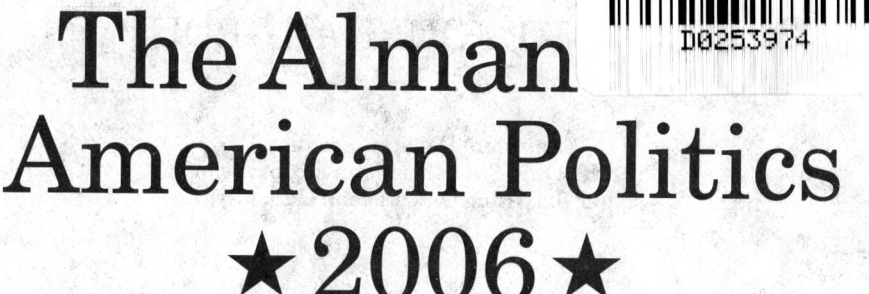

The Alman
American Politics
★ 2006 ★

THE **Senators,** THE **Representatives**
AND THE **Governors:**
THEIR **Records** AND **Election Results,**
THEIR **States** AND **Districts**

Michael Barone
Richard E. Cohen

National
Journal
—GROUP—

Washington, D.C.

NATIONAL JOURNAL GROUP

Printed in the United States of America by United Book Press. Database design by Directional Data, Inc.; composition by Fry Communications Inc. Distributed to the trade by the University of Chicago Press.

Original cover concept by Adrian O. Constantyn. Photographs by Richard A. Bloom, Liz Lynch and Bruce Reedy. For information regarding photographs, contact: National Journal, 600 New Hampshire Ave., N.W., Washington, D.C. 20037; 202-739-8400. All rights reserved.

The Almanac of American politics. — 1972 –

v. : ill. ; 24 cm.

Biennial
Published by Gambit 1972– ; by National Journal 1988–

ISSN: 0362-076X
ISBN: 0-89234-111-4 (2006)
ISBN: 0-89234-112-2 (pbk. : 2006)

1. United States. Congress—Biography. 2. United States. Congress—Committees. 3. Election districts—United States—Handbooks, manuals, etc. I. Barone, Michael. II. Ujifusa, Grant. III. Matthews, Douglas.

JK1012 .A44
328.73/005   70-160417

THE ALMANAC OF AMERICAN POLITICS 2006

Author
Michael Barone

Co-Author
Richard E. Cohen

Editor
Charles Mahtesian

Founding Editor
Grant Ujifusa

Research Associates
Peter Bell, Jessica Brady, Josh Kraushaar

Researcher
Thomas Rains

Editorial Interns
Sarah John, Ben Leubsdorf, Shaina Martinez

Editorial Assistance
Clare Lochary

Photo Editor
Liz Lynch

Presidential Election Results
Polidata

State Maps
Polidata

Congressional Election Results
Election Data Services Inc.

TABLE OF CONTENTS

6   Contents

12   **Contents**

GUIDE TO USAGE

The following guide provides a brief description of each section and a list of sources from which information was derived, both of which serve as a road map to understanding the meaning behind the figures. Some of the data will be updated regularly on the Almanac website. For information on how to subscribe to this free service, please see the insert card toward the middle of the book. Data in each category below is generated for *The Almanac of American Politics* by Polidata from data compiled by the 2000 Census, unless otherwise noted. Figures released by the Census Bureau may vary slightly from those used by the Almanac due to different methods of data aggregation or tabulation.

The People

Population. All population figures, excluding voter registration, are from the Census Bureau, www.census.gov. Census estimates as of July 1, 2004 are used for each state; Census estimates as of July 1, 2003 are used for cities. Official April 1, 2000 figures are used for district population.

Area Size. Area size is in square miles, including water.

State Native. Refers to persons born in their state of residence as a % of all persons.

Non-Citizen. Refers to persons foreign born and not a citizen as a % of all persons.

Language. Refers to the % of households speaking that language. The abbreviation *Other Eur.* refers to Other Indo-European languages. **Race and Ethnic Origin.** For the 2000 Census, the Census Bureau asked people what their race or ethnic origin was. Race, as defined by the Census, reflects the individual respondent's perception of his or her racial identity and does not reflect any biological or anthropological definition. The basic racial categories are: American Indian or Alaska Native (designated in the box as *Native Am.*); Asian; Native Hawaiian or other Pacific Islander (*Hawaiian*); Black or African American; White; Two or more races (*Two + races*); Other non-Hispanic persons (*Other*). The race statistics used in the Almanac are drawn from respondents reporting only one race category, but the book also includes a total for those who responded to more than one race category. Hispanic origin is defined as an ethnicity, and includes those who classified themselves in one of three specific Hispanic categories (Cuban, Mexican, Puerto Rican) or as of "other Spanish/Hispanic origin." Persons of Latino or Hispanic origin may be of any race for Census purposes, but the Almanac includes only non-Hispanic Blacks in the Black population category and only non-Hispanic Whites in the White population category, so that the percentages add to 100%. The figures in the box are as a % of all persons in a state or congressional district.

Ancestry. Ancestry refers to ethnic origin or descent; categories are drawn from Census-designated possible groups. The question was intended by the Census to provide data for groups that were not included in the Hispanic origin and race questions; thus it does not reflect diversity within Hispanic and Asian subgroups. The % figure is calculated by using the average number of responses to estimate the % of the population that shares this ancestry characteristic. NOTE: The *USA* designation refers to "American" as a unique ethnicity, if it was provided alone as a response without any other ethnicity. *Subsaharan* refers to the Census category of Subsaharan African. *West Indian* excludes Hispanic groups.

Military Veterans. Refers to persons who were in the Armed Forces previously as a % of voting age persons. *Gulf War %* includes all veterans with service after 1990, but does not include those who also served in Vietnam.

Urban/Rural Population. Refers to the % of total population that lives in areas defined as urban or rural by the Census Bureau.

Education. *H.S. Grad* refers to persons with a high school diploma or higher, as a % of persons 25 years and older. *College Grad* refers to persons with a bachelor's degree or higher, as a % of persons 25 years and older.

Industry.   Refers to industry of occupation. The figure is of persons employed by that particular industry as a % of employed persons 16 years or older. Abbreviations: *Agri* (agriculture, forestry, fishing and mining); *Con* (construction); *Fin* (finance, insurance and real estate); *Info* (information); *Mfg* (manufacturing, durable and non-durable); *Prof* (professional and related services, including health and education); *Public* (public administration); *Trade* (trade, wholesale and retail); *Other* (primarily entertainment, recreation, hotel and food services).

Occupation.   Refers to type of job within industry. The figure is the % of employed persons 16 years and older in these occupations. *White collar* refers to management, professional, sales and administrative occupations. *Blue collar* refers to construction, production and transportation occupations. *Gray collar* refers to the balance of employed persons not classified as white or blue collar, such as farming, fishing and forestry or health care, protective service, food prep and personal care occupations.

Work Sector.   Refers to a classification of worker by economic sector. The figure is the % of employed persons 16 years and older. Abbreviations: *Private* (private for profit/not for profit wage/salary employers); *Govt* (federal, state and local government); *Self* (self-employed); *Family* (unpaid family workers).

Unemployment.   Unemployed civilians as a % of persons 16 years and older and as a % of the labor force.

Household Income/Poverty Status.   *Household Income* refers to household income in 1999, as a % of all households. *Poverty* status refers to % of persons below the poverty line.

Home Value.   Refers to self-estimated market value of owner-occupied units as % of owner-occupied housing units for which value was specified.

State Information.   Each legislature is referred to according to the proper name of its legislative body, followed by a breakdown by party membership. Partisan composition figures are as of April 6, 2005.

Legislative Term Limits.   Refers to whether a state has term limits for state legislators.

Registered Voters.   Refers to the number of registered voters by party, as close as possible to the November 2004 election. The individual states' election bureaus or political parties provide these figures. Some states have no voter registration. *D* refers to Democrat; *R* refers to Republican; *O* refers to independent, unaffiliated and minor parties.

Cook Partisan Voting Index.   Refers to the Partisan Voting Index (PVI) as used by Charlie Cook, Washington's foremost political handicapper. The PVI is designed to provide a quick overall assessment of generic partisan strength. For this volume, the PVI includes an average of the 2000 and 2004 presidential elections in the district as the partisan indicator. The PVI value is calculated by a comparison of the district average for the party nominee, compared to the 2004 national value for the party nominee. *The calculations are based upon the two-party vote.* The national values for 2004 are George W. Bush 51.2% and John Kerry 48.8%. The PVI value indicates a district with a partisan base above the national value for that party's 2004 presidential nominee. Thus a district with an R+15 is a district that voted 15 percentage points (as an average of its 2000 and 2004 presidential vote) higher for Bush than the national value of 51.2%. Similarly, a district with a D+15 is a district that voted 15 percentage points (as an average of its 2000 and 2004 presidential vote) higher for Kerry than the national value of 48.8%. An X +00 indicates an evenly balanced district.

Biography.   This section lists when each governor, senator and representative was elected or appointed, date and place of birth, home, college education and degrees obtained (if any), religion, marital status and, if applicable, spouse's name. The number of terms listed reflects full, elected terms. Also listed is a brief outline of the politician's past elected offices, professional career and military service and his or her office addresses and telephone numbers. Committee and subcommittee assignments, as of June 3, 2005, are provided as well. (Note: On many committees, the chairman and ranking minority member are ex officio members of each subcommittee on which they do not hold a regular assignment.)

Ratings

Group Ratings.   The congressional rating statistics of 10 interest groups provide an idea of a legislator's general ideology and the degree to which the legislator represents different groups' interests. Not just a record of liberal/conservative voting behavior, these ratings come from a range of groups concerned with everything from single issues (environmental concerns) to the political interests of a particular sector (e.g., business). The order of the groups is such that the more "liberal" groups are on the left and the more "conservative" are on the right. Four groups, ACLU, ITIC, NTLC, and CHC provide one rating for the two-year congressional session. Following is a general description of each organization.

ADA   Americans for Democratic Action

Liberal: Since its founding in 1947, ADA members have pushed for legislation designed to curtail rising defense spending, prevent encroachments on civil liberties and promote international human rights. The ADA uses 20 votes from the 108th Congress based on a broad spectrum of issues for its vote analysis.

ACLU   American Civil Liberties Union

Pro-individual liberties: ACLU seeks to protect individuals from legal, executive and congressional infringement on basic rights guaranteed by the Bill of Rights. The ACLU ratings are published for every Congress.

AFS   American Federation of State, County and Municipal Employees (AFSCME)

Liberal labor: As the nation's largest public service employees union, representing more than 1.4 million members, AFSCME is committed to improving working conditions through collective bargaining. The AFSCME voting records are based on a representative sample of roll call votes from the 108th Congress.

LCV   League of Conservation Voters

Environmental: Formed in 1970, LCV is the national, non-partisan arm of the environmental movement. LCV works to elect pro-environmental candidates to Congress. LCV ratings are based on key votes concerning energy, environment and natural resource issues.

ITIC   Information Technology Industry Council

High-tech industry: ITIC represents the leading U.S. providers of information technology products and services. ITIC's mission is to help shape policies that advance electronic commerce, open new markets, rely on market-based solutions, and foster innovation.

NTU   National Taxpayers Union

Pro-taxpayer rights: NTU is the nation's largest and oldest taxpayers' rights group, representing 350,000 members in all 50 states. NTU analyzes every roll call vote taken during both sessions of Congress that significantly affects federal taxes, spending, debt, or regulatory impact.

COC   Chamber of Commerce of the United States

Pro-business: Founded in 1912 as a voice for organized business, COC represents local, regional and state chambers of commerce in addition to trade and professional organizations.

ACU   American Conservative Union

Conservative: Since 1971, ACU ratings have provided a means of gauging the conservatism of members of Congress. Foreign policy, social and budget issues are their primary concerns.

NTLC   National Tax-Limitation Committee

Pro-tax limitation: NTLC was organized in 1975 to seek constitutional and other limits on taxes, spending and deficits. These ratings are based on budget issue votes and bills that would have a major impact on long-term government taxing and spending programs.

CHC   Christian Coalition

Conservative: Pro-family citizen organization and national lobby founded in 1989 working for family-friendly public policy on a local, state and national level with over 2 million members.

National Journal Ratings.   *National Journal's* rating system establishes an objective method of analyzing congressional voting. A panel of *National Journal* editors and staff initially compiled a list of congressional roll call votes and classified them as either economic, social or foreign policy-related. The interrelationship of these votes was shown by a statistical procedure called "principal components analysis," which revealed which "yea" votes and which "nay" votes fit a liberal or a conservative pattern. The votes in each of the three subject areas were computer-weighted to reflect the degree they fit the common pattern. All members of Congress who participated in at least half of the votes in each area received ratings; those who missed more that half the votes were not scored (shown as *). Absences and abstentions were not counted.

Members of Congress were then ranked according to relative liberalism and conservatism. Finally, they were assigned percentiles showing their rank relative to others in their chamber. Percentile scores range from a minimum of 0 to a maximum of 99. Because some members voted liberal or conservative on every roll call, however, there are ties at the liberal and conservative ends of each scale. For that reason, the maximum percentiles often turn out to be less than 99.

Election Results

Listed for each member of the House are results of the 2004 general, runoff and primary elections, as well as the 2002 general elections (results of any special elections are also listed). Gubernatorial and senatorial results are presented in a like manner. Votes and percentages are included, indicating the margin of victory (due to the process of rounding up and rounding down, some totals may equal more or less than 100%). Candidates receiving less than 4% of the total vote are grouped together and listed as "Other." Election returns were collected from the individual states. Where a state abbreviation and district number appear in parenthesis next to an election year, this indicates that the member ran in a differently numbered congressional district that year.

Prior Winning Percentage.   This feature provides winning percentage of the vote in past elections; in Senate profiles, the word "House" indicates the election that year was for the U.S. House. If no percentage is provided for an election year, it indicates that the member lost or did not run for reelection that year; generally this will occur where there has been a gap in service. An odd election year (e.g. 2001) indicates a special election; two elections in the same year indicate a special and a general election.

Presidential Vote.   The 2000 and 2004 presidential votes are included for each state. Results of the 2004 presidential primaries were provided by the Federal Election Commission; caucus results are not provided. The 2000 and 2004 presidential votes are included here for each congressional district. The 2000 presidential vote reflects the vote within the new district lines in effect for the 2002 election. The 2004 presidential vote reflects the vote within the district lines in effect for the 2004 election. The presidential vote by congressional district is estimated by Polidata, from information collected from state and local election offices. Only seven states provide district-level presidential vote data; by necessity, other results are aggregated from precinct-level returns. Voting data from districts with split precincts and centrally counted absentee votes thus should be considered estimates; the allocation of these unassigned votes is determined by Polidata. While estimates of votes are included in each district, the percentage values generally provide the more reliable information. The votes for minor party candidates are included where available but are not consistent across all 50 states. The total of the congressional district votes may not add up to the total state vote, because some votes (overseas, military and some absentee and early votes) are not assigned to a congressional district and because county election office reports sometimes conflict with reports from state election authorities.

Campaign Finance

All data are derived from candidates' campaign finance reports and party reports available from the Federal Election Commission (FEC). The dollar figure, in parentheses to the right of the election results, represents the candidates' net disbursements (expenditures) for the period beginning January 1, 2003, and ending December 31, 2004. These figures may not include candidate loans that have been repaid, nor does it include any corrections or amendments filed with the FEC after June 2005.

Abbreviations

ABC	Americans for Better Childcare Act	IC	Independent Conservative
AC	American Constitution Party (CO)	Ind	Independence Party
ACLU	American Civil Liberties Union	IAP	Independent American Party (NV)
ACP	A Connecticut Party	IR	Independent-Republican Party (MN)
ACU	American Conservative Union		
ADA	Americans for Democratic Action, Americans with Disabilities Act	ISTEA	Intermodal Surface Transportation Efficiency Act
AFDC	Aid to Families with Dependent Children	IVP	Independent Voters Party
		L	Liberal Party
AFS	American Federation of State, County & Municipal Employees (AFSCME)	LCV	League of Conservation Voters
		LHOB	Longworth House Office Building
		Lib	Libertarian Party
AI	Alaska Independent Party	LU	Liberty Union
AID	Agency for International Development	NAFTA	North American Free Trade Agreement
ANWR	Arctic National Wildlife Refuge	NARAL	National Abortion Rights Action League
AS	American Samoa		
BGH	Bovine Growth Hormone	NEA	National Endowment for the Arts
BL	Better Life Party	NFIB	National Federation of Independent Business
C	Conservative Party (NY)		
CAFE	Corporate Average Fuel Economy	NL	Natural Law Party
CFA	Consumer Federation of America	NP	Non-Partisan
CFC	Conscience for Congress	NPA	No Political Affiliation
CCP	Change Congress Party	NRCC	National Republican Congressional Committee
CHC	Christian Coalition		
CHOB	Cannon House Office Building	NRSC	National Republican Senatorial Committee
CIA	Central Intelligence Agency		
CNP	Constitution Party	NTLC	National Tax-Limitation Committee
CPF	Constitution Party of Florida	NTU	National Taxpayers Union
COC	Chamber of Commerce of the United States	NTX	No New Taxes Party (MN)
		PDP	Popular Democratic Party (PR)
COLA	Cost of Living Adjustment	P & F	Peace and Freedom Party (CA)
DCCC	Democratic Congressional Campaign Committee	PJ	Peace and Justice Party (NY)
		PNTR	Permanent Normal Trade Relations
DFL	Democratic-Farmer-Labor Party (MN)	POP	Populist Party
		PR	Puerto Rico
DLC	Democratic Leadership Council	PRG	Progressive Party
DNC	Democratic National Committee	Ref	Reform Party
DSCC	Democratic Senatorial Campaign Committee	RHOB	Rayburn House Office Building
		RLDS	Reorganized Church of the Latter Day Saints
DSOB	Dirksen Senate Office Building		
EMILY	EMILY's List (Early Money is Like Yeast)	RMM	Ranking Minority Member
		RNC	Republican National Committee
ERISA	Employee Retirement Income Security Act	RP	Republican Moderate Party (AK)
		RSOB	Russell Senate Office Building
FEC	Federal Election Commission	RTL	Right-to-Life Party
FERC	Federal Energy Regulatory Commission	S	Capitol Building Room, Senate side
		SCH	School Choice Party
GATT	General Agreement on Tariffs & Trade	SDI	Strategic Defense Initiative
		SOC	Socialist Party
Green	Green Party	UAW	United Auto Workers
H	Capitol Building Room-House side	UCIT	United Citizens Party (SC)
HMO	Stop HMO Abuses Party	VNS	Voter News Service
HSOB	Hart Senate Office Building	WIC	Women and Infant Children
I	Independent	WF	Working Families

Key Votes of the 108th Congress

Key Votes.   The Key Votes section attempts to illustrate a legislator's stance on important votes where he or she must vote for or against a national issue. The process grossly oversimplifies the legislative system where months of debate, amendment, pressure, persuasion, and compromise go into a final floor vote. However, the voting record remains the best indication of a member's general ideologies and position on specific issues. Following is a list of key votes used. A member who was absent, voted present, or who was not in office at the time of a particular vote receives an "*". Roll-call data were drawn from Congressional Observer Publications at www.proaxis.com/cop, a private legislative tracking company.

House Votes, 108th Congress:

1. **Drilling in ANWR** (HR 6) Permit oil drilling in 2,000 acres of the Arctic National Wildlife Refuge. April 10, 2003. (226-202) (D: 30-171; R: 196-30; I: 0-1)
2. **Approve Bush Tax Cuts** (HR 2) Approve the conference report on the tax-cut package that would reduce taxes by $350 billion through 2013. May 23, 2003. (231-200) (D: 7-198; R: 224-1; I: 0-1)
3. **Medicare/Rx Bill** (HR 1) Approve the conference report on Medicare prescription drug benefit legislation. November 22, 2003. (220-215) (D: 16-189; R: 204-25; I: 0-1)
4. **Bar Overtime Pay Regs.** (HR 5006) Bar funds to implement new federal regulations for overtime pay. September 9, 2004. (223-193) (D: 200-0; R: 22-193; I: 1-0)
5. **DC School Vouchers** (HR 2765) Provide funds for private school vouchers in the District of Columbia. September 9, 2003. (209-208) (D: 3-192; R: 206-15; I: 0-1)
6. **Ban Human Cloning** (HR 534) Prohibit human cloning and impose criminal sanctions. February 27, 2003 (241-155) (D: 42-139; R: 198-16; I: 1-0)
7. **Restrict Gun Liability** (HR 1036) Restrict liability lawsuits against manufacturers and sellers of firearms and ammunition. April 9, 2003. (285-140) (D: 63-137; R: 221-3; I: 1-0)
8. **Ban Partial-Birth Abortion** (HR 760) Ban the procedure that opponents describe as "partial-birth" abortion and impose criminal sanctions for those who perform the procedure. June 4, 2003. (282-139) (D: 62-133; R: 220-5; I: 0-1)
9. **Ban Same-Sex Marriage** (HJRes 106) Amend the Constitution to ban same-sex marriage. September 30, 2004. (227-186; failed to receive two-thirds approval required for ratification) (D: 36-158; R: 191-27; I: 0-1)
10. **Fund Iraq War** (HR 3289) Approve the fiscal 2004 supplemental appropriations bill providing $87 billion for U.S. military operations and reconstruction aid to Iraq and Afghanistan. October 17, 2003. (303-125) (D: 83-118; R: 220-6; I: 0-1)
11. **Bar Cuba Embargo Funds** (HR 5025) Prohibit funds to enforce the economic embargo of Cuba. September 22, 2004. (188-225) (D: 162-37; R: 25-188; I: 1-0)
12. **Intelligence Reorg.** (HR 10) Reorganize U.S. intelligence agencies and create a national intelligence director. October 8, 2004. (282-134) (D: 69-125; R: 213-8; I: 0-1)

Senate Votes, 108th Congress:

1. **Ban Drilling in ANWR** (SConRes 23) Strike a provision in the fiscal 2004 budget resolution that would provide procedural protection for legislation authorizing oil drilling in the Arctic National Wildlife Refuge. March 19, 2003 (52-48) (D: 43-5; R: 8-43; I: 1-0)
2. **Approve Bush Tax Cuts** (HR 2) Approve the conference report on the tax-cut package that would reduce taxes by $350 billion through 2013. May 23, 2003. (50-50; Vice President Dick Cheney broke the tie) (D: 2-46; R: 48-3; I: 0-1)
3. **Medicare/Rx Bill** (HR 1) Approve the conference report on Medicare prescription drug benefit legislation. November 25, 2003. (54-44) (D: 11-35; R: 42-9; I: 1-0)
4. **Bar Overtime Pay Regs.** (S 1637) Bar funds to implement new federal regulations for overtime pay. May 4, 2004. (52-47) (D: 46-1; R: 5-46; I: 1-0)
5. **Energy Bill** (HR 6) Cloture motion to end debate on the conference report on the comprehensive energy bill. November 21, 2003. (58-39; after the motion failed to receive

the required 60 votes, Majority Leader Bill Frist switched his vote in favor so that he might move to reconsider the vote later) (D: 13-32; R: 44-7, I: 0-1)

6. **Support Roe v. Wade** (S 3) Express the sense of the Senate in support of the Supreme Court's decision in *Roe v. Wade*, which legalized abortion. March 12, 2003. (52-46) (D: 42-5; R: 9-41; I: 1-0)

7. **Ban Partial-Birth Abortion** (S 3) Ban the procedure that opponents describe as "partial-birth" abortion, and impose criminal sanctions for those who perform the procedure. March 13, 2003. (64-33) (D: 16-29; R: 48-3; I: 0-1)

8. **Assault Weapons Ban** (S 1805) Extend for 10 years the ban on the sale and possession of assault weapons. March 2, 2004. (52-47) (D: 41-6; R: 10-41; I: 1-0)

9. **Ban Same-Sex Marriage** (SJRes 40) Cloture motion to end debate on a proposed constitutional amendment to ban same-sex marriage. July 14, 2004. (48-50; failed to receive required 60 votes) (D: 3-43; R: 45-6; I: 0-1)

10. **Ban Bunker-Buster bomb** (S 2400) Prohibit use of $37 million for the Energy Department's nuclear penetrator "bunker-buster" program. June 15, 2004. (42-55) (D: 41-5; R: 1-50)

11. **Fund Iraq War** (S 1689) Approve the fiscal 2004 supplemental appropriations bill providing $87 billion for U.S. military operations and reconstruction aid to Iraq and Afghanistan. October 17, 2003. (87-12) (D: 37-11; R: 50-0; I: 0-1)

12. **Restrict Missile Defense** (S 2400) Restrict deployment of a national missile defense system. June 17, 2004. (42-57) (D: 40-7; R: 1-50; I: 1-0)

American Politics in The Networking Era

By Michael Barone

On the surface, the 2004 election looked very much like the 2000 election. George W. Bush was again running against a liberal Democrat who had spent much of his career in the Senate and who had clinched his nomination by early victories in Iowa and New Hampshire. In November, 47 of the 50 states and the District of Columbia voted for the candidate of the same party as they had in 2000. Only three states switched, New Hampshire to the Democrats, Iowa and New Mexico to the Republicans. Bush won again, this time without a court battle. Republicans ended up with majorities in both houses of Congress. But in many ways, the 2004 campaign was very different from 2000. It produced a different kind of politics, a politics that reflects the character of the post-industrial, networking age we live in.

For changes in politics resemble changes in the larger society. For several decades now, we have seen the change from industrial America to post-industrial America, from an industrial nation characterized by centralization and large command-and-control organizations to a post-industrial, Information Age nation characterized by decentralization and network-connected organizations. This is an America where Microsoft overtakes IBM, where FedEx overtakes the U.S. Postal Service, where Wal-Mart overtakes Sears. It is an America whose network-connected Special Forces overthrow the Taliban in Afghanistan and whose network-connected Army and Marines overthrow Saddam Hussein in Iraq. It is an America where the abolition of guaranteed welfare has produced higher incomes and greater independence for the target population, where network-connected police forces have cut crime by more than half in New York City and shown the way toward vast reductions in crime across the nation. Our private sector and important parts of our public sector have moved from industrial command-and-control America to post-industrial, Information Age, network-connected America. In 2004, our politics followed.

The Politics of Networking   This was an election whose outcome cannot be dismissed as a fluke. It was an election in which most voters and most partisan activists on both sides believed that big things were at stake. It was an election in which the outcome by no means seemed certain: John Kerry led in the polls during a good portion of the time from March 2, when he clinched the Democratic nomination, to Election Day, November 2. It was an election that both sides believed would be determined by turnout. They had good reasons to think so.

The 1990s saw a decline in ticket splitting and a convergence of the two parties' percentages in presidential and congressional voting. Bill Clinton was re-elected with 49% of the vote in 1996, while the popular vote for the House that year was 49% Republican and 48.5% Democratic. In 1998, the popular vote for the House was 49% Republican and 48% Democratic. In 2000, both Al Gore and George W. Bush won 48% of the vote, while the popular vote for the House was again 49% Republican to 48% Democratic. The House vote in 2002 was a little different, 51% Republican and 46% Democratic.

But polling in late 2003 and for most of 2004 indicated a very close presidential race. Bush strategist Karl Rove keeps a card in his pocket showing that the percentage of voters who were behaviorally "independent" declined from 15% in 1988 to 7% in 2002. The strategy that Rove designed and that Bush-Cheney '04 campaign manager Ken Mehlman executed was geared not to persuading the undecided and weakly committed voters, but to turning out the maximum number of Republicans. The Kerry campaign and other Democrats likewise saw their main task as turning out the party faithful.

Both parties succeeded. Total turnout increased by 16%—a historic increase. In 2000, 105 million Americans voted; in 2004, 122 million did. Turnout as a percentage of eligible voters increased from 51% in 2000 to 61% in 2004—again a historic increase. This was particularly extraordinary because turnout usually doesn't rise in rematches. In 1956, when Dwight Eisenhower ran against Adlai Stevenson for the second time, turnout increased only slightly; it decreased as a percentage of eligible voters. In 1996, when Bill Clinton faced a decorated World War II veteran for a second time, turnout declined in total numbers and, even more, as a percentage of eligibles. But in 2004, in the second contest between George W. Bush and a Democrat who had served in Vietnam and spent much of his career in the Senate, turnout zoomed upward.

But if both parties succeeded in raising turnout, one party was more successful than the other. Kerry won 16% more votes than Gore did. Bush won 23% more votes in 2004 than he did in 2000. The number of voters for the Democratic nominee increased from 51 million to 59 million. The number of Bush voters increased from 50 million to 62 million.

The parties went about raising their turnout in different ways. The Democrats depended on labor unions, as they had in the past, and on the turnout efforts of billionaire-funded "527" organizations. (These are named after a section of the Internal Revenue Code, and a number of these groups were funded by rich men like George Soros, who spent $27 million trying to defeat George W. Bush. Thank goodness the McCain-Feingold campaign finance law got the Big Money out of politics.) These groups relied on paid workers supervised by command-and-control organizations. They concentrated on black neighborhoods in central cities and on university towns—areas where new voters would likely vote 90% Democratic. This was traditional, industrial-era politics, well executed. The Democratic groups met their turnout goals and more; if they had performed this well in 2000, Gore would have won by a large margin.

The Bush campaign was different. Its architect was Rove, who remained in the White House and advised President Bush on policy as well as politics; its structural engineer was Mehlman, who created an organization unlike any seen before, a networking organization that far surpassed what the Democrats were doing. In mid-2003, when former Vermont Gov. Howard Dean surged ahead of other Democrats in fundraising and in the polls, much attention was given to campaign manager Joe Trippi's use of the Internet. He used it to bring volunteers and money into the campaign, and to allow Dean supporters to add their own words, literally, in the campaign blog. Many political supporters were impressed, and rightly so, that the Dean campaign amassed a list of 600,000 e-mail addresses. But few reporters at the time took note of the number of e-mail addresses the Bush campaign had collected: 6 million.

Over two years, the Bush campaign built an organization of 1.4 million active volunteers. This was unprecedented. By way of comparison, the Democratic National Committee has said it enlisted 233,000 volunteers during the 2004 campaign. The Bush volunteers worked not just in heavily Republican neighborhoods—only 15% of Republican voters, Mehlman calculated, live in precincts that vote 65% or more Republican. Instead, they went everywhere, especially to rural counties, many of them slow-growing places where most politicians figure there are no more votes to be won, and to the fast-growing exurban areas at the edges of metropolitan areas, where most of the young families moving in tend to be Republican. Just as Sam Walton figured he could make huge profits selling things to people in low-income rural areas and in low-fashion exurbs, so Mehlman calculated that he could wring votes out of areas that most political strategists and political reporters ignored.

To make sure that those volunteers were achieving their goals, Mehlman established metrics—numerical goals, measured by third parties. Every week, the leaders of the local, state, and national organizations got reports on whether those metrics had been achieved. Productive volunteers were given positive reinforcement, sometimes a call from Mehlman himself. Unproductive volunteers were replaced or persuaded to do more. Mehlman's management was very much like former Mayor Rudolph Giuliani's management of the New York City Police Department: Precinct commanders were given goals—low crime numbers—which were independently validated. Those who produced were promoted; those who failed lost their jobs. As a result, crime in New York was cut by more than 50%—more than even Giuliani thought was possible. This is not command-and-control management, but management by networking, by holding people accountable and letting them learn from each other how to do better. And in post-industrial America, it got better results than command-and-control management. In crucial states with the largest volunteer organizations, the numbers speak as loudly as Giuliani's—turnout rose 28% from 2000 in fast-growing Florida and 20% in slow-growing Ohio.

The Bush campaign used connections—networks—to recruit volunteers and identify voters. The campaign built on existing connections—religious, occupational, voluntary—to establish contacts. If a Bush volunteer was a Hispanic accountant active in the Boy Scouts, the campaign would reach out through him to other Hispanics, accountants and their clients, and Boy Scout volunteers. Of course, the campaign put much effort into contacting people in religious groups—particularly evangelical Christians, but also Catholics and Orthodox Jews. And the Bush campaign reached out to people with shared affinities who tend to be Republicans. The campaign consulting firms National Media and TargetPoint identified Republican-leaning groups—Coors beer and bourbon drinkers, college football TV viewers, Fox News viewers, people with caller ID—and devised ways to connect with them. As Thomas Edsall and James Grimaldi wrote in *the Washington Post* after the election, "Surveys of people on these consumer data lists were then used to determine 'anger points' (late-term abortion, trial lawyer fees, estate taxes) that coincided with the Bush agenda for as many as 32 categories of voters, each identifiable by income, magazine subscriptions, favorite television shows, and other 'flags.' Merging this data, in turn, enabled those running direct-mail, precinct-walking, and phone-bank programs to target each voter with a tailored message."

Presidential campaigns from 1968 up through 2000 spent most of their time, money, and psychic energy on devising television ads to appeal to undecided and weakly committed voters. Bush-Cheney '04 spent unprecedented amounts of time, money, and psychic energy on networking—making connections with voters—through advertising, to be sure, but also through personal contact. The Democrats' turnout drive depended on paid workers persuading strangers to get out and vote. The Republicans' turnout drive depended on volunteers persuading people with whom they had something in common to get out and vote. In industrial America, the Democrats' way may have been more effective. In Information Age America, the Bush campaign's strategy was more effective.

In his book *Bowling Alone*, Harvard professor of public policy Robert Putnam argued that America is suffering from a decline in social-connectedness—in people voluntarily working and playing together, being active in those voluntary associations that Alexis de Tocqueville identified as one of the defining characteristics of democracy in America in the 1830s. The Bush campaign, by assembling a core of 1.4 million volunteers, increased social-connectedness in America in an important way. Anyone who has volunteered and worked actively for a political campaign knows that it is a way to make new friends, to establish ties with people with whom you will work together again, on political campaigns but also on community projects and in voluntary associations of all kinds. Volunteer campaign work has reverberations over the years. Rove and Mehlman believed that it was possible to build such a large volunteer organization, but only for an incumbent president whom people had come to know well and admire, or even love. The Republicans will not have an incumbent to campaign for in 2008. But the 2004 Bush campaign created a quantum of social-connectedness that the Republican nominee in 2008 can build on, a long-lasting asset for the Republican Party.

Forging a Majority   In the process, the Bush campaign reshaped the electorate. People who have voted once are more likely to vote than are people who have never voted. The Bush campaign added more people to the electorate in 2004 than the Democrats did, and that achievement is likely to reverberate in elections to come. It could even lead to the kind of natural majority for the party that the Democrats built in the 1930s and the Republicans built in the 1890s, majorities that pretty much prevailed for more than 30 years.

Recall that total turnout increased 16% in 2004. This was extraordinary: Increases in turnout in presidential years have averaged only 7% in the last 110 years, if one puts to one side the larger increases in the years from 1916 to 1928, when women were entering the electorate for the first time. Massive increases in turnout have the potential to reshape the electorate and create a new majority for a party that adds many more new voters than its rival. Over the 110 years preceding 2004, again disregarding 1916 to 1928, turnout increased by more than 14% in only four elections. Two of those four elections resulted in a new national majority for the winning party. The two that did not produce natural majorities were in 1992 and 1952. Turnout in 1992 was up 14% from 1988, and Clinton won this three-way race with 43% of the vote. That gave Clinton a chance to build a majority party. But this politically gifted president failed to do so. After his first two years, and in response to his tax increase and to the health care finance plan promoted by Hillary Rodham Clinton, Republicans won majorities in the Senate and, for the first time in 40 years, in the House of Representatives. Clinton failed to get 50% of the vote in 1996, and Gore, his vice president, failed to do so in 2000. Democrats did not win 50% of the vote in the House elections of 1994, 1996, 1998, and 2000. And these were all years of apparent peace and apparent prosperity, the most favorable atmosphere in which an incumbent party can run. In a counterfactual world without Ross Perot or Ralph Nader, Clinton and Gore might have won majorities in 1996 and 2000—but very small majorities, and we don't live in a counterfactual world. Now, the Democrats will not be able to run as the incumbent presidential party in a time of peace and prosperity until 2012 at the earliest.

The year when turnout increased the most was 1952, when it rose 26% over 1948. That was the year in which the G.I. generation entered the electorate in great numbers. Over the preceding 12 years, they had been fighting a war, moving around the country to work in defense industries, going to college on the G.I. Bill, trying to scrape up money for a down payment on a house. Then, in 1952, faced with the choice of two attractive candidates after 20 years of Democratic presidents, they started voting in a rush. The 1952 turnout produced a victory for Dwight Eisenhower, but he made no effort and apparently had no inclination to build a natural majority for his party.

That was not true of Franklin D. Roosevelt. He won re-election in 1936 over Alfred Landon by 61% to 37%, in an election in which turnout rose 15% from four years before. Roosevelt won 22% more votes than he had in 1932—almost exactly the same percentage by which George W. Bush increased his vote take from 2000 to 2004. Roosevelt reshaped the electorate, adding millions of voters in the big cities and cementing them to his Democratic coalition of Western progressives (mostly Republican in the 1920s) and Southern whites (solid Democrats until the 1950s) that became the dominant force in American politics for a long generation. Roosevelt reshaped the electorate, in part, by adopting new political tactics appropriate to an industrial America caught in economic depression. Democratic machines had not previously dominated the politics of all big cities—Chicago had two-party competition, and Philadelphia was solidly Republican in the 1920s. But Roosevelt's welfare programs and his cultivation of machine politicians, combined with the popularity of his New Deal in the cities, meant that the machines, sometimes with helpful subsidies from government, could roll up huge majorities simply by turning out anyone they could find (and perhaps some they couldn't) in now monopartisan constituencies. In addition, the labor law that Roosevelt signed in 1935 permitted the rapid growth of industrial unions starting in 1937 and continuing through World War II, and those unions became powerful turnout machines for the Democrats.

The other instance was the election of 1896, when turnout increased 15% over 1892, and Republican William McKinley was elected over populist Democrat William Jennings Bryan by 51% to 47%. McKinley received a startling 37% more votes than the incumbent Republican president, Benjamin Harrison, had four years before. Mostly, this election is remembered for Bryan's brilliant oratory and his fervent advocacy of "free silver"—in effect, inflation—as the savior of the farmer. But McKinley's platform of hard money and protective tariffs had more appeal to workers and immigrants in the growing big cities. McKinley's campaign, managed by Sen. Mark Hanna of Ohio and future Vice President Charles Dawes, pioneered new tactics to appeal directly to the big- and small-city masses and won votes the Republicans had never won before. McKinley did not win big—his advantage was almost identical to that of Bush over Kerry in 2004—but he did succeed in reshaping the electorate and setting forth policies that would continue to increase Republican support in the years following. For a long generation, until the Depression of the 1930s, the Republicans were the natural majority party in the country.

Interestingly, neither McKinley nor Roosevelt was considered a sure winner during the fiercely waged campaigns of 1896 and 1936—another similarity to 2004. Bryan was the candidate of the party in the White House, a party that had won more popular votes for president in four of the five preceding elections, and his oratory and appeal to farmers seemed likely to add more. Few foresaw how the push by Hanna and Dawes to recruit voters in the cities and factory towns would reshape the electorate. As for Roosevelt, he faced a mostly hostile press, and many of his critics doubted that he could hold together what seemed to them an unwieldy coalition of opposites. Republicans, after all, had won big majorities in three of the four preceding elections. Random-sampling polling had just been developed: George Gallup published his first scientific poll in October 1935, and his later surveys showed Roosevelt leading. But many observers had more faith in the familiar *Literary Digest* mail-in poll, which showed Roosevelt trailing Republican Landon.

The 1896 and 1936 elections reshaped the American electorate, in ways that produced natural majorities for the winning party. The winning parties succeeded, in part, by inventing new political techniques appropriate to the times. The 2004 election has also reshaped the American electorate, in part through the invention of new political techniques. It is too early to say that it produced a natural majority for the winning party. But it has laid the groundwork.

The votes in 1896 and 1936 were harbingers of long-lasting majority coalitions for their parties. Political strategist Rove, who has often identified McKinley and the coalition he built as a model, hoped that the vote in 2004 would be, as well.

Like Clinton's election with 43% of the vote in 1992, Bush's election with 48% of the vote in 2000 gave the winner an opportunity to build a majority for his party. So far, Bush has succeeded where Clinton failed. In the 2002 elections, Republicans ousted the Democratic majority in the Senate and increased their majority in the House. No incumbent president's party had increased its number of seats in both houses in an off-year election since Roosevelt's Democrats did it in 1934. In 2004, Bush was re-elected by 51% to 48%, and Republicans increased their margins in the Senate and the House; the popular vote for the House was 50.1% to 48%. Note that Republicans won these admittedly small majorities not in times of apparent peace and apparent prosperity, but in times when the nation was under attack and facing war, and when the economy was in recession or was in what was widely, though inaccurately, described as a jobless recovery. In other words, the Republicans were facing the voters in 2002 and 2004 in a more unfavorable posture than the Democrats had had in 1996, 1998, and 2000. The Democrats, in the more favorable posture, failed to win majorities. The Republicans, in a less favorable posture, succeeded in winning majorities.

In this space four years ago, we described America as "the 49% nation," evenly split between the two parties, with voters divided especially along lines of religious belief and observance. That division remains, but the numbers have changed. America is now, perhaps momentarily, or perhaps at the beginning of a long period, a 51% nation, a majority—a narrow majority—Republican nation. The evidence is there in Bush's re-election victory, in the Republicans' popular-vote majorities in the 2002 and 2004 elections to the House, in the 2004 National Election Pool exit poll that showed party identification at 37% Democratic and 37% Republican, compared with the 39%-to-35% Democratic advantage registered in the Voter News Service exit polls in 1996 and 2000. Clinton had the chance to forge a majority for his party. He failed. Bush had the chance to forge a majority for his party. He succeeded.

The Reshaped Electorate   The new shape of this enlarged electorate can be gauged by comparisons of numbers from the NEP exit poll in 2004 against the VNS exit-poll numbers in previous elections. In 2004, the adjusted NEP figures showed party identification at 37% Republican and 37% Democratic. This is in contrast to the Democrats' 39%-to-35% edge in 1996 and 2000 and their much larger party-identification advantages in the 1970s and 1980s. This was the first election in which Republicans achieved parity in party identification since the invention of random-sample polling in the 1930s. In other words, this was the most Republican electorate any American under age 80 has ever seen. It was also a conservative electorate; 34% identified themselves as conservative versus 21% who said they were liberal. That's a 5-percentage-point increase since 2000 in the number of self-identified conservatives.

Much of the campaigning—the candidates' appearances, the advertising, the organizational work—was concentrated in the battleground states. In October, they numbered 13 (Colorado, Florida, Iowa, Maine, Michigan, Minnesota, Nevada, New Hampshire, New Mexico, Ohio, Oregon, Pennsylvania, and Wisconsin), as the campaigns winnowed the list by striking off states that seemed hopelessly out of reach. Nine of these states have had lower-than-average population growth since 2000, and four—Michigan, Ohio, Pennsylvania, and Wisconsin—have had highly visible losses of manufacturing jobs. Overall turnout in these battleground states was up 20%, and both Bush and Kerry increased their party's total votes over 2000 by 22%. In fast-growing Florida, Bush turnout was up 36% and Democratic turnout up 23%. Bush's 537-vote edge in 2000 was transformed into a 381,000-vote advantage in 2004. In Ohio, which was plagued by manufacturing-job losses and Republicans' state tax increases, Bush faced less-favorable terrain. Democratic turnout went up 25%, and Republican turnout went up 22%—enough for Bush to hold a state that he had carried in 2000 by 166,000 votes; he won Ohio by 119,000 votes this time. In the battleground states generally, and particularly in Florida and Ohio, Kerry needed to do better to win, and didn't.

The reason that Kerry needed to do better to win is that the states that the Democrats conceded as safe for Bush had more electoral votes, 213, than the states the GOP conceded to Kerry, 179. And in both sets of states, the same pattern prevailed: The Bush vote rose more than the Democratic vote. Bush's popular vote increased 23% in the safe Bush states and 22% in the safe Kerry states. Kerry's vote increased 15% over Gore's in the safe Bush states and only 12% in the safe Kerry states. Bush carried the safe Bush states by 56% to 41% in 2000 and by 59% to 40% in 2004. Gore carried the safe Kerry states by 56% to 39% in 2000, and Kerry carried them by 56% to 43%. In sum: The 2004 results showed the red states getting redder and the blue states getting less blue.

All of this means that as long as something like the current contours of support prevail, Republicans start off a future presidential campaign with more electoral votes on their "safe" list than Democrats and have the potential to add more states to their target list. Of the safe Bush states, only one, Missouri, with 11 electoral votes, went to the president by a result as narrow as 53% to 46%. In contrast, three safe Kerry states, Delaware, New Jersey, and Washington, with a total of 29 electoral votes, were that close.

Religion is, as pointed out in previous *Almanacs*, the great divider, the demographic variable that correlates with voting behavior—and what matters is not only religious denomination, but also degree of observance. Pundits made much of Rove's claim that turnout of white evangelical Protestants in 2000 was 4 million less than expected and of his determination to get them to the polls in 2004. He probably did, but they don't seemed to have increased their percentage of the electorate much; they were 23% of voters in the 2004 NEP exit poll; the 2000 VNS exit poll didn't have the same category. Bush won 78% of their votes this time, and so they were indispensable to his victory; but so were others. Bush's percentage among all Protestants was up 3 percentage points, to 59%; among Catholics, up 5 points, to 52% (against the first Catholic nominee since 1960); among Jews, up 6 points, to 25%; among those with no religion, up 1 point, to 31%. Those who said they attended religious services weekly voted 61% for Bush, up just 1 point; those who said they never attended voted 36% for Bush, up 4 points. Protestant weekly churchgoers voted 70% for Bush, and Catholic weekly congregants, 56%; Protestants who attended less often voted 56% for Bush, and Catholics who did so voted 49% for Bush. So the reshaping of the electorate has slightly reduced the polarization along religious lines.

If there is a religion gap within the American electorate, there is also a marriage gap—a gap that is far wider than the oft-touted gender gap. Married people voted 57% to 42% for Bush; unmarried people voted 58% to 40% for Kerry. Those who said they were gay, lesbian, or bisexual voted 23% for Bush, just 2 percentage points less than in 2000, despite his support for a constitutional amendment banning same-sex marriage.

But if the Bush campaign has reshaped the electorate and made it more Republican, the changing racial or ethnic composition of the country will, over time, tend to make it more Democratic. That is the argument made by Ruy Teixeira and John Judis in their thoughtful, if optimistically titled book, *The Emerging Democratic Majority*. The results of the 2004 election among Hispanics, Asians, and African-Americans do not provide much support for their thesis. To be sure, the leaders of Hispanic and Asian groups, like the leaders of black groups, are overwhelmingly Democratic. But the Bush campaign evidently was able to establish connections—create new networks—to reach Hispanic and Asian voters.

Hispanics are potentially the fastest-growing segment of the electorate—13% of the total population, 17% of the population under age 18, between 6% and 8% of the 2004 electorate. Bush and Rove, from their days in Texas, have been targeting Hispanics for conversion. Democrats have hoped that Hispanics would become, like African-Americans, a solidly Democratic voting bloc, so that registration and turnout drives among Hispanics would produce a reliable harvest of Democratic votes.

There is some dispute as to how Hispanics voted in 2004. The NEP exit poll reported that 44% of Hispanics voted for Bush, up from 35% in the VNS exit poll in 2000. But NEP later revised its Texas figures (reducing Bush's percentage there from 59% to 49%, which was his share of the Hispanic vote when he ran for reelection as governor in 1998), which lowered the national Bush percentage to 42%; NBC recrunched the numbers and came up with a 40% figure. The *Los Angeles Times* exit poll showed Bush with 45% of Hispanics. Democratic psephologist Ruy Teixeira put Bush's Hispanic percentage at 39%. A poll by the Willie Velasquez Institute put Bush's Hispanic percentage at 33%. Pro-Bush 527 consultant Richard Nadler reviewed the NEP figures and came up with 38%. A post-election Annenberg survey put the number at 41%. Taking into account the various exit polls and surveys, it seems prudent to estimate that Bush won about 40% of the Hispanic votes in 2004, about a 5-percentage-point increase from 2000.

The first thing to be said about this is that a 40% vote from Hispanics is much closer to Bush's percentage among whites, 58%, than it is to the 11% that the NEP exit poll said Bush won among blacks. If Democrats turn out 100 black voters, they're likely to generate a popular vote margin of 78; if they turn out 100 Hispanics, the likely popular vote margin is only 20: a big difference. The second thing is that Bush clearly increased his percentage among Hispanics from 2000 to 2004, and almost certainly by something more than among the electorate as a whole. The third thing is that there is a wide variance among Hispanic voters across the country. This is what we should expect, for Hispanics are from a wide variety of countries—about 67% have roots in Mexico, but there are wide regional variations within that country of 106 million people—and they have encountered very different political environments where they have settled. Black Americans vote pretty much the same all over the country: the NEP exit polls show 80% or more of blacks voting for John Kerry in every state in which they are measured except Oklahoma and Washington. Hispanics are different: NEP exit polls show them voting 56% for Bush in Florida, 49% in Texas, 44% in New Mexico, 43% in Arizona, 43% in New Jersey, 39% in Nevada, 32% in California, 24% in New York and 23% in Illinois. The tentative conclusion here is that Hispanics tend to vote pretty much like their neighbors, more Republican in Republican environments like Texas and Florida, more Democratic in Democratic environments in Los Angeles, New York City and Chicago. Hispanics in central Los Angeles tend to vote much more Democratic than Hispanics in Santa Ana, in Orange County. West Texas counties which are one-third or one-quarter Hispanic keep voting 70% or more for George W. Bush as Hispanics enter the electorate. The NEP data show Hispanics voting 74% for Bush in Oklahoma and 80% for Kerry in Massachusetts; admittedly these are small sample sizes, but given the large percentages the numbers are unlikely to be too far off the mark—and are not all that much different from how their non-Hispanic neighbors were voting.

Something similar may be happening with the even more disparate Asian electorate. National NEP data show Asians voting 44% for Bush, up 3 percentage points from 2000. In the two states with the largest numbers of Asians, NEP shows them voting 48% for Bush in Hawaii—where Filipino- and Japanese-Americans have long shown a tendency to leave the Democratic Party to vote for incumbent Republican presidents—and 34% for Bush in California, not far off his percentages in the San Francisco Bay Area and Los Angeles County, where most of California's Asians live.

The picture is quite different for African-American voters. Nationally, NEP showed them voting only 11% for Bush, up just 2 percentage points from 2000, although it does seem likely that the Democratic Party won't be able to count on the same 90% level of support from blacks that it has come to expect since the election of 1964. In any case, blacks are not a growing segment of the electorate, as Hispanics and Asians are and will continue to be for some time. And Hispanics and Asians are not lining up with African-Americans as a single, overwhelmingly Democratic bloc of people of color. Something rather different is going on, something more like the political progress of the immigrants of the period from 1840 to 1924.

Taking Exception to American Exceptionalism   The 2004 campaign refuted two assumptions that just about every prognosticator and participant believed, that higher turnout would benefit the Democrats and that the Republicans would raise much more money than the Democrats. We have already seen that the Bush campaign's networking politics produced far more additional votes than the Democrats' command-and-control organizations. Now consider the fact that the Democrats raised more money. The Kerry campaign, the Democratic National Committee and the anti-Bush 527 organizations spent some $344 million on ads during the campaign, while the Bush campaign, the Republican National Committee and pro-Bush 527 organizations spent some $289 million. No one, including the Democrats themselves, expected that they would outraise the Republicans. No one expected that gushers of money would flow into Howard Dean's campaign over the Internet, and then, once he won the Iowa caucuses, to John Kerry's campaign. Few expected the funders of the anti-Bush 527s to spend as lavishly as they did.

What motivated those who gave so much money? Animosity toward George W. Bush. Few Dean contributors had even heard of him before they mouse-clicked their money his way; few Kerry contributors were suffused with affection for their man; the billionaires who funded the 527s made it plain that their goal was the defeat of George W. Bush and that they didn't care much about the Democratic nominee. Very many Democratic voters felt the same. The NEP poll showed that 59% of Bush voters cast their votes for him rather than against his opponent, while 70% of Kerry voters were voting more against Bush than for Kerry—and this seven months after Kerry clinched the Democratic nomination and had a chance to gain their affections. In this space two years ago the argument was advanced that both Bill Clinton and George W. Bush have personal characteristics which those on the opposite side of the cultural divide absolutely loathe, and that this has contributed to the polarization of the electorate and the vitriolic tone of the political debate. The vitriol heaped on Bush during the long campaign certainly provides support to that argument.

Not all Democratic voters shared this Bush hatred. Some large number simply preferred Kerry or would have preferred just about any other Democratic nominee on the issues. But the Bush haters managed to control the tone of the campaign. Howard Dean's full-throated opposition to the Iraq war and his frequently voiced contempt for Bush propelled this former Governor of Vermont with a moderate record on some issues to the number one position in the polls for the nomination by July 2003. His continued strength in the polls through the rest of the year surely prompted John Kerry and John Edwards to vote against the $87 billion supplemental appropriation for Iraq in November 2003. In debates all the Democratic candidates except Joseph Lieberman vied to see who could sound the loudest note of contempt for Bush. Bush bashing was so much a part of the air prominent Democrats breathed that they sought out and celebrated Michael Moore, the filmmaker who charged that Bush was a "deserter" and proclaimed on his website that "Americans are the stupidest people in the world." Democratic candidate Wesley Clark invited Moore to speak at his campaign rallies; a dozen Democratic senators and the Democratic National Chairman attended the Washington premiere of Moore's film *Fahrenheit 9/11*; at the Democratic National Convention delegates cheered Moore and he was seated in Jimmy Carter's presidential box on opening night.

During the primary season, hostility toward Bush seemed to energize volunteers and voters. The orange-stocking-capped Perfect Stormers thronging the streets of Des Moines and the crossroads of rural Iowa for Howard Dean seemed a veritable army, and Kerry and to a lesser extent Edwards drew large and enthusiastic crowds in Iowa and New Hampshire. But turnout in the Democratic caucuses and primaries did not set any records, with the single exception of New Hampshire, which turned out to be the only state that voted for George W. Bush in 2000 and against him in 2004. According to the Committee for the Study of the American Electorate, turnout in the Democratic primaries up through March 2, the day Kerry clinched the nomination, was the lowest in terms of percentage of eligible voters of any year since 1972, with the exceptions of 1996, when Bill Clinton ran unopposed, and 2000, when Al Gore clinched the nomination after Iowa and New Hampshire. Bush haters may have been eager to get out and vote. But other Democrats evidently weren't.

The division of Democrats between Bush haters and other Democrats reflected a more basic division. This was a division on American exceptionalism, the idea that this is a special and specially good country, an idea endorsed by political leaders of both parties for generations, by Theodore Roosevelt and Franklin Roosevelt, John Kennedy and Ronald Reagan. In early 2004 pollster Scott Rasmussen asked voters two questions that measure belief in American exceptionalism. Is this basically a fair and decent country, or not? Would the world be better off if more countries were more like America, or not? About two-thirds of all voters answered yes to both questions. About 80% of Bush voters answered yes to both. But Kerry voters were split down the middle, with about equal numbers answering yes and no. Republicans were united, American exceptionalists full of love or at least affection for the president. Democrats were divided, some seething with resentment of Bush and not inclined to think their country was a special place, others opposed to Bush but inclined to think this is a special and specially good country.

This posed problems for the Kerry campaign. In an election in which turnout was the key, it had to rally two very different groups of Democrats to the polls. Bush hatred seemed indispensable to winning the nomination, but it did not seem enough to win the general election. In this context, it is not surprising that, two weeks after clinching the nomination, John Kerry told an audience in Huntington, West Virginia, "I did actually vote for the $87 billion before I voted against it." Bill Clinton may have the skills to sound two different notes convincingly to two differing constituencies, but few other politicians do. John Kerry may have more than his share of the common politician's penchant to try to please people on all sides of an issue. But any Democratic nominee would have faced the same problem.

If the primary campaign tilted Democrats toward the Bush haters, so did their reliance in the general election campaign on the billionaire-funded 527 organizations. George Soros and most of the other big contributors were fervent, even feverish Bush haters, and the television spots their organizations put on the air seethed with Bush hatred. They may have made Bush haters feel good, but they seem to have been off-putting to voters in the middle of the electorate and they may have inspired Bush lovers to even greater support of their president. Kerry campaign strategists wanted more pro-Kerry spots on the air. But they evidently obeyed the law that prohibited coordination with the people running the 527 organizations; George Soros and Steve Bing, not Mary Beth Cahill or Robert Shrum, called the shots. Post-election surveys showed the anti-Bush 527 ads not to have been very persuasive and identified as the most persuasive 527 spots one run by the Swift Boat Veterans for Truth (on which more in the next section) and "Ashley's Story," a spot featuring Bush comforting an 11-year-old girl whose mother was murdered on September 11. The 527 organizations did not run spots defending Kerry on the Swift Boat Vets' charges; as Harold Ickes, who was running one of the 527 organizations, said the issue seemed "a matter so personal to Senator Kerry, so much within his knowledge. Who knew what the facts were?" The Democrats were hurt by having several command-and-control organizations that were barred from networking with each other.

Kerry strategists evidently understood that too much Bush hatred could hurt their cause: They sought to quiet the Bush haters at the Democratic National Convention. But the Bush haters' dominance of the long primary campaign and the Bush hatred sounded incessantly by the 527 organizations was unmistakable. The sheer mass of Bush haters in the Democratic coalition made it risky for Kerry to take up the theme of American exceptionalism, with all its appeal to the broad mass of the American people. Voters full of love or at least affection for George W. Bush streamed to the polls in larger numbers than voters full of contempt for him.

The deep split in the Democratic constituency, between Democrats who share the common belief in American exceptionalism and Bush haters who are made uncomfortable by any mention of it, could be an enduring problem for the Democratic party. George W. Bush will not be on the ballot again, but he is likely to be the central figure in the 2006 elections, and he could be a reference point for candidates for the Democratic nomination in 2008, as Ronald Reagan was in 1988.

Politics doesn't stand still. The 2004 campaign gave Republicans a head start in networking politics, but they will not have Bush as their leader in 2008. Democrats can learn from the Republican success and try to imitate their networking tactics. What is plain is that the 2004 campaign has taken us into a new political era, untrodden ground where the pathway is not clear and the effect of taking the next step cannot be known.

The Shape of the Political Future   Political numbers suggest the shape of the political future. Suggest, but not determine. The 2004 election results give us some very hard numbers: this was an election which was fiercely contested, in which both sides were highly motivated to win and employed their most skillful and experienced political operators in their attempts to do so, in which huge amounts of money were raised spent and in which record numbers of votes were cast. The results show narrow Republican victories. George W. Bush won the electoral vote 286-252 (counting for John Kerry the evidently carelessly cast Minnesota electoral vote for John Edwards) and the popular vote 51%-48%. Republicans hold a margin of 55-45 in the Senate and 232-203 in the House (counting in each house the Vermont Independent with the Democrats). But scratch just a little bit beneath the surface and you come up with numbers that suggest that the Republican position is a little stronger than the electoral and popular vote for president and the party's margins in the Senate and House would suggest.

Start with the Senate. George W. Bush carried 31 of the 50 states, which elect 62 senators. There are nine Republican senators elected from states carried by John Kerry and 16 Democratic senators from states carried by George W. Bush. Many of these were from states that were close in the presidential election. But when we look to see how many senators are from states where their presidential nominee got less than 47% of the vote—from where their party might be an electoral drag—we find that there are 11 Democrats and only three Republicans. That suggests there is more pressure from the ultimate source, the voters, on Democrats to vote with Bush and the Republicans than there is on Republicans to vote against Bush and with the Democrats.

Does the Senate have this Republican tilt because of its disproportionate representation of the smallest states and its vast under representation of the largest? Not exactly. The 11 largest states, those with 15 or more electoral votes, split only 6-5 for John Kerry. The 12 smallest states, those with 3 or 4 electoral votes, split 6-6. It is the 27 states in the middle, with between 5 and 13 electoral votes, that gave Bush his advantage; he carried 20 of them and Kerry carried only seven.

If Bush carried 62% of the constituencies that elect senators, he also carried 59% of the constituencies that elect congressmen. These are the results shown by Polidata, which calculated the presidential vote by congressional district for the *Almanac of American Politics* and the *Cook Political Report*. These numbers surprised even some political pros; even after the presidential results came in, White House chief strategist Karl Rove estimated that Bush carried 248 districts. But the Polidata numbers showed that Bush carried 255 districts, John Kerry only 180. In all, 41 House Democrats represent districts carried by Bush and 18 House Republicans represent districts carried by Kerry. The differences between the parties are even starker when we look at the number of members whose presidential nominee got less than 47% of the vote in their districts—in other words, in districts where the incumbent's party identification might start to be a political problem. There are only five Republicans from districts where Bush got less than 47%, but there are 29 Democrats from districts where Kerry got less than 47%. The House has 227 Republicans—above the 218 majority—from districts where Bush got 47% or more. It has only 173 Democrats from districts where Kerry got 47% or more. This helps to explain why on several important issues voted on in early 2005 House Republicans held together more of their members than did House Democrats, despite aggressive and skillful leadership by Minority Leader Nancy Pelosi and Minority Whip Steny Hoyer.

It must strike many readers as monstrously unfair that Bush carried 59% of the districts while winning only 51% of the popular vote. After all, these are districts created under the equal population standard, based on the results of the 2000 Census which in November 2004 was not very far out of date. And it is unfair, but not entirely so. As political scientists have shown, in almost any districting plan a popular vote winner will tend to carry a percentage of districts larger than his percentage of the vote. That is one reason Bush carried so many districts. Another reason is gerrymandering, at which Republicans were more successful in the 2000 Census cycle than Democrats. Republican gerrymanders in Florida, Pennsylvania and Michigan overbalanced Democratic gerrymanders in Georgia, North Carolina and Maryland. House Majority Leader Tom DeLay's 2003 Republican gerrymander in Texas added to the Republican advantage. But bipartisan incumbent protection plans also increased the number of Bush districts: if you go to some trouble to draw districts to protect incumbent Republicans in California, New York, Illinois, Ohio and New Jersey, as redistricters did (even as they went to some trouble to draw districts to protect incumbent Democrats), you will probably increase the number of Bush 2004 districts above what politically blind plans would produce.

But there is a third factor explaining the large number of Bush districts: the Voting Rights Act. Under the prevailing interpretation of this act, redistricters are obliged to maximize the number of districts with majorities or near-majorities of blacks and Hispanics. That means that redistricters bunch very large numbers of heavily Democratic precincts into a few districts and keep them out of adjacent districts where the political balance is much closer. The Voting Rights Act, thus interpreted, tends to result in the election of more blacks and Hispanics and fewer Democrats: little wonder that in the 1990 and 2000 cycles Republican legislators made common cause with black Democratic colleagues in some southern states on redistricting. The Polidata figures showed that John Kerry won 80% or more of the vote in 20 districts. The number of districts in which George W. Bush won 80% or more of the vote: zero. A lot of Kerry votes in those 22 districts could have been put to work electing Democrats in adjacent districts, but thanks to the Voting Rights Act they were not available for such duty.

The implications? In the long run, Republicans are well positioned to increase their numbers in both Senate and House. Most of the Democrats representing heavily Bush districts win because of personal popularity or moderate voting records. But when they retire, Republicans may well succeed them. In the short run, very few Republicans run great political risk by supporting Bush programs. But significantly more Democrats do by opposing them.

The Party of the Future   Let us slice the electorate another way. Since the days of Franklin D. Roosevelt, Democrats have depended heavily on winning majorities in the nation's largest counties. In Roosevelt's day those were almost all Northern, central city counties; today they are concentrated in the largest population states in all regions and include suburban as well as central city counties (the fifth largest county in the Census's 2004 estimates is Orange County, California). In 2004 John Kerry carried the 100 largest counties, as determined by 2004 Census estimates, by a popular vote margin of 6.5 million. Since his popular vote deficit nationally was 3.0 million, that means he lost the nation's 3,042 smallest counties by 9.4 million votes. Kerry's big margins here were obtained through excellent registration and turnout drives run by the Democratic party and by anti-Bush 527 organizations. At least in target states, they reached all their goals and in some cases exceeded them, and it was in central city counties and university town counties that most of their efforts were directed.

But they succeeded more in some places than others. If you stratify the 100 largest counties by percentage population growth between 2000 and 2004, you find very different pictures in fast-growing and slow-growing counties. In the 25 counties whose population increased by 7% or more—rapid population growth over four years—George W. Bush actually won a popular vote plurality of 617,000 votes. He carried 16 of these 25 counties. Next, look at those 27 counties whose population rose between 3.0% and 6.9%: John Kerry carried 17 of these 27 counties and won a popular vote plurality of 1,031,000. If you add these two groups together, you have something not far from an even balance among the 52 fastest-growing of the 100 largest counties. Bush carried 26 of these 52 counties and his average percentage per county was 49.9%. Kerry had a popular vote plurality of 413,000 in these counties, all and more of which came from Los Angeles County, which grew 4.4% and gave Kerry an 831,000-vote plurality. Without Los Angeles County, Bush would have had a 400,000-vote plurality in this group.

It was the large counties with slow growth or with population loss that Kerry racked up his big popular vote majorities. In the 30 counties that grew between .0% and 2.9%—rather slow population growth—Kerry won a popular vote plurality of 3,027,000 votes. He carried 27 of these counties, losing only DuPage County, Illinois, Tulsa County, Oklahoma, and Pinellas County, Florida. Finally in the 18 of the 100 largest counties which lost population between 2000 and 2004, Kerry carried 16 of them (losing only Jefferson County, Alabama, and Hamilton County, Ohio) and amassed a popular vote margin of 3,074,000 votes. Taking the slow-growth and the population-loss counties together, you find Kerry carrying 43 of these 48 counties and amassing a popular vote margin of 6,101,000.

The good news for the Democratic party was that it was able to produce such stunning pluralities from half the nation's 100 largest counties. The bad news is that these counties are losing population and that it is not clear that the Democrats' registration and turnout efforts can be substantially improved there. Will they be able to summon up the enthusiasm among workers and voters which was so apparent in the 2004 cycle when George W. Bush is no longer on the ballot? Will they be able to produce similar turnouts in the 2006 offyear cycle? Is the reservoir of potential voters running dry? Look at the list of counties whose populations declined by 2% or more between 2000 and 2004: Wayne County, Michigan; Baltimore City, Maryland; Allegheny County, Pennsylvania; Philadelphia County, Pennsylvania; Cuyahoga County, Ohio; Suffolk County, Massachusetts; Hamilton County, Ohio; San Francisco County, California (down 4.2%). Democrats did an excellent job increasing their turnout in each of these counties in 2004. Can they duplicate it in 2006 or 2008?

A different picture emerges when we look at the Census Bureau's list of the 100 fastest-growing counties between 2000 and 2004 (the list excludes counties under 10,000 because very small population increases can register as large percentages). These 100 counties accounted for 25% of the nation's total population increase in those years: 3.1 million of the total 12.2 million population increase. Only five of these counties, by the way, appear on the list of the 100 largest counties: Collin County, Texas; Will County, Illinois; Riverside County, California; Clark County, Nevada; and Gwinnett County, Georgia. If the 100 largest, and especially the 50 largest counties, are heavily Democratic, these 100 fastest-growing counties are overwhelmingly Republican: 97 of these 100 counties voted for George W. Bush. The only exceptions were Clark County, Nevada, where the Bush percentage of 47% was large enough to enable him to carry the state; and St. Lucie County, Florida and Hoke County, North Carolina, where Bush won 48% and 47% of the vote. The average Bush percentage in these 100 counties was 57.2% and he carried them by a popular vote margin of 1,815,000 votes—more than half his national popular vote margin.

This is not, of course, as large as the margin by which John Kerry carried the 100 largest counties. But it is a margin that is likely to increase over time, and can easily be increased even more by the kind of organizational effort mounted by the Bush campaign in 2004. These are for the most part exurban counties, the fast-growing edges of usually fast-growing metro areas, far from the established centers of culture and commerce, places that are building their own cultural and commercial and religious centers anew. The people heading out to these exurbs are heading out past Saks Fifth Avenue to Wal-Mart, out past left-leaning mainline Protestant churches to new megachurches with giant parking lots, out past the left-trending public schools of the inner suburbs to new schools which they can establish in their own image. Democratic analysts who have predicted an emerging majority for their party pass over the exurbs on the grounds there aren't all that many people there, and they have something of a point. But there are more than there used to be, and there will be even more tomorrow, and the 2004 election results show that they produce Republican votes far in excess of what any analysis of the past would suggest. These analysts might also object that many of these 100 fastest-growing counties are in states that are already safely Republican, notably Texas and Georgia. But Texas was once a Democratic state and Georgia as recently as 1992 voted for Bill Clinton. Exurban counties played a vital role in carrying Florida, Ohio, Virginia and North Carolina for George W. Bush and for Republican upsurges in Colorado and Minnesota in 2002. Continued rapid growth in the exurban Inland Empire and the Central Valley may even make California winnable for Republicans, as the San Francisco Bay area population stagnates and Latinos trend, as they did in 2004, Republican.

It is perhaps too much to say that the 2004 election results in the 100 largest counties and in the 100 fastest-growing counties mean that the Democrats are the party of the past and the

Republicans the party of the future. But they do suggest that the Republicans will have an easier time and the Democrats a harder time in increasing their turnout over the levels which, in 2004, were impressive on both sides but which also produced a Republican victory.

Old Media and New Media   If American politics doesn't stand still, neither do the media through which Americans gain their understanding of politics and government. In the last quarter-century, with a quantum leap in the 2004 campaign, American political media moved from centralization to decentralization. In 1980 most Americans got most of their information about politics and government from the three broadcast TV networks, ABC, CBS and NBC. Those networks' news organizations in turn took their guidance in very large part from two newspapers: *The New York Times* and *The Washington Post*. For the purposes of this essay, call them Old Media. Of course other media outlets were of some importance—metropolitan area newspapers, radio networks, news magazines. But the days when regional newspapers had great political influence, like the *Chicago Tribune* in the 1930s and 1940s, were gone. *Time* and *Life* magazines, once the advocates of a liberal Republicanism, had taken on other coloration. But the three broadcast networks and the *Times* and the *Post* had an influence that far outweighed them.

The people running and working for these news organizations believed they had a responsibility to present the news accurately and fairly and, for the most part, worked hard to do so. But it was also a fact that their personnel was overwhelmingly Democratic and liberal: surveys show that in 1992, 89% of the people in leading Washington media voted for Bill Clinton. Inevitably this has some effect on the news they present. As *The Washington Post's* David Broder explained in his book *Behind the Front Page*, journalists look for stories where they expect to find them. They decide what is news on the basis of how they think the world works. Democrats and Republicans, liberals and conservatives, moderates and those farther off to the left or the right—not always, not on every issue, but at least sometimes, on some issues—differ on where they expect to find news and how they think the world works. They will have these differences even when they are trying hard to be fair and objective. One broadcast network news executive, asked whether the fact that 90% of his people were Democrats affected their work product, replied that it did not: they had professional standards, they were capable of objectivity. Then, asked whether that meant that the work product would be identical if 90% of his people were Republicans, he said, "No. Then it would be biased."

In 1980 Old Media did not have much competition. You could have gotten a pretty good idea of what Americans were learning about the fall presidential campaigns if you had been able to sit each day in five rooms: the two rooms where the Democratic and Republican candidates' campaign staffs held their morning meetings and determined their message of the days and the three rooms, all of them on the West Side of Manhattan, where the three broadcast networks' producers and anchors met to determine the lineup and story lines of their evening newscasts. Cable news had only started to exist: CNN presented its first news program on June 1, 1980; it was available to just 1.7 million households. Talk radio did not exist. The FCC's fairness doctrine which required stations to give equal time to different points of view was not repealed until 1987. The Internet was a project being developed by a Pentagon agency, DARPA, with some help from tech-minded members of Congress including the congressman from the 4th District of Tennessee, Al Gore.

Flash forward to 2004. Old Media continues to exist, and continues to be staffed by people about 90% of whom are Democrats. The best description of the effects of that was made by Mark Halperin in ABC News's *The Note*, a daily Internet posting, on February 10, 2004. "Like every other institution, the Washington and political press corps operate with a good number of biases and predilections. They include, but are not limited to, a near-universal shared sense that liberal political positions on social issues like gun control, homosexuality, abortion, and religion are the default, while more conservative positions are 'conservative positions.' They include a belief that government is a mechanism to solve the nation's problems; that more taxes on corporations and the wealthy are good ways to cut the deficit and raise money for social spending and don't have a negative affect on economic growth; and that emotional examples of suffering (provided by unions or consumer groups) are good ways to illustrate economic statistic stories. . . . The press, by and large, does not accept President Bush's justifications for the Iraq war—in any of its [weapons of mass destruction], imminent threat, or evil-doer formulations. It does not understand how educated, sensible people could possibly be wary of multilateral institutions or friendly, sophisticated European allies. It does not accept the proposition that the Bush tax cuts helped the economy by stimulating summer spending. It remains fixated on the unemployment rate. It believes President Bush is 'walking a fine line' with regards to the gay marriage issue, choosing between 'tolerance' and his 'right-wing base.' It still has a hard time understanding how, despite the drumbeat of conservative grass-top complaints about overspending and deficits, President Bush's base remains extremely and loyally devoted to him—and it looks for every opportunity to find cracks in that base. . . . The worldview of the dominant media can be seen in every frame of video and every print word choice that is currently being produced about the presidential race."

This description of Old Media will ring true to many readers and false to many others: it is, however, the view of as sophisticated and knowledgeable an observer of Old Media as any and, coming from an Old Media source, an admission against interest. Here there is disagreement only with the final sentence. For in 2004 the worldview of dominant media was not reflected in every video and every print word choice and every radio soundbite that was produced about the presidential race. Old Media had competition, from New Media. The cable news audience had vastly expanded in the preceding quarter-century, and CNN had competition from MSNBC and Fox News Channel, which in the 2004 cycle had more viewers than CNN and MSNBC put together. Talk radio had become a vibrant source of political information and argumentation. And the blogosphere—weblogs sent out over the Internet—provided an additional source of information and networking.

New Media personnel has leaned toward the right of the political spectrum. Not entirely and not uniformly; but enough to provide a counterweight to Old Media. CNN and MSNBC personnel may have a world view little different from that of the three broadcast networks, but Fox News Channel employs a much higher percentage of Republicans than the broadcast networks, yet a percentage that is almost certainly lower than that of Democrats there (and Fox's polling firm is headed by a Democrat). Conservative talk radio hosts have a far larger audience than liberals, large enough that liberals felt obliged to start Air America in 2004 as a counterweight.

The blogosphere presents a more complicated picture. Two of the most viewed websites are run by left Democrats, dailykos.com, run by Democratic consultant Markos Moulitsas, and atrios.blogspot.com, run by economist Duncan Black. They provided a forum where Democrats and opponents of the Iraq war could exchange ideas, hone arguments and establish contact with Democratic campaigns. In the 2004 campaign cycle, Howard Dean's campaign made effective use of the Internet, raising money and attracting volunteers rapidly and effectively. The left blogosphere and the Dean campaign shaped the tone and content of the debate in the contest for the Democratic presidential nomination and in John Kerry's campaign after he clinched the Democratic nomination in March 2004. Hundreds of thousands, perhaps more than 1 million, people were able to make their voices heard and their opinions count, thanks to the Internet.

The right blogosphere was different. The focus of its hatred was not so much on Democrats or John Kerry as it was Old Media. Instapundit.com, run by University of Tennessee law professor Glenn Reynolds, supported George W. Bush on the Iraq war and gun control, but opposed his views on abortion, same-sex marriage and embryonic stem-cell research. The proprietors of two websites followed avidly by conservatives, Andrew Sullivan of andrewsullivan.com and Mickey Kaus of kausfiles.com, endorsed John Kerry, although with some disdain. The three bloggers who put out powerlineblog.com and Hugh Hewitt of hughhewitt.com supported Bush pretty much down the line, but added their own emphases and concentrated much of their fire on Old Media.

The interplay of Old Media and New Media in the 2004 can be seen in how they handled two issues: the Swift Boat Veterans for Truth's charges about John Kerry's service in Vietnam and activities thereafter, and Dan Rather's report about George W. Bush's service in the Texas Air National Guard.

Kerry had spoken often of his military record in the primary season and after he clinched the Democratic nomination; he was accompanied by veterans who had served on the same boat with him, most of whom praised his service and supported his campaign. The Swiftvets (as the organization refers to itself on its website) held its first news conference in May, at which veterans who had served in the larger squadron criticized Kerry's service and the statements he made to the Senate Foreign Relations Committee in 1971; eventually most of the veterans in the squadron and one veteran in Kerry's boat endorsed the Swiftvets' charges. They got little or no coverage in Old Media. They received more notice in New Media, on conservative websites and on talk radio programs. The Kerry campaign decided not to respond and made his military service the central theme of the Democratic National Convention in late July. Shortly afterward, the Swiftvets announced their first television ads criticizing Kerry. The ads were covered by Fox News and got wide circulation in New Media. Many of the differences between the Swiftvets and the veterans supporting Kerry involved differing recollection of events that had occurred 36 years before in the heat of combat, differences that would certainly be hard and probably be impossible for any non-observer to resolve. But that was not entirely true. Kerry had claimed repeatedly to have spent Christmas or Christmas Eve 1968 on a secret mission to Cambodia; in an article in the *Boston Herald* in 1979, on the Senate floor in 1986, to the Associated Press in 1992. The Swiftvets said he was never in Cambodia. On August 11 Kerry spokesman Michael Meehan abandoned the claim that Kerry had been in Cambodia in Christmas 1968; he said he had been on missions there in 1969. No corroborative evidence of this has appeared, even from Kerry's boatmates who supported him; one said they had been near the Cambodian border.

On August 19 Kerry addressed the charges against him, and Old Media began covering the Swiftvets' charges, though not as exhaustively as many in New Media were. After the election, Kerry campaign strategists said that the Swiftvets charges did hurt him. It's possible they might have scripted the Democratic National Convention, Kerry's moment of maximum exposure, differently if they had thought that these charges would become a major issue. Whether you credit the Swiftvets' charges or not, this is an issue which had some impact on the campaign and which would not have emerged if Old Media still had a monopoly.

On September 8, Dan Rather aired charges on CBS's *60 Minutes II* that Bush had failed to perform his duties in the Texas Air National Guard. The charges were based largely on documents dated 1972 that CBS put on its website. Before midnight Atlanta lawyer Harold McDougald posted on freerepublic.com, a conservative website, a note pointing out that the documents were in proportionately shaped fonts, not in general use in 1972. "I am saying these documents are forgeries, run through a copier for 15 generations to make them look old. This should be pursued aggressively." It was. At 6:30 a.m. on September 9 in St. Paul, Minnesota, Scott Johnson reprinted that posting under the heading "The Sixty-First Minute" on powerlineblog.com and asked readers for information. It came pouring in, from document experts, typography experts and people who had typed National Guard documents in 1972. Almost all of it discredited the documents. Later that morning blogger Charles Johnson in California duplicated the CBS documents using Microsoft Word with default settings and then electronically overlaid this copy with the CBS document on littlegreenfootballs.com; they matched exactly. Bill Gates founded Microsoft in 1975. It took CBS 11 more days before it admitted it couldn't authenticate the documents, and in fact never had. But its story, which obviously had the potential to damage Bush, was undermined in less than 24 hours. CBS asked outsiders to investigate the incident, and Dan Rather retired as anchor of CBS Evening News in March 2005, a year earlier than he had planned. A quarter-century before, perhaps even as recently as 2000, the documents would have been widely accepted as genuine and probably never challenged: the Old Media monopoly at work. But in 2004 they were quickly discredited by New Media and it was CBS, not Bush, which had its reputation damaged.

The changes in the media are apparent in a Pew Research Center survey conducted in 2004; the poll showed a 6% increase between 2002 and 2004 in cable news consumption and a 4% increase for Internet news, but only a 2% increase for nightly network news over the same period. A November post-election survey by Pew found that use of the Internet as a primary source of news about presidential candidates and the campaign had grown 10% since 2000—twice as fast as television as a whole. Mistrust of the media was much higher in 2004 than in 2000, with Republicans much more likely to mistrust Old Media outlets than Democrats. The increasing importance of New Media and the partial eclipse of Old Media in the 2004 campaign cycle seems, on balance to have helped George W. Bush and the Republicans. The left blogosphere pushed Democrats toward a vitriolic critique of Bush, which did not result in victory, while the right blogosphere sowed mistrust of Old Media, which undermined its negative coverage of Bush. But there is no guarantee that the interplay between Old Media and New Media will help one side or the other in future elections. What is clear is this: You might have been able to cover the 1980 presidential campaign in five rooms. But you could not cover the 2004 presidential campaign in 100 rooms. The political media have moved from centralized command-and-control toward a more decentralized networking model. The consequences for the future are unclear.

President

George W. Bush (R)

Elected 2000, term expires Jan. 2009, 2d term; b. July 6, 1946, New Haven, CT; home, Crawford, TX; Yale U., B.A. 1968, Harvard U., M.B.A. 1975; Methodist; married (Laura).

Military Career: TX Air Natl. Guard, 1968–73.

Elected Office: TX Gov., 1994–2000.

Professional Career: Founder & CEO, Bush Exploration Oil & Gas Co., 1975–87; Sr. Advisor, Bush Presidential Camp., 1988; Managing Gen. Partner, Texas Rangers baseball org., 1989–98.

Vice President

Richard (Dick) B. Cheney (R)

Elected 2000, term expires Jan. 2009, 2d term; b. Jan. 30, 1941, Lincoln, NE; home, Casper, WY; U. of WY, B.A. 1965, M.A. 1966; United Methodist; married (Lynne).

Elected Office: U.S. House of Reps., 1978–89

Professional Career: Spec. Asst. to the Dir. of OEO, 1969–70; White House Staff Asst., 1971; Asst. Dir., Cost of Living Cncl., 1971–73; V.P., Bradley, Woods & Co., 1973–74; Dep. Asst. to Pres. Gerald Ford, 1974–75; White House Chief of Staff, 1975–77; U.S. Secy. of Defense, 1989–93; Sr. Fellow, American Enterprise Inst., 1993–95; Chmn. & CEO, Halliburton Co., 1993–2000.

The People		Race/Ethnic Origin			Military veterans: 26,403,703 (12.6%)	
Pop. 2004 (est):	293,655,404	194,552,774	69.1%	White	WWII: 20.5%	Korea: 13.6%
Pop. 2000:	281,421,906	33,947,837	12.1%	Black	Vietnam: 31.7%	Gulf War: 10.2%
Pop. 1990:	248,709,873	10,123,169	3.6%	Asian	**Most populous cities (2003):**	
Change 1990–2000:	Up 13.2%	2,068,883	0.7%	Native Am.	1. New York	8,085,742
% of U.S. total:	100.0%	353,509	0.1%	Hawaiian	2. Los Angeles	3,819,951
Area size:	3,794,083 sq. mi.	4,602,146	1.6%	Two+ races	3. Chicago	2,869,121
State Native:	60.0%	467,770	0.2%	Other	4. Houston	2,009,690
Non-citizen:	6.6%	35,305,818	12.5%	Hisp. Origin	5. Philadelphia	1,479,339
Language		**Ancestry**				
English: 81.1%	Spanish: 10.2%	German: 12.0%		Irish: 8.5%	Urban population: 79.0%	
Other Eur.: 5.2%		English: 6.8%		USA: 5.7%	Rural population: 21.0%	
		Italian: 4.4%				

Education		Work Sector		Home Value	
H.S. Grad:	80.4%	Private: 78.5%	Govt: 14.6%	<50k: 14.9%	50-100k: 29.6%
College Grad:	24.4%	Self: 6.6%	Family: 0.3%	100-200k: 35.2%	200-300k: 11.2%
Industry		Unemployment: 5.7%		300-500k: 6.1%	>500k: 2.9%
Agri: 1.9%	Con: 6.8%	**Household Income**		Median: $111,800	
Fin: 6.9%	Info: 3.1%	<15k: 15.8%	15-35k: 25.6%		
Mfg: 19.3%	Prof: 29.2%	35-50k: 16.5%	50-100k: 29.7%		
Public: 4.8%	Trade: 15.3%	100-150k: 7.7%	>150k: 4.6%		
Other: 12.7%		Median: $41,994			
Occupation		Poverty status: 12.4%			
Blue collar: 24.1%	White collar: 60.3%				
Gray collar: 15.6%					

2004 Presidential Vote

George W. Bush (R) 62,040,606   (50.7%)
John Kerry (D) 59,028,109   (48.3%)
Other 1,217,895   (1.0%)

2000 Presidential Vote

George W. Bush (R) 50,456,169   (47.8%)
Al Gore (D) 50,996,116   (48.4%)
Ralph Nader (Green) 2,831,066   (2.7%)

★ ALABAMA ★

Beginnings matter, and Alabama had its beginnings in two surges of settlement. One was from the north, when Jacksonian farmers from Tennessee surged into the red clay hills from which their hero, Andrew Jackson, expelled the Creek and other Indians. You can see their early Greek Revival buildings in historic Huntsville, surrounded by the boom town that has grown up around the Marshall Space Center, but Jacksonian Alabama is anything but cool and classical: the settlers brought the fighting faith of the Scots-Irish, a hot-spirited willingness to fight to the death against any perceived insult or threat. The other surge of settlement into Alabama came a few years later, as entrepreneurial Southern planters brought slaves in to pick cotton in the fertile Black Belt (so named for its soil) east and west of Montgomery in the middle of the state. The interplay between the offspring of these two streams of settlers has been the stuff of Alabama politics ever since.

The Jacksonians' fighting spirit led them to join the planters and support secession; the first Confederate Congress convened and Jefferson Davis took the oath of office as president of the Confederacy in the Greek Revival Alabama Capitol in February 1861. After the Civil War, Alabama like other southern states became solidly Democratic, but with an angry populist accent. Birmingham, with its solid-iron Red Mountain, became the South's first steel producer in the 1880s. Alabama politics in the first half of the 20th century was a struggle between angry populists who favored New Deal government spending to help the little guy—Senator and Supreme Court Justice Hugo Black, Senators Lister Hill and John Sparkman, Governor "Kissin' Jim" Folsom—and the local economic potentates they called the "Big Mules" and the plantation owners of the Black Belt.

Then Alabama became one of the birthplaces of the civil rights movement. Down the hill from the Capitol is the Dexter Avenue Baptist Church, where in December 1956 the 27-year-old Martin Luther King Jr. led the boycott that began when Montgomery seamstress Rosa Parks refused to move to the back of the bus. A hundred miles north in Birmingham, while King was held in jail, Birmingham Police Commissioner Bull Connor (then Alabama's Democratic National Committeeman) ordered police dogs and fire hoses to be turned on peaceful demonstrators in May 1963. Four months later four girls were killed when a bomb exploded in Birmingham's 16th Street Baptist Church (bombers were convicted in 1977, 2001 and 2002). In March 1965 a civil rights marcher was murdered in Montgomery two weeks after police beat dozens at Selma's Pettus Bridge; another activist was shot and killed in Lowndes County that August. These events had reverberations far beyond Alabama: in June 1963 John Kennedy endorsed what would become the Civil Rights Act of 1964, and in March 1965 Congress passed the Voting Rights Act. But, like the state's Confederate heritage, they are no longer controversial but are commemorated and promoted as tourist attractions by the state, in Maya Lin's circular Civil Rights Memorial in Montgomery, the Civil Rights Institute on 16th Street in Birmingham, the Pettus Bridge in Selma and the Dexter Avenue in Montgomery.

While Alabamians like Parks were leading the nation toward civil rights, Alabama's leading politician of the time, George Wallace, was leading the other way. Elected governor in 1962, he made national news in June 1963 by standing in a schoolhouse door and pretending to defy a federal court desegregation order. In 1964 Wallace ran in northern Democratic presidential primaries against Lyndon Johnson; in 1968 he ran for president as a third-party candidate and won 13.5% of the vote. He ran in the Democratic primaries again in 1972 and was partially paralyzed by a gunshot wound while campaigning in May; he took delegates to the national convention, and did not lose his force as a national politician until he lost to Jimmy Carter in the March 1976 Florida primary. But he remained the key figure in Alabama for three decades, running his first wife to succeed him in 1966 (she died in mid-term), regaining the governorship again in 1970 and (when second terms were allowed) in 1974, then running and winning one last time in 1982. He spent his last sad years apologizing for his acts, meeting with the student he tried to block in the schoolhouse door, and proclaiming, "The South has changed, and for the better," until his death in September 1998.

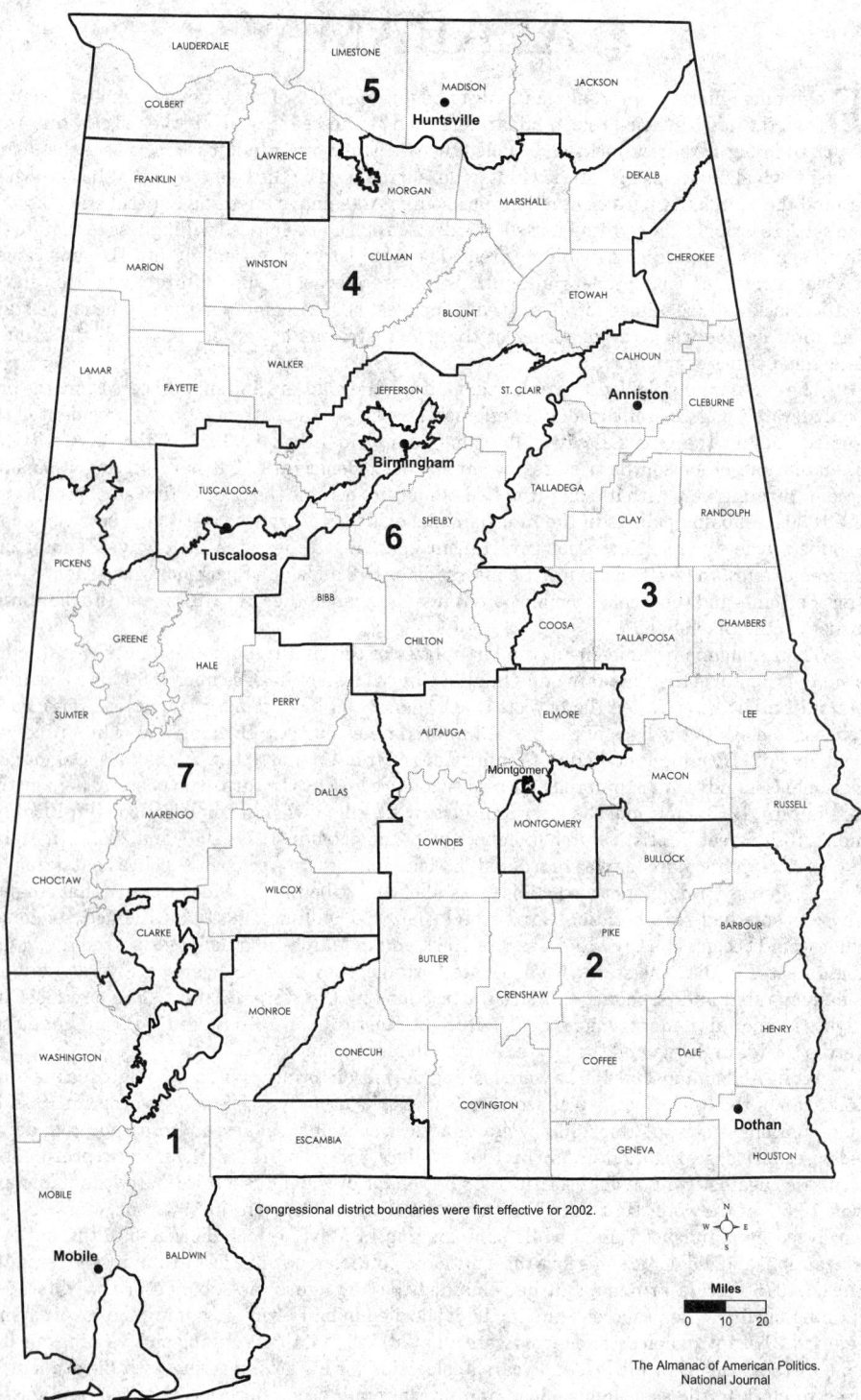

Congressional district boundaries were first effective for 2002.

Miles
0   10   20

The Almanac of American Politics.
National Journal

In the Wallace years, Alabama lost important ground. While Atlanta was peacefully deseg-regating and beginning three decades of vibrant white-collar growth, Birmingham was violently resisting the civil rights movement, only to see the shrinkage of its once substantial blue-collar base—the steel industry—and an outflow of talented people of all races. The state's economy, regarded as progressive when manufacturing was the leading edge of growth, seemed backward at the end of the Wallace era.

Alabama's economy enjoyed no Atlanta-like boom in the Wallace years, and politically Wallace delayed for a generation the rise of the Republicans in Alabama and the non-metropolitan South. But Alabama's economy has moved ahead recently, most notably with the Mercedes plant, now under expansion, in Tuscaloosa and the new Honda plant in Talladega. And since Wallace's last election, Alabama has developed a two-party politics and, in presidential elections, has completed its transformation from one of the nation's most Democratic states to one of its most Republican. But state politics remains competitive. On one side of this political conflict are the Democrats: Their voting base is Alabama's large black minority and the institu-tional base is the state's well organized teachers' unions and trial lawyers. On the other side are the Republicans: Their voting base is white evangelical Protestants and their institutional base is small businessmen and the affluent young families filling the fast-growing suburban areas outside Birmingham, Montgomery, Mobile and Huntsville—groups that are fractious and not well organized. The Republicans have tended to prevail, by large margins in presidential and Senate and state Supreme Court elections and by narrow margins in races for governor and statewide downballot offices. But the Democrats have fought back hard, holding onto the legislature and, since Wallace left office, bringing ethics charges against one Republican gover-nor which led to his conviction and removal from office (Guy Hunt in 1993), defeating another (Fob James in 1998) and twice contesting election results with dubious legal arguments (the Democratic runoff in 1986 and the general election in 2002).

Slowly, a new Alabama is growing along the state's Interstate highways—Alabama ranks number one in the percentage of workers who drive to work—and in the suburban sprawl beyond Birmingham, Montgomery, Mobile and Huntsville. The exceedingly close 2002 race for governor between Democrat Don Siegelman and Republican Bob Riley showed the close division between two Alabamas. Siegelman carried the central cities, the Black Belt and many of the poor-white rural counties in the north. This was the coalition of blacks and poor whites the political scientist V.O. Key, Jr., longed for in his mid-century classic *Southern Politics*. But it was not enough to win. Riley carried prospering small counties along the Interstates near the Georgia and Florida borders and the area around the space/high-tech center of Huntsville. By an even greater margin, he carried the fast-growing suburban counties. Eight Alabama counties grew by more than 25% in the 1990s, and Riley carried seven of them 62%–35%, with a 59,000-vote margin, although they cast only 14% of total votes. The other 59 counties went 51%–47% for Siegelman, enough for a 55,000-vote margin, but not quite enough to win.

Since Riley's election, Alabama politics has been as turbulent as ever. One controversy raged over Chief Justice Roy Moore's installation in July 2001 of a huge monument with the Ten Commandments in the Supreme Court building. In 2002 a federal judge ruled that unconstitu-tional, and an appeals court affirmed the judgment and ordered him to remove the statue in 2003. Moore refused; the other eight justices complied; the Alabama Court of the Judiciary removed Moore in November 2003 and the Supreme Court declined to hear his appeal in 2004. Another controversy came when Bob Riley put on the ballot a referendum on a $1.2 billion tax increase. Riley argued that his changes would reduce taxes on low-income people and that such a move was in line with Christian morality. Alabama's Jacksonians did not buy it: the proposition was defeated 67%–33%, and won by unimpressive margins even in black-majority counties and the state capital. It won only 14% in Winston County, an independent-minded hill county which seceded from secessionist Alabama during the Civil War. There was more controversy in Novem-ber 2004, when it turned out that voters rejected by a 50.1%–49.9% margin Amendment 2 that would have overturned both the state's 1901 provision requiring racial segregation in schools and a 1950s provision saying there was "no right" to public schools. The state Christian Coalition and economic conservatives argued that removing the latter provision could spark a lawsuit, like those brought successfully in many states, requiring a new school aid formula and higher taxes. So the result should not be taken as a yearning for a return to segregated schools; Amendment 2's sponsor said he might sponsor another amendment repealing only the 1901 provision.

The People		Race/Ethnic Origin			Military veterans: 447,397 (13.5%)	
Pop. 2004 (est):	4,530,182	3,125,819	70.3%	White	WWII: 17.5%	Korea: 14.0%
Pop. 2000:	4,447,100	1,150,076	25.9%	Black	Vietnam: 32.9%	Gulf War: 11.6%
Pop. 1990:	4,040,587	30,989	0.7%	Asian	**Most populous cities (2003):**	
Change 1990–2000:	Up 10.1%	21,618	0.5%	Native Am.	1. Birmingham	236,620
% of U.S. total:	1.6%	1,059	0.0%	Hawaiian	2. Montgomery	200,123
Pop. rank:	23d of 50	39,086	0.9%	Two+ races	3. Mobile	193,464
Area size:	52,419 sq. mi.	2,623	0.1%	Other	4. Huntsville	164,237
State Native:	73.4%	75,830	1.7%	Hisp. Origin	5. Tuscaloosa	79,294
Non-citizen:	1.2%	**Ancestry**				
Language		USA: 14.8%		English: 6.8%	Urban population: 55.4%	
English: 94.2%	Spanish: 3.1%	Irish: 6.7%		German: 5.0%	Rural population: 44.6%	
Other Eur.: 1.8%		Scotch-Irish: 1.7%				

Education		Work Sector		Legislature	
H.S. Grad:	75.3%	Private: 77.9%	Govt: 15.5%	Senate	25 D 10 R
College Grad:	19.0%	Self: 6.2%	Family: 0.3%	House	63 D 42 R
Industry		Unemployment: 6.2%		Legislative Term Limits: No	
Agri: 1.9%	Con: 7.6%	**Household Income**		**Registered Voters**	
Fin: 5.8%	Info: 2.2%	<15k: 22.5%	15-35k: 28.4%	No party registration	
Mfg: 23.7%	Prof: 26.4%	35-50k: 16.5%	50-100k: 24.9%		
Public: 5.2%	Trade: 15.8%	100-150k: 4.9%	>150k: 2.7%		
Other: 11.4%		Median: $34,135			
Occupation		Poverty status: 16.1%			
Blue collar: 30.3%	White collar: 55.4%	**Home Value**			
Gray collar: 14.3%		<50k: 28.4%	50-100k: 38.3%	100-200k: 24.7%	200-300k: 5.2%
		300-500k: 2.3%	>500k: 1.1%	Median: $76,700	

Presidential politics   George W. Bush carried Alabama by 56%–42% in 2000 and 62%–37% in 2004. Bush lost all but one of the black-majority counties in the Black Belt and, narrowly, two nearby counties; in the exurban counties outside Birmingham, Montgomery and Mobile, he won 76% to 81% of the vote. Alabama whites voted 80%–19% for George W. Bush and Alabama blacks voted 91%–6% for John Kerry. So foreordained was the Alabama result that neither candidate set foot in the state except for Bush's visit to see Hurricane Ivan damage; the Bush campaign dispatched volunteers to Florida for the last week.

Alabama's presidential primary is in June—too late to count for much. An attempt to change the date failed in 1999.

2004 Presidential Vote
Bush (R) 1,176,394   (62%)
Kerry (D)...................... 693,933   (37%)
Nader (I) 6,701   (0%)
Other.............................. 6,387   (0%)

2004 Democratic Presidential Primary
Kerry (D)...................... 164,021   (75%)
Uncommitted (D) 38,223   (17%)
Kucinich (D) 9,076   (4%)
Other.............................. 7,254   (3%)

2000 Presidential Vote
Bush (R) 941,173   (56%)
Gore (D) 692,611   (42%)
Nader (Green) 18,323   (1%)
Other.............................. 14,165   (1%)

Congressional districting   The Democrats in control of redistricting in Alabama in 2002 did a pretty good job of helping their party in drawing the boundaries of the state's seven congressional districts—but not good enough to add to the two seats they have held since 1994. They marginally strengthened Democrat Bud Cramer in the 5th District and reduced the black percentage in the majority-black 7th District. The biggest change was to the 3d District, where incumbent Republican Bob Riley was leaving to

109th Congress Lineup
5 R   2 D

108th Congress Lineup
5 R   2 D

run for governor. The 3d was made significantly more Democratic by the subtraction of fast-growing St. Clair County east of Birmingham and the addition of part of Montgomery County, including the area around the Capitol. The black percentage was raised from 25% to 32%, the second highest in the state. But Republican Mike Rogers still won narrowly in the 2002 open seat contest and easily held the seat in 2004.

Governor

Bob Riley (R)

Elected 2002, term expires Jan. 2007, 1st term; b. Oct. 3, 1944, Ashland; home, Ashland; U. of AL, B.A. 1965; Baptist; married (Patsy).

Elected Office: Ashland City Cncl., 1972–76; U.S. House of Reps., 1996–2002.

Professional Career: Owner, egg & poultry co.; Rancher; Owner, Midway Transit, 1965–present.

Office: Alabama State Capitol, 600 Dexter Ave., Montgomery, 36130, 334-242-7100; Fax: 334-353-0004; Web site: www.governor.state.al.us.

Election Results

2002 general	Bob Riley (R)	672,225	(49%)
	Don Siegelman (D)	669,105	(49%)
	Other	25,273	(2%)
2002 primary	Bob Riley (R)	262,851	(74%)
	Steve Windom (R)	63,775	(18%)
	Tim James (R)	30,871	(9%)
1998 general	Don Siegelman (D)	760,155	(58%)
	Fob James (R)	554,746	(42%)

Bob Riley, elected governor of Alabama by a 3,120-vote margin in 2002, grew up in Clay County, off the beaten track east of Birmingham, where his family had lived for seven generations. Riley attended the University of Alabama during its desegregation in 1963 and after graduation returned home with a business degree; he and his brother started selling eggs door-to-door. Eventually, that became a large egg and poultry company; he also ran a grocery store, owned an airport, a pharmacy and sold real estate. He ended up with a car dealership (Midway Ford and Chrysler), a trucking company (Midway Transit), half a shopping center and a cattle farm, and served on the Ashland city council. In 1996, when the 3d District's Democratic congressman ran unsuccessfully for the Senate, Riley ran for the House. He started off little known outside Clay County, but he was a strong and energetic campaigner, a supporter of school prayer, term limits, tax cuts and a balanced budget amendment and an opponent of abortion, gun control and racial quotas. Riley won 50%–47%—a key victory in keeping the House Republican that year.

In the House, Riley had a solidly conservative voting record; he said he came to Washington intending to be bipartisan, but his first three months made him "become the most partisan person on Capitol Hill." He fought to save jobs at the Anniston Army Depot and got a $4 billion armored vehicle repair project and an $800 million incinerator for destruction of military gases. Riley had serious competition in 1998 from former Democratic state Chairman Joe Turnham, but he spent $845,000 of his own money and won 58%–42%. Unopposed in 2000, he ran for governor in 2002.

The incumbent was Don Siegelman, a Democrat elected by 58%–42% in 1998 over embattled incumbent Republican Fob James. Siegelman's main policy was a lottery to fund education, but voters later rejected the lottery 54%–46% in an October 1999 referendum. "I have no Plan B," Siegelman said, and state spending on education was cut, with universities and K-12 lobbies fighting over shares of a shrinking pie. Siegelman had success in attracting automakers

Honda and Hyundai to the state and convinced voters to approve a ballot proposition for $425 million in bonds to fund road and bridge building. But he continued to have trouble on education funding. A special session in mid-2001 rejected his entire proposal; another in December 2001 passed $140 million in business and telephone taxes. Siegelman was also troubled by scandal. In September 1999, he was embarrassed when two young aides were revealed to have been getting tickets fixed. A 1998 campaign contributor and adviser pleaded guilty in October 2001 to Medicaid fraud. In 2002, it was revealed that Siegelman's personal finances were under investigation by a joint state-federal task force, and in June 2003 a former Siegelman aide and a lobbyist pleaded guilty to bribery for buying a utility trailer and a motorcycle at about the time Siegelman obtained such items.

Riley beat Lieutenant Governor Steve Windom 74%–18% in the June 2002 primary. George W. Bush came to Alabama the next month for a $4 million fundraiser; overall, Riley outspent the incumbent. The issues were pretty squarely posed. Siegelman said in May that he still favored a lottery, but his Plan B appeared to be raising taxes on business; in October 2002, anticipating victory, he called for a special session for that purpose. Riley charged that state government was "sinking into a quicksand of corruption and fraud." He called the lottery "the return of a bad idea." He opposed tax increases and called for limiting spending to the prior year's revenues. He called for a new model for economic development, aimed at using the University of Alabama at Birmingham and other universities as magnets for biotech, high-tech and research industries and creating incentives for small business. He called for a commission to recommend changes in the 1901 Constitution to give local governments more power to pass local laws that do not require approval by the legislature. In late summer, Riley was running ahead in polls, but in September he made several blunders and his standing fell. He stumped one day with National Rifle Association president Charlton Heston; the next day it was revealed that the NRA endorsed Siegelman (as it does all incumbents who oppose gun control). Then Riley aides hinted that Heston might have been affected by Alzheimer's disease. And contrary to a promise Riley made during a debate, his campaign finance disclosure did not list the names of those who paid $50,000 to get their pictures taken with President Bush.

This turned out to be the closest gubernatorial race in the nation in 2002. Siegelman won overwhelmingly among black voters and his denunciations of corporations who opposed his business tax increase probably helped him carry heavily white rural counties in northwestern Alabama. He carried Birmingham's Jefferson County and Montgomery County, but by narrower margins than in 1998. Riley won by big margins in fast-growing suburban counties. He ran far ahead of the 1998 Republican showing in his old congressional district, and around three widely separated cities—Huntsville in the north, Dothan in the southeast and Mobile, Siegelman's hometown, in the south. On election night, a clerical error in rapidly-growing and heavily Republican Baldwin County on the Gulf coast credited Siegelman with 7,000 more votes than he actually received, which put him ahead in the statewide count. Both Riley and Siegelman proclaimed themselves winners. Siegelman refused to recognize the 7,000-vote error in Baldwin County and called for a statewide recount which could take months and indicated he would not relinquish the governor's office. Only after two weeks, on November 18, did he concede.

Facing a $675 million budget shortfall and a Democratic legislature, Riley cut spending and came up with a broad-based proposal to transform state finances. It would eliminate many of the earmarkings in Alabama's 1901 constitution (now, with 772 amendments, the longest in the world) and raise state and local taxes by $1.2 billion by 2008. High- and middle-income earners would pay more; so would farmers and timberland owners, whose taxes are held down by constitutional provisions; cigarette and bank taxes would be increased; utility taxes would be lowered. In return for support from the Alabama Education Association's head Paul Hubbert—a candidate for governor in 1990 and a key player in Alabama politics before and since—Riley agreed to maintain spending on teacher pay and to put the increased revenue into a non-earmarked Alabama Excellence Initiative. Why did a politician who was elected on a no-tax-increase program back such a plan? Riley said he was influenced by North Carolina Democratic Congressman Bobby Etheridge, who described how his state increased education spending in the 1960s and now had much higher test scores than Alabama. And he considered it a matter of

Christian obligation. "When I read the New Testament, there are three things we're asked to do: That's love God, love each other and take care of the least among us."

Supporting Riley were the state Democratic party, Hubbert and the AEA and some leaders of the insurance, banking, utility and consumer products industry. In opposition were the state Republican party, timber companies, the state Christian Coalition and national organizations like Americans for Tax Reform and the American Conservative Union. As state Republican Chairman Marty Connors described the situation, "We've got a conservative, evangelical Christian Republican governor, trying to get a massive turnout of black voters to pass a tax increase so he can raise taxes on Republican constituents." Turnout in the September 2003 referendum was high — only 6% below the November 2002 general election. The result was unambiguous. Riley's proposal was rejected 67%–33%. It was approved in only 12 Black Belt counties and lost by more than 3–1 in most small counties in north Alabama.

For 2004 Riley proposed more cuts and foreswore broad-based tax increases; the cigarette tax, some fees and oil and gas severance taxes were increased. As revenues suddenly increased, the state ended the fiscal year with a $150 million surplus. Riley's accountability package—for example, reporting of PAC-to-PAC transfers—was rejected by the legislature. Riley's response: "Teacher and public employee unions dictate too much of what happens in the legislature." Riley called a special session to cut the increases in health insurance for state employees and, with Hubbert's support, got a bill he signed into law. In the meantime, other controversies raged. Chief Justice Roy Moore was removed from the state Supreme Court after refusing to obey a federal court order to remove his Ten Commandments monument from the court's building. A jury verdict against Exxon Mobil for shortchanging the state on natural gas royalties was cut from $11.9 billion to $3.6 billion by a judge; Exxon Mobil appealed to the state supreme court.

Riley's September 2003 referendum prompted some Republicans to consider opposing Riley when he comes up for reelection in 2006. One possible candidate: ousted Chief Justice Roy Moore. In spring 2005 Riley had not decided whether he would run again. The most prominent Democratic candidate was Lieutenant Governor Lucy Baxley, whose husband Bill Baxley ran unsuccessfully for governor in 1978 and 1986; she declared her candidacy in May 2005. Siegelman also was considering running again.

Senior Senator

Richard Shelby (R)

Elected 1986, seat up 2010, 4th term; b. May 6, 1934, Birmingham; home, Tuscaloosa; U. of AL, B.A. 1957, LL.B. 1963; Presbyterian; married (Annette).

Elected Office: AL Senate, 1970–78; U.S. House of Reps., 1978–86.

Professional Career: Practicing atty., 1963–78; City Prosecutor, Tuscaloosa, 1963–71; U.S. Magistrate 1966–70; Spec. Asst. to U.S. Atty. Gen., 1969–71.

DC Office: 110 HSOB, 20510, 202-224-5744; Fax: 202-224-3416; Web site: shelby.senate.gov.

State Offices: Birmingham, 256-731-1384; Huntsville, 256-772-0460; Mobile, 251-694-4164; Montgomery, 334-223-7303; Tuscaloosa, 205-759-5047.

Committees: *Aging (Special). Appropriations*: Commerce, Justice & Science (Chmn.); Defense; Homeland Security; Labor, Health and Human Services, Education & Related Agencies; State, Foreign Operations & Related Programs; Transportation, Treasury, the Judiciary, HUD & Related Agencies. *Banking, Housing & Urban Affairs* (Chmn.): Economic Policy; Housing & Transportation.

Group Ratings

	ADA	ACLU	AFS	LCV	ITIC	NTU	COC	ACU	NTLC	CHC
2004	20	11	14	0	83	65	88	84	85	100
2003	10	—	0	5	—	72	82	75	—	—

National Journal Ratings

	2003 LIB	—	2003 CONS		2004 LIB	—	2004 CONS
Economic	40%	—	58%		42%	—	57%
Social	0%	—	59%		16%	—	81%
Foreign	35%	—	62%		0%	—	67%

Key Votes of the 108th Congress

1. Ban Drilling in ANWR	N	5. Energy Bill	Y	9. Ban Same-Sex Marriage	Y
2. Approve Bush Tax Cuts	Y	6. Support Roe v. Wade	N	10. Ban Bunker-Buster Bomb	N
3. Medicare/Rx Bill	Y	7. Ban Partial-Birth Abortion	Y	11. Fund Iraq War	Y
4. Bar Overtime Pay Regs.	N	8. Assault Weapons Ban	N	12. Restrict Missile Defense	N

Election Results

2004 general	Richard Shelby (R)	1,242,200	(68%)	($1,922,646)
	Wayne Sowell (D)	595,018	(32%)	($4,869)
	Other	1,848	(0%)	
2004 primary	Richard Shelby (R)	unopposed		
1998 general	Richard Shelby (R)	817,973	(63%)	($1,890,484)
	Clayton Suddith (D)	474,568	(37%)	($15,723)

Prior Winning Percentages: 1992 (65%); 1986 (50%); 1984 House (97%); 1982 House (97%); 1980 House (73%); 1978 House (94%)

Richard Shelby, Alabama's senior senator, has had a political career going back more than 30 years. Shelby grew up in Birmingham, the son of a steelworker. After earning two degrees from the University of Alabama, he stayed in Tuscaloosa and went into law practice with Walter Flowers, who was later a conservative Democratic congressman; Shelby was well enough politically connected to be elected state senator in 1970, at 36. When Flowers ran, unsuccessfully, for the Senate in 1978, Shelby ran for his House seat. The critical contest was the Democratic runoff against Chris McNair, a black legislator whose daughter had been killed in the 1963 Birmingham church bombing. The district had the highest black percentage in Alabama at the time; Shelby won 59%–41%. In the House Shelby had a conservative voting record, opposing the Voting Rights Act extension and the Martin Luther King Holiday. He ran for the Senate in 1986 and won the primary with 51% after getting then-Secretary of State (later Governor) Don Siegelman to withdraw. In the general, he ran ads against Republican Jeremiah Denton, a retired admiral who had been a prisoner of war in Vietnam, for voting to cut Social Security and owning two Mercedes (not a likely negative now, with the Mercedes plant in Tuscaloosa County). Shelby won by 7,000 votes.

As one of half a dozen or so conservative southern Democrats in the Senate, Shelby at first attracted little notice. He voted for the confirmation of Clarence Thomas and for the Gulf War resolution. He voted against the campaign finance bill supported by almost all Democrats and he voted for the Strategic Defense Initiative. In 1992, he was re-elected 65%–33%; this broke the jinx on a seat which, before Shelby's election in 1986, had four occupants in 10 years.

Shelby broke with the Democratic Party soon after Bill Clinton took office. At a meeting with Vice President Al Gore, he turned to 19 Alabama TV cameras and opposed the Clinton program as "high on taxes, low on spending cuts." In response, it was announced that a multi-million dollar space facility would be built not in Alabama but in Texas (it eventually went up in Alabama). But, as Clinton's ratings slid downward, this only raised Shelby's popularity ratings to the highest level in the state, making a politician previously known more for his suppleness of maneuver now appear an embattled defender of principle. Relentlessly, Shelby voted against the administration again and again and lined up with Republicans on almost every partisan issue. The day after Republicans regained control of the Senate in 1994, Shelby announced he was switching parties and increased the Republican majority to 53–47. Republicans happily allowed him to keep his seniority on the Banking Committee and gave him seats on Appropriations and its Defense Subcommittee and on Intelligence as well.

This is the path that led Shelby to the chairmanship of the Intelligence Committee in 1997 and which made him, as ranking minority member on the committee, an important policymaker after September 11. Shelby took an adversarial posture toward the intelligence agencies during the Clinton years and in the Bush years as well. He criticized and helped kill Anthony Lake's nomination as CIA director in 1997. He called the Wye River Memorandum's use of CIA officers to monitor compliance "troubling," and promised to investigate the use of American-made satellites by the Chinese to gather military intelligence. Soon after September 11, Shelby stopped just short of calling for the resignation of CIA Director George Tenet, who was appointed by Clinton and retained by Bush. He had evidently found Tenet excessively defensive in 1997 of his predecessor John Deutch for downloading classified material onto his personal laptop and was negatively impressed when, after India conducted three underground nuclear tests, Tenet told him. "We didn't have a clue." He was also concerned about the lack of information on the February 1993 World Trade Center bombing, the 1996 bombing of Khobar Towers, the 1998 attacks on the embassies in Kenya and Tanzania and the 2000 attack on the *U.S.S. Cole*. "I got to thinking, 'I wonder what else they're missing big time.'" In June 2004, when Tenet announced his resignation, Shelby said, "This is not a surprise to me at all. What was a surprise was that he held onto the job as long as he did."

Shelby was mostly supportive of the Bush administration's conduct of the war on terrorism. In December 2001, he was one of ten senators signing a letter saying, "it is imperative that we plan to eliminate the threat from Iraq." But he clashed with the two Intelligence Committee chairmen, Bob Graham and Porter Goss, in the joint investigations of the intelligence community. He helped push their choice as staff director aside and install his own original choice. At first he opposed the appointment of an independent 9/11 commission as unnecessary, but in September 2002, nearing the end of the 107th Congress (and his tenure on the Intelligence Committee), he changed his mind. The organization of the families of September 11 victims insisted that Shelby and John McCain be given veto power over Republican Leader Trent Lott's two nominations to the independent commission. In September 2002, he complained, "We've made some adjustments, but the cultures have not changed between all the intelligence agencies. . . . I don't believe they're sharing information. There's no fusion, no central place yet to do it." He called for a separate Director of National Intelligence, a position later taken by the 9/11 Commission and in the intelligence reorganization approved by Congress in December 2004. That bill included a Shelby proposal to give the DNI ombudsman access to all intelligence for analytical reviews.

One other controversy remains from Shelby's service on the Intelligence Committee. Shortly after a June 2002 closed committee hearing, CNN reported the contents of two NSA intercepts received before September 11 but not analyzed until after. The administration argued these were harmful leaks, and an FBI investigation began. In August 2004 Fox News's Carl Cameron told FBI investigators that Shelby told him the contents of the classified intercepts in June 2002, and earlier the *Washington Post* reported that Shelby was a target of the probe. But no prosecution was brought, and the Justice Department referred the matter to the Senate Ethics Committee. In 2004 Shelby said, "I have never knowingly—and that is a very important word, and I've been told to use that by Senate counsel, by other counsel—that I have never knowingly, intentionally, willfully disclosed classified information. I think most people know that, believe that." As of May 2005, the Ethics Committee had taken no action.

On domestic issues, Shelby has compiled a mostly conservative record. But he is not a free market purist. Despite his party switch he has remained friendly with trial lawyers, who usually support Democrats in Alabama. He opposed his colleague Jeff Sessions' amendment to cap lawyers' fees in tobacco cases, and insists tort reform should be only a state issue. He voted against a 2004 bill to protect gun manufacturers from liability for actions of users of their products. He was the only Senate Republican to vote against financial services deregulation in November 1999 and opposed allowing federally-insured banks to sell real estate or insurance. He opposed the 1999 law barring one branch of a financial services company from sharing personal data with another only if a client affirmatively opts out; he favors an opt in provision, which would allow sharing of information only for those clients who affirmatively authorize it. He opposes federal preemption of stricter state privacy laws. He has worked for repeal of the Public Utility Holding Company Act and opposes the current Community Reinvestment Act. Shelby became chairman of the Banking Committee in January 2003, and on a hotly-lobbied issue supported defining stock options as expenses, a measure opposed by the high-tech industry.

When the Financial Accounting Standards Board voted to require expensing and the House voted by a wide margin to overturn its ruling, Shelby together with ranking Democrat Paul Sarbanes blocked action in the Banking Committee, and the FASB action became effective in June 2005.

Shelby also serves on the Appropriations Committee, where he looks out for Alabama interests. He authored a law allowing airliners to fly from Alabama to Dallas's in-town Love Field and, with Washington's Patty Murray, fashioned a compromise on Mexican trucks. The House wanted to keep them inside a zone within 20 miles of the border; the Bush administration wanted to let them in, subject to inspections, as required under NAFTA. Shelby and Murray won agreement that they can come in only at entry points where inspectors are on duty, that their drivers' licenses must be subject to electronic verification and that they must be insured by a company licensed in the U.S. He has sponsored amendments channeling some $310 million over and above Alabama's highway allotments, into the Corridor X highway which runs northwest from Birmingham. When the sock industry in Ft. Payne's DeKalb County—the "sock capital of the world," with 150 sock mills—was hurt by the Trade Act of 2002, he held up a trade bill to get protection from socks mended in the Caribbean and in November 2004 got country-of-origin labeling for imported and domestic socks. In 2004 he obtained $20 million for the University of Southern Alabama's cancer research institute and $3.5 million to refurbish the Vulcan statue on Birmingham's Red Mountain—a favorite target of John McCain.

Shelby's party switch caused him no trouble in increasingly Republican Alabama. "I think people at times like some independence. They like independent thought, not someone to be a rubber stamp for either party. I sit up here, and who am I accountable to? Only the people of Alabama." He was reelected 63%–37% in 1998 over a retired ironworker who mortgaged his pickup truck to pay the $2,672 filing fee. For the 2004 election, he accumulated some $11 million, more than any other incumbent than New York's Charles Schumer. His opponent, Alabama's first black Senate nominee, was a telephone claims representative for the Social Security Administration in Birmingham. Shelby spent only $2.3 million of his money, and won 68%–32%, running behind in only nine black-majority counties in the Black Belt.

Junior Senator

Jeff Sessions (R)

Elected 1996, seat up 2008, 2d term; b. Dec. 24, 1946, Hybart; home, Mobile; Huntingdon Col., B.A. 1969, U. of AL, J.D. 1973; Methodist; married (Mary).

Military Career: Army Reserves, 1973–86.

Elected Office: AL Atty. Gen., 1994–96.

Professional Career: Practicing atty., 1973–75, 1977–81, 1993–94; Asst. U.S. Atty., 1975–77; U.S. Atty., 1981–93.

DC Office: 335 RSOB, 20510, 202-224-4124; Fax: 202-224-3149; Web site: sessions.senate.gov.

State Offices: Birmingham, 205-731-1500; Huntsville, 256-533-0979; Mobile, 251-414-3083; Montgomery, 334-244-7017.

Committees: *Armed Services:* Airland; Readiness & Management Support; Strategic Forces (Chmn.). *Budget. Health, Education, Labor & Pensions:* Education & Early Childhood Development; Employment & Workplace Safety; Retirement Security & Aging. *Judiciary:* Administrative Oversight & the Courts (Chmn.); Corrections & Rehabilitation; Crime & Drugs; Immigration, Border Security & Citizenship; Terrorism, Technology & Homeland Security. *Joint Economic Committee.*

Group Ratings

	ADA	ACLU	AFS	LCV	ITIC	NTU	COC	ACU	NTLC	CHC
2004	10	0	14	0	100	82	88	96	93	100
2003	0	—	0	5	—	78	100	90	—	—

National Journal Ratings

	2003 LIB	—	2003 CONS		2004 LIB	—	2004 CONS
Economic	0%	—	82%		11%	—	84%
Social	0%	—	59%		16%	—	81%
Foreign	0%	—	78%		0%	—	67%

Key Votes of the 108th Congress

1. Ban Drilling in ANWR	N	5. Energy Bill	Y	9. Ban Same-Sex Marriage	Y
2. Approve Bush Tax Cuts	Y	6. Support Roe v. Wade	N	10. Ban Bunker-Buster Bomb	N
3. Medicare/Rx Bill	Y	7. Ban Partial-Birth Abortion	Y	11. Fund Iraq War	Y
4. Bar Overtime Pay Regs.	N	8. Assault Weapons Ban	N	12. Restrict Missile Defense	N

Election Results

2002 general	Jeff Sessions (R)	792,561	(59%)	($5,115,730)
	Susan Parker (D)	538,878	(40%)	($1,185,718)
	Other	21,584	(2%)	
2002 primary	Jeff Sessions (R)	unopposed		
1996 general	Jeff Sessions (R)	786,436	(52%)	($3,862,359)
	Roger Bedford (D)	681,651	(45%)	($2,284,801)
	Other	31,306	(2%)	

Jeff Sessions, Alabama's junior senator, grew up in the state's Black Belt, walked to school barefoot and is the son of a country store owner. He graduated from Huntingdon College and the University of Alabama Law School, practiced law in a small town near the Tennessee Valley, became a federal prosecutor and then practiced law in Mobile. He was appointed U.S. Attorney in 1981, at 35, where he became known as a tough, aggressive prosecutor, and served for 12 years. In 1985, he was nominated for federal judge, but was attacked by liberals for "gross insensitivity" in racial matters for prosecuting vote fraud cases. With Alabama's Senator Howell Heflin voting against him in the Judiciary Committee, his nomination never went to the floor. In 1994, Sessions challenged state Attorney General Jimmy Evans, who had successfully prosecuted Governor Guy Hunt the year before, and won 57%–43%. In March 1995, when Heflin announced his retirement, Sessions started running for his seat; he became the favorite among the seven Republicans and four Democrats.

Sessions started early, avoiding debates and controversy, and relying on his base in south-ern Alabama—territory that not long ago cast almost no Republican primary votes. Long-distance carrier executive Sid McDonald spent more than $1 million and attacked Sessions. From Birmingham north, it was a close race: McDonald led in the June 4 primary by 30%–29%. But in the rest of the state, Sessions led 48%–12%, for a 38%–22% statewide margin. In the runoff, McDonald extended his lead north from Birmingham, 54%–46%, but almost half the votes were cast farther south, and there Sessions led 73%–27%, for a 59%–41% win.

The Democratic nominee, trial lawyer and state Senator Roger Bedford, was financed by trial lawyers and endorsed by key public employee unions and black organizations—the heart of today's Alabama Democratic Party. In the past, Democratic primaries had turnouts of nearly 1 million, with the advantage going to moderate or conservative candidates, like Glen Browder, the 3d District congressman. But only 315,000 voted in the June 4 Democratic primary in 1996, about half of them black; Bedford led Browder 45%–29%. In the June 25 runoff, Browder attacked Bedford for supporting NAFTA and gambling, and for being backed by trial lawyers, but Bedford had more money. With a low turnout of 230,000, Bedford won 62%–38%. In the general Bedford was competitive in fundraising and seemed the better campaigner. He opposed abortion, gun control, and gays in the military. Sessions avoided debates and attacked the Democrat as a Ted Kennedy backer and for leading the battle against tort reform in the Alabama Senate in 1996. Sessions won 52%–45%, running best in the suburbanizing counties around Alabama's cities; Bedford carried the Black Belt and many rural counties in the north.

In the Senate, Sessions has a very conservative voting record. In 2003 he co-sponsored John McCain's bill to prohibit earmarked appropriations. He was one of 21 senators in 2004 to oppose the $318 transportation bill as too expensive, and in May 2004 he told Huntsville lobbyists the outlook was "dicey" for increasing the administration's NASA budget. In early 2004 he also called for reopening the Medicare/prescription drug law passed in December 2003. He serves on the Judiciary Committee which once rejected his own nomination, and in 2003 complained, "I'm angry and passionate about the way the Democrats refused to let the Senate vote on these judgeships." One was for Alabama Attorney General Bill Pryor; he received a recess appointment in February 2004, and Sessions called on Bush to nominate him again in 2005. In 2004 he co-sponsored a bill to prevent interstate transportation of children to have abortions. But Sessions also has taken on some causes that are not labeled conservative. With Edward Kennedy he co-sponsored a bill to combat sexual assault in prisons. And in 2002 he co-sponsored a bill to reduce the ratio between the amount of powder cocaine and the amount of crack cocaine required to justify a five-year sentence and to reduce mandatory minimum sentences for minor players in drug offenses.

Sessions has not sponsored major legislation, but has had considerable success in inserting provisions that set new federal policy into bills likely to pass. With Bob Graham and Mitch McConnell, Sessions succeeded in putting into the 2001 tax cut a provision expanding Section 529 plans to allow parents and grandparents to contribute up to $250,000 for college expenses into investment accounts if authorized by states. Into the 2003 Medicare/prescription drug bill, Sessions inserted a provision for higher Medicare reimbursement for rural hospitals; he threatened to vote against the measure unless this was retained in conference committee. It was, providing $738 million to Alabama — more than any other state except Texas and Florida. In the 2004 defense authorization, Sessions and Charles Schumer included a provision giving the Justice Department authority to prosecute employees of civilian contractors supporting the U.S. military overseas; this was prompted by the Abu Ghraib abuses. He also got a provision increasing military life insurance payoffs to $325,000 (later raised to $350,000) and providing two years' salaries and benefits for the families of military personnel killed in hostile action. Sessions also inserted $16.5 million for the Cairns Army Airfield Hangar complex at Fort Rucker.

Other Sessions achievements include a 2004 law to make it easier to develop and get FDA approval of drugs for minor animals, such as Alabama catfish. After Hurricane Ivan devastated southern Alabama timberlands, Sessions inserted into the corporate tax bill a provision giving landowners who sell timber in small quantities the same tax advantages of those who sell timber in bulk. The 2004 special education bill included a Sessions provision giving school districts the authority to establish uniform discipline policies for all schools—and to be relieved of the Education Department's complex requirements for special ed discipline.

In 2002 Sessions was opposed by Democrat Susan Parker, a fundraiser for colleges, who beat trial lawyer Julian Phillips in the June runoff after Phillips argued that he could handle issues of importance to women and children because he was the father of three and Parker had no children; Parker replied that she had had a miscarriage and her doctor advised her not to have children. Parker had the support of teachers' unions, but Sessions outspent her 4–1. In October, she took note of the travails of New Jersey's Democratic Senator Bob Torricelli and attacked Sessions for seeking a provision, not passed, which would allow a group of investors to escape a $15 million debt owed to Lloyds of London. "Just like the Torch [Torricelli's nickname], Sessions tried to sneak in a bailout for millionaires who gave him money," she said, and then proceeded to dump thousands of dollars onto the floor at a press conference. A clever tactic, but it availed her little. Sessions won 59%–40%, even as Republican Bob Riley was being elected governor by just a narrow margin. Parker carried two Tennessee River counties in the north and 12 Black Belt counties in the center of the state but Sessions carried everything else.

FIRST DISTRICT

Rep. Jo Bonner (R)

Elected 2002, 2d term; b. Nov. 19, 1959, Selma; home, Mobile; U. of AL, B.A. 1982, U. of AL Law Schl. 1988; Episcopalian; married (Janee).

Professional Career: Sr. Aide, U.S. Rep. Sonny Callahan, 1984–02.

DC Office: 315 CHOB, 20515, 202-225-4931; Fax: 202-225-0562; Web site: www.bonner.house.gov.

District Offices: Foley, 251-943-2073; Mobile, 251-690-2811.

Committees: *Agriculture* (14th of 25 R): Department Operations, Oversight, Nutrition & Forestry; General Farm Commodities & Risk Management. *Budget* (7th of 22 R). *Science* (16th of 24 R): Energy; Space & Aeronautics.

Group Ratings

	ADA	ACLU	AFS	LCV	ITIC	NTU	COC	ACU	NTLC	CHC
2004	0	0	13	9	90	59	100	95	67	100
2003	5	—	0	5	—	61	97	92	—	—

National Journal Ratings

	2003 LIB	—	2003 CONS		2004 LIB	—	2004 CONS
Economic	9%	—	84%		13%	—	87%
Social	5%	—	87%		24%	—	76%
Foreign	11%	—	80%		0%	—	96%

Key Votes of the 108th Congress

1. Drilling in ANWR	Y	5. DC School Vouchers	Y	9. Ban Same-Sex Marriage	Y
2. Approve Bush Tax Cuts	Y	6. Ban Human Cloning	Y	10. Fund Iraq War	Y
3. Medicare/Rx Bill	Y	7. Restrict Gun Liability	Y	11. Bar Cuba Embargo Funds	*
4. Bar Overtime Pay Regs.	N	8. Ban Partial-Birth Abortion	Y	12. Intelligence Reorg.	Y

Election Results

2004 general	Jo Bonner (R)	161,067	(63%)	($1,015,702)
	Judy McCain Belk (D)	93,938	(37%)	($442,141)
	Other	159	(0%)	
2004 primary	Jo Bonner (R)	unopposed		
2002 general	Jo Bonner (R)	108,102	(60%)	($1,713,019)
	Judy McCain Belk (D)	67,507	(38%)	($472,383)
	Other	3,078	(2%)	

The People		Race/Ethnic Origin	Ancestry	
Area size:	7,182 sq. mi.	67.8% White	USA: 12.4%	Irish: 6.7%
Urban population:	64.4%	28.0% Black	English: 6.6%	
Rural population:	35.6%	1.0% Asian	**2004 Presidential Vote**	
Pop. 2000:	635,300	1.0% Native Am.	Bush (R) 168,817	(64%)
Median income:	$34,739	0.0% Hawaiian	Kerry (D) 91,832	(35%)
Poverty status:	16.9%	0.9% Two+ races	Other 1,922	(1%)
Military veterans:	14.3%	0.1% Other	**2000 Presidential Vote**	
		1.3% Hispanic Origin	Bush (R) 138,938	(60%)
			Gore (D) 86,142	(37%)
			Other 4,798	(2%)
			Cook Partisan Voting Index: R +12	
Occupation	Blue collar: 29.7%	White collar: 54.7%	Gray collar: 15.6%	

Mobile, the port where the Tombigbee and Alabama rivers flow into the Gulf of Mexico, was long a key point on the American frontier. Spanish after the Revolutionary War, it was wrested away by threats of war from Secretary of State John Quincy Adams. During the Civil War, it was one of the major Confederate ports; here in 1864 Admiral David Farragut, while steaming into the harbor lashed to his mast, cried, "Damn the torpedoes! Full speed ahead." Today, Mobile is full of graceful signs of its slightly exotic past. Behind the docks and rail lines are downtown buildings and old houses with Spanish motifs, French accents, or tropical Art Deco lines. Further inland are neighborhoods with spacious houses, often with double porches, overhung by huge live oaks, graced with Spanish moss. Mobile is a Gulf Coast version of Charleston or a smaller, more comfortable New Orleans, with a taste for shellfish and spicy food and an even older Mardi Gras, which the locals have been celebrating since 1703. As befits a frontier city with a martial past, Mobile is bristling with arms: One of the city's proudest possessions is the battleship *U.S.S. Alabama*, moored at the head of Mobile Bay, with its guns aimed out toward the Gulf. Mobile's economy was based originally on docks and shipyards, factories and terminals, but with a determination to impose touches of beauty on its hot, flat landscape. Its economy has been thriving at the shipyards, chemical plants, and a new cruise terminal. The capital improvements include Mobile's State Docks, which serves Alabama's booming Mercedes, Honda, and Hyundai auto-production factories. But after opposition from local activists worried about safety, Exxon Mobil withdrew plans to build a giant offshore liquefied natural gas terminal.

Mobile is the focus of Alabama's 1st Congressional District, which extends north along the lazily flowing Tombigbee and Alabama Rivers, near the old forts and mansions. Monroeville was the home of great writers—Truman Capote and his childhood playmate, Harper Lee, whose *To Kill a Mockingbird* is set here; and Winston Groom, author of *Forrest Gump*. Also here are surviving backcountry settlements of blacks and Cajans (who may or may not be descended from Louisiana Cajuns) and Creek Indians. Once cotton fields, this is now timber land, a major contributor to Alabama's economy, though many stands were devastated by Hurricane Ivan in September 2004. To the south, along the shores of the Gulf of Mexico, are the fast-growing condominium communities in Baldwin County, one of the two fastest-growing counties in Alabama; the glorious Gulf beaches are one of the South's best-kept secrets. For years, this southern seaboard of the Confederacy and the Union has been one of the most hawkish parts of America, and today it is solidly Republican in national elections.

The congressman from the 1st District is Jo Bonner, a Republican first elected in 2002. Bonner grew up in Selma and is just a little too young to remember the days when it was the focus of the civil rights movement; his father, who died when he was 13, was a probate judge appointed by the relatively moderate Governor Albert Brewer. Bonner graduated from the University of Alabama in 1982 and two years later started working as a campaign press secretary for Sonny Callahan, a gregarious nine-term Republican who rose to become an Appropriations subcommittee chairman. In 1989, Bonner was promoted to chief of staff and later moved his family back to Mobile, where he became the rare top aide permanently stationed in the district. That background left Bonner well positioned when Callahan announced his retirement just three months before the June 2002 primary.

Bonner's strongest opponent in the in the seven-candidate Republican primary had a similar background: Tom Young had been the chief of staff to Senator Richard Shelby for 12 years. Like Bonner, Young had his former boss's endorsement and showed a knack for campaign fundraising: the two raised more than $2 million between them. With help from their bosses, each raised lots of money from Washington lobbyists; some complained about the pressure to choose sides. Young contrasted his experience on intelligence and defense policy with Bonner's focus on more mundane constituent-service work. Bonner responded by arguing that the Washington-based Young had more connections in Washington than in southern Alabama; he jibed that Young should have been welcomed at a luncheon for "new Mobilians." Young outspent Bonner by $300,000 and was helped by ads from the pro-tax cut Club for Growth, but Bonner led in the June 4 primary 40%–20%. In the June 25 runoff Bonner was endorsed by the Republicans who ran third, fourth and fifth; he won 62%–38%. In a district held by Republicans since 1964, when Barry Goldwater swept Alabama, Bonner beat Democratic businesswoman Judy McCain Belk, who contributed more than $300,000 to her campaign, by a 60%–38% margin—almost the same as George W. Bush's margin in 2000.

In the House, Bonner cast a solidly conservative voting record and made few waves as a party loyalist. He opposed on-shore LNG terminals for Mobile, but proposed an off-shore option for the future. In a rematch against Belk, Bonner won by a 63%–37% margin, a margin very close to Bush's 2004 margin in the district. Starting before the 2004 election, he pushed to get Callahan's seat on Appropriations but failed to get it. Back home, Bonner has succeeded Callahan as host of the weekly "Gulf Coast Congressional Report," which has aired since 1972 and bills itself as the longest-running televised public service program hosted by a member of Congress. He seems likely to have a lengthy tenure in this safely Republican seat.

SECOND DISTRICT

Rep. Terry Everett (R)

Elected 1992, 7th term; b. Feb. 15, 1937, Dothan; home, Enterprise; Dale County H.S.; Baptist; married (Barbara).

Military Career: Air Force, 1955–59.

Professional Career: Newspaper reporter, 1959–61, 1966–68; Businessman, 1961–64; Editor & Publisher, 1968–88; Real estate developer, 1988–92; Owner & Pres., *Union Springs Herald*, 1988–2003.

DC Office: 2312 RHOB, 20515, 202-225-2901; Fax: 202-225-8913; Web site: www.house.gov/everett.

District Offices: Dothan, 334-794-9680; Montgomery, 334-277-9113; Opp, 334-493-9253.

Committees: *Agriculture* (4th of 25 R): General Farm Commodities & Risk Management; Specialty Crops & Foreign Agriculture Programs (Vice Chmn.). *Armed Services* (6th of 34 R): Strategic Forces (Chmn.); Tactical Air & Land Forces. *Permanent Select Committee on Intelligence* (4th of 12 R): Oversight; Technical & Tactical Intelligence. *Veterans' Affairs* (3d of 16 R): Oversight & Investigations.

Group Ratings

	ADA	ACLU	AFS	LCV	ITIC	NTU	COC	ACU	NTLC	CHC
2004	0	5	13	9	78	54	100	92	86	100
2003	10	—	0	5	—	65	90	88	—	—

National Journal Ratings

	2003 LIB	—	2003 CONS		2004 LIB	—	2004 CONS
Economic	19%	—	80%		25%	—	74%
Social	14%	—	85%		0%	—	91%
Foreign	23%	—	71%		25%	—	68%

Key Votes of the 108th Congress

1. Drilling in ANWR	Y	5. DC School Vouchers	Y	9. Ban Same-Sex Marriage	Y
2. Approve Bush Tax Cuts	Y	6. Ban Human Cloning	Y	10. Fund Iraq War	Y
3. Medicare/Rx Bill	Y	7. Restrict Gun Liability	Y	11. Bar Cuba Embargo Funds	N
4. Bar Overtime Pay Regs.	N	8. Ban Partial-Birth Abortion	Y	12. Intelligence Reorg.	Y

Election Results

2004 general	Terry Everett (R)	177,086	(71%)	($1,937,038)
	Charles James (D)	70,562	(28%)	($1,320)
	Other	299	(0%)	
2004 primary	Terry Everett (R)	unopposed		
2002 general	Terry Everett (R)	129,233	(69%)	($1,076,731)
	Charles Woods (D)	55,495	(30%)	
	Other	3,237	(2%)	

Prior Winning Percentages: 2000 (68%); 1998 (69%); 1996 (63%); 1994 (74%); 1992 (49%)

The People		Race/Ethnic Origin	Ancestry	
Area size:	10,608 sq. mi.	67.0% White	USA: 15.7%	English: 6.2%
Urban population:	50.1%	29.4% Black	Irish: 5.9%	
Rural population:	49.9%	0.6% Asian	**2004 Presidential Vote**	
Pop. 2000:	635,300	0.4% Native Am.	Bush (R) 170,427	(67%)
Median income:	$32,460	0.0% Hawaiian	Kerry (D) 84,043	(33%)
Poverty status:	17.2%	0.9% Two+ races	Other 1,091	(0%)
Military veterans:	15.1%	0.1% Other	**2000 Presidential Vote**	
		1.5% Hispanic Origin	Bush (R) 137,168	(61%)
			Gore (D) 84,435	(38%)
			Other 3,061	(1%)
			Cook Partisan Voting Index: R +13	

Occupation   Blue collar: 29.5%   White collar: 55.1%   Gray collar: 15.4%

The thick green countryside is everywhere in southern Alabama. Even in Montgomery the stone and brick buildings that rise in the irregular downtown grid do not mask the contours of the hills or hide the lush foliage. You can look downhill from the restored Greek Revival Capitol toward Dexter Avenue Baptist Church where the young Martin Luther King Jr. was pastor in the 1950s, or out past the impressive Carolyn Blount Theater where the Alabama Shakespeare Festival is held toward new subdivisions and shopping malls, and you can easily imagine when this land was covered with cotton fields and pine trees. The atmosphere is even more rural in southeast Alabama's Wiregrass region, named for the stiff native grass, in the fishing town of Eufaula along the Chattahoochee River, around the town of Dothan, past Daleville and the Army's Fort Rucker (the home of Army aviation flight training) to Enterprise, site of the Boll Weevil Monument that commemorates the insect that destroyed two-thirds of the cotton crop here in 1915 and then spread throughout the South. Timber is an important resource here these days, and peanuts are now the main crop in the area surrounding Dothan; the district ranks second in the nation in acres harvested for peanuts.

The 2d Congressional District of Alabama covers the southeast corner of the state. It includes most of the city of Montgomery, but only a small part of Montgomery County; Democratic redistricters put the rest (which includes the Capitol and many black precincts), into the 3d District in an attempt to make that seat more Democratic. The result left the 2d heavily Republican. The Montgomery County precincts in the 2d together with suburban Elmore and Autauga Counties vote heavily Republican; so does the area around Dothan and Houston County in the Wiregrass region. These places heavily outvote the district's Black Belt counties—Lowndes, the site of Hyundai's first U.S. plant, Bullock, with a large black majority, and Barbour on the Georgia border, which was George Wallace's home base. It would be a mistake to see these preferences as purely racial, however. The civil rights laws of the 1960s have long since been accepted. Blacks here tend to support a larger and more generous government, and hence vote Democratic. Alabama whites tend to take a hard line on defense and crime, want government to promote traditional cultural values and hence vote Republican.

The congressman from the 2d District is Terry Everett, a businessman from the Wiregrass first elected in 1992. He grew up in the Wiregrass region and served in Air Force Intelligence in Germany in the 1950s, where he learned Russian, then worked as a sports and police beat reporter and circulation manager for southern Alabama newspapers. He bought some newspapers himself and sold them for far more, and ended up heading a S&L and owning a large farm and real estate development firm. In 1992, when he decided to run for the seat being vacated by 28-year incumbent Republican Bill Dickinson, he was far from the favorite. But he beat two career politicians, a Montgomery legislator in the Republican primary and, in the general, state Treasurer George C. Wallace, son of the former governor (Wallace, now a Republican, is an elected Public Service Commissioner). Everett spent $600,000 of his own money and, echoing an old George Wallace slogan, called on voters to, "Send them a message, not a politician." Everett carried the Montgomery area and the Wiregrass but lost the Black Belt and rural areas.

Everett's voting record is mostly conservative; he shows a practical-minded concern about local issues and demonstrates a real impact on some issues. A prime example is peanuts: In 1995, he formed a Peanut Caucus and on the Agriculture Committee held out against the Freedom to Farm Act until he got the peanut program continued, though with a 10% cut in the support price and a lower national quota. On the 2002 farm bill, Everett chaired the Specialty Crops and Foreign Agriculture Programs Subcommittee, which placed him in a strong position to advocate the interests of peanut farmers. When he concluded that Congress would no longer support the 30 cents per pound peanut subsidy, Everett worked with Saxby Chambliss and Sanford Bishop of Georgia on a compromise that reduced imports and guaranteed quota farmers 10 cents per pound, with new farmers receiving a fallback option of government purchase at 18 cents. That Everett was able to get the House to accept a $3.5 billion (over 10 years) program shows his skill in protecting the interests of local farmers. Everett, himself a holder of a peanut quota, estimated that he would get $30,000 over five years from the new program. The new program developed record yields for the district's peanut crop, though the number of farmers fell a bit. On another issue, he echoed the district's populist tradition when he filed a bill to require two months public notice before corporations could give big pay raises to their top executives.

Everett has also worked on military and veterans' issues. As a Veterans Affairs subcommittee chairman in 1999, he took credit for a $1.7 billion increase for veterans' health care spending plus the opening of four new national cemeteries. In 2003, Everett became chairman of the Armed Services Strategic Forces Subcommittee, where he sought to shift funding priorities "from longer-term efforts to those that will provide more immediate benefit to the war fighter" in Iraq, including space-based military capabilities.

Everett has been reelected easily against poorly-funded challengers.

THIRD DISTRICT

Rep. Mike Rogers (R)

Elected 2002, 2d term; b. July 16, 1958, Hammond, IN; home, Anniston; Jacksonville St. U., B.A. 1981, M.P.A. 1984, Birmingham Schl. of Law, J.D. 1991; Baptist; married (Beth).

Elected Office: Calhoun Cnty. Commission, 1986–90; AL House of Reps., 1994–2002, Min. Ldr., 1998–2000.

Professional Career: Practicing atty., 1991–2002; Owner, auto lot.

DC Office: 514 CHOB, 20515, 202-225-3261; Fax: 202-226-8485; Web site: www.house.gov/mike-rogers/.

District Offices: Anniston, 256-236-5655; Montgomery, 334-277-4210; Opelika, 334-745-6221.

Committees: *Agriculture* (15th of 25 R): Conservation, Credit, Rural Development & Research; Livestock & Horticulture; Specialty Crops & Foreign Agriculture Programs. *Armed Services* (27th of 34 R): Readiness; Strategic Forces. *Homeland Security* (13th of 19 R): Economic Security, Infrastructure Protection & Cybersecurity; Emergency Preparedness, Science & Technology; Management, Integration & Oversight (Chmn.).

Group Ratings

	ADA	ACLU	AFS	LCV	ITIC	NTU	COC	ACU	NTLC	CHC
2004	10	0	13	9	90	49	100	88	73	100
2003	5	—	0	5	—	58	97	92	—	—

National Journal Ratings

	2003 LIB	—	2003 CONS		2004 LIB	—	2004 CONS
Economic	26%	—	73%		26%	—	74%
Social	17%	—	79%		25%	—	73%
Foreign	0%	—	89%		17%	—	78%

1. Drilling in ANWR	Y	5. DC School Vouchers	Y	9. Ban Same-Sex Marriage	Y
2. Approve Bush Tax Cuts	Y	6. Ban Human Cloning	Y	10. Fund Iraq War	Y
3. Medicare/Rx Bill	Y	7. Restrict Gun Liability	Y	11. Bar Cuba Embargo Funds	N
4. Bar Overtime Pay Regs.	N	8. Ban Partial-Birth Abortion	Y	12. Intelligence Reorg.	Y

Election Results

2004 general	Mike Rogers (R)	150,411	(61%)	($1,893,588)
	Bill Fuller (D)	95,240	(39%)	($240,774)
	Other	133	(0%)	
2004 primary	Mike Rogers (R)	unopposed		
2002 general	Mike Rogers (R)	91,169	(50%)	($1,638,145)
	Joe Turnham (D)	87,351	(48%)	($1,010,933)
	Other	2,703	(2%)	

The People		Race/Ethnic Origin	Ancestry	
Area size:	7,988 sq. mi.	64.9% White	USA: 15.9%	Irish: 6.0%
Urban population:	53.3%	32.2% Black	English: 5.8%	
Rural population:	46.7%	0.6% Asian	**2004 Presidential Vote**	
Pop. 2000:	635,300	0.3% Native Am.	Bush (R) 146,380	(58%)
Median income:	$30,806	0.0% Hawaiian	Kerry (D) 103,456	(41%)
Poverty status:	18.8%	0.7% Two+ races	Other 1,501	(1%)
Military veterans:	13.4%	0.1% Other	**2000 Presidential Vote**	
		1.2% Hispanic Origin	Bush (R) 112,320	(52%)
			Gore (D) 101,431	(47%)
			Other 3,769	(2%)
			Cook Partisan Voting Index: R + 4	

Occupation	Blue collar: 33.1%	White collar: 51.7%	Gray collar: 15.2%

Forty years ago, Lineville, Alabama, in the red hills of Clay County, was Ku Klux Klan country, with whites determined to resist race-mixing and blacks intimidated by threats of violence. More recently in Lineville, integrated crowds regularly cheer integrated high school teams, and people of all races work amicably together, though they tend to pray separately on Sundays. Lineville's progress perhaps echoes that of America's most integrated institution, the military, for the small town produced more men and women per capita for Operation Desert Storm than any other community in the nation. In 2003 Alabama was the nation's top contributor of National Guard personnel and in 2005, there were about 1,300 Alabama National Guard troops deployed in Iraq; Clay County has one of the highest concentrations of Guard enlistments and reservists in the state.

The 3d Congressional District of Alabama is centered geographically and perhaps spiritually in Lineville. The military presence is unmistakable: Calhoun County is home to the Anniston Army Depot and formerly home to Fort McClellan, which survived several rounds of base closings until it was finally closed in 1999. Horseshoe Bend is where Andrew Jackson won a climactic battle against the Upper Creek Indians. Fort Mitchell, a 19th century frontier military outpost, is the site of a national military cemetery sometimes referred to as the "Arlington of the South." Phenix City, across the Chattahoochie River from Georgia's Fort Benning, served as a "sin city" in the 1940s and 1950s with virtually every imaginable vice for pleasure-seeking soldiers, a place so sleazy that General George Patton threatened to level it with his tanks; today, the huge military installation plays a more constructive role in the local economy. There are other places of distinction in the 3d: Tuskegee, home of Booker T. Washington's Tuskegee Institute; Auburn, home of Auburn University and its renowned sports teams and veterinary school; Talladega, home of the Alabama Institute for the Deaf and Blind, which is perhaps America's most user-friendly city for the disabled. NASCAR fans know it as the home of a famed speedway and for the International Motorsports Hall of Fame—the Cooperstown of auto racing. This looks and feels like rural country, though few people here make a living off their farms. Instead, they drive to work at Tyson Foods or Wal-Mart or in dozens of small- or medium-sized factories.

Politically, this was long one of the heartlands of the Democratic Party, the home of populist white Democrats—patriotic supporters of the military, cautious supporters of some domestic programs—who won power so often in the House and Senate. But the cotton mills have closed, and interstates have brought in new businesses, including a huge Honda assembly plant in Talladega County, where solid wages boosted local personal income by 22% in the three years after it opened. Except for Tuskegee's Macon County and the portions of Montgomery County added by the 2002 redistricting, the area has become Republican, though Democrats have remained competitive in some state elections.

The congressman from the 3d is Mike Rogers, a Republican first elected in 2002—the second Republican Mike Rogers in the House (the other is from the 8th District of Michigan). The Alabama Mike Rogers is a fifth generation resident of Calhoun County who, at the age of 28 in 1986, was the first Republican elected to the county commission. In 1994, he won a seat in the Alabama House and in his second term, he became Minority Leader. In 2002, the 3d District's congressman, Bob Riley, ran successfully for governor. Democrats had their eye on this district; their redistricting plan had increased the black percentage from 25% to 32%. Rogers decided to run anyway and won the Republican nomination easily. But he had stiff competition from Democrat Joe Turnham, Jr., who served three years as state party chairman and challenged Riley unsuccessfully in 1998.

In a strenuous campaign, Turnham and Rogers tried to "out-Bubba" each other. Turnham called for a congressional auto racing caucus and demanded that Rogers prove he had hunting and fishing licenses. Rogers touted his working class values and support from the National Rifle Association; he is an abortion opponent who supports a constitutional amendment for prayer in public school. He promised to focus on education and local economic development, notably for shuttered Fort McClellan. Turnham attacked Rogers for supporting free trade and called him a "career politician." Though both national parties targeted the district, Turnham did not risk bringing in national Democrats to campaign for him in this socially conservative district, while Rogers got frequent visits from national Republican leaders. Speaker Dennis Hastert promised him a seat on the Armed Services Committee, where he could protect the interests of the Anniston Army Depot. The contrast in national party support was evident in Rogers's big fundraising advantage. Still, the election was close: Rogers won by only a 50%–48% margin. Rogers did well in his base, Calhoun County, where he got 60% of the vote and a margin of more than 7,000 votes. In contrast, Turnham lost Lee County, his home, by a 52%–46% margin, and carried the district's portion of Montgomery County by only 57%–42% and a margin of some 4,000 votes.

In the House Rogers has a conservative voting record. He bucked the Bush administration and won local praise by opposing the free trade agreement with Morocco on the grounds that it would reduce local textile and apparel jobs. On the Armed Services Committee he opposed a new round of base closings and won House passage of a bill to assure that universities would provide fair access to their facilities for military recruiters and ROTC personnel.

In this ancestrally Democratic district, Rogers worked hard to entrench himself and raise money to discourage strong Democratic opposition in 2004. He drew a credible challenger in Democrat Bill Fuller, the former state human resources commissioner and an 18-year veteran of the state House, where he chaired the Ways and Means Committee. Fuller called for limits on outsourcing of jobs and criticized Rogers for supporting the 2003 Medicare/prescription drug law; Rogers boasted of the law's increased payments for Alabama's rural hospitals. Though national and state Democrats hyped Fuller's prospects, he was inadequately funded and his campaign never posed a serious threat. Sadly, on the weekend before the election, Fuller's antebellum home, which also was his campaign headquarters, burned down and he broke his knee jumping from the second floor. Rogers won 61%–39%, carrying 11 of the 13 counties; he won 73% in Calhoun County. He seems to have made this a safe Republican district.

FOURTH DISTRICT

Rep. Robert Aderholt (R)

Elected 1996, 5th term; b. July 22, 1965, Haleyville; home, Haleyville; Birmingham-Southern Col., B.A. 1987, Samford U., J.D. 1990; Congregationalist; married (Caroline).

Professional Career: Haleyville Municipal Judge, 1992–96; Asst. Legal Advisor, Gov. Fob James, 1995–96.

DC Office: 1433 LHOB, 20515, 202-225-4876; Fax: 202-225-5587; Web site: www.aderholt.house.gov.

District Offices: Cullman, 256-734-6043; Gadsden, 256-546-0201; Jasper, 205-221-2310.

Committees: *Appropriations* (21st of 37 R): Interior, Environment & Related Agencies; Military Quality of Life & Veterans Affairs & Related Agencies (Vice Chmn.); Transportation, Treasury, HUD, the Judiciary & District of Columbia.

Group Ratings

	ADA	ACLU	AFS	LCV	ITIC	NTU	COC	ACU	NTLC	CHC
2004	0	0	14	9	67	49	100	92	70	100
2003	10	—	0	0	—	61	89	88	—	—

National Journal Ratings

	2003 LIB	—	2003 CONS	2004 LIB	—	2004 CONS
Economic	0%	—	91%	27%	—	72%
Social	17%	—	79%	0%	—	91%
Foreign	23%	—	71%	4%	—	93%

Key Votes of the 108th Congress

1. Drilling in ANWR	Y	5. DC School Vouchers	Y	9. Ban Same-Sex Marriage	Y
2. Approve Bush Tax Cuts	Y	6. Ban Human Cloning	Y	10. Fund Iraq War	Y
3. Medicare/Rx Bill	Y	7. Restrict Gun Liability	Y	11. Bar Cuba Embargo Funds	N
4. Bar Overtime Pay Regs.	N	8. Ban Partial-Birth Abortion	Y	12. Intelligence Reorg.	Y

Election Results

2004 general	Robert Aderholt (R)	191,110	(75%)	($735,352)
	Carl Cole (D)	64,278	(25%)	($25,496)
	Other	336	(0%)	
2004 primary	Robert Aderholt (R)	unopposed		
2002 general	Robert Aderholt (R)	139,705	(87%)	($662,595)
	Tony Hughes McLendon (Lib)	20,858	(13%)	

Prior Winning Percentages: 2000 (61%); 1998 (56%); 1996 (50%)

The People		Race/Ethnic Origin	Ancestry	
Area size:	8,524 sq. mi.	90.4% White	USA: 21.3%	Irish: 8.2%
Urban population:	26.5%	5.1% Black	English: 6.8%	
Rural population:	73.5%	0.2% Asian	**2004 Presidential Vote**	
Pop. 2000:	635,300	0.4% Native Am.	Bush (R) 186,509	(71%)
Median income:	$31,344	0.0% Hawaiian	Kerry (D) 73,504	(28%)
Poverty status:	14.7%	0.8% Two+ races	Other 1,741	(1%)
Military veterans:	12.9%	0.0% Other	**2000 Presidential Vote**	
		3.0% Hispanic Origin	Bush (R) 141,285	(61%)
			Gore (D) 87,062	(37%)
			Other 4,240	(2%)
			Cook Partisan Voting Index: R +16	

Occupation	Blue collar: 40.8%	White collar: 46.0%	Gray collar: 13.2%

The Appalachians' corduroy ridges, dividing the Atlantic coast from the interior, are America's coal-and-steel industrial spine, from the black coal country of western Pennsylvania to the red hill country of northern Alabama. Here rose America's two premier steel cities, Pittsburgh and Birmingham. Around both, and for many miles in between them, is the country settled by feisty Scots-Irish farmers in the years between the Revolution and the Civil War. In valley land accessible to railroads are the great steel factories built in the 80 years after the Civil War and smaller factories that produce underwear and tires, glass and chemicals, socks and chickens. Politically, the two regions were separated by the Civil War: Western Pennsylvania was overwhelmingly Republican until the 1930s, while northern Alabama was solidly Democratic through the 1950s. But they shared the same political impulses—populist on economics, conservative on culture—which made them both Democratic heartlands during the New Deal and in congressional politics for years afterwards. Now they seem to have traded partisan allegiances: Western Pennsylvania is Democratic, though less solidly so when the Democrats emphasize cultural liberalism; northern Alabama has moved toward the Republicans, even though it has benefited from massive federal public works programs, and the movement is most pronounced in counties close to Birmingham and along the interstates.

Alabama's 4th Congressional District is a collection of small towns—Cullman, Jasper, Russellville, Fort Payne, Albertville—with gritty Gadsden, population 37,000, as the biggest city. Sandwiched between Huntsville to the north and Birmingham to the south, the 4th crosses the state and the Appalachian ridges, from the Georgia line to the Mississippi line near lightly populated rural counties. This is Alabama's premier Scots-Irish district, with the lowest black percentage of the state's seven congressional districts.

The congressman from the 4th District is Robert Aderholt (pronounced *ADD-er-holt*), a Republican first elected in 1996 to replace 30-year Democrat Tom Bevill, a senior Appropriations member and benefactor of great federal projects, including the Tennessee-Tombigbee Waterway project. Aderholt is from Winston County, the one ancestrally Republican county in north Alabama, which opposed secession in the Civil War and declared itself the Free State of Winston. His father was a circuit judge for more than 30 years; his wife's father was a state senator and state commissioner of Agriculture and Industry. In 1992, Aderholt was appointed Haleyville municipal judge; in 1995, he became a top aide to Governor Fob James. With that pedigree, he decided to run for Congress when Bevill retired. As Republican nominee, he faced Democratic state Senator Bob Wilson Jr., who called himself a Democrat "in the Tom Bevill tradition." But in this culturally conservative district, Aderholt didn't hedge on cultural issues. Against abortion, gun control and same-sex marriage, and for school prayer, he said, "We want to go to Washington to deliver a message, and that is, don't mess with our traditional family values." He attacked Wilson for his support from unions and trial lawyers, and invited Newt Gingrich to the district. This was a nationally targeted race, seriously contested, and Aderholt won 50%–48%—one reason Republicans held their House majority in 1996.

Recognizing Aderholt's electoral vulnerability, Republican leaders put him on Appropriations; he has brought home more highway and sewer money than most Republicans. And he hasn't forgotten the social issues. After Alabama's ousted Chief Justice Judge Roy Moore called for a new law to prevent federal judges from interfering with public displays of the Ten Commandments, Aderholt sponsored legislation to work toward that goal. "The acknowledgment of God is not a legitimate subject of review by the federal courts," Aderholt said. When the state's public health department required clinics to offer patients morning-after birth control pills, Aderholt joined the local Christian Coalition and got HHS Secretary Tommy Thompson to clarify that the federal government does not mandate emergency contraception services.

Aderholt's voting record is generally conservative, but he is not a reliable free trade vote. He supported quotas on steel imports and sponsored a bill assessing additional antidumping duties on foreign steel in 1999, and he reached out further to industrial unions with his vote against PNTR with China. But after George W. Bush was elected—and after Aderholt got protection for the local sock industry (Fort Payne, with 150 plants, proclaims itself the Sock Capital of the World)—he voted for trade promotion authority in 2002. In the 108th Congress he opposed free trade agreements with Chile, Morocco and Singapore but voted in favor of the U.S.-Australia Free Trade Agreement. Back home, when a group of local paleontologists found in an inactive mine a large trove of fossil tracks that were believed to date back more than 300 million years, Aderholt moved to provide federal protection for the site.

Aderholt faced serious challenges in 1998 and 2000, but has won easily ever since. 2004 Democratic nominee Carl Cole, a recent University of Alabama Law School graduate, said Aderholt "sides with big business over the real people" and drove 20,000 miles across the district in his campaign. But Aderholt pointed out that Cole would cast his first vote in the House "for San Francisco liberal Nancy Pelosi, who's for gay marriage, opposes the rights of gun owners and is for partial birth abortions." Aderholt won, 75%–25%. He appears to have entrenched himself in what used to be a swing seat.

FIFTH DISTRICT

Rep. Bud Cramer (D)

Elected 1990, 8th term; b. Aug. 22, 1947, Huntsville; home, Huntsville; U. of AL, B.A. 1969, J.D. 1972; Methodist; widowed.

Military Career: Army, 1972; Army Reserves, 1976–78.

Professional Career: Instructor, U. of AL Law Schl., Dir., Clinical Studies Program, 1972–73; Madison Cnty. Asst. Dist. Atty., 1973–75; Practicing atty., 1975–80; Madison Cnty. Dist. Atty., 1981–90; Founder, Natl. Children's Advocacy Ctr., 1985.

DC Office: 2368 RHOB, 20515, 202-225-4801; Fax: 202-225-4392; Web site: www.cramer.house.gov.

District Offices: Decatur, 256-355-9400; Huntsville, 256-551-0190; Tuscumbia, 256-381-3450.

Committees: *Appropriations* (17th of 29 D): Military Quality of Life & Veterans Affairs & Related Agencies; Science, State, Justice, Commerce & Related Agencies. *Permanent Select Committee on Intelligence* (5th of 9 D): Oversight (RMM); Technical & Tactical Intelligence.

Group Ratings

	ADA	ACLU	AFS	LCV	ITIC	NTU	COC	ACU	NTLC	CHC
2004	75	25	63	36	89	26	86	50	18	58
2003	45	—	75	35	—	28	89	56	—	—

National Journal Ratings

	2003 LIB	—	2003 CONS	2004 LIB	—	2004 CONS
Economic	51%	—	49%	50%	—	49%
Social	53%	—	46%	48%	—	51%
Foreign	53%	—	47%	54%	—	45%

Key Votes of the 108th Congress

1. Drilling in ANWR	Y	5. DC School Vouchers	N	9. Ban Same-Sex Marriage	Y
2. Approve Bush Tax Cuts	Y	6. Ban Human Cloning	Y	10. Fund Iraq War	Y
3. Medicare/Rx Bill	Y	7. Restrict Gun Liability	Y	11. Bar Cuba Embargo Funds	Y
4. Bar Overtime Pay Regs.	Y	8. Ban Partial-Birth Abortion	Y	12. Intelligence Reorg.	Y

Election Results

2004 general	Bud Cramer (D)	200,999	(73%)	($588,838)
	Gerald Wallace (R)	74,145	(27%)	($12,610)
	Other	315	(0%)	
2004 primary	Bud Cramer (D)	37,573	(90%)	
	Michael Williams (D)	4,393	(10%)	
2002 general	Bud Cramer (D)	143,029	(73%)	($770,032)
	Stephen Engel (R)	48,226	(25%)	($13,593)
	Other	3,916	(2%)	

Prior Winning Percentages: 2000 (89%); 1998 (70%); 1996 (56%); 1994 (50%); 1992 (66%); 1990 (67%)

The People		Race/Ethnic Origin	Ancestry	
Area size:	4,689 sq. mi.	77.7% White	USA: 16.1%	Irish: 8.0%
Urban population:	59.4%	16.9% Black	English: 7.6%	
Rural population:	40.6%	1.0% Asian	**2004 Presidential Vote**	
Pop. 2000:	635,300	0.9% Native Am.	Bush (R) 167,552	(60%)
Median income:	$38,054	0.0% Hawaiian	Kerry (D) 110,633	(39%)
Poverty status:	12.5%	1.4% Two+ races	Other 2,225	(1%)
Military veterans:	14.0%	0.1% Other	**2000 Presidential Vote**	
		2.0% Hispanic Origin	Bush (R) 131,608	(54%)
			Gore (D) 106,685	(44%)
			Other 5,241	(2%)
			Cook Partisan Voting Index: R + 6	
Occupation	Blue collar: 29.6%	White collar: 57.1%	Gray collar: 13.3%	

Twice this century, the federal government has transformed the northern Alabama counties along the Tennessee River. The first time was when it created the Tennessee Valley Authority in 1933. Proposed by Nebraska Senator George Norris, a favorite of President Franklin Roosevelt, TVA took the World War I federal munitions plant at Muscle Shoals on the unnavigable Tennessee River, and built a series of dams to control flooding and produce cheap hydroelectric power. This was backward country then: Poor white farmers scratched an existence out of hardscrabble land, were housed in shacks without electricity or running water, and lived off a diet that produced pellagra and rickets. The TVA was intended to showcase what an enlightened, generous federal government could do. The second major federal project here was the space program. After the Soviets put up Sputnik in 1957, the Redstone Arsenal in Huntsville became the nation's major missile development center—the first of the large U.S. ballistic missiles were developed here. On the grounds of Redstone, NASA built its Marshall Space Flight Center in the 1960s and the Huntsville-Decatur area soon achieved high-tech critical mass. With leadership from Werner von Braun and other German engineers, Redstone and Marshall built Explorer 1, the first American orbiting satellite, the Mercury-Redstone vehicle that boosted astronaut Alan Shepard into suborbital flight and the Saturn V rocket that sent man to the moon. In the 1970s, Marshall produced Skylab and developed the Space Shuttle's main engines and solid rocket boosters. In 1990, it helped launch the Hubble Space Telescope. The Boeing research center here has been a prime contractor for the space station. Boeing also produces its Delta IV booster out of its local factory in Decatur. Fifty years ago Huntsville was a sleepy town huddled around a well-preserved early 19th century residential district. Today it is the center of Alabama's third-largest and fast-growing metro area.

The 5th Congressional District of Alabama takes in most of the state's TVA and space counties. TVA and the space program were primarily Democratic projects, and for years most voters here were staunch New Deal Democrats, liberal on economics and not much interested in race, like the longtime Senator John Sparkman, the party's vice presidential nominee in 1952. But professional and technical people in the space business tend to combine high-tech and traditional values, and this made much of northern Alabama marginal-to-Republican country in the 1990s. This district has never elected a Republican to Congress, but it has voted Republican for president since the defeat of Jimmy Carter, and in the mid-1990s, it had seriously contested congressional elections.

The congressman from the 5th District is Bud Cramer, a Democrat first elected in 1990. He grew up in Huntsville, served as an Army tank officer after law school, and beat the incumbent district attorney in 1980, at 33. In 1985, he set up the Child Advocacy Center, a child-friendly environment for abused children. When Congressman Ronnie Flippo ran unsuccessfully for governor in 1990, Cramer ran for Congress. He won the general election by a 2–1 margin.

In the House, Cramer has been a tireless booster of the beleaguered Space Station and a leading advocate of a spending boost for missile defense. In the TVA tradition, he supported the Democratic leadership on key issues. But his votes for the Clinton budget and tax package in 1993 and for the Clinton crime bill with its gun control provisions were unpopular locally and in

1994, against Texas Republican Bill Archer's son-in-law, he was reelected by only a 50%–49% margin. Since then, Cramer has avoided liberal votes on most visible issues. With his seat on Appropriations, he has successfully pursued a nonpartisan approach of federal dollars and contracts. The September 11 attacks provided an additional financial boost: Cramer got $23 million for bomb squad training at the Redstone Arsenal. He also was an early supporter of the proposal to create a national intelligence director to oversee the complex intelligence bureaucracy. Child abuse is another issue that has long been of concern to Cramer: As a district attorney, he set up the National Child Advocacy Center, a child-friendly environment for abused children that has trained thousands of caregivers and case workers since opening in 1985. "We are the Mayo Clinic there in Huntsville of child abuse," he boasted. In Congress, Cramer set up a $5 million federal program to encourage similar centers across the country. But the pork-busting Citizens Against Government Waste has listed many of Cramer's local projects in its "Pork Alert" listing, with a salute, "This Bud's for you!"

Cramer's overall voting record remains in the middle of the House. But he has voted conservative on key issues, ranging from the Republicans' impeachment inquiry of Bill Clinton to the ban on partial-birth abortions and needle exchanges.

After the 2000 election, Cramer was said to be under consideration for a job in the Bush administration and later was touted as a possible challenger to Jeff Sessions in the 2002 Senate campaign. But he was not appointed by Bush and in May 2001 he said he wouldn't run for the Senate. Before and after the 2002 election, Cramer was strikingly coy about persistent rumors that he might switch parties. "I don't plan on switching parties right now," or, "at this time," he would say. Amid this speculation, Democratic leadership gave him a seat on the Intelligence Committee. Since then, he has been sounding more like a loyal Democrat. When asked in mid-2004 about switching parties, he told the *Huntsville Times,* "I am right where I need to be." After winning 56%–42% in 1996, he has been reelected by much wider margins. He won 73%–27% in 2004, even as George W. Bush was carrying every county in the 5th District.

SIXTH DISTRICT

Rep. Spencer Bachus (R)

Elected 1992, 7th term; b. Dec. 28, 1947, Birmingham; home, Birmingham; Auburn U., B.A. 1969, U. of AL, J.D. 1972; Baptist; married (Linda).

Military Career: Natl. Guard, 1969–71.

Elected Office: AL Senate, 1983–84; AL House of Reps., 1984–87.

Professional Career: Owner, Lumber Co.; Practicing atty., 1972–92; AL Repub. Party Chmn., 1991–92.

DC Office: 442 CHOB, 20515, 202-225-4921; Fax: 202-225-2082; Web site: www.house.gov/bachus.

District Offices: Birmingham, 205-969-2296; Northport, 205-333-9894.

Committees: *Financial Services* (5th of 37 R): Capital Markets, Insurance & Government Sponsored Enterprises; Financial Institutions & Consumer Credit (Chmn.). *Judiciary* (11th of 23 R): Courts, the Internet & Intellectual Property; The Constitution. *Transportation & Infrastructure* (10th of 41 R): Aviation; Highways, Transit & Pipelines; Railroads.

Group Ratings

	ADA	ACLU	AFS	LCV	ITIC	NTU	COC	ACU	NTLC	CHC
2004	5	0	0	0	90	62	100	96	84	92
2003	10	—	0	15	—	63	96	92	—	—

National Journal Ratings

	2003 LIB	—	2003 CONS		2004 LIB	—	2004 CONS
Economic	0%	—	91%		17%	—	80%
Social	5%	—	87%		20%	—	77%
Foreign	0%	—	89%		25%	—	68%

Key Votes of the 108th Congress

1. Drilling in ANWR	Y	5. DC School Vouchers	Y	9. Ban Same-Sex Marriage	Y
2. Approve Bush Tax Cuts	Y	6. Ban Human Cloning	Y	10. Fund Iraq War	Y
3. Medicare/Rx Bill	Y	7. Restrict Gun Liability	Y	11. Bar Cuba Embargo Funds	N
4. Bar Overtime Pay Regs.	N	8. Ban Partial-Birth Abortion	Y	12. Intelligence Reorg.	Y

Election Results

2004 general	Spencer Bachus (R)	264,819	(99%)	($1,376,103)
	Other	3,224	(1%)	
2004 primary	Spencer Bachus (R)	45,448	(87%)	
	Phillip Jauregui (R)	7,000	(13%)	
2002 general	Spencer Bachus (R)	178,171	(90%)	($747,977)
	J. Holden McAllister (Lib)	19,639	(10%)	

Prior Winning Percentages: 2000 (88%); 1998 (72%); 1996 (71%); 1994 (79%); 1992 (52%)

The People		Race/Ethnic Origin	Ancestry	
Area size:	4,649 sq. mi.	88.8% White	USA: 14.5%	English: 10.1%
Urban population:	62.1%	7.7% Black	Irish: 8.1%	
Rural population:	37.9%	0.9% Asian	**2004 Presidential Vote**	
Pop. 2000:	635,300	0.3% Native Am.	Bush (R) 248,095	(78%)
Median income:	$46,946	0.0% Hawaiian	Kerry (D) 69,449	(22%)
Poverty status:	8.1%	0.7% Two+ races	Other 722	(0%)
Military veterans:	12.9%	0.0% Other	**2000 Presidential Vote**	
		1.6% Hispanic Origin	Bush (R) 200,818	(74%)
			Gore (D) 67,975	(25%)
			Other 3,997	(1%)
			Cook Partisan Voting Index: R +25	
Occupation	Blue collar: 22.1%	White collar: 67.7%	Gray collar: 10.2%	

Birmingham, once one of America's booming industrial cities, then the site of violence in the civil rights revolution, now has future prospects far more hopeful than seemed possible not long ago. This is a new city by southern standards: Before the Civil War there was nothing here but a few creeks running below Red Mountain. But Red Mountain is almost pure iron ore, and by 1890, Birmingham had the South's largest steel mills. In the early 20th century, as the statue of Vulcan, Roman god of fire and metalworking, looked out over the smokestack-rich valley, Birmingham seemed the most up-to-date and progressive city in the South. But the worldwide overcapacity in steel and technological obsolescence at home sent the American steel industry into long-term decline starting in the 1950s. Meanwhile, industrial Birmingham's political leaders plotted to avoid desegregation, and the city's violent reaction to civil rights—Police Commissioner (and Democratic National Committeeman at the time) Bull Connor set dogs and fire hoses against peaceful demonstrators, and Ku Klux Klansmen bombed the 16th Street Baptist Church, killing four young girls in 1963—made a vivid impression over the new medium of television news, spurring the Civil Rights Act of 1964, and created a reputation from which Birmingham still suffered a generation later. The convictions in May 2001 and May 2002 of the last surviving suspects in the church bombing triggered renewed criticism of J. Edgar Hoover's FBI for its lack of vigilance in the case; that incident became the topic of *Four Little Girls*, a film documentary by Spike Lee. More bad publicity resulted when the Vulcan statue deteriorated, a victim of age and the icon of a deteriorating industry; federal money restored it and the statue has been returned to its pedestal.

But in recent years Birmingham has worked to improve race relations and has developed a new economic base to generate growth. Health care is one major industry: Birmingham has some of the largest and most advanced medical care centers in the South, and is especially renowned for its sports medicine facilities and specialists. Banking is the other: While Atlanta's banks foundered and were acquired by outsiders, Birmingham became the largest southern banking center after Charlotte, North Carolina, with headquarters of SouthTrust (which recently merged with Charlotte-based Wachovia), AmSouth Bancorp, Regions Financial, and Compass Bancshares. But city leaders worry that downtown may become "irrelevant," and white movement to newer suburbs has arguably increased racial polarization. The city's population has declined by 100,000 since 1960 and was 74% black in 2000. Whites have been moving out of Birmingham's Jefferson County southeast to Shelby County, which grew 44% in the 1990s—the fastest growth in the state—and is now 90% white. As a result, Jefferson County, once more Republican than most of Alabama, votes Democratic in close statewide elections, while Shelby County is one of the most Republican counties in the state.

The 6th Congressional District of Alabama, which once included all of Birmingham and most of Jefferson County, is now the suburban Birmingham-area district and strongly Republican. It includes parts of Jefferson County (such as prosperous Mountain Brook), and stretches southwest to Tuscaloosa and south along Interstate 65 halfway to Montgomery. In 2002, the Democratic line-drawers made it even more Republican, removing the last part of Birmingham and some black precincts in Tuscaloosa, and adding most of fast-growing St. Clair County north of Shelby County. Today, this is one of the most Republican districts in the nation: it voted 74% for George W. Bush in 2000—his second best district (the first was the Nebraska 3d) outside of Texas. In 2004, it broke even harder for Bush, giving him 78% and ranking as his second-best district in the nation.

The congressman from the 6th District is Republican Spencer Bachus (pronounced *BACK-us*). A Birmingham native, he owned a sawmill company and practiced law; he boasts that he was a good enough trial lawyer to have produced four straight acquittals in murder trials. Elected to the state legislature in 1982, he was an activist—though one of very few Republicans. After running unsuccessfully for attorney general in 1990, he became Republican state chairman. When the 6th District was radically redrawn in 1992, he won a Republican runoff and defeated incumbent Ben Erdreich, a moderate Democrat.

Bachus has a mostly, though not totally, conservative voting record and has been an aggressive lawmaker and investigator. As chairman of Banking's oversight subcommittee, he discovered that the Community Development Financial Institute, which Bill Clinton established in 1994, directed $11 million in loans to four banks with ties to Hillary Rodham Clinton without proper documentation; the two top CDFI officials resigned as a consequence. With George W. Bush in the White House, Bachus has had a less adversarial role as chairman of the Financial Institutions and Consumer Credit Subcommittee, although he was an early critic of then-Securities and Exchange Commission chairman Harvey Pitt. He helped to enact changes in the Fair Credit Reporting Act, which provided consumers additional access to their credit reports and helped to cut back on identity theft, but also stripped away some state law privacy protections. He led hearings on the NCAA's investigations of rules compliance by university athletic programs, including complaints that the University of Alabama and Auburn University had been unfairly placed on probation; Bachus criticized the association for failure to allow open hearings in its review process. He has been something of a maverick on foreign policy. In the 1990s, Bachus became an unlikely crusader for international debt relief for poor Third World nations. He joined a broad coalition of domestic and international activists in a one-day fast to demand action, which ultimately proved successful. In early 2002, he criticized the Bush administration's dealings with the genocidal regime in Sudan. Later that year, he was a prime backer of the Sudan Peace Act, which threatens diplomatic reprisals and supports rebel groups. He also urged Bush to stop payment of oil revenues to the Sudanese government.

In 2004, Bachus faced an infrequent primary challenge: Phillip Jauregui, the lawyer for ousted Alabama Chief Justice Roy Moore. This looked like a conflict between religious and business conservatives but Bachus emphasized his conservative credentials and proudly noted that he had the lowest ACLU rating in the Alabama delegation; he won 87%–13%. In November, he was unopposed. Bachus has voiced interest in a statewide race, and could be a Senate candidate if Richard Shelby or Jeff Sessions retires.

SEVENTH DISTRICT

Rep. Artur Davis (D)

Elected 2002, 2d term; b. Oct. 9, 1967, Montgomery; home, Birmingham; Harvard U., B.A. 1990, J.D. 1993; Lutheran; single.

Professional Career: Asst. U.S. atty., 1994–1998, Practicing atty., 1998–2002

DC Office: 208 CHOB, 20515, 202-225-2665; Fax: 202-226-9567; Web site: www.house.gov/arturdavis/.

District Offices: Birmingham, 205-254-1960; Demopolis, 334-287-0860; Livingston, 205-652-5834; Selma, 334-877-4414; Tuscaloosa, 205-752-5380.

Committees: *Budget* (10th of 17 D). *Financial Services* (27th of 32 D): Capital Markets, Insurance & Government Sponsored Enterprises; Housing & Community Opportunity; Oversight & Investigations.

Group Ratings

	ADA	ACLU	AFS	LCV	ITIC	NTU	COC	ACU	NTLC	CHC
2004	75	70	75	64	90	12	71	24	6	33
2003	90	—	100	60	—	23	50	32	—	—

National Journal Ratings

	2003 LIB	—	2003 CONS		2004 LIB	—	2004 CONS
Economic	60%	—	40%		60%	—	40%
Social	67%	—	31%		64%	—	35%
Foreign	70%	—	27%		66%	—	33%

Key Votes of the 108th Congress

1. Drilling in ANWR	N	5. DC School Vouchers	N	9. Ban Same-Sex Marriage	Y
2. Approve Bush Tax Cuts	N	6. Ban Human Cloning	Y	10. Fund Iraq War	N
3. Medicare/Rx Bill	N	7. Restrict Gun Liability	Y	11. Bar Cuba Embargo Funds	N
4. Bar Overtime Pay Regs.	Y	8. Ban Partial-Birth Abortion	Y	12. Intelligence Reorg.	Y

Election Results

2004 general	Artur Davis (D)	183,408	(75%)	($1,068,606)
	Steve Cameron (R)	61,019	(25%)	
	Other	211	(0%)	
2004 primary	Artur Davis (D)	58,793	(88%)	
	Albert Turner (D)	8,061	(12%)	
2002 general	Artur Davis (D)	153,735	(92%)	($1,441,878)
	Lauren Orth McCay (Lib)	12,100	(7%)	

The People		Race/Ethnic Origin	Ancestry	
Area size:	8,780 sq. mi.	35.5% White	USA: 7.1%	English: 3.7%
Urban population:	72.2%	61.7% Black	Irish: 3.5%	
Rural population:	27.8%	0.6% Asian	**2004 Presidential Vote**	
Pop. 2000:	635,300	0.2% Native Am.	Kerry (D) 160,875	(64%)
Median income:	$26,672	0.0% Hawaiian	Bush (R) 88,433	(35%)
Poverty status:	24.7%	0.6% Two+ races	Other 233	(0%)
Military veterans:	11.6%	0.1% Other	**2000 Presidential Vote**	
		1.3% Hispanic Origin	Gore (D) 158,580	(66%)
			Bush (R) 78,670	(33%)
			Other 1,827	(1%)
			Cook Partisan Voting Index: D +17	

Occupation	Blue collar: 28.6%	White collar: 53.4%	Gray collar: 18.0%

Alabama celebrates its black heritage more than any other state, building striking memorials to the civil rights movement in Montgomery and Birmingham, commemorating with dignified restraint a history that was full of raucous hatred and moving sacrifice. Blacks first came here as slaves; the last slave ship to the United States, the *Clotilde*, docked in Mobile in 1859, where its cargo was then set free. Blacks were part of the great migration into the cottonlands after the Jacksonians swept the Indians out of the Southeast and sent them on their Trail of Tears to what is now Oklahoma. Today, Alabama's rural blacks are still clustered in the Black Belt of fertile dark soil across the center of the state. In Selma, founded by Alabama's one vice president, William Rufus King, Sheriff Jim Clark's troops beat up peaceful marchers on the Edmund Pettus Bridge in demonstrations that led to the march on Montgomery and the 1965 Voting Rights Act. All 10 of Alabama's majority-black counties are in the rich farm country of the Black Belt but most Alabama blacks now live in urban areas—one-quarter in metropolitan Birmingham.

The 7th Congressional District of Alabama was created in 1992 as a black-majority district. It includes Black Belt counties where the Alabama and Tombigbee Rivers flow past old plantations, plus part of Tuscaloosa, home of the University of Alabama, and nearby Vance, site of a Mercedes factory. But most of its people are in Birmingham and surrounding Jefferson County. The 2002 redistricting removed part of Montgomery County and black-majority Lowndes County just to the west, and more of Birmingham and Jefferson County were added. The district's black percentage dropped from 70% to 62% and more than 40% of the residents were new, but it remained solidly Democratic.

The congressman from the 7th District is Artur Davis, first elected at age 35 in 2002. Davis grew up in Montgomery and was raised by his mother and grandmother. He graduated from Harvard and Harvard Law School, then returned to Alabama. After working as an intern in the Southern Poverty Law Center and as a clerk to federal Judge Myron Thompson, he served four years as an assistant U.S. attorney. Later, he practiced law in Birmingham. In 2000, he challenged 7th District incumbent Earl Hilliard in the Democratic primary. He criticized the incumbent's controversial trip to Libya, taken despite the State Department ban on travel in what was then a terrorist state, and argued that Hilliard failed to aid his financially pressed district. Davis ran a vigorous campaign, but lost 58%–34%.

In 2002 Davis ran again, in the altered district. Much of the dialogue focused on race and Middle East politics. Campaign surrogates for Hilliard questioned whether Davis was "black enough" to represent the district. Referring to Davis' background as a federal prosecutor, Hilliard claimed that, "the only thing [Davis] has done for black people is put them in jail." Davis framed the debate as a generational battle between old-style black machine politics and a fresher, more effective approach. One key to Davis's victory appeared to be strong financial backing from supporters of Israel: Hilliard was one of only 21 House members to vote against a resolution supporting Israel's fight against terrorism, just weeks after Palestinian suicide bombers killed hundreds of Israelis. Otherwise, the two candidates had relatively few major policy differences. In the June 4 primary, Hilliard led Davis by only 46%–43% and was forced into a runoff. Hilliard took the offensive with an unsubstantiated charge that Davis had been the target of a date-rape accusation and ran an ad that depicted Davis as "for sale" to cigar-smoking fat cats. Several Congressional Black Caucus members, plus Al Sharpton, came in to campaign for Hilliard; some criticized the Democratic leadership for its perceived lack of support for the incumbent. Davis accused Hilliard of being divisive and called for "healing." Outspending Hilliard by nearly $180,000, Davis won the June 25 runoff 56%–44%. He had no trouble winning in November.

In the House Davis quickly reached out to other Black Caucus members, though some tensions remained from Hilliard's allies. Davis has a moderate voting record for House Democrats, with a less liberal ranking than Hilliard. He focused on rural issues—environmentally unsafe landfills, inadequate supplies of doctors and hospitals. Working with a bipartisan coalition, he called for trade protection to level the playing field with China; his particular concerns were the steel and catfish industries. Following a visit to Israel, he said that the United States must remain "an engaged partner to our ally Israel," and he discussed common bonds between American blacks and Jews.

Davis told local audiences that blacks must move beyond a preoccupation with race. "Too many of us, black and white, are teaching our children first and foremost about what separates us," he said. He also criticized national Democrats—including John Kerry's presidential campaign—for calling on black lawmakers only to rally black voters. In the 2004 primary, Davis was challenged by Albert Turner, a son of a leader of Selma's "Bloody Sunday" march. Turner criticized Davis for not giving sufficient priority to Black Belt needs and called him a self-promoter. With endorsements from most leading local Democrats, Davis won 88%–12%, a bigger margin than even he expected. In the general, against former NASA engineer Steve Cameron, who said he wanted to recruit more black Christians to the Republican Party, Davis won 75%–25%. He has said he plans to run for statewide office in the future. He told the *Mobile Register* in 2005 that he would not challenge Senator Jeff Sessions in 2008 or run for governor against a Democratic incumbent; Davis also said he would run for Senate if Richard Shelby decides not to run for reelection in 2010.

★ ALASKA ★

With 16% of the nation's land area and 0.22% of the nation's population, Alaska is America in the Arctic, a state created by a federal government which it now often resents and an individualistic society that has responded to its unique situation in creative ways that commend themselves to the attention of what Alaskans call the Lower 48 or, more simply, Outside. Alaska would not be American at all but for the expansive dream of Secretary of State William Seward, who took advantage of a fleeting opportunity to create an American Pacific empire by purchasing it from Russia in 1867 for $7.2 million. The Alaska Territory owed most of its early growth to decisions made by the federal government. It started growing feverishly with the Klondike gold rush in 1897, just as William McKinley reaffirmed the gold standard. Anchorage, the major city here, had its beginnings in 1913 as the chief worksite of the federal government's Alaska Railroad. The Alcan Highway, connecting Alaska to the Lower 48, was built by the Army in the grim war days of 1942, when the Aleutian island of Attu was held by the Japanese, the only part of the United States occupied by a foreign enemy since the War of 1812. During the Cold War, Alaska was the only state abutting the Soviet Union, across the Bering Strait and over the North Pole. Even today Alaska remains militarily strategic, and the military remains a major presence at Fort Richardson and Elmendorf Air Force Base near Anchorage and Fort Wainwright and Eielson Air Force Base near Fairbanks, and the Pentagon in 2004 installed interceptors for the national missile defense system at Fort Greely 100 miles southeast. Alaska's giant size remains hard for Americans to comprehend: If superimposed on the Lower 48, it would stretch from Florida to southern California to Lake Superior. One-third of Alaskans have no access to the state's roads and are reachable only by boat or airplane; Alaska has, per capita, six times the number of pilots and 14 times the number of airplanes as the rest of the nation, and 663 registered airports. Yet only 655,000 of 293.7 million Americans live here, more than 40% in the Anchorage area, the rest in Fairbanks in the interior and Juneau in the Panhandle and scattered in small towns and Native settlements over millions of acres of stunning scenery and bleak tundra.

Statehood was won in 1959, after a valiant campaign. But statehood did not end federal decision-making power over Alaska—or the widespread resentment of it. Alaska's economy at statehood depended on fishing, oil production in Cook Inlet around Anchorage and the military—all federally regulated or controlled. Less than a decade later, however, Alaska's economy and public life were reshaped by the discovery of North Slope oil. It began suddenly, accidentally: On the day after Christmas 1967, at Prudhoe Bay on the Arctic coast, an undulating roar as loud as four jumbo jets directly overhead drew a crowd of 40 men, heavily clothed against the 30-below weather, to an oil rig. Suddenly a natural gas flare shot 30 feet straight up: This was the great 12 billion barrel North Slope oil field. Earlier oil companies had drilled seven dry wells on Prudhoe Bay, and Arco chief executive Robert Anderson wouldn't have ordered this last try, except that he had a drilling rig nearby. This was the greatest oil strike ever in the United States and the beginning of much of today's Alaska.

Finding oil in Prudhoe Bay was something like finding it on the moon. It was not clear in 1967 who owned the oil or how it could be taken out. The Statehood Act of 1959 provided for the

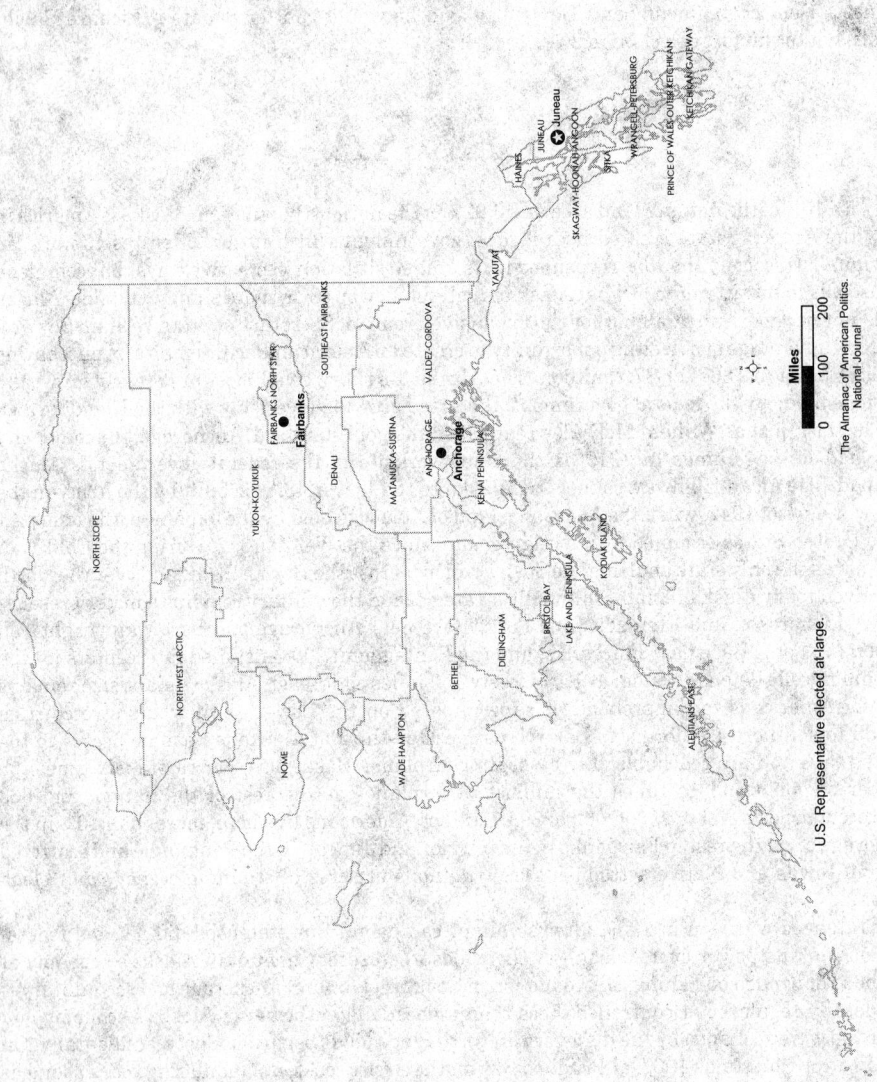

NORTH SLOPE

NORTHWEST ARCTIC

NOME

YUKON-KOYUKUK

FAIRBANKS NORTH STAR
Fairbanks

SOUTHEAST FAIRBANKS

DENALI

MATANUSKA-SUSITNA

VALDEZ-CORDOVA

ANCHORAGE
Anchorage

KENAI PENINSULA

WADE HAMPTON

BETHEL

DILLINGHAM

BRISTOL BAY

LAKE AND PENINSULA

KODIAK ISLAND

ALEUTIANS EAST

YAKUTAT

HAINES

JUNEAU
★ Juneau

SKAGWAY-HOONAH-ANGOON

SITKA

WRANGELL-PETERSBURG

PRINCE OF WALES-OUTER KETCHIKAN

KETCHIKAN GATEWAY

Miles
0   100   200

The Almanac of American Politics.
National Journal

U.S. Representative elected at-large.

state to choose its own public lands, but only after settling Native land claims. Congress, not Alaska, settled such claims in the 1971 Alaska Native Claims Act which set up 12 regional and 220 village Native corporations, gave them $962 million and time to select their own 44 million acres, and ended the Interior Department's freeze that enabled the state to stake claims to mineral-rich acreage. The only feasible way to get the oil out—the Arctic Ocean ice only breaks up in late July for six weeks—was a pipeline. But that was opposed by environmentalists for fear it would destroy the delicate permafrost and interfere with caribou migrations. Development-minded Alaskans got a pipeline bill through Congress in 1973, by just a one-vote margin in the Senate, but the pipeline had to be built on stilts and wasn't opened until 1977, and Congress banned oil exports to Japan and other obvious East Asian markets. Then in 1980, after brilliant lobbying by environmentalists, Congress passed—over the objections of Alaska's two senators and in the face of tears from its Congressman-at-Large Don Young—the Alaska Lands Act, which set aside 159 million acres as national parks, national monuments or wilderness: One-third of the state was protected from development. Much, if not all, of this was for the best. The pipeline came on line just as oil prices were approaching their peak, thus generating maximum revenues to the state, which gets 100% of the royalties. The environment was protected much better than it would have been without the environmentalists' safeguards—while there have been complaints about pipeline and oil field safety, operations are good by industrial standards. The caribou herd has risen from 3,000 animals to 32,000 and the Natives got more autonomy than the non-Native majority of Alaskans would have given them. With oil providing more than 80% of its revenue, the state abolished its income tax in 1980 and created a low-tax regime that has helped Alaska to grow even as oil revenues and military spending declined.

Wisely, Alaska did not squander its windfall. In 1976, Governor Jay Hammond persuaded the legislature to establish a Permanent Fund for most of the oil revenues. Each year it presents every one-year resident with a dividend of 20% of the average of profits for the preceding five years—$1,107 in 2003, $919 in 2004. More important, even though $13 billion has been paid in dividends, most of the money has been invested. The North Slope is producing less than half as much oil as in the late 1980s, but the Permanent Fund was worth $27.4 billion in 2004, and most of its income now comes from investments rather than oil. Some speculated that Alaska voters would pressure legislators for bigger payouts. But Alaskans have acted like investors: They want their dividend checks not just now, but in the future. In 1999, after Governor Tony Knowles proposed tapping the Permanent Fund, voters rejected the change by an 83%–17% margin. In spring 2004, Governor Frank Murkowski urged the legislature to use earnings from the Permanent Fund to balance the budget. But the state Senate balked, and it turned out that sharply rising oil prices pushed the state's budget into surplus.

Similarly, the 12 regional Native Corporations created by the Alaska Native Claims Act have proved to be successful, not just in providing income for Natives, but in helping them preserve Native traditions and adapt to Alaska's market economy at their own pace. On Indian reservations in the Lower 48, all land is held by the tribe and supervised by the government; elections held on the political model have produced a winner-take-all politics that is too often corrupt and incapable of pursuing long-range strategies. The corporate model, on the other hand, allows the Alaska Native corporations' management more continuity in office—though some have made bad decisions and been thrown out. But the cumulative voting method, by which a minority can get a seat on the board, has produced management that is sensitive to all opinions. Huge windfalls are avoided because 70% of profits from mineral sales are shared by all corporations. But the corporation itself, not a distant federal bureaucracy, is left with the choice of how much ancestral land to retain and how much to exploit economically. Individual Natives can make the transition from their traditional communal economy, living on subsistence fishing and hunting, or make their way in the market economy; 43% of Natives now live in Anchorage, Fairbanks, Juneau, Matanuska-Susitna or the Kenai Peninsula. The 12 regional Native corporations and the 30 village corporations in 2001 had revenues of $2.9 billion, paid $52.1 million in dividends, had payrolls of $434 million and gave $9.3 million to charities and $4.1 million to scholarships. Under federal law Native corporations are eligible for sole-source Pentagon contracts with no upper limit, and two corporations now contract to provide civilian guards for domestic military installations.

Not all is rosy here. Native villages in the bush have essentially no private sector economy, and rates of alcoholism and suicide remain high. In the solemn mien so typical of Natives, one may be seeing the memory of great kill-offs by disease, which struck Native villages as recently as the 1920s. Native subsistence hunting was threatened by a 1989 state Supreme Court decision that struck down the subsistence preference for fishing and hunting by rural residents. The legislature refused to pass a constitutional amendment allowing it, and in 1999 the Interior Department took over regulation of fishing (it has regulated hunting since 1990) and shut down commercial and sports fishing for a time to protect Natives' subsistence. But in the long run, Natives have made great progress. A May 2004 report by Native organizations showed dramatic improvements since statehood in Native Alaskans' incomes, health and education levels. The credit for that is widely shared; as Julie Kitka of the Alaska Federation of Natives said, "It's fascinating to see a lot of the success that's occurred, based on lots of people's actions—Congress, the state, Alaskans, Natives, corporations, tribes." Alaska's senior Senator Ted Stevens put in a January 2004 appropriation a provision to set up a commission to revise the legal and law enforcement system in rural Alaska and to create an economic development commission to promote private sector investment there. This would be done through Stevens's Denali Commission, which has worked to improve public health standards in the bush.

Still the federal government continues to make decisions that shape Alaska's economy—and not always Alaska's way, despite the clout of Stevens, senator since 1968, and Don Young, Congressman-at-Large since 1973. They have failed to get approval of oil drilling in a small sliver of the Arctic National Wildlife Refuge—an area the size of Washington-area Dulles International Airport in an area the size of Delaware—although it was on the verge of being approved in 1989 when the Exxon *Valdez* ran aground in Prince William Sound in March 1989. Prospects for approval looked better in 2005 but Governor Frank Murkowski warned that "people should not be sharpening drill bits" yet. Environmental groups have made ANWR oil drilling one of their main issues in their direct-mail fundraising even though ANWR is estimated to have between 9 and 16 billion barrels of oil, the most by far in any untapped U.S. oil field. George W. Bush backed it in his 2000 presidential campaign and put it into his energy bill; it passed the House, with strong support from the Teamsters Union, by a 223–206 margin in August 2001, but was blocked in the Senate in 2002 and again in 2003.

In the meantime, they had unexpected success in 2004 on the proposal for a natural gas pipeline. For years gas has been burned off at the wellhead or pumped back into the ground in the North Slope—there is an estimated 30 trillion cubic feet in Prudhoe Bay and another 70 trillion cubic feet elsewhere on the Slope. The long-unpassed energy bill included provisions for a federal loan guarantee of up to 80% of the cost of a gas pipeline, but as it continued to languish Stevens in October 2004 inserted the proposal into the unstoppable military construction appropriation. He omitted the price floor provision guaranteeing the oil companies a minimum price for their gas, but did provide rapid permit approval and avoidance of judicial review; he directed that the pipeline be built across Alaska and not, as some have proposed, east into the Canadian Arctic. Governor Murkowski, Stevens's colleague in the Senate from 1981 to 2002, accepted two proposals—one from the three North Slope oil companies, another from a pipeline company with Native corporations involved—to build the pipeline, and he urged that the state take an equity interest in the project as well. In February 2005 the Federal Energy Regulatory Commission issued standards requiring fair bidding opportunities for small and large companies seeking pipeline access to encourage more exploration of possible gas supplies. Before construction begins, the state must contract with a developer and Canadian regulators will need to act if the pipeline is to go from southern Alaska into Canada. But with oil and natural gas prices high, the pipeline suddenly seemed a real possibility.

Alaska remains heavily dependent on oil and on the federal government, so there is some reason for unease about its economy. Fishing, its largest employer, is a troubled industry. Tourism, the number two employer, is on the rise, with some 1.4 million tourists spending $2 billion a year—some arrive on cruise ships and others head to Denali National Park and Mount McKinley. Tourism is the mainstay of the old Russian-settled capital of Sitka and of the private sector economy in Juneau. Another spur is the air freight business. The Anchorage airport, near the top of the world, is seven hours from New York, Tokyo and London, and is a major cargo transfer point for UPS, FedEx, Northwest Airlines and the U.S. Postal Service. More all-cargo, wide-bodied aircraft move through Anchorage International than any other U.S. airport. The state receives hundreds of millions of dollars every year in "Stevens money"— construction, highway, sewer and harbor projects shepherded by Senator Stevens, chairman of the Appropriations Committee in 1997–2001 and 2003–05 and the most senior Republican in the Senate. Don Young, chairman of the Infrastructure Committee since 2001, sponsors projects as well, including two huge proposed bridges, one to tiny Ketchikan and the other from Anchorage to the largely uninhabited land two miles across Knik Arm. Yet for all its federal help, this is a low-tax, low-regulation state, which has been attracting independent-spirited, entrepreneurial-minded young families; Alaska has the nation's third-youngest population, although its small elderly population is growing (up from 4% to 6% in the 1990s). Big institutions don't run things here: Unions, politically pivotal 25 years ago, are much less so now, and the oil companies, while not unpopular, weren't able to stop higher state oil taxes. The biggest private employers now are not the oil companies, but Safeway and Providence Alaska Medical Center: This is an economy that buzzes with small business success.

Politically, Alaska is heavily Republican, with a libertarian streak. In national politics, it has been solidly Republican since the 1970s because national Democrats have favored locking up natural resources. George W. Bush carried Alaska 59%–28% in 2000 and 61%–36% in 2004, carrying even the traditionally Democratic Panhandle and the Native-majority bush country beyond Anchorage and Fairbanks. No Democrat has been elected to Congress since 1974, and if one came close in 2004, it was in unusual circumstances: Senator Frank Murkowski, elected governor in 2002, promptly appointed his daughter, state Senator Lisa Murkowski, to his U.S. Senate seat. That prompted a proposed state constitutional amendment revoking the appointive power from the governor. It passed, and it almost enabled former Governor Knowles, the Democrats' strongest candidate in years, to beat Lisa Murkowski. But she won 49%–46%. In state races, persona may matter more than party: Frank Murkowski was the first Republican nominee elected governor since 1978. The legislature is solidly Republican, and tends to be more solidly conservative than any governor. Referendums show Alaskans to be increasingly conservative, though with a libertarian tinge: In 1998, they voted for medical marijuana, English-only and a ban on same-sex marriage, though a ban on wolf snaring was defeated. In 2000, they rejected an initiative that would not only have legalized marijuana but would have paid restitution to those convicted of marijuana offenses. In 2004 they rejected medical marijuana once again and rejected a ban on bear baiting.

Regional differences persist. Anchorage is much like a prosperous Rocky Mountains' metropolis with longer summer days and winter nights; it is affluent and booming, with an unusually high percentage of working women. Politically, it is solidly Republican. So are the smaller settlements in a 200-mile arc around Anchorage, which have been growing even more rapidly: the Matanuska-Susitna Valley (one of the few places in Alaska where farming is possible), Seward, the Kenai peninsula and the little port of Valdez at the southern terminus of the pipeline. Fairbanks, Alaska's second-largest city, is a pipeline and mineral service center deep in the interior, unprotected from Arctic winds in winter and crowds of mosquitoes and, in 2004, huge wildfires bellowing smoke, in the brief but hot summer. It tends to vote Republican, too.

The old Alaska, first settled by Russians, can be seen in the towns of the Panhandle and in the capital of Juneau, located on an inlet of the Pacific up against a steep mountain. These are historically Democratic, but variable these days; in the 2002 gubernatorial election, Ketchikan voted for Murkowski, champion of logging in the Tongass, while Juneau, the capital, voted for Lieutenant Governor Fran Ulmer, the city's former mayor. Juneau is a remote site for most Alaskans, reachable only by harrowing and often-cancelled plane rides through the fjords, and there have been efforts to move the capital to a site near Anchorage. Alaskans voted to do so in

1974, but rejected proposals to pay for it in 1978 and 1982. Juneau, threatened with the loss of 40% of its economy, has had no trouble raising up to $1 million to keep state government there. Juneau defeated a proposal to move all state government by 55%–45% in 1994 and a proposal to move the legislature by 67%–33% in 2002. Mostly Democratic is the bush, the villages where Natives—Athabaskans, Aleuts, Yupiks, Inupiats—are the large majority. Natives make up 16% of Alaska's population and nearly 50% in the vast lands north and west of Anchorage and Fairbanks. They are greatly outnumbered and outvoted on many issues, and yet are the object of awed respect for their achievement in building viable civilizations with impressive art traditions in such a forbidding environment.

The People		Race/Ethnic Origin			Military veterans: 71,552 (16.4%)	
Pop. 2004 (est):	655,435	423,788	67.6%	White	WWII: 7.9%	Korea: 6.9%
Pop. 2000:	626,932	21,073	3.4%	Black	Vietnam: 41.2%	Gulf War: 18.4%
Pop. 1990:	550,043	24,741	3.9%	Asian	**Most populous cities (2003):**	
Change 1990–2000:	Up 14.0%	96,505	15.4%	Native Am.	1. Anchorage	270,951
% of U.S. total:	0.2%	3,181	0.5%	Hawaiian	2. Juneau	31,187
Pop. rank:	48th of 50	30,454	4.9%	Two+ races	3. Fairbanks	30,970
Area size:	663,267 sq. mi.	1,338	0.2%	Other	4. Sitka	8,876
State Native:	38.1%	25,852	4.1%	Hisp. Origin	5. Ketchikan	7,453
Non-citizen:	2.7%	**Ancestry**				
Language		German: 12.5%		Irish: 8.1%	Urban population: 65.7%	
English: 82.6%	Asian: 3.9%	English: 7.2%		USA: 4.3%	Rural population: 34.3%	
Spanish: 3.9%		Norwegian: 3.2%				

Education		Work Sector		Legislature	
H.S. Grad:	88.3%	Private: 64.9%	Govt: 26.8%	Senate	12 R 8 D
College Grad:	24.7%	Self: 8.0%	Family: 0.3%	House	26 R 14 D
Industry		Unemployment: 8.6%		Legislative Term Limits: No	
Agri: 4.9%	Con: 7.3%	**Household Income**		**Registered Voters**	
Fin: 4.6%	Info: 2.7%	<15k: 10.6%	15-35k: 21.6%	D: 71,506	(15.1%)
Mfg: 12.2%	Prof: 29.3%	35-50k: 16.0%	50-100k: 35.7%	R: 118,008	(24.9%)
Public: 10.7%	Trade: 14.2%	100-150k: 11.4%	>150k: 4.6%	O: 284,413	(60.0%)
Other: 14.2%		Median: $51,571			
Occupation		Poverty status: 9.4%			
Blue collar: 22.4%	White collar: 60.5%	**Home Value**			
Gray collar: 17.1%		<50k: 12.1%	50-100k: 17.7%	100-200k: 51.4%	200-300k: 13.7%
		300-500k: 4.0%	>500k: 1.2%	Median: $137,400	

Presidential politics   In presidential elections, Alaska votes Alaska issues, but this was not always so: In 1960 and 1968, its votes came eerily close to the national average. Since then it has voted against the national Democrats: in 1980, the year of the Alaska Lands Act, it gave only 26% of its votes to Jimmy Carter, who in some places ran behind Libertarian Ed Clark. In 1992, Ross Perot won 28% here, his second-best showing in the country. In 2000, George W. Bush won 59%–28%, but Ralph Nader got 10% of the vote—his best showing in the country. There was a big gender gap: men voted 65%–24% for Bush, which recalls the plaint of Alaskan women who are outnumbered by men: "The odds are good but the goods are odd." In 2004 Bush

2004 Presidential Vote		
Bush (R)	190,889	(61%)
Kerry (D)	111,025	(36%)
Nader (POP)	5,069	(2%)
Other	5,615	(2%)

2000 Presidential Vote		
Bush (R)	167,398	(59%)
Gore (D)	79,004	(28%)
Nader (Green)	28,747	(10%)
Other	10,411	(4%)

got 61% and John Kerry improved on Al Gore's showing with 36%: Democratic nominees tend to do better here if they do not bear the burden of the environmental policies of an incumbent Democratic administration.

Alaska has no presidential primary. Party true believers tend to dominate the caucuses. In the January 1996 straw poll or "beauty contest," Alaska Republicans voted 33% for Pat

Buchanan, 31% for Steve Forbes, and 17% for Bob Dole. This gave Buchanan the confidence and verve he showed weeks later in Louisiana, where he beat Phil Gramm, and in other early contests climaxed by his win in New Hampshire on February 20. But Buchanan got only 2% here in November 2000. In November 1999, the Republican Party committee voted 39–36 to hold precinct caucuses and a straw poll on January 24, 2000. About 4,000 Alaskans voted, and George W. Bush led Forbes by 5 votes. Alaska, unlike Florida, didn't have a recount. In 2004, Democrats here, like Democrats Outside, rallied early to John Kerry.

Governor

Frank Murkowski (R)

Elected 2002, term expires Dec. 2006, 1st term; b. Mar. 28, 1933, Seattle, WA; home, Fairbanks; U. of Santa Clara, 1951–53, Seattle U., B.A. 1955; Catholic; married (Nancy).

Military Career: Coast Guard, 1955–56.

Elected Office: U.S. Senate, 1980–2002.

Professional Career: Pacific Natl. Bank of Seattle, 1957–58; Natl. Bank of AK, 1959–67; Commissioner, AK Dept. of Econ. Devel., 1966–70; Pres., AK Natl. Bank of the North, 1971–80.

Office: P.O. Box 110001, Juneau, 99811, 907-465-3500; Fax: 907-465-3532; Web site: www.gov.state.ak.us.

Election Results

2002 general	Frank Murkowski (R)	129,279	(56%)
	Fran Ulmer (D)	94,216	(41%)
	Other	7,989	(3%)
2002 primary	Frank Murkowski (R)	50,838	(70%)
	Wayne Ross (R)	18,852	(26%)
	Other	2,558	(4%)
1998 general	Tony Knowles (D)	112,879	(51%)
	Robin Taylor (write-in)	43,571	(20%)
	John Lindauer (R)	39,331	(18%)
	Ray Metcalfe (RP)	13,540	(6%)
	Other	10,856	(5%)

Frank Murkowski, elected governor in 2002, grew up in Seattle and Ketchikan, the logging town in the Panhandle, where his father was a banker. He went to college in California and Seattle, served in the Coast Guard, worked in a Seattle bank, then returned to Alaska while it was still a territory. He worked for a bank in Wrangell and Anchorage, then at 32 was appointed Commissioner of Economic Development by Governor Walter Hickel. He ran for Congress and lost 55%–45% to incumbent Democrat Nick Begich in 1970, then was president of a bank in Fairbanks for nine years. In 1980, he ran for the Senate and won a six-candidate Republican primary with 59% of the vote. In the Democratic primary incumbent Mike Gravel lost to liberal Clark Gruening, grandson of one of Alaska's first two senators. Murkowski campaigned against environmental restriction groups and called Gruening a "no growther"—not a popular position: Jimmy Carter, who signed the Alaska Lands Act that year, got only 26% of Alaskans' votes. Murkowski won 54%–46%.

In the Senate, Murkowski took a seat on the Energy and Natural Resources Committee, which he chaired from 1995 to June 2001. In 1991, he helped secure a ban on drift net fishing in international waters and the lifting of the ban on Alaska oil exports to Asia in 1995. Usually he worked in tandem with senior colleague Ted Stevens, though they differed on a few issues—commercial fishing in Glacier Bay National Park and subsistence hunting and fishing.

Murkowski's great frustrations came on issues involving opposite ends of Alaska—logging in the Tongass National Forest near Ketchikan and oil drilling in the Arctic National Wildlife Reserve. Murkowski opposed Clinton administration attempts to stamp out logging in the Tongass, but the amount of timber taken there still declined 75% in the 1990s. He managed to get enough logging for one sawmill in Ketchikan, and more logging was allowed by the Bush administration. Clinton vetoed a bill allowing ANWR drilling in 1995, and Murkowski's attempts to pass it as part of an energy bill in 2001 and 2002 were unsuccessful. In April 2002, he was able to get only 46 votes to stop the filibuster threatened by several Democrats, far short of the needed 60; Murkowski and Stevens said that they would have had 51 votes for passage had it come to the floor. A ploy to win votes by using some of the revenues for health benefits for retired steel workers fell even farther short. Murkowski proved more successful getting into the energy bill tax credits estimated at $20 billion for a natural gas pipeline from the North Slope (where gas is now pumped back into the ground) to Fairbanks and then east through Canada to the Lower 48. But despite Murkowski's yeoman efforts, the energy bill did not pass.

Murkowski was reelected to the Senate in 1998 by 74%–20%. There is little doubt that he could have won reelection in 2004. But he evidently found his Senate career frustrating. He had devoted thousands of hours to the ANWR and Tongass issues, with little success. Democrats had a Senate majority in 2001, when he was making his decision to run for governor, so he was no longer a chairman, and term limits would have forced him out of the top Republican spot on the Energy Committee in 2003; on Finance, his other major committee, he ranked behind Charles Grassley and Orrin Hatch and figured he wouldn't have a shot at that chair for eight more years, when he would be 77. He had seriously considered running against Democratic Governor Tony Knowles in 1998, and in 2002 Knowles was prevented from running by term limits. So in October 2001, by a press release from his Senate office, he announced he was running for governor.

During Knowles's governorship the state was faced with serious fiscal problems. Alaska gets 80% of its state revenues from royalties on oil, and Prudhoe Bay production was running at about half the levels of the mid-1980s. As oil prices fell, the state faced unpalatable choices: cut spending on services, institute a state income or sales tax or spend some of the income of the Permanent Fund, thereby reducing Alaskans' annual dividends. The voters strongly rejected the third alternative, 83%–17%, in a 1999 referendum, and were obviously hostile to the second. So the legislature imposed stringent cuts and the budget was balanced by drawing on the Constitutional Budget Reserve—money set aside earlier from the Permanent Fund. In April 2002, the state budget was facing an $865 million shortfall; by Election Day, it was routinely described as $1 billion. It was widely predicted that the $2.1 billion Constitutional Budget Reserve would be drawn down to zero during the next governor's four-year term.

In the Republican primary Murkowski beat Anchorage lawyer Wayne Ross 70%–26%. The Democratic nominee was Lieutenant Governor Fran Ulmer, who had a career in Alaska politics almost as long as Murkowski's. She moved from Wisconsin to Juneau in the early 1970s and, while still in her 20s, was a policy adviser to Governor Jay Hammond, in the years when he established the Permanent Fund. She was mayor of Juneau from 1983–85, won election to the state House in 1986 and, as a two-term lieutenant governor, worked closely with Knowles.

Murkowski and Ulmer took diametrically opposed positions on Alaska's future. Murkowski said that Alaska should look to greater production of oil and natural gas for economic growth and state revenue. Ulmer said the state should try to diversify its economy. Murkowski opposed new taxes and talked about cutting spending. Ulmer called for caps on spending, plus a "parachute plan" to institute a statewide tax when the Constitutional Budget Reserve fell below $1 billion. "My commitment is to protect the dividend, control spending and get this state moving," Murkowski said; he counseled against "gloom and doom" about the $1 billion shortfall. He called for building roads and other transportation infrastructure—roads from Skagway to Juneau, along the Bradfield Canal near Wrangell, from Anchorage to Bristol Bay, to Cordova, from King Cove to Cold Bay and to remote mining prospect towns like Donlin Creek and Pogo, plus a bridge over Knik Arm near Anchorage and an Alaska-Canada Railroad. Ulmer questioned how Murkowski could pay for these projects and said his approach to the budget was "don't worry, be happy."

Jay Hammond, though a Republican, cut spots for Ulmer in which he charged that Murkowski's reliance on unproven oil and gas revenues would leave state government with no choice but to take money from the Permanent Fund dividend. Murkowski countered that Ulmer had sponsored two amendments to use Permanent Fund earnings for ongoing state government.

They did agree on some things: Both opposed moving the legislature from Juneau and both promised not to tap the Permanent Fund without a referendum. In ads Murkowski showed Ulmer gleefully casting Alaska's votes for Bill Clinton at the Democratic National Convention and Ulmer chided Murkowski for giving up 22 years of seniority in the Senate.

Polls showed a close race, but Murkowski won by a solid 56%–41% margin. The margin was just about the same in greater Anchorage, which cast 39% of the state's votes (55%–42%), although Anchorage used to be the state's Republican stronghold. Now, the greatest Republican strength is in fast-growing areas around Anchorage—the Kenai Peninsula and Valdez (65%–31% Murkowski) and the Matanuska Valley (68%–28%), where voters have a strong libertarian, anti-tax streak. Greater Fairbanks also went for the Republican (57%–39%), and Murkowski carried the Kodiak-Bristol Bay area (54%–43%). The Bush, as usual, was heavily Democratic (66%–29% Ulmer), but in the formerly Democratic Panhandle the race was even (49%–49%): Murkowski's big margin in Ketchikan neutralized Ulmer's big margin in Juneau.

Murkowski took office December 2 and for the next two years his approval ratings were low. Under a law passed by the legislature over Knowles's veto, he was permitted to appoint his successor in the Senate—on December 20, he chose his daughter, Lisa, a controversial move to say the least. Also controversial were Murkowski's budget cuts—$138 million of vetoes in 2003, including an end to the $44 million longevity bonus for seniors (originally passed to get them to stay in the state)—and his advocacy of a sales tax. In December 2003 Murkowski announced a budget with tax increases on cigarettes and cruise ship passengers. In January 2004 he called for creation of a commission to authorize spending of a limited amount of Permanent Fund income— something he had not campaigned on. The House voted to tap the Permanent Fund but the Senate balked, despite Murkowski threats to cut spending on education, public radio and television (very widely relied on in Alaska) and the Alaska Marine Highway Service. A special session called in June voted a cigarette tax increase but refused to touch the Permanent Fund. By July it was apparent that higher oil prices would produce a budget surplus; Murkowski cut only $5 million with vetoes. The Permanent Fund dividend dropped from $1,107 to $919.

Murkowski's goal of a natural gas pipeline suddenly became much closer in October 2004, when Senator Ted Stevens inserted a pipeline provision into the military construction appropriation. The provision did not include the price floor the three North Slope oil companies had sought, but it did offer loans up to 80% of the pipeline cost, streamlined permitting and judicial review and state control of in-state use of gas. It rejected the route through Canada's Mackenzie River delta in the Arctic which Murkowski had always opposed, and approved a route south into much of Alaska and then through Canada. Murkowski quickly began setting out terms for a state contract with two consortiums, one including the North Slope oil companies and another including a pipeline company and Native corporations; his proposal for the state to acquire an ownership interest was enthusiastically seconded by Stevens. To encourage exploration of possible gas supplies, the Federal Energy Regulatory Commission's pipeline standards issued in February 2005 require fair bidding opportunities on pipeline access for small and large companies. Many obstacles remain, but Murkowski seems determined to get the pipeline built and make his contribution as one of the builders of Alaska's infrastructure.

Senior Senator

Ted Stevens (R)

Appointed Dec. 1968, seat up 2008, 6th full term; b. Nov. 18, 1923, India-napolis, IN; home, Girdwood; U.C.L.A., B.A. 1947, Harvard, LL.B. 1950; Episcopalian; married (Catherine).

Military Career: Army Air Corps, 1943–46 (WWII).

Elected Office: AK House of Reps., 1964–68.

Professional Career: Practicing atty., 1950–53, 1961–68; U.S. Atty., 1953–56; U.S. Dept. of Interior, Legis. Cnsl., 1956–58, Asst. to Secy., 1958–60, Solicitor, 1960–61.

DC Office: 522 HSOB, 20510, 202-224-3004; Fax: 202-224-2354; Web site: stevens.senate.gov.

State Offices: Anchorage, 907-271-5915; Fairbanks, 907-456-0261; Juneau, 907-586-7400; Kenai, 907-283-5808; Ketchikan, 907-225-6880; Wasilla, 907-376-7665.

Committees: *President Pro Tempore. Appropriations*: Commerce, Justice & Science; Defense (Chmn.); Homeland Security; Interior & Related Agencies; Labor, Health and Human Services, Education & Related Agencies; Transportation, Treasury, the Judiciary, HUD & Related Agencies. *Commerce, Science & Transportation* (Chmn.): Aviation; Consumer Affairs, Product Safety & Insurance; Disaster Prevention & Prediction; Fisheries & the Coast Guard; Global Climate Change & Impacts; National Ocean Policy Study; Science & Space; Surface Transportation & Merchant Marine; Technology, Innovation & Competitiveness; Trade, Tourism & Economic Development. *Homeland Security & Governmental Affairs*: Federal Financial Management, Govt. Information & International Security; Investigations (Permanent); Oversight of Govt. Management, the Federal Workforce & the District of Columbia. *Rules & Administration*.

Group Ratings

	ADA	ACLU	AFS	LCV	ITIC	NTU	COC	ACU	NTLC	CHC
2004	20	0	0	0	92	67	100	92	88	83
2003	10	—	22	5	—	71	91	70	—	—

National Journal Ratings

	2003 LIB	—	2003 CONS	2004 LIB	—	2004 CONS
Economic	24%	—	73%	18%	—	78%
Social	48%	—	51%	34%	—	63%
Foreign	22%	—	68%	0%	—	67%

Key Votes of the 108th Congress

1. Ban Drilling in ANWR	N	5. Energy Bill	Y	9. Ban Same-Sex Marriage	Y
2. Approve Bush Tax Cuts	Y	6. Support Roe v. Wade	Y	10. Ban Bunker-Buster Bomb	N
3. Medicare/Rx Bill	Y	7. Ban Partial-Birth Abortion	Y	11. Fund Iraq War	Y
4. Bar Overtime Pay Regs.	N	8. Assault Weapons Ban	N	12. Restrict Missile Defense	N

Election Results

2002 general	Ted Stevens (R)	179,438	(78%)	($2,295,429)
	Frank Vondersaar (D)	24,133	(11%)	($1,049)
	Jim Sykes (Green)	16,608	(7%)	
	Other	9,369	(4%)	
2002 primary	Ted Stevens (R)	64,315	(89%)	
	Mike Aubrey (R)	7,997	(11%)	
1996 general	Ted Stevens (R)	177,893	(77%)	($2,711,710)
	Jed Whittaker (Green)	29,037	(13%)	
	Theresa Obermeyer (D)	23,977	(10%)	

Prior Winning Percentages: 1990 (66%); 1984 (71%); 1978 (76%); 1972 (77%); 1970 (60%)

No other senator fills so central a place in his state's public and economic life as Ted Stevens of Alaska; quite possibly no other senator ever has. "They sent me here," Stevens said in one impassioned debate, "to stand up for the state of Alaska." Stevens is now President Pro Tempore of the Senate, and thus third in line for the presidency. He is the chairman of the Commerce Committee and in 2005 stepped down after 6 ½ years as chairman of the Appropriations Committee; he has chaired or been ranking member on the Defense Appropriations Subcommittee for 20 years. He has also been for a quarter century the leading public policymaker for and about Alaska. "We ask for special consideration," Stevens is not too shy to say, "because no one else is that far away, no one else has the problems that we have or the potential that we have, and no one else deals with the federal government day in and day out the way we do." Probably more than any other senator, Stevens has shaped the public institutions and private economy of his state—and he doesn't seem finished yet.

Stevens grew up in Indiana and California in very modest surroundings, served in World War II flying C-46s and C-47s, graduated from UCLA and Harvard Law, then moved to Alaska in 1950, driving up the Alaska Highway with his new bride. He was U.S. attorney in Fairbanks and worked in the Interior Department in Washington. In 1962, he ran for the Senate and lost to Democrat Ernest Gruening by a 58–42% margin. He then served in the legislature in Juneau and was appointed to the Senate by Governor Walter Hickel in December 1968, at 45. He quickly gained a seat on Appropriations and worked on Alaska issues of all description. He has not been entirely successful. He could not stop the Alaska Lands Act in 1980 and has failed repeatedly to win approval of oil drilling in the Arctic National Wildlife Refuge, though prospects looked better in the 109th Congress. But he played a major role on the Native Claims Act in 1971 and got the oil pipeline through by one vote in 1973. In 1995, he and Frank Murkowski finally secured the repeal of the 1977 law forbidding exports of Alaskan oil, thus opening up the obvious East Asian markets. And in 2004 he secured approval of loan guarantees for a natural gas pipeline.

On non-Alaska issues, Stevens has a moderate voting record. On defense, he worked for years with ranking Democrat Daniel Inouye—another decorated World War II veteran who has represented an offshore state since the 1960s—to support robust defense spending and has been a staunch advocate of missile defense. He has worked hard to fund the National Guard, to raise military salaries and to keep troops in readiness. He was one of the few senators to express concerns about whether the fall 2004 intelligence bill would impair military operations. On the Commerce committee, looking ahead to becoming chairman in 2005, he said he would work to revise the 1996 telecom act. He is concerned about providing a level playing field for companies that provide similar services over different mediums. He is particularly concerned about the Universal Service Fund which provides money for underserved communities and wants more companies to contribute to it. "My number one priority in the rewrite of the communications laws will be to preserve the universal service system and make it work in the 21st century." Public radio has a larger audience in Alaska than in any other state—commercial radio is unprofitable in the Bush—and Stevens has been a strong supporter of public radio and television.

For years Stevens has been known for—and seems to want to be known for—his terrible temper. When he succeeded Mark Hatfield as Appropriations Committee chairman in 1997, he told his colleagues, "Senator Hatfield had the patience of Job and the disposition of a saint. I don't. The watch has changed. I'm a mean, miserable SOB." Some of this, at least, is an act: Stevens gets along with appropriators of all parties, at least if they do their homework and respect his prerogatives. He does not take kindly to those who vote against what he considers Alaska's interests for what he considers frivolous or bogus reasons. In the debate over oil drilling in the Arctic National Wildlife Refuge in March 2003, he said, "I have never broken a commitment in my life. I make this commitment: People who vote against this today are voting against me, and I will not forget it." But that may not mean direct retaliation; as Stevens put it on another occasion, "There are those people I am not going to go out of my way to help." For years John McCain has taken to the floor and bitterly attacked Stevens's Alaska projects as unjustified pork. But Stevens contributed to McCain's 2004 campaign.

At some point, probably in the 1990s, Alaskans began referring matter-of-factly to funding for federal projects as "Stevens money." He argues that Alaska has special needs and special handicaps and therefore deserves special treatment. "Congress has not awakened to the fact that we've got a state with one-fifth the land in this country. My mission is to try to make Congress understand that the promise of statehood is that we should have the ability to establish a workable private-enterprise economy in the areas of Alaska that want it. And that's basically 90% of the state." His prowess is legendary. In 1998, Stevens sought a land trade for a seven-mile road through the Izembeck National Wildlife Refuge—which the Clinton Interior Department wanted to declare off-limits—so that the tiny Aleutian village of King Cove would have access to medical facilities. The administration offered three alternatives; Stevens took all three: $37.7 million for an airport road, medical clinic and doctor and nurse. In 1998, he set up the Denali Commission (Denali is the Native name of Mount McKinley), which funds infrastructure projects—water and sewer, electricity—in central Alaska, to the tune of $38 million in 2001, $45 million in 2002 and $48 million in 2003. When a Stevens aide showed Stevens an *Anchorage Daily News* article about a volunteer group that had raised $6,000 to promote a string of public-use huts linked by hiking trails, he thought it was a good idea and, without consulting the group, put in $500,000 for a backcountry hut network at Snow River near Seward. "That's crazy!" exulted the group's vice president. "There's, like, tears in my eyes." It could be argued that Stevens is less a legislator than he is a philanthropist in the mode of John D. Rockefeller or Andrew Carnegie, although of course he is not spending his own money.

In 2003 Stevens inserted into the appropriations bill provisions limiting judicial review of timber sales in the Tongass National Forest (in December 2003 the Bush administration opened up 3% of it to logging), $17 million for anti-alcohol funding (taking some away from the Alaska Federation of Natives and giving it to the Village Safety Public Officer programs), $5.5 million to the National Energy Technology Laboratory at the University of Alaska in Fairbanks, $7.75 million for wildfire fighting and protection (including $2 million to Anchorage to combat the spruce bark beetle), $1 million to consider Alaskan claims to rights-of-way on federal lands under RS 2477, $350,000 for the Alaska Mountain and Wilderness Huts Association (the huts on hiking trails project), $74 million for safe water and sanitation in Bush villages, $35 million for Denali Commission rural health clinics, $10 million for the Alaska Fisheries Marketing Board (created in a 2002 appropriation), $16.8 million for sea lion research at the Alaska SeaLife Center (a pollock fishery was closed because of a decline in number of sea lions). This is, of course, a partial list.

Stevens was just as active in 2004. The defense appropriation in July included 200 seasonal visas for Japanese technicians to evaluate salmon eggs; the Japanese will only buy them if they are Japanese-inspected and without those sales some fisheries would be unprofitable. The agriculture appropriation in October contained $2 million for the Denali Commission plus a provision making eligible for 75% grants the Tri-Valley Community Center in Healy, the Cold Climate Housing Research Center in Fairbanks and the Fairbanks Allied Health Learning Center. A rider to the Interior appropriation in October included a provision allowing out-of-staters to exercise subsistence hunting and fishing rights for Natives physically unable to do so. The November 2004 omnibus spending bill included $150,000 for a botanical garden in Anchorage, $900,000 for an aquarium in Ketchikan and $525,000 to upgrade a quarry in Nome. Even Stevens's critics concede that he does not shovel money into projects willy-nilly. He shifts money around if he thinks it is not well spent and, past the age of 80, he is still prepared to defend every single project on the merits.

Since the framing of the Native Claims Act—perhaps the most creative legislation concerning American aboriginal peoples—Stevens has continued to work tirelessly to help Alaska Natives, who vote heavily Democratic in most elections. They have voted overwhelmingly for Stevens in recent elections, but he could win without their support easily. He skillfully elicits consensus with Native leaders when opinion is divided, getting more health and sanitation aid to bush villages and funding for health research on fetal alcohol syndrome and cancers common among Natives, and to gain preference in federal contracting for Native corporations. At the same time, Stevens is not uncritical of Native leaders. In October 2002, he urged the Alaska Federation of Natives not to funnel their requests for federal money through the 229 individual village-based tribes granted official status by the Clinton administration, but to consolidate federal requests so that "the very, very poor communities that don't have that ability to hire consultants, to hire grantsmen, people to write applications," get assistance. In a January 2004 appropriation, he set up a commission to draw up a new legal and governmental system for rural Alaska and an economic development commission funded through the Denali Commission to "promote private sector investment to reduce poverty in economically distressed rural villages."

He evidently wants to prevent the emergence of a separate Native legal system. As he said on the Alaska Public Radio Network, "The road they're on now is the road to the destruction of statehood, because the Native population is increasing at a much greater rate than the non-Native population. I don't know if you realize that. And they want to have total jurisdiction over anything that happens in a village without regard to state law and without regard to federal law."

Stevens played a crucial role in the 1970s in getting the oil pipeline approved. Now in this decade he has played a similar role for the proposed natural gas pipeline. For years oil drillers in Prudhoe Bay have been pumping natural gas back into the ground; there are an estimated 30 trillion cubic feet there and another 70 trillion cubic feet elsewhere on the North Slope—all undeliverable to customers without a pipeline. Pipeline provisions had been included in the 2001 and 2003 energy bills—a loan guarantee of 80% of construction costs, a price floor for the producers, accelerated depreciation, limited judicial review—but the energy bill remained stalled for other reasons. In October 2004 Stevens decided to insert the pipeline provisions, except for the price floor, into the must-pass military construction appropriation; he also got accelerated depreciation into the corporate tax bill. The rider specified a route through central Alaska, not directly east into Canada, and provided for in-state use of gas. Governor Frank Murkowski quickly solicited contracts from two consortiums, one being the three North Slope oil companies, the other a pipeline company with Native corporation participation; Stevens endorsed Murkowski's proposal that the state have an equity share. There are still other barriers to overcome—federal and Canadian regulatory approval, private financing—but the gas pipeline, for the first time, seems likely to be built.

Stevens's work has not gone unappreciated. In January 2000, he was named Alaskan of the Century. In July 2000, Anchorage Airport was named the Ted Stevens International Airport and the Challenger Center in Kenai became the Ted and Catherine Stevens Center for Space Science Technology. Stevens was criticized in a December 2003 *Los Angeles Times* story for investing in local Alaskan properties with his brother-in-law and for providing help to co-investors and a tenant (one of the Native corporations) in buildings he co-owned. Stevens insisted he was a "passive investor" and said, "I have never helped anyone to achieve financial gain for myself or anyone else." In fact Stevens has a long record of helping Alaskans of all kinds, especially the Native corporations, on many projects; as he said, "I have helped Alaskans without regard to race, religion, sex, party, financial circumstance—without qualification."

Stevens has been re-elected easily. In the August 1996 Republican primary a banker and former legislator spent $1.3 million of his own money and charged that Stevens was insufficiently conservative. Stevens won 59%–27%. His Democratic opponent that year blamed Stevens for her husband's failure to pass the Alaska bar on 22 separate tries; even Democratic Governor Tony Knowles announced he was voting for Stevens, who won 77%–13%. In November 2002 his Democratic opponent, a denizen of the hip town of Homer, charged that Stevens was part of a government conspiracy to keep him under constant surveillance. Stevens was reelected 78%–11% margin, carrying all but three precincts. He campaigned actively for his 22-year colleague Frank Murkowski in the 2002 governor race and for his new colleague, Murkowski's daughter Lisa Murkowski, in the 2004 Senate race. No one doubts he can be reelected again in 2008.

Junior Senator

Lisa Murkowski (R)

Appointed Dec. 2002, seat up 2010, 1st full term; b. May 22, 1957, Ketchikan; home, Anchorage; Willamette U., 1975–77, Georgetown U., B.A. 1980, Willamette U., J.D. 1985; Catholic; married (Verne Martell).

Elected Office: AK House of Reps., 1998–02.

Professional Career: Anchorage Dist. Court Clerk's Office, atty., 1987–89; Practicing atty., 1989–98.

DC Office: 709 HSOB, 20510, 202-224-6665; Fax: 202-224-5301; Web site: murkowski.senate.gov.

State Offices: Anchorage, 907-271-3735; Bethel, 907-543-1639; Fairbanks, 907-456-0233; Juneau, 907-586-7400; Kenai, 907-283-5808; Ketchikan, 907-225-6880; Wasilla, 907-376-7665.

Committees: *Energy & Natural Resources*: Energy; Public Lands & Forests; Water & Power (Chmn.). *Environment & Public Works*: Fisheries, Wildlife & Water; Transportation & Infrastructure. *Foreign Relations*: African Affairs; East Asian & Pacific Affairs (Chmn.); European Affairs; International Economic Policy, Export & Trade Promotion. *Indian Affairs*.

Group Ratings

	ADA	ACLU	AFS	LCV	ITIC	NTU	COC	ACU	NTLC	CHC
2004	35	0	43	0	92	59	94	74	88	83
2003	20	—	22	11	—	71	86	70	—	—

National Journal Ratings

	2003 LIB	—	2003 CONS		2004 LIB	—	2004 CONS
Economic	43%	—	56%		43%	—	55%
Social	47%	—	52%		37%	—	62%
Foreign	39%	—	54%		0%	—	67%

Key Votes of the 108th Congress

1. Ban Drilling in ANWR	N	5. Energy Bill	Y	9. Ban Same-Sex Marriage	Y
2. Approve Bush Tax Cuts	Y	6. Support Roe v. Wade	Y	10. Ban Bunker-Buster Bomb	N
3. Medicare/Rx Bill	Y	7. Ban Partial-Birth Abortion	Y	11. Fund Iraq War	Y
4. Bar Overtime Pay Regs.	Y	8. Assault Weapons Ban	N	12. Restrict Missile Defense	N

Election Results

2004 general	Lisa Murkowski (R)	149,773	(49%)	($5,465,098)
	Tony Knowles (D)	140,424	(46%)	($5,768,963)
	Other	18,118	(6%)	
2004 primary	Lisa Murkowski (R)	45,710	(58%)	
	Mike Miller (R)	29,313	(37%)	
	Wev Shea (R)	2,857	(4%)	
	Other	748	(1%)	
1998 general	Frank Murkowski (R)	165,227	(74%)	($911,926)
	Joseph Sonneman (D)	43,743	(20%)	($26,091)
	Other	12,837	(6%)	

Lisa Murkowski became Alaska's sixth U.S. senator when Governor Frank Murkowski, her father, appointed her in December 2002 to fill the vacancy caused by his own resignation. She grew up in Ketchikan in Alaska's Panhandle and in Fairbanks, the second of six children. In her senior year of high school she worked five weeks as an intern in Senator Ted Stevens's Washington office. She attended Willamette University in Salem, Oregon, and graduated from Georgetown in 1980, the year her father was first elected to the Senate, and graduated from Willamette law school in 1985. She served as an Anchorage District Court attorney and worked for an Anchorage law firm for eight years, then established her own law practice. In 1998 she was elected to the state House from a north Anchorage district including her neighborhood of Government Hill.

Alaska's state government depends heavily on revenues from North Slope oil, and in early 2002 was facing a budget shortfall of $1.1 billion. Murkowski was one of the leaders of a bipartisan Fiscal Policy Caucus that sought tax increases-a position opposite to that of her father, who was running for governor on a platform of no new taxes. In March 2002 the House Finance Committee passed a package that included spending $900 million from the Permanent Fund, the first such spending since the Fund was created in 1977; that was eventually defeated. But Murkowski pushed hard for increasing the alcohol tax from 3 cents a drink to 10 cents. She fought fiercely—when another legislator proposed an amendment with a much smaller increase, she said, "I'm gonna kill somebody!"—and the tax was passed in May, giving Alaska the nation's highest alcohol tax. Some conservatives referred to her and her allies as RIMs, "Republican invertebrate moderates." She also angered conservatives when she was one of five Republicans to vote against a bill restricting publicly funded abortions. At the time she said, "I may have a very short-lived political future here. But you know, I've got great kids and a great husband, and I'm going to have a good heart, and I'm going to stand up for the women of the state of Alaska, and I'm going to vote no." But she has also said that abortion should be legal only when a mother's life is in danger or in cases of rape and incest, and in March 2003 said she was against partial-birth abortion. Nonetheless, Alaska Right to Life opposed her in 1998, claiming, "She is not pro-life."

Conservatives opposed her reelection in 2002, and against conservative Nancy Dahlstrom, who attacked her for favoring tax increases and tapping the Permanent Fund, she won by only 486–429—a margin of 57 votes. During this period she evidently stayed at arm's length from her father, who easily won the nomination for governor. "We have always maintained very separate identities at least for the time I have been in the legislature," Lisa Murkowski said. "I haven't called him for counseling and typically he doesn't offer." During and after the primary, she ran for House speaker. In November 2002, Republican House members chose the more conservative Pete Kott of Eagle River for that post and Murkowski for House majority leader.

That was just two days after Frank Murkowski had been elected governor. There were two years left in the Senate term to which he had been elected, and Republican legislators had seen to it that he, and not outgoing Democratic Governor Tony Knowles, would appoint his successor. Earlier in the year, they passed over Knowles's veto a law barring a governor from appointing a successor until five days after the vacancy occurred. Murkowski said he wanted to appoint someone who had legislative experience, was young enough and reelectable enough to serve for many years, who knew and shared his views on Alaska issues. On November 15 he unveiled a short list of 26 potential nominees, not all of whom met all his criteria. Many were experienced politicians, but some had different backgrounds—General Joseph Ralston, NATO Supreme Commander who had served in Alaska and was registered to vote there, as an Independent; retired General Mark Hamilton, President of the University of Alaska; Jerry Hood, secretary-treasurer of Teamsters Local 959 and a former Democrat who had become a Republican (and supported Murkowski for governor in 2002); Francis Hurley, the retired Catholic Archbishop of Anchorage; John Troxel, an Anchorage plastic surgeon; incoming state Senate Majority Leader Ben Stevens, son of Ted Stevens. Also on the list was House Majority Leader Lisa Murkowski. As she later recalled, "We had a conversation and he said, 'Your name keeps coming up. Are you interested in going back to Washington?' I confirmed that that was one of those things that everyone in Alaska office would think to as kind of the highlight of a political career. So basically he asked if I wanted to have my name continue on the list, and I said yes." Frank Murkowski interviewed some of those on the short list and promised a decision by December 10. But he had not yet made up his mind when he left for a 10-day trip to Washington that day. On December 17, he said the short list had been narrowed down.

On December 20, Governor Murkowski appointed state Representative Murkowski as senator. "Above all, I felt the person I appoint to the remaining two years of my term should be someone who shares my basic philosophy, my values, but particularly one who shares on the issues of Alaska matters that are before us," he said. "Someone whose judgment I trust in representing the state and all of its people." This was the first time a governor had appointed his daughter, or for that matter his child, to the Senate. Most Republicans and many Democrats said nice things about the new senator. But there was some disapproval, even from the Republican side. Jim Whitaker, an ally of Murkowski in the Alaska House, said her appointment "is nepotism and therefore contrary to the democratic principles of representative government. An action of this type undermines the public trust and is therefore of great concern." All of which cast a shadow on her prospects for winning a full term in November 2004.

In the Senate, Lisa Murkowski had a moderate voting record, considerably closer to the middle of the road than her father. She got seats on the Energy, Environment, Veterans and Indian Affairs Committees. In March 2003 she was disappointed when the Senate voted down oil drilling in the Arctic National Wildlife Refuge. She was more upbeat in November 2003, when the Senate unanimously passed the Healthy Forests Act, authorizing fuel reduction treatment-cutting down disease- or insect-infested trees-in national forests; she worked to make sure that it included the Kenai peninsula forests infested by the spruce bark beetle. Her biggest success came in October 2004, when she sponsored the inclusion in the must-pass military construction appropriation of provisions from the stalled energy bill authorizing an Alaska gas pipeline; but the real mover was Ted Stevens, in his last months as Appropriations Chairman. This included 80% loan guarantees, accelerated depreciation, expedited permitting and judicial review, but did not include the price floor protecting the operators from a fall in gas prices. Like many Alaskans, she was critical of the Patriot Act and called for greater judicial discretion in deciding whether federal officers could obtain "any tangible thing." She opposed driver's license standards in the 2004 intelligence bill as a prelude to a national identity card. She worked, with Stevens's help, to get 200 seasonal visas for Japanese experts to evaluate Alaska salmon eggs, needed to keep one salmon fishery economically viable.

No Alaska Republican senator had ever been defeated, but Murkowski entered the 2004 campaign in weak condition. She had primary opposition from conservative former legislator Mike Miller, who attacked her stands on abortion, the Second Amendment and the income tax; Miller was even supported by her father's lieutenant governor, Loren Leman. Murkowski was much better financed and had the support of Stevens and Congressman-at-Large Don Young, but she won the primary by only a 58%–37% margin-not a strong performance for an incumbent senator.

Her opponent in the general election was former Governor Tony Knowles, the most success-ful Alaska Democrat in recent times. A Vietnam veteran and Yale classmate and friend of George W. Bush, Knowles ran a restaurant in Anchorage and was twice elected the city's mayor in the 1980s. In 1994 he was elected governor in a multi-candidate field with 41% of the vote; in 1998 he won a second term, again against divided opposition, with 51%. Knowles strongly supported oil drilling in ANWR and the gas pipeline; he criticized Murkowski for not including the price floor and said that, as a Democrat, he would have a better chance of attracting votes on ANWR. National Republicans responded with an ad featuring John Kerry and saying he "wouldn't know a caribou if it dropped in for a bowl of Boston clam chowder," and Murkowski offered him space in her office to lobby for ANWR oil drilling. Knowles criticized Murkowski for not supporting full funding—that is, appropriating as much as was authorized—for veterans' health care and spotlighted a 49–48 vote (actually, on that occasion a 60-vote supermajority was needed). Stevens responded by saying that Murkowski supported $1.2 billion for veterans' health in committee. In October 2004 he said that, knowing what he did now, he would not have voted for war in Iraq; Murkowski said she would have.

Looming over the campaign was the issue of nepotism. Knowles's pollster said that 54% found it a convincing reason to vote against Murkowski, and she trailed, usually by narrow margins, during most polls conducted during the campaign. Frank Murkowski's job rating as governor suffered after his 2003 budget cuts; particularly grating was his cutting of the $250 per month Longevity Bonus for seniors. Organizers obtained 50,000 signatures for Ballot Measure No. 4, to ban governors from appointing new senators; it passed in November with 56% of the vote. Against this Republicans raised the issue of party and seniority. Stevens said Alaska would be hurt if Democrats gained a majority in the Senate, and Young said, "I do believe there's a lot of merit to Lisa being elected for the benefit of the state. Everybody says, 'Ted can work with the minority,' and, yes, he can. But there's a difference between working with the minority as a minority member and working in the majority and being chairman." They also made the point that Murkowski, at 47, would have a chance of amassing much more seniority than Knowles, at 61, would.

This was one of the national Democrats' best chances of picking up a Republican seat, but this Republican state ended up giving its Republican junior senator a full term, by a 49%–46% margin. Like her father in the 2002 governor's race, Murkowski ran behind by a wide margin in the Bush and a lesser margin in the Panhandle. In historically Republican Anchorage and Fairbanks, Murkowski ran only narrowly ahead. Her winning margins came in south central Alaska, in the fast-growing arc around Anchorage.

Representative-At-Large

Don Young (R)

Elected Mar. 1973, 16th full term; b. June 9, 1933, Meridian, CA; home, Fort Yukon; Yuba Jr. Col., A.A. 1952, Chico St. Col., B.A. 1958; Episcopalian; married (Lu).

Military Career: Army, 1955–57.

Elected Office: Fort Yukon City Cncl., 1960–64; Fort Yukon Mayor, 1964–68; AK House of Reps., 1966–70; AK Senate, 1970–73.

Professional Career: School teacher, Fort Yukon, 1960–68; Riverboat captain, 1960–68.

DC Office: 2111 RHOB, 20515, 202-225-5765; Fax: 202-225-0425; Web site: www.house.gov/donyoung.

District Offices: Anchorage, 907-271-5978; Fairbanks, 907-456-0210; Juneau, 907-586-7400; Kenai, 907-283-5808; Ketchikan, 907-225-6880; Mat-Su, 907-376-7665.

Committees: *Homeland Security* (2d of 19 R): Economic Security, Infrastructure Protection & Cybersecurity; Prevention of Nuclear & Biological Attack. *Resources* (2d of 27 R): Energy & Mineral Resources; Fisheries & Oceans. *Transportation & Infrastructure* (Chmn. of 41 R).

Group Ratings

	ADA	ACLU	AFS	LCV	ITIC	NTU	COC	ACU	NTLC	CHC
2004	0	5	0	0	67	54	100	95	84	84
2003	5	—	13	0	—	60	93	83	—	—

National Journal Ratings

	2003 LIB	—	2003 CONS		2004 LIB	—	2004 CONS
Economic	16%	—	83%		17%	—	83%
Social	21%	—	78%		30%	—	69%
Foreign	31%	—	69%		38%	—	61%

Key Votes of the 108th Congress

1. Drilling in ANWR	Y	5. DC School Vouchers	Y	9. Ban Same-Sex Marriage	Y
2. Approve Bush Tax Cuts	Y	6. Ban Human Cloning	Y	10. Fund Iraq War	Y
3. Medicare/Rx Bill	Y	7. Restrict Gun Liability	Y	11. Bar Cuba Embargo Funds	N
4. Bar Overtime Pay Regs.	*	8. Ban Partial-Birth Abortion	Y	12. Intelligence Reorg.	N

Election Results

2004 general	Don Young (R)	213,216	(71%)	($1,747,897)
	Thomas Higgins (D)	67,074	(22%)	
	Timothy Feller (Green)	11,434	(4%)	
	Other	8,272	(3%)	
2004 primary	Don Young (R)	unopposed		
2002 general	Don Young (R)	169,685	(75%)	($1,378,269)
	Clifford Greene (D)	39,357	(17%)	($980)
	Russell DeForest (Green)	14,435	(6%)	

Prior Winning Percentages: 2000 (70%); 1998 (63%); 1996 (59%); 1994 (57%); 1992 (47%); 1990 (52%); 1988 (63%); 1986 (57%); 1984 (55%); 1982 (71%); 1980 (74%); 1978 (55%); 1976 (71%); 1974 (54%); 1973 (51%)

Don Young has been Alaska's congressman-at-large since 1973. He was once tugboat captain on the Yukon and is the only licensed mariner in Congress—in his words, "not one of these smooth, namby-pamby politicians." He is a hot-tempered, salty-tongued true believer, given to malapropisms ("Pribilof's dog" and "bladderdash") and tough talk (when a Texas congressman blocked a motion for unanimous consent on an airline bill, Young replied, "Those in Texas will not fly; may you walk and may you die in the desert"). Young grew up in rural California, served in the Army and graduated from college, then moved to Alaska, captained his tugboat and was elected mayor of Fort Yukon. He was elected to the legislature in 1966 and ran for Congress in 1972. His opponent, incumbent Nick Begich, was killed in a plane crash in October and was reelected posthumously; Young won the March 1973 special election to succeed him. Young is not a free-market conservative—he casts many liberal economic votes—but he is a cultural and foreign policy conservative, and an unceasing advocate of what he considers Alaska's interests.

For his first 21 years in the House, Young was in the minority, outvoted on what was then the Interior Committee and often on the floor by environmentalists—whom he once called a "self-centered bunch, the waffle-stomping, Harvard-graduating, intellectual idiots." Since the Republicans won their House majority in 1994, he has been a committee chairman, and one with ambitious objectives which he has not always achieved. He steered to passage in the House bills allowing oil drilling in the Arctic National Wildlife Refuge in 1995 and 2001, only to see them defeated or bottled up in the Senate. His attempts to roll back some environmental rulings, like allowing logging in the Tongass National Forest, were frustrated in the 1990s by vetoes by Bill Clinton, or by adverse votes cast by Republicans from the Northeast, Florida and Arizona. But he also showed a talent for consensus. In 1997, he passed, by 419–1, the National Wildlife Improvement Act, which sets new guidelines for the nation's 500-plus wildlife refuges. The bill, endorsed by Clinton and environmental groups, allows for recreational activities that are compatible with the refuges' conservation mission. In May 2000 he got the House to pass, by a 315–102 vote, the Conservation and Reinvestment Act, to dedicate royalties from offshore oil and gas wells to provide federal dollars for state purchases of land. His original version would require that $3 billion be spent every year, independent of the appropriations process, for 15 years; Alaska would be guaranteed $163 million a year in compensation for the environmental costs of oil drilling, more than all but two other states. Other money was directed to urban parks, to increase support in the House. Many conservative Republicans opposed this as a federal power grab, and it was not a popular cause in the Senate, which passed a scaled-down version which authorized $12 billion over six years, subject to appropriators, with about $50 million a year for Alaska. In 2004 Young was backing a similar version, with $175 million for Alaska; but Alaska Republicans concerned about rights of private property holders opposed it.

After the 2000 election, Young was term-limited out of the Resources Committee chairmanship and became chairman of Transportation and Infrastructure instead. It was a different sort of assignment; as he has said, "On the Resources Committee I like to say I was in charge of everything God made, and now on Transportation I'm in charge of everything man made." Under his predecessor Bud Shuster, Transportation had become the largest and arguably the most bipartisan committee in the House, because Shuster made sure every cooperating member received plenty of highway (or mass transit) projects and fought ruthlessly to keep transportation money flowing directly from the gasoline and airplane fuel taxes without any review by the Appropriations Committees. Young lost some skirmishes with the appropriators in 2001 and 2002, but maintained Shuster's bipartisan approach.

His biggest task was to reauthorize Shuster's masterpiece, the 1998 $218 billion TEA-21 surface transportation act, which expired in 2003. In November 2003 Young presented his TEA-LU (named after his wife Lu) version, with $375 billion in spending. It was financed with an increase in the gas tax—retroactive indexing, he said, to the last time the gas tax was increased in 1993, and indexed to rise in the future. But the Bush administration and the House Republican administration were stoutly opposed to any gas tax increase. The administration set a limit of $256 billion; the Senate in early 2004 approved a $318 billion bill. In March 2004 the Transportation Committee approved Young's $375 billion package by voice vote, but Young promised the House leadership not to bring it to the floor; and in early April the House approved a $275 billion bill, without Young's gas tax increase. The Senate bill readjusted the funding formula, to give some states more money per dollar of gas tax revenue; the House bill didn't. The conference committee split the difference at $284 billion, a number the administration threatened to veto. The expiration date of TEA-21 was extended, and extended again, as conferees and the administration failed to agree. John McCain argued against the many earmarked highway projects and called for formula changes (Arizona got 90 cents for each dollar of revenue under the old formula, and 92 cents under the Senate formula; Alaska got $6.60), while Richard Shelby of Alabama wanted $319 billion in spending and wanted to shift mass transit money to highways; with Senate Democrats all voting against agreement, the conference was stymied.

Problems proliferated. There was reaction against the Alaska earmarks Young included, especially against his $200 million for a bridge from Anchorage across Knik Arm to a largely uninhabited area and a $100 million bridge from Ketchikan to an island with its airport, which could be reached more rapidly by the local ferry: "bridges to nowhere," critics said. Colorado's Marilyn Musgrave, resisting Young's tax increase, was rebuked. "I have never had a man talk to me the way Mr. Young talked to me," she said. Earlier, Young said, "I have the pencil, and I can erase something very quickly if things don't go the way I'd like." At one point it was discovered that the February 2004 omnibus spending bill subtracted earmarked projects from formula funds: the Alaska delegation had to scramble to get them back. At the end of 2004 the transportation bill remained unreauthorized, and with no clear solution in sight. But it seemed that Young's drive for a gas tax increase was dead, and the ability of the Transportation Committee to roll the House leadership was unclear.

Young had to deal with other contentious issues after September 11. There was sharp conflict over the details of emergency aid for Amtrak, over provisions for federal aid to the airlines and over whether airport security personnel should be federal workers. Even after the Senate voted 100–0 for federalization, Young and the Republican leadership held out for federal supervision of private contractors—the system used in Israel and Europe. But the pressure for action was too great, and when the Bush White House made it clear there would be no presidential veto, federalization prevailed. Young also fought the Bush administration on arming airline pilots. He and Florida Rep. John Mica introduced a bill to do so in April 2002, and watered it down by limiting it to 2% of pilots and making it a two-year test program. But in July 2002, Oregon Democrat Peter DeFazio passed an amendment gutting those provisions, and the bill passed by the veto-proof margin of 310–113. The Senate did the same by 87–6 in September, and the administration was overruled. In summer 2004 Young and committee Democrats moved to require national biometric identification standards for personnel at U.S. airports; in October they pressed legislation to implement recommendations of the 9/11 Commission. In the midst of this, Young was stopped, mistaken for a suspected terrorist, another Don Young, in September 2004. "Apparently the guy is not a nice person. They had a reason for doing that and that is their job . . . It was sort of a shock, though. I'm the chair of the Transportation Committee. I actually behaved myself."

Young has two more years as chairman of Transportation. He is ninth in House seniority, and third among Republicans, and remains unashamed of his support of Alaska projects. "If I had not done fairly well for our state, I'd be ashamed of myself." He remains responsive to Alaska opinion. After the Alaska legislature and the Anchorage Assembly passed resolutions against the Patriot Act, he voted to repeal part of it and said that it was "not really thought out."

Young has had his ups and downs with Alaska voters over the years, with significant opposition in 1978, 1984, 1986, 1990 and 1992. For years, the *Anchorage Daily News*' criticisms hurt him in that usually Republican city, and his reputation for abrasiveness and arrogance became such a problem that he cut an apology spot in 1992, when he was trailing in the polls. It worked—he has not had electoral trouble since. His work over the years on Native causes (he has pushed constantly for more federal jobs for Natives, as promised in the Alaska Native Claims Act) have enabled him to win by large margins even in the usually heavily Democratic Bush. In the last three elections, against weak opposition, he was reelected by 70%–17%, 75%–17%, and 71%–22% margins.

★ ARIZONA ★

Youth and age, new and old: Arizona is home to America's oldest continuous community and is one of America's fastest-growing and most rapidly changing states. The Hopi Indians, living as shepherds on plateaus east of the Grand Canyon, have not changed much in perhaps 500 years. They have spurned Christianity since 1680, when they killed the local Franciscan priests and burned their churches; more recently they have been involved in land disputes with the far more numerous Navajo. The Hopi are the oldest Arizonans; the newest are moving in every day, into subdivisions rising up out of the empty desert east, north, and west of Phoenix, hemmed in only by dry river beds, upcroppings of mountains, and Indian reservation boundaries.

For Arizona is one of America's boom states. Its population grew 52% from 1990 to 2003, second only to Nevada; Maricopa County, which has 61% of the state's people, is the fourth most populous county in the nation (and, spreading far out from Phoenix, the 14th largest in area). It is a state with an economy now sophisticated and decentralized enough that there is no easy explanation, as there once was, of how and why Arizona grows. The first explanation was copper: The dome of the state Capitol dome is encased in copper; one of Arizona's leading public figures was Lewis Douglas, copper heir and congressman, Franklin D. Roosevelt's first budget director and Harry Truman's ambassador to Britain. In those years Arizona depended heavily on the federal government, and on politicians like Carl Hayden, Democratic congressman from statehood in 1912 and senator from 1927–69, whose public works projects watered Arizona's cotton, citrus and cattle farms. Then, in the decades after World War II, businessmen, lawyers, developers and water companies, notably the Salt River Project, built an Arizona based on something like the opposite of New Deal principles: With minimal government and precious little regulation of business, a welcoming of new technological ideas and shunning of new cultural liberalism; like Disneyland, a more gleaming and spotless embodiment of old values than America had ever been. Their political champion was Barry Goldwater, Phoenix city council member and senator and the nation's Mr. Conservative for much of the 1950s and 1960s. He helped to make Arizona Republican, the only state to vote Republican for president in every election from 1952 to 1992.

This Arizona has grown phenomenally, from 700,000 people at the end of World War II to 3.6 million in 1990 and then to 5.6 million in 2003. It is growth based on high-tech and low taxes. It is not growth based on an influx of elderly retirees—Arizona may have Sun City, but just 13% of its residents are over 65, compared to 12% nationally. Nor is it based on farming subsidized by cheap water, since thirsty cotton farms are being phased out for urban users who outbid them; the Valley around Phoenix lost nearly half its farmland between 1975 and 2000. It also is not based on (though it is helped by) immigration: Arizona has attracted immigrants from Mexico and Latin America eager for entry-level jobs, so eager that many cross the lightly guarded border in the desert even at the risk of death. More than anything else, the engine of Arizona's growth has been technology: Phoenix has been attracting high-tech industries since Motorola built a research center for military electronics there in 1948. Big employers include Honeywell, Raytheon, Motorola, Intel, Avnet and Northrop Grumman. Defense industries are important here: Arizona ranked number seven in Defense Department contracts in 2003. The state counts two Air Force bases and a Marine Air Station plus the huge Barry M. Goldwater Range over which many of America's pilots have been trained. And for all its growth, Arizona still produces two-thirds of the nation's copper. The state's economy kept humming while much of the nation was in recession and newcomers kept streaming in—many from across the border. With border control strengthened in California and Texas, the Arizona desert in Cochise and Santa Cruz Counties has become the major entry point for illegal immigrants. The Tucson sector alone accounted for 42% of Border Patrol arrests in 2004, some 1,350 a day along just 260 miles of frontier. Some 9% of the state's population now are illegal immigrants, second only to California. Anger at the flood of illegals led to the passage in 2004 of Proposition 200, denying welfare benefits to illegals and requiring government employees to report any illegal immigrant, despite opposition from prominent officeholders, business groups and local media. But the vote was a

District 2 is highlighted for visibility.

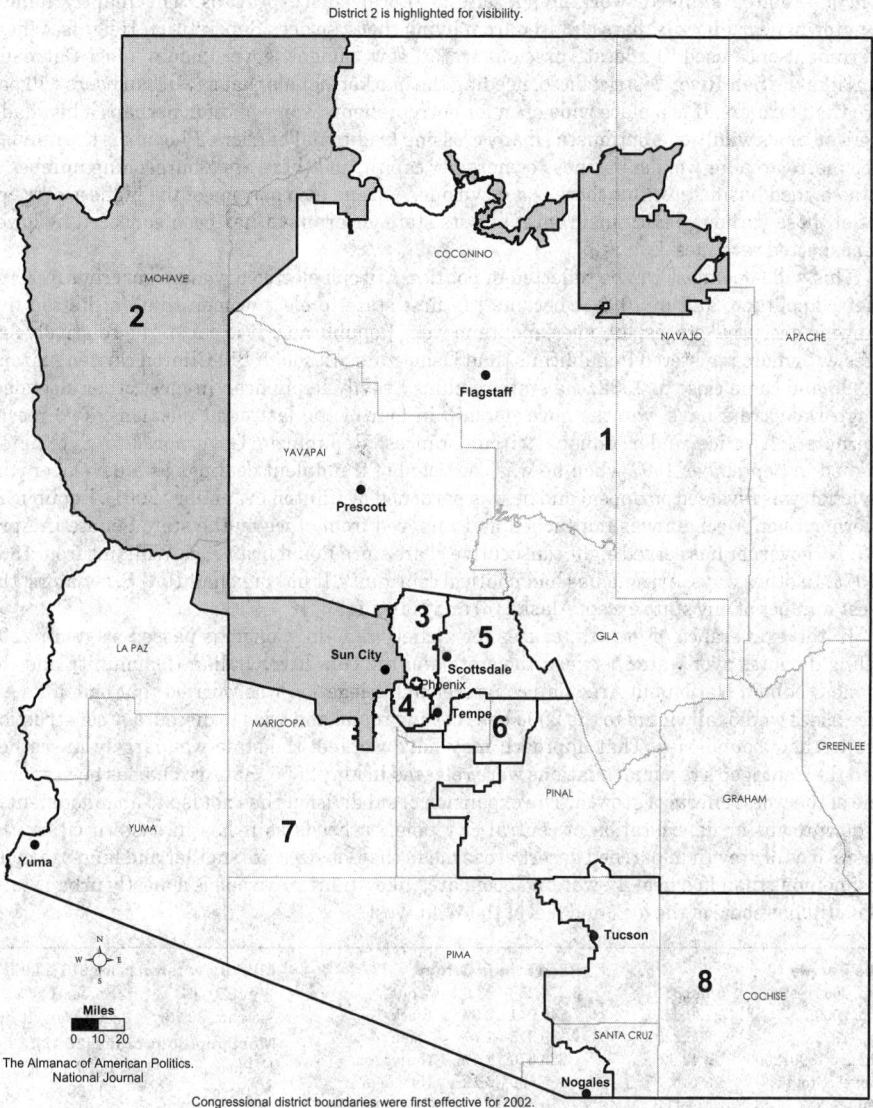

The Almanac of American Politics.
National Journal

Congressional district boundaries were first effective for 2002.

less than overwhelming 56%–44%, with most Democrats against and most Republicans for; interestingly, 56% of whites and 47% of Latinos voted yes.

Arizona is a place where the private sector is expanding and the public sector, if not shriveling away, is yielding ground. State taxes were cut sharply in the 1990s and there's been little increase since. Arizona pioneered in providing choice in education, with America's largest proportion of charter schools (some 20% of the total) and the for-profit University of Phoenix, based here but with branches in many states, which leases space and hires working-age adults to teach job-related skills to working-age adults. Local choice prevails: The inaptly named Youngtown, near Phoenix, bars children from living there; so does Superstition Heights. Where government once used to allocate precious water, now "shadow governments" (Joel Garreau's term) like the Salt River District do so, heeding the market signals that say urban users will pay more than farmers. It is a place wide open for entrepreneurs, some of them perhaps a bit shady, others at times wildly overoptimistic, many crossing traditional barriers. Phoenix is the number three metro area for women business owners per capita, and there are a burgeoning number of Latino-owned businesses. But there is a downside. Arizona also has one of the highest percentages of those without health insurance, and its state government has been squeezed by lower than expected revenues.

This wide-openness can be reflected in politics. Arizona elected a woman governor in 2002, Janet Napolitano, and in 1998 it became the first state to elect women to all of its top five statewide executive offices; all but Napolitano were Republicans. It is one of the relatively few states with more registered Republicans than Democrats. Although Bill Clinton carried Arizona in 1996 and came close in 1992, the state remains heavily Republican in most other elections, though Democrats have won the governorship in four of the last eight elections. Two recent governors left office under unusual circumstances: Republican Governor Fife Symington resigned in September 1997 when he was convicted of fraudulent dealings as a developer (the conviction was reversed on appeal and he was pardoned by Clinton in January 2001). Republican Governor Evan Mecham was impeached and removed from office by the state Senate in April 1987. No governor has served eight consecutive years since Republican Jack Williams from 1966 to 1974. In other ways, Arizona has had political continuity. It has only had 10 U.S. senators, the lowest number of any state except Alaska (6) and Hawaii (5).

In the exuberance of growth, causes for anxiety remain. Congress passed a law in 2004 settling disputes over water between the state and the Gila River Indian Community and the Tohono O'odham Nation but Arizona's congressional delegation was worried that one of its Air Force bases would fall victim to the 2005 base closing round and tried to discourage construction close to their boundaries. That approach may have worked: the state was largely unscathed when the Pentagon's recommendations were released in May 2005. But Arizona has been spared some of the worst effects of growth. The expansion of subdivisions has not led to abandonment of old downtowns or deterioration of central city neighborhoods as it has in eastern cities; the imperatives of growth in parched desert areas mean that lot sizes are smaller and land use more parsimonious than in a heavily-watered boom area like Atlanta. Arizona is a mostly urban state, but it still has some of the look and feel of the Wild West.

The People		Race/Ethnic Origin			Military veterans: 562,916 (14.9%)	
Pop. 2004 (est):	5,743,834	3,274,258	63.8%	White	WWII: 21.3%	Korea: 14.7%
Pop. 2000:	5,130,632	149,941	2.9%	Black	Vietnam: 30.7%	Gulf War: 10.4%
Pop. 1990:	3,665,228	89,315	1.7%	Asian	**Most populous cities (2003):**	
Change 1990–2000:	Up 40.0%	233,370	4.5%	Native Am.	1. Phoenix	1,388,416
% of U.S. total:	1.8%	5,639	0.1%	Hawaiian	2. Tucson	507,658
Pop. rank:	20th of 50	76,372	1.5%	Two+ races	3. Mesa	432,376
Area size:	113,998 sq. mi.	6,120	0.1%	Other	4. Glendale	232,838
State Native:	34.7%	1,295,617	25.3%	Hisp. Origin	5. Scottsdale	217,989
Non-citizen:	9.0%	**Ancestry**				
Language		German: 12.2%		English: 8.1%	Urban population: 88.2%	
English: 73.6%	Spanish: 18.5%	Irish: 8.0%		USA: 3.7%	Rural population: 11.8%	
Other Eur.: 3.4%		Italian: 3.4%				

Education		Work Sector		Legislature	
H.S. Grad:	81.0%	Private: 78.1%	Govt: 15.2%	Senate	18 R 12 D
College Grad:	23.5%	Self: 6.4%	Family: 0.3%	House	38 R 22 D
Industry		Unemployment: 5.6%		Legislative Term Limits: Yes	
Agri: 1.5%	Con: 8.7%	**Household Income**		**Registered Voters**	
Fin: 7.9%	Info: 2.8%	<15k: 14.9%	15-35k: 27.9%	D: 914,264	(34.6%)
Mfg: 15.2%	Prof: 28.3%	35-50k: 17.5%	50-100k: 28.9%	R: 1,055,252	(39.9%)
Public: 5.4%	Trade: 15.6%	100-150k: 6.9%	>150k: 3.9%	O: 673,815	(25.5%)
Other: 14.7%		Median: $40,558			
Occupation		Poverty status: 13.9%			
Blue collar: 21.9%	White collar: 61.2%	**Home Value**			
Gray collar: 16.9%		<50k: 13.0%	50-100k: 31.4%	100-200k: 39.7%	200-300k: 9.5%
		300-500k: 4.5%	>500k: 1.9%	Median: $109,400	

Presidential politics   Far from the media centers of the East Coast, Arizona has tried every so often to make itself another Iowa or New Hampshire in presidential politics, with little success. In 1972 it had an early Democratic primary, the improbable winner of which was Republican-turned-Democrat New York Mayor John Lindsay. But he went nowhere anyplace else. In 1996 Arizona tried to set its primary for the same date as New Hampshire; when that failed the state set it one week later. The intended beneficiary was Republican Phil Gramm, running with the support of Arizona's John McCain. But Gramm pulled out of the race a week before New Hampshire, and Arizona became a battleground between Bob Dole, who now had McCain's support; Pat Buchanan, who urged his followers to "mount up and ride" after his narrow victory in New Hampshire; and Steve Forbes, who peppered the state with ads boosting his flat tax and attacking Washington politicians. Buchanan's campaigning in gun-slinger costume wearing a black hat was a bit too much, and he finished third, with 27%; it was clear he had no chance to win the nomination. Dole finished second with 30%; Forbes won 33% and all the delegates, after which his campaign, like that of his fellow easterner Lindsay a quarter-century before, went nowhere.

2004 Presidential Vote		
Bush (R)	1,104,294	(55%)
Kerry (D)	893,524	(44%)
Badnarik (Lib)	11,856	(1%)
Other	2,911	(0%)

2004 Democratic Presidential Primary		
Kerry (D)	101,809	(43%)
Clark (D)	63,256	(26%)
Dean (D)	33,555	(14%)
Edwards (D)	16,596	(7%)
Lieberman (D)	15,906	(7%)
Other	3,896	(2%)

2000 Presidential Vote		
Bush (R)	781,652	(51%)
Gore (D)	685,341	(45%)
Nader (Green)	45,645	(3%)
Other	19,268	(1%)

In 2000, Arizona tried again. McCain had irritated local Republicans enough that Governor Jane Hull and other party leaders endorsed George W. Bush. McCain, however, won a solid victory in his home state in the February primary, but it was overshadowed by his victory the same day in Michigan, made possible because, in a state with no party registration, 20% of Republican primary voters were self-identified Democrats. Arizona Democrats ran and paid for their own primary in March, because the state's February date was outside the "window" permitted by national Democratic Party rules. They allowed voting by Internet, and about 35,000 Arizonans mouse-clicked their choices; another 20,000 voted by mail; still others voted by computer or paper ballot at the polls. But the Internet voting was not flawless and the primary didn't matter because Al Gore had already clinched the nomination. In 2004 a regular primary was held one week after New Hampshire, on February 3, the same day as Delaware, Missouri, New Mexico, North Dakota, Oklahoma and South Carolina. John Kerry and Wesley Clark were the only candidates who targeted the state, and Kerry got 43% of the vote to Clark's 26%. Only 603,000 voted in a state of 5.6 million people.

In the 1990s, Arizona suddenly became competitive in presidential general elections. The national trend toward Clinton-Gore Democrats in the very largest metropolitan areas was operative in Phoenix and Maricopa County; once very heavily Republican, it was closely divided in 1996 and 2000. In 1996 Bill Clinton carried the state by a 47%–44% margin—the first Democrat to carry the state since Harry Truman in 1948. The winning issue was not Medicare—Arizona does not have an especially large elderly population, and the air seemed to go out of the Medicare issue in mid-October. Rather, it was the environment: Arizona's mostly metropolitan voters want to preserve the environment, not make a living off it as most voters in sparsely populated Western states do. Clinton's staging of the announcement of a Utah land preserve at the Grand Canyon may have carried Arizona single-handedly (it may also have defeated the only Democratic congressman in Utah at the time). Clinton went on to create new National Monuments in Arizona—four in 2000 alone—perhaps in the hope of aiding Al Gore. But George W. Bush won 51%–45%. He carried not only Phoenix and Maricopa County, as Republican nominees had in 1992 and 1996, but also the smaller counties outside the Phoenix and Tucson metro areas, which they had not.

Polls in spring and summer 2004 showed Arizonans closely divided, and John Kerry's campaign targeted the state. But Bush pulled ahead here after the Republican National Convention. In September, on a visit to Arizona, Teresa Heinz Kerry was asked about her husband's poor showing in local polls. "Oh, who cares?" she said. "You know, one state is not a whole [country]." Bush won 55%–44% in a record turnout. Once again Bush carried Maricopa County and the part of the state beyond the Phoenix and Tucson metro areas.

Congressional districting

Arizona gained two House seats in the 2000 Census, after gaining one each in the Censuses of 1960, 1970, 1980 and 1990: In 40 years it has moved from two districts to eight. This time redistricting was done not by the legislature but by a five-member Arizona Independent Redistricting Commission, a body created by the passage of Proposition 106 in November 2000.

109th Congress Lineup	
6 R	2 D

108th Congress Lineup	
6 R	2 D

Two Republican and two Democratic legislators appoint four members, and the fifth, to be neither a Democrat nor a Republican, is picked by the other four. The commission held 66 hearings and meetings and in October 2001 approved a plan closely resembling a suggestion made in *The Almanac of American Politics 2002*. Democrats were disappointed because it didn't create a competitive seat in the Phoenix area; commissioners said such a district could be created only by drawing grotesque lines that, in their view, would be gerrymandering. Actually, the Democrats came off fairly well, especially in a state in which, absent Proposition 106, Republicans would have controlled redistricting: One new district was heavily Democratic and the other evenly split between the parties; a Democrat won the former and a Republican the latter.

An explanation may be due for the odd shape of the 2d District. The demographically and politically similar areas of Mohave County and western Maricopa County are connected by a thin band of La Paz County (9 voters showed up there in both 2002 and 2004), and then Mohave County is connected by a strip that runs along the bottom of the Grand Canyon to the Hopi Reservation. The Hopi have had disputes for many years with the far more numerous Navajo, whose reservation surrounds theirs, and the commission evidently thought the Hopi should have a congressman who doesn't also represent the Navajo. The Navajo sued to get the lines redrawn but did not succeed.

Governor

Janet Napolitano (D)

Elected 2002, term expires Jan. 2007, 1st term; b. Nov. 29, 1957, New York City; home, Phoenix; Santa Clara U., B.A. 1979, U. of VA, J.D. 1983; Methodist; single.

Elected Office: AZ Atty. Gen., 1998–02.

Professional Career: Clerk, U.S. Appeals Ct. Judge Mary Schroder, 1983–84; Practicing atty., 1984–93; AZ U.S. atty., 1994–98.

Office: State Capitol, 1700 W. Washington, Phoenix, 85007, 602-542-4331; Fax: 602-542-7601; Web site: www.governor.state.az.us.

Election Results

2002 general	Janet Napolitano (D)	566,284	(46%)
	Matt Salmon (R)	554,465	(45%)
	Richard Mahoney (I)	84,947	(7%)
	Other	20,415	(2%)
2002 primary	Janet Napolitano (D)	128,702	(57%)
	Alfredo Gutierrez (D)	50,377	(22%)
	Mark Osterloh (D)	31,422	(14%)
	Mike Newcomb (D)	14,373	(6%)
1998 general	Jane Dee Hull (R)	620,188	(61%)
	Paul Johnson (D)	361,552	(36%)
	Other	35,876	(4%)

Janet Napolitano, a Democrat, in 2002 became the second woman in a row to be elected governor of Arizona. Napolitano was born in New York City and grew up in Pittsburgh and Albuquerque, where her father helped establish the University of New Mexico Medical School. She graduated from Santa Clara University and the University of Virginia Law School, and moved to Phoenix in 1983 to clerk for Judge Mary Schroeder, currently the chief judge on the 9th Circuit Court of Appeals. She practiced corporate law, volunteered as an attorney for the state Democratic party and later joined the team of lawyers representing Anita Hill at the Clarence Thomas confirmation hearings in October 1991. In 1993 she was appointed U.S. Attorney for Arizona where she served until she ran for attorney general in 1998; she was elected by a 50%–47% margin in a year in which the top five statewide offices were all won by women, with Napolitano the only Democrat among them. As attorney general, she got plenty of good publicity. She pursued Qwest for its bad telephone service on charges of consumer fraud. She negotiated a $217 million settlement with Arthur Andersen on behalf of investors. She sued Ford for explosions in Crown Victoria police cars and reduced the number of open child abuse and neglect cases from 6,000 to 700.

By October 2001 Napolitano's work as attorney general had earned her a 55% positive job rating, and she was obviously running for governor (incumbent Jane Hull was term limited). She was motivated, she said, after she was diagnosed with breast cancer in 2000 and after having a successful mastectomy; she wanted to work on health care. She announced in January 2002 and then in April 2002 presented the 6,000 nominating petitions and 6,000 $5 contributions that qualified her for financing under the Clean Elections Act passed by voters in 1998. She received public financing of $409,000 for the September primary and $615,000 for the general election. She campaigned as a "conservative Democrat" and was criticized as "too Republican" by one primary opponent. But she was able to enlist the help of the fire fighters' union and the United Food and Commercial Workers to amass her nominating petitions and $5 contributions.

The leading Republican candidate was former Congressman Matt Salmon, who was first elected in 1994 and kept his promise to serve just three terms by retiring in 2000. His high point in the House came in November 1998 when he announced he would not vote for Newt Gingrich for Speaker—a move that prompted Gingrich's resignation three days after the election. Salmon is a Mormon who did missionary work in Taiwan, speaks Mandarin Chinese, rides a Harley Davidson and fronts an Elvis cover band. Both candidates won their primaries by wide margins. Napolitano led former state Senator Alfredo Gutierrez 57%–22% and Salmon led Secretary of State Betsey Bayless 56%–30%. In the race as an Independent was Richard Mahoney, a Democrat elected Secretary of State in 1990, who qualified for the Clean Elections Act money. He attacked both nominees. "Are Matt and Janet going to take on the oil companies or the special interests? Tweedledum and Tweedledee, Salmon and Napolitano." He portrayed himself as more conservative on fiscal issues than Salmon and more liberal on cultural issues than Napolitano.

In the general election, Napolitano relied on her record as attorney general and called for closing loopholes and cutting spending to make up the budget shortfalls; she supported the death penalty. Salmon opposed tax increases—"I will not raise taxes, go after shared revenues or make cuts in the classroom"—and announced a Workforce 2010 plan to create 500,000 jobs paying more than $40,000. The tone of their campaigns was different. Napolitano was businesslike and stressed her experience. Salmon said he wanted to bring God back into government and his ads showed him with his wife and four children (Napolitano is unmarried). The Clean Elections Act played a role: Salmon declined the Clean Elections money, and raised his own, more slowly than he had hoped. But the proceeds he got from a George W. Bush fundraiser were a mixed blessing: The law requires the state to pay candidates who have accepted the Clean Elections funding (and the concomitant limitations on spending) an amount equal to what candidates who decline the Clean Elections Act money raise above its limits. So every dollar Bush raised for Salmon above that amount put a dollar in Napolitano's campaign treasury.

This proved to be a very close election. Napolitano led on election night and Wednesday by 25,000 votes, but it took time to count 200,000 early ballots, mostly from the Phoenix and Tucson areas. On Sunday Napolitano led by 11,000 votes with just 11,000 more to count, and Salmon conceded. Salmon carried Phoenix's Maricopa County, but by only 48%–44%. Napolitano won Tucson's Pima County 52%–39%. In the smaller counties, the "conservative Democrat" led 46%–44%. Overall, Napolitano won 46%–45%, with 7% for Mahoney.

Napolitano faced a Republican legislature, but was able to pass most of her budget in 2003 with help from moderate Republicans; she negotiated with Senate President Ken Bennett, while she worked with rank-and-file House Republicans who refused to follow the lead of Speaker Jake Flake. She was sharply criticized for not following usual procedures when she renamed Squaw Peak and a Phoenix freeway after Lori Piestewa, an Arizona soldier slain in Iraq. In June 2003 she launched CopperRx, a program of discounts on prescription drugs for seniors and the disabled; only 15,000 enrolled that year, and in January 2004 she dropped the $9.95 enrollment fee and enrollments went up to 30,000 by June, when estimated savings for individuals totaled $3.2 million. In January 2004 she had to deal with a long standoff in a hostage-taking in a state prison; her actions were criticized by some Republicans. In 2004 she presented a $7.3 billion budget with no tax increases and $500 million of borrowing. Once again, working in different ways with Senate and House Republicans, she got it passed. It included $25 million for all-day kindergarten in 150 schools serving low-income pupils, which she pressed for hard. It also included money to purchase land near Arizona's military bases, to prevent development which would make them more vulnerable in the 2005 base closing round. She also agreed on tax breaks for landowners who clear forests (Arizona was in its seventh year of drought) and doubled spending on forest crews and child abuse prevention. She signed a law requiring plaintiffs to get an expert opinion before their lawyers could file a medical malpractice suit. In 2003 she had vetoed an increase in unemployment benefits when unions complained about restrictions; in 2004 the legislature passed the increase without restrictions, and she signed it. She did not succeed in getting a statewide rating system for preschools or tax law changes. She vetoed a bill requiring a 24-hour waiting period for abortions.

"People are rejecting the notion that you can say no to everything and still grow a state," Napolitano said after passage of the 2004 budget. "This is a new day in Arizona." But not all were pleased by the new day. Several Republican legislators who supported Napolitano on the budget and other issues were defeated by conservatives in the September 2004 primary. In November Republicans increased their margin in the Senate to 18–12, and though their margin in the

House was reduced to 38–22, there were fewer moderates there for Napolitano to work with. Observers speculated that the new legislature might pass the abortion waiting period, business tax cuts (including a phase out of the business personal property tax), a ban on same-sex marriage and increased tax credits for private school fees. Looking ahead in 2004, Napolitano said her goals were to attract more high-wage jobs, finding ways to aid seniors and building up a rainy day fund. Another pressing problem was water. In April 2004 the general manager of the Central Arizona Project attacked her for not meeting with his organization and for not pushing for the reopening of a desalination plant near Yuma to produce some of the water the United States is obliged by treaty to transfer to Mexico. That would mean less diversion of Colorado River Water and less chance of the federal Interior Department declaring an emergency and shutting off delivery of Colorado River water to CAP. In November 2004 Napolitano ordered state agencies to reduce water usage by 5% and called for new water conservation efforts and new authority and more money for the Department of Water Resources. "We're the second fastest growing state in the country and we're in the ninth year of drought. In the end, we're going to need conservation, we're going to need to fight for Colorado River water, we're going to have to work with our agricultural community and help them find other technologies."

Napolitano has consistently said that she will run for reelection in 2006, although some national Democrats would like her to run against Senator Jon Kyl instead. Traveling around the state in 2004, obviously with an eye to running for governor, was Republican Congressman J. D. Hayworth but in March 2005 he said he would stay in Congress. Other possible candidates in mid-2005 were state Senate President Ken Bennett and Secretary of State Jan Brewer; party officials were also recruiting Marilyn Quayle, wife of former Vice President Dan Quayle, and U.S. Surgeon General Richard Carmona, a Tucson doctor.

Senior Senator

John McCain (R)

Elected 1986, seat up 2010, 4th term; b. Aug. 29, 1936, Panama Canal Zone; home, Phoenix; U.S. Naval Acad., B.S. 1958, Natl. War Col., 1973–74; Episcopalian; married (Cindy).

Military Career: Navy, 1958–80 (Vietnam).

Elected Office: U.S. House of Reps., 1982–1986.

Professional Career: Dir., Navy Senate Liaison Ofc., 1977–81.

DC Office: 241 RSOB, 20510, 202-224-2235; Fax: 202-228-2862; Web site: mccain.senate.gov.

State Offices: Phoenix, 602-952-2410; Tempe, 480-897-6289; Tucson, 520-670-6334.

Committees: *Armed Services*: Airland (Chmn.); Personnel; Readiness & Management Support; Seapower. *Commerce, Science & Transportation*: Aviation; Global Climate Change & Impacts; Surface Transportation & Merchant Marine; Trade, Tourism & Economic Development. *Indian Affairs* (Chmn.).

Group Ratings

	ADA	ACLU	AFS	LCV	ITIC	NTU	COC	ACU	NTLC	CHC
2004	35	22	29	67	100	77	67	72	80	83
2003	35	—	22	53	—	72	61	75	—	—

National Journal Ratings

	2003 LIB	—	2003 CONS	2004 LIB	—	2004 CONS
Economic	50%	—	49%	49%	—	48%
Social	0%	—	59%	44%	—	55%
Foreign	39%	—	54%	49%	—	49%

Key Votes of the 108th Congress

1. Ban Drilling in ANWR	Y	5. Energy Bill	N	9. Ban Same-Sex Marriage	N
2. Approve Bush Tax Cuts	N	6. Support Roe v. Wade	N	10. Ban Bunker-Buster Bomb	N
3. Medicare/Rx Bill	N	7. Ban Partial-Birth Abortion	Y	11. Fund Iraq War	Y
4. Bar Overtime Pay Regs.	N	8. Assault Weapons Ban	N	12. Restrict Missile Defense	N

Election Results

2004 general	John McCain (R)............................... 1,505,372	(77%)	($2,140,807)
	Stuart Starky (D)............................... 404,507	(21%)	($12,716)
	Other... 51,798	(3%)	
2004 primary	John McCain (R)........................... unopposed		
1998 general	John McCain (R)............................... 696,577	(69%)	($2,461,900)
	Ed Ranger (D) 275,224	(27%)	($371,439)
	Other... 41,479	(4%)	

Prior Winning Percentages: 1992 (56%); 1986 (60%); 1984 House (78%); 1982 House (66%)

For many Americans John McCain is the closest thing our politics has to a national hero, a presidential candidate widely admired in 2000 and an independent leader of great force in the years after. His personal story is a dramatic one, told beautifully by Robert Timberg in *The Nightingale's Song* and by McCain himself and Mark Salter in the 1999 bestseller *Faith of My Fathers*. McCain is the son and grandson of Navy admirals, a decorated Navy pilot himself who was shot down over Vietnam and who spent five years, most of it in pain and torture, in Communist prisoner of war camps. He refused to be let out ahead of those who had been in longer when he was offered release because of his father's rank. McCain returned to the United States in March 1973. His final assignment in the Navy was as Senate liaison. In 1980 he retired and moved to Arizona, his wife's home state; in 1982 he ran for an open House seat. Attacked as an outsider, he responded, "The longest place I ever lived in was Hanoi." He led 32%–26% in a four-way primary, and won the 1982 and 1984 general elections and then the 1986 Senate contest easily.

In his first years in the Senate he had a low profile. His first major issue was one on which he had considerable expertise: Vietnam. In the early 1990s McCain worked hard with John Kerry, also a decorated Vietnam veteran, on the special committee investigating charges that American POWs or MIAs remained in Vietnam; they found no evidence of any. With Kerry he supported ending the trade embargo on, and pressed for, establishing diplomatic relations with Vietnam. But his support for reconciliation with our former enemies has not dimmed his memories of how his captors treated his fellow prisoners of war. On the Armed Services Committee, McCain has called for more defense spending and insisted military interventions be designed to achieve victory; he criticized the Clinton administration for using air power alone and ruling out ground troops in Bosnia and for not using "all necessary force" in Kosovo.

McCain's other major committee assignment is Commerce, which handles heavily lobbied regulatory issues. McCain's impulse on these is toward deregulation, and he obviously has a distaste for the political deal-making and log-rolling that is so common. It appears to be his view that members of Congress, like members of the military, should serve the national interest honorably and without reference to political considerations. He has a distaste for what he considers pork barrel spending, and sometimes tries to halt passage of what he considers pork-laden bills; that provides him plenty of material for his self-deprecating jokes about how unpopular he is with many colleagues. On the big issue before Commerce in the 1990s, telecommunications, he took little part in shaping the 1996 legislation and voted against it, arguing that it did not effectively ensure competition. "The whole Telecommunications Act was a disaster," he said in November 2002.

The issue McCain is most closely identified with is campaign finance regulation. His interest came from his experience as one of the "Keating Five" senators investigated for meeting in 1987 with regulators on behalf of Charles Keating's Arizona savings and loan. Democrats kept McCain in the case, though he had done nothing for Keating; as the one Republican involved, he thus made the scandal bipartisan. Ultimately he was cited for nothing more than bad judgment. Vindicated by reelection in 1992, in the majority after the election of 1994, he sought out

Democrat Russ Feingold, whose campaign finance bill had gotten nowhere that year. The McCain-Feingold bills went through several transformations. The 1998 bill purported to ban soft money contributions to political parties and to limit "issue ads" run by independent organizations within 60 days of an election. It was fiercely opposed as an infringement of free speech and as a threat to the Republican Party by Mitch McConnell of Kentucky. Majority Leader Trent Lott yanked the bill from the Senate floor in February 1998; it returned in September, after the House passed a similar bill, but could summon up no more than 52 votes and died. In September 1999, after the House passed a similar bill again, McCain and Feingold introduced a new version that attacked soft money but did not address issue ads. The obvious intent was to get a bill to conference and generate enough public support that McConnell and other Republican opponents would have to back down. But in October McConnell, noting that McCain had charged that the current campaign finance system produces corruption, challenged McCain to name senators who had been corrupted. McCain refused to name names and said the system was corrupt in general. Against McConnell's filibuster a few days later, McCain and Feingold were able to summon up only 55 votes for cloture, five short of the 60 needed, and the bill was taken off the floor.

His work on campaign finance and his record of service in Vietnam provided solid credentials for the presidential campaign he embarked on in 1999. He wisely decided to avoid the Iowa caucuses (McCain had long campaigned against ethanol subsidies as pork) and concentrated on New Hampshire, where he traveled around the state in his "Straight Talk Express" bus. At first only a few reporters traveled with him and crowds were sparse. But it soon became clear McCain was striking a chord. To increasingly large and fervent crowds he told his personal story in self-deprecating terms, and pledged, "I will never tell you a lie." He was asked to autograph hundreds of copies of *Faith of My Fathers*. He talked about defense and foreign policy issues—the only candidate to spend much time doing so—and invariably called for campaign finance reform. On the campaign bus, McCain was always available to answer reporters' questions and banter with the press, while making fun of his aides and consultant Mike Murphy (who later called the press "our constituency"). McCain did not have much support from politicians. Only four fellow senators endorsed him (Jon Kyl, Chuck Hagel, Fred Thompson and Mike DeWine). Back home, Arizona Governor Jane Hull, apparently because of abrasive treatment by McCain, endorsed George W. Bush; *The Arizona Republic* wrote editorials warning of McCain's "volcanic" temper. But the strength of feeling among his ever-larger crowds was palpable. Bush predicted victory in New Hampshire, but on February 1 McCain beat him by an impressive 49%–31% margin. Suddenly he became, if not the frontrunner, at least the most admired of either party's presidential candidates.

From there the "Straight Talk Express" had mixed success. It went down to South Carolina, where both the Republican establishment and Christian conservatives lined up with Bush in 2000. The campaigning got negative but what hurt even more was his failure to win over self-identified Republicans. His emphasis on campaign finance reform and his criticisms of Bush's tax plan for giving too much to the rich helped with independents, but sounded like enemy talk to Republicans. On February 18 Bush won 53%–42% in South Carolina, in what turned out to be as decisive a victory as his father's there had been 12 years before. The New Hampshire and South Carolina results were templates for what happened elsewhere; in New Hampshire and other Northeastern states McCain ran about even with Bush among self-identified Republicans and way ahead among self-identified independents and self-identified Democrats; in South Carolina and other states outside the Northeast, Bush ran way ahead among Republicans and behind among independents and Democrats. On February 22 McCain won in Arizona and, in a big 50%–43% upset, in Michigan.

McCain might have done better if he had emphasized other issues on which he had consistently taken stands in line with most Republicans' thinking—defense, tax cuts (he had an interesting tax cut plan himself, but he spent less time on it than on attacking Bush's), abortion, Social Security individual investment accounts. Instead, after South Carolina, he gave a speech in Virginia Beach attacking the religious right and in an offhand comment on the bus called Pat Robertson and Jerry Falwell "forces of evil." As he explained the next day, this was sarcastic "Luke Skywalker talk," which reporters often heard on the bus but which rarely appeared in their reports. But to many Christian conservatives, a large segment of the Republican primary vote, it sounded like angry hostility; McCain lost in Virginia and Washington on February 29. On Super Tuesday, March 7, McCain won in Massachusetts, Connecticut, Rhode Island and Vermont. But he lost decisively in New York, Ohio and California and "suspended" his campaign on March 9. Much attention was focused on the fact that he did not "endorse" Bush; when they finally met in Pittsburgh in May reporters practically had to extract the word from his mouth. He made it clear he did not want to be nominated for vice president and said he wanted no cabinet post, making the plausible argument that he operated better as his own man than as someone else's appointee. He insisted on having his wife Cindy McCain, not Jane Hull, head the Arizona delegation to the convention, and he gave a moving, elegiac speech that ended as if in a minor key.

Some defeated presidential candidates sulk in their tents; McCain became more legislatively active than ever—and increasingly likely to ally himself with Democrats and oppose most Republicans. His first priority was the campaign finance bill; he had campaigned for Republican House candidates and tried, with some success, to get them to support it. In January 2001 he threatened to tie up the Senate unless Majority Leader Trent Lott set aside two weeks of debate on the issue. In March 2001, after two weeks of remarkably civilized but spirited debate, during which McCain and Feingold fended off several poison-pill amendments, the legislation passed April 2 by a 59–41 vote. An amendment by Fred Thompson and Dianne Feinstein was passed to raise limits on individual contributions from $1,000 to $2,000, but the bill retained the soft-money ban and limit on issue ads prior to the election, which some senators fear will be struck down by the courts as an unconstitutional ban of free speech. The House, which twice had passed similar bills, took up the issue in June 2001. But after the Republican leadership's rule was defeated—a very rare event indeed—Speaker Dennis Hastert pulled the bill from the floor. Supporters tried to get the 218 signatures needed for a discharge petition. For months the number hovered just under 218, but in January 2002 the signatures were obtained. The House passed its version of the bill in February 2002 by a 240–189 vote, and the bill became law in March 2002; most of it was upheld by the Supreme Court. But McCain didn't rest on his victory. He was furious that the Bush administration didn't appoint a Democrat designated by Tom Daschle to a seat on the Federal Election Commission; the holdover Democrat was voting with the Republicans and passing regulations which McCain argued undercut the bill; one was to define the word "solicitation" as "ask" rather than as "request, suggest or recommend." In June he threatened to block all nominations until Bush made the appointment, and in October 2002 he invoked the Congressional Review Act to try to overturn the new regulations and also filed a lawsuit against the FEC.

On other issues, McCain voted with the Democrats in July 2001 on HMO regulation. He was the only Republican to vote against the water projects bill in October, charging that it contained $1.2 billion of special projects earmarked for districts. He appeared in ads in Colorado and Oregon for ballot propositions requiring background checks for sales at gun shows. In 2002, after campaign finance regulation passed the Senate, he worked with many Democrats again. He, John Edwards and Edward Kennedy sponsored an HMO regulation bill. He supported embryonic stem-cell research. With John Kerry he proposed CAFE standards for all cars and light trucks of 36 miles per gallon by 2015. He was one of two Republicans to vote against the conference report on the tax cut in May and, after Jim Jeffords switched parties, he invited Tom Daschle to a friendly visit to his vacation home near Sedona; speculation abounded that McCain would switch parties too, and liberals writing in *The Washington Monthly* and *The New Republic* argued that he would be the strongest Democratic nominee for president. But he turned that talk aside. And he took strong stands with George W. Bush and most Republicans on some issues— the nomination of his tobacco bill adversary John Ashcroft, repeal of ergonomics regulations, the May 2001 budget resolution, and allowing Mexican trucks into the United States.

McCain strongly supported Bush in the war on terrorism after September 11. In October 2001 he urged more ground troops in Afghanistan, and in December 2001 he was one of 10 members of Congress to sign a letter urging that Iraq be the next target. He called for the government to run airline security and he co-sponsored a bill with Ernest Hollings that effectively decided the issue; it passed 97–0 in October 2001. But he also proposed that screeners be fireable without regard to civil service rules—the position Bush insisted on and Democrats, to their political detriment, opposed on the homeland security bill in 2002. He called for a special commission to investigate intelligence failures before September 11, a proposal opposed for months by the Bush administration, and said that former Senators Gary Hart and Warren Rudman should serve on it. The final version of the law provided, at the insistence of relatives of September 11 casualties, that McCain and Richard Shelby get a veto over Trent Lott's appointees to the commission; McCain's attempts to get Lott to appoint Rudman failed. In 2002 he did much less campaigning for Republicans than in 2000, making appearances in tandem with promotion of his latest book *Worth the Fighting For* and only on behalf of Republicans who had supported his brand of campaign finance regulation; in September, he appeared with Richard Gephardt in support of the generic drug bill and said it was "very, very likely" that Republicans would lose their majority in the House.

They didn't and in fact regained their majority in the Senate, making McCain chairman of the Commerce committee again. There he promoted the bill he co-sponsored with Joseph Lieberman to reduce carbon dioxide emissions; it got 43 votes on the floor of the Senate in 2003. In March 2004 he threatened to hold hearings on steroid use in baseball, and in December he said that he would file legislation in January to limit steroid use unless the baseball team owners and players' union agreed to do so. On Armed Services he persisted in his campaign against the proposed purchase of Boeing 767s as aerial refueling tankers and in his attacks on Pentagon improprieties. He questioned the fallback from Fallujah in April 2004. He also continued to call for a larger army and more troops in Iraq. "I have strenuously argued for larger troop numbers in Iraq, including the right kind of troops—linguists, special forces, civil affairs, etc. There are very strong differences of opinion between myself and Secretary Rumsfeld on that issue." In December 2004 he said he had "no confidence" in Rumsfeld but did not call on him to resign—an ominous note in that McCain is in line to become chairman of the committee in January 2007. He pushed for adoption of the 9/11 Commission's recommendations for changes in the intelligence community, but failed in October to get appropriations power for the Intelligence Committee. He opposed the constitutional amendment to ban same-sex marriage as "antithetical in every way to the core philosophy of Republicans. It usurps from the states a fundamental authority they have always possessed and imposes a federal remedy for a problem that most states believe does not confront them." On all these issues he was at odds with the Bush administration.

Two issues with an Arizona dimension on which McCain has worked are water and Indians. With Jon Kyl and the state's House delegation, he worked to pass the Arizona Water Settlements Act, resolving disputes between the state and Indian tribes and between the federal government over water rights. It allocated 47% of the state's Colorado River water to Indian tribes, notably the Gila River Indian Community and the Tohono O'odham Nation, who could lease it to cities in Arizona. This was the most far-reaching Indian water settlement in history. The Senate passed it in October 2004, as the presidential campaign was raging, and the House passed it in November, after it was over. McCain served as chairman of the Indian Affairs Committee in 1995–97 and became chairman again in January 2005. In February 2004, after the *Washington Post* reported that lobbyist Jack Abramoff and publicist Michael Scanlon, both with strong Republican connections, had received $45 million in fees from Indian tribes, McCain demanded a hearing. It was held in September and McCain was fierce in his denunciation: "What sets this tale apart, what makes it truly extraordinary, is the extent and degree of the apparent exploitation and deceit."

Heading into the 2004 presidential campaign McCain was a major national figure, with high positives and very low negatives among Democrats as well as Republicans, a leading Republican who was nonetheless at odds with the Bush White House on many issues. The press, always enchanted with him, gave him plenteous coverage. As John Kerry, his fellow Vietnam veteran, clinched the Democratic nomination in March 2004, there was speculation that he would ask McCain to be his vice presidential nominee. Polls showed Kerry-McCain running far ahead of Bush-Cheney. After some days of speculation and some talks with Kerry, he firmly rejected the idea. "I am a pro-life, deficit hawk, free trade Republican," he said. Bush chief strategist Karl Rove sat down for a talk with McCain's 2000 strategist John Weaver, an old adversary from Texas politics, and made peace. In June 2004 McCain appeared with Bush at

Fort Lewis, Washington, and at a campaign stop in Nevada and McCain endorsed him strongly. After press stories that suggested Bush would drop Dick Cheney from the ticket, McCain made a campaign appearance with Cheney. When the Swift Boat Veterans for Truth ads appeared against John Kerry, McCain called them "dishonorable" and said they should be dropped from the air. When Bush declined to join that demand, he didn't press the issue further, and conceded that, "Everybody is accountable for what they do, and certainly John Kerry is accountable for what he did after the war, and people can make a judgment." He said that he had advised Kerry to avoid mentioning the war, as he had done in his 2000 campaign, and to let others do it. In August he asked Kerry to stop running an ad showing him criticizing Bush in 2000; Kerry did so. On Monday night at the Republican National Convention McCain delivered another eloquent speech unequivocally endorsing Bush. "He has been tested and has risen to the most important challenge of our time, and I salute him." And he took a swipe at the "disingenuous filmmaker" Michael Moore, who was then sitting in the press section, to the delight of the delegates.

McCain made common cause with Bush not only on the campaign trail but on some important issues. McCain complained that heavy spending by mostly anti-Bush 527 organizations of millions of dollars of soft money violated McCain-Feingold. The Bush campaign took the same position, filing a complaint with the FEC in March 2004 and joining McCain in a lawsuit in August to force the FEC to act. In September McCain and Feingold filed a bill to limit the use of soft money by 527s and promised to push it forward in 2005. On immigration—a raging issue in Arizona—McCain said, "The truth is, border enforcement alone does not work." With Congressman Jim Kolbe and Jeff Flake he sponsored a guest worker law, which would provide six-year temporary worker visas and three-year visas for those who are here illegally now. He also co-sponsored with Jon Kyl a bill to fund border security measures. He recognized Arizona voters' anger. "The nation has lost control of its southern border, and Arizona is paying the price through transient traffic, violence in our streets and deaths in our deserts." But he opposed Proposition 200, cutting off public benefits to illegal immigrants, arguing that it would "delay, possibly derail, the search for a solution." It passed, but with a less than overwhelming 56% of the vote. One week after the election McCain went to the White House to work with Bush on a guest worker bill for 2005. And he supported him on Social Security and tax changes as well.

Will McCain run for president in 2008? In May 2004 he said, "This is all so transient. It could all end tomorrow. My philosophy is to just go, go like hell. Like Teddy Roosevelt did it. Full bore." In November 2004 he told the Manchester *Union Leader*, "I'm not ruling it out, but I'm not ruling it in." McCain has obvious strengths as a presidential candidate, and some weaknesses. He is widely respected and has relatively few detractors, though some of them are in his own party; on many issues he is in line with culturally conservative Republicans, but those are not the issues he likes to emphasize or on which he shows the greatest fervor; his appeal to Independents and Democrats is undoubtedly greater than George W. Bush's, and his popularity with the press is very much greater, but those things may change if and when he clinches the Republican nomination. He will turn 72 in August 2008, a year younger than Ronald Reagan was when he was reelected in 1984; he continues to maintain a very active, indeed hyperkinetic, schedule. He might be entitled to argue that voters shouldn't count the five and a half years he spent in Hanoi. McCain could turn out to be a much less polarizing candidate in a general election than either Bush or Bill Clinton; in 2004, he said, "In all candor, I really don't think the country is polarized at all. We've got to stop polarizing ourselves in Washington in a vain attempt to polarize the nation." But he could be polarizing for some in the Republican primaries.

McCain's appeal in general elections, and the irritation he evokes in some conservatives, have been apparent in Arizona. He won his Senate seat in 1986 by 60%–40% and in 1992, after the Keating Five investigation, he was re-elected 56%–32%. In 1998 he won by an impressive 69%–27%, carrying the heavily Democratic Apache County 54%–42% and winning the Hispanic vote 52%–42%. In late 2002 and early 2003 the Club for Growth encouraged Congressman Jeff Flake to challenge him in the Republican primary; Flake decided not to. In November 2004 McCain was reelected 77%–21%, while Bush was carrying the state 55%–44%.

Junior Senator

Jon Kyl (R)

Elected 1994, seat up 2006, 2d term; b. Apr. 25, 1942, Oakland, NE; home, Phoenix; U. of AZ, B.A. 1964, L.L.B. 1966; Presbyterian; married (Caryll).

Elected Office: U.S. House of Reps., 1986–94.

Professional Career: Practicing atty., 1966–86; Chmn., Phoenix Chamber of Commerce, 1984–85.

DC Office: 730 HSOB, 20510, 202-224-4521; Fax: 202-224-2207; Web site: kyl.senate.gov.

State Offices: Phoenix, 602-840-1891; Tucson, 520-575-8633.

Committees: *Republican Policy Committee Chairman.* *Finance*: Health Care; Social Security & Family Policy; Taxation & IRS Oversight (Chmn.). *Judiciary*: Administrative Oversight & the Courts; Crime & Drugs; Immigration, Border Security & Citizenship; Intellectual Property; Terrorism, Technology & Homeland Security (Chmn.).

Group Ratings

	ADA	ACLU	AFS	LCV	ITIC	NTU	COC	ACU	NTLC	CHC
2004	5	0	0	0	92	89	88	100	98	100
2003	10	—	0	16	—	79	96	90	—	—

National Journal Ratings

	2003 LIB	—	2003 CONS		2004 LIB	—	2004 CONS
Economic	24%	—	73%		2%	—	96%
Social	0%	—	59%		0%	—	84%
Foreign	0%	—	78%		0%	—	67%

Key Votes of the 108th Congress

1. Ban Drilling in ANWR	N	5. Energy Bill	Y	9. Ban Same-Sex Marriage	Y
2. Approve Bush Tax Cuts	Y	6. Support Roe v. Wade	N	10. Ban Bunker-Buster Bomb	N
3. Medicare/Rx Bill	Y	7. Ban Partial-Birth Abortion	Y	11. Fund Iraq War	Y
4. Bar Overtime Pay Regs.	N	8. Assault Weapons Ban	N	12. Restrict Missile Defense	N

Election Results

2000 general	Jon Kyl (R)	1,108,196	(79%)	($2,503,674)
	William Toel (I)	109,230	(8%)	($21,491)
	Vance Hansen (Green)	108,926	(8%)	
	Barry J. Hess, II (Lib)	70,724	(5%)	
2000 primary	Jon Kyl (R)	unopposed		
1994 general	Jon Kyl (R)	600,999	(54%)	($4,138,203)
	Sam Coppersmith (D)	442,510	(40%)	($1,577,556)
	Scott Grainger (Lib)	75,493	(7%)	

Prior Winning Percentages: 1992 House (59%); 1990 House (61%); 1988 House (87%); 1986 House (65%)

Jon Kyl, Arizona's junior senator, was first elected to the House in 1986 and to the Senate in 1994. His father John Kyl was a Republican congressman from Iowa (1959–65, 1967–73), who eventually lost his seat in reapportionment; Jon Kyl moved to a state that, in effect, was gaining the Republican seats that Great Plains states like Iowa were losing. Kyl went to college and law school in Arizona, practiced law in Phoenix, worked on Republican campaigns and headed the Phoenix Chamber of Commerce; he won the heavily Republican 4th District seat in 1986 by beating former (1973–77) Congressman John Conlan, who had support from the religious right, 60%–28%.

In the House, Kyl was a leader among Republicans on missile defense, the balanced budget amendment, and for disclosing the names of House members with overdrafts on the House bank—one of the causes that destabilized Democrats' control of the House in the years running up to 1994. By that time, Kyl was running for the Senate seat held for three terms by Democrat

Dennis DeConcini, whose reputation was stained by his involvement in the Keating Five scandal. Kyl had no primary opposition and the further good fortune that one-term Congressman Sam Coppersmith won the September 13 Democratic primary by only 59 votes of 255,000 cast after a two-week recount. Kyl, with far more money, ran ads with home movie texture showing him traveling through the desert countryside, dressed in jeans and working on ranches, while talking about how he and his wife first fell in love with the state (he has climbed Camelback Mountain "more than 1,000 times"). Coppersmith stressed his support for abortion rights and said he would welcome a campaign visit from Bill Clinton. Kyl won easily, 54%–40%.

Kyl has a solidly conservative voting record. Quietly, he has become a major force on defense policy. He is perhaps the Senate's biggest champion of a missile defense system. A 1996 speech he made in Europe on the future of NATO impressed Margaret Thatcher and Henry Kissinger, who accepted his invitation to a conference at the Arizona Biltmore. In 1997 he led, with Jesse Helms, the losing fight against the Chemical Weapons Convention. Learning from that experience, he organized the winning fight to reject the Comprehensive Test Ban Treaty, submitted by Bill Clinton to the Senate in September 1997. Starting in 1998, Kyl studied the details and worked to persuade Republican colleagues to oppose the treaty. In May 1999 he told Majority Leader Trent Lott that he had 34 solid votes against, enough to prevent ratification, but Helms, the Foreign Relations chairman, insisted that Kyl get more before he would let the treaty come to the floor. All 45 Democrats, unaware in the increasingly partisan Senate of Kyl's efforts, wrote Helms in July demanding the treaty be brought forward by September. Helms replied dismissively that he would not do so until he got action on the Kyoto treaty and amendments to the ABM treaty. In September North Dakota Democrat Byron Dorgan promised to "plant myself on the floor like a potted plant" until the CTBT was considered. The ranking Foreign Relations Democrat still thought that 25 Republicans could be persuaded to vote for the treaty, and concurred when Lott promised to bring it up in October. Only then did Senate Democrats and the Clinton White House begin to discover that they had conspired to defeat their own treaty. Kyl had done his work well: The CTBT did not even get a majority, much less the required two-thirds, as it was defeated 48–51. "Our success," Kyl said, "depended on being quiet about what we did." Kyl continues to press forward on missile defense. He urged George W. Bush to abrogate the treaty, and when Senate Democrats on the Armed Services Committee tried to cut missile defense funds in May 2002 he was quick to respond, pointing out that Iran had just successfully tested an 800-mile-range missile. Kyl strongly supported the Bush administration on Afghanistan and Iraq. When Edward Kennedy attacked Bush in March 2004 for misusing intelligence on Iraq, Kyl replied, "The reality is, no one was duped. We were all working off the same data. Reasonable people reached different conclusions about what to do based on a commonly understood set of facts. There was nothing devious about that. One need not veer off into conspiracy theories to explain honest differences of opinion about policies."

On Judiciary Kyl ranks behind Chairman Arlen Specter, former Chairman Orrin Hatch and Charles Grassley in seniority and is chairman of the Terrorism, Technology and Homeland Security Subcommittee. Before September 11 he and ranking Democrat Dianne Feinstein co-sponsored a bill to prepare defenses for attacks by terrorists with chemical and biological weapons, and in November 2001 they introduced a bill to establish a comprehensive lookout database, which would combine information from the CIA, the FBI and the State Department and make it available to border and consular personnel. In 2003 and 2004 the subcommittee held extensive hearings on border security, narcoterrorism, database security, domestic terrorist recruitment and the influence of Wahhabism. In 2004 Kyl's bill passed the Senate to include terrorists not known to be affiliated with a group in the Patriot Act, and he held hearings on other potential changes in the law. He has pointed out how lax State Department visa policies—notably the Visa Express program in Saudi Arabia, which delegated visa issuance to travel agents—enabled most of the September 11 hijackers to enter the country and how the State Department resisted any tightening of procedures.

On other Judiciary issues, Kyl has worked to beef up the Border Patrol and to track legal immigrants who overstay their visas. He also has worked for more federal reimbursement of states and localities for the costs of hospitalizing and incarcerating illegal aliens. He offered amendments to the DNA bill to allow law enforcement access to DNA samples voluntarily submitted by convicts and to allow into the national database DNA samples of those acquitted or arrested but never charged. In November 2004, when cultural conservative groups tried to block Specter from becoming Judiciary chairman, Kyl, who was next in line, avoided public comment.

Water is one of the most sensitive issues in Arizona. For years Kyl worked, mostly behind the scenes, on settling Indian claims to Colorado and Gila River water and the dispute between the federal government and the state of Arizona of how much the state must pay the feds for the Central Arizona Project, completed in 1993 at a cost of $3.6 billion. The stakeholders were many and the stakes were huge; some of the litigation had been ongoing for 20 years. With John McCain as co-sponsor and with the support of the entire Arizona House delegation, Kyl succeeded in passing the Arizona Water Settlement Act in 2004. It settled Indian lawsuits against Arizona and New Mexico and set Arizona's reimbursement to the federal government at $1.65 billion. It allocated 47% of the state's Colorado River water to Indian tribes, notably the Gila River Indian Community and the Tohono O'odham Nation, who could lease it to cities in Arizona. This was the most far-reaching Indian water settlement in history.

Kyl is not an active seeker of publicity, and is far less well known in Arizona and Washington than his colleague McCain. He is pleasant and unassuming, but can surprise: He is a big fan of race cars and has been seen driving the lead car around the track in a warm-up lap at the Phoenix International Raceway. He became the chairman of the Republican Steering Committee in 2001 and, moving up in the leadership, chairman of the Republican Policy Committee in 2003. In June 2000 Kyl was interviewed as a possible vice presidential nominee by Dick Cheney, whom he had chosen as a kind of model when he came to the House, but he ultimately recommended against his own selection.

Kyl had no difficulty winning reelection in 2000: No Democrat filed to run against him and he won 79% of the vote against an Independent, a Green Party candidate and a Libertarian. When he first ran for the Senate in 1994, he said he would probably serve only two terms, and in July 2001 he said, "It was my intention then, and it's probably still my intention, although I'm not going to make any decisions for another three or four years." But he held a fundraiser with Rudy Giuliani in February 2005 and Bill Frist in March. He had $2.5 million in his Senate campaign account and seemed to be as active as ever. One Democrat positioning himself as a candidate was real estate developer and state Democratic Chairman Jim Pederson, who spent $1.8 million of his own money on rebuilding the party in 2003 and 2004; the results were disappointing, as the Democrats failed to make Arizona competitive in the presidential race and made no significant gains in legislative races. If Kyl does not run, possible Republican candidates include Congressmen Jeff Flake, John Shadegg and J. D. Hayworth.

FIRST DISTRICT

Rep. Rick Renzi (R)

Elected 2002, 2d term; b. June 11, 1958, Ft. Monmouth, NJ; home, Flagstaff; N. AZ. U., B.S. 1980, Catholic U., J.D. 2002; Catholic; married (Roberta).

Professional Career: Admin., Defense Dept, 1984–89; Owner, Patriot Insurance Co., 1989–2002; Owner, Renzi & Campbell Dev. Inc., 1994–2002; Owner, Renzi Vino vineyard, 1998-present.

DC Office: 418 CHOB, 20515, 202-225-2315; Fax: 202-226-9739; Web site: www.house.gov/renzi/.

District Offices: Casa Grande, 520-705-2181; Flagstaff, 928-213-3434; Prescott, 928-708-9120; Show Low, 928-537-2800.

Committees: *Financial Services* (30th of 37 R): Capital Markets, Insurance & Government Sponsored Enterprises; Financial Institutions & Consumer Credit; Housing & Community Opportunity. *Permanent Select Committee on Intelligence* (12th of 12 R): Intelligence Policy; Oversight; Terrorism, Human Intelligence, Analysis & Counterintelligence. *Resources* (18th of 27 R): Forests & Forest Health.

Group Ratings

	ADA	ACLU	AFS	LCV	ITIC	NTU	COC	ACU	NTLC	CHC
2004	10	5	25	18	90	51	95	88	81	100
2003	10	—	0	5	—	57	90	88	—	—

National Journal Ratings

	2003 LIB	—	2003 CONS		2004 LIB	—	2004 CONS
Economic	33%	—	64%		40%	—	59%
Social	0%	—	95%		28%	—	70%
Foreign	31%	—	65%		25%	—	68%

Key Votes of the 108th Congress

1. Drilling in ANWR	Y	5. DC School Vouchers	Y	9. Ban Same-Sex Marriage	Y
2. Approve Bush Tax Cuts	Y	6. Ban Human Cloning	Y	10. Fund Iraq War	Y
3. Medicare/Rx Bill	Y	7. Restrict Gun Liability	Y	11. Bar Cuba Embargo Funds	N
4. Bar Overtime Pay Regs.	N	8. Ban Partial-Birth Abortion	Y	12. Intelligence Reorg.	Y

Election Results

2004 general	Rick Renzi (R)	148,315	(59%)	($2,207,249)
	Paul Babbitt (D)	91,776	(36%)	($1,274,852)
	John Crockett (Lib)	13,260	(5%)	
2004 primary	Rick Renzi (R)	unopposed		
2002 general	Rick Renzi (R)	85,967	(49%)	($1,557,104)
	George Cordova (D)	79,730	(46%)	($606,443)
	Edwin Porr (Lib)	8,990	(5%)	

The People		Race/Ethnic Origin	Ancestry	
Area size:	58,714 sq. mi.	58.4% White	German: 10.3%	English: 8.7%
Urban population:	55.5%	1.2% Black	Irish: 7.1%	
Rural population:	44.5%	0.5% Asian	**2004 Presidential Vote**	
Pop. 2000:	641,329	22.1% Native Am.	Bush (R) 139,221	(54%)
Median income:	$32,979	0.1% Hawaiian	Kerry (D) 117,673	(46%)
Poverty status:	20.3%	1.2% Two+ races	Other 1,726	(1%)
Military veterans:	15.7%	0.1% Other	**2000 Presidential Vote**	
		16.4% Hispanic Origin	Bush (R) 102,068	(51%)
			Gore (D) 91,920	(46%)
			Other 7,931	(4%)
			Cook Partisan Voting Index: R + 2	
Occupation	Blue collar: 25.6%	White collar: 53.5%	Gray collar: 20.9%	

Beyond Phoenix and the Valley of the Sun, Arizona is a vast state of stunning beauty: The awe-inspiring Grand Canyon, the subtle pastel hues of the Painted Desert, the sheer cliff walls of Canyon de Chelly, the still waters of Lake Powell, the mountainous pine forests around Flagstaff, the rust-and-rosy red rocks of Sedona. It is also the home of man-made landmarks: The celebrated U.S. 66, now mostly superseded by Interstate 40 (though you can still take the exit ramp and ride on the old unmarked 66 in Holbrook and Winslow and Williams); the old gold mining camp of Prescott, home since 1888 of America's oldest annual rodeo; Jerome, a mining town built improbably on hillside stilts, now reborn as an artist colony; plus old copper mining towns like Globe.

All of these places are in the 1st Congressional District of Arizona, which includes over half the state and is larger than Pennsylvania. It covers most of northern Arizona, except for Mohave County and the Hopi Indian Reservation and a narrow band of land connecting them. It reaches south to the northern edges of the Phoenix and Tucson metro areas. The 1st is the home of the nation's largest and fastest-growing Indian population: 22% of its residents identify themselves as American Indians. There are many reservations here—Fort Apache, San Carlos, Zuni—but by far the largest is the Navajo Nation in the northeast. The Hopi are excluded because they have a long and angry boundary dispute with the Navajo and agreed to be part of the 2d District. The Hualapai and Havasupai are also carefully excluded. Most of the Navajo are in (oddly) Apache County, with the rest in Navajo and Coconino Counties. They have a history of fiercely contested tribal elections and, alas, considerable corruption; their winner-take-all political governance does not seem to have served the community well: Unemployment has run close to 50%, nearly 60% are without phone service and 30% live without running water or electricity.

Environmental stewardship is an everyday issue for residents of this part of Arizona. Near Flagstaff firefighters thin forests by tree-cutting and controlled burns. In Page, north of the Grand Canyon, townspeople making money off Lake Powell opposed the Sierra Club's proposal to get rid of Glen Canyon Dam and the lake. But the biggest story in recent years was the Rodeo-Chediski fires near Show Low in east central Arizona. Two separate blazes in the summer of 2002 merged into the largest wildfire in Arizona history, and consumed 470,000 acres and destroyed 467 homes.

The 1st District was designed to be closely divided between the two parties. But there are sharp divisions within the district itself. The copper mining counties (Greenlee, Graham, Gila) are historically Democratic and still register that way, but tend to vote Republican. Apache County, with its Navajo majority, has been heavily Democratic; Coconino County, which includes Flagstaff, part of the Navajo Reservation, the college town of Flagstaff and New Age haven Sedona, is increasingly Democratic. Prescott and Yavapai County are heavily Republican. Prescott in heavily Republican Yavapai County is where Barry Goldwater always began his Arizona campaigns. In 2002 this was an open seat, and was fiercely contested.

The congressman from the 1st District is Rick Renzi, a Republican elected in 2002 in his first bid for elective office. Renzi grew up in Sierra Vista, Arizona, near Fort Huachuca and the Mexican border, and graduated from Northern Arizona University in Flagstaff. During the campaign, he billed himself as a "hometown, Flagstaff boy," but he has spent most of his life outside the district. In 1986 he moved to Virginia to work for the Defense Department and in 1989 he started an insurance business in Virginia. In 2002, he received a law degree from Catholic University in Washington. Since 1991, he and his family have lived in a $765,000 house with five acres in Burke, Virginia, where he was a registered voter. In 1999 he declared himself an Arizona resident; he registered to vote as an independent in Santa Cruz County, near the Mexican border, where he owned some animals and a vineyard that has produced small quantities of wine. Soon after the Arizona Independent Redistricting Commission announced the new congressional map, Renzi bought a $216,000 house in Flagstaff, where he owned a real estate investment firm, and registered there, this time as a Republican.

This new seat attracted plenty of candidates—six Republicans, seven Democrats and two Libertarians—some, like Renzi, with only weak links to the district. Renzi quickly established himself as the frontrunner among Republicans by spending more than $500,000 of his own money for an early advertising blitz, which the *Arizona Daily Sun* described as "light on issues, heavy on pretty images." He claimed to have worked on legislation for Congressman Jim Kolbe and Senator Jon Kyl; he was an unpaid intern for two months in his office in 1999, an annoyed Kyl said. The father of 12 children (each of whose names begin with "R"), Renzi opposed abortion and supported gun rights and a flat tax. He won the Republican primary with 24% of the vote, carrying Yavapai and Coconino Counties—Prescott, Sedona, Flagstaff—plus Pinal County in the south. In the Democratic primary, two candidates were familiar in Washington. Stephen Udall, a former Apache County Attorney, is a cousin of Congressmen Mark Udall of Colorado and Tom Udall of New Mexico and of Senator Gordon Smith of Oregon. Fred Duval was a Clinton administration official. But the Democratic nominee was George Cordova, a venture capitalist and political neophyte who did grass roots campaigning on the Indian reservations. He won the primary with 22% of the vote, carrying Navajo County where he had family ties, plus Gila and Pinal Counties to the south. So in this district with 641,000 people, 100,000 voted in the primaries, and the winners each won 11,000 votes.

In the general, Cordova supported abortion rights, a prescription drug benefit, and environmental protection; Renzi was a stronger supporter of using force against Iraq. But the key to the outcome was skillful opposition research. After the September primary, the NRCC quickly launched an intense attack on Cordova for four failed ventures in the 1980s that left behind a trail of lawsuits, tax liens and court-adjudicated debts. More than $2 million of Republican ads and a total of $4 million spent on Renzi's behalf weakened Cordova, on whose behalf national

Democrats spent about $1 million. Renzi won 49%–46%. Cordova carried the three counties with large Navajo populations, but Renzi led 61%–33% in Yavapai, which cast one-third of the votes, and led in the southern part of the district.

In the House, Renzi made few waves and usually voted with conservatives, especially on cultural issues. He focused his attention on topics with a local impact. One of his bills proposed an exchange of more than 56,000 acres of Forest Service and private lands to expand the Flagstaff airport; this would have been the largest such transfer in Arizona history. Renzi said that the proposal, which was backed by Senators John McCain and Jon Kyl, was for "the greater good" of northern Arizona. But it bogged down because of disputes about other federal lands proposals. Renzi also worked hard on Indian issues. He urged officials to locate a Veterans' Affairs hospital in the Navajo Nation, which would be the first ever on an Indian reservation. With Housing Subcommittee chairman Bob Ney, he held a hearing on the reservation to get first-hand evidence of the poverty. That led to enactment of his bill to reduce the risk to lenders for housing of Native Americans. Barney Frank, ranking Democrat on the Financial Services Committee, gave credit to Renzi for focusing attention on Indian housing problems.

In 2004, Renzi ranked high on the Democrats' target list. Democratic challenger Paul Babbitt, former mayor of Flagstaff and the brother of former Interior Secretary and Arizona Governor Bruce Babbitt, criticized Renzi as a Republican loyalist. But there was some local resentment over Bruce Babbitt's actions as Interior Secretary. In contrast, there was great local appreciation for Renzi's work on Indian issues; he won important endorsements, including that of the Navajo Nation. In Yavapai County and in the southern part of the district, Renzi ran about even with George W. Bush—enough for a narrow win, if repeated district-wide. But in Indian country he ran far ahead of Bush. He carried Apache County with 56% of the vote; Bush got only 35% there. He carried Navajo County with 67%; Bush got only 53% there. And he lost Coconino County, Babbitt's home turf, by only 112 votes out of 51,000 cast; Bush got only 43% there. The result was a stunning 59%–36% victory for Renzi.

In December, the Federal Election Commission released a staff audit claiming numerous financial irregularities in his 2002 campaign, including the use of "impermissible corporate funds" from two companies that he owns. Renzi disputed the charges and insisted the money in question was his own and that it was a personal loan.

SECOND DISTRICT

Rep. Trent Franks (R)

Elected 2002, 2d term; b. June 19, 1957, Uravan, CO; home, Glendale; Ottawa University, 1989–90; Baptist; married (Josie).

Elected Office: AZ House of Reps., 1984–86.

Professional Career: Director, AZ Governor's Office for Children, 1987–88; Exec. Director, AZ Family Research Institute, 1989–93; Writer-commentator, AZ radio station KTKP; Co-owner, Franks Brothers Independent Drilling; Pres.-CEO, Liberty Petroleum Corp.

DC Office: 1237 LHOB, 20515, 202-225-4576; Fax: 202-225-6328; Web site: www.house.gov/franks.

District Office: Glendale, 623-776-7911.

Committees: *Armed Services* (28th of 34 R): Readiness; Strategic Forces. *Judiciary* (22d of 23 R): The Constitution.

Group Ratings

	ADA	ACLU	AFS	LCV	ITIC	NTU	COC	ACU	NTLC	CHC
2004	0	0	0	0	90	85	95	100	100	100
2003	10	—	0	5	—	78	93	92	—	—

National Journal Ratings

	2003 LIB	—	2003 CONS	2004 LIB	—	2004 CONS
Economic	9%	—	84%	0%	—	95%
Social	5%	—	87%	0%	—	91%
Foreign	11%	—	80%	7%	—	93%

Key Votes of the 108th Congress

1. Drilling in ANWR Y	5. DC School Vouchers Y	9. Ban Same-Sex Marriage Y
2. Approve Bush Tax Cuts Y	6. Ban Human Cloning Y	10. Fund Iraq War Y
3. Medicare/Rx Bill Y	7. Restrict Gun Liability Y	11. Bar Cuba Embargo Funds N
4. Bar Overtime Pay Regs. N	8. Ban Partial-Birth Abortion Y	12. Intelligence Reorg. Y

Election Results

2004 general	Trent Franks (R)	165,260	(59%)	($738,525)
	Randy Camacho (D)	107,406	(39%)	($101,998)
	Other	6,637	(2%)	
2004 primary	Trent Franks (R)	45,261	(64%)	
	Rick Murphy (R)	25,871	(36%)	
2002 general	Trent Franks (R)	100,359	(60%)	($555,648)
	Randy Camacho (D)	61,217	(37%)	($40,206)
	Edward Carlson (Lib)	5,919	(4%)	

The People

Area size:	20,391 sq. mi.
Urban population:	89.0%
Rural population:	11.0%
Pop. 2000:	641,329
Median income:	$42,432
Poverty status:	8.9%
Military veterans:	19.6%

Race/Ethnic Origin
78.4% White
2.1% Black
1.7% Asian
2.0% Native Am.
0.1% Hawaiian
1.4% Two+ races
0.1% Other
14.2% Hispanic Origin

Ancestry
German: 14.6%   English: 9.4%
Irish: 9.3%

2004 Presidential Vote
Bush (R) 182,326 (61%)
Kerry (D) 112,620 (38%)
Other 1,634 (1%)

2000 Presidential Vote
Bush (R) 119,386 (56%)
Gore (D) 86,251 (41%)
Other 5,760 (3%)

Cook Partisan Voting Index: R + 9

Occupation   Blue collar: 22.2%   White collar: 60.3%   Gray collar: 17.5%

Beyond the reach of metropolitan Phoenix and Tucson, much of Arizona looks as it did a century ago. Some is intentionally preserved in its natural state, such as the sere uplands of the Hopi Indian Reservation; other places maintain a timeless western look, like Wickenburg, the oldest Arizona town north of Tucson. Still others preserve antiquated ways of life, such as the polygamist community of Colorado City, just south of Utah, which prosecutes open polygamists. In some cases, nature and settlement juxtapose jarringly: the real London Bridge has been transplanted to Lake Havasu City, a retirement community on the Colorado River.

All these areas are part of the 2d Congressional District of Arizona, which stretches from the west side of Phoenix to cover the northwest corner of the state, from Hoover Dam and Lake Mead to the western suburbs of Phoenix, where 80% of its voters live. Astride Grand Avenue, the only diagonal street in the rigorous grid of metro Phoenix, is the mushrooming suburb of Glendale, not so long ago just a crossroads but with 219,000 people in 2000. Just west in the former desert are Peoria, as Middle American as its namesake in Illinois, and the huge retirement community of Sun City, where locals obsessively prune their Seussian hedges. The 2d also includes the fast-growing corridor along the westbound I-10 Papago Freeway, past Luke Air Force Base—the largest fighter training wing in the Air Force and the only active duty F-16 training base in the U.S.—to the once open spaces of Goodyear and Buckeye. The 2d also includes the Hopi Indian Reservation, connected to the rest of the district by a narrow, oddly shaped corridor that runs along the bottom of the Grand Canyon.

This is Republican territory. The retirees here remember—and upwardly-striving, family-oriented young migrants who have populated these new towns in the desert still try to live—the culturally conservative, Ozzie-and-Harriet lifestyle of the 1950s. Culture, more than affluence, which by national standards is not all that striking here, accounts for their political conservatism. Similarly Republican are the new cities along the Colorado River.

The congressman from the 2d District is Trent Franks, a Republican first elected in 2002. He grew up in Colorado, attended college only briefly and started his own oil and gas exploration business. His political career began when he won a single term in the Arizona House in 1984; he was known for wearing a tie tack in the shape of the feet of a fetus. In 1987 he was the director of the Governor's Office for Children under Governor Evan Mecham, a conservative Republican who was impeached and removed from office in April 1988. He was a consultant to Pat Buchanan's presidential campaign and in 1989 became executive director of the Arizona Family Research Institute, an organization associated with James Dobson's Focus on the Family. Franks led the campaign for an unsuccessful 1992 ballot initiative to limit abortion rights and designed the state's 1997 scholarship tax credit legislation, a much-litigated measure that ultimately was upheld by the U.S. Supreme Court. The plan provides tax credits for donations to non-profits to help families pay for private education. He was a school-choice advocate and an abortion opponent on Family Life radio. In 1994, he ran for the open 4th District seat and trailed John Shadegg in the Republican primary, 43%–30%.

In April 2002, Republican Congressman Bob Stump, first elected in 1976, announced he was retiring and endorsed Lisa Atkins, his chief of staff throughout his congressional career. When the campaign started, Franks was not considered in the top tier of candidates. But his base of Christian conservatives and abortion opponents (plus more than $300,000 of his own money) made him a contender. Franks spent heavily on radio ads; he also benefited from the distribution of a voter guide by the religious conservative Center for Arizona Policy, which describes itself as "the only organization in Arizona actively fighting in the legislature and media for conservative, traditional views on gambling, homosexuality and pornography." Franks called for overturning *Roe v. Wade* and for constitutional protection to fetuses. He endorsed a flat tax as a step toward eliminating the federal income tax, individual investment accounts under Social Security, tougher enforcement of immigration laws and minimal federal involvement in health care. In a contest that operated mostly under the political radar, Franks's base of activists made the difference. He finished first with 28% of the vote, only 797 votes ahead of Atkins, who got 26%. In November he won 60%–37%.

In the House, Franks became the most conservative member of the Arizona delegation. He got 21 co-sponsors for his Children's Hope Act, which was based on his 1997 state scholarship tax credit. He showed his outsider stripes by proposing that service on the Appropriations Committee be limited to a maximum of three terms in 10 years; redundantly, he commented that he had no interest in serving on Appropriations. He said he voted against the highway bill because it was bloated and also short-changed Arizona. But he succumbed to pressure from Republican leaders, and earned their gratitude, by switching his vote to support the Medicare/prescription drug bill while the roll call was held open for nearly three hours. On the Armed Services Committee, he worked to secure $27 million for Arizona to buy land adjacent to Luke Air Force Base in order to curtail housing development, and he worked to locate at Luke the new F-35 joint strike fighter planes. Franks got $4 million for a new highway bypass at the Hoover Dam as part of a broader traffic and security project.

Franks faced a competitive primary in September 2004 against Rick Murphy, a free-spending radio station owner, who criticized Franks for abandoning his conservative principles by supporting the Medicare/prescription drug bill. Murphy was endorsed by several local Republican officials who complained about their lack of contact from Franks; he attacked Franks for abandoning his promise not to take money from political action committees. Franks won 64%–36%—a wide margin, but less than incumbents usually get over primary challengers. He narrowly lost Mohave County, but he took 68% in Maricopa, which cast 76% of the total vote. In November Franks won 59%–39%, a downtick from 2002: more evidence he needs to pay closer attention to his district.

THIRD DISTRICT

Rep. John Shadegg (R)

Elected 1994, 6th term; b. Oct. 22, 1949, Phoenix; home, Phoenix; U. of AZ, B.A. 1972, J.D. 1975; Episcopalian; married (Shirley).

Military Career: Air Natl. Guard, 1969–75.

Professional Career: Practicing atty., 1975–94; US Spec. Asst. Atty. Gen., 1983–90; Spec. Cnsl., AZ House Republican Caucus, 1991–92; Cnsl., AZ Wildlife Conservation, 1992.

DC Office: 306 CHOB, 20515, 202-225-3361; Fax: 202-225-3462; Web site: johnshadegg.house.gov.

District Office: Phoenix, 602-263-5300.

Committees: *Republican Policy Committee Chairman. Energy & Commerce* (13th of 31 R): Energy & Air Quality; Environment & Hazardous Materials; Health.

Group Ratings

	ADA	ACLU	AFS	LCV	ITIC	NTU	COC	ACU	NTLC	CHC
2004	0	5	0	0	90	81	95	100	100	100
2003	20	—	13	5	—	83	90	100	—	—

National Journal Ratings

	2003 LIB	—	2003 CONS	2004 LIB	—	2004 CONS
Economic	37%	—	62%	0%	—	95%
Social	30%	—	65%	9%	—	85%
Foreign	0%	—	89%	0%	—	96%

Key Votes of the 108th Congress

1. Drilling in ANWR	Y	5. DC School Vouchers	Y	9. Ban Same-Sex Marriage	Y
2. Approve Bush Tax Cuts	Y	6. Ban Human Cloning	Y	10. Fund Iraq War	Y
3. Medicare/Rx Bill	N	7. Restrict Gun Liability	Y	11. Bar Cuba Embargo Funds	N
4. Bar Overtime Pay Regs.	N	8. Ban Partial-Birth Abortion	Y	12. Intelligence Reorg.	Y

Election Results

2004 general	John Shadegg (R)	181,012	(80%)	($794,256)
	Mark Yannone (Lib)	44,962	(20%)	
2004 primary	John Shadegg (R)	unopposed		
2002 general	John Shadegg (R)	104,847	(67%)	($814,461)
	Charles Hill (D)	47,173	(30%)	($11,694)
	Other	3,731	(2%)	

Prior Winning Percentages: 2000 (64%); 1998 (65%); 1996 (67%); 1994 (60%)

The People		Race/Ethnic Origin	Ancestry	
Area size:	599 sq. mi.	78.5% White	German: 14.5%	Irish: 10.0%
Urban population:	96.5%	2.3% Black	English: 8.6%	
Rural population:	3.5%	2.1% Asian	**2004 Presidential Vote**	
Pop. 2000:	641,329	1.2% Native Am.	Bush (R) 150,511	(58%)
Median income:	$48,108	0.1% Hawaiian	Kerry (D) 107,881	(41%)
Poverty status:	8.7%	1.6% Two+ races	Other 1,612	(1%)
Military veterans:	13.4%	0.1% Other	**2000 Presidential Vote**	
		14.1% Hispanic Origin	Bush (R) 114,259	(54%)
			Gore (D) 89,308	(43%)
			Other 6,140	(3%)
			Cook Partisan Voting Index: R + 6	
Occupation	Blue collar: 17.7%	White collar: 68.2%	Gray collar: 14.1%	

In May 1998 Barry Goldwater died at his home in the Phoenix suburb of Paradise Valley. His life had spanned almost the whole history of Arizona. He was born on New Year's Day 1909, when Arizona was still a territory, and he could remember when it was the "baby state," with fewer people than every other state but Delaware, Wyoming and Nevada. When he returned from World War II, Paradise Valley was still empty land and Phoenix—founded after the Civil War as a hay market for cavalry horses at Fort McDowell 40 miles away—was not much more than a tiny outpost of American civilization in a sizzling desert. Today Arizona has 5.6 million people, with 3.4 million in metropolitan Phoenix; the city has been transformed from a frontier outpost to a diversified high-tech center, an example of how creativity and ingenuity can build a sophisticated city with relatively minimalist government and low taxes.

Like Los Angeles and San Francisco, Phoenix is dotted with mountains that rise grandly from the plains and are kept as undeveloped parkland. Some, such as Shaw Butte in the shadow of I-17, contain archeological evidence that Indians used them as a base for sophisticated astronomical observations. From Camelback Mountain, 1,800 feet above Phoenix and Paradise Valley, you can with equal awe get a sense of what this land was originally like and an understanding of how impressively Phoenix has grown. East of Camelback, subdivisions were often built with grass and greenery; in the affluent areas north of Camelback and spreading out Scottsdale Road and the Black Canyon Freeway, the natural desert look is more common. In 1999, the master-planned community of Anthem opened 35 miles north of downtown; it is expected to grow to 50,000 within a decade. Grass is discouraged, and often banned by subdivision covenant; planting anything but desert flora is frowned upon. The architecture of the houses tends toward unadorned stucco with picture windows facing away from the sun; the idea is to suggest that there is a horse corral over in the next lot and sometimes, especially in the northern edges of Phoenix, there is.

The 3d Congressional District of Arizona includes the northern part of Phoenix plus Paradise Valley, bounded on the south by a zigzag line that approximates the Arizona Canal. The 3d also includes, 20 miles north of downtown Phoenix, the communities of New River, Cave Creek and Carefree (so named in 1955 by developers who hoped to lure retirees). Here the stores are more likely to feature horse feed than designer clothes—but that is changing fast, as metro Phoenix moves inexorably north, bringing with it more upscale malls in the adobe vernacular. This is an affluent, and comfortably Republican, district.

The congressman from the 3d District is John Shadegg, first elected in 1994, with a fine Arizona Republican pedigree. His father, Stephen Shadegg, managed Barry Goldwater's first campaign for the Senate in 1952, when Goldwater upset Senate Majority Leader Ernest McFarland; in those pre-fax, pre-email days, the older Shadegg helped deliver campaign press releases. The younger Shadegg is a lawyer who served as special assistant to the state attorney general and a special counsel to the Arizona House Republican Caucus. When Jon Kyl ran for the Senate in 1994, Shadegg ran for his House seat and won 43% in the Republican primary, to 30% for Trent Franks (now the 2d District congressman), and 21% for a county supervisor. He won the general election easily, 60%–36%.

In the House, Shadegg has been a consistent conservative who has been willing to stick to principle. As one of the firebrand 1994 Republican freshmen, he held firm against Democratic policies and often rebelled against his own party's leadership. He refused to back the balanced budget amendment without a three-fifths supermajority for tax increases, in defiance of Speaker Newt Gingrich. When he chaired the House's Republican Study Committee, Shadegg and his group agreed to support the annual budget resolution but they insisted—with occasional success—that appropriators strictly comply with budget limits; when he gave up the post in 2003, he contended that the RSC's influence had grown and its membership had increased to about 70. In 2002, a *Washingtonian* magazine poll of House staffers placed him high on the list of members with the "strongest backbone." His anti-leadership stands cost him a seat on Ways and Means in 1997; it went to J.D. Hayworth instead. But he got a seat on Energy and Committee where, at the request of Speaker Dennis Hastert, he worked to write an alternative HMO bill. Shadegg's version gave House Republicans some cover when they were pressured to support the more sweeping Norwood-Dingell alternative. Later, that approach helped to broker Norwood's split from Dingell and his return as a party regular. In November 2003, Shadegg and Norwood were the only Republicans serving on Energy and Commerce, or Ways and Means, who voted against the Medicare/prescription drug bill.

Even with his independence, Shadegg has gained influence and respect among his colleagues. He was given the dicey assignment of serving on the Ethics Committee panel that reviewed charges by Nick Smith of Michigan that party leaders had used undue pressure to seek his vote on the 2003 Medicare bill. He worked diligently with others to produce the unanimous report that Smith's charges were overstated. At the 2004 national Republican convention, Shadegg urged delegates to call *USA Today* to protest the paper's hiring of film producer Michael Moore as a columnist for the week. In January 2005, Shadegg ran unopposed to replace Christopher Cox as chairman of the Republican Policy Committee.

He has shown his independence at home: In 2004, he opposed the tax increase for Phoenix-area transportation (which passed anyway), but he supported higher taxes on business to pay for full-day kindergarten for all Arizona children. Shadegg has won re-election each time with at least 64% of the vote against weak opponents. He has made known his interest in running for the Senate if either John McCain or Jon Kyl retires. But his growing influence in the House may give him second thoughts.

FOURTH DISTRICT

Rep. Ed Pastor (D)

Elected Sept. 1991, 7th full term; b. June 28, 1943, Claypool; home, Phoenix; AZ St. U., B.A. 1966, J.D. 1974; Catholic; married (Verma).

Elected Office: Maricopa Cnty. Bd. of Supervisors, 1976–91.

Professional Career: High schl. teacher, 1966–69; Asst., AZ Gov. Castro, 1975.

DC Office: 2465 RHOB, 20515, 202-225-4065; Fax: 202-225-1655; Web site: www.house.gov/pastor.

District Office: Phoenix, 602-256-0551.

Committees: *Chief Deputy Minority Whip. Appropriations* (14th of 29 D): Energy & Water Development & Related Agencies; Transportation, Treasury, HUD, the Judiciary & District of Columbia.

Group Ratings

	ADA	ACLU	AFS	LCV	ITIC	NTU	COC	ACU	NTLC	CHC
2004	100	84	100	100	38	7	29	4	0	16
2003	80	—	100	90	—	21	37	21	—	—

National Journal Ratings

	2003 LIB	—	2003 CONS		2004 LIB	—	2004 CONS
Economic	74%	—	25%		85%	—	14%
Social	77%	—	23%		86%	—	12%
Foreign	84%	—	16%		90%	—	9%

Key Votes of the 108th Congress

1. Drilling in ANWR	N	5. DC School Vouchers	N	9. Ban Same-Sex Marriage	N
2. Approve Bush Tax Cuts	N	6. Ban Human Cloning	N	10. Fund Iraq War	N
3. Medicare/Rx Bill	N	7. Restrict Gun Liability	N	11. Bar Cuba Embargo Funds	Y
4. Bar Overtime Pay Regs.	Y	8. Ban Partial-Birth Abortion	N	12. Intelligence Reorg.	N

Election Results

2004 general	Ed Pastor (D)	77,150	(70%)	($624,271)
	Don Karg (R)	28,238	(26%)	
	Gary Fallon (Lib)	4,639	(4%)	
2004 primary	Ed Pastor (D)	unopposed		
2002 general	Ed Pastor (D)	44,517	(67%)	($679,772)
	Jonathon Barnert (R)	18,381	(28%)	($3,112)
	Amy Gibbons (Lib)	3,167	(5%)	

Prior Winning Percentages: 2000 (69%); 1998 (68%); 1996 (65%); 1994 (62%); 1992 (66%); 1991 (56%)

The People		Race/Ethnic Origin	Ancestry		
Area size:	199 sq. mi.	29.3% White	German: 5.8%	Irish: 4.0%	
Urban population:	99.5%	7.5% Black	English: 3.4%		
Rural population:	0.5%	1.3% Asian	**2004 Presidential Vote**		
Pop. 2000:	641,329	2.4% Native Am.	Kerry (D) 71,805	(62%)	
Median income:	$30,624	0.1% Hawaiian	Bush (R) 43,967	(38%)	
Poverty status:	25.6%	1.5% Two+ races	Other 930	(1%)	
Military veterans:	9.6%	0.1% Other	**2000 Presidential Vote**		
		58.0% Hispanic Origin	Gore (D) 57,198	(63%)	
			Bush (R) 31,542	(35%)	
			Other 2,598	(3%)	
			Cook Partisan Voting Index: D +14		
Occupation	Blue collar: 35.7%	White collar: 43.8%	Gray collar: 20.5%		

Phoenix is a new American metropolis, grown to huge metropolitan size within most Americans' lifetimes. Yet it is also an ancient city, or built on top of one. The Arizona Canal, several miles north of downtown Phoenix, runs along the route of a canal built about 600 years ago by the Hohokam people. They distributed irrigated water diverted from the Salt River in its wet moments to farmers in what Phoenicians today call the Valley of the Sun and made sophisticated astronomical observations from the mountains that jut up from the plains. This society disappeared, for reasons that are not known, less than half a century before the Spaniards arrived in North America. So today's Phoenix is the second civilization to grow in this desert. Its growth is recent. Phoenix and Maricopa County had 331,000 people in 1950 and 3.4 million in 2003. Half a century ago, Phoenix spread half a dozen miles north, west and east of the downtown and only a few miles south. Downtown was its single office and main shopping district, and people blew fans over boxes of ice to keep cool. Today from downtown Phoenix's office towers the city seems to spread as far as the eye can see, including other clumps of office towers to the north and northwest.

The 4th Congressional District of Arizona is centered on downtown Phoenix. It covers downtown, the Capitol in a rundown neighborhood a couple of miles to the west, and busy Sky Harbor International Airport in an industrial corridor several miles east. It includes most of southern Phoenix and its boundaries follow approximately the southern and western city limits; it extends as far north as Bethany Home Road and Northern Avenue. Geographically it covers most of the land between South Mountain and Camelback Mountain. The district was designed to be one of Arizona's two Hispanic districts; its population in 2000 was 58% Hispanic. The typical Latino neighborhood here is a collection of 1940s and 1950s bungalows, spaced out by empty lots. Here Habitat for Humanity built South Ranch, the largest low-income subdivision built by the organization in the U.S.; the idea was to cluster poor homeowners together and encourage them to stave off neighborhood decline collectively. Politically this is a solidly Democratic district, the most Democratic in Arizona.

The congressman from the 4th District is Ed Pastor, a Democrat who won a 1991 special election to replace Morris Udall at a time when the district's boundaries were quite different. He grew up in Claypool, a mining town in Gila County, where his parents "taught me the value of education, the need of tolerance and the responsibility of community service. But especially they taught me the reward of a hard day's work." Pastor is a career politician who does not seek much public attention. After teaching high school, he got a law degree at Arizona State, worked as an assistant to Governor Raul Castro in 1975, then was elected in 1976 to the Maricopa County Board of Supervisors, where he served until elected to Congress. In 1991, he beat Republican Pat Connor 56%–44%. He has not faced stiff competition since then.

Pastor has been a faithful follower of the Democratic leadership and has a mostly liberal voting record. He supported NAFTA, despite strong labor opposition, but he opposed normal trade relations with China. He vigorously opposed Arizona's English Only law and supports bilingual ballots, but says, "everyone acknowledges that English is the common language of our country." In 2002 he sponsored legislation to provide amnesty to immigrants who were in the U.S. prior to January 2000. After a trip to Cuba where he met with Fidel Castro for three hours in 2002, he urged the immediate end of the trade embargo. In July 2004, he narrowly lost in the Appropriations Committee on his proposal to remove a provision that prohibited banks from allowing the use of Mexican *matricula consular* identity cards.

Much of Pastor's work has been on the Appropriations Committee, where he often delivers projects of the kind that John McCain labels "pork." Home state demands on him and Appropriations Republican Jim Kolbe have been great because neither Arizona senator is an appropriator. On the Energy and Water Development and the Transportation Subcommittees, he does bring home the bacon—$32 million for the Rio Salado (Salt River) project to control flooding and restore wildlife habitat in Phoenix, $75 million for a light-rail transit project in Phoenix, $26.3 million for air traffic control facilities at the city airport, and $3 million for improvements to a visitors facility at the Grand Canyon. In 2000 he won enactment of his proposal to authorize a new international port of entry at the border in Yuma, with conveyance of 330 acres to the Greater Yuma Port Authority; the project was designed to relieve congestion that often caused delays of several hours for commercial vehicles at San Luis five miles to the west. Pastor is "not a headline maker," editorialized *The Arizona Republic.* "He is a congressman from the old school, congenial, collaborative, attuned to the needs of his district, with no grand ambitions other than helping his constituents."

In the 2004 presidential campaign, he was an early supporter of Dick Gephardt, but backed John Kerry in the Arizona primary after Gephardt dropped out. Kerry named him a co-chairman of the Democratic National Committee.

FIFTH DISTRICT

Rep. J.D. Hayworth (R)

Elected 1994, 6th term; b. July 12, 1958, High Point, NC; home, Scottsdale; NC St. U., B.A. 1980; Baptist; married (Mary).

Professional Career: Sports Reporter/Anchor: WPTF–TV Raleigh, NC, 1980–81; WYFS–TV Greenville, SC, 1981–86; WLWT–TV, Cincinnati, OH, 1986–87; KTSP–TV Phoenix, AZ, 1987–94; Insurance agent & PR consultant, 1994.

DC Office: 2434 RHOB, 20515, 202-225-2190; Fax: 202-225-3263; Web site: www.house.gov/hayworth.

District Office: Scottsdale, 480-926-4151.

Committees: *Resources* (16th of 27 R): Forests & Forest Health; Water & Power. *Ways & Means* (11th of 24 R): Health; Oversight; Social Security.

Group Ratings

	ADA	ACLU	AFS	LCV	ITIC	NTU	COC	ACU	NTLC	CHC
2004	5	0	0	0	90	75	100	96	97	91
2003	10	—	0	5	—	64	97	88	—	—

National Journal Ratings

	2003 LIB	—	2003 CONS		2004 LIB	—	2004 CONS
Economic	0%	—	91%		12%	—	88%
Social	24%	—	71%		15%	—	84%
Foreign	35%	—	64%		23%	—	76%

Key Votes of the 108th Congress

1. Drilling in ANWR	Y	5. DC School Vouchers	Y	9. Ban Same-Sex Marriage	Y
2. Approve Bush Tax Cuts	Y	6. Ban Human Cloning	Y	10. Fund Iraq War	Y
3. Medicare/Rx Bill	Y	7. Restrict Gun Liability	Y	11. Bar Cuba Embargo Funds	N
4. Bar Overtime Pay Regs.	N	8. Ban Partial-Birth Abortion	Y	12. Intelligence Reorg.	Y

Election Results

2004 general	J.D. Hayworth (R)	159,455	(59%)	($1,356,723)
	Elizabeth Rogers (D)	102,363	(38%)	($4,898)
	Other	6,189	(2%)	
2004 primary	J.D. Hayworth (R)	43,166	(79%)	
	Roselyn O'Connell (R)	11,296	(21%)	
2002 general	J.D. Hayworth (R)	103,870	(61%)	($1,482,389)
	Craig Columbus (D)	61,559	(36%)	($351,955)
	Other	4,383	(3%)	

Prior Winning Percentages: 2000 (61%); 1998 (53%); 1996 (48%); 1994 (55%)

The People		Race/Ethnic Origin	Ancestry	
Area size:	1,423 sq. mi.	76.8% White	German: 14.3% Irish: 9.5%	
Urban population:	97.2%	2.7% Black	English: 9.0%	
Rural population:	2.8%	3.3% Asian	**2004 Presidential Vote**	
Pop. 2000:	641,329	1.8% Native Am.	Bush (R)	152,576 (54%)
Median income:	$51,780	0.2% Hawaiian	Kerry (D)	127,811 (45%)
Poverty status:	8.4%	1.7% Two+ races	Other	1,620 (1%)
Military veterans:	12.4%	0.2% Other	**2000 Presidential Vote**	
		13.3% Hispanic Origin	Bush (R)	121,462 (54%)
			Gore (D)	97,604 (43%)
			Other	7,635 (3%)
			Cook Partisan Voting Index: R + 4	

Occupation	Blue collar: 14.2%	White collar: 73.1%	Gray collar: 12.7%

As metropolitan Phoenix grows over the expanse of the Valley of the Sun, around and beyond the mountains that block the passage of the grid streets from the plains below, it has encompassed and absorbed the crossroads towns that were separate and distinct—and much smaller—communities 50 years ago. Two such are Tempe and Scottsdale. Tempe is east of downtown Phoenix, south of the Arizona Canal. It was founded in 1871 as Hayden's Ferry, by the father of the future Senator (1927–69) Carl Hayden and was renamed in 1879 for an ancient Greek vale. The old town nucleus centered on Arizona State University; both the town and university have expanded greatly. The University is home of the Fiesta Bowl, which sits astride a rise with a fine view of much of metropolitan Phoenix; the town is relatively affluent, with 158,000 people in 2000, an increase from 7,600 in 1950. Then there is Scottsdale, east of the affluent part of Phoenix and north of the Salt River Indian Reservation; it now juts far north and encompasses Frank Lloyd Wright's Taliesin West, which was beyond the reach of electricity and telephone lines when it was built in the 1940s. Scottsdale features luxury shopping malls, the new Buffalo Bill Historical Center, plus the WestWorld equestrian center. But it tries to retain an Old Western look, with hitching posts for SUVs and Mercedes. Scottsdale has 202,000 people, as compared to, well, zero in 1940; it shows up first in the 1950 Census, with 2,000.

The 5th Congressional District of Arizona includes Tempe, Scottsdale and the northeast corner of Maricopa County—Fountain Hills, the Salt River and Fort McDowell Indian Reservations and part of the Tonto National Forest. Politically, this is a Republican district, though not quite as much as it was a dozen years ago; some affluent people here, like so many in coastal metropolises, have been attracted to the Democrats by their stands on cultural issues.

The congressman from the 5th District is J.D. Hayworth, a conservative Republican who grew up in North Carolina and moved up the hierarchy of local TV stations as a sportscaster, from Raleigh to Greenville to Cincinnati and then, in 1987, to Phoenix. Hayworth is 6'5", speaks with a booming voice and had a certain resemblance—help in some quarters, a hindrance in others—to Rush Limbaugh. (After stomach surgery for a gastric bypass in 2003, he lost more than 100 pounds and became practically svelte; coincidentally or otherwise, he toned down his rhetoric at roughly the same time.) Certainly he was well known when he ran for the House in 1994 and won the five-way Republican primary with 45% of the vote. In the general, he attacked first-term Democrat Karan English for voting for the Clinton tax increase and framed the race as "between a citizen who pays taxes and a career politician who raises them." In what was the old

6th District, he carried Maricopa County 65%–32%, enough to overcome English's support on the Indian reservations and around Flagstaff, and won 55%–41%.

Hayworth became a strong voice and a solid vote in the new majority. He seemed to irritate Democrats more than just about any other Republican. Veteran Democrat David Obey told him, "You are one of the most impolite members I have ever seen in my service in this House." Hayworth usually has supported the Republican leadership, even as other 1994 colleagues have led rebellions. One exception has been his vigorous advocacy of Indians and their needs, from health services to their freedom to operate casinos. He reaped his reward for loyalty when Newt Gingrich gave him a seat on Ways and Means. On that committee Hayworth organized a bipartisan coalition to oppose taxes on Indian gambling. In fall 2001, he was a year ahead of George W. Bush in calling for Treasury Secretary Paul O'Neill to resign, arguing that he wasn't sufficiently supportive of the economic stimulus proposal. In 2003, he filed a bill to prevent the Internal Revenue Service from challenging depreciation in the motor-sports industry. With Representative Darlene Hooley, he sponsored a bill to ban the use of ephedra and dietary supplements with its ingredient, which has had serious health effects on athletes. The House defeated his amendment to block Social Security payments to Mexican immigrants who have not met eligibility requirements. Hayworth opposed Bush's proposal for an expanded guest-worker program until border controls are more effective; he accused Mexico of acting as "an accomplice" in illegal immigration. At home, he supported enactment in 2004 of the settlement of claims by the Gila River Indian community to water from the Colorado River, in exchange for reduction of Arizona's debt to the federal government for the building of the Central Arizona Project canal. The transfer of more than 650,000 acre-feet of water was the largest tribal water settlement in the nation's history, and was supported by the entire Arizona delegation.

As he gained seniority, Hayworth continued to speak his mind. He attacked the "controlled burns" that got out of control at Los Alamos and the North Rim of the Grand Canyon as "misguided management," calling instead for thinning and timber harvesting. Democrats were infuriated during the debate on campaign-finance reform when he backed campaign restrictions on "enemies of the state," which Hayworth said referred to contributors from China. He became a prominent spokesman for the party on the talk-show circuit and had frequent ribald exchanges with radio personality Don Imus in the morning. In November 2002 he ran for chairman of the Republican Conference, touting his skill as a communicator. He said he had toned down his combative image and that his wife had persuaded him to listen more and talk less. "Righteous indignation can come across at times as a snarl. You have to have a positive image to focus on." But Deborah Pryce defeated Hayworth in a three-candidate contest 133–61.

The 2002 redistricting removed the Indian counties from his district and made it more safely Republican; Hayworth has said he regrets losing northeast Arizona and he continues to take an interest in Indian issues. Perhaps it is because he is interested in running statewide: in 2004 he traveled the state, and speculation was rife that he would run against Governor Janet Napolitano in 2006. "Hayworth has spent a political career being wildly underestimated by his opponents," *The Arizona Republic* editorialized. But in March 2005, he said he would stay in Congress.

SIXTH DISTRICT

Rep. Jeff Flake (R)

Elected 2000, 3d term; b. Dec. 31, 1962, Snowflake; home, Mesa; Brigham Young U., B.A. 1986, M.A. 1987; Mormon; married (Cheryl).

Professional Career: Pub. Plcy. Exec., Shipley, Smoak & Henry, 1987–89; Exec. Dir., Fndt. for Democracy (Namibia), 1989–90; Owner, Interface Pub. Affairs, 1990–92; Exec. Dir., The Goldwater Inst., 1992–99.

DC Office: 424 CHOB, 20515, 202-225-2635; Fax: 202-226-4386; Web site: www.house.gov/flake.

District Office: Mesa, 480-833-0092.

Committees: *International Relations* (14th of 27 R): Africa, Global Human Rights & International Operations; Oversight & Investigations (Vice Chmn.). *Judiciary* (17th of 23 R): Commercial & Administrative Law; Crime, Terrorism & Homeland Security; Immigration, Border Security & Claims. *Resources* (17th of 27 R): Forests & Forest Health.

Group Ratings

	ADA	ACLU	AFS	LCV	ITIC	NTU	COC	ACU	NTLC	CHC
2004	15	20	13	9	90	90	81	96	92	92
2003	25	—	13	5	—	90	67	88	—	—

National Journal Ratings

	2003 LIB	—	2003 CONS		2004 LIB	—	2004 CONS
Economic	51%	—	49%		32%	—	67%
Social	37%	—	61%		36%	—	61%
Foreign	44%	—	55%		47%	—	51%

Key Votes of the 108th Congress

1. Drilling in ANWR	Y	5. DC School Vouchers	Y	9. Ban Same-Sex Marriage	Y
2. Approve Bush Tax Cuts	Y	6. Ban Human Cloning	Y	10. Fund Iraq War	Y
3. Medicare/Rx Bill	N	7. Restrict Gun Liability	Y	11. Bar Cuba Embargo Funds	Y
4. Bar Overtime Pay Regs.	N	8. Ban Partial-Birth Abortion	Y	12. Intelligence Reorg.	Y

Election Results

2004 general	Jeff Flake (R)	202,882	(79%)	($675,055)
	Craig Stritar (Lib)	52,695	(21%)	
2004 primary	Jeff Flake (R)	33,784	(59%)	
	Stan Barnes (R)	23,186	(41%)	
2002 general	Jeff Flake (R)	103,094	(66%)	($265,350)
	Deborah Thomas (D)	49,355	(32%)	($22,209)
	Other	3,888	(2%)	

Prior Winning Percentages: 2000 (54%)

The People		Race/Ethnic Origin	Ancestry	
Area size:	724 sq. mi.	76.6% White	German: 14.1%	English: 10.2%
Urban population:	96.8%	1.9% Black	Irish: 8.6%	
Rural population:	3.2%	1.8% Asian	**2004 Presidential Vote**	
Pop. 2000:	641,329	0.8% Native Am.	Bush (R) 188,372	(64%)
Median income:	$47,976	0.2% Hawaiian	Kerry (D) 102,902	(35%)
Poverty status:	7.7%	1.4% Two+ races	Other 1,352	(0%)
Military veterans:	15.8%	0.1% Other	**2000 Presidential Vote**	
		17.2% Hispanic Origin	Bush (R) 118,278	(61%)
			Gore (D) 72,093	(37%)
			Other 3,942	(2%)
			Cook Partisan Voting Index: R +12	

Occupation   Blue collar: 22.6%   White collar: 63.3%   Gray collar: 14.2%

The metropolis of Phoenix is exceedingly young. Barry Goldwater, born in 1909, grew up knowing people who remembered when the Valley of the Sun—or the Valley, as most people say—was virtually empty, with a few parched settlements set above the dry riverbed. As late as 1950, only 106,000 people lived in Phoenix and 331,000 in all of Maricopa County. But the air conditioner and military technology transformed Phoenix from a sleepy whistlestop to today's high-rise-studded metropolis, with 1.3 million people in Phoenix and 3.4 million in Maricopa. This is not, as some people think, a giant retirement village, nor is it overrun by crooked land salesmen and fast-buck artists, though Phoenix has attracted its share of each.

The second largest city in Maricopa County is Mesa, south of the Salt River and east of Phoenix. It was founded by Mormons in 1878 on a square mile; it was laid out Salt Lake City-style on broad streets with huge blocks holding just four home sites, using canals built by Indians 1,100 years earlier. A gleaming white Mormon Temple was built in 1927, one of the few in the United States then. In 1950, Mesa had 17,000 people, enough to make it Arizona's third largest city. In 2000, it had 396,000 people, more than Minneapolis or Pittsburgh, though few people back east have ever heard of it.

The 6th Congressional District of Arizona is made up of Mesa and Chandler, Gilbert and Queen Creek to the south; it crosses the Pinal County line and includes fast-growing bedroom communities such as Apache Junction, Gold Camp and Sun Lakes. Growth has been constant here: In the 1990s Gilbert zoomed from a rail siding and a dot on the map to 110,000 people. The 6th includes some high-income precincts (interestingly, Asians lead whites in income in Chandler and Gilbert), but the district's cultural tone is resolutely middle class, hard-working and churchgoing. By most measures it is the most Republican district in Republican Arizona.

The congressman from the 6th District is Jeff Flake, a Republican elected in 2000, and something of a maverick—or, to some in House leadership, a "flake." A fifth-generation Arizonan, he is a practicing Mormon who was born and raised on a ranch in Snowflake; the town was named after his great-great grandfather. The fifth of 11 children, Flake served as a Mormon missionary in South Africa and Zimbabwe and graduated from Brigham Young University. In 1987 he moved to Washington, D.C., and worked in a lobbying firm. He returned to southern Africa to serve as executive director of the Foundation for Democracy, which monitored democratic progress in Namibia. Following Namibian independence in 1990 and two more years in Washington representing Namibian companies, he returned to Arizona and became executive director of the Goldwater Institute, where he led the fight for Arizona's charter school law.

In 2000, when Congressman Matt Salmon kept his pledge to serve only three terms (he lost narrowly for governor in 2002), he handpicked Flake to succeed him. Flake faced four opponents in a hard-fought September primary, in which he was the most conservative candidate. Flake had the support of several prominent Republican state leaders and was bolstered by more than $200,000 from the Club for Growth. Flake won with 32% of the vote to 24% for Phoenix Councilman Sal DiCiccio. In the general, Flake won 54%–42% over Democrat David Mendoza, a longtime lobbyist for public employees.

Flake promised to serve no more than three terms and to "continue to rock the boat," much as Salmon had for six years. Less than a month after he took office, Flake—who favors replacing the income tax with a national sales tax—said that it would be a mistake for George W. Bush to limit his proposed tax cut to the "easy things," such as repeal of the marriage penalty, and estate and gift taxes. In July 2001 the House passed, 240–186, his amendment to lift restrictions on travel by U.S. citizens to Cuba. But House Republican leaders and the Bush administration strongly opposed this and removed it in conference committee. In early 2002, Flake organized the bipartisan Cuba Working Group to review the U.S. embargo of Cuba. That summer the House again passed his proposal to lift the travel ban. But all legislative provisions on Cuba later were stricken from that year's appropriations bill. Flake has taken lonely stands. He was one of two members who voted in 2001 against a bill to punish Sudan for its human right abuses; Flake said he had seen in Africa the adverse impact of economic sanctions on poor nations. He was one of 33 Republicans who voted against final approval of the Bush education bill and one of 25 who opposed the Medicare/prescription drug bill.

As he gained experience, Flake became more independent. He vowed never to ask appropriators for a dollar for any item or local project while he served in the House. When appropriators responded with his list of requests for the military, he responded that requests solely for defense were legitimate; he left the door open to making requests of other committees. He urged George W. Bush to veto the "bloated" highway bill and continued to press to end the embargo on Cuba, but in September 2004 he withdrew his amendment to lift the travel ban after pressure from House leadership. With Jim Kolbe and John McCain, he co-sponsored a guest worker law, which would provide six-year temporary worker visas and three-year visas for those who are here illegally now. Back home, he formed a political committee to call for repeal of Arizona's publicly financed elections. He criticized the law, passed in a 2000 referendum, as "nothing more than welfare for politicians" and said that taxpayer money should not finance attack ads.

Flake was reelected easily in 2002. He gave some thought to challenging McCain in the 2004 Senate primary, but decided not to. Instead he faced a serious primary challenge himself. Former state Senator Stan Barnes called Flake "fringe, libertarian and just a bit kooky" and attacked him on immigration issues; this was one of two primary challenges to Arizona Republican incumbents financed by supporters of greater restrictions on immigration. Flake won 59%–41%—not an overwhelming margin for an incumbent. He had no Democratic opponent in November. Days after the election he announced that he would abandon his term-limit pledge. "As much as I hate to admit making a mistake, I made a big one here." He has been mentioned as a possible Senate candidate if one of Arizona's senators retires.

SEVENTH DISTRICT

Rep. Raul Grijalva (D)

Elected 2002, 2d term; b. Feb. 19, 1948, Tucson; home, Tucson; U. of AZ, B.A. 1985; Catholic; married (Ramona).

Elected Office: Tucson Unified Schl. Dist. Governing Bd., 1974–86; Pima Cnty. Bd. of Supervisors, 1988–2002.

Professional Career: Asst. Dean of Hisp. Affairs, U. of AZ., 1987.

DC Office: 1440 LHOB, 20515, 202-225-2435; Fax: 202-225-1541; Web site: www.house.gov/grijalva.

District Offices: Tucson, 520-622-6788; Yuma, 928-343-7933.

Committees: *Education & the Workforce* (18th of 22 D): Education Reform; Employer-Employee Relations. *Resources* (16th of 22 D): Energy & Mineral Resources (RMM); Water & Power. *Small Business* (10th of 15 D): Workforce, Empowerment & Government Programs.

Group Ratings

	ADA	ACLU	AFS	LCV	ITIC	NTU	COC	ACU	NTLC	CHC
2004	100	95	100	100	30	11	10	0	0	0
2003	100	—	100	100	—	25	20	8	—	—

National Journal Ratings

	2003 LIB	—	2003 CONS		2004 LIB	—	2004 CONS
Economic	92%	—	0%		97%	—	3%
Social	84%	—	13%		88%	—	0%
Foreign	94%	—	0%		98%	—	0%

Key Votes of the 108th Congress

1. Drilling in ANWR	N	5. DC School Vouchers	N	9. Ban Same-Sex Marriage	N
2. Approve Bush Tax Cuts	N	6. Ban Human Cloning	N	10. Fund Iraq War	N
3. Medicare/Rx Bill	N	7. Restrict Gun Liability	N	11. Bar Cuba Embargo Funds	Y
4. Bar Overtime Pay Regs.	Y	8. Ban Partial-Birth Abortion	N	12. Intelligence Reorg.	N

Election Results

2004 general	Raul Grijalva (D)	108,868	(62%)	($618,854)
	Joseph Sweeney (R)	59,066	(34%)	
	Dave Kaplan (Lib)	7,503	(4%)	
2004 primary	Raul Grijalva (D)	unopposed		
2002 general	Raul Grijalva (D)	61,256	(59%)	($544,081)
	Ross Hieb (R)	38,474	(37%)	($131,282)
	John Nemeth (Lib)	4,088	(4%)	

The People		Race/Ethnic Origin	Ancestry	
Area size:	22,891 sq. mi.	38.6% White	German: 7.8% Irish: 5.4%	
Urban population:	83.6%	2.8% Black	English: 4.8%	
Rural population:	16.4%	1.3% Asian	**2004 Presidential Vote**	
Pop. 2000:	641,329	5.3% Native Am.	Kerry (D) 105,532	(57%)
Median income:	$30,828	0.1% Hawaiian	Bush (R) 79,674	(43%)
Poverty status:	21.8%	1.3% Two+ races	Other 1,155	(1%)
Military veterans:	13.3%	0.1% Other	**2000 Presidential Vote**	
		50.6% Hispanic Origin	Gore (D) 74,176	(58%)
			Bush (R) 49,343	(38%)
			Other 5,271	(4%)
			Cook Partisan Voting Index: D +10	

Occupation	Blue collar: 26.8%	White collar: 51.4%	Gray collar: 21.8%

Southern Arizona, though technically part of Mexico for hundreds of years, was never a home to Hispanic civilization like northern New Mexico. Here the hot desert land was inhabited mainly by Indians who kept their native ways and language until English-speaking whites came in on cavalry horses, miners' wagons and railroad cars in the late 19th century. This was after the 1854 Gadsden Purchase—$10 million to Mexico for 30,000 square miles of desert—cleared the way for a southern transcontinental railroad. Today's Hispanic Arizonans are mostly descendants of later immigrants from Mexico, some who came over the border in the sleepier days before World War II, when *la frontera* was scarcely patrolled, and many more who have come since the 1980s to partake in the dazzling economic growth that has served as both an attraction and an example to so many *norteno* Mexicans.

The 7th Congressional District of Arizona was designed to be the state's second Hispanic district; its population in 2000 was 51% Hispanic. It is a collection of four distant communities connected by many square miles of uninhabited Sonoran desert. One is the suburb of Tolleson just west of downtown Phoenix. The second is the heavily Latino west side of Tucson. The third is Yuma, located at a Colorado River crossing in an irrigated agricultural valley, often the hottest place in the country. The fourth is the Mexican border town of Nogales, 94% Hispanic and near many maquiladora plants, long an entry point for illegal drugs and the scene of many illegal border crossings in recent years. The twin smuggling tides—drugs and people—have inflicted damage on the fragile desert ecosystem. In an interesting example of international cooperation the sister cities of Nogales, Arizona and Nogales, Sonora have signed an agreement to respond jointly to fire and hazardous material emergencies. Out in the desert there is the Organ Pipe Cactus National Monument, the Tohono O'odham Indian Reservation and the Barry M. Goldwater Air Force Range (the largest aerial gunnery range after Nevada's Nellis Air Force Range), which is twice the size of Delaware; 95% of it is not used for target practice as it is the habitat of the endangered Sonoran pronghorn antelope. Near Nogales, wilderness and wildlife— including endangered species such as the jaguar, peregrine falcon, Chiricahua leopard frog, and Mexican spotted owl—have been protected in the Tumacacori Highlands. With its brutal desert heat, the Baboquivari trail that runs north to the Tohono O'odham nation has been the deadliest immigrant crossing in the nation. Politically, the 7th is one of two solidly Democratic districts in Arizona.

The congressman from the 7th District is Raul Grijalva, a Democrat first elected in 2002. He grew up in Tucson and graduated from the University of Arizona; he has lived in the city all his life and has deep roots in the immigrant community on the city's southwest side. He was the director of El Pueblo Neighborhood Center, and an assistant dean for Hispanic student affairs at the University of Arizona. In 1974 he was elected to the Tucson school board and served 12 years. In 1988 he was elected a Pima County Supervisor and served 14 years. As supervisor he backed an effort to extend medical and dental benefits to the same-sex domestic partners of county employees and focused on affordable healthcare, family and children services and growth. Developers and builders helped elect him to office in 1988, but his support for planned growth and impact fees quickly alienated them.

In 2002, the Democratic primary would obviously determine who would be the new congressman, and Grijalva entered with a home court advantage: 64% of the primary votes were cast in Pima County. His chief opponent was state Senator Elaine Richardson, who was endorsed by EMILY's List and spent more than $500,000 on ads. She criticized him for wasting taxpayer money on a $3.8 million contract to survey all the manholes in Pima County. Although outspent nearly 3–1, Grijalva had a well-organized grassroots effort and endorsements from labor unions, teachers' unions and the Sierra Club. Mocking his opponent's national funding, Grijalva created "Adelita's List," the name an allusion to the independent women who fought in the Mexican Revolution. He opposed any "privatization" of Social Security or increase in the retirement age. His proposals for immigration reform included an amnesty provision plus a comprehensive border policy with legalization, economic development, cost recovery, infrastructure enhancement and environmental protection. He won the primary with 41% to Richardson's 21%. In Pima County, Grijalva got 54% of the vote. Using the campaign slogan, "It's all about the love," he won easily in November and his daughter Adelita won a seat on the school board.

In the House, Grijalva's voting record is strongly liberal. On the Education and Workforce Committee, he promoted the "much improved" bipartisan agreement on the Individuals with Disabilities Education Act, and urged full funding. As an alternative to George W. Bush's immigration plan, he co-sponsored with Senator Edward Kennedy the SOLVE (Safe, Orderly, Legal Visas and Enforcement) Act, which would legalize millions of workers who have been in the United States for five years and who can prove that they have worked and paid taxes for at least two of those years. Grijalva joined Tucson activists in calling for an investigation of alleged Border Patrol abuse and mistreatment of illegal immigrants, including excessive force and racial profiling. He worked with other members of the Arizona delegation to resolve disputes over water rights with Indian reservations.

Grijalva initially endorsed Howard Dean for president, and worked actively on his campaign. In a fiery speech at the 2004 Democratic convention, he was one of three speakers who nominated John Edwards for vice president and he asked, "Mr. Bush, where is the compassion?" He was reelected easily in 2004; his Republican challenger called for the military to shoot illegal aliens seeking to cross the border.

EIGHTH DISTRICT

Rep. Jim Kolbe (R)

Elected 1984, 11th term; b. June 28, 1942, Evanston, IL; home, Tucson; Northwestern U., B.A. 1965, Stanford U., M.B.A. 1967; United Methodist; divorced.

Military Career: Navy, 1968–69 (Vietnam), Naval Reserves, 1970–77.

Elected Office: AZ Senate, 1976–82.

Professional Career: Asst., IL Bldg. Authority Architect, 1970–72; Asst., IL Gov. Ogilvie, 1972–73; Vice Pres., land planning firm; Real estate consultant.

DC Office: 237 CHOB, 20515, 202-225-2542; Fax: 202-225-0378; Web site: www.house.gov/kolbe.

District Offices: Sierra Vista, 520-459-3115; Tucson, 520-881-3588.

Committees: *Appropriations* (6th of 37 R): Foreign Operations, Export Financing & Related Programs (Chmn.); Homeland Security.

Group Ratings

	ADA	ACLU	AFS	LCV	ITIC	NTU	COC	ACU	NTLC	CHC
2004	20	40	13	9	90	49	100	56	65	46
2003	15	—	0	5	—	59	97	60	—	—

National Journal Ratings

	2003 LIB	—	2003 CONS		2004 LIB	—	2004 CONS
Economic	9%	—	84%		23%	—	76%
Social	51%	—	49%		58%	—	42%
Foreign	50%	—	49%		55%	—	44%

Key Votes of the 108th Congress

1. Drilling in ANWR	Y	5. DC School Vouchers	Y
2. Approve Bush Tax Cuts	Y	6. Ban Human Cloning	N
3. Medicare/Rx Bill	Y	7. Restrict Gun Liability	Y
4. Bar Overtime Pay Regs.	N	8. Ban Partial-Birth Abortion	N

9. Ban Same-Sex Marriage	N
10. Fund Iraq War	Y
11. Bar Cuba Embargo Funds	N
12. Intelligence Reorg.	Y

Election Results

2004 general	Jim Kolbe (R)	183,363	(60%)	($1,146,714)
	Eva Bacal (D)	109,963	(36%)	($99,691)
	Other	10,443	(3%)	
2004 primary	Jim Kolbe (R)	36,039	(57%)	
	Randy Graf (R)	26,686	(43%)	
2002 general	Jim Kolbe (R)	126,930	(63%)	($865,996)
	Mary Ryan (D)	67,328	(34%)	($292,398)
	Other	6,170	(3%)	

Prior Winning Percentages: 2000 (60%); 1998 (52%); 1996 (69%); 1994 (68%); 1992 (67%); 1990 (65%); 1988 (68%); 1986 (65%); 1984 (51%)

The People		Race/Ethnic Origin	Ancestry	
Area size:	9,057 sq. mi.	73.9% White	German: 14.4%	English: 9.7%
Urban population:	87.3%	3.0% Black	Irish: 9.1%	
Rural population:	12.7%	2.1% Asian	**2004 Presidential Vote**	
Pop. 2000:	641,329	0.8% Native Am.	Bush (R) 167,647	(53%)
Median income:	$40,656	0.1% Hawaiian	Kerry (D) 147,300	(46%)
Poverty status:	10.5%	1.8% Two+ races	Other 1,886	(1%)
Military veterans:	19.1%	0.1% Other	**2000 Presidential Vote**	
		18.2% Hispanic Origin	Bush (R) 123,585	(50%)
			Gore (D) 114,055	(46%)
			Other 10,814	(4%)
			Cook Partisan Voting Index: R + 1	

Occupation	Blue collar: 16.5%	White collar: 66.7%	Gray collar: 16.8%

Arizona's first frontier was just south of today's Tucson, where Franciscan friars built San Xavier del Bac mission in the 18th century. To the east the late 19th century mining towns of Tombstone and Bisbee sprang up on desert mountainsides, where miners dug up gold and silver and much of America's copper; Cochise County, which includes those two towns, was the most populous county when Arizona became the 48th state in 1912. Here the white man last subdued the Indians, when the Apache leader Geronimo faced the U.S. Army in 1900. In the last decade Cochise County has been an active frontier again. After the Border Patrol reduced illegal crossings in California and Texas, Mexicans wishing to enter the United States came to Agua Prieta, just across the border from the town of Douglas. There they fan out, cross the border and use the area's numerous roads, mountain trails and ranch lands to get to Tucson and Phoenix. The Border Patrol's Tucson sector has become the most active on the border, with 230,000 illegal aliens apprehended in 2004, almost double the population of Cochise County; more were apprehended that year in Arizona than in California, New Mexico and Texas combined. Numerous border-crossers are found dead in the mountains and the desert; in winter Border Patrol officers carry blankets and heat packs to treat cases of hypothermia.

One of their destinations is Tucson, Arizona's second metropolis, much smaller, more rough-hewn and politically less conservative than Phoenix. Tucson is a high-tech city and home of the University of Arizona. It is also a tourist destination, with famed resorts. For nearly 40 years, Tucson was the political base of the brothers Udall: Stewart, congressman in the 1950s, Interior secretary in the 1960s, now an Arizona lawyer again; Morris, congressman for 30 years and Interior Committee chairman, who retired in 1991 because of Parkinson's disease and died in 1998. Now their sons, Tom and Mark Udall, represent New Mexico and Colorado districts; a cousin, Stephen Udall, finished second in the 2002 primary in Arizona's 1st District.

The 8th Congressional District of Arizona includes all of Tucson except the Latino west side that is in the 7th District. The 8th also includes the eastern half of surrounding Pima County and much southeastern Arizona desert real estate: All of Cochise County (including Tombstone and Bisbee), Douglas and Sierra Vista near Fort Huachuca, site of the Army Military Intelligence Center, the training site for military interrogators; and very small portions of Santa Cruz and Pinal Counties. Politically it is closely divided, voting narrowly for George W. Bush in 2000 and 2004.

The congressman from the 8th District is Jim Kolbe, a Republican first elected in 1984. He was born in Evanston, Illinois, moved to Arizona at age 5 and grew up on a cattle ranch in Sonoita. He graduated from Northwestern and Stanford Business School, served in the Navy in Vietnam, became an assistant to Illinois' Republican Governor Richard Ogilvie in 1972, and moved back to Arizona shortly thereafter and went into real estate. In 1976 he was elected to the Arizona Senate. In 1982 he ran in the 5th District and lost to Democrat Jim McNulty 50%–48%. In 1984 he ran again and beat him 51%–48%.

Kolbe's voting record on economics has been mostly conservative; he ranks near the middle of the House on cultural and foreign issues. He is a strong booster of free trade and of the maquiladora program, in which U.S.-made components shipped to Mexico for assembly can reenter the U.S. without paying full duty. He was one of the Republican leaders in the successful fight to pass NAFTA in the House in November 1993. He supported GATT, trade promotion authority and the WTO and has called for a free-trade zone covering Central America. In 2000, he was one of the leading House spokesmen for normal trade relations with China; in 2002, he opposed steel import quotas. He favors eliminating U.S. farm subsidies but said, "We will not do so unilaterally." In November 2004, at his suggestion, Tucson hosted a session of the Andean trade talks with Colombia, Ecuador, Peru and Bolivia.

Immigration has become the hottest local issue: "On a list of 10 issues," Kolbe has said, "it would be one through seven or one through eight." In April 2002 he called for using more military troops, including National Guard units, on the border. In May 2002 he proposed that the INS be split into three parts, with function-specific units to be folded into the Justice, State and Labor Departments. At his insistence, the CIS (formerly INS) has only roving checkpoints in Arizona, to preserve "the element of surprise." In April 2004 he and Senators John McCain and Jon Kyl sponsored a bill to spend $4 billion on technology to secure the borders; he wants tamper-proof, biometric, machine-readable identity cards for immigrants. At the same time, he has said, "We do not currently have an enforceable law" and that attempts to control immigration and stepped-up law enforcement is "spitting in the wind." To solve the larger problem, Kolbe, with McCain and the 6th District's Jeff Flake have co-sponsored a guest worker law, which would provide six-year temporary worker visas and three-year visas for those who are here illegally now.

Another Kolbe cause is individual investment accounts in Social Security. In May 2002, he said the debate was moving backward, and when Republican candidates in the 2002 cycle, on the advice of NRCC chairman Tom Davis, attacked "privatization" (by which they meant Bill Clinton's 1999 proposal for government investment of Social Security payroll taxes), he said, "A plague on all of them. We ought to be focused on acknowledging the long-term problem and the options that we might look at that would save Social Security. One has to look at the debate and say this will be a tough thing to do in the next several years." In 2005, he co-sponsored a bill with Democrat Allen Boyd to establish personal retirement accounts, the only bipartisan plan currently on the table.

From 1997–2000, Kolbe was Appropriations subcommittee chairman with jurisdiction over the Treasury, the White House and the Postal Service. In 2001 he switched to the chairmanship of the Foreign Operations Subcommittee. He devoted particular attention to Pakistan, where he visited Afghan refugee camps in May 2001. After September 11 he called for lifting sanctions on Pakistan and setting it specific tasks in the war on terrorism; he also called for lifting the restrictions on imports of Pakistani textiles and other products. He was disturbed in November 2002 when it became clear that Pakistan had shipped nuclear technology to North Korea, and said that the 1994 Agreed Framework with North Korea was "effectively ended." In May 2002 he inserted $200 million additional aid to Israel into a supplemental; at Colin Powell's suggestion he added $50 million for Palestinian relief. He has supported the Bush administration on Iraq but, with McCain, opposed the Pentagon policy of not releasing photographs of the coffins of slain Americans. He has pushed for more funding for global AIDS programs—$2.3 billion in 2004.

On cultural issues Kolbe is often liberal. He angered many Republicans by supporting funding for the National Endowment for the Arts and was one of the few Republicans to vote against the partial-birth abortion ban. He opposed the Bush policy on stem-cell research. He voted for the Defense of Marriage Act and in July 1996, pressured by an impending article in *The Advocate*, announced that he is gay. This had little apparent impact on the 1996 election, in which he beat Morris Udall's chiropractor 69%–26%. He supported hate crimes legislation before the Matthew Shepard slaying and said afterward, "Thank God Wyoming has the death penalty." In July 1998 he opposed Joel Hefley's amendment to overturn Clinton's order banning discrimination against homosexuals in federal employment. Republican leaders got Hefley to agree not to offer his amendment to Kolbe's appropriation; when it came up later, Kolbe helped persuade 63 Republicans to vote against it. He voted against the constitutional amendment to ban same-sex marriage, saying it was a matter for the states.

In 1998 Kolbe won reelection over former Tucson Mayor Tom Volgy by only 52%–45%, and many wondered whether his sexual orientation was a hidden liability. In August 2000 Kolbe was the first openly gay speaker at a Republican National Convention. As he spoke about the importance of free trade, his assigned topic and one on which he had a strong record, several members of the Texas delegation in the front took off their cowboy hats and bowed their heads in prayer. Kolbe said he didn't notice. In September he easily dispatched a primary opponent by 79%–21%. In November 2000 against former state Senator George Cunningham he won by a solid 60%–35%. Redistricting did not hurt Kolbe, and in November 2002 he beat a Tucson prosecutor 63%–34%.

Kolbe had tougher competition in the September 2004 Republican primary from state Representative Randy Graf. He opposed Kolbe's guest worker bill and called for tougher border enforcement, with "a role for the military." He supported Protect Arizona Now's Proposition 200, which passed 56%–44% in November, and argued that Kolbe had been ineffective in protecting the border. Kolbe, evidently disturbed by his polling, ran tough attack ads against Graf in the weeks before the primary. Kolbe won 57%–43%—an unimpressive margin for a 20-year incumbent in a primary. His hometown support in Tucson stayed strong; he won 60%–40% in Pima County. But Graf carried Cochise County 53%–47%. In November he won by a wider margin 60%–36%.

★ ARKANSAS ★

Two weeks after the 2004 election, four American presidents journeyed to Little Rock, Arkansas, to open the $165 million William J. Clinton Presidential Center. George H.W. Bush and George W. Bush gave gracious tribute to the president who defeated the former and was succeeded by the latter, and Jimmy Carter added words of praise. The Clinton Center is the largest of our presidential libraries, and the first with electronic records as well as paper documents; in its alcoves are exhibits and electronic connections to what the 42d president considers his great achievements along with a treatment of "the politics of persecution," Bill Clinton's take on the impeachment controversy. But not all is serious here: Clinton the hearty eater decreed that there be space on the grounds for picnics and cookouts. Bill Clinton may not

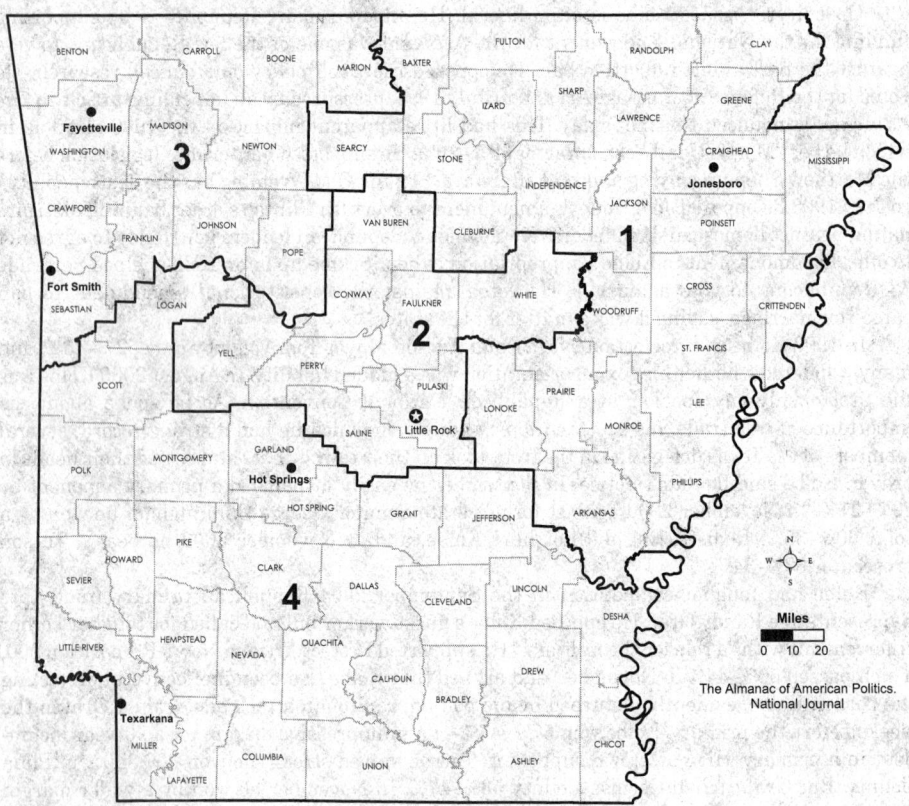

Congressional district boundaries were first effective for 2002.

The Almanac of American Politics.
National Journal

have returned to live in Arkansas (nor did eight other presidents return to their home states), but he clearly is Arkansas's most distinguished politician and a man whose articulateness and earthiness, outsized ambitions and overly visible faults are redolent of the state from which he began his unlikely ascent to national and international prominence. Clinton still has his detractors in Arkansas, but as his presidential center opened most Arkansans considered him an outstanding or above average president. As one said when he left Little Rock for Washington in January 1993, "I distinctly remember thinking that this was finally going to wipe away the stain left by Faubus"—the governor whose disobedience of an order desegregating Little Rock's Central High School prompted President Dwight D. Eisenhower to dispatch federal troops to enforce it in 1957. Clinton certainly did that—no small accomplishment, but the scandals associated with him, if they did not bring him down, tarnished the reputations of many other Arkansans.

Arkansas, like Clinton, began life without many advantages. In area, it's the smallest state between the Mississippi River and the Pacific; in population, it's the smallest state in the South; it has not been blessed with any great natural resource—unless you count flame-retarding bromine, of which it produces half the world supply—or any growing major industry. Arkansas is the land left over when Louisiana and Missouri were carved out of the Louisiana Purchase and what is now Oklahoma was fenced off as Indian Territory. Settled by poor farmers with large families, few slaves, and little cash, it has had no Atlanta or Dallas or even Memphis to be a focus of growth. Arkansas has the third lowest income levels of any state, the second lowest percentage of college graduates and the second lowest percentage of Internet use. But its manufacturing economy—food processing, aerospace, auto parts, medical and construction equipment—has recovered smartly from the 2001 recession and the Clinton Center should bring in a steady stream of tourists. Growth is concentrated in the booming northwest corner of the state, in Little Rock and in counties along the Interstate highways; Arkansas is the only southern state without a big auto plant. Yet it has high hopes of getting Toyota to build a plant in Marion, across the Mississippi from Memphis, which already has a cluster of auto parts factories; voters in 2004 approved a proposition authorizing state bonds for such a project. Arkansas prides itself on being a traditional values state—58% of adults are married, higher than any other state except Idaho and Utah. But the divorce rate has also been higher than average, prompting Governor Mike Huckabee to declare "a state of marital emergency" and, in February 2005, to convert his marriage into a covenant marriage. In 2004 voters passed 74%–26% an amendment prohibiting same-sex marriage and civil unions.

As the late Arkansas political scientist Diane Blair noted, Arkansas never had a power elite of great plantation owners or economic robber barons. That has left it a heritage without honored traditions or tight standards, but has also made Arkansas a land of great opportunities, where talented people can move up fast, amassing huge fortunes by taking break-through ideas and making them work. Sam Walton believed that rural and small town America would support a chain of giant discount stores which, through tough bargaining with vendors and ultra-quick distribution, could undersell competitors, but through demanding management and employee profit-sharing could embody small town friendliness and service. Walton was the richest American when he died in April 1992, and Wal-Mart today is the largest private employer in the world, with a payroll of 1.4 million. Jack Stephens and his late brother Witt started an investment banking house in Little Rock specializing in underwriting municipal bonds and investing in businesses that are a mix of private enterprise, government subsidies and public regulation; their success—and political connections in Arkansas and elsewhere—amassed a billion dollar fortune. Don Tyson took his father's chicken business and made it one of the biggest food producers in America. Another big Arkansas operation is J.B. Hunt's trucking empire. These business giants have cultivated a down-home, laid-back style, but they have also skillfully united their interests with those of the state's politicians, including Bill Clinton.

Politically, Arkansas was long solidly Democratic, with Republican pockets in the mountains in the northwest. For years it produced politicians who accumulated great seniority and power in Washington—longtime House Ways and Means Chairman Wilbur Mills, Senators John McClellan and William Fulbright, who represented the state for a total of 65 years from the 1940s to the 1970s, and Senators Dale Bumpers and David Pryor, who served a total of 42 years from the 1970s to the 1990s. But in the 108th Congress, Arkansas was represented by two freshman senators and four House members with an average of four years of seniority—the delegation with the least clout of any state according to *Roll Call*. Republicans have won top of the line races occasionally—Winthrop Rockefeller, Sr., was elected governor in 1966 and 1968, following Orval Faubus, and Frank White beat Bill Clinton in 1980. The northwest 3d Congressional District has elected Republican congressmen since 1966, though Clinton came close to winning it in 1974, when he was 28. But Republicans have not had sustained political success, and the legislature is still overwhelmingly Democratic—one of the last in the South to be so (the others are Mississippi and Louisiana).

Nonetheless there is an underlying trend. Like the rest of the nation as a whole, Arkansas was carried by Bill Clinton in 1992 and 1996 and voted for George W. Bush in 2000 and 2004. At the state level there is robust two-party competition. Republican Mike Huckabee has been governor since 1996, and Republican Tim Hutchinson was elected senator that year. But Democrat Blanche Lincoln was elected to the Senate in 1998 and reelected in 2004, and in 2002 Democrat Mark Pryor, David Pryor's son, defeated Hutchinson. That makes Arkansas as the only southern state with two Democratic senators; there are only two others from the rest of the South. Generational and demographic change on balance favor Republicans. In 2004 John Kerry led George W. Bush among Arkansans over 60 by 52%–48% and won by a similar margin among those under 30. But among the great mass of voters age 30 to 59 Bush led by 59%–40%. Demographically, the fastest growth has been in the Little Rock metro area and in northwest Arkansas around Bentonville. In 2004 metro Little Rock cast about one-quarter of the state's votes and the Bentonville area one-eighth; metro Little Rock voted 51%–48% and the Bentonville area 62%–37% for George W. Bush.

The People		Race/Ethnic Origin			Military veterans: 281,714 (14.1%)	
Pop. 2004 (est):	2,752,629	2,100,135	78.6%	White	WWII: 20.1%	Korea: 13.3%
Pop. 2000:	2,673,400	416,615	15.6%	Black	Vietnam: 32.0%	Gulf War: 10.5%
Pop. 1990:	2,350,725	19,892	0.7%	Asian	**Most populous cities (2003):**	
Change 1990–2000:	Up 13.7%	16,702	0.6%	Native Am.	1. Little Rock	184,053
% of U.S. total:	1.0%	1,494	0.1%	Hawaiian	2. Fort Smith	81,562
Pop. rank:	33d of 50	30,364	1.1%	Two+ races	3. Fayetteville	62,078
Area size:	53,179 sq. mi.	1,332	0.0%	Other	4. North Little Rock	59,687
State Native:	63.9%	86,866	3.2%	Hisp. Origin	5. Jonesboro	57,435
Non-citizen:	1.9%	**Ancestry**				
Language		USA: 13.2%		Irish: 7.9%	Urban population: 52.4%	
English: 93.5%	Spanish: 4.0%	German: 7.7%		English: 6.5%	Rural population: 47.6%	
Other Eur.: 1.6%		French: 1.6%				

Education		Work Sector		General Assembly		
H.S. Grad:	75.3%	Private: 76.8%	Govt: 14.9%	Senate	27 D 8 R	
College Grad:	16.7%	Self: 7.8%	Family: 0.4%	House	72 D 28 R	
Industry		Unemployment: 6.1%		Legislative Term Limits: Yes		
Agri: 3.7%	Con: 7.0%	**Household Income**		**Registered Voters**		
Fin: 4.8%	Info: 2.2%	<15k: 22.0%	15-35k: 31.7%	No party registration		
Mfg: 25.3%	Prof: 25.0%	35-50k: 17.5%	50-100k: 22.8%			
Public: 4.3%	Trade: 16.3%	100-150k: 3.8%	>150k: 2.2%			
Other: 11.3%		Median: $32,182				
Occupation		Poverty status: 15.8%				
Blue collar: 31.6%	White collar: 52.8%	**Home Value**				
Gray collar: 15.6%		<50k: 34.1%	50-100k: 40.2%	100-200k: 19.8%	200-300k: 3.6%
		300-500k: 1.6%	>500k: 0.7%	Median: $67,400	

Presidential politics   Arkansas has voted for the winners of the last nine presidential elections. It voted 53% for Bill Clinton in 1992 and 54% in 1996, his best and eighth-best percentages those years. In 2000, it voted only 46% for Al Gore, his 29th-best state, and in 2004, only 44% for John Kerry, his 33d best. George W. Bush won 51% here in 2000, his lowest percentage in the South except of course for Florida; he won 54% in 2004. For a brief moment in mid-October, polls showed a tight race here. Bush already had headquarters across the state and ran radio ads, while Kerry and the Democrats went on TV and Bill Clinton returned to the state on Halloween. But Bush, who narrowly lost two of Arkansas's congressional districts in 2000, carried all four in 2004.

The Arkansas presidential primary, held in May, attracts little attention; nor did it in 1992 when it was held on Super Tuesday. There is no party registration requirement and Republican turnout has typically been very low.

2004 Presidential Vote		
Bush (R)	572,898	(54%)
Kerry (D)	469,953	(45%)
Nader (POP)	6,171	(1%)
Other	5,923	(1%)
2004 Democratic Presidential Primary		
Kerry (D)	177,754	(67%)
Uncommitted (D)	61,800	(23%)
Kucinich (D)	13,766	(5%)
LaRouche (D)	13,528	(5%)
2000 Presidential Vote		
Bush (R)	472,940	(51%)
Gore (D)	422,768	(46%)
Nader (Green)	13,421	(1%)
Other	12,652	(1%)

Congressional districting   In April 2001, the boundaries of Arkansas's four congressional districts were adjusted slightly by the Democratic legislature to meet the equal-population standard. Because it didn't split counties, the legislature's plan had the highest population difference in the nation between the districts—6,698 people—but it also contained a backup provision that if a court found the plan invalid, it would be repealed and 4,400 voters would be shifted between districts; a court challenge did not materialize. Governor Mike Huckabee, lacking the votes to prevent an override of his veto, let the plan become law without his signature.

109th Congress Lineup	
3 D	1 R

108th Congress Lineup	
3 D	1 R

Governor

Mike Huckabee (R)

Assumed office, July 1996, term expires Jan. 2007, 2d full term; b. Aug. 24, 1955, Hope; home, Little Rock; Ouachita Baptist U., B.A. 1975, Southwestern Baptist Theological Seminary, 1976–80; Baptist; married (Janet).

Elected Office: AR Lt. Gov., 1993–96.

Professional Career: Advertising Dir., Focus, 1976–80; Baptist Minister, 1980–92; Pres., ACTS–TV, 1983–86; Pres., KBSC–TV, 1987–92; Pres., Cambridge Comm., 1992–96.

Office: State Capitol, Rm. 250, Little Rock, 72201, 501-682-2345; Fax: 501-682-3597; Web site: www.state.ar.us/governor.

Election Results

2002 general	Mike Huckabee (R)	427,082	(53%)
	Jimmie Lou Fisher (D)	378,250	(47%)
2002 primary	Mike Huckabee (R)	78,803	(85%)
	Doyle Cannady (R)	13,434	(15%)
1998 general	Mike Huckabee (R)	421,989	(60%)
	Bill Bristow (D)	272,923	(39%)
	Other	11,099	(2%)

Mike Huckabee has been governor of Arkansas since July 1996. Like Bill Clinton, Huckabee was born in Hope; unlike Clinton, he grew up there. Clinton was elected governor of Arkansas Boys State in 1963, Huckabee in 1972. Huckabee had a profound spiritual experience at 15, while on a two-week youth fellowship program at Cape Kennedy—the first time he had been outside Arkansas. Clinton went off to Georgetown and Yale Law School; Huckabee graduated from Ouachita Baptist University at 19 and attended Southwestern Baptist Theological Seminary in Fort Worth for four years. In the 1980s, Huckabee was a Baptist minister in Pine Bluff and then Texarkana; in both towns he started a 24-hour television station, where he produced documentaries and hosted a program called *Positive Alternatives*. In 1989, he became president of the Arkansas Baptist Convention, with a membership of 490,000.

Huckabee's first stab at politics was running against Senator Dale Bumpers in 1992; he lost 60%–40%. Then, after Jim Guy Tucker replaced Bill Clinton as governor, Huckabee ran in a special election for lieutenant governor. It was July 1993, the Clinton tax plan and gays in the military had been in the headlines, and Huckabee beat pro-Clinton Democrat Nate Coulter 51%–49%. He was re-elected 59%–41% in November 1994. In October 1995, after David Pryor said he was retiring from the Senate, Huckabee announced for the seat and led in the polls. But in May 1996, Tucker was convicted on one count of arranging nearly $3 million in fraudulent loans. Tucker promised to resign July 15; on that day, claiming he had a good case on appeal, he hesitated, then finally in the early evening he resigned. Huckabee, who had already bowed out of the Senate race, had insisted Tucker resign and handled the transition gracefully but firmly.

Despite facing a heavily Democratic legislature, Huckabee has had some significant achievements as governor. He is most proud of the ARKids First plan providing health insurance for parents of children above the Medicaid income limits. It requires a small co-payment, to avoid the stigma of being a handout; Huckabee wanted to offer parents the choice of ARKids First or Medicaid, which the Clinton administration overruled in July 2000, so he rolled the two plans into one. Huckabee boasts that the program has given insurance to 70,000 kids who didn't have it and that Arkansas ranks number one in the decrease of percentage of residents without health insurance. In his first term, he cut income taxes and passed a taxpayer's bill of rights for property owners; he supported a successful ballot measure to raise the sales tax 0.5% to fund a $300 homestead property tax credit. He signed a law requiring women to receive information about abortion 24 hours before the procedure and mailed a letter to school superintendents reminding them of a child's right to engage in "personal or group prayer."

In 1998, against Democrat Bill Bristow, an attorney representing state trooper Danny Ferguson in the case Paula Jones brought against Clinton, Huckabee was elected to a full term by a 60%–39% margin. Budget cuts in 2001 cut out most of a promised $3,000 increase for teachers and cut health services programs, but Huckabee, at the time, remained opposed to tax increases. He was popular enough that prominent Democrats declined to run in 2002; only in March 2002 did Democrats came up with a candidate, state Treasurer Jimmie Lou Fisher, who had announced she would retire from this minor office after 22 years and return home to Paragould, where her mother was in bad health. A onetime staffer for freshman Governor Bill Clinton, she was regarded as an exceedingly nice person, always welcome at Democratic get-togethers, but not a strong candidate. But she came close to winning. Huckabee started making astonishing mistakes; his job rating plummeted from 70% to 50%. Huckabee had a penchant for granting pardons; one felon he paroled in 1996 committed a murder in Missouri. In July 2001, he commuted the sentence of the stepson of an administrative aide in the governor's office whose criminal record went back to 1972. In June 2002, he fired the head of the AASIS (Arkansas Administrative Statewide Information System) project, who promptly told reporters he and other employees had been pressured for campaign contributions and that Huckabee had tried to stifle news of cost overruns—nearly 100%—during the election year. Huckabee also had been in the practice of receiving large gifts; he reported a total of $112,000 in 1999, which included $23,000 in clothes from one state appointee. Huckabee responded—in an election year!—with a lawsuit to allow him to receive more gifts and another lawsuit to stop the state ethics commission from investigating him.

Another self-inflicted wound came in March 2002, when Huckabee's wife announced she was running for secretary of state. Janet Huckabee was known for her daredevil antics—bungee jumping, skydiving, jet skiing, kayaking—and for her oversight of the two-year renovation of the Governor's Mansion, a time when the Huckabees lived in a triple-wide on the mansion grounds. She insisted on a 24-hour state police detail while campaigning across the state; when that was challenged, she at first said she had no control over it, then promised to pay the cost, then said she would pay only up to $500. Meanwhile, Jimmie Lou Fisher, with teachers' union support, called for spending $133 million more for education; she said she would find the money from waste, fraud and abuse, or perhaps from a lottery (though she opposed one). She got more mileage by attacking AASIS and criticizing Huckabee's grants of clemency and acceptance of gifts. Mike Huckabee won by only 53%–47%, while Janet Huckabee lost 62%–38%. Huckabee called the campaign "a kidney stone that takes six months to pass."

Another obstacle appeared. In November 2002 the state Supreme Court ruled that Arkansas's school finance system was unconstitutional and ruled it must be changed by January 2004: one of many such rulings in which state courts take control of education policy. Huckabee tussled with the legislature, which declined to pass a budget until he called a special session; he announced in August 2003 he would not run against Senator Blanche Lincoln in 2004, but would concentrate instead on education. Huckabee's solution was consolidation of school districts with less than 1,500 pupils. Local school superintendents and rural voters vehemently opposed this; the state Senate approved consolidation for districts with less than 500 pupils, but the state House would have none of it. Huckabee protested, "I do not want to be the second Arkansas governor to step on, in this case, the Capitol steps rather than a school campus and to openly and publicly defy a court order." Huckabee called a special session in December 2003, and fought for consolidation with what legislators called "bullying tactics." In January 2004 the state Supreme Court hired two former justices as special masters to redesign school finance if the legislature failed to act; consultants had already proposed an $847 million increase to the $1.7 billion state education budget. In February 2004 the House approved a $377 million sales tax increase, with consolidation of districts with less than 350 pupils; Huckabee let it become law without his signature. Criticized for supporting the largest tax increase in Arkansas history, Huckabee said, "Pure conservatism means lean and responsible government, not mean and irresponsible government." By the end of the session, 19 of 21 bills he proposed became law including one merging the state's Health and Human Services departments together and another altering the funding formula for state colleges.

Huckabee made news in other ways. Diagnosed with Type II diabetes in 2003, he lost some 110 pounds over the next year or so. He quit eating fried foods and sweets and started exercising regularly; he showed his progress by toting a 90-pound girl around a school gym. In May 2004 he started a Healthy Arkansas initiative, to discourage bad eating habits and smoking; no smoking was allowed within 25 feet of state buildings, and the state started paying for nicotine patches. Parents were given children's health report cards. He started a Get Five fruits and vegetables a day initiative and eschewed an old favorite, fried Twinkies. Huckabee said he wanted government to "model healthy behavior," but he still opposed a ban on smoking in restaurants. His weight down from 280 pounds to 170, Huckabee was profiled in *People* magazine, accompanied by a photo of him holding a pair of his old pants. He wrote a best-selling book titled *Quit Digging Your Grave with a Knife and Fork* and went on television to promote it.

Huckabee campaigned hard for George W. Bush in 2004. But despite Bush's victory in Arkansas, Republicans lost two seats in the state House. Huckabee is term-limited and cannot run again in 2006; he has been mentioned as a possible candidate for president in 2008, though he downplayed any national aspirations. "It is not a big focus of my life right now." Republican candidates to succeed him as governor include Lieutenant Governor Win Rockefeller, whose father was elected governor in 1966 and 1968, and former Congressman Asa Hutchinson, who served as undersecretary of the Department of Homeland Security until resigning in March 2005. In June 2005 the Democratic frontrunner was Attorney General Mike Beebe.

Senior Senator

Blanche Lincoln (D)

Elected 1998, seat up 2010, 2d term; b. Sept. 30, 1960, Helena; home, Horseshoe Lake; U. of AR, 1979–80, Randolph Macon Col., B.S. 1982; Episcopalian; married (Steve).

Elected Office: US House of Reps., 1992–96

Professional Career: Staff Asst., U.S. Rep. Bill Alexander, 1982–84; Lobbyist & govt. affairs rep., 1985–91.

DC Office: 355 DSOB, 20510, 202-224-4843; Fax: 202-228-1371; Web site: lincoln.senate.gov.

State Office: Little Rock, 501-375-2993.

Committees: *Aging (Special). Agriculture, Nutrition & Forestry*: Forestry, Conservation & Rural Revitalization (RMM); Production & Price Competitiveness; Research, Nutrition & General Legislation. *Finance*: Social Security & Family Policy; Taxation & IRS Oversight.

Group Ratings

	ADA	ACLU	AFS	LCV	ITIC	NTU	COC	ACU	NTLC	CHC
2004	95	67	100	67	92	16	71	20	23	16
2003	75	—	89	32	—	20	78	20	—	—

National Journal Ratings

	2003 LIB	—	2003 CONS	2004 LIB	—	2004 CONS
Economic	56%	—	42%	65%	—	31%
Social	56%	—	43%	53%	—	46%
Foreign	60%	—	35%	61%	—	36%

Key Votes of the 108th Congress

1. Ban Drilling in ANWR	Y	5. Energy Bill	Y	9. Ban Same-Sex Marriage	N
2. Approve Bush Tax Cuts	N	6. Support Roe v. Wade	Y	10. Ban Bunker-Buster Bomb	Y
3. Medicare/Rx Bill	Y	7. Ban Partial-Birth Abortion	Y	11. Fund Iraq War	Y
4. Bar Overtime Pay Regs.	Y	8. Assault Weapons Ban	Y	12. Restrict Missile Defense	Y

Election Results

2004 general	Blanche Lincoln (D)	580,973	(56%)	($5,816,913)
	Jim Holt (R)	458,036	(44%)	($148,682)
2004 primary	Blanche Lincoln (D)	231,037	(83%)	
	Lisa Burks (D)	47,010	(17%)	
1998 general	Blanche Lincoln (D)	385,878	(55%)	($3,122,776)
	Fay Boozman (R)	292,906	(42%)	($1,093,007)
	Other	21,860	(3%)	

Prior Winning Percentages: 1994 House (53%); 1992 House (70%)

Blanche Lambert Lincoln was elected to the Senate in 1998 after showing something close to perfect political pitch in her 1990s electoral career. She grew up in Helena, on the flat rice lands of eastern Arkansas, where her father and brother are the sixth and seventh generations running a farm raising rice, wheat, soybeans, and cotton, and where she stayed in public schools after they were integrated. Cheerful, active, endowed with good political sense, she lists her hobbies as duck hunting, fishing and yard sales. After college, in 1982, she worked as a staffer for 1st District Congressman Bill Alexander, then after two years worked as a lobbyist for, among others, Billy Broadhurst—Gary Hart's host on the 1987 *Monkey Business* cruise. In 1992, she moved back to Arkansas and, as Blanche Lambert (she was married in 1993) ran against Alexander, sensing he was in trouble. He had lost a leadership race in 1986, was named in a lawsuit for a $308,000 debt and had 487 overdrafts totaling $208,000 on the House bank. "I'll promise you one thing," the 31-year-old challenger said, "I can sure enough balance my checkbook." She won the primary 61%–39%, carrying 23 of 25 counties.

In the House, Lincoln compiled a moderate voting record and got a seat on the Commerce Committee. She saw Japan open its market to Arkansas rice and denounced the Supplemental Security Income program that provided disability checks to kids who act up in school. She supported much of the Contract with America in 1995. But when the moratorium on regulations threatened duck hunting season and national wildlife refuges were closed, she got laws changed to ensure it wouldn't happen again. Her re-election margin in 1994 was only 53%–47%, but she seemed well positioned to hold the seat when, in January 1996, she announced that she was pregnant with twin boys and would not run for reelection because of the strain of campaigning in an Arkansas summer during a difficult pregnancy.

When Senator Dale Bumpers announced he would not run for reelection in 1998, Lincoln got into the race. She flashed snapshots of her twins and ran ads showing her overseeing mealtime, balancing one twin on her lap, bouncing the other on her knee, laying her head on her husband's shoulder. "Daughter, wife, mother, congresswoman . . . Living our rock-solid Arkansas values." In the primary, she faced Attorney General Winston Bryant, the Democratic nominee in the 1996 Senate race. She led by an impressive 45%–27% in the May primary, with 64% in her old 1st District, which cast nearly one-third of the votes. She won the June runoff 62%–38%.

In the general election, Lincoln stanched the Republican tide that had been running since Bill Clinton left the state. The Republican nominee was Fay Boozman, an ophthalmologist from Rogers in northwest Arkansas who attended the same church as Republican Senator Tim Hutchinson. Boozman had a profound religious experience in 1992, sold his medical practice, and ran for the state Senate; there he was the champion of the partial-birth abortion ban. Boozman called on Bill Clinton to resign and ran tough comparative ads on Lincoln. He said the Bible dictated his anti-tax philosophy and made a serious gaffe when he said it is rare for women to get pregnant by rape because fear triggers a hormonal change that blocks conception. Lincoln won 55%–42%; Boozman carried the northwest corner of the state and little else. She was the youngest woman ever elected to the Senate.

Lincoln's voting record has been a bit to the left of the midpoint of the Senate; she was one of nine Democrats to form a moderate caucus, similar to the House's Blue Dogs, in February 2000. Working with her 1st District successor, Marion Berry, she promoted farm exports, joining the WTO caucus in October 1999 and in May 2000 visiting Cuba, which, before Fidel Castro, purchased much of Arkansas's rice. She described Castro as "very cordial" and "still very much in command and in control," accepted two boxes of cigars, worth $1,250, and strongly supported ending the embargo on trade in Cuba. She voted for the partial-birth abortion ban, saying it was "always a difficult vote." In February 2001, Lincoln got a seat on the Finance Committee and played an important role in some key votes in the closely divided Senate. In March 2001 she was one of six Democrats to vote to kill the Clinton ergonomics regulations and one of six Democrats to vote for non-severability on campaign finance (which threatened to get the whole bill declared unconstitutional). On the Finance Committee, she and other moderates negotiated with Chairman Charles Grassley and ranking member Max Baucus to get two provisions into the committee bill: to make the child care tax refundable to those who pay no income tax and to create a new 10% income bracket. She was one of 12 Democrats to vote for the tax cut in May 2001, but she voted against the Bush budget also in May 2001.

In 2003 and 2004 Lincoln continued to work to make the child tax credit totally refundable, and succeeded in conference in September 2004. She was also successful in extending the 10% bracket and relief from the marriage penalty. In the conference committee on the corporate tax bill, she won provisions for $20 million writeoffs for low-budget movie and TV production companies operating in low-income areas and scholarships and stipends for nurses who agree to work in areas with shortages of health care workers. She worked for a $20 million cap on small businesses that qualify for industrial development bonds, tax breaks for production of electricity from municipal solid and agricultural wastes and tax credits for producers of biodiesel.

Lincoln was one of five Democrats who voted to support the Bush administration's repeal of the Clinton administration's New Source Review pollution regulations. She supported the Iraq war but later criticized the administration for miscalculations and mismanagement. In 2004 she proposed a soldiers' bill of rights, including full disability and retirement benefits and retirement at 55 for reservists. She was the only Arkansas Democrat to vote for the Medicare/prescription drug bill supported by Bush in 2003. "I thought the good outweighed the bad. We really focused on the neediest and sickest." But in 2004 she co-sponsored a bill to eliminate health savings accounts and to authorize the government to negotiate with pharmaceutical companies. While she joined other Democrats in filibustering the nomination of Miguel Estrada and other appeals court nominees, Lincoln supported the nomination of Arkansan Leon Holmes after he was criticized for years-ago comments on abortion; he was confirmed 51–46. She worked with Republican Congressman Dan Burton to aid U.S. citizens (usually children abducted by a parent) who have been kidnapped and held in Saudi Arabia.

Never far from her mind are the rice farmers of Arkansas's Delta. She was one of two Democrats to vote against the farm bill in February 2002, because she said it was not generous enough to cotton and rice farmers; she also worked with Olympia Snowe of Maine to change the softwood lumber agreement with Canada. She fought unsuccessfully against limits on farm subsidies. Three rice farms in Stuttgart and Helena were among the top five recipients of farm subsidies in the country, with $106 million from 1996–2001, the largest concentration of subsidies in the United States. She has supported the $16 million Grand Prairie irrigation project, to replace water that rice farmers get from the nearly depleted alluvial aquifer. In February 2005, she issued a Rural Report Card and said that George W. Bush failed the rural voters who supported him by proposing budget cuts to agriculture programs, rural health care and rural law enforcement.

National Republicans, anticipating a Bush victory in Arkansas in 2004, hoped to target Lincoln. But Governor Mike Huckabee in August 2003 said he wouldn't run against her, and former Congressman Asa Hutchinson made no move to leave his number two post in the Department of Homeland Security. That left the Republican nomination to state Senator Jim Holt, who raised only $106,000. But Lincoln took nothing for granted. She raised $6.4 million, an Arkansas record. He said she was too busy to help John Kerry. "I'm going to focus on my own race. I need to keep the seat and keep it Democratic. If I keep my focus on Democratic values in Arkansas, I think it will help Senator Kerry. Democrats will get out and vote." Holt emphasized his opposition to same-sex marriage, which Arkansans voted 74%–26% to prohibit in November, and Lincoln's vote against the federal Family Marriage Amendment. "It's been his one, only consistent message. I haven't heard him talking about anything else," she complained. "There's many issues we've talked about, but the overwhelmingly large issue is the marriage amendment," Holt said. Lincoln ran 11% ahead of Kerry and won 56%–44%, losing 20 of Arkansas's 75 counties, mostly in the northwest. "If we had just had $500,000 or $1 million more we would have won this race," Holt said afterward. Lincoln, reflecting on Democrats' losses after her own victory, said, "Sometimes you have to condense down your values and message into something that makes sense. I think Democrats will work a lot on that. I know I did. I stood up in my caucus on several occasions when I differed with the party and told them it was important to move down the field and get things done as opposed to just standing in opposition."

Junior Senator

Mark Pryor (D)

Elected 2002, seat up 2008, 1st term; b. Jan. 10, 1963, Fayetteville; home, Little Rock; U. of AR, B.A. 1985, J.D. 1988; Christian; married (Jill).

Elected Office: AR House of Reps., 1990–94; AR Atty. Gen., 1998–02.

Professional Career: Practicing atty., 1988–96.

DC Office: 217 RSOB, 20510, 202-224-2353; Fax: 202-228-0908; Web site: pryor.senate.gov.

State Office: Little Rock, 501-324-6336.

Committees: *Commerce, Science & Transportation*: Aviation; Consumer Affairs, Product Safety & Insurance (RMM); Science & Space; Surface Transportation & Merchant Marine; Technology, Innovation & Competitiveness; Trade, Tourism & Economic Development. *Ethics (Select)*. *Homeland Security & Governmental Affairs*: Investigations (Permanent); Oversight of Govt. Management, the Federal Workforce & the District of Columbia. *Small Business & Entrepreneurship*.

Group Ratings

	ADA	ACLU	AFS	LCV	ITIC	NTU	COC	ACU	NTLC	CHC
2004	85	56	86	67	92	13	71	20	13	16
2003	70	—	100	42	—	19	61	30	—	—

National Journal Ratings

	2003 LIB	—	2003 CONS	2004 LIB	—	2004 CONS
Economic	62%	—	37%	56%	—	43%
Social	55%	—	44%	56%	—	42%
Foreign	60%	—	35%	67%	—	31%

Key Votes of the 108th Congress

1. Ban Drilling in ANWR	Y	5. Energy Bill	Y	9. Ban Same-Sex Marriage	N
2. Approve Bush Tax Cuts	N	6. Support Roe v. Wade	N	10. Ban Bunker-Buster Bomb	Y
3. Medicare/Rx Bill	N	7. Ban Partial-Birth Abortion	Y	11. Fund Iraq War	Y
4. Bar Overtime Pay Regs.	Y	8. Assault Weapons Ban	Y	12. Restrict Missile Defense	Y

Election Results

2002 general	Mark Pryor (D)	434,890	(54%)	($4,414,148)
	Tim Hutchinson (R)	369,069	(46%)	($5,063,923)
2002 primary	Mark Pryor (D)	unopposed		
1996 general	Tim Hutchinson (R)	445,942	(53%)	($1,604,014)
	Winston Bryant (D)	400,241	(47%)	($1,577,838)

Mark Pryor, the junior senator from Arkansas elected in 2002, is one of six children of former senators now serving in the Senate; the others are Christopher Dodd of Connecticut, Robert Bennett of Utah, Evan Bayh of Indiana, Lincoln Chafee of Rhode Island and Lisa Murkowski of Alaska (Jon Kyl of Arizona is the son of a congressman; Edward Kennedy's two brothers and Elizabeth Dole's husband were senators). His grandmother, Susie Newton Pryor, was the first woman in Arkansas to run for office when women got the vote. Mark Pryor grew up in southern Arkansas, the Washington area and Little Rock: His father, David Pryor, was elected to the House in 1966, lost a Senate race in 1972 and was elected governor in 1974 and 1976 and then senator in 1978. Mark Pryor graduated from the University of Arkansas and its law school in the 1980s. He practiced law in Little Rock and was elected to the Arkansas House in 1990 and 1992; in 1998, he was elected state attorney general, at 35 the youngest attorney general in the nation (but not in Arkansas history: Bill Clinton won the office at 30). In 1995 he was diagnosed with clear-cell sarcoma, a rare form of cancer. He underwent tendon transplant surgery in his left heel in 1996; the cancer has not returned.

As attorney general, he tried to curb telemarketing and worked for "Do Not Call" legislation. He claimed to save the state $243 million in attorneys' fees in the tobacco settlement. He pushed for legislation to increase penalties for single-incident nursing home accidents (regulating nursing homes also was a big issue for young Congressman David Pryor in the 1960s) and to strengthen background checks for long-term care employees. He worked to reduce utility rates and to remove unsafe baby products from licensed day care centers. In July 2002, he filed a brief in the state Supreme Court defending Arkansas's school financing system as constitutional and urging the court to overturn a lower court ruling that some said would cost the state $800 million a year; the Supreme Court ruled against him, but not until after he was elected senator.

In July 2001, Pryor announced that he would run against Senator Tim Hutchinson, the first Republican to win an Arkansas Senate seat since 1879, who was elected in 1996 to replace the retiring David Pryor. A Baptist minister, owner of a radio station and founder of a Christian school in Rogers, Hutchinson represented that conservative area in the legislature from 1984 and then for two terms as 3d District congressman. Hutchinson's conservative voting record would ordinarily have made him a favorite for reelection. But in June 1999, Hutchinson filed for divorce from his wife of 29 years, and in August 2000, he married Randi Fredholm, a former member of his House staff. For some senators, this would not have hurt politically. But for a Christian conservative, who criticized Bill Clinton strongly during the impeachment crisis, it was a severe handicap.

Pryor never mentioned Hutchinson's divorce and remarriage and instructed his pollster not to ask questions about them. When asked about Hutchinson's marital problems, he said, "They are what they are. Let the voters decide." But one recurrent theme in his campaign was "Tim Hutchinson has changed"—even though Hutchinson's positions on issues had not changed much, if at all. Pryor campaigned on his support for Second Amendment rights, repeal of the estate tax, increased military spending and, in October, of the Iraq war resolution. In 1998, he had run as a "pro-choice" candidate, but in 2002 he emphasized his belief that abortion was wrong except in cases of rape, incest or saving the life of the mother. But he avoided saying whether or not *Roe v. Wade* should be overturned. He attacked Hutchinson for working for special interests, especially the pharmaceutical companies, and for supporting plans that would risk Social Security benefits; he said he was "way too conservative" for Arkansas. But he carefully avoided identification with the national Democratic party, and made a point of being unavailable and elsewhere when Clinton paid visits to the state.

Pryor's ads were some of the most artful of the 2002 cycle. One showed him, his wife and their two children saying grace before a meal. Then Pryor, holding a Bible, said, "The most important lessons in life are in this book right here." The Pryors belonged to an evangelical church in Little Rock and sent their children to a private Christian school. He turned down an invitation to appear with Hutchinson on *Meet the Press*, explaining that voters wouldn't be able to watch "because they're in church Sunday morning." In another ad, Jill Pryor says laughingly, "I love my husband, but he's cheap." "You know me as Arkansas Attorney General, but I'm also my father's son," said Pryor, in one ad showing him with his father. He explained that not every Democratic idea is good and not every Republican idea is bad. He asked a meeting of municipal leaders in June to pray for George W. Bush. "I think he has done a pretty good job on the war on terrorism. He has a tremendous burden, an inhuman burden."

Against these ads, the Hutchinson ads showing his walking the halls on Capitol Hill or even those showing him playing with his three-year-old grandson were no match. Bush's visits to Arkansas to campaign for Hutchinson did not succeed, as they did in other southern states, in nationalizing the race. During the campaign Randi Hutchinson said, "I just think when a person goes into the voting booth, they look at issues that affect them and not someone else's personal life." But Pryor pulled ahead in polls in mid-year and never really fell behind. On the Sunday before the election, a story broke that the Pryors had employed an illegal immigrant. Pryor campaign aides found the woman that night; they persuaded her to sign an affidavit that she had been asked whether she was a legal immigrant and had said she was, and provided documents proving that. They went over to her house and photocopied a Social Security and regular resident card and provided them to the press. Two days after the election, the woman told Little Rock's *El*

Latino that she had signed the affidavit under pressure and denied that she had provided documents to the Pryors when she was hired. The story seems to have had little effect, and the generally anti-Democratic *Arkansas Democrat-Gazette* treated it lightly. In any case, Pryor won 54%–46%, a solid victory in a year when Democrats lost their majority in the Senate. A survey by pollster John Zogby showed that 12% said Hutchinson's divorce affected their vote—enough by itself to explain his drop from 53% in 1996 to 46% in 2002. Hutchinson's losses were particularly great in his home area. In 1996, he had won 65%–35% in the current 3d Congressional District; in 2002, he carried the 3d District by only 56%–44%.

Pryor entered the Senate ranked 100th in seniority. He got a seat on the Governmental Affairs Committee, on which his father had served. With his senior colleague Blanche Lincoln, he was one of five Democrats voting to uphold George W. Bush's repeal of the Clinton New Source Review EPA regulations. But he voted against oil drilling in the Arctic National Wildlife Refuge. In March 2003 he voted for the partial-birth abortion ban and supported an amendment, which failed, granting an exception if the mother's physical health is at risk. He opposed an amendment by Dianne Feinstein that would allow an exception for a mother's mental health. He also voted against a resolution supporting *Roe v. Wade*. He supported the filibuster of the judicial nomination of Miguel Estrada and others, but voted for Timothy Tymkovich for the 10th Circuit and, with Lincoln, supported Arkansan Leon Holmes for the 8th Circuit. At the all-night judicial filibuster in November 2003 he read from Robert Caro's *Master of the Senate* at 3 a.m. He voted against the Federal Marriage Amendment in July 2004, explaining that it's an issue that should be left to the states, but supported the amendment on the ballot in November 2004 banning same-sex marriage in Arkansas.

In 2003 Pryor voted against the omnibus appropriations bill which contained $300 million for Arkansas projects and against the $350 billion Bush tax cut. "I just can't support these budgets that send our deficits and national debt soaring out of control." He opposed the Bush Medicare/prescription drug bill. He attended hearings diligently on the Armed Services Committee and expressed concern that the National Guard was being overworked. He had success sponsoring a bill to allow combat pay to be considered as taxable income in calculating the earned income tax and child tax credits; this had the effect of lowering soldiers' taxes. He took care to get Charles Grassley and Max Baucus of the Finance Committee as co-sponsors; the bill passed. He also passed in the Senate a bill to help families get thorough information quickly about family members wounded in combat. And he used the Armed Services seat to push a nanotechnology initiative, with emphasis on Arkansas. He lost his seat after Democrats lost seats on the committee after the 2004 election: he called it "an involuntary departure."

Pryor is one of four Democratic senators from the South and seems acutely aware of the party's weakness in his region. On the issue of guns, he told the Democratic Leadership Conference, "Silence is an admission of guilt. If you don't talk about what your position is on guns, guess what? You're for gun control." He endorsed John Kerry in June 2004, months after he clinched the Democratic nomination, and suggested he go hunting in Arkansas. He admitted that the two "have a little different approach on some issues. But I'm comfortable with him as a person and a leader." Pryor comes up for reelection in 2008.

FIRST DISTRICT

Rep. Marion Berry (D)

Elected 1996, 5th term; b. Aug. 27, 1942, Bayou Meto; home, Gillett; U. of AR, B.S. 1965; Methodist; married (Carolyn).

Professional Career: Pharmacist, 1965–67; farmer, 1968–present; AR Soil & Water Conservation Comm., 1986–94, Chmn. 1992; Special Asst. to the Pres., Domestic Policy Cncl., White House, 1993–96.

DC Office: 2305 RHOB, 20515, 202-225-4076; Fax: 202-225-5602; Web site: www.house.gov/berry.

District Offices: Cabot, 501-843-3043; Jonesboro, 870-972-4600; Mountain Home, 870-425-3510.

Committees: *Appropriations* (29th of 29 D): Energy & Water Development & Related Agencies; Homeland Security.

Group Ratings

	ADA	ACLU	AFS	LCV	ITIC	NTU	COC	ACU	NTLC	CHC
2004	60	37	100	45	22	11	45	36	9	53
2003	85	—	100	40	—	28	47	48	—	—

National Journal Ratings

	2003 LIB	—	2003 CONS		2004 LIB	—	2004 CONS
Economic	59%	—	41%		57%	—	42%
Social	55%	—	45%		52%	—	48%
Foreign	73%	—	25%		68%	—	30%

Key Votes of the 108th Congress

1. Drilling in ANWR	Y	5. DC School Vouchers	N	9. Ban Same-Sex Marriage	Y
2. Approve Bush Tax Cuts	N	6. Ban Human Cloning	Y	10. Fund Iraq War	N
3. Medicare/Rx Bill	N	7. Restrict Gun Liability	Y	11. Bar Cuba Embargo Funds	Y
4. Bar Overtime Pay Regs.	Y	8. Ban Partial-Birth Abortion	Y	12. Intelligence Reorg.	Y

Election Results

2004 general	Marion Berry (D)	162,388	(67%)	($947,839)
	Vernon Humphrey (R)	81,556	(33%)	($23,836)
2004 primary	Marion Berry (D)	unopposed		
2002 general	Marion Berry (D)	129,701	(67%)	($1,315,408)
	Tommy Robinson (R)	64,357	(33%)	($142,244)

Prior Winning Percentages: 2000 (60%); 1998 (100%); 1996 (53%)

The People		Race/Ethnic Origin	Ancestry	
Area size:	17,521 sq. mi.	80.2% White	USA: 15.3%	Irish: 7.5%
Urban population:	44.5%	16.6% Black	German: 6.8%	
Rural population:	55.5%	0.3% Asian	**2004 Presidential Vote**	
Pop. 2000:	668,360	0.4% Native Am.	Bush (R) 127,179	(52%)
Median income:	$28,940	0.0% Hawaiian	Kerry (D) 115,994	(47%)
Poverty status:	18.5%	0.9% Two+ races	Other 3,020	(1%)
Military veterans:	13.8%	0.0% Other	**2000 Presidential Vote**	
		1.6% Hispanic Origin	Gore (D) 109,160	(50%)
			Bush (R) 105,547	(48%)
			Other 5,482	(2%)
			Cook Partisan Voting Index: D + 1	

Occupation	Blue collar: 35.0%	White collar: 48.8%	Gray collar: 16.2%

The Mississippi Delta, the flat, mushy, river-crossed lowland on both sides of the great river, was some of the country's first industrial farmland. This land was uncultivated in most of the 19th Century, when plows were still pulled by mules and muddy flatlands were impassable. Then, about a century ago, big landowners used machines to drain the marshlands and persuaded poor blacks to move here to tend fields of cotton, rice, and later, soybeans. The results were bountiful agriculture and impoverished people. Around 1940, the Delta began to change slowly: the first minimum wage and war industry jobs up North drew young people out of the Delta and the mechanical cotton picker forced many off the farms. But this land—stretching flat as far as the eye can see, past rows of telephone poles and ribbons of asphalt that shimmer in the heat—remains poor by national standards and the people are undereducated and underemployed. Local rice farmers are among the largest recipients of federal farm subsidies: three farms in Phillips and Arkansas Counties that were among the top five subsidy farms in the country received $105 million from 1996–2001. The local rice fields also attract enough ducks to make Arkansas the nation's most productive for mallard hunters. But there are signs of change in the region. Several big auto parts plants have been built in Marion, across the Mississippi River from Memphis, and Arkansas is hoping that Toyota will choose the site for its seventh North American plant.

The 1st Congressional District of Arkansas includes most of the state's Delta lands and stretches west to the cool green Ozarks. The largest city in the district is Jonesboro, whose cheap labor and flat land has made it an industrial hub for food-processing companies like Nestle and Frito-Lay. The Delta with its large black population is the most Democratic part of the Arkansas; some of the hill counties are ancestrally Republican, and there is a Republican trend in Jonesboro and in Lonoke County, which is part of the Little Rock metro area. The result is that the 1st District is closely divided in national politics: it voted 50%–48% for Al Gore in 2000 but 52%–47% for George W. Bush in 2004.

The congressman from the 1st District is Marion Berry, a Democrat who was first elected in 1996. He is the type of folksy small-town southern Democrat that was prominent in Congress when Democrats were in control: "a pharmacist and a farmer, the owner of a loud laugh," profiled the *Arkansas Democrat-Gazette*. Berry grew up in Bayou Meto in Arkansas County in the Delta. When his rice-farming father suggested that he study something else, he earned a pharmacy degree in Little Rock, where he made some political connections, and then ran a pharmacy for two years. He also has been a family farmer since 1968, with a net worth of more than $1 million; he and his family have received more than $100,000 annually in federal farm subsides since 1996. As governor, Bill Clinton, when advocating changes in the state's water policy, appointed him to the Arkansas Soil & Water Conservation Commission in 1986; in 1993, as president, Clinton appointed him White House liaison to the Agriculture Department. Berry returned to Arkansas in 1996, after Congresswoman—now, Senator—Blanche Lincoln announced she would not run for re-election because she was pregnant with twins. Berry had tough opposition for the seat. Against Tom Donaldson, a 28-year-old deputy prosecutor in Crittenden County (Marion, West Memphis) who spent little money but ran rural radio ads criticizing Berry for accepting farm subsidies, Berry won the primary runoff by only 52%–48%. In the general, Berry faced Republican Warren Dupwe, a former Jonesboro city attorney. They sparred over Medicare; both candidates opposed abortion rights and gun control and favored a balanced budget. Berry outspent Dupwe nearly 2–1 and, in a district that has never elected a Republican, won 53%–44%.

Berry's cooperation with Democratic leaders earned him a slot on the Appropriations Committee. His voting record is moderate (especially on cultural issues) to liberal; a Blue Dog Democrat, he supported the balanced budget amendment and said he wanted to pay off the national debt and save Social Security and Medicare. He voted against Republican tax cuts because they are "just borrowing money from our children and grandchildren." With his background, Berry was a natural as co-founder of Democrats' Prescription Drug Task Force and he has pursued his interest in health care. He complained that Republicans put in loopholes to his proposal to allow the re-importation of prescription drugs from other nations. He eagerly stepped forward to criticize George W. Bush's Medicare/prescription drug bill. In October 2003, he was one of three House Democrats appointed to the House-Senate conference committee, all of whom complained of being shut out of the negotiations in which they said that they could be helpful. The enacted bill was "the sorriest piece of legislation" that Congress ever enacted, Berry said. "It is nothing but an expedited way to make it legal to cheat and steal from old people." He visited Cuba with Lincoln to promote an end to the trade embargo, so that Arkansas farmers could sell rice and feed products there. He actively supported the nuclear waste depository in Yucca Mountain in Nevada, and argued that additional nuclear waste from two local Entergy Corp. reactors could be dumped into the Arkansas River.

Berry has declined opportunities to run statewide, citing health and family responsibilities. He has been reelected easily: In 2004 he won 67%–33%, carrying all 26 counties. After the election, he criticized the Democrats' presidential nominating process for favoring Northeast liberals; he also said presidential nominee John Kerry "would have made a good president, but was a lousy candidate."

SECOND DISTRICT

Rep. Vic Snyder (D)

Elected 1996, 5th term; b. Sept. 27, 1947, Medford, OR; home, Little Rock; Willamette U., B.A. 1975, U. of OR, M.D. 1979, U. of AR, J.D. 1988; Methodist; married (Betsy Singleton).

Military Career: Marine Corps, 1967–69 (Vietnam).

Elected Office: AR Senate, 1990–96.

Professional Career: Practicing physician, 1982–present.

DC Office: 1330 LHOB, 20515, 202-225-2506; Fax: 202-225-5903; Web site: www.house.gov/snyder.

District Office: Little Rock, 501-324-5941.

Committees: *Armed Services* (9th of 28 D): Military Personnel (RMM); Readiness. *Veterans' Affairs* (5th of 12 D): Health.

Group Ratings

	ADA	ACLU	AFS	LCV	ITIC	NTU	COC	ACU	NTLC	CHC
2004	95	75	75	91	90	15	57	20	6	8
2003	85	—	100	95	—	25	52	17	—	—

National Journal Ratings

	2003 LIB	—	2003 CONS		2004 LIB	—	2004 CONS
Economic	64%	—	36%		65%	—	34%
Social	75%	—	25%		68%	—	31%
Foreign	56%	—	44%		64%	—	35%

Key Votes of the 108th Congress

1. Drilling in ANWR	N	5. DC School Vouchers	N	9. Ban Same-Sex Marriage	N
2. Approve Bush Tax Cuts	N	6. Ban Human Cloning	*	10. Fund Iraq War	Y
3. Medicare/Rx Bill	N	7. Restrict Gun Liability	N	11. Bar Cuba Embargo Funds	Y
4. Bar Overtime Pay Regs.	Y	8. Ban Partial-Birth Abortion	N	12. Intelligence Reorg.	Y

Election Results

2004 general	Vic Snyder (D)	160,834	(58%)	($880,496)
	Marvin Parks (R)	115,655	(42%)	($574,023)
2004 primary	Vic Snyder (D)	unopposed		
2002 general	Vic Snyder (D)	142,752	(93%)	($440,566)
	Ed Garner (Write-in)	10,874	(7%)	

Prior Winning Percentages: 2000 (58%); 1998 (58%); 1996 (52%)

The People		Race/Ethnic Origin	Ancestry	
Area size:	6,045 sq. mi.	75.6% White	USA: 11.7%	German: 8.4%
Urban population:	66.2%	19.4% Black	Irish: 7.9%	
Rural population:	33.8%	0.9% Asian	**2004 Presidential Vote**	
Pop. 2000:	666,058	0.4% Native Am.	Bush (R) 145,392	(51%)
Median income:	$37,221	0.0% Hawaiian	Kerry (D) 134,478	(48%)
Poverty status:	12.7%	1.1% Two+ races	Other 2,785	(1%)
Military veterans:	14.5%	0.1% Other	**2000 Presidential Vote**	
		2.4% Hispanic Origin	Bush (R) 116,075	(49%)
			Gore (D) 112,720	(48%)
			Other 6,817	(3%)
			Cook Partisan Voting Index: R + 0	

Occupation	Blue collar: 25.0%	White collar: 60.5%	Gray collar: 14.5%

Little Rock has been the capital, largest city and central focus of Arkansas for more than a century, and now is the home of the nation's largest presidential library. It is one of those capitals located at its state's geographical center and, in a state that has no other metropolis, it stands out. For a long moment, Little Rock became internationally famous. That was in September 1957, when Governor Orval Faubus, eager for a third term, sent in the National Guard to block a desegregation order at Central High School. President Dwight D. Eisenhower sent in U.S. troops and federalized the National Guard to enforce the order, and Little Rock became a synonym for bigotry around the world. Forty years later, the Little Rock Nine who had integrated the high school returned for an anniversary commemoration with President Bill Clinton. "It was Little Rock that made racial equality a driving obsession in my life," he said, and added that American life still was in too many ways segregated. Also speaking was Republican Governor Mike Huckabee, who said, "Today we come to say once and for all that what happened here 40 years ago was simply wrong." Most impressive were the Little Rock Nine themselves and what these graying adults had achieved: Their occupations included writer, managing director of an investment bank, real estate broker, chairman of a university psychology department, magazine publisher, financial specialist for the Department of Defense, teacher, public relations specialist and journalist.

Little Rock is also the political center of Arkansas. It may not be upscale by national standards, but it is in Arkansas. Little Rock sets the tone of the public life of its state as do only a few other state capitals—Boston, Providence, Atlanta, Denver, Honolulu. It is home to the *Arkansas Democrat-Gazette*, the feisty, conservative paper whose editor Paul Greenberg christened Clinton "Slick Willie." It is home to the state government, to the Peabody Little Rock hotel and the long-defunct Madison Guaranty Savings & Loan. On the east bank of the Arkansas River is the Clinton Presidential Center and Park, designed to promote local economic revitalization and with architecture evocative of a "bridge to the 21st century." It was opened in November 2004 during a rainy outdoor ceremony attended by the current and three former presidents.

The 2d Congressional District of Arkansas includes Little Rock, with its large black and affluent white neighborhoods, and North Little Rock, a kind of industrial suburb across the Arkansas River known informally for years as Dog Town. It also includes surrounding Saline and Faulkner Counties that have grown rapidly as people move farther out on the freeways, and a couple of hill counties. In the 1990s, the Little Rock area was trending Republican, and fast-growing Saline County to the southwest was heavily Republican. In 2004, with turnout up sharply, George W. Bush got 63% of the vote in Saline County and 59% in Faulkner, but John Kerry won 55% in Little Rock's Pulaski County. Overall, the district gave Bush a 51%–48% margin—the same as in the national popular vote.

The congressman from the 2d District is Vic Snyder, a Democrat first elected in 1996. He has held the seat longer than any member since legendary Ways and Means chairman Wilbur Mills, who served 38 years and retired in 1976. Snyder is an unusual politician, "an inveterately private man in a public profession, quite content to be all alone," wrote the *Arkansas Democrat-Gazette*. He grew up fatherless in Medford, Oregon, dropped out of Willamette University, and at

20 signed up in the Marine Corps and served in Vietnam. Then he returned to Oregon for college and medical school, became a practicing physician, and went on medical missions in Thailand, Honduras, Sierra Leone and Sudan. He got a law degree, but never practiced law. In 1990, he was elected to the state Senate and made news when he called for repeal of Arkansas's anti-sodomy law and when he refused to accept a pension.

When the incumbent retired in 1996, Snyder, consulting no one, decided to run for Congress. He campaigned as a reformer, promising not to accept a congressional pension until the establishment of an equitable system for federal employees. His main Democratic opponents had more political backgrounds, but in a 51%–49% upset, Snyder won the June runoff over Pulaski County prosecutor Mark Stodola, who was a strong Clinton supporter. Against Republican lawyer Bud Cummins, Snyder continued to sound reform themes while outspending him. Snyder won narrowly, 52%–48%.

Snyder's voting record is close to the center of the House Democrats, which is liberal for this district and the most liberal in the Arkansas delegation. He voted for needle exchanges, against the partial-birth abortion ban, and was the only House member from Arkansas to favor a bill permitting victims of gun violence to sue the manufacturer and seller of the firearm. In 2004 he opposed a state constitutional amendment to ban same-sex marriage; the ballot measure passed 75%–25%. But Snyder has bragged of supporting more moderate measures—the balanced budget, tax cuts, a strong education system—and has stressed his military record and service on the Armed Services Committee. He helped to organize the bipartisan Cuba working group to push the House to end the trade embargo of Cuba and the ban on travel there; he was the only Democrat from Arkansas to vote for trade promotion authority in 2001. He criticized the Bush administration for failure to provide increased security for embassies overseas and was the only Arkansas member to vote against authorizing Bush to use military force against Iraq. After the war began, he visited Iraq and called for more support of U.S. troops, but he criticized the Pentagon for failing to inform Congress of prison abuses. In March 2004, he sponsored legislation establishing separate medals for service in Afghanistan and Iraq; it was later signed into law by George W. Bush. Snyder has been active on internal House issues: He unsuccessfully sought changes in Democratic rules to spread committee assignments more equitably among members. He challenged as a possible violation of the House's anti-bribery rule the practice of interest groups that notify members that they will include an upcoming vote in their legislative scorecard. And he spoke out against members—mostly Democrats—who wanted to give governors the power to appoint new House members in the event of a catastrophic attack on the Capitol. He also wants to amend the Constitution to permit foreign-born citizens to serve as President.

Since his initial tight election, he has been reelected with at least 58% of the vote. In 2004, Republican challenger Marvin Parks aligned himself with George W. Bush and criticized Snyder for being out of touch with local views, especially on issues such as abortion and gay marriage. Although he raised more than $500,000, Parks had little national Republican support. Parks was criticized for taking a $4,000 monthly salary from his campaign, and for driving three miles out of his way each day he served in the legislature to collect an additional $16,400 in state reimbursement. Parks carried Saline and Faulkner Counties, but Snyder won 58%–42%. In endorsing Snyder, the *Democrat-Gazette* wrote, "While we may abhor some of his political stances, there is no doubting the sincerity with which he takes them. Or his patriotism . . . We're endorsing an honorable opponent today, not his politics."

THIRD DISTRICT

Rep. John Boozman (R)

Elected Nov. 2001, 2d full term; b. Dec. 10, 1950, Shreveport, LA; home, Rogers; U. of AR, 1969–72, Southern Col. of Optometry, O.D. 1977; Baptist; married (Cathy).

Elected Office: Rogers School Bd., 1994–2001.

Professional Career: Optometrist, 1977–2001.

DC Office: 1519 LHOB, 20515, 202-225-4301; Fax: 202-225-5713; Web site: www.boozman.house.gov.

District Offices: Fayetteville, 479-442-5258; Ft. Smith, 479-782-7787; Harrison, 870-741-6900.

Committees: *International Relations* (22d of 27 R): Africa, Global Human Rights & International Operations; Middle East & Central Asia. *Transportation & Infrastructure* (26th of 41 R): Aviation; Highways, Transit & Pipelines; Water Resources & Environment. *Veterans' Affairs* (10th of 16 R): Economic Opportunity (Chmn.); Oversight & Investigations.

Group Ratings

	ADA	ACLU	AFS	LCV	ITIC	NTU	COC	ACU	NTLC	CHC
2004	10	5	0	0	90	61	100	96	81	100
2003	10	—	0	5	—	60	97	88	—	—

National Journal Ratings

	2003 LIB	—	2003 CONS		2004 LIB	—	2004 CONS
Economic	9%	—	84%		17%	—	80%
Social	17%	—	79%		0%	—	91%
Foreign	23%	—	71%		34%	—	63%

Key Votes of the 108th Congress

1. Drilling in ANWR	Y	5. DC School Vouchers	Y	9. Ban Same-Sex Marriage	Y
2. Approve Bush Tax Cuts	Y	6. Ban Human Cloning	Y	10. Fund Iraq War	Y
3. Medicare/Rx Bill	Y	7. Restrict Gun Liability	Y	11. Bar Cuba Embargo Funds	Y
4. Bar Overtime Pay Regs.	N	8. Ban Partial-Birth Abortion	Y	12. Intelligence Reorg.	Y

Election Results

2004 general	John Boozman (R)	160,629	(59%)	($543,281)
	Janice Judy (D)	103,158	(38%)	($353,822)
	Other	7,016	(3%)	
2004 primary	John Boozman (R)	unopposed		
2002 general	John Boozman (R)	141,478	(99%)	($651,062)

Prior Winning Percentages: 2001 (56%)

The People		Race/Ethnic Origin	Ancestry	
Area size:	8,661 sq. mi.	87.3% White	USA: 11.8%	German: 10.0%
Urban population:	54.4%	2.0% Black	Irish: 8.8%	
Rural population:	45.6%	1.4% Asian	**2004 Presidential Vote**	
Pop. 2000:	672,756	1.2% Native Am.	Bush (R) 171,853	(62%)
Median income:	$33,915	0.2% Hawaiian	Kerry (D) 100,656	(36%)
Poverty status:	13.7%	1.6% Two+ races	Other 3,449	(1%)
Military veterans:	14.3%	0.1% Other	**2000 Presidential Vote**	
		6.3% Hispanic Origin	Bush (R) 138,977	(60%)
			Gore (D) 86,739	(37%)
			Other 7,691	(3%)
			Cook Partisan Voting Index: R +11	

Occupation	Blue collar: 32.0%	White collar: 53.0%	Gray collar: 14.9%

The northwest corner of Arkansas has become one of America's boom areas—the nation's number one growth area in 2003, according to the Milken Institute—with major corporate headquarters and dozens of small factories, tourist attractions and retirement developments in the Ozarks, some of America's richest families and growing numbers of hard-working Hispanic immigrants—about 20% of the population of Springdale and Rogers in 2000. It is one of the fastest-growing populations in the nation and home to the handsome University of Arkansas in Fayetteville and the mountain-bound resort town of Eureka Springs. All this would have seemed unlikely during most of the 20th century, when these rounded green mountains and pleasant wide valleys, farmhouses and small towns seemed left behind. But the friendly atmosphere and strong religious faith of these communities have proved to be assets, not liabilities, conducive to economic creativity and personal serenity. There have also been touches of genius. Sam Walton, who opened his first Wal-Mart on the town square of Bentonville (it's now a small museum), had the inspiration to build a retail chain in tradition-minded small towns and rural areas using sophisticated computerized management; it made him the richest man in America, though he still drove a pickup truck and kept the corporate headquarters in a deliberately unsnazzy building in Bentonville. Don Tyson took his family chicken business and made Tyson Foods, in its sparkling headquarters outside Springdale, the world's leading chicken producer and processor. Other firms have flocked in, especially to do business with Wal-Mart, and the area is attracting a diverse group of new residents, from upscale executives buying lavish homes in gated communities to 20,000 Hispanics and 6,000 Marshall Islanders seeking work in booming local industries.

The 3d Congressional District covers Northwest Arkansas, including Bentonville, Fayetteville and Springdale, plus Fort Smith on the Oklahoma line. It extends as far east as Marion County, home to Ranger Boats, the renowned manufacturer of tournament-quality fishing boats. Its population rose 30% in the 1990s and another 7% from 2000 to 2003—more than Arkansas's other three districts. Politically, this area has been the most Republican part of Arkansas since the Civil War, for there were few slaves here and much suspicion of planters. The area became more Republican in the 1950s, and a Republican congressman, John Paul Hammerschmidt, was elected here in 1966. He was strong enough even in Democratic 1974 to beat Bill Clinton, then 28, in his first election, though Clinton did get an impressive 48% of the vote. Lately this area has become even more Republican, as Christian conservatives have entered politics and new migrants and millionaires have voted heavily Republican. After voting narrowly for Clinton in 1992 and narrowly against him in 1996, the 3d twice voted strongly for George W. Bush.

The congressman from the 3d District is John Boozman (it's pronounced like Bozeman, Montana), a Republican who won a special election in November 2001. He replaced Asa Hutchinson, who had resigned in August to head the Drug Enforcement Administration. A graduate of the University of Arkansas, where he was an offensive guard for the football team, Boozman became an optometrist in Rogers, part of rapidly growing Benton County. He served two terms on the local school board, and he worked for his brother Fay's unsuccessful campaign for the U.S. Senate in 1998.

To win the House seat, Boozman prevailed in three close contests in two months, even though he was outspent in each. In the wide-open primary, Boozman had the endorsement of Governor Mike Huckabee and was the only Republican to support George W. Bush's decision to permit limited federal funding of stem-cell research. His chief opponent initially, former state Representative Jim Hendren, was damaged by revelations that he had a lengthy extramarital affair; Boozman ended up in a runoff against state Senator Gunner DeLay, who raised little funds and had little support from local politicians (but is a cousin of then-House Majority Whip Tom DeLay, who stayed neutral). In the three-week runoff, neither candidate spent heavily and turnout remained low. With a stronger grass-roots organization, Boozman won 57%–43%. The winner of the Democratic runoff was state Representative Mike Hathorn, a 28-year-old lawyer who, local Democrats hoped, could prevail with his Clinton-like personality. But House Democrats did little to help his campaign and only in the closing days of the campaign ran TV and radio ads that criticized Boozman's support for Social Security "privatization" and, despite his endorsement by the NRA, his allegedly weak support of the right to bear arms. Boozman ran ads emphasizing his "guarantee" of Social Security benefits. He won 56%–42%, with help from a sophisticated Republican voter-turnout operation.

Arriving in Washington for the first time in his life, Boozman was appointed to the Republican task force that prepared a bill for prescription drugs for seniors. With Roy Blunt of Missouri, he created a water quality committee to get money from the Environmental Protection Agency for the White and Elk Rivers, both vital to local tourism and economic development. He showed his independence of the White House by voting to remove the embargo on trade with Cuba and to import prescription drugs from Canada; he opposed Bush's immigration proposal as amnesty for illegal aliens. Boozman also sponsored bills to abolish the tax code and to display the Ten Commandments in the House and Senate chambers. A devout evangelical Christian, he wants to weaken restrictions on churches' political activities. On the Transportation Committee, he filed a proposal to give more flexibility to federal regulations setting maximum hours of service for truckers. He is an enthusiastic member of the I-49 caucus, who want to connect the existing I-540 from Fort Smith to Bentonville with interstates running north to Kansas City and south to Texarkana and New Orleans.

In the 2004 campaign, he was opposed by surprisingly well-funded Democratic state Representative Janice Judy, the owner of a pizza restaurant in Fayetteville, who sought to energize Democratic base voters. Boozman criticized her opposition to a constitutional amendment to ban same-sex marriage and civil unions in Arkansas. He won comfortably, 59%–38%, running 3% behind George W. Bush. Unique in the new South, he is the only Republican in his state delegation.

FOURTH DISTRICT

Rep. Mike Ross (D)

Elected 2000, 3d term; b. Aug. 2, 1961, Texarkana; home, Prescott; U. of AR, B.A. 1987; Methodist; married (Holly).

Elected Office: Nevada County Quorum Court, 1983–85; AR Senate, 1990–2000.

Professional Career: Chief of Staff, AR Lt. Gov. Winston Bryant, 1984–89; Owner, Holly's Health Mart, 1993–present.

DC Office: 314 CHOB, 20515, 202-225-3772; Fax: 202-225-1314; Web site: www.house.gov/ross.

District Offices: El Dorado, 870-881-0681; Hot Springs, 501-520-5892; Pine Bluff, 870-536-3376; Prescott, 870-887-6787.

Committees: *Energy & Commerce* (26th of 26 D): Commerce, Trade & Consumer Protection; Energy & Air Quality.

Group Ratings

	ADA	ACLU	AFS	LCV	ITIC	NTU	COC	ACU	NTLC	CHC
2004	65	40	88	36	60	13	62	44	9	53
2003	80	—	100	45	—	25	50	40	—	—

National Journal Ratings

	2003 LIB	—	2003 CONS	2004 LIB	—	2004 CONS
Economic	57%	—	42%	56%	—	44%
Social	57%	—	43%	54%	—	45%
Foreign	70%	—	27%	57%	—	42%

Key Votes of the 108th Congress

1. Drilling in ANWR	Y	5. DC School Vouchers	N	9. Ban Same-Sex Marriage	Y
2. Approve Bush Tax Cuts	N	6. Ban Human Cloning	Y	10. Fund Iraq War	Y
3. Medicare/Rx Bill	N	7. Restrict Gun Liability	Y	11. Bar Cuba Embargo Funds	Y
4. Bar Overtime Pay Regs.	Y	8. Ban Partial-Birth Abortion	Y	12. Intelligence Reorg.	Y

Election Results

2004 general	Mike Ross (D) .... unopposed		($756,922)
2004 primary	Mike Ross (D) .... unopposed		
2002 general	Mike Ross (D) 119,633	(61%)	($2,050,221)
	Jay Dickey (R) 77,904	(39%)	($2,029,545)

Prior Winning Percentages: 2000 (51%)

The People		Race/Ethnic Origin	Ancestry	
Area size:	20,951 sq. mi.	71.0% White	USA: 14.0%	Irish: 7.3%
Urban population:	44.7%	24.4% Black	English: 5.7%	
Rural population:	55.3%	0.4% Asian	**2004 Presidential Vote**	
Pop. 2000:	666,226	0.5% Native Am.	Bush (R) 128,474	(51%)
Median income:	$29,675	0.0% Hawaiian	Kerry (D) 118,825	(48%)
Poverty status:	18.5%	0.9% Two+ races	Other 2,840	(1%)
Military veterans:	13.9%	0.0% Other	**2000 Presidential Vote**	
		2.7% Hispanic Origin	Gore (D) 114,149	(49%)
			Bush (R) 112,341	(48%)
			Other 6,083	(3%)
			Cook Partisan Voting Index: D + 0	

Occupation	Blue collar: 34.9%	White collar: 47.8%	Gray collar: 17.2%

West from the Delta flatlands along the Mississippi River, where the water-soaked fields produce America's largest rice crop, across small cities with antique pasts like Pine Bluff and El Dorado, southern Arkansas runs west to the Ouachita Mountains and the border town of Texarkana, where the main street divides two states and Texan Ross Perot grew up five blocks west of Arkansas. This is the northwestern corner of the Deep South. It includes the state's largest black population, a reminder that parts of southern Arkansas were once plantation country; there is also oil production, a reminder that this is the beginning of the Southwest. It includes the Crater of Diamonds State Park, the source of the 4.24 carat Kahn canary diamond which Hillary Rodham Clinton wore to her husband's second inauguration as president. The broiler chicken industry looms large in these parts, and the accent is clearly Arkansan: El Dorado, Nevada and Lafayette are all pronounced with long As and accents on the penultimate syllable, and Ouachita is, with a bow to the original French rendition of the Indian name, *waSHEEta*. The district also includes the little railroad-crossing, county seat town of Hope, where President Bill Clinton and his first White House Chief of Staff Mack McLarty were classmates at Miss Mary's kindergarten, and where Governor Mike Huckabee grew up a decade later; and Hot Springs, the spa resort and gambling haven where Clinton's stepfather sold Buicks, his mother bet on the horses, and he excelled in high school as he began his climb from southern Arkansas obscurity to world prominence.

The 4th Congressional District occupies almost all of the southern geographical half of Arkansas, from the Mississippi River to the Ouachita Mountains, the Delta to Texarkana. It is historically a Democratic district, and one that for most of the 20th century elected young men to the House and kept them there for years, to cut deals with the Democratic leadership and bring home the bacon. During the 1990s, it had a very different congressional politics: Bipartisan, with rancorous debates on national issues followed by narrow election victories. But this may be one part of the South returning to its heritage.

The congressman from the 4th District is Mike Ross, a Democrat who in 2000 defeated four-term Republican Jay Dickey, the only House Republican outside California who was defeated that year. A fifth-generation Arkansan, Ross was born in Texarkana. He graduated from Hope High School and from the University of Arkansas at Little Rock. He got his start in local politics in 1982 as a travel aide for Bill Clinton's successful bid to recover from his 1980 loss and recapture the governorship. Then, while in college, he served on the staff of Lieutenant Governor Winston Bryant and was executive director of the Arkansas Youth Suicide Prevention Commission. Ross also sold insurance and worked as a sales manager for a pharmaceutical company. He owns Holly's Health Mart in rural Prescott, where he lives with his wife Holly, who is the store's pharmacist. He was elected to the state Senate in 1990 and served for a decade until term limits forced him out; then he ran for Congress. This was perhaps the only district in the nation where impeachment played a pivotal role in 2000. Dickey, representing Clinton's boyhood homes, had voted for impeachment, and Clinton vowed to get back at him. Although Dickey often was a thorn in the Republican leadership's side, Ross tied him to the Republican leadership and argued that "the real Jay Dickey" voted to cut Medicare and Social Security to fund tax cuts for the rich. Dickey responded that Ross was getting his script from "his liberal masters in Washington." Clinton had an impact: He helped raise $300,000 for Ross at fundraisers, orchestrated endorsements from administration officials with Arkansas roots, and campaigned for Ross in Pine Bluff on the Sunday before the election. There were plenty of independent expenditures as well, by pharmaceutical groups against Ross and by labor unions against Dickey. Ross won, 51%–49%.

In the House, Ross joined the Blue Dogs and he became a vocal proponent of prescription drug legislation, often citing his experiences as a small-town pharmacist. On the Financial Services Committee, he got approval in 2002 of his proposal to remove Arkansas's constitutional limit on interest rates, which local bankers and consumer groups agreed had made financing difficult. His action won wide support from political leaders in Arkansas, which is the only remaining state to mandate such terms. But national banking interests voiced concerns about separate aspects of his measure, and it died when Congress adjourned. Although Ross voted in October 2002 for the use of force in Iraq, he later questioned whether the U.S. should finance reconstruction after the ouster of Saddam Hussein. "We have a duty and an obligation to finish the job we started," he wrote in November 2003, "but other countries . . . should share in providing troops and the cost of post-war Iraq." Back home, Ross feuded with Huckabee. He accused the governor of running the Delta Regional Authority as a "slush fund", but refrained from criticizing specific local projects. Ross is an enthusiastic member of the I-49 caucus; construction is beginning south of Texarkana, to connect it with New Orleans, and Ross is seeking funding for building in north across the Ouachita Mountains to Fort Smith. Ross cultivates his "country boy" image, including regular skeet shooting from the back of his pick-up truck.

Dickey decided to run again in 2002 and Ross seemed to face a serious challenge. Both candidates again raised substantial sums, but the Republican's campaign stumbled from the start. Dickey refused, as he had in the past, to accept funds from political action committees, but the Republicans' campaign committee got him to back down. Dickey constantly reminded voters that he had delivered federal money to them from his Appropriations Committee seat and carried a pledge from Speaker Dennis Hastert that he would get his seat back. Ross criticized Republican leaders for reversing after the 2000 election the appropriators' tentative decision to send $4 million to the district. Hastert defended the action, in an interview with the *Arkansas Democrat-Gazette*: "If we had a Republican in there, we could deliver the money. Jay is the one who worked for it. Ross wasn't even on the committee." Dickey complained to his friend Warren Stephens about news coverage in the publisher's *Pine Bluff Commercial.* The publisher's sympathetic response led the editor to resign in a well-publicized protest. Ross won by a convincing 61%–39% margin.

That seems to have made the 4th a safe Democratic district again, after more than a decade of fierce partisan contests. Ross had no Republican opposition in 2004, and Dickey became a Washington lobbyist. After the election, Ross won a seat on the Energy and Commerce Committee. He had encouraged speculation that he might run for governor in 2006, when Huckabee will be ineligible to run, but in January 2005 Ross said he would stay in Congress.

★ CALIFORNIA ★

KAL-ee-for-nee-ah, as its current governor pronounces the name, more faithful to the original Spanish than any of his predecessors except perhaps Romualdo Pacheco, who served 10 months in 1875, is America's largest state, a nation-state really, with an economy larger than all but five nations. It is the site of the world's most advanced cutting-edge technology, yet it is a place with plenty of Third World neighborhoods and it greeted the 21st century with Third World-like rolling blackouts of electricity. Its growth has been awesome: The Census Bureau estimated that there were 35.9 million Californians in 2004, far ahead of second-place Texas's 22.5 million; metro Los Angeles had 17.3 million people, second only to metro New York's 20.7 million, and the San Francisco Bay area had 7.1 million, not so far behind Chicagoland's 9.4 million. The Central Valley and mountain counties had 6.7 million people; if this were a separate state it would rank 13th in population, yet it has only 19% of the population of California. San Diego County, with 2.9 million people the sixth largest county in the United States, contains only 8% of Californians. California owes this preeminence not to natural advantage but to human ingenuity. Los Angeles, with little in the way of natural resources and no natural harbor, is the nation's leading port and second-biggest manufacturer, as well as the world's entertainment center. The Bay area, which once lived by exporting food, is now the world's leader in computers and high tech. California has grown not because it had to but because people wanted it to. It has not grown without contradictions. California loves its physical environment, but also has the largest urban sprawl in the United States; it likes to think of itself as the America of the future, even as it watches the electricity flicker out; it likes to see itself as the political leader of the nation, but lives now with a president who did not come close to winning here and has a public sector that in important ways—in its public schools, fiscal condition, electricity regulation—has been deeply dysfunctional. California today is generally Democratic, well off to the left on cultural issues, secular more than religious. If it could imagine itself leading the nation when Bill Clinton was president, it is all too conscious that the nation is not following its lead now that George W. Bush has succeeded Clinton. And in recalling Governor Gray Davis and electing Arnold Schwarzenegger in his place, California in 2003 went some distance toward following the nation's example.

Most of all California has been a state that is always transforming itself, whose economy has been transformed several times over, whose population has been transformed by one group of newcomers after another and whose politics is periodically transformed with the suddenness of an earthquake. If other states have changed gradually on an analog scale over the years, California has changed sharply on a digital scale: this is quantum theory physics, not wave theory. So it has been from its American beginning. In 1848, when California passed from Mexico to the United States by the Treaty of Guadalupe Hidalgo, this was an almost entirely empty land, inhabited by a few thousand Indians and Mexicans and by a few hundred American soldiers and men on the make. Then in 1849 gold was found in Sutter's Mill and thousands arrived in the Gold Rush; within months San Francisco became one of America's 25 largest cities. The big money was made not by the miners but by the grocers and dry goods merchants who provisioned them, like the Big Four—Crocker, Hopkins, Huntington, Stanford—who built the Central and Southern Pacific Railroads. The railroads sold off vast chunks of the Central Valley to large farming operations and enticed settlers with low fares to newly-platted suburbs in the Los Angeles Basin. Engineers built great aqueducts that stretched hundreds of miles, from the Hetch Hetchy Valley in Yosemite to San Francisco and from the Owens River to Los Angeles, without which these metropolises with 24.4 million people could not exist. Early 20th century California was affluent and cultured, with great universities already, Berkeley and Stanford, and fine museums and libraries; it was America's window on the Pacific, alert to developments in China and Japan, Hawaii and the Philippines, eager to extend America's economic reach and military strength, but still, as Carey McWilliams wrote, an "island" separated from the rest of the country. Then in World War II California became one of the great defense industry states, building ships and

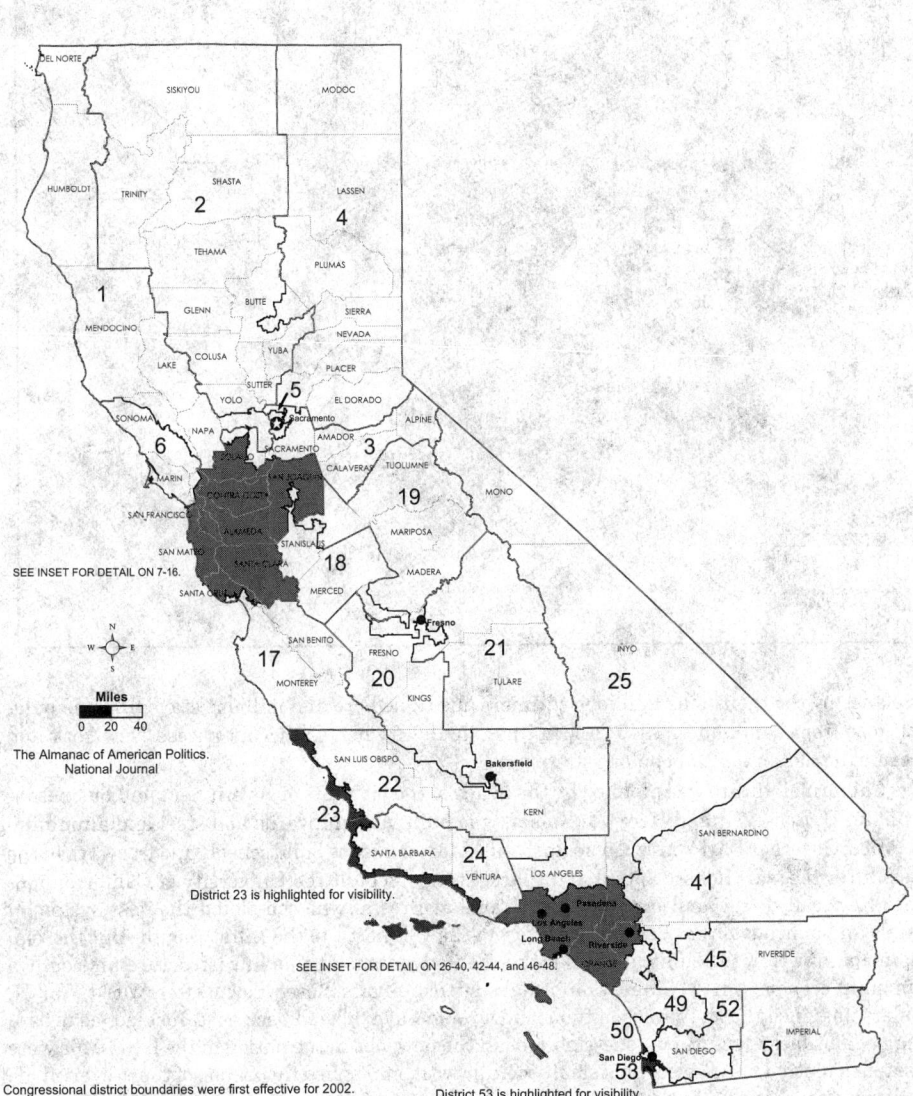

DEL NORTE

SISKIYOU

MODOC

HUMBOLDT

TRINITY

SHASTA

LASSEN

2

4

TEHAMA

PLUMAS

1

GLENN

BUTTE

SIERRA

MENDOCINO

COLUSA

YUBA

NEVADA

LAKE

SUTTER

PLACER

YOLO

5

SONOMA

NAPA

SOLANO

Sacramento

EL DORADO

6

MARIN

AMADOR

ALPINE

SAN FRANCISCO

CONTRA COSTA

SAN JOAQUIN

CALAVERAS

3

TUOLUMNE

ALAMEDA

STANISLAUS

19

MONO

SAN MATEO

SANTA CLARA

18

MARIPOSA

SANTA CRUZ

MERCED

MADERA

SEE INSET FOR DETAIL ON 7-16.

Fresno

N

W E

S

17

SAN BENITO

FRESNO

21

INYO

MONTEREY

20

25

Miles

KINGS

TULARE

0   20   40

The Almanac of American Politics.
National Journal

SAN LUIS OBISPO

Bakersfield

22

KERN

23

SANTA BARBARA

24

SAN BERNARDINO

District 23 is highlighted for visibility.

VENTURA

LOS ANGELES

41

Pasadena

Los Angeles

Riverside

Long Beach

45

RIVERSIDE

SEE INSET FOR DETAIL ON 26-40, 42-44, and 46-48.

49

52

50

Congressional district boundaries were first effective for 2002.

51

IMPERIAL

San Diego

SAN DIEGO

53

District 53 is highlighted for visibility.

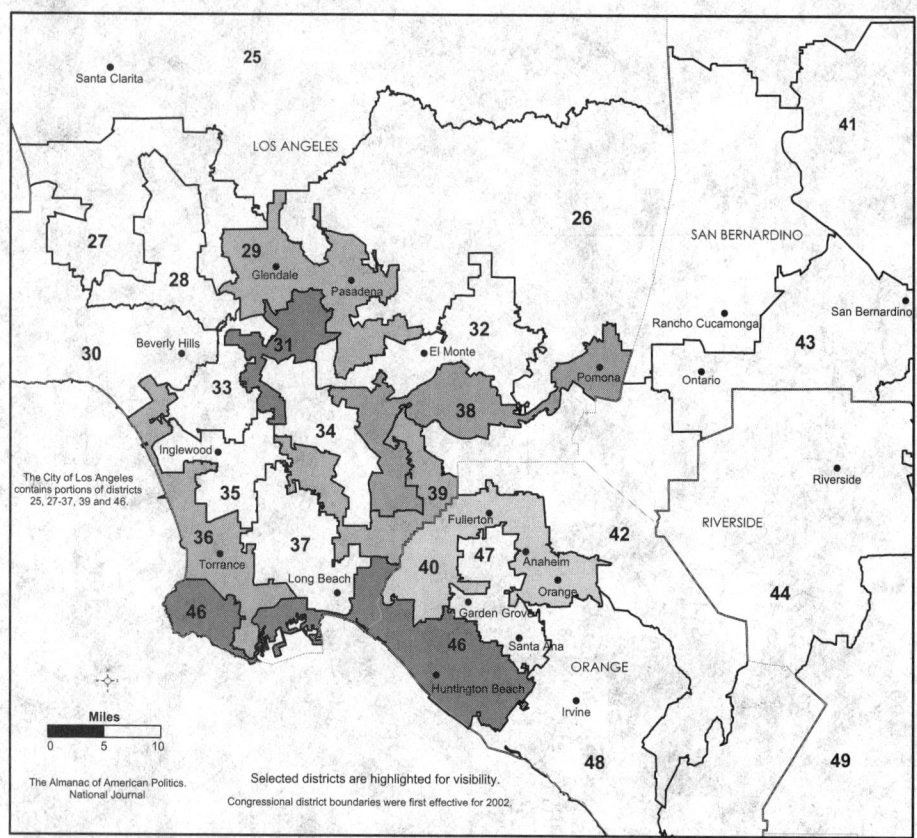

The City of Los Angeles contains portions of districts 25, 27-37, 39 and 46.

Miles
0   5   10

The Almanac of American Politics.
National Journal

Selected districts are highlighted for visibility.

Congressional district boundaries were first effective for 2002.

airplanes by the thousands. Millions of Americans came here and millions stayed: The population rose from 7 million in 1940 to 17 million in 1963, when California passed New York and became the nation's most populous state.

California's future was planned by the heads of the big units of government and business—Franklin D. Roosevelt and Henry J. Kaiser, who built vast shipyards and steel and aluminum factories; Governor Earl Warren, who husbanded tax monies to build schools and freeways in the years after the war; Robert Sproul and Clark Kerr, who built the University of California into what Kerr called "the multiversity;" Governor Pat Brown, who completed the vast system of canals and aqueducts that brought water from the wet north to the thirsty south. But the real engine of growth was the little people who took advantage of this infrastructure and built a humming economy on it. When California's defense plants closed down after World War II, leaders imagined that hundreds of thousands would have to head back east. Instead, as urbanologist Jane Jacobs points out, one-eighth of all the new jobs in the nation in the late 1940s were created in metro Los Angeles. This small-scale growth, multiplied thousands of times over, made California the nation's largest state. And this infusion of new people transformed California politically. Before World War II this was a Republican state, with progressive leanings; political struggles took place inside the Republican Party. The in-rush of the G.I. generation, with its allegiance to the New Deal, the building for the first time here of auto and steel factories with unionized work forces, made California a two-party state. Warren's progressive Republicans still were dominant through the mid-1950s, but with the election of Democratic Governor Pat Brown in 1958, a group of talented liberal Democrats took over. Things turned sour in the mid-1960s, when student rebellions starting in Berkeley in 1964 and the Watts riot of 1965 upset the New

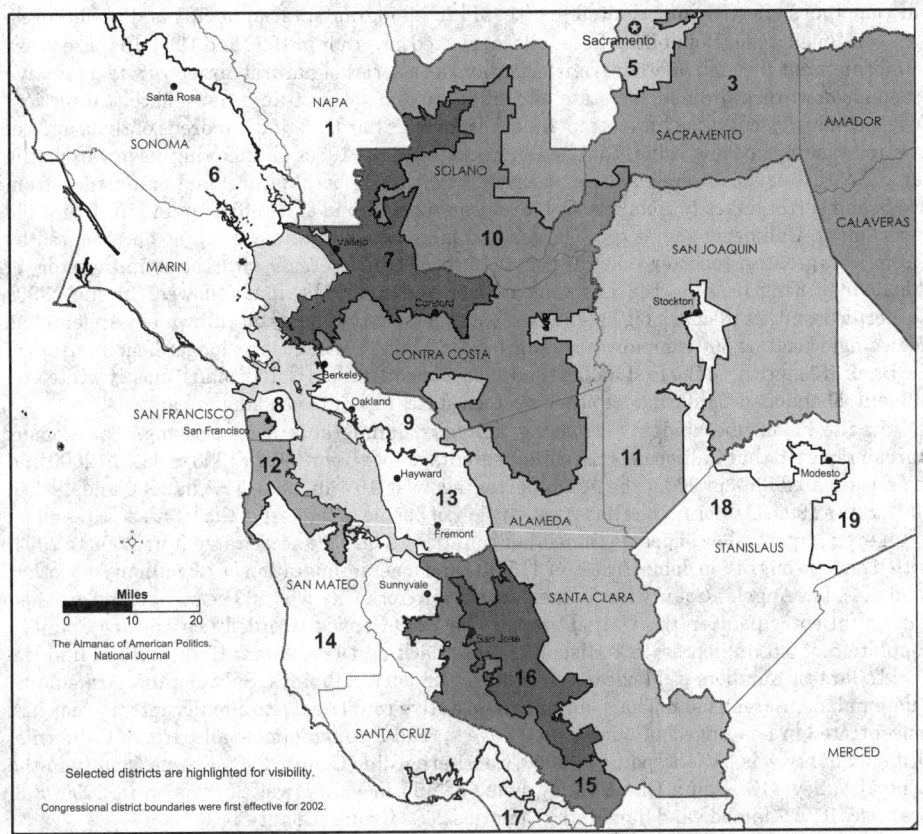

Deal order. Californians responded by calling in a disillusioned New Dealer espousing the conformist cultural conservatism of the G.I. generation, Ronald Reagan, who presaged the course the nation would follow in the 1980s.

California veered off on a different path in the 1970s, electing Jerry Brown as governor, entranced for a time by his idiosyncratic version of Baby Boomer liberalism (though he was too old to be a Boomer himself), as the World War II generation started to die out and California received a new infusion of migrants, well-educated whites attracted to the state's groovy lifestyle and, little noticed at first, Mexicans and other Latin Americans looking for work. Voters in time soured on Brown's liberalism: They passed Proposition 13 in 1978, banning property tax increases in a state where rapidly rising housing values were the chief source of people's wealth; they decried his spraying of Medfly-infested crops with an overly-effective insecticide that peeled paint on houses; they ousted, after he left office, three of his Supreme Court nominees who had overturned death penalty verdicts and struck down tough-on-crime laws. Brown, with Californian creativity, has reinvented himself as the law-and-order mayor of Oakland and in 2006, at 68, is running for attorney general.

When Brown left Sacramento, politics and government more or less disappeared from TV stations' newscasts and voters' minds. In the 1980s, with Reagan as president and quiet Republican George Deukmejian as governor, California's defense industry boomed and Silicon Valley flowered off I-280 south of San Francisco. Public policy was mostly set by Willie Brown, speaker of the California Assembly from 1980 to 1995 and later mayor of San Francisco, and the Democratic legislature furthered the causes of their clients—teachers' unions, trial lawyers and the criminal defense bar. The response was government by referendum, usually a clumsy matter but sometimes effective, on criminal justice, aid to immigrants, racial quotas and preferences. This continued under Republican Pete Wilson, elected governor in 1990 and 1994. In these years California went through another transformation, as a series of natural disasters and a massive economic downturn drained the state of confidence and set it off in a new political direction. Defense industry cutbacks hit metropolitan Los Angeles hard, costing hundreds of thousands of jobs and sending housing values that had skyrocketed in the 1980s plummeting downward in the early 1990s. Television screens were absorbed by disasters both natural and manmade—from floods and earthquakes to riots and O.J. Simpson. Long proud of its efficient and incorruptible government, California saw it grow larger and increasingly dysfunctional, as documented by California's greatest reporter, Lou Cannon, in his book *Official Negligence*, the definitive story of the Rodney King beating, the Los Angeles riot and the trials that followed. In the 1990s California lost its trademark big businesses to mergers, so that today downtown Los Angeles has not a single Fortune 500 company headquarters and San Francisco is no longer headquarters of the Bank of America. In the first half of the 1990s, about 2 million Californians, mostly white and affluent, abandoned California for other western states or went even farther back east.

In the meantime, and in increasing numbers, immigrants keep arriving. The Census Bureau reported that California's Hispanic percentage rose from 26% in 1990 to 32% in 2000 and to an estimated 35% in 2003; the Asian percentage was 10% in 1990, 11% in 2000 and 12% in 2003. Since 1990, California has had a net outflow of people to the rest of the United States offset by an even larger inflow of people from other countries. The pace accelerated from 2000 to 2004, with a net out-migration domestically of 415,000 and a net in-migration of 1.2 million from other countries. Los Angeles County has become what New York City was 100 years ago, the greatest immigrant entry point in the United States. The 2000 Census recorded Los Angeles County's population of 9.5 million as 45% Hispanic, 10% Black and 12% Asian. Here you can find the world's largest numbers of Mexicans, Iranians, Samoans, Filipinos, Salvadorans, Armenians, Guatemalans, Koreans and Thais outside their native countries. And immigrants are not just concentrated in Los Angeles County; they have spread through almost all parts of California. Orange County was 31% Hispanic in 2000, San Bernardino County 39%, Fresno County in the Central Valley 44%. Santa Clara Valley, home of Silicon Valley, was 26% Asian in 2000, San Francisco 31%, Alameda and San Mateo Counties 20%, Orange County 14%.

These immigrants have come to California to participate in an economy that has been growing for most of the last 25 years. Twice during that period it has suffered severe shocks: sharp declines in defense spending shook the Los Angeles area in the early 1990s and the sudden collapse of the dot.com boom shook the San Francisco Bay area a decade later. But underneath the defense buildup and the tech boom, little noticed, and still continuing, California's small business economy has been growing and prospering, despite high taxes and heavy-handed regulation. But not as much as it might have; there is lots of evidence that businesses are fleeing to other Western states to escape California's highest-in-the-nation workmen's comp premiums, second-highest capital gains tax rate, third-highest personal income tax rate and fifth-highest minimum wage. In many ways this is a two-tier economy. California imports high-skill Americans and some foreigners—especially from Taiwan, China and India—and exports low-skill and retired Americans, and it imports very large numbers of low-skill Latinos and Asians to work in a rapidly growing service economy. This leaves a population with an income and education gap: California has more high-income people and more in poverty than anywhere else in the country; it has a higher than average percentage of people who have college degrees and people who haven't graduated from high school. But low-income people are not just hovering at the bottom; they are working their way up, or their children are. Latinos or Asians own four in ten small businesses in Los Angeles County. Statistics which show the lowest quintile of earners with barely increased incomes are misleading; today's lowest quintile of earners in California 10 years ago were living in some other country, making far less than they do now. California's population and economy are continuing to grow faster than the nation's.

How do these new Californians fit into, and affect, California politics? In the hard economic times of the early 1990s Governor Pete Wilson discovered that the state was spending billions on illegal immigrants and their children—for welfare (though Latinos in poverty apply for welfare much less than anyone else), for schools and for prison spaces. In 1994, uncertain of re-election against state Treasurer Kathleen Brown, Jerry Brown's sister, he supported Proposition 187, which denied non-emergency state government spending on illegal aliens and their children. In speeches Wilson was careful to differentiate between legal and illegal immigrants, and voters did too; at least one-third of Hispanic voters voted for 187, which passed by a wide margin. But campaign ads make a much greater impression than politicians' careful statements in a state where TV news coverage of politics and government is miniscule. Wilson's ad showing Mexicans running across the border, with the announcer proclaiming ominously, "They just keep coming," was taken by many as a slur, suggesting that all Latinos were more interested in welfare than work, which stung all the more because it is simply not true—Hispanic males have the highest work force participation rate of any measured group.

The result was that Latino turnout increased and Latinos increasingly turned to the Democratic Party. The Latino vote increased from 10% of the vote in 1994 to 14% in 1998, and Gray Davis beat Republican Dan Lungren among Hispanics by 78%–16%—a huge drop for Republicans, since Wilson got almost 40% of the Latino vote in 1990. In 2000 Hispanics again cast 14% of California's votes, and voted 68%–29% for Al Gore. But as memories of the 187 campaign dim—some current Latino voters were not even in California then—Latinos have produced smaller margins for Democrats. In 2002 Gray Davis carried them by 65%–24%; in October 2003, Lieutenant Governor Cruz Bustamante carried them by only 21% over Arnold Schwarzenegger; NEP's exit poll showed John Kerry leading George W. Bush 63%–34% in 2004. That last number may understate Bush's support, since between 2000 and 2004 he gained 6% to 8% in seven congressional districts with large numbers of middle class Latinos.

Asian immigrants are even more of a political puzzle. In the early 1990s Asians cast Republican margins, perhaps out of recoil from the 1992 riot, after the establishment showed great solicitude for the needs of the rioters but little sympathy for the Korean shopkeepers who were their victims. Later in the decade, Asians seemed to move toward Democrats, as Bill Clinton and Al Gore (remember his visit to the Buddhist temple in Hacienda Heights) courted them assiduously. The 2000 exit polls were in conflict: VNS showed Asians for Gore by only 48%–47% while the *Los Angeles Times* exit poll showed them giving Gore a 63%–33% margin. The 2004 NEP poll, showing Kerry carrying Asians 66%–34%, tends to confirm the *Times's* numbers.

This Democratic trend among Latinos was one of two trends that moved California toward the Democrats in the 1990s; the other was the increasing prominence of cultural issues like abortion and gun control on which most affluent Californians in the big metropolitan areas have liberal views. Between 1980 and 1990 Republicans won seven of nine contests for president, senator and governor and nearly won another. From 1990 to 2002 Democrats won nine of ten such contests, the one exception being Wilson's reelection in 1994. Another key factor was Bill Clinton. After winning California in 1992 with 46% of the vote, Clinton understood that if he could lock up California's 54 electoral votes (it now has 55) he would be a long way toward being assured of re-election. He courted the state with dozens of appearances, with special attention to California issues and projects, with assiduous cultivation of Hollywood celebrities and Silicon Valley cybermillionaires. He carried the state 51%–38% in 1996. Clinton's combination of moderation on economic issues and liberalism on cultural issues was a perfect fit for a critical block of California voters, the affluent professionals and techies who support abortion rights and gun control and who are increasingly fearful of the prominence of Christian conservatives in the national and to some extent the state Republican party. Affluent Americans increasingly are not moored to any one locality, but can choose where they live, from an array of places with widely different cultural atmospheres. Those who espouse traditional values and have traditional religious views tend to pick metropolises like Atlanta, Dallas and Houston; those with liberation-minded values and secular or non-Christian religious attitudes tend to pick Los Angeles and the San Francisco Bay area. The quantum of all these personal decisions over the last decade made Georgia and Texas more Republican and made California more Democratic.

The Democratic trend in California reached its peak in 1998 when Gray Davis was elected governor by a 58%–38% margin and in 2000 when Al Gore carried the state 53%–42% over

George W. Bush, even though Bush spent $20 million on California media and Gore not a penny. In the same years, Democratic Senators Barbara Boxer and Dianne Feinstein were both reelected by far wider margins than six years before. In 2002, with Clinton far less prominent, the Democrats' fortunes ebbed a bit in California. Gray Davis, with low job ratings after the 2001 electricity crisis, was reelected by only a 47%–42% margin. Democrats won every statewide downballot office for the first time since 1882, but not by overwhelming margins: their candidates' percentages varied from 45% to 51%, while Republicans' percentages varied from 40% to 45%, and conservative firebrand Tom McClintock came within 17,000 votes of being elected controller.

In retrospect, these numbers presaged the huge turnaround in state politics that occurred in 2003, when Davis was recalled as governor and Arnold Schwarzenegger elected to replace him. Yet as late as June 2003 this scenario seemed exceedingly unlikely. He governed as a centrist, frequently vetoing or blocking measures sought by the left-leaning Democratic legislature. But he failed to hold back spending enough when the dot.com boom brought in huge gushers of revenue in 1998 and 1999, and he stuck to the flawed electricity deregulation plan adopted by a unanimous legislature and his Republican predecessor until it produced blackouts and huge costs to the state. Davis was no one's first choice for anything; his appeal was that he was centrist and competent. But when the fiscal and electricity crisis cast doubt on those essentials he was vulnerable. He won only 47% of the vote against the stumbling campaign of Bill Simon in 2002. And when the voters had an unexpected opportunity to vote him up or down, in October 2003, only 45% stuck with him and voted no on recall.

Davis represented an apotheosis of a political governing class which, thanks to its political competence and to California voters' faithfulness to a party which stood for liberal cultural values, had insulated itself largely from public control. The California legislature was the first in the nation to develop a large staff and to use the advantages of incumbency to protect against opposition; redistricting plans were adopted which reduced toward zero the chance of change in party control of seats. Davis capitalized on an apathetic electorate and an uninterested press to win elections by delivering the simple message that the opposition was unacceptable. But politicians who insulate themselves from public retaliation risk widespread revolt when things go sour. That is what happened in California in 2003.

The recall was a project of the right wing of the Republican party, which had been singularly unsuccessful since the retirement of Governor George Deukmejian in 1990. But the beneficiary was not the culturally conservative right-wingers but the culturally liberal Arnold Schwarzenegger. He was not without his own political credentials: he spent fall 2002 campaigning for his own Proposition 49, which called for after-school programs to keep kids busy in those hours from 3:00 to 6:00 p.m. when so many of their parents are not home; it passed 57%–43%. The recall's original organizers had little money and their petition drive seemed doomed to failure in February 2003. But then Congressman Darrell Issa, a car alarm millionaire who had run and lost in the 1998 Senate primary, poured in money of his own. And discontent with Davis rose when he signed a bill (after vetoing others) authorizing driver's licenses for illegal aliens and unilaterally increased the license plate fee by 2% of vehicle value. Petition forms were circulated over the Internet; shoppers in mall parking lots, usually disdainful of petition gatherers, stood in line to sign; by July it was apparent that enough signatures would be obtained to force a recall election. California law provides that in a recall election voters also get to choose who will succeed to the office if the incumbent is recalled; a relatively low number of signatures is required, and only a plurality is needed to win. Conservative state Senator Tom McClintock plunged in on July 24 while Schwarzenegger kept his own counsel. He was committed, he said, to publicizing his latest movie, *Terminator 3*, in July 2003; he would decide later. On August 6, he proceeded to NBC's Burbank studio for a taping of *The Tonight Show*. The political advisers he had assembled, veterans of Pete Wilson's campaigns, believed he was not going to run. He surprised them and just about everyone else when he said he would. The next day, Issa dropped out; 1984 Los Angeles Olympics organizer Peter Ueberroth, a moderately well-known Republican, got in. California Democratic leaders, desperate to keep Davis in office and unable to characterize the pro-abortion rights, pro-gun control, pro-gay-rights Schwarzenegger as a far right conservative, pressured state officeholders not to put their names on the replacement ballot. The threat was that anyone who did would be blackballed in the 2006 primary contest to succeed Davis. The idea was to convince Democratic voters that the only way to maintain Democrats' hold on the governorship was to vote no on recall. But Lieutenant Governor Cruz Bustamante ran anyway. A moderate from the Central Valley, Bustamante had few connections with the hyperpolitical leftish Latino politicians from Los Angeles County. But he adopted their policies, including driver's licenses for illegal aliens, and made mistakes. When Bustamante accepted contributions from Indian gambling tribes, Schwarzenegger cited it as evidence of Democrats' allegiance to special interests.

Polls are not a good guide to voters' feelings on unfamiliar issues and unanticipated contests, and the *Los Angeles Times's* polls in particular seemed, as in the past, to have an unduly Democratic sample. Despite the *Times's* Thursday-before-the-election stories about Schwarzenegger's gropings of women some years before, the recall was approved in October 2003 by 55% of voters and opposed by 45%—2% less than the percentage Davis had won 11 months before. On the replacement ballot Schwarzenegger won 49% of the vote to 32% for Bustamante and 14% for McClintock; a solid majority in this Democratic state had voted for a Republican. Turnout was actually up from 2002—from 7.5 million to 9.0 million—and Schwarzenegger received more votes in 2003, 4.2 million, than Davis had in 2002, 3.5 million. The Edison/Mitofsky exit poll showed 60% of whites, 46% of Latinos and 27% of blacks voting for recall. So did 24% of Democrats, 24% of liberals and 45% of union members. Voters with graduate degrees—the core of Democratic support along with blacks and Latinos—voted 55% to keep Davis in office; voters with less levels of education voted to throw him out. The San Francisco Bay area, which voted 57%–29% for Davis in 2002, voted 64%–36% against recall. But Los Angeles County, which voted 56%–35% for Davis, voted only 51%–49% against recall. The margins for recall were overwhelming in the rest of Southern California (69%–31%) and the rest of the state (64%–36%). Schwarzenegger led Bustamante among almost all segments of the electorate except blacks and Latinos; the latter voted only 52% for Bustamante and 31% for Schwarzenegger.

Schwarzenegger's election meant the end of insider politics in California and the beginning of plebiscitary politics. Television stations rushed to set up news bureaus in Sacramento and newspapers headlined state government news: Schwarzenegger is the first governor since Jerry Brown to get such news coverage. Taking advantage of it, he ordered an audit of state government and forced the legislature to repeal driver's licenses for illegal immigrants; he vetoed another version of the bill in September 2004. He forced changes in workmen's comp laws. He put on the March 2004 ballot two measures to allow the state to borrow money to meet budgetary needs and requiring a balanced budget. At first they languished in the polls, but Schwarzenegger campaigned for them vigorously and they passed with 63% and 71% of the vote. At the same time, 66% of voters rejected Democratic legislators' amendment to make it easier to raise taxes. In March 2004 he forced the legislature to accept his budget by using his star power and threatening to take the issue to the people. Schwarzenegger had his successes in November 2004 referenda as well. A measure he backed promising $3 billion for stem-cell research passed 59%–41%. A measure to relax the "three strikes and you're out" law, which had been leading in the polls, lost 53%–47% after Schwarzenegger campaigned against it. A measure to limit tort actions passed 59%–41%. Indian tribes' attempts to augment their casino businesses were rejected by 77% and 84% of the voters. A telephone tax for emergency medical funding was rejected by 72%. And a measure to mandate health insurance coverage for small businesses was rejected, though by only 51%–49%. California voters seemed to be in line with their new Republican governor.

In January 2005 Schwarzenegger went on the offensive, attacking the heart of the political system, by demanding action on four issues and, again, threatening to take them to the people in November 2005. They included a nonpartisan board of retired judges to redistrict California's congressional and legislative districts, automatic across-the-board spending cuts if spending grew faster than revenues, merit pay for teachers and defined contribution 401(k)-like pensions for state employees. Democrats responded with a push to put their own issues on the ballot, including a minimum wage increase. As Schwarzenegger raised their issues, his popularity declined from stratospheric to something less: his job approval hovered around 55%. He had become just another partisan figure, Democrats said. But a partisan figure with the kind of approval Pete Wilson had in his best years and that Ronald Reagan had during his governorship and presidency, when California seemed more a Republican than a Democratic state.

To be sure, in the 2004 presidential race California confirmed its Democratic status. John Kerry carried the state 54%–44%, a margin similar to Al Gore's 53%–42% in 2000. But there was a regional split. Outside the San Francisco Bay area, Bush cut the Democratic margin from 50%–45% in 2000 to 50%–49% in 2004. Bush made significant gains among Jews in Los Angeles County, among Latinos in the Los Angeles metro area and in the Central Valley and from increasing turnout in the Inland Empire of Riverside and San Bernardino Counties. But in the San Francisco Bay area, Democratic and left-wing enthusiasm produced a surge in turnout, even though the metro area population scarcely increased, and increased Gore's 64%–30% margin to Kerry's 69%–29%. No other major metro area in the country is nearly so Democratic; the closest is metro Washington, D.C., which voted 61%–38% for Kerry. Long-term population trends probably work for Republicans: between 2000 and 2004 population rose only 1% in the Bay Area and 4% in Los Angeles County, while it rose faster in more Republican areas, 7% in the rest of Southern California and 6% in the rest of the state. There is a divide here, a divide that runs within metropolitan areas, between heavily Democratic coastal California, full of the very rich and very poor, which is mostly built up and tends to support limits on local growth, and much more Republican interior California, the more middle class territory from the southern desert and Inland Empire east of Los Angeles County and running up the Central Valley and the foothills of the Sierra Nevada, which is growing much more rapidly.

California in the early 21st century is very much like New York in the early 20th century: the nation's largest state, its greatest immigrant magnet, with its most productive and creative economy. But it seems to lack two things which enabled New York over the first half of the 20th century to develop its full potential and become a national leader, to create an image of itself as an "empire state" in which every citizen could take pride. One is a coherent and competent civic and political elite. The other is a pattern to interweave the newcomers into the American fabric. Schwarzenegger can be seen as supplying what is missing on both counts. He has been an eminently successful entrepreneur in California's most visible business: he took an impressive physique, what are at best unorthodox good looks and a well-nigh incomprehensible accent and made himself, as he likes to recall, the number one box office movie star in Hollywood. And he has shown how a penniless immigrant can rise to any heights—well, almost any, until the Constitution is amended to allow immigrants to run for president—in the country and the state that he celebrates as the greatest in the world. He has cultivated a wide acquaintanceship among California's business elites and has drawn on a wide range of talent in all walks of life. He seems to be trying to institutionalize his success by restructuring state government and state politics. But to do that he depends, for the moment, on his personal appeal.

One other thing California lacks is rooted in the dominant *laissez faire* cultural style in California: letting people do pretty much anything they want (except smoke cigarettes). But tolerance can segue into indifference, and it does not necessarily translate into a sense of common identity and purpose. The California of Earl Warren, Pat Brown and Ronald Reagan had a kind of nationalism, a shared vision of itself, like the New York of Theodore Roosevelt, Al Smith, Franklin D. Roosevelt, Fiorello LaGuardia and Thomas Dewey. That has been missing in the California of today. Instead, articulate elites, focusing on changing demography, paint a vision of California as a "multicultural" polity, with a Third World majority (or approaching it) of "people of color." But the immigrants of today's California are no more a single united mass striving to overthrow the system than were the immigrants of New York 100 years ago; they came to the United States not to change this country but to become part of it. California businesses and political elites, like those in the United States generally, have responded to these newcomers with racial quotas and preferences, which cast doubt on their achievements, and with bilingual education, which consigns them to low-wage jobs. Policies designed to address the problems faced by blacks in the 1960s and 1970s are ill-suited to the needs of immigrants in the 1990s and 2000s. Schwarzenegger has not chosen to challenge these policies. But his own example points the other way, toward the lessons taught by the New York elites of a century ago: that immigrants can move forward to become leaders in America.

The People		Race/Ethnic Origin			Military veterans: 2,569,340 (10.4%)	
Pop. 2004 (est):	35,893,799	15,816,790	46.7%	White	WWII: 20.5%	Korea: 13.7%
Pop. 2000:	33,871,648	2,181,926	6.4%	Black	Vietnam: 32.4%	Gulf War: 9.8%
Pop. 1990:	29,760,021	3,648,860	10.8%	Asian	**Most populous cities (2003):**	
Change 1990–2000:	Up 13.6%	178,984	0.5%	Native Am.	1. Los Angeles	3,819,951
% of U.S. total:	12.0%	103,736	0.3%	Hawaiian	2. San Diego	1,266,753
Pop. rank:	1st of 50	903,115	2.7%	Two+ races	3. San Jose	898,349
Area size:	163,696 sq. mi.	71,681	0.2%	Other	4. San Francisco	751,682
State Native:	50.2%	10,966,556	32.4%	Hisp. Origin	5. Long Beach	475,460
Non-citizen:	15.9%	**Ancestry**				
Language		German: 8.0%		Irish: 6.3%	Urban population: 94.5%	
English: 62.2%	Spanish: 22.4%	English: 6.1%		Italian: 3.5%	Rural population: 5.5%	
Asian: 8.6%		USA: 2.7%				

Education		Work Sector		Legislature	
H.S. Grad:	76.8%	Private: 76.5%	Govt: 14.7%	Senate	25 D 15 R
College Grad:	26.6%	Self: 8.5%	Family: 0.4%	Assembly	48 D 32 R
Industry		Unemployment: 6.9%		Legislative Term Limits: Yes	
Agri: 1.9%	Con: 6.2%	**Household Income**		**Registered Voters**	
Fin: 6.9%	Info: 3.9%	<15k: 14.0%	15-35k: 22.9%	D: 7,120,425	(43.0%)
Mfg: 17.8%	Prof: 30.1%	35-50k: 15.2%	50-100k: 30.7%	R: 5,745,518	(34.7%)
Public: 4.5%	Trade: 15.2%	100-150k: 10.4%	>150k: 6.9%	O: 3,691,330	(22.3%)
Other: 13.4%		Median: $47,493			
Occupation		Poverty status: 14.2%			
Blue collar: 21.2%	White collar: 62.7%	**Home Value**			
Gray collar: 16.1%		<50k: 5.1% 50-100k: 11.3% 100-200k: 34.0% 200-300k: 20.8%			
		300-500k: 17.8% >500k: 11.0% Median: $198,900			

Presidential politics   George W. Bush's chief strategist Karl Rove itched to make California a target state in 2000 and 2004. It just seems too large to ignore: 54 electoral votes in 2000, 55 in 2004, one-fifth of those needed to win the presidency. In 2000 Rove poured $20 million of California-raised money into ads on California TV stations. Al Gore's campaign, coolly assessing the polls, put in nothing at all, and won 53%–42%. Gore's California victory owed something to its increasing number of Latino voters and their distaste, rooted in California politics, for Republicans; it owed much to Californians' affection for and assiduous cultivation by Bill Clinton; it owed much as well to the liberal attitude on cultural issues here—abortion and gun control and the environment—which has trumped any desire for lower taxes. In 2004 Rove and Bush campaign manager Ken Mehlman kept a close eye on California, with a view toward putting money in and forcing Democrats to compete in this huge state if the race grew close here. Perhaps if Bush had won the first two

2004 Presidential Vote		
Kerry (D)	6,745,485	(54%)
Bush (R)	5,509,826	(44%)
Badnarik (Lib)	50,165	(0%)
Other	145,328	(1%)

2004 Democratic Presidential Primary		
Kerry (D)	2,002,539	(64%)
Edwards (D)	614,441	(20%)
Kucinich (D)	144,954	(5%)
Dean (D)	130,892	(4%)
Sharpton (D)	59,326	(2%)
Other	155,457	(5%)

2000 Presidential Vote		
Gore (D)	5,861,203	(53%)
Bush (R)	4,567,429	(42%)
Nader (Green)	418,707	(4%)
Other	118,517	(1%)

debates and maintained the national lead he enjoyed in September, they would have targeted California. After all, the memory of the 1994 campaign and Proposition 187 had faded among Latinos, Clinton was no longer head of the Democratic party, Bush's Israel policies had brought him new admirers among Jewish voters and Arnold Schwarzenegger's election as governor—and his wholehearted support of Bush—had projected a new image of the Republican party in the Golden State. But none of these things changed enough minds to make California close. Bush reduced his loss in Los Angeles County from 63%–32% to 63%–36% and increased his margin in the rest of Southern California from 52%–44% to 56%–43%. In the rest of the state outside the Bay Area, he increased his margin from 51%–43% to 54%–44%. But the Democratic margin in the San Francisco Bay Area increased from 64%–30% to 69%–29%. The result was that John Kerry carried California by 54%–44%.

Some oldtimers can still recall when California's June primary was the national tiebreaker. This state was the center of national attention when Nelson Rockefeller lost here to Barry Goldwater in 1964, when Robert Kennedy and Eugene McCarthy slugged it out in 1968— Kennedy won and was murdered by a Palestinian terrorist on primary night—and when George McGovern edged Hubert Humphrey in 1972. California was all the more important because it was winner-take-all in both parties: Voters chose between slates pledged to each candidate, and whoever won a plurality won every vote in the largest delegation in each party's convention. But since the 1980s nominations have been sewed up a lot earlier than June, and California for some time was an irrelevancy.

For 1996 California moved its presidential primary from the first week in June to March 26; that was still too late to make any difference. So in 2000 it moved it to March 7. That was still a problem. California's all-party primary, adopted by referendum and overturned three months later by the U.S. Supreme Court, allowed anyone, not just registered Democrats or Republicans, to vote for a Democrat or a Republican. But Secretary of State Bill Jones, a Republican, came up with a computer-assisted double counting procedure, which would allow a total of just registered Democrats' votes to be counted for Democratic delegates. Under those rules, Al Gore won 34% of all votes and 80% of those cast for a Democrat; George W. Bush won 29% and John McCain 23% of all votes. Among those voting for Republicans, Bush led McCain 52%–43%. In 2004 California voted on March 2, for John Kerry; this was the day Kerry clinched the Democratic nomination. In September 2004 Governor Arnold Schwarzenegger signed a bill rescheduling the presidential primary in June.

Congressional districting   California has gained House seats in every Census going back to 1850, when it became a state; over that century and a half it has grown from 2 seats to 53, the most of any state in history. But California grew less rapidly in the early 1990s, and so it gained only 1 seat from the 2000 Census, the first time in a century it has not gained 2 or more. The tradition of partisan redistricting goes way back: Republicans drew the lines to their advantage in the 1940s and 1950s, Democrats in the 1960s, 1970s and 1980s, as the California House delegation grew from 23 in the 1940s to 30, 38, 43, 45 and 52. The great genius of redistricting here was Democratic Congressman Phillip Burton, who dominated the line-drawing for House seats and for the state Senate and Assembly as well (and intervened behind the scenes in other states too); his 1982 plan, slightly revised for 1984–90, left Democrats in secure control of the delegation even though he died in 1983. In the 1990s neither party had full control. Governor Pete Wilson, after hard-nosed bargaining with the Democratic legislature, persuaded the state Supreme Court to adopt a plan drawn up by his appointed commission in 1992. This was a relatively evenhanded plan, with generally regular boundaries; the fact that Democrats had a 32–20 margin in the delegation after the 2000 election reflected the party's strength in most parts of the state, not any acuity in drawing district lines.

109th Congress Lineup
33 D   20 R
108th Congress Lineup
33 D   20 R

The assumption after the 2000 election was that California would produce a Democratic redistricting plan. Democrats held the governorship and controlled the state Senate 26–14 and the Assembly 50–30. But that is not what happened; for the second decade in a row California ended up with a plan that gave neither party any great advantage. Democrats picked up four California seats from Republicans in 2000 and entered the process with a 32–20 edge in the delegation. They could have weakened several Republican incumbents, but that would have made it harder to safeguard the four incumbents who won in 2000. And they had to do something about the Central Valley seat held by Gary Condit, world-famous for his affair with the slain intern Chandra Levy in 2001. With his moderate record, Condit had held a seat that leaned

Republican in other races. It would have to be made more Democratic if Democrats hoped to keep it. The key player for Democrats was Michael Berman, brother of Congressman Howard Berman and a redistricting expert who had worked with Phil Burton on redistricting in the 1970s and 1980s. He came out of retirement and was hired as a redistricting consultant by House and state Senate Democrats, at $20,000 per incumbent. As Congresswoman Loretta Sanchez said, "Twenty thousand is nothing to keep your seat. I spend $2 million every election. If my colleagues are smart, they'll pay their $20,000 and Michael will draw the district they can win in."

Term limits played a role in convincing Berman and the Democrats not to maximize the number of Democratic seats. Assemblymen are limited to six years in office, state senators to eight; incumbents, especially assemblymen, spend much of their time plotting to run for other offices. As a result, it was not at all clear that there were 41 Democratic votes in the Assembly for plans that would protect incumbent congressmen and state senators, most of whom feared competition in the primary much more than in the general election. In February 2001 Berman met with five House Republicans, including David Dreier, who spoke for most of his California colleagues, and NRCC Chairman Tom Davis, who is also a redistricting buff. They agreed on the outline of a deal: Democrats would protect all incumbents, strengthen the Condit seat and take the new seat created by reapportionment; Republicans would get 20 seats for 19 of their incumbents in which the Bush 2000 percentage was at least 50%. It was understood that Long Beach Republican Steve Horn, nearly beaten in 2000 and surrounded by mostly Democratic territory, would have to be sacrificed to create a new Hispanic Democratic seat, and that Republicans would get a new seat in the Central Valley. In turn, Republicans would get Republican legislators to vote for the plan, with a view toward getting the two-thirds vote necessary to block a ballot initiative on the subject in 2002. This angered some Sacramento Republicans, who wanted to take their chances in court or with an initiative, and it angered Ways and Means Chairman Bill Thomas, who argued that a plan that put most Latino voters in safe Democratic districts would not give Republicans an incentive to develop ties to Latinos which would be necessary if the party is ever to be a majority in the state again.

While Berman was busy drawing the lines in his Beverly Hills office, Republicans were busy building support for the deal. Howard Berman, who spoke for other delegation Democrats on redistricting, of course favored the deal. The National Republican Congressional Committee chartered a private plane to fly Berman to Washington, where he met at the White House with Karl Rove, who endorsed the plan. Davis secretly flew to Sacramento and lobbied Assembly Republicans. In August 2001 the plan was unveiled; Berman sent out copies to all incumbents, Republicans as well as Democrats, with personal notes. There was never much chance that it would not be approved. In the Assembly only 28 of the 50 Democrats voted for it initially, but some switched their votes and with Republican help it was passed with a two-thirds margin. In the Senate 24 of the 26 Democrats voted for it and it easily got the two-thirds. The plan was signed by Governor Gray Davis September 27. To criticism by Republicans that they should have tried to undermine Democrats via the courts or the ballot box, Tom Davis said, "Our view is that we are trying to control the House in 2002. A bird in the hand is worth two in the bush. Democrats were in control, and they were generous in giving us a 20th District." To national Democrats who hoped for redistricting gains in California, Howard Berman said, "Sometimes the cautious move is the smart move. Time will tell. But I'm convinced we made the right decision, given the vagaries of politics and unanticipated decisions. . . . We will have a massive Democratic majority in the delegation for the rest of the decade." California Democrats had already done enough for the national party, they said, converting the 26–26 delegation elected in 1994 to 33–20. As for Republicans, by 2005 their 20 California members included the chairmen of the Appropriations, Armed Services, Homeland Security, Resources, Rules and Ways and Means committees.

The plan itself has the elegance one would expect of the nation's foremost redistricter. Where the district shapes are contorted, there is often a demographic as well as political rationale: the 23d District, which connects a thin band of Pacific Coast in Ventura, Santa Barbara and San Luis Obispo Counties, collects a constituency with common interests and proclivities, quite different from those of the voters in the interior of those counties who were placed in the 22d and 24th Districts. Naturally there were some complaints. Moderate Democrat

Ellen Tauscher complained that she was given a too Democratic district; she wanted one that matched her moderate record. Latino groups complained that only one additional Hispanic district was created. The Mexican American Legal Defense and Educational Fund filed a lawsuit against the plan, honing in on the fact that it reduced the Hispanic percentages in the districts held by Howard Berman and Bob Filner. In all, 23 of the 26 Latino legislators backed the plan; weighing in against MALDEF also was former Speaker Antonio Villaraigosa. The suit was dismissed in June 2002.

The plan was condemned by many journalists and political scientists for protecting incumbents and reducing competition. In 2002 in these 53 seats—12% of the nation's total—only one was seriously contested, the Condit seat; in 2004, only one was arguably seriously contested, the open 20th in the Central Valley. But political trends over the course of a decade can make uncompetitive seats competitive: the political divisions of 2000 will not necessarily stay locked in place forever. In January 2005 Governor Arnold Schwarzenegger took direct aim at California's redistricting plans, condemning them because not a single one of the 153 congressional and legislative seats up in 2004 had changed partisan hands. He called on the legislature to set up a nonpartisan commission of retired judges to redistrict the seats once again. Republicans in the U.S. House delegation applauded the idea generally, but argued that only the state legislative seats should be redistricted in mid-decade.

Governor

Arnold Schwarzenegger (R)

Elected Oct. 2003, term expires Jan. 2007, 1st term; b. July 30, 1947, Thal, Austria; home, Pacific Palisades; U. of WI-Superior, B.A. 1979; Catholic; married (Maria Shriver).

Military Career: Austrian Army, 1965–66.

Professional Career: Bodybuilder, 1965–80; Chairman of the President's Council on Physical Fitness and Sports, 1990–93; Actor, 1970–2003.

Office: State Capitol Bldg., Sacramento, 95814, 916-445-2841; Fax: 916-445-4633; Web site: www.governor.ca.gov.

Election Results

2003 special	Arnold Schwarzenegger (R)	4,206,284	(49%)
	Cruz Bustamante (D)	2,724,874	(32%)
	Tom McClintock (R)	1,161,287	(13%)
	Other	565,470	(7%)
2002 general	Gray Davis (D)	3,533,490	(47%)
	Bill Simon (R)	3,169,801	(42%)
	Peter Camejo (Green)	393,036	(5%)
	Other	379,984	(5%)
2002 primary	Gray Davis (D)	1,755,276	(81%)
	Anselmo Chavez (D)	179,301	(8%)
	Charles Pineda, Jr. (D)	139,121	(6%)
	Mosemarie Boyd (D)	95,857	(4%)
1998 general	Gray Davis (D)	4,858,817	(58%)
	Dan Lungren (R)	3,216,749	(38%)
	Other	306,305	(4%)

Arnold Schwarzenegger, movie actor and entrepreneur, was elected governor of California in October 2003. He grew up in Graz, Austria, where his father was a police officer. At 13 he told his parents, "I want to be the best built man in the world." At 14, he started training; at 15, he studied psychology; at 17, he started competing in bodybuilding contests. Drafted into the Austrian army, he went off base to win the Mr. Europe Junior contest in Stuttgart, Germany; his superiors put him in the brig, then decided to let him spend the rest of his military career building his body. In 1966, at 19, he won the Mr. Europe competition in London. He lost a Mr. Universe contest that year but won in 1967. There were three organizations holding Mr. Universe contests; by 1970 he had won them all. In 1970 he won the Mr. Olympia contest for the first of seven times and was generally hailed as the strongest man in the world.

In the course of these competitions, Schwarzenegger came to California in September 1968 with $20 in his pocket. After listening to presidential candidates Richard Nixon and Hubert Humphrey, he decided he preferred the Republican. In between his training, he started buying commercial properties in Santa Monica. In 1970 he got a bit part in a movie called *Hercules in New York* and in 1977 was the chief subject of the documentary *Pumping Iron*. In 1978 he published an autobiography, *Arnold: The Education of a Bodybuilder*. He got a business degree from the University of Wisconsin at Superior in 1979. In 1982 he starred in *Conan the Barbarian*, the first in a string of box office hits that included *The Terminator*, *Predator*, *Total Recall*, and *True Lies*. In 1986 this Republican movie star married television journalist Maria Shriver, daughter of Sargent Shriver, first head of the Peace Corps and the Great Society's antipoverty program, and Eunice Kennedy Shriver, founder of Special Olympics. Schwarzenegger was active in promoting physical fitness among underprivileged children; from 1990 to 1993 he was chairman of George H. W. Bush's Council on Physical Fitness and Sports, and in 1995 he established the National Inner City Games Foundation. He became involved with the successful LA's BEST after-school program and in 2002 sponsored a ballot proposition to establish a state after-school program; it provided that no money be spent until available in the budget. Proposition 49 passed 57%–43%. It won 62% in Los Angeles County, 58% in the rest of Southern California, 54% in the San Francisco Bay Area and 53% in the rest of the state.

Not many noticed, but Proposition 49 got 491,000 more votes than Governor Gray Davis did as he won reelection by a 47%–42% margin the same day. There was speculation that Schwarzenegger might run for governor in 2006, but many noted that his liberal positions on cultural issues—pro-choice on abortion, pro-gun control, pro-civil unions for gays and lesbians— might make it difficult for him to win a Republican primary. But there turned out to be another path to the governorship. In February 2003, after the state deficit was projected to be between $26 and $35 billion, and Davis mulled tax increases, conservative activist Ted Costa of People's Advocate started a movement to recall Davis. California law provides that a recall election must be called if petitions are filed with signatures amounting to 12% of the votes most recently cast for the office; with turnout low in 2002, that meant 897,000 signatures. Costa said he had hundreds of thousands of dollars pledged for a petition drive, but in March and April it seemed to falter as polls showed most voters critical of Davis but opposed to recall. Then in May 2003 Congressman Darrell Issa, who made millions from a car alarm business, started pumping $1.7 million into the recall effort. After the July 4 weekend, organizers said they had 1.2 million signatures; on July 16 they were sent to county officials and on July 23 the secretary of state said the petitions qualified. Lieutenant Governor Cruz Bustamante set the election for October 7; voters would decide whether to recall Davis and could choose from a list of candidates who would replace him if he were recalled. Anyone could file by paying a $3,500 fee and filing 65 signatures by August 9. Would Schwarzenegger run? He said he had to promote *Terminator 3* and would only decide after that. On August 3 and 4 Davis filed lawsuits trying to get the recall called off or delayed; on August 5 the state AFL-CIO urged Democrats not to put their names on the replacement ballot. On the morning of August 6 Senator Dianne Feinstein, whom some Democrats wanted as a backup to hold the governorship if Davis was recalled, announced she would not run. That afternoon Schwarzenegger went to Burbank to tape *The Tonight Show*; his political consultants believed he would announce he was not running; he shocked them when he said he was. A few hours later Bustamante broke ranks with other Democratic leaders and announced he was running on the replacement ballot. Within 24 hours Issa withdrew from the race. In all, 135 candidates qualified for the replacement ballot. But the ranks of serious candidates soon dwindled. Bill Simon, the Republican businessman who had lost to Davis in 2002, ended his campaign August 23. 1984 Olympics organizer Peter Ueberroth ended his September 9. By mid-September it was clear that there were three serious candidates on the replacement ballot,

Schwarzenegger, Bustamante and state Senator Tom McClintock, a fiscal and cultural conservative who had lost the 2002 race for state controller by only a 45.4%–45.1% margin. On September 15, a three-judge panel of the Ninth Circuit federal appeals court postponed the election to March 2004 at the urging of the ACLU; but on September 23 a full 11-judge panel ordered the recall to go ahead on October 7.

Throughout the campaign, in campaign rallies and in televised debates, Schwarzenegger made few specific proposals, but said that Davis must be removed, taxes must not be increased and spending needed to be cut. His campaign organized monster rallies which attracted thousands and where he spoke only briefly and did not mingle with the crowd. Davis rallies were sparsely attended, mainly by Democratic party and union officials; Bustamante, who announced his candidacy by fax, scarcely campaigned at all. On October 2 the *Los Angeles Times* ran a story alleging that Schwarzenegger had groped various women some years ago. Recall advocates had considered the *Times's* coverage biased against their cause—its poll showed much more anti-recall sentiment than other public polls—and saw this as another attempt to keep Gray Davis in office. Schwarzenegger admitted that he had "behaved badly sometimes" and apologized. But the stories failed to stop the tide. Davis, elected 58%–38% in 1998 and reelected 47%–42% in 2002, was recalled 55%–45%. On the replacement ballot Schwarzenegger won 49% of the vote, Bustamante 32% and McClintock 13%. The San Francisco Bay Area voted 64%–36% against recall, but Los Angeles County rejected it by only 51%–49%, though Davis had won 56% there 11 months before. Southern California voted 69% and the rest of the state voted 64% for recall. Schwarzenegger trailed Bustamante 46%–33% in the Bay Area, but led him 45%–37% in Los Angeles County, 60%–21% in Southern California and 52%–25% in the rest of the state.

Democrats were bitter over losing control of state government in this generally Democratic state after holding it for only five years of the preceding 21; some even threatened to recall Schwarzenegger in 2004. But Davis conceded graciously and ordered his appointees to cooperate with the new administration. On November 17 Schwarzenegger became governor and made state government suddenly visible; Los Angeles and San Francisco TV stations scrambled to open Sacramento bureaus. Schwarzenegger ordered a performance review of state government and plunged into the business of budget making. He pressed the legislature for repeal of the law Davis signed providing driver's licenses for illegal immigrants; he said he would sign a measure with sufficient security guarantees. He also repealed Davis's car tax increase and used deficiency appropriations to help local governments; they agreed to give up $1.3 billion in each of the next two years in return for a constitutional amendment making it harder for the state to take over local revenues. He got two constitutional amendments put on the March 2004 primary ballot: one to authorize $15 billion of debt to cover the current budget deficit, another to require a balanced budget in out-years. Both trailed in the polls, but after Schwarzenegger started campaigning for them, the first passed with 63% of the vote and the second with 71%; at the same time, voters rejected 66%–34% Democratic legislators' attempt to make it easier to raise taxes. In April 2004, by threatening to take the issue to the voters, he got the legislature to make changes in workmen's comp law without the rate regulation Democrats were seeking. In May 2004 he accepted Speaker Fabian Nunez's electricity bill allowing utilities to buy electricity through long-term contracts but gave businesses less ability to buy power directly than Schwarzenegger wanted. In May 2004 he released a $99 billion budget with deficits that seemed likely to be $8 billion over two years. It called for higher payments from Indian casinos and cuts in pay and benefits for state employees. Unlike his Republican predecessors Ronald Reagan and Pete Wilson, he refused to support a tax increase in a budget crisis. "Higher taxes have no place in our California recovery." California requires budgets to be approved by two-thirds votes in the legislature, so they always represent something of a consensus; after negotiations broke down, Schwarzenegger signed a $105 billion budget July 31.

Schwarzenegger campaigned for some Republican legislative candidates in fall 2004, but none won. Democrats held Silicon Valley seats in the state Senate and Assembly by 64%–34%, and held two coastal seats, in Santa Barbara County and in Palos Verdes and Long Beach, with 53%. Schwarzenegger had his successes in November 2004 referenda. A measure he backed promising $3 billion for stem-cell research passed 59%–41%. His measure to protect local government revenues from state takeover was approved 84%–16%. A measure to relax the "three strikes and you're out" law, which had been leading in the polls, lost 53%–47% after Schwarzenegger campaigned against it. A measure to limit tort actions passed 59%–41%. Indian tribes' attempts to augment their casino businesses were rejected by 77% and 84% of the voters. A telephone tax for emergency medical funding was rejected by 72%. And a measure to mandate health insurance coverage for small businesses was rejected, though by only 51%–49%. California voters seemed to be in line with their new Republican governor.

In January 2005 Schwarzenegger proposed a $111 billion budget, with cuts in scheduled increases in health care, transportation and school aid. To cries of protest he said, "Year after year, politicians have promised increases in health care, increases in education, increases in pensions, increases in this, increases in that. My administration and every legislature loves to give those kinds of things. But we don't have the money." Perhaps even more important, he went on the offensive, attacking the heart of the political system, by demanding action on four issues and, again, threatening to take them to the people in November 2005. They included a nonpartisan board of retired judges to redistrict California's congressional and legislative districts, automatic across-the-board spending cuts if spending grew faster than revenues, merit pay for teachers and defined contribution 401(k)-like pensions for state employees. All four threaten the roots of Democratic institutional power. Schwarzenegger said, "We're going right where all the evil is, and we're going to fix it." Redistricting would put more Democrats (and Republicans) at risk of losing their seats, and Democrats might not be guaranteed the permanent majorities they have had under the current plan. Across-the-board spending cuts would give the governor huge leverage in budget negotiations and would repeal the provision the teacher unions got voters to pass guaranteeing a certain level of spending for education. Merit pay for teachers, furiously opposed by teacher unions, would further reduce the power of one of the Democrats' key supporting institutions. Defined contribution pension plans would reduce, over time, the power of CalPERS, which invests California's pension money and is one of the biggest institutional investors in the country; Democrats have dominated CalPERS and have used its leverage to influence the acts of major corporations. In early 2005 the Democratic legislature seemed certain to reject those measures; in June, Schwarzenegger called a November 2005 special election to get voters to approve them. Three of his favored measures qualified for the ballot: one would give the governor new authority to cut spending, another called for an increase in the service required before teachers could receive tenure and a third would create a non-partisan board of retired judges the authority to redistrict state legislative boundaries. Schwarzenegger dropped his initiative to overhaul the state employee pension system and got rid of the merit pay proposal. Democratic legislators and public employees vigorously opposed his plans, criticizing their cost; Schwarzenegger said the election was a "fantastic bargain" for taxpayers. "For a buck and a quarter per citizen, you can fix a broken system and save the state billions of dollars."

Schwarzenegger is a national figure of considerable prominence. He was one of the featured speakers at the 2004 Republican National Convention, where he lauded George W. Bush. "America is back. Back from the attack on our homeland, back from the attack on our economy and back from the attack on our way of life. We are back because of the perseverance, character and leadership of the 43d president of the United States, George W. Bush." And he got tough on Democrats. "To those critics who are so pessimistic about our economy, I say: Don't be economic girlie men." He said he was too busy to campaign much for Bush, but appeared with him in California and a few days before the election flew into Columbus to appear with him in what turned out to be the key state of Ohio. Schwarzenegger is ineligible to run for president under the Constitution, but has backed a constitutional amendment to allow immigrants to serve as president after they have been citizens for 20 years.

Will Schwarzenegger run for a full term in 2006? Some in California think he won't if he fails to achieve victories on his reform packages in November 2005. But he seems to have a zest for the job and not to have been intimidated by the attacks that have been launched his way.

Senior Senator

Dianne Feinstein (D)

Elected 1992, seat up 2006, 2d full term; b. June 22, 1933, San Francisco; home, San Francisco; Stanford U., B.A. 1955; Jewish; married (Richard C. Blum).

Elected Office: San Francisco Bd. of Supervisors, 1970–78, Pres., 1970–71, 1974–75, 1978; San Francisco Mayor, 1978–88.

Professional Career: CA Women's Parole Bd., 1960–66.

DC Office: 331 HSOB, 20510, 202-224-3841; Fax: 202-228-3954; Web site: feinstein.senate.gov.

State Offices: Fresno, 559-485-7430; Los Angeles, 310-914-7300; San Diego, 619-231-9712; San Francisco, 415-393-0707.

Committees: *Appropriations*: Agriculture, Rural Development & Related Agencies; Defense; Energy & Water; Homeland Security; Interior & Related Agencies; Military Construction & Veterans Affairs (RMM). *Energy & Natural Resources*: Energy; Public Lands & Forests; Water & Power. *Intelligence (Select)*. *Judiciary*: Administrative Oversight & the Courts; Constitution, Civil Rights & Property Rights; Crime & Drugs; Immigration, Border Security & Citizenship; Intellectual Property; Terrorism, Technology & Homeland Security (RMM). *Rules & Administration*.

Group Ratings

	ADA	ACLU	AFS	LCV	ITIC	NTU	COC	ACU	NTLC	CHC
2004	100	78	100	100	50	14	65	4	2	0
2003	90	—	89	79	—	15	39	5	—	—

National Journal Ratings

	2003 LIB	—	2003 CONS		2004 LIB	—	2004 CONS
Economic	60%	—	39%		65%	—	31%
Social	67%	—	32%		82%	—	0%
Foreign	74%	—	22%		61%	—	36%

Key Votes of the 108th Congress

1. Ban Drilling in ANWR	Y	5. Energy Bill	N	9. Ban Same-Sex Marriage	N
2. Approve Bush Tax Cuts	N	6. Support Roe v. Wade	Y	10. Ban Bunker-Buster Bomb	Y
3. Medicare/Rx Bill	Y	7. Ban Partial-Birth Abortion	N	11. Fund Iraq War	Y
4. Bar Overtime Pay Regs.	Y	8. Assault Weapons Ban	Y	12. Restrict Missile Defense	Y

Election Results

2000 general	Dianne Feinstein (D)	5,932,522	(56%)	($10,346,170)
	Tom Campbell (R)	3,886,853	(37%)	($4,378,283)
	Other	804,233	(8%)	
2000 primary	Dianne Feinstein (D)	3,759,560	(52%)	
	Tom Campbell (R)	1,697,208	(23%)	
	Ray Haynes (R)	679,034	(9%)	
	Bill Horn (R)	453,630	(6%)	
	Other	759,405	(10%)	
1994 general	Dianne Feinstein (D)	3,977,063	(47%)	($14,407,179)
	Michael Huffington (R)	3,811,501	(45%)	($29,969,695)
	Other	714,500	(8%)	

Prior Winning Percentages: 1992 (54%)

Dianne Feinstein, California's senior senator, is a Democrat first elected in 1992. Feinstein grew up in San Francisco, in lush Presidio Heights, graduated from Stanford and later studied criminology. She was appointed by Governor Pat Brown to the women's parole board in 1960, at 27. In 1969 she was elected to the San Francisco County Board of Supervisors—the city's council—and twice ran for mayor and lost. As president of the board, she became mayor in 1978 when Mayor George Moscone and Supervisor Harvey Milk were murdered by former Supervisor Dan White; she discovered Moscone's body and showed steadiness and a sense of command that calmed the city. She was elected to full terms in 1979 and 1983. In 1984, Walter Mondale seriously considered her for vice president, but passed over her for Geraldine Ferraro because of qualms about the business dealings of her husband, Richard Blum. Feinstein presided gracefully that year over the Democratic National Convention in San Francisco—while Ferraro juggled questions about *her* family's business. In fact, Feinstein and Blum's investments have thrived; the Capitol Hill newspaper *Roll Call* estimated their net worth in 2003 at $32 million, the twelfth highest in Congress.

Feinstein left the mayor's office in 1987, ineligible for a third full term, and ran for governor in 1990. She won the Democratic primary impressively, then lost 49%–46% to Pete Wilson. When Wilson appointed Orange County state Senator John Seymour—an unknown and bland choice—to replace him in the Senate, Feinstein quickly announced for the seat, even though the 1992 race was for only the last two years of Wilson's term, and she could have run for the seat being vacated by Alan Cranston the same year. She had primary competition from Gray Davis, then state controller, who ran an ad against her campaign finance practices comparing her to Leona Helmsley. Feinstein won 58%–33% and her relations with Davis, elected governor in 1998 and 2002 and recalled in 2003, were not always warm; she appeared in two spots for him in the 2003 recall campaign that did not mention his name. In the 1992 general election, nothing worked for the hapless Seymour—not his switches to pro-choice on abortion and anti-offshore oil drilling, not his attacks on Feinstein's arguably tricky financing of her 1990 gubernatorial campaign (which resulted in a $190,000 fine), not fears of immigration, not Seymour's tending to agricultural interests. Feinstein won 54%–38%, coming close even in Seymour's southern California base.

In the Senate, Feinstein kept a certain distance from the Clinton administration, negotiating for changes before voting for the 1993 budget, voting against NAFTA, withdrawing her support of the Clinton health care plan in May 1994, condemning Bill Clinton's "I did not have sexual relations with that woman, Miss Lewinsky" comment which she had heard in person. She had two significant legislative achievements in her first two years. One was the attachment of the assault weapons ban to the 1994 crime bill. When Idaho's Larry Craig argued that her definition of assault weapons was not rigorous enough and challenged her knowledge of firearms, she responded by saying: "I know something about what firearms can do; I came to be mayor of San Francisco as a product of assassination." Her other major achievement was a California Desert Protection Act. Similar measures had been stymied by the state's Republican senators as too restrictive, but now that there was no Republican senator, Feinstein managed it through enactment.

Feinstein has a moderate to liberal voting record, and has differed on some issues from her colleague and Bay area neighbor Barbara Boxer. Feinstein sponsored the Y2K liability act opposed by trial lawyers, for example, and voted to repeal the marriage penalty and the estate tax. She supported the 2001 Bush tax cut and voted for the Iraq war resolution in October 2002 and the $87 billion supplemental in November 2003. She took the lead in supporting school vouchers for the District of Columbia in 2003. "As a former mayor, I also believe that local leaders should have an opportunity to experiment with programs that they believe are right for their area." She supported the Medicare/prescription drug bill in November 2003. When she ran for governor in 1990 she emphasized her support of the death penalty and of abortion rights, and on the Judiciary Committee she has taken tough stands. Before September 11, Feinstein and Jon Kyl co-sponsored a bill to prepare defenses for attacks by terrorists with chemical and biological weapons. After the attacks, she proposed a six-month moratorium on new student visas. College and university presidents squawked; there were 548,000 foreign students in the country in 2000–01, pumping $11 billion into the economy, much of it directly into universities. In October she said she was willing to drop the moratorium if colleges and universities would verify compliance with the visas. She and Kyl came forward with a bill to establish a central database of visa holders and other aliens in the country, to bar entry for people from nations that sponsor terrorism, to require the INS and the State Department to create biometric visa cards and passports, to require foreign nations to supply airlines with passenger manifest lists and to lift the 45-minute deadline for INS inspection of incoming foreigners. This was more stringent than a similar measure sponsored by Edward Kennedy and Sam Brownback. In December the two versions were melded and it was signed into law by Bush in May 2002.

Feinstein sought to crack down on Internet piracy of movies in 2003 and blocked for a time reauthorization of the moratorium on Internet taxation. She has sought to limit the sale of pseudophedrine to 9 grams to choke off the illegal meth trade. She opposed the Bush immigration plan in January 2004, arguing that it "could be a magnet for more illegal immigrants." She has criticized Mexico for not granting extradition of criminal defendants to the United States. In 2000 she introduced a bill to require licensing of all guns and in 2004 pressed fervently for reauthorization of the 1994 assault weapons ban. George W. Bush had said in 2000 that he would sign such a bill, but despite Feinstein's frequent pleas did nothing to bring it forward; the act expired in September 2004. With Patty Murray she co-sponsored an unsuccessful amendment in March 2004 which would have imposed multiple penalties for homicides causing the death of a fetus, but would not have defined the latter as a separate crime. With Harry Reid, she blocked an Indian Affairs Committee bill to reduce state supervision of Indian gambling. With Orrin Hatch, she got 54 senators to sign a letter calling for more embryonic stem-cell research. She has joined other Judiciary Committee Democrats in opposing and filibustering several Bush nominees to federal appeals court. In 2002 she and Boxer blocked the nomination of Orange County Congressman Christopher Cox to the Ninth Circuit Court of Appeals, a bench so liberal that it is frequently reversed 9–0 by the Supreme Court. With Boxer, she made an arrangement with the Bush administration to set up six-member panels to decide on the potential merits of federal trial judges in California; three members were appointed by each side, and four votes is required for approval of a nominee. This bypasses the two senior Republicans in the House delegation, Bill Thomas and Jerry Lewis, to whom the White House customarily looks when both state's senators are of the opposition party.

Feinstein voted for the Iraq war resolution in October 2002—an act unpopular with many California Democrats. In January 2003 she said U.S. troop deployments in the area were "deeply disturbing" in what she said was the absence of proof that Iraq had weapons of mass destruction. Hours after Colin Powell spoke at the United Nations in February 2003 she took a different view: "I no longer think inspections are going to work." In April 2004 she said she was misled into voting for the war by an exaggeration of the threat, and regretted her vote. In December 2004 she called on Bush to "tell the American people the truth" that troops would be required in Iraq for many years. But in January 2005 she introduced Condoleezza Rice to the Foreign Relations Committee and warmly supported her nomination to be secretary of state. On nuclear weapons, Feinstein in 2003 and 2004 sought to deny funding to studies of the Robust Nuclear Earth Penetrator (the bunker buster bomb) and the Advanced Concepts Initiative (a low-yield nuclear bomb). On the Intelligence Committee, she called for a single national intelligence director in 2002, long before the 9/11 Commission recommended one and voted in September 2004 to confirm Porter Goss as CIA director. But in November she said the changes he was making could have "a significant and negative effect on the agency."

Feinstein has a seat on Appropriations, where she can funnel money to California, and on Energy and Natural Resources, where she works on water issues. She has worked for several years to revive the CALFED water program, a series of projects—raising Shasta Dam, building a new reservoir in Colusa County, buying up and flooding islands in the Sacramento River Delta and providing fish screens there. She was blocked in 2001 and 2002 by Republicans from other western states who thought California was drawing too much water from the Colorado River water until a January 2003 change. In 2003 and 2004 she worked with House Resources Chairman Richard Pombo to reauthorize CALFED and to protect water quality in San Francisco Bay and the Sacramento Delta. She also worked with Pombo and with Western Republican senators in 2003 to get passage of a compromise Healthy Forests Act. She managed to protect California's strict emissions standards on small engines from federal preemption in 2003 and 2004, with help from Governor Arnold Schwarzenegger.

Feinstein has had only one serious challenge since she was first elected in the Senate, in the Republican year of 1994 from one-term Congressman Michael Huffington. In 1992 Huffington spent $3 million of his own money to unseat an 18-year incumbent in the Republican primary in the Santa Barbara area House seat. In 1994 he spent nearly $30 million of his own money against Feinstein. He pulled even in polls in September, and Feinstein was clearly flustered and angry that she could not count on heavily outspending him. Huffington slipped when it was revealed that he and his wife Arianna Huffington, now an outspoken liberal, employed an illegal alien as a nanny. On the Thursday before the election, it was revealed that Feinstein, despite her earlier denials, had employed a woman whose work permit had expired; but the news media ran stories saying that federal officials cast doubt on whether the woman was an illegal. That probably made the difference. Feinstein won 47%–45%. She carried Los Angeles County 52%–40% and the San Francisco Bay area 63%–30%, offsetting Huffington's margins in Southern California and the rest of the state.

Since 1994 Feinstein has gotten pretty solid ratings in the polls. In late 1997 she gave some thought to running for governor; in 2003 some Democrats tried to persuade her to put herself on the replacement ballot in the recall election. But both times she declined to seek the office she lost in 1990. In 2000 she was opposed by Republican Congressman Tom Campbell, a libertarian Stanford Law professor who had nearly won the 1992 nomination to run against Barbara Boxer and who, in a more Republican California than it is now, might have won. Campbell took a conservative line on economics and supported abortion rights. In 1999 and 2000, his big issue was drugs: he favored more treatment and less imprisonment, and called for use of heroin in drug treatments. Campbell was outspent by $10.3 million to $4.4 million, and his stand on drugs failed to make inroads among Democrats. Feinstein won 56%–37%, carrying all major regions of the state. She won 5,932,000 votes, the most popular votes cast for a senator in American history, a record eclipsed by Barbara Boxer in 2004. Feinstein has made it plain she will run for reelection in 2006; in December 2004 she said, "There's no doubt I'm running,. I've been effective. I've been a strong senator for California." Absent an opponent who can self-finance as Michael Huffington did or who can raise the kind of money Arnold Schwarzenegger has, she is a heavy favorite for reelection.

Junior Senator

Barbara Boxer (D)

Elected 1992, seat up 2010, 3d term; b. Nov. 11, 1940, Brooklyn, NY; home, Greenbrae; Brooklyn Col., B.A. 1962; Jewish; married (Stewart).

Elected Office: Marin Cnty. Bd. of Supervisors, 1976–82; U.S. House of Reps., 1982–92.

Professional Career: Stockbroker & researcher, 1962–65; Journalist, *Pacific Sun*, 1972–74; Dist. aide, U.S. Rep. John Burton, 1974–76.

DC Office: 112 HSOB, 20510, 202-224-3553; Fax: 415-956-6700; Web site: boxer.senate.gov.

State Offices: Fresno, 559-497-5109; Los Angeles, 213-894-5000; Sacramento, 916-448-2787; San Bernardino, 909-888-8525; San Diego, 619-239-3884; San Francisco, 415-403-0100.

Committees: *Commerce, Science & Transportation*: Aviation; Consumer Affairs, Product Safety & Insurance; National Ocean Policy Study (RMM); Surface Transportation & Merchant Marine. *Environment & Public Works*: Superfund & Waste Management (RMM); Transportation & Infrastructure. *Foreign Relations*: International Operations & Terrorism; Near Eastern & South Asian Affairs (RMM); Western Hemisphere, Peace Corps & Narcotics Affairs.

Group Ratings

	ADA	ACLU	AFS	LCV	ITIC	NTU	COC	ACU	NTLC	CHC
2004	95	75	100	100	67	18	56	4	5	0
2003	95	—	100	89	—	16	22	10	—	—

National Journal Ratings

	2003 LIB	—	2003 CONS		2004 LIB	—	2004 CONS
Economic	82%	—	10%		75%	—	24%
Social	85%	—	0%		82%	—	0%
Foreign	90%	—	0%		82%	—	16%

Key Votes of the 108th Congress

1. Ban Drilling in ANWR	Y	5. Energy Bill	N	9. Ban Same-Sex Marriage	N
2. Approve Bush Tax Cuts	N	6. Support Roe v. Wade	Y	10. Ban Bunker-Buster Bomb	Y
3. Medicare/Rx Bill	N	7. Ban Partial-Birth Abortion	N	11. Fund Iraq War	N
4. Bar Overtime Pay Regs.	Y	8. Assault Weapons Ban	Y	12. Restrict Missile Defense	Y

Election Results

2004 general	Barbara Boxer (D)	6,955,728	(58%)	($14,886,426)
	Bill Jones (R)	4,555,922	(38%)	($7,802,657)
	Other	541,643	(4%)	
2004 primary	Barbara Boxer (D)	unopposed		
1998 general	Barbara Boxer (D)	4,410,056	(53%)	($13,737,548)
	Matt Fong (R)	3,575,078	(43%)	($10,764,892)
	Other	326,771	(4%)	

Prior Winning Percentages: 1992 (48%); 1990 House (68%); 1988 House (73%); 1986 House (74%); 1984 House (68%); 1982 House (52%)

Barbara Boxer, California's junior senator, was first elected in 1992 and reelected in 1998. She grew up in Brooklyn, where she was a victim of sexual harassment by a college professor and was refused work as a stockbroker. She and her husband moved to San Francisco in 1965 and then, in search of affordable housing, to Marin County in 1968. In 1968 she volunteered for Eugene McCarthy's presidential campaign; in 1970 she and some neighbors formed the Marin Alternative, to oppose the Vietnam War and a subdivision planned for a wetland near Sir Francis Drake Boulevard. Marin County was only on its way to being trendy then; the overall political tone was liberal Republican, but heading left: it was one of the few parts of the country where George McGovern won a higher percentage in 1972 than Hubert Humphrey had in 1968 and where abortion rights supporter Gerald Ford got a larger percentage margin over abortion critic Jimmy Carter in 1976 than Richard Nixon had over McGovern; in contrast, Marin voted 73%–25% for John Kerry in 2004. In 1972 Boxer ran for the Board of Supervisors and lost to an incumbent Republican. She then worked for Democratic Congressman John Burton. In 1976, when women candidates were more accepted, she ran again for the board and won. When Burton retired unexpectedly in 1982, she ran for the House and was easily elected. She made many splashes in the House, unearthing the Air Force's $7,622 coffee pot in 1984, denouncing the Gulf war with more ardor than just about anyone and leading a march of women on the Senate when Anita Hill was testifying against Clarence Thomas.

In the 1980s it seemed improbable that anyone as liberal as Boxer could be elected senator from California, which had after all voted Republican for president in all but one election from 1952 to 1988. But now Boxer has been elected three times, by decisive and rising margins. In 1992 she started off as neither the best-known nor the best-financed candidate, but this turned out to be the year of the woman, in which the enthusiasm of the feminist left produced important victories for Democratic women. Boxer won the June 1992 Democratic primary with 44% of the vote, to 31% for Lieutenant Governor Leo McCarthy, and 22% for Congressman Mel Levine. Her general election opponent was Bruce Herschensohn, a Los Angeles TV and radio commentator, backer of a flat tax and offshore oil drilling and opponent of abortion. Herschensohn had edged Silicon Valley moderate Congressman Tom Campbell 38%–36% in the primary, with the help of then-Palm Springs Mayor Sonny Bono, who won 17%. The Boxer-Herschensohn race was a battle of opposites, the far left versus the far right of the American electoral spectrum. Boxer was helped by the collapse of the Bush candidacy in California, by hearty support from Feinstein and by the revelation by state Democratic political director Bob Mulholland during the last week of the campaign that Herschensohn attended nightclubs that featured nude dancers.

Boxer's voting record has been strongly liberal, among the most liberal in the Senate in *National Journal's* ratings. She is perhaps the personification of the feminist left, and is one of the strongest proponents of abortion rights in the Senate; she has vehemently opposed the partial-birth abortion ban. But she was also a staunch defender of Bill Clinton. In 1998, the senator who had marched across the Capitol to protest the cross-examination of Anita Hill, found little to believe in the charges against Clinton until he admitted their truth, and even then limited her condemnation to a perfunctory statement combined with a total commitment to defeat impeachment. And in 1999 the crusader against the Gulf War resolution solidly backed the bombing campaign against Serbia. In September 2001 she supported the use of force in Afghanistan. But in October 2002 she voted against the use of force in Iraq, and she voted against the $87 billion supplemental appropriation in October 2003. She has often charged that the Bush administration diverted its attention from Al Qaeda to Iraq. But she supported the act denouncing Syria in November 2003. "We don't want to go to war with Syria. We just want to say in a truthful way, 'These are things that you've been doing wrong. Please meet these markers.'"

Boxer has supported gun control and has sponsored amendments to require childproof safety locks on all handguns and to ban sales of guns to people who are intoxicated. But in summer 2002 she and Kentucky Republican Jim Bunning emerged as the Senate's leading advocates of allowing airline pilots to carry guns. Boxer argued that pilots could be trusted with that responsibility and that they could protect passengers against terrorists. The measure was initially opposed by the Bush administration but, after the House passed it, it passed the Senate by a wide margin. In April 2004 Boxer and Bunning charged that the TSA was stalling on implementation and urged it be speeded up. "TSA has slow-walked the program from day one, denying thousands of pilots their right to be trained in this program and denying the American people the additional security they deserve." Also in 2003 Boxer warned of the danger to airliners from shoulder-fired missiles and called for installation of anti-missile devices on all airliners and beefed up Coast Guard and National Guard patrolling in airport perimeters. She co-sponsored a bill passed by the Commerce committee in 2004 to provide $500 million for rail and mass transit safety. She has opposed the partial-birth abortion ban and oil drilling in the Arctic National Wildlife Refuge. In January 2004 she called for testing of all cows slaughtered in the U.S. to prevent an outbreak of mad cow disease.

Boxer was frustrated when Republicans during the Clinton years held up nominations to the Ninth Circuit Court of Appeals, currently the most liberal in the country. In spring 2001 she opposed the nomination of Orange County Congressman Christopher Cox to the Ninth Circuit; when Dianne Feinstein said she might oppose him too, Cox withdrew. She and Feinstein worked to set up a procedure to give them approval of all federal district judges in California.

Boxer has weighed in on all manner of California issues. As California was hit by rolling electricity blackouts in early 2001, she proposed a windfall profits tax on energy producers and, with Feinstein, sponsored a bill to impose temporary price controls on wholesale electric power suppliers. But she split with Feinstein by backing the two Oregon senators' unsuccessful amendment to the bankruptcy reform bill that would have barred PG&E and Southern California Edison from discharging their debts in bankruptcy; a few weeks later PG&E sought bankruptcy protection. She and Anna Eshoo sponsored similar bills to require FERC to order refunds of up to $9 billion to California consumers. In 2004 she called for the resignation of FERC members who refused to order immediate refunds. She has joined Oregon Democrat Ron Wyden in his attacks on FTC members who have not taken action against West Coast gasoline price increases which they said were the result of oil company mergers. She criticized the Bush administration for opposing $10 million in funding for preserving California's 21 Franciscan missions built between 1769 and 1823. In June 2001, when Jesse Helms amended the education bill to bar funds for school districts that exclude the Boy Scouts, she successfully pressed a substitute which requires equal access to all youth groups; this would allow San Francisco and other California districts to keep excluding the Boy Scouts, which ban gays from the organization. When San Francisco Mayor Gavin Newsom was performing same-sex marriages in February 2004, she avoided endorsing his acts and said, "I have always been very strongly for domestic partnerships. I think the California law is a very good, workable law." She joined with Dianne Feinstein in May 2004 in calling for federal prosecutors to seek the death penalty for a defendant accused of killing a San

Francisco police officer with an AK-47; San Francisco District Attorney Kamala Harris, whom Boxer had supported, had declined to seek the death penalty.

During her first three years in the Senate Boxer's job ratings were among the Senate's lowest. But California with its large metro areas trended sharply toward the Democrats in the mid-1990s, and in early 1997 Boxer's job rating was up to 50%. Prominent Republicans—Congressman Tom Campbell, San Diego Mayor Susan Golding, 1994 Senate nominee Michael Huffington—decided not to run against her in 1998. In the all-party primary, state Treasurer Matt Fong edged businessman (and now Congressman) Darrell Issa. On paper Fong was a strong candidate, with an Asian heritage and a moderate record on issues; his mother March Fong Eu, a Democrat, was California's secretary of state from 1974 to 1994. But Boxer raised $15 million and campaigned long and hard. She launched an ad campaign attacking Fong for his ambiguous stances on issues like abortion. She guarded herself from contact with reporters so she would not have to answer questions about Bill Clinton; the president's brother-in-law Tony Rodham was then married to her daughter Nicole. Fong attacked her for the hypocrisy of her stand on the Clinton scandals. But he spoke hesitantly and unconvincingly in the sound bites that are the staple of California politics and never succeeded in raising much money. For much of September and October he was off the air, while Boxer was pounding the airwaves mercilessly. Boxer won 53%–43%. She won 61% of the vote in Los Angeles County and 63% in the San Francisco Bay area, and trailed not far behind in Southern California and the rest of the state—an impressive performance for a Democrat dismissed a few years before as too left wing for much of the state.

Boxer says that before September 11 she had decided not to seek a third term in 2004. But when House Majority Leader Tom DeLay six months after the attacks criticized Democrats for criticizing the Bush administration, she changed her mind. "Then I got really fearful for my country. The greatest thing about our country is that we're free and that we debate and we talk." She began raising impressive amounts of money, and once again many well-known Republicans declined to make the race. The best-known candidate against her, Bill Jones, had been elected secretary of state by narrow margins in 1994 and 1998; but he was not well known outside his home base in Fresno County. He had the endorsement but not the active support of Governor Arnold Schwarzenegger. Nonetheless he won the March 2004 primary with 45% of the vote, to 20% for former U.S. Treasurer Rosario Marin and 11% for former Assemblyman Howard Kaloogian; Marin made a close race of it in Los Angeles County and Southern California, but Jones won by wide margins in the rest of the state. This turned out not to be a seriously contested race. George W. Bush's political advisers may still have been miffed that Jones in 2000 retracted his primary endorsement of Bush and endorsed John McCain; in any case, national Republicans made no effort to pump in the huge amounts of money needed to make a California Republican competitive. Boxer spent $16 million to Jones's $7 million; Boxer ran no attack ads, as she had done in 1998, while Jones ran no TV ads at all in September and October. Boxer, elected with 48% of the vote in 1992 and 53% in 1998, won 58% in 2004—almost a perfect arithmetical progression upward. Jones won only 38%. Boxer won 67% of the vote in Los Angeles County and 70% in the San Francisco Bay area; she ran narrowly ahead in Southern California and almost precisely even in the rest of the state. Running in a presidential year, she won 6,955,000 votes—more popular votes than any other senator had ever won in American history, far ahead of Dianne Feinstein's previous records set in 1992 and 2000.

Boxer seems to have taken this huge victory in the nation's largest state as a mandate to speak out. In January 2005, as the electoral vote count was read out to a joint session of Congress, she was the one senator to protest the award of Ohio's electoral votes to George W. Bush. She remembered that four years before no senator had protested the Florida vote even though several members of the House had, and she said she regretted not having protested then. Her protest triggered the dissolution of the joint session and a debate in each of the two Houses—for one hour in the Senate, rather longer in the House. The Senate voted 74–1 to accept the Ohio count, with Boxer was the one dissenter; the House voted 267–31 on the same question. "I hate inconveniencing my friends, but I think it's worth a couple of hours to shine some light on these issues," Boxer said. Later in January, after her California colleague Dianne Feinstein escorted Condoleezza Rice to the Foreign Relations Committee hearing on her nomination to be secretary of state, Boxer attacked Rice stingingly. Her "loyalty to the mission," Boxer said, "overwhelmed your respect for the truth." Speaking of the troops, she said, "You sent them in there because of weapons of mass destruction. Later the mission changed when there were none." Rice responded, "I really hope you will refrain from impugning my integrity. I really hope that you will not imply that I take the truth lightly." In these exchanges Boxer seemed to emerge as the most aggressive and articulate challenger of the Bush administration in the Senate.

FIRST DISTRICT

Rep. Mike Thompson (D)

Elected 1998, 4th term; b. Jan. 24, 1951, St. Helena; home, St. Helena; CA St. U., B. A. 1982, M. A. 1996.; Catholic; married (Janet).

Military Career: Army, 1969–73 (Vietnam).

Elected Office: CA Senate, 1990–98.

Professional Career: Supervisor, Beringer Winery; CA Assembly fellow, 1982–83; Chief of Staff, CA Assemblyman Lou Papan, 1984–87; Chief of Staff, CA Assemblywoman Jacqueline Speier, 1987–90.

DC Office: 231 CHOB, 20515, 202-225-3311; Fax: 202-225-4335; Web site: mikethompson.house.gov.

District Offices: Eureka, 707-269-9595; Fort Bragg, 707-962-0933; Napa, 707-226-9898; Yolo, 530-662-5272.

Committees: *Ways & Means* (15th of 17 D): Health; Select Revenue Measures.

Group Ratings

	ADA	ACLU	AFS	LCV	ITIC	NTU	COC	ACU	NTLC	CHC
2004	90	75	88	91	90	11	48	13	6	7
2003	90	—	100	90	—	31	50	24	—	—

National Journal Ratings

	2003 LIB	—	2003 CONS		2004 LIB	—	2004 CONS
Economic	66%	—	32%		62%	—	38%
Social	73%	—	26%		86%	—	12%
Foreign	75%	—	21%		83%	—	16%

Key Votes of the 108th Congress

1. Drilling in ANWR	N	5. DC School Vouchers	N	9. Ban Same-Sex Marriage	N
2. Approve Bush Tax Cuts	N	6. Ban Human Cloning	N	10. Fund Iraq War	N
3. Medicare/Rx Bill	N	7. Restrict Gun Liability	Y	11. Bar Cuba Embargo Funds	Y
4. Bar Overtime Pay Regs.	Y	8. Ban Partial-Birth Abortion	N	12. Intelligence Reorg.	N

Election Results

2004 general	Mike Thompson (D)	189,366	(67%)	($1,272,329)
	Lawrence Wiesner (R)	79,970	(28%)	($28,993)
	Pamela Elizondo (Green)	13,635	(5%)	
2004 primary	Mike Thompson (D)	unopposed		
2002 general	Mike Thompson (D)	118,669	(64%)	($1,037,781)
	Lawrence Wiesner (R)	60,013	(32%)	($85,419)
	Kevin Bastian (Lib)	6,534	(4%)	

Prior Winning Percentages: 2000 (65%); 1998 (62%)

The People		Race/Ethnic Origin	Ancestry	
Area size:	12,195 sq. mi.	71.2% White	German: 11.3%	Irish: 9.0%
Urban population:	76.0%	1.3% Black	English: 8.9%	
Rural population:	24.0%	3.9% Asian	**2004 Presidential Vote**	
Pop. 2000:	639,087	2.4% Native Am.	Kerry (D) 173,926	(60%)
Median income:	$38,918	0.2% Hawaiian	Bush (R) 111,754	(38%)
Poverty status:	15.3%	2.9% Two+ races	Other 5,508	(2%)
Military veterans:	13.4%	0.2% Other	**2000 Presidential Vote**	
		17.9% Hispanic Origin	Gore (D) 131,376	(52%)
			Bush (R) 98,506	(39%)
			Other 24,220	(10%)
			Cook Partisan Voting Index: D +10	

Occupation	Blue collar: 20.9%	White collar: 58.3%	Gray collar: 20.8%

The North Coast of California is unlike any other place in America. It is the only part of the Lower 48 states first settled by Russians, who built Fort Ross in 1812; they sold it in 1841 to a Swiss named John Augustus Sutter, whose discovery of gold near Sacramento started the Gold Rush eight years later. It is the only part of the world with large numbers of redwood trees, shooting up in the moist and drizzly air hundreds of feet toward the sky. It is wet country, and for years it has been one of America's prime lumbering areas: Eureka and smaller lumber towns are filled with filigreed Victorian houses and old lumber mills, saloons and waterfront hotels. It has moved on to other crops: in sunny valleys sealed off from the Coast Range, some of the nation's premium wine grapes grow on ridges, and Mendocino County has been known since the late 1960s for its premier marijuana fields. Thirty years ago, there were only 20 wineries in Napa Valley. Today, there are several hundred, with more just west of the ridges in Sonoma County; wineries were a favorite investment for Silicon Valley millionaires. Some of the land here has been planted in olive trees, and local olive production has grown to more than $100 million annually. These valleys were some of California's earliest literary haunts: Robert Louis Stevenson took his honeymoon near Calistoga in Napa, and Jack London owned a giant house in Sonoma that mysteriously burned down in 1913.

The 1st Congressional District of California consists of most of the North Coast from Mendocino County on north and Napa County and the eastern edge of Sonoma County—Healdsburg and the Alexander Valley and part of Sonoma Valley—plus part of the Yolo County flatlands to the east, including the University of California at Davis and industrial West Sacramento. The North Coast lumbering area from Mendocino on north, once filled with rough-hewn working men, was historically Democratic country; but their business became hostage to concern about the northern spotted owl, and the area backlashed toward the Republicans on environmental issues. As the timber industry waned, veterans of the counterculture settled in Mendocino County and along the coast, and the area became Democratic again. Inland, the wine-growing country around Healdsburg and in Napa County was Republican in the 1970s, but now partakes of the San Francisco Bay area's liberal consensus. The 2001 redistricting removed Fairfield and Travis Air Force Base from the district and added Davis and gritty West Sacramento, both heavily Democratic. This district changed partisan hands four times during the 1990s, thanks largely to splits among Democrats. But it is heavily Democratic now.

The congressman from the 1st District is Mike Thompson, a Democrat first elected in 1998. Thompson grew up in the Napa Valley town of St. Helena, dropped out of high school, served in the Army in Vietnam and earned a Purple Heart. Later, he got a bachelor and master's degree from what has become California State University-Chico, owned a vineyard and worked as a maintenance supervisor for Beringer, a big winery in the valley. In 1982 he was chosen an Assembly Fellow, and from 1984–90 was chief of staff to two Bay Area Assembly members. In 1990, he was elected to the first of two terms in the state Senate, where he chaired the Budget Committee.

In 1998, facing California's legislative term limits, Thompson decided to run for the House seat held, precariously, by Republican Frank Riggs, who had been elected in 1990, 1994 and

1996. Thompson looked like a serious challenger who could unite Democrats, and in January 1998 Riggs announced he was running for Barbara Boxer's Senate seat; with no name identification beyond the district and little money, he withdrew in April. Thompson faced weak opposition and won support from almost every interest group that matters in the 1st: unions, medical providers, vintners, oil and timber interests, environmental restriction advocates, law enforcement groups, fishermen. His issue stands—opposition to oil drilling off the California coast, support of abortion rights and the death penalty—were broadly popular. He won the June primary easily, 78%–22%, and won the general by 62%–33%.

In the House, Thompson has voted and styled himself as a moderate Democrat. He joined both the New Democrats and the Blue Dogs, and pledged bipartisanship. With Republican George Radanovich, he started the House Wine Caucus. On behalf of the wine industry, he lost a battle with conservative senators and beer and alcohol wholesalers on a bill giving states new power to restrict sales over the Internet. He joined Jerry Lewis on a proposal to create a $1 billion pool to help pay for making buildings more resistant to earthquakes. Mindful of local businesses, he voted to override Bill Clinton's veto of the estate tax repeal. Before deciding to vote for normal trade relations with China, he got the Clinton White House to resolve a nine-year battle over a local zip code. But he voted against trade promotion authority. In June 2001, the House passed his bill to finance salmon habitat restoration projects. After the massive fish kill caused by flooding of the Klamath River in late 2002, he proposed emergency aid to local communities and a long-term water conservation program.

Thompson has been a close ally of Minority Leader Nancy Pelosi and has been seen as a rising star among House Democrats. But his ambitions to head the Democratic Congressional Campaign Committee after the 2002 election was frustrated after his trip, with David Bonior and Jim McDermott, to Baghdad in September 2002, on which Bonior criticized George W. Bush and opposed the use of force in Iraq and McDermott suggested that Saddam Hussein was more credible than Bush. Thompson, who did not appear on television, said that he went to get first-hand information on the consequences of war and to urge Iraq to comply with demands for inspections. But polls suggested that Bonior's and McDermott's comments moved many voters away from the Democratic party, and they also angered many Democrats who supported Bush's stand against Saddam Hussein. In an opinion article in the *Washington Post,* Thompson wrote, "I never expected conservative partisans to try to use my State Department-licensed trip to fuel their own propaganda machine." He won reelection easily, but it was obvious that making Thompson chairman of House Democrats' campaign committee would give Republican candidates in every close race in the country a talking point, and no more was heard about his candidacy for that position.

Thompson got a consolation prize, a seat on the Budget Committee. He retreated deliberately to obscurity in the House, working chiefly on district issues, including proposals to resolve land disputes with area Indian tribes and to designate new wilderness areas in the Coast Range, which drew broad local support. After the 2004 election, he was again mentioned as a possible DCCC chairman, but many Democrats were still wary, and he was put in charge of the DCCC's incumbent protection program. He also won a seat on the Ways and Means Committee. He has been reelected without difficulty.

SECOND DISTRICT

Rep. Wally Herger (R)

Elected 1986, 10th term; b. May 20, 1945, Yuba City; home, Marysville; American River Comm. Col., A.A. 1967, CA St. U., 1968–69; Mormon; married (Pamela).

Elected Office: CA Assembly, 1980–86.

Professional Career: Rancher; Owner, Herger Gas Inc., 1969–80.

DC Office: 2268 RHOB, 20515, 202-225-3076; Fax: 202-226-0852; Web site: www.house.gov/herger.

District Offices: Chico, 530-893-8363; Redding, 530-223-5898.

Committees: *Ways & Means* (4th of 24 R): Human Resources (Chmn.); Trade.

Group Ratings

	ADA	ACLU	AFS	LCV	ITIC	NTU	COC	ACU	NTLC	CHC
2004	5	5	0	0	100	75	100	100	95	92
2003	5	—	0	5	—	68	97	88	—	—

National Journal Ratings

	2003 LIB	—	2003 CONS		2004 LIB	—	2004 CONS
Economic	0%	—	91%		0%	—	95%
Social	0%	—	95%		0%	—	91%
Foreign	30%	—	70%		25%	—	68%

Key Votes of the 108th Congress

1. Drilling in ANWR	Y	5. DC School Vouchers	Y	9. Ban Same-Sex Marriage	Y
2. Approve Bush Tax Cuts	Y	6. Ban Human Cloning	Y	10. Fund Iraq War	Y
3. Medicare/Rx Bill	Y	7. Restrict Gun Liability	Y	11. Bar Cuba Embargo Funds	Y
4. Bar Overtime Pay Regs.	N	8. Ban Partial-Birth Abortion	Y	12. Intelligence Reorg.	Y

Election Results

2004 general	Wally Herger (R)	182,119	(67%)	($580,670)
	Mike Johnson (D)	90,310	(33%)	($6,297)
2004 primary	Wally Herger (R)	unopposed		
2002 general	Wally Herger (R)	117,747	(66%)	($719,053)
	Mike Johnson (D)	52,455	(29%)	($9,422)
	Other	8,783	(5%)	

Prior Winning Percentages: 2000 (66%); 1998 (63%); 1996 (61%); 1994 (64%); 1992 (65%); 1990 (64%); 1988 (59%); 1986 (58%)

The People		Race/Ethnic Origin	Ancestry	
Area size:	21,977 sq. mi.	76.2% White	German: 11.8%	English: 9.0%
Urban population:	67.7%	1.2% Black	Irish: 8.9%	
Rural population:	32.3%	3.6% Asian	**2004 Presidential Vote**	
Pop. 2000:	639,087	1.9% Native Am.	Bush (R) 173,528	(62%)
Median income:	$33,559	0.1% Hawaiian	Kerry (D) 102,254	(37%)
Poverty status:	17.0%	2.8% Two+ races	Other 3,980	(1%)
Military veterans:	15.7%	0.2% Other	**2000 Presidential Vote**	
		14.0% Hispanic Origin	Bush (R) 150,196	(61%)
			Gore (D) 81,861	(33%)
			Other 13,609	(6%)
			Cook Partisan Voting Index: R +13	

Occupation	Blue collar: 23.2%	White collar: 54.9%	Gray collar: 21.9%

Rising 14,000 feet over low foothills and the Central Valley, visible for 100 miles, is the snow-capped volcanic cone of Mount Shasta, one of a string of (supposedly) burnt-out volcanoes that march up and down the Pacific Coast states. This is the far northern end of California, where truck traffic on Interstate 5 is the only reminder of the choked metropolitan areas where most of the state's people live. This is lumber country mostly, where the mountains that rise on all sides—the Coast Range to the west, the Sierra Nevada to the east, the scattered mountains sealing off the Central Valley north of Redding—are carpeted with trees: rough flannel-shirt, two-lane-road country that was left behind economically when Los Angeles and San Francisco boomed after World War II. North of Shasta, the tiny town of Weed became a logging center and a noted locale for racial integration a half-century ago, but the loss of jobs has led younger blacks as well as whites to move out. Further south are the flat farm fields of the Sacramento Valley, spread across the 50 miles between the Sierra Nevada and the Coast Range. For more a decade, this northern end of California has been attracting people, mostly young families who come here to raise their children in a small town atmosphere, but also retirees looking for a calm atmosphere and low cost of living. This is one part of California that remains overwhelmingly white Anglo.

The 2d Congressional District of California covers most of this area. The district has three major population areas. One is around Redding, south of Mount Shasta. The second is further south, at the edge of the Sierra foothills, around the Butte County communities of Paradise and Chico, home to a state university campus and Sierra Nevada Pale Ale. Still further south are the farm counties of Colusa (the leading rice-producing county in the nation, and a source of local prosperity with its locally cultivated rice hybrids), Yuba and Sutter, not far north of Sacramento. The region has a Democratic heritage, but is culturally conservative, angry at the diktats of urban environmentalists. Until 1980, it elected rough-and-ready Democrats who pulled strings in Sacramento and Washington to build roads and dams. Since then it has elected abstemious Republicans who have solidly conservative voting records and tend to local needs. George W. Bush won 62% of the vote here in 2004, his best showing in a northern California district.

The congressman from the 2d District is Republican Wally Herger, a Republican first elected in 1986. He grew up in the farm country north of Sacramento and worked as a rancher and propane gas company owner. In 1980 he was elected to the California Assembly. In 1986 he was elected to the House after winning solid margins over the mayor of Redding in the primary and a Shasta County supervisor in the general. He has served quietly on the Ways and Means Committee, favoring balanced budgets and lower taxes. When federal budget deficits disappeared in the late 1990s, Herger was a leader of the battle to create lock boxes for the surpluses in the Social Security and Medicare trust funds; that discussion became moot with the return of big deficits. In 2001 he took over as chairman of the Human Resources Subcommittee, which gave him responsibility for reauthorizing the 1996 welfare act. The House has repeatedly passed the bill that he and other Ways and Means Republicans wrote to increase work requirements for recipients and incentives for states to reduce caseloads; it included provisions to encourage marriage and other Bush administration recommendations. But few House Democrats supported his version, and it has died in the Senate, where Democrats have demanded more money for the states; meanwhile, the landmark 1996 law has had several temporary extensions. With encouragement from Majority Leader Tom DeLay, he has proposed an overhaul of foster care to give states more flexibility to prevent abuse of children who become lost in the system. Herger ranks fourth in seniority among committee Republicans, but does not seem likely to be a candidate to succeed Bill Thomas as chairman.

On local issues, Herger tends to local water projects, lamenting the failure to shore up levees to prevent floods, and opposing the Central Valley Project for legislating "a permanent drought." He called for exemption of flood control programs from the Endangered Species Act. With Greg Walden of Oregon, he proposed full compensation of farmers and related businesses that suffered damages from the Klamath River flooding, but he rejected environmentalists' calls for management controls of the fisheries, which he called part of "an anti-agriculture agenda." He joined other California Republicans in urging the Forest Service to scale back controls on Sierra wildlife preservation because of the fire risk. In 2000, he helped to enact a five-year program to aid about 750 counties that have suffered from a loss of revenue from timber sales; in 2005, he worked to extend the relief. Herger advocated increased basing of Global Hawk unmanned spy planes at Beale Air Force Base, which already housed the older U-2 and SR-71 reconnaissance aircraft; the huge base, whose rocky pastures were used before June 1944 to practice the Normandy invasion and to simulate combat in a fake European town, is about 40 miles north of Sacramento and military officials are unhappy about the increased local development.

In this district, Herger has nothing to fear politically other than nuisance candidates. Since 1990, he has been consistently reelected with more than 60% of the vote against weak Democratic opponents, in what has become one of the safest Republican districts in the nation. In the 2002 primary, he won 89% of the vote against two opponents who criticized him for failing to support the gold standard and for backing free trade.

THIRD DISTRICT

Rep. Dan Lungren (R)

Elected 2004, 1st term; b. Sept. 22, 1946, Long Beach; home, Folsom; Notre Dame U., A.B. 1968, Georgetown U., J.D. 1971; Catholic; married (Bobbi).

Elected Office: U.S. House of Reps.1978–88; CA Atty. Gen. 1990–98.

Professional Career: Staff, U.S. Sen. George Murphy, 1969–70; Staff, U.S. Sen. Bill Brock, 1971; Spec. asst. RNC, 1971–72; Practicing atty., 1973–78.

DC Office: 2448 RHOB, 20515, 202-225-5716; Fax: 202-226-1298; Web site: www.house.gov/lungren.

District Office: Gold River, 916-859-9906.

Committees: *Budget* (14th of 22 R). *Homeland Security* (10th of 19 R): Economic Security, Infrastructure Protection & Cybersecurity (Chmn.); Intelligence, Information Sharing & Terrorism Risk Assessment; Prevention of Nuclear & Biological Attack. *Judiciary* (8th of 23 R): Crime, Terrorism & Homeland Security; Immigration, Border Security & Claims.

Group Ratings and Key Votes: Newly Elected

Election Results

2004 general	Dan Lungren (R)	177,738	(62%)	($1,407,970)
	Gabe Castillo (D)	100,025	(35%)	($98,284)
	Other	9,310	(3%)	
2004 primary	Dan Lungren (R)	35,595	(39%)	
	Rico Oller (R)	32,728	(36%)	
	Mary Ose (R)	21,469	(23%)	
	Other	1,693	(2%)	
2002 general	Doug Ose (R)	121,732	(62%)	($659,095)
	Howard Beeman (D)	67,136	(34%)	($63,747)
	Other	6,050	(3%)	

Prior Winning Percentages: 1986 (73%); 1984 (73%); 1982 (69%); 1980 (72%); 1978 (54%)

The People		Race/Ethnic Origin	Ancestry	
Area size:	3,422 sq. mi.	74.4% White	German: 12.4% Irish: 9.0%	
Urban population:	86.4%	4.3% Black	English: 8.9%	
Rural population:	13.6%	5.9% Asian	**2004 Presidential Vote**	
Pop. 2000:	639,088	0.8% Native Am.	Bush (R)	176,512 (58%)
Median income:	$51,313	0.3% Hawaiian	Kerry (D)	123,671 (41%)
Poverty status:	8.5%	3.5% Two+ races	Other	2,936 (1%)
Military veterans:	15.7%	0.2% Other	**2000 Presidential Vote**	
		10.7% Hispanic Origin	Bush (R)	142,946 (55%)
			Gore (D)	107,690 (41%)
			Other	9,820 (4%)
			Cook Partisan Voting Index: R + 7	
Occupation	Blue collar: 18.4%	White collar: 67.8% Gray collar: 13.8%		

Until recently, Sacramento was chiefly the metropolis of a fertile valley that produced a marvelous variety of crops: rice, plums, almonds, olives, asparagus, pears, hops, beans, celery, onions, potatoes, plus caviar-yielding sturgeon in pools of filtered water. The farmlands remain, and the capital city flourishes as a center of government; greater Sacramento is one of the fastest-growing metro areas in the country. Almost all the growth has been away from the flood plain of the Sacramento River, in the higher land east of the city that eventually turns into hills rising toward the Sierra Nevadas. Here is the Mother Lode country in Amador and Calaveras Counties, which filled up with people in the Gold Rush days, when Mark Twain was inspired to write his story about the famous jumping frog of Calaveras County. Only in recent decades has Calaveras County had more than the 16,000 people who lived there in Twain's time. In Rancho Cordova, local leaders have worked to create a development plan with a new downtown in place of aging strip malls. But some things have not changed. When an animal-rights group called for cancellation of the annual Jumping Frog Jubilee, a local official said that the frogs are not tortured and that the jubilee would continue.

The 3d Congressional District of California includes much of suburban Sacramento, some territory in Solano County to the west and some of the Mother Lode country in Amador and Calaveras Counties to the east, where it reaches over the Sierras to Alpine County, the smallest county in California (1,190 people in 2004) with the state's highest mountain ridge line, and the Nevada line. Its ungainly shape contains only a little territory that was in the old district before 2001 redistricting. More than 80% of the people in the district live in Sacramento County, in suburbs like Carmichael, Citrus Heights and Arden-Arcade and the old town of Folsom. Historically Sacramento was Democratic. But in the 1980s and 1990s, Sacramento County, with its rapid private-sector growth, became more Republican. The 3d District voted 58% for George W. Bush in 2004 and has become a safe Republican seat.

The congressman from the 3d District is Dan Lungren, first elected here in 2004 but with previous experience in the House. Lungren grew up in Long Beach, and his father was Richard Nixon's personal physician; young Dan worked on the staffs of Senators George Murphy and Bill Brock. After a few years of law practice in Long Beach, he unsuccessfully challenged a "Watergate baby" in 1976, then came back and won rather easily in 1978 with a boost from the anti-tax Proposition 13. He entered a freshman class that included Dick Cheney, Newt Gingrich, and Jerry Lewis and Bill Thomas from California; one unsuccessful Republican who failed to win a seat that year was George W. Bush. During his first decade in Congress, Lungren focused on criminal code reform from his perch on the House Judiciary Committee; he was a member of the Conservative Opportunity Society, the influential group of young House conservatives founded in 1983 by Gingrich. He played a key role on major immigration legislation in 1986, which was enacted despite major reservations from Mexican-American groups, the Democratic leadership and the Reagan administration. In 1989 he was nominated as state treasurer but was not confirmed by the state Senate, despite court challenges; in 1990, he was elected to the first of two terms as California attorney general. After losing 58%–38% to Democrat Gray Davis in the 1998 race for governor, Lungren worked in the Sacramento area as a visiting professor and radio talk show host and joined a Washington-based law firm. When he returned to Congress, it not only had become a very different place with its Republican majority, but he found himself representing a district nearly 400 miles north of his old one.

In 2004 3d District incumbent Republican Doug Ose honored his pledge to retire after serving three terms, and Lungren ran for the seat. His toughest competition was in the Republican primary, in which he faced Mary Ose, the incumbent's sister, and state Senator Rico Oller. The contest split the California delegation, with the 4th district's John Doolittle backing Oller and Ways and Means Chairman Bill Thomas supporting Lungren. Ose, a real estate developer, raised more than $2 million, much of it from her own pocket, but despite an almost 2-to-1 fundraising advantage over both Oller and Lungren, she won only 23% of the votes. Oller, with a geographic base in Amador and Calaveras Counties, attacked Lungren as soft on immigration; Lungren ran an ad with praise from Gingrich for his work on the 1986 immigration bill. It took a week of counting absentee ballots to determine the outcome, but Lungren beat Oller 39%–36%. Oller was well ahead in Amador and Calaveras Counties, but in Sacramento County, which cast

82% of the total vote, Lungren led Oller 42%–32%. The general election was no contest. Lungren criticized his successor as attorney general, Bill Lockyer, for not immediately stopping San Francisco Mayor Gavin Newsom from issuing marriage licenses to same-sex couples and said he his first act in Congress would be to introduce legislation banning same-sex marriage. He won 62%–35%.

Lungren returned to Washington with well-defined positions on crime, abortion and same-sex marriage. An opponent of abortion, Lungren supports capital punishment and has been an uncompromising advocate for California's "three-strikes" mandatory-minimum sentencing law. He claimed credit for his previous service in determining seniority and became eighth ranking Republican on the Judiciary Committee and 10th ranking Republican on Homeland Security and chairman of the latter's Economic Security, Infrastructure Protection, and Cybersecurity Subcommittee. And on the Judiciary Committee he could get help learning the ropes from veteran communications director Jeff Lungren, his son.

FOURTH DISTRICT

Rep. John Doolittle (R)

Elected 1990, 8th term; b. Oct. 30, 1950, Glendale; home, Rocklin; U. of CA at Santa Cruz, B.A. 1972, U. of the Pacific, J.D. 1978; Mormon; married (Julia).

Elected Office: CA Senate, 1980–90, Repub. Caucus Chmn., 1987–90.

Professional Career: Practicing atty., 1978–80.

DC Office: 2410 RHOB, 20515, 202-225-2511; Fax: 202-225-5444; Web site: www.house.gov/doolittle.

District Office: Granite Bay, 916-786-5560.

Committees: *Republican Conference Secretary. Appropriations* (26th of 37 R): Agriculture, Rural Development, FDA & Related Agencies; Energy & Water Development & Related Agencies (Vice Chmn.); Interior, Environment & Related Agencies. *House Administration* (4th of 6 R).

Group Ratings

	ADA	ACLU	AFS	LCV	ITIC	NTU	COC	ACU	NTLC	CHC
2004	0	0	13	9	89	55	90	92	85	100
2003	5	—	0	0	—	62	93	78	—	—

National Journal Ratings

	2003 LIB	—	2003 CONS	2004 LIB	—	2004 CONS
Economic	36%	—	63%	17%	—	80%
Social	5%	—	87%	0%	—	91%
Foreign	0%	—	89%	4%	—	93%

Key Votes of the 108th Congress

1. Drilling in ANWR	Y	5. DC School Vouchers	Y	9. Ban Same-Sex Marriage	Y
2. Approve Bush Tax Cuts	Y	6. Ban Human Cloning	Y	10. Fund Iraq War	Y
3. Medicare/Rx Bill	Y	7. Restrict Gun Liability	Y	11. Bar Cuba Embargo Funds	N
4. Bar Overtime Pay Regs.	N	8. Ban Partial-Birth Abortion	Y	12. Intelligence Reorg.	Y

Election Results

2004 general	John Doolittle (R)	221,926	(65%)	($912,648)
	David Winters (D)	117,443	(35%)	($2,061)
2004 primary	John Doolittle (R)	unopposed		
2002 general	John Doolittle (R)	147,997	(65%)	($979,438)
	Mark Norberg (D)	72,860	(32%)	($7,548)
	Other	7,649	(3%)	

Prior Winning Percentages: 2000 (63%); 1998 (63%); 1996 (60%); 1994 (61%); 1992 (50%); 1990 (50%)

The People		Race/Ethnic Origin	Ancestry	
Area size:	17,159 sq. mi.	83.8% White	German: 13.1%	English: 11.2%
Urban population:	67.4%	1.2% Black	Irish: 10.1%	
Rural population:	32.6%	2.3% Asian	**2004 Presidential Vote**	
Pop. 2000:	639,088	1.1% Native Am.	Bush (R) 216,838	(61%)
Median income:	$49,387	0.1% Hawaiian	Kerry (D) 132,267	(37%)
Poverty status:	8.7%	2.4% Two+ races	Other 4,119	(1%)
Military veterans:	16.6%	0.2% Other	**2000 Presidential Vote**	
		8.9% Hispanic Origin	Bush (R) 172,169	(59%)
			Gore (D) 104,437	(36%)
			Other 15,633	(5%)
			Cook Partisan Voting Index: R +11	

Occupation   Blue collar: 19.6%   White collar: 63.1%   Gray collar: 17.3%

California sprang suddenly into existence: The Gold Rush of 1849 was followed by statehood and the creation of the first 27 counties in 1850. The new state's first boom area was the Mother Lode country in the foothills of the Sierras above Sacramento. Mining camps the size of eastern cities grew up in vacant valleys locked amid steep hills, with thousands of would-be millionaires gathered to find gold—though most of those who actually got rich did so by catering to miners' needs. In Placerville, John Studebaker had a buggy shop, Phillip Armour ran a butcher shop and Mark Hopkins had a dry goods store. The biggest mine in California was sunk in Grass Valley in 1857 and worked for half a century. But long before that, most of the Mother Lode country emptied out, leaving ghost towns and villages with hundreds of deserted houses: an antique vacation country left behind in time.

When local residents celebrated the sesquicentennial, the area had been resurrected as a booming exurban and tourist mecca. "The American River near Coloma becomes a virtual freeway of whooping rafters on summer weekends," reported *USA Today*. "The Mother Lode also offers modern-day prospectors an intriguing pastiche of bed-and-breakfast inns, musty antique stores and such blink-and-you'll-miss-'em outposts as Volcano, Fiddletown, Rough and Ready"—named after President Zachary Taylor. Thousands of Californians—many of them families from smog-filled, middle-class suburbs of the Los Angeles Basin and the San Francisco Bay area—looking for a more pleasant, small-town, orderly environment, have found it along fast-flowing creeks where the '49ers camped. For the past three decades, populations of these counties have risen sharply. Placer County, which includes Sacramento suburbs and part of the Mother Lode country, grew 78% from 1990 to 2004, more than any other county in California. It also has a higher percentage of registered Republicans than any other county. Politically, this growth has changed the Mother Lode country from Democratic to Republican. In 1976, nine Mother Lode counties from Sierra to Mariposa cast 118,000 votes and voted 50%–47% for Jimmy Carter over Gerald Ford: close to the California average. In 2004 they cast 370,000 votes and voted 61% for George W. Bush—a percentage closer to Idaho's than California's. The culture here could not be much different than what prevails less than 50 miles away in the Bay Area.

The 4th Congressional District of California consists of the northern half of the Mother Lode country and the Placer County suburbs of Sacramento, plus a small slice of Sacramento County. It extends northward through thinly populated mountain counties to the Oregon line. Most of its residents live within the I-80 corridor, clustered near the Sacramento County line in suburban places like Roseville (the district's most populous city) and Rocklin, or in the Mother Lode country from Placerville to Nevada City. Some 33% of its people live in areas classified as rural, the largest percentage of the state's 53 districts.

The congressman from the 4th District is John Doolittle, a Republican first elected in 1990. Doolittle grew up in the Los Angeles area and went to high school in Cupertino, in what now is Silicon Valley. His conservatism was annealed in the fires of adversity: He graduated from the University of California at Santa Cruz in 1972, when the campus was 97% for George McGovern. After law school he moved to the edge of the Sacramento metro area where the foothills begin, and in 1980 was elected to the state Senate at 30. When the Republican incumbent retired in

1990 in a district that then stretched from the Mother Lode country to Stockton, Doolittle ran for the seat. He had tougher competition than expected from Democrat Patricia Malberg, who was pro-choice on abortion, against nuclear power and for defense spending cuts; he won by just 50%–46%.

As a freshman, Doolittle was one of the Republicans' Gang of Seven, who were the advance guard for Newt Gingrich's 1994 revolution. In the Republican House, Doolittle chaired a subcommittee the Democrats who represented this area would have relished: Water and Power. But his agenda resembled theirs only in his support for the Auburn Dam, which he and other Sacramento area congressmen for decades have wanted to build on the American River, 35 miles east of Sacramento. Doolittle insisted on a design that could supply water to the Mother Lode but for years he deadlocked with a combination of environmentalists and spending opponents led by the 5th District's Robert Matsui. Doolittle contended that alternative plans by the Army Corps of Engineers to repair and strengthen the Folsom Dam, which was completed in 1955, would be a waste of money. In 2001, Doolittle gave up the subcommittee to join the Appropriations Committee, where he has gotten many millions of dollars for projects for his district, including land acquisition, wastewater treatment facilities and restoration projects in the Lake Tahoe basin. That increased leverage helped Doolittle to finally reach a deal with Matsui in 2003, with an agreement to raise the Folsom Dam by seven feet and to spend $135 million on upstream water projects that Doolittle would largely determine. The once fiscally tight-fisted Doolittle had loosened up, and Sacramento got its long-sought flood protection. Because Congress does not operate in an ideal world, he told a local reporter, "I work with what I've got." The onetime foes became something of a mutual admiration society, and Doolittle noted after Matsui died the progress that they made in addressing local issues. After the reorganization of Appropriations subcommittees in 2005, Doolittle became vice-chairman of the Energy and Water Subcommittee.

On other issues, the iPod-toting Doolittle has taken a consumer interest in copyright policy. He introduced with Rick Boucher a bill to permit fair use copying of certain communications software; it would weaken the anti-circumvention rules of a 1998 copyright law and brought criticism from the motion picture industry. They also organized the Personal Technology Freedom Coalition. With Zoe Lofgren, he filed a bill on behalf of film preservationists and archivists to make it easier to restore old movies without having to pay copyright fees.

Doolittle has worked closely with Majority Leader Tom DeLay on several issues, including opposing the Shays-Meehan campaign finance bill. (Critics said that the duo preferred a "do little and delay" Congress.) During the 2002 debate, he described its partisan impact in apocalyptic terms. "If this passes, we lose the House. We may not lose it this time. . . . This is literally the survival of the Republican Party that is going on right now." As a leader of House conservatives, Doolittle was a co-founder of the Conservative Action Team, since renamed the Republican Study Committee, which has become a force in attempting to limit domestic spending. After the 2002 election, he was elected without opposition as secretary of the House Republican Conference; this is the lowest ranking position in the party leadership, but it gives him a seat at leadership meetings and he has used it to become the leadership liaison to House conservatives. He gained unwanted attention with news reports in 2004 that he had been a beneficiary of the fundraising largess of lobbyist Jack Abramoff and that Doolittle's wife Julie, who runs a fund-raising firm, was among those subpoenaed by a grand jury investigating Abramoff.

Back home he defeated Malberg in a 1992 rematch and has won more than 60% of the vote since. In 2002, against an active primary opponent who called the Auburn Dam a "boondoggle" and favored Shays-Meehan, he won 78%–22%. The outspoken Doolittle strongly opposed Governor Arnold Schwarzenegger's proposal for nonpartisan redistricting, dismissing it as "self-defeating" for Republicans and "stupid" in its goal of seeking more moderates.

FIFTH DISTRICT

Rep. Doris Matsui (D)

Elected March 2005, 1st term; b. Sept. 25, 1944, Poston, AZ; home, Sacramento; U. of CA at Berkeley, B.A. 1966; United Methodist; widowed.

Professional Career: Transition team, President-elect Bill Clinton, 1992–93; Dep. Asst. to the Pres., Dep. Dir. of Public Liaison, White House, 1993–98; Lobbyist, 1998–2005.

DC Office: 2310 RHOB, 20515, 202-225-7163; Fax: 202-225-0566; Web site: www.house.gov/matsui.

District Office: Sacramento, 916-498-5600.

Committees: *Rules* (4th of 4 D): Rules & Organization of the House.

Group Ratings and Key Votes: Newly Elected

Election Results

2005 special	Doris Matsui (D)	56,175	(68%)	($941,224)
	Julie Padilla (D)	7,158	(9%)	
	John Thomas Flynn (R)	6,559	(8%)	
	Serge Chernay (R)	3,742	(5%)	
	Other	8,841	(11%)	
2004 general	Robert Matsui (D)	138,004	(71%)	
	Mike Dugas (R)	45,120	(23%)	
	Other	10,263	(5%)	
2004 primary	Robert Matsui (D)	unopposed		
2002 general	Robert Matsui (D)	92,726	(70%)	($867,352)
	Richard Frankhuizen (R)	34,749	(26%)	($5,692)
	Other	4,103	(3%)	

The People		Race/Ethnic Origin	Ancestry		
Area size:	150 sq. mi.	43.4% White	German: 7.5%	Irish: 5.9%	
Urban population:	99.7%	14.4% Black	English: 5.3%		
Rural population:	0.3%	14.9% Asian	**2004 Presidential Vote**		
Pop. 2000:	639,088	0.8% Native Am.	Kerry (D)	125,378	(61%)
Median income:	$36,719	0.8% Hawaiian	Bush (R)	77,788	(38%)
Poverty status:	19.7%	4.7% Two+ races	Other	2,172	(1%)
Military veterans:	12.2%	0.3% Other	**2000 Presidential Vote**		
		20.8% Hispanic Origin	Gore (D)	113,987	(60%)
			Bush (R)	66,011	(35%)
			Other	9,239	(5%)
			Cook Partisan Voting Index: D +14		
Occupation	Blue collar: 20.1%	White collar: 62.9%	Gray collar: 17.0%		

Sacramento, capital of the nation's largest state, focus of California's third-largest media market (19th in the nation), home of a national sports franchise (the NBA's Sacramento Kings) and an 18-mile light rail system, is no longer just a small city with a lot of civil servants and a vegetable-packing economy. It is a vibrant American metropolis, with some of the nation's highest job growth. Sacramento started as a river port on the sluggish waters of the Sacramento and American rivers. It was the destination of many overland migrants, the site of Sutter's Fort, where John Augustus Sutter found the gold that set off the Gold Rush of 1849, and the western terminus of the Pony Express in 1860. This was the natural choice at the time to be California's capital, halfway between the San Francisco Bay and the Mother Lode country in the foothills of the Sierras, and in the middle of California's vast valley. Agriculture continues to be important today in Sacra-tomato (as some call it): it has the world's largest almond processing plant.

In the old days, government was not a big business. Just a few lobbyists hung out in saloons on K or J streets, the governor's mansion was a musty antique, and the 100-plus degree summers emptied out what there was of the city. But air conditioning has replaced awnings, freeways and shopping malls have followed the city's growth east and north toward the Sierra foothills and affluence has made this one of America's higher income metropolitan areas. In the 1980s metropolitan Sacramento grew 35% and in the 1990s by 22%, so that it now has 1.8 million people, about the same as metro Cincinnati or Kansas City. Some high-tech firms have moved east from Silicon Valley, with Intel and Hewlett-Packard housing large campuses, and Bay Area refugees have welcomed less expensive and more comfortable living standards. Government expanded, too, and platoons of lobbyists, lawyers and consultants have set up permanent shop here, and new hotels have been built to serve them. Today, 1,000 registered lobbyists prowl the halls of the Capitol. The closing of Mather and McClellan Air Force Bases appeared to have little economic impact. As Sacramento has grown, this once Democratic, pro-government, working-class bastion has become closer to an upscale Sun Belt boomtown. In 1966, Sacramento was just about the only part of California beyond the Bay Area that stuck with Pat Brown over challenger Ronald Reagan. But when John Kerry carried California 54%–44% in 2004, he carried Sacramento County by only 49.6%–49.3%. In the 2003 recall election, 60% of county voters voted to remove Gray Davis, and Schwarzenegger won 52% of the vote on the replacement ballot. The election of Schwarzenegger brought unprecedented public attention plus a dose of Hollywood to the capital.

The 5th Congressional District of California consists of the center of metropolitan Sacramento, all of the city of Sacramento and some of its close-in suburbs. The 5th contains affluent neighborhoods on older grid streets and scattered low-income black, Mexican-American and Hmong neighborhoods, plus new condominiums north of the American River and middle-class subdivisions south of downtown. Sacramento's neighborhoods are more ethnically diverse than those of any other big city in California, according to the Public Policy Institute of California. This is the solidly Democratic part of metro Sacramento, and the 5th is the most Democratic district in the great valley from Bakersfield north to Oregon.

The congresswoman from the 5th is Doris Matsui, who won a special election in March 2005 to replace her late husband Robert Matsui. He died of complications from a rare blood disorder on January 1, after serving 13 terms as a senior member of the House Ways and Means Committee and was a confidant to Nancy Pelosi as chairman of the Democratic Congressional Campaign Committee. As an infant, Robert Matsui and his family were among the West Coast Japanese Americans forced into internment camps in 1942; he was first elected to the House in 1978 and was one of the lead sponsors of the 1988 Japanese American redress law that apologized for the internment policy and provided monetary compensation for every survivor of the camps and for so-called "voluntary evacuees." Doris Matsui was herself born in an Arizona internment camp and was a well-known figure during her husband's career in Congress. She grew up in Dinuba in Fresno County and graduated from UC-Berkeley; in Sacramento she chaired the board of the local public television station and participated in many civic organizations. After working on Bill Clinton's presidential campaign, she joined his presidential transition team and then served as his deputy director of public liaison, where she coordinated relationships with both the public and private sectors on economic and budget priorities. When she left the White House in 1998, she became a senior adviser and director of government relations and public policy at the Washington law firm of Collier Shannon Scott.

A few days after the Washington and Sacramento memorial services for Robert Matsui, Doris Matsui announced that she would run in the March 8 special election. "People lose their spouses every day and make decisions about what they'll do next. I'm no different than anyone else," she said. She had strong support from Minority Leader Nancy Pelosi, and other prominent Sacramento Democrats decided not to run. None of her 10 opponents in the nonpartisan contest had significant political experience or name recognition. Matsui emphasized her support for local water projects and said that she opposed George W. Bush's proposal for personal retirement accounts in Social Security; she opposed the war in Iraq but supported maintaining U.S. troops there to avoid a political vacuum. Her investment in a partnership with a long-time friend who was a Sacramento land developer sparked a brief flurry of criticism, but she emphasized that her husband had nothing to do with the deal and that there was no conflict of interest. Some called the contest a "coronation," but the lack of competition surely reflected the respect the Matsuis had won over the years. Doris Matsui won the all-party primary with 68% of the vote to 9% for the runner up. She became the fourth House member, and the third Californian, in the 109th Congress who had won election immediately after the death of their husbands. Pelosi rewarded her with a seat on the Rules Committee.

SIXTH DISTRICT

Rep. Lynn Woolsey (D)

Elected 1992, 7th term; b. Nov. 3, 1937, Seattle, WA; home, Petaluma; U. of San Francisco, B.S. 1981; Presbyterian; divorced.

Elected Office: Petaluma City Cncl., 1985–92, Vice Mayor, 1986, 1991.

Professional Career: Human Resources Mgr., Harris Digital Telephone, 1969–80; Owner, Woolsey Personnel Svc., 1980–92.

DC Office: 2263 RHOB, 20515, 202-225-5161; Fax: 202-225-5163; Web site: woolsey.house.gov.

District Offices: San Rafael, 415-507-9554; Santa Rosa, 707-542-7182.

Committees: *Education & the Workforce* (7th of 22 D): Education Reform (RMM); Workforce Protections. *Science* (4th of 20 D): Energy.

Group Ratings

	ADA	ACLU	AFS	LCV	ITIC	NTU	COC	ACU	NTLC	CHC
2004	95	94	100	100	22	14	0	8	0	8
2003	100	—	100	95	—	29	12	8	—	—

National Journal Ratings

	2003 LIB	—	2003 CONS		2004 LIB	—	2004 CONS
Economic	84%	—	15%		89%	—	8%
Social	92%	—	0%		88%	—	0%
Foreign	94%	—	0%		94%	—	4%

Key Votes of the 108th Congress

1. Drilling in ANWR	N	5. DC School Vouchers	*	9. Ban Same-Sex Marriage	N
2. Approve Bush Tax Cuts	N	6. Ban Human Cloning	N	10. Fund Iraq War	N
3. Medicare/Rx Bill	N	7. Restrict Gun Liability	N	11. Bar Cuba Embargo Funds	Y
4. Bar Overtime Pay Regs.	Y	8. Ban Partial-Birth Abortion	N	12. Intelligence Reorg.	N

Election Results

2004 general	Lynn Woolsey (D)	226,423	(73%)	($562,533)
	Paul Erickson (R)	85,244	(27%)	($6,309)
2004 primary	Lynn Woolsey (D)	99,970	(84%)	
	Renn Vara (D)	19,039	(16%)	
2002 general	Lynn Woolsey (D)	139,750	(67%)	($803,235)
	Paul Erickson (R)	62,052	(30%)	($10,187)
	Other	7,761	(4%)	

Prior Winning Percentages: 2000 (64%); 1998 (68%); 1996 (62%); 1994 (58%); 1992 (65%)

The People		Race/Ethnic Origin	Ancestry	
Area size:	2,119 sq. mi.	76.1% White	German: 11.1%	Irish: 10.6%
Urban population:	89.8%	2.0% Black	English: 9.8%	
Rural population:	10.2%	3.7% Asian	**2004 Presidential Vote**	
Pop. 2000:	639,087	0.6% Native Am.	Kerry (D) 226,051	(70%)
Median income:	$59,115	0.2% Hawaiian	Bush (R) 90,432	(28%)
Poverty status:	7.7%	2.7% Two+ races	Other 4,574	(1%)
Military veterans:	12.2%	0.2% Other	**2000 Presidential Vote**	
		14.5% Hispanic Origin	Gore (D) 178,746	(62%)
			Bush (R) 87,082	(30%)
			Other 21,514	(7%)
			Cook Partisan Voting Index: D +21	
Occupation	Blue collar: 17.2%	White collar: 68.0%	Gray collar: 14.8%	

When the Golden Gate Bridge was opened in 1937, San Francisco was one of the nation's best-known cities, but few knew much about the land beyond the bridge's north pier head. There were fewer than 50,000 people in Marin County then and another 65,000 just to the north in Sonoma County. For San Franciscans, Marin was known for the ferry terminus in Sausalito, a fishing village and art colony, and as the beginning of the Redwood Empire, with its giant trees in Muir Woods, which has a dense concentration of spotted owls. Near the Bay and adjacent to the I-580 bridge is the state prison at San Quentin, one of the oldest in the nation, with its famous gas chamber and crowded Death Row; plans to overhaul the facility led to local calls to demolish it and use the valuable land for more commercial enterprises. Farther north is the Point Reyes peninsula for many recreational outdoor activities, and the wine country of Sonoma County, sunny valleys protected from the fog by the Coast Range. In one such valley was Santa Rosa, site of agronomist Luther Burbank's laboratory, a town that looked Middle American enough to be the set for dozens of movies. Politically, the area was then typical of the nation: traditionally Republican, but favoring Franklin D. Roosevelt in the 1930s.

Today this part of California is far more populous, with a population of 246,000 people in Marin County and 468,000 in the faster-growing Sonoma, affluent beyond the dreams of post-World War II Americans and extreme in its cultural attitudes, and with relatively few racial minorities compared to other counties in the San Francisco Bay Area. Until it was surpassed by the Silicon Valley in the late 1990s, it was the nation's most expensive housing market. Santa Rosa is thriving, thanks to the wine and telecommunications industries. Trendy Marin, with its hot tubs and its fashionable people getting in touch with themselves, became a national carica-ture: economically affluent, culturally liberationist; this was the home of "American Taliban" John Walker Lindh. When the war in Iraq began, "many of the same people who marched against the Vietnam War have held nightly peace vigils," Tom Edsall of *The Washington Post* reported. They included a group of feminists who "bared witness" by using their nude bodies to spell out "PEACE." After a while such an image feeds on itself; a place like Marin attracts affluent people who share its values, while those who don't, go elsewhere—in the Bay Area to the more conser-vative San Ramon Valley, beyond the mountains east of Oakland. Indeed the Bay Area as a whole seems to attract liberals and repel conservatives, just as the Dallas-Fort Worth Metroplex does the opposite. And Marin and Sonoma are attracting the most liberal of the liberal—averse to traditional religion, derisive of traditional sexual and marriage mores, viscerally anti-military.

The 6th Congressional District of California includes all of Marin County and all of Sonoma County except for its rural eastern border. Marin and Sonoma Counties have been transformed politically over the past generation. In 1980 they voted for Ronald Reagan over Jimmy Carter by a 47%–36% margin. Then they moved left and voted in 1988 for Michael Dukakis over George H. W. Bush by 57%–41%. Now Republicans seem almost an endangered species here: in 2004 the two counties voted for John Kerry over George W. Bush by a 69%–29% margin. The public dialogue here is increasingly monopartisan and, in this community priding itself on its tolerance, barely a dissenting word is heard.

The congresswoman from the 6th District is Lynn Woolsey, a Democrat first elected in 1992 when Barbara Boxer was elected to the Senate. Woolsey grew up in the Pacific Northwest, moved to Marin and was a housewife with three children under 6 when her marriage ended in 1968. She went on welfare, got a low-paying job and left her children with 13 different babysitters in a year. Deliverance appeared in the form of a job with a high-tech startup firm where she rose to become a top executive. She remarried and moved to a house in Petaluma where her mother could live and look after the kids. She put herself through business school at night, earned a degree in human resources and started her own personnel service. In 1984 Woolsey won a seat on the Petaluma Council. In 1992 she won the House seat in a nine-candidate primary with 26%, well ahead of 19% for the runner-up. In the general she faced liberal Republican Assemblyman Bill Filante. But he had surgery for a brain tumor and stopped campaigning; she won 65%–34%.

An apt representative of her district, Woolsey has one of the most liberal voting records in the House. As one of the few former welfare recipients in Congress, she co-chaired a Democratic task force on welfare. She opposed the 1996 welfare law and calls for easing work requirements and providing more child care; she wants mothers to be able to stay at home until their children are 11. She lobbied against banning gays in the military, accompanied by her son who is gay. Republicans sought to embarrass Democrats by calling for a vote on Woolsey's bill to revoke the federal charter for the Boy Scouts because the group excludes gays; her bill was defeated 362–12. She has lost House votes on amendments to prohibit religious organizations from discrimination in hiring in federal programs. On the 2001 education bill, she sought to make improved teacher quality a top priority, but she voted against the final House-Senate deal; she has failed in efforts to make funding for disabled students mandatory. She introduced a "Go Girl" bill to bridge the digital divide between the genders. On the Science Committee, Woolsey worked to increase federal support for alternative energy sources. During debate on the Homeland Security Department, the House passed her amendment to create an independent Homeland Security Institute to provide technological guidance. She wants to repeal portions of the Patriot Act on civil liberties grounds, and sponsored a resolution in January 2005 for the immediate withdrawal of U.S. troops from Iraq. Woolsey sought the Appropriations seat that her Bay Area neighbor Nancy Pelosi relinquished in 2003. But Pelosi awarded the two vacancies on the committee that year to members from the South.

At home, she worked to expand the protected area around the Point Reyes National Seashore by purchasing easements from nearby farmers and barring them from selling their land to nonagricultural users. The House authorized $15 million for her proposal to renovate the immigration complex on Angel Island—now a state park in the Bay not far from Golden Gate Bridge, but a place where countless Chinese arrivals were detained in deplorable conditions—and turn it into an Ellis Island of the West. In February 2004, she apologized for intervening on behalf of the son of an office aide who was convicted as a rapist; the victim rejected the gesture.

Woolsey has been easily reelected. She had a rare challenge in the 2002 primary from Santa Rosa Mayor Mike Martini, the founder of a winery in Sebastopol, who criticized her for lack of leadership, excessively liberal votes and failure to bring sufficient funds to the district. Woolsey responded that she had delivered $430 million since 1997, and defended on civil-liberties grounds her October 2001 vote against increased federal powers to track down terrorists; she won 80%–20%. In May 2005, term-limited Assemblyman Joe Nation, who lost to Woolsey in the 1992 open seat primary, announced that he would challenge her in 2006.

SEVENTH DISTRICT

Rep. George Miller (D)

Elected 1974, 16th term; b. May 17, 1945, Richmond; home, Martinez; San Francisco St. U., B.A. 1968, U. of CA at Davis, J.D. 1972; Catholic; married (Cynthia).

Professional Career: Legis. aide, CA Senate Majority Ldr., 1969–74; Practicing atty., 1972–74.

DC Office: 2205 RHOB, 20515, 202-225-2095; Fax: 202-225-5609; Web site: www.house.gov/georgemiller.

District Offices: Concord, 925-602-1880; Richmond, 510-262-6500; Vallejo, 707-645-1888.

Committees: *Democratic Steering Committee Co-Chair. Education & the Workforce* (RMM of 22 D). *Resources* (2d of 22 D): Water & Power.

Group Ratings

	ADA	ACLU	AFS	LCV	ITIC	NTU	COC	ACU	NTLC	CHC
2004	100	95	100	100	33	11	21	4	3	7
2003	100	—	100	85	—	23	18	8	—	—

National Journal Ratings

	2003 LIB	—	2003 CONS		2004 LIB	—	2004 CONS
Economic	92%	—	0%		96%	—	3%
Social	92%	—	0%		88%	—	0%
Foreign	94%	—	0%		98%	—	0%

Key Votes of the 108th Congress

1. Drilling in ANWR	N	5. DC School Vouchers	N	9. Ban Same-Sex Marriage	N
2. Approve Bush Tax Cuts	N	6. Ban Human Cloning	N	10. Fund Iraq War	N
3. Medicare/Rx Bill	N	7. Restrict Gun Liability	N	11. Bar Cuba Embargo Funds	Y
4. Bar Overtime Pay Regs.	Y	8. Ban Partial-Birth Abortion	N	12. Intelligence Reorg.	N

Election Results

2004 general	George Miller (D)	166,831	(76%)	($571,957)
	Charles Hargrave (R)	52,446	(24%)	
2004 primary	George Miller (D)	unopposed		
2002 general	George Miller (D)	97,849	(71%)	($402,021)
	Charles Hargrave (R)	36,584	(26%)	
	Other	3,943	(3%)	

Prior Winning Percentages: 2000 (76%); 1998 (77%); 1996 (72%); 1994 (70%); 1992 (70%); 1990 (61%); 1988 (68%); 1986 (67%); 1984 (66%); 1982 (67%); 1980 (63%); 1978 (63%); 1976 (75%); 1974 (56%)

The People		Race/Ethnic Origin	Ancestry	
Area size:	443 sq. mi.	43.2% White	German: 7.5%	Irish: 6.7%
Urban population:	98.7%	16.8% Black	English: 5.6%	
Rural population:	1.3%	13.3% Asian	**2004 Presidential Vote**	
Pop. 2000:	639,088	0.5% Native Am.	Kerry (D) 153,988	(67%)
Median income:	$52,778	0.6% Hawaiian	Bush (R) 72,994	(32%)
Poverty status:	10.0%	3.9% Two+ races	Other 2,300	(1%)
Military veterans:	12.5%	0.3% Other	**2000 Presidential Vote**	
		21.4% Hispanic Origin	Gore (D) 139,421	(66%)
			Bush (R) 64,477	(31%)
			Other 6,824	(3%)
			Cook Partisan Voting Index: D +19	
Occupation	Blue collar: 22.7%	White collar: 60.1%	Gray collar: 17.1%	

The journey inward from the Pacific Ocean to the vast flatness of California's Central Valley passes through a wondrous variety of terrain. The traveler starts at the Golden Gate, with the lush green Presidio on one side and the bluff of the Marin mountains on the other; through the waters of San Francisco Bay, looked down upon by ridges above the East Bay on one side and the cone of Mount Tamalpais on the other; through the narrow Carquinez Strait to Suisun Bay, with its sloughs and marshes, fed by the sluggish waters of the Sacramento and San Joaquin Delta; and finally past the mountains and waters, to the flat, fertile expanse of California's great interior. This is not a journey most tourists make, but it was a familiar route to the first Americans in California and it passes by much of the industrial base of the Bay Area. On the east side of the bay is Richmond, developed almost instantaneously during World War II when Henry J. Kaiser built a shipyard in its deep-water port and 91,000 people from all over the country were put to work building ships for the Pacific theater; what became known as Rosie the Riveter Memorial Park is now a national park, and the city now has a 36% black population and is attracting high-tech spinoffs. Across Carquinez Strait is Vallejo, named for a Mexican general and member of the first California Senate, the site from 1853 to 1996 of the giant Mare Island Naval Shipyard, now being redeveloped, where 41,000 worked during World War II. Farther up the bay, on the south, is Concord, the largest city in the county, whose city officials were unique in that they lobbied the Pentagon to close the mostly unused Concord Naval Weapons Station; they wanted to use the land for business and residential development, which is banned beyond the urban limit that Contra Costa County voters imposed in 1990. The Defense Department complied and included the site on the 2005 base closure list. These shores are the industrial part of the Bay area, with tank farms and refineries. The towns are among the most ethnically diverse in the country, with large percentages of blacks, Hispanics and Asians and large numbers of Filipinos in Vallejo and other towns.

The 7th Congressional District of California includes most of this passage, from Richmond to Vallejo (the 7th's largest city), Hercules, Martinez and Pittsburg. It also proceeds inland through the intermountain interstices of Contra Costa County to include part of Concord and northeast from Vallejo over the sloughs and up I-80 to include Vacaville, on flat land beneath Vaca Mountain. Politically, this industrial area was blue-collar, labor union Democratic back in the days when San Francisco, with its larger white-collar population, often voted Republican. Today housing values have risen, as they have just about everywhere in the Bay Area, but it remains heavily Democratic, liberal on most issues. But not as leftish as San Francisco Democrats: Contra Costa voters in March 2004 rejected 54%–46% a ballot measure which would have banned Wal-Mart super centers here.

The congressman from the 7th District is George Miller, one of three remaining Democrats of the Watergate class of 1974 (the others are James Oberstar and Henry Waxman), the first baby-boom liberal to chair a House committee. He is heir to a tradition of Bay Area working class politics. His father was chairman of the state Senate Finance Committee; when he died in 1969, Miller lost the race to succeed him, but became a staffer for Senate Leader (and later San Francisco Mayor) George Moscone. Miller was a protégé of San Francisco Congressman Phillip Burton, who did so much to establish liberal hegemony in the House in the 1970s. To his work Miller brings an aggressiveness and zest for political combat reminiscent of Burton. He is a strong backer of protecting the environment against what he sees as greedy private sector operators and of furthering the causes of labor unions. Like Burton, Miller has grasped for top party leadership posts but hasn't made it. But he has learned a legislator's virtues of patience, timing and creativity.

Miller began the 1990s in a position of power, able to advance his causes forward; in the mid-1990s he found himself defending yesterday's gains and trying to prevent losses; in 2001 he found himself working with a Republican president on one of his top priorities. In 1991 he became chairman of the Interior Committee (he renamed it Natural Resources in 1993 and Republicans renamed it Resources in 1995) and proceeded, in his words, "to kick ass and take names." He had long crusaded against water reclamation projects that provided cheap water to farmers. In 1992, amid a California drought, he passed a Central Valley Project law that raised farmers' prices closer to those of urban users and imposed environmental restrictions, over the

fierce opposition of Central Valley politicians and Governor Pete Wilson. He passed the California desert bill, with Senator Dianne Feinstein, in October 1994; it was the last major legislation
of the Democratic Congress.

For several years in the minority he worked more to prevent change than to make change.
He helped to stymie John Doolittle's attempt to revise the Central Valley Project and was part of
the coalition opposing the Auburn Dam sought by Doolittle and others from the Sacramento
area. He harshly criticized Republicans for trying to change the Endangered Species Act, EPA
regulations, the bans on Arctic National Wildlife Refuge oil drilling and Tongass National Forest
logging and for commercial sponsorship of national parks; for the most part, he was successful,
with help from the Clinton administration. He won with Republican Don Young in 2000 a major
expansion of the Land and Water Conservation Fund, although the Senate scuttled a more
sweeping version.

The election of George W. Bush unexpectedly returned Miller to the center ring. He replaced
the retired Bill Clay as ranking Democrat on the Education and the Workforce Committee. The
incoming chairman, John Boehner, recommended that Bush include Miller and other Democrats
in a pre-inauguration meeting in Austin. They struck up a cordial relationship; Bush started
calling Miller "Big George." Miller is a Democrat who doesn't always follow the dictates of the
teacher's unions; he seems genuinely concerned that too many American children are getting a
rotten education. "My first concern has always been children. I look at the number of poor
children who have been denied a chance at a real educational opportunity. This has to rank first
and foremost." He came to believe that Bush shared that concern. Miller wanted more spending
on education, but he also wanted more rigorous standards, with consequences. Boehner and
Miller worked on a bipartisan basis on a committee that has usually had bitter partisan
divisions. The committee bill provided more money and required uniform standards, though not
the NAEP tests favored by Miller. The bill passed the House in May 2001 384–45. A different
version passed the Senate in June 2001. At the bill signing in January 2002 Bush took care to
praise Miller for his contributions. Miller has not been entirely happy with the way the administration implemented the law, however. He has continually complained that the administration
and Congress have not appropriated the full amounts authorized (though that is standard
practice on many programs). But he has also said that there has been progress by minority and
poor students—his goal in the first place.

Miller has fought the Bush administration and committee Republicans on many issues. He
has sponsored a bill to allow unions to be recognized as bargaining representatives by securing
signatures on cards and requiring arbitration of initial contracts: a cause going nowhere in a
Republican or probably in a Democratic House. He worked to defeat the Department of Labor
overtime regulations and lost on the floor. In February 2004 he got the House to vote 227–179 to
extend unemployment benefits for six months, and was pleased when Federal Reserve Chairman Alan Greenspan said extending benefits was "not a bad idea"; committee Chairman John
Boehner objected that the states already had money to do this and that Miller's measure was
ineffective because benefits weren't extended through the Labor Department; the argument was
settled when the Senate failed to adopt Miller's approach. In 2004 he proposed, as an alternative
to Ways and Means Chairman Bill Thomas's corporate tax bill, an American Jobs Plan that read
like a Democratic wish list: rollbacks of incentives for outsourcing jobs, $40 billion of research
and development spending, doubling of Pell grants, a federal broadband program, extension of
unemployment benefits. He has called for consolidation of college loans and wants to encourage
more colleges to participate in the direct loan program. When George W. Bush proposed to
increase Pell grants by $500 over five years, Miller said, "My first instinct is to say, 'Show me the
money,' because this administration has a track record of broken promises on education funding."

Education and Workforce has had a history of being a committee sharply split on partisan
lines from the 1960s to 1990s. But on the 2001 education bill Boehner worked closely with Miller,
and in 2004 and early 2005 he seemed prepared to do that again on the issue of pensions. Miller
praised Boehner for raising the subject in 2004, and in September 2004 the House placed on an
appropriation Miller's amendment to require the Pension Benefit Guaranty Corporation to
disclose corporate pension funding levels to participants. When United Airlines threatened to

terminate its pension plan in August 2004 and let the PBGC take over its obligations, Miller urged that it not do so. As the PBGC deficit doubled in 2004 to $23 billion, Miller warned of the possibility of "an S&L style taxpayer bailout of the agency to the tune of billions of dollars has increased." In October 2004 he sponsored a bill, "as a public marker," to freeze for five years the pensions of corporate executive who terminate employee pension plans or vastly reduce benefits. In early 2005, Boehner said he would work on pension law in terms that suggested a bipartisan approach might be possible. He defeated Miller's motion to give committee Democrats the power to call oversight hearings, but joined him in demanding an inspector general's investigation of the Department of Education's $241,000 contract with commentator Armstrong Williams.

In local matters, Miller supported the anti-Wal-Mart ballot measure in Contra Costa and worked to reduce the number of slot machines in the Lytton Band of Pomo Indians casino in San Pablo from 5,000 to 2,500, though he had passed in 2000 an amendment freeing the casino from federal and state restrictions; Senator Dianne Feinstein in January 2005 moved to rescind the 2000 measure.

Miller has been reelected by wide margins in this very Democratic district every two years.

EIGHTH DISTRICT

Rep. Nancy Pelosi (D)

Elected June 1987, 9th full term; b. Mar. 26, 1940, Baltimore, MD; home, San Francisco; Trinity Col., B.A. 1962; Catholic; married (Paul).

Professional Career: CA Dem. Party, Northern Chmn., 1977–81, St. Chmn., 1981–83; DSCC Finance Chmn., 1985–87; PR exec., Ogilvy & Mather, 1986–87.

DC Office: 2371 RHOB, 20515, 202-225-4965; Fax: 202-225-8259; Web site: www.house.gov/pelosi.

District Office: San Francisco, 415-556-4862.

Committees: *Minority Leader.*

Group Ratings

	ADA	ACLU	AFS	LCV	ITIC	NTU	COC	ACU	NTLC	CHC
2004	100	90	100	100	70	8	35	8	3	8
2003	100	—	100	90	—	21	34	16	—	—

National Journal Ratings

	2003 LIB	—	2003 CONS	2004 LIB	—	2004 CONS
Economic	92%	—	0%	93%	—	6%
Social	89%	—	10%	88%	—	0%
Foreign	70%	—	27%	81%	—	18%

Key Votes of the 108th Congress

1. Drilling in ANWR	N	5. DC School Vouchers	N	9. Ban Same-Sex Marriage	N
2. Approve Bush Tax Cuts	N	6. Ban Human Cloning	N	10. Fund Iraq War	N
3. Medicare/Rx Bill	N	7. Restrict Gun Liability	N	11. Bar Cuba Embargo Funds	Y
4. Bar Overtime Pay Regs.	Y	8. Ban Partial-Birth Abortion	N	12. Intelligence Reorg.	N

Election Results

2004 general	Nancy Pelosi (D)	224,017	(83%)	($1,240,543)
	Jennifer Depalma (R)	31,074	(12%)	($5,704)
	Leilani Dowell (P&F)	9,527	(4%)	
	Other	5,446	(2%)	
2004 primary	Nancy Pelosi (D)	unopposed		
2002 general	Nancy Pelosi (D)	127,684	(80%)	($966,946)
	G. German (R)	20,063	(13%)	($7,130)
	Jay Pond (Green)	10,033	(6%)	
	Other	2,661	(2%)	

Prior Winning Percentages: 2000 (85%); 1998 (86%); 1996 (84%); 1994 (82%); 1992 (82%); 1990 (77%); 1988 (76%); 1987 (63%)

The People		Race/Ethnic Origin	Ancestry	
Area size:	114 sq. mi.	42.9% White	Irish: 6.9%	German: 6.4%
Urban population:	100.0%	8.6% Black	English: 5.1%	
Rural population:	0.0%	28.7% Asian	**2004 Presidential Vote**	
Pop. 2000:	639,088	0.3% Native Am.	Kerry (D) 244,009	(85%)
Median income:	$52,322	0.5% Hawaiian	Bush (R) 40,558	(14%)
Poverty status:	12.2%	2.9% Two+ races	Other 4,024	(1%)
Military veterans:	6.8%	0.3% Other	**2000 Presidential Vote**	
		15.7% Hispanic Origin	Gore (D) 196,878	(77%)
			Bush (R) 37,737	(15%)
			Other 20,869	(8%)
			Cook Partisan Voting Index: D +36	

Occupation	Blue collar: 11.9%	White collar: 72.9%	Gray collar: 15.1%

On February 20, 1915, Governor Hiram Johnson and Mayor James Rolph led 150,000 people onto the grounds of the Panama-Pacific International Exposition to see the Spanish-Italian baroque style building built on reclaimed land in what became San Francisco's Marina district. The Exposition ostensibly celebrated the completion of the Panama Canal, but it was clearly intended to show off San Francisco's recovery from the 1906 earthquake. It also spotlighted San Francisco as the central focus of an America that was becoming, with its acquisition of Hawaii and the Philippines and its interest in an open-door policy with China and trade with Japan, a power in the Pacific. The Exposition set the physical style of San Francisco: It encouraged the use of Mediterranean color, accent and detail that characterizes most post-Victorian houses and commercial structures in The City (as the *San Francisco Examiner* called it for years). It created the picturesque Marina district, whose old buildings were among those damaged in the 1989 earthquake, and today's tourist waterfront around Fisherman's Wharf and Ghirardelli Square. This San Francisco has many facets: On a sunny day it looks almost tropical, with brown mountains baking in the sun and light shining off the pastel stucco buildings; when the clouds scud in from the Pacific, it can look sinister, full of dark corners where a private detective's partner might be ambushed by a pretty girl. The buildings can be majestic, like the monumental Beaux Arts City Hall, or tawdry, like the hotels of the Tenderloin; it is a city that looks exotic at first but, when you look closely, can only be American.

San Francisco has been a dynamic city, capable of great growth, carrying the American tradition of tolerance of diversity to new lengths; it grew from nothing to a major city in the single year of 1850; its American origins are obvious from the regular grids of streets named after politicians and local developers. The San Francisco of 1915 was proud of the writers who had flourished there—Jack London, Ambrose Bierce, Frank Norris—and of the hometown traditions of the arts and crafts movement, just as San Francisco later would have a Herb Caen-ish pride in the beats of the 1950s North Beach, the hippies who thronged Haight-Ashbury in 1967, and the gays of Castro in the 1970s and since. Over the years, the city's booming economy, based initially on food processing, but now on finance, high-tech and clothing (Levi Strauss, The Gap) attracted talented newcomers, weighted increasingly toward those who find its liberation-minded cultural attitudes congenial.

Politically, San Francisco was a progressive Republican town, like the two men who led the way into the Exposition. The sour-tempered Hiram Johnson made his name as a reformer throwing out crooked city politicians; his administration gave California primary elections, referenda and recall, and strong civil service laws. "Sunny Jim" Rolph, mayor from 1911–30 and then governor, built the civic center, parks, schools, streetcars and the Hetch Hetchy aqueduct—the antique infrastructure of San Francisco today. Sympathetic to the conservation movement, willing to deal with organized labor in a union town that had America's only general strike in 1934, tolerant of the diversity of California, these progressive Republicans were the recognizable ancestors of, though certainly not identical to, the latter-day San Franciscans who became increasingly liberal and even radical.

But San Francisco's hipness can be overstated. For if its distinctive style attracted liberal singles and gays in increasing numbers, its economic dynamism on the Pacific Rim has attracted Asians—as indeed San Francisco did from 1850 until immigration was shut off by the Chinese Exclusion Act in 1882. The city has elected strong liberal politicians—notably, Mayor George Moscone and openly gay Supervisor Harvey Milk, who were shot to death in 1978 by a political opponent who was acquitted of murder by a liberal jury on the bizarre theory that he had been crazed by junk food. Over the next decade, the city's cultural liberalism was tempered by Mayor Dianne Feinstein, who vetoed a same-sex marriage ordinance and opposed commercial rent control. In 1995, Willie Brown, ousted after 15 years as speaker of the Assembly, returned home and was elected mayor. After reaping admiring publicity following his takeover of the office, Brown's record turned dismal. While the affluent neighborhoods were enriched with new Silicon Valley millionaires, the Chinese, Filipino and other Asian immigrants in the southern and western parts of the city were beleaguered by high taxes that supported the pampered public employee unions. He won praise for Operation Scrub Down to clean the downtown streets. After sparking protests for his crackdown on the homeless, the term-limited Brown stepped down in 2003. As his successor, San Francisco passed over the radical Matt Gonzalez and installed Gavin Newsom, who in February 2004 started issuing marriage licenses to same-sex couples, more than 4,000 in all, although California voters outlawed same-sex marriage and the courts declined to overturn that law. The state Supreme Court ordered him to stop after a month, and later declared that Newsom had exceeded his authority and that the marriages were "void and of no legal effect from their inception."

The 8th Congressional District of California takes in four-fifths of San Francisco, all but the southwest corner. It includes all of San Francisco's high-rise downtown, the crowded and bustling Chinatown, Telegraph, Nob and Russian Hills, North Beach (which was once really a beach), Pacific Heights (which is still on heights) and the Marina District (which does not have a very big marina). In the valleys are the mostly black Fillmore and Western Addition areas; the 8th is 9% black, 16% Hispanic and 29% Asian—the second highest Asian percentage of any district outside Hawaii. The 8th also has the gay Castro district and Noe Valley, Haight-Ashbury, once the bedraggled center of hippiedom and now another yup-and-coming San Francisco neighborhood, and Portrero Hill with its restored houses overlooking downtown. Farther south are the old residential areas overlooking I-280, with pastel houses strewn along grid streets that hug the steep hills. The district is overwhelmingly Democratic and voted 85%–14% for John Kerry in 2004.

The 8th District is represented by Nancy Pelosi, a Democrat with deep political roots and enormous ambition, who was first elected in June 1987 and is now the House minority leader. She has the energy and shrewdness of one who has handled the most delicate political chores, and the charm and unflappability of one who is the mother of five children. Pelosi grew up in Maryland; her father, Thomas D'Alesandro, served in the House from 1939–47 and was mayor of Baltimore for 12 years after that, and her brother, Thomas D'Alesandro Jr., was mayor from 1967 to 1971. Married to a successful San Francisco businessman, she was California Democratic Party chairman in the early 1980s. Since the 1960s, San Francisco's congressional politics were dominated by Phillip Burton, an old-fashioned labor-liberal Democrat. But Burton died in 1983 and his widow Sala, elected to succeed him, died in 1987. With deathbed encouragement from Sala Burton, Pelosi ran and won 35%–31% in the special against gay supervisor Harry Britt.

Pelosi has taken the lead on important issues of local sensitivity. One is human rights, especially in China. After the Tiananmen Square massacre, she sponsored an amendment to give Chinese students the right to remain in the United States; George H.W. Bush vetoed it. In 1991 she became the lead sponsor of the bill to condition China's Most Favored Nation status on human rights reforms; the House overrode Bush's veto but it was upheld in the Senate. After that, Pelosi led the annual fight against normal trade relations and sharply criticized China. She said that Bill Clinton was either in denial or ill-informed about what's going on in China. When Clinton in 1999 agreed to terms for China's entry into the World Trade Organization, Pelosi led even more furious opposition to normal trade relations with China. Although bitter about the setbacks, she vowed to maintain her human rights vigil. She has done all this at some political risk: Pelosi's position is by no means universally popular with Asian Americans in her district; many think the U.S. should trade and negotiate quietly with China. One of her chief adversaries on the issue is her San Francisco neighbor, Senator Dianne Feinstein; their houses are just a few blocks apart. In addition to working with some Republicans on China, she usually cooperated with chairman Porter Goss as the senior Democrat on the Intelligence Committee, especially after the September 11 attacks. She joined in the committee's report that, while the intelligence community did not have specific evidence in advance, it did have information that was clearly relevant to the attacks, particularly when considered for its collective significance.

On other issues Pelosi has an almost perfectly liberal voting record. She has worked to restore welfare for legal immigrants, and has supported needle exchanges for HIV/AIDS prevention. She has been a leader in encouraging family planning and environmental protection overseas. At home, Pelosi has been reelected by huge margins.

Her move into the leadership was persistent, shrewd and well-organized. In hopes that Democrats would regain House control in 2000, she ran a vigorous campaign against Steny Hoyer to become majority whip—raising more than $3 million for her party's candidates. Although she was not running "as a woman," she said, "the fact that I am a woman is an enhancement because we absolutely must have diversity in the leadership." Unfortunately for Democrats and Pelosi, Republicans kept control and Tom DeLay remained majority whip. When David Bonior decided in 2001 to run for governor of Michigan and step down as minority whip, Pelosi and Hoyer ran leadership campaigns again, this time in a real contest. Pelosi said that Democrats needed to refocus on grassroots organization, money and message. Supporters played up her potential to become a celebrity—"a glamorous grandmother who knocks people off their feet," as Hawaii's Neil Abercrombie put it. With nearly unanimous support from the 32 California Democrats, and showing that she knew how to whip and count her supporters, Pelosi won by a convincing 118–95.

As whip, Pelosi moved quickly to assert herself, sometimes independently from Minority Leader Dick Gephardt. She sparked controversy when she contributed $10,000 to Representative Lynn Rivers in a redistricting-forced Michigan primary against John Dingell—the ranking Democrat on Energy and Commerce, who had been a strong supporter of Hoyer for whip. Normally, party leaders do not take sides in such elections. Dingell handily won the primary. Her biggest conflict came in fall 2002 when she actively encouraged opponents of the resolution authorizing the use of force in Iraq, which Gephardt had enthusiastically endorsed with George W. Bush at the White House. Pelosi contended that supporters had not made the case for using force, and that she had seen no evidence that Iraq "poses an imminent threat to our nation." To the surprise of many, her efforts helped win 126 Democratic votes against the resolution, while only 81 backed the position of Gephardt, which also was backed by Democratic Caucus chairman Martin Frost. In retrospect, that split signaled the transition in the caucus. Once the disappointing 2002 election results were in and Gephardt said that he was stepping down, Pelosi had all but locked up the support of a majority of the caucus. Frost announced his candidacy with warnings that the selection of Pelosi might create a "permanent minority party;" he withdrew from the contest a day later, conceding that he could not win. Harold Ford made a belated, quixotic bid designed to appeal to a combination of blacks and New Democrats, but Pelosi won 177–29.

As Democratic leader in the House, she brought a burst of energy—and favorable press coverage—to a party that badly needed it. She showed hands-on management in selecting members for House committee vacancies and developing a Democratic message designed to highlight the shortcomings of the Bush agenda. There were bruised feelings over some committee assignments, but even allies of Hoyer and Frost credited her with bringing a breath of fresh air and enthusiasm to party deliberations. As Republicans pressed their agenda, Pelosi declared that Democrats would take "a party position" in opposition to the Republican Medicare/prescription drug bill. But 16 Democrats voted for the final deal in November 2003, providing the critical margin for passage; she was largely silent about the renegades, many of whom were responding to local pressures. This was a painful lesson for Pelosi in the limited power of the minority leader in the House. She called President Bush an "incompetent" leader for his handling of the war in Iraq. Working with Robert Matsui as chairman of the DCCC, she tirelessly traveled the country raising money and boosting local candidates. If she became Speaker, Pelosi pledged, she would reform the House to give a greater voice to all members and assure fairness. She cited Democratic gains of open seats in Kentucky and South Dakota in special elections in early 2004 as proof that the political tide was turning their way. But the three-seat loss in the November election turned out to be yet another crushing disappointment for House Democrats, though Pelosi noted that they won a net gain apart from the effects of the 2003 Texas redistricting. She also cast some of the blame on the presidential campaign of John Kerry. That increased the personal stakes for Pelosi in the 2006 election; historically, opposition parties have usually gained seats in offyear elections, though that was not the case in 1998 and 2002. In early 2005, she firmly insisted that House Democrats would not sit down with Republicans on Social Security until they removed personal retirement accounts from discussion.

NINTH DISTRICT

Rep. Barbara Lee (D)

Elected April 1998, 4th full term; b. July 16, 1946, El Paso, TX; home, Oakland; Mills Col., B.A. 1973, U. of CA at Berkeley, M.A. 1975; no religious affiliation; divorced.

Elected Office: CA Assembly, 1990–96; CA Senate, 1996–98.

Professional Career: Chief of Staff, U.S. Rep. Ron Dellums, 1975–87.

DC Office: 1724 LHOB, 20515, 202-225-2661; Fax: 202-225-9817; Web site: www.house.gov/lee.

District Office: Oakland, 510-763-0370.

Committees: *Financial Services* (13th of 32 D): Domestic and International Monetary Policy, Trade & Technology; Housing & Community Opportunity. *International Relations* (13th of 23 D): Africa, Global Human Rights & International Operations; Western Hemisphere.

Group Ratings

	ADA	ACLU	AFS	LCV	ITIC	NTU	COC	ACU	NTLC	CHC
2004	95	100	100	100	30	16	5	0	0	7
2003	100	—	100	95	—	28	17	8	—	—

National Journal Ratings

	2003 LIB	—	2003 CONS		2004 LIB	—	2004 CONS
Economic	87%	—	9%		94%	—	5%
Social	92%	—	0%		88%	—	0%
Foreign	89%	—	8%		98%	—	0%

Key Votes of the 108th Congress

1. Drilling in ANWR	N	5. DC School Vouchers	N	9. Ban Same-Sex Marriage	N
2. Approve Bush Tax Cuts	N	6. Ban Human Cloning	N	10. Fund Iraq War	N
3. Medicare/Rx Bill	N	7. Restrict Gun Liability	N	11. Bar Cuba Embargo Funds	Y
4. Bar Overtime Pay Regs.	Y	8. Ban Partial-Birth Abortion	N	12. Intelligence Reorg.	N

Election Results

2004 general	Barbara Lee (D)	215,630	(85%)	($783,143)
	Claudia Bermudez (R)	31,278	(12%)	($482,942)
	Other	8,131	(3%)	
2004 primary	Barbara Lee (D)	unopposed		
2002 general	Barbara Lee (D)	135,893	(81%)	($911,962)
	Jerald Udinsky (R)	25,333	(15%)	
	Other	5,691	(3%)	

Prior Winning Percentages: 2000 (85%); 1998 (83%); 1998 (67%)

The People		Race/Ethnic Origin	Ancestry	
Area size:	152 sq. mi.	35.2% White	German: 5.9%	English: 5.1%
Urban population:	99.9%	26.0% Black	Irish: 5.0%	
Rural population:	0.1%	15.4% Asian	**2004 Presidential Vote**	
Pop. 2000:	639,088	0.4% Native Am.	Kerry (D) 228,642	(86%)
Median income:	$44,314	0.4% Hawaiian	Bush (R) 33,450	(13%)
Poverty status:	16.9%	3.6% Two+ races	Other 4,082	(2%)
Military veterans:	8.4%	0.4% Other	**2000 Presidential Vote**	
		18.7% Hispanic Origin	Gore (D) 184,030	(79%)
			Bush (R) 31,464	(13%)
			Other 18,868	(8%)
			Cook Partisan Voting Index: D +38	

Occupation	Blue collar: 17.3%	White collar: 69.0%	Gray collar: 13.7%

Oakland and Berkeley, on the East Bay opposite San Francisco, stand today on one of the lushest sites in America, overlooking the Bay Bridge and the Golden Gate, basking in the sunshine that is more common here than across the Bay. Both cities are the homes of great institutions, but in different ways they are also museum pieces, antiques from a moment in the 1960s when both, especially Berkeley, gained identities that became hard to shake. Berkeley was founded as a university town, named after the 18th century Irish philosopher Bishop George Berkeley, for his proclamation, "Westward the course of empire takes its way." Famous for years as the home of first-rate scholarship at the University of California, Berkeley became famous politically in 1964 as the home of student rebellion when the Free Speech Movement, protesting an administrator's refusal to let students set up a card table to sign up volunteers for Lyndon B. Johnson's campaign, led to months of riots, student strikes and classroom confrontation. In 1969, students led protests at "People's Park," a lot owned by the university, and Governor Ronald Reagan sent in the National Guard to protect state property from conversion to a playground: an episode in which both sides relished the confrontation. Berkeley in the 1960s gave birth to a street culture that still exists. Its denizens made common cause with the Black Panthers, a violent quasi-political criminal gang from nearby Oakland, and smoked marijuana with the Hell's Angels motorcycle gang, also once based in Oakland. Berkeley's city council features bizarre political wars in which Democrats who are very liberal by national standards are the right wing; in March 2004, council members deferred to advice not to urge impeachment of George W. Bush and instead demanded a censure for a litany of grievances. The campus, with its view of the Bay, remains beautiful, and old buildings like the shingled Claremont Hotel are grand. But Berkeley has had little commercial development, and its public facilities have a low-maintenance, almost Third World look.

Oakland has a different history, centered around commerce and building its own civic institutions (Gertrude Stein was wrong: there is a there there). It became the western terminus of the transcontinental railroad in 1870 and was connected by ferry to San Francisco; it has always had heavy industry, and its port today is the busiest on the bay. The docks attracted young roustabouts like the writer Jack London, after whom a downtown square is named; civic affairs were run by the local elite, like the Knowland family who owned the *Oakland Tribune*. With the Bay Area's largest black community, Oakland spawned the Black Panthers in the 1960s; blacks took control of city government in the 1970s and the *Tribune* in the 1980s. Onto the scene came Jerry Brown, governor of California 20 years earlier, unsuccessful presidential candidate in 1976, 1980 and 1992; in 1998, he ran an unorthodox campaign for mayor, and won. Brown irritated local factions by firing department heads and ignoring longstanding alliances, but he seemed to take seriously his mission of propelling Oakland to the prominence its geographic position suggests it can occupy. He sounded like a conservative, with his tough talk on crime and advocacy of big commercial development projects that drove up rents; he set up a military high school. Crime rates dropped and the local economy thrived, partly with the growth of middle-income refugees from the exorbitant housing costs of San Francisco.

The 9th Congressional District of California consists of Oakland and Berkeley, plus Castro Valley. It has the largest black percentage of any northern California district (26% in 2000, down from 32% in 1990); almost as high were its percentages of Hispanics (19%) and Asians (15%). Politically, it may be the most activist left-wing district in the nation. It voted 86%–13% for John Kerry.

The congresswoman from the 9th District is Barbara Lee, a Democrat first chosen in an April 1998 special election. She grew up in Texas and the San Fernando Valley, graduated from Mills College in Oakland, got a degree in social work at Berkeley and has brought that training to her work since then. She started a community mental health center in Berkeley and then worked as a staffer for 12 years for Congressman Ronald Dellums, a liberal Democrat who became chairman of the Armed Services Committee. In 1990 Lee was elected to the California Assembly; in 1996, she was elected to the California Senate. After Dellums announced he was resigning, he endorsed Lee as his successor, and she won the special election with 67% of the vote.

In the House, Lee stands at the far left of the ideological spectrum. She wants to reduce the nation's weapons stockpiles and cut Pentagon spending sharply. She won enactment of her bill to require that federal cancer data collection include information on benign brain tumors in order to assist health research. In May 2001, the International Relations Committee passed her amendment to reverse the Bush policy on denying funding to international groups who offer abortion counseling of services, but later that month the House voted to strike the language from the State Department authorization bill. In negotiations with chairman Henry Hyde, she increased support for international AIDS programs, but later criticized administration emphasis on abstinence programs. Lee became co-chair of the Progressive Caucus. After a visit to Cuba, she called for steps to end the 40-year embargo of Castro's island; the House accepted her amendment to lift restrictions on education travel to Cuba. On the Financial Services Committee, she urged steps to increase consumer knowledge of financial decisions. For her district, she got $27 million to dredge the busy port of Oakland for container ships.

Lee has consistently opposed military action. She criticized Bill Clinton's bombing of Iraq in 1998. As most Democrats voted to authorize bombing of Serbia in 1999, Lee was the only House member to oppose a resolution supporting U.S. troops. In September 2001 she was the only member of Congress to vote against the resolution authorizing the use of force in response to the terrorist attacks. Her vote brought a torrent of national attention and protest, but there were supportive rallies in her district. She received threats of violence and the Capitol police provided her with 24-hour protection. During debate in October 2002 on whether to authorize the use of force in Iraq, Lee offered an alternative calling for diplomatic rather than military action; it was defeated 355–72. In 2003, the House defeated her amendment for a study of intelligence failures on claims of weapons of mass destruction. She called for an independent probe of the Bush administration's role in the ouster of Haiti President Jean-Bertrand Aristide. After a January 2005 visit to Sudan, she joined a bipartisan condemnation of the continuing genocide and urged disinvestment in companies that do business there.

Lee has been reelected easily. Lee won the 2002 primary 85%–15% over an opponent who criticized her vote against military force.

TENTH DISTRICT

Rep. Ellen Tauscher (D)

Elected 1996, 5th term; b. Nov. 15, 1951, Newark, NJ; home, Alamo; Seton Hall U., B.A. 1973; Catholic; divorced.

Professional Career: Wall Street Invest. Banker, 1974–88, NYSE member, 1977–79; Founder & CEO, Registry Cos., 1992–96.

DC Office: 1034 LHOB, 20515, 202-225-1880; Fax: 202-225-5914; Web site: www.house.gov/tauscher.

District Offices: Antioch, 925-757-7187; Fairfield, 707-428-7792; Walnut Creek, 925-932-8899.

Committees: *Armed Services* (13th of 28 D): Projection Forces; Strategic Forces; Terrorism, Unconventional Threats & Capabilities. *Transportation & Infrastructure* (15th of 34 D): Aviation; Highways, Transit & Pipelines; Water Resources & Environment.

Group Ratings

	ADA	ACLU	AFS	LCV	ITIC	NTU	COC	ACU	NTLC	CHC
2004	100	75	100	100	70	12	48	16	3	0
2003	90	—	100	100	—	29	40	16	—	—

National Journal Ratings

	2003 LIB	—	2003 CONS		2004 LIB	—	2004 CONS
Economic	71%	—	27%		71%	—	28%
Social	78%	—	20%		78%	—	19%
Foreign	57%	—	42%		79%	—	20%

Key Votes of the 108th Congress

1. Drilling in ANWR	N	5. DC School Vouchers	N	9. Ban Same-Sex Marriage	N
2. Approve Bush Tax Cuts	N	6. Ban Human Cloning	N	10. Fund Iraq War	Y
3. Medicare/Rx Bill	N	7. Restrict Gun Liability	N	11. Bar Cuba Embargo Funds	Y
4. Bar Overtime Pay Regs.	Y	8. Ban Partial-Birth Abortion	N	12. Intelligence Reorg.	N

Election Results

2004 general	Ellen Tauscher (D)	182,750	(66%)	($780,196)
	Jeff Ketelson (R)	95,349	(34%)	($159,219)
2004 primary	Ellen Tauscher (D)	unopposed		
2002 general	Ellen Tauscher (D)	126,390	(76%)	($860,031)
	Sonia Harden (Lib)	40,807	(24%)	

Prior Winning Percentages: 2000 (53%); 1998 (53%); 1996 (49%)

The People		Race/Ethnic Origin	Ancestry	
Area size:	1,085 sq. mi.	65.4% White	German: 10.7%	Irish: 9.1%
Urban population:	96.5%	5.7% Black	English: 8.2%	
Rural population:	3.5%	9.1% Asian	**2004 Presidential Vote**	
Pop. 2000:	639,088	0.4% Native Am.	Kerry (D) 169,373	(59%)
Median income:	$65,245	0.4% Hawaiian	Bush (R) 117,037	(40%)
Poverty status:	6.3%	3.7% Two+ races	Other 3,098	(1%)
Military veterans:	13.4%	0.2% Other	**2000 Presidential Vote**	
		15.0% Hispanic Origin	Gore (D) 145,996	(55%)
			Bush (R) 109,149	(41%)
			Other 9,273	(4%)
			Cook Partisan Voting Index: D + 9	

Occupation	Blue collar: 17.8%	White collar: 69.0%	Gray collar: 13.2%

In the 1950s, when the streets of San Francisco and Oakland were already crowded, the rolling grasslands on the east of the mountain ridges, over the hill and through the tunnel from Oakland, were still mostly empty. In the years since, they have filled up. Freeways took the first commuters through the Caldecott Tunnel to the woodsy trail-like roads of Orinda and Lafayette; I-580 brought people east from the southern East Bay towns to the Amador Valley and Livermore, site of one of the nation's nuclear laboratories; I-680 running north-south provided a spine for businesses and shopping centers up and down the San Ramon Valley, from burgeoning Concord through Walnut Creek in Contra Costa County and points south; BART stations in Walnut Creek and Orinda took commuters to downtown San Francisco. Not all of the inhabitable areas are filled in yet, and local voters have passed measures to keep growth inside an urban limit. But what has evolved in this sunny land, shielded by the mountains from the ocean fogs and rains, is an advanced civilization of highly skilled and educated people. Affluent and generally tolerant of—if a little put off by—what happens in San Francisco, they are respectful of economic markets and wary of government, but concerned about preserving a physical environment that is one of America's most pleasant.

This remains the heart of the 10th Congressional District of California. The 2001 redistricting removed the San Ramon Valley south of Walnut Creek, the last Republican-leaning part of the San Francisco Bay area, and added part of the Sacramento River Delta and part of booming Solano County to the north—Fairfield (now the largest city in the 10th) and nearby Travis Air Force Base and Suisun City. This made the district more working-class and Democratic. In 2004 John Kerry carried the district 59%–40%—a solid margin, but nothing his like one-sided margins in the San Francisco and Oakland-Berkeley districts.

The congresswoman from the 10th District is Ellen Tauscher, a Democrat first elected in 1996. Tauscher grew up in New Jersey, where her father ran a grocery store; at 25, she held a seat on the New York Stock Exchange, where she was a stock trader and investment banker. In 1989, she and her then-husband, owner of Vanstar (formerly ComputerLand), moved to California. After a difficult childbirth plus trouble finding quality childcare for her daughter, Tauscher started the ChildCare Registry, the first company to offer (for $140) background information on child-care providers. In 1996 she ran against two-term Republican Congressman Bill Baker, a fiscal conservative who was also a tart-tongued conservative on cultural issues. She ran as a moderate Democrat and spent liberally of her own money, some $1.7 million in all. Baker ran ads comparing her to a lottery winner buying a congressional seat. Tauscher's ads called Baker an "extremist" on gun control, abortion and the environment. This proved a winning combination, though only barely. Tauscher won 49%–47%.

In the House, Tauscher has a more moderate and activist bipartisan voting record than other Bay Area Democrats—"Tauscherism," as *Time* called it. She voted for the Republicans' impeachment inquiry resolution and called on Bill Clinton to stop "legal hairsplitting and speak plain English to the American people." On transportation issues, she has taken the lead for the region on behalf of both highway projects and Bay Area transit plans; her priorities have included widening congested Highway 4 on the East Bay. Though a mid-level member of the minority party, she said she had the ability to make bipartisan deals: "I feel like I'm back on Wall Street. If you have a sensory touch that can tell there's a deal in the room—and I have a great one—you can get things done." Alone among Bay Area Democrats, she favored normal trade relations with China; after initially opposing trade promotion authority, which disappointed the high-tech industry, she voted for the final House-Senate deal. Tauscher joined the moderate Blue Dog Democrats and the New Democrat Coalition; in 2005, she became chair of the New Democrats, with a pledge to find new areas of collaboration, including a greater emphasis on national security, but lamented that Republicans were not amenable. "We want bipartisanship. Unfortunately, the majority [party] doesn't share that."

On the Armed Services Committee, Tauscher was an early advocate of improving America's homeland security and the nation's ability to deal with the threat of terrorism, which led her to join a bipartisan group urging creation of the Homeland Security Department. She supported use of force in Iraq. She criticized the failure of the Pentagon to provide information to Congress, including the quality of intelligence in Iraq plus required reports of nonproliferation programs. The House defeated her amendments to reduce funds for the Energy Department's Robust Nuclear Earth Penetrator program. She led Democratic calls to increase military forces, including 40,000 in increased Army troop levels. Worried about the future of Travis, which is home of

13,000 jobs and is a center of the Air Mobility Command, she called the "precipitous rush to close bases . . . just irresponsible." She opposed proposals to close Buchanan Field airport in Concord and convert it to commercial development, including an option for 6,000 residences. The public need is "to increase the aviation capacity, not decrease it," she said.

Among Democrats, Tauscher showed her centrism and independence with early support for Steny Hoyer against San Francisco's Nancy Pelosi in the 2001 contest for majority whip. That did not please many local colleagues and may have been one reason the redistricters removed the San Ramon Valley from her district. While most Democrats would welcome getting a more Democratic district, Tauscher complained and accused other Democrats of giving her a district where her moderate voting record would be a liability. In the old 10th District, Tauscher had competitive re-election contests. In 1998, Charles Ball, a national-security analyst at the Lawrence Livermore National Laboratory, put together a serious platform and raised $1 million to Tauscher's $1.3 million. The national Republican Party spent another $500,000 on ads attacking Tauscher on taxes. She won 53%–43%. In 2000 she won 53%–44% against community banker Claude Hutchison. In 2002 she was the only California Democrat without Republican opposition. In 2004, she easily defeated an opponent who criticized her for partisanship. Tauscher does not discourage speculation that she might run if either of California's Democratic senators steps down, but neither has shown any inclination to do so and the crowd of aspirants is growing. Despite her Wall Street background, she called Republican proposals for personal retirement accounts in Social Security "ill-advised."

ELEVENTH DISTRICT

Rep. Richard Pombo (R)

Elected 1992, 7th term; b. Jan. 8, 1961, Tracy; home, Tracy; CA Polytechnic Inst., 1979–82; Catholic; married (Annette).

Elected Office: Tracy City Cncl., 1990–92.

Professional Career: Cattle rancher; Co–founder, Citizens Land Alliance, 1986.

DC Office: 2411 RHOB, 20515, 202-225-1947; Fax: 202-226-0861; Web site: www.house.gov/pombo.

District Offices: San Ramon, 925-866-7040; Stockton, 209-951-3091.

Committees: *Agriculture* (3d of 25 R): Department Operations, Oversight, Nutrition & Forestry; Livestock & Horticulture. *Resources* (Chmn. of 27 R).

Group Ratings

	ADA	ACLU	AFS	LCV	ITIC	NTU	COC	ACU	NTLC	CHC
2004	0	0	0	0	80	61	95	100	86	92
2003	5	—	0	5	—	64	97	88	—	—

National Journal Ratings

	2003 LIB	—	2003 CONS		2004 LIB	—	2004 CONS
Economic	0%	—	91%		7%	—	92%
Social	17%	—	79%		9%	—	85%
Foreign	23%	—	71%		25%	—	68%

Key Votes of the 108th Congress

1. Drilling in ANWR	Y	5. DC School Vouchers	Y	9. Ban Same-Sex Marriage	Y
2. Approve Bush Tax Cuts	Y	6. Ban Human Cloning	Y	10. Fund Iraq War	Y
3. Medicare/Rx Bill	Y	7. Restrict Gun Liability	Y	11. Bar Cuba Embargo Funds	N
4. Bar Overtime Pay Regs.	N	8. Ban Partial-Birth Abortion	Y	12. Intelligence Reorg.	Y

Election Results

2004 general	Richard Pombo (R)	163,582	(61%)	($1,017,709)
	Gerald McNerney (D)	103,587	(39%)	($154,701)
2004 primary	Richard Pombo (R)	unopposed		
2002 general	Richard Pombo (R)	104,921	(60%)	($1,471,650)
	Elaine Shaw (D)	69,035	(40%)	($595,298)

Prior Winning Percentages: 2000 (58%); 1998 (61%); 1996 (59%); 1994 (62%); 1992 (48%)

The People		Race/Ethnic Origin	Ancestry	
Area size:	2,316 sq. mi.	64.1% White	German: 11.4%	Irish: 8.3%
Urban population:	90.1%	3.4% Black	English: 7.5%	
Rural population:	9.9%	8.7% Asian	**2004 Presidential Vote**	
Pop. 2000:	639,088	0.5% Native Am.	Bush (R) 151,397	(54%)
Median income:	$61,996	0.2% Hawaiian	Kerry (D) 127,102	(45%)
Poverty status:	8.8%	3.2% Two+ races	Other 2,306	(1%)
Military veterans:	12.0%	0.2% Other	**2000 Presidential Vote**	
		19.7% Hispanic Origin	Bush (R) 125,876	(53%)
			Gore (D) 106,354	(45%)
			Other 5,882	(2%)
			Cook Partisan Voting Index: R + 3	

Occupation   Blue collar: 19.1%   White collar: 67.6%   Gray collar: 13.3%

People from back East looking for clues about California might consider avoiding Beverly Hills and Nob Hill and taking a look at the Central Valley directly east of San Francisco. This is an old part of California with much recent growth. Stockton on the San Joaquin River was a Gold Rush trading town founded in 1847, named after Robert Stockton, the second U.S. military governor of California, who captured Santa Barbara and Los Angeles from Mexico and proclaimed California U.S. territory. The Central Valley around Stockton, criss-crossed with railroads and canals, became one of the world's greatest agriculture areas; the San Joaquin River channel was deepened to 37 feet and Stockton today is the Central Valley's ocean port. The rich farming attracted immigrants from all over: Mexicans coming up Route 99 joined North Dakotans flocking to the town of Lodi; Italian and Yugoslav immigrants bringing their Old World crops; Yankees and Okies bringing their distinct churches and systems of belief; and Southeast Asian refugees crowd into the older streets of Stockton. In the 1990s, Stockton positioned itself to take advantage of the region's economic strength by turning into a warehouse and distribution center for northern California. This growth came even though the farm economy was threatened by moves toward reducing water subsidies, the difficulty of attracting migrant workers for harvests and declines in crop prices. But it may benefit because many of its crops (especially, fruits and vegetables) are not subject to the vagaries of federal controls, though cotton remains a big producer here. And the Central Valley has also become a suburb: with the high cost of living in San Francisco, Bay Area workers with modest incomes are increasingly buying cheaper houses around Tracy and Stockton and commuting to work past the windmills of Altamont on I-580. Stockton's San Joaquin County had a population increase of 17% from 2000 to 2004, while the Bay area's population rose only 1%.

The 11th Congressional District of California includes much of this area plus the Bay Area suburbia of San Ramon Valley in Contra Costa County. The central part of Stockton is not in the district; rather, it is connected by a thin corridor to the 18th District further south in the valley. But the 11th does include northwest Stockton and most of the rest of San Joaquin County—Tracy, Lodi, Manteca. Connected to this is the adjacent town of Brentwood in Contra Costa County, the fastest-growing city in the Bay Area in the 1990s. The farm town of Morgan Hill anchors the far southern edge of the 11th in Santa Clara County. The San Ramon Valley towns—Danville and San Ramon in Contra Costa County and Dublin and Pleasanton in Alameda County, are much more affluent than the Central Valley parts of the district. Politically, both parts are Republican. The political heritage of the Central Valley is Democratic, and it produced two House Democratic whips, John McFall in the late 1970s and Tony Coelho in the late 1980s. But it has been moving toward Republicans on cultural issues and on farm interests' hostility to environmental restrictions. The San Ramon Valley is the most Republican part of the Bay Area, but not very Republican by national standards, fairly liberal on cultural issues but conservative on economics. This district voted 54% for George W. Bush in 2004.

The congressman from the 11th District is Richard Pombo, a Republican first elected in 1992, a leader of the property rights movement in Congress and the chairman of the House Resources Committee. Pombo grew up in Tracy, studied agricultural business at Cal Poly Pomona, worked on the family ranch and served on the Tracy city council for two years. Tracy is Pombo country. He is the second of five sons of his father Ralph; each has a first name beginning with "R" so that they could share the family cattle brand, "RP." The large Pombo Real Estate firm was founded by his uncle. Joe Pombo Parkway was named after his grandfather, who was a dairyman. Richard Pombo got interested in politics during a dispute over a railroad right of way. Running in a seat without an incumbent, he was elected to the House by defeating a pro-choice moderate in the Republican primary and then beating the wife of state Senator (now Insurance Commissioner) John Garamendi 48%–46% in the general. Even in his official photos, he often wears a cowboy hat and boots, some of which are eel and ostrich skin. "I'm not going to fit in too well, because I'm anything but politically correct," Pombo predicted.

With a consistently conservative voting record, he fought with environmentalists on the Resources Committee and with subsidy advocates on Agriculture. Once in the majority, he took charge of the unsuccessful effort to rewrite the Endangered Species Act; he held hearings with stories of absurd regulations and filed a bill to compensate landowners whose property values declined greatly. The Sierra Club called Pombo an "eco-thug." Environmentalists complained that a chemical industry lobbyist wrote his pesticide bill, but Pombo denied any ethical impropriety. He chaired the Western Caucus, which sought to speak with a unified conservative voice on water and property rights issues. Pombo found common ground with Barney Frank (who once called him a "low-rent Pat Buchanan") on one issue: winning $24 million for a military base in Portugal's Azores. Pombo's grandparents came from the islands, as have many of Frank's constituents.

In January 2003, the Republican Steering Committee, to the surprise of many, made Pombo chairman of the Resources Committee after Jim Hansen retired from Congress. The next two Republicans in seniority were already chairmen of other committees; Pombo was 11th in seniority. But Pombo was the first to start running for the post; he worked the hardest and he had the vital support of Majority Leader Tom DeLay plus the Californians on the Steering Committee. Jim Saxton, the most senior member of the panel who wanted the job, was ruled out as too sympathetic to environmentalists. Pombo's victory left some hard feelings among other committee members who sought the chairmanship, including John Duncan and Joel Hefley.

As chairman, Pombo did not change his views but he surprised many by reaching out to others. He "has earned a reputation as a lawmaker willing to engage in tough negotiations with opponents in order to get legislation passed," wrote Margaret Kriz of *National Journal*. A prime example was Pombo's role in the 2003 enactment of the Healthy Forests initiative of George W. Bush, which was designed to thin forests to reduce the risk of additional huge fires. Pombo negotiated for hours with Senator Dianne Feinstein to reach agreement on a broadly backed bill. Forming what some termed California's new political odd couple, he also worked with Feinstein on the CALFED bill to resolve continuing differences over regulation of water projects in California. On the major energy bill, which died in the Senate, he wrote sections to open development of federal lands, including the controversial proposal to permit oil and gas drilling on the Alaska National Wildlife Refuge. He continued to push to remove restrictions on logging and off-road vehicles from the controversial Wild Sky bill surrounding the Mount Baker area northeast of Seattle. Pombo remains a prime foe of environmental activists, but the committee's ranking Democrat Nick Rahall has said, "The chairman has been fair-minded, while at the same time keeping his views clearly known." He also used his chairmanship on district problems. He convinced officials of the Justice Department to back down and compensate San Joaquin Valley water districts with $16.7 million for excessive regulation that required them to conserve water to protect endangered fish. Pombo retains big goals. He wants to overhaul the National Environmental Policy Act to relax restrictions on new projects, and he wants to encourage oil and gas drilling on some federal lands. And he remains fixated on what first got him started: revising the Endangered Species Act so that it is less intrusive, arbitrary and litigious; he has gained an ally in Central Valley Democrat Dennis Cardoza.

Back home, the 2001 redistricting changed the district so much that half the district was new to Pombo, and he faced his first serious reelection challenge in 2002. Democrats nominated Elaine Shaw, a corporate lawyer and political newcomer who hired several political aides of Ellen Tauscher, who had represented the San Ramon Valley since 1996. She called Pombo "a conservative without the compassion," and said Pombo's opposition to abortion rights and environmental protection were too extreme for the new district. But she received little assistance from national Democrats. Pombo won 60%–40%. In San Joaquin County, which cast 56% of the vote, he won 65% of the vote. He got 57% in Contra Costa County, 53% in Santa Clara County and 51% in Alameda County. In 2004, he won easily against a wind energy engineer.

Pombo created controversy when he used his franking privilege to send favorable newsletters on environmental accomplishments to districts of Republicans in close races. Partisan exchanges failed to resolve whether the practice violated House rules. But he appears to have managed the combination of a sharply revised district and an unexpected chairmanship, as he seeks to deliver on his conservative philosophy that may not be especially popular in some parts of his district.

TWELFTH DISTRICT

Rep. Tom Lantos (D)

Elected 1980, 13th term; b. Feb. 1, 1928, Budapest, Hungary; home, San Mateo; U. of WA, B.A. 1949, M.A. 1950, U. of CA, Ph.D. 1953; Jewish; married (Annette).

Professional Career: Economist, Bank of America, 1952–53; TV Commentator, San Francisco, 1955–63; Dir. of Intl. Programs, CA St. U., 1962–71; Advisor, U.S. Sen. Joseph R. Biden Jr., 1978–79; Mbr., Pres. Task Force on Defense & Foreign Policy, 1976; Prof., San Francisco St. U., 1950–80.

DC Office: 2413 RHOB, 20515, 202-225-3531; Web site: www.house.gov/lantos.

District Office: San Mateo, 650-342-0300.

Committees: *Government Reform* (2d of 17 D): Energy & Resources; National Security, Emerging Threats & International Relations. *International Relations* (RMM of 23 D).

Group Ratings

	ADA	ACLU	AFS	LCV	ITIC	NTU	COC	ACU	NTLC	CHC
2004	95	72	100	100	12	9	37	9	0	9
2003	80	—	100	95	—	19	28	12	—	—

National Journal Ratings

	2003 LIB	—	2003 CONS		2004 LIB	—	2004 CONS
Economic	79%	—	20%		84%	—	16%
Social	77%	—	22%		85%	—	15%
Foreign	64%	—	35%		75%	—	24%

Key Votes of the 108th Congress

1. Drilling in ANWR	N	5. DC School Vouchers	N	9. Ban Same-Sex Marriage	N
2. Approve Bush Tax Cuts	N	6. Ban Human Cloning	N	10. Fund Iraq War	Y
3. Medicare/Rx Bill	N	7. Restrict Gun Liability	N	11. Bar Cuba Embargo Funds	Y
4. Bar Overtime Pay Regs.	Y	8. Ban Partial-Birth Abortion	*	12. Intelligence Reorg.	N

Election Results

2004 general	Tom Lantos (D)	171,852	(68%)	($1,190,646)
	Mike Garza (R)	52,593	(21%)	
	Pat Gray (Green)	23,038	(9%)	($44,685)
	Other	5,116	(2%)	
2004 primary	Tom Lantos (D)	63,323	(74%)	
	Ro Khanna (D)	17,107	(20%)	
	Maad Abu-Ghazalah (D)	5,678	(7%)	
2002 general	Tom Lantos (D)	105,597	(68%)	($937,721)
	Michael Moloney (R)	38,381	(25%)	
	Maad Abu-Ghazalah (Lib)	11,006	(7%)	($165,522)

Prior Winning Percentages: 2000 (75%); 1998 (74%); 1996 (72%); 1994 (67%); 1992 (69%); 1990 (66%); 1988 (71%); 1986 (74%); 1984 (70%); 1982 (57%); 1980 (46%)

The People		Race/Ethnic Origin	Ancestry	
Area size:	363 sq. mi.	48.2% White	Irish: 8.2%	German: 7.4%
Urban population:	99.9%	2.5% Black	Italian: 6.4%	
Rural population:	0.1%	28.5% Asian	**2004 Presidential Vote**	
Pop. 2000:	639,088	0.2% Native Am.	Kerry (D) 193,689	(72%)
Median income:	$70,307	0.9% Hawaiian	Bush (R) 73,740	(27%)
Poverty status:	5.4%	3.6% Two+ races	Other 2,646	(1%)
Military veterans:	8.9%	0.3% Other	**2000 Presidential Vote**	
		15.7% Hispanic Origin	Gore (D) 164,490	(67%)
			Bush (R) 70,468	(29%)
			Other 11,103	(5%)
			Cook Partisan Voting Index: D +22	

Occupation	Blue collar: 14.6%	White collar: 72.8%	Gray collar: 12.6%

Running south from San Francisco is the Peninsula, which connects the city with the mainland of the United States. This is geologically interesting, and active, country: The San Andreas Fault runs just east of the Coast Range, underneath the reservoirs that store San Francisco's water supply. To the west are green mountains running down into the foggy ocean. To the east is a zone of flat land between mountain and bay, an unbroken chain of suburbs and urban settlement, with light industry and salt flats along the bay front, and residential neighborhoods and some commercial strips from the Bayshore Freeway up through the Junipero Serra Freeway atop the mountain ridge. Historically, the Peninsula has seemed separate from San Francisco. But Daly City and Pacifica on the ocean are a kind of extension of San Francisco's old working class districts, with boxy houses on streets looking out on the ocean or the freeway; now they are the home of many of the Bay Area's Asian immigrants and Asian supermarkets. Pacific Islanders, too: the mainland's biggest concentration of Samoans is in Daly City and the biggest concentration of Tongans in San Bruno; King Taufa'ahau Tupou IV of Tonga has a house in the high-income suburb of Hillsborough. On the Bay side is South San Francisco which, a sign on the side of San Bruno Mountain proclaims, is "the Industrial City." Actually, these days it is post-industrial, for it is here that Herb Boyer and Bob Swanson sketched on a napkin their plans for the first biotechnology company, Genentech; they bought space in an old warehouse on the waterfront near a Bethlehem Steel plant; today the area is one large biotech campus, with lawns, parkways and earth-tone office complexes, the center of the biotech industry. Further south, between the Bayshore Freeway and I-280, there are middle-class suburbs that are now also cities with office complexes—Millbrae, Burlingame, San Mateo, San Carlos.

The 12th Congressional District of California consists of these northern Peninsula suburbs plus the southwest quadrant of San Francisco—the city's middle-income Sunset district, with older houses amid unburied telephone and electric wires, lying on curving hills that were once sand dunes, and affluent St. Francis's Wood and West Portal. It is an ethnically and racially diverse, economically productive part of America; 29% of its residents are Asian—the third highest of any district outside Hawaii—and another 16% are Hispanic. The economic orientation here was historically toward San Francisco, then south toward the Silicon Valley, now to its own burgeoning biotech industries. Income levels are among the highest in the state, very far above average. Politically, the Peninsula historically was a bastion of progressive Republicanism, a lively force in California from the election of Governor Hiram Johnson in 1910 until the liberal Democratic breakthrough in 1958. But that tradition is only a memory now. In national and California elections the 12th District is now overwhelmingly Democratic.

The congressman from the 12th District, Tom Lantos, has several distinctions, but none more important than the fact that he is the only Holocaust survivor ever to serve in Congress. Lantos was born in Hungary and grew up in Budapest. In 1944, as a teenager, he was sent to a labor camp, escaped, was captured and beaten, escaped again, then lived with his aunt in a building whose occupants were protected by Swedish diplomat Raoul Wallenberg. His wife Annette, his childhood sweetheart, also survived by going into hiding and escaping to Switzerland with fake documents; these two Holocaust survivors have two daughters and 17 grandchildren. Lantos immigrated to the United States and graduated from the University of Washington and got a Ph.D. in economics at Berkeley. He taught economics at San Francisco State, made money as an investor and appeared on television as a foreign policy expert. He had the political insight to challenge a Republican incumbent in the Peninsula in 1980, a Republican year nationally though not so much here; he has shown great capacity for publicizing his crusades in congressional hearings and on television. In January 2005 he traveled to Auschwitz to attend a UN celebration of the liberation of the concentration camps there 60 years before.

Lantos has spent much of his time in the House on foreign policy and is now ranking minority member on the International Relations Committee. Unlike other Bay Area Democrats, he has not brought to his work an instinctive mistrust of American policy or doubts of American good intentions. He founded the Congressional Human Rights Caucus, focusing on Communist regimes as well as the right-wing dictatorships other liberal Democrats denounced. During the collapse of Communism, Lantos stayed in close touch with Eastern Europe, especially Hungary, as new democracies rose up; in 1990 he was the first American official to visit Albania since 1946. He sponsored the first U.S. aid to the newly free countries of Eastern Europe and strongly backed NATO expansion. He has attacked human rights violations in China, opposes normalizing of Chinese trade status and in September 2000 sponsored a resolution urging that Beijing not be selected as the site of the 2008 Olympics. He is among the most enthusiastic supporters of Israel and called for economic sanctions against Iraq back in 1988 for its gassing of the Kurds; he continued to support sanctions against Iraq in 2000 when other Bay area members tried to end them. He helped lead the debate in favor of the Iraq war resolution in October 2002, although he had urged that it be debated after the election.

Lantos opposed U.S. participation in the United Nations conference on racism in Durban in September 2001. "We have a group of countries hell-bent on hijacking a noble and worthwhile event into yet another forum for Israel-bashing and for the most extreme form of antisemitism to gain global notoriety." But when the Oil for Food scandal broke in May 2004 he said that the UN had taken some action to prevent abuses and that members of the Security Council, including the U.S., had much of the responsibility. In 2004 he sponsored a bill to keep off the Human Rights Commission nations that violate human rights themselves. In April 2002 he introduced a resolution expressing "solidarity with Israel in its fight against terrorism," co-sponsored by Majority Whip Tom DeLay. They delayed it at the request of the White House, but it passed 352–21 in May 2002. He worked with committee Chairman Henry Hyde to get $1.3 billion to fight AIDS around the world in December 2001 and $3 billion as down payment on the $15 billion pledged by George W. Bush in May 2003; he and Hyde worked out language giving preference on funding to organizations that emphasize on abstinence from extramarital sex. Lantos has sought to make the federal government pay employees called up for military service amounts lost because of lower military pay. He founded the Humanity in Action Capitol Hill fellowships for foreign interns.

Lantos was among the first members of Congress to visit Libya since the 1960s in January 2004 and hailed Muammar el-Qaddafi's renunciation of weapons of mass destruction; he said Libya had "turned the corner" but called for a measured response in line with Libyan actions. He proposed converting 25% of military aid to Egypt to economic assistance. He got the House to pass in October 2004 a bill suspending aid to Ethiopia and Eritrea until they settled their border dispute. He got the House to vote for $300 million in humanitarian relief in Sudan, with two-thirds targeted at Darfur; when debt relief and aid were resumed there after the government agreed to a truce with Sudanese People's Liberation Army forces in the south, he said that should be put on hold until the government stopped the killing in Darfur. "What is keeping the international community from intervening in the Darfur crisis? I hesitate to ask, because I hate to think that the answer is the same double standard that stayed our hand in Rwanda in the 1990s." He said African Union forces were inadequate and called for a UN civilian protection mandate led by the African Union mission and enforced by NATO-led troops. In January 2004 he became the first member of Congress to visit Libya since the 1960s; when he went to North Korea in January 2005, he praised Libya for abandoning its nuclear weapons program and encouraged North Korea to do the same. "They indicated that they view their nuclear program as important, but I had the very strong impression that they are ready to discuss the matter because they understand that we are determined to do so. . . . There is no conceivable reason for anyone to expect a significant change in U.S. policy toward the Korean peninsula." When George W. Bush called for doubling aid to Palestinians in February 2005, Lantos said he would delay the aid until Arab countries made promised contributions.

Lantos spent $1.7 million on his 1980 and 1982 campaigns and has won easily ever since. He helped his son-in-law Dick Swett get elected from the 2d District of New Hampshire in 1990 and 1992; Swett lost to Charlie Bass in 1994 and in the 1996 Senate race, as did Lantos's daughter Katrina Swett in the 2d District House race in 2002. In 2004 Lantos had his first primary opposition in the 12th District since 1992, from two candidates who criticized his support of the war in Iraq. To that he said, "Had I been older and had I been in power, clearly I would have preferred in the mid-30s preempting Hitler because the Second World War cost slightly over 50 million innocent lives." He won with 74% of the vote.

THIRTEENTH DISTRICT

Rep. Pete Stark (D)

Elected 1972, 17th term; b. Nov. 11, 1931, Milwaukee, WI; home, Fremont; MIT, B.S. 1953, U. of CA at Berkeley, M.B.A. 1960; Unitarian; married (Deborah).

Military Career: Air Force, 1955–57.

Professional Career: Founder, Beacon Savings & Loan Assn., 1961; Founder & Pres., Security Natl. Bank, Walnut Creek, 1963–72.

DC Office: 239 CHOB, 20515, 202-225-5065; Fax: 202-226-3805; Web site: www.house.gov/stark.

District Office: Fremont, 510-494-1388.

Committees: *Ways & Means* (2d of 17 D): Health (RMM); Human Resources. *Joint Committee on Taxation* (5th of 5 Reps.).

Group Ratings

	ADA	ACLU	AFS	LCV	ITIC	NTU	COC	ACU	NTLC	CHC
2004	90	100	100	100	11	13	5	0	0	7
2003	100	—	100	95	—	28	17	8	—	—

National Journal Ratings

	2003 LIB	—	2003 CONS		2004 LIB	—	2004 CONS
Economic	92%	—	0%		98%	—	0%
Social	92%	—	0%		88%	—	0%
Foreign	81%	—	17%		98%	—	0%

Key Votes of the 108th Congress

1. Drilling in ANWR	N	5. DC School Vouchers	N	9. Ban Same-Sex Marriage	N
2. Approve Bush Tax Cuts	N	6. Ban Human Cloning	N	10. Fund Iraq War	N
3. Medicare/Rx Bill	N	7. Restrict Gun Liability	N	11. Bar Cuba Embargo Funds	Y
4. Bar Overtime Pay Regs.	Y	8. Ban Partial-Birth Abortion	N	12. Intelligence Reorg.	N

Election Results

2004 general	Pete Stark (D)	144,605	(72%)	($455,735)
	George Bruno (R)	48,439	(24%)	($31,883)
	Mark Stroberg (Lib)	8,877	(4%)	
2004 primary	Pete Stark (D) .... unopposed			
2002 general	Pete Stark (D)	86,495	(71%)	($438,055)
	Syed Mahmood (R)	26,852	(22%)	($51,307)
	Other...	8,376	(7%)	

Prior Winning Percentages: 2000 (70%); 1998 (71%); 1996 (65%); 1994 (65%); 1992 (60%); 1990 (58%); 1988 (73%); 1986 (70%); 1984 (70%); 1982 (61%); 1980 (55%); 1978 (65%); 1976 (71%); 1974 (71%); 1972 (53%)

The People		**Race/Ethnic Origin**	**Ancestry**		
Area size:	281 sq. mi.	38.4% White	German: 6.9%	Irish: 5.7%	
Urban population:	99.3%	6.3% Black	English: 4.8%		
Rural population:	0.7%	28.2% Asian	**2004 Presidential Vote**		
Pop. 2000:	639,088	0.4% Native Am.	Kerry (D)	153,598	(71%)
Median income:	$62,415	0.8% Hawaiian	Bush (R)	60,559	(28%)
Poverty status:	7.1%	4.5% Two+ races	Other	2,378	(1%)
Military veterans:	9.6%	0.3% Other	**2000 Presidential Vote**		
		21.1% Hispanic Origin	Gore (D)	126,477	(67%)
			Bush (R)	55,803	(30%)
			Other	6,472	(3%)
			Cook Partisan Voting Index: D +22		

Occupation   Blue collar: 22.3%   White collar: 66.8%   Gray collar: 10.9%

The East Bay is the workaday, unglamorous side of the San Francisco Bay area—a narrow strip of land between San Francisco Bay and the surprisingly high mountains that rise just to the east. The shoreline is not picturesque, with its closed-down Navy bases, docks, airports and salt evaporators; the Bay Bridge, bisected by Yerba Buena Island, cuts an inspiring figure, but the San Mateo Bridge to the south is at best utilitarian. Six decades ago, when the shipyards of Richmond and the Navy yard in Oakland were buzzing, the East Bay south of Oakland was still largely uninhabited farm fields. In the postwar years, it filled up, south along the old Route 17: San Leandro, originally settled by Portuguese; Hayward with its Cal State University campus and seafood industry; Union City with its rail yards; Fremont, home of the NUMMI auto plant where Chevrolets and Toyotas are produced together; and Newark, with dozens of manufacturing plants that range from salt processing to computer network servers. Hit hard by the dot-com bust, the East Bay has shown some life in high-tech and health care. Underneath is the Hayward Fault, not as famous as the San Andreas, but just as dangerous.

The 13th Congressional District of California is made up of this string of East Bay towns in Alameda County, with lower income than the Peninsula towns across the Bay. The district is racially and ethnically mixed in the California manner. Fremont is home to the Little Kabul neighborhood of Afghans; Koreans and other Asians have moved in large numbers not only to Fremont, but to Hayward and other East Bay towns. The district is 28% Asian—the fourth highest Asian percentage in any district outside Hawaii—21% Hispanic and 6% black. This has long been a Democratic area, and it has become more Democratic than ever: in 2004, John Kerry got 71% of the vote here.

The congressman from the 13th District is Pete Stark, a liberal Democrat and product of the peace movement of the 1960s, first elected in 1972. Stark grew up in Wisconsin, served in the Air Force, got an engineering degree at MIT and an M.B.A. at Berkeley, and in 1961 started a bank in

Walnut Creek. He attracted attention, and accounts, all over the Bay Area when he put a giant peace symbol atop the bank headquarters and peace symbols on all checks. In 1972 he ran for Congress, spending his own money freely; he beat an 81-year-old incumbent in the primary 56%–22% and held on in the McGovern undertow to win the general with 53%. By his third term he had a safe seat back home and was on Ways and Means, on which he now is the second ranking Democrat; he chaired its Health Subcommittee from 1985 to 1995.

Stark brought to that post a desire to use government powers to make health care more available. In the majority, his record was mixed. He did expand Medicare benefits and provided COBRA benefit continuation to younger workers. But his major achievement was the Catastrophic Health Care Act of 1988, which created a new benefit for Medicare recipients, then was repealed by an overwhelming vote in 1989 after an outpouring of public protest: the problem was that its tax on the high-income elderly was very unpopular while benefits seemed puny. He has supported universal health insurance in various forms.

In the minority, Stark has mostly criticized and found few areas of agreement with Republicans, and has had testy personal dealings. He was one of two votes against the 1996 Kennedy-Kassebaum bill, on the grounds it did not include mental health coverage and extended patent protection for a drug. When George W. Bush presented his proposal for prescription drug coverage for seniors, Stark countered with a plan that would guarantee affordable and comprehensive coverage for all seniors under Medicare. "Our legislation will not be cheap," he conceded. But other than criticism from the sidelines, he played little role in the debate on the Medicare/prescription drug bill in 2003. He led the second-guessers when new cost projections revealed that the 10-year cost had ballooned to $720 billion. "I told you so. We can't trust numbers provided by administration officials," he said. He continued to push to permit reimportation of prescription drugs and opposed trade agreements that barred that.

During his long tenure (1995–2004) as the senior Democrat on the Joint Economic Committee, Stark produced reports that criticized Republican policies. He was one of two House members to vote against repeal of the 3% telephone excise tax and one of three who opposed the resolution denouncing the Ninth Circuit Court of Appeals decision declaring the Pledge of Allegiance unconstitutional. In March 2003 he called the bombing of Iraq "an act of extreme terrorism." He co-sponsored a plan to reinstate the military draft, and was on the losing side of a 402–2 vote on the proposal in October 2004. He cited the experience of World War II, when "it was everyone's patriotic duty and our country was better for it."

Stark has a habit of making provocative comments about other members. After he incorrectly stated at a committee hearing in May 2001 that all children of Republican Conference chairman J.C. Watts had been born out of wedlock, Watts confronted him in the House chamber and Stark reportedly gave a flippant response that further angered Watts. At a hearing on prescription drug coverage in February 2003, he said that George W. Bush did not have to pay a penny when he went to Alcoholics Anonymous to quit drinking (Bush has never said that he attended AA or that he was an alcoholic). In July 2003, when committee Democrats gathered in a room adjacent to the Ways and Means room and Chairman Bill Thomas called the Capitol Police to evict them, Stark called Thomas a "fascist." The *San Francisco Chronicle* reported "rumblings that it might be time for the veteran Congressman to retire," but Stark said, "I've got to keep running. I've got 2-year-old twins and I've got to get them through college. Our retirement plan is good, but it ain't that good."

Stark is next in line on Ways and Means to ranking Democrat Charles Rangel, and there has been talk that, should Rangel retire, another committee Democrat might challenge Stark for Rangel's post; would Minority Leader Nancy Pelosi protect her Bay Area colleague? There was speculation in the district that Stark's outspoken remarks might prompt a serious primary challenge in 2004, but well-known local politicians showed no interest in running in 2004, and Stark seems even at his most flamboyant to be expressing the views of most Democrats in the district.

FOURTEENTH DISTRICT

Rep. Anna Eshoo (D)

Elected 1992, 7th term; b. Dec. 13, 1942, New Britain, CT; home, Atherton; Canada Col., A.A. 1975; Catholic; divorced.

Elected Office: San Mateo Cnty. Bd. of Supervisors, 1982–92, Pres., 1986.

Professional Career: Chmn., San Mateo Cnty Dem. Party, 1980; Chief of Staff, CA Assembly Speaker, 1981.

DC Office: 205 CHOB, 20515, 202-225-8104; Fax: 202-225-8890; Web site: www.eshoo.house.gov.

District Office: Palo Alto, 650-323-2984.

Committees: *Energy & Commerce* (10th of 26 D): Health; Telecommunications & the Internet. *Permanent Select Committee on Intelligence* (6th of 9 D): Intelligence Policy; Technical & Tactical Intelligence (RMM).

Group Ratings

	ADA	ACLU	AFS	LCV	ITIC	NTU	COC	ACU	NTLC	CHC
2004	100	79	100	100	78	13	38	12	6	10
2003	90	—	100	100	—	28	24	17	—	—

National Journal Ratings

	2003 LIB	—	2003 CONS	2004 LIB	—	2004 CONS
Economic	92%	—	0%	87%	—	13%
Social	89%	—	10%	86%	—	12%
Foreign	73%	—	25%	79%	—	20%

Key Votes of the 108th Congress

1. Drilling in ANWR	N	5. DC School Vouchers	N	9. Ban Same-Sex Marriage	N
2. Approve Bush Tax Cuts	N	6. Ban Human Cloning	N	10. Fund Iraq War	N
3. Medicare/Rx Bill	N	7. Restrict Gun Liability	N	11. Bar Cuba Embargo Funds	Y
4. Bar Overtime Pay Regs.	Y	8. Ban Partial-Birth Abortion	*	12. Intelligence Reorg.	N

Election Results

2004 general	Anna Eshoo (D)	182,712	(70%)	($939,389)
	Chris Haugen (R)	69,564	(27%)	($52,623)
	Brian Holtz (Lib)	9,588	(4%)	
	Other	24	(0%)	
2004 primary	Anna Eshoo (D)	unopposed		
2002 general	Anna Eshoo (D)	117,055	(68%)	($863,431)
	Joseph Nixon (R)	48,346	(28%)	($45,158)
	Andrew Carver (Lib)	6,277	(4%)	

Prior Winning Percentages: 2000 (70%); 1998 (69%); 1996 (65%); 1994 (61%); 1992 (57%)

The People		Race/Ethnic Origin	Ancestry	
Area size:	1,030 sq. mi.	59.6% White	German: 9.7%	English: 8.3%
Urban population:	93.6%	3.0% Black	Irish: 7.2%	
Rural population:	6.4%	16.0% Asian	**2004 Presidential Vote**	
Pop. 2000:	639,088	0.3% Native Am.	Kerry (D) 188,864	(68%)
Median income:	$77,985	0.7% Hawaiian	Bush (R) 83,326	(30%)
Poverty status:	6.4%	2.7% Two+ races	Other 3,981	(1%)
Military veterans:	9.5%	0.3% Other	**2000 Presidential Vote**	
		17.5% Hispanic Origin	Gore (D) 155,165	(62%)
			Bush (R) 84,637	(34%)
			Other 12,451	(5%)
			Cook Partisan Voting Index: D +18	

Occupation	Blue collar: 12.1%	White collar: 77.1%	Gray collar: 10.8%

Silicon Valley is a place and a state of mind, an area that had no distinctive identity three decades ago but which people all over the world have recognized, admired and tried to imitate. In the 1980s and 1990s Silicon Valley emerged as the center of America's computer industry, a place where creative minds have developed products that large corporations never thought would sell. Its beginnings can be traced back to 1939, when William Hewlett and David Packard started their electronics firm in a Palo Alto garage, or perhaps to 1891, when Stanford University was founded on the estate of a California governor and senator. Not every aspect of the computer business is centered here. Microsoft, routinely disparaged in every Palo Alto espresso shop and bar, is up in Redmond, Washington, and IBM is off in Armonk, New York. But Silicon Valley is where most of the giants, and very much of the creativity, of the high-tech business—as well as the ghosts of dot-coms whose stock has melted down to zero—have been based.

How did Silicon Valley come to be where it is? One reason is Stanford, the students it attracts and produces, and fact that it has always encouraged profit-making activity by faculty. Another is venture capital, widely available from innovation-minded old San Francisco money, dispensed mostly from nondescript office buildings on Sand Hill Road off I-280 on the reclaimed flatlands along San Francisco Bay. A third, perhaps the greatest, is that Silicon Valley is the kind of place where smart young innovators like to live. Elite law and medical school graduates head to the prestigious, high-salary jobs of central cities; but techies are free to live in this pleasant, healthy environment. Sheltered by hills from coastal fogs and rains, Silicon Valley boasts a sunny climate with perceptible but gentle seasons, perfect for year-round outdoor sports; there may well be more jogging trails and bicycle paths here than anywhere else in the country. There is a sort of pure Americana here: these communities were rustic but never poor, rural but never bigoted, country-like but still easily accessible to the luxuries of civilization. People here were ahead of the rest of the nation in fighting for the environment, in favoring natural over processed foods and in indulging in regular exercise. And they have been quick to adapt to change. In the 1970s Silicon Valley thrived when the semiconductor business took off. In the 1980s, in the face of threats from Japanese firms, Silicon Valley shifted to microprocessors and personal computers. In the 1990s, when PCs became a low-profit commodity business, Silicon Valley shifted to the Internet. Yahoo and Hotmail reportedly were conceived at Buck's restaurant, the networking nexus in Woodside. When the Internet bubble burst in March 2000, Silicon Valley fell on hard times. By one estimate, it lost 127,000 jobs, more than half of the total created between 1998 and 2000. Stock prices plummeted and real estate prices have too, though they are still the highest in the nation; the Valley actually lost population from 2000 to 2003. Billions in paper wealth disappeared, and technology exports from California fell from $61 billion in 2000 toward $40 billion in 2002. The question became whether Silicon Valley still had the ability to adapt. In 2004 the Valley seemed to be on the upturn, with rising profits and Google's hugely successful public offering. No one knows what the next big thing in high-tech will be, but there are still lots of people working in Silicon Valley's bland office parks or in someone's garage who think they're on the way to it, and perhaps some are.

The 14th Congressional District of California includes much of Silicon Valley, with Menlo Park, Palo Alto, home of Stanford, and most of Redwood City, where tech office parks went up on the old salt flats and large condominium projects followed. Further south along El Camino Real are Mountain View, Los Altos and Sunnyvale (the district's largest city). There are some ultra-wealthy enclaves here: Woodside, with its 1850s country store and mansions dotting the hills; Portola Valley and Los Altos Hills, with stark contemporary homes overlooking the Bay. Atherton, with its stone-walled lots, ranked as the most expensive zip code in the nation in 2004, with a median home-sale price of $2.5 million. Over the mountains it includes the little town of Half Moon Bay, with its pumpkin farms rising over the ocean, and the mountains where imposing redwoods grow within five miles of spectacular beaches. The 14th's political heritage is progressive: a sort of environmentalist, dovish, healthy-lifestyle, but entrepreneurial Republicanism, typified by former Congressmen Pete McCloskey, Ed Zschau and Tom Campbell, each of whom quit the House to run unsuccessfully for the Senate between 1982 and 2002. But this kind of Republican is virtually extinct, and Silicon Valley has become heavily Democratic. It is liberal on cultural issues and was enchanted by the attention it received from Bill Clinton and Al Gore. In 2004 George W. Bush got only 30% of the vote here.

The congresswoman from the 14th District is Anna Eshoo, a Democrat first elected in 1992. Born back East, she is the only member of Congress of Assyrian descent. She was a full time homemaker, then chaired the San Mateo County Democratic Party and was elected to the San Mateo Board of Supervisors in 1982. In 1988, she ran for the House against Tom Campbell. The two spent a total of $2.5 million, and Eshoo was the first congressional candidate to distribute videotapes to voters. Campbell won 52%–46%. But in 1992 he ran for the Senate and Eshoo ran for the House again. In the primary she beat an assemblyman redistricted out of his seat by 40%–36%. In the general, Eshoo outspent her opponent and won 57%–39%. She has not faced a serious challenge for reelection.

In the House, Eshoo's voting record has been mostly liberal and occasionally moderate on foreign policy. She was a bit nervous in 1993 about supporting the Clinton budget and tax package, which hit this high-income area hard, and hesitated before supporting NAFTA and fast track. She joined Republicans and high-tech interests on securities litigation, liability relief for Y2K computer problems, normal trade relations with China and electronic signatures. Despite local pressure, she voted against trade promotion authority. Eshoo has been among the House Democrats willing to pursue bipartisan deals. On Energy and Commerce, she has worked with Joe Barton to get quicker FDA regulatory approval for medical devices. With Richard Baker, she passed a House bill to oppose the FASB accounting board proposal to charge stock options against earnings, which would hit hard in Silicon Valley. With John Shimkus, she won House passage of a bill for enhanced 911 service as part of a national cell phone tracking system.

With Minority Leader Nancy Pelosi's help, Eshoo got a seat on the Intelligence Committee. They have been close friends and confidants since they first met at a Democratic event in the Bay Area in the early 1970s, and their families have spent time together. Eshoo was part of Tim Roemer's short-lived campaign for the chairmanship of the Democratic National Committee.

FIFTEENTH DISTRICT

Rep. Mike Honda (D)

Elected 2000, 3d term; b. June 27, 1941, Walnut Creek; home, San Jose; San Jose St. U., B.S. 1969, B.A. 1970, M.A. 1973; Protestant; widowed.

Elected Office: San Jose Unified Sch. Bd., 1981–90; Santa Clara Cnty. Bd. of Supervisors, 1990–96; CA Assembly, 1996–2000.

Professional Career: Peace Corps, 1965–67; Elem. sch. principal, 1978–90.

DC Office: 1713 LHOB, 20515, 202-225-2631; Fax: 202-225-2699; Web site: www.house.gov/honda.

District Office: Campbell, 408-558-8085.

Committees: *Science* (8th of 20 D): Energy (RMM); Space & Aeronautics. *Transportation & Infrastructure* (22d of 34 D): Aviation; Coast Guard & Maritime Transportation; Highways, Transit & Pipelines.

Group Ratings

	ADA	ACLU	AFS	LCV	ITIC	NTU	COC	ACU	NTLC	CHC
2004	95	94	100	100	40	13	39	10	0	8
2003	95	—	100	100	—	24	20	8	—	—

National Journal Ratings

	2003 LIB	—	2003 CONS		2004 LIB	—	2004 CONS
Economic	92%	—	0%		88%	—	12%
Social	87%	—	12%		88%	—	0%
Foreign	94%	—	0%		86%	—	13%

Key Votes of the 108th Congress

1. Drilling in ANWR	N	5. DC School Vouchers	N	9. Ban Same-Sex Marriage	N
2. Approve Bush Tax Cuts	N	6. Ban Human Cloning	N	10. Fund Iraq War	N
3. Medicare/Rx Bill	N	7. Restrict Gun Liability	N	11. Bar Cuba Embargo Funds	Y
4. Bar Overtime Pay Regs.	Y	8. Ban Partial-Birth Abortion	N	12. Intelligence Reorg.	N

Election Results

2004 general	Mike Honda (D)	154,385	(72%)	($539,475)
	Raymond Chukwu (R)	59,953	(28%)	($84,998)
2004 primary	Michael Honda (D) .... unopposed			
2002 general	Mike Honda (D)	87,482	(66%)	($840,384)
	Linda Hermann (R)	41,251	(31%)	($30,470)
	Other..	4,289	(3%)	

Prior Winning Percentages: 2000 (54%)

The People		Race/Ethnic Origin	Ancestry	
Area size:	289 sq. mi.	47.1% White	German: 8.0%	Irish: 6.3%
Urban population:	99.3%	2.4% Black	English: 6.1%	
Rural population:	0.7%	29.2% Asian	**2004 Presidential Vote**	
Pop. 2000:	639,088	0.3% Native Am.	Kerry (D) 145,007	(63%)
Median income:	$74,947	0.3% Hawaiian	Bush (R) 82,742	(36%)
Poverty status:	6.6%	3.2% Two+ races	Other 2,903	(1%)
Military veterans:	8.4%	0.2% Other	**2000 Presidential Vote**	
		17.2% Hispanic Origin	Gore (D) 124,880	(60%)
			Bush (R) 74,974	(36%)
			Other 7,108	(3%)
			Cook Partisan Voting Index: D +14	

Occupation	Blue collar: 16.9%	White collar: 73.6%	Gray collar: 9.6%

The broad valley of Santa Clara County around San Jose a few decades ago was mostly orchards and vineyards. Sheltered by mountains from the chilly ocean fogs, with soil incredibly fertile once it was irrigated, this valley produced peaches, plums, prunes, apricots and grapes and made San Jose half a century ago the nation's biggest fruit-packing center. Today, subdivisions, shopping centers and office buildings have replaced almost all the orchards, and San Jose and Santa Clara County have a population of 1.68 million people. San Jose, with a growing downtown, an arena for its National Hockey League team, and a population of 898,000, has become a major American city. San Jose and some towns to the west are part of Silicon Valley, which has no official boundaries. Local planners have explored a light-rail transit system.

The 15th Congressional District consists of the central slice of Santa Clara County. It includes 295,000 people in San Jose, about one-third of the city's population and nearly half of the district's; for the most part these are San Jose's affluent neighborhoods. West of San Jose, the district includes the cities of Santa Clara and Cupertino, where Steve Jobs started Apple in a garage in the 1970s and where the company is still headquartered, Los Gatos and Campbell. The district also includes the salt flats of San Jose, site of the Great America theme park not far from where a huge Lockheed plant was once the nation's largest defense contractor, the heavily Asian city of Milpitas and, far to the south, connected by a swath of mountains, Gilroy, the garlic capital of the United States. Outside of Hawaii, this district has the highest percentage of Asians in the nation (29.2%); in Cupertino, where nearly a majority are Asians, their political influence has become a force and has stirred controversy. Politically, this area was once marginal territory but is now heavily Democratic. John Kerry got 63% of the vote here in 2004.

The congressman from the 15th District is Mike Honda, a Democrat first elected in 2000. A Japanese American, Honda was born in Walnut Creek and spent his early childhood in a World War II internment camp in Colorado. He received bachelor's and master's degrees from San Jose State University and served two years in the Peace Corps in El Salvador. In 1971, San Jose Mayor Norman Mineta appointed him to the city Planning Commission. From 1978 to 1986, Honda was a principal at two area elementary schools; during these years he was elected to the

San Jose Unified School Board and later to the Santa Clara County Board of Supervisors. In 1996, he was elected to the first of two terms in the California Assembly. He worked to reduce classroom sizes and increase teacher benefits, and to secure an apology from Japan for its wartime atrocities against other Asian nations. For relaxation, the once-shy Honda sings karaoke.

In 2000 15th District Congressman Tom Campbell, the last Republican elected in the San Francisco Bay area, decided to run against Senator Dianne Feinstein. At first Honda was reluctant to run for the House, even though California's term limits meant that a third term in the Assembly would be his last. Days before the filing deadline, he told supporters that he would not run for the open seat. But persuasive telephone calls from several leading House Democrats and, finally, from Bill Clinton changed his mind. One reason for his initial reluctance was the prospect of running against former Carter administration Pentagon official Bill Peacock, a venture capitalist who was ready to spend $1 million of his own money and had gotten significant endorsements. But the primary was no contest: Honda won 67% to 24% for Peacock. His Republican opponent was Republican Assemblyman Jim Cunneen. A Campbell protégé, Cunneen was strongly supported by national Republican leaders; the contest seemed likely to be one of the year's most competitive. Cunneen favored liberal positions on cultural issues; as a former global corporate affairs manager for Applied Materials he was able to get support from many Silicon Valley capitalists. He tried to depict the contest as a referendum on the old economy versus the new economy. Honda, despite his close ties to unions, supported normal trade relations with China, which was strongly backed by the high tech industry. Honda won 54%–42%.

Honda has been among the most liberal members of the House. With Senator John Ensign, he formed the Wireless Task Force to encourage better understanding of spectrum issues and support for innovative technologies. He helped to enact the Cyber Security Research and Development Act, which funds training and programs to protect computer data and networks. He also was a major architect of the Nanotechnology Research and Development Act of 2003 to improve planning and encourage the development of networked facilities, which involve the manipulation of molecules at the atomic level; this has become a booming technology in the Bay Area. He publicized the cause of American POWs from World War II who were taken on "hell ships" as slave laborers in Japan, and sought apologies from Japan and its companies that profited from them; the 1951 peace treaty with Japan waived the rights of Americans to file such suits. Later, he signed on to an amendment with Dana Rohrabacher to prevent the State Department from opposing the POWs in court, but the amendment disappeared in conference committee after it passed both the House and Senate. He sponsored a bill to protect 275 Korean immigrants in California who unknowingly received green cards that were initially obtained through bribery. Honda cast one of the three votes against the resolution condemning the Ninth Circuit decision that found the words "under God" in the Pledge of Allegiance unconstitutional.

Honda breezed to reelection in 2002 and 2004. In 2003, he demanded an apology from North Carolina's Howard Coble, who said the internment of Japanese Americans in World War II was necessary to protect them. During the 2004 presidential campaign, he advised John Kerry on Asian-American issues. After the election, he successfully campaigned to become one of five vice-chairs of the Democratic National Committee, where he planned to continue his outreach to immigrant communities and serve as a "bridge" between Chairman Howard Dean and House Democrats.

SIXTEENTH DISTRICT

Rep. Zoe Lofgren (D)

Elected 1994, 6th term; b. Dec. 21, 1947, San Mateo; home, San Jose; Stanford U., B.A. 1970, U. of Santa Clara Law Schl., J.D. 1975; Protestant; married (John Collins).

Elected Office: Santa Clara Bd. of Supervisors, 1980–94.

Professional Career: Staff Asst., U.S. Rep. Don Edwards, 1970–78; Practicing atty., 1978–80; Prof., U. of Santa Clara Law Schl., 1981–94.

DC Office: 102 CHOB, 20515, 202-225-3072; Fax: 202-225-3336; Web site: www.house.gov/lofgren.

District Office: San Jose, 408-271-8700.

Committees: *Homeland Security* (9th of 15 D): Economic Security, Infrastructure Protection & Cybersecurity; Intelligence, Information Sharing & Terrorism Risk Assessment (RMM); Management, Integration & Oversight. *House Administration* (3d of 3 D). *Judiciary* (7th of 17 D): Courts, the Internet & Intellectual Property; Immigration, Border Security & Claims.

Group Ratings

	ADA	ACLU	AFS	LCV	ITIC	NTU	COC	ACU	NTLC	CHC
2004	95	89	100	100	60	16	33	12	3	8
2003	85	—	100	100	—	28	26	13	—	—

National Journal Ratings

	2003 LIB	—	2003 CONS		2004 LIB	—	2004 CONS
Economic	92%	—	0%		86%	—	13%
Social	83%	—	16%		88%	—	0%
Foreign	84%	—	14%		85%	—	14%

Key Votes of the 108th Congress

1. Drilling in ANWR	N	5. DC School Vouchers	N	9. Ban Same-Sex Marriage	N
2. Approve Bush Tax Cuts	N	6. Ban Human Cloning	N	10. Fund Iraq War	N
3. Medicare/Rx Bill	N	7. Restrict Gun Liability	N	11. Bar Cuba Embargo Funds	Y
4. Bar Overtime Pay Regs.	Y	8. Ban Partial-Birth Abortion	*	12. Intelligence Reorg.	N

Election Results

2004 general	Zoe Lofgren (D)	129,222	(71%)	($598,739)
	Douglas McNea (R)	47,992	(26%)	($244)
	Other	5,067	(3%)	
2004 primary	Zoe Lofgren (D)	unopposed		
2002 general	Zoe Lofgren (D)	72,370	(67%)	($524,128)
	Douglas McNea (R)	32,182	(30%)	($1,826)
	Other	3,434	(3%)	

Prior Winning Percentages: 2000 (72%); 1998 (73%); 1996 (66%); 1994 (65%)

The People		Race/Ethnic Origin	Ancestry	
Area size:	232 sq. mi.	31.9% White	German: 5.7%	Irish: 4.6%
Urban population:	98.7%	3.4% Black	English: 4.2%	
Rural population:	1.3%	23.4% Asian	**2004 Presidential Vote**	
Pop. 2000:	639,088	0.4% Native Am.	Kerry (D) 125,415	(63%)
Median income:	$67,689	0.4% Hawaiian	Bush (R) 70,190	(36%)
Poverty status:	9.8%	2.8% Two+ races	Other 2,089	(1%)
Military veterans:	7.6%	0.2% Other	**2000 Presidential Vote**	
		37.6% Hispanic Origin	Gore (D) 109,632	(64%)
			Bush (R) 57,160	(33%)
			Other 4,832	(3%)
			Cook Partisan Voting Index: D +16	

Occupation	Blue collar: 24.7%	White collar: 60.9%	Gray collar: 14.4%

With more people than San Francisco, a tradition of high-tech innovation that rivals any on earth, and now a major league sports team, San Jose has great claims on national attention and respect. Yet San Jose does not bulk as large in the national consciousness as it should. At the southern end of the Bay, it remains in the shadow of the city on the Golden Gate. San Francisco is every tourist's idea of a city: geographically compact, with picturesque public transportation, old-time and new immigrant groups, an economy historically based on heavy industry and sea trade, a large city bureaucracy and a monumental city hall. San Jose is quite different. It got its start as a farm-market town, with canneries and fruit-packing operations for the produce from the surrounding fertile plains. It sits not on the Bay, but on the Southern Pacific line above the marshes and salt evaporators; its major transportation arteries are the freeways—U.S. 101, Interstates 280, 680 and 880, California 17—that encircle its revitalized downtown.

Starting in the 1950s, San Jose has grown out in every direction, developers hip-hopping across the farmland, putting up subdivisions faster sometimes than the few city employees could update the street map. Economically, San Jose has been sustained by everything from its traditional agriculture to manufacturing to the high-tech businesses that are centered in Silicon Valley towns just to the west but are omnipresent here: an American city, 21st century style. Local planners see redevelopment of North San Jose as a potential growth area for high-tech businesses. They have thought about trying to attract the economically struggling Oakland Athletics to San Jose, and they have suggested a 16-mile extension of BART from Fremont to San Jose. For many years San Jose had Northern California's largest Mexican-Americans community, many of whom were farm workers; now there is a major immigrant presence, with large numbers from Latin America and East and South Asia. Nearly half of all Santa Clara County residents speak a language other than English at home, mostly Spanish, Vietnamese or Chinese; one in three are foreign-born.

The 16th Congressional District of California consists of about two-thirds of San Jose, plus nearby unincorporated area to the south; 92% of its residents live inside the jagged city limits of San Jose. It includes the old and new downtowns and the heavily Mexican-American areas to the east. This is the most heavily Hispanic district in the Bay Area (38%); it is also heavily Asian (23%), with the largest concentration of Vietnamese in the U.S (the next highest district is the Orange County-based 47th). Politically, it is solidly Democratic; John Kerry won here 63%–36%. Its future leanings depend on the trends among Latinos and Asians, who are not necessarily as favorable to big government as black voters.

The congresswoman from the 16th District is Zoe Lofgren, a Democrat first elected in 1994. Lofgren grew up in the Bay Area, where her father was a Teamster truck driver and her mother worked for the Machinists Union. She graduated from Stanford and Santa Clara law school and was a staffer for eight years to Congressman Don Edwards; as a law student, she worked for him while he was a leader on the Judiciary Committee that voted to impeach Richard Nixon. In 1980 she was elected to the Santa Clara County Board of Supervisors. When Edwards retired, Lofgren ran for the seat. Her chief Democratic opponent, former San Jose Mayor Tom McEnery, started off better known. But Lofgren raised almost twice as much money, with the support of the national women's organizations and women in the California delegation. She won the primary 45%–42%, and easily won the general.

Edwards, her predecessor, never spent a day in the minority during 32 years in the House. To Lofgren's surprise, that's where she found herself and has remained. Nonetheless she has had some impact, and her voting record, while mostly liberal, includes some bipartisan free market positions responsive to local businesses. Working with David Dreier, she won expanded allotments in the H-1B visa program for high-tech workers. She pushed for looser controls on encryption exports, securities litigation limitation and relaxation of trade restraints on supercomputers: all big Silicon Valley causes. In 2004, she worked with Mac Thornberry to bolster the cyber-security responsibilities of the Homeland Security Department, but their House-passed plan was dropped in the conference committee with the Senate. She has cosponsored bipartisan legislation to impose criminal penalties for "spyware" violations. When the

House split 210–210 on a proposal to restrict government spying on library records, Lofgren was the only member to vote "present;" the amendment went too far in preventing legitimate law-enforcement searches, she said.

Her more partisan efforts have taken several directions. After backing normal trade relations with China, she opposed trade promotion authority. She voted to repeal the estate tax in June 2003 but her position changed in April 2005 when she voted against repeal. In 2001, the Republicans' energy plan included her proposal to accelerate the development of fusion as an energy source, but she voted against the overall bill. When Republicans brought up a bill to make it a separate offense to injure or kill a fetus while committing a crime against a pregnant woman, she offered an alternative simply to make it a crime to attack a pregnant woman, without conferring rights to the fetus; that lost 229–196.

Lofgren has had no trouble winning reelection. After the 2002 election, she ran for vice chairman of the Democratic Caucus. But Nancy Pelosi, also from the Bay Area, had already been elected minority leader, and the Congressional Black Caucus was pressing to have one of its members in the leadership. Lofgren got 53 votes to 95 for James Clyburn and 56 for Gregory Meeks. As chair of the California Democratic delegation, she led efforts to oppose the recall in 2003 of Governor Gray Davis. In 2005, Pelosi appointed Lofgren to a vacancy on the House Administration Committee.

SEVENTEENTH DISTRICT

Rep. Sam Farr (D)

Elected June 1993, 6th full term; b. July 4, 1941, San Francisco; home, Carmel; Willamette U., B.S. 1963; Episcopalian; married (Shary).

Elected Office: Monterey Cnty. Bd. of Supervisors, 1975–80, Chmn., 1979; CA Assembly, 1980–93.

Professional Career: Peace Corps, Colombia, 1963–65; Staff, CA Assembly, 1965–75.

DC Office: 1221 LHOB, 20515, 202-225-2861; Fax: 202-225-6791; Web site: www.farr.house.gov.

District Offices: Salinas, 831-424-2229; Santa Cruz, 831-429-1976.

Committees: *Appropriations* (22d of 29 D): Agriculture, Rural Development, FDA & Related Agencies; Military Quality of Life & Veterans Affairs & Related Agencies.

Group Ratings

	ADA	ACLU	AFS	LCV	ITIC	NTU	COC	ACU	NTLC	CHC
2004	100	95	100	100	50	11	43	4	0	7
2003	95	—	100	95	—	28	23	16	—	—

National Journal Ratings

	2003 LIB — 2003 CONS	2004 LIB — 2004 CONS
Economic	83% — 16%	89% — 8%
Social	92% — 0%	88% — 0%
Foreign	94% — 0%	90% — 9%

Key Votes of the 108th Congress

1. Drilling in ANWR	N	5. DC School Vouchers	N	9. Ban Same-Sex Marriage	N
2. Approve Bush Tax Cuts	N	6. Ban Human Cloning	N	10. Fund Iraq War	N
3. Medicare/Rx Bill	N	7. Restrict Gun Liability	N	11. Bar Cuba Embargo Funds	Y
4. Bar Overtime Pay Regs.	Y	8. Ban Partial-Birth Abortion	N	12. Intelligence Reorg.	N

Election Results

2004 general	Sam Farr (D)	148,958	(67%)	($616,323)
	Mark Risley (R)	65,117	(29%)	($144,619)
	Other	9,150	(4%)	
2004 primary	Sam Farr (D)	65,809	(91%)	
	Art Dunn (D)	6,401	(9%)	
2002 general	Sam Farr (D)	101,632	(68%)	($565,220)
	Clint Engler (R)	40,334	(27%)	($1,532)
	Other	7,330	(5%)	

Prior Winning Percentages: 2000 (69%); 1998 (65%); 1996 (59%); 1994 (52%); 1993 (52%)

The People		Race/Ethnic Origin	Ancestry	
Area size:	5,386 sq. mi.	46.3% White	German: 7.6%	English: 6.3%
Urban population:	90.0%	2.6% Black	Irish: 6.3%	
Rural population:	10.0%	4.8% Asian	**2004 Presidential Vote**	
Pop. 2000:	639,088	0.4% Native Am.	Kerry (D)	149,029 (66%)
Median income:	$49,234	0.3% Hawaiian	Bush (R)	75,005 (33%)
Poverty status:	13.3%	2.5% Two+ races	Other	3,144 (1%)
Military veterans:	10.4%	0.3% Other	**2000 Presidential Vote**	
		42.9% Hispanic Origin	Gore (D)	124,580 (60%)
			Bush (R)	68,717 (33%)
			Other	14,819 (7%)
			Cook Partisan Voting Index: D +17	

Occupation	Blue collar: 19.7%	White collar: 55.4%	Gray collar: 24.9%

The California coast around Monterey Bay is for many a working definition of paradise. This kernel of California, where Spanish and then Mexicans governed a virtually empty land and Californians set up their first state capital, still makes a fine living off the land and sea, as it has for 150 years. The locale for *The Grapes of Wrath* and many other John Steinbeck novels, the fields around Salinas supply much of the nation's lettuce and cauliflower. Nearby, the fields around Castroville supply almost all of its artichokes, and the vast greenhouses around Watsonville supply a goodly portion of its roses. The fishing fleet and the 18 now-closed canneries of Monterey are no longer a major industry, but they have generated a new industry: Cannery Row is refurbished with upscale shops and hotels, and the magnificent Monterey Bay Aquarium is one of California's top tourist destinations. The Monterey Bay area has become the nation's language learning capital, with the Defense Language Institute, AT&T Language Line Services and Cal State's Monterey Bay Center for Intensive Language and Culture on the site of Fort Ord, which was closed in 1994. There are other attractions on the Monterey peninsula: the Pebble Beach golf courses, Del Monte Lodge, and Carmel, whose restrictive laws—no house numbers, no door-to-door mail delivery, no live entertainment, no stop lights, no cutting trees without city council permission—reflect an effort to maintain the atmosphere of nearly a century ago, when it really was an artists' colony. But plans to give to public use the four miles of beachfront from Fort Ord have been stifled by bureaucracy and environmental cleanup.

   The 17th Congressional District of California includes all the coast of Monterey Bay and follows the stunning Big Sur coastline south along the steep slopes almost to William Randolph Hearst's castle, San Simeon, past some of the most beautiful scenery in America; to the north along Monterey Bay, it extends past Watsonville to Santa Cruz and the last boardwalk amusement park on the West Coast. The district extends inland, into sunny valleys sheltered from ocean mists, and covers some of the nation's richest farmland. In San Benito County is Hollister, where tens of thousands of motorcyclists assemble annually at an oval dirt racetrack for the Independence Rally. Most of the farm workers are Latino (mainly Mexican), and in the 1990s the district's Latino population rose from 31% to 43%—the largest increase in any Northern California district. The Census also showed that the gap between rich and poor in Monterey County widened in the 1990s: More than 2,000 homes were valued at more than $1 million, while the county ranked seventh statewide in the share of households below the poverty line; of course many of these people were living in much greater poverty in other countries a decade earlier. This area is a prime example of how the California coast has trended Democratic. Forty years ago this was a solidly Republican area, dominated politically by the landowners in Salinas and the townspeople who sympathize with them, plus retirees in Santa Cruz and the Monterey peninsula. But an influx of liberation-minded young people, attracted less by the economy than by the atmosphere, moved the coast to the left. In 2002, Santa Cruz officials in front of City Hall gave away medical marijuana in defiance of a law enforcement crackdown. The University of California branch at Santa Cruz is so liberal that it has changed the political balance of the whole county. As late as 1980, Monterey and Santa Cruz Counties were voting less Democratic than the nation. But since 1984 they have become steadily more Democratic than the nation, and each now exceeds the Democratic presidential vote by more than 10%. In 2004 John Kerry won by 66%–33% a district that was carried four times by Ronald Reagan.

The congressman from the 17th is Sam Farr, a Democrat first elected in June 1993. A fifth-generation Californian, he grew up in Monterey County, where his father was a state senator for many years. Farr signed up for the Peace Corps after college, learned Spanish at the Monterey Institute of International Studies and served two years in Colombia. He was a California Assembly staffer for a decade, became a Monterey County supervisor in 1975, and was elected to the Assembly in 1980. There, he wrote one of the nation's strictest oil spill liability laws. In 1993 17th District Congressman Leon Panetta resigned to become Office of Management and Budget director, and Farr ran for the House. He entered the race as the overwhelming favorite, and in the all-party primary won 26% to beat two other Democrats who had 19% and 14%. But in the runoff, after the Clinton budget and tax increase had been introduced, he had trouble against Republican Bill McCampbell, whom Panetta had defeated 72%–24% seven months earlier. Farr won, but by just 52%–43%.

In the House, Farr has a solidly liberal voting record. In voting against trade promotion authority, Farr cited the Clinton administration's failure to restrict imports of cut flowers from Colombia, which compete with a major local industry. On the Appropriations Committee, Farr has focused on two major local concerns: farming and military bases. He helped to negotiate the final agreement that conveyed the former Fort Ord to civilian hands, and he took the lead in refusing to permit the Navy to establish a practice bombing range near Big Sur. Working with Senator Patrick Leahy, he led a successful effort in 2003 to repeal a little-noted provision of an appropriations bill that would have allowed poultry and beef to be raised on non-organic food but still be labeled organic. George W. Bush signed his bill to add 55,000 acres to Big Sur wilderness area. Farr co-chaired the Oceans Caucus to improve oceans-related policymaking, including job protection in the fishing industry. Combining those two interests, he filed with Senator Richard Durbin a bill to prohibit cruise ships from dumping waste or other contaminants within a 12-mile coastal zone. He also filed a bill to encourage research on sea otters. Jumping the gun a bit, he circulated a paper that proposed turning Fort Hunter Liggett into part of a new national forest if it was closed in the 2005 base closing round; as it turned out, the facility was spared. He mocked Bush's Social Security plan as "a guaranteed lottery ticket."

Farr was elected to a full term in 1994 against McCampbell by only 52%–44%. Since then California has moved toward the Democrats and he has been reelected easily. His ability to work well with diverse interests has made Farr an influential member on statewide issues; he has been a close ally of Minority Leader Nancy Pelosi.

EIGHTEENTH DISTRICT

Rep. Dennis Cardoza (D)

Elected 2002, 2d term; b. March 31, 1959, Merced; home, Atwater; U. of MD, B.A. 1982, CA St. U. Stanislaus; Catholic; married (Kathleen McLoughlin).

Elected Office: Atwater City Cncl., 1984–86; Merced City Cncl., 1994–95; CA Assembly, 1996–2002.

Professional Career: Agribusiness owner.

DC Office: 435 CHOB, 20515, 202-225-6131; Fax: 202-225-0819; Web site: www.house.gov/cardoza.

District Offices: Merced, 209-383-4455; Modesto, 209-527-1914; Stockton, 209-946-0361.

Committees: *Agriculture* (7th of 21 D): Department Operations, Oversight, Nutrition & Forestry; Livestock & Horticulture. *International Relations* (23d of 23 D): International Terrorism & Nonproliferation; Middle East & Central Asia. *Resources* (17th of 22 D): Forests & Forest Health; Water & Power.

Group Ratings

	ADA	ACLU	AFS	LCV	ITIC	NTU	COC	ACU	NTLC	CHC
2004	85	55	88	64	40	16	65	25	9	25
2003	80	—	100	70	—	27	50	44	—	—

National Journal Ratings

	2003 LIB	—	2003 CONS		2004 LIB	—	2004 CONS
Economic	60%	—	40%		59%	—	41%
Social	62%	—	37%		59%	—	41%
Foreign	61%	—	39%		71%	—	29%

Key Votes of the 108th Congress

1. Drilling in ANWR	N	5. DC School Vouchers	N	9. Ban Same-Sex Marriage	N
2. Approve Bush Tax Cuts	N	6. Ban Human Cloning	N	10. Fund Iraq War	Y
3. Medicare/Rx Bill	N	7. Restrict Gun Liability	Y	11. Bar Cuba Embargo Funds	Y
4. Bar Overtime Pay Regs.	Y	8. Ban Partial-Birth Abortion	N	12. Intelligence Reorg.	Y

Election Results

2004 general	Dennis Cardoza (D)	103,732	(68%)	($809,014)
	Charles Pringle (R)	49,973	(33%)	($11,095)
2004 primary	Dennis Cardoza (D)	unopposed		
2002 general	Dennis Cardoza (D)	56,181	(51%)	($1,648,539)
	Dick Monteith (R)	47,528	(43%)	($1,042,288)
	Other	5,884	(5%)	

The People		Race/Ethnic Origin	Ancestry	
Area size:	3,101 sq. mi.	39.1% White	German: 6.2%	Irish: 4.8%
Urban population:	91.3%	5.6% Black	English: 4.0%	
Rural population:	8.7%	8.9% Asian	**2004 Presidential Vote**	
Pop. 2000:	639,088	0.7% Native Am.	Bush (R) 80,157	(50%)
Median income:	$34,211	0.3% Hawaiian	Kerry (D) 79,764	(49%)
Poverty status:	22.7%	3.2% Two+ races	Other 1,677	(1%)
Military veterans:	10.1%	0.2% Other	**2000 Presidential Vote**	
		41.9% Hispanic Origin	Gore (D) 77,908	(53%)
			Bush (R) 65,105	(44%)
			Other 3,690	(3%)
			Cook Partisan Voting Index: D + 3	

Occupation   Blue collar: 31.0%   White collar: 46.0%   Gray collar: 23.1%

The Central Valley of California is a miraculous man-made landscape, an outdoor factory stretching as far as the eye can see. Nature created the vast flatlands, rimmed by mountains rising surreally in the distant haze. But man in the last century has disciplined the land with a remorseless mile-square grid of roads, and the sluggish-flowing California Aqueduct and dozens of arrow-straight canals; pipes fitted with valves and gauges to pump water and fertilizer and pesticides to the fields in measured quantities give an air of industrial precision. The crops grow in carefully spaced rows, filling the fields; the rich soil and the irrigated water are too precious to waste on decoration or flower gardens. Farming here has been a business, not a way of life; in the 19th century the land was not given to 160-acre homesteaders, but sold to thousands-of-acres capitalist enterprises.

The Central Valley in recent years has become one of California's surprise boom areas, growing not just crops but people. Middle-income employees in the San Francisco Bay area drive east at the end of the day on I-580, past surreal windmills whirling on the bare hills of the Altamont pass, across the Westlands fields to modestly priced homes in Modesto, the town immortalized (when it was much smaller) in *American Graffiti* and made famous more recently as the home of Gary Condit and Scott Peterson. Warehouses and factories have sprung up on land that, for all its farming value, is cheaper than industrial land in the Bay Area, and some croplands have been given over to pasture, as subsidized water was cut off from cultivators of cotton, and water prices move slowly toward market levels far above those of government subsidy. The result is not stagnation but growth, and a more well-rounded economy; the Central Valley south of Sacramento grew 8% from 2000 to 2003 while the San Francisco Bay area grew only 0.8%. But there are costs. Traffic is a problem, air pollution on bad days approaches coastal metropolitan levels and the pace of life has become more hectic.

The 18th Congressional District of California includes a large chunk of the Central Valley from Stockton, south to Modesto and through Merced County to the fringes of Fresno. The political tradition here had been Democratic: Democrats in Washington and Governor Pat Brown in California built the irrigation canals and authorized the water subsidies; Democrats owned the McClatchy newspapers, the predominant Valley chain; Democrats staffed the Bank of America, long the dominant financial force here; on the walls of insider law firms were signed pictures of Franklin D. Roosevelt and Pat Brown, not Ronald Reagan and Pete Wilson. But the Central Valley is the part of California with the highest proportion of families and children, and there is a natural cultural conservatism here, shared by successful local politicians. In the 1980s and 1990s the Central Valley trended Republican, and even Latinos here are less heavily Democratic than in Los Angeles. The 18th District is still modestly Democratic, because of very careful redistricting. The old Central Valley district had voted 53% for George W. Bush in 2000. By removing much of Stanislaus County and adding a corridor along I-5 in San Joaquin County, including the central part of Stockton, the Bush 2000 vote dropped to 44%; in 2004 Bush carried the district 50%–49%.

The congressman from the 18th District is Dennis Cardoza, a Democrat first elected in a 2002 contest that drew international attention because of the notoriety of his predecessor, Gary Condit. Cardoza grew up in Merced and Stanislaus Counties and graduated from the University of Maryland; he is, by the way, not of Latin American but of Portuguese descent (like Jim Costa of the adjacent 20th District, Devin Nunes of the 21st and Richard Pombo of the 11th, all in the Central Valley). In the mid-1980s Cardoza worked as an aide to Condit, then an assemblyman, assisted Condit's 1989 special election campaign and served on his Washington staff. In 1997 Cardoza was elected to the Assembly; he undoubtedly would have remained loyal to Condit had Chandra Levy, a Modesto resident who was working as an intern in the executive branch, not disappeared in Washington in April 2001. Her disappearance generated saturation media coverage; it was revealed that Condit had a relationship with her, though he steadfastly denied it was sexual in nature. In those pre-September 11 days, the Levy case suddenly became top news; Condit was harried by reporters and cameramen as he left his Adams Morgan apartment or walked from the Capitol to the Rayburn Building. For constituents, the case was a revelation. Condit had always portrayed himself as a family man, the son of a preacher; his wife was well known and beloved in the Modesto area. Now it appeared that Condit had been living another life in Washington, dating young women and acting decidedly unlike a family man.

After September 11 Condit disappeared from the cable news networks, but the question remained whether he would seek reelection. Cardoza was careful not to criticize Condit or question his actions at a time when his conduct with Levy generated worldwide speculation. But national and local Democrats urged him to enter the contest because they feared that Condit could not survive a general election. Cardoza entered the race in October; Senators Dianne Feinstein and Barbara Boxer endorsed him, as did many members of the House delegation. To Condit, though, Cardoza's decision to challenge him was a betrayal. In the primary, Cardoza won 53%–39%. Condit led 48%–46% in his base of Stanislaus County, but Cardoza clobbered him in San Joaquin County, 60%–25%. The embittered Condit all but disappeared from the airwaves, but filed a libel suit against celebrity columnist Dominick Dunne, which was settled in March 2005 for cash and an apology.

For Cardoza the election was not over. Republicans nominated state Senator Dick Monteith, whose seat included 73% of the congressional district; he claimed Cardoza was too liberal for an agriculture-oriented constituency. Cardoza allies responded by citing his business-oriented reputation in the Legislature. Cardoza tried to mollify Condit supporters, but Condit would not speak to him and predicted that Monteith would win in November. Monteith pledged to oppose "privatizing" Social Security, but Cardoza replied that Monteith had supported personal retirement accounts. In October, Condit's children released a letter that harshly criticized Cardoza and urged citizens to vote against him; Cardoza won anyway, 51%–43%. Stockton made the difference. Monteith led 49%–47% in Merced County and 48%–44% in Stanislaus County. But Cardoza led 67%–27% in San Joaquin County, a 10,000-vote margin that wiped out Monteith's 2,000-vote lead elsewhere.

In the House, Cardoza cast a Condit-like independent and centrist voting record, and gravitated to the obvious issues of agriculture and resources. He cosponsored with Majority Whip Roy Blunt a bill to promote improved federal-state cooperation during farm disasters. He called for a foster care commission, an interest that he shares with Majority Leader Tom DeLay. He bucked environmentalists and worked with Resources Committee chairman Pombo on farmer-friendly revisions to the Endangered Species Act, including changes in designating critical habitat; perhaps not coincidentally, he no longer serves on the Resources Committee. In another signal that he had problems with Minority Leader Nancy Pelosi, Cardoza sought but failed to win a seat on the Armed Services Committee. Instead, he joined International Relations.

Cardoza won reelection handily. He helped on fundraising for other Blue Dog Democrats, and became their communications co-chairman in 2004.

NINETEENTH DISTRICT

Rep. George Radanovich (R)

Elected 1994, 6th term; b. June 20, 1955, Mariposa; home, Mariposa; CA Polytechnic U., B.S. 1978; Catholic; married (Ethie).

Elected Office: Mariposa Cnty. Planning Comm., 1982–86, Chmn., 1985–86; Mariposa Cnty. Bd. of Supervisors, 1989–92.

Professional Career: Farmer; Founder & Owner, Radanovich Winery, 1986–2003.

DC Office: 438 CHOB, 20515, 202-225-4540; Fax: 202-225-3402; Web site: www.radanovich.house.gov.

District Offices: Fresno, 559-449-2490; Turlock, 209-656-8660.

Committees: *Energy & Commerce* (18th of 31 R): Commerce, Trade & Consumer Protection; Energy & Air Quality; Telecommunications & the Internet. *Resources* (9th of 27 R): National Parks; Water & Power (Chmn.).

Group Ratings

	ADA	ACLU	AFS	LCV	ITIC	NTU	COC	ACU	NTLC	CHC
2004	0	0	0	0	100	69	100	100	84	91
2003	5	—	0	5	—	63	96	92	—	—

National Journal Ratings

	2003 LIB	—	2003 CONS		2004 LIB	—	2004 CONS
Economic	0%	—	91%		9%	—	88%
Social	22%	—	77%		20%	—	77%
Foreign	23%	—	71%		0%	—	96%

Key Votes of the 108th Congress

1. Drilling in ANWR	Y	5. DC School Vouchers	Y	9. Ban Same-Sex Marriage	Y
2. Approve Bush Tax Cuts	Y	6. Ban Human Cloning	Y	10. Fund Iraq War	Y
3. Medicare/Rx Bill	Y	7. Restrict Gun Liability	Y	11. Bar Cuba Embargo Funds	N
4. Bar Overtime Pay Regs.	N	8. Ban Partial-Birth Abortion	Y	12. Intelligence Reorg.	Y

Election Results

2004 general	George Radanovich (R)	155,354	(66%)	($919,414)
	James Bufford (D)	64,047	(27%)	
	Larry Mullen (Green)	15,863	(7%)	
2004 primary	George Radanovich (R)	unopposed		
2002 general	George Radanovich (R)	106,209	(67%)	($646,981)
	John Veen (D)	47,403	(30%)	
	Other	4,190	(3%)	

Prior Winning Percentages: 2000 (65%); 1998 (79%); 1996 (67%); 1994 (57%)

The People		Race/Ethnic Origin	Ancestry	
Area size:	6,781 sq. mi.	59.9% White	German: 10.0%	English: 7.3%
Urban population:	80.6%	3.4% Black	Irish: 6.9%	
Rural population:	19.4%	4.4% Asian	**2004 Presidential Vote**	
Pop. 2000:	639,088	1.0% Native Am.	Bush (R) 151,603	(61%)
Median income:	$41,225	0.1% Hawaiian	Kerry (D) 93,918	(38%)
Poverty status:	14.8%	2.8% Two+ races	Other 2,308	(1%)
Military veterans:	12.4%	0.2% Other	**2000 Presidential Vote**	
		28.2% Hispanic Origin	Bush (R) 125,465	(58%)
			Gore (D) 84,559	(39%)
			Other 6,823	(3%)
			Cook Partisan Voting Index: R +10	

Occupation	Blue collar: 22.0%	White collar: 59.3%	Gray collar: 18.8%

The city of Fresno started as a farm-marketing center—one high-income neighborhood is called Fig Garden because that's what it used to be—and as a tourists' stop-off point on the way to Yosemite National Park. But it has long since grown out north, east and west from its old downtown, and its economy has diversified. Like all the Central Valley, Fresno has always been ethnically diverse, with a telephone book that reads like the United Nations; it has America's second largest Armenian community, after Los Angeles. Its already large Latino population has more than doubled in the past 20 years, and Fresno County was 44% Hispanic in 2000; Asians, including Chinese, Filipinos, Vietnamese and Hmong, were 8% of the county's population. The city grew a lusty 29% from 1990 to 2004, despite high unemployment rates, violent teenage gangs and air pollution that made the Sierra Nevada invisible on many days. Tighter border patrolling has encouraged illegal Mexican immigrants to remain in Fresno County year round, even during the off season for farm work; migrants have been crowding into trailers and makeshift homes on formerly vacant farmland. Historically, Fresno was a Democratic town, the prime Democratic bastion in the Central Valley south of Sacramento. But in the 1990s it moved toward the Republicans. It voted for Bob Dole and twice for George W. Bush, Republican governor candidates Dan Lungren in 1998 and Bill Simon in 2002, who all lost statewide. This is one part of California that has trended toward Republicans, when coastal California was moving the other way.

The 19th Congressional District of California includes nearly half of Fresno, the relatively affluent north side of the city, and the farm towns of Madera County to the north. This is one of the two heavily populated parts of the district. The other nearly 100 miles away is the northern and eastern half of Stanislaus County, including the northern edge of Modesto and towns like

Turlock, Riverbank and Oakdale. These two areas are linked and surrounded by mountainous Mariposa and Tuolumne Counties, including Sierra foothills, the peaks of the Sierra Nevada and Yosemite National Park. Gold was once prospected in these butterfly-filled hills and a chain of mining camps ran along what is now Highway 49.

The congressman from the 19th District is George Radanovich, a Republican first elected in 1994. Radanovich is the son of Croatian immigrants, with relatives all over the Valley. He worked on the family farm, served on the Mariposa County Planning Commission in the 1980s and won a seat on the Board of Supervisors in 1989. In 1986, after studying local microclimates, he opened the first winery in Mariposa County and made it work; the Radanovich Winery shipped 4,000 cases annually of sauvignon blanc, merlot, zinfandel and cabernet sauvignon. In 1992 he ran for Congress, losing the primary 33%–30% to 28-year-old Tal Cloud, who lost to incumbent Democrat Richard Lehman 47%–46%. In 1994, Radanovich, an easy winner in this primary, attacked Lehman for supporting the Clinton administration and California Democrat George Miller's efforts to raise the price of Valley water. Radanovich won 57%–40% in the widest defeat of a non-freshman incumbent that year.

In the House, where Radanovich was elected president of his 74-member freshmen Republican class, he has a mostly conservative voting record that briefly turned a bit moderate as he contemplated statewide office. In 1996 he passed with David Bonior an amendment to require Turkey to acknowledge the Armenian genocide of 1915; Turkey spurned aid under such conditions. In 2000, Radanovich secured $90 million in aid for Armenia—one of the largest recipients of U.S. aid; but Speaker Dennis Hastert acceded to Bill Clinton's personal appeal to abandon another resolution that recognized the Armenian genocide. In 2004, the House initially approved a similar resolution by Democrat Adam Schiff, but Hastert and other Republican leaders insisted on dropping it as an amendment from a foreign aid bill. Radanovich was more enthusiastic about supporting trade promotion authority after George W. Bush became president.

On the Energy and Commerce Committee, Radanovich worked to deal with hydroelectric problems in the Sierra Nevadas. On the Resources Committee, he chaired in 2003 the National Parks, Recreation and Public Lands Subcommittee—a useful assignment for the representative of Yosemite; he pledged a greater local voice in planning for the parks but his proposed changes in the master plan for Yosemite encountered widespread opposition, and he made changes before the House passed the bill. Radanovich's earlier criticism of the plan to overhaul operations at Yosemite led its superintendent to resign. He enacted his proposal to improve the remote schools serving families that work at the park. He faced opposition from John Doolittle and Wally Herger on his proposal designating the 318-mile Highway 49 as a national heritage corridor; property rights advocates worried that private landowners would lose their rights and Radanovich modified the plan. In 2005, he took over as chairman of the Water and Power Subcommittee.

Back home, Radanovich has won reelection easily. After his initial pledge to serve only 10 years in the House, he said that he needed "some flexibility" to accomplish his priorities and he suffered no apparent retribution. He explored a race against Senator Barbara Boxer in 2004, but decided to hold onto his safe seat in the House. He suffered a black eye when the *Fresno Bee* in July 2004 published a lengthy report about the collapse of his winery, which left several investors short hundreds of thousands of dollars while Radanovich continued to own the land and other assets; the story raised the question of whether the investors' losses amounted to a gift to Radanovich contrary to House rules. Radanovich refused to cooperate with the *Bee's* six-month investigation, and an aide said that the newspaper was representing the views of "unhappy investors."

TWENTIETH DISTRICT

Rep. Jim Costa (D)

Elected 2004, 1st term; b. April 13, 1952, Fresno; home, Fresno; CA State U. Fresno, B.A. 1974; Catholic; single.

Elected Office: CA Assembly, 1978–94; CA Senate, 1994–2002.

Professional Career: Consultant, 2002–04.

DC Office: 1004 LHOB, 20515, 202-225-3341; Fax: 202-225-9308; Web site: www.house.gov/costa.

District Offices: Bakersfield, 661-869-1620; Fresno, 559-495-1620.

Committees: *Agriculture* (14th of 21 D): Department Operations, Oversight, Nutrition & Forestry; General Farm Commodities & Risk Management; Livestock & Horticulture. *Resources* (19th of 22 D): Energy & Mineral Resources; Water & Power. *Science* (17th of 20 D): Space & Aeronautics.

Group Ratings and Key Votes: Newly Elected

Election Results

2004 general	Jim Costa (D)	61,005	(53%)	($1,937,317)
	Roy Ashburn (R)	53,231	(47%)	($1,093,429)
2004 primary	Jim Costa (D)	24,338	(73%)	
	Lisa Quigley (D)	8,925	(27%)	
2002 general	Cal Dooley (D)	47,627	(64%)	($642,724)
	Andre Minuth (R)	25,628	(34%)	($503,230)
	Other	1,515	(2%)	

The People		Race/Ethnic Origin	Ancestry	
Area size:	4,989 sq. mi.	21.4% White	German: 3.2%	Irish: 2.7%
Urban population:	91.2%	7.2% Black	USA: 2.3%	
Rural population:	8.8%	5.6% Asian	**2004 Presidential Vote**	
Pop. 2000:	639,088	0.7% Native Am.	Kerry (D) 58,534	(51%)
Median income:	$26,800	0.1% Hawaiian	Bush (R) 56,045	(48%)
Poverty status:	32.2%	1.7% Two+ races	Other 1,023	(1%)
Military veterans:	8.1%	0.2% Other	**2000 Presidential Vote**	
		63.1% Hispanic Origin	Gore (D) 57,790	(55%)
			Bush (R) 46,058	(44%)
			Other 1,844	(2%)
			Cook Partisan Voting Index: D + 5	

Occupation	Blue collar: 27.2%	White collar: 37.8%	Gray collar: 35.0%

California's Central Valley by car seems a monotonous landscape: mile after mile of farmland with mile-square grid roads, cut across by diagonal railroads and canals, with an occasional cluster town. The land is hilly and gets more water near the Sierra Nevada, and this is where you find the larger cities. On the other side is the Westlands, where the land is flatter and the water scarcer. Here the land was always developed and sold in large plots, and it has some of the world's largest farming operations today. And it produces plenty: alfalfa, cantaloupes, cotton, grapes, lima beans, olives, peaches, plums, raisins, sugar beets, tomatoes, walnuts, wheat. The owners are a hardy lot, but like most entrepreneurs they have been happy to have government help over the years: crop price supports (in the case of cotton), agricultural research, exceptions to the immigration laws, irrigation systems and (most important) subsidized water. They have fought hard against liberals' efforts at change, from Governor Jerry Brown's attempts to encourage Cesar Chavez's United Farm Workers in the 1970s to former House Natural Resources Committee Chairman George Miller's 1992 law to draw off more water to the Sacramento delta and charge higher prices for it in the Valley. But the greatest threats could come from conservatives: In a free market for water, Los Angeles users might outbid the farmers. And the Republican-controlled Congress has declined to approve guest worker programs pushed by Valley members.

The 20th Congressional District of California includes most of the Westlands of the Central Valley, from Bakersfield to a point northwest of Fresno. Its irregular boundaries were drawn to maximize the Hispanic population and Democratic percentage, so the 20th includes the old downtown neighborhoods of both Bakersfield and Fresno, but not their more affluent neighborhoods; it includes heavily Latino towns like Delano, long Chavez's headquarters and recently the site of a potentially large natural gas discovery, but the 20th does not include more Anglo places like Tulare. Just 36% of Fresno's population is included within the 20th and just 18% of Bakersfield's; the district's Hispanic population is 63%, about double that in other Central Valley districts. This is the most Democratic Valley seat between Sacramento and Los Angeles. While the Valley has been trending Republican, redistricting made this district less so; but in 2004 Bush won 48% of the vote here.

The congressman from the 20th District is Jim Costa, a Democrat elected in 2004. Costa was born in Fresno and worked on the family farm. In 1978 he was elected to the Assembly where he known as a moderate Democrat. In 2002 he was forced to retire because of term limits. He turned down an opportunity that year to run in the less familiar 18th District against the politically vulnerable Gary Condit; he founded a consulting firm instead. In 2004 20th District Democrat Cal Dooley retired after 14 years. Costa entered the race and started off with wide name recognition, because his former state Senate district covered the entire congressional district. But in the March primary, he faced a bruising challenge from Lisa Quigley, chief of staff to Dooley. Quigley grew up in the Central Valley, but she hadn't lived in the district in nearly two decades since she left for the University of California at Berkeley and a career on Capitol Hill. Costa, a third-generation family farmer and a Fresno native, questioned her residency and her agricultural credentials. Quigley, who was endorsed by Dooley and national abortion-rights groups, bashed Costa's legislative record and painted him as a special interest lobbyist. In the final days Quigley ran ads mentioning Costa's 1986 arrest for soliciting a prostitute and a 1994 incident in which police found drug paraphernalia in his home. Costa shrugged off the attacks and won the primary by an unexpectedly large 73%–27%.

In the general, Costa began as a clear favorite in this Democratic-leaning district. But state Senator Roy Ashburn, the Republican nominee, ran a formidable campaign. He focused on cultural issues, including same-sex marriage, hoping to win Latino votes. He criticized Costa for supporting tax policies that he said hurt low-income families. He brought in Vice President Dick Cheney, Speaker Dennis Hastert and Governor Arnold Schwarzenegger and benefited from $1.5 million in ads from the National Republican Congressional Committee that claimed, "Jim Costa — he's gonna cost ya." But Costa's lengthy legislative record didn't readily lend itself to the "liberal" label. He criticized Ashburn as an "extreme partisan" who would be a tool of the Republican leadership. In a relatively low turnout, Costa won 53%–47%. In Fresno County, which cast 42% of the vote, he won 61%–39%. Costa also carried Bakersfield-centered Kern County, 55%–45%. Ashburn won in the geographically central Kings County 61%–39%, but its 29% of the vote was too little to make a difference. After the election, Ashburn attacked the 22d District's Bill Thomas and other Republican moderates for "sabotaging" his efforts. Thomas responded that the district lines made it "unwinnable" for a Republican against a Democrat like Costa.

In the House, Costa got seats on Agriculture and Resources, both of obvious relevance to the Valley, and on the Science Committee.

TWENTY-FIRST DISTRICT

Rep. Devin Nunes (R)

Elected 2002, 2d term; b. Oct. 1, 1973, Tulare; home, Visalia; Col. of the Sequoias, A.D. 1993, CA Poly. U., B.S. 1995, M.A. 1996; Catholic; married (Elizabeth).

Elected Office: Col. of the Sequoias Governing Bd., 1996–2002.

Professional Career: State Dir., USDA Rural Dev., 2001

DC Office: 1017 LHOB, 20515, 202-225-2523; Fax: 202-225-3404; Web site: www.nunes.house.gov/.

District Offices: Clovis, 559-323-5235; Visalia, 559-733-3861.

Committees: *Ways & Means* (24th of 24 R): Human Resources; Oversight.

Group Ratings

	ADA	ACLU	AFS	LCV	ITIC	NTU	COC	ACU	NTLC	CHC
2004	0	0	0	0	100	59	100	96	81	100
2003	5	—	0	5	—	61	100	92	—	—

National Journal Ratings

	2003 LIB	—	2003 CONS		2004 LIB	—	2004 CONS
Economic	21%	—	75%		12%	—	88%
Social	5%	—	87%		31%	—	67%
Foreign	11%	—	80%		22%	—	77%

Key Votes of the 108th Congress

1. Drilling in ANWR	N	5. DC School Vouchers	Y
2. Approve Bush Tax Cuts	Y	6. Ban Human Cloning	Y
3. Medicare/Rx Bill	Y	7. Restrict Gun Liability	Y
4. Bar Overtime Pay Regs.	N	8. Ban Partial-Birth Abortion	Y

9. Ban Same-Sex Marriage	Y
10. Fund Iraq War	Y
11. Bar Cuba Embargo Funds	N
12. Intelligence Reorg.	Y

Election Results

2004 general	Devin Nunes (R)	140,721	(73%)	($667,520)
	Fred Davis (D)	51,594	(27%)	
2004 primary	Devin Nunes (R)	unopposed		
2002 general	Devin Nunes (R)	87,544	(70%)	($1,213,781)
	David LaPere (D)	32,584	(26%)	($19,827)
	Other	4,070	(3%)	

The People		Race/Ethnic Origin	Ancestry	
Area size:	8,090 sq. mi.	46.4% White	German: 7.7%	English: 5.6%
Urban population:	79.9%	2.1% Black	Irish: 5.5%	
Rural population:	20.1%	4.9% Asian	**2004 Presidential Vote**	
Pop. 2000:	639,088	0.9% Native Am.	Bush (R) 133,004	(65%)
Median income:	$36,047	0.1% Hawaiian	Kerry (D) 68,501	(34%)
Poverty status:	20.7%	2.2% Two+ races	Other 1,646	(1%)
Military veterans:	10.6%	0.2% Other	**2000 Presidential Vote**	
		43.4% Hispanic Origin	Bush (R) 107,645	(60%)
			Gore (D) 65,268	(37%)
			Other 5,120	(3%)
			Cook Partisan Voting Index: R +13	

Occupation	Blue collar: 22.0%	White collar: 52.8%	Gray collar: 25.2%

Fresno, in California's Central Valley, between the flat Westlands and the Sierras, is a city agricultural and industrial, middle American and ethnically diverse. It is a creation of the industrial age, founded by the Central Pacific Railroad; its city fathers bred the local wine grape, developed the raisin industry and introduced the Smyrna fig. These are not all of Fresno's crops, which include cotton, lima beans, tomatoes, cantaloupes, plums, peaches and alfalfa. Fresno

County produces more farm products in dollar value than any other county in the United States. Central Valley agriculture is industrial in its precision, its thoroughness and its ownership by large corporations. The vineyards outside Fresno radiate in mechanical precision, with vines just 10 feet apart and exposed to the relentless summer sun: nothing romantic or quaint about it. Times have been good here: The weak dollar of recent years has boosted farm exports, as has the apparent break in the longstanding local drought; large citrus groves benefited from hurricanes in Florida, and nuts have found new export markets. The city of Fresno started as a farm-marketing center and as a tourists' stop-off point on the way to Yosemite National Park. It has long since grown out north, east and west from its old downtown, and its economy has diversified. New homebuilders can barely keep up with the demand by farm workers.

The 21st Congressional District of California covers most of Fresno County east of Fresno and all of Tulare County to the south; 42% of the population is in Fresno County and 58% in Tulare. Here and there amid the farm fields are small cities— Visalia (fast-growing, and the largest in the district), Tulare, Clovis, Reedley, Porterville. Past Kings Canyon and Sequoia National Parks loom the giant peaks of the Sierra Nevada, including Mount Whitney, at 14,494 feet, the highest point in California and in the lower 48 states. This part of the Central Valley had vigorous growth in the 1990s; the district is 43% Hispanic. In 2004, George W. Bush got 65% of the vote, his second highest percentage in a California district.

The congressman from the 21st District is Devin Nunes, a Republican first elected in 2002. He grew up in Tulare County, on a dairy farm that has been in his family for three generations. He graduated from Cal Poly in San Luis Obispo with degrees in agriculture and worked on the dairy farm. He is politically well connected. In 1998, at 25, he ran for the House in the 20th District and finished second in the primary, losing by just 52%–48%. In 2000 he was Tulare County campaign chairman for the 22d District's Bill Thomas, chairman of the Ways and Means Committee. In 2001, with help from Thomas, he was appointed California director of rural development for the Agriculture Department.

When California's redistricting plan was unveiled in September 2001, there was no incumbent in the 21st District, and Nunes moved quickly to run. He was supported by Thomas and in time by nine other California Republican incumbents—half the state Republican delegation. His $5,000 contribution from Thomas opened doors in Washington, and many in the pharmaceutical and insurance industries supported him. At home he won the endorsement of the California Farm Bureau, the state's largest farm organization and a powerful voice in Central Valley politics. But Nunes had serious primary competition. The best known candidate was Jim Patterson, the conservative former mayor of Fresno, who was endorsed and well-financed by the Club for Growth. Another serious candidate was Assemblyman Mike Briggs, who worked on agriculture issues in Sacramento and expected the Farm Bureau's support. Briggs was criticized for being one of only four Republicans to cross the aisle and vote for the state budget in 2001; he defended his vote by saying he got large tax breaks for farmers. Nunes had help in Fresno County, when he won the endorsement of *The Fresno Bee*. There were few differences on policy. All three said that agriculture was their top priority and promised to seek new water sources. All called for cuts in taxes and government regulations. All endorsed expanded guest worker programs. Nunes won with 37% of the vote, to 33% for Patterson and 26% for Briggs. In his base of Tulare County, which cast 49% of the Republican votes, Nunes led with 46% of the vote. In Fresno County he finished third with 27%, but his two opponents divided the vote: Patterson got 37% and Briggs 30%. Nunes won in November 70%–26%.

Nunes began what could be a lengthy House career with seats on Agriculture and Resources, both well-suited for the new district, plus a very good friend as chairman of Ways and Means. He had a conservative voting record: not too extreme, but not so moderate as Thomas's. He joined Roy Blunt's whip team, and Speaker Dennis Hastert tapped him for a group of about a dozen House members who meet informally with him each week. He worked to prevent a trade dispute when South Korea banned the import of local oranges because of what Nunes said was an unwarranted report of a fungus. In January 2005, his well-placed friends maneuvered to get Nunes a seat on Ways and Means, but he took an immediate leave of absence until there was an opening. Meanwhile, he became chairman of the National Parks, Recreation and Public Lands

Subcommittee at Resources. But he received his permanent seat on Ways and Means in May after Rob Portman of Ohio exited the House, and Ways and Means, to become trade representative. Nunes benefited from a strategically rapid response. Within minutes of the White House announcement on Portman, Nunes issued a statement staking his claim. Ohio Republicans objected and stated that the seat ought to be given to an Ohioan but they had been outmaneuvered by Nunes and his patron Bill Thomas. The only downside was that Nunes was forced to relinquish his National Parks subcommittee gavel. Also with Thomas, Nunes has criticized the state's redistricting map, saying, "I realize that this doesn't make me popular among people who don't want their districts changed." He was an early backer of Arnold Schwarzenegger's proposed referendum for a new non-partisan plan.

Like most California members of both parties, he was reelected by a wide margin.

TWENTY-SECOND DISTRICT

Rep. Bill Thomas (R)

Elected 1978, 14th term; b. Dec. 6, 1941, Wallace, ID; home, Bakersfield; San Francisco St. U., B.A. 1963, M.A. 1965; Baptist; married (Sharon).

Elected Office: CA Assembly, 1974–78.

Professional Career: Prof., Bakersfield Commun. Col., 1965–74.

DC Office: 2208 RHOB, 20515, 202-225-2915; Fax: 202-225-8798; Web site: billthomas.house.gov.

District Offices: Bakersfield, 661-327-3611; San Luis Obispo, 805-549-0390.

Committees: *Ways & Means* (Chmn. of 24 R). *Joint Committee on Taxation* (Chmn. of 5 Reps.).

Group Ratings

	ADA	ACLU	AFS	LCV	ITIC	NTU	COC	ACU	NTLC	CHC
2004	5	0	0	0	100	54	100	88	72	76
2003	5	—	0	15	—	62	100	80	—	—

National Journal Ratings

	2003 LIB	—	2003 CONS		2004 LIB	—	2004 CONS
Economic	9%	—	84%		20%	—	79%
Social	40%	—	58%		41%	—	59%
Foreign	38%	—	60%		23%	—	76%

Key Votes of the 108th Congress

1. Drilling in ANWR	Y	5. DC School Vouchers	Y	9. Ban Same-Sex Marriage	Y
2. Approve Bush Tax Cuts	Y	6. Ban Human Cloning	Y	10. Fund Iraq War	Y
3. Medicare/Rx Bill	Y	7. Restrict Gun Liability	Y	11. Bar Cuba Embargo Funds	N
4. Bar Overtime Pay Regs.	N	8. Ban Partial-Birth Abortion	Y	12. Intelligence Reorg.	Y

Election Results

2004 general	Bill Thomas (R)	unopposed		($1,493,678)
2004 primary	Bill Thomas (R)	unopposed		
2002 general	Bill Thomas (R)	120,473	(73%)	($1,591,853)
	Jaime Corvera (D)	38,988	(24%)	($10,426)
	Other	4,824	(3%)	

Prior Winning Percentages: 2000 (72%); 1998 (79%); 1996 (66%); 1994 (68%); 1992 (65%); 1990 (60%); 1988 (71%); 1986 (73%); 1984 (71%); 1982 (68%); 1980 (71%); 1978 (59%)

The People		Race/Ethnic Origin	Ancestry		
Area size:	10,454 sq. mi.	66.8% White	German: 10.7%	Irish: 8.1%	
Urban population:	82.5%	5.6% Black	English: 7.8%		
Rural population:	17.5%	2.9% Asian	**2004 Presidential Vote**		
Pop. 2000:	639,088	0.9% Native Am.	Bush (R) 180,584	(68%)	
Median income:	$41,801	0.1% Hawaiian	Kerry (D) 82,356	(31%)	
Poverty status:	13.7%	2.5% Two+ races	Other 2,747	(1%)	
Military veterans:	14.8%	0.2% Other	**2000 Presidential Vote**		
		21.0% Hispanic Origin	Bush (R) 141,156	(64%)	
			Gore (D) 73,338	(33%)	
			Other 5,043	(2%)	
			Cook Partisan Voting Index: R +16		

Occupation	Blue collar: 23.1%	White collar: 57.8%	Gray collar: 19.1%

Bakersfield, at the apex of the southern end of California's Central Valley, has been the focus of great migrations four times—in a gold rush in 1885, when oil was discovered here in 1899, during the 1930s when the Okies drove their jalopies from the Dust Bowl of Oklahoma and Kansas and Texas across the Southwest on U.S. 66, and again in the 1980s and 1990s, when Bakersfield and Kern County grew more rapidly than California's biggest metro areas. Bakersfield's oil rigs pump more oil than is produced annually in Oklahoma, but the migration that made the deepest imprint was in the 1930s. The Okies drove over one thousand miles of brown landscape, then through the Tehachapi Pass, and found this vast green valley, with its irrigated fields and its eucalyptus-shaded towns, the richest farming country in the world. The story is told vividly in John Steinbeck's *The Grapes of Wrath*, though his vision of the Okies as workers eager to join together with their fellow proletarians and rise up against their bosses did not get the picture quite right. More accurate is Dan Morgan's *Rising in the West*, which shows the strong Pentecostal beliefs that drove many migrants and, unlike Steinbeck, explains how they prospered in California.

The area around Bakersfield has become the one Southern-accented part of California, the home of country singers Buck Owens and Merle Haggard and a thriving contemporary country music scene, culturally conservative with a strong drive toward discipline and little empathy for the therapy that is so common in Los Angeles, 110 miles south. But Bakersfield's uniqueness may be diluted as southern California spreads north: developers are planning a town of 70,000 on valley land where I-5 plunges downhill from the Tejon Pass.

The 22d Congressional District of California, the southernmost district in the Central Valley, includes most of Bakersfield and Kern County, most of the land area of San Luis Obispo County, over the mountains to the west, and a slice of northern Los Angeles County including half the desert town of Lancaster. At the eastern end in the desert is Edwards Air Force Base where Chuck Yeager flew the X-1 and where the Space Shuttle has frequently landed; not far away is Mojave, the end of the Twenty Mule Team Trail where borate from Death Valley was loaded onto trains. The district's boundaries are designed to maximize the Hispanic percentage of the next-door 20th District, but the population of the 22d is still 21% Hispanic. The 22d includes most of Bakersfield and its surroundings, oil fields and high-income subdivisions, and Kern County desert and mountain communities. The rich farmland produces most of the olives grown in the United States and is the nation's largest dairy-producing region. Politically, Kern County was Democratic territory in the early 1960s—when, for that matter, so was Oklahoma. By the late 1960s, both had become solidly Republican in national politics, and today both seem Republican up and down the ticket. The inland portion of San Luis Obispo County has always been Republican. George W. Bush won 64% of the vote here in 2000 and 68% in 2004, in both cases his best showing in any California district.

The congressman from the 22d District is Bill Thomas, a Republican first elected in 1978 and now chairman of the House Ways and Means Committee. Thomas grew up in Idaho and in Orange County; his father was a union plumber and his parents never graduated from high school; he lived for a time in public housing. He graduated from San Francisco State and taught political science from 1965 to 1974 in the community college in Bakersfield. In 1974 he was elected to the Assembly, a conservative in a liberal-run legislature; when Congressman Bill Ketchum died after the 1978 primary, Thomas ran as the relative moderate at the party convention and won the seat. In his first year in Washington he roomed with another young professor just elected to the House, Newt Gingrich. He is bright and testy; he has, wrote Faye Fiore in the *Los Angeles Times*, "an intellect so sharp he is considered one of the brightest members of the House and a temper so mercurial some say he may be one of the meanest." In *Washingtonian's* 2004 poll of congressional staffers, Thomas was number one in the "meanest," "brainiest," "hottest temper" and "workhorse" categories. Thomas says, "Other people have other skills, interpersonal maybe, or [they're] backslappers, or whatever they do. My stock in trade has always been knowledge." Some of that may have come from being beaten again and again by Democrats on elections issues. On the House Administration Committee he was the Republicans' point man on the challenge to Indiana's 8th District result in 1985, in which the Democrats voted in their man though the state authorities said the Republican had won—"rape," said Thomas, who added that if Republicans ever got a majority, "We will not be civilized. We will not assume it's business as usual. We will not go back to playing the lackey." He was also attacked by conservatives for being too moderate, and in December 1992 Gingrich and others ran Paul Gillmor of Ohio against him for ranking-member on House Administration; Thomas won by only 12 votes. "That particular event changed his life. It taught him, in a very serious way, that leadership in the House is a team sport," said Gingrich later.

Now things are different. After Republicans won the majority in 1994, Thomas received two tough assignments from Gingrich. As chairman of House Administration, Thomas managed the Republicans' bills reducing the House budget by $50 million, reducing committee staffs by one-third, providing an independent audit of the House and applying to Congress the laws it applies to others. He opposed Democratic campaign finance measures and proposed his own.

On Ways and Means, and as chairman of its Health Subcommittee, Thomas has been the majority Republicans' lead man on Medicare. He studied the issue intensively, rising at 4:00 a.m. to crack the books, and reflected on the situation of his parents (his mother was killed and his father gravely injured in a Kern County car crash). Thomas played a lead role in the Medicare changes and spending cuts—including steps to give senior citizens additional private insurance options—that were enacted as part of the Clinton-Republican Congress budget agreement of May 1997. In June 2000 and again in 2002 he pushed to passage bills to provide a stand-alone prescription drug benefit for seniors; this allowed Republican House members to say they had passed a bill while the Senate Democrats hadn't. He returned to the issue in 2003.

Throughout 2000 Thomas was running, quietly, for Ways and Means chairman. Chairman Bill Archer, limited to six years by Republicans' term limits, was retiring from Congress. The next committee Republican in seniority was Phil Crane, who had not been nearly as productive legislatively; in March 2000 Crane admitted he had a problem with alcohol, and spent some weeks in treatment. Thomas's problem was his temper. He takes pride in his knowledge, and has shown contempt for those with less. Even his hobbies are unsociable: he likes to disassemble and reassemble old cars and take apart computers. Thomas recognized the problem and assured Republican leaders that he would contain his temper. Crane had backing from some economic and religious conservatives, but Thomas got the backing of Speaker Dennis Hastert, even though both he and Crane are from Illinois. Thomas was the choice of the Republican Steering Committee, a choice ratified by the Republican Conference.

As chairman, Thomas moved first on taxes. Immediately after the September 11 attacks, Thomas began talking about a cut in capital gains tax to stimulate the economy. In October he put together a $100 billion stimulus package that passed the House in October 216–214. In November and December Thomas denounced Tom Daschle and Trent Lott when they insisted that Thomas's negotiating guidelines would violate Senate rules; the package did not pass the Senate until March 2002. In June 2002, after the World Trade Organization declared the Extraterritorial Income Exclusion an illegal export subsidy, Thomas started working on a bill to replace it with a tax credit for multinational corporations and other changes in the tax code, including higher taxes on U.S. subsidiaries of foreign corporations.

While Thomas was working on the 2001 economic stimulus package, he was also working to renew trade promotion authority, which had lapsed in 1994. He was criticized for not negotiating with Democrats Charles Rangel and Sander Levin, the ranking members on the committee and its Trade Subcommittee, who wanted to require labor and environmental provisions in trade agreements. Instead he negotiated with junior committee Democrats Bill Jefferson and John Tanner. The bill was passed by a 26–13 vote in committee in October. During the next two months, he struggled to get the Democratic votes necessary for passage even while trying to hold Republicans together on the stimulus package; he got some Democratic votes by supporting more Trade Adjustment Assistance health care spending. Trade promotion authority passed the House December 6 by a 215–214 as Speaker Dennis Hastert kept the roll call on past the usual time limit so that Thomas and Tom DeLay could round up a majority. In all, 23 Republicans voted against, 21 Democrats for: a very small number from a party that from the 1830s through the 1970s had free trade as one of its major causes. In May 2002 the Senate passed a trade package including trade promotion authority, approval of an Andean trade agreement and Trade Adjustment Assistance; the House had passed separate bills on each; the Senate bill also included the Dayton-Craig amendment barring any trade agreements that repealed trade retaliation laws. Thomas again scuffled with the Senate over the rules for the conference committee and pressed for a rule for consideration in the House which many opposed as overly constricting. The leadership pulled the rule from the floor June 20 for lack of votes; it was approved June 26 by 215–214. The conference committee was settled in a late night meeting between Thomas and Senate Finance Chairman Max Baucus; the Senate got $12 billion in Trade Adjustment Assistance and health care provisions opposed by Thomas, the House got rid of Dayton-Craig. The conference report passed the House 215–212 on July 26 and the Senate 64–34 on August 1.

Through all this furious activity Thomas depended largely on Republican support and had little contact with Ways and Means ranking Democrat Charles Rangel or with other ranking Democrats on the committee. The level of mistrust built up was reflected in an incident on July 18, 2003. The committee was considering a bipartisan pension bill put together by Rob Portman and Ben Cardin. Thomas asked for a quick vote, before Democrats had time to read the measure; Democrats objected and called for a full reading of the bill. All Democrats but Pete Stark walked out and sat in an anteroom as Thomas made sarcastic comments. Thomas called on Capitol Police to remove Democrats from the anteroom; they refused. In the committee room Stark said he doubted the full measure was being read. Committee Republican Scott McInnis told Stark to "shut up." "Oh, you think you are big enough to make me," Stark said. "You little wimp. I said come over here and make me. I dare you. You are a little fruitcake." Thomas ordered the reading suspended; Stark objected. Thomas said his objection was too late; Stark called him a "fascist." In the full House Democrats objected loudly. "Pretty petty, I think, on both sides," said Speaker Dennis Hastert. Thomas at first refused to apologize. Then on July 24 he went on the floor and tearfully admitted to "poor judgment," being "just plain stupid." "As my mother would have put it, when they were passing out moderation, you were hiding behind the door. . . . As members, you deserve better judgment from me, and you'll get it."

Some thought this embarrassing incident would impair Thomas's ability to push through major legislation. But it didn't. Thomas had already, on June 27, gotten the House to pass his Medicare/prescription drug bill by one vote. The Senate passed a different bill that day, and the conference committee proceeded rockily. Thomas allowed only two Democrats, Senators Max Baucus and John Breaux, to take part in deliberations—"a coalition of the willing." In August Senate Finance Chairman Charles Grassley ordered his staffers to boycott meetings for a week after Thomas refused to make a deal on rural health care providers, one of Grassley's great concerns. In September the conference reached agreement on some issues, but in October Grassley complained of being "ridiculed" by Thomas. Thomas presented his own version of the legislation, which included nationwide private sector competition for government Medicare; later he considered making changes in that. At one meeting he so berated HHS Secretary Tommy Thompson that George W. Bush called Speaker Dennis Hastert and demanded that he rein in Thomas. Senate Democrats and rural state members like Grassley bridled at private sector competition for fear that it would not be available outside big metropolitan areas. On November

12 Senate Majority Leader Bill Frist, a member of the conference committee, and Hastert stepped in with a compromise, limiting private sector competition to four metro areas and one region starting only in 2008. Thomas, furious, stomped out of the meeting room and said he was flying home. He returned that evening after phone calls from Hastert and DeLay. On November 15 tentative agreement was reached; provisions included a $70 billion subsidy to employers so that seniors would maintain their retiree coverage (this netted the bill the support of AARP), discount cards available in 2004 and 2005 and a Medicare benefit beginning in 2006 and tax breaks for high-deductible health savings accounts. On November 22 this package was brought to the House floor. It was opposed by most Democrats and by some conservative Republicans who opposed creation of an expensive new entitlement. In the first 15 minutes, 24 Republicans voted against the bill and only 7 Democrats for it; the roll call remained stuck at 218–216 against. Hastert and DeLay kept the roll call open for a record two hours and 51 minutes as they and others tried to switch Republican votes. They suggested that Democrats might bring forward the Senate version with reimportation of prescription drugs, a more expensive and politically unstoppable entitlement. Eventually Idaho's Butch Otter and Arizona's Trent Franks switched and, with others also then moving, the bill passed 220–215. Democratic leaders understandably complained about the leadership's tactics, but the Senate also passed the bill and it became law.

Thomas had less success on the tax portions of the energy bill. He and Charles Grassley disagreed in 2003 on tax subsidies: Grassley wanted to promote ethanol and wind energy, while Thomas wanted incentives for the Alaska natural gas pipeline and for small oil producers with old wells like those in Kern County. The Senate was unable to pass the measure, and Thomas refused to append it to the corporate tax bill in October 2004.

The corporate tax bill came to the fore after the U.S. Extraterritorial Income Exclusion, an export tax break, was ruled illegal by the WTO, which authorized the European Union to issue $4 billion in trade sanctions on the United States if it was not repealed by January 2004. Thomas responded with a bill in July 2002 which was opposed by major exporters like Boeing and Caterpillar and did not go forward. In 2003 Thomas faced a rival bill, sponsored by Phil Crane and Charles Rangel, which directly subsidized exporting manufacturers; it quickly attracted support from many Democrats and from Illinois Republican Don Manzullo, who was disturbed by manufacturing job losses in his district. In July 2003 Thomas offered his alternative, with $190 billion in tax cuts and $70 billion from tax increases (the repeal of the ETI providing $50 billion). The different approaches were summarized by *National Journal*: "Thomas's idea was to use the money from the repeal of the export subsidy to reform tax law on overseas income in ways that would make all multinational companies more competitive globally. By contrast, Rangel and Crane had proposed targeting all new tax breaks to industries that had benefited from the ETI subsidy." When that approach failed to get support, Thomas reduced the tax cuts to $110 billion in October and incorporated a Senate provision allowing overseas profits repatriated within six months to be taxed at 7% (the Senate had 5.25%) rather than the 35% corporate rate, which the Thomas bill reduced to 32%. Defined as manufacturers were producers of software and movies, oil and gas refiners and huge construction firms like Bechtel and Halliburton. This bill was marked up in October but was still opposed by Manzullo and, he said, 25 conservatives. The EU voted in November to phase in sanctions in March 2004, but Manzullo's conservatives and most Democrats kept it short of a majority, and in March Thomas came forward with another version. Here Thomas banned sale-in-lease-out arrangements with local governments, long a target of the Treasury, and changed the 5.2 cent ethanol exemption from the gasoline tax to an income tax credit: both counted as revenue increases. But the latter was opposed by farm state members and Thomas missed an April deadline for going to the floor. To attract more support in May Thomas included two measures, a tobacco buyout with FDA regulation (popular in North Carolina, Virginia and Kentucky) and, at the suggestion of Tom DeLay, deductions for state sales taxes for taxpayers in states without income taxes (Florida, Texas, Washington, Tennessee, New Hampshire, Alaska, Nevada, South Dakota, Wyoming). Thomas included a measure allowing churches more leeway in expressing political opinions without endangering their tax-exempt status, but dropped it when advocates said it was worth less than nothing.

In the conference committee in October, Thomas refused to consider amendments not championed by the 41 conferees and conducted the sessions in public. Dropped from the Senate version were FDA regulation of tobacco (but not the tobacco buyout) and disapproval of the Labor Department's overtime regulations. Charity car sales were limited as well as sales-in-lease-out transactions barred. The bill passed on October 7 280–141; the Senate chimed in four days later. As *National Journal* wrote, "Thomas accomplished much of his goal, according to business and Capitol Hill sources, through a combination of shrewd negotiating and digging deep to find additional sources of revenue."

Thomas has been reelected easily every two years in his heavily Republican district. In the 1990s he was California House Republicans' point man on redistricting issues. After the November 1998 election, when it became clear that Democrats would control redistricting, Thomas concocted a ballot proposition in 1999 that would turn redistricting over to the California Supreme Court (most of whose justices were appointed by Republicans) and also cut legislators' salaries. The House Republicans' campaign committee, fearful that it could lose eight seats in redistricting, put up $1.3 million to get it on the ballot. But in December 1999 the state Supreme Court ruled it was invalid because it included two subjects. Thomas then split the proposal into two separate initiatives, but in March 2000 the campaign committee declined to put up any more money to get it on the ballot. In 2001 NRCC chairman Tom Davis, acting with the approval of White House political strategist Karl Rove, and David Dreier met directly with California Democratic redistricting consultant Michael Berman and made a deal: Berman would draw a plan with safe seats for all but one of California's Republican incumbents and would make the state's one new seat safely Republican in return for Republican support in the legislature for the plan, which would also provide safe seats for 33 California Democrats. Thomas was the lone member of the delegation who argued against the deal: he feared it would put most of the state's Latinos in Democratic districts, where Republicans would have no incentives to win them over, and he preferred to take his chances on a court challenge to a Democratic plan. But his advice wasn't followed. In 2004, unopposed at home, he gave $1.2 million to other Republican candidates.

In January 2005, as George W. Bush was preparing to make personal retirement accounts in Social Security his number one domestic legislative priority, Thomas suggested a different and broader approach. He argued that personal accounts on their own "cannot, given the politics of the House and the Senate," be passed by both chambers. "Sometimes elevating it to a larger, universal solution makes it easier because you bring more people to the table. The problem with Social Security, narrowly, is that it becomes more of a partisan issue than you would like." He suggested consideration of a value added tax which, he argued, would make the United States more competitive in world trade. "The United States is the world's largest importer and the world's largest exporter, and our tax system is out of sync with the rest of the world. We pay their social costs; they don't pay ours. That at least needs to be examined." As for the payroll tax, "Why go back to the same old solution? When it was 2%, doubling it wasn't a big problem. Now that it's 12%, we actually are dealing with a job killer. The higher the payroll tax the fewer people are hired. Why does that have to be the way we solve the financing problem? Let's find revenue that doesn't continue to kill jobs but also meets our basic needs." He suggested that a flat tax or the single-rate "fair tax" promoted by John Linder would be politically unacceptable. Again in February and March 2005, Thomas seemed to be suggesting melding the Social Security and tax reform issues which the Bush White House wanted handled separately. In his third (and last, unless term limits are waived) term as Ways and Means chairman, Thomas was thinking big. As for his role, he was asked in November 2004 if he would like to see the size of Ways and Means Committee reduced. "Yeah," he said, "I'd like to see it reduced to one."

TWENTY-THIRD DISTRICT

Rep. Lois Capps (D)

Elected March 1998, 4th full term; b. Jan. 10, 1938, Ladysmith, WI; home, Santa Barbara; Pacific Lutheran U., B.S. 1959, Yale U., M.A. 1964, U. of CA at Santa Barbara, M.A. 1990; Lutheran; widowed.

Professional Career: Staff nurse, Visiting Nurses Assn., 1963–64; Head nurse, Yale New Haven Hospital, 1960–63; Instructor, Santa Barbara City Col., 1983–95; Nurse, Santa Barbara Schl. Dist., 1979–96.

DC Office: 1707 LHOB, 20515, 202-225-3601; Fax: 202-225-5632; Web site: www.house.gov/capps.

District Offices: Oxnard, 805-385-3440; San Luis Obispo, 805-546-8348; Santa Barbara, 805-730-1710.

Committees: *Budget* (7th of 17 D). *Energy & Commerce* (17th of 26 D): Energy & Air Quality; Environment & Hazardous Materials; Health.

Group Ratings

	ADA	ACLU	AFS	LCV	ITIC	NTU	COC	ACU	NTLC	CHC
2004	100	80	100	100	60	9	24	0	0	7
2003	100	—	100	100	—	22	33	12	—	—

National Journal Ratings

	2003 LIB	—	2003 CONS		2004 LIB	—	2004 CONS
Economic	87%	—	9%		89%	—	8%
Social	84%	—	13%		86%	—	12%
Foreign	80%	—	19%		89%	—	10%

Key Votes of the 108th Congress

1. Drilling in ANWR	N	5. DC School Vouchers	N	9. Ban Same-Sex Marriage	N
2. Approve Bush Tax Cuts	N	6. Ban Human Cloning	N	10. Fund Iraq War	*
3. Medicare/Rx Bill	N	7. Restrict Gun Liability	N	11. Bar Cuba Embargo Funds	Y
4. Bar Overtime Pay Regs.	Y	8. Ban Partial-Birth Abortion	N	12. Intelligence Reorg.	N

Election Results

2004 general	Lois Capps (D)	153,980	(63%)	($1,009,290)
	Don Regan (R)	83,926	(34%)	($148,631)
	Other	6,391	(3%)	
2004 primary	Lois Capps (D)	unopposed		
2002 general	Lois Capps (D)	95,752	(59%)	($1,461,132)
	Beth Rogers (R)	62,604	(39%)	($1,844,444)
	Other	3,866	(2%)	

Prior Winning Percentages: 2000 (53%); 1998 (55%); 1998 (53%)

The People		Race/Ethnic Origin	Ancestry	
Area size:	2,479 sq. mi.	48.7% White	German: 8.3%	English: 7.2%
Urban population:	98.0%	1.9% Black	Irish: 6.5%	
Rural population:	2.0%	4.9% Asian	**2004 Presidential Vote**	
Pop. 2000:	639,088	0.5% Native Am.	Kerry (D) 147,361	(58%)
Median income:	$44,874	0.2% Hawaiian	Bush (R) 101,817	(40%)
Poverty status:	15.7%	2.0% Two+ races	Other 3,464	(1%)
Military veterans:	11.0%	0.1% Other	**2000 Presidential Vote**	
		41.7% Hispanic Origin	Gore (D) 119,795	(53%)
			Bush (R) 90,550	(40%)
			Other 13,574	(6%)
			Cook Partisan Voting Index: D + 9	
Occupation	Blue collar: 20.3%	White collar: 57.3%	Gray collar: 22.4%	

Santa Barbara is one of California's most paradisiacal places, a collection of red tile roofs and leafy live oaks, sheltered by towering mountains just above the sea. The impression is a bit misleading, for Santa Barbara has its problems, and its Spanish style is a creation not of 18th century Mission culture, but of the 20th century. Most of its white stucco buildings were put up after a 1925 earthquake leveled much of the town and the most distinguished of the Spanish Revival buildings were designed by an architect with the marvelously un-Latin name of George Washington Smith. Santa Barbara, like Disneyland, does not reproduce the past but presents a bigger, more attractive, cleaner version of it, maintained not by a company but by an architectural review board. But Santa Barbara's affluence isn't ersatz. This has long been one of the nation's richest retirement communities, and one determined to preserve its environment and serenity. Both features came under threat spectacularly in 1969, when an underwater oil well ruptured, coating the beach with oil; pictures of the oil slick in the channel and of volunteers trying to wash oil off grounded birds, helped to launch the environmental movement. Almost all the wells are closed now (though some old 19th century wells still send globs of oil to the beach at nearby Summerland), but the oil spill did leave a residue in Santa Barbara's politics—and helped obscure the fact that the environment also causes some of Santa Barbara's problems, as when in early 2005 torrential storms caused mud slides and destroyed many homes. This was once a mostly Republican community, uninterested in redistribution of wealth, but very concerned about the environment (it has built the nation's largest desalination plant) and moderate to liberal on cultural issues. Like most of coastal California, it moved decisively to the left in the past decade. But some of those changes have not gone smoothly, as pressures grew to split Santa Barbara into two counties of roughly equal population: a proposed Mission County to the west and north, which would be more conservative; and the residue in the more liberal Santa Barbara County.

The 23d Congressional District of California is a thin strip of Pacific coastline, from two to 12 miles deep, from the industrial ports of Oxnard and Port Hueneme southeast of Santa Barbara to the north end of San Luis Obispo County on the Big Sur coast, just north of William Randolph Hearst's San Simeon. There are nodes of populated territory. The largest city is Oxnard, in Ventura County, which is anything but upscale, with a large number of immigrants; overall the district is 42% Hispanic. Santa Barbara and nearby Montecito are far more upscale. Much of the Santa Barbara coastline is occupied by Vandenberg Air Force Base, which launches unmanned government and commercial satellites into polar orbit. The largest towns in northern Santa Barbara County, like San Luis Obispo to the north, are pleasant, comfortable places, as untrendy as you can find in coastal California. This was a marginal district, seriously contested several times in the 1990s. Now, after redistricting, it is safely Democratic.

The congresswoman from the 23d District is Lois Capps, a Democrat first chosen in a March 1998 special election to replace her late husband Walter Capps. Lois Capps grew up in Wyoming and Montana, the daughter of a Lutheran minister; she graduated from college with a nursing degree and was head nurse at Yale New Haven Hospital where she met Walter Capps, a student at Yale Divinity School. In 1964 he became a professor at the University of California at Santa Barbara. Lois Capps became the head elementary school nurse for the Santa Barbara school system, director of the county's teenage pregnancy and parenting project and a part-time instructor at Santa Barbara City Community College. In 1994, when Republican Michael Huffington gave up the seat after one term to run for the Senate, Walter Capps ran and lost 49.3%–48.5% to Andrea Seastrand, a conservative Republican assemblywoman from San Luis Obispo County. Capps ran again in 1996 and won 48%–44%, but died of a heart attack in October 1997. Speaker Newt Gingrich encouraged the candidacy of Assemblyman Brooks Firestone—an heir to the Firestone tire fortune and successful winemaker and a centrist in favor of abortion rights and gun control. But also running was Assemblyman Tom Bordonaro, the favorite of Christian conservatives. Bordonaro, a paraplegic since a car accident in college, emphasized his "blue-collar roots and common values" and attacked Firestone's wealthy status. Tom DeLay steered about $30,000 to Bordonaro. Lois Capps ran with support from many of Walter Capps's admirers as well as from labor and environmental groups. In the January 1998 all-party primary she finished first with 45%, to 29% for Bordonaro and 25% for Firestone. In the runoff Bordonaro suffered from lingering animosity of Firestone supporters plus voter backlash against the outside groups' advertising. Capps won by a surprisingly large 53%–45% margin. The same two candidates were on the ballot in November. But national Republicans had few hopes of winning this time, and it was not a priority race. Capps won 55%–43%.

With her seat on Energy and Commerce and background as a health care professional, Capps has focused on HMO regulation and protecting the privacy of medical records, including genetic tests. She began as less of a down-the-line liberal than her husband, and she scored more legislative successes than the typical California Democrat. After she voted for normal trade relations with China, the Teamsters claimed that Capps betrayed them and withdrew their endorsement. When George W. Bush took over, she patched things up with labor by opposing trade promotion authority and her voting record became more liberal. She stood by George W. Bush's side during a White House signing ceremony of her bill to attract more students into the nursing profession. When the AARP endorsed Bush's Medicare prescription drug bill, Capps said that she was "stunned and offended" and resigned from the group. In 2004, the House passed her amendment for a comprehensive inventory of oil and gas resources beneath the Outer Continental Shelf; she opposed the Bush administration plan for drilling in the Los Padres National Forest. She gained unwanted national attention after getting funds for gang-related tattoo removal in San Luis Obispo. The $50,000 program initially received little attention at home, but it became the butt of jokes and criticism from national conservative and anti-pork groups. Capps defended the program for working with "people in our community to help erase this social stigma."

In 2000, Capps had serious competition from moderate Republican Mike Stoker, a former Santa Barbara County Supervisor and California Agricultural Labor Relations Board chairman. Capps had a big fundraising edge and won 53%–44%. In 2002, after redistricting, she won 59%–39%. After promising in 1998 to serve only three terms, she announced in 2003 that she would run again in 2004. Voters showed little reaction and she was reelected easily. Her biggest problem in the 2004 campaign was that law enforcement officials discovered that a former finance director had embezzled $200,000 from her campaign.

TWENTY-FOURTH DISTRICT
Rep. Elton Gallegly (R)

Elected 1986, 10th term; b. Mar. 7, 1944, Huntington Park; home, Simi Valley; Los Angeles St. Col., 1962–63; Protestant; married (Janice).

Elected Office: Simi Valley City Cncl., 1979–80; Simi Valley Mayor, 1980–86.

Professional Career: Owner, real estate firm.

DC Office: 2427 RHOB, 20515, 202-225-5811; Fax: 202-225-1100; Web site: www.house.gov/gallegly.

District Offices: Solvang, 805-686-2525; Thousand Oaks, 805-497-2224.

Committees: *International Relations* (5th of 27 R): Asia & the Pacific; Europe & Emerging Threats (Chmn.). *Judiciary* (5th of 23 R): Courts, the Internet & Intellectual Property; Immigration, Border Security & Claims. *Permanent Select Committee on Intelligence* (5th of 12 R): Technical & Tactical Intelligence; Terrorism, Human Intelligence, Analysis & Counterintelligence. *Resources* (4th of 27 R): National Parks.

Group Ratings

	ADA	ACLU	AFS	LCV	ITIC	NTU	COC	ACU	NTLC	CHC
2004	0	5	0	0	100	57	100	96	76	83
2003	5	—	0	10	—	62	97	88	—	—

National Journal Ratings

	2003 LIB	—	2003 CONS	2004 LIB	—	2004 CONS
Economic	19%	—	81%	22%	—	78%
Social	15%	—	84%	9%	—	85%
Foreign	31%	—	65%	39%	—	59%

Key Votes of the 108th Congress

1. Drilling in ANWR	Y	5. DC School Vouchers	Y	9. Ban Same-Sex Marriage	Y
2. Approve Bush Tax Cuts	Y	6. Ban Human Cloning	*	10. Fund Iraq War	Y
3. Medicare/Rx Bill	Y	7. Restrict Gun Liability	Y	11. Bar Cuba Embargo Funds	N
4. Bar Overtime Pay Regs.	N	8. Ban Partial-Birth Abortion	Y	12. Intelligence Reorg.	Y

Election Results

2004 general	Elton Gallegly (R)	178,660	(63%)	($551,059)
	Brett Wagner (D)	96,397	(34%)	($207,432)
	Other	9,321	(3%)	
2004 primary	Elton Gallegly (R)	unopposed		
2002 general	Elton Gallegly (R)	120,585	(65%)	($427,481)
	Fern Rudin (D)	58,755	(32%)	
	Other	5,666	(3%)	

Prior Winning Percentages: 2000 (54%); 1998 (60%); 1996 (60%); 1994 (66%); 1992 (54%); 1990 (58%); 1988 (69%); 1986 (68%)

The People		Race/Ethnic Origin	Ancestry	
Area size:	4,157 sq. mi.	68.6% White	German: 11.7%	English: 9.0%
Urban population:	94.2%	1.6% Black	Irish: 8.8%	
Rural population:	5.8%	4.4% Asian	**2004 Presidential Vote**	
Pop. 2000:	639,088	0.5% Native Am.	Bush (R) 165,430	(56%)
Median income:	$61,453	0.1% Hawaiian	Kerry (D) 127,875	(43%)
Poverty status:	7.2%	2.2% Two+ races	Other 3,473	(1%)
Military veterans:	13.1%	0.2% Other	**2000 Presidential Vote**	
		22.3% Hispanic Origin	Bush (R) 140,755	(54%)
			Gore (D) 112,436	(43%)
			Other 9,220	(4%)
			Cook Partisan Voting Index: R + 5	

Occupation   Blue collar: 17.1%   White collar: 67.8%   Gray collar: 15.1%

On a golden mountainside, looking westward over a valley hemmed in by mountains north and south, five United States presidents gathered in November 1991 to dedicate the Ronald Reagan Library. This was the first time in 202 years that five presidents stood together in one place—one which the Founding Fathers probably did not imagine would ever be American and yet today seems quintessentially so. Simi Valley, famous a few months later as the site of the trial of police officers accused of assaulting Rodney King, is a product of the 1960s, the expansive and still optimistic postwar years when the vast stream of migrants who had come from all over the United States to Los Angeles spread beyond city and county limits to fill up barren valleys between golden mountains. They brought a willingness to work hard, high competence and high tech, an appreciation of the local environment and a distaste for crime and rioting that seemed all too common in the Los Angeles basin they left behind. Simi Valley is just one of several communities in the valleys of Ventura County, west of Los Angeles, that have been filling up with people leaving Los Angeles and the San Fernando Valley and building new communities in what had been orange and lemon groves. Ventura County "is part of an attempt by lots of very desirable areas to control growth," said author Joel Kotkin. "It's an elitist strategy. The irony is that the elitists are so numerous that they prompt growth by themselves." To the south, in another valley, is Thousand Oaks, one of the safest large cities in the nation. Farther west in Pleasant Valley is Camarillo; in inland valleys still farther west are Santa Paula and Ojai. Academy Award nominee *Sideways*, which dealt with the abundant consumption of local wines by two friends, was filmed in nearby Buellton. Looking out toward these valleys and to the

Pacific beyond at the Reagan Library are 55 million pages of presidential documents and a large piece of the Berlin Wall, which Reagan urged Mikhail Gorbachev to tear down and which fell two years later.

The 24th Congressional District of California includes all of the interior of Ventura County and of Santa Barbara County to the west, plus a stretch of the Ventura County coastline including the Santa Monica Mountains and Point Mugu Naval Weapons Test Center. The Santa Barbara County interior is lightly inhabited; it includes the small towns of Lompoc, Solvang and Santa Ynez, near Reagan's beloved cabin in the mountains. It shares both Vandenberg Air Force Base and the Channel Islands with the 23d District. Most of the population is in eastern Ventura County. Politically, these areas are solidly Republican. The district voted 56% for George W. Bush in 2004.

The congressman from the 24th District is Elton Gallegly, a Republican first elected in 1986. He grew up in the working class (and now entirely Latino) suburb of Huntington Park in Los Angeles County, dropped out of college and became a real estate broker. In 1979 he was elected to the Simi Valley city council, became mayor in 1980, then was elected to Congress in 1986. In 1992, when redistricting moved much of Republican Robert Lagomarsino's district into the new Ventura County-based seat, Gallegly moved fast to push Lagomarsino into running in the district to the north, where he lost the primary to Michael Huffington's $3 million campaign.

Gallegly has a moderate-to-conservative voting record and has played a role on major issues. He has been active on immigration. He called for a constitutional amendment to deny citizenship to babies of illegal immigrants, a tougher Border Patrol, an end to welfare for illegal immigrants and a tamperproof identification card for legal aliens. In 1996, he got the House to pass his amendment allowing states to deny education to children who are illegal immigrants. On other issues, he passed a law to allow government agencies to give away their dogs— superannuated drug-sniffers and guard dogs—to their handlers. After pressure from local citrus growers, he decided in the final hours to support normal trade relations with China. In 2004 he passed a resolution calling on the United Nations to take action to respond to the threat that Burma poses to Southeast Asia. The House defeated his amendment to prevent federal spending on bear-baiting to assist hunters. Locally, he worked hard to save the Point Mugu Navy base, threatened with closure in 1996 and, with 18,000 related jobs, Ventura County's largest employer; he worked to get a wing of 16 E-2 radar planes assigned there, plus two new C-130s to fight forest fires. Point Mugu was slated to gain jobs according to the Pentagon's May 2005 base closure and realignment list.

Gallegly, a non-lawyer, has passed up several opportunities to chair a Judiciary subcommittee and declined to serve as a House manager during the Senate impeachment trial of Clinton. In 2003, he was one of several senior members of the Resources Committee who were passed over when Richard Pombo became chairman. In January 2005 he became chairman of the Europe Subcommittee of International Relations, with an expanded jurisdiction that includes tracking of terrorist threats in the world. His strongest recent reelection challenge came in 2000; Gallegly won 54%–41% over corporate attorney Michael Case, who attacked his views on abortion and guns. He spent a few days campaigning for governor in the 2003 recall, but withdrew because he lacked name recognition.

TWENTY-FIFTH DISTRICT

Rep. Buck McKeon (R)

Elected 1992, 7th term; b. Sept. 9, 1938, Los Angeles; home, Santa Clarita; Brigham Young U., B.S. 1985; Mormon; married (Patricia).

Elected Office: William S. Hart Schl. District Bd., 1979–87; Santa Clarita Mayor, 1987–88; Santa Clarita City Cncl., 1988–92.

Professional Career: Small businessman; Owner, Howard & Phil's Western Wear, 1973–00; Chmn., Valencia Natl. Bank, 1987–88.

DC Office: 2351 RHOB, 20515, 202-225-1956; Fax: 202-226-0683; Web site: www.house.gov/mckeon.

District Offices: Palmdale, 661-274-9688; Santa Clarita, 661-254-2111.

Committees: *Armed Services* (8th of 34 R): Readiness; Tactical Air & Land Forces. *Education & the Workforce* (3d of 27 R): 21st Century Competitiveness (Chmn.); Employer-Employee Relations.

Group Ratings

	ADA	ACLU	AFS	LCV	ITIC	NTU	COC	ACU	NTLC	CHC
2004	0	0	13	9	90	62	100	88	73	92
2003	10	—	0	0	—	59	97	80	—	—

National Journal Ratings

	2003 LIB	—	2003 CONS		2004 LIB	—	2004 CONS
Economic	9%	—	84%		5%	—	93%
Social	37%	—	61%		28%	—	70%
Foreign	21%	—	79%		17%	—	78%

Key Votes of the 108th Congress

1. Drilling in ANWR	Y	5. DC School Vouchers	Y	9. Ban Same-Sex Marriage	Y
2. Approve Bush Tax Cuts	Y	6. Ban Human Cloning	Y	10. Fund Iraq War	*
3. Medicare/Rx Bill	Y	7. Restrict Gun Liability	Y	11. Bar Cuba Embargo Funds	N
4. Bar Overtime Pay Regs.	N	8. Ban Partial-Birth Abortion	Y	12. Intelligence Reorg.	Y

Election Results

2004 general	Buck McKeon (R)	145,575	(64%)	($954,938)
	Tim Willoughby (D)	80,395	(36%)	($47,171)
2004 primary	Buck McKeon (R)	unopposed		
2002 general	Buck McKeon (R)	80,775	(65%)	($757,256)
	Bob Conaway (D)	38,674	(31%)	($6,995)
	Frank Consolo (Lib)	4,887	(4%)	

Prior Winning Percentages: 2000 (62%); 1998 (75%); 1996 (62%); 1994 (65%); 1992 (52%)

The People		Race/Ethnic Origin	Ancestry	
Area size:	21,622 sq. mi.	57.2% White	German: 10.3% Irish: 7.6%	
Urban population:	88.2%	7.9% Black	English: 7.1%	
Rural population:	11.8%	3.7% Asian	**2004 Presidential Vote**	
Pop. 2000:	639,087	0.9% Native Am.	Bush (R) 142,052	(59%)
Median income:	$49,002	0.2% Hawaiian	Kerry (D) 96,355	(40%)
Poverty status:	12.6%	2.7% Two+ races	Other 3,057	(1%)
Military veterans:	12.7%	0.2% Other	**2000 Presidential Vote**	
		27.1% Hispanic Origin	Bush (R) 108,627	(56%)
			Gore (D) 81,893	(42%)
			Other 5,055	(3%)
			Cook Partisan Voting Index: R + 7	

Occupation Blue collar: 23.6% White collar: 60.3% Gray collar: 16.1%

One tragedy of the 1994 Northridge earthquake was at the intersection of the I-5 and Route 14 freeways at the north edge of the San Fernando Valley, where an overpass collapsed and a motorcycle patrolman hurtled to his death. Destruction of the interchange had an economic and personal impact for months afterwards, for the settled area of Los Angeles County no longer ends at the mountains at the northern rim of the San Fernando Valley. It continues along Route 14 past the mountain-surrounded city of Santa Clarita, with 168,000 people in 2004 and home of the Six Flags Magic Mountain theme park, and 25 miles beyond, where the mountains stop at the San Andreas Fault and the desert stretches out low and flat. This is the Antelope Valley, with huge aerospace plants and military bases around the fast-growing towns of Palmdale and Lancaster, where more than 253,000 people live and where there has been a resurgence of specialty farm crops such as baby carrots, organic onions and parsnips. The long runways of Palmdale airport remain a little-used alternative to crowded LAX. Beyond the Antelope Valley the desert stretches for miles, with clumps of human settlement—Edwards Air Force Base, where Chuck Yeager flew the X-1 and where the Space Shuttle has frequently landed, and the desert towns of Victorville and Barstow on I-15.

The 25th Congressional District of California covers all of these areas (though it shares Edwards AFB with the 22d). It is enormous, geographically the largest in the state, extending far to the north, across the almost uninhabited Mojave Desert and mountains, to include Death Valley and the Owens Valley, the starting point of the Los Angeles Aqueduct, one of the glories of early 20th century engineering. The military occupies hundreds of thousands of acres with its China Lake Naval Air Weapons Station, the Goldstone deep space communications complex, and the battlefield training center at Fort Irwin. It then swings north to include mountainous Inyo and Mono Counties. But less than 10% of the district's people live in this vast expanse. Politically, this is a solidly Republican district.

The congressman from the 25th District is Howard "Buck" McKeon, a Republican first elected in 1992. He grew up in Southern California, graduated from Brigham Young University and was a co-owner of Howard and Phil's Western Wear, a family business that expanded to 52 stores in California, Arizona, Nevada and Utah in the early 1990s, but closed in 2000. McKeon was the first mayor of Santa Clarita when it was incorporated in 1987. He ran for the new House seat in 1992 and won the crucial primary 40%–38% over Assemblyman Phil Wyman, who once proposed to ban the allegedly satanic practice of recording certain words into songs backwards.

McKeon became Republican freshman class president and helped abolish four select committees in 1993. With a seat on the Armed Services Committee, he worked to save local defense jobs—this was the production base for the B-1 and B-2 bombers and the SR-71 spy plane. He helped get new contracts for the X-33, the next generation Space Shuttle and the Joint Strike Fighter; at his urging, the Pentagon is building part of the fighter in the Antelope Valley. He tried to authorize more B-2s and got NASA to perform Space Shuttle modifications to Air Force Base Plant 42 in Palmdale.

He has been a leader at the Education and the Workforce Committee. After the 1998 election, he briefly considered a challenge to Majority Leader Dick Armey, but concluded that Armey would prevail. In 2001 McKeon lost out to John Doolittle for an Appropriations seat; instead he became chairman of the 21st Century Competitiveness Subcommittee, which deals mostly with higher education issues. In handling the renewal of the higher education bill, he advocated steps that would penalize hundreds of universities and colleges that have raised tuition much faster than inflation, and pointed to expensive luxuries on many campuses. "We can no longer stand idly by while our nation's students, the future of our country, are being priced out of the promise of higher education." Many schools and Democrats complained loudly that he was advocating price controls. McKeon disagreed, responding that he simply was calling for removal of federal aid from schools that push their rates too high; but in the face of opposition from the Bush administration he later abandoned the proposal, claiming that many colleges had moved to rein in tuition hikes. In 2004, he enacted the Assistive Technology Act to benefit individuals with disabilities. With John Boehner term-limited as Education Committee chairman after 2006, McKeon may well succeed him, since more senior Republicans seem more interested in other chairmanships—Tom Petri is in line to chair Transportation then and Pete Hoekstra already chairs Intelligence.

McKeon has been re-elected without serious opposition, but now he must travel long distances to keep in touch with all his constituents. At the National Republican Congressional Committee, he ran the STOMP grass roots campaign to mobilize voters.

TWENTY-SIXTH DISTRICT

Rep. David Dreier (R)

Elected 1980, 13th term; b. July 5, 1952, Kansas City, MO; home, San Dimas; Claremont McKenna Col., B.A. 1975, Claremont Grad. Schl., M.A. 1976; Christian Scientist; single.

Professional Career: Corp. Relations Dir., Claremont McKenna Col., 1976–78; Mktg. Dir., Industrial Hydrocarbons, 1978–80; V.P., Dreier Development Co., 1985–present.

DC Office: 233 CHOB, 20515, 202-225-2305; Fax: 202-225-7018; Web site: dreier.house.gov.

District Office: Glendora, 626-852-2626.

Committees: *Chairman, Committee on Rules. Rules* (Chmn. of 9 R): Legislative & Budget Process; Rules & Organization of the House.

Group Ratings

	ADA	ACLU	AFS	LCV	ITIC	NTU	COC	ACU	NTLC	CHC
2004	5	10	0	0	100	52	100	88	70	66
2003	5	—	0	0	—	64	100	88	—	—

National Journal Ratings

	2003 LIB	—	2003 CONS		2004 LIB	—	2004 CONS
Economic	21%	—	75%		17%	—	80%
Social	42%	—	58%		42%	—	57%
Foreign	38%	—	62%		45%	—	54%

Key Votes of the 108th Congress

1. Drilling in ANWR	Y	5. DC School Vouchers	Y	9. Ban Same-Sex Marriage	N
2. Approve Bush Tax Cuts	Y	6. Ban Human Cloning	Y	10. Fund Iraq War	Y
3. Medicare/Rx Bill	Y	7. Restrict Gun Liability	Y	11. Bar Cuba Embargo Funds	N
4. Bar Overtime Pay Regs.	N	8. Ban Partial-Birth Abortion	Y	12. Intelligence Reorg.	Y

Election Results

2004 general	David Dreier (R)	134,596	(54%)	($1,338,730)
	Cynthia Matthews (D)	107,522	(43%)	($25,535)
	Randall Weissbuch (Lib)	9,089	(4%)	
2004 primary	David Dreier (R)	53,368	(84%)	
	S. Sonny Sardo (R)	10,502	(16%)	
2002 general	David Dreier (R)	95,360	(64%)	($637,925)
	Marjorie Mikels (D)	50,081	(33%)	($64,363)
	Other	4,089	(3%)	

Prior Winning Percentages: 2000 (57%); 1998 (58%); 1996 (61%); 1994 (67%); 1992 (58%); 1990 (64%); 1988 (69%); 1986 (72%); 1984 (71%); 1982 (65%); 1980 (52%)

The People		Race/Ethnic Origin	Ancestry	
Area size:	755 sq. mi.	52.7% White	German: 9.6%	English: 7.5%
Urban population:	98.8%	4.4% Black	Irish: 6.9%	
Rural population:	1.2%	15.2% Asian	**2004 Presidential Vote**	
Pop. 2000:	639,088	0.3% Native Am.	Bush (R) 148,352	(55%)
Median income:	$58,968	0.1% Hawaiian	Kerry (D) 117,532	(44%)
Poverty status:	8.4%	2.6% Two+ races	Other 3,202	(1%)
Military veterans:	10.5%	0.2% Other	**2000 Presidential Vote**	
		24.4% Hispanic Origin	Bush (R) 127,468	(53%)
			Gore (D) 105,023	(44%)
			Other 7,044	(3%)
			Cook Partisan Voting Index: R + 4	

Occupation	Blue collar: 17.3%	White collar: 70.7%	Gray collar: 12.0%

It was the great route west to California in the first half of the 20th century: Passengers on the Santa Fe railroad's *Super Chief* or motorists on U.S. 66, after hours and days in barren desert, descended through the Cajon Pass into the Los Angeles Basin, then moved in a stately procession beneath the 10,000-foot snow-capped San Gabriel Mountains, marveling at orange groves and exotic plants. The railroad and highway ran through a line of towns built by Midwestern Protestants as independent communities and now mostly high-income suburbs with their own civic institutions: Claremont, home of the academically renowned Claremont Colleges; La Verne and Glendora and San Dimas with its rodeo and horse trails; Monrovia and Arcadia, site of the Santa Anita race track and the Los Angeles County Arboretum; and, a few miles from the tracks, luxurious San Marino, home of the Huntington Library, one of the world's great museums and scholarly institutions. Today, the traveler arriving in Los Angeles can see the same sights, if the air is clear, much more quickly as the jet glides down the flight path to LAX.

The 26th Congressional District of California covers this territory in the San Gabriel Valley. It includes, east of Claremont, the newer San Bernardino cities of Upland, Montclair and Rancho Cucamonga, home of the minor league baseball team the Quakes who play at a stadium called the Epicenter. It also includes the new suburb of Walnut to the south and, far to the west, connected by the San Gabriel Mountains, the mountain-enclosed suburb of La Canada-Flintridge, home of NASA's Jet Propulsion Laboratory. Historically, the towns running east from Los Angeles have been heavily Republican. But many of these towns now have large Hispanic and Asian populations—Arcadia, San Dimas and Walnut have sizable Chinese populations—and have become Democratic. The communities in the 26th District, however, have remained pretty heavily Republican, even San Marino, whose population was 49% Asian in 2000. George W. Bush won 55% of the vote here in 2004.

The congressman from the 26th District is David Dreier, a Republican first elected in 1980 and chairman of the House Rules Committee. Dreier grew up in Kansas City, Missouri, then spent a decade mostly on the Claremont McKenna campus, as a student and administrator, before he was elected to Congress in 1980. Dreier first ran in 1978, at 25, and lost to Democratic incumbent Jim Lloyd. He beat Lloyd in 1980 and in 1982 beat fellow Republican Wayne Grisham after they were redistricted together. At that point, Dreier evidently decided never to be pressed for funds again; he raised plenty and spent little, which takes more self-discipline than one might think. After the 2002 campaign he had $2.5 million cash on hand, the highest in the House.

Dreier personifies the intellectually rigorous conservatism and free market economics that has thrived at Claremont and maintains a California cheerfulness and good humor characteristic of California—even after serving for 14 years in the minority, chiefly on the Rules Committee, where Republicans were outnumbered 9–4 and lost almost every vote. Now Dreier is on the long end of the 9–4 split, and the complaints are coming from the Democrats.

Rules chairmen, once upon a time independent operators, have become an operating part of the House leadership since Democrats instituted election of committee chairmen in 1974 and Republicans did so in 1994. Rules sets the terms for debate and limits the amendments that can be offered—an essential procedural function in a legislature with 435 members, and one which can be and often is used to shape substantive outcome. The 9–4 ratio and the careful selection of members guarantee the chairman and leadership control over committee votes, but over time it must be tempered by a sense of fairness: An outraged minority party can store up grievances and wait for a chance to overturn a rule on the floor. In 1999 and 2000, Dreier's Rules Committee produced 229 rules, and not one was defeated on the floor; in 2003 and 2004, the committee produced 169 rules, and again not one was defeated on the floor. He also led a bipartisan process that reduced the number of standing House rules from 51 to 28, and expanded the Subcommittee on Technology and the House. After September 11, he opposed conducting congressional sessions electronically and helped establish the Select Committee on Homeland Security for the 108th Congress. In 2003 he pushed through rules changes to allow the speaker to adjust, in case of a catastrophic attack, the number of House members required for a quorum. In April 2004 he led the House in passing a law setting a 45-day limit for special elections to fill vacancies if more than 100 seats are declared vacant by the speaker. In September 2004 he circulated a draft rule allowing the speaker in case of catastrophe to hold extended quorum calls and then declare vacancies and set an emergency quorum; Democrats criticized this for not allowing minority party input, and scholars questioned its constitutionality. But the House passed the emergency quorum rule on January 4.

Dreier also has a policy agenda: free trade, high-tech and San Gabriel Valley water. He was one of the leading advocates of normal trade relations with China, and led the fight for many months when it seemed short of votes. Days before the vote, to counter complaints about China's suppression of religious freedom, he circulated a carefully worded letter from Billy Graham seeming to favor open trade ties; normal trade relations with China passed 237–197 in May 2000. In 2001 and 2002 he worked to pass trade promotion authority, which had lapsed in 1994. On high-tech, he was one of the chief sponsors, with the Silicon Valley's Zoe Lofgren, of increasing the number of H1-B visas. He has pushed for changing the Export Administration Act by changing the standard that determines whether high-performance computers can be exported; he argues that the MTOPS standard is obsolete. Dreier has threatened to use his chairmanship to strip from bills measures he opposes, such as an Internet gambling ban (he is against all Internet regulation) and the Northeast Dairy Compact. In March 2003 he and Anna Eshoo sponsored a bill to provide transparency and information about corporations' issuance of stock options but which did not require expensing of options. In response to France's opposition to the United States on Iraq, Dreier in March 2003 suggested increasing the number of immigration slots to citizens of France, so that more of its most talented citizens can come to the United States.

Dreier has taken a role in Republican party politics. He serves on the Republican Steering Committee and twice served as parliamentarian at the Republican National Convention, in which capacity he produced the rationale for the three-day "rolling roll call." He supported George W. Bush early in the 2000 race for president; they have been acquainted since Dreier sat next to Bush at a training school for Republican congressional candidates in 1978. That year neither won; 22 years later they were elected and became Rules Committee chairman and President. Dreier took the lead for the Republican delegation on redistricting in 2001, and played a part in reaching agreement with Democratic redistricter Michael Berman under which 19 of the 20 Republican incumbents got safe districts in return for Republican support in the California legislature. That helped Dreier, whose district was becoming more Hispanic and more Democratic; he was reelected by 57%–40% in 2000, his closest margin since 1980. In August 2003 he supported Arnold Schwarzenegger for governor in the recall election and appeared with him at almost every campaign rally. In the six weeks between Schwarzenegger's election October 7 and his inauguration, Dreier acted as head of his 65-member transition team in Sacramento, missing House votes. In November 2003 he declined to run against Senator Barbara Boxer.

Election year 2004 seemed likely to be routine for Dreier. He was opposed by a conservative in the March primary who attacked him on trade and illegal immigration; Dreier won 84%–16%. He went to Texas to campaign for Rules member Pete Sessions in his campaign against ranking Rules Democrat Martin Frost; they had been put in the same district by Tom DeLay's redistricting plan. But in August 2004 Los Angeles radio talk show hosts John Kobylt and Ken Chiampou, who had been inveighing against illegal immigration, started a Fire Dreier campaign. In September they held a rally outside Dreier's office with his Democratic opponent, who in all spent only $26,000. Dreier protested, "I take a back seat to no one on the issue of illegal immigration, yet I'm being painted as a coyote," and he sponsored a bill to provide 700 new border guards and a fraudproof Social Security card. Dreier spent $1.3 million and won by the reduced margin of 54%–43%, the first time since 1980 he finished with under 57%. He ran slightly behind George W. Bush, who carried the district 55%–44%.

In January 2005 the House Republican Conference clarified its rules to permit Dreier to continue to serve as Rules Chairman. Dreier pushed through new House rules, strongly attacked by Democrats, which changed ethics committee procedures to make it easier to create investigative subcommittees and to allow members to contest letters of admonishment. On the first day of the session Dreier filed a bill to increase penalties on employers of illegal immigrants and provide a plastic Social Security card with a picture; it was supported by T.J. Bonner, president of the Border Patrol employees' union and co-sponsored by Democrat Silvestre Reyes, the former head of the Border Patrol in El Paso, Texas. Dreier opposed Arnold Schwarzenegger's February proposal to redistrict all the state's legislative districts; Dreier argued that the congressional district boundary lines should stay in place until after the 2010 Census. Critics pointed out that his district is mostly surrounded by Democratic districts, and a neutral redrawing of the lines could give him a significantly more Democratic district.

TWENTY-SEVENTH DISTRICT

Rep. Brad Sherman (D)

Elected 1996, 5th term; b. Oct. 24, 1954, Los Angeles; home, Sherman Oaks; U.C.L.A., B.A. 1974, Harvard U., J.D. 1979; Jewish; single.

Elected Office: CA St. Board of Equalization, 1990–95, Chmn., 1991–95.

Professional Career: Accountant, 1980–90.

DC Office: 1030 LHOB, 20515, 202-225-5911; Fax: 202-225-5879; Web site: www.house.gov/sherman.

District Office: Sherman Oaks, 818-501-9200.

Committees: *Financial Services* (11th of 32 D): Capital Markets, Insurance & Government Sponsored Enterprises; Domestic and International Monetary Policy, Trade & Technology; Financial Institutions & Consumer Credit. *International Relations* (8th of 23 D): Africa, Global Human Rights & International Operations; International Terrorism & Nonproliferation (RMM). *Science* (14th of 20 D): Energy; Space & Aeronautics.

Group Ratings

	ADA	ACLU	AFS	LCV	ITIC	NTU	COC	ACU	NTLC	CHC
2004	95	85	100	100	30	9	33	4	0	15
2003	90	—	100	100	—	24	30	9	—	—

National Journal Ratings

	2003 LIB	—	2003 CONS	2004 LIB	—	2004 CONS
Economic	87%	—	9%	75%	—	24%
Social	81%	—	19%	84%	—	15%
Foreign	87%	—	12%	71%	—	28%

Key Votes of the 108th Congress

1. Drilling in ANWR	N	5. DC School Vouchers	N	9. Ban Same-Sex Marriage	N
2. Approve Bush Tax Cuts	N	6. Ban Human Cloning	N	10. Fund Iraq War	N
3. Medicare/Rx Bill	N	7. Restrict Gun Liability	N	11. Bar Cuba Embargo Funds	N
4. Bar Overtime Pay Regs.	Y	8. Ban Partial-Birth Abortion	N	12. Intelligence Reorg.	N

Election Results

2004 general	Brad Sherman (D)	125,296	(62%)	($871,672)
	Robert Levy (R)	66,946	(33%)	
	Eric Carter (Green)	8,956	(4%)	
2004 primary	Brad Sherman (D)	unopposed		
2002 general	Brad Sherman (D)	79,815	(62%)	($713,658)
	Robert Levy (R)	48,996	(38%)	($20,104)

Prior Winning Percentages: 2000 (66%); 1998 (57%); 1996 (49%)

The People		Race/Ethnic Origin	Ancestry	
Area size:	152 sq. mi.	44.9% White	German: 6.3%	Irish: 5.0%
Urban population:	99.7%	4.5% Black	English: 4.6%	
Rural population:	0.3%	10.5% Asian	**2004 Presidential Vote**	
Pop. 2000:	639,088	0.3% Native Am.	Kerry (D) 130,567	(59%)
Median income:	$46,781	0.1% Hawaiian	Bush (R) 86,397	(39%)
Poverty status:	13.4%	3.1% Two+ races	Other 3,034	(1%)
Military veterans:	8.4%	0.2% Other	**2000 Presidential Vote**	
		36.5% Hispanic Origin	Gore (D) 117,120	(60%)
			Bush (R) 70,557	(36%)
			Other 6,568	(3%)
			Cook Partisan Voting Index: D +13	

Occupation	Blue collar: 19.9%	White collar: 66.2%	Gray collar: 13.9%

The San Fernando Valley, in the early 20th century when the movie business was young, was a vast expanse of empty land, annexed to Los Angeles in 1915; moviemakers, looking for filming sites for a western, drove past the vacant lots of Westwood, up narrow roads through the Santa Monica Mountains and over into the vast Valley, sheltered from ocean breezes and rain-bearing clouds by the mountains. Since then this vast bowl of land has been transformed, first into 1950s suburbia, then into a postmodern city of its own, economically vital and yeastily ethnic. Even in its suburban years, the San Fernando Valley was not entirely residential: big factories—the General Motors Van Nuys assembly plant, the Anheuser Busch brewery, Rockwell (now, Boeing) and Litton (now, Northrop Grumman) defense plants—provided jobs. In those years this was fast-growing, family-friendly territory; politically, it was turf fought over hard by Republicans and Democrats. By the 1970s young white Anglo families were fleeing, as the Los Angeles Unified School District was hit by a busing order. There is plenty of upscale territory left in the uplands in the rims of the Valley, in Granada Hills and Tarzana; the office blocks and mini-malls show unmistakable signs of affluence. In what had been the culturally arid Valley, lounges and bars have become prevalent. Urban planners hope to revive Panorama City, which was the busy center of the Valley during the 1950s. In the inner lowlands of the Valley, new immigrants have moved in to Reseda and Van Nuys. Some old neighborhoods have become rough enclaves, with youth gangs and boarded-up houses and apartments weakened by the Northridge earthquake; Iranians and Chinese, Mexicans and Koreans, Israelis and Filipinos are keeping other neighborhoods solidly middle-class. Even this multiethnic Valley has been unhappy to be linked with the city of Los Angeles, whose liberal-dominated Council imposes high taxes and irksome regulations that have stopped in the Valley the kind of vibrant economic growth seen in independent municipalities like Burbank and Glendale; a Valley secession movement arose and the issue was put on the November 2002 ballot, and the Valley voted 51%–49% for it. But it needed a majority in all of Los Angeles to pass, and failed.

The 27th Congressional District of California on the map looks like an inverted "U" over the San Fernando Valley, between the Santa Monica and San Gabriel mountains. On the east it includes part of Burbank, famous as the home of the NBC studios and Disney's headquarters. Just to the north are the Sunland and Tujunga neighborhoods at the base of the San Gabriel Mountains. The larger part of the district is on the western side of the Valley, including most of Granada Hills, Northridge, Van Nuys and Tarzana. This is a diverse district indeed, 37% Hispanic and 11% Asian, roughly half of whom are Filipino or Korean. The district remains solidly Democratic.

The congressman from the 27th District is Brad Sherman, a Democrat first elected in 1996. Sherman grew up in Monterey Park, in the San Gabriel Valley east of Los Angeles; he started working on Democratic campaigns at age 6, licking stamps and stuffing envelopes for Congressman George Brown, and he set up his own stamp-wholesaling firm at 14. He graduated with high honors from UCLA, worked as an accountant, then went to Harvard Law School and practiced tax law in L.A. He always had the political bug, and in 1990 was elected to the state Board of Equalization. This four-member body is a sort of tax court; Sherman's district was most of Los Angeles County. He was known as a stickler for detail, a "tax nerd," as one former staffer said, who used the office with a keen scent for political advantage. But he irritated cartoonists with a ruling that exempted them from the state tax on artwork but not on illustrations; they set up a website, the Sherman Gallery, in which they vied in caricaturing the balding and bespectacled Sherman.

Sherman decided to run for Congress, and moved his residence from Santa Monica to Sherman Oaks, when Anthony Beilenson retired after 20 years in the House in 1996. Sherman had an active Republican opponent, businessman Rich Sybert. Both of these self-financers (Sherman spent $578,000 of his own money) stressed their moderation. Sherman ran against Newt Gingrich and the Republican Congress, but he also supported the death penalty, wanted racial quotas and preferences phased out and favored tough measures on illegal immigration. Sybert stressed his independence of Gingrich, favoring abortion rights and environmental protections. Sybert was intense, Sherman a bit humorous (he handed out combs to voters, saying "You'll be able to use it more than I can"). Sherman won 49%–44%.

In the House, Sherman's voting record has been notably more moderate than those of most other Los Angeles County Democrats. One of the few CPAs in Congress, he serves on the Financial Services Committee. During debate on corporate accountability, he offered an amendment to require accounting firms that audit publicly held companies to carry liability insurance to cover investor losses caused by their errors; the amendment was defeated. He objected to proposals that blocked new Financial Accounting Standards Board rules requiring companies to treat stock options as an expense. Sherman was one of the few Los Angeles politicians who said that the Valley was not getting its fair share of spending from the city of Los Angeles, but he did not take a position on Valley secession. In October 2002 he voted for the use of force in Iraq, after initially backing language to urge more support from the United Nations. On the International Relations Committee, he is ranking Democrat of the International Terrorism and Nonproliferation Subcommittee. The House accepted his "Halliburton" amendment to require competitive bidding procedures for the procurement of oil from Iraq, but a conference committee later dropped it. He sought to limit the use of franked mailings by House committee chairmen. He filed a proposal to modify the Presidential Succession Act to make it unlikely that a leader of the Legislative Branch could become president.

Sherman has won reelection easily, even after redistricting gave him a district that was two-thirds new to him. The first lines, drawn by Michael Berman, brother of 28th District Congressman Howard Berman, were objected to by Sherman. The Bermans made some accommodations, and Sherman ended up with district that was 37% Hispanic and Berman with one that was 56% Hispanic. So far, he has not had serious Latino opposition. But Arnold Schwarzenegger's proposed redistricting referendum could place Sherman at greater risk.

TWENTY-EIGHTH DISTRICT

Rep. Howard Berman (D)

Elected 1982, 12th term; b. Apr. 15, 1941, Los Angeles; home, N. Hollywood; U.C.L.A., B.A. 1962, LL.B. 1965; Jewish; married (Janis).

Elected Office: CA Assembly, 1973–82, Maj. Ldr., 1974–79.

Professional Career: Practicing atty., 1967–72.

DC Office: 2221 RHOB, 20515, 202-225-4695; Fax: 202-225-3196; Web site: www.house.gov/berman.

District Office: Van Nuys, 818-994-7200.

Committees: *International Relations* (2d of 23 D): Middle East & Central Asia; Oversight & Investigations. *Judiciary* (2d of 17 D): Courts, the Internet & Intellectual Property (RMM); Immigration, Border Security & Claims.

Group Ratings

	ADA	ACLU	AFS	LCV	ITIC	NTU	COC	ACU	NTLC	CHC
2004	90	90	100	73	50	14	29	0	3	7
2003	85	—	100	70	—	23	34	13	—	—

National Journal Ratings

	2003 LIB	—	2003 CONS		2004 LIB	—	2004 CONS
Economic	92%	—	0%		88%	—	12%
Social	92%	—	0%		83%	—	16%
Foreign	64%	—	36%		75%	—	25%

Key Votes of the 108th Congress

1. Drilling in ANWR	N	5. DC School Vouchers	N	9. Ban Same-Sex Marriage N
2. Approve Bush Tax Cuts	N	6. Ban Human Cloning	N	10. Fund Iraq War Y
3. Medicare/Rx Bill	N	7. Restrict Gun Liability	N	11. Bar Cuba Embargo Funds Y
4. Bar Overtime Pay Regs.	Y	8. Ban Partial-Birth Abortion	N	12. Intelligence Reorg. N

Election Results

2004 general	Howard Berman (D)	115,303	(71%)	($902,390)
	David Hernandez (R)	37,868	(23%)	($32,611)
	Kelley Ross (Lib)	9,339	(6%)	
2004 primary	Howard Berman (D)	33,702	(82%)	
	Charles Coleman (D)	7,448	(18%)	
2002 general	Howard Berman (D)	73,771	(71%)	($758,236)
	David Hernandez (R)	23,926	(23%)	($8,953)
	Kelley Ross (Lib)	5,629	(5%)	

Prior Winning Percentages: 2000 (84%); 1998 (82%); 1996 (66%); 1994 (63%); 1992 (61%); 1990 (61%); 1988 (70%); 1986 (65%); 1984 (63%); 1982 (60%)

The People		Race/Ethnic Origin	Ancestry	
Area size:	78 sq. mi.	31.4% White	German: 3.7%	Irish: 3.2%
Urban population:	99.9%	4.1% Black	English: 2.9%	
Rural population:	0.1%	5.9% Asian	**2004 Presidential Vote**	
Pop. 2000:	639,087	0.2% Native Am.	Kerry (D) 125,351	(71%)
Median income:	$40,439	0.1% Hawaiian	Bush (R) 49,220	(28%)
Poverty status:	19.1%	2.4% Two+ races	Other 2,011	(1%)
Military veterans:	5.9%	0.2% Other	**2000 Presidential Vote**	
		55.6% Hispanic Origin	Gore (D) 112,332	(73%)
			Bush (R) 36,762	(24%)
			Other 5,021	(3%)
			Cook Partisan Voting Index: D +25	

Occupation	Blue collar: 26.2%	White collar: 58.0%	Gray collar: 15.8%

A hiker looking north from the crest of the Santa Monica Mountains in 1910 would have seen spread out, almost totally empty and barren, 20 miles wide and 12 miles deep, the San Fernando Valley. Separated by the Cahuenga Pass from rapidly growing Los Angeles and Hollywood, the Valley was bought up in massive tracts by civic leaders even as they were urging city engineer William Mulholland to build a huge 250-mile aqueduct from the Owens Valley to give Los Angeles water and persuading the city in 1915 to annex 200 square miles of the Valley. In the years after World War II, this was modern suburbia, filled with *Leave It to Beaver* families. Today the San Fernando Valley is postmodern urban, with a look you can see in exaggerated form in Disney headquarters buildings in Burbank or Universal City's CityWalk shopping mall: The driver topping the crest today sees office towers looming out over slightly hazy air, shopping centers, occasional palm trees, lines of grid streets stretching out into the distance beyond stucco subdivisions and the squat factory and warehouse buildings that have made Los Angeles County a top manufacturing locale. The Valley has aged, sometimes gracefully; homeowners in Van Nuys, Sun Valley and Granada Hills are now forming preservation districts, maintaining the antic architecture of the Valley in the 1950s.

The people in the Valley have also changed. The white Anglo families with stay-at-home moms in the 1950s have been replaced by hard-working Latino families, with children waiting at the bus stops for schools and parents juggling two jobs. But there is continuity: These remain places where people work hard and try to raise children who will have better chances and make better livings than they have. Pacoima, at the northern end of the Valley, where Rodney King was pulled over and beaten and arrested, is mostly Latino. Farther south, in Canoga Park, Van Nuys and Burbank, was the industrial base—the aircraft and GM assembly plants—of the Valley in the 1950s and 1960s; the GM plants were shut down in the 1980s and only one of the defense plants, the old Rocketdyne plant now owned by Boeing, remains open, and a Neiman Marcus is going up across the street. Less visible are the hundreds of small factories and multimedia plants where thousands of jobs have been created. The lower income areas here are farther from the central city; the southern rim of the Valley, around Studio City and North Hollywood, is still heavily Jewish and is attracting new families who often send their kids to religious schools; there is a trendy and lively shopping strip along Ventura Boulevard. People with money cluster near the rims of the mountains around the Valley; those less well off settle on the flatlands beyond.

The 28th Congressional District of California consists of about half of the San Fernando Valley and some of the mountains in the south. It includes parts of Van Nuys and several miles of land on either side of the Hollywood Freeway from where it comes through the Cahuenga Pass from Hollywood up to the junction with the Golden State Freeway; much of the northern end of the Valley around the Golden State, including Pacoima and the small city of San Fernando, is in the district. Mulholland Drive, which runs along the crest of the Santa Monica Mountains and the Ventura Freeway, forms the southern border until the district dips south to Hollywood Boulevard. Within these borders are affluent North Hollywood, Studio City, Sherman Oaks and Encino, with big houses on twisting streets overlooking the Valley and just above the shops of Ventura Boulevard. The population of the district in 2000 was 56% Hispanic; the central and northern parts are much more Hispanic, while the southern end has a large Jewish population. But Hispanics are still not the majority voting bloc here; many are not citizens, many are children or young people not yet in the voting stream; and the tradition among Hispanics today, as among Italians 100 years ago, is to trust family and hard work, not politics and government, to get ahead. The high Democratic percentages here are due as much to Jewish as to Latino voters, who both trended Democratic in the late 1990s, one group in response to the emergence of the Christian right, the other in response to the campaign for cutting off aid to illegal aliens which suggested, incorrectly, that Latinos are interested more in welfare than hard work. The trend now may be a little bit in the other direction: George W. Bush's percentage here rose from 24% in 2000 to 28% in 2004.

The congressman from the 28th District is Howard Berman, one of the most aggressive and creative members of the House—and one of the most clear-sighted operators in American politics. He grew up in Los Angeles in modest circumstances, got interested in politics in high school and went to UCLA where he became friends with Henry Waxman, his ally in politics ever since. At UCLA law school he got an internship at the California Assembly. "I was assigned to the Assembly Agriculture Committee. It was dealing with farm labor issues and Cesar Chavez's movement. From then on, I was hooked." Just a few years later he and Waxman were elected to the Assembly, Waxman in 1968 from the Westside, Berman in 1972 by beating the Assembly Republican leader in a Hollywood Hills district. This was the beginning of the so-called Berman-Waxman political machine—not so much a precinct organization as a group of consultants who raised money, redrew district lines and endorsed candidates through direct mail; a key player was Berman's brother Michael Berman, who became an expert on redistricting and who drew the new lines in 2001. "We don't have a machine any more, if we ever did," Howard Berman said in 2004. "We just helped some friends." Their core constituency was liberal Westside Jews. Berman became Assembly Majority Leader in his first term. In 1980 he tried to unseat Speaker Leo McCarthy; ultimately both lost to Willie Brown, who served 15 years. Berman's consolation prize was a Valley-based congressional seat in 1982. The machine fell on hard times in the 1990s, as Republicans wrested away control of redistricting and the feminist left became the Democratic Party's driving force. Since then, Berman has been a political force on his own, with a record that is mostly but not always liberal.

Berman has been an active legislator even more than a political operator, and on all manner of issues, but not one who gets much publicity. On foreign policy, he started off less as a Vietnam War dove than as a backer of Israel. For a decade he floor-managed foreign aid authorization bills, defending aid to many countries as well as Israel. With Henry Hyde he wrote the law authorizing embargoes on nations that condone terrorism; in April 1990 he called for sanctions on Iraq, four months before Saddam Hussein invaded Kuwait. Berman voted for the Gulf War resolution, but was understandably critical of the Bush administration—if it had followed his advice there might well have been no need for war. He is supportive of organized labor and opposed trade promotion authority. Berman passed a law banning the double-issuing of U.S. passports to coddle Arab countries that refuse to honor passports with Israeli marks. He offered an amendment to revoke normal trade relations with China if it attacks, invades or blockades Taiwan and, when that was rejected, voted against it. Berman played a critical role in winning passage by a wide margin of the Iraq war resolution in October 2002. He strongly supported military action against Iraq, and in September he came out from behind the scenes and organized a group of Democrats who shared his views. They broke off from the negotiations between Republicans and John Spratt, who ended up offering an alternative to the administration's resolution, and talked directly to the Bush administration. He didn't seek the permission of Minority Leader Richard Gephardt but Berman's discussions led to Gephardt's agreement with the administration on the terms of the resolution—talks that undercut the demands of Spratt, Minority Whip Nancy Pelosi and Senate Foreign Relations Chairman Joseph Biden. In 2004, after the Presbyterian Church USA called for divestment of stock of firms doing business in Israel Berman wrote a letter, signed by 14 prominent members of both parties, calling the action "irresponsible, counterproductive and morally bankrupt." It "leads us to only one conclusion: the Presbyterian Church has knowingly gone on record calling for jeopardizing the existence of the State of Israel."

Immigration is another issue on which Berman has been a major legislator. In 1988 he sponsored the provision allowing 20,000 immigrant visas for migrants without close relatives here, to be selected randomly by computer—"Berman visa applications," they are called. He secured in 1990 more family reunification slots, expediting the immigration of Soviet Jews (a vivid presence in L.A.), and gaining amnesty provisions for more family members to remain in this country. In 2001 Berman, Lucille Roybal-Allard and Chris Cannon sponsored a bill to offer legal status to illegal immigrants 18 to 21 who had graduated from American high schools and enrolled in college. In 2003 he worked out a farm workers bill with Cannon and Senators Larry Craig and Edward Kennedy. Worked out laboriously with farm organizations and farm workers unions, it would legalize temporary agricultural workers, provide for good working conditions and allow them eventually to become legal residents; it was set aside as George W. Bush proposed a broader guest worker program with different terms, but it was reintroduced in January 2005.

In 1999 Berman took the ranking position on the Courts and Intellectual Property Subcommittee of Judiciary, one of vital importance to Hollywood interests. There he passed an anticybersquatting law to discourage pouncing on website names. In 2002 he filed a bill to enable copyright owners—primarily the record companies—to use technology to stop people from using peer-to-peer services to copy music; compact discs could contain software that would hack into people's P2P software. It was supported by subcommittee Chairman Howard Coble, but opposed vigorously by tech companies and music users as "vigilante legislation." In 2003 Berman co-sponsored with John Conyers and Lamar Smith a bill to create new judgeships to determine copyright royalty rates and distribution of royalties and to remedy defects in Copyright Arbitration Royalty Panels. It passed the House unanimously in March 2004 and the Senate unanimously in October and was signed into law in November. In 2003 Berman, Conyers and Smith also sponsored a bill providing for criminal penalties of mass downloaders of music and requiring file-sharing software to contain warnings of security risk. In July 2004 Berman was unable to prevent an amendment to the bill allowing firms to sell software that could delete offensive passages from movie DVDs; Berman still supported the overall bill which was approved by the Judiciary Committee in September 2004.

In 2003 Berman and Republican Buck McKeon assembled 300 co-sponsors for a bill that would eliminate the Government Pension Offset and the Windfall Elimination Provision of Social Security; he argued that those provisions reduced benefits earned by private sector workers who took late-career jobs as teachers or other government employees not covered by Social Security. He and McKeon reintroduced the measure in January 2005. From 1997 to 2003 Berman was the ranking Democrat on the House ethics committee. During his tenure, few complaints were filed for partisan reasons. After he left the committee in 2003, that no longer was the case. Berman opposed the Republican changes in ethics rules including the elimination of admonishments for conduct unbecoming a member of Congress—the action taken by the ethics committee against Majority Leader Tom DeLay in 2004, even as it declared that he had violated no House rule.

Berman is not the most senior member of the California delegation, but he is the go-to guy on many state issues. One California Assembly lobbyist said of him, "He's the conscience and dad of the delegation. In this era of term limits and turnover, Howard Berman is the constant. He has a vast institutional knowledge of issues in both Congress and the legislature that is rare these days." One issue on which he was the dad of the delegation was redistricting. California gained one seat in the 2000 Census and Democrats controlled the process. Michael Berman was hired as redistricting consultant by all U.S. House and state Senate Democrats at $20,000 per member. Because Assembly members are limited to three two-year terms, these other Democrats couldn't count on Assembly Democrats to draw them favorable districts. The Bermans and Republican David Dreier and House Republican campaign chairman Tom Davis, an expert on redistricting himself, made a deal: 19 of the 20 House Republicans would get safe Republican districts and a new Republican district would be created in return for Republican votes for the plan in the state legislature. National Democrats were angry that Democrats didn't pick up more than one district. But Howard Berman defended the deal. "Sometimes the cautious move is the smart move. Time will tell. But I'm convinced that we made the right decision, given the vagaries of politics and unanticipated decisions," he said. When the lines were unveiled in August 2001, the biggest controversy came over the San Fernando Valley. Brad Sherman, the Democrat from the 27th District, claimed that Howard Berman had been given too much of his territory south of Ventura Boulevard, while Sherman would be given too many Hispanics to have a secure seat over the decade. "Howard Berman stabbed me in the back," Sherman said. At first Berman was dismissive but agreed to negotiate. Adjustments were made in the lines, and Sherman's district ended up 37% Hispanic and Berman's 56%. The Mexican American Legal Defense Fund immediately took the plan to court, arguing that seats in the San Fernando Valley and San Diego tended to reduce Hispanic representation. The court approved the plan in June 2002.

In any case, Hispanics are not a majority of voters in this district and are not likely to be before 2010, and Berman has in fact worked on issues like farm labor and immigration long before he had any significant number of Hispanic constituents. Against Republican David

Hernandez, a proponent of Valley secession, he won 71%–23% in both 2002 and 2004. In October 2004 he endorsed former Assembly Speaker Antonio Villaraigosa in his successful race against Los Angeles Mayor James Hahn, even though he had endorsed no one in the race between those two candidates in 2001. "Antonio believes, as I do, that we need more police. The more cops we have on the street, the safer Los Angeles will be. And I think we need to look at how the city is being run. I still believe the San Fernando Valley is not getting the services it is entitled to."

TWENTY-NINTH DISTRICT

Rep. Adam Schiff (D)

Elected 2000, 3d term; b. June 22, 1960, Framingham, MA; home, Burbank; Stanford U., B.A. 1982; Harvard U., J.D. 1985; Jewish; married (Eve).

Elected Office: CA Senate, 1996–00.

Professional Career: Prosecutor, U.S. Atty. Gen. Ofc., L.A., CA 1987–93; Practicing atty. 1986–87, 1995–96.

DC Office: 326 CHOB, 20515, 202-225-4176; Fax: 202-225-5828; Web site: www.house.gov/schiff.

District Office: Pasadena, 626-304-2727.

Committees: *International Relations* (18th of 23 D): Middle East & Central Asia; Oversight & Investigations. *Judiciary* (14th of 17 D): Courts, the Internet & Intellectual Property.

Group Ratings

	ADA	ACLU	AFS	LCV	ITIC	NTU	COC	ACU	NTLC	CHC
2004	95	80	100	100	70	12	43	12	0	23
2003	100	—	100	100	—	23	33	20	—	—

National Journal Ratings

	2003 LIB	—	2003 CONS		2004 LIB	—	2004 CONS
Economic	87%	—	9%		75%	—	24%
Social	76%	—	23%		73%	—	25%
Foreign	64%	—	35%		62%	—	36%

Key Votes of the 108th Congress

1. Drilling in ANWR	N	5. DC School Vouchers	N	9. Ban Same-Sex Marriage	N
2. Approve Bush Tax Cuts	N	6. Ban Human Cloning	N	10. Fund Iraq War	N
3. Medicare/Rx Bill	N	7. Restrict Gun Liability	N	11. Bar Cuba Embargo Funds	N
4. Bar Overtime Pay Regs.	Y	8. Ban Partial-Birth Abortion	N	12. Intelligence Reorg.	Y

Election Results

2004 general	Adam Schiff (D)	133,670	(65%)	($955,782)
	Harry Scolinos (R)	62,871	(30%)	($605,280)
	Other	10,291	(5%)	
2004 primary	Adam Schiff (D)	unopposed		
2002 general	Adam Schiff (D)	76,036	(63%)	($712,072)
	Jim Scileppi (R)	40,616	(33%)	
	Ted Brown (Lib)	4,889	(4%)	

Prior Winning Percentages: 2000 (53%)

The People		Race/Ethnic Origin	Ancestry	
Area size:	102 sq. mi.	39.1% White	Armenian: 10.6% German: 6.2%	
Urban population:	99.4%	5.9% Black	English: 5.5%	
Rural population:	0.6%	23.7% Asian	**2004 Presidential Vote**	
Pop. 2000:	639,088	0.2% Native Am.	Kerry (D) 136,796	(61%)
Median income:	$43,895	0.1% Hawaiian	Bush (R) 83,448	(37%)
Poverty status:	14.5%	4.7% Two+ races	Other 3,097	(1%)
Military veterans:	6.8%	0.2% Other	**2000 Presidential Vote**	
		26.1% Hispanic Origin	Gore (D) 119,396	(58%)
			Bush (R) 79,210	(38%)
			Other 7,671	(4%)
			Cook Partisan Voting Index: D +12	

Occupation   Blue collar: 16.0%   White collar: 70.2%   Gray collar: 13.8%

In the early years of the 20th century, when Los Angeles was growing rapidly, on its way to become one of America's major cities, its richest citizens settled not on the beach (too clammy and cold) or on the west side (too dusty and remote), but in communities they built at the base of the San Gabriel Mountains that rise 10,000 feet above the city, their snow-capped peaks visible most of the year. The premier such community was Pasadena, with its institutions of national stature—the Rose Bowl and the Rose Parade, Cal Tech; its premier structure is its baroque-domed City Hall. Pasadena and South Pasadena have proudly preserved their bungalow neighborhoods, and Pasadena preserved and rebuilt the 80-year old curving Colorado Boulevard Bridge over Arroyo Seco. More middle class is Glendale, north of downtown Los Angeles, site of Forest Lawn Cemetery and Dreamworks Animation; just west, beneath the Verdugo Mountains, is Burbank (named not for botanist Luther Burbank but for a local dentist-developer), famous now for the NBC Studios, ABC Studios, Warner Brothers, and Disney, plus many small entertainment multimedia companies as well. With their lower taxes and business-friendly attitude, and despite earlier loss of aerospace jobs, Glendale and Burbank are booming while inside the city limits of high-tax and high-regulation Los Angeles, Hollywood has become seedy and plagued by commercial buildings with huge vacancy rates.

The 29th Congressional District of California includes Pasadena, South Pasadena, Glendale and the eastern half of Burbank. Historically, these were solidly Republican cities, but they have become more Democratic in recent years, for various reasons—Pasadena because of affluent voters' cultural liberalism and a growing black community; Glendale because of large communities of Armenians (the nation's largest), Iranians, Koreans and Filipinos; Burbank from the trendiness of show business. The district also includes, south of South Pasadena, cities with large Asian populations: Vietnamese in San Gabriel, Chinese in Alhambra, Temple City and the northern edge of Monterey Park (which calls itself the nation's first Chinese suburb). This is one of California's polyglot districts—26% Hispanic, 24% Asian, 11% Armenian and 6% black. Once mostly Republican country, it is now solidly Democratic, casting only 38% of its votes for George W. Bush in 2000 and 37% in 2004.

The congressman from the 29th District is Adam Schiff, a Democrat elected in fierce 2000 over Republican James Rogan in what was the most expensive House race ever. Schiff's father was a traveling salesman, and Schiff grew up throughout the country, graduating from high school in northern California, and went on to Stanford and Harvard Law School. From 1987 to 1993, he worked in the U.S. attorney's office in Los Angeles. He ran for the Assembly and lost three times, twice to Rogan. But in 1996 he was elected to the state Senate, where he became its youngest member. In his first two years, he authored dozens of measures that Governor Pete Wilson signed into law, including landmark school textbook legislation. Schiff also taught political science at Glendale Community College.

Rather than seeking reelection as a state senator, Schiff ran for the House. This was one of the few House races in which the impeachment of Bill Clinton was an important issue. Rogan was a leading player in the Judiciary Committee's deliberations, and a persuasive voice for the case against Clinton. He obviously knew that supporting impeachment carried political risks; he had won reelection in 1998 by just 51%–46%. Entertainment mogul—and Clinton pal—David Geffen promised to raise millions to oppose him. The Schiff-Rogan race became a fundraising contest; the candidates, buoyed by responses to direct mail, raised more than $10 million combined, and more was spent independently by Clinton lovers and Clinton haters. Rogan had no apologies for his work on impeachment. The candidates disagreed on health care, abortion, gun control and taxes. Rogan branded his opponent as a traditional tax-and-spend liberal, who would "run naked through the Treasury, spending everything he can." Schiff attacked Rogan for calling abortion a "Holocaust" for the African-American community and saying that the Ku Klux Klan "couldn't do a better job on committing genocide on African Americans." They also battled for the support of more than 67,000 local Armenians. Rogan was a lead sponsor of a House resolution commemorating their genocide from 1915 to 1923 by the Ottoman Turks; he was promised a floor vote in October 2000, but Speaker Dennis Hastert reneged after phone calls from Clinton and his foreign policy appointees. Schiff cosponsored a state Senate resolution declaring "a day of remembrance of Armenian genocide," and got $400,000 from state taxpayers to produce a documentary about Armenian issues. Schiff said that Rogan's focus on Washington led him to ignore local problems. He won by a surprisingly large 53%–44% margin.

In the House, Schiff's voting record has been moderate, especially on foreign policy. He joined the Blue Dog Democrats and said that he was ready to work across party lines. On the Justice Department reauthorization bill, he won approval for annual reports on U.S. citizens detained because of suspected terrorist ties, plus steps to make it easier for states to gain access to a federal DNA data base. He helped to enact the bill to make "identity theft" a crime. On the bill to implement recommendations of the 9/11 Commission, he was the only Democrat voting with Judiciary Committee Republicans on added immigration restrictions; the final bill included his provisions to establish new penalties for developing a "dirty bomb," and to give new tools to law enforcement to crack down on weapons of mass destruction. On International Relations, he took up the cause of Armenian genocide, and called it a "symbolic victory" when the House passed a foreign aid bill with his provision, even though Hastert later insisted on its removal. He stirred complaints from liberal constituents when he supported the Patriot Act, and he voted for the use of force in Iraq, though he later criticized intelligence gathering. With New York's Steve Israel, Schiff created a Democratic study group on nonproliferation and made that a personal priority, including efforts to secure nuclear materials in the former Soviet Union so that they terrorists don't gain access to them. On local issues, he wants to expand the Santa Monica Mountains National Recreation Area. With neighboring Republican David Dreier, he restored $50 million to preserve the Mars surveyor program, which is based at the Jet Propulsion Lab in La Canada-Flintridge, just north of Pasadena.

Redistricting made the 29th District more Democratic, and Schiff was easily reelected in 2002 and 2004.

THIRTIETH DISTRICT

Rep. Henry Waxman (D)

Elected 1974, 16th term; b. Sept. 12, 1939, Los Angeles; home, Los Angeles; U.C.L.A., B.A. 1961, J.D. 1964; Jewish; married (Janet).

Elected Office: CA Assembly, 1968–74.

Professional Career: Practicing atty., 1965–68.

DC Office: 2204 RHOB, 20515, 202-225-3976; Fax: 202-225-4099; Web site: www.house.gov/waxman.

District Office: Los Angeles, 323-651-1040.

Committees: *Energy & Commerce* (2d of 26 D): Energy & Air Quality; Health; Oversight & Investigations. *Government Reform* (RMM of 17 D).

Group Ratings

	ADA	ACLU	AFS	LCV	ITIC	NTU	COC	ACU	NTLC	CHC
2004	100	95	100	100	40	8	20	0	0	15
2003	95	—	100	80	—	24	34	13	—	—

National Journal Ratings

	2003 LIB	—	2003 CONS		2004 LIB	—	2004 CONS
Economic	92%	—	0%		94%	—	6%
Social	92%	—	0%		83%	—	16%
Foreign	84%	—	14%		88%	—	11%

Key Votes of the 108th Congress

1. Drilling in ANWR	N	5. DC School Vouchers	N	9. Ban Same-Sex Marriage	N
2. Approve Bush Tax Cuts	N	6. Ban Human Cloning	N	10. Fund Iraq War	N
3. Medicare/Rx Bill	N	7. Restrict Gun Liability	N	11. Bar Cuba Embargo Funds	Y
4. Bar Overtime Pay Regs.	Y	8. Ban Partial-Birth Abortion	N	12. Intelligence Reorg.	N

Election Results

2004 general	Henry Waxman (D)	216,682	(71%)	($453,715)
	Victor Elizalde (R)	87,465	(29%)	($262,130)
2004 primary	Henry Waxman (D)	unopposed		
2002 general	Henry Waxman (D)	130,604	(70%)	($509,690)
	Tony Goss (R)	54,989	(30%)	

Prior Winning Percentages: 2000 (76%); 1998 (74%); 1996 (68%); 1994 (68%); 1992 (61%); 1990 (69%); 1988 (72%); 1986 (88%); 1984 (63%); 1982 (65%); 1980 (64%); 1978 (63%); 1976 (68%); 1974 (64%)

The People		Race/Ethnic Origin	Ancestry	
Area size:	388 sq. mi.	76.4% White	German: 8.4%	English: 6.8%
Urban population:	97.5%	2.6% Black	Irish: 6.8%	
Rural population:	2.5%	8.8% Asian	**2004 Presidential Vote**	
Pop. 2000:	639,088	0.2% Native Am.	Kerry (D) 220,181	(66%)
Median income:	$60,713	0.1% Hawaiian	Bush (R) 109,014	(33%)
Poverty status:	9.0%	3.3% Two+ races	Other 3,660	(1%)
Military veterans:	8.3%	0.3% Other	**2000 Presidential Vote**	
		8.3% Hispanic Origin	Gore (D) 199,282	(68%)
			Bush (R) 81,336	(28%)
			Other 11,464	(4%)
			Cook Partisan Voting Index: D +20	

Occupation   Blue collar: 6.9%   White collar: 84.4%   Gray collar: 8.7%

The Westside: The term was not much used 20 years ago, but is now shorthand for what might be the biggest and flashiest concentration of affluence in the world. It is the heartland of one of America's most productive and creative industries and one of the nation's major exports, show business. The first moviemakers came here earlier in the century, looking for a place to shoot silent films where the sunlight was more dependable than in Astoria, Queens, or Englewood, New Jersey. They found it in Hollywood, a suburb just annexed by burgeoning Los Angeles when the first movie studio was built in 1911. In 1923 came the Hollywood sign, overlooking the soon-famous intersection of Hollywood and Vine. By the 1930s, big studio lots were scattered around town, over the mountains in Burbank or out toward the ocean in Westwood and Culver City. Miraculously, the studio bosses of that era—most of them Jewish immigrants with little ancestral experience of America—created a popular culture that was universally accessible and embodied the American spirit in a way that still captures the imagination.

Showbiz still sets the tone for the Westside. It remains tremendously profitable, and not just for the big studios which are owned by large conglomerates; there are thousands of entrepreneurs, actors, writers and craftsmen who are the best in the world at what they do and who tend to cluster on the Westside because so many of the others they do business with are here. Many people on the Westside like to portray themselves as artists in a garret, willing to risk starving to make art and speak truth to bourgeois society. But their yen for fashionable new moral standards often make them disdainful of the ordinary people who are the market of mass entertainment.

Showbiz rejoiced in the election of Bill Clinton and in his frequent forays into California and obvious fascination with entertainers; it rejected with fury the notion that there was something wrong about his affair with a White House intern (from the Westside, it turns out) or with lying under oath in a sexual harassment case in a federal court. It responded with rage to George W. Bush and the war in Iraq; but its shrill endorsements of his opponent probably inspired more votes for Bush than against him.

Not everyone on the Westside is in show business, of course. Los Angeles ranks first in the nation in percentage of people who work at home and this is a place where thousands of small entrepreneurs, manufacturers, and inventors and marketers of everything imaginable helped spark the huge growth of the Los Angeles Basin, and there are even traces of pre-show business Los Angeles money, which is also plentiful. There are large numbers of singles and gays here. The Fairfax neighborhood remains solidly middle-class Jewish—though many of its Jews today are recent Russian immigrants. The Westside was the home of a former president who does not at all exemplify its politics, Ronald Reagan; before his Alzheimer's disease worsened, he kept his office on the former Fox lot that is now Century City. It is the center of the second-largest Jewish community in the United States, as well as the focus of the 1980s immigration of Iranians to the United States (6% of the district population is of Iranian ancestry). It is also the locus of some of America's most expensive residential real estate, where people buy houses for multiples of $1 million, knock down the structure and build something new for more millions, and of one of the world's premier high-priced shopping areas—Rodeo Drive, once a quite ordinary shopping street.

The 30th Congressional District of California contains most of Westside Los Angeles plus territory to the west. It includes the Fairfax neighborhood east to La Brea Avenue, heavily gay West Hollywood, Beverly Hills and the heavily Jewish Los Angeles neighborhoods to the south, Westwood and UCLA, Bel Air and Brentwood, Santa Monica and the whole 27 miles of Malibu on the ocean; most of the workload of the California Coastal Commission comes from Malibu. The district also includes the western end of the San Fernando Valley, the high-income neighborhoods of Woodland Hills and Chatsworth up against the mountains that rim the Valley. And it includes the high-income suburbs of Hidden Hills, Calabasas, Agoura Hills and Westlake Village, nestled amid mountains along the Ventura Freeway west of the San Fernando Valley. This is a mostly high-income district, with a large number of Jews and immigrants from Russia and Iran, but by today's definitions it is the least diverse district in metro Los Angeles. Only 3% of its residents in 2000 were black; no L.A. County district has a lower percentage. Only 8% of its residents are Hispanic, by a considerable margin the lowest percentage in southern California. Many Latinos work in the district, but few are interested in paying the prices for housing that has been bid up by rich people who can't imagine living anywhere else. Politically, the 30th District is heavily Democratic, but perhaps not quite as heavily as is generally believed. In 2000 it cast only 28% of its votes for George W. Bush, but in 2004 he got 33% here, even as his percentages declined in the San Francisco Bay area. One reason is the response of many Jewish voters to his support for Israel and policy of overthrowing or undermining tyranny in the Middle East. Bush's share of the vote rose from 20% to 42% in Beverly Hills, where the showbiz celebrities living in the rolling hills north of Sunset Boulevard are outnumbered by the Iranian Jews in the flatlands south of Wilshire.

The congressman from the 30th District is Henry Waxman, a Democrat first elected in 1974, one of the ablest members of the House, a shrewd political operator who is a skilled and idealistic policy entrepreneur. There is no Westside glitz about him: He grew up over his family's store in Watts, his personal demeanor is quiet, and he has never attended the Oscars ceremony. He graduated from UCLA and its law school, where he met Howard Berman, his longtime political ally and colleague. He moved up rapidly in politics by spying openings before others did and taking advantage of them. He ran against Assemblyman Lester McMillan in the mostly Jewish Fairfax area in 1968, at 28, and won 64% in the primary. From 1971–72 he chaired the redistricting committee, a good place to make friends, but he went to Congress in 1974 in a district designed, he points out, not by his committee but by a court. Waxman's biggest break in Congress came after the 1978 election, when he was elected chairman of the Commerce Committee's Health and Environment Subcommittee. This was one of the first times House Democrats decided to ignore seniority in handing out subcommittee chairs. Nevertheless, Waxman argued his case on the issues and—in a move quite unprecedented at the time, though common in Sacramento then and soon in Washington—made campaign contributions to other Democrats on the full committee, and won the post, 15–12, over the widely respected Richardson Preyer of North Carolina.

The campaign contributions were no accident. In the 1970s and 1980s Waxman and Berman built their own political machine in Los Angeles. Its power came not from patronage but from fundraising and savvy. They raised huge sums on the Westside for favored candidates. For them they put out carefully targeted direct mail, with hundreds of customized letters and endorsement slates sent out to different lists of people. In the apolitical commonwealth of California, where television advertising is exceedingly expensive and people seem to avoid politics, this made them critical though not always successful players. But in 1992 their machine foundered; since then, Waxman has rarely taken an active role in Los Angeles area politics, though he did endorse former Assembly Speaker Antonio Villaraigosa in his successful race against Los Angeles Mayor James Hahn in 2005.

As part of the Democratic majority and chairman of a key subcommittee from 1978 to 1994, Waxman was a major national policymaker, usually from behind the scenes. In 1981 and 1982 he prevented the Reagan administration and Commerce Committee Chairman John Dingell from revising the Clean Air Act; biding his time, he worked to strengthen the law in its 1990 revision. Another great Waxman project was expanding Medicaid for the poor. Between 1984 and 1990, he got coverage for all poor children up to 18, all children under seven and pregnant women in families under 133% of poverty income. This helped raise Medicaid from 9% to 14% of state spending in the 1980s, and helps to explain why Waxman was so disliked by many governors because many of these mandates were unfunded. Waxman had less success on reforming national health care. He wanted to move to something like a single-payer program and supported the Clinton plan but to no avail. He has secured more funding for AIDS research, important in the 30th District with its large gay population. In early 1994, in widely publicized hearings, he lined up the chief executive officers of leading tobacco companies and accused them of adding nicotine and other substances to cigarettes and of lying in their testimony. All this had no immediate legislative result, and when Thomas Bliley of Virginia became Commerce Committee chair, the hearings stopped. But Waxman brought the tobacco issue into public view, and he helped to inspire the lawsuits against tobacco companies which have resulted in the biggest redistribution of corporate assets—from the tobacco companies to state governments and trial lawyers—in history.

Waxman reacted with dismay to the Republican takeover of Congress, but with no slackening of effort. He gave up the ranking position on the Health Subcommittee to become ranking Democrat on the Government Reform Committee. There he sharply attacked Chairman Dan Burton's investigation of Clinton campaign misdeeds, arguing that Burton had given himself unprecedented subpoena power and was misusing it, and he emerged as perhaps the House's most articulate defender of Bill Clinton against scandal charges. In 2001, Waxman switched from being a defender of the White House to being a critic, frequently writing letters to Burton calling for investigations. There is an apologetic note in his comment about this course. "I'm doing what I think I ought to be doing. It's not what I'd like to be doing." In May 2001 he and John Dingell asked the GAO for the names of company executives who had been consulted by Vice President Dick Cheney's energy task force. In June he asked Burton to seek the names. In July the GAO sent a letter to Cheney asking for the names, the first such demand letter the GAO had ever sent; Cheney declined. In February 2002 the GAO brought a lawsuit against Cheney. In December 2002 a federal judge ruled against the GAO, and the agency declined to appeal. In response to the collapse of Enron in 2001, he wrote to Burton in February 2002 demanding an investigation of Enron's political activities; it turned out that there were connections with both to the Clinton administration (the company's support of the Kyoto Protocol, the administration's actions to help Enron's Dabhol electricity plant in India) and the Bush administration (the energy task force, FERC appointments, the company's position on the corporate Alternative Minimum Tax).

In January 2003 the House Republicans' term limits removed Burton as chairman and the Republican leadership installed Tom Davis, who promised a more constructive chairmanship and on occasion worked together with Waxman on issues. Nevertheless Waxman indefatigably wrote letters, called for GAO investigations and invoked the 1920s seven-member rule, which entitles any seven members of the committee to seek information from the executive branch. He noted that the 2003 Medicare prescription drug bill "will set up a dynamic in the future that requires us to add more revenue," and, when the cost proved to be higher than the $400 billion claimed when the bill was passed, sought internal administration estimates by March 2004. When those were denied he and 18 other committee Democrats filed suit in May. In July 2004 he and Louise Slaughter pointed out that HHS's list of pharmacies accepting Medicare discount cards contained many inaccuracies. With Davis, he sponsored a bill to block Internet prescriptions from doctors who had never seen the patients. With Carolyn Maloney, he proposed an amendment to restore non-prescription sale of morning after contraceptive drugs. When 150 NIH scientists were told they were under scrutiny by conservatives for research projects involving Asian prostitutes in San Francisco and women's responses to pornography, he called the notifications "intimidation" and "scientific McCarthyism." In February 2004 he and Sherrod Brown asked 10 pharmaceutical companies to reveal how much they paid in consulting fees and stock options to NIH scientists; this and other inquiries resulted in a stricter NIH policy on ethics and disclosure in February 2005, of which Waxman said he approved.

Since mid-2003 Waxman has issued continual criticisms of Halliburton and other government contractors in Iraq, pointing out relentlessly that Vice President Dick Cheney was once Halliburton's CEO. In September 2003 he accused the administration of "putting the interests of companies like Halliburton and Bechtel over the interests of the American taxpayer and the Iraqi people." In December he set up an Internet line for tips on Halliburton misdeeds. In June 2004 he questioned a fall 2002 decision to award a $1.8 million contract to Halliburton, which he said Cheney influenced. In October 2004 he said an investigation of U.S. management of Iraqi oil revenue should come before any investigation of the UN Oil for Food program. In November 2004 he said State Department documents showed that Halliburton employees tried to extract bribes for fuel contracts.

"If I were chairman, it would be a lot different. The biggest things that we're not taking up are oversight issues, in a lot of areas where I think we should be very, very active," Waxman said in 2004. He mentioned the flawed intelligence about yellowcake uranium in Niger, the Valerie Plame incident and Halliburton contracts. The committee did hold hearings on contracting in Iraq in March 2004, for which Waxman commended Davis. They worked together on investigations on mad cow disease and D.C. drinking water, and on the bipartisan project of changing the Postal Service. But Waxman blistered Davis in a seven-page letter for investigating former National Security Adviser Sandy Berger in July 2004; Berger said then that he only inadvertently took classified documents out of the National Archives, but in 2005 he admitted that he took them on purpose. Waxman oversees minor as well as major issues. He and other Democrats demanded an investigation of EPA's rules on industrial laundries and regulations on hydraulic fracturing oil drilling, arguing in both cases that there was political influence. In January 2005 he called for a GAO investigation of how a flawed HHS report on obesity was allowed to be released. When flu vaccine turned out to be widely unavailable because of the disqualification of the British firm Chiron, Waxman and Davis demanded records of Chiron's contacts with the FDA and British regulators; Waxman later said the FDA ignored "repeated opportunities" to fix Chiron's problems. When Davis called for restoring the executive branch's reorganization powers and for reducing the number of appointments requiring congressional confirmation, Waxman strongly disagreed.

Waxman has always won re-election easily, and has contributed generously to other Democrats' campaigns. Redistricting added Malibu and the San Fernando Valley to his district but it is still very heavily Democratic; the lines were drawn by Howard Berman's brother, Michael Berman.

THIRTY-FIRST DISTRICT

Rep. Xavier Becerra (D)

Elected 1992, 7th term; b. Jan. 26, 1958, Sacramento; home, Eagle Rock; Stanford U., B.A. 1980, J.D. 1984; Catholic; married (Carolina Reyes).

Elected Office: CA Assembly, 1990–92.

Professional Career: Staff Atty., Legal Assistance Corp. of Central MA; Dist. Dir., CA Sen. Art Torres, 1986; CA Dep. Atty. Gen., 1987–90.

DC Office: 1119 LHOB, 20515, 202-225-6235; Fax: 202-225-2202; Web site: www.house.gov/becerra.

District Office: Los Angeles, 213-483-1425.

Committees: *Ways & Means* (11th of 17 D): Human Resources; Social Security.

Group Ratings

	ADA	ACLU	AFS	LCV	ITIC	NTU	COC	ACU	NTLC	CHC
2004	95	95	100	100	70	9	29	0	0	8
2003	95	—	100	90	—	23	31	12	—	—

National Journal Ratings

	2003 LIB — 2003 CONS		2004 LIB — 2004 CONS	
Economic	92%	— 0%	97%	— 2%
Social	87%	— 12%	84%	— 15%
Foreign	83%	— 16%	88%	— 12%

Key Votes of the 108th Congress

1. Drilling in ANWR	N	5. DC School Vouchers	N	9. Ban Same-Sex Marriage	N
2. Approve Bush Tax Cuts	N	6. Ban Human Cloning	N	10. Fund Iraq War	N
3. Medicare/Rx Bill	N	7. Restrict Gun Liability	N	11. Bar Cuba Embargo Funds	Y
4. Bar Overtime Pay Regs.	Y	8. Ban Partial-Birth Abortion	N	12. Intelligence Reorg.	N

Election Results

2004 general	Xavier Becerra (D)	89,363	(80%)	($623,023)
	Luis Vega (R)	22,048	(20%)	
2004 primary	Xavier Becerra (D)	26,308	(89%)	
	Mervin Leon Evans (D)	3,103	(11%)	
2002 general	Xavier Becerra (D)	54,569	(81%)	($441,254)
	Luis Vega (R)	12,674	(19%)	

Prior Winning Percentages: 2000 (83%); 1998 (81%); 1996 (72%); 1994 (66%); 1992 (58%)

The People		Race/Ethnic Origin	Ancestry	
Area size:	40 sq. mi.	9.8% White	USA: 1.6%	German: 1.5%
Urban population:	100.0%	4.2% Black	Irish: 1.3%	
Rural population:	0.0%	13.8% Asian	**2004 Presidential Vote**	
Pop. 2000:	639,088	0.3% Native Am.	Kerry (D) 92,894	(77%)
Median income:	$26,093	0.1% Hawaiian	Bush (R) 26,054	(22%)
Poverty status:	30.1%	1.5% Two+ races	Other 1,815	(2%)
Military veterans:	3.7%	0.2% Other	**2000 Presidential Vote**	
		70.2% Hispanic Origin	Gore (D) 79,560	(77%)
			Bush (R) 19,400	(19%)
			Other 4,156	(4%)
			Cook Partisan Voting Index: D +30	

Occupation	Blue collar: 33.7%	White collar: 44.1%	Gray collar: 22.2%

Surrounding downtown Los Angeles are neighborhoods just now becoming antique, as mid-20th century buildings stop looking familiar and start taking on the patina of the historic. Downtown LA, with its 1980s marble slabs and pink cylinders jutting up to 70 stories from what was once a low-rise business district, has become surprisingly pedestrian-friendly, with attractive plazas like the one around the dazzlingly redesigned Los Angeles Library. But downtown is detached from the neighborhoods around, which change character with every new immigration flow. South of downtown is the garment district, with factories in nondescript buildings, an economically vibrant area with high rents and one of the reasons Los Angeles has become the largest manufacturing city in America today; the anti-sweatshop movement has struggled to maintain new facilities here, while attempting to compete with overseas manufacturers. To the north is Lincoln Heights, a heavily Hispanic area centering on the busy shopping street of North Broadway where residents have been fighting gangs and graffiti, and the neighborhoods of Highland Park and Eagle Rock, white middle-class 30 years ago, now mostly Latino but with Asians as well. West of downtown are Pico Union, an entry point for new immigrants; lower Sunset Boulevard; University Park, which surrounds the University of Southern California campus; and Thai Town along Hollywood Boulevard between Normandie and Western. Lower Sunset Boulevard and Echo Park have become lively shopping strips filled with that rare L.A. commodity: pedestrians. Hollywood has long had a seedy look—it has not sprouted the office buildings you can see in Burbank or Glendale, because of Los Angeles's high taxes and daffy regulations— but has recently been spiffed up.

Almost all of these areas, centering geographically on Dodger Stadium, are part of California's 31st Congressional District. In Los Angeles's booming 1980s these neighborhoods were suddenly thronged with immigrants, more thickly populated than a quarter-century before, with small houses and garden apartments full of large families and many children. In the 1990s, the population surge stopped and this became the slowest-growing district in California, as the newcomers of the decade before moved out to middle class neighborhoods and as incoming immigrants spread more evenly around the Los Angeles Basin. This remains a district of immigrants, though: It ranks first in the nation with its non-citizens (41%) and last in the nation in homes where English is spoken (21%). The population here is 70% Hispanic and 14% Asian.

The congressman from the 31st District is Xavier Becerra, a Democrat first elected in 1992. He grew up in Sacramento, went to college and law school at Stanford, worked for legal services, then worked for state Senator Art Torres and Attorney General John Van de Kamp, and married a Harvard Medical School graduate who became vice president of California's largest health-care foundation. In 1990 he was elected to the Assembly. In 1992, when Edward Roybal, California's first Latino congressman, announced late in the game that he was retiring, Becerra jumped into the race. His main Latino competitor, Leticia Quezada, was a member of the Los Angeles school board, a powerful engine for publicity. But Becerra had the endorsements of Roybal and County Supervisor Gloria Molina. In a primary in which only 33,000 voters turned out, Becerra won with 32% to 22% for Quezada. His 10,417 votes effectively made him the representative of more than half a million people.

In the House, he has been a consistent liberal. His pleasant and businesslike manner combined with his obvious ambition could make him a force in the House, but his views have limited his effectiveness in a Republican House. He said declaring English as the official language "sends a message of intolerance for those trying to learn English." He opposed a law to allow local law enforcement agents to enter pacts with the Department of Justice to enforce immigration laws. He opposed restrictions on bilingual education and Republican efforts to stop census sampling techniques.

On the Ways and Means Committee, Becerra advocated tax changes to prevent the overseas exodus of jobs in the entertainment industry, including a tax credit for labor costs of independent film producers. He supported normal trade relations with China and won House approval of his resolution supporting reunification efforts between North and South Korea. His support for free-trade deals with Chile and Singapore led to local protests by union activists, but he demanded changes in the labor standards in the Central American Free Trade Agreement. He opposed expansion of Los Angeles International Airport and favors development of outlying airports. He enacted a bill renaming a Western Avenue post office for the late singer Nat King Cole. He sponsored a bill that would forgive student loans for graduates who work as librarians in poor neighborhoods. On Social Security, he objected when Ways and Means chairman Bill Thomas suggested race or gender could be among the factors used for determining future Social Security benefits.

Becerra ran for mayor of Los Angeles in 2001. But he did not raise enough money to establish name recognition outside his district and was overshadowed by former Assembly Speaker Antonio Villaraigosa. Villaraigosa reportedly said he would drop out if Becerra agreed not to run again for the House even if he lost the Mayor's race; Becerra was not interested in such a deal. In the primary, Becerra was scarcely a presence in the ad wars and he finished fifth, with 6% of the vote, far behind Villaraigosa's 30% and James Hahn's 25%; Hahn won the runoff. Among the 21% of voters who were Hispanic, Villaraigosa led Becerra 62%–17%. Post-election analyses noted that Becerra damaged his standing among Latino leaders with negative campaign telephone calls.

While Villaraigosa ran again in 2005 and defeated Hahn, Becerra seems content to move up the seniority ladder at Ways and Means. In March 2005, he took pride in his selection by House leaders to fill the seat on the board of regents of the Smithsonian Institution, which had been left vacant by the death of Robert Matsui. "The Smithsonian museums are among this country's most endearing treasures and I look forward to helping maintain and enhance their coveted works of art." He earlier called for a commission to study creation of a new museum of the American Latino, which would be located on the National Mall and would be part of the Smithsonian.

THIRTY-SECOND DISTRICT

Rep. Hilda Solis (D)

Elected 2000, 3d term; b. Oct. 20, 1957, Los Angeles; home, El Monte; CA St. Polytechnic U., B.A. 1979; U. of S. CA, M.A. 1981; Catholic; married (Sam Sayyad).

Elected Office: CA Assembly, 1992–94; CA Senate 1994–00.

Professional Career: Editor, White House Ofc. of Hispanic Affairs, 1980–81; Management Analyst, Ofc. of Management & Budget, 1981.

DC Office: 1725 LHOB, 20515, 202-225-5464; Fax: 202-225-5467; Web site: solis.house.gov.

District Offices: East Los Angeles, 323-307-9904; El Monte, 626-448-1271.

Committees: *Energy & Commerce* (22d of 26 D): Energy & Air Quality; Environment & Hazardous Materials (RMM).

Group Ratings

	ADA	ACLU	AFS	LCV	ITIC	NTU	COC	ACU	NTLC	CHC
2004	100	95	100	100	40	8	25	0	0	7
2003	100	—	100	100	—	23	21	8	—	—

National Journal Ratings

	2003 LIB	—	2003 CONS	2004 LIB	—	2004 CONS
Economic	92%	—	0%	94%	—	5%
Social	92%	—	0%	88%	—	0%
Foreign	94%	—	0%	98%	—	0%

Key Votes of the 108th Congress

1. Drilling in ANWR	N	5. DC School Vouchers	N	9. Ban Same-Sex Marriage	N
2. Approve Bush Tax Cuts	N	6. Ban Human Cloning	N	10. Fund Iraq War	N
3. Medicare/Rx Bill	N	7. Restrict Gun Liability	N	11. Bar Cuba Embargo Funds	Y
4. Bar Overtime Pay Regs.	Y	8. Ban Partial-Birth Abortion	N	12. Intelligence Reorg.	N

Election Results

2004 general	Hilda Solis (D)	119,144	(85%)	($527,054)
	Leland Faegre (Lib)	21,002	(15%)	
2004 primary	Hilda Solis (D)	unopposed		
2002 general	Hilda Solis (D)	58,530	(69%)	($450,512)
	Emma Fischbeck (R)	23,366	(27%)	($20,031)
	Michael McGuire (Lib)	3,183	(4%)	

Prior Winning Percentages: 2000 (79%)

The People		Race/Ethnic Origin	Ancestry	
Area size:	93 sq. mi.	14.8% White	German: 3.1%	Irish: 2.5%
Urban population:	100.0%	2.6% Black	English: 2.2%	
Rural population:	0.0%	18.4% Asian	**2004 Presidential Vote**	
Pop. 2000:	639,087	0.3% Native Am.	Kerry (D) 99,286	(62%)
Median income:	$41,394	0.1% Hawaiian	Bush (R) 58,341	(37%)
Poverty status:	18.0%	1.4% Two+ races	Other 1,756	(1%)
Military veterans:	6.3%	0.1% Other	**2000 Presidential Vote**	
		62.3% Hispanic Origin	Gore (D) 96,217	(67%)
			Bush (R) 45,018	(31%)
			Other 3,057	(2%)
			Cook Partisan Voting Index: D +17	

Occupation   Blue collar: 32.7%   White collar: 51.3%   Gray collar: 16.0%

Anyone interested in the future of America and today's immigrants should drive straight east from downtown Los Angeles on I-10, the San Bernardino Freeway, through the string of suburbs that grew up in the 1940s and 1950s. These were once white middle-class communities, with grid streets of stucco houses above the dry riverbeds; they were filled with Midwest and East Coast migrants who discovered California during World War II and decided to stay, or who learned of its golden reputation from the new medium of television in the days before smog became part of the language. The atmosphere then was Midwestern, cheerful, busy, with children always underfoot. The next generation resulted in almost a complete population turnover here, but some things remained the same. Mexican-Americans spread out from their original East Los Angeles base to become majorities in blue-collar suburbs like El Monte, Baldwin Park, Azusa and West Covina, all with many more residents than in their Anglo days. Chinese and other Asians are the majority in Monterey Park and 49% of the population in Rosemead. *New York Times* food maven R.W. Apple Jr. described "a memorable week in the gastronomic trenches" of the local Asian restaurant scene, and reported that "it is easier to buy bok choy than iceberg" in Monterey Park. Almost every neighborhood here is mixed, with people whose origins are in different continents and cultures. The new people here have upgraded the neighborhoods, bringing in energy and money, the enthusiasm of the young and the community-spiritedness of the homeowner. There are busy shops with new signs, newly painted homes with carefully tended gardens, neighborhoods still filled with children whose parents believe in traditional values. When blacks and Latinos were rioting in South Central and Hollywood in 1992, East Los Angeles and the San Gabriel Valley were quiet and orderly. Some time later in this century, novels will be written about these immigrant suburbs, which will surely tell more about the human condition than stories about the clueless youth of Beverly Hills.

The 32d Congressional District of California covers much of this territory. It includes part of East Los Angeles and a small part of Los Angeles, most of Monterey Park and all of Rosemead, El Monte, Baldwin Park, Azusa, West Covina and Covina. It is 62% Hispanic and 18% Asian—the second-highest Asian percentage and one of the lowest percentages of non-Hispanic whites in southern California. Politically, the new Latinos and Asians have been up for grabs. In the early 1990s Asians, dismayed that the civic elite seemed more interested in ministering to the complaints of rioters than compensating the store owners whose property was ruined and lives threatened, moved toward the Republicans. In the middle 1990s Latinos, because of Republican immigration and welfare laws removing aid to legal immigrants—and because Republican campaign ads suggested Latinos were more interested in welfare than work—moved heavily toward the Democrats; Asians moved a bit in the same direction. Republicans Arnold Schwarzenegger and Tom McClintock together won nearly half of the Latino vote in the 2003 recall of Gray Davis as governor, according to exit polls. This was assumed to be a heavily Democratic district when it was created by the 2001 redistricting. But it voted 50.2% to recall Gray Davis in October 2003, and 13 months later its percentage for George W. Bush rose from 31% to 37%: at least a considerable part of the Latino vote seems to be up for grabs.

The congresswoman from the 32d District is Hilda Solis, a Democrat first elected in 2000. She is the daughter of a Teamsters Union shop steward from Mexico and an assembly line worker from Nicaragua who met while taking citizenship courses in Los Angeles. She graduated from California State Polytechnic University in 1979 and from the University of Southern California. She worked in the Carter White House's Office of Hispanic Affairs. Solis began her career as an elected official in 1984 when she won a seat on the Rio Hondo Community College Board of Trustees. She was elected to the Assembly in 1992, and in 1994 became the first Latina elected to the state Senate. Her work for environmental justice led the John F. Kennedy Library Foundation to give her a Profiles in Courage Award. In 2000, she ran against Congressman Matthew Martinez. He was originally elected in 1982 with the support of Congressman Howard Berman and Henry Waxman; he lost support among feminist and labor activists by voting for a ban on late-term abortions and fast-track trade authority and helping to stall gun control. Solis was endorsed by labor unions, EMILY's List, the Sierra Club, Senator Barbara Boxer and Congresswoman Loretta Sanchez. Martinez was supported by colleagues Lucille Roybal-Allard and Grace Napolitano; Berman and Waxman, no longer much involved in local politics, were neutral. Solis raised four times as much money as Martinez and had hundreds of volunteers from reinvigorated unions and local grass-roots organizations. The contest was caustic; she won 62%–29%, and had no Republican opposition. After the primary, a bitter Martinez switched parties, but his efforts to urge Latinos to vote Republican fell flat.

In the House, Solis has been among the most liberal members. Viewing her role in Republican-controlled Washington as mostly defensive, she opposed the Bush administration's fiscal policy and fought proposals to weaken worker safety regulations. She complained that the Nielsen television ratings undercounted Latinos. Solis showed her good standing with Nancy Pelosi by becoming the fourth California Democrat to gain a highly-sought seat on the Energy and Commerce Committee, and is ranking Democrat on its Environment and Hazardous Materials Subcommittee—a good fit with her career work.

Solis has scored some legislative successes. She was among the early sponsors of the bill to give citizenship eligibility to immigrants who have served a year in the military, which George W. Bush signed in November 2003; previous law required three years of service. She enacted a bill for the Interior Department to restore the water flow of the San Gabriel River and study ways to create more green space and urban recreation areas. Recalling childhood picnics and noting that many of her constituents don't have the luxury to visit Yosemite, she told the *Los Angeles Times,* "It's part of me, part of my soul . . . .We haven't paid attention to it." She enacted another bill in 2003 to name a post office in Duarte for Francisco Martinez Flores, a Marine who was among the first casualties in the Iraq war. She broke her earlier alliance and had bitter arguments with Loretta Sanchez by backing Hector De La Torre against her sister Linda Sanchez in the 2002 primary for the new 39th District. She was easily reelected in 2002 and 2004.

THIRTY-THIRD DISTRICT

Rep. Diane Watson (D)

Elected June 2001, 2d full term; b. Nov. 12, 1933, Los Angeles; home, Los Angeles; U.C.L.A., B.A. 1954, CA State L.A., M.A. 1968, Claremont U., Ph.D. 1987; Catholic; single.

Elected Office: L.A. Bd. of Education, 1975–78; CA Senate, 1978–98.

Professional Career: Teacher & school psychologist, 1954–75; lecturer, CA State L.A. & CA State Long Beach; U.S. Ambassador, Micronesia 1999–2001.

DC Office: 125 CHOB, 20515, 202-225-7084; Fax: 202-225-2422; Web site: www.house.gov/watson.

District Office: Los Angeles, 323-965-1422.

Committees: *Government Reform* (11th of 17 D): Criminal Justice, Drug Policy & Human Resources; Energy & Resources (RMM). *International Relations* (19th of 23 D): Africa, Global Human Rights & International Operations; Asia & the Pacific; International Terrorism & Nonproliferation.

Group Ratings

	ADA	ACLU	AFS	LCV	ITIC	NTU	COC	ACU	NTLC	CHC
2004	85	89	100	82	67	10	16	0	0	7
2003	100	—	100	90	—	28	21	13	—	—

National Journal Ratings

	2003 LIB — 2003 CONS		2004 LIB — 2004 CONS	
Economic	92%	0%	95%	4%
Social	90%	8%	88%	0%
Foreign	84%	14%	83%	17%

Key Votes of the 108th Congress

1. Drilling in ANWR	N	5. DC School Vouchers	N	9. Ban Same-Sex Marriage	N
2. Approve Bush Tax Cuts	N	6. Ban Human Cloning	N	10. Fund Iraq War	N
3. Medicare/Rx Bill	N	7. Restrict Gun Liability	N	11. Bar Cuba Embargo Funds	Y
4. Bar Overtime Pay Regs.	Y	8. Ban Partial-Birth Abortion	N	12. Intelligence Reorg.	N

Election Results

2004 general	Diane Watson (D)	166,801	(89%)	($259,663)
	Bob Weber (Lib)	21,513	(11%)	
2004 primary	Diane Watson (D)	unopposed		
2002 general	Diane Watson (D)	97,779	(83%)	($1,481,123)
	Andrew Kim (R)	16,699	(14%)	
	Other	3,971	(3%)	

Prior Winning Percentages: 2001 (75%)

The People		Race/Ethnic Origin	Ancestry	
Area size:	48 sq. mi.	19.9% White	German: 2.8%	Irish: 2.4%
Urban population:	100.0%	29.9% Black	English: 2.1%	
Rural population:	0.0%	12.1% Asian	**2004 Presidential Vote**	
Pop. 2000:	639,088	0.2% Native Am.	Kerry (D) 172,382	(83%)
Median income:	$31,655	0.1% Hawaiian	Bush (R) 33,132	(16%)
Poverty status:	23.5%	2.8% Two+ races	Other 2,631	(1%)
Military veterans:	6.5%	0.4% Other	**2000 Presidential Vote**	
		34.6% Hispanic Origin	Gore (D) 148,978	(83%)
			Bush (R) 24,214	(14%)
			Other 6,067	(3%)
			Cook Partisan Voting Index: D +36	
Occupation	Blue collar: 17.8%	White collar: 63.9%	Gray collar: 18.4%	

One of the myths of the Los Angeles riots of 1992 and 1965 is that black Angelenos live in conditions of isolation and poverty. Some do. But in levels of income and in degree of residential integration with non-blacks, Los Angeles blacks rank among the top in the United States. Its black-owned businesses have the highest revenues of any city in the nation. Californians have historically shown less prejudice toward blacks than most Americans, and job opportunities in Los Angeles—up to and including the office of mayor for 20 years—have been plenteous for blacks. This is apparent in the hills just west of Crenshaw, an Art Deco neighborhood built in the 1920s and 1930s in vacant flat land southwest of downtown LA and the birthplace of West Coast hip-hop music. Here, in Baldwin Hills, where on clear days you can see the towers of downtown and the snow-capped San Gabriel Mountains beyond, is a high-income black neighborhood, one of the strongest in the country. Near Windsor Hills along Slauson Avenue, other comfortable black-majority neighborhoods have been built. In the more rundown Crenshaw area, former L.A. Laker Magic Johnson built his successful multiplex theaters. With Olympic Boulevard as its main street, Koreatown has become a center for the city's cultural and business life; Aroma, a large new futuristic shopping center and spa along Wilshire Boulevard, caters to affluent Koreans. On the site of the old Ambassador Hotel, the Los Angeles Unified School District decided to build a school rather than approve retail shops. To the north at Hollywood Boulevard, near the tourist mecca of the famed Grauman's Chinese Theatre, a huge new complex includes the Kodak Theater, which hosts the Oscars plus many live entertainment shows.

This part of Los Angeles is the heart of the 33d Congressional District, which runs from the Golden State Freeway southwest to Culver City and almost to the Pacific Ocean. It includes most of Koreatown, centered on Western Avenue and Olympic Boulevard, and includes some of Hollywood and the affluent Los Feliz neighborhoods to the east. It is 35% Hispanic, 30% black and 12% Asian, with a sizable Korean population. But many Latinos are not citizens or registered voters, and most likely a majority of Democratic primary voters here are black, though that may no longer be true in 2010. Politically, this is one of the most Democratic districts in the nation: John Kerry got 83% of the vote here in 2004. Affluent, well-educated blacks seem if anything to be culturally more liberal than low-income black voters who may have closer ties to church and tradition. Many have profited on the way up from some form of government intervention—a student loan, a public sector job, racial quotas and preferences—and many still hold public sector jobs.

The congresswoman from the 33d District is Diane Watson, first elected in a June 2001 special election. She grew up in Los Angeles and graduated from UCLA. She worked as an elementary school teacher, school psychologist and lecturer at Cal State Los Angeles. Watson began her political career in 1975 as the first black woman elected to the Los Angeles Board of Education, where she worked on school desegregation issues. Three years later, she ran for the state Senate, again becoming the first black woman in that body. She served as chairman of the Health and Human Services Committee for 17 years before term limits forced her to retire in 1998. She stirred controversy in 1989 when she defended legislative perks that have since been outlawed; she argued that legislators deserved special treatment because they were not "ordinary people." In 1999, Watson was confirmed as U.S. Ambassador to Micronesia; she returned home to run in the special election to replace Julian Dixon, who died in December 2000.

In that contest, which effectively was decided in the Democratic primary, her chief opponents were state Senator Kevin Murray and Councilman Nate Holden. Watson's theme was familiarity. Murray argued that, at 41 and 26 years younger than Watson and 30 years younger than Holden, he could build seniority; Watson countered by campaigning with her 91-year-old mother. Watson was funded by EMILY's List; in the waning days of the race, she was backed by Magic Johnson. Murray was endorsed by Dixon's widow Bettye, Maxine Waters, Henry Waxman and Howard Berman. Holden was endorsed by outgoing Mayor Richard Riordan. Watson won 33% of the vote, to 26% for Murray and 17% for Holden. On her victory night, she angrily attacked the party leaders who opposed her. In the June runoff, she won 75%–20% over a Republican who spent $709,000 of her own money on her campaign.

Watson has a solidly liberal voting record. She drew protests from California dentists by sponsoring a bill to prohibit the use of mercury amalgams in dental fillings; Watson responded that the California legislature had banned mercury thermometers and was reviewing the use of dental amalgams. Later, she demanded that Kellogg stop placing a Spiderman toy in its cereal boxes because it contained a mercury battery. She strongly opposed President Bush's nomination of California Supreme Court Justice Janice Rogers Brown to the federal appeals court in the District of Columbia: "This Bush nominee has such an atrocious civil rights record that she makes Clarence Thomas look like Thurgood Marshall." On the International Relations Committee, she was an observer of the 2003 presidential recall election in Venezuela. She joined other Black Caucus members in calling for United Nations monitors of the 2004 U.S. presidential election. In November 2004, she gained attention when she claimed that she had tipped off federal agents to an alleged terror plot at an Albany, New York mosque; law enforcement authorities said that they had launched a sting operation months earlier. Watson is ranking Democrat on the Government Reform Subcommittee on Energy and Resources.

If Governor Arnold Schwarzenegger gains approval of his redistricting referendum, small shifts of lines in this district could have a major impact for ethnic groups in a primary here.

THIRTY-FOURTH DISTRICT

Rep. Lucille Roybal-Allard (D)

Elected 1992, 7th term; b. June 12, 1941, Los Angeles; home, Los Angeles; CA State L.A., B.A. 1965; Catholic; married (Edward Allard).

Elected Office: CA Assembly, 1986–92.

DC Office: 2330 RHOB, 20515, 202-225-1766; Fax: 202-226-0350; Web site: www.house.gov/roybal-allard.

District Office: Los Angeles, 213-628-9230.

Committees: *Appropriations* (21st of 29 D): Homeland Security; Labor, Health and Human Services, Education & Related Agencies. *Standards of Official Conduct* (4th of 5 D).

Group Ratings

	ADA	ACLU	AFS	LCV	ITIC	NTU	COC	ACU	NTLC	CHC
2004	100	95	100	100	40	8	35	0	0	7
2003	100	—	100	90	—	20	27	8	—	—

National Journal Ratings

	2003 LIB	—	2003 CONS		2004 LIB	—	2004 CONS
Economic	92%	—	0%		97%	—	3%
Social	92%	—	0%		88%	—	0%
Foreign	88%	—	11%		82%	—	18%

Key Votes of the 108th Congress

1. Drilling in ANWR	N	5. DC School Vouchers	N	9. Ban Same-Sex Marriage	N
2. Approve Bush Tax Cuts	N	6. Ban Human Cloning	N	10. Fund Iraq War	N
3. Medicare/Rx Bill	N	7. Restrict Gun Liability	N	11. Bar Cuba Embargo Funds	Y
4. Bar Overtime Pay Regs.	Y	8. Ban Partial-Birth Abortion	N	12. Intelligence Reorg.	N

Election Results

2004 general	Lucille Roybal-Allard (D)	82,282	(74%)	($572,055)
	Wayne Miller (R)	28,175	(26%)	
2004 primary	Lucille Roybal-Allard (D)	unopposed		
2002 general	Lucille Roybal-Allard (D)	48,734	(74%)	($449,244)
	Wayne Miller (R)	17,090	(26%)	

Prior Winning Percentages: 2000 (85%); 1998 (87%); 1996 (82%); 1994 (81%); 1992 (63%)

The People		Race/Ethnic Origin	Ancestry		
Area size:	59 sq. mi.	11.4% White	German: 2.0%	USA: 1.9%	
Urban population:	100.0%	4.4% Black	Irish: 1.5%		
Rural population:	0.0%	5.5% Asian	**2004 Presidential Vote**		
Pop. 2000:	639,088	0.3% Native Am.	Kerry (D) 82,942	(69%)	
Median income:	$29,863	0.1% Hawaiian	Bush (R) 35,926	(30%)	
Poverty status:	26.0%	0.9% Two+ races	Other 1,654	(1%)	
Military veterans:	4.8%	0.1% Other	**2000 Presidential Vote**		
		77.2% Hispanic Origin	Gore (D) 76,876	(72%)	
			Bush (R) 27,384	(26%)	
			Other 1,901	(2%)	
			Cook Partisan Voting Index: D +23		

Occupation   Blue collar: 40.0%   White collar: 43.7%   Gray collar: 16.4%

A block from the 452-foot white tower of Los Angeles's "modern architecture" City Hall—long the symbol of the city, but now less spectacular than the nearby Westin Bonaventure Hotel and dwarfed by 60- and 70-story postmodern marble slabs and pink cylinders a few blocks away—is the huge retail shopping street of Broadway. The sidewalks are thronged with Latinos, the signs are mostly in Spanish, the merchandise is often strewn on tables: this could be Mexico City or Lima. It is Latin America transplanted a block from a gleaming symbol of Yankee propriety and gaudy emblems of North American prosperity. Broadway is neither the geographical nor spiritual center of Los Angeles's Latino communities and it is just one of many shopping and dining areas. But it is an emblem of the entry-level Latino neighborhoods of the nation's second-largest city, the places where many immigrants, not only from Mexico but from Central and South America, come to find a cheap place to live—doubling and tripling up with other families and single newcomers, close enough to drive an old car to work in factories and warehouses that fill so much of the acreage south and east of downtown.

Broadway and many of these entry-level neighborhoods are part of the 34th Congressional District of California. It includes downtown and Boyle Heights, once an entry neighborhood for Irish and Jewish immigrants and for the last 40 years predominantly Mexican-American. Near the Hollywood Freeway is the Cathedral of Our Lady of the Angels, the $190 million center of the nation's largest and most ethnically diverse Roman Catholic archdiocese, which Cardinal Roger Mahony dedicated as an "anchor for the ages." Another new landmark is the Walt Disney Concert Hall, home of the Los Angeles Philharmonic. Even though prostitution and drug sales flourish in other areas not far from City Hall, the commercial revival has spurred residential development in the central business district, with both new housing and renovations. The 34th also includes the giant factories south of downtown along the Southern Pacific Railroad and Santa Ana Freeway and it takes in part of East Los Angeles. To the south it includes the garment factories of Vernon and the 1940s working-class suburbs: Huntington Park—with its vibrant shopping strip on the wide Pacific Boulevard and with a youthful population that has more than doubled since 1980—Bell and Bell Gardens, Commerce, Maywood and Cudahy, all of which are now heavily Latino. To the south are the more affluent suburbs of Bellflower, which was a prime shopping area decades ago and recently has started a comeback, and Downey, home of the Boeing (formerly Rockwell) plant that built the space shuttle. Bisecting much of the district is the concrete-lined Los Angeles River, which civic activists want to convert to an artificial lake with giant rubber dams. The drenching rainstorms of 2004–05 helped to fill the LA basin's water supply and sharply reduced the days with dangerous smog levels.

The 34th District is 77% Hispanic, the highest percentage in any California district. Politically, this area is heavily Democratic, but with just 4% black residents the 34th is less Democratic than some neighboring districts. It is not clear what the future political preferences of people here will be, for the large majority of adults here do not vote. In 2004, in a constituency of 639,000 people, only 120,000 voted in the general election, far less than the 333,000 who voted in the Westside 30th District.

The congresswoman from the 34th District is Lucille Roybal-Allard, first elected in 1992, the daughter of 30-year Congressman Edward Roybal. His roots were in New Mexico, not Mexico, and in 1949 he was the first Latino elected to the Los Angeles city council. Lucille Roybal-Allard dreamed of a show business career as a teenager and later worked as a department store clerk and for non-profit organizations. After raising a family—her two children are both lawyers—she entered politics at age 45, with the encouragement of local activists. She was elected to the Assembly in 1986. She entered the 1992 House race before her father announced his retirement in the adjacent district, and she easily won, with 75% in the primary and 63% in the general election.

The first Mexican-American woman elected to Congress, Roybal-Allard has compiled a solidly liberal voting record. On the Appropriations Committee, where her father had been a subcommittee chairman, she has worked on immigration issues. On other issues, she won House passage of an amendment to allow breastfeeding in national parks and museums. She has sought to focus on underage drinking, including a call for higher taxes on alcohol and restraints on advertising. She secured $2.5 million for an anti-gang program for Boyle Heights and East LA. In June 2004, the House passed her amendment to prevent the privatizing of services for immigration information officers or investigators. With Republican Chris Cannon, she filed a bill to provide in-state college tuition for children of illegal immigrants. In December 2004, she was selected for the ethics panel to review charges against Representative Jim McDermott, which stem from a lawsuit that John Boehner filed against him for the 1996 taping of a cell-phone call between Boehner and Newt Gingrich.

Back home, in her office at the Edward R. Roybal Federal Building, Roybal-Allard sponsors health fairs and workshops on home buying and U.S. citizenship. She wants to revive downtown's former Red Car trolley line, a five-mile loop that would include Staples Center and Chinatown, with possible expansion to USC to the south and Echo Park to the north. She has been reelected without difficulty.

THIRTY-FIFTH DISTRICT

Rep. Maxine Waters (D)

Elected 1990, 8th term; b. Aug. 15, 1938, St. Louis, MO; home, Los Angeles; CA State L.A., B.A. 1970; Christian; married (Sidney Williams).

Elected Office: CA Assembly, 1976–90.

Professional Career: Head Start teacher, 1966; Dpty., City Councilman David Cunningham, 1973–76.

DC Office: 2344 RHOB, 20515, 202-225-2201; Fax: 202-225-7854; Web site: www.house.gov/waters.

District Office: Los Angeles, 323-757-8900.

Committees: *Chief Deputy Minority Whip. Financial Services* (3d of 32 D): Domestic and International Monetary Policy, Trade & Technology; Financial Institutions & Consumer Credit; Housing & Community Opportunity (RMM). *Judiciary* (9th of 17 D): Courts, the Internet & Intellectual Property; Crime, Terrorism & Homeland Security; Immigration, Border Security & Claims.

Group Ratings

	ADA	ACLU	AFS	LCV	ITIC	NTU	COC	ACU	NTLC	CHC
2004	95	100	100	91	20	11	12	4	0	16
2003	100	—	100	95	—	23	17	13	—	—

National Journal Ratings

	2003 LIB	—	2003 CONS		2004 LIB	—	2004 CONS
Economic	92%	—	0%		80%	—	19%
Social	92%	—	0%		88%	—	0%
Foreign	94%	—	0%		98%	—	0%

Key Votes of the 108th Congress

1. Drilling in ANWR	N	5. DC School Vouchers	N	9. Ban Same-Sex Marriage	N
2. Approve Bush Tax Cuts	N	6. Ban Human Cloning	*	10. Fund Iraq War	N
3. Medicare/Rx Bill	N	7. Restrict Gun Liability	N	11. Bar Cuba Embargo Funds	Y
4. Bar Overtime Pay Regs.	*	8. Ban Partial-Birth Abortion	N	12. Intelligence Reorg.	N

Election Results

2004 general	Maxine Waters (D)	125,949	(81%)	($330,980)
	Ross Moen (R)	23,591	(15%)	($3,540)
	Other	6,867	(4%)	
2004 primary	Maxine Waters (D)	unopposed		
2002 general	Maxine Waters (D)	72,401	(78%)	($262,943)
	Ross Moen (R)	18,094	(19%)	($75,114)
	Other	2,912	(3%)	

Prior Winning Percentages: 2000 (87%); 1998 (89%); 1996 (86%); 1994 (78%); 1992 (83%); 1990 (79%)

The People		Race/Ethnic Origin	Ancestry	
Area size:	55 sq. mi.	10.4% White	German: 2.0% Irish: 1.7%	
Urban population:	100.0%	34.1% Black	Subsaharan: 1.6%	
Rural population:	0.0%	5.6% Asian	**2004 Presidential Vote**	
Pop. 2000:	639,088	0.2% Native Am.	Kerry (D)	130,764 (79%)
Median income:	$32,156	0.3% Hawaiian	Bush (R)	33,110 (20%)
Poverty status:	26.4%	1.8% Two+ races	Other	1,726 (1%)
Military veterans:	7.2%	0.2% Other	**2000 Presidential Vote**	
		47.4% Hispanic Origin	Gore (D)	118,450 (82%)
			Bush (R)	24,495 (17%)
			Other	2,262 (2%)
			Cook Partisan Voting Index: D +33	

Occupation   Blue collar: 28.3%   White collar: 53.0%   Gray collar: 18.7%

Los Angeles in the years just after World War II was the fastest growing metropolitan area in America. If a traveler deplaning today at LAX could suddenly put himself in the postwar Los Angeles of 50 years ago, he would see quite a different city. LAX, today the nation's third-busiest airport, with eight central terminals, was then a small airfield, standing amid open country. The mile-square grids east, north and south of the airport were just filling up with rapidly built subdivisions. North of the airport on open fields you would find the spanking new middle class Westchester subdivision; just beyond you would see the wetlands along Ballona Creek, where Howard Hughes took his Spruce Goose, the largest airplane ever built, up for its one and only flight. Inglewood, the rapidly growing suburb just east of the airport around the Hollywood Park Race Track, was filling up with the young families of people who had moved to Los Angeles during or after the war—workers in the giant aircraft factories or in the small factories built by entrepreneurs manufacturing products that Californians got from factories back East before the war. Inglewood would become a focus of sports fans when the Forum opened in 1967, the home of the Los Angeles Lakers for 32 years. In Hawthorne, just to the south, home of a big Northrop Grumman plant, future celebrities were growing up—Sonny Bono and the Beach Boys. Gardena, east of Hawthorne, was famous for its legal poker clubs and its Japanese American residents, back from the wartime internment camps. East of Gardena is the part of Los Angeles called South Central or, more recently, South Los Angeles, after the city council in 2003 officially renamed this community to rid it of the stigma as a place of gang wars and race riots. In the days of residential segregation, much of this area was the home of Los Angeles's black community, its numbers greatly expanded by migration from the South during and after the war. Here you could find the Central Avenue entertainment district, at whose clubs and theaters you could see the likes of Ella Fitzgerald, Sarah Vaughn, Billy Eckstine, Duke Ellington, Louis Armstrong, Count Basie, Dizzy Gillespie and Charlie Parker. Later, it was the epicenter of L.A.'s two postwar riots, in the Watts district of Los Angeles in 1965 and at the corner of Florence and Normandie in 1992. In the last 20 years, Latinos have been buying houses here, which are among the cheapest in the metro area—only five L.A. zip codes have median prices below $200,000—and new businesses have been cropping up in garages and small factories.

The 35th Congressional District of California today is made up of all these areas, with a landscape and populations very different from what you would have found 50 years ago. At its west and east ends are two of the Los Angeles area's great transportation facilities. One is LAX and the cluster of hotels and office buildings all around; the swooping arches of LAX's theme building, intended in 1961 to symbolize the jet era, are now an historic landmark, like Disneyland's Tomorrowland or the *Jetsons*, an antique version of a surpassed future. In December 2004 the Los Angeles Council approved Mayor James Hahn's $11 billion expansion plan, which includes $500 million for soundproofing and other measures to placate nearby communities. The other is the Alameda Corridor, the 20-mile rail express line connecting the ports of Los Angeles and Long Beach with rail distribution points near downtown Los Angeles in a trench 33 feet below ground, built between 1997 and 2002 at a cost of $2.4 billion. Westchester, once all white, now is home to many blacks and Latinos. Inglewood, once all white, later mostly black, is now 46% Hispanic; it also has a school system that is producing some of the state's highest test scores. Hawthorne, with more Hispanics than whites or blacks, is home of the Western Museum of Flight. Gardena still has its poker clubs and a large Asian population. South Los Angeles, an almost entirely black neighborhood at the time of the Watts riot, now is home to more Hispanics than blacks: the 35th District's population in 2000 was 34% black and 47% Hispanic. Since the 1992 riot, local businesses have revived though it still has high crime rates and plenty of mistrust of local police, exacerbated in February 2005 when a policeman shot a 13-year-old boy who was stopped after a freeway chase and backed his stolen car toward police officers and into their cruiser. Politically, this is an overwhelmingly heavily Democratic district.

The congresswoman from the 35th District is Maxine Waters, a Democrat first elected in 1990. She grew up in St. Louis, one of 13 children; she has said, "I know all about welfare. I remember the social workers peeking in the refrigerator and under the beds." She moved to California in 1961; she worked in a garment factory and raised two children, got a sociology degree at California State University in Los Angeles and became an assistant Head Start teacher after the Watts riot of 1965. She likes to call herself "The Organizer", and has shown the capacity to draw big supportive crowds to her protests over the years. From 1973 to 1976 she worked on the staff of a Los Angeles councilman. In 1976 she won a seat in the California Assembly. She became a Democratic national committeewoman in 1980 and Phil Burton consulted her on the 1982 redistricting. When Augustus Hawkins retired in 1990 after 28 years in the House and 28 years in the California Assembly, Waters was the obvious choice for the seat and won it easily.

Waters comes from a background of poverty and believes with fervor in federal aid for the poor and for racial preferences to help blacks overcome years of slavery, segregation and discrimination; she has favored drastic reductions in defense spending. She was one of six members who voted against supporting the Gulf War once it started, asking how urban gang members could be expected to stop fighting when America's own leaders were waging battles. In March 2003 she was one of 11 members who voted against the resolution to support the troops in Iraq after battle began. She brings to her work a fury that is almost palpable, and an insistence that she will assert herself regardless of protocol, partly perhaps a result of anger but also a weapon she uses shrewdly to get both publicity and results. "I don't have time to be polite," she says, beginning her House career by getting herself included in a post-riot White House meeting with George H. W. Bush. The Los Angeles riot was occasion for both Waters' best and worst moments. She flew home immediately and roused the Department of Water and Power to restore water to the riot area, and was effective in gaining provisions to the post-riot emergency act that eventually made it through Congress and was signed into law. But she also suggested rioters were morally justified and claimed ominously, "Los Angeles is under siege," she said. "The violence could spill over to many other cities in this country."

Waters isn't afraid to step on toes in pursuit of her legislative agenda. She is a chief deputy Democratic whip. She has produced specific legislation and pushed Section 108 loan guarantees to cities for economic and infrastructure development. To the terrorism insurance bill she added an amendment for a 50% discount on deposit insurance premiums for low-income people with lifeline bank accounts. In a rare legislative success in the Republican House, Waters sponsored an amendment to triple spending for the erasure of the debts of poor nations, mostly in Africa; many Republicans agreed, and it passed 216–211. She has sponsored bills to repeal mandatory minimum sentences for drug crimes, and charges that the war on drugs has created "apartheid."

Her husband, a former professional football player and Mercedes Benz salesman, became Bill Clinton's ambassador to the Bahamas. But she voted against the crime bill rule in August 1994 when the administration desperately needed votes. Waters said she "could not vote for a crime bill that sweepingly expands the death penalty to include sixty new crimes." In 1996 and 1997, she attracted attention for pushing the theory, supported in a story in the *San Jose Mercury News* (later repudiated by the paper), that the CIA had worked with Nicaraguan Contras to import crack cocaine into South Central Los Angeles. During the Judiciary Committee's Clinton impeachment inquiry, she assailed "trumped-up charges" and said Kenneth Starr was "guilty" of "raw, unmasked, unbridled hatred and meanness that drives this impeachment coup d'etat."

Waters is a force to be reckoned with in L.A. politics as well. Other politicians are eager to be included on her Progressive Connections slates that are mailed out to many thousand black voters. Politicians pay to be included—a common California practice. In the April 2001 primary for city attorney Councilman Mike Feuer paid $10,000 to be on the slate and ran even in black areas with Deputy Mayor Rocky Delgadillo. But Feuer wouldn't pay $25,000 to be on the slate for the June runoff; Delgadillo paid $35,000 and got 65% in black areas. For mayor in 2001 she strongly supported City Attorney James Hahn over former Assembly Speaker Antonio Villaraigosa. Hahn is the son of Kenneth Hahn, Los Angeles County Supervisor for 40 years, whose work for black constituents made him beloved among black voters. Hahn won with the support of 80% of black voters and 60% of white voters; Hispanics heavily favored Villaraigosa. After Hahn won, Waters approached banker and *LA Focus* owner Jheryl Busby and insisted he fire columnist Najee Ali, who had backed Villaraigosa. Busby fired Ali in July 2001. Ali sued Busby, and Busby's attorney said Busby "told me he needs a positive relationship with Waters because of her ability to help him with his bank and other business interests." (Waters is on the Financial Services Committee). But Waters sharply opposed Hahn in February 2002 when he urged the 10-member Police Commission not to reappoint Chief Bernard Parks. Waters wrote an opinion article strongly criticizing Hahn. "The city of Los Angeles deserves better leadership than he has shown. His father would not be proud of that. . . . Mr. Mayor it is you—not Chief Parks—who has failed to earn the right to serve a second term." In March 2005 she supported Villaraigosa against Hahn. "Jimmy Hahn is not Kenny Hahn. We gave him a chance. He's failed, so we're moving on." She was one of the most visible opponents of an Inglewood referendum to permit a Wal-Mart superstore; it was defeated 61%–39% April 2004 in a turnout of 11,000 in a city of 115,000. Waters was one of the few officials to oppose November 2004's Measure A, a .5% sales tax increase to pay for more police officers; it failed to get the needed two-thirds majority and got less than 50% in South Los Angeles. She opposed Hahn's LAX expansion plan and drew more than 1,000 to protest the proposed closing of the trauma unit in King/Drew hospital, a county facility which, a *Los Angeles Times* investigation found, is much more costly than other hospitals because of high spending per patient, high payments to injured and absentee employees and high fees to doctors.

Waters has been reelected without difficulty. The 2001 redistricting removed some black areas from the district and added Westchester, LAX and Lawndale, which do not have large black percentages. The one potential threat to her tenure is the rising Hispanic percentage in the district; blacks are still a majority of Democratic primary voters, but that may no longer be true in 2010. Her strong support of James Hahn over Antonio Villaraigosa in the 2001 Los Angeles mayor race risked angering Latino voters; the late labor leader Miguel Contreras said that many Latinos in her district felt that she "played the race card against the Latino candidate." Her support of Villaraigosa in 2005 may have soothed any angry feelings on this. She is one of many Democrats who has sought a seat on the Appropriations, but with Republicans in control open seats have been scarce, and she has not been successful yet.

THIRTY-SIXTH DISTRICT

Rep. Jane Harman (D)

Elected 2000, 3d term; b. June 28, 1945, New York, NY; home, Venice; Smith Col., B.A. 1966, Harvard U., J.D. 1969; Jewish; married (Sidney).

Elected Office: U.S. House of Reps., 1992–98.

Professional Career: Legis. Dir., U.S. Sen. John Tunney, 1972–73; Chief Cnsl. & Staff Dir., Senate Judiciary Subcmtee., 1973–77; Dep. Cabinet Secy., White House, 1977; Defense Dept. Special Cnsl., 1979; Harman Intl. Industries, Corp. Secy., 1985–92, Dir., 1990–92; Practicing atty., 1970–72, 1982–92; Regents Prof., U.C.L.A., 1999.

DC Office: 2400 RHOB, 20515, 202-225-8220; Fax: 202-226-7290; Web site: www.house.gov/harman.

District Offices: El Segundo, 310-643-3636; Wilmington, 310-549-8282.

Committees: *Homeland Security* (5th of 15 D): Emergency Preparedness, Science & Technology; Intelligence, Information Sharing & Terrorism Risk Assessment; Prevention of Nuclear & Biological Attack. *Permanent Select Committee on Intelligence* (RMM of 9 D).

Group Ratings

	ADA	ACLU	AFS	LCV	ITIC	NTU	COC	ACU	NTLC	CHC
2004	95	68	88	91	80	16	55	13	12	16
2003	85	—	100	100	—	25	45	20	—	—

National Journal Ratings

	2003 LIB	—	2003 CONS		2004 LIB	—	2004 CONS
Economic	66%	—	34%		66%	—	33%
Social	73%	—	26%		71%	—	29%
Foreign	70%	—	27%		73%	—	26%

Key Votes of the 108th Congress

1. Drilling in ANWR	N	5. DC School Vouchers	N	9. Ban Same-Sex Marriage		*
2. Approve Bush Tax Cuts	N	6. Ban Human Cloning	N	10. Fund Iraq War		N
3. Medicare/Rx Bill	N	7. Restrict Gun Liability	N	11. Bar Cuba Embargo Funds		Y
4. Bar Overtime Pay Regs.	Y	8. Ban Partial-Birth Abortion	N	12. Intelligence Reorg.		N

Election Results

2004 general	Jane Harman (D)	151,208	(62%)	($763,781)
	Paul Whitehead (R)	81,666	(33%)	($68,635)
	Other	11,170	(5%)	
2004 primary	Jane Harman (D)	unopposed		
2002 general	Jane Harman (D)	88,198	(61%)	($1,206,046)
	Stuart Johnson (R)	50,328	(35%)	($158,318)
	Mark McSpadden (Lib)	5,225	(4%)	

Prior Winning Percentages: 2000 (48%); 1996 (52%); 1994 (48%); 1992 (48%)

The People		Race/Ethnic Origin	Ancestry	
Area size:	122 sq. mi.	48.4% White	German: 8.0%	Irish: 6.6%
Urban population:	100.0%	4.1% Black	English: 6.2%	
Rural population:	0.0%	13.4% Asian	**2004 Presidential Vote**	
Pop. 2000:	639,087	0.3% Native Am.	Kerry (D) 154,010 (59%)	
Median income:	$51,633	0.4% Hawaiian	Bush (R) 103,425 (40%)	
Poverty status:	12.7%	2.9% Two+ races	Other 3,558 (1%)	
Military veterans:	8.8%	0.3% Other	**2000 Presidential Vote**	
		30.3% Hispanic Origin	Gore (D) 130,752 (57%)	
			Bush (R) 88,619 (39%)	
			Other 9,423 (4%)	
			Cook Partisan Voting Index: D +11	

Occupation	Blue collar: 16.1%	White collar: 71.1%	Gray collar: 12.8%

For many southern Californians, there is no better place to be than the beach. It is not a perfect environment: In the morning there may be mists, the winter air is damp and clammy, even in summer the weather can be chilly, the water is never very warm and is sometimes polluted. But for many this is echt-California, and in this democratic polity, there is a beach to suit the taste of just about everyone, many of them with their unique piers and athletes, especially volleyball. The funkiest of all is Venice, with its beach houses plus some expensive new mansions jammed together, its long-stagnant canals dug by a developer in 1904 and paved over in the late 1920s to make way for cars, and the boardwalk where skateboarding got its start and roller blade sports are *de rigueur*. To the south is Marina Del Rey, with sleek modern apartment complexes and expensive yacht moorings, and, south of LAX, El Segundo, named for Chevron's second oil refinery; now it has big office buildings. Next are Manhattan Beach, one of the favorites four decades ago of the Beach Boys who grew up a couple of miles inland in Hawthorne, and tiny Hermosa Beach, with tightly packed frame houses, originally the homes of elderly retirees, now filled with the young and would-be young. Many of the beaches enforce no-smoking rules. Farther south are the flower-planted rises of Redondo Beach and the larger city of Torrance, whose vast inland expanse is the home of the North American headquarters of both Honda and Toyota (and to large Korean and Japanese communities). Just to the east, overlooking L.A.'s eerily modern container port, are Wilmington and San Pedro, once working-class, but moving up as well.

The 36th Congressional District of California includes most of this beach territory, from Venice south to San Pedro (both of which are within the Los Angeles city limits, though the area in between is not). California today is mostly multiethnic, but the beach communities are still, as if in the 1950s, filled mostly with white Anglos. This is one of four California districts that were made more Democratic by redistricting to accommodate a Democrat who narrowly replaced a Republican in 2000. This area is still leery of taxes, but culturally it is libertarian—against restrictions or even aspersions on its various lifestyles. This has been one of America's leading defense and aerospace areas, where Howard Hughes built planes half a century ago and where so much of the 1980s defense buildup took place. With its many military and space operations, Boeing is the largest private employer in the area, including its assembly operation in El Segundo. There was speculation that Los Angeles Air Force Base, which has no runways but works closely with nearby aerospace companies, might be a target for base closing but it did not appear on the Pentagon's May 2005 base closure list.

The congresswoman from the 36th District is Democrat Jane Harman, who regained the seat in 2000 that she held for six years before running for governor in 1998. Born in New York City, she grew up in Los Angeles as the daughter of a Westside physician and was in the gallery as a volunteer usher when John F. Kennedy was nominated at the 1960 Democratic National Convention in Los Angeles. She graduated from Smith College and Harvard Law School, when women were still rare there. In the 1970s, she worked for California Senator John Tunney and the Senate Judiciary Committee. She served in the Carter White House and as a special counsel in the Defense Department. Later, she practiced law and worked as a lobbyist in Washington.

Harman is one of the richest members of Congress; her husband Sidney Harman is founder of audio-equipment maker Harman International Industries, and she has spent large amounts of her own money on her campaigns.

In 1992, the "year of the woman," she campaigned as "pro-choice and pro-change," defeating a pro-life Republican woman 48%–42% in a new district; she was narrowly reelected in 1994 and 1996. (Nearly a decade later, the Federal Election Commission found that Harman received $21,000 in illegal contributions from Hughes Aircraft in her 1994 campaign, but ruled that the violation was not deliberate.) She decided late to run for governor in 1998 and spent more than $20 million, including $15 million of her own money, but finished a disappointing third among Democrats, far behind Gray Davis. Congressional and state Democrats lobbied her hard to reclaim her former House seat, which Republican Steven Kuykendall narrowly won in 1998. Kuykendall supported abortion rights and took liberal stands on environmental issues; many Democrats believed that only Harman could defeat him. She attacked Kuykendall for failing to support the Democrats' proposal for a prescription drug benefit in Medicare and for voting to repeal the estate tax, and tried to tie him to House Republican leaders. She stressed her earlier House record, economically somewhat conservative and culturally liberal. Kuykendall was hurt by the lack of appeal of George W. Bush in coastal California. This was a race targeted by both parties, with each candidate spending nearly $2 million. After more than a week of absentee ballot counting, Kuykendall conceded; Harman won 48%–47%.

On her return to the House, Harman joined Energy and Commerce. Her voting record has been among the most conservative of Democrats from California. Harman disappointed many Democrats by voting for the final version of trade promotion authority after initially opposing it; she cited improved worker training provisions. After September 11, her focus turned to national security. On the Intelligence Committee, she became ranking Democrat of the new Terrorism and Homeland Security Subcommittee. Working closely with chairman Saxby Chambliss, she criticized the CIA, FBI and National Security Agency for moving too slowly to share information and respond to terrorism threats. She was an early supporter of a Department of Homeland Security and she voted for the use of force in Iraq.

Nancy Pelosi, who was ranking Democrat on Intelligence, chose Harman to replace her after the 2002 election, despite a vigorous campaign by Sanford Bishop. At Pelosi's request, Harman took a leave of absence from Energy and Commerce. She agreed with the thrust of the 9/11 Commission's recommendations to give more authority to a national intelligence director and to unify intelligence resources. She worked closely with new chairman Pete Hoekstra and Senate Governmental Affairs Chairman Susan Collins in getting Congress to pass the intelligence reorganization bill in December 2004. Harman's bipartisanship and pragmatism occasionally rankled other Democrats on the committee and in the House. In February 2005, she called for a ban on torture by U.S. interrogators and a prohibition on transfer of detainees to countries that engage in torture.

Harman has been reelected easily since 2000, winning 62%–33% in 2004.

THIRTY-SEVENTH DISTRICT

Rep. Juanita Millender-McDonald (D)

Elected March 1996, 5th full term; b. Sept. 7, 1938, Birmingham, AL; home, Carson; U. of Redlands, B.S. 1979, CA State L.A., M.Ed. 1981; Baptist; married (James).

Elected Office: Carson City Cncl., 1990–92; Carson Mayor Pro–Tem, 1991–92; CA Assembly, 1992–96.

Professional Career: Teacher & Schl. Admin., 1981–90.

DC Office: 2445 RHOB, 20515, 202-225-7924; Fax: 202-225-7926; Web site: www.house.gov/millender-mcdonald.

District Office: Torrance, 310-538-1190.

Committees: *House Administration* (RMM of 3 D). *Small Business* (2d of 15 D): Tax, Finance & Exports (RMM). *Transportation & Infrastructure* (12th of 34 D): Aviation; Coast Guard & Maritime Transportation; Highways, Transit & Pipelines.

Group Ratings

	ADA	ACLU	AFS	LCV	ITIC	NTU	COC	ACU	NTLC	CHC
2004	75	82	100	73	44	8	35	9	0	20
2003	85	—	100	65	—	23	30	10	—	—

National Journal Ratings

	2003 LIB	—	2003 CONS		2004 LIB	—	2004 CONS
Economic	85%	—	14%		75%	—	25%
Social	75%	—	25%		88%	—	0%
Foreign	87%	—	13%		86%	—	14%

Key Votes of the 108th Congress

1. Drilling in ANWR	N	5. DC School Vouchers	N	9. Ban Same-Sex Marriage	N
2. Approve Bush Tax Cuts	N	6. Ban Human Cloning	*	10. Fund Iraq War	N
3. Medicare/Rx Bill	N	7. Restrict Gun Liability	N	11. Bar Cuba Embargo Funds	*
4. Bar Overtime Pay Regs.	Y	8. Ban Partial-Birth Abortion	N	12. Intelligence Reorg.	N

Election Results

2004 general	Juanita Millender-McDonald (D)	118,823	(75%)	($307,056)
	Vernon Van (R)	31,960	(20%)	
	Herb Peters (Lib)	7,535	(5%)	
2004 primary	Juanita Millender-McDonald (D)	27,047	(65%)	
	Albert Robles (D)	7,800	(19%)	
	Peter Mathews (D)	6,802	(16%)	
2002 general	Juanita Millender-McDonald (D)	63,445	(73%)	($244,632)
	Oscar Velasco (R)	20,154	(23%)	($14,093)
	Herb Peters (Lib)	3,413	(4%)	

Prior Winning Percentages: 2000 (82%); 1998 (85%); 1996 (85%); 1996 (27%)

The People		Race/Ethnic Origin	Ancestry	
Area size:	75 sq. mi.	16.6% White	German: 3.2% Irish: 2.7%	
Urban population:	100.0%	24.8% Black	English: 2.4%	
Rural population:	0.0%	11.1% Asian	**2004 Presidential Vote**	
Pop. 2000:	639,088	0.3% Native Am.	Kerry (D)	126,068 (74%)
Median income:	$34,006	1.4% Hawaiian	Bush (R)	43,160 (25%)
Poverty status:	25.2%	2.4% Two+ races	Other	2,281 (1%)
Military veterans:	8.1%	0.2% Other	**2000 Presidential Vote**	
		43.2% Hispanic Origin	Gore (D)	112,235 (76%)
			Bush (R)	31,832 (22%)
			Other	3,712 (3%)
			Cook Partisan Voting Index: D +27	

Occupation	Blue collar: 29.0%	White collar: 53.5%	Gray collar: 17.5%

Long Beach, founded in 1888, with 475,000 people in 2003, would be a major metropolis almost anywhere but in Los Angeles County, where it seems just the largest of many suburbs. But it has an identity of its own. Started as a beach resort, it soon became a port when Los Angeles civic leaders decided that if their town were to be a world-class city it must have a world-class harbor; nature not having provided one, they built it where the Los Angeles River flows into the ocean at the western edge of Long Beach. By 1909, Los Angeles had annexed the harbor towns of San Pedro and Wilmington on the other side of the river; over the next decades the two cities persuaded federal government to dredge channels and build a breakwater and turning basins. Long Beach was developing other businesses as well. It sprouted oil derricks in the 1920s and briefly became one of the nation's big oil producers; it was the site of major aircraft plants in the 1940s and after. Since then, the Los Angeles-Long Beach port has become the nation's largest, the fastest-growing major cargo center in the world, with huge steel-gray container ships pulling quietly up to enormous automated loading facilities—a 21st century contrast to the rotting docks of New York and San Francisco. The length of three football fields, these ships unload a daily average of 12,000 containers, which is nearly half of the nation's containerized goods and is vital for its commerce; from there, about half of the cargo leaves by rail along the new $2.5 billion, high-speed 20-mile Alameda Corridor to the large rail yards near downtown Los Angeles. Although the cargo has faced a huge increase in inspections since September 11, including scanning at the port of all high-risk containers, cargo security remains a major problem. Long Beach's naval station was closed in the 1990s and there were job losses at the huge McDonnell Douglas aircraft; Boeing, the new owner, announced in January 2005 that it would stop producing commercial jets here. But small businesses have grown, and Long Beach's beachfront has thrived; the *Queen Mary,* converted into a floating hotel, is a big tourist attraction, and there is a glittering array of high-rises along the beach.

The 37th Congressional District of California includes 80% of the city of Long Beach (but not the harbor), and Signal Hill, surrounded by Long Beach, where the oil rigs are still pumping. It includes two industrial suburbs of Compton and Carson. Compton switched from all-white to all-black in the 1960s and in the 1980s became heavily Latino and economically depressed; lately it has been mentioned as a possible site for an Indian casino. Carson, with recent subdivisions amid freeway interchanges and tank farms, has a multiethnic population. The district includes the south end of South Central Los Angeles, including the Watts tower near which the riot of 1965 broke out. In 2000 the district's population was 25% black and 43% Hispanic, but many of the Hispanics are not U.S. citizens and do not vote here. It is a heavily Democratic district.

The congresswoman from the 37th District is Juanita Millender-McDonald, first chosen in a 1996 special election. She was born in Alabama, raised a family in Carson, and earned a bachelor's degree in 1979, at 40. She worked as a teacher and editor/writer for the Los Angeles Unified School District and was manuscript editor for *IMAGES*, a state textbook designed for young women to enhance self-esteem. She later became director of gender equity programs for the district and was appointed to the National Commission on Teaching and America's Future. In 1990 she was elected to the Carson City Council. In 1992 she ran for the Assembly and beat an incumbent in the primary.

Her opening to run for Congress came in December 1995, when two-term Congressman Walter Tucker was convicted of extortion and tax fraud as mayor of Compton and sentenced to 27 months in federal prison. A special election was set for the following March, the same day as the regular primary; since no Republican ran, it determined the winner. Already running and better known was Assemblyman Willard Murray, who had been chief of staff to former Congressman Mervyn Dymally. But with help from EMILY's List, Millender-McDonald raised much more money. Murray had other problems, including his support for building a prison for Compton, which voters there turned down 87%–13%. Millender-McDonald won the nine-candidate special with 27% to 20% for Murray.

In the House, Millender-McDonald has a liberal voting record. She got a seat on the Transportation and Infrastructure Committee, where she made the Alameda Corridor her chief priority. She backed the Chinese government-owned China Ocean Shipping Company's bid to build a container terminal at the former Long Beach Naval Air Station. But despite its likely benefits for the port, she voted against normal trade relations with China because of its human rights abuses. She created a congressional Goods Movement Caucus to focus on shipping issues, especially problems related to the Long Beach port, and she called for more security funding at the ports. She co-chaired the Caucus on Women's Issues, where she focused on the impact of proposed Social Security reform and led opposition to the bill making it a crime to harm a fetus during an assault on a pregnant woman. In January 2005 Minority Leader Nancy Pelosi named Millender-McDonald as ranking Democrat on the House Administration Committee.

She has easily won re-election. Despite the fact that 40% of the district was new to her in 2002, she had modest competition. In the 2002 primary she beat Peter Mathews by a 78%–22% margin. In 2004, Mathews ran again and lost the primary 65%–16% with Carson businessman Albert Robles getting 19%. Millender-McDonald easily won the general each time. She may face a serious Latino challenger before the decade is out, and could face even greater jeopardy if the proposed redistricting referendum of Arnold Schwarzenegger gains approval. In October 2004, her son Keith McDonald, a Los Angeles water district official, was convicted of extortion in a case involving municipal contracts; Millender-McDonald was not implicated.

THIRTY-EIGHTH DISTRICT

Rep. Grace Napolitano (D)

Elected 1998, 4th term; b. Dec. 4, 1936, Brownsville, TX; home, Norwalk; Brownsville H.S.; Catholic; married (Frank).

Elected Office: Norwalk City Cncl., 1986–92; Norwalk Mayor, 1989–92; CA Assembly, 1992–98.

Professional Career: Employee, Ford Motor Co., 1970–1992.

DC Office: 1609 LHOB, 20515, 202-225-5256; Fax: 202-225-0027; Web site: www.napolitano.house.gov.

District Office: Santa Fe Springs, 562-801-2134.

Committees: *International Relations* (17th of 23 D): Europe & Emerging Threats; Western Hemisphere. *Resources* (13th of 22 D): Water & Power (RMM).

Group Ratings

	ADA	ACLU	AFS	LCV	ITIC	NTU	COC	ACU	NTLC	CHC
2004	95	80	100	100	40	9	33	0	0	15
2003	95	—	100	90	—	20	24	8	—	—

National Journal Ratings

	2003 LIB	—	2003 CONS		2004 LIB	—	2004 CONS
Economic	92%	—	0%		96%	—	3%
Social	84%	—	13%		84%	—	15%
Foreign	93%	—	6%		85%	—	14%

Key Votes of the 108th Congress

1. Drilling in ANWR	N	5. DC School Vouchers	N	9. Ban Same-Sex Marriage	N
2. Approve Bush Tax Cuts	N	6. Ban Human Cloning	N	10. Fund Iraq War	N
3. Medicare/Rx Bill	N	7. Restrict Gun Liability	N	11. Bar Cuba Embargo Funds	Y
4. Bar Overtime Pay Regs.	Y	8. Ban Partial-Birth Abortion	N	12. Intelligence Reorg.	N

Election Results

2004 general	Grace Napolitano (D)	unopposed		($273,757)
2004 primary	Grace Napolitano (D)	26,632	(79%)	
	Michael Manzo (D)	7,122	(21%)	
2002 general	Grace Napolitano (D)	62,600	(71%)	($283,868)
	Alex Burrola (R)	23,126	(26%)	
	Other	2,301	(3%)	

Prior Winning Percentages: 2000 (71%); 1998 (68%)

The People		Race/Ethnic Origin	Ancestry	
Area size:	105 sq. mi.	13.6% White	German: 2.7% Irish: 1.8%	
Urban population:	100.0%	3.6% Black	English: 1.8%	
Rural population:	0.0%	10.2% Asian	**2004 Presidential Vote**	
Pop. 2000:	639,088	0.3% Native Am.	Kerry (D) 106,652	(65%)
Median income:	$42,488	0.1% Hawaiian	Bush (R) 54,869	(34%)
Poverty status:	16.3%	1.4% Two+ races	Other 1,846	(1%)
Military veterans:	6.8%	0.1% Other	**2000 Presidential Vote**	
		70.6% Hispanic Origin	Gore (D) 104,612	(70%)
			Bush (R) 41,706	(28%)
			Other 2,929	(2%)
			Cook Partisan Voting Index: D +20	

Occupation   Blue collar: 34.1%   White collar: 50.7%   Gray collar: 15.2%

One of the great population surges in the United States is the upward social movement of the hundreds of thousands of immigrants in the Los Angeles Basin, from crowded entry-level neighborhoods out on freeways to the suburbs. It is visible east and southeast of Los Angeles, in suburbs that over a generation have changed from solidly white Anglo to largely Latino. Many people here have made their way up working in small smokeless factories along railroad tracks and near river beds, beneath roaring freeways and on grid streets near stucco garden apartment blocks and in small business offices and stores; these have made Los Angeles the nation's top manufacturing metro area, surpassing Chicago in recent years. Their values resemble those of working-class Americans of the 1960s: pro-family and respectful of traditional personal morals (L.A.-area Latinos have lower than average divorce rates), patriotic and hard-working (Latino males have the highest work force participation of any measured group and the incomes of U.S.-born Los Angeles County Latinos are at the county average).

Vast numbers of these new residents live in the 38th Congressional District of California, where the percentage of Hispanics in 2000 was 71%, the second highest of any California district. This is a swath of Los Angeles County anchored by four primarily Hispanic suburbs. To the northwest is Montebello (Italian for "beautiful hill"), a working-class suburb just beyond East Los Angeles, where there is a cultural divide between Americanized residents and the "TJ" crowd that acts as though they are still in Tijuana; heavy traffic on the Union Pacific tracks here has produced calls to place the rail line underground to minimize dangers and routine interference. To the east is La Puente, a center of the light manufacturing economy that created hundreds of thousands of jobs in the Los Angeles Basin, and in which increasing numbers of small businesses are owned by Asians, Latinos and blacks. Farther east is the old town of Pomona, the district's largest city, now much expanded and site of the Los Angeles County Fair, but long troubled by gang wars. To the south are Norwalk, a rail crossroad astride the Santa Ana Freeway, 63% Hispanic, and Santa Fe Springs.

The congresswoman from the 38th District is Grace Napolitano, a Democrat first elected in 1998. Napolitano grew up in the Lower Rio Grande Valley of Texas, married at 18, and had five children and moved to California by the time she was 23. She worked as a secretary at Ford Motor Company for 22 years. After her first husband died, she married Frank Napolitano and in 1980 they started a pizzeria business. She served on the city council in Norwalk from 1986 to 1992 and served one term as mayor, becoming the first Latino to hold each position. In 1992 she was elected to the California Assembly from a seat that covered much of this congressional district.

Term-limited in 1998, she got the opportunity to run for Congress when 16-year incumbent Esteban Torres announced three days before the filing deadline that he was retiring. Torres's surprise move seemed designed to promote the election of Jamie Casso, his son-in-law and chief of staff, who immediately announced his candidacy. But Napolitano was not deterred. She convinced the state AFL-CIO to vote an "open endorsement," although the executive board had backed Casso, and Torres had been a senior United Auto Workers official in the 1960s.

Napolitano and Casso waged a fierce campaign. She criticized him for not living in the district; he criticized her $180,000 loan to her campaign at an unusual 18% interest rate. Torres was featured prominently in Casso's campaign literature and appearances. Napolitano had the financial backing of national women's organizations, including EMILY's List, plus the benefit of higher name identification. The two candidates had few differences on major issues; Napolitano signed a pledge to serve only three terms. Napolitano won the primary by 618 votes. Her victory in November was routine.

In the House, she has a generally liberal voting record. As the new chairman of the Congressional Hispanic Caucus in 2005, she urged efforts to reshape the way that the Democratic Party reaches out to Hispanic voters. But Napolitano has shown the ability to get a lot done on issues that are often not associated with the Hispanic community. On the Resources Committee, where she is ranking Democrat on the Water and Power Subcommittee, Napolitano was active in the reauthorization in 2004 of the California Bay-Delta water allocation program, which featured unusual bipartisanship among Californians, including Resources Committee Chairman Richard Pombo. "The key to solving California's water problems is in building partnerships, working together and bringing all parties to the table," she said when the measure was passed. In committee, Napolitano removed the 25% limit on how much of the federal total for new water conservation projects can go to CALFED; she later sponsored her own version of the bill that removed approval of additional projects outside California. With Pennsylvania's Tim Murphy, she co-founded the congressional Mental Health Caucus, on which Napolitano focused on the needs of veterans. She initially became interested in mental health issues after reading a report that showed comparatively high suicide rates among Hispanic girls. "Mental health is treatable. But we [the Latino community] have a stigma attached to it. We don't want to see it, we don't want to hear it, we don't want to feel it. We hide it." She blamed, in part, the "macho mentality."

Napolitano's work has played well at home. She has not been seriously challenged for reelection. In February 2003, she abandoned her earlier pledge and announced she plans to run for reelection two more times and then retire after serving five terms. In November 2004, she was the only Democrat in California who was reelected without opposition.

THIRTY-NINTH DISTRICT

Rep. Linda Sanchez (D)

Elected 2002, 2d term; b. Jan. 28, 1969, Orange; home, Lakewood; U. of CA, B.A. 1991, U.C.L.A., J.D. 1995; Catholic; married (Mark Valentine).

Professional Career: Practicing atty., 1995–98; Exec. Secy. Treas. of Orange Cnty. AFL-CIO, 2000–02.

DC Office: 1007 LHOB, 20515, 202-225-1012; Fax: 202-226-1012; Web site: www.house.gov/lindasanchez.

District Office: Lakewood, 562-429-8499.

Committees: *Government Reform* (14th of 17 D): Criminal Justice, Drug Policy & Human Resources; National Security, Emerging Threats & International Relations. *Judiciary* (15th of 17 D): Courts, the Internet & Intellectual Property; Immigration, Border Security & Claims. *Small Business* (12th of 15 D).

Group Ratings

	ADA	ACLU	AFS	LCV	ITIC	NTU	COC	ACU	NTLC	CHC
2004	100	95	100	100	22	8	20	0	0	0
2003	100	—	100	95	—	21	24	8	—	—

National Journal Ratings

	2003 LIB	—	2003 CONS		2004 LIB	—	2004 CONS
Economic	92%	—	0%		97%	—	2%
Social	92%	—	0%		83%	—	17%
Foreign	89%	—	8%		83%	—	16%

Key Votes of the 108th Congress

1. Drilling in ANWR	N	5. DC School Vouchers	N	9. Ban Same-Sex Marriage	N
2. Approve Bush Tax Cuts	N	6. Ban Human Cloning	N	10. Fund Iraq War	N
3. Medicare/Rx Bill	N	7. Restrict Gun Liability	N	11. Bar Cuba Embargo Funds	Y
4. Bar Overtime Pay Regs.	Y	8. Ban Partial-Birth Abortion	N	12. Intelligence Reorg.	N

Election Results

2004 general	Linda Sanchez (D)	100,132	(61%)	($782,521)
	Tim Escobar (R)	64,832	(39%)	($772,577)
2004 primary	Linda Sanchez (D)	unopposed		
2002 general	Linda Sanchez (D)	52,256	(55%)	($1,074,253)
	Tim Escobar (R)	38,925	(41%)	($218,239)
	Richard Newhouse (Lib)	4,165	(4%)	

The People		**Race/Ethnic Origin**	**Ancestry**	
Area size:	65 sq. mi.	21.0% White	German: 4.3%	Irish: 3.3%
Urban population:	100.0%	6.1% Black	English: 3.0%	
Rural population:	0.0%	9.5% Asian	**2004 Presidential Vote**	
Pop. 2000:	639,088	0.3% Native Am.	Kerry (D) 102,660	(59%)
Median income:	$45,307	0.3% Hawaiian	Bush (R) 70,635	(40%)
Poverty status:	15.7%	1.5% Two+ races	Other 2,110	(1%)
Military veterans:	7.1%	0.1% Other	**2000 Presidential Vote**	
		61.2% Hispanic Origin	Gore (D) 98,478	(62%)
			Bush (R) 56,067	(36%)
			Other 3,390	(2%)
			Cook Partisan Voting Index: D+13	

Occupation   Blue collar: 31.2%   White collar: 55.0%   Gray collar: 13.9%

In the years just after World War II much of southeast Los Angeles County was farmland—citrus groves, dairy farms. Then in the next two decades subdivisions were built and new cities incorporated so that what had been a few separate towns separated by farmland became one continuous swatch of suburbia. The separate towns were different in character. Whittier, founded by Midwestern Quakers, was the hometown of Richard Nixon, a young lawyer thinking about running for Congress in early 1946 who was inaugurated as vice president of the United States seven years later. South Gate and Lynwood, with new auto and other factories, filled up with newcomers from the South. Lakewood, just north of Long Beach, was built up so rapidly in the 1950s from former lima bean fields that it was featured in *Life* magazine as one of the first mass-produced suburbs. Other towns grew later; there were still dairy farms in Cerritos in the 1970s.

The 39th Congressional District of California is made up of a heterogeneous and oddly shaped collection of these suburbs. It is shaped like a U. On the east end of the U are two-thirds of Whittier, all of South and West Whittier and La Mirada. The bottom end of the U includes Lakewood, the classic fast-growing post-war suburb, and in former dairy country, Cerritos, Artesia and Hawaiian Gardens. The west end of the U includes South Gate, Lynwood, Paramount and the eastern fringe of South Central Los Angeles: these were once working class white, then mostly black, then heavily Latino. The district's population is 61% Hispanic and 10% Asian. At a local motor vehicle office, the written exam can be taken in 33 languages. As this area grew in the postwar years it was pretty closely divided between the parties. But in the 1990s it trended Democratic. This new district was created by redistricting in 2001, and was intended to be a safe seat for California Democrats. It voted 62%–36% for Al Gore in 2000 but only 59%–40% for John Kerry in 2004.

The congresswoman from the 39th District is Linda Sanchez, a Democrat first elected in 2002, and the junior member of the first pair of sisters ever elected to Congress. They are the oldest and youngest of seven children of Ignacio Sanchez, a machinist, and Maria Macias. Loretta Sanchez, who is nine years older, was elected to the House in 1996 when she unseated Republican Robert Dornan in an Orange County district. Linda Sanchez graduated from Berkeley and UCLA law school. She became a civil rights lawyer and was executive secretary-treasurer of the Orange County Federation of Labor. "She's definitely the more liberal one," Loretta said. Linda later explained to the *Los Angeles Times* the key to the family's success. "Immigrants have more hope. They seek out opportunities more than people who have things . . . .[My parents] were very forward-looking. They saw the value of education." Their five other siblings include two business owners, a mortgage broker, a securities broker, and a civil engineer.

When the district lines were unveiled, Linda Sanchez was one of six Democrats who ran. Her most important asset was her sister's support. Linda Sanchez tapped Loretta's extensive fundraising network, walked precincts with her and appeared in a television commercial with her. In the Spanish language ad, their mother urged voters to send both of her daughters to Capitol Hill. All this gave Linda Sanchez an advantage over her two chief opponents, who started off better known—two-term Assemblywoman Sally Havice and South Gate Councilman Hector De La Torre, who had worked several years in Washington as a legislative aide and Labor Department official. There were few differences between them on major issues, and the campaign turned negative in the closing weeks. Sanchez's labor ties helped her build a strong voter turnout operation; the L.A. County AFL-CIO endorsed both Sanchez and Havice. With help from her sister, Sanchez was endorsed by then-Minority Whip Nancy Pelosi. Her opponents replied that Sanchez had received no endorsements from other Latino members of Congress; Hilda Solis, whom Loretta Sanchez backed in her first House race in 1998, endorsed De La Torre. They charged that Linda Sanchez was a political opportunist who changed her name and residence to run in the newly-created district; like her sister, Sanchez had used her non-Latino married name until she started to run for the House. Sanchez won with 33% of the vote, to 29% for De La Torre and 19% for Havice. Afterwards the Long Beach *Press-Telegram* attacked Sanchez's tactics: "It may have been the only way for Sanchez to win, as an unemployed labor activist with little political experience, but the tactics were deceptive, dishonest and mean." This district is not as Democratic as the four other LA-based Hispanic-majority districts, and Sanchez's negative primary campaign may have hurt her. Republican Tim Escobar, a financial adviser and former Army helicopter pilot, said Sanchez was an inexperienced liberal extremist; he quoted the bitter remarks of her primary opponents. But Sanchez won 55%–41%.

In the House, the election of the two sisters generated largely flattering national press coverage. But it waned after it became evident that their service in the minority party in the House limited their influence and activity. Linda Sanchez has a strongly liberal voting record. With Republican Jack Quinn, she filed the "Bullying Prevention for School Safety and Crime Reduction Act," with federal funds to help stop bullying; she got the proposal included in the Justice Department authorization bill, but it died in the Senate. Other legislative priorities included an increase in small-business loan limits from $35,000 to $50,000, and reimbursement of states for the cost of incarcerating illegal immigrants who have committed crimes in this country. She called for the State Department to investigate the murder of a U.S. Teamsters activist who was working to organize truck drivers in El Salvador. She attacked the House Republican proposal to deny drivers' licenses to undocumented immigrants, for "using national security as a facade to alienate law-abiding and taxpaying immigrants."

In 2004, Escobar ran again and spent $773,000, more than three times as much money as in his first race and more than the total spent by Sanchez. But she had a bigger win this time, 61%–39%, and attributed the improvement to her efforts as an incumbent.

FORTIETH DISTRICT

Rep. Ed Royce (R)

Elected 1992, 7th term; b. Oct. 12, 1951, Los Angeles; home, Fullerton; CA State Fullerton, B.A. 1977; Catholic; married (Marie).

Elected Office: CA Senate, 1982–92.

Professional Career: Tax Mgr., 1979–82.

DC Office: 2202 RHOB, 20515, 202-225-4111; Fax: 202-226-0335; Web site: www.royce.house.gov.

District Office: Fullerton, 714-992-8081.

Committees: *Financial Services* (8th of 37 R): Capital Markets, Insurance & Government Sponsored Enterprises; Financial Institutions & Consumer Credit; Oversight & Investigations. *International Relations* (8th of 27 R): Africa, Global Human Rights & International Operations (Vice Chmn.); International Terrorism & Nonproliferation (Chmn.); Oversight & Investigations.

Group Ratings

	ADA	ACLU	AFS	LCV	ITIC	NTU	COC	ACU	NTLC	CHC
2004	15	0	13	18	80	85	90	96	97	92
2003	10	—	0	10	—	69	87	92	—	—

National Journal Ratings

	2003 LIB	—	2003 CONS		2004 LIB	—	2004 CONS
Economic	41%	—	57%		41%	—	59%
Social	24%	—	71%		0%	—	91%
Foreign	11%	—	80%		17%	—	78%

Key Votes of the 108th Congress

1. Drilling in ANWR	Y	5. DC School Vouchers	Y	9. Ban Same-Sex Marriage	Y
2. Approve Bush Tax Cuts	Y	6. Ban Human Cloning	Y	10. Fund Iraq War	Y
3. Medicare/Rx Bill	Y	7. Restrict Gun Liability	Y	11. Bar Cuba Embargo Funds	N
4. Bar Overtime Pay Regs.	N	8. Ban Partial-Birth Abortion	Y	12. Intelligence Reorg.	Y

Election Results

2004 general	Ed Royce (R)	147,617	(68%)	($736,717)
	Tilman Williams (D)	69,684	(32%)	
2004 primary	Ed Royce (R)	unopposed		
2002 general	Ed Royce (R)	92,422	(68%)	($845,661)
	Christina Avalos (D)	40,265	(29%)	($10,452)
	Other	3,955	(3%)	

Prior Winning Percentages: 2000 (63%); 1998 (63%); 1996 (63%); 1994 (66%); 1992 (57%)

The People		Race/Ethnic Origin	Ancestry	
Area size:	102 sq. mi.	49.3% White	German: 9.3%	English: 6.8%
Urban population:	100.0%	2.2% Black	Irish: 6.8%	
Rural population:	0.0%	15.6% Asian	**2004 Presidential Vote**	
Pop. 2000:	639,088	0.3% Native Am.	Bush (R) 138,766	(60%)
Median income:	$54,356	0.4% Hawaiian	Kerry (D) 88,631	(39%)
Poverty status:	10.2%	2.4% Two+ races	Other 2,740	(1%)
Military veterans:	10.1%	0.2% Other	**2000 Presidential Vote**	
		29.6% Hispanic Origin	Bush (R) 119,443	(56%)
			Gore (D) 86,460	(41%)
			Other 5,886	(3%)
			Cook Partisan Voting Index: R + 8	

Occupation Blue collar: 22.1% White collar: 64.5% Gray collar: 13.4%

Orange County is the fifth most populous county in the United States, having grown steadily from 130,000 in 1940 to 703,000 in 1960, 1.9 million in 1980, 2.8 million in 2000 and just a hair under 3 million, 2,988,000 in 2004. It is now a community with the patina of maturity—in some places an aging community, fraying around the edges. The county can no longer double its population, as it did for several decades, when Disneyland sprung up on empty land and mile-square grids of orange groves and bean fields were transformed into one suburban subdivision, shopping center or office tower after another. Although developers have plans for a few more huge projects in the next decade, "We're outta land. We don't have any dirt left," a real estate analyst told the *Los Angeles Times* in 2003. A distinctive civilization was implanted here by ranchers and farmers, who settled the place and then gave way to Cold War aerospace engineers: mostly white and middle-class, confident of its traditional values and its market capitalism, proud of American principles and American military might. Orange County has been transformed in the years since by its openness to economic and ethnic change. Its economy was constantly reshaped by the inevitable upheavals of capitalism. There is no single industry here that is responsible for the prosperity of Orange County. It was hit hard by the defense cutbacks and recession of the early 1990s but it bounced back, pitched forward by new startups and small entrepreneurial successes not anticipated by government or corporate planners.

Always Republican, Orange County became a symbol of conservatism first in California and then nationally. This was a solid base for Ronald Reagan in his campaigns for governor and president. In 1988 its 317,000-vote plurality for George H. W. Bush was his largest in any county in the nation. Orange County's conservatism reflected a belief in technological progress and traditional values as unyielding as the mile-square grid the county's founders imposed on most of its land, a belief in the market economies that had produced such local wonders as Disneyland and the area's advanced military technologies. But problems developed. In 1994, the county government declared bankruptcy because of the county treasurer's sloppy investment and bookkeeping practices; shortly afterwards, the Disney company shelved plans for a $2 billion resort development that would have doubled the size of Disneyland. Orange County has rebounded, and so has Disney, which in 2001 opened its California Adventure amusement park on Disneyland property. Over the years Orange County has become racially and ethnically more diverse; contrary to the images presented in the TV series *The OC*, the all-white Orange County stereotype is now thoroughly out of date. Orange County's population in 2003 was 32% Hispanic and 16% Asian. And those percentages seem likely to rise; the median age of non-Hispanic whites was 40 while for Hispanics it was 25. In 2000 the county gave George W. Bush only a 149,000-vote margin; four years later, his margin was up to 222,000 votes, still well below his father's margin 16 years before.

The 40th Congressional District of California, located entirely in Orange County, consists of acreage that was mostly farmland when Disneyland was being laid out. At the geographic center is Fullerton, with its own branch of Cal State University, and named after rail executive George Fullerton, who extended the railroad there; to the southwest are Buena Park, home of Knott's Berry Farm, the earliest theme park (1940), plus Cypress, Los Alamitos, La Palma, Stanton, and parts of Garden Grove and Westminster. Southeast of Fullerton the district includes most of Placentia, a part of eastern Anaheim and all of Villa Park and Orange, the district's largest city. Overall the 40th District is 30% Hispanic, 16% Asian (primarily Korean, Vietnamese and Filipino) and 2% black.

The congressman from the 40th District is Ed Royce, a Republican first elected in 1992. His life almost precisely covers the area's growth. He grew up in Fullerton; he was in the Young Americans for Freedom at Cal State Fullerton and was the head of Youth for Reagan in California during his 1976 challenge to Gerald Ford. He worked several years as a tax and capital projects manager for a cement company. In 1982, a bunch of conservative legislators known as "the Cave Men" took him to a Black Angus restaurant—no avocado and sprout sandwiches for them—and persuaded him to run for the state Senate. He won at age 31. When the legislature refused to pass his bill allowing crime victims to object to trial delays, giving grand juries more power and ending shopping for juries, he put it on the ballot as an initiative and it passed by a wide margin. In 1992 Royce ran for the House. With the blessing of Orange County Republican leaders, he was unopposed in the Republican primary and easily won the general.

In the House, Royce has a conservative voting record, though a bit less so on economic issues. He co-chaired the House "porkbusters," risking others' wrath by opposing appropriations bills with dubious projects. With John McCain, he estimated that spending bills following the September 11 attacks had $14 billion in pork. His proposal to ensure that nonprofit religious organizations have access to all necessary financial resources was a forerunner of George W. Bush's faith-based initiative. On the Financial Services Committee, he worked with Paul Kanjorski to expand lending authority for credit unions.

As chairman for eight years of the International Relations Subcommittee on Africa and an ardent free-trader, Royce backed an Africa free trade bill with ranking Ways and Means Democrat Charles Rangel; it came at a time when, after three decades of economic stagnation and dictatorship, several African countries were moving toward market economics and democracy. Displaying legislative creativity, he helped steer the bill to enactment. When Congress passed trade promotion authority, it revised the bill to raise the cap on duty-free apparel imports from Africa. In 2004, he shepherded another revision to extend the period for duty-free treatment of imports. Although Royce had never set foot in Africa before he became chairman, he was widely praised for learning about the continent. His other initiatives on Africa included steps to encourage oil production while also promoting human rights, and encouragement of the Bush Administration to stop the genocide in Sudan. "The days of Africa being the lowest rung on the U.S. foreign policy ladder are ending," he said in 2004. Royce also has a strong interest in Asia; he co-chairs the Congressional Caucus on India and Indian Americans and urges stronger strategic and trade relationships between the United States and India. George W. Bush signed his bill establishing Radio Free Afghanistan as a tool in the fight against terrorism; later, with Zoe Lofgren, he filed a proposal for more open communication in Vietnam. In January 2005, Royce became chairman of the Subcommittee on International Terrorism and Nonproliferation, and said that he would focus on the spread of radical Islam.

Royce has been reelected by wide margins. After redistricting in 2001, half of the district was new to him, but he won 68% of the vote in 2002 and 2004.

FORTY-FIRST DISTRICT

Rep. Jerry Lewis (R)

Elected 1978, 14th term; b. Oct. 21, 1934, Seattle, WA; home, Redlands; U.C.L.A., B.A. 1956; Presbyterian; married (Arlene).

Elected Office: CA Assembly, 1968–78.

Professional Career: Insurance exec., 1959–78; Field rep., U.S. Rep. Jerry Pettis, 1968.

DC Office: 2112 RHOB, 20515, 202-225-5861; Fax: 202-225-6498; Web site: www.house.gov/jerrylewis.

District Office: Redlands, 909-862-6030.

Committees: *Appropriations* (Chmn. of 37 R).

Group Ratings

	ADA	ACLU	AFS	LCV	ITIC	NTU	COC	ACU	NTLC	CHC
2004	0	0	13	9	90	49	100	88	67	76
2003	5	—	0	5	—	58	100	84	—	—

National Journal Ratings

	2003 LIB	—	2003 CONS		2004 LIB	—	2004 CONS
Economic	9%	—	84%		20%	—	79%
Social	30%	—	65%		31%	—	67%
Foreign	31%	—	65%		17%	—	78%

Key Votes of the 108th Congress

1. Drilling in ANWR	Y	5. DC School Vouchers	Y	9. Ban Same-Sex Marriage	Y
2. Approve Bush Tax Cuts	Y	6. Ban Human Cloning	Y	10. Fund Iraq War	Y
3. Medicare/Rx Bill	Y	7. Restrict Gun Liability	Y	11. Bar Cuba Embargo Funds	N
4. Bar Overtime Pay Regs.	N	8. Ban Partial-Birth Abortion	Y	12. Intelligence Reorg.	Y

Election Results

2004 general	Jerry Lewis (R)	181,605	(83%)	($1,450,053)
	Peymon Mottahedek (Lib)	37,332	(17%)	
2004 primary	Jerry Lewis (R)	unopposed		
2002 general	Jerry Lewis (R)	91,326	(67%)	($645,070)
	Keith Johnson (D)	40,155	(30%)	
	Other	4,052	(3%)	

Prior Winning Percentages: 2000 (80%); 1998 (65%); 1996 (65%); 1994 (71%); 1992 (63%); 1990 (61%); 1988 (70%); 1986 (77%); 1984 (85%); 1982 (68%); 1980 (72%); 1978 (61%)

The People		Race/Ethnic Origin	Ancestry	
Area size:	13,350 sq. mi.	63.5% White	German: 11.7%	English: 8.4%
Urban population:	89.4%	5.3% Black	Irish: 8.3%	
Rural population:	10.6%	3.7% Asian	**2004 Presidential Vote**	
Pop. 2000:	639,087	1.0% Native Am.	Bush (R) 149,673	(62%)
Median income:	$38,721	0.2% Hawaiian	Kerry (D) 89,424	(37%)
Poverty status:	15.2%	2.7% Two+ races	Other 2,729	(1%)
Military veterans:	16.1%	0.2% Other	**2000 Presidential Vote**	
		23.4% Hispanic Origin	Bush (R) 114,498	(56%)
			Gore (D) 83,584	(41%)
			Other 5,116	(3%)
			Cook Partisan Voting Index: R + 9	
Occupation	Blue collar: 25.0%	White collar: 57.3%	Gray collar: 17.8%	

Over the last quarter-century the great American movement west has turned back east, at least in California. As settlement reached the Pacific Coast, young families looking for affordable houses, neighborhoods and schools, where traditional values are respected, moved away from the liberation-minded and high-crime coast and toward the sunny, often hot, valleys inland. This impulse has resulted in rapid growth in the Central Valley, the repopulation of the Mother Lode country in the foothills of the Sierras and the startling growth in the Inland Empire at the eastern end of the Los Angeles Basin, around San Bernardino and Riverside, and east and north past the mountain rims into the High Desert. This Inland Empire, generally defined as San Bernardino and Riverside Counties, though other definitions abound—grew from 1.6 million people in 1980 to 2.6 million in 1990, 3.2 million in 2000 and 3.8 million in 2004.

The 41st Congressional District covers some of the Inland Empire and the desert beyond the mountains. It includes most of the land area of San Bernardino County, which with 20,052 square miles is the largest county in the United States and is more than twice the size of New Jersey. Nearly half its population is concentrated in its southwest corner, in the Inland Empire, including the northern and eastern edges of San Bernardino and all of Loma Linda, Redlands, Highland, Yucaipa—small towns founded by pious Midwesterners at the base of 10,000-foot mountains. It also includes towns in Riverside County just to the south—Calimesa, Beaumont, Banning, San Jacinto. East of the mountains is the vast Mojave Desert, mostly uninhabited, but with growing clusters of population. In the Victor Valley are Hesperia and Apple Valley, new towns in the desert with 129,000 people between them. Roy Rogers and Dale Evans lived for years on a ranch here, with their stuffed horses Trigger, Buttermilk and Bullet in a nearby museum. The district includes the mountain country around Lake Arrowhead and Big Bear

Lake, Desert Hot Springs, the rustic town north of posh Palm Springs, and Twentynine Palms and the huge Twentynine Palms Marine Corps Base, the largest Marine base in the world and the Marines' leading live-fire training facility. This fast-growing area is Republican country—56%–41% for George W. Bush in 2000, 62%–37% in 2004.

The congressman from the 41st District is Jerry Lewis, a Republican first elected in 1978 and now chairman of the Appropriations Committee. Lewis grew up in San Bernardino, worked as a lifeguard and graduated from UCLA. (He maintains his swimming skills, and once saved former Speaker Jim Wright off the shore of Hawaii.) He was an insurance agent in Redlands, a joiner in civic causes, and was elected to the local school board in the early 1960s. He was elected to the California Assembly in 1968, at 34. In 1978, the incumbent congressman retired and Lewis was elected to the House. In 1980, he got a seat on the Appropriations Committee, where bipartisan cooperation was the norm, enabling even minority members to confer favors on their districts. With a small city background and an accommodationist attitude toward Democrats, he steadily won leadership positions—chairman of the Republican Research Committee in 1984, chairman of the Republican Policy Committee in 1986, Republican Conference chairman in 1988, and seemed headed towards the minority leader post. But a small group of young conservatives around Newt Gingrich resented Lewis's cooperation with Democrats and believed that Republicans could break out of the minority if they confronted Democrats more. In March 1989 the minority whip position came open when Dick Cheney was appointed Secretary of Defense. Lewis considered running, but declined; Gingrich won by an 87–85 vote. In December 1992 Dick Armey, with support from Gingrich, challenged Lewis for the Conference chairmanship and won 88–84. Those two votes put in place the two top leaders of the Republican majority that emerged after November 1994.

Lewis recovered from that setback, and when Republicans won their majority in 1994, he became chairman of the VA-HUD Appropriations Subcommittee—a member of the "college of cardinals," as Appropriations subcommittee chairmen are known. Here he got his agencies' attention by reporting a bill making deep cuts in NASA, including closing the Goddard space center in Greenbelt, Maryland. Goddard was saved, but Lewis forced other cuts at NASA. In 1999 Lewis became chairman of the Defense Subcommittee, with the largest share of federal spending of any of the 13 subcommittees. He attracted attention when the subcommittee voted unanimously to cut $1.8 billion for building the first six of the Air Force's F-22s. This was a bolt out of the blue, and something that would not have happened had Gingrich still been speaker—the F-22 is produced in a Lockheed Martin plant in Gingrich's former district. Lewis was disturbed by a report that the Air Force had been spending money on programs Congress never authorized, including an $800 million military communications satellite and updates to the C-5. He argued that the F-22 was a Cold War super weapon, whose high cost left the Air Force as "very close to a broken branch" of the military, and he pointed out that the old F-15 did just fine in the spring 1999 bombing of Kosovo, while the Air Force was short of tankers and radar-jamming aircraft there. Funds were restored by the Senate, but the program was cut by $500 million and the Pentagon's attention was gained. Lewis continued to promote the Predator unmanned air vehicle, which had been tested on the Mojave Desert; this proved to be of prime importance in Afghanistan and Iraq.

In August 2001 Lewis said that he would press for the $18.4 billion George W. Bush had requested over the original $310.5 billion. On the morning of September 11, the subcommittee was debating an increase in funding for counterterrorism when news of the attacks came; members quickly left the Capitol. In November a $317 billion defense appropriation was passed. It did not include funding for transformation of defense programs; Lewis said that appropriations bills should not be the vehicle for major policy changes, although he had arguably used the process for that on the F-22. In June 2002 Lewis steered a $354.7 billion defense appropriation to passage in the House. In October the final $355.4 billion appropriation was passed. In 2003 and 2004 the defense appropriations bill were approved in a smooth process. The House accepted a $368 billion conference report in September 2003, with Iraq left to be dealt with in a supplemental. Bowing to the Senate and civil liberties groups, Lewis eliminated the Pentagon's Total Information Awareness program in the U.S. early in the year, and the House acceded in having five rather than six Virginia class submarines built over five years. In early 2004 Lewis warned Defense Secretary Donald Rumsfeld that "people will be targeting our budget in a serious way." But the House passed a $417 billion appropriation in June, including $25 billion for Iraq; Lewis insisted that only $1 billion of that, rather than all, as the administration had sought, be available for flexible use. The conference report was approved a month later.

As an appropriator, Lewis has been unapologetic about channeling funds into his district. One special beneficiary has been Loma Linda University, whose medical center got $26 million for medical research in 2000. Some are sentimental projects. Lewis got $1 million to rebuild the Perris Hill Plunge, a WPA-built pool where he was a lifeguard and taught dozens of children to swim; he helped to get another $1 million for the Jerry Lewis Community Center in his hometown of Highland. In December 2003 he got $40 million for district projects, which included national forest protection and emergency watershed protection in the Inland Empire. Local projects included $13.7 million for a new dining hall at Twentynine Palms, $3 million for Loma Linda University space radiation cancer research, $1.1 million to remove arsenic in the Mojave Desert, $3 million for the I-15/Tippecanoe interchange in San Bernardino, $11 million for the restoration of the 1918 Santa Fe Depot in San Bernardino. Drought and bark beetles have threatened the San Bernardino National Forest, and Lewis responded in 2004 by raising aid from $1 million to $24 million a year. "I don't know exactly if it will be $20 million a year or $50 million a year, but I know Congress will be there for the forest," he said. It was $30 million in 2005. He got $14.5 million for rehabilitating the runway at San Bernardino International Airport, the former Norton Air Force Base. Lewis intervened when the Fish and Wildlife Service kept objecting to the construction of a 100-acre soccer and football complex in San Bernardino, for fear it would threaten the San Bernardino kangaroo rat. Lewis wrote to the Interior Department, "This is a rat we're talking about."

Lewis has been reelected easily in this solidly Republican and fast-growing district. In the 1990s Lewis, noticing the rising Hispanic population, took Spanish lessons and spent time with a family in Mexico City to learn the language. But Latinos were not the only constituency to which he paid heed. Appropriations Chairman Bill Young reached the end of House Republicans' six-year term limit in 2004, and Lewis, third in seniority among committee Republicans, sought the chairmanship. So did the more senior Ralph Regula, who voted less often with the House leadership, and the less senior Hal Rogers. The House Republican leadership urges aspirants to chairmanships to raise money for fellow Republicans; Regula, who refused to accept PAC contributions, contributed little before 2004; Rogers, at a meeting in July 2004, came forward with a check for $300,000, at which point Lewis proffered his own check for $600,000. In all, he contributed $1.35 million to Republicans in the 2004 cycle. The Republican Steering Committee interviewed all three in January 2005 and, after Speaker Dennis Hastert said it was a marginal difference, chose Lewis. In February Lewis, following a suggestion by Majority Leader Tom DeLay, reduced the number of subcommittees from 13 to 10. The District of Columbia and Legislative Subcommittees, each of which handled small sums, were disbanded; the VA-HUD subcommittee was split up between two other subcommittees. The big loser was Ernest Istook of Oklahoma, who had embarrassed the leadership by his handling of the Transportation Subcommittee, which went to Joe Knollenberg; James Walsh, formerly chairman of VA-HUD, was rewarded with the Military Quality of Life Subcommittee, which took over military construction, and was formerly headed by Knollenberg.

FORTY-SECOND DISTRICT

Rep. Gary Miller (R)

Elected 1998, 4th term; b. Oct. 16, 1948, Huntsville, AR; home, Diamond Bar; Mt. San Antonio Col. 1971, 1988–89; Christian; married (Cathy).

Military Career: Army, 1967–1968.

Elected Office: Diamond Bar City Cncl., 1989–95; Diamond Bar Mayor, 1992; CA Assembly, 1995–98.

Professional Career: Businessman, real estate developer, G. Miller Development Co., 1971–98.

DC Office: 1037 LHOB, 20515, 202-225-3201; Fax: 202-226-6962; Web site: www.house.gov/garymiller.

District Offices: Brea, 714-257-1142; Mission Viejo, 949-470-8484.

Committees: *Financial Services* (21st of 37 R): Capital Markets, Insurance & Government Sponsored Enterprises; Financial Institutions & Consumer Credit; Housing & Community Opportunity (Vice Chmn.). *Transportation & Infrastructure* (17th of 41 R): Highways, Transit & Pipelines; Railroads; Water Resources & Environment.

Group Ratings

	ADA	ACLU	AFS	LCV	ITIC	NTU	COC	ACU	NTLC	CHC
2004	0	0	0	0	90	70	100	100	92	100
2003	5	—	0	5	—	68	100	91	—	—

National Journal Ratings

	2003 LIB	—	2003 CONS	2004 LIB	—	2004 CONS
Economic	0%	—	91%	7%	—	92%
Social	0%	—	95%	0%	—	91%
Foreign	21%	—	77%	10%	—	86%

Key Votes of the 108th Congress

1. Drilling in ANWR	Y	5. DC School Vouchers	Y	9. Ban Same-Sex Marriage	Y
2. Approve Bush Tax Cuts	Y	6. Ban Human Cloning	*	10. Fund Iraq War	Y
3. Medicare/Rx Bill	Y	7. Restrict Gun Liability	Y	11. Bar Cuba Embargo Funds	N
4. Bar Overtime Pay Regs.	N	8. Ban Partial-Birth Abortion	Y	12. Intelligence Reorg.	Y

Election Results

2004 general	Gary Miller (R)	167,632	(68%)	($421,841)
	Lewis Myers (D)	78,393	(32%)	
2004 primary	Gary Miller (R)	unopposed		
2002 general	Gary Miller (R)	98,476	(68%)	($443,707)
	Richard Waldron (D)	42,090	(29%)	
	Other	4,680	(3%)	

Prior Winning Percentages: 2000 (59%); 1998 (53%)

The People

Area size:	317 sq. mi.
Urban population:	98.7%
Rural population:	1.3%
Pop. 2000:	639,088
Median income:	$70,463
Poverty status:	6.0%
Military veterans:	9.6%

Race/Ethnic Origin

54.4% White
2.9% Black
15.9% Asian
0.3% Native Am.
0.2% Hawaiian
2.4% Two+ races
0.2% Other
23.8% Hispanic Origin

Ancestry

German: 10.2%   Irish: 7.4%
English: 7.4%

2004 Presidential Vote

Bush (R)	164,998	(62%)
Kerry (D)	98,108	(37%)
Other	2,578	(1%)

2000 Presidential Vote

Bush (R)	139,655	(59%)
Gore (D)	92,169	(39%)
Other	5,157	(2%)

Cook Partisan Voting Index: R +10

Occupation   Blue collar: 15.2%   White collar: 74.1%   Gray collar: 10.7%

The fastest growth in the Los Angeles metropolitan area over the last 25 years has been in the Inland Empire at eastern end of the Los Angeles Basin. Mostly orange groves and dairy farms a few decades ago, this territory now is the site of a booming economy, personal upward mobility, and ethnic and cultural harmony. The main ingredient of this economic growth has been small entrepreneurial businesses, usually started by people with no particular connections or advantages—often, of Asian or Latino immigrant background. California has never been a land of leisure, as stereotype would have it, but rather a place for hard work, where the fertility of the soil and the productivity of the people have prospered with considerable effort and tolerance toward newcomers. California hasn't always welcomed people from distant places: anti-Asian sentiment expressed itself in the Chinese Exclusion Act of 1882 and the Japanese American internment camps of 1942–44. But since World War II this has been one of the least prejudiced and most welcoming places on earth, which helps to explain why it has received more immigrants than any other state.

The 42d Congressional District of California is one place where such trends are visible. It is centered in the Inland Empire on the point where Los Angeles, San Bernardino and Orange Counties come together. In San Bernardino County it includes Chino, site of a low-security prison, and Chino Hills, incorporated in 1991 and full of new subdivisions for commuters who battle the heavy traffic to L.A. and Orange Counties. In Los Angeles County it includes Diamond Bar, where the local high school had the best College Board scores in the world on the calculus exam, and La Habra Heights and the eastern part of Whittier. Nearly two-thirds of the district's population is in Orange County. Here it includes Yorba Linda, site of the birthplace of Richard Nixon in 1913 (when only 40,000 people lived in Orange County, short of the 2,987,000 in 2004) and the site now of his presidential library; Brea and La Habra to the west; the eastern part of Anaheim; and, connected only by the uninhabited Santa Ana Mountains, the newer condominium communities of Mission Viejo and Rancho Santa Margarita. Ethnically diverse, its residents are 24% Hispanic and 16% Asian, believers still in traditional values (the 42d has the highest percentage of married people in the state), working their way up through the private sector—and leaning toward Republicans. The 2001 redistricting made this district slightly more Republican; in 2004, George W. Bush won 62% here.

The congressman from the 42d District is Gary Miller, a Republican first elected in 1998. He was born in Arkansas but grew up in Whittier. In his early 20s he became a homebuilder and developed planned communities. He began his public service in 1988 when he was appointed to the Diamond Bar Municipal Advisory Council. A year later, after Diamond Bar was incorporated, Miller was elected to the city council and served as mayor. In 1995 he was elected to the Assembly in a special election to replace Republican Paul Horcher, who was recalled after he supported Democrat Willie Brown for Assembly speaker. In 1997 he decided to run for the House against scandal-tarred incumbent Jay Kim, who lived just two blocks away in Diamond Bar. Kim and his wife had pleaded guilty to accepting and concealing $230,000 in illegal campaign contributions. In March 1998 Kim was sentenced to house arrest, confined to the House and his apartment in suburban Virginia, and was required to wear an electronic bracelet around his ankle for two months. As a result, he could not campaign back home. Miller was endorsed by Governor Pete Wilson; the National Republican Congressional Committee, which normally endorses incumbents, remained neutral. Miller emphasized standard Republican themes—lower taxes, tougher penalties for crime, improved local education—and largely financed his own campaign. The result was unambiguous. Two-thirds of the votes in the all-party primary were cast for Republican candidates, and Miller won 48% to 26% for Kim. Democrats did not pose a serious challenge in November; Miller won 53%–41%.

Miller has a very conservative voting record in the House and has advanced some original proposals. He sponsored anti-spam legislation in the California Assembly well before it became a notorious problem; in Congress, he sponsored a bill to allow Internet Service Providers to decide whether they want to allow spamming and, if not, to give them a cause of action against spammers, with $500 per message in damages. A Civil War buff who discovered that nearly 20% of the major battle sites have been lost, he successfully sponsored a bill to preserve Civil War battlefields by authorizing matching grants to local governments and nonprofits for unprotected sites. On a contemporary conflict, he called for inclusion of a ban on driver's licenses for illegal immigrants in the 2004 intelligence reorganization bill. As the only California Republican on the Transportation and Infrastructure Committee, Miller had the daunting task of representing the state's diverse interests on the highway bill. His own transportation priorities included the extension from Pasadena to Montclair of the light-rail Gold Line, improvements along the Riverside Freeway and road and rail grade separations across the metropolitan area. He worked with the Fish and Wildlife Service to help remove three nesting pairs of gnatcatchers from the proposed site of a new high school. He also helped to arrange the controversial transfer of Richard Nixon's presidential papers from the National Archives in College Park, Maryland, to the Nixon Library. "It's been 30 years. I think it's appropriate to have it all in here, and the family wants it here," he said of the Yorba Linda site.

Miller has been easily reelected against token opposition. He has shared his Virginia apartment with his daughter Elizabeth, an activist with Witness for Peace; he reports, "We have some very interesting discussions at the dinner table."

FORTY-THIRD DISTRICT

Rep. Joe Baca (D)

Elected Nov. 1999, 3d full term; b. Jan. 23, 1947, Belen, NM; home, Rialto; CA State L.A., B.A., 1971; Catholic; married (Barbara).

Military Career: Army, 1966–68.

Elected Office: CA Assembly, 1992–98; CA Senate, 1998–99.

Professional Career: Community affairs rep., General Telephone and Electric, 1974–89; Co-owner, Interstate World Travel, 1989-present.

DC Office: 328 CHOB, 20515, 202-225-6161; Fax: 202-225-8671; Web site: www.house.gov/baca.

District Office: San Bernardino, 909-885-2222.

Committees: *Agriculture* (5th of 21 D): Department Operations, Oversight, Nutrition & Forestry (RMM). *Financial Services* (22d of 32 D): Capital Markets, Insurance & Government Sponsored Enterprises; Financial Institutions & Consumer Credit.

Group Ratings

	ADA	ACLU	AFS	LCV	ITIC	NTU	COC	ACU	NTLC	CHC
2004	90	70	100	82	40	10	43	12	0	16
2003	85	—	100	50	—	22	40	25	—	—

National Journal Ratings

	2003 LIB	—	2003 CONS		2004 LIB	—	2004 CONS
Economic	61%	—	39%		77%	—	22%
Social	65%	—	34%		68%	—	31%
Foreign	75%	—	21%		78%	—	21%

Key Votes of the 108th Congress

1. Drilling in ANWR	Y	5. DC School Vouchers	N	9. Ban Same-Sex Marriage	N
2. Approve Bush Tax Cuts	N	6. Ban Human Cloning	*	10. Fund Iraq War	Y
3. Medicare/Rx Bill	N	7. Restrict Gun Liability	Y	11. Bar Cuba Embargo Funds	Y
4. Bar Overtime Pay Regs.	Y	8. Ban Partial-Birth Abortion	N	12. Intelligence Reorg.	N

Election Results

2004 general	Joe Baca (D)	86,830	(66%)	($450,287)
	Ed Laning (R)	44,004	(34%)	($40,391)
2004 primary	Joe Baca (D)	unopposed		
2002 general	Joe Baca (D)	45,374	(66%)	($511,550)
	Wendy Neighbor (R)	20,821	(30%)	($6,379)
	Other	2,145	(3%)	

Prior Winning Percentages: 2000 (60%); 1999 (51%)

The People		Race/Ethnic Origin	Ancestry		
Area size:	193 sq. mi.	23.4% White	German: 4.6%		Irish: 3.4%
Urban population:	99.3%	12.4% Black	English: 3.0%		
Rural population:	0.7%	3.1% Asian	**2004 Presidential Vote**		
Pop. 2000:	639,087	0.4% Native Am.	Kerry (D) 79,946		(58%)
Median income:	$37,390	0.3% Hawaiian	Bush (R) 55,952		(41%)
Poverty status:	20.7%	1.9% Two+ races	Other 1,497		(1%)
Military veterans:	8.9%	0.2% Other	**2000 Presidential Vote**		
		58.3% Hispanic Origin	Gore (D) 76,710		(64%)
			Bush (R) 41,272		(34%)
			Other 2,293		(2%)
			Cook Partisan Voting Index: D +13		

Occupation	Blue collar: 36.2%	White collar: 46.4%	Gray collar: 17.4%

The gateway to the Los Angeles Basin for decades was San Bernardino, situated on flat land where the route through the twisting, windy Cajon Pass took passengers on the Santa Fe Railroad and motorists on U.S. 66 from the hot and dusty desert to the greener, tree-lined Los Angeles basin. There were orange groves around the little railroad towns and vineyards to the west; this was an agricultural zone until World War II, when Henry J. Kaiser built the West Coast's first major steel mill between the Santa Fe and Southern Pacific lines in Fontana, just west of San Bernardino. Today, these lands have largely filled up. This Inland Empire, as it is called, may be where the smog piles up against the mountains, but it also has some of the lowest real estate prices in the Los Angeles Basin and an energetic small business economy. Business growth has been spurred by huge distribution and warehouse centers that service overseas cargos from the Long Beach port. Wal-Mart has viewed local sites as prime opportunities for its Supercenters.

The 43d Congressional District of California includes most of San Bernardino and Colton and the towns running west—Rialto; Fontana, where many new businesses supplanted the steel mill closed in 1994 (and reassembled in China) and property values have increased sharply; and Ontario, with its expanded airport. Every year Ontario celebrates the 4th of July at the longest picnic table in the world. San Bernardino's economy turned downward after the closure of Norton Air Force Base and the Santa Fe rail repair yard. But the base is now San Bernardino's new airport, and the city has built a new baseball stadium and Northrop Grumman has opened a new Missile Engineering Center here. Politically this area—and San Bernardino County, in general—trended Republican in the 1980s, as the cultural liberalism of California Democrats repelled family-oriented residents. But as the economy slowed in the early 1990s, and California's growing Latino population (the district was 58% Hispanic in 2000) and its continuing aversion to Republicans shifted it farther to the left, the district trended to the Democrats. It remains Democratic, but perhaps is becoming less so: George W. Bush's percentage here increased from 34% in 2000 to 41% in 2004, his second biggest increase in California's 53 districts.

The congressman from the 43d District is Joe Baca, a Democrat first elected in November 1999. He was born in Belen, New Mexico, the youngest of 15 children. His family moved to Barstow, California, in the desert, when he was four years old. His father worked as a laborer for the Santa Fe Railroad; Baca shined shoes at age 10 and later sold newspapers and worked as a janitor. He served in the Army as a paratrooper during the Vietnam War, but did not see combat. After graduating from California State University at Los Angeles, Baca moved to the San Bernardino area, where he spent 15 years as a community affairs representative for General Telephone and Electric and was elected four times to the San Bernardino Community College board. After two unsuccessful campaigns, the persistent Baca was elected to the Assembly in 1992. He became speaker pro tempore of the Assembly, the first Latino to serve in this capacity in California. He earned a reputation as a hard worker, introducing more bills than any other member in his first year, but his aggressiveness rubbed some colleagues the wrong way. A moderate to conservative Democrat, he worked to reduce welfare rolls, lower taxes on middle-income earners and increase penalties for drug dealers. Facing term limits in 1998, he threatened to run in the primary against veteran Congressman George Brown. Instead he ran for the state Senate, spending $2 million to raise his local profile.

His opportunity came in July 1999, when Brown died in his 18th term. His widow Marta Macias Brown ran for the seat. Widows of members had won in 35 of the last 36 such races, but Minority Leader Richard Gephardt refused her request to clear the field, and Baca ran. Baca won the endorsement of organized labor and had a base among Latino voters. Brown attacked Baca for his endorsement by the National Rifle Association. Baca won the all-party primary with 32% of the vote; Brown got 30%, losing by 518 votes. The Republican nominee was real estate developer Elia Pirozzi, who in 1998 lost to Brown 55%–40%. Baca emphasized his centrist voting record and his support for targeted tax cuts, a minimum wage increase and abortion rights. Brown did not endorse Baca. In a light turnout, Baca won 51%–45%.

In the House, Baca had the most conservative voting record of any Latino from California and one of the more conservative voting records of California Democrats. He lobbied for a seat on the Rules Committee, and complained that he had been "bypassed" after Gephardt filled openings there with an African-American from Florida and a white from Massachusetts; Nancy Pelosi, too, did not accommodate his request for a higher-profile assignment. After extensive review, he opposed the resolution authorizing the use of force in Iraq. Baca has called for more enforcement of decency standards on Spanish-language broadcast media, and he wants controls on video games that depict nudity, sexual conduct or other content deemed harmful to minors. In June 2004, he protested inland sweeps of illegal immigrants in southern California by Border Patrol agents; Homeland Security Department officials admitted that the sweeps violated agency policy. In 2005, he became vice-chairman of the Hispanic Caucus, and hoped to become a national spokesman on Hispanic issues; he has worked to promote Hispanic representation in corporate boardrooms. He also moved up to ranking Democrat on the Agriculture Subcommittee on Department Operations, Oversight, Dairy, Nutrition and Forestry and said that he will focus on dairy and nutrition policy; dairy production is the chief agricultural business in his district.

In 2000, former Congressman Jay Kim said he was interested in running for this seat: Kim had pleaded guilty to three misdemeanor charges of accepting illegal campaign contributions in 1997, and was beaten in an adjacent district in the 1998 primary by Gary Miller. Republican party officials urged a reluctant Pirozzi to run a third time. Pirozzi beat Kim 80%–20% in the March primary, and Baca beat Pirozzi 60%–35%. With redistricting changes, the district became significantly more Democratic and less competitive. Campaign season attacks on Baca by Los Angeles radio talk show hosts John Kobylt and Ken Chiampou for his stands on illegal aliens had little impact. One Baca son was elected to the Assembly in 2004, and another son has his eye on a seat there.

FORTY-FOURTH DISTRICT

Rep. Ken Calvert (R)

Elected 1992, 7th term; b. June 8, 1953, Corona; home, Corona; Chaffey Col., 1972–73; San Diego St. U., B.A. 1975; Protestant; divorced.

Professional Career: Restaurant owner, 1975–80; Real estate broker, 1980–92; Chmn., Riverside Cnty. Repub. Party, 1984–88.

DC Office: 2201 RHOB, 20515, 202-225-1986; Fax: 202-225-2004; Web site: www.house.gov.calvert.

District Offices: Riverside, 909-784-4300; San Clemente, 949-496-2343.

Committees: *Armed Services* (15th of 34 R): Projection Forces; Tactical Air & Land Forces. *Resources* (7th of 27 R): Water & Power. *Science* (6th of 24 R): Space & Aeronautics (Chmn.).

Group Ratings

	ADA	ACLU	AFS	LCV	ITIC	NTU	COC	ACU	NTLC	CHC
2004	0	0	14	9	89	48	100	88	70	92
2003	5	—	0	5	—	59	100	92	—	—

National Journal Ratings

	2003 LIB	—	2003 CONS		2004 LIB	—	2004 CONS
Economic	9%	—	84%		21%	—	78%
Social	21%	—	78%		31%	—	67%
Foreign	11%	—	80%		25%	—	68%

Key Votes of the 108th Congress

1. Drilling in ANWR	Y	5. DC School Vouchers	Y	9. Ban Same-Sex Marriage	Y
2. Approve Bush Tax Cuts	Y	6. Ban Human Cloning	Y	10. Fund Iraq War	Y
3. Medicare/Rx Bill	Y	7. Restrict Gun Liability	Y	11. Bar Cuba Embargo Funds	N
4. Bar Overtime Pay Regs.	N	8. Ban Partial-Birth Abortion	Y	12. Intelligence Reorg.	Y

Election Results

2004 general	Ken Calvert (R)	138,768	(62%)	($687,467)
	Louis Vandenberg (D)	78,796	(35%)	($6,196)
	Other	7,559	(3%)	
2004 primary	Ken Calvert (R)	49,107	(86%)	
	David Rizzo (R)	8,132	(14%)	
2002 general	Ken Calvert (R)	76,686	(64%)	($643,408)
	Louis Vandenberg (D)	38,021	(32%)	
	Phill Courtney (Green)	5,756	(5%)	

Prior Winning Percentages: 2000 (74%); 1998 (56%); 1996 (55%); 1994 (55%); 1992 (47%)

The People		Race/Ethnic Origin	Ancestry	
Area size:	549 sq. mi.	51.3% White	German: 9.5% Irish: 7.0%	
Urban population:	97.7%	5.5% Black	English: 6.8%	
Rural population:	2.3%	4.8% Asian	**2004 Presidential Vote**	
Pop. 2000:	639,088	0.5% Native Am.	Bush (R) 139,476	(59%)
Median income:	$51,578	0.3% Hawaiian	Kerry (D) 94,374	(40%)
Poverty status:	12.1%	2.4% Two+ races	Other 2,562	(1%)
Military veterans:	11.2%	0.2% Other	**2000 Presidential Vote**	
		35.0% Hispanic Origin	Bush (R) 101,897	(53%)
			Gore (D) 84,048	(44%)
			Other 5,143	(3%)
			Cook Partisan Voting Index: R + 6	

Occupation   Blue collar: 26.0%   White collar: 59.3%   Gray collar: 14.6%

Riverside was a sleepy town of 34,000, a couple hours' drive from Los Angeles, when Richard and Pat Nixon were married there in 1940 in the gaudy Mission Inn, with its bell towers, altars, fountains, rotunda, stained-glass windows and wrought-iron grilles. Riverside was not much larger, with 46,000 people, when Ronald and Nancy Reagan spent their honeymoon at the Mission Inn a dozen years later, in 1952. Riverside then was a citrus center, a market town amid orange groves, where the local agricultural college developed among other things, the navel orange. Today the Mission Inn is still doing business, but Riverside has changed completely. The city has expanded to some 281,000 people, and Riverside County, which had 105,000 people in 1940, had 1.9 million in 2004, more than doubling since 1980. Much of that growth came in the Inland Empire around Riverside, where the flat Los Angeles Basin plains are interrupted by oddly shaped hills and ridges, and the vegetation has an other-worldly air; it has used as the backdrop for reality TV shows. This has been a boom part of California, where modest-income families found new houses in inexpensive developments and small businesses expanded might-ily; it was hit hard by the recession of the early 1990s but rebounded with strong growth. Near Moreno Valley the former March Air Force Base has become a regional hub for the shipping giant DHL.

The 44th Congressional District of California, which covers much of this area, has been one of the fastest-growing congressional districts in the nation in the past two decades. Some 40% of its residents live in the city of Riverside and most others in nearby towns like Corona and Norco, the home of a Naval Surface Warfare Center, which evaluates weapons systems. In May 2005, the Pentagon recommended closing the base; a 2004 study commissioned by Norco reported that closure would cost Corona and Norco more than $300 million a year and result in a loss of 3,300 local jobs. The district includes the eastern edge of Orange County all the way to the ocean, much of it uninhabited mountainsides but also including San Clemente, where Richard Nixon lived after he resigned the presidency, and half of San Juan Capistrano, to which the swallows famously return on the same day each spring. This is a solidly Republican district.

The congressman from the 44th District is Ken Calvert, a Republican first elected in 1992. Calvert grew up in Corona; during college, he was a congressional intern at the Senate Watergate hearings of 1973. Later, he ran the family restaurant back home and in 1980 entered the commercial real estate business. In 1982, at 29, he ran for Congress in a district that included almost all the geographic expanse of Riverside County and lost a nine-candidate primary to Al McCandless by 868 votes. In 1992 he ran in a new district and won the primary with 28% of the vote. His Democratic opponent was Mark Takano, an eighth grade teacher with institutional support from teachers' unions and financial support from Japanese Americans. In a district where George H.W. Bush beat Bill Clinton by 797 votes, Calvert beat Takano by 519 votes.

In the House, Calvert has compiled a moderate-to-conservative voting record. He ran into trouble back home soon after he was elected, when the Riverside *Press-Enterprise* reported that he had been stopped by police with a convicted prostitute in his car; Calvert apologized, and said that he was upset because his wife had divorced him the month before and his father had recently committed suicide. It was, as he said, "an extremely embarrassing situation," of which his opponents rushed to take advantage. Calvert won the 1994 primary 51%–49%, with only an 884-vote margin, against business professor Joseph Khoury. Takano, running again in the general, ran an ad with the song "The Liar" and accused him of "flagrant womanizing." But the Republican tide of the year showed up in the election results, with Calvert winning 55%–38%.

Since 1995, Calvert has worked quietly as a subcommittee chairman, and usually has been a Republican team player. In 2001, Calvert took over as chairman of the Water and Power Subcommittee at Resources, which distributes public works projects. He focused intensively on building support for reauthorization of the vital water supply program (CALFED) for California's Central Valley. During the middle of the water fight, Calvert was one of several contenders seeking to chair the Resources Committee in 2003, but he lost to fellow Californian Richard Pombo, who was backed by Tom DeLay; he kept the Water and Power chairmanship. With help from Pombo, Calvert negotiated with Senator Dianne Feinstein, and they reached a compromise among the competing users, including new levees and recycling projects. After the bill was finally enacted in October 2004, southern California was deluged with rain for months, perhaps a sign of celestial gratification. With the water issues largely resolved, he switched in 2005 to become chairman of Science's Space and Aeronautics Subcommittee, which could be a boost for local aerospace firms. In the meantime, he joined the Armed Services Committee, where he advocated the interests of local defense contractors and the area's shrinking military facilities, including March Air Reserve Base in Riverside, which has the longest runway in California. With Democrat Paul Kanjorski, he sponsored a bill to prohibit national banks and their subsidiaries from acting as real estate brokers or managers.

Calvert increased his margins in Republican primaries from 56%–35% in 1998 to 58%–25% in 2000 and 70%–25% in 2002; he has not had serious Democratic opposition. In early 2003 he said he would not keep his 1992 pledge to serve only 12 years; he was reelected easily anyway in 2004.

FORTY-FIFTH DISTRICT

Rep. Mary Bono (R)

Elected April 1998, 4th full term; b. Oct. 24, 1961, Cleveland, OH; home, Palm Springs; U. of S. CA, B.F.A. 1984; Protestant; married (Glenn Baxley).

Professional Career: Gen. Mgr., Bono restaurant, 1986–90.

DC Office: 405 CHOB, 20515, 202-225-5330; Fax: 202-225-2961; Web site: www.house.gov/bono.

District Offices: Hemet, 909-658-2312; Palm Springs, 760-320-1076.

Committees: *Energy & Commerce* (21st of 31 R): Commerce, Trade & Consumer Protection; Energy & Air Quality; Environment & Hazardous Materials; Health.

Group Ratings

	ADA	ACLU	AFS	LCV	ITIC	NTU	COC	ACU	NTLC	CHC
2004	35	25	13	18	90	51	100	56	77	84
2003	10	—	0	10	—	55	93	72	—	—

National Journal Ratings

	2003 LIB	—	2003 CONS	2004 LIB	—	2004 CONS
Economic	36%	—	64%	35%	—	65%
Social	49%	—	50%	56%	—	44%
Foreign	42%	—	57%	50%	—	50%

Key Votes of the 108th Congress

1. Drilling in ANWR	Y	5. DC School Vouchers	Y	9. Ban Same-Sex Marriage	N
2. Approve Bush Tax Cuts	Y	6. Ban Human Cloning	Y	10. Fund Iraq War	Y
3. Medicare/Rx Bill	Y	7. Restrict Gun Liability	Y	11. Bar Cuba Embargo Funds	Y
4. Bar Overtime Pay Regs.	N	8. Ban Partial-Birth Abortion	Y	12. Intelligence Reorg.	Y

Election Results

2004 general	Mary Bono (R)	153,523	(67%)	($501,088)
	Richard Meyer (D)	76,967	(33%)	($262,288)
2004 primary	Mary Bono (R)	51,429	(86%)	
	John Barker (R)	8,422	(14%)	
2002 general	Mary Bono (R)	87,101	(65%)	($582,769)
	Elle Kurpiewski (D)	43,692	(33%)	($312,387)
	Other	2,740	(2%)	

Prior Winning Percentages: 2000 (59%); 1998 (60%); 1998 (64%)

The People		Race/Ethnic Origin	Ancestry	
Area size:	6,062 sq. mi.	50.1% White	German: 8.9%	English: 7.1%
Urban population:	89.9%	6.3% Black	Irish: 6.6%	
Rural population:	10.1%	2.8% Asian	**2004 Presidential Vote**	
Pop. 2000:	639,088	0.6% Native Am.	Bush (R) 132,288	(56%)
Median income:	$40,468	0.2% Hawaiian	Kerry (D) 101,679	(43%)
Poverty status:	15.0%	1.9% Two+ races	Other 2,102	(1%)
Military veterans:	14.5%	0.1% Other	**2000 Presidential Vote**	
		38.0% Hispanic Origin	Bush (R) 93,802	(51%)
			Gore (D) 85,427	(47%)
			Other 4,029	(2%)
			Cook Partisan Voting Index: R + 3	

Occupation	Blue collar: 23.1%	White collar: 53.2%	Gray collar: 23.7%

From the air two decades ago, a night flight east from Los Angeles showed the lights of 10 million persons' streets and houses and then almost perfect darkness: a vast metropolis surrounded by almost uninhabited territory. Today the sprinkled pattern of white lights has spread into the Inland Empire around Riverside and San Bernardino and is multiplying outward into the desert. The Inland Empire has filled up with instant towns like family-oriented Moreno Valley, which did not exist in 1980 and had 157,000 people in 2004. Over the 10,000-foot San Jacinto Mountains, desert communities have boomed: Palm Springs, once the lone winter resort for the stars and now popular for its retro architecture such as flying-saucer roofs and steel-and-glass buildings, is one of a string of communities along Highway 111 and Frank Sinatra and Bob Hope Drives. Among rich retirees, the vogue for the coast lessened as beach cities filled up with roller bladers and rent control crusaders; the clean, dry, roomy desert, where the days are almost always crystal clear and the sky usually blue and cloudless, became more attractive, and, with everything air-conditioned, a comfortable year-round home. Two presidents retired to the desert here: Dwight Eisenhower in Palm Desert for the winters and Gerald Ford in nearby Rancho Mirage. The population is nearly 300,000 for the entire corridor if you count Indio and Coachella, the heavily Latino and fast-growing cities in the agricultural Coachella Valley, which has 75% of the country's date palms and features camel races at its annual date festival; *Rolling Stone* magazine called the launch of the annual music festival in Coachella one of the 50 greatest moments in rock history.

The 45th Congressional District of California covers almost all the desert in Riverside County from Blythe on the Nevada border to Palm Springs. The Joshua Tree National Park, with its high desert sands, is a popular tourist spot, with growing real estate values in nearby towns. About half its population lives west of the 10,000-foot peak that looms above Palm Springs, in fast-growing Moreno Valley and socially conservative Murrieta and in the old town of Hemet surrounded by surreal landscape. This area tends to vote Republican; it voted 51% for George W. Bush in 2000 and 56% in 2004.

The congresswoman from the 45th District is Mary Bono, who won the seat in April 1998 after the death of her husband Sonny Bono, onetime showbiz celebrity and mayor of Palm Springs. He was on a family vacation when he died in a skiing accident in South Lake Tahoe, California. Mary Bono grew up as Mary Whitaker in South Pasadena, where she was an accomplished gymnast; she remains a fitness buff, a certified personal fitness instructor who has studied karate and Tae Kwan Do. She met Sonny Bono when she was celebrating her college graduation at his Los Angeles restaurant in 1984; they were married two years later. Before her campaign, she had no political experience and was little known in Washington. She was strongly encouraged to run for the seat by House Republican leaders who believed that only she could avert a divisive Republican primary and that she had the best chance to hold the seat. In the special election, she faced actor Ralph Waite, best known as Pa Walton in *The Waltons*. Waite was hurt during the brief campaign because he kept a commitment to play Willy Loman in *Death of a Salesman* six times a week in a New Jersey theater. The campaign's biggest controversy came when Sonny's 83-year-old mother said that her son would have opposed Mary's candidacy, preferring that she care for their children. But it was no contest. Bono won 64%–29%, a bigger margin than Sonny's two victories.

Bono has a moderate voting record, especially on social and foreign issues; the least conservative voting record of California Republicans. Her initial legislative priority was passage of Sonny's bill to restore the Salton Sea, an artificial body of water in the desert created when a canal burst in 1905; it has been shrinking in recent decades, increasing the salinity of the water and the pollution from agricultural runoff. Although some Democrats objected to taking funds from other California projects, Mary Bono initially secured $13.4 million for what became the Sonny Bono Salton Sea National Wildlife Refuge. She later pushed for engineering projects to reduce the heavy salinity of the lake and to assure continuing sources of fresh water; if successful, one result could be to avoid further deterioration of air quality in Southern California. Final costs likely would exceed $1 billion. With her seat on the Energy and Commerce Committee, she worked on a bill to require companies to expense their employee stock options. Other committee work included her legislation to crack down on invasive computer "spyware", which she discovered when purple gorillas kept appearing on her home computer after her two teen-agers inadvertently downloaded the software; in October 2004, the House passed her bill. Bono, who collects about $100,000 annually from her late husband's royalties, has opposed legislation to relax controls on digital piracy.

Mary Bono has been easily reelected. She was considered a possible candidate for Barbara Boxer's Senate seat in 2004: Sonny Bono ran for the seat in 1992, and finished third in the Republican primary. She also was mentioned as the possible new head of the Recording Industry Association of America, but she decided to remain in the House.

FORTY-SIXTH DISTRICT

Rep. Dana Rohrabacher (R)

Elected 1988, 9th term; b. June 21, 1947, Coronado; home, Huntington Beach; Long Beach St. Col. B.A. 1969, U. of S. CA, M.A. 1975; Baptist; married (Rhonda).

Professional Career: Radio & print journalist, 1970–80; Sr. Speechwriter, Special Asst. to Pres. Reagan, 1981–88.

DC Office: 2338 RHOB, 20515, 202-225-2415; Fax: 202-225-0145; Web site: www.house.gov/rohrabacher.

District Office: Huntington Beach, 714-960-6483.

Committees: *International Relations* (7th of 27 R): Asia & the Pacific; Oversight & Investigations (Chmn.). *Science* (5th of 24 R): Research; Space & Aeronautics.

Group Ratings

	ADA	ACLU	AFS	LCV	ITIC	NTU	COC	ACU	NTLC	CHC
2004	15	10	13	18	40	80	85	91	94	84
2003	15	—	0	5	—	72	80	88	—	—

National Journal Ratings

	2003 LIB	—	2003 CONS		2004 LIB	—	2004 CONS
Economic	21%	—	75%		41%	—	58%
Social	40%	—	58%		36%	—	61%
Foreign	51%	—	48%		25%	—	68%

Key Votes of the 108th Congress

1. Drilling in ANWR	Y	5. DC School Vouchers	Y	9. Ban Same-Sex Marriage	Y
2. Approve Bush Tax Cuts	Y	6. Ban Human Cloning	Y	10. Fund Iraq War	Y
3. Medicare/Rx Bill	Y	7. Restrict Gun Liability	Y	11. Bar Cuba Embargo Funds	N
4. Bar Overtime Pay Regs.	N	8. Ban Partial-Birth Abortion	Y	12. Intelligence Reorg.	Y

Election Results

2004 general	Dana Rohrabacher (R)	171,318	(62%)	($517,315)
	Jim Brandt (D)	90,129	(33%)	($85,456)
	Tom Lash (Green)	10,238	(4%)	
	Other	5,005	(2%)	
2004 primary	Dana Rohrabacher (R)	69,132	(84%)	
	Robert Dornan (R)	13,630	(16%)	
2002 general	Dana Rohrabacher (R)	108,807	(62%)	($380,008)
	Gerrie Schipske (D)	60,890	(35%)	($228,084)
	Keith Gann (Lib)	6,488	(4%)	

Prior Winning Percentages: 2000 (62%); 1998 (59%); 1996 (61%); 1994 (69%); 1992 (55%); 1990 (59%); 1988 (64%)

The People		Race/Ethnic Origin	Ancestry	
Area size:	825 sq. mi.	62.8% White	German: 10.7%	English: 8.5%
Urban population:	99.9%	1.4% Black	Irish: 8.4%	
Rural population:	0.1%	15.4% Asian	**2004 Presidential Vote**	
Pop. 2000:	639,088	0.3% Native Am.	Bush (R) 168,158	(57%)
Median income:	$61,567	0.3% Hawaiian	Kerry (D) 122,991	(42%)
Poverty status:	7.8%	2.6% Two+ races	Other 3,734	(1%)
Military veterans:	11.3%	0.2% Other	**2000 Presidential Vote**	
		16.9% Hispanic Origin	Bush (R) 145,729	(55%)
			Gore (D) 110,984	(42%)
			Other 9,413	(4%)
			Cook Partisan Voting Index: R + 6	

Occupation	Blue collar: 15.4%	White collar: 72.7%	Gray collar: 11.9%

In the 1950s, when the Beach Boys were at Hawthorne High School, surfers would drive far down the coast to the vast expanse of Huntington Beach in Orange County to catch a wave. This was empty country then, vegetable fields and orange groves, with nary a freeway or shopping center in sight. Today a long stretch of the beach itself is eerily empty, with swampland across the highway where surfers' pickups are parked, but the rest of the 42-mile shoreline of Orange County is pretty much filled in. Pricey coastal resorts have become a popular destination. Huntington Beach is a city of 194,000, a mixture of family subdivisions and garden apartments and home of the International Surfing Museum. To the north is Westminster, the center of the nation's most prominent Vietnamese-American community, with miles of malls where all the shops have Vietnamese names and the area has its own Vietnamese-language daily newspaper. Southeast along San Diego Freeway is Fountain Valley, the central focus of many Asian-owned high-tech businesses, an engine of Southern California growth. Near the coast is Costa Mesa, site of South Coast Plaza's luxury stores. Out on the beach in Huntington Beach you can see the curving coastline to the west, past the port of Los Angeles and Long Beach to where the mountains of the seismically active and economically upscale Palos Verdes Peninsula rise above the water. Using "cold ironing" technology, plans are underway to cut air pollution from tankers in the busy port complex by equipping at least two BP tankers into onshore electricity so that they can shut down their diesel engines.

The 46th Congressional District of California includes all of this beachfront plus the Long Beach Harbor area and the Palos Verdes Peninsula. It also includes territory inland: the eastern end of Long Beach and next-door Seal Beach, areas settled by many retirees, most of Westminster, all of Fountain Valley, Costa Mesa, the southwest corner of Santa Ana and a tiny slice of Los Angeles. Over most of the distance the eastern part of the district is connected to the Palos Verdes Peninsula by just a thin strip of beach or the port area. Politically, the two ends of the district connected by this narrow corridor are solidly Republican, from high-income Palos Verdes to Westminster: Vietnamese there are mostly conservative, angry at America not for going into Vietnam but for leaving it. This is no longer the monoracial Orange County of the 1960s: the district's population is 17% Hispanic and 15% Asian.

The congressman from the 46th District is Dana Rohrabacher, a Republican first elected in 1988. He calls himself a surfer Republican and sports an American flag surfboard. He grew up in southern California, went to college and experimented with drugs, and once had a folk band called the Goldwaters. He was a press aide in the 1976 and 1980 Reagan presidential campaigns, wrote editorials for the *Orange County Register* and was a speechwriter in the Reagan White House. He returned to Southern California in 1988 when Long Beach-based Congressman Dan Lungren decided not to run again (Lungren was elected attorney general in 1990 and 1994, and in 2004 was elected to the House again in the 3d District 400 miles away). Rohrabacher, with fundraising help from Oliver North, won the primary with 35% of the vote, to 22% for an Orange County supervisor and 20% for Steve Horn, who later represented a Long Beach-based district. After redistricting in 1992, Rohrabacher tussled with Robert Dornan and won, running in this heavily Republican district while Dornan ran in the inland seat which, after a quixotic presidential campaign, he lost in 1996.

A self-styled free spirit, Rohrabacher likes to make waves in the House. His Web site once featured the motto: "Fighting for freedom and having fun." His voting record can be unpredictable, especially on cultural issues. That helps to explain why he remains assigned to second-level committees, but he has made the most of his opportunities. As chairman of the Science Subcommittee on Space and Aeronautics, he worked for the single-stage-to-orbit vehicle. After the *Columbia* disaster in February 2003, he quickly noted that he had raised questions about the safety of the aging space shuttle. He said that a manned space flight to repair the Hubble space telescope was not worth the risk. In December 2004, George W. Bush signed his bill to promote the development of the commercial human space flight industry; the law is aimed at protecting the fledgling space travel industry from overregulation and provides relief from legal liability.

In 2005, after House Republicans' six-year term limit clicked in, Rohrabacher left the Space chairmanship and became chairman of the Oversight and Investigations Subcommittee on International Relations, an area where he already had stirred the waters. As a White House aide, he traveled in November 1988 with a mujahedeen militia unit for one week. "Half of our group was napalmed," he said. Soon after the September 11 attacks, he visited the exiled King of Afghanistan in Rome, encouraged him to return to Kabul and promised that the United States would oust the Taliban and help rebuild Afghanistan. He visited liberated Afghanistan in April 2002 and complained that the Pentagon imposed too many limits on his visit. Rohrabacher has been a long-time critic of China's rulers and strongly opposed normal trade relations. In 2001, the House soundly defeated his attempts to block expanded trade with China and Vietnam. Despite the Bush administration's criticism that it would violate the peace treaty, he won House passage of his amendment to allow World War II prisoners of war to sue Japanese companies for enslaving them. In July 2002, after a lengthy delay while he paced the House floor, he cast one of the final votes that secured the passage by one vote of trade promotion authority for President Bush. He went through a similar routine in November 2003 before finally voting for the Medicare/prescription drug bill; in exchange, Republican leaders gave him a vote on his bill to require hospitals to report potential illegal immigrants to the Homeland Security Department. In 2004, with in-vitro fertilization and at age 56, he and wife Rhonda became the parents of triplets. Later he became an advocate of embryonic stem-cell research.

Rohrabacher has been routinely reelected by wide margins. In 2002 his Democratic opponent was Gerrie Schipske, a nurse practitioner and attorney who lost to Republican Steve Horn in 2000 in the old 38th District by only 48%–47%. But this was a much less Democratic district; Schipske raised only one-third as much money as in 2000, and Rohrabacher won 62%–35%. In the 2004 primary, he was challenged by his former colleague Robert Dornan, who had become a radio talk-show host. Rohrabacher won 84%–16%.

FORTY-SEVENTH DISTRICT

Rep. Loretta Sanchez (D)

Elected 1996, 5th term; b. Jan. 7, 1960, Lynwood; home, Santa Ana; Chapman U., B.A. 1982, American U., M.B.A. 1984; Catholic; divorced.

Professional Career: Mgr. & Financial Analyst, Orange Cnty. Transp. Auth., 1984–87; Asst. Vice Pres., Fieldman, Rolapp & Assoc., 1987–90; Assoc., Booz, Allen & Hamilton, 1990–93; Principal, Amiga Advisors.

DC Office: 1230 LHOB, 20515, 202-225-2965; Fax: 202-225-5859; Web site: www.house.gov/sanchez.

District Office: Garden Grove, 714-621-0102.

Committees: *Armed Services* (11th of 28 D): Military Personnel; Strategic Forces. *Homeland Security* (2d of 15 D): Economic Security, Infrastructure Protection & Cybersecurity (RMM); Emergency Preparedness, Science & Technology; Intelligence, Information Sharing & Terrorism Risk Assessment. *Joint Economic Committee.*

Group Ratings

	ADA	ACLU	AFS	LCV	ITIC	NTU	COC	ACU	NTLC	CHC
2004	100	79	100	82	50	11	40	12	0	9
2003	90	—	100	95	—	24	34	8	—	—

National Journal Ratings

	2003 LIB	—	2003 CONS		2004 LIB	—	2004 CONS
Economic	76%	—	23%		79%	—	21%
Social	76%	—	24%		78%	—	19%
Foreign	73%	—	25%		77%	—	22%

Key Votes of the 108th Congress

1. Drilling in ANWR	N	5. DC School Vouchers	N	9. Ban Same-Sex Marriage	N
2. Approve Bush Tax Cuts	N	6. Ban Human Cloning	*	10. Fund Iraq War	Y
3. Medicare/Rx Bill	N	7. Restrict Gun Liability	N	11. Bar Cuba Embargo Funds	Y
4. Bar Overtime Pay Regs.	Y	8. Ban Partial-Birth Abortion	N	12. Intelligence Reorg.	N

Election Results

2004 general	Loretta Sanchez (D)	65,684	(60%)	($1,837,079)
	Alex Coronado (R)	43,099	(40%)	($356,372)
2004 primary	Loretta Sanchez (D)	unopposed		
2002 general	Loretta Sanchez (D)	42,501	(61%)	($1,290,368)
	Jeff Chavez (R)	24,346	(35%)	($47,054)
	Paul Marsden (Lib)	2,944	(4%)	

Prior Winning Percentages: 2000 (60%); 1998 (56%); 1996 (47%)

The People

Area size:	55 sq. mi.
Urban population:	100.0%
Rural population:	0.0%
Pop. 2000:	639,087
Median income:	$41,618
Poverty status:	19.1%
Military veterans:	5.2%

Race/Ethnic Origin

17.3% White
1.5% Black
13.9% Asian
0.3% Native Am.
0.4% Hawaiian
1.3% Two+ races
0.1% Other
65.3% Hispanic Origin

Ancestry

German: 3.5%   Irish: 2.5%
English: 2.3%

2004 Presidential Vote

Bush (R)	56,226	(50%)
Kerry (D)	54,623	(49%)
Other	1,393	(1%)

2000 Presidential Vote

Gore (D)	59,515	(56%)
Bush (R)	43,752	(41%)
Other	2,257	(2%)

Cook Partisan Voting Index: D + 5

Occupation   Blue collar: 37.9%   White collar: 40.9%   Gray collar: 21.2%

When Walt Disney began planning Disneyland in the late 1940s, he did not have to drive far from downtown Los Angeles before finding agricultural land. Dairy farms and orange groves covered most of southeast Los Angeles County and adjacent Orange County, which had only 216,000 people in 1950. As Disneyland opened there in 1955 and became a vast success, the area around it—a mass of flat land surrounded by mountains and sea—found itself directly in the path of the most explosively growing metropolitan area in the United States. With 2,987,000 people in 2004, it is now the nation's fifth-largest county, just a bit ahead of San Diego County.

Just as Orange County was once transformed by newcomers from Los Angeles County and the Midwest, so it is again being transformed by immigrants, from Mexico and other parts of Latin America, and from Vietnam, Taiwan, Korea and other parts of East Asia. By 1990 the county's population was 23% Hispanic and 10% Asian; in 2000, the figures were 31% Hispanic and 14% Asian. Some of these new Orange County residents are direct migrants: Santa Ana, the county seat, is a major arrival point for immigrants from Mexico, and its population 76% Hispanic. Others have moved out along the freeways, like so many southern Californians before them, working hard at jobs, commuting on freeways and living in stucco subdivisions like anyone else. There are concentrations in various places—Latinos in Santa Ana and much of Anaheim; Vietnamese in Westminster and Garden Grove, who comprise the largest expatriate Vietnamese community in the nation—but many of these new Californians are just speckled through the county. These changes have made for some political wobble, but until the mid-1990s not very much: Asians were split between the parties and few Latinos were registered to vote. After the 1994 approval of Proposition 187, which sought to deny most social services to illegal immigrants, many more Latinos began voting, and initially were voting Democratic; evidence suggests Asians voted increasingly for Democrats too.

The 47th Congressional District of California is the geographic heart of Orange County. About half its people live in Santa Ana, in neighborhoods full of large families and many workers. The district includes most of Garden Grove, with many Latinos and Vietnamese, and most of Anaheim, with many Latinos. It includes many Orange County landmarks—Anaheim Stadium, Disneyland and Disney's California Adventure, opened in 2001. The population of the district is 65% Hispanic and 14% Asian (primarily Vietnamese). This core area has always been the most Democratic part of Orange County; the movement of Latinos to Democrats made it more Democratic in the 1990s. But it is not overwhelmingly Democratic like most majority-Hispanic districts in Los Angeles County. In 2003 the district voted 62% to recall Democratic Governor Gray Davis. George W. Bush, who lost the district 56%–41% to Al Gore in 2000, won it 50%–49% over John Kerry in 2004. This was the biggest rise in percentage for Bush in any of California's 53 districts. It represents a considerable increase in Bush support from Latinos and probably from Vietnamese, who turned out in large numbers in 2004 to elect one of their own as a Republican assemblyman; he promised to make Garden Grove a "Communist-free zone."

The congresswoman from the 47th District is Loretta Sanchez, a Democrat first elected in 1996. Sanchez was raised in Anaheim by Mexican immigrant parents and graduated from Chapman University in Orange. She worked as a financial analyst, providing advice to public agencies and private businesses; she established her own firm in the early 1990s. For a time she and her husband lived in affluent Palos Verdes Estates, far from Orange County, but in 1994 she ran for the city council in Anaheim under her married name, Loretta Sanchez-Brixey, and lost. In 1996, she ran for the House, this time as Loretta Sanchez, against one of the loudest voices of American conservatism, Robert Dornan. In the primary against three Anglo male Democrats, she won with 35% of the vote. Her primary victory attracted little attention, not even from Dornan. But she shrewdly counted on increasing Latino turnout. Sanchez calculated that she could attract contributions from the many enemies that Dornan had made over a political career that went back to 1976 and included a quixotic presidential campaign that took him far from Orange County during 1995 and 1996. Bill Clinton came to Santa Ana late in the campaign to stump for Sanchez, and may have made the difference. She won by 984 votes, 47%–46%. In response to great cheering in the White House and many liberal precincts came bellows of rage from Dornan and charges of vote fraud. Using the privileges afforded to former members, he regularly appeared on the House floor trying to convince his former colleagues to call for a special election; Democrats charged that he was abusing his privileges by promoting a personal agenda and the House voted to bar him from the floor after a heated discussion between Dornan and New Jersey Democrat Bob Menendez. Finally, in February 1998, the House Administration Committee upheld Sanchez's victory.

After the election Sanchez was named general co-chairwoman of the Democratic National Committee to lead a Hispanic voter registration drive, and Al Gore tapped her as honorary chair of his political action committee. But that proved a mixed blessing for both Sanchez and her party. She scheduled a fundraiser during the 2000 Democratic National Convention at Hugh Hefner's Playboy Mansion. Gore and many House Democrats—including other Latinos, from whom she had kept her distance—said that she was undermining the party's image. At first quietly, then more bluntly, she was urged to choose a new site and warned that she was jeopardizing her political future. Belatedly she relented and moved the event to Universal Studio's City Walk.

In the House, Sanchez's voting record leaned to the Democratic middle. Vietnam has been a focus: Accompanying Clinton on his November 2000 visit to Vietnam, she met with dissidents to discuss human rights. Her plans to return in 2004 were blocked when she was denied an entry visa because her visit "would not serve Vietnam-U.S. relations." She sends newsletters in Vietnamese to the local community. On the Armed Services Committee, she has worked to bring jobs to local high tech firms; in 2004, the House passed her provision for the Pentagon to study the loss of civilian income by reservists on active duty. She wants to update the sexual assault crimes in the Uniform Code of Military Justice so that it complies with federal sexual assault crimes. She became the number two Democrat on the Homeland Security Committee, where she has focused on port security, including her proposal for a secure, long-range automated vessel tracking system.

Sanchez has been reelected comfortably. In 2002 she angered some Latino Democrats when she worked hard to elect her sister Linda Sanchez in the new 39th District. That may not be her only foray into politics beyond the 47th District; ever ambitious, Sanchez has said that she might like to be a senator some day. For a few days in August 2003, she floated her name as a Democratic candidate in the governor recall election.

FORTY-EIGHTH DISTRICT

Rep. Christopher Cox (R)

Elected 1988, 9th term; b. Oct. 16, 1952, St. Paul, MN; home, Newport Beach; U. of S. CA, B.A. 1973, Harvard U., M.B.A., J.D., 1977; Catholic; married (Rebecca).

Professional Career: Clerk, U.S. Court of Appeals, Judge Herbert Choy, 1977–78; Practicing atty., 1978–86; Lecturer, Harvard Bus. Schl., 1982–83; Sr. Assoc. Cnsl., White House, 1986–88.

DC Office: 2402 RHOB, 20515, 202-225-5611; Fax: 202-225-9177; Web site: www.cox.house.gov.

District Office: Newport Beach, 949-756-2244.

Committees: *Homeland Security* (Chmn. of 19 R).

Group Ratings

	ADA	ACLU	AFS	LCV	ITIC	NTU	COC	ACU	NTLC	CHC
2004	5	5	0	0	100	78	95	100	94	92
2003	5	—	0	5	—	70	97	92	—	—

National Journal Ratings

	2003 LIB	—	2003 CONS		2004 LIB	—	2004 CONS
Economic	17%	—	81%		0%	—	95%
Social	13%	—	86%		31%	—	67%
Foreign	0%	—	89%		7%	—	92%

Key Votes of the 108th Congress

1. Drilling in ANWR	Y	5. DC School Vouchers	Y	9. Ban Same-Sex Marriage	N
2. Approve Bush Tax Cuts	Y	6. Ban Human Cloning	Y	10. Fund Iraq War	Y
3. Medicare/Rx Bill	Y	7. Restrict Gun Liability	Y	11. Bar Cuba Embargo Funds	N
4. Bar Overtime Pay Regs.	N	8. Ban Partial-Birth Abortion	Y	12. Intelligence Reorg.	Y

Election Results

2004 general	Christopher Cox (R)	189,004	(65%)	($1,038,914)
	John Graham (D)	93,525	(32%)	($1,994)
	Other	8,343	(3%)	
2004 primary	Christopher Cox (R)	unopposed		
2002 general	Christopher Cox (R)	122,884	(68%)	($736,225)
	John Graham (D)	51,058	(28%)	($10,030)
	Other	5,607	(3%)	

Prior Winning Percentages: 2000 (66%); 1998 (68%); 1996 (66%); 1994 (72%); 1992 (65%); 1990 (68%); 1988 (67%)

The People		Race/Ethnic Origin	Ancestry	
Area size:	301 sq. mi.	68.0% White	German: 11.3%	English: 9.3%
Urban population:	99.9%	1.4% Black	Irish: 8.3%	
Rural population:	0.1%	12.7% Asian	**2004 Presidential Vote**	
Pop. 2000:	639,087	0.2% Native Am.	Bush (R) 178,739	(58%)
Median income:	$69,663	0.2% Hawaiian	Kerry (D) 123,664	(40%)
Poverty status:	6.3%	2.7% Two+ races	Other 3,364	(1%)
Military veterans:	10.3%	0.2% Other	**2000 Presidential Vote**	
		14.7% Hispanic Origin	Bush (R) 156,340	(58%)
			Gore (D) 106,809	(39%)
			Other 7,421	(3%)
			Cook Partisan Voting Index: R + 8	

Occupation   Blue collar: 10.1%   White collar: 79.8%   Gray collar: 10.1%

If you drove south on the Santa Ana and San Diego Freeways in Orange County 30 years ago, once you got past Santa Ana and John Wayne Airport you would have found yourself in open land for the next 25 miles, a vacant landscape of flat plains and low mountains, all beneath the 4,600-foot Trabuco Peak in the distance. This was the land of the Irvine Ranch, purchased by Gold Rush merchant James Irvine from the Sepulveda and Yorba families and maintained as a ranch until the early 1970s, the last large plot of vacant land in metro Los Angeles. Irvine sold some of it to create the cities of Santa Ana and Tustin, but in the 1970s there was still this great swath of land, 10 miles along the Pacific Coast and 22 miles inland to the mountains, where the freeway traveler could see what the California the first American settlers saw looked like. As Orange County grew up to the limits of the Irvine Ranch, the Irvine family realized that they owned immensely valuable land. In 1959 they donated a site for the University of California at Irvine and in the 1970s they sold the rest of the property to developers. The resulting city of Irvine was a planned community, with eight-lane parkways, huge office parks and shopping malls and attractive subdivisions and condominiums. Irvine has attracted high-tech and high-growth businesses, highly educated and affluent people, including Asian immigrants; in 2000, 10% of its 143,000 residents were Chinese, enough to support a Chinese supermarket and a Chinese-language library. Irvine is one planned city that respects free market economics; the new expressways on the Irvine Ranch land were built by private companies and paid for by tolls. Now the last piece of Irvine, the El Toro Marine Corps Air Station that closed in 1999, is, as Orange County voters decided in a 2002 referendum, being developed as a Great Park, with 3,800 acres of open space, 3,600 homes and 3 million square feet of commercial and industrial space. Efforts by then-Los Angeles Mayor James Hahn to have the land developed as an airport were angrily rebuffed by the Navy, which auctioned off the property online for $649 million in February 2005.

Irvine is set amid a raft of affluent communities, except for low-income and 76% Hispanic Santa Ana. To the north is Tustin, an older town built on Irvine land. To the south is Newport Beach, one of California's richest cities; Newport Harbor is chock full of expensive boats, and Newport Beach is the setting for the TV program, *The OC*. To the east is Lake Forest; the name used to be El Toro, and some residents now complain that it has few lakes or forests. To the southeast, on the ocean is Laguna Beach with its art galleries and cute shops, and more conventionally affluent Dana Point. Inland are new affluent communities—Laguna Niguel, Laguna Hills, Laguna Woods.

The 48th Congressional District of California is centered geographically on the Irvine Ranch lands and includes all of these communities. Politically, this is a conservative area, and for a long time it was one of the most Republican districts in the United States. In the 1990s, like most of metro Los Angeles, it trended to the Democrats, but it is still Republican, but far from the most Republican district in the state; it voted 58% for George W. Bush in 2000 and 2004.

The congressman from the 48th District is Christopher Cox, a Republican first elected in 1988; in June 2005, he was nominated by George W. Bush to chair the Securities and Exchange Commission. Cox grew up in St. Paul, Minnesota, graduated from the University of Southern

California in three years, went to Harvard Law and Business Schools jointly, clerked for a Ninth Circuit judge in Hawaii, practiced law at a big firm in Orange County, then was part of the Reagan White House counsel's staff. In fall 1987 he had lunch in the White House Mess with Dana Rohrabacher, then a speechwriter. Cox told him that Orange County Congressman Robert Badham had announced he was retiring; Rohrabacher said Dan Lungren was vacating his Long Beach seat. That day they decided to run for the seats. Cox was one of 14 Republican candidates for the safe Republican seat. With the support of Oliver North, Robert Bork and members of the Irvine family, he won the primary with 31% of the vote. He has since won primary and general elections without difficulty. Cox's intellect and range of interests are impressive: from the former Soviet Union (he and his father published an English translation of *Pravda* from 1984 to 1988) to lobbying for more local control of highway funds.

With the Republican victory in 1994, Cox came into his own, becoming chairman of the Republican Policy Committee and a leading legislator on many fronts. On the first day of the new Congress, he led the move to end baseline budgeting. Another specialty is tort law. He wrote the securities litigation reform to prevent predatory suits against high-tech and other companies, which got two-thirds support in both houses and was the only bill passed over Bill Clinton's veto in his first term. His bill to limit appeals of death penalties became law in April 1995. With Democratic Senator Ron Wyden of Oregon, he won enactment in 1998 of an important proposal for the emerging marketplace— the Internet Tax Freedom Act, which placed a three-year moratorium on state and local governments from imposing special taxes on electronic commerce. It was renewed for two years in November 2001 and December 2004. In January 2003 Cox and Wyden sponsored a bill to make it permanent. Cox has sponsored another Internet-related bill, to create an Office of Global Internet Freedom in the Board of International Broadcasting, to monitor state censorship of the Internet, to deploy technology to defeat efforts to block access to sites and to keep track of companies which sell China and other dictatorships technology to block sites. Cox wrote a thesis at Harvard in 1977 on double taxation of corporate dividends, and beginning in 1992 he has sponsored bills to end double taxation. He welcomed George W. Bush's proposal to do just that in January 2003, and the cut passed later that year.

He also chaired the special committee investigating technology transfers from U.S. companies to China. Thanks to Cox and ranking Democrat Norman Dicks, this investigation was conducted on a bipartisan basis, without leaks, and produced a unanimous report documenting an extensive operation by China to acquire military technology, including nuclear weapons design, by groups with links to the Chinese military or state intelligence service. It faulted the policies of the Reagan, Bush and Clinton administrations; Cox won much bipartisan praise over his handling of the report.

After the September 11 attacks, some members speculated about what would have happened if United Flight 93 had not been downed in Pennsylvania but had struck the Capitol: hundreds of congressmen and senators might have been killed or disabled. Vacancies in the Senate can be filled by gubernatorial appointments of successors, but under the Constitution vacancies in the House can be filled only by elections, which usually takes several months. Cox took the lead among Republicans on the issue. Cox co-chaired the bipartisan Continuity of Government Commission which started meeting in September. Speaker Dennis Hastert did not consider the issue a priority and wanted members to consider solutions which could be achieved by changing House rules and passing statutes before considering a constitutional amendment. In January 2003 Cox proposed three changes in House rules which were adopted with bipartisan support. The first would allow the speaker to designate successors in the event of a vacancy; that would allow the new speaker to convene the House. The second provided that the speaker could adjourn the House at any time of imminent danger; this overrode the rule that the speaker could not adjourn the House when a measure was being considered. The third allowed the House to adjust the number of its members after a catastrophic attack; the House cannot go into session without a majority of members, and so if many members were disabled, it could not act. In April 2004 he worked with Rules Chairman David Dreier and got the House to pass a law setting a 45-day limit for special elections to fill vacancies if more than 100 seats are declared vacant by the speaker, but the Senate did not act on this.

Cox has often been mentioned as a candidate for statewide office, but has never run. George Will suggested he would be a good choice for vice president. During the House Republican turmoil in late 1998, Cox twice showed interest in running for speaker but he backed off each time. In early 2001 Cox was on the verge of being nominated to be a judge on the Ninth Circuit Court of Appeals. But Senator Barbara Boxer opposed him and in May 2001, after Jim Jeffords announced he was switching parties, he withdrew his name from consideration even as other Republicans were running active campaigns for what they assumed would soon be a vacant seat.

In January 2003 Cox sought the chairmanship of the Government Reform Committee. He was less senior than Christopher Shays, but Shays seemed unlikely to be picked because of his role on the campaign finance regulation bill passed over the leadership's opposition. The Republican Steering Committee passed over both of them and picked Tom Davis. Instead, Cox was named chairman of the Select Committee on Homeland Security. In October 2003 he prepared a bill requiring that first responder grants be ranked by DHS's information analysis wing based on the likelihood of a threat; this was resisted by the department, but a similar approach was taken by ranking Democrat Jim Turner. In July 2004 his BioShield bill became law; it provided for $5.6 billion over 10 years to purchase and stockpile vaccines and antidotes that would be needed after a bioattack. In September 2004 he proposed a set jurisdiction for the committee, which was opposed by Transportation Chairman Don Young and Commerce Chairman Joe Barton. In November Speaker Dennis Hastert supported making the committee permanent, and in January 2005 it got jurisdiction over the TSA, border security, infrastructure protection, some Customs functions and port security. Barton persuaded a closed Republican conference to give Commerce jurisdiction over cybersecurity by a 65–59 vote, and the Coast Guard remained under Transportation.

On June 2, 2005, Bush nominated Cox to chair the Securities and Exchange Commission; he was to replace William Donaldson, who announced the previous day his resignation at the end of June. Bush cited Cox's background as a securities lawyer plus his congressional experience in curbing securities lawsuits. Some business lobbyists welcomed the nomination because of unhappiness over Donaldson's increased regulatory activism; consumer groups were wary of Cox. Although the SEC chairmanship typically has not been a political stepping stone, Franklin D. Roosevelt promoted William O. Douglas to the Supreme Court after he served as SEC chairman during the New Deal. Cox became the second ambitious House Republican leader in the 109th Congress to be tapped by the White House: Representative Rob Portman was confirmed as the Bush administration's trade representative in April 2005. Republicans would be almost certain to hold Cox's Orange County seat in a special election.

FORTY-NINTH DISTRICT

Rep. Darrell Issa (R)

Elected 2000, 3d term; b. Nov. 1, 1953, Cleveland, OH; home, Vista; Sienna Heights U., B.A. 1976; Antioch Orthodox Christian; married (Kathy).

Military Career: Army, 1970–72; 1976–80.

Professional Career: Founder & Pres., Directed Electronics, 1982–99.

DC Office: 211 CHOB, 20515, 202-225-3906; Fax: 202-225-3303; Web site: www.issa.house.gov.

District Offices: Temecula, 909-693-2447; Vista, 760-599-5000.

Committees: *Government Reform* (15th of 23 R): Energy & Resources (Chmn.); Federal Workforce & Agency Organization. *International Relations* (13th of 27 R): Europe & Emerging Threats; International Terrorism & Nonproliferation (Vice Chmn.); Middle East & Central Asia. *Judiciary* (16th of 23 R): Courts, the Internet & Intellectual Property; Immigration, Border Security & Claims.

Group Ratings

	ADA	ACLU	AFS	LCV	ITIC	NTU	COC	ACU	NTLC	CHC
2004	0	5	0	0	100	57	100	92	81	84
2003	5	—	0	10	—	60	97	87	—	—

National Journal Ratings

	2003 LIB — 2003 CONS	2004 LIB — 2004 CONS
Economic	9% — 84%	15% — 84%
Social	22% — 77%	25% — 73%
Foreign	38% — 62%	34% — 63%

Key Votes of the 108th Congress

1. Drilling in ANWR	Y	5. DC School Vouchers	Y	9. Ban Same-Sex Marriage	Y
2. Approve Bush Tax Cuts	Y	6. Ban Human Cloning	Y	10. Fund Iraq War	Y
3. Medicare/Rx Bill	Y	7. Restrict Gun Liability	Y	11. Bar Cuba Embargo Funds	N
4. Bar Overtime Pay Regs.	N	8. Ban Partial-Birth Abortion	Y	12. Intelligence Reorg.	Y

Election Results

2004 general	Darrell Issa (R)	141,658	(63%)	($882,952)
	Mike Byron (D)	79,057	(35%)	($69,035)
	Other	5,751	(3%)	
2004 primary	Darrell Issa (R)	unopposed		
2002 general	Darrell Issa (R)	94,594	(77%)	($326,416)
	Karl Dietrich (Lib)	26,891	(22%)	($27,792)
	Other	1,012	(1%)	

Prior Winning Percentages: 2000 (61%)

The People

Area size:	1,778 sq. mi.
Urban population:	90.3%
Rural population:	9.7%
Pop. 2000:	639,087
Median income:	$46,445
Poverty status:	11.9%
Military veterans:	15.3%

Race/Ethnic Origin

57.9% White
5.0% Black
3.5% Asian
0.9% Native Am.
0.5% Hawaiian
2.5% Two+ races
0.2% Other
29.5% Hispanic Origin

Ancestry

German: 10.7%   Irish: 7.9%
English: 7.8%

2004 Presidential Vote

Bush (R)	149,283	(63%)
Kerry (D)	86,998	(36%)
Other	2,389	(1%)

2000 Presidential Vote

Bush (R)	114,193	(59%)
Gore (D)	75,561	(39%)
Other	5,217	(3%)

Cook Partisan Voting Index: R +10

Occupation   Blue collar: 24.4%   White collar: 58.1%   Gray collar: 17.5%

The California coast between Los Angeles and San Diego has never entirely filled up with development—and never will as long as the Marine Corps retains custody of Camp Pendleton, the giant training base just south of the Orange-San Diego County line. The land along the coast and inland in northern San Diego County, usually referred to as North County, was largely empty territory a quarter century ago—never fertile enough to produce a large farm community, never endowed with much manufacturing, never actively promoted as a retirement community. But North County has been growing rapidly since then. Today about one million people live here, and who can blame them? For this is one of America's most beautiful and comfortable environments, with ocean and mountain scenery, sunny and warm weather, no rural poverty and low crime. Here, amid dry but not desert landscape, you can see miles of rolling hills, with occasional surrealistic trees and sagebrush-like bushes; mountains clump up not in ridges, but here and there, seemingly at random. This land has attracted thousands of new migrants—many, but by no means all, retirees.

The 49th Congressional District of California occupies the northern part of San Diego County and the southwestern corner of Riverside County. It was the fastest-growing California district in the 1990s, with a population increase of 35%. On the coast next to Camp Pendleton is Oceanside, a lower-middle-income town heavily dependent on the base; local business declined in early 2003 when thousands of residents went off to war. Inland is Vista, a higher-income community. About 40% of the district's population is in these two areas. About 30% are in small communities in North County, including a small portion of San Diego. Another 30% are in Riverside County. Here is the instant city of Temecula: a corner-grocery town serving a vineyard district in the mid-1980s, it is now the center of an area with more than 100,000 people, mostly commuters attracted by low-priced homes and traditional values, but with 3,000 employed by Guidant, recently purchased by Johnson & Johnson. To the north are the older communities of Lake Elsinore, Canyon Lake and Perris. Politically, this is a heavily Republican area, which rarely elects Democrats to any office; it voted 63% for George W. Bush in 2004, the third highest percentage in California's 53 districts. People here are affluent enough to identify with the party of property, conventional enough in their personal lives to identify with what describes itself as the party of traditional values.

The congressman from the 49th District is Darrell Issa (pronounced *EYE-sah*), a Republican first elected in 2000. He grew up in a Lebanese-Christian family in a heavily Jewish neighborhood of Cleveland, and graduated from Sienna Heights University in Adrian, Michigan. To compensate for dyslexia, he studies hard and attempts to memorize prepared statements. After his Army service, Issa started the Viper car alarm company in Cleveland, moved the business to North County and renamed it Directed Electronics, where it became the world's largest manufacturer of vehicle security systems, with the industry's largest R&D budget. The firm, the first with a programmable personal computer system, made him a fortune estimated at $200 million as he found a way to capitalize legally on America's high crime rates. He became active in the high-tech industry, serving as chairman of the Consumer Electronics Association. In the early 1990s he turned to politics, contributing to Republicans and chairing the 1996 campaign to pass Proposition 209, which banned state use of racial quotas and preferences. In 1998 he ran for the Senate seat of Barbara Boxer and spent $9.8 million of his own money. But he lost the Republican primary 45%–40% to Matt Fong.

In November 1999, when North County incumbent Ron Packard announced his retirement, it was obvious that his successor would be chosen in the Republican primary. Although there were 10 candidates, the race turned into a bruising two-man contest between Issa and state Senator Bill Morrow; former Congressman Robert Dornan expressed interest in a comeback attempt, but he deferred to his son, Mark Dornan, who trailed well behind. Morrow questioned Issa's business practices. Issa raised questions about his opponent's honesty. On most issues, the candidates took similar positions; they supported streamlining government, opposed abortion and favored rebuilding the military. Issa spent $1.5 million of his own money on the primary, and beat Morrow 46%–30%. In the fall the Democratic nominee disconnected his phone and abandoned his campaign because his party, predictably, gave him little support. Issa won 61%–28%.

In the House, Issa's voting record was relatively moderate, especially on foreign issues. He became unusually active on overseas issues. On the eve of George W. Bush's decision to start the military action in Afghanistan, Issa joined Democrat Robert Wexler, who is Jewish, in a visit to several Middle East nations to build support for the United States. During that trip, he suggested that he was the victim of racial profiling when he was kept off an Air France flight to Paris; the airline claimed that he was late. After he hesitatingly voted for a House resolution expressing solidarity with Israel, he voiced reservations about its lack of evenhandedness. In December 2001, the issue of terrorism hit especially close to home: two members of the militant Jewish Defense League were charged with plotting to blow up Issa's office in San Clemente and a Culver City mosque.

At the start of his second term, he won a seat on Energy and Commerce that he had sought as a freshman. He won House passage of his bill for a new water project from the Santa Margarita River to serve Camp Pendleton. In January 2005, he took a leave of absence from Energy and Commerce, so that he could rejoin the International Relations and Judiciary Committees, where he reclaimed his seniority. Issa has sought to cut back on illegal immigrants in the United States and to prevent them from getting driver's licenses. He also joined the Government Reform Committee, where as a new member he became chairman of the Energy and Resources Subcommittee; he planned to use his technology experience to oversee federal programs.

Issa considered running against Boxer in 2004, but decided not to. In May and June 2003 he spent $1.7 million of his own money on the campaign to get the signatures needed for a special election to recall Governor Gray Davis; without his money the drive would have failed. He also hinted that he would run for governor on the replacement ballot but, when Arnold Schwarzenegger entered the field just before the deadline, Issa tearfully announced that he would not run. He had been weakened by Democratic charges against him that were linked to decades-old news reports of possible criminal activity in Ohio; a judge had dismissed the prosecutor's charges. After Schwarzenegger won, Issa made known his interest in running for lieutenant governor in 2006. He was an early supporter of Schwarzenegger's non-partisan redistricting proposal.

FIFTIETH DISTRICT

Rep. Randy (Duke) Cunningham (R)

Elected 1990, 8th term; b. Dec. 8, 1941, Los Angeles; home, San Diego; U. of MO, B.A. 1964, M.S. 1965, National U., M.B.A. 1985; Christian; married (Nancy).

Military Career: Navy, 1966–87 (Vietnam).

Professional Career: Teacher, Hinsdale H.S., 1965–66; Businessman, 1987–90.

DC Office: 2350 RHOB, 20515, 202-225-5452; Fax: 202-225-2558; Web site: www.house.gov/cunningham.

District Office: Escondido, 760-737-8438.

Committees: *Appropriations* (16th of 37 R): Defense; Labor, Health and Human Services, Education & Related Agencies. *Permanent Select Committee on Intelligence* (3d of 12 R): Technical & Tactical Intelligence; Terrorism, Human Intelligence, Analysis & Counterintelligence (Chmn.).

Group Ratings

	ADA	ACLU	AFS	LCV	ITIC	NTU	COC	ACU	NTLC	CHC
2004	5	0	13	9	100	54	100	92	81	100
2003	5	—	0	15	—	62	97	92	—	—

National Journal Ratings

	2003 LIB	—	2003 CONS	2004 LIB	—	2004 CONS
Economic	27%	—	71%	26%	—	73%
Social	5%	—	87%	9%	—	85%
Foreign	0%	—	89%	33%	—	66%

Key Votes of the 108th Congress

1. Drilling in ANWR	Y	5. DC School Vouchers	Y	9. Ban Same-Sex Marriage	Y
2. Approve Bush Tax Cuts	Y	6. Ban Human Cloning	Y	10. Fund Iraq War	Y
3. Medicare/Rx Bill	Y	7. Restrict Gun Liability	Y	11. Bar Cuba Embargo Funds	N
4. Bar Overtime Pay Regs.	N	8. Ban Partial-Birth Abortion	Y	12. Intelligence Reorg.	Y

Election Results

2004 general	Randy (Duke) Cunningham (R)	169,025	(58%)	($939,542)
	Francine Busby (D)	105,590	(36%)	($212,406)
	Other	14,713	(5%)	
2004 primary	Randy (Duke) Cunningham (R)	unopposed		
2002 general	Randy (Duke) Cunningham (R)	111,095	(64%)	($770,722)
	Del Stewart (D)	55,855	(32%)	($19,713)
	Other	5,751	(3%)	

Prior Winning Percentages: 2000 (64%); 1998 (61%); 1996 (65%); 1994 (67%); 1992 (56%); 1990 (46%)

The People		Race/Ethnic Origin	Ancestry	
Area size:	365 sq. mi.	65.8% White	German: 11.5%	English: 8.8%
Urban population:	97.8%	1.8% Black	Irish: 8.6%	
Rural population:	2.2%	10.3% Asian	**2004 Presidential Vote**	
Pop. 2000:	639,087	0.3% Native Am.	Bush (R) 169,935	(55%)
Median income:	$59,813	0.2% Hawaiian	Kerry (D) 135,007	(44%)
Poverty status:	8.1%	2.6% Two+ races	Other 2,891	(1%)
Military veterans:	13.4%	0.2% Other	**2000 Presidential Vote**	
		18.8% Hispanic Origin	Bush (R) 136,311	(54%)
			Gore (D) 107,436	(43%)
			Other 8,996	(4%)
			Cook Partisan Voting Index: R + 5	

Occupation	Blue collar: 15.7%	White collar: 70.8%	Gray collar: 13.5%

Soledad Mountain looms over La Jolla, the affluent San Diego neighborhood, overlooking the Pacific Ocean to the west, the hills of San Diego and, past them, the flat expanse of Miramar Marine Corps Air Station. Here a visitor to San Diego can stand in the sunshine and see the Blue Angels perform aerial stunts. It is a sight no one could have seen half a century before: Miramar then was a small airfield, military planes could do nothing like those stunts and San Diego, even after heavy activity in its Navy bases in World War II, was still a urban small center well to the south. Most of the land you would see looking east and north from Soledad Mountain was empty landscape. Since then San Diego has grown to become the nation's seventh-largest city. Development has jumped over Miramar, where plans are underway to locate a national veterans' cemetery, to the inland communities of Escondido and San Marcos and over the old Del Mar race track on the coast to Encinitas and Carlsbad. These are pleasant and affluent communities, attractively planned, many with red tile roofs that contrast with the tan hillsides. Local officials continue to explore sites to replace the San Diego airport, which is on a small piece of downtown land with little room for expansion.

The 50th Congressional District of California covers much of this part of San Diego County. About 40% of its population is in the city of San Diego, including most of scenic La Jolla, hillside Clairemont, Carmel Valley and University City to the west and, north of Miramar, Mira Mesa, Rancho Penasquitos and part of Rancho Bernardo. About 25% are on or near the coast, from Del Mar, where a 1,000 foot pier was opened in 1917 but washed away in 1926, to Encinitas and Carlsbad, home of the La Costa resort. Just inland is affluent Rancho Santa Fe, with its multi-million dollar mansions set amid rolling hills and lush greenery. About 30% of the people are in Escondido and San Marcos. Politically, this is Republican territory, more so as one gets away from the coast; it voted 55% for George W. Bush in 2004.

The congressman from the 50th District is Randy (Duke) Cunningham, a Republican first elected in 1990. Born the day after Pearl Harbor, he taught and coached swimming in Hinsdale, Illinois, and San Diego; in 1966, at 25, he joined the Navy and became one of the most decorated pilots in the Vietnam War. He then trained pilots at Miramar in the Top Gun program; he retired from the Navy in 1987 and started a business in San Diego. In 1990 he ran in a Democratic district against Congressman Jim Bates, who had been charged with sexual harassment. Cunningham beat a former ambassador to Qatar in the Republican primary 46%–30% and in the general beat Bates 46%–45%. In 1992, faced with a choice of districts to run in, he passed up the marginal and culturally more liberal area on the coast and ran here. Incumbent Bill Lowery, a Republican who had 300 overdrafts at the House bank, withdrew from the race, and Cunningham comfortably won the primary and general. He has not been seriously challenged since then.

Cunningham has a generally conservative voting record. He arrived just in time for the Gulf War debate and in his first years worked to make Filipino Gulf war veterans eligible to apply for U.S. citizenship (San Diego is home to a sizable Filipino community) and to prevent base closings in the San Diego area. In May 2005, the Pentagon's base closure recommendation list spared all major local installations but Cunningham was dismayed by the BRAC commission chairman's suggestion that the Marine Corps Recruit Depot San Diego might be added to the list. Cunningham was one of four congressmen who in October 1992 met with George H.W. Bush and prompted him to ask questions about Bill Clinton's student trip to Moscow and Eastern Europe, an issue that hurt the Republican ticket. After Republicans gained the majority in 1994, he switched to the Appropriations Committee and has assignments on its two subcommittees with the largest budgets: Defense and Labor-HHS-Education. He has been a forceful advocate of more defense spending. Cunningham has pressed for stricter enforcement of immigration laws and sponsored a "no frills prison act." He successfully opposed efforts to terminate registration with the Selective Service, is a leading advocate of the constitutional amendment to bar flag desecration and co-sponsored legislation to ensure that military overseas ballots are counted. During the October 2002 debate on authorizing the use of force in Iraq, which he strongly supported, he broke down in tears as he recounted the sacrifices that members of the armed services make during war. When Secretary of Defense Donald Rumsfeld testified about the budget in February 2005, Cunningham said that he was "very concerned" about proposed cuts in the F/A-22 Raptor and raised doubts about continued support of the F-35 joint strike fighter, which he called "an inferior airplane." On his limited work outside of Appropriations, after a decade-long effort, he passed in 2004 a bill to exempt current and retired law enforcement officers from state laws that prohibit the carrying of concealed handguns. In 2005, he took over as chairman of the Intelligence Subcommittee on Human Intelligence and Counterintelligence, an assignment that Republican leaders said was an ideal fit with his military experience.

FIFTY-FIRST DISTRICT

Rep. Bob Filner (D)

Elected 1992, 7th term; b. Sept. 4, 1942, Pittsburgh, PA; home, San Diego; Cornell U., B.A. 1963, Ph.D. 1973, U. of DE, M.A. 1969; Jewish; married (Jane Merrill).

Elected Office: San Diego Schl. Bd., 1979–83, Pres., 1982–83; San Diego City Cncl., 1987–92, Dpty. Mayor, 1991.

Professional Career: Prof., San Diego St. U., 1970–92; Legis. Asst., U.S. Sen. Hubert Humphrey, 1974; Legis. Asst., U.S. Rep. Don Fraser, 1975.

DC Office: 2428 RHOB, 20515, 202-225-8045; Fax: 202-225-9073; Web site: www.house.gov/filner.

District Offices: Chula Vista, 619-422-5963; Imperial, 760-355-8800.

Committees: *Transportation & Infrastructure* (9th of 34 D): Aviation; Coast Guard & Maritime Transportation (RMM); Railroads. *Veterans' Affairs* (2d of 12 D): Health.

Group Ratings

	ADA	ACLU	AFS	LCV	ITIC	NTU	COC	ACU	NTLC	CHC
2004	95	93	100	73	33	10	22	9	0	15
2003	100	—	100	95	—	24	17	8	—	—

National Journal Ratings

	2003 LIB	—	2003 CONS	2004 LIB	—	2004 CONS
Economic	92%	—	0%	73%	—	26%
Social	92%	—	0%	88%	—	0%
Foreign	94%	—	0%	96%	—	3%

Key Votes of the 108th Congress

1. Drilling in ANWR	N	5. DC School Vouchers	N	9. Ban Same-Sex Marriage	N
2. Approve Bush Tax Cuts	N	6. Ban Human Cloning	N	10. Fund Iraq War	N
3. Medicare/Rx Bill	N	7. Restrict Gun Liability	N	11. Bar Cuba Embargo Funds	Y
4. Bar Overtime Pay Regs.	Y	8. Ban Partial-Birth Abortion	N	12. Intelligence Reorg.	*

Election Results

2004 general	Bob Filner (D) 111,441	(62%)	($657,867)
	Michael Giorgino (R) 63,526	(35%)	($111,778)
	Other 5,912	(3%)	
2004 primary	Bob Filner (D) 33,046	(77%)	
	Daniel Ramirez (D)............................. 10,074	(23%)	
2002 general	Bob Filner (D) 59,541	(58%)	($905,137)
	Maria Garcia (R) 40,430	(39%)	($113,569)
	Other... 2,816	(3%)	

Prior Winning Percentages: 2000 (68%); 1998 (99%); 1996 (62%); 1994 (57%); 1992 (57%)

The People		Race/Ethnic Origin	Ancestry		
Area size:	4,896 sq. mi.	21.3% White	German: 4.2%	Irish: 3.3%	
Urban population:	95.6%	9.4% Black	English: 2.9%		
Rural population:	4.4%	12.4% Asian	**2004 Presidential Vote**		
Pop. 2000:	639,087	0.5% Native Am.	Kerry (D) 100,062	(53%)	
Median income:	$39,243	0.6% Hawaiian	Bush (R) 85,762	(46%)	
Poverty status:	16.3%	2.4% Two+ races	Other 1,731	(1%)	
Military veterans:	12.2%	0.2% Other	**2000 Presidential Vote**		
		53.3% Hispanic Origin	Gore (D) 85,561	(57%)	
			Bush (R) 61,008	(41%)	
			Other 3,819	(3%)	
			Cook Partisan Voting Index: D + 7		

Occupation	Blue collar: 23.5%	White collar: 54.7%	Gray collar: 21.8%

San Diego, at one corner of the continental United States, not so long ago a small Navy town known for its good harbor and splendid weather, is now a major metropolis, a city of 1.26 million people and the center of a metro area of 2.93 million. It is also, to its sometime discomfort, one of the largest cities anywhere directly on an international border and between countries with strikingly different economic conditions, political systems and cultural traditions. On a daily basis, agents for the Border Patrol play a cat-and-mouse game with illegal immigrants trying to make the crossing. Nearly 70,000 were apprehended in a roughly 12-month period in 2004, but perhaps three times as many crossed the border in this area without being captured.

This is the busiest border crossing in the world, but most of San Diego seems to look away, toward the ocean. Tijuana looks to the United States, to the lower-income part of San Diego—the industrial zone on brown hills in Otay Mesa and San Ysidro, the industrial suburbs of Chula Vista and National City and the grid streets south of downtown and behind the harbor in San Diego itself. Many children from Mexico cross the border daily to attend public and private schools. Latinos are scattered in various parts of the city, in the southern corridor and in Encanto and Chollas Park in the east. Oddly, there is not much evidence of Mexican style in San Diego—less even than in Los Angeles, as if the border city was insisting on its Yanqui origins, just as San Diego's civic leaders bridled at the idea of a bi-national airport on the border, even though their single-runway airport is unable to meet demand and has major barriers to growth. Even the city's favorite symbol, the red Tijuana Trolley that takes tourists from downtown to the San Ysidro-Tijuana border station, is as resolutely Yanqui as Main Street in Disneyland.

The 51st Congressional District of California covers all of California's border with Mexico, including the southeast corner of San Diego, National City and Chula Vista on San Diego Bay, and San Ysidro and Otay Mesa, which are part of the city of San Diego, connected to the rest by lines running down the harbor. The 51st also extends east to the Arizona border to include all of Imperial County, with its string of farms and towns running south from the Salton Sea to Mexicali, Mexico. The water comes from the Colorado River through the All-American Canal; the Salton Sea was created when the canal burst in 1905 and water flowed into the lowest part of the desert. A new state law imposes a tax on water use in San Diego to pay for restoration of the sea. With farm land being turned into moderately priced subdivisions, rapidly growing Imperial County in 2000 had 142,000 people, 72% Hispanic; Mexicali has 790,000. District-wide, 73% of the people live in San Diego, National City and Chula Vista, 19% in Imperial County and only 8%

in the rest. Minorities make up 80% of the population: 53% Hispanic, 12% Asian (mainly Filipino) and 9% black. This was created to be a solidly Democratic district, but may be becoming less so: Al Gore won 57% of the vote here, but John Kerry won only 53%.

The congressman from the 51st District is Bob Filner, a Democrat first elected in 1992. Filner grew up in New York City and was a Freedom Rider in 1961, imprisoned for two months in Mississippi. He earned a Ph.D. at Cornell, taught history at San Diego State and directed the Lipinsky Institute for Judaic Studies; he took time off to work on Senator Hubert Humphrey's staff in the 1970s, was elected to the San Diego school board in 1979 and to the city council in 1987. The 1992 redistricting created a new Democratic seat in San Diego County, and Filner decided to run. He was strongly backed by local activists although he had two better-known rivals. Filner won the primary with 26%, to 23% for Waddie Deddeh, state senator and assemblyman since 1966; 20% for Jim Bates, four-term congressman defeated in 1990 after being disciplined for sexual harassment; and 19% for Juan Carlos Vargas.

Filner is politically savvy, with some original ideas about policy, aggressive in articulating his views, and has one of the most liberal voting records in the House. As the number two Democrat on the Veterans' Affairs Committee, Filner has become a vocal advocate of veterans' rights, a popular cause in a district of many military retirees. He wants to pay benefits to merchant mariners who served during World War II and often encountered hazardous conditions. In 1998, Filner was one of only five House members to vote against both parties' impeachment inquiries. In July 2001, he forced a House vote on a Social Security issue, to prohibit spending to implement the final report of Bush's Commission to Strengthen Social Security which proposed various forms of individual investment accounts; the vote was almost entirely on party lines. He voted against the use of force in Iraq; in September 2002, in a joint appearance on C-SPAN, Filner and Joe Wilson of South Carolina engaged in a heated argument after Filner stated that the U.S. had supplied biological and chemical weapons to Saddam Hussein in the past. Wilson angrily accused Filner of being "viscerally anti-American." Filner, citing his experience as a Freedom Rider, later said, "I've been beaten up and thrown in jail by better people than Joe Wilson." In 2004, he was the only member of the California delegation not to sign a letter seeking a waiver from a Clean Air Act provision requiring the state to add oxygenates to fuel; while the delegation felt that this would increase fuel costs, Filner saw an opportunity for ethanol made from sugar cane grown in Imperial County. He supported truckers blockading the border because of long waits they were facing, but he opposed an expansion of the border station at San Ysidro because he feared that I-5 construction would split the community geographically. He opposed the planned triple-fencing project at the westernmost stretch of the border because of environmental concerns.

In the 1996 primary, Filner was again opposed by Juan Carlos Vargas, by then on the San Diego Council. Filner won, but by just 55%–45%. The 2001 redistricting plan removed heavily Latino parts of San Diego but the addition of Imperial County resulted in an increase in Hispanic percentage from 51% to 53%. In the 2002 primary, Filner was challenged by Danny Ramirez, an Imperial County businessman. Filner won 70%–30%. In Imperial County, which cast one-quarter of the vote, Ramirez led 60%–40%. But Filner won 70%–30% in San Diego County. Filner won the general election 58%–39%. Early in 2005, Vargas, who was term-limited in the Assembly, said he was planning to challenge Filner for a third time. Although he would have an ethnic advantage, Imperial County Hispanics have known little of Vargas, and Filner may benefit from his constituent work there.

FIFTY-SECOND DISTRICT

Rep. Duncan Hunter (R)

Elected 1980, 13th term; b. May 31, 1948, Riverside; home, Alpine; U. of MT, U. of CA, Western St. U., B.S.L & J.D. 1976; Baptist; married (Lynne).

Military Career: Army, 1969–71 (Vietnam).

Professional Career: Practicing atty., 1976–80.

DC Office: 2265 RHOB, 20515, 202-225-5672; Fax: 202-225-0235; Web site: www.house.gov/hunter.

District Office: El Cajon, 619-579-3001.

Committees: *Armed Services* (Chmn. of 34 R).

Group Ratings

	ADA	ACLU	AFS	LCV	ITIC	NTU	COC	ACU	NTLC	CHC
2004	5	0	13	9	60	56	95	87	84	100
2003	10	—	0	10	—	58	83	88	—	—

National Journal Ratings

	2003 LIB	—	2003 CONS	2004 LIB	—	2004 CONS
Economic	21%	—	75%	31%	—	69%
Social	5%	—	87%	0%	—	91%
Foreign	23%	—	71%	14%	—	85%

Key Votes of the 108th Congress

1. Drilling in ANWR	Y	5. DC School Vouchers	Y	9. Ban Same-Sex Marriage	*
2. Approve Bush Tax Cuts	Y	6. Ban Human Cloning	Y	10. Fund Iraq War	Y
3. Medicare/Rx Bill	Y	7. Restrict Gun Liability	Y	11. Bar Cuba Embargo Funds	N
4. Bar Overtime Pay Regs.	N	8. Ban Partial-Birth Abortion	Y	12. Intelligence Reorg.	Y

Election Results

2004 general	Duncan Hunter (R)	187,799	(69%)	($1,058,126)
	Brian Keliher (D)	74,857	(28%)	($14,828)
	Other	8,782	(3%)	
2004 primary	Duncan Hunter (R)	unopposed		
2002 general	Duncan Hunter (R)	118,561	(70%)	($761,970)
	Peter Moore-Kochlacs (D)	43,526	(26%)	
	Michael Benoit (Lib)	6,923	(4%)	

Prior Winning Percentages: 2000 (65%); 1998 (76%); 1996 (65%); 1994 (64%); 1992 (53%); 1990 (73%); 1988 (74%); 1986 (77%); 1984 (75%); 1982 (69%); 1980 (53%)

The People		Race/Ethnic Origin	Ancestry	
Area size:	2,129 sq. mi.	72.9% White	German: 12.5%	Irish: 9.1%
Urban population:	93.6%	3.7% Black	English: 8.5%	
Rural population:	6.4%	5.4% Asian	**2004 Presidential Vote**	
Pop. 2000:	639,087	0.7% Native Am.	Bush (R) 177,055	(61%)
Median income:	$52,940	0.3% Hawaiian	Kerry (D) 108,806	(38%)
Poverty status:	8.1%	3.2% Two+ races	Other 2,509	(1%)
Military veterans:	16.0%	0.2% Other	**2000 Presidential Vote**	
		13.7% Hispanic Origin	Bush (R) 143,081	(57%)
			Gore (D) 98,633	(40%)
			Other 7,833	(3%)
			Cook Partisan Voting Index: R + 9	
Occupation	Blue collar: 18.2%	White collar: 67.7%	Gray collar: 14.1%	

San Diego began as a port, but today most metropolitan area residents live out of sight of the sea, in hilltop neighborhoods inland that look out over distant ridges and freeways or in warm, sunny valleys amid the mountains which become denser and higher as one travels east from the Pacific. There is a discernible difference in attitudes and values between those who have settled inland and those nearer the ocean, part of the split that became critical in California's political struggles and culture wars since the 1980s. In San Diego, both groups tend to identify as Republicans, and coastal people may be more affluent. But those who settle inland are more likely to be conventionally religious and to have traditional moral values; they tend to be more supportive of the military and assertive foreign policy; they are more dubious about the ability of government to shape poor citizens' lives. They are more conservative on most of the cultural and foreign issues of recent times, and therefore more reliably Republican: When oceanfront voters in San Diego shifted sharply toward Democrats in the 1990s, the movement was much less among voters inland. Inland San Diego County produced higher percentages for George W. Bush in 2004 than in 2000, while coastal San Diego County did not.

The 52d Congressional District of California takes in many of the inland San Diego suburbs and most of the mountain and desert interior of San Diego County. It includes the part of San Diego north of I-8 and east of I-15; Santee, an East County city of 53,000; El Cajon, which has the nation's second largest (after the Detroit area) community of Chaldeans, Catholic Arabs from Iraq, who own half of San Diego County's independent retail convenience stores and are known for their toughness—it was not easy being a Christian in Saddam Hussein's Iraq. It includes high-income Poway, north of San Diego, and more modest La Mesa, east of San Diego. The mountains and the desert to the east are lightly inhabited. In the mountains is tiny Alpine with one Indian casino and another sought by a tribe with a membership of seven adults and one child. In the desert is the town of Borrego Springs amid the giant Anza-Borrego Desert State Park. This East County area was swept by horrific fires in October and November 2003, which killed 17 people and destroyed more than 2,400 homes. Politically, this is a solidly Republican district.

The congressman from the 52d District is Duncan Hunter, a Republican first elected in 1980, an upset winner in the Reagan landslide who is now chairman of the Armed Services Committee. He grew up on a ranch outside Riverside, where his father was a real estate developer. He dropped out of college to serve in the Army, and was awarded a Bronze Star for his service in 24 helicopter combat assaults in Vietnam. He graduated from Western State University law school in 1976 and started a legal practice in San Diego's Barrio Logan. In 1980 his father urged him to run against Democratic Congressman Lionel Van Deerlin in what had been a safe Democratic district. But it was a Republican year in southern California and Hunter won 53%–47%. "Your real campaign is just starting," his father told him. "You've got to get on Armed Services." He did, and redistricting gave him a safe Republican seat. In the 1980s he was part of the group of young conservative Republicans around Newt Gingrich, but he concentrated on military issues.

On the committee, Hunter supported the Reagan defense buildup and was ardent backer of the Strategic Defense Initiative, which had few backers in the services or among senior committee members, and of the 600-ship Navy. After the 1994 election he failed in his attempt to get into the Republican leadership when he lost the Conference chairmanship to John Boehner. But he became chairman of the Military Procurement Subcommittee. He worked to accelerate development of the F-22, arguing that the Navy needed a stealth-equipped carrier plane. He argued for building more B-2s and against reducing the number of B-1s. He tried to push the Pentagon to build more nuclear submarines and match apparent Russian gains in quiet technology. He argued that the Pentagon had too many procurement officials who held up weapons development, and he inserts in each year's defense authorization amendments requiring that their numbers be reduced by 25,000; by 2002 the number had been reduced from 300,000 to 190,000.

Hunter argued for many years that the Clinton administration cut defense spending far too much, and he was willing to buck the Republican leadership and the incoming Bush administration to get more spending. He was disappointed with the increase in the first Bush budget, and in November 2001 called for a $32 billion increase in current spending, and said the administration was trying to "conduct an aggressive Ronald Reagan foreign policy with a Jimmy Carter defense budget." By January 2002 he was asking the Bush administration for a $50 billion increase in the next fiscal year; later, when the administration called for a $45 billion increase, he said he wanted $30 billion more than that.

In 2000 Hunter passed up a chance to run for the committee chairmanship but got the position two years later. Chairman Floyd Spence was rotated off as chairman because of House Republicans' six-year term limit; Hunter supported the next most senior member, Bob Stump, over Curt Weldon. Hunter said that he would be a candidate if Stump lost in the Republican Steering Committee; Stump won by one vote. On April 26, 2002, Stump announced that he was retiring because of poor health; that day Hunter said, "I'll be working hard for the chairmanship position." Weldon was considering running, but on May 20 withdrew and endorsed Hunter. During much of the rest of the year Stump was absent and Hunter was chairing committee meetings. In January 2003 he revised the subcommittee structure, establishing a new subcommittee on emerging threats and giving the other subcommittees jurisdiction based on service activities rather than Pentagon procedures.

On some issues Hunter has been at odds with the Bush administration. He said that the campaign in Afghanistan, fought with no area air bases, showed the need for more B-2s and B-1s. He called for more F-22s than the Pentagon wanted and was an enthusiastic supporter of the Joint Strike Fighter. He said there was a danger that the military was no longer capable of fighting two wars at the same time and he argued that Defense Secretary Donald Rumsfeld's plans for transforming the military should be accompanied by a buildup in troops. In November 2002 he argued that the administration's budget request still left the military $30 billion behind on modernization projects. In November 2002 he got the administration to back down on the issue of full retirement and disability benefits for veterans with Purple Hearts or injured during training or hazardous duty. Hunter has also frustrated the Senate: Senator Richard Lugar charged that he and Weldon took money away from the Nunn-Lugar program to dismantle Russian weapons of mass destruction to pay for weapons programs. "It is not the House," said Lugar, "it is two people."

In 2003 Hunter supported the administration budget request but disagreed with the cancellation of the Crusader armed vehicle and tried to postpone the 2005 base closing round. He added more B-1s and B-2s and authorization for a new bomber. Hunter has long favored restrictions on trade—he opposed NAFTA, GATT, normal trade relations with China and trade promotion authority and endorsed Patrick Buchanan in the 1996 presidential primaries—and in 2001 he barred the Army from buying berets made in China. In the 2003 defense authorization he increased the percentage of purchases that must be bought in America; this was opposed by the administration and led to a long deadlock with the Senate. On transformation he said, "Everybody has a different idea of what transformation means. The lesson of Iraq is some of the old and some of the new." In September 2003 Hunter and ranking Democrat Ike Skelton backed a permanent increase in the Army from 485,000 to 525,000. In early 2004 Hunter lined up House Republicans to back George W. Bush's $421 billion defense spending request against other claims on the money and called for a new international agency to keep weapons from terrorists. He supported Defense Secretary Donald Rumsfeld during the clamor about the Abu Ghraib abuses in May 2004 and pointedly refused to hold hearings on the subject as the Senate Armed Services Committee was doing.

Hunter played a major role on the intelligence reorganization bill in late 2004. In October Joint Chiefs Chairman Richard Myers told him that the new director of national intelligence could use his budgetary power to interrupt the flow of intelligence to the battlefield; Hunter urged him to put that in writing, which he did. At a closed-door meeting of House Republican leaders November 20 Hunter demanded changes in the intelligence bill that had come out of the conference committee, because the Senate had removed White House language assuring the secretary of defense power over military intelligence. He said that troops in the field would be imperiled and noted that his son Duncan Duane Hunter, who enlisted in the Marine Corps after September 11, was serving in Iraq. Also, Judiciary Committee Chairman James Sensenbrenner wanted to insert provisions on driver's licenses and asylum. Speaker Dennis Hastert pulled the bill from the floor and negotiations commenced. On December 6 Hunter accepted language proposed by Senator Susan Collins, that the bill "respects and does not abrogate the statutory responsibilities of the heads of departments," and the administration agreed to issue regulations maintaining the flow of intelligence from aircraft and satellites to troops in the field.

In 2005 Hunter again supported administration requests but sought more. He and Skelton questioned whether the Navy would have enough ships. He insisted the refueling tankers be built by an American firm. He hailed the award of a contract for the X-Craft Sea Fighter, a catamaran that can travel at 50 knots and deliver Special Forces teams to shore, a project he and Duke Cunningham had been pushing for several years.

Hunter was angered by the large number of illegal immigrants in the early 1990s, and at one point he called for using military aircraft for "deep deportation" of illegal immigrants. He wrote the 1997 law requiring the 14-mile, 15-foot high fence along the Mexican border from the Pacific Ocean to Otay Mountain; the inland 10 miles was built despite the threat to the endangered California gnat catcher and Least Bell's vireo. When the California Coastal Commission rejected the plan to build the remaining four miles to the ocean because it would fill in gulleys and interrupt the flow of a stream, Hunter denounced the decision as "nutty." In February 2005 he managed to include an override of this state decision in Sensenbrenner's driver's license and asylum bill. But San Diego's natural environment can cause problems. The border fence has reduced illegal immigration but seems to have led to more immigration in East County and Imperial County, and hundreds of illegal immigrants have died of thirst in the desert or by drowning in the All-American Canal. In 2000 Poway resident John Hunter, Duncan Hunter's younger brother, organized volunteers to put bottles of water in the desert to keep illegal immigrants from dying of thirst. Duncan Hunter thought it was a good idea and got Bureau of Land Management permits for his brother's project. And Duncan Hunter has been touched by nature too. In October 2003 his house in Alpine was engulfed by the wildfire; everything was destroyed, he reported, except an old station wagon he had been trying to get rid of.

Hunter has been routinely reelected by wide margins.

FIFTY-THIRD DISTRICT

Rep. Susan Davis (D)

Elected 2000, 3d term; b. Apr. 13, 1944, Cambridge, MA; home, San Diego; U.of CA at Berkeley, B.A. 1964, U. of NC, M.A. 1968; Jewish; married (Steven).

Elected Office: San Diego School Bd., 1983–92; CA Assembly, 1994–2000.

Professional Career: Devel. Assoc., KPBS Radio, 1980–82.; Exec. Dir., Aaron Price Fellows, 1990–94.

DC Office: 1224 LHOB, 20515, 202-225-2040; Fax: 202-225-2948; Web site: www.house.gov/susandavis.

District Office: San Diego, 619-280-5353.

Committees: *Armed Services* (16th of 28 D): Military Personnel; Readiness. *Education & the Workforce* (15th of 22 D): 21st Century Competitiveness; Education Reform.

Group Ratings

	ADA	ACLU	AFS	LCV	ITIC	NTU	COC	ACU	NTLC	CHC
2004	100	75	100	100	70	12	43	4	3	7
2003	90	—	100	100	—	22	33	16	—	—

National Journal Ratings

	2003 LIB	—	2003 CONS		2004 LIB	—	2004 CONS
Economic	87%	—	9%		75%	—	24%
Social	78%	—	20%		78%	—	19%
Foreign	61%	—	37%		72%	—	27%

Key Votes of the 108th Congress

1. Drilling in ANWR	N	5. DC School Vouchers	N	9. Ban Same-Sex Marriage	N
2. Approve Bush Tax Cuts	N	6. Ban Human Cloning	N	10. Fund Iraq War	Y
3. Medicare/Rx Bill	N	7. Restrict Gun Liability	N	11. Bar Cuba Embargo Funds	Y
4. Bar Overtime Pay Regs.	Y	8. Ban Partial-Birth Abortion	N	12. Intelligence Reorg.	N

Election Results

2004 general	Susan Davis (D)	146,449	(66%)	($387,177)
	Darin Hunzeker (R)	63,897	(29%)	($68,081)
	Other	11,090	(5%)	
2004 primary	Susan Davis (D)	unopposed		
2002 general	Susan Davis (D)	72,252	(62%)	($582,445)
	Bill VanDeWeghe (R)	43,891	(38%)	($742,535)

Prior Winning Percentages: 2000 (50%)

The People		Race/Ethnic Origin	Ancestry		
Area size:	251 sq. mi.	51.0% White	German: 8.8%	Irish: 7.4%	
Urban population:	99.9%	7.2% Black	English: 6.3%		
Rural population:	0.1%	8.3% Asian	**2004 Presidential Vote**		
Pop. 2000:	639,087	0.5% Native Am.	Kerry (D)	146,160	(61%)
Median income:	$36,637	0.4% Hawaiian	Bush (R)	89,890	(38%)
Poverty status:	20.2%	3.1% Two+ races	Other	2,953	(1%)
Military veterans:	12.1%	0.3% Other	**2000 Presidential Vote**		
		29.4% Hispanic Origin	Gore (D)	114,435	(58%)
			Bush (R)	74,526	(37%)
			Other	9,944	(5%)
			Cook Partisan Voting Index: D +12		

Occupation	Blue collar: 16.3%	White collar: 64.6%	Gray collar: 19.1%

When the United States was dictating the terms of the Treaty of Guadalupe Hidalgo in 1848, after its successful war with Mexico, it made sure the southern boundary of its new California territory was just south of the port of San Diego. This is one of three splendid natural harbors on the Pacific Coast and in 1914 the Marine Corps established a base on North Island. This was just the first of many military bases in San Diego, with its mild climate, deep harbor and plentiful land for aircraft maneuvers. This has been the major West Coast U.S. Navy base for more than 50 years, and home to 22,000 active duty Navy and Marine personnel on shore, with $7.5 billion in payroll and contract grants, the second largest Navy port behind Norfolk. Also based here are the retired aircraft carriers *Midway* and *Constellation*, plus the *Ronald Reagan*, which is the Navy's newest carrier, with a flight deck that covers 4.5 acres.

The port and Navy base in the sheltered harbor remain the central focus of a metropolis that has grown tenfold over that time and now stretches far inland and to the north. On one side is downtown, booming with postmodern buildings like the Horton Plaza amid a few well-preserved early 20th century relics like the Spreckels Theatre. Across the harbor, on the sand spit that guards it against the ocean, is the white frame castle of the Hotel Del Coronado, with its surprisingly dark wooden interior—the U.S.'s largest wooden structure and a favored resort of past American presidents; the town of Coronado has long been a favorite retirement place for Navy admirals and captains. But San Diego is not all harbor and Navy. To the north, the Pacific waves pound against the beach beneath erose cliffs of unique rock formations that stride up and down the coast. Here stand some of San Diego's great cultural institutions: the Scripps Institute of Oceanography, the University of California San Diego campus, the Salk Institute and the Torrey Pines reserve, home of this unique, wide-spreading pine tree. To the south are raffish Mission Beach, Ocean Beach, with its strong rip currents, and Point Loma, overlooking the entrance to the harbor. The weather—a sunny 70 degrees most of the time—has lured tourists and new residents to San Diego. But this is a working town as well, a sophisticated high-tech center with around 200,000 full and part-time students at its colleges and universities and growing biotech, electronics, software and telecommunications industries. It is a manufacturing center as well, with maquiladora factories clustering near the Mexican border.

The 53d Congressional District of California—the first and only 53d Congressional District in American history—consists of the center of San Diego, the San Diego beaches from Blacks Beach to Ocean Beach, the port that has become the home of several cruise lines, La Jolla beach (but not its interior) and Balboa Park. It includes the heavily Latino neighborhoods south and east of downtown, the Gaslamp District, with its glitzy night-life scene that has driven out most of the porn shops and the older neighborhoods of University Heights and East San Diego. Altogether, 85% of the district population is inside the San Diego city limits. It also includes Coronado and Imperial Beach, just north of the Mexican border, and the inland suburbs of La Presa and Lemon Grove, site of a celebrated school-desegregation case in the 1930s. Historically, this was a Republican district, but after Coastal California's trend toward cultural liberalism in the 1990s and the 2001 redistricting, it is now solidly Democratic. The Hispanic percentage is 29%, and John Kerry carried the district 61%–38%. Also in 2004, a local election captured national attention when surfer and write-in candidate Donna Frye fell about 2,000 votes short of defeating Mayor Dick Murphy with her outsider appeal and forced a three-month review of the vote; more than 5,500 ballots for her were disallowed because voters neglected to fill in the oval bubble next to the write-in, as required by state law. In April 2005, as the SEC and the U.S. Attorney's Office investigated whether he and other city officials concealed a $1.4 billion pension deficit from investors, Murphy announced his resignation. A special election was scheduled and Frye announced her candidacy.

The congresswoman from the 53d District is Susan Davis, a Democrat first elected in 2000. She grew up in Richmond, California, graduated from the University of California at Berkeley and got a degree in social work at the University of North Carolina. Her father and husband have both been physicians. She moved to San Diego in 1973 and became president of the local League of Women Voters and a community producer for the local public television station. In 1983 she was elected to the San Diego school board. In 1990, she became the executive director of the Aaron Price Fellows Program, which helps teach leadership and citizen skills to high school students. She returned to politics in 1994, winning the first of three terms in the California Assembly. Barred from a fourth term by term limits, Davis in 2000 challenged Republican Brian Bilbray, who had won three close elections. She portrayed him as a conservative, even though he took liberal positions on abortion and the environment and made a point of not attending the Republican National Convention. He supported John McCain's campaign finance regulation bill and said that he was comfortable with votes to impeach a president he called "a perpetual liar." She attacked Bilbray for supporting bills that would deny citizenship to U.S.-born children of illegal immigrants and that would allow private insurers to provide prescription drug benefits to seniors; she called for coverage under Medicare. The AFL-CIO ran so much advertising on her behalf that Davis requested it stop. Bilbray criticized Davis for her handling of utility deregulation, but Davis won 50%–46%.

In the House, she has had a moderate-to-liberal voting record, leaning to the center on foreign policy. Assigned to the Armed Services and Education and the Workforce committees, her priorities included higher military pay, increased aid for school districts with a large military presence, increased student loans and incentives for better teachers. She angered organized labor and some Democratic activists by voting for trade promotion authority, one of only 21 House Democrats to do so. She called the vote "agonizing," but in the interests of a city that has been built on trade; organized labor rescinded its endorsement. She crusaded against dietary supplements that contain the herbal stimulant ephedra, which has been said to cause heart attacks and strokes, and introduced legislation removing them from the marketplace. San Diego-based Metabolife was a leading producer of the supplements; the Food and Drug Administration eventually banned ephedra in 2004. With Republican Ginny Brown-Waite, she won House passage of a bill to increase the maximum loan amount that the Veterans Administration approves for home mortgages. Davis has been reelected easily.

★ COLORADO ★

At the Front Range of the Rocky Mountains, Colorado is also at the front edge of economic, cultural and political change. Colorado is an island of 4.6 million people surrounded by the sea of the Great Plains and the ramparts of the Rockies. With vistas of vast emptiness, it is mostly an urban state: More than half its people live in metropolitan Denver and four-fifths in the urban strip paralleling the Front Range, where the Rockies rise suddenly from the mile-high plateau. And its very ruggedness is inviting more settlement. While the eastern plains continue to lose population, the valley-crevices between the mountains are being filled with second-home condominiums and ranchettes and the rolling land on three sides of metro Denver is being platted into subdivisions.

Colorado started off with a boom, and its recent history has been punctuated by booms—and then by pauses of moderate growth. The first boom came with the discovery of gold and silver in the Rockies. Evidence of this mining boom still can be seen in the opera houses and storefronts of Cripple Creek and Central City, Aspen and Telluride, built when Denver was just a village on the creek that is the South Platte River. Then Denver grew, as a meatpacking, banking and manufacturing center, and also as the state capital and regional headquarters of the federal government. After that came the boom of the high-energy-price 1970s, when the Denver skyline sprouted new buildings overlooking the Capitol's golden dome and entrepreneurs built ever more ski resorts and year-round mountain condominiums.

Colorado's economy sagged during the low-energy-price 1980s but, based more on telecommunications and high-tech than energy, boomed again in the 1990s. The visible signs of this boom are still all around—in the skyscrapers of downtown Denver, bearing at various times, the names of Qwest and TCI and other telecommunications and high-tech companies; in the retro Coors Field baseball park set amid Denver's LoDo, where warehouses have been renovated into restaurants and clubs; in the startling architecture of the Denver International Airport far out in the plains; in the sprawling Denver Tech Center south of the city; in the fast-growing tracts of subdivisions and office parks in Douglas County south of Denver, the fastest-growing American county from 1990 to 2003. Colorado's economy grew robustly in the 1990s and the state attracted well-educated newcomers from around the country, with many from California; it ranked number one in high-tech workers per capita and third in venture capital financing per capita. In 2001 and 2002 it painfully shed high-tech jobs, but it remains among the top five states in economic development and venture capital, with high salaries and low unemployment. With its relatively young and highly educated population and its stunning environment, Colorado is also the leanest state, with the lowest percentage of obesity, and arguably the healthiest. In the mile high (or more) air, Coloradans like to ride, jog, bike and, of course, ski. There are bike paths not only in Denver but also in the mountains, and Governor Bill Owens started a campaign to urge people to eschew elevators and climb stairs.

Colorado has been reshaped, economically and politically, by its successive waves of new residents. The conservative and boosterish Colorado of the 1960s was transformed by a wave of liberal young migrants in the 1970s who swept the state's politics by calling for environmental protections and slow growth and eventually reached the national stage—slow-growth Governor Dick Lamm, Senator Gary Hart, Congresswoman Patricia Schroeder, Congressman Tim Wirth. Democrats held the governorship for 24 years but Republicans held the legislature. Then, in the 1990s, a new wave of migrants—tech-savvy, family-oriented cultural conservatives looking for an environment to prosper—moved Colorado politics to the right. In the 1990s, public school enrollment rose 14%, while private school enrollment was up 33% and the number of home-schooled children tripled. If the spirit of the 1970s newcomers was embodied in Boulder, with its pedestrian mall, outdoor sports shops and vegetarian restaurants, dominated politically by environmentalist liberals, the spirit of the 1990s newcomers was embodied in Colorado Springs, the home of the Air Force Academy, Fort Carson and Focus on the Family, and dominated politically by religious and family-oriented conservatives. Both of these politically very different

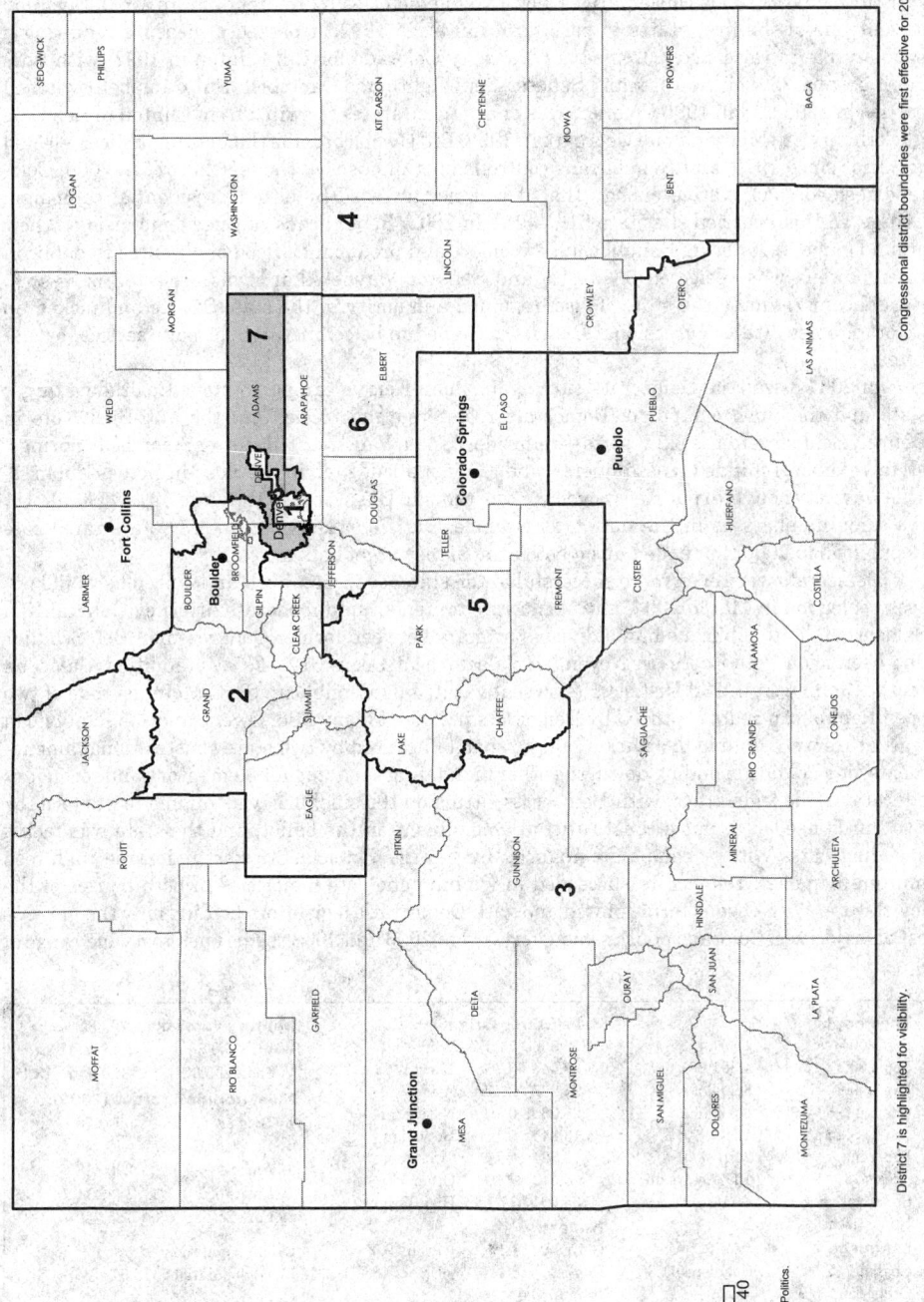

Congressional district boundaries were first effective for 2002.

District 7 is highlighted for visibility.

Miles

0   20   40

The Almanac of American Politics,
National Journal

communities have some reason to believe that they exemplify the state; elections here can be seen as political contests to determine which one does.

In the early 1990s conservatives won two big victories by referendum. In 1990, Colorado became one of the first states to pass term limits; in 1992, it passed a measure requiring a popular vote to raise taxes. Democrats did carry Colorado for Bill Clinton in 1992 (with Ross Perot getting 23% of the vote) and Senator Ben Nighthorse Campbell. But Campbell switched parties in 1995 and in 1996 Colorado was one of three states to switch from Clinton to Bob Dole (the others were Montana and Georgia). In 1998, Bill Owens became the first Republican elected governor since 1970, and Republicans controlled both houses of the legislature. In 2000, Colorado seemed conservative enough that it was not targeted by either presidential campaign; George W. Bush carried the state 51%–42%. In 2002, Republicans put new emphasis on their ground game, registering Republican newcomers and producing a flood of absentee Republican votes. Owens was reelected 63%–34% and Senator Wayne Allard was reelected 51%–46%. Republicans retained the state House, regained a majority in the state Senate and picked up Colorado's new 7th Congressional District, designed to be competitive for both parties, by 121 votes.

In 2004 it was the Democrats' turn again. John Kerry's campaign made Colorado a target state and the Bush campaign. Democrats registered and turned out the anti-Bush vote in Denver, Boulder and the ski resorts—Telluride, Aspen, Vail, Crested Butte, Steamboat Springs, all full of liberal-minded trustfunders—and ran just about even in the close-in Denver suburbs. This was not enough to put Kerry over the top, though: Bush carried the state 52%–47%, almost the same numbers as in the nation as a whole. But Colorado was the only state rated safe Republican in 2000 that ended up on both campaigns' target lists in 2004.

Democrats were even more successful at the state level. Campbell announced he would not seek reelection in March 2004, and Democrats united around moderate Attorney General Ken Salazar while Republicans had a divisive primary between former Congressman Bob Schaffer and beer scion Pete Coors. In November Salazar beat Coors 51%–47%. In addition, Salazar's brother John won the 3d District House seat vacated by Republican Scott McInnis—one of two open Republican seats captured by Democrats in 2004. Meanwhile, Owens and the Republican legislature were unable to attack a budget shortfall caused by two state constitutional amendments, one holding spending down, the other mandating spending for elementary and secondary education. The legislature, with Democrats sitting on the sidelines, was unable to produce the two-thirds needed to put a constitutional amendment on the ballot, and the state was facing spending cuts. With a campaign financed by heiress Patricia Stryker and three high-tech multimillionaires, Democrats succeeded in winning one-vote majorities in both houses of the legislature. With Owens term-limited and with Democratic legislators holding only the narrowest of majorities, Colorado politics going forward in 2006 and 2008 seems open to a wide range of possibilities.

The People		**Race/Ethnic Origin**			**Military veterans:** 446,385 (13.9%)	
Pop. 2004 (est):	4,601,403	3,202,880	74.5%	White	WWII: 15.0%	Korea: 11.3%
Pop. 2000:	4,301,261	158,443	3.7%	Black	Vietnam: 36.3%	Gulf War: 13.1%
Pop. 1990:	3,294,394	93,277	2.2%	Asian	**Most populous cities (2003):**	
Change 1990–2000:	Up 30.6%	28,982	0.7%	Native Am.	1. Denver	557,478
% of U.S. total:	1.5%	3,845	0.1%	Hawaiian	2. Colorado Springs	370,448
Pop. rank:	24th of 50	72,721	1.7%	Two+ races	3. Aurora	290,418
Area size:	104,094 sq. mi.	5,512	0.1%	Other	4. Lakewood	142,474
State Native:	41.1%	735,601	17.1%	Hisp. Origin	5. Fort Collins	125,740
Non-citizen:	5.9%	**Ancestry**			Urban population: 84.5%	
Language		German: 16.3%		Irish: 9.0%	Rural population: 15.5%	
English: 82.5%	Spanish: 11.3%	English: 8.8%		USA: 3.8%		
Other Eur.: 3.9%		Italian: 3.5%				

Education		Work Sector		General Assembly	
H.S. Grad:	86.9%	Private: 78.1%	Govt: 13.9%	Senate	18 D 17 R
College Grad:	32.7%	Self: 7.7%	Family: 0.3%	House	35 D 30 R
Industry		Unemployment: 4.3%		Legislative Term Limits: Yes	
Agri: 2.0%	Con: 9.1%	**Household Income**		**Registered Voters**	
Fin: 7.7%	Info: 4.9%	<15k: 11.9%	15-35k: 23.8%	D: 942,025	(30.4%)
Mfg: 14.0%	Prof: 28.7%	35-50k: 17.0%	50-100k: 33.1%	R: 1,118,597	(36.1%)
Public: 4.6%	Trade: 15.2%	100-150k: 9.1%	>150k: 5.2%	O: 1,037,239	(33.5%)
Other: 13.8%		Median: $47,203			
Occupation		Poverty status: 9.3%			
Blue collar: 21.0%	White collar: 64.5%	**Home Value**			
Gray collar: 14.5%		<50k: 6.0% 50-100k: 13.4% 100-200k: 48.1% 200-300k: 19.3%			
		300-500k: 9.4% >500k: 3.8% Median: $160,100			

Presidential politics   Colorado was a battleground state in 2004, as it was in the three-way race in 1992 (it was one of Ross Perot's best states) and was not in 2000. George W. Bush and John Kerry both paid several visits to the state; both campaigns ran TV ads here, and both parties launched major organizational efforts. The Democrats seem to have been more successful: they increased their margins by 34,000 votes in Denver and 33,000 in Boulder County, while Bush margins went up only 17,000 in El Paso County and 12,000 in Douglas County.

2004 Presidential Vote		
Bush (R)	1,101,255	(52%)
Kerry (D)	1,001,732	(47%)
Nader (Ref)	12,718	(1%)
Other	13,925	(1%)

2000 Presidential Vote		
Bush (R)	883,748	(51%)
Gore (D)	738,227	(42%)
Nader (Green)	91,434	(5%)
Other	27,959	(2%)

One additional fillip in Colorado was Amendment 36, financed by Jorge Klor de Alva, a California multimillionaire who runs a for-profit university in Brazil, which would have split Colorado's 9 electoral votes in proportion to its popular vote. In addition, it stated it would take effect immediately, i.e., when the electoral votes were cast in December 2004. Proponents said it would more accurately reflect voters' views and would serve as an example to the rest of the nation (Maine and Nebraska already give the winner in each congressional district an electoral vote, but this has not ever resulted in a split in those states' electoral votes.) Amendment 36 was vociferously opposed by Governor Bill Owens and other Republicans as an attempt to steal four electoral votes from George W. Bush, and others raised the specter of litigation over the immediate applicability clause determining the outcome of the 2004 presidential race. But as it became clear that John Kerry was contesting the state, and as polls showed him running even (most Colorado public polls in 2002 and 2004 seemed to lean Democratic), some Democrats decided that they would rather go for the full nine electoral votes rather than settle for the additional one they would get under Amendment 36 for carrying the state. Democratic Senate nominee Ken Salazar opposed the amendment, and support in polls slipped from 51% in mid-September to 36% in late October. The amendment was defeated 65%–35%; it lost in both Republican and Democratic counties. That likely dooms similar efforts in other states: partisans on both sides will oppose it in a closely divided state, while partisans of the minority party in a safe state will find it hard to muster enough votes to pass.

Colorado has had an early March presidential primary since 1992, when Jerry Brown won it. It has not attracted much attention since; in 2003, to save money, the legislature voted to eliminate its presidential primary in 2004.

Congressional districting

109th Congress Lineup
4 R   3 D
108th Congress Lineup
5 R   2 D

Colorado gained a House seat from the 2000 Census, just as it did from the Censuses of 1970 and 1980. Republicans would have controlled the redistricting process, except that they lost control of the state Senate in 2000. When the legislature proved unable to reach a compromise, a state court judge selected a Democrat-designed plan. The judge did not make major changes in the existing districts, but Republicans still responded angrily—they wanted the new district drawn in the fast-growing Republican counties on the south side of Denver. Instead, the newly created 7th District was anchored in the inner Denver suburbs to the north of the city—making it highly competitive for both parties.

The Republicans' one-seat takeover of the Senate in 2002 gave them another opportunity to take a crack at the congressional map. They prepared a new map, then introduced and passed it in late May 2003, in the final days of the legislative session. The new Republican map significantly strengthened 7th District Republican Bob Beauprez, who won in 2002 by 121 votes, the closest margin in the nation. They also increased the Republican base of the 3d District. Attorney General (now Senator) Ken Salazar sued in the Colorado courts, and in December 2003 the state Supreme Court threw out the new plan on the grounds that the state constitution prohibited more than one plan every 10 years; it rejected the argument that the court that drew the plan left it open for the legislature to act. Beauprez still won reelection by a comfortable margin.

Governor

Bill Owens (R)

Elected 1998, term expires Jan. 2007, 2d term; b. Oct. 22, 1950, Ft. Worth, TX; home, Aurora; Austin St. U., B.S. 1973; U. of TX, M.P.A. 1975; Catholic; married (Frances).

Elected Office: CO House of Reps., 1982–88; CO Senate, 1988–94; CO Treasurer, 1994–98.

Professional Career: Consultant, Touche Ross & Co., 1975–77; Project Mgr., Gates Corp., 1977–80, Assoc. Dir., 1980–82; Exec. Dir., CO trade assn., 1982–95.

Office: 136 State Capitol, Denver, 80203, 303-866-2471; Fax: 303-866-2003; Web site: www.state.co.us.

Election Results

2002 general	Bill Owens (R)	884,583	(63%)
	Rollie Heath (D)	475,373	(34%)
	Other	52,646	(4%)
2002 primary	Bill Owens (R)	unopposed	
1998 general	Bill Owens (R)	648,202	(49%)
	Gail Schoettler (D)	639,905	(48%)
	Other	33,200	(3%)

Bill Owens is now in the last two years of his second term as governor of Colorado. Owens grew up in Fort Worth, Texas, and was appointed a congressional page by Congressman Jim Wright, whom Owens's father had supported in his first victory in 1954. He went to Austin State University, where he demonstrated with a red-white-and-blue armband against anti-Vietnam war demonstrators, and to the University of Texas's Lyndon B. Johnson School, where he was one of the few Republicans during the Watergate scandal. He moved to Colorado and went to work for an oil producers association. In 1982, he was elected to the state House and in 1988 to the state Senate. In 1994, he was elected state treasurer.

In 1998 he ran for governor. Over the preceding 24 years Colorado had had only two governors, both Democrats, liberal environmentalist Dick Lamm and moderate Roy Romer. Owens won the Republican nomination over Senate President Tom Norton 59%–41%. In the general election, against Lieutenant Governor Gail Schoettler, Owens won 49%–48%.

In his first term, Owens delivered on many of his promises, though not always as some Republicans liked. In 1999, with a big campaign treasury and support from Romer and Denver Mayor Wellington Webb, he got voters to back a $1.7 billion transportation bond issue, which he claimed would finance $4.4 billion of transportation projects. Much of that money was being spent on T-REX, a rebuilding of the jammed I-25 and I-70 in Denver, scheduled for completion in 2006. After the shootings at Columbine High School in April 1999, Owens called for changes in police tactics and longer school hours for teenagers. Owens and the legislature sidetracked a pending concealed-carry law, and Owens backed a referendum that passed in 2000 requiring background checks for all sales at gun shows.

One of Owens's major issues was education reform. His proposal to expand the use of state assessment tests and to send to parents performance-based report cards for each school was loudly opposed by Democrats and teachers' unions but, after Owens got support from the Denver Public Schools, was passed by the Republican legislature in 2000. The report cards, rating schools as excellent, high, average, low or unsatisfactory, are the most explicit in the nation. While using TABOR and line item vetoes to rein in spending, he was able to get full funding for K-12 schools for four years in a row.

He also got the legislature to cut the income tax from 5% to 4.75%, and later to 4.63%. As revenues started coming in lower than expected in 2001 and 2002, he imposed across-the-board spending cuts and froze construction budgets. He passed paycheck protection for state employees, so that union leaders had to get positive authorization of dues payments every year; as a result, 70% of members left the Colorado Association of Public Employees.

In the 2002 election year Owens had high job ratings, plenty of funding and weak opposition. Against Democrat Rollie Heath, a strong liberal who had been president of asbestos-maker Johns Manville when it declared bankruptcy in 1982, Owens was reelected 63%–34%, carrying 60 of 64 counties. Democrats regained their majority in the state Senate, but Owens attracted national attention: he was called "America's Best Governor" in a cover story in *National Review*, got favorable coverage on the *Wall Street Journal* editorial page and appeared on Fox News and CNN.

But he ran into trouble in 2003 and 2004. In September 2003 he separated from his wife of 28 years, which sparked criticism from some local cultural conservatives. In November 2003 he backed Referendum A, for $2 billion in bonds to to store Western Slope water for distribution in the Front Range. Western Slope residents including Republican Congressman Scott McInnis and environmentalists including Democratic Congressman Mark Udall opposed it; the Farm Bureau and business interests backed it. But it lost 67%–33%, running behind in every county. Other Owens initiatives were overruled by courts. A federal court overturned a Pledge of Allegiance law in August 2003 and the Colorado Supreme Court overturned the legislature's congressional redistricting in December 2003. In June 2004, that court overturned Owens's school vouchers law. But that same month he signed a law setting up an institute to establish charter schools in any district; the state, under a 1993 charter law, already had more than 100 charter schools. Owens also signed a law giving in-state students a $2,400 voucher for tuition at any Colorado college or university. Owens also signed laws encouraging basic health insurance policies and health savings accounts.

In 2004 the state faced serious fiscal problems, not from lack of revenue but from a clash between two referenda passed by the state's voters: TABOR, which limited spending growth to the increase in inflation and population growth and mandated tax refunds, and Amendment 23, passed in 2000 by a 53%–47% margin, which mandated increases in K-12 spending. The combined effect of the two was to squeeze out spending on other programs. To put changes in either TABOR or Amendment 23 on the ballot required two-thirds majorities in the legislature. Majority Republicans were split over whether to allow inroads into TABOR; minority Democrats voted against most proposals and favored a citizens' initiative whose supporters decided not to put it on the ballot. Owens proposed to use funds from securitizing the state's tobacco settlement money, but was unable to get the legislature to agree in May 2004. Efforts at further negotiations failed up through the September 2004 deadline.

It was against that backdrop that Democrats won one-vote majorities in both houses of the legislature in November 2004, picking up one seat in the Senate and five in the House; they were assisted by a campaign financed by high-tech millionaires Jared Polis and Tim Gill and heiress Patricia Stryker and by a labor campaign run by the AFL-CIO's Colorado President Steve Adams. Accompanying that win were Democratic victories for Attorney General Ken Salazar in the Senate race and his brother John Salazar in the Republican-held 3d Congressional District. Democrats argued that the Republicans failed to solve the state's fiscal problem and instead concentrated on cultural issues, like the Pledge of Allegiance law, a resolution supporting the Family Marriage Amendment and a bill restricting teaching on homosexuality in schools. Owens also lost on a referendum for a Denver area sales tax increase for a FasTracks light rail project much larger than the one he backed as part of T-REX. After the election, Owens joined incoming Speaker Andrew Romanoff and argued that taxpayers should forego some TABOR refunds in return for a small income tax cut; Owens also continued to push for his tobacco payments plan. In March, Owens reached agreement with Romanoff and Senate President Joan Fitz-Gerald to place a referendum on the November ballot to divert $3.1 billion in taxpayer refunds from TABOR to social services. He said he will campaign with Democrats to win passage of the measure; anti-tax activists, including Grover Norquist, said they will oppose it.

After Colorado Republicans' success in the 2002 election, Owens was frequently mentioned as a future presidential candidate. Colorado Democrats' success in the 2004 election obviously casts a pall over his chances, although he can still point to some important policy achievements. He is not eligible to run for a third term in 2006. Among the Republicans mentioned as possible successors are former Speaker Lola Spradley, Congressman Bob Beauprez, former Congressman Scott McInnis and University of Denver President (and former Owens appointee) Marc Holtzman. Among the Democrats are Senator Ken Salazar, tech millionaire Rutt Bridges, head of the Bighorn Center for Public Policy, who contributed heavily to the Democratic campaigns in 2002, former state Senator Mike Feeley, state Senator Ken Gordon, 2002 nominee Rollie Heath, 1998 nominee Gail Schoettler, Denver District Attorney Bill Ritter, Romanoff and Chris Romer, son of former Governor Roy Romer.

Senior Senator

Wayne Allard (R)

Elected 1996, seat up 2008, 2d term; b. Dec. 2, 1943, Fort Collins; home, Loveland; CO St. U., D.V.M. 1968; Protestant; married (Joan).

Elected Office: CO Senate, 1982–90; US House of Reps., 1990–96.

Professional Career: Veterinarian, 1968–present; Loveland City Health Officer, 1970–78; Owner, Allard Animal Hosp., 1970–90.

DC Office: 521 DSOB, 20510, 202-224-5941; Fax: 202-224-6471; Web site: allard.senate.gov.

State Offices: Colorado Springs, 719-634-6071; Denver, 303-220-7414; Durango, 970-375-6311; Grand Junction, 970-245-9553; Loveland, 970-461-3530; Pueblo, 719-545-9751.

Committees: *Appropriations*: District of Columbia; Energy & Water; Homeland Security; Interior & Related Agencies; Legislative Branch (Chmn.); Military Construction & Veterans Affairs. *Banking, Housing & Urban Affairs*: Financial Institutions; Housing & Transportation (Chmn.); Securities & Investment. *Budget*.

Group Ratings

	ADA	ACLU	AFS	LCV	ITIC	NTU	COC	ACU	NTLC	CHC
2004	5	22	0	0	100	84	94	96	98	100
2003	10	—	0	0	—	81	100	85	—	—

National Journal Ratings

	2003 LIB	—	2003 CONS		2004 LIB	—	2004 CONS
Economic	18%	—	77%		2%	—	96%
Social	0%	—	59%		0%	—	84%
Foreign	39%	—	54%		0%	—	67%

Key Votes of the 108th Congress

1. Ban Drilling in ANWR	N	5. Energy Bill	Y	9. Ban Same-Sex Marriage	Y
2. Approve Bush Tax Cuts	Y	6. Support Roe v. Wade	N	10. Ban Bunker-Buster Bomb	N
3. Medicare/Rx Bill	Y	7. Ban Partial-Birth Abortion	Y	11. Fund Iraq War	Y
4. Bar Overtime Pay Regs.	N	8. Assault Weapons Ban	N	12. Restrict Missile Defense	N

Election Results

2002 general	Wayne Allard (R)	717,893	(51%)	($5,223,592)
	Tom Strickland (D)	648,130	(46%)	($5,160,517)
	Other...	50,059	(3%)	
2002 primary	Wayne Allard (R) .... unopposed			
1996 general	Wayne Allard (R)	750,325	(51%)	($2,233,429)
	Tom Strickland (D)	677,600	(46%)	($2,894,916)
	Other...	41,686	(3%)	

Prior Winning Percentages: 1994 House (72%); 1992 House (58%); 1990 House (54%)

Wayne Allard, Colorado's Republican senator, was first elected to the House in 1990 and to the Senate in 1996. Allard grew up in the northern end of the Front Range, the son of a cattle rancher and developer, attended veterinary school, then in 1970 started a veterinary practice in Loveland—a lively business in an area with vast feedlots. His father was a Democrat—Allard's colleague Edward Kennedy remembers him from the 1960 campaign—and a friend of conservative Democratic Congressman Wayne Aspinall, but both father and son switched parties after Aspinall was defeated by a liberal in the 1972 primary. In 1982, Allard was elected to the state Senate, where he succeeded in limiting the length of legislative sessions to 120 days, so legislators would be more in touch with their constituents. In 1990, when Congressman Hank Brown ran for the Senate, Allard ran for the House in the 4th District, which covered much of the High Plains and the northern end of the Front Range. Against a former local university president and legislator, Allard won a 54% victory. He was easily re-elected in 1992 and 1994 and, when Brown retired from the Senate after just one term, Allard ran for the seat.

Allard's voting record was one of the most conservative in the House. He was scarcely the most prominent candidate going into 1996, but others better known declined to run—former Senator Gary Hart, Governor Roy Romer, former Governor Dick Lamm. In the August 13 primary, Allard won 57%–43% over Attorney General Gale Norton, now George W. Bush's Interior Secretary.

The Democratic nominee was Tom Strickland, who had more money and sophistication, but Allard ended up with more votes. Strickland held fundraisers with Robert Redford and Gloria Steinem and attacked Allard's "Neanderthal" positions on the environment; Allard said he was interested in "sound science" rather than emotional appeals, more local decision-making and less bureaucracy. Allard ran ads attacking Strickland for defending clients with environmental problems, including one company trying to build a medical waste incinerator in a poor Denver neighborhood. Allard won 51%–46%.

Allard has a very conservative voting record in the Senate and prides himself on having returned $2.7 million in office funds to the Treasury since 1991. He is not much of a headline-maker. "I try not to be on the front burner of every issue that comes through." As ranking member and former chairman of the Armed Services Strategic Forces Subcommittee, he strongly supported missile defense and pushed to develop space-based radar and defenses for space-based assets. In 2004 he called for the Pentagon to rely more on smaller, cheaper satellites and he sponsored a bill to end the University of California's management of the security-troubled Los Alamos National Laboratory. Prompted by complaints from the mother of a cadet, he investigated charges of rape and sexual mistreatment at the Air Force Academy and insisted on an amendment establishing an independent panel to determine who was responsible for "the atmosphere that was conducive to recent acts of sexual misconduct." Allard has acted when other outrages come to his attention: in 2004 he got a plane to return an Afghan-American who had suffered a heart attack in Afghanistan and he convinced the ATF to investigate the arson of a Habitat for Humanity house he was working on in Colorado.

Allard gets low ratings from national environmental groups, but has done much work on his own environmental causes. With 2d District Democrat Mark Udall, he has worked successfully to create a wildlife refuge at Rocky Flats, a much-polluted nuclear plant near Denver that closed in 1989; this was modeled on his action as a House member, when he joined with Democrat Patricia Schroeder to make the Rocky Mountain Arsenal site a wildlife refuge. One of Allard's most interesting proposals is a ban on the interstate shipment of roosters for cockfighting. He explains: "I'm a veterinarian. I've never supported the idea of animal fighting. My training is not to encourage that kind of treatment of animals with no purpose other than fighting."

One of Allard's few moments in the national spotlight came in 2004, when he was the lead Senate sponsor of the Family Marriage Amendment sponsored in the House by Colorado's Marilyn Musgrave. "The courts are driving a redefinition of marriage, contrary to democratic principles," he argued. The amendment fell far short of the 67 votes needed; Allard was defeated 48–50 on a procedural vote. But he was upbeat. "I feel like it was a very strong first vote," he said. "If they technically want to make that argument I guess they can on the number of votes, but I think it is a win." In 2004 he was mentioned as a possible chairman of the Budget Committee; he ended up with a seat on the Appropriations Committee.

In his 2002 reelection race, Allard faced the same opponent as in 1996, Tom Strickland. Polls showed he remained relatively little known, perhaps because he has kept his promise to visit all 63 of Colorado's counties—64 since the creation of Broomfield County in November 2001—every year, even though 10 of those counties have 80% of the state's population. Allard was not troubled by his low name identification. "At the end of the day, there are work horses, and there are show horses. As a veterinarian, I know the difference." There was a vast contrast in style between the rural and stolid Allard and the urban and urbane Strickland: The candidate of the simple rural areas versus the candidate of the sophisticated urban core in a mostly suburban state. Strickland said his favorite food (in landlocked Colorado) was sushi; Allard said his was his wife's Crisco cherry pie. Allard constantly called Strickland a lawyer-lobbyist; Strickland called Allard a far right-winger and ran ads saying he lived in a right-wing "Wayne's World." Strickland described himself as a conservative Democrat, ready and able to work with senators in both parties; he called for broader access to health care and a $12,000 per year deduction for college tuition.

Much of the campaign dialogue focused on corporate wrongdoing and the candidates' involvement in it. Some of the accusations came in the candidates' 13 debates, but voters saw it more in the independent expenditure ads. Over the summer, the bulk was run by liberal groups against Allard; the Club for Growth and the NRA chimed in with ads against Strickland later. Strickland accused Allard of promoting the 1999 acquisition by Qwest of USWest, which had turned out badly, and criticized him for buying 50 shares of Qwest one day after the acquisition was announced. Allard responded that in 1998 Strickland made a profit of $25,000 in one day because he was let in to the IPO of Global Crossing (which later failed). Allard called Strickland a liberal "elitist" who had worked for a company that wanted to build a medical waste incinerator in north Denver in the late 1980s.

In the end, even though many public polls showed Strickland leading, the result was exactly the same as in 1996: Allard won 51%–46%. The percentage and the contours of support were strikingly similar to George W. Bush's 2004 Colorado victory. Allard was shellacked in Denver and Boulder and carried the old-line suburban Jefferson and Arapahoe Counties with only 51% and 52% of the vote. But he won 65% in fast-growing Douglas County, where the turnout was up 40% from the last off-year election, and 66% in Colorado Springs's El Paso County. Strickland carried some fashionable resort areas in the Western Slope and a few Hispanic counties in the south; Allard won large margins in most of the Western Slope and most of the Eastern Plains counties. Strickland carried metro Denver 51%–45%, but Allard carried the rest of the state 57%–39%.

Allard has long said that he intended to serve only two terms. After 6th District Rep. Tom Tancredo renounced his term limit pledge in September 2002, Allard, asked whether he would run again, said, "I may or may not. I don't want to talk about what I'll be doing six years from now. I don't see me running again." In December 2004 he said he still plans to keep his term-limits promise. But his new Appropriations seat may provide him with a reason to run for reelection. In March 2005, Congressman Mark Udall said he is preparing to run for this seat in 2008.

Junior Senator

Ken Salazar (D)

Elected 2004, seat up 2010, 1st term; b. March 2, 1955, Alamosa; home, Denver; CO College, B.A. 1977; U. of MI, J.D. 1981; Catholic; married (Hope).

Elected Office: CO Atty. Gen., 1998–2004.

Professional Career: Practicing atty., Exec. Dir., CO Nat. Resources Dept., 1990–94; Chairman, Rio Grande Compact Comm., 1995–98.

DC Office: 702 HSOB, 20510, 202-224-5852; Fax: 202-228-5036; Web site: salazar.senate.gov.

State Offices: Colorado Springs, 719-328-1100; Denver, 303-455-7600; Durango, 970-259-1710; Fort Collins, 970-224-2200; Grand Junction, 970-241-6631; Pueblo, 719-542-7550.

Committees: *Agriculture, Nutrition & Forestry*: Forestry, Conservation & Rural Revitalization; Marketing, Inspection & Product Promotion. *Energy & Natural Resources*: Energy; National Parks; Water & Power. *Veterans' Affairs.*

Group Ratings and Key Votes: Newly Elected

Election Results

2004 general	Ken Salazar (D)	1,081,188	(51%)	($9,886,551)
	Pete Coors (R)	980,668	(47%)	($7,858,598)
	Other	45,616	(2%)	
2004 primary	Ken Salazar (D)	173,167	(73%)	
	Mike Miles (D)	63,973	(27%)	
1998 general	Ben Nighthorse Campbell (R)	829,370	(62%)	($3,045,982)
	Dottie Lamm (D)	464,754	(35%)	($1,818,801)
	Other	33,111	(3%)	

Ken Salazar was elected to the Senate in 2004, the first Democratic senator elected in Colorado since 1992. Salazar grew up in Conejos County, in the San Luis Valley in south central Colorado, on a 217-acre ranch and farm owned by his family since 1850. He was one of eight children; the family spoke Spanish at home, though Ken was fluent in English thanks to his three older brothers—one of whom, John Salazar, was elected to the House in 2004. The San Luis Valley is one of the oldest parts of Colorado, settled by Spanish-speaking people who came north from New Mexico; it has also been one of the poorest, and the Salazars did not have electricity when Ken was growing up. He spent two of his teen years in a Catholic seminary, but decided not to become a priest. Instead, he graduated from Colorado College and the University of Michigan Law School. Then he moved to Denver and practiced law. But when he was married in 1985, the wedding was at Our Lady of Guadalupe Church in Conejos, the oldest church in Colorado.

In 1987, as he was on the brink of making partner in his Denver law firm, Salazar was asked by incoming Governor Roy Romer to be his chief legal counsel, and accepted. He developed knowledge of water law—always important in Colorado politics—and negotiated a compromise between the Southern Utes and EPA in an air pollution case. In 1990 Romer appointed him head of the state Department of Natural Resources. With a Republican state legislator he drafted Amendment 8, which, after voters approved it in 1990, created the Great Outdoors Colorado program using lottery proceeds for parks and land preservation. In 1994 he resigned and joined a Denver law firm; Senator Ben Nighthorse Campbell, then still a Democrat, recommended him for a post in the Bureau of Land Management, but he evidently wasn't interested. In 1998, when Attorney General Gale Norton—now Interior Secretary—was barred from running because of term limits, Salazar ran for attorney general. It was a Republican year and he was expected to lose to Colorado Springs District Attorney John Suthers. But he won by a 50%–47% margin, making him the first Hispanic elected to statewide office in Colorado. After the Columbine massacre in April 1999 he worked with Republican Governor Bill Owens on a youth violence summit and for a ballot measure on gun shows; he pushed for release of investigation documents. He supported Owens on vouchers and flexibility in spending federal funds; some Democrats grumbled that he wasn't partisan enough.

In 2002 Salazar was reelected 58%–38%, even as Owens was winning by a wider margin. In 2003 he opposed Owens and the Republicans on congressional redistricting, and prevailed in the Colorado Supreme Court. He also opposed Owens's Referendum A, for $2 billion in bonds for water storage facilities, which was defeated 67%–33% and lost in all 64 counties. In late 2003 and early 2004 it was widely assumed that Salazar would run for governor in 2006; with his moderate record and his talents as a conciliator he seemed a strong candidate.

No one at that time expected him to run against Campbell, whose Senate seat was up in 2004 and who seemed determined to run for a third term. Indeed Democrats struggled to come up with a candidate against Campbell; former Senator Gary Hart and Congressman Mark Udall decided they weren't interested. Campbell was distinctive as the only Native American in the Senate, only the eighth to serve in Congress; he was the sponsor of the Native American Graves Protection and Repatriation Act of 1990 and the Indian Tribal Regulatory and Development commission in 2000 and chief congressional backer of the National Museum of the American Indian, and appeared in full headdress at the opening ceremonies on the Mall in September 2004. Campbell had been elected to the House from rural Colorado in 1986 and to the Senate as a Democrat in 1992 and, tired of attacks from Denver and Boulder liberals, switched to the Republican Party in March 1995. With his distinctive flair and moderate voting record, he seemed likely to win again in 2004. But in February 2004 stories appeared suggesting a kickback scheme involving one of his top aides, and in March he suddenly announced he was retiring for health reasons.

Campbell's retirement set off a scramble for his seat. The strongest candidate seemed to be Governor Bill Owens but on March 9 he announced he would not run. The next day Democratic Congressman Mark Udall and former Republican Congressman Bob Schaffer announced they were running. Also in was Democrat Rutt Bridges, a software millionaire and geophysicist who originated Colorado's popular do-not-call registry in 2001. Then on March 10, Salazar announced that he was running. He was accompanied by former Governor Dick Lamm and Denver Mayor John Hickenlooper—and by Udall and Bridges, who announced that they were no longer running and were supporting Salazar. On the Republican side, Schaffer thought he had the support of high-ranking party officials, including Owens. But many Republicans believed that with his strong conservative record on cultural issues and his base far from metro Denver, Schaffer would be hard to sell statewide. They encouraged Pete Coors, chairman of the Coors brewing company and a longtime backer of Republican and conservative causes, to run; when Coors became a candidate, Schaffer's campaign reacted angrily. What had looked like a race with a strong Republican nominee and a fractious Democratic primary became, within a few days, a race with a strong Democratic nominee and a fractious Republican primary. Actually, Salazar did have a primary opponent, former Army Ranger and State Department officer Mike Miles, who backed universal health care and said he would "de-Halliburton" Iraq. Miles's leftish views won him a majority at the activist-filled Democratic state convention but Salazar won the August primary 73%–27%.

Coors had a more difficult time. A familiar figure from his appearances in Coors beer ads, he was less than adept in debates; Schaffer flustered him by recalling his proposals to lower the drinking age and pointing out that he couldn't name the Prime Minister of Canada (Paul Martin). Schaffer supporters pointed to Coors ads showing scantily clad women and the company's sponsorship of Denver's gay PrideFest and provision of benefits for same-sex couples. "I'm not trying to be an advocate for the lifestyle, I'm trying to be in business," Coors explained. In

July he announced that he was changing the company's health insurance which was paying for abortions. Just before the August primary Coors lent $400,000 of his own money to his campaign; he won the primary 61%–39%.

Up to the August primary, Salazar raised more money and Coors spent more; in the fall, the Democrats' Senate campaign committee put more money into this race than its Republican counterpart. Salazar kept distant from the Kerry campaign, avoiding joint appearances in Colorado and opposing Amendment 36, which would have split the state's nine electoral votes in proportion to the popular vote. He proclaimed himself "an independent voice for the people of Colorado" and asked the Sierra Club and other independent expenditure groups to stay out of the state. But Salazar also engaged in edgy attacks: Coors was "fronting for his drug company backers," his company was "one of Colorado's biggest polluters" and cut 900 jobs. He attacked Coors for supporting Referendum A in 2003; he favored the death penalty while Coors was opposed. Coors hit Salazar for his various stances on vouchers; Salazar hit Coors for conflicting statements on the 2002 Bush education act. Other differences were more predictable: Coors was for the Family Marriage Amendment, Salazar against; Coors backed Bush on the Iraq war (though in October he suggested he might not vote for it if he had known what we did then), while Salazar called him a "rubber stamp" for Bush in the war on terrorism. Salazar, like Kerry, would rescind the Bush tax cut on top earners; Coors ran an ad on taxes showing Salazar and Kerry together. Salazar was attacked by independent groups for acting as a lawyer for polluters and for taking money from casino interests. Their frequent debates could be fractious. Coors: "I'm a businessman; my opponent is a bureaucrat. I'm a job creator, and my opponent is a litigator." Salazar: "You know, he says we have too many lawyers in the United States Senate. Many of them—in fact, more than half—are Republicans. My point of view, Pete, is that we have too many multimillionaires in the United States Senate."

Republicans won almost all the close Senate races in 2004—but not this one. Salazar came out ahead 51%–47%—almost the same margin by which George W. Bush beat John Kerry in the state. Coors lost all of the suburban Denver counties except Douglas County; Salazar ran about even on the Western Slope, even as his brother John was winning the 3d Congressional District there. Coors ran far behind Bush in areas with large Hispanic populations. Salazar, along with Florida's Mel Martinez, became the first Hispanic in the Senate since Joseph Montoya of New Mexico lost in 1976, but he rejected the role of group tribune: "I sometimes bristle when people say I'm the first Hispanic elected statewide or I would be the first Hispanic senator in 30 years. I'm an American, and I represent all the people in the state." As a potentially pivotal vote in the new Senate, Salazar expressed cautious support for Bush on immigration, but not much on Social Security: "Replacing the guarantee of benefits through Social Security with a roll of the dice on the stock market seems like a dangerous proposition."

Salazar's actions in his first months in office were hard to predict. During the campaign he indicated he would not oppose Bush on judicial nominations but in December 2004, he suggested he would join other Democrats in filibustering appeals court nominees. He introduced Alberto Gonzales at his confirmation hearings for Attorney General and was one of only six Democrats to vote for him. In March, he called for Bush to withdraw controversial judicial nominees, including William Myers, whom he had endorsed for the 9th Circuit Court of Appeals in 2004 while sitting as Colorado's attorney general. In a conference call with reporters that same month, he refused to rule out a bid for governor in 2006.

FIRST DISTRICT

Rep. Diana DeGette (D)

Elected 1996, 5th term; b. July 29, 1957, Tachikawa, Japan; home, Denver; CO Col., B.A. 1979, N.Y.U., J.D. 1982; Presbyterian; married (Lino Lipinsky).

Elected Office: CO House of Reps., 1992–96, Asst. Min. Ldr., 1994–95.

Professional Career: Practicing atty., 1982–96.

DC Office: 1527 LHOB, 20515, 202-225-4431; Fax: 202-225-5657; Web site: www.house.gov/degette.

District Office: Denver, 303-844-4988.

Committees: *Chief Deputy Minority Whip. Energy & Commerce* (16th of 26 D): Commerce, Trade & Consumer Protection; Health; Oversight & Investigations.

Group Ratings

	ADA	ACLU	AFS	LCV	ITIC	NTU	COC	ACU	NTLC	CHC
2004	90	95	100	100	60	11	37	0	0	15
2003	90	—	100	90	—	27	31	13	—	—

National Journal Ratings

	2003 LIB	—	2003 CONS		2004 LIB	—	2004 CONS
Economic	85%	—	14%		83%	—	16%
Social	92%	—	0%		88%	—	0%
Foreign	64%	—	35%		89%	—	10%

Key Votes of the 108th Congress

1. Drilling in ANWR	N	5. DC School Vouchers	N	9. Ban Same-Sex Marriage	N
2. Approve Bush Tax Cuts	N	6. Ban Human Cloning	N	10. Fund Iraq War	N
3. Medicare/Rx Bill	N	7. Restrict Gun Liability	N	11. Bar Cuba Embargo Funds	Y
4. Bar Overtime Pay Regs.	Y	8. Ban Partial-Birth Abortion	N	12. Intelligence Reorg.	N

Election Results

2004 general	Diana DeGette (D)	177,077	(73%)	($620,599)
	Roland Chicas (R)	58,659	(24%)	($16,968)
	Other	5,193	(2%)	
2004 primary	Diana DeGette (D)	unopposed		
2002 general	Diana DeGette (D)	111,718	(66%)	($787,840)
	Ken Chlouber (R)	49,884	(30%)	($114,832)
	Other	6,962	(3%)	

Prior Winning Percentages: 2000 (69%); 1998 (67%); 1996 (57%)

The People		Race/Ethnic Origin	Ancestry	
Area size:	173 sq. mi.	54.3% White	German: 11.6% Irish: 7.8%	
Urban population:	100.0%	10.1% Black	English: 6.9%	
Rural population:	0.0%	2.7% Asian	**2004 Presidential Vote**	
Pop. 2000:	614,465	0.7% Native Am.	Kerry (D) 180,064	(68%)
Median income:	$39,658	0.1% Hawaiian	Bush (R) 81,265	(31%)
Poverty status:	13.7%	1.9% Two+ races	Other 2,817	(1%)
Military veterans:	11.3%	0.2% Other	**2000 Presidential Vote**	
		30.0% Hispanic Origin	Gore (D) 134,187	(61%)
			Bush (R) 72,455	(33%)
			Other 14,430	(7%)
			Cook Partisan Voting Index: D +18	
Occupation	Blue collar: 20.4%	White collar: 64.3% Gray collar: 15.3%		

Denver is serious about being the mile high city: in 2003, to reflect more accurate surveying, the state moved three feet the 1909 plaque on the steps of the gold-domed Capitol that proclaims the elevation of 5,280 feet. Denver is situated a few miles from where the High Plains yield to the sharp peaks of the Front Range of the Rockies, on no historic trade route and with a fresh water supply adequate for a town one-tenth of its size. With 557,000 people, the city has been the economic and cultural capital for 100 years of the whole Rocky Mountain region. On top of its Old West heritage and early 20th century elegance, Denver has developed an exuberant postmodern style. The National Western Stock Show held here every year and the LoDo entertainment district redeveloped near the railyards along the South Platte evoke the Old West; the Capitol, the spacious parks, the aspens which line so many streets, give the city a lush, burnished air, in contrast to the dry high plains and the stark Rocky peaks. Amid its downtown grid, slanted on a 45-degree angle to align with the South Platte and the railroads, are the skyscrapers of the 1970s energy and 1990s high-tech booms, plus the new-old Coors Stadium, Elitch Gardens amusement park and the expanded Museum of Nature and Science. Rather than losing population as many central cities have, it has gained people since 1990; most of its neighborhoods have vitality, including the black neighborhoods of northeastern Denver, filled with well-maintained 1950s bungalows, and the Hispanic quarter northwest of downtown. But more than three-quarters of the metro area's people now live in the suburbs, and Denver has disproportionate numbers of singles and cultural liberals who value an urban and physically active lifestyle, in the gentrified areas south of the Capitol and the rich neighborhood where the Tattered Cover, among the nation's premier independent book stores, sits opposite posh Cherry Creek Shopping Center.

Denver has become the liberal heart of Colorado, heavily Democratic as the state has mostly voted Republican, strongly liberation-minded on cultural issues, cautiously liberal on economic issues. Though it remains majority Anglo, it has elected Hispanic and black mayors for the past two decades. In the early 1970s, Denver liberals were hostile to growth and boosterism; today's Denver, from Cherry Creek to LoDo, has shown that growth can produce more of the distinctiveness that people here appreciate, and the 2000–03 downturn has shown that there are things worse than growth. Civic pride is rampant: At the start of the 21st century, boosters noted that Denver was ranked among the nation's top 10 cities in its business climate, livability, libraries, and bikeways. In the lower downtown near Coors Field, dilapidated bars have been replaced by art galleries over the past decade. The down side is apparent if you are stalled in traffic on still-being-widened I-25 and its horrendous interchange with usually congested I-70. In November 2004, voters easily approved a sales tax increase to pay for the "FasTracks" expansion of commuter rail and bus service across the metro area.

The 1st Congressional District of Colorado includes all of Denver and extends northeast to take in Denver International Airport, encompassing places with warehouses and trucking terminals on main streets and curved-street subdivisions behind. The 2002 redistricting added affluent suburbs, long-settled Englewood and newly settled Cherry Hills Village, in Arapahoe County. This remains a heavily Democratic district, and counts most of metro Denver's blacks and Hispanics, singles and gays: The percentage of households with married couples and children has been among the lowest in America, and was lower in 2000 than in 1990. In an era when cultural attitudes are a better clue to voting behavior than economic status, this district, politically marginal in the 1970s, is solidly Democratic.

The congresswoman from the 1st District is Diana DeGette, a Democrat elected in 1996. DeGette is a fourth-generation Denverite (though she was born on a military base in Japan) who went away to law school, returned to practice employment law and became involved in politics. In 1992, at 35, she was elected to the Colorado House, where she was surprisingly productive for a member of the minority. She sponsored a "bubble" bill placing a zone of protection around abortion clinics and their clients, which the Supreme Court upheld in 2000.

In 1995, Congresswoman Patricia Schroeder announced she was retiring after 24 years in the House, where she became a pioneer of the feminist left. Today, in a place like Denver, the feminist left is the heart of the Democratic Party (as the religious right is the heart of the Republican Party in Colorado Springs) and DeGette—feminist, organizationally adept and legislatively creative—has become a worthy successor to Schroeder. DeGette has a very liberal voting record but she has shown on the Commerce Committee, as she did in Denver, some legislative successes even though in the minority. She has focused especially on health care issues. She won House passage of an amendment to ensure that organ-transplant legislation recognizes the needs of children; the House passed the controversial measure with bipartisan support. She supported President Bill Clinton on trade relations with China but returned to organized labor's graces by opposing trade promotion authority in 2002. When John Hickenlooper took office as Denver mayor in 2003, DeGette urged him to reverse outgoing Mayor Wellington Webb's decision to cut back on the city's lobbying in Washington. Teaming with Republican Mike Castle of Delaware, she formed a broad bipartisan coalition to expand federal funds for stem cell research and remove President George W. Bush's restrictions; in May 2005, they won majority support but Bush promised a veto. She opposed the war in Iraq, and said that Bush's handling had created a "credibility gap." DeGette backed Steny Hoyer in his unsuccessful leadership race against Nancy Pelosi; when Hoyer became Minority Whip he named DeGette a floor whip. Although Democrats have had few victories on the House floor, DeGette seeks opportunities for parliamentary mischief and has deliberately moved into a role as a party strategist.

In 2002, DeGette fared impressively against credible primary and general election opponents. Ramona Martinez, a 15-year term-limited member of the Denver City Council and a Democratic National Committeewoman, criticized DeGette for having lost touch with the district. DeGette moved her family back to Denver from the Maryland suburbs in 2001 and won by an unexpectedly large 73%–27% margin. In November 2002 she faced Republican Ken Chlouber, a rural state senator known for folksy humor and a flame-painted pickup truck, who won the Teamsters' endorsement. His outgoing personality was not nearly outgoing enough in this Democratic district: DeGette won 66%–30%. She won reelection in 2004 without serious opposition, and talked in Washington of the lessons of Democrats' 2004 successes in Colorado.

SECOND DISTRICT

Rep. Mark Udall (D)

Elected 1998, 4th term; b. July 18, 1950, Tucson, AZ; home, Boulder; Williams Col., B.A. 1972; no religious affiliation; married (Maggie L. Fox).

Elected Office: CO House of Reps., 1996–98.

Professional Career: CO Outward Bound Course Dir., 1975–85, Exec. Dir., 1985–95.

DC Office: 115 CHOB, 20515, 202-225-2161; Fax: 202-226-7840; Web site: www.house.gov/markudall.

District Office: Westminster, 303-650-7820.

Committees: *Armed Services* (25th of 28 D): Military Personnel; Readiness. *Resources* (15th of 22 D): Forests & Forest Health; Water & Power. *Science* (6th of 20 D): Environment, Technology & Standards; Space & Aeronautics (RMM).

Group Ratings

	ADA	ACLU	AFS	LCV	ITIC	NTU	COC	ACU	NTLC	CHC
2004	100	72	100	100	80	13	53	8	3	16
2003	80	—	100	100	—	33	32	14	—	—

National Journal Ratings

	2003 LIB	—	2003 CONS		2004 LIB	—	2004 CONS
Economic	92%	—	0%		71%	—	29%
Social	77%	—	22%		73%	—	25%
Foreign	69%	—	31%		70%	—	29%

Key Votes of the 108th Congress

1. Drilling in ANWR	N	5. DC School Vouchers	*	9. Ban Same-Sex Marriage	N
2. Approve Bush Tax Cuts	N	6. Ban Human Cloning	N	10. Fund Iraq War	N
3. Medicare/Rx Bill	N	7. Restrict Gun Liability	N	11. Bar Cuba Embargo Funds	Y
4. Bar Overtime Pay Regs.	Y	8. Ban Partial-Birth Abortion	N	12. Intelligence Reorg.	Y

Election Results

2004 general	Mark Udall (D)	207,900	(67%)	($885,440)
	Stephen Hackman (R)	94,160	(30%)	($10,262)
	Other	7,304	(2%)	
2004 primary	Mark Udall (D)	unopposed		
2002 general	Mark Udall (D)	123,504	(60%)	($776,268)
	Sandy Hume (R)	75,564	(37%)	($34,430)
	Other	6,454	(3%)	

Prior Winning Percentages: 2000 (55%); 1998 (50%)

The People		Race/Ethnic Origin	Ancestry	
Area size:	5,664 sq. mi.	78.9% White	German: 16.9%	Irish: 9.8%
Urban population:	87.3%	1.0% Black	English: 9.1%	
Rural population:	12.7%	3.2% Asian	**2004 Presidential Vote**	
Pop. 2000:	614,465	0.5% Native Am.	Kerry (D) 188,538	(58%)
Median income:	$55,204	0.1% Hawaiian	Bush (R) 132,642	(41%)
Poverty status:	7.4%	1.5% Two+ races	Other 1,975	(1%)
Military veterans:	11.2%	0.1% Other	**2000 Presidential Vote**	
		14.7% Hispanic Origin	Gore (D) 126,607	(52%)
			Bush (R) 103,518	(43%)
			Other 13,107	(5%)
			Cook Partisan Voting Index: D + 8	

Occupation	Blue collar: 20.2%	White collar: 66.3%	Gray collar: 13.5%

Nestled right up against the Front Range of the Rockies is Boulder, the home of the 29,000-student University of Colorado, once billed by its convention bureau as "a combination of lycra-clad athletes, New Age artists, and thoughtful intellectuals sipping cappuccinos." Dubbed the "adventure capital of the U.S.," Boulder is one of the nation's leading centers for bungee jumping, mountain biking, snowshoe running, rock and ice climbing, downhill skiing, land surfing and hot-air ballooning. It has been called the nation's number one town for outdoor sports by *Outdoor* magazine. It is also the home of the Buddhist Naropa Institute and the Boulder School of Massage Therapy. All of which is suggested by the terrain: The grid streets of Boulder literally look up at craggy peaks rising to 14,000 feet from a mile-high plain stretching farther east than the eye can see.

The 2d Congressional District of Colorado is centered on Boulder. It includes most of Boulder County and extends west along Interstate 70 on its awesome course through the mountains as it takes in some lightly-populated but picturesque Rocky Mountains acreage, including the old mining town of Central City, the nearby casino mecca of Black Hawk, and the lodges and resorts of Vail. The district contains some of the northwest suburbs of Denver—Northglenn, Federal Heights, Lafayette and most of Westminster and Thornton—and the old Rocky Flats nuclear weapons plant, now being converted to a national wildlife refuge. The plant, where plutonium triggers were once manufactured, was home to the notorious Building 771—once known as the "most dangerous building in America" because of its immeasurably high levels of radioactive contamination. Also in the district is Broomfield County, which separated from Boulder County to become Colorado's 64th and newest county in 2001. Greater Boulder has grappled with the effects of commercial and residential "growth management," as development is restricted to just 1% annually and open space is protected by a "blue line" barrier, causing housing prices to soar. Politically, the Metro North area is marginal while Boulder is heavily Democratic and the mountain counties have been trending Democratic. Overall, this remains one of a half dozen safe Democratic districts in the Rocky Mountain states.

The congressman from the 2d District is Mark Udall, a Democrat elected in a close race in 1998. Udall is the son of longtime (1961–91) Arizona Congressman Morris Udall, who ran for president in 1976 and died in December 1998, and the nephew of Stewart Udall, who served in the House before his brother and was Interior secretary from 1961–68. "I can remember the excitement I felt sitting in a corner of Stewart's kitchen listening to my father, Stewart, Bob McNamara, Bobby Kennedy and Justice Douglas talk about the issues of the day, and there was a sense of optimism and sense of involvement and sense of meaning," Mark recalls. He is also a cousin of Oregon Senator Gordon Smith, a Republican, and of New Mexico Congressman Tom Udall, a Democrat also elected in 1998. Another Udall ran in the new Arizona 1st District in 2002, but lost the Democratic nomination. "Vote for the Udall nearest you," as Mark put it.

Soon after college, Udall moved to Boulder to work for the Colorado Outward Bound School and headed it for 10 years. He is an accomplished mountaineer (though he didn't quite make it to the top of Mount Everest), rock climber and kayaker. In 1996, he ran for the state House, and with his family and ideological connections raised 40% of his money out of state and won. In 1998, Udall ran when incumbent Democratic Congressman David Skaggs retired. Republicans nominated Bob Greenlee, mayor of Boulder, who put more than $1 million of his own money into his campaign; Udall stressed environmental protection, growth management and education. Greenlee ran well in the Metro North suburbs, but even with all his involvement in local government and charities in Boulder, he still lost Boulder County, where nearly half the votes were cast, 56%–41%. That gave Udall a 50%–47% victory.

With seats on the Resources and Science Committees and his co-chairmanship of the Renewable Energy Caucus, Udall has focused on the West and environmental issues. Three months after George W. Bush took office, Udall called his energy policy a "war on the West." He opposed the Interior Department's decision to permit western states to designate roads across thousands of acres of federal land that might otherwise be designated as wilderness areas. He cited his father's regret over supporting the Tonkin Gulf resolution in 1964, as he explained his October 2002 opposition to the resolution authorizing force against Iraq. A year later, he opposed as a "blank check" the $87 billion bill to finance the war, which he called "one hell of a mess."

Udall has had relatively easy re-elections. His 2000 challenger spent $450,000 of her own money, but national Republicans did not target the district, and Udall won 55%–39%. Udall has often been mentioned as a contender for statewide office. He declined to run against Senator Ben Nighthorse Campbell in 2003, but when Campbell suddenly announced his retirement in March 2004, he announced in March that he was running even if it meant a contested primary. "I am reminded of what Ben Campbell said, 'You prepare to compete and you don't get to pick your opponents.'" Within 24 hours he changed his mind and appeared with Attorney General Ken Salazar as he announced his candidacy and endorsed him. After this "shortest Senate campaign in history," he told the *Denver Post*, "I was deeply disappointed personally . . . Some people suggested that I was risk-averse or that I blinked." Salazar, unencumbered with serious primary opposition, won in November. That leaves Udall as a potential serious candidate for senator in 2008, when incumbent Wayne Allard has said he may not seek another term. In March 2005, Udall said he would run for reelection and then prepare to run for the Senate in 2008.

THIRD DISTRICT

Rep. John Salazar (D)

Elected 2004, 1st term; b. July 21, 1953, Alamosa; home, Manassa; Adams St. Col., B.A. 1981; Catholic; married (Mary Lou).

Military Career: Army Criminal Investigations Unit, 1973–76.

Elected Office: CO House, 2002–04.

Professional Career: Farmer.

DC Office: 1531 LHOB, 20515, 202-225-4761; Fax: 202-226-9669; Web site: www.house.gov/salazar.

District Offices: Alamosa, 719-587-5105; Durango, 970-375-3264; Grand Junction, 970-245-7107; Pueblo, 719-543-8200.

Committees: *Agriculture* (15th of 21 D): General Farm Commodities & Risk Management; Livestock & Horticulture. *Transportation & Infrastructure* (34th of 34 D): Aviation; Water Resources & Environment.

Group Ratings and Key Votes: Newly Elected

Election Results

2004 general	John Salazar (D)	153,500	(51%)	($1,625,022)
	Greg Walcher (R)	141,376	(47%)	($1,562,081)
	Other	8,770	(3%)	
2004 primary	John Salazar (D)	unopposed		
2002 general	Scott McInnis (R)	143,433	(66%)	($567,940)
	Denis Berckefeldt (D)	68,160	(31%)	
	Other	6,379	(3%)	

The People		Race/Ethnic Origin	Ancestry	
Area size:	54,100 sq. mi.	74.6% White	German: 13.6%	English: 9.0%
Urban population:	61.0%	0.7% Black	Irish: 8.1%	
Rural population:	39.0%	0.5% Asian	**2004 Presidential Vote**	
Pop. 2000:	614,467	1.4% Native Am.	Bush (R) ... 171,115	(55%)
Median income:	$35,970	0.1% Hawaiian	Kerry (D) ... 135,755	(44%)
Poverty status:	12.8%	1.2% Two+ races	Other ... 3,787	(1%)
Military veterans:	15.3%	0.1% Other	**2000 Presidential Vote**	
		21.5% Hispanic Origin	Bush (R) ... 140,191	(54%)
			Gore (D) ... 102,100	(39%)
			Other ... 19,585	(7%)
			Cook Partisan Voting Index: R + 6	
Occupation	Blue collar: 25.0%	White collar: 56.1%	Gray collar: 18.9%	

On a clear night from the air, they look like tiny mottled veins with small clots here and there, thicker near Denver but never very bright: These are the lights of the civilization Americans have built on the Western Slope of the Rockies in Colorado. The lights follow the trails of valley roads and mountainside switchbacks. The nodes mark the dozens of little towns built during mining boom years: The gold rush of the 1870s, the uranium boom of the 1950s, and the oil shale boomlet of the 1970s. The Western Slope—everything west of the Front Range, with dozens of peaks over 14,000 feet—has always blocked east-west movement; except for mining and now skiing, few would have followed the Ute Indians and settled here. The miners who tracked gold and silver and lead ores also built Victorian towns with opera houses and gingerbread storefronts in Aspen and Telluride in valleys and defiles scarcely accessible to the outside world. Now, many of these towns have been restored by ski resort operators and joined by dozens of new condominiums and shopping malls. Cries of overdevelopment have followed.

The political map of the Western Slope is as diverse as its history. Aspen and Telluride, with Victorian houses and counter-cultural substrata, are liberal and Democratic; Crested Butte and Steamboat Springs, with contemporary condominiums, formerly Republican, are now Democratic as well. The rough-handed mining area around Grand Junction, where piles of tailings still crackle with radioactivity, Glenwood Springs, with its old hot springs hotel once visited by President Taft, and the northwest corner of the state, where people remember the oil shale boom with nostalgia, are hostile to environmentalists and heavily Republican. Thus high-income areas, with lots of liberal-minded trustfunders, are the lead Democratic areas, while modest-income, working-class towns are the lead Republican areas on the Western Slope.

The 3d Congressional District of Colorado is the state's largest—roughly the size of Arkansas—and includes most of the Western Slope. Redistricters in 2002 removed some of the resort and mining towns like Vail and Leadville and moved the district east of the Front Range to include the small industrial city of Pueblo. There, on the banks of the Arkansas River, the Rockefellers built large steel factories before World War I to make barbed wire and rails; now, this blue-collar town has attracted large medical centers and some industrial plants. Pueblo is heavily Democratic and so are the counties on the plains and in the San Luis Valley to the south. These inhabitants are Hispanic, not Mexican-American: Spanish-speaking people have been living here, as in northern New Mexico, for 350 years. Politically, the 3d District has been moving to the right, voting for Bill Clinton in 1992 but for Bob Dole in 1996 and George W. Bush in 2000 and 2004. On balance, it is a Republican district, but it can be unpredictable.

The new congressman from the 3d District is John Salazar, a Democrat and the older brother of Senator Ken Salazar; both were first elected in 2004. They are the third pair of brothers in the 109th Congress. The Salazar brothers grew up on a family ranch without electricity in the San Luis Valley, east of the Front Range just north of the New Mexico border. After high school, John Salazar served in the Army, including a tour of duty in a criminal investigations unit overseas. After his service he returned to Colorado and got a business degree from Adams State College. He settled on the ranch, which has been in his family since 1850, and developed a seed potato farming operation that grows millions of potatoes in huge fields; he was active in the Colorado Certified Seed Growers and on state farming boards. When a private developer in the mid-1990s tried to buy up water rights in the San Luis Valley to ship it to the Denver area, Salazar organized a citizens' revolt. Ken Salazar had held high state office from the 1980s and was elected Attorney General in 1998; John Salazar did not run for office until 2002, when he was elected to the state House. During his tenure, he sought unsuccessfully to limit water transfers between basins.

When six-term Republican Congressman Scott McInnis announced his retirement in September 2003, Salazar moved quickly to run. Rather than emphasizing his Hispanic heritage, he called himself a farmer. And wisely in this district, he cast himself as a pragmatic centrist and a friendly guy, not a partisan Democrat. But he proved to be a good fundraiser and won labor endorsements which helped him win 69% of the delegate votes in the May 2004 state party convention and had no opposition in the August primary. Meanwhile, five candidates battled for the Republican nomination. Former state Department of Natural Resources Director Greg Walcher narrowly beat McInnis's brother-in-law, state Representative Matt Smith, 32%–31%. Walcher, considered the most socially conservative of the candidates, was the only one who in 2003 supported Governor Bill Owens's Referendum A. This measure would have authorized $2 billion in bonds for water storage projects, and was highly unpopular in the Western Slope, where voters feared it would transfer their water to the Front Range. McInnis, among others, opposed it; it was defeated by a 67%–33% margin statewide and 85%–15% on the Western Slope. John Salazar, who was state co-chairman of the anti-Referendum A campaign, hammered the issue relentlessly; Walcher said after the referendum's defeat that he had not actually supported it, but he was working for Owens at the time and had said that the proposal "could be really good for the Western Slope."

Walcher accused Salazar of being a pro-tax liberal and attempted to tie him to Democratic presidential nominee John Kerry. But Salazar proved to be an elusive target. Though he supported abortion rights and opposed a constitutional amendment banning same-sex marriage, the folksy, cowboy-hat wearing Democrat crafted a moderate image by keeping Kerry at a safe distance, embracing tax cuts for farmers and ranchers and supporting estate tax repeal. He also sported an "A" rating from the National Rifle Association for co-sponsoring legislation to allow gun owners to carry concealed weapons and for opposing renewal of the federal assault weapons ban. Both candidates highlighted their agricultural credentials: When Walcher, a peach grower, skipped a debate by claiming he had to harvest his peaches, Salazar responded that he had managed to attend despite the responsibility of running a 2,000-acre farm. Late in the campaign, Walcher angered his opponent with ads claiming that Salazar supported amnesty for illegal immigrants, and subsidized tuition for their children.

In November Salazar won 51%–47%; this was one of only two Republican-held open seats in the nation won by a Democrat in the general election. He won 16 of the 29 counties and ran far ahead of John Kerry in Pueblo and in the Hispanic counties on the plains and in the San Luis Valley. Salazar also won the Grand Junction area and the mining counties in the northwest, but by fewer votes. Salazar carried the ski resort counties with percentages similar to Kerry's. In Washington, Salazar said that his priorities would be affordable health care, veterans' benefits, rural economic development and water. He could be a Republican target in 2006, but he will have a chance to use the advantages of incumbency to his benefit.

FOURTH DISTRICT

Rep. Marilyn Musgrave (R)

Elected 2002, 2d term; b. Jan. 27, 1949, Greeley; home, Ft. Morgan; CO St. U., B.A. 1972; First Assembly of God; married (Steve).

Elected Office: Ft. Morgan Schl. Bd., 1990–94; CO House of Reps., 1994–98; CO Senate, 1998–2002.

DC Office: 1507 LHOB, 20515, 202-225-4676; Fax: 202-225-5870; Web site: www.house.gov/musgrave.

District Offices: Greeley, 970-352-4037; Las Animas, 719-456-0925; Loveland, 970-663-3536; Sterling, 970-522-1788.

Committees: *Agriculture* (17th of 25 R): General Farm Commodities & Risk Management. *Education & the Workforce* (17th of 27 R): Education Reform; Employer-Employee Relations. *Resources* (26th of 27 R): Fisheries & Oceans; National Parks. *Small Business* (8th of 18 R): Rural Enterprises, Agriculture & Technology; Workforce, Empowerment & Government Programs (Chmn.).

Group Ratings

	ADA	ACLU	AFS	LCV	ITIC	NTU	COC	ACU	NTLC	CHC
2004	0	0	0	0	90	77	100	100	97	100
2003	15	—	13	5	—	81	93	100	—	—

National Journal Ratings

	2003 LIB — 2003 CONS		2004 LIB — 2004 CONS	
Economic	41%	57%	12%	88%
Social	5%	87%	0%	91%
Foreign	0%	89%	4%	93%

Key Votes of the 108th Congress

1. Drilling in ANWR	Y	5. DC School Vouchers	Y	9. Ban Same-Sex Marriage	Y
2. Approve Bush Tax Cuts	Y	6. Ban Human Cloning	Y	10. Fund Iraq War	Y
3. Medicare/Rx Bill	N	7. Restrict Gun Liability	Y	11. Bar Cuba Embargo Funds	N
4. Bar Overtime Pay Regs.	N	8. Ban Partial-Birth Abortion	Y	12. Intelligence Reorg.	Y

Election Results

2004 general	Marilyn Musgrave (R)	155,958	(51%)	($3,314,507)
	Stan Matsunaka (D)	136,812	(45%)	($868,439)
	Bob Kinsey (Green)	12,739	(4%)	($6,946)
2004 primary	Marilyn Musgrave (R)	44,649	(78%)	
	Bob Faust (R)	12,553	(22%)	
2002 general	Marilyn Musgrave (R)	115,359	(55%)	($1,249,564)
	Stan Matsunaka (D)	87,499	(42%)	($959,962)
	Other	7,097	(3%)	

The People		Race/Ethnic Origin	Ancestry		
Area size:	31,048 sq. mi.	79.4% White	German: 20.3%	English: 8.7%	
Urban population:	75.1%	0.7% Black	Irish: 8.4%		
Rural population:	24.9%	1.1% Asian	**2004 Presidential Vote**		
Pop. 2000:	614,466	0.5% Native Am.	Bush (R)	180,017	(58%)
Median income:	$43,389	0.1% Hawaiian	Kerry (D)	128,002	(41%)
Poverty status:	10.9%	1.2% Two+ races	Other	2,637	(1%)
Military veterans:	12.3%	0.1% Other	**2000 Presidential Vote**		
		17.0% Hispanic Origin	Bush (R)	145,056	(57%)
			Gore (D)	92,602	(36%)
			Other	16,271	(6%)
			Cook Partisan Voting Index: R + 9		

Occupation	Blue collar: 24.0%	White collar: 59.8%	Gray collar: 16.2%

The High Plains of eastern Colorado are dusty brown, gently rolling grasslands that seem flat but actually slope imperceptibly up toward the Rocky Mountains. The land is fertile, but dry; rainfall is rare, the rivers are just a trickle most of the year, and in many places groundwater is equally scarce. It is fine wheat country when irrigated and one of the foremost beef cattle regions. But it has been squeezed in recent decades between declining prices for wheat and declining demand for beef and increased prices for water because of high demand in Denver and along the Front Range. Bitter confrontations continue over who gets access to the South Platte River. Local farmers are now finding that the value of their water rights to metro Denver far exceeds what they hope to gain by farming; their neighbors condemn them for selling out and betraying a way of life that seems destined to decline. The prairie lands and small towns of the High Plains have small reminders of their past: The Pawnee National Grasslands, where antelope, coyotes and prairie dogs still roam, and Burlington's 1905 carousel, one of the few with the original paint. But the free market that once peopled the High Plains with farmers and ranchers and made it the scene of farm protests and revolts is now causing it to empty out and revert to untamed land, ready again for now increasingly numerous buffalo.

The 4th Congressional District of Colorado contains almost all of the High Plains plus the medium-sized and fast-growing area around Greeley, Fort Collins and Loveland—the northern end of the densely populated Front Range, off I-25 toward Cheyenne, Wyoming. It includes all of fast-growing Larimer County just east of the mountains and reaches into Boulder County to pick up the city of Longmont. Fort Collins became a center for California transplants seeking a different lifestyle at start-up telecommunications firms, and appeared to survive the dot.com bust by spending its money on infrastructure instead of corporate incentives. Fort Collins also is home to a Centers for Disease Control and Prevention lab that conducts cutting-edge research in the war against bio-terrorism. To the east is Weld County, somewhat less fast-growing and more conservative in its politics. By heritage and usually by inclination, this is Republican territory: It was evenly split in 1992, but later gave solid margins to Bob Dole and George W. Bush.

The congresswoman from the 4th District is Marilyn Musgrave, first elected in 2002; she replaced Bob Schaffer, a Republican who reluctantly abided by his pledge to limit himself to three terms and who lost the Republican Senate nomination in 2004 to Pete Coors. Musgrave grew up in rural Weld County, where she worked as a waitress, cleaned houses and cared for children. She first became interested in politics when a liberal teacher in her high school government class inspired her with his interest in issues. She pursued her interest in social studies at Colorado State, where she found herself increasingly disturbed by socialist ideas. She and her husband Steve, whom she married at college, started a hay-stacking business. Musgrave was first elected to public office in 1990 as a member of the Fort Morgan school board and in 1994, she was elected to the state House. In 1998, she successfully challenged a popular Democratic state senator. In the statehouse, she earned a reputation as an honest, but uncompromising social conservative. She was one of the legislature's strongest Second Amendment supporters, an advocate of tax cuts and a sponsor of bills opposing abortion, same-sex marriage and adoptions by same-sex parents.

When Schaffer announced in November 2001 he would retire, Musgrave became the immediate front-runner to replace him. In the Republican primary, she was opposed by a Greeley lawyer who criticized her focus on cultural issues. Musgrave won Schaffer's backing, and easily won the primary 65%–35%. In the general, she faced state Senator Stan Matsunaka of Loveland who, after the Democrats won a one-seat majority in the Senate in 2000, thwarted many of her legislative initiatives. Matsunaka had considered running for governor, but decided not to take on popular incumbent Bill Owens; national Democrats recruited him because of history of winning over Republican voters in Larimer County. Matsunaka emphasized his fiscal conservatism and his support for gun ownership rights and at every opportunity depicted Musgrave as an ineffective extremist and as a zealot on cultural issues. But Musgrave raised more money and criticized Matsunaka's record on tax issues. At the end of the campaign, voters could be excused for thinking that Matsunaka's name was "Stan Taxsunaka" or "Stan the Tax Man." Musgrave won 55%–42% and carried all 18 counties. In Larimer County, which cast about 45% of the vote, Musgrave won 50%–47%. In the eastern plains, she won overwhelmingly.

In the House, Musgrave quickly made a name for herself with her independent style and outspoken conservatism. After only three months in office, she drew attention when she wrote a letter to Speaker Dennis Hastert that criticized the pork-barrel habits of Public Works and Transportation Committee Chairman Don Young and called his proposal to raise the gas tax "ill-timed." That caught Young's attention: On the House floor, he walked across an aisle toward her and, as she recounted, "he proceeded to browbeat me." Later, he rejected her requests for highway projects in her district. She then opposed the Bush Medicare/prescription drug bill as too expensive. During the extended three-hour roll call, Hastert urged her to switch her vote, but she waved off his entreaties. Later that night she told George W. Bush too that she was a firm "no" vote. When Denver Democrat Diana DeGette praised her independence, she joked that she might have to reconsider her vote. In late 2003 Musgrave moved into the national spotlight as the lead sponsor of the Federal Marriage Amendment banning same-sex marriage, to reverse what she called "the modern assault on marriage." Musgrave dismissed gay rights advocates who called her an extremist, and she added that her views were well known to her constituents. On the eve of the Republican convention, *Newsweek* listed her as the only House member and the only woman in its group of seven Republican stars. When the House in September 2004 fell 49 votes short of the required two-thirds support to pass the constitutional amendment, Musgrave called it "a victory to me that we had a vote."

Musgrave's reelection race proved closer than expected. At the last minute Matsunaka decided to run again. He was even more heavily outspent than in 2002; Musgrave called him "the same old Stan." But he benefited from independent advertising that harshly criticized Musgrave for voting to cut veterans' benefits, including a TV spot that depicted her taking money from a dead soldier's pocket. Matsunaka declined to defend the ad but said it was accurate about her record. The NRCC spent about $1 million to bail out Musgrave. Usually incumbents increase their margin of victory in their second race. But Musgrave won this time by only 51%–45%, about half her percentage margin in 2002. She lost Larimer County by 49%–46%, and in Larimer, Boulder and Weld Counties, which cast 84% of the district's votes, she led by only 49%–47%. Most of her margin came from the sparsely populated eastern plains, which she carried 64%–33%. In February 2005, she campaigned for and got a seat on the Resources Committee; she also won a seat on the Republican Steering Committee. But her narrow 2004 win raises the question of whether Democrats will target this seat in 2006—and whether the close vote has chastened this conviction politician.

FIFTH DISTRICT

Rep. Joel Hefley (R)

Elected 1986, 10th term; b. Apr. 18, 1935, Ardmore, OK; home, Colorado Springs; OK Baptist U., B.A. 1957; OK St. U., M.S. 1962; Baptist; married (Lynn).

Elected Office: CO House of Reps., 1976–78; CO Senate, 1978–86.

Professional Career: Exec. Dir., Community Planning & Research Cncl., 1966–86.

DC Office: 2372 RHOB, 20515, 202-225-4422; Fax: 202-225-1942; Web site: www.house.gov/hefley.

District Office: Colorado Springs, 719-520-0055.

Committees: *Armed Services* (3d of 34 R): Readiness (Chmn.); Terrorism, Unconventional Threats & Capabilities.

Group Ratings

	ADA	ACLU	AFS	LCV	ITIC	NTU	COC	ACU	NTLC	CHC
2004	15	5	25	9	56	77	90	92	84	92
2003	10	—	13	15	—	71	77	84	—	—

National Journal Ratings

	2003 LIB	—	2003 CONS	2004 LIB	—	2004 CONS
Economic	48%	—	51%	40%	—	60%
Social	24%	—	71%	0%	—	91%
Foreign	45%	—	55%	32%	—	67%

Key Votes of the 108th Congress

1. Drilling in ANWR	Y	5. DC School Vouchers	Y	9. Ban Same-Sex Marriage	Y
2. Approve Bush Tax Cuts	Y	6. Ban Human Cloning	Y	10. Fund Iraq War	Y
3. Medicare/Rx Bill	Y	7. Restrict Gun Liability	Y	11. Bar Cuba Embargo Funds	N
4. Bar Overtime Pay Regs.	N	8. Ban Partial-Birth Abortion	Y	12. Intelligence Reorg.	Y

Election Results

2004 general	Joel Hefley (R)	193,333	(71%)	($93,332)
	Fred Hardee (D)	74,098	(27%)	($8,949)
	Other	6,627	(2%)	
2004 primary	Joel Hefley (R)	unopposed		
2002 general	Joel Hefley (R)	128,118	(69%)	($100,786)
	Curtis Imrie (D)	45,587	(25%)	
	Biff Baker (Lib)	10,972	(6%)	($32,333)

Prior Winning Percentages: 2000 (83%); 1998 (73%); 1996 (72%); 1994 (100%); 1992 (71%); 1990 (66%); 1988 (75%); 1986 (70%)

The People		Race/Ethnic Origin	Ancestry	
Area size:	7,732 sq. mi.	77.4% White	German: 16.1% Irish: 9.1%	
Urban population:	85.7%	5.7% Black	English: 8.9%	
Rural population:	14.3%	2.2% Asian	**2004 Presidential Vote**	
Pop. 2000:	614,467	0.7% Native Am.	Bush (R)	190,190 (66%)
Median income:	$45,454	0.2% Hawaiian	Kerry (D)	93,684 (33%)
Poverty status:	8.3%	2.5% Two+ races	Other	3,248 (1%)
Military veterans:	19.9%	0.2% Other	**2000 Presidential Vote**	
		11.1% Hispanic Origin	Bush (R)	151,751 (63%)
			Gore (D)	74,940 (31%)
			Other	13,116 (5%)
			Cook Partisan Voting Index: R +16	

Occupation	Blue collar: 21.3%	White collar: 63.2%	Gray collar: 15.5%

In 1893, Katherine Lee Bates took the cog railway up from Colorado Springs to the top of 14,110-foot Pikes Peak and, looking out at the purple mountain's majesty above amber waves of grain, wrote the lines of "America the Beautiful." Pike's Peak, espied by Zebulon Pike in 1806, and Colorado Springs, with the Garden of the Gods and the Broadmoor Hotel, have been tourist attractions for more than 100 years. In the second half of the 20th century, Colorado Springs, safe in the vastness of North America, has also become a great American military fortress, the home of Fort Carson, the site of the Air Force Academy; Peterson Air Force Base, site of space-based defense research; and Schriever Air Force Base, formerly Falcon AFB but renamed in 1998 for General Bernard A. Schriever, a pioneer in the development of ballistic missile programs.

Around them, Colorado Springs has built a high-tech, innovative economy. And with the arrival of Dr. James Dobson's Focus on the Family in 1994 and other Christian organizations, it has been a center of conservative Christianity, the home of Colorado's young conservatism, the counterpoint to Denver's aging liberalism. This was the birthplace of Colorado's anti-tax initia- tives and of Amendment 2, which in 1992 repealed city gay rights ordinances but was overturned by the U.S. Supreme Court. More recently, Colorado Springs conservative activists have had some local opposition; the city even passed a tax increase to fund purchases of open land. But overall, this is one of America's most Republican metropolitan areas: Colorado Springs's El Paso County in 2004 cast more votes than Denver County, and its 83,000-vote margin for George W. Bush almost counterbalanced Denver's 96,000-vote margin for John Kerry.

The 5th Congressional District consists of Colorado Springs and El Paso County, plus all or most of four mountain counties to the west. One of them, Lake County, includes the old mining town of Leadville and usually votes Democratic. But 87% of the district's population is in El Paso County and in effect this is the Colorado Springs congressional district. The 5th District is the most Republican district in Colorado and one of the most Republican in the nation.

The congressman from the 5th District is Joel Hefley, a Republican first elected in 1986. Hefley grew up in Oklahoma, received his college and graduate degrees there and originally came to Colorado seeking work as a cowboy. He moved to Colorado Springs in 1965, became a professional civic leader, and was elected to the legislature in 1976; he served two years in the state House and eight in the Senate. In 1986, he was elected to the U.S. House when incumbent Ken Kramer ran unsuccessfully for the Senate; Hefley won a two-candidate primary with 57% and the general election with 70%. He is now the third ranking Republican on the Armed Services Committee; in 2003, he resigned from Resources in protest after the less senior Richard Pombo received the chairmanship.

Hefley is one of Congress's artists, making sketches of life on Capitol Hill, drawing political cartoons, and sculpting bronze statues depicting Western scenes. He came to Congress just as defense cutbacks were beginning; he has always backed spending more on defense, and has been a particularly staunch supporter of missile defense. As chairman of the Armed Services Subcom- mittee on Military Installations and Facilities, which has jurisdiction over base closings, he opposed the Clinton administration's request for new rounds of closings. As chairman of the Readiness Subcommittee since nine days after September 11, he has had to deal with many serious issues. In June 2004 he asked the Pentagon to explain why the death of an Iraqi general was attributed to natural causes rather than homicide. On base closings, he led the subcommit- tee in voting in May 2004 to suspend the scheduled 2005 base closing round for at least two years. He has been successful in getting money for military installations in the Colorado Springs area, including $17.9 million for a Peterson Air Force Base airlift control flight facility and $21.5 million for an Air Force Academy hospital addition.

Hefley is not afraid to take lonely positions and to buck the Republican leadership. Of Majority Leader Tom DeLay he says, "He lets me know repeatedly I'm not part of his team, and that's fine. I don't want to be part of his team." He often offers amendments to cut appropriations by 1% and in September 2004 stripped dozens of transportation projects off an appropriation because they had not been authorized. "It's just an exercise to illustrate that you ought to do it by the proper procedure." He was one of three Republicans to vote against the budget resolution in May 2001 and one of 12 Republicans who voted against it in 2003. He was the only member of the Colorado delegation not to support aid to ill Rocky Flats workers in 2004. He favors abolishing the income tax and the IRS and moving to a flat or sales tax. He has backed a number of other so-far lost causes—blocking the Clinton administration ban on discrimination against gay federal workers, passing a federal law like Colorado's grant of immunity to polluters who voluntarily disclose their violations, setting a 10-year term for federal judges.

In 2001 Hefley was named chairman of the House ethics committee—a job no member wants. In July 2002 he presided over the tumultuous hearings on the expulsion of Ohio Democrat James Traficant, who had been convicted of taking bribes. The committee voted unanimously to expel Traficant for a "continuing pattern and practice of official misconduct." Hefley and ranking Democrat Howard Berman presented the committee's case on the floor and members voted to expel their boisterous colleague by a 420–1 vote (the 1 was Gary Condit).

In June 2004 Texas Democrat Chris Bell, defeated in his primary thanks to DeLay's redistricting plan, filed three charges against DeLay. These were viewed by many Republicans as a breach of the unspoken agreement between the parties since 1997 that no harassing charges would be filed. Obliged to consider the charges, Hefley said, "Three charges have been filed against DeLay. I'll handle those in the ethics committee like I would handle anything else. He knows I would not use this as a way to get back at him for our disagreements." In October the committee voted to admonish DeLay on two of the charges—the least serious discipline it could have taken—and found that he had not broken House rules. He also was admonished for offering to support Michigan Republican Nick Smith's son in a primary if Smith would vote for the Medicare bill; Smith himself was rebuked for making comments based on "speculation or exaggeration" and for failing to cooperate fully during the probe. A week later DeLay was admonished for granting lobbyists special access at a golf fundraiser, "an appearance of impropriety under House standards of conduct." These were unanimous decisions, and Hefley appeared to work closely with ranking Democrat Alan Mollohan. Afterwards, some Republicans expressed anger that DeLay was disciplined just a few weeks before the election, while some Democrats said he got off too lightly. After the election Hefley and Mollohan called for the chairman and ranking member to be given power of subpoena. "I'm not getting any threats from the leadership," Hefley said a few days after the decisions, but later he said, "I've been attacked; I've been threatened." In January 2005, Hefley issued a statement criticizing the ethics rules changes proposed by Republican leadership; not long afterwards, with his term up as Ethics chairman, Speaker Dennis Hastert replaced him with Doc Hastings.

At home, the only threat to Hefley's tenure came in the 2002 redistricting. Democrats wanted to divide El Paso County, but his wife, State Representative Lynn Hefley, successfully advocated keeping the entire county in one district. In the *Colorado Springs Gazette* she argued that Colorado Springs needed a single member of Congress because it would guarantee the district a seat on the House Armed Services Committee; the court which drew up the redistricting plan concurred with her that the community interest surrounding the military made it "imperative that El Paso County" not be split. Hefley then won easy reelection. He raised only $100,000 for his 2004 campaign, but again won easily.

In 2003 there were rumors that Hefley would retire because of his estrangement from the House Republican leadership and they resurfaced in early 2005. Hefley dismissed the speculation. "Unless I announce differently," he said in a February statement. "I think it is fair to assume that I am planning on running for reelection."

SIXTH DISTRICT

Rep. Tom Tancredo (R)

Elected 1998, 4th term; b. Dec. 20, 1945, Denver; home, Littleton; U. of N. CO, B.A. 1968; Presbyterian; married (Jackie).

Elected Office: CO House of Reps., 1976–81

Professional Career: Jr. high teacher, 1968–81; Regional rep., U.S. Dept. of Education, 1981–93; Pres., Independence Inst., 1993–98

DC Office: 1130 LHOB, 20515, 202-225-7882; Fax: 202-226-4623; Web site: www.house.gov/tancredo.

District Office: Centennial, 720-283-9772.

Committees: *International Relations* (11th of 27 R): Africa, Global Human Rights & International Operations; International Terrorism & Nonproliferation. *Resources* (15th of 27 R): Forests & Forest Health; Water & Power.

Group Ratings

	ADA	ACLU	AFS	LCV	ITIC	NTU	COC	ACU	NTLC	CHC
2004	10	5	25	0	60	81	95	100	94	100
2003	25	—	13	5	—	84	77	96	—	—

National Journal Ratings

	2003 LIB	—	2003 CONS		2004 LIB	—	2004 CONS
Economic	46%	—	54%		13%	—	87%
Social	30%	—	65%		17%	—	81%
Foreign	46%	—	52%		14%	—	85%

Key Votes of the 108th Congress

1. Drilling in ANWR	Y	5. DC School Vouchers	Y	9. Ban Same-Sex Marriage	Y
2. Approve Bush Tax Cuts	Y	6. Ban Human Cloning	Y	10. Fund Iraq War	N
3. Medicare/Rx Bill	N	7. Restrict Gun Liability	Y	11. Bar Cuba Embargo Funds	N
4. Bar Overtime Pay Regs.	N	8. Ban Partial-Birth Abortion	Y	12. Intelligence Reorg.	Y

Election Results

2004 general	Tom Tancredo (R)	212,778	(59%)	($1,178,724)
	Joanna Conti (D)	139,870	(39%)	($827,526)
	Other	5,093	(1%)	
2004 primary	Tom Tancredo (R)	unopposed		
2002 general	Tom Tancredo (R)	158,851	(67%)	($475,451)
	Lance Wright (D)	71,327	(30%)	($6,476)
	Other	7,323	(3%)	

Prior Winning Percentages: 2000 (54%); 1998 (56%)

The People

Area size:	4,111 sq. mi.	
Urban population:	84.7%	
Rural population:	15.3%	
Pop. 2000:	614,466	
Median income:	$73,393	
Poverty status:	2.7%	
Military veterans:	13.6%	

Race/Ethnic Origin
87.7% White
1.9% Black
2.6% Asian
0.4% Native Am.
0.1% Hawaiian
1.5% Two+ races
0.1% Other
5.8% Hispanic Origin

Ancestry
German: 18.9%   Irish: 10.9%
English: 10.5%

2004 Presidential Vote
Bush (R) 223,156 (60%)
Kerry (D) 144,683 (39%)
Other 2,553 (1%)

2000 Presidential Vote
Bush (R) 169,205 (60%)
Gore (D) 104,126 (37%)
Other 7,580 (3%)

Cook Partisan Voting Index: R +10

Occupation   Blue collar: 13.2%   White collar: 77.4%   Gray collar: 9.4%

Two generations ago, most people in metro Denver lived in the city itself; at the city limits, the tree-shaded sidewalks gave way to the empty High Plains. Today, more than three-quarters of metro Denver residents live outside the city, some in long-settled suburbs, some in huge new subdivisions raised up in the 1990s and 2000s on bare rolling land with magnificent views of the Rockies. You can see the boundaries to these areas in Littleton, originally a small, long-settled suburb just south of Denver, but now extending to vast new tracts; this is the site of the massacre at Columbine High School in April 1999. Just south of Littleton is Douglas County, which until the 1970s was a sparsely populated patch of the High Plains just east of the Front Range. From 1990 to 2003 it was the fastest-growing county in the United States, as young families moved into 35-acre "ranchettes," or huge subdivisions around Castle Rock and Parker just south of the Denver Tech Center, and took high-paying telecommunications jobs at local employers Echo Star and AT&T Broadband, now a part of Comcast. In 2000 it was the nation's most affluent county in median household income ($84,645) and had the smallest percentage of people living in poverty (1.8%). This is Patio Land, as David Brooks has described, with a high-tech economy, a highly educated population with relatively conservative cultural values, family men and women who want to create a safe, comfortable environment for their children with the serenity if not the close personal ties of the traditional small town and the economic vibrancy and creativity of the great metropolis. "The fastest-growing regions of the country tend to have the highest concentrations of children. Young families move away from what they perceive as disorder, vulgarity and danger and move to places like Douglas County," Brooks wrote in *The New York Times*.

The 6th Congressional District of Colorado is centered on Littleton and Douglas County. To the west, it includes much of Jefferson County, including part of affluent Evergreen in the mountains. To the east, it includes much of Arapahoe County and, southeast, Elbert County, long empty land but now sprouting new subdivisions on the high plains. Redistricting in 2002 changed the 6th District more than any previously existing district in Colorado. The subtraction of closer-in suburbs in Jefferson and Arapahoe Counties and the addition of Douglas County made the 6th much more Republican, and this is now Colorado's second most Republican district.

The congressman from the 6th District is Tom Tancredo (pronounced *tan-CRAY-doe*), a self-described religious right Republican, who was first elected in a turbulent 1998 campaign. Tancredo grew up on the north side of Denver, taught junior high school civics, and in 1976, at 30, was elected to the state House. He was part of a group called "the Crazies," who zeroed out the sales tax on food and utilities, the inheritance tax and the auto safety inspection tax. In 1981, he became head of the regional office of the Education Department, and cut its staff by two-thirds. A lapsed Catholic who began attending an evangelical Presbyterian church in 1990, he became in 1993 head of the Independence Institute, a libertarian think tank in Golden.

When the 6th District incumbent retired in 1998, Tancredo, an energetic and voluble speaker, jumped into the race. He had four opponents in the Republican primary, spanning the ideological spectrum. Tancredo campaigned by walking the district and running radio ads the last 10 days; his big break was an endorsement by former Senator Bill Armstrong (1979–91), a religious conservative who has stayed politically active. Armstrong's endorsement was worth 5% of the vote, Tancredo said, and he needed it: He defeated moderate Bill Schroeder 25%–22%. In the general election, Tancredo was smeared by a self-financing 70-year-old Democrat, who ran a TV ad linking Tancredo with a white supremacist militia. But Tancredo won comfortably, 56%–42%.

Tancredo drew attention from the start. He declined to attend a Clinton White House reception for new members. Then came the shootings at Columbine High School, six blocks from Tancredo's house. An outcry arose for new gun controls. Tancredo, a Second Amendment supporter, pointed out that Colorado has stronger gun-control laws than the federal government. Gun control measures failed to pass; Tancredo was the only Colorado House member to vote for the National Rifle Association's bill.

In November 2003, he was one of 25 House Republicans to vote against the final version of the Medicare/prescription drug bill, which he said would trigger a "catastrophic fiscal crisis", but immigration is the chief cause that has exercised Tancredo. He is the leading voice in Congress for tougher border enforcement and increased immigration regulation and heads the 71-member

Congressional Immigration Caucus. After September 11, he crusaded for stricter border controls to keep out terrorists. In April 2002, in an editorial meeting with *The Washington Times,* Tancredo earned the enmity of the White House by charging that George W. Bush's "open door" border policy was a threat to national security. Tancredo said that Bush strategist Karl Rove called him disloyal and told him, "Don't ever darken the doorstep of the White House." But six months later, Tancredo was invited to the White House for the signing of the Sudan Peace Act, which he co-sponsored. Democratic National Chairman Terry McAuliffe called Tancredo "the true Republican voice on immigration policy."

While Bush was calling for a legalized guest worker program, Tancredo remained relentless. He opposed proposals to grant regularized status to illegal immigrants who entered the country illegally or overstayed visas and proposed an amendment to the Colorado constitution to deny state services to illegal immigrants. He called for taxes on the checks that immigrants send to their families that have remained south of the border. At the Republican convention he criticized the platform's "open-border policy" for pandering to corporate desires for cheap labor. He set up a PAC that funded anti-immigration challengers to incumbent House members Chris Cannon and Jim Kolbe for which he was rebuked by Majority Leader Tom DeLay. Tancredo said that DeLay told him: "You're finished, kaput. You cannot think of making a career in this place." When Bush suggested in March 2005 that the Minuteman Project activists who patrolled the Arizona-Mexico border were "vigilantes", Tancredo told them, "You are not vigilantes, you are heroes in my book."

Tancredo's views obviously have made him controversial, and in 2000 he was reelected by the not overwhelming margin of 54%–42%. Redistricting made reelection in 2002 much easier; he won 67%–30%. In September 2002, he renounced his pledge to serve only three terms, and said he would run again to pursue his campaign to change immigration laws. In 2004 well-financed Democrat Joanna Conti criticized him as ineffective. Tancredo won 59%–39%, running behind George W. Bush. He got just 56% and 57% in Arapahoe and Jefferson Counties, as well as 65% in Douglas County.

After the election, Tancredo stirred local waters when he criticized as "self-serving" bills naming a lake and a conservation area for retiring Senator Ben Nighthorse Campbell and Representative Scott McInnis. He is not likely to win a popularity contest among his fellow Republicans or in the Bush White House, but his immigration caucus has increased its numbers and he is a force to be reckoned with on immigration issues. He has talked about running for president, but recognized that his candidacy would be "so audacious in one way, and so idiotic in another"; in February 2005, he did a two-day tour of New Hampshire. "What I'm trying to do is stir the pot on immigration so the serious candidates in the next presidential race have to face it wherever they go," he said. "The only way I would be a candidate is if they all weasel out."

SEVENTH DISTRICT

Rep. Bob Beauprez (R)

Elected 2002, 2d term; b. Sept. 22, 1948, Lafayette; home, Arvada; U. of CO, B.S. 1970; Catholic; married (Claudia).

Professional Career: Dairy farmer, 1970–90; Banker, 1990–2002; Chair, CO Rep. Party, 1999–2002.

DC Office: 5041 CHOB, 20515, 202-225-2645; Fax: 202-225-5278; Web site: www.house.gov/beauprez/.

District Office: Wheat Ridge, 303-940-5821.

Committees: *Ways & Means* (21st of 24 R): Human Resources; Oversight.

Group Ratings

	ADA	ACLU	AFS	LCV	ITIC	NTU	COC	ACU	NTLC	CHC
2004	5	5	0	0	90	72	100	92	95	100
2003	5	—	0	10	—	68	100	88	—	—

National Journal Ratings

	2003 LIB	—	2003 CONS	2004 LIB	—	2004 CONS
Economic	0%	—	91%	9%	—	88%
Social	24%	—	71%	31%	—	67%
Foreign	31%	—	65%	25%	—	68%

Key Votes of the 108th Congress

1. Drilling in ANWR	Y	5. DC School Vouchers	Y	9. Ban Same-Sex Marriage	Y
2. Approve Bush Tax Cuts	Y	6. Ban Human Cloning	Y	10. Fund Iraq War	Y
3. Medicare/Rx Bill	Y	7. Restrict Gun Liability	Y	11. Bar Cuba Embargo Funds	N
4. Bar Overtime Pay Regs.	N	8. Ban Partial-Birth Abortion	Y	12. Intelligence Reorg.	Y

Election Results

2004 general	Bob Beauprez (R)	135,571	(55%)	($2,970,799)
	Dave Thomas (D)	106,026	(43%)	($1,125,677)
	Other	6,167	(2%)	
2004 primary	Bob Beauprez (R)	unopposed		
2002 general	Bob Beauprez (R)	81,789	(47%)	($1,827,119)
	Mike Feeley (D)	81,668	(47%)	($1,147,759)
	Other	9,422	(3%)	

The People

Area size:	1,265 sq. mi.
Urban population:	97.7%
Rural population:	2.3%
Pop. 2000:	614,465
Median income:	$46,149
Poverty status:	8.9%
Military veterans:	14.1%

Race/Ethnic Origin

68.9% White
5.8% Black
2.9% Asian
0.6% Native Am.
0.1% Hawaiian
1.9% Two+ races
0.1% Other
19.6% Hispanic Origin

Ancestry

German: 16.0%   Irish: 8.9%
English: 8.4%

2004 Presidential Vote

Kerry (D)	130,984	(51%)
Bush (R)	122,772	(48%)
Other	1,150	(0%)

2000 Presidential Vote

Gore (D)	103,592	(50%)
Bush (R)	101,632	(49%)
Other	2,783	(1%)

Cook Partisan Voting Index: D + 2

Occupation   Blue collar: 23.8%   White collar: 62.6%   Gray collar: 13.6%

The inner circle of suburbs around Denver was developed in the 1950s, 1960s and 1970s. West of Denver, on broad avenues running toward the mountains, is Lakewood, where growth was sparked by the Denver Federal Center; affluent in the south, more marginal near the Denver city limits, a place not of uniformity but of suburban diversity. Out to the west is the town of Golden, with the old Colorado School of Mines and the Coors brewery. To the north are Arvada (which is shared with the 2d District) and Wheat Ridge, middle-income suburbs with an increasing number of Latinos. On the other side of Denver, to the east of the now-closed Stapleton Airport, is Aurora, as vast as Lakewood, and somewhat newer, with its huge regional mall and an increasing number of middle class blacks. East of Aurora are rolling, empty plains that stretch to the Kansas line.

The 7th Congressional District of Colorado, newly created for the 2002 elections, covers parts of three counties and most of the inner Denver suburbs. The bulk of its land area, but only 15% of its voters, are in Adams County, which includes the industrial zone along the South Platte River and the Rocky Mountain Arsenal National Wildlife Refuge. Adams County has long been the most Democratic of the suburban Denver counties, but its political future cannot be predicted safely: This empty area is likely to fill up with new subdivisions in the next decade. Aurora, partly in Adams County with a larger part in Arapahoe County, has long been Republican. But with more black and Latino residents, it has been trending Democratic. Lakewood and the other towns in Jefferson County (or Jeffco, as people call it) is perhaps Colorado's premier political battleground. Long solidly Republican, it is now more marginal. And it is crucial here: Jeffco has 62% of the 7th District's voters. The judge who handed down the redistricting plan deliberately chose to make the 7th evenly divided between the parties, and so it has been. The areas within its boundaries voted 50%–49% for Al Gore in 2000 and 51%–48% for John Kerry in 2004, and in the 2002 House election this was the most closely divided district in the nation.

The congressman from the 7th District is Bob Beauprez, who won the 2002 election by exactly 121 votes out of 173,000 cast. Beauprez is a third-generation Coloradoan, whose Belgian-born grandfather immigrated and earned the money to bring the rest of his family to America by shoveling coal into the giant furnaces at a local power plant. When that work destroyed his eyesight, he bought 80 acres of land and became a farmer. Beauprez's father became a nationally recognized breeder of registered Hereford beef cattle, and later diversified into dairy cattle. Beauprez graduated from the University of Colorado and in 1990, after the family sold the dairy farm, he bought a small community bank wavering on the verge of collapse. By 2001, he was chairman and CEO of Heritage Bank, with 13 locations in Denver's northern suburbs and more than $300 million in assets. Beauprez also turned the state Republican Party around. When he became state chairman in 1999, the party had a $130,000 debt; when he resigned to run for the House in 2002, it was $700,000 in the black.

Despite his record for the party and his close ties to Governor Bill Owens, Beauprez faced a crowded Republican primary. He had not run for office before and began with low name recognition. One opponent was Lieutenant Governor Joe Rogers, who had publicly feuded with Owens. Another was Owens's former policy chief, Rick O'Donnell, who won most straw polls. Also running was former state senator and former ambassador to Bahrain, Sam Zakhem. Zakhem eventually faded and Rogers was hurt when state auditors probed his finances. O'Donnell accused Beauprez of "trying to buy" the contest with his own $350,000 but in light voting, Beauprez defeated O'Donnell 38%–31%, with 18% for Zakhem and 13% for Rogers. In the less negative Democratic primary, former state senate Minority Leader Mike Feeley defeated Jeffco District Attorney Dave Thomas 56%–44%. The fall campaign revolved around economic issues—Social Security reform, health care, corporate responsibility. On most issues, each candidate reflected his national party. The contest remained exceedingly close to the very end; a visit from George W. Bush in the final days surely helped Beauprez—and anything that helped him was enough to make the difference. In the crucial Jeffco vote, Beauprez won 49%–46%. Districtwide, that gave Beauprez his 121-vote win.

His mainstream voting record in the House won the gratitude of the House Republican leadership, especially in contrast to the often prickly independence of the state's other Republicans. Beauprez called for enactment of the House-passed energy bill, and blamed the Senate's failure to follow for soaring gasoline prices and the nation's trade imbalance. On the Transportation Committee, he got $45 million in projects for his district, more than three times any other Colorado member.

In May 2003 the Republican legislature drew a new redistricting plan designed to make the 7th more Republican; it removed Lakewood and much of Jefferson County and added heavily Republican parts of Arapahoe County and raised the Bush 2000 percentage from 49% to 54%. (Beauprez claimed unconvincingly that he knew nothing about the changes). The plan was challenged by Attorney General (now Senator) Ken Salazar and was ruled in violation of the state constitution by the state Supreme Court in December 2003. Beauprez, who had said he would gladly run within the existing lines, seemed nonplussed. His opponent in 2004 was Jeffco District Attorney Dave Thomas, who ran second in the 2002 Democratic primary. This district started off at the top of the national Democrats' target list. But Thomas's connection to the Columbine High School shooting investigation hurt him politically. In September 2004, Salazar's office released a report implicating Thomas in the failure to disclose information about the killings. Days after the shootings, Thomas attended a meeting with Jefferson County law enforcement officials where it was decided to withhold information authorities had about the Columbine gunmen that predated the shooting. Thomas said he had nothing to do with the decision but press coverage was unsympathetic. Thomas's name identification, previously an asset, had become a liability, and national Democrats downplayed the race; Beauprez ended up raising three times as much money. Beauprez emphasized his voting record, including his support of the Bush Medicare/prescription drug bill, which he said "may not be perfect, but it is a big step forward" for seniors. This time, Beauprez won handily: 56%–42% in Jeffco, and 55%–43% overall.

After the election, Beauprez, banking on his party loyalty, eagerly sought and gained a seat on the Ways and Means Committee. But in March he began exploring a run for governor in 2006, frustrating House Republican leaders who had directed large sums of money into his reelection effort in a marginal seat and then placed him on an A-list committee.

★ CONNECTICUT ★

Connecticut is by many measures the nation's highest-income state and quite likely the wealthiest, not through any natural advantage but by virtue of its own pluck. Through most of its history this small chunk of rocky terrain has been isolated and insular, and politically Connecticut has been an odd duck, one of the last to renounce an established church (in 1818) and one of the last to impose an income tax (in 1991), one of the last to back the Federalist Party (1816) and one of the few to vote to re-elect Herbert Hoover (1932). Life here still bears the imprint of the original 17th century settlers, even though most Connecticut residents today are descendants of Catholic immigrants who arrived here between 1840 and 1924. Connecticut was founded by Puritans who found Massachusetts too lenient and backsliding; Connecticut Yankees for years were flintier and more unyielding, more tight-fisted and set in their ways, than their Bay State brethren.

These characteristics yielded economic advantage. Connecticut's affluence came not from any windfall but from a knack for tinkering and making good use of savings. In 1831, Alexis de Tocqueville was struck by how this spot on the map gave America "the clock-peddler, the schoolmaster, and the senator. The first gives you time, the second tells you what to do with it, and the third makes your law and civilization." Connecticut made clocks of wood and metal and hats of felt; it produced combs, cigars, clocks, silk thread, pins, matches, furniture; it invented and still manufactures Pez candy in Orange, Pepperidge Farm bread and Nivea cream in Norwalk, the Stanley Powerlock tape measure in New Britain and the Wiffle Ball in Shelton. Connecticut, one of the least violent parts of America, has always specialized in arms. The quintessential Connecticut Yankee, Eli Whitney, was the inventor not only of the cotton gin but also of rifles with interchangeable parts. Connecticut has been an arms maker ever since Samuel Colt won a War Department contract to manufacture guns for the Mexican-American War; during the Reagan defense buildup of the 1980s it produced Air Force jets and Army helicopters and, in the Electric Boat Shipyard in New London, most of the Navy's nuclear submarines. These arms industries, like Connecticut's civilian manufacturers, depend heavily on meticulous work. For years, the state was the center of the brass industry, the nation's main producer of precision instruments. Through decades of immigration Connecticut workers never lost the Yankee knack: Connecticut ranks second in new patents per capita, and a Milken Institute study ranked Connecticut number three among states in its ability to excel in the information economy. Over the years Connecticut has accumulated capital and invested shrewdly, with great skill at assessing risk; it is the home of several of the nation's great insurance companies, and its laws are uniquely friendly to creditors and harsh on bankrupts.

But for all its successes, Connecticut may be finding its success hard to sustain. Connecticut has never entirely recovered from the recession of the early 1990s. Its insurance companies were hit by huge casualty losses, and cuts in defense spending cost Connecticut nearly 150,000 manufacturing jobs. Connecticut's small central cities—New Haven, Hartford, Bridgeport—have been plagued by crime and have lost manufacturing jobs and people; in 1950 those three cities had 500,000 people in a state of 2.0 million, while in 2004 they had 389,000 in a state of 3.5 million. Connecticut's post-1990 economic growth has been concentrated in two corners of the state, on opposite sides of the invisible divide that separates Yankee fans and Red Sox fans. In the

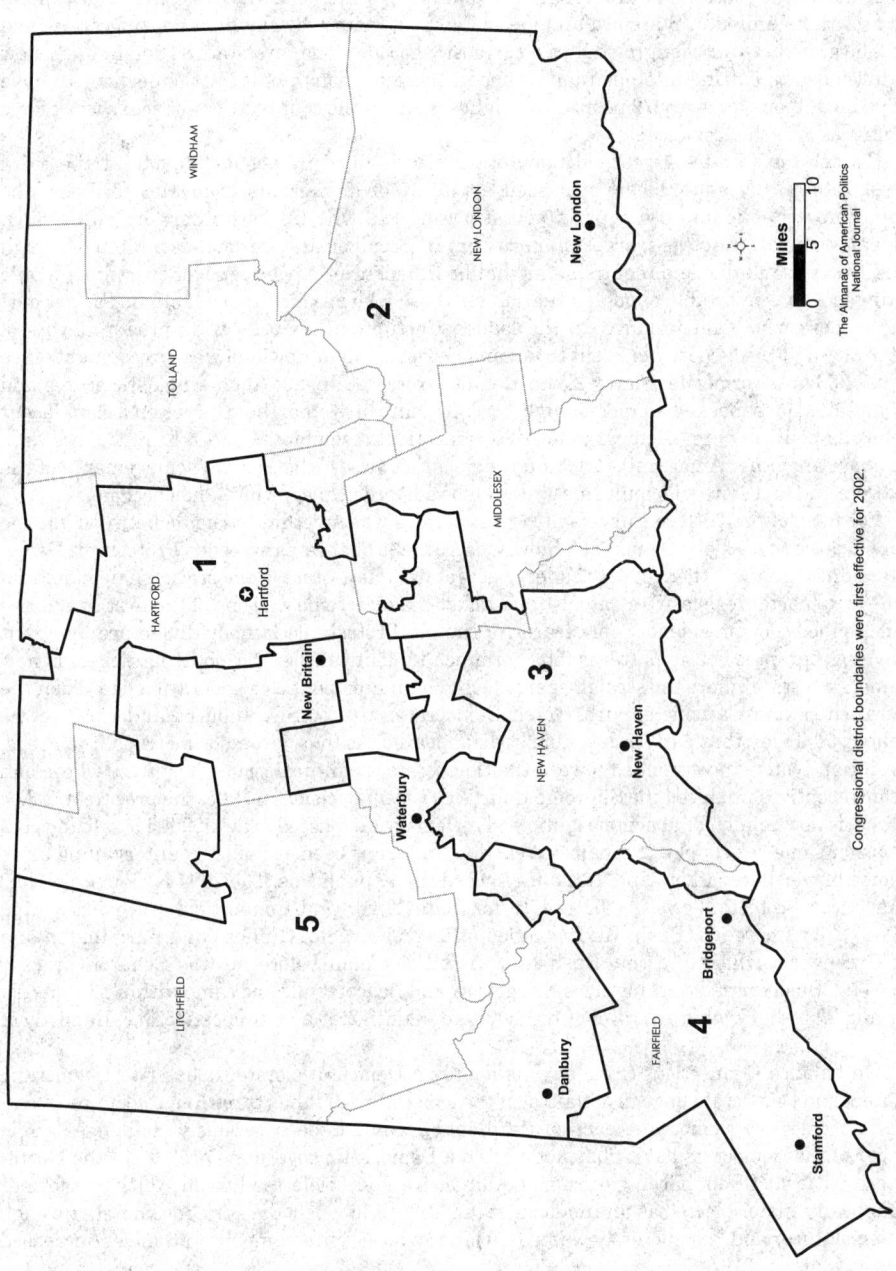

WINDHAM

NEW LONDON

New London

TOLLAND

MIDDLESEX

HARTFORD

1

Hartford

New Britain

3

NEW HAVEN

New Haven

Waterbury

LITCHFIELD

5

Bridgeport

Danbury

FAIRFIELD

4

Stamford

Miles

0   5   10

The Almanac of American Politics
National Journal

Congressional district boundaries were first effective for 2002.

southeast is the state's biggest employer and taxpayer, the Foxwoods Resort Casino, opened in 1992, run by a battery of lawyers and lobbyists and developers working for the 650-member Mashantucket Pequot tribe; its big competitor is Mohegan Sun, owned by the 1,600-member Mohegans. In the southwest Stamford has become a major financial services center. But population growth is limited in Stamford and lower Fairfield County by sky-high housing prices and limits on growth. Otherwise growth has been most vigorous along Interstate 84 and Route 2; new subdivisions are cutting into open land, though there is enough of it for Connecticut to have 47,000 horses, one for every 72 people, the highest ratio in the country. Connecticut's work force is aging, as over the last decade.

Connecticut's 18-to-34-year-old population has declined by about 200,000, at the third fastest rate of any state. There has been an influx of immigrants from Mexico, Peru, the Dominican Republic and other parts of Latin America, who fill jobs others let go begging; Hispanics are now the state's largest minority group. Small business growth is inhibited by high taxes, heavy regulation and requirements that health insurance policies cover every imaginable contingency: a comfortable enough situation for those who are already well off, but a "get out" sign to those who want to move up the ladder. Corruption has been widespread; mayors of Waterbury and Bridgeport were sent to jail and Governor John Rowland was forced out of office in July 2004. As former legislator Kevin Rennie wrote, "Affluence, high scholastic scores and verdant hills have masked an increasingly corrupt political system that thrives on a complacent public and political elite." Demographically, Connecticut resembles Western Europe more than just about any other American state, and the question arises whether the achievements of the tinkerers and investors who built this state can be sustained given what it has become.

For most of the 20th century, Connecticut politics was an ethnic struggle between Yankee Republicans and Catholic Democrats. Slowly, as Catholic birthrates exceeded Protestant, Democrats gained ground; their great leader was John Bailey, state Democratic chairman from 1946–75, a master legislative strategist and ticket-balancer, who was one of the first to endorse John Kennedy for president. Some traces of the old Protestant-Catholic divide are apparent today in geographic voting patterns, but not much in political rhetoric; splitting tickets is now common in a state where the straight-party lever dominated politics a generation ago. Then the central cities and Catholic suburbs voted Democratic, the WASPy suburbs and rural towns Republican. Today that pattern has almost disappeared. As in other major metropolitan areas, high-income voters have trended toward the Democrats on cultural issues. The state whose ban on contraceptives produced the Supreme Court's *Griswold* decision in 1965, the precursor of *Roe v. Wade*, is now solidly for abortion rights, and its legislature passed a law in 2005 legalizing civil unions for same-sex couples. Perhaps in reaction, there has been a smaller countervailing move by some blue-collar workers and Catholics toward the Republicans. The 2004 NEP exit poll has Connecticut Protestants voting 52%–47% for John Kerry and Connecticut Catholics voting 53%–47% for George W. Bush. Kerry carried affluent Fairfield, Guilford and Farmington and lost Greenwich, where Prescott Bush was First Selectman before he was Senator, by only 52%–47%. Bush carried working class Naugatuck and Beacon Falls and came within 161 votes of carrying Waterbury, where a crowd of 100,000 waited until 2:00 a.m. to cheer John F. Kennedy in 1960.

On balance Connecticut these days is mostly a Democratic state. It has two Democratic senators and Democrats have firm control of the legislature. If it has three Republican congressmen and only two Democrats, each of the Republicans has been seriously challenged while neither of the Democrats has. It has not elected a Democratic governor since 1986—the Northeastern pattern of Republican governors obtains here—but it elected Lowell Weicker, a former Republican senator elected as an Independent in 1990, who pushed a state income tax through the legislature, and his successor John Rowland, who despite campaign promises increased taxes as well.

The People		Race/Ethnic Origin			Military veterans: 310,069 (12.1%)	
Pop. 2004 (est):	3,503,604	2,638,845	77.5%	White	WWII: 25.4%	Korea: 15.3%
Pop. 2000:	3,405,565	295,571	8.7%	Black	Vietnam: 29.6%	Gulf War: 6.3%
Pop. 1990:	3,287,116	81,564	2.4%	Asian	**Most populous cities (2003):**	
Change 1990–2000:	Up 3.6%	7,267	0.2%	Native Am.	1. Bridgeport	139,664
% of U.S. total:	1.2%	958	0.0%	Hawaiian	2. New Haven	124,512
Pop. rank:	29th of 50	52,896	1.6%	Two+ races	3. Hartford	124,387
Area size:	5,543 sq. mi.	8,141	0.2%	Other	4. Stamford	120,107
State Native:	57.0%	320,323	9.4%	Hisp. Origin	5. Waterbury	108,130
Non-citizen:	5.6%	**Ancestry**				
Language		Italian: 13.7%		Irish: 12.2%	Urban population: 87.7%	
English: 78.8%	Other Eur.:10.6%	English: 7.6%		German: 7.3%	Rural population: 12.3%	
Spanish: 8.4%		Polish: 6.2%				

Education		Work Sector			General Assembly	
H.S. Grad:	84.0%	Private: 79.9%		Govt: 13.3%	Senate	24 D 12 R
College Grad:	31.4%	Self: 6.5%		Family: 0.2%	House	99 D 52 R
Industry		Unemployment: 5.2%			Legislative Term Limits: No	
Agri: 0.4%	Con: 6.0%	**Household Income**			**Registered Voters**	
Fin: 9.8%	Info: 3.3%	<15k: 12.0%		15-35k: 19.7%	D: 671,656	(34.2%)
Mfg: 18.7%	Prof: 32.1%	35-50k: 14.4%		50-100k: 33.6%	R: 449,727	(22.9%)
Public: 4.0%	Trade: 14.4%	100-150k: 11.7%		>150k: 8.5%	O: 844,433	(43.0%)
Other: 11.2%		Median: $53,935				
Occupation		Poverty status: 7.9%				
Blue collar: 19.9%	White collar: 65.6%	**Home Value**				
Gray collar: 14.5%		<50k: 2.5%	50-100k: 14.2%	100-200k: 48.6%	200-300k: 17.7%	
		300-500k: 10.2%	>500k: 6.7%	Median: $160,600		

Presidential politics   Why does the nation's highest income state vote Democratic for president? Because liberal stands on cultural issues have trumped the hunger for tax cuts among most of these often cynical voters; because most people here regard themselves as members of ethnic groups with a historic Democratic heritage; because, in 2000, Connecticut's own Joe Lieberman was on the Democratic ticket. The Gore-Lieberman ticket carried Connecticut 56%–38%, better than Kerry-Edwards's 54%–44% in 2004. Over the years Connecticut has oscillated between the parties, moving toward Republicans in the 1970s and 1980s as cultural conflicts split the old Democratic majority, moving toward Democrats in the 1990s in response to the 1990–91 recession and also out of increasing distaste for Southern-accented Republican conservatism. They may have moved a little the other way here in 2004. Bush carried 61 of Connecticut's 169 cities and towns, up from 43 in 2000, and his 44% here was the best his party has run since his father carried the state 52%–47% in 1988.

2004 Presidential Vote

Kerry (D)	857,488	(54%)
Bush (R)	693,826	(44%)
Nader (I)	12,969	(1%)
Other	14,486	(1%)

2004 Democratic Presidential Primary

Kerry (D)	75,860	(58%)
Edwards (D)	30,844	(24%)
Lieberman (D)	6,705	(5%)
Dean (D)	5,166	(4%)
Kucinich (D)	4,133	(3%)
Other	7,315	(6%)

2000 Presidential Vote

Gore (D)	816,015	(56%)
Bush (R)	561,094	(38%)
Nader (Green)	64,452	(4%)
Other	17,920	(1%)

Connecticut's presidential primary, though held fairly early in the process, has not been quite early enough and has made little difference. Edward Kennedy won here in 1980, Gary Hart in 1984, Jerry Brown in 1992, John McCain in 2000; but they fared no better than the Federalists Connecticut favored in 1816. Connecticut's Democratic primary has never produced a president: Al Gore and John Kerry won in 2000 and 2004 but were not elected.

Congressional districting   Connecticut has devised a bipartisan process for redistricting.

109th Congress Lineup
3 R   2 D

108th Congress Lineup
3 R   2 D

Two Republicans and two Democrats from each house of the legislature meet and try to draw lines; if they are approved by a two-thirds vote in both chambers, they become law. Otherwise, a ninth member is chosen by the other eight, and they try to reach consensus. It worked in 1991, when a plan that made minimal changes in the congressional district lines was approved. And it worked in 2001, with a nudge from the state Supreme Court, when the task was much harder: Connecticut lost one of its six seats in the 2000 Census, and two incumbents had to be put together in one district. Legislators of both parties said they wanted a "fair fight" between a Republican and a Democrat. Some Democrats called for dividing the 2d District in eastern Connecticut, which Republican Rob Simmons won from veteran incumbent Democrat Sam Gejdenson in 2000. But Simmons argued that eastern Connecticut had been a single district since 1843, and the commission moved in another direction.

The commission decided to create a new seat out of the 5th District represented by Democrat Jim Maloney and the 6th District represented by Republican Nancy Johnson. The narrow and elongated 5th, the only district to have boundaries with all the others, seemed to many the obvious district to eliminate. But the commissioners haggled over precisely what boundaries would set up a fair fight. Maloney wanted to keep the three biggest cities in the 5th in the new district: Danbury, his hometown, and Waterbury and Meriden had a community of interest, because they were linked by I-84, had a common labor market and had been in the same district for 37 years. But some Republicans tried to put Danbury into the heavily Republican 4th District. Johnson insisted on keeping her hometown of New Britain, even though it is heavily Democratic and she had not always carried it. The four-member commission failed to come up with a plan by the September 2001 deadline, and it appointed as its tie-breaker 79-year-old former Speaker Nelson Brown, a Republican, who had served in the same capacity 10 years before. The commission tried out various plans, but couldn't reach agreement by a November 30 deadline. Then the issue went to the state Supreme Court, but the commissioners asked for an extension and the court granted one to December 21. Ninety minutes before the deadline the commission reached unanimous agreement. Some 27,000 of Waterbury's residents were put into the 3d District, but otherwise Maloney kept his three cities. Johnson kept New Britain. Both incumbents said they were happy. Johnson ended up winning 54%–43%, drawing on personal strength after 20 years of incumbency; this is a seat a Democrat could certainly win some time in the next decade.

Governor

M. Jodi Rell (R)

Assumed office July 2004, term expires Jan. 2007, 1st term; b. June 16, 1946, Norfolk, VA; home, Brookfield; Attended Old Dominion U., Western CT St. U.; Protestant; married (Louis).

Elected Office: CT House of Reps., 1989–1994; Lt. Gov., 1994–2004.

Office: 210 Capitol Ave., Hartford, 06106, 860-566-4840; Fax: 860-566-4677; Web site: www.state.ct.us/governor.

Election Results

2002 general	John Rowland (R)	573,958	(56%)
	Bill Curry (D)	448,984	(44%)
2002 primary	John Rowland (R)	unopposed	
1998 general	John Rowland (R)	628,707	(63%)
	Barbara Kennelly (D)	354,187	(35%)
	Other	16,641	(2%)

M. Jodi Rell, a Republican, became governor of Connecticut in July 2004 after the resignation of her predecessor John Rowland. Rell was born Mary Carolyn Reavis and grew up in Norfolk, Virginia. Her mother died when she was 7, and her father remarried; she spent summers with relatives in North Carolina, picking tobacco and driving a truck. A teenage boyfriend nicknamed her Jodi, after actress Joey Heatherton. She attended Old Dominion University and dropped out to marry her husband, Louis Rell, a Navy pilot. After military service, he became a pilot with TWA, and the Rells moved to Parsippany, New Jersey, and then to an 1843 house with views of wild turkeys, deer and foxes in Brookfield, Connecticut. (Airline pilots can live where they want, and neither New Jersey nor Connecticut had a state income tax when the Rells moved there.) Before her children were born, Rell worked as an office clerk for an investment firm in Danbury. Then she became a stay-at-home mom, active in the PTA and a volunteer for the local Republican party. She took classes at Western Connecticut State University but did not graduate. In 1984 Brookfield state Representative David Smith, an Eastern pilot, told Rell he was not running for reelection and that he wanted her to run for the seat. After twice rejecting the idea, she agreed. Connecticut has small legislative districts, and this one was heavily Republican; she was elected with 64%. At a campaign event, she met John Rowland, then a 27-year-old state representative, who was running for Congress and beat a Democratic incumbent that Reagan landslide year.

In the state House Rell supported tax cuts and fiscal responsibility. Her maternal manner helped weld the minority Republicans together as a solid block. House Minority Leader Robert Ward describes how: "When it appeared that most of us were supporting something that was good for the state, a good Republican issue, and say 90% of us were behind it, she knew if she could get us to 100% we'd be a more effective voice. That became known as 'Rell's Rule.' " Rell's rule helped her move up on the leadership ladder, to become Assistant Minority Leader and Deputy Minority Leader. In 1994 Rowland, running for governor, asked Rell to be his lieutenant governor candidate. The Rowland-Rell ticket won a narrow victory in a three-way race in 1994, then was reelected with 63% of the vote in 1998 and 56% in 2002. As lieutenant governor, Rell presided over the state Senate, where she was regarded as businesslike and fair. Rowland named her his chief liaison to municipalities, and she traveled to all 169 Connecticut cities and towns. By all accounts she was not part of Rowland's inner circle. She continued to live in Brookfield, where she rose each morning at 5:30 a.m. and started the day with a two-hour walk, listening to tapes; she was known for writing personal notes, baking brownies for her staff, delivering rye bread to a sick friend.

Other scandals made much more news during the Rowland administration. In September 1999 former state Treasurer Paul Silvester, a Republican appointed by Rowland, pleaded guilty to federal charges arising out of a scheme to steer state pension funds to conspiring investment firms in return for campaign contributions. In October 2000 some Silvester aides and investment firm executives were indicted. In December 2000 Rowland met with Enron executives and their consultant, a big Rowland contributor, and a few days later the Connecticut Resources Recovery Authority (the state trash agency) agreed to pay Enron $220 million for a fuel cell facility which would buy energy from CRRA's trash-to-energy facility for $2 million a month for 11 years; when Enron went bankrupt in December 2001, the state was out $220 million, and municipal trash collection fees had to be raised. Democrats demanded that Peter Ellef, CRRA head and Rowland's co-chief of staff, resign. Criticism also focused on the other co-chief of staff, who had a long-term relationship with a woman who lobbied for CRRA and raised money for Rowland. Rowland fired both co-chiefs of staff in March 2002. In March 2003, Rowland's former deputy chief of staff pleaded guilty to accepting bribes. In December 2003 charges surfaced that Rowland had accepted gifts from contractors who had received $100 million-plus no-bid contracts and from appointees for his family's cottage on Bantam Lake in Litchfield—a new heating system, a front stepping-stone, custom-made cabinets, gutter work, a $3,600 hot tub. Rowland said he hadn't received gifts and that the cabinets had been purchased off the shelf at Home Depot. On December 12, 2003, Rowland admitted that he had lied about the cottage renovations. On January 7, 2004, he delivered a six-minute speech about "my own personal nightmare."

Rowland's poll numbers plummeted to a record low. Not only Democrats but some Republicans said he should resign or be impeached. Three newspapers called for his resignation. After his December 12 announcement, Rell said, "I feel sick at heart. I'm disappointed and I'm angry." The state House set up a Select Committee of Inquiry to consider Rowland's impeachment and set a deadline of June 30. On June 18 the state Supreme Court ruled that Rowland had to testify before the committee. On June 21 Rowland announced he would resign on July 1. In December he pleaded guilty to income tax evasion.

At noon on July 1 Rell walked up the steps of the Capitol and was sworn in as governor. She was still little known to the public. "Today, we begin to restore faith, integrity and honor to our government," she said. "It is our solemn obligation. It will be our lasting legacy." House Majority Leader James Amann said she was "the right person at the right time." Rell announced that she would accept no gifts of any kind; she donated T-shirts and caps to the state or charities. She demanded that all appointees submit resignations, and proceeded to fire four commissioners and accept another's resignation. She installed an ethics lawyer in the governor's office, ordered a review of contracting provisions, announced a zero tolerance policy on ethics violations and banned lobbyists from her office. In October she suspended four transportation managers after irregular contracting procedures were discovered. She worked to change procedures at the State Ethics Commission. In January 2004, polls showed that 70% of voters had no opinion of Rell; in June her favorable job rating was just 34%. It rose rapidly, to 73% in August, 77% in September, 80% in November.

Before becoming governor, Rell said her priorities were job creation, holding the line on government spending, changing the rules for medical malpractice cases and relieving traffic. She was pro-choice on abortion, in favor of embryonic stem-cell research, against a constitutional ban on same-sex marriage. The Democratic legislature had passed in April a no-tax-increase budget by veto-proof majorities. By summer the state was running a surplus, because of $400 million in one-time revenues, Rell said; she described the state's economy as "very fragile." In December she said the state faced a deficit of $1.3 billion; Democrats said it was more like $600 or $700 million. Democrats seemed poised to pass a millionaire's tax, which Rell had opposed and which Rowland had vetoed. They also seemed likely to provide $10 to $20 million in state money for stem-cell research. In January 2005 Rell presented an ethics package banning contributions from contractors and lobbyists; some Democrats were calling for public financing of campaigns. She refused to commute the death sentence of serial killer Michael Ross and threatened to veto a proposed bill that would abolish the death penalty.

In December Rell was diagnosed with breast cancer and days after Christmas underwent a mastectomy. Against doctors' advice she went to the Capitol to deliver a State of the State address on January 5 as legislators of both parties applauded and wept. Her job rating fell from 83% in January to 74% in February—still stellar. Rell refused to say whether she would run for a full term in 2006. When reporters pressed her, she said, "Go ask Dick Blumenthal. Why do I have to decide?" In early 2005 Blumenthal, who won wide publicity for his work on tobacco and securities cases, seemed to be uninterested in running, as did Senator Christopher Dodd. But during 2004 New Haven Mayor John DeStefano and Stamford Mayor Dannel Malloy of Stamford raised more than $1 million each, and Secretary of State Susan Bysiewicz raised $770,000. So the likelihood is that Rell, if she runs, will have serious competition.

Senior Senator

Christopher Dodd (D)

Elected 1980, seat up 2010, 5th term; b. May 27, 1944, Willimantic; home, East Haddam; Providence Col., B.A. 1966, U. of Louisville, J.D. 1972; Catholic; married (Jackie Clegg).

Military Career: Army Reserves, 1969–75.

Elected Office: U.S. House of Reps., 1974–80.

Professional Career: Peace Corps, Dominican Republic, 1966–68; Practicing atty., 1972–74.

DC Office: 448 RSOB, 20510, 202-224-2823; Fax: 202-228-1683; Web site: dodd.senate.gov.

State Office: Wethersfield, 860-258-6940.

Committees: *Banking, Housing & Urban Affairs*: Financial Institutions; Housing & Transportation; Securities & Investment (RMM). *Foreign Relations*: African Affairs; European Affairs; International Economic Policy, Export & Trade Promotion; Western Hemisphere, Peace Corps & Narcotics Affairs (RMM). *Health, Education, Labor & Pensions*: Bioterrorism & Public Health Preparedness; Education & Early Childhood Development (RMM); Employment & Workplace Safety. *Rules & Administration* (RMM).

Group Ratings

	ADA	ACLU	AFS	LCV	ITIC	NTU	COC	ACU	NTLC	CHC
2004	100	78	100	100	50	12	41	4	0	0
2003	95	—	100	84	—	15	32	15	—	—

National Journal Ratings

	2003 LIB — 2003 CONS		2004 LIB — 2004 CONS	
Economic	68%	— 30%	79%	— 13%
Social	79%	— 15%	77%	— 19%
Foreign	74%	— 22%	74%	— 25%

Key Votes of the 108th Congress

1. Ban Drilling in ANWR	Y	5. Energy Bill	N	9. Ban Same-Sex Marriage	N
2. Approve Bush Tax Cuts	N	6. Support Roe v. Wade	Y	10. Ban Bunker-Buster Bomb	Y
3. Medicare/Rx Bill	N	7. Ban Partial-Birth Abortion	N	11. Fund Iraq War	Y
4. Bar Overtime Pay Regs.	Y	8. Assault Weapons Ban	Y	12. Restrict Missile Defense	Y

Election Results

2004 general	Christopher Dodd (D)	945,347	(66%)	($3,938,132)
	Jack Orchulli (R)	457,749	(32%)	($1,462,401)
	Other	21,630	(2%)	
2004 primary	Christopher Dodd (D)	unopposed		
1998 general	Christopher Dodd (D)	628,306	(65%)	($4,442,567)
	Gary A. Franks (R)	312,177	(32%)	($1,478,307)
	Other	23,974	(2%)	

Prior Winning Percentages: 1992 (59%); 1986 (65%); 1980 (56%); 1978 House (70%); 1976 House (65%); 1974 House (59%)

Christopher Dodd was almost born into politics, one of six senators who are children of former senators (Lisa Murkowski, Mark Pryor, Evan Bayh, Lincoln Chafee and Bob Bennett are the others). His father Thomas Dodd, a prosecutor at the Nuremberg trials, was elected to the House in 1952, when Chris was eight; he lost a Senate race to Prescott Bush, George W. Bush's grandfather, in 1956, then won in 1958. Chris Dodd served in the Peace Corps in the Dominican Republic from 1966–68. In 1967 the older Dodd was censured by the Senate for misuse of funds; he ran as an independent in 1970 and Chris Dodd managed his campaign, in which he finished behind Republican Lowell Weicker and Democrat Joseph Duffey, for whom Yale Law School student Bill Clinton was working as a volunteer. Almost immediately after law school, Chris Dodd ran for the House in the open-seat eastern Connecticut 2d District and, in the Watergate year of 1974, won comfortably. He was re-elected easily and in 1980 outmaneuvered fellow

Watergate Democrat Toby Moffett to get the Democratic nomination to succeed Senator Abraham Ribicoff; he won that race by a wide margin.

Dodd, who speaks fluent Spanish, has often played a role on Latin American issues. On the Western Hemisphere Subcommittee in the 1980s he took the lead in opposing U.S. military aid to El Salvador's government and aid to the Nicaraguan contras. He has long backed freer travel to Fidel Castro's Cuba and an end to the embargo on trade with Cuba. But he opposed the language in the House Republicans' June 2000 bill on lifting the embargo on food and medicine, which he said would restrict the president's ability to open up travel to Cuba. Dodd threatened a filibuster on the issue, and prevented it from being passed in June 2000 with the aid package that included the Clinton administration's $1 billion-plus Plan Colombia. In October, with some grumbling, he voted for the bill lifting the embargo, which passed by a wide margin. In contrast to his wariness of U.S. military aid in Central America in the 1980s, he supported Plan Colombia, to provide equipment and military training to Colombians fighting the FARC guerrillas. In September 2002 he called for international cooperation to disarm Saddam Hussein but said that lacking that, "I don't think we have any choice but to act alone." He voted for the Iraq war resolution in October 2002 but later had second thoughts. In November 2003, when the turnover to Iraqis in June 2004 was announced, Dodd said, "The good news is that they're doing it. The bad news is that it took so long to do it. Iraqi people have to choose their own leaders." In September 2004, he said of the Iraqi war resolution, "There wouldn't have been a vote if we knew then what we know now. Only the threat of weapons of mass destruction caused us to vote as we did." Would he vote for it again? "Of course not."

Connecticut, with its big insurance companies, has long been a creditor state, and one that is leery of trial lawyers. In 1995 Dodd was the chief Democratic sponsor of the securities litigation bill sought by high-tech companies and fought by trial lawyers. When Bill Clinton vetoed it, Dodd immediately started lobbying Senate and House Democrats, and both houses in December 1995 voted to override. He was a lead sponsor of the product liability bill vetoed by Clinton in May 1996. In March 2002 he and Jon Corzine sponsored a bill to prohibit accountants performing audits from providing many consulting and non-audit services and to allow them to provide tax consulting only if approved by the audit committee; in December 2003 he and Corzine sponsored a bill to ban short-term trading by mutual fund insiders and to require disclosure of the amount each investor pays for operating expenses. Dodd supported the bill to limit class action lawsuits, but cast a critical vote against cloture in October 2003 when he said Republican leaders were not addressing his concerns. He voted for the measure when it passed in February 2005.

Dodd was the lead Democratic sponsor of the terrorism bill, which passed the Senate in June 2002. His original version would have had the government pay for the first $10 billion of terrorism claims each year and then 90% of the rest. The House version, passed in December 2001, required insurers to repay the government and provided full coverage of only the first $1 billion of damage. In lengthy negotiations, Dodd managed to get a bill limiting claims to a sliding scale of percentages of premiums and placing a surcharge on all commercial insurance if companies' claims exceeded a sliding scale of limits. But there was intense argument over the House's provision shielding property owners from pain and suffering damages in lawsuits. Finally Dodd's compromise was accepted by the Republicans, consolidating lawsuits in a single federal court and setting up rigid tests for holding property owners liable.

Dodd has a cheerful manner, seems unfazed by opposition and approaches debates with an affable air, deflating opponents' indignation and suggesting that they are all in this game together. In November 1994 he made an attempt to get a position in the national spotlight after Jim Sasser, who had expected to run for Senate majority leader, was defeated for reelection by Bill Frist. Dodd spent a month campaigning among colleagues for the minority leadership and lost to Tom Daschle by just 24–23. Dodd was promptly asked by Bill Clinton to be Democratic National Committee chairman. Dodd performed ably in public debates and set-tos with Republican Chairman Haley Barbour, but was embarrassed in October 1996 when he followed White House orders to stonewall on charges that DNC top-level fundraiser John Huang raised millions in illegal foreign contributions. Dodd left the chairmanship in January 1997. In 2000 he lobbied hard to get his junior colleague Joe Lieberman nominated for vice president, assuring Jesse Jackson, NEA head Bob Chase, and AFL-CIO President John Sweeney that Lieberman was a good Democrat. In 2003 Dodd gave some consideration to running for president in 2004, but in March 2003 announced he would not and endorsed Lieberman. After the defeat of Tom Daschle in November 2004, he made soundings to run for majority leader but did not when it became quickly apparent that Harry Reid had the votes.

In April 2004, when Robert Byrd cast his 17,000th Senate vote, Dodd joined other senators of both parties in praising him. "I do not think it is an exaggeration at all to say to my friend from West Virginia that he would have been a great senator at any moment. Some were right for the time. Robert C. Byrd, in my view, would have been right at any time. He would have been right at the founding of the country. He would have been in the leadership crafting the Constitution. He would have been right during the great conflict of civil war in this nation." Protests came in from right and left because of some parts of Byrd's record. Dodd quickly apologized. "I could have chosen better words. I wasn't thinking about his vote against the Civil Rights Act of 1964 or his involvement in the Ku Klux Klan—both of which he has apologized for profusely. Nonetheless actions and words can sting and hurt. I should have been more careful about this. I apologize for that."

As ranking member on and then as chairman of the Senate Rules Committee, Dodd worked with Mitch McConnell on the elections procedure bill that just about everyone thought was necessary after the Florida controversy. Both sides accepted many provisions, but there were significant differences between the House bill passed in December 2001 and the Senate bill passed in April 2002. Most matters were agreed on: Provisional voting, computerized voter lists, improved access to the polls for the disabled, $3.9 billion to help states upgrade their equipment. But approval was delayed over disagreement over whether first-time voters who register by mail should have to show driver's licenses. Finally it was agreed that they could use utility bills, bank statements, paychecks, government documents with their names and addresses instead, and the bill was signed in October 2002. In June 2003, in response to demands that the Russell Senate Office Building be renamed, he proposed a bill setting standards and restrictions for naming places on the Senate side of the Capitol. He has sought more portraits of women and blacks there.

Dodd was one of the chief sponsors of the Family and Medical Leave Act, vetoed by George H. W. Bush but signed in 1993 by Bill Clinton. Dodd has sponsored an immigration bill to make sure that employers seeking L-1 and H-1B visas have made efforts to hire Americans first. In September 2003 he added $1.2 billion for special education to an appropriations bill, to be financed by extending expiring Customs fees. In February 2004 he sponsored a bill to bar the use of federal funds to buy goods and services produced by overseas workers. In June 2002, when the Bureau of Indian Affairs approved tribal designation for Connecticut's Eastern Pequots, Dodd joined other Connecticut elected officials in opposing a new casino in the state. Dodd and Lieberman tried to get the Senate to agree to a one-year moratorium on recognition of new Indian tribes and lost 80–15. In September Dodd met with tribal leaders and said that BIA's designation process had to be fixed. On another state issue, Dodd has worked to preserve the old Coltsville complex in Hartford, where the Colt .45 was made, the telegraph first conceptualized and jet engine technology first developed.

Dodd was reelected by 65%–32% in 1998 over former Congressman Gary Franks, one of the few black Republicans to serve in Congress. In 2004 he faced fashion entrepreneur Jack Orchulli who spent $1.38 million of his own money on the campaign. Dodd won 66%–32%, carrying all but five of Connecticut's 169 cities and towns. In November 2004 there was speculation that Dodd might run for governor of Connecticut in 2006 but in spring 2005 he didn't seem interested.

Junior Senator

Joe Lieberman (D)

Elected 1988, seat up 2006, 3d term; b. Feb. 24, 1942, Stamford; home, New Haven; Yale U., B.A. 1964, LL.B. 1967; Jewish; married (Hadassah).

Elected Office: CT Senate, 1970–80, Maj. Ldr., 1974–80; CT Atty. Gen., 1982–88.

Professional Career: Practicing atty., 1967–70, 1980–82

DC Office: 706 HSOB, 20510, 202-224-4041; Fax: 202-224-9750; Web site: lieberman.senate.gov.

State Office: Hartford, 860-549-8463.

Committees: *Armed Services*: Airland (RMM); Personnel; Seapower. *Environment & Public Works*: Clean Air, Climate Change & Nuclear Safety; Fisheries, Wildlife & Water; Transportation & Infrastructure. *Homeland Security & Governmental Affairs* (RMM). *Small Business & Entrepreneurship.*

Group Ratings

	ADA	ACLU	AFS	LCV	ITIC	NTU	COC	ACU	NTLC	CHC
2004	75	83	86	100	80	14	79	0	3	0
2003	70	—	100	42	—	15	25	0	—	—

National Journal Ratings

	2003 LIB	—	2003 CONS		2004 LIB	—	2004 CONS
Economic	66%	—	33%		62%	—	37%
Social	75%	—	24%		82%	—	0%
Foreign	*	—	*		55%	—	43%

Key Votes of the 108th Congress

1. Ban Drilling in ANWR	Y	5. Energy Bill	N	9. Ban Same-Sex Marriage	N
2. Approve Bush Tax Cuts	N	6. Support Roe v. Wade	Y	10. Ban Bunker-Buster Bomb	Y
3. Medicare/Rx Bill	*	7. Ban Partial-Birth Abortion	N	11. Fund Iraq War	Y
4. Bar Overtime Pay Regs.	Y	8. Assault Weapons Ban	Y	12. Restrict Missile Defense	N

Election Results

2000 general	Joe Lieberman (D)	828,902	(63%)	($3,786,665)
	Phil Giordano (R)	448,077	(34%)	($1,080,020)
	Other	34,282	(3%)	
2000 primary	Joe Lieberman (D)	unopposed		
1994 general	Joe Lieberman (D)	723,842	(67%)	($4,017,520)
	Jerry Labriola (R)	334,833	(31%)	($166,064)
	Other	20,989	(2%)	

Prior Winning Percentages: 1988 (50%)

Joseph Lieberman, Connecticut's junior senator, was first elected to the Senate in 1988 and was the Democratic nominee for vice president in 2000. Lieberman grew up in Stamford, the son of a liquor store owner, and was interested in politics early on; he remembers coming home from school at age nine eager to watch the televised Kefauver hearings. He graduated from Yale College and Yale Law School, became chairman of the *Yale Daily News* and worked summers for Senator Abraham Ribicoff and the Democratic National Committee. His political ambitions were no secret— other students called him "the Senator." In college he wrote an admiring yet revealing biography of that quintessential political boss John Bailey, Connecticut Democratic chairman from 1946–1975. Writing a book that was intellectually honest enough to pass academic scrutiny but tactful enough not to displease a man who could make or break his political career was a challenge, and Lieberman met it. At the same time, he was not afraid to challenge the political establishment. He helped found a reform and anti-war Caucus of Connecticut Democrats; in 1970 he ran for state Senate in New Haven against state Senate Majority Leader Edward Marcus, and won with help from, among others, a Yale Law student volunteer named Bill

Clinton. In 1980 he ran for an open House seat and lost 52%–46% in a Republican year. In 1982 he was elected Connecticut attorney general, where he took action against fake charities, crooked car dealers and gouging merchants.

In 1988 Lieberman challenged Senator Lowell Weicker, another maverick, but of a different sort. Weicker was well to the left of most Republicans on economic and cultural issues; Lieberman was to the right of most Democrats on cultural issues and foreign policy. Lieberman is an Orthodox Jew—he didn't attend the convention that nominated him for senator because it was held on Saturday, and sent in videotape instead—and a believer that "we in government should look to religion as a partner, as I think the Founders of our country did." He ran witty ads, one showing a bear sleeping through work—a nice take-off on the growling but erratic Weicker. Lieberman won 50%–49%.

Lieberman has made a distinctive mark in foreign policy. He was one of the leaders in the fight for the Gulf War resolution in January 1991, and without his earnest but vehement support it might not have passed. Presciently, he called for "final victory" over Saddam Hussein. He is a strong supporter of Israel but favored F-15 sales to Saudi Arabia in 1992. He has strongly opposed Fidel Castro's regime in Cuba—a difference between him and his colleague Christopher Dodd—and in May 2001 sponsored with Jesse Helms a bill to give $100 million to Cuban opposition groups. After September 11 he strongly supported the war against terrorism in Afghanistan and in December 2001 was one of 10 members who signed a letter urging George W. Bush to target Iraq next. And his vision is broader: in January 2002 he urged the administration to move its putative allies in the Arab world toward political freedom to prevent a "theological iron curtain" behind which terrorism can build. In May 2002, when Tom DeLay introduced a resolution supporting Israel in the House, Lieberman introduced one in the Senate, but with fewer condemnations of Palestinian leaders. While running for president in July 2003, he criticized Democrats for attacking Bush and continued to steadfastly support him on Iraq. With Chuck Hagel, he introduced a bill to provide $1 billion yearly to promote democratic institutions, development aid for infrastructure and help for small enterprises in the Middle East and Central Asia. After the pictures of Abu Ghraib abuses were circulated in May 2004, he and John McCain wrote in *The Washington Post*: "We will have exponentially magnified the mistakes made in Abu Ghraib if we allow these abuses to destroy our goal of a free and democratic Iraq. Success in Iraq remains possible, and it is more necessary now than ever." They called for more troops in Iraq, decried the April retreat from Fallujah and insisted the handover of power to Iraqis must be genuine. In July 2004 he and Jon Kyl revived the Committee on the Present Danger, which actively supported prosecuting the Cold War in the 1950s and resisting Soviet advances in the 1970s.

On economic issues, Lieberman has backed capital gains tax cuts for small business ("you can't be pro-jobs and anti-business") and urged Bill Clinton to sign the 1996 welfare bill—both stands opposed by many Democrats. He opposed the Bush tax cut in May 2002 and the post-September 11 stimulus package in January 2002. He preferred instead cuts in depreciation and a 10-day sales tax holiday. In May 2002 he called for delay of scheduled future tax cuts.

From the platform of the Governmental Affairs Committee, Lieberman also made points on environmental issues. He attacked the Bush administration for refusing to cap wholesale electricity prices during California's electricity crisis. In November 2001 he threatened to filibuster against oil drilling in the Arctic National Wildlife Refuge. He subpoenaed documents from the Bush Interior and Agriculture departments and EPA on scalebacks of Clinton environmental regulations. With McCain, increasingly a legislative partner, he has sponsored bills to reduce carbon dioxide and other emissions with an economy-wide cap and to sanction emissions trading; one version was rejected 55–43 in October 2003. He called Bush's leadership on emissions "feeble" and said his energy policy was "mired in crude oil."

Lieberman has spoken out eloquently on moral issues. In 1995 he joined with *Book of Virtues* author William Bennett and criticized gangsta rap records, and shamed Time Warner into selling their Interscope label; in 1998 they said the purchaser, Seagram, failed to keep its promises to clean up the words, and gave it a Silver Sewer award. In highly publicized Commerce Committee hearings in September 2000 he denounced the marketing of violent movies, music and video games with children. But during that fall campaign, after he attended a Hollywood fundraiser and spoke of being a "noodge" to the industry, Bennett criticized him for abandoning their fight against obscenity and violence. One thing that made Lieberman an attractive running mate for Al Gore was the fact that he was one of the few Democrats who was not a lockstep defender of Bill Clinton. He was dismayed by Clinton's August 17, 1998, speech in which he grudgingly admitted lying about the Lewinsky affair for seven months. When the Senate resumed in September, Lieberman took the floor and said, "Such behavior is . . . wrong and unacceptable and should be followed by some measure of public rebuke and accountability." But he was persuaded by Senate Minority Leader Tom Daschle not to call for censure, and he stopped well short of backing impeachment or resignation. Lieberman has long believed, as he said in 2002, that "faith-based groups can help government solve pressing social problems." But he opposed the faith-based charities bill the House passed in July 2001, and with Rick Santorum developed a different approach, based on tax incentives for corporate giving, for matching by banks of poor people's "development accounts," plus charitable deductions of up to $400 a year for taxpayers who take the standard deduction. He has supported gun control measures, but worked to get a gun produced by Connecticut-based Colt removed from the 1994 assault weapon ban and voted against making lawsuits against gunmakers non-dischargeable in bankruptcy.

Lieberman played a key—and frustrating—role on the issue of homeland security. He became convinced well before George W. Bush that there should be a cabinet department combining the government agencies involved in homeland security, and in October 2001 he sponsored a bill to create one. Then, in June 2002, Bush came out with his proposal for such a department. Lieberman said, with good reason, that Bush's plan resembled his own, and drafted a bill in July 2002. But in late August Bush said that the personnel provisions of Lieberman's bill would not give him sufficient flexibility to manage the department. The main issue was whether the president could get rid of unions in divisions of the department. Lieberman argued that his version allowed removal on a case-by-case basis if there was a showing that union rights were a threat to national security. Bush administration spokesmen said that such civil service procedures were too cumbersome and that Lieberman's version actually reduced the president's ability to move employees out of unions. For most of September there was a standoff in the Senate; in October, the bill was pulled for a while for consideration of the Iraq war resolution and other issues. Lieberman evidently had a 51-vote majority for his version, but Republicans were able to keep it from coming to the floor. Democrats, in refusing to give in to Bush's demands, were being faithful to their longtime supporters, the government employee unions. But the issue played a major role in the defeats of Senators Max Cleland in Georgia and Jean Carnahan in Missouri. After the election, Democrats meekly conceded most of the issue.

After his presidential candidacy ended in February 2004, he returned to work vigorously in the Senate. He reacted positively to the recommendations of the 9/11 Commission on intelligence restructuring. He and committee Chairman Susan Collins introduced a bill that adopted many of them, including a national intelligence director with control over 2/3 of the intelligence budget and the power to move personnel and assets among intelligence agencies, and the creation of a National Counterterrorism Center. It passed the Senate 96–2 in October 2004. The House took a different view. Speaker Dennis Hastert pulled the bill off the floor in November because of opposition by committee chairmen. In December the House and Senate agreed on a version that included a provision recognizing the existing military chain of command. Lieberman said, "No one has been ultimately responsible for the deadly mistakes that have been made. This legislation changes all of that. The dots will be connected. And I hope, pray and believe that we will never have to suffer through another attack like the one we did suffer on September 11, 2001." Other Lieberman legislation: a bill with Orrin Hatch to give incentives to companies developing antidotes and vaccines against bioterrorism, a bill with John McCain to impose the hard money requirements of McCain-Feingold on the 527 organizations which spent so freely in the 2004 campaign and a proposal that the United States maintain a global system of warning against tsunamis.

Lieberman's distinctive positions on issues and his differences with Democrats on many issues, his independence of mind and civility of spirit helped him to win the nomination for vice president in 2000 and to fall far short of winning the nomination for president in 2004. Al Gore's decision to make him his vice presidential nominee in 2000 was history-making: He was the first Jew on a major party ticket in American history. Gore knew Lieberman from the Senate, where they were friends. But two things probably pushed Gore toward his choice: Lieberman's reputation for probity and denunciation of Clinton, which gave the ticket some insulation from the Clinton scandals, and Lieberman's moderate record on many issues and undoubted ability. Another asset proved to be Lieberman's fervent avowals of religious faith and that it has a rightful place in politics; what might have been resented from a Christian conservative seemed attractive coming from an Orthodox Jew.

Overall, Lieberman was clearly an asset to the ticket. His poll ratings were high, and if there was general agreement that Dick Cheney excelled at the October 6 vice presidential debate, Lieberman also performed well; some observers wondered whether the order of the tickets should be reversed. Lieberman's Judaism seems not to have hurt the ticket anywhere, and it probably helped in crucial Florida; he made memorable campaign appearances in heavily Jewish Broward and Palm Beach Counties, which together voted 65%–32% for Gore-Lieberman. But there was some tension between positions Lieberman had taken before August 2000 and what he said during the campaign. He had questioned racial quotas and preferences, and refused to oppose Proposition 209 in California in 1996, which banned racial quotas and preferences by paraphrasing the Civil Rights Act of 1964. Lieberman told the Black Caucus at the Democratic convention, to great applause, that he had voted against abolishing racial set asides in transportation contracts. Lieberman had supported vouchers for students in the failing District of Columbia schools; he told teachers' union leaders that he was for demonstration vouchers, but overall wanted to put money into public schools. He had said that Social Security was headed on a disastrous course and needed an injection of funds from private markets; in the campaign he said that the transition costs for George W. Bush's plan were too high. In the Florida controversy, Lieberman took what to some was a surprisingly partisan role—though of course this was a quintessentially partisan issue. On Sunday interview shows he said that he and Gore would never challenge legitimately cast military absentee ballots. But on the preceding Friday night, lawyers working for the Gore-Lieberman ticket did precisely that.

He returned to the Senate as a major national figure—and one self-evidently eager to run for president in 2004. He even got into a post-mortem argument with Gore over campaign strategy. In August 2002 he said, "Al said some things in the campaign that were not the logical continuation of things—his voting record in the Senate and his career in public service. The people versus the powerful unfortunately left that track and gave a different message, which may have been caused by the pressure that the Nader campaign was giving us. But I think it was not the New Democratic approach." Gore responded in a *New York Times* opinion article that people versus the powerful was "the right choice." Lieberman kept to his pledge not to run if Gore did, and he began active fundraising and campaigning only after Gore announced in December 2002 he would not run. Lieberman started off ahead in the polls. But that just reflected his name identification, and there remained his chief problem, that he was out of step with most active Democrats on the war on terrorism and was unable to create a mass Democratic constituency which took his view. Lieberman supported Bush on going into Afghanistan and going into Iraq, and he supported him not just perfunctorily or after the fact, but was in fact urging these actions, fervently and cogently, before Bush acted. He was one of the most prominent voices calling for the remaking of the Middle East and the encouragement of democracy and human rights in the region.

He stuck to those positions in spring and summer 2003 even as Howard Dean attracted a mass constituency over the Internet and rose in the polls, and as other candidates echoed his stringent criticism of Bush on Iraq. In August 2003 Lieberman said, "I share the anger of my fellow Democrats with George Bush and the wrong direction he has taken our nation. But the answer to his outdated, extremist ideology is not to be found in outdated extremes of our own. That path will not solve the challenges of our time and it could well send us Democrats back to the political wilderness for a long time." He added that nominating Dean was "a ticket to nowhere." He told unions that foreign trade is good for the American economy and criticized John

Kerry for "ambivalence" on Iraq. He presented a tax program in October, to raise taxes on the wealthy and lower them on the middle class. And he cautioned Democrats not to abandon the policies of Bill Clinton, who "made our party once again fiscally responsible, pro-growth, strong on values, for middle-class tax cuts, and Howard Dean is against all of these."

Like other hawkish candidates—Gore in 1988, McCain in 2000—Lieberman decided to avoid dovish Iowa. He was stung in December 2003 when Gore endorsed Dean, with no notice to Lieberman. "I don't have anything to say today about Al Gore's sense of loyalty, I really don't, and I have no regrets about the loyalty that I had to him when I waited until he decided whether he would run to make my decision because that was the right thing to do," he said. While Dean, Kerry, John Edwards and Dick Gephardt were attracting attention in Iowa, Lieberman spent the month before the January 27 primary entirely in New Hampshire, living in a basement apartment, chatting with voters over coffee, speaking to groups wherever he could. But Dean was attracting far more volunteers and far larger crowds and Kerry, after his come-from-behind victory in Iowa, was also far better organized. "We have JOE-mentum," the always cheerful Lieberman proclaimed, but it wasn't enough. He finished fifth in New Hampshire, with 9% of the vote. For another week he persisted in campaigning for the February 3 primaries in Delaware, Oklahoma, Arizona, Missouri, New Mexico and South Carolina. But the best he could do was a second-place finish in Delaware, with 11% of the vote. He announced the end of his campaign election night in an Arlington, Virginia, hotel. Lieberman did not formally endorse Kerry, whom he had known at Yale, until May, and at the Democratic National Convention he was perhaps the only speaker to refer to "the liberation of Iraq."

Lieberman's days of major influence in Democratic presidential politics are apparently over, but he remains an important and active senator. In Connecticut he has remained widely popular. He was reelected 67%–31% in 1994 and, while he was also running for vice president, by 63%–34% in 2000. He seems unbeatable in any general election. But he could be vulnerable to a challenger on the left in a Democratic primary. His advantage here is that he is widely popular among other Democratic officeholders and party officials in the state, and it's not clear that a challenger could get the support in the Democratic state convention necessary to get a ballot position. But thanks to an open primary law passed in 2003, candidates for statewide office and Congress now can qualify for the primary ballot by getting signatures from 2% of registered party members.

FIRST DISTRICT

Rep. John Larson (D)

Elected 1998, 4th term; b. July 22, 1948, Hartford; home, E. Hartford; Central CT St. U., B.S. 1971; Catholic; married (Leslie).

Elected Office: E. Hartford Bd. of Ed., 1977–79; E. Hartford Town Cncl., 1979–83; CT Senate, 1983–95, Pres. Pro-Tem 1986–95.

Professional Career: H.S. teacher, 1972–77; Insurance broker, 1977–98; Sr. Fellow, Yale Bush Ctr., 1995–1998.

DC Office: 1005 LHOB, 20515, 202-225-2265; Fax: 202-225-1031; Web site: www.house.gov/larson.

District Office: Hartford, 860-278-8888.

Committees: *Ways & Means* (16th of 17 D): Select Revenue Measures; Trade.

Group Ratings

	ADA	ACLU	AFS	LCV	ITIC	NTU	COC	ACU	NTLC	CHC
2004	100	83	100	100	40	10	38	16	0	9
2003	100	—	100	90	—	23	21	16	—	—

National Journal Ratings

	2003 LIB	—	2003 CONS	2004 LIB	—	2004 CONS
Economic	74%	—	25%	75%	—	24%
Social	82%	—	18%	76%	—	23%
Foreign	89%	—	8%	94%	—	4%

Key Votes of the 108th Congress

1. Drilling in ANWR	N	5. DC School Vouchers	N	9. Ban Same-Sex Marriage	N
2. Approve Bush Tax Cuts	N	6. Ban Human Cloning	N	10. Fund Iraq War	N
3. Medicare/Rx Bill	N	7. Restrict Gun Liability	N	11. Bar Cuba Embargo Funds	Y
4. Bar Overtime Pay Regs.	Y	8. Ban Partial-Birth Abortion	*	12. Intelligence Reorg.	N

Election Results

2004 general	John Larson (D) 198,802	(73%)	($604,516)
	John Halstead (R) 73,601	(27%)	
2004 primary	John Larson (D) .... unopposed		
2002 general	John Larson (D) 134,698	(67%)	($565,840)
	Phil Steele (R) 66,968	(33%)	

Prior Winning Percentages: 2000 (72%); 1998 (58%)

The People		Race/Ethnic Origin	Ancestry	
Area size:	673 sq. mi.	71.6% White	Italian: 12.1% Irish: 11.1%	
Urban population:	93.4%	12.6% Black	English: 6.9%	
Rural population:	6.6%	2.4% Asian	**2004 Presidential Vote**	
Pop. 2000:	681,113	0.2% Native Am.	Kerry (D) 187,089	(60%)
Median income:	$50,227	0.0% Hawaiian	Bush (R) 121,263	(39%)
Poverty status:	9.6%	1.7% Two+ races	Other 5,809	(2%)
Military veterans:	12.0%	0.2% Other	**2000 Presidential Vote**	
		11.4% Hispanic Origin	Gore (D) 178,977	(62%)
			Bush (R) 96,411	(33%)
			Other 13,731	(5%)
			Cook Partisan Voting Index: D +14	
Occupation	Blue collar: 19.7%	White collar: 65.8%	Gray collar: 14.5%	

In 1871, Mark Twain moved to Hartford to become director of an insurance company, and in time became the Connecticut capital's most famous citizen. Hartford, already more than two centuries old, home of the nation's longest circulating newspaper (since 1764), *The Hartford Courant*, boyhood home of the financier J. P. Morgan, was becoming the nation's best-known insurance center. This was not what the harsh Puritans who founded Hartford had in mind, but Connecticut's Yankees turned out to be shrewd businessmen. Thanks to the broad Connecticut River, Hartford also became a seaport; its merchants, prevented from trading and writing marine insurance by Thomas Jefferson's Embargo Act of 1807, turned to writing fire insurance and using the capital they had accumulated in the Napoleonic Wars to finance their ventures. One was Samuel Colt's gun factory just south of downtown Hartford, which became one of the nation's great arms plants.

Insurance and arms are still economic mainstays of Hartford, Connecticut's capital and the center of its largest metropolitan area. Insurance carriers account for 17% of local jobs; The Phoenix Companies, which includes Phoenix Life Insurance, and the Hartford Financial Services Group are among the two largest employers. Across the river is the Pratt & Whitney jet engine plant in East Hartford, cornerstone of Connecticut-based United Technologies; even though its local work force is less than one-fourth its size in 1980, it still builds engines for more than 600 customers around the world. The small central city of Hartford is otherwise in bad shape, its high-crime neighborhoods abandoned and bedraggled, its school system deeply troubled. Many words have been written about the sad decline of this once rich city, but a few numbers make the case: where 177,000 people lived in 1950 there were 124,000 in 2000. Today, its population is 41% Hispanic and 38% black. In its latest hope for an incarnation, the city in 2002 selected Eddie Perez as its first Hispanic Mayor, who described Hartford as "a Latin city," with challenges and opportunities, including the Adriaen's Landing convention center which opened in June 2005 near the riverfront. Beyond Hartford, the metropolitan area is mostly affluent and growing slowly, spread out over pleasant hills.

The 1st Congressional District of Connecticut is centered on Hartford. On the map it looks like a lobster claw. The claw extends west, excluding some affluent suburbs from the district while including small towns and part of Torrington in the north. Southwest of Hartford, the district includes the industrial town of Bristol, where along a two-lane country road is the sprawling headquarters of ESPN, the 24-hour cable network that revolutionized sports broadcasting. East of the Connecticut River are East Hartford, home of the Pratt & Whitney plant, and more affluent suburbs. Politically, the Hartford area has long been more Democratic than the rest of Connecticut: Hartford is something like Boston, a commercial metropolis more statist than its surroundings. It owes some of its Democratic character to longtime state (1946–75) and national (1961–68) Democratic chairman John Bailey, an old-fashioned political boss with a scandal-free career who promoted a raft of first-class candidates.

The congressman from the 1st District is John Larson, a Democrat first elected in 1998 to replace Barbara Kennelly (Bailey's daughter), who ran unsuccessfully for governor. Larson grew up in the Mayberry Village public housing project in East Hartford, one of eight children; his father was a fireman at Pratt & Whitney, and his mother worked at the state Capitol. He graduated from Central Connecticut State, taught high school and coached athletics; he then became an insurance agent. He comes from a political family—his brother Timothy became mayor of East Hartford—and in 1982, at 34, John Larson was elected to the state Senate. Four years later he was Senate president. There Larson sponsored one of the nation's first family medical leave laws, a prototype for the law sponsored by Senator Christopher Dodd and signed by Bill Clinton in 1993. He seemed headed for the governorship, and in 1994 he won the party designation at the state convention. But Comptroller Bill Curry built an organization of unionists and liberal activists, and beat him 55%–45% in the primary.

When Kennelly announced her retirement, Larson ran against Secretary of State Miles Rapoport, from more affluent West Hartford, who had the support of unions, the Sierra Club, and the Connecticut Citizens Action group. Rapoport led in polls and fundraising. But Larson raised impressive sums as well, built a local organization, did lots of door-to-door campaigning, and benefited from the support of Hartford Mayor Mike Peters. Larson won by 46%–43%. Rapoport won in the northwest part of the district, including Hartford, West Hartford and Bloomfield; Larson carried most of the rest, with a big vote in East Hartford. The general election was vigorously contested by Kevin O'Connor, a 31-year-old former law clerk and SEC lawyer who was endorsed by the *Hartford Courant*, but Larson won 58%–41%.

In the House Larson's voting record places him near the center of his party. He voted against normal trade relations with China, he said, because of a promise he had made to labor unions. Larson actively opposed authorizing the use of force in Iraq; he worried that unilateral action would unite the Arab world against the United States. In 2004, he added a provision to the defense bill to reimburse soldiers and their families who have purchased body armor before deploying to Iraq. He got $21 million in the 2004 omnibus appropriation to help build in East Hartford a National Center for Aerospace Leadership. As ranking Democrat for two years on the House Administration Committee, he responded to colleagues' concerns and questions about how to run their offices, and worked with Capitol officials on security. When the House approved a bipartisan package of steps to reconstitute Congress in the event of a catastrophic attack on its members, it defeated proposals by Larson to give states additional time to fill vacancies. This former history teacher took an unusual interest in the institution—pushing successfully for the Library of Congress to write an illustrated, narrative history of the House, to match the fine history of the Senate written by Senator Robert Byrd. He was forced to give up his committee post in 2005, when Minority Leader Nancy Pelosi tapped him for a seat on the Ways and Means Committee. Even before joining that panel, Larson had denounced the 2003 Medicare/ prescription drug law as a "masquerade" that benefits pharmaceutical firms and big business.

In 2000 Larson faced a celebrity challenger in former World Wrestling Federation champion Bob Backlund, but this was to be no repeat of the Jesse Ventura phenomenon. Backlund had little experience in public life, raised little money, and lost every town as he was defeated 72%–28%. Two years later, Larson won with 67% against the brother of Robert Steele, who won two terms in the eastern Connecticut 2d District in the 1970s. In 2004 he won 73%–27%.

SECOND DISTRICT

Rep. Rob Simmons (R)

Elected 2000, 3d term; b. Feb. 11, 1943, New York, NY; home, Stonington; Haverford Col., B.A. 1965, Harvard U., M.A. 1979; Episcopalian; married (Heidi Paffard).

Military Career: Army, 1965–69 (Vietnam); Army Reserves, 1969–2000.

Elected Office: CT House of Reps., 1990–2000.

Professional Career: Operations Ofcr., CIA, 1969–79; Staff, Sen. John Chafee, 1979–81; Staff Dir., Sel. Cmte. on Intelligence, 1981–85; Visiting Lecturer, Yale U., 1985–95; Teaching asst., U. of CT, 1988–91.

DC Office: 215 CHOB, 20515, 202-225-2076; Fax: 202-225-4977; Web site: www.house.gov/simmons.

District Office: Norwich, 860-886-0139.

Committees: *Armed Services* (16th of 34 R): Projection Forces; Readiness. *Homeland Security* (12th of 19 R): Emergency Preparedness, Science & Technology; Intelligence, Information Sharing & Terrorism Risk Assessment (Chmn.); Prevention of Nuclear & Biological Attack. *Transportation & Infrastructure* (19th of 41 R): Coast Guard & Maritime Transportation; Highways, Transit & Pipelines; Railroads.

Group Ratings

	ADA	ACLU	AFS	LCV	ITIC	NTU	COC	ACU	NTLC	CHC
2004	55	45	38	64	80	42	86	40	65	46
2003	20	—	38	70	—	58	80	52	—	—

National Journal Ratings

	2003 LIB	—	2003 CONS		2004 LIB	—	2004 CONS
Economic	47%	—	53%		52%	—	47%
Social	57%	—	42%		56%	—	43%
Foreign	53%	—	47%		43%	—	56%

Key Votes of the 108th Congress

1. Drilling in ANWR	N	5. DC School Vouchers	N	9. Ban Same-Sex Marriage	N
2. Approve Bush Tax Cuts	Y	6. Ban Human Cloning	Y	10. Fund Iraq War	Y
3. Medicare/Rx Bill	Y	7. Restrict Gun Liability	Y	11. Bar Cuba Embargo Funds	N
4. Bar Overtime Pay Regs.	Y	8. Ban Partial-Birth Abortion	N	12. Intelligence Reorg.	Y

Election Results

2004 general	Rob Simmons (R)	166,412	(54%)	($2,516,937)
	Jim Sullivan (D)	140,536	(46%)	($1,056,756)
2004 primary	Rob Simmons (R)	unopposed		
2002 general	Rob Simmons (R)	117,434	(54%)	($1,861,492)
	Joe Courtney (D)	99,674	(46%)	($1,233,222)

Prior Winning Percentages: 2000 (51%)

The People		Race/Ethnic Origin	Ancestry	
Area size:	2,143 sq. mi.	88.6% White	Irish: 13.3%	Italian: 10.2%
Urban population:	66.7%	3.3% Black	English: 10.2%	
Rural population:	33.3%	1.7% Asian	**2004 Presidential Vote**	
Pop. 2000:	681,113	0.5% Native Am.	Kerry (D) 180,235	(54%)
Median income:	$54,498	0.0% Hawaiian	Bush (R) 147,819	(44%)
Poverty status:	5.8%	1.5% Two+ races	Other 6,208	(2%)
Military veterans:	14.6%	0.1% Other	**2000 Presidential Vote**	
		4.3% Hispanic Origin	Gore (D) 162,762	(54%)
			Bush (R) 119,184	(40%)
			Other 19,587	(6%)
			Cook Partisan Voting Index: D + 8	

Occupation   Blue collar: 20.9%   White collar: 62.9%   Gray collar: 16.2%

Eastern Connecticut, one of the longest-settled parts of the United States, had great, and sometimes painful, change in recent years—a change comparable to those of the 1640s or 1810s or 1950s. When the Puritan settlers from Massachusetts and England arrived, these flinty hills were the home of small Indian tribes, whose numbers were decimated by warfare and even more by disease. This was never fertile farming country, but New London and Norwich were among the 13 colonies' leading workshops and ports. Not long after, factories developed around mills in little villages on the fast-flowing Quinebaug and Shetucket Rivers. Sandbars kept oceangoing ships out of the rivers, but they docked at New London. Norwich was the home of Samuel Huntington, signer of the Declaration of Independence, and the president of the Continental Congress in 1781 when the nation officially was named the United States of America. In the mid-20th century new technology shaped the area. Four nuclear power plants were built here, more than in any similarly populated part of the United States. In Groton, the "Submarine Capital of the World" across the Thames River from New London and downriver from the Coast Guard Academy, is General Dynamics' Electric Boat Company, which built the nuclear submarines that may very well have deterred nuclear war. New London is also the site of the Coast Guard Museum; the local congressional delegation passed a measure in 2004 barring its relocation.

In the 1990s, this local economy was in trouble. Nuclear plants were wearing out and being shut down across the country. After the end of the Cold War much of the Electric Boat work force was laid off, though some remained to work on the next-generation Virginia-class submarine; the base is home port to more than 20 subs, still the nation's most active submarine port, and about 10,000 employees. The area's economic base then shifted to entertainment. Some of that was tourism—Mystic Seaport and the Coast Guard Academy. Much more important was the Foxwoods Casino, built by the 650-member Mashantucket Pequot tribe and opened in 1992. Foxwoods is now the largest casino in the world, and with hotels, golf courses and a convention center, it is the largest employer in Connecticut. With the Mohegan Sun casino (the second largest casino in the world), opened near Norwich in 1996, gambling establishments now provide more tax dollars to the state than any insurance or defense company.

The 2d Congressional District of Connecticut includes most of the eastern part of the state, centering on the small cities of New London and Norwich, including mill towns and the University of Connecticut town of Storrs nestled in the rocky hills to the north. The 2d also stretches west to the outskirts of Hartford, and to antique-filled small towns like Essex and Old Lyme on Long Island Sound. For many years this was a politically marginal district, with close battles between Yankee Republicans and Catholic Democrats. More recently it has trended Democratic and has become volatile, with substantial votes for Ross Perot and Ralph Nader.

The congressman from the 2d District is Rob Simmons, a Republican first elected in 2000. Simmons grew up in New York City and enlisted in the Army after graduating from Haverford College in 1965; he spent 19 months in Vietnam, where he earned two Bronze Stars. In 1969 he joined the CIA, working as an operations officer for a decade, including five years on assignment in East Asia. Simmons joined the staff of Senator John Chafee in 1979 and was staff director for the Senate Intelligence Committee from 1981–85. When he left Washington, he said that he never expected to return. He earned a master's in public policy administration from the Kennedy School of Government and was a doctoral candidate in political science at the University of Connecticut. He was an associate fellow of Yale's Berkeley College, where he taught military intelligence; he also chaired the Stonington Police Commission. Simmons served five terms in a Democratic-leaning district in the General Assembly, voting against the state's new income tax. He remained in the Army Reserve, with the rank of colonel.

In 2000, Simmons ran against 20-year Democratic Congressman Sam Gejdenson, starting out with little name recognition. Gejdenson portrayed him as too conservative for the district. Simmons said Gejdenson was too entrenched in Washington, where he was ranking minority member of the International Relations Committee, and was out of touch with the district—living in his wife's home in a gated community in the 3d District. When House Democratic strategists realized in October that Gejdenson was in trouble, they sent money in, but it was too late. Simmons won by 2,860 votes—51%–49%. Simmons was one of only two successful House Republican challengers that year.

In the House, Simmons has a voting record near the center of the House, a bit more liberal on cultural issues than on defense; he describes himself, accurately, as "one of the most independent Republicans." On trade promotion authority, he delayed long before casting his vote and then voted against because, he said, it had inadequate labor and environmental protections. He was one of 12 House Republicans to vote against changes in the Head Start program and one of five who opposed final approval of the partial-birth abortion ban. When he led an effort to seek more money for Amtrak, Appropriations subcommittee chairman Ernest Istook retaliated by denying Simmons local transportation projects; House Republican leaders later chastised Istook, and he apologized.

Simmons serves on the Armed Services Committee, where he has sought to protect jobs at Electric Boat. After September 11, he used his background in Army intelligence to advise colleagues on how the military and Congress might have avoided the attacks. He has avidly sought, but has not won, a seat on the Intelligence Committee; still, he is permitted to attend classified briefings and receive classified materials. Since the Cold War ended, he said, terrorists have been able to roam more freely and intelligence agencies have relied more on technical data than on human expertise. Simmons strongly backed authorizing war in Iraq. He added an amendment to the intelligence bill permitting the CIA to reimburse overseas agents for personal liability insurance.

With the next round of base realignment and closing looming, in January 2005 he took a junior position on the Armed Services Readiness Subcommittee in anticipation of hearings on the issue; he promised to fight to protect the Navy submarine base in New London from closing. But in May, the base appeared on the Pentagon's list of bases recommended for closure. Simmons reacted quickly. Less than two weeks later, he introduced an amendment to delay the closure by two years; it failed 316–112. He lobbied the Pentagon, enlisting the help of the Navy's top submarine commander, and held hearings on the need for more submarines.

Also in 2005, Simmons was a skeptic about Social Security reform. "Why stir up a political hornet's nest. . . . when there is no urgency?" he said to *The Washington Post*. "When does the program go belly up? 2042. I will be dead by then."

The 2d District voted for Al Gore in 2000 and John Kerry in 2004, and not surprisingly Democrats have targeted Simmons. The Democratic candidate in 2002 was former state Representative Joseph Courtney, the unsuccessful 1998 nominee for lieutenant governor. Courtney ran on the standard Democratic themes of Social Security, prescription drug coverage for seniors and against the Bush tax cut. Friends of the Earth endorsed Simmons, saying that he had the most pro-environment record of the freshmen Republicans. Courtney gained ground late in the campaign, but Simmons won 54%–46%. In 2004, the story was similar. After winning a contested primary, Jim Sullivan challenged Simmons's support for the war in Iraq, criticized the Medicare/prescription drug law and tax cuts that Simmons backed and demanded that he return contributions from Majority Leader Tom DeLay. Simmons distanced himself from the national Republican platform, and won some labor and environmental endorsements. Simmons again won 54%–46%, carrying 55 of the 65 cities and towns. Sullivan's only big margin was in Storrs; Simmons lost New London and Norwich but carried the surrounding towns by larger margins. The fate of the New London submarine base is likely to play a prominent role in the 2006 election; Courtney said in March 2005 he planned to challenge Simmons again.

THIRD DISTRICT

Rep. Rosa DeLauro (D)

Elected 1990, 8th term; b. Mar. 2, 1943, New Haven; home, New Haven; Marymount Col., B.A. 1964, London Sch. of Econ., 1962–63, Columbia U., M.A. 1966; Catholic; married (Stanley Greenberg).

Professional Career: Exec. Asst., New Haven Mayor Frank Logue, 1976–77; Exec. Asst. & Develop. Admin., City of New Haven, 1977–79; Chief of Staff, U.S. Sen. Christopher Dodd, 1980–87; Exec. Dir., Countdown '87, 1987–88; Exec. Dir., EMILY's List, 1989.

DC Office: 2262 RHOB, 20515, 202-225-3661; Fax: 202-225-4890; Web site: www.house.gov/delauro.

District Offices: Durham, 860-344-1159; New Haven, 203-562-3718; Stratford, 203-378-9005.

Committees: *Democratic Steering Committee Co-Chair. Appropriations* (11th of 29 D): Agriculture, Rural Development, FDA & Related Agencies (RMM); Labor, Health and Human Services, Education & Related Agencies. *Budget* (4th of 17 D).

Group Ratings

	ADA	ACLU	AFS	LCV	ITIC	NTU	COC	ACU	NTLC	CHC
2004	100	80	100	100	40	8	29	4	0	15
2003	100	—	100	95	—	22	30	16	—	—

National Journal Ratings

	2003 LIB	—	2003 CONS		2004 LIB	—	2004 CONS
Economic	87%	—	9%		89%	—	8%
Social	84%	—	13%		86%	—	12%
Foreign	81%	—	17%		87%	—	12%

Key Votes of the 108th Congress

1. Drilling in ANWR	N	5. DC School Vouchers	N	9. Ban Same-Sex Marriage	N
2. Approve Bush Tax Cuts	N	6. Ban Human Cloning	N	10. Fund Iraq War	N
3. Medicare/Rx Bill	N	7. Restrict Gun Liability	N	11. Bar Cuba Embargo Funds	Y
4. Bar Overtime Pay Regs.	Y	8. Ban Partial-Birth Abortion	N	12. Intelligence Reorg.	N

Election Results

2004 general	Rosa DeLauro (D)	200,638	(72%)	($714,890)
	Richter Elser (R)	69,160	(25%)	($21,416)
	Other	7,182	(3%)	
2004 primary	Rosa DeLauro (D)	unopposed		
2002 general	Rosa DeLauro (D)	121,557	(66%)	($686,768)
	Richter Elser (R)	54,757	(30%)	($81,050)
	Charles Pillsbury (Green)	9,050	(5%)	($102,890)

Prior Winning Percentages: 2000 (72%); 1998 (71%); 1996 (71%); 1994 (63%); 1992 (66%); 1990 (52%)

The People		Race/Ethnic Origin	Ancestry	
Area size:	485 sq. mi.	76.1% White	Italian: 18.7%	Irish: 12.5%
Urban population:	96.6%	11.5% Black	German: 6.7%	
Rural population:	3.4%	2.5% Asian	**2004 Presidential Vote**	
Pop. 2000:	681,113	0.2% Native Am.	Kerry (D) 174,382	(56%)
Median income:	$49,752	0.0% Hawaiian	Bush (R) 128,960	(42%)
Poverty status:	8.8%	1.5% Two+ races	Other 5,980	(2%)
Military veterans:	11.8%	0.2% Other	**2000 Presidential Vote**	
		8.0% Hispanic Origin	Gore (D) 168,196	(60%)
			Bush (R) 96,446	(34%)
			Other 15,455	(6%)
			Cook Partisan Voting Index: D +12	

Occupation	Blue collar: 21.1%	White collar: 64.7%	Gray collar: 14.2%

The beginnings of Connecticut's defense industry came more than two centuries ago, in 1798, when Eli Whitney, a young Yale graduate, won an order from the federal government to produce 10,000 muskets at $13.40 each. Six years before, Whitney had invented the cotton gin, which revolutionized the South but for years only embroiled him in a patent suit. On the musket contract, he was determined to make a profit right off, so he set up a system of interchangeable parts and invented a milling machine and gauges: The beginning of standardized American manufacturing. It was also the beginning of New Haven as a manufacturing center, for Whitney set up his factory along a small, rapidly flowing river just north of this town, established more than 150 years before as a religious haven for strict Puritans. For the next 150 years or so, the town mass-produced rifles, clocks, locks, hardware and toys—anything its tinkerers and entrepreneurs could fashion. Today there are few factories left in New Haven, and Connecticut's defense contracts have been cut way back; the Sikorsky plant in Stratford, west of New Haven, lost the contract to produce the new Marine One helicopter in January 2005. Southern Connecticut around New Haven is mostly prosperous, with scores of mostly small technology and biomedical firms. But the city itself, with significant crime rates and many neighborhoods scarred by abandoned homes, has been abandoned to a considerable extent: it had 164,000 people in 1950 and 125,000 in 2003. Yale, with its Gothic spires and redbrick halls, has always been the visual focus of the city, and now is New Haven's largest employer. Although there has been some revival in recent years, sparked by Yale's homebuyers' program of incentives to faculty and staff and by $1 billion in local investments by biotech firms, the economic vitality of the region is centered outside the city limits. New Haven, however, has a new historic claim. It was the birthplace of George W. Bush in 1946, and he lived his first two years on Hillhouse Avenue in a building that now houses the economics department.

The 3d Congressional District of Connecticut covers the New Haven metropolitan area, which has long since spread beyond the narrow city limits over the hills of what were once Yankee villages and countryside; New Haven cast only 12% of its votes in 2004. For many years the 3d was a marginal district, changing partisan hands in the 1980s as well as the 1940s and 1950s. But it has moved to the Democratic side and is now a strongly Democratic district.

The congresswoman from the 3d District is Rosa DeLauro, first elected in 1990. She is well connected in New Haven and Washington. She grew up in New Haven's Wooster Square. Both her parents were elected as New Haven aldermen; her mother, Luisa DeLauro, retired in 1999 after 35 years as New Haven's longest-serving alderman. Rosa DeLauro's husband, Stanley Greenberg, was Bill Clinton's chief pollster from 1991–94 and worked for Al Gore in 2000 and John Kerry in 2004. Rosa DeLauro has been in politics nearly all of her life. She was a development administrator in New Haven in the 1970s, chief of staff to Senator Christopher Dodd from 1980–87, then spent a year working to stop U.S. military aid to Nicaraguan contras before going on to become director of EMILY's List, the feminist campaign fundraising group. In 1990, when 3d District incumbent Bruce Morrison ran for governor, DeLauro ran for Congress and won 52%–48% over anti-tax and anti-abortion legislator Tom Scott, after spending an impressive $957,000.

DeLauro has had the most liberal voting record in the Connecticut delegation, and became one of the Democratic leadership's loudest champions on the floor. Like most House Democratic leaders, she voted against NAFTA and normal trade relations with China. She has been an active and enthusiastic supporter of feminist issues. A cancer survivor, she sponsored the law to require 48-hour hospital stays for mastectomies and argued for insurance coverage of early-detection tests of cervical cancer. She has sought unsuccessfully to remove abortion restrictions on federal employees' health benefits. As a member of the committee that drafted in 2002 the bill creating the Homeland Security Department, she embarrassed House Republican leaders by winning a vote to prevent the department from contracting with corporations that move overseas for tax purposes; the House-Senate conference committee later watered down that provision. When she added similar language in committee to an appropriation bill in 2004, she lost a floor vote on procedural grounds. DeLauro organized the House's food safety caucus, and she has sought to increase its relevance in the era of security fears by demanding increased steps to prevent bioterrorism. She wants fast food and chain restaurants to display nutrition information on their menus.

She remains an active and intense political strategist, "a live wire whose words rush out like sparks," wrote the *New York Times*. She has run twice for chairman of the Democratic Caucus and suffered two painfully close losses. In 1998, she lost 108–97 to Martin Frost, but Dick Gephardt then named her an assistant to the leader to work on the party message. In 2002 she lost by 104–103 to Bob Menendez after an intense yearlong contest. The deciding vote was cast for Menendez by Mike Feeley of Colorado, whose election was in question at the time; it later turned out that he lost his race and so was never actually a member of Congress. DeLauro was an active and early supporter of Nancy Pelosi in her races for minority whip and minority leader, and she was probably hurt in her own race by the reluctance of some Democrats to put so many liberal women in the party leadership. But she has found other opportunities for leadership. Pelosi named her as co-chair of the Democratic Steering Committee, which assigns members to House committees. In 2004, working in close coordination with the Kerry campaign, DeLauro led the drafting panel of the Democratic Platform Committee.

DeLauro's last serious competition in the 3d District came in 1992, when she won a rematch against Scott 66%–34%. She has been reelected easily since then. She has expressed her interest in running for the Senate when there was talk that Joseph Lieberman's or Christopher Dodd's seats might become open. In 2002 and 2004 she defeated Richter Elser, an openly gay restaurateur who became a bread truck driver, by 66%–30% and 72%–25%.

FOURTH DISTRICT

Rep. Christopher Shays (R)

Elected Aug. 1987, 9th full term; b. Oct. 18, 1945, Darien; home, Bridgeport; Principia Col., B.A. 1968, NYU, M.B.A. 1974, M.P.A. 1978; Christian Scientist; married (Betsi).

Elected Office: CT House of Reps., 1974–87.

Professional Career: Peace Corps, Fiji, 1968–70; Aide, Trumbull Mayor, 1971–72.

DC Office: 1126 LHOB, 20515, 202-225-5541; Fax: 202-225-9629; Web site: www.house.gov/shays.

District Offices: Bridgeport, 203-579-5870; Norwalk, 203-866-6469; Ridgefield, 203-438-5953; Shelton, 203-402-0426; Stamford, 203-357-8277.

Committees: *Financial Services* (19th of 37 R): Capital Markets, Insurance & Government Sponsored Enterprises; Housing & Community Opportunity. *Government Reform* (Vice Chmn. of 23 R): Federalism & the Census; National Security, Emerging Threats & International Relations (Chmn.). *Homeland Security* (5th of 19 R): Management, Integration & Oversight; Prevention of Nuclear & Biological Attack.

Group Ratings

	ADA	ACLU	AFS	LCV	ITIC	NTU	COC	ACU	NTLC	CHC
2004	70	50	50	82	80	52	86	38	73	53
2003	30	—	25	90	—	59	77	52	—	—

National Journal Ratings

	2003 LIB	—	2003 CONS		2004 LIB	—	2004 CONS
Economic	48%	—	51%		53%	—	47%
Social	58%	—	41%		61%	—	38%
Foreign	54%	—	45%		55%	—	44%

Key Votes of the 108th Congress

1. Drilling in ANWR	N	5. DC School Vouchers	Y	9. Ban Same-Sex Marriage	N
2. Approve Bush Tax Cuts	Y	6. Ban Human Cloning	N	10. Fund Iraq War	Y
3. Medicare/Rx Bill	Y	7. Restrict Gun Liability	N	11. Bar Cuba Embargo Funds	Y
4. Bar Overtime Pay Regs.	N	8. Ban Partial-Birth Abortion	Y	12. Intelligence Reorg.	Y

Election Results

2004 general	Christopher Shays (R)	152,493	(52%)	($2,255,210)
	Diane Farrell (D)	138,333	(48%)	($1,542,410)
2004 primary	Christopher Shays (R)	unopposed		
2002 general	Christopher Shays (R)	113,197	(64%)	($919,160)
	Stephanie Sanchez (D)	62,491	(36%)	($110,699)

Prior Winning Percentages: 2000 (58%); 1998 (69%); 1996 (60%); 1994 (74%); 1992 (67%); 1990 (77%); 1988 (72%); 1987 (57%)

The People		Race/Ethnic Origin	Ancestry	
Area size:	539 sq. mi.	70.9% White	Italian: 13.5%	Irish: 11.6%
Urban population:	95.9%	10.9% Black	German: 7.1%	
Rural population:	4.1%	3.2% Asian	**2004 Presidential Vote**	
Pop. 2000:	681,113	0.1% Native Am.	Kerry (D) 162,166	(52%)
Median income:	$66,598	0.0% Hawaiian	Bush (R) 143,280	(46%)
Poverty status:	7.4%	1.7% Two+ races	Other 4,121	(1%)
Military veterans:	10.0%	0.3% Other	**2000 Presidential Vote**	
		12.8% Hispanic Origin	Gore (D) 148,022	(53%)
			Bush (R) 120,140	(43%)
			Other 10,219	(4%)
			Cook Partisan Voting Index: D + 5	

Occupation   Blue collar: 15.5%   White collar: 71.8%   Gray collar: 12.7%

No one in colonial America imagined that the rocky shore of southern Connecticut on Long Island Sound would some day lodge one of the largest concentrations of wealth in the world. The soil was stony, the terrain unaccommodating, the harbors not as convenient as those in New York and Rhode Island and Massachusetts. Yet that is what has happened. For 200 years this was the home of unnoticed Yankee farmers, sailors and tinkerers; then, factories were built on its fast-running stream. In the 19th century, Bridgeport became famous as the home of P.T. Barnum, and around that same time rich New Yorkers began taking the train north to country houses in Connecticut. In the 20th century, Greenwich and other Yankee villages clustered around commuter railroad stations became the home of some of New York's elite. Greenwich has beautifully manicured hills, elaborately simple boat docks, carefully casual roads, good manners and dull haircuts, over a dozen private clubs and 12 private schools—and houses which are routinely sold for more than $3 million and then torn down to make way for grander mansions. Starting in the 1950s, New York-based CEOs, eager to minimize their own commutes and avoid New York income taxes, moved their headquarters out to Greenwich and further, and today there are more than a dozen corporations with sales over $1 billion headquartered here, including General Electric in Fairfield and several large firms in Stamford. Greenwich, sometimes referred to as "Wall Street by the Sea" for its proliferation of hedge fund offices and financial firms, is closest to New York and commands the highest commercial rents of all these places.

The 4th Congressional District covers Connecticut along Long Island Sound, from industrial Bridgeport to affluent Greenwich, and goes inland to Ridgefield, Redding, Monroe and Oxford. It includes bustling and pricey Stamford, woodsy Darien, modest Norwalk, artsy-craftsy Westport, Fairfield and then Bridgeport, an odd duck, an industrial and low-income town, though spruced up when the state-financed Harbor Yard sports complex opened for minor league baseball. The basic political balance has been the same since the 1940s, when the heavily affluent suburbs out-voted Bridgeport and elected Republican Clare Boothe Luce to the House. More than the rest of Connecticut, the 4th is oriented to New York rather than Hartford or Boston. People here watch New York TV stations: They are Yankee, not Red Sox, fans; their political attitudes are shaped by what is happening in the City as much as in Hartford. Opposition to high taxes helped former Governor John Rowland to win by big margins here. But the influence of Christian conservatives in the Republican party has repelled Episcopalians and other mainline Protestants here, and they have been increasingly voting Democratic. This is the district where George H. W. Bush grew up and one which he carried in 1988 and 1992. But George W. Bush lost it in 2000 and 2004.

The 4th District's congressman, Christopher Shays, is a product of the upscale towns and he has been a pivotal Republican in the House. Shays grew up in Darien. After college he and his wife volunteered for the Peace Corps and served in Fiji; after graduate school he was elected to the Connecticut House in 1974, at 29, and served for 12 years. He was elected to Congress in a 1987 special election by beating a culturally conservative Democrat from Bridgeport. Shays is a pleasant man with a stubborn streak and considerable legislative savvy; his voting record is near the middle of the House, a bit left on cultural issues. When he feels strongly, he will risk everything: He registered for conscientious objector status during the Vietnam War, and says he would not have served if drafted; as a legislator, he went to jail for seven days in 1986 to protest judicial system corruption; he is one of two congressmen (the other is Frank Wolf) who have made trips to Iraq on their own, without guides from the Defense Department.

Despite his dissent from many Republicans' views—on campaign finance reform, abortion, gun control, subsidies to the arts, gay rights, the minimum wage, defense spending, Census sampling—he was a partisan Republican from the time he was ignored by the House's Democratic leaders and impressed by a speech in Connecticut by a backbencher named Newt Gingrich. The first major bill of the Republican Congress was managed by Shays: the Congressional Accountability Act, imposing on Congress the laws it imposes on others, passed unanimously on the first day. Shays supported Gingrich on ethics charges and warned him of the other leaders' attempted coup in 1997. But he soured on Republican leaders after they went to great lengths to sink his Shays-Meehan campaign finance bill. On some big issues he was solidly with George W. Bush: He voted for trade promotion authority and to authorize the use of force in Iraq. After the ouster of Saddam Hussein, Shays made several visits to Iraq to meet with local groups, and he typically returned with suggestions for the Bush administration. In 2002, he became a leading supporter of Bush's proposal for a Homeland Security Department and he helped to defeat an amendment to permit its employees to join unions. In 2004, he pressed harder than most House Republicans wished to enact the intelligence-reform recommendations of the 9/11 Commission; that success was another personal achievement.

Shays's great cause has been campaign finance regulation. As enacted in March 2002, his Shays-Meehan bill—or McCain-Feingold, as it was known in the Senate and more widely— banned in federal elections soft money from corporations, labor unions and wealthy individuals and prohibited issue advocacy ads within 60 days of an election. Although the House passed the bill 240–189, all but 41 House Republicans voted against it, with many contending it was harmful to their party. The conflict caused bitter divisions and anger by Republicans toward Shays. Anne Northup of Kentucky said that Shays's constant criticism of opponents of the legislation as corrupt was "making it very hard to vote your conscience." Shays defended the new law in federal court; after lengthy review, the Supreme Court in December 2003 upheld most of the provisions. Then, he turned his attention to abolishing the Federal Election Commission and creating a more assertive agency to enforce the nation's campaign finance laws. On other domestic issues, he chaired a bipartisan group that filed the Climate Stewardship Act, to focus attention on global warming and set a schedule to reduce harmful emissions. He fought unsuccessfully to extend the ban on assault weapons. And in November 2004 he spoke out against proposed House Republican rules changes to remove the requirement that a party leader step down after being indicted. "The power has gotten to our heads," he said.

After the November 2002 election, the chairmanship of the Government Reform Committee was open, and Shays was next in line in seniority. He actively sought the post; he argued that it was best suited for him and that his work on campaign finance ought not to be held against him. But he clearly was not popular with the Republican leadership, and the Steering Committee chose Tom Davis of Virginia, who had done a brilliant job for four years maintaining the Republican majority at the National Republican Congressional Committee. Shays retained the chairmanship of the Government Reform subcommittee with the most far-reaching investigative authority, on national security issues.

Back home, Shays had opposition from Democrats who have attacked him for supporting Gingrich and, in 2000, from a Republican primary opponent who said he was too independent and too liberal. Until 2004, none caused him serious difficulty. But Shays faced an armful of a challenge that year from Democrat Diane Farrell, the First Selectman of Westport. Farrell got extensive financial support from House Democrats and argued that Shays was a "rubber stamp" for Bush and House Republican leaders. National Republicans found themselves in the curious position of citing and defending Shays's independence based on roll-call vote analysis. Farrell also said that his focus on national and international issues had resulted in Shays losing touch with local concerns such as traffic jams on I-95. He cited the grants that he had obtained to show that he had not forgotten local causes. Shays had campaign help from Rudy Giuliani, John McCain and Governor Jodi Rell, but—to the dismay of the NRCC—he ordered the campaign committee not to run ads attacking Farrell. His endorsers included the League of Conservation Voters, Human Rights Campaign Fund, and the Veterans' of Foreign Wars. Hillary Rodham Clinton, Howard Dean, Lowell Weicker and Nancy Pelosi made appearances for Farrell. Both candidates were well-funded but Shays won by the narrow margin of 52%–48%. He carried 13 of the 17 cities and towns, losing narrowly in Norwalk, Stamford and Westport and by a big margin in Bridgeport. In affluent Greenwich, Darien, New Canaan and Wilton he ran 8% or 9% ahead of George W. Bush. Farrell left the door open to another run.

Shays returned to the House with less than a full embrace from his party colleagues, some of whom view him as a sanctimonious troublemaker. He stepped down as vice chairman of the Budget Committee—with a nudge from Republican leaders unhappy over his failure to support the budget resolution in 2004. His call for Majority Leader Tom DeLay's resignation in April 2005 compounded his isolation. Apart from the Government Reform Committee, his current committee posts are remarkably junior for such a senior member. But he has repeatedly shown that he can get a lot done without official title, but with legislative skill, persistence, and hard work.

FIFTH DISTRICT

Rep. Nancy Johnson (R)

Elected 1982, 12th term; b. Jan. 5, 1935, Chicago, IL; home, New Britain; U. of Chicago, 1951–53, Radcliffe Col., B.A. 1957, U. of London, 1957–58; Unitarian; married (Theodore).

Elected Office: CT Senate, 1976–82.

Professional Career: Pres., Sheldon Community Guidance Clinic; Adjunct Prof., Central CT St. Col., 1968–71.

DC Office: 2409 RHOB, 20515, 202-225-4476; Fax: 202-225-4488; Web site: www.house.gov/nancyjohnson.

District Offices: Danbury, 203-790-6856; Meriden, 203-630-1903; New Britain, 860-223-8412; Waterbury, 203-573-1418.

Committees: *Ways & Means* (3d of 24 R): Health (Chmn.); Human Resources. *Joint Committee on Taxation* (3d of 5 Reps.).

Group Ratings

	ADA	ACLU	AFS	LCV	ITIC	NTU	COC	ACU	NTLC	CHC
2004	45	40	0	55	100	54	100	56	69	41
2003	35	—	25	70	—	54	79	57	—	—

National Journal Ratings

	2003 LIB	—	2003 CONS	2004 LIB	—	2004 CONS
Economic	49%	—	51%	47%	—	53%
Social	57%	—	42%	59%	—	41%
Foreign	46%	—	52%	49%	—	50%

Key Votes of the 108th Congress

1. Drilling in ANWR	N	5. DC School Vouchers	Y	9. Ban Same-Sex Marriage	N
2. Approve Bush Tax Cuts	Y	6. Ban Human Cloning	N	10. Fund Iraq War	Y
3. Medicare/Rx Bill	Y	7. Restrict Gun Liability	Y	11. Bar Cuba Embargo Funds	Y
4. Bar Overtime Pay Regs.	N	8. Ban Partial-Birth Abortion	N	12. Intelligence Reorg.	Y

Election Results

2004 general	Nancy Johnson (R)	168,268	(60%)	($1,241,036)
	Theresa Gerratana (D)	107,438	(38%)	($128,229)
	Other	5,741	(2%)	
2004 primary	Nancy Johnson (R)	unopposed		
2002 general	Nancy Johnson (R)	113,626	(54%)	($3,752,161)
	Jim Maloney (D)	90,616	(43%)	($2,075,621)
	Other	5,212	(3%)	

Prior Winning Percentages: 2000 (63%); 1998 (58%); 1996 (50%); 1994 (64%); 1992 (70%); 1990 (74%); 1988 (66%); 1986 (64%); 1984 (64%); 1982 (52%)

The People		**Race/Ethnic Origin**	**Ancestry**	
Area size:	1,282 sq. mi.	80.2% White	Italian: 14.5% Irish: 12.7%	
Urban population:	85.9%	5.2% Black	German: 8.2%	
Rural population:	14.1%	2.1% Asian	**2004 Presidential Vote**	
Pop. 2000:	681,113	0.2% Native Am.	Kerry (D)	153,616 (49%)
Median income:	$53,118	0.0% Hawaiian	Bush (R)	152,504 (49%)
Poverty status:	7.7%	1.5% Two+ races	Other	5,325 (2%)
Military veterans:	11.9%	0.3% Other	**2000 Presidential Vote**	
		10.5% Hispanic Origin	Gore (D)	146,599 (52%)
			Bush (R)	121,424 (43%)
			Other	13,887 (5%)
			Cook Partisan Voting Index: D + 4	

Occupation	Blue collar: 22.4%	White collar: 62.9%	Gray collar: 14.6%

Over the years, Connecticut's stony soil has become the home of some of the most affluent people in the nation and the world. This is true even in the hills of northwest Connecticut, off the interstates and far from Connecticut's small urban capital of Hartford and its sometime booming edge city of Stamford. Here are exquisite Yankee towns like Washington and Kent, once prosperous in the post-Revolutionary era when Connecticut's ship owners accumulated capital and invested it in factories and mills, and now the "anti-Hamptons," a country-home mecca for ultra-rich New Yorkers seeking to avoid the glitz of Southampton and East Hampton. Not far away are small industrial cities like New Britain, America's ball bearing capital for years; Meriden, which turned from ivory combs, clocks, cutlery, and silver, to producing electrical signaling equipment, jewelry, biotech filters, and nuclear instruments; Waterbury, once the nation's largest producer of brass, where political corruption and economic malaise resulted in the state taking over its finances in 2001; and Danbury, once the nation's leading producer of hats, but now a growing corporate headquarters with an eclectic mix of recent immigrants from South America, the Caribbean and Southeast Asia. Over the hills from Hartford are Avon and Simsbury, booming towns that have become comfortable bedroom communities and the home of champion international ice-skaters.

The 5th Congressional District of Connecticut covers much of the western side of the state, dipping down to include the northern towns of Fairfield County. It has two arms that reach into the hills of central Connecticut—one to Democratic Meriden, and the other to the affluent and Republican-leaning Farmington Valley suburbs of Hartford. This district was carefully drawn by a bipartisan redistricting commission to provide a "fair fight" between two incumbents forced into the same district because Connecticut lost a House seat in the 2000 Census.

The congresswoman from the 5th District is Nancy Johnson, a Republican first elected in 1982. She grew up in Chicago, the daughter of a Republican state legislator, came east to school, then lived in New Britain as a doctor's wife and a teacher, raising three children while active in charitable and community affairs. She was elected to the Connecticut Senate in 1976 from a heavily Democratic district. When 6th District Congressman Toby Moffett ran against Senator Lowell Weicker in 1982, Johnson won the House seat, defeating Bill Curry, then a 30-year-old nuclear freeze organizer and later a Clinton White House aide and twice unsuccessful Democratic candidate for governor.

Johnson is the third-ranking member of Ways and Means and chairs its Health Subcommittee. Her record has been fairly liberal on cultural issues and consciously moderate elsewhere, but market-oriented on much of her committee work. For years, she has been one of the most active and productive legislators in the House. In 1993 and 1994 she opposed the Clinton health care plan, enduring gratuitous and sexist insults from then-subcommittee Chairman Pete Stark in hearings, and her efforts contributed to its demise. Her efforts to reshape Medicare included sponsoring the first preventive health care benefits for seniors and measures to strengthen community hospitals, nursing homes and Medicare Choice plans. She was the lead Republican sponsor in 1997 of enactment of the CHIP health coverage for uninsured children. Her work in 2003 on the Medicare/prescription drug law was a major milestone, both for herself and her party. It was passed with scant specific direction from the Bush White House, after months of closed-door negotiations among a dozen congressional leaders and key committee players, all of them Republicans, except for Democratic Senators Max Baucus and John Breaux. Johnson, the only woman in that group and the only moderate Republican, brought an understanding of the policy and partisan impact of complicated provisions. A key part of the final agreement that received relatively little attention was Johnson's program for chronic disease management for seniors, including steps to assure proper coordination of medication and medical treatment.

On Ways and Means Johnson also worked to increase the Independent Living program for older foster care children and to help fathers on welfare get jobs and develop parental skills. In 2002, the House passed her resolution urging Major League Baseball to implement a mandatory program to test for steroid use; two years later, she got results. And she responded to constituent unhappiness over the decision of New Britain-based Stanley Works to reincorporate in Bermuda to save $30 million annually in federal taxes, by introducing a bill imposing a moratorium on such actions. In early 2005, she said that Social Security changes were urgently needed and supported personal retirement accounts.

Johnson has on occasion bucked the House Republican leadership. She voted against the Contract with America crime package, has supported abortion rights (Johnson harshly criticized Bush's executive order reimposing a ban on federal aid to international organizations that discuss abortion), was one of the first Republicans to sign a discharge petition for the Shays-Meehan campaign finance bill and introduced legislation to prevent oil drilling in the Arctic National Wildlife Refuge. But she also cooperated often with Speaker Newt Gingrich, and that caused her electoral trouble in 1996, when she chaired the House ethics committee during its investigation of charges brought by Democrats against him. Her opponent called her "an enabler and participant in the right-wing Republican agenda," and national liberal groups targeted the district. Johnson readily admitted that her role on the ethics committee "absolutely hurt me" in the election, which she won 50%–49%. In March 2004, a bit later than other Connecticut Republicans, she called on Gov. John Rowland to resign. In November 2004 she opposed the move to drop the requirement that House Republican leaders step aside after an indictment. With Christopher Shays and Rob Simmons, she opposed the recognition by the Bureau of Indian Affairs of the Schaghticoke Tribal Nation, which hoped to open a casino in western Connecticut.

In 2002, this senior lawmaker was faced with redistricting and the unpleasant task of running against feisty Democratic colleague Jim Maloney. Although the new district was drawn evenly—in both geographic and partisan terms—from the old districts, Johnson entered the contest with some clear-cut advantages: She was a more experienced legislator, with a longer record of performance; she was a better fundraiser, including the most funds received from the pharmaceutical and hospital industries by any House candidate that cycle. In addition, Maloney didn't help his cause by reaffirming a pledge not to seek another term in 2004. Neither contender held anything back, with the *Hartford Courant* describing Johnson as "a pit bull in pearls," and Maloney as "the bulky junkyard dog of Connecticut politics." Maloney depicted Johnson as an ally of the powerful who failed to defend the weak. Johnson stressed her ability to cross party lines and the respect accorded her in Washington. Johnson won a comfortable 54%–43% victory, carrying 37 of the 41 cities and towns. So complete was Johnson's victory that she led Maloney 50%–48% in his old district; in her old district, she won 59%–39%. In 2004 she won 60%–38%, carrying every city and town but tiny Cornwall and her heavily Democratic hometown of New Britain. She likely will hold this seat as long as she wants it, but it should be a competitive district if she does not run.

Johnson faces a more immediate decision on whether and how to run for the Ways and Means chairmanship in 2006, when Bill Thomas will be term-limited and she will be 71. Although there is little doubt that she has the political and policy skills required for the job, the difficulties that she endured in chairing the ethics committee may be a warning of the challenges that confront a pragmatic moderate seeking to steer a course through the polarized House. So she may defer to the more senior Clay Shaw.

★ DELAWARE ★

Delaware, the first state to ratify the Constitution, the second smallest state in area, sixth smallest in population, is a small corner of America, with some considerable claims on the national attention. The mouth of the Delaware River was explored by Henry Hudson, and the Dutch and Swedes built settlements on the west bank in the 1630s. But the three counties of Delaware owe their separate existence to the politics of the proprietors of William Penn's colony of Pennsylvania, and to Delawareans' own speed in ratifying the Constitution which made it literally the "First State."

Through most of its history, Delaware has been unusually affluent. It had the nation's highest income levels during the early 20th century and high incomes in the prosperous 1990s. It houses, in beautiful cobblestone mansions in its chateau country, many members of the most numerous wealthy family in America, the du Ponts. Delaware's ethnic and racial mixture is much like that along the rest of the East Coast and not that much different than the nation's, though with fewer than average Hispanics and Asians; there is a mixture here of suburbs, old immigrant neighborhoods, urban black neighborhoods, attractive beach towns and farmlands. Sussex County in southern Delaware is a world of its own. It produces more chickens than any other county in the country (chickens outnumber people by a 300–1 ratio in Delaware), and also thousands of tons of processed chicken dung (or "broiler litter"). Its beach communities are bustling with growth and zooming housing values, and there is a move toward historic preservation in the old towns inland.

The central focus of Delaware's economy for two centuries was the business started when Eleuthere Irenee du Pont, the practical, business-minded son of a dreamy, idealistic French immigrant, built a gunpowder mill on the banks of Brandywine Creek in 1802. This was the first enterprise of the family du Pont, and it expanded to become one of America's great munitions and chemical companies. It grew especially rapidly during World War I, generating so much capital that the company bought a huge block of stock in General Motors in the 1920s and controlled GM for thirty years while it was America's largest corporation. DuPont capital also financed what was arguably the world's finest research and development program. In the years during and

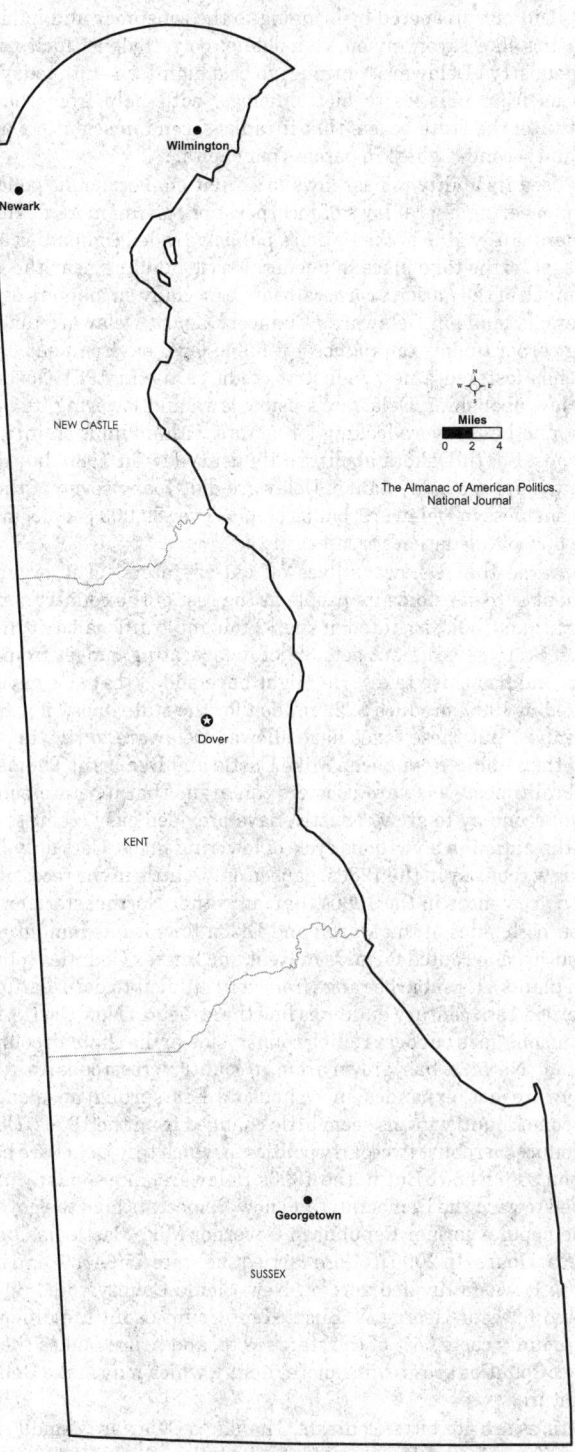

Wilmington

Newark

NEW CASTLE

Miles
0   2   4

The Almanac of American Politics.
National Journal

Dover

KENT

Georgetown

SUSSEX

U.S. Representative elected at-large.

after World War II, DuPont prospered by bringing to the consumer and industrial market new synthetics and plastics like rayon, nylon, cellophane, polyethylene, lucite and teflon: "Better Living Through Chemistry." Delaware continues to be a high-tech state today, although DuPont has shifted its focus from plastics to biotechnology, with help from the state's Delaware Biotechnology Institute; the state boasts that it ranks second in scientists and engineers with Ph.D.'s per capita and second-highest in patents per capita.

Delaware has used its ability to pass laws to set national economic policy. In the late 19th century, it passed pioneering liberal laws of incorporation, giving more flexibility and power to managers and owners. Fully 50% of the nation's publicly traded companies are incorporated in Delaware—their legal births take place in a federal-style building near the Capitol in Dover—which means that much of the nation's corporate law, especially on mergers and acquisitions and unfriendly takeovers, is made in Delaware's Chancery Court. Delaware takes care in choosing judges and writing corporate law to produce a reliable legal environment. In the last quarter-century Delaware has fostered a new industry: credit cards. In 1981 Governor Pete du Pont pushed through a law abolishing Delaware's usury laws and lowering its bank franchise tax. Inflation was high, and banks were looking for a state with no limit on interest to locate their credit card operations. South Dakota abolished its usury law in 1980, but didn't have a labor force large enough to support many banks; Delaware did. Today seven of the 10 biggest credit card companies do business in Delaware; banks employ over 32,000 people, more than any other industry and issue 60% of the nation's credit cards.

Some critics charge that Delaware lives off out-of-staters. "The organizing principle of Delaware government is to subsidize its people at the rest of the country's expense," wrote the *New Republic*'s Jonathan Chait, irritated at the $2 toll and traffic jams at the tollbooths on the Delaware Turnpike. State government gets 3% of its operating budget from the tolls and 22% from corporate fees and franchise taxes. He might have added that slot machines at Delaware race tracks, legalized in 1996, produce $222 million for the state, most of it from out-of-staters, another 9% of revenues. But these taxes have allowed Delaware to levy no sales tax and, first under du Pont and then under Republican Mike Castle and Democrat Thomas Carper, to lower its income tax several times. Delaware boosters can argue that its state policies have enabled America's industrial economy to grow robustly, have provided easy credit to millions of Americans and have led the nation in a virtuous cycle of lowering taxes. Certainly Delaware has done well: Its economy grew robustly in the 1980s, paused only a little in the recessions of 1990–91 and 2001; its population grew more in the 1990s than any other Northeastern or Midwestern state.

Delaware is on both sides of the Mason and Dixon line; it has immigrant communities in Wilmington and southern-accented farmers in Kent and Sussex Counties (plus Latino migrants working in chicken plants); its suburbs range from very affluent to not-so-affluent in New Castle County. Well-preserved 18th century buildings line the streets of New Castle, the state capital in 1776–77, while mansions gaze out over rolling countryside in the chateau country in Centreville, north of Wilmington. Newark has grown from a country crossroads to a small city as the University of Delaware has expanded; new housing has sprung up along U.S. 40 west of Wilmington while some country towns seem little changed from the 1950s. Delaware's considerable variety has produced a robust two-party politics in which tiny Delaware has often voted very much like the nation as a whole. But in the 1990s Delaware, like so many of America's largest metro areas, trended toward the Democrats, and now Democrats hold the governorship and both Senate seats, while popular former Republican Governor Mike Castle has held onto the state's single seat in the U.S. House. In 2000 Al Gore carried the state 55%–42% and in 2004 John Kerry carried it 53%–46%. It was a divided verdict. New Castle County voted 60% for Kerry, while Sussex County voted 60% for George W. Bush; Kent County split the difference with 56% for Bush. New Castle County casts 64% of the state's vote, and hence makes the state Democratic; but Kent and Sussex Counties are growing more rapidly, which may make Delaware once again a bellwether in the future.

Delaware elections are not bitter contests. Thanks to Delaware's small size there is still an intimacy to politics here. Most of Delaware is reached (though politically ignored) by Philadelphia TV, so personal campaigning is still important. Successful Delaware politicians are almost always nice people; they couldn't get elected otherwise. Then there is Delaware's unique custom, on the Thursday after the election of "Return Day," when winning and losing candidates— opponents ride in the same car—come back to the Sussex County seat of Georgetown to receive the bipartisan cheers of the voters and, literally, bury a hatchet in a box of Lewes beach sand. Not a bad example for the nation.

The People

Pop. 2004 (est):	830,364			
Pop. 2000:	783,600			
Pop. 1990:	666,168			
Change 1990–2000:	Up 17.6%			
% of U.S. total:	0.3%			
Pop. rank:	45th of 50			
Area size:	2,489 sq. mi.			
State Native:	48.3%			
Non-citizen:	3.3%			

Race/Ethnic Origin

567,973	72.5%	White
148,435	18.9%	Black
16,110	2.1%	Asian
2,324	0.3%	Native Am.
234	0.0%	Hawaiian
10,222	1.3%	Two+ races
1,025	0.1%	Other
37,277	4.8%	Hisp. Origin

Language

English: 88.1%	Spanish: 5.4%
Other Eur.: 4.6%	

Ancestry

Irish: 12.6%	German: 10.9%
English: 9.2%	Italian: 7.1%
USA: 4.6%	

Military veterans: 84,289 (14.3%)

WWII: 19.2%	Korea: 13.7%
Vietnam: 31.7%	Gulf War: 10.1%

Most populous cities (2003):

1. Wilmington	72,051
2. Dover	32,808
3. Newark	29,821
4. Milford	6,991
5. Seaford	6,948

Urban population: 80.0%
Rural population: 20.0%

Education

H.S. Grad:	82.6%
College Grad:	25.0%

Industry

Agri: 1.1%	Con: 7.4%
Fin: 11.6%	Info: 1.9%
Mfg: 18.0%	Prof: 28.6%
Public: 5.2%	Trade: 14.3%
Other: 11.9%	

Occupation

Blue collar: 22.0%	White collar: 62.9%
Gray collar: 15.1%	

Work Sector

Private: 81.1%	Govt: 13.8%
Self: 5.0%	Family: 0.2%
Unemployment: 5.1%	

Household Income

<15k: 12.2%	15-35k: 23.5%
35-50k: 16.9%	50-100k: 33.3%
100-150k: 9.4%	>150k: 4.6%
Median: $47,381	
Poverty status: 9.2%	

Home Value

<50k: 9.7%	50-100k: 26.0%	100-200k: 47.9%	200-300k: 11.3%
300-500k: 3.7%	>500k: 1.4%	Median: $122,000	

General Assembly

Senate	13 D 8 R
House	25 R 15 D

Legislative Term Limits: No

Registered Voters

D: 245,328	(43.9%)
R: 182,710	(32.7%)
O: 130,903	(23.4%)

Presidential politics Delaware has been competitive in presidential elections since the Federalists were battling the Jeffersonians. Until 2000, it could claim to be the nation's presidential bellwether: It had voted for every winner from 1952 to 1996, the longest winning streak of any state. But in 2000 and, to a lesser extent, 2004, Delaware voted distinctly more Democratic than the rest of the nation. The New Castle County suburbs, like other affluent parts of major metropolitan areas, tilted toward the Democrats and away from the Republicans on cultural issues. This leaves Delaware, more affluent than the nation, as also more Democratic. The 2004 Bush campaign, advertising in the Philadelphia market in pursuit of Pennsylvania's 21 electoral votes, also covered most of Delaware and, to add the rest, bought time in the tiny Salisbury, Maryland, market that reaches Kent and Sussex Counties; but only by a stretch could it be said that Delaware was a target state in 2004.

In 1996 Delaware vied for attention by holding its presidential primary February 24, just four days after New Hampshire. But New Hampshire Republicans put pressure on candidates to ignore Delaware, and only Steve Forbes and Alan Keyes showed up here. For 2000 Republicans decided to hold a primary on February 9,

2004 Presidential Vote

Kerry (D)	200,152	(53%)
Bush (R)	171,660	(46%)
Nader (I)	2,153	(1%)
Other	1,225	(0%)

2004 Democratic Presidential Primary

Kerry (D)	16,787	(50%)
Lieberman (D)	3,706	(11%)
Edwards (D)	3,674	(11%)
Dean (D)	3,462	(10%)
Clark (D)	3,165	(10%)
Other	2,497	(8%)

2000 Presidential Vote

Gore (D)	180,638	(55%)
Bush (R)	137,081	(42%)
Nader (Green)	8,288	(3%)
Other	1,863	(1%)

nine days after New Hampshire. George W. Bush, who spent two full days in Delaware, led with 51%, well ahead of John McCain (25%) and the still-remembered Forbes (20%). The Democratic primary, held February 5, was outside the Democrats' rules and neither candidate campaigned, and only 11,000 voters turned out; Al Gore led Bill Bradley 57%–40%. In 2004, Delaware scheduled its primary one week after New Hampshire, on February 3, but it was only one of several states voting that day. Joseph Lieberman, endorsed by Senator Tom Carper, Lieutenant Governor John Carney and Treasurer Jack Markell, paid several trips to Delaware. Other candidates were scarcer. John Kerry won the primary with 50% of the vote; Lieberman ran second with 11%, in what amounted to a tie with John Edwards, Howard Dean and Wesley Clark.

Governor

Ruth Ann Minner (D)

Elected 2000, term expires Jan. 2009, 2d term; b. Jan. 17, 1935, Slaughter Neck; home, Milford; G.E.D. 1968; Methodist; widowed.

Elected Office: DE House of Reps., 1974–82; DE Senate, 1982–92; DE Lt. Gov. 1992–2000.

Professional Career: Owner, Roger Minner Towing, 1969-present; Receptionist, Gov. Sherman Tribbitt, 1973.

Office: Tatnall Bldg., Dover, 19901, 302-744-4101; Fax: 302-739-2775; Web site: www.state.de.us/governor.

Election Results

2004 general	Ruth Ann Minner (D)	185,687	(51%)
	Bill Lee (R)	167,115	(46%)
	Other	12,206	(3%)
2004 primary	Ruth Ann Minner (D)	unopposed	
2000 general	Ruth Ann Minner (D)	191,484	(59%)
	John M. Burris (R)	128,436	(40%)
	Other	3,263	(1%)

Ruth Ann Minner, a Democrat, was elected governor in 2000. She was born in Slaughter Neck in southern Delaware, the daughter of a sharecropper; one grandfather was an oysterman and a grandmother a midwife. She dropped out of high school to work on the farm, and got married at 17. In 1967, her husband died; at 32, she was left with three sons and no high school diploma. She worked as an agricultural worker and a librarian, got her GED, and in 1972 landed a job as a receptionist in the office of Governor Sherman Tribbitt. In 1974 she ran for the state House ("Tribbitt Greeter Will Seek Office" read the headline in *The Evening Journal*) and, in one of Delaware's small districts (they average 20,000 residents today), won. In 1982 she was elected to the state Senate. In the legislature, she helped build the state's open space protection program, worked on education and public safety and chaired a commission that reorganized state agencies. She also married again, and she and her husband started a car-towing business; he died in 1991, but her sons still run the business. In 1992 she ran for lieutenant governor as Democratic Congressman-at-Large Tom Carper's running mate, but the offices are elected separately. She won 61% of the vote in 1992 and 70% in 1996.

Minner was the favorite in the 2000 election and was unopposed in the Democratic primary. The Republicans had a close primary between former state Senate Majority Leader John Burris and former Judge Bill Lee. Some 27,000 voters voted in the Republican primary; Burris won by exactly 46 votes. Both nominees were from southern Delaware, and both were generally regarded as moderates. Minner ran as a successor to Carper, who had continued former Governor Pete du Pont's policy of cutting income taxes even as, helped by the state's surging economy, he increased state spending by 40%. Burris attacked the state's education testing program, which produced high fail rates among students; Minner said it was an improvement over the past, but called for extra classes for failing students on afternoons and Saturdays, rather than summer school.

Minner was ahead in polls all along; she won 59%–40%. At first, the state's fiscal situation looked good enough that she backed a 2% pay increase in May 2001. But by December she was cutting back. She imposed a hiring freeze in March 2002, lifted it in June, and then reimposed it in November. In fall 2002 she started making $35 million in cuts and asked school districts to give back $10 million; in January 2003 that turned out to be unnecessary when windfall revenue—a $47 million abandoned property settlement, a $4 million fee from Goldman Sachs— came in. In 2004 revenue started coming in at a brisk pace, and Minner got the first pay raise in 18 months for state employees, a $10 million program to carry out the recommendations of a cancer task force, $1 million for all-day kindergarten and a $30 million New Economy Initiative, a sort of venture capital fund. She failed to get the legislature to increase the cigarette tax, but did get it to pass a law banning smoking in public buildings, including restaurants and bars; she failed to get a ban on discrimination on the basis of sexual orientation. She opposed expansion of gambling. She put in place a Liveable Delaware program, to steer development to places where public services exist or are planned and to encourage historic preservation. She delayed implementation of the three-tier high school diploma program and created a Delaware Teachers Corps program.

During her first term Minner faced controversies about the state police and corrections system. In 2001 the state NAACP demanded the firing of the state police chief. In 2002 white troopers brought a lawsuit claiming they were the victims of racial quotas. In 2002 a woman trooper who had wanted to be assigned to the governor's detail filed a lawsuit claiming sexual harassment. In July 2004 an inmate was injured in a fight and, according to a lawsuit he filed, denied proper medical treatment. Two days later a prison counselor was abducted and raped by a rapist sentenced to 699 years; the convict was shot dead by a sharpshooter. Minner responded, "There are problems at every prison. This isn't something that is unique to Delaware. In prisons, you almost expect this to happen. The people who work in our prisons are doing an outstanding job." She said she was talking about the training of prison personnel, but many thought her words were brusque. In October 2004 the counselor filed a lawsuit, claiming that the prison was understaffed and that the incident was preventable; it turned out that Minner's legal counsel had rejected a $3.9 million settlement.

The incident played a major part in the 2004 campaign. Minner's Republican opponent was retired Judge Bill Lee, the narrow loser of the 2000 primary, and well known for his role presiding over the trial of Thomas Capano, an adviser to Governor Tom Carper, for killing Anne Marie Fahey in 1996. Lee called for doing away with the three-tier diploma, revamping the state's educational tests, better enforcement of environmental laws and new revenue sources that wouldn't inhibit growth. But he also criticized Minner's handling of the state police and prisons and was endorsed by police and prison guard groups. In October the Republican Governors Association ran an ad recounting the July abduction and rape, accusing Minner of resisting an independent investigation and dismissing the incident. Democrats were outraged; Senator Joseph Biden rallied to Minner's side and her campaign ran negative ads in response. On Election Day Minner had a bandaged finger, injured inadvertently, she said, by Lee's handshake the day before. Observers had expected Minner to win easily. But the result was close. She won by just 51%–46%, carrying New Castle County and losing Kent and Sussex Counties.

Minner is limited to two terms as governor and has said she will not seek another office. "I'll serve until my term is up. And then I'll retire and enjoy my family more."

Senior Senator

Joseph Biden (D)

Elected 1972, seat up 2008, 6th term; b. Nov. 20, 1942, Scranton, PA; home, Wilmington; U. of DE, B.A. 1965, Syracuse U., J.D. 1968; Catholic; married (Jill).

Elected Office: New Castle Cnty. Cncl., 1970–72.

Professional Career: Practicing atty., 1968–72.

DC Office: 201 RSOB, 20510, 202-224-5042; Fax: 202-224-0139; Web site: biden.senate.gov.

State Offices: Milford, 302-424-8090; Wilmington, 302-573-6345.

Committees: *Foreign Relations* (RMM): East Asian & Pacific Affairs; European Affairs (RMM); International Operations & Terrorism. *Judiciary*: Antitrust, Competition Policy & Consumer Rights; Corrections & Rehabilitation; Crime & Drugs (RMM); Immigration, Border Security & Citizenship; Intellectual Property; Terrorism, Technology & Homeland Security.

Group Ratings

	ADA	ACLU	AFS	LCV	ITIC	NTU	COC	ACU	NTLC	CHC
2004	95	86	100	83	45	15	62	0	6	16
2003	75	—	100	95	—	15	32	26	—	—

National Journal Ratings

	2003 LIB	—	2003 CONS		2004 LIB	—	2004 CONS
Economic	82%	—	10%		93%	—	0%
Social	77%	—	22%		69%	—	30%
Foreign	60%	—	35%		69%	—	29%

Key Votes of the 108th Congress

1. Ban Drilling in ANWR	Y	5. Energy Bill	N	9. Ban Same-Sex Marriage	N
2. Approve Bush Tax Cuts	N	6. Support Roe v. Wade	*	10. Ban Bunker-Buster Bomb	Y
3. Medicare/Rx Bill	N	7. Ban Partial-Birth Abortion	*	11. Fund Iraq War	Y
4. Bar Overtime Pay Regs.	Y	8. Assault Weapons Ban	Y	12. Restrict Missile Defense	Y

Election Results

2002 general	Joseph Biden (D)	135,253	(58%)	($3,152,762)
	Raymond Clatworthy (R)	94,793	(41%)	($1,983,141)
2002 primary	Joseph Biden (D)	unopposed		
1996 general	Joseph Biden (D)	165,465	(60%)	($2,466,499)
	Raymond Clatworthy (R)	105,088	(38%)	($1,126,427)
	Other	5,038	(2%)	

Prior Winning Percentages: 1990 (63%); 1984 (60%); 1978 (58%); 1972 (51%)

Joseph Biden, Delaware's longest-serving senator, was first elected in 1972, at age 29 (he reached the constitutional age of 30 by the time he took office); he has spent most of his life as a senator. Biden grew up in the suburbs of Wilmington in a middle class home; his father was a car salesman and one grandfather was a state senator in Pennsylvania. As a teenager he had a stutter, but taught himself to deliver a speech to his whole school; he is now one of the Senate's most fluent orators. He married and started a family while still in law school. After school he moved back to the Wilmington suburbs, practiced law, and in 1970, at 27, was elected to the New Castle County Council. In 1972 he ran for the Senate against a popular incumbent who seemed ready to retire, while this young challenger had energy, an attractive extended family and an ability to connect with voters' emotions. He won 51%–49%. A month later his wife and daughter were killed in an auto accident; his two young sons were injured. He thought about resigning, but was persuaded to serve, and began his practice, kept to this day, of commuting from his home near Wilmington on Amtrak, 80 minutes to and from Washington every day. He remains a familiar figure in, and one familiar with, his constituency (and to Amtrak employees).

In the Senate, Biden has a moderate-to-liberal voting record. For many years he did much of his most visible work on the Judiciary Committee, which he chaired from 1987–95 and served as ranking Democrat on from 1981–87 and 1995–97. The issues that arise here—abortion, flag-burning, capital punishment, crime control—cut deeply, and for years the cultural liberals in the Democratic Party differed sharply on most of them from the constituents Biden saw in Delaware every day. As chairman, Biden presided over the most contentious Supreme Court confirmation hearings in history. In his 1987 hearings, nominee Robert Bork set a high standard for intellectual seriousness, but some of his opponents used his candor to vote against him, from which Biden's attempts to construct an honestly based, anti-Bork rationale proved politically indistinguishable; no other nominee since has testified so frankly. The 1991 hearings on Clarence Thomas exploded when someone leaked charges of sexual harassment by Anita Hill against the nominee. Biden was bitterly criticized for covering up this information, but he had shared it with committee members, who agreed that Hill's initial unwillingness to testify publicly meant that any reference to it would be unfair to Thomas. Once the story was out though, Hill and then Thomas testified to fascinated television audiences; Thomas was confirmed, over Biden's opposition.

In the middle of the Bork hearings came a climactic moment for Biden, who in 1987 started running for president. He hoped to inspire a new generation as John Kennedy had inspired his. But Biden decided to leave the race when a Michael Dukakis staffer leaked an "attack video" showing similarities between Biden's stump speech about his background and a speech by British Labour Party leader Neil Kinnock. Paraphrasing someone else's words is not a political crime—most political discourse is conducted in familiar shorthand terms—but Biden in dramatizing his background actually distorted it, for unlike Kinnock he did not rise from working class roots, and unlike in Britain, upward social mobility is a common experience in the United States. In 1988, Biden was stricken by an aneurysm on the night of the New Hampshire primary; he was rushed to the hospital and nearly died, but has recovered fully.

After the Thomas hearings, Biden seemed defensive about attacks from the feminist left, then the greatest source of activism in the Democratic Party, just as the religious right has been in the Republican Party. He sought out women to serve on Judiciary and worked hard on the 1994 Violence Against Women Act; he helped renew it in 2000, although the Supreme Court declared part of it unconstitutional. He has been the sponsor in Judiciary of the bankruptcy bill, backed strongly by Delaware's MBNA and other credit card issuers, which was vetoed by Bill Clinton in 2000. It was brought up again in 2001 with a president ready to sign it, and versions passed both the Senate and the House. But there were two contentious issues blocking final passage. One was the homestead exemption; the Senate voted to limit it to $125,000, but the House version allowed unlimited exemptions once a home had been owned for two years (Florida and Texas have unlimited exemptions, and some bankrupts hold onto $5 million houses). Biden agreed to accept the House version. The other issue was Charles Schumer's amendment making fines incurred by anti-abortion protesters undischargeable in bankruptcy. On this, Biden would not yield. In November 2002 the bill, with a version of the Schumer provision was defeated in the House when 87 anti-abortion Republicans spurned the leadership's pleas and defeated the bill. In 2005, Biden again voted for the Schumer amendment, which failed, but also voted for the final bankruptcy bill. "This bill establishes unprecedented protections for child support and alimony, making bankruptcy part of the enforcement system for women and children, who now will be at the head of the line, in front of every other creditor. Is this bill perfect? No. But over several congresses it has earned the kind of bipartisan consensus only balanced legislation can achieve."

Biden has also used his seat on Judiciary to combat what he considers harmful drugs. In April 2003 he amended an Amber Alert bill with a version of the RAVE Act, with prison terms up to nine years for club owners sponsoring raves at which Ecstasy and other illegal drugs are used. In October 2004 he persuaded the Senate to pass a bill criminalizing steroid precursors like androstenedione, the supplement used by baseball slugger Mark McGwire; it was reconciled with the House version and became law. In December 2004 Biden threatened to sponsor legislation addressing drug use in baseball if Major League Baseball failed to clamp down. Biden has weighed in on another sports institution, the BCS college football bowl system.

Biden became ranking Democrat on the Foreign Relations Committee in 1997 and chairman in June 2001. To the surprise of many, he entered into a constructive working relationship with Chairman Jesse Helms. When democracy in the former Yugoslavia was thwarted by state-led terrorism and when multilateral instrumentalities proved ineffective, Biden was among the strongest voices to call for lifting the arms embargo on Bosnia and training Bosnian Muslims, demanding that the United States and NATO investigate war crimes there, and arguing for NATO air strikes.

To the incoming Bush administration he was friendly but sometimes critical. Then Biden became chairman of Foreign Relations in June 2001 and America was attacked on September 11. In the weeks following the attack Biden praised Bush for being "patient, resolute and cautious." In October some Republicans attacked him when he told the Council on Foreign Relations that the bombing campaign in Afghanistan "plays into every stereotypical criticism of us that we're this high-tech bully that thinks from the air we can do whatever we want to do." But Biden was not endorsing that criticism, rather he was calling for ground troops to be sent in soon, as indeed they were. In July and August 2002 he held two days of hearings on Iraq, with administration witnesses. In August he said the United States has "no choice but to eliminate" Saddam Hussein and that "probably" it means war with Iraq. He conferred frequently with Secretary of State Colin Powell and pushed for the U.S. to bring the issue to the United Nations; he said a unilateral attack would be the "single worst option." In late September 2002, he and ranking Republican Richard Lugar were working to bring forward a resolution that would authorize the president to take action to remove weapons of mass destruction, but not Saddam Hussein himself, only after exhausting diplomatic options. Bush opposed this, and forestalled Biden and Lugar by getting agreement on terms of a resolution from Trent Lott, Dennis Hastert and Richard Gephardt. Biden voted for it in October 2002.

Biden continued to campaign against missile defense and opposed abrogation of the ABM Treaty. But Bush's withdrawal from the treaty did not prevent the May 2002 nuclear disarmament treaty, which Biden hailed as "an important step forward." Biden traveled widely as chairman and seems to have been taken into the confidence of the administration: Condoleezza Rice encouraged him to sound out Iranian diplomats at the United Nations when they requested a meeting. As ranking minority member he does not, of course, have as much power as he did as chairman. But he has worked closely with the new chairman, Richard Lugar, and has said that he and Lugar are in agreement on a great many issues. Biden was often critical of the administration performance on Iraq. In June 2003 he said Bush should "level with the American people" about the cost and length of the Iraq commitment; he was angry when administration officials refused to put a price tag on the effort. In August 2003 he said he did not regret his vote for the war, but added, "There's nothing international about this until we get NATO in there and we get Islamic forces in there." He said the administration was filled with "control freaks who are allowing their ideology to get in the way of common sense," and mentioned Dick Cheney. "Neoconservatives seem to have captured the heart and mind of the president and they're controlling the foreign policy agenda [which] puts a premium on the use of unilateralist power. . . . I disagree with those in my own party who have not yet faced the reality of the post-9/11 world and believe we can only exercise power if we act multilaterally." With John Kerry, he sponsored the measure to increase taxes on the top 1% to pay for the $87 billion Iraq supplemental, but unlike Kerry he voted for it in October 2003.

In April 2004, looking ahead to the June 30 turnover of power, he said, "Our goal should be to take the 'American face' off the occupation so that we are not blamed for everything that doesn't go right in Iraq." He said that Bush should call a summit conference of allies and broaden the coalition. After disclosure of the Abu Ghraib abuses, he said that the U.S. should release every prisoner it could and "bulldoze down that damn prison." In June 2004 he sponsored a resolution, adopted by voice vote, calling on the U.S. to create a democracy caucus at the United Nations. Biden has urged caution on Iran and has called for the U.S. to engage in unilateral negotiations with North Korea and seek a non-aggression pact.

Biden remains an everyday figure in Delaware and has tended to its most local needs. He has worked to protect Dover Air Force Base and its C-5s and C-17s against closing. Sussex

County is America's number one chicken-producing county, and he held up a bill for favorable trade status for Russia when that country blocked the import of U.S. chickens. And naturally he has supported Amtrak funding. On his daily commutes, he has come to know the Amtrak crew members personally and hosts an annual Christmas dinner for the crews.

Biden's most visible gift is an articulateness that can verge on the mellifluous; he can inspire, but can also drone on at great length (being elected a senator at 29 does not curb a tendency to verbosity). But this has not reduced the appreciation most Delawareans have for his admirable personal qualities. He was re-elected by wide margins in 1984, 1990 and 1996. His 1996 opponent Raymond Clatworthy was a Naval Academy graduate, Marine aviator and businessman who walked, rode a bicycle and rollerbladed through the state, raised $1 million and questioned the sale of Biden's house to an executive of MBNA, the big credit card company whose top executives gave generously to Biden's campaign. But Biden won 60%–38%. In 2002 Clatworthy ran again and raised $1.8 million: Evidently Biden has raised the hackles of many Republicans across the country, and you can raise money by direct mail against him. Clatworthy argued that he would support George W. Bush more fully on defense and foreign policy and called for $1,500 child tax credits and individual investment accounts in Social Security. This time the result was a little closer: Biden won 58%–41%, the same margin he had in 1978. He actually lost Kent County, which includes Dover, and only narrowly carried Sussex County; together the two counties cast 37% of the state's votes, up from 33% in 1996.

Will Biden run for president? It was a question raised in the runups to 1992, 2000 and 2004. He made little move to run in 1992 or 2000. In January 2003 he said he would decide by fall 2003. In early August he said he was confident he could beat George W. Bush. But on August 11 he announced he was not running. Biden said he was not sure he could raise $9 million by January; as it turned out, Howard Dean raised far more money, in large part through the Internet, while Biden was likely expecting to rely on traditional Democratic contributors. In 2004 Biden campaigned for John Kerry, whom he has known since 1972, when they both hired the same political consultant. Biden was frequently mentioned as a possible secretary of state if Kerry had been elected, but said he liked serving in the Senate. But he said in June 2005 that he plans to run for president in 2008. "My intention is to seek the nomination," he said on *Face the Nation.* "I know I'm supposed to tell you, you know, that I'm not sure. But if, in fact, I think that I have a clear shot at winning the nomination by this November or December, then I'm going to seek the nomination."

Junior Senator

Thomas Carper (D)

Elected 2000, seat up 2006, 1st term; b. Jan. 23, 1947, Beckley, WV; home, Wilmington; OH St. U., B.A. 1968, U. of DE, M.B.A. 1975; Presbyterian; married (Martha).

Military Career: Navy, 1968–73 (Vietnam); Naval Reserves, 1973–91.

Elected Office: DE Treas., 1976–82; U.S. House of Reps., 1982–92; DE Gov. 1992–2000.

Professional Career: Industrial Devel. Specialist, DE Div. of Econ. Devel., 1975–76.

DC Office: 513 HSOB, 20510, 202-224-2441; Fax: 202-228-2190; Web site: carper.senate.gov.

State Offices: Dover, 302-674-3308; Georgetown, 302-856-7690; Wilmington, 302-573-6291.

Committees: *Aging (Special). Banking, Housing & Urban Affairs*: Financial Institutions; Housing & Transportation; Securities & Investment. *Environment & Public Works*: Clean Air, Climate Change & Nuclear Safety (RMM); Transportation & Infrastructure. *Homeland Security & Governmental Affairs*: Federal Financial Management, Govt. Information & International Security (RMM); Investigations (Permanent); Oversight of Govt. Management, the Federal Workforce & the District of Columbia.

Group Ratings

	ADA	ACLU	AFS	LCV	ITIC	NTU	COC	ACU	NTLC	CHC
2004	95	56	100	83	67	17	71	12	16	16
2003	75	—	89	89	—	16	70	10	—	—

National Journal Ratings

	2003 LIB	—	2003 CONS		2004 LIB	—	2004 CONS
Economic	56%	—	42%		89%	—	10%
Social	59%	—	37%		70%	—	26%
Foreign	58%	—	41%		64%	—	34%

Key Votes of the 108th Congress

1. Ban Drilling in ANWR	Y	5. Energy Bill	N	9. Ban Same-Sex Marriage	N
2. Approve Bush Tax Cuts	N	6. Support Roe v. Wade	Y	10. Ban Bunker-Buster Bomb	Y
3. Medicare/Rx Bill	Y	7. Ban Partial-Birth Abortion	Y	11. Fund Iraq War	Y
4. Bar Overtime Pay Regs.	Y	8. Assault Weapons Ban	Y	12. Restrict Missile Defense	Y

Election Results

2000 general	Thomas Carper (D)	181,387	(56%)	($2,608,942)
	William V. Roth Jr. (R)	142,683	(44%)	($4,366,884)
	Other...	2,144	(1%)	
2000 primary	Thomas Carper (D) .... unopposed			
1994 general	William V. Roth Jr. (R)	111,088	(56%)	($2,310,474)
	Charles M. Oberly III (D)	84,554	(42%)	($1,561,440)
	Other...	3,387	(2%)	

Prior Winning Percentages: 1990 House (66%); 1988 House (68%); 1986 House (66%); 1984 House (59%); 1982 House (52%)

Democrat Thomas Carper was elected Delaware's junior senator in 2000, after already serving 24 years in statewide elective office. Carper grew up in Southside Virginia and Ohio and went to college in Ohio. He first came to Delaware as an ensign in the Navy, then returned to get his M.B.A. after service in Southeast Asia, where he served as a mission commander piloting submarine-hunting planes. In 1976, he was elected state treasurer, at 29; he ran for Congress in 1982 and beat a scandal-tarred incumbent. In the House, Carper had a moderate voting record and worked to let banks into the securities business and to prevent ocean sludge dumping, both causes supported by Delaware constituencies. In 1992, when Republican Governor Mike Castle had served his two allotted terms and ran for Congress, Carper ran for governor and won the general election with 65% of the vote.

As governor, Carper pursued an agenda in many ways more conservative than liberal. He continued his Republican predecessor Pete du Pont's policy of cutting taxes, reducing income tax rates about 10% and also cutting small business and utility taxes. Revenues kept gushing in from Delaware's strong economy, and he increased the "rainy day" fund and boosted the state's credit rating to an historic high even as state spending rose 40% in eight years. He inherited Castle's standard-based education reform, raised standards, started testing students in 1998 and provided public school choice, instituted charter schools and passed a teacher accountability bill in 2000. He was re-elected by 70%–30% over then-Treasurer Janet Rzewnicki. Barred from a third term, he was an obvious candidate for the Senate seat held by Republican William Roth since 1970.

This was a battle of positives. Both candidates had very high approval ratings, and both were familiar figures to many voters; they brought a combined total of 58 years in statewide office to the race. Roth had a record of achievements that paid direct benefits to people in this generally affluent state: The Kemp-Roth tax cut of 1981, the Roth IRAs enacted in 1997, the reform of the Internal Revenue Service passed in 1998, $2.3 billion for Amtrak capital improvements in 1998 and $10 billion in bonds in 2000. Roth's main problem was that he was 79 in 2000. When Carper announced his candidacy in September 1999, a poll showed him ahead 48%–38%. He was careful not to campaign negatively against Roth or to attack him for his age, but his slogan "A Senator for Our Future" spotlighted the contrast between their ages. Carper's 16-hour days of campaigning at factories, bowling alleys and parades was a contrast with Roth, who stayed in Washington legislating much of the time and made a dwindling number of campaign appearances with his trademark St. Bernards. As Roth unveiled initiatives—Amtrak funding, a program to aid states to pay for prescription drugs for low-income seniors—Carper suggested that Roth's tax cuts were too large and his prescription drug plan too stingy. Roth, able to raise large sums as Finance chairman, outspent Carper by $4.3 million to $2.5 million, but the Democratic Party spent some $4 million of soft money in Delaware, more than evening the score. In October, Roth fainted twice on the campaign trail, once in full view of cameras. Polls showed the race close to even in September and October, but in November Carper won by a solid 56%–44% margin.

In the Senate, Carper has a moderate voting record and supports centrist proposals. He voted with Republicans on farm spending and the tax cut in budget resolution votes in April 2001. With five Republicans and five other Democrats he moved unsuccessfully to condition the Bush tax cut on deficit reduction. In June 2001 he and Judd Gregg got $125 million for public school choice programs and $400 million for charter schools. He voted with Jim Jeffords to impose on old power plants the standards of the Clean Air Act. But he also put forward, with Lincoln Chafee, John Breaux and Max Baucus, a milder bill that would not impose those standards on old plants when remodeled and require 2001 levels of carbon dioxide by 2012. He has worked for reauthorization of the 1996 welfare act, with higher work requirements, funding for transitional jobs, funding for abstinence programs and more funding for child care. Since September 11 he has pressed for more spending on rail security, and he has sought $30 billion in bond financing for railroad projects.

Carper has taken the lead on several issues. One is Postal Service reform, where he and Governmental Affairs Chairman Susan Collins collaborated on a bill to allow more flexibility on rates and worksharing with private firms, but only on a profitable basis; it did not pass in 2004 but seemed likely to come forward in 2005. He worked with Lamar Alexander, another former governor, on the extension of the moratorium on Internet taxation, to preserve existing state taxes on DSL and Voice Over Internet Protocol. He also collaborated with Alexander on a bill to limit emissions not only of sulphur dioxide, nitrous oxide and mercury (as in the Bush Clear Skies bill), but also carbon dioxide, with a cap and emissions trading. He worked with Mary Landrieu to add amendments to the D.C. school voucher bill, to ban schools from charging additional tuition and limiting eligibility to students in failing schools. He strongly supported the bill limiting class actions and was angry when Majority Leader Bill Frist refused to allow non-germane amendments in July 2004; that killed the bill for the year, but it was passed in February 2005. He declined to vote on the tobacco buyout because he owns tobacco-growing land in North Carolina. Delaware is the only state without a National Park Service facility, and in August 2004 Carper proposed a Coastal Heritage Park, to consist of four interpretive centers in Wilmington, Port Penn, Little Creek and Lewes.

Carper has been "bitterly disappointed" by the reduction of the number of centrist Democratic senators after the 2002 and 2004 elections. In November 2004 he speculated that centrist Republicans might be readier to collaborate after the reelection of George W. Bush and said that passage of an asbestos bill would help. "A victory like that, early on, on a contentious issue . . . where our views have moderated the finished product will help set the tone for progress on other contentious issues." On Social Security, in December 2004 he said, "I don't think it's sufficient for Democrats just to say no." But in January 2005 he added, "The better part of valor [would be] for the administration to present their proposal. Let us read it and understand it. . . . I don't rule out at some point having private accounts."

Carper comes up for reelection in 2006, 30 years after his first statewide election victory. In mid-2005 no serious opponent had emerged.

Representative-At-Large

Michael Castle (R)

Elected 1992, 7th term; b. July 2, 1939, Wilmington; home, Wilmington; Hamilton Col., B.A. 1961, Georgetown U., LL.B. 1964; Catholic; married (Jane).

Elected Office: DE House of Reps., 1966–68; DE Senate, 1968–76, Minority Ldr., 1975–76; DE Lt. Gov., 1980–84; DE Gov., 1984–92.

Professional Career: Practicing atty., 1964–80; DE Dep. Atty. Gen., 1965–66.

DC Office: 1233 LHOB, 20515, 202-225-4165; Fax: 202-225-2291; Web site: www.house.gov/castle.

District Offices: Dover, 302-736-1666; Georgetown, 302-856-3334; Wilmington, 302-428-1902.

Committees: *Education & the Workforce* (4th of 27 R): 21st Century Competitiveness; Education Reform (Chmn.). *Financial Services* (6th of 37 R): Capital Markets, Insurance & Government Sponsored Enterprises; Domestic and International Monetary Policy, Trade & Technology; Financial Institutions & Consumer Credit.

Group Ratings

	ADA	ACLU	AFS	LCV	ITIC	NTU	COC	ACU	NTLC	CHC
2004	50	30	25	73	67	52	85	52	60	38
2003	40	—	25	70	—	50	76	44	—	—

National Journal Ratings

	2003 LIB	—	2003 CONS		2004 LIB	—	2004 CONS
Economic	52%	—	47%		50%	—	49%
Social	59%	—	40%		57%	—	42%
Foreign	46%	—	52%		45%	—	54%

Key Votes of the 108th Congress

1. Drilling in ANWR	N	5. DC School Vouchers	Y	9. Ban Same-Sex Marriage	N
2. Approve Bush Tax Cuts	Y	6. Ban Human Cloning	N	10. Fund Iraq War	Y
3. Medicare/Rx Bill	Y	7. Restrict Gun Liability	N	11. Bar Cuba Embargo Funds	N
4. Bar Overtime Pay Regs.	N	8. Ban Partial-Birth Abortion	Y	12. Intelligence Reorg.	Y

Election Results

2004 general	Michael Castle (R)	245,978	(69%)	($902,706)
	Paul Donnelly (D)	105,716	(30%)	($4,429)
	Other	4,351	(1%)	
2004 primary	Michael Castle (R)	unopposed		
2002 general	Michael Castle (R)	164,605	(72%)	($760,161)
	Michael Miller (D)	61,011	(27%)	($13,202)
	Other	2,789	(1%)	

Prior Winning Percentages: 2000 (68%); 1998 (66%); 1996 (70%); 1994 (71%); 1992 (55%)

Michael Castle, a Republican first elected in 1992, is Delaware's congressman-at-large. A direct descendant of Benjamin Franklin, he grew up in Delaware, the son of a DuPont patent lawyer. After college and law school, he returned to be a deputy attorney general. In 1966, at 27, local Republicans urged him to run for the state House in a Democratic seat; the competitive Castle was elected. Two years later he was elected to the state Senate, and in time became minority leader. He left the legislature in 1976 to practice law in Wilmington; he still lives there, in the same house, and commutes to Washington. In 1980 Governor Pete du Pont asked him to run for lieutenant governor; he did and won. He was elected governor in 1984 and 1988. In 1992, barred from running for re-election by term limits, he traded jobs with Democratic Congressman-at-Large Thomas Carper. Castle won the Republican primary for Congress by 56%–30% over state Treasurer Janet Rzewnicki, and won the general election 55%–43% over former Senate candidate and Lieutenant Governor S. B. Woo.

At that point it seemed unlikely that Castle, as a moderate member of a conservative minority party, could be influential; yet he was. He was a leader of the bipartisan freshmen who offered their own budget cuts. In August 1994 he withdrew his support from the crime bill when he thought Democrats overreached; then, at Newt Gingrich's suggestion, he led a group of moderate Republicans to negotiate with the Clinton administration. This delivered a stinging rebuke to Democrats—it broke their majority apart, in fact—and yet ultimately produced a crime bill with less spending on prevention but with the gun control provisions that Castle, unlike most Republicans, supported.

Castle has a voting record at the middle of the House; he was one of the 10 Republicans to support Clinton administration positions on most issues, has been a leader of the informal Tuesday Group which meets for lunch on Wednesdays (don't ask) and is the president of the Republican Main Street Partnership. He voted for the 2001 Bush tax cut with some ambivalence; he had voted against repeal of the estate tax and wanted the tax cuts made contingent. In September 2002 he said moderate Republicans would vote against the Labor-HHS appropriations unless more money was available for appropriations, and forced an extra $3.5 billion. He initially opposed the 2003 tax cut, but voted for it when it was reduced to $350 billion, with $20 billion in aid to the states. He voted against the budget resolution in March 2004 because it "does not address real reform, shared restraint and elimination of waste." Castle is cautious about tax cuts, because he wants to reduce deficits and is pessimistic about holding down spending. "If you go through the Republican Conference, you'll find almost no one who is pure in this. The whole idea of balancing the budget by cutting spending is somebody's wish list. It's highly unlikely to happen."

Castle chairs the Education Reform Subcommittee, and while he may support higher spending than some other Republicans, he also questions the worth of programs originally fashioned by Democrats. That was evident in his work on the No Child Left Behind Act in 2001 and on Head Start in 2003. Castle's bill, passed in subcommittee and full committee in June 2003, maintained the core program. But he cited studies showing that the progress Head Start children make tends to disappear by third or fourth grade, and he inserted provisions requiring more teaching of literacy and academics. He also had a provision allowing eight states to get waivers to fashion their own programs. This brought down a storm of criticism from Democrats and from Head Start employees, who said these measures would gut a program that was a proven success. Castle persevered. The bill was pulled off the floor once, then passed in July 2003 by only a 217–216 vote; one Republican was brought in fresh from an auto accident. The Senate HELP committee passed a version cutting out the pilot projects but the bill did not receive a floor vote in 2003. Castle took a similar approach on reauthorization of the Carl Perkins vocational education act. His measure required states to impose new academic standards and accountability measures and merged the funding of Perkins grants and Tech-Prep but it also failed to get a floor vote. There was somewhat less controversy over reauthorization of the IDEA special education act, which expired in 2002. Castle's version passed the House 251–171 in April 2003. There were serious differences with the Senate bill passed in May 2004, but they were reconciled in November. The school lunch and WIC bill was least controversial. It included a 5-state test of expanding eligibility for free lunches to those at 185% of poverty level and allowing more states to increase access to fruits and vegetables, and passed with wide bipartisan support in June 2004 and was signed into law.

Castle serves on the Financial Services Committee, which is of great importance to Delaware. His special project there has been coins. He sponsored the 1997 law establishing commemorative quarters, with different designs for each state. He sponsored the Sacagawea dollar coin, more successful than its Susan B. Anthony predecessor. In 2004 he sponsored a bill for new dollar coins, with likenesses of each president replacing Sacagawea and the Statue of Liberty replacing the eagle. The bill did not come to the floor in 2004, but may in 2005. The coins have done more than just encouraging numismatics. The government makes a profit off seignorage, the difference between the value of the metal and the face value of the coin; the state quarters have brought in a cool $4 billion. In January 2005 Castle's bill to limit the number of Congressional Gold Medals to two a year was one of the first bills to pass the House in the 109th Congress.

Castle served on the Intelligence Committee and was part of the joint Senate-House hearings on intelligence failures before September 11; he endorsed the joint report. He also called for biometric identification of all foreigners entering the United States and for biometric identification for Americans who choose it. He was a co-sponsor of James Sensenbrenner's immigration measures included in the House intelligence bill in 2004, but dropped in conference.

Castle supports embryonic stem cell research. In 2004 he and Diana DeGette co-sponsored a bill to permit and fund research on stem cells obtained, with written consent, from embryos created for fertility treatment or about to be discarded. This, like the more restrictive Bush position, is somewhere in between allowing and forbidding all stem cell research.

Castle is a strong supporter of Amtrak and opposed the Bush administration's 2003 plan to divide it into three units. He negotiated a $1.225 billion compromise funding level in 2003 and in 2004, and naturally opposed the defunding proposed in Bush's 2005 budget. He has also criticized the Department of Homeland Security for spending virtually no money on railroad security. He and Rob Andrews sought to cut the $8 million for dredging the Delaware River another five feet in July 2003, but lost 213–194 as Philadelphians pushed strongly for it.

Castle has been re-elected by wide margins in Delaware, 68%–31% in 2000, 72%–27% in 2002, 69%–30% in 2004, when his opponent was a Head Start family services worker. He has often been mentioned as a candidate for the Senate in this small state, and said that he would have run if Republican Senator William Roth had retired in 1994. But Roth chose to run then and again in 2000 when, at 79, he lost. But even if Roth had not run, Castle might not have. "As time has evolved, I have grown to like my role in the House," he said in 1998. In October 2004 he said, "I want to do it more today than perhaps I've ever wanted to do it."

★ DISTRICT OF COLUMBIA ★

The District of Columbia, the seat of government of the most powerful and affluent nation in the history of the world, is a beautiful city of great achievements and astonishing contrasts—but not one which has always been blessed with competent local government. For most of a century it was governed directly by Congress, not an ideal state of affairs. In 1974 the District got self-government. But for 16 out of the 20 years from 1978–98 the District government was run by Mayor Marion Barry, a talented politician but disastrous mayor. Under him the District was a dysfunctional polity, a city with above-average incomes and a vibrant commercial property base, but with a local government so bloated with employees yet so indifferent to its responsibilities that it destroyed one marginal neighborhood after another. Now things are different. The District's population decline has slowed; crime is sharply down; affluent professionals and eager immigrants are flowing in, gentrifying and giving vitality to neighborhoods long given up to decline—Columbia Heights, Logan Circle, Shaw. There are still problems: The outflow of middle class blacks from the District to the suburbs continues, and some neighborhoods, especially east of the Anacostia River, continue to be plagued by crime and flight. But most of the city is safer and more prosperous than it was a decade ago.

The problem of how to govern the nation's capital is not new. In 1787 the framers of the Constitution, familiar with contemporary London and Paris mobs and remembering how crowds had threatened Congress in Philadelphia, purposely gave the new federal government control of the 10-mile-square enclave that came to be called the District of Columbia (the portion across the Potomac River was retroceded to Virginia in 1846). Over the years Congress kept control, for its own advantage and, later, out of distrust of the city's large black population. Blacks have consistently made up one-quarter of the population of Washington and surrounding counties since the 1790s, and the city was a center for free blacks even before the Civil War and Emancipation. Radical Republicans gave the District self-government in the era of Reconstruction in 1871, but Governor Alexander "Boss" Shepherd in building great public works spent the District into bankruptcy, and the experiment ended in 1874. Later, Washington's vast growth, starting with the New Deal and World War II, resulted in the growth of large, mostly white suburbs, and blacks became a larger percentage of the city's population—a majority in the 1960 Census. Amid the 1960s civil rights revolution, it began to seem absurd to deny the vote to Washington. So in 1964, District residents began to cast three electoral votes for president, in 1968 they were allowed to vote for school board, in 1971 they finally got to elect a non-voting delegate to Congress and in 1974, they got home rule and could vote for a mayor and city council.

The results were tragic. Marion Barry, a man of great ability and charm, inherited a government that was already overlarge and undermanaged, and over the years made it more so. He raised money from public employee unions and real estate developers and increasingly won votes from poor blacks by attacking any critic as racist. In January 1990, he was arrested in a D.C. hotel using crack cocaine, and was prosecuted and sent to jail. Later that year voters chose a reform-minded mayor, Sharon Pratt Kelly, but she flinched when it came time to cut the payroll. Barry, out of prison and elected to the council in 1992, ran for mayor in 1994 and won the Democratic primary with 47% to 37% for Councilman John Ray and only 13% for Kelly. Against Republican Carol Schwartz, a longtime council member, Barry won 56%–42% in November.

In the meantime, the District had changed. Even as the District payroll was peaking—at 51,300 in 1992—the District's population was falling, and becoming more white. Washington's population fell from 802,000 in 1950 to 572,000 in 2000. In the 1950s and 1960s, the District saw white flight; in the Barry years, it saw black flight. The District lost 6% of its population in the 1990s, as blacks headed to majority-black Prince George's County and other suburbs, where three-quarters of Washington-area blacks live. At the same time, Ward 3 and gentrifying neighborhoods near downtown grew in population, so that the black percentage of the population has declined from a peak of 71% in 1970 to 60% in 2000. With higher turnout in affluent areas, whites may now cast half or almost half of the District's votes. But the electorate remains overwhelmingly Democratic: In 2004, John Kerry carried the District over George W. Bush by an 89%–9% margin. Whites voted for Kerry 80%–19%—a higher percentage than in any state. Bush got over 20% of the vote in only 14 of 142 precincts, and over 30% in only two.

But the District's fiscal crisis after Barry's return in 1995 led Congress to take most of the government out from under his control. This was not a hostile takeover: House Speaker Newt Gingrich appointed as chairman of the D.C. subcommittee Tom Davis, a Republican congressman from Northern Virginia long sympathetic to the District, and Davis worked closely with the District's elected delegate, Eleanor Holmes Norton. They got Congress to establish a five-member financial control board in April 1995, and the control board's CFO, Anthony Williams, hacked away at the payroll, reformed management practices and literally cleaned up messes in District government offices.

When Barry announced in May 1998 that he wouldn't run again, four council members joined the race — Schwartz and three Democrats. Then there was a move, encouraged by *The Washington Post*, to draft Anthony Williams. He was an unlikely candidate. He grew up in Los Angeles, a speechless foster child adopted when he was 3. He was once an alderman in New Haven, Connecticut; when he took the CFO job in 1995, he moved first to Virginia and only later to Washington's Foggy Bottom. Williams had a history of changing course: He participated in anti-Vietnam war demonstrations, enlisted in the Air Force and served, then applied for conscientious objector status and got an honorable discharge. After seven years he graduated with honors from Yale, started an antique map business, then got degrees from Harvard Law and the Kennedy School and worked in Connecticut, Boston and St. Louis. Always dressed in a bow tie, diffident in crowds, he did not seem to have a political touch. But that may have been an asset. In the Democratic primary Williams beat Councilman Kevin Chavous 50%–35%, and in the general he beat Schwartz 66%–30%. The control board immediately delegated power to the new mayor, and in fall 2000, judges returned control of most District departments to the city.

There were still problems. Williams did not get along well with the council, the Police Department's homicide division was in disarray, and the child welfare agency seemed to do little to help neglected children. D.C. General Hospital was closed down. Tourism declined after September 11. But in spring 2002 Williams seemed headed to easy reelection without serious opposition. Then it was discovered that most of Williams's 10,000 election petition signatures were fraudulent. Embarrassed and fined, he launched a write-in campaign. His major opponent was another write-in, Willie Wilson, pastor of a 7,000-member church in Anacostia and a spiritual counselor to Marion Barry. Barry's support turned out to be a dead weight in much of the city; Williams won the September 10 primary 66%–22%. In the general, he again faced Schwartz, also nominated by write-ins; Williams won 61%–34%.

In his second term Williams boasted of adding beds to homeless shelters, putting money into an affordable housing trust fund and fixing agencies which had long been operating under court order; the Corrections Department was freed from court control for the first time in 33 years. He took a cue from cities such as Chicago and sought control of the school system but the city council in July 2004 blocked his plan to turn the school board into an appointed body. Instead the council extended the tenure of the current hybrid board of five elected and four appointed officials to 2008, at which time all school board seats will return to elected status. Williams protested when the Homeland Security Department raised the terrorism threat level in August 2004; streets were closed and 14 vehicle checkpoints were established around Capitol Hill. "This is a living, breathing city; this isn't just a dead, static piece of concrete. We can't continue to close streets without doing death to commerce in this city, to tourism in this city, to a tax base in this city that provides all the services people need." He was pleased when the threat level was lowered in November 2004 and the checkpoints removed. Williams was pleased as well when in September 2004 Major League Baseball decided to move the Montreal Expos to move to Washington, provided the city built a new stadium to replace Robert F. Kennedy stadium, where the 2005 season would be played. Williams proposed a $440 million stadium at Buzzards Point, on the Anacostia River, in a neighborhood of empty lots and little-used industrial sites. But many council members bridled at the cost, and Council President Linda Cropp delayed the project. Finally, the council approved, but only with critical votes cast by council members defeated in the September 2004 Democratic primary.

Those defeats reflected opposition to the mayor and trends in District government in Anacostia, the poor wards east of that river; one of the winners was Marion Barry, who was returned to the council by Ward 8. It was unclear whether the District might try to return to the kind of governance it received in the era of Barry—and risk the same dire consequences. In May 2005 it was also unclear whether Williams would run for a third term in 2006. He told *The Washington Post* he wasn't sure if he had "the energy, the tenacity, the discipline, the focus" to serve a third term. If he runs, he seems likely to have serious opposition. Possible candidates included: Council members David Catania, Linda Cropp, Jack Evans, Adrian Fenty and Vincent Orange; lobbyist Michael Brown (son of former Democratic National Chairman and Commerce Secretary Ron Brown), former D.C. Democratic party chairman A. Scott Bolden, and former U.S. Attorney Eric Holder Jr.

The People		Race/Ethnic Origin			Military veterans: 44,484 (9.7%)	
Pop. 2004 (est):	553,523	159,178	27.8%	White	WWII: 22.1%	Korea: 14.4%
Pop. 2000:	572,059	340,088	59.4%	Black	Vietnam: 29.5%	Gulf War: 10.4%
Pop. 1990:	606,900	15,039	2.6%	Asian	**Most populous cities (2003):**	
Change 1990–2000:	Down 5.7%	1,274	0.2%	Native Am.	1. Washington	563,384
% of U.S. total:	0.2%	273	0.0%	Hawaiian		
Area size:	68 sq. mi.	9,584	1.7%	Two+ races	Urban population: 100.0%	
State Native:	39.2%	1,670	0.3%	Other	Rural population: 0.0%	
Non-citizen:	9.0%	44,953	7.9%	Hisp. Origin		
Language		**Ancestry**				
		Irish: 4.3%		German: 4.2%		
English: 81.0%	Spanish: 9.1%	English: 3.9%		Subsaharan: 2.5%		
Other Eur.: 6.2%		Italian: 1.9%				

Education		Work Sector		Registered Voters	
H.S. Grad:	77.8%	Private: 68.7%	Govt: 25.9%	D: 286,084	(74.5%)
College Grad:	39.1%	Self: 5.2%	Family: 0.1%	R: 30,179	(7.9%)
Industry		Unemployment: 10.7%		O: 67,656	(17.6%)
Agri: 0.1%	Con: 3.9%	**Household Income**			
Fin: 7.4%	Info: 6.4%	<15k: 20.7%	15-35k: 23.7%		
Mfg: 5.1%	Prof: 36.8%	35-50k: 14.2%	50-100k: 24.9%		
Public: 15.0%	Trade: 6.9%	100-150k: 8.4%	>150k: 8.0%		
Other: 18.4%		Median: $40,127			
Occupation		Poverty status: 20.2%			
Blue collar: 10.0%	White collar: 73.9%	**Home Value**			
Gray collar: 16.1%		<50k: 1.9% 50-100k: 19.4% 100-200k: 42.4% 200-300k: 12.0%			
		300-500k: 14.5% >500k: 9.7% Median: $153,500			

2004 Presidential Vote

Kerry (D)	202,970	(89%)
Bush (R)	21,256	(9%)
Nader (I)	1,485	(1%)
Other	1,875	(1%)

2000 Presidential Vote

Gore (D)	171,923	(85%)
Bush (R)	18,073	(9%)
Nader (Green)	10,576	(5%)
Other	1,322	(1%)

Delegate

Eleanor Holmes Norton (D)

Elected 1990, 8th term; b. June 13, 1937, Washington, D.C.; home, Washington, D.C.; Antioch Col., B.A. 1960, Yale, M.A. 1963, LL.B. 1964; Episcopalian; divorced.

Professional Career: Asst. Legal Dir., ACLU, 1965–70; New York City Human Rights Comm., 1970–77; Equal Empl. Oppor. Comm., 1977–81; Sr. Fellow, The Urban Inst., 1981–82; Prof., Georgetown U. Law Ctr., 1982–present.

DC Office: 2136 RHOB, 20515, 202-225-8050; Fax: 202-225-3002; Web site: www.norton.house.gov.

District Offices: Washington, D.C., 202-678-8900; Washington, D.C., 202-783-5065.

Committees: *Government Reform* (17th of 17 D): Federal Workforce & Agency Organization; Regulatory Affairs. *Homeland Security* (8th of 15 D): Emergency Preparedness, Science & Technology; Prevention of Nuclear & Biological Attack. *Transportation & Infrastructure* (5th of 34 D): Aviation; Economic Development, Public Buildings & Emergency Management (RMM); Water Resources & Environment.

Election Results

2004 general	Eleanor Holmes Norton (D)	202,027	(91%)	($213,604)
	Michael Andrew Monroe (R)	18,296	(8%)	
	Other	890	(0%)	
2004 primary	Eleanor Holmes Norton (D)	unopposed		
2002 general	Eleanor Holmes Norton (D)	119,268	(93%)	($168,650)
	Patricia Kidd (I)	7,733	(6%)	

Prior Winning Percentages: 2000 (90%); 1998 (90%); 1996 (90%); 1994 (89%); 1992 (85%); 1990 (62%)

Eleanor Holmes Norton, who was first elected delegate from the District of Columbia in 1990, grew up in Washington. She graduated from Antioch and Yale Law School, worked for the ACLU and the New York City Commission on Human Rights, and was head of the Equal Employment Opportunity Commission in the Carter administration. Afterward, she taught law at Georgetown. When the delegate seat came open in 1990, she ran and drew criticism because her husband hadn't filed their income taxes for several years. But in the primary she edged past city Councilwoman Betty Anne Kane, 39%–33%. Norton has been re-elected easily since.

In the House, she had the difficult and sometimes vexing task of responding to the fiscal collapse of the District government just as Republicans took over Congress. She has been hard-working, competent, intellectually honest, able to get along with opponents as well as fellow partisans and willing to take personal and political risks. She established good relations with Republicans active on District matters before 1994, even though she led the drive, much resented by Republicans in 1993 and repealed by them in 1995, to give her and the four territorial delegates to the House—all of whom were then Democrats—votes on most legislation in the House. In 1995, she worked with Tom Davis and Newt Gingrich to create the fiscal control board to superintend District finances; in 1997, she and Davis came up with the package that rescued District finances and removed control over most of the District government from Marion Barry. It also included tax breaks for downtown and some other areas. In return, the District gave up the $660 million federal payment for a $198 million "contribution," which, Norton argues, should in the long run remove the District from the close superintendency of Congress. But in May 2004 she and metro Washington congressmen of both parties proposed an $800 million, indexed federal payment; Mike DeWine, chairman of the Senate subcommittee with jurisdiction, promised hearings.

Norton understands that statehood for the District is improbable—it was defeated 277–153 by a Democratic Congress in 1993—and has sought voting representation in Congress. But she opposed proposals by Republicans Ralph Regula and Dana Rohrabacher to count the District as part of Maryland for purposes of House representation. As for the proposal by northern Virginia's Tom Davis, with whom she has worked closely on District affairs, to increase the House temporarily by two new members — one from the District and one from the state entitled under the statutory formula to the 436th seat (which under the 2000 Census happens to be heavily Republican Utah) — she has argued that it is moot because Utah will get a new seat soon anyway. She has protested vigorously when Congress has made decisions for the District, as in September 2004 when the House voted to repeal the District's ban on handguns ("that we are here discussing this matter is yet a new low"). She also objected in November 2004 to the amendment, added by Democratic Senator Mary Landrieu, that would require the city to offer surplus school property to public charter schools for at least 25% less than the appraised value before selling it to anyone else. But here, as on her opposition to school vouchers and school choice for D.C. students, she has so far been frustrated. In 2004 she sponsored a bill to prevent the administration from using the District as one of its test cities for private health insurance under Medicare.

Despite her lack of a floor vote, Norton has effectively moved District legislation in the House. She successfully pushed the Southeast Federal Center Public-Private Development Act which provided a coordinated approach to the area around the Washington Navy Yard; this has resulted in new federal and private sector buildings near the Navy Yard.

After the terrorism threat level was raised in August 2004, streets around the Capitol were closed and 14 vehicle checkpoints established. Norton exploded, "We concede this makes it easier for security. You want to make it really easier? Close down all the streets! Close down the city! You can make it real safe." When the terrorism threat level was lowered in November and the checkpoints dismantled, she said, "while I am pleased that change is on the way, we will not be satisfied until the nation's capital no longer looks like an armed camp." But she concedes there is a need to balance interests here. "I recognize this is perhaps the highest-target city in the world. But we have to remember that we are fighting to preserve security and freedom, not one or the other."

Norton has been regularly reelected with 90% or more of the vote.

★ FLORIDA ★

For a moment in history, a moment that lasted 36 days, Florida was the center of the political world, the state whose vote count would determine who would become president of the United States, the most evenly balanced political state in the nation. To students of political history this seemed astonishing. Sixty years before, Florida was the smallest Southern state, with just 5 congressional districts and 7 electoral votes, overwhelmingly Democratic. In 2000 it was the fourth-largest state in the nation, with 23 congressional districts and 25 electoral votes—and about to get 2 more from the 2000 Census. Only 12 years earlier, Florida had voted 61% for then-Vice President George Bush, who carried 66 of its 67 counties. Military-minded Southerners in the northern part of the state, affluent retirees on the Gulf Coast, middle-class conservatives in Tampa Bay and Orlando and around Disney World, Cubans in Miami and Dade County—all voted Republican, easily outnumbering the state's scattered black communities and its Jewish voters concentrated in Broward and Palm Beach Counties on the Gold Coast. But by 2000 Florida had become a state with political divisions as deep and political preferences as starkly different as any in the nation. Broward and Palm Beach on the Gold Coast voted 65%–33% for Al Gore; Escambia, Santa Rosa and Okaloosa Counties, on the western end of the Panhandle around what is called, perhaps unkindly, the Redneck Riviera, voted 68%–30% for George W. Bush. During the 2004 presidential campaign the focus again was on Florida more than any other state, as Republicans and Democrats brought in their nominees and organized to register new voters and get them to vote by absentee ballot or on Election Day. This time Florida turned out not to be close: John Kerry got 23% more votes there than Al Gore, but George W. Bush got 36% more and carried the state 52%–47%. Florida was only 1% less Republican than New Jersey was Democratic, though New Jersey was on no one's list of battleground states. Yet Florida, the fourth largest state, was still closely enough divided—much more closely than the three larger states, that it remains crucial, for both parties. The story of how Florida became the pivot of American politics is a story of growth and change, and over the past 60 years Florida has grown more rapidly and changed more vividly than just about any other part of the United States.

Florida has an exotic past. It is the only Atlantic Coast state that was not part of the colonial United States; through the exertions of John Quincy Adams and Andrew Jackson it was acquired from Spain in 1819. Starting off as a forgotten swamp and semitropical resort, Florida has emerged as almost an empire of its own, a prototype in many ways of America's future, with an international flavor and sometimes almost with its own foreign policy. Pivotal has been the rise of air conditioning: in 1950 only 20% of Florida houses had it, in 2000, 95% did. For many years, Florida was the place which millions of retirees looked forward to: the sunny, year-round warmth after eternal gray skies over winter factories and dark offices. But in the 1980s and 1990s Florida's population of children grew rapidly as young couples, from the South, from various points north and from Latin America, chose to raise their families and make their livings in a booming economy, with jobs and opportunities in communities that did not exist a generation ago. For refugees from Cuba and Haiti and immigrants from all over the Caribbean and Latin America, Florida has been a land of freedom and security from authoritarian regimes and totalitarian police states. For Americans and foreigners of all kinds—some 80 million of them— Florida is the place to visit, with lively attractions, year-round swimming, restaurants and rooms to suit every taste and pocketbook. Yet all is not sunny: crime is down, but still a threat; the economic future is, as always, uncertain; the melting pot seems to work slowly and Florida's Hispanic population seems often to live in a world apart.

Florida is a creation not of America's elite—though a few millionaires like Henry Flagler and Marcus Plant pioneered tourism here—but a place for which ordinary people have voted with their feet. Before World War II it was the least populous state in the South, with 1.4 million people, isolated, disease-ridden, bigoted, with phosphate mines but no mineral resources, not much agriculture outside its citrus groves, and hardly any manufacturing at all. Today, Florida has 17 million people. It is a state one-fifth of whose economy is based on tourism in a country

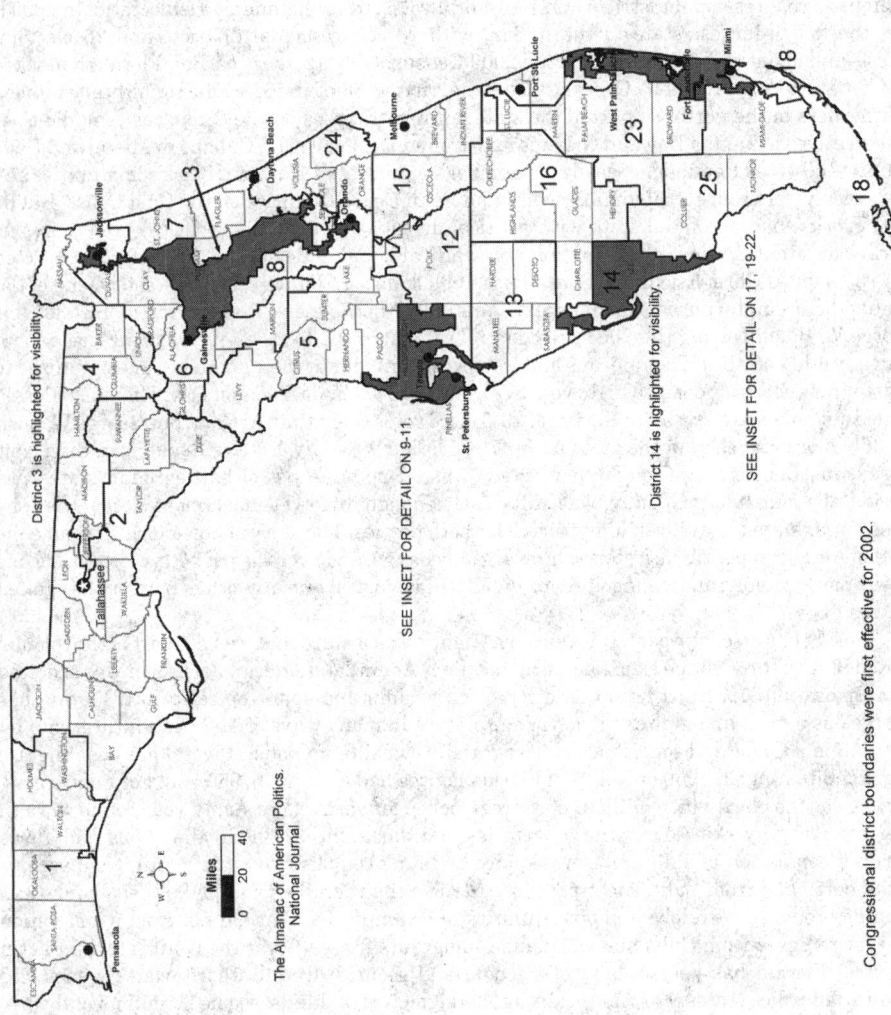

District 3 is highlighted for visibility.

SEE INSET FOR DETAIL ON 9-11.

District 14 is highlighted for visibility.

SEE INSET FOR DETAIL ON 17, 19-22.

Congressional district boundaries were first effective for 2002.

The Almanac of American Politics.
National Journal.

Miles
0   20   40

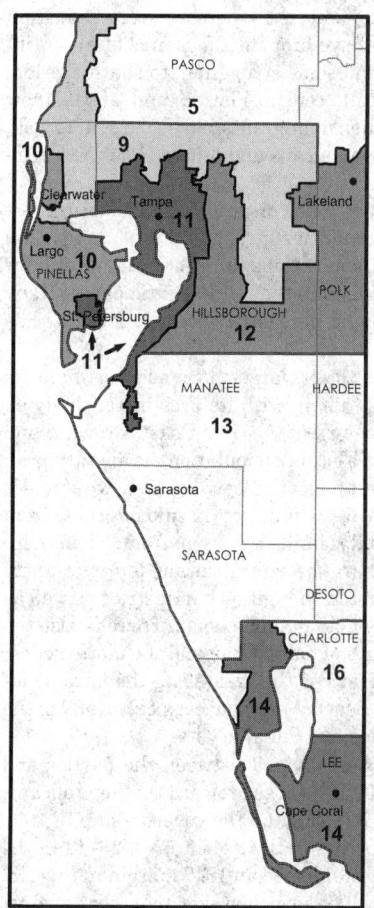

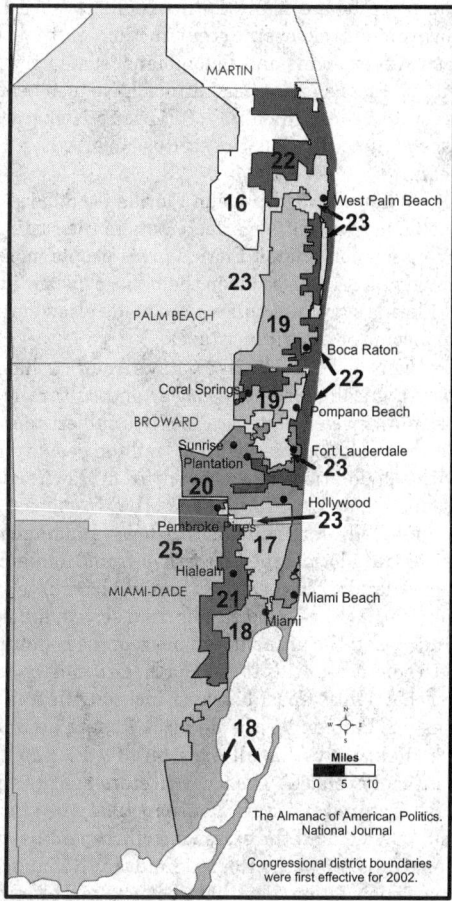

where tourism is one of the great growth industries; a state with an economy based on services in a country increasingly service-oriented; the state with the largest proportion of elderly and retired citizens in a country where an increasing percentage will live many years in retirement; a state also with a growing number of school children in a country which, replenished by immigration, is growing faster and more robustly than any other advanced nation. It is a state continually replenished with people from out of state, two-thirds of them from the United States, one-third from foreign countries: enough that at present rates of growth Florida seems likely to pass New York as the third largest state in the 2010 Census.

Florida in recent years has had one of America's most buoyant economies—it has gained jobs consistently over the last 10 years except during the three months after September 11—though its economic base often seems a mystery to outsiders. This is an economy based heavily on small business—98% of businesses have fewer than 100 employees and in the 1990s Florida ranked number one in small business starts—with a significant high-tech sector (fifth in the country) and retirees, who account for 52% of Florida's consumer spending and pay 47% of its property taxes (though some of this may be in jeopardy, as retirees head to other states). Florida's economy is also based on international merchandise trade, which increased from $24 billion in 1987 to $81 billion in 2004; while foreign investment increased from $9.5 billion to $34.3 billion in 2002. Miami for three decades has been the economic and commercial capital of Latin America, as well as its mecca for political exiles. You can fly nonstop from Miami to just about any place in Latin America, both English and Spanish are commonly understood, and it has been the one place where many Latins could be sure their money and their persons were safe from government takeover. Recent ructions in their countries have brought thousands of Argentinians, Venezuelans and Colombians, some very affluent and some struggling, to south Florida; Puerto Ricans and other Latinos have also been moving into central Florida, and Cubans now account for less than half of Florida's Hispanics. And other immigrants have come in as well, especially to the Gold Coast: Russians, Arabs, Haitians, Jamaicans and others from the Caribbean.

What may be fragile in Florida is civil society; Florida can be disorderly and chaotic. Most people here do not have deep roots in the state, most communities sprang into existence within living memory and, if Florida gives people more freedom and options than they may ever have imagined, it has also given them more disruption and crime than they surely anticipated. Many of Florida's great fortunes were made elsewhere, and brought here partly because the state has no income or inheritance taxes.

This new Florida, like today's America, has no real center. Its largest urban focus, Miami, is geographically off to one corner and culturally uniquely Cuban, with its eyes increasingly on Latin America and its local politics subject to ridicule. The rest of the Gold Coast, Broward and Palm Beach Counties, with 2.9 million people (one-sixth of Florida's population), is also atypical, with a population drawn heavily from New York (the largest migration between any two states is from New York to Florida) and other Northeastern metro areas, plus non-Latino migrants from Miami-Dade, large numbers of Jews, and huge retiree condos lining the ocean front. Then there is Central Florida, the I-4 corridor from Tampa-St. Petersburg through citrus and tourist country and Orlando. This is mostly family, not retiree, country, living off high-tech industries as well as tourism: A year-round rather than seasonal megalopolis of 4.8 million people. There is also the Gulf Coast, the affluent and burgeoning communities south of Tampa Bay and the more modest retirement counties to the north. Growing even more rapidly is the area along the hard-sand-beach Atlantic Coast between Jacksonville and Daytona Beach. Very Southern culturally is the western Panhandle, the Redneck Riviera around Pensacola and Panama City.

Politically, this all adds up to a Florida that is closely divided between the parties and politically volatile. The trend in state politics since the 1990s has been toward the Republicans, who captured the state House in 1994, the state Senate in 1996, and the governorship in 1998 and now hold all the statewide offices and have big majorities in the legislature—26–14 in the Senate, 84–36 in the House. Similarly, Republicans have established an 18–7 margin in the U.S. House delegation. They have been helped by term limits (which soon, however, may work against them) and by shrewdly adapting to local terrain. Redistricting, which Republicans influenced in 1992 and controlled in 2002, helped: heavily black and Jewish areas are concentrated in a few districts, to the point that two-thirds of Democrats holding legislative and House seats are black or Jewish.

The trend in national politics in the 1990s was toward the Democrats. Bill Clinton lost the state by only 41%–39% in 1992 and carried it 48%–42% in 1996. Al Gore actually had a higher percentage when he lost the state by the excruciating margin of 48.85%–48.84%. Most of the change was due to movement toward Democrats on the Gold Coast and in the I-4 corridor from Tampa-St. Petersburg to Orlando. Drops in crime and welfare rolls deprived Republicans of issues in these metro areas as they did in the big metro areas of the Northeast, industrial Midwest and West Coast, and after 1995 the tax issue was taken off the table; cultural issues like abortion and gun control favored Democrats. Also, the increasing Jewish population in Broward and Palm Beach Counties moved the Gold Coast toward Democrats; Joe Lieberman campaigned there and drew enthusiastic crowds in 2000. In the I-4 corridor, what had been a big Republican margin for Bush in 1988 was transformed to a Clinton margin in 1996 and a standoff in 2000. The biggest drop in the Republican percentage in any county in Florida between 1988 and 2000 was in Osceola County, which contains part of Disney World and the Disney-sponsored "new town" of Celebration. In the 1980s, Disney World was still an epitome of traditional conservative values; by 2000, Disney was hosting Gay Day.

The closeness of Florida's political divisions was shown not only in the 2000 presidential race but in the two most recent races for Senate seats opened up by the retirement of two popular senators, Republican Connie Mack III and Democrat Bob Graham, whose appeal crossed party lines. In 2000, when Mack retired, Insurance Commissioner and former Democratic Congressman Bill Nelson beat Republican Congressman Bill McCollum 51%–46%. In 2004, when Graham retired, Republican former HUD Secretary and Orange County Commission Chairman Mel Martinez beat former state Education Commissioner Betty Castor 49%–48%. Both winners made inroads in the other party's strongholds. Nelson, with his Florida roots and accent, lost the part of the state outside the Gold Coast and the I-4 corridor by only 52%–46%. Martinez, who was born in Cuba and came to the United States as a teenager, ran ahead of George W. Bush among Miami-Dade's Cubans and lost the Gold Coast by only 57%–41%.

After the U.S. Supreme Court made its decision in December 2000, Florida Democrats promised that voters' rage would redound against Jeb Bush in 2002, when he ran for reelection as governor, and in fall 2002 DNC Chairman Terry McAuliffe said that the Florida governor's race was the national party's number one priority. Yet his job approval rating remained around 55% throughout the campaign and he won by a 56%–43% margin. At the same time, Republican Charlie Crist was elected attorney general, replacing the last Democrat holding a non-federal statewide office, and Republican margins in the U.S. House delegation and the state Senate and House were increased. Then came the 2004 presidential election. Democrats concentrated on registering blacks and increasing turnout in Broward and Palm Beach Counties. But Republicans built an effective statewide organization manned by some 109,000 volunteers, who made 3 million voter contacts on Election Day and increased Republican turnout just about everywhere. The Bush campaign may have been helped by the fact that Florida was badly hit by four hurricanes in August and September; Governor Jeb Bush and also his brother the president got great credit for their response. And Florida's economy, unlike those of other battleground states like Ohio, Michigan and Pennsylvania, was humming along. But the organization may have made the difference. Bush won 2.9 million votes in Florida in 2000 and 3.9 million in 2004. He did not increase his percentage much in the Gold Coast—which he lost 60%–38% in 2000 and 59%–40% in 2004—but he prevented Democrats from increasing their popular vote margin there. In the I-4 corridor Bush led 51%–49% in 2000 and 54%–46% in 2004, increasing a 50,000-vote margin to 230,000 votes. And in the rest of the state, Bush increased his 2000 popular vote margin from 316,000 votes to 524,000. In counties with small populations, with more trailer parks than gated communities, with more swampland than sandy beaches, the Bush percentage rose by 4% to 12%.

But this was not the last struggle in Florida politics. Jeb Bush, after two successful and controversy-strewn terms as governor, is ineligible to run for a third in 2006. In early 2005 multiple Republicans and Democrats were lining up to run for only the second open seat race for governor in 20 years. And Senator Bill Nelson comes up for reelection, with several strong potential rivals. There is no rest for the weary in Florida politics.

Two more things are worth noting about Florida politics. The first is that politics here is not driven by an elderly population terrified of losing government benefits. To be sure, the elderly are a larger percentage of the electorate here than in any other state, 19% in 2004, but the difference is not overwhelming; most new residents come here to work, not to retire. Florida has the five congressional districts with the most Social Security recipients in the nation; Republican congressmen with elderly districts who have supported changes in the Social Security system have been reelected in all but one case by wide margins. In 2000 and 2004 George W. Bush called for personal retirement accounts in Social Security and according to exit polls carried the over 65 vote in Florida by a 52%–46% and 51%–48%. The elderly tend to vote in line with long-established partisan preferences, not in panicky response to the latest proposal on Social Security.

The second point is that the environment is an increasingly important issue in Florida, but one that may not cut in a partisan way. People come to Florida partly because of the kind of place it is; migrants from New York or Illinois may not have cared much about environmental issues when they lived there, but they came to Florida in large part because of the climate and setting, and don't want to see oil drilled on the Gulf Coast or the Everglades paved over. This is a change from history. The Everglades were seen as a nuisance for years. In 1845, when Florida was admitted to the Union, the legislature called for "reclaiming" the Everglades, and in 1850 Congress passed the Swamp and Overflowed Lands Act. The Army Corps of Engineers started building a dike across Lake Okeechobee in 1930 and for nearly 50 years worked to straighten the Kissimmee River and build dikes and channels to reclaim land for farming. But with the 1947 publication of *The Everglades: River of Grass* by Marjory Stoneman Douglas, who died in 1998 at 108, Floridians began to appreciate the Everglades, which is essentially a flow of water south, from the Kissimmee River near Disney World, through Lake Okeechobee down to Florida Bay and the Gulf of Mexico.

The People		Race/Ethnic Origin			Military veterans: 1,875,597 (15.2%)	
Pop. 2004 (est):	17,397,161	10,458,509	65.4%	White	WWII: 25.6%	Korea: 15.0%
Pop. 2000:	15,982,378	2,264,268	14.2%	Black	Vietnam: 28.0%	Gulf War: 9.2%
Pop. 1990:	12,937,926	261,693	1.6%	Asian	**Most populous cities (2003):**	
Change 1990–2000:	Up 23.5%	42,358	0.3%	Native Am.	1. Jacksonville	773,781
% of U.S. total:	5.7%	6,887	0.0%	Hawaiian	2. Miami	376,815
Pop. rank:	4th of 50	236,954	1.5%	Two+ races	3. Tampa	317,647
Area size:	65,755 sq. mi.	28,994	0.2%	Other	4. St. Petersburg	247,610
State Native:	32.7%	2,682,715	16.8%	Hisp. Origin	5. Hialeah	226,401
Non-citizen:	9.2%	**Ancestry**				
Language		German: 9.5%		Irish: 8.3%	Urban population: 89.3%	
English: 76.2%	Spanish: 15.7%	English: 7.4%		USA: 6.4%	Rural population: 10.7%	
Other Eur.: 6.3%		Italian: 5.0%				

Education		Work Sector		Legislature	
H.S. Grad:	79.9%	Private: 79.8%	Govt: 13.7%	Senate	26 R 14 D
College Grad:	22.3%	Self: 6.2%	Family: 0.3%	House	84 R 36 D
Industry		Unemployment: 5.5%		Legislative Term Limits: Yes	
Agri: 1.3%	Con: 8.0%	**Household Income**		**Registered Voters**	
Fin: 8.1%	Info: 3.1%	<15k: 16.3%	15-35k: 28.7%	D: 4,261,249	(41.4%)
Mfg: 12.6%	Prof: 28.7%	35-50k: 17.4%	50-100k: 27.2%	R: 3,892,492	(37.8%)
Public: 5.2%	Trade: 17.5%	100-150k: 6.3%	>150k: 4.1%	O: 2,148,030	(20.9%)
Other: 15.6%		Median: $38,819			
Occupation		Poverty status: 12.5%			
Blue collar: 21.1%	White collar: 61.1%	**Home Value**			
Gray collar: 17.8%		<50k: 16.5%	50-100k: 38.7%	100-200k: 32.1%	200-300k: 7.1%
		300-500k: 3.6%	>500k: 2.1%	Median: $93,200	

Presidential politics   Going into the 2004 campaign, just about every strategist and pundit thought that Florida would be crucial once again, and very narrowly decided. Crucial it certainly was: George W. Bush would not have won without Florida's 27 electoral votes. But narrowly decided it turned out not to be. Bush's .01% percentage margin in 2000 ballooned into a 5.01% margin—larger than the percentage margins in 10 other states. Bush was declared the winner in Florida at 11:39 p.m. by ABC, at 11:43 by CBS, at 11:51 by Fox, at 12:10 by CNN and at 12:24 by NBC and MSNBC.

Bush's biggest gains were among minorities. According to the NEP exit poll, whites voted 57% for Bush, the same as in 2000; blacks voted 13% for Bush, up 6% from 2000; Latinos voted 56% for Bush, up 7% from 2000. The Latino numbers are all the more remarkable, since he seems to have lost ground among still heavily Republican Cuban-Americans; he seems to have done particularly well among Nicaraguans and surprisingly well among Puerto Ricans. Osceola

2004 Presidential Vote
Bush (R) 3,964,522   (52%)
Kerry (D)..................... 3,583,544   (47%)
Nader (Ref) 32,971   (0%)
Other.......................... 28,773   (0%)

2004 Democratic Presidential Primary
Kerry (D)...................... 581,672   (77%)
Edwards (D) 75,703   (10%)
Sharpton (D)................... 21,031   (3%)
Dean (D) 20,834   (3%)
Kucinich (D) 17,198   (2%)
Other.......................... 37,324   (5%)

2000 Presidential Vote
Bush (R) 2,912,790   (49%)
Gore (D)...................... 2,912,253   (49%)
Nader (Green) 97,488   (2%)
Other.......................... 40,579   (1%)

County, which includes part of Disney World, has a rapidly expanding Latino population; it voted for Al Gore in 2000 and for Bush in 2004. Jews voted 80%–20% for John Kerry, but Bush's share was up from 2000; despite increased voter turnout, Broward and Palm Beach Counties produced lower Democratic popular vote margins. In the heavily Jewish 19th and 20th Congressional Districts, Bush's percentage rose from 27% to 34% and from 31% to 36%.

Florida has had a presidential primary in March for many years; since 1988 it has been part of Southern Super Tuesday. In recent years, as one of many states voting on a single day, it has attracted less attention. In 2004 it came too late to matter: the primary was held March 9, but John Kerry clinched the Democratic nomination on March 2.

It should be noted that Florida's Democratic electorate differs markedly from what it was the last time the Florida primary was the center of national attention, in 1976. Then, 67% of Florida's voters were registered Democrats; voters in north Florida, segregationist in the 1960s and hawkish in the 1970s were still almost all registered Democrats. That is why George Wallace won the 1972 Florida presidential primary and why he was still a strong candidate in 1976. In November 2004 only 41% of Florida's voters were registered Democrats (38% were registered Republicans). This is a much smaller and much more liberal pool. The large mass of urban and suburban Democrats—in 2004, 31% of registered Democrats were in the three Gold Coast counties and 28% in the I-4 corridor—are not that much different from registered Democrats in big northern states. There are still some north Florida counties where many who vote Republican in general elections are still registered as Democrats; some conspiracy theorists argued that there must have been vote fraud because so many registered Democrats voted for George W. Bush, but they have been voting for Republicans in general elections for years. Unless they change their registration, they will not be eligible to vote in the Republican primaries for governor and senator in 2006 and president in 2008.

Congressional districting   Florida has gained congressional districts from every Census since 1930, when it was still the smallest state in the South: in

109th Congress Lineup
18 R   7 D
108th Congress Lineup
18 R   7 D

1930 it elected four House members; in the 2000 Census it gained two seats, for a total of 25. In 2002, the redistricting process was controlled by Republicans; they agreed on a plan and passed it in March 2002. Disagreement between the House and Senate was resolved when senators agreed to create a district tailor-made for House Speaker Tom Feeney; the other new district was tailor-made for Mario Diaz-Balart, chairman of the House Congressional Districting Committee. When Democratic Attorney General Bob Butterworth failed to pass it along to the Department of Justice for Voting Rights Act review, Governor Jeb Bush sent it there in May 2002. Democrats filed lawsuits against the plan in state and federal courts. The Justice Department approved the plan on June 7. A state court on June 17 dismissed the suit and said the federal court had jurisdiction. On July 9, in time for the filing deadline, a three-judge federal court approved the plan.

This was one of the most successful partisan redistrictings of the 2002 cycle. Feeney and Diaz-Balart were both elected to the House by wide margins. Karen Thurman was defeated by Republican state Senator Ginny Brown-Waite. Two senior Republicans, Bill Young of St. Petersburg and Clay Shaw of Fort Lauderdale, were strengthened; both represented areas which were among the first in Florida to elect Republican congressmen, but which had become more Democratic in the 1980s and 1990s. Democrat Allen Boyd of the 2d District was weakened. The seats of the three black Democrats and two Latino Republicans were protected, although the black percentage in Alcee Hastings's 23d District was reduced. The 2002 plan produced a delegation of 18 Republicans and 7 Democrats, a lopsided Republican majority in a state that was evenly divided in the 2000 presidential election. Florida now has the third largest Republican delegation in the House; its 18 Republican congressmen are almost as numerous as California's 20 and Texas's 21. In 2004 Democrats called for an independent redistricting panel to handle redistricting, something they had not considered when they had control; Republicans, who might have backed it then, showed no interest.

Governor

Jeb Bush (R)

Elected 1998, term expires Jan. 2007, 2d term; b. Feb. 11, 1953, Midland, TX; home, Miami; U. of TX, B.A. 1974; Catholic; married (Columba).

Elected Office: FL Commerce Secy., 1987–88.

Professional Career: Pres. & COO, Codina Group, 1981–94; Founder & Chmn., Foundation for Florida's Future, 1995–98.

Office: The Capitol, Tallahassee, 32399, 850-488-4441; Fax: 850-487-0801; Web site: www.state.fl.us.

Election Results

2002 general	Jeb Bush (R)	2,856,845	(56%)
	Bill McBride (D)	2,201,427	(43%)
2002 primary	Jeb Bush (R)	unopposed	
1998 general	Jeb Bush (R)	2,192,105	(55%)
	Buddy MacKay (D)	1,773,054	(45%)

Jeb Bush, son of President George H. W. Bush and brother of President George W. Bush, was elected governor of Florida in 1998 and 2002. Jeb grew up in Midland and Houston, Texas. He majored in Latin American studies at the University of Texas and there met his wife, Columba, who is originally from Mexico. He speaks Spanish fluently—but with more of a Mexican than Cuban accent, he notes. In 1981 he moved to Miami and started a real estate development company. For a year or so, he was Commerce secretary under Republican Governor Bob Martinez. With a well-known name and strong convictions on issues, he decided to run against Governor Lawton Chiles in 1994, vanquishing competition in the Republican primary and leading in polls during most of the fall. Chiles started emphasizing his "cracker" roots and called himself "the he-coon [who] always walks before the light of day." The result was a 51%–49% Chiles victory.

Bush immediately started running again. While his positions on issues did not change much, his approach and his tone did. The consensus in Florida had been moving for some time toward Bush and now Bush came some distance toward the consensus. He entered 1998 as the heavy favorite for governor while Democrats inflicted damage on themselves. Democrats noisily looked for alternatives to the likely nominee, Lieutenant Governor Buddy MacKay, though MacKay had received good press for his work in office and nearly beat Connie Mack for senator in 1988. Bush won 55%–45%.

As governor, Bush has worked relentlessly to put into place, with the help of Republican legislatures, a series of programs that cut tax rates, encourage market provision of services in welfare, health care and education, and end racial discrimination by government. An example of the last is Bush's One Florida program, to curtail quotas and set-asides in state contracts, get rid of quotas and preferences in state colleges and universities and replace them by guaranteeing places in the state's 10 public colleges to the top 20% of every high school graduating class. It was initially a response to the effort by Ward Connerly, sponsor of California's 1996 Proposition 209 which outlawed state government racial quotas and preferences, to put a similar proposition on the Florida ballot, which Bush said would start a "war." One Florida prompted sit-ins in Bush's office by black legislators and lawsuits that were eventually dismissed. But predictions that the policy would reduce the number of blacks and other minorities in state universities have been proven wrong: the percentage of minorities admitted rose from 33% in 1999 to 35% in 2004. And those admitted were better prepared, thanks to efforts to improve education in lower grades and to quadruple the number of minorities taking the PSAT. As Bush said in December 2004, "In Florida we don't push unprepared children forward. Nor do we separate them by racial classification. We maintain that the best way to ensure minority participation in higher education is to provide the same opportunities and support to all students and to hold all students to the same standards."

On education, Bush moved to seek accountability in schools before Congress passed the No Child Left Behind Act in 2001. His A-Plus program set up a series of tests and provided that students in schools found to be failing after a period of time could obtain vouchers to be used to attend other public or private schools. This was vigorously opposed by teacher unions and passed over their opposition. By 2003, some 24,000 students were receiving vouchers; perhaps more important, test scores had risen throughout the state far more than many education profession-als had predicted. The threat of competition elicited better performance from thousands of teachers and students. To shore up middle schools, where test scores improved less, Bush signed a bill in 2004 providing reading coaches for middle school teachers and in 2005 he proposed more standardized tests and graduation requirements for middle schools similar to those of high schools. Bush also pushed for an innovative policy on pre-kindergarten. In 2002 he got voters to approve a voluntary pre-K program and in 2004 the legislature passed a bill he signed, with standards for class size, curriculum and teacher certification; it provided vouchers and encour-aged private school rather than public school pre-K. Bush's major setback on education was the passage by a 52%–48% margin in November 2002 of Amendment 9, a teacher union-backed measure requiring that class size be reduced to 18 in grades K-3, 22 in grades 4–8 and 25 in grades 9–12 in 2010. Bush argued that this would cost an extra $27 billion and that studies had shown that reducing class size produced little gain in achievement. He proposed his own program for $2.8 billion over five years to build 12,000 new classrooms. In March 2003 he called for repeal of Amendment 9, but failed to get it; 60% of the year's increase in education spending went for reducing class size. By December 2004 it appeared that the state would have to add at least 30,000 new teachers to the current total of 160,000, and school districts were having trouble finding math, science and special education applicants.

Since his first years in office, Bush moved persistently to reduce tax rates, with considerable success. Florida's rapid population growth has increased demands on government, but lower taxes have arguably spurred economic growth which has generated revenues to provide higher spending. The state's tourism industry suffered in the aftermath of September 11, but had fully recovered by 2004, and the state's economy suffered little from the recession that hurt many other states. In 2000 Bush succeeded in cutting taxes by $500 million, while increasing highway spending and putting up money for the Everglades restoration program. In 2001 he pressed for more tax cuts, and in October called a special session of the legislation to cut spending to account for a budget shortfall; the intangibles tax cut was delayed. In January 2002 his budget provided just a 1% increase in spending. The 2004 budget included $220 million in tax cuts, more than half for businesses, and Bush vetoed $349 million in spending proposals. In January 2005 he pro-posed a $61 billion budget, with increases in most programs; one-third of the increases were for education, with half of those for reducing class size.

Medicaid is a major expense for Florida state government. In 2001 Bush negotiated rebates with pharmaceutical companies saving 15% on the Medicaid budget. In 2004 he signed a bill requiring insurance companies to offer health savings accounts to small business and got the legislature to authorize HMOs in Medicaid. In January 2005 he proposed "empowered care"—with Medicaid recipients given certain funds, depending on their medical conditions, and HMOs and other private insurers competing to provide coverage. He also sought to get HMOs to provide in-home care rather than nursing home care to the eligible elderly.

In January 2002 the Bushes signed an agreement to implement the Everglades restoration plan approved by Congress by spending $7.8 billion over 30 years to restore 2.4 million acres and provide an extra 1.7 billion gallons of fresh water yearly to south Florida. He got his brother George W. Bush in his 2004 budget to increase Everglades spending from $28 to $67 million and to provide $40 million to begin buying out the Collier family's right to drill for oil in the Big Cypress National Preserve. After Democrats complained about inaction, Jeb Bush in October 2004 proposed to borrow $1.5 billion to build eight projects over seven years, to be run by the South Florida Water Management District rather than the Army Corps of Engineers.

Jeb Bush has been judged in Florida largely on his record in state government, but national political commentators have treated him largely as the brother of the 2000 presidential nominee and the 43d president. Jeb Bush did not take a highly visible role in the 2000 presidential campaign. When it became clear that there would be a battle over the Florida results, he recused himself from the three-member board of elections, substituting Agriculture Commissioner Bob Crawford, a Democrat who had endorsed George W. Bush; charges that he orchestrated Secretary of State Katherine Harris' decisions to certify George W. Bush as the winner foundered for lack of evidence. He did say that he would sign a proclamation by the Florida legislature that the Republican electors had won, but there was nothing to back the charges that somehow the governor of Florida had stolen the election for his brother. The day after the election was decided, he appeared with officials of both parties and announced the formation of a bipartisan commission to study Florida's election procedures. In March 2001 it came forward with its recommendations, including getting rid of punch card ballots, leasing optical scanning equipment for all counties for the 2002 election and setting a uniform standard for recounts; these were embodied in a bill signed in May 2001. Voting machine problems occurred in the September 2002 primary, but there were no significant problems in 2004, when George W. Bush's Florida margin was far too large to provide any basis for challenge.

After the 2000 Florida controversy, Democratic National Chairman Terry McAuliffe declared that Jeb Bush would be the party's number one target in 2002, and many Democrats predicted a surge of turnout against him from Democrats convinced their party had been cheated of the presidency. Bush had additional problems as well. In 2002 it was reported that the Department of Children and Families had lost track of some 500 children under its supervision, and that three had died; the agency head resigned in August 2002. But Bush's job rating remained well above 50% in 2001 and 2002, and Democrats had a hard time finding a candidate.

On September 4, 2001, former Attorney General and Dade County State's Attorney Janet Reno announced she was running. Reno, as a Miami-Dade liberal, seemed well positioned to win votes from blacks and women in the Democratic primary but, despite her travels around the state in a red pickup truck, less well positioned to win vital votes in the general election. Two other declared candidates, state Senator Darryl Jones and state Representative Lois Frankel, also represented core Democratic constituencies and seemed to have little general election appeal. Democratic insiders and the teacher unions found another candidate in Bill McBride, from 1992 to 2001 managing partner of Tampa's Holland & Knight, the largest law firm in Florida. McBride grew up in the small town of Leesburg, the son of a TV repairman; he gave up a football scholarship after his knee was injured and worked his way through school; he left law school to enlist in the Marine Corps and was awarded a Bronze Star for his service in Vietnam. He was endorsed by the state AFL-CIO in April 2002. Reno called for health care and schooling for preschoolers; McBride called for a 50-cent increase in the cigarette tax to increase spending on education. In the weeks before the September 10 primary McBride was running even with Reno in the polls. McBride led in the first count by 8,196 votes out of 1.3 million cast, and was certified as the winner September 12. But Miami-Dade County, where Reno led by a wide margin, had not prepared to handle the new voting equipment, and was still counting votes. Florida's revised election laws require a recount if the margin is less than 0.5% of the vote, and Reno demanded a recount as the vote hovered just outside that. On September 17 Miami-Dade votes came in; Reno, still behind by 4,794 votes, 44.4%–44.0% conceded and endorsed McBride. But his campaign had lost a week of an already short general election campaign.

The chief issue in the general election turned out to be Amendment 9, the teacher union measure to reduce class size. Proponents said it would cost only $4 billion over seven years; Bush cited a state government study saying that it would cost $27 billion—a huge amount in a state whose budgets have been hovering around $50 billion. Bush strongly opposed it and proposed his own program for $2.8 billion over five years to build 12,000 new classrooms. McBride, who called Bush's A-plus program a "mirage" and an "illusion" and his testing program "foolish," strongly supported it. Under state law the estimated cost of a ballot proposition has to be put on the ballot; but a Florida judge, in a move that would not surprise those who remember the 2000 Florida ballot controversy, ruled it unnecessary. At one point Bush seemed to stumble on the issue. On

October 3, in a Capitol conversation with three Pensacola area legislators witnessed by a Gannett News Service reporter, Bush talked about how he would respond if Amendment 9 passed. "We're going to have to cut nursing homes. So I've got a couple of devious plans if this thing passes. . . . We might want to have another look at it." The next day his words were in Gannett's *Pensacola News Journal* and a tape of him speaking them was on the paper's website. But McBride stumbled even more. Bush proceeded to bombard television viewers with ads citing his accomplishments and attacking McBride for saying different things to different audiences, hinting that he was a hidden liberal indebted to the teachers' unions and charging that his proposal to eliminate Bush's testing would cost the state $2.5 billion in federal aid. On October 22 the candidates appeared in a debate moderated by *Meet the Press* host Tim Russert. Bush answered questions with mastery of knowledge of state government. McBride was charmingly talkative but unspecific. When Russert asked him whether Amendment 9 would cost $3 billion as some proponents claimed or $27 billion as Bush claimed, McBride said it was "somewhere in between the $8 billion and the $27 billion" and conceded it could cost $12 to $15 billion. His response gave credence to Bush ads that charged that McBride's overexpansion at Holland & Knight showed that as an executive he was overly optimistic and inclined to overspending.

Bush won by the impressive margin of 56%–43%. He carried Hispanic precincts throughout the state and had huge margins in Cuban areas in Miami-Dade County. He lost ground compared to 1998 in Tallahassee and in small north Florida counties with universities, prisons or other state facilities: his Service First overhauls of the state personnel system and privatization of non-core functions of state agencies made him unpopular with public employee unions. Bush lost the Gold Coast by only 54%–46%; he carried the I-4 corridor by a solid 58%–41% and carried the other counties in the south 62%–37% and in the north 59%–40%. Republican Charlie Crist was elected attorney general over Democrat Buddy Dwyer 53%–47%, completing the Republican sweep of statewide offices. Republican margins were increased in the state Senate to 26–14 and the state House to 81–39.

Bush continued to make national headlines in his second term. Acting under a law passed by the legislature, he ordered Terri Schiavo's feeding tube inserted in October 2003; Florida courts ruled this unconstitutional in a series of decisions in 2004, and ultimately Schiavo died after she was denied food and water in March 2005. In August and September 2004 Florida was hit by a record four devastating hurricanes. Bush traveled indefatigably around the state, and his relief efforts resulted in 62% job approval. He successfully pressed Congress for $2 billion of disaster relief in September and $11 billion in November. In November he proposed rebates on property taxes for homeowners whose homes were uninhabitable. That was voted in December, along with rebates on second and third deductibles; high deductibles had been instituted after Hurricane Andrew in 1992, but it was never envisaged that homeowners would have to pay more than one deductible a year. The legislature also voted a $1,500 sales tax breaks for buyers of replacement mobile homes. Curiously, the hurricane proved to be a windfall for state government, with recovery and construction activity generating some $3 billion in increased revenues over two years, to help Florida's already booming economy.

Jeb Bush has been mentioned, since he started running for governor in 1993, as a possible presidential candidate. As governor, he has had some international experience, on business and tourism promotion trips to Central America, Mexico and Canada and on no less than four trips to Israel. In January 2005, his brother sent him and Secretary of State Colin Powell to Indonesia and other countries stricken by the December 26, 2004 tsunami. But this son and brother of presidents seemed to rule a presidential run out, at least for 2008. "I'm not going to run for president in 2008," he told reporters in October 2004. "I'll go back to Miami and I'll figure out what I'm going to do. But it isn't going to be running for president, I promise." But he has not promised not to run for vice president, and will be just 53 when he leaves office as governor; he could conceivably run for president as late as 2020, when he will turn 67.

The open governor race in 2006 seemed sure in early 2005 to attract many candidates. Among the Republicans mentioned were statewide officials: Lieutenant Governor Toni Jennings, Attorney General Charlie Crist and Chief Financial Officer Tom Gallagher. Among the Democrats mentioned were Congressman Jim Davis, state Representative Rod Smith, Democratic state Chairman Scott Maddox, and Anthony Shriver, Miami Beach-based head of the Best Buddies organization, son of Sargent and Eunice Kennedy Shriver and brother-in-law of California Governor Arnold Schwarzenegger.

Senior Senator

Bill Nelson (D)

Elected 2000, seat up 2006, 1st term; b. Sept. 29, 1942, Miami; home, Melbourne; Yale U., B.A. 1965; U. of VA, J.D. 1968; Protestant; married (Grace Cavert).

Military Career: U.S. Army, 1968–70; U.S. Army Reserves, 1965–71.

Elected Office: FL House of Reps., 1972–78; U.S. House of Reps., 1978–90; FL Treasurer, Insurance Comm. & Fire Marshal, 1994–2000.

Professional Career: Practicing atty., 1970–79, 1991–94; Legis. asst., FL Gov. Reubin Askew, 1971; Crew member, Space Shuttle Columbia, 1986.

DC Office: 716 HSOB, 20510, 202-224-5274; Fax: 202-228-2183; Web site: billnelson.senate.gov.

State Offices: Coral Gables, 305-536-5999; Davie, 954-693-4851; Fort Myers, 239-334-7760; Jacksonville, 904-346-4500; Orlando, 407-872-7161; Tallahassee, 850-942-8415; Tampa, 813-225-7040; West Palm Beach, 561-514-0189.

Committees: *Aging (Special). Armed Services*: Airland; Emerging Threats & Capabilities; Readiness & Management Support; Strategic Forces (RMM). *Budget. Commerce, Science & Transportation*: Aviation; Disaster Prevention & Prediction; Science & Space (RMM); Trade, Tourism & Economic Development. *Foreign Relations*: International Operations & Terrorism (RMM); Near Eastern & South Asian Affairs; Western Hemisphere, Peace Corps & Narcotics Affairs.

Group Ratings

	ADA	ACLU	AFS	LCV	ITIC	NTU	COC	ACU	NTLC	CHC
2004	80	67	100	100	64	9	65	4	10	16
2003	80	—	100	79	—	14	48	20	—	—

National Journal Ratings

	2003 LIB	—	2003 CONS		2004 LIB	—	2004 CONS
Economic	82%	—	10%		79%	—	13%
Social	65%	—	34%		82%	—	0%
Foreign	60%	—	35%		55%	—	43%

Key Votes of the 108th Congress

1. Ban Drilling in ANWR	Y	5. Energy Bill	N	9. Ban Same-Sex Marriage	N
2. Approve Bush Tax Cuts	N	6. Support Roe v. Wade	Y	10. Ban Bunker-Buster Bomb	N
3. Medicare/Rx Bill	N	7. Ban Partial-Birth Abortion	N	11. Fund Iraq War	Y
4. Bar Overtime Pay Regs.	Y	8. Assault Weapons Ban	Y	12. Restrict Missile Defense	N

Election Results

2000 general	Bill Nelson (D)	2,989,487	(51%)	($6,535,832)
	Bill McCollum (R)	2,705,348	(46%)	($8,664,112)
	Other	161,896	(3%)	
2000 primary	Bill Nelson (D)	692,147	(78%)	
	Newall J. Daughtrey (D)	105,650	(12%)	
	David B. Higginbottom (D)	95,492	(11%)	

Prior Winning Percentages: 1988 House (61%); 1986 House (73%); 1984 House (61%); 1982 House (71%); 1980 House (70%); 1978 House (61%)

Bill Nelson was elected Florida's junior senator in 2000, after nearly 30 years in politics. He grew up in Melbourne, on what is now the Space Coast, the son of a developer and real estate investor who died when he was 14; Nelson likes to recall that his great-grandfather arrived in Florida from Denmark on boat as a stowaway. From his family home, Rock Point, he could see rockets blast off from what is now the Kennedy Space Center in the 1950s and 1960s. Nelson was active in student government and has always been something of a straight arrow; he doesn't drink, smoke or swear. He went to the University of Florida for two years, then graduated from Yale and the University of Virginia law school. He served two years in the Army, then returned to Melbourne and briefly practiced law and worked on the staff of Governor Reubin Askew. In 1972, at 30, he was elected to the state House of Representatives.

In 1978, when Republican Congressmen Louis Frey retired, Nelson ran for Congress, from a seat that then included the Space Coast's Brevard County and most of Orlando's Orange County. His religious faith and traditional values, his indefatigable campaigning and folksy manner helped make him popular in an area that was trending Republican. He won the seat 61%–39% and in five succeeding elections won between 61% and 73% of the vote, in a district that voted 29% for Michael Dukakis in 1988. On the Science Committee, he got his fellow Democrats to vote him rather than the more liberal George Brown chairman of the Space Subcommittee—obviously of prime importance to the district. Nelson not only boosted the space program in every possible way, he also rode the space shuttle *Columbia* himself, in early January 1986. Less than two weeks later the *Challenger* exploded. After the *Columbia* was lost in February 2003, he called for continued manned space flight despite the risks. "Americans are explorers and adventurers by nature," he said. "We never want to give that up."

In 1989, with the support of leading Florida Democrats, Nelson set out to run against Republican Governor Bob Martinez, who was not faring well in polls. But in early 1990, some Democrats became antsy about Nelson's prospects and persuaded Lawton Chiles, who had retired from the Senate in 1988 after three terms, to run. Chiles was always far ahead, and won the September primary 69%–31%. Nelson returned to his 77-acre oceanfront home in Melbourne, his political career seemingly over. But in 1994 he found an opening when state Insurance Commissioner Tom Gallagher, a Republican, ran for governor. Nelson was elected in November to an office whose full title was Treasurer, Insurance Commissioner and State Fire Marshal, and proceeded to make a highly publicized activist record.

Nelson was obviously setting himself up to run for higher statewide office, and his opening came in March 1999, when Republican Senator Connie Mack said he would not run for reelection in 2000. Mack's retirement left a seat up for grabs in a state that, as election night viewers learned in November 2000, was very closely divided between the parties. And Republicans had a rough primary contest—always a problem in a state with a late September primary and, before the law changed in 2002, an even later October runoff if no candidate gets a majority. The contestants were 20-year, Orlando-based Congressman Bill McCollum, one of the House's impeachment managers, and Tom Gallagher, then Florida education commissioner. Not until June 2000, after a meeting with Governor Jeb Bush and state Republican Chairman Al Cardenas, did Gallagher take himself out of the race, to run for insurance commissioner, the office he had relinquished to Nelson in 1994. A possible problem for Nelson was the independent candidacy of Willie Logan, a veteran African-American legislator whom Democrats had ousted as Speaker-designate in January 1998 on the grounds that he wasn't raising enough money. But Logan, who was getting 5% in many polls, ended up winning just 1.4% in November.

Washington observers considered the race a contest over the wisdom of impeachment but mostly it was a battle of competing styles. Nelson, running his fourth statewide race in 10 years, always led in polls. His easygoing, folksy manner contrasted favorably with McCollum's stiff, often aggressive manner. McCollum, with a long conservative record on abortion and gun control, attempted to modulate his positions, but only succeeded in antagonizing his base; his charge that Nelson was a "liberal" and a proponent of "class warfare" proved unconvincing. This was the most expensive Senate race in Florida history, with the two candidates spending over $15 million between them; Nelson won 51%–46%. Nelson won 60%–37% in the Gold Coast, almost exactly the same margin as in the presidential race. In the I-4 corridor, which included McCollum's district and most of the district Nelson had represented in the House, Nelson won 51%–46%; superior name identification was not Nelson's only advantage. In the rest of the state Nelson lost by only 52%–46%, compared to the 55%–42% margin by which Al Gore lost there. Folksiness and Florida roots counted.

In the Senate, Nelson voted on the Budget Committee to limit the Bush tax cut, then voted against it on the floor in May 2001. In 2001 and 2002 he tried to amend the terrorism insurance bill to put limits on insurance rate increases and to guarantee continued coverage; in June 2002 he was defeated 70–24. He lamented that his experience as an insurance regulator was unappreciated. "Nobody understands anything about insurance here at the federal level, so there's a big education effort that has got to be made." In March 2004 he agreed with John Kerry's call for a delay in military base closings and an increase of 40,000 troops. After exposure of the Abu Ghraib abuses, he said he thought that orders for them came from higher up, but was not sure how high.

On the Foreign Relations and Armed Services committees, Nelson kept pushing with Pat Roberts to get Iraq to provide information about Scott Speicher, the Navy pilot shot down in 1991 who was classified as Missing In Action; Speicher's family lives in Orange Park, near Jacksonville. In February 2004 he recommended a multilateral peacekeeping force for Haiti, and in April 2004 became the first member of Congress to meet with heads of its provisional government since the resignation in February of Jean-Bertrand Aristide. In June 2004 he called on the OAS and the Carter Center to review the purchase of an untested voting system by the Hugo Chavez government in Venezuela; in January 2005, with two Senate colleagues, he met with Chavez, who told him he would cooperate in keeping Colombian FARC guerrillas from reaching sanctuary in Venezuela. Nelson voted for the Iraq war resolution in October 2002, but in May 2004 said he regretted the vote. "I received incorrect intelligence information."

Nelson serves on the Commerce subcommittee with jurisdiction over the space program, where he has strongly supported the space shuttle. After the loss of *Columbia*, he called for accelerated development of a reusable space vehicle to ferry astronauts to the Space Station. When George W. Bush proposed sending spacecraft to the Moon by 2020 and Mars by 2030, Nelson praised the idea but said funding was insufficient. When the committee was considering reauthorization of the space program in September 2004, Nelson passed an amendment calling on NASA to report to Congress on the costs of extending the space shuttle past 2010, but did not get approval of another amendment requiring NASA to find laid-off shuttle workers similar jobs in the agency. Facing the prospect of cuts in shuttle spending and safety concerns in November 2004, he said, "I'm not feeling comfortable at all. I am very distressed when they start whacking jobs—which is exactly what I said they were going to do, start whacking jobs at the Kennedy Space Center." After weeks of study, he voted against the Medicare/prescription drug bill in November 2003 and said in August 2004, "When seniors see how miniscule the coverage is and the costs escalate, there will be a lot of moaning and groaning. People will demand change." He voted against the constitutional amendment banning same-sex marriage on the grounds it "could limit civil rights—including inheritance and hospital visitation—for a whole class of people." He has promoted physical fitness programs, and in 2001 urged Major League Baseball to pay pensions to 29 former Negro League players; in 2004 MLB agreed. In July 2004 he called for an independent audit of Florida's new touch-screen voting machines. After hurricanes hit Florida in August and September 2004, he pushed successfully to get $1 billion of agricultural assistance in the homeland security appropriation; he questioned the inclusion of Miami-Dade County as a disaster area after Frances because it had suffered little damage. In November he blasted FEMA for not providing enough housing for victims of Charley in Charlotte, DeSoto and Hardee Counties.

In 2004 he was mentioned several times as a possible running mate for John Kerry, but tended to defer to his senior colleague Bob Graham. In January 2005 he made it clear that he wanted to run for reelection and not for governor in 2006. Elected with 51% of the vote, and as one of only four Democratic senators representing the 11 Confederate states, he is an obvious Republican target. In January 2005 he opposed George W. Bush's Social Security plan. "By linking benefits to a volatile stock market, privatization shifts the risk to seniors and weakens Social Security's guaranteed safety net. In the wake of recent cases of corporate laundering, we all know too well the dangers of relying on stocks for retirement." After the Pentagon limited access to military bases for the Boy Scouts, apparently in response to criticism of their policy of excluding gays and requiring belief in God, Nelson introduced a resolution supporting the Scouts and embarked on a tour of Florida in their support. "There is no way, shape or form that the U.S. military should be separated from the Boy Scouts. They're not going to stop the Boy Scouts from using military facilities."

In June 2005, Congresswoman Katherine Harris, who decided not to run for the Senate in 2004 after consultations with White House strategist Karl Rove, announced she would run against Nelson in 2006. Governor Jeb Bush, probably the strongest possible Republican candidate, has indicated time and again that he is not interested in running. This is likely to be a high-spending race—Nelson has said he needs to raise $18 million—and could be one of the most fiercely contested in the 2006 cycle.

Junior Senator

Mel Martinez (R)

Elected 2004, seat up 2010, 1st term; b. Oct. 23, 1946, Sagua La Grande, Cuba; home, Orlando; FL St. U., B.A. 1969, J.D. 1973; Catholic; married (Kitty).

Elected Office: Orange County chairman, 1998–2001.

Professional Career: Practicing atty.; Secy., U.S. Dept. of Housing and Urban Dev., 2001–03.

DC Office: 317 HSOB, 20510, 202-224-3041; Fax: 202-228-5171; Web site: martinez.senate.gov.

State Offices: Coral Gables, 305-444-8332; Orlando, 407-254-2573.

Committees: *Aging (Special). Banking, Housing & Urban Affairs*: Financial Institutions; Housing & Transportation; Securities & Investment. *Energy & Natural Resources*: Energy; National Parks; Water & Power. *Foreign Relations*: African Affairs (Chmn.); International Economic Policy, Export & Trade Promotion; Western Hemisphere, Peace Corps & Narcotics Affairs.

Group Ratings and Key Votes: Newly Elected

Election Results

2004 general	Mel Martinez (R)	3,672,864	(49%)	($12,836,836)
	Betty Castor (D)	3,590,201	(48%)	($11,472,071)
	Other	166,829	(2%)	
2004 primary	Mel Martinez (R)	522,994	(45%)	
	Bill McCollum (R)	360,474	(31%)	
	Doug Gallagher (R)	158,360	(14%)	
	Johnnie Byrd (R)	68,982	(6%)	
	Other	55,121	(5%)	
1998 general	Bob Graham (D)	2,436,402	(62%)	($5,094,581)
	Charlie Crist (R)	1,463,749	(38%)	($1,487,498)

Mel Martinez, a Republican, was elected Florida's junior senator in 2004. Melquiades Martinez grew up in the Cuban countryside, near Sagua La Grande, where his father made his living as a veterinarian inseminating cows. After a neighboring 16-year-old was shot by a firing squad for dealing with the underground, Martinez's parents sent him to the United States in February 1962, as part of Operation Pedro Pan, a Catholic Church program that brought 14,000 unaccompanied children to the United States. He stayed in a camp along the St. John's River west of St. Augustine, then was taken in as a foster child by Eileen and Walt Young of Orlando, still unable to speak much English; later he was taken in by June and Jim Berkmeyer. Martinez attended Orlando Junior College and worked at a Publix supermarket; his parents arrived in 1966, and he bought them a used Chevy. He transferred to Florida State, graduated from its college and law school and practiced law in Orlando with Orlando Mayor Bill Frederick's firm. A Democrat in college and law school, he became a Republican in 1979. As one of the few bilingual lawyers in town, he got many Spanish-speaking clients. As a personal injury plaintiff's lawyer, Martinez made lots of money and became head of the Florida Academy of Trial Lawyers. He and his college roommate, Ken Connor, started a personal injury practice; Connor ran for governor in 1994 as a pro-life Republican and asked Martinez to be his running mate. Jeb Bush won the primary with 46% of the vote and Connor finished fifth with 9%, but Martinez was noticed. In 1998 Martinez ran for chairman of the Orange County government and in a nonpartisan three-way race won by a wide margin. He sought to deny zoning changes that would result in overcrowded schools and replaced the fire chief for failing to achieve racial diversity. In 2000 Martinez, a Cuban-American not involved in Cuban-American politics in Miami, was named co-chairman of George W. Bush's Florida campaign, and after the election he was appointed Secretary of Housing and Urban Development.

In December 2003 he resigned as HUD secretary to run for the Senate. There he set up a $1.7 billion tax credit program for investors building affordable housing and a $1 billion program to help 650,000 low-income families make down payments over five years; spending on Section 8 housing vouchers increased from $12 billion to $18 billion. But his attempt to streamline the closing process on housing purchases was unsuccessful. Martinez traveled extensively and was constantly available to Spanish language television and radio media; he commented not only on HUD programs but in defense of administration domestic and foreign policy generally.

Up through 2003 he was a distant observer of politics in Florida, where Senator Bob Graham's seat came up for reelection in 2004. Graham was widely popular, a long-term fixture in Florida politics, first elected to the legislature in 1966, elected governor in 1978 and 1982 and to the Senate in 1986, 1992 and 1998, all by wide margins. In May 2003 he announced he was running for president and embarked on campaigning in Iowa, New Hampshire and other locales. When asked whether he would run for reelection to the Senate, he would say he did not anticipate doing so. Suddenly a Senate seat that had seemed to be safe seemed to be open. Graham's apparent withdrawal from the Senate race led many Republicans and Democrats to run, the latter all insisting that they would withdraw if he decided to run for reelection. Curiously, the candidates who seemed to be gearing up most impressively in early 2003 ended up dropping out in the fall. Republican Congressman Mark Foley raised $3.2 million by June 30, far more than the $670,000 raised by former Congressman Bill McCollum, who lost 51%–46% to Democrat Bill Nelson in 2000. On the Democratic side, Congressman Allen Boyd by July 2003 had assembled a first-rate campaign team; Boyd had the kind of moderate record that had enabled Democrats like Graham, former Governor and Senator Lawton Chiles and former Governor Reubin Askew to dominate Florida politics for years even as the state trended Republican. In summer 2003 a South Florida newspaper wrote that Foley was gay; Foley held a press conference and said he would not discuss his sexual orientation. Then in September, saying that he needed to take care of his sick father, he withdrew from the Senate race and announced for reelection to the House. In early October Graham withdrew from the presidential race but left his intentions in the Senate race unclear. Later that month Boyd withdrew from the Senate race and announced for reelection to the House.

This left both parties with candidates and potential candidates whose ability to win many party leaders doubted. On the Democratic side Broward County Congressman Peter Deutsch was running hard: he was well financed but had a liberal voting record and a strong partisan edge that seemed unlikely to go over well statewide; former Miami-Dade County Mayor Alex Penelas had strong support from Cuban-Americans but uncertain appeal statewide; Congressman Alcee Hastings, who had been impeached and removed as a federal judge, was talking about running. On the Republican side, McCollum was an active and earnest campaigner but had already demonstrated in 2000 that he was capable of running 3% behind George W. Bush; businessman Doug Gallagher was ready to spend his own money, but was unknown; Congresswoman Katherine Harris, who was expressing interest in the race, was well known for her role as secretary of state in the 2000 Florida recount controversy, but was a target who would clearly attract a huge response from Democratic moneygivers and activists. So both parties found other candidates who ended up winning their nominations. Democrats found Betty Castor, a former legislator from Tampa, elected state education commissioner in 1986 and 1990 and later president of the University of South Florida. White House strategist Karl Rove met with Harris, who decided not to run after serving only one House term, while Senators George Allen and Rick Santorum met with Mel Martinez and urged him to run. Martinez had earlier expressed interest in running for governor in 2006—a better natural fit for his executive experience than a run for the Senate. But in December 2003 Martinez resigned as HUD Secretary and announced he was running for the Senate. He quickly raised sufficient money to make himself competitive.

Both parties' primaries proved fractious. McCollum attacked Martinez as a trial lawyer and as a "failed" HUD secretary. To the first charge Martinez replied, "I'm proud of what I did as a lawyer helping people, fighting big insurance companies. There is nothing in my life I would run away from." Martinez ran a nine-minute spot showing him as a teenager in a refugee camp, old home movie footage and a statement by George W. Bush: "The American dream is alive and well, and Mel Martinez represents it all." Doug Gallagher spent $6.3 million on ads calling his opponents "the M&M boys" and citing his accomplishments in business and diabetes research. In the week before the August 31 primary, Martinez ads attacked McCollum as "anti-family" because of his support of embryonic stem cell research and said he was appeasing "the radical homosexual lobby" because of his support of a hate crimes bill. In a debate McCollum called the ads "despicable" and said Martinez was "unfit" to serve; Governor Jeb Bush phoned Martinez on the subject, and Martinez pulled the ads over the weekend. Polls had consistently showed Martinez ahead, with many undecided. But Martinez won big, with 45% of the vote, to 31% for McCollum and 14% for Gallagher. Martinez won 79% in Miami-Dade County, where Cuban-Americans make up a large share of registered Republicans; he beat McCollum 59%–18% in the Gold Coast but also by 40%–37% in the I-4 corridor (both candidates' home turf), and 41%–32% in the rest of the state. McCollum declined to endorse Martinez until 13 days after the primary. But two days after the primary, Martinez went to New York and spoke in prime time to the Republican National Convention. "Only in America can a 15-year-old boy arrive on our shores alone, not speaking the language—with a suitcase and the hope of a brighter future—and rise to serve in the Cabinet of the president of the United States. And only in America can that same young boy today stand one step away from making history as the first Cuban-American to serve in the United States Senate."

The Democratic primary was just as fractious. Deutsch, an aggressive spokesman for Al Gore during the 2000 Florida controversy, attacked Penelas for not supporting Gore vigorously enough. In ads he attacked Castor for not taking enough action against Sami al-Arian, a professor at the University of South Florida, who was indicted on terrorism charges in 2003. Castor argued that she had put al-Arian on paid leave in 1996 but, after no charges were brought against him, allowed him to be reinstated. Castor avoided attacks on her primary opponents and, on her specialty issue, attacked the 2002 education act as fundamentally flawed; she said little about abortion. Public polls showed Castor leading throughout the race. Statewide Castor won with 58% of the vote to 28% for Deutsch and 10% for Penelas; Deutsch carried the Gold Coast, but by only 47%–36%, while Castor led in the I-4 Corridor 70%–18% and in the rest of the state 66%–22%.

Throughout September and October public polls showed the race a dead heat. There was plenty of contrast between the candidates on issues—the Iraq war, abortion, stem-cell research, Cuba, tax cuts, Social Security, education. Both sides spent plenty of money—Martinez $12.8 million, Castor $11.4 million. But it was a hard environment in which to get messages through: Florida airwaves were filled with ads by the presidential candidates and 527 organizations and by backers and opponents of a medical malpractice ballot measure, and local newscasts in late August and most of September were dominated by the four hurricanes that swept through the state. The Senate candidates differed on hurricane relief: Martinez called for tax-exempt development bonds for the areas worst hit and for zero interest loans to help damaged businesses; Castor called for incentives for insurance companies to open their disaster relief funds and for FEMA to pay insurance deductibles for afflicted homeowners. Martinez accused Castor of going soft on the "terrorist cell" in the University of South Florida and ran an ad featuring a retired INS agent criticizing Castor. Castor said Martinez's ads were "despicable" and said she was the only one who had taken any action against al-Arian. She ignored John Kerry and featured Bob Graham; she depicted herself as independent and Martinez as a rubber stamp for George W.

Bush. The Human Rights Campaign ran an ad, aimed at Martinez's opposition to hate crimes legislation, featuring pictures recalling the murders of James Byrd in Texas and Matthew Shepard in Wyoming. In the final days Castor ran ads charging Martinez with ethical improprieties at HUD. Both also ran positive ads—Martinez more bio spots on his rise from Cuba and the refugee camp, Castor on her work on education. In their second debate, Castor said she would not have supported the Iraq war resolution knowing what she did now and Martinez said he would.

On election night, the returns showed a very close race, and Castor claimed a recount would be needed. But when more complete returns came in the next morning, she conceded. Martinez won by less than 100,000 votes, 49%–48%; Castor led 57%–41% in the Gold Coast, and the I-4 corridor produced a 49%–49% tie; Martinez won 56%–42% in the rest of the state. Martinez ran ahead of Bush among Cuban-Americans. Some were unhappy with the Bush administration's limits on trips that could be made and remittances that could be sent to Cuba, measures supported by Martinez; but the prospect of a Cuban-American senator proved attractive even to some Cubans who voted for John Kerry. Martinez carried Latino voters 60%–39%, better than Bush's 56%–43%; he carried Miami-Dade County 49.2%–49.0% while Bush lost it 53%–47%. Martinez ran 1% behind Bush in the rest of the Gold Coast, 4% behind in the I-4 corridor and 3% behind in the rest of the state—but it was enough to win.

So Martinez joined Democrat Bill Nelson in the Senate. Nelson was no stranger to him: as far back as 1978, Martinez had campaigned for Nelson in his first race for the House. He got seats on the Foreign Relations, Banking and Energy committees. Martinez promised to work on local issues—getting a veterans hospital for Orlando, the nation's largest metropolitan area without one; alleviating traffic in central Florida—and he said that, as a former trial lawyer and a Republican, he would try to be an "honest broker" on medical malpractice. "I know that there's a need for people to be helped when they have a serious problem but I also know there are tremendous abuses in the system." He flew to the Middle East to monitor the Palestinian elections in January 2005 and in his maiden speech in February 2005 he defended Attorney General Alberto Gonzalez. He took a lead role in March 2005 on the bill seeking federal judicial review in the case of Terri Schiavo but was embarrassed after he unknowingly handed to Democrat Tom Harkin a memo, drafted by one of his staffers, that made mention of the political advantages presented by the case.

FIRST DISTRICT

Rep. Jeff Miller (R)

Elected Oct. 2001, 2d full term; b. June 27, 1959, St. Petersburg; home, Chumuckla; U. of FL, B.A. 1984; Methodist; married (Vicki).

Elected Office: FL House of Reps., 1998–2001.

Professional Career: Real estate broker, Henry Co. homes; Owner, Jeff Miller Real Estate; deputy sheriff.

DC Office: 324 CHOB, 20515, 202-225-4136; Fax: 202-225-3414; Web site: jeffmiller.house.gov.

District Offices: Ft. Walton Beach, 850-664-1266; Pensacola, 850-479-1183.

Committees: *Armed Services* (20th of 34 R): Readiness; Terrorism, Unconventional Threats & Capabilities. *Veterans' Affairs* (9th of 16 R): Disability Assistance & Memorial Affairs (Chmn.); Health.

Group Ratings

	ADA	ACLU	AFS	LCV	ITIC	NTU	COC	ACU	NTLC	CHC
2004	5	0	13	0	90	82	100	100	100	100
2003	15	—	13	10	—	84	83	96	—	—

National Journal Ratings

	2003 LIB	—	2003 CONS		2004 LIB	—	2004 CONS
Economic	37%	—	62%		0%	—	95%
Social	24%	—	71%		0%	—	91%
Foreign	11%	—	80%		8%	—	91%

Key Votes of the 108th Congress

1. Drilling in ANWR	Y	5. DC School Vouchers	Y	9. Ban Same-Sex Marriage	Y
2. Approve Bush Tax Cuts	Y	6. Ban Human Cloning	Y	10. Fund Iraq War	Y
3. Medicare/Rx Bill	N	7. Restrict Gun Liability	Y	11. Bar Cuba Embargo Funds	*
4. Bar Overtime Pay Regs.	N	8. Ban Partial-Birth Abortion	Y	12. Intelligence Reorg.	Y

Election Results

2004 general	Jeff Miller (R)	236,604	(77%)	($279,318)
	Mark Coutu (D)	72,506	(23%)	($33,000)
2004 primary	Jeff Miller (R)	unopposed		
2002 general	Jeff Miller (R)	152,635	(75%)	($956,353)
	Bert Oram (D)	51,972	(25%)	($13,951)

Prior Winning Percentages: 2001 (66%)

The People		Race/Ethnic Origin	Ancestry	
Area size:	5,241 sq. mi.	78.0% White	USA: 10.7%	German: 8.8%
Urban population:	77.5%	14.0% Black	Irish: 8.5%	
Rural population:	22.5%	1.9% Asian	**2004 Presidential Vote**	
Pop. 2000:	639,295	0.9% Native Am.	Bush (R) 231,199	(72%)
Median income:	$36,738	0.1% Hawaiian	Kerry (D) 88,686	(28%)
Poverty status:	13.1%	2.0% Two+ races	Other 2,135	(1%)
Military veterans:	21.7%	0.2% Other	**2000 Presidential Vote**	
		3.0% Hispanic Origin	Bush (R) 173,896	(69%)
			Gore (D) 78,469	(31%)
			Cook Partisan Voting Index: R +19	
Occupation	Blue collar: 24.4%	White collar: 57.1%	Gray collar: 18.6%	

The "Redneck Riviera" is the affectionate local name for the Gulf Coast beaches of Florida's Panhandle, stretching from Pensacola east to Destin. This has been military country ever since John Quincy Adams persuaded Spain to sell Florida to the U.S. in 1819 to get the port of Pensacola. In October 1861, the Union defeated the Confederates in a battle to control Santa Rosa Island, the outermost spit of land protecting Pensacola Bay. A quarter century later, the site of that clash, Fort Pickens, became Apache warrior Geronimo's prison. In the 20th century, the Pensacola Naval Air Station was turned into the nation's first naval aviation training base, giving birth to carrier aviation. Today, about 20,000 people are employed at Eglin Air Force Base, which spreads over three counties and, with approximately 100,000 square miles of airspace stretching over the Gulf of Mexico to the Florida Keys, is considered the largest air base in the free world. Eglin developed the BLU-82 "Daisy Cutter" bomb that was used in Afghanistan, and this was the test site for the largest conventional bomb in the U.S. arsenal, the 21,000-pound ordnance referred to as the "Mother of All Bombs."

The western panhandle of Florida, closer to Memphis than to Miami, is culturally part of Dixie. Until recently, it was economically backward and heavily dependent on the military. As the South has become more prosperous, however, the shore has attracted vacationing and retiring Southerners to its vast, fine-grained white sand beaches, perhaps the finest in the Lower 48, and its pleasant inlet-filled bays; it also has become a leading spring break destination for college students. The region has long been culturally and economically conservative, with a strong pro-military bent.

The 1st Congressional District of Florida is so far west that it's in the Central time zone. Pensacola's Escambia County, where about half the district's people live, is the state's westernmost county. The time zone issue became a sore point in 2000, when TV networks announced that Florida's polls had closed at 7 p.m. Eastern time, though they were still open in the Panhandle, and then declared Al Gore the winner of Florida's electoral votes 10 minutes before the Panhandle's polls had closed; without that misinformation, a few thousand votes might have been cast for George W. Bush here and made the whole Florida controversy unnecessary. The district's shoreline runs from Pensacola, adjoining the Alabama border, through Fort Walton Beach and all the way to the west side of Destin; from there, a string of more affluent beach towns is in the 2d District. Inland, the 1st stretches further east, taking in rural Walton, Holmes and Washington Counties. The population here has grown steadily, with young civilians, not just military retirees, moving in and shifting attention towards education and quality-of-life issues. In 2004, four massive hurricanes roared through the region, with devastating effect: in Pensacola alone, 45,000 homes were deemed unlivable.

With the most military veterans of any district in the nation, the 1st District is strongly Republican. It voted 69%–31% for George W. Bush in 2000 and 72%–28% in 2004. In April 2004, a columnist for the *Pensacola News Journal* wrote that it was time to consider creation of a separate state, or independent commonwealth, of West Florida. "We don't have much in common with the people inhabiting what I call peninsular Florida," wrote Jerry Maygarden. "I'm convinced that the further south you drive, the further north you get."

The congressman from the 1st District is Jeff Miller, a Republican who won a special election in October 2001. The son of a pioneering farm family that settled in central Florida in the mid-1800s, Miller grew up in Levy County, where his parents raised cattle. He graduated from the University of Florida and became an aide to the state's long-time agriculture commissioner, Democrat Doyle Conner. In 1998 he moved to Santa Rosa County, his wife's family's home, and began to sell real estate. Also in 1998, a year after he switched to the Republican Party, he ran his first campaign, challenging a Republican incumbent state representative who had received some negative press after an altercation with a state trooper. Miller won 53%–47% out of only 6,000 votes cast (a lot of people here still are registered Democrats though they almost always vote Republican).

The 1st District House seat came open when incumbent Joe Scarborough, one of the most outspoken members of the Republican Class of 1994 and now a talk show host on MSNBC, announced in May 2001 that he would resign in September. Miller quickly became the favorite of national party leaders. Sensitive to coastal interests, the candidates claimed to be ardent environmentalists, an unusual twist in a Republican primary. Miller's best-known opponent was state Representative Randy Knepper, chief of staff to the district's former Democratic Congressman Earl Hutto, who retired in 1994. On the weekend before the July 24 primary, Scarborough endorsed Miller as "a strong voice for northwest Florida." In the six-candidate contest, Miller got 54% to only 15% for Knepper, just behind the 16% for businessman Michael Francisco, a decorated combat pilot. National Democrats made no perceptible effort to win this seat that they held less than seven years earlier, and Miller won the October general election by 66%–28% over a former Republican.

In the House, Miller has compiled a conservative record. In contrast to the vocal Scarborough, he gained a reputation for being soft-spoken and a good listener. He won seats on the Armed Services and Veterans' Affairs committees, obvious assignments for this district. He made multiple visits to U.S. troops in Afghanistan and Iraq and praised the conduct of the war; he accompanied Bush cabinet officials to visit military and veterans' facilities in northwest Florida. Like other local officials, he was optimistic that the area's bases would survive the base-closing review; his optimism proved well-founded when none of the four installations in Escambia and Santa Rosa Counties appeared on the Pentagon's list of recommended base closures in May 2005. In 2004, when Democrats were seeking to force a House vote on Miller's bill to provide a 100% annuity to surviving military spouses, he convinced Republican leaders to call up the bill and avoid a partisan conflict; the measure was passed into law. Miller was more independent when he voted against the Medicare/prescription drug bill. He joined Senator Bill Nelson in seeking a review by the Environmental Protection Agency of a 1994 decision that allowed toxic chemicals to collect in the aquifer that supplies drinking water to Pensacola, and he continued to oppose oil and gas drilling in the eastern Gulf of Mexico. He sponsored a bill to place the face of Ronald Reagan on the half-dollar coin. With a group of former federal officials, Miller called for denying pensions to members of Congress who have been expelled from office.

In the 2002 primary, Miller faced a rematch with special election primary runner-up Francisco, who criticized his lack of military experience. Miller won 64%–36%. Democrats have run token challengers against him.

SECOND DISTRICT

Rep. Allen Boyd (D)

Elected 1996, 5th term; b. June 6, 1945, Valdosta, GA; home, Monticello; N. FL Jr. Col., A.A. 1966, FL St. U., B.S. 1969; Methodist; married (Cissy).

Military Career: Army 1969–71 (Vietnam).

Elected Office: FL House of Reps., 1989–96.

Professional Career: Farmer.

DC Office: 1227 LHOB, 20515, 202-225-5235; Fax: 202-225-5615; Web site: www.house.gov/boyd.

District Offices: Panama City, 850-785-0812; Tallahassee, 850-561-3979.

Committees: *Appropriations* (25th of 29 D): Agriculture, Rural Development, FDA & Related Agencies; Military Quality of Life & Veterans Affairs & Related Agencies.

Group Ratings

	ADA	ACLU	AFS	LCV	ITIC	NTU	COC	ACU	NTLC	CHC
2004	70	35	88	45	90	23	75	46	23	50
2003	70	—	86	60	—	30	71	42	—	—

National Journal Ratings

	2003 LIB	—	2003 CONS	2004 LIB	—	2004 CONS
Economic	57%	—	43%	53%	—	47%
Social	59%	—	40%	52%	—	48%
Foreign	59%	—	41%	44%	—	56%

Key Votes of the 108th Congress

1. Drilling in ANWR	Y	5. DC School Vouchers	N	9. Ban Same-Sex Marriage	Y
2. Approve Bush Tax Cuts	N	6. Ban Human Cloning	*	10. Fund Iraq War	Y
3. Medicare/Rx Bill	Y	7. Restrict Gun Liability	*	11. Bar Cuba Embargo Funds	N
4. Bar Overtime Pay Regs.	Y	8. Ban Partial-Birth Abortion	Y	12. Intelligence Reorg.	Y

Election Results

2004 general	Allen Boyd (D)	201,577	(62%)	($2,064,646)
	Bev Kilmer (R)	125,399	(38%)	($1,132,998)
2004 primary	Allen Boyd (D)	unopposed		
2002 general	Allen Boyd (D)	152,164	(67%)	($588,785)
	Tom McGurk (R)	75,275	(33%)	($35,916)

Prior Winning Percentages: 2000 (72%); 1998 (100%); 1996 (59%)

The People		Race/Ethnic Origin	Ancestry	
Area size:	11,141 sq. mi.	71.5% White	USA: 10.3%	English: 8.0%
Urban population:	62.1%	22.1% Black	Irish: 7.9%	
Rural population:	37.9%	1.2% Asian	**2004 Presidential Vote**	
Pop. 2000:	639,295	0.5% Native Am.	Bush (R) 181,300	(54%)
Median income:	$34,718	0.0% Hawaiian	Kerry (D) 153,164	(46%)
Poverty status:	16.5%	1.3% Two+ races	Other 1,346	(0%)
Military veterans:	15.3%	0.1% Other	**2000 Presidential Vote**	
		3.3% Hispanic Origin	Bush (R) 132,275	(53%)
			Gore (D) 118,758	(47%)
			Cook Partisan Voting Index: R + 2	

Occupation	Blue collar: 19.3%	White collar: 61.7%	Gray collar: 19.1%

For most of the 36 days from November 7 to December 12, 2000, Tallahassee was the center of the political universe. Many wondered why this small city, in the middle of swampy lowlands and far from Florida's booming cities and beachfronts, should be the capital of the nation's fourth-largest state. The answer is that it was chosen back when Florida's modest population lived mostly along the state's northern tier, placing Tallahassee, more or less, at the state's center of gravity. Ralph Waldo Emerson, visiting Tallahassee in the 19th century, called it a "grotesque place, rapidly settled by public officers, land speculators and desperadoes." Today the countryside around Tallahassee is distinctly Dixie: Cotton fields, soft pine stands, catfish farms, large families, small towns with big churches. Until recently, Tallahassee was little more than a Spanish-mossed county seat with a handsome Creole capitol, built in 1845 and preserved opposite its 1977 skyscraper replacement, and a pair of state universities. Since the 1980s, however, Tallahassee has spread out and become a middling-sized city, with a tight-knit and sometimes fractious political and legal elite, bringing a taste of newly urbanized Florida to the state's north. Tallahassee has not yet attained the critical mass of Sacramento, Austin, or Albany, but perhaps it is on its way as the state legislature inches closer to professional status.

The 2d Congressional District of Florida is centered on Tallahassee, and extends along the Gulf coast west to Destin and east to the Suwanee River, which empties into the Gulf in the only part of Florida where the beach is still undeveloped. In Gulf County, the pristine bay and large dunes of Port St. Joe have been described as the nation's best beach. Inland, the 2d runs north to the Alabama and Georgia borders, and far enough east to be within an hour's drive of Jacksonville. Historically, this was Democratic country, Jeffersonian and segregationist. Today, it is still mostly Democratic, though for different reasons: More than one in three Tallahassee area jobs are in city and state government, three times the statewide level. The district, 22% black, includes Gadsden County, the state's only black-majority county. Growth is spreading south into Wakulla County, which grew 91% from 1990 to 2004, more than all but three others in Florida. There is similar growth along the beach areas near Destin which have attracted affluent families to "new urbanist" communities like Seaside and Rosemary Beach. But for all this recent growth, this is the part of Florida with the highest percentage of native Floridians.

With state government, two universities and many public employee union members, Tallahassee and Leon County have voted solidly for Democratic presidential nominees; the Florida law that establishes Leon County as the venue for election cases clearly favors Democrats. Beyond Leon County, which casts nearly 40% of the district's votes, partisan performance is less predictable. Gadsden County is heavily Democratic; the Gulf beach areas tend to be Republican. The 2d District has voted twice for George W. Bush, but in 2002 it gave a hefty margin to Democrat Bill McBride over Governor Jeb Bush, who is disliked by most public employee unions.

The congressman from the 2d District is Allen Boyd, a Democrat first elected in 1996. A lifelong farmer, Boyd grew up in Monticello in Jefferson County just east of Tallahassee. He served in Vietnam and graduated from Florida State. His political career began when he won a special election to the state House in 1989. Boyd decided to run for the House in 1996 when Pete Peterson, a moderate Democrat and Vietnam prisoner-of-war, retired after three terms, saying he believed in term limits. In a high-turnout Democratic primary, Boyd won 48% of the vote to 26% for Leon County Commissioner Anita Davis. Boyd easily won the runoff 64%–36%. In the general, Boyd campaigned with Blue Dog conservative Democrats and outspent the Republican by 2–1 to win a solid 59%–40% victory.

In the House, Boyd has worked as a behind the scenes consensus builder. With one of the House's most centrist voting records, he called himself a "moderate Democrat with a social conscience." He was unperturbed when animal rights advocates picketed the Annual Boyd Family Dove Hunt, and was the only Florida Democrat to vote for an amendment that helped kill the 1999 gun control bill. He opposed George W. Bush's 2001 tax cut but voted to repeal the Clinton administration's ergonomics regulation. Later, he opposed trade promotion authority, but he voted to authorize the use of force in Iraq, though he said that he wanted Bush to get a United Nations resolution before launching the invasion. In 2003 he was one of 16 House Democrats who voted for the Medicare/prescription drug bill; Minority Leader Nancy Pelosi voiced her unhappiness to Boyd. With Republican John Peterson of Pennsylvania, Boyd chairs the Rural Caucus. As a member of the Appropriations Committee, he has delivered largess to local universities, farmers and military facilities.

In December 2004, Boyd attracted attention and created some heartburn among Democrats when he replaced Charlie Stenholm in co-sponsoring with Republican Jim Kolbe on a bipartisan Social Security package including personal retirement accounts and lower benefits; he said that he would seek additional Democratic supporters, but he was slow to find them in the House. His goal, he said, was "a fair balance between preserving the basic benefit of Social Security while also encouraging individual responsibility." In February 2005, Moveon.org ran television ads in Boyd's district criticizing Bush's proposals.

Boyd has been easily reelected. In 2002, despite unfavorable redistricting changes, Boyd won 67%–33%. In early 2003, after Senator Bob Graham launched a presidential campaign, Boyd made moves to run for the Senate, all the while saying that he would not run if Graham sought reelection. By July Boyd had raised significant money and had a team of consultants in place. In early October Graham ended his presidential candidacy, but did not say whether he would run for reelection; later in the month Boyd announced he would not run for the Senate. In November Graham announced he was retiring.

In 2004, Boyd was challenged by state Representative Bev Kilmer, a former Democrat and an author of books about business and management. She raised substantial funds with prominent campaign supporters, including Laura Bush and Speaker Dennis Hastert. She said she would support George W. Bush's agenda on defense, terrorism, health care and the economy. Boyd countered that he sometimes supported Bush, but said that voters wanted somebody who would be independent and represent their interests. He won handily, 62%–38%, despite losing big in the two western counties along the beach and running even in Panama City's Bay County; he won 71% of the vote in Leon County. Boyd kept his distance from the presidential race—a wise move since Bush twice carried the 2d District. After the 2004 election, he hosted a closed-door meeting at his farm in which state party leaders and likely statewide candidates in 2006 reviewed the party's recent plight and their options going forward.

THIRD DISTRICT

Rep. Corrine Brown (D)

Elected 1992, 7th term; b. Nov. 11, 1946, Jacksonville; home, Jacksonville; FL A&M, B.S. 1969, M.S., 1971; Baptist; single.

Elected Office: FL House of Reps., 1982–92.

Professional Career: Prof., FL Commun. Col., 1977–82, Guidance Counselor, 1982–92.

DC Office: 2444 RHOB, 20515, 202-225-0123; Fax: 202-225-2256; Web site: www.house.gov/corrinebrown.

District Offices: Jacksonville, 904-354-1652; Orlando, 407-872-0656.

Committees: *Transportation & Infrastructure* (8th of 34 D): Aviation; Coast Guard & Maritime Transportation; Railroads (RMM). *Veterans' Affairs* (4th of 12 D): Health.

Group Ratings

	ADA	ACLU	AFS	LCV	ITIC	NTU	COC	ACU	NTLC	CHC
2004	90	67	100	100	40	11	37	8	0	25
2003	95	—	100	90	—	22	33	17	—	—

National Journal Ratings

	2003 LIB	—	2003 CONS		2004 LIB	—	2004 CONS
Economic	79%	—	20%		78%	—	21%
Social	71%	—	29%		72%	—	28%
Foreign	88%	—	11%		72%	—	27%

Key Votes of the 108th Congress

1. Drilling in ANWR	N	5. DC School Vouchers	N	9. Ban Same-Sex Marriage	*
2. Approve Bush Tax Cuts	N	6. Ban Human Cloning	*	10. Fund Iraq War	N
3. Medicare/Rx Bill	N	7. Restrict Gun Liability	Y	11. Bar Cuba Embargo Funds	N
4. Bar Overtime Pay Regs.	Y	8. Ban Partial-Birth Abortion	N	12. Intelligence Reorg.	Y

Election Results

2004 general	Corrine Brown (D) .... unopposed			($13,932)
2004 primary	Corrine Brown (D)	46,285	(81%)	
	Prince Brown (D)	10,639	(19%)	
2002 general	Corrine Brown (D)	88,462	(59%)	($438,810)
	Jennifer Carroll (R)	60,747	(41%)	($229,103)

Prior Winning Percentages: 2000 (58%); 1998 (55%); 1996 (61%); 1994 (58%); 1992 (59%)

The People		Race/Ethnic Origin	Ancestry	
Area size:	2,097 sq. mi.	38.4% White	USA: 6.4%	German: 5.2%
Urban population:	89.7%	49.3% Black	Irish: 4.9%	
Rural population:	10.3%	1.6% Asian	**2004 Presidential Vote**	
Pop. 2000:	639,295	0.3% Native Am.	Kerry (D) 151,466	(65%)
Median income:	$29,785	0.0% Hawaiian	Bush (R) 81,778	(35%)
Poverty status:	21.5%	2.1% Two+ races	Other 42	(0%)
Military veterans:	14.2%	0.2% Other	**2000 Presidential Vote**	
		8.0% Hispanic Origin	Gore (D) 110,501	(65%)
			Bush (R) 59,144	(35%)
			Cook Partisan Voting Index: D +16	

Occupation	Blue collar: 26.6%	White collar: 51.8%	Gray collar: 21.6%

Before the Civil War, most of Florida was still an uncharted watery wilderness, festooned with exotic greenery, inhabited by unusual animals: a part of the United States so far out of the experience of most Americans as to seem foreign. As late as 1940, Florida had the smallest population of any southern state, and most of the people here lived in classic Dixie rural counties with small courthouse towns, where civic affairs were run by the richest white men; blacks lived in poorly constructed, unpainted shotgun shacks propped up on blocks, with little money and no vote. This was a land of swamps, lakes and orange groves, of Marjorie Kinnan Rawlings's Cross Creek, where she wrote the great children's classic *The Yearling*, and the Florida of the broad St. Johns River, one of the few North American rivers that flows (if only sluggishly) north, through orange grove country to the port of Jacksonville, which was for many years Florida's largest city.

The 3d Congressional District of Florida occupies much of this swampy terrain. The district was created in 1992 to be north Florida's black majority seat, and has had three sets of boundaries. The district borders five Republican-held districts, each of which was designed to shift as many Democrats as possible to the 3d to strengthen Republicans elsewhere. In its current form it follows the St. Johns River upstream from center city Jacksonville to downtown Orlando, reaching out to pluck additional minority and Democratic voters from Sanford, where Amtrak's Auto Train unloads its Florida-bound travelers, and Gainesville, home of the University of Florida. Along the way, the district takes in smaller black settlements, such as lettuce-producing Zellwood, and Eatonville, home of author Zora Neale Hurston. In time, this relatively unpopulated, lake-filled region may see itself become Florida's next development frontier but for now, the 3d District is growing more slowly than the rest of the state. The district is 49% black—the third-highest of any Florida district—and 8% Hispanic. It is solidly Democratic.

The congresswoman from the 3d District is Corrine Brown, a Democrat first elected in 1992. She grew up in Jacksonville, taught at the community college, was a guidance counselor and in 1982 was elected to the Florida House. With her Jacksonville base, she was the clear favorite in 1992. In the Democratic primary, she faced white talk radio host Andy Johnson, who called himself "the blackest candidate in the race." Brown led 43%–31% in the primary and won 64%–36% in the runoff; she won the general 59%–41%.

Brown has compiled a liberal record on most issues. In this district where many voters work at military bases she tends to support high defense spending; she argues that the military can be a source of opportunity. On the Veterans Committee she sought additional veterans cemeteries for Florida, which is the home to more veterans than any other state except California; new cemeteries were approved for Jacksonville and Sarasota in 2003. On the Transportation and Infrastructure Subcommittee, she was active on legislation to strengthen security at the ports. She called for increased security for passenger and freight rail.

Brown has had spirited campaign opposition, which is unusual for Florida incumbents. Her most difficult contest came in 1998, with her problems largely of her own making. That April the *St. Petersburg Times* reported that she received $10,000 from Baptist minister Henry Lyons, who had since been indicted on theft charges; she said the money was for his help in a rally. In June the same paper reported that her daughter, attorney and EPA employee Shantrel Brown, was given a $50,000 Lexus by agents of African millionaire Foutanga Sissoko; he had been imprisoned in Miami on federal charges of paying an illegal gratuity to a Customs Service officer, and Brown worked furiously to get him released, lobbying Attorney General Janet Reno to have him deported to Africa to continue his humanitarian work. A third charge was that she kept a jazz singer on her payroll as a "congressional outreach specialist," who occasionally visited the district from her New York City home. Brown reacted with fury: she filed a criminal contempt charge against the *Times* reporters with the Capitol Police, claiming they "accosted" her and their questions made her cry. A federal prosecutor said there was not enough to indict them for impeding a member of Congress. These charges attracted national Republican attention. They had a presentable candidate: Bill Randall, also black, a former General Motors manager who had become a minister; he opposed abortion, favored local control of schools and school vouchers. The charges hurt Brown: she won by only 55%–45%.

But the ramifications were not finished. The Congressional Accountability Project requested that the House ethics committee investigate the $10,000 contribution and the Lexus gift; her daughter later sold the car and gave the proceeds to charity. In September 2000 the committee concluded that Brown "demonstrated, at the least, poor judgment and created substantial concerns regarding both the appearance of impropriety and the reputation of the House," but dropped the case because it was unable to question key witnesses, including Sissoko. She faced a vigorous reelection challenge from Republican Jennifer Carroll, a retired Navy officer with 20 years of service, who criticized Brown for lack of vision and an inability to work with people. Brown, who called Carroll "a zero" and "a Republican puppet," was outspent by Carroll, who is also black. But Brown had help from an October campaign rally with Bill Clinton and a strong grass-roots organization. Brown won 58%–42%. During the presidential recount, Brown was insistent that voting irregularities discriminated against black voters. In 2002 Carroll again challenged Brown. But local Republicans were not enthusiastic about Carroll's candidacy in this heavily Democratic district. "I would rather not give Corrine Brown an excuse to go through another massive voter turnout exercise, in which she is very talented," Duval County Republican chairman Tom Slade told the *Jacksonville Free Press*. Brown won 59%–41%, again with huge leads in the Jacksonville and Orlando. Brown was unopposed in 2004.

In that year's presidential election, she repeated her criticism of the 2000 presidential campaign recount and rallied Democrats with warnings that "Jeb Bush and his people are willing to do anything to deliver this state to the Republicans." Her outspoken partisan views got her in trouble in the House. In February 2004, she criticized a briefing on the Haiti crisis by saying that administration representatives were "a bunch of white men," and reportedly said, "you all look alike to me." After Republican Henry Bonilla said that she should resign, Brown apologized, but she continued to call the Haiti policy racist. In July, under parliamentary pressure, she rescinded her comment to the House that Republicans "stole the election" in 2000.

Barring unexpected problems, she appears secure until the next redistricting.

FOURTH DISTRICT

Rep. Ander Crenshaw (R)

Elected 2000, 3d term; b. Sept. 1, 1944, Jacksonville; home, Jacksonville; U. of GA, B.A. 1966, U. of FL, J.D. 1969; Episcopalian; married (Kitty).

Elected Office: FL House of Reps., 1972–78; FL Senate 1986–93.

Professional Career: Investment banker, 1980–2000.

DC Office: 127 CHOB, 20515, 202-225-2501; Fax: 202-225-2504; Web site: crenshaw.house.gov.

District Offices: Jacksonville, 904-598-0481; Lake City, 386-365-3316.

Committees: *Appropriations* (34th of 37 R): Foreign Operations, Export Financing & Related Programs; Homeland Security; Military Quality of Life & Veterans Affairs & Related Agencies. *Budget* (3d of 22 R).

Group Ratings

	ADA	ACLU	AFS	LCV	ITIC	NTU	COC	ACU	NTLC	CHC
2004	0	0	13	9	90	50	100	92	77	84
2003	5	—	0	5	—	60	97	92	—	—

National Journal Ratings

	2003 LIB	—	2003 CONS		2004 LIB	—	2004 CONS
Economic	9%	—	84%		17%	—	80%
Social	21%	—	78%		17%	—	81%
Foreign	0%	—	89%		10%	—	86%

Key Votes of the 108th Congress

1. Drilling in ANWR	Y	5. DC School Vouchers	Y	9. Ban Same-Sex Marriage	Y
2. Approve Bush Tax Cuts	Y	6. Ban Human Cloning	Y	10. Fund Iraq War	Y
3. Medicare/Rx Bill	Y	7. Restrict Gun Liability	Y	11. Bar Cuba Embargo Funds	N
4. Bar Overtime Pay Regs.	N	8. Ban Partial-Birth Abortion	Y	12. Intelligence Reorg.	Y

Election Results

2004 general	Ander Crenshaw (R) .... unopposed		($279,540)
2004 primary	Ander Crenshaw (R) 48,129	(90%)	
	Deborah Katz Pueschel (R) 5,368	(10%)	
2002 general	Ander Crenshaw (R) .... unopposed		($311,183)

Prior Winning Percentages: 2000 (67%)

The People

		Race/Ethnic Origin	Ancestry	
Area size:	4,368 sq. mi.	77.8% White	USA: 9.7%	German: 9.0%
Urban population:	78.2%	13.5% Black	Irish: 8.7%	
Rural population:	21.8%	2.4% Asian	**2004 Presidential Vote**	
Pop. 2000:	639,295	0.3% Native Am.	Bush (R) 227,431	(69%)
Median income:	$43,947	0.1% Hawaiian	Kerry (D) 100,414	(31%)
Poverty status:	9.1%	1.5% Two+ races	Other 744	(0%)
Military veterans:	17.1%	0.1% Other	**2000 Presidential Vote**	
		4.2% Hispanic Origin	Bush (R) 154,615	(66%)
			Gore (D) 80,227	(34%)
			Cook Partisan Voting Index: R +16	

Occupation   Blue collar: 20.6%   White collar: 64.8%   Gray collar: 14.7%

With a metropolitan area of 1.2 million people, Jacksonville is beginning to overcome its reputation as Florida's overlooked city. Not long ago, Jacksonville was considered a backwater, dominated by insurance and smelly paper mills. It now boasts a National Football League franchise, the Jaguars; bold new skyscrapers looming above a wide river; and a shopping mall that overshadows gridded streets and tiny shotgun houses. The city received favorable reviews when it hosted the 2005 Super Bowl, even though it has far fewer hotel rooms than the usual sites; to meet the demands for lodging, cruise ships docked in the harbor, which has grown as a destination for cargo and passenger operations. The wide freeways sidestep primeval wetlands on their way to huge beachfront subdivisions. With the Mayport Naval Station and the Naval Air Station, Jacksonville has a significant military employment base (they are two of the top three metro area employers). Shrewd marketing has lured big-name private sector companies; Jacksonville has the headquarters of Winn-Dixie supermarkets and railway giant CSX and has big operations of Publix supermarkets, UPS and Bank of America. The metro area grew 33% from 1990 to 2004.

The 4th Congressional District of Florida includes much of Jacksonville (minus the mostly black neighborhoods, which are in the 3d District) as well as a northern tier of counties along the Georgia border that runs all the way west to Tallahassee. This northern tier is sleepy territory punctuated by small towns like White Springs, Lake City, and Raiford (home to a big state prison); it is criss-crossed by Interstates 10 and 75. Some 70% of the population is in Jacksonville and Nassau County, just to the north. The boosterish Jacksonville civic culture and significant military presence make the 4th a pro-business, pro-military and pro-Republican district. George W. Bush won 66% of the vote here in 2000 and 69% in 2004, both his second highest percentages in any Florida district.

The congressman from the 4th District is Ander Crenshaw, a Republican first elected in 2000. He grew up in Jacksonville and attended the University of Georgia on a basketball scholarship, then graduated from the University of Florida law school. His wife's father, Claude Kirk, was elected governor, the first Republican since Reconstruction, in 1966, then defeated in 1970. Crenshaw was elected to the state House in 1972 and served for six years until he ran unsuccessfully for secretary of state; he then became an investment banker. In 1980 he ran for the Senate and finished third of six in the 1980 Republican primary won by Paula Hawkins. From 1986 until 1993 he served in the state Senate, and in 1992 became the first Republican state Senate president in 118 years. He ran for governor in 1994 but ran fourth in the primary, far behind Jeb Bush, who narrowly lost to Chiles in November. Crenshaw's opportunity to run for the House came in 2000 when Republican Tillie Fowler announced that she would honor her promise to serve only four terms. Crenshaw was promptly endorsed by local Republican leaders, which discouraged several other potential candidates. He won the primary 70%–30% and the general election 67%–31%.

In the House, Crenshaw is a reliable conservative. Although his tall frame makes him hard to miss in a crowd, he has not sought attention. He has cited approvingly the comment by Ronald Reagan: "There's no limit to what you can do as long as you don't care who gets the credit." He displayed his political savvy by becoming freshman class liaison to the Republican leadership, which admitted him to weekly leadership meetings, and he became friends with Majority Leader Tom DeLay and Majority Whip Roy Blunt. In his second term, he won a seat on Appropriations where his top priorities were the district's large military and veterans' facilities. He helped the Pentagon get $115 million for the Marine Corps to buy 1,100 acres on and near Blount Island north of Jacksonville for its maritime prepositioning program. He pushed hard to pass a bill for new veterans' cemeteries in Jacksonville and Sarasota, which George W. Bush signed in November 2003, and he fought for expanded disability coverage for Gulf War veterans. He enacted a bill to add more than 8 acres of sand dunes to the Timucuan Ecological and Historical Preserve north of the Nassau River. In January 2005, he described as "short-sighted, short-term thinking," reports that the *USS John F. Kennedy,* which was scheduled for an overhaul in Mayport, might instead be decommissioned. "Our national security demands at least 12 carriers, if not more." He later discussed his concerns for 30 minutes with Bush. Although the Navy did not formally call for retirement of the carrier, one of only two that is oil-powered, it revealed that it planned to reduce its carriers to 11; in April 2005, the Navy announced it was canceling a $378 million overhaul of the ship. But Crenshaw attached a provision to the 2005 emergency supplemental that would delay plans to decommission the *Kennedy.*

Crenshaw has been reelected twice without general election opposition. He obviously has a safe seat, and in mid-2005 seemed unlikely to run for senator or governor in 2006.

FIFTH DISTRICT

Rep. Ginny Brown-Waite (R)

Elected 2002, 2d term; b. Oct. 5, 1943, Albany, NY; home, Brooksville; S.U.N.Y. Albany, B.S. 1976, Russell Sage Col., M.S. 1984; Catholic; married (Harvey).

Elected Office: Hernando Cnty. Commissioner, 1990–92; FL Senate, 1992–2002.

Professional Career: Small business owner; Legis. Dir., NY Senate, 1972–90.

DC Office: 414 CHOB, 20515, 202-225-1002; Fax: 202-226-6559; Web site: www.house.gov/brown-waite/.

District Offices: Brooksville, 352-799-8354; Dade City, 352-567-6707.

Committees: *Financial Services* (27th of 37 R): Capital Markets, Insurance & Government Sponsored Enterprises; Financial Institutions & Consumer Credit; Housing & Community Opportunity. *Government Reform* (16th of 23 R): Criminal Justice, Drug Policy & Human Resources; Regulatory Affairs (Vice Chmn.). *Veterans' Affairs* (12th of 16 R): Disability Assistance & Memorial Affairs; Economic Opportunity (Vice Chmn.).

Group Ratings

	ADA	ACLU	AFS	LCV	ITIC	NTU	COC	ACU	NTLC	CHC
2004	5	0	0	0	100	68	100	96	86	100
2003	10	—	0	5	—	56	87	88	—	—

National Journal Ratings

	2003 LIB	—	2003 CONS		2004 LIB	—	2004 CONS
Economic	17%	—	81%		33%	—	67%
Social	13%	—	86%		15%	—	84%
Foreign	35%	—	64%		17%	—	78%

Key Votes of the 108th Congress

1. Drilling in ANWR	Y	5. DC School Vouchers	Y	9. Ban Same-Sex Marriage	Y
2. Approve Bush Tax Cuts	Y	6. Ban Human Cloning	Y	10. Fund Iraq War	Y
3. Medicare/Rx Bill	Y	7. Restrict Gun Liability	Y	11. Bar Cuba Embargo Funds	N
4. Bar Overtime Pay Regs.	N	8. Ban Partial-Birth Abortion	Y	12. Intelligence Reorg.	Y

Election Results

2004 general	Ginny Brown-Waite (R)	240,315	(66%)	($787,436)
	Robert Whittel (D)	124,140	(34%)	($140,742)
2004 primary	Ginny Brown-Waite (R)	unopposed		
2002 general	Ginny Brown-Waite (R)	121,998	(48%)	($922,944)
	Karen Thurman (D)	117,758	(46%)	($1,907,181)
	Other	14,915	(6%)	

The People		Race/Ethnic Origin	Ancestry
Area size:	4,801 sq. mi.	87.7% White	German: 13.0% Irish: 10.5%
Urban population:	64.5%	4.5% Black	English: 10.1%
Rural population:	35.5%	0.8% Asian	**2004 Presidential Vote**
Pop. 2000:	639,295	0.3% Native Am.	Bush (R) 221,259 (58%)
Median income:	$34,815	0.0% Hawaiian	Kerry (D) 156,632 (41%)
Poverty status:	10.6%	0.9% Two+ races	Other 1,948 (1%)
Military veterans:	21.5%	0.1% Other	**2000 Presidential Vote**
		5.6% Hispanic Origin	Bush (R) 147,231 (54%)
			Gore (D) 124,982 (46%)
			Cook Partisan Voting Index: R + 5

Occupation	Blue collar: 26.1%	White collar: 55.2%	Gray collar: 18.7%

Over the past quarter century, Florida's urban areas have grown in almost every direction, occupying the high ground between the swamps that still take up much of the state's peninsula. The pattern of development is evident in counties to the north and east of St. Petersburg and

Tampa, where subdivisions, trailer parks and shopping centers with Eckerd drug stores and Publix and Winn-Dixie supermarkets sprang up in what previously were sleepy little towns and farm areas with low brick buildings baking in the Florida sun. This area—a haven for manatees, the unusual and beloved sea mammal—has seen suburban development run up the spines of U.S. 19, just off the Gulf Coast, and U.S. 41 and I-75 inland alongside orange groves. Though there are plenty of working people here, this is mainly retirement country; residents are comfortable though not usually affluent. One of every four residents is over 65, and Citrus and Hernando County have a higher percentage of military veterans than any other Florida county but one; Citrus County has the second-highest percentage of retirees (33%) in the state. Drawn by plenteous lakes, green scenery and a pleasant climate, retirees from Michigan, Indiana and Ohio flocked here by taking Interstate 75 south—a pattern distinct from the retirees who drove Interstate 95 from the Boston-Washington corridor to such destinations as Palm Beach, Fort Lauderdale and Miami.

The 5th Congressional District of Florida occupies much of this fast-growing area. The beach areas in Levy, Citrus and Hernando Counties are largely undeveloped; the bulk of the population lives inland, in such places as Citrus Springs in Citrus County, Brooksville in Hernando County, Zephyrhills and Land o' Lakes in Pasco County, and Clermont in Lake County. More than two-thirds of the population is in Pasco, Hernando and Citrus Counties; Sumter County is growing rapidly in part due to a massive retirement community known as the "Villages," which is split between the 5th and 6th Districts. The district has 251,000 Social Security recipients, more than any other district in the country. Politically, this is marginal territory. The district lines were drawn by Republicans in 2002 to make the district more Republican; they raised the Bush 2000 percentage from 46% to 54%. That percentage went up to 58% in 2004, as volunteers in the Bush campaign registered new Republicans and made sure they voted absentee or on election day. The results are plain from the numbers. In Pasco County turnout was up 31% from 2000 to 2004, and the Bush percentage rose from a losing 48% to a winning 54%.

The congresswoman from the 5th District is Ginny Brown-Waite, a Republican first elected in 2002. She grew up in Albany, New York, and graduated from State University of New York at Albany and from Russell Sage College. She worked for two decades as a Republican staffer for the New York state Senate. She moved to Spring Hill in 1987, worked as a health care consultant and became active in politics. In 1990 she was elected to the Hernando County Commission. In 1992 she was elected to the state Senate, after attracting attention for her successful efforts to block a local mining company's controversial plan to burn hazardous waste. As a member of the Senate congressional redistricting committee, Brown-Waite was well positioned to shape the 5th District boundaries. Republican leaders had asked her to run for the House in 1996, but she didn't think the district was winnable; in 2002, she helped to draw a district that was, and she gave it a try.

In the primary, health care consultant Don Gessner said he was the only "true conservative" and he criticized Brown-Waite's willingness to vote across party lines. His attacks had some resonance, but she won 58%–42%. In the general, she faced Democratic incumbent Karen Thurman, who won the district in 1992 after serving as chairman of the state Senate congressional redistricting committee. This was one of the most competitive contests in the country, targeted by both national parties. Abortion was a key area of disagreement. Both said they supported abortion rights, but Brown-Waite highlighted Thurman's vote against the partial-birth abortion ban as evidence of Thurman's fealty to the Democratic party line. Brown-Waite criticized Thurman for voting against the Republicans' prescription drug bill; Thurman called it a "sham." Thurman outspent Brown-Waite 2-to-1 but Brown-Waite benefited from a late visit by George W. Bush and the strong showing of Governor Jeb Bush, who carried every county in the district. Brown-Waite won 48%–46%. This was an election decided by redistricting: Thurman carried the parts of the district she had previously represented, which cast 49% of the votes, by a 52%–43% margin. But Brown-Waite carried the new parts of the district 53%–41%.

In the House, Brown-Waite had a mostly conservative voting record. On the Budget Committee, she styled herself as a fiscal hawk in demanding spending restraint. But she took a different approach at the Veterans' Affairs Committee, where she worked hard to expand benefits. The House passed her proposal to reduce long waits for veterans to get medical treatment, and she cosponsored another bill for faster filling of prescriptions. She helped to broker the deal to permit disabled retirees to receive both their pensions and their full veterans disability benefits. When France opposed military action in Iraq, Brown-Waite proposed removal of the remains of World War II veterans buried in France. As the Social Security debate opened in 2005, she was cautious as she told Bush that she "won't drink the Kool Aid;" she was one of five Republicans to vote against the bill to get federal courts to review the case of Terri Schiavo in March 2005.

Her narrow win in 2002 placed Brown-Waite high on the worry list for House Republicans campaign experts in 2004. But several prime candidates, including Thurman, decided not to run. Democrats nominated a former Republican who had never voted before and demanded that she return $14,000 in contributions from Majority Leader Tom DeLay. Brown-Waite won 66%–34%.

SIXTH DISTRICT

Rep. Cliff Stearns (R)

Elected 1988, 9th term; b. Apr. 16, 1941, Washington, DC; home, Ocala; George Washington U., B.S. 1963; Presbyterian; married (Joan).

Military Career: Air Force, 1963–67.

Professional Career: Data Control Systems Inc., 1967–68; Negotiator, CBS, 1969–70; Pres., Stearns House Inc., 1972–present.

DC Office: 2370 RHOB, 20515, 202-225-5744; Fax: 202-225-3973; Web site: www.house.gov/stearns.

District Offices: Gainesville, 352-337-0003; Ocala, 352-351-8777; Orange Park, 904-269-3203.

Committees: *Energy & Commerce* (5th of 31 R): Commerce, Trade & Consumer Protection (Chmn.); Oversight & Investigations; Telecommunications & the Internet. *Veterans' Affairs* (4th of 16 R): Health (Vice Chmn.).

Group Ratings

	ADA	ACLU	AFS	LCV	ITIC	NTU	COC	ACU	NTLC	CHC
2004	0	0	0	0	78	77	100	96	97	100
2003	5	—	0	15	—	73	90	88	—	—

National Journal Ratings

	2003 LIB	—	2003 CONS	2004 LIB	—	2004 CONS
Economic	37%	—	62%	17%	—	80%
Social	17%	—	79%	0%	—	91%
Foreign	50%	—	50%	17%	—	78%

Key Votes of the 108th Congress

1. Drilling in ANWR	Y	5. DC School Vouchers	Y
2. Approve Bush Tax Cuts	Y	6. Ban Human Cloning	Y
3. Medicare/Rx Bill	Y	7. Restrict Gun Liability	Y
4. Bar Overtime Pay Regs.	N	8. Ban Partial-Birth Abortion	Y

9. Ban Same-Sex Marriage	Y
10. Fund Iraq War	Y
11. Bar Cuba Embargo Funds	N
12. Intelligence Reorg.	Y

Election Results

2004 general	Cliff Stearns (R)	211,137	(64%)	($283,334)
	David Bruderly (D)	116,680	(36%)	($118,904)
2004 primary	Cliff Stearns (R)	unopposed		
2002 general	Cliff Stearns (R)	141,570	(65%)	($332,419)
	David Bruderly (D)	75,046	(35%)	($58,524)

Prior Winning Percentages: 2000 (100%); 1998 (100%); 1996 (67%); 1994 (100%); 1992 (65%); 1990 (59%); 1988 (54%)

The People		Race/Ethnic Origin	Ancestry	
Area size:	3,026 sq. mi.	78.9% White	German: 10.7%	Irish: 9.1%
Urban population:	69.4%	11.9% Black	English: 8.9%	
Rural population:	30.6%	2.2% Asian	**2004 Presidential Vote**	
Pop. 2000:	639,295	0.3% Native Am.	Bush (R) 210,101	(61%)
Median income:	$36,846	0.0% Hawaiian	Kerry (D) 136,622	(39%)
Poverty status:	13.4%	1.4% Two+ races	Other 838	(0%)
Military veterans:	18.3%	0.1% Other	**2000 Presidential Vote**	
		5.2% Hispanic Origin	Bush (R) 142,489	(58%)
			Gore (D) 102,179	(42%)
			Cook Partisan Voting Index: R + 8	

Occupation　Blue collar: 21.7%　White collar: 61.4%　Gray collar: 16.9%

The flat grasslands of central Florida, once bypassed by southbound tourists heading for the coast, has over the past two decades become a prime growth area in this high-growth state. Central Florida's economy once depended on farming, on tourists getting off the interstate, and on state institutions, most notably the University of Florida in Gainesville. Then retirees began settling in places like the bluegrass country around Ocala, one of America's prime horse-breeding grounds, and Leesburg, perched on a narrow spit of land between Lake Griffin and Lake Harris. Initially, these areas were studded with trailer parks and mobile home developments, but the 1990s brought more upscale development, albeit nothing approaching the high-rise apartments and gated communities that line the coasts further south. Some of this development is at the intersection of Lake, Marion and Sumter counties in the rapidly expanding "Villages" retirement community. This part of central Florida grew by 62% from 1990 to 2004.

　　The 6th Congressional District of Florida includes much of central Florida and also part of the Jacksonville metropolitan area, connected by a thin strip of lightly populated counties. In the south it includes parts of Marion and Sumter Counties, around Ocala, and a corner of Lake County. In the north it includes the western part of Jacksonville's Duval County and most of Clay County just to the south. In between it includes most of Alachua County and Gainesville, home of the University of Florida, where students from wealthier parts of Florida study in a town with many flimsy houses from the impoverished South of 50 years ago; here they can become part of a Florida elite bonded by shared memories of the Gator Growl festivities. On balance, this is a Republican district. The Gainesville area is the exception: Alachua is one of the few Florida counties to regularly vote Democratic, but the most heavily Democratic precincts are located in the 3d District. The country around Ocala and the Villages in the south is pretty heavily Republican; western Jacksonville and Clay County, with many military retirees, are even more Republican. In 2002 Governor Jeb Bush won 77% of the vote in Clay County, his highest percentage in any of Florida's 67 counties. Overall the 6th District voted 58% for George W. Bush in 2000 and 61% in 2004.

　　The congressman from the 6th District is Cliff Stearns, a Republican first elected in 1988. Stearns grew up and attended public schools in Washington, D.C., and served in the Air Force. In 1972 he went into Florida real estate and ended up owning five motels, three restaurants and other property. He was "someone who works in the community, goes to church with his neighbors, and doesn't live in Tallahassee," as he put it in his 1988 campaign, when he beat the favorite, state House Speaker Jon Mills, 54%–46%. "I was elected to put the federal government on a diet," Stearns said, and went on to compile a conservative voting record, though a bit less so on foreign policy. Since losing a low-level leadership contest in 1994, he has been an occasional maverick. He opposed IMF funding and normal trade relations with China. In the cliffhanger vote in December 2001 on trade promotion authority, Stearns was among a handful of Republicans who paced the House floor and delayed casting their vote until it became clear that their party needed them. He complains about the growth in the federal deficit since George W. Bush took office. "We used to be the party of accountability and fiscal responsibility," he said. He wants to end the automatic cost-of-living increases for members of Congress.

Stearns has become an active legislator. On the Veterans Committee, he sponsored a research center on Gulf War syndrome and won new medical facilities and benefits for disabled vets. On Energy and Commerce, he has worked on health care and Internet policy. He enacted a bill that encourages states to permit asthmatic children to carry and self-administer medication at school. After failing to win the chairmanship of the Telecommunications Subcommittee, Stearns became chairman of the revamped Commerce, Trade and Consumer Protection Subcommittee, where he has taken on many Internet issues. In 2004, he won House passage of the bill to restrict abuses of computer spyware; he got committee approval of database protection legislation, but ran into jurisdictional squabbles with Howard Coble at the Judiciary Committee. His Do-Not-Call Implementation Act became law, authorizing the Federal Trade Commission to establish a national registry of consumers who opt out of telemarketing calls. He also helped to enact the anti-spam law that requires most commercial e-mail to be labeled and have a valid return address. He has proposed creation of a Federal Boxing Commission, with enforcement of uniform standards, and he held hearings on the U.S. Olympic Committee and on problems in college athletics, including gambling and recruitment. Although some critics contend that he has not done enough on oversight of highway and product-safety issues, committee Democrats have been surprised by his relatively nonpartisan and productive course. As a senior member of Energy and Commerce, Stearns could become a player when the chairmanship next is in play.

Stearns has not suffered from breaking a 1988 promise to serve only six terms. After running unopposed in 1998 and 2000, he was reelected easily in 2002 and 2004.

SEVENTH DISTRICT

Rep. John Mica (R)

Elected 1992, 7th term; b. Jan. 27, 1943, Binghamton, NY; home, Winter Park; Miami-Dade Commun. Col., A.A. 1965, U. of FL, B.A. 1967; Episcopalian; married (Patricia).

Elected Office: FL House of Reps., 1976–80.

Professional Career: Exec. Dir., Palm Beach & Orange Cnty. Govt. Charter Study Commissions, 1970–74; Pres., MK Development, 1975–92; A.A., U.S. Sen. Paula Hawkins, 1981–85; Partner, Mica, Dudinsky & Assoc., 1985–92.

DC Office: 2313 RHOB, 20515, 202-225-4035; Fax: 202-226-0821; Web site: www.house.gov/mica.

District Offices: Deltona, 386-860-1499; Maitland, 407-657-8080; Ormond Beach, 386-676-7750; Palatka, 386-328-1622; Palm Coast, 386-246-6042; St. Augustine, 904-810-5048.

Committees: *Government Reform* (6th of 23 R): Criminal Justice, Drug Policy & Human Resources; Federal Workforce & Agency Organization (Vice Chmn.). *House Administration* (3d of 6 R). *Transportation & Infrastructure* (7th of 41 R): Aviation (Chmn.); Highways, Transit & Pipelines; Railroads.

Group Ratings

	ADA	ACLU	AFS	LCV	ITIC	NTU	COC	ACU	NTLC	CHC
2004	0	0	13	9	100	53	100	84	78	100
2003	10	—	0	5	—	61	97	92	—	—

National Journal Ratings

	2003 LIB — 2003 CONS		2004 LIB — 2004 CONS	
Economic	9%	84%	13%	85%
Social	21%	78%	25%	73%
Foreign	0%	89%	17%	78%

Key Votes of the 108th Congress

1. Drilling in ANWR	Y	5. DC School Vouchers	Y	9. Ban Same-Sex Marriage	Y
2. Approve Bush Tax Cuts	Y	6. Ban Human Cloning	Y	10. Fund Iraq War	Y
3. Medicare/Rx Bill	Y	7. Restrict Gun Liability	Y	11. Bar Cuba Embargo Funds	N
4. Bar Overtime Pay Regs.	N	8. Ban Partial-Birth Abortion	Y	12. Intelligence Reorg.	Y

Election Results

2004 general	John Mica (R) .... unopposed		($256,103)
2004 primary	John Mica (R) .... unopposed		
2002 general	John Mica (R) 142,147	(60%)	($1,756,115)
	Wayne Hogan (D) 96,444	(40%)	($4,659,352)

Prior Winning Percentages: 2000 (63%); 1998 (100%); 1996 (62%); 1994 (73%); 1992 (56%)

The People		Race/Ethnic Origin	Ancestry	
Area size:	2,221 sq. mi.	81.3% White	German: 11.7% Irish: 10.6%	
Urban population:	86.7%	8.8% Black	English: 9.9%	
Rural population:	13.3%	1.4% Asian	**2004 Presidential Vote**	
Pop. 2000:	639,295	0.3% Native Am.	Bush (R) 204,454	(57%)
Median income:	$40,525	0.0% Hawaiian	Kerry (D) 155,302	(43%)
Poverty status:	10.1%	1.1% Two+ races	Other 964	(0%)
Military veterans:	17.6%	0.1% Other	**2000 Presidential Vote**	
		6.9% Hispanic Origin	Bush (R) 143,672	(54%)
			Gore (D) 122,818	(46%)
			Cook Partisan Voting Index: R + 4	
Occupation	Blue collar: 20.3%	White collar: 63.2%	Gray collar: 16.4%	

In 1513, Spanish explorer Ponce de Leon headed to Florida, hoping to discover the Fountain of Youth; instead, he found Ponte Vedra Beach, located just south of modern-day Jacksonville. A few decades later and a little farther south, Spanish colonists founded St. Augustine, the oldest permanent European settlement in North America—42 years older than Jamestown, Virginia, and 55 years older than the Plymouth colony in Massachusetts. But near long-settled St. Augustine are a Northrop Grumman aircraft plant and some of the newest communities in America. St. Johns and Flagler Counties, the two coastal counties between Jacksonville and Daytona Beach, grew 24% and 39% between 2000 and 2004; Flagler County was the fastest growing county in the nation between 2003 and 2004. Some of the communities here are old: John D. Rockefeller used to winter in Ormond Beach, and cars have been zooming on Daytona's rock-hard beach for decades. Nearby DeLand is a mecca for skydivers, while Heathrow, just off Interstate 4, serves as the home base of the American Automobile Association. Other places are much newer, instant cities: the Palm Coast development on the beach in Flagler County and Deltona, built inland on a drained swamp in Volusia County.

The 7th Congressional District of Florida covers the Atlantic coast for nearly 100 miles, from Ponte Vedra Beach to Daytona Beach. Inland it includes Deltona and affluent Seminole County suburbs of Orlando as well as the timber center of Palatka. Nearly two-thirds of the population is in the south, around Orlando, Deltona and Daytona Beach. The political tendencies in this area are mixed. Seminole County and St. Augustine's St. Johns County are affluent and heavily Republican. Palm Coast's Flagler County is marginal; Daytona Beach's Volusia County leans Democratic, but about 40% of it is in the 24th District. On balance, this is a Republican district, but not overwhelmingly so.

The congressman from the 7th District is John Mica, a Republican first elected in 1992. He grew up in south Florida, in a bipartisan political family: His younger brother Dan Mica was a Democratic congressman from Palm Beach County from 1978 to 1988, when he lost a primary for U.S. Senate; another brother, David Mica, worked for Democratic Governor Lawton Chiles and became executive director for the Florida Petroleum Council. John Mica made a small fortune by turning 360 feet of New Smyrna beachfront into a real estate business. He was elected to the state House in 1976 and served four years, worked on Senator Paula Hawkins's staff from 1981 to 1985, and then became a lobbyist. He ran for the House when this district was created after the 1990 Census. After he was attacked in the Republican primary as an insider representing special interests, he said, "Some of the finest folks I've met are lobbyists." He won the primary 53%–34%. In the general election, against an opponent he attacked as a liberal backed by trial lawyers and labor unions, he won 56%–44%. He has since been reelected easily.

Mica took office as a consistent conservative and a brash reformer, leading the charge to abolish House select committees and to make public the names of those signing petitions to discharge legislation. When Republicans took control of the House, Mica became chairman of Government Reform's Civil Service Subcommittee. There he helped pass the White House Accountability Act of 1996, imposing on the White House, just as a Republican-pushed law imposed on Congress, the laws that are imposed on the private sector. One exception to his image as a congressional tightwad: he was an early backer of the Congressional Visitors Center, whose cost estimates have risen; he called CVC critics a "chorus of prima donnas." Mica has said that his biggest issue is fighting drugs. In 2004, he held a hearing on prescription-drug abuse, including the painkiller OxyContin.

When Mica took over in 2001 as chairman of the Aviation Subcommittee at Transportation and Infrastructure, he pledged faster building of runways across the nation. But after the September 11 attacks he focused on security. After congressional leaders moved within days to pass a bill to aid the airlines, Mica played a major role in designing the next legislation: improved screening at all airports. The Senate, by 100–0, approved a bill that federalized the screeners. Mica and House Republicans objected to a complete federal takeover and sought to preserve some role for the private sector. In November 2001 Mica and others reached a deal that that allows airports to opt out of the federal system after three years if they meet certain standards. A few months later Mica found himself in the middle of another post-September 11 conflict. With Transportation Committee chairman Don Young, Mica introduced a bill to permit commercial airline pilots to carry guns in the cockpit. The bill was initially opposed by the Bush administration and the Senate; airlines worried about the risks of having firearms aboard planes. Mica brought to the floor a bill permitting a few pilots to carry the weapons during a two-year demonstration period. But the House, to his surprise, voted 310–113 voted to allow all pilots to carry guns. The Senate agreed by an 87–6 margin. The Bush administration acquiesced to what was obviously the popular will. In reauthorizing the Federal Aviation Administration, he worked to give it a more corporate structure. During an April 2004 hearing on steps toward private airport screening, Mica raised alarms about gaps in security. He later called for legislation to mandate advanced technology, including biometrics. When Congress passed intelligence reform in the 2004 lame-duck session, it included some aviation-security provisions from Mica, including demands for quicker action by the Homeland Security Department.

Mica takes an interest in local transportation issues, especially in the traffic-clogged Orlando area. He has fought for mass transit in the area; he got $9 million in start-up funds for a commuter rail system in Central Florida. He worked to keep simulation training command for all four branches of the military in Orlando, where it has spawned many local businesses.

In 2002, Mica faced a serious challenge at home from Democrat Wayne Hogan, a Jacksonville trial lawyer who spent $2.7 million of his own money on his campaign. Redistricting had made the district a bit more Republican, but more than half of the voters were new to Mica. Hogan, part of the legal team that won Florida's settlement with the tobacco industry, from which he netted $54 million, said that he would fight for "ordinary families against powerful interests." Mica responded that Hogan was trying to buy the seat, and that his pledge not to take contributions from political action committees was like "Rockefeller saying he won't take food stamps." Mica won comfortably, 60%–40%, carrying all six counties. In 2004, Mica ran unopposed.

EIGHTH DISTRICT

Rep. Ric Keller (R)

Elected 2000, 3d term; b. Sept. 5, 1964, Johnson City, TN; home, Orlando; E. TN St. U., B.S. 1986, Vanderbilt U., J.D. 1992; Methodist; divorced.

Professional Career: Practicing atty., 1992–2000.

DC Office: 419 CHOB, 20515, 202-225-2176; Fax: 202-225-0999; Web site: www.keller.house.gov.

District Offices: Eustis, 888-642-1211; Ocala, 888-642-1211; Orlando, 407-872-1962.

Committees: *Education & the Workforce* (12th of 27 R): 21st Century Competitiveness; Education Reform; Workforce Protections. *Judiciary* (15th of 23 R): Courts, the Internet & Intellectual Property; Crime, Terrorism & Homeland Security. *Small Business* (12th of 18 R): Tax, Finance & Exports.

Group Ratings

	ADA	ACLU	AFS	LCV	ITIC	NTU	COC	ACU	NTLC	CHC
2004	0	0	0	0	90	70	100	100	100	91
2003	5	—	0	15	—	66	96	91	—	—

National Journal Ratings

	2003 LIB	—	2003 CONS		2004 LIB	—	2004 CONS
Economic	0%	—	91%		5%	—	93%
Social	14%	—	85%		9%	—	85%
Foreign	0%	—	89%		10%	—	86%

Key Votes of the 108th Congress

1. Drilling in ANWR	Y	5. DC School Vouchers	*	9. Ban Same-Sex Marriage	Y
2. Approve Bush Tax Cuts	Y	6. Ban Human Cloning	Y	10. Fund Iraq War	Y
3. Medicare/Rx Bill	Y	7. Restrict Gun Liability	Y	11. Bar Cuba Embargo Funds	N
4. Bar Overtime Pay Regs.	N	8. Ban Partial-Birth Abortion	Y	12. Intelligence Reorg.	Y

Election Results

2004 general	Ric Keller (R)	172,232	(61%)	($292,257)
	Stephen Murray (D)	112,343	(39%)	($62,420)
2004 primary	Ric Keller (R)	unopposed		
2002 general	Ric Keller (R)	123,497	(65%)	($1,038,656)
	Eddie Diaz (D)	66,099	(35%)	($218,651)

Prior Winning Percentages: 2000 (51%)

The People		Race/Ethnic Origin	Ancestry	
Area size:	1,158 sq. mi.	69.9% White	German: 10.7%	Irish: 9.0%
Urban population:	91.7%	7.2% Black	English: 8.6%	
Rural population:	8.3%	3.0% Asian	**2004 Presidential Vote**	
Pop. 2000:	639,295	0.3% Native Am.	Bush (R) 160,722	(55%)
Median income:	$41,568	0.1% Hawaiian	Kerry (D) 133,328	(45%)
Poverty status:	9.4%	1.6% Two+ races	Other 261	(0%)
Military veterans:	14.9%	0.3% Other	**2000 Presidential Vote**	
		17.6% Hispanic Origin	Bush (R) 119,139	(54%)
			Gore (D) 102,538	(46%)
			Cook Partisan Voting Index: R + 3	

Occupation   Blue collar: 19.3%   White collar: 63.6%   Gray collar: 17.2%

Who would have supposed 40 years ago that the most popular tourist destination in the world would rise amid the swamps and orange groves of central Florida? The answer: Walt Disney, and just about no one else. In the mid-1960s, Disney looked at the map and decided that the intersection of I-4 and Florida's Turnpike, the "crossroads of Florida," just a few miles southwest of Orlando, was the perfect place for the vast theme park he was planning. The spirit of this place was set by a man who never lived here but created something now taken for granted. Disney conceived the first theme park in the flatlands of Orange County, California, in 1955, but he perfected it in the 17,000 acres of swamp and lakes in Florida's Orange County that his associates had stealthily snapped up and where Disney World opened in 1971. With the invention of the theme park, Disney also pioneered sophisticated communications, utility, and waste-disposal methods—all out of sight and underground. Yet Disney World is not just an engineering marvel; it requires some 56,000 people with know-how and earnest cheerfulness to entertain its 40 million-plus visitors. Walt Disney World set the model for the private corporation handling functions historically run by cities—a model that would be followed, on a much smaller scale, by countless gated developments nationwide. But Disney World is hardly the only site that has made Orlando one of the world's great tourist destinations: other popular theme parks here include Sea World and Universal Studios; Cape Canaveral is less than 40 miles away. The high-tech economy also has moved into the business world of Greater Orlando; defense contractor Lockheed Martin has a big missile facility here. Continuing growth has fueled what may be uphill efforts to control the sprawl in one of the nation's booming areas.

The 8th Congressional District of Florida includes parts of Orlando and surrounding Orange County and most of the enormous Walt Disney World complex, including the Disney new urbanist town of Celebration. It includes most of the southeast and southwest parts of Orlando and adjoining suburbs; the heavily black areas of central Orlando are in the 3d District, which stretches all the way to Jacksonville. More than three-quarters of the district's residents live in Orange County. The rest live in a ribbon of territory to the northwest, past Lake Apopka to little market towns like Mount Dora and Umatilla in Lake County that seem insulated from the booming metro area; around here, turtles, alligators and river otters go about their lives underneath cypress trees draped with Spanish moss. Nearby is Silver Springs, where tourists can view the world's largest formation of clear artesian springs from glass-bottomed boats—a theme park from an earlier era. Beyond that is the horse farm country of Marion County, around Ocala. In the 1980s the Orlando area was heavily Republican, but in the 1990s it moved perceptibly toward national Democrats. The 8th District was designed to be a Republican district, and changed significantly in redistricting. Some 18% of the district's residents are Hispanic, most of them not Cuban Republicans, but Puerto Ricans and people with roots in other parts of Latin America; many work in the tourism industry. Up through 2000 they tended to vote Democratic, but in 2002 they favored Governor Jeb Bush, and in 2004 seem to have trended toward George W. Bush.

The congressman from the 8th District is Ric Keller, a Republican first elected in 2000 in one of the closest races in the country but comfortably reelected since then. He was born in Tennessee but grew up mostly in Orlando, in a one-bedroom house with his brother, sister, mother and grandmother. With financial help from Pell grants, he graduated first in his class at East Tennessee State University, then graduated from Vanderbilt law school. In 1992 he moved to Orlando and practiced law and quickly earned conservative credentials. His firm served as general counsel to a business coalition that won passage of changes in tort law in the Florida legislature.

When Congressman Bill McCollum decided to run for the Senate in 2000, Keller ran for the House. He had tough primary competition from state Representative Bill Sublette, who boasted of delivering state funds to the area and was supported by most local Republican leaders. With greater name recognition, Sublette led in most polls. Keller focused on issues like abortion and gun owners' rights. Sublette led Keller in the September primary 43%–31%. In the October 3 runoff, Keller was helped by $400,000 in contributions and issue ads by the conservative Club for Growth. Keller won the runoff 52%–48%. In the five-week general election, Keller again was considered the underdog against Linda Chapin, former Orange County Commission chairman, who argued that her moderate views plus her experience as a county official put her more in line with district voters. Keller played up his anti-tax views and outsider status, while Republican ads lampooned Chapin for providing frills for the county jail and other local facilities, including $150,000 for palm trees. Keller's 50.8%–49.2% win was a great disappointment to House Democratic leaders, who had long expected Chapin to win. It may have been decided by the personal touch: Keller's folksy, self-deprecating style made him "an easy man to like," wrote the *Orlando Sentinel*.

In the House, Keller has mostly been a reliable conservative. His strong support for tax cuts plus his advocacy of increased education funding for the disadvantaged made him "a bootstrap conservative," in the *Sentinel's* words. On oil drilling in the Gulf of Mexico and the Clinton administration's proposed regulations on arsenic in drinking water, he surprised many by voting against the Republican leadership. Keller has become active in his committee work. On Judiciary, he has carved a niche in the tort-reform wars by authoring the House-passed "Cheeseburger bill," which prohibits most obesity-related lawsuits against the food industry. "The gist of this legislation is there should be common sense in the food court, not blaming other people in the legal court," he explained. When critics complained that there have been few such lawsuits, and the legislation is a solution in search of a problem, Keller responded that legal activists already had begun their forum-shopping. He also won committee approval of his proposal for a one-year suspension of the license of any lawyer who has filed three or more frivolous lawsuits in the same federal court. On Education and the Workforce, he pushed for increases in Pell grants, especially for low-income students, and he joined Democrats in opposing a Bush administration proposal to change the funding formula. He helped to enact bipartisan changes in the special education program, including paperwork reduction and sanctions against students who bring a gun to school. He also worked to bring a successful end to the more than decade-long fight to get a VA hospital for Orlando, the largest metropolitan area without one.

In 2002, national Democrats were enthusiastic about their nominee, Eddie Diaz, a Puerto Rican-born former Orlando policeman who was gravely wounded while his partner was killed in a shootout. Diaz's lack of campaign experience and his modest fundraising skills hampered his effort; his campaign never caught fire. Keller, a relentless campaigner and fundraiser, reached out to the Hispanic community. In a major disappointment for Democrats, Keller won 65%–35%. In 2004, he faced Stephen Murray, a political newcomer and former manager of a computer-game software company. After Murray ran an ad about Keller's divorce, he responded, "This is a sleazy, bogus 11th-hour personal attack by a sleazy, desperate candidate who just moved here from California and has no support whatsoever." Keller won 61%–39%. In 2000, he pledged to serve only four terms.

NINTH DISTRICT

Rep. Michael Bilirakis (R)

Elected 1982, 12th term; b. July 16, 1930, Tarpon Springs; home, Palm Harbor; U. of Pittsburgh, B.S. 1959, U. of FL, J.D. 1963; Greek Orthodox; married (Evelyn).

Military Career: Air Force, 1951–55.

Professional Career: Steelworker, 1955–59; Govt. contract negotiator, 1959–60; Petroleum engineer, 1960–63; Aerospace Industries admin., 1963–1969; Practicing atty., 1969–82.

DC Office: 2408 RHOB, 20515, 202-225-5755; Fax: 202-225-4085; Web site: www.house.gov/bilirakis.

District Offices: Palm Harbor, 727-773-2871; Tampa, 813-960-8173.

Committees: *Energy & Commerce* (3d of 31 R): Energy & Air Quality; Health; Telecommunications & the Internet. *Veterans' Affairs* (Vice Chmn. of 16 R): Oversight & Investigations (Chmn.).

Group Ratings

	ADA	ACLU	AFS	LCV	ITIC	NTU	COC	ACU	NTLC	CHC
2004	5	0	13	18	90	59	100	92	81	100
2003	5	—	0	20	—	64	93	92	—	—

National Journal Ratings

	2003 LIB	—	2003 CONS	2004 LIB	—	2004 CONS
Economic	41%	—	59%	38%	—	62%
Social	30%	—	65%	9%	—	85%
Foreign	21%	—	77%	10%	—	86%

Key Votes of the 108th Congress

1. Drilling in ANWR	Y	5. DC School Vouchers	Y	9. Ban Same-Sex Marriage	Y
2. Approve Bush Tax Cuts	Y	6. Ban Human Cloning	Y	10. Fund Iraq War	Y
3. Medicare/Rx Bill	Y	7. Restrict Gun Liability	Y	11. Bar Cuba Embargo Funds	N
4. Bar Overtime Pay Regs.	N	8. Ban Partial-Birth Abortion	Y	12. Intelligence Reorg.	Y

Election Results

2004 general	Michael Bilirakis (R) .... unopposed			($596,389)
2004 primary	Michael Bilirakis (R) 44,579	(84%)		
	Joseph Stanley (R) 8,189	(16%)		
2002 general	Michael Bilirakis (R) 169,369	(71%)		($816,932)
	Chuck Kalogianis (D) 67,623	(29%)		($307,568)

Prior Winning Percentages: 2000 (82%); 1998 (100%); 1996 (69%); 1994 (100%); 1992 (59%); 1990 (58%); 1988 (100%); 1986 (71%); 1984 (79%); 1982 (51%)

The People		Race/Ethnic Origin	Ancestry	
Area size:	800 sq. mi.	85.2% White	German: 13.3%	Irish: 11.2%
Urban population:	93.8%	3.5% Black	English: 9.2%	
Rural population:	6.2%	1.8% Asian	**2004 Presidential Vote**	
Pop. 2000:	639,296	0.2% Native Am.	Bush (R) 196,837	(57%)
Median income:	$40,742	0.0% Hawaiian	Kerry (D) 148,694	(43%)
Poverty status:	8.6%	1.1% Two+ races	Other 953	(0%)
Military veterans:	17.2%	0.1% Other	**2000 Presidential Vote**	
		7.9% Hispanic Origin	Bush (R) 146,735	(54%)
			Gore (D) 124,242	(46%)
			Cook Partisan Voting Index: R + 4	
Occupation	Blue collar: 17.6%	White collar: 68.0%	Gray collar: 14.4%	

Half a century ago, the land north of St. Petersburg and Tampa was scarcely inhabited. Behind the barrier island of beaches, the land along the Gulf shore was swampy; further inland was dense, semitropical forest spotted with lakes. Over the years, development has moved up the coast and inland via the major highways, first to Clearwater and Tarpon Springs in Pinellas County and then up the once-empty coast of Pasco County. Much of this area originally was designed for retirees, offering everything from condominiums to garden apartments to trailer parks to what is probably the largest array of Medicare HMO plans in the nation. But it has attracted others. Clearwater, in Pinellas County north of St. Petersburg, in 2000 had a higher percentage of senior citizens than any other city over 100,000, but it is also the spiritual headquarters for the Church of Scientology, which has transformed its downtown by buying 200 businesses and building a $50 million Mediterranean Revival-style Scientology religious center. Businesses have sprouted in northern Pinellas County and inland off the I-75 corridor; nearly half of Pasco County's workers commute to jobs in other counties. The people who settled here in recent decades brought their ancestral political beliefs with them: In the 1950s and 1960s, only white-collar retirees could afford to buy new places in Florida, and they were heavily Republican. As Florida retirements became more feasible for people with modest incomes in the 1970s and 1980s, the partisan balance shifted toward Democrats. In the 1990s, young in-migrants with professional and technical backgrounds flooded the area; their political independence has turned this into one of Florida's most politically marginal areas. In 2004 Republican organizers brought out a lot of new voters, many of them Christian conservatives.

The 9th Congressional District of Florida covers part of the area north of St. Petersburg and north and east of Tampa. It includes the string of towns on the coast of Pasco County—Holiday, New Port Richey, Bayonet Point, Hudson. In Pinellas County to the south, the 9th includes Tarpon Springs, an old resort first settled by Greek sponge divers a century ago, the affluent neighborhoods of mid- and upper-level managers in East Lake, the young commuter families of Oldsmar, the bayside community of Safety Harbor and Clearwater. The district also includes the northern Tampa suburbs in Hillsborough County and much of the eastern part of the county, including part of strawberry-growing Plant City (named not for plants but for Tampa pioneer Henry B. Plant). The borders were drawn by Republican redistricters to produce a district that would elect a Republican. The district gave Jeb Bush a big margin in 2002 and voted 54% for George W. Bush in 2000 and 57% in 2004.

The congressman from the 9th District is Michael Bilirakis, a Republican first elected in 1982. He grew up near Pittsburgh; he served in the Air Force, and then worked his way through college, toiling in a steel mill. He also worked for the government in Washington and an aerospace contractor in Florida, then practiced law. He believes strongly that Americans can work their way up, with occasional government assistance (like the G.I. Bill that helped him through school). Originally a Democrat, he switched to the Republican Party in 1980, and in 1982, when this district was created, he won though the seat had been designed for a Democrat.

Bilirakis has a moderate record on economics and is more conservative on other issues. Early in his career, Bilirakis won a seat on the Commerce committee, and starting in 1995 he held one of the most potentially powerful chairmanships in Congress, that of the Health and Environment Subcommittee. He managed to retain it in 2001, despite House Republicans' six-year term limit, by arguing that it had been reconfigured to merely the Health Subcommittee and thus wasn't the same subcommittee any more. He kept the chair until January 2005, but he was passed over for chairman of the full committee in February 2004, when Billy Tauzin resigned his position, in favor of the less senior Joe Barton.

In 1993 and 1995, Bilirakis sponsored a bill which tried to make health insurance portable and to stop insurers from denying coverage for pre-existing conditions; it was put aside in 1994 in the debate over the Clinton health care plan, but something very like it was passed in 1996, known from its Senate sponsors as Kennedy-Kassebaum. He served on the Medicare Commission and was part of the majority that supported the Breaux-Thomas premium support plan; a version of that has been supported by George W. Bush and Bilirakis played a role in Medicare legislation. Bilirakis also sponsored a bill to provide a state-based prescription drug benefit for the poorest and sickest Medicare beneficiaries. This became the Republican party's plan, and again Bush supported something quite similar. Bilirakis supported the Dingell-Norwood HMO regulation bill, and was its only supporter placed on the conference committee by Speaker Dennis Hastert. In 2003 he worked to drop the few Medicare-covered prescription drugs from the formula used to calculate physicians' annual increases and sought cooperation from state agencies in an investigation of Medicaid fraud. He supported the 2003 Medicare/prescription drug bill and opposed reimportation of prescription drugs from Canada. In 2004 he questioned NIH's Roadmap priority-setting process and said the agency "lacks transparency"; he denounced NIH for allowing its scientists to have lucrative consulting contracts with pharmaceutical and biotech companies.

Bilirakis is also vice-chairman of the Veterans Committee. He sponsored a 1997 law to provide "forgotten widows" of veterans with a minimum annuity of $165 a month, and a 1999 law to enable severely disabled military retirees to collect retirement as well as disability benefits. For most of his congressional career, Bilirakis has backed a center to treat veterans with spinal cord injuries; the $17 million Tampa facility opened in February 2002. In 2003 he got approval of a bill allowing veterans to collect disability as well as retirement payments; it would be phased in for 10 years and limited to veterans with disabilities rated at 60% or more. In March 2004 he criticized the Veterans Affairs Department for testing a $472 million computer system at the Bay Pines VA hospital in St. Petersburg, the second largest veterans' hospital in the nation; in June, the department admitted it may never work. In seven Congresses, Bilirakis has introduced bills that would deny congressmen their pay if they fail to pass appropriations bills by the beginning of the fiscal year.

Bilirakis had no Democratic opponent in 1998 or 2000. In 2002, he was reelected 71%–29%. In early 2004 he said he would run for just one more term; he won the primary with 84% of the vote and had no Democratic opponent. In January 2005, his son, state Representative Gus

Bilirakis, who is term-limited in 2006, said he would run to succeed his father; by June he had endorsements from Majority Whip Roy Blunt and National Republican Congressional Committee Chairman Tom Reynolds. In early 2005 former state Senator John Grant, who has support from religious conservatives, said he might run. Also mentioned as possible candidates were state Senator Victor Crist, former state Senator Jack Latvala, and former state House Speaker Johnnie Byrd.

TENTH DISTRICT

Rep. Bill Young (R)

Elected 1970, 18th term; b. Dec. 16, 1930, Harmarville, PA; home, Largo; ; Baptist; married (Beverly).

Military Career: Army Natl. Guard, 1948–57.

Elected Office: FL Senate, 1960–70, Min. Ldr., 1966–70.

Professional Career: Aide, U.S. Rep. William Cramer, 1957–60.

DC Office: 2407 RHOB, 20515, 202-225-5961; Fax: 202-225-9764; Web site: www.house.gov/young.

District Offices: Largo, 727-581-0980; St. Petersburg, 727-893-3191.

Committees: *Appropriations* (2d of 37 R): Defense (Chmn.); Military Quality of Life & Veterans Affairs & Related Agencies.

Group Ratings

	ADA	ACLU	AFS	LCV	ITIC	NTU	COC	ACU	NTLC	CHC
2004	10	0	25	9	67	48	95	87	62	91
2003	10	—	0	15	—	59	93	91	—	—

National Journal Ratings

	2003 LIB	—	2003 CONS		2004 LIB	—	2004 CONS
Economic	33%	—	67%		35%	—	64%
Social	39%	—	60%		35%	—	65%
Foreign	0%	—	89%		16%	—	83%

Key Votes of the 108th Congress

1. Drilling in ANWR	Y	5. DC School Vouchers	Y	9. Ban Same-Sex Marriage	Y
2. Approve Bush Tax Cuts	Y	6. Ban Human Cloning	*	10. Fund Iraq War	Y
3. Medicare/Rx Bill	Y	7. Restrict Gun Liability	Y	11. Bar Cuba Embargo Funds	N
4. Bar Overtime Pay Regs.	N	8. Ban Partial-Birth Abortion	Y	12. Intelligence Reorg.	Y

Election Results

2004 general	Bill Young (R)	207,175	(69%)	($681,749)
	Bob Derry (D)	91,658	(31%)	($85,865)
2004 primary	Bill Young (R)	unopposed		
2002 general	Bill Young (R)	unopposed		($487,592)

Prior Winning Percentages: 2000 (76%); 1998 (100%); 1996 (67%); 1994 (100%); 1992 (57%); 1990 (100%); 1988 (73%); 1986 (100%); 1984 (80%); 1982 (100%); 1980 (100%); 1978 (79%); 1976 (65%); 1974 (76%); 1972 (76%); 1970 (67%).

The People		Race/Ethnic Origin	Ancestry	
Area size:	448 sq. mi.	88.0% White	German: 14.0%	Irish: 11.6%
Urban population:	100.0%	3.6% Black	English: 10.2%	
Rural population:	0.0%	2.3% Asian	**2004 Presidential Vote**	
Pop. 2000:	639,295	0.3% Native Am.	Bush (R) 158,082	(51%)
Median income:	$37,168	0.0% Hawaiian	Kerry (D) 150,761	(49%)
Poverty status:	8.9%	1.3% Two+ races	**2000 Presidential Vote**	
Military veterans:	18.3%	0.1% Other	Gore (D) 137,286	(51%)
		4.4% Hispanic Origin	Bush (R) 133,004	(49%)
			Cook Partisan Voting Index: D + 1	

Occupation Blue collar: 19.9%   White collar: 64.9%   Gray collar: 15.2%

St. Petersburg was first settled in the 1870s, reached by railroad in 1888 and in 1892 named, after a coin toss, by one of the rail partners, Pyotr Dementyev, for his native city in Russia; if his partner had won the toss, it would have been named Detroit. For decades, it was known as the American city with the largest percentage of elderly residents, sitting on its green park benches and playing shuffleboard. In the early 1900s, *St. Petersburg Times* editor W. L. Straub sought to reverse the industrialization of the waterfront, establishing the parks that continue to define the city's character. Starting out on the grid streets facing Tampa Bay, St. Petersburg later spread toward the Gulf Coast as the migration of retirees accelerated. Mostly from the North and modestly affluent, the newcomers adapted easily to a city whose civic tone was set by the *St. Petersburg Times* and its longtime owners Nelson and Henrietta Poynter: Sober, good-humored, supportive of clean government and civil rights. More recently, retirees have come to prefer homes in less urbanized settings, and St. Petersburg has become a more conventional central city, with a larger working population, more families and minorities, and more office buildings and civic attractions—the Salvador Dali Museum, the Florida International Museum, the Museum of Fine Arts. The new balance has brought new politics. White-collar Yankee retirees in the 1940s and 1950s made St. Petersburg and surrounding Pinellas County the first Republican county in ancestrally Democratic Florida. Then, in the early 1970s Social Security was vastly increased and indexed to inflation and St. Petersburg basked in prosperity. More workers came to afford a Florida retirement, the affluent moved farther down the Gulf Coast, and St. Petersburg trended Democratic in the 1970s and 1980s. The whole of St. Petersburg and Pinellas County are now pretty well built up, with new projects replacing old buildings in downtown St. Pete and elsewhere; except for the county containing the Florida Keys, this was the slowest growing county in the state between 1990 and 2003.

The 10th Congressional District is the only Florida district entirely within one county. It includes all of Pinellas County south of Clearwater except for heavily black precincts in south St. Petersburg, which are part of the Tampa-based 11th District. It includes all the Pinellas County beach communities on the barrier islands facing the Gulf from Belleair Beach to Mullet Key and, north of Clearwater, includes middle-class Dunedin and pricey Palm Harbor in the north to the new subdivisions of Largo in the center of the peninsula. In 2004 it voted 51% for George W. Bush.

The congressman from the 10th District is Bill Young, a Republican first elected in 1970, the most senior Republican in the House. Young grew up in a dirt-poor Pennsylvania coal town. His first home was a shotgun shack that was swept down a river when he was 6; at 16 he was shot in a hunting accident. The family moved to Florida, and Young dropped out of high school to support his ill mother by hauling concrete blocks and mixing mortar; at 25 he applied for a job as an insurance salesman, and ultimately ran a successful insurance agency. In the 1950s he worked for St. Petersburg's first Republican congressman, William Cramer. Young was elected to the state Senate in 1960, at 29, and was the lone Republican there. When Cramer ran for the U.S. Senate in 1970, Young ran for his House seat and won.

Young has a moderate to conservative voting record. Early on, Young got a seat on Appropriations, where he, like many Republicans, worked closely with the Democratic chairmen. Young's special project has been the bone marrow donor program, originated by Dr. Robert Good of All Children's Hospital in St. Petersburg. Working from his seat on the Defense Subcommittee, he originally placed the program in the Pentagon; in 1987 it started off with $2.1 million; by 2005 it had matched nearly 20,000 patients with one of 5.5 million volunteers.

Despite his seniority, Young did not become full committee chairman after Republicans won their majority in 1994. Speaker-designate Newt Gingrich passed over him and two more senior Republicans for being too accommodating to Democrats. With some reason: after 34 years as a minority party legislator Young's instincts were bipartisan. "I came into the majority party with this strong conviction that every member of Congress has been elected by their constituents and should be given respect. I've tried to deal with anybody on that basis, whether it is a first-term freshman or a 20-year veteran." Young says that Gingrich offered him the job, but that he preferred to chair the Defense Subcommittee, on which he had done much of his work. In that post he worked to produce bipartisan appropriations out of the spotlight; he has said he knew every dime that goes into secret "black" military and intelligence operations.

In 1998 Young considered retiring, but at the end of the year he was suddenly catapulted into the Appropriations chairmanship. It happened three days after the November election, when Gingrich decided to resign; Appropriations Chairman Bob Livingston quickly became the Speaker-designate, and Young became chairman.

In 2001 and 2002 Young was caught between demands by OMB Director Mitch Daniels that spending be held down to Bush administration limits and demands by appropriators for more spending. For the most part he came down on Bush's side. On the antiterrorism supplemental in November 2001 he reluctantly backed the administration and the Republican leadership, but warned that committee members might vote for more. When the administration proposed an end to earmarking money for members' projects (there were 7,803 earmarks in 2001, totaling $15 billion), Young demurred. In early May 2002 he proposed to add $2.5 billion to the $27.3 billion emergency spending bill, but after a meeting where George W. Bush expressed his "disappointment" and stormier sessions with Daniels and Speaker Dennis Hastert, Young held to the $27.3 billion level, partly through accounting legerdemain—$1.8 billion of defense spending was put on a contingency basis. Later $383 million of airline bailout money that seemed unlikely to be used was put into the next fiscal year. In September he tried to get Hastert to move the $130 billion Labor-HHS appropriation to the floor under an open rule, to see if the Bush limits would be accepted by the House; Hastert declined, and work on appropriations was not completed until early 2003. After the November election, House Republicans adopted a new rule requiring Appropriations subcommittee chairmen—the college of cardinals—to be approved by the Republican Steering Committee. This was seen as a move to rein in appropriators; when it passed by a close voice vote, Young did not call for a roll call vote. "I could not let that meeting conclude with the Speaker having lost."

Young resolved to make the appropriations process go more smoothly in 2003 and managed to pass all 13 bills through the House by early September. But delays in the Senate and in resolving differences between the chambers resulted in the postponement of final action until January 2004 on an omnibus package with 7 of the bills. In 2004, appropriators got a late start because the House and Senate could not agree on a budget resolution. In June 2004, leading a coalition of appropriators and Democrats, Young beat a proposal to impose budget caps on spending. The House passed more appropriations bills than the Senate in the summer and fall, but Young agreed to a continuing resolution and an omnibus appropriation bill after the election. The House also was able to pass disaster relief after Florida was hit by four hurricanes in August and September. In early September Congress approved $2 billion; in early October another $11.6 billion was included in the military construction appropriation. Finally the House approved the omnibus appropriation in November, but not until after Tom DeLay pressured Young into including an extra $300 million for NASA.

Like other appropriators, Young has worked on projects in his district. "I don't appropriate for my state or my district for junk. I don't think anybody can really complain about the value of what we do," he has said. And he adds, "I try to make sure things that are needed in the whole state of Florida are taken care of." But anti-pork lobbyists like Keith Ashdown of Taxpayers for

Common Sense agree that he has not put too much money into his area. "I'd probably put him at the top of the list of people in Congress I most admire. If you could clone him 434 times, the Congress would be a better place."

The November 2004 omnibus contained some $180 million for local projects. And as chairman of the Defense Appropriations Subcommittee before and after his six years as full committee chairman, he has taken an interest in local defense facilities. The 2004 omnibus included $72 million in local defense projects. MacDill Air Force Base in Tampa, just across the bay from St. Petersburg, is the headquarters of Central Command and Special Operations Command. Young has pushed through a $25 million intelligence and operations center and $78 million for a conference center for SOCOM and $31 million for more family housing and a new headquarters for CentCom. MacDill has been thought to be in jeopardy because few planes are based there; Young was pleased when the Air Force announced it would station 32 of the 100 KC-767 aerial refueling tankers built by Boeing at MacDill in June 2003 and dismayed when the Boeing project was held up by the Senate in December 2003.

In the 1970s Young persuaded Congress and Gerald Ford to build the Bay Pines Veterans Medical Center in St. Petersburg, now the second largest VA hospital. In February 2004 he called for an investigation of poor care there and held hearings the next month; the hospital's chief of staff was promptly transferred elsewhere. In October 2003 he persuaded the House to vote 399–0 to end the practice of charging military personnel in military hospitals $8.10 a day for meals. In October 2004 the Veterans Affairs Department gave speedy approval to a Fisher House for families of wounded military personnel at the Haley Veterans Medical Center in Tampa. He has said that his final goal is to establish a federal law enforcement center in downtown St. Petersburg.

After the 2004 election, House Republicans' term limits ended Young's tenure as Appropriations chairman. He said that some members wanted to get him a waiver, but he turned them down. "I'll still have the influence, without the administrative headaches." The Center for Biodefense and Emerging Infectious Diseases at NIH in Bethesda, Maryland, is to be named for Young; the Bay Pines Veterans Medical Center will be too, but, at his insistence, only after he is no longer in Congress.

The trend toward Democrats in Pinellas County has not posed any political threat to Young. But Republican redistricters in 2002 wanted to make it more Republican anyway, so that the party will have a good chance to hold the seat if Young is not a candidate. Young said he simply wanted a compact district. He was reelected unopposed in 2002 and by a 69%–31% margin in 2004. Asked in December 2004 if he would retire, he said, "I'm still energetic, I still have all my faculties about me. I still have a role to play."

ELEVENTH DISTRICT

Rep. Jim Davis (D)

Elected 1996, 5th term; b. Oct. 11, 1957, Tampa; home, Tampa; Wash. & Lee U., B.A. 1979, U. of FL, J.D. 1982; Episcopalian; married (Peggy).

Elected Office: FL House of Reps., 1988–96, Maj. Ldr. 1994–96.

Professional Career: Practicing atty., 1982–96.

DC Office: 409 CHOB, 20515, 202-225-3376; Fax: 202-225-5652; Web site: www.house.gov/jimdavis.

District Offices: St. Petersburg, 727-867-5301; Tampa, 813-354-9217.

Committees: *Energy & Commerce* (20th of 26 D): Commerce, Trade & Consumer Protection; Energy & Air Quality; Health.

Group Ratings

	ADA	ACLU	AFS	LCV	ITIC	NTU	COC	ACU	NTLC	CHC
2004	90	60	88	100	80	16	48	4	8	15
2003	85	—	100	100	—	27	41	25	—	—

National Journal Ratings

	2003 LIB	—	2003 CONS		2004 LIB	—	2004 CONS
Economic	76%	—	24%		69%	—	31%
Social	69%	—	30%		73%	—	25%
Foreign	55%	—	45%		62%	—	36%

Key Votes of the 108th Congress

1. Drilling in ANWR	N	5. DC School Vouchers	N	9. Ban Same-Sex Marriage	N
2. Approve Bush Tax Cuts	N	6. Ban Human Cloning	N	10. Fund Iraq War	Y
3. Medicare/Rx Bill	N	7. Restrict Gun Liability	N	11. Bar Cuba Embargo Funds	N
4. Bar Overtime Pay Regs.	Y	8. Ban Partial-Birth Abortion	Y	12. Intelligence Reorg.	Y

Election Results

2004 general	Jim Davis (D)	191,780	(86%)	($630,804)
	Robert Johnson (Lib)	31,579	(14%)	($32,700)
2004 primary	Jim Davis (D)	unopposed		
2002 general	Jim Davis (D)	unopposed		($385,272)

Prior Winning Percentages: 2000 (85%); 1998 (65%); 1996 (58%)

The People		Race/Ethnic Origin	Ancestry	
Area size:	460 sq. mi.	48.3% White	German: 7.6%	Irish: 6.6%
Urban population:	99.6%	27.4% Black	English: 5.8%	
Rural population:	0.4%	2.0% Asian	**2004 Presidential Vote**	
Pop. 2000:	639,295	0.3% Native Am.	Kerry (D) 145,831	(58%)
Median income:	$33,559	0.1% Hawaiian	Bush (R) 103,748	(41%)
Poverty status:	17.5%	1.7% Two+ races	Other 1,764	(1%)
Military veterans:	13.1%	0.2% Other	**2000 Presidential Vote**	
		20.0% Hispanic Origin	Gore (D) 120,926	(61%)
			Bush (R) 77,367	(39%)
			Cook Partisan Voting Index: D +11	
Occupation	Blue collar: 21.2%	White collar: 61.4%	Gray collar: 17.4%	

Tampa, one of America's boomtowns, has a history that goes back not much more than a century. Its industrial past can be traced to 1886, when Cuban cigarmakers left Key West for what became the Ybor City neighborhood. Then Tampa became the major embarkation port for U.S. troops in the Spanish-American War of 1898. It also became a major citrus distribution center. The old industrial city developed along the waterfront, where today you can find what is billed as the world's longest sidewalk (6.5 miles along Bayshore Boulevard); you can also see the 13 minarets on the Arabian-style Tampa Bay Hotel built by railroad and real-estate tycoon Henry B. Plant in the 1890s (now part of the University of Tampa). For a time, Tampa was Florida's one industrial city. Now, it has a diversified economy: A healthy service sector, the University of Tampa and the University of South Florida, and tourist attractions led by Busch Gardens. Tampa's subdivisions and condominiums, office towers and low-rise commercial buildings have spread inland across swamps and lowlands.

Through all of this, and in contrast to St. Petersburg with its many retirees, Tampa has remained a city of families and young people; seniors account for only about one in eight residents here, an unusually low percentage for Florida. As Tampa expands, its blue-collar character is quickly moving upscale. In January 2005, Donald Trump announced a 52-story luxury condominium on the Hillsborough River in the city. Tampa is also an important military center. MacDill Air Force Base, on the south side of Tampa jutting into Tampa Bay, is the headquarters of Central Command, which ran the Persian Gulf War and the campaigns in Afghanistan and Iraq, and of Special Operations Command. Generals Norman Schwarzkopf and Tommy Franks, retired after their successful commands in the same gated community in Tampa.

The 11th Congressional District of Florida is centered on Tampa, but has irregular boundaries. It includes most of the city of Tampa and close-in suburbs, the east shore of Tampa Bay, plus two areas across Tampa Bay. One is the heavily black and lower-income neighborhoods south of Central Avenue in St. Petersburg. The other is a strip of Manatee County bordering Tampa Bay that includes working-class neighborhoods in Memphis, Palmetto and Bradenton, as well as the world headquarters of the Tropicana juice company. Connecting them is the distinctive Sunshine Skyway Bridge, a four-mile span completed in 1987 that has come to symbolize the Tampa Bay area. The district has a population that is 27% black and 20% Hispanic, making it the most heavily minority district in Florida outside the Gold Coast and the Jacksonville-to-Orlando 3d District. While Hillsborough County as a whole voted for George W. Bush in 2000 and 2004, the 11th District cast solid majorities for Al Gore and John Kerry.

The congressman from the 11th District is Jim Davis, a Democrat first elected in 1996. Davis grew up in Tampa as the grandson of a former mayor, returned after law school, and was elected in 1988, at 31, to the state House. There he showed insider skills and interests; after the 1994 election, he was elected majority leader—the most recent Democrat to hold that job, since Republicans won a majority in 1996. That year, Congressman Sam Gibbons decided to retire after 34 years. Davis was far from the best-known candidate, but he showed great skill at raising money and was the only one running TV ads for the September primary. Sandy Freedman, Tampa's mayor from 1986 to 1995, led Davis in the primary 35%–25%. Both supported the balanced budget amendment, the 1996 welfare act and called for more managed care. Davis won the runoff 56%–44% and in the general faced Republican Mark Sharpe, who had given Gibbons two close contests. He attacked Davis as a fan of higher taxes and a career politician. Davis insisted he was a New Democrat, supporting the Defense of Marriage Act and opposing the penny-per-pound sugar tax on the Florida ballot. Davis won by a solid 58%–42%.

Davis's record has moved toward the center of the House, especially on foreign policy. He was elected the Democratic freshman class president. After securing a deal to liberalize trade in manufactured fertilizers, whose chief U.S. shipping port is Tampa, Davis voted for normal trade relations with China. He voted for trade promotion authority after he got protection for Florida citrus. In February 2003 he was the first member of Congress from Florida to openly travel to Castro's Cuba. He became an outspoken proponent of permitting the Cuban government to purchase U.S. food and for relaxing travel restrictions to the island; he remained a supporter of the overall trade embargo. Republican Lincoln Diaz-Balart called Davis's trip "a disgrace," but Davis said that the United States "should not be in the business of separating families." Despite vociferous opposition, the House in September 2004 passed two Davis amendments to liberalize travel to Cuba, including "people to people" exchanges plus family visits. In 2003, he got a seat on the Energy and Commerce Committee after being "deeply, deeply disappointed" over his failure to win it in 2001. He worked with Republican Charlie Bass on what they called a compromise proposal to tighten carbon dioxide emissions. He proposed a bill to spend $200 million in 10 years on new plants that filter salt from seawater.

In February 2005 Davis announced that he was running for governor in 2006. He had talked of running for governor in 2002, but decided not to. He is one of the few prominent Democratic officeholders in Florida with a relatively moderate record of the sort that enabled Reubin Askew, Lawton Chiles and Bob Graham to win statewide office in the 1970s, 1980s and 1990s. It seems likely that Democrats will hold this House seat. In March 2005, state Senator Les Miller and lawyer Scott Farrell had announced they were running and Hillsborough County Commissioner Kathy Castor, whose mother Betty Castor lost the Senate race to Mel Martinez in 2004, announced in April she would run.

TWELFTH DISTRICT

Rep. Adam Putnam (R)

Elected 2000, 3d term; b. July 31, 1974, Bartow; home, Bartow; U. of FL, B.S. 1995; Episcopalian; married (Melissa).

Elected Office: FL House of Reps., 1996–00.

Professional Career: Rancher, Putnam Groves, Inc.

DC Office: 1213 LHOB, 20515, 202-225-1252; Fax: 202-226-0585; Web site: www.adamputnam.house.gov.

District Office: Bartow, 863-534-3530.

Committees: *Budget* (4th of 22 R). *Rules* (5th of 9 R): Rules & Organization of the House (Vice Chmn.).

Group Ratings

	ADA	ACLU	AFS	LCV	ITIC	NTU	COC	ACU	NTLC	CHC
2004	0	0	0	0	100	66	100	100	86	100
2003	5	—	0	5	—	61	97	92	—	—

National Journal Ratings

	2003 LIB	—	2003 CONS		2004 LIB	—	2004 CONS
Economic	27%	—	71%		5%	—	93%
Social	17%	—	79%		20%	—	80%
Foreign	21%	—	79%		17%	—	78%

Key Votes of the 108th Congress

1. Drilling in ANWR	Y	5. DC School Vouchers	Y	9. Ban Same-Sex Marriage	Y
2. Approve Bush Tax Cuts	Y	6. Ban Human Cloning	Y	10. Fund Iraq War	*
3. Medicare/Rx Bill	Y	7. Restrict Gun Liability	Y	11. Bar Cuba Embargo Funds	N
4. Bar Overtime Pay Regs.	N	8. Ban Partial-Birth Abortion	Y	12. Intelligence Reorg.	Y

Election Results

2004 general	Adam Putnam (R)	179,204	(65%)	($700,625)
	Bob Hagenmaier (D)	96,965	(35%)	($54,002)
2004 primary	Adam Putnam (R)	42,605	(92%)	
	Robert Wirengard (R)	3,546	(8%)	
2002 general	Adam Putnam (R) .... unopposed			($350,343)

Prior Winning Percentages: 2000 (57%)

The People		Race/Ethnic Origin	Ancestry	
Area size:	2,096 sq. mi.	72.1% White	German: 9.9%	USA: 9.8%
Urban population:	84.3%	13.0% Black	Irish: 8.4%	
Rural population:	15.7%	1.1% Asian	**2004 Presidential Vote**	
Pop. 2000:	639,296	0.3% Native Am.	Bush (R) 167,216	(58%)
Median income:	$37,769	0.0% Hawaiian	Kerry (D) 119,825	(42%)
Poverty status:	12.4%	1.3% Two+ races	Other 798	(0%)
Military veterans:	17.0%	0.1% Other	**2000 Presidential Vote**	
		12.0% Hispanic Origin	Bush (R) 121,083	(55%)
			Gore (D) 99,826	(45%)
			Cook Partisan Voting Index: R + 5	
Occupation	Blue collar: 26.1%	White collar: 55.9%	Gray collar: 18.0%	

With their skyscrapers rising over bays and rivers, the great gleaming cities of Florida are found near the Atlantic or Gulf coasts. But the most expansive inland county in the state, billed as the heart of central Florida, is Polk County. It is filled with modest lakes and small and medium-sized cities: Lakeland, Bartow, Lake Wales, Winter Haven, Frostproof and Haines City. It is the part of Florida most dependent on agriculture: strawberries, cattle and citrus remain economic mainstays, though periodic freezes have convinced some orange growers to move south or to produce tomatoes instead. Turpentine distilleries, dependent on the big stands of pine, and phosphate mining businesses can be found as well. There are more manufacturing jobs here proportionately than almost anywhere else in Florida (though still not very many). Retired *Ladies Home Journal* editor Edward Bok built the most prominent landmarks here: the gothic Bok Tower and the surrounding Mountain Lake Sanctuary and gardens. But the area has not become a major retiree haven; it grew 23% between 1990 and 2004—rapid growth in most of the country, but not in Florida. About half the growth here has been a large influx of Latinos. Three devastating hurricanes struck this area hard in 2004 and caused the loss of thousands of jobs for migrant and seasonal laborers, especially those who work on tomato and citrus crops.

The 12th Congressional District of Florida includes almost all of Polk County. This was the home of Spessard Holland and Lawton Chiles, two legendary Democrats who each served as governor and senator. Even today, there are more registered Democrats than Republicans, but Polk County, like most of the Deep South, increasingly votes Republican, and Chiles lost Polk County to Jeb Bush when he was reelected in 1994. The 12th District also includes a sliver of Osceola County and the rapidly growing suburbs just east of Tampa in Hillsborough County— places like Brandon, home to strip malls and younger, pro-business families. Overall this district, historically Democratic, is becoming reliably Republican. It voted 55% for George W. Bush in 2000 and 58% in 2004.

The congressman from the 12th District is Adam Putnam, a Republican first elected in 2000. He was the youngest member of the House from January 2001 until the January 2005 swearing in of Patrick McHenry of North Carolina. He grew up in Polk County, a fifth-generation member of a Bartow family, graduated from the University of Florida and worked in his family's citrus and cattle business. In 1996, at 22, he was elected to the state House, where as Agriculture Committee chairman he supported a "sovereign lands" bill that would have given shoreline property on inland waters to adjacent property owners and that was strongly opposed by environmental groups. In 2000, when incumbent Charles Canady retired at age 46, keeping his pledge to serve only four terms, Putnam was unopposed in the Republican primary. Putnam supported most parts of the Republican agenda. He opposed abortion and gun control, wanted to lower the capital gains tax and favored personal retirement accounts in Social Security and favored missile defense. In his first election, Putnam had a tougher than expected challenge from auto-dealer and first-time candidate Michael Stedem; he said that Putnam did not have enough life experience for the job. Stedem's message gained some traction; Putnam was ridiculed in the press. "Putnam is 26 and looks as if he's going on 13," wrote Daniel Ruth of the *Tampa Tribune* in October 2000, in a story headlined, "Opie runs for Congress." But Putnam won the seat 57%–43%.

With one notable exception, Putnam has been a reliable conservative vote. That one case was the December 2001 vote on trade promotion authority, where an evidently conflicted Putnam sided with the citrus industry, despite considerable pressure from party leaders and from George W. Bush on Air Force One a week before the vote. When the bill returned to the House a few months later to resolve final details, Putnam voted in favor after he got what he viewed as a stronger commitment to protect citrus interests. Putnam had another memorable ride with Bush three months earlier. On the morning of September 11, 2001 he was with Bush during a visit to an elementary school in Sarasota when word came of the attacks on the World Trade Center towers. After their rapid and steeply-banking exit and before they landed at Barksdale Air Force Base in Louisiana, Bush called in Putnam and the 13th District's Dan Miller for a briefing of his options that morning. The two congressmen returned to Washington on another plane. He urged the EPA to relax restrictions on phosphogypsum, a waste product of fertilizer manufacturing; industry studies have concluded that it could be used in landfills and roadbeds. On immigration, an important local issue, Putnam supported Bush's guest worker proposal, based partly on his own family's hiring experiences. After the 2004 hurricanes, he helped to get $500 million in disaster relief for his state's agricultural industry.

In 2003 he became chairman of the Technology, Information Policy, Intergovernmental Relations and Census Subcommittee on Government Reform, making him the youngest subcommittee chair in the post-World War II era. As chairman, Putnam worked to reduce the risk of cyberterrorism, and passed an amendment to the 2004 intelligence bill that required federal agencies to emphasize information security in planning new systems. His party faithfulness was rewarded when Speaker Dennis Hastert in September 2004 named Putnam to a seat on the House Rules Committee, which had become open when Porter Goss resigned to become director of the CIA; he was the first new member that Hastert picked for Rules in the six years that he had been Speaker. Putnam was forced to relinquish his chairmanship, but the new assignment moved him closer to leadership operations. At home, he has been reelected easily.

THIRTEENTH DISTRICT

Rep. Katherine Harris (R)

Elected 2002, 2d term; b. April 5, 1957, Key West; home, Sarasota; Agnes Scott Col., B.A. 1979, Harvard U. Kennedy Schl. of Gov., M.P.A. 1996; Presbyterian; married (Anders).

Elected Office: FL Senate, 1994–98; FL Secy. of State, 1998–2002.

DC Office: 116 CHOB, 20515, 202-225-5015; Fax: 202-226-0828; Web site: www.harris.house.gov.

District Offices: Bradenton, 941-747-9081; Sarasota, 941-951-6643.

Committees: *Financial Services* (29th of 37 R): Capital Markets, Insurance & Government Sponsored Enterprises; Domestic and International Monetary Policy, Trade & Technology; Housing & Community Opportunity. *Homeland Security* (15th of 19 R): Economic Security, Infrastructure Protection & Cybersecurity; Emergency Preparedness, Science & Technology; Management, Integration & Oversight. *International Relations* (20th of 27 R): Middle East & Central Asia; Western Hemisphere.

Group Ratings

	ADA	ACLU	AFS	LCV	ITIC	NTU	COC	ACU	NTLC	CHC
2004	0	0	0	0	100	72	100	92	86	100
2003	5	—	0	15	—	60	97	88	—	—

National Journal Ratings

	2003 LIB	—	2003 CONS		2004 LIB	—	2004 CONS
Economic	17%	—	81%		5%	—	93%
Social	17%	—	79%		28%	—	70%
Foreign	11%	—	80%		25%	—	68%

Key Votes of the 108th Congress

1. Drilling in ANWR	Y	5. DC School Vouchers	Y	9. Ban Same-Sex Marriage	Y
2. Approve Bush Tax Cuts	Y	6. Ban Human Cloning	Y	10. Fund Iraq War	Y
3. Medicare/Rx Bill	Y	7. Restrict Gun Liability	Y	11. Bar Cuba Embargo Funds	N
4. Bar Overtime Pay Regs.	N	8. Ban Partial-Birth Abortion	Y	12. Intelligence Reorg.	Y

Election Results

2004 general	Katherine Harris (R)	190,477	(55%)	($3,556,976)
	Jan Schneider (D)	153,961	(45%)	($655,790)
2004 primary	Katherine Harris (R)	unopposed		
2002 general	Katherine Harris (R)	139,048	(55%)	($3,298,146)
	Jan Schneider (D)	114,739	(45%)	($336,796)

The People		Race/Ethnic Origin	Ancestry	
Area size:	2,948 sq. mi.	86.0% White	German: 14.1%	English: 10.8%
Urban population:	89.4%	4.4% Black	Irish: 10.2%	
Rural population:	10.6%	0.8% Asian	**2004 Presidential Vote**	
Pop. 2000:	639,295	0.2% Native Am.	Bush (R) 200,932	(56%)
Median income:	$40,187	0.0% Hawaiian	Kerry (D) 156,727	(43%)
Poverty status:	9.4%	0.8% Two+ races	Other 2,642	(1%)
Military veterans:	19.2%	0.1% Other	**2000 Presidential Vote**	
		7.7% Hispanic Origin	Bush (R) 152,725	(54%)
			Gore (D) 127,751	(46%)
			Cook Partisan Voting Index: R + 4	

Occupation	Blue collar: 21.0%	White collar: 58.5%	Gray collar: 20.5%

When the Ringling Brothers made a success of the circus they founded in the 1880s, they needed a place for performers and animals to rest during the winter months. They settled on the bayfront village of Sarasota, located behind a barrier island on the Gulf of Mexico. It was just far enough north to be reachable by railroad, just far enough south to be semitropical so the elephants would not get sick and die. Here, on the calm Sarasota Bay, John Ringling established the Ringling Museum of Art, a huge sculpture garden and his own Venetian palace, the Ca'd'Zan; next door, his brother Charles built a pair of neoclassical revival mansions made of pink Georgia marble, now part of New College of Florida. After World War II, the balmy Gulf Coast attracted new settlers—affluent, well-educated Republicans from WASPy, upper-crust suburbs in the north. The population exploded, with Manatee and Sarasota Counties leaping from 63,000 in 1950 to 651,000 in 2003. This part of Florida is no longer a winter community for snow birds from the North; it has generated its own economy, one with considerably more vitality than and just as much diversity as the places from which its residents have come.

The 13th Congressional District of Florida runs from just below Tampa Bay to Charlotte Harbor, north of Fort Myers. It includes all of Sarasota County, which accounts for just over half the district's population, and all of lightly populated, rural DeSoto and Hardee Counties, most of Manatee County to the north and an adjoining sliver of Charlotte County to the south. The barrier islands include much idyllic beachfront, from sleepy Anna Maria down through pricey Longboat Key and Lido Key to more casual Siesta Key. The bayfront area, along the Intracoastal Waterway, is lined with high rises and often clogged with traffic, running from Bradenton south to Sarasota. Below that, Venice—established in 1920 as a speculative land venture by the Brotherhood of Locomotive Engineers and, since 1960, the winter quarters for the circus—sits directly on the ocean. Though some high-tech firms diversify the economy, this remains a place of tourists and well-off retirees: 29% of the population is over 65, and it has 182,000 Social Security recipients, third highest of all U.S. congressional districts. For many years, the 13th District was heavily Republican, and it remains that way in party registration, but like the affluent northern suburbs from which so many of its voters came, it trended toward the Democrats in the 1990s. George W. Bush has carried this district, but with just 54% of the vote in 2000 and 56% in 2004.

The congresswoman from the 13th District is Katherine Harris, a Republican first elected in 2002 and a political figure of renown before her election to the House. She grew up in Bartow in Polk County, where her grandfather Ben Hill Griffin Jr. was one of Florida's largest landowners, with thousands of acres of citrus grove and cattle range; he was also politically influential, and the University of Florida football stadium is named for him. Harris interned for Congressman Andy Ireland in college, graduated from Agnes Scott College in Georgia, and studied art and other courses in Europe. She moved to Sarasota and worked as a commercial real estate executive and in marketing for IBM and became a patron of the arts. In 1994, she was elected to the state Senate in what was then the most expensive legislative race in state history. In 1998 she ran against the incumbent secretary of state, who was backed by Governor Jeb Bush, and won the primary 61%–39% and then the general election 54%–46%. In 1999, the legislature voted to remove the office from the Cabinet and make it an appointive rather than elective position. So Harris was a lame duck on election night 2000, as the votes coming in showed that the presidential race in Florida was going to be extremely close. Florida law gave Harris the responsibility of certifying the election and declaring the winner of the state's electoral votes. When she vowed to certify the results one week after Election Day, as state law required, lawyers for Al Gore sued for more time. Two weeks later, when Harris did certify Bush as the winner, Gore sued her again, claiming she acted before all the recounts were complete. Democratic critics charged that her actions were biased; Republicans hailed her for adhering to the letter of the law and for ultimately certifying Bush, by 537 votes, as winner in accordance with state law.

Harris had an obvious political opening when 13th District Congressman Dan Miller kept his promise to retire after serving 10 years. When she announced in October 2001 that she was running, her primary opponent, former local TV anchor John Hill, filed a lawsuit arguing that under Florida law she could not run until she resigned as secretary of state. She quickly resigned and won the primary 68%–32%. In the general election she faced Democrat Jan Schneider, who graduated from Yale Law School in 1973, the same year as Bill and Hillary Rodham Clinton. She worked in Washington as a lawyer and lobbyist for 25 years and, after moving to Florida in 1999, she played a bit role in the 2000 Florida controversy when she interviewed allegedly disenfranchised voters in Palm Beach County. She repeated Democrats' charges that Harris had not followed the law in November and December 2000, and she questioned whether the nation was "adopting a 'might is right' policy" in dealing with Iraq. Harris opposed oil drilling in the Gulf of Mexico, supported personal retirement accounts in Social Security and supported current law on abortion, although she calls herself pro-life. She made the case for her decisions in 2000 in her book, *Center of the Storm,* which was released in October. When she went on a national publicity tour, Schneider criticized her for leaving the district; Harris said she had pleaded with the publisher to release the book much later. Harris won 55%–45%. Given her name identification and 10-to-1 money advantage, this was not a huge margin.

In the House, Harris was usually a reliable conservative and a focus of interest, but she did not immediately exercise much influence. She passed her first bill through the House in October 2003: the American Dream Downpayment Act, which had bipartisan support and was designed to assist first-time, low-income homebuyers. In August 2004, she gained attention when she told an audience in Venice that she learned from classified information that more than 100 potential attacks against the nation had been thwarted since September 11. Pressed for more details, Harris, who limited her contacts with reporters in Washington, demurred; "I probably said too much." The next day she expressed regret over her claim of a threat to the power grid in Carmel, Indiana, but she stood by her general statement. In October and November 2003 she entertained the idea of running for the Senate seat being vacated by Democrat Bob Graham. But after talking with White House chief strategist Karl Rove, she said that she would not run after having served only one term in the House. In 2004 campaign she again attracted articulate opposition. Some Democratic leaders encouraged Christine Jennings, a retired Sarasota bank president, to run, but Schneider ran again and won the primary 47%–38%. Schneider called for rolling back tax cuts and stopping the flow of jobs overseas; Harris defended George W. Bush's handling of the economy and the war. In the presidential battleground state, she again became a focus of attention. In October, a driver drove his car onto a sidewalk toward her and nearly struck her while she was waving to voters a week before the election; he was charged with aggravated assault with a deadly weapon. Once again, Harris won 55%–45%.

Florida's 17 other Republican House members ran ahead of Bush in their districts, while Harris ran slightly behind. Nonetheless in June 2005 she announced that she would run against Senator Bill Nelson in 2006. No doubt the controversy she generated in 2000 will enable both her and Nelson to raise large sums in Florida and nationally in a Harris-Nelson race. An open House seat could result in a competitive contest, but the Republican nominee would be favored.

FOURTEENTH DISTRICT

Rep. Connie Mack (R)

Elected 2004, 1st term; b. Aug. 12, 1967, Fort Myers; home, Fort Myers; U. of FL, B.S. 1993; Catholic; married (Ann).

Elected Office: FL House, 2000–03.

Professional Career: Marketing consultant, 1994–2004.

DC Office: 317 CHOB, 20515, 202-225-2536; Fax: 202-226-0439; Web site: www.house.gov/mack.

District Offices: Fort Myers, 239-322-4677; Naples, 239-774-8035.

Committees: *Budget* (20th of 22 R). *International Relations* (24th of 27 R): Middle East & Central Asia; Western Hemisphere. *Transportation & Infrastructure* (36th of 41 R): Coast Guard & Maritime Transportation; Water Resources & Environment.

Group Ratings and Key Votes: Newly Elected

Election Results

2004 general	Connie Mack (R)	226,662	(68%)	($1,854,028)
	Robert Neeld (D)	108,672	(32%)	($25,275)
2004 primary	Connie Mack (R)	27,526	(36%)	
	Carole Green (R)	24,767	(32%)	
	Andy Coy (R)	17,089	(22%)	
	Frank Schwerin (R)	7,465	(10%)	
2002 general	Porter Goss (R)	unopposed		($90,189)

The People		Race/Ethnic Origin	Ancestry	
Area size:	1,718 sq. mi.	83.8% White	German: 14.5%	Irish: 11.0%
Urban population:	90.7%	5.1% Black	English: 10.2%	
Rural population:	9.3%	0.7% Asian	**2004 Presidential Vote**	
Pop. 2000:	639,295	0.2% Native Am.	Bush (R) 222,234	(62%)
Median income:	$42,541	0.0% Hawaiian	Kerry (D) 136,049	(38%)
Poverty status:	8.8%	1.0% Two+ races	Other 2,631	(1%)
Military veterans:	19.8%	0.1% Other	**2000 Presidential Vote**	
		9.0% Hispanic Origin	Bush (R) 163,750	(61%)
			Gore (D) 103,118	(39%)
			Cook Partisan Voting Index: R +10	

Occupation	Blue collar: 21.1%	White collar: 59.6%	Gray collar: 19.3%

On the edge of the tropics, in a physical environment once teeming with diseases and inhospitable to advanced civilization three generations ago, Florida's Gulf Coast has sprung up as a model for retirement living. Early on, there were only a few white settlements here; one was Fort Myers, built in 1850 as an Army base to help get rid of the Seminole Indians. The fort achieved its goal: In 1858, the last Seminoles were sent west on boats. For another century after that, this corner of Florida was mostly deserted. But in time, it became resort country, thanks to its wide, white-sand beaches with gentle breakers; the inlets and broad estuaries that are perfect for boating; and the wetlands graced with exotic birds. Thomas Edison had his winter home in Fort Myers, Henry Ford used to visit here. Tourists came to a beach thick with sea shells on nearby Sanibel and Captiva islands. But the local economy could not support many permanent residents, and at the beginning of World War II, there were only 68,000 people living on the Gulf Coast from Bradenton south to Naples.

By 2004, there were 1.6 million. The climate and environment, and the fact that Florida has no state income or inheritance tax, had attracted waves of affluent suburbanites from the Midwest and Northeast. Developers like Barron Collier, who built the Tamiami Trail across the soggy Everglades and designed Naples with the wealthy in mind (and gave his name to Collier

County, the richest and from 1990 to 2003 the third fastest-growing in Florida), were determined to avoid the high-rise canyons that line the Atlantic from Palm Beach to Miami. Their alternative was to construct low-rise, city-style developments, such as Cape Coral, with canals in most backyards, and thinly paved roads along the sand spits next to the sultry, lapping waves of the Gulf, and luxurious boutique towns like Naples, set amidst preserved coastal islands, St. Augustine grass and banyan trees. This is very much retirement country, for those who can afford it. Although much of this area was damaged in 2004 by multiple hurricanes, there was no appreciable slowdown in new residential or commercial development; Fort Myers prepared to open a new airport terminal.

The 14th Congressional District of Florida occupies the southern half of the habitable Gulf Coast below Tampa Bay; it grew by almost 40% in the 1990s, largely from retirees, who account for more than one of every four residents. The 14th includes a small part of Port Charlotte and Charlotte County, all of Lee County and the coastal strip of Collier County including Naples and Marco Island. Two-thirds of the district's residents live in Lee County, in places like Fort Myers, Bonita Springs and Sanibel and Captiva Islands. In a state where Republican registration rates often understate Republican voting strength, the 14th District counts 50% of its electorate as registered Republicans. Just 28% are registered Democrats, the lowest percentage of any Florida district.

The congressman from the 14th District is Connie Mack IV, a Republican elected in 2004, whose father Connie Mack III held the same seat for three terms in the 1980s and was elected to the Senate in 1988 and 1994. His great-grandfather and best-known forebear was Philadelphia Athletics baseball owner and manager Cornelius McGillicuddy, who shortened his name to Connie Mack. Connie Mack IV graduated from the University of Florida after seven years and worked as a marketing consultant. In 2000 he was elected to the state House from a district in Broward and Palm Beach Counties, along the Atlantic Ocean front from Hollywood to Boca Raton, by a 56%–44% margin; he was reelected with only Libertarian opposition 79%–21% in 2002. In the Florida House Mack formed the anti-tax Freedom Caucus, which fought against increased state spending and in favor of lower taxes. As chairman of the Victims' Compensation Coalition, a political action committee, he helped lead a 2003 statewide petition drive to place a measure on the ballot to limit attorneys' fees in personal injury and malpractice cases. To political observers Mack seemed a logical candidate to succeed 22d District Republican Clay Shaw when he retires.

But Porter Goss, congressman since 1988 and chairman of the House Intelligence Committee since 1997, was not running for reelection in the 14th District; in July 2004 Goss was nominated to be Director of the CIA and, after his confirmation by the Senate, resigned from the House in September 2004. Mack resigned from the state House in October 2003 and moved across the state to Lee County and ran for the seat his father had represented. He faced three opponents in the August 31 Republican primary: state Representative Carole Green from Lee County, Lee County Commissioner Andy Coy and Naples physician Frank Schwerin. Mack raised $1.4 million for the primary, outpacing his nearest Republican rival by more than 2–1, and blanketed southwestern Florida with TV ads. His opponents attacked him as a carpetbagger who hadn't lived in the 14th District since he was a teenager and had moved there simply to run for Congress. Mack, who refused interviews with reporters and responded only to written questions, countered that he was the only candidate who had been born and raised in the district.

Green was endorsed by the *Fort Myers News-Press* and by Mariel Goss, wife of Porter Goss. Editorialists were dismissive of Mack's qualifications, as well as his carpetbagging. "What a hoot," wrote the *Palm Beach Post,* which noted that his marketing consulting included sending Hooters girls to charity events. Mack's opponents claimed that he was an inexperienced lightweight who spoke only in platitudes. Mack accused Green of taking campaign money from an HMO while working on health care legislation; she responded that Mack had taken money from the same company. The four Republicans differed little on the issues. All campaigned as conservatives and all supported George W. Bush's war on terrorism and tax cuts. Mack campaigned as a budget hawk and said that national security would top his agenda. While he opposed abortion, he broke with the Bush administration on federal funding of embryonic stem-cell research. He also supported reimportation of prescription drugs from Canada; the 14th District has the fourth highest number of Social Security recipients in the nation.

Mack won the primary with 36% of the vote; Green narrowly carried Lee County, which cast 73% of the total vote, but fell short district-wide with 32%; Coy won 22% and Schwerin 10%. In November Mack won 68%–32%. He got seats on the Budget and International Relations committees, and on the Transportation and Infrastructure Committee, where he said he would work to widen I-75, on which he said he would work with Broward County freshman Democrat Debbie Wasserman Schultz, with whom he served in Tallahassee. In January 2005 George W. Bush named his father to co-chair a commission to study tax reform and make recommendations by the summer.

FIFTEENTH DISTRICT

Rep. Dave Weldon (R)

Elected 1994, 6th term; b. Aug. 31, 1953, Amityville, NY; home, Palm Bay; S.U.N.Y. Stony Brook, B.A. 1978, S.U.N.Y. Buffalo, M.D. 1981; Christian; married (Nancy).

Military Career: Army Medical Corps, 1981–87, Army Reserves, 1987–92.

Professional Career: Practicing physician, 1987–94.

DC Office: 2347 RHOB, 20515, 202-225-3671; Fax: 202-225-3516; Web site: www.house.gov/weldon.

District Office: Melbourne, 321-632-1776.

Committees: *Appropriations* (30th of 37 R): Labor, Health and Human Services, Education & Related Agencies; Science, State, Justice, Commerce & Related Agencies (Vice Chmn.).

Group Ratings

	ADA	ACLU	AFS	LCV	ITIC	NTU	COC	ACU	NTLC	CHC
2004	0	0	13	9	90	54	100	91	78	100
2003	5	—	0	5	—	62	93	92	—	—

National Journal Ratings

	2003 LIB	—	2003 CONS	2004 LIB	—	2004 CONS
Economic	9%	—	84%	16%	—	84%
Social	30%	—	65%	17%	—	83%
Foreign	11%	—	80%	0%	—	96%

Key Votes of the 108th Congress

1. Drilling in ANWR	Y	5. DC School Vouchers	Y	9. Ban Same-Sex Marriage	Y
2. Approve Bush Tax Cuts	Y	6. Ban Human Cloning	Y	10. Fund Iraq War	Y
3. Medicare/Rx Bill	Y	7. Restrict Gun Liability	Y	11. Bar Cuba Embargo Funds	N
4. Bar Overtime Pay Regs.	N	8. Ban Partial-Birth Abortion	Y	12. Intelligence Reorg.	Y

Election Results

2004 general	Dave Weldon (R)	210,388	(65%)	($733,711)
	Simon Pristoop (D)	111,538	(35%)	($54,355)
2004 primary	Dave Weldon (R)	unopposed		
2002 general	Dave Weldon (R)	146,414	(63%)	($721,859)
	Jim Tso (D)	85,433	(37%)	($51,697)

Prior Winning Percentages: 2000 (59%); 1998 (63%); 1996 (51%); 1994 (54%)

The People		Race/Ethnic Origin	Ancestry	
Area size:	3,253 sq. mi.	77.8% White	German: 12.2%	Irish: 10.6%
Urban population:	89.6%	7.3% Black	English: 9.7%	
Rural population:	10.4%	1.6% Asian	**2004 Presidential Vote**	
Pop. 2000:	639,295	0.3% Native Am.	Bush (R) 195,076	(57%)
Median income:	$39,397	0.0% Hawaiian	Kerry (D) 146,914	(43%)
Poverty status:	9.8%	1.4% Two+ races	Other 2,128	(1%)
Military veterans:	19.4%	0.2% Other	**2000 Presidential Vote**	
		11.3% Hispanic Origin	Bush (R) 141,242	(54%)
			Gore (D) 121,611	(46%)
			Cook Partisan Voting Index: R + 4	

Occupation	Blue collar: 21.5%	White collar: 58.4%	Gray collar: 20.1%

When Cape Canaveral was chosen as the nation's rocket testing site in the 1940s, there were only 20,000 people in all of Brevard County, which stretches along 63 miles of the coast north and south of the Cape. It was a backward place reliant on fishing and citrus-growing, chosen because it was on the sunny Atlantic coast: rockets here have to be launched eastward so that spent parts fall into the ocean. The Brooklyn Dodgers' spring-training home of Vero Beach, located 60 miles south of Canaveral in Indian River County, remained segregated through the mid-1950s, until Dodger executives used an ingenious method to flex their economic muscle in the service of integration: They stamped the team's name on 20,000 dollar bills and told players and reporters to spend them freely at local establishments. Local officials got the message, easing off on Jim Crow, at least when Jackie Robinson and his teammates were in town. Today, the region has come a long way. Brevard County has 519,000 people, and the Kennedy Space Center attracts 2 million visitors annually. Brevard County is a prototype of America's future, with no city center but plenty of shopping centers along strip highways, with a white-collar, service economy, knitted together by interest in the space program, which constitutes 16% of local jobs. Even with cutbacks in NASA launches, some from the Cape Canaveral Air Force Station, development continued strong. Proximity to Disney World has spawned growth in the cruise business, including Disney's mega-ships.

The 15th Congressional District of Florida includes much, but not all of the Space Coast. Its northern end is at Cape Canaveral itself, but most of the Space Center facilities, including the visitors' center, are in the 24th District just to the north. It runs south along the Atlantic Coast and includes all of Indian River County; among the bigger towns are Cocoa Beach, Melbourne, Palm Bay and Vero Beach. To the west the district also includes all but a small piece of Osceola County; the population here is just south of Disney World and concentrated around Kissimmee and St. Cloud. This is the fastest-growing part of the district, with a rapidly increasing Puerto Rican and Latino population. The district also includes the northern tip of Polk County. In between are trackless swamp and ranch lands traversed by Florida's Turnpike. The population here is a mixture of young workers and retirees, plus military families stationed at Patrick Air Force Base, home of the 45th Space Wing. In 2004, the area suffered heavy damage from three hurricanes. Politically, the district leans Republican. In 2004, George W. Bush won more easily here than in 2000. The Bush campaign worked intensively on the new Latino voters in Osceola County; Bush lost the county 52%–48% in 2000 but carried it 52%–47% in 2004.

The congressman from the 15th District is Dave Weldon, a Republican first elected in 1994. Weldon grew up on Long Island, went to medical school in Buffalo, and served in the Army as a major at Fort Stewart, Georgia. In 1987, he joined Melbourne Internal Medicine Associates in Florida; two years later, he founded the Space Coast Family Forum "to promote family-friendly issues and positions." In 1994 Weldon ran for the House when moderate Democrat Jim Bacchus retired after two terms; he was considered a weak candidate because of his strong conservative views on cultural issues. But he led the seven-candidate Republican primary with 24% of the vote, and in the runoff won 54%–46% over moderate Carole Jordan. Democrats ran Sue Munsey, a former Republican and Space Coast Chamber of Commerce head who supported abortion rights. Weldon called for phasing out welfare and banning abortion; he won 54%–46%. Speaker

Newt Gingrich, whom Weldon called an "idol," gave him a seat on the Science Committee and made him vice chairman of the Space and Aeronautics Subcommittee.

Weldon has a conservative voting record. He started off defending the Kennedy Space Center and promoting the space shuttle, protecting their funding even when NASA funding was going down. But in time he moved from defending to transforming the program. With Senator Bob Graham, he passed a bill in 1998 to move toward commercialization of space. The idea was to increase U.S. commercial launching capacity, by using antiquated (and disposable) ballistic missiles. Still, commercial competition and the response to the loss of the space shuttle Columbia in February 2003, may bring long-term challenges to the Cape Canaveral area. Even before the shuttle blew up over Texas, Weldon complained that budget cuts were "slowly killing space exploration" and that NASA requirements are "fluid" and its designs "overly complex"; he cited reduced spending as a factor in the failure of two Mars missions. In 2002, he co-authored with writer William Proctor *Moongate,* a sci-fi novel about a Brevard County congressman who chairs the House Space Committee and gains the power to cure many ills through genetic engineering.

Weldon favors increased defense spending, a 17% flat tax, school vouchers and education IRAs. Citing labor and human rights abuses plus undercutting of the U.S. space launch industry, he voted against normal trade relations with China; but he voted for trade promotion authority. Weldon has been a leader in the campaign to ban cloning, including embryonic stem cell research. When the House passed his anti-cloning bill, Weldon noted that it does not restrict research on adult stem cells. The House passed his amendment to bar the issuance of patents on human organisms. On a more practical matter, he won a change in House rules to drop the restrictions on members who are physicians from earning income from their medical practice. In 2003, Weldon got a seat on the Appropriations Committee, where he gained an opportunity to have more direct impact on NASA's budget. When the committee reorganized, he became vice-chairman of the Science, State and Justice Subcommittee. In 2004, he used his committee position, over strong objections from abortion advocates, to enact a provision to block states and localities from requiring health care providers and insurers to provide abortion services.

Weldon's reputation for outspoken conservatism has inspired strong electoral opposition, but he has survived with comfortable margins. In 2002, Weldon beat a primary opponent who criticized him for violating his term-limit pledge by 83%–17%. He briefly considered a run for the Senate in 2004, but backed off when other conservatives entered the contest. He was reelected by a 65%–35% margin.

SIXTEENTH DISTRICT

Rep. Mark Foley (R)

Elected 1994, 6th term; b. Sept. 8, 1954, Newton, MA; home, West Palm Beach; attended Palm Beach Commun. Col., 1974; Catholic; single.

Elected Office: Lake Worth City Commissioner, 1977–83; Vice Mayor, 1983–84; FL House of Reps., 1990–92; FL Senate, 1992–94.

Professional Career: Restaurateur, 1974–84; Real estate broker, 1984–90.

DC Office: 104 CHOB, 20515, 202-225-5792; Fax: 202-225-3132; Web site: www.house.gov/foley.

District Offices: Palm Beach Gardens, 561-627-6192; Port Charlotte, 941-627-9100; Port St. Lucie, 772-878-3181.

Committees: *Ways & Means* (15th of 24 R): Select Revenue Measures; Trade.

Group Ratings

	ADA	ACLU	AFS	LCV	ITIC	NTU	COC	ACU	NTLC	CHC
2004	25	10	0	9	100	56	100	68	76	84
2003	5	—	0	20	—	59	97	80	—	—

National Journal Ratings

	2003 LIB	—	2003 CONS		2004 LIB	—	2004 CONS
Economic	27%	—	71%		33%	—	65%
Social	42%	—	56%		52%	—	47%
Foreign	44%	—	55%		25%	—	68%

Key Votes of the 108th Congress

1. Drilling in ANWR	Y	5. DC School Vouchers	Y	9. Ban Same-Sex Marriage	N
2. Approve Bush Tax Cuts	Y	6. Ban Human Cloning	Y	10. Fund Iraq War	Y
3. Medicare/Rx Bill	Y	7. Restrict Gun Liability	Y	11. Bar Cuba Embargo Funds	N
4. Bar Overtime Pay Regs.	N	8. Ban Partial-Birth Abortion	Y	12. Intelligence Reorg.	Y

Election Results

2004 general	Mark Foley (R)	215,563	(68%)	($1,839,746)
	Jeff Fisher (D)	101,247	(32%)	
2004 primary	Mark Foley (R) .... unopposed			
2002 general	Mark Foley (R)	176,171	(79%)	($902,644)
	Jack McLain (CPF)	47,169	(21%)	($2,587)

Prior Winning Percentages: 2000 (60%); 1998 (100%); 1996 (64%); 1994 (58%)

The People		Race/Ethnic Origin	Ancestry	
Area size:	5,249 sq. mi.	81.8% White	German: 12.3%	Irish: 11.3%
Urban population:	84.5%	5.8% Black	English: 9.7%	
Rural population:	15.5%	1.0% Asian	**2004 Presidential Vote**	
Pop. 2000:	639,295	0.3% Native Am.	Bush (R) 183,339	(54%)
Median income:	$39,408	0.0% Hawaiian	Kerry (D) 154,632	(46%)
Poverty status:	10.0%	1.0% Two+ races	Other 1,312	(0%)
Military veterans:	18.9%	0.1% Other	**2000 Presidential Vote**	
		10.1% Hispanic Origin	Bush (R) 141,029	(53%)
			Gore (D) 124,752	(47%)
			Cook Partisan Voting Index: R + 2	
Occupation	Blue collar: 21.8%	White collar: 57.5%	Gray collar: 20.6%	

Urban Florida has fanned far across the swamplands from its original nuclei in beachfront resort communities. Once, metro Palm Beach was a narrow stretch along Lake Worth; now it runs inland almost halfway to Lake Okeechobee. Thus Palm Beach has spread out from its original locus around the posh Breakers Hotel and the Addison Mizner villas, across Lake Worth and well beyond West Palm Beach: These are now just neighborhoods within a vast metropolitan area. Old beach towns, such as Hobe Sound, located northward along the ocean, have become the hub of very affluent developments that stretch all the way to Stuart in Martin County. Farther north, near the old town of Fort Pierce, are larger but more modest developments like Port St. Lucie. Here, spring training sites compete for baseball franchises that direct millions of dollars to local economies.

The 16th Congressional District of Florida stretches from the Atlantic almost to the Gulf of Mexico; it is one of the most oddly designed districts in the nation. In 2000, before redistricting, 44% of the 16th District's vote was cast in Palm Beach County; after redistricting, just 15% was cast there. On the Atlantic Coast it includes most of Martin County, with its very affluent towns of Stuart and Hobe Sound; much of St. Lucie County, where it includes the new developments of Port St. Lucie and Hutchinson Island and the white neighborhoods of Fort Pierce; and just a bit of Palm Beach County—Tequesta, its northernmost beach town, inland Royal Palm Beach and Wellington, a town for rich horse fanciers. By a thin corridor of land this Atlantic Coast area is connected to rural territory north and west of Lake Okeechobee: here huge farms produce citrus, tomatoes and other vegetables or support large dairy herds; the only population cluster is around Sebring, with its car racing track. This area is connected by the swamps of eastern Charlotte County with the Gulf Coast towns of Port Charlotte and Punta Gorda, on the wide Peace River where it empties into Port Charlotte and the Gulf of Mexico.

The congressman from the 16th District is Mark Foley, a Republican first elected in 1994. Foley was born in Massachusetts, moved to Florida at age 3, dropped out of Palm Beach

Community College and opened The Lettuce Patch restaurant in Lake Worth at 20. He was active in politics, working for Democratic Congressman Paul Rogers; he was a real estate broker and served on civic boards. Foley was elected to the Lake Worth City Commission in 1977, at 23, to the state House as a Republican in 1990, and to the state Senate from a Democratic district in 1992. When Republican Congressman Tom Lewis retired, Foley won a three-way primary with 61% of the vote. In the general, he outraised the Democrat and outpolled him 58%–42%.

In the House, Foley's political skills caught the eye of leadership early on but Foley also displayed an independent streak, with a record on cultural issues that leans to the left. He has concentrated on issues with particular local resonance, including immigration and agriculture. He pushed to deport imprisoned illegal immigrants, and to amend the Constitution so that children born here are not automatically citizens; he also worked to increase the number of immigrants admitted as farmworkers.

On the Ways and Means Committee he worked with Sander Levin to give additional preventive screening tests to Medicare beneficiaries. Foley was one of only 23 House Republicans—and the only one on Ways and Means—to oppose trade promotion authority during the initial vote. He cited opposition from local citrus farmers; the leadership was angry because Foley's stand forced them to seek votes from members who had much weaker holds on their districts. (Citrus farmers have major clout, though the industry has little bearing on the vast majority of Floridians, because the state has 25 House members). But Foley voted in favor of the final deal on trade promotion authority. Speaker Dennis Hastert tapped Foley to lead an entertainment task force for House Republicans to sell themselves to Hollywood; his work extended from escorting actors across Capitol Hill to shepherding a treaty that protects creative work from Internet piracy and opposing legislative limits on "violent" material. He got a General Accounting Office report into scandals involving cemeteries and crematoria, which he used to call for greater federal regulation of death-care providers. In the 2003 Medicare/prescription drug bill, he added a provision to revise payment for shoes with inserts or custom-made shoes for individuals with diabetes. He opposed the Central American Free Trade Agreement because of its damage to the sugar industry. After the hurricane onslaught of 2004, which hit St. Lucie County especially hard, Foley worked to gain assistance, including tax relief, for badly-hit areas; he demanded an investigation of the delays in restoring electric power and he proposed legislation to allow insurance companies to create special funds for disasters. On the intelligence reorganization bill that passed in the lame-duck session after the 2004 election, he worked with Gary Ackerman to successfully add a provision to make it easier to deport war criminals and torturers from the United States.

Foley complained about the new shape the district took in 2002 redistricting, but used it as an opportunity to become better known outside the West Palm Beach media market; he has often been available to speak to local stations or cable news networks. In early 2003 he was preparing to run for Bob Graham's Senate seat. In May, rumors that Foley is gay surfaced in several newspaper stories; in response, he held a news conference where he said he will not discuss his sexual orientation. But in September 2003, he abandoned the contest to spend more time with his ailing parents; he said that the reports about his sexual orientation had nothing to do with his decision, and he soon endorsed Mel Martinez in the Republican primary. He had no problem retaining his House seat. Foley was mentioned as a possible challenger to Senator Bill Nelson in 2006, but early polling showed that he was not among the frontrunners.

SEVENTEENTH DISTRICT

Rep. Kendrick Meek (D)

Elected 2002, 2d term; b. Sept. 6, 1966, Miami; home, Miami; FL A&M U., B.S. 1989; Baptist; married (Leslie).

Elected Office: FL House of Reps., 1994–98; FL Senate, 1998–2002.

DC Office: 1039 LHOB, 20515, 202-225-4506; Fax: 202-226-0777; Web site: http://kendrickmeek.house.gov.

District Offices: Miami Gardens, 305-690-5905; Pembroke Pines, 954-450-6767.

Committees: *Armed Services* (22d of 28 D): Readiness; Tactical Air & Land Forces. *Homeland Security* (15th of 15 D): Intelligence, Information Sharing & Terrorism Risk Assessment; Management, Integration & Oversight (RMM).

Group Ratings

	ADA	ACLU	AFS	LCV	ITIC	NTU	COC	ACU	NTLC	CHC
2004	85	79	100	100	50	11	45	9	3	10
2003	85	—	100	85	—	22	47	18	—	—

National Journal Ratings

	2003 LIB	—	2003 CONS		2004 LIB	—	2004 CONS
Economic	71%	—	27%		74%	—	26%
Social	80%	—	19%		88%	—	0%
Foreign	65%	—	34%		73%	—	27%

Key Votes of the 108th Congress

1. Drilling in ANWR	N	5. DC School Vouchers	N	9. Ban Same-Sex Marriage	*
2. Approve Bush Tax Cuts	N	6. Ban Human Cloning	N	10. Fund Iraq War	N
3. Medicare/Rx Bill	N	7. Restrict Gun Liability	N	11. Bar Cuba Embargo Funds	N
4. Bar Overtime Pay Regs.	Y	8. Ban Partial-Birth Abortion	N	12. Intelligence Reorg.	*

Election Results

2004 general	Kendrick Meek (D) .... unopposed	($488,407)
2004 primary	Kendrick Meek (D) .... unopposed	
2002 general	Kendrick Meek (D) .... unopposed	($286,738)

The People		Race/Ethnic Origin	Ancestry
Area size:	99 sq. mi.	18.4% White	West Indian: 20.3% USA: 4.7%
Urban population:	100.0%	55.2% Black	Italian: 2.4%
Rural population:	0.0%	1.5% Asian	**2004 Presidential Vote**
Pop. 2000:	639,296	0.2% Native Am.	Kerry (D) 178,605 (83%)
Median income:	$30,426	0.0% Hawaiian	Bush (R) 35,642 (17%)
Poverty status:	23.3%	3.1% Two+ races	**2000 Presidential Vote**
Military veterans:	7.2%	0.3% Other	Gore (D) 145,341 (85%)
		21.2% Hispanic Origin	Bush (R) 26,081 (15%)
			Cook Partisan Voting Index: D +35
Occupation	Blue collar: 24.0%	White collar: 52.5% Gray collar: 23.5%	

North from downtown Miami, alongside the railroad tracks that Henry Flagler built shortly after Miami was founded in 1896, and alongside Interstate 95, Miami's main north-south artery, is the city's largest black community, stretching from the Miami Arena in downtown Miami north through Allapattah and Liberty City, to the brightly painted minarets and Moorish arches of Opa-Locka. This has been a kind of frontierland in Miami, the scene where hostilities between Miami's blacks and its Cuban-American majority have played out. Many Miami blacks have resented the economic upward mobility and political strength of the Cubans, the first generation of which rose while still speaking mostly Spanish, and of other Latinos—including the Haitians in Little Haiti, the Creole-speaking community whose heart is in N.E. 54th Street, north of downtown—who have been moving upward as well. The Elian Gonzalez affair reminded many local blacks of the refugee status granted to Cubans even as many black Haitians were deported without notice or turned away at the shore. This animosity is reflected in partisan politics: Blacks in Miami-Dade County vote more than 90% Democratic, while Cuban Americans have voted 70% to 80% Republican.

The 17th Congressional District of Florida covers much of northeast Miami-Dade County right up to Biscayne Boulevard; it does not include the affluent enclaves facing Biscayne Bay or the beach towns north of Miami Beach nor does it include heavily Latino Hialeah to the west. Within its borders is the historic, socially active Greater Bethel AME Church in Overtown; the district also includes part of Hollywood and other communities in southern Broward County, with fewer blacks, but still very heavily Democratic. Some 55% of the 17th District's residents are black, the highest percentage of any Florida district, which explains why this district has the lowest number of registered Republicans—just 41,000—of any Florida district. In November 2004 Democratic activists complained that Republican observers were intimidating Haitian-Americans at polling places in Little Haiti; Republicans, in turn, accused Democrats of harassment by threatening voters who backed George W. Bush.

The congressman from the 17th is Kendrick Meek, a Democrat first elected in 2002. He is the son of his predecessor, Carrie Meek, who was first elected when the district was created in something like its present form in 1992. She is the granddaughter of a slave and was elected to the state legislature in 1978, when Kendrick Meek was 12. In July 2002, just two weeks before the filing deadline, Carrie Meek announced that she would not run again and promised to work "24 hours a day, seven days a week" to elect her son. It turned out not to require that much effort: the timing of her announcement left little time for a candidate to emerge against her son and no Democrat or Republican filed to run against him.

But Kendrick Meek would have been a formidable candidate even without the succession scheme. He served as a page in the Florida legislature when his mother was elected. At Florida A&M in Tallahassee he was president of state College Young Democrats. After receiving his degree in criminology, he worked as a captain in the Highway Patrol and became security aide to Lieutenant Governor Buddy MacKay. He was elected to the Florida House in 1994, at 28, and to the Florida Senate in 1998; in each case he took on longtime, respected incumbents and waged contentious campaigns to oust them. He attracted nationwide attention in January 2000 for staging a 25-hour sit-in at the lieutenant governor's office to protest Governor Jeb Bush's "One Florida" executive orders, which called for ending the use of racial preferences in state contracting and university admissions. Meek failed to change Bush's mind, but his act of political theater helped spark the largest-ever protest march on the state Capitol two months later. In 2002 he was well known as the chief proponent of the class size initiative which qualified for the November ballot and which, despite the opposition of Bush, was approved 52%–48%; after the election, Bush met with Meek and said he would cooperate with him on implementing the measure. The Meeks are not the first mother-son combination in the House. In 1952 Oliver Bolton, an Ohio Republican, was elected to the House from a district adjoining the one which had been represented by his mother Frances Bolton since 1940 and by his father Chester Bolton before that.

In Washington, Democratic leaders were impressed by Meek's political and fundraising skills and predicted a bright future for him; he was comfortable in front of the camera, especially with appeals to young voters. His voting record was toward the center of House Democrats, especially on foreign policy issues. He filed a bill to make it easier for Haitians to become permanent residents and urged the Bush administration not to take sides in the conflict on the island. He promoted minority home ownership. He failed to win his mother's seat on Appropriations, but served on the Armed Services Committee, where he criticized chairman Duncan Hunter for not pursuing more aggressively the Abu Ghraib prison scandal in Iraq. He was the first freshman chosen to serve on the Homeland Security Committee. As chairman of the John Kerry campaign in Florida, he worked long hours in the Fort Lauderdale headquarters and won praise from Kerry despite the election setback. "We did a good job, but the other side did a better job," said Meek after the returns came in—as good a succinct summary of what happened in 2004 as anyone has made.

In 2004 Meek had no major party opposition.

EIGHTEENTH DISTRICT

Rep. Ileana Ros-Lehtinen (R)

Elected Aug. 1989, 8th full term; b. July 12, 1952, Havana, Cuba; home, Miami; Miami-Dade Comm. Col., A.A. 1972, FL Intl. U., B.A. 1975, M.S. 1986, U. of Miami, Ph.D. 2004; Catholic; married (Dexter).

Elected Office: FL House of Reps., 1982–86; FL Senate, 1986–89.

Professional Career: Teacher, Principal & Owner, Eastern Academy Elem. Schl., 1978–85.

DC Office: 2160 RHOB, 20515, 202-225-3931; Fax: 202-225-5620; Web site: www.house.gov/ros-lehtinen.

District Office: Miami, 305-275-1800.

Committees: *Budget* (13th of 22 R). *Government Reform* (4th of 23 R): Energy & Resources; National Security, Emerging Threats & International Relations. *International Relations* (6th of 27 R): Middle East & Central Asia (Chmn.); Western Hemisphere.

Group Ratings

	ADA	ACLU	AFS	LCV	ITIC	NTU	COC	ACU	NTLC	CHC
2004	15	17	0	9	78	56	95	80	78	90
2003	5	—	0	15	—	60	90	83	—	—

National Journal Ratings

	2003 LIB	—	2003 CONS		2004 LIB	—	2004 CONS
Economic	27%	—	73%		35%	—	65%
Social	36%	—	63%		49%	—	50%
Foreign	20%	—	80%		46%	—	53%

Key Votes of the 108th Congress

1. Drilling in ANWR	Y	5. DC School Vouchers	Y	9. Ban Same-Sex Marriage	*
2. Approve Bush Tax Cuts	Y	6. Ban Human Cloning	*	10. Fund Iraq War	Y
3. Medicare/Rx Bill	Y	7. Restrict Gun Liability	Y	11. Bar Cuba Embargo Funds	N
4. Bar Overtime Pay Regs.	N	8. Ban Partial-Birth Abortion	Y	12. Intelligence Reorg.	N

Election Results

2004 general	Ileana Ros-Lehtinen (R)	143,647	(65%)	($859,083)
	Sam Sheldon (D)	78,281	(35%)	($11,882)
2004 primary	Ileana Ros-Lehtinen (R)	unopposed		
2002 general	Ileana Ros-Lehtinen (R)	103,512	(69%)	($446,561)
	Ray Chote (D)	42,852	(29%)	
	Other	3,423	(2%)	

Prior Winning Percentages: 2000 (100%); 1998 (100%); 1996 (100%); 1994 (100%); 1992 (67%); 1990 (60%); 1989 (53%)

The People		Race/Ethnic Origin	Ancestry	
Area size:	3,196 sq. mi.	29.7% White	German: 4.0%	English: 3.5%
Urban population:	99.1%	5.7% Black	Irish: 3.3%	
Rural population:	0.9%	0.9% Asian	**2004 Presidential Vote**	
Pop. 2000:	639,295	0.1% Native Am.	Bush (R) 127,746	(54%)
Median income:	$32,298	0.0% Hawaiian	Kerry (D) 107,073	(46%)
Poverty status:	19.3%	0.7% Two+ races	**2000 Presidential Vote**	
Military veterans:	6.6%	0.1% Other	Bush (R) 109,596	(57%)
		62.7% Hispanic Origin	Gore (D) 83,524	(43%)
			Cook Partisan Voting Index: R + 4	

Occupation   Blue collar: 20.6%   White collar: 60.1%   Gray collar: 19.3%

A century ago it was a tiny tropical village where the Miami River empties into Biscayne Bay. Today it is a world city, not just America's "Gateway to Latin America" but the "Capital of the Americas," as welcoming signs proclaim. The surrealistic high-rises of Brickell Boulevard, the reminders of the 1920s in the pseudo-Spanish Villa Vizcaya and the winding lanes of Coral Gables, the shimmer of orange and pink neon signs in the hot night air: the lights of the grid streets stretching for miles and then abruptly turning to darkness at the bayfront or the Everglades: This is Miami today. It lives on the cusp of two civilizations, North American and Latin American, with different traditions, styles and sensibilities converging in this one place, despite some friction, toward an amalgam with the strengths of both. Miami has become commercially and economically the capital of Latin America, the one place from which it is easiest to fly directly to any other part of Latin America, where top business and banking services are available to a sophisticated Spanish-speaking (and usually also English-speaking) clientele.

The 1980s TV program *Miami Vice* showed the underside of Miami, the air of menace in streets where many are armed and vast quantities of drugs and cash regularly change hands and killings are not at all unusual. The news columns have focused on violence: The riots in 1980 and 1989; the late 1990s shenanigans of the city's politicians, when corruption charges were lodged at several officeholders (and the mayor thrown out after the courts ruled that vote fraud produced his winning margin); and on the controversy over six-year-old Elian Gonzalez in 2000. But the negatives are often exaggerated. What is striking about Miami is less its vices than its virtues—the vitality and creativity of entrepreneurs and artists, the cosmopolitan sophistication of people living and prospering in two (or more) cultures, the successful Americanization of Cubans and other Latinos who make up more than half of Miami-Dade County's population, together with the retention of a cultural flavor that is linked to the past but headed fast into the future.

John Quincy Adams believed that Cuba would inevitably become a part of the United States. That never happened, but many of Cuba's people have become Americans, and the focus of Cuban America has been Miami, ever since the first refugees fled Fidel Castro in 1959. That caused some resentment among the previous majority. In the 1960s, as the Cuban population grew, the tone of Miami civic life was set by the large Jewish community and the liberal voice of the *Miami Herald*: Dade County was the one liberal bastion in a state dominated by George Wallace Democrats and rising conservative Republicans. But the Cubans, implacably opposed to the totalitarian Castro and estranged by John F. Kennedy's betrayal of their cause at the Bay of Pigs, entered the voting stream heavily Republican.

In the early 1960s Cubans were a noisy minority in the Miami area; now they are dominant in a Latino majority in Miami-Dade County (as Dade County was renamed in 1997). In 2000, the population of Miami-Dade was 57% Hispanic and 19% black, leaving Anglo whites a fading minority; the city has the highest percentage of immigrants of any large city in the world. South Florida's Jewish community has mostly moved north to Broward and Palm Beach Counties. Little Havana around Calle Ocho (Southwest 8th Street in English) is now home to many Nicaraguans, Hondurans and Peruvians; its annual spring carnival has featured the world's largest paella (serving 300,000 people) and the longest conga line (four miles). Latinos in Miami-Dade tend to go to school at Miami-Dade Community College (one of the nation's largest)and Florida International University, and start businesses or join the professions in Miami's vibrant economy.

Politically, Miami-Dade has been volatile. It voted 57%–38% for Bill Clinton in 1996, after he signed the Helms-Burton Act and responded angrily to the shooting down of two Brothers to the Rescue planes. But it soured on him after he suspended Helms-Burton and clashed with the Cuban community during the Elian Gonzalez affair. The Elian case soured Cuban Americans on the Clinton administration, and Democrats generally. Al Gore, despite overwhelming support from Miami-Dade's blacks and Jews, carried the county by only 53%–46%. In 2004, Bush's share of the Cuban-American vote declined, partly because younger Cubans are not so focused on Fidel Castro, partly through resentment of the limits placed on visits and remittances sent to Cuba. At the same time Democrats did a good job of turning out more blacks in the county. The result was that Kerry carried Miami-Dade 53%–47%; Bush's percentage rose 2% in Florida as a whole but only 0.3% in Miami-Dade County.

The 18th Congressional District of Florida is one of Miami-Dade's three Hispanic-majority districts. It is 63% Hispanic and only 6% black. The district includes most of the city of Miami, which is the home of only 16% of the county's residents. It follows Calle Ocho west to heavily Hispanic West Miami and Westchester. It includes most of metro Miami's high-income residential areas—Coral Gables, with luxurious streets laid out in the 1920s with Spanish, French country and even Chinese style houses; Cocoplum, the gated community with huge houses of rich Cuban-Americans with docks for their boats; the postmodern apartment buildings and upscale hotels along Brickell Boulevard; and Key Biscayne, with its high-rise apartments mostly owned by Latin Americans in need of a safe harbor if their countries are threatened with revolution or confiscation. The district also includes parts of Miami Beach: South Beach, where old art deco hotels that used to house elderly retirees and have become the crowded home to the glitziest celebrities of North America, Latin America and Europe; the high-rises along Collins Avenue facing the ocean; and the increasingly Latino neighborhoods around 63d Street to the north. South of Miami, the district is connected to the Florida Keys by U.S. 1, the sturdier successor to Henry Flagler's "folly" of a railway that was built on an archipelago of calcified outcroppings and destroyed, two decades after its construction, by a hurricane in 1935. The highway ends in bustling, tropical Key West, the southernmost city in the continental United States. Key West was long accessible only by sea, and treasures from shipwrecks along the miles of coral reefs once provided its residents the highest per capita income in the nation. Key West has attracted famous residents—Ernest Hemingway, Tennessee Williams, Jimmy Buffett—and a large gay population, many living in quaint clapboard bungalows called "conch houses." The gay communities in Key West and Miami Beach are solidly Democratic, and they have begun to exercise clout: Gay leaders in Miami-Dade spearheaded a successful effort to reject a countywide gay-rights repeal ordinance in 2002. Overall the 18th is Republican, but George W. Bush's percentage here in 2004 was lower than in 2000.

The congresswoman from the 18th District is Ileana Ros-Lehtinen, the first Cuban-American and the first Hispanic woman elected to Congress, in August 1989. She was born in Havana, came to Miami at 7, graduated from Miami-Dade Community College and Florida International University. She became a teacher, then was the owner of a private school. In December 2004, she got her doctorate in education from the University of Miami; she wrote her dissertation on the views of House members regarding national testing for high school students. She was elected to the Florida House in 1982, at 30, and to the state Senate in 1986; while there, she met her husband Dexter Lehtinen, who also served in both houses of the legislature and as U.S. attorney in Miami during the first Bush administration. Ros-Lehtinen ran for the House in the special election after the death of Claude Pepper, one of the most enduring liberals in American politics and a staunch opponent of Castro. It was an acrimonious contest, with voting almost entirely on ethnic lines: exit polls showed that 96% of blacks and 88% of non-Hispanic whites voted for Democrat Gerald Richman, while 90% of Hispanics voted for Ros-Lehtinen. Overall, Ros-Lehtinen won 53% of the vote. With a much more heavily Latino district since 1992, she has won without serious opposition.

Ros-Lehtinen has a mixed voting record: moderate on economics and cultural policy, more conservative on foreign issues. She refused to sign the Contract with America, and was a harsh critic of Republican attempts to pass English-only legislation, to cut off welfare for legal immigrants and to reduce the immigration quota for relatives of U.S. citizens. She has been the chief sponsor of the Child Custody Protection Act, to bar the transport of minors across state lines for abortions; the House twice passed it, but it died each time in the Senate because, she said, the chamber is "controlled by the abortion lobby."

Ros-Lehtinen serves on the International Relations Committee, where much of her energy has been devoted to Cuban and Latin issues. She strongly backed the Cuban Democracy Act and the 1996 Helms-Burton law that tightened sanctions against Fidel Castro. She has opposed amendments to appropriations bills by farm state Republicans to relax the trade embargo on Cuba; these have been passed by the House, but Republican leaders have seen to it that they have been deleted in conference. But she and her Cuban-American allies have been losing ground on their overriding cause: the U.S. embargo of Cuba that has been in effect since 1961.

Even though George W. Bush firmly supports the embargo, its opponents—a coalition of liberal Democrats, farm state Republicans and foreign policy left-wingers—have been gaining strength. As chairwoman of the Middle East and Central Asia Subcommittee, she has been a booster of Israel and initiated the 2003 law that imposed additional economic sanctions on Syria. Ros-Lehtinen has been quietly running an intensive campaign to become chairman of International Relations in 2007, when term limits would have forced Henry Hyde to step down; he announced in April 2005 that he would not seek reelection to the House in 2006. With her affable personality, she has the opportunity to gain the most influential chairmanship ever for any woman in the House or Senate.

Ros-Lehtinen was re-elected without opposition from 1994 through 2000. In 2004 she won 65%–35%. Dexter Lehtinen, who was severely wounded as an Army Ranger during the Vietnam war, was an outspoken campaign critic of Kerry for his 1971 testimony against the war.

NINETEENTH DISTRICT

Rep. Robert Wexler (D)

Elected 1996, 5th term; b. Jan. 2, 1961, Queens, NY; home, Boca Raton; U. of FL, B.A. 1982, George Washington U., J.D. 1985; Jewish; married (Laurie).

Elected Office: FL Senate, 1990–96.

Professional Career: Practicing atty., 1985–96.

DC Office: 213 CHOB, 20515, 202-225-3001; Fax: 202-225-5974; Web site: www.wexler.house.gov.

District Offices: Boca Raton, 561-988-6302; Margate, 954-972-6454.

Committees: *International Relations* (9th of 23 D): Europe & Emerging Threats (RMM); International Terrorism & Nonproliferation. *Judiciary* (12th of 17 D): Courts, the Internet & Intellectual Property.

Group Ratings

	ADA	ACLU	AFS	LCV	ITIC	NTU	COC	ACU	NTLC	CHC
2004	95	74	100	100	50	9	37	0	0	15
2003	95	—	100	100	—	25	27	12	—	—

National Journal Ratings

	2003 LIB	—	2003 CONS		2004 LIB	—	2004 CONS
Economic	80%	—	19%		92%	—	7%
Social	84%	—	16%		86%	—	14%
Foreign	81%	—	17%		67%	—	33%

Key Votes of the 108th Congress

1. Drilling in ANWR	N	5. DC School Vouchers	N	9. Ban Same-Sex Marriage	N
2. Approve Bush Tax Cuts	N	6. Ban Human Cloning	N	10. Fund Iraq War	N
3. Medicare/Rx Bill	N	7. Restrict Gun Liability	N	11. Bar Cuba Embargo Funds	*
4. Bar Overtime Pay Regs.	Y	8. Ban Partial-Birth Abortion	N	12. Intelligence Reorg.	Y

Election Results

2004 general	Robert Wexler (D)	.... unopposed		($939,363)
2004 primary	Robert Wexler (D)	.... unopposed		
2002 general	Robert Wexler (D)	 156,747	(72%)	($650,528)
	Jack Merkl (R)	 60,477	(28%)	($25,784)

Prior Winning Percentages: 2000 (72%); 1998 (100%); 1996 (66%)

The People		Race/Ethnic Origin	Ancestry	
Area size:	234 sq. mi.	77.5% White	Italian: 9.0%	German: 8.4%
Urban population:	99.6%	6.1% Black	Irish: 7.6%	
Rural population:	0.4%	2.0% Asian	**2004 Presidential Vote**	
Pop. 2000:	639,295	0.1% Native Am.	Kerry (D) 210,695	(66%)
Median income:	$42,237	0.0% Hawaiian	Bush (R) 107,348	(34%)
Poverty status:	7.7%	1.4% Two+ races	**2000 Presidential Vote**	
Military veterans:	16.6%	0.3% Other	Gore (D) 191,382	(73%)
		12.7% Hispanic Origin	Bush (R) 71,544	(27%)
			Cook Partisan Voting Index: D +21	

Occupation	Blue collar: 17.1%	White collar: 67.1%	Gray collar: 15.7%

When the first millionaires came to Palm Beach in the 1920s to winter in their new Addison Mizner pseudo-Mediterranean mansions, and as the first real estate speculators arrived in Miami, there was virtually nothing man-made between these two cites. In 1920, Dade, Broward and Palm Beach Counties boasted a mere 66,000 residents. In 1990, 4.0 million people lived in the 5- to 15-mile strip between the Atlantic Ocean and the protected Everglades, a number that grew to 5.4 million in 2004. The contrast between the 1920s and today is especially striking in Boca Raton, where Mizner built in 1926 what is now the Boca Raton Hotel and Club. Its azure fountains and red-tiled roofs, its pseudo-Moorish columns and pink stucco walls bespeak a vision of a holiday Florida, a bit mannered and antique to today's eye, but still exuberant. Boca Raton has grown inland and is still solidly affluent, but it has become more functional and workaday. Affluent retirees from the Northeast and Canada ("snow birds") live in unadorned high-rise towers, enjoying the weather and the lack of a state income tax.

The 19th Congressional District of Florida includes former swampland and citrus groves in Palm Beach and Broward Counties. It does not touch the ocean at all, kept inland by the majority-black 23d District, which collects poorer black neighborhoods just behind the Intracoastal Waterway, and the 22d District, which ties together more affluent (and more Republican) oceanside precincts. The boundaries of the 19th District are erose and irregular, obviously drawn with an eye to political advantage; the Republicans who controlled the redistricting process were happy to pack heavily Democratic precincts into the 19th. It extends north from Fort Lauderdale to Okeechobee Boulevard in unglamorous but booming West Palm Beach; the district also takes in the towns of Margate, Mission Bay and Boca Raton. What ties these communities together is that they have large Jewish populations and vote heavily Democratic. Senior citizens are an especially important voting bloc here: the 19th ranks second among all 435 congressional districts in the number of Social Security recipients. In the past Democrats have concentrated on increasing turnout in the big condominiums in the confidence that they would produce huge Democratic majorities. But George W. Bush's Israel and Middle East policies seem to have won over many Jewish voters here. His percentage in the district rose from 27% in 2000 to 34% in 2004, the biggest rise in any Florida district and one of the biggest in the nation.

The congressman from the 19th is Robert Wexler, a Democrat first elected in 1996. Wexler grew up in Florida from age 10, and after law school went into practice in Boca Raton. In 1990, at 29, he was elected to the state Senate. When Democrat Harry Johnston retired, Wexler was one of three Democratic legislators who jumped into the race. In the September primary he led with 47% to 29% for state Senator Peter Weinstein. The October 1 runoff was bitter. Wexler won 65%–35%; afterwards Weinstein filed a $10 million defamation suit against him, citing an unflattering picture of Weinstein in a Wexler TV ad (the suit soon was dropped). In this heavily Democratic district, Wexler won the general 66%–34%.

Wexler has a fairly liberal voting record in the House and a flair for gaining attention. Wexler made his greatest mark as an ardent defender of Bill Clinton during impeachment. Producers of cable shows are always looking for someone who can be relied on to take one side of an issue and to bring energy to the broadcast: one look at Wexler convinced bookers that he would fill the bill, and he seemed to turn down few invitations. He was the only member of the House in attendance at the Wye River accords with Israeli leader Benjamin Netanyahu and Palestinian chairman Yasir Arafat in October 1998. An orthodox Jew, he said in December 2002 that Israel was engaged in full-scale war, and that it was time for the United States to force the ouster of terrorist leaders in the Mideast, including Arafat and Saddam Hussein; he voted for the Iraq war resolution in 2002. On the International Relations Committee, he lost a party-line vote in September 2003 in an effort to force the Bush administration to turn over a report from the Joint Chiefs of Staff on lessons learned from the ouster of Saddam. On the Judiciary Committee he was the only Democrat to favor a three-year pilot program giving temporary visas to an unlimited number of foreign workers for seasonal farm work.

Wexler appeared often on cable TV news during the Florida vote controversy in 2000 and in 2004 he relentlessly demanded that Florida election officials provide paper printouts from touch-screen voting machines to assure a credible paper trail and avoid what he continued to argue was the theft of the 2000 election. In 2005, Wexler again became a frequent face on national news shows when he broke ranks with his party and introduced his own Social Security bill, a measure that would impose a 6% tax on income above the current $90,000 cap. Democratic leaders were unhappy with his defection but Wexler said, "My allegiance to seniors is greater than my allegiance to the Democratic party."

Despite frequent rumors, Wexler has not run for statewide office. In 2002 it was revealed that he had a complex financial arrangement involving a loan and stock ownership with an airline security investor who was charged with stock fraud. Wexler voiced regret about his corporate dealings. He has been reelected without difficulty.

TWENTIETH DISTRICT

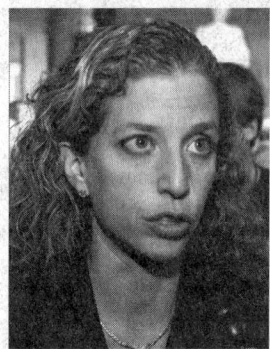

Rep. Debbie Wasserman Schultz (D)

Elected 2004, 1st term; b. Sept. 27, 1966, Queens, NY; home, Weston; U. of FL, B.A. 1988, M.A. 1990; Jewish; married (Steve).

Elected Office: FL House, 1992–2000; Min. leader pro tem., 1999–2000; FL Sen., 2000–04.

Professional Career: State legislative aide, 1989–1992.

DC Office: 118 CHOB, 20515, 202-225-7931; Fax: 202-226-2052; Web site: www.house.gov/schultz.

District Offices: Aventura, 305-936-5724; Pembroke Pines, 954-437-3936.

Committees: *Financial Services* (31st of 32 D): Capital Markets, Insurance & Government Sponsored Enterprises; Domestic and International Monetary Policy, Trade & Technology; Oversight & Investigations.

Group Ratings and Key Votes: Newly Elected

Election Results

2004 general	Debbie Wasserman Schultz (D)	191,195	(70%)	($1,468,898)
	Margaret Hostetter (R)	81,213	(30%)	($35,045)
2004 primary	Debbie Wasserman Schultz (D)	unopposed		
2002 general	Peter Deutsch (D)	unopposed		($683,827)

The People		Race/Ethnic Origin	Ancestry	
Area size:	218 sq. mi.	66.9% White	Italian: 7.9%	German: 7.7%
Urban population:	99.7%	7.9% Black	Irish: 7.5%	
Rural population:	0.3%	2.3% Asian	**2004 Presidential Vote**	
Pop. 2000:	639,295	0.2% Native Am.	Kerry (D)	183,510 (64%)
Median income:	$44,034	0.0% Hawaiian	Bush (R)	104,039 (36%)
Poverty status:	9.6%	1.6% Two+ races	**2000 Presidential Vote**	
Military veterans:	11.3%	0.3% Other	Gore (D)	161,154 (69%)
		20.6% Hispanic Origin	Bush (R)	72,553 (31%)
			Cook Partisan Voting Index: D +18	

Occupation   Blue collar: 16.0%   White collar: 69.4%   Gray collar: 14.6%

Fort Lauderdale, back when Connie Francis made it famous in the 1960 spring break movie *Where the Boys Are*, was just a small town with a strip of motels along the beach and some nice houses fronting canals. Now it is a more stylish beach resort and the center of a sprawling metropolitan area, where the visitor bureau website announces, "Fort Lauderdale is no longer 'Where the boys are,' but where well-heeled Europeans, sophisticated Northerners and laid-back Midwesterners come to relax and vacation." In 1950, Fort Lauderdale and Broward County had 183,000 people; in 2004 they had 1.8 million. The land from the strip of beach along the Atlantic Ocean west to the Sawgrass Expressway and the Everglades Wildlife Management Area has filled up with subdivisions, shopping centers, office complexes, warehouses and trucking terminals. Broward County is no longer just vacation country; it is also a major port and business center with high-tech companies and startups that have become national giants, including Blockbuster Video.

As it has grown, the ethnic composition of Broward County has changed. In the 1950s, it was understood that Jews couldn't buy houses or rent hotel rooms this far north of Miami. Today, after four decades of Cubans moving into the Miami area and many Jews moving out, Broward County is the most heavily Jewish part of Florida, indeed one of the most heavily Jewish parts of the United States. Nearer the coast, especially in the huge high-rises of Hollywood and Hallandale, most of Broward's Jews are retirees from New York and other Northeastern metro areas. But inland, in towns like booming Davie, Plantation and Sunrise that didn't exist a few decades ago, there are many young Jewish parents raising families in communities that pride themselves on fine schools and high property values. Places like Weston, a 15,000-home development built on 16 square miles on the edge of the Everglades, drew affluent transplants to its gated communities, including, in Weston's case, many from Venezuela. This is one reason that in the 1990s the number of children in Florida rose more rapidly than the number of seniors, with school enrollment rising more than 35% in Broward alone.

The 20th Congressional District of Florida includes much of southeastern Broward County and the northern Biscayne Bay shoreline in Miami-Dade. Precinct by precinct, its computer generated borders are drawn to include heavily Democratic and Jewish areas; with its large gay and lesbian community, Wilton Manors trails only Provincetown, Massachusetts and Guerneville, California in its proportion of same-sex households. It includes much of Fort Lauderdale, Hollywood and Dania Beach on the coast, but its biggest blocks of territory are inland, around Davie, Plantation, Sunrise and Weston. In Miami-Dade County, it includes the shores of Biscayne Bay both on the Miami and Miami Beach side, with expensive homes and huge high-rises. This is a strongly Democratic district. But some significant number of Jewish voters did swing toward George W. Bush over his first term; his percentage in the district rose from 31% in 2000 to 36% in 2004.

The congresswoman from the 20th District is Debbie Wasserman Schultz, a Democrat elected in 2004. She accomplished the unusual feat of winning her seat in Congress without a primary opponent or a significant general election foe. She grew up on Long Island, where she ran for student council every year and always lost. After getting her bachelor's and master's degrees in political science from the University of Florida, in 1992, at age 26, she became the state's youngest woman ever elected to the state House. Many of her constituents treat her like a granddaughter. She served eight years in the state House, including two years as minority leader, followed by four years in the state Senate. She calls herself "a pragmatic liberal" but sponsored a controversial law to require an equal number of men and women on state boards and a bill which failed to pass requiring that dry cleaners and some other businesses charge the same prices for women as for men. She learned to compromise: After failing to pass a proposal to require fences around swimming pools, she won a requirement to give owners a choice among several safety options, including a pool cover or door alarm.

When 20th District incumbent Peter Deutsch ran for the Democratic nomination for Bob Graham's open Senate seat, Wasserman Schultz moved to replace him in Congress, as she had earlier replaced him in Tallahassee. She began laying the groundwork early. In July 2003, more than a year before the primary, she announced she had raised $115,000. By February 2004 she had lined up endorsements from Minority Leader Nancy Pelosi and six of Florida's seven House

Democrats. Wasserman Schultz ultimately collected more than $1 million for what turned out to be an uncompetitive race and in June 2004 pledged to give $100,000 to the Democratic Congressional Campaign Committee, a staggeringly large contribution from a non-incumbent.

Most of her campaign views were conventionally liberal. Wasserman Shultz called for repeal of the Bush tax cuts, a reduction in the budget deficit, greater use of diplomacy, improved prescription drug coverage and gay and abortion rights. Against a Republican who attacked the "homosexual agenda" in the public schools, Wasserman Schultz won 70%–30%. Wasserman Schultz said that her primary choice for a committee assignment was Energy and Commerce, where she hoped to take Deutsch's slot. But that was a long shot for a freshman, even with her ambition, insider savvy, and fundraising skills. Instead, she was placed on Financial Services.

TWENTY-FIRST DISTRICT

Rep. Lincoln Diaz-Balart (R)

Elected 1992, 7th term; b. Aug. 13, 1954, Havana, Cuba; home, Miami; U. of S. FL, B.S. 1977, Case Western Reserve U., J.D. 1979; Catholic; married (Cristina).

Elected Office: FL House of Reps., 1986–89; FL Senate 1989–92.

Professional Career: Practicing atty., 1979–92; Asst. FL Atty., 1983–84.

DC Office: 2244 RHOB, 20515, 202-225-4211; Fax: 202-225-8576; Web site: www.house.gov/diaz-balart.

District Office: Miami, 305-470-8555.

Committees: *Rules* (2d of 9 R): Legislative & Budget Process (Chmn.).

Group Ratings

	ADA	ACLU	AFS	LCV	ITIC	NTU	COC	ACU	NTLC	CHC
2004	10	11	0	9	90	57	84	83	77	90
2003	10	—	0	15	—	58	90	75	—	—

National Journal Ratings

	2003 LIB	—	2003 CONS		2004 LIB	—	2004 CONS
Economic	33%	—	64%		38%	—	62%
Social	30%	—	70%		47%	—	53%
Foreign	11%	—	80%		38%	—	62%

Key Votes of the 108th Congress

1. Drilling in ANWR	Y	5. DC School Vouchers	Y	9. Ban Same-Sex Marriage	*
2. Approve Bush Tax Cuts	Y	6. Ban Human Cloning	*	10. Fund Iraq War	Y
3. Medicare/Rx Bill	Y	7. Restrict Gun Liability	Y	11. Bar Cuba Embargo Funds	N
4. Bar Overtime Pay Regs.	N	8. Ban Partial-Birth Abortion	Y	12. Intelligence Reorg.	N

Election Results

2004 general	Lincoln Diaz-Balart (R)	146,507	(73%)	($451,555)
	Frank Gonzalez (Lib)	54,736	(27%)	($12,719)
2004 primary	Lincoln Diaz-Balart (R)	unopposed		
2002 general	Lincoln Diaz-Balart (R)	unopposed		($404,300)

Prior Winning Percentages: 2000 (100%); 1998 (75%); 1996 (100%); 1994 (100%); 1992 (100%)

The People		Race/Ethnic Origin	Ancestry	
Area size:	140 sq. mi.	21.0% White	USA: 3.2%	German: 2.6%
Urban population:	99.9%	6.5% Black	West Indian: 2.6%	
Rural population:	0.1%	1.8% Asian	**2004 Presidential Vote**	
Pop. 2000:	639,295	0.1% Native Am.	Bush (R) 127,326	(57%)
Median income:	$41,426	0.0% Hawaiian	Kerry (D) 96,232	(43%)
Poverty status:	13.0%	0.8% Two+ races	**2000 Presidential Vote**	
Military veterans:	4.8%	0.2% Other	Bush (R) 104,888	(58%)
		69.7% Hispanic Origin	Gore (D) 76,322	(42%)
			Cook Partisan Voting Index: R + 6	
Occupation	Blue collar: 22.6%	White collar: 63.6%	Gray collar: 13.9%	

Miami's Cuban-American community has been one of America's most dynamic over the last 40 years, growing from 50,000 in 1960, the year after Fidel Castro took over Cuba, to well over 1 million today. Over those years, the Cuban-American neighborhoods centered along 8th Street—Calle Ocho—expanded to the southwest, west and northwest. In the 1980s, development reached outward to the Homestead extension of Florida's Turnpike. In the 1990s, Cuban-Americans moved out and beyond Hialeah, whose now-closed racetrack was constructed in the 1920s beyond the edge of urban development; Hialeah's 90% Hispanic population is the highest in the Miami area. The suburbs of Miami have spread through former swampland, with planned communities and subdivisions leading to streets that fan out around lakes and golf courses.

The 21st Congressional District of Florida is an irregular rectangle about 20 miles long and two to six miles wide on the western side of settled territory in Miami-Dade County and southern Broward County. In Miami-Dade it includes Kendall and Cutler, southwest of Miami, and Westwood Lakes and Sweetwater, directly to the west. It includes low-income Hialeah and nearby Miami Lakes, developed in the 1960s by future Senator Bob Graham and his brothers. In Broward County the 21st District includes much of Miramar and Pembroke Pines. It includes such landmarks as Florida International University and Miami International Airport which, with new concourses, ranks third in the nation for overseas travel. The population of the district is 70% Hispanic, the highest of any Florida district, but only 58% of these are of Cuban origin. Cuban voters continue to be very heavily Republican; other Latino voters are less so, but by no means overwhelmingly Democratic. Many here do not vote at all: The 21st has the lowest number of registered voters of any Florida district. There are relatively few Hispanics in the Broward County portion of the district, which tends to vote Democratic. Overall, this is a Republican district, but one that sometimes votes for Democrats who support the Cuban community. In 2004, some Cuban-Americans—typically, the more recent arrivals—were unhappy with the Bush administration's tightened restrictions on travel and remittances to Cuba, but others supported any steps that kept dollars from Castro. As a result the Bush percentage declined from 58% in 2000 to 57% in 2004.

The congressman from the 21st District is Lincoln Diaz-Balart, a Republican first elected when the district was created in 1992. Diaz-Balart was born in Cuba where his grandfather, father and uncle served in the Cuban Congress; the family left Cuba in 1959, shortly after Castro took over and after their house was looted and burned while they were vacationing in Paris. His aunt was the former wife of Fidel Castro and the mother of Castro's only recognized child. Diaz-Balart started off as a poverty lawyer and a Democrat, but switched parties. He was elected to the state House as a Republican in 1986 and to the state Senate in 1989, a year after his younger brother Mario was elected to the state House. (Unlike Mario, who is now the congressman from the 25th District, Lincoln Diaz-Balart was not born in the United States and is ineligible to be President.) The Diaz-Balarts are sometimes called the "Cuban Kennedys": one other brother is a TV anchorman on Telemundo and another is an investment banker. In 1989 Jorge Mas Canosa's Cuban American National Foundation convinced Diaz-Balart not to run against Ileana Ros-Lehtinen in the special election to replace Claude Pepper. In 1992 the organization endorsed him in the 21st. State Senator Javier Souto, also Cuban-born, opposed him in the primary, charging that Diaz-Balart was backed by wealthy contributors and was not a lifelong Republican. Diaz-Balart won 69%–31%.

Diaz-Balart has a voting record that is rather liberal on economics, veering far from market principles on issues from the minimum wage to NAFTA, though he has said he believes a hemispheric common market is inevitable. He was one of three Republican incumbents who refused to sign the Contract with America in 1994, and he voted against the Republican welfare bills because of their provisions denying benefits to legal immigrants. Many older Cubans who have not taken U.S. citizenship because they hoped some day to return to Cuba are dependent on Supplemental Security Income and other aid. He persevered, and his bill to restore SSI benefits to legal immigrants passed.

Diaz-Balart, who shares a birthday with Castro, hopes that he will return some day to his freed homeland (Castro refers to the Diaz-Balarts as "his most repulsive enemies" and "miserable Judases"). Naturally he has favored sanctions against Cuba, and when the Clinton administration announced in 1995 that it would no longer give automatic safe haven to Cuban refugees and instead would return them to Cuba, Diaz-Balart was arrested while protesting this switch. He wrote the section of the Helms-Burton Act codifying the embargo against Cuba. During the Elian Gonzalez controversy, Diaz-Balart closely advised the Miami family—he gave the six-year-old a black Labrador puppy—and he was a prominent spokesman for the local community. Although farm state Republicans, working with Democrats, have gotten the House to pass bills relaxing the trade embargo on Cuba, Diaz-Balart has worked to assure the Bush administration's unyielding opposition to significant trade openings to Cuba. With other Cuban-Americans and their allies, he created the House's Cuba Democracy Group, as a counterpoint to the trade-opening Cuba Working Group. As chairman of the Rules Subcommittee on Homeland Security, he worked with Speaker Dennis Hastert to make the full committee permanent. He is vice-chairman and next in line to chair the Rules Committee, but the chairman is selected by the Speaker and some Republicans contend that Diaz-Balart is too independent for the post. He calls Democrat Claude Pepper, who chaired Rules in the 1980s, a "role model."

Diaz-Balart has had no problem winning reelection. He has not faced a Democratic opponent since 1998. In 2004, he won 73%–27% against a Libertarian candidate.

TWENTY-SECOND DISTRICT

Rep. Clay Shaw (R)

Elected 1980, 13th term; b. Apr. 19, 1939, Miami; home, Ft. Lauderdale; Stetson U., B.S. 1961, U. of AL, M.B.A. 1963, Stetson U., J.D. 1966; Catholic; married (Emilie).

Elected Office: Ft. Lauderdale City Commissioner., 1971–73; Ft. Lauderdale Vice Mayor, 1973–75, Mayor, 1975–80.

Professional Career: Practicing atty., 1966–68; Ft. Lauderdale Chief Prosecutor, 1968–69; Assoc. Municipal Judge, 1969–71.

DC Office: 1236 LHOB, 20515, 202-225-3026; Fax: 202-225-8398; Web site: www.house.gov/shaw.

District Offices: Ft. Lauderdale, 954-522-1800; West Palm Beach, 561-832-3007.

Committees: *Ways & Means* (2d of 24 R): Oversight; Social Security; Trade (Chmn.). *Joint Committee on Taxation* (2d of 5 Reps.).

Group Ratings

	ADA	ACLU	AFS	LCV	ITIC	NTU	COC	ACU	NTLC	CHC
2004	10	0	13	9	90	49	100	80	68	84
2003	10	—	0	15	—	57	90	80	—	—

National Journal Ratings

	2003 LIB	—	2003 CONS	2004 LIB	—	2004 CONS
Economic	27%	—	71%	17%	—	80%
Social	30%	—	65%	40%	—	59%
Foreign	40%	—	58%	25%	—	68%

Key Votes of the 108th Congress

1. Drilling in ANWR	Y	5. DC School Vouchers	Y	9. Ban Same-Sex Marriage	Y
2. Approve Bush Tax Cuts	Y	6. Ban Human Cloning	Y	10. Fund Iraq War	Y
3. Medicare/Rx Bill	Y	7. Restrict Gun Liability	Y	11. Bar Cuba Embargo Funds	N
4. Bar Overtime Pay Regs.	N	8. Ban Partial-Birth Abortion	Y	12. Intelligence Reorg.	Y

Election Results

2004 general	Clay Shaw (R)	192,581	(63%)	($1,237,966)
	Robin Rorapaugh (D)	108,258	(35%)	($9,800)
	Other	5,887	(2%)	
2004 primary	Clay Shaw (R)	unopposed		
2002 general	Clay Shaw (R)	131,930	(61%)	($1,968,153)
	Carol Roberts (D)	83,265	(38%)	($1,138,776)

Prior Winning Percentages: 2000 (50%); 1998 (100%); 1996 (62%); 1994 (63%); 1992 (52%); 1990 (98%); 1988 (66%); 1986 (100%); 1984 (66%); 1982 (57%); 1980 (55%)

The People		Race/Ethnic Origin	Ancestry	
Area size:	500 sq. mi.	82.3% White	German: 11.7% Irish: 11.0%	
Urban population:	99.2%	3.8% Black	Italian: 9.5%	
Rural population:	0.8%	1.7% Asian	**2004 Presidential Vote**	
Pop. 2000:	639,295	0.1% Native Am.	Kerry (D)	169,161 (52%)
Median income:	$51,200	0.0% Hawaiian	Bush (R)	153,265 (48%)
Poverty status:	7.1%	1.2% Two+ races	**2000 Presidential Vote**	
Military veterans:	14.9%	0.2% Other	Gore (D)	135,868 (52%)
		10.7% Hispanic Origin	Bush (R)	123,302 (48%)
			Cook Partisan Voting Index: D + 4	
Occupation	Blue collar: 16.0%	White collar: 69.4%	Gray collar: 14.7%	

The barrier islands of Florida's Gold Coast have been developed in spasms of speculative frenzy, not just as vacation places and retirement homes but as embodiments of dreams and fantasies. Consider Palm Beach, the great beach resort of the 1920s, where rich WASPs would leave their snow-covered Tudor or Georgian mansions and live in Addison Mizner's pseudo-Mediterranean confections. Or Boca Raton, where Mizner built the Boca Raton Hotel in 1926. Or Fort Lauderdale, a tiny town when Clyde Beatty brought his circus there for the winter in the 1930s (locals complained about the roaring lions) and then, from the 1950s to the 1980s, the favored winter break beach resort of college students. Starting in the 1970s, high-rise condominiums sprouted up and down the Atlantic coast of Broward and Palm Beach Counties. In recent years the old town centers have been revived. Palm Beach remains, as it has been since the 1920s, the precinct of the very rich, including Rush Limbaugh, who broadcasts from there. Boca Raton now sports the stylish Mizner Park, a collection of upscale stores on a walking street. Downtown Fort Lauderdale is the home of new condominiums and museums, the Museum of Art Fort Lauderdale, the Museum of Discovery and Space, the Broward Center for the Performing Arts and the International Swimming Hall of Fame.

The 22d Congressional District of Florida covers most of the Atlantic oceanfront in Palm Beach and Broward Counties, from Jupiter in Palm Beach County to Fort Lauderdale in Broward County. It is rarely more than a few miles wide and in some places it is not much wider than the barrier islands separated from the mainland by the Indian River and Lake Worth. But it also has jagged salients that extend several miles inland. The district, a testament to the advances made in redistricting software, was drawn by Republican redistricters to provide a safe seat for Republican Congressman Clay Shaw after he barely won reelection in 2000. The Miami-Dade County portion of the district was removed, as was heavily Democratic Hollywood in Broward County. Inland salients in Broward County brought in Republican precincts in

Plantation and Coral Springs. Much new territory was added in Palm Beach County—an inland finger in wealthy Boca Raton, a long strand parallel to the oceanfront of affluent areas from Delray Beach to Glen Ridge (here the 22d surrounds the heavily black 23d district on three sides) and an inland slice in north Palm Beach County including parts of Palm Beach Gardens and Jupiter. The resulting district is affluent, elderly, with a large Jewish population politically very active in condominium groups.

The congressman from the 22d District is Clay Shaw, a Republican first elected in 1980. Shaw grew up in Fort Lauderdale, practiced law and served as a judge and councilman; in 1975, at 36, he became the city's mayor. In 1980 he ran for the House in a very differently shaped district, and had the good fortune of seeing the Democratic incumbent lose his primary. Shaw won the seat handily and held it despite the Fort Lauderdale area's increasing Democratic tilt. For eight years he served on the Judiciary Committee, working on drug and crime bills. In July 1988 he switched to Ways and Means.

In the Republican Congress Shaw has taken on big issues—first welfare, then Social Security, now trade. After Republicans won control in 1994, Shaw became chairman of the Way and Means subcommittee handling welfare. His little-noticed 1993 bill, to end the federal entitlement to welfare and take most recipients off the rolls and require them to work after two years, was part of the Contract with America and became one of House Republicans' major priorities. Shaw's bills were passed twice in 1995, in somewhat different form, and vetoed twice by Bill Clinton. In early 1996 House Republicans hoped that Bob Dole could use the welfare issue against Clinton. By July 1996 they decided that Dole was likely to lose anyway, and so decided to pass welfare reform a third time, giving Dole an issue if Clinton vetoed it again and giving House Republicans an accomplishment if Clinton signed it. They had no idea what he would do, but in the end he signed, and a major change in American public policy was made.

After the 1998 election, Shaw, then representing the House district with the nation's highest percentage of those 65 and over, became chairman of the Social Security Subcommittee. He said he wanted to reform the system and preserve it for baby boomers' retirements. In 2000, Shaw focused on the earnings tax on Social Security recipients; he managed to pass a bill repealing it for Social Security recipients age 65 to 69. In 2003 he got the House to pass a bill restricting representative payees for Social Security recipients and in 2004 one to prevent government agencies and businesses from putting Social Security numbers on checks or driver's licenses. He helped pass another bill allowing active duty National Guard and Reserve troops to make penalty-free withdrawals from their retirement accounts and sponsored a measure to create a loan program for deployed reservists' families. In 2004 he proposed giving workers the option of 2% or 3% personal accounts over and above Social Security; they would be financed by government borrowing and currently scheduled Social Security benefits would be guaranteed. Shaw argued that his was the only approach that would make the system solvent and allow personal investment, and that using part of the Social Security tax for personal retirement accounts was politically unfeasible. "In my plan I don't cut benefits and I don't raise taxes. There is no way the Congress or the president is going to approve a plan that cuts benefits." That didn't prevent Democrats from making automated phone calls in the district charging Shaw with privatization and reducing future benefits 47%.

After terms limits forced him to relinquish the Social Security chairmanship (he remains on the subcommittee), Shaw became chairman of the Trade Subcommittee in January 2005; he ranks just behind Ways and Means Chairman Bill Thomas, on whom the six-year term limit falls after the 2006 election. He said his top priority was approval of the Central American Free Trade Agreement, loudly opposed by organized labor; other trade issues on his agenda included competition from Brazilian citrus and Mexican tomatoes. At home, Shaw worked for many years on what became the $7.8 billion Everglades Restoration Act, passed in October 2000, and objected in 2004 when EPA proposed to let partially treated sewage into waterways during rainstorms. He led the Florida delegation in objecting to the funding formula in the transportation bill in April 2004, but they lost on the floor 254–170. Shaw also objected when the city of Miami was named the designee of homeland security funds for South Florida and its officials allocated only 10% for Broward County; Broward officials refused the money in protest. He fought to split the South Florida federal judicial district in two when judges proposed closing Fort Lauderdale's federal courthouse.

In 2000 Shaw faced the strongest opposition since he first won the seat, from state Representative Elaine Bloom, who had a base in the condominiums and raised large sums from national liberal and feminist groups. With both candidates buying Miami and West Palm Beach television, this was one of the most expensive House races in the country: Bloom spent $2.4 million and Shaw $3 million. That was the year Joe Lieberman and his mother were campaigning often in the condos, spurring record turnout. This turned out to be one of the closest races in the country. The initial count showed Shaw ahead by 599 votes; the mechanical recount required by Florida law didn't change the margin. Bloom sought a hand count, but the three county boards of canvassers, willing to order hand counts for Al Gore, declined to do so in this race (Miami-Dade did hand count six precincts, three chosen by each candidate). Shaw ran far ahead, 58%–42%, in Palm Beach County and carried his home base in Broward County by 55%–45%. He lost in the Miami-Dade County portion 67%–33%. So it was hardly surprising that Republican redistricters removed the Miami-Dade portion from the district.

Shaw had an easier time of it in 2002 and 2004. In 2002 his opponent was Palm Beach County Commissioner Carol Roberts, chiefly known as one of the three members of the board of canvassers in November and December 2000 who sought to count dimpled chads as votes for Al Gore. Shaw won 61%–38%. In 2004 Shaw had another opponent who proved able to raise money nationally. Wilton Manors Mayor Jim Stork, owner of two bakery-cafes, was helped by his partner, a Massachusetts philanthropist, and raised $1 million from gay rights advocates across the country; he was aided by Barney Frank, Nancy Pelosi, Howard Dean's Democracy for America and the DailyKos weblog. In August Shaw filed a complaint with the FEC over ads for his bakery that Stork was running on local cable TV. Then in mid-August, Stork, 37, suspended his campaign, saying he had experienced fatigue and was undergoing medical testing. On September 17 he said he was withdrawing from the race because of a "heart-related condition." State law allowed the Democratic party to name another candidate, but Stork's withdrawal letter was not received until September 24 and Secretary of State Glenda Hood, after consulting with Palm Beach and Broward County officials, said it was too late to change the ballot; military and overseas ballots had already been sent out. Two Palm Beach County Democratic officials sued, and a judge in Tallahassee allowed the Democrats to nominate another candidate. Some suggested 20th District Congressman Peter Deutsch, defeated in the August 31 primary for U.S. senator, but state law seemed to bar that, and Democrats named Robin Rorapaugh, a Deutsch aide. Ballots marked for Stork were deemed marked for her. Shaw responded to all this by donating $300,000 to the NRCC. Shaw won 63%–35%. In March 2005, state Senator Ron Klein announced he would run against Shaw in 2006; within a month of his candidacy, Klein had raised over $150,000.

TWENTY-THIRD DISTRICT

Rep. Alcee Hastings (D)

Elected 1992, 7th term; b. Sept. 5, 1936, Altamonte Springs; home, Miramar; Fisk U., B.A. 1958, Howard U., 1958–60, FL A&M, J.D. 1963; Methodist; single.

Elected Office: Broward Cnty. Circuit Court Judge, 1977–79.

Professional Career: Practicing atty., 1964–77; Federal Judge, U.S. District Court, 1979–89.

DC Office: 2353 RHOB, 20515, 202-225-1313; Fax: 202-225-1171; Web site: www.alceehastings.house.gov.

District Offices: Ft. Lauderdale, 954-733-2800; West Palm Beach, 561-684-0565.

Committees: *Permanent Select Committee on Intelligence* (2d of 9 D): Oversight; Terrorism, Human Intelligence, Analysis & Counterintelligence. *Rules* (3d of 4 D): Legislative & Budget Process (RMM).

Group Ratings

	ADA	ACLU	AFS	LCV	ITIC	NTU	COC	ACU	NTLC	CHC
2004	55	88	100	36	33	12	21	0	3	7
2003	100	—	100	90	—	24	19	21	—	—

National Journal Ratings

	2003 LIB	—	2003 CONS		2004 LIB	—	2004 CONS
Economic	92%	—	0%		92%	—	8%
Social	92%	—	0%		88%	—	0%
Foreign	70%	—	27%		74%	—	26%

Key Votes of the 108th Congress

1. Drilling in ANWR	N	5. DC School Vouchers	N	9. Ban Same-Sex Marriage	*
2. Approve Bush Tax Cuts	N	6. Ban Human Cloning	N	10. Fund Iraq War	N
3. Medicare/Rx Bill	N	7. Restrict Gun Liability	N	11. Bar Cuba Embargo Funds	N
4. Bar Overtime Pay Regs.	Y	8. Ban Partial-Birth Abortion	N	12. Intelligence Reorg.	N

Election Results

2004 general	Alcee Hastings (D)	.... unopposed		($947,430)
2004 primary	Alcee Hastings (D)	 49,284	(74%)	
	Keith Clayborne (D)	 17,106	(26%)	
2002 general	Alcee Hastings (D)	 96,347	(77%)	($325,685)
	Charles Laurie (R)	 27,986	(23%)	($13,501)

Prior Winning Percentages: 2000 (76%); 1998 (100%); 1996 (73%); 1994 (100%); 1992 (59%)

The People		Race/Ethnic Origin	Ancestry	
Area size:	3,703 sq. mi.	29.4% White	West Indian: 16.2% USA: 5.0%	
Urban population:	97.9%	51.2% Black	German: 4.1%	
Rural population:	2.1%	1.2% Asian	**2004 Presidential Vote**	
Pop. 2000:	639,295	0.2% Native Am.	Kerry (D) 155,915	(76%)
Median income:	$31,309	0.1% Hawaiian	Bush (R) 50,138	(24%)
Poverty status:	21.9%	3.9% Two+ races	Other 28	(0%)
Military veterans:	9.1%	0.4% Other	**2000 Presidential Vote**	
		13.7% Hispanic Origin	Gore (D) 130,518	(80%)
			Bush (R) 33,034	(20%)
			Cook Partisan Voting Index: D +29	

Occupation	Blue collar: 25.8%	White collar: 48.0%	Gray collar: 26.2%

In the morning shadow of the high-rise condominiums that line the Atlantic Ocean, behind the quiet waters that separate the barrier islands from the mainland, usually a few blocks off of old U.S. 1 and behind the railroad lines, are the black neighborhoods of South Florida's Gold Coast. They are gatherings of older stucco homes and commercial storefronts, ranging from enclaves of upper-middle-class residents to rundown slums. These neighborhoods, populated by the working poor and with relatively few seniors, are overlooked by most tourists.

The 23d Congressional District of Florida gathers together many of South Florida's black neighborhoods in a geographically contrived, but demographically coherent, constituency. Geographically most of the district is in the Everglades, east and south of Lake Okeechobee. This is a land of swamps and drainage canals, with some farms and citrus groves—and very few people, some in migrant worker camps, some on the Miccosukee Indian Reservation, some in places like Southwest Ranches, where residents have blocked new roads and street lights. Almost all of the people in the district live within four narrow tentacles that extend east from the Everglades and get close to but never reach the Atlantic Ocean. The northernmost reaches into St. Lucie County and takes in black neighborhoods in Fort Pierce. In northern Palm Beach County a tentacle reaches past high-income Wellington into West Palm Beach and then continues south along the railroad tracks and U.S. 1 to Delray Beach, which has a big Haitian community. The most heavily populated tentacle reaches east into Broward County to take in heavily black areas in Lauderhill, Fort Lauderdale, Pompano Beach and Deerfield Beach; Haitian groups here lobbied for a ballot in Creole. Farther south in Broward County there is a much smaller tentacle that reaches into parts of fast-growing Miramar and Pembroke Pines, including Century Village, the retirement development known for its politically powerful, liberal associations led by "condo commandos." (The Del Boca Vista subdivision in *Seinfeld* tweaked such places for their neighborhood busybodies and early-bird dinner deals). Overall, the population is 51% black and 14% Hispanic. This is a heavily Democratic district.

The congressman from the 23d District is Alcee Hastings, a Democrat first elected in 1992, the only member of Congress ever to have been impeached and removed from office as a federal judge. Hastings is charming but hard-edged, the only child of a hotel maid from Orlando, who later worked as a domestic for wealthy families across the nation. He practiced law, finished fourth in the five-candidate Democratic primary when he ran for the U.S. Senate in 1970, and was confirmed as a federal judge in 1979. Hastings was charged with conspiring with a friend to take a $150,000 bribe and give two convicted swindlers light sentences. A Miami jury acquitted Hastings in 1983, but the friend was convicted. The 11th Circuit Court of Appeals called for impeachment in 1987 and referred the case to Congress. Hastings was impeached by the House by a vote of 413–3 and convicted by the Senate, 69–26. In the House, John Conyers, senior member of the Congressional Black Caucus, made the case for impeachment; a panel of 12 senators heard the case, and Hastings was removed in 1989. Footnote: In 1997, after the Department of Justice in investigating the FBI crime lab found that an agent falsely testified against Hastings, he and Conyers moved to reopen the case. Nothing came of that, raising a question: Can a removed federal judge be restored to office?

After his removal Hastings was unapologetic. In 1990 he ran an abortive campaign for governor, then lost the primary for secretary of state. When the 23d District was created, he entered that race and led in the primary 28%–27%. In the October runoff he faced Palm Beach County legislator Lois Frankel, who blasted Hastings for his record; he responded, "The bitch is a racist." Hastings was helped by a ruling by federal Judge Stanley Sporkin that his removal from office was invalid since the full Senate did not hear the charges; the Supreme Court later ruled to the contrary in a case involving another federal judge, but by that time Hastings was in Congress. He won the runoff 58%–42%, with voting closely following racial lines. He won the general election 59%–31%.

In the House, he treated colleagues pleasantly and respectfully. His voting record has been the most liberal in the Florida delegation. He focused on international issues, and strongly supported the U.S. intervention in Kosovo but opposed the use of force in Iraq. Naturally, Hastings's opinion was sought when the subject of impeachment arose, and it was exuberantly given. He saw Bill Clinton's impeachment as being driven by prosecutors, like the judges in his own case, abusing their powers: "In my case, they nullified a jury. In this case, they are nullifying an election." He moved to impeach Independent Counsel Kenneth Starr; his motion was voted down 340–71. He serves on the House Rules Committee. In 2004, with the support of Speaker Dennis Hastert, he was elected president of the Organization for Security and Cooperation in the pan-European Parliamentary Assembly.

After the 2002 election, he said that he would run for the Senate if Bob Graham did not seek reelection, 34 years after his first Senate race. But later Hastings said that he changed his mind because of his important assignments in the House. He has been reelected easily, in part because of his responsiveness to local concerns: his congressional website offers Creole and Spanish versions.

TWENTY-FOURTH DISTRICT

Rep. Tom Feeney (R)

Elected 2002, 2d term; b. May 21, 1958, Abington, PA; home, Oviedo; PA St. U., B.A. 1980, U. of Pittsburgh, J.D. 1983; Presbyterian; married (Ellen).

Elected Office: FL House of Reps., 1990–94, 1996–2002, Speaker, 2000–02.

Professional Career: Practicing atty., 1983–2002.

DC Office: 323 CHOB, 20515, 202-225-2706; Fax: 202-226-6299; Web site: www.house.gov/feeney.

District Offices: Orlando, 407-208-1106; Port Orange, 386-756-9798; Titusville, 321-264-6113.

Committees: *Financial Services* (24th of 37 R): Capital Markets, Insurance & Government Sponsored Enterprises; Financial Institutions & Consumer Credit. *Judiciary* (21st of 23 R): Crime, Terrorism & Homeland Security; The Constitution. *Science* (17th of 24 R): Space & Aeronautics.

Group Ratings

	ADA	ACLU	AFS	LCV	ITIC	NTU	COC	ACU	NTLC	CHC
2004	0	0	0	0	90	82	100	100	100	100
2003	10	—	14	10	—	74	93	100	—	—

National Journal Ratings

	2003 LIB	—	2003 CONS	2004 LIB	—	2004 CONS
Economic	27%	—	73%	0%	—	95%
Social	24%	—	71%	0%	—	91%
Foreign	21%	—	77%	4%	—	93%

Key Votes of the 108th Congress

1. Drilling in ANWR	Y	5. DC School Vouchers	Y	9. Ban Same-Sex Marriage	Y
2. Approve Bush Tax Cuts	Y	6. Ban Human Cloning	Y	10. Fund Iraq War	Y
3. Medicare/Rx Bill	N	7. Restrict Gun Liability	Y	11. Bar Cuba Embargo Funds	N
4. Bar Overtime Pay Regs.	N	8. Ban Partial-Birth Abortion	Y	12. Intelligence Reorg.	Y

Election Results

2004 general	Tom Feeney (R)	.... unopposed		($705,578)
2004 primary	Tom Feeney (R)	.... unopposed		
2002 general	Tom Feeney (R)	 135,576	(62%)	($1,853,423)
	Harry Jacobs (D)	 83,667	(38%)	($3,989,408)

The People		Race/Ethnic Origin	Ancestry	
Area size:	1,915 sq. mi.	80.0% White	German: 12.4% Irish: 10.5%	
Urban population:	91.2%	6.3% Black	English: 9.3%	
Rural population:	8.8%	2.0% Asian	**2004 Presidential Vote**	
Pop. 2000:	639,295	0.3% Native Am.	Bush (R) 188,973	(55%)
Median income:	$43,954	0.0% Hawaiian	Kerry (D) 153,130	(45%)
Poverty status:	8.7%	1.4% Two+ races	Other 476	(0%)
Military veterans:	17.1%	0.2% Other	**2000 Presidential Vote**	
		9.8% Hispanic Origin	Bush (R) 133,531	(53%)
			Gore (D) 116,502	(47%)
			Cook Partisan Voting Index: R + 3	
Occupation	Blue collar: 19.4%	White collar: 65.3% Gray collar: 15.3%		

In 1960, central Florida was a sleepy place: Orlando was a small city surrounded by citrus groves; the Atlantic Coast from Cape Canaveral north was a quiet winter vacation spot, with small motels lining U.S. 1 or along the beach on Highway A1A. Then two outsiders transformed this part of America, and made it in two different ways a leader in the world: John F. Kennedy and Walt Disney. Kennedy promised in 1961 to put a man on the moon before the end of the decade, and the Kennedy Space Center was built on an island near Cape Canaveral. This part of

Florida suddenly became the Space Coast, from which Americans traveled directly to the moon. Disney in 1971 opened Disney World southwest of Orlando, near the Intersection of I-4 and Florida's Turnpike. Other theme parks followed, and metro Orlando became the number one tourist destination in the world. In the process, the populations of metro Orlando and the Space Coast have more than tripled since the 1960s. People from all over the United States and, more recently, immigrants from Latin America and elsewhere, have come here in large numbers and, with the aid of ubiquitous air conditioning, have transformed sleepy backwaters into vibrant metropolitan areas. This is a part of Florida that has attracted many more young families and people in their working years than retirees: people who have built all-American communities where there used to be orange groves and swamps.

The 24th Congressional District of Florida has about half its population in the Orlando area, much of it in affluent Orange and Seminole County suburbs north and northeast of Orlando— all of Oviedo and parts of Maitland and Altamonte Springs. The other half is on the coast. The 24th includes the northern half of Brevard County, including the main grounds of the Space Center itself, the Canaveral National Seashore and the county seat of Titusville; the economy here has diversified to include commercial and military satellites, plus the East Coast surfing capital in nearby Cocoa Beach (which is in the 15th District). It also contains the southern half of Volusia County, including part of Daytona Beach, where NASCAR is a big employer and Bike Week and Speed Week are held every year, and New Smyrna Beach, founded as a colony by Andrew Turnbull, a Scotch doctor, where you can see the ruins of an 1820s sugar mill. In between is Ponce de Leon Inlet, near which 22 people were bitten by sharks in the summer of 2001: the sort of thing that made national news before September 11. This is as close as Florida gets to a typical suburban district: There are higher than average numbers of homeowners, families with children, working women and white-collar employees. This is on balance a Republican district; it voted 53% for George W. Bush in 2000 and 55% in 2004.

The congressman from the 24th District is Tom Feeney, a Republican first elected in 2002 who was a prominent political player in the Bush versus Gore machinations in Florida. His political career has been marked by ambition, impulsiveness and a quick rise through the ranks but with some bumps along the way. He grew up in Pennsylvania, the son of schoolteachers, and was an unsuccessful candidate to be a delegate for Ronald Reagan in 1980. After graduating from Penn State and University of Pittsburgh law school, he moved to Florida and practiced real estate law. In 1990 he was elected to the state House, where his early focus was on education. In 1994 Jeb Bush picked him as his lieutenant governor candidate. The statewide race was a sobering experience. Democrats zeroed in on Feeney's conservative voting record—he opposed abortion rights and favored school prayer and vouchers—and attacked him as an extremist bent on injecting religion into the public schools. Bush and Feeney lost to Lawton Chiles and Buddy MacKay 51%–49%.

In an April 1996 special election, Feeney was returned to the state House, in which Republicans won a majority that November. In November 2000, he became Speaker and suddenly found himself in the national spotlight. During the 36-day presidential recount he aggressively challenged the rulings of the Florida Supreme Court and supported Secretary of State Katherine Harris. When it was unclear whether the U.S. Supreme Court would review the Florida court's second decision, Feeney called a special session of the House to appoint presidential electors for Bush; that became moot after the U.S. Supreme Court decision on December 12. As Speaker, Feeney took a lead role on congressional redistricting. Central Florida's population had increased robustly in the 1990s, and it was the part of the state most obviously entitled to one of the two additional seats Florida had picked up in the 2000 Census. Feeney immediately started to run in the new 24th District and was unopposed in the Republican primary.

The Democratic nominee was Harry Jacobs, a wealthy trial lawyer who in November 2000 filed a lawsuit challenging the validity of some 16,000 absentee ballots in Seminole County. The weakness of the lawsuit was that even Jacobs conceded that the overwhelming majority of the ballots were valid, and there was no way to distinguish those that weren't from those that were. A trial judge appointed by a Democratic governor dismissed it. Jacobs spent $3.2 million of his own money on his 2002 campaign. He boasted about his work as a public school teacher and attacked Feeney's "questionable ethics." Feeney said that Jacobs tried to disenfranchise military voters with his lawsuit in 2000. He won 62%–38%.

In the House, Feeney usually sides with conservatives. On the Judiciary Committee, he enacted a controversial proposal to restrict judges from imposing sentences in sexual assault cases that are more lenient than federal guidelines. The question, he said, "is who should decide: the elected representatives of the people, or the individual judges." Chief Justice William Rehnquist criticized the proposal as an "unwarranted and ill-considered effort to intimidate individual judges." Liberal lawmakers criticized the proposal, but many voted for it as part of the bill to create a nationwide "Amber Alert" system to recover abducted children. Feeney also sponsored a bill to prohibit federal judges from citing foreign laws in their rulings. After the death of Ronald Reagan, he called the former president "our Moses." Although he made an exception for NASA, he joined other conservatives who said that the federal government was spending too much money; "When push comes to shove, conservatives are becoming more willing to say, 'You'll have to get to 218 [votes] without us.'" Feeney ignored the pleas of Republican leaders, including George W. Bush, to vote for the Medicare/prescription drug bill in November 2003; while asking for his vote, Bush reportedly hung up when Feeney told him that he came to Washington to cut entitlements, not increase them. When the Ethics Committee admonished Tom DeLay in October 2004, Feeney said that the majority leader "stands strong as our leader." He secured a change in House rules to remove the prohibition on referring to the Senate or individual Senators. "The rule was antiquated," he said.

Feeney won a second term without opposition.

TWENTY-FIFTH DISTRICT

Rep. Mario Diaz-Balart (R)

Elected 2002, 2d term; b. Sept. 25, 1961, Ft. Lauderdale; home, Miami; U. of S. FL; Catholic; married (Tia).

Elected Office: FL House of Reps., 1988–92, 2000–02; FL Senate, 1992–00.

Professional Career: A.A., Miami Mayor Xavier Suarez, 1985–88; Public relations executive.

DC Office: 313 CHOB, 20515, 202-225-2778; Fax: 202-226-0346; Web site: www.house.gov/mariodiaz-balart.

District Offices: Miami, 305-225-6866; Naples, 239-348-1620.

Committees: *Budget* (11th of 22 R). *Transportation & Infrastructure* (28th of 41 R): Aviation; Coast Guard & Maritime Transportation; Highways, Transit & Pipelines.

Group Ratings

	ADA	ACLU	AFS	LCV	ITIC	NTU	COC	ACU	NTLC	CHC
2004	5	11	0	0	80	72	95	96	92	100
2003	5	—	0	10	—	67	93	92	—	—

National Journal Ratings

	2003 LIB	—	2003 CONS	2004 LIB	—	2004 CONS
Economic	0%	—	91%	9%	—	88%
Social	24%	—	71%	47%	—	53%
Foreign	0%	—	89%	17%	—	78%

Key Votes of the 108th Congress

1. Drilling in ANWR	Y	5. DC School Vouchers	Y	9. Ban Same-Sex Marriage	*
2. Approve Bush Tax Cuts	Y	6. Ban Human Cloning	Y	10. Fund Iraq War	Y
3. Medicare/Rx Bill	Y	7. Restrict Gun Liability	Y	11. Bar Cuba Embargo Funds	N
4. Bar Overtime Pay Regs.	N	8. Ban Partial-Birth Abortion	Y	12. Intelligence Reorg.	N

Election Results

2004 general	Mario Diaz-Balart (R) .... unopposed			($322,024)
2004 primary	Mario Diaz-Balart (R) .... unopposed			
2002 general	Mario Diaz-Balart (R)	81,845	(65%)	($999,322)
	Annie Betancourt (D)	44,757	(35%)	($155,450)

The People		Race/Ethnic Origin	Ancestry	
Area size:	4,724 sq. mi.	24.3% White	USA: 3.8%	West India: 3.7%
Urban population:	94.4%	10.0% Black	German: 3.2%	
Rural population:	5.6%	1.6% Asian	**2004 Presidential Vote**	
Pop. 2000:	639,295	0.1% Native Am.	Bush (R) 122,342	(56%)
Median income:	$44,489	0.0% Hawaiian	Kerry (D) 95,001	(44%)
Poverty status:	13.7%	1.4% Two+ races	**2000 Presidential Vote**	
Military veterans:	6.0%	0.2% Other	Bush (R) 88,308	(55%)
		62.4% Hispanic Origin	Gore (D) 72,050	(45%)
			Cook Partisan Voting Index: R + 4	

Occupation   Blue collar: 20.8%   White collar: 61.7%   Gray collar: 17.5%

An interconnected sea of wetlands once covered 8.9 million acres of southern Florida, stretching from present-day Orlando down to the peninsula's southern tip. It was once a coherent ecosystem, a "river of grass" in which water moved slowly down a gentle slope to the ocean, buffering plants and animals from meteorological extremes, and providing different micro-environments for flora and fauna based on an inch or two gained or lost in elevation. It was long a dream of Florida's white settlers to control this land and make it more useful, but for decades this goal proved elusive. It took three attempts between 1915 and the late 1920s to build the Tamiami Trail from Miami to Tampa; to this day, it is one of only two roads that cross the South Florida interior from coast to coast. Over time man managed to reshape the Everglades. In 1948, Congress approved the Central and South Florida Project, which authorized the construction of 1,000 miles of canals and 720 miles of levees to channel and drain the Everglades. Since that time, about half of the original ecosystem has been turned over to agriculture and housing, and the amount of water discharged into the ocean has fallen by 70%. Floridians later began to question the wisdom of government policy and called for restoration of the Everglades. State politicians of both parties began to take notice, and called for change. So did officials of the Clinton administration. In 2000 they all came together in agreement, and Congress passed a law to restore the Everglades, authorizing $7.8 billion over 30 years. Then came the hard part. No one is actually sure how to accomplish the goals, but in 2002 President George W. Bush and his brother Jeb signed an agreement to proceed and the Army Corps of Engineers was set to work.

A century of meddling has produced an often-surreal landscape. Farmers came to the Fakahatchee Strand in the early 20th century, but they found that crops would not grow reliably, and livestock often escaped, leaving a legacy of feral, mean-spirited swamp pigs. Timbering came next, until there were no more trees to chop down. Then the timber barons sold their land to real estate speculators who made hundreds of millions of dollars duping customers into buying wretched plots for $10 a month, using patently false promises, spying on their customers' private conversations in their hotel rooms and driving potential buyers to remote areas of the site and threatening to let them walk home if they did not sign a contract. Much of the landholdings became an untamed state park.

The 25th Congressional District of Florida sprawls almost all the way across this uninhabitable portion of South Florida, connecting population centers near (but not on) each of Florida's two coasts. About 13% of its residents live in Collier County, in new housing wedged between decidedly upscale Naples and the wild Everglades and in the farm town of Immokalee. The large majority live in western and southern edges of metropolitan Miami, never very far from the swamps. Here you can drive out on roads past the subdivisions and find strawberry, tomato and citrus farms; the trees thin out and then the road just ends, and the Everglades begin. During the 1990s this area's population grew by 52%. The towns in the northern part of Miami-Dade are heavily Cuban and Latino—Hialeah Gardens, Tamiami, Kendale Lakes, South Miami Heights, Cutler Ridge. Farther south the 25th takes in low-income agricultural areas along South Dixie

Highway (U.S. 1), like Princeton and Naranja, as well as a few older tourist attractions, like the Metrozoo, Monkey Jungle and Coral Castle. Even further south is what was once the country town of Homestead. Before 1992, Homestead Air Force Base was a major employer here. But in August 1992 Hurricane Andrew hit Homestead, leaving massive property destruction; Homestead was leveled and the Air Force Base closed. In one of his last acts as president, Bill Clinton rejected a plan to convert the base to a commercial airport, citing environmental concerns. Instead, 700 acres were transferred to the county for use by developers, resulting in a new boomtown, with residential developments, shops, hospitals, parks and schools, plus a Coast Guard base; NASCAR has an annual race at the speedway. Politically, this area leans Republican, thanks to the allegiance of its many Cuban Americans (though this is the least Cuban of the three South Florida Hispanic majority districts).

The congressman from the 25th District is Mario Diaz-Balart, a Republican first elected in 2002. His father, Rafael Lincoln Diaz-Balart, served as majority leader in pre-revolution Cuba's House of Representatives. His uncle and grandfather also served in the Cuban House. His aunt was once married to Fidel Castro. He comes from a prominent family sometimes called "the Cuban Kennedys," which seems to have politics in its blood. One of his three older brothers is Lincoln Diaz-Balart, congressman from the 21st District just to the east. Mario Diaz-Balart, unlike Lincoln, was born in the United States after his family fled Cuba.

Even for a scion of one of Miami's most prominent political families, Mario Diaz-Balart's ascent has been impressive. He dropped out of the University of South Florida at 24 to work for former Miami Mayor Xavier Suarez and was elected in 1988 to the Florida House. In 1992, at 31, he became the youngest person ever elected to the Florida Senate. Soon after that, Diaz-Balart was named chairman of the Senate Ways and Means Committee, where he quickly established a reputation as a budget hawk. His 1995 order calling for state agencies to cut spending by 25% earned him the nickname "The Slasher"—a moniker he wore with pride. The eight-year term limit forced him from the state Senate in 2000, so he again ran for the Florida House and was elected. He was no ordinary freshman, though. Diaz-Balart requested and received the chairmanship of the congressional redistricting committee. The resulting plan included a central Florida district tailored to Speaker Tom Feeney and this western Miami-Dade district tailored for Diaz-Balart.

The election proved anticlimactic. Diaz-Balart went to court and eliminated all his would-be Republican opponents. In the general election he coasted to victory over Democratic state Representative Annie Betancourt, a former social worker and the widow of a Bay of Pigs veteran. Betancourt's campaign was underfinanced and she remained largely unknown; Diaz-Balart was well financed and had support from teachers and other unions. Betancourt called to end the "failed" embargo of Cuba in a way "that doesn't pander to the Cuban regime but likewise doesn't punish the Cuban people." This was a bold move in a strongly anti-Castro constituency. Diaz-Balart did not pursue the issue vigorously, perhaps because he sensed that the growing population of non-Cuban Latinos in south Florida are less concerned about Castro. He won 65%–35%.

In the House, he has had a more conservative voting record than brother Lincoln on economic and foreign policy and has been a moderate on cultural issues. He got on the Budget and Transportation and Infrastructure committees. With fellow freshmen Tom Feeney and Jeb Hensarling, he founded Washington Waste Watchers, to combat government waste, fraud and abuse. He also organized the Congressional Hispanic Conference, a Republican alternative to the Democrats' Congressional Hispanic Caucus. By working with other freshmen, he helped to reduce the number of supporters of legislation to relax the travel ban to Cuba. When 36 Democrats opposed the confirmation of Alberto Gonzales as Attorney General, Diaz-Balart responded, "It is no surprise Hispanic support for Democrats keeps eroding." He got the Federal Emergency Management Agency to postpone implementation of new flood maps in the town of Golden Gate that would have raised residential insurance rates. Unopposed in 2004, he made contributions and campaign appearances for freshmen in competitive races elsewhere.

★ GEORGIA ★

Georgia and Atlanta—the megacity whose metropolitan area spreads out over the red clay hills of 20 of Georgia's 159 counties—have been one of the great boom areas of America over the last dozen years and have been the site as well of one of the great political transformations of the first decade of the 21st century. From 1990 to 2004, Georgia's population grew by 36%, the sixth highest rate of population growth among states, the highest east of Colorado, and the highest rate of growth for Georgia since the 1870s, when Atlanta rose literally from the ashes of the Civil War and Henry Grady's New South sprang into being. Atlanta and Georgia have been in many ways, for many years, the center of the South, at least since General William Tecumseh Sherman marched here in 1864. This is where John Stith Pemberton invented Coca-Cola, where Margaret Mitchell wrote *Gone With the Wind*, where Martin Luther King Jr. grew up, and where most of the civil rights organizations that changed America were headquartered. But in growth and flamboyance, Georgia for decades was outdazzled by other parts of the South—by Texas with its oil wells and high-tech industries, by Florida with Miami Beach and Disney World, even by North Carolina with its Research Triangle and college basketball champions.

Since 1990, however, Georgia has grown faster than any of them. The 2000 Census recorded it as the tenth-largest state—the first time it has been in the top 10 since the Census of 1850—and the 2004 Census estimates placed it ninth, ahead of New Jersey. Most of this growth has come in the booming Atlanta metropolitan area, not in the core city, but amid the hills of suburban counties for almost 100 miles around. Atlanta, long a regional capital, has become a world city, a status suitably memorialized when it hosted the 1996 Summer Olympics, and re-emphasized every day as travelers all over the world watch the news from the CNN Broadcast Center.

Neither Atlanta's rise to world eminence nor its role as the capital of the South was inevitable. This was only a small, though well located, railroad crossroads when it was burned by Sherman's troops on their "march to the sea." Richmond, Charleston and New Orleans all had stronger claims to being the central focus of the South a century ago. But in the 20th century two figures imprinted Atlanta on the national imagination. One was Margaret Mitchell, whose 1936 novel *Gone with the Wind* inspired the 1939 movie. The other was Martin Luther King Jr., reared in Atlanta and based there during most of his career, as a leader and ultimately the national symbol of the civil rights revolution that changed the South and the nation. Linking the two was Atlanta's business community, notably Robert Woodruff, who headed Coca-Cola from 1932–60 and made Coke a worldwide enterprise. Perhaps aware that a world company could not indefinitely be associated with racial segregation, Woodruff and William Hartsfield, mayor from 1937–61, cooperated with blacks and promoted Atlanta as "the city too busy to hate." Hartsfield's successor, Ivan Allen, elected in 1961 and 1965, supported the Civil Rights Act of 1964, as Peachtree Center and the first atriumed Hyatt Regency were going up in downtown Atlanta.

This new Atlanta was growing up amid a mostly rural, deeply segregationist Georgia that as late as 1960 cast the second-highest Democratic percentage of any state for president: Hatred of Sherman was still strong. Political contests typically matched Atlanta-supported moderates against rural-supported segregationists, and the latter invariably won: Georgia's electoral votes were cast for Barry Goldwater in 1964 and George Wallace in 1968. Then came change in the person of Jimmy Carter, a one-term state senator who was elected governor in 1970 with a rural base as well as conspicuous black support. On taking office he proclaimed a reconciliation of the races and installed a portrait of Martin Luther King Jr. in the Capitol. Carter thus became one of the first politicians from the rural South to celebrate and honor the civil rights revolution and in the process set himself on the road to being elected president in 1976.

Since then, Georgia and Atlanta have seen an in-migration of black Americans. The state's population was 29% black in 2000, the highest figure since 1950; the state has more blacks than any other state except New York and Texas, and will surpass them soon if present trends continue. The presence of nine historically black colleges, of large numbers of prominent black public officials and businessmen, the growth of middle- and upper-income predominantly black

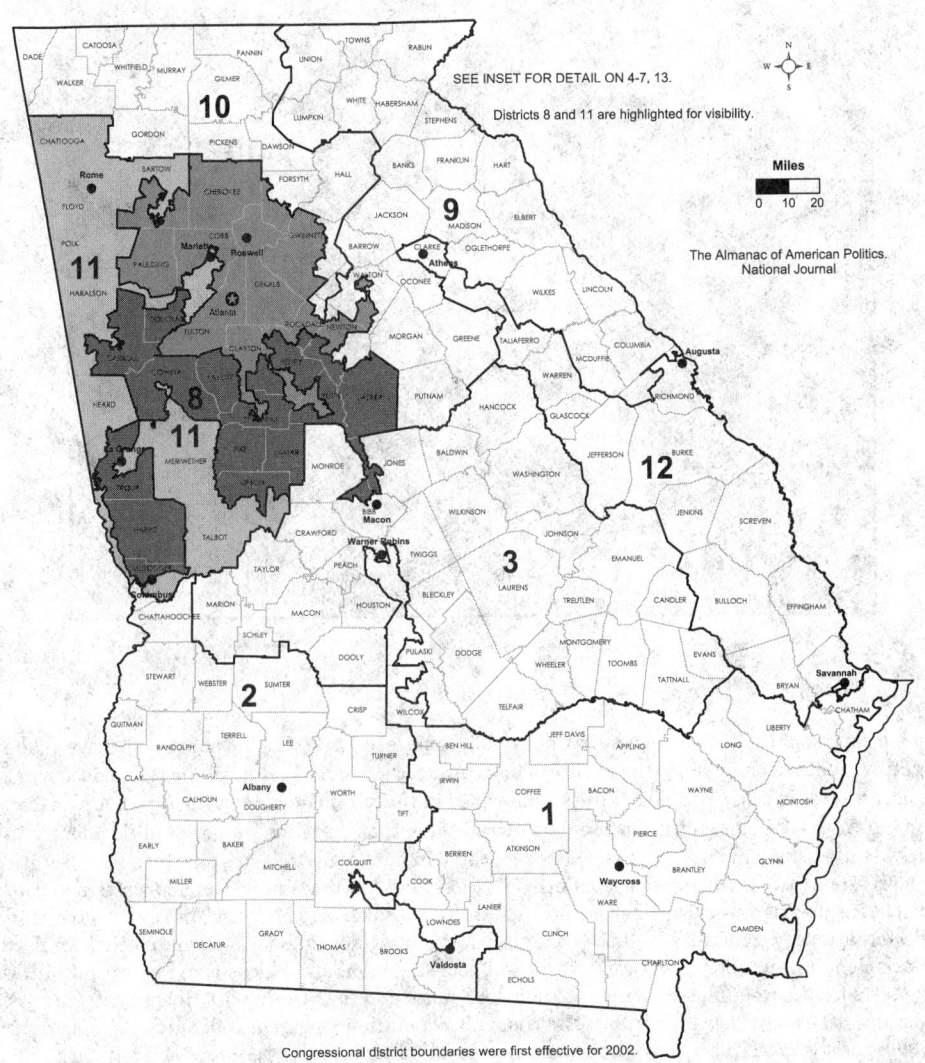

SEE INSET FOR DETAIL ON 4-7, 13.

Districts 8 and 11 are highlighted for visibility.

Miles
0 10 20

The Almanac of American Politics.
National Journal

Congressional district boundaries were first effective for 2002.

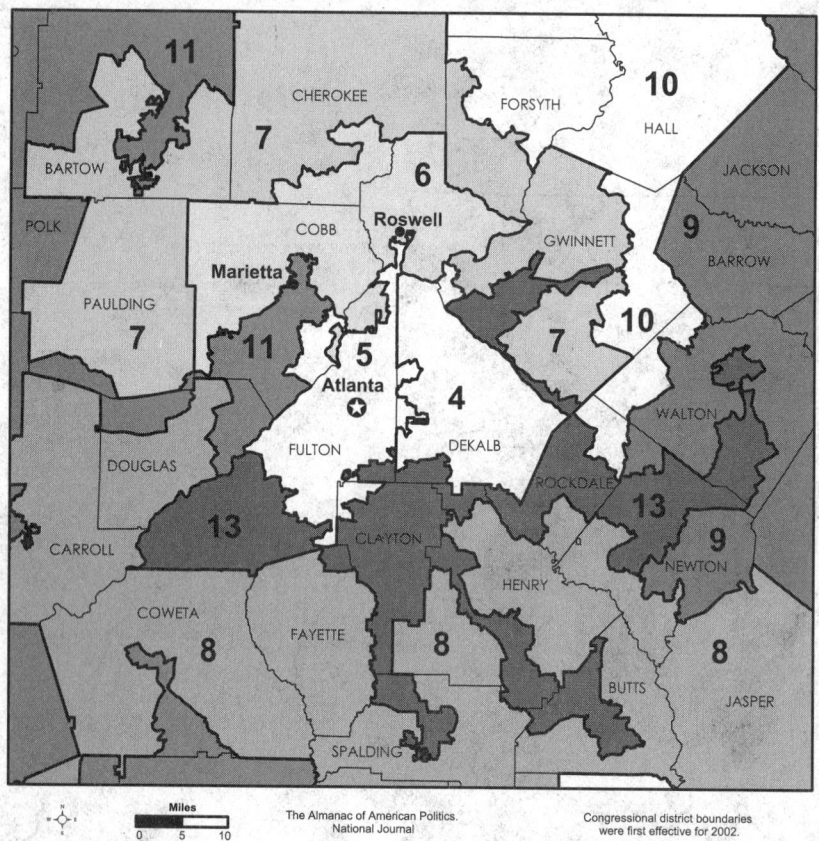

Miles
0   5   10

The Almanac of American Politics.
National Journal

Congressional district boundaries
were first effective for 2002.

suburban neighborhoods in DeKalb County and, more recently, Cobb County—all have made
metro Atlanta in some sense the capital of black America. Arguably, Georgia has developed what
Charles Moskos and John Sibley Butler described in their book on race in the Army, *All We Can
Be*, an Anglo-African culture, a merger of traditions that were long associated intimately in
private life but rigidly and even violently separated in public. Georgia has four black Democratic
congressmen, two from non-black majority districts, and Andrew Young won in a white-majority
district as long ago as 1972; black Democrats Thurbert Baker and Michael Thurmond have been
elected attorney general and labor commissioner statewide; in 2004 Georgia elected its first
black Republican state representative since Reconstruction, and blacks came in second in the
contests for the Republican nomination for the Senate and the 8th District House seat. Georgia
also has been attracting immigrants: Its Hispanic population rose from 109,000 to 435,000 in the
1990s, and three Latino legislators were elected in 2002; both parties were actively targeting
Latinos in 2004.

Demographic change and economic change in Georgia have been followed by political
change, to the point that this once heavily Democratic state now seems to be solidly Republican.
In retrospect, this change seems to have been a long time coming. It was delayed by the presence
of politically skillful Southern and Georgia Democrats with rural bases—George Wallace, who
carried the state in 1968; Jimmy Carter, who sent it in a different direction in 1970, and carried it
solidly in 1976 and 1980; Carter's successors as governor, each of whom served for eight years,
George Busbee, Joe Frank Harris and Zell Miller; by Bill Clinton, who carried the state
43.5%–42.9% in 1992 and lost it by only 47%–46% in 1996. Then, in 2000, a sign of change:

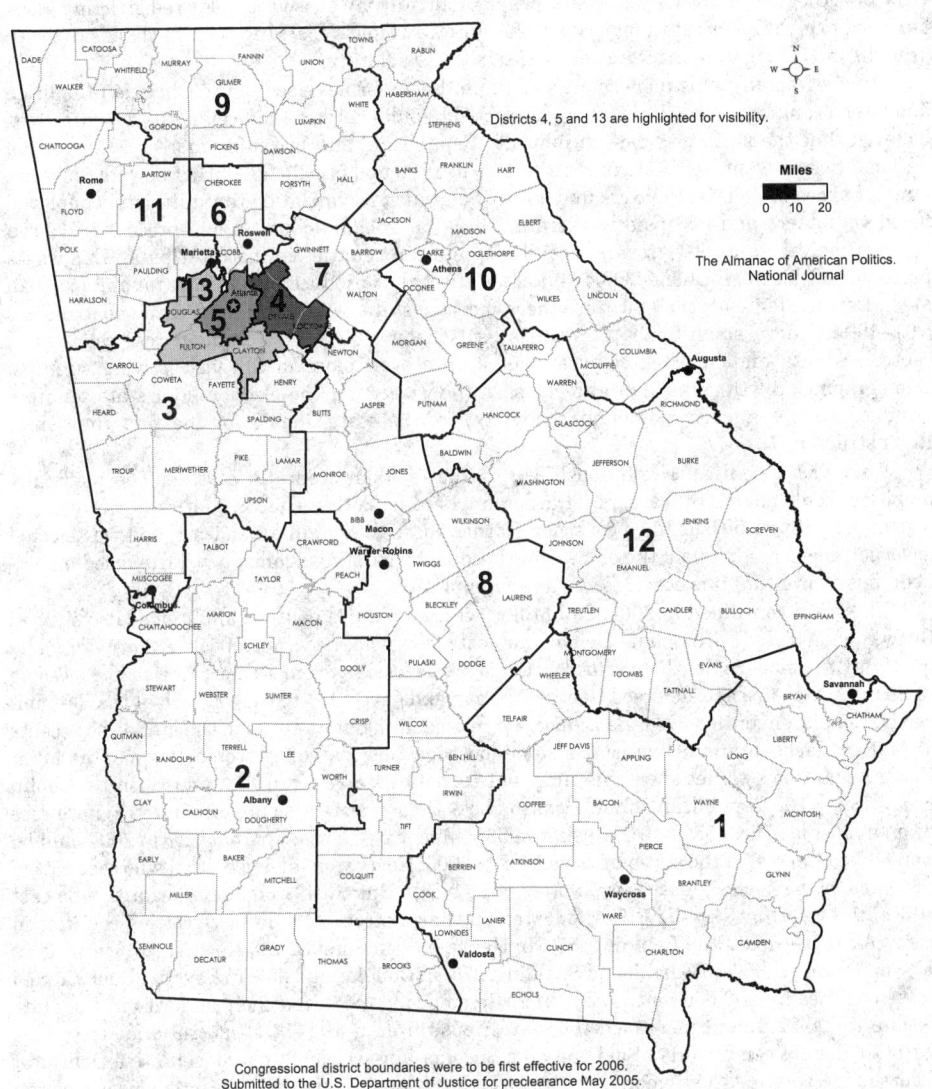

Districts 4, 5 and 13 are highlighted for visibility.

Miles
0   10   20

The Almanac of American Politics.
National Journal

Congressional district boundaries were to be first effective for 2006.
Submitted to the U.S. Department of Justice for preclearance May 2005.

George W. Bush carried Georgia by a solid 55%–43% margin. Bush carried metro Atlanta (which cast 53% of the state's votes) by 52%–45% and the rest of Georgia, historically Democratic, by a resounding 57%–41%. Sherman was a thing of the past.

Going into the 2002 elections, Democrats seemed well positioned. Roy Barnes, an activist governor with strong ties to Atlanta's business community, raised $19 million for his campaign and was mentioned as a possible vice presidential or even presidential candidate. Senator Max Cleland was well known as a veteran who had lost both legs and an arm in Vietnam. The Democratic legislature, led by 28-year Speaker Tom Murphy passed complex redistricting plans designed to give Democrats a majority of the state's 13 House seats (up from 11 thanks to 1990s growth) and to lock in Democratic majorities in the legislature.

Arrayed against this juggernaut was Ralph Reed, former head of the Christian Coalition and later a campaign consultant, who was elected Republican state chairman in May 2001. Reed believed that the state was demographically Republican, and becoming more so: Republican national tickets went from 43% in 1992 to 47% in 1996 and 55% in 2000. He knew he could not match Barnes in dollars, so he created an on-the-ground organization that ultimately deployed 3,000 volunteers and 500 paid workers to knock on 150,000 doors in 600 precincts. He ran registration drives in fast-growing heavily Republican counties in metro Atlanta. This was a prototype of the Bush-Cheney 2004 volunteer effort that produced votes in rural and exurban areas Democrats never thought were there. Former state Senator Sonny Perdue beat Barnes 51%–46%; Congressman Saxby Chambliss beat Cleland 53%–46%. Turnout rose robustly in central Atlanta and in black counties, but it rose even more in the fast-growing suburbs: Demographic growth translated into votes. In the week after the election, four state senators switched parties and gave Republicans control of the state Senate for the first time since Reconstruction.

This was a political revolution of a sort that seldom occurs in a state. The politically ambitious could ponder the careers of Barnes and Perdue. Both started in politics as canny young legislators with ambitions to be governor. Barnes chose to remain a Democrat and was elected governor, then couldn't hold the office. Now Perdue, by winning against a well-financed incumbent, has shown that it is easier to win as a Republican.

The trend continued in 2004. Zell Miller, with no further political ambitions, also showed the way. Frustrated with Senate Democrats' obstructionism, he wrote a book, *A National Party No More* ("the modern South and rural America are as foreign to our Democratic leaders as some place in Asia or Africa"), endorsed George W. Bush and gave a rip-roaring speech at the Republican National Convention. Georgia Democrats reviled him, but he spoke in the authentic accents of Andrew Jackson and delivered the same message Georgia voters would two months later. Georgia was not a target state this time, but turnout rose 28% anyway, and Bush beat John Kerry 58%–41%. Republican Johnny Isakson beat Democrat Denise Majette in the Senate race by an almost identical 58%–40%. Bush won 56% in metro Atlanta, up from 52% in 2000, and he won 60% in the rest of the state, up from 57% in 2000. Kerry won among blacks, who cast 25% of the votes, by 88%–12%; most Kerry voters were black. But Bush won among whites, who cast 70% of the votes, by 76%–23%. Turnout was up sharply from 2000 in fast-growing counties in metro Atlanta—up 67% in Paulding, 65% in Henry, 59% in Forsyth and Newton, 45% in Walton, 41% in Cherokee, 38% in Carroll and Spalding, 37% in Douglas and 25% in Fayette. Bush carried these counties by 200,000 votes, 72%–27%. Republicans increased their majority in the state Senate to 34–22 and transformed the state House from a 102–77 Democratic majority to a 99–80–1 Republican majority. Said outgoing Speaker Terry Coleman, a conservative Democrat from south Georgia, "The Democratic party, as it has been traditionally, has problems in Georgia unless we get back to the sensible center."

Georgia's Republican party has problems as well, problems of governance. Metro Atlanta Republicans tend to want low taxes, but also generous spending on roads and limits on sprawling growth—you can see new subdivisions from the Kennesaw Mountain battlefield. Rural Georgia Republicans tend to be inspired by cultural and often religious conservatism, and are hungry for public works projects in areas that have seen far less growth than metro Atlanta. Governor Sonny Perdue seems to have defused one controversy, over the state flag. Barnes in 2001 persuaded the legislature to get rid of the Confederate battle flag, adopted as the state flag in 1956, for his own blue background design. Perdue in 2003 promoted a new red, white and blue flag, designed by among others Jimmy Carter. In the 2002 campaign he had promised a referendum on the flag; he persuaded the legislature to call one for the March 2004 presidential primary, but the legislators allowed voters to chose only the 2001 or 2003 designs; the 2003 model won 73%–27%. Perhaps Georgia is ready to move on.

The People		Race/Ethnic Origin			Military veterans: 768,675 (12.8%)	
Pop. 2004 (est):	8,829,383	5,128,661	62.6%	White	WWII: 13.5%	Korea: 10.8%
Pop. 2000:	8,186,453	2,331,465	28.5%	Black	Vietnam: 34.4%	Gulf War: 15.4%
Pop. 1990:	6,478,216	171,513	2.1%	Asian	**Most populous cities (2003):**	
Change 1990–2000:	Up 26.4%	17,670	0.2%	Native Am.	1. Atlanta	423,019
% of U.S. total:	2.9%	3,278	0.0%	Hawaiian	2. Augusta	193,316
Pop. rank:	10th of 50	87,364	1.1%	Two+ races	3. Columbus	185,702
Area size:	59,425 sq. mi.	11,275	0.1%	Other	4. Savannah	127,573
State Native:	57.8%	435,227	5.3%	Hisp. Origin	5. Athens	102,498
Non-citizen:	5.0%	**Ancestry**				
Language		USA: 11.6%		English: 7.0%	Urban population: 71.7%	
English: 88.6%	Spanish: 6.0%	Irish: 6.7%		German: 6.0%	Rural population: 28.3%	
Other Eur.: 3.2%		Italian: 1.7%				

Education		Work Sector			General Assembly	
H.S. Grad:	78.6%	Private: 78.9%		Govt: 15.0%	Senate	34 R 22 D
College Grad:	24.3%	Self: 5.9%		Family: 0.3%	House	99 R 80 D 1 I
Industry		Unemployment: 5.4%			Legislative Term Limits: No	
Agri: 1.4%	Con: 7.9%	**Household Income**			**Registered Voters**	
Fin: 6.5%	Info: 3.5%	<15k: 16.0%		15-35k: 24.9%	No party registration	
Mfg: 20.8%	Prof: 27.0%	35-50k: 16.7%		50-100k: 30.1%		
Public: 5.0%	Trade: 15.8%	100-150k: 7.8%		>150k: 4.6%		
Other: 11.9%		Median: $42,433				
Occupation		Poverty status: 13.0%				
Blue collar: 26.5%	White collar: 59.5%	**Home Value**				
Gray collar: 14.0%		<50k: 16.9%	50-100k: 32.8%	100-200k: 34.4%	200-300k: 9.3%	
		300-500k: 4.7%	>500k: 1.9%	Median: $100,600		

Presidential politics   For many years Georgia seemed to vote against General Sherman, shunning Republican presidential candidates even when states less ravaged by Sherman's troops, like next-door South Carolina and Alabama, embraced them. It was the second most Democratic state for John Kennedy in 1960, voted for opponents of the Civil Rights Act of 1964 (Barry Goldwater in 1964 and George Wallace in 1968), delivered big margins for Jimmy Carter in both 1976 and 1980 and voted heavily Republican only in 1972, 1984 and 1988. A residual anti-Sherman vote in rural Georgia can perhaps explain why Bill Clinton carried the state outside metro Atlanta in 1992 and lost it by only 2% in 1996. But no more. George W. Bush carried Georgia by wide margins and the half of the state outside metro Atlanta by even wider margins in 2000 and 2004. It will take a major shift of opinion to make Democrats competitive for Georgia's electoral votes again.

2004 Presidential Vote
Bush (R) 1,914,254   (58%)
Kerry (D).................... 1,366,149   (41%)
Badnarik (Lib)................ 18,387   (1%)

2004 Democratic Presidential Primary
Kerry (D)...................... 293,225   (47%)
Edwards (D) 259,361   (41%)
Sharpton (D).................. 39,123   (6%)
Dean (D) 11,320   (2%)
Kucinich (D) 7,699   (1%)
Other.......................... 16,110   (3%)

2000 Presidential Vote
Bush (R) 1,419,720   (55%)
Gore (D)..................... 1,116,230   (43%)
Other.......................... 47,258   (2%)

Georgia's presidential primary comes early in the cycle and has been of some importance. In 1992 Governor Zell Miller had it scheduled one week before Super Tuesday in order to help Clinton, and it did: Clinton won solidly to balance losses in Maryland and Colorado the same day. In 1996 and 2000, Georgia was of little importance except as a measure of turnout: Democratic turnout fell from 622,000 in 1988 to 284,000 in 2000, while Republican turnout rose from 400,000 to 643,000. In the March 2, 2004, primary Democratic turnout zoomed to 627,000, as there was no Republican contest. John Edwards visited Georgia five times after the Iowa caucuses and John Kerry only once, but Kerry beat Edwards 47%–41%. Edwards carried white voters and won 101 of the 159 counties, but Kerry carried black voters and carried Atlanta's Fulton County and the two majority-black counties in the Atlanta metro area by 47,000 votes—more than his 33,000-vote statewide plurality. Edwards's loss here made it plain that he had no chance to win the nomination and would be hard pressed to win other Southern states, and he withdrew from the race.

Congressional districting

109th Congress Lineup	
7 R	6 D

108th Congress Lineup	
8 R	5 D

After the 1990 and 2000 Censuses, Georgia Democrats pushed through convoluted redistricting plans—arguably the most convoluted in the nation each time—to guarantee majorities for their party in the state's House delegation. Both times they failed. In the 1990s, Speaker Thomas Murphy tried to end the career of Newt Gingrich and strengthen incumbent Democrats. Instead, what was a 9–1 Democratic delegation in October 1992 was 8–3 Republican in April 1995, and Gingrich was Speaker of the House. A court-ordered redistricting in 1995 left virtually all incumbents with safe seats, and the balance remained 8–3. In 2001 the Democrats tried again, drawing several plans and negotiating among themselves. This time the boundaries were even more convoluted, and Democrats had a bit more success. But only a bit—plus some unintended consequences. Congressman Saxby Chambliss, placed in the new 1st District with fellow Republican Jack Kingston, ran for the Senate and beat incumbent Max Cleland. The new 11th and 12th Districts, created to elect Democrats, elected Republicans instead, and Democrats only narrowly won the new 3d District. The new 13th District did elect a black Democrat, Georgia's fourth, but the delegation remained Republican by an 8–5 margin. And Georgia's plan prompted the House Republicans' campaign committee head Tom Davis to push successfully for a similarly convoluted Republican gerrymander in Pennsylvania, one which netted the Republicans more gains than the Democrats achieved in Georgia.

Still, the Democrats' 2001 plan must be admired for its creativity. The 13th District sends narrow tentacles into 11 metro Atlanta counties to unite black neighborhoods along strip highways or in town centers with majority-black Clayton County just south of Atlanta. The new 11th District made a stab, though unsuccessful, at creating a Democratic district in Republican northwest Georgia by excluding fast-growing mostly white areas and sending in tentacles to south Cobb County with its increasing population. The 12th District for the most part has a regular shape and yet connects black neighborhoods in cities as distant as Savannah, Augusta and Athens. Heavily Republican areas are packed into five districts—the 6th and 7th on the north side of metro Atlanta, the 8th on the south side, the 9th and 10th in north Georgia—which voted 70% to 77% for George W. Bush in 2004 and are among the most Republican in America.

But this work of art likely will not endure. In March 2004, a court redrew the district lines for the state House and state Senate, which helped the Republicans increase their Senate margin and gain control of the state House in November. In February 2005, Republicans in control of the governorship and the legislature worked with congressional Republicans in Washington to make redistricting of the U.S. House districts one of their top priorities; freshman Congressmen Lynn Westmoreland and Tom Price had previously served as legislative leaders in Atlanta. Moving more deliberately and facing far less Democratic obstructionism than Republicans encountered in Texas in 2003, they passed the plan in March with a few Republican defections and with limited Democratic support; federal review was mandatory under the Voting Rights Act, and Democratic leaders said that they would file court challenges. Another difference between Texas and Georgia: Georgia Republicans could argue they had popular support for redrawing the congressional map since they campaigned on the issue in 2002 and 2004.

The new 2005 plan strengthens Republican Phil Gingrey in the 11th District; it weakens Democrats Jim Marshall and John Barrow of the 3d and 12th Districts, though each Democrat appeared to have a possibility to retain his seat. By extending farther west into central Georgia, the 12th District lost its white liberals in the university town of Athens. From the Republicans' perspective, the most significant changes are the straightening of district lines and the splitting of far fewer precincts and counties (from 34 to 18) under the new map. Indeed, the severely gerrymandered lines in many of the old districts had become something of an embarrassment for Democrats and made it more difficult for them to defend their existing map. Another significant revision is that the 3d District (renumbered as the 8th) dips deeper into south Georgia and the overall map returns to the design of three districts in the southern part of the state.

Despite initial speculation that the new map would force some incumbents to run against each other, the map left a clearly defined district for each of the 7 Republicans and 6 Democrats. But by appearing to entrench Gingrey in the 11th and posing risks for the delegation's two white Democrats, the map opened the door to a variation of the 8–3 Republican-controlled delegation from much of the previous decade; each of the state's four African-American House Democrats appeared secure, with the 13th District in metro Atlanta gaining far less convoluted boundaries. Republicans quietly worked with some of the African-American congressional Democrats to accommodate their personal concerns with the new districts. By raising the black population in the redrawn 12th District from 42% to 45%, the 2005 map increases the chances of an African-American candidate in a Democratic primary; it also leaves open the prospect that the district could be competitive in a general election.

Governor

Sonny Perdue (R)

Elected 2002, term expires Jan. 2007, 1st term; b. Dec. 20, 1946, Perry; home, Bonaire; U. of GA, D.V.M 1971; Baptist; married (Mary).

Military Career: Air Force, 1971–74 (Vietnam).

Elected Office: GA Senate, 1990–2001; Maj. Ldr. 1994–97.

Professional Career: Veterinarian; owner, Houston Fertilizer and Grain; owner, Perdue Inc.; owner, AgroStar.

Office: 203 State Capitol, Atlanta, 30334, 404-656-1776; Fax: 404-657-7332; Web site: www.gov.state.ga.us.

Election Results

2002 general	Sonny Perdue (R)	1,041,677	(51%)
	Roy Barnes (D)	937,062	(46%)
	Other	47,122	(2%)
2002 primary	Sonny Perdue (R)	259,966	(51%)
	Linda Schrenko (R)	142,911	(28%)
	Bill Byrne (R)	108,586	(21%)
1998 general	Roy Barnes (D)	941,076	(52%)
	Guy Millner (R)	790,201	(44%)
	Other	61,531	(3%)

Sonny Perdue, the first Republican governor of Georgia since Reconstruction, grew up on his family's farm in Bonaire, near Warner Robins in central Georgia. He was a high school football quarterback and earned a veterinarian degree at the University of Georgia, where he was a walk-on football player. He served in the Air Force from 1971 to 1974, practiced as a veterinarian for two years in North Carolina, then returned to Georgia and started a fertilizer and grain business and a trucking firm near Warner Robins. In the 1980s he served on Houston County zoning boards. In 1990 he was elected to the state Senate as a Democrat; he was easily reelected and was elected Senate majority leader in 1994 and Senate president pro tem in 1997. In 1998 he announced that he was switching parties and running for reelection as a Republican; he said his values were not the same as Bill Clinton's and those of other Democrats and that his efforts to change the party had not worked. He was stripped of his leadership posts and staff, but was reelected as a Republican with 70% of the vote. In December 2001, after his Senate seat had been hacked up in redistricting, he resigned his seat and announced he was running for governor.

He had taken on the daunting task of running against Governor Roy Barnes, elected in 1998 after a 22-year legislative career and an unsuccessful 1990 run for governor. Barnes, a conservative-sounding Democrat from suburban Cobb County, won the office by a 52%–44% margin over businessman Guy Millner and had pushed through an ambitious program. In 1999 he persuaded the legislature to create the Georgia Regional Transportation Authority that gave him control over transportation and development in the 20-county metro Atlanta area, with $300 million to allow local governments to purchase land and maintain it as open space. He got a $640 million property tax cut and HMO regulation and got the legislature to outlaw video poker. In 2000 he produced an education reform plan that required annual testing and held teachers accountable for results, with bonuses for some and adverse consequences for others; it also ended tenure for newly-hired teachers. In January 2001 Barnes persuaded the legislature to replace the Confederate battle flag, which had been chosen the state flag in 1956, and replace it with a design in which the state seal occupied most of the flag and which included at the bottom small depictions of five flags that have flown over the state, including the battle flag. One by one he antagonized many groups—Confederate battle flag lovers, the Georgia Association of Education, video poker operators, opponents of the Northern Arc highway he wanted to build north of Atlanta.

On all this Perdue capitalized. He called for dismantling the Office of Education Accountability, and relying less on yearly tests and state standards and more on local teachers and parents to enforce standards. He called for a constitutional amendment to require 2/3 supermajorities of legislators to use surplus revenue for anything but tax cuts or paying down state debt. He attacked Barnes for the Democrats' highly partisan redistricting of state legislative and U.S. House seats. Coming from south (or at least central) Georgia, he employed a rural strategy. "We're trying to capture the basic voting instincts of the non-metro voter," he said. He also promised a referendum on the state flag. This worked in tandem with state Republican Chairman Ralph Reed's program of building Republican organizations and volunteer corps not just in heavily Republican metro Atlanta counties, but also in 70 target counties outside the metro area. With a big turnout and solid majorities outside metro Atlanta, Perdue won the August primary with 51% of the vote, just enough to avoid a runoff.

Barnes still had a positive job approval and outspent Perdue $19 million to $3 million. But he was put on the defensive when the Georgia Association of Educators refused to endorse anyone for governor and endorsed Republican Kathy Cox, another opponent of the Barnes education reform, for school superintendent. Barnes put a hold on the Northern Arc and, curiously, said that Augusta National Golf Club should admit women as members. Still, it was a shock on election night when Perdue beat Barnes 51%–46%. Barnes led very narrowly in metro Atlanta, 49%–48%, but Perdue won the rest of the state 55%–43%—just 2% below George W. Bush's 2000 showing there. There were two electoral keys to Perdue's victory. One was the rural strategy. Barnes carried only 41 of the 159 counties, most of them either central city or very small rural counties, down from 118 in 1998. The other factor was increased turnout in the fast-growing suburbs. Turnout was up 13% statewide and 15% in metro Atlanta. It was up far more in the heavily Republican fast-growing counties—up 60% in Forsyth, 49% in Paulding, 40% in Henry, 34% in Cherokee, 32% in Walton, 28% in Newton, 25% in Fayette, 19% in Gwinnett, 13% in Cobb. These counties gave Perdue a 116,000-vote margin, more than his statewide margin of 104,000 votes.

It turned out to be a Republican victory up and down the line. Within a week of the election four Democratic state senators switched parties and gave Republicans a 30–26 margin in the Senate.

All was not easy for Perdue once in office. He cut some $1.7 billion of projected spending and still got the legislature to raise the cigarette tax; he vetoed local projects sponsored by Democratic legislators. He found savings in postponing school class size reductions. His ethics bill failed in the House. With help from Jimmy Carter, he proposed a new design for the state flag, with a red, white and blue background similar to the first Confederate flag (but wholly unlike the familiar battle flag); this and Barnes's 2001 flag, but not the Confederate battle flag, were put on the March 2004 ballot, and voters approved the Carter-Barnes flag 73%–27%. In October 2003 he and Carter hosted a "family discussion" on race at the Carter Center; Perdue recounted how he grew up with African-Americans and how he and his wife brought black foster children into their household from 1998 to 2000. In 2004 Perdue proposed no tax increases and again started off cutting projected spending. The Medicaid rolls were cut and recipients channeled into HMO-type programs. For teachers he proposed a 2% pay increase and tax deductions for purchases of school supplies; for parents he obtained a four-day holiday from sales taxes on school supplies, clothes and computers. When lottery revenues threatened to be insufficient to fund HOPE college scholarships, Perdue called for them to be limited to students with top SAT scores; the legislature stopped that. Georgia has the lowest SAT scores of any state, but one reason is that it has the highest participation rate: more proof of the popularity of Zell Miller's HOPE scholarships. The 2004 budget was approved in a special session in June 2003.

Transportation spending in recent years has been directed disproportionately outside metro Atlanta; Perdue sponsored a Fast Forward transportation bond issue, with proceeds to go the express lanes for buses and HOV lanes in Fulton and Cobb Counties. House Democrats again rejected Perdue's ethics package. Perdue signed a bill to protect 40,000 acres of state-owned forest and told a Latino group he was amenable to in-state tuition though not HOPE scholarships for students who were the children of illegal immigrants.

Perdue has periodically conducted barnstorming tours of the state; on one such trip, in April 2004, he announced that two more Democratic legislators had switched to the Republican party. He had even more success in the 2004 election. As George W. Bush was carrying the state with 58% of the vote, Republicans raised the majority in the state Senate to 34–22 and transformed a 77–102 deficit in the state House to a 99–80–1 majority. The new majorities help Perdue get his legislation passed: in February, he signed a medical malpractice bill that capped pain-and-suffering awards and punished frivolous lawsuits. A month later, he signed a bill requiring a 24-hour waiting period for women seeking an abortion and parental notification for minors. In May he signed two bills strengthening ethics rules. But he angered some black legislators when he signed a bill requiring voters to show government-issued photo identification at the polls.

Perdue comes up for reelection in 2006. Likely Democratic candidates include Lieutenant Governor Mark Taylor and Secretary of State Cathy Cox, both from south Georgia. April 2005 polls showed Cox running about even with Perdue and Taylor running 13 points behind Perdue; but then Perdue was running far behind Roy Barnes in the polls taken during September and October 2002.

Senior Senator

Saxby Chambliss (R)

Elected 2002, seat up 2008, 1st term; b. Nov. 10, 1943, Warrenton, NC; home, Moultrie; U. of GA, B.A. 1966, U. of TN, J.D. 1968; Episcopalian; married (Julianne).

Elected Office: U.S. House of Reps., 1994–2002.

Professional Career: Practicing atty., 1968–94.

DC Office: 416 RSOB, 20510, 202-224-3521; Fax: 202-224-0103; Web site: chambliss.senate.gov.

State Offices: Atlanta, 404-763-9090; Augusta, 706-738-0302; Savannah, 912-232-3657.

Committees: *Agriculture, Nutrition & Forestry* (Chmn.). *Armed Services*: Airland; Personnel; Readiness & Management Support; Seapower. *Intelligence (Select)*. *Rules & Administration*.

Group Ratings

	ADA	ACLU	AFS	LCV	ITIC	NTU	COC	ACU	NTLC	CHC
2004	5	0	0	0	82	83	93	96	95	100
2003	5	—	11	0	—	74	91	90	—	—

National Journal Ratings

	2003 LIB	—	2003 CONS		2004 LIB	—	2004 CONS
Economic	0%	—	82%		10%	—	89%
Social	0%	—	59%		0%	—	84%
Foreign	46%	—	52%		0%	—	67%

Key Votes of the 108th Congress

1. Ban Drilling in ANWR	N	5. Energy Bill	Y	9. Ban Same-Sex Marriage	Y
2. Approve Bush Tax Cuts	Y	6. Support Roe v. Wade	N	10. Ban Bunker-Buster Bomb	N
3. Medicare/Rx Bill	Y	7. Ban Partial-Birth Abortion	Y	11. Fund Iraq War	Y
4. Bar Overtime Pay Regs.	N	8. Assault Weapons Ban	N	12. Restrict Missile Defense	N

Election Results

2002 general	Saxby Chambliss (R)	1,071,153	(53%)	($7,743,004)
	Max Cleland (D)	931,857	(46%)	($9,116,775)
	Other	26,981	(1%)	
2002 primary	Saxby Chambliss (R)	300,371	(61%)	
	Bob Irvin (R)	132,132	(27%)	
	Robert Brown (R)	59,109	(12%)	

Prior Winning Percentages: 2000 House (59%); 1998 House (62%); 1996 House (53%); 1994 House (63%)

Saxby Chambliss, the senior senator from Georgia, was elected in 2002 after serving four terms in the House. Chambliss grew up in Shreveport, Louisiana, the son of an Episcopalian minister, went to college in Georgia, and practiced business and agriculture law in Moultrie starting in 1968. In 1992 he ran for the House and lost the Republican primary; in 1994 he was the sole Republican candidate, while Democrats, as in days of yore, had a multi-candidate contest. The winner was Craig Mathis, the 32-year-old son of Congressman (1971–81) Dawson Mathis. Chambliss won 63%–37%.

In the House, Speaker Newt Gingrich saw that Chambliss got the committee assignments he needed most—Armed Services, to look after Warner Robins Air Force Base near Macon, and Agriculture, to protect subsidies for peanut farmers in the counties to the south. In 2001 he helped draft the farm bill provisions that phased out the peanut quota program—evidently he concluded there was just not enough support to maintain it—but to compensate quota holders.

In November 1998, Speaker-designate Bob Livingston put Chambliss on the Budget Committee and named him vice chairman; in July 1999 Budget Chairman John Kasich announced his retirement and Chambliss started a campaign for the post. In July 2000, after Senator Paul Coverdell died suddenly, Chambliss considered running in the November election to replace him; he had also considered running for governor in 1998. Speaker Dennis Hastert persuaded him to stay in the House, and Chambliss came away feeling he would get the Budget chair. But he had competition from Jim Nussle of Iowa; the Republican Steering Committee interviewed both candidates and in December 2000 picked Nussle. Chambliss got an Agriculture subcommittee chairmanship and Hastert made him head of a working group on terrorism. After September 11, Hastert made that into an Intelligence Subcommittee on Terrorism and Homeland Security.

These were obviously good political credentials for a Senate candidacy, and Chambliss had two other reasons to consider challenging Democratic Senator Max Cleland in 2002. One was Cleland's narrow 49%–48% margin of victory in 1996 and Georgia's Republican trend, evident in George W. Bush's 55%–43% margin there in 2000. The other was the uncertainty of his House seat. Democratic redistricters passed a plan in September 2001 that left him with two unpleasant options: run in a primary against Savannah-based 1st District Republican incumbent Jack Kingston or in the new Democratic-leaning 3d District. The Bush White House and campaign committee Chairman Bill Frist urged Chambliss to run for the Senate, and in October 2001 he announced he would.

Chambliss was not an initial favorite to win. Cleland had a compelling biography. After college he volunteered for the Army and went to Vietnam in 1967; he lost both legs and his right arm when a loose grenade exploded. In 1982 he was elected Georgia secretary of state and was reelected three times by wide margins. In October 1995, after Senator Sam Nunn announced his retirement after four terms, he ran for the Senate and beat Republican businessman Guy Millner 49%–48%. He served on the Armed Services Committee and had a moderate voting record by the standards of some Democratic senators. But in 2001 and 2002 he tended to stick with the close-knit Democratic Caucus while his new colleague, Zell Miller, dissented vociferously on issues from the tax cut to the Department of Homeland Security personnel rules. On the Republican side, Chambliss won the August 2002 primary 61%–27%, carrying all but two of Georgia's 159 counties. "From Rabun Gap to Tybee Light, voters continue to tell me that Max Cleland is too liberal for Georgia," he said on primary election night.

Cleland's two major strengths—his sacrifice in Vietnam and his support from the highly popular Miller—seemed formidable. Cleland supporters noted that Chambliss had received four student deferments in the 1960s and then was found ineligible for service because of a bad knee. Moreover, Cleland pointed out, he voted for the use of military force in Iraq in 1998, in Kosovo in 1999, in the war on terrorism in September 2001 and against Iraq in October 2002. Miller, in ads, told voters of Cleland's "rock solid Georgia values." But that did not deter Chambliss from launching sharp attacks. He ran a series of 10-second spots, mentioning Cleland's opposition to an amendment banning aid for schools that barred the Boy Scouts, his votes against the partial-birth abortion ban, his support of school clinics passing out morning-after pills without parental permission, his vote against confirming Attorney General John Ashcroft, his vote against speeding elimination of the marriage penalty—all ending with an apparently astounded announcer asking, "Why would he do that?" Chambliss burnished his own national security issues by talking of his work on Armed Services and the Terrorism Subcommittee.

But probably the most important issue was homeland security. Cleland stood with other Senate Democrats in opposing the degree of flexibility over work rules in the new department. The dispute occupied the Senate for much of October and prevented passage of the bill. On the other side, standing loudly in his support of Bush and his opposition to the other Senate Democrats was Zell Miller. Chambliss ran an ad, much attacked in the press, showing pictures of Osama Bin Laden, Saddam Hussein and Max Cleland, and saying that Cleland "voted against the President's vital homeland security efforts 11 times." Against this, Cleland's ads attacking Chambliss for opposing an increase in the minimum wage and financing children's health insurance, for cutting student loans and school aid for the disabled, were weak stuff. In an October 27 debate, Cleland, echoing John Randolph of Roanoke on Henry Clay, said that the Osama Bin Laden ad was "like a mackerel in the moonlight—it both shines and stinks at the same time." But Cleland's record in Vietnam did not inoculate him against charges that he had given short shrift to homeland security.

The tide of opinion, as measured by very late polls, was moving toward Chambliss. George W. Bush visited the state three times in his behalf, with visits to Atlanta and Savannah the Saturday before the election. On Election Day Chambliss won 53%–46%, a much bigger margin than just about anyone expected for either candidate. Chambliss, though from south Georgia, carried metro Atlanta 52%–47%, running ahead of Republican governor candidate Sonny Perdue, and he carried the rest of Georgia 54%–45%. It was a slightly stronger showing than Paul Coverdell made running for reelection to the Senate four years before, primarily because of increased turnout and increasing Republican percentages in the outer counties of metro Atlanta. In the three black-majority counties of 20-county metro Atlanta (Fulton, DeKalb and Clayton), turnout was up 26,000 from 1998 and the Democratic margin up 34,000. But in the other 17 counties, turnout was up 123,000 and the Republican margin was up 40,000.

In the Senate Chambliss has had a conservative voting record and has taken a lead role on several issues. He served as chairman of the Immigration Subcommittee of Judiciary, and in 2003 succeeded in passing a law modifying L-1 visas, so that international companies who bring in foreign employees cannot shop them out to other employers. He continued to be favorable to firms seeking more H-1B visas for high-tech foreign employees. He also pressed to change the law so that immigrants seeking to stay in the U.S. through the lottery procedure are not disqualified if the immigration authorities fail to process their applications on time; he was prompted by the case of divinity student Charles Nyaga, a Kenyan living in Cobb County, who was threatened with deportation. In February 2004 he called for "total overhaul" of immigration, but conceded that wasn't practicable. He sounded favorable to George W. Bush's proposal for a guest worker program, at least for farm workers, but unlike some Democrats who back similar proposals he argued that putting such workers on the road to citizenship unfairly rewards those who broke the law. With Edward Kennedy he sought an extension of the deadline for citizens from visa waiver countries to have biometric identification from October 2004 to November 2006. In October 2004 he moved to have jurisdiction over immigration stay in Judiciary rather than migrate to the Homeland Security panel.

Chambliss is also a member of the Armed Services Committee. Alert to the needs of Georgia military bases, he sought to require a recommendation of seven of the nine members of any base closing commission to list a base not recommended for closure by the secretary of defense. He sponsored a law to grant posthumous U.S. citizenship to foreign soldiers killed in combat; he was inspired by the case of 19-year-old Colombian Diego Rincon of Rockdale County. In December 2003 Armed Services Chairman John Warner named him to investigate sexual harassment at the Air Force Academy. Chambliss supported the Bush administration on Iraq, but in November 2003 voted to have the $20 billion in reconstruction aid classed as a loan rather than a grant. He strongly supported the nomination of his House Intelligence Committee colleague Porter Goss to be head of the CIA and called for a unified Intelligence Command in the Pentagon to interface with the new National Intelligence Director.

In January 2005 Chambliss became chairman of the Agriculture Committee, as more senior Republicans on the committee opted for other chairmanships or leadership posts. But the farm bill does not come up for reauthorization until 2007. He has been a backer of Rep. John Linder's Fair Tax, a 23% retail sales tax to replace all income taxes. He also sought to bar states from requiring catalytic converters on lawn mowers under 50 horsepower (Briggs & Stratton produces them in Statesboro).

In the 2004 campaign Chambliss took aim at John Kerry. "When you have a 32-year history of voting to cut defense programs and cut defense systems, folks in Georgia are going to look beyond what he says and look at his voting record." Kerry and his strong backer Max Cleland expressed outrage that a man who had not been qualified for military service because of a "trick knee" could criticize them, but most Georgia voters evidently gave greater weight to Chambliss's arguments.

Chambliss comes up for reelection in 2008.

Junior Senator

Johnny Isakson (R)

Elected 2004, seat up 2010, 1st term; b. Dec. 28, 1944, Atlanta; home, Marietta; U. of GA, B.B.A. 1966; Methodist; married (Dianne).

Military Career: GA Air Natl. Guard, 1966–72.

Elected Office: GA House of Reps., 1976–90, Repub. Ldr., 1983–90; GA gubernatorial candidate, 1990; GA Senate, 1993–96; U.S. House of Reps., 1999–2004.

Professional Career: Northside Realty, 1967–99, Pres., 1979–99; Co-chair, Dole GA presidential campaign, 1988, 1996; Chmn., GA Board of Ed., 1997.

DC Office: 120 RSOB, 20510, 202-224-3643; Fax: 202-228-0724; Web site: isakson.senate.gov.

State Office: Atlanta, 770-661-0999.

Committees: *Environment & Public Works*: Clean Air, Climate Change & Nuclear Safety; Superfund & Waste Management. *Health, Education, Labor & Pensions*: Education & Early Childhood Development; Employment & Workplace Safety (Chmn.); Retirement Security & Aging. *Small Business & Entrepreneurship. Veterans' Affairs.*

Group Ratings (as Member of U.S. House of Representatives)

	ADA	ACLU	AFS	LCV	ITIC	NTU	COC	ACU	NTLC	CHC
2004	5	0	0	0	88	78	100	95	84	92
2003	5	—	0	5	—	65	100	88	—	—

National Journal Ratings (as Member of U.S. House of Representatives)

	2003 LIB	—	2003 CONS	2004 LIB	—	2004 CONS
Economic	31%	—	68%	9%	—	91%
Social	24%	—	71%	28%	—	72%
Foreign	0%	—	89%	17%	—	83%

Key Votes of the 108th Congress (as Member of U.S. House of Representatives)

1. Drilling in ANWR	Y	5. DC School Vouchers	Y	9. Ban Same-Sex Marriage	Y
2. Approve Bush Tax Cuts	Y	6. Ban Human Cloning	Y	10. Fund Iraq War	Y
3. Medicare/Rx Bill	Y	7. Restrict Gun Liability	Y	11. Bar Cuba Embargo Funds	N
4. Bar Overtime Pay Regs.	N	8. Ban Partial-Birth Abortion	Y	12. Intelligence Reorg.	Y

Election Results

2004 general	Johnny Isakson (R)	1,864,202	(58%)	($8,038,200)
	Denise Majette (D)	1,287,690	(40%)	($2,391,248)
	Other	69,089	(2%)	
2004 primary	Johnny Isakson (R)	346,670	(53%)	
	Herman Cain (R)	170,370	(26%)	
	Mac Collins (R)	133,952	(21%)	
2000 special	Zell Miller (D)	1,413,224	(58%)	($2,533,746)
	Mack Mattingly (R)	920,478	(38%)	($1,093,408)
	Other	94,540	(4%)	

Prior Winning Percentages: 2002 House (80%); 2000 House (75%); 1999 House (65%)

Johnny Isakson, a Republican, was elected Georgia's junior senator in 2004. Isakson grew up outside Atlanta, in south Fulton County; his father drove a Greyhound bus and his parents bought old houses, renovated them and sold them for a profit. Isakson graduated from the University of Georgia and served in the Air National Guard. He went to work for Northside Realty in 1967 and eventually became president of the firm. He volunteered for Barry Goldwater in 1964 and Richard Nixon in 1972, and in 1974 he ran for the state House as a Republican and lost. In 1976 he ran again and won, and in 1983 became Minority Leader. He ran for governor in 1990 and lost 53%–45% to Zell Miller. Two years later he was elected to the state Senate. In 1996 he ran statewide again, and lost the Republican runoff for senator to self-financing businessman Guy Millner, who lost in November to Max Cleland 49%–48%. In December 1996 Miller appointed Isakson head of the state Board of Education. His partisan political career seemed over, but it would be revived by two timely retirements.

In November 1998 Newt Gingrich announced that he was stepping down as Speaker and would resign from the House. That opened up a vacancy in the heavily Republican 6th District which included much of the northern suburbs plus Atlanta's affluent Buckhead neighborhood. Isakson was by far the best known of the six candidates in the February 1999 nonpartisan election. He raised $1 million and spent $500,000 of his own money and won the seat with 65% of the vote, to 25% for Christina Jeffrey, a local history professor whom Gingrich had hired and then fired as House historian. In the House Isakson served on the Transportation Committee, where he pushed for a rapid transit line for the overburdened Georgia 400 corridor on the north side and talked up high-speed rail service from Atlanta to Richmond. On the Education Committee he was named to the Web-Based Education Commission and took a leading role in negotiations of the No Child Left Behind Act, working to give schools more discretion in using funds. Committee Chairman John Boehner credited Isakson for the provision requiring that 25% of technology funds be used for teacher classroom training.

Isakson passed up a chance to run against Cleland in 2002, but when Zell Miller announced his retirement in January 2003, Isakson announced for the seat a week later. For months he had no well-known opponent but eventually he had two serious competitors in the Republican primary. One was Herman Cain, who grew up in a black neighborhood in Atlanta, worked for Pillsbury and Burger King, then became CEO and owner of Omaha-based Godfather's Pizza. In 1994, as president of the National Restaurant Association, Cain attended one of Bill Clinton's meetings on health care and denounced the Clinton plan. Afterwards he left the company, became a motivational speaker and returned to Atlanta. The other was Congressman Mac Collins of the 8th District, which includes the southern edge of metro Atlanta and some still mostly rural and small town counties to the south. Cain and Collins were both solid conservatives and abortion rights opponents, and they made abortion a major issue. During the primary, Isakson said he opposed abortion rights except in cases of incest, rape or to save the mother's life; he received an 82% rating from the National Right to Life Committee in the 108th Congress. But he had voted against the Mexico City policy preventing foreign aid money from funding abortions, in favor of importation of RU-486 and to allow servicewomen to have abortions at their own expense in military hospitals. He had a reputation as an abortion rights supporter: in the 1996 Senate primary, he irked religious conservatives when he appeared in a TV ad opposing a constitutional amendment banning abortion, saying, "I will not vote to amend the Constitution to make criminals of women and their doctors. I trust my wife, my daughter and the women of Georgia to make the right choices."

That may have made him unacceptable in a Republican primary then; it was not so disqualifying in 2004. Isakson had taken care to keep in friendly touch with religious conservatives. In 2004 he was endorsed by a former president of the Georgia Christian Coalition and the current president predicted the anti-abortion vote would be divided between the three candidates. His opponents nonetheless attacked him on the issue. Collins called him "a certified moderate," and Cain, in a TV spot, said, "There's a big difference between me and Johnny Isakson. And it's not just the color of our eyes." Cain also backed a consumption tax and individual investment accounts in Social Security; Collins criticized Isakson for favoring an extension of the date for the turnover of sovereignty in Iraq. Isakson called for staying the course in Iraq, tax reform and support of Bush judicial nominees. He favored pushing ahead with the base closing commission and opposed a guest worker program that would put illegal immigrants ahead of legal ones on the way to citizenship. One of the big differences between the candidates was money. With his business contacts, Isakson raised $5.5 million for the primary; Cain spent $3 million, much of it his own money and Collins only $1.9 million. Between May and the July 20 primary, Isakson was on the air, mostly with biographical spots.

Early on, most observers thought this race would end with a runoff. But Isakson got 53% of the vote to 26% for Cain and 21% for Collins. It was not just an Atlanta area victory: Isakson won 55% in metro Atlanta and 52% in the rest of the state. Moreover, this was the first state primary in which more Georgians chose the Republican ballot (650,000) over the Democratic (625,000). Indeed, Georgia Democrats had a hard time coming up with a candidate for a seat held by a Democrat—albeit, one who usually voted with Republicans in the Senate and supported George W. Bush for reelection. The Democratic race came down to two late entering candidates, 4th District Congresswoman Denise Majette and businessman Cliff Oxford. Both had their weaknesses. Majette had served just one term after her upset victory over Cynthia McKinney in the 2002 primary, and she had a solidly liberal voting record. Oxford was accused of spousal abuse by a former wife, though she supported his candidacy. Oxford spent $1 million of his own money, but in a primary in which a majority of votes appear to have been cast by blacks, Majette led 41%–21%. In the August runoff Majette won 59%–41%. In both contests Majette had big leads in metro Atlanta but ran behind in the rest of the state—not a good harbinger for November.

This was one of the two 2004 Senate races which the in party expected to lose (the other was Illinois, where Republican Peter Fitzgerald retired). Zell Miller, as he had promised in January 2003, backed neither candidate; he had appointed Majette to a judgeship in 1993 and Isakson as head of the Board of Education in 1996. Through most of the fall Isakson continued to run positive ads; in the last two weeks he attacked Majette's liberal voting record, including her vote against the $87 billion supplemental appropriation for Iraq. Majette criticized Isakson for not voting the funding the full amounts authorized by No Child Left Behind. It was no surprise when Isakson won 58%–40%, almost exactly the same margin by which George W. Bush beat John Kerry in the state. Majette carried only 19 of 159 counties—Atlanta's Fulton County and the two black-majority counties in metro Atlanta, the counties including the central cities of Athens, Columbus and Augusta and 12 Black Belt rural counties.

FIRST DISTRICT

Rep. Jack Kingston (R)

Elected 1992, 7th term; b. Apr. 24, 1955, Bryan, TX; home, Savannah; U. of GA, B.S. 1977; Episcopalian; married (Libby).

Elected Office: GA House of Reps., 1984–92.

Professional Career: Insurance agent, 1979–92.

DC Office: 2242 RHOB, 20515, 202-225-5831; Fax: 202-226-2269; Web site: www.house.gov/kingston.

District Offices: Baxley, 912-367-7403; Brunswick, 912-265-9010; Savannah, 912-352-0101; Warner Robins, 478-923-8987.

Committees: *Republican Conference Vice Chairman. Appropriations* (13th of 37 R): Agriculture, Rural Development, FDA & Related Agencies; Defense.

Group Ratings

	ADA	ACLU	AFS	LCV	ITIC	NTU	COC	ACU	NTLC	CHC
2004	0	0	13	9	90	64	100	96	84	92
2003	10	—	0	0	—	64	97	92	—	—

National Journal Ratings

	2003 LIB	—	2003 CONS		2004 LIB	—	2004 CONS
Economic	21%	—	79%		0%	—	95%
Social	14%	—	85%		0%	—	91%
Foreign	11%	—	80%		0%	—	96%

Key Votes of the 108th Congress

1. Drilling in ANWR	Y	5. DC School Vouchers	Y	9. Ban Same-Sex Marriage	Y
2. Approve Bush Tax Cuts	Y	6. Ban Human Cloning	Y	10. Fund Iraq War	Y
3. Medicare/Rx Bill	Y	7. Restrict Gun Liability	Y	11. Bar Cuba Embargo Funds	N
4. Bar Overtime Pay Regs.	N	8. Ban Partial-Birth Abortion	Y	12. Intelligence Reorg.	Y

Election Results

2004 general	Jack Kingston (R)	.... unopposed		($783,347)
2004 primary	Jack Kingston (R)	.... unopposed		
2002 general	Jack Kingston (R)	 103,661	(72%)	($819,954)
	Don Smart (D)	 40,026	(28%)	($21,768)

Prior Winning Percentages: 2000 (69%); 1998 (100%); 1996 (68%); 1994 (77%); 1992 (58%)

The People		Race/Ethnic Origin	Ancestry	
Area size:	12,071 sq. mi.	71.0% White	USA: 15.3%	English: 7.2%
Urban population:	57.9%	22.5% Black	Irish: 7.0%	
Rural population:	42.1%	0.9% Asian	**2004 Presidential Vote**	
Pop. 2000:	629,761	0.3% Native Am.	Bush (R) 158,216	(68%)
Median income:	$36,158	0.1% Hawaiian	Kerry (D) 72,658	(31%)
Poverty status:	14.8%	1.0% Two+ races	Other 691	(0%)
Military veterans:	15.8%	0.1% Other	**2000 Presidential Vote**	
		4.1% Hispanic Origin	Bush (R) 119,133	(64%)
			Gore (D) 65,744	(35%)
			Other 1,524	(1%)
			Cook Partisan Voting Index: R +15	

Occupation   Blue collar: 30.2%   White collar: 53.3%   Gray collar: 16.5%

Georgia's South Atlantic coast, long one of the poorest parts of the country, was settled in the 1730s by James Oglethorpe as Britain's 13th coastal colony as a refuge and reformatory for convicts. It did not take long for the sea islands and lowlands along the wide rivers and inlets to become plantation country. It is here where General William Tecumseh Sherman and his troops famously set their sights when they marched from Atlanta in 1864. Without supplies or lines of communication, they burned plantation houses, destroyed crops and captured the Confederacy's leader (the Jefferson Davis Memorial in Ocilla marks the spot where Union troops nabbed him in May 1865); when their march was complete, they left behind memories of property destroyed and slaves freed, which were handed down as family lore for more than a century.

The 1st Congressional District of Georgia includes much of the southeast and south part of the state. It includes the state's whole Atlantic coast and runs approximately to Interstate 75 and from the Ocmulgee and Altamaha Rivers in the north to the Florida border in the south. It takes in a sliver of Savannah, most of which is now in the 12th District, and all of the Sea Islands, which house a vibrant resort economy with efforts to preserve the African-American Gullah culture and its eponymous West African-originated language; with natural protection from protesters, Sea Island hosted in 2004 the G-8 summit of world leaders. One of those coastal communities is the historic black settlement of Pin Point, nine miles southeast of Savannah. Its 300 citizens are mostly descendants of the first slaves here and its most famous son is Supreme Court Justice Clarence Thomas. In central Georgia, a salient of the 1st District thrusts north nearly to Macon to take in part of Warner Robins, adjoining Warner Robins Air Force Base; another salient thrusts west to include Moultrie, the home town of Senator Saxby Chambliss. There are a few modest-sized cities like Brunswick, a World War II shipbuilding center and now site of the 1,500-acre Federal Law Enforcement Training Center, and Waycross, a railroad junction town and gateway to the Okefenokee Swamp, the largest swamp in North America. Much of the district is rural, with cotton and tobacco fields and softwood forests inhabited by wild hogs and bears. Appling County and Berrien County are known for their turpentine and bell peppers. Many popular films have been produced in the region, including *Glory* and *Forrest Gump*. This was Democratic country for a century after General Sherman's troops marched through Georgia, but voters here are solidly conservative on most issues. For two decades this part of south Georgia voted for national Republicans but Georgia Democrats; since 2000, it has voted solidly Republican for governor and senator, as well.

The congressman from the 1st District is Jack Kingston, a Republican first elected in 1992. Kingston grew up in Texas, Ethiopia, and Athens, Georgia, the son of a professor. After college he moved to Savannah and became a commercial insurance agent. In 1984 he was elected to the Georgia House, at 29, and served eight years. In 1992, when Democrat Lindsay Thomas retired to work on the Atlanta Summer Olympics, Kingston ran for Congress. Against Democrat Barbara Christmas, a school principal, he won decisively—58%–42%, with a 2–1 margin in his home base of Savannah and Chatham County. He has not been seriously challenged since then.

In the House, Kingston has a mostly conservative voting record and has tended to district interests. He parted company with Bill Clinton on trade issues, notably NAFTA, GATT and normal trade relations for China, and he decries the World Trade Organization; but he voted to give trade promotion authority to George W. Bush. He serves on the Agriculture Subcommittee of Appropriations, where he has worked for district interests. In 2003, he became chairman of the Appropriations Legislative Branch Subcommittee, an influential post with colleagues but one whose more than $4 billion budget produces many headaches. He was on the firing line for the huge cost overruns of the underground Capitol Visitors Center, whose initial cost estimate (in 1991) of $71 million has ballooned to more than $400 million, and counting. He also has managed the rapid growth in the Capitol police force. But he lost his chairmanship in 2005 when his subcommittee was eliminated in an Appropriations Committee restructuring.

Kingston also has pursued leadership activities. As head of the Republicans' "theme team," which coordinates the party's national message on the House floor and at home, he became a spokesman on late-night television shows. In November 2002 he defeated Melissa Hart of Pennsylvania to win election as vice-chairman of the Republican Conference—the party's fifth-highest leadership post—he stepped up his role in setting the party's message. At the start of the Iraq war, he wrote a letter to Defense Secretary Rumsfeld urging cancellation of the Pentagon's contract with a U.S. subsidiary of a food catering company based outside Paris. "My colleagues and I abhor the idea of continuing to pour American dollars into a French-based firm," Kingston wrote. He proposed an "academic bill of rights" to, as Kingston said, safeguard a student's right to "get an education rather than an indoctrination." In 2004 he played a key role in convincing House Republican leadership to back the $10 billion tobacco buyout, which ended the quota system in place since 1938.

On local issues, Kingston has fought for historic preservation and looked after local military facilities. His district annually is among the largest recipients of funds from the military construction spending bill, including $188 million in October 2004. Concerned about the impact of a base-closing process, he urged local groups to make sure that "everything is up to date." As an appropriator and co-chairman of the Congressional Waterways Caucus, he has brought millions of dollars to improve the water flow of the Savannah River and complete the Sidney Lanier drawbridge in Brunswick. He reached out to the black community with $450,000 from the Interior Department to preserve the remnants of slave cabins on Cumberland Island.

Kingston considered but turned down opportunities to run for the Senate in 2002 and 2004. With two first-term Republican senators now representing Georgia, he may not have that opportunity again. He was reelected without opposition in 2004.

SECOND DISTRICT

Rep. Sanford Bishop (D)

Elected 1992, 7th term; b. Feb. 4, 1947, Mobile, AL; home, Albany; Morehouse Col., B.A. 1968, Emory U., J.D. 1971; Baptist; divorced.

Military Career: Army, 1970–71.

Elected Office: GA House of Reps., 1976–90; GA Senate, 1990–92.

Professional Career: Practicing atty., 1971–92.

DC Office: 2429 RHOB, 20515, 202-225-3631; Fax: 202-225-2203; Web site: www.house.gov/bishop.

District Offices: Albany, 229-439-8067; Columbus, 706-320-9477; Dawson, 229-995-3991; Valdosta, 229-247-9705.

Committees: *Appropriations* (28th of 29 D): Homeland Security; Military Quality of Life & Veterans Affairs & Related Agencies.

Group Ratings

	ADA	ACLU	AFS	LCV	ITIC	NTU	COC	ACU	NTLC	CHC
2004	55	56	75	36	60	14	79	35	3	46
2003	75	—	100	35	—	22	57	48	—	—

National Journal Ratings

	2003 LIB	—	2003 CONS	2004 LIB	—	2004 CONS
Economic	59%	—	41%	54%	—	46%
Social	59%	—	41%	61%	—	39%
Foreign	70%	—	27%	57%	—	43%

Key Votes of the 108th Congress

1. Drilling in ANWR	Y	5. DC School Vouchers	N	9. Ban Same-Sex Marriage	Y
2. Approve Bush Tax Cuts	N	6. Ban Human Cloning	Y	10. Fund Iraq War	Y
3. Medicare/Rx Bill	N	7. Restrict Gun Liability	Y	11. Bar Cuba Embargo Funds	*
4. Bar Overtime Pay Regs.	Y	8. Ban Partial-Birth Abortion	Y	12. Intelligence Reorg.	Y

Election Results

2004 general	Sanford Bishop (D)	129,984	(67%)	($761,275)
	Dave Eversman (R)	64,645	(33%)	($25,277)
2004 primary	Sanford Bishop (D)	unopposed		
2002 general	Sanford Bishop (D)	unopposed		($306,022)

Prior Winning Percentages: 2000 (54%); 1998 (57%); 1996 (54%); 1994 (66%); 1992 (64%)

The People		Race/Ethnic Origin	Ancestry	
Area size:	9,887 sq. mi.	50.3% White	USA: 12.2%	English: 5.0%
Urban population:	58.6%	44.5% Black	Irish: 4.7%	
Rural population:	41.4%	0.6% Asian	**2004 Presidential Vote**	
Pop. 2000:	629,735	0.3% Native Am.	Bush (R) 108,128	(54%)
Median income:	$29,354	0.1% Hawaiian	Kerry (D) 92,769	(46%)
Poverty status:	22.5%	0.8% Two+ races	Other 571	(0%)
Military veterans:	12.7%	0.1% Other	**2000 Presidential Vote**	
		3.5% Hispanic Origin	Bush (R) 84,854	(51%)
			Gore (D) 81,684	(49%)
			Other 1,160	(1%)
			Cook Partisan Voting Index: R + 1	

Occupation	Blue collar: 31.1%	White collar: 50.2%	Gray collar: 18.7%

Before the Civil War, the southwest corner of Georgia was plantation country. It was in this part of Georgia that Confederates ran the Andersonville military prison, which within 14 months killed more than 13,000 of the 45,000 Union soldiers confined there, through disease, poor sanitation, malnutrition, overcrowding and exposure; they are remembered at the National Prisoner of War Museum at Andersonville, dedicated to all Americans who have endured wartime captivity. The military has been unscathed by base closings and remains a presence here, most notably at Fort Benning, the Army's third largest installation and home of the Army Infantry School. But today the region is mostly farmland: Cotton fields, peanut acreage (this is the nation's top peanut producing district), pecan groves, pine lands. In the south, near the Florida border, is the Cairo birthplace of baseball's black pioneer Jackie Robinson, plus the Plantation Trace area around Thomasville, where rich Northerners have come to shoot quail and ducks in winters since the 1880s—a part of Georgia memorialized in Tom Wolfe's *A Man in Full.* A bit to the north is Albany, with several factories, a civil rights museum and the site of Martin Luther King Jr.'s least successful civil rights protests in the 1960s. Not far from Albany, between upland pine stands and bottomland habitats, lies the Chickasawatchee Swamp, one of the Southeast's largest freshwater swamps and home to rare plant species such as the needle palm and the green fly orchid. Two counties north is the village of Plains, the home since childhood of Jimmy Carter. This is hardscrabble country: As recently as World War II most rural residents lived in clapboard cabins without power or running water, eking a living out of over-tilled soil.

This is the land of Georgia's 2d Congressional District. The 2d came out of the radical redistricting of September 2001 with the least changed boundaries of any district in the state. There is some splitting of cities at the edges: The 2d includes about two-thirds of Valdosta and nearly a third of Columbus and Muscogee County. Redistricting raised the black percentage of the district from 40% to 45% and thus made it more Democratic. But George W. Bush won a small majority here in 2000 and by a wider 54%–46% in 2004.

The congressman from the 2d District is Sanford Bishop, a Democrat first elected in 1992. Bishop grew up in Mobile, Alabama, where his father was a state college president. He went to Morehouse College in Atlanta, where he was student body president in 1968 and sang at Martin Luther King Jr.'s funeral. He was an award-winning student at Emory Law School, then served in the Army. After a year in New York he settled in Columbus, practiced law, and was elected to the state legislature in 1976, at 29. He served there until 1990, when he was elected to the Georgia Senate. In 1992 he ran for the House against Democratic incumbent Charles Hatcher, who revealed he had 819 overdrafts on the House bank. Bishop defeated Hatcher in the runoff 53%–47%, and won the general election 64%–36%.

Bishop describes himself as "a moderate conservative on fiscal issues and a 'traditionalist' on so-called family issues." His style is not confrontational, and his voting record has been among the most conservative in the Congressional Black Caucus. After first voting for the assault weapons ban, he switched, joined the NRA and started hunting doves. He joined the conservative Blue Dog Democrats, and supported the balanced budget, school prayer, partial-birth abortion ban and anti-flag burning amendments. He was one of 10 House Democrats to vote for George W.Bush's tax cuts in 2001. He voted for the partial-birth abortion ban and the constitutional amendment to ban gay marriage, but opposed a federal court-stripping bill on gay-rights issues. He works to protect local military bases, like the School of the Americas that trains Latin American soldiers at Fort Benning, which was renamed the Western Hemisphere Institute for Security Cooperation. In 2002, the NAACP gave him a "C" on its report card for House votes but he got an "A" in 2004.

In 2003, after Nancy Pelosi turned down his bid to become ranking Democrat on the Intelligence Committee, Bishop won a long-sought seat on Appropriations. In 2004, he claimed credit for $133 million to the Albany Marine Corps base for development of amphibious assault vehicles, $83 million for projects at Fort Benning and $10 million for Moody Air Force Base. He also has been active on farm programs, working with Republicans on the 1996 Freedom to Farm Act to fashion a "market-oriented, no-net cost" program for peanuts. In 2002, he helped to craft the scaled-back program for peanut support, which was based on a combination of phasing out quotas and price guarantees. On the Intelligence Committee, he urged the appointment of additional minorities to intelligence and diplomatic agencies.

In 2000 Bishop faced serious reelection competition from Dylan Glenn, a former aide to George H.W. Bush and RNC staffer. The unprecedented contest between two African-Americans in a rural, majority-white district was strikingly lacking in racial overtones. Bishop largely ignored the challenger and ran on his record, while Glenn offered the perspective of a new generation focusing on economic growth. Bishop won 54%–47%. He was unopposed in 2002 and won 67%–33% in 2004.

THIRD DISTRICT

Rep. Jim Marshall (D)

Elected 2002, 2d term; b. March 31, 1948, Ithaca, NY; home, Macon; Princeton U., B.A. 1972, Boston U., J.D. 1977; Catholic; married (Camille).

Military Career: Army, 1968–70 (Vietnam).

Elected Office: Macon Mayor, 1995–99.

Professional Career: Mercer U. Law Professor, 1979–95, 1999–2002.

DC Office: 515 CHOB, 20515, 202-225-6531; Fax: 202-225-3013; Web site: www.house.gov/marshall.

District Offices: Dublin, 478-296-2101; Macon, 478-464-0255.

Committees: *Agriculture* (9th of 21 D): General Farm Commodities & Risk Management; Specialty Crops & Foreign Agriculture Programs. *Armed Services* (21st of 28 D): Projection Forces; Readiness; Terrorism, Unconventional Threats & Capabilities.

Group Ratings

	ADA	ACLU	AFS	LCV	ITIC	NTU	COC	ACU	NTLC	CHC
2004	55	15	63	64	40	26	55	48	29	75
2003	70	—	88	55	—	22	48	28	—	—

National Journal Ratings

	2003 LIB	—	2003 CONS		2004 LIB	—	2004 CONS
Economic	58%	—	41%		57%	—	43%
Social	50%	—	50%		47%	—	52%
Foreign	57%	—	43%		53%	—	46%

Key Votes of the 108th Congress

1. Drilling in ANWR	Y	5. DC School Vouchers	N	9. Ban Same-Sex Marriage	Y
2. Approve Bush Tax Cuts	Y	6. Ban Human Cloning	Y	10. Fund Iraq War	*
3. Medicare/Rx Bill	Y	7. Restrict Gun Liability	Y	11. Bar Cuba Embargo Funds	N
4. Bar Overtime Pay Regs.	Y	8. Ban Partial-Birth Abortion	Y	12. Intelligence Reorg.	Y

Election Results

2004 general	Jim Marshall (D)	136,273	(63%)	($1,307,926)
	Calder Clay (R)	80,435	(37%)	($1,054,493)
2004 primary	Jim Marshall (D)	unopposed		
2002 general	Jim Marshall (D)	75,394	(51%)	($1,006,764)
	Calder Clay (R)	73,866	(49%)	($2,014,777)

The People

Area size:	11,003 sq. mi.
Urban population:	48.8%
Rural population:	51.2%
Pop. 2000:	629,748
Median income:	$31,433
Poverty status:	19.9%
Military veterans:	13.1%

Race/Ethnic Origin

56.2% White
39.8% Black
0.5% Asian
0.2% Native Am.
0.0% Hawaiian
0.7% Two+ races
0.1% Other
2.6% Hispanic Origin

Ancestry

USA: 15.2%   English: 5.4%
Irish: 4.8%

2004 Presidential Vote

Bush (R)	125,362	(55%)
Kerry (D)	99,930	(44%)
Other	755	(0%)

2000 Presidential Vote

Bush (R)	98,100	(52%)
Gore (D)	89,374	(47%)
Other	1,766	(1%)

Cook Partisan Voting Index: R + 3

Occupation   Blue collar: 32.5%   White collar: 48.9%   Gray collar: 18.7%

Macon, the hub of central Georgia, is a city proud of its restored houses and its Japanese cherry trees, of which it has 20 times as many as Washington, D.C. It is the home of music legends Otis Redding, Little Richard and the Allman Brothers, and of the Harriet Tubman Historical and Cultural Museum. To the east and west are the farm and forest lands of central Georgia. Much of this land was the site of General William Tecumseh Sherman's 1864 march from Atlanta to the sea. To the east are Toombs County, home of fragrant Vidalia onions, Claxton in tiny Evans County, which has for nearly a century been home to two of the nation's prime fruitcake makers, and Twiggs, Wilkinson and Washington Counties, which are among the world's major sources of kaolin, a clay used for china and ceramics. A short drive north on Interstate 75 is Juliette, an old mill town that's too small for most maps; it is the place where many scenes in the movie *Fried Green Tomatoes* were filmed.

The 3d Congressional District of Georgia includes almost all of Macon and Bibb County and stretches east and west, almost all the way to Fort Stewart near Savannah in the east and almost all the way to Fort Benning near Columbus in the west. About one-third of its votes are cast in the five-county Macon metro area. This was Democratic country from the time of Sherman's march until the civil rights revolution of the 1960s; every single county in the district voted for John Kennedy in 1960. Today the political balance is different. More than 70% of whites usually vote Republican; about 90% of blacks usually vote Democratic. So the political leanings of any district in this part of Georgia depend on the racial percentages. The boundaries of the current 3d District were drawn by a Democratic legislature and approved by a Democratic governor; 40% of district residents are black, which makes this a pretty evenly divided district. George W. Bush carried it with a small majority in 2000 and by a more comfortable 55%–44% in 2004.

The congressman from the 3d District is Jim Marshall, first elected in 2002. The son and grandson of Army generals, he grew up at several Army posts. He graduated from high school in Mobile, Alabama, and went on to Princeton but interrupted his education to enlist in the Army and volunteer for infantry combat in Vietnam. He served there in the elite Airborne Ranger reconnaissance platoon, was wounded in combat and awarded two Bronze Stars and a Purple Heart. After military service, he graduated from Princeton and Boston University Law School. He joined the faculty of Mercer University law school in Macon, practiced business law and became active in Democratic politics. His wife Camille is a federal bankruptcy trustee. In his first political contest, Marshall was elected mayor of Macon in 1995. He made his first run for Congress in 2000 against Saxby Chambliss in the old 8th District, which covers much of the same territory as the current 3d. He campaigned almost exclusively on prescription drugs for seniors, and lost 59%–41%.

When Democrats drew the new 3d District, Marshall quickly entered the contest and made his military experience the centerpiece of his campaign. Against three opponents in the Democratic primary, his toughest competitor was politically-connected attorney Chuck Byrd, whose father Garland Byrd was lieutenant governor from 1959–63. Byrd ran as a conservative in the Sam Nunn tradition and as an opponent of abortion but Marshall carried Bibb County solidly and won 54% of the total vote, enough to avoid a runoff. In the general election, Marshall faced Bibb County Commissioner Calder Clay, an energetic fundraiser who claimed Marshall was too liberal for the district. Marshall kept emphasizing his military record; Clay had not served in the military. Both supported George W. Bush on Iraq, but they differed on abortion and Social Security. Each candidate got a pledge of a seat on the House Armed Services Committee. In one of 2002's closest contests, Clay carried most of the eastern counties and the Warner Robins area. But Marshall won 61%–39% in Bibb County and 50.5%–49.5% overall.

It didn't take long for Marshall to get noticed within the Democratic Caucus. In March 2003, on the day after hostilities began in Iraq, Marshall showed up, uninvited, to a press conference convened by a group of anti-war House Democrats. "The time for debate is past," he announced. He then invoked an obscure House rule to cancel a Democratic Caucus meeting organized to debate war alternatives. After a September 2003 visit to Iraq, he criticized news coverage of the war for focusing disproportionately on the coalition's "death, mistakes and setbacks"; he said the "Pentagon's version is far closer to reality" than the media's portrayal. In an *Atlanta Journal-Constitution* opinion article, he urged Democrats to "carefully avoid using the language of failure" which he said could be "unforgivably self-fulfilling." The following Christmas, he secretly returned to Iraq to visit some of the most dangerous areas, observe the conditions, and thank U.S. soldiers. "As I look through these eyes at each of you, I see myself," he told the GIs. "My time in the Army and especially my time in combat stands out as unique. I cherish it. You will too."

Marshall's voting record is near the center of the House. He avidly backed "concurrent receipt" legislation to permit veterans to receive full retirement pay plus disability compensation at the same time; within months, Republicans took up and passed a modified version. At home, he organized a coalition of small cigarette manufacturers to oppose the merger of R.J. Reynolds and Brown & Williamson, whose Macon plant closed after the merger went through.

In 2004, Marshall turned down pleas from national and state Democrats to run for the Senate seat left open by Zell Miller's retirement. Instead, he faced a rematch with Calder Clay, who supported John Linder's national sales tax plan. While Clay had visits from a string of Republican leaders, Marshall kept his distance from John Kerry and congressional Democrats. He defended himself from attacks that he was not doing enough to protect Social Security by pointing to his support for the Democratic Blue Dogs' budget alternative. Marshall was the only Democratic candidate endorsed by Miller, who called him "the kind of Democrat we need to keep in Washington." In an unexpectedly strong showing, Marshall won 63%–37%, carrying all 29 counties; he won 74%–26% in Bibb County, which cast 20% of the vote. But the March 2005 redistricting may give Marshall cause to think about running statewide. By reducing the black population in his district (renumbered as the 8th District) from 40% to 33%, Republicans bolstered their chances of taking this seat. Their best hope appeared to be former Representative

Mac Collins, who ran unsuccessfully in 2004 for the Republican Senate nomination; conveniently, the redistricters placed his home in the north end of Marshall's redrawn district, and Collins voiced interest in running.

FOURTH DISTRICT

Rep. Cynthia McKinney (D)

Elected 2004, 1st term; b. Mar. 17, 1955, Atlanta; home, Stone Mountain; U. of S. CA, B.A. 1978; Catholic; divorced.

Elected Office: GA House of Reps., 1988–92; U.S. House of Reps., 1992–2002.

Professional Career: Diplomatic Fellow, Spelman Col., 1984; Atlanta Bd. of Health Svcs. Plng. Cncl., 1990–92; Adjunct Prof., Agnes Scott Women's Col., 1991–92.

DC Office: 320 CHOB, 20515, 202-225-1605; Fax: 202-226-0691; Web site: www.house.gov/mckinney.

District Offices: Atlanta, 404-320-2001; Decatur, 404-633-0927.

Committees: *Armed Services* (27th of 28 D): Military Personnel; Terrorism, Unconventional Threats & Capabilities. *Budget* (14th of 17 D).

Group Ratings and Key Votes: Newly Elected

Election Results

2004 general	Cynthia McKinney (D)	157,461	(64%)	($569,680)
	Catherine Davis (R)	89,509	(36%)	($39,874)
2004 primary	Cynthia McKinney (D)	48,512	(51%)	
	Liane Levetan (D)	19,723	(21%)	
	Cathy Woolard (D)	18,164	(19%)	
	Connie Stokes (D)	4,972	(5%)	
	Other	4,218	(4%)	
2002 general	Denise Majette (D)	118,045	(77%)	($1,917,879)
	Cynthia Van Auken (R)	35,202	(23%)	($69,681)

Prior Winning Percentages: 2000 (61%); 1998 (61%); 1996 (58%); 1994 (66%); 1992 (73%)

The People		Race/Ethnic Origin	Ancestry	
Area size:	254 sq. mi.	32.0% White	English: 5.4%	German: 4.6%
Urban population:	99.6%	53.1% Black	Irish: 4.2%	
Rural population:	0.4%	4.2% Asian	**2004 Presidential Vote**	
Pop. 2000:	629,690	0.2% Native Am.	Kerry (D) 183,190	(72%)
Median income:	$49,307	0.0% Hawaiian	Bush (R) 70,600	(28%)
Poverty status:	10.5%	1.7% Two+ races	**2000 Presidential Vote**	
Military veterans:	10.7%	0.2% Other	Gore (D) 140,767	(69%)
		8.5% Hispanic Origin	Bush (R) 58,338	(29%)
			Other 4,107	(2%)
			Cook Partisan Voting Index: D +23	

Occupation	Blue collar: 19.6%	White collar: 67.4%	Gray collar: 13.0%

In 1920, when Gutzom Borglum began sculpting Jefferson Davis, Robert E. Lee and Stonewall Jackson into the side of Stone Mountain, the huge outcropping of granite was a day's drive into the country from central Atlanta and was soon to become a rallying point for the Ku Klux Klan. Even when the memorial (the largest single piece of sculpture in the world) was completed in 1972, suburban development barely reached this far. But today, after three decades of some of the most explosive metropolitan growth in the country, DeKalb County, which Stone Mountain overlooks, is part of the core of the Atlanta metropolitan area, and this monument to the Confederacy sits in one of the most cosmopolitan and liberal constituencies in the South. Not far from Stone Mountain is Emory University, just beyond the old mansions of Druid Hills. A few miles away are the Centers for Disease Control and Prevention, one of the federal government's superb research institutions. All around in north DeKalb County are affluent suburbs, including much of Atlanta's Jewish community, with voting habits much more liberal than in other suburbs. South DeKalb has been transformed from mostly rural territory 30 years ago to one of the nation's largest collections of affluent black neighborhoods, rivaled only by Prince George's County, Maryland. Its population grew by 22% in the 1990s. By 2000 the county had pretty well filled up, and growth slowed, but demand for housing has given DeKalb the fastest-growing new-home sales prices in metro Atlanta. These demographic changes have moved DeKalb County's politics well to the left: It was a Republican county when rural Georgia was almost all Democratic in the 1960s, now it is the most heavily Democratic major county in Georgia, considerably more than next-door Fulton County which includes central Atlanta; in 2004 DeKalb voted 73%–27% for John Kerry, his best percentage except for one tiny rural county in all the 159 counties of Georgia.

The 4th Congressional District of Georgia consists of almost all of DeKalb County plus a small slice of the more Republican Gwinnett County to the northeast. The 4th and next-door 5th Districts are the most Democratic districts in Georgia, giving both Al Gore and Kerry huge majorities.

Back in place as the congresswoman from the 4th District is Cynthia McKinney, a Democrat who reclaimed her seat in 2004 after serving previously from 1992 to 2002. McKinney grew up in Atlanta; she recalls riding on her father's shoulders as a child in civil rights marches. Her father, Billy McKinney, was one of the first blacks on the Atlanta police force and was elected to the legislature in 1973. Cynthia McKinney went to college in California, taught at Spelman College, Clark Atlanta University, and Agnes Scott College. In 1988, she was elected to the Georgia House. She got a seat on the legislature's 1991 redistricting committee and worked long and hard to draw new black-majority districts. In 1992 she ran in the new 11th District, which stretched from south DeKalb all the way to Savannah. She led the Democratic primary with 31%, then won the runoff with 56%. Her first decade in the House was marked by a very liberal voting record, a confrontational style and a habit of making racially provocative statements that alienated members on both sides of the aisle. She complained when White House guards in 1996 and again in 1998 did not recognize her or treat her like other members of Congress: "I am absolutely sick and tired of having to have my appearance at the White House validated by white people." During the 2000 campaign, following a complaint by black Secret Service agents, her office issued a statement attacking Al Gore's low "Negro tolerance level" and accused him of rarely having more than one black agent with him.

McKinney focused much of her legislative work on Africa, which she called "the forgotten and ignored continent." She called for respect for human rights and hailed new African leaders who are willing to allow the private sector to get involved in economic development. She described IMF agreements as a "cruel hoax" because they require countries to spend money on repayment of loans they can never pay off rather than on health care and education. McKinney's bombastic reaction to the events of September 11 proved to be her undoing. She publicly apologized to a Saudi prince after Mayor Rudolph Giuliani refused his $10 million donation because he suggested that pro-Israel U.S. policy contributed to the attacks. In April 2002 she charged that George W. Bush "may" have had prior knowledge of the September 11 attacks and did not act on it because the war on terrorism would boost the defense stocks of associates of his father. Senator Zell Miller called her comments "loony."

In 2002 Denise Majette resigned her judgeship and ran against McKinney in the August Democratic primary. During the campaign it was revealed that one-third of McKinney's contributions over the past five years had come from donors with apparently Arab-American or Muslim names; at least 18 of her donors were officers of Muslim foundations under investigation by the FBI or people who had voiced support for Palestinian and Lebanese terrorist organizations or had made inflammatory statements about Jews. Majette received substantial contributions from supporters of Israel, many of them from outside Georgia. The national media treated the contest as a proxy battle on Middle East policy; it was also a contest between conflicting styles of black leadership. McKinney attacked Majette as "a Democrat in name only" and a tool of white interests. She accused her of "flip-flopping" on affirmative action because Majette did not support reparations for descendants of slaves. Majette, for the most part, declined to return fire, preferring instead to focus on domestic issues and criticism of McKinney's constituent service record. Majette won 58%–42%—a resounding repudiation for an incumbent. "We united this district. My opponent had divided it for 10 long years," Majette said. In the bitter end, McKinney's father blamed the defeat on, as he put it, "J-E-W-S."

McKinney considered running for President on the Green Party ticket in 2004. She also considered running against Majette. Then Majette suddenly announced that she was running for the Senate seat being vacated by Zell Miller, and McKinney decided to run for her old seat. Her comeback campaign was as subdued as her exit was memorable. In what local observers termed a "stealth" campaign, she steered clear of controversy, refrained from making contentious statements, and rarely made television appearances. She even avoided mailing campaign brochures to the majority-white, northern DeKalb County precincts that voted overwhelmingly against her in 2002. Instead, McKinney relied on a loyal grassroots base that had never abandoned her. Opposed in the Democratic primary by three state senators and a former Atlanta City Council president, she won 51% and thus was nominated without a runoff. McKinney won the general election with 64% of the vote, running well behind John Kerry. Minority Leader Pelosi denied her request to credit her with 10 years of seniority for committee assignments; the normal practice is to give former members precedence only over other freshmen who have not previously served in the House.

FIFTH DISTRICT

Rep. John Lewis (D)

Elected 1986, 10th term; b. Feb. 21, 1940, Troy, AL; home, Atlanta; Amer. Baptist Theol. Seminary, B.A. 1961, Fisk U., B.A. 1963; Baptist; married (Lillian).

Elected Office: Atlanta City Cncl., 1981–86.

Professional Career: Chmn., Student Nonviolent Coord. Cmte., 1963–66; Field Foundation, 1966–67; Community Organization Dir., Southern Regional Cncl., 1967–70; Exec. Dir., Voter Educ. Project, 1970–76; Assoc. Dir., ACTION, 1977–80; Community Affairs Dir., Natl. Coop. Bank, 1980–82.

DC Office: 343 CHOB, 20515, 202-225-3801; Fax: 202-225-0351; Web site: www.house.gov/johnlewis.

District Office: Atlanta, 404-659-0116.

Committees: *Senior Chief Deputy Minority Whip. Ways & Means* (6th of 17 D): Health; Oversight (RMM).

Group Ratings

	ADA	ACLU	AFS	LCV	ITIC	NTU	COC	ACU	NTLC	CHC
2004	100	100	100	100	30	14	10	4	0	7
2003	90	—	100	100	—	26	17	9	—	—

National Journal Ratings

	2003 LIB	—	2003 CONS		2004 LIB	—	2004 CONS
Economic	92%	—	0%		98%	—	0%
Social	92%	—	0%		88%	—	0%
Foreign	94%	—	0%		94%	—	0%

Key Votes of the 108th Congress

1. Drilling in ANWR	N	5. DC School Vouchers	N	9. Ban Same-Sex Marriage	N
2. Approve Bush Tax Cuts	N	6. Ban Human Cloning	N	10. Fund Iraq War	N
3. Medicare/Rx Bill	N	7. Restrict Gun Liability	N	11. Bar Cuba Embargo Funds	Y
4. Bar Overtime Pay Regs.	Y	8. Ban Partial-Birth Abortion	N	12. Intelligence Reorg.	N

Election Results

2004 general	John Lewis (D) .... unopposed	($547,098)
2004 primary	John Lewis (D) .... unopposed	
2002 general	John Lewis (D) .... unopposed	($537,597)

Prior Winning Percentages: 2000 (77%); 1998 (79%); 1996 (100%); 1994 (69%); 1992 (72%); 1990 (76%); 1988 (78%); 1986 (75%)

The People		Race/Ethnic Origin	Ancestry	
Area size:	254 sq. mi.	34.4% White	English: 5.4%	German: 4.5%
Urban population:	99.5%	55.7% Black	Irish: 4.4%	
Rural population:	0.5%	2.2% Asian	**2004 Presidential Vote**	
Pop. 2000:	629,727	0.2% Native Am.	Kerry (D) 176,332	(72%)
Median income:	$39,725	0.0% Hawaiian	Bush (R) 65,488	(27%)
Poverty status:	19.7%	1.2% Two+ races	Other 1,759	(1%)
Military veterans:	9.5%	0.2% Other	**2000 Presidential Vote**	
		6.1% Hispanic Origin	Gore (D) 136,606	(70%)
			Bush (R) 55,605	(28%)
			Other 3,232	(2%)
			Cook Partisan Voting Index: D +23	
Occupation	Blue collar: 16.7%	White collar: 68.1%	Gray collar: 15.2%	

Venture out of the quiet of the Ebenezer Baptist Church or the shade of Martin Luther King Jr.'s boyhood home two blocks away and into the steamy heat of the sun on Auburn Avenue—Sweet Auburn—and you can see, a mile away, downtown Atlanta's atrium-skyscrapers towering in their glory. They are evidence of the wealth and vibrant growth of the commercial capital of the South, the metropolis that has grown up where there was little more than a railroad junction at the time of the War Between the States. But the awesome achievement that is downtown Atlanta is overshadowed by the revolution made in very large part by a man who grew up on Auburn Avenue, where people who never felt air-conditioning moved slowly in the sweltering heat, and around Morehouse and Spelman colleges, where proud professionals struggled and worked hard to raise their families. Atlanta's white establishment, led by Mayors William Hartsfield and Ivan Allen and Coca-Cola's Robert Woodruff, deserve credit for abandoning segregation, but it was King and other civil rights leaders who took the risks that led them to do so. Atlanta's city fathers acted out of good will, but also with an eye for the economic growth of their city, which they knew would be hurt by violent resistance.

Yet, sadly, not all is entirely well in Atlanta. Downtown Atlanta's primacy in office buildings is being eclipsed by north-side edge cities in Buckhead and along I-285. Many of Atlanta's black neighborhoods today have been abandoned by families who have headed to subdivisions in DeKalb, Cobb and Douglas Counties, leaving the central city with vacant housing and street crime. But Atlanta also has its glories: The headquarters of world-girdling Coca-Cola and CNN, the gigantic Hartsfield-Jackson Atlanta International Airport, the modern Martin Luther King Jr. Center that depicts the triumphs of the civil rights movement, the Jimmy Carter Presidential Center, the antique Cyclorama that shows Atlanta burning during the Civil War, and the stadiums and sports facilities built for the 1996 Summer Olympics.

The 5th Congressional District of Georgia includes most of Atlanta, including much of the posh and Republican Buckhead neighborhood in the north, plus the suburbs of East Point to the south. It also extends a tentacle north along Route 400 to include a part of Roswell and another northwest to include a small part of Cobb County. Redistricting in 2002 reduced the district's black population from 62% to 56% but the 5th remains overwhelmingly Democratic—72% for John Kerry in 2004.

The congressman from the 5th District is John Lewis, who made history a long generation ago as a hero of the civil rights movement, as he recounted in his 1998 autobiography, *Walking With the Wind*. A sharecropper's son from Troy, Alabama, he was seized by religious fervor as a child, preaching in the barnyard, determined to be a minister. Lewis was the first in his family to finish high school; he wrote to Ralph Abernathy for help in suing for the right to enter Troy State

College; he met Martin Luther King Jr. when he was 18. In 1959, at 19, he helped organize the first lunch-counter sit-in, which was received with open hostility hard to imagine today. In 1960, the day after John Kennedy was elected, Lewis sat in the Krystal Diner in Nashville while a waitress poured cleansing powder down his back and water over his food; he went to talk to the manager, who turned a fumigating machine on him. In May 1961, he was on the first of the Freedom Rides, riding buses as they were attacked and burned; he was viciously beaten in Rock Hill, South Carolina and Montgomery, Alabama. He spoke at the 1963 March on Washington, criticizing Kennedy liberals for inaction on civil rights and calling for massive help for the poor. In 1964, he helped coordinate the Mississippi Freedom Project. In 1965, he led the Selma-to-Montgomery march to petition for voting rights and was beaten by policemen who fractured his skull. Modestly, quietly, maintaining his poise and good judgment under harsh circumstances, Lewis was one of the people who risked their lives many times to make the civil rights revolution happen. He worked for Robert Kennedy for president in 1968, and was with him in Indianapolis when they heard King was killed, and in Los Angeles just before Kennedy himself was shot.

Lewis's first foray into electoral politics was unsuccessful: He ran in 1977 to replace Andrew Young in the House and was soundly beaten by Wyche Fowler (but ran ahead of Republican Paul Coverdell, who beat Fowler in the 1992 Senate election). After winning a seat on the Atlanta Council in 1981, Lewis ran for Congress in 1986, and trailed Julian Bond 47%–35% in the primary. But even though Bond won more than 60% of the black vote, Lewis won the runoff by assembling a coalition of poor blacks and affluent whites: "Vote for the tugboat, not the show-boat" was his slogan, stressing his hard work on local issues. He has been re-elected easily since.

Lewis has been a strong partisan, with one of the most liberal voting records in the House. Usually quiet, he can speak in the cadences of black preachers, as he did on the Gulf War resolution in January 1991 and the impeachment of Bill Clinton in December 1998. He is the Democrats' senior chief deputy whip, a member of the leadership, and has a seat on Ways and Means. Only occasionally does he defect from his party, as when he opposed the 1994 crime bill because of his disapproval of capital punishment. He furiously voiced his disappointment when Republicans captured the House in 1994 and argued passionately against the Republican welfare bills.

Lewis has worked to commemorate the civil rights revolution in which he played such a large part. He got a federal building in Atlanta named for Martin Luther King Jr. and got the route from Selma to Montgomery designated a National Historic Trail. He has said affirmative action should move from race to class as a criterion, but he has stoutly defended racial quotas and preferences and opposed school vouchers for low-income children in Washington, D.C. He passed a Minority Health and Health Disparities Research and Education Act, setting up a research center at the National Institutes of Health. He spotlighted what he charged was racial profiling in Customs searches at airports. For many years he sponsored legislation to authorize an African-American history museum on the Mall; co-sponsored by Georgia Republican Jack Kingston and Senator Sam Brownback, it finally became law in December 2003. In 2004 he sponsored a law to exchange lands with the Martin Luther King, Jr. National Historic Site.

In August 1999, Lewis declared that he was running for majority whip should Democrats win a House majority; Nancy Pelosi and Steny Hoyer had already started lining up support. But not all Congressional Black Caucus members supported him, and Lewis left the race (which turned out to be academic) in July 2000. In 2004 he and Martin Frost celebrated the long history of mutual support of American blacks and Jews. In March 2004 he testified against a constitutional amendment to ban same-sex marriage. "We have been down this road before in this country. The right to liberty and happiness belongs to each of us and on the same terms, without regard to either skin color or sexual orientation."

Lewis was reelected without opposition in 2002 and 2004.

SIXTH DISTRICT

Rep. Tom Price (R)

Elected 2004, 1st term; b. Oct. 8, 1954, Lansing, MI; home, Roswell; U. of MI, B.A. 1976, M.D. 1979; Presbyterian; married (Betty).

Elected Office: GA Senate, 1996–2004; Maj. Ldr., 2002–03.

Professional Career: Practicing orthopedic surgeon, 1979–2002; Asst. prof., Emory U., 2002-present.

DC Office: 506 CHOB, 20515, 202-225-4501; Fax: 202-225-4656; Web site: www.house.gov/tomprice.

District Office: Marietta, 770-565-4990.

Committees: *Education & the Workforce* (21st of 27 R): 21st Century Competitiveness; Workforce Protections. *Financial Services* (34th of 37 R): Domestic and International Monetary Policy, Trade & Technology; Financial Institutions & Consumer Credit; Oversight & Investigations.

Group Ratings and Key Votes: Newly Elected

Election Results

2004 general	Tom Price (R)	unopposed		($2,283,545)
2004 runoff	Tom Price (R)	28,180	(54%)	
	Robert Lamutt (R)	23,959	(46%)	
2004 primary	Tom Price (R)	29,144	(35%)	
	Robert Lamutt (R)	23,176	(28%)	
	Chuck Clay (R)	17,705	(21%)	
	Roger Hines (R)	7,645	(9%)	
	Alfred Beverly (R)	3,187	(4%)	
	Other	1,965	(2%)	
2002 general	Johnny Isakson (R)	163,203	(80%)	($541,913)
	Jeff Weisberger (D)	41,043	(20%)	

The People		Race/Ethnic Origin	Ancestry	
Area size:	441 sq. mi.	83.0% White	German: 11.1%	English: 11.0%
Urban population:	97.8%	6.9% Black	Irish: 10.1%	
Rural population:	2.2%	4.0% Asian	**2004 Presidential Vote**	
Pop. 2000:	629,725	0.2% Native Am.	Bush (R) 229,990	(70%)
Median income:	$75,611	0.0% Hawaiian	Kerry (D) 96,456	(29%)
Poverty status:	3.7%	1.2% Two+ races	Other 1,225	(0%)
Military veterans:	12.1%	0.2% Other	**2000 Presidential Vote**	
		4.5% Hispanic Origin	Bush (R) 174,414	(68%)
			Gore (D) 77,646	(30%)
			Other 6,303	(2%)
			Cook Partisan Voting Index: R +19	

Occupation	Blue collar: 11.2%	White collar: 79.7%	Gray collar: 9.1%

In the red clay hills north of Atlanta, over the past four decades an almost wholly new metropolitan quarter has grown up as affluent Atlanta has spread out past the I-285 Perimeter into territory that was once just farms, small towns and little factory cities. Where there were perhaps 100,000 people in the 1950s, there are more than 1 million today. No longer is downtown Atlanta the only focus: The edge cities of Perimeter Center and the area near Cumberland Mall are now not just for shopping; they are major office centers, rivaling downtown Atlanta in square footage. Cobb County is the headquarters of Home Depot and the Weather Channel. Farther out, in the fast-growing northern part of Fulton County, are the affluent suburbs of Alpharetta and Roswell. Yet for all this economic and demographic change, this Golden Crescent north of the Perimeter and between I-75 in Cobb County and I-85 in Gwinnett County outwardly does not seem to have changed greatly: The buildings are tree-shaded, and lush foliage and large-lot requirements have given most of the communities a woodsy look.

The 6th Congressional District of Georgia occupies a large portion of this Golden Crescent north of Atlanta, including the bulk of north and west Cobb County, almost all of Fulton County north of the Perimeter and a slice of Cherokee County including Woodstock. This seat was in effect created after the 1990 Census, and its boundaries were contracted in the 2001 redistricting in response to additional population growth. It would surely surprise Georgians a generation or two ago to learn that one of their congressional districts, with a median income exceeding $75,000, would rank among the nation's richest and most educated: Now the 6th and the 7th, which surrounds it on the north, east and west, both do. It is one of several heavily Republican Georgia districts, and the political tension here tends to be between economic and cultural conservatives. The cultural signals are mixed: In 1993, the Cobb County commission passed a resolution that "lifestyles advocated by the gay community" were incompatible with local values. That resolution eventually expired and was not renewed. More recently, in April 2002, the county's board of education required placement of stickers on high school biology textbooks with the disclaimer, "Evolution is a theory, not a fact, regarding the origin of living things. This material should be approached with an open mind, studied carefully, and critically considered."

The congressman from the 6th District is Tom Price, a Republican elected in 2004. Price grew up in Michigan and graduated from the University of Michigan and its medical school; his father and grandfather were physicians. He did his residency in orthopedic surgery at Emory Medical School and moved to Roswell, where he was involved in civic affairs and was president of the Rotary Club. Working closely with the Medical Association of Georgia, he campaigned locally against the Clinton health care plan. When a seat opened in the state Senate in 1996, he was elected and quickly moved up the leadership ranks to become Majority Leader when Republicans won a majority after some party switches right after the 2002 election.

In January 2003, 6th District Congressman Johnny Isakson announced he was running for the Senate seat being vacated by Zell Miller. The contest for this heavily Republican open seat was hard-fought and big-spending. Three state senators were running—Price from Fulton County (which has 38% of the district's population) and Robert Lamutt and Chuck Clay from Cobb County (which has 55% of the district's population). Price spent $499,000 of his own money and contrasted his work in medicine with the legal and business careers of his two main opponents. He highlighted his fiscal conservatism and strong support for limiting jury awards in malpractice suits, a position that won him considerable support from the medical community. Calling the federal income tax "broken," he advocated 7th District Republican John Linder's national retail sales tax. He said that he had "a surgeon's mentality . . . . I get things done." Price led the first round of the primary with 35% (with 63% in Fulton County and only 21% in Cobb); Lamutt made it into the runoff with 28% to 21% for Chuck Clay in the battle of Cobb County senators.

Lamutt, who cited his success in creating an assets management firm and gave $1.5 million to his campaign, criticized Price as a "special interest" candidate because he raised large sums from fellow doctors. He attacked Price's 2003 support for a 25-cent state tax increase on a pack of cigarettes. Price defended his vote as a tool to reduce local property taxes. "Bob Lamutt helped cigarette makers but voted against tax relief for you," a Price ad said. In the runoff the Cobb vote was nearly twice as large as in Fulton. But Price got 79% in Fulton County and held Lamutt to 59% in Cobb; with the small vote in Cherokee County split nearly evenly, Price won 54%–46%. Lamutt was one of two candidates in Georgia runoffs endorsed by former Speaker Newt Gingrich, who represented this district from 1992 until his resignation in 1999; both lost. With obstetrician Phil Gingrey and dentists Linder and Charlie Norwood, Price is the fourth medical professional in the Georgia Republican delegation. He was assigned to the Financial Services and Education and the Workforce committees.

SEVENTH DISTRICT

Rep. John Linder (R)

Elected 1992, 7th term; b. Sept. 9, 1942, Deer River, MN; home, Duluth; U. of MN, B.S. 1964, D.D.S., 1967; Presbyterian; married (Lynne).

Military Career: Air Force, 1967–69.

Elected Office: GA House of Reps., 1974–80, 1982–90.

Professional Career: Practicing dentist, 1969–82; Founder & Pres., Linder Financial Corp., 1977–92.

DC Office: 1026 LHOB, 20515, 202-225-4272; Fax: 202-225-4696; Web site: linder.house.gov.

District Offices: Canton, 770-499-1888; Duluth, 770-232-3005.

Committees: *Homeland Security* (7th of 19 R): Economic Security, Infrastructure Protection & Cybersecurity; Management, Integration & Oversight; Prevention of Nuclear & Biological Attack (Chmn.). *Ways & Means* (20th of 24 R): Oversight; Select Revenue Measures.

Group Ratings

	ADA	ACLU	AFS	LCV	ITIC	NTU	COC	ACU	NTLC	CHC
2004	0	0	0	0	100	69	100	100	89	83
2003	5	—	0	5	—	68	100	92	—	—

National Journal Ratings

	2003 LIB — 2003 CONS	2004 LIB — 2004 CONS
Economic	0% — 91%	17% — 83%
Social	5% — 87%	16% — 83%
Foreign	0% — 89%	10% — 86%

Key Votes of the 108th Congress

1. Drilling in ANWR	Y	5. DC School Vouchers	Y	9. Ban Same-Sex Marriage	Y
2. Approve Bush Tax Cuts	Y	6. Ban Human Cloning	Y	10. Fund Iraq War	Y
3. Medicare/Rx Bill	Y	7. Restrict Gun Liability	Y	11. Bar Cuba Embargo Funds	N
4. Bar Overtime Pay Regs.	N	8. Ban Partial-Birth Abortion	Y	12. Intelligence Reorg.	Y

Election Results

2004 general	John Linder (R)	unopposed		($746,763)
2004 primary	John Linder (R)	unopposed		
2002 general	John Linder (R)	138,997	(79%)	($2,214,265)
	Michael Berlon (D)	37,124	(21%)	

Prior Winning Percentages: 2000 (100%); 1998 (69%); 1996 (64%); 1994 (58%); 1992 (51%)

The People		Race/Ethnic Origin	Ancestry	
Area size:	1,220 sq. mi.	82.4% White	USA: 11.9%	English: 9.5%
Urban population:	85.9%	6.9% Black	German: 9.4%	
Rural population:	14.1%	3.8% Asian	**2004 Presidential Vote**	
Pop. 2000:	629,706	0.2% Native Am.	Bush (R) 225,342	(76%)
Median income:	$63,455	0.0% Hawaiian	Kerry (D) 72,100	(24%)
Poverty status:	4.5%	1.1% Two+ races	Other 521	(0%)
Military veterans:	12.1%	0.1% Other	**2000 Presidential Vote**	
		5.4% Hispanic Origin	Bush (R) 154,575	(70%)
			Gore (D) 60,082	(27%)
			Other 6,694	(3%)
			Cook Partisan Voting Index: R +23	
Occupation	Blue collar: 20.6%	White collar: 69.1%	Gray collar: 10.3%	

In the last two decades, greater Atlanta has grown out in every direction, south past the airport, west over the Chattahoochee, north past far Buckhead and the Perimeter Mall, and east and northeast past Stone Mountain. The outer suburbs north of Atlanta have grown fastest of all: A semi-circular ring that stretches from Paulding County in the west, with its starter homes for young families, to Gwinnett County to the east, with its more mature neighborhoods of affluent professionals and entrepreneurs. The closer-in portion of Gwinnett, near I-85, with their older shopping districts, have been attracting Georgia's largest concentration of Hispanics and also middle class blacks; the county's rapidly growing school system boasts that its students speak more than 100 languages. Republicans responded by taking to door-to-door campaigning and Democrats by staging rallies among local Latinos. Recently, several of Atlanta's outer counties decided to link up with urban bus lines for the first time, after shunning them for years. But further out, downtown Atlanta seems very far away, both physically—it is 30 to 50 miles, and more than an hour of clogged rush-hour driving, to Peachtree Street—and in state of mind. For many, Atlanta is something that whizzes by on the way to Hartsfield-Jackson Atlanta International Airport.

The growth here is hard to overstate. Gwinnett County cast 21,000 votes in 1972 and 243,000 in 2004, not so far behind Fulton County (336,000), which includes central Atlanta, or DeKalb County (276,000) just to the east. Forsyth County, with golf courses and expensive subdivisions, was the third fastest growing county in the United States in the 1990s; it grew another 34% between 2000 and 2004. Paulding County, with 30%, was the 10th fastest growing county in 2000–04. These counties were once rural, low-income and heavily Democratic; now they are full of strivers and achievers, with many religious conservatives and many economic conservatives, and relatively few liberals and Democrats. The big local issue has been the Northern Arc highway proposed by Governor Roy Barnes; commuters between Forsyth and Cherokee Counties ached for relief, but others opposed the new highway, and Barnes was defeated not least by Forsyth and Cherokee, which voted a combined 71%–25% for his Republican opponent Sonny Perdue.

The 7th Congressional District of Georgia owes its existence to the rapid growth here in the 1990s; it was a new crescent-shaped district created by Democratic redistricters with a few odd twists to cordon off Republican votes from districts they hoped to win. It includes almost all of Paulding and Cherokee Counties, plus large parts of Bartow, Forsyth and Gwinnett Counties. More than half the population and half the votes are in Gwinnett County. This was George W. Bush's best Georgia district in 2000, when he won 70% of the vote here, and second best in 2004 when he won 76%.

The congressman from the 7th District is John Linder, a Republican first elected in 1992 in the old 4th District (which combined north DeKalb County and half of Gwinnett). After a court-ordered redistricting, he moved in 1996 to the 11th District (which stretched from Gwinnett to Athens and the South Carolina border). Like many in the Georgia delegation, Linder grew up elsewhere, in his case Minnesota, where he went to college and dental school. After two years in the Air Force he moved to greater Atlanta and practiced dentistry for 13 years. In 1977 he started Linder Financial Corporation, a lending institution for entrepreneurial ventures in the South. In 1974, at 32, he was elected to the Georgia House, where he served all but two of the next 16 years. In 1990 he challenged Congressman Ben Jones and lost 52%–48%. After the 1992 redistricting, Linder ran again in the 4th, where he ran first in a six-candidate primary and won the runoff with 62% of the vote. In the general, he faced Democratic state Senator Cathey Steinberg and, in a race that broke along national party lines, won 51%–49%.

From this tenuous beginning Linder quickly became an important congressman. For a time he was a close ally to Newt Gingrich. They went back a ways: In 1975 Linder, Gingrich and Paul Coverdell began meeting to try to build a strong Georgia Republican Party, surely not imagining that within 20 years they would be Congressman, Speaker and Senator. A decade later, they were setting political strategy for congressional Republicans. Now, only Linder survives in office. But they built a strong local party base.

Linder has a calm, sometimes humorous demeanor; his views are solidly conservative—though a bit more Wall Street than Main Street. After Republicans won control, Gingrich gave Linder a seat on the House Rules Committee and called on him often to preside over contentious debates. After the 1996 election, Gingrich chose Linder as chairman of the National Republican Congressional Committee. He excelled at fundraising, and relentlessly prevailed on incumbents to contribute to Republican challengers. He did a good job at recruiting candidates and shared the assumption of most observers that Republicans would gain seats as the out party in an off-year election. But one of his ads misfired: At the behest of Gingrich, it raised the trust and impeachment issues against Bill Clinton. While run in only a few districts, the ad was publicized nationally; it yielded a minimum of gain and a maximum of pain. When Republicans lost five seats, Linder was in deep trouble. He said the problem was the lack of a "strong message," which "was not my responsibility"—an obvious reference to Gingrich. Gingrich said that the next NRCC chairman would be elected by the conference rather than appointed by the speaker. Tom Davis of Virginia, a highly competent election buff, started running for the job, with the support of Whip Tom DeLay. Linder reacted bitterly: "I remember when Newt Gingrich's wife left a press conference in tears when he blamed her. So I don't think he has any compunction about blaming me." That was Thursday, two days after the election. Gingrich announced his resignation late on Friday; 12 days later, Linder lost to Davis 130–77.

Taking a far lower profile, Linder resumed his legislative work and got on well with the new Republican leadership: Rules is not a committee for a party rebel. Linder turned his attention toward the fight for fundamental tax reform. With more than 50 co-sponsors, including DeLay, his FairTax plan would abolish all federal income taxes, including payroll taxes, and replaces them with a single 23% national retail sales tax, with no exceptions for food or medical expenses but a monthly rebate for low-income citizens. As Linder explains, "the FairTax gives the American people control over their own lives again by allowing them to keep 100% of their pay checks and shielding their personal information from bureaucrats." Late in the 2004 campaign, however, many Democratic candidates sought to turn the issue in their favor with alarming descriptions of increased costs for consumers. Linder spoke up for his Republican co-sponsors, especially Senate candidate Jim DeMint of South Carolina. "I'm thrilled to have the Democrats out there defending the current [tax] system," he said. By Election Day, the furor had died down, and George W. Bush listed tax reform as one of his second-term priorities. Linder has longed to serve as chairman of Rules, but Speaker Hastert in January 2005 deferred that opportunity when he decreed that the six-year limit on committee chairmen did not apply and gave David Dreier of California another term as head of Rules. Linder obviously was disappointed, but he did not cause a fuss; he left the committee and got a seat on Ways and Means.

In 2002, Linder was unexpectedly inconvenienced by the redistricting plan drawn by Georgia Democrats. Although the new 7th appeared tailor-made for him, he found himself in a primary contest with Representative Bob Barr, who had served a district northwest of Atlanta. The new 7th had only 18% of Barr's old district, and most Republicans expected that he would run in the new 11th, which contained more of his old seat and which in fact ended up electing a Republican, albeit narrowly. Linder had represented, at one time or another, most of Gwinnett County, and one-third of his old 11th District was in the new 7th. The race was a contrast of styles, not of voting records. Linder campaigned as a political insider who quietly got things done. Barr, an early advocate of the impeachment of Bill Clinton, campaigned as a champion of conservative principle. Linder had more local financial support; Barr had contributors across the nation. The campaign grew bitter, and there were some odd moments. Two weeks before the primary Barr, long an advocate of Second Amendment rights, was handling a gun at a supporter's house when it went off and shattered a glass door. But the final result was unambiguous. Linder won 64%–36%. Linder won 74% in Gwinnett County, which cast 57% of the votes.

Linder's local priorities include funding for the Centers for Disease Control and Prevention. He was unopposed in 2004.

EIGHTH DISTRICT

Rep. Lynn Westmoreland (R)

Elected 2004, 1st term; b. April 2, 1950, Atlanta; home, Grantville; Attended GA State U., 1969–71; Baptist; married (Joan).

Elected Office: GA House of Reps., 1992–2004; Min. Ldr. 2000–03.

Professional Career: Real estate developer; Owner, L.A.W. Builders, 1982-present.

DC Office: 1118 LHOB, 20515, 202-225-5901; Fax: 202-225-2515; Web site: http://www.house.gov/westmoreland/.

District Office: Newnan, 770-683-2033.

Committees: *Government Reform* (19th of 23 R): Energy & Resources (Vice Chmn.); Regulatory Affairs. *Small Business* (17th of 18 R): Regulatory Reform & Oversight; Workforce, Empowerment & Government Programs. *Transportation & Infrastructure* (39th of 41 R): Aviation; Railroads.

Group Ratings and Key Votes: Newly Elected

Election Results

2004 general	Lynn Westmoreland (R)	227,524	(76%)	($1,943,512)
	Silvia Delamar (D)	73,632	(24%)	($28,846)
2004 runoff	Lynn Westmoreland (R)	34,250	(55%)	
	Dylan Glenn (R)	27,485	(45%)	
2004 primary	Lynn Westmoreland (R)	43,005	(46%)	
	Dylan Glenn (R)	35,276	(38%)	
	Mike Crotts (R)	10,596	(11%)	
	Tom Mills (R)	4,926	(5%)	
2002 general	Mac Collins (R)	142,505	(78%)	($781,503)
	Angelos Petrakopoulos (D)	39,422	(22%)	

The People		Race/Ethnic Origin	Ancestry	
Area size:	3,553 sq. mi.	82.8% White	USA: 15.6%	English: 8.8%
Urban population:	58.5%	12.5% Black	Irish: 8.7%	
Rural population:	41.5%	1.3% Asian	**2004 Presidential Vote**	
Pop. 2000:	629,700	0.2% Native Am.	Bush (R) 231,269	(73%)
Median income:	$52,406	0.0% Hawaiian	Kerry (D) 83,292	(26%)
Poverty status:	6.3%	0.9% Two+ races	Other 102	(0%)
Military veterans:	15.4%	0.1% Other	**2000 Presidential Vote**	
		2.1% Hispanic Origin	Bush (R) 157,703	(69%)
			Gore (D) 67,192	(29%)
			Other 4,098	(2%)
			Cook Partisan Voting Index: R +21	
Occupation	Blue collar: 27.5%	White collar: 60.7%	Gray collar: 11.8%	

Running south from Atlanta, within an hour or so by car, you leave behind the newest parts of Georgia—like Henry County, the sixth-fastest growing county in America from 2000–04—and come upon some of the most traditional. Henry County's flourishing residential, commercial and industrial development has risen near its seven I-75 interchanges and has benefited from its proximity to Hartsfield-Jackson Atlanta International Airport. To the west is the old courthouse town of Fayetteville, now surrounded by new suburbs, whose Holliday-Dorsey-Fife House is thought to have inspired the columned architecture of Tara in Margaret Mitchell's *Gone With the Wind*. Further west metro Atlanta is spreading through the countryside to Newnan and Carrollton, further east to Jasper County, further south past tourist-appealing Barnesville to Thomaston. Even farther to the southwest is yet another Georgia, the small industrial city of Columbus and next-door Fort Benning, long the home of the Army's Infantry School; it is the place where General George Marshall's talents were first noted and where he kept his little black book with a list of gifted officers whom he would make generals in World War II.

Much of this territory is within the 8th Congressional District of Georgia. On the map it looks like an unsightly splatter. In metro Atlanta, it is divided by tentacles of territory in the new, "majority minority" 13th District. One way to think of it is that it contains most of the white areas of a ring around the southern edge of metro Atlanta, with tentacles reaching down to include heavily white portions in the outskirts of Columbus and Macon. Politically, this is conservative country, with young tradition-minded families with busy breadwinners and with a heavy military background. People here are upwardly mobile, but not necessarily at the upper end of the income scale. The ancestral politics of most of this area was Democratic, but that is as much a part of history now as Tara; this is one of the most heavily Republican congressional districts in Georgia, and in the country.

The congressman from the 8th District is Lynn Westmoreland, a Republican elected in 2004. Westmoreland grew up in the Atlanta area, left Georgia State University after two years and became a real estate broker and homebuilder in Fayette County. After losing two races for the state senate, Westmoreland was elected in 1992 to the Georgia House, where he founded the Conservative Policy Caucus, a group of fiscally conservative, anti-tax lawmakers; longtime House Speaker Tom Murphy once called him "a braying jackass." In 2000 he was elected House Minority Leader and in that position refused to agree to tax increases, even when it meant defying newly elected Republican Governor Sonny Perdue. In 2003, Westmoreland led a public fight against Perdue's budget, which would have increased the cigarette tax by 25 cents to cover the state deficit; instead, he called for belt-tightening on spending.

In 2004 8th District Congressman Mac Collins ran for the Senate seat being vacated by Zell Miller. Westmoreland faced a choice between staying in Georgia, where he stood to become Speaker if Republicans won a majority in the state House (as they did), or taking advantage of a rare opportunity to run for a safe Republican open seat in the U.S. House. He chose the latter and ran on an anti-spending platform. The primary race became a contest between him and Dylan Glenn, a former staffer for George H.W. Bush and Perdue. Glenn, who is black and from Columbus, had run twice in the 2d District; he lost the Republican nomination 53%–47% in 1998 and lost to Democratic incumbent Sanford Bishop by the same margin in November 2000. Glenn was endorsed by former Congressmen Jack Kemp and J. C. Watts and by former Speaker Newt Gingrich, who argued in what he later said was a personal letter to Westmoreland's wife that a Glenn victory would "strengthen us in our area of greatest weakness" and that Republicans needed "representation from every aspect of America." Senator Saxby Chambliss and four current Georgia House members endorsed Westmoreland. In the July primary, Westmoreland led Glenn 46%–38%. He won 60% of the vote in his base in Fayette and Coweta Counties; Glenn led in the three counties nearest his home base in Columbus. During the three weeks between the primary and the August runoff, Glenn accused Westmoreland of taking excessive gifts from lobbyists (with an ad that depicted his opponent as a hog), while Westmoreland labeled Glenn a "Washington insider" with an inflated resume. Westmoreland won 55%–45%, carrying 12 of the 18 counties.

Westmoreland said he would focus on the district's need for improved highways and light-rail service to Atlanta, plus the needs of Hartsfield airport and the airlines. He said he hoped that the newly Republican-controlled legislature in Atlanta would redraw congressional district lines to create more compact districts, even though that might make the 8th more competitive in general elections; in March 2005, the legislature passed a new congressional map designed by a 23-year-old legislative aide to Westmoreland.

NINTH DISTRICT

Rep. Charlie Norwood (R)

Elected 1994, 6th term; b. July 27, 1941, Valdosta; home, Evans; GA S. U., B.S. 1964, Georgetown U., D.D.S. 1967; Methodist; married (Gloria).

Military Career: Army, 1967–69 (Vietnam).

Professional Career: Small businessman, 1969–present; Practicing dentist, 1969–93; Pres., GA Dental Assn., 1983.

DC Office: 2452 RHOB, 20515, 202-225-4101; Fax: 202-226-0776; Web site: www.house.gov/norwood.

District Offices: Augusta, 706-733-7066; Toccoa, 706-886-2776.

Committees: *Education & the Workforce* (7th of 27 R): Workforce Protections (Chmn.). *Energy & Commerce* (9th of 31 R): Energy & Air Quality; Health.

Group Ratings

	ADA	ACLU	AFS	LCV	ITIC	NTU	COC	ACU	NTLC	CHC
2004	0	0	0	0	62	85	100	100	100	100
2003	10	—	13	10	—	76	87	96	—	—

National Journal Ratings

	2003 LIB	—	2003 CONS		2004 LIB	—	2004 CONS
Economic	41%	—	57%		0%	—	95%
Social	0%	—	95%		0%	—	91%
Foreign	23%	—	71%		24%	—	75%

Key Votes of the 108th Congress

1. Drilling in ANWR	Y	5. DC School Vouchers	Y	9. Ban Same-Sex Marriage	Y
2. Approve Bush Tax Cuts	Y	6. Ban Human Cloning	Y	10. Fund Iraq War	Y
3. Medicare/Rx Bill	N	7. Restrict Gun Liability	Y	11. Bar Cuba Embargo Funds	N
4. Bar Overtime Pay Regs.	N	8. Ban Partial-Birth Abortion	Y	12. Intelligence Reorg.	*

Election Results

2004 general	Charlie Norwood (R)	197,869	(74%)	($905,590)
	Bob Ellis (D)	68,462	(26%)	($113,330)
2004 primary	Charlie Norwood (R)	unopposed		
2002 general	Charlie Norwood (R)	123,313	(73%)	($1,143,213)
	Barry Irwin (D)	45,974	(27%)	($14,404)

Prior Winning Percentages: 2000 (63%); 1998 (60%); 1996 (52%); 1994 (65%)

The People		Race/Ethnic Origin	Ancestry	
Area size:	7,124 sq. mi.	81.2% White	USA: 16.8%	English: 8.1%
Urban population:	34.1%	13.6% Black	Irish: 7.8%	
Rural population:	65.9%	1.2% Asian	**2004 Presidential Vote**	
Pop. 2000:	629,762	0.3% Native Am.	Bush (R) 200,604	(72%)
Median income:	$39,987	0.0% Hawaiian	Kerry (D) 75,971	(27%)
Poverty status:	11.2%	0.9% Two+ races	Other 1,224	(0%)
Military veterans:	13.9%	0.1% Other	**2000 Presidential Vote**	
		2.6% Hispanic Origin	Bush (R) 141,065	(66%)
			Gore (D) 67,451	(32%)
			Other 4,025	(2%)
			Cook Partisan Voting Index: R +19	
Occupation	Blue collar: 32.8%	White collar: 53.5%	Gray collar: 13.7%	

Northeastern Georgia is a land where the coastal plains and cotton fields yield first to gently rolling hills, then finally near the North Carolina border to the Appalachian Mountains. For most of its history, this has been quiet rural country, with courthouse towns and a few small cities, mostly forgotten by national elites, bypassed even by General Sherman on his march to the sea. But in the last two decades, economic growth has radiated outward from Atlanta and has spread across much of the region. The effects can be seen as far away as the old city of Augusta, on the Savannah River across from South Carolina. Founded in 1735, with an old Cotton Exchange and mansions untouched by Sherman, it is rich in history. It is also a center for newer industries, which are replacing the paper industry and the nuclear industry that has abandoned the Savannah River weapons site over the border in South Carolina. Augusta is the home of the Augusta National Golf Club, the site of the Masters tournament every year, its entrance barely visible off four-lane Washington Road.

The 9th Congressional District of Georgia includes most of the northeast corner of the state, with a few prominent exceptions. It includes most of the Augusta area but not heavily black precincts in Augusta itself and it excludes the liberal enclave of Athens, home of the University of Georgia—both were included in the 12th District by Democratic redistricters to create a new Democratic seat. There are new retiree communities and second-home developments in the mountains in the northern part of the district, and there is rapid growth in its west end, in Walton and Barrow Counties, which are part of metro Atlanta. Barrow was once a sleepy rural county, notable mainly as the home of longtime (1933–71) Senator Richard Russell. Columbia County, next to Augusta, and Oconee County, next to Athens, are particularly affluent and rapidly growing. Voters here prefer traditional values over liberal values; several counties have rejected ballot propositions to end prohibition of alcohol. This is an overwhelmingly Republican district, in national politics and, since 2002, in state elections as well.

The congressman from the 9th District is Charlie Norwood, a Republican first elected in 1994. Norwood grew up in Valdosta, went to college and dental school, served in the Army in Vietnam and at Fort Gordon, then practiced dentistry in Augusta. He was president of the Georgia Dental Association and also started small businesses—Northwood Tree Nursery and Park Avenue Fabrics. In 1993 he decided to sell his dental practice and run against Congressman Don Johnson, a freshman elected in 1992. Johnson came under scathing criticism when he broke a campaign promise to vote against any tax increase and supported the Clinton budget and tax package in 1993. Norwood's toughest race in 1994 turned out to be the primary; he came from behind to beat Ralph Hudgens in the runoff 51%–49%. When Johnson said he wanted Bill Clinton or Al Gore to visit the 10th District only if "they are coming down to endorse my opponent," Norwood invited Clinton and offered to pay his plane fare. Norwood won 65%–35%, as Johnson took one of the worst lickings of a non-scandal-tarred incumbent in recent history.

Norwood generally has had a conservative voting record, though he is less ideological than other Republicans in the Georgia delegation. In 1997, he emerged from obscurity to become one of the House's most influential members. The reason was PARCA, the Patient Access to Responsible Care Act, regulating health maintenance organizations, which Norwood pushed with great vehemence. In his dental practice, Norwood was in an HMO for three years and decided, "This was no way to go." He assembled 230 co-sponsors, including 90 Republicans. Large businesses and the Chamber of Commerce predicted it would raise insurance costs by 35%. HMOs and the Blues also opposed it. The American Medical Association, American Dental Association and American College of Emergency Physicians came out in favor, as did most Democrats. As momentum grew, Newt Gingrich appointed a Republican working group headed by then-Chief Deputy Whip Dennis Hastert. Norwood judged that he couldn't pass his full bill, and so was ready to compromise. The working group's bill did not include the right to sue, but did permit emergency room visits without previous approval and allowed patients to appeal decisions to an outside arbitrator. The Patient Protection Act passed 216–210; but the Senate did not act. In the 106th Congress, Hastert had become speaker but he could no longer stop the tide once Norwood signed on with senior Democrat John Dingell on the patients' bill of rights. When Norwood-Dingell passed 275–151 in October 1999. Norwood became many Democrats' favorite Republican, and Clinton embraced the bill as "a major victory for every family." Then something unexpected happened. The next year featured all sorts of negotiations: Republican-Democratic, House-Senate, Congress-White House. But the bill remained logjammed. Unwilling to add further burdens to the courts, Republicans correctly gambled that momentum for HMO regulation had waned. Many Democrats moved on to their new health-care issue, prescription drug coverage for seniors. In 2001, his former allies were miffed when Norwood unexpectedly went to the White House and agreed to a deal with George W. Bush on a new version of the bill that permitted employers to limit their liability. House Republicans passed that plan amid cries from Democrats that Norwood had sold out his principles; the Senate Democratic majority had no interest in cutting a deal.

Despite his work on this issue, Norwood's standing has remained strong among leadership Republicans. As chairman of the Workforce Protections panel on the Education and the Workforce Committee, he pressed for tougher enforcement by the Labor Department of union disclosure forms. Norwood latched onto a new issue when he joined foes of illegal immigration in filing a bill requiring local police to deport aliens who have violated immigration law, especially those who are convicted criminals; growing problems with aliens in north Georgia produced an enthusiastic local response. When critics called his CLEAR Act (Clear Law Enforcement for Alien Removal Act) "anti-immigration," Norwood responded that they should "stand up for immigrants, not criminals."

Norwood faced tough electoral competition in 1996 after a court-ordered redistricting made the district 38% black; he won by only 52%–48%. As the champion of PARCA and as an excellent fundraiser, he did not attract such strong competition in later cycles. The new boundaries established for 2002 all but guaranteed easy reelection but in September 2004 Norwood revealed that he had suffered from an incurable lung condition, idiopathic pulmonary fibrosis, since 1998 and was at the top of the list for lung transplant surgery. The pending operation forced him to remain in Washington; the surgery was performed successfully in northern Virginia in October. Despite being unable to return home to campaign, Norwood won 74%–26%. Norwood was able to return to the district in March 2005, though he was unable to shake hands with constituents for fear of infection. He has said he fully expects to seek reelection in 2006; his Democratic opponent could be John Barrow of the 12th District, whose Clarke County base was moved into the 10th in the March 2005 redistricting. But Barrow seems more likely to run in the new 12th District, which includes a larger portion of his old district.

TENTH DISTRICT

Rep. Nathan Deal (R)

Elected 1992, 7th term; b. Aug. 25, 1942, Millen; home, Clermont; Mercer U., B.A. 1964, J.D. 1966; Baptist; married (Sandra).

Military Career: Army, 1966–68.

Elected Office: Hall Cnty. Juvenile Court Judge, 1971–72; GA Senate, 1980–92, Pres. Pro-Tem, 1989–90, 1991–92.

Professional Career: Hall Cnty. Atty., 1966–70; Asst. Dist. Atty., NE Judicial Circuit, 1970–71; Practicing atty., 1971–92.

DC Office: 2133 RHOB, 20515, 202-225-5211; Fax: 202-225-8272; Web site: www.house.gov/deal.

District Offices: Dalton, 706-226-5320; Gainesville, 770-535-2592; Lafayette, 706-638-7042.

Committees: *Energy & Commerce* (7th of 31 R): Commerce, Trade & Consumer Protection; Environment & Hazardous Materials; Health (Chmn.).

Group Ratings

	ADA	ACLU	AFS	LCV	ITIC	NTU	COC	ACU	NTLC	CHC
2004	0	0	0	0	70	78	94	100	97	92
2003	5	—	0	5	—	69	93	88	—	—

National Journal Ratings

	2003 LIB	—	2003 CONS		2004 LIB	—	2004 CONS
Economic	0%	—	91%		0%	—	95%
Social	0%	—	95%		0%	—	91%
Foreign	23%	—	71%		16%	—	84%

Key Votes of the 108th Congress

1. Drilling in ANWR	Y	5. DC School Vouchers	Y	9. Ban Same-Sex Marriage	Y
2. Approve Bush Tax Cuts	Y	6. Ban Human Cloning	Y	10. Fund Iraq War	Y
3. Medicare/Rx Bill	Y	7. Restrict Gun Liability	Y	11. Bar Cuba Embargo Funds	N
4. Bar Overtime Pay Regs.	N	8. Ban Partial-Birth Abortion	Y	12. Intelligence Reorg.	Y

Election Results

2004 general	Nathan Deal (R) .... unopposed	($372,286)
2004 primary	Nathan Deal (R) .... unopposed	
2002 general	Nathan Deal (R) .... unopposed	($307,161)

Prior Winning Percentages: 2000 (75%); 1998 (100%); 1996 (66%); 1994 (58%); 1992 (59%)

The People		Race/Ethnic Origin	Ancestry	
Area size:	3,820 sq. mi.	85.4% White	USA: 17.8%	Irish: 8.3%
Urban population:	52.0%	3.3% Black	English: 7.8%	
Rural population:	48.0%	0.7% Asian	**2004 Presidential Vote**	
Pop. 2000:	629,702	0.3% Native Am.	Bush (R) 197,988	(77%)
Median income:	$42,037	0.0% Hawaiian	Kerry (D) 58,876	(23%)
Poverty status:	10.3%	0.8% Two+ races	Other 1,235	(0%)
Military veterans:	12.2%	0.1% Other	**2000 Presidential Vote**	
		9.4% Hispanic Origin	Bush (R) 134,619	(69%)
			Gore (D) 54,633	(28%)
			Other 4,614	(2%)
			Cook Partisan Voting Index: R +23	

Occupation   Blue collar: 36.9%   White collar: 51.4%   Gray collar: 11.7%

In the last years of the 20th century, the hills and mountains of north Georgia suddenly became one of the boom areas of the South. This was a sharp turn in their history: Since the Cherokee were driven out early in the 19th century this was poor country, where small farmers scratched a living off rocky land. It was devastated by the Civil War, by General Sherman's troops and because so many young men who left to fight for the Confederacy (and a few who left from mountain counties to fight for the Union) never returned. After the war, not much changed for a while. Most communities lived in isolation; roads with hairpin curves led to remote hills where until very recently moonshine stills were more common than summer cabins (the novel *Deliverance* was a thinly-disguised portrait of life along the Coosawatee River in Gilmer and Murray Counties, though the movie was filmed on the Chattooga River in Rabun County). In time, textile mills began springing up along the railroads, poultry production became a big business around Gainesville, and in Dalton the craft tradition of tufted bedspread handiwork was transformed into the world's largest carpet industry, producing 60% of the world's tufted carpet. But these were low-wage industries and all white; there had never been many slaves here and there are few blacks here today.

Since the 1980s, there has been a rush of change. Interstate highways have brought north Georgia in easy range of the world-city of Atlanta; the carpet industry has become more high-tech; small manufacturing is booming, with higher-skill work replacing low-tech mills; vacation and retirement communities have been built in mountains and around lakes. Agribusiness remains important, with huge poultry processors in Hall County around Gainesville. The carpet industry still plays a key economic role, too: The area economy is vulnerable to fluctuations in new construction activity. Once rural counties are now part of the booming ring around Atlanta, and Lake Sidney Lanier, named for the 19th century poet who wrote *Song of the Chattahoochee*, is the most visited lake served by the Army Corps of Engineers. So tight are the labor markets that tens of thousands of Latinos from Texas, Mexico and other Latin countries have come to Dalton, Gainesville and the area around to snap up the jobs the boom is creating; this area now has nearly three times as many Hispanics as blacks.

The 10th Congressional District covers most of northwest Georgia, snaking far enough south to take fast-growing parts of counties on the east edge of metro Atlanta—Gwinnett, Walton, Rockdale. Its northern tier of counties borders North Carolina, Tennessee and Alabama, much of it in the Chattanooga—not the Atlanta—media market. Here are some of the few mountainous parts of Georgia, where within living memory the major product was moonshine whiskey and which in the days of the Democratic Solid South had a robust two-party politics. Today the Democratic history of most of this region is forgotten and this is a solidly Republican area in national and state elections; when north Georgia native and lifelong Democrat Zell Miller backed George W. Bush in 2004, he was only doing as his neighbors do.

The congressman from the 10th District is Nathan Deal, first elected in 1992 as a Democrat, who switched parties and became a Republican in April 1995. Deal grew up in Gainesville, went to Mercer University, then served in the Army from 1966–68; he returned home to practice "street level law," with offices always on the ground floor, and public offices a young lawyer takes as civic duty: Assistant district attorney, juvenile court judge, county attorney. In 1980, at 38, he was elected to the state Senate as a Democrat. Jimmy Carter was still president, the legislature was overwhelmingly Democratic; it would have been quixotic to run as a Republican. A capable legislator, he twice was elected Senate president pro tem. In 1992, when Democrat Ed Jenkins retired from Congress, Deal ran and defeated a Republican abortion opponent with 59% of the vote.

In the House, Deal opposed the new Clinton administration's economic policies, voting against the 1993 budget, for the line-item veto and balanced budget amendment. Many saw Deal as a potential party-switcher, but while campaigning in 1994 he said, "If I choose to switch during the term, I think the honest thing to do is resign and have a special election." He beat an underfunded Republican, but with a slightly lower percentage than two years before. In early 1995, he worked with other Democrats to offer an alternative to the Republicans' welfare reform package. On April 3, Deal said how pleased he was by Democrats' support for that plan. Two days later, he was unhappy with Democrats' opposition to tax cuts and with senior Democrats' criticisms of Clean Water Act revisions he had won on a bipartisan committee vote. On April 10, back home in Gainesville, Deal announced he was a Republican—but he did not resign and run in a special election. He said the national Democratic Party was unwilling to admit it was "out of touch with mainstream America," and "I think that it is important that at some point you get away from the schizophrenia I have had to deal with." Democrats were stunned, and Newt Gingrich was clearly delighted; Deal was rewarded with a seat on the Commerce Committee.

Deal's voting record is mostly conservative. Although he has not been a reflexive Republican, he has not made dramatic breaks from the party line either. He filed a bill to cut up to 10% of congressional salaries if the budget is not balanced. Working with the Federation for American Immigration Reform, he sponsored higher penalties for illegal aliens plus citizenship restrictions on their U.S.-born children, and he opposed the Bush administration's study of legalization of immigrants from Mexico. But he made some accommodation to a district with a rapidly growing Hispanic population by backing increased spending for bilingual education; a majority of school children in Dalton are Hispanic. He also focused on the problems faced by Lake Lanier because of heavy use and Georgia's water shortage, and he won House passage of a $75 million water project for north Georgia, which would include 47 miles of water lines. On the Telecommunications and the Internet Subcommittee, he was the leading proponent of "a la carte" proposals to give cable television subscribers greater choice. He called his plan "a step toward protecting the American family from indecency;" opponents said that the proposal could lead to higher prices and fewer programming choices. In 2005, he accrued enough seniority to become chairman of the Subcommittee on Health at Energy and Commerce.

Deal has not faced serious opposition from either party since 1995, and he has been unopposed the past two cycles.

ELEVENTH DISTRICT

Rep. Phil Gingrey (R)

Elected 2002, 2d term; b. July 10, 1942, Augusta; home, Marietta; GA Inst. of Tech., B.S. 1965, Med. Col. of GA, M.D. 1969; Catholic; married (Billie).

Elected Office: Marietta Schl. Bd., 1993–97; GA Senate, 1998–2002.

Professional Career: Practicing obstetrician, 1976-present.

DC Office: 119 CHOB, 20515, 202-225-2931; Fax: 202-225-2944; Web site: www.house.gov/gingrey/.

District Offices: Carrollton, 770-836-8130; Marietta, 770-429-1776.

Committees: *Rules* (9th of 9 R): Legislative & Budget Process.

Group Ratings

	ADA	ACLU	AFS	LCV	ITIC	NTU	COC	ACU	NTLC	CHC
2004	5	0	0	0	89	72	100	96	92	100
2003	5	—	0	5	—	60	100	88	—	—

National Journal Ratings

	2003 LIB	—	2003 CONS		2004 LIB	—	2004 CONS
Economic	9%	—	84%		15%	—	84%
Social	0%	—	95%		9%	—	85%
Foreign	0%	—	89%		10%	—	86%

Key Votes of the 108th Congress

1. Drilling in ANWR	Y	5. DC School Vouchers	Y	9. Ban Same-Sex Marriage	Y
2. Approve Bush Tax Cuts	Y	6. Ban Human Cloning	Y	10. Fund Iraq War	Y
3. Medicare/Rx Bill	Y	7. Restrict Gun Liability	Y	11. Bar Cuba Embargo Funds	N
4. Bar Overtime Pay Regs.	N	8. Ban Partial-Birth Abortion	Y	12. Intelligence Reorg.	Y

Election Results

2004 general	Phil Gingrey (R)	120,696	(57%)	($2,254,633)
	Rick Crawford (D)	89,591	(43%)	($280,307)
2004 primary	Phil Gingrey (R)	unopposed		
2002 general	Phil Gingrey (R)	69,260	(52%)	($1,819,423)
	Roger Kahn (D)	64,922	(48%)	($3,683,359)

The People		Race/Ethnic Origin	Ancestry	
Area size:	3,750 sq. mi.	61.7% White	USA: 13.7%	Irish: 6.3%
Urban population:	72.3%	28.2% Black	English: 5.7%	
Rural population:	27.7%	1.2% Asian	**2004 Presidential Vote**	
Pop. 2000:	629,730	0.2% Native Am.	Bush (R) 121,610	(55%)
Median income:	$37,582	0.0% Hawaiian	Kerry (D) 97,105	(44%)
Poverty status:	13.8%	1.1% Two+ races	Other 427	(0%)
Military veterans:	12.8%	0.2% Other	**2000 Presidential Vote**	
		7.2% Hispanic Origin	Bush (R) 93,359	(51%)
			Gore (D) 85,542	(47%)
			Other 2,632	(1%)
			Cook Partisan Voting Index: R + 3	

Occupation	Blue collar: 33.4%	White collar: 52.3%	Gray collar: 14.3%

Northwest Georgia, home of the Cherokee Nation before they were sent west in the 1830s on the Trail of Tears, has been manufacturing country for the last century. There were once hundreds of textile mills and dozens of carpet mills located near the supply of natural cotton and along the railroad lines heading southwest at the base of the southern Appalachian chain. The late 19th century propagandists of the New South hailed factories as the vanguard of technological progress, and in fact the factories produced a higher standard of living than farms on this stubborn land. But mill work put scant premium on education or the cultivation of civic virtues and did little to bring in higher-skill white-collar work. All-white hiring practices maintained racial segregation in mostly white north Georgia. Today, this area is developing a different kind of economy, as metro Atlanta spreads out highways north and west into what used to be mill towns. Floyd County is home to an auto-parts manufacturing cluster; places like the textile mill town of LaGrange or the carpet mill town of Rome are seeing change as well, as Latino immigrants have become a major part of the mill work force.

The 11th Congressional District of Georgia includes much of this part of the state, taking in small industrial towns and rural cotton, poultry and cattle-producing areas and a cluster of older suburbs around Atlanta. It stretches from Rome in the north to the outer reaches of Columbus in the south (which, like Augusta, Macon, Savannah and Valdosta, is divided among districts). The 11th includes part of Bartow County, enough to include the Democratic stronghold of Cartersville, and has a tentacle that extends past fast-growing subdivisions into parts of central and south Cobb County near I-285 just west of Atlanta that have many black residents and voted out local Republicans in 2004. This slice of the district includes most of Marietta, where Lockheed Martin builds the F-22 Raptor and the C-130 cargo plane. Directly west of Atlanta is Carrollton, once the home of an untenured West Georgia College professor who in his third try became a Republican congressman: Newt Gingrich. The 11th also includes heavily black Meriwether County, home of Warm Springs, where Franklin Roosevelt recuperated from polio in the 1920s and died in April 1945. The boundaries here are contorted, drawn with an eye to political advantage by Democratic redistricters, and an affront to the notions of compactness or communities of interest. Northwest Georgia generally is Republican, but the redistricters were careful to exclude the most heavily Republican areas in metro Atlanta suburbs, and to add to the district Democratic areas, like south Cobb County and Meriwether County. The result is a district that is not Democratic, but competitive between the parties. George W. Bush carried it with 51% in 2000 and 55% in 2004; it still votes Democratic in some state elections. The obvious target of this redistricting was Cobb County-based Republican Congressman Bob Barr, who had represented much of this area since 1994. The controversial Barr decided to run instead in the new 7th District, very little of which he had represented, and lost in the Republican primary to fellow incumbent John Linder.

But the Democrats' redistricting plan failed to achieve its objective here. The congressman from the 11th is Republican Phil Gingrey, a physician first elected in his party's sweep of Georgia in 2002. Gingrey grew up in Augusta, graduated from Georgia Tech, and returned home to attend the Medical College of Georgia. After his medical training in Georgia hospitals, he settled in Marietta, where he set up an obstetrics and gynecology practice and delivered more than 5,200 babies. During his spare time, he served on the local school board, and was chosen as chairman. In 1998, he was elected to the state Senate, where he had a reputation as a staunch social conservative but one who could work with Democrats on other issues.

When Barr decided not to run in the 11th, Gingrey got into the race, and faced tough competition in both the primary and general election. The issue differences were small among the three candidates in the Republican primary. Gingrey, who is Catholic, styled himself as the only native Georgian. Cecil Staton, an ordained Baptist minister, vowed to view all legislation from the perspective of the traditional family. Barr supported Bob Herriott, a pilot for Delta Airlines. In the primary, Gingrey won 40% of the vote to 32% for Staton and 28% for Herriott. The bitter September runoff revolved around their respective religions and allegations by Staton that Gingrey supported homosexual causes. Voters who knew Gingrey from his state Senate tenure didn't buy it; he won 64%–36%, carrying every county. The Democrats, meanwhile, had their own brawl featuring former Congressman (1983–1995) Buddy Darden, and Roger Kahn, a millionaire beer distributor who in 2000 lost to Barr 55%–45%. Kahn was a good friend of House Speaker Tom Murphy, and Darden was close to Governor Roy Barnes; by the end of 2002, all four had been defeated. Darden was the first one out, losing 52%–48%. The general election was another negative contest. Kahn accused Gingrey of seeking special favors for cocaine-dealing felons and violent criminals who had assaulted police officers. He spent $2.8 million from his own pocket, and complained that national Democrats did not give him more help. Spending $600,000 of his own money, Gingrey portrayed Kahn as a wealthy liquor distributor posing as a modest farmer. With a boost from the Georgia Republican tide and the National Republican Congressional Committee, Gingrey won 52%–48%.

In the House, Gingrey got seats on the Armed Services and Education Committees and became an active member of the majority. In May 2003, the House passed his bill authorizing funding to agencies that aid runaway and homeless youths; it also funded George W. Bush's initiative to create maternal group homes. After Bush signed it into law in October, Gingrey claimed he was the first freshman that year to get substantive legislation passed. During a pre-Christmas visit to Iraq, he explored ways to improve training and equipment to protect troops against insurgent attacks. He filed a bill to reduce reporting requirements for federally licensed firearm dealers. In dozens of local town hall meetings, he enthusiastically supported the new prescription drug benefit for seniors, which he said should end "the days of forgoing, rationing and splitting pills." He sought and failed to get a seat on the Ways and Means Committee at the start of the 109th Congress but got a seat on the Rules Committee.

Democrats claimed they would seriously contest Gingrey in 2004 but he had an easier than expected reelection. He raised $2.3 million, much of it from the medical community. The campaign of his opponent, conservative Democrat Rick Crawford, failed to impress national Democrats. Gingrey won 57%–43%, and in Bartow, Carroll and Floyd Counties raised his percentage from 68% to 70%. But he lost Cobb County 52%–48%, evidently because of the increased number of black voters there. The Republican-controlled redistricting in early 2005 was designed, in part, to shore up Gingrey by giving him all of Bartow County. With the loss of much of south Cobb County and a reduction in his district's black population from 28% to 12%, Gingrey may be immune from another serious Democratic challenge.

TWELFTH DISTRICT

Rep. John Barrow (D)

Elected 2004, 1st term; b. Oct. 31, 1955, Athens; home, Athens; U. of GA, B.A. 1976, Harvard Law Schl., J.D. 1979; Baptist; married (Victoria).

Elected Office: Athens-Clarke City-Co. comm., 1990–2004.

Professional Career: Practicing atty., 1981–2004.

DC Office: 226 CHOB, 20515, 202-225-2823; Fax: 202-225-3377; Web site: www.house.gov/barrow.

District Offices: Athens, 706-613-3232; Augusta, 706-722-4494; Savannah, 912-354-7282.

Committees: *Agriculture* (16th of 21 D): General Farm Commodities & Risk Management; Livestock & Horticulture; Specialty Crops & Foreign Agriculture Programs. *Education & the Workforce* (22d of 22 D): 21st Century Competitiveness; Workforce Protections. *Small Business* (13th of 15 D): Rural Enterprises, Agriculture & Technology (RMM); Workforce, Empowerment & Government Programs.

Group Ratings and Key Votes: Newly Elected

Election Results

2004 general	John Barrow (D)	113,036	(52%)	($1,866,177)
	Max Burns (R)	105,132	(48%)	($2,798,725)
2004 primary	John Barrow (D)	28,110	(51%)	
	Doug Haines (D)	15,808	(29%)	
	Tony Center (D)	8,122	(15%)	
	Caine Cortellino (D)	2,585	(5%)	
2002 general	Max Burns (R)	77,479	(55%)	($925,706)
	Charles Walker (D)	62,904	(45%)	($1,120,201)

The People		Race/Ethnic Origin	Ancestry	
Area size:	5,265 sq. mi.	51.9% White	USA: 8.8%	Irish: 5.8%
Urban population:	74.5%	42.3% Black	English: 5.8%	
Rural population:	25.5%	1.4% Asian	**2004 Presidential Vote**	
Pop. 2000:	629,735	0.2% Native Am.	Kerry (D) 120,563	(54%)
Median income:	$31,108	0.1% Hawaiian	Bush (R) 103,295	(46%)
Poverty status:	21.7%	1.1% Two+ races	Other 698	(0%)
Military veterans:	13.5%	0.1% Other	**2000 Presidential Vote**	
		2.9% Hispanic Origin	Gore (D) 95,845	(54%)
			Bush (R) 80,665	(45%)
			Other 2,636	(1%)
			Cook Partisan Voting Index: D + 5	

Occupation	Blue collar: 28.0%	White collar: 53.6%	Gray collar: 18.4%

In Georgia, the focus is usually on Atlanta. But Georgia also has some gracious smaller cities, with roots deep in the past. One is Savannah, the state's first capital, which by the 1830s was one of America's booming cotton ports; it languished after the Civil War, living off paper mills and chemical plants in the 20th century, while impoverished blacks on the islands a few miles away still spoke Gullah dialects. Then, a few decades ago, preservationists started restoring houses and churches on the grid punctuated by 24 squares that James Oglethorpe had laid out more than 200 years before. Today Savannah is one of the most graciously preserved cities in the country, and a major tourism mecca thanks to the popularity of John Berendt's *Midnight in the Garden of Good and Evil*, a somewhat-based-on-facts story of eccentricity and murder on the bestseller lists for four years in the 1990s. The city actively competes with neighboring—and equally well-preserved—Charleston, South Carolina, not only for tourists but for shipping. Another such city is Augusta, upriver on the Savannah River, founded in 1735 as a fur-trading post, home of the Medical College of Georgia since 1835 and boyhood home of President Woodrow Wilson, with its own Cotton Exchange and Riverwalk. A third such city is Athens, on the smaller Oconee River, site of the gracious campus of the University of Georgia since 1801 and home to the rock bands R.E.M. and the B-52s, graceful Greek Revival mansions, boxwood gardens and magnolias.

The 12th Congressional District of Georgia, newly created by the Democratic redistricting of 2001, combines almost all of Savannah (but only some of its suburbs), four-fifths of Augusta (but not much of its suburbs) and all of Athens into a long slim district that extends some 230 miles. The 12th is sometimes referred to as Georgia's "higher education district"—because nearly a dozen universities and colleges are concentrated within its boundaries. It is two or three counties deep along the Savannah River from Savannah to Augusta, then runs northwest in a narrowing finger from Augusta to Athens. There is, of course, a political explanation for the shape of the district. The district carefully excludes the heavily Republican suburbs of Savannah's Chatham County (in the 1st District), the heavily Republican suburbs of Augusta in Columbia County and heavily Republican Oconee County outside Athens (in the 9th District). It also carefully excludes most of Hunter Army Airfield near Savannah and Fort Gordon near Augusta. It contains the Depression-wracked farm country near Augusta that Erskine Caldwell chronicled in his scandalous bestseller, *Tobacco Road*; the titular dirt thoroughfare, which led to a small port on the Savannah River, is now paved and passes a nondescript mix of residential and commercial areas. White areas were excluded and black areas included so that the population of the district was 42% black. It was designed to be safely Democratic; it voted for Al Gore in 2000 and John Kerry in 2004.

The congressman from the 12th District is a Democrat, John Barrow, who was one of only two successful challengers to House Republican incumbents in 2004. Barrow claims seven generations of Georgians in his family; his father handled school desegregation cases as a Superior Court judge in the Athens area. A graduate of the University of Georgia and Harvard Law School, Barrow became a trial lawyer who made his name in local politics by winning four terms as an Athens-Clarke city-county commissioner. In 2004 he decided to run against Republican Max Burns, who had won an upset victory in the district in 2002. Burns won by waging a vigorous campaign but he also had help from the Democrats. The district had been designed by state Senate Majority Leader Charles Walker to elect his son, Charles "Champ" Walker Jr., from Augusta. As the campaign progressed, young Walker's credibility eroded after local newspapers reported a past littered with failed business ventures and run-ins with the law. Burns said that the district needed "honest and ethical representation." On Election Day, Burns beat Champ Walker 55%–45% and Charles Walker Sr. lost his legislative seat. Burns was an obvious Democratic target in 2004, and House Republican leaders gave him all the help they could.

Barrow had to work hard to win. Although most Democratic voters here are black, all four candidates in the Democratic primary were white. Barrow raised more than $700,000 and, with the endorsements of former Senator Max Cleland, the Sierra Club and the Georgia AFL-CIO, was able to extend his appeal beyond his home base. He won 51% of the vote and all 14 counties, enough to avoid a runoff. In the general election, Barrow focused on Burns's support of a national retail sales tax to replace the income tax; he attacked the proposal as a tax increase that "just doesn't add up for Georgia families," and labeled it "the Max Tax." Burns replied that Barrow distorted the proposal; he called Barrow a "liberal trial attorney" controlled by "Atlanta party bosses," who "would let France determine our national defense policy." Barrow criticized Burns for supporting the Medicare prescription drug bill and ran an ad that claimed Burns had cut funding for Georgia's rural hospitals. Barrow also mocked Burns for inaccurately claiming he helped create the Homeland Security Department. He distanced himself from John Kerry and the national Democratic party. Burns sought to turn the focus to same-sex marriage, an issue on which Barrow struggled to find a consistent position; this debate occurred against the backdrop of a proposed state constitutional amendment banning same-sex marriage. The amendment was approved by 76%–24% on the November ballot; it passed by only 52%–48% in Clarke County, the closest margin in any of the state's 159 counties.

But this was not enough to save Burns: Barrow won 52%–48%. Burns ran well in rural areas, winning eight of the 14 counties, but Barrow won big margins among the heavily black electorates in the three counties which cast two-thirds of the district's votes—62% in Richmond, 58% in Chatham, and 58% in Clarke. Another local Democratic victory: Charles Walker Sr., while under federal indictment, regained his Senate seat. But Barrow's political life was made more difficult by the March 2005 redistricting, which moved his Clarke County base into the heavily Republican 10th District. Barrow said that he would run in the new district that included the largest part of his former district, which would place him in the new 12th. He could face challenges from two former House members. Democrat Denise Majette, who served one term in an Atlanta-area seat before her unsuccessful Senate bid in 2004, raised the possibility of a primary challenge. And Burns announced in May 2005 that he would run for the seat, even though it is more Democratic than the district that he represented for two years.

THIRTEENTH DISTRICT

Rep. David Scott (D)

Elected 2002, 2d term; b. June 27, 1946, Aynor, SC; home, Atlanta; FLA&M U., B.A. 1967, U. of PA, M.B.A. 1969; Baptist; married (Alfredia).

Elected Office: GA House of Reps., 1974–82; GA Senate, 1982–2002.

Professional Career: Founder and Pres., Dayn-Mark Advertising, 1979-present.

DC Office: 417 CHOB, 20515, 202-225-2939; Fax: 202-225-4628; Web site: house.gov/davidscott.

District Office: Jonesboro, 770-210-5073.

Committees: *Agriculture* (8th of 21 D): General Farm Commodities & Risk Management; Livestock & Horticulture; Specialty Crops & Foreign Agriculture Programs. *Financial Services* (26th of 32 D): Capital Markets, Insurance & Government Sponsored Enterprises; Housing & Community Opportunity; Oversight & Investigations.

Group Ratings

	ADA	ACLU	AFS	LCV	ITIC	NTU	COC	ACU	NTLC	CHC
2004	75	65	86	64	70	19	78	30	11	33
2003	75	—	88	50	—	23	60	36	—	—

National Journal Ratings

	2003 LIB	—	2003 CONS		2004 LIB	—	2004 CONS
Economic	55%	—	45%		58%	—	42%
Social	67%	—	33%		66%	—	34%
Foreign	61%	—	37%		62%	—	36%

Key Votes of the 108th Congress

1. Drilling in ANWR	N	5. DC School Vouchers	N	9. Ban Same-Sex Marriage	Y
2. Approve Bush Tax Cuts	Y	6. Ban Human Cloning	N	10. Fund Iraq War	Y
3. Medicare/Rx Bill	Y	7. Restrict Gun Liability	Y	11. Bar Cuba Embargo Funds	Y
4. Bar Overtime Pay Regs.	Y	8. Ban Partial-Birth Abortion	N	12. Intelligence Reorg.	Y

Election Results

2004 general	David Scott (D)	unopposed		($980,333)
2004 primary	David Scott (D)	42,498	(84%)	
	William Ogletree (D)	8,340	(16%)	
2002 general	David Scott (D)	70,011	(60%)	($1,505,191)
	Clay Cox (R)	47,405	(40%)	($639,841)

The People		Race/Ethnic Origin	Ancestry	
Area size:	784 sq. mi.	42.1% White	USA: 8.2%	Irish: 5.1%
Urban population:	92.1%	40.7% Black	English: 4.6%	
Rural population:	7.9%	5.1% Asian	**2004 Presidential Vote**	
Pop. 2000:	629,732	0.2% Native Am.	Kerry (D) 136,912	(64%)
Median income:	$43,429	0.0% Hawaiian	Bush (R) 76,327	(36%)
Poverty status:	11.2%	1.5% Two+ races	Other 123	(0%)
Military veterans:	12.4%	0.2% Other	**2000 Presidential Vote**	
		10.2% Hispanic Origin	Gore (D) 91,895	(57%)
			Bush (R) 66,576	(41%)
			Other 3,392	(2%)
			Cook Partisan Voting Index: D +12	
Occupation	Blue collar: 29.6%	White collar: 55.9%	Gray collar: 14.5%	

Many great landmarks of the civil rights movements, the headquarters of major civil rights organizations and the campuses of six historically black colleges are all in the central city of Atlanta. The city's cohesive and talented black community, more than any other, provided the leadership and inspiration for the civil rights movement which changed America so much for the better. In the 1960s, Atlanta's blacks were clustered in ghetto neighborhoods on the south and west side of the city; the north side of Atlanta and the suburbs in every direction were heavily or entirely white. Today, a long generation after the great days of the civil rights movement, blacks have moved outward from Atlanta in almost all directions in one of the nation's fastest-growing metro areas. The central city of Atlanta has an increasing white percentage, as whites move into affluent Buckhead and the thriving communities of Midtown Atlanta, while the crime-ridden ghettoes in south and west Atlanta lose population. But this is a story not of failure but of success: members of metro Atlanta's thriving black middle class have been moving out to many other parts of the Atlanta metro area—to south DeKalb County to the east, to Clayton County directly south of the city and Hartsfield-Jackson Atlanta International Airport, to southwest Fulton County outside Atlanta, to eastern Cobb and Douglas Counties to the west.

The 13th Congressional District of Georgia, newly created in the 2001 redistricting, can rightfully be depicted as the most geographically grotesque district in the country. Yet it can be defended as a collection of areas into which Atlanta area blacks have been moving or are likely to be moving in the next 10 years—Sweet Auburn marching south to the suburbs. Its nucleus is Clayton County, heavily dependent on the airport and almost all of which is in the district: a county that voted for George Wallace in 1968 but now has the highest black percentage of any metro Atlanta county. It includes southwest Fulton County and small slices of south Fulton and DeKalb Counties. Then there are the tentacles that thrash out in several directions. One extends south from Clayton into Spalding County to black neighborhoods in the old county seat of Griffin. Another extends southeast along I-75 into the middle of Henry and Butts Counties. To the east, another tentacle moves to include most of Rockdale County and east into Newton County and northward to Walton County. From Rockdale, another particularly tenuous tentacle hugs the Gwinnett County line and then heads northeast along the I-85 and Buford Highway low-income corridor in high-income Gwinnett County. The result is a district whose perimeter might well be as long as the combined boundaries of the state of Georgia and whose lines an area freeway driver may cross over a dozen times a day. In 2000, the population of this district was 41% black and 10% Hispanic; the latter is the highest percentage in any Georgia district. This is a Democratic district that voted for Al Gore in 2000 and John Kerry in 2004.

The congressman from the 13th District is David Scott, a Democrat first elected in 2002. Born in rural South Carolina, he grew up around the country—in Scranton, Pennsylvania, Scarsdale, New York, and Daytona Beach, Florida. He graduated from Florida A&M and the Wharton School of Finance. He was elected to the Georgia House in 1974 and to the Georgia Senate in 1982; there he chaired the Rules Committee. Since 1979 he has owned the Dayn-Mark Advertising Company, which creates and places radio, television and print advertising.

In 2002 Scott ran for the new 13th District seat, though he lived near Midtown Atlanta. It was obvious that the primary would be decisive in this heavily Democratic district. Four other Democrats ran, the best known of whom was former state party chairman David Worley, who nearly defeated Newt Gingrich in 1990. Scott, however, was far more familiar to most voters, after more than a quarter-century in the legislature. His brother-in-law Hank Aaron, baseball's home run king and an Atlanta icon, co-chaired his campaign. Scott brought his advertising expertise to the campaign, plastering the Interstates with eye-catching billboards. His chief competitors, Worley and state Senator Greg Hecht of Clayton County, were both white, and ran ads against each other; racial appeals seem to have played little part in the campaign. Scott won the primary without a runoff, with 54% of the vote and at least 50% in every county but one. The son of a minister and grandson of a deacon, Scott credited God and said that "a divine hand worked with us." He won the general election 60%–40%—not a huge margin, but a decisive one. He lost five counties in the eastern part of the district by narrow margins, while carrying Clayton County, which cast 36% of the votes, by a 67%–31%.

In the House, Scott's voting record was far more centrist than that of an Atlanta liberal. His business background and nearly three decades' experience in representing multiracial, multiethnic constituencies were unique credentials to bring to the Congressional Black Caucus and the House. Scott joined the Blue Dogs group of moderate Democrats, and showed no reluctance about going his own way. In May 2003, he was one of seven House Democrats to vote for final passage of the Bush tax cut. In June 2004, he was one of 11 Democrats who angered their party leaders by joining Republicans on a procedural vote in support of the buyout of tobacco farmers, which Scott helped to write before it reached the House floor. He split with most of his party by voting for the constitutional amendment to ban same-sex marriages. On the Financial Services Committee, Scott criticized predatory lenders that exploit would-be homeowners in poor communities but he was reluctant to pass new laws to eliminate favorable interest deals. "There are peculiar issues in each state that are different," he said.

In 2004, Scott encountered a weak opponent in the primary and ran unopposed in the general. Although Scott never faced serious jeopardy from the 2005 redistricting, the result appears to make his district travels easier by making the 13th more compact. The black population of the new seat barely changed and it remains centered in Clayton County, but it lost several of its rural tentacles and it gained south Cobb County.

★ HAWAII ★

Times are suddenly good again in Hawaii. The 1990s were a terrible decade for this island state. Its gross state product declined from 1992 to 1998, the number of jobs peaked in 1991, foreign investment plummeted, bankruptcies zoomed, home sales dropped and welfare caseloads increased. Labor force participation declined as the number of young adults fell and the number of elderly rose: Hawaii seemed to be getting old and tired. The early 1990s recession in California and the decade-long recession in Japan had a devastating effect on the mainstay of Hawaii's economy— tourism. The number of visitors peaked at 7 million in 1990, dropped to 6.1 million in 1993, and did not reach 7 million again until 2000: it was 6.9 million in 2001 and estimated at 6.4 million in 2002: September 11 really hurt. Sugar plantations and the Dole pineapple plantation in Lanai closed down. Agriculture, Hawaii's economic mainstay before tourism, employed just 12,000 Hawaiians in 2000. The military and the federal government have also been important to Hawaii's economy, but the number of military personnel and civilian federal employees fell from 97,800 in 1988 to 67,750 in 2000. But by 2004 Hawaii's economy had come back. Tourism rose back to 6.9 million in 2004, as Japan's economy recovered and the mainland U.S. economy surged. More tourists were from Eastern U.S. (east of the Rockies), and they stayed longer and spent more than Western U.S. tourists; destination weddings and extended family anniversaries became more common. Housing prices zoomed upward—the median sale price was over $500,000 on Maui and just under that on Oahu—and the construction industry boomed. Military cutbacks ended after September 11 and deployments overseas followed. Hawaii's small high-tech sector grew while Silicon Valley contracted. This economic turnaround coincided with a political turnaround, the election of Republican Linda Lingle as governor in 2002 after Democrats had held the office and controlled state government for 40 years. The question now is whether Hawaii can sustain it economic boom and at the same time preserve the defining characteristics that have made Hawaii strong and tolerant in the six decades since Pearl Harbor.

Hawaii was settled only about a thousand years ago by Polynesians who paddled across vast Pacific expanses in small outrigger canoes; when Captain Cook came here in 1776, he found his Maori interpreter from New Zealand could understand Hawaiian. On these geologically young islands, teeming with food and seldom inconvenienced by bad weather, Hawaiians built a fierce civilization, with harsh taboos and cannibalism as well as alluring music and dance. The islands were united politically in 1779 by King Kamehameha I, who ate one of his rivals and maintained the old culture. In 1819, within a year of his death, his consort Kaahumanu outlawed the Hawaiian religious taboos and welcomed the American missionary Hiram Bingham. New England missionaries and their trader cousins came—while British and Russian ships occasionally put into port—and established the predominant culture. By the 1850s, laborers from China, Japan, Portugal and the Philippines streamed in to work the sugar and pineapple plantations. American planters and businessmen bridled at the caprices of the royal family and, in January 1893, with the help of U.S. Marines, ousted Queen Liliuokalani from the Iolani Palace and called on the United States to annex Hawaii. President Grover Cleveland demurred, and Hawaii for five years was a republic; President William McKinley annexed it in July 1898.

This history is a source of regret for some; an *Onipa'a* ceremony remembering Liliuokalani's overthrow was staged by John Waihee, the first governor of Native Hawaiian descent, in January 1993, with the American flag conspicuously absent. Yet Hawaii is a civilization both American and Pacific, which has created a better life for its citizens than almost any other island or native commonwealth. Its ethnic mixing began a century ago when disease reduced the native Hawaiians to 45,000; they shared Liliuokalani's Hawaii with 3,000 Americans, 20,000 Chinese and 25,000 Japanese.

To that Americana, each group has made positive contributions. The Asian migrant laborers brought traditions of hard work, family loyalty and group solidarity that found expression most vividly in the performance of the 442d "Go for Broke" Regimental Combat Team, made up mostly of sons of Japanese immigrants, which became the most decorated unit in U.S. military history. The Yankee spirit has been evident in Hawaii's commercial success and in its attachment to the

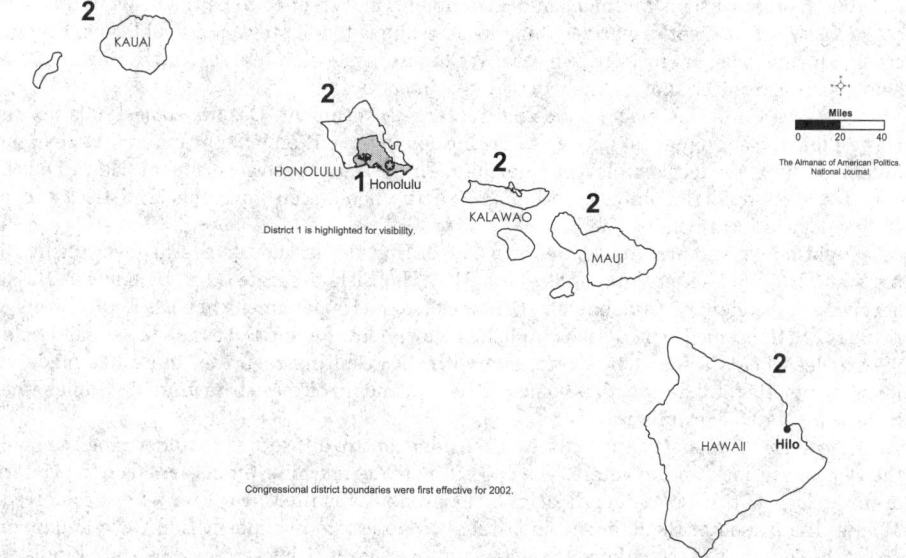

District 1 is highlighted for visibility.

Congressional district boundaries were first effective for 2002.

The Almanac of American Politics
National Journal

rule of Anglo-American law. The Hawaiian spirit is alive in the vitality of the *aloha* ambience, the welcoming of others despite their differences, and a willingness to absorb the teachings of others while maintaining a certain Polynesian attitude toward life. When the Japanese attacked Pearl Harbor in December 1941, no one in Hawaii or on the mainland doubted that this was part of America. Ironically, it was Hawaii's super-American tolerance that inspired segregationist Southern Democrats to block its admission to the Union for years. Today, Hawaiians retain pride in their ethnic heritage—or heritages: About half of non-military weddings are "out" marriages and most babies are of mixed ethnicity. In the 2000 Census, 18% of Hawaiians identified themselves as being of two races and 7% said three or more. Some 23% described themselves as at least partly Native Hawaiian—nearly 225,000 descendants of the 45,000 Native Hawaiians of the mid 19th century. By census category, Hawaii in 2000 was 41% Asian, 23% white, 2% black, 9% Native Hawaiian or Pacific Islander and 7% Hispanic. But those categories seem artificial when looking at Hawaii. Local experts identify Hawaiians by ethnicity and give estimates of the size of each group: Hawaiian 22%, Caucasian 21%, Japanese 18%, Filipino 12%, Chinese 5%. The 2004 NEP exit poll classified the electorate as 42% white, 26% Asian, 10% Latino, 1% black and 22% "other."

Before 1960, Hawaii seemed to be Republican; after all, southern Democrats were blocking statehood and championing racial segregation. John Kennedy carried it in 1960 by just 115 votes. But from 1962 to 2002, its politics was dominated by a Democratic machine which had its beginning in the 1950s, when returning World War II veterans like Daniel Inouye, Spark Matsunaga and George Ariyoshi joined forces with former mainlander John Burns, who as a policeman during the war helped prevent persecution of Japanese Americans. They allied themselves with the then-powerful International Longshoremen's and Warehousemen's Union, and cemented the allegiance of Japanese American voters. The Burns-Inouye machine built on the grievances against the *haole* (a pejorative word for white) owners of the big companies and triumphed. Inouye was elected as a Democrat to the House in 1959 and to the Senate in 1962; Burns was elected governor in 1962, and for 40 years the office was passed down in lineal succession to George Ariyoshi, John Waihee and Benjamin Cayetano—a balanced ticket, of Japanese, Native Hawaiian and Filipino descent. As agriculture and the docks became less important, the ILWU's power waned; it has been replaced by the strongly Democratic public employee unions. Voting has long tended to run along ethnic lines. Japanese Americans, used to working in organizations in unions and government, have tended to be the heart of the Democratic Party; whites, with relatively high incomes, have tended toward Republicans; Filipinos, often in menial jobs, are heavily Democratic; Chinese, somewhat less so; Native Hawaiians, are heavily Democratic but not as likely to be active in politics.

Over the years this machine has built a large government. Despite some 1990s tax cuts, Hawaii had the third highest per capita tax burden in the nation in 2000 and by far the highest number of state and local employees per capita. This is centralized government: Hawaii has five counties (with one, Honolulu, covering 72% of the population), one school district and one statewide health care plan.

Eight public and private entities own 69% of Hawaii's land: The federal government 16%, the state 29%, and six private landowners 24%. The Bishop Estate (Mrs. Bishop was the last surviving descendant of Kamehameha I), now called the Kamehameha Schools Estate, owns 8%. A 1984 U.S. Supreme Court decision upheld a Hawaii law forcing the estate to sell land held in 99-year leaseholds when they expire, and with the resulting cash the estate has made vast investments. Its total net worth is some $10 billion, and its purpose is to fund the Kamehameha Schools for Native Hawaiians.

The sluggish economy, high taxes and insider control all worked to undermine the hold of the Democratic machine on voters. The opposition to the machine, often carried on in primaries or in the form of third party candidacies by longtime Honolulu Mayor Frank Fasi, coalesced in 1998 in the person of Republican Linda Lingle. She lost to incumbent Ben Cayetano by only 50%–49% and in 2000 Republicans made gains in state legislative races. In 2002 Lingle won 52%–47% but union-backed Democrats made gains in both the primary and general elections; they gained more seats in 2004.

Hawaii has great potential. It is still the favorite tourist destination of the Japanese, who throng to the King Kamehameha Hula Competition every June. It still has great potential as a central Pacific emporium—the stability of the American flag and dollar, the heritage of tolerance and openness to diversity that is second to none, the wondrous climate and physical beauty of these islands.

Hawaii may face problems also from the Native Hawaiian sovereignty movement. Consciousness of native ancestry grew in the 1990s: Many more Hawaiians claimed Native Hawaiian ancestry in the 2000 Census than before, partly because of the new option of claiming multiple races. More people are learning the Hawaiian language. The centennials of the overthrow of Queen Liliuokalani (1993) and of U.S. annexation of Hawaii (1998) inspired demonstrations and expressions of bitterness over the end of the Hawaiian kingdom; a Hawaiian who claims he is still living under the pre-1893 constitution filed a lawsuit in the World Court. A state sovereignty commission met for two years and in 1996 sponsored a referendum of Native Hawaiians; 73% of those eligible (with some native blood) voted yes on the question, "Shall the Hawaiian people elect delegates to propose a native Hawaiian government?" The problem is that no one is quite sure what sovereignty means—independence, a commonwealth status like Puerto Rico's, Indian tribal status? In February 2000 the U.S. Supreme Court declared unconstitutional the 1978 Hawaii state constitutional amendment setting up Native-Hawaiian-only elections for the Office of Hawaiian Affairs, which administers a $400 million trust fund. That decision casts doubt on other provisions of the 1978 amendment, including the Hawaiian Homes Commission and the recognition of native gathering rights on private property. The bill granting Native Hawaiians Indian status was passed in the U.S. House in September 2000, but was not acted on by the Senate, and its advocates considered it effectively killed by the election of George W. Bush.

The People		Race/Ethnic Origin			Military veterans: 120,587 (13.1%)	
Pop. 2004 (est):	1,262,840	277,091	22.9%	White	WWII: 17.6%	Korea: 12.0%
Pop. 2000:	1,211,537	20,829	1.7%	Black	Vietnam: 34.5%	Gulf War: 13.2%
Pop. 1990:	1,108,229	494,149	40.8%	Asian	**Most populous cities (2003):**	
Change 1990–2000:	Up 9.3%	2,539	0.2%	Native Am.	1. Honolulu	380,149
% of U.S. total:	0.4%	108,441	9.0%	Hawaiian	2. Hilo CDP	40,759
Pop. rank:	42d of 50	218,700	18.1%	Two+ races	3. Kailua CDP	36,513
Area size:	10,931 sq. mi.	2,089	0.2%	Other	4. Kaneohe CDP	34,970
State Native:	56.9%	87,699	7.2%	Hisp. Origin	5. Waipahu CDP	33,108
Non-citizen:	7.0%	**Ancestry**				
Language		German: 4.6%		Irish: 3.5%	Urban population: 91.6%	
English: 65.7%	Asian: 29.1%	English: 3.4%		Portuguese: 3.2%	Rural population: 8.4%	
Spanish: 2.7%		Italian: 1.4%				

Education		Work Sector		Legislature	
H.S. Grad:	84.6%	Private: 70.9%	Govt: 21.0%	Senate	20 D 5 R
College Grad:	26.2%	Self: 7.6%	Family: 0.4%	House	41 D 10 R
Industry		Unemployment: 5.9%		Legislative Term Limits: No	
Agri: 2.3%	Con: 6.0%	**Household Income**		**Registered Voters**	
Fin: 7.0%	Info: 2.5%	<15k: 12.5%	15-35k: 21.9%	No party registration	
Mfg: 9.8%	Prof: 28.5%	35-50k: 15.7%	50-100k: 33.3%		
Public: 8.1%	Trade: 15.4%	100-150k: 11.1%	>150k: 5.4%		
Other: 20.5%		Median: $49,820			
Occupation		Poverty status: 10.7%			
Blue collar: 17.5%	White collar: 60.3%	**Home Value**			
Gray collar: 22.2%		<50k: 2.3% 50-100k: 7.4% 100-200k: 26.8% 200-300k: 27.6%			
		300-500k: 26.3% >500k: 9.6% Median: $249,300			

Presidential politics   Hawaii's presidential voting over the years has been the product of two, sometimes countervailing, forces. One is the Islands' historic preference for the Democratic party. This helps explain why Hawaii voted Democratic when few other states did in 1980 and 1988. The other is an inclination to support incumbents in a state that takes patriotism very seriously, in part because the patriotism of so many of its citizens was once unjustly questioned and in part because, in these heavily fortified Pacific islands, foreign threats may seem more menacing. This helps explain why Hawaii supported Ronald Reagan solidly in 1984 and came close to voting for Gerald Ford in 1976, though it wasn't nearly enough to help George

2004 Presidential Vote
Kerry (D) 231,708   (54%)
Bush (R) 194,191   (45%)
Cobb (Green) 1,737   (0%)
Other 1,377   (0%)

2000 Presidential Vote
Gore (D) 205,286   (56%)
Bush (R) 137,845   (37%)
Nader (Green) 21,623   (6%)
Other 3,197   (1%)

H. W. Bush in 1992: Ross Perot's military background, and the presence of Hawaiian Orson Swindle among his top leaders, gave him 14% and helped Bill Clinton carry Hawaii 48%–37%. In 1996 and 2000, as in 1968 and 1980, both those forces were moving in the same direction, and Hawaii voted 57%–32% for Clinton and 56%–37% for Al Gore.

In 2004, Hawaii's two countervailing forces were in tension and suddenly, in late October, this state which had given the Democrat a 19% majority four years before and which had seen campaign ads only on national cable shows, was a battleground state. The *Honolulu Star-Bulletin* and the *Honolulu Advertiser* both ran polls showing the state a dead heat. The polls and attendant reporting suggested that Filipino and Japanese Americans, usually heavily Democratic, were leaning toward the Commander-in-Chief. On October 29 Al Gore appeared at a Filipino concert in Kalihi and, well briefed, noted that John Kerry favored higher benefits for Filipino World War II veterans and supported a Native Hawaiian federal recognition bill that would create a process for sovereignty. Kerry gave satellite TV interviews, Bill Clinton was interviewed by four Hawaii TV reporters and Democratic National Chairman Terry McAuliffe held a conference call with Hawaii reporters. Governor Linda Lingle stepped up her campaigning for George W. Bush. On October 31 Dick Cheney flew into Honolulu at 10 p.m. "I was in the neighborhood and I thought I'd stop by and say, 'Aloha,'" he said (actually, he flew 8,270 miles to make the appearance). "Some candidates may take Hawaii for granted—President Bush and I take it seriously." He left two hours after he arrived. No presidential or vice presidential nominee had campaigned in Hawaii since Richard Nixon did in 1960 to keep his pledge to campaign in all 50 states. Now there was a battle for Hawaii's four electoral votes.

It was a battle Kerry won. The race was closest on Oahu, which Kerry carried by only a 51%–48% margin. He led 60%–39% on Kauai and 61%–38% on Maui and the Big Island for a statewide margin of 54%–45%. This is contrary to the usual pattern (Maui usually votes more Republican than Oahu), and the NEP exit poll showed unusual patterns of support: whites 58%–42% for Kerry, Latinos 54%–46% for Kerry, Asians only 52%–48% for Kerry. Kerry carried all but five precincts on the Big Island, all but one on Kauai and all but two on Maui. On Oahu, Bush carried the affluent Kahala and Koko Head areas, but ran behind on the Windward Coast where Republicans usually do best in legislative races. Instead he carried most of Oahu west of Honolulu, places like Aiea, Waipahu, Wahiawa, Ewa and Kapolei, around the big military bases of Pearl Harbor and Schofield Barracks, areas that voted mostly for Democrats in the legislative races.

Hawaii chooses presidential delegates by caucus. Sometimes insurgent candidates have been able to swamp thinly-attended meetings and win, as Jesse Jackson and Pat Robertson did in 1988. Between 1992 and 2000, frontrunners won. In 2004 Dennis Kucinich campaigned twice in the state and two days before the caucus attracted a crowd of 200 in a Honolulu theater. Fewer than 4,000 appeared at the caucus, and the preference poll gave John Kerry 46% and Kucinich 30%; Kerry got 12 delegates and Kucinich 8.

Congressional districting

109th Congress Lineup
2 D
108th Congress Lineup
2 D

Hawaii has two congressional districts: The 1st includes urban Honolulu (city elections now cover all of Oahu) and extends westward to Pearl Harbor and the rural area beyond; the 2d includes the rest of Oahu and the Neighbor Islands. Both districts have long elected Democrats and, despite the death of the 2d District's Patsy Mink in September 2002, both continued to do so in 2002, in a 2003 special election and in 2004. The Democratic legislature made minor and politically insignificant changes for 2002.

Governor

Linda Lingle (R)

Elected 2002, term expires Dec. 2006, 1st term; b. June 4, 1953, St. Louis, MO; home, Honolulu; CA St. U. at Northridge, B.A. 1975; Jewish; divorced.

Elected Office: Maui Cnty. Cncl., 1980–90; Mayor, Maui Cnty., 1990–98.

Professional Career: Founder and editor, *Moloka'i Free Press*, 1977–80.

Office: State Capitol, Executive Chambers, Honolulu, 96813, 808-586-0034; Fax: 808-586-0006; Web site: www.hawaii.gov/gov.

Election Results

2002 general	Linda Lingle (R)	197,009	(52%)
	Mazie Hirono (D)	179,647	(47%)
2002 primary	Linda Lingle (R)	70,808	(90%)
	John Carroll (R)	7,616	(10%)
1998 general	Benjamin J. Cayetano (D)	204,206	(50%)
	Linda Lingle (R)	198,952	(49%)
	Other	4,398	(1%)

Linda Lingle is the first woman elected governor of Hawaii and the first Republican elected since 1959. She grew up in the St. Louis area and Los Angeles's San Fernando Valley; after graduating from California State University at Northridge in 1975, she moved to Hawaii, where her father owned a Ford dealership. She worked for the Teamsters and Hotel Workers unions in Honolulu and then founded the *Moloka'i Free Press* on that island, which is part of Maui County. In 1980 she was elected to the Maui Council and for six years represented Molokai and for four more held an at-large seat. She was elected mayor of Maui in 1990 over former Mayor and House Speaker Elmer Carvalho and reelected in 1994 over a 40-year member of the Council.

In 1998 she ran for governor. She hailed what she called "the Maui miracle"—job growth in at least one part of Hawaii—and said, "It's time for a change, and change is about joining the other 49 states with economic revitalization that is taking place across the country." Lingle led in polls throughout the campaign, but incumbent Ben Cayetano appealed to Hawaii's ethnic groups and Democratic tradition. In August, Lingle accused the Cayetano campaign of spreading the false rumor that she is gay (she has been divorced twice). The outcome may have been determined by Lingle's decision to take state matching funds and abide by a $2.7 million spending limit; she was heavily outspent by Cayetano in the last two weeks. Cayetano won 50%–49%.

Lingle immediately set out to run again. She became Republican state chairman, traveled around the state and built an organization much stronger than what she had in 1998; in 2000, Republicans made notable gains in state House seats. She raised plenty of money, much of it from the mainland and changed the mindset in Hawaii that Democratic victories were inevitable. In the meantime, Cayetano struggled with budget problems. In April 2001 teachers in the state's single public school district went out on strike seeking a 22% raise. Prominent Democrats were caught up in scandals. Against this backdrop, Lingle led in the polls from the start. She set out a detailed platform with specific pledges. She was by no means conservative on all issues; she called for 20% of energy to come from renewable sources by 2020 and backed Native Hawaiian groups' claims for some form of sovereignty. She favored parental consent for abortions and a partial-birth abortion ban, but did not oppose abortion rights altogether. But the chief theme of her campaign was change. "We've got to break our reputation as a place where you've got to know someone to get things done."

Meanwhile Democrats were in disarray. The initial party insider favorite, Honolulu Mayor Jeremy Harris, was accused of violating fundraising laws and was ruled by a court to be ineligible to run until he resigned as mayor in March 2002. He suspended his campaign for two months, and then withdrew from the race in May. Lieutenant Governor Mazie Hirono, who had been running for mayor, entered the race for governor. She was part of the ruling Democratic machine, and there were two candidates who were running as outsiders. Then-state Representative Ed Case, a cousin of Steve Case, then head of AOL Time Warner (the Cases are an old Hawaii family), ran as "an independent, moderate, clean candidate who is change-oriented." He said that Hirono was a spear-carrier for the status quo with no plan for meaningful change. Also running was Andy Anderson, a former Republican who lost two previous races for governor and who had also served 20 years in the legislature. Both Case and Anderson were regarded as archenemies by the Democratic machine and the powerful public employees union, which campaigned furiously for Hirono. It was just barely enough. She won the September 21 primary with 41% of the vote to 39% for Case and 18% for Anderson. Democratic turnout was down 8% from 1994, the last year with seriously contested primaries, while Republican turnout, even though Lingle did not have a strong opponent, was up 44%.

Hirono had an appealing life story. She was born in Japan and raised by a single mother who came to Hawaii to escape an abusive husband. As a legislator from 1980 to 1994 she worked for the law that forced big landowners like the Bishop Estate to sell land rather than lease it; as lieutenant governor from 1994 to 2002 she worked to set up a state-owned workmen's comp insurer. When Lingle ran an ad highlighting Hawaii's poor test scores, low rate of job creation and growing poverty, Hirono said that Lingle was "always putting our people down." But Democrats remained on the defensive on corruption and Hirono was far behind Lingle in fundraising. With the Democrats no longer seen as inevitable winners, and after the Harris fundraising charges, many business interests were no longer ponying up for the party that had held the governorship for 40 years. Ethnic balance for once helped Republicans; they had a ticket with a white Caucasian and a Native Hawaiian, Lingle and retired Judge James "Duke" Aiona, while the Democrats had a ticket with two Japanese Americans, Hirono and former state Senator Matt Matsunaga.

Hirono did manage to narrow the gap by appealing to the party loyalties and by now ancient memories that had rallied late victories for Cayetano in 1998 and Waihee in 1986. But it all wasn't quite enough. She won 52%–47%. She carried Oahu, which cast 70% of the vote, 53%–46% and ran only narrowly ahead in Maui, 50%–47%, and the Big Island, 51%–47%; she lost only in Kauai, which cast only 6% of the votes, by 58%–41%.

Lingle proclaimed her governorship a "New Beginning" and held a series of talk-story town meetings around the state, eating stew and rice and listening to citizens' complaints. With Democrats controlling the state Senate 20–5 and the state House 36–15, she had little leverage with the legislature. It put Hawaii in a consortium of six states purchasing prescription drugs, under the label Hawaii Rx Plus. Hawaii reportedly has the highest use of crystal meth of any state; the legislature passed and Lingle signed a law penalizing landlords whose properties are used as "ice houses" and spending $14 million on prevention and education. Because of the large number of convictions Lingle called for a new prison on the Big Island. The legislature did not act on Lingle's calls for changes in workmen's comp and reducing business fees, but she set up a www.eHawaii.gov website to make applying for permits easier. Hawaii has the nation's highest gas prices, and the legislature passed a law capping wholesale prices; Lingle criticized it and claimed it would lead to higher prices, and its effective date was postponed until September 2005. The legislature overrode Lingle's veto of a raise for 23,000 white-collar state employees. Lingle signed a five-year extension of technology tax credits, but resisted spending on the State Private Investment Fund, set up to use $36 million in contingent tax funds as security for bonds to be used to invest in venture capital projects; Hawaii has already spawned something of a high-tech sector. Lingle pushed for the 20/20 bill passed in June 2004, requiring 20% of Hawaii's electricity to be produced from renewable sources by 2020; the current figure was 7%, and the law required steps increases over the years. In September 2004 she signed a bill requiring that 85% of gas sold in Hawaii would have to be 10% ethanol by April 2006; the law created incentives of up to $2 in tax credits and rebates for every $1 invested in ethanol plants which, it was hoped, would use Hawaii sugar to produce the ethanol.

Lingle came to office determined to change education in Hawaii. She called for the creation of seven local school boards, instead of a statewide board, which would require a constitutional amendment, and she called for giving school principals control over 90% of operational money. She also called for allocating money for schools not according to the number of pupils but according to a new formula taking into account special education spending and students' incomes. The legislature rejected the constitutional amendment, but in April 2004 passed a bill with a new spending formula and giving principals power to oversee 70% of operational money. Lingle vetoed it, and asked for five changes; the legislature overrode the veto in May. Lingle also signed a bill creating a new junior kindergarten program for children turning five after August 1. Lingle said she would work on charter schools in 2005.

Not all of Lingle's stands pleased her (few) fellow Republicans. She said Oahu should raise taxes to finance its $2.64 billion light-rail system. In July 2004 she spoke movingly of Hawaii's homeless people, visible in Waikiki and in the Neighbor Islands as well, and called for building 17,000 units of affordable housing in five years; she identified state land as sites for some of the housing, and the legislature gave her $100 million in bonding authority. She supported the Native Hawaiian recognition legislation supported by the Hawaii delegation, made moves to reduce the waiting list of Native Hawaiians applying to live on homestead lands and accelerated payments to the state Office of Hawaiian Affairs from revenues from former kingdom lands. She increased to $4 million state spending on preserving Hawaii's many endangered species and stamping out invasive species. Lingle was disappointed in November 2004 when George W. Bush failed to carry the state and Republicans lost, in some cases by agonizingly small margins, five seats in the state House: Democrats started 2005 with 20–5 and 41–10 majorities in the legislature. But Lingle's popularity in polls remained high and her chances in the 2006 election seemed reasonably good. One possible opponent is Hirono, her 2002 opponent.

Senior Senator

Daniel Inouye (D)

Elected 1962, seat up 2010, 8th term; b. Sept. 7, 1924, Honolulu; home, Honolulu; U. of HI, B.A. 1950, George Washington U., J.D. 1952; United Methodist; married (Margaret).

Military Career: Army, 1943–47 (WWII).

Elected Office: HI House of Reps., 1954–58; HI Senate, 1958–59; U.S. House of Reps., 1959–62.

Professional Career: Honolulu Dpty. Public Prosecutor, 1953–54.

DC Office: 722 HSOB, 20510, 202-224-3934; Fax: 202-224-6747; Web site: inouye.senate.gov.

State Offices: Hilo, 808-935-0844; Honolulu, 808-541-2542; Kauai, 808-245-4611; Kona, 808-935-0844; Maui, 808-242-9702; Molokai, 808-642-0203.

Committees: *Appropriations*: Commerce, Justice & Science; Defense (RMM); Energy & Water; Homeland Security; Labor, Health and Human Services, Education & Related Agencies; Military Construction & Veterans Affairs; State, Foreign Operations & Related Programs. *Commerce, Science & Transportation* (Co-Chmn): Aviation; Fisheries & the Coast Guard; National Ocean Policy Study; Surface Transportation & Merchant Marine (RMM). *Indian Affairs. Rules & Administration.*

Group Ratings

	ADA	ACLU	AFS	LCV	ITIC	NTU	COC	ACU	NTLC	CHC
2004	100	56	100	100	45	7	50	8	6	0
2003	85	—	100	53	—	12	40	11	—	—

National Journal Ratings

	2003 LIB	—	2003 CONS		2004 LIB	—	2004 CONS
Economic	65%	—	34%		79%	—	13%
Social	74%	—	25%		82%	—	0%
Foreign	56%	—	43%		64%	—	34%

Key Votes of the 108th Congress

1. Ban Drilling in ANWR	N	5. Energy Bill	N	9. Ban Same-Sex Marriage	N
2. Approve Bush Tax Cuts	N	6. Support Roe v. Wade	Y	10. Ban Bunker-Buster Bomb	Y
3. Medicare/Rx Bill	N	7. Ban Partial-Birth Abortion	N	11. Fund Iraq War	Y
4. Bar Overtime Pay Regs.	Y	8. Assault Weapons Ban	Y	12. Restrict Missile Defense	Y

Election Results

2004 general	Daniel Inouye (D)	313,629	(76%)	($1,768,886)
	Cam Cavasso (R)	87,172	(21%)	($57,123)
	Other	14,546	(4%)	
2004 primary	Daniel Inouye (D)	157,367	(94%)	
	Brian Evans (D)	8,051	(5%)	
	Other	2,437	(1%)	
1998 general	Daniel Inouye (D)	315,252	(79%)	($1,375,601)
	Crystal Young (R)	70,964	(18%)	
	Other	11,908	(3%)	

Prior Winning Percentages: 1992 (57%); 1986 (74%); 1980 (78%); 1974 (83%); 1968 (83%); 1962 (69%); 1960 House (74%); 1959 House (68%)

The largest figure in Hawaii's public life remains Senator Daniel K. Inouye, who has held elective office here since before Hawaii attained statehood in 1959, and before. Inouye (pronounced *in-NO-ay*) grew up in Honolulu, the son of Japanese immigrants; his ambition was to become a surgeon. He served in the 442d Regimental Combat Team in World War II, in which capacity he earned 15 medals and citations and, in the last days of the war, lost his right arm. Unsure of what to do, recovering in a Michigan veterans' hospital, he asked a Kansas veteran whose right arm had been shattered what his plans were; the man said he was going to law school, would run for the legislature and "when the opportunity presents itself, I am going to Congress": It was Bob Dole. They served together two years in the House and 28 in the Senate. Inouye graduated from the University of Hawaii and George Washington University Law School, then became a leader of a group of young veterans who took over Hawaii's creaking Democratic party. He was elected to the territorial legislature in 1954, the House in 1959, and the Senate in 1962. He was keynoter at the turbulent 1968 Democratic National Convention, a tenacious member of the Senate Watergate Committee in 1973–74 and the first chairman of the Senate Intelligence Committee, in 1976. Inouye believes in the Senate, the Democratic Party, Hawaii, the armed services, and Native Americans—among other things. He is the third most senior member of the Senate, after Robert Byrd and Edward Kennedy. In June 2000 he was awarded the Congressional Medal of Honor.

Inouye is co-chairman of the Senate Commerce Committee, a title that says something about his friendship with Ted Stevens of Alaska, the committee's chairman since January 2005. Inouye and Stevens also serve together on Appropriations, on which they are the second ranking members of their parties; Stevens was chairman until the Republicans' term limits forced him out, and Inouye ranks behind Robert Byrd. They have served together as chairman and ranking member, depending on which one's party is in the majority, on the Defense Appropriations Subcommittee since 1989. These positions give enormous clout to two senators in office since the 1960s from the two states most recently admitted to the Union, both with their own special claims on the federal government; their friendship can be gauged by the fact that Republican Stevens contributed money to Democrat Inouye's campaign. Inouye's voting record has generally been very liberal, but not always. On foreign and defense issues he is close to the center of the Senate. He and Hawaii colleague Daniel Akaka were two of the four Democrats who joined all Republicans in 1998 in seeking to deploy a ballistic missile defense system; the Clinton administration's opposition to deployment was based in part on an intelligence estimate that there will be no missile threat within the next 10 years to the continental 48 states—which seems to exclude Hawaii and Alaska from the "common defense" the Constitution promises. He has opposed the Bush administration also on occasion, as when in January 2003 he and Stevens characterized Defense Secretary Donald Rumsfeld's decision to defer funding for two Army Stryker combat brigades as contrary to laws passed by Congress.

Inouye has long used his seat on Appropriations to fund projects he finds worthy, from his alma mater of George Washington University to Native Hawaiian education. From 1998 to 2003 he steered $1.4 billion to military projects in Hawaii. He helped to persuade the Navy that the *U.S.S. Missouri's* final berth would be at Pearl Harbor and got $4.5 million for the Smithsonian Astrophysical Observatory at Hilo. When asked how he could do that, he said, "I've been in the

Senate 42 years. Unless I'm a real dud, I should have learned something." There are sound military reasons for much of this: Hawaii occupies a forward geographical position, and the U.S. has shut down other facilities in the Pacific since the end of the Cold War. The 2005 defense appropriation contained $496.7 million for Hawaii projects, many of them high-tech: an Army high-tech intelligence center, telemedicine research at Tripler Army Medical Center, the Maui Space Surveillance System, the Pacific Missile Range Facility on Kauai. Inouye has also shown creativity in stitching together a public/private partnership to refurbish Ford Island and the Pearl Harbor area. "It was something that had to be done because public taxpayers' moneys were not available," Inouye explained. It started when Inouye got a provision passed in 1999 allowing the Navy to enter such contracts. It came to fruition in July 2003 with the signing, presided over by Inouye, of a contract by the Navy, Fluor Hawaii and the Hunt Building Company to build what will ultimately be a $650 million project, including Navy housing, office space, restaurants, a museum, commercial developments and training facilities; it would add 2,000 rental units to the tight Oahu real estate market. Inouye may also have inspired the Aloha Stabilization Agreement, a February 2004 project labor agreement between the Hawaii Building and Construction Trades Council and Fluor and Hunt. One can see Inouye is thinking ahead in small legislation, such as the 2004 authorization of a study of establishing a Pacific Region of the Department of Homeland Security, an appropriation amendment passed by voice vote of $20 million to integrate federal coastal and ocean mapping activities.

Like Ted Stevens, Inouye takes a kind of proprietary interest in the public policy of his home state, with a sense of responsibility for its long-term development and character. Seemingly small matters can get Inouye's attention. In 2004, after a court overturned as inconsistent with federal law Hawaii's law prohibiting para-sailing, jet skis and other recreational vessels from waters south of Maui during Humpback whale birthing season, he inserted into the omnibus appropriation a provision authorizing the Hawaii law. He also got $7.2 million for two sugar growers on Kauai and Maui who suffered $18 million in crop damage due to high winds and heavy rainfall.

Inouye chaired the Indian Affairs Committee from 1989–94 and again in 2001, and was moved by the tragic history. Inouye evidently sees many analogies between the condition of mainland Indians and Native Hawaiians. He was a co-sponsor of the 1993 law in which the United States apologized for overthrowing the Hawaiian monarchy. He supported the Hawaiian Homes Commission Act and in 2000 finally secured funding for Native Hawaiians purchasing property in the Home Lands, the 200,000 acres set aside in 1920 for a permanent homeland for Native Hawaiians. On the heated issue of Native Hawaiian sovereignty, some Native Hawaiian activists consider him lukewarm. Since 2000 he has worked with his colleague Daniel Akaka on Native Hawaiian recognition legislation, which has been approved by committee but has never reached the floor and seems likely to be opposed by the Bush administration.

On the Commerce Committee, Inouye was long involved in communications issues and tends to favor government regulation over markets. Like Stevens, he has been a backer of the Universal Service Fund. He and Stevens were successful in October 2004 in preventing the transfer of jurisdiction over TSA and the Coast Guard from Commerce to the Governmental Affairs Committee.

Honolulu is a long two flights from Washington, and Inouye's local influence has varied, but is generally great. He is part of the faction of Hawaii's Democratic party that held the governorship from 1962 to 2002. In 2002 he vigorously supported Lieutenant Governor Mazie Hirono in her nearly successful attempt to extend this 40-year string. He has complained that the Bush administration was not consulting him on Hawaii judicial nominations. Inouye has always been re-elected by wide margins. His greatest trouble came in 1992, when Republican Rick Reed ran an ad with tapes of Inouye's longtime barber, a woman who made charges about events many years before. On Election Day, Inouye won with a much reduced percentage, 57%, to 27% for Reed and 14% for the Green Party's Linda Martin. He was reelected by huge margins in 1998 (79%–18%) and 2004 (76%–21%). In 2004 both he and his colleague Daniel Akaka turned 80, but both said they intended to continue in the Senate. When asked whether Inouye would retire, Congressman Neil Abercrombie said, "May that day not come for many years. Someone will take his position, but not his place." But Democratic legislators did explore the possibility of depriving Republican Governor Linda Lingle of the power to fill a Senate vacancy.

Junior Senator

Daniel Akaka (D)

Appointed May 1990, seat up 2006, 2d full term; b. Sept. 11, 1924, Honolulu; home, Honolulu; U. of HI, B.Ed. 1952, M.A. 1966; Congregationalist; married (Mary Mildred).

Military Career: Army Corps of Engineers, 1945–47 (WWII).

Elected Office: U.S. House of Reps., 1976–90.

Professional Career: Public schl. teacher, principal & admin., 1953–71; Dir., HI Office of Econ. Oppor., 1971–74; Asst., HI Gov. Ariyoshi, 1975–76; Dir., Progressive Neighborhoods Program, 1975–76.

DC Office: 141 HSOB, 20510, 202-224-6361; Fax: 202-224-2126; Web site: akaka.senate.gov.

State Offices: Hilo, 808-935-1114; Honolulu, 808-522-8970.

Committees: *Armed Services:* Airland; Personnel; Readiness & Management Support (RMM). *Energy & Natural Resources:* Energy; National Parks (RMM); Public Lands & Forests. *Ethics (Select). Homeland Security & Governmental Affairs:* Federal Financial Management, Govt. Information & International Security; Investigations (Permanent); Oversight of Govt. Management, the Federal Workforce & the District of Columbia (RMM). *Indian Affairs. Veterans' Affairs* (RMM).

Group Ratings

	ADA	ACLU	AFS	LCV	ITIC	NTU	COC	ACU	NTLC	CHC
2004	95	75	100	100	42	10	29	5	5	0
2003	90	—	100	84	—	16	30	15	—	—

National Journal Ratings

	2003 LIB	—	2003 CONS		2004 LIB	—	2004 CONS
Economic	68%	—	30%		90%	—	7%
Social	79%	—	15%		82%	—	0%
Foreign	79%	—	14%		99%	—	0%

Key Votes of the 108th Congress

1. Ban Drilling in ANWR	N	5. Energy Bill	N	9. Ban Same-Sex Marriage	N
2. Approve Bush Tax Cuts	N	6. Support Roe v. Wade	Y	10. Ban Bunker-Buster Bomb	Y
3. Medicare/Rx Bill	N	7. Ban Partial-Birth Abortion	N	11. Fund Iraq War	Y
4. Bar Overtime Pay Regs.	Y	8. Assault Weapons Ban	Y	12. Restrict Missile Defense	Y

Election Results

2000 general	Daniel Akaka (D)	251,215	(73%)	($428,516)
	John Carroll (R)	84,701	(25%)	($97,407)
	Other	9,707	(3%)	
2000 primary	Daniel Akaka (D)	13,857	(91%)	
	Art P. Reyes (D)	1,317	(9%)	
1994 general	Daniel Akaka (D)	256,189	(72%)	($1,017,872)
	Maria M. Hustace (R)	86,320	(24%)	($29,293)
	Richard O. Rowland (Lib)	14,393	(4%)	

Prior Winning Percentages: 1990 (54%); 1988 House (89%); 1986 House (76%); 1984 House (82%); 1982 House (89%); 1980 House (90%); 1978 House (86%); 1976 House (80%)

Daniel Akaka is the first senator of Native Hawaiian descent and Hawaii's second senator of Chinese descent. Born four days after Daniel Inouye, he served in the Army Corps of Engineers in the 1940s, went to college, taught school and became a principal. In 1971, at 47, he became director of the Hawaii antipoverty program; in 1975, he became an assistant to Governor George Ariyoshi. The next year, when both of Hawaii's congressmen ran for the Senate, he was elected to the House, where he served quietly on the Appropriations Committee. In May 1990, after the death of Senator Spark Matsunaga, Governor John Waihee appointed Akaka to the Senate. He has thus been an integral part of the dominant Democratic organization and a quiet but diligent worker on Hawaii issues for nearly 30 years.

Akaka, though a member of Congress since 1976, is not well known in Washington. "I do much of my work with members in committees," he said. "I do it that way because it works, it's where you find out whether you have heavy opposition, which could cause you to change tactics or not even bring [the issue] up." Akaka has a mostly liberal voting record, somewhat less so on foreign and defense issues; he and Inouye were two of the four Democrats supporting deployment of a ballistic missile defense system in 1998. Hawaii, out in the Pacific, is much more vulnerable to North Korean missiles than the U.S. mainland.

Much of Akaka's time has been spent on the issue of Native Hawaiian sovereignty. He was the sponsor of the 1993 Apology Resolution, signed by Bill Clinton, in which the United States acknowledged as illegal the overthrow of the Kingdom of Hawaii in 1893 and the denial of Native Hawaiians' right to self-determination. In 1998 and 1999 he pushed the Clinton administration to recognize Native Hawaiians as an aboriginal people with whom the U.S. has a special relationship, as it does with Indian tribes. But in February 2000 the U.S. Supreme Court ruled that the Hawaii Constitution provision limiting voting for the Office of Hawaiian Affairs to those of Native Hawaiian descent was unconstitutional racial discrimination; the Clinton administration assertion of a special relationship was rejected. Other lawsuits were brought against OHA activities. In response, in July 2000 Akaka introduced a native recognition bill, which would recognize Native Hawaiians as an indigenous people with a right to self-determination and set up a process for formation of a Native Hawaiian governing body to have, as many Indian tribes do, a government-to-government relationship with the United States. Thanks to the energetic efforts of Congressman Neil Abercrombie, this passed the House in September 2000. But in the Senate some Republicans objected to unanimous consent, and it died there in December. Akaka brought the bill up again in 2001 and it was passed by Inouye's Indian Affairs Committee in July. It had passed the House committee in May 2001, but House Republican leaders refused to bring it to the floor. In the Senate, Akaka had lobbying help from Alaska Native and American Indian groups, but a hold was placed on the bill by a Republican perhaps influenced by the opposition of some Native Hawaiians, who argue that it would make them wards of the government.

In April 2004 the bill, with some changes, was approved by the Indian Affairs Committee, but again faced a hold, apparently by Jon Kyl of Arizona. Akaka tried to attach it to the class action bill in June and July, but Majority Leader Bill Frist would not allow non-germane amendments. Akaka protested, "This we consider a bipartisan bill. Our governor supports it. Our state legislature supports it and the majority of our citizens support it. It is effectively blocked by a few senators who refused to acknowledge Native Hawaiians as an indigenous people." The House Resources Committee voted unanimously for the bill in September. Akaka's colleague Daniel Inouye put it on an appropriation as an amendment. But Kyl was vigorous in his opposition. "Persons of different races, who live together in the same society, would be subject to different legal codes. This would not produce racial reconciliation in Hawaii. Instead, it is a recipe of permanent racial conflict." In October Akaka and Inouye agreed to drop the bill in return for a promise, made by Frist and Kyl as well, that the bill would come to the floor before August 7, 2005.

Other Akaka causes include the 1995 law for a review of World War II service records with a view to awarding higher medals to deserving Asian Americans (under this, Senator Daniel Inouye was awarded the Congressional Medal of Honor in 2000), a law making permanent the waiver of visa requirements from certain countries including Japan (2 million Japanese visit Hawaii every year). He pushed through a doubling of Pu'uhonua O Honauna National Historical Park on the Big Island. He has taken a lead role on the 1989 and 1994 laws to protect whistleblowers in government and in 2001 and 2004 co-sponsored others to overturn what he thought were incorrect court decisions. With Susan Collins, he sponsored the successful move to enhance dental and vision benefits for federal employees; they also sponsored a bill to allow federal employees to switch their investments in the Thrift Savings Plan at any time, not just during open seasons. After disclosure of irregular practices by mutual funds in 2003, Akaka co-sponsored a bill requiring disclosure of brokerage commissions and requiring them to be counted in the expense ratios of funds; it also required that 75% of their boards be independent of management. He approved when the SEC required independent directors in 2004. He and George Allen sponsored a bill for $2 million for economics education in public schools. He was one of the nine senators (Inouye was another) voting against the homeland security bill in November 2002, arguing that it gave the government too much power to compile information about citizens and failed to protect the rights of whistleblowers. He supported oil drilling in the Arctic National Wildlife Refuge, perhaps out of solidarity with colleagues from Alaska, who like Hawaiians often feel resentment that policy is made for their states by mainlanders who have little knowledge and understanding of their needs.

Akaka had one tough election in 1990—indeed the only Senate election in Hawaii that has generated any suspense since 1976. His opponent, Republican Congresswoman Pat Saiki, conceded that Akaka was congenial, but suggested he was ineffective and not too bright. Akaka struck back with ads attacking drugs and his work to end the use of the island of Kahoolawe as a target range. The Democratic organization worked hard; Akaka won 54%–45%. Akaka was reelected by 72%–24% in 1994 and by 73%–25% in 2000. In 2004 he said he expected to run for reelection in 2006, when he turns 82. Akaka hailed the election in 2004 in Illinois of Barack Obama, who was born in Hawaii and spent part of his childhood there. When Obama visited Honolulu Akaka said, "I like to think of him as a member of our delegation."

FIRST DISTRICT

Rep. Neil Abercrombie (D)

Elected 1990, 8th term; b. June 26, 1938, Buffalo, NY; home, Honolulu; Union Col., B.A. 1959, U. of HI, M.A.1964, Ph.D. 1974; no religious affiliation; married (Nancie Caraway).

Elected Office: HI House of Reps., 1974–78; HI Senate, 1978–86; U.S. House of Reps., 1986–87; Honolulu City Cncl., 1988–90.

Professional Career: College prof., 1959–63; Probation Officer, Marin Cnty., CA, 1964–67; Sociologist, 1967–74; Asst. prof., HI Loa Col., 1979–80; Consultant, 1983–87, 1989–90; Asst., HI Superintendent of Educ., 1987–88.

DC Office: 1502 LHOB, 20515, 202-225-2726; Fax: 202-225-4580; Web site: www.house.gov/abercrombie.

District Office: Honolulu, 808-541-2570.

Committees: *Armed Services* (6th of 28 D): Readiness; Tactical Air & Land Forces (RMM). *Resources* (7th of 22 D): Fisheries & Oceans; Forests & Forest Health; National Parks.

Group Ratings

	ADA	ACLU	AFS	LCV	ITIC	NTU	COC	ACU	NTLC	CHC
2004	85	95	86	73	30	9	32	0	5	7
2003	95	—	100	85	—	23	30	12	—	—

National Journal Ratings

	2003 LIB — 2003 CONS	2004 LIB — 2004 CONS
Economic	70% — 30%	74% — 25%
Social	90% — 8%	88% — 0%
Foreign	81% — 17%	91% — 7%

Key Votes of the 108th Congress

1. Drilling in ANWR	Y	5. DC School Vouchers	N	9. Ban Same-Sex Marriage	N
2. Approve Bush Tax Cuts	N	6. Ban Human Cloning	N	10. Fund Iraq War	N
3. Medicare/Rx Bill	N	7. Restrict Gun Liability	N	11. Bar Cuba Embargo Funds	Y
4. Bar Overtime Pay Regs.	Y	8. Ban Partial-Birth Abortion	N	12. Intelligence Reorg.	N

Election Results

2004 general	Neil Abercrombie (D)	128,567	(63%)	($1,055,643)
	Dalton Tanonaka (R)	69,371	(34%)	($213,639)
	Other	6,243	(3%)	
2004 primary	Neil Abercrombie (D)	unopposed		
2002 general	Neil Abercrombie (D)	131,673	(73%)	($673,054)
	Mark Terry (R)	45,032	(25%)	
	Other	4,028	(2%)	

Prior Winning Percentages: 2000 (69%); 1998 (62%); 1996 (50%); 1994 (54%); 1992 (73%); 1990 (60%); 1986 (30%)

The People		Race/Ethnic Origin	Ancestry	
Area size:	326 sq. mi.	17.7% White	German: 3.8%	English: 2.9%
Urban population:	99.3%	1.9% Black	Irish: 2.8%	
Rural population:	0.7%	53.6% Asian	**2004 Presidential Vote**	
Pop. 2000:	606,718	0.1% Native Am.	Kerry (D) 110,702 (53%)	
Median income:	$50,798	6.6% Hawaiian	Bush (R) 99,256 (47%)	
Poverty status:	9.7%	14.4% Two+ races	**2000 Presidential Vote**	
Military veterans:	13.0%	0.2% Other	Gore (D) 100,403 (55%)	
		5.4% Hispanic Origin	Bush (R) 70,674 (39%)	
			Other 10,211 (6%)	
			Cook Partisan Voting Index: D + 7	

Occupation	Blue collar: 15.7%	White collar: 63.8%	Gray collar: 20.5%

Tourists in Honolulu see the airport and adjacent Hickam Air Force Base, the *Arizona* monument in Pearl Harbor, perhaps the downtown with its wondrously Victorian Iolani Palace, and of course Waikiki, with its 40-story hotels rising within a few feet of one another. This is tight-packed Hawaii, between the 3,000-foot Koolau Range and the beaches and harbor, where tropical bungalows and garden apartments house Hawaiians of all incomes. Here are Hawaii's largest shopping centers and its state university; here are neighborhoods where the rich overlook the ocean and neighborhoods where the relatively poor are packed into people-clogged streets. Hawaii's topography also jams cars into just a few freeways and avenues, where traffic slows during rush hour and the *aloha* spirit is sorely tested. For much of the last decade Hawaii's high taxes and high land and utility costs have limited growth, but by 2004 the tourism business was reaching record levels, and the local economy has once again been growing. The University of Hawaii opened a medical school with an Asian-Pacific focus.

All of these areas are in the 1st District of Hawaii. It is mostly built up now, with well-established neighborhoods, and is growing less rapidly than the rest of the state. Politically, the neighborhoods around Honolulu's downtown and the university campus are middle and lower income and usually Democratic. To the west, around the harbor, are many military families in modest neighborhoods who may vote for Democrats but can be attracted to Republicans, including George W. Bush in 2004. To the east, past Waikiki, around Diamond Head and out to the Kahala and Koko Head beach areas, is higher-income territory, often voting for Hawaii Republicans as well as for Bush.

The congressman from the 1st District is Neil Abercrombie, a Democrat with a graying beard who used to sport a ponytail. He has been called an aging hippie but he has bench-pressed 260 pounds in the House gym; he debates with an aggressiveness and bombast tempered by enthusiasm and good humor. After college in upstate New York, he taught school, moved to Hawaii, earned a Ph.D. in American studies, and at various times worked as a waiter, custodian and probation officer. In those years he got to know Illinois Senator Barack Obama's parents before Obama was born. Abercrombie was elected to the Hawaii legislature in 1974 and served 12 years. Abercrombie first came to the House in 1986, when he won a special election, and served only three months; he lost a primary for the full term to Democrat Mufi Hanneman (now mayor of Honolulu) who then lost to Republican Pat Saiki. When she ran for the Senate in 1990, Abercrombie won a three-way primary for the House seat and won the general election easily.

Abercrombie is one of the distinctive and often delightful figures in the House. His voting record is mostly, but not entirely, liberal. He serves on the Armed Services Committee and sees no contradiction between his protests of war, and votes for military spending in Hawaii and elsewhere. But he still gets things done on Armed Services. "I see my work on Armed Services as a fulfillment of my principles and the motivating force of my life. I never opposed the military. . . . It's not about pro-war or anti-war, but how do you keep the peace." As ranking Democrat on the Tactical Air and Land Forces Subcommittee, Abercrombie has helped to get $3 billion in military construction for Hawaii, which became strategically more important with the closing of facilities elsewhere in the Pacific. He convinced Fluor Hawaii and the Hunt Building Company, which signed a 50-year contract to modernize and maintain 7,800 Army housing units, to accept the building trades as bargaining agent. He got a Navy admiral to commit to keeping nuclear submarine jobs in Hawaii, but endorsed a later plan to move some subs to Guam. He also has worked to assure adequate funding for Micronesia and the Marshall Islands 2,500 miles to the southwest in the Pacific.

On other issues Abercrombie is not always predictable. He co-sponsored repeal of the estate tax—there are a lot of small businesses in Hawaii, he said. Despite Hawaii's trade interests, he voted against normal trade relations with China and opposed trade promotion authority. He filed a bill to allow businesses to write off the travel costs of spouses on business trips—Hawaii has lots of hotels. He sought ways to use the Pentagon budget to combat the extinction of Hawaii's endemic animals and plants by invasive species.

In September 2000, he won a surprising victory as House sponsor of a bill to recognize Native Hawaiians as an indigenous people with a right to self-determination. The Senate Indian Affairs Committee, chaired by Daniel Inouye, approved the bill, but some Republicans objected when it was brought to the floor the next month, and the bill died. Since then, the House Republican leadership has not allowed the bill to come to the floor, though the Resources Committee unanimously approved it in September 2004. He sponsored a bill to end racial profiling in the 27 states, including Hawaii, which do not have such laws.

The 1st District is usually solidly Democratic, but in 1994 Abercrombie had serious competition from Orson Swindle, Marine Corps pilot and Vietnam POW, a national leader of Ross Perot's United We Stand America, and later member of the Federal Communications Commission. Swindle charged that Abercrombie was too dovish, but Abercrombie raised more money and won 54%–43%. Swindle ran again in 1996, labeled Abercrombie a far left hippie and called for big spending cuts. Abercrombie narrowly outspent him, and won by only 50%–46%. Since then, he has been reelected by overwhelming margins.

SECOND DISTRICT

Rep. Ed Case (D)

Elected Nov. 2002, 1st full term; b. Sept. 27, 1952, Hilo; home, Honolulu; Williams Col., B.A. 1975, U. of CA Hastings Col. of Law, J.D. 1981; Protestant; married (Audrey).

Elected Office: Manoa Neighborhood Bd., 1985–89; HI House of Reps., 1999–2002, Maj. Ldr., 1999–2000.

Professional Career: Practicing atty., 1983–2002; L.A., Sen. Spark Matsunaga, 1975–78; Clerk, HI Supreme Ct. Chief Justice William Richardson, 1981–82.

DC Office: 115 CHOB, 20515, 202-225-4906; Fax: 202-225-4987; Web site: www.house.gov/case.

District Office: Honolulu, 808-541-1986.

Committees: *Agriculture* (6th of 21 D): Conservation, Credit, Rural Development & Research; Livestock & Horticulture (RMM). *Budget* (13th of 17 D). *Small Business* (8th of 15 D): Regulatory Reform & Oversight; Rural Enterprises, Agriculture & Technology; Tax, Finance & Exports.

Group Ratings

	ADA	ACLU	AFS	LCV	ITIC	NTU	COC	ACU	NTLC	CHC
2004	90	65	88	100	70	19	50	20	17	8
2003	95	—	100	90	—	29	48	24	—	—

National Journal Ratings

	2003 LIB — 2003 CONS		2004 LIB — 2004 CONS	
Economic	64%	35%	61%	38%
Social	84%	13%	64%	35%
Foreign	56%	43%	58%	42%

Key Votes of the 108th Congress

1. Drilling in ANWR	N	5. DC School Vouchers	N	9. Ban Same-Sex Marriage	N
2. Approve Bush Tax Cuts	N	6. Ban Human Cloning	N	10. Fund Iraq War	Y
3. Medicare/Rx Bill	N	7. Restrict Gun Liability	N	11. Bar Cuba Embargo Funds	N
4. Bar Overtime Pay Regs.	Y	8. Ban Partial-Birth Abortion	N	12. Intelligence Reorg.	Y

Election Results

2004 general	Ed Case (D)	133,317	(63%)	($784,823)
	Mike Gabbard (R)	79,072	(37%)	($484,160)
2004 primary	Ed Case (D)	73,705	(95%)	
	John Gentile (D)	4,121	(5%)	
2003 special	Ed Case (D)	33,002	(44%)	($124,973)
	Matt Matsunaga (D)	23,050	(30%)	
	Colleen Hanabusa (D)	6,046	(8%)	
	Barbara Marumoto (R)	4,497	(6%)	
	Bob McDermott (R)	4,298	(6%)	
	Other	4,681	(6%)	
2002 special	Ed Case (D)	23,576	(51%)	
	John Mink (D)	16,624	(36%)	
	John Carroll (R)	1,933	(4%)	
	Other	2,754	(6%)	

The People

Area size:	10,605 sq. mi.
Urban population:	83.8%
Rural population:	16.2%
Pop. 2000:	604,819
Median income:	$48,686
Poverty status:	11.7%
Military veterans:	13.3%

Race/Ethnic Origin

28.0% White
1.5% Black
28.0% Asian
0.3% Native Am.
11.3% Hawaiian
21.7% Two+ races
0.2% Other
9.0% Hispanic Origin

Ancestry

German: 5.4%   Portuguese: 4.2%
Irish: 4.0%

2004 Presidential Vote

Kerry (D)	120,633	(56%)
Bush (R)	94,860	(44%)
Other	1,214	(1%)

2000 Presidential Vote

Gore (D)	104,830	(56%)
Bush (R)	67,118	(36%)
Other	14,577	(8%)

Cook Partisan Voting Index: D+10

Occupation   Blue collar: 19.3%   White collar: 56.7%   Gray collar: 24.0%

The 2d District of Hawaii includes not only the Neighbor Islands but most of Oahu's acreage beyond the old limits of Honolulu. It has Wheeler Army Airfield and the farmlands north of Pearl Harbor, between two jagged chains of mountains that lift the island out of the sea. Over the mountains to the west on Oahu is the Leeward Coast—calm, sultry and lightly populated; over the mountains to the northeast is the Windward Coast with many prosperous and Republican subdivisions in and around Kaneohe and Kailua. The 137 islands have distinct personalities. Hawaii, the Big Island, is the size of Connecticut and boasts huge cattle ranches, the active volcano of Kilauea, which started erupting in 1983 and had not stopped as of early 2005, and Mauna Kea, the highest mountain in the world if you count from its base far under the ocean to the peak; tourists are told that it is bad luck to take pieces of lava home, and many send them back. On the north shore, with heavy rainfall and tropical foliage, is the old port of Hilo and Hawaii's macadamia nut industry; this is a blue-collar Democratic area in a natural wonderland. On the Kona Coast, where there is little rainfall and the landscape is dominated by lava flows, there are retirement condominiums and a higher-income, more Republican population. Maui, favored more by North American than Asian tourists, has dozens of luxury condominiums and vast upscale resorts. Workers are employed chiefly in tourism, the military, social services and agriculture. Kauai, much of which was devastated by Hurricane Iniki in 1992, is the least developed and most agricultural of the main islands; parts of it have the nation's highest rainfall, while others seldom get wet. Its large farm work force—a reminder of what most of Hawaii was like a century ago—makes it the most Democratic of the islands.

The congressman from the 2d District is Ed Case, a Democrat who managed to win two elections after the November 2002 general election and still get sworn in with the new Congress in January 2003. A fourth-generation Hawaiian, his father founded the local chapter of the Association for Retarded Citizens; his mother was a librarian and was elected to the Hawaii School Advisory Council. He is a cousin of former AOL Time-Warner chairman Steve Case. Ed Case attended local schools before venturing to the Mainland, where he graduated from Williams College and Hastings Law School in San Francisco. He spent three years on Capitol Hill as an aide to Senator Spark Matsunaga. After returning home, he became a partner in a Honolulu law firm, where he specialized in land and commercial law. He narrowly lost when he ran for the state House in 1986 and the state Senate in 1988. Finally he was elected to the state House in 1994, where he was majority leader in 1999 and 2000.

The year 2002 was an extraordinarily busy campaign year for Case by any measure. On September 21 he lost the gubernatorial primary to Lieutenant Governor Mazie Hirono by a 41%–39% margin. He ran as a reformer in a state where the dominant Democratic machine, which held the governorship for 40 years, was being buffeted by criticism for overspending and corruption. Then 2d District Congresswoman Patsy Mink, first elected in 1964, defeated in a Senate primary in 1976 and elected again to the House in 1990, died on September 28. State law prohibited changes in the general election ballot after September 26, and so Mink's name remained on the ballot. On November 5 she was posthumously reelected 56%–40% against Republican state Representative Bob McDermott.

This was the first of three elections in two months for this district. Outgoing Governor Ben Cayetano called a special election for November 30 to fill the remaining five weeks of the term. It was a winner-take-all contest, in which 12 Democrats, 13 Republicans and 16 candidates of other parties filed to run. The initial favorite was John Mink, Patsy Mink's widower, who said that he wanted to honor the work of his former wife and keep her office together. Case, running as a reformer with more moderate views on economic and labor issues than other Hawaii Democrats, won a surprising 51% of the votes to John Mink's 36%. Case never took the oath of office for the 107th Congress, but he did accrue seniority over other incoming freshmen. And he was able to run as the incumbent in the January 4 special election to fill Patsy Mink's seat in the 108th Congress. In all, 44 candidates filed to run in this winner-take-all contest. Case's chief opponent was former Democratic state Senator Matt Matsunaga, a son of the late Spark Matsunaga and the Democratic nominee for lieutenant governor in November 2002. Case said that he could support unilateral military action against Iraq only if there was "a clear and present danger" against the United States; Matsunaga ran election-eve ads claiming that Case supported the legalization of marijuana and lower pay for teachers. Case defeated Matsunaga 44%–30%, winning decisively in Kauai, where the Case family has roots, and on the Big Island.

In the House, Case's voting record is near the center of the Democratic Party, a bit more conservative on foreign issues. He enacted a bill to double the size of the Kilauea Point National Wildlife Refuge, which is the habitat for many stream species and water birds. He sought $7 million to fight coqui frogs, a small invasive species that emits a piercing sound and has created a state of emergency on the Big Island. He urged the National Park Service to make repairs at the visitors center of the *USS Arizona* Memorial, which was built on poor soil and is sinking.

In November 2004, Case was opposed by Honolulu councilman Mike Gabbard, who stressed his opposition to same-sex marriages; Case dismissed him as a single-issue candidate and won 63%–37%. After the election, he said that he would not challenge Governor Lingle in 2006, but that he would run for the Senate when one of the seats becomes open; Senators Daniel Inouye and Daniel Akaka turned 80 within four days of each other in September 2004.

★ IDAHO ★

Idaho, with just 1.3 million people, tucked off near the northwest edge of the country, has been an American success story of late. Since 1990 its population has grown by 38%, more than all but four other states, thanks to technological progress and economic creativity. Idaho's growth has tapered off a bit after 2000, but it still has a robust economy. Its biggest businesses are big: J.R. Simplot is one of the nation's largest potato processors; Micron Technology, the state's number one private employer, is a leader in semiconductors; Albertson's is the nation's second largest supermarket chain; Morrison-Knudsen, the huge contractor. And dozens of smaller high-tech and service businesses have sprung up. From California, a few highly publicized liberal entertainment personalities and a much larger number of conservative engineers and entrepreneurs have come to Idaho for a fresh environment and fresh start, clean air and few crowds, and no cumbersome or expensive regulations, where family lifestyles are still prevalent, traditional values respected and traditional rules enforced.

The wilderness is never far away in Idaho, nor is the experience of the first settlers. Towering over the state Capitol in Boise is the vast peak of Shafer Butte, and not far away are impassable mountains of the Frank Church River of No Return Wilderness, the largest wilderness area outside Alaska and the Salmon River, at 425 miles the longest undammed river in the Lower 48. Idaho was the last North American area European pioneers—fur traders—set eyes on. In the 1840s, New England Yankees led by ministers made their way west on the Oregon Trail through southern Idaho. Idaho's northern panhandle, an extension of Washington's Columbia Valley, was first settled by miners seeking gold and silver, then by loggers seeking timber. Mormons moved north from Utah and settled eastern Idaho. But federal water reclamation projects first authorized in 1894 brought the most settlers, and they transformed the barren Snake River Valley into some of the nation's best volcanic soil-enriched farmland, which with its warm days and cool nights proved ideal for the Burbank russet potato. Idaho potatoes are ideal for baked potatoes and frozen french fries, developed and sold on a handshake to McDonald's by J. R. Simplot and the basis of his billion dollar fortune. Fresh in family lore are the people who pioneered this state, built the first towns and farms, established the first churches and schools and became its community leaders. Yet Idaho is also cosmopolitan. It exports potatoes—mostly frozen french fries—across the Pacific Rim, and its high-tech companies have competitors all over the world. If Idaho politicians used to concentrate on water and maintaining irrigation, now they also work to curb Canadian potato imports and South Korean semiconductor subsidies.

Not so long ago Idaho was a state of farms and small towns; Boise, the pleasant state capital, was just the largest of the small towns. Today Idaho is increasingly urbanized. Most of its people live in just five counties, in and around Boise, Idaho Falls, Pocatello and Coeur d'Alene. One-third live in the Boise's Treasure Valley, which has been growing rapidly, with big increases in the towns west of Boise—Eagle, Meridian, Middleton, Nampa. There have been large influxes from California and from Mexico and other parts of Latin America. Idaho's Hispanic population grew by 92% in the 1990s and is now 8% of the total; driver's license exams are given in English, Spanish, Serbo-Croatian, Russian, Arabic and Vietnamese. Here the political trend has been very much toward the Republicans: The newcomers are from Orange County, not San Francisco, and they seek not cultural liberation, but an environment in which they can raise their children in traditional lifestyles.

At the same time, small counties that have depended on mining and grazing have been hurting. But they think of themselves not as downtrodden employees of absentee corporations needing a protective federal government, but as pioneering entrepreneurs who need to get a bloated, bossy federal government off their backs. The federal government owns 62% of Idaho's land, and most Idahoans were furious at how President Bill Clinton's appointees managed it. The Clinton administration's proposal to stop roadbuilding in about one-third of national forest land was bitterly opposed. Federal limitations on grazing on public lands have squeezed cattle ranchers already hurt by declining beef consumption and lower prices. Similarly, potato farmers

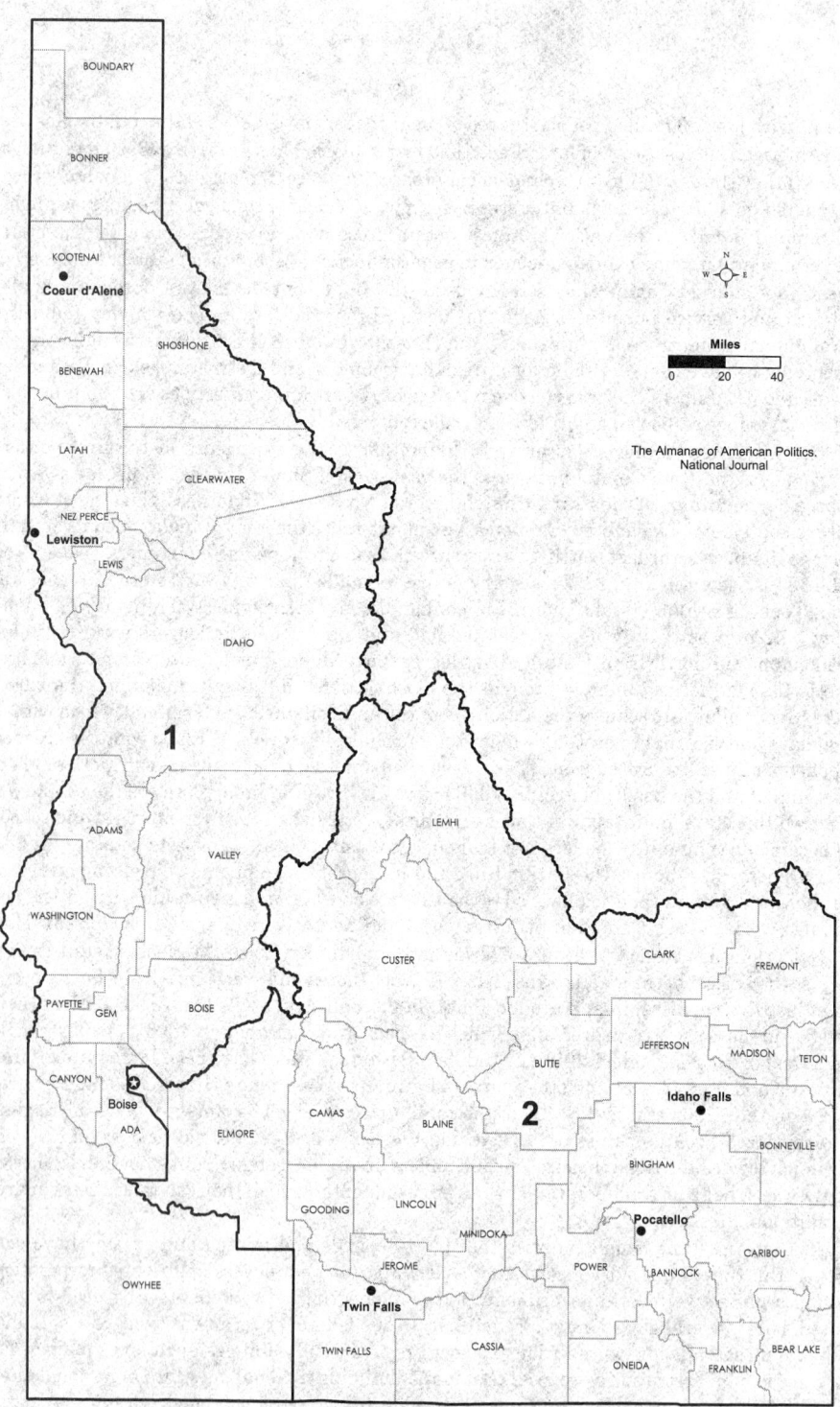

BOUNDARY

BONNER

KOOTENAI
Coeur d'Alene

SHOSHONE

BENEWAH

LATAH

CLEARWATER

NEZ PERCE
Lewiston

LEWIS

IDAHO

1

ADAMS

VALLEY

LEMHI

WASHINGTON

CUSTER

CLARK

FREMONT

JEFFERSON

MADISON

TETON

PAYETTE

GEM

BOISE

BUTTE

CANYON

Boise

ADA

ELMORE

CAMAS

BLAINE

2

Idaho Falls

BONNEVILLE

BINGHAM

GOODING

LINCOLN

MINIDOKA

Pocatello

OWYHEE

JEROME

POWER

BANNOCK

CARIBOU

Twin Falls

TWIN FALLS

CASSIA

BEAR LAKE

ONEIDA

FRANKLIN

N
W   E
S

Miles

0   20   40

The Almanac of American Politics.
National Journal

Congressional district boundaries were first effective for 2002.

dependent on irrigated water were enraged when the *Idaho Statesman* and local environment restriction advocates called for breaching dams on the Snake River to protect salmon.

The political result of all these things was to make a heavily Republican state more Republican. George W. Bush—against breaching the Snake River dams, dubious about the reintroduction of grizzlies and the prohibition of roadbuilding in the national forests, eager to cut taxes on entrepreneurs—carried Idaho by a 67%–28% margin in 2000. Bush reversed some of the Clinton environmental programs, giving national forest regional managers more flexibility in approving commercial use and streamlining approval of forest thinning. But economic problems and state spending cuts produced new issues in 2002, when Republican Governor Dirk Kempthorne was reelected by only 56%–42% and Democrats gained seats in the legislature. In 2004 Bush carried Idaho by 68%–30%, with a slightly higher percentage and a slightly smaller percentage margin than in 2000. Each time he carried every county but Blaine County, with Sun Valley and its rich newcomers. Bush's percentage held steady in Boise's Ada County and fell in Blaine County (perhaps John Kerry's visit to his wife's home in Sun Valley to go skiing helped); he ran stronger in the Snake River Valley but his percentage fell in most rural northern counties, where the environmental policies of the Clinton administration were no longer an irritant.

The People		Race/Ethnic Origin			Military veterans: 136,584 (14.8%)	
Pop. 2004 (est):	1,393,262	1,139,291	88.0%	White	WWII: 18.6%	Korea: 12.6%
Pop. 2000:	1,293,953	4,889	0.4%	Black	Vietnam: 32.3%	Gulf War: 13.5%
Pop. 1990:	1,006,749	11,641	0.9%	Asian	**Most populous cities (2003):**	
Change 1990–2000:	Up 28.5%	15,789	1.2%	Native Am.	1. Boise	190,117
% of U.S. total:	0.5%	1,200	0.1%	Hawaiian	2. Nampa	64,269
Pop. rank:	39th of 50	18,261	1.4%	Two+ races	3. Idaho Falls	51,507
Area size:	83,570 sq. mi.	1,192	0.1%	Other	4. Pocatello	51,009
State Native:	47.2%	101,690	7.9%	Hisp. Origin	5. Meridian	41,127
Non-citizen:	3.3%	**Ancestry**				
Language		German: 13.8%		English: 13.3%	Urban population: 66.4%	
English: 88.4%	Spanish: 7.4%	Irish: 7.3%		USA: 6.1%	Rural population: 33.6%	
Other Eur.: 2.7%		Norwegian: 2.6%				

Education		Work Sector		Legislature	
H.S. Grad:	84.7%	Private: 73.8%	Govt: 16.4%	Senate	28 R 7 D
College Grad:	21.7%	Self: 9.3%	Family: 0.5%	House	57 R 13 D
Industry		Unemployment: 5.7%		Legislative Term Limits: No	
Agri: 5.8%	Con: 8.1%	**Household Income**		**Registered Voters**	
Fin: 5.1%	Info: 2.3%	<15k: 15.8%	15-35k: 30.3%	No party registration	
Mfg: 17.8%	Prof: 27.2%	35-50k: 19.1%	50-100k: 27.6%		
Public: 5.1%	Trade: 16.2%	100-150k: 4.8%	>150k: 2.5%		
Other: 12.5%		Median: $37,572			
Occupation		Poverty status: 11.8%			
Blue collar: 25.0%	White collar: 56.7%	**Home Value**			
Gray collar: 18.3%		<50k: 12.3%	50-100k: 36.3%	100-200k: 39.5%	200-300k: 7.5%
		300-500k: 2.8%	>500k: 1.6%	Median: $102,100	

Presidential politics   Idaho is one of the most Republican states in national politics. George W. Bush and Bob Dole carried it easily; in 1992 Bill Clinton only narrowly beat out Ross Perot for second place, 28%–27%. It was Bush's third best state in both 2000 and 2004. Idaho saw John Kerry, on his visit to Sun Valley, and Dick Cheney, at a Boise fundraiser, in 2004, but not the president. British Prime Minister Tony Blair, in his July 2003 speech to Congress, said that he would like to visit people in Idaho, and Senator Larry Craig complained to Bush that Blair would get there before he did; Bush promised to visit in 2005. Interestingly, Kerry raised almost as much money in Idaho as Bush, most of it from Sun Valley and Boise liberals.

Since 1988, Idaho's presidential primary has been held in late May and has been little noticed elsewhere.

2004 Presidential Vote		
Bush (R)	409,235	(68%)
Kerry (D)	181,098	(30%)
Badnarik (Lib)	3,844	(1%)
Other	4,199	(1%)

2004 Democratic Presidential Primary		
Kerry (D)	25,921	(82%)
None (D)	2,479	(8%)
Kucinich (D)	1,568	(5%)
Sharpton (D)	927	(3%)
LaRouche (D)	590	(2%)

2000 Presidential Vote		
Bush (R)	336,937	(67%)
Gore (D)	138,637	(28%)
Nader (Green)	12,292	(2%)
Other	13,749	(3%)

Congressional districting   Idaho has two congressional districts, which split Boise between them. After the 2000 Census, a bipartisan commission drew new boundaries. It moved the boundary of the districts in Boise about a mile to the west, along Cole Road—a minor and uncontroversial change.

109th Congress Lineup
2 R
108th Congress Lineup
2 R

Governor

Dirk Kempthorne (R)

Elected 1998, term expires Jan. 2007, 2d term; b. Oct. 29, 1951, San Diego, CA; home, Boise; U. of ID, B.A. 1975; Methodist; married (Patricia).

Elected Office: Boise Mayor, 1986–93; U.S. Senate, 1992–98.

Professional Career: Exec. Asst. to Dir., ID Dept. of Public Lands, 1976–78; Exec. V.P., ID Home Builders Assn., 1978–81; Campaign Mgr., Phil Batt for Gov., 1982; ID Public Affairs Mgr., FMC Corp, 1983–86.

Office: P.O. Box 83720, Boise, 83720, 208-334-2100; Fax: 208-334-2175; Web site: www.state.id.us/gov.

Election Results

2002 general	Dirk Kempthorne (R)	231,566	(56%)
	Jerry Brady (D)	171,711	(42%)
	Other	8,200	(2%)
2002 primary	Dirk Kempthorne (R)	95,882	(66%)
	Milt Erhart (R)	37,523	(26%)
	Walter Bayes (R)	6,873	(5%)
	Raynelle George (R)	5,271	(4%)
1998 general	Dirk Kempthorne (R)	258,095	(68%)
	Robert C. Huntley (D)	110,815	(29%)
	Other	12,338	(3%)

Dirk Kempthorne was elected governor of Idaho in 1998 after six years in the U.S. Senate. He was born in San Diego, grew up in Spokane, Washington, and graduated from the University of Idaho. He has spent most of his adult life in the political arena, starting in state government, then working for the Idaho Home Builders Association and FMC Corporation. He managed Phil

Batt's unsuccessful gubernatorial campaign in 1982 (Batt finally won in 1994) and was mayor of Boise for seven boom years from 1986–93. Kempthorne was elected to the Senate seat vacated in 1992 by two-term incumbent Republican Steve Symms and over tough competition from Democratic Congressman Richard Stallings. A Mormon and a conservative on abortion and gun control, Stallings was a three-time congressman from the eastern Idaho 2d District. Kempthorne won with 57%, barely carrying the northern panhandle, but running far ahead in the Boise market and carrying the Mormon areas in the east.

Kempthorne started off 100th in seniority in a Democratic Senate, concentrating on the nonstarter issue of unfunded mandates. But after the 1994 Republican victory, Majority Leader Bob Dole made Kempthorne's unfunded mandates bill S.1, the first order of legislative business. Kempthorne impressed colleagues with his knowledge of detail and his willingness to face off with West Virginia Senator Robert Byrd, who fought mightily against the bill as an infringement of congressional prerogatives; it passed the Senate easily with bipartisan support.

Then Idaho beckoned. Phil Batt, elected at 67, decided to retire after a long career in state politics and one successful four-year term as governor. In September 1997, Batt announced his decision to step down; in October 1997, Kempthorne announced he was running. He was willing to give up what easily could have been a lifetime Senate seat for a more limited tenure as governor. Once Kempthorne was in, the race was essentially over. Former state Supreme Court Justice Robert Huntley ran, he said, to maintain two-party competition. Kempthorne won 68%–29%, carrying every county but the one including Sun Valley.

In 1999 he proclaimed "the Generation of the Child" and got the legislature to pass a $5.5 million Idaho Reading Initiative and scholarships for 3.0 high school graduates at in-state colleges. He passed a voluntary immunization registry bill. He worked on a four-state salmon recovery program and entered a Memorandum of Understanding with Indian tribes as part of the Northwest Power Planning Council's sub-basin planning process. He got funding for a Rural Idaho Initiative, with state money for projects in the non-booming parts of Idaho.

In his first three years, Kempthorne and the legislature cut taxes several times. But by late 2001 revenues came in under expectations, and there were rounds of cuts in planned increases in public schools and actual cuts in higher education. The state tapped the Budget Stabilization Fund and tobacco settlement money and state employees were laid off; $200 million in projected spending was cut. He opposed giving state businesses the benefit of George W. Bush's 30% immediate depreciation allowance. Many members of the overwhelmingly Republican legislature complained that Kempthorne was aloof and uninvolved. They were unhappy when in early 2002 Kempthorne vetoed their repeal of term limits; the voters upheld the repeal by a narrow margin in November. Kempthorne had articulate opposition that year from Democrat Jerry Brady, owner of the *Idaho Falls Post Register*, the state's second largest newspaper, whose great-grandfather James Brady had been elected governor as a Republican in 1908. Brady spent $320,000 of his own money and attacked Kempthorne for cutting education spending in a "formulaic" and "lazy" way. He criticized Kempthorne for ousting Fish and Game Commissioner Rod Sando and said the commission was subservient to farmers and ranchers; he said he would appoint new members nominated by sportsmen. Kempthorne protested that he had only cut planned increases in school spending and that he would permit no further education cuts.

Kempthorne won by the reduced margin of 56%–42%. He lost the counties containing Sun Valley and Pocatello, three northern panhandle counties and, surprisingly, Boise's Ada County, where voters presumably know him best. Republican margins in the legislature were reduced to 28–7 and 54–16. Facing a budget shortfall in January 2003, Kempthorne proposed the largest tax increase in state history; after battling with conservatives, he signed into law a one-cent sales tax increase in April. He got the legislature to approve $70 million of bonds for colleges and universities by supporting projects around the state. He vetoed tax breaks for renewable energy, saying they would lose too much revenue. He reached an agreement with other governors on expanding the Bonneville power grid. He signed a ban on smoking in restaurants. In May 2004 he reached an agreement with the Interior Department and the Nez Perce tribe on water rights, in which the tribe waived a portion of its water rights in return for protection of salmon and other benefits; it was approved by Congress when Senator Larry Craig inserted it into the omnibus spending bill in November 2004.

Kempthorne became chairman of the National Governors Association in August 2003 and said the most important issue before state governments was the rising cost of long-term care. In June 2003 he was described in news accounts as the leading candidate to succeed EPA Administrator Christine Todd Whitman; but he may have been too open about his interest, and Utah Governor Mike Leavitt got the job. He was also said to be a possible choice for the cabinet after the November 2004 election, but no call came. Republicans gained three seats in the Idaho House in 2004, and Kempthorne announced he would propose a highway bond program. Energy-conscious, Kempthorne in November 2004 started using a Suburban SUV that ran on fuel that was 85% ethanol, produced from potatoes by a Simplot plant in Idaho. In December 2004 J. R. Simplot and his wife donated their hilltop house overlooking Idaho to the state for use as a governor's mansion.

During the 2002 campaign Kempthorne said he planned to serve only two terms as governor. But in March 2004 he said he wouldn't reveal his plans for 2006. He finally cleared things up in his January 2005 State of the State Address, when he said he would not seek a third term. Waiting in the wings were two Republicans, Lieutenant Governor Jim Risch and 1st District Congressman Butch Otter, who first ran for governor in 1978. On the Democratic side, Jerry Brady, the 2002 nominee, said he would run and state Senate Minority Leader Clint Stennett was a possible candidate.

Senior Senator

Larry Craig (R)

Elected 1990, seat up 2008, 3d term; b. July 20, 1945, Midvale; home, Payette; U. of ID, B.A. 1969; United Methodist; married (Suzanne).

Military Career: Army Natl. Guard, 1970–74.

Elected Office: ID Senate, 1974–80; U.S. House of Reps., 1980–90.

Professional Career: Rancher, farmer.

DC Office: 520 HSOB, 20510, 202-224-2752; Fax: 202-228-1067; Web site: craig.senate.gov.

State Offices: Boise, 208-342-7985; Coeur d'Alene, 208-667-6130; Idaho Falls, 208-523-5541; Lewiston, 208-743-0792; Pocatello, 208-236-6817; Twin Falls, 208-734-6780.

Committees: *Aging (Special)*. *Appropriations*: Agriculture, Rural Development & Related Agencies; Energy & Water; Homeland Security; Interior & Related Agencies; Labor, Health and Human Services, Education & Related Agencies; Military Construction & Veterans Affairs. *Energy & Natural Resources*: Energy; Public Lands & Forests (Chmn.); Water & Power. *Veterans' Affairs* (Chmn.).

Group Ratings

	ADA	ACLU	AFS	LCV	ITIC	NTU	COC	ACU	NTLC	CHC
2004	5	11	0	0	83	76	88	96	95	100
2003	5	—	0	0	—	73	91	90	—	—

National Journal Ratings

	2003 LIB — 2003 CONS		2004 LIB — 2004 CONS	
Economic	0%	— 82%	11%	— 84%
Social	0%	— 59%	0%	— 84%
Foreign	39%	— 54%	0%	— 67%

Key Votes of the 108th Congress

1. Ban Drilling in ANWR	N	5. Energy Bill	Y	9. Ban Same-Sex Marriage	Y
2. Approve Bush Tax Cuts	Y	6. Support Roe v. Wade	N	10. Ban Bunker-Buster Bomb	N
3. Medicare/Rx Bill	Y	7. Ban Partial-Birth Abortion	Y	11. Fund Iraq War	Y
4. Bar Overtime Pay Regs.	N	8. Assault Weapons Ban	N	12. Restrict Missile Defense	N

Election Results

2002 general	Larry Craig (R)	266,215	(65%)	($3,045,521)
	Alan Blinken (D)	132,975	(33%)	($2,170,928)
	Other	9,354	(2%)	
2002 primary	Larry Craig (R)	unopposed		
1996 general	Larry Craig (R)	283,532	(57%)	($2,992,451)
	Walt Minnick (D)	198,422	(40%)	($2,140,878)
	Other	15,279	(3%)	

Prior Winning Percentages: 1990 (61%); 1988 House (66%); 1986 House (65%); 1984 House (69%); 1982 House (54%); 1980 House (54%)

Larry Craig, Idaho's senior senator, was first elected to the House in 1980 and to the Senate in 1990. Born on a ranch homesteaded by his grandfather in 1899, he was first elected to the state Senate in 1974, at 29, and served six years before running for the U.S. House. In 1990, when Senator James McClure retired, he was elected to the Senate; he won the Republican primary with 59% of the vote and the general election with 61%. In his early years in Congress, Craig was a well-informed and persistent critic of Western lands policies favored by environmentalists or, as he once put it, "environmental extremism." He opposed Bill Clinton's efforts to revise the Mining Act of 1872 and increase grazing fees and the Clinton proposal to introduce grizzly bears into Idaho's Bitterroot Range. He opposed expansion of the Craters of the Moon National Monument, and sponsored a bill to create certain requirements for presidents to declare national monuments, as Clinton frequently did. He also opposed breaching the Snake River dams to allow salmon to swim more easily upstream and sponsored a bill to require the Fish and Wildlife Service to consider many factors, including the effect on farming, when it makes decisions on salmon protection programs.

As chairman of the Public Lands and Forests Subcommittee Craig worked to change the policies and institutional culture of the Forest Service. In the 1990s it reduced by nearly 80% the timber harvest on public lands, and in the process eliminated the livelihoods of many in small towns in Idaho and the West. While attacking Clinton policies publicly, he also worked behind the scenes with Oregon Democrat Ron Wyden to come up with a bipartisan alternative. In the wake of the summer 2000 wildfires that raged in Idaho, he strongly criticized the Clinton administration for failing to fund fire prevention and called for $240 million for federal agencies to remove timber and brush. He sponsored a reorganization bill to streamline planning procedures, limit court challenges to local people who commented during the planning process, and forbid deviations from the plan once adopted. It would allow states and private organizations, with congressional approval, to take over management of National Forest and Bureau of Land Management lands. He opposed the Clinton regulation to ban construction of roads in national forests and supported the Bush administration's attempts to repeal it. He also backed the Bush administration's 2002 proposal to give regional managers power to approve commercial or recreational use without protracted environmental impact statements and the Bush Healthy Forest Initiative streamlining approval of forest thinning.

Over the years he has moved from provoking controversy to forging consensus. "There are a lot of people who would like to cast me in comments that I've made over the years, and made 10 or 15 years ago. What I suggest is that they see the actions I've taken over the last decade, actions that I think have been extremely progressive, open and inclusive." Once an opponent of new wilderness area designations, he agreed in November 2004 to support the Boulder-White Clouds wilderness area sponsored by 2d District Congressman Mike Simpson and the Owyhee Canyonlands wilderness proposal, worked out after lengthy negotiations with his Senate colleague Mike Crapo, the Owyhee County commissioners, local landowners, in-state environmentalists and the Shoshone-Paiute Tribe.

Another Craig cause is nuclear waste. He has been pushing relentlessly for the government to meet its commitment to establish a permanent nuclear waste repository at Yucca Mountain in Nevada. Opposition came from Nevada's two senators and from Bill Clinton, who carried Nevada twice by narrow margins after promising to veto bills to establish a temporary waste facility there. In July 2002, Craig's efforts came to fruition: George W. Bush signed a resolution establishing the repository. In March 2002 he inserted into the energy bill a Nuclear Power 2010 program for the Energy Department, and in March 2003 he got Energy Committee Chairman Pete Domenici to insert into the energy bill a $1.2 billion nuclear reactor for the INEEL laboratory in Butte County. And he worked to get compensation for downwinders, residents of four Idaho counties subjected to radiation from above-ground nuclear weapons tests in Nevada in the 1950s.

Craig has taken on a variety of national issues. He was a lead sponsor of the constitutional amendment to require a balanced budget in the House in 1982 and in the Senate in 1995. He has supported free trade measures but he co-sponsored a May 2002 amendment with Minnesota Senator Mark Dayton to trade promotion authority which would have allowed Congress to separately examine provisions of any trade agreement that affect trade remedy laws; that passed 61–38 but was dropped in conference committee after Bush threatened a veto. Craig has opposed what he considers dumping of Korean microchips (Micron is Idaho's biggest employer) and Canadian softwood lumber. He opposed the Central American Free Trade Agreement because it would allow more sugar imports and insisted that sugar should be considered only in the Doha Round, not in regional trade agreements. In 2004 he sponsored with Dayton a bill imposing tariffs on milk protein concentrates. Craig has supported opening up trade with Cuba, once a big purchaser of Idaho lentils and peas, and in February 2004, he and 1st District Congressman Butch Otter visited Cuba. He opposed the Bush administration proposal to require payment in advance for Cuban purchases.

Craig was chairman of the Special Committee on Aging in 2003 and 2004, and sponsored a bill with Evan Bayh of Indiana to enable seniors to purchase state-approved long-term care policies. He warned that he might support federal regulation of assisted living facilities if state regulation proved ineffective. In January 2005 he became chairman of the Veterans Affairs Committee. In the gun control debate after the 1999 Columbine murders, he sponsored a bill to allow (but not force) unlicensed sellers at gun shows to conduct background checks. In July 2002 he, John McCain, Edward Kennedy and Charles Schumer were an "odd duck" coalition sponsoring a bill to improve the National Instant Check background check system; they want to make sure that it includes all those convicted of crimes or otherwise ineligible to buy guns. In March 2004 he sponsored the bill to protect gun manufacturers from lawsuits seeking money for injuries committed by gun users. It seemed to have a majority, but when liberals attached to it a reauthorization of the assault weapons ban, he successfully killed the whole measure; he was pleased when the assault weapons ban expired in September 2004. That same year he sponsored a bill, backed by liberals and conservatives, to repeal or limit portions of the USA PATRIOT Act.

Craig has used his seat on the Appropriations Committee to advance Idaho projects. In November 2004 he attached to the omnibus bill the agreement worked out by the Interior Department, Governor Dirk Kempthorne and the Nez Perce tribe settling water claims on the Snake River. He obtained funding for a new tower at Boise's airport and $245,000 for an aging study and $900,000 for a Center for Environmental Science and Economic Development at Boise State University.

In the 1990s Craig was chairman of an informal committee whose members seemed to win most leadership positions. After Senator Bob Dole's resignation in June 1996, Craig was elected chairman of the Republican Policy Committee, the number four leadership position. In December 2000 Craig was challenged for this position by the more senior and more conciliation-minded Pete Domenici, and Craig just barely hung on, 26–24. Term limits prevented him from running again in 2002. He considered running for whip in the fall, but evidently became convinced that Mitch McConnell had the votes and did not run.

Winning reelection is ordinarily not difficult for an Idaho Republican, but Craig has had to run twice against Democrats who largely self-financed their campaigns. In 1996 building materials tycoon Walt Minnick spent $945,000 of his own money and attacked Craig sharply for backing Governor Phil Batt's nuclear waste compact. Craig responded by rafting down the river with his family and running ads predicting toxic desolation if the nuclear waste compact was not carried out. Craig won 57%–40%. In 2002 retired investment banker Alan Blinken, owner of a Sun Valley house who registered to vote there in 2001, spent $1.5 million of his own money on the campaign. Blinken had points against him: he had been Clinton's ambassador to Belgium and had lived for many years in New York City. But he boasted that he owned eight pistols, eight rifles and eight shotguns, "and I use them all. I'm a gun-totin' Idaho Democrat." Blinken said he could bring "good paying" jobs to Idaho and attacked Craig for voting in favor of certain interests shortly after receiving campaign contributions from them. Craig defended his votes as being in line with long-held principles and on many issues said that Blinken's stands showed he doesn't understand life in Idaho. Craig spent more than $3 million and Idaho did not drift far from its usual voting habits. Craig won 65%–33%; he carried 43 counties and Blinken carried the county that includes Sun Valley. He drew mention as a possible Cabinet appointee in November 2004, but he wasn't asked and is considered likely to run for a fourth term in 2008.

Junior Senator

Mike Crapo (R)

Elected 1998, seat up 2010, 2d term; b. May 20, 1951, Idaho Falls; home, Idaho Falls; Brigham Young U., B.A. 1973, Harvard U., J.D. 1977; Mormon; married (Susan).

Elected Office: ID Senate, 1984–92, Senate Ldr., 1988–92; U.S. House of Reps., 1992–98.

Professional Career: Practicing atty., 1977–92.

DC Office: 239 DSOB, 20510, 202-224-6142; Web site: crapo.senate.gov.

State Offices: Boise, 208-334-1776; Caldwell, 208-455-0360; Coeur D'Alene, 208-664-5490; Idaho Falls, 208-522-9779; Lewiston, 208-743-1492; Pocatello, 208-236-6775; Twin Falls, 208-734-2515.

Committees: *Agriculture, Nutrition & Forestry*: Forestry, Conservation & Rural Revitalization (Chmn.); Research, Nutrition & General Legislation. *Banking, Housing & Urban Affairs*: Financial Institutions; International Trade & Finance (Chmn.); Securities & Investment. *Budget. Finance*: International Trade; Social Security & Family Policy; Taxation & IRS Oversight. *Indian Affairs*.

Group Ratings

	ADA	ACLU	AFS	LCV	ITIC	NTU	COC	ACU	NTLC	CHC
2004	10	11	0	0	83	66	94	92	95	100
2003	5	—	0	0	—	73	91	89	—	—

National Journal Ratings

	2003 LIB	—	2003 CONS		2004 LIB	—	2004 CONS
Economic	0%	—	82%		11%	—	84%
Social	0%	—	59%		0%	—	84%
Foreign	39%	—	54%		0%	—	67%

Key Votes of the 108th Congress

1. Ban Drilling in ANWR	N	5. Energy Bill	Y	9. Ban Same-Sex Marriage	Y
2. Approve Bush Tax Cuts	Y	6. Support Roe v. Wade	N	10. Ban Bunker-Buster Bomb	N
3. Medicare/Rx Bill	Y	7. Ban Partial-Birth Abortion	Y	11. Fund Iraq War	Y
4. Bar Overtime Pay Regs.	N	8. Assault Weapons Ban	N	12. Restrict Missile Defense	N

Election Results

2004 general	Mike Crapo (R)	499,796	(99%)	($1,031,912)
	Other	4,136	(1%)	
2004 primary	Mike Crapo (R)	unopposed		
1998 general	Mike Crapo (R)	262,966	(70%)	($1,563,811)
	Bill Mauk (D)	107,375	(28%)	($241,443)
	Other	7,833	(2%)	

Prior Winning Percentages: 1996 House (69%); 1994 House (75%); 1992 House (61%)

Mike Crapo (pronounced *CRAY-poe*) is a Republican elected to the House in 1992 and the Senate in 1998. He grew up in Idaho Falls, graduated from Brigham Young University and Harvard Law School, and is a faithful Mormon who was named a bishop in the church at 31. A former congressional intern, he was elected to the state Senate at 33 in 1984, two years after leukemia took his older brother Terry's life. Terry Crapo had been state House majority leader and a rising star in state politics; the two were close and Mike Crapo decided to follow in his brother's path to the legislature. He became state Senate leader in 1988 and ran for the House in 1992, campaigning against all tax increases, for spending cuts, a balanced budget amendment and the line-item veto—the Contract with America two years early. He won the primary 68%–32%. "Cowboy Democrat" J. D. Williams, the state controller, ran on a "put America first" stand on industrial policy and trade. Crapo won 61%–35%.

With a self-professed "passion for reform," Crapo became Republican freshman class leader and championed institutional reforms—on discharge petitions, select committees, closed rules, closed committee meetings, open voting—many of which were adopted after Republicans won control in 1994. Like many Republicans, he favored simple, hard-and-fast rules—a balanced budget, term limits, across-the-board discretionary spending cuts (excluding Social Security)—to force tough decisions. He sponsored the deficit reduction lock box bill that passed the House in 1995; he served on Agriculture as it passed the Freedom To Farm Act. He was a founding member of the Congressional Water Caucus and a member of the fabled Congressional Boot Caucus, an informal group of Western lawmakers who wear boots; he is co-chairman of the Congressional Sportsman's Caucus and the Senate Nuclear Cleanup Caucus. His overall voting record has been very conservative, with some exceptions on economics. He opposed NAFTA in 1993 but supported PNTR with China in 2000. In 2002, he voted in favor of trade promotion authority. He has criticized many recent trade agreements for accepting limits on U.S. agricultural exports as leverage for opening up access for other products, but has said that negotiators did less of that at the WTO meetings in Seattle and Cancun.

In 1997 Crapo, who prides himself on returning to Idaho Falls to be with his family every weekend, faced a career choice that many House members would like to face. In September Governor Phil Batt announced his retirement and in October Senator Dirk Kempthorne said he would run for governor. Within days Crapo announced he would run for the Senate. His opponent was former Democratic chairman and Boise trial lawyer Bill Mauk. Idaho, one-quarter Mormon, had never elected a Mormon senator; this time it did. Crapo led in polls by a wide margin and won 70%–28%, carrying every county.

In his first years in the Senate, Crapo became chairman of the subcommittee with jurisdiction over the troubled Superfund program and many EPA programs. He worked on the farm bill in 2001 and 2002, and helped write the conservation provisions; he sought to free farmers taking part from complying with federal water standards. He was troubled with the bill's dairy provisions, which he said would take money away from Western producers and give it to Eastern dairies; Idaho has a growing dairy industry. He passed a bill providing $1 million for small Idaho communities to comply with federal water quality standards, and seeks to extend it to the whole nation. He sponsored the Senate version of the Healthy Forests Restoration Act. He worked on changing the Endangered Species Act, and in November 2004 he produced a draft bill directing the Interior Secretary to set deadlines based on specific criteria. He promised to keep working on the issue, though he was leaving the Environment Committee in January 2005. "I am heartened by the consensus that ESA should produce more obvious benefits for species."

In the Senate and in working on issues in Idaho, Crapo has met with groups with very different views and has tried to forge consensus. "If you have collaborative decision-making, instead of creating a forum where people conflict, you have a table where people can create win-win solutions." Of Crapo, Oregon Democrat Ron Wyden said, "He is not a showboat. He is somebody who day in and day out is always a constructive force for sensible public policy." He rounded up support from California and Oregon colleagues for a plan that would give Idaho funding for salmon recovery proportionate to that of the Pacific Coast states; when Idaho was left off a list of states eligible for the Wildlife Habitat Incentives Program, he quickly got it put on. With Harry Reid of Nevada he got the Senate in June 2002 to pass unanimously a bill providing for continuous production of the American Eagle Silver Bullion Coin by having the Treasury replenish its silver supply on the open market. Blanks for coins are manufactured at Sunshine Minting Inc. in Coeur d'Alene and Idaho's Silver Valley mines produce $70 million of silver per year. Crapo opposed reintroduction of grizzly bears to the Bitterroot Mountains and breaching the Snake River dams and opposed spring drawdowns on lower Snake River dams; he wrote a bill to compensate businesses around the Dworshak Reservoir for summer drawdowns to help migrating salmon. He has worked to get compensation for downwinders, residents of four Idaho counties subjected to radiation from above-ground nuclear weapons tests in Nevada in the 1950s, and worked on the Snake River Water Rights Act, which was passed as part of the omnibus appropriation in November 2004.

From 2001 to 2004 he worked to forge a consensus on the Owyhee Canyonlands wilderness proposal with the Owyhee County Commissioners, landowners and cattlemen, environmental groups and the Shoshone-Paiute Tribe. In November 2004, consensus resulted—199,000 acres formerly off limits would be opened to fence-building and pipelines, with independent review of BLM decisions; 517,000 acres would be set aside as wilderness and 384 miles of rivers would be protected, and open to hikers and boaters; the habitat of the California bighorn sheep and sage grouse would be protected. His Idaho colleague Larry Craig promised to steer it through his Public Lands and Forests Subcommittee in 2005.

On other issues, Crapo and Craig supported the DREAM Act, allowing young illegal aliens to earn temporary resident status by graduating from high school and enrolling in college. They both opposed a provision blocking disposal of radioactive sludge in cement containers at INEEL and the Savannah River Site; they said INEEL would not do any of this.

Crapo had expressed interest in a federal district judgeship but sought reelection in 2004; he had no Democratic opponent and won with 99% of the vote.

FIRST DISTRICT

Rep. Butch Otter (R)

Elected 2000, 3d term; b. May 3, 1942, Caldwell; home, Star; Col. of ID, B.A. 1967; Catholic; divorced.

Military Career: ID Natl. Guard, 1967–73.

Elected Office: ID House of Reps., 1972–76; ID Lt. Gov., 1986–2000.

Professional Career: Rancher; Dir., Food Products Div., Pres., Simplot Livestock, Pres., Simplot Intl., 1963–1993.

DC Office: 1711 LHOB, 20515, 202-225-6611; Fax: 202-225-3029; Web site: www.house.gov/otter.

District Offices: Boise, 208-336-9831; Coeur d'Alene, 208-667-0127; Lewiston, 208-298-0030; Nampa, 208-466-4503.

Committees: *Energy & Commerce* (26th of 31 R): Commerce, Trade & Consumer Protection; Energy & Air Quality; Environment & Hazardous Materials.

Group Ratings

	ADA	ACLU	AFS	LCV	ITIC	NTU	COC	ACU	NTLC	CHC
2004	5	20	0	0	90	82	95	100	100	92
2003	20	—	0	5	—	71	97	84	—	—

National Journal Ratings

	2003 LIB	—	2003 CONS		2004 LIB	—	2004 CONS
Economic	21%	—	75%		15%	—	84%
Social	40%	—	58%		36%	—	61%
Foreign	51%	—	48%		51%	—	48%

Key Votes of the 108th Congress

1. Drilling in ANWR	Y	5. DC School Vouchers	Y	9. Ban Same-Sex Marriage	Y
2. Approve Bush Tax Cuts	Y	6. Ban Human Cloning	Y	10. Fund Iraq War	N
3. Medicare/Rx Bill	Y	7. Restrict Gun Liability	Y	11. Bar Cuba Embargo Funds	Y
4. Bar Overtime Pay Regs.	N	8. Ban Partial-Birth Abortion	Y	12. Intelligence Reorg.	Y

Election Results

2004 general	Butch Otter (R)	207,662	(70%)	($512,498)
	Naomi Preston (D)	90,927	(31%)	($15,152)
2004 primary	Butch Otter (R)	48,986	(78%)	
	Jim Pratt (R)..	13,433	(22%)	
2002 general	Butch Otter (R)	120,743	(59%)	($997,441)
	Betty Richardson (D)	80,269	(39%)	($476,354)
	Other..	5,129	(2%)	

Prior Winning Percentages: 2000 (65%)

The People		Race/Ethnic Origin	Ancestry	
Area size:	39,972 sq. mi.	89.0% White	German: 15.4%	English: 10.6%
Urban population:	65.8%	0.3% Black	Irish: 8.2%	
Rural population:	34.2%	0.9% Asian	**2004 Presidential Vote**	
Pop. 2000:	648,774	1.2% Native Am.	Bush (R) 215,069	(69%)
Median income:	$38,364	0.1% Hawaiian	Kerry (D) 94,915	(30%)
Poverty status:	11.0%	1.5% Two+ races	Other 3,540	(1%)
Military veterans:	15.5%	0.1% Other	**2000 Presidential Vote**	
		6.8% Hispanic Origin	Bush (R) 171,364	(68%)
			Gore (D) 70,523	(28%)
			Other 11,983	(5%)
			Cook Partisan Voting Index: R +19	

Occupation	Blue collar: 26.2%	White collar: 56.1%	Gray collar: 17.7%

The 1st District of Idaho stretches from the Nevada border to Canada, including some of usually Republican Boise and all of the panhandle, historically Democratic but more recently leaning Republican. It includes two of Idaho's big growth areas, the western suburbs of Boise and the Coeur d'Alene area to the north in Kootenai County; high-tech and tourism have fueled the economy. In Nampa, whose population nearly doubled in the 1990s and replaced Pocatello as Idaho's second-largest city, commercial developers have taken over land outside Boise that not long ago grew wheat and alfalfa. Subdivisions with as many as 1,000 homes are being constructed in nearby Meridian, the fastest-growing city in Idaho, as city planners struggle to upgrade their infrastructure. Some old-timers worry that their areas may become a new version of San Jose or Orange County, but support for property rights remain strong here. Politically, the 1st District is overwhelmingly Republican. Northern mining counties were once the district's Democratic base; now it is the university town of Moscow. But every county here voted for George W. Bush in 2000 and 2004.

The congressman from the 1st District is C.L. "Butch" Otter, a Republican first elected in 2000 and something of a free spirit. His father was a journeyman electrician and lifelong Democrat. He entered an abbey to pursue the priesthood but quickly decided that was not his calling; in 1967, he graduated from the College of Idaho. He went to work for his then father-in-law, billionaire J.R. Simplot, at the J.R. Simplot Company, one of the largest potato processors in the world, owner of the largest feedlot in the nation, and an early investor in Micron Technology. In 1972 he was elected to the state House. Otter ran for governor in 1978, finishing third in the Republican primary. In 1986, he was elected lieutenant governor, and served under three governors until he was elected to Congress. Otter, a wealthy ranch owner after his 1993 divorce, believes strongly in gun ownership and property rights. But he is not the social conservative that other Idaho Republicans have been. In 1992, he won the "Mr. Tight Jeans" contest at the Rockin' Rodeo bar in Boise. While he opposes abortion, he believes that the government should stay out of people's lives. He wants to check the power of the Environmental Protection Agency. This isn't a surprise: As a ranch owner, Otter has been charged three times by the EPA for violating the Clean Water Act; in 2001, he paid a fine of $50,000 for dredging and filling wetlands without a permit. But violating federal environmental regulations is not necessarily the worst offense in Idaho.

In 2000, when Helen Chenoweth-Hage kept her pledge to limit herself to three terms, a venomous Republican primary ensued between Otter and Dennis Mansfield, who founded the

Christian conservative group Idaho Family Forum. Mansfield's supporters highlighted Otter's 1993 drunk-driving conviction, following which he agreed to perform 72 hours of community service and attend 16 hours of an alcohol treatment program; he apologized and went on a speaking tour to youngsters across Idaho. One of Mansfield's ads stated: "Just what we need in Washington—another bad example for our children." But Otter had the support of most Republican insiders, including Governor Dirk Kempthorne and 29 of 31 state senators. Mansfield, running as a political outsider, backed term limits and was endorsed by the Wall Street-based Club for Growth. With help from a late get-out-the-vote campaign by the National Rifle Association and local farming and ranching interests—plus a more than 3–1 fundraising advantage—Otter won all 19 counties and defeated Mansfield 48%–27%. He easily won the general, 65%–31%.

In the House, Otter occasionally broke with conservatives on cultural issues and foreign policy. He was criticized locally when he called for a 10-year study of how to control development in the state's vast wild areas, rather than work as other members of the delegation have to develop consensus among those with different views; Idaho is one of two Western states without a federal wilderness area. He sought $50 million to restore salmon habitat in Idaho rivers. In 2001, he was one of three House Republicans to vote against the USA Patriot Act. Later, six House Republicans co-sponsored Otter's bill to repeal parts of the statute. In July 2004 he sponsored an amendment with independent Bernie Sanders to prevent authorities from using the Patriot Act to demand information on book buyers and library users; he lost on a tie vote after Republican leaders held the roll call open for 23 extra minutes to turn the outcome their way. "You win some, and some get stolen," Otter said. He called airport "pat-down" screening procedures degrading to women.

In 2002, Otter faced a re-election challenge from Betty Richardson, who was U.S. Attorney for Idaho during the Clinton administration. She called Otter too conservative for his constituents, but conceded that national Democrats were too liberal for Idaho. Otter modified his earlier position on Social Security, and said that investment in private accounts should be for amounts above the payroll deduction. Richardson spent plenty of money and carried two counties surrounding the University of Idaho, but Otter won 59%–39%. He was reelected in 2004 with 70% of the vote. In mid-2005 he was running for governor in 2006 and looked likely to have a strong primary opponent in Lieutenant Governor Jim Risch. If Otter does not run for reelection, Republicans seem likely to hold this district.

SECOND DISTRICT

Rep. Mike Simpson (R)

Elected 1998, 4th term; b. Sept. 8, 1950, Burley; home, Blackfoot; UT St. U., 1968–72; WA U. Dental Schl., D.D.S. 1977; Mormon; married (Kathy).

Elected Office: Blackfoot City Cncl., 1980–84; ID House of Reps., 1984–98, Speaker, 1993–98.

Professional Career: Practicing dentist, 1977–98.

DC Office: 1339 LHOB, 20515, 202-225-5531; Fax: 202-225-8216; Web site: www.house.gov/simpson.

District Offices: Boise, 208-334-1953; Idaho Falls, 208-523-6701; Pocatello, 208-478-4160; Twin Falls, 208-734-7219.

Committees: *Appropriations* (31st of 37 R): Energy & Water Development & Related Agencies; Interior, Environment & Related Agencies (Vice Chmn.); Military Quality of Life & Veterans Affairs & Related Agencies. *Budget* (17th of 22 R).

Group Ratings

	ADA	ACLU	AFS	LCV	ITIC	NTU	COC	ACU	NTLC	CHC
2004	0	11	13	9	80	55	95	92	65	75
2003	10	—	0	5	—	58	97	88	—	—

National Journal Ratings

	2003 LIB	—	2003 CONS		2004 LIB	—	2004 CONS
Economic	31%	—	68%		23%	—	76%
Social	47%	—	53%		42%	—	58%
Foreign	11%	—	80%		17%	—	78%

Key Votes of the 108th Congress

1. Drilling in ANWR	Y	5. DC School Vouchers	*	9. Ban Same-Sex Marriage	Y
2. Approve Bush Tax Cuts	Y	6. Ban Human Cloning	Y	10. Fund Iraq War	Y
3. Medicare/Rx Bill	Y	7. Restrict Gun Liability	Y	11. Bar Cuba Embargo Funds	N
4. Bar Overtime Pay Regs.	N	8. Ban Partial-Birth Abortion	Y	12. Intelligence Reorg.	Y

Election Results

2004 general	Mike Simpson (R)	193,704	(71%)	($498,082)
	Lin Whitworth (D)	80,133	(29%)	($68,209)
2004 primary	Mike Simpson (R)	unopposed		
2002 general	Mike Simpson (R)	135,605	(68%)	($320,236)
	Edward Kinghorn (D)	57,769	(29%)	($12,467)
	Other	5,508	(3%)	

Prior Winning Percentages: 2000 (71%); 1998 (53%)

The People		Race/Ethnic Origin	Ancestry	
Area size:	43,598 sq. mi.	87.1% White	English: 16.0%	German: 12.2%
Urban population:	67.0%	0.5% Black	Irish: 6.4%	
Rural population:	33.0%	0.9% Asian	**2004 Presidential Vote**	
Pop. 2000:	645,179	1.2% Native Am.	Bush (R) 194,166	(69%)
Median income:	$36,934	0.1% Hawaiian	Kerry (D) 86,183	(30%)
Poverty status:	12.6%	1.3% Two+ races	Other 2,665	(1%)
Military veterans:	14.0%	0.1% Other	**2000 Presidential Vote**	
		8.9% Hispanic Origin	Bush (R) 165,559	(67%)
			Gore (D) 68,055	(28%)
			Other 12,319	(5%)
			Cook Partisan Voting Index: R +19	
Occupation	Blue collar: 23.8%	White collar: 57.3%	Gray collar: 18.9%	

The 2d District of Idaho, from central Boise east to the Utah and Wyoming borders, is one of America's most Republican districts. It's also one of the most picturesque. The thick forests, mountain ranges and river valleys close by the Montana border are strongly Republican and suspicious of government. Southeast Idaho is part of the Mormon heartland, and the LDS presence runs deep; eastern Idaho's first Mormon settlements were in Franklin, Bear Lake and Caribou Counties. The old frontier and railroad town of Pocatello was once a Democratic outpost, home to unionized rail workers, a liberal college campus and a far more diverse population than the surrounding parts (Idaho State University used to be known as the place where Mormon kids went to lose their religion). But Pocatello has moved in a Republican direction as union strength declined and the conservative Mormon influence increased. Fifty miles north on I-15, Idaho Falls serves as the metropolis for a vast region stretching from West Yellowstone, Wyoming to the Salmon River Mountains. The nearby Idaho National Engineering and Environmental Laboratory, a massive facility that occupies 890 square miles and employs more than 8,000 workers, is located on a windswept, desolate range—exactly why the federal government selected the site in the 1940s to test nuclear reactors. West of INEEL, in the year-round resort community of Sun Valley (Blaine County), celebrities from Bill Gates and Arnold Schwarzenegger to John Kerry and Teresa Heinz have spurred rapid development, which has led to calls for restrictions on growth. Blaine is in the one Idaho county that voted for Kerry, 59%–40%. The other counties in

the 2d District voted for George W. Bush by percentages that range between 61% (Teton County) and 92% (Madison County). The district also includes the east side of Boise.

The congressman from the 2d District is Mike Simpson, a Republican first elected in 1998 when incumbent Mike Crapo ran successfully for the Senate. Simpson grew up in Blackfoot, became a dentist and joined his father's practice there. He was elected to the city council in 1980 and to the state House in 1984; he didn't declare himself as a Republican until then and was opposed by the local Republican organization. In 1993 he became Speaker, but kept up his dental practice as well. In the legislature he was known as a moderate in a conservative House, affable and able to get differing sides together. When Governor Phil Batt announced he would retire in 1998, Simpson wanted to run for his office; Senator Dirk Kempthorne's decision to seek the office closed that option. Crapo's decision to run for Kempthorne's Senate seat opened up the House seat for Simpson.

There was a serious contest for the district. In the Republican primary, state Representative Mark Stubbs called for lower payroll taxes; he had opposed nuclear programs at INEEL, while Simpson wanted more work at the facility. But the big issue was term limits. Simpson refused to take a pledge to serve only three terms; the other candidates did. Term limits advocates spent large sums against Simpson. Angry at these ads, Batt endorsed Simpson five days before the election. Simpson ran ads against "outsiders" and "out-of-state folk." Simpson beat Stubbs, 47%–41%. The Democratic nominee was Richard Stallings, a former history professor elected to the House in 1984 and re-elected three times; in 1992 he ran against Kempthorne for the Senate and lost 57%–43%. Stallings talked about his conservative voting record in the House, called for more education spending and pointed with anxiety at falling farm commodity prices. Simpson wanted a smaller federal role in education; he favored tax cuts and individual investment accounts in Social Security. Simpson won 53%–45%, losing the most visible parts of the district—Pocatello, Sun Valley, Boise—but carrying just about everything else.

In the House, Simpson has been relatively moderate for a western Republican. In his first two years, he set out to build relationships with each of his 434 colleagues—preferably, he said, in one-on-one informal conversations. But he did not get to know all of them—the House is a big place—and that reinforced his opposition to term limits. More than most western Republicans, he has reached out to Democrats on economic and social issues. The *Idaho Statesman* called him "a savvy and solutions-oriented lawmaker." He helped to establish a bipartisan caucus to talk about the trade-related needs of farmers and ranchers. He called for a middle ground on resource issues, but criticized the Clinton administration for acting unilaterally to expand the Craters of the Moon National Monument and filed a bill to prevent similar actions. George W. Bush signed two of his bills; one, to protect hunting rights in the expanded portions of the Craters of the Moon monument, and the other to overhaul a job-training program for veterans. To promote a delicate balance between economic development and a project of the Nature Conservancy, Simpson advanced a proposal for a huge and long-discussed land transfer in Custer County, including a slice of the Sawtooth National Recreation Area. "I want your grandchildren to be able to enjoy the White Clouds like I did when I was young," he told a local group. In 2003, he showed his skills as a party insider when he got a seat on the Appropriations Committee.

Simpson has been reelected without difficulty.

★ ILLINOIS ★

At the beginning of the 20th century Chicago seemed destined to be the center of America. This brash new city on the lake had grown from 112,000 residents in 1860, when it was host to the Republican Convention that nominated Illinois's Abraham Lincoln, to 1.4 million when it hosted the Columbian Exposition in 1893 and 1.7 million in 1900. "Make no little plans," Chicago architect Daniel Burnham exhorted. And Chicago was making vast plans: building grand parks on the lakefront, erecting America's first downtown of skyscrapers, building expansive retail palaces, becoming the headquarters of the new American Medical and American Bar Associations, creating a great university from scratch on the Exposition's Midway Plaisance, housing union agitators and their liberal advocate Clarence Darrow as well as corporate leaders and attorneys who bested them, hosting the Democratic Convention of 1896 that nominated 36-year-old William Jennings Bryan after his "cross of gold" speech, and becoming the headquarters of the brilliant campaign Mark Hanna waged for William McKinley that beat Bryan in the fall. Chicago started with the advantage of a great location, where the Great Lakes meet the prairies of the vast Mississippi Valley, and Chicago's entrepreneurs made it the hub of the nation's railroad network and the center of the nation's trade in lumber, grain and meat, as William Cronon describes in *Nature's Metropolis*.

A century later, Chicago is the nation's third-largest metropolis, sometimes overshadowed by and often ignored by the media of coastal New York and Los Angeles, but still a productive and creative world-city. Illinois, after near-zero population growth in the 1970s and 1980s, saw its population rise 11% from 1990 to 2004, more than other big states like New York, Pennsylvania, Ohio or Michigan. In commerce, Chicago remains a prime producer and processor of food products, the nation's number one manufacturing center with the strongest white-collar and service economy between the coasts, the home of the world's greatest commodities exchanges and futures markets. O'Hare Airport, promoted and nurtured by longtime (1955–76) Mayor Richard J. Daley and long one of the world's busiest airports, is one of its great hubs of commerce. But for the most part Chicago was established not by government but by markets; it has always been a free enterprise city, settled by pioneers from New England and Kentucky, by immigrant Irishmen who dug the first canal connecting Lake Michigan and the Illinois River, and by railroad promoters who saw its potential as the great connecting point between East and West, the Great Lakes and the Mississippi Valley. Its factories, built where iron ore from Great Lakes freighters and coal from inland hills came together, attracted migrants from near and far. Today many of the old factories have been closed or demolished, and some of the Chicago area's biggest corporations have had problems. But Chicago's economy, based on finance and commodities, manufacturing and food, and undergirded by thousands of small firms, continues to thrive. The O'Hare area rivals downtown Chicago in number of jobs; central city neighborhoods north and south of the Loop are attracting new affluent residents; Latinos are thronging to the Chicago area and adding vitality to tired old neighborhoods.

Chicago and Illinois produced no presidents in the 20th century, but they have produced crucial votes and pivotal politicians. The list starts with Charles Dawes, a 30-year-old lawyer sent to Chicago by Hanna to manage McKinley's campaign—later he was a World War I general, the first Budget Bureau (now Office of Management and Budget) director, and vice president under Calvin Coolidge. Next comes Chicago lawyer Harold Ickes, who was Franklin Roosevelt's great Interior secretary. Prominent Illinois Republicans have included House Speaker Joseph Cannon, Senate Republican Leader Everett Dirksen, Senator Charles Percy and House Republican Leader Robert Michel; prominent Democrats have included Governor Adlai Stevenson, Mayor Richard J. Daley and Ways and Means Chairman Dan Rostenkowski. For most of the 20th century, Illinois was a key political battleground, closely divided between (usually) Democratic Chicago and (mostly) Republican Downstate, with the growing ring of suburbs around Chicago becoming increasingly pivotal. Its mixture of blacks and whites and Hispanics, immigrants and pioneers, city-dwellers and suburbanites and farmers, the affluent and the impoverished, heavy industry and high-tech, make it a rough proxy for the nation. For a century Illinois was a political

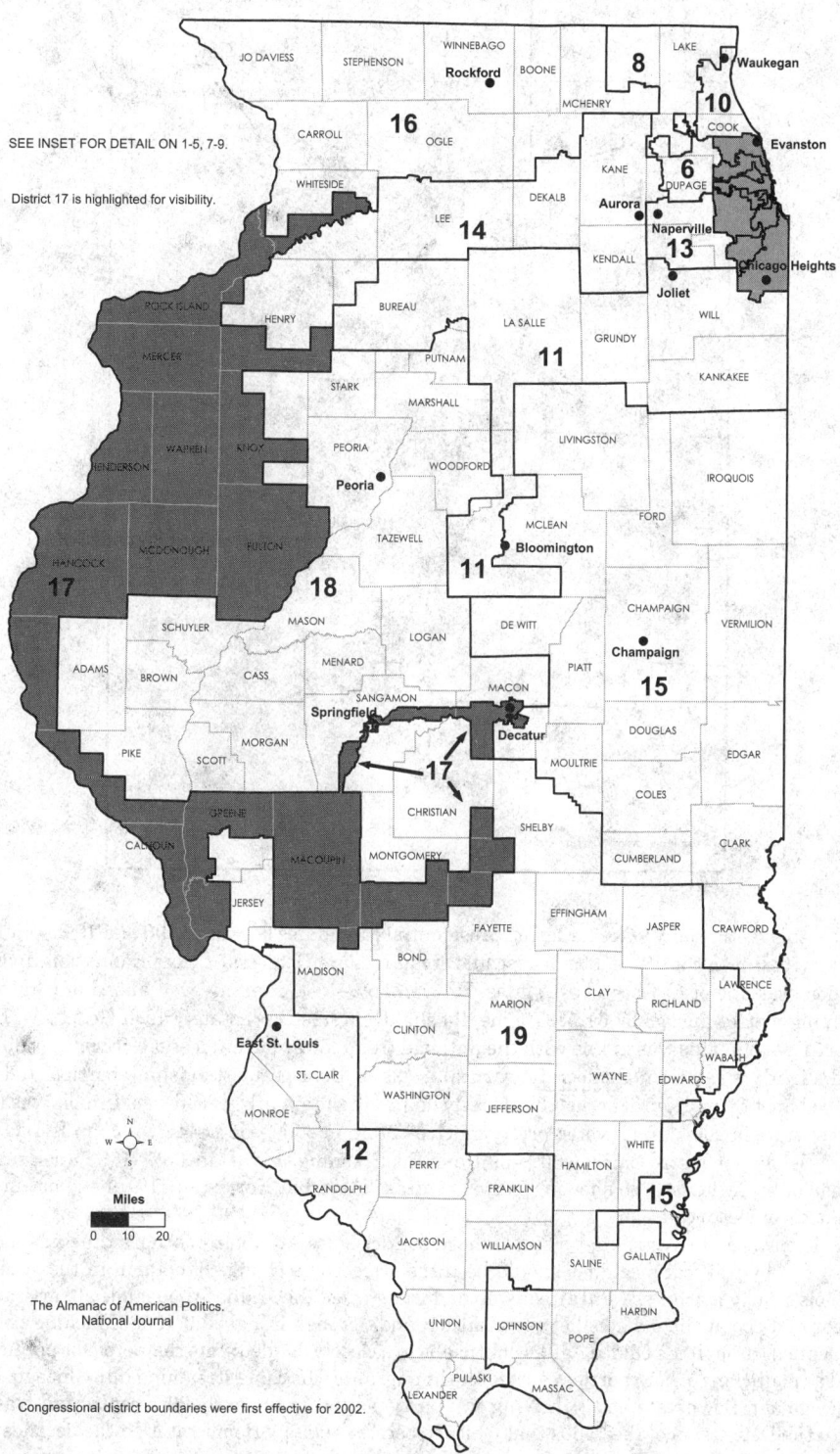

SEE INSET FOR DETAIL ON 1-5, 7-9.

District 17 is highlighted for visibility.

Miles
0 10 20

The Almanac of American Politics.
National Journal

Congressional district boundaries were first effective for 2002.

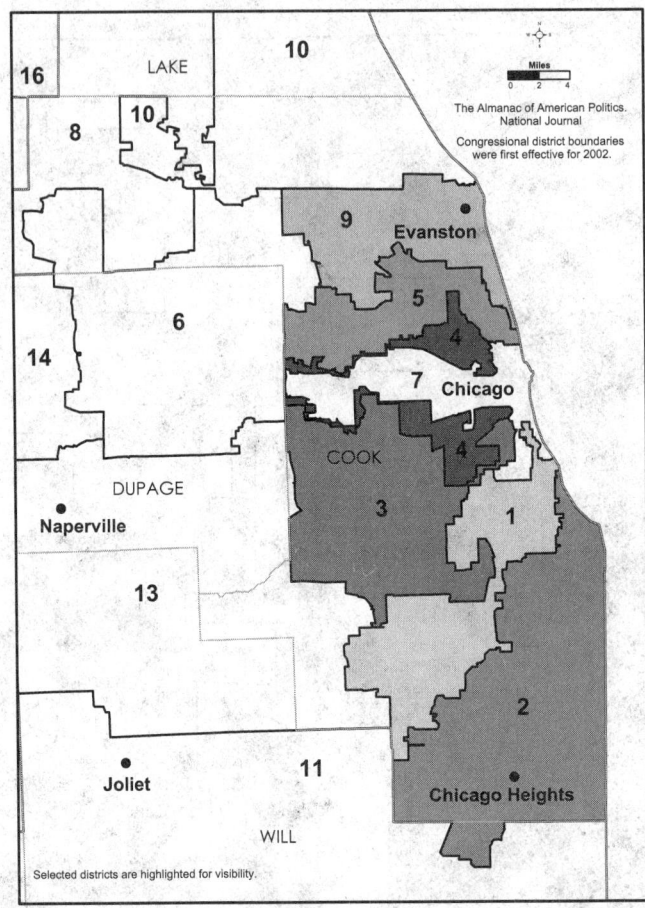

Selected districts are highlighted for visibility.

bellwether, voting only twice for losing presidential candidates between 1896 and 1996—in 1916 and 1976. But in the 1990s Illinois became steadily more Democratic than the nation. In 2000 Illinois was one of Al Gore's best states. He won 55%–43%, running even ahead of Clinton in winning metro Chicago by 61%–37%; he did slightly worse Downstate, which George W. Bush won 51%–46%. This was in line with the national trend toward Clinton and Gore in the suburbs and slightly away from Democrats in rural areas; if Democrats' stands on abortion and gun control hurt them in rural areas, they clearly helped in the suburbs of Chicago. Illinois was not a target state in 2004, and it voted pretty much as it did in 2000—55%–44% for John Kerry, with Kerry leading in metro Chicago 60%–39% and Bush leading Downstate 55%–45%. Bush ran 3% ahead of his father's 1988 showing in Downstate Illinois, but Kerry ran 11% ahead of Michael Dukakis in metro Chicago.

It may seem strange that a state whose politics since Abraham Lincoln's time has mostly been run by political machines should be transformed by a change of opinion in the suburbs. Illinois's party machines were already up and going when they rallied thousands of partisans to cheer and boo at the debates between Lincoln and Stephen Douglas in 1858. Machine politics continued through the Gilded Age as politicians in a closely divided state competed for public jobs and as politicians of both parties courted the immigrants who came streaming into Chicago. Both Chicago and Downstate had a thriving two-party politics in the early 20th century; it was not until the Depression of the 1930s that Chicago became reliably Democratic. In the decades that followed, the suburbs, wary of Chicago, became Republican and developed machines of their own. Starting in 1950, Illinois's political trends were set by reactions to the political officeholder most visible to the voters, who was not the governor off in remote Springfield and certainly not the senators who have to work "out of town" in Washington, but the mayor of Chicago. It was only through the herculean efforts of mayor and party boss Richard J. Daley that John F. Kennedy was able to win Illinois by exactly (or so it was certified) 8,858 votes out of 4.7 million cast—a turnout that has been exceeded since only in 1984, 1992 and 2004. In the 1970s, reaction against Daley was key to the rise of James Thompson, who as U.S. Attorney successfully prosecuted machine denizens and served as governor from 1976 to 1990. For most of the 1980s the dominant figure was Mayor Harold Washington, the able black mayor who was vociferously opposed by white politicians in the "council wars." Suburbanites, repelled by the hubbub and out of fear that Chicago's demands might increase their taxes, voted heavily Republican.

The dominant figure since his election in 1989 has been Mayor Richard M. Daley. Like his father, he seems to know the city block by block, and has worked to beautify it—planting thousands of trees and encouraging handsome wrought-iron fences. The old political machine which his father so ably led is no more, but Daley has used the powers of office to propitiate the black politicians who at first seemed to be obdurate opponents; he has been reelected by overwhelming majorities. He has kept on good terms with presidents of both parties. Daley's luster has extended to his party. His example as the state's leading Democrat undoubtedly helped ease the way for suburbanites to move toward Democrats over the last 15 years.

What has resulted is a turnover of state government from Republicans to Democrats. In 1994 Republican Governor Jim Edgar was reelected and Republicans won majorities in both houses of the legislature. They lost their House majority in 1996 and their Senate majority in 2002. Democrat Richard Durbin was elected to the Senate in 1996 and easily reelected in 2002. In 1998 Republican Secretary of State George Ryan was elected governor and Republican Peter Fitzgerald beat ethics-challenged Senator Carol Moseley Braun but both had political problems. Ryan's top aides in the Secretary of State office were implicated in a bribery scandal; Ryan prudently decided not to run for reelection in 2002 and after leaving office was indicted in December 2003. The Republican nominee to succeed him, Attorney General Jim Ryan, was no relation, but having the same last name did not help him; he lost to Chicago Congressman Rod Blagojevich, who had the advantage of a name that no one could confuse with Ryan, 52%–45%. Blagojevich carried metro Chicago 57%–40% while losing Downstate 52%–46%: the key was the suburbs. In 2003 Senator Peter Fitzgerald, who had criticized George Ryan and many other Republican leaders, decided not to seek reelection; Democratic state senator and University of Chicago Law Professor Barack Obama won the seat by 70%–27%, the most one-sided Senate victory in Illinois history. His margin may have been a factor in the defeat of 8th District Congressman Philip Crane, the most senior House Republican, in what once had been an overwhelmingly Republican suburban district.

Democrats did have some problems. Disagreement between Blagojevich and Speaker Michael Madigan resulted in a budget passed 54 days late. Disagreements between Blagojevich and Daley also made headlines. Republicans gained one seat each in the state Senate and state House. But Illinois these days seems to be a solidly Democratic state, the only one of the nine largest states in which Democrats hold the governorship, both Senate seats, both houses of the legislature and a majority of the U.S. House seats.

The People		Race/Ethnic Origin			Military veterans: 1,003,572 (10.9%)	
Pop. 2004 (est):	12,713,634	8,424,140	67.8%	White	WWII: 22.7%	Korea: 14.4%
Pop. 2000:	12,419,293	1,856,152	14.9%	Black	Vietnam: 30.1%	Gulf War: 9.0%
Pop. 1990:	11,430,602	419,916	3.4%	Asian	**Most populous cities (2003):**	
Change 1990–2000:	Up 8.6%	18,232	0.1%	Native Am.	1. Chicago	2,869,121
% of U.S. total:	4.4%	3,116	0.0%	Hawaiian	2. Aurora	162,184
Pop. rank:	5th of 50	153,996	1.2%	Two+ races	3. Rockford	151,725
Area size:	57,914 sq. mi.	13,479	0.1%	Other	4. Naperville	137,894
State Native:	67.1%	1,530,262	12.3%	Hisp. Origin	5. Joliet	123,570
Non-citizen:	7.5%	**Ancestry**				
Language		German: 15.1%		Irish: 9.3%	Urban population: 87.8%	
English: 80.3%	Spanish: 9.6%	Polish: 5.8%		English: 5.1%	Rural population: 12.2%	
Other Eur.: 7.1%		Italian: 4.6%				

Education		Work Sector		General Assembly	
H.S. Grad:	81.4%	Private: 81.8%	Govt: 12.7%	Senate	31 D 27 R 1 I
College Grad:	26.1%	Self: 5.3%	Family: 0.3%	House	65 D 53 R
Industry		Unemployment: 6.0%		Legislative Term Limits: No	
Agri: 1.1%	Con: 5.7%	**Household Income**		**Registered Voters**	
Fin: 7.9%	Info: 3.0%	<15k: 13.8%	15-35k: 23.2%	No party registration	
Mfg: 22.0%	Prof: 29.5%	35-50k: 16.2%	50-100k: 32.3%		
Public: 4.0%	Trade: 14.9%	100-150k: 9.0%	>150k: 5.4%		
Other: 11.9%		Median: $46,590			
Occupation		Poverty status: 10.7%			
Blue collar: 24.0%	White collar: 61.8%	**Home Value**			
Gray collar: 14.3%		<50k: 11.2%	50-100k: 26.1%	100-200k: 39.7%	200-300k: 13.6%
		300-500k: 6.6%	>500k: 2.8%	Median: $127,800	

Presidential politics Illinois's presidential primary, for years held fittingly on or around St. Patrick's Day, clinched the nominations for Republican victors Gerald Ford in 1976, Ronald Reagan in 1980 and George Bush in 1988, and Democratic victors Jimmy Carter in 1980, Walter Mondale in 1984 and Bill Clinton in 1992. In 1988 the Democratic nomination would probably have been clinched here for Michael Dukakis, except for the dominance of two Illinois candidates, Paul Simon and Jesse Jackson. But as more states voted earlier, Illinois has voted too late to decide any nomination.

In the 1990s, as Republican margins in the suburban Collar Counties dwindled and in suburban Cook County disappeared, Illinois became a solidly Democratic state in presidential politics. Bush strategists in 2004 kept an eye out for favorable developments in California, with its 55 electoral votes, but they didn't pay attention to Illinois, with its 21.

2004 Presidential Vote
Kerry (D)..................... 2,891,550   (55%)
Bush (R) 2,345,946   (44%)
Badnarik (Lib)................. 32,442   (1%)
Other........................... 4,384   (0%)

2004 Democratic Presidential Primary
Kerry (D)...................... 873,230   (72%)
Edwards (D) 131,966   (11%)
Braun (D) 53,249   (4%)
Dean (D) 47,343   (4%)
Sharpton (D)................... 36,123   (3%)
Other.......................... 75,604   (6%)

2000 Presidential Vote
Gore (D)..................... 2,589,026   (55%)
Bush (R) 2,019,421   (43%)
Nader (Green) 103,759   (2%)
Other......................... 29,902   (1%)

Congressional districting Illinois lost one of its 20 House seats in the 2000 Census, and control of redistricting was split between the Democratic state House and the then-Republican state Senate and governor. In similar circumstances, the 1980s and 1990s redistricting plans had been drawn by courts, with results that were politically unpredictable and unpalatable to incumbents: in 1992, four incumbents lost their primaries. Things worked differently in

109th Congress Lineup
10 D   9 R

108th Congress Lineup
10 R   9 D

2001. Speaker Dennis Hastert and 3d District Democrat William Lipinski started negotiating early, to produce an incumbent-protection plan that would pass both houses of the legislature. Before the Census data came in, it was assumed that the 5th District would be eliminated, since Democratic incumbent Rod Blagojevich had announced that he was running for governor. But the Census figures showed that the 5th District and adjacent districts in Chicago, swelled with new immigrants, had gained population, while rural southern Illinois had lost population. Mayor Richard M. Daley let it be known that he would not like to see Chicago lose a seat.

So Hastert and Lipinski concocted a new plan taking a district away from southern Illinois. The victim was 19th District Democratic Congressman David Phelps, a former professional gospel singer with little seniority and a somewhat conservative voting record. His hometown was connected by a narrow band of land on the eastern edge of the state with the central Illinois 15th District held by Republican Tim Johnson. Phelps had no clout in the legislature, and the Hastert-Lipinski plan became law in May 2001. Phelps sued unsuccessfully and then ran, also unsuccessfully, against Republican incumbent John Shimkus in the new 19th District. Why were Lipinski, Daley and Speaker Michael Madigan willing to sacrifice a fellow Democrat and lose their party's 10–10 parity in the House delegation? Because the low-seniority Phelps could do little for them in the House, while Hastert had been generous in using his powers as Speaker to aid Daley, Lipinski and other Chicago Democrats on Chicago issues and projects. Maintaining a Republican majority that would keep Hastert in the speakership was in the interests of Chicago Democrats.

The resulting map is a nightmare for those who believe redistricting plans should have compact and competitive districts. Aside from Phelps and perhaps Shimkus, every other incumbent was strengthened. And the resulting district lines are grotesque. The 17th District, long confined to west central Illinois, now has a narrow finger extending to downtown Springfield and Decatur. The 15th District in central Illinois has a long narrow tentacle along the eastern border of the state, then snakes south to the Kentucky border. Hastert's 14th District extends from the Chicago suburbs to a point six miles from the Iowa border. Incumbents were accommodated in the most minute fashion. A small portion of Livingston County was added to Jerry Weller's 11th District so his parents could vote for him. Complicated boundaries were drawn to Philip Crane's 8th District so that his Palatine office would still be in his district (he lost anyway in 2004). Jesse Jackson Jr.'s 2d District was extended southward to be nearer to Peotone, the site for the proposed third Chicago airport that he has been tirelessly promoting. Lipinski lost a heavily black ward in Chicago and majority-Hispanic Cicero and in return got the white Bridgeport neighborhood that is the homeland of the Daleys and some heavily white suburbs (he engineered the nomination of his son to succeed him in 2004).

In 2005, Congressman Rahm Emanuel, the newly-installed chairman of the Democratic Congressional Campaign Committee, sought to revisit the issue of the state's congressional map; the idea was to draw a new map to retaliate for post-2002 Republican redistricting efforts in Colorado, Georgia and Texas. But the legislature didn't seem to have much interest in drawing new lines and neither did a majority of the Democratic congressional delegation. In March, the idea was shelved.

Governor

Rod Blagojevich (D)

Elected 2002, term expires Jan. 2007, 1st term; b. Dec. 10, 1956, Chicago; home, Chicago; Northwestern U., B.A. 1979, Pepperdine U., J.D. 1983; Eastern Orthodox; married (Patti).

Elected Office: IL House of Reps., 1992–96; U.S. House of Reps., 1996–2002.

Professional Career: Practicing atty., 1984–96; Asst. Cook County Atty., 1986–88.

Office: State Capitol, 207 Statehouse, Springfield, 62706, 217-782-6830; Fax: 217-524-1676; Web site: www.illinois.gov/gov.

Election Results

2002 general	Rod Blagojevich (D)	1,847,040	(52%)
	Jim Ryan (R)	1,594,960	(45%)
	Other	96,883	(3%)
2002 primary	Rod Blagojevich (D)	457,197	(37%)
	Paul Vallas (D)	431,728	(34%)
	Roland Burris (D)	363,591	(29%)
1998 general	George H. Ryan (R)	1,714,094	(51%)
	Glenn Poshard (D)	1,594,191	(47%)
	Other	50,420	(2%)

Rod Blagojevich was elected governor of Illinois in 2002, the first Democrat elected to the office since 1972, when Blagojevich was in high school. He grew up in Chicago, the son of a Serbian immigrant who worked at the A. Finkl & Sons steel works on the North Side; his mother worked as a ticket-taker for the Chicago Transit Authority. He lived in a five-room walkup near Cicero and Armitage and worked as a shoeshine boy and a dishwasher on the Alaskan pipeline. Blagojevich (pronounced *blah-GOY-eh-vich*) graduated from Northwestern and Pepperdine Law School and was a Golden Gloves boxer. A fine athlete, he runs marathons and climbs perilous mountains. He practiced law and worked two years in State's Attorney Richard M. Daley's office. But he got his start in politics through his father-in-law, 33d Ward Alderman and Democratic Ward Committeeman Richard Mell. Mell was first elected alderman in 1975; he delivered the highest ward percentage for Mayor Jane Byrne in 1983, against Harold Washington and Richard M. Daley, and was a foe of Washington in the 1980s "council wars"; he is currently chairman of the Council's Rules Committee. In 1988 Blagojevich met Mell's daughter Patti at a Mell fundraiser, and in 1990 they were married. In 1988 he got a job on Mell's staff; in 1992 he was elected to the Illinois House. His opportunity to run for the U.S. House came after Republican Michael Flanagan upset Ways and Means Chairman Dan Rostenkowski in 1994. Flanagan, who had little backing, was obviously a one-termer. In 1996 Blagojevich outspent Flanagan and won 64%–36%.

The initial impulse for Blagojevich's gubernatorial candidacy may have come from uncertainty about redistricting. It was fairly clear early on that Illinois would lose a seat in the 2000 Census, and most politicians assumed one of the Chicago districts would have to go—and Blagojevich's 5th District was vulnerable because it could easily be sliced up by its neighbors and was not represented by a black or Hispanic. Moreover, it was apparent that unpopular incumbent Republican Governor George Ryan, embroiled in scandal, would be hard put to win a second term. Blagojevich in July 2001 announced that he was running for governor. He plunged ahead, although the redistricting plan passed two months earlier had preserved his 5th District in almost identical form.

There were crowded races in both parties' March 2002 primaries. In the Democratic primary, Blagojevich faced former Chicago schools CEO Paul Vallas and former Attorney General Roland Burris. Burris was relying on his appeal to black voters, Vallas on his record in improving

Chicago's public schools, although he had left office at odds with his original patron, Mayor Richard M. Daley. In metro Chicago Vallas led with 38% of the vote to 32% for Burris and 29% for Blagojevich. But Blagojevich won 56% of the vote Downstate, for a 37%–34%–29% victory over Vallas and Burris. There was more acrimony on the Republican side. All three candidates vied to distance themselves from George Ryan. State Senator Patrick O'Malley campaigned as an outspoken conservative. Lieutenant Governor Corinne Wood, a supporter of abortion rights, said her two rivals were "too extreme" because they opposed abortion. Jim Ryan, no relation to the incumbent, well known from his years as DuPage County State's Attorney and state Attorney General, was pummeled from both sides. But he won convincingly, with 45% of the vote to 28% for O'Malley and 27% for Wood.

Ordinarily in Illinois politics it is an advantage to have an Irish name shared by other successful politicians. Candidates named Ryan, Hynes or Hines, or Cullerton are often elected to downballot state and Cook County offices without much difficulty and can easily become serious contenders for the top positions. But in 2002 it was not an advantage to be a Ryan. Jim Ryan was at pains to distinguish himself from George Ryan; his campaign signs said simply "Jim." In July 2002 Jim Ryan called on George Ryan to resign; in September George Ryan called Jim Ryan "a lousy candidate"; Jim Ryan said the governor "ran the worst administration in the history of Illinois." Jim Ryan lamented that Blagojevich was not being hurt by his ties to machine politicians. But Richard Mell was not a political liability in 2002 and Mayor Daley, the chairman of Blagojevich's campaign, was a decided political asset.

Blagojevich campaigned for "changing the old way of doing business—an obvious attack on George Ryan. Always ahead in the polls, he got support from big lobby groups which usually back Republicans—the Illinois State Medical Society, the Illinois Retail Merchants Association—and raised $25 million, far more than Jim Ryan. The only surprise about the outcome was that it was a bit closer than expected. Blagojevich won 52%–45%; he carried metro Chicago by a solid 57%–40% and lost Downstate by only 52%–46%—a good return on the time and money he spent there. On election night, held at the A. Finkl & Sons steel works, Blagojevich, a big Elvis Presley fan, said he was "all shook up" and full of "a whole bunch of hunk o', hunk o' burnin' love for each one of you." Democrats captured a majority in the state Senate, and Chicagoan Emil Jones succeeded longtime Republican leader Pate Philip as Senate Majority Leader; Democratic State Chairman and Speaker Michael Madigan remained in charge of the Chicago House. Federal investigators, led by U.S. Attorney Patrick Fitzgerald—an out-of-stater nominated by Republican Senator (and George Ryan critic) Peter Fitzgerald—zeroed in on George Ryan, and in December 2003 he was indicted on bribery charges; 59 other people involved in the scandal had already been convicted.

Democrats were in control of state government for the first time since 1976, and Democrats with friendly ties to Chicago politicians for the first time since 1968. But all was not harmony. "Illinois has voted for change," Blagojevich proclaimed, and proceeded to oppose the kind of pork spending which George Ryan had lavished on legislators of both parties. As co-chairman of his transition team he named former Governor Jim Thompson, a Republican who had built his career on opposition to the Chicago machine. He announced that he would govern from Chicago, and traveled to the gritty state capital of Springfield only rarely (a not unheard of procedure: current or recent governors of California, New York and Illinois have spent more time in Los Angeles, New York City and Chicago rather than their state capitals than most voters would guess). He hired his law school roommate from California and a former top aide to Senator Charles Schumer and Mayor Michael Bloomberg of New York as top aides in a state where politics is an intensely parochial matter. Senate Minority Leader Frank Watson said, "He's taken us on. He's taken the constitutional officers on. Maybe in his eyes that builds him up. But it tears the process down." Senate Majority Leader Emil Jones said, "Well, he does a pretty good job of communicating—if I read the papers in time." Blagojevich's response: "The system has to change. I know it, I presume you know it and I know the people know it. We are going to keep fighting to change this system, a system that has way too much cynicism, a system that has too many misplaced priorities and a system that spends the people's money with reckless disregard."

On many issues the new governor prevailed. In 2003 he vetoed one ethics package passed by the legislature and got it to pass a much stronger version. He succeeded in keeping his promise not to allow increases in the sales or income taxes. He got steep cuts in some programs and an increase in education spending; borrowing $10 billion to shore up pension systems freed $2 billion for operating expenses. He got changes in the death penalty law, and got the legislature to strike a provision on police perjury which was supported by Emil Jones but opposed by police unions. Richard M. Daley's plan for vastly expanding O'Hare Airport—the mayor's absolute number one priority—was approved. The minimum wage was increased. But there were clashes along the way, with Secretary of State Jesse White over spending for his office, with Michael Madigan over the 2004 budget. In 2004 Blagojevich and Jones were allies on the budget, with Madigan and Senate Republican leaders as their adversaries seeking cuts in education and Medicaid: scrambled political alignments reminiscent of the city-states of Renaissance Italy.

Riverboat gambling has become a big business in Illinois, and state government faces current gambling issues. In May 2004, one day after Mayor Daley called for a city-run casino in Chicago, Blagojevich abruptly rejected the proposal; he said that gambling should be confined to depressed riverfront areas. At the same time, Attorney General Lisa Madigan, Michael Madigan's daughter, abruptly blocked the Illinois Gaming Board's award of a bankrupt casino's license to a company that wanted to build a new casino at Rosemont, next to O'Hare Airport. Blagojevich sponsored the first state-run program to enable people to buy prescription drugs from Canada, Britain and Ireland and ignored the FDA's pleas that he cease and desist; but by November 2004 only a few seniors had signed up. In October 2003 he hired historian Richard Norton Smith to head the troubled Lincoln President Library and Museum in Springfield, which "very frankly has failed every expectation" and "got unfortunately caught up in politics and patronage" under George Ryan. In the Chicago area most interstates are named after politicians and road builders; Blagojevich named I-88 after Ronald Reagan. In 2004 Blagojevich considered naming a state (non-alcoholic) beverage in return for money.

During most of 2003 and 2004 Blagojevich's job approval remained at or above 50%, far better than his predecessor's. But in 2005 his poll ratings dropped amid news reports about alleged cronyism in his administration and favors for campaign donors. A family feud with his powerful father-in-law, Alderman Richard Mell, also drew considerable attention; in May, Blagojevich said that by confronting Mell over a disputed landfill operation he had shown "testicular virility." The Republicans' gain of one seat each in the state House and Senate in November 2004 were of little political significance in the legislature, since the chief battles there have been between Democrats. Blagojevich continued to raise large sums of money and it is not clear, given Republicans' difficulties in coming up with a substitute candidate for U.S. senator in 2004, whether he will face a serious Republican challenger in 2006. As early as November 2002 Blagojevich was already talking with Democratic allies about a six-year plan to run for president in 2008; little was heard of that in 2003 and 2004, but a solid reelection victory may revive the prospect.

Senior Senator

Richard Durbin (D)

Elected 1996, seat up 2008, 2d term; b. Nov. 21, 1944, E. St. Louis; home, Springfield; Georgetown U., B.S. 1966, J.D. 1969; Catholic; married (Loretta).

Elected Office: U.S. House of Reps., 1982–96.

Professional Career: Staff, Lt. Gov. Paul Simon, 1969–72; Legal Cnsl., IL Sen. Judiciary Cmte., 1972–82; Prof., S. IL Schl. of Medicine, 1978–82.

DC Office: 332 DSOB, 20510, 202-224-2152; Fax: 202-228-0400; Web site: durbin.senate.gov.

State Offices: Chicago, 312-353-4952; Marion, 618-998-8812; Springfield, 217-492-4062.

Committees: *Minority Whip. Appropriations*: Agriculture, Rural Development & Related Agencies; Defense; District of Columbia; Labor, Health and Human Services, Education & Related Agencies; Legislative Branch (RMM); State, Foreign Operations & Related Programs; Transportation, Treasury, the Judiciary, HUD & Related Agencies. *Judiciary*: Constitution, Civil Rights & Property Rights; Corrections & Rehabilitation (RMM); Immigration, Border Security & Citizenship; Intellectual Property; Terrorism, Technology & Homeland Security. *Rules & Administration*.

Group Ratings

	ADA	ACLU	AFS	LCV	ITIC	NTU	COC	ACU	NTLC	CHC
2004	95	89	100	83	58	8	47	4	5	0
2003	95	—	100	89	—	14	35	10	—	—

National Journal Ratings

	2003 LIB	—	2003 CONS		2004 LIB	—	2004 CONS
Economic	93%	—	0%		90%	—	7%
Social	79%	—	15%		82%	—	0%
Foreign	79%	—	14%		95%	—	1%

Key Votes of the 108th Congress

1. Ban Drilling in ANWR	Y	5. Energy Bill	N	9. Ban Same-Sex Marriage	N
2. Approve Bush Tax Cuts	N	6. Support Roe v. Wade	Y	10. Ban Bunker-Buster Bomb	Y
3. Medicare/Rx Bill	N	7. Ban Partial-Birth Abortion	N	11. Fund Iraq War	Y
4. Bar Overtime Pay Regs.	Y	8. Assault Weapons Ban	Y	12. Restrict Missile Defense	Y

Election Results

2002 general	Richard Durbin (D)	2,103,766	(60%)	($4,979,865)
	Jim Durkin (R)	1,325,703	(38%)	($794,634)
	Other	57,382	(2%)	
2002 primary	Richard Durbin (D)	unopposed		
1996 general	Richard Durbin (D)	2,384,028	(56%)	($4,966,804)
	Al Salvi (R)	1,728,824	(41%)	($4,696,065)
	Other	137,870	(3%)	

Prior Winning Percentages: 1994 House (55%); 1992 House (57%); 1990 House (66%); 1988 House (69%); 1986 House (68%); 1984 House (61%); 1982 House (50%)

Richard Durbin, Illinois's senior senator, is a Democrat first elected to the House in 1982 and the Senate in 1996. Durbin grew up in East St. Louis, and for almost all his adult life has been in politics: Right out of law school he joined Paul Simon's staff when he was lieutenant governor (1969–73), then was a state Senate staffer in the 1970s. He lost two races for office in the 1970s, but in 1982 won the nomination to oppose Republican Congressman Paul Findley, who had characterized himself as Yasir Arafat's best friend in Congress; that helped Durbin raise large sums from Israel supporters. Durbin won that race, got a seat on the Agriculture Committee and then moved to Appropriations, where in 1993 he became chairman of the Agriculture Subcommittee. Durbin's father died of lung cancer when he was 14, and Durbin's most prominent achievement in the House was the 1988 ban on smoking on domestic airline flights; he followed that up by trying to limit tobacco subsidies and in 1994 moved unsuccessfully to direct the FDA to regulate tobacco as a health hazard.

Durbin won his Senate seat in 1996 after his onetime employer Senator Paul Simon announced his retirement; the race may have looked more attractive because Democrats had lost control of the House in 1994 and because Durbin's own margins in the 1992 and 1994 House races were fairly close. Raising more than $1 million, he outspent former state Treasurer (and current Lieutenant Governor) Pat Quinn in the March 1996 primary and won 65%–30%. In the general he faced trial lawyer and abortion opponent Al Salvi and won 56%–41%.

In the Senate, Durbin has compiled a liberal voting record, though he has supported welfare reform and the death penalty. He has been an active and dependable Democratic partisan on the floor and on cable news networks. After the defeat of Tom Daschle in 2004 and the elevation of Harry Reid as minority leader, Durbin became minority whip—a natural promotion since he has held the floor for Democrats on many seriously contested issues. He serves on the Judiciary Committee and has been a strong opponent of the Bush judicial nominees whom the Democrats have chosen to oppose. In his early years there he attempted to move his goal of gun control incrementally forward. But many Democrats have concluded that gun control helped defeat Al Gore in 2000 and these moves have not been successful. While serving in the House, Durbin favored restrictions on abortion, including the Hyde Amendment and the Human Life amendment. But in the Senate he has opposed restrictions on abortion, including the partial-birth abortion ban; he said it should include an exception for health of the mother. This has caused some controversy among his fellow Catholics. In April 2004 the priest at his home church in Springfield said that he wouldn't give Holy Communion to Durbin; he said that earlier leafletters had subjected him to a "rather uncomfortable atmosphere" there. Durbin responded, "It troubles me to have some members of the Church—and I'm not pointing to the clergy now, I'm really speaking to laypeople—who have appointed themselves the policemen of the church." In June 2004 he presented a report showing how senators voted on positions taken by the U.S. Conference of Catholic Bishops, including international and domestic issues beyond abortion; it showed Democratic senators, including John Kerry, Edward Kennedy and Durbin himself with records above 60%.

On other domestic issues, Durbin has had a very strong pro-union voting record, but split with them on trade, supporting NAFTA in the House and normal trade relations with China in the Senate: Illinois is a big exporter. In the wake of September 11, Durbin proposed $1.8 billion for more security on trains and on rail bridges and tunnels and for national standards for state-issued driver's licenses; in 2004 he called for more spending on air traffic controllers than the Bush administration proposed.

Durbin took a lead role on asbestos legislation in 2003. Called on by Illinois-based businesses to support a bill establishing quick recovery for injured plaintiffs and reducing the burden on businesses only tangentially connected with asbestos, he negotiated with Judiciary Committee Chairman Orrin Hatch. But Durbin insisted on a "collateral source" amendment which would grandfather in existing asbestos cases and settlements—a poison pill, in the view of the National Association of Manufacturers. His amendment was not approved and an asbestos bill was not passed. In July 2003 Minority Leader Tom Daschle asked Durbin to be the Democrats' point man on medical malpractice, and he successfully blocked action on the legislation. In November 2003 Durbin opposed the energy bill because of the provisions relieving liability for MTBE; Hastert said he was doing the bidding of the trial lawyers, but in any case the legislation did not pass.

Durbin voted against the Gulf War resolution in January 1991 and the Iraq war resolution in October 2002, though he voted to authorize the use of force in Iraq when Bill Clinton was president in February 1998. In July 2003 he took to the Senate floor to charge that the Bush White House was trying to push him off the Intelligence Committee; some Republican senators said that Durbin may have disclosed classified information. In June and July 2004 he charged that there are "those in the Bush administration who are misinterpreting or ignoring intelligence, who are misusing intelligence and who are setting up their own intelligence-gathering agencies that actually compete with the CIA." He unsuccessfully called on White House staffers to testify before the Intelligence Committee. In September 2004 he called for a special committee to investigate government contracts in Iraq and Afghanistan. In June 2005, Durbin was at the center of a storm over remarks he made from the Senate floor concerning detainees at Guantanamo Bay. Citing an FBI report that described the mistreatment of some prisoners, Durbin likened the American interrogators to "Nazis, Soviets in their gulags, or some mad regime—Pol Pot or others—that had no concern for human beings." His over-the-top comments dominated the news cycle for days; Durbin said he regretted any misunderstanding over his remarks. When that failed to quell the furor, a few days later he issued an emotional apology from the Senate floor.

Durbin was mentioned briefly in 2000 as a possible vice presidential nominee; he said that he had been contacted by the Gore campaign in June and asked for information, but had called back four days later to say they he did not want to be considered. He was reelected 60%–38% in 2002 against an opponent who raised very little money; the parties' Senate campaign committees are unwilling to put money into a long shot race in a large state like Illinois when they can target races in much smaller states with much less money. In March 2004 Durbin was asked by John Kerry to be a co-chairman of the Democratic National Committee and to speak for the ticket on the campaign trail. This time he was not much mentioned as a vice presidential nominee and played only a small role—introducing his soon-to-be colleague Barack Obama—at the Democratic National Convention. In Washington he continues to live in what some call an "animal house" with Senate colleague Charles Schumer and Congressmen George Miller and William Delahunt.

Junior Senator

Barack Obama (D)

Elected 2004, seat up 2010, 1st term; b. Aug. 4, 1961, Honolulu, HI; home, Chicago; Attended Occidental College, 1979–81; Columbia U., B.A. 1983; Harvard Law Schl., J.D. 1991; United Church of Christ; married (Michelle).

Elected Office: IL Senate, 1996–2004.

Professional Career: Dir., Illinois Project Vote!, 1992; Practicing atty.; Lecturer, U. of Chicago, 1993–2004.

DC Office: 713 HSOB, 20510, 202-224-2854; Fax: 202-228-4260; Web site: obama.senate.gov.

State Offices: Chicago, 312-886-3506; Marion, 618-997-2402; Springfield, 217-492-5089.

Committees: *Environment & Public Works*: Clean Air, Climate Change & Nuclear Safety; Fisheries, Wildlife & Water. *Foreign Relations*: African Affairs; East Asian & Pacific Affairs; International Economic Policy, Export & Trade Promotion; Near Eastern & South Asian Affairs. *Veterans' Affairs*.

Group Ratings and Key Votes: Newly Elected

Election Results

2004 general	Barack Obama (D)	3,595,299	(70%)	($14,532,493)
	Alan Keyes (R)	1,389,850	(27%)	($2,545,325)
	Other	153,158	(3%)	
2004 primary	Barack Obama (D)	655,923	(53%)	
	Daniel Hynes (D)	294,717	(24%)	
	Blair Hull (D)	134,453	(11%)	
	Maria Pappas (D)	74,987	(6%)	
	Gery Chico (D)	53,433	(4%)	
	Other	29,483	(2%)	
1998 general	Peter Fitzgerald (R)	1,709,041	(50%)	($17,678,198)
	Carol Moseley-Braun (D)	1,610,496	(47%)	($7,200,895)
	Other	74,984	(2%)	

Barack Obama, Illinois's junior senator, was a national political celebrity even before he was elected to the Senate in November 2004. His background is unusual, quite different from that of most black politicians, yet as quintessentially American as that of Tiger Woods. Obama's father was from Kenya, his mother from Kansas; they met in Hawaii, where her parents had gone to live and where Barack Jr. was born in 1961. When he was 2, Obama's father left to get a degree at Harvard, then returned to Kenya where he was a prominent politician and then, after a downward spiral, died in an auto accident in 1982; Obama recalls meeting him only once, when he was 10. Obama's mother married an Indonesian, and the family moved there; he attended both Muslim and Catholic schools for two years, then went back to Hawaii to attend Punahou Academy and live with his maternal grandparents. Hawaii was even then very much a multiracial background, but Obama mused long about his background, as he recounted in his 1995 autobiography *Dreams from My Father: A Story of Race and Inheritance*. He went east to college, first to Occidental College in Los Angeles, then to Columbia University in New York. After graduation he worked as a community organizer in Chicago from 1985 to 1988. He then attended Harvard Law School, where he graduated *magna cum laude* and was the first black president of the *Harvard Law Review* (and was also a classmate of Bush 2004 campaign manager and Republican National Chairman Ken Mehlman). He and his wife, also a Harvard Law graduate, then moved to Chicago, her hometown, where in 1993 he became a lecturer at the University of Chicago law school.

Politics always seems to have been on his mind. In 1992 he worked on voter registration for the Democratic ticket. In 1996 he ran for the state Senate and was unopposed in the decisive Democratic primary. Next came a political misstep: in 2000 he ran in the primary against 1st District Democratic Congressman Bobby Rush, who the year before had lost the February 1999 race for mayor to incumbent Richard M. Daley by 72%–28%. Obama was attacked for missing a vote on a gun control measure sought by Daley and Governor George Ryan because he was in Hawaii, visiting family, and one of his daughters was ill. Rush was endorsed by Bill Clinton and won 61%–30%. Obama compiled an impressive record in the state Senate. He played important roles in welfare legislation, on the earned income tax credit and on the 2003 ethics legislation. In 2003 he pushed successfully for a law requiring electronic recording of interrogations and confessions in homicide cases; prosecutors resisted it, but he argued persuasively that it would insure convictions in the large majority of cases.

Looming not too far ahead was the 2004 Senate race. Illinois has one of the earliest filing deadlines and state primaries in the nation, in December 2003 and in March 2004 in this case, and the incumbent senator, Republican Peter Fitzgerald, was obviously in trouble. Elected in 1998 in large part because of the ethical shortcomings of incumbent Democrat Carol Moseley Braun, he had compiled an attractive record on ethics himself, challenging Ryan on the financing of the Abraham Lincoln Library and Museum, bringing in an out-of-stater, Patrick Fitzgerald (no relation) as U.S. Attorney in Chicago, opposing cozy political deals by old-style politicians. But Fitzgerald would have to run in an increasingly Democratic state, and without the support of leading Illinois Republicans; in November 2002 Congressman Ray LaHood said, "I'm thinking about trying to make sure that Peter has an opponent" in the Republican primary, and the Republican state committee declined to support Fitzgerald for reelection. In 1998 Fitzgerald had largely self-financed his campaign, but his wealth would have been serious diminished by another such race, and in April 2003 he announced he would not seek reelection.

With Democratic Senator Richard Durbin comfortably reelected in 2002 and still in the prime of life, it seemed that another Illinois Senate seat would not come open for many years, perhaps a generation, so a host of candidates—eight Democrats and eight Republicans, many of them capable of self-financing a campaign—entered the 2004 race. Initially Obama did not stand out among them. As an African-American he had an edge with black voters, who would probably make up 25% of the primary electorate. But some prominent black politicians, notably Bobby Rush, endorsed other candidates, though Obama was backed by state Senate Majority Leader Emil Jones, 2d District Congressman Jesse Jackson Jr. and 1984 and 1988 presidential candidate Jesse Jackson Sr. His positions on issues were not particularly distinctive among Illinois Democrats—he favored abortion rights, background checks on all gun sales, and was willing to filibuster Bush judicial nominees. He was for civil unions but against same-sex marriage inasmuch as it is widely opposed in many parts of the country; he backed only the middle-class Bush tax cuts and favored pay-as-you-go budgeting, which is consistent with tax increases on the wealthy.

Other candidates seemed better positioned. State Comptroller Dan Hynes, elected to that office in 1998 at age 30, from a prominent Cook County Democratic family, was backed by Cook County Board President John Stroger and Cook County Commissioner John Daley, brother of Mayor Richard M. Daley. Blair Hull, who sold his trading firm to Goldman-Sachs in 1999 for $531 million, had contributed $260,000 to Governor Rod Blagojevich in 2002 and announced that he was willing to spend $40 million of his own money on his campaign. He imitated Blagojevich's 2002 tactic by buying Downstate TV starting in June 2003 and spent $29 million by the March primary, including $75 a day for anyone who would put up a lawn sign. Also running were Cook County Treasurer Maria Pappas and former Chicago School Board President Gery Chico, each with plausible claims on the nomination. But Hull turned out to have serious problems. It was revealed that he had struck his first wife in the shin in 1998 and that she had sought a protection order, calling him "a violent man with an ungovernable temper." His lead in the polls collapsed. Hynes was unable to translate his support from prominent officeholders in the face of Obama's poised performances in endorsement meetings. Obama's opposition to the Iraq war resolution and his dismissive criticism of some Bush policies helped establish a bond with the Bush-hating Deaniacs of his party. And he had some other endorsements—a $10,000 contribution from Michael Jordan and an ad featuring Sheila Simon, daughter of former (1984–96) Senator Paul Simon, a fondly remembered and thoughtful politician who had died in December 2003. Obama was endorsed by the *Chicago Tribune*, no reflexive backer of Democrats, as "one of the strongest Democratic candidates Illinois has seen in some time"—something of a slap in the face to Senator Durbin and Governor Blagojevich. The March primary was a blowout victory for Obama. He won 53% of the vote in an eight-candidate race, to 24% for Hynes, 11% for Hull, 6% for Pappas and 4% for Chico. In metro Chicago, where 74% of the votes were cast, and where the race received the most coverage in the free media, Obama led Hynes 63%–17%. Hull, benefiting from his early ads, won a plurality of 24% Downstate, but that didn't matter. As Obama said on election night, "I think it is fair to say the conventional wisdom was we could not win. We didn't have enough money. We didn't have enough organization. There was no way that a skinny guy from the South Side with a funny name like Barack Obama could ever win a statewide race. Sixteen months later we are there." Moreover, the primary turnout showed huge Democratic strength. Some 1,242,000 voted in the Democratic primary, while only 661,000 voted in the Republican primary—just a tad bit over the 656,000 votes Obama won.

The Senate race was over except for the shouting—but there turned out to be quite a lot of that. The Republican nominee was Jack Ryan, who led the eight-candidate field with 35% of the vote and, like Obama, had an attractive life story. He had graduated from Harvard Law and Harvard Business Schools, made a fortune working for Goldman Sachs and had then gone to teach in an inner city school. He and Obama might have had a series of civil exchanges on the issues. But Ryan, like Hull, had a divorce problem. Before the primary he released the records of his California divorce from television actress Jeri Ryan, except for some passages which he said would be harmful to his nine-year-old son. After the primary the *Chicago Tribune* pressed for full disclosure. In June a California judge agreed. It turned out that Ryan had pressed his former wife, against her wish, to go to sex clubs in Paris. Republican party leaders were furious that Ryan had not told them of this vulnerability, and pressed him to get out of the race. After an agonizing interval he did—and then the Republicans had to figure out who to put in his place. The candidates who lost the primary proved either unwilling or unacceptable. Former Chicago Bears coach Mike Ditka thought about it, and said no.

While this was going on, Obama delivered the keynote speech at the Democratic National Convention. In quietly elegant prose, with echoes of the rhythms of black preachers, Obama proclaimed to delegates of a party that tends to divide its ranks into discrete constituencies, "There's not a liberal America and a conservative America, there is the United States of America. There's not a black America and white America and Latino America and Asian America, there is the United States of America." Drawing on his own experiences campaigning in Illinois, he said,

"We worship an awesome God in the Blue States, and we don't like federal agents poking around in our libraries in the Red States. We coach Little League in the Blue States, and yes, we've got some gay friends in the Red States." And, echoing Bill Cosby, he spoke about the black community. "Go into any inner city neighborhood, and folks will tell you that government alone can't teach our kids to learn—they know that parents have to teach, that children can't achieve unless we raise their expectation and turn off the television sets and eradicate the slander that says a black youth with a book is acting white. They know these things." Immediately, and not without justification, commentators were hailing this state senator from Hyde Park as a national leader and possible future president.

Republicans still did not have a candidate against him, and it was clear none could do very well. As Peter Fitzgerald said, "Taking the Republican nomination in Illinois for the U.S. Senate would be akin to accepting a cancer transplant." Cultural conservatives, including 16th District Congressman Don Manzullo, put forward the name of Alan Keyes, the fiery conservative who had run for president in 1996 and 2000. Keyes is a Harvard Ph.D. who believes that the purpose of America is defined by the Declaration of Independence and that abortion is a violation of the Declaration's principle of respect for life, liberty and the pursuit of happiness. He had run for the Senate twice before, in Maryland, losing 62%–38% to Paul Sarbanes in 1988 and 71%–29% to Barbara Mikulski in 1992. Inconveniently, he still lived in Maryland and in 2000 had sharply criticized Hillary Rodham Clinton's move into New York to run for the Senate. But this was different, Keyes said; he was being invited to run by the Illinois Republican party. On August 4 he became its nominee.

In a state where liberal cultural views had moved critical suburban votes to the Democrats, Keyes chose to campaign primarily on abortion and same-sex marriage. Polls showed Obama with huge majorities, and the state Republican party sent out mailers omitting Keyes's name. Former Governor Jim Thompson said he wouldn't vote for him; former Governor Jim Edgar and Speaker Dennis Hastert said they'd vote for the Republican ticket; Manzullo said he was still for Keyes, but "I don't like the way he says some things"; state Republican Chairman Judy Baar Topinka said one of his comments was "idiotic." In mid-October the FEC fined Keyes $23,000 for receiving $180,000 in illegal donations to his 2000 presidential campaign. Obama meanwhile was confident enough to contribute $283,000 to other campaigns and send volunteers into Wisconsin to campaign for the Kerry-Edwards ticket.

Obama won 70%–27%, the widest victory margin in Illinois history. Keyes carried 9 heavily Republican counties in southern Illinois; Obama carried the other 93. Obama carried blacks 92%–8% and whites 66%–31%; he won 70% or more from all income groups; Keyes carried Republicans by only 56%–40% and, in a state where there are almost as many liberals as conservatives, carried conservatives by only 61%–33%. Keyes declined to call Obama with congratulations, saying it would be a "false gesture," and promised to remain active in Illinois politics. Obama appeared on *Meet the Press* and *This Week* and was featured on the cover of *Newsweek*. Obama predicted this attention would be fleeting, and his voting record in the Senate is likely to be less distinctive from those of his Democratic colleagues than his speech at the Convention was to standard Democratic oratory. Still he stands out, and seems likely to be a major American politician for a generation to come.

FIRST DISTRICT

Rep. Bobby Rush (D)

Elected 1992, 7th term; b. Nov. 23, 1946, Albany, GA; home, Chicago; Roosevelt U., B.A. 1973, U. of IL, M.A. 1994, McCormick Seminary, M.A. 1998; Baptist; married (Carolyn).

Military Career: Army, 1963–68.

Elected Office: Chicago City Alderman, 1983–92; 2d Ward Committeeman, 1984–present.

Professional Career: Member, Student Non–Violent Coord. Cmte., 1966–68; Co–founder, IL Black Panther Party, 1968; Med. Clinic Dir., 1970–1973; insurance agent, 1978–83.

DC Office: 2416 RHOB, 20515, 202-225-4372; Fax: 202-226-0333; Web site: www.house.gov/rush.

District Office: Chicago, 773-224-6500.

Committees: *Energy & Commerce* (9th of 26 D): Commerce, Trade & Consumer Protection; Health; Telecommunications & the Internet.

Group Ratings

	ADA	ACLU	AFS	LCV	ITIC	NTU	COC	ACU	NTLC	CHC
2004	100	100	100	91	30	11	24	0	3	15
2003	95	—	100	85	—	23	29	8	—	—

National Journal Ratings

	2003 LIB	—	2003 CONS		2004 LIB	—	2004 CONS
Economic	68%	—	32%		81%	—	18%
Social	92%	—	0%		88%	—	0%
Foreign	89%	—	8%		91%	—	7%

Key Votes of the 108th Congress

1. Drilling in ANWR	N	5. DC School Vouchers	N	9. Ban Same-Sex Marriage	N
2. Approve Bush Tax Cuts	N	6. Ban Human Cloning	N	10. Fund Iraq War	N
3. Medicare/Rx Bill	N	7. Restrict Gun Liability	N	11. Bar Cuba Embargo Funds	Y
4. Bar Overtime Pay Regs.	Y	8. Ban Partial-Birth Abortion	N	12. Intelligence Reorg.	N

Election Results

2004 general	Bobby Rush (D)	212,109	(85%)	($361,032)
	Raymond Wardingley (R)	37,840	(15%)	
2004 primary	Bobby Rush (D)	unopposed		
2002 general	Bobby Rush (D)	149,068	(81%)	($299,460)
	Raymond Wardingley (R)	29,776	(16%)	
	Other	4,812	(3%)	

Prior Winning Percentages: 2000 (88%); 1998 (87%); 1996 (86%); 1994 (76%); 1992 (83%)

The People		Race/Ethnic Origin	Ancestry	
Area size:	99 sq. mi.	27.3% White	Irish: 7.1%	German: 6.2%
Urban population:	100.0%	65.2% Black	Polish: 4.5%	
Rural population:	0.0%	1.4% Asian	**2004 Presidential Vote**	
Pop. 2000:	653,647	0.1% Native Am.	Kerry (D)	234,086 (83%)
Median income:	$37,222	0.0% Hawaiian	Bush (R)	47,533 (17%)
Poverty status:	19.7%	1.0% Two+ races	Other	565 (0%)
Military veterans:	10.8%	0.1% Other	**2000 Presidential Vote**	
		4.8% Hispanic Origin	Gore (D)	213,244 (84%)
			Bush (R)	39,400 (15%)
			Other	2,097 (1%)
			Cook Partisan Voting Index: D +35	
Occupation	Blue collar: 21.6%	White collar: 61.3%	Gray collar: 17.1%	

The South Side of Chicago has been the nation's largest urban black community for nearly a century now. A hundred years ago there were just a few blocks where black families from the

South could settle; this ghetto grew rapidly with the first influx of blacks from the Mississippi Delta in the 1910s. By the 1920s the South Side was well established, a center of blues music in America and of black-owned businesses. Politically, the South Side was a heavily Republican constituency throughout those years; the comfortable white Protestants who settled in solid brick houses here believed in the party of Yankee propriety, and the blacks had faith in the party of Lincoln. This was one of the heartlands of the Republican Party, represented in the House in the 1920s by Appropriations Chairman Martin Madden. After Madden died in the Appropriations Committee room in 1928, the 1st District elected Oscar DePriest, the first black elected to the House in the 20th century. Blacks remained faithful to the party of Lincoln even during the Depression, voting for Herbert Hoover and DePriest in 1932.

The New Deal and the racial liberalism of New Dealers like Eleanor Roosevelt and Interior Secretary Harold Ickes (both former Republicans themselves) attracted blacks to the Democratic Party, and black Democrat Arthur Mitchell beat DePriest in 1934. The South Side has been Democratic ever since. For 40 years it was a cooperative part of Chicago's Democratic machine; then, after the death of longtime Congressman William Dawson, it rebelled against Mayor Richard J. Daley. The South Side seemed to take over the city when Congressman Harold Washington was elected mayor in 1983 and 1987. After Washington died in November 1987, other black South Side politicians flailed at each other, even though Chicago's electorate peaked at about 40% black (because so many blacks have been moving to the suburbs) and black candidates need non-black voters to win.

The 1st Congressional District of Illinois includes about half of Chicago's black South Side community plus many suburbs beyond. The lines were sharply redrawn by the 2001 redistricting—only 54% of the new district was in the old 1st—since the 1st and adjacent 2d Districts each needed to add about 100,000 people. The 1st has a northern salient that includes some of Chicago's first black neighborhoods plus the Gothic spires of the University of Chicago and the mansions of Kenwood, once the home of Chicago's Jewish aristocracy and more recently the headquarters of the Nation of Islam and home to its leader, Louis Farrakhan. It includes most of the South Side from Stony Island west almost to the city limit and from 60th Street to 95th—miles and miles of bungalow neighborhoods, with single-family houses lining arrow-straight streets. In neighborhoods such as Englewood, which lost more than half of its population after 1970, thousands of private residential homes have been built with federal support in recent years in hopes of creating a new black middle-class community; some have been placed on vacant lands or in abandoned buildings that housed gangs. Redistricting added the heavily black 18th Ward and gave up the mostly white 19th Ward to the 3d District. From there a narrow neck connects the 1st with a still mostly white collection of suburbs, starting with Blue Island and fanning southwest to Palos Heights, Orland Park and Oak Forest. The 1st remains overwhelmingly Democratic: Only 15% for George W. Bush in 2000, his weakest district in Illinois that year, and just 17% for him in 2004.

The congressman from the 1st District is Bobby Rush, a man who has gone through several transformations. He grew up on the North Side, a Boy Scout whose mother was a Republican precinct captain. In the Army he became involved in the Student Non-Violent Coordinating Committee in the South, then went AWOL. He founded the Illinois Black Panthers, with its "Power to the People" slogan; there he recruited Fred Hampton, who became chairman but was later killed in a raid by police in 1969; the next day, police raided Rush's family's apartment, but he wasn't there. Rush served six months in prison for illegal possession of firearms, but also during his time with the Black Panthers he had run a medical clinic that developed the nation's first mass sickle cell anemia testing program. "I don't repudiate any of my involvement in the Panther party—it was part of my maturing," Rush later said. Lately, he has commemorated the anniversary of the raid by holding a job fair to promote the future. In 1983 he was elected 2d Ward alderman and became a strong Harold Washington supporter. In 1992, he challenged Congressman Charles Hayes, an older generation politician with a union background. Just before the primary it was revealed that Hayes had 716 overdrafts on the House bank. Rush won 42%–39%.

In the House, Rush has a liberal voting record; he serves on the Energy and Commerce Committee. Rush's rhetoric has toned down over the years, and his more deliberate style contrasts sharply with his days as a Panther. Gun violence caused great pain to Rush in 1999, when his son Huey Rich—who was born three weeks before the 1969 police raid, and, although raised by an aunt, had recently grown close to his father—was murdered by a man wielding a handgun as he returned to his South Side home with his fiancée. The experience moved him spiritually to the point that he was ordained as a Baptist minister, and he founded in October 2002 a church in the depressed Englewood community. In the 108th Congress, he ran for chairman of the Congressional Black Caucus, but Elijah Cummings of Maryland defeated him. In July 2004, he was arrested when he sought to block the front door of the Sudan embassy in Washington.

Rush waged a quixotic mayoral campaign in 1999 against Richard M. Daley, of whom he has sometimes been a harsh critic. During the campaign, he attacked the mayor for tolerating police brutality, inadequate mass-transit service and "cronyism." House colleagues Jesse Jackson Jr. and Danny Davis were at his side, but only three of the 50 aldermen endorsed him. Rush insisted that he wanted to build a multiracial coalition, but for practical purposes his only chance was with black voters. Daley's record was too popular and his financial advantage overwhelming. Daley won the February primary by 72%–28%, with nearly 45% of the black vote and the support of many prominent black ministers.

After that pounding, Rush found himself challenged in the primary in 2000 by two state senators—Donne Trotter and the then little-known Barack Obama. Obama waged an active campaign, but was attacked for being absent from the legislature for two months and missing a vote on a gun control bill. He was on a family trip to Hawaii that was extended after his daughter got sick, he said—South Side voters may not have known that Obama grew up in Hawaii and may have had little sympathy for a candidate who escaped a Chicago January for Hawaii's sunny climate. Rush was also helped by an endorsement from Bill Clinton and beat Obama 61%–30%. Surely not by coincidence, redistricting shifted Obama's Hyde Park home two blocks outside the new lines and removed the 19th Ward that he had carried. Rush has been routinely reelected since then. In the 2004 Senate primary, he was campaign chairman for free spending ($29 million) self-financer Blair Hull, who finished third; after the primary he warmly supported Obama.

SECOND DISTRICT

Rep. Jesse Jackson Jr. (D)

Elected Dec. 1995, 5th full term; b. Mar. 11, 1965, Greenville, SC; home, Chicago; NC A&T, B.S. 1987, Chicago Theological Seminary, M.A. 1990, U. of IL, J.D. 1993; Baptist; married (Sandra).

Professional Career: Civil rights activist; Pres., Keep Hope Alive PAC, 1989–90; V.P., Operation PUSH, 1991–95; Field Dir., Natl. Rainbow Coalition, 1993–95.

DC Office: 2419 RHOB, 20515, 202-225-0773; Fax: 202-225-0899; Web site: www.house.gov/jackson.

District Office: Homewood, 708-798-6000.

Committees: *Appropriations* (23d of 29 D): Foreign Operations, Export Financing & Related Programs; Labor, Health and Human Services, Education & Related Agencies.

Group Ratings

	ADA	ACLU	AFS	LCV	ITIC	NTU	COC	ACU	NTLC	CHC
2004	100	100	100	100	20	11	14	0	0	15
2003	100	—	100	100	—	29	17	8	—	—

National Journal Ratings

	2003 LIB	—	2003 CONS		2004 LIB	—	2004 CONS
Economic	87%	—	9%		89%	—	8%
Social	92%	—	0%		88%	—	0%
Foreign	94%	—	0%		97%	—	2%

Key Votes of the 108th Congress

1. Drilling in ANWR	N	5. DC School Vouchers	N	9. Ban Same-Sex Marriage	N
2. Approve Bush Tax Cuts	N	6. Ban Human Cloning	N	10. Fund Iraq War	N
3. Medicare/Rx Bill	N	7. Restrict Gun Liability	N	11. Bar Cuba Embargo Funds	Y
4. Bar Overtime Pay Regs.	Y	8. Ban Partial-Birth Abortion	N	12. Intelligence Reorg.	N

Election Results

2004 general	Jesse Jackson Jr. (D)	207,535	(88%)	($527,367)
	Stephanie Sailor (Lib)	26,990	(12%)	
2004 primary	Jesse Jackson Jr. (D)	106,506	(89%)	
	Mel Reynolds (D)	7,103	(6%)	
	Anthony Williams (D)	5,159	(4%)	
	Other	1,516	(1%)	
2002 general	Jesse Jackson Jr. (D)	151,443	(82%)	($749,704)
	Doug Nelson (R)	32,567	(18%)	($9,249)

Prior Winning Percentages: 2000 (90%); 1998 (89%); 1996 (94%); 1995 (76%)

The People		Race/Ethnic Origin	Ancestry	
Area size:	192 sq. mi.	25.6% White	German: 5.8%	Polish: 4.4%
Urban population:	99.9%	62.0% Black	Irish: 4.4%	
Rural population:	0.1%	0.6% Asian	**2004 Presidential Vote**	
Pop. 2000:	653,647	0.1% Native Am.	Kerry (D) 230,613	(84%)
Median income:	$41,330	0.0% Hawaiian	Bush (R) 43,822	(16%)
Poverty status:	15.2%	1.2% Two+ races	Other 353	(0%)
Military veterans:	11.7%	0.1% Other	**2000 Presidential Vote**	
		10.4% Hispanic Origin	Gore (D) 204,372	(82%)
			Bush (R) 41,005	(17%)
			Other 2,455	(1%)
			Cook Partisan Voting Index: D +35	
Occupation	Blue collar: 23.8%	White collar: 60.1%	Gray collar: 16.1%	

Chicago is a great center of both commerce and industry, and if its white-collar offices are heavily concentrated in the Loop, its blue-collar heavy industries are most visible on the far South Side. This Chicago, diminished in importance economically today, is historically significant and, with the remnants of its great hulking factories around Lake Calumet and the nearby rail yards, has a certain undeniable majesty. Thomas Geoghegan, who writes more poetically than a lawyer ought to be able to, has told in his book, *Which Side Are You On?*, of the fights to wrest severance benefits and pension rights for the workers whose steel mills shut down, of the decline in the labor movement in a place where it got much of its inspiration. This is where the Pullman strike of 1894 was broken by federal troops and where policemen killed 10 union supporters in the Little Steel strike of 1937. Over the years, Chicago grew around the tight ethnic neighborhoods where workers went home at shift break each afternoon or midnight; today they are mostly empty buildings that suburbanites speed past on the Calumet and Dan Ryan Expressways; a local historic preservation group has listed the Hillett Iron Ore Unloaders, built in 1912 and resembling a giant preying mantis, as endangered structures.

The 2d Congressional District of Illinois includes much of Chicago's old South Side industrial area, Comiskey Park and many Cook County suburbs to the south. The district reaches north to include Jackson Park, where the Columbian Exposition of 1893 was held, and the South Shore neighborhood to the south, once heavily Jewish and now home to middle-class blacks. The district includes all of Chicago south of 95th Street and east of I-57, including the old industrial area around Lake Calumet. The Chicago portion of the 2d is overwhelmingly black, though many blacks, especially young parents fleeing Chicago public schools, are moving into suburbs directly to the south—Harvey, Dolton, Markham. Farther south are economically revitalized Homewood and Flossmoor, with significant Jewish populations, high-income Olympia Fields, the planned town of Park Forest, and Chicago Heights, home town of America's premier political reporter for more than four decades, David Broder. In the south is Ford Heights; once a steel-industry hub known as East Chicago Heights, it is now the nation's leader in single mothers per capita, the vast majority of whom live in public housing. The 2d District now has more people in the suburbs than in Chicago; the district spills slightly into Will County, to include Governors State University in University Park. These extensions reduced the black percentage from 76% to 62%, but the district remains middle class and still one of the most Democratic in the nation.

The congressman from the 2d District is Jesse Jackson Jr., a Democrat first elected at age 30 in December 1995, son of civil rights activist and 1984 and 1988 presidential candidate Jesse Jackson. Jesse Jackson Jr. was born in Greenville, South Carolina, while his father was marching to Selma; he went to the St. Albans School in Washington, then to North Carolina A&T (as did his father), and got a masters degree at Chicago Theological Seminary and a law degree at the University of Illinois. He worked for his father's Rainbow Coalition and did not run for office until the spectacular rise and fall of Congressman Mel Reynolds, who was hailed nationally when he defeated the anti-Semitic Gus Savage in the 1992 primary and then disgraced when he was convicted and sentenced to five years in prison for having sexual relations with a teenage campaign worker. Jackson had serious competition in the 1995 special election from Emil Jones, then a legislator for 23 years and now the state Senate President, who had the support of Mayor Richard M. Daley. Jones emphasized his clout and political experience; Jackson said being his father's son was a lifetime of political experience. He talked of bringing dollars to the South Side and, echoing the argument Dan Rostenkowski made to Mayor Richard J. Daley in 1957, said, "The only way one grows into leadership in Congress is to get elected young enough that you become speaker of the House or chairman of the Ways and Means Committee." Jackson won the primary 46%–37% and easily won the special general election.

In the House, Jackson has combined liberal advocacy with careful attention to the interests of his district and a steady advancement of his own influence. He called for a single-payer universal health care system. He waged unexpectedly fierce opposition to the Crane-Rangel bill to relax trade restrictions on Africa, saying that he feared exploitation of African workers. Charles Rangel, a longtime ally of the senior Jackson, was furious—calling the attack on the Ways and Means Committee bill "unprofessional." The bill was enacted, but the dispute badly split the Congressional Black Caucus. In the 108th Congress, he filed only one legislative bill, but nine constitutional amendments with proposed 21st century rights such as "health care of equal high quality," "decent, safe, sanitary and affordable housing," and "full employment and balanced economic growth." He plans to keep introducing his amendments "as long as I am alive and in Congress." All would be unlikely of passage even in a Democratic Congress.

Jackson has worked on local projects, notably the proposal for a third Chicago area airport in Peotone, 45 miles south of the Loop and just south of the 2d District along Interstate 57. The fight pitted him against fellow Democrats, including former Congressman William Lipinski, the great protector of Midway Airport in his 3d District, and Daley, whose number one priority is expansion of O'Hare. Jackson's allies have included Republicans Henry Hyde, who is worried about O'Hare noise over his suburban 6th District, and former Senator Peter Fitzgerald, who sought unsuccessfully to prevent O'Hare expansion.

With his seat on the Appropriations Committee, he seems content to remain in the House. "His ultimate goal is to become the first black speaker of the House," reported the Chicago *Daily Herald*. In December 2002, Jackson seemed to finally close the door on mayoral speculation. "I'm not interested in the job of mayor of Chicago," he told the *Chicago Tribune*. "I'm not interested in it today, I'm not interested in it tomorrow. I'm not ever going to be interested in being the mayor of the city of Chicago." But his increasingly sharp criticism of Mayor Richard M. Daley in 2005 led to speculation that perhaps he was interested; in May 2005, a *Tribune*/WGN-TV poll showed a 40%–37% Jackson lead in a head-to-head match with Daley, with 23% undecided.

Jackson has been careful not to exploit his huge name recognition or to be seen as exclusively the "black issues" congressman. The movement of middle-class blacks to the suburbs reduces his core constituency but Jackson's advocacy of the Peotone airport suggests he has anticipated this and is set on representing a mostly suburban, mostly black district for some time. In the 2004 primary, he had a rematch with Reynolds, who sought a comeback following his prison time. Reynolds said that his opponent was "born with a platinum picket sign in his mouth;" he made a futile attempt for the support of his former patron, Mayor Daley, who at the time called Jackson "a good congressman." Jackson got 89% to 6% for Reynolds. In the presidential primary, Jackson was an early supporter of Howard Dean, and campaigned for him in the early battleground state of South Carolina; he dismissed Al Sharpton as "not running seriously." These various actions all reinforce the notion that Jackson is building clout and connections for the long term, an often successful approach in Illinois.

THIRD DISTRICT

Rep. Daniel Lipinski (D)

Elected 2004, 1st term; b. July 15, 1966, Chicago; home, Western Springs; Northwestern U., B.S. 1988, Stanford U., M.A. 1989, Duke U., Ph.D. 1998; Catholic; married (Judy).

Professional Career: Asst. professor, U. of TN, 2001–04.

DC Office: 1217 LHOB, 20515, 202-225-5701; Fax: 202-225-1012; Web site: www.house.gov/lipinski.

District Offices: Chicago, 312-886-0481; LaGrange, 708-352-0524.

Committees: *Science* (12th of 20 D): Energy; Research. *Small Business* (4th of 15 D): Tax, Finance & Exports; Workforce, Empowerment & Government Programs (RMM).

Group Ratings and Key Votes: Newly Elected

Election Results

2004 general	Daniel Lipinski (D) 167,034	(73%)	($49,004)
	Ryan Chlada (R) 57,845	(25%)	
	Other... 5,077	(2%)	
2004 primary	William Lipinski (D) .... unopposed		
2002 general	William Lipinski (D) .... unopposed		($419,270)

The People		Race/Ethnic Origin	Ancestry	
Area size:	126 sq. mi.	68.2% White	Irish: 14.2%	Polish: 13.5%
Urban population:	100.0%	5.8% Black	German: 11.0%	
Rural population:	0.0%	2.8% Asian	**2004 Presidential Vote**	
Pop. 2000:	653,647	0.1% Native Am.	Kerry (D) 144,657	(59%)
Median income:	$48,048	0.0% Hawaiian	Bush (R) 100,257	(41%)
Poverty status:	8.3%	1.7% Two+ races	Other 533	(0%)
Military veterans:	10.9%	0.1% Other	**2000 Presidential Vote**	
		21.3% Hispanic Origin	Gore (D) 131,650	(58%)
			Bush (R) 91,471	(40%)
			Other 4,913	(2%)
			Cook Partisan Voting Index: D +10	
Occupation	Blue collar: 27.6%	White collar: 58.1%	Gray collar: 14.3%	

A century ago, Finley Peter Dunne's fictional Mr. Dooley pontificated on matters political in a saloon on Archery Road. This was, and is, Archer Avenue on the South Side of Chicago, one of the radial streets that cut across what was once open prairie near the Loop and out the Chicago River and the Chicago and Sanitary Ship Canal. Archer Avenue was one of the paths of outward migration and upward mobility for the children and grandchildren of Chicago's ethnic and cultural groups, and still is. (Even today, in Archer Heights, you can scarcely go a block without hearing someone speaking Polish). Italians from the river wards along the Canal moved west; the South Side Irish moved west and south along Cicero Avenue toward Oak Lawn; the Bohemians (as they were called then; now Czechs) were heavily concentrated in the neat bungalows of industrial suburbs like Berwyn. Today, Latinos are driving these same avenues, up before dawn to arrive at large factories and small, or heading to the Loop on the CTA or to "edge city" jobs out the expressways or the Tollway, then home past storefronts with Spanish signs to carefully refurbished old bungalows. Midway Airport, Chicago's main airport before O'Hare opened in 1955 and now a low-cost facility, has been expanding its terminals and parking lots squeezed into the heart of a busy commercial area on the southwest side.

The 3d Congressional District of Illinois consists of much of this territory, crisscrossed by the Canal, the radial streets and the railroad lines and switching yards so common in this, the center of the nation's rail network. It includes much of the Bungalow Belt; in his book, *The Lost City,* Alan Ehrenhalt describes the houses as "so close together that one had to make a special effort even to notice the side of the building. Driving down the street, what you saw was one front after another, and the fronts, clean and well-laid in dark-brown brick by Swedish and Italian immigrant masons, always looked good." The 3d also includes the far southwest edge of Chicago and most of Berwyn; Riverside, with its early 20th century prairie-style houses; a few older affluent suburbs like Western Springs and the more recent and middle-income expanses of Oak Lawn and Palos Hills. The 3d was one of the Illinois districts least changed by the 2001 redistricting, which was no coincidence—the lead negotiator of the bipartisan deal was the 3d District's William Lipinski. Retained were the Archer Avenue neighborhoods where Poles defiantly cling to their heritage with more than 20 weekend schools teaching Polish to local kids and adults. Added was a narrow corridor to the famed Bridgeport neighborhood, the lifetime home of the late Mayor Richard J. Daley and the storied Irish stronghold that produced four other Chicago mayors. Politically, this is marginal territory: ancestrally Democratic, culturally conservative, multiethnic and viscerally patriotic. Of the seven districts that include parts of Chicago, this has cast the highest percentages, though well short of majorities, for George W. Bush.

The congressman from the 3d District is Dan Lipinski, elected in 2004, son of Congressman Bill Lipinski, who represented the district for 22 years. Dan Lipinski grew up in Chicago, in the 23d Ward, and first served as a campaign volunteer for his father in 1979. He graduated from Northwestern and got advanced degrees in political science at Stanford and Duke. He also worked on the staffs of four House Democrats from Illinois, though not on his father's, and was an American Political Science Association congressional fellow for the House Democratic Policy Committee. He wrote his doctoral thesis on the topic of congressional newsletters (*Congressional Communication,* published by the University of Michigan Press); at the beginning of 2004, he was an assistant professor of political science at the University of Tennessee in Knoxville. His skimpy campaign resume does not list his scholarly or teaching experiences, nor his out-of-state connections; they might not have been great selling points in the 3d District.

Bill Lipinski filed for reelection in December 2003 and was nominated without opposition in the March 2004 primary. There were widespread rumors that he was going to give up his seat, but on June 10, when asked by the *Chicago Sun-Times* whether he planned to remain on the November 2004 ballot, he replied, "That's my plan." Perhaps it was then, but on August 13 he announced he would not seek reelection. "I want to come back to Chicago and spend more time with my wife," he explained. "When you live three days in one city and four days in another, it takes you away. I want to slow down the march of time." The deadline for replacing a withdrawing candidate was August 26; a meeting was scheduled for August 17 for the 19 ward and township Democratic committeemen in the 3d District, who would choose the new nominee by weighted vote. Among them were 11th Ward Committeeman John Daley, Cook County Commissioner, son of the late Mayor Richard J. Daley and brother of Mayor Richard M. Daley; 13th Ward Committeeman Michael Madigan, Speaker of the Illinois House and father of Illinois Attorney General Lisa Madigan; 14th Ward Committeeman Edward Burke, who succeeded his father as 14th Ward Alderman and whose wife is a judge on the Illinois Appeals Court; 19th Ward committeeman Tom Hynes, former Cook County Assessor and father of Illinois Comptroller Dan Hynes; and 23d Ward Committeeman Bill Lipinski: Politics is a family business in Chicago. Bill

Lipinski advanced his son's name and said, "I'm optimistic, but one never knows in politics until the votes are counted." It did not take long to count them: Dan Lipinski was nominated without opposition. To charges that the nomination was rigged, one participant dryly noted that anyone could have run.

Dan Lipinski, who had not lived in Illinois for 15 years, quickly reestablished his residency. But at his first press conference, he stumbled: He admitted that he rooted for North Side Chicago's baseball Cubs since he was three years old, rather than the South Side White Sox— this in a city that has two separate St. Patrick's Day parades, one downtown and one on the South Side. A local legislator signaled Lipinski from the back of the room to cut off his politically embarrassing remarks. It did not matter much. In the solidly Democratic 3d District, the Democratic nomination is tantamount to election. But local critics charged that Bill Lipinski had further predetermined the outcome by putting up a stooge as the Republican nominee. Ryan Chlada, the 26-year-old college dropout and bar owner who won the Republican nomination unopposed, was a political ally of former Cicero Mayor Betty Loren-Maltese, who was serving prison time for racketeering. Chlada had four relatives on the Cicero payroll; Bill Lipinski had long worked closely with Cicero Republicans. Chlada avoided publicity, had no website, filed no reports with the FEC (legal, if you don't raise or spend much money) and was unknown to local Republicans; the Cook County Republican chairman said he was a sham candidate. Unsurprisingly, Dan Lipinski won, 73%–25%.

Dan Lipinski said that he would be "not really that different from my father," who was the most conservative Democrat in the Illinois delegation and focused on local transportation projects, especially Midway Airport, which generates more jobs than any other 3d District employer. His experience as a diabetic plus a recent hospitalization for a broken hip after a bicycle fall made him aware of the need to improve the health care system, he said, though he disagreed with his father's support for nationalized health care. Lipinski said he opposed same-sex marriage and opposed abortion except when the mother's life is at stake; he named Ronald Reagan as his political hero. Local Democrats and Republicans both said that they might challenge him in 2006.

FOURTH DISTRICT

Rep. Luis Gutierrez (D)

Elected 1992, 7th term; b. Dec. 10, 1953, Chicago; home, Chicago; NE IL U., B.A. 1975; Catholic; married (Soraida).

Elected Office: Chicago City Alderman, 1986–92, Pres. Pro Tem, 1989–92.

Professional Career: Teacher, Puerto Rico, 1977–78; Social Wkr., Chicago Dept. of Children & Family Svcs., 1979–83; Advisor, Chicago Mayor Harold Washington, 1984–86.

DC Office: 2367 RHOB, 20515, 202-225-8203; Fax: 202-225-7810; Web site: luisgutierrez.house.gov.

District Offices: Northside Chicago, 773-384-1655; Southside Chicago, 312-666-3882.

Committees: *Financial Services* (5th of 32 D): Domestic and International Monetary Policy, Trade & Technology; Financial Institutions & Consumer Credit; Oversight & Investigations (RMM). *Veterans' Affairs* (3d of 12 D): Health.

Group Ratings

	ADA	ACLU	AFS	LCV	ITIC	NTU	COC	ACU	NTLC	CHC
2004	90	83	100	100	30	9	22	0	0	8
2003	90	—	100	95	—	22	31	8	—	—

National Journal Ratings

	2003 LIB	—	2003 CONS		2004 LIB	—	2004 CONS
Economic	92%	—	0%		98%	—	0%
Social	83%	—	16%		88%	—	0%
Foreign	93%	—	6%		88%	—	11%

Key Votes of the 108th Congress

1. Drilling in ANWR	N	5. DC School Vouchers	N	9. Ban Same-Sex Marriage	N
2. Approve Bush Tax Cuts	N	6. Ban Human Cloning	N	10. Fund Iraq War	N
3. Medicare/Rx Bill	N	7. Restrict Gun Liability	N	11. Bar Cuba Embargo Funds	N
4. Bar Overtime Pay Regs.	Y	8. Ban Partial-Birth Abortion	N	12. Intelligence Reorg.	N

Election Results

2004 general	Luis Gutierrez (D) 104,761	(84%)	($233,086)
	Tony Cisneros (R) 15,536	(12%)	
	Jacob Witmer (Lib) 4,845	(4%)	
2004 primary	Luis Gutierrez (D) .... unopposed		
2002 general	Luis Gutierrez (D) 67,339	(80%)	($805,574)
	Tony Cisneros (R) 12,778	(15%)	
	Maggie Kohls (Lib) 4,396	(5%)	

Prior Winning Percentages: 2000 (89%); 1998 (82%); 1996 (94%); 1994 (75%); 1992 (78%)

The People		Race/Ethnic Origin	Ancestry	
Area size:	39 sq. mi.	18.4% White	Polish: 5.0%	German: 3.4%
Urban population:	100.0%	3.7% Black	Irish: 3.1%	
Rural population:	0.0%	1.7% Asian	**2004 Presidential Vote**	
Pop. 2000:	653,647	0.1% Native Am.	Kerry (D) 105,419	(79%)
Median income:	$35,935	0.0% Hawaiian	Bush (R) 27,684	(21%)
Poverty status:	20.2%	1.4% Two+ races	Other 809	(1%)
Military veterans:	4.3%	0.1% Other	**2000 Presidential Vote**	
		74.5% Hispanic Origin	Gore (D) 93,266	(79%)
			Bush (R) 23,809	(20%)
			Other 317	(0%)
			Cook Partisan Voting Index: D +31	
Occupation	Blue collar: 39.2%	White collar: 43.5%	Gray collar: 17.3%	

Just west of the Loop, the Chicago River splits into North and South Branches, both penetrating the heart of old neighborhoods where immigrants fresh off the boat first got their start in Chicago. The South Branch is the guts of Chicago, the site of one of Western civilization's astonishing engineering feats: in 1900 the course of the river was reversed so that sewage flowed Downstate through a canal rather than out into Lake Michigan. Just blocks away was Maxwell Street, then thronged with market stalls, long the arrival neighborhood for Chicago's Jews; not far away, in an Italian-American neighborhood on Halsted Street, was Jane Addams's Hull House, the original settlement house, where social workers told new immigrants not how to rebel against middle-class American mores but how to live up to them. To the south were Pilsen, arrival neighborhood for the Bohemians (Czechs), and the Irish neighborhoods along Archer Avenue. To the north was Milwaukee Avenue, the main street of Polish-Americans and Ukrainian-Americans for a century now.

Today, many of these places are arrival neighborhoods again, mostly for Chicago's wide variety of Hispanic immigrants. On the South Side, in the old river wards, is Chicago's Mexican-American community, extending west into the once Bohemian suburb of Cicero (famous as a haven for Al Capone's mobsters in the 1920s) and to Pilsen; this is the largest community of Mexican-Americans in the nation outside California. On the North Side are many Puerto Ricans and other Hispanics. In the 1990s, Chicago's Hispanic population increased from 545,000 to 754,000, by far the largest Latino concentration north of Texas and Florida and between the two coasts, and not all that much less than the 1.1 million blacks in Chicago. Spanish-language radio stations have become a local force.

The 4th Congressional District of Illinois is the Hispanic-majority district created in 1992 and altered somewhat by the 2001 redistricting. With the South Side Mexican-American and the North Side Puerto Rican communities separated by the West Side black ghetto, the solution was the creation of one of the most bizarrely-shaped congressional districts in the country. Essentially these two Latino communities, defined by careful boundaries to maximize the Hispanic percentage, are connected by a thin line of territory stretching around the West Side black-majority 7th District to meet at the Cook-DuPage County line. The district is sandwiched between the 5th District to the north and the 3d District to the south; it is shaped something like a pair of earmuffs. More than 95% of the votes are in Chicago or Cicero. The latest redistricting raised the Hispanic share of the district population to 75% (75% of these Hispanics are Mexican; 10% are Puerto Rican). Even so, because many have not become citizens and some who have do not vote, Latinos may be only a bare majority of the electorate; the total turnout here is about half of that in nearby suburban districts.

The congressman from the 4th District is Luis Gutierrez, a Democrat who has held the seat since its creation in 1992. He is of Puerto Rican descent, grew up in Chicago and returned for two years to Puerto Rico as a teacher after college. Back in Chicago, he worked as a cab driver and social worker. In 1983 he ran for 32d Ward committeeman against Dan Rostenkowski, and lost decisively. Then he became a staffer for Mayor Harold Washington, ran for alderman in 1984 and lost; in 1986 he ran again and won in one of two new Hispanic-majority aldermanic seats. After Washington died, Gutierrez backed Richard M. Daley in the 1989 election to succeed him. In the 1992 primary race for the new 4th Congressional District seat, rival alderman Juan Solis called Gutierrez a machine candidate; Gutierrez won anyway, 60%–40%. After easily winning a rematch in 1994, Gutierrez has not had serious competition since.

In the House, Gutierrez's in-your-face style has produced mixed results. As a freshman, his outspoken opposition to congressional pay raises and his appearance on a *60 Minutes* broadcast—in which he called the House "the belly of the beast" and charged that Democratic leaders stifled reform and that some freshmen Democrats "sold out"— was not well received. "I've gotten my rear end kicked around here," Gutierrez told *The Washington Post*; a leadership staffer said Gutierrez "will never get a choice committee" and "will always end up on the Banking Committee." True enough, though he's moved into the senior ranks of what is now the Financial Services Committee. In a return visit to *60 Minutes*, he was not repentant but he did say, "I'm more careful" in speaking out. Gutierrez has staked out liberal positions and has been more a commentator than a legislative craftsman. In the Hispanic Caucus, he has cheered on efforts to restore food stamp eligibility and other benefits to legal immigrants. He filed another bill to grant automatic citizenship to immigrants in military combat. In May 2004, when George W. Bush's proposal to permit guest workers to seek U.S. citizenship appeared dead in the water, Gutierrez said, "The ball is in your court, Mr. President." At his urging, Governor Rod Blagojevich created a state commission to investigate the threats to day laborers injured or killed during their work. Gutierrez has been passionate about giving independence to Puerto Rico. He vehemently opposed the Navy's bombing exercises on the island of Vieques off Puerto Rico's coast. He was twice arrested with others for protesting inside the bombing range on Vieques, and later complained of "inhumane" treatment.

Gutierrez often takes the posture of the political rebel, but he has been capable of making accommodations with the locally powerful. Locally, Gutierrez also consolidated Chicago's previously fractious Democratic politicians so as to maximize Latino influence. That could prove helpful if Gutierrez runs for mayor in the future, as some have speculated.

FIFTH DISTRICT

Rep. Rahm Emanuel (D)

Elected 2002, 2d term; b. Nov. 29, 1959, Chicago; home, Chicago; Sarah Lawrence Col., B.A. 1981; Northwestern U., M.A. 1985; Jewish; married (Amy).

Professional Career: Pol. Dir., DCCC, 1985–86; Natl. Campaign Dir., DCCC, 1988; Sr. White House adviser, 1993–99; Investment bank dir., 1999–2002.

DC Office: 1319 LHOB, 20515, 202-225-4061; Fax: 202-225-5603; Web site: www.house.gov/emanuel.

District Office: Chicago, 773-267-5926.

Committees: *DCCC Chairman. Ways & Means* (17th of 17 D): Health; Human Resources.

Group Ratings

	ADA	ACLU	AFS	LCV	ITIC	NTU	COC	ACU	NTLC	CHC
2004	100	70	100	100	60	8	29	0	0	8
2003	95	—	100	95	—	23	39	20	—	—

National Journal Ratings

	2003 LIB	—	2003 CONS		2004 LIB	—	2004 CONS
Economic	77%	—	23%		89%	—	8%
Social	75%	—	24%		78%	—	22%
Foreign	70%	—	27%		85%	—	14%

Key Votes of the 108th Congress

1. Drilling in ANWR	N	5. DC School Vouchers	N	9. Ban Same-Sex Marriage	N
2. Approve Bush Tax Cuts	N	6. Ban Human Cloning	N	10. Fund Iraq War	Y
3. Medicare/Rx Bill	N	7. Restrict Gun Liability	N	11. Bar Cuba Embargo Funds	Y
4. Bar Overtime Pay Regs.	Y	8. Ban Partial-Birth Abortion	N	12. Intelligence Reorg.	N

Election Results

2004 general	Rahm Emanuel (D)	158,400	(76%)	($689,463)
	Bruce Best (R)	49,530	(24%)	
2004 primary	Rahm Emanuel (D)	60,821	(83%)	
	Mark Fredrickson (D)	12,255	(17%)	
2002 general	Rahm Emanuel (D)	106,514	(67%)	($2,971,514)
	Mark Augusti (R)	46,008	(29%)	($217,731)
	Frank Gonzalez (Lib)	6,913	(4%)	

The People		Race/Ethnic Origin	Ancestry	
Area size:	58 sq. mi.	65.9% White	Polish: 13.5%	German: 11.5%
Urban population:	100.0%	2.2% Black	Irish: 9.9%	
Rural population:	0.0%	6.5% Asian	**2004 Presidential Vote**	
Pop. 2000:	653,647	0.2% Native Am.	Kerry (D) 161,348	(67%)
Median income:	$48,531	0.0% Hawaiian	Bush (R) 79,349	(33%)
Poverty status:	8.5%	2.2% Two+ races	Other 1,539	(1%)
Military veterans:	6.7%	0.2% Other	**2000 Presidential Vote**	
		23.0% Hispanic Origin	Gore (D) 143,106	(66%)
			Bush (R) 73,793	(34%)
			Other 885	(0%)
			Cook Partisan Voting Index: D +18	
Occupation	Blue collar: 21.5%	White collar: 64.9%	Gray collar: 13.6%	

Few places in America today have more variety—ethnic and cultural—than the North Side of Chicago. This has been the homeland of one immigrant group after another and the chosen neighborhoods of all manner of successful middle-class people. Wooden workingman's cottages from the late 19th century give way to sturdy huge brick houses of the early 1900s and then to the prairie bungalows of the 1920s and white-shuttered, orange-brick colonials of the 1950s. Chicago was America's number one immigrant destination for Poles, Lithuanians, Czechs, Slovaks, Ukrainians and Romanians; something about the heavy dull clouds of the long winters, the short hot summers, a climate suited to potatoes and cabbage and other hardy vegetables, may have reminded them of central and eastern Europe. By the late 1980s, upwardly mobile immigrants from Mexico and Guatemala, Korea and the Philippines moved in; the 1990s witnessed new rounds of immigrants from Poland and Ukraine, plus Pakistan and India. Family ties, webs of acquaintance that reach back to ancestral villages, have made the North Side of Chicago a natural port of entry for Eastern bloc migrants, even as newcomers establish new family ties and webs of relationships extending to Latin America and Southeast Asia.

The 5th Congressional District of Illinois covers an oddly shaped slice of Chicago's North Side, running from the lakefront to the suburbs directly south of O'Hare Airport. It was not apparent in early 2001 that the 5th District would survive redistricting: with the incumbent running for governor, it seemed convenient for the bipartisan redistricters to slice up the district. But the 2000 Census results showed a big population increase in Chicago's immigrant neighborhoods. Mayor Richard M. Daley insisted that Chicago should retain all its districts; the May 2001 plan left the boundaries of the 5th mostly undisturbed. It was carefully drawn to put most Hispanics in the 4th District just to the south, but otherwise it reflects the full variety of the North Side. It includes Chicago's most glamorous lakefront apartments facing the Oak Street beach and the gentrified neighborhoods of Old Town, where old houses and factories are being converted into upscale condominiums, and nearby Lincoln Park, which has the highest median household income of Chicago's 77 community areas. It takes in baseball's famed Wrigley Field, the Polish-American and Ukrainian-American neighborhoods around Milwaukee Avenue, and the old Italian neighborhoods running west on Grand Avenue. It includes, a couple of blocks from the Chicago River, the grand old church of St. Stanislaus Kostka—a traditional center of the Polish community since the 19th century but now with Masses in Spanish—and the residence across Pulaski Park of Dan Rostenkowski, chairman of the House Ways and Means Committee from 1981 to 1994, for whom the district was designed in 1992. It reaches the Cook County suburbs, beyond River Grove and Franklin Park into Schiller Park and Northlake. This is a solidly Democratic district.

The congressman from the 5th District is Rahm Emanuel, a Democrat elected in 2002 when Rod Blagojevich gave up the seat and ran successfully for governor. Emanuel grew up in Chicago, the son of an Israeli immigrant; he graduated from Sarah Lawrence and from Northwestern. Tony Coelho recruited him to join the staff of the Democratic Congressional Campaign Committee in 1985. He worked for Mayor Richard M. Daley, before joining Bill Clinton's presidential campaign in 1991. He was rewarded with a high-level staff post in the Clinton White House, where he gained wide respect for his political savvy but drew criticism, even from allies, for an arrogant and abrasive style. In 1999 he left the White House and returned to Chicago where he made millions as an investment banker. His decision to seek Blagojevich's seat was greeted with disdain by those who had toiled for years in the vineyards of local Chicago politics. His strongest opponent was former state Representative Nancy Kaszak, who lost the 1996 primary to Blagojevich; she portrayed Emanuel as an interloper with few ties to the district. But Emanuel had his own local connections. He was endorsed by Daley and by labor unions (despite his support of NAFTA), and he raised large sums—nearly $2 million for the primary—from his extensive Chicago and national Democratic fundraising networks. Emanuel benefited from controversy two weeks before the primary, when a local Polish-American leader supporting Kaszak charged that Emanuel served in the Israeli army in 1991 during the Gulf War and suggested he had dual loyalties. The charge was false—Emanuel is a U.S. citizen who volunteered as a civilian at an Israeli supply base—and Kaszak's campaign was thrown off-stride. Emanuel won 50%–39%, with large majorities on the Lakefront and in Lincoln Park. He carried all of the 13 wards in the district, except for the heavily Polish 30th. In the general election, Emanuel faced a feisty challenger who attacked him as overly ambitious, but the result was never in doubt; he won 67%–29%. That made him the district's fourth congressman in a decade; before he was indicted and eventually served prison time, Rostenkowski served this area for 36 years.

In his first term in the House, Emanuel cut an unusually high-profile figure. Even before winning election in 2002, he strategized for the national party, met with the national media and sought a prime committee assignment: Rosty's old haunt at Ways and Means. Although he failed—freshmen seldom get on Ways and Means—his aggressiveness, political skills and fundraising prowess quickly made him a congressman to watch. "He's very strategic, very good at message, smart on the legislative process, and disciplined," said Democrat Jan Schakowsky, who represents the neighboring 9th District. In March 2004, working with Representative Rosa DeLauro, Emanuel asked the General Accounting Office to investigate whether the Bush administration had improperly promoted the new Medicare law; two months later, they were the first Democrats to applaud the GAO decision that the HHS's "video news releases" about the new prescription drug benefit violated federal law. He also showed skill in working across the aisle. He cosponsored with Representative Gil Gutknecht the House-passed bill allowing Americans to import prescription drugs from other nations. "Few members here have Rahm's energy, or know what reporter to talk to at *The New York Times,*" Gutknecht marveled. NRCC chairman Tom Reynolds became Emanuel's chief co-sponsor of a proposal to spend billions of dollars to clean up the Great Lakes. "He came to me, and I liked his concept," Reynolds said. "I think that Hillary [Rodham Clinton] told him he should get to know me."

In the highly competitive House, the peripatetic Emanuel was careful not to seem overly ambitious. "The legislative process is a people business," he said. "You are part of a group, and you try to get to know people." But he made another run to convince Minority Leader Nancy Pelosi that he was ready for a Ways and Means seat and in January 2005 he got one. After the death of Robert Matsui, the DCCC chairman in the 2004 cycle, Emanuel was named as his replacement, thus chairing the committee on which he had once been a staffer. With his quick start, Emanuel has shown that he is a member to watch.

SIXTH DISTRICT

Rep. Henry Hyde (R)

Elected 1974, 16th term; b. Apr. 18, 1924, Chicago; home, Wood Dale; Georgetown U., B.S. 1947, Loyola U., J.D. 1949; Catholic; widowed.

Military Career: Navy, 1944–46 (WWII); Naval Reserves, 1946–68.

Elected Office: IL House of Reps., 1966–74, Maj. Ldr., 1971–72.

Professional Career: Practicing atty., 1950–75.

DC Office: 2110 RHOB, 20515, 202-225-4561; Fax: 202-225-1166; Web site: www.house.gov/hyde.

District Office: Addison, 630-832-5950.

Committees: *International Relations* (Chmn. of 27 R). *Judiciary* (2d of 23 R): Courts, the Internet & Intellectual Property.

Group Ratings

	ADA	ACLU	AFS	LCV	ITIC	NTU	COC	ACU	NTLC	CHC
2004	15	0	13	9	90	51	95	75	78	91
2003	10	—	0	5	—	60	93	87	—	—

National Journal Ratings

	2003 LIB	—	2003 CONS		2004 LIB	—	2004 CONS
Economic	0%	—	91%		41%	—	58%
Social	17%	—	83%		34%	—	65%
Foreign	0%	—	89%		4%	—	93%

Key Votes of the 108th Congress

1. Drilling in ANWR	Y	5. DC School Vouchers	Y	9. Ban Same-Sex Marriage	Y
2. Approve Bush Tax Cuts	Y	6. Ban Human Cloning	*	10. Fund Iraq War	Y
3. Medicare/Rx Bill	Y	7. Restrict Gun Liability	*	11. Bar Cuba Embargo Funds	N
4. Bar Overtime Pay Regs.	N	8. Ban Partial-Birth Abortion	Y	12. Intelligence Reorg.	Y

Election Results

2004 general	Henry Hyde (R)	139,627	(56%)	($804,197)
	Christine Cegelis (D)	110,470	(44%)	($193,947)
2004 primary	Henry Hyde (R)	unopposed		
2002 general	Henry Hyde (R)	113,174	(65%)	($839,199)
	Tom Berry (D)	60,698	(35%)	

Prior Winning Percentages: 2000 (59%); 1998 (67%); 1996 (64%); 1994 (73%); 1992 (66%); 1990 (67%); 1988 (74%); 1986 (75%); 1984 (75%); 1982 (68%); 1980 (67%); 1978 (66%); 1976 (61%); 1974 (53%)

The People		Race/Ethnic Origin	Ancestry	
Area size:	215 sq. mi.	75.3% White	German: 16.7% Irish: 11.0%	
Urban population:	100.0%	2.7% Black	Polish: 9.4%	
Rural population:	0.0%	8.1% Asian	**2004 Presidential Vote**	
Pop. 2000:	653,647	0.1% Native Am.	Bush (R)	139,028 (53%)
Median income:	$62,640	0.0% Hawaiian	Kerry (D)	121,344 (47%)
Poverty status:	4.3%	1.3% Two+ races	**2000 Presidential Vote**	
Military veterans:	9.6%	0.1% Other	Bush (R)	126,254 (53%)
		12.5% Hispanic Origin	Gore (D)	103,616 (44%)
			Other	6,945 (3%)
			Cook Partisan Voting Index: R + 3	

Occupation	Blue collar: 20.2%	White collar: 69.5%	Gray collar: 10.3%

In World War II, what is now the nation's second-busiest airport was an apple orchard on which a defense plant was built (hence its current three-letter code: ORD). To the east was the Forest Preserve along the Des Plaines River, to the west little suburban villages strung along rail lines, separated by cornfields. But in the 1940s, Chicago politicians, in search of a new airport site, annexed the orchard and named it after a World War II airman awarded the Medal of Honor, who got a military appointment from the feds after his father turned state's evidence against Al Capone and was gunned down. Mayor Richard J. Daley opened O'Hare in 1955 and promoted its development, correctly concluding that a great airport could maintain in the 20th century the economic strength Chicago gained from railroad stations and rail yards in the 19th century. For years O'Hare has been America's number one or two airport in passenger traffic, and number one in combined passenger and cargo traffic; it has done much to maintain Chicago as the most vibrant center of commerce in the Midwest. Mayor Richard M. Daley's plans to reconfigure the runways and expand the airport are aimed at maintaining that preeminence. They are not popular, however, with the suburbs that surround O'Hare on all sides and are almost as densely settled as the bungalow wards of the city. Politically, these suburbs were for many years solidly Republican, convinced that civic virtues could best be realized by opposing the party of City Hall in Chicago and that economic growth could best be assured by opposing the party that backed stifling government regulation. But in the 1990s they became less Republican, as voters here recoiled from the national party's cultural conservatism.

The 6th Congressional District of Illinois includes O'Hare and much of the suburban area to its west. Most of the district is in DuPage County, the second largest county in Illinois. It includes the string of long-settled suburbs due west of the Loop: Elmhurst, Villa Park, Lombard, Glen Ellyn, Wheaton, plus the newer suburbs along I-290 and Lake Street: Bensenville, Addison, Wood Dale, Bloomingdale. Economically, this remains high-income territory; culturally, it is now cautiously moderate or even liberal. Politically, it has become less overwhelmingly Republican. In 1988 George Bush carried DuPage by 124,000 votes, with 68% of the vote, but in 2004 George W. Bush carried the county by only 39,000, with 54% of the vote—which tells you in a nutshell why the elder Bush carried Illinois in 1988 and the younger Bush twice wrote it off.

The congressman from the 6th District is Henry Hyde, chairman of the House International Relations Committee and one of the most respected and intellectually honest members of the House. Hyde springs from Chicago earth, was raised a Catholic and a Democrat; he was an all-city basketball center and played against basketball great George Mikan; he went off to college at Georgetown and enlisted in the Navy and served at Lingayen Gulf. After the war, he finished college and law school, practiced law in Chicago, and in 1958 switched parties, convinced that Republicans were more in line with his anti-Communist beliefs. He ran for the House in 1962 in northwest Chicago and lost 53%–47% to incumbent Roman Pucinski. He was elected to the Illinois House in 1966 and in the Democratic year of 1974 was elected to the U.S. House, where he now is the second-oldest member (next to Ralph Hall) and the fourth most senior Republican (behind Bill Young, Ralph Regula and Don Young).

He first made his name in the House as an abortion opponent, attaching to appropriations bills his amendments prohibiting the use of federal funds to pay for most abortions. "I look for the common thread in slavery, the Holocaust and abortion," he said in 1998. "To me, the common thread is dehumanizing people." In 1976 he passed the first Hyde amendment, banning abortions financed by Medicaid. It has remained in force ever since, though states can spend their own money on abortions, and some do; exceptions for saving the life of the mother, and victims of rape and incest were added in 1993. Hyde is concerned about born as well as unborn children. He was one of the few Republicans who supported the family leave bill, and has sponsored bills to expand the number of women eligible for pregnancy benefits under the children's health insurance program. He opposes assisted suicide as part of a "culture of death" and sponsored the bill passed by the House to criminalize the prescription of lethal drugs to terminally ill patients contemplating ending their lives.

On many occasions, Hyde has proven himself one of the most eloquent members of the House. His speeches against term limits and in favor of the flag-burning amendment are classics; his evisceration of the nuclear freeze resolution helped turn the tide on foreign policy in the House in the 1980s. He defended the Reagan administration on Iran-Contra and in the process said, somewhat to his embarrassment in the impeachment debate, that to condemn all lying "seems to me too simplistic. In the murkier grayness of the real world, choices must often be made." Three major Hyde measures passed both houses but were vetoed by Bill Clinton: the partial-birth abortion ban, product liability and tort law changes.

None of these challenges he had faced before was as great or as public as the challenge of impeachment, when he chaired the Judiciary Committee. From the first, Hyde had little taste for the subject, yet realized he had the responsibility to handle it. Early in 1998, he said that any impeachment resolution must be bipartisan if it were to be credible, but it became clear by September that many Democrats were determined to defend Clinton at every turn. Democrats resisted his resolution for an impeachment inquiry but felt obliged to advance one of their own. All Republicans and 31 Democrats voted for the Republican resolution. Clinton defenders tried to put Hyde on the defensive. In September, an online publication, *Salon*, reported that Hyde had had an affair 30 years before; "youthful indiscretions," Hyde responded. As the facts of Clinton's conduct became known, Hyde decided that the president had lied under oath in a District Court proceeding, and that that could not be forgiven. He ran the fractious hearings with scrupulous fairness, and even with occasional humor. His summation to the House was genuinely eloquent, and impeachment was voted on two of four counts.

Then came the historic march of Hyde and the 12 other House managers to the Senate presided over by Chief Justice William Rehnquist. The managers were pitted against Clinton's professional litigators, and the discomfort of almost all senators was obvious. Remembering his own experience in combat, he summoned up memories of Americans who had fallen in battle and urged the senators to uphold the rule of law. But Democrats did not waver, and the articles of impeachment were rejected.

After the 2000 election he tried to get House Republican leaders to waive the six-year term limit on chairmanships, arguing that he had lost one year of chairing Judiciary to impeachment. But they declined; instead, at age 76, Hyde got the International Relations chairmanship. This was a far less partisan assignment for Hyde, who agreed with committee senior Democrat Tom

Lantos on many foreign policy issues, including support for the Iraq war, support for Israel, door-opening to Vietnam, economic aid to Afghanistan, aiding third world nations fighting AIDS and increased funding for public diplomacy overseas after September 11.

Hyde has continued to work on other issues. Much of his district lies under O'Hare flight paths, and he has championed a third Chicago-area airport in Peotone in Will County; in this, his chief ally has been the 2d District's Jesse Jackson Jr. He was the only House Republican from Illinois not to endorse a federal bailout for United Airlines. He supported the bankruptcy bill, and unexpectedly found himself at odds with the House's pro-life movement that he had been instrumental in creating. When he painstakingly negotiated in 2002 a deal with Senator Charles Schumer on the Democrat's amendment to the bankruptcy bill to make it more difficult for abortion-clinic protestors to declare bankruptcy to avoid paying court fines or damages, many conservative colleagues said that Hyde had been too accommodating, and the bill died that year.

Although his mind has remained sharp, Hyde has slowed physically and has appeared frail in recent years; back surgery in March 2003 forced him to use a wheelchair. In 2004, he was held to a 56%–44% victory over information technology consultant Christine Cegelis, his smallest margin since he was first elected. With committee term limits set to conclude in 2006 his second chairmanship, he announced on April 18, his 81st birthday, that he would retire at the end of the term. He will take with him the bipartisan respect accorded to an iconic and principled lawmaker. Although his successor likely will be a Republican, Democrats back home will be more competitive than when Hyde first took this seat. Likely Republican candidates include state Senator Peter Roskam, who lost the 13th District House primary to Judy Biggert in 1998, state Senator Carole Pankau of Roselle and former DuPage County Recorder J.P. "Rick" Carney. On the Democratic side, Wheaton arbitrator Peter O'Malley announced he would run and 2004 nominee Cegelis said she would run again.

SEVENTH DISTRICT

Rep. Danny Davis (D)

Elected 1996, 5th term; b. Sept. 6, 1941, Parkdale, AR; home, Chicago; AR AM&N Col., B.A. 1961, Chicago St. U., M.S. 1968, Union Inst., Ph.D. 1977; Baptist; married (Vera).

Elected Office: Chicago City Alderman, 1979–90; Cook Cnty. Commissioner, 1990–96.

Professional Career: Teacher, Chicago Public Schls., 1962–69; Health Care Planner, 1969–79.

DC Office: 1526 LHOB, 20515, 202-225-5006; Fax: 202-225-5641; Web site: www.house.gov/davis.

District Offices: Broadview, 708-345-6857; Chicago, 773-533-7520.

Committees: *Education & the Workforce* (17th of 22 D): Education Reform; Select Education. *Government Reform* (9th of 17 D): Criminal Justice, Drug Policy & Human Resources; Federal Workforce & Agency Organization (RMM). *Small Business* (6th of 15 D): Tax, Finance & Exports; Workforce, Empowerment & Government Programs.

Group Ratings

	ADA	ACLU	AFS	LCV	ITIC	NTU	COC	ACU	NTLC	CHC
2004	90	100	88	100	60	8	30	0	3	15
2003	100	—	100	100	—	26	19	8	—	—

National Journal Ratings

	2003 LIB	—	2003 CONS		2004 LIB	—	2004 CONS
Economic	83%	—	17%		81%	—	19%
Social	92%	—	0%		88%	—	0%
Foreign	94%	—	0%		89%	—	10%

Key Votes of the 108th Congress

1. Drilling in ANWR	N	5. DC School Vouchers	N	9. Ban Same-Sex Marriage	*
2. Approve Bush Tax Cuts	N	6. Ban Human Cloning	N	10. Fund Iraq War	N
3. Medicare/Rx Bill	N	7. Restrict Gun Liability	*	11. Bar Cuba Embargo Funds	Y
4. Bar Overtime Pay Regs.	Y	8. Ban Partial-Birth Abortion	N	12. Intelligence Reorg.	N

Election Results

2004 general	Danny Davis (D)	221,133	(86%)	($438,680)
	Antonio Davis-Fairman (R)	35,603	(14%)	($43,718)
2004 primary	Danny Davis (D)	84,950	(82%)	
	Anita Rivkin-Carothers (D)	15,190	(15%)	
	Other	3,191	(3%)	
2002 general	Danny Davis (D)	137,933	(83%)	($215,233)
	Mark Tunney (R)	25,280	(15%)	($51,387)
	Other	2,543	(2%)	

Prior Winning Percentages: 2000 (86%); 1998 (93%); 1996 (83%)

The People		Race/Ethnic Origin	Ancestry	
Area size:	59 sq. mi.	27.3% White	German: 5.6%	Irish: 5.2%
Urban population:	100.0%	61.6% Black	Italian: 2.9%	
Rural population:	0.0%	3.8% Asian	**2004 Presidential Vote**	
Pop. 2000:	653,647	0.1% Native Am.	Kerry (D) 227,018	(83%)
Median income:	$40,361	0.0% Hawaiian	Bush (R) 45,071	(17%)
Poverty status:	24.0%	1.2% Two+ races	Other 887	(0%)
Military veterans:	8.0%	0.1% Other	**2000 Presidential Vote**	
		5.8% Hispanic Origin	Gore (D) 199,064	(83%)
			Bush (R) 38,196	(16%)
			Other 1,985	(1%)
			Cook Partisan Voting Index: D +35	

Occupation   Blue collar: 15.5%   White collar: 70.6%   Gray collar: 13.9%

The cross-country flyer on a lucky day can get a clear view of the biggest man-made cityscape between the Atlantic and Pacific Oceans: Chicago's Loop. High-rise buildings were pioneered a century ago in the Loop—named in 1897 for the quadrilateral the elevated train forms around the city's center—by architects like Louis Sullivan and Daniel Burnham. International School modernists built their most impressive collection of buildings here and along Lake Shore Drive in the years after World War II; in recent years, postmodernists have decorated the Chicago River and reinvented the skyscraper. The Loop now spreads beyond the El, up the wondrous shopping street of North Michigan Avenue with a peak at the John Hancock Tower plus the new Millennium Park and band shell along the lakefront, and west beyond the commodities exchanges to the Sears Tower on the Chicago River. This is the face Chicago likes to present to the world: giant structures rising where the prairies meet the inland sea, a vast concentration of brains and muscle, the nerve center of the markets of the nation and the world.

Behind the lakefront, where the air traveler sees the grid spread out below with occasional radials, are the muscle and sinew, gristle and fat of the city. There are parts that do not work so well: houses and apartment buildings are abandoned; commercial space stands empty and vandalized; giant, crime-racked housing projects, like the Robert Taylor Homes off the Dan Ryan Expressway, built by Mayor Richard J. Daley in the 1960s (he preferred low-rise projects, but the feds wouldn't finance them) and now torn down by Mayor Richard M. Daley. The West Side of Chicago, the vast acres directly west of the Loop, for years was a dreadful slum, with some areas almost emptied out; the decay spread west to the Austin neighborhood, just before the border of upper-income—and for decades racially integrated—Oak Park. In the 1990s, there was some revival. The United Center, the erstwhile home court of Michael Jordan, sparked commercial development of the West Side, and lower crime rates raised the value of land once again.

The 7th Congressional District of Illinois contains the Loop and most of the North Michigan corridor and the Near North Side, where the infamous Cabrini-Green housing project has been replaced by new, mixed-market housing. It goes south, past landmark museums, controversially renovated Soldier Field stadium and 19th century Prairie Avenue mansions to take in a few of the heavily black South Side neighborhoods chronicled in the groundbreaking 1945 book *Black Metropolis*. Its heart, demographically and spiritually, is the black ghetto of the West Side, more depopulated and socially disorganized than the South Side. To the west, just outside city limits, are Oak Park, the boyhood home of Ernest Hemingway and location of the Frank Lloyd Wright home and museum and many of his prairie-style houses; River Forest; and the much more modest Maywood, which is black-majority; plus Broadview and Hillside, site of a one-lane Chicago expressway bottleneck known as the Hillside Strangler. As with the South Side districts, redistricting in 2001 added nearly 100,000 people to the 7th and reduced slightly the share of black population, but did not change the basic contours. Just under two-thirds of the people here are black; there are relatively few Hispanics, since Latino neighborhoods were carefully placed in the 4th District.

The congressman from the 7th District is Danny Davis, a Democrat first elected in 1996 after two unsuccessful tries in the 1980s. Davis grew up on a cotton farm in Arkansas, graduated from college there, then moved to Chicago and worked as a teacher, assistant principal and guidance counselor in Chicago public schools. For 10 years, he ran a community health project on the West Side. He was elected alderman in the 29th Ward on the boundary of Oak Park in 1979 and supported Mayor Harold Washington in the council wars of the 1980s. In 1990 he was elected a Cook County commissioner; in 1991 he made a quixotic run for mayor against Richard M. Daley; he lost his 29th Ward committeeman post to a Daley-backed challenger in 2000.

In 1996, when Cardiss Collins retired after nearly 24 years in the House, Davis decided to run for the House again. His major opponents were 3d Ward Alderman Dorothy Tillman, a Daley ally, and 37th Ward Alderman Ed Smith. Davis campaigned as a big-government liberal, calling for a $7.60 minimum wage, affirmative action, and a national health care plan. Davis won with 33%. He won the general with ease and has not faced a serious challenge since then.

In the House, Davis has a very liberal voting record. He has opposed income tax cuts, even when advocated by Bill Clinton. He opposed the sugar program as corporate welfare (Chicago is the nation's leading candy manufacturer). On the Government Reform Committee, he has worked with a bipartisan coalition led by chairman Tom Davis that has pressed for changes in the Postal Service. With his wife Vera, who is president of the West Side NAACP, Davis advocated a local program to increase from its existing 28% the share of black home ownership in his district by offering credit counseling and innovative forms of mortgage financing. Davis also has taken a deep interest in the problems of former convicts seeking to transition back to the mainstream.

Davis speaks in an impressive sepulchral tone, and his self-evident sincerity and concern for the poor have helped him to some success in a mostly conservative House. With conservative Republican Mark Souder, he proposed the Public Safety ex-Offender Self-Sufficiency Act, to use tax credits to encourage transitional housing and job training for former prisoners. "Within three years, 60% to 70% of the people who get out of the penitentiary are rearrested," he says. "That's just recycling misery and poverty, and reinforcing the inability of our society to salvage."

EIGHTH DISTRICT

Rep. Melissa Bean (D)

Elected 2004, 1st term; b. Jan. 22, 1962, Chicago; home, Barrington; Oakton Comm. Col., A.A. 1982, Roosevelt U., B.A. 2002; Serbian Orthodox; married (Alan).

Professional Career: Technology and sales consultant, 1982–2004.

DC Office: 512 CHOB, 20515, 202-225-3711; Fax: 202-225-7830; Web site: www.house.gov/bean.

District Office: Schaumburg, 847-519-3434.

Committees: *Financial Services* (30th of 32 D): Capital Markets, Insurance & Government Sponsored Enterprises; Domestic and International Monetary Policy, Trade & Technology. *Small Business* (14th of 15 D): Tax, Finance & Exports; Workforce, Empowerment & Government Programs.

Group Ratings and Key Votes: Newly Elected

Election Results

2004 general	Melissa Bean (D)	139,792	(52%)	($1,586,829)
	Phil Crane (R)	130,601	(48%)	($1,618,074)
2004 primary	Melissa Bean (D)	26,740	(78%)	
	William Scheurer (D)	7,518	(22%)	
2002 general	Phil Crane (R)	95,275	(57%)	($834,585)
	Melissa Bean (D)	70,626	(43%)	($320,956)

The People		Race/Ethnic Origin	Ancestry	
Area size:	646 sq. mi.	78.8% White	German: 19.5%	Irish: 11.0%
Urban population:	96.1%	3.2% Black	Polish: 8.3%	
Rural population:	3.9%	5.6% Asian	**2004 Presidential Vote**	
Pop. 2000:	653,647	0.1% Native Am.	Bush (R) 153,245	(56%)
Median income:	$62,762	0.0% Hawaiian	Kerry (D) 121,710	(44%)
Poverty status:	4.4%	1.2% Two+ races	**2000 Presidential Vote**	
Military veterans:	10.6%	0.1% Other	Bush (R) 131,967	(56%)
		10.8% Hispanic Origin	Gore (D) 98,664	(42%)
			Other 6,954	(3%)
			Cook Partisan Voting Index: R + 5	

Occupation	Blue collar: 21.8%	White collar: 67.3%	Gray collar: 10.9%

Schaumburg may not be nationally known, but it is one of America's major corporate headquarters cities and one of several edge cities northwest of Chicago. Sixty years ago this was farmland, half a dozen miles beyond the orchard that is now O'Hare Airport. Today, Schaumburg—near the intersection of the Northwest Tollway and I-290, with lots of office space and Woodfield Mall and miles of subdivisions, with some moderately priced apartments—is the site of the headquarters of Motorola and Zurich American Insurance; nearby are the headquarters of Sears and Kemper Insurance. Yet Schaumburg yearns for traditions. It has built a performing arts center, formed an orchestra for young people, and has built from scratch a traditional downtown.

The 8th Congressional District of Illinois is made up of Schaumburg and dozens of similar communities to the north, on the hilly lakelands north and northwest of Chicago. Just to the north are Palatine and country-manor Barrington Hills (in-between Inverness is connected by a narrow corridor to the 10th District). The district includes the rapidly-growing western half of Lake County, with little lake communities being surrounded by new suburbs like Deer Park and Volo, and also includes the Lake Michigan town of Zion at the Wisconsin border. To the west, the 8th includes about half of fast-growing McHenry County. The tone of life is not elite, but people here are affluent. Culturally, this is part of the great rural Midwest perhaps more than it is of yeasty, lusty Chicago, though it lacks much regional identity other than the "northwest suburbs." Economically, its suspicion of government and trade restrictions has declined, as Motorola has become the victim of overseas competition, which has caused job upheaval in Schaumburg. Historically, this area was one of the most Republican places in the nation. In the past decade, like other suburban Chicago areas, it moved toward the Democrats, and if the 8th is still one of Illinois's most Republican districts, as measured by its support of George W. Bush in 2000 and 2004, it is far less Republican than districts with similar demographics in Texas or Georgia.

The new congresswoman from the 8th District is Melissa Bean, who on her second attempt defeated Phil Crane, one of only two Republican incumbents defeated in 2004. Bean grew up in Park Ridge, where her father owned a company that manufactured conveyor belts. She attended a local community college, then worked from home as a business consultant in technology sales, training executives at Motorola and other companies how to develop marketing and sales campaigns. She served on the local PTA and volunteered for Crane's Democratic challenger in 2000; two years later, she ran for the seat herself. When Bean challenged Crane in 2002, she got little assistance from national Democrats. But she held him to 57%, the second-lowest performance of his long career, and never stopped campaigning. In 2004, her energetic campaign offered a vivid contrast to Crane's sluggish and late-starting effort. Downplaying her party identification and keeping her distance from Democratic leaders, she handed voters jelly beans to help them remember her name, framed her candidacy as "a fresh start," and consistently talked about the need for a vigorous new voice. In this Republican district, she sharply attacked Crane for having lost touch back home and showing little influence in Washington; her attacks were directed at Crane rather than the Republican majority.

Crane was the senior Republican in the House, first elected in November 1969 to succeed Donald Rumsfeld, who resigned to become director of the antipoverty program in the Nixon administration. In 1980 he ran for president, hoping, as the truer libertarian, to cut in on the elderly Ronald Reagan's support and then take it over when the Reagan candidacy faded. But his strategy failed and through the 1980s he seemed embittered and unfocused; he was not part of the young conservative movement in the House led by Jack Kemp, Newt Gingrich and Trent Lott. He was challenged in the Republican primary in 1994 by Peter Fitzgerald, later U.S. senator, and beat him by only 40%–33%. As Trade Subcommittee chairman, he supported NAFTA, GATT, fast track, and normal trade relations with China. But when the chairmanship of the full Ways and Means Committee came open after the 2000 election, Crane was passed over by the Republican Steering Committee. After Bean's strong performance in 2002, Speaker Dennis Hastert and other Republicans urged Crane to do more constituency work. "A lot of people are worried that the November surprise could be Phil Crane," Ray LaHood told *The Hill* in June 2004.

Bean's energetic campaign also benefited from dissatisfaction with the scandal-ridden Illinois Republican party and from the unpopularity of Republican Senate nominee Alan Keyes. She supported the war in Iraq, opposed the Bush tax cuts and favored abortion rights. Crane tried to depict Bean as an inexperienced newcomer who would be unable to deliver federal dollars for the district: but this is not a district with visible infusions of federal money. In September, Crane took a hit when the public radio program "Marketplace" reported that he was among Congress's most frequent travelers; he defended his trips as necessary to his committee work. But his critics noted the lobbyist-paid golf fees and spa treatments for his wife. "The least that he could do is bring back more to the district than a tan," Bean joked, as her campaign flooded the district with comic mailings featuring computer-generated pictures of the incumbent vacationing in exotic locales.

In October, the *Chicago Tribune*, historically Republican and still less liberal than most other big metro area newspapers, endorsed Bean. Crane "has used his seat in Congress as a cozy sinecure." Bean "will, unlike Crane, pay close attention to the folks back home." Crane complained, "I have been busting my hump for about five straight weeks" in the campaign. But that wasn't enough. Bean won 52%–48%. She won 56%–44% on her home turf of Cook County, won 50.3%–49.7% in Lake County and trailed 49%–51% in McHenry County, running in each case well ahead of usual Democratic percentages, though behind Senator Barack Obama. Crane was an unusually bitter loser, refusing to speak to Bean or to arrange for the usually routine post-election transfer of district cases and other office files. Bean immediately became a top Republican target for 2006; the list of possible candidates for a seat that had been occupied for more than three decades was lengthy. But Bean will have the advantages of incumbency and constituency service, and her showing and Obama's confirm that it is no longer impossible for Democrats to win in this historically Republican territory.

NINTH DISTRICT

Rep. Jan Schakowsky (D)

Elected 1998, 4th term; b. May 26, 1944, Chicago; home, Evanston; U. of IL, B.S. 1965; Jewish; married (Robert Creamer).

Elected Office: IL House of Reps., 1990–98.

Professional Career: Founder, Natl. Consumers Unite, 1969–73; Prog. Dir., IL Public Action, 1976–85; Exec. Dir., IL State Cncl. of Sr. Citizens, 1985–90.

DC Office: 1027 LHOB, 20515, 202-225-2111; Fax: 202-226-6890; Web site: www.house.gov/schakowsky.

District Offices: Chicago, 773-506-7100; Evanston, 847-328-3399; Park Ridge, 847-298-2128.

Committees: *Chief Deputy Minority Whip. Energy & Commerce* (21st of 26 D): Commerce, Trade & Consumer Protection (RMM); Environment & Hazardous Materials; Oversight & Investigations.

Group Ratings

	ADA	ACLU	AFS	LCV	ITIC	NTU	COC	ACU	NTLC	CHC
2004	100	95	100	100	20	13	5	0	0	7
2003	100	—	100	100	—	27	20	8	—	—

National Journal Ratings

	2003 LIB	—	2003 CONS		2004 LIB	—	2004 CONS
Economic	92%	—	0%		89%	—	8%
Social	92%	—	0%		88%	—	0%
Foreign	94%	—	0%		97%	—	2%

Key Votes of the 108th Congress

1. Drilling in ANWR	N	5. DC School Vouchers	N	9. Ban Same-Sex Marriage	N
2. Approve Bush Tax Cuts	N	6. Ban Human Cloning	N	10. Fund Iraq War	N
3. Medicare/Rx Bill	N	7. Restrict Gun Liability	N	11. Bar Cuba Embargo Funds	Y
4. Bar Overtime Pay Regs.	Y	8. Ban Partial-Birth Abortion	N	12. Intelligence Reorg.	N

Election Results

2004 general	Jan Schakowsky (D)	175,282	(76%)	($1,068,961)
	Kurt Eckhardt (R)	56,135	(24%)	($2,624)
2004 primary	Jan Schakowsky (D)	unopposed		
2002 general	Jan Schakowsky (D)	118,642	(70%)	($864,506)
	Nicholas Duric (R)	45,307	(27%)	($32,750)
	Other	4,887	(3%)	

Prior Winning Percentages: 2000 (76%); 1998 (75%)

The People		Race/Ethnic Origin	Ancestry	
Area size:	78 sq. mi.	62.5% White	German: 10.5% Polish: 8.4%	
Urban population:	100.0%	10.7% Black	Irish: 8.2%	
Rural population:	0.0%	12.3% Asian	**2004 Presidential Vote**	
Pop. 2000:	653,647	0.2% Native Am.	Kerry (D) 175,288	(68%)
Median income:	$46,531	0.1% Hawaiian	Bush (R) 81,138	(32%)
Poverty status:	11.0%	2.6% Two+ races	Other 677	(0%)
Military veterans:	8.0%	0.3% Other	**2000 Presidential Vote**	
		11.5% Hispanic Origin	Gore (D) 155,529	(67%)
			Bush (R) 71,064	(31%)
			Other 4,331	(2%)
			Cook Partisan Voting Index: D +20	

Occupation	Blue collar: 16.1%	White collar: 69.8%	Gray collar: 14.0%

"Make no little plans," commanded architect Daniel Burnham, who made no little plans for the Chicago lakefront. The glorious parks he designed are among America's urban jewels, and the row of high-rise apartment buildings—some austere works of masters of the International style, some in traditional styles evocative of some other place and time, some sleek Art Deco works of the 1920s and 1930s—are a splendid accompaniment. Behind the lakefront is all the diversity of Chicago. In sturdy brick houses, with scarcely a shoehorn's space between them, or in stubby apartment buildings, are ethnic and racial groups of all sorts, from Argentineans to Slavs, Plains Indians to Indian plainsmen. In the 1970s the neighborhoods behind the lakefront seemed to be getting grimier and heading downhill. But since the late 1980s, they have been busy gentrifying, as young couples and gays, professionals and entrepreneurs renovate old houses and open new businesses. Today this part of Chicago has as much urban energy and lively diversity as any place in America.

The lakefront has long been the most heavily Jewish part of Chicago. The local Jewish community, prominent for more than a century, has never been as much a force for big government as in New York, nor is it connected as much to a glamorous industry as in Los Angeles. Yet these Jewish voters' liberal impulses have been strong: the 19th century impulse to resist state authority and imposition of cultural uniformity and the 20th century impulse to increase state responsibility for individuals' lives. Chicago's North Side Jews, on the lakefront or in neighborhoods like Rogers Park and nearby suburbs like Skokie and Niles, have been a solidly Democratic voting bloc, involved with—but skeptical of—the old Democratic machine. In city politics since the 1980s Jewish voters and lakefront liberals of all backgrounds have been a key swing group.

The 9th Congressional District of Illinois covers most of Chicago's lakefront, from just north of Diversey Harbor past the thriving Asian and orthodox Jewish communities in West Rogers Park and on to Evanston, founded by Methodists to promote temperance (a cause that never prospered in Chicago). The home of Northwestern University, Evanston has moved gracefully from historic Yankee Republican-ness to trendy post-graduate Democratic-ness; a developer's plan for a local marina was rejected due to fears of excessive growth. From Evanston and nearby Wilmette (which is shared with the 10th), the 9th presses inland through heavily Jewish Skokie to Morton Grove and Niles and includes most of Des Plaines. The district extends west to once rock-solid Republican territory—Park Ridge, with its characteristic Chicago brick houses in orderly rows, where Hillary Rodham Clinton grew up at 235 Wisner, and the cluster of office buildings and interchanges in Rosemont, next to O'Hare Airport. Though much less Republican than it was before the 1990s, this territory lowered the district's Democratic percentage. But this remains an overwhelmingly Democratic district.

The congresswoman from the 9th District is Jan Schakowsky, a Democrat elected in 1998 and an outspoken progressive, one of the leftmost members of the Democratic Caucus. She grew up in Rogers Park and worked two years as a teacher; in 1969 she formed National Consumers Unite and worked for date-of-freshness labels on dairy products and other food. Later she joined Illinois Public Action, a consumer group; in 1985 she became executive director of the Illinois

State Council of Senior Citizens. She organized the 1989 protest to Dan Rostenkowski's Medi-care catastrophic health care bill for seniors because of its financing, which resulted in televised pictures of him fleeing from elderly protestors and led Congress to repeal the benefit. In 1990 she was elected to the state House from Evanston and Skokie.

In 1998 Schakowsky was selected in the Democratic primary to replace Sidney Yates, who had represented the lakefront in Congress for all but two of the preceding 50 years. Her strategy was to run from the left—"I don't think I can be defined as too far left in a district like this"—and to build a volunteer organization. With ads in college papers, she got 400 young people to apply for 20 field organizer jobs; they set about identifying Schakowsky voters. She also raised $1.4 million, with help from EMILY's List. Against state Senator Howard Carroll, who had the support of most Democratic ward committeemen and attacked her opposition to the death penalty, Schakowsky's 1,500 workers, 250 from unions, helped to give her a 45%–34% win. She easily won the general election.

In the House, Schakowsky has one of the most liberal voting records. She called for expand-ing Medicare to cover everybody—single payer government health insurance—and has advanced a proposal to have a government-run investment fund that taxpayers could use to supplement Social Security. As ranking Democrat on the Commerce, Trade and Consumer Protection Subcommittee, Schakowsky has pursued her public advocacy. In a letter to the Consumer Product Safety Commission, she urged the recall of yo-yo balls, a water-filled toy with a long cord that has resulted in hundreds of reports of injuries. To encourage food safety, she filed a bill to create a national database of school food suppliers.

Schakowsky has worked with party leaders on electoral strategy, gaining their support to expand her training program for political organizers. An early supporter of Nancy Pelosi for party whip, Schakowsky was rewarded with a chief deputy whip slot. Her contacts with national liberal groups have helped her to become a major party fundraiser. When the McCain-Feingold law ended big soft-money contributions after the 2002 election, Schakowsky helped to assemble the House Democrats' program to expand contributions from small donors.

Schakowsky briefly considered a run for the Senate in 2004 but decided to remain in the House. In March 2004 her husband Robert Creamer, longtime head of Illinois Public Action Fund, was indicted on bank and tax fraud charges. She said she was unaware of his financial problems, but took herself out of the running to chair the Democratic Congressional Campaign Committee.

TENTH DISTRICT

Rep. Mark Kirk (R)

Elected 2000, 3d term; b. Sept. 15, 1959, Champaign; home, Kenilworth; Universidad Nacional Autonoma de Mexico, 1977–78, Cornell U., B.A. 1981, London Sch. of Econ., M.Sc. 1982; Georgetown U., J.D. 1992; Congre-gationalist; married (Kimberly Vertolli-Kirk).

Military Career: U.S. Naval Reserve, 1989-present.

Professional Career: Parliamentary aide, British House of Commons, 1981–83; A.A., U.S. Rep. John E. Porter, 1984–89; Staffer, World Bank, 1990–91; Spec. Asst., U.S. Dept. of State, 1991–93; Practicing atty., 1993–95; Counsel, U.S. House Cmte. on Intl. Relations, 1995–2000.

DC Office: 1717 LHOB, 20515, 202-225-4835; Fax: 202-225-0837; Web site: www.house.gov/kirk.

District Offices: Deerfield, 847-940-0202; Waukegan, 847-662-0101.

Committees: *Appropriations* (33d of 37 R): Foreign Operations, Export Financing & Related Programs; Military Quality of Life & Veterans Affairs & Related Agencies; Science, State, Justice, Commerce & Related Agencies.

Group Ratings

	ADA	ACLU	AFS	LCV	ITIC	NTU	COC	ACU	NTLC	CHC
2004	45	32	25	55	78	56	90	63	65	69
2003	10	—	0	80	—	58	89	63	—	—

National Journal Ratings

	2003 LIB	—	2003 CONS		2004 LIB	—	2004 CONS
Economic	50%	—	50%		50%	—	50%
Social	53%	—	46%		58%	—	42%
Foreign	45%	—	54%		44%	—	55%

Key Votes of the 108th Congress

1. Drilling in ANWR	N	5. DC School Vouchers	Y	9. Ban Same-Sex Marriage	N
2. Approve Bush Tax Cuts	Y	6. Ban Human Cloning	Y	10. Fund Iraq War	Y
3. Medicare/Rx Bill	Y	7. Restrict Gun Liability	Y	11. Bar Cuba Embargo Funds	*
4. Bar Overtime Pay Regs.	N	8. Ban Partial-Birth Abortion	N	12. Intelligence Reorg.	Y

Election Results

2004 general	Mark Kirk (R)	177,493	(64%)	($1,653,529)
	Lee Goodman (D)	99,218	(36%)	($88,520)
2004 primary	Mark Kirk (R) .... unopposed			
2002 general	Mark Kirk (R)	128,611	(69%)	($1,436,056)
	Henry Perritt (D)	58,300	(31%)	($473,270)

Prior Winning Percentages: 2000 (51%)

The People		Race/Ethnic Origin	Ancestry	
Area size:	252 sq. mi.	75.2% White	German: 14.4%	Irish: 9.9%
Urban population:	99.6%	5.3% Black	Polish: 7.3%	
Rural population:	0.4%	5.9% Asian	**2004 Presidential Vote**	
Pop. 2000:	653,647	0.1% Native Am.	Kerry (D) 150,267	(53%)
Median income:	$71,663	0.0% Hawaiian	Bush (R) 134,536	(47%)
Poverty status:	4.8%	1.1% Two+ races	**2000 Presidential Vote**	
Military veterans:	10.5%	0.2% Other	Gore (D) 134,149	(51%)
		12.3% Hispanic Origin	Bush (R) 123,982	(47%)
			Other 6,097	(2%)
			Cook Partisan Voting Index: D + 4	

Occupation   Blue collar: 14.4%   White collar: 75.9%   Gray collar: 9.7%

Since 1855, when the Chicago & Northwestern opened the railroad line from downtown Chicago north along the lakeshore, the North Shore suburbs along Lake Michigan have been the favorite residence for Chicago's elite. The North Shore starts in Evanston, and goes on to Wilmette and Winnetka and Glencoe, then crosses into the eastern Lake County towns of Highland Park and Lake Forest—each with a slightly different personality, each long established, mightily prosperous and with a patina of age. Not far from the gritty, monosyllabic city, these are communities of pleasant, affluent, well-educated people living in an environment whose natural beauty—the long water vista and blue light off the lake, the gentle hills and fine trees—is kept carefully disciplined. Corporate headquarters fit comfortably here, including Baxter Healthcare, Abbott Laboratories, Allstate Insurance, plus Goelitz Confectionary Company, which produced Ronald Reagan's jelly beans. This is also the home of the Great Lakes Naval Training Center.

The 10th Congressional District of Illinois is the North Shore district, starting on the Wilmette lakefront, running north to the city of Waukegan (once famous as the home of comedian Jack Benny) and almost to the Wisconsin border. The district goes inland to Northbrook and Deerfield through what for many years were cornfields. Farther inland are suburbs like Arlington Heights, developed in the 1950s and 1960s on the Northwestern railroad line, and Wheeling, developed in the 1970s near I-294. To the north is Libertyville, near where the Adlai Stevensons, the late presidential candidate and his son the former senator, owned what is now one of the last farms only a few miles from Lake Michigan. With the big movement toward Democrats in the Chicago suburbs in the 1990s, this establishment Republican district voted narrowly for Al Gore in 2000 and by a slightly larger margin for John Kerry in 2004.

The congressman from the 10th District is Mark Kirk, a Republican first elected in 2000. Kirk was born in downstate Illinois but grew up mostly in Kenilworth, on the Lake between Wilmette and Winnetka. He graduated from Cornell and the London School of Economics, worked as a staffer in Congressman John Porter's Washington office and became the chief of staff in just three years. Kirk left Capitol Hill in 1990 and moved on to a number of Washington jobs, first at the World Bank, then as a State Department aide working on the Central American peace process. After two years of international law practice, he served four years as counsel to the House International Relations Committee. He is also a commander in the Naval Reserves, serving as an aviator with tours of duty in Turkey, Serbia, Bosnia, Haiti, and Panama. In flights during the Gulf War, he was a frequent target of Iraqi guns; he continues to work one weekend each month at the Pentagon's "war room," monitoring intelligence reports.

In 1999, when Porter announced his retirement, Kirk returned home to the 10th District, where he was one of 11 competitors in the Republican primary. This contest included six millionaires who spent nearly $4 million of their own money. Kirk did not spend nearly as much, but he had great advantages: the endorsement of the highly popular Porter, the fact that he was the only candidate with moderate views on cultural issues and his greater experience in government. His 31% put him well ahead of the 15% for R.R. Donnelley & Sons printing company heiress Shawn Margaret Donnelley, and the 14% for Northbrook Mayor Mark Damisch. Democrats nominated state Representative Lauren Beth Gash. Both Kirk and Gash campaigned as candidates in the Porter mold, promising to carry on his fiscally conservative, culturally moderate record. Gash tried to downplay Kirk's years in Washington, touting her own legislative experience while talking about Social Security and prescription drugs. But Kirk won 51%–49%.

In the House, Kirk has compiled a centrist voting record, though a bit more conservative on foreign issues. He said that he wanted to strengthen moderate Republicans with a libertarian approach. His familiarity with the workings of the House and a helpful connection enabled him to get a seat on the Appropriations Committee. His explanation for the assignment: "Three words—J. Dennis Hastert."

In 2004, Kirk worked with Republican deficit hawks on steps to limit federal spending; the House passed his amendment that requires the Congressional Budget Office to publish an annual report that compares projected annual spending for entitlements to the actual spending in the preceding year. Citing intelligence failures in Iraq, the well-informed Kirk pushed for reform of the intelligence community. "For the president, it's incumbent on him to say mistakes were made and it's incumbent on him to fix it," he said. With Democrat Jesse Jackson Jr. and backed by the Everglades Foundation, he fought unsuccessfully in the Appropriations Committee to end subsidized loans for storage by sugar processing companies; Chicago-area candy producers have complained that high sugar prices forced them to cut thousands of jobs. He filed the "American Heroes Act" proposal for a statue in the new Capitol Visitors Center to commemorate the victims of the United Airlines flight that crashed in Pennsylvania after passengers struggled with terrorists to prevent them from reaching their target, which was probably the Capitol. Back home, he facilitated expansion of the North Chicago Veterans Affairs Medical Center, a neighbor to the naval training base. He pushed for O'Hare expansion and opposed a proposal for suburban rail commuters to subsidize the beleaguered Chicago Transit Authority. He worked with the 5th District's Rahm Emanuel on a sweeping package to clean up Lake Michigan.

In the 109th Congress, Kirk chaired the mainstream Republicans' Tuesday Group, and said that Congress should reflect the nation's preponderant moderates. He spoke out against House Republicans' "DeLay rule" change to drop the requirement that an indicted party leader must automatically step down from the post; the proposal was dropped.

Kirk has won reelection relatively easily. Running against an openly gay candidate in 2002, he was endorsed by the Human Rights Campaign for his support of gay rights, and by the Sierra Club and Planned Parenthood. Kirk seems headed for a lengthy career like Porter's, though like Porter he needs to be mindful of a serious primary challenge from a conservative. With the defeat of Phil Crane and the retirement of Henry Hyde, Kirk will likely become the "go to" Republican in the northern suburbs.

ELEVENTH DISTRICT

Rep. Jerry Weller (R)

Elected 1994, 6th term; b. July 7, 1957, Streator; home, Morris; U. of IL, B.S. 1979; Christian; married (Zury Rios Sosa).

Elected Office: IL House of Reps., 1988–94.

Professional Career: Farmer; Aide, U.S. Rep. Tom Corcoran, 1980–81; Aide, U.S. Agriculture Secy. John Block, 1981–85.

DC Office: 108 CHOB, 20515, 202-225-3635; Fax: 202-225-3521; Web site: weller.house.gov.

District Office: Joliet, 815-740-2028.

Committees: *International Relations* (17th of 27 R): International Terrorism & Nonproliferation; Western Hemisphere (Vice Chmn.). *Ways & Means* (12th of 24 R): Select Revenue Measures; Trade.

Group Ratings

	ADA	ACLU	AFS	LCV	ITIC	NTU	COC	ACU	NTLC	CHC
2004	15	0	13	9	100	57	100	84	70	84
2003	5	—	0	10	—	64	97	88	—	—

National Journal Ratings

	2003 LIB	—	2003 CONS		2004 LIB	—	2004 CONS
Economic	0%	—	91%		27%	—	72%
Social	5%	—	87%		43%	—	56%
Foreign	23%	—	71%		39%	—	59%

Key Votes of the 108th Congress

1. Drilling in ANWR	Y	5. DC School Vouchers	Y	9. Ban Same-Sex Marriage	Y
2. Approve Bush Tax Cuts	Y	6. Ban Human Cloning	Y	10. Fund Iraq War	Y
3. Medicare/Rx Bill	Y	7. Restrict Gun Liability	Y	11. Bar Cuba Embargo Funds	N
4. Bar Overtime Pay Regs.	N	8. Ban Partial-Birth Abortion	Y	12. Intelligence Reorg.	Y

Election Results

2004 general	Jerry Weller (R)	173,057	(59%)	($1,792,779)
	Tari Renner (D)	121,903	(41%)	($315,600)
2004 primary	Jerry Weller (R)	unopposed		
2002 general	Jerry Weller (R)	124,192	(64%)	($1,600,389)
	Keith Van Duyne (D)	68,893	(36%)	($30,233)

Prior Winning Percentages: 2000 (56%); 1998 (59%); 1996 (52%); 1994 (61%)

The People

Area size:	4,284 sq. mi.
Urban population:	78.2%
Rural population:	21.8%
Pop. 2000:	653,647
Median income:	$47,800
Poverty status:	8.4%
Military veterans:	12.5%

Race/Ethnic Origin

83.7% White
7.8% Black
0.8% Asian
0.1% Native Am.
0.0% Hawaiian
0.9% Two+ races
0.1% Other
6.7% Hispanic Origin

Ancestry

German: 18.4%   Irish: 11.8%
Italian: 6.0%

2004 Presidential Vote

Bush (R)	162,779	(53%)
Kerry (D)	140,619	(46%)
Other	1,018	(0%)

2000 Presidential Vote

Bush (R)	128,280	(50%)
Gore (D)	122,979	(48%)
Other	7,269	(3%)

Cook Partisan Voting Index: R + 1

Occupation   Blue collar: 29.4%   White collar: 55.3%   Gray collar: 15.3%

The low-lying land west and south of Chicago, where sluggishly flowing rivers run circles around industrial sites, is a great divide over which French explorers portaged the easiest path from the inland oceans of the Great Lakes to the Mississippi River valley. Today there is still a kind of borderland here, as the factories and shopping centers and subdivisions stop somewhere past the

Cook County line and downstate prairies begin, cornfields bisected by highways and railroads radiating out from the Loop and the rail yards of the nation's transportation hub. Politically, this is a borderland as well, between the traditionally Democratic Chicago metropolitan area, with its hard-bitten machine politics, and heavily Republican Downstate Illinois, with its tradition of governance by local civic leaders that stretches back to the days of Abraham Lincoln.

The 11th Congressional District of Illinois covers much of this borderland. It includes most of Will County, the fastest-growing of the large suburban Chicago counties, and its county seat of Joliet—politically marginal territory. Once a canal boat town, and later the producer of one-third of America's wallpaper, Joliet now has two big prisons and a 75,000-seat NASCAR racetrack; it owes its current prosperity and growing tourist locales in part to riverboat gambling. Farther west, on bluffs above the Illinois River heading down to the Mississippi, are the factory towns of Ottawa and LaSalle and, to the south, Streator; this is LaSalle County, also politically marginal (it was Barack Obama's first Illinois campaign stop after the Democratic National Convention). South of Joliet is Kankakee, a county seat amid rich prairie earth on the Illinois Central main line; this is Republican territory. Redistricting in 2001 removed from the 11th the southernmost townships of Cook County, which were increasingly Democratic, and added two ungainly-looking appendages. One goes west to rural Bureau County; the other heads south at the intersection of I-80 and I-39 and includes most of Bloomington in McLean County, one of the faster-growing Downstate counties. Another addition was a small corner of Livingston County, which includes the home of the parents of the 11th District's congressman. The 2001 redistricting made this district more Republican than its 1990s incarnation; George W. Bush won here with 53% in 2004.

The congressman from the 11th District is Jerry Weller, a hard-working, politically savvy Republican who won the seat in 1994. Weller grew up on a farm, where his family raised hogs. Out of college, he was a staffer to Congressman Tom Corcoran and Agriculture Secretary John Block; in the mid-1980s he returned to Illinois and was elected to the state House in 1988. In 1994, when Democratic Congressman George Sangmeister retired, Weller was one of six Republicans and seven Democrats to run for the seat. He called for reforming health care via market-based principles and promoting markets for ethanol fuels and soybean inks; he was proud of replacing the "granny tax" on nursing home residents with a cigarette tax as a way to pay for health care. Against Democrat Frank Giglio, a 20-year state legislator, who said of Congress, "Wouldn't this be a nice way to finish my career?" Weller won 61%–39%.

In the House, Weller quickly showed impressive insider skills. In 1996 he ran hard for a seat on the Ways and Means Committee, arguing that no one there represented Chicago. With help from Dennis Hastert, then chief deputy whip, he succeeded. He became a prime sponsor of ending the marriage penalty. He backed several other tax cuts, including the end of the Social Security earnings limit on seniors, which Bill Clinton signed; plus elimination of the estate tax, which Clinton opposed and George W. Bush signed, though on a phased schedule and with a sunset date. Later, he was an early advocate of making the 2001 tax cuts permanent. As he gained seniority on Ways and Means, he worked with the high-tech industry to expand tax credits for education and training expenses.

Weller did not neglect local concerns. With Democrat Jesse Jackson Jr., he promoted the third Chicago-area airport proposed for Peotone, 45 miles south of Chicago and a few miles north of Kankakee, which he insisted should be under Will County's authority; he also supported improvements at O'Hare. But he opposed Jackson's proposal for a new casino in Lynwood in southern Cook County. He got the new veterans' cemetery in Elwood named after Abraham Lincoln.

Weller has been active in internal House Republican politics, with mixed success. He lost a race for Republican Conference secretary in 1997 and withdrew from a race for chairman of the Policy Committee in 1998. When Speaker-designate Bob Livingston stunned everyone by announcing his retirement, Weller worked the phones for Hastert, along with Tom DeLay and Tom Davis, and helped Hastert win the speakership within hours. In early 2001, he was named finance chairman of the NRCC but suffered another setback to his leadership ambitions in November 2002, when Tom Reynolds defeated him for House Republicans' campaign committee chairmanship 119–90.

Weller gained unusual attention in 2004 when he announced his engagement to Zury Rios Sosa, a Guatemalan congresswoman and the daughter of Jose Efrain Rios Montt, who seized power in that country in 1982 in a military coup that was followed with a bloody revolt and thousands of deaths. Weller said that his personal life was a private matter, and criticized as "disgraceful" Democrats who criticized the background of his fiancée, whom he met at a reception hosted by the U.S. Ambassador in Guatemala. But that didn't stop Tari Renner, Weller's Democratic opponent in 2004. Renner, a McLean County Board member and political science professor at Illinois Wesleyan University, demanded that Weller give up his seat on the International Relations Committee and its Western Hemisphere Subcommittee. Weller got a unanimous Federal Election Commission ruling that Sosa could take part in his campaign, even though she is a foreign national. Renner also criticized Weller for lockstep support of George W. Bush; Weller referred to his opponent simply as "the college professor." House Democrats hoped that Weller's fiancée's background would hurt him, but he won 59%–41%. He carried seven of the eight counties, including 58%–42% in Will, which cast nearly half the total vote; Renner carried his home county, McLean, 53%–47%. Weller and Sosa were married on November 20 at a Guatemalan mansion guarded by tight security.

TWELFTH DISTRICT

Rep. Jerry Costello (D)

Elected Aug. 1988, 9th full term; b. Sept. 25, 1949, E. St. Louis; home, Belleville; Belleville Area Col., A.A. 1971, Maryville Col., B.A. 1973; Catholic; married (Georgia).

Elected Office: Chmn., St. Clair Cnty. Bd. of Supervisors, 1980–88.

Professional Career: Dir., IL Court Svcs. & Probation, 1973–80; Chmn., Region's Cncl. of Govts., 1980–84.

DC Office: 2269 RHOB, 20515, 202-225-5661; Fax: 202-225-0285; Web site: www.house.gov/costello.

District Offices: Belleville, 618-233-8026; Carbondale, 618-529-3791; Chester, 618-826-3043; E. St. Louis, 618-397-8833; Granite City, 618-451-7065; West Frankfort, 618-937-6402.

Committees: *Science* (2d of 20 D): Energy. *Transportation & Infrastructure* (4th of 34 D): Aviation (RMM); Railroads; Water Resources & Environment.

Group Ratings

	ADA	ACLU	AFS	LCV	ITIC	NTU	COC	ACU	NTLC	CHC
2004	70	45	88	64	10	15	38	36	12	61
2003	80	—	100	70	—	34	38	44	—	—

National Journal Ratings

	2003 LIB	—	2003 CONS		2004 LIB	—	2004 CONS
Economic	63%	—	37%		62%	—	38%
Social	55%	—	44%		53%	—	46%
Foreign	61%	—	37%		67%	—	33%

Key Votes of the 108th Congress

1. Drilling in ANWR	N	5. DC School Vouchers	N	9. Ban Same-Sex Marriage	Y
2. Approve Bush Tax Cuts	N	6. Ban Human Cloning	Y	10. Fund Iraq War	N
3. Medicare/Rx Bill	N	7. Restrict Gun Liability	Y	11. Bar Cuba Embargo Funds	Y
4. Bar Overtime Pay Regs.	Y	8. Ban Partial-Birth Abortion	Y	12. Intelligence Reorg.	N

Election Results

2004 general	Jerry Costello (D)	198,962	(69%)	($637,567)
	Erin Zweigart (R)	82,677	(29%)	($15,983)
	Other	4,796	(2%)	
2004 primary	Jerry Costello (D)	56,397	(90%)	
	Kenneth Wiezer (D)	6,265	(10%)	
2002 general	Jerry Costello (D)	131,580	(69%)	($466,184)
	David Sadler (R)	58,440	(31%)	

Prior Winning Percentages: 2000 (100%); 1998 (60%); 1996 (72%); 1994 (66%); 1992 (71%); 1990 (66%); 1988 (53%); 1988 (51%)

The People		Race/Ethnic Origin	Ancestry	
Area size:	4,556 sq. mi.	79.7% White	German: 18.6%	Irish: 8.7%
Urban population:	76.7%	16.3% Black	English: 6.6%	
Rural population:	23.3%	0.8% Asian	**2004 Presidential Vote**	
Pop. 2000:	653,647	0.2% Native Am.	Kerry (D) 152,055	(52%)
Median income:	$35,198	0.0% Hawaiian	Bush (R) 139,710	(48%)
Poverty status:	15.0%	1.0% Two+ races	Other 1,600	(1%)
Military veterans:	15.3%	0.1% Other	**2000 Presidential Vote**	
		1.8% Hispanic Origin	Gore (D) 144,548	(54%)
			Bush (R) 116,724	(43%)
			Other 7,634	(3%)
			Cook Partisan Voting Index: D + 5	

Occupation   Blue collar: 26.2%   White collar: 55.1%   Gray collar: 18.7%

The nation's two mightiest rivers, the Mississippi and Missouri, their waters roiling together, join just a few miles above St. Louis and just a few miles below Alton, Illinois. Most views of this center of the Mississippi Valley focus on the Gateway Arch and the buildings of downtown St. Louis. But the Mississippi shoreline of Illinois is worthy of attention as well. Alton's 19th century buildings recall its turbulent history, when it was the home of the anti-slavery agitator Elijah Lovejoy, who was murdered by a mob. More recently it was the longtime home of conservative crusader and columnist Phyllis Schlafly. Nearby in Hartford, Lewis and Clark spent five months preparing their team and collecting supplies for their journey westward. Just across from the Gateway Arch is East St. Louis, where dozens of rail lines and highways funnel into bridges over the river. Once a rail and stockyards center second only to Chicago, East St. Louis is now almost entirely black and one of America's poorest and most troubled cities, a half-abandoned slum with one of the nation's highest crime rates and a rapidly declining tax base, almost entirely dependent on a riverboat casino and an adjacent waterfront hotel for its tax revenue. After peaking at 82,000 in 1960, its population is now less than 32,000—down 9,000 in the 1990s. East St. Louis is in St. Clair County, long heavily Democratic; Alton is in Madison County, politically more marginal and famous as a prime locale for trial lawyers to file tort suits. George W. Bush came here in January 2005 to campaign for changes in tort law.

South of East St. Louis and the industrial area around Belleville, the river counties are lightly inhabited, but they were not always unimportant. This was the site of the French Kaskaskia settlement that became Illinois's first capital in 1818, but repeated flooding turned it into an island and reduced its population to 9 people and many more egrets. Farther south, the river abuts coal country and is not far from Carbondale, once a coal center but now, as the home of Southern Illinois University, bustling with students from Downstate Illinois and Chicago. The land here is sometimes known as Egypt, the southern end of Illinois where the Ohio River meets the Mississippi: flat, fertile farmland, protected by giant man-made levees because it is susceptible to yearly floods. The marshy landscape has created the Sinkhole Plain, with more than 10,000 sinkholes. There is more than a touch of Dixie here: The unofficial capital of Egypt, Cairo (pronounced *KAY-roh*), is a declining town closer to Mississippi than to Chicago. In his 1842 work, *American Notes*, Charles Dickens described the town in these unflattering terms: "The hateful Mississippi circling and eddying before it, and turning off upon its southern course a slimy monster hideous to behold; a hotbed of disease, an ugly sepulchre, a grave uncheered by any gleam of promise: a place without one single quality, in earth or air or water, to commend it: such is this dismal Cairo." A more enticing locale not far from Cairo is the Shawnee National Forest, which has preserved Native American sites that are 10,000 years old; the Cherokee Nation left here in the 1830s on its devastating forced march to Oklahoma, which became known as the Trail of Tears.

The 12th District of Illinois covers all of this riverfront from Alton south to Cairo, with some inland territory as well. Most of its population is in the Metro East area in St. Clair and Madison Counties. The largest employer in southern Illinois is Scott Air Force Base near Belleville, where local officials hoped that a relocation of planes for the 932d Airlift Wing would give the facility protection in the 2005 base-closing review. Senator Richard Durbin admitted that "things looked pretty bleak"; Governor Rod Blagojevich lobbied for the base with top Pentagon officials after the 2004 election. When the Defense Department's recommendations were released in May 2005, there was joy in Belleville: Scott ended up gaining 797 jobs and 12 refueling tankers.

The congressman from the 12th District is Jerry Costello, a Democrat first elected in 1988. He grew up in a St. Clair County political family, worked for the courts after college, then became chairman of the St. Clair County Board of Supervisors. He waited with some impatience for the retirement of Congressman Mel Price, first elected in 1944; Price died in office in April 1988. Experienced, well connected, supported by organized labor, Costello was the obvious successor. Yet he received only 51% of the votes in the special election and 53% for a full term.

Costello is a practical-minded politician with a voting record more liberal on economics than on cultural and foreign issues. Seniority has moved him toward top posts on the Science plus Transportation and Infrastructure Committees, where he is ranking Democrat on the Aviation Subcommittee. Concern over their local economic impact led him to oppose the Clean Air Act and NAFTA. He voted against authorizing to use force against Iraq in January 1991 and October 2002; his son was a paratrooper during the 1991 war. Costello was instrumental in creating the Mid-America Airport at Scott Air Force Base; although it has no scheduled airline service, local officials have taken steps to make it a cargo hub. Attempting to revive his district's largely dormant high-sulfur coal mines, he authored several provisions for expanded clean-coal research and development that the House included in its 2003 energy bill; he also got $18 million from the House Appropriations Committee for a projected FutureGen clean coal power plant, which is designed to burn coal without releasing pollutants. Costello has worked for authorization in highway legislation of a $1.6 billion Mississippi River bridge slightly north of the current congested bridge on Interstate 70, which would require hundreds of millions more for highway relocation; the existing Poplar Street bridge serves three interstates in the St. Louis area.

For a while, a cloud hung over Costello. In 1996 federal prosecutors indicted and won a conviction of Amiel Cueto, Costello's longtime friend and business partner, for trying to stop an investigation of a gambling operation run by a client and for conspiring to get himself installed as St. Clair County state's attorney. Although a federal judge ruled that Costello was an unindicted co-conspirator and government attorneys said he was a silent partner in a plan to build an Indian casino, Costello denied it all. In 2004 the chief prosecutor said that Costello was never the target of the investigation.

Costello was opposed in 1998 by Bill Price, an orthopedic surgeon and son of Mel Price, who switched parties and ran as a Republican. Costello won by a solid 60%–40%. Since then, he has been reelected without significant opposition. In 2004 Costello was reelected against a 28-year-old opponent, whose 1993 Ford Mustang died three times on the campaign trail, 69%–29%.

THIRTEENTH DISTRICT

Rep. Judy Biggert (R)

Elected 1998, 4th term; b. Aug. 15, 1937, Chicago; home, Hinsdale; Stanford U., B.A. 1959, Northwestern U., J.D. 1963; Episcopalian; married (Rody).

Elected Office: Hinsdale Bd. of Ed., 1982–85; IL House of Reps., 1992–98.

Professional Career: Clerk, U.S. Ct. of Appeals, 1963–64; Practicing atty., 1975–98.

DC Office: 1317 LHOB, 20515, 202-225-3515; Fax: 202-225-9420; Web site: judybiggert.house.gov.

District Office: Willowbrook, 630-655-2052.

Committees: *Education & the Workforce* (9th of 27 R): Education Reform; Workforce Protections (Vice Chmn.). *Financial Services* (18th of 37 R): Capital Markets, Insurance & Government Sponsored Enterprises; Domestic and International Monetary Policy, Trade & Technology (Vice Chmn.); Financial Institutions & Consumer Credit. *Science* (11th of 24 R): Energy (Chmn.); Environment, Technology & Standards. *Standards of Official Conduct* (2d of 5 R).

Group Ratings

	ADA	ACLU	AFS	LCV	ITIC	NTU	COC	ACU	NTLC	CHC
2004	35	30	0	18	100	60	100	64	70	61
2003	10	—	13	25	—	58	100	64	—	—

National Journal Ratings

	2003 LIB	—	2003 CONS		2004 LIB	—	2004 CONS
Economic	27%	—	71%		33%	—	65%
Social	52%	—	47%		57%	—	43%
Foreign	46%	—	52%		55%	—	44%

Key Votes of the 108th Congress

1. Drilling in ANWR	Y	5. DC School Vouchers	N	9. Ban Same-Sex Marriage	N
2. Approve Bush Tax Cuts	Y	6. Ban Human Cloning	N	10. Fund Iraq War	Y
3. Medicare/Rx Bill	Y	7. Restrict Gun Liability	Y	11. Bar Cuba Embargo Funds	Y
4. Bar Overtime Pay Regs.	N	8. Ban Partial-Birth Abortion	Y	12. Intelligence Reorg.	Y

Election Results

2004 general	Judy Biggert (R)	198,823	(65%)	($542,733)
	Gloria Schor Andersen (D)	106,525	(35%)	($42,129)
2004 primary	Judy Biggert (R)	46,861	(100%)	
	Other	231	(0%)	
2002 general	Judy Biggert (R)	139,546	(70%)	($464,054)
	Thomas Mason (D)	59,069	(30%)	

Prior Winning Percentages: 2000 (66%); 1998 (61%)

The People		Race/Ethnic Origin	Ancestry	
Area size:	362 sq. mi.	81.6% White	German: 16.5%	Irish: 13.1%
Urban population:	98.8%	4.9% Black	Polish: 10.0%	
Rural population:	1.2%	6.6% Asian	**2004 Presidential Vote**	
Pop. 2000:	653,647	0.1% Native Am.	Bush (R) 175,705	(55%)
Median income:	$71,686	0.0% Hawaiian	Kerry (D) 142,397	(45%)
Poverty status:	2.9%	1.2% Two+ races	**2000 Presidential Vote**	
Military veterans:	9.9%	0.1% Other	Bush (R) 148,621	(55%)
		5.5% Hispanic Origin	Gore (D) 113,450	(42%)
			Other 7,166	(3%)
			Cook Partisan Voting Index: R + 5	

Occupation   Blue collar: 15.8%   White collar: 74.9%   Gray collar: 9.4%

Most residents of Chicagoland now live not in the city but in the suburbs, and increasingly not even in Cook County but in the Collar Counties all around. DuPage County, straight west of Chicago, had 103,000 residents in 1940; in 2003, there were 925,000, with new subdivisions still springing up at the western edges. Nor are these just bedroom communities. Since 1970 DuPage County has generated nearly half the new jobs in metro Chicago. Here in Oak Brook are the headquarters of Ace Hardware, Federal Signal, the Spiegel catalog, Molex and, most famously, McDonald's and its Hamburger University, an 80-acre campus where more than 73,000 trainees have received Bachelor of Hamburgerology degrees since it was founded in 1961. Nearby are gracefully older railroad commuter towns like Hinsdale and Downers Grove, but also Naperville, once a country village, now an edge city, with a school district ranked number one in the world in science in an international exam and a top-rated public library. The Argonne National Laboratory has sparked numerous private research firms along the Sanitary and Ship Canal, the Des Plaines River and the Illinois and Michigan Canal, built way back in 1848.

The 13th Congressional District of Illinois includes the southern part of DuPage County (including Oak Brook, Downers Grove and Naperville), a small section of southwest corner of Cook County and the northern slice of Will County (including Bolingbrook, Romeoville and Lockport). Politically, this has been a heavily Republican area, suspicious of the motives and operations of Chicago Democrats, devoted to free enterprise and hostile to higher taxes. Republican margins shrunk in DuPage County as the Chicago suburbs became more Democratic in the 1990s, but the 13th District has not been in danger of going Democratic.

The congresswoman from the 13th District is Judy Biggert, a Republican first elected in 1998. She grew up in Kenilworth, on the affluent North Shore (as did Mark Kirk of the 10th District), graduated from New Trier Township High School, Stanford and Northwestern Law School and clerked for a federal appeals judge. She raised four children in Hinsdale, practicing estate and real estate law out of her home, served on the Hinsdale Township Board of Education, was chairman of the Visiting Nurses Association of Chicago—a "former car pool mom and assistant soccer coach," as her campaign put it. In 1992 she was elected to the state House, and was soon part of the leadership.

Biggert started running for the U.S. House in 1997 when incumbent Republican Harris Fawell announced his retirement; he endorsed her in November 1997. She said she supported abortion rights and opposed most gun control measures for constitutional reasons, though she had campaigned for gun control in 1992. She had primary opposition from state Representative Peter Roskam, who moved into the district to run. Biggert put in $402,000 of her own money and got support from Planned Parenthood and the Human Rights Campaign. She won the March 1998 primary by 45%–40% and the November the general election 61%–39%.

In the House, Biggert has had a moderate voting record on cultural issues but has been more conservative on economic and foreign matters. On the Education and the Workforce Committee, she was the prime sponsor of a bill to allow employees to take compensatory time rather than overtime, a measure she said would allow flexibility especially necessary for working mothers. The House passed similar bills in 1996 and 1997, but in June 2003 the AFL-CIO lobbied heavily against it, and the Republican leadership cancelled a roll call after it was apparent they didn't have the votes. A year later Biggert and other committee members sought to amend the transportation bill to remove Davis-Bacon and other labor provisions inconsistent with committee policy. Less controversially, she and Harold Ford passed a bill to allow church pension plans to pool their funds in collective trusts.

Biggert has been a strong supporter of the Argonne National Laboratory. In 2002 she gathered 64 cosponsors, including others with national laboratories in their districts, for her bill to reorganize the Energy Department's Office of Science in line with the American Physical Society's recommendations to emphasize energy research. In February 2004 she sponsored a bill authorizing $180 million for university nuclear science and engineering programs, and later she inserted a 65% funding increase for the Office of Science into the energy bill. In June 2004 she sponsored a bill to fund the Energy Department with $165 million over three years to build a supercomputer with a sustained performance of 100 trillion teraflops (floating-point operations per second). It passed the House and, in different form, the Senate and became law in November

2004. Biggert has also sponsored bills to make sure homeless children get schooling, to help children with eating disorders and to finance school construction. She has paid heed to local issues, getting Lake Michigan water for Downers Grove when wells were contaminated there.

Biggert's attempts to move into the Republican leadership have been less successful. In November 2000 she ran for secretary of the Republican Conference and lost to Barbara Cubin of Wyoming, 122–73. In July 2002, when Cubin was moving up to another position, she ran for one day for the same post, but withdrew when it became clear that John Doolittle of California had the votes. In October 1999 Biggert abandoned her pledge to serve only three terms. She has been reelected easily ever since. In July 2004 Republican leaders asked if she wanted the vacant nomination for the U.S. Senate; she passed.

FOURTEENTH DISTRICT

Rep. Dennis Hastert (R)

Elected 1986, 10th term; b. Jan. 2, 1942, Aurora; home, Yorkville; Wheaton Col., B.A. 1964, N. IL U., M.A. 1967; Protestant; married (Jean).

Elected Office: IL House of Reps., 1980–86.

Professional Career: H.S. teacher & coach, 1965–80.

DC Office: 235 CHOB, 20515, 202-225-2976; Fax: 202-225-0697; Web site: www.house.gov/hastert.

District Offices: Batavia, 630-406-1114; Dixon, 815-288-0680.

Committees: *Speaker of the House.*

Group Ratings and Key Votes: Speaker does not usually vote.

Election Results

2004 general	Dennis Hastert (R)	191,616	(69%)	($5,013,947)
	Ruben Zamora (D)	87,590	(31%)	($18,028)
2004 primary	Dennis Hastert (R)	unopposed		
2002 general	Dennis Hastert (R)	135,198	(74%)	($2,970,554)
	Laurence Quick (D)	47,165	(26%)	($18,136)

Prior Winning Percentages: 2000 (74%); 1998 (70%); 1996 (64%); 1994 (76%); 1992 (67%); 1990 (67%); 1988 (74%); 1986 (52%)

The People		Race/Ethnic Origin	Ancestry	
Area size:	2,866 sq. mi.	74.0% White	German: 18.9%	Irish: 9.9%
Urban population:	86.2%	4.6% Black	English: 6.0%	
Rural population:	13.8%	1.8% Asian	**2004 Presidential Vote**	
Pop. 2000:	653,647	0.1% Native Am.	Bush (R) 158,428	(55%)
Median income:	$56,314	0.0% Hawaiian	Kerry (D) 125,269	(44%)
Poverty status:	7.0%	1.0% Two+ races	Other 1,828	(1%)
Military veterans:	10.3%	0.1% Other	**2000 Presidential Vote**	
		18.5% Hispanic Origin	Bush (R) 129,745	(54%)
			Gore (D) 101,369	(42%)
			Other 7,428	(3%)
			Cook Partisan Voting Index: R + 5	

Occupation	Blue collar: 26.8%	White collar: 59.9%	Gray collar: 13.3%

A few dozen miles beyond the Loop there is an invisible line marking two different Chicagos. One is the Chicago dominated by blacks and descendants of the vast immigrations of 1840–1924 and 1970–2000, a Chicago where certain loyalties are taken for granted: loyalty to ethnic group, to church (usually the Catholic Church, often with an ethnic prefix), and to party (almost always the Democrats). This Chicago is a gritty city, where personal cheerfulness and courtesy lighten up days otherwise as cold and impersonal as the gray winter sky. The other Chicago is the beginning of the Great Plains, originally a white Anglo-Saxon Protestant Chicago, a place whose residents are products of the first great wave of immigration to America. The tone of this Chicago is lighter, its streets and highways cleaner and neater, its daily life generally free from evidence of unpleasantness and deprivation. Ronald Reagan grew up in Downstate Illinois within the orbit of this Chicago (though he did live in the city briefly), and its spirit helped to characterize his presidency. His migration to southern California, incidentally, is not atypical: You can see in the geometric grids and Republican voting patterns of Orange County or Phoenix almost exact replicas of the grids and patterns in Chicago's suburban Collar Counties, transported to the once-empty Southwest on the Atchison, Topeka & Santa Fe or out the old U.S. 66 from their beginnings in Chicago's Loop.

The 14th Congressional District of Illinois straddles this line between metropolitan Chicago and Downstate Illinois. It gets as close as 30 miles to Chicago's Loop, in western DuPage County, with two great Chicagoland landmarks—Cantigny, the estate of Colonel Robert McCormick, longtime publisher of the *Chicago Tribune*, and FermiLab, the world's fastest energy particle accelerator and employer of some 2,500 people—icons of political conservatism and high technology within two miles of each other. The 14th also contains the Fox River Valley and its industrial cities of Elgin and Aurora, now the third-largest city in Illinois, plus antique St. Charles with its annual Scarecrow Festival; local debates rage over whether to tear down the dams on the Fox River. To the south is Kendall County, the fastest-growing county in Illinois, where new subdivisions are growing up outside the old town of Yorkville. Farther west, amid what may be the world's richest cornfields, the 14th passes through DeKalb, long the world's leading manufacturer of barbed wire, and goes on to Lee County, including Reagan's boyhood home in Dixon. Since the 2001 redistricting, the 14th moves farther west, almost to the Mississippi River, to include farmlands in parts of Whiteside, Bureau and Henry Counties. This was traditionally some of the most heavily Republican territory in the country. Northern Illinois was settled when Chicago was just a frontier village by Yankees from Ohio, Indiana, Upstate New York and New England, and by Germans emigrating after the failed revolutions of 1848: people who formed the heart of the Republican Party from its founding in 1854 and who would form the core of the Grand Army of the Republic a few years later. Their descendants, in this extension of Chicagoland, remain mostly Republican today.

The congressman from the 14th District is Dennis Hastert, a Republican first elected in 1986, and since 1999 the 51st Speaker of the House of Representatives. He comes from the Fox River Valley, outside the Chicago metro orbit when he was growing up, but now part of its booming outer edge. His great-grandfather emigrated from Luxembourg to Aurora, on the Fox River, in the 19th century, to work on the railroads. His father, originally an embalmer, opened a feed supply business in Oswego. Denny and his two younger brothers hoisted 100-pound bags and delivered milk in the early morning; his parents also had a restaurant where he worked as a fry cook. At high school in Oswego—then a rural town, now exploding with subdivisions—he wrestled and played football. He graduated from Wheaton College, a religious school in nearby DuPage County, and then he became a high school teacher at Yorkville High School, a few miles south of Oswego. There he taught history and coached wrestling for 16 years and met his wife, a physical education teacher. But his experience was not entirely local. In summers he traveled as a teacher for the YMCA or other groups to Japan, Colombia, Venezuela, Europe and the Soviet Union. And as a wrestling coach he excelled. His team won the state championship and he was named the national coach of the year in 1976; he can still remember the names and records of all of his wrestlers. He tries to attend the NCAA wrestling tournament every year. He owns nine antique vehicles, including two fire engines and a pickup truck; he likes to carve duck decoys and fish for walleye in the Fox River.

After a trip to Washington in 1978, when Democrats had a 2–1 majority in the House, Hastert got involved in politics, interning with state Senator John Grotberg. In 1980 he finished third in an Illinois House primary; then the incumbent became fatally ill and Hastert was chosen to take his place on the November ballot and was elected. After the March 1986 primary,

Grotberg, at that point a member of Congress, was fatally stricken with cancer and Hastert again was chosen by the party as a replacement. The election was unusually close, but Hastert won 52%–48%.

In his early years in the House, Hastert had a conservative voting record and made few waves. But he gained valuable experience. He got a seat on the Commerce committee and on the subcommittees handling health, energy and telecommunications issues. He built a relationship with Minority Leader Robert Michel, from the 18th District of Illinois. He worked together with Tom DeLay of Texas for Illinois's Ed Madigan in the race for minority whip in March 1989; Madigan lost by just two votes to an upstart from Georgia named Newt Gingrich. In 1994 he was chief organizer for DeLay's campaign for whip, the one leadership post won by a non-Gingrichite after the big Republican gains that fall. Afterwards Hastert was named chief deputy whip and shared an office and staff with DeLay. If he had not stopped in the hall to answer a reporter's question, he would have been in the line of fire when a crazed killer stormed into DeLay's office in July 1998.

To his work Hastert brought the habits of a coach, listening long to colleagues' goals and complaints, sizing up their character and capacity, then insisting firmly on a course of action when he reached a judgment. He operated with minimal ego and a bear-like friendliness, putting his arm around a colleague when asking advice or seeking intelligence; increasingly he was looked to by other leaders to help Republicans reach consensus and to negotiate difficult issues with Democrats, particularly health care. In 1997 he helped put together the Republicans' Medicare bill. Gingrich made him head of a task force that hammered out a patients' rights bill, which was passed by the House in August 1998. Over the years, Hastert has continued his trips abroad, including to Japan, and has been supportive of free trade; central Illinois, where the largest company is Caterpillar, produces more exports than just about anywhere else in the country.

Then suddenly one day in December 1998 he was chosen Speaker of the House. Speaker Newt Gingrich announced his retirement three days after the November election. Members scrambled for leadership positions, and Hastert was urged to run against Majority Leader Dick Armey. But Hastert had pledged to support him and, when he asked to be released from the pledge, Armey said no; so he kept his word and didn't run for a position he probably could have won. Then on December 19, just before the House voted on impeachment, Speaker-designate Bob Livingston announced his retirement too. Gingrich told Hastert, "You are the only one in this conference who could pull this body together. You are going to have to be the next speaker of the House." At 1 p.m. he announced; by the end of the day he had more than 100 votes, and the speakership.

Some called him "the accidental Speaker," but he has served as Speaker longer than anyone since Tip O'Neill and his fitness for the job has long since ceased to be in question. In many ways he resembles O'Neill, who likely would never have been Speaker but for the death of Hale Boggs in a plane crash in 1972. Like O'Neill, Hastert is tall and heavy, is from a modest background, speaks in a rough and tumble manner but has a sophisticated understanding of politics and a more than sufficient command of policy; and like O'Neill he is a tough partisan and a man of his word. He is a backslapper who continually listens to other members—in the words of the *Wall Street Journal's* Paul Gigot, "the rumpled, enormous Speaker who doesn't approach members so much as engulf them."

As Speaker, Hastert has been good at tactics. In his first four years, working with Majority Leader Dick Armey and Majority Whip Tom DeLay, Hastert's leadership team brought to the floor 558 rules—the resolutions that set the terms and conditions of debate— and lost on only two. But Hastert, though he has none of the grandiose vision of Newt Gingrich, has also been good at strategy. The House passed financial services deregulation and, after negotiations with White House Chief of Staff John Podesta (whom Hastert had known in college), an appropriations bill. He backed Clinton's Plan Colombia in June 2000 and agreed in August 2000 to allow a minimum wage increase in return for tax relief for small business; in October 2000 he canceled a vote on a resolution condemning Turkey's 1915–23 massacres of Armenians in response to pleas from the White House.

All the while, Hastert kept his eye on the 2000 elections. He effectively lobbied some Republicans in marginal seats, like Upstate New York's Amo Houghton, to stay on rather than retire; he allowed members with Democratic-leaning districts to cast votes against the leadership that would be useful at home. He used the tool of the Republicans' six-year term-limit on chairmanships to get those competing for spots opening up to raise money for Republican candidates and helped the Battleground 2000 program raise some $21 million. His quiet pursuit of a modest legislative strategy let Republican candidates emphasize their own local issues—a far cry from Gingrich's nationalized Contract With America campaign in 1994. His Republicans did hold their majority, narrowly, on November 7.

With a Republican president, Hastert's role changed. Legislative priorities would be set mainly by the White House; the House's job was to pass administration-backed legislation so that the President could put pressure on the always shaky Senate. As White House Chief of Staff Andrew Card said, "He has basically made sure that the president doesn't have to be presented any legislation that would split our party and compromise the president's objectives for policy." Hastert's relations with Bush have been good (though he refused to deal with White House staff on the transportation bill in 2003–04) but not subservient: he was careful to protect his members and wary lest the White House water down legislation too much in negotiations with the Senate. In spring 2001 the House quickly passed the Bush tax cut and education bill. In July and August 2001—when Bush's job rating was hovering around 50% and there were only 222 House Republicans, four more than a majority—Hastert had a spectacular record. The House passed the Bush energy program, including drilling in the Arctic National Wildlife Refuge and not including an increase in auto mileage standards. In 2000, Republican Charlie Norwood had gotten 68 Republicans to join him and almost all Democrats on his HMO regulation bill. In July 2001 Hastert developed and gathered votes for a Republican alternative and in the meantime the White House negotiated with Norwood, who agreed to George W. Bush's terms, much to the dismay of many of his allies. A Bush veto threat—and the existence of a plausible alternative that might pass—persuaded Norwood to compromise; the House passed an HMO regulation bill acceptable to Republicans and for which they could claim credit.

On September 11, the mood of the House changed. Hastert and Gephardt, together with Senate leaders Tom Daschle and Trent Lott were taken to a secure location far from the Capitol and emerged with much closer bonds. But Hastert also continued to forge a record that Republicans could run on in 2002. He got the House to pass a Republican bill providing prescription drugs for seniors; the Democratic Senate never passed a bill on the issue. Republicans went to the floor to give the president trade promotion authority with fewer than 218 commitments and, with little Democratic help, prevailed by 215–214 in December 2001 and then again by 215–212 in July 2002. When the corporate misdeeds of Enron, WorldCom and other companies filled the headlines, Hastert saw that the issue could be political poison for Republicans. The House passed a corporate accountability bill fashioned by Financial Services Chairman Michael Oxley in April 2002, but it was attacked in the press and by Democrats as too lenient. In July, Hastert pressed Oxley and other Republicans to pass the bill sponsored by Senator Paul Sarbanes (and passed 97–0 by the Senate), to put in place legislation and take a political issue off the calendar; Oxley and others resisted, but Hastert prevailed, and House Republicans could go home in the August recess and say they had acted against corporate misconduct. Hastert's power increased when he got the Republican Conference to require Appropriations subcommittee chairmen to be approved by the party's Steering Committee—additional leverage for the leadership interested in holding spending within limits in its continuing institutional battle against appropriators interested in controlling the level of spending themselves.

In 2003 Hastert concentrated on adding a prescription drug benefit to Medicare. As one of his aides said, "This is the thing he thinks will keep us in the majority for a while." The Bush White House wanted to have the benefits provided entirely by private insurers, outside the Medicare structure; Hastert waved that off as a nonstarter. The Senate first passed a bill to the liking of Democrats like Edward Kennedy. House Ways and Means Chairman Bill Thomas drafted a different measure, with health savings accounts and nationwide competition between Medicare and private insurers. The conference committee worked for many days, with clashes between Thomas and Senate Finance Chairman Charles Grassley. Hastert stepped in at many points and finally pressed Thomas to drop the nationwide competition. Thomas walked out and said he was going to fly home to California; Hastert insisted he come back. Competition was limited to a few geographic areas, and the AARP promptly endorsed the bill. When it came to the floor in November 2003, Hastert hoped that many Democrats would support it, but only a few did, and with many conservatives opposed to the creation of a new entitlement, Hastert decided to hold the 15-minute roll call open until he could switch enough votes. It was held open for nearly three hours—an unprecedented amount, and one criticized by Democrats; John Dingell said, "Never have I seen such a grotesque, arbitrary and gross abuse of power." Hastert was more taciturn. "I wasn't about to give it up until we got it done," he said. "Our job was to get people on board. It took some time."

Other tasks proved more difficult. In spring 2004 Hastert squeezed out narrow majorities for a budget resolution which would not require that tax cuts be offset by spending cuts. The Senate, because of the votes of four Republican senators, took the opposite stand, and the two versions were never reconciled. Hastert was frustrated. "The House of Representatives tried to bow and scrape and do everything we could to go along with the Senate. Our members will not be tied down." And he attacked John McCain, one of the four Republican senators. But that left room for Hastert to get the House to vote to extend the child tax credit, repeal the marriage penalty and make permanent the 10% bracket. Hastert was also at odds with the Senate on intelligence issues. In early 2004 he refused to allow a 60-day extension of the deadline for the 9/11 Commission's report, but eventually backed down. The commission's report in July 2004 recommended major changes in intelligence, and a bill sponsored by Susan Collins and Joseph Lieberman won near-unanimous support in the Senate. The House took a different view. The Republican leadership in September unveiled a bill with provisions making it easier to deport immigrants involved in terrorism, to monitor terrorism suspects with no known organizational affiliation and to increase the penalties for false statements in terrorism cases. Judiciary Chairman James Sensenbrenner added other immigration measures, including a requirement that states not issue driver's licenses to illegal aliens.

Hastert spent much time trying to reconcile the two and even flew to Maine for a 7 a.m. meeting with Collins in October. No bill was passed before the election. On November 20 Hastert held a meeting of House committee chairmen and found them unwilling to accept the Senate version. He was particularly moved by Armed Services Chairman Duncan Hunter's belief that it would endanger troops in the field. Enough Democrats were ready to vote for the Senate version for it to pass the House, but Hastert announced he would keep the bill off the floor because it did not have the support "of a majority of the majority." He prodded the White House to resolve the differences and got Dick Cheney to come to the Capitol to mediate. In December Hunter agreed on a provision that stated that the military chain of command would not be altered by the new National Intelligence Director, and Sensenbrenner's provisions were put aside, with a promise that they could be attached to the first must-pass legislation of 2005. The bill passed 336–75.

There have been headaches for Hastert. He has had to deal with the Transportation Committee's insistence on a highway bill more expensive than the Senate's and far more expensive than the Bush administration wanted; that issue was not resolved in 2004. He had to deal with a breakdown in the ethics truce the two parties' leaders agreed on in the late 1990s. "I said to Gephardt at the time, 'Lookit, when people have misused their office or done something wrong we need to go forward with an ethics charge, but to use the ethics committee as a political football I think is wrong, and we shouldn't do it.'" The truce was broken in June 2004, when Texas Democrat Chris Bell, defeated in his primary after redistricting, filed a complaint against Tom DeLay for, among other things, allegedly offering to support Nick Smith's son in the race to succeed him if Smith voted for the Medicare prescription drug bill. Smith didn't vote for the bill, his son lost in the Republican primary and Smith's story changed during the investigation. But the committee did vote in late September 2004 to admonish DeLay—the lightest sanction possible—for conduct putting the House in a bad light. Democrats crowed, and many Republicans believed the offense was too loosely defined. Hastert moved to change the rule after the election, but backed down when many Republicans complained. He also moved to change the

Republican Conference rule requiring a member to resign a leadership position if indicted; some DeLay aides had been indicted by the Travis County, Texas, district attorney, a liberal Democrat who had brought what turned out to be a baseless indictment against Senator Kay Bailey Hutchison in 1993; many Republicans feared he would do the same thing to DeLay.

Hastert is the dominant force on the Republican Steering Committee which names committee chairmen. He has used that position to reward some members and punish others. In January and February 2005 the Steering Committee removed ethics committee Chairman Joel Hefley—it's normal for ethics chairmen to serve just two terms, Hastert said—and Veterans Committee Chairman Christopher Smith, who was seen as unresponsive to the leadership and supportive of too much spending. In contrast, Hastert decreed that the usual six-year term limit on chairmanships did not apply to Rules Committee Chairman David Dreier.

It has become apparent that for all his bear hugs, his penchant for listening to members, his Midwestern plainspokenness, Hastert is a formidable, aggressive and partisan leader, of the kind often found in Illinois politics. Like a good coach, he has an appreciation for the talents of his players; but like a good coach, he wants very much to win. In his readable and sometimes acerbic autobiography *Speaker* he noted, "There is a perception in the liberal press that [Tom] DeLay calls the shots and I march to his instructions. That's what the Democrats would like people to believe." But no one with any knowledge of the House believes that any more. As Hastert went on slyly, "They try to demonize Tom all the time, and that just makes things a little bit easier for me." In 2004 he had harsh words for John McCain on the budget issue and, in his book, for Hillary Rodham Clinton for seeking too much money for New York. He issued a sharp statement criticizing Clinton National Security Adviser Sandy Berger for removing classified documents from the National Archives. "Mr. Berger apparently skirted the law and removed highly classified documents, purportedly in his pants . . . and then proceeded to lose or destroy some of them. Was Mr. Berger trying to cover up facts regarding the intelligence failures during his watch?" During the 2004 campaign he expressed scorn for John Kerry as a legislator. "I've fought a lot of battles on education, on health care, and a lot of times I've been nose to nose with a guy like [Edward] Kennedy. I didn't agree with him on everything, but we've been nose to nose in battle and I respect him for his positions. I've never really encountered John Kerry on positions. It's just kind of, all of a sudden, he's there." In September 2004, when asked if Al Qaeda would operate more comfortably if Kerry were elected, Hastert said, "That's my opinion, yes."

Amid all this work on legislation and national politics, Hastert has become a power in Illinois politics. He has worked closely with Mayor Richard M. Daley on any number of projects and Daley obviously appreciates having a Chicago-area Speaker of the House. In May 2001, Hastert and 3d District Democrat William Lipinski reached agreement on a congressional redistricting plan which strengthened almost all of the state's incumbents. Hastert has strongly supported Daley's plans to expand O'Hare Airport, pressing for crucial legislation in the House, and has exacted from Daley a promise that the expanded airport will have expressway access on its western edge, nearer to Hastert's district. He has strongly backed the purchase of Chicago-headquartered Boeing's 767 as replacements for aging air tankers.

Hastert has told friends that he yearns to retire from the hectic pace of the speakership; he has sold his house on the Fox River and lives on a farm nearby in Kendall County, where he paints duck decoys and has a 1954 fire engine in the barn. But there is no demand for him to move on. In January 2003 House Republicans voted to repeal their eight-year term-limit on speakers. In December 2004 George W. Bush said to him, "I hope you're going to run again. We need you." The challenges continue. In early 2005 he still faced deadlock on the transportation bill that so many members wanted. Sensenbrenner's immigration proposals would have to be considered when the Iraq supplemental came up; his requirement that "a majority of the majority" must approve a bill before he will bring it up could doom Bush's rather different immigration proposals, which are unpopular with many Republican members. With Bush calling for changes in Social Security, Hastert said pointedly, "You can't just go, 'Hocus pocus, here's a package we're going to pass on Social Security.' It needs a lot of vetting. . . . We're deluding ourselves if we think we're going to do this on a unilateral basis. It has to be on a bipartisan basis." His formula for doing business seems unchanged. In January 2005 he said, "My goal is to work across the aisle as much as I can. . . . I have to bring my caucus together too. And if I'm forced to do everything with just Republican votes, which sometimes we end up doing, then I have to make sure that all our people are on board." He added that he would stay as Speaker "as long as I can be effective and as long as the president wants me to serve and my members want me to serve."

Hastert won easily in 2004; he's never been reelected with less than 64%.

FIFTEENTH DISTRICT

Rep. Tim Johnson (R)

Elected 2000, 3d term; b. July 23, 1946, Champaign; home, Sidney; U. of IL, B.A. 1969, U. of IL, J.D. 1972; Assembly of God; divorced.

Elected Office: Urbana City Council, 1971–76; IL House of Reps., 1976–2000.

Professional Career: Practicing atty., Johnson, Frank, Frederick & Walsh.

DC Office: 1229 LHOB, 20515, 202-225-2371; Fax: 202-226-0791; Web site: www.house.gov/timjohnson.

District Offices: Bloomington, 309-663-7049; Champaign, 217-403-4690; Charleston, 217-348-6759; Mt. Carmel, 618-262-8719.

Committees: *Agriculture* (10th of 25 R): General Farm Commodities & Risk Management. *Science* (14th of 24 R): Environment, Technology & Standards; Research. *Transportation & Infrastructure* (21st of 41 R): Aviation; Highways, Transit & Pipelines.

Group Ratings

	ADA	ACLU	AFS	LCV	ITIC	NTU	COC	ACU	NTLC	CHC
2004	40	40	38	45	80	46	86	64	65	84
2003	30	—	50	75	—	56	79	56	—	—

National Journal Ratings

	2003 LIB	—	2003 CONS		2004 LIB	—	2004 CONS
Economic	51%	—	48%		52%	—	47%
Social	51%	—	48%		48%	—	51%
Foreign	49%	—	50%		51%	—	48%

Key Votes of the 108th Congress

1. Drilling in ANWR	N	5. DC School Vouchers	N	9. Ban Same-Sex Marriage	Y
2. Approve Bush Tax Cuts	Y	6. Ban Human Cloning	Y	10. Fund Iraq War	Y
3. Medicare/Rx Bill	Y	7. Restrict Gun Liability	Y	11. Bar Cuba Embargo Funds	Y
4. Bar Overtime Pay Regs.	Y	8. Ban Partial-Birth Abortion	Y	12. Intelligence Reorg.	Y

Election Results

2004 general	Tim Johnson (R)	178,114	(61%)	($428,750)
	David Gill (D)	113,625	(39%)	($100,106)
2004 primary	Tim Johnson (R)	unopposed		
2002 general	Tim Johnson (R)	134,650	(65%)	($398,949)
	Joshua Hartke (D)	64,131	(31%)	
	Carl Estabrook (Green)	7,836	(4%)	($25,004)

Prior Winning Percentages: 2000 (53%)

The People		Race/Ethnic Origin	Ancestry		
Area size:	10,122 sq. mi.	88.5% White	German: 18.8%	Irish: 9.2%	
Urban population:	64.2%	5.7% Black	English: 8.4%		
Rural population:	35.8%	2.3% Asian	**2004 Presidential Vote**		
Pop. 2000:	653,647	0.2% Native Am.	Bush (R) 174,928	(59%)	
Median income:	$38,583	0.0% Hawaiian	Kerry (D) 121,814	(41%)	
Poverty status:	11.7%	1.0% Two+ races	Other 2,227	(1%)	
Military veterans:	12.4%	0.1% Other	**2000 Presidential Vote**		
		2.2% Hispanic Origin	Bush (R) 148,176	(54%)	
			Gore (D) 116,436	(42%)	
			Other 9,616	(4%)	
			Cook Partisan Voting Index: R + 6		

Occupation	Blue collar: 26.3%	White collar: 57.7%	Gray collar: 16.0%

South from Chicago, the Illinois Central Railroad heads to the city of New Orleans on a railbed elevated a few feet above the rich black soil of the Illinois prairie, topsoil reaching down not just inches but feet. This land dazzled its first settlers, who were used to land that had to be cleared of trees and stumps before it could be plowed; this treeless prairie could be cultivated almost immediately, and with bounteous results. Today this remains farming country, made up not of small family farms but of large commercial operations, typically of 1,000 acres or more. Cultivating this soil is a business, requiring informed decisions about crop selection, maximizing yields, proper pesticides, marketing decisions, watching farm export prospects and, except for the early years of the 1996 Freedom to Farm Act, taking advantage of government programs. The prairie landscape of eastern Illinois is marked by only a few towns, the largest of which are the sites of universities (the University of Illinois in Champaign-Urbana and Illinois Wesleyan and Illinois State in Bloomington-Normal). Politically, these prairie lands incline much more to the party of former House Speaker Joseph Cannon, a Republican from the manufacturing city of Danville east of Urbana, than to that of Vice President Adlai Stevenson, a Democrat from Bloomington, who served under *laissez-faire* Democrat Grover Cleveland and was the grandfather of the Adlai Stevenson nominated by Democrats for president in 1952 and 1956.

The 15th Congressional District of Illinois occupies much of this prairie, beginning 60 miles from Chicago, where the Illinois Central heads south into Iroquois County and covering some 130 miles south to the old National Road and U.S. 40, traditionally the line between northern Republican and southern Democratic Downstate Illinois. The biggest city here is Champaign-Urbana and the district also includes Normal, though next-door Bloomington was removed by the 2001 redistricting. Redistricting also added, south of the prairie, a narrow corridor of land extending more than 100 miles along the Wabash River border with Indiana as far south as the Ohio River, with an extension to the town of Eldorado. The university towns are somewhat liberal but the prairie counties have long been Republican, and this on balance is a Republican district.

The congressman from the 15th District is Tim Johnson, a Republican first elected in 2000. Johnson grew up in Champaign and graduated from the University of Illinois and its law school. He was elected to the Urbana City Council while still in law school and served there four years before winning election to the state House in 1976. In the legislature, Johnson worked his way up to deputy majority leader. He is a trial lawyer and managed a small local farm operation until he sold it in April 2005.

Johnson's chance to run for Congress came after incumbent Republican Tom Ewing announced his retirement in October 1999. Ewing and Speaker Dennis Hastert had been close friends in Congress and previously in the state House, and Ewing was part of the team that backed Hastert for speaker and then closely advised him in his early months in that office. But Hastert was evidently unhappy that Ewing delayed his retirement announcement until his 29-year-old son Sam could move back to the district from Texas to launch his own candidacy. The Speaker endorsed state Representative Bill Brady, the scion of a prominent real estate family from Bloomington. But Johnson had more political experience than either and was a ferocious campaigner. The primary results broke along regional lines. Brady won his base of McLean County, 62%–20% over Johnson. In Champaign, Johnson led Brady, 61%–28%. Johnson carried seven of the 11 counties; he won 44% of the vote, to 36% for Brady and 17% for Ewing. Against Illinois State University instructor Mike Kelleher in the general, the voting pattern was similar: Kelleher narrowly won his home of McLean County, while Johnson again took Champaign and nine of the 11 counties, winning 53%–47% overall.

In the House, Johnson compiled a moderate voting record, with maverick tendencies and notable independence from Hastert, which helps to explain his modest committee assignments compared to other Illinois Republicans. He has taken issue with the Bush administration's environmental record and voted against opening the Alaska National Wildlife Refuge to oil drilling, winning him reelection endorsement from the League of Conservation Voters. He called his vote in favor of the use of force in Iraq "the most difficult decision of my political career."

Johnson makes a point of keeping in touch with the grass roots, making what he says are 200 calls to constituents on most days. "That's 90% of the job," he said. He delivered to Illinois State University a $165,000 grant for its Physical Education Obesity Prevention and Lifestyle Enhance (PEOPLE) program, and told organizers that the funds were "just the first round." He also got a grant for the Cra-Wa-La program in Lawrenceville for mentoring children of prisoners.

Since redistricting Johnson has won easily against weak opposition. In October 2002 he announced that he had changed his mind and renounced the term-limit pledge he made during his first campaign. In March 2003 he was hospitalized after a car accident near a church where he was scheduled to speak; he suffered a fractured rib and punctured lung but delivered the speech anyway, before seeking medical treatment.

SIXTEENTH DISTRICT

Rep. Don Manzullo (R)

Elected 1992, 7th term; b. Mar. 24, 1944, Rockford; home, Egan; American U., B.A. 1967, Marquette U., J.D. 1970; Baptist; married (Freda).

Professional Career: Practicing atty., 1970–92; author.

DC Office: 2228 RHOB, 20515, 202-225-5676; Fax: 202-225-5284; Web site: www.house.gov/manzullo.

District Offices: Crystal Lake, 815-356-9800; Rockford, 815-394-1231.

Committees: *Financial Services* (16th of 37 R): Capital Markets, Insurance & Government Sponsored Enterprises; Domestic and International Monetary Policy, Trade & Technology. *Small Business* (Chmn. of 18 R).

Group Ratings

	ADA	ACLU	AFS	LCV	ITIC	NTU	COC	ACU	NTLC	CHC
2004	5	5	13	0	90	72	100	100	92	100
2003	10	—	0	0	—	63	97	84	—	—

National Journal Ratings

	2003 LIB	—	2003 CONS	2004 LIB	—	2004 CONS
Economic	0%	—	91%	29%	—	70%
Social	30%	—	65%	0%	—	91%
Foreign	45%	—	55%	33%	—	66%

Key Votes of the 108th Congress

1. Drilling in ANWR	Y	5. DC School Vouchers	Y	9. Ban Same-Sex Marriage	Y
2. Approve Bush Tax Cuts	Y	6. Ban Human Cloning	Y	10. Fund Iraq War	Y
3. Medicare/Rx Bill	Y	7. Restrict Gun Liability	Y	11. Bar Cuba Embargo Funds	*
4. Bar Overtime Pay Regs.	N	8. Ban Partial-Birth Abortion	Y	12. Intelligence Reorg.	Y

Election Results

2004 general	Don Manzullo (R) 204,350	(69%)	($1,078,353)
	John Kutsch (D) 91,452	(31%)	($2,911)
2004 primary	Don Manzullo (R) .... unopposed		
2002 general	Don Manzullo (R) 133,339	(71%)	($945,291)
	John Kutsch (D) 55,488	(29%)	($45,808)

Prior Winning Percentages: 2000 (67%); 1998 (100%); 1996 (60%); 1994 (71%); 1992 (56%)

The People		Race/Ethnic Origin	Ancestry	
Area size:	4,158 sq. mi.	85.7% White	German: 21.8%	Irish: 10.0%
Urban population:	78.4%	5.3% Black	English: 6.7%	
Rural population:	21.6%	1.3% Asian	**2004 Presidential Vote**	
Pop. 2000:	653,647	0.2% Native Am.	Bush (R) 168,303	(55%)
Median income:	$48,960	0.0% Hawaiian	Kerry (D) 133,701	(44%)
Poverty status:	7.3%	1.0% Two+ races	Other 1,539	(1%)
Military veterans:	12.8%	0.1% Other	**2000 Presidential Vote**	
		6.5% Hispanic Origin	Bush (R) 141,878	(54%)
			Gore (D) 113,020	(43%)
			Other 8,163	(3%)
			Cook Partisan Voting Index: R + 4	

Occupation   Blue collar: 29.7%   White collar: 57.2%   Gray collar: 13.0%

The far northwest corner of Illinois is one of the heartlands of the Republican Party. Here in the town square of Freeport, some 15,000 people came to hear Abraham Lincoln and Stephen Douglas in one of their seven debates in 1858, the one on the terrain most partial to Lincoln. Settled by New England Yankees, northern Illinois was one of the strongest Republican constituencies in 1860 and for years after. Not far away, on a little river once navigable by Mississippi River steamboats, is Galena, one of the earliest settlements in northern Illinois, the home of Ulysses S. Grant before he became general and then president. Once larger than Chicago, Galena is now a tourist attraction. The largest city here is Rockford, on the Rock River, settled by Swedes as well as Yankees, one of America's leading furniture manufacturers at one time, then a major center for machine tools. Today, manufacturing accounts for nearly one-quarter of all jobs in the metro area and there are more than 1,400 manufacturers.

Politically, northern Illinois, perhaps repelled by Democratic Chicago, remained steadfastly Republican for many years; it backed Herbert Hoover in 1932, Barry Goldwater in 1964 and George H.W. Bush in 1992 when most of America and Illinois were going the other way. But in recent years the trend here has been the other way. In 2004 George W. Bush ran ahead of his father's 1988 percentages in almost every Illinois county south of Champaign. But he ran far behind in metro Chicago and behind in every one of the state's three northern tiers of counties, carrying all but two of them but not by margins large enough to carry the state.

The 16th Congressional District of Illinois consists of much of the northwest part of the state. It includes the hilly, almost mountainous country around Galena and the Mississippi River, and the flatter plains in the farming counties to the east and south. Rockford remains the biggest city, but the fastest-growing part of the district is in the east, where it contains part of McHenry County and all of Boone County, two of the fastest-growing counties in Illinois since 1990.

The congressman from the 16th District is Donald Manzullo, a Republican first elected in 1992. He grew up in Rockford, where his father ran a grocery store, and his father and brother owned Manzullo's Famous Italian Restaurant from 1953 until it closed in December 2004. While in college in Washington in the mid-1960s Manzullo worked for Republican candidates and he started practicing law in Illinois in 1970. He lives on a cattle-breeding farm, writes poetry and books on constitutional law, and ran a radio talk show; he and his wife home-schooled their three children until high school and started the Northern Illinois Crisis Pregnancy Center. Manzullo ran for Congress in 1990 and lost the primary 54%–46% to a moderate, who after revelations of personal problems then lost the general to Democrat John Cox. Cox favored increased taxes, opposed capital punishment and was hurt when heavily Republican McHenry County was added in redistricting. Manzullo ran again and, with support from conservative Christians, beat a moderate 56%–44% in the primary. In the general election, Cox campaigned for higher taxes; Manzullo for a 10% across-the-board income tax cut. Manzullo won with 56% of the vote.

Manzullo is now chairman of the Small Business Committee, a post he won over New York's Sue Kelly after the 2000 campaign. He has used the committee to hold hearings on all manner of issues, in Washington and around the country. He journeyed to West Yellowstone, Montana, in January 2002, to hold a hearing in which he encouraged allowing snowmobiles in Yellowstone National Park; several Rockford-area factories produce snowmobile parts. Manzullo came to Congress as a market conservative and a strong supporter of free trade, and he supported NAFTA, GATT, the WTO and normal trade relations with China. He criticized the Bush administration's imposition of steel tariffs in March 2002 and cited Rockford manufacturers' increased costs; he worked to exclude products like tool-grade steel from the tariffs. But he has been dismayed by job local losses in manufacturing—some 13,000 in the Rockford area since 2000—which he attributes to Chinese competition. In February 2004, when White House Council of Economic Advisers Chairman Gregory Mankiw said, "Outsourcing is just a new way of doing international trade," Manzullo said his remarks "were insensitive and they were wrong." He complained to Federal Reserve Chairman Alan Greenspan, "I'd like to know, my constituents would like to know, what are the new jobs, when are they going to created, what sectors are they involved in?" In November 2004 he said the Bush administration should do more to shore up the defense industrial base.

Manzullo was particularly exercised when funding for the SBA's 7(a) program lapsed in January 2004; the SBA had previously guaranteed lenders 75% if the borrower defaulted on loans up to $750,000. Stories appeared about hapless entrepreneurs in Chicago and Rockford newspapers, and Manzullo demanded reinstatement of the program. But the Bush administration insisted on abolishing the SBA subsidy and funding the program with higher fees to borrowers and lenders. In June 2004 Manzullo got the House, 281–137, to add $79 million to the SBA budget but the funds would not go straight to 7(a). The SBA reauthorization foundered on this issue, but in November 2004 Manzullo and Senate Chairman Olympia Snowe got the administration to agree on increased fees, with increases in the amounts of loans; Manzullo was agreeable since 7(a) lending remained strong after the authorization expired on October 1.

Small Business has a very small jurisdiction and the Ways and Means Committee a very large one, and in 2003 and 2004 Manzullo found himself at odds with Ways and Means Chairman Bill Thomas. In 2003 Manzullo threatened not to vote for the Medicare prescription drug bill because Thomas had not responded to one of his letters. In June 2004 Manzullo was one of 23 Republicans who voted against Thomas's corporate tax bill and even voted against the rule bringing the measure to the floor; he argued that the measure provided far too little relief for small businesses including Subchapter S corporations. For some months it appears that Manzullo and Thomas did not speak, though they communicated through intermediaries. Manzullo explained, "Members of Congress see the world through the people they represent. Thomas does not represent a heavy, heavy manufacturing base. We are creatures of our constituents."

Manzullo has worked on local projects, and sponsored a $300,000 study of a rail-to-truck facility in Rochelle, then introduced Union Pacific officials to the town where they are now building a $180 million facility. He helped obtain $5.65 million from NIST for Rockford's EIGER*lab*, a city-state-university center for the study of advanced manufacturing technologies like micromachining, with startup assistance available, which opened in May 2004 in an old Ingersoll Machine Tool building in Rockford. Manzullo entered Illinois's airport wars by arguing that any third Chicago-area airport should be based in Rockford.

In June 2004, after Republican Senate nominee Jack Ryan left the race, Manzullo and Rockford state Senator Dave Syverson were among those who urged that Republicans nominate former presidential candidate (and Maryland resident) Alan Keyes. Keyes was nominated, and turned out to be a disastrous candidate, and was repudiated by many Republican pols. In October Manzullo said he still supported him but admitted, "I don't like the way he says some things." Manzullo will reach the end of House Republicans' six-year term limit on chairmanships in December 2006, and does not seem to be in line for a subcommittee chair on his other committee, Financial Services. There has been speculation he will not run again in 2006. If so, possible candidates include Republican Syverson and Rockford Mayor Doug Scott, a Democrat.

SEVENTEENTH DISTRICT

Rep. Lane Evans (D)

Elected 1982, 12th term; b. Aug. 4, 1951, Rock Island; home, Rock Island; Augustana Col., B.A. 1974, Georgetown U., J.D. 1978; Catholic; single.

Military Career: Marine Corps, 1969–71.

Professional Career: Practicing atty., 1978–82.

DC Office: 2211 RHOB, 20515, 202-225-5905; Fax: 202-225-5396; Web site: www.house.gov/evans.

District Offices: Decatur, 217-422-9150; Galesburg, 309-342-4411; Moline, 309-793-5760.

Committees: *Armed Services* (4th of 28 D): Readiness; Tactical Air & Land Forces. *Veterans' Affairs* (RMM of 12 D): Disability Assistance & Memorial Affairs; Economic Opportunity.

Group Ratings

	ADA	ACLU	AFS	LCV	ITIC	NTU	COC	ACU	NTLC	CHC
2004	95	80	100	82	10	9	38	4	0	7
2003	95	—	100	95	—	25	30	13	—	—

National Journal Ratings

	2003 LIB	—	2003 CONS	2004 LIB	—	2004 CONS
Economic	81%	—	18%	75%	—	24%
Social	78%	—	20%	78%	—	19%
Foreign	81%	—	17%	87%	—	12%

Key Votes of the 108th Congress

1. Drilling in ANWR	N	5. DC School Vouchers	N	9. Ban Same-Sex Marriage	N
2. Approve Bush Tax Cuts	N	6. Ban Human Cloning	N	10. Fund Iraq War	N
3. Medicare/Rx Bill	N	7. Restrict Gun Liability	N	11. Bar Cuba Embargo Funds	Y
4. Bar Overtime Pay Regs.	Y	8. Ban Partial-Birth Abortion	N	12. Intelligence Reorg.	N

Election Results

2004 general	Lane Evans (D)	172,320	(61%)	($752,444)
	Andrea Lane Zinga (R)	111,680	(39%)	($270,256)
2004 primary	Lane Evans (D)	unopposed		
2002 general	Lane Evans (D)	127,093	(62%)	($774,108)
	Peter Calderone (R)	76,519	(38%)	($45,275)

Prior Winning Percentages: 2000 (55%); 1998 (52%); 1996 (52%); 1994 (55%); 1992 (60%); 1990 (67%); 1988 (65%); 1986 (56%); 1984 (57%); 1982 (53%)

The People		Race/Ethnic Origin	Ancestry		
Area size:	8,289 sq. mi.	87.3% White	German: 18.2%		Irish: 9.0%
Urban population:	71.1%	7.2% Black	English: 7.7%		
Rural population:	28.9%	0.6% Asian	**2004 Presidential Vote**		
Pop. 2000:	653,647	0.2% Native Am.	Kerry (D) 148,562		(51%)
Median income:	$35,066	0.0% Hawaiian	Bush (R) 139,251		(48%)
Poverty status:	12.5%	1.0% Two+ races	Others................. 1,333		(0%)
Military veterans:	14.4%	0.1% Other	**2000 Presidential Vote**		
		3.7% Hispanic Origin	Gore (D) 146,548		(54%)
			Bush (R) 119,563		(44%)
			Other 7,807		(3%)
			Cook Partisan Voting Index: D + 5		

Occupation	Blue collar: 29.9%	White collar: 51.7%	Gray collar: 18.4%

Illinois's western prairies are some of America's richest agricultural land. They were first settled by Yankees coming overland from northern Indiana and Ohio and Upstate New York. After 1848, Germans left their homeland in search of better opportunities and settled this land that in so many ways resembles the flat, orderly plains of northern Germany. All these migrants farmed quarter-sections and built small towns, with banks and stores, community churches and libraries. As farming expanded, so did the need for agricultural equipment. Entrepreneurs and investors built farm machinery factories, and the Quad Cities of the Mississippi—Davenport and Bettendorf, Iowa, and Rock Island and Moline, Illinois—became one of the nation's biggest agricultural equipment manufacturing centers. These plants were unionized in the 1930s and 1940s, and in post-World War II America their wages went up as the demand for ever more sophisticated machines rose among the Midwest's government-subsidized farmers. But eventually the cost of subsidies rose too high and the market had its revenge. In the early 1980s farm profits vanished, land values declined and orders for new machinery and equipment dried up. The result was a depression in western Illinois and neighboring Iowa, and a political swing toward the Democrats and away from the Republicans who had been the ancestral party in most of this area. In the 1990s the Democratic tide receded a bit, but this was still one of the few parts of rural America carried by Al Gore in 2000. Recent job losses—in Galesburg, Maytag closed a factory with 1,600 jobs despite local tax breaks—and wildly oscillating farm prices have helped Democrats maintain majorities here.

The 17th Congressional District of Illinois includes the state's portion of the Quad Cities plus several rural counties to the south: All of the Mississippi River border with Iowa and south almost to St. Louis. But that is not the entire district, for redistricting in 2001 changed its shape considerably. Removed were counties north and directly east of Rock Island and Moline. Added was a thin strip of land along the Mississippi River and the lower Illinois River. Connected to that was an extension that includes rural Macoupin County and a tentacle heading east, plus a very thin strip of land that includes central Springfield (but not the state Capitol building) and, some miles further east, a portion of Decatur. Decatur is home to Archer Daniels Midland, the largest agricultural processor in the world and a key promoter of ethanol. It would be fairly easy to drive directly from any part of the 17th District to another, but only if you crossed over into the 18th or 19th Districts. To drive from one end of the 17th to the other while remaining entirely inside the district would take many more miles and many, many more hours than to drive from Chicago to the southern tip of Illinois in Cairo. There is, of course, a good political explanation for this weird configuration. Illinois's redistricting was a largely bipartisan, incumbent-protection project, negotiated by Speaker Dennis Hastert and 3d District Democrat William Lipinski. For many years Republicans hoped that the Republican counties outlying Rock Island and Moline in the 17th District would outvote those Democratic towns and oust local Democratic Congressman Lane Evans, who was first elected in something of a fluke in 1982 and then was helped by the Democratic trend in the Farm Belt in the 1980s; he later survived several serious challenges. So the current 17th was drawn to help Evans: the Republican counties east and north of the Quad Cities were removed; the Mississippi River corridor casts few votes; Macoupin County is historically Democratic; central Springfield and Decatur are solidly Democratic. The old 17th district gave George W. Bush a 6% margin in 2000; the new 17th gave Al Gore a 10% margin.

Lane Evans, first elected in 1982, is now the ranking minority member on the Veterans Affairs Committee. He grew up in Rock Island, the son of a union firefighter. He joined the Marine Corps in 1969 after high school and served two years, then went to college and law school and worked as a legal services lawyer. In 1982, he ran for Congress—a seemingly quixotic race against longtime incumbent Republican Tom Railsback. But Railsback lost his primary to a conservative and the economically hard-pressed district voted 53% for Evans.

He calls himself a "populist" rather than a liberal; by most standards, his voting record is solidly liberal and one of the most pro-union in the House. But he was one of 31 Democrats who voted for the Republicans' impeachment inquiry in October 1998, though he later voted against impeachment. He was a strong opponent of NAFTA, GATT and normal trade relations with China. He fervently favored higher agricultural subsidies during his five-year tenure on the Agriculture Committee, but left that post to take a seat on Armed Services in 1988. There, his major cause has been a ban on land mines, which continue to injure thousands of people years after wars are over.

Evans has devoted much time to veterans' issues. He worked hard for years to get compensation for veterans who claimed they were harmed by exposure to Agent Orange, and ultimately succeeded. In 1994 he began to investigate what he and others have characterized as Gulf War syndrome. In 2004, working with Veterans Committee Chairman Christopher Smith, Evans helped pass bills to increase assistance to homeless veterans, to fund research on complex multi-trauma injuries in combat, to increase G.I. Bill benefits for apprenticeships and on the job training programs, to expand VA home loans and to give the Veterans Administration more flexibility in paying medical professionals. He has sponsored bills to further address Post-Traumatic Stress Disorder and other mental health concerns of veterans. But the House Republican leadership abruptly removed Smith as committee chairman in January 2005, and it is not clear whether the new chairman, Steve Buyer, will work in harmony with Evans as Smith did.

In the years of agricultural unrest and high unemployment in western Illinois, Evans was re-elected by wide margins. In the 1990s he had closer calls. After he defeated Republican Mark Baker, a former TV anchor, in 2000, Rock Island County Republicans filed a complaint with the FEC alleging that Evans had illegally coordinated his campaign with two purportedly independent committees. In February 2004, after settlement efforts failed, the FEC filed an unusual suit in federal court charging that the 17th District Victory Fund and the Rock Island Democratic Central Committee spent some $330,000, two-thirds of it raised from unions which could not legally contribute directly to Evans, at "the direction of and in close coordination with" Evans's campaign manager. The FEC said that the Victory Fund had no charter, bylaws, members, meetings or office space in the district and that contributions to it were solicited by Evans campaign officials. Evans said the charges were "baseless" but at one point conceded "mistakes." Local Republicans compared the situation to the scandal around former Republican Governor George Ryan, but there was little resemblance: that was a case of bribery, carefully concealed, whereas the Evans case rests on the degree of coordination between committees openly committed to the same cause.

In May 1998 Evans announced he had Parkinson's disease, which was diagnosed in 1995 after he found he could not wave with his left hand at a Labor Day rally in Galesburg. In 1998 he said he could not stand long without pain or smile easily, but could still jog and that he had lost weight under doctor's orders. In 2000 he spent much of his ad budget talking about his Parkinson's disease; one showed him jogging and saying, "If you hear someone say they're worried about Lane Evans, tell them you saw him running today and he's doing just fine." In 2002 little was heard of his illness. But in 2004 his Republican opponent, onetime Quad Cities TV anchor Andrea Zinga, raised it loudly. By this time Evans had trouble getting up from a chair and pouring a soft drink, and he had speech therapy once a week to prevent "lazy tongue," though he said he still went out running some mornings and regularly traveled throughout the district and traveled to Europe for the 2004 ceremonies commemorating D Day. But Zinga said he was not physically fit to serve. "People who are on the medications he is on may have trouble with judgment, which can be worsened by excitement or stress." Evans assured friendly audiences, "I may be slow, but I know which way to go." Evans was the first Downstate congressman to endorse Barack Obama in the 2004 Senate primary, and Obama recalled that after a campaign tour of the district with Evans, "For those concerned about Lane's health, don't worry. I couldn't keep up with him." Tom Schroeder, the executive director of the Rock Island County Council on Addictions, said, "The next time you hear some washed up TV news reader spouting mean-spirited and hurtful garbage about our congressman, tell her to go straight to some place really hot that rhymes with bell." Evans refused to debate Zinga until she apologized and said, "I'm a better congressman now that I have had this tragedy happen. I can understand what families are going through."

How did this issue play? Parkinson's disease produces physical infirmity but no mental impairment, and Evans's heavy schedule in the district suggested he was far from incapacitated. He was reelected 61%–39%, carrying every county but Adams, a heavily Republican county included in this district only because it was the essential land bridge between two swaths of Democratic territory. Speculation inevitably arises as to what would happen if Evans does not run again. Possible Democratic candidates include Phil Hare, his district director since 1982, Rock Island Mayor Mark Schweibert, state Senator John Sullivan and Clarence Darrow, grandson and namesake of the great lawyer, who served as a lawyer in the Marine Corps and moved to the area proclaiming an interest in politics.

EIGHTEENTH DISTRICT

Rep. Ray LaHood (R)

Elected 1994, 6th term; b. Dec. 6, 1945, Peoria; home, Peoria; Canton Jr. Col., 1963–65, Bradley U., B.S. 1971; Catholic; married (Kathy).

Elected Office: IL House of Reps., 1982.

Professional Career: Jr. High Schl. Teacher, 1971–77; Dir., Rock Island Youth Svcs., 1972–74; Chief Planner, Bi–state Planning Comm., 1974–76; Dist. A.A., U.S. Rep. Tom Railsback, 1977–82; Dist. A.A., U.S. Rep. Bob Michel, 1983–90, Chief of Staff, 1990–94.

DC Office: 1424 LHOB, 20515, 202-225-6201; Fax: 202-225-9249; Web site: www.house.gov/lahood.

District Offices: Jacksonville, 217-245-1431; Peoria, 309-671-7027; Springfield, 217-793-0808.

Committees: *Appropriations* (27th of 37 R): Agriculture, Rural Development, FDA & Related Agencies (Vice Chmn.); Homeland Security; Science, State, Justice, Commerce & Related Agencies. *Permanent Select Committee on Intelligence* (2d of 12 R): Oversight; Terrorism, Human Intelligence, Analysis & Counterintelligence.

Group Ratings

	ADA	ACLU	AFS	LCV	ITIC	NTU	COC	ACU	NTLC	CHC
2004	20	6	25	18	80	45	85	71	63	92
2003	15	—	0	20	—	51	89	76	—	—

National Journal Ratings

	2003 LIB	—	2003 CONS		2004 LIB	—	2004 CONS
Economic	44%	—	55%		46%	—	54%
Social	42%	—	56%		45%	—	55%
Foreign	40%	—	58%		52%	—	48%

Key Votes of the 108th Congress

1. Drilling in ANWR	Y	5. DC School Vouchers	Y	9. Ban Same-Sex Marriage	Y
2. Approve Bush Tax Cuts	Y	6. Ban Human Cloning	Y	10. Fund Iraq War	Y
3. Medicare/Rx Bill	Y	7. Restrict Gun Liability	Y	11. Bar Cuba Embargo Funds	N
4. Bar Overtime Pay Regs.	Y	8. Ban Partial-Birth Abortion	Y	12. Intelligence Reorg.	N

Election Results

2004 general	Ray LaHood (R)...................................	216,047	(70%)	($955,764)
	Steve Waterworth (D)	91,548	(30%)	($4,519)
2004 primary	Ray LaHood (R).............................	unopposed		
2002 general	Ray LaHood (R).............................	unopposed		($1,051,220)

Prior Winning Percentages: 2000 (67%); 1998 (100%); 1996 (59%); 1994 (60%)

The People		Race/Ethnic Origin	Ancestry	
Area size:	8,302 sq. mi.	90.0% White	German: 21.2%	Irish: 9.7%
Urban population:	68.0%	6.4% Black	English: 8.8%	
Rural population:	32.0%	0.9% Asian	**2004 Presidential Vote**	
Pop. 2000:	653,647	0.2% Native Am.	Bush (R) 181,058	(58%)
Median income:	$41,934	0.0% Hawaiian	Kerry (D) 130,669	(42%)
Poverty status:	8.9%	0.9% Two+ races	Other 1,954	(1%)
Military veterans:	14.2%	0.1% Other	**2000 Presidential Vote**	
		1.5% Hispanic Origin	Bush (R) 159,475	(54%)
			Gore (D) 128,411	(43%)
			Other 7,464	(3%)
			Cook Partisan Voting Index: R + 5	

Occupation	Blue collar: 24.7%	White collar: 59.1%	Gray collar: 16.2%

Old vaudeville bookers, presented with a new act, used to ask, "Will it play in Peoria?" The implication was that if an act went over in this small city on the bluffs above the Illinois River, 154 miles from Chicago and 171 miles from St. Louis, it would go over just about anywhere. In the first half of this century, Peoria did seem pretty typical of America. If its citizens were mostly of British or German descent, with a small percentage of blacks, that was the image of ordinary America that prevailed through the 1960s, despite the great immigrations of 1880–1924 and the northward urban migrations of southern rural blacks of 1940–1965. But Peoria's economy, arguably typical at mid-century, is less so today. This is still a heavy manufacturing town, dominated by big plants that produce farm machinery and earth-moving equipment. Its biggest employer is Caterpillar, the world's leading producer of earth-moving and construction equipment, and one of America's major exporters. There are more than just memories here of the sharp divide between blue collar and white collar, union and management, Democrat and Republican—the basis of the class warfare politics that was the norm in heavy industrial metropolises of the Great Lakes region starting with the sit-down strikes of the late 1930s. But the blue-collar workers now are not as numerous and the unions not as strong. The Peoria area went through terrible times in the 1980s, as big farm machinery plants laid off workers and even closed down. Then Caterpillar, struck by the United Auto Workers in 1992, hired replacement workers and continued to operate—not without some friction and inefficiency, but profitably—something unheard of a decade or more earlier. Not until March 1998 did union members approve a settlement, pretty much on the company's terms. In 2004, the Environmental Protection Agency cited Caterpillar as a good citizen for donating smog-reducing equipment to Peoria school buses, with hopes for expanding the program nationwide. There was no population growth here in the 1990s, and Peoria slipped from 3d to 5th among the largest cities in Illinois.

The 18th Congressional District of Illinois, variously configured, has been the Peoria district since the 1940s. It has been represented by two national Republican leaders: from 1933–49 by Everett McKinley Dirksen, who was elected senator in 1950 and was Senate Republican leader from 1959–69, and Robert Michel, congressman from 1957–95 and Republican House leader from 1981–95. The 18th's boundaries currently extend south along the Illinois River and east to include half of Springfield (including the state Capitol) and west within a few miles of Iowa, away from historically Republican Peoria toward the historically marginal counties of central Illinois. It is the home of Eureka College, which dedicated the Ronald Reagan Peace Garden in honor of its 1932 graduate and the end of the Cold War that he helped to achieve.

The congressman from the 18th District is Ray LaHood, a Republican elected in 1994. LaHood grew up in Peoria, the grandson of an immigrant from Lebanon and son of a restaurant manager. He worked his way through school, spent six years teaching in Catholic schools, then moved to Rock Island, where he worked with delinquent teens and became a staffer for Congressman Tom Railsback. He served in the Illinois House in 1982, then worked for Congressman Michel in Peoria and, from 1990–94, was his chief of staff in Washington. When Newt Gingrich pointedly declined to rule out running against Michel for Republican leader after the 1994 election, Michel decided to retire. LaHood ran to replace his boss, and in the Republican primary beat state Representative Judy Koehler, 50%–40%. LaHood's Democratic opponent was Douglas Stephens, a labor lawyer and small businessmen, who held Michel to 52% in 1982. In a Republican year, LaHood carried all but one county and won 60%–39%.

LaHood's voting record has been toward the middle of the House. An odd man out under Speaker Gingrich, LaHood became more visible during and after Gingrich's final days as speaker. He was one of only three Republicans who did not sign the Contract with America; he had reservations about voting for tax cuts until the budget was balanced. He filled a niche by frequently presiding over the House. With his experience in monitoring the floor for Michel, LaHood's evenhanded rulings, his surefooted mastery of parliamentary procedure and his determination to maintain decorum were widely appreciated. Most famously, he presided over the impeachment of Bill Clinton.

When Dennis Hastert replaced Gingrich as speaker, LaHood suddenly was well placed with House leaders. With Hastert's support, he has seats on the Appropriations and Intelligence committees. As a self-styled deficit hawk, he supported a freeze in federal spending. He seized on the disputed 2000 count in Florida as an opportunity to advance his cause of abolishing the Electoral College and replacing it with a national popular vote count. But the moment passed without action. After September 11, he refused to join critics who complained that the government was targeting people of Middle Eastern descent and he voted for the use of force against Iraq. He was the only House member to speak out against the creation of the commission to investigate the causes of the September 11 attacks. When the House debated the commission's proposed reforms of intelligence operations, LaHood opposed them for "creating another bureaucracy." He has been active in internal House politics. In 2002, he considered running for majority whip, but he decided not to when it became clear that Roy Blunt had locked up the votes. Two years later, when he lost a bid for the Intelligence Committee chairmanship, LaHood said that he would not agree to Hastert's requirement that he give up his Appropriations seat. When lame duck Democrat Chris Bell of Texas filed an ethics complaint against Tom DeLay, LaHood pleased Republicans when he called for a House rule to prohibit such actions by departing members; but opposition from Mark Kirk, another Illinois Republican, defeated the proposal.

LaHood has been re-elected by wide margins throughout his district, and he has been outspoken about problems among Illinois Republicans. When Senator Peter Fitzgerald attacked Hastert for not imposing federal bidding requirements on the Abraham Lincoln Library project, LaHood told the *Chicago Sun-Times*, "I'm thinking about trying to make sure that Peter has an opponent" in the Republican primary. "I think we can do better than him." Fitzgerald retired. When court records opened by court order revealed that 2004 Senate nominee Jack Ryan took his former wife to sex clubs, LaHood said that he should leave the race; Ryan did. After LaHood said in early 2004 that Phil Crane was in reelection jeopardy because he "has not really worked" his district, LaHood complained that Democrats were making misleading use of the quote. But Crane lost; LaHood was right again. In 2005, LaHood began touring the state to explore a run for governor in 2006.

NINETEENTH DISTRICT

Rep. John Shimkus (R)

Elected 1996, 5th term; b. Feb. 21, 1958, Collinsville; home, Collinsville; West Point Military Acad., B.S. 1980, Christ Col., Teaching Cert., 1990, S. IL U., M.B.A. 1997; Lutheran; married (Karen).

Military Career: Army 1980–85; Army Reserves, 1985–present.

Elected Office: Collinsville Township Trustee, 1989–93; Madison Cnty. Tres., 1990–96.

Professional Career: High schl. teacher, 1986–90.

DC Office: 513 CHOB, 20515, 202-225-5271; Fax: 202-225-5880; Web site: www.house.gov/shimkus.

District Offices: Centralia, 618-532-9676; Collinsville, 618-344-3065; Harrisburg, 618-252-8271; Olney, 618-392-7737; Springfield, 217-492-5090.

Committees: *Energy & Commerce* (11th of 31 R): Energy & Air Quality; Health; Telecommunications & the Internet.

Group Ratings

	ADA	ACLU	AFS	LCV	ITIC	NTU	COC	ACU	NTLC	CHC
2004	20	5	14	0	90	66	95	88	94	100
2003	10	—	13	10	—	64	90	84	—	—

National Journal Ratings

	2003 LIB	—	2003 CONS	2004 LIB	—	2004 CONS
Economic	39%	—	60%	44%	—	56%
Social	42%	—	56%	25%	—	73%
Foreign	23%	—	71%	45%	—	54%

Key Votes of the 108th Congress

1. Drilling in ANWR	Y	5. DC School Vouchers	Y	9. Ban Same-Sex Marriage	Y
2. Approve Bush Tax Cuts	Y	6. Ban Human Cloning	Y	10. Fund Iraq War	Y
3. Medicare/Rx Bill	Y	7. Restrict Gun Liability	Y	11. Bar Cuba Embargo Funds	Y
4. Bar Overtime Pay Regs.	N	8. Ban Partial-Birth Abortion	Y	12. Intelligence Reorg.	Y

Election Results

2004 general	John Shimkus (R)	213,451	(69%)	($544,784)
	Tim Bagwell (D)	94,303	(31%)	($38,229)
2004 primary	John Shimkus (R)	unopposed		
2002 general	John Shimkus (R)	133,956	(55%)	($2,144,611)
	David Phelps (D)	110,517	(45%)	($1,278,758)

Prior Winning Percentages: 2000 (63%); 1998 (61%); 1996 (50%)

The People		Race/Ethnic Origin	Ancestry	
Area size:	11,646 sq. mi.	94.0% White	German: 21.6% USA: 8.8%	
Urban population:	52.2%	3.5% Black	Irish: 8.6%	
Rural population:	47.8%	0.5% Asian	**2004 Presidential Vote**	
Pop. 2000:	653,647	0.2% Native Am.	Bush (R)	192,678 (61%)
Median income:	$38,955	0.0% Hawaiian	Kerry (D)	123,172 (39%)
Poverty status:	9.1%	0.7% Two+ races	Other	1,287 (0%)
Military veterans:	14.4%	0.1% Other	**2000 Presidential Vote**	
		1.1% Hispanic Origin	Bush (R)	164,541 (56%)
			Gore (D)	121,210 (41%)
			Other	7,621 (3%)
			Cook Partisan Voting Index: R + 8	

Occupation	Blue collar: 28.2%	White collar: 55.4%	Gray collar: 16.4%

Southern Illinois is a land of prairies, of flat, treeless land sloping imperceptibly down to the Ohio and Mississippi Rivers. It was settled almost entirely from the south by farmers coming overland from Kentucky, such as Abraham Lincoln's family. Just beyond the Ohio River, they found hilly terrain, some of which turned out to have coal deposits. To the north they must have been astonished, after miles of thick forest, to see the great American prairie stretch before them, a vast sea of empty land extending past the horizon. The prairie lands proved wondrously rich, and were soon crisscrossed by rail lines taking their produce away and bringing in products of industrial civilization from St. Louis, Chicago and points east. About the same time, vast coal deposits were found in southern Illinois, producing one mining town after another: This was the home turf of John L. Lewis, the imperious leader of the United Mine Workers for half a century and, in the late 1930s and early 1940s, one of the most powerful and eloquent figures in American public life.

The 19th Congressional District of Illinois, which extends more than 200 miles up and down and across the state, covers all or part of 30 counties in the rich agricultural heartland of southern Illinois—most of the land area of the state south of Springfield, from the Ohio River to the Mississippi. Much of it is south of the old National Road, which became U.S. 40 and is paralleled by Interstate 70, the traditional boundary between the part of Downstate Illinois settled by Southerners and that settled by Yankees, and also the boundary between traditional Democrats and traditional Republicans. Its boundaries are jagged, and seemingly without rational geographic basis, but there is a rational political explanation for them. The biggest voting blocs are in Madison, Clinton and Washington Counties, which are part of the St. Louis metropolitan area, and the Sangamon County suburbs of Springfield, the state capital. The district also includes the coal mining area around Mount Vernon, the sparsely settled counties along the Ohio River and prairie counties along U.S. 40 and south of Springfield.

The congressman from the 19th District is John Shimkus, a Republican first elected in 1996. Shimkus grew up in Collinsville, in Madison County. His father was an installer for Illinois Bell, and his mother a township trustee; he is of Lithuanian descent, as is his predecessor in the House, Democratic Senator Richard Durbin. Shimkus graduated from West Point, trained in the Army as a ranger and paratrooper, studied in California, then came back to Collinsville to teach high school. Almost immediately he began running for local office. In 1988 he ran for the Madison County Board, and lost; in 1989 he was elected Collinsville Township Trustee. In 1990, at 32, he beat a 12-year incumbent and was elected Madison County Treasurer, the only Republican countywide officer. He ran for the House against Durbin in 1992, and lost 57%–43%, a closer margin for Durbin than in his previous campaigns. In 1996, when Durbin ran for the Senate, Shimkus easily won the Republican primary with 51% against seven other candidates. In the general election he faced state Representative Jay Hoffman. Both were anti-abortion, anti-gun control, and pro-balanced budget amendment. Hoffman raised more money and had the benefit of AFL-CIO ads but Shimkus won by 50.3%–49.7%. The following August, after taking classes part-time for six years, he received an MBA from Southern Illinois University.

In the House, Shimkus's voting record has been a bit right of center. He got a seat on the Commerce Committee and used it to sponsor one small but locally important piece of legislation: his amendment that qualified the soybean-diesel fuel blend B-20 for the alternative fuels program. The Clinton administration opposed it, arguing that any standard diesel fuel engine would qualify. But Shimkus got it enacted. He got the White House in May 2004 to scuttle proposed Environmental Protection Agency rules to control mercury emissions from coal-fired generators.

In October 2004, Shimkus returned from a visit to Iraq and criticized the news media for not fully reporting the conditions there. By not reporting good news—that passenger airplanes were flying into the Baghdad airport, for example—he said the press was hurting the morale of the U.S. military. Shimkus remains a lieutenant colonel on active duty in the Army Reserves, and occasionally teaches at West Point. On an internal assignment, the former high school teacher took the chairmanship of the House page board and imposed stricter review procedures for applicants.

Illinois lost one House seat in the 2000 Census. When the state's redistricting plan was produced by Speaker Dennis Hastert and 3d District Democrat William Lipinski, they decided to eliminate the 19th District seat held since 1998 by David Phelps, a conservative Democrat and former professional gospel singer from far south Illinois. Phelps decided to run against Shimkus in the new 19th, of which Shimkus had been representing 63% of the voters and Phelps 34%. Chicago-based Democrats, interested in colleagues who could help them with O'Hare expansion and other Chicago priorities, did not care much about Phelps. The result was a spirited contest. The candidates disagreed on whether the Bush tax cuts should be made permanent, on trade promotion authority, on prescription drugs. The AFL-CIO spent more than $1.5 million attacking Shimkus; Shimkus was helped by campaign ads paid by the pharmaceutical industry. But the numbers were all for Shimkus. In the portions of the district he had represented he won 59%–41%, with a popular vote margin of 29,000. Phelps, in the portions he had represented, won by only 53%–47%, with a popular vote margin of 5,000. Overall Shimkus won 55%–45%. He was reelected easily in 2004. But the seat could be contested if Shimkus runs for another office; in 1996, he said he would limit himself to 12 years in the House.

★ INDIANA ★

On Memorial Day every year the nation's eyes turn to Indianapolis, the center of a state with the nation's most distinctive nickname—Hoosier—and some of its least distinctive borders, for a sports spectacle celebrating the knack for tinkering and the taste for powerful machines that make the Midwest the nation's manufacturing center: the Indianapolis 500. This combination of sports and manufacturing is symbolic of Indiana's strengths and successes. The image of its manufacturing base and sports heritage seems as antique as the bricks with which the Indianapolis Speedway was originally paved, though all but one yard at the start/finish line has long since been asphalted. Throughout the 1990s, Indiana's manufacturing economy was humming and becoming increasingly high-skill, high-employment and high-tech. The Speedway is literally at the center of American manufacturing: Almost precisely half the country's manufacturing jobs are east of Indiana and the other half west, almost half are north and half south. Indiana itself has the nation's highest percentage of workers in manufacturing (20%) and is second in percentage of gross product attributable to manufacturing. It is the number two steel producer with its giant, heavily automated steel mills on the south shore of Lake Michigan and mini-mills scattered across the state. Indiana leads the nation in making elevators, refrigerators, engines, engine-electrical equipment, recreational vehicles, mobile homes, and truck and bus bodies. It gave the world canned pork and beans, tomato juice, the Coca-Cola bottle and Alka-Seltzer. Nor are Indiana's days of innovation over. Just as it has attracted new teams and events to Indianapolis's sports facilities, the small factories set amidst farm landscape or at the edge of small cities have become centers of advanced manufacturing innovation. The Eli Lilly company and Purdue and Indiana Universities are pouring venture capital into biotechnology and life sciences. And in 2005 Purdue undergraduates won the Rube Goldberg Machine Contest for the third year in a row.

But there is one downside to a manufacturing economy: It is subject to sharp contraction in times of recession. The economic slowdown of 2000–02 was not by historic standards a major one. But it cost the state some 180,000 jobs, and led to large numbers of bankruptcies and foreclosures. State government revenue fell well below expectations, and taxes were raised. The long-term trajectory of the state is unclear.

Culturally, Indiana is like an earlier America; it retains some of the old norms that in the 1920s and 1930s brought sociologists Robert and Helen Lynd in their search for the typical American place to "Middletown" (actually Muncie). Ethnically, Indiana seems like an earlier America too: Except for the steel area around Gary—really an extension of the Chicago metropolitan area—Indiana has relatively few descendants from the 1840–1924 wave of immigration and only a small flow of recent Hispanic or Asian immigrants. But it does have religious diversity, with 109 denominations according to the Glenmary Center; only six states have more. The major metropolitan area, Indianapolis, now has 1.5 million people but still doesn't have the big singles and gay neighborhoods of larger cities. What it does have is one of the nation's largest founda-

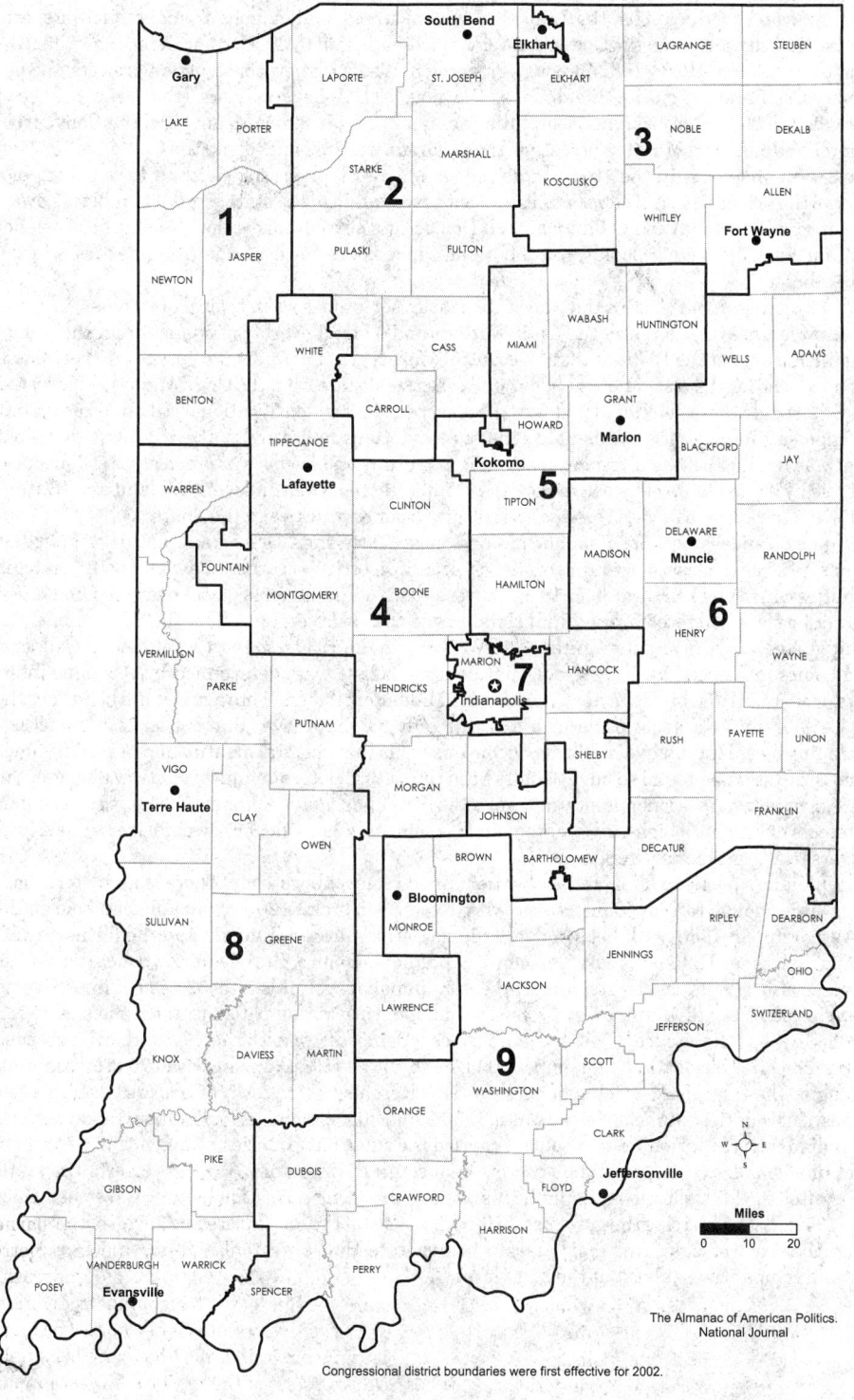

The Almanac of American Politics.
National Journal

Congressional district boundaries were first effective for 2002.

tions, the Lilly Endowment (which gives much of its money locally) and a willingness to create and innovate. In the 1980s, the Lilly Endowment urged Indianapolis to make itself a sports center. The city attracted the Colts professional football team to the Hoosier Dome (now the RCA Dome). In the late 1990s, Indianapolis's downtown filled with new construction projects: the pro basketball Pacers' Conseco Fieldhouse, the new NCAA headquarters (the lease has been extended to 2039), a conservatory and the Indiana State Museum. Meanwhile, the Convention Center and Eiteljorg Museum of Native American Art were expanded and the Circle Center Mall filled with shoppers. In the 1990s Indianapolis Mayor Stephen Goldsmith, a Republican, pioneered the privatization of city services and cut taxes, while in the state Capitol four blocks away, Governors Evan Bayh and O'Bannon, both Democrats, also cut taxes. Government has been not a drain on the private economy, but a booster. Since 2000, however, the trend has been in the other direction.

The partisan patterns in Indiana state politics sometimes seem typical of an older America, with preferences anchored in the Civil War era and a small overlay of change from the union-organizing days of the 1930s. Indiana's cultural conservatism has kept it Republican in presidential elections for the last generation, but it was a crucial state from the Civil War to the New Deal in the struggles between Republicans and Democrats. Party identification was handed down like religious affiliation—the Lynds noted that Presbyterians had little to do with Methodists, but that was nothing next to divisions between Republicans and Democrats—in a state still peopled largely by descendants of its original settlers, Yankees from Ohio and New England and "Butternuts" (as they were called in the Civil War years) from Kentucky and the South.

Most Yankees became Republicans and most Butternuts Democrats, and that split has persisted over generations and can still be seen in election returns today. Of the 26 Indiana counties carried by Bill Clinton in 1996, 18 were south of Indianapolis, most near the Ohio River. The others are clustered around industrial towns that were organized by the CIO unions, the United Steelworkers and the United Auto Workers, in the 1930s. In the 1920s the Lynds, liberal academics influenced by Marx's idea that political beliefs were determined by economic interests, were puzzled why the factory workers in "Middletown" didn't vote against the bosses; in the 1930s and since in some parts of industrial Indiana they have. But not so in other cities, including metro Indianapolis. Why not? One answer is that cultural identity and personal values tend to be permanent and so have usually been the critical determinants of political allegiance in an America where economic status can often be changeable. Another is that the economic interests of Indiana's high-skill workers and its small and large factory owners are not nearly as adversarial as academics suppose.

Indiana's partisan allegiances have remained remarkably steady. There is an historic base here large enough to allow Democrats to win: Evan Bayh broke a 20-year Republican hold on the governorship in 1988, with his strongest support from southern Indiana and the far northwest industrial zone. His successor, Democrat O'Bannon—from a Butternut town near the Ohio River—with similar moderate policies beat Indianapolis's Goldsmith 52%–47% in 1996 and Congressman David McIntosh by 57%–42% in 2000, with voting patterns much the same as in 1988. In 2004 Republican Mitch Daniels beat Democrat Joe Kernan, who had succeeded O'Bannon after his death in September 2003, but by 53%–45%. Daniels carried 75 of 92 counties, losing in the three Lake Michigan counties and Kernan's home town of South Bend, in a few industrial counties (Muncie, Terre Haute, Evansville) and one university county (Bloomington), in Indianapolis's Marion County (but he carried the suburban counties by much wider margins) and nine smaller counties, all but two of them south of Interstate 70 which bisects the state.

After the 2004 elections, Republicans were in as strong a position as they have been since the 1950s, with control of the governorship, both houses of the legislature and seven of the state's nine U.S. House seats. But their margin in the state House was only 52–48, and Democrats remain competitive, at least at the state level.

The People		Race/Ethnic Origin			Military veterans: 590,476 (13.1%)	
Pop. 2004 (est):	6,237,569	5,219,373	85.8%	White	WWII: 19.7%	Korea: 13.7%
Pop. 2000:	6,080,485	505,462	8.3%	Black	Vietnam: 31.3%	Gulf War: 9.3%
Pop. 1990:	5,544,159	58,424	1.0%	Asian	**Most populous cities (2003):**	
Change 1990–2000:	Up 9.7%	13,654	0.2%	Native Am.	1. Indianapolis	783,438
% of U.S. total:	2.2%	1,573	0.0%	Hawaiian	2. Fort Wayne	219,495
Pop. rank:	14th of 50	61,115	1.0%	Two+ races	3. Evansville	117,881
Area size:	36,418 sq. mi.	6,348	0.1%	Other	4. South Bend	105,540
State Native:	69.3%	214,536	3.5%	Hisp. Origin	5. Gary	99,961
Non-citizen:	1.9%	**Ancestry**				
Language		German: 17.6%		USA: 9.3%	Urban population: 70.8%	
English: 91.7%	Spanish: 4.1%	Irish: 8.4%		English: 6.9%	Rural population: 29.2%	
Other Eur.: 3.1%		Polish: 2.3%				

Education		Work Sector			General Assembly	
H.S. Grad:	82.1%	Private: 83.4%		Govt: 10.9%	Senate	33 R 17 D
College Grad:	19.4%	Self: 5.4%		Family: 0.3%	House	52 R 48 D
Industry		Unemployment: 4.9%			Legislative Term Limits: No	
Agri: 1.4%	Con: 6.6%	**Household Income**			**Registered Voters**	
Fin: 5.7%	Info: 2.1%	<15k: 14.3%		15-35k: 27.2%	No party registration	
Mfg: 28.0%	Prof: 25.6%	35-50k: 17.9%		50-100k: 31.5%		
Public: 3.3%	Trade: 15.2%	100-150k: 6.3%		>150k: 2.8%		
Other: 12.0%		Median: $41,567				
Occupation		Poverty status: 9.5%				
Blue collar: 31.4%	White collar: 54.0%	**Home Value**				
Gray collar: 14.6%		<50k: 15.7%	50-100k: 40.6%	100-200k: 34.5%	200-300k: 6.1%	
		300-500k: 2.2%	>500k: 0.9%	Median: $92,500		

Presidential politics   Democrats are not, however, competitive in Indiana's presidential politics; the one time they have carried the state since 1936 was in 1964. Since then it has been close only in 1976, when Gerald Ford beat Jimmy Carter here by 53%–46%, and in 1996, when Bob Dole beat Bill Clinton 47%–42%. George W. Bush won here 57%–41% in 2000 and, with big percentage increases in small counties, 60%–39% in 2004. So Indiana sees little of presidential candidates in election year autumns. Nor does it see much of them in spring or summer: Indiana's May presidential primary has not been influential since 1968. Only if Evan Bayh is on the Democratic ticket is Indiana likely to be seriously contested in 2008.

2004 Presidential Vote
Bush (R)	1,479,438	(60%)
Kerry (D)	969,011	(39%)
Badnarik (Lib)	18,058	(1%)
Other	1,495	(0%)

2004 Democratic Presidential Primary
Kerry (D)	231,047	(73%)
Edwards (D)	35,651	(11%)
Dean (D)	21,482	(7%)
Clark (D)	17,437	(5%)
Kucinich (D)	7,003	(2%)
Other	4,591	(1%)

2000 Presidential Vote
Bush (R)	1,245,836	(57%)
Gore (D)	901,980	(41%)
Other	51,489	(2%)

Congressional districting   Indiana lost one congressional district in the 2000 Census, and that required significant changes in district lines that had

109th Congress Lineup	
7 R	2 D

108th Congress Lineup	
6 R	3 D

stayed pretty much the same for 20 years. In charge were Democrats, who then had the governorship and a majority in the state House, though Republicans had a majority in the state Senate; Indiana law provides that if the House and Senate cannot agree, the decision goes to a five-member commission, with the tie-breaking member appointed by the governor. In May 2001, the commission adopted a plan largely identical to that passed by the state House. Democrats hoped to retain the four seats they held and improve their chances in at least one more. But as happens often with redistricting, the results were disappointing. In the marginal 2d District Tim Roemer retired in 2002, and Republican Chris Chocola picked up the seat. In 2004 Republican Mike Sodrel beat incumbent Democrat Baron Hill in the 9th District. Hill was one of the few incumbents to lose to a challenger in 2004; the district, marginal in state politics, voted heavily for George W. Bush.

Governor

Mitch Daniels (R)

Elected 2004, term expires Jan. 2009, 1st term; b. April 7, 1949, Monongahela, PA; home, Indianapolis; Princeton U., B.A. 1971; Georgetown U., J.D. 1979; Presbyterian; married (Cheri).

Professional Career: Advisor, Mayor of Indianapolis Richard Lugar, 1971–76; Chief of Staff, U.S. Sen. Lugar, 1976–82; Exec. Dir., NRSC, 1983–84; senior adv., White House, 1985–87; CEO, Hudson Institute, 1987–90; executive, Eli Lilly, 1990–2001; Dir., OMB, 2001–02.

Office: 206 State House, Indianapolis, 46204, 317-232-4567; Fax: 317-232-3443; Web site: www.in.gov/gov.

Election Results

2004 general	Mitch Daniels (R)	1,302,907	(53%)
	Joe Kernan (D)	1,113,879	(45%)
	Other	31,717	(1%)
2004 primary	Mitch Daniels (R)	335,228	(66%)
	Eric Miller (R)	169,930	(34%)
2000 general	Frank O'Bannon (D)	1,232,525	(57%)
	David McIntosh (R)	908,285	(42%)
	Other	38,458	(1%)

Mitch Daniels, elected governor of Indiana in 2004, grew up in Indianapolis and graduated from Princeton and Georgetown law school. He worked as a staffer for Richard Lugar when he was mayor of Indianapolis in the early 1970s, as chief of staff for Lugar from 1976 to 1983 when he was in the Senate, and then as political director in the Reagan White House. In 1987, he returned to Indianapolis to work at the Hudson Institute and then went to work for the Eli Lilly company in 1990 where he climbed high in its ranks to president of Lilly's North American pharmaceutical operations; when he resigned to reenter government in 2001, he made $27 million from liquidating his stock holdings. He reentered government at the top level, as George W. Bush's Director of the Office of Management and the Budget. There he developed a reputation for cutting spending and for having disdain for members of Congress, whose motto he said should be, " 'Don't just stand there. Spend something.' This is the only way they feel relevant." Bush insiders referred to him as "the Blade"; Senator Robert Byrd called him "Little Caesar." Senator Ted Stevens said the only way he could fix his relationship with Congress was to "go home to Indiana."

Which is what he did, in May 2003. Daniels's family had remained in Indianapolis, he was tired of commuting on weekends and he saw an opportunity to run for governor. Democrats had held the office in mostly Republican Indiana since 1988—first Evan Bayh, elected in 1988 and 1992, then Frank O'Bannon, elected in 1996 and 2000. For most of that time Bayh and O'Bannon cut taxes, cut the welfare rolls and instituted education testing. O'Bannon's 21st Century Research and Development Fund issued grants for high-tech startups. But after the 2001 recession cost the state jobs and revenues plummeted, O'Bannon was forced to take a different course. In 2002 funding for the R&D Fund was cut off and the sales tax raised. Out-year deficits loomed. Small scandals were exposed—DMV employees selling black market IDs, a state contracting official accepting favors, child protective workers filing false reports. Lieutenant Governor Joseph Kernan, a Vietnam veteran and POW for 11 months and a popular three-term mayor of South Bend, was widely assumed to be the strongest Democrat to succeed the term-limited

O'Bannon. But in December 2002 Kernan shocked just about everyone by announcing that he would not run. "I just want to have a beer in my back yard on a Tuesday night. I've got a great job. I've enjoyed it, but I want to go back to South Bend." That left the Democratic field to former Democratic state and national Chairman Joe Andrew and state Senator Vi Simpson.

Soon after he returned home, Daniels announced he was running for governor. All but one of the Republicans then running, including 2000 nominee David McIntosh, left the race and endorsed him. Bush, on a visit to the state, referred to "my man Mitch," and in time Dick Cheney, Laura Bush and Andy Card made appearances for him. He campaigned around the state in checked shirts and sweaters, traveling in an RV with supporters' signatures all over it; he touched down in every one of Indiana's 92 counties and eventually visited each of them three times.

Then in September 2003 Frank O'Bannon was found in his hotel room in Chicago paralyzed by a stroke. Two days later, Kernan was sworn in as acting governor. Three days after that, on September 13, O'Bannon died and Kernan became governor in his own right. He handled the tragic transition gracefully and, perhaps inevitably, reconsidered his decision not to run in 2004. In November he announced he was running; quickly Andrew and Simpson ended their campaigns and supported him, as did Indianapolis Mayor Bart Peterson, often mentioned as a potential candidate himself.

From there on in it was a two-man race, although Daniels did have primary opposition. While his former boss George W. Bush was put on the defensive about losses of manufacturing jobs nationally, Daniels was attacking Kernan and local Democrats for losses of manufacturing jobs in Indiana and said it was time for a "new crew." He called for tax breaks for new business property investments, new hires and research and development. He said he would put more emphasis on winning federal grants. He said he would create a state agriculture department and would provide tougher enforcement of child support obligations. Daniels opposed drug reimportation and favored an online referral service to match patients with drug discount programs. He called for health savings accounts for state employees and credits for employees who stop smoking and stay fit.

Kernan called for lower property taxes and for tax abatements for new business on a case-by-case basis. He endorsed full-day kindergarten. He criticized Daniels for his budget cuts as OMB Director, and for signing off on foreign contracts and job outsourcing; he blamed Indiana job losses on federal trade policy. He dropped a state contract with a company based in India to process unemployment claims. He charged that I-69 from Indianapolis to Evansville would have been built if Daniels had put in the money; Daniels said it had to be financed as a toll road.

Daniels had modest leads in polls during most of the campaign and won 53%–45%. He carried metro Indianapolis 57%–42% but ran behind in northern Indiana and Kernan's home town of South Bend. In southern rural counties, places where people are used to voting Democratic in state races, he ran farther behind Bush than in the north. Republicans increased their margin in the state Senate to 33–17 and converted a 51–49 deficit in the state House to a 52–48 majority: it was the first time Republicans had won control of state government since 1986. Fiscal problems loomed: state government faced a $645 million deficit and owed $710 million in back payments to schools, universities and local governments. He proposed a temporary tax increase on those earning more than $100,000, but that angered conservatives. There were successes in his first legislative session: With the assistance of business interests, he convinced lawmakers to enact daylight-savings time to stop Indiana from being one of three states that does not go on daylight-savings time. He created a state economic development corporation to replace the Department of Commerce and a new inspector general post for ethics; he also got a small funding increase for schools, a voter identification bill, and a methamphetamine crackdown.

Senior Senator

Richard Lugar (R)

Elected 1976, seat up 2006, 5th term; b. Apr. 4, 1932, Indianapolis; home, Indianapolis; Denison U., B.A. 1954, Rhodes Scholar, Oxford U., M.A. 1956; Methodist; married (Charlene).

Military Career: Navy, 1957–60.

Elected Office: Indianapolis Bd. of Schl. Commissioners, 1964–67; Indianapolis Mayor, 1968–75.

Professional Career: Mgr., family farm; V.P. & Treas., Thomas L. Green & Co., 1960–67; Prof., U. of Indianapolis, 1976.

DC Office: 306 HSOB, 20510, 202-224-4814; Fax: 202-228-0360; Web site: lugar.senate.gov.

State Offices: Evansville, 812-465-6313; Ft. Wayne, 260-422-1505; Indianapolis, 317-226-5555; Jeffersonville, 812-288-3377; Valparaiso, 219-548-8035.

Committees: *Agriculture, Nutrition & Forestry*: Forestry, Conservation & Rural Revitalization; Marketing, Inspection & Product Promotion; Research, Nutrition & General Legislation. *Foreign Relations* (Chmn.).

Group Ratings

	ADA	ACLU	AFS	LCV	ITIC	NTU	COC	ACU	NTLC	CHC
2004	20	0	0	0	100	70	100	84	95	100
2003	10	—	13	5	—	73	96	80	—	—

National Journal Ratings

	2003 LIB	—	2003 CONS		2004 LIB	—	2004 CONS
Economic	0%	—	82%		35%	—	64%
Social	0%	—	59%		47%	—	52%
Foreign	0%	—	78%		0%	—	67%

Key Votes of the 108th Congress

1. Ban Drilling in ANWR	N	5. Energy Bill	Y	9. Ban Same-Sex Marriage	Y
2. Approve Bush Tax Cuts	Y	6. Support Roe v. Wade	N	10. Ban Bunker-Buster Bomb	N
3. Medicare/Rx Bill	Y	7. Ban Partial-Birth Abortion	Y	11. Fund Iraq War	Y
4. Bar Overtime Pay Regs.	N	8. Assault Weapons Ban	Y	12. Restrict Missile Defense	N

Election Results

2000 general	Richard Lugar (R)	1,427,944	(67%)	($4,251,603)
	David L. Johnson (D)	683,273	(32%)	($1,179,029)
	Other	33,992	(1%)	
2000 primary	Richard Lugar (R)	unopposed		
1994 general	Richard Lugar (R)	1,039,625	(67%)	($4,688,326)
	James Jontz (D)	470,799	(31%)	($472,788)
	Other	33,144	(2%)	

Prior Winning Percentages: 1988 (68%); 1982 (54%); 1976 (59%)

Richard Lugar, still running 5K races at the annual Dick Lugar Run and Walk in Indianapolis, has a career in public life going back to the late 1950s, when as a young Navy officer he prepared intelligence briefings for Chief of Naval Operations Arleigh Burke and briefed President Eisenhower over closed-circuit television. Now he is the first Indiana senator ever elected to a fourth or fifth term and a powerful voice on foreign policy. Lugar grew up in Indianapolis, near his family's farm and food machinery firm, which was founded in 1893. He was an Eagle Scout, a straight-A student at Denison College and a Rhodes scholar. After military service Lugar returned to the family business, was elected to the school board in 1964, then was elected mayor of Indianapolis in 1967, at 35. As mayor, he consolidated the city and county into Unigov, which brought in tax resources and suburban voters, keeping the city both solvent and Republican (until 1999, when a Democrat was finally elected mayor). In the late 1960s, Lugar bucked fashion and called for fewer rather than more federal programs and became known as Richard Nixon's favorite mayor. This was not a political asset in the Watergate year of 1974, when Lugar ran against Senator Birch Bayh, father of his current junior colleague, and lost 51%–46%. But in the more favorable climate of 1976 and against a weaker Democratic incumbent, Vance Hartke, Lugar won 59%–40%.

Throughout his public life, Lugar's strength has been that he has followed where his stubborn convictions and his considerable intellect led, regardless of political risk or reward: He has plenty of accomplishments but also some disappointments. His lone course has served him well in Indiana, but has had mixed results in the Senate and in the national arena. He is a conservative on some, but not all, of the hot-button issues of today's conservative activists; he is solidly anti-abortion but voted for background checks at gun shows in 1999. He was an internationalist even in the mid-1990s when Bill Clinton's attention to foreign issues was episodic and some Republicans were opposing his foreign interventions. Lugar started off in the Senate leading the 1978 filibuster to defeat the AFL-CIO's labor law reform bill, although unions were then big in Indiana. He strongly supported NAFTA in 1993, in a Midwest manufacturing state where many thought foreigners were taking their jobs. He ran for president in 1996 on his own platform and without any concessions to the political shorthand or the TV sensibility of the day, but his candidacy made little impact. Lugar based his campaign on "nuclear security and fiscal sanity"—deterring nuclear terrorism and backing a 17% national sales tax. But he got little coverage, and finished 7th in Iowa and 5th in New Hampshire and soon left the race.

Lugar's great interest is foreign policy. In January 2003, he became chairman of the Foreign Relations Committee, a post he also held from January 1985 to January 1987. In 1985 he quickly took command over a committee sharply divided between Jesse Helms and liberal Democrats. Lugar was in the middle, backing Contra aid and favoring sanctions on South Africa. He took the lead on the Philippines, quickly concluding that Ferdinand Marcos's 1986 election "victory" over Corazon Aquino was fraudulent and, at a decisive point, calling on Marcos to leave office. Helms had allowed him to become chairman in 1985, despite his lower seniority, because of a campaign promise in 1984 to take the chairmanship of the Agriculture Committee. But after Republicans lost their Senate majority in 1986, Helms said he was no longer bound by his promise and invoked seniority; Lugar took the issue to the Republican Conference, but lost a vote there. So Helms was ranking minority member from 1987 to 1995 and 2001 to 2003 and chairman from 1995 to 2001, while Lugar waited. Helms left Lugar off conference committees and seldom communicated with him; Lugar led the fight to ratify the Chemical Weapons Agreement over Helms' opposition in April 1997, and won. Lugar has favored the arms control treaties about which many conservatives have been skeptical—INF in 1988, START I in 1992, START II in 1996. He supported NATO expansion and U.S. payment of U.N. dues. But in October 1999, he joined other Republicans in voting against the Comprehensive Test Ban Treaty, arguing that the U.S. must keep testing to maintain its nuclear arsenal.

His greatest achievement was passage in 1991 of the Nunn-Lugar Cooperative Threats Reduction program to pay Russia, Ukraine, Belarus and Kazakhstan to dismantle and destroy their nuclear weapons and some chemical and biological weapons as well, to prevent them from falling into the hands of hostile powers or terrorists. Lugar has gotten some notice for this work—he and Nunn have been nominated for the Nobel Peace Prize and an Indianapolis TV station filmed a documentary of him inspecting weapons in Russia—but probably not enough. As of 2004, the Nunn-Lugar program had deactivated 6,462 nuclear warheads, 550 ICBMs, 459 ICBM silos, 13 ICBM mobile missile launchers, 135 bombers, 733 nuclear SAMs, 408 submarine missile launchers, 530 SLCMs, 27 nuclear submarines and 194 nuclear test tunnels; all nuclear weapons have been removed from Ukraine, Belarus and Kazakhstan. A nerve gas destruction facility has been built at Shchuchye, Russia. Since September 11 Lugar has called for a Nunn-Lugar approach to prevent chemical and biological weapons throughout the world from falling into the hands of terrorists. In October 2004, legislation was signed extending Nunn-Lugar to Albania. Amid charges by John Kerry that the Bush administration slighted Nunn-Lugar, Lugar credited the administration with getting $10 billion for the program from the other members of the Group of Eight, with establishing the Global Threat Reduction Initiative to secure radioactive materials globally, with the ending of weapons of mass destruction programs in Libya, and with the IAEA Additional Protocol and UN Resolution 1540 requiring states to criminalize proliferation.

Lugar kept a vigilant eye on Iraq throughout the 1990s. Starting in August 1990, he called for an end to Saddam Hussein's regime and said that Saddam might have to be killed and U.S. ground troops needed to accomplish that. But he has not necessarily been a team player for the Bush administration. In summer 2002, he and then-Chairman Joseph Biden conducted hearings on Iraq to which the administration declined to send witnesses. In September 2002 he and Biden drafted their own resolution, which limited the authorization geographically and required the administration either to obtain a U.N. resolution or to certify to Congress that its efforts at the U.N. had failed; this was bypassed when House Democratic Leader Dick Gephardt and Senators Joe Lieberman and Evan Bayh agreed with the administration on a resolution. In late 2002 Lugar complained that he had not been briefed on postwar plans for Iraq. In April 2004 he said the administration "failed to communicate" its plans to Congress and argued that the June 30 turnover to Iraqis was too soon and said the Army needed to be increased by 80,000 soldiers. In a May 2004 speech he said, "Unless the United States commits itself to a sustained program of repairing and building alliances, expanding trade, pursuing resolutions to regional conflicts, supporting democracy and development worldwide, and controlling weapons of mass destruction, we are likely to experience acts of catastrophic terrorism." In September 2004 he said the failure to spend more than $1 billion of $18 billion appropriated for Iraqi reconstruction was the result of a "lack of planning." When John Kerry seized on some of his comments as evidence of administration failure, Lugar objected, saying in October 2004, "I don't think Senator Kerry's use of my name or John McCain or even Colin Powell will make any difference in the election. I think it's unfortunate. He's tried to use Lugar, McCain, Powell, other people to buttress a point of view, and usually with words that are out of context."

As chairman, Lugar has been at arm's length from the administration and has worked cooperatively with ranking Democrat Joseph Biden. When tougher standards for students visas were proposed, he pointed out that we are competing with other countries for foreign students and called witnesses from Purdue and Indiana Universities, which are among the top 20 universities in foreign student enrollment. But he does not always go along with established authorities. In May and July 2004 he held hearings on Third World nations' corrupt use of World Bank funds. And after the dubious elections held in Ukraine in November 2004 he said, "A concerted and forceful program of election day fraud and abuse was enacted with either the leadership or the cooperation of government authorities"—an echo of his denunciation of Marcos's electoral fraud in the Philippines in 1986. When the Republican leadership moved in July 2004 to change the Foreign Relations committee's classification to open up seats for senior members, he resisted, saying that the current members were excellent.

Lugar was chairman of the Agriculture Committee from 1995 to 2001. He liked to point out that he was the only working farmer on the committee—his 604 acres, thanks to Unigov, is inside the city of Indianapolis—and he played a key role in the 1996 passage of the Freedom to Farm Act, which purported to phase out over seven years the farm subsidies of which he had long been a critic. But low crop prices starting in 1998 resulted in disaster relief payments that kept in place something very much like the old subsidy system. In October 2001 he opposed the House farm bill with its big increases for historically subsidized crops, and proposed his own bill, guaranteeing up to 80% of income of qualified farmers, but at far less cost. But with key Senate races in states with historically subsidized farmers, the Senate passed a farm bill similar to the House's and George W. Bush signed it.

In Indiana, Lugar has remained vastly popular. His most recent victory margins have been 68%–32% in 1988, 67%–31% in 1994 and 67%–32% in 2000—pretty monotonous. The last was won against a respectable opponent who raised little money; Lugar nevertheless agreed to meet in three Lincoln-Douglas style debates. He seems likely to win reelection in 2006 if he runs; if he serves out that term, he will have served twice as long as any Indiana senator before him.

Junior Senator

Evan Bayh (D)

Elected 1998, seat up 2010, 2d term; b. Dec. 26, 1955, Shirkieville; home, Indianapolis; IN U., B.S. 1978, U. of VA, J.D. 1981; Episcopalian; married (Susan).

Elected Office: IN Secy. of State, 1986–88; IN Gov., 1988–96.

Professional Career: Practicing atty., 1981–86, 1997–98; Visiting Prof., Indiana U., 1997–98.

DC Office: 463 RSOB, 20510, 202-224-5623; Fax: 202-228-1377; Web site: bayh.senate.gov.

State Offices: Evansville, 812-465-6500; Fort Wayne, 260-426-3151; Hammond, 219-852-2763; Indianapolis, 317-554-0750; Jeffersonville, 812-218-2317; South Bend, 574-236-8302.

Committees: *Aging (Special). Armed Services*: Airland; Emerging Threats & Capabilities; Readiness & Management Support. *Banking, Housing & Urban Affairs*: Financial Institutions; International Trade & Finance (RMM); Securities & Investment. *Intelligence (Select). Small Business & Entrepreneurship.*

Group Ratings

	ADA	ACLU	AFS	LCV	ITIC	NTU	COC	ACU	NTLC	CHC
2004	90	56	100	100	92	25	65	20	25	33
2003	75	—	89	74	—	26	48	30	—	—

National Journal Ratings

	2003 LIB	—	2003 CONS	2004 LIB	—	2004 CONS
Economic	59%	—	40%	58%	—	39%
Social	59%	—	37%	70%	—	26%
Foreign	54%	—	44%	53%	—	46%

Key Votes of the 108th Congress

1. Ban Drilling in ANWR	Y	5. Energy Bill	N	9. Ban Same-Sex Marriage	N
2. Approve Bush Tax Cuts	N	6. Support Roe v. Wade	Y	10. Ban Bunker-Buster Bomb	N
3. Medicare/Rx Bill	N	7. Ban Partial-Birth Abortion	Y	11. Fund Iraq War	Y
4. Bar Overtime Pay Regs.	Y	8. Assault Weapons Ban	Y	12. Restrict Missile Defense	N

Election Results

2004 general	Evan Bayh (D)	1,496,976	(62%)	($2,250,428)
	Marvin Scott (R)	903,913	(37%)	($2,242,526)
	Other	27,344	(1%)	
2004 primary	Evan Bayh (D)	unopposed		
1998 general	Evan Bayh (D)	1,012,244	(64%)	($3,914,375)
	Paul Helmke (R)	552,732	(35%)	($642,784)
	Other	23,641	(1%)	

Evan Bayh (pronounced *BY*) was elected in 1998 to the Senate seat his father Birch Bayh first won in 1962 when Evan was just 6. He grew up mostly in Washington, graduated from Indiana University and the University of Virginia Law School, then returned to Indiana to practice law—and politics. His father, a charismatic candidate, beat three serious opponents: Incumbent Senator Homer Capehart in 1962, later-Deputy Attorney General William Ruckelshaus in 1968, and future Senator Richard Lugar in 1974. But in 1980, with Evan helping run the campaign, he lost to Dan Quayle. In 1986, at 30, Evan Bayh was elected secretary of state, often a stepping-stone office. In 1988, at 32, he ran for governor. Republicans had held the office and controlled most of Indiana state government for 20 years. However, their smoothly run machine had grown sluggish: The Republican nominee promised innovation, but Bayh was a young and fresh face. As governor, he balanced the budget, cut taxes and piled up a $1.6 billion budget surplus. He trimmed a deficit in state pension plans and sliced Medicaid spending. He claimed credit for the creation of 350,000 jobs, as Indiana's manufacturing economy revived. He did less to reform education and other government services, but he was immensely popular when he left office.

It was widely expected that Bayh would run for the Senate in 1998, and in December 1996, incumbent Republican Dan Coats announced he would not run for reelection. Bayh's 1998 opponent was Fort Wayne Mayor Paul Helmke, who had backed tax increases in Fort Wayne and who even had kind words for the Clintons, whom he had known since law school; he narrowly won the Republican primary with 35% against two more conservative candidates. Helmke argued that Bayh "still comes across a little the empty suit." But Bayh's platform—a balanced budget, saving Social Security, raising education standards and a "fairer, flatter" tax— preempted the Hoosier political center. He ran ads showing his wife extolling his accomplishments, saying he "cracked down on deadbeat dads, sponsored Indiana's fatherhood initiative . . . worked to make our schools safer and drug-free and to move people from welfare to work." Bayh won 64%–35%, carrying 88 of 92 counties, although it is a victory that probably never would have happened if Birch Bayh had not beaten Homer Capehart by 10,000 votes 36 years before—one election can make a big difference.

In the Senate, Bayh has pursued the issues he campaigned on. If his father had a mostly liberal voting record, Evan Bayh has been one of the most moderate Democrats. He has irritated important Democratic constituency groups. He voted for normal trade relations with China in 2000. In 2004 he took a somewhat different approach, sponsoring a trade bill that would allow countervailing duties on China and other non-market countries and revive Super 301 actions. He voted in 1999 and 2003 to ban partial-birth abortions; he says he opposes abortion personally, but in most instances doesn't want to impose his religious beliefs on others; as governor, he vetoed an 18-hour waiting period. He was one of two Democrats and one of only 21 senators to vote against allowing the importing of foreign price-controlled prescription drugs in July 2000. This was portrayed as truckling to Eli Lilly, one of Indiana's biggest employers and on whose board Bayh served in 1997–98, but his stand was vindicated when HHS Secretary Donna Shalala declined to enforce the law later in the year. In March 2005 he voted to give the federal government authority to negotiate lower drug prices.

In May 2000, Bayh and Connecticut Senator Joe Lieberman sponsored a revision of the basic federal aid to education act, which would increase spending by $35 billion over five years, target poor-performing school districts, foster English proficiency among immigrants, promote public school choice and demand accountability of teachers and students. Many of these measures became part of the Bush education bill, for which Bush gave Bayh some of the credit. But Bayh voted against the Bush tax cut, voted against the confirmation of Attorney General John Ashcroft and criticized the Bush energy package. With Tom Carper, he sponsored a welfare reauthorization bill that would raise the work week to 40 hours and the work participation rate to 70%, and also provide grants to nonprofits and faith-based organizations to encourage men to take responsibility for their children. He has had a penchant for spotting early problems that make headlines later. In January 2004 he and Larry Craig introduced a bill to require the CDC to estimate need for vaccines and to buy back unused doses; later in the year there was a flu vaccine shortfall but the bill was not passed. In May 2004 he got the Armed Services Committee to vote $610 million for more humvees that could be armored (the vehicles are produced in South Bend but armored in Fairfield, Ohio); this became a hot issue in December 2004 when Defense Secretary Donald Rumsfeld was asked about the armor by a reservist in Iraq.

Bayh serves on the Intelligence and Armed Services Committees and has backed the Bush administration in the war on terrorism. After September 11 he said that Congress should "think carefully about a more proactive response to terrorism. We should think carefully about some of the prohibitions that have been put in place the last 30 years." He was one of the Democrats who early on indicated he would support a resolution authorizing military force in Iraq and continued to support the administration in 2003 and 2004. But when Rumsfeld came before Armed Services after publication of the Abu Ghraib abuse photos, he asked him if he might step down to "demonstrate how seriously we take the situation and therefore help to undo some of the damage to our reputation." Rumsfeld replied, "That's possible." He supported the intelligence overhaul bill recommended by the 9/11 Commission and sponsored an amendment to allow the Intelligence Committee to set its own priorities.

After then-Lieutenant Governor Joe Kernan said in December 2002 he wouldn't run for governor in 2004, some Democrats wanted Bayh to run, but he said no a month later. His reelection was never in doubt. He won 62%–37%, with a slightly lower percentage than in 1998, carrying 86 of 92 counties, but with the highest number of popular votes ever for an Indiana senator—a considerable achievement as George W. Bush was carrying the state 60%–39%.

Birch Bayh ran for president in 1976 and Evan Bayh has often been mentioned as a candidate for national office. In July 2000, he was on Al Gore's short list of vice presidential possibilities. But leaders of feminist organizations opposed him because of his vote for a partial-birth abortion ban. In June 2001, he announced he wouldn't run for president in 2004; it would keep him away for too long from his young children. But he held the door open for a vice presidential nomination. In July 2003 he was asking, "Do we want to vent or do we want to govern?" and as the Democratic National Convention convened said he, Blanche Lincoln and Tom Carper would start a "Third Way" think tank. Since February 2001, he has been chairman of the moderate Democratic Leadership Council, which helped foster the national career of Bill Clinton. After the November 2004 election Bayh seemed open to running for president in 2008. "I do think that whatever's right for the Democratic party and right for the American people will be found in the center, both geographically and ideologically. National security, economic growth, making government accountable and fiscal discipline, and then showing we're in tune with middle American values—I think that's the right approach."

FIRST DISTRICT

Rep. Peter Visclosky (D)

Elected 1984, 11th term; b. Aug. 13, 1949, Gary; home, Merrillville; IN U. Northwest, B.S. 1970, U. of Notre Dame, J.D. 1973, Georgetown U., LL.M. 1982; Catholic; divorced.

Professional Career: Practicing atty., 1973–76, 1983–84; Aide, U.S. Rep. Adam Benjamin, 1976–82.

DC Office: 2256 RHOB, 20515, 202-225-2461; Fax: 202-225-2493; Web site: www.house.gov/visclosky.

District Office: Merrillville, 219-795-1844.

Committees: *Appropriations* (8th of 29 D): Defense; Energy & Water Development & Related Agencies (RMM).

Group Ratings

	ADA	ACLU	AFS	LCV	ITIC	NTU	COC	ACU	NTLC	CHC
2004	95	75	100	91	20	11	35	4	0	30
2003	85	—	100	70	—	20	37	20	—	—

National Journal Ratings

	2003 LIB — 2003 CONS		2004 LIB — 2004 CONS	
Economic	70%	— 30%	74%	— 26%
Social	67%	— 31%	63%	— 36%
Foreign	75%	— 21%	82%	— 17%

Key Votes of the 108th Congress

1. Drilling in ANWR	N	5. DC School Vouchers	N	9. Ban Same-Sex Marriage	N
2. Approve Bush Tax Cuts	N	6. Ban Human Cloning	N	10. Fund Iraq War	Y
3. Medicare/Rx Bill	N	7. Restrict Gun Liability	N	11. Bar Cuba Embargo Funds	Y
4. Bar Overtime Pay Regs.	Y	8. Ban Partial-Birth Abortion	Y	12. Intelligence Reorg.	N

Election Results

2004 general	Peter Visclosky (D)	178,406	(68%)	($1,076,753)
	Mark Leyva (R)	82,858	(32%)	($20,755)
2004 primary	Peter Visclosky (D)	unopposed		
2002 general	Peter Visclosky (D)	90,443	(67%)	($755,668)
	Mark Leyva (R)	41,909	(31%)	($11,956)
	Other	2,759	(2%)	

Prior Winning Percentages: 2000 (72%); 1998 (73%); 1996 (69%); 1994 (56%); 1992 (69%); 1990 (66%); 1988 (77%); 1986 (73%); 1984 (71%)

The People		Race/Ethnic Origin	Ancestry	
Area size:	2,443 sq. mi.	69.8% White	German: 13.8% Irish: 8.9%	
Urban population:	87.0%	18.2% Black	Polish: 7.3%	
Rural population:	13.0%	0.8% Asian	**2004 Presidential Vote**	
Pop. 2000:	675,562	0.2% Native Am.	Kerry (D)	148,698 (55%)
Median income:	$44,087	0.0% Hawaiian	Bush (R)	118,417 (44%)
Poverty status:	10.5%	1.0% Two+ races	Other	2,214 (1%)
Military veterans:	13.4%	0.1% Other	**2000 Presidential Vote**	
		10.0% Hispanic Origin	Gore (D)	141,163 (56%)
			Bush (R)	104,917 (42%)
			Other	4,759 (2%)
			Cook Partisan Voting Index: D + 8	

Occupation	Blue collar: 31.2%	White collar: 53.1%	Gray collar: 15.7%

At the southernmost shore of Lake Michigan is a part of America made by steel. Here, in the northwest corner of Indiana, where the water highway of the Great Lakes comes closest to the rail highway of the transcontinental railroads, America's leading capitalists a century ago identified an ideal site for manufacturing steel. On empty sand dunes United States Steel, then the nation's largest corporation, founded Gary in 1906 and named it for the company's chairman, Chicago Judge Elbert Gary. For nearly 70 years the steel mills attracted a diverse work force, like Chicago and quite unlike the rest of Indiana: Irish, Poles, Czechs, Ukrainians and blacks from the American South. Politics here has always been turbulent, from the Communist-led long and unsuccessful steel strike of 1919 to the racially polarized politics of the 1960s and 1970s. The tone of public life—the clash between union stewards and management foremen, between blacks and eastern European ethnics, between the stalwarts of different factions vying for control of Gary's massive City Hall—was always abrasive, like the clash of steel on steel.

Steel brought sudden growth and sudden depression to northwest Indiana. The massive storefronts built on Gary's aptly named Broadway bear witness to the confidence and exuberance of the 1920s. But today they stand vacant—vandalized, whole blocks burned down—witness to steel layoffs and crime waves. The steel mills went cold during the Depression of the 1930s, but were thronged with workers during World War II, and in the years afterward their massiveness helped create the illusion that life in the steel towns of Gary, Hammond and East Chicago would go on forever just like it was in the 1950s. But technological advances inevitably replaced increasingly expensive workers with increasingly efficient machines. And the efforts to seal off the U.S. steel market from the world inevitably failed. The oil crunch of 1979 was the catalyst for change, reducing the demand for large-sized autos, the biggest customer for steel. Steel employed 70,000 workers in northwest Indiana in 1979, 35,000 a few years later, 23,000 in 2001. Obsolete mills were closed, old mills modernized and new ones built that cut the number of man-hours needed by two-thirds. Just-in-time methods were introduced, management and high-skill workers cooperated to engineer higher-quality, less expensive steel to meet customers' needs. For the last decade, Indiana has been the number one or two steel-producing state. The steel tariffs imposed by George W. Bush in March 2002 were followed by a rise in steel prices, but steel producers complained and sought exemptions, and the tariffs were dropped 20 months later.

As the steel industry was changing, Gary was falling almost into ruins. As long ago as 1967, Gary elected a black mayor, Richard Hatcher, who was determined to use city government to cure poverty. But high crime rates gave Gary the national distinction as the "Murder Capital" for nine consecutive years with the most homicides per capita, and led to white flight to the suburbs. The city's population fell 12% in the 1990s to 102,000, far below its peak of 170,000; in nearby Hammond, with many Hispanic immigrants, the population loss was much less. Local officials tried to promote the city's airport as a third Chicago area airport, but with only limited success.

Indiana's 1st Congressional District stretches from Gary and Hammond along the Lake Michigan shore, east almost to Michigan City. It includes Lake County, 25% black and 12% Hispanic in 2000, and Porter County to the east, which includes Valparaiso, known locally as Valpo, notable for its annual Popcorn Festivals, honoring longtime resident and developer of 300 popcorn hybrids, Orville Redenbacher. The 2001 redistricting added three small Republican-leaning counties south of Gary, but nearly three-quarters of the population is in Lake County. This remains the most Democratic district in Republican Indiana, as it has been since the United Steelworkers' organizing drives of the late 1930s.

The congressman from the 1st District is Pete Visclosky, a Democrat first elected in 1984. Visclosky grew up in Lake County (his father was mayor of Gary in the early 1960s), went to college there and law school at Notre Dame. He practiced law, and then worked for six years for 1st District Congressman Adam Benjamin. Benjamin died suddenly in 1982 and Visclosky returned to Indiana. In 1984 he ran against Katie Hall, a black state senator who had been given the 1982 nomination—and thus the election, in this Democratic district—by Mayor Hatcher, then district party chairman. But Hall was able to win only 33% of the 1984 primary vote; Visclosky had 34% and another white candidate got 31%. In two later primaries Visclosky twice beat Hall by more than 20%.

Visclosky's voting record has trended moderate and he concentrates much of his effort on projects to help the local economy, especially the steel industry. He has a solid pro-union voting record. He is a leader of the Congressional Steel Caucus and has been vigilant in monitoring surges in steel imports. When George W. Bush was elected with critical help from steel-producing areas, Visclosky had greater leverage, and Bush did impose steel import quotas. But when the quotas were removed, Visclosky protested that Bush "stabbed the American steelwork-ers in the back." Visclosky, meanwhile, sought health benefits for unemployed and retired workers whose steel companies were unable to pay them, and he again called for closer monitor-ing of imports.

As ranking Democrat on the Appropriations Subcommittee on Energy and Water Develop-ment, Visclosky has secured federal funding for projects in his district. He pushed through an exception to the Johnson Act, making Lake Michigan waters eligible for gambling and thus allowing riverboat casinos for Gary. In 2004, he took credit for a $4 million appropriation for expanded commuter rail service to Chicago. He has worked with local communities to encourage economic and recreational development along the lakeshore.

In heavily Republican 1994, with an opponent who spent more than $100,000, Visclosky lost some conservative suburbs and won by just 56%–44%. Since then he has won without difficulty, by 68%–32% in 2004.

SECOND DISTRICT

Rep. Chris Chocola (R)

Elected 2002, 2d term; b. Feb. 24, 1962, Jackson, MI; home, Bristol; Hillsdale Col., B.L.S. 1984, Thomas Cooley Law Schl., J.D. 1988; Presbyterian; married (Sarah).

Professional Career: Foreign Exchange Trader, 1984–87; Mngr. and CEO, CTB Intl., 1988–2002.

DC Office: 510 CHOB, 20515, 202-225-3915; Fax: 202-225-6798; Web site: www.house.gov/chocola/.

District Offices: Logansport, 574-753-4700; South Bend, 574-251-0596.

Committees: *Budget* (22d of 22 R). *Ways & Means* (23d of 24 R): Select Revenue Measures.

Group Ratings

	ADA	ACLU	AFS	LCV	ITIC	NTU	COC	ACU	NTLC	CHC
2004	5	0	0	0	100	75	100	96	92	92
2003	5	—	0	10	—	65	100	92	—	—

National Journal Ratings

	2003 LIB	—	2003 CONS		2004 LIB	—	2004 CONS
Economic	9%	—	84%		9%	—	88%
Social	5%	—	87%		20%	—	77%
Foreign	0%	—	89%		4%	—	93%

Key Votes of the 108th Congress

1. Drilling in ANWR	Y	5. DC School Vouchers	Y	9. Ban Same-Sex Marriage	Y
2. Approve Bush Tax Cuts	Y	6. Ban Human Cloning	Y	10. Fund Iraq War	Y
3. Medicare/Rx Bill	Y	7. Restrict Gun Liability	Y	11. Bar Cuba Embargo Funds	N
4. Bar Overtime Pay Regs.	N	8. Ban Partial-Birth Abortion	Y	12. Intelligence Reorg.	Y

Election Results

2004 general	Chris Chocola (R)	140,496	(54%)	($1,480,546)
	Joe Donnelly (D)	115,513	(45%)	($700,728)
	Other	3,346	(1%)	
2004 primary	Chris Chocola (R)	36,847	(84%)	
	Tony Zirkle (R)	7,043	(16%)	
2002 general	Chris Chocola (R)	95,081	(50%)	($1,697,816)
	Jill Thompson (D)	86,253	(46%)	($1,535,962)
	Sharon Metheny (Lib)	7,112	(4%)	

The People		Race/Ethnic Origin	Ancestry	
Area size:	3,719 sq. mi.	84.4% White	German: 18.3%	Irish: 8.8%
Urban population:	72.8%	8.1% Black	USA: 6.4%	
Rural population:	27.2%	0.8% Asian	**2004 Presidential Vote**	
Pop. 2000:	675,766	0.3% Native Am.	Bush (R) 146,000	(56%)
Median income:	$40,381	0.0% Hawaiian	Kerry (D) 112,671	(43%)
Poverty status:	9.5%	1.3% Two+ races	Other 1,964	(1%)
Military veterans:	13.5%	0.1% Other	**2000 Presidential Vote**	
		5.0% Hispanic Origin	Bush (R) 128,803	(53%)
			Gore (D) 107,344	(44%)
			Other 5,276	(2%)
			Cook Partisan Voting Index: R + 4	

Occupation   Blue collar: 34.7%   White collar: 50.7%   Gray collar: 14.6%

When Notre Dame University was founded in 1842, Catholics were still a rarity in most of America and certainly rare on the limestone-bottomed plains of northern Indiana. This was still farm country and South Bend no more than a crossroads on the St. Joseph River. But by the

1920s, both had grown. Notre Dame, thanks to its football team, "the Fighting Irish," was the most famous Catholic university in the land, and South Bend was a significant industrial city, home of Studebaker and Bendix and dozens of other factories. In the past 50 years, Notre Dame has grown in size and reputation, but South Bend has had the experience of many Midwestern industrial cities: In the 1960s, Studebaker went out of business, in the early 1980s there were big layoffs at big factories, and in the early 1990s there were well-publicized layoffs in nearby Elkhart. But these high-visibility job losses were accompanied by the much less visible creation of jobs in small factories throughout the region. The work here requires more skill than did the old assembly lines, and the products must be more responsive to just-in-time prime contractors or computer-inventory retailers. In the late 1990s, many employers had trouble filling job openings, and the economic base was more secure than when it depended on the fate of two or three big companies. There have been painful layoffs since then as part of the nation's continuing industrial shrinkage, but nothing like the agony of 20 years before.

The 2d Congressional District of Indiana is centered on South Bend, which for three decades has seen plenty of close congressional contests. This is an industrial and ethnic city—with one of the nation's largest percentage of Hungarian-Americans, plus a growing community of Mexicans—that has long been Democratic; so is LaPorte County around Michigan City. Elkhart County to the east is heavily Republican and conservative—there used to be a six-foot Ten Commandments monument in front of Elkhart City Hall until an ACLU lawsuit led to its removal. The 2d District also includes several counties on the limestone plains to the south down past the Wabash River. This is an area rural in appearance but with much small manufacturing; politically, it has been part of the Republican heartland since the party was created in the 1850s. Moderate Democrat Tim Roemer represented this area for 12 years before he retired in 2002; he later gained renown as a member of 9/11 Commission. Indiana Democrats drew the lines of the 2d to maximize their chance to hold it by including Democratic Michigan City, excluding much of heavily Republican Elkhart County and adding the industrial town of Kokomo at its southern edge. But Roemer did not run for reelection in 2002, and the partisan lines were not enough to elect a Democrat.

The congressman from the 2d District is Chris Chocola, a Republican elected in the 2002 open-seat contest. Chocola grew up in Williamston, Michigan, graduated from Hillsdale College and Thomas Cooley Law School in Michigan, and became chief executive of his family's agricultural equipment manufacturing business, which he sold in 2002. With a net worth of $15 million, he ranked 20th on *Roll Call*'s list of the 50 wealthiest members of Congress in 2004. In 2000, he ran against Roemer in the old 3d District and held him to a 52%–47% victory. When Roemer announced that he would not run again, Chocola was the obvious Republican nominee in the new 2d District. Democrats rallied around Jill Long Thompson, who as Jill Long served three terms in the old Fort Wayne-based 4th District before losing in 1994 and serving as an undersecretary of the Agriculture Department in the Clinton administration. The campaign was bitterly contested. Chocola derided career politicians and highlighted his background in business. Democrats assailed him for living a mile outside the district. Thompson struck a populist note against her CEO opponent and walked the 100 miles from Kokomo to South Bend to get acquainted with the district. She criticized Chocola as a threat to Social Security because of his support of personal retirement accounts. "Eventually, I'd like to see the entire system privatized," Chocola had said during his 2000 campaign. In 2002, he said he would "support our president in making sure that 20-year-olds find a way to get Social Security." Democrats mined his record as chairman of CTB International to portray him as the embodiment of corporate greed. The North American Free Trade Agreement was an especially contentious issue. Chocola, who said his company conducted nearly 40% of its business overseas, defended free trade. Thompson argued that NAFTA cost the state 30,000 jobs. Chocola's support for NAFTA resulted in a key endorsement from the Indiana Farm Bureau; he also benefited from two campaign visits by George W. Bush. Chocola won 50%–46%.

Chocola has had a strongly conservative voting record and Republican leadership has usually been able to rely on his support. He sponsored a bill, with 54 co-sponsors, to create the crime of "eco-terrorism," damage to property that is aimed at influencing public opinion on environmental issues. One objective was to respond to destruction of vehicles at SUV dealerships: Humvees and Hummer H2s are produced by AMGeneral in South Bend (Chocola himself campaigns in a red Humvee). With Mark Souder of the neighboring 3d District, Chocola sought to increase military research and purchase of armored Humvee vehicles for Iraq. In the 109th Congress, Chocola made a successful bid for a Ways and Means seat.

Democrats targeted this district in 2004, but challenger Joe Donnelly raised less than half as much money as Thompson had in 2002. Donnelly, a local businessman, compared himself to Roemer and said that he would be more independent of his party than Chocola had been. But the tone of debate was polite and the DCCC made the district a low priority. Bush narrowly carried South Bend's St. Joseph County and Chocola got 49% of the vote there. With big margins in the southern counties, Chocola won overall 54%–45%. Chocola seems to be in strong shape in this district; Democrats are looking to convince St. Joseph County prosecutor Michael Dvorak to run.

THIRD DISTRICT

Rep. Mark Souder (R)

Elected 1994, 6th term; b. July 18, 1950, Ft. Wayne; home, Ft. Wayne; IN U., B.S. 1972, Notre Dame U., M.B.A. 1974; Protestant; married (Diane).

Professional Career: Furniture salesman, 1976–83; Staff Dir., U.S. House Select Cmte. on Children, Youth & Families, 1984–89; Legis. Dir., U.S. Sen. Dan Coats, 1989–91, Dep. Chief of Staff, 1991–93.

DC Office: 2231 RHOB, 20515, 202-225-4436; Fax: 202-225-3479; Web site: www.house.gov/souder.

District Offices: Ft. Wayne, 260-424-3041; Goshen, 574-533-5802; Winona Lake, 574-269-1940.

Committees: *Education & the Workforce* (6th of 27 R): Education Reform; Select Education. *Government Reform* (8th of 23 R): Criminal Justice, Drug Policy & Human Resources (Chmn.); Government Management, Finance & Accountability; Regulatory Affairs. *Homeland Security* (8th of 19 R): Economic Security, Infrastructure Protection & Cybersecurity; Intelligence, Information Sharing & Terrorism Risk Assessment.

Group Ratings

	ADA	ACLU	AFS	LCV	ITIC	NTU	COC	ACU	NTLC	CHC
2004	5	5	13	18	90	57	100	88	81	100
2003	5	—	0	5	—	62	100	92	—	—

National Journal Ratings

	2003 LIB	—	2003 CONS		2004 LIB	—	2004 CONS
Economic	19%	—	80%		32%	—	67%
Social	5%	—	87%		25%	—	73%
Foreign	35%	—	65%		25%	—	68%

Key Votes of the 108th Congress

1. Drilling in ANWR	Y	5. DC School Vouchers	Y	9. Ban Same-Sex Marriage	Y
2. Approve Bush Tax Cuts	Y	6. Ban Human Cloning	Y	10. Fund Iraq War	*
3. Medicare/Rx Bill	Y	7. Restrict Gun Liability	Y	11. Bar Cuba Embargo Funds	N
4. Bar Overtime Pay Regs.	N	8. Ban Partial-Birth Abortion	Y	12. Intelligence Reorg.	Y

Election Results

2004 general	Mark Souder (R)	171,389	(69%)	($238,176)
	Maria Parra (D)	76,232	(31%)	($18,761)
2004 primary	Mark Souder (R)	46,583	(79%)	
	William Larsen (R)	12,210	(21%)	
2002 general	Mark Souder (R)	92,566	(63%)	($518,717)
	Jay Rigdon (D)	50,509	(34%)	($131,458)
	Other	3,531	(2%)	

Prior Winning Percentages: 2000 (62%); 1998 (63%); 1996 (58%); 1994 (55%)

The People		Race/Ethnic Origin	Ancestry	
Area size:	3,292 sq. mi.	87.6% White	German: 22.8%	USA: 8.4%
Urban population:	65.1%	5.6% Black	Irish: 7.1%	
Rural population:	34.9%	0.9% Asian	**2004 Presidential Vote**	
Pop. 2000:	675,457	0.2% Native Am.	Bush (R) 172,919	(68%)
Median income:	$44,013	0.0% Hawaiian	Kerry (D) 79,674	(31%)
Poverty status:	7.8%	1.1% Two+ races	Other 737	(0%)
Military veterans:	11.9%	0.1% Other	**2000 Presidential Vote**	
		4.5% Hispanic Origin	Bush (R) 147,106	(66%)
			Gore (D) 73,775	(33%)
			Other 3,682	(2%)
			Cook Partisan Voting Index: R +16	

Occupation	Blue collar: 35.9%	White collar: 51.7%	Gray collar: 12.4%

The northeast corner of Indiana, in the center of a flat agricultural and manufacturing area, can claim to be the center of Middle America. Its first settlers were of New England Yankee stock, establishing orderly communities with public schools and even colleges. They were joined by German immigrants, who built tidy farms and their own civic institutions. In the northern part of the state there are hills and lakes, and the strange swamp that is the central focus of Gene Stratton Porter's children's classic, *A Girl of the Limberlost*. The one large city here, Fort Wayne, was built on the flat terrain along the Maumee River that flows to Toledo, Ohio. It grew as a factory town, surging ahead and then falling back as large factories, often tied to the auto industry, opened and closed over the years. As much as anything else, this part of Indiana is a place where people make things. Northwest of Fort Wayne on U.S. Route 33, Elkhart County is a manufacturing hub where local companies make everything from pharmaceuticals to musical instruments—oboes, bassoons, piccolos. The county is best known as the nation's manufacturing center for recreational vehicles ("I represent the biggest gas guzzling district in the U.S.," says the congressman), a business that flourished after the September 11 attacks as travelers stayed closer to home. Neighboring Kosciusko County is renowned for medical supplies; residents have been making orthopedic devices in Warsaw for at least a century. This also is a surprisingly diverse area. Its eclectic population mix includes a concentration of Amish that ranks with those in central Ohio and Lancaster Pennsylvania, plus Bosnians, Somalis and the nation's largest population of dissident Burmese.

The 3d Congressional District of Indiana consists of most of eight counties in the northeast part of the state; all are heavily Republican. This part of Indiana has been heavily Republican since the Civil War, though it has sometimes veered Democratic in times of economic distress. The seat recently has had members who have gone on to other high positions: Dan Quayle, who was elected here in 1976, then was elected senator and vice president, and Dan Coats, a Quayle aide, who was elected here in 1980, succeeded to Quayle's Senate seat and was appointed ambassador to Germany by George W. Bush.

The congressman from the 3d District is Mark Souder (pronounced *SOW-dur*), a Republican first elected in 1994. Souder grew up in Grabill, 10 miles from Fort Wayne, where his Amish great-great-grandfather's family settled. There the family started Souders of Grabill in 1907, originally a harness shop and now a furniture store and manufacturer of store fixtures. As an undergraduate at Indiana University, he wore a button, "I'm proud to be a square." Souder worked in the furniture business, returned to Grabill, then went to work in 1984 for Coats, as staff director of the House Select Committee on Children, Youth and Families. He moved with Coats to the Senate in 1989, where he served as his legislative director. In 1993, he returned to Fort Wayne and started running against Democrat Jill Long, who had won a special election to succeed Coats when he was appointed to the Senate. With a moderate record and a farm background, she was not an easy target. But Souder, after winning a six-candidate primary with 40%, raised more money. When the state Republican ticket ran far ahead of the Democrats, Souder won a 55%–45% victory.

Souder says that he is "most defined by the fact that I'm an evangelical Christian." In Washington, despite his solidly conservative views, he has been a rebel in the House, especially against his own party's leaders. His independence frequently leaves senior Republicans muttering. As a leader of the Conservative Action Team, Souder challenged House appropriators for excessive spending, including the close-to-home House members' office allowances. He voted against the balanced budget amendment because it did not require a supermajority to raise taxes. More recently, he has displayed a greater interest in financing projects back home, including a windmill museum near Kendallville. In the 2004 omnibus appropriation, he inserted a requirement for the Veterans' Administration to reexamine its plan to eliminate in-patient services at its Fort Wayne facility.

Souder has been active on drug issues and blamed Bill Clinton's "half-hearted" anti-drug message for increased drug use by teens. He proposed a bill pre-empting state laws that allow marijuana for medicinal purposes. As chairman of the Government Reform subcommittee dealing with criminal justice and drug policy, Souder held hearings on growing addiction to methamphetamines, and he blamed weak enforcement in the 1990s for reviving drug abuse problems. He protested to Washington-area officials about Metro ads supporting marijuana legalization.

Souder opposed normal trade relations with China because trade should be "a leverage in foreign policy," but he voted to give trade promotion authority to George W. Bush. He has worked for years to ensure that faith-based programs are eligible for federal funds, a cause that Bush has pursued. With Democrat Brian Baird, he formed a National Parks Caucus to assure adequate funding; but the League of Conservation Voters continued to rate him poorly. In September 2004, the House passed his bill to rescind the District of Columbia's ban on gun ownership, but it died in the Senate.

Souder has been comfortably re-elected since 1994 against poorly funded opponents. In 2002, former Fort Wayne Mayor Paul Helmke, challenged him in the primary. With support from the League of Conservation Voters, Helmke ran as a moderate and criticized Souder's use of congressional perks. Souder said that Helmke, had been a liberal mayor and called him "a Clinton clone." He carried all eight counties to win by 60%–37%. His string of weak Democratic challengers continued in 2004 when stage fright forced Democratic challenger Maria Parra to walk off the stage during a campaign debate. "I'm not used to being in front of the camera," Parra said. "I was just overwhelmed." She lost, 69%–31%.

FOURTH DISTRICT

Rep. Steve Buyer (R)

Elected 1992, 7th term; b. Nov. 26, 1958, Rensselaer; home, Monticello; The Citadel, B.S. 1980, Valparaiso U., J.D. 1984; Methodist; married (Joni).

Military Career: Army, 1984–87, 1990–91 (Persian Gulf); Army Reserves, 1980–84, 1987–present.

Professional Career: IN Dep. Atty. Gen., 1987–88; Vice Chmn., White Cnty. Repub. Party, 1988–90; Practicing atty., 1988–92.

DC Office: 2230 RHOB, 20515, 202-225-5037; Fax: 202-225-2267; Web site: www.house.gov/buyer.

District Offices: Bedford, 812-277-9590; Monticello, 574-583-9819; Plainfield, 317-838-0404.

Committees: *Energy & Commerce* (17th of 31 R): Health. *Veterans' Affairs* (Chmn. of 16 R).

Group Ratings

	ADA	ACLU	AFS	LCV	ITIC	NTU	COC	ACU	NTLC	CHC
2004	5	0	0	9	90	56	100	96	84	90
2003	10	—	0	5	—	68	97	92	—	—

National Journal Ratings

	2003 LIB	—	2003 CONS		2004 LIB	—	2004 CONS
Economic	39%	—	61%		25%	—	75%
Social	13%	—	87%		17%	—	83%
Foreign	35%	—	64%		9%	—	91%

Key Votes of the 108th Congress

1. Drilling in ANWR	Y	5. DC School Vouchers	Y	9. Ban Same-Sex Marriage	Y
2. Approve Bush Tax Cuts	Y	6. Ban Human Cloning	Y	10. Fund Iraq War	Y
3. Medicare/Rx Bill	Y	7. Restrict Gun Liability	Y	11. Bar Cuba Embargo Funds	N
4. Bar Overtime Pay Regs.	N	8. Ban Partial-Birth Abortion	Y	12. Intelligence Reorg.	Y

Election Results

2004 general	Steve Buyer (R)	190,445	(69%)	($509,517)
	David Sanders (D)	77,574	(28%)	($15,480)
	Other	6,117	(2%)	
2004 primary	Steve Buyer (R)	52,921	(66%)	
	Dennis Hardy (R)	10,862	(13%)	
	Mike Campbell (R)	8,403	(10%)	
	Brian Paasch (R)	8,305	(10%)	
2002 general	Steve Buyer (R)	112,760	(71%)	($924,869)
	Bill Abbott (D)	41,314	(26%)	($21,634)
	Other	3,934	(2%)	

Prior Winning Percentages: 2000 (61%); 1998 (63%); 1996 (65%); 1994 (70%); 1992 (51%)

The People		Race/Ethnic Origin	Ancestry	
Area size:	4,033 sq. mi.	93.6% White	German: 17.0%	USA: 11.7%
Urban population:	68.2%	1.3% Black	Irish: 8.9%	
Rural population:	31.8%	1.5% Asian	**2004 Presidential Vote**	
Pop. 2000:	675,617	0.2% Native Am.	Bush (R) 196,010	(69%)
Median income:	$45,947	0.0% Hawaiian	Kerry (D) 85,179	(30%)
Poverty status:	8.0%	0.8% Two+ races	Other 1,700	(1%)
Military veterans:	13.0%	0.1% Other	**2000 Presidential Vote**	
		2.6% Hispanic Origin	Bush (R) 156,747	(66%)
			Gore (D) 74,660	(31%)
			Other 5,739	(2%)
			Cook Partisan Voting Index: R +17	

Occupation	Blue collar: 29.6%	White collar: 56.5%	Gray collar: 13.9%

The landscape of central Indiana is some of the most prosaic in the United States, mostly flat, with neat farms and frame-bungalowed towns, looking mostly unchanged from many years ago. Across this landscape run some of the nation's chief transportation arteries. The earliest was the old National Road, from Baltimore to St. Louis, which was paralleled by U.S. 40 in the 1930s. Also here are the great east-west rail lines, on which famed railroad passenger trains like the old *Wabash Cannonball* rumbled along Indiana's Wabash River. Today the *Cannonball* no longer runs: People bounce around the Midwest on commuter airlines from small city to hub, and U.S. 40 has been replaced for through traffic by Interstate 70. The landscape still looks rural, and there are some large farms. But the economy here is more industrial, with small factories at crossroads and in courthouse towns. This is a part of America with little heritage from the early waves of immigration, relatively few blacks, and only a handful of Latin and Asian immigrants. Traditional cultural values have not been shaken so much here as in other parts of the nation.

The 4th Congressional District of Indiana covers much of this territory, running from Indiana's northern plains to its southern hills. It includes all or part of 12 counties in western Indiana, including the far western edge of Indianapolis and Marion County, and extends south past (but not including) Bloomington to Lawrence County, which was the source of the limestone used to rebuild the Pentagon after the September 11 attacks. The largest city is Lafayette, where the main business is Purdue University, Indiana's land-grant college and the alma mater of C-SPAN founder Brian Lamb. Growing and prosperous, Lafayette tends to vote Republican.

Even more Republican are the small counties and the suburban territory outside Indianapolis—places like fast-growing Hendricks County, which delivered 73% for George W. Bush in 2004.

The 4th District's congressman is Steve Buyer (pronounced *BOO-yer*), a Republican elected in 1992. Buyer grew up in White County, graduated from The Citadel, served in the Army, worked in Indianapolis and started a family law practice in Monticello, where he joined all the civic organizations. As a lieutenant colonel in the Army reserve, he was called to active duty in fall 1990, serving as legal adviser at a prisoner-of-war camp in the Persian Gulf. Buyer was enraged that most House Democrats, including then-Congressman Jim Jontz, voted against the war. After Buyer returned to Indiana, where he was White County Republican vice chairman, he began making speeches around the Hoosier heartland attacking Jontz on his Gulf War stand. Jontz was a skilled politician, but Buyer won 51%–49%.

As a mainstream conservative, Buyer has made a legislative mark in the House. On the Veterans' Affairs Committee, he has spent much time on the lingering effects of Gulf War illness—which Buyer says is incorrectly referred to as "Gulf War syndrome." He successfully co-sponsored legislation that allows the Veterans Administration to compensate Gulf War vets suffering from chronic disabilities resulting from undiagnosed illnesses that became manifest to a degree of 10% or more within a year of that war—a real departure in veterans' law. In 2004, he led an investigation that uncovered lapses in the hiring process for medical practitioners at VA hospitals. When he chaired the Military Personnel Subcommittee on Armed Services, he won enactment of what military officials call the greatest expansion of health care benefits for military retirees in at least three decades. But Buyer later took issue with Veterans Committee chairman Chris Smith over the implementation of that law, contending that some wealthy veterans had taken advantage of the new the benefits, causing costs to soar. In January 2005, the Republican Steering Committee voted Smith out of the Veterans' Affairs Committee chairmanship, evidently because of his opposition to the leadership on budget and labor issues, and installed Buyer. So after 12 years in the House he is a committee chairman.

Still in the Army Reserves, Buyer was called to duty again in March 2003 during the war with Iraq. He returned home, collected his gear and had received a leave of absence from Speaker Dennis Hastert. But the Army later notified Buyer that his high-profile status jeopardized both him and his Army colleagues; he was not deployed. Later, it was revealed that the brigade to which he had been assigned was among those blamed for the prisoner abuse scandal at the Abu Ghraib complex near Baghdad. In 2004, he was promoted to colonel by George W. Bush.

Buyer can be blunt. In 2004, when he learned that House Democrats had requested that the United Nations send "monitors" for the presidential election, he furiously forced a vote stating the House's opposition. Later that year, he circulated a proposal to bar reporters from the Speaker's Lobby behind the House chamber on the ground that lawmakers—from both parties—needed more space to meet privately with each other; the idea went nowhere.

Probably his most self-assured—and politically successful—strategy was his handling of redistricting in 2002. Democratic redistricters sliced up Buyer's old 5th District so that its remains were grafted onto seven of Indiana's nine surviving districts. Left without a seat, Buyer picked the one that happened to be the most heavily Republican, that happened to include his hometown of Monticello (population 5,723) and that had the least senior member of the delegation—first-term Republican Brian Kerns. This district, the new 4th, was 97% new to Buyer. It included seven of the 13 counties and 68% of the population from Kerns' old 7th District. Buyer charged Democrats with trying to end his career because of his work as a manager of the impeachment of Bill Clinton and in the Florida recount. He emphasized that Kerns's home in Vigo County was 70 miles outside the new 4th, and argued that he should run against the 8th District's John Hostettler. Kerns said Buyer should run elsewhere, and when he didn't, Kerns seemed dumbfounded. Kerns's reelection effort moved in fits and starts. In a peculiar campaign incident, Kerns claimed to witness the September 11 airplane crash into the Pentagon while he was driving to the Capitol. When subsequent inquiry raised questions about whether Kerns had been in the area, he responded, "Who knows?" With Buyer outraising Kerns by more than 3–1, the result wasn't close. Buyer bested Kerns 55%–30%, and carried every county. Buyer won easily in November 2002 and November 2004.

FIFTH DISTRICT

Rep. Dan Burton (R)

Elected 1982, 12th term; b. June 21, 1938, Indianapolis; home, Indianapolis; IN U., 1958–59, Cincinnati Bible Seminary, 1959–60; Protestant; widowed.

Military Career: Army, 1956–57, Army Reserves, 1957–62.

Elected Office: IN House of Reps., 1966–68, 1976–80; IN Senate, 1968–70, 1980–82.

Professional Career: Real estate broker; Founder, Dan Burton Insurance Agency, 1968.

DC Office: 2185 RHOB, 20515, 202-225-2276; Fax: 202-225-0016; Web site: www.house.gov/burton.

District Offices: Indianapolis, 317-848-0201; Marion, 765-662-6770.

Committees: *Government Reform* (3d of 23 R): Criminal Justice, Drug Policy & Human Resources; National Security, Emerging Threats & International Relations. *International Relations* (4th of 27 R): Asia & the Pacific (Vice Chmn.); Western Hemisphere (Chmn.). *Veterans' Affairs* (5th of 16 R).

Group Ratings

	ADA	ACLU	AFS	LCV	ITIC	NTU	COC	ACU	NTLC	CHC
2004	0	0	0	0	80	65	95	100	92	100
2003	20	—	13	10	—	71	93	96	—	—

National Journal Ratings

	2003 LIB	—	2003 CONS		2004 LIB	—	2004 CONS
Economic	45%	—	55%		13%	—	85%
Social	23%	—	76%		0%	—	91%
Foreign	31%	—	65%		34%	—	63%

Key Votes of the 108th Congress

1. Drilling in ANWR	Y	5. DC School Vouchers	Y	9. Ban Same-Sex Marriage	Y
2. Approve Bush Tax Cuts	Y	6. Ban Human Cloning	*	10. Fund Iraq War	Y
3. Medicare/Rx Bill	N	7. Restrict Gun Liability	Y	11. Bar Cuba Embargo Funds	N
4. Bar Overtime Pay Regs.	N	8. Ban Partial-Birth Abortion	*	12. Intelligence Reorg.	Y

Election Results

2004 general	Dan Burton (R)	228,718	(72%)	($777,535)
	Katherine Carr (D)	82,637	(26%)	($10,229)
	Other	7,008	(2%)	
2004 primary	Dan Burton (R)	83,136	(86%)	
	George Holland (R)	8,825	(9%)	
	Victor Wakley (R)	4,287	(4%)	
2002 general	Dan Burton (R)	129,442	(72%)	($844,159)
	Katherine Carr (D)	45,283	(25%)	($25,551)
	Other	5,130	(3%)	

Prior Winning Percentages: 2000 (70%); 1998 (72%); 1996 (75%); 1994 (77%); 1992 (72%); 1990 (63%); 1988 (73%); 1986 (68%); 1984 (73%); 1982 (65%)

The People		Race/Ethnic Origin	Ancestry	
Area size:	3,291 sq. mi.	93.2% White	German: 18.7%	USA: 9.6%
Urban population:	74.5%	2.6% Black	Irish: 9.1%	
Rural population:	25.5%	1.3% Asian	**2004 Presidential Vote**	
Pop. 2000:	675,577	0.3% Native Am.	Bush (R) 233,215	(71%)
Median income:	$52,800	0.0% Hawaiian	Kerry (D) 91,955	(28%)
Poverty status:	5.2%	0.9% Two+ races	Other 1,506	(0%)
Military veterans:	12.9%	0.1% Other	**2000 Presidential Vote**	
		1.6% Hispanic Origin	Bush (R) 187,489	(69%)
			Gore (D) 80,945	(30%)
			Other 5,110	(2%)
			Cook Partisan Voting Index: R +20	

Occupation	Blue collar: 24.4%	White collar: 63.2%	Gray collar: 12.4%

Indianapolis is one of America's most symmetrical cities, sited in almost the exact center of Indiana, centered on Monument Circle with eight avenues radiating like wheel spokes. A hundred years ago, it was a compact city, with everybody living within walking distance or a buggy ride of the circle in the center of downtown; even Indianapolis's one president, Benjamin Harrison, lived not far away in a mansion on North Meridian Street. But today's Indianapolis is spread out in all directions, and the metropolitan area includes nine counties smack in the center of Indiana. The most explosive growth has been in the most affluent quarter, to the north, where the fields of Carmel and Fishers in Hamilton County have filled with subdivisions, shopping centers and corporate headquarters. Hamilton County, directly north of Indianapolis's Marion County, was the fastest-growing county in the state in the 1990s, when its population rose 68%; it is now the fifth largest county in the state. Hamilton County had five banks in 1969; now there are 21, as many as in Marion County. The affluent establishment of Indianapolis is increasingly located here north of the city limits. The city of Carmel was one of the top zip codes for political donors in 2002; it was the only zip code outside New York, Chicago, California, Texas and the D.C. area that made the top 35. In 2004, residents cut their political donations back by more than half. These are not wealthy suburbs with a penchant for Democrats: Hamilton County is the most Republican county in Indiana and one of the most Republican in the nation. It voted 74%–24% for George W. Bush in 2004. The news show *60 Minutes* once referred to Noblesville, the county seat, as "arguably the most Republican spot on earth."

The 5th Congressional District of Indiana includes Hamilton County and other prosperous parts of metropolitan Indianapolis—the northern fringes of the city itself, Hancock County just to the east (where the U.S. Lawn Mower Racing Association's championship is held every September), and parts of less affluent but still conservative Shelby and Johnson Counties to the south. It juts northward from Hamilton County to include part of Kokomo and, in the north, Wabash and Huntington Counties, which are a cradle of vice presidents: Thomas Marshall, Woodrow Wilson's vice president, was from North Manchester in Wabash County, and Dan Quayle, the first George Bush's vice president, spent his high school years and later practiced law in Huntington (which was in the Fort Wayne-based district when Quayle represented it in the House).

The congressman from the 5th District is Dan Burton, an active and enthusiastic Republican first elected to the House in 1982. He has been running for office since he was in his 20s. He had a horrific childhood: His father was abusive and left the family, his mother worked as a waitress and bought the kids' clothes at Goodwill, his father ultimately kidnapped his mother and went to jail, and the kids were sent to the county home. "I think part of my aggressive nature is because of my childhood," Burton told author Studs Terkel in an interview for *Hope Dies Last*. "The highest moment of hope in my childhood was when we finally got away from my father. When I was five, six years old, my mother used to stand between me and him when he'd start to beat me and take the blows. I was black and blue from my neck to my ankles." As a teenager, Burton earned money shining shoes and at 18 enlisted in the Army. He never finished college but made his way up as a real estate broker and insurance salesman. He also ran for public office, often unsuccessfully. He was elected to the Indiana House in 1966, 1976 and 1978 and to the Indiana Senate in 1968 and 1980; he lost races for Congress in 1970 and 1972 and finally won in 1982 when a Republican legislature created a heavily Republican suburban seat.

For years, Burton was regarded by many Democrats as a nut, excitably pursuing lost causes. He opposed sanctions on South Africa, backed UNITA in Angola and Renamo in Mozambique, offered dozens of spending cuts that were overwhelmingly defeated, and pushed for universal mandatory AIDS testing. He has spent much time investigating the alleged link between thimerosal, a mercury-based vaccine preservative, and autism. He contends his grandson's autism was caused by thimerosal, and in December 2002, he bitterly criticized the Department of Homeland Security bill provision ending lawsuits against vaccine makers. He has held hearings on vaccine safety and pressed for the removal of thimerosal. In May 2004, he criticized the Institutes of Medicine ("pawns for the pharmaceutical industry") when they found no link between thimerosal and autism. His position on the issue puts him at odds with one of his district's major employers, Indianapolis-based Eli Lilly and Co., the company that developed thimerosal.

But Burton has also been vindicated by events for some stands that were widely scorned, from his hard-line opposition to the Soviet Union to his lonely vote against the later-repealed Catastrophic Health Care Act of 1988. In November 2003, Burton was one of the 25 Republican House members who voted against the Medicare/prescription drug bill. He argued that the drug benefit would cost too much, and the day before the vote, he warned that the bill would not meet seniors' expectations for coverage: "Wait until they find out what's in this turkey. It isn't Thanksgiving yet."

Burton has had some significant legislative successes but his biggest achievement was the Helms-Burton Act. It was a response to the Cuban Air Force's downing of the "Brothers to the Rescue" planes and stated that foreign companies could be sued in American courts if, as part of business deals with Fidel Castro's regime, they took over property expropriated from American owners. Helms-Burton passed both houses in fall 1995 and was signed by Bill Clinton, but Clinton then delayed its full implementation.

As chairman of the Government Reform Committee, he conducted tumultuous hearings on the Clinton-Gore campaign finance scandals from 1997 to 2000. Many Republicans were queasy about having Burton conduct the hearing; they felt he was too excitable and vulnerable to attack by Democrats and remembered with dismay his 1994 speech questioning whether White House counsel Vincent Foster had been murdered and his body moved. Burton promised a bipartisan approach but encountered early and fierce opposition; ranking Democrat Henry Waxman, one of the brainiest Democrats in the House, set the tone, calling it "a partisan witch hunt." Burton helped that impression along when, in reference to Clinton, he told *The Indianapolis Star* editorial board in April 1998, "This guy's a scumbag. That's why I'm after him." Burton faced great resistance —some 90 witnesses took the Fifth Amendment or left the country—and perhaps official retaliation: In July 1997, the FBI subpoenaed Burton's finance records of his House campaigns. Burton worked doggedly to get hold of memos to Attorney General Janet Reno with recommendations on dealing with Clinton-Gore campaign fundraising irregularities, or worse; he was still seeking them in 2002, when the Bush administration claimed executive privilege. In May 2000, when it was revealed that White House e-mails from 1996–98 sought in the investigation had been erased, Burton angrily sought an investigation, an independent counsel and he sent a criminal referral to the Justice Department; the e-mail stonewall continued until the end of the Clinton presidency. Burton has also tried to get internal Justice documents about an FBI scandal in which agents covered up evidence of crime by mobster informants in Boston from the 1960s to the 1980s; when his efforts were opposed by the Bush administration, erstwhile critic Barney Frank said, "I see now a genuine intellectual integrity in his approach."

Burton had to relinquish the Government Operations chairmanship in January 2003 because of House Republicans' six-year limit on committee chairmen; he was seeking the chairmanship of what was then the Middle East and South Asia Subcommittee of International

Relations, but Chairman Henry Hyde was said to have doubts about whether he should get it. In the 109th Congress, Burton chairs the Western Hemisphere Subcommittee.

On International Relations, Burton has bucked the tide on several issues. He opposed normalization of relations with Vietnam. He moved to reduce aid to India, because of its treatment of the Sikhs and Kashmiris, whose American diaspora contributed heavily to his 1996 campaign; he has been a steady backer of Pakistan.

For all the pasting Burton has taken from the national press, he has never been in trouble for re-election—not even when it was revealed in 1998 that he had fathered an illegitimate son some 15 years before. The woman had not notified Burton until her companion, long presumed to be the father, left her five years later. Burton took a blood test and afterward paid child support. Redistricting changed the shape of the district considerably, and changed the number too. But any district that contains Hamilton County will be heavily Republican, and Burton has won reelection without difficulty.

SIXTH DISTRICT

Rep. Mike Pence (R)

Elected 2000, 3d term; b. June, 7, 1959, Columbus; home, Elwood; Hanover Col., B.A. 1981, IN U., J.D. 1986; Protestant; married (Karen).

Professional Career: Practicing atty., 1986–91; Pres., IN Policy Review Fndt., 1991–93; Radio broadcaster, Network Indiana, 1992–99; Host, Pub. Affairs TV, UPN-23, 1995–99.

DC Office: 426 CHOB, 20515, 202-225-3021; Fax: 202-225-3382; Web site: mikepence.house.gov.

District Office: Anderson, 765-640-2919.

Committees: *Agriculture* (12th of 25 R): General Farm Commodities & Risk Management; Livestock & Horticulture. *International Relations* (18th of 27 R): Middle East & Central Asia; Oversight & Investigations. *Judiciary* (18th of 23 R): Courts, the Internet & Intellectual Property; Crime, Terrorism & Homeland Security.

Group Ratings

	ADA	ACLU	AFS	LCV	ITIC	NTU	COC	ACU	NTLC	CHC
2004	0	0	0	0	89	78	100	100	100	100
2003	10	—	13	10	—	76	96	96	—	—

National Journal Ratings

	2003 LIB	—	2003 CONS		2004 LIB	—	2004 CONS
Economic	36%	—	64%		0%	—	95%
Social	5%	—	87%		0%	—	91%
Foreign	11%	—	80%		4%	—	93%

Key Votes of the 108th Congress

1. Drilling in ANWR	Y	5. DC School Vouchers	Y	9. Ban Same-Sex Marriage	Y
2. Approve Bush Tax Cuts	Y	6. Ban Human Cloning	Y	10. Fund Iraq War	Y
3. Medicare/Rx Bill	N	7. Restrict Gun Liability	Y	11. Bar Cuba Embargo Funds	N
4. Bar Overtime Pay Regs.	N	8. Ban Partial-Birth Abortion	Y	12. Intelligence Reorg.	Y

Election Results

2004 general	Mike Pence (R)	182,529	(67%)	($1,010,228)
	Melina Fox (D)	85,123	(31%)	($50,071)
	Other	4,397	(2%)	
2004 primary	Mike Pence (R)	unopposed		
2002 general	Mike Pence (R)	118,436	(64%)	($1,214,879)
	Melina Fox (D)	63,871	(34%)	($342,987)
	Other	3,346	(2%)	

Prior Winning Percentages: 2000 (51%)

The People		Race/Ethnic Origin	Ancestry		
Area size:	5,572 sq. mi.	93.4% White	German: 16.8%		USA: 12.7%
Urban population:	59.3%	3.8% Black	English: 7.7%		
Rural population:	40.7%	0.5% Asian	**2004 Presidential Vote**		
Pop. 2000:	675,669	0.2% Native Am.	Bush (R)	177,214	(64%)
Median income:	$39,002	0.0% Hawaiian	Kerry (D)	97,781	(35%)
Poverty status:	9.7%	0.8% Two+ races	Other	2,096	(1%)
Military veterans:	13.6%	0.1% Other	**2000 Presidential Vote**		
		1.3% Hispanic Origin	Bush (R)	148,415	(58%)
			Gore (D)	100,231	(40%)
			Other	5,090	(2%)
			Cook Partisan Voting Index: R +11		

Occupation   Blue collar: 35.0%   White collar: 49.7%   Gray collar: 15.3%

Muncie, Indiana, became famous as the "Middletown" that sociologists Robert and Helen Lynd lived in and reported on in 1924–25 and again in 1935, and where a team of sociologists investigated again in 1976–78. The Lynds were attracted to Muncie by its typicalness—"every small city from Maine to California," said *Life* magazine. But it wasn't exactly: It was a factory town in a country still almost half rural, it was almost entirely Protestant and Northern in a country one-quarter Catholic and one-third Southern. Muncie was more typical in being culturally homogeneous but economically riven. In the 1920s Muncie celebrated its common values and was loath to admit its economic disparities; in the 1930s the latter came out into the open when Muncie, like much of the industrial Midwest, was unionized in what were sometimes violent uprisings. Workers who were joining CIO unions and voting for Democrats fiercely opposed the business elite—local bankers, merchants, executives at General Motors and the Ball family's glass company. Partisan politics took on the sharp, bitter tone of a struggle for wealth between two rival classes whose claims seemed irreconcilable. Echoes of this class-warfare politics reverberate only faintly today. They grow louder with local economic distress, as Muncie suffered years ago in layoffs at GM and when the Ball headquarters moved to Colorado in 1998. And there are higher Democratic percentages in towns with union traditions, like Muncie and Anderson, than in others such as Richmond. But Indiana's more recent prosperity, based on high-skill manufacturing, has brought something like a political consensus here for tax cuts, trimmed budgets and quiet support of traditional values, with strong support for candidates of either party who agree. Basketball is the civic religion here. Indiana has nine of the nation's 10 largest high school gyms; The Fieldhouse, in New Castle near the Indiana Basketball Hall of Fame, is number one. Also at hand is Tom Raper Inc. in Richmond, the nation's largest RV dealer.

The 6th Congressional District of Indiana covers most of the east-central part of the state. It includes Muncie and Anderson, with their big GM factories, in the north; and Richmond, founded by a major branch of American Quakers and the home of their Earlham College. In the north and south are suburban fringes of Fort Wayne and Cincinnati. Redistricting in 2001 added some rural counties to the north and south, and removed parts of Shelby and Johnson Counties outside Indianapolis. The district is solidly Republican in presidential politics and but has been a swing district in some state races.

The congressman from the 6th District is Mike Pence, a Republican first elected in 2000. He grew up in Columbus and graduated from Hanover College and Indiana University Law School, then practiced law; he is an evangelical Christian. Starting before he was 30, he ran as the Republican nominee for this seat in 1988 and 1990 against longtime Democratic Congressman (1975–95) Philip Sharp, then wrote an article after the second contest called "Confessions of a Negative Campaigner," in which he apologized for running negative advertisements. He was president of the conservative Indiana Policy Review Foundation, a think tank based in Fort Wayne, and began broadcasting "The Mike Pence Show," a conservative talk radio program that was syndicated statewide starting in 1994 and lasting until he launched his 2000 campaign.

The seat opened up when Republican Congressman David McIntosh challenged Governor Frank O'Bannon. In the six-candidate Republican primary, Pence beat state Representative Jeff Linder, 44%–24%. Robert Rock, Anderson lawyer and son of former Lieutenant Governor Robert Rock, had a closer contest in the Democratic primary, 30%–23%. The general became complicated when Bill Frazier, a former Republican state senator and four-time loser against Sharp, entered the race as an independent after the primary. All three candidates opposed abortion rights and gun control, and supported increased military spending; Frazier tried to tap into populist sentiment. Rock, a former Marine, attacked Pence for not serving in the military (Pence was 13 when the draft was abolished and U.S. troops left Vietnam) and supported tax cuts for middle-income families. Pence called for across-the-board tax cuts, and reform of Medicare financing. Pence won 51% to 39% for Rock and 9% for Frazier.

Pence quickly made his mark as one of the House's more conservative members. He antagonized the business community by abandoning the bankruptcy bill because he objected to a provision on abortion. As the only House member to become a plaintiff in the lawsuit challenging the constitutionality of the McCain-Feingold campaign finance law, Pence said that Senator John McCain was "so deep in bed with the Democrats that his feet are coming out of the bottom of the sheets." He was one of 33 House Republicans to vote against final action on George W. Bush's education bill, and one of 25 to oppose the Medicare/prescription drug bill as too costly and he claimed vindication when budget estimates subsequently showed that costs had soared. "Out here in heartland America, there's not a lot of enthusiasm for the politics of entitlements," he said. He did vote for the big-spending farm bill in 2002, conceding, "I don't have clean hands." Pence sponsored the House-passed resolution in July 2004 that deplored the United Nations for "misuse of the International Court of Justice" in a ruling on the Israeli-Palestinian conflict. He was the first House member to install a radio studio in his office.

In the 109th Congress, Pence took over as chairman of the Republican Study Committee, and promoted greater attention to the party's conservative message. "We win as conservatives when we communicate," Pence said. "If you can't communicate, you can't govern." He placed a strong emphasis on the need to control federal spending, advocating changes in how Congress handles the budget. Pence's group worked with Majority Whip Roy Blunt and Budget Committee Chairman Jim Nussle to impose procedural roadblocks on appropriations bills that exceed annual spending limits. Although some House insiders dismissed the outcome as a "fig leaf," Pence contended that the change would increase budget discipline. He opposed any Social Security reforms that would raise taxes. Showing that he could reach beyond the usual conservative themes, he joined Democrat Albert Wynn in filing a bill to repeal the 2002 campaign reform law, which he said was a violation of First Amendment rights. Although that proposal probably is a lost cause for now, Pence showed that he wanted to be taken seriously in shaping the policy debate. When he took the chairmanship, Pence stepped down as a deputy whip but his RSC activism could lead to a future bid for a Republican leadership post. Pence was reelected by wide margins in 2002 and 2004.

SEVENTH DISTRICT

Rep. Julia Carson (D)

Elected 1996, 5th term; b. July 8, 1938, Louisville, KY; home, Indianapolis; attended Martin U., IU-Purdue at Indianapolis; Baptist; divorced.

Elected Office: IN House of Reps., 1972–76; IN Senate, 1976–90; Marion Cty. Center Township Trustee, 1991–96.

Professional Career: Secy., UAW, 1962–63; Legis. Aide, U.S. Rep. Andy Jacobs, 1965–72.

DC Office: 1535 LHOB, 20515, 202-225-4011; Fax: 202-225-5633; Web site: www.juliacarson.house.gov.

District Office: Indianapolis, 317-283-6516.

Committees: *Financial Services* (10th of 32 D): Financial Institutions & Consumer Credit; Housing & Community Opportunity. *Transportation & Infrastructure* (26th of 34 D): Economic Development, Public Buildings & Emergency Management; Highways, Transit & Pipelines; Railroads.

Group Ratings

	ADA	ACLU	AFS	LCV	ITIC	NTU	COC	ACU	NTLC	CHC
2004	75	94	100	64	12	7	29	0	0	25
2003	95	—	100	95	—	21	33	9	—	—

National Journal Ratings

	2003 LIB	—	2003 CONS		2004 LIB	—	2004 CONS
Economic	75%	—	25%		92%	—	8%
Social	82%	—	18%		81%	—	19%
Foreign	88%	—	11%		*	—	*

Key Votes of the 108th Congress

1. Drilling in ANWR	N	5. DC School Vouchers	N	9. Ban Same-Sex Marriage	N
2. Approve Bush Tax Cuts	N	6. Ban Human Cloning	*	10. Fund Iraq War	N
3. Medicare/Rx Bill	N	7. Restrict Gun Liability	N	11. Bar Cuba Embargo Funds	Y
4. Bar Overtime Pay Regs.	Y	8. Ban Partial-Birth Abortion	N	12. Intelligence Reorg.	N

Election Results

2004 general	Julia Carson (D)	121,303	(54%)	($419,603)
	Andy Horning (R)	97,491	(44%)	($25,303)
	Other	4,381	(2%)	
2004 primary	Julia Carson (D)	30,915	(89%)	
	Bob Hidalgo (D)	3,652	(11%)	
2002 general	Julia Carson (D)	77,478	(53%)	($1,099,924)
	Brose McVey (R)	64,379	(44%)	($1,105,370)
	Other	3,983	(3%)	

Prior Winning Percentages: 2000 (59%); 1998 (58%); 1996 (53%)

The People		Race/Ethnic Origin	Ancestry	
Area size:	265 sq. mi.	63.0% White	German: 12.3%	Irish: 7.8%
Urban population:	99.7%	29.4% Black	USA: 7.8%	
Rural population:	0.3%	1.3% Asian	**2004 Presidential Vote**	
Pop. 2000:	675,674	0.2% Native Am.	Kerry (D) 130,779	(58%)
Median income:	$36,522	0.0% Hawaiian	Bush (R) 93,347	(42%)
Poverty status:	13.5%	1.5% Two+ races	**2000 Presidential Vote**	
Military veterans:	12.6%	0.2% Other	Gore (D) 109,800	(55%)
		4.4% Hispanic Origin	Bush (R) 84,362	(43%)
			Other 3,795	(2%)
			Cook Partisan Voting Index: D + 9	

Occupation	Blue collar: 26.2%	White collar: 57.7%	Gray collar: 16.1%

Indianapolis, radiating outward from the Soldiers and Sailors statue in Monument Circle, is precisely at the center of Indiana, dominating it as few other cities do a state. It is the political and governmental capital, industrial and financial center, and the intellectual center of Indiana as well. It is symmetrically laid out: Just to the west of the circle is the state Capitol, to the north is the American Legion headquarters, to the east is the City-County building, and to the south is the Circle Center mall, and the RCA Dome (formerly Hoosier Dome). Farther out are some classic and some new Indianapolis institutions: the Indiana University Medical Center, the Convention Center, the Eiteljorg Museum of Native American and Western Art and the new Indiana State Museum, Conseco Fieldhouse and NCAA headquarters. Indianapolis has become the nation's amateur sports capital, especially for basketball, and one of the most popular places for religious conventions. Eli Lilly and Company has expanded its already large corporate presence. The city has the world's biggest children's museum.

Politically, Indianapolis has long had robust competition in national as well as local races. Republicans held the mayor's office from 1967, when Richard Lugar won it, until 1999, when Stephen Goldsmith retired and became a top adviser to George W. Bush. Lugar expanded

Indianapolis's city limits to include all of Marion County in UniGov, which made it a solidly Republican constituency then; Goldsmith became a national innovator in privatization, by putting services up for bid he saved taxpayers money and spurred city employees to come up with innovations. But more recently affluent young people have been moving to counties farther out, and Marion County has been trending Democratic. In 2004, Marion County voted for John Kerry by 51%–49%, even as seven surrounding suburban counties gave Bush 70% to 75% of their votes.

Indiana's 7th Congressional District includes most of Indianapolis and Marion County. It includes all of Center Township, a Democratic stronghold with a large black population and gentrified middle class, but does not include all of the affluent, Republican northern edge of the county. It extends west to include Speedway, where the Indianapolis 500 has been held on a 2.5 mile track since 1911, and southward and east to modest neighborhoods, including Amtrak's largest repair yard in Beech Grove; Mexicans, whose population nearly tripled in size during the 1990s, are the newest immigrant group. Within these boundaries, the 7th District leans Democratic, and it gave Bill Clinton, Al Gore and John Kerry solid margins.

The congresswoman from the 7th District is Julia Carson, a Democrat first elected in 1996. Carson was born to an unmarried teenage mother and grew up in poverty, working as a waitress, newspaper deliverer and summer farm laborer; she can remember going to the welfare office for a ration of cornmeal and lard. As a divorced mother, she raised two children and then two grandchildren. In 1965 she was hired away from her job as a secretary at UAW Local 550 by newly elected Congressman Andy Jacobs to do casework in his Indianapolis office. When his election prospects looked dim in 1972 (he did lose, but won the seat back two years later), he encouraged Carson to run for the state House; she won, then was elected to the state Senate in 1976. In 1990 she was elected as Center Township trustee, the position responsible for running welfare in central Indianapolis. In 1996, when Jacobs retired, Carson decided to run. She won his endorsement and that of the local Democratic organization. She was outspent by former prosecutor and party chairman Ann DeLaney, but won the primary 49%–31%. The Republican nominee was Virginia Blankenbaker, a stockbroker and state senator. In this race between two grandmothers, both were more liberal than many in their parties, pro-choice on abortion and against the death penalty. Many commentators wondered whether a black Democrat could beat a white Republican in this district, but Carson raised and spent almost as much as Blankenbaker; she won 53%–45%.

Carson has compiled a liberal voting record, but chronic health problems have limited her activity. She was sworn into office from her hospital bed after heart surgery in January 1997, and was hospitalized in December 1999 with a serious case of pneumonia. In 2004, she missed close to 200 House votes, complaining of a lack of energy; her doctor imposed a diet and exercise regimen, and halted her weekly commute to Washington. She worked with Senator Richard Lugar to enact a bill wiping away bureaucratic roadblocks to child health insurance. In the House, Carson sometimes has been unpredictable. One of the last House members to decide how to vote on normal trade relations with China, she spent the final hours before the vote chatting with Clinton for 45 minutes at the White House (but refusing to tell him how she would vote), listening to union officials, and then talking to CNN. Her vote for the measure left organized labor steaming, but its Indiana officials supported her reelection because they liked her overall record. In November 2001, human-rights concerns caused her to agonize over the anti-terrorism bill, which she finally supported. She voted against trade promotion authority and against the use of force in Iraq.

Carson has faced serious competition at home. In 2002, redistricting made the district slightly more welcoming for Republican candidates; public affairs specialist and former Senate Republican aide Brose McVey ran, saying that Indianapolis needs "a congressman with energy and creativity" and that Carson was "out of step with her own constituency." Carson cited the federal funds that she delivered for local development and anti-violence programs; she said that Congress should put "the skids on the tax cuts" until the economy strengthened. McVey raised large amounts from the local business community and received national Republican backing in an ad that accused Carson of not paying her property taxes on time from 1997 to 2001. During their final pre-election debate, Carson walked off the stage to protest "the lowest common denominator" and "racial polarization" campaign run by McVey. Using that message to motivate her strong grass-roots network, Carson won 53%–44%. In 2004 her Republican opponent raised little money and was unable to arrange joint appearances; when the *Indianapolis Star* endorsed Carson, he protested outside its offices and burned a copy of the newspaper. Still, Carson won by only 54%–44%, suggesting that there is an entrenched anti-Carson (as well as a pro-Carson) vote. Carson, who said during the campaign that her work was not limited to votes in the House, returned to the hospital an hour after her victory speech but claimed that she was visiting a friend. She accused political rivals of fueling speculation about her health.

EIGHTH DISTRICT

Rep. John Hostettler (R)

Elected 1994, 6th term; b. July 19, 1961, Evansville; home, Blairsville; Rose-Hulman Inst. of Tech., B.S. 1983; Baptist; married (Beth).

Professional Career: Mechanical Engineer, S. IN Gas & Electric Co., 1983–94.

DC Office: 1214 LHOB, 20515, 202-225-4636; Fax: 202-225-3284; Web site: www.house.gov/hostettler.

District Offices: Covington, 765-793-2161; Evansville, 812-465-6484; Terre Haute, 812-232-0523; Vincennes, 812-882-0632.

Committees: *Armed Services* (10th of 34 R): Projection Forces; Readiness. *Judiciary* (13th of 23 R): Immigration, Border Security & Claims (Chmn.); The Constitution.

Group Ratings

	ADA	ACLU	AFS	LCV	ITIC	NTU	COC	ACU	NTLC	CHC
2004	20	10	25	9	60	73	81	88	100	100
2003	35	—	38	15	—	79	87	88	—	—

National Journal Ratings

	2003 LIB	—	2003 CONS		2004 LIB	—	2004 CONS
Economic	48%	—	51%		35%	—	64%
Social	30%	—	65%		20%	—	77%
Foreign	51%	—	48%		45%	—	54%

Key Votes of the 108th Congress

1. Drilling in ANWR	N	5. DC School Vouchers	Y	9. Ban Same-Sex Marriage	N
2. Approve Bush Tax Cuts	Y	6. Ban Human Cloning	Y	10. Fund Iraq War	Y
3. Medicare/Rx Bill	N	7. Restrict Gun Liability	Y	11. Bar Cuba Embargo Funds	N
4. Bar Overtime Pay Regs.	N	8. Ban Partial-Birth Abortion	Y	12. Intelligence Reorg.	Y

Election Results

2004 general	John Hostettler (R)	145,576	(53%)	($494,781)
	Jon Jennings (D)	121,522	(45%)	($1,504,920)
	Other	5,680	(2%)	
2004 primary	John Hostettler (R)	unopposed		
2002 general	John Hostettler (R)	98,952	(51%)	($573,220)
	Bryan Hartke (D)	88,763	(46%)	($395,840)
	Other	5,150	(3%)	

Prior Winning Percentages: 2000 (53%); 1998 (52%); 1996 (50%); 1994 (52%)

The People		Race/Ethnic Origin	Ancestry	
Area size:	7,132 sq. mi.	93.7% White	German: 18.1%	USA: 11.9%
Urban population:	58.1%	3.7% Black	Irish: 8.1%	
Rural population:	41.9%	0.6% Asian	**2004 Presidential Vote**	
Pop. 2000:	675,564	0.2% Native Am.	Bush (R) 170,390	(62%)
Median income:	$36,732	0.0% Hawaiian	Kerry (D) 104,625	(38%)
Poverty status:	10.7%	0.8% Two+ races	Other 2,006	(1%)
Military veterans:	13.9%	0.1% Other	**2000 Presidential Vote**	
		0.9% Hispanic Origin	Bush (R) 144,848	(56%)
			Gore (D) 106,850	(42%)
			Other 4,808	(2%)
			Cook Partisan Voting Index: R + 9	

Occupation	Blue collar: 31.9%	White collar: 51.9%	Gray collar: 16.2%

"Evansville," wrote John Bartlow Martin in 1947, "is the capital of a tri-state area comprising the neglected tag ends of Indiana, Kentucky and Illinois." It was a factory town then, building car parts and refrigerators, drawing workers from Kentucky, Tennessee and the picturesque but not very fertile hills of southern Indiana. It has seen hard times, such as the terrible flood of March 1997, but it also has Indiana's first riverboat casino and claims to have the nation's second largest street festival, second only to New Orleans's Mardi Gras celebration. In 2004, defective equipment at a coal-fired power plant in Princeton resulted in the spewing of nitrogen oxide emissions across the border into Illinois, and forced Cinergy Corporation to spend nearly $2 billion to repair that and similar generators.

Evansville is one of two major focuses of the 8th Congressional District, which covers most of southwest and west central Indiana. The other, in Vigo County, is Terre Haute, an old manufacturing town and the boyhood home of Socialist Eugene Debs. It hosts a maximum-security penitentiary, which includes the only federal death chamber, where Oklahoma City bomber Timothy McVeigh was executed in June 2001. This southwest corner of Indiana was the first part of the state settled by whites. Vincennes, now a small town on the banks of the Wabash River, was once the metropolis of Indiana, and Scottish philanthropist and visionary Robert Owen established the town of New Harmony downstream. Owen's son was the first congressman from the area, elected in 1842 and 1844. Southern Indiana is ancestrally Democratic, just as northern Indiana is ancestrally Republican; these southern counties were hostile to the Civil War. In New Deal times, workers in Evansville moved again toward the Democrats.

The result has been a very close political balance, and this district has become known as the "Bloody Eighth" for its tight congressional races. At one point in the 1970s it elected four different congressmen in four successive elections. In 1984, the state certified the Republican as the winner by exactly 34 votes, but the Democratic U.S. House, in a fight that left many Republican members bitterly aggrieved, overturned the result. Since then, it has been as fiercely contested as ever. The trend in presidential politics, however, is away from national Democrats: Bill Clinton twice carried it by 2%, but in 2000 George W. Bush won 56% followed by 62% in 2004.

The congressman from the 8th District is John Hostettler, a Republican first elected in 1994, an ingenuous and idealistic man who seems miscast in politics. Hostettler is from Posey County, just west of Evansville; he went to Rose-Hulman Institute of Technology in Terre Haute and in 1983 became a Southern Indiana Gas & Electric Company engineer. He had never run for office, but in 1994, at 33, he was the Republican nominee vying to run against 12-year incumbent Democrat Frank McCloskey. Hostettler's great strength was his support from anti-abortion and Christian fundamentalist groups. His biggest fundraiser was a $100-per-family fried chicken dinner with Marilyn Quayle. He attacked McCloskey on taxes, gay rights, gun control, the environment, school prayer, his 65 overdrafts at the House bank, and constantly referred to him as "Frank McClinton." McCloskey accused Hostettler of wanting to outlaw all abortions and called him "John McGingrich." McCloskey carried Evansville and the university town of Bloomington—then but not now in the district—by microscopic margins, but Hostettler carried most of the rural counties and won 52%–48%.

In the House, Hostettler has been a conservative willing to buck conventional political wisdom and his party leadership. He and fellow Indiana freshman Mark Souder were the only two Republicans to vote against the balanced budget amendment in 1995 because it did not require a supermajority to raise taxes. He opposed term limits, saying that he was against amending the Constitution unless there is no alternative. In 2000 Hostettler was one of three members to vote against the Violence Against Women Act in September; the other two weren't running for reelection. Opposed to "hate crimes" legislation, he asked, "What crime is motivated out of love? We should not create a federal thought police." He was one of six House Republicans to vote against authorizing force against Iraq; he kept a low profile on the vote, but argued on the House floor that it would set "an ominous precedent" that the "rest of the world could justifiably follow," and that Iraq was not an imminent threat.

Hostettler has been a leading voice for social conservatives. He won House approval of his amendment to prohibit federal enforcement of the court order to remove a replica of the Ten Commandments from the state courthouse in Alabama. In 2004, the House passed his bill preventing federal courts from examining the constitutionality of the Defense of Marriage Act. On the Armed Services Committee, Hostettler has been a strong support for missile defense, including airborne laser shooting ballistic missiles and solid-state lasers fired from jet fighters. He opposed a change in the highway formula which would have given Indiana more money but which would not have maintained the commitment to build I-69 from Indianapolis to Evansville. As chairman of Judiciary's Immigration subcommittee since January 2003, he has been at odds with the Bush administration over the guest worker proposal.

Hostettler has repeatedly faced serious Democratic opposition. Refusing to raise PAC money, he is among the few incumbents who sometimes gets outspent in reelection contests. In 1996 he eked out a 50%–48% victory. In 2000, he faced Paul Perry, an Evansville orthopedic surgeon who spent $350,000 of his own money. The undertow of the Democrats' national ticket in the rural and small town area was strong that year; Hostettler won 53%–45%. In 2002, Hostettler showed once again that he is a politician who goes his own way, and creates good breaks for himself. Democrats hoped that state House Speaker John Gregg from Vigo County would run in the district he helped draw; Gregg unexpectedly said no, as did Paul Perry and, just before the filing deadline, former Congressman McCloskey. That left the inexperienced Brian Hartke, the nephew of Indiana's former three-term Senator (1959–1977) Vance Hartke. Hostettler's biggest problems, it seemed, were himself and the *Evansville Courier & Press*. In September 2002, Hostettler said on a local radio program that he would no longer give interviews to the local newspaper because of what he considered unfair coverage of his August meeting in Washington with breast-cancer survivors; during that session, he offended some by discussing controversial studies that link abortion and breast cancer. On Election Day, Hostettler won, 51%–46%. In 2004, Democrats enthusiastically promoted Jon Jennings, a pro-life, pro-gun former Justice Department official and assistant to basketball coach Bobby Knight at Indiana University. Republicans mocked Jennings as a carpetbagger because he had lived in Boston for 10 years as a scout for the Boston Celtics basketball team, some of whose leaders campaigned for him, and roughly half of his campaign funds came from Massachusetts. Jennings returned fire by calling Hostettler a "Washington insider," but the result was familiar: Although outspent by more than 2-to-1, Hostettler won a bit bigger than usual, 53%–45%. Hostettler scored a big gain by taking Evansville's Vanderburgh County 50%–48% plus big margins in the other 14 counties, mostly in rural areas where he was bolstered by support in churches.

He appeared unaffected politically by his guilty plea in Kentucky in August 2004 for carrying a loaded semiautomatic handgun at a security checkpoint in the Louisville airport four months earlier. The judge suspended a 60-day sentence, barred him from carrying a gun in Kentucky for two years, and prevented him from purchasing a gun during that period anywhere except in Indiana or Washington, D.C. Hostettler called his action a "stupid mistake."

NINTH DISTRICT

Rep. Mike Sodrel (R)

Elected 2004, 1st term; b. Dec. 17, 1945, Louisville, KY; home, New Albany; Attended IN U. SE; Christian; married (Marquita).

Military Career: Army Natl. Guard, 1966–73.

Professional Career: Sodrel Truck Lines, Owner, 1987–2004; Sodrel Logistics, 2000–04.

DC Office: 1508 LHOB, 20515, 202-225-5315; Fax: 202-226-6866; Web site: www.house.gov/sodrel.

District Offices: Bloomington, 812-330-1543; Jasper, 812-482-9864; Jeffersonville, 812-288-3999; Seymour, 812-523-8050; Versailles, 812-689-7300.

Committees: *Science* (20th of 24 R): Energy; Research. *Small Business* (14th of 18 R): Regulatory Reform & Oversight; Rural Enterprises, Agriculture & Technology. *Transportation & Infrastructure* (32d of 41 R): Highways, Transit & Pipelines; Railroads.

Group Ratings and Key Votes: Newly Elected

Election Results

2004 general	Mike Sodrel (R)	142,197	(49%)	($1,546,877)
	Baron Hill (D)	140,772	(49%)	($1,634,699)
	Other	4,541	(2%)	
2004 primary	Mike Sodrel (R)	unopposed		
2002 general	Baron Hill (D)	96,654	(51%)	($1,144,666)
	Mike Sodrel (R)	87,169	(46%)	($1,626,646)
	Other	5,134	(3%)	

The People		Race/Ethnic Origin	Ancestry		
Area size:	6,670 sq. mi.	94.0% White	German: 19.9%	USA: 12.2%	
Urban population:	52.3%	2.3% Black	Irish: 8.7%		
Rural population:	47.7%	0.9% Asian	**2004 Presidential Vote**		
Pop. 2000:	675,599	0.2% Native Am.	Bush (R)	171,926	(59%)
Median income:	$39,011	0.0% Hawaiian	Kerry (D)	117,647	(40%)
Poverty status:	10.5%	0.9% Two+ races	Other	1,568	(1%)
Military veterans:	13.0%	0.1% Other	**2000 Presidential Vote**		
		1.5% Hispanic Origin	Bush (R)	142,694	(56%)
			Gore (D)	106,417	(42%)
			Other	4,288	(2%)
			Cook Partisan Voting Index: R + 7		
Occupation	Blue collar: 34.4%	White collar: 50.6%	Gray collar: 15.0%		

The southeastern corner of Indiana was a busy place when settlers rafted down the Ohio River in the early 19th century. They were mostly Southerners, "Butternuts," from across the river in Kentucky or over the mountains in Virginia, and they built the first large Indiana settlements. Today, you can see their work in the marvelous old buildings of Madison, now quiet but once one of the busiest ports on the Ohio River. Farther down the river is Corydon, from 1816–25 the state capital. The early 19th century buildings here have been well preserved because these towns were bypassed first by the railroads, then by U.S. routes and interstate highways, and they certainly are remote from major airports. The river remains an artery of commerce, but utilitarian barges have replaced steamers, except for riverboat casinos.

Butternut Indiana retained its affection for things Southern into the Civil War and beyond. Local politician Jesse Bright was expelled from the U.S. Senate in 1862 for "supporting the rebellion." To this day, the hills along the Ohio River typically vote Democratic, as do the Indiana suburbs of Louisville. But to the east, Indiana is now filling up with migrants from Cincinnati—a

Yankee and German abolitionist bastion in Jesse Bright's time, an overwhelmingly Republican stronghold in ours—who are moving the southeast corner of Indiana away from its ancestral party.

The 9th Congressional District of Indiana is made up of most of the state's Ohio River counties. It includes tiny Milan, home to the championship high school of *Hoosiers* movie fame, and the Indiana University campus in the rolling hills of Democratic-leaning Bloomington. To the east is Batesville, home of the Batesville Casket Company, which makes the caskets used for U.S. military personnel who die in the line of duty. Most of the district is ancestrally Democratic and culturally conservative; much of it has recently been trending Republican, particularly in the suburbs of Cincinnati.

The congressman from the 9th District is Mike Sodrel, the only Republican in 2004 to defeat a Democratic incumbent who was not the victim of redistricting. Sodrel grew up in New Albany in a family that had been in the transport business since his great-grandfather traveled the Ohio River on a flatboat. He attended Indiana University Southeast, started a company called the Free Enterprise System in 1976, then purchased Sodrel Truck Lines from his family. In 2000, he added a third business, Sodrel Logistics. He was also a chairman of the Southern Indiana Chamber of Commerce. In 2002, Sodrel ran against 9th District incumbent Democrat Baron Hill and fell short, 51%–46%. As a first-time candidate and without attracting much local or national attention, he spent $1 million of his own money on his campaign. He blamed his defeat in part on the national party's refusal to provide him with adequate support.

In 2003 he said he would not run again. But national Republicans said they would give him more support in a second race; he was on the tarmac when George W. Bush visited Indianapolis, and Dick Cheney, Tom DeLay, Tommy Thompson and Dennis Hastert were scheduled for Sodrel fundraisers. He campaigned in a semitrailer truck leased from his company with a loudspeaker blaring "Courtesy of the Red, White and Blue." Ultimately the NRCC spent $1 million on this race. Sodrel opposed abortion and campaigned on the theme of "traditional moral values." He supported a federal constitutional amendment to ban gay marriage and criticized Hill for opposing it; Hill argued that the issue should be left to the states. He attacked Hill for opposing legislation to strip courts of their jurisdiction to review cases involving the Pledge of Allegiance and for his increasing support of the Democratic leadership. Sodrel backed the administration's tax cuts as a necessary economic stimulus. Hill, a member of the moderate Democratic Blue Dogs who had turned down a possible run for governor in 2004, favored limited tax cuts when the federal budget was in surplus; but he opposed Bush's subsequent tax cuts, saying that he wasn't "going to vote for tax cuts that aren't paid for." Hill cited his support for "pay as you go" budget rules, but Sodrel criticized him for withdrawing support for a balanced budget constitutional amendment. Sodrel supported tolls as a way to pay for a new Ohio River bridge near Louisville, one of the most expensive federal highway projects being planned; Hill staunchly opposed tolls.

Sodrel won 49.5%–49.0%, with a popular vote margin of 1,425. He ran about even in the Democratic-leaning counties that are part of the Louisville metro area; Hill won Bloomington's Monroe County 58%–39%. The Cincinnati suburban counties went for Sodrel, and he carried all but two of the more rural counties. Democrats demanded a recount in three counties, because voting machines of the type used there malfunctioned in a county outside the district; Republicans charged that votes were cast in Monroe County by voters to whom mail was returned as undeliverable. But the recounts changed little, and Hill conceded in early December. This is one district where the result can be attributed to George W. Bush's coattails: Bush ran ahead of his 2000 performance here and carried every county in the district except Monroe; he won 59%–40% districtwide. This in a district represented for 40 years by Democrats; Hill's predecessor, Lee Hamilton, was first elected in 1964 and rose to become chairman of the Foreign Affairs Committee before his retirement in 1998. Hill said in May 2005 that he intended to seek a rematch in 2006. If Democrats want to regain a majority in the House, they need to retake districts like this one.

★ IOWA ★

As Americans were surging westward in the 1840s, Iowa was filling up with Yankee farmers and German immigrants, watching as wagon trains headed to the Oregon Trail and the Mormon thousands mustered by Brigham Young headed from the Mississippi across the rolling hills to Council Bluffs on the Missouri and then west. Iowa was a young state then, proud of its hundreds of schools and dozens of colleges, sending more than its share of young men back east to fight for the cause of the Union. After that war Iowans built a solid civilization based on farming, farm-machine manufacturing and meat processing that resisted the blandishments of William Jennings Bryan's populism and cheap money, and Iowa became one of the most solidly Republican states in the nation.

But starting around 1900, Iowa grew old. "If you build it, they will come" was the theme from the movie *Field of Dreams*, set in Iowa, and in the 19th century, Iowans built a model society. Yet for most of the 20th century very few people came. Iowa's commercial and financial center remained stuck in the railroad hub of Chicago, its economy failed to diversify and develop the dense manufacturing base of the Great Lakes states, and its young people started to move east or west to make their fortunes. Iowa's population, up from 674,000 in 1860 to 2.2 million in 1900, increased only slowly, and has not reached 3 million to this day: In 1900, Iowa had 11 congressional districts and California 7; now Iowa has 5 and California 53. Iowa's solid Capitol—a memorial to its Civil War dead—and its courthouses, its sturdy but mostly old housing stock, give testimony to Iowa's strengths but also bespeak its lack of dynamism. Even its great economic achievement—the development of high-tech, ever more productive, but also less labor-intensive agriculture—has made this a state that did not grow much. Iowa is number one in pork, number one in corn, and number one in soybeans, but it is down near the bottom in population growth.

Indeed, for much of the 20th century, Iowa has been a culturally and politically countercyclical state, headed in just the opposite direction of the rest of the nation—determinedly, with confidence in its own chipper rectitude, unembarrassedly out of step. In the industrial New Deal era, it stayed mostly agricultural and Republican, even as Des Moines radio announcer Ronald Reagan became an enthusiastic Roosevelt Democrat and headed to Hollywood. Iowa partook little of postwar economic growth. It was dovish during the Vietnam War and after. In the 1980s, as Reagan, by then a conservative Republican, became president, Iowans watched helplessly as farm prices and land values plummeted downward, farm implement factories closed and 5% of its citizens left; its population fell more than any other state except West Virginia. Self-pity became the dominant note of Iowa's politics, as voters sought protection from the vagaries of the market even as commercial real estate and stock prices boomed elsewhere. By 1988, once-Republican Iowa had become one of the most Democratic states, sending presidential caucus winner Dick Gephardt's politics solidly to the left and producing the second-highest percentage for Michael Dukakis in November.

In the 1990s, Iowa and the nation converged. If its economic rebellion against America's move toward free markets failed in the 1980s, its cultural qualms about America's move away from traditional values may have set an example for the rest of the country in the 1990s. For Iowa has managed to combine over the years steady habits and tolerance of diversity. The farm population continued to drop in the 1990s; from 1982 to 1997, the number of Iowans whose principal occupation was farming dropped from 86,000 to 56,000. Subsidies keep some farmers going, and farm prices boomed in 2004, but most of the money goes to a few large farms, and today many of Iowa's farmers are part-timers, with full-time jobs and just a little side income from the farm. In the 1990s, Iowa grew in other ways. Its high level of literacy and good work habits have produced white-collar and high-tech growth in and around its pleasant small cities, especially in Des Moines and Cedar Rapids, even as many old factories have closed. The state's population fell 4.7% in the 1980s but grew by 5.4% in the 1990s, the biggest percentage increase since the 1910s. And if educated young Iowans still often leave the state, immigrants are coming in—Mexicans to work in the big new meatpacking factories, Serbian and Bosnian refugees who

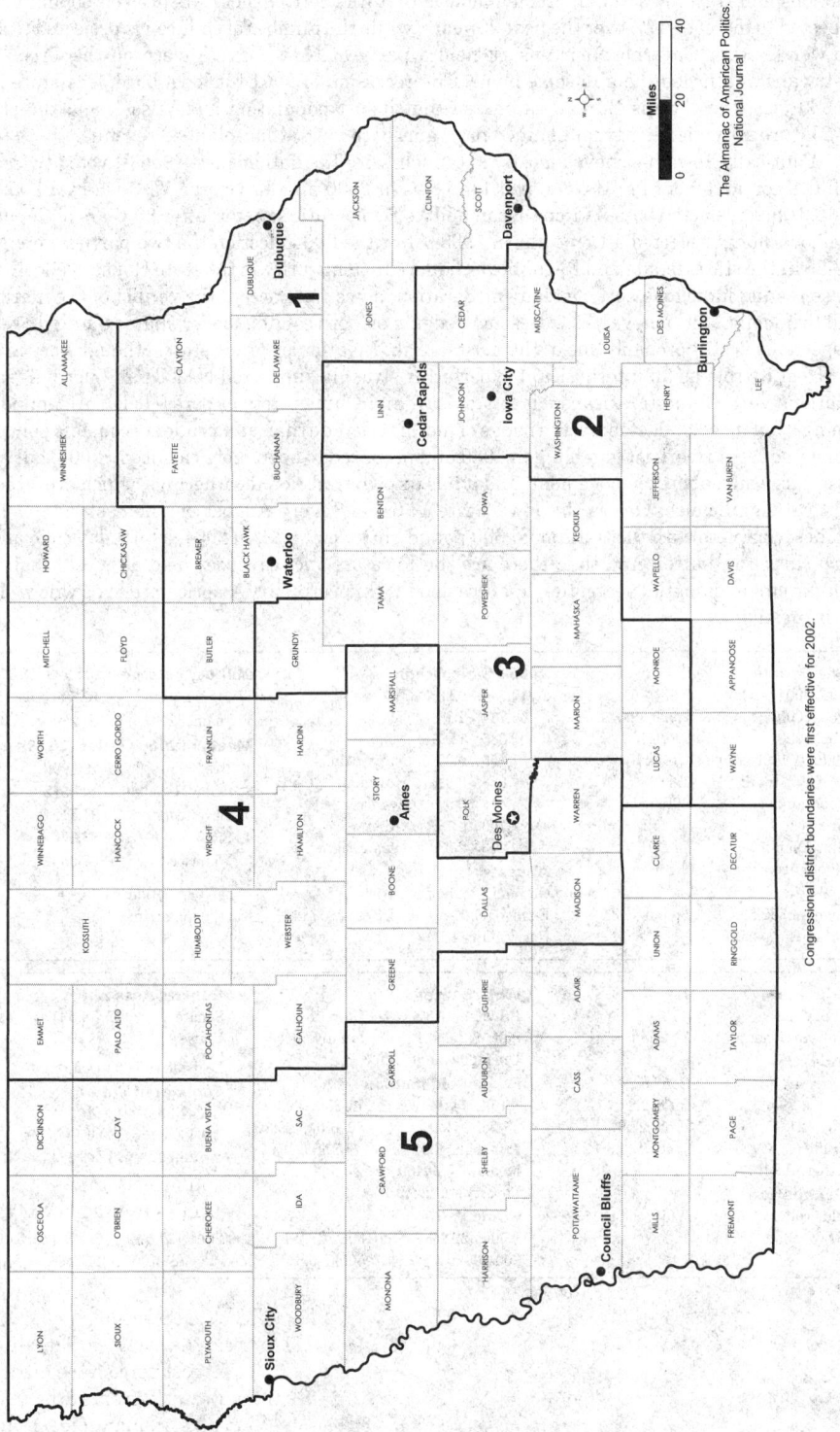

The Almanac of American Politics.
National Journal

Congressional district boundaries were first effective for 2002.

find jobs and stay. Iowa's main problem now is that it is getting older: Its over-65 population is expected to increase 47% over the next 20 years, while the number of children is projected to fall. No wonder that Governor Tom Vilsack held a party at New York's Tavern on the Green for ex-Iowans and urged them to come home. The recession of 2001 hit Iowa hard: The state lost 10,000 jobs, the Census Bureau estimated that it lost population and Vilsack and the state legislature struggled to pay for planned programs with lower-than-planned revenue.

Politically, Iowa has moved mostly in tandem with the nation since 1990. It voted twice for Bill Clinton and went for Al Gore by 4,144 votes in 2000 and for George W. Bush by 10,059 in 2004. It has reelected both its Republican and its Democratic senator; after 30 years of Republican governors, it elected a Democrat in 1998. After the 2004 election the two parties were tied 25–25 in the state Senate and Republicans had a 51–49 majority in the state House. Collectively these results indicate a sort of steady moderation, a desire to accept the verdict of the markets and to honor traditional values with some hedging on both counts. Iowa remains quirky in some respects. It is still probably one of the most dovish, isolationist-prone states, though very much aware of its role as an international exporter: It strongly supported NAFTA and normal trade relations with China (Mexicans eat lots of corn and Chinese lots of pork). It is thrift-minded, seeing a balanced budget more as a badge of moral rectitude than as a prudent economic policy. It pioneered legal riverboat gambling in 1989 and prepared to open more casinos in 2004, but also has a large anti-abortion movement. And it has its own traditional gatherings, which are often of political significance. One is the Iowa State Fair held every August on the east side of Des Moines, complete with the traditional 600-pound butter cow and, in 2004, a birthday cake and a barn carved in butter. And then there are the Iowa precinct caucuses held on a cold night in January in presidential years, the first occasion in which ordinary Americans decide who will be their president.

The People		**Race/Ethnic Origin**			**Military veterans:** 292,020 (13.3%)	
Pop. 2004 (est):	2,954,451	2,710,344	92.6%	White	WWII: 22.6%	Korea: 15.6%
Pop. 2000:	2,926,324	60,744	2.1%	Black	Vietnam: 31.4%	Gulf War: 8.3%
Pop. 1990:	2,776,755	36,345	1.2%	Asian	**Most populous cities (2003):**	
Change 1990–2000:	Up 5.4%	7,955	0.3%	Native Am.	1. Des Moines	196,093
% of U.S. total:	1.0%	888	0.0%	Hawaiian	2. Cedar Rapids	122,542
Pop. rank:	30th of 50	25,472	0.9%	Two+ races	3. Davenport	97,512
Area size:	56,272 sq. mi.	2,103	0.1%	Other	4. Sioux	83,876
State Native:	74.8%	82,473	2.8%	Hisp. Origin	5. Waterloo	67,054
Non-citizen:	2.1%	**Ancestry**				
Language		German: 26.0%		Irish: 9.8%	Urban population: 61.1%	
English: 92.5%	Spanish: 3.7%	English: 6.9%		USA: 4.9%	Rural population: 38.9%	
Other Eur.: 2.6%		Norwegian: 4.1%				

Education		**Work Sector**		**General Assembly**	
H.S. Grad:	86.1%	Private: 77.8%	Govt: 13.6%	Senate	25 R 25 D
College Grad:	21.2%	Self: 8.2%	Family: 0.4%	House	51 R 49 D
Industry		Unemployment: 4.2%		Legislative Term Limits: No	
Agri: 4.4%	Con: 6.2%	**Household Income**			
Fin: 6.7%	Info: 2.8%	<15k: 14.9%	15-35k: 29.0%	**Registered Voters**	
Mfg: 21.9%	Prof: 27.8%	35-50k: 19.0%	50-100k: 29.8%	D: 641,232	(30.4%)
Public: 3.4%	Trade: 15.6%	100-150k: 4.9%	>150k: 2.4%	R: 645,881	(30.6%)
Other: 11.1%		Median: $39,469		O: 823,122	(39.0%)
Occupation		Poverty status: 9.1%			
Blue collar: 27.0%	White collar: 57.2%	**Home Value**			
Gray collar: 15.8%		<50k: 22.9%	50-100k: 42.2%	100-200k: 27.5%	200-300k: 5.0%
		300-500k: 1.8%	>500k: 0.6%	Median: $82,100	

Presidential politics   On a frosty evening in January every four years, more than 100,000 Iowans troop to caucuses in some 1,986 precincts and begin the process of choosing a president of the United States. The precinct caucuses were scheduled early in the cycle for 1972 by Democratic doves who wanted more leverage for their views, and that year they started George McGovern on his way to the Democratic nomination. But the caucuses have had other, unanticipated consequences. In 1976, Jimmy Carter's strategist Hamilton Jordan determined that intensive campaigning could produce a surprise victory that could make a little-known candidate a national contender: Without Iowa and the next-week New Hampshire primary, Carter would never have become president.

2004 Presidential Vote		
Bush (R)	751,957	(50%)
Kerry (D)	741,898	(49%)
Nader (I)	5,973	(0%)
Other	7,080	(0%)
2000 Presidential Vote		
Gore (D)	638,517	(49%)
Bush (R)	634,373	(48%)
Nader (Green)	29,374	(2%)
Other	13,299	(1%)

Then, for 20 years, the Iowa caucuses were less nomination-determinative. In 1980, George H.W. Bush's intensive campaigning gave him a victory among Republicans, while Carter, still profiting from his 1976 contacts, trounced Senator Edward Kennedy. But Bush lost the nomination to Ronald Reagan, and Carter lost in November. In 1984 Democratic favorite Walter Mondale won 49% of the "delegate strength" (Democrats don't compute the actual number of votes), but the momentum went to the 17% second place finisher Gary Hart, though Mondale did win the nomination. In 1988, Iowa failed to pick the winners on either side: Dick Gephardt capitalized on Iowa's economic woes to win among Democrats, while George H.W. Bush finished in third place behind Kansas Senator Bob Dole and televangelist Pat Robertson among Republicans—a sign of the rising strength of Christian conservatives here. But Gephardt and Dole lost in New Hampshire, and neither was nominated. In 1992, Iowa went dark: No Democrat challenged Iowa's Tom Harkin here, and Pat Buchanan began his campaign against Bush in New Hampshire. In 1996, Dole had the support of leading Republicans, led by Governor Terry Branstad and Senator Charles Grassley, and farm state roots as well: Dole's very narrow victory was an omen of the weakness of his candidacy later.

In 2000, Iowa moved its caucus date back to Monday, January 24, when New Hampshire surprised everyone by scheduling its primary for Tuesday, February 1. And in 2000, Iowa turned out to be important again. George W. Bush won the August 1999 straw poll at Ames with 31% of the vote, to 21% for Steve Forbes and 14% for Elizabeth Dole; Dole soon dropped out, as did Dan Quayle and Lamar Alexander, while Pat Buchanan left the Republican party altogether and, as the Reform party candidate in November, won 0.4% of the popular vote. In January Bush won the caucuses with 41% of the vote while Forbes got 30%, not the upset victory he needed. Both got a share of religious conservatives, as did Alan Keyes, who was third with 14%. On the Democratic side the race was between Al Gore and Bill Bradley. In his 1988 campaign, Gore skipped what he called "madness" in "the small state of Iowa"; in June 1997 he was proclaiming, "I love Iowa," and in November 1998, he was on the phone congratulating Tom Vilsack before Vilsack himself realized he had been elected governor. Gore did not get Vilsack's support—he stayed carefully neutral—but Gore did get vigorous support from Vilsack's wife, from Senator Tom Harkin and, perhaps most important, from Iowa's labor unions. Gore won in "delegate strength" with 63% to Bradley's 35%. That gave Gore momentum in New Hampshire, which he won eight days later, by only 50%–46%. With five weeks to the next Democratic contest, Bradley dropped out and Gore was the nominee.

Iowa was dispositive in 2004 as well. George W. Bush had no opposition: this was the Democrats' show. The leader in Iowa polls from summer 2003 through the second week of January 2004 was Howard Dean. His opposition to the war in Iraq was popular among Iowa's overwhelmingly dovish caucusgoers; his thousands of out-of-state volunteers seemed to have built the best turnout organization. But as the new year opened, Democrats suddenly confronted the possibility that they could actually defeat George W. Bush, and the question for many became not who could most stridently criticize for the president and his policies but who could defeat him. Al Gore's December 9 endorsement of Dean didn't help Dean with the party regulars and union operatives who had won the caucuses for Gore four years before; Dean's comment that the December 13 capture of Saddam Hussein "has not made America safer" raised doubts about his electability. Dean's irritated outshouting of a 68-year-old Republican questioner in Oelwein January 11 was a breach of Iowa manners; his poll numbers immediately started plummeting. The question was who would rise. Dick Gephardt, supported by private sector unions and veterans of his campaign 16 years before, failed to gather new adherents. John Edwards, endorsed by the *Des Moines Register*, had only a few chipper out-of-staters organizing things. John Kerry, who mortgaged his Boston house for $6.4 million and put all his efforts into Iowa, had the best organization, led by 2002 congressional candidate John Norris, the endorsement of Christie Vilsack—the governor was again technically neutral—and a message. Just days before the caucuses he was joined by a Green Beret whom he had rescued in the waters of Vietnam. Kerry proclaimed that he could stand up to Bush on Iraq because he had volunteered and been decorated in Vietnam.

That was enough for victory on caucus night—and the nomination. Howard Dean's 3,500 orange-stocking-capped Perfect Stormers were swarming in the streets of Des Moines. But Kerry got the votes. Under Iowa Democrats' procedures, the supporters of candidates who fail to meet a 15% threshold of the votes in any precinct can choose to caucus for another candidate; this gives a premium to front-runners and penalizes also-rans. Entry polls at the caucuses showed Kerry well ahead, with Edwards, Dean and Gephardt trailing. But Edwards had shrewdly targeted supporters of Dennis Kucinich and their support helped swell his numbers in the final standings, while Dean and Gephardt, failing to make the threshold in many precincts, saw their numbers dwindle below the entry poll. The final results, in delegate strength: Kerry 38%, Edwards 32%, Dean 18%, Gephardt 11%. Gephardt soon left the race; Dean was effectively finished even before he emitted his famous scream on caucus night; Edwards was left to finish second or third to Kerry until Kerry clinched the nomination six weeks and one day later. But it was Iowa Democrats—some 122,000 of them—who did the deciding.

Iowa has been a closely contested state in three of the last four presidential elections and has cast percentages for the two parties close to their national averages in all four. One reason is that Iowa Democrats have used the competitive caucuses in 2000 and 2004 and the strong organization developed by Senator Tom Harkin in his 1996 and 2002 campaigns to develop a strong voter turnout organization. They have been especially effective in getting votes cast by mail in early voting (which started September 23 in 2004). This enabled Democrats to carry the state in 2000—Al Gore lost among those who cast their votes on election day but won because of absentees—and to come very close four years later. But in 2004, more quietly and without the hoopla of a presidential caucus fight, Iowa Republicans also developed a strong organization. In November 2004 this resulted in increased Republican popular vote margins (or decreased Democratic margins) in 72 of Iowa's 99 counties. Democrats produced hefty popular vote margins increases in the counties including Iowa City (the University of Iowa) and Cedar Rapids (Quaker Oats) and smaller increases in the counties including Ames (Iowa State University) and Newton (Maytag). But Republicans produced a hefty increase in Pottawatomie County (east of Omaha, Nebraska) and Dallas and Warren Counties (both Des Moines suburbs) and actually produced improved popular vote margins in the counties including Des Moines (the state capital) and Davenport (Oscar Mayer). Moreover, Republicans increased their popular vote margins in most of Iowa's unglamorous and non-growing rural counties, especially in western Iowa: a considerable political achievement, delivering Iowa's seven electoral votes to George W. Bush.

Iowa's first-in-the-nation status has been preserved by Democratic, but not by Republican, party rules; these are under challenge by Michigan Senator Carl Levin and others. And one does indeed search the text of the Constitution in vain for the provision that requires that Iowa and New Hampshire vote first. But chances are that, come summer 2006, Iowa is going to be seeing lots of the Democrats and Republicans who are thinking about running for president. It proved determinative of party nominations in the last two cycles and candidates who have ignored it (Gore in 1988, John McCain in 2000, Joe Lieberman and Wesley Clark in 2004) have finished out of the money.

Congressional districting   Iowa's congressional district lines are drawn by the nonpartisan Legislative Services Bureau and then approved by the (Democratic in 2002) governor and (Republican in 2002) legislature—a process that is praised by many critics of partisan gerrymandering and bipartisan incumbent protection plans. But it is not entirely apolitical. The Legislative Service Bureau is not supposed to take past voting patterns or legislator's place of residence into account, and in good Iowa fashion, they don't. But the governor and legislators can and do. In May 2001, the Iowa Senate rejected the Legislative Service Bureau's first plan; Republicans said the population disparities were too large, but Democrats contended that Republicans thought it was politically damaging to them. So a special session was called in June to consider the Bureau's second plan. That plan placed Republican congressmen Jim Nussle and Jim Leach in the same district and separated Des Moines from suburban Dallas and Warren Counties, with which it arguably has a community of interests. Indeed, with the exception of the 5th District in western Iowa, all the districts combine very disparate parts of Iowa. Nevertheless Democratic Governor Vilsack and the Republican legislature approved the plan. Two incumbents moved their residences, Leach into the 2d District, most of which he had been representing, and Democrat Leonard Boswell into Des Moines in the new 3d District, whose incumbent, Republican Greg Ganske, was running for the Senate.

The Iowa plan did produce more strenuous competition than was seen in most states, in 2002. Four of the five districts were contested seriously by both Democrats and Republicans that year, and the 5th had a spirited Republican primary. Still, no incumbent was defeated, and in 2004 only one district was seriously contested, and four of five incumbents improved their percentages.

109th Congress Lineup	
4 R	1 D

108th Congress Lineup	
4 R	1 D

Governor

Tom Vilsack (D)

Elected 1998, term expires Jan. 2007, 2d term; b. Dec. 13, 1950, Pittsburgh, PA; home, Mt. Pleasant; Hamilton Col., B.A. 1972, Albany Law Schl., J.D. 1975; Catholic; married (Christie).

Elected Office: Mt. Pleasant Mayor, 1987–92; IA Senate, 1992–98.

Professional Career: Practicing atty., 1975–98.

Office: State Capitol, Des Moines, 50319, 515-281-5211; Fax: 515-281-6611; Web site: www.governor.state.ia.us.

Election Results

2002 general	Tom Vilsack (D)	540,449	(53%)
	Doug Gross (R)	456,612	(45%)
	Other	28,741	(3%)
2002 primary	Tom Vilsack (D)	unopposed	
1998 general	Tom Vilsack (D)	500,231	(52%)
	Jim Ross Lightfoot (R)	444,787	(47%)
	Other	11,397	(1%)

Tom Vilsack, the only Democratic governor Iowa has had since 1968, was elected in 1998 and reelected in 2002. He was orphaned at birth, was adopted and grew up in Pittsburgh, where his father lost all his money and his mother succumbed to alcoholism, graduated from Hamilton College and Albany law school in Upstate New York, visited Iowa courting his wife and decided to live there. They moved to Mount Pleasant in southeast Iowa where he joined his father-in-law's law firm and won notable verdicts for farmers defrauded in the Prairie Grain Elevator case and in a class action that returned $13 million to 86,000 insurance policyholders (average: $151 each). His political career began inauspiciously. In 1987, he was elected mayor of Mount Pleasant after the incumbent was shot and killed during a council meeting by a disgruntled citizen. He was elected to the state Senate in 1992 with 50% of the vote. He nearly retired from the state Senate in 1996, but decided to stay; now he is governor.

In 1998 Vilsack was an upset winner in both the Democratic primary and in the general election. Republicans had held the governorship for 30 years; they had just gained control of the state House in 1994 and the state Senate in 1996. The state had a record surplus, unemployment was down to 3% and it was widely assumed Republicans would win again. In the Democratic primary, Vilsack was endorsed by the United Auto Workers and upset former state Supreme Court Justice Mark McCormack, who ran as a moderate, 51%–48%. In the general election, he faced former Congressman Jim Ross Lightfoot, who had held Senator Tom Harkin to a 52%–47% victory in 1996. Vilsack called for upgrading education and attracting agribusinesses to make Iowa "the Silicon Valley of food." Lightfoot advocated tax cuts and ran negative ads. On election night, Vice President Al Gore called Vilsack to tell him he'd won; Vilsack was watching *All the President's Men* instead of the televised results. His margin was 52%–47%.

The legislature remained in Republican hands, so Vilsack did not achieve some of his goals—such as an increase in the minimum wage. But he got increases in teacher pay and greatly increased the number of children in the children's health insurance program. In April 2000, the legislature repealed Vilsack's order banning discrimination in state employment against gays, lesbians and transsexuals; Vilsack vetoed that and in the fall 22 legislators sued, charging he exceeded his powers—a state judge declared Vilsack's order invalid. Vilsack vetoed a waiting period for abortions and signed a health insurance regulation law without the right to sue he had sought. He championed a Vision Iowa program, to build community attractions like the Gladbrook theater, the America's River Project in Dubuque, the Mid-American Convention Center in Council Bluffs and a steam-powered carousel in his own Mount Pleasant. Perhaps most controversial was the recommendation, embraced by Vilsack, of a bipartisan commission that Iowa should recruit 310,000 foreign workers to settle in the state. Iowa had a low unemployment rate and a relatively elderly population; more workers seemed necessary to keep its economy growing. He proposed a 10-year $600 yearly tax credit for graduates of Iowa colleges who stayed in the state.

But Iowa's economy stopped growing in 2000, and little more was heard about encouraging immigration. Instead, the focus was on cutting state spending when expected revenues failed to flow in. Cuts began in 2001; in February 2002, Vilsack dipped into the state's rainy day fund. State employees were furloughed or given retirement buyouts. That was the situation as Vilsack sought to be the first Iowa Democratic governor reelected since 1966. The candidates for the Republican nomination were not well known. State Representative Steve Sukup, owner of a family farm equipment business, called for a $20 million tax cut. Robert VanderPlaats, a Sioux City businessman and head of a children's physical rehabilitation nonprofit, called for thoroughgoing tax reform. Doug Gross, a late entry, had been a staffer for Governor Robert Ray and chief of staff to Governor Terry Branstad; he charged Vilsack with mismanaging the budget. Gross won the Republican nomination with 36% of the vote—just above the 35% threshold required to keep the nomination from going to a state party convention—while Sukup and VanderPlaats, with different geographic bases, got 32% each. In the general, Vilsack, as the incumbent and with strong support from labor unions, had more money and attacked Gross for being a $300,000 lawyer-lobbyist whose firm represented hog lot producers who opposed proposals for local regulation of hog lots. This is a (literally) sulphurous issue in some communities. Polls in late June showed the race even. But Vilsack's attacks enabled him to pull ahead, and in November, he won by a 53%–45% margin, carrying 68 of Iowa's 99 counties.

In January 2003 Vilsack called for creation of an Iowa Values Fund, to use federal economic development money to provide money for companies to add or retain workers. Republicans, in control of both houses of the legislature, balked. But in a June 2003 special session the Republicans agreed to establish the Values Fund in return for business tax cuts and changes in workmen's comp. Vilsack signed the bill but line-item vetoed the tax cuts and workmen's comp changes. Speaker Christopher Rants and Senate President Stewart Iverson immediately sued, arguing that the line-item veto applies only to appropriations, not policy bills. They lost in a lower court, and Iowa Department of Economic Development director Michael Blouin started approving Values Fund projects. By May 2004 Vilsack said the Fund had aided 127 businesses, retaining or adding nearly 10,000 jobs and stimulating $1.3 billion in capital investment. Examples included $500,000 to Archer Daniels Midland and a French company for a Cedar Rapids plant to use corn syrup to produce baker's yeast, $5 million to Phytodyne of Ames to commercialize a gene targeting system and $100,000 to H.J. Heinz as part of a $4 million project to improve the process of filling ketchup bottles in Muscatine. In June 2004 the Iowa Supreme Court ruled that Vilsack's line-item veto was illegal and declared the whole law void. In a September special session, legislators agreed to a $100 million tranche to keep the Values Fund going for the fiscal year. But conservative Republicans grumbled that the state should not be in the investing business, while liberal state Representative Ed Fallon joined Iverson in skepticism about claims of job creation and pointed out that aided businesses were only pledging to create or retain jobs.

On other issues, the legislature rejected Vilsack's proposals to apply the sales tax to services to provide money for schools and to raise the cigarette tax 60 cents for health care programs; it provided $109 million more for schools, not the $137 million Vilsack asked. Vilsack vetoed bills declaring the killing of a fetus a crime and capping non-economic damages in medical malpractice cases; the state Senate rejected an openly gay Vilsack appointee to the state education board. Vilsack signed the first state law banning thimerosal, an additive to vaccines that some activists, though not the National Academies' Institute of Medicine, argue produces autism. In May the legislature and Vilsack approved new gambling casinos; 10 applications were filed by November.

While all this was ongoing, Vilsack was a central figure in the Iowa presidential caucuses and in the speculation about the vice presidential nomination. As in 2000, he stayed neutral in the caucuses, but his wife Christie Vilsack endorsed the winning candidate. By March Vilsack was frequently mentioned as a possible vice presidential nominee, and was telling national reporters how he would like to have a "conversation" with Vice President Dick Cheney and that the "administration has pursued the most shortsighted, breathtakingly misguided economic policy of any in my lifetime." He was vetted by the Kerry people and joined Kerry July 4 on the last leg of a Midwestern bus tour. Articulate and pleasant, a solid partisan Democrat with a nonpartisan air, nationally prominent but without a troublesome congressional voting record, Vilsack seemed attractive to many. But the nomination went to John Edwards instead. In November Vilsack had the satisfaction of seeing his Democrats gain seats in the legislature. The Senate ended up in a 25–25 tie, and the Republican majority in the House was reduced to 51–49. The new legislative leaders stressed the need for bipartisanship. Vilsack called for ending the deductibility of federal income taxes, in return for other tax cuts; Rants disagreed. Remaining on the table were a possible cigarette tax increase and the fate of the Iowa Values Fund.

In his 1998 and 2002 campaigns Vilsack promised to serve only two terms as governor. But his ambitions may go farther. After the November election, he said he might be interested in becoming Democratic national chairman, but when many Democrats made it clear that they did not want the new chairman to run for president in 2008, he withdrew from the race. It's possible that he might run for president; a Vilsack candidacy might clear the field in Iowa, as Tom Harkin's candidacy did in 1992, but it's not clear whether that would make him a more viable candidate than Harkin turned out to be.

Iowa has only had three governor's elections in the last 40 years in which the incumbent was not running, 1968, 1982 and 1998; 2006 will evidently be the fourth. In spring 2005, possible Democratic candidates included Fallon, Secretary of State Chet Culver, IDED director and former Congressman Michael Blouin, Shenandoah Mayor Greg Connell and state Senate Democratic Leader Michael Gronstal. Possible Republicans included Rants, VanderPlaats, state Senate Republican President Jeff Lamberti and Congressman Jim Nussle.

Senior Senator

Charles Grassley (R)

Elected 1980, seat up 2010, 5th term; b. Sep. 17, 1933, New Hartford; home, New Hartford; U. of N. IA, B.A. 1955, M.A. 1956, U. of IA, 1957–58; Baptist; married (Barbara).

Elected Office: IA House of Reps., 1958–74; U.S. House of Reps., 1974–80.

Professional Career: Farmer.

DC Office: 135 HSOB, 20510, 202-224-3744; Fax: 202-224-6020; Web site: grassley.senate.gov.

State Offices: Cedar Rapids, 319-363-6832; Council Bluffs, 712-322-7103; Davenport, 563-322-4331; Des Moines, 515-284-4890; Sioux City, 712-233-1860; Waterloo, 319-232-6657.

Committees: *Agriculture, Nutrition & Forestry*: Marketing, Inspection & Product Promotion; Production & Price Competitiveness. *Budget*. *Finance* (Chmn.): Long-Term Growth & Debt Reduction; Social Security & Family Policy. *Judiciary*: Administrative Oversight & the Courts; Antitrust, Competition Policy & Consumer Rights; Crime & Drugs; Immigration, Border Security & Citizenship; Terrorism, Technology & Homeland Security. *Joint Committee on Taxation* (Vice Chmn. of 5 Sens.).

Group Ratings

	ADA	ACLU	AFS	LCV	ITIC	NTU	COC	ACU	NTLC	CHC
2004	20	11	14	0	100	69	100	96	90	100
2003	5	—	11	0	—	72	100	80	—	—

National Journal Ratings

	2003 LIB	—	2003 CONS		2004 LIB	—	2004 CONS
Economic	0%	—	82%		29%	—	70%
Social	0%	—	59%		19%	—	71%
Foreign	0%	—	78%		33%	—	61%

Key Votes of the 108th Congress

1. Ban Drilling in ANWR	N	5. Energy Bill	Y	9. Ban Same-Sex Marriage	Y
2. Approve Bush Tax Cuts	Y	6. Support Roe v. Wade	N	10. Ban Bunker-Buster Bomb	N
3. Medicare/Rx Bill	Y	7. Ban Partial-Birth Abortion	Y	11. Fund Iraq War	Y
4. Bar Overtime Pay Regs.	N	8. Assault Weapons Ban	N	12. Restrict Missile Defense	N

Election Results

2004 general	Charles Grassley (R)	1,038,175	(70%)	($6,403,445)
	Arthur Small (D)	412,365	(28%)	($135,503)
	Other	28,688	(2%)	
2004 primary	Charles Grassley (R)	unopposed		
1998 general	Charles Grassley (R)	648,480	(68%)	($2,781,940)
	David Osterberg (D)	289,049	(30%)	($165,429)
	Other	10,378	(1%)	

Prior Winning Percentages: 1992 (70%); 1986 (66%); 1980 (54%); 1978 House (75%); 1976 House (57%); 1974 House (51%)

Charles Grassley, the senior senator from Iowa, was first elected to the Senate in 1980. He grew up on a farm in Butler County near Waterloo; his parents switched to the Republican party when Franklin Roosevelt ran for a third term in 1940. He graduated from the University of Northern Iowa and, while in graduate school, ran for the state House in 1956 and lost by 70-some votes. Two years later he ran again and was elected, at 25; while in the legislature he worked as a sheet metal shearer and an assembly line worker. He won an open U.S. House seat in the Democratic year of 1974 and a Senate seat by beating incumbent Democrat John Culver, in 1980.

Grassley combines political shrewdness with a seeming naiveté that at some level is surely genuine. He describes himself as "just a hog farmer from New Hartford," and says, "I don't know how you're going to have a strong farm economy if we don't have some farmers in Congress. I can't tell you how many people I have to tell that food doesn't grow on grocery shelves." Starting in 1997, he led the Senate in consecutive roll call votes; the last one he missed came when he was inspecting flood damage in Iowa in 1993. He goes back home to Iowa just about every weekend, helps his son run the 710-acre family farm and holds open meetings in every one of Iowa's 99 counties each year.

Three issues guided Grassley's early record in Congress: Thrift, agriculture and dovishness on defense. He is ever alert for abuse of power. His first major legislation was the 1986 Federal False Claims Act, which authorizes suits for fraud on behalf of the government; he says it brought in $12 billion by 2004. He long sponsored the bill to apply to Congress the same laws it applies to others, and was the chief sponsor of the Congressional Accountability Act of 1995. He is a strong supporter of free trade and has worked from Washington to Seattle to open up markets for agricultural products; he strongly supported normal trade relations with China and managed trade promotion authority to passage in May 2002. He supported the Australia Free Trade Agreement and pushed for action on the Central American Free Trade Agreement, which he argues will knock down tariffs on U.S. agricultural imports. Grassley also proposed an amendment to the Caribbean Basin Initiative to limit the import of duty-free ethanol only partly produced in the Caribbean, lest it give an advantage to Brazil. Grassley supported both the Freedom to Farm Act of 1996 and subsequent emergency payments and loan provisions for farmers. He has tried to limit the amount farmers can receive under the farm acts (the big sums tend to go to cotton growers) and has sought to redefine agricultural cooperatives. He opposed the May 2002 farm bill, since the final version lacked his amendment to ban meatpacker ownership of livestock and had higher limits on subsidies than the $275,000 he had persuaded the Senate to vote for. "A number of folks have been saying this is a good bill, and I'd say those folks are part right. It's a good bill if you're a cotton and rice producer. The problem is, we don't grow those commodities in my state of Iowa." He continues to oppose meatpacker ownership of livestock (state law bans it in Iowa) and has pushed for country-of-origin labeling of meat. In 1991, he was one of two Republicans to vote against the Gulf war resolution. He does not echo other Republicans' calls for more defense spending and is quick to seize on Pentagon outrages.

Since January 2003 Grassley has been chairman of the Senate Finance Committee; he also held the post from January to June 2001. There he had worked for the childcare tax credit, enacted in 1997, and to reinstate the deductibility of interest on student loans. He seeks favorable treatment for ethanol and biomass; in 1998, he got the ethanol tax credit extended to 2007. In 2004 he and Blanche Lincoln successfully sought tax incentives for biodiesel—diesel fuel made partly with soybean oil or recycled cooking oil. As chairman in May 2001 and again in May 2003, he rounded up bipartisan support for the Bush tax cuts.

Grassley was one of the lead players on the Medicare/prescription drug act of 2003. The year before he had been chief sponsor of the "tripartisan" prescription drug plan (it was co-sponsored by John Breaux and Jim Jeffords), but it failed to get the required 60 votes. In 2003 he worked with ranking Democrat Max Baucus to put together the Senate bill that got the approval even of Edward Kennedy. A different version passed the House, and after an abrasive conference committee Grassley successfully worked to sell the new version on the Senate floor. Throughout the process he was careful to look after the interests of rural health care providers and to seek changes in the Medicare reimbursement formula which had Iowa receiving the lowest reimbursement per beneficiary of any state. After the bill was passed, he defended it against continuing Democratic attacks. He complained, "the drug discount card has been the target of a deliberate campaign to discredit it and confuse seniors." He continued to closely monitor the workings of Medicare and Medicaid. He spotlighted an Inspector General report that hospitals had been overcharged by drug companies, contrary to a provision requiring Medicare providers to get the lowest available price and complained that state waiver proposals were undermining Medicaid guarantees. He questioned CMS's oversight of fraud and abuse and sponsored a bill to insure that low-income seniors get $800 a year to pay for Medicare Part B premiums. When Merck withdrew Vioxx from the market in September 2004, he expressed concerns that the FDA may have been "footdragging" on the drug and suppressing an internal report on the drug. He summoned Merck's president, the FDA's acting commissioner and Vioxx critic David Graham to testify.

He supported income averaging for farmers in the late 1990s and in 2004 urged the IRS to publicize it. On the 2004 corporate tax bill he and Baucus sought to prevent municipal transit agencies from using leveraged lease transactions that he said cost the government at least $22 billion in revenue. In September 2004 he held up the bill reauthorizing individual tax cuts to get passage of the corporate tax bill; it was needed to get rid of EU sanctions which were hurting Iowa exporters. After the 2004 election he said that comprehensive tax reform would be "difficult." "I'm not one to spend a lot of time tilting at windmills." He said that it was a "missed opportunity" that George W. Bush had not talked more about the issue in the campaign. His own priorities were to make the 2001 and 2003 tax cuts permanent, to close loopholes, to shield the middle class from tax increases and to reduce the tax burden on savings and investment. On tax and Medicare issues, his preference has been to seek bipartisan agreement, usually with Baucus, and then to salvage as much of the Senate approach as he can in conference with the often acerbic House Ways and Means Chairman Bill Thomas.

On the Judiciary Committee, Grassley was for years the chief sponsor of the bankruptcy bill which failed because of a provision on abortion; it finally passed in 2005 and Bush signed it in April. "The free ride is over for people who have higher incomes and can repay their debts," he said. He took special care to see that Chapter 12, applying to farmers, would allow them to reorganize their debt without creditors' consent. Large issues claim much of Grassley's attention, but he is willing to devote much time to smaller issues as well. He worked on the money-laundering bill after September 11 and said of bank lobbyists, "They are being very unpatriotic in their approach." In 2004 he asked the 9/11 Commission to looking into Saudi transactions made through FleetBoston and Riggs Bank.

For more than 20 years, Grassley has been the most popular politician in Iowa. As he said in the runup to the 2004 election, "I commune with Iowans on a regular basis and I think they know that, they appreciate it and they don't feel like Washington has gone to my head. I suppose if I don't get smug and overconfident, I'll be reelected." In 1986, he became the first Iowa senator to win re-election in 20 years, with a record 66% of the vote. In 1992, he broke the record when he won 70%–27%, carrying all 99 counties. In 1998, against a Democrat who campaigned by taking trips down Iowa rivers, he won 68%–30%, carrying all 99 counties again. Against a Democrat with whom he served in the legislature in the early 1970s, he was reelected in 2004 by 70%–28%. He carried all 99 counties again, from Johnson County and its college town Iowa City (53%–43%) to heavily Dutch-American Sioux County (92%–7%). He has now served Iowa longer in the Senate than anyone but William B. Allison, whose record he will beat if he serves until June 2016, three months before he turns 83.

Junior Senator

Tom Harkin (D)

Elected 1984, seat up 2008, 4th term; b. Nov. 19, 1939, Cumming; home, Cumming; IA St. U., B.S. 1962, Catholic U., J.D. 1972; Catholic; married (Ruth).

Military Career: Navy, 1962–67; Naval Reserves, 1969–72.

Elected Office: U.S. House of Reps., 1974–84.

Professional Career: Practicing atty., 1972–74; Staff Aide, House Select Cmte. on U.S. Involvement in SE Asia, 1973–74.

DC Office: 731 HSOB, 20510, 202-224-3254; Fax: 202-224-9369; Web site: harkin.senate.gov.

State Offices: Cedar Rapids, 319-365-4504; Davenport, 563-322-1338; Des Moines, 515-284-4574; Dubuque, 563-582-2130; Sioux City, 712-252-1550.

Committees: *Agriculture, Nutrition & Forestry* (RMM). *Appropriations*: Agriculture, Rural Development & Related Agencies; Commerce, Justice & Science; Defense; Labor, Health and Human Services, Education & Related Agencies (RMM); State, Foreign Operations & Related Programs; Transportation, Treasury, the Judiciary, HUD & Related Agencies. *Health, Education, Labor & Pensions*: Bioterrorism & Public Health Preparedness; Education & Early Childhood Development; Employment & Workplace Safety. *Small Business & Entrepreneurship.*

Group Ratings

	ADA	ACLU	AFS	LCV	ITIC	NTU	COC	ACU	NTLC	CHC
2004	100	89	100	83	50	10	59	8	3	0
2003	95	—	100	68	—	16	32	15	—	—

National Journal Ratings

	2003 LIB	—	2003 CONS		2004 LIB	—	2004 CONS
Economic	80%	—	19%		79%	—	13%
Social	85%	—	0%		81%	—	18%
Foreign	90%	—	0%		86%	—	8%

Key Votes of the 108th Congress

1. Ban Drilling in ANWR	Y	5. Energy Bill	Y	9. Ban Same-Sex Marriage	N
2. Approve Bush Tax Cuts	N	6. Support Roe v. Wade	Y	10. Ban Bunker-Buster Bomb	Y
3. Medicare/Rx Bill	N	7. Ban Partial-Birth Abortion	N	11. Fund Iraq War	N
4. Bar Overtime Pay Regs.	Y	8. Assault Weapons Ban	Y	12. Restrict Missile Defense	Y

Election Results

2002 general	Tom Harkin (D)	554,278	(54%)	($6,897,168)
	Greg Ganske (R)	447,892	(44%)	($5,392,510)
	Other	20,905	(2%)	
2002 primary	Tom Harkin (D)	unopposed		
1996 general	Tom Harkin (D)	634,166	(52%)	($6,070,137)
	Jim Ross Lightfoot (R)	571,807	(47%)	($2,439,679)

Prior Winning Percentages: 1990 (54%); 1984 (55%); 1982 House (59%); 1980 House (60%); 1978 House (59%); 1976 House (65%); 1974 House (51%)

Tom Harkin, a Democrat first elected to the Senate in 1984, is an accomplished veteran of Capitol Hill who still brings the attitude of the aggrieved outsider to his work. Harkin grew up poor in a rural town, where his father was a coal miner and his mother, a Slovenian immigrant, died when he was 10. His desire to use government to help those who are struggling comes not from academic theory, but from tough personal experience. He worked his way through college and law school, and spent five years in the Navy during the 1960s, ferrying planes from Vietnam for repair. Returning there in 1970 as an aide to Congressman Neal Smith, he discovered the infamous "tiger cages" prison cells. After a narrow loss in 1972, Harkin ran for Congress again in 1974 and invented "work days," a campaign technique widely imitated since: He spent a day working at each of a dozen or so local jobs. He won and then held the seat with solid percentages. Well before the 1984 election, he cornered the Democratic nomination to run against Senator Roger Jepsen. In the midst of Iowa's farm depression of the 1980s, Harkin was elected with 55% of the vote.

Harkin served as chairman of the Agriculture Committee from June 2001 to January 2003 and steered to passage the 2002 farm bill. This was a considerable achievement, and one out of line with his previous record. His earlier initiative was the 1987 Harkin-Gephardt supply management farm bill, which would have raised overall food costs in order to benefit small farmers. But it was a nonstarter even in the 1980s, when Iowa farmers were hurting. In 1996, Harkin opposed the Freedom to Farm Act, which purported to phase out farm subsidies. But starting in 1998, Congress approved disaster relief every year for farmers, which had much the same economic effect. Harkin supported these efforts and worked to make conservation payments an entitlement and to promote the use of ethanol and alcohol fuels. Farm exports are important to Iowa, and Harkin, despite his warm feelings for labor unions, voted, apparently with some reluctance, for NAFTA in 1993 and normal trade relations with China in 2000. But he and Charles Grassley sought to stop the importation of Brazilian ethanol tariff-free through El Salvador.

On taking the chairmanship in June 2001, Harkin worked to fashion a farm bill that would restore much of the subsidies (and end the need, supporters said, for annual disaster relief) and that could win bipartisan support. His top goals were to increase conservation programs, come up with a formula for countercyclical aid and fight concentration in agribusiness. In November 2001, Harkin introduced his bill, with no limit on subsidies (though Harkin had proposed one) and more spending for conservation and food stamps (to secure votes from non-farm states). The bill was defeated in December 2001, but revived and passed in February 2002, with increased but limited subsidies for grain and cotton and a doubling of conservation money in an expanded Conservation Security Program. The total cost was estimated at $73.5 billion over 10 years. Harkin put in subsidies to discourage the use of irrigated water and added dairy and peanut provisions that won votes from New England and the Deep South; it passed 58–40. It included a ban on meatpackers owning livestock—a key issue for Iowa Republican Charles Grassley. The bill went to conference committee, in which the House Republicans, led by Larry Combest from cotton-farming west Texas, insisted on higher subsidy limits and deletion of the ban on meatpacker ownership of livestock. Harkin brought the bill back and got the Senate to pass it.

Harkin continues to follow farm issues closely. He put a hold on the nomination of an Iowa farmer to an Agriculture undersecretary post, saying the man cheated the federal Farm Service Agency. He pointed to security shortcomings in the department's Plum Island animal disease research laboratory. He complained that the administration ignored the usual income and payment limitations in Florida disaster relief in October 2004. For much of 2003 and 2004 he criticized Agriculture Secretary Ann Veneman's Conservation Security Program regulations as tardy and narrow. In October 2004 he held up the corporate tax bill to protest an appropriation that paid for $2.8 billion in drought aid by deferring conservation spending and the dropping of FDA regulation of tobacco; he got a non-binding resolution to restore the conservation money. After the 2004 election, he said the administration had made some progress on conservation.

Apart from agriculture, Harkin's greatest impact has probably been on health policy. Two of his sisters died from breast cancer and one brother of thyroid cancer; another brother became deaf at age nine. Harkin was a key player in shaping the Americans with Disabilities Act of 1990. This was a great achievement, one that required overcoming resistance based on cost and qualms about the real-world effect of regulations, to build a bipartisan coalition with the first Bush administration. At a 2003 hearing he pressed the cause of the disabled on Secretary of State Colin Powell; the result was $2.5 million in grants for disability rights in developing countries, a Disability Advisor at State and a requirement that AID grantees provide access for the disabled. As chairman and ranking Democrat on the Labor-HHS Appropriations Committee, Harkin worked creatively and determinedly to double the budget for the National Institutes of Health over five years—strengthening one of America's greatest research institutions in a way that may be remembered gratefully 50 or 100 years from now. He also sponsored a national institute on alternative medicine. "We need a new paradigm in American health care, a prevention paradigm," he said in 2004, and sponsored a multi-part bill to encourage better nutrition and fitness. Provisions passed include requiring schools to set nutritional standards for food available during the school day, making Harkin Fresh Fruit and Vegetable grants to schools permanent.

Another Harkin crusade has been opposition to the Bush administration's overtime regulations. Several times he persuaded a majority of senators to vote to block the regulations, but the House disagreed and the regulations took effect in August 2004.

On foreign policy, Harkin's views seem to have been shaped by the Vietnam War. He was a vocal opponent of Contra aid in the 1980s and of the Gulf War resolution in 1991, bringing a lawsuit against President George H.W. Bush to prevent him the use of force without congressional approval. But he favored the threat of force in Haiti in 1994. He voted to authorize the use of force in Iraq in 1998, when Bill Clinton sought it, and in October 2002, when George W. Bush did. But as the violence continued in Iraq, he said in December 2003, it "may not be Vietnam, but, boy, it sure smells like it." In May 2004 he said the Abu Ghraib prison abuses reminded him of the tiger cages in Vietnam, and "I believe it's time to fire the secretary of defense." On the campaign trail, he responded in August 2004 to Dick Cheney's attacks on John Kerry by saying, "When I hear this coming from Dick Cheney, who was a coward, who would not serve during the Vietnam war, it makes my blood boil. He'll be tough, but he'll be tough with someone else's kid's blood." And in September he said, "If, God forbid, another attack happens here, I see the president using that as a linchpin to reinstate the draft."

Harkin has been a force in Iowa politics. His fervent stands on issues and his hard-edged campaigning give him a large base of strong supporters and a large base of strong detractors as well. He has never won by a large margin but in his career he has beaten no less than five members of Congress—according to his office, more than anyone else in history—while never winning more than 55% of the vote in his Senate campaigns. He ran for president in 1992. In angry phrases, with a Trumanesque zest, Harkin preached that George H.W. Bush and the Republicans helped only the rich and that government must get involved to help the poor and middle class. But organized labor withheld an early endorsement despite his 90%-plus AFL-CIO voting record—a great tactical victory for Bill Clinton. Harkin's sweep of the Iowa caucuses February 10, actually an impressive testimonial to his home state popularity, was mostly discounted by the media. He finished with only 10% in New Hampshire; though he won the Minnesota and Idaho caucuses March 3, he got only 7% in South Carolina March 7 after campaigning there with Jesse Jackson, and quit the race.

In Iowa Harkin has built a strong political organization that helped him win reelection in 1990—the first time Iowa has elected a Democratic senator to a second full term—1996 and 2002. In 2000 he endorsed Al Gore in the Iowa precinct caucuses and appeared with him all over the state—an important factor in Gore's smashing victory.

In 2002 Harkin's opponent was Congressman Greg Ganske, a Des Moines plastic surgeon who had upset 36-year incumbent Neal Smith in 1994 and had been one of the lead supporters of HMO regulation in the House. Ganske won the June 2002 primary, but by an unimpressive 59%–41% margin over a more conservative candidate. Against Harkin, Ganske argued that his work on HMO regulation showed that he could work on a bipartisan basis for solutions to problems. Harkin argued that with his seniority he could best serve Iowa's interests. Harkin attacked Ganske for supporting "privatization" of Social Security and touted passage of the farm bill; Ganske said it gave too much in subsidies to southern cotton and rice farmers and didn't include a ban on meatpacker ownership of livestock. Polls showed the race fairly close after the June primary. But Harkin had far more money and, for the first time, the endorsement of the Iowa Farm Bureau Federation.

Then, in September, scandal struck. A Des Moines Democrat and former Harkin staffer, who changed his registration to Republican and contributed $50 to Ganske, attended a meeting of Ganske fundraisers with a tape recorder in his pocket. After the meeting, he turned it over to a 21-year-old Harkin campaign staffer. A transcript was leaked to a political reporter by "Democratic sources." Harkin's campaign manager said his campaign had nothing to do with it. That lie was exposed and by the end of the week, the campaign manager resigned and Harkin apologized. At the candidates' next debate angry words flowed. Many observers speculated that in squeaky-clean Iowa this caper would cost Harkin votes. Perhaps it did, but not very many. Harkin's campaign and the Iowa Democratic party also ran an effective, high-tech voter registration and turnout operation, with volunteers equipped with Palm Pilots and wireless transmission devices; they appear to have maximized the Democratic vote not only in factory towns but in rural counties Democrats usually don't carry. Harkin won 54%–44%. Regional patterns of support evident in Harkin's 1990 and 1996 runs were not evident in 2002. He carried Des Moines, Cedar Rapids and all of Iowa's significant cities except Council Bluffs, but he won in most rural areas as well, carrying 79 of Iowa's 99 counties—far more than the 50 he carried in 1996 or the 63 he carried in 1990.

Harkin seemed likely to be a key figure in the 2004 Iowa presidential precinct caucuses. As he noted, "Every candidate I have supported in Iowa has gone on to be the nominee of our party." In May 2003 he organized the first of 10 Hear It From the Heartland meetings, each featuring a different presidential candidate. Most attended his September 2003 Harkin Steak Fry. For months he did not endorse. He seemed cool toward his Senate colleague John Kerry, more friendly to Dick Gephardt who won the Iowa caucuses in 1988 (when Harkin was neutral), displeased that Wesley Clark decided not to campaign in Iowa and impressed by Howard Dean's campaign. On January 9, just ten days before the caucuses, he endorsed Dean. It proved not a big help: Dean's standing in the polls started declining a few days later. He finished third and on election night Harkin awkwardly cheered on stage as he watched Dean deliver "the scream" speech.

FIRST DISTRICT

Rep. Jim Nussle (R)

Elected 1990, 8th term; b. June 27, 1960, Des Moines; home, Manchester; Luther Col., B.A. 1983, Drake U., J.D. 1985; Lutheran; married (Karen).

Professional Career: Practicing atty., 1985–86; Delaware Cnty. Atty., 1986–1990.

DC Office: 303 CHOB, 20515, 202-225-2911; Fax: 202-226-5051; Web site: nussle.house.gov.

District Offices: Davenport, 563-326-1841; Dubuque, 563-557-7740; Manchester, 563-927-5141; Waterloo, 319-235-1109.

Committees: *Budget* (Chmn. of 22 R). *Ways & Means* (8th of 24 R): Trade.

Group Ratings

	ADA	ACLU	AFS	LCV	ITIC	NTU	COC	ACU	NTLC	CHC
2004	15	5	13	0	90	56	95	80	81	92
2003	15	—	13	0	—	62	90	88	—	—

National Journal Ratings

	2003 LIB	—	2003 CONS		2004 LIB	—	2004 CONS
Economic	33%	—	64%		38%	—	62%
Social	24%	—	71%		36%	—	61%
Foreign	23%	—	71%		39%	—	59%

Key Votes of the 108th Congress

1. Drilling in ANWR	Y	5. DC School Vouchers	Y	9. Ban Same-Sex Marriage	Y
2. Approve Bush Tax Cuts	Y	6. Ban Human Cloning	Y	10. Fund Iraq War	Y
3. Medicare/Rx Bill	Y	7. Restrict Gun Liability	Y	11. Bar Cuba Embargo Funds	Y
4. Bar Overtime Pay Regs.	Y	8. Ban Partial-Birth Abortion	Y	12. Intelligence Reorg.	Y

Election Results

2004 general	Jim Nussle (R)	159,993	(55%)	($1,622,743)
	Bill Gluba (D)	125,490	(43%)	($524,168)
	Other	4,571	(2%)	
2004 primary	Jim Nussle (R)	unopposed		
2002 general	Jim Nussle (R)	112,280	(57%)	($1,692,794)
	Ann Hutchinson (D)	83,779	(43%)	($1,020,908)

Prior Winning Percentages: 2000 (55%); 1998 (55%); 1996 (53%); 1994 (56%); 1992 (50%); 1990 (50%)

The People		Race/Ethnic Origin	Ancestry	
Area size:	7,291 sq. mi.	92.1% White	German: 31.5%	Irish: 11.1%
Urban population:	66.3%	3.8% Black	English: 6.0%	
Rural population:	33.7%	0.8% Asian	**2004 Presidential Vote**	
Pop. 2000:	585,302	0.2% Native Am.	Kerry (D) 157,380 (53%)	
Median income:	$38,727	0.0% Hawaiian	Bush (R)............. 138,073 (46%)	
Poverty status:	10.1%	1.0% Two+ races	Other 2,381 (1%)	
Military veterans:	13.8%	0.1% Other	**2000 Presidential Vote**	
		2.0% Hispanic Origin	Gore (D) 135,856 (52%)	
			Bush (R)............. 116,588 (45%)	
			Other 7,737 (3%)	
			Cook Partisan Voting Index: D + 5	

Occupation	Blue collar: 28.3%	White collar: 55.7%	Gray collar: 16.0%

Northeast Iowa, along the Mississippi River and westward, has some of the loveliest landscape in America. Here the Mississippi flows past green bluffs, then broadens out in great quiet pools and flows past picturesque towns. A century and a half ago settlers surged west of the Mississippi. Germans stopped at the river bluffs reminiscent of their native land and built neat farmhouses and substantial towns. Inland, on the rolling hills portrayed with surprisingly little exaggeration in the paintings of Iowa's Grant Wood, and in the more open territory to the west, New England and Midwestern Yankees built their characteristic farmhouses, barns, town halls, church spires and small colleges. Railroad builders, headquartered in Chicago, extended their networks of steel rails over the plains and rivers. You can see the stamp of these pioneers today, though the old ethnic folkways have faded and giant barges and riverboat casinos have replaced the old river steamboats; much of this is in the Silos and Smokestacks National Heritage Area. Davenport, on the hills over the Mississippi River still has the look of the city where Ronald Reagan got his first radio job more than 60 years ago; in order to maintain its riverfront heritage, the city has refused to erect flood walls along the Mississippi which brought the ire of FEMA Director Joseph Allbaugh during the April 2001 flood season. German Catholics settled Dubuque, whose giant Victorian courthouse looks down on the Mississippi and up at the Fenelon Place Elevator that rides up the bluff. Farther west is Waterloo, which grew rapidly after 1900 as the John Deere tractor factory expanded and the eight-floor Rath factory became the largest meat-packing plant in the world; Rath closed in 1984 and Deere had thousands of layoffs, but Waterloo has rebounded somewhat with new businesses from telemarketing to a high-tech Iowa Beef Processing (IBP) factory, acquired by Tyson Foods in 2001.

The 1st Congressional District covers much of northeast Iowa, including the Mississippi riverfront from the antique town of McGregor south to Davenport, Iowa's part of the Quad Cities and heading west 100 miles as far as Butler County. There is considerable political variation here. Davenport and next-door Bettendorf were historically Republican, but in 2000 and 2004, like much of eastern Iowa, they voted narrowly for Al Gore and John Kerry. Dubuque, heavily German Catholic, was for years Iowa's most Democratic city, and still is sometimes unless abortion is the issue. But the rural counties along the river and farther west—more German Protestant, Scandinavian and Yankee—were traditionally Republican. Waterloo and Cedar Falls, originally Republican, trended sharply Democratic in the troubled 1980s. Overall this district is pretty evenly balanced and was a key battleground in the 2000 and 2004 presidential races. At one point George W. Bush and John Kerry were campaigning within blocks of each other in Davenport (thieves took advantage of the distraction and robbed three local banks).

The congressman from the 1st District is Jim Nussle, first elected in 1990, at 30 the youngest member of the 102d Congress, and now chairman of the House Budget Committee. Nussle grew up in Chicago, then moved back to his native Iowa to attend a Lutheran college (he is Danish-American and speaks Danish; he has a Great Dane PAC) and law school. In the small town way, he soon became Delaware County attorney, known for prosecuting a local day care employee for child abuse. He coupled his anti-abortion stance with support for helping expectant mothers with the expenses of parenthood. When Republican Congressman Tom Tauke ran for the Senate in 1990, Nussle ran for his seat, narrowly winning the Republican primary and then facing a better-financed Democrat. He won 50%–49%, one of the closest margins in the country that year.

Nussle quickly became one of the leaders of the nascent Republican revolution. He was one of the Gang of Seven, a group of freshman Republican reformers who attacked the Democratic leadership. In October 1991 he made national news by donning a paper bag over his head on the House floor to protest Democratic leaders' refusal to make full disclosure of House bank overdrafts. He voted against agricultural appropriations, to the dismay of senior Iowa Democrats, and moved to cut congressional salaries 5% every year the federal budget is not balanced. For 1992, redistricting put Nussle into a district with Democratic incumbent Dave Nagle. Nagle had represented more of the new district's territory, but Nussle won again by 50%–49%. In 1994 Nagle tried again, and Nussle won more easily, 56%–43%.

After the 1994 election, Speaker Newt Gingrich appointed Nussle chairman of the transition to Republican rule: From paper bag to power in just three years. Nussle froze hiring, demanded detailed accountings, and supervised an overhaul of House administration. He also got a seat on Ways and Means. But Nussle had an unexpectedly tough time of it in the 1996 election. He vastly outspent Democrat Donna Smith, a 17-year Dubuque County supervisor, but she hammered home his closeness to Gingrich, and attacked "Georgia Jim" for supporting big hog feedlots. Nussle won by just 53%–46%.

After that election, Nussle sounded a much less revolutionary note. He was passed over by Gingrich for the chair of the Republicans' campaign committee and in July 1997 he ran for Conference vice chairman against Jennifer Dunn, Gingrich's choice; he lost 129–85.

In July 1999, when John Kasich announced his retirement from the House, Nussle said he would run for Budget chairman. His main competitor was Saxby Chambliss of Georgia, who held the leadership spot on the committee and thought he had a commitment from the leadership. But Majority Leader Dick Armey, who tangled with Chambliss on base closings and peanut subsidies, strongly backed Nussle, and the House leadership picked him in January 2001.

As chairman, Nussle vowed not to pass a phony budget resolution with spending figures so low appropriators would ignore them, and he worked closely with Appropriations members and took care to consult committee Democrats. But he was largely guided by the recommendations of the Bush administration. In the May 2001 budget conference committee, he abandoned the emergency reserve fund that was opposed by appropriators and ruled in violation of the budget law by the Senate parliamentarian. In the conference he got a low budget number, while Senate Budget Chairman Pete Domenici got money allotted for a Medicare reserve fund, health insurance for the uninsured and restoration of Medicare cuts. The House passed the conference report 221–207 in May 2001. In 2002, things were different because the Senate, by now with a Democratic majority, never passed a budget resolution. In the post-election session in November 2002, he exerted his power as Budget chairman when others had agreed to allow states to keep $2.7 billion of children's health insurance money they had not spent; Nussle heard about it at 12:30 a.m. and killed it by 2:00.

When Nussle first became chairman, there was a surplus; but no longer. "You can wake up one day and have a balanced budget, September 10, and then wake up the next day and have everything completely turned around." In 2003 he sought across-the-board spending cuts, but he was quickly shot down. He did insert into the budget resolution a requirement that committees prepare reports on waste and fraud in their programs. In 2004 he prepared a budget resolution that froze non-security-related spending and provided for continuation of the marriage penalty elimination, child tax credit and 10% bracket. When local religious leaders interested in helping AIDS sufferers in Africa complained, he increased international spending from $26.5 billion to $29.3 billion. His resolution passed 215–212 in March, with 10 Republicans voting against. With the concurrence of the Republican leadership, he did not include the pay-as-you-go provision that was in the Senate budget resolution. In conference the Senate insisted on this; Nussle and the House leadership were agreeable to pay-as-you-go for spending, but not for tax cuts. And so there was no budget resolution adopted by both houses. Other Nussle goals were achieved. The

Medicare reimbursement formula was rewritten in the Medicare bill, which he said would give Iowa $438 million more over 10 years. And he got $45 million for the Julien Dubuque Bridge and Southwest Arterial.

Nussle was reelected with 55% of the vote in 1998 and 2000—not large margins for an incumbent. The June 2001 redistricting plan removed the western parts of Nussle's old 2d District and added three counties, two of which he had represented in the early 1990s. But the other—Scott County—was the largest in the new, renumbered 1st District, and included Davenport and Bettendorf, Iowa's half of the bi-state Quad Cities. Scott County was also the home of incumbent Republican Jim Leach, who decided to move to Iowa City and run in the new 2d District. Scott County was also the home base of Nussle's 2002 Democratic opponent, Ann Hutchinson. She appeared to be a strong candidate, and this was a first-tier race for both parties. Hutchinson had been mayor of Bettendorf since 1988; she boasted that she turned a $4 million budget deficit into a $4 million surplus. Just before announcing, she switched her party registration from Republican to Democratic; she said she had registered Republican in 1988 to vote for a friend in a state Senate primary. She accused Nussle of being a Washington insider who voted for big corporate interests and attacked him on prescription drugs and "privatization" of Social Security; he said he was against "privatization" but wanted to add options for savings and investment for younger workers. Nussle won 57%–43% and carried every county, including Scott County by a 56%–44% margin.

As a result, this was not a first-tier race in 2004. Nussle was opposed by Bill Gluba, of Davenport, who had run against Leach in 1982 and 1988. Nussle won by the reduced margin of 55%–43%. Again he carried every county, and in most ran 9% or more ahead of Bush; but he won just 53% in Scott County. During 2004 Nussle made appearances throughout the state, with an eye on running for governor in 2006; Republicans' six-year term limit means he would have to give up the Budget chairmanship in any case. Gluba said he would run in the 1st again. This could very well be a seriously contested district in 2006.

SECOND DISTRICT

Rep. Jim Leach (R)

Elected 1976, 15th term; b. Oct. 15, 1942, Davenport; home, Iowa City; Princeton U., B.A. 1964, Johns Hopkins U., M.A. 1966, London Schl. of Econ., 1966–68; Episcopalian; married (Elisabeth).

Professional Career: Staff Asst., U.S. Rep. Donald Rumsfeld, 1965–66; U.S. Foreign Svc., 1968–69, 1971–72 (Arms Control & Disarmament Agency); A.A. to Dir., U.S. Office of Econ. Opp., 1969–70; Pres., Flamegas Co., 1973–76; Chmn. of the Bd., Adel Wholesalers, Inc., 1973–76; Dir., Fed. Home Loan Bank Bd., Midwest Reg., 1975–76.

DC Office: 2186 RHOB, 20515, 202-225-6576; Fax: 202-226-1278; Web site: www.house.gov/leach.

District Offices: Burlington, 319-754-1106; Cedar Rapids, 319-363-4773; Iowa City, 319-351-0789; Ottumwa, 641-684-4024.

Committees: *Financial Services* (2d of 37 R): Domestic and International Monetary Policy, Trade & Technology. *International Relations* (2d of 27 R): Asia & the Pacific (Chmn.); Western Hemisphere.

Group Ratings

	ADA	ACLU	AFS	LCV	ITIC	NTU	COC	ACU	NTLC	CHC
2004	55	55	50	55	90	37	94	43	57	38
2003	50	—	63	90	—	39	70	40	—	—

National Journal Ratings

	2003 LIB	—	2003 CONS	2004 LIB	—	2004 CONS
Economic	53%	—	46%	51%	—	49%
Social	59%	—	40%	61%	—	38%
Foreign	55%	—	45%	61%	—	39%

Key Votes of the 108th Congress

1. Drilling in ANWR	N	5. DC School Vouchers	N	9. Ban Same-Sex Marriage	N
2. Approve Bush Tax Cuts	N	6. Ban Human Cloning	N	10. Fund Iraq War	Y
3. Medicare/Rx Bill	Y	7. Restrict Gun Liability	Y	11. Bar Cuba Embargo Funds	Y
4. Bar Overtime Pay Regs.	Y	8. Ban Partial-Birth Abortion	Y	12. Intelligence Reorg.	Y

Election Results

2004 general	Jim Leach (R)	176,684	(59%)	($479,605)
	Dave Franker (D)	117,405	(39%)	($122,489)
	Other	5,792	(2%)	
2004 primary	Jim Leach (R)	unopposed		
2002 general	Jim Leach (R)	108,130	(52%)	($780,586)
	Julie Thomas (D)	94,767	(46%)	($1,342,801)
	Other	4,274	(2%)	

Prior Winning Percentages: 2000 (62%); 1998 (57%); 1996 (53%); 1994 (60%); 1992 (68%); 1990 (100%); 1988 (61%); 1986 (66%); 1984 (67%); 1982 (59%); 1980 (64%); 1978 (64%); 1976 (52%)

The People		Race/Ethnic Origin	Ancestry		
Area size:	7,684 sq. mi.	92.4% White	German: 24.0%	Irish: 10.4%	
Urban population:	66.0%	2.0% Black	English: 7.3%		
Rural population:	34.0%	1.5% Asian	**2004 Presidential Vote**		
Pop. 2000:	585,241	0.2% Native Am.	Kerry (D)	171,561	(55%)
Median income:	$40,121	0.0% Hawaiian	Bush (R)	135,991	(44%)
Poverty status:	9.9%	1.0% Two+ races	Other	3,090	(1%)
Military veterans:	13.0%	0.1% Other	**2000 Presidential Vote**		
		2.7% Hispanic Origin	Gore (D)	141,487	(53%)
			Bush (R)	113,255	(43%)
			Other	11,581	(4%)
			Cook Partisan Voting Index: D + 7		

Occupation	Blue collar: 26.5%	White collar: 58.6%	Gray collar: 14.9%

Eastern Iowa is a land little known to outsiders. It is a land of rolling hills and deep river valleys, of undulant farm fields and big skies, of prosperous small towns and grain elevators and factories. Even political writers, who come to Iowa by the thousands for the quadrennial precinct caucuses tend to hang out in Des Moines and to do their reporting there or in small counties within an hour's drive; this is a lot bigger state than New Hampshire, and driving from Des Moines east to the second largest city, Cedar Rapids, takes more than two hours—only worth it for some major event. Eastern Iowa was not accessible even to candidate George W. Bush in 2000, since his campaign plane was too big to land in any of the airports here. So Al Gore ran well in eastern Iowa—it was one of the few parts of the country where he carried most rural counties— and carried the state by 4,000 votes. But by 2004 a local airline runway had been extended and George W. Bush improved his showing enough to carry Iowa by 10,000 votes.

Cedar Rapids, the metropolis in these parts, has high-tech employers and contemporary office buildings; it boomed in the 1990s, and per capita income, adjusted for the local cost of living, is among the nation's highest. Yet traditional industries still make themselves known: Go down by the river and you can't miss the smell of burnt oats coming from the Quaker Oats factory. Nearby Coralville is building a $180 million indoor rain forest; Congress voted $50 million for it in January 2004. More controversial is the proposal to build a Muslim youth camp behind the Coralville reservoir. Iowa City, just to the south, is a university town complete with trendy bookstores and vegetarian eateries; the University of Iowa is known for its Writer's Workshop. Travel farther afield, and you will come on increasing oddities. Rural Cedar County, the birthplace of Herbert Hoover, reported a tie on election night 2000, the only county in the nation to do so; a recount gave Al Gore a 4,033–4,031 vote lead. In 2004 George W. Bush carried it 4,869–4,747—a 122-vote landslide. Bentonsport, in Van Buren County near the Missouri border, was mostly bought up by the county's conservation board in the 1970s, and restored; now it is an artists' and craftsmen's colony. Conesville, in Muscatine County near the Mississippi, has an Hispanic majority—the only city in Iowa that does—attracted at first by farm work in the fields and more recently by the IBP plant in nearby Columbus Junction. Anamosa, in Jones County just east of Cedar Rapids, features the house painted by Anamosa native Grant Wood in *American Gothic*—the models for the two figures were his dentist and his sister, who died only in 1990—and you can have your picture taken there too. The oddest of all is Iowa's newest city, incorporated in 2001, Vedic City. It's just outside Fairfield, in Jefferson County, where followers of the Maharishi Mahesh Yogi built Maharishi University in 1973, where believers in transcendental meditation study and meditate and practice yogic flying (the first step is hopping around). There's a political angle too: TM followers supported John Hagelin of the Natural Law party for president in 1996, and he won 21% of the vote in Jefferson County in 1996 and 15% in 2000. Hagelin didn't run in 2004 and his votes evidently went to John Kerry, who carried the county.

All these parts of eastern Iowa are in the state's 2d Congressional District. It is by most measures Iowa's most Democratic congressional district, thanks in large part to big Democratic majorities in Iowa City's Johnson County; Cedar Rapids's Linn County has also been inclined toward the Democrats in recent years.

The congressman from the 2d District is, however, a Republican, Jim Leach, first elected in 1976, and chairman of the House Banking Committee from 1995 to 2001. Leach grew up in Davenport, where his family owned propane gas and wholesale businesses. He has a bipartisan political heritage: a great-grandfather was president of a Republican state Senate, and a Democratic grandfather was head of the Iowa branch of the WPA in the 1930s and hired Grant Wood to paint murals. Leach graduated from Princeton, studied Soviet politics at Johns Hopkins and the London School of Economics. He worked for Donald Rumsfeld in his House office in 1965–66 and at the Office of Economic Opportunity in 1969–70 (like Rumsfeld he wrestled at Princeton). In between he became a Foreign Service officer in 1968, then was assigned to the Arms Control and Disarmament Agency and served in the United Nations when George Bush was U.S. ambassador there. In 1973, Leach resigned after Richard Nixon fired special prosecutor Archibald Cox and returned to the family businesses in Davenport. In 1974 he ran for the House against incumbent Democrat Edward Mezvinsky and in that Democratic year lost by only a 54%–46% margin. In 1976 he ran again and beat Mezvinsky 52%–48%. A believer in free enterprise with hands-on experience in a regulated business, Leach remains market-oriented on most economic issues. But he is leery of tax cuts: he was the only Republican to vote against the May 2003 Bush tax cuts. On cultural issues, he looks with favor on international family planning and abortion rights. On foreign policy, like many Iowa Republicans, he has shown caution about asserting U.S. military power, but supported the Gulf War resolution in 1991 and continued deployment of troops in Bosnia in 1997. He voted against the Iraq war resolution in October 2002, one of six House Republicans to do so; he said his major concern was the possible use of Iraq's biological weapons.

On the Banking Committee (now Financial Services), Leach was one of the few who predicted the S&L crisis of the late 1980s: He warned early on that allowing the states to liberate their savings and loans from investment limits while maintaining federal deposit insurance and not increasing capital requirements would lead to trouble. His greatest achievement was the November 1999 passage of financial services deregulation, tearing down the 1933 Glass-Steagall Act wall between commercial and investment banks, authorizing financial holding companies and allowing them to own insurance companies. This bill was the focus of most of his chairmanship; his efforts were blocked by the insurance industry in 1996 and his bill was yanked from the floor by the leadership in March 1998. House Republicans impose a six-year limit on committee chairmanships, and so Leach lost the Banking Committee chair in January 2001. He remains a senior member, and one concerned about government-sponsored enterprises Fannie Mae and Freddie Mac. "Full privatization is a bit radical, particularly for the moment," he said in October 2004. But he added, "If they are to maintain a privileged position in the market, it must be made clear that their obligations to the public trust must come first."

Since 2001 Leach has been chairman of what is now the Asia and the Pacific Subcommittee of International Relations, on which he had been ranking minority member from 1985 to 1993. In 2001, he took care to warn Chinese officials that the United States would worry about China's intentions toward Taiwan as long as it kept missiles aimed there. But he and Henry Hyde opposed conservatives who wanted to bring up the Taiwan Security Enhancement Act that passed the House but not the Senate in 2000; they argued that Taiwan could depend on George W. Bush to protect its interests. On Iraq he said in November 2004, "The United States now is obligated to try to make things better in Iraq and we can't leave without making them better." But in a lecture at Iowa State University in October 2004 he seemed to be criticizing the Bush administration. "At this time in history pride is more dangerous than greed. In shunning embarrassment, politicians refuse to acknowledge errors, either explicitly with words or implicitly through policy adjustments." He has argued for restraint in dealing with Iran. In 2004 Leach was a major supporter of the North Korea Human Rights Act and the Comprehensive Peace in Sudan Act. He decried the terrorism of the Tamil Tigers in Sri Lanka before the Boxing Day tsunami directed world attention to that country. With Lynn Woolsey and Todd Platts he moved to keep open the National War College's Peacekeeping Institute. Leach is in line to become chairman of the International Relations Committee after the 2006 election, provided he is reelected and Republicans maintain their majority.

At home, Iowa's much-praised nonpartisan redistricting system put Leach in jeopardy of losing his seat in 2002. He had won without difficulty from 1978 to 1994, and his one serious challenge came in 1996, after the Whitewater hearings, when Bill Clinton juiced up a campaign by a former state senator who held Leach to a 53%–46% win. The 2001 redistricting plan sliced up his district and forced Leach to make a tough choice: He could either run in the new 1st District, which included Scott County, his home and the county that supplied almost all of his victory margin in 1996, or he could run in the new 2d District, where over half the votes were cast in Johnson and Linn Counties (Iowa City and Cedar Rapids) which Leach lost in 1996. Leach decided to run in the 2d, which contained more of his old district than the new 1st, and, characteristically, sold his house in Davenport and bought one in Iowa City, which he calls "the cultural heartbeat of the state."

Leach attracted a formidable opponent, Julie Thomas, a Cedar Rapids pediatrician since 1974 who had lobbied state legislators on laws like the one banning drive-by deliveries. She said she decided to run because Leach wouldn't endorse universal health care coverage for children. Thomas ran an aggressive, politically savvy campaign, on what were standard Democratic themes in 2002: against "privatization" of Social Security, for a prescription drug benefit under Medicare, for reimportation of drugs from Canada, against trade promotion authority, against tort reform (which earned her the opposition of the American Medical Association PAC). She far outraised Leach—ultimately by $1.3 million to $780,000 (Leach refuses to accept contributions from PACs or from contributors outside Iowa). This was Al Gore's best Iowa district, and to Democrats she argued: Vote for a real Democrat.

Lack of money forced Leach to pull ads off the air during the summer, while Thomas was able to keep them coming. "We've almost reversed roles. I'm running the challenger's campaign. I go to all the events. I'm everywhere. She spends most of her time on the telephone, what Democrats call dialing for dollars. It's smart politics. I just happen to be uncomfortable with it. I'm confident I'll be the most outspent Republican incumbent." But Leach was assisted by the spending of others, for whom this was a top tier race. The League of Conservation Voters, appreciative of his environmental record, spent $200,000 on ads to help him. He had the endorsements of the Iowa State Education Association, the Iowa Farm Bureau Federation and the Human Rights Campaign—not groups usually found in the same room. In September 2002, Leach took to the floor of the House and denounced the nationalization of campaigns, and went over to NRCC chairman Tom Davis and asked him not to buy ads in his district. "I think he looked at me as if I'm naive," Leach said later; the campaign committee, seeing polls that showed Leach's early wide leads narrowing, spent money on anti-Thomas ads all through October.

This turned out to be the closest House race in a state with much more than its national share of close races that year. Leach won 52%–46%. He carried Linn County, Thomas's home base, by 52%–46% and Johnson County by 51%–48%. Thomas carried industrial Ottumwa and Fort Madison and Keokuk on the lower Mississippi River. In 2004 Democrats did not target the district, and Leach won 59%–39%, carrying every county.

THIRD DISTRICT

Rep. Leonard Boswell (D)

Elected 1996, 5th term; b. Jan. 10, 1934, Harrison Cnty., MO; home, Davis City; Graceland Col., B.A. 1969; Reorganized Latter Day Saints; married (Dody).

Military Career: Army, 1956–76 (Vietnam).

Elected Office: IA Senate, 1984–96, Pres., 1992–96.

Professional Career: Farmer.

DC Office: 1427 LHOB, 20515, 202-225-3806; Fax: 202-225-5608; Web site: www.house.gov/boswell.

District Office: Des Moines, 515-282-1909.

Committees: *Agriculture* (18th of 21 D): General Farm Commodities & Risk Management; Livestock & Horticulture. *Permanent Select Committee on Intelligence* (4th of 9 D): Terrorism, Human Intelligence, Analysis & Counterintelligence (RMM). *Transportation & Infrastructure* (17th of 34 D): Aviation; Railroads.

Group Ratings

	ADA	ACLU	AFS	LCV	ITIC	NTU	COC	ACU	NTLC	CHC
2004	80	60	88	55	90	17	55	20	14	38
2003	80	—	100	70	—	24	45	27	—	—

National Journal Ratings

	2003 LIB	—	2003 CONS		2004 LIB	—	2004 CONS
Economic	61%	—	38%		57%	—	42%
Social	61%	—	38%		62%	—	37%
Foreign	66%	—	32%		53%	—	46%

Key Votes of the 108th Congress

1. Drilling in ANWR	N	5. DC School Vouchers	N	9. Ban Same-Sex Marriage	N
2. Approve Bush Tax Cuts	N	6. Ban Human Cloning	N	10. Fund Iraq War	N
3. Medicare/Rx Bill	N	7. Restrict Gun Liability	Y	11. Bar Cuba Embargo Funds	Y
4. Bar Overtime Pay Regs.	Y	8. Ban Partial-Birth Abortion	Y	12. Intelligence Reorg.	Y

Election Results

2004 general	Leonard Boswell (D)	168,007	(55%)	($1,545,133)
	Stan Thompson (R)	136,099	(45%)	($862,304)
2004 primary	Leonard Boswell (D)	unopposed		
2002 general	Leonard Boswell (D)	115,367	(53%)	($1,316,037)
	Stan Thompson (R)	97,285	(45%)	($895,163)
	Other	3,333	(2%)	

Prior Winning Percentages: 2000 (63%); 1998 (57%); 1996 (49%)

The People		Race/Ethnic Origin	Ancestry	
Area size:	7,034 sq. mi.	90.1% White	German: 20.7%	Irish: 9.6%
Urban population:	73.1%	3.2% Black	English: 7.7%	
Rural population:	26.9%	1.9% Asian	**2004 Presidential Vote**	
Pop. 2000:	585,305	0.4% Native Am.	Bush (R) 154,919	(50%)
Median income:	$43,176	0.0% Hawaiian	Kerry (D) 154,652	(50%)
Poverty status:	8.0%	1.1% Two+ races	Other 2,443	(1%)
Military veterans:	12.7%	0.1% Other	**2000 Presidential Vote**	
		3.2% Hispanic Origin	Gore (D) 132,890	(49%)
			Bush (R) 131,319	(48%)
			Other 7,226	(3%)
			Cook Partisan Voting Index: D + 1	

Occupation   Blue collar: 23.5%   White collar: 62.0%   Gray collar: 14.5%

Iowa, which today seems very much in the middle of the country, was once part of the West. It was not only the home of sober farmers and pious burghers, but also the eastern terminus of the first Transcontinental Railroad, a way stop for people in a hurry to get across the Great Plains to the Rockies and the Pacific Northwest. Those who stayed behind were determined to use the wealth accumulated by methodical husbandry of their fertile farmlands to implant firmly the glories of Western civilization. You can feel that impulse today in Des Moines when you look across the river from downtown at the Victorian Capitol, its gold dome above a Corinthian pediment, or Terrace Hill, the beautifully restored governor's mansion, atop a hill overlooking the Raccoon River. The nearby Living History Farms, which recreate Indian villages, frontier towns and turn-of-the-century farms, show the effort the new settlers made to put their imprint on the environment.

The 3d Congressional District covers 12 counties in central Iowa, including Des Moines's Polk County and extends mostly to the east. It is the only Iowa district that does not border another state or a mighty river on the east or west. Some 65% of its votes are cast in Polk County, but it does not include Dallas or Warren Counties which are in the Des Moines metropolitan area. Des Moines remains classically Middle America, even as it spreads into the countryside and even as Iowa farm counties' population continues to decline. The area has become a sanctuary for people from around the nation who are seeking a family-friendly urban life style. Insurance, agricultural supply, and printing and service businesses are expanding in office centers downtown and at freeway interchanges; Iowans are driving 100 miles or more to fill the shopping malls at cities' edges. Plans to bring a riverboat casino to Des Moines were scuttled when a suburban casino agreed to pay $13 million to the city. The remainder of the district is largely rural, with no city larger than 30,000. But these small towns continue to house some giant manufacturing plants. Pella (9,800) is the home of the Pella window and door maker, which employs 3,000 workers. The famed Amana colonies, which were founded in 1855 by the Community of True Inspiration, German pietists who have retained many of their old customs, is the home of the Amana appliance business; in 2001, Newton (population 15,000) appliance-maker Maytag acquired Amana in a marriage of two of the state's largest manufacturers. Polk County has historically voted Democratic, but has become more Republican as its white collar businesses grow and its blue collar businesses fade; the rural counties here have mostly been historically Republican. The result is a district split right down the middle, about as evenly divided as any in the nation: 49%–48% for Al Gore in 2000, 49.7%–49.6% for George W. Bush in 2004.

The congressman from the 3d District is Leonard Boswell, a Democrat first elected in 1996, the only new Iowa Democrat elected to the House since 1986. He is not the stereotypical Democrat, however. Boswell grew up on farms in Ringgold and Decatur Counties, near the Missouri border. He was drafted in 1956, at 22, and was a private in the Army. He re-enlisted, graduated first in his class in both fixed wing and helicopter flying school, served two years in Vietnam, and retired as a lieutenant colonel in 1976; he was a teacher at the Army command college at Fort Leavenworth, Kansas. Boswell settled down on his Decatur County farm and became head of the local Farmers' Co-op. He managed to keep it out of bankruptcy during the farm depression of the 1980s and decided to go into politics. He was elected state senator from a six-county Republican district in 1984, served as chairman of Appropriations and, after 1992, Senate president; he was the Democratic nominee for lieutenant governor in 1994.

In 1996, Boswell ran for an open seat in the old 3d District, whose Republican congressman was running against Senator Tom Harkin. The district was largely rural and extended across the southern tier of Iowa from the Mississippi River to within one county of the Missouri. Boswell flew his four-seater Piper Comanche 250 around the district and called for balancing the budget, higher education aid and protections against Medicare reductions, all to be financed with Pentagon cuts and elimination of Medicare waste. Poweshiek County attorney Mike Mahaffey ran as a moderate Republican. Boswell was endorsed by the Farm Bureau, which usually backs Republicans. He raised more money than Mahaffey and, like other Democrats, ran ads attacking Newt Gingrich and the Republican Medicare plan. The result was a 49%–48% Boswell victory.

Boswell got a seat on Agriculture and, amid dropping farm prices, continued to support the Freedom to Farm Act. Along with all of the delegation's Republicans, he voted for normal trade relations with China, the world's biggest market for pork. His voting record has consistently placed him in the most conservative quadrant of House Democrats. Focusing on health care, he has called for expanded tax breaks for insurance coverage. Assigned to the Intelligence Committee, his extensive military background and security clearance left him well positioned to investigate the nation's response to terrorism. He voted to authorize military action in Iraq, but later criticized the Bush administration for not spending enough money for counter-terrorism.

The non-partisan June 2001 redistricting plan drawn by the Legislative Service Bureau left Boswell with a dilemma. Only seven of the 27 counties and 24% from the population in his former district were moved to the new 3d District. Decatur County was one of eight counties moved to western Iowa's new, heavily Republican 5th District. The other option was to move to the new 2d District, which leans Democratic but where he would have faced a tough contest against incumbent Republican Jim Leach. Boswell decided to move to Des Moines and run in the 3d. But Democratic state Senator Matt McCoy had already said he would run in the Polk County district; local fundraising events for Boswell by Minority Leader Dick Gephardt eventually convinced him to defer. Republican challenger Stan Thompson was less accommodating. A Des Moines lawyer who worked for George W. Bush in the 2000 Iowa caucuses, Thompson argued that Boswell was out of step with the new district's geography and philosophy. He cited the incumbent's votes against Bush's tax bill and trade promotion authority. Thompson ran a credible campaign and won several endorsements, including a joint designation with Boswell from the Farm Bureau. Boswell won by a 53%–45% margin.

After that election, Boswell said that he would break his pledge to limit himself to four terms. "I made a mistake," he explained to the *Des Moines Register*. "It seemed like sort of the popular thing, and I was O.K. with it." Thompson challenged him again. "It's time we elect a congressman who is on the way up and not one on the way out," he said. Boswell criticized Thompson as beholden to House Republican leaders. Although he did not endorse Howard Dean for the 2004 presidential nomination, Dean's campaign raised $70,000 for Boswell. In departures from the 2002 campaign, Thompson won endorsements from the Iowa Farm Bureau and from the *Register*, which praised his energy and job-creating proposals, and said that Boswell had become "almost so low-key he is no longer heard." This time, Boswell won 55%–45% and carried Polk County 57%–43%.

FOURTH DISTRICT

Rep. Tom Latham (R)

Elected 1994, 6th term; b. July 14, 1948, Hampton; home, Alexander; Wartburg Col., 1966–67, IA St. U., 1967–70; Lutheran; married (Kathy).

Professional Career: Farmer; Bank Teller/Bookkeeper, 1970–72; Independent Insurance Agent, 1972–74; Hartford Insurance Mktg. Rep., 1974–76; Co-Owner, Latham Seed Co., 1976–present.

DC Office: 2447 RHOB, 20515, 202-225-5476; Fax: 202-225-3301; Web site: www.tomlatham.gov.

District Offices: Ames, 515-232-2885; Clear Lake, 641-357-5225; Fort Dodge, 515-573-2738.

Committees: *Appropriations* (19th of 37 R): Agriculture, Rural Development, FDA & Related Agencies; Energy & Water Development & Related Agencies; Homeland Security.

Group Ratings

	ADA	ACLU	AFS	LCV	ITIC	NTU	COC	ACU	NTLC	CHC
2004	10	5	13	9	100	49	100	72	70	92
2003	5	—	13	5	—	57	97	88	—	—

National Journal Ratings

	2003 LIB	—	2003 CONS		2004 LIB	—	2004 CONS
Economic	33%	—	64%		37%	—	62%
Social	17%	—	79%		36%	—	61%
Foreign	40%	—	58%		49%	—	51%

Key Votes of the 108th Congress

1. Drilling in ANWR	Y	5. DC School Vouchers	Y	9. Ban Same-Sex Marriage	Y
2. Approve Bush Tax Cuts	Y	6. Ban Human Cloning	Y	10. Fund Iraq War	Y
3. Medicare/Rx Bill	Y	7. Restrict Gun Liability	Y	11. Bar Cuba Embargo Funds	Y
4. Bar Overtime Pay Regs.	N	8. Ban Partial-Birth Abortion	Y	12. Intelligence Reorg.	Y

Election Results

2004 general	Tom Latham (R)	181,294	(61%)	($988,369)
	Paul Johnson (D)	116,121	(39%)	($287,843)
	Other	151	(0%)	
2004 primary	Tom Latham (R)	unopposed		
2002 general	Tom Latham (R)	115,430	(55%)	($1,546,043)
	John Norris (D)	90,784	(43%)	($1,258,631)
	Other	7,512	(3%)	

Prior Winning Percentages: 2000 (69%); 1998 (100%); 1996 (65%); 1994 (61%)

The People		Race/Ethnic Origin	Ancestry	
Area size:	15,833 sq. mi.	94.7% White	German: 27.1%	Norwegian: 9.1%
Urban population:	50.5%	0.8% Black	Irish: 8.9%	
Rural population:	49.5%	1.1% Asian	**2004 Presidential Vote**	
Pop. 2000:	585,305	0.2% Native Am.	Bush (R) 155,587	(51%)
Median income:	$38,242	0.0% Hawaiian	Kerry (D) 148,331	(48%)
Poverty status:	8.9%	0.6% Two+ races	Other 2,711	(1%)
Military veterans:	13.1%	0.1% Other	**2000 Presidential Vote**	
		2.5% Hispanic Origin	Bush (R) 131,391	(49%)
			Gore (D) 129,280	(48%)
			Other 8,506	(3%)
			Cook Partisan Voting Index: D + 0	
Occupation Blue collar: 27.2%	White collar: 56.2%	Gray collar: 16.6%		

Central Iowa is where the Great Plains begin—a land of farm fields marked off by straight roads every mile and rolling slightly upward to the west, punctuated by occasional crossroads towns and grain elevators, with a sky that seems to fill the eyes. Pioneers coming here in the 1840s and 1850s found prairie grass whose roots were two feet thick and girded trees with grubbing machines that cut off their roots below ground. Central Iowa has some of the world's most productive soil, and it has also had some of its most productive and creative agricultural scientists and farmers. A monument to one of them is the 12-foot statue of Norman Borlaug in his home town of Cresco, in Howard County near the Minnesota border, by Karen Novak, another Cresco native. This is long-settled land now, and Iowans' productivity means that there are fewer people living here on farms than there were 50 and 100 years ago. But its towns and small cities remain centers of creativity. One is Ames, in Story County, home of Iowa State University, and home of Iowa Republicans' straw poll that has launched several Republican presidential contests. Ames is part of the growth zone around Des Moines, 30 miles south; so is Boone County to the west. Directly west of Des Moines and its most affluent suburbs is Dallas County, the fastest-growing county in Iowa in the 1990s. To the south is Madison County, famous for the wooden covered bridges that gave their name to a best-selling novel and movie; in 2002 one of the bridges caught fire and burned, and so now there are only five left. Toward the north is Mason City, the boyhood home of *The Music Man* author Meredith Wilson. Algona in rural Kossuth County opened a museum with a replica of the prisoner of war camp that housed more than 10,000 Germans during World War II. In nearby Winnebago County is Winnebago Industries, which manufactures motor homes and recreation vehicles on computer-controlled assembly lines with robotic equipment; the main factory in Forest City employs more than 3,000 workers.

The 4th Congressional District includes all these parts of central and northern Iowa. Drawn by the Legislative Service Bureau and approved by the legislature and governor, the 4th District covers 28 counties. It does not include Des Moines, but counties around Des Moines cast more than one-third of its votes. Like Iowa, the 4th District is closely divided politically: George W. Bush carried the district 49%–48% in 2000 and 51%–48% in 2004.

The congressman from the 4th District is Tom Latham, a Republican first elected in 1994. Latham grew up on a farm in Franklin County, near Alexander (population 165) where his family has owned a seed company—a very Iowa business—since 1947. For years Latham was active in Republican politics, attending the national convention and serving as a farm adviser to Congressman Fred Grandy. In 1994 Grandy ran against Governor Terry Branstad and lost a close primary, and Latham ran for the House. His Democratic opponent Sheila McGuire had been one of 47 health care professionals to sit on an advisory panel for Hillary Rodham Clinton's health care plan; Latham opposed it. He won 61%–39%.

In the House, Latham has a moderately conservative record and has usually been a quiet member who avoids the national spotlight. He has pursued local interests on the Appropriations Committee and its Agriculture Subcommittee. With the support of independent producers seeking fair pricing, he won a requirement that packers report prices they pay for livestock. He strongly opposed legislation to permit states to allow physician-assisted suicide. He talked of his 87-year-old father who has Alzheimer's disease and said, "We could question what the value of that life is, but to my mother . . . that is her life every day, is to go to the home, visit my father, and there is extraordinary quality there." Latham has generally supported the Bush administration. On behalf of manufacturers of lightweight trailers, he sought an exemption from federal reporting rules pertaining to recalls. In November 2004, he criticized the Senate Appropriations Committee, where Tom Harkin is a senior Democrat, for reducing funds needed to complete the National Animal Disease Center in Ames, which he described as essential to "agro-terrorism" prevention.

Redistricting split Latham's old 5th District between the new 4th and 5th, and he chose to run in the 4th, which includes his home in Franklin County, rather than in the 5th, which is much more Republican. The result was his first competitive campaign since he was elected. Latham had not been an active fundraiser and Democrats targeted the race. Their nominee was John Norris, former chief of staff to Governor Tom Vilsack and, in 2003 and 2004, John Kerry's Iowa manager in the precinct caucuses. Norris talked about jobs, education and Social Security and sounded the theme of working hard for "Iowa's working families;" he attacked Latham for supporting Republican positions on taxes and health care. He was an aggressive campaigner and raised more than $1 million. But Latham won by a relatively comfortable 55%–43%, winning all 28 counties—though, only by 9 votes in Ames's Story County, which cast the most votes. Angry at Latham's negative ads, Norris refused to make the customary election-night concession call to Latham. Latham responded that Norris attacked him from the start, and forced him to respond. In 2004 Latham won 61%–39% over a farmer and former legislator.

Latham has been mentioned as a possible statewide candidate. If he does not seek reelection, the 4th District will likely be seriously contested again.

FIFTH DISTRICT

Rep. Steve King (R)

Elected 2002, 2d term; b. May 28, 1949, Storm Lake; home, Kiron; NW MO St. U., 1967–70; Catholic; married (Marilyn).

Elected Office: IA Senate, 1996–2002.

Professional Career: Construction co. owner, 1975–2002.

DC Office: 1432 LHOB, 20515, 202-225-4426; Fax: 202-225-3193; Web site: www.house.gov/steveking.

District Offices: Council Bluffs, 712-325-1404; Sioux City, 712-224-4692; Storm Lake, 712-732-4197.

Committees: *Agriculture* (16th of 25 R): Conservation, Credit, Rural Development & Research; General Farm Commodities & Risk Management; Livestock & Horticulture. *Judiciary* (20th of 23 R): Immigration, Border Security & Claims; The Constitution. *Small Business* (10th of 18 R): Regulatory Reform & Oversight; Rural Enterprises, Agriculture & Technology.

Group Ratings

	ADA	ACLU	AFS	LCV	ITIC	NTU	COC	ACU	NTLC	CHC
2004	5	0	0	0	90	78	100	96	97	100
2003	10	—	0	10	—	64	96	92	—	—

National Journal Ratings

	2003 LIB	—	2003 CONS		2004 LIB	—	2004 CONS
Economic	21%	—	79%		9%	—	88%
Social	21%	—	78%		0%	—	91%
Foreign	0%	—	89%		10%	—	86%

Key Votes of the 108th Congress

1. Drilling in ANWR	N	5. DC School Vouchers	Y	9. Ban Same-Sex Marriage	Y
2. Approve Bush Tax Cuts	Y	6. Ban Human Cloning	Y	10. Fund Iraq War	Y
3. Medicare/Rx Bill	Y	7. Restrict Gun Liability	Y	11. Bar Cuba Embargo Funds	N
4. Bar Overtime Pay Regs.	N	8. Ban Partial-Birth Abortion	Y	12. Intelligence Reorg.	Y

Election Results

2004 general	Steve King (R)	168,583	(63%)	($553,171)
	Joyce Schulte (D)	97,597	(37%)	($59,976)
2004 primary	Steve King (R)	unopposed		
2002 general	Steve King (R)	113,257	(62%)	($650,612)
	Paul Shomshor (D)	68,853	(38%)	($91,855)

The People		Race/Ethnic Origin	Ancestry	
Area size:	18,429 sq. mi.	93.7% White	German: 26.8%	Irish: 9.2%
Urban population:	49.4%	0.6% Black	English: 6.7%	
Rural population:	50.6%	0.9% Asian	**2004 Presidential Vote**	
Pop. 2000:	585,171	0.4% Native Am.	Bush (R) 167,387	(60%)
Median income:	$36,773	0.0% Hawaiian	Kerry (D) 109,974	(39%)
Poverty status:	8.9%	0.7% Two+ races	Other 2,428	(1%)
Military veterans:	14.0%	0.0% Other	**2000 Presidential Vote**	
		3.6% Hispanic Origin	Bush (R) 141,820	(57%)
			Gore (D) 99,004	(40%)
			Other 7,623	(3%)
			Cook Partisan Voting Index: R + 8	

Occupation	Blue collar: 29.5%	White collar: 53.3%	Gray collar: 17.2%

Sioux City, one of the oldest market towns on the Great Plains, is situated picturesquely, nestled below and running up the loess bluffs above the Missouri River. Although still the largest city on the Plains west of Des Moines and north of Omaha, Sioux City has not grown much in the past five decades. Its original economic base has become obsolete, and so has some of the city itself: The waterfront, once raucous with boatmen and stockyard workers, is now quiet; the downtown stores have been replaced by shopping malls at the edge of town where people still spend a day doing a season's shopping and then drive for hours back home. The stockyards, which employed thousands and slaughtered millions of hogs during their peak years in the 1920s, have closed. But there are still many hogs in western Iowa, more than anywhere else in the nation. Instead of meeting sellers in the markets of the Sioux City stockyard, packers now contract directly with large farms and build their modern slaughterhouses nearby; Tyson Foods has facilities in Buena Vista and Crawford Counties.

Sioux City is the largest city in the 5th Congressional District of Iowa, which covers the western part of the state from Minnesota to Missouri. This is the state's largest congressional district, the one with the most 4-H members and the nation's top hog-and-pig producing district. The 2001 redistricting removed 15 counties centered around Fort Dodge and added 17 counties centered around Council Bluffs; the shift moved incumbent Tom Latham's home to the new 4th District, and he decided to run there. Council Bluffs houses the mansion of General Grenville Dodge, who in 1859 lobbied Illinois lawyer Abraham Lincoln on the need for a transcontinental railroad; Lincoln got it through Congress in 1863, Dodge became its chief engineer, and the city became its eastern terminus when it was completed in 1869. Surrounded by beef grazing territory, where federal intrusion has long been resented, Council Bluffs looks west across the Missouri River to Omaha, taking on the culturally more conservative tone of Nebraska and the conservative politics of the *Omaha World-Herald*. In Crawford County, Denison houses the Donna Reed Heritage Museum that commemorates the former Hollywood film-star and middle-America mom. This is by far the most Republican district in Iowa and George W. Bush twice carried it by wide margins.

The congressman from the 5th District is Steve King, a Republican who won the open seat in 2002. He was born in Storm Lake in western Iowa and attended Northwest Missouri State University. He founded the King Construction Company in 1975. He began his political career in 1996, at 47, when he was elected to the state Senate where he quickly gained a reputation as a conservative's conservative. He opposed abortion, racial quotas and preferences and same-sex marriage. He sponsored Iowa's "God and Country" bill, which would require Iowa schools to recognize that the United States "has derived its strength from biblical values," and was a driving force behind the state's English-only law. In 2000, King filed suit to repeal Governor Tom Vilsack's executive order banning workplace discrimination based on sexual orientation. On economic matters, King was just as resolute. He supported repeal of the state's inheritance tax, backed a 15% state income tax reduction and a national right-to-work law.

In 2002 there were four main contenders in the Republican primary. King ran as a strong conservative and the only rural candidate and called for limiting federal control over local schools. King led in the June primary with 30% of the vote. Because nobody received the required 35% of the primary vote, the nomination was determined by a special party convention three weeks later. The 533 voting delegates needed three ballots to select a winner. King led on each ballot and defeated House Speaker Brent Siegrist of Council Bluffs 272–253 in the final round, marking the first time in 38 years that Iowans used a convention to select a congressional nominee. The general election outcome was never in doubt. Democrat Paul Shomshor attempted to paint King as too conservative for the district, and won the endorsement of the *Omaha World-Herald*—perhaps because his home city of Council Bluffs had not elected a member to Congress since the 1920s—but he fell far short, 62%–38%. *National Review* called King the "Great Right Hope."

In the House, King has a firmly conservative record and became the most conservative member of the Iowa delegation, but he did not emerge as the outspoken leader that some had expected. He voted for the 2003 Medicare/prescription drug bill, which contained higher Medicare reimbursement rates for Iowa. He characterized the revelations of abuse of Iraqi prisoners at Abu Ghraib as "hazing," especially compared to abuses suffered by Americans in Iraq. The House defeated his amendment to limit the United States contribution to the United Nations to the largest assessment of any other Security Council member. He also was turned down on his amendment to fund Justice Department enforcement of a 1996 law that forbids localities from preventing police officers from reporting immigration information to the federal government. On local issues, he called for expansion of "value-added agriculture," including biotechnology and ethanol, to strengthen the local economy. He joined Christian conservatives who demanded that the Iowa Supreme Court display a donated copy of the Ten Commandments. He listed his top local projects as the dredging of Storm Lake and expanding Highway 20 to a four-lane road from near Storm Lake to Sioux City. "I told my wife I don't get to die until they're done," King said of the two projects.

In November 2004 he carried all but one small county and won 63%–37% over a Democrat who said King's comments on Abu Ghraib and immigration policy "embarrass" Iowa.

★ KANSAS ★

What's the Matter With Kansas? is the title of a 2004 bestseller by Kansas native Thomas Frank. His argument is that Kansas's economy is in sharp decline but that Kansas voters have been hornswoggled into voting against their economic interests by big business operatives operating undercover through Christian evangelists. Never mind that Frank's home town, which he cites as evidence of economic decline, is in Johnson County, economically booming suburban country just west of Kansas City, Missouri, and that Kansas's unemployment rate has been well below the national average; and never mind that it's arguable whether government spending programs help low income people. Frank might as well complain about rich people on the Upper East Side of New York voting against their economic interests by opposing candidates who would cut their high taxes. Kansans, like Upper East Siders, are entitled to vote on whatever basis they want, and if their views on cultural issues trump their short-term economic interest, as they do in both cases, they still are entitled to be respected as rational decision-makers, however misguided you might think they are. It's their decision.

Frank has a better point when he says, "Kansas may be the land of averageness, but it is a freaky, militant, outraged averageness." For the history of seemingly placid Kansas—it actually is flatter than a pancake, geographers announced in 2004 after comparing its geography to an IHOP product—has been punctuated by uprisings, intellectual and violent, by moments of anger and rage sweeping through the tall sheaves like a tornado wind. Kansas literally began in a moment of violence, the Bleeding Kansas of the 1850s that led proximately to the terrible war that split the whole nation. The trigger was the Kansas-Nebraska Act of 1854, which left to local settlers the question of whether this new Kansas Territory would be a free or slave state. Pro-slavery "bushwhackers" rode over the line from Missouri, stealing elections and writing a pro-slavery constitution. But much larger numbers of free-soil "jayhawkers" from New England and the New England-Yankee-settled Great Lakes states put down roots and, despite the massacres of the mad John Brown, prevailed and established their own law and order. This was a civil war before the Civil War and, as Wichita State historian Charles Miner points out, one conducted by literate people who produced mountains of documents that have not been fully mined by historians.

Kansas's effect on national politics was tumultuous: The Democratic Party was split, the Republican Party was created, and the nation was plunged into Civil War. The ultimate effect on Kansas was calming: The anti-slavery majority bent the soil to the plow and built small towns thick with schools, churches and colleges, to the point that in the 1939 color movie, *The Wizard of Oz*, the Kansas scenes were shot in dreary black and white as the image of dull, prim, old-fashioned Middle America, while the scenes in imaginary Oz were shot in brilliant color. But the rebellious impulse did not totally die out. Kansans' livelihoods were always at risk: Hailstorms, grasshopper invasions, dry seasons or a drop in world farm prices could mean disaster for thousands. The high-rainfall 1880s attracted hundreds of thousands of new settlers to Kansas; the low-rainfall 1890s produced a bust and a populist rebellion. "What you farmers should do,"

Miles
0 10 20

The Almanac of American Politics.
National Journal

Congressional district boundaries were first effective for 2002.

said orator Mary Ellen Lease, "is to raise less corn and more hell." For a few years in the 1890s, and then in farm rebellions of the 1930s, 1950s and 1970s, Kansans did, but afterwards always returned to jayhawker Republicanism.

Kansas remains Republican in the 21st century, but not in quite the same old way. Its most famous politician, Bob Dole, still returns occasionally to his small hometown of Russell, out on the plains. But Kansas' population is increasingly metropolitan. Some 51% of Kansans live in just five counties, which include Kansas City, Lawrence, Topeka and Wichita, and in 78 of the 100 other counties the population declined between 2000 and 2004. A majority of Kansans are in or within easy reach of metropolitan Kansas City, which has a diverse economy that is by no means dependent on farming. Small towns on the plains see their city halls and post offices padlocked and high schools closed because of low attendance; some towns have bought land to be distributed free to homesteaders, others have courted call centers. But at the same time new office complexes and corporate headquarters are rising amidst the affluent suburbs of Johnson County, which has one of the highest job growth rates in the country. The smaller metropolitan area of Wichita, while less diversified, has an economy built on its role as the world's leading producer of small airplanes: Here many World War II planes were built and here today Cessna, Bombardier, Raytheon and other manufacturers make 53% of the general aviation aircraft in the world. Hispanics are flocking to work in meatpacking factories in towns like Dodge City, Garden City and Liberal, whose populations in 2000 were more than 40% Hispanic; Hispanics accounted for nearly half of Kansas's population growth in the 1990s; Wichita Mayor Carlos Mayans was born in Cuba. There is no warrant today for shooting the Kansas scenes in black and white.

This transformation has had political consequences. Some 40% of Kansas's votes in 2004 were cast in the mostly suburban counties from Kansas City west to Topeka, and another 15% in Wichita's Sedgwick County. If rural Kansas once produced farm rebellions, these urban and suburban Kansans have produced their own kind of rebellion. Since the mid-1990s Kansas has had a kind of three-party politics—conservative Republicans versus moderate Republicans versus Democrats. Republican Governor Bill Graves, elected in 1994 and 1998, favored abortion rights and gun control; he was fiercely opposed by conservative Republicans in the legislature. Graves beat back a conservative challenge in the 1998 Republican primary by nearly 3–1, but conservatives won a majority on the state school board and in 1999 issued guidelines that treated evolution as a theory. That aroused a national uproar and was reversed in 2001, and in 2003 moderate Republicans took leadership posts in the legislature. The Republican split opened the way for Democrats, who captured the 3d Congressional District seat in 1998 by beating a conservative who was hated by suburban moderates and the governorship in 2002 when Democrat Kathleen Sebelius beat conservative Treasurer Tim Shallenburger. Conservatives won victories in the August 2004 legislative primaries and gained a 6–4 majority over moderate Republicans and Democrats on the state school board, where the board planned to revisit the science guidelines in May 2005.

But Kansas has not moved toward Democrats in national politics. In voted 58%–37% for George W. Bush in 2000 and 62%–37% in 2004. Its two Republican senators were both first elected in 1996, when Bob Dole resigned and Nancy Landon Kassebaum retired. Sam Brownback reflects the views of Kansas's conservatives and Pat Roberts of its moderates, but they seem to work in harmony unlike their local equivalents. Kansas has not elected a Democratic senator since 1932—the only state that hasn't. Three of the state's four House seats have gone to Republicans essentially uncontested, although Democrats represented two of them in the 1980s and early 1990s.

The People		Race/Ethnic Origin			Military veterans: 267,452 (13.5%)	
Pop. 2004 (est):	2,735,502	2,233,997	83.1%	White	WWII: 21.2%	Korea: 13.1%
Pop. 2000:	2,688,418	151,407	5.6%	Black	Vietnam: 32.6%	Gulf War: 10.9%
Pop. 1990:	2,477,574	46,301	1.7%	Asian	**Most populous cities (2003):**	
Change 1990–2000:	Up 8.5%	22,322	0.8%	Native Am.	1. Wichita	354,617
% of U.S. total:	1.0%	1,154	0.0%	Hawaiian	2. Overland Park	160,368
Pop. rank:	32d of 50	42,508	1.6%	Two+ races	3. Kansas City	145,757
Area size:	82,277 sq. mi.	2,477	0.1%	Other	4. Topeka	122,008
State Native:	59.5%	188,252	7.0%	Hisp. Origin	5. Olathe	105,274
Non-citizen:	3.3%	**Ancestry**				
Language		German: 19.5%		Irish: 8.7%	Urban population: 71.4%	
English: 89.7%	Spanish: 6.0%	English: 8.1%		USA: 6.7%	Rural population: 28.6%	
Other Eur.: 2.6%		French: 2.3%				

Education		Work Sector		Legislature		
H.S. Grad:	86.0%	Private: 76.3%	Govt: 15.5%	Senate	30 R 10 D	
College Grad:	25.8%	Self: 7.8%	Family: 0.4%	House	83 R 42 D	
Industry		Unemployment: 4.2%		Legislative Term Limits: No		
Agri: 3.8%	Con: 6.5%	**Household Income**		**Registered Voters**		
Fin: 6.1%	Info: 3.3%	<15k: 14.9%	15-35k: 27.8%	D: 454,478	(26.8%)	
Mfg: 20.3%	Prof: 29.1%	35-50k: 18.1%	50-100k: 29.9%	R: 783,068	(46.2%)	
Public: 4.4%	Trade: 14.8%	100-150k: 6.1%	>150k: 3.2%	O: 456,819	(27.0%)	
Other: 11.6%		Median: $40,624				
Occupation		Poverty status: 9.9%				
Blue collar: 24.9%	White collar: 59.7%	**Home Value**				
Gray collar: 15.5%		<50k: 27.3%	50-100k: 35.6%	100-200k: 28.6%	200-300k: 5.6%	
		300-500k: 2.2%	>500k: 0.7%	Median: $81,000		

Presidential politics

Except for 1964, when it narrowly favored Lyndon Johnson over Barry Goldwater, Kansas has voted Republican for president throughout the last 60 years. In 2000 and 2004 George W. Bush carried 103 of its 105 counties, losing only those containing the old industrial city of Kansas City and the university town of Lawrence. Bush's percentage rose from 58% to 62%, and rose by more in most rural counties. But it rose only a little in suburban Johnson County and fell in Douglas County, dominated by the university town of Lawrence. Kansas is so one-sidedly Republican that it sees little of presidential candidates. But on May 17, 2004, both George W. Bush and John Kerry came to Topeka and, in separate appearances,

2004 Presidential Vote		
Bush (R)	736,456	(62%)
Kerry (D)	434,993	(37%)
Nader (I)	9,348	(1%)
Other	6,959	(1%)

2000 Presidential Vote		
Bush (R)	622,332	(58%)
Gore (D)	399,276	(37%)
Nader (Green)	36,086	(3%)
Other	14,522	(1%)

commemorated the *Brown v. Board of Education* decision, which outlawed Topeka's segregated schools.

In 1996 the state legislature voted to cancel the April primary and none have been held since.

Congressional districting

109th Congress Lineup
3 R   1 D

108th Congress Lineup
3 R   1 D

In 2002 Republicans had full control of redistricting in Kansas for the first time since the 1960s, but did not use it to partisan advantage. Why? As one legislator put it, "What's ground zero with reapportionment? I'd say it's Lawrence." In the previous plan, Lawrence, midway between Kansas City and Topeka, and home of the University of Kansas, was in the 3d District captured by Democrat Dennis Moore in 1998 and held in 2000. The 3d District had to shed 61,000 people, and the obvious partisan move was to remove Lawrence, which Moore carried by wide margins, and place it in the heavily Republican 2d District, where incumbent Republican Jim Ryun would be unbeatable anyway. But Lawrence civic leaders insisted that Lawrence be kept together in the 3d District—they wanted the university to be in the same district as its hospital in Kansas City—and Republicans in the state House in March 2002 passed a plan splitting the city but keeping most of it, including the university, in the 3d. The state Senate in April 2002 passed a different plan, promoted by national Republicans, which extended the western 1st District all the way to the southeast corner of the state. But the House's plan prevailed and was adopted in June.

Governor

Kathleen Sebelius (D)

Elected 2002, term expires Jan. 2007, 1st term; b. May 15, 1948, Cincinnati, OH; home, Topeka; Trinity Col., B.A. 1970, U. of KS, M.P.A. 1977; Catholic; married (Gary).

Elected Office: KS House of Reps., 1986–94; KS Insurance Commissioner, 1994–2002.

Professional Career: KS Dept. of Corrections, 1975–77; Dir., KS Trial Lawyers Assoc., 1977–87.

Office: State Capitol, 2d Fl., Topeka, 66612, 785-296-3232; Fax: 785-296-7973; Web site: www.ksgovernor.org.

Election Results

2002 general	Kathleen Sebelius (D)	441,858	(53%)
	Tim Shallenburger (R)	376,830	(45%)
2002 primary	Kathleen Sebelius (D)	unopposed	
1998 general	Bill Graves (R)	544,882	(73%)
	Tom Sawyer (D)	168,243	(23%)
	Other	29,540	(4%)

Kathleen Sebelius was elected governor of Kansas in 2002, the second Democratic woman to win the office (the first was Joan Finney in 1990). Sebelius grew up in Cincinnati, where her father John Gilligan was elected to the city council in 1953, when she was 5. Campaigns were very much a part of her life. Her father was elected to Congress in a usually Republican district in the very Democratic year of 1964; he was defeated in 1966 by Robert Taft Jr., father of Ohio's current Governor Bob Taft: They have something to talk about at governors' conferences. John Gilligan was elected governor of Ohio in 1970 and in 1971 pushed through the state's first income tax. A man of wry humor, he was given to self-deprecating statements; when asked at the Ohio State Fair in 1972 whether he would join the sheep-shearing, he said, "I shear taxpayers, not sheep." Comments like this helped defeat him in 1974 by a 49%–48% margin. Still active and a member of the Cincinnati school board in 2002, he had the satisfaction of being the first governor to see his daughter elected governor.

Kathleen Sebelius graduated from Trinity College in Washington, D.C., where she met her husband, the son of Kansas Republican Congressman (1969–81) Keith Sebelius. After graduation the Sebeliuses moved to Topeka, where they live just 12 blocks from the state Capitol. Kathleen Sebelius worked for the state trial lawyers association and in 1986 was elected to the state House as a Democrat. With a Topeka base and a name well known in western Kansas, she was elected state Insurance Commissioner in 1994. It was a position held since its creation by Republicans, and by just three men over the preceding 50 years.

Sebelius's moderate image and her political savvy made her the obvious Democrat to run for governor in 2002, and she had no primary opposition. Term-limited Governor Bill Graves was a moderate who engaged in fierce feuds with conservatives in the Republican party, and there was a rip-roaring battle for the Republican nomination. Attorney General Carla Stovall, the choice of the moderate wing, announced in 2001 and raised over $500,000. But in April 2002, she let it be known that she was leaving the race, just two months before the filing deadline. That left moderates with no candidate against conservative state Treasurer Tim Shallenburger, a strong opponent of abortion who pledged not to increase taxes and said he would cut state spending by 10%. Quickly state Senate President Dave Kerr and Wichita Mayor Bob Knight jumped in. State House Speaker Kent Glasscock, Stovall's running mate, jumped to Knight's ticket and tried to bring Stovall's money with him. But the one conservative beat the two moderates. Shallenburger won the August primary with 41% of the vote to 30% for Kerr and 26% for Knight.

The general election provided a clear contrast on issues. Sebelius promised a top-to-bottom review of state government and refused to pledge she would veto any tax increase. "No one is talking about a tax increase," she said in an October debate. "We need to do more with less." She favored abortion rights, opposed capital punishment and favored banning concealed weapons except for retired law enforcement officers. She picked a Republican, a retired Cessna executive, for her running mate. She called for a $1,000 increase in per pupil spending and said she would institute character education in schools. She proved to be an excellent fundraiser and spent $3.2 million to Shallenburger's $1.5 million. Graves waited until six weeks after the primary to grudgingly endorse Shallenburger, and the Kansas Farm Bureau in September decided to stay neutral. Sebelius made one slip when she said that Missouri's underfunded highways were "much more terrifying to me than the attacks on the World Trade Center," but she quickly apologized. She got some mileage attacking Shallenburger for calling her, in a fundraising letter, "a lying dangerous liberal who will ruin our schools and endanger our children." Polls showed her well ahead all along, and she won 53%–45%. She carried most counties in eastern Kansas and lost heavily Republican Johnson County by only 52%–46%. She ran only about even in the Wichita area, but carried most rural counties west of the 100th meridian, long regarded as the boundary between the fertile Midwest and the arid West.

Sebelius's victory plus gains by Republican moderates left conservative Republicans even more out of power than ever. Sebelius retained Graves's budget director and appointed a Republican as secretary of administration. Her top-to-bottom review of state government resulted, she said, in $76 million in savings; but this included $40 million raised by tax amnesties and $10 million in higher fees. Still, there were no tax increases in 2003. Trouble came in December 2003 when a trial judge in Shawnee County ruled on a suit brought by Dodge City and Salina in 1999 that Kansas's school funding formula was unconstitutional; Sebelius and the legislature were given until July 2004 to come up with changes. In January 2004 Sebelius announced a balanced budget but then added that she favored a $300 million increase in education spending and proposed increases in the sales, income and property taxes to pay for it. She wanted to increase spending by $250 per pupil over three years and start all-day kindergarten for low-income children. A coalition of moderate Republicans and Democrats in the House passed a $155 million tax increase, but the Senate rejected it; the Senate passed $82 million in transportation borrowing, but the House rejected that.

The Shawnee County trial judge replied with an angry opinion and ordered that nothing at all be spent on schools after July 1, even though the case was on appeal to the state supreme court. The issue undoubtedly overshadowed the August 2004 primaries, which were held under separate rules. The Republican state chairman, a moderate, ruled that unaffiliated voters as well as registered Republicans could vote in the Republican primary; but a conservative district chairman sued, and the state supreme court ruled that only registered Republicans could vote, even though unaffiliated as well as Democrats could vote in the Democratic primary. That may have made a difference, as conservative Republicans made significant gains in the primary, including the defeat of the two moderate co-sponsors of the tax increase in the state House. Also defeated were four of six Republicans who voted against a ban on same-sex marriage. Conservatives swept the field in party posts in the December 2004 district conventions. In early January 2005, the field was set for battle, as all sides waited for the Supreme Court to act. Speaker Doug Mays said, "Voters didn't appreciate the legislature trying to raise taxes last time and don't want it to happen again." Sebelius said, "Unless the court says everything is fine, which is a possibility, my guess is we'll have to look for additional resources." In January 2005, the state supreme court ruled that the legislature had inadequately funded education and ordered it to come up with a solution by April. With spending cuts, Sebelius and legislators came to an agreement to add $127 million to the state's $2.7 billion education budget.

On other issues, Sebelius worked for a new Indian gambling casino in Kansas City, which was delayed by Mays. Sebelius's program to provide more flexibility on pay raises for state employees was bitterly criticized by public employee unions; former Republican Governor Mike Hayden, a Sebelius appointee, said she could do more on this than a Republican could. Sebelius signed a bill to allow young illegal immigrants who graduated from high school and were admitted to college in-state tuition rates—proof that neither side in Kansas politics is reflexively hostile to the state's growing Hispanic population. In November 2004 Sebelius joined Illinois Governor Rod Blagojevich's I-SaveRx plan to enable citizens to buy reimported prescription drugs from Canada, Britain and Ireland, and she proposed a $50 million plan to provide health insurance for low-income uninsured with a 50 cent increase in the cigarette tax. In December 2004 the state Supreme Court declared the state's death penalty law unconstitutional.

Sebelius comes up for reelection in 2006. Possible Republican opponents include Mays and Congressman Jerry Moran. Both sides in this race would seem to have weaknesses, Sebelius because of her advocacy of a tax increase, the Republicans because of the likelihood of a rough primary fight between the party's moderate and conservative branches.

Senior Senator

Sam Brownback (R)

Elected 1996, seat up 2010, 2d full term; b. Sept. 12, 1956, Garnett; home, Topeka; KS St. U., B.S. 1978, U. of KS, J.D. 1982; Catholic; married (Mary).

Elected Office: U.S. House of Reps., 1994–96.

Professional Career: Radio broadcaster, KKSU, 1978–79; Practicing atty., 1982–86, 1993; Prof., KS St. U. Law Schl., 1982–86; Ogden & Leonardville City Atty., 1983–86; KS Secy. of Agriculture, 1986–93; White House Fellow, Office of USTR, 1990–91.

DC Office: 303 HSOB, 20510, 202-224-6521; Fax: 202-228-1265; Web site: brownback.senate.gov.

State Offices: Garden City, 620-275-1124; Overland Park, 913-492-6378; Pittsburg, 620-231-6040; Topeka, 785-233-2503; Wichita, 316-264-8066.

Committees: *Appropriations*: Agriculture, Rural Development & Related Agencies; Commerce, Justice & Science; District of Columbia (Chmn.); Military Construction & Veterans Affairs; State, Foreign Operations & Related Programs; Transportation, the Judiciary, HUD & Related Agencies. *Judiciary*: Antitrust, Competition Policy & Consumer Rights; Constitution, Civil Rights & Property Rights (Chmn.); Corrections & Rehabilitation; Immigration, Border Security & Citizenship; Intellectual Property. *Joint Economic Committee*.

Group Ratings

	ADA	ACLU	AFS	LCV	ITIC	NTU	COC	ACU	NTLC	CHC
2004	15	11	0	17	100	78	94	96	93	100
2003	5	—	11	0	—	72	100	90	—	—

National Journal Ratings

	2003 LIB	—	2003 CONS		2004 LIB	—	2004 CONS
Economic	18%	—	77%		5%	—	91%
Social	0%	—	59%		19%	—	71%
Foreign	39%	—	54%		0%	—	67%

Key Votes of the 108th Congress

1. Ban Drilling in ANWR	N	5. Energy Bill	Y	9. Ban Same-Sex Marriage	Y
2. Approve Bush Tax Cuts	Y	6. Support Roe v. Wade	N	10. Ban Bunker-Buster Bomb	N
3. Medicare/Rx Bill	Y	7. Ban Partial-Birth Abortion	Y	11. Fund Iraq War	Y
4. Bar Overtime Pay Regs.	N	8. Assault Weapons Ban	N	12. Restrict Missile Defense	N

Election Results

2004 general	Sam Brownback (R)	780,863	(69%)	($2,476,585)
	Lee Jones (D)	310,337	(27%)	($102,931)
	Other	37,822	(3%)	
2004 primary	Sam Brownback (R)	286,839	(87%)	
	Arch Naramore (R)	42,880	(13%)	
1998 general	Sam Brownback (R)	474,639	(65%)	($1,719,612)
	Paul Feleciano Jr. (D)	229,718	(32%)	($39,500)
	Other	22,879	(3%)	

Prior Winning Percentages: 1996 (54%); 1994 House (66%)

Sam Brownback grew up on a farm in Anderson County, some 50 miles from Kansas City; he has family roots in Osawatomie, a center of evangelical abolitionism in the bleeding Kansas of the 1850s. He was student body president at Kansas State University and briefly worked as a farm broadcaster. After law school, he practiced law for four years in Manhattan, Kansas, in the 1980s; he was appointed secretary of the state Board of Agriculture in 1986 and served until it was abolished in 1993. He was a White House Fellow, working from 1990–91 for Special Trade Representative Carla Hills. In March 1994, after 2d District Democrat Jim Slattery ran for governor, Brownback announced for Congress, condemning "a welfare system that discourages the work ethic and encourages the disintegration of families and a government that can't say no to spending or yes to reform." He won the three-way House primary; in the general, he faced John Carlin, governor from 1978–86. Brownback won 66%–34%, carrying every county.

Brownback was one of the enthusiastic 1994 freshmen who tried to shake up the House. He pushed successfully to reduce Congress's own budget. He headed a group of "New Federalists," which sought to abolish three cabinet departments. He backed the McCain-Feingold campaign finance bill and in 1995 spoke at Ross Perot's United We Stand convention denouncing "influence peddling" in Washington. On immigration, he played a key role in separating the legal and illegal immigration issues, which led to passage of a tough measure against illegal immigrants but no major reductions in the number of legal immigrants.

On May 15, 1996, Bob Dole surprised just about everyone when he announced he was resigning from the Senate on June 11. On May 17, Brownback said he would seek the seat, noting, "They are size 25 shoes that even Michael Jordan couldn't fill." Governor Bill Graves' choice to fill the vacancy, Lieutenant Governor Sheila Frahm, delayed ten days before accepting. Then Brownback decided to run. There were strong differences between the two on issues. She was pro-choice on abortion, he was pro-life. Brownback accused her of voting as a state legislator to raise taxes $500 million; she criticized his "slash and burn" approach to federal spending. In the August primary, Brownback won 55%–42%. In the general election for the remaining two years of Dole's term, Brownback faced a Democrat with a great political name, Wichita stockbroker Jill Docking, wife of a former lieutenant governor whose father and grandfather both served as governor. Docking promised "Kansas common sense" and likened herself to Kassebaum. Brownback campaigned on the 3 R's: "Reduce, reform and return. Reduce the size and scope of the federal government. Reform the Congress. Return to the basic values that built the country: Work and family and the recognition of a higher moral authority." He promised to serve only two terms—presumably two full terms. Both candidates spent liberally, and some fall polls showed the race close. But Brownback won by the convincing though not overwhelming margin of 54%–43%.

Brownback has a conservative voting record in the Senate and has taken on many issues because of his strong moral views; his hero is William Wilberforce, the parliamentarian who led the fight to end the slave trade. "I think every life is sacred and beautiful, whether it's the unborn or whether it's Ted Kennedy," he has said. "I really try to reach out and work with anybody and everybody I can." After September 11, Brownback and Kennedy co-sponsored a bill to strengthen the nation's borders. It provided for an automatic entry and exit system, the development of biometric identifiers and tracking of foreign students and called for greater sharing of information about potential terrorists by the INS, State Department and intelligence agencies. The bill became law in May 2002. He has had less success in banning human cloning, an issue he became interested in while working as state agriculture secretary. His bill, co-sponsored by Mary Landrieu, would ban reproductive human cloning and the cloning of embryos for use in research; as a fallback, he called for a six-month moratorium on cloning. But he was denied a freestanding vote and a competing bill sponsored by Dianne Feinstein and Arlen Specter passed instead.

Prior to the 109th Congress, Brownback had a seat on Foreign Relations and was chairman of the East Asian and Pacific Affairs Subcommittee. After September 11, he worked to ease sanctions against Pakistan and urged a tough approach on Iraq; he called the Iraqi National Congress, a group shunned by many in the State Department and the CIA, "invaluable in the fight to rid the world of Saddam's threat." He led the fight for the Sudan Peace Act of 2002 and has worked to end slavery and the civil war there; he and Congressman Frank Wolf visited refugee camps in Darfur in June 2004. In 2003 he secured passage of the Syrian Accountability and Lebanese Sovereignty Act and got the Bush administration to withdraw its opposition. He co-sponsored the North Korea Refugee Act with Edward Kennedy and in December 2002 said, "If hell is the absence of God, I think you can see North Korea is the closest place to that on Earth." Using his seat on Appropriations, he added $1.5 million in 2003 and $3 million in 2004 for programs to encourage democracy in Iran and $2 million in 2004 for a human rights conference on North Korea; also he removed the requirement that AID get approval from the Egyptian government for pro-democracy projects there. He criticized the State Department for not helping rescue American children abducted by Saudi parents. In June 2004 he criticized China for "trampling on the autonomy" of Hong Kong and threatened that export controls might have to be extended to Hong Kong as well as China. He has supported the Bush administration on Iraq, but in fall 2003 said half the $20 billion for reconstruction should be in loans not grants.

In 2003 and 2004 Brownback used his chairmanship of the Science Subcommittee of Commerce to hold hearings on cloning, genetic testing and pornography addiction. He sponsored a bill to provide $25 million for prizes for private sector successes in space and called for research on asteroids that might hit the Earth. He hailed the Bush administration for bringing a WTO action against Airbus, and said that if European subsidies to Airbus were not removed, U.S. subsidies to Boeing should be considered. He worked with Joseph Lieberman to discourage violence and pornography in movies and rock music. In 2004 he tried, ultimately unsuccessfully to increase the fine on broadcasters for indecency to $500,000. On taxes, he said in April 2004, "I think we need fundamental tax reform—flat, or a consumption-based tax system." With Congressman John Lewis, he worked to authorize the African-American Museum on Washington's Mall, and he sponsored a resolution apologizing to Native Americans for past government misdeeds.

Brownback was elected to a full six-year term in 1998 by a 65%–32% margin after well-known candidates declined to run. In November 2002 Brownback announced he would run again, and Democrats had a hard time finding a candidate to run against him. Former Congressman and Agriculture Secretary Dan Glickman bowed out in September 2003; Governor Kathleen Sebelius wasn't interested. The winner of the August 2004 primary withdrew from the race. "Just tired, I guess," he said. Brownback was reelected 69%–27%, carrying 104 of Kansas's 105 counties. After the 2004 elections, some conservatives were talking about Brownback running for president. Michael Horowitz of the Hudson Institute has made the case: "In temperament, vision and faith, Sam Brownback is closer to George Bush than to any member of Congress. Like the president—and Ronald Reagan—his positions are seen by adversaries to spring from decency rather than meanness of spirit. For these and other reasons many conservative and religious leaders intend for him to become a serious candidate to succeed the president."

Junior Senator

Pat Roberts (R)

Elected 1996, seat up 2008, 2d term; b. Apr. 20, 1936, Topeka; home, Dodge City; KS St. U., B.A. 1958; United Methodist; married (Franki).

Military Career: Marine Corps, 1958–62.

Elected Office: U.S. House of Reps., 1980–96.

Professional Career: Co–owner, editor, *The Westsider* (AZ newspaper) 1962–67; A.A., U.S. Sen. Frank Carlson, 1967–68; A.A., U.S. Rep. Keith Sebelius, 1968–80.

DC Office: 109 HSOB, 20510; 202-224-4774; Fax: 202-224-3514; Web site: roberts.senate.gov.

State Offices: Dodge City, 620-227-2244; Overland Park, 913-451-9343; Topeka, 785-295-2745; Wichita, 316-263-0416.

Committees: *Agriculture, Nutrition & Forestry*: Marketing, Inspection & Product Promotion; Production & Price Competitiveness; Research, Nutrition & General Legislation. *Armed Services*: Emerging Threats & Capabilities; Readiness & Management Support; Strategic Forces. *Ethics (Select)*. *Health, Education, Labor & Pensions*: Bioterrorism & Public Health Preparedness; Employment & Workplace Safety; Retirement Security & Aging. *Intelligence (Select)* (Chmn.).

Group Ratings

	ADA	ACLU	AFS	LCV	ITIC	NTU	COC	ACU	NTLC	CHC
2004	15	22	0	0	100	71	100	92	93	100
2003	15	—	11	0	—	72	100	80	—	—

National Journal Ratings

	2003 LIB	—	2003 CONS		2004 LIB	—	2004 CONS
Economic	29%	—	68%		31%	—	65%
Social	0%	—	59%		19%	—	71%
Foreign	22%	—	68%		0%	—	67%

Key Votes of the 108th Congress

1. Ban Drilling in ANWR	N	5. Energy Bill	Y	9. Ban Same-Sex Marriage	Y
2. Approve Bush Tax Cuts	Y	6. Support Roe v. Wade	N	10. Ban Bunker-Buster Bomb	N
3. Medicare/Rx Bill	Y	7. Ban Partial-Birth Abortion	Y	11. Fund Iraq War	Y
4. Bar Overtime Pay Regs.	N	8. Assault Weapons Ban	N	12. Restrict Missile Defense	N

Election Results

2002 general	Pat Roberts (R)	641,075	(83%)	($1,038,984)
	Steven Rosile (Lib)	70,725	(9%)	
	George Cook (Ref)	65,050	(8%)	($3,473)
2002 primary	Pat Roberts (R)	233,642	(84%)	
	Tom Oyler (R)	45,491	(16%)	
1996 general	Pat Roberts (R)	652,677	(62%)	($2,305,898)
	Sally Thompson (D)	362,380	(34%)	($659,066)
	Other	37,243	(4%)	

Prior Winning Percentages: 1994 House (77%); 1992 House (68%); 1990 House (63%); 1988 House (100%); 1986 House (75%); 1984 House (76%); 1982 House (68%); 1980 House (62%)

Pat Roberts is from a fine Kansas Republican background. His abolitionist great-grandfather "arrived in Kansas with a flat-bed press, a six-gun and a Bible" and founded Kansas' second-oldest newspaper, the *Oskaloosa Independent*, and his father, Wes Roberts, was briefly Republican National Committee chairman during the Eisenhower years. Pat Roberts has spent most of his adult life preparing for the place he is in now. After four years in the Marine Corps and five years running an Arizona newspaper, he worked for two years as an aide to Senator Frank Carlson and 12 years as chief aide to 1st District Congressman Keith Sebelius, Bob Dole's successor in the House and the father-in-law of Democratic Governor Kathleen Sebelius. When Sebelius retired in 1980, Roberts won the seat with 56% in a three-candidate Republican primary. For 14 years, in the minority in the House, he concentrated on farm issues, learning their intricacies and minutiae, traveling in a van to keep in touch with constituents in a district so large that it took two weeks to visit every county seat. His voting record was moderate, and he looked after Kansas interests.

In January 1995 Roberts became chairman of the House Agriculture Committee. He had long believed that the huge subsidies of the early 1980s would never return. Faced with Republican budget parameters, Roberts fashioned a Freedom to Farm bill designed to phase out subsidies over seven years. In September 1995 his bill failed in committee when Southern Republicans eager to protect cotton, rice and peanut subsidies voted against it. But in November 1995, Roberts persuaded Agriculture conferees to include most of his bill in the 1996 budget reconciliation bill, which Bill Clinton vetoed. He agreed to maintain cotton and rice marketing loans and managed to preserve the Conservation Reserve Program, which is popular in Kansas. But overall this was the biggest change in agriculture policy since the New Deal act of 1933. Roberts' new bill passed the Agriculture Committee 29–17 in January 1996, the full House in February, and became law in April. But after the Asian financial collapse in 1997, world crop prices fell and Congress started voting disaster relief to farmers every year—the subsidies in another form.

Amid this furious legislative activity, one of Kansas' Senate seats came open when in November 1995 Nancy Landon Kassebaum announced her retirement. At first Roberts said he was too busy working on the farm bill and declined to run. When the bill's fortunes improved, he announced his candidacy in January 1996; the law seemed likely to remove much of the power of the committee, and under new Republican rules he was limited to three terms as chairman. He won the August primary with an overwhelming 78% in a four-way race. In the general election he faced state Treasurer Sally Thompson and won easily, 62%–34%. Thus Roberts became the first House member to give up a committee chairmanship to run for the Senate since Lister Hill in 1938 (and Hill got appointed to his Senate seat).

Roberts is on the Senate Agriculture Committee and has spent much time on farm issues. The Freedom to Farm Act worked well in 1997, and farmers seemed pleased to be able to decide what crops to plant without getting government approval. But in 1998 crop prices plunged—in line with the long-run trend of falling prices for basic commodities—and some demanded a return to the old system. Roberts resisted that, and bills were passed to give temporary aid and accelerate $4.5 billion in payments and give farmers an extra $4 billion in disaster assistance. In 2000 the pattern continued: Roberts argued that increased subsidies for crop insurance would mean less need for yearly assistance and argued that limiting production would not raise prices because the U.S. accounts for less than one-fifth of world production. The problem seems intractable. The number of family farmers continues to fall in places like western Kansas, where farm communities are tending to disappear, yet prices are not sufficient to maintain many operations.

The Freedom to Farm Act came up for reauthorization in 2002, and this time Roberts was not chairman of an Agriculture Committee but the fifth-ranking member of the minority. He admitted the Freedom to Farm Act "didn't work out as anybody would have hoped," and with Thad Cochran pushed for farm savings accounts: The federal government would match farmers up to $10,000 a year in their accounts, which could be drawn on when, for any reason, farm income was below average. But in committee that was rejected in favor of Chairman Tom Harkin's approach: Revival of countercyclical subsidies when crop prices are low, plus a larger conservation reserve program and inclusion of previously uncovered crops. Harkin prevailed on the Senate floor 58–40 in February 2002; Roberts wasn't even on the conference committee. "I've never seen such partisanship in a farm bill," Roberts said. "This policy fails farmers." He argued that it would provide no aid when production was low and crop prices rose, which is exactly what happened when drought struck the Great Plains in summer 2002. Roberts has tried to encourage farm exports in many ways, opposing cargo preferences, urging passage of trade promotion authority and replenishment of IMF funds. He was a lead sponsor of the 2000 law to end the embargo on food to Cuba, and he and Kansas colleague Sam Brownback sponsored the 1999 law allowing the president to lift the embargo on India and Pakistan and in 2000 sought to end food sanctions altogether. He supported normal trade relations with China and met with Fidel Castro in Cuba in 2000. In November 2003 he was promoting conservation tillage, or no-till farming, which leaves more carbon in the ground and could qualify farmers for credits if carbon trading were used. "The Kansas prairie is a great big carbon sponge. If you pay farmers to maintain these conservation projects, you'd be able to clean up the environment." In September 2004 he said that Brazil's cotton complaint to the WTO was "the most serious, full-frontal assault on the U.S. farm program in our history." In January 2005 he let the less senior Saxby Chambliss became chairman of Agriculture so he could keep the chairmanship of the Intelligence Committee; the farm bill does not come up for reauthorization until 2007.

In 1999 Roberts was named chairman of the new Emerging Threats and Capabilities Subcommittee of Armed Services. He began his first hearing by saying, "I want to know what keeps you awake at night." In hearings that attracted little attention, he probed the nation's vulnerability to terrorists and predicted that targets would be "selected for their symbolic value, like the World Trade Center in the heart of Manhattan." He warned of the dangers of information and biological warfare. When he heard the news on September 11 while driving to work, he thought. "Oh, my God. It's just exactly what we predicted." He was driving in front of the Capitol when United flight 93 would have hit it if that was its intended target. He gave strong support to the Bush administration on Iraq.

In January 2003 Roberts became chairman of the Intelligence Committee. There were signs of increasing partisanship there; in October 2002 ranking Democrat Jay Rockefeller had said that if Democrats were to regain their majority he would diminish the entire traditionally bipartisan staff and replace them with partisan appointees. Roberts started off favorably disposed toward CIA Director George Tenet and in summer 2003 resisted Democratic calls for investigation of how administration officials used intelligence on Iraq and for declassification of the 28 pages of the White House report which were classified. In November Fox News's Sean Hannity obtained a memo prepared by Democratic committee staffers saying that in the hearings on pre-March 2003 Iraq intelligence they should "pull the majority along" on getting information out and then in early 2004 should "pull the trigger" and use it to attack the Bush administration. Majority Leader Bill Frist demanded an apology on behalf of Roberts and the committee's weekly meeting was cancelled. Rockefeller tried to mend relations, but refused to apologize; the next day he said he was "profoundly surprised" by a November 13 opinion article in *The Washington Post* written by Roberts. "The Democrats planned to undermine the integrity of the committee by conducting a partisan attack, which threatens to destroy the credibility of an institution that has served the U.S. Senate and the nation well for nearly 30 years. I oppose them, and for this I make no apologies," Roberts wrote.

Roberts said that there would be a meeting on the intelligence authorization and that hearings would go on in 2004. In January 2004 the Senate and House Intelligence Committee reported that the CIA did not seriously consider the possibility that Saddam Hussein had no weapons of mass destruction. Roberts said, "It was like a runaway train. Once it left the station, it kept going faster and faster. Some analysts may have been trying to slow it down, but it just kept going."

In April 2004 Roberts proposed that the Intelligence Committee take over from Armed Services oversight of Defense Department intelligence operations. "You're rolling a pin-free grenade down the halls of the Pentagon," he conceded; the proposal was resisted. After the 9/11 Commission recommended changes in intelligence organizations, including a new national intelligence director, Roberts and committee Republicans came up with their own proposal, to abolish the CIA and arrange its functions in three component organizations under a new national intelligence director. The CIA opposed this; the White House had not been informed, and was frosty to the idea; John Kerry mentioned the proposal favorably; the 9/11 Commission was neutral. But soon thereafter there was bipartisan agreement in the Senate on the proposal made by the Governmental Affairs Committee's Susan Collins and Joseph Lieberman; it was not entirely accepted in conference committee with the House. Roberts's verdict: "It is no secret that I believe we should have gone farther. What it fails to do is to create a leader of the intelligence community who is clearly in charge and as a result is fully accountable." Roberts supported the nomination in summer 2004 of his House counterpart, Porter Goss, to be the new CIA Director; he turned down the chairmanship of the Agriculture Committee in January 2005 to remain chairman of Intelligence.

In 2004, for the fourth time, Roberts was voted the funniest senator in *Washingtonian's* biennial poll of congressional staffers. "I think Kansas is where the humor comes from. Something in the chlorine."

Roberts came up for re-election in 2002. No Democrat filed to run against Roberts and against Libertarian and Reform party candidates he won 83% of the vote.

FIRST DISTRICT

Rep. Jerry Moran (R)

Elected 1996, 5th term; b. May 29, 1954, Great Bend; home, Hays; U. of KS, B.S. 1976, J.D. 1981; Methodist; married (Robba).

Elected Office: KS Senate, 1988–96, Majority Ldr., 1995–96.

Professional Career: Operations Officer, Consolidated State Bank, 1975–77; Mgr., Farmers State Bank & Trust Co., 1977–78; Practicing atty., 1981–96; Instructor, Ft. Hays St. U., 1986.

DC Office: 2443 RHOB, 20515, 202-225-2715; Fax: 202-225-5124; Web site: www.house.gov/moranks01.

District Offices: Hays, 785-628-6401; Hutchinson, 620-665-6138; Salina, 785-309-0572.

Committees: *Agriculture* (6th of 25 R): Conservation, Credit, Rural Development & Research; Department Operations, Oversight, Nutrition & Forestry; General Farm Commodities & Risk Management (Chmn.). *Transportation & Infrastructure* (16th of 41 R): Aviation; Highways, Transit & Pipelines; Railroads. *Veterans' Affairs* (6th of 16 R): Disability Assistance & Memorial Affairs (Vice Chmn.); Health.

Group Ratings

	ADA	ACLU	AFS	LCV	ITIC	NTU	COC	ACU	NTLC	CHC
2004	10	10	0	9	78	68	95	92	92	100
2003	25	—	25	10	—	66	90	92	—	—

National Journal Ratings

	2003 LIB	—	2003 CONS		2004 LIB	—	2004 CONS
Economic	46%	—	54%		38%	—	61%
Social	42%	—	56%		27%	—	73%
Foreign	46%	—	52%		47%	—	51%

Key Votes of the 108th Congress

1. Drilling in ANWR	Y	5. DC School Vouchers	Y	9. Ban Same-Sex Marriage	Y
2. Approve Bush Tax Cuts	Y	6. Ban Human Cloning	Y	10. Fund Iraq War	Y
3. Medicare/Rx Bill	N	7. Restrict Gun Liability	Y	11. Bar Cuba Embargo Funds	Y
4. Bar Overtime Pay Regs.	N	8. Ban Partial-Birth Abortion	Y	12. Intelligence Reorg.	Y

Election Results

2004 general	Jerry Moran (R)	239,776	(91%)	($349,807)
	Jack Warner (Lib)	24,517	(9%)	
2004 primary	Jerry Moran (R)	unopposed		
2002 general	Jerry Moran (R)	189,976	(91%)	($393,078)
	Jack Warner (Lib)	18,585	(9%)	

Prior Winning Percentages: 2000 (89%); 1998 (81%); 1996 (73%)

The People		Race/Ethnic Origin	Ancestry	
Area size:	57,576 sq. mi.	84.5% White	German: 23.2%	English: 7.3%
Urban population:	52.4%	2.1% Black	USA: 7.2%	
Rural population:	47.6%	0.9% Asian	**2004 Presidential Vote**	
Pop. 2000:	672,091	0.4% Native Am.	Bush (R) 199,554	(72%)
Median income:	$34,869	0.0% Hawaiian	Kerry (D) 73,309	(26%)
Poverty status:	11.0%	1.1% Two+ races	Other 3,962	(1%)
Military veterans:	13.4%	0.1% Other	**2000 Presidential Vote**	
		10.9% Hispanic Origin	Bush (R) 177,857	(67%)
			Gore (D) 76,448	(29%)
			Other 12,514	(5%)
			Cook Partisan Voting Index: R +20	

Occupation   Blue collar: 28.5%   White collar: 52.8%   Gray collar: 18.8%

"A prairie is not any old piece of flatland in the Midwest," writes Kansas-born reporter Dennis Farney. "No, a prairie is wine-colored grass, dancing in the wind. A prairie is a sun-splashed hillside, bright with wild flowers. A prairie is a fleeting cloud shadow, the song of the meadowlark. It is the wild land that has never felt the slash of the plow." This prairie once covered almost all of Kansas. Now only a little virgin prairie can still be found, in the Flint Hills region west and south of Topeka, where the waist-deep sea of grass still waves in the wind as it did when the pioneers on the Santa Fe Trail went west through here some 150 years ago; the Tallgrass Prairie National Preserve was created in 1996 to protect this unique landscape. Much of it was grazing land, first for buffalo, then for the cattle driven to Kansas railheads like Abilene and Dodge City in the 1870s and 1880s. This brief moment in history has been recaptured with varying accuracy in movies over a much longer span, and commemorated in the Boot Hill Museum of Dodge City, where Wyatt Earp Boulevard is the main street.

Then, after the harsh winter of 1886–87 wiped out the cattle herds, came the plow and barbed wire (commemorated in LaCrosse's Barbed Wire Museum), which enabled farmers to keep livestock out of their wheat fields and later became the foundation for a cheap telephone system. The farmers also brought to this vacant landscape Yankee civilization, with its schools and churches, and some foreign traditions as well, like the Cathedral of the Plains built by German Catholics. Now this civilization is threatened. "My great-grandparents and grandparents were part of the stream of settlers who migrated to western Kansas after the Civil War to become wheat farmers," writes James Dickenson in his elegiac *Home on the Range*. "They broke the virgin sod, erected houses, barns, schools, churches and towns, and made the area one of the most agriculturally productive in the world. A little more than a century later, the population has ebbed away from this area and many of the farms, schools, churches and towns lie vacant, dilapidated and boarded up like old boomtowns." The average age of Kansas farmers now is approaching 60. But there are also signs of new life. Some towns are attracting new residents by giving away lands as homesteads, and big meatpacking plants in Dodge City, Garden City and Liberal (the "Golden Triangle of meatpacking") have attracted large numbers of Hispanic immigrants; nearly two-thirds of the school children in these counties are Hispanic. Wind farms are being built on prairie land, though some worry about their effect on the tallgrass.

The 1st Congressional District consists of most of this expanse of Kansas, almost everything from the Flint Hills and Abilene west. Its 66 full counties (it also contains parts of three others; only the Nebraska 3d District has more counties) increased from 76,000 people in 1870 to 570,000 in 1890; but it has not grown much since then and is only 625,000 today. With its aging population, it has the most hospitals of any district in the nation. Kansas now has more "frontier counties," with between two and six people per square mile, than it did in 1890. The "Big First," which now stretches 350 miles east from the Colorado border, is also district of firsts: it has more farms and more acres in grain sorghum production than any other, and more cattle than all but one (again, Nebraska's 3d). Politically, the 1st District is heavily Republican. It voted better than 2–1 for George W. Bush in 2000 and by nearly 3–1 in 2004, and his county percentages were as high as 85%. But it also voted narrowly for Democratic Governor Kathleen Sebelius, whose late father-in-law, Republican Keith Sebelius, represented the district in the House for 14 years.

The congressman from the 1st District is Jerry Moran, a Republican first elected in 1996. Moran grew up in Plainville in Rooks County and got his start in politics as an intern for Keith Sebelius; he got a seat at the hearings on the impeachment of Richard Nixon. Moran worked as a banker for four years before attending the University of Kansas Law School. He practiced law and was elected to the state Senate in 1988 where, as chairman of Judiciary, he pushed to give judges greater flexibility on juvenile crime. In 1995 he became state Senate majority leader. When Congressman Pat Roberts ran for the Senate in 1996, Moran stepped into the 1st District race and, with the help of Republican leaders, avoided serious primary competition. He won 76% of the vote in the primary, which was tantamount to election.

Moran's voting record has been sporadically moderate on economic and foreign issues, and he has sometimes gone his own way in pursuing district causes. In response to Moran's pressure, the Agriculture Department reversed a decision to stop helping rural communities get visas for overseas doctors; at the same time, he attacked the Bush administration for failing to increase Medicare reimbursement for rural hospitals. He praised the 2002 farm bill for improving the safety net to farmers. But as a senior member of the Agriculture Committee, he worried about the "unhealthy" divisiveness caused by limitations on farm payments. He criticized U.S. trade negotiators for not fighting hard enough against European farm subsidies. To the dismay of Speaker Dennis Hastert, he "ran and hid" as one of the 25 House Republicans who opposed the Medicare/prescription drug bill in November 2003 because it did not reduce drug prices. "I have never been under such pressure to vote contrary to what I thought was right as I was with this vote," Moran later wrote. Despite continuing opposition from Republican leaders, he has been a leader in bipartisan efforts to bar the Treasury Department from enforcing sanctions against the sale of food and medicine to Cuba; he called the embargo "a failed policy."

Each year, Moran has logged about 50,000 miles around the district (people here expect to see their congressman without driving to the next county over). He was reelected in 1998 with a record 81% of the vote and has had no Democratic opponent since. In 2005 he was reportedly exploring a run for governor in 2006. In April he told Republican officials that he had decided against running but in June, he told the *Kansas City Star* that he might change his mind and run for governor after all.

SECOND DISTRICT

Rep. Jim Ryun (R)

Elected 1996, 5th term; b. Apr. 29, 1947, Wichita; home, Lawrence; U. of KS, B.A. 1970; Presbyterian; married (Anne).

Professional Career: U.S. Olympian, Track & Field, 1964, 1968, 1972; Founder & Dir., Jim Ryun Running Camps, 1976–present; Rancher, 1983–present.

DC Office: 1110 LHOB, 20515, 202-225-6601; Fax: 202-225-7986; Web site: www.ryun.house.gov.

District Offices: Pittsburg, 316-232-6100; Topeka, 785-232-4500.

Committees: *Armed Services* (12th of 34 R): Military Personnel; Readiness; Tactical Air & Land Forces. *Budget* (2d of 22 R). *Financial Services* (14th of 37 R): Capital Markets, Insurance & Government Sponsored Enterprises (Vice Chmn.); Financial Institutions & Consumer Credit.

Group Ratings

	ADA	ACLU	AFS	LCV	ITIC	NTU	COC	ACU	NTLC	CHC
2004	5	0	0	0	90	70	100	96	97	100
2003	15	—	13	0	—	79	97	100	—	—

National Journal Ratings

	2003 LIB	—	2003 CONS	2004 LIB	—	2004 CONS
Economic	37%	—	62%	16%	—	84%
Social	0%	—	95%	9%	—	85%
Foreign	0%	—	89%	9%	—	91%

Key Votes of the 108th Congress

1. Drilling in ANWR	Y	5. DC School Vouchers	Y	9. Ban Same-Sex Marriage	Y
2. Approve Bush Tax Cuts	Y	6. Ban Human Cloning	Y	10. Fund Iraq War	Y
3. Medicare/Rx Bill	N	7. Restrict Gun Liability	*	11. Bar Cuba Embargo Funds	N
4. Bar Overtime Pay Regs.	N	8. Ban Partial-Birth Abortion	Y	12. Intelligence Reorg.	Y

Election Results

2004 general	Jim Ryun (R)	165,325	(56%)	($1,136,464)
	Nancy Boyda (D)	121,532	(41%)	($1,105,838)
	Other...	7,579	(3%)	
2004 primary	Jim Ryun (R) .... unopposed			
2002 general	Jim Ryun (R)	127,477	(60%)	($431,532)
	Dan Lykins (D)	79,160	(38%)	($38,926)
	Other...	4,340	(2%)	

Prior Winning Percentages: 2000 (67%); 1998 (61%); 1996 (52%)

The People		Race/Ethnic Origin	Ancestry	
Area size:	14,318 sq. mi.	87.3% White	German: 19.3%	Irish: 9.1%
Urban population:	59.8%	4.9% Black	English: 8.2%	
Rural population:	40.2%	1.0% Asian	**2004 Presidential Vote**	
Pop. 2000:	672,102	1.2% Native Am.	Bush (R) 176,764	(59%)
Median income:	$37,855	0.1% Hawaiian	Kerry (D) 117,924	(39%)
Poverty status:	11.2%	1.7% Two+ races	Other 4,103	(1%)
Military veterans:	14.6%	0.1% Other	**2000 Presidential Vote**	
		3.8% Hispanic Origin	Bush (R) 144,721	(54%)
			Gore (D) 109,133	(41%)
			Other 13,723	(5%)
			Cook Partisan Voting Index: R + 7	

Occupation	Blue collar: 26.1%	White collar: 57.6%	Gray collar: 16.3%

The green plains of eastern Kansas have seen more than their share of American history. Here, on bluffs above the Missouri River, Fort Leavenworth was built in 1827, famous in later years for its war college and military prison and now the oldest U.S. fort west of the Mississippi. In the 1850s, newly founded towns along the Kansas River and along the Missouri line were the centers of Bleeding Kansas, where the pro-slavery bushwhackers set up a state capital in tiny Lecompton and anti-slavery New Englanders set up their stronghold down the river at Lawrence. Farther up the river is Manhattan, home of Kansas State University, and Fort Riley, once an outpost against the Indians, then a major Army base often threatened with closure. In May 2005, the Pentagon delivered good news: not only was Fort Riley spared from closure, it will be the headquarters of the 1st Infantry Division. Topeka, the state capital, sits here on a low bluff above the river; it was this city whose system of legal segregation was overturned in the 1954 landmark case, *Brown v. Board of Education*. Farther south, on the Missouri border, are the hills called "the Balkans." Here coal miners, often of Eastern European origin, lived in and near towns like Pittsburg and Girard, once a center of American socialism, where Clarence Darrow and Upton Sinclair made pilgrimages; the local paper, *Appeal to Reason*, had circulation of 750,000 across the nation. Population loss is not as great here as in western Kansas. The Topeka area and the Balkans have had slow growth, but coal-bed methane gas wells have been a growth industry in southeast Kansas. The area around Lawrence has been booming as, in effect, the perimeter of metropolitan Kansas City.

These disparate areas, Topeka and Manhattan, Fort Riley and Fort Leavenworth, the wheat-growing counties and the Balkans—most of eastern Kansas except the Kansas City metropolitan area—make up the 2d Congressional District. The 2002 redistricting added Miami

County and a part of Lawrence west of Iowa Street, but not the University of Kansas campus. The heritage of most of this area has been Republican ever since the jayhawks defeated the bushwhackers once the votes were counted honestly in the 1850s. Yet Democrats in recent decades have been competitive in state races, especially in Topeka. For 20 of the years from 1970–94, Democrats held the 2d District seat. Since then, it has voted for strongly conservative Republicans by comfortable margins.

The congressman from the 2d District is Jim Ryun, famous more than 30 years before he ran for Congress. He grew up in Wichita, where in 1965 he was the first high-schooler to break the four-minute mile; he made the cover of *Sports Illustrated*. His 3:55.3 time remained the world record for high schoolers until 2001. He was a star runner at the University of Kansas, and ran in the Olympics of 1964, 1968 and 1972; he won a silver medal and set world records for the mile, half-mile and 1500-meter runs. After his competitive athletic career, he operated a sports camp, was a motivational speaker for corporations and Christian groups, wrote two books, started a sports management firm and worked with a hearing aid company that produced a "Sounds of Success" program to help hearing-impaired children achieve their potential. His four children all became competitive runners, and one outran her boss—George W. Bush—in the three-mile President's Fitness Challenge race at Fort McNair in 2002. His son Ned has run a program to encourage political activity by home-schooled children.

In 1996, when 2d District freshman Sam Brownback ran for the Senate seat suddenly vacated by Bob Dole, Ryun decided to run for the House. He was opposed in the Republican primary by former Topeka Mayor Douglas Wright and Cheryl Brown Henderson, whose father was the plaintiff in *Brown v. Board*. Wright called Ryun an "extremist" and predicted that Ryun couldn't win the general. Ryun campaigned for tax cuts and opposed abortion rights. While the press treated Ryun as something of an oddity, Republican voters didn't: He won 62% of the vote. In the general, Ryun was outspent by trial lawyer John Frieden. Democrats circulated "Courtship Makes a Comeback," written by Ryun and his wife for Focus on the Family. It told how any young man wanting to date Ryun's daughters has to call him and ask permission. Again there was ridicule, with the press calling Dr. Ruth to mock the Ryuns' practices. However absurd these beliefs may seem to Upper East Side Manhattan or Malibu sophisticates, they were not political poison in Manhattan, Kansas. Ryun won 52%–45%.

In the House, Ryun has a very conservative voting record. Unlike former athletes like Jack Kemp and Bill Bradley, he has not sought the spotlight. He was a leader of anti-abortion forces who opposed the bankruptcy reform bill because of a provision put in by the Senate which made fines for certain abortion protesters undischargeable in bankruptcy; he also bucked Republican leaders by voting against the Medicare/prescription drug bill in 2003. Ryun, who suffered 50% hearing loss because of childhood measles, wants to provide hearing aids to those with disabilities. On the Armed Services Committee, he backed increased military spending. An outspoken supporter of Taiwan, he won House passage of his amendment to improve its defense against China. Concerned about Fort Riley, he sought to delay the 2005 base-closing process, and worked to bring money in for base improvements.

In 2004, he had his first competitive reelection contest since he came to Congress. After switching parties, Democratic challenger Nancy Boyda complained that Republicans had grown too conservative and criticized Ryun's votes for school vouchers and his lack of support for public schools. Ryun attacked her for participating in protests against the war in Iraq. Despite spending heavily, including nearly $300,000 of her own money, Boyda lost 56%–41%, winning only in historically Democratic Crawford County in the Balkans.

THIRD DISTRICT

Rep. Dennis Moore (D)

Elected 1998, 4th term; b. Nov. 8, 1945, Anthony; home, Lenexa; U. of KS, B.A. 1967; Washburn U. Law Schl., J.D. 1970; Protestant; married (Stephene).

Military Career: Army, 1970; Army Reserves, 1971–73.

Elected Office: Johnson Cnty. Dist. Atty., 1976–88; Johnson Cnty. Comm. Coll. Bd. of Trustees, 1993–98.

Professional Career: Asst. KS Atty. Gen., 1971–73; Practicing atty., 1973–76, 1989–98.

DC Office: 1727 LHOB, 20515, 202-225-2865; Fax: 202-225-2807; Web site: www.house.gov/moore.

District Offices: Kansas City, 913-621-0832; Lawrence, 785-842-9313; Overland Park, 913-383-2013.

Committees: *Budget* (2d of 17 D). *Financial Services* (14th of 32 D): Capital Markets, Insurance & Government Sponsored Enterprises; Financial Institutions & Consumer Credit; Oversight & Investigations.

Group Ratings

	ADA	ACLU	AFS	LCV	ITIC	NTU	COC	ACU	NTLC	CHC
2004	90	60	88	82	100	18	62	20	14	30
2003	90	—	100	95	—	23	52	24	—	—

National Journal Ratings

	2003 LIB	—	2003 CONS	2004 LIB	—	2004 CONS
Economic	63%	—	36%	61%	—	39%
Social	69%	—	30%	65%	—	35%
Foreign	61%	—	37%	59%	—	40%

Key Votes of the 108th Congress

1. Drilling in ANWR	N	5. DC School Vouchers	N	9. Ban Same-Sex Marriage	N
2. Approve Bush Tax Cuts	N	6. Ban Human Cloning	N	10. Fund Iraq War	Y
3. Medicare/Rx Bill	N	7. Restrict Gun Liability	N	11. Bar Cuba Embargo Funds	Y
4. Bar Overtime Pay Regs.	Y	8. Ban Partial-Birth Abortion	N	12. Intelligence Reorg.	Y

Election Results

2004 general	Dennis Moore (D)	184,050	(55%)	($2,362,887)
	Kris Kobach (R)	145,542	(43%)	($1,191,231)
	Other	6,147	(2%)	
2004 primary	Dennis Moore (D)	unopposed		
2002 general	Dennis Moore (D)	110,095	(50%)	($1,871,416)
	Adam Taff (R)	102,882	(47%)	($1,050,226)
	Other	6,412	(3%)	

Prior Winning Percentages: 2000 (50%); 1998 (52%)

The People		Race/Ethnic Origin	Ancestry	
Area size:	787 sq. mi.	79.6% White	German: 18.0%	Irish: 10.5%
Urban population:	94.7%	8.8% Black	English: 9.0%	
Rural population:	5.3%	2.6% Asian	**2004 Presidential Vote**	
Pop. 2000:	672,124	0.6% Native Am.	Bush (R)	186,476 (55%)
Median income:	$51,118	0.0% Hawaiian	Kerry (D)	150,598 (44%)
Poverty status:	7.8%	1.5% Two+ races	Other	3,262 (1%)
Military veterans:	12.1%	0.1% Other	**2000 Presidential Vote**	
		6.8% Hispanic Origin	Bush (R)	152,832 (53%)
			Gore (D)	122,463 (42%)
			Other	13,452 (5%)
			Cook Partisan Voting Index: R + 4	

Occupation	Blue collar: 17.3%	White collar: 70.4%	Gray collar: 12.3%

Though its central city is in Missouri, 40 percent of metropolitan Kansas City's residents now live west of the state line in Kansas. Some are in Kansas City, Kansas, (or KCK as it is sometimes called) where the low-lying land near the Missouri River used to house one of the nation's largest stockyards. This is still a working-class town with a few dilapidated looking streets and lots of modest frame houses, new Latino neighborhoods, the largest black neighborhood and the oldest Catholic ethnic neighborhoods in Kansas. Kansas City's Wyandotte County was 28% black and 16% Hispanic in 2000. South of Kansas City and Wyandotte is Johnson County, much more affluent and more than three times larger than Wyandotte, separated from the affluent Kansas City, Missouri, neighborhood around the old Country Club Plaza shopping center by just a single small street. The newer neighborhoods are arrayed along the interstates, as subdivisions have replaced croplands. They have grown to the point that Overland Park, Olathe, Shawnee and Lenexa are among the largest cities in the state. These suburbs are not just residential; Applebee's restaurant chain, a J.C. Penney catalog center, as well as lots of thriving small businesses, are in Johnson County. But capitalism produces creative destruction: Sprint, headquartered here, merged with Nextel and moved its corporate headquarters to Northern Virginia. Politically, Wyandotte County has an old Democratic machine politics, while Johnson County has long been heavily Republican, but with plenty of voters moderate or even liberal on cultural issues and fierce fights between moderate and conservative Republicans.

The 3d Congressional District of Kansas consists of Johnson County, Wyandotte County and part of Douglas County to the west including the portion of Lawrence that is the home of the University of Kansas campus. More than two-thirds of its people live in Johnson County, which grew by 27% in the 1990s and had a $62,000 median household income. This is an affluent metropolitan district in a rough-hewn, historically rural state.

The congressman from the 3d District is Dennis Moore, a Democrat first elected in 1998. Moore grew up in Wichita, where his father Warner Moore ran for Congress in the 4th District and lost the general by only 50.3%–49.7% in 1958. Moore went to college and law school in Kansas, served in the Army and practiced law in Johnson County. In 1976, at 31, he was elected Johnson County district attorney and was twice re-elected. He went into private law practice, and was elected to the local community college board in 1993.

In 1998, when national Democrats were recruiting a candidate to run against conservative Republican incumbent Vince Snowbarger, Moore's electoral success made him a natural choice. Snowbarger made "trust" his major theme, but ran few if any ads on what he'd done positively. The contest attracted independent expenditure campaigns, with the Sierra Club and the AFL-CIO spending heavily on TV ads, mailings and phone banks to elect Moore. Moore won 52%–48%, carrying Kansas City and Lawrence by wide margins, but his key wins came in the affluent, long-settled suburbs in northeast Johnson County.

In the House, Moore joined the Blue Dogs and moderate Democrats who sought to straddle party lines. To the dismay of organized labor, he voted for normal trade relations with China and trade promotion authority. He filed a bill, with 175 cosponsors, to authorize the HHS Secretary to negotiate fair prescription-drug prices for Medicare beneficiaries.

Republicans have tried to recapture this seat, but have been hampered by the bitter division between conservative and moderate Kansas Republicans. In 2000, the primary was between tax-cutting state Representative Phill Kline and Greg Musil, an Overland Park councilman with support from moderates and the backing of National Republican Congressional Committee Chairman Tom Davis. Kline won the primary 50%–37%. In the general, Kline did a more effective job than Snowbarger had in rallying moderate Republican leaders, but Moore appealed to moderates by portraying himself as a fiscal conservative and a crime-fighter. The result was similar to 1998: Moore won 50%–47%. The scenario changed slightly in 2002. This time, the NRCC supported reconstructive surgeon Jeff Colyer, the anti-abortion candidate, against United Airlines pilot and former Naval F-18 aviator Adam Taff, who supported abortion rights. Colyer outspent him 2-to-1, but Taff got a late endorsement from Governor Bill Graves and unexpectedly won the primary, 52%–48%. Republicans coalescéd behind Taff, who emphasized his military experience and top-secret clearance, but it didn't help that NRCC Chairman Davis earlier had said Taff is "a nice kid, but he's got no clue." Taff was significantly outspent and did not run negative ads. He carried Johnson County by 53%–44% but lost overall, 50%–47%. His backers complained that NRCC support was too little and too late. And as it turned out, Republican redistricters also had inadvertently helped Moore by keeping part of Douglas County in the district.

In 2004, Taff ran again. But he lost the primary to Kris Kobach, a conservative former Overland Park councilman and a top aide to Attorney General John Ashcroft who helped to create the Justice Department program to collect information about foreign visitors following the September 11 attacks. With strong support from Christian conservatives, Kobach matched Taff in the primary and, after a one-week recount, won the primary by 207 votes. In the general, both candidates spent abundantly and Kobach appealed aggressively to his base, but Moore had his biggest win yet: 55%–43%. He took 70% of the vote in Wyandotte County and 68% in Douglas County; he even prevailed 50%–48% in Johnson County, which cast 74% of the total vote.

Demographics pretty much guarantee that this district will continue to be seriously contested. Johnson County continues to grow rapidly, while Wyandotte County has been losing population. Moore has appealed to enough Republican voters to hold the seat but he probably is not secure enough to avoid seriously contested challenges for as long as he runs.

FOURTH DISTRICT

Rep. Todd Tiahrt (R)

Elected 1994, 6th term; b. June 15, 1951, Vermillion, SD; home, Goddard; SD Sch. of Mines, 1969–71; Evangel Col., B.A. 1975; SW MO St. U., M.B.A. 1989; Assembly of God; married (Vicki).

Elected Office: KS Senate, 1992–94.

Professional Career: Project Engineer, Zenith Corp., 1978–81; Proposal Mgr., Boeing Co., 1981–94.

DC Office: 2441 RHOB, 20515, 202-225-6216; Fax: 202-225-3489; Web site: www.house.gov/tiahrt.

District Office: Wichita, 316-262-8992.

Committees: *Appropriations* (17th of 37 R): Defense; Transportation, Treasury, HUD, the Judiciary & District of Columbia. *Permanent Select Committee on Intelligence* (10th of 12 R): Oversight; Terrorism, Human Intelligence, Analysis & Counterintelligence.

Group Ratings

	ADA	ACLU	AFS	LCV	ITIC	NTU	COC	ACU	NTLC	CHC
2004	5	0	13	9	88	60	100	92	81	100
2003	5	—	13	0	—	63	100	92	—	—

National Journal Ratings

	2003 LIB	—	2003 CONS		2004 LIB	—	2004 CONS
Economic	0%	—	91%		16%	—	83%
Social	5%	—	87%		23%	—	77%
Foreign	0%	—	89%		4%	—	93%

Key Votes of the 108th Congress

1. Drilling in ANWR	Y	5. DC School Vouchers	Y	9. Ban Same-Sex Marriage	Y
2. Approve Bush Tax Cuts	Y	6. Ban Human Cloning	Y	10. Fund Iraq War	Y
3. Medicare/Rx Bill	Y	7. Restrict Gun Liability	Y	11. Bar Cuba Embargo Funds	N
4. Bar Overtime Pay Regs.	N	8. Ban Partial-Birth Abortion	Y	12. Intelligence Reorg.	Y

Election Results

2004 general	Todd Tiahrt (R)	173,151	(66%)	($491,456)
	Michael Kinard (D)	81,388	(31%)	($15,083)
	Other	7,376	(3%)	
2004 primary	Todd Tiahrt (R)	unopposed		
2002 general	Todd Tiahrt (R)	115,691	(61%)	($1,132,104)
	Carlos Nolla (D)	70,656	(37%)	($686,952)
	Other	4,616	(2%)	

Prior Winning Percentages: 2000 (54%); 1998 (58%); 1996 (50%); 1994 (53%)

The People		Race/Ethnic Origin	Ancestry	
Area size:	9,596 sq. mi.	81.0% White	German: 17.7%	English: 8.0%
Urban population:	78.8%	6.8% Black	Irish: 7.9%	
Rural population:	21.2%	2.4% Asian	**2004 Presidential Vote**	
Pop. 2000:	672,101	1.1% Native Am.	Bush (R) 173,643	(64%)
Median income:	$40,917	0.0% Hawaiian	Kerry (D) 93,129	(34%)
Poverty status:	9.6%	2.0% Two+ races	Other 3,783	(1%)
Military veterans:	14.0%	0.1% Other	**2000 Presidential Vote**	
		6.6% Hispanic Origin	Bush (R) 146,921	(59%)
			Gore (D) 91,232	(37%)
			Other 10,918	(4%)
			Cook Partisan Voting Index: R +12	

Occupation   Blue collar: 28.3%   White collar: 57.0%   Gray collar: 14.6%

Wichita is the largest Kansas-only metropolitan area, smaller than million-plus metro Kansas City, but a Great Plains metropolis of the magnitude of Omaha or Tulsa, and still growing. It began as a farm market town and grew with local oil and gas discoveries in the 1920s. But its real impetus came during World War II and the years just after, when aircraft factories sprouted up here on the Kansas plains and Wichita suddenly became the nation's major producer of small planes. Today the big four—Cessna, Raytheon, Boeing, Bombardier—are all located here. In the early 1990s, general aviation was hurt by the recession and by lawsuits that held manufacturers liable for planes they had produced years, even decades, before. A few years later, Wichita recovered: The demand for small planes was robust, and a federal limit on liability enlivened the industry. But the September 11 attacks were a severe blow to the airline industry and, therefore, to Wichita which lost some 12,000 jobs. Some shifted to health care, as Wichita has become a regional center in the Great Plains pattern, as people from miles around come to the metropolis for treatment. In 2004, the Navy gave the area a boost with a contract for 100 modified 737's to hunt submarines. More good news came with the opening of Cessna's huge hangar center to service business jets.

Kansas' 4th Congressional District is centered around Wichita, covering wheat-growing areas to the east and west, but with most of its people in Wichita and Sedgwick County. Politically, it has voted Republican in federal elections but has voted Democratic occasionally in state contests.

The congressman from the 4th District is Todd Tiahrt (pronounced *TEE-hart*), a Republican first elected in 1994. He grew up on a farm in South Dakota, went to the same high school as South Dakota Senator Tim Johnson, played football for the South Dakota School of Mines and Technology and graduated from Evangel College. In 1976 he moved to the Wichita area to be closer to his wife's family and worked at Zenith as a project engineer and at Boeing as a proposal manager on the Space Station, Air Force One, KC-135, B-52, B-1, B-2, A-67, YF-22 and Comanche helicopter programs. In 1990 he went to the courthouse to file to run for the Kansas House and decided he was a Republican; he lost that race by eight votes. His grandfather raised him to be a Democrat, but he found his strong religious views were more in line with Republicans. In 1992 he was elected to the Kansas Senate, where his great cause was a concealed weapons law.

In 1994 Tiahrt decided to run against Democratic Congressman Dan Glickman, who had served for 18 years: one of the reasons Democrats held majorities in the House so long was because talented politicians held Republican-leaning districts like this for many years. Tiahrt ran ads showing Glickman's face morphing into Bill Clinton's, and attacked him for voting for gun control in the 1994 crime bill. With his base among Wichita's numerous religious conservatives, who had taken over the local Republican Party, he assembled a corps of 1,800 volunteers, many from church contacts. Glickman outspent him more than 3-to-1 and continued to run relatively well in high-income Republican precincts, but he suffered serious losses in middle-income areas in Sedgwick County. Tiahrt won a solid 53%–47% victory.

In the House, Tiahrt has a solidly conservative voting record, and has been a close ally of Tom DeLay. He has sponsored measures that help aircraft manufacturers, including accelerated depreciation for non-commercial sales and support for the Air Force's proposal to buy KC-767 aerial refueling tankers from Boeing. He sided with aerospace workers in opposing George W. Bush's proposal to change rules on overtime pay. He proposed eliminating the Department of Energy and transferring nuclear weapons storage and waste disposal to the Pentagon, to no effect. He tried to zero out—and later, to reduce—AmeriCorps, but with no success. On Appropriations, he won approval of his proposal to bar enforcement of certain record-keeping requirements for gun dealers. He kept the pressure on Metro officials in the Capitol region to make sure that their signs included the correct name of Ronald Reagan Washington National Airport. In response to a federal investigation of Wichita-area construction sites, Tiahrt proposed to overhaul the Occupational Safety and Health Administration so that the relationship between builders and OSHA was less adversarial. In November 2004, in conference he added $1 million to the omnibus appropriations bill at the request of Wichita's police chief; the police department was running out of money to investigate the "BTK" serial killer, who had resurfaced earlier that year. In March 2005, police announced an arrest in the case. By agreeing to his funding request, "The Republican leadership helped to catch a serial killer," Tiahrt said. "It's one of the top 10 most gratifying things I've done since I got to Congress."

Democrats targeted Tiahrt during his early years with well-financed opponents, but he finally may have locked up the district. In 2000, Wichita attorney and former Glickman aide Carlos Nolla ran a tougher-than-expected challenge against him. Tiahrt won 54%–42%, sweeping all 12 counties. In a rematch two years later, Nolla doubled his fundraising with support from national Hispanics, and said that Tiahrt was beholden to pharmaceutical companies, but he lost 61%–37%. In 2004, the Democratic nominee was poorly funded and got little attention. Tiahrt has sought to move up the political ladder. He considered running for governor in 2002, but backed off. In the House, he pushed for Roy Blunt to appoint him as chief deputy whip, but the job went to the more junior Eric Cantor of Virginia. Blunt later named Tiahrt as his liaison to the Appropriations Committee.

★ KENTUCKY ★

Kentucky is a state that in many ways remains close to its beginnings. This is, literally, a Jeffersonian commonwealth: It is one of four commonwealths (the others are Virginia, Pennsylvania and Massachusetts) and when the first settlers came here, in the years Thomas Jefferson was writing his *Notes on Virginia*, it was part of Virginia. Kentucky was admitted to the Union in 1792, when Jefferson was secretary of state; when Jefferson was aroused at the Federalists' anti-sedition acts, he ghostwrote the Kentucky Resolutions in 1798. Kentucky's largest county is named after Jefferson and what has long been its largest city after the monarch to whom he was credentialed as ambassador to France, Louis XVI. To this day, Kentucky still has a constitution informed by a Jeffersonian jealousy of power. Its one-term limit on governors was raised to two only in 1995; it limited it state legislature to one 60-day session every two years until 2001, so that much important business was done in special sessions; every governor must swear that he or she has not participated in a duel (remember what Jefferson thought of Aaron Burr). Kentucky for many long years favored the Democratic Party, which can trace its ancestry at least tenuously back to Jefferson. But here too there has been change recently. George W. Bush

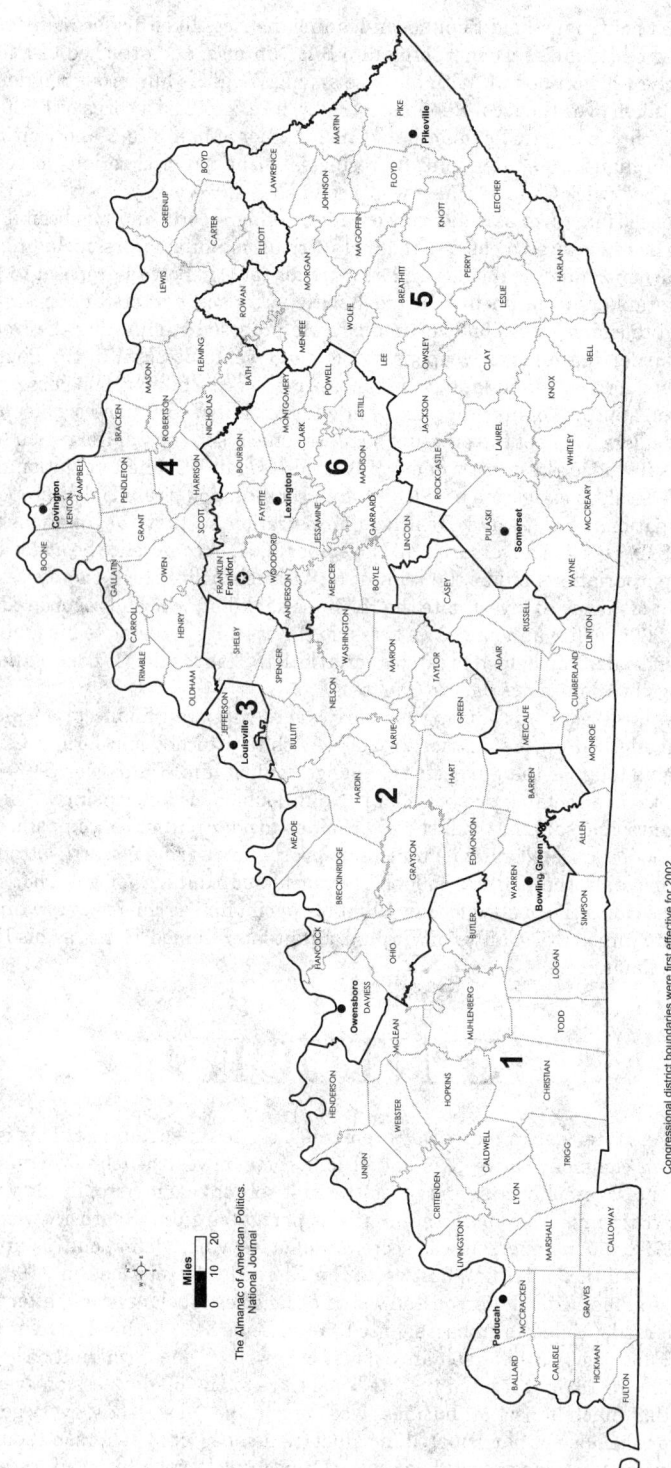

The Almanac of American Politics.
National Journal

Miles
0 10 20

Congressional district boundaries were first effective for 2002.

carried Kentucky twice, after it was carried twice, by diminishing margins, by William Jefferson Clinton. Both of Kentucky's senators and five of its six House members are Republicans; a Republican was elected governor in 2003, for the first time since 1967, and Republicans have had a majority in the state Senate since 1999.

The agrarian Jefferson would approve of Kentucky's demography, which is still quite rural, with well under half its population in the big metropolitan areas of Louisville, Lexington and the Northern Kentucky area across the Ohio River from Cincinnati. And the tobacco planters who once presided over what one historian called "the alcoholic republic" might not entirely disapprove of a Kentucky economy that remained for years heavily dependent on century-old industries such as whiskey (Bourbon County, where the beverage was invented in the 18th century, is in Kentucky), tobacco (Kentucky is the nation's number two producer after North Carolina, and it has the largest number of tobacco farms) and coal. But change is coming here too. Kentucky ranks number one in percentage of smokers, but the city-county council voted a ban on smoking in public places in Lexington, the site of Kentucky's burley market, and the buyout of already dwindling tobacco quotas voted by Congress in 2004 will likely result in the end of tobacco farming in the Appalachian mountains and a shift of production to central and western Kentucky. Louisville's Brown & Williamson Tobacco was absorbed by R. J. Reynolds, based in North Carolina. Employment is sharply down in coal and tobacco, and Kentucky has big plants producing appliances, Toyotas, Ford trucks and Lexmark printers; it also has big companies that specialize in things not traditionally Kentuckian, such as Humana health services and Ashland Inc. oil company. Still, this is an economy that did not partake in much of the bounteous growth of the 1990s and in which manufacturing jobs declined after 2000.

Many of the buildings here are old: The small-town 19th century courthouses, the cabins in the coal mining Appalachians, the unpainted houses in the soggy lowlands beneath the levees by the Mississippi River. Kentucky is the home of some of the nation's oldest traditions, from bourbon to bluegrass music to religious revivals (the Disciples of Christ got their start in the enormous revival at Cane Ridge in 1801); it was the home of the inventor of Mother's Day in 1887 and a Louisville restaurant that claims credit for inventing the cheeseburger. Some things have changed. Satellite dishes and four-lane highways have brought modern civilization into hollows and lowland farms that lacked indoor plumbing and electricity within living memory and farmers have begun to diversify their crops; Eastern Kentucky farmers raise goats for meat production and the state touts its grape vineyards and fruit orchards. But people in this state still have a strong attachment to place and family; the continuity is real. Kentucky's population has grown just 42% over the past 50 years; few outsiders have moved in, though the number increased in the 1990s, so today's Kentuckians are mostly descendants of settlers who poured over the mountains in the 40 years after Daniel Boone made his way through the Cumberland Gap in 1775, when Kentucky's population rose from 73,000 in the Census of 1790 to 564,000 in 1820.

There has long been hearty, though lopsided, political competition here, with most of the 120 counties voting today as they did in the Civil War era. The eastern mountains were pro-Union and remain Republican, except for counties where coal miners were organized by the United Mine Workers in the 1930s; the Bluegrass region and the western end of the state were slaveholding territory and Democratic, though they have shifted to Republicans in the last decade. Louisville, with many German immigrants, was an anti-slavery town, and for years flirted with Republicans; Jefferson County recently has voted narrowly Democratic, though by margins small enough to be offset by Republican margins in fast-growing suburban Oldham and Bullitt Counties. For years, all this meant Democratic party control, with the real battle in the primary. For nearly half a century there was almost a two-party system within the dominant party, with factions going back to the 1938 primary when Senate Majority Leader (and later Vice President) Alben Barkley was challenged by Governor (and later Senator and baseball commissioner) "Happy" Chandler. Barkley's faction was later led by Governor (1959–63) Bert Combs and by Governor (1971–74) and Senator (1974–99) Wendell Ford. But as Louisville *Courier-Journal* reporter Al Cross notes, factional gave way to money, with rich Democrats elected governor over most of the last 20 years—John Y. Brown Jr. in 1979, Wallace Wilkinson in 1987 and Brereton

Jones in 1991. Partisan competition since has been sharper. Democrat Paul Patton was only narrowly elected in 1995 and in 2003, when the term-limited Patton was tarred by scandal, Republican Ernie Fletcher beat Attorney General (now Congressman) Ben Chandler, the grandson of "Happy" Chandler, by a 55%–45% margin.

The change has been most pronounced in congressional elections. Much of this has been the work of Senator Mitch McConnell, first elected in 1984. McConnell helped line up candidates who carried three formerly Democratic congressional districts in 1994 and 1996; he provided key support for Senator Jim Bunning's 6,766-vote win in 1998 and helped capture the 6th District vacated by Bunning's opponent that year as well. Now only the 6th District is represented by a Democrat, Ben Chandler, who replaced Governor Ernie Fletcher in a 2004 special election not long after Chandler lost the governor's race. In July and August 1999 party switches gave Republicans a 20–18 margin in the state Senate, where they were outnumbered 30–8 in 1990; the state House is just 57–43 Democratic. The biggest Republican triumph came in the 2000 presidential race. Al Gore initially targeted Kentucky, which is just north of his home state of Tennessee and which the Clinton-Gore ticket carried twice. But Kentucky was part of the rural trend away from Clinton Democrats and toward Republicans in the 1990s, and Gore had taken stands seen as hostile to the state's leading industries—tobacco, coal and automobiles. Early polls showed Bush far ahead, and Gore took his ads off Kentucky stations and took the state off his schedule. Bush swept the state, 57%–41%. In 2004 Kentucky was never on anyone's list of battleground states and Bush won 60%–40%. If Bush's politics of decentralized government and confident nationalism can be called Jeffersonian, then Kentucky in 2000 and 2004 voted in line with its Jeffersonian roots.

The People		Race/Ethnic Origin			Military veterans: 380,618 (12.5%)	
Pop. 2004 (est):	4,145,922	3,608,013	89.3%	White	WWII: 18.9%	Korea: 13.5%
Pop. 2000:	4,041,769	293,639	7.3%	Black	Vietnam: 32.6%	Gulf War: 10.8%
Pop. 1990:	3,685,296	29,368	0.7%	Asian	**Most populous cities (2003):**	
Change 1990–2000:	Up 9.6%	7,939	0.2%	Native Am.	1. Louisville	699,017
% of U.S. total:	1.4%	1,275	0.0%	Hawaiian	2. Lexington	266,798
Pop. rank:	25th of 50	37,750	0.9%	Two+ races	3. Owensboro	54,312
Area size:	40,409 sq. mi.	3,846	0.1%	Other	4. Bowling Green	50,663
State Native:	73.7%	59,939	1.5%	Hisp. Origin	5. Covington	42,687
Non-citizen:	1.3%	**Ancestry**				
Language		USA: 17.3%		German: 10.5%	Urban population: 55.7%	
English: 94.4%	Spanish: 2.7%	Irish: 8.6%		English: 8.0%	Rural population: 44.3%	
Other Eur.: 2.0%		Scotch-Irish: 1.4%				

Education		Work Sector		Legislature	
H.S. Grad:	74.1%	Private: 78.5%	Govt: 14.4%	Senate	22 R 15 D 1 I
College Grad:	17.1%	Self: 6.7%	Family: 0.4%	House	57 D 43 R
Industry		Unemployment: 5.7%		Legislative Term Limits: No	
Agri: 3.3%	Con: 7.2%	**Household Income**		**Registered Voters**	
Fin: 5.4%	Info: 2.2%	<15k: 22.3%	15-35k: 29.2%	D: 1,618,928	(57.5%)
Mfg: 23.6%	Prof: 26.6%	35-50k: 16.4%	50-100k: 24.9%	R: 1,011,972	(36.0%)
Public: 4.3%	Trade: 15.5%	100-150k: 4.6%	>150k: 2.6%	O: 184,251	(6.5%)
Other: 12.0%		Median: $33,672			
Occupation		Poverty status: 15.8%			
Blue collar: 30.7%	White collar: 54.1%	**Home Value**			
Gray collar: 15.2%		<50k: 27.3%	50-100k: 38.9%	100-200k: 26.1%	200-300k: 5.1%
		300-500k: 1.9%	>500k: 0.8%	Median: $79,600	

Presidential politics   Kentucky's solid backing of George W. Bush in 2000 was all the more remarkable because Kentucky has usually been a competitive state when Democrats run a Southerner or two on its ticket, as in such widely separated years as 1952, 1976, 1980, 1992 and 1996. In 2004, when the Democrats nominated a Massachusetts liberal, Kentucky was even more one-sided. Bush lost Jefferson County 50%–49% and carried 108 of the 119 other counties; Kerry carried just 11 counties in the eastern mountains. Bush's percentage increased robustly in the southeastern mountains, in the Bluegrass region around Lexington and in the Jackson Purchase in far western Kentucky; he lost ground appreciably only in some northeastern mountain counties. Bush carried voters in all age and income groups; he won 71% among white evangelical or born again Protestants, who made up 45% of the electorate.

Kentucky was part of the Super Tuesday primary in March 1988, but switched back to a May date in 1992, so that state and presidential contests can be held on the same day. It has had no effect on the outcome of the presidential contest.

2004 Presidential Vote		
Bush (R)	1,069,439	(60%)
Kerry (D)	712,733	(40%)
Nader (I)	8,856	(0%)
Other	4,832	(0%)

2004 Democratic Presidential Primary		
Kerry (D)	138,175	(60%)
Edwards (D)	33,403	(15%)
Uncommitted (D)	21,199	(9%)
Lieberman (D)	11,062	(5%)
Dean (D)	8,222	(4%)
Other	17,855	(8%)

2000 Presidential Vote		
Bush (R)	872,520	(57%)
Gore (D)	638,923	(41%)
Nader (Green)	23,118	(1%)
Other	9,465	(1%)

Congressional districting   Kentucky's 1991 redistricting plan, drawn by Democrats after the state lost one House seat in the 1990 Census, was intended to protect Democratic incumbents, but instead produced a delegation that was 5–1 Republican by 1996. Party control of the legislature in 2001 was split. House Democrats prepared a plan that would have chopped off the east end of the 1st District and added Owensboro to it, making it more difficult for Republican Ed Whitfield. Senate Republicans were prepared to pass the incumbent Republicans' plan that would have added heavily Republican Oldham County to the 3d District to strengthen Anne Northup. The impasse continued through January 2002, delaying the January 29 filing deadline for candidates. On February 1, the legislature finally adopted a compromise plan that changed the lines very little. With one important exception: It removed increasingly Republican suburban Shelby County from the 4th District and added three and one-half traditionally Democratic counties.

109th Congress Lineup
5 R   1 D

108th Congress Lineup
5 R   1 D

Governor

Ernie Fletcher (R)

Elected 2003, term expires Dec. 2007, 1st term; b. Nov. 12, 1952, Mt. Sterling; home, Lexington; U. of KY, B.S. 1974, M.D. 1984; Baptist; married (Glenna).

Military Career: Air Force, 1974–80.

Elected Office: KY House of Reps., 1994–96; U.S. House of Reps., 1998–2003.

Professional Career: Practicing physician, 1984-present; CEO, St. Joseph Medical Foundation, 1997–99.

Office: State Capitol, 700 Capitol Ave., Frankfort, 40601, 502-564-2611; Fax: 502-564-2517; Web site: gov.state.ky.us.

Election Results

2003 general	Ernie Fletcher (R)	596,284	(55%)
	Ben Chandler (D)	487,159	(45%)
2003 primary	Ernie Fletcher (R)	90,912	(57%)
	Rebecca Jackson (R)	44,084	(28%)
	Steve Nunn (R)	21,167	(13%)
	Other	2,365	(1%)
1999 general	Paul Patton (D)	352,099	(61%)
	Peppy Martin (R)	128,788	(22%)
	Gatewood Galbraith (Ref)	88,930	(15%)
	Other	6,934	(1%)

There is no question who ordinarily stands at the apex of Kentucky politics: The governor. The governor's appointment powers are wide; until the passage of a constitutional amendment in 2000, the legislature met in regular session for only 60 days in even-numbered years. Beginning in 2001, the legislature began meeting for 30 days in odd-numbered years also but the governor still can shift around line items in the state budget and call special sessions. Kentucky's governor, elected in 2003, is Ernie Fletcher, a Republican who grew up in Mount Sterling, about an hour's drive east of the state capitol. Fletcher got an engineering degree from the University of Kentucky, was an Air Force pilot for five years, intercepting Soviet aircraft; then he went to medical school, practiced medicine, and was CEO of a company that managed medical practices. He did volunteer medical work in India and was a lay minister. In 1994 he was elected to the Kentucky House. In 1996 he won the Republican primary—by exactly 4 votes—and ran against Democratic Congressman Scotty Baesler, a tobacco farmer and onetime University of Kentucky basketball star. With help from national Republicans, Fletcher raised and spent nearly as much as the incumbent and ran a spirited campaign. He lost 56%–44%, but kept his taste for campaigning.

When Baesler ran for the Senate in 1998, Fletcher decided to run for Congress again and won 53%–46%. In the House, Fletcher established a conservative record and became an activist legislator. Unlike other recent Republican doctors elected to the House who have taken on HMOs, he worked to craft the less sweeping Republican alternative on HMO regulation. He advocated the successful ed-flex bill to give the states greater flexibility in education spending, a measure he will surely come to appreciate more in his new position. He twice won reelection; in 2002, no Democrat filed to run.

Kentucky is one of five states that hold governor's elections in odd years, which enabled Fletcher to run in 2003 without the risk of giving up his House seat, a necessary consideration in a state where Republicans last won the governorship in 1967. He did not have a clear path to the nomination. He faced two serious candidates, former Jefferson County Judge-Executive (the county and Louisville city governments were merged in 2003) Rebecca Jackson and state Representative Steve Nunn, the son of Louie Nunn, the state's last Republican governor. Jackson stressed her credentials as an executive and zeroed in on outgoing Governor Paul Patton; she called for his resignation during his scandal-plagued second-term. In early 2002 Patton seemed at the summit of his career; he became head of the National Governors Association in July and he was seen as a likely and formidable candidate against Senator Jim Bunning in 2004. Then, in September 2002, the owner of a nursing home in Hickman County sued Patton for sexual harassment. At first Patton denied her charges, but when the Louisville *Courier-Journal* obtained phone records showing 440 calls from Patton's office to Conner's home and office, he admitted that they had had an "inappropriate personal relationship," but denied that he had used state government to retaliate. Not surprisingly this was the biggest Kentucky news story of the year. The state's two U.S. attorneys and state Attorney General Ben Chandler announced they were investigating. A few days after his confession Patton said, "I do not anticipate, in the foreseeable future, any involvement in the political process, including the U.S. Senate race." Republicans ran ads for the November 2002 legislative races urging voters to "stand up to Paul Patton and the scandals in Frankfort"; Patton's chief of staff had been indicted for violating campaign finance laws in the 1995 election.

In January 2003, Patton's lieutenant governor, Steve Henry, announced his withdrawal from the governor's race. "I'm part of an administration," he said. "In the end, that would have been used against me." But he had other troubles: the federal government had sued Henry, a surgeon, for overbilling Medicare and Medicaid. That left Attorney General Ben Chandler, House Speaker Jody Richards and health care entrepreneur Bruce Lunsford as the most serious candidates in the Democratic primary.

The Patton administration scandals gave the Republicans field a strong theme to run on but Fletcher and Nunn, both of whom campaigned as agents of change, became enmeshed in legal struggles. Fletcher's original choice for lieutenant governor, Hunter Bates, a former top aide to Senator Mitch McConnell, was disqualified after a lawsuit successfully challenged his eligibility. The Kentucky constitution requires that the governor and lieutenant governor must have lived in the state for six years when elected; Bates had moved back to the state less than two years before. Steve Nunn's choice for lieutenant governor, Bob Heleringer, then sued to prevent Fletcher from choosing another running mate, a gambit which, if successful, would have made Fletcher himself ineligible for the nomination. The state supreme court ruled in Fletcher's favor and he then named U.S. Attorney Steve Pence—who had been prosecuting Steve Henry in the overbilling case before resigning—as Bates's replacement.

Among Republican primary voters, the legal maneuvering appeared to hurt Nunn far worse than Fletcher. Fletcher won a solid 57% victory, with 28% for Jackson and just 13% for Nunn. State Senator Virgil Moore finished fourth with 2%. Fletcher showed his greatest strength in the counties he represented in Congress and racked up 84% in Lexington's Fayette County, his home. In the general, Fletcher faced Attorney General Ben Chandler, the grandson of former Governor and Senator (and pro baseball commissioner) A.B. "Happy" Chandler. Ben Chandler had narrowly won the nomination over House Speaker Jody Richards 50%–47% after weathering a tough primary season as the main target of Lunsford, who spent more than $8 million, much of it attacking Chandler as a career politician. Lunsford withdrew his candidacy four days before the May 20 primary and backed Richards after the Chandler campaign ran a tough ad stating Lunsford didn't care about the abuse of a patient in one of his nursing homes; he eventually endorsed Fletcher in the general.

Chandler, who was unpopular with some insiders but popular with voters for his prosecution of Patton's chief of staff and two union leaders, reminded voters that he had taken on Patton and had "convicted corrupt politicians." But Fletcher, as the nominee of the party that hadn't held the governor's office in over three decades, had the more persuasive argument. He promised to "clean up the mess in Frankfort." In the background loomed a $300 million budget deficit facing the next governor. Both Fletcher and Chandler promised to address the shortfall by cutting waste, abuse and fraud in state government. Fletcher also signed a pledge not to raise taxes. In June, the Republican Governors Association released a poll showing Fletcher with a 7-point lead, the first time, noted political reporter Al Cross of the *Courier-Journal*, that any Republican gubernatorial nominee had ever led in a published poll in Kentucky. Chandler focused on job losses and national Republican economic policies, a questionable tack considering George W. Bush's popularity in Kentucky (he would win 60% in 2004). Chandler also hammered Fletcher for a 2003 congressional vote against reimportation of prescription drugs from Canada; he said Fletcher was too close to drug manufacturers, who were big contributors to Fletcher while he was in Congress.

Fletcher won 55% to 45%, carrying 86 of 120 counties. He carried Northern Kentucky, won Lexington's Fayette County 54%–46% and only narrowly lost Louisville's Jefferson County 51%–49%; Fletcher ran weakest in traditionally Democratic areas, the Pennyrile to the west and in the coal-mining eastern mountain counties. He outspent Chandler $5.7 million to $3.8 million and was assisted by close to $2 million in television ads bought by the RGA. His win capped a decade-long Republican surge that, by the end of 2004, left Republicans in control of both Senate seats, 5 of 6 House seats, and a majority in the state Senate. Republicans also in 2003 won two state offices that had been in Democratic control since 1971—secretary of state and commissioner of agriculture—and picked up 7 state House seats to the narrow the Democratic margin to 57–43.

Kentucky governors begin their terms in December and by mid-January 2004 Fletcher could point to several accomplishments. He reduced the number of executive branch cabinets that operate state government, abolished the mismanaged Kentucky Racing Commission and replaced it with a Kentucky Horse Racing Authority, and balanced the 2004 budget with $302 million in spending cuts. But his first year as governor failed to achieve much beyond that. The legislature adjourned in April without having passed a budget, divided over Fletcher's proposal to overhaul the state's tax code. The state teachers association voted to strike in October in response to Fletcher's 2005 state health plan, which they claimed would increase out-of-pocket costs. Fletcher had to call the legislature back into special session in October; the final plan that emerged cost close to $200 million more than Fletcher's original and the strike was averted. In November, death penalty opponents sought an opinion from the Kentucky Board of Medical Licensure as to whether Fletcher, still a licensed doctor, violated medical guidelines by signing a death warrant for a convicted killer. The board unanimously dismissed the complaint, saying that the governor had acted as a governor, not a doctor, when he signed the order. Fletcher also attracted additional unwanted attention in June when the state police plane taking him to the funeral of Ronald Reagan was nearly shot down by two F-16 fighters in Washington airspace after air defense officials were unable to identify the aircraft; the incident caused the evacuation of thousands from the U.S. Capitol and the Supreme Court building.

Senior Senator

Mitch McConnell (R)

Elected 1984, seat up 2008, 4th term; b. Feb. 20, 1942, Sheffield, AL; home, Louisville; U. of Louisville, B.A. 1964, U. of KY, J.D. 1967; Baptist; married (Elaine Chao).

Elected Office: Jefferson Cnty. Judge Exec., 1977–84.

Professional Career: Chief Legis. Asst., U.S. Sen. Marlow Cook, 1968–70; Dpty. Asst. U.S. Atty. Gen., 1974–75.

DC Office: 361-A RSOB, 20510, 202-224-2541; Fax: 202-224-2499; Web site: mcconnell.senate.gov.

State Offices: Bowling Green, 270-781-1673; Ft. Wright, 859-578-0188; Lexington, 859-224-8286; London, 606-864-2026; Louisville, 502-582-6304; Paducah, 270-442-4554.

Committees: *Majority Whip. Agriculture, Nutrition & Forestry*: Marketing, Inspection & Product Promotion; Production & Price Competitiveness (Chmn.); Research, Nutrition & General Legislation. *Appropriations*: Agriculture, Rural Development & Related Agencies; Commerce, Justice & Science; Defense; Energy & Water; Military Construction & Veterans Affairs; State, Foreign Operations & Related Programs (Chmn.). *Rules & Administration*.

Group Ratings

	ADA	ACLU	AFS	LCV	ITIC	NTU	COC	ACU	NTLC	CHC
2004	15	0	14	0	100	71	94	96	90	100
2003	10	—	0	0	—	76	100	84	—	—

National Journal Ratings

	2003 LIB	—	2003 CONS		2004 LIB	—	2004 CONS
Economic	0%	—	82%		11%	—	84%
Social	0%	—	59%		19%	—	71%
Foreign	0%	—	78%		0%	—	67%

Key Votes of the 108th Congress

1. Ban Drilling in ANWR	N	5. Energy Bill	Y	9. Ban Same-Sex Marriage	Y
2. Approve Bush Tax Cuts	Y	6. Support Roe v. Wade	*	10. Ban Bunker-Buster Bomb	N
3. Medicare/Rx Bill	Y	7. Ban Partial-Birth Abortion	Y	11. Fund Iraq War	Y
4. Bar Overtime Pay Regs.	N	8. Assault Weapons Ban	N	12. Restrict Missile Defense	N

Election Results

2002 general	Mitch McConnell (R)	731,679	(65%)	($5,336,099)
	Lois Combs Weinberg (D)	399,634	(35%)	($2,244,035)
2002 primary	Mitch McConnell (R)	unopposed		
1996 general	Mitch McConnell (R)	724,794	(55%)	($5,031,293)
	Steven L. Beshear (D)	560,012	(43%)	($2,073,794)
	Other	22,240	(2%)	

Prior Winning Percentages: 1990 (52%); 1984 (50%)

Mitch McConnell is Kentucky's senior senator, the architect of its 7–1 Republican congressional delegation and Senate majority whip; his wife is Labor Secretary Elaine Chao. He grew up in Alabama, where he overcame polio, and at age 13 moved to Louisville. He has been in politics almost his whole career. He was an intern for Senator John Sherman Cooper in 1964 and, after finishing law school, became a staffer for Senator Marlow Cook. He moved back to Louisville and in 1977, at 35, won by a narrow margin the office that had been Cook's political stepping stone, Jefferson County judge-executive. In 1981 he was re-elected, again narrowly. In 1984 he ran for the Senate, against incumbent Dee Huddleston. McConnell ran ads showing bloodhounds sniffing for Huddleston in vacation locales where he had collected fees for speeches while the Senate was in session. McConnell won by 5,169 votes of 1.2 million cast.

Many senators go to Washington and over the years become less conservative; McConnell has become more so. As his longtime adversary on campaign finance regulation, John McCain, has said, "There are few things more daunting in politics than the determined opposition of Senator McConnell." He has taken on tough assignments on occasion: As Ethics Committee chairman in 1995, he led the investigation of Bob Packwood for sexual harassment (the committee recommended expulsion, and Packwood ultimately resigned). He has often opposed trial lawyers, backing product liability and medical malpractice laws that would reduce their leverage and sponsoring the auto choice plan that would let car owners pay less for insurance by disclaiming pain and suffering damages. McConnell served on Foreign Relations until 1992, then switched to Appropriations and in 1994 became chairman of the Foreign Operations Subcommittee. In that capacity he has had much to say about foreign aid. He has strongly supported aid to Israel. In June 2003 he and Dianne Feinstein called for the U.S. to expel the ambassador from dictatorial Burma.

McConnell's greatest expertise is on campaign finance. He first got interested while teaching a night course at the University of Louisville, and his thinking at first was quite different from what it is now. In 1990 he drafted a bill that would have banned PACs, cut in half out-of-state donations and banned soft money. But in a few years he came to believe that these provisions and those in the various bills sponsored by John McCain and Russ Feingold are unconstitutional infringements of free speech. He disputes the notions that campaign ads are some kind of pollution and that too much is spent on them. In 1994 he spoke all night to filibuster a campaign finance bill, "the only true all-night filibuster in the last 12 years," he said in 1999. In October 1999, with more than 40 senators on his side, he killed a version of the McCain-Feingold campaign finance bill. In March 2001, McCain insisted on bringing campaign finance forward again, and despite McConnell's efforts, managed to pass his measure. But as McConnell pointed out, it did not include many provisions in previous McCain-Feingold bills, including public subsidies for candidates and voluntary spending limits. McCain's bill was also amended by a doubling of the limit on individual contributions—something McConnell supported.

In 2001 the House Republican leadership blocked consideration of the similar Shays-Meehan bill. But after the implosion of Enron, Shays and Meehan got enough signatures on a discharge petition to bring their bill to the floor, and it passed in February 2002. For more than a month, McConnell put forward 13 "technical corrections," and Majority Leader Tom Daschle refused to bring the issue to the floor until he and McCain settled their differences. The bill passed on March 27, and immediately McConnell filed a lawsuit charging it was unconstitutional. In May 2003 a deeply divided three-judge federal court issued 1,700 pages of opinions and upheld some provisions of the law but not others. In December 2003 the Supreme Court upheld almost all the provisions of the bill. "There won't be any less speech or money spent. Dramatically more will be spent, just in a different way," McConnell predicted, and warned that 527 organizations would raise and spend huge amounts of money, as indeed they did. More quietly, as ranking member of the Rules Committee, McConnell helped put together the bipartisan Help America Vote Act.

McConnell's interest in elections is not just theoretical. He ran for chairman of the NRSC and lost to Phil Gramm in 1990 and in 1992 by one vote; he won the post in November 1996. But he was unable to get Republican senators to contribute as much to campaigns as Democratic senators did in 1998 and the party gained no seats. In the 2000 cycle, he had tougher sledding; Republicans lost five of the five closest races, and the result was a 50–50 split that put Democrats in position to gain a majority when Jim Jeffords left the Republican party in May 2001.

McConnell has had more success in building up Kentucky's long ailing Republican Party. He helped Ed Whitfield pick up the 1st District and Republican legislative candidates win in western Kentucky in 1994. He backed Anne Northup in her win in Louisville's 3d District in 1996. In 1998 McConnell strongly backed Jim Bunning's candidacy for the Senate. In 2000 McConnell helped the Bush campaign target and carry Kentucky; he backed the ballot proposition to merge the Jefferson County and Louisville city governments. He helped to persuade two Democratic state senators to switch parties in July and August 1999, which gave Republicans a 20–18 margin in the state Senate. In 2000 he helped them hold that majority. In November 2002 the Republicans increased their majority to 21–17. In 2003 he helped support the gubernatorial candidacy of Congressman Ernie Fletcher and was pleased when Fletcher beat Democrat Ben Chandler 55%–45%. And in 2004 he helped rescue his colleague Jim Bunning's campaign.

McConnell has frequently used his seat on Appropriations to insert riders that help Kentucky and channel aid to the state. He has also worked hard on tobacco issues. In 2003 he was working for a buyout of tobacco quotas from farmers, and said he would support FDA regulation of tobacco in order to get it. "This is a marriage of convenience. The two issues needed to be married if we were going to get either one out of the U.S. Senate." In July 2004 the Senate voted 78–15 to add the buyout and FDA regulation to the must-pass corporate tax bill. But the House refused to support FDA regulation, and in October 2004 the Senate backed the tobacco buyout without it and passed the corporate tax bill by 69–17.

McConnell has now won reelection three times. In 2002 McConnell's opponent was Lois Combs Weinberg, daughter of former (1959–63) Governor Bert Combs. She had the support of the state's Democratic establishment, but memories of her father, one of the state's most notable governors, had evidently dimmed. In the primary she faced former 1st District Congressman Tom Barlow, who spent only $6,000; he lost the May primary by only 958 votes out of 461,000 cast—50.1%–49.9%—by winning 74%–26% in his old congressional district. After that, national Democrats put little money into the race. McConnell refused to debate and ran ads showing how he had done things for Kentuckians—helping the widow of a police officer killed in the line of duty, getting compensation for the families of workers sickened by radiation poisoning at the Paducah uranium plant. McConnell spent $5.3 million to Weinberg's $2.2 million and won 65%–35%, carrying 112 of 120 counties, losing only in a few Democratic strongholds in the eastern mountains.

Back in Washington, he won another election a week later, to become majority whip. He had been campaigning for months among colleagues and his only opponent, Larry Craig, dropped out several days before the contest. In December, when Trent Lott was criticized for his comments at Strom Thurmond's 100th birthday party, McConnell was at first his strongest public defender, suggesting on December 15 that Lott might resign from the Senate if ousted (which would mean a Democrat would get his seat and the Republicans would no longer have a majority) and threatening that if Democrats moved to censure Lott, he would amend the motion to add censure of some Democrats' comments. But on December 20 he privately recommended to Lott that he "step down as soon as possible"; McConnell did not challenge Bill Frist for the majority leadership, and urged Rick Santorum not to either. McConnell advised Frist, who was relatively unversed in Senate procedures; in June 2003 he and House Whip Roy Blunt started attending each others' whip meetings. As the intelligence reorganization bill was being considered in October 2004, McConnell and Democratic Whip Harry Reid worked on reorganizing the Senate to account for intelligence and homeland security changes. They agreed to elevate the Homeland Security Committee and strengthen the Intelligence Committee, but they did not accept the 9/11 Commission's recommendation to give the latter both authorizing and appropriations functions.

After Republicans gained four Senate seats in the 2004 election, McConnell looked ahead to a new form of bipartisanship: "The key now will be whether there are a group of Democrats willing to join with most Republicans in a coalition of the center-right." He declined to join in the laments about partisan divisiveness in Washington. "I'm amazed at all the hand-wringing over the level of discourse and partisanship. It leads me to believe that nobody has read any history. The level of divisiveness now is really quite mild when it's compared with numerous periods in our history." Bill Frist has long maintained that he would not run for reelection in 2006, and McConnell made no secret that he wanted to succeed him as majority leader; in September 2004 third-ranking Republican Rick Santorum let it be known he would not seek the post, but in March 2005 there was talk that former Majority Leader Trent Lott might.

Junior Senator

Jim Bunning (R)

Elected 1998, seat up 2010, 2d term; b. Oct. 23, 1931, Campbell Cnty.; home, Southgate; Xavier U., B.S. 1953; Catholic; married (Mary).

Elected Office: Ft. Thomas City Cncl., 1977–79; KY Senate, 1979–83; U.S. House of Reps., 1986–98.

Professional Career: Pro baseball player, 1950–71; Investment broker & agent, 1960–86.

DC Office: 316 HSOB, 20510, 202-224-4343; Fax: 202-228-1373; Web site: bunning.senate.gov.

State Offices: Ft. Wright, 859-341-2602; Hazard, 606-435-2390; Hopkinsville, 270-885-1212; Lexington, 859-219-2239; Louisville, 502-582-5341; Owensboro, 270-689-9085.

Committees: *Banking, Housing & Urban Affairs*: Economic Policy (Chmn.); Financial Institutions; Securities & Investment. *Budget. Energy & Natural Resources*: Energy; Water & Power. *Finance*: Health Care; International Trade; Social Security & Family Policy.

Group Ratings

	ADA	ACLU	AFS	LCV	ITIC	NTU	COC	ACU	NTLC	CHC
2004	15	0	14	0	100	69	100	100	90	100
2003	10	—	11	0	—	73	100	85	—	—

National Journal Ratings

	2003 LIB	—	2003 CONS		2004 LIB	—	2004 CONS
Economic	0%	—	82%		11%	—	84%
Social	0%	—	59%		0%	—	84%
Foreign	0%	—	78%		0%	—	67%

Key Votes of the 108th Congress

1. Ban Drilling in ANWR	N	5. Energy Bill	Y	9. Ban Same-Sex Marriage	Y
2. Approve Bush Tax Cuts	Y	6. Support Roe v. Wade	N	10. Ban Bunker-Buster Bomb	N
3. Medicare/Rx Bill	Y	7. Ban Partial-Birth Abortion	Y	11. Fund Iraq War	Y
4. Bar Overtime Pay Regs.	N	8. Assault Weapons Ban	Y	12. Restrict Missile Defense	N

Election Results

2004 general	Jim Bunning (R)	873,507	(51%)	($6,075,399)
	Daniel Mongiardo (D)	850,855	(49%)	($3,104,981)
2004 primary	Jim Bunning (R)	96,545	(84%)	
	Barry Metcalf (R)	18,395	(16%)	
1998 general	Jim Bunning (R)	569,817	(50%)	($3,746,540)
	Scotty Baesler (D)	563,051	(49%)	($3,841,950)
	Other	12,546	(1%)	

Prior Winning Percentages: 1996 House (68%); 1994 House (74%); 1992 House (62%); 1990 House (69%); 1988 House (74%); 1986 House (55%)

Jim Bunning, a Republican elected to the Senate in 1998, is the first player elected to the Baseball Hall of Fame to serve in Congress. Bunning grew up in Northern Kentucky, just across the Ohio River from Cincinnati. He started in minor league baseball in 1950, but at his father's insistence finished high school and college. He made the majors in 1956 and the next year became the only pitcher to strike out Ted Williams three times in one game. Bunning threw a no-hitter for the Detroit Tigers in 1958 and pitched a perfect game for the Philadelphia Phillies on Father's Day 1964; he also played for the Pittsburgh Pirates and the Los Angeles Dodgers. He retired in 1971 with a 224–184 record, a 3.24 ERA and 2,855 strikeouts; he was the second pitcher (Cy Young was the first) to achieve 1,000 strikeouts and 100 wins in both the American and the National Leagues. He was inducted into the Baseball Hall of Fame in August 1996. He is a family man, with nine children (two sets of twins) and at last count 35 grandchildren and 2 great-grandchildren; his son David Bunning, after 10 years as a federal prosecutor, was unanimously confirmed as a federal judge in February 2002. Jim Bunning and fellow pitcher Robin Roberts set up the Major League Baseball Players Association and hired Marvin Miller in 1966, when the minimum player salary was $6,000; in 2002, however, he was criticizing the players for not accepting a salary cap, the big metro area teams for not accepting revenue sharing and the owners for not opening their books. He has long been in favor of repealing baseball's exemption from the antitrust laws.

The skill, energy and aggressiveness he showed in baseball—Bunning registered one of the highest totals in baseball history for hitting batters—he brought to politics in his native northern Kentucky. He was elected to the Fort Thomas City Council in 1977, to the state Senate in 1979, and won a respectable 44% against Martha Layne Collins in the 1983 race for governor (the best showing for a Republican gubernatorial candidate between 1971 and 1995). When incumbent 4th District Congressman Gene Snyder retired in 1986, Bunning won the seat with 55% of the vote. He served six years on the ethics committee, starting off in March 1992 by leading the charge against the House bank overdraft scandal. In September 1993, he called Bill Clinton "the most corrupt, the most amoral, the most despicable person I've ever seen in the presidency."

In February 1997, Senator Wendell Ford announced he would retire in 1998, and Bunning, with typical aggressiveness, made plans to run for his seat. The Democratic nominee was Lexington Congressman Scotty Baesler, who was still known as a star on one of Adolph Rupp's University of Kentucky basketball teams in the early 1960s.

Baesler emerged from the primary ahead of Bunning in the polls but out of money; Bunning, with extensive help from Senator Mitch McConnell, had plenty of money. Bunning ran an ad showing actors thanking Baesler, in Spanish and (with subtitles) Chinese, for voting for NAFTA and for normal trade relations with China. This was perhaps the country's closest race for months. And, despite Kentucky's early poll closing times and rapid count, it was not until late in the evening that Bunning was declared the winner. His margin was 49.7%–49.2%, or 6,766 votes.

Bunning has compiled one of the most conservative voting records in the Senate. He has taken bipartisan initiatives on occasion. In 2002 he teamed up with Democrat Barbara Boxer to get approval of arming pilots. In March 2004, he and Boxer complained about the TSA's delaying in approving pilots and sponsored a bill to require training within 90 days of application. He joined Paul Sarbanes on a bill to crack down on property owners who falsely claim flood damage.

Bunning has worked on many Kentucky issues. He has criticized the Energy Department's cleanup of the USEC uranium enrichment plant in Paducah, ongoing since 1988, on which $823 million had been spent by 2003. He has been especially angry at DOE's failure to compensate workers stricken with radiation-related disease. He held several hearings on the issue and blocked the nomination of the agency's CFO to get attention. In December 2003 he supported the workers' union's efforts to get laid-off workers hired by the new contractor with continued pension and service credit. In March 2004 he noted that only one claim had been filled in four years. In June 2004 he got a unanimous vote to put in the defense authorization an amendment moving the compensation process to the Labor Department and to have the government rather than private contractors compensate workers. It was part of the final bill passed in October 2004. "It guarantees a willing payer and will ensure that these claims are processed in a timely manner." The first Kentucky claimant got $125,000 in December 2004; Bunning pointed out that there were 24,000 claims pending and only 30 had been acted on.

Bunning came up for reelection in 2004. For some time it seemed he would face Governor Paul Patton, ineligible to seek a third term in 2003. But in September 2002 Patton admitted that he had had an affair with a nursing home operator who sued him that month for sexual harassment; she accused him of sending in state inspectors to close down her business after she broke off the affair. Patton, after denying the affair, admitted it after phone records showed 440 calls from his office to her home or business; a few days later he announced, unsurprisingly, that he would not run for the Senate. Other well known Democrats—Lieutenant Governor Steve Henry, Treasurer Jonathan Miller, 4th District Congressman Ken Lucas—dropped out for one or another reason. That left Bunning the heavy favorite. But he ended up facing a serious challenge from state Senator Daniel Mongiardo. Mongiardo, a physician from the eastern mountains, had beaten a longtime incumbent for one state Senate seat, then won another that Republicans had redistricted three hours away from his home; he started off by putting $168,000 of his own money into his campaign. Bunning raised and spent $6.5 million in all, but the Democratic Senatorial Campaign Committee started spending money on Mongiardo in July. Mongiardo got ammunition from what some considered Bunning's strange behavior. He refused to give the press advance notice of his appearances—Kentucky Republicans believe the state's dominant paper, the Louisville *Courier-Journal*, is biased against them—and traveled with a security guard, because of "classified briefings that I have received in the U.S. Senate," Bunning said. At one campaign stop (Mongiardo staffers videotaped Bunning on the stump) Bunning said that Mongiardo looked like one of Saddam Hussein's sons. Bunning ran ads attacking Mongiardo on national security, taxes and as a "Medicaid millionaire." Mongiardo promised to reduce the cost of health care and called for reimportation of prescription drugs from Canada; his ads pointed out that Bunning accepted $75,000 from pharmaceutical PACs. Mongiardo said he was against abortion and same-sex marriage and in favor of gun rights.

The contest came to a head in the single debate October 11. Bunning participated on video from Washington, where he said he needed to be to vote in the Senate. Democrats complained loudly about this because Bunning read his opening and closing statements from a teleprompter, though that did not violate the agreed on rules. Bunning accused Mongiardo and his staff of passing on "horrible rumors" about his health (he was 73) and asked for an apology. "I hope that you are healthy," Mongiardo said, and accused Bunning of behavior "unbecoming of a U.S. senator. You have conduct that has been unbecoming of a Kentucky gentleman. People are reaching, searching for an excuse." Bunning apologized for "an inappropriate comment," presumably the Saddam Hussein comment. Both continued in that vein in post-debate comments. "When we went to Fancy Farm," Bunning said, referring to the traditional July political gathering in Graves County, "my wife was black and blue from their staff or someone connected with the Mongiardo campaign—absolutely running into her." He said that members of the media were hostile because they "don't believe the same way I believe." Mongiardo said, "Senator Bunning has the history and record of throwing high, hard fastballs and we were ready for a beanball. Senator Bunning's arrogance and his mean-spiritedness prevents him from seeing the impact of his policies on the people of Kentucky." The commentary continued from others. The *Courier-Journal* editorialized, "Is he, as he ages, just becoming a more concentrated version of himself: more arrogant, more prickly? Certainly that would be a normal occurrence. Or is his increased belligerence an indication of something worse? Has Senator Bunning drifted into territory that indicates a serious health concern?" Republicans were also throwing punches at Mongiardo. State Senate President David Williams said he had a "limp wrist," and another state senator said Mongiardo "is not a gentleman. I'm not even sure the word 'man' applies to him." A constitutional amendment to ban same-sex marriage was on the ballot, and passed in November 75%–25%.

The DSCC shrewdly poured money into this race, $466,000 in five days in October alone, and the polls tightened; a Democratic poll showed Bunning leading by only 47%–39% and a Bunning poll showed him ahead by the not entirely reassuring margin of 50%–39%. Bunning provided his critics with more material on October 21 when asked about a unit of Army Reserve soldiers in Iraq who refused an order to deliver fuel because they said their trucks were lightly armored. Bunning said he was unaware of the incident. "Let me explain something. I don't watch the national news, and I don't read the paper. I haven't done that for the last six weeks. I watch Fox News to get my information." This might have been taken as a statement of how busy he was during campaign season or as a response to what he saw as press bias.

On November 2 Bunning just barely squeaked to victory, 51%–49%, as George W. Bush was carrying the state 60%–40%. Mongiardo ran far ahead of John Kerry in his home area in the eastern mountains—30% ahead in his home of Perry County—and 12% to 22% ahead in the ring of counties around Lexington. But Bunning was rescued, as he had been in 1998, by his strong showing in his home area, the three counties of Northern Kentucky, where he won 66.5% of the vote (to Bush's 66.6%), and which he carried by 48,000 votes, more than double his statewide margin of 22,000. Bunning, asked whether he had made mistakes, said, "Sure we made mistakes. Everybody makes mistakes. The only time I've ever been perfect was for about two hours and 10 minutes on June 21, 1964."

FIRST DISTRICT

Rep. Ed Whitfield (R)

Elected 1994, 6th term; b. May 25, 1943, Hopkinsville; home, Hopkinsville; U. of KY, B.S. 1965, J.D. 1969; Methodist; married (Connie).

Military Career: Army Reserves, 1967–73.

Elected Office: KY House of Reps., 1973–75.

Professional Career: Practicing atty., 1969–79; Owner, Rhodes Oil Co., 1975–79; Cnsl., Seaboard System Railroad, 1979–83; V.P., CSX, 1983–91; Cnsl., Interstate Commerce Comm., 1991–93.

DC Office: 301 CHOB, 20515, 202-225-3115; Fax: 202-225-3547; Web site: www.house.gov/whitfield.

District Offices: Henderson, 270-826-4180; Hopkinsville, 270-885-8079; Paducah, 270-442-6901; Tompkinsville, 270-487-9509.

Committees: *Energy & Commerce* (8th of 31 R): Energy & Air Quality; Oversight & Investigations (Chmn.); Telecommunications & the Internet.

Group Ratings

	ADA	ACLU	AFS	LCV	ITIC	NTU	COC	ACU	NTLC	CHC
2004	5	5	13	27	100	54	100	88	70	100
2003	10	—	13	5	—	60	100	88	—	—

National Journal Ratings

	2003 LIB	—	2003 CONS		2004 LIB	—	2004 CONS
Economic	33%	—	64%		40%	—	60%
Social	36%	—	64%		17%	—	81%
Foreign	30%	—	70%		34%	—	63%

Key Votes of the 108th Congress

1. Drilling in ANWR	Y	5. DC School Vouchers	Y	9. Ban Same-Sex Marriage	Y
2. Approve Bush Tax Cuts	Y	6. Ban Human Cloning	Y	10. Fund Iraq War	Y
3. Medicare/Rx Bill	Y	7. Restrict Gun Liability	Y	11. Bar Cuba Embargo Funds	N
4. Bar Overtime Pay Regs.	N	8. Ban Partial-Birth Abortion	Y	12. Intelligence Reorg.	Y

Election Results

2004 general	Ed Whitfield (R)	175,972	(67%)	($557,233)
	Billy Cartwright (D)	85,229	(33%)	
2004 primary	Ed Whitfield (R)	unopposed		
2002 general	Ed Whitfield (R)	117,600	(65%)	($828,894)
	Klint Alexander (D)	62,617	(35%)	($544,511)

Prior Winning Percentages: 2000 (58%); 1998 (55%); 1996 (54%); 1994 (51%)

The People		Race/Ethnic Origin	Ancestry	
Area size:	12,058 sq. mi.	89.7% White	USA: 19.5%	English: 7.8%
Urban population:	36.5%	7.2% Black	Irish: 7.7%	
Rural population:	63.5%	0.3% Asian	**2004 Presidential Vote**	
Pop. 2000:	673,629	0.2% Native Am.	Bush (R) 180,446	(63%)
Median income:	$30,360	0.0% Hawaiian	Kerry (D) 102,346	(36%)
Poverty status:	16.5%	0.9% Two+ races	Other 1,866	(1%)
Military veterans:	12.9%	0.1% Other	**2000 Presidential Vote**	
		1.5% Hispanic Origin	Bush (R) 147,486	(58%)
			Gore (D) 101,551	(40%)
			Other 3,961	(2%)
			Cook Partisan Voting Index: R +10	

Occupation	Blue collar: 37.3%	White collar: 46.6%	Gray collar: 16.0%

The point where the Ohio River flows into the Mississippi—the intersection Huckleberry Finn and Jim missed in the fog—must have struck early settlers as a site for a great city. But no Pittsburgh or St. Louis grew up on this fertile black soil. Instead, the Kentucky land west of the dammed-up Tennessee and Cumberland rivers, bought from the Chickasaw Indians by General Andrew Jackson and Governor Isaac Shelby in 1818—the Jackson Purchase, it is still called— was settled by farmers. Most people here today are the descendants of these farmers, with memories of earlier generations living in family lore. Just to the east of the Tennessee and the Cumberland rivers is the Pennyrile (after pennyroyal, a common variety of local wild mint), a land of low hills and small farms, where you find the west Kentucky coal fields, the site of much strip mining in recent years. Here is Lyon County, founded by Matthew "Spitting" Lyon, who earned his epithet while a congressman from Vermont, and who later represented western Kentucky from 1803 to 1811. These areas are separated by the Land Between the Lakes, the boating and recreational haven created by the damming of the Tennessee and Cumberland Rivers just before the debouche into the Ohio; this is the fastest-growing area in these parts, as the Jackson Purchase and the Pennyrile struggle economically. The biggest problem is the USEC uranium enrichment plant, under federal cleanup since 1988 and slated to be closed; in the meantime the government has been slow to compensate workers stricken with radiation-related sickness.

The 1st Congressional District of Kentucky is made up of the Jackson Purchase and much of the Pennyrile, plus a line of counties stretching some 200 miles east of the Mississippi in the mountains along the Tennessee border and then north toward the center of the state. There is a distinctive Southern atmosphere here—in the crops that are grown, in historically low wage levels, and in the fact that the big city that people look to is more often Nashville than Louisville. Turkey hunting has become a big business here. The Jackson Purchase and the Pennyrile are ancestrally Democratic; Paducah produced one of the most enduring Democratic politicians of this century, Alben Barkley, whose career from 1912 to 1956 included 14 years in the House, 24 in the Senate and four as vice president; he was Senate majority and minority leader, keynoted four Democratic National Conventions, and died while delivering the peroration at Washington and Lee University's mock political convention in 1956. But the hills far from the Mississippi are Republican country and this, combined with the Republican trend that reached north from Dixie to Paducah, has made the 1st District seriously contested territory in state elections—and one of the longtime Democratic rural areas solidly that went solidly for George W. Bush in 2000 (58%) and 2004 (63%). In the close Senate election of 2004, Republican Jim Bunning won 48% in the Jackson Purchase and most state legislators elected in the region were Republicans.

The congressman from the 1st District is Ed Whitfield, a Republican first elected in 1994. Whitfield grew up in Hopkinsville and Madisonville, in a family with Pennyrile roots going back before 1800. He served in the Army Reserves, practiced law in Hopkinsville, and was elected to the legislature in 1973 as a Democrat where he was something of an insider; former Governor (1963–67) Edward Breathitt was best man at his wedding. After one term in Frankfort, Whitfield ran an oil distributorship in the west Kentucky coalfields, then in 1979 moved to Washington to become an executive for the Seaboard and CSX railroads. He was legal counsel to the chairman of the Interstate Commerce Commission from 1991–93, when he returned to west Kentucky and ran for Congress as a Republican. He was returning to a district that since Barkley's time had been represented by quiet, long-serving, conservative Democrats. But the one-term incumbent, Tom Barlow, was a free-spirited supporter of the Clinton administration. Encouraged to run by Senator Mitch McConnell, Whitfield turned aside criticism that he was carpetbagging and concentrated on attacking Barlow's vote for the Clinton budget and tax increase. With help from the mountain counties added by redistricting, and running strongly in the Pennyrile, Whitfield won a 51%–49% win in the big Republican sweep of 1994.

In the House, Whitfield has a moderate-to-conservative voting record and a seat on the Energy and Commerce Committee. One major concern has been aid to workers exposed to radiation at the USEC plant in Paducah; overriding appropriators, Whitfield won $150,000 lump sum payments and medical benefits for thousands of affected workers. He also overcame objections from the Bush administration to cleaning up the site, which is projected to cost more than $3 billion and last more than another decade. He voted for normal trade relations with China after the Chinese agreed to lower tariffs on imported tobacco, and he voted for trade promotion authority. He supported the tobacco buyout bill, which handsomely benefited local farmers. The House passed his bill to discourage "doctor shopping" by addicts of prescription drugs, through the use of an electronic data base in which each state would participate to monitor people who cross state lines to buy pharmaceuticals. A thoroughbred owner, Whitfield co-sponsored legislation to ban the killing of horses for meat. In January 2005, he became chairman of the Oversight and Investigati ns Subcommittee at Energy and Commerce, and cited it as an opportunity to "identify and correct some inequities that are particularly unfair to the American public."

Whitfield has entrenched himself to the point that he is no longer much of a Democratic target. In 1996, when lawyer Dennis Null opposed him, Whitfield carried 18 of the district's 31 counties, including Paducah, which he lost in 1994, and won 54%–46%. In 1998, Tom Barlow ran again, this time with a lightly funded "grass roots" campaign. Whitfield won 55%–45%. In 2000, Whitfield increased his margin to 58%–42%, carrying for the first time several counties in the far western corner. In 2001 state House Democrats trie d to make the district more Democratic by removing the eastern counties and adding Owensboro, but that was blocked by state Senate Republicans. Since then, Whitfield has won easily. This longtime Democratic stronghold now seems to be a safe Republican seat.

SECOND DISTRICT

Rep. Ron Lewis (R)

Elected May 1994, 6th full term; b. Sept. 14, 1946, South Shore, KY; home, Cecilia; U. of KY, B.A. 1969, Morehead St. U., M.A. 1981; Southern Baptist; married (Kayi).

Military Career: Navy OCS, 1972.

Professional Career: Heavy Equip. Sales Rep., 1975–80; Baptist Minister, 1980–present; Prof., Watterson Col., 1980–85; Owner, Alpha Christian Bookstore, 1985–94.

DC Office: 2418 RHOB, 20515, 202-225-3501; Fax: 202-226-2019; Web site: www.house.gov/ronlewis.

District Offices: Bowling Green, 270-842-9896; Elizabethtown, 270-765-4360; Owensboro, 270-688-8858.

Committees: *Ways & Means* (14th of 24 R): Social Security; Trade.

Group Ratings

	ADA	ACLU	AFS	LCV	ITIC	NTU	COC	ACU	NTLC	CHC
2004	5	0	13	9	90	58	95	84	89	100
2003	15	—	13	10	—	62	97	88	—	—

National Journal Ratings

	2003 LIB	—	2003 CONS	2004 LIB	—	2004 CONS
Economic	33%	—	64%	31%	—	68%
Social	22%	—	77%	17%	—	81%
Foreign	0%	—	89%	7%	—	93%

Key Votes of the 108th Congress

1. Drilling in ANWR	Y	5. DC School Vouchers	Y	9. Ban Same-Sex Marriage	Y
2. Approve Bush Tax Cuts	Y	6. Ban Human Cloning	Y	10. Fund Iraq War	Y
3. Medicare/Rx Bill	Y	7. Restrict Gun Liability	Y	11. Bar Cuba Embargo Funds	N
4. Bar Overtime Pay Regs.	N	8. Ban Partial-Birth Abortion	*	12. Intelligence Reorg.	Y

Election Results

2004 general	Ron Lewis (R)	185,394	(68%)	($688,898)
	Adam Smith (D)	87,585	(32%)	
2004 primary	Ron Lewis (R)	unopposed		
2002 general	Ron Lewis (R)	122,773	(70%)	($553,116)
	David Williams (D)	51,431	(29%)	

Prior Winning Percentages: 2000 (68%); 1998 (64%); 1996 (58%); 1994 (60%); 1994 (55%)

The People		Race/Ethnic Origin	Ancestry	
Area size:	7,669 sq. mi.	90.6% White	USA: 18.7%	German: 9.2%
Urban population:	47.2%	5.7% Black	Irish: 8.5%	
Rural population:	52.8%	0.7% Asian	**2004 Presidential Vote**	
Pop. 2000:	673,224	0.2% Native Am.	Bush (R) 190,612	(65%)
Median income:	$35,724	0.1% Hawaiian	Kerry (D) 100,580	(34%)
Poverty status:	13.3%	1.0% Two+ races	Other 2,065	(1%)
Military veterans:	13.7%	0.1% Other	**2000 Presidential Vote**	
		1.7% Hispanic Origin	Bush (R) 152,236	(62%)
			Gore (D) 90,086	(37%)
			Other 4,288	(2%)
			Cook Partisan Voting Index: R +13	

Occupation   Blue collar: 35.2%   White collar: 49.6%   Gray collar: 15.1%

In the 1770s and 1780s, Americans began settling the limestone-soiled country of central Kentucky, staking out towns like Bardstown and Elizabethtown and starting academies and colleges; they were well-settled when Stephen Foster wrote "My Old Kentucky Home" just before the Civil War. That conflict tore deeply here: This part of Kentucky gave birth to Abraham Lincoln and in the Civil War it lost thousands of soldiers, Union and Confederate; it would suffer disproportionate casualties in the 20th century wars as well. This area is the home of several Kentucky landmarks—Fort Knox, the nation's gold depository; some of the nation's largest bourbon distilleries; and Mammoth Cave, the world's largest accessible cavern, near Bowling Green. And Kentucky culture is more broadly disseminated than one might think: Japanese executives at the five Japanese-owned plants in Bardstown feel at home there because Stephen Foster's songs, apparently well adapted to Japanese tones, are universally known in Japan. In 2004, a Japanese blue-grass band played at a bluegrass festival in Owensboro.

The 2d Congressional District of Kentucky consists of much of the territory south and southwest of Louisville, starting with fast-growing Spencer County southeast of Louisville and proceeding south to Bowling Green and west along the Ohio River to Owensboro, the home of the International Bluegrass Music Museum and a port with warehouses that receive aluminum alloys to make lightweight engine parts. Much of this is rural and small-town country, where most people have family roots that go back generations and a connection with the past not often found in big metropolitan areas. Civil War loyalties are reflected in the election returns here; Kentucky was deeply split on secession, and a color-coded map of the current 2d District would show various splotches of counties pro-South and splotches pro-Union. For many years, the balance of opinion here favored the Democrats. But in the 1990s, the Civil War gave way to the culture war, and opinion moved toward the Republicans. In 2000 and 2004 this was George W. Bush's best district in Kentucky.

The congressman from the 2d District is Ron Lewis, a Republican first elected in a May 1994 special election that had national implications. Lewis was born in a log cabin and raised in eastern Kentucky; he worked his way through Morehead State as a laborer at Armco Steel. He worked in the highway department, at a state hospital, then served in the Navy. In 1980, he became a Baptist minister; in 1985 he started a Christian bookstore in Elizabethtown, two counties south of Louisville; he was the opposite of a political insider. Then, in March 1994, Democratic Congressman William Natcher died. He was chairman of the Appropriations Committee and a politician of a very old school, so hard-working and conscientious that he never missed a roll call vote in 41 years. Though the district voted for George H.W. Bush in 1992, Democratic leaders assumed they would win: They handpicked former state Senate President Joe Prather. Before the election, Prather even flew to Washington to go apartment hunting. But they failed to account for the national and local conservative trend. The NRCC spent $200,000, while Prather raised campaign money belatedly and asserted that he was quite a different sort of Democrat than Bill Clinton. Lewis won a solid 55%–45% victory.

In the House, Lewis has a solidly conservative voting record and is attentive to local concerns. He co-sponsored emergency farm relief and pushed for precision agriculture research. He backed tobacco buyout proposals, phasing out tobacco price supports and providing a mandatory buyout of tobacco farmers' entitlements. With a seat on the Ways and Means Committee, Lewis—who doesn't drink—took up the cause of local distillers and got more than 60 co-sponsors on his bill to reduce the excise tax on liquor by 26%. But by the time the lobbying campaign was in full gear, the budget surplus had disappeared. He cited his own experience as the father of an adopted child to oppose stem-cell research on embryos. Concerned about exposure of Fort Knox to the base-closing commission in 2005, Lewis got $200 million for the Army to spend on housing at what has become mostly a training facility. After the 9th Circuit appeals court ruled that the Pledge of Allegiance was unconstitutional, Lewis sponsored a bill that would allow two-thirds majorities in the House and Senate to override Supreme Court rulings that overturn federal statutes. In May 2004 he sponsored a roundtable discussion in Campbellsville that described for two other Ways and Means members how the community recovered from the closing of a textile factory a few years earlier by bringing in new employers to fill the openings.

In 1994, many Democrats assumed that Lewis's special election victory was aberrational and that Democratic Owensboro Mayor David Adkisson would win in November. But Lewis projected sincerity, and his strong religious views and opposition to the Clinton tax increase and health care plan were pluses. Lewis won by a resounding 60%–40% margin. In 1998, Lewis reversed his 1994 campaign pledge to serve no more than four full terms, announcing he had changed his mind. But he said he would still vote for term limits. Breaking the pledge caused barely a ripple back home. Since then, he has easily defeated little-known and poorly-funded challengers.

His growing seniority has increased his influence in the House and at Ways and Means, where he works on his promises to cut the capital gains tax to 15% and fix the long-term financing of Social Security.

THIRD DISTRICT

Rep. Anne Northup (R)

Elected 1996, 5th term; b. Jan. 22, 1948, Louisville; home, Louisville; St. Mary's Col., B.A. 1970; Catholic; married (Robert).

Elected Office: KY House of Reps., 1987–96.

DC Office: 2459 RHOB, 20515, 202-225-5401; Fax: 202-225-5776; Web site: northup.house.gov.

District Office: Louisville, 502-582-5129.

Committees: *Appropriations* (20th of 37 R): Labor, Health and Human Services, Education & Related Agencies (Vice Chmn.); Military Quality of Life & Veterans Affairs & Related Agencies; Transportation, Treasury, HUD, the Judiciary & District of Columbia.

Group Ratings

	ADA	ACLU	AFS	LCV	ITIC	NTU	COC	ACU	NTLC	CHC
2004	5	0	25	9	89	49	100	83	67	92
2003	10	—	0	5	—	55	97	88	—	—

National Journal Ratings

	2003 LIB	—	2003 CONS	2004 LIB	—	2004 CONS
Economic	26%	—	73%	37%	—	62%
Social	5%	—	87%	36%	—	64%
Foreign	0%	—	89%	25%	—	68%

Key Votes of the 108th Congress

1. Drilling in ANWR	Y	5. DC School Vouchers	Y
2. Approve Bush Tax Cuts	Y	6. Ban Human Cloning	Y
3. Medicare/Rx Bill	Y	7. Restrict Gun Liability	Y
4. Bar Overtime Pay Regs.	N	8. Ban Partial-Birth Abortion	Y

9. Ban Same-Sex Marriage	Y
10. Fund Iraq War	Y
11. Bar Cuba Embargo Funds	N
12. Intelligence Reorg.	Y

Election Results

2004 general	Anne Northup (R)	197,736	(60%)	($3,339,760)
	Tony Miller (D)	124,040	(38%)	($1,221,092)
	Other	6,363	(2%)	
2004 primary	Anne Northup (R)	unopposed		
2002 general	Anne Northup (R)	118,228	(52%)	($3,221,714)
	Jack Conway (D)	110,846	(48%)	($1,539,362)

Prior Winning Percentages: 2000 (53%); 1998 (52%); 1996 (50%)

The People		Race/Ethnic Origin	Ancestry	
Area size:	379 sq. mi.	76.0% White	German: 14.8% Irish: 10.4%	
Urban population:	98.3%	19.1% Black	USA: 8.8%	
Rural population:	1.7%	1.4% Asian	**2004 Presidential Vote**	
Pop. 2000:	674,032	0.2% Native Am.	Kerry (D)	167,440 (51%)
Median income:	$39,468	0.0% Hawaiian	Bush (R)	160,772 (49%)
Poverty status:	12.4%	1.3% Two+ races	**2000 Presidential Vote**	
Military veterans:	13.7%	0.2% Other	Gore (D)	141,337 (50%)
		1.8% Hispanic Origin	Bush (R)	134,234 (48%)
			Other	5,628 (2%)
			Cook Partisan Voting Index: D + 2	
Occupation	Blue collar: 23.7%	White collar: 62.0%	Gray collar: 14.3%	

At the falls of the Ohio River, Americans more than 200 years ago founded one of their first inland metropolises, the river port and industrial city of Louisville (pronounced *LOOuhv'l*). The city has always retained an air of the South; when Kentucky decided not to secede in 1861, the decision was not unanimous, and the culture of tidewater Virginia is still visible in the Louisville lawn party. Steamboats are tied up in front of Louisville's downtown, primed to follow the channel around the falls of the Ohio that prompted George Rogers Clark to found the town in 1778. Mint juleps are served on the verandas of mansions, especially (but not only) during Kentucky Derby week in May; horse racing is a preoccupation throughout the year. Although the Ohio River is crossed with many bridges and the accent across the river in Indiana may sound the same to outsiders, Louisville partakes of the cavalier culture that second sons of big landowners from England brought to Virginia in the 17th century and their heirs brought over the Appalachians to the valleys of Kentucky in the 18th century.

Louisville is Kentucky's largest city, though in the 2000 Census it was ranked number two, behind Lexington, which includes all of Fayette County. One of the arguments that persuaded voters in November 2000 by a 54%–46% margin to consolidate the city and surrounding Jefferson County is that it would make Louisville number one again; the merger took effect in January 2003. Louisville has not been growing as rapidly as many other Southern and Midwestern cities. Its economy is in many ways pre-postindustrial: It produces cigarettes and whiskey, large appliances and automobiles. But it is also the headquarters of Humana health services and of Yum! Brands, which owns KFC, Pizza Hut, Taco Bell and Long John Silver's and is expanding most rapidly in China. It has a new medical services center downtown, as well as the Muhammad Ali Center and the Owsley Brown Frazier Historical Arms Museum. The Louisville Bats's Slugger Field, opened in April 2000 on the riverfront, has attracted $100 million in development nearby. But this growth is less than in the ring of Kentucky counties around Jefferson County, whose populations increased from 40% to 118% from 1990 to 2004, or in the counties across the river in Indiana. Louisville has not yet attracted large numbers of immigrants, but has an interesting variety—Vietnamese, Bosnians, Cubans, Chinese, Indians, Koreans, Mexicans.

The 3d Congressional District of Kentucky includes all but a dozen or so precincts of Louisville-Jefferson County. There is a large black population in the West End of Louisville and just south of the old city limits and a lower-income white population along the strip highway that leads to Fort Knox. The suburbs to the east tend to be affluent; little elite neighborhoods— Mockingbird Valley, Glenview, Ten Broeck—nestled in the hills above the Ohio River. Louisville has long been an odd duck in Kentucky politics. If its elite were Virginia cavaliers, many of its burghers were Germans and Pennsylvanians who made this river town a Republican and anti-slavery island in a secessionist and pro-slavery sea. That tradition helps explain why Republican Mitch McConnell was able to get elected Jefferson County judge-executive in 1977 and 1981 when the state was electing Democrats to most other offices. In the 1990s Louisville, like so many bigger metro areas, trended toward the Democrats, even as the rest of Kentucky trended Republican. The 3d District voted by narrow margins for Al Gore in 2000 and John Kerry in 2004, while the state's other five districts all voted twice for George W. Bush.

The congresswoman from the 3d District is Anne Northup, a Republican first elected in 1996. She grew up in a large Catholic family in Louisville—she has nine sisters and one brother—and has raised six children of her own. She was elected to the Kentucky House in a 1987 special election, where she became the number one critic of tobacco in the capital of the nation's number two tobacco state. In 1996 she decided to run for Congress, against freshman Democrat Mike Ward, an "old Democrat" who won the seat by 425 votes in 1994, when 12% voted for an anti-abortion third candidate. In a year when almost all Democrats and most Republicans ran cookie-cutter campaigns, Northup showed originality in strategy and tactics. Ward ran behind his party ticket and Northup won 50.3%–49.7%, a margin of 1,299 votes.

In Washington, Northup was singled out by the leadership and was one of two Republican freshmen to get a seat on Appropriations. Her voting record is somewhat moderate on economic and foreign issues and conservative on cultural issues. She opposes abortion and claims the district is "more pro-life than pro-choice."

Despite her votes against spending generally, Northup has used her seat on Appropriations to bring in what she estimated in 2000 as "approaching $500 million" into her district—a "fair share" she called it. In January 2004 her earmarks for the district totaled roughly $26 million. On another issue, Northup journeyed to China in January 2002 to try to get the Chinese to lift their limit on the number of Chinese babies that can be adopted by Americans. In July 2003 she sponsored a bill to assist 1,000 families whose adoptions of Chinese children had been delayed by the SARS epidemic.

Northup's biggest project in dollar terms is the building of two new bridges over the Ohio River, one downtown that would also replace the "spaghetti junction" intersection of Interstates 64, 65 and 71, and one in eastern Jefferson County connecting I-265 in Kentucky and Indiana. Projected to cost $2 billion, this is the second biggest pending highway project in the nation, after metro Washington's Woodrow Wilson Bridge. She favored building both bridges at the same time, lest the eastern bridge be delayed indefinitely, and DOT prioritized the combined project for accelerated environmental review in October 2002. In February 2004 Governor Ernie Fletcher committed $118 million of state money over three years and praised Northup's efforts. A few days later Senator Jim Bunning said one of the Louisville bridges needed to be delayed to build a new bridge connecting Northern Kentucky to Cincinnati. Northup said he was "confused" and "mistaken." She went on, "I don't think he realized the status of this project—and that it's one project. There is going to be no diversion of money. It's not as though anyone, including Jim, could divert those dollars." In April 2004 Northup got $49 million in the transportation bill for the bridges, bringing the total of federal money she secured for the project up to $110 million, but the highway bill stalled. In October 2004, just as a designer for the downtown bridge was selected, Northup, running for reelection, noted, "Right now it's slated to be a 19-year project. With the right funding it could be 10. It could be a 40-year project if the money starts to dribble out." In February 2005 she voiced support for the project Bunning wanted—a $750 million bridge to replace the 40-year-old span that carries traffic from two interstate highways across the Ohio River. But the Louisville area bridges, it seems, will still come first. Meanwhile, the $49 million in bridge money that Northup had won in 2004 was trimmed to $34 million when the highway bill was reintroduced.

The 3d District has been seriously contested in every election since 1992. In 1998, former Attorney General Chris Gorman challenged Northup; he attacked her for voting with Newt Gingrich 95% of the time and for her vote for the Republican version of HMO regulation. Northup raised over $1.6 million, almost three times as much as Gorman. She won 52%–48%. In 2000 Northup was opposed by state Representative Eleanor Jordan, from the heavily black West End of Louisville and won 53%–44%.

In 2002 Northup faced Jack Conway, 33, deputy cabinet secretary to then-Governor Paul Patton. He was her first opponent who had no legislative record she could attack. Northup spent $3.2 million, raising $1.8 million from individuals and $1 million from PACs. Conway, with much help from Patton (who called him "the closest thing I've seen in Kentucky to Jack Kennedy"), raised $508,000 by the end of 2001, more than any other Democrat challenging a Republican incumbent, and $1.5 million in all. Conway's theme was that Northup was more conservative than voters thought. Northup called Conway a state bureaucrat "who has never held a private sector job," and said, "This is no time for fast-talking, inexperienced approaches to the challenges that face this country." Conway was hurt when, in September 2002, Patton admitted to having an affair with a nursing home operator who sued, claiming he had state inspectors close down her business after she broke off the affair. Patton's job rating in Jefferson County dropped sharply, and Patton withdrew from politicking; Democrats said he otherwise would have raised another $100,000 for Conway. In debate Conway declined to renounce him: "I'm disappointed, deeply. But he's my friend, and I am not gonna pull an Al Gore, and I am not the type of person who runs away from their friends when times are tough." Northup won 52%–48%, with a 7,382-vote margin.

Democratic leaders wanted Conway to run again but Conway said in November 2003 that the party apparatus was too weak and that he would not run. Jefferson County Circuit Clerk Tony Miller, fresh from defeat as the lieutenant governor nominee of Speaker Jody Richards in the Democratic gubernatorial primary, announced he would challenge Northup—part of the old courthouse crowd, Northup said. Northup campaigned on her work securing the Ohio River bridges, airport expansion, a new veterans hospital and after-school and tutoring projects. Miller attacked her stands on economic issues, Iraq, health care and Social Security. He supported light rail; she said it would be a "disaster" for the Ohio River bridges. Both supported the state constitutional amendment to ban same-sex marriage (it was approved 60%–40% in Jefferson County) but Northup attacked him for opposing the similar federal constitutional amendment. A Louisville *Courier-Journal* poll in September showed her leading only 47%–40%, but the same poll in October showed her up 57%–33%. By November Northup had spent $3.3 million and Miller $1.2 million. This time, prominent Democrats endorsed Northup: Metro Councilwoman Denise Bentley in May and her 1998 opponent Chris Gorman in October. She won 60%–38%, her biggest margin ever, in a district George W. Bush lost 49%–51%. In December, Democrat Jerry Abramson, the very popular Metro mayor, let it be known that he voted for her too.

FOURTH DISTRICT

Rep. Geoff Davis (R)

Elected 2004, 1st term; b. Oct. 26, 1958, Montreal, Canada; home, Hebron; U.S.M.A., B.S. 1981; Baptist; married (Pat).

Military Career: Army, 1976–87.

Professional Career: Technology consultant, 1989–2004; Owner, Republic Consulting, 1992–2004.

DC Office: 1541 LHOB, 20515, 202-225-3465; Fax: 202-225-0003; Web site: www.geoffdavis.house.gov.

District Offices: Ashland, 606-324-9898; Fort Mitchell, 859-426-0080.

Committees: *Armed Services* (34th of 34 R): Strategic Forces; Terrorism, Unconventional Threats & Capabilities. *Financial Services* (36th of 37 R): Capital Markets, Insurance & Government Sponsored Enterprises; Housing & Community Opportunity; Oversight & Investigations.

Group Ratings and Key Votes: Newly Elected

Election Results

2004 general	Geoff Davis (R)	160,982	(54%)	($2,959,526)
	Nick Clooney (D)	129,876	(44%)	($1,448,282)
	Other	5,069	(2%)	
2004 primary	Geoff Davis (R)	13,957	(58%)	
	Kevin Murphy (R)	7,672	(32%)	
	John King (R)	2,434	(10%)	
2002 general	Ken Lucas (D)	87,776	(51%)	($1,451,062)
	Geoff Davis (R)	81,651	(48%)	($874,453)
	Other	2,308	(1%)	

The People		Race/Ethnic Origin	Ancestry	
Area size:	5,770 sq. mi.	95.1% White	German: 17.6%	USA: 13.6%
Urban population:	59.7%	2.2% Black	Irish: 10.4%	
Rural population:	40.3%	0.5% Asian	**2004 Presidential Vote**	
Pop. 2000:	673,588	0.2% Native Am.	Bush (R) 195,055	(63%)
Median income:	$40,150	0.0% Hawaiian	Kerry (D) 111,049	(36%)
Poverty status:	11.4%	0.8% Two+ races	Other 2,547	(1%)
Military veterans:	13.0%	0.1% Other	**2000 Presidential Vote**	
		1.1% Hispanic Origin	Bush (R) 152,856	(61%)
			Gore (D) 92,768	(37%)
			Other 6,060	(2%)
			Cook Partisan Voting Index: R +12	
Occupation	Blue collar: 29.6%	White collar: 56.0%	Gray collar: 14.3%	

The commonwealth of Kentucky has gone to court more than once to assert its claim to all of the Ohio River up to its northern bank: This is one of the northernmost extensions of the South. The Ohio sees many different parts of Kentucky. Ashland, near the West Virginia border, is industrial, the home of Ashland Oil; the river here is bound in by tight hills that hold smoke and soot close in the air. Farther down the river, the country is more bucolic: Here Eliza fled across the ice floes in Harriet Beecher Stowe's *Uncle Tom's Cabin*. Farther west, between Louisville and Cincinnati, are counties that still look like they're in the 19th century. But metropolitan growth obtrudes. Oldham County, just upriver from Louisville, has some of Kentucky's oldest homes, though the horse country is also sprouting affluent subdivisions; this is by far the most affluent county in the state. The three Northern Kentucky counties across the river from Cincinnati—Campbell, Kenton and fast-growing Boone—are urban and suburban. Overlooking the suspension bridge built by John Roebling 16 years before the Brooklyn Bridge are new buildings on the Covington waterfront while Newport is sprucing up, and office buildings and new subdivisions are rising on the hills in Boone County above the river and near the Cincinnati-Northern Kentucky International Airport. The lowering of fares by Delta Air Lines in early 2005 was good news for the airport, which is a Delta hub. Controlled for decades by an organized crime syndicate based in Cleveland, Newport, with its panoramic view of the Cincinnati skyline plus its entertainment and nightlife, has become a regional hot spot; local features include the aquarium, Labor Day fireworks on the river, and its hometown status for one-time Republican presidential candidate Gary Bauer.

The 4th Congressional District of Kentucky spans all these variations of Ohio River country; it also includes lightly populated counties just inland. Economically, it runs the gamut from coal mining towns to rich suburbs. Politically, it has some of the most Democratic counties in America, like mountain-bound Elliott County (70%–30% for John Kerry in 2004), and some of the most Republican territory in Kentucky, like Oldham County (69%–30% for George W. Bush). The three northern Kentucky counties across the river from Cincinnati cast nearly half the district's votes, and they too are heavily Republican; in 2004, Bush won the district, 63%–36%.

The congressman from the 4th District is Geoff Davis, a Republican elected in 2004. He grew up in Pittsburgh and graduated from West Point. He was an Army ranger and served as a helicopter flight commander, then directed Army air operations enforcing the peace between Israel and Egypt. After 11 years in the Army, he moved to Fort Worth, Texas, then to Northern Kentucky, where in 1992 he started a consulting firm that advised companies on how to streamline manufacturing technology. In 2002 he ran against Congressman Ken Lucas, a conservative Democrat first elected in 1998 when Jim Bunning vacated the seat to run for the Senate, and lost 51%–48% after receiving very little assistance from the national party. After some hesitation, Lucas decided to honor his pledge to serve only three terms and announced his retirement in November 2003.

That left Davis the frontrunner in this heavily Republican district, and he won the May primary with 58% of the vote. But he had a formidable challenge from Democrat Nick Clooney, famous locally as a newspaper columnist and television commentator and derivatively well-known as the father of actor George Clooney and brother of the late singer Rosemary Clooney. George Clooney appeared at fundraisers for his father and got Paul Newman, Kevin Costner and Catherine Zeta-Jones to write checks for his campaign. Dick Cheney and Dennis Hastert came into the district on Davis's behalf and this time the National Republican Congressional Committee poured in large sums to help Davis compete with the cash coming in from Beverly Hills. Davis said his opponent had more in common with the people of Southern California than with those in northern Kentucky. "Hollywood versus the Heartland" is how he described the contest; national Republicans called the Democrat, "Looney Clooney." Clooney said he was a moderate and supported the Bush tax cuts and opposed same-sex marriage and abortion except when the mother's life was in danger. He stayed away from the Democratic National Convention in Boston. The Davis campaign unearthed columns Clooney had written over a period of 15 years in *The Cincinnati Post* and *The Kentucky Post*, including a 1998 column in which he criticized gun ownership; Davis, in contrast, said he was a lifetime member of the National Rifle Association membership and supported gun ownership rights.

Even with Clooney's Hollywood connections, Davis had a big fundraising advantage: he spent $2.6 million to Clooney's $1.5 million. Davis won 54%–44%. Clooney carried 10 of the 24 counties, though they were mostly in the rural and mining areas in the eastern end of the district. In the three Cincinnati-area suburban counties, which cast 50% of the total vote, Davis led 57%–41%. Clooney said that his political career was finished.

Davis got seats on the Armed Services and Financial Services Committees, which cater to his experience. In this solidly Republican district he is likely to be a favorite for reelection in 2006.

FIFTH DISTRICT

Rep. Harold Rogers (R)

Elected 1980, 13th term; b. Dec. 31, 1937, Barrier; home, Somerset; U. of KY, B.A. 1962, J.D. 1964; Baptist; married (Cynthia).

Military Career: Army Natl. Guard, 1957–64.

Professional Career: Practicing atty., 1964–69; Pulaski–Rockcastle Commonwealth's Atty., 1969–80.

DC Office: 2406 RHOB, 20515, 202-225-4601; Fax: 202-225-0940; Web site: www.house.gov/rogers.

District Offices: Hazard, 606-439-0794; Prestonburg, 606-886-0844; Somerset, 606-679-8346.

Committees: *Appropriations* (4th of 37 R): Homeland Security (Chmn,); Transportation, Treasury, HUD, the Judiciary & District of Columbia.

Group Ratings

	ADA	ACLU	AFS	LCV	ITIC	NTU	COC	ACU	NTLC	CHC
2004	0	5	13	9	90	50	100	88	73	92
2003	5	—	0	0	—	60	97	88	—	—

National Journal Ratings

	2003 LIB	—	2003 CONS		2004 LIB	—	2004 CONS
Economic	21%	—	75%		20%	—	79%
Social	5%	—	87%		19%	—	80%
Foreign	23%	—	71%		25%	—	68%

Key Votes of the 108th Congress

1. Drilling in ANWR	Y	5. DC School Vouchers	Y	9. Ban Same-Sex Marriage	Y
2. Approve Bush Tax Cuts	Y	6. Ban Human Cloning	Y	10. Fund Iraq War	Y
3. Medicare/Rx Bill	Y	7. Restrict Gun Liability	Y	11. Bar Cuba Embargo Funds	N
4. Bar Overtime Pay Regs.	N	8. Ban Partial-Birth Abortion	Y	12. Intelligence Reorg.	Y

Election Results

2004 general	Harold Rogers (R) .... unopposed		($737,589)
2004 primary	Harold Rogers (R) 26,909	(91%)	
	Billy Wilson (R) 2,566	(9%)	
2002 general	Harold Rogers (R) 137,986	(78%)	($480,850)
	Sidney Jane Bailey (D) 38,254	(22%)	

Prior Winning Percentages: 2000 (74%); 1998 (78%); 1996 (100%); 1994 (79%); 1992 (55%); 1990 (100%); 1988 (100%); 1986 (100%); 1984 (76%); 1982 (65%); 1980 (67%)

The People		Race/Ethnic Origin	Ancestry	
Area size:	10,759 sq. mi.	97.1% White	USA: 29.5%	English: 6.8%
Urban population:	21.3%	1.1% Black	Irish: 5.7%	
Rural population:	78.7%	0.3% Asian	**2004 Presidential Vote**	
Pop. 2000:	673,670	0.2% Native Am.	Bush (R) 159,489	(61%)
Median income:	$21,915	0.0% Hawaiian	Kerry (D) 102,142	(39%)
Poverty status:	28.1%	0.6% Two+ races	Other 1,911	(1%)
Military veterans:	10.0%	0.0% Other	**2000 Presidential Vote**	
		0.7% Hispanic Origin	Bush (R) 131,494	(57%)
			Gore (D) 97,104	(42%)
			Other 3,423	(1%)
			Cook Partisan Voting Index: R + 8	

Occupation   Blue collar: 35.3%   White collar: 48.4%   Gray collar: 16.3%

The mountains of eastern Kentucky have been a special place since Daniel Boone came through the Cumberland Gap in 1775. As Virginians poured through and created their version of a Tidewater civilization in the Bluegrass country, the people who settled the mountain counties and the Cumberland Plateau, most of them of Irish Protestant or Border Scot descent, brought different values—an assertive egalitarianism, loyalty to family and community, and passionate willingness to defend honor by feuds or violence. Most of the people in the mountains today are descendants of families who settled there in the two or three generations after Boone. Handed down are living memories of the old ways of doing things from the time not so far distant when there was little contact here with the outside world and the ties to the rest of American civilization were secured mainly by school primers and the King James Bible. Only when people's lives have been changed and uprooted by outside events and institutions have their basic political attitudes been changed—and with a lasting imprint. The first agent of such change here was the Civil War; the second was the great United Mine Workers organizing drives in the coalmines around the 1930s. The Civil War made the mountains and the Cumberland Plateau a stronghold of the Republican Party. This was never slave territory—hardly any blacks have ever lived here, yet communities and families were riven by the rebellion of the South. People have not forgotten: The counties around Somerset and Corbin in south central Kentucky cast some of the highest Republican percentages in the nation, election after election.

Then came coal. Early in the 20th century, vast seams of coal were discovered under the Kentucky mountains; representatives of eastern capitalists (including the young Franklin D. Roosevelt) began prowling through these hills, hiring town lawyers to buy up mineral rights from unsuspecting farmers, building industrial slum towns in hollows and creek beds beneath glowering, heavily forested mountainsides. Coal mining was harsh and deadly work: Mine accidents, black lung disease and simple exhaustion killed tens of thousands of miners, while low wages and company stores kept them poor. Then John L. Lewis's United Mine Workers came in and something like open warfare followed, with neither mine operators nor union organizers loath to use violence and threats. The union mostly won in eastern Kentucky and in the short run raised wages and built hospitals for miners and their families; in the longer run, the UMW phased out many jobs in the mines in return for job security and health benefits, as use of oil expanded. Today there are just over 400 mines in Kentucky, a drop from over 2,000 25 years ago. Politically, the UMW counties in the eastern part of the state became heavily Democratic. In the mid-1960s Lyndon B. Johnson came to eastern Kentucky and cited the poverty here in pushing for his Appalachian and anti-poverty bills. The high energy prices of the 1970s sparked strip mining, and eastern Kentucky's economy moved upward; the lower energy prices of the 1980s and 1990s were something of a setback; high coal prices in 2004 stepped up the pace at existing mines, but the big mining companies who increasingly control production were wary of opening new mines. Most eastern coal counties have lost population since 1980, but life here today is much closer to the ordinary American standard of living than it was in Johnson's time. There is less insularity and less defensiveness, and more celebration of heritage, as in the Hillbilly Days Festival that draws 100,000 people every June to Pikeville; the mine-scarred hills of Harlan

County are now a mecca for all terrain vehicles. Income levels are low, but so is the cost of living. The biggest problem in recent years in these parts has been abuse of OxyContin and other painkilling drugs, which led to huge federal raids in 2004.

The 5th Congressional District of Kentucky includes much of the Cumberland Plateau and most of the eastern mountains, a mixture of heavily Republican and heavily Democratic territory. There are huge political differences here between counties separated by just a mountain ridge or two, evidence of the depth of Civil War and United Mine Workers political loyalties, and only somewhat modulated by the trend toward George W. Bush in the coal country. Jackson County, which Bill Clinton visited on his "poverty tour" in 1999, voted 84%–15% for Bush in 2004; a few counties over, Knott County (where 95% of registered voters are Democrats) voted 63%–36% for John Kerry. On one matter there is widespread agreement: More people here identify their ancestry as "American" than any other congressional district in the nation. The 5th District, created in the 1991 redistricting and modified just slightly in 2001, spans these lines and combines most of two former districts, one heavily Democratic and the other heavily Republican. But overall this is a solidly Republican district—57% for Bush in 2000, 61% in 2004.

The congressman from the 5th District is Harold Rogers, a Republican first elected in 1980. Rogers grew up in Wayne County, went off to the University of Kentucky and served in the National Guard, then practiced law in Somerset; in 1969, at 34, he was elected Pulaski-Rockcastle Commonwealth's Attorney. In 1979 he was the Republican nominee for lieutenant governor. In 1980, when the 5th District congressman retired, Rogers was one of 11 Republicans in the primary; he won with 23% in the primary (Kentucky has no runoffs) and then easily in November. His toughest race came in 1992, with redistricting. At first his likely opponent was 7th District incumbent Chris Perkins, longtime Congressman Carl Perkins's son; but then Perkins retired at 37, before it was revealed he had 514 overdrafts on the House bank. Rogers ended up facing state Senator John Doug Hays of Pike County, whose grandfather Doug "Sawloggin" Hays was state senator before him. Hays attacked Rogers for supporting trickle-down economics and argued that as a Democrat he could get more money for the district. Rogers countered by pointing to his ongoing efforts to build the $250 million Cumberland Gap twin tunnels and Harlan County flood projects. Rogers won with 55% of the vote. He won 71% in his old 5th District, which cast 52% of the new district's votes.

Rogers is now the fourth ranking Republican on the Appropriations Committee. From 2001 until 2003, he was chairman of its Transportation Subcommittee. In February 2003 he became the first chairman of the Homeland Security Appropriations Subcommittee. His voting record is mostly, but not always, conservative. Representing a low-income district, he is sympathetic to some spending bills. Rogers represents a district that has long been hungry for federal aid, and does not have a uniformly conservative record on economic issues. He supported most of the Contract with America, but prevented the zeroing out of several programs—the Appalachian Regional Commission, the Legal Services Corporation—by straightforwardly negotiating deals, then sticking to them. And of course he has worked on projects for eastern Kentucky. Over the years he has worked to provide $162 million to protect the solvency of the funds for the United Mine Workers Combined Benefit Fund. After he became chairman of the Transportation Subcommittee, Kentucky became the fourth highest state in transportation funding per capita.

Even before September 11, Rogers was lamenting that most airport screeners were not U.S. citizens. After Congress voted to federalize airport screeners, he kept close watch in the new TSA, insisting that it get rid of the Argenbright Security firm, objecting when it got around Congress's 45,000-employee cap by classifying 9,000 five-year workers as temporary.

In 2002 and 2003 he obtained $16 million for anti-drug initiatives. The December 2004 appropriation included $150 million for law enforcement and economic development in eastern and southern Kentucky, including $8 million for the Operation UNITE drive against OxyContin abuse, $10 million for the Harold Rogers Prescription Drug Monitoring Program and $3 million for the Rural Law Enforcement Technology and Training Center in Hazard. Two days after the 2004 election, Rogers hosted a summit meeting in Somerset featuring Homeland Security Secretary Tom Ridge and Governor Ernie Fletcher. The Daniel Boone Parkway, from London to Hazard, has been renamed the Hal Rogers Parkway.

Since 1992, Rogers has been re-elected by overwhelming margins, carrying even the most Democratic counties. In 2002 he set up a leadership PAC and contributed $600,000 to Republican candidates and party organizations. Many Republicans urged him to run for governor in 2003, but in March 2002 he said he could do more for the state from his current position. In 2004 he won the Republican primary 91%–9% and was unopposed in the general election. He donated some $423,000 to 64 Republican candidates during the 2004 cycle, and sent $5,000 to the South Dakota Republican party and $1,000 to Missouri governor candidate Matt Blunt, son of House Republican Whip Roy Blunt. After the 2004 election he was one of three senior appropriators who sought the chairmanship of the Appropriations Committee. Rogers said he would impose a "sweeping attitudinal change of the entire committee," crack down on earmarks, negotiate aggressively with the Senate and impose fundraising quotas on members. All this may have pleased the Steering Committee, but not enough; the chair went to the more senior Jerry Lewis.

SIXTH DISTRICT

Rep. Ben Chandler (D)

Elected Feb. 2004, 1st full term; b. Sept. 12,1959, Versailles; home, Versailles; U. of KY, B.A. 1983, J.D. 1986; Presbyterian; married (Jennifer).

Elected Office: KY Auditor, 1991–95; KY Atty. Gen. 1995–2004.

Professional Career: Practicing atty., 1986–91.

DC Office: 1504 LHOB, 20515, 202-225-4706; Fax: 202-225-2122; Web site: www.house.gov/chandler.

District Office: Lexington, 859-219-1366.

Committees: *Agriculture* (21st of 21 D): General Farm Commodities & Risk Management; Specialty Crops & Foreign Agriculture Programs. *International Relations* (22d of 23 D): Europe & Emerging Threats; Middle East & Central Asia. *Transportation & Infrastructure* (30th of 34 D): Aviation; Highways, Transit & Pipelines.

Group Ratings (Only Served Partial Term)

	ADA	ACLU	AFS	LCV	ITIC	NTU	COC	ACU	NTLC	CHC
2004	70	18	83	100	100	14	55	—	19	—
2003	—	—	—	—	—	—	—	—	—	—

National Journal Ratings (Only Served Partial Term)

	2003 LIB	—	2003 CONS	2004 LIB	—	2004 CONS
Economic	*	—	*	69%	—	30%
Social	*	—	*	51%	—	49%
Foreign	*	—	*	52%	—	48%

Key Votes of the 108th Congress (Only Served Partial Term)

1. Drilling in ANWR	*	5. DC School Vouchers	*	9. Ban Same-Sex Marriage	Y
2. Approve Bush Tax Cuts	*	6. Ban Human Cloning	*	10. Fund Iraq War	*
3. Medicare/Rx Bill	*	7. Restrict Gun Liability	*	11. Bar Cuba Embargo Funds	N
4. Bar Overtime Pay Regs.	Y	8. Ban Partial-Birth Abortion	*	12. Intelligence Reorg.	Y

Election Results

2004 general	Ben Chandler (D)	175,355	(59%)	($1,623,086)
	Tom Buford (R)	119,716	(40%)	($137,072)
	Other	4,146	(1%)	
2004 primary	Ben Chandler (D)	unopposed		
2004 special	Ben Chandler (D)	84,168	(55%)	
	Alice Forgy Kerr (R)	65,474	(43%)	
	Other	2,592	(2%)	
2002 general	Ernie Fletcher (R)	115,622	(72%)	($1,238,265)
	Gatewood Galbraith (I)	41,753	(26%)	($18,697)
	Other	3,313	(2%)	

The People		Race/Ethnic Origin	Ancestry	
Area size:	3,775 sq. mi.	87.1% White	USA: 15.3%	English: 9.5%
Urban population:	71.3%	8.2% Black	German: 9.3%	
Rural population:	28.7%	1.2% Asian	**2004 Presidential Vote**	
Pop. 2000:	673,626	0.2% Native Am.	Bush (R) 182,787	(58%)
Median income:	$37,544	0.0% Hawaiian	Kerry (D) 128,967	(41%)
Poverty status:	13.2%	1.1% Two+ races	Other 2,505	(1%)
Military veterans:	11.7%	0.1% Other	**2000 Presidential Vote**	
		2.1% Hispanic Origin	Bush (R) 145,606	(55%)
			Gore (D) 109,602	(42%)
			Other 7,282	(3%)
			Cook Partisan Voting Index: R + 7	

Occupation	Blue collar: 25.8%	White collar: 58.8%	Gray collar: 15.4%

With its white picket fences, horse farms and Georgian brick house-filled small towns, the rolling plateau of the Bluegrass country almost plumb in the middle of Kentucky is the part of interior America longest settled by English speakers: Lexington was founded in 1775; the town of Hopewell was renamed Paris in 1789 out of gratitude for French help during our Revolution and in a salute to theirs (though the county name remained Bourbon even after Louis XVI was guillotined). Tobacco farming started here in the 1770s, horse racing in 1787, and the first whiskey distillery, in Bourbon County, was built in 1790. Tobacco, whiskey and racehorses remained the staples of the Bluegrass economy for six generations until 1956, when IBM built its typewriter plant in Lexington. IBM's arrival "really was the beginning of Lexington's industrial revolution," as University of Kentucky historian Carl Cone put it. But capitalism, as Joseph Schumpeter wrote, is a process of creative destruction. The PC eventually outclassed the typewriter, and the IBM plant was put on the block. The big employer here became Lexmark International, an independent IBM spinoff that makes inkjet and laser printers. Another mainstay of the local economy is the Toyota plant, built in the 1980s, in Georgetown, a town with early 19th century houses and lush countryside, just one county north of Lexington and west of Paris; auto parts and suppliers have naturally moved in nearby as an adjunct to the Georgetown plant, which can produce 500,000 cars annually. The engineering school at the University of Kentucky has created additional manufacturing job opportunities. Lexington, which includes all of Fayette County, grew by a sprightly 18% between 1990 and 2004, and the 2000 Census showed it the largest city in Kentucky, just ahead of Louisville. But Louisville voters decided to merge the city and Jefferson County, and in January 2003 Louisville became number one again.

The 6th Congressional District of Kentucky includes Lexington and the surrounding counties—a natural unit, unlike some other Kentucky districts. Lexington casts 40% of the votes. It was the home base of the Whig Party's great leader Henry Clay, but in the 150 years after his death, the Bluegrass country was mostly Democratic. In the 1990s the area became more Republican, and George W. Bush carried the district in 2000 and 2004.

The congressman from the 6th District is Ben Chandler, a Democrat who won a special election in February 2004. He grew up in Versailles, in the horse country just west of Lexington, the grandson of A.B. "Happy" Chandler, the former governor and senator who for five years was commissioner of baseball before eventually serving another term as governor. His father owned a local newspaper. Ben Chandler got his bachelor's and law degree from the University of Kentucky and practiced law for five years. In 1991 he was elected state auditor and in 1995 and 1999 attorney general. In that job he made a name for himself by prosecuting corrupt politicians. But he, like other Kentucky Democrats, was hurt in 2002 when Governor Paul Patton admitted an extramarital affair with a woman who owned a nursing home and who was given preferential treatment by the state. In 2003 Chandler ran for governor and beat Speaker Jody Richards in the Democratic primary by a 50%–47% margin. But he lost the general election to 6th District Congressman Ernie Fletcher 55%–45%. Fletcher resigned the 6th District House seat on December 9.

Chandler quickly decided that if he could not defeat Fletcher, he would try to succeed him. He won the Democratic nomination without opposition, and Republicans picked low-profile state Senator Alice Forgy Kerr, whose brother Larry Forgy was the unsuccessful Republican nominee for governor in 1995. Both candidates supported the war in Iraq and a constitutional amendment to ban same-sex marriage and opposed amnesty for illegal aliens, but they disagreed on state and national taxes. Chandler attacked Republicans for not supporting reimportation of prescription drugs from Canada, promised to fight for additional veterans benefits and to defend a local VA hospital from efforts to close it. Although he was glad to accept House Democrats' fundraising help, Chandler kept his distance from Minority Leader Nancy Pelosi; "It's a lie to say that I'll do what she wants." Kerr ran as a solid supporter of George W. Bush. Chandler scored an unexpectedly easy victory, 55%–43%, carrying 14 of the 16 counties, with a 55%–43% margin in Fayette County. Kerr won only two exurban counties south of Lexington. Polls showed that Chandler won back the support of many traditionally Democratic older voters who had supported Republican candidates in recent years. The biggest change from his November defeat, said a Chandler adviser, was that the special election was not a referendum on Paul Patton. This was the first time since 1991 that Democrats captured a Republican seat in a special election; national Democrats celebrated Chandler's victory as a good omen for their hopes of recapturing the House in November 2004. National chairman Terry McAuliffe said it was a sign of Bush's unpopularity in the South. But Republicans credited the outcome to Chandler's smart campaign and high name recognition. Out-party candidates tend to do well in special elections, since they can argue that they will serve local interests and their opponents cannot plausibly claim that their victories will result in a change of party control. Democrats did not win any Chandler-like victories in House seats in November 2004.

In the House, Chandler had a moderate voting record, which was a bit more liberal on economic issues. In November, he was challenged by state Senator Tom Buford, who supported Bush on nearly every issue. Chandler won again, 59%–40%. He has seats on the Agriculture, International Relations, and Transportation and Infrastructure committees. His victories in 2004 kept alive Kentucky's record of electing at least one Democrat to Congress every year since Andrew Jackson founded the party in 1828.

★ LOUISIANA ★

Louisiana often seems to be America's banana republic, with its charm and inefficiency, its communities interlaced by family ties and its public sector sometimes laced with corruption, with its own indigenous culture and its tradition of fine distinctions of class and caste. It is a state with an economy uncomfortably like that of an underdeveloped country, based on pumping minerals out of soggy ground and shipping grain produced in the vast hinterland drained by its great river, an economy increasingly dependent on businesses typical of picturesque Third World countries—tourism (now the second largest industry, hard hit by September 11) and gambling. Its politics too has a Third World quality, with its own peculiar election laws and a heritage of no-holds-barred conflict and demagoguery no other state can match: what other state has produced a Huey Long or an Edwin Edwards? Louisiana has a hereditary rich class and a large low-wage working class. It has conservative cultural attitudes: Louisiana and Utah have the

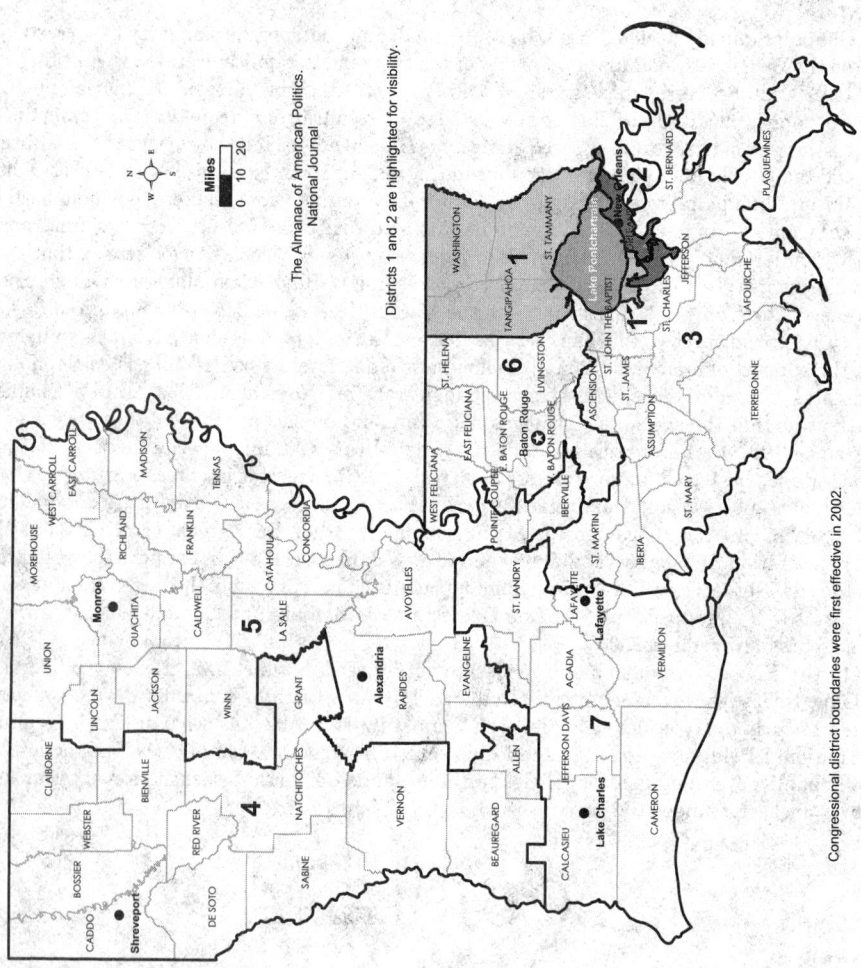

N

Miles
0 10 20

The Almanac of American Politics.
National Journal

Districts 1 and 2 are highlighted for visibility.

Congressional district boundaries were first effective in 2002.

most restrictive abortion laws in the U.S.—its partial-birth abortion ban and optional "Choose Life" license plates have been ruled illegal by federal courts—and Louisiana in 1997 became the first state to offer covenant marriages, in which spouses would agree not to be covered by no-fault divorce laws. But Louisiana also has a lazy tolerance of rule-breaking, and feels more like the Caribbean or the Mediterranean than the North Atlantic or the Pacific Rim. This is not an entirely original observation. Four decades ago, A. J. Liebling described Louisiana as an outpost of the Levant along the Gulf of Mexico. Most of the United States faces east toward the vast Atlantic Ocean or west toward the vast Pacific; Louisiana faces south, to the Gulf of Mexico and the steamy heat and volatile societies of the Caribbean and Latin America.

New Orleans preserves the look and feel it had as a French and Spanish outpost in the New World. Traditions of centralized control and easygoing corruption, classic traits of colonialism, are part of this heritage. The *dirigiste* tradition comes from the fact that Louisiana is the only state whose law is based not on the common law of England but on the Napoleonic Code of France; the concept of civil liberties has shallower roots in Louisiana than in the other 49 states. Here abstract ideals have been overshadowed by the practical need for centralized action. This Delta land—much of it below sea level, soggy, swampy, laced with tributaries and offshoots of the Mississippi and other major rivers like the Atchafalaya—requires vast capital expenditures for levees and drainage and causeways.

The economy that grew up in these rich Delta lands has always been based on raw materials. Antebellum Louisiana produced and exported sugar, rice and cotton in enough abundance to generate the wealth which built grand plantation houses behind alleys of oaks running in from the Mississippi, and to make New Orleans the nation's fifth largest city by the time of the Civil War. Then came oil, found in the great Spindletop strike just over the Texas line in 1901 and in salt domes in Louisiana not long after, followed by the huge Baton Rouge refinery that became the training ground for generations of top oil executives. When energy prices boomed after the oil shocks of 1973 and 1981, Louisiana, like an oil-rich Third World country, boomed too, reaching up toward national income levels, generating 500,000 new jobs between 1972 and 1981. But it lost 150,000 jobs in the next six years as oil prices crashed and the rig count dropped by two-thirds and energy taxes fell from 41% of state government revenues in 1982 to 9% in 1996. Louisiana's economy has never regained much forward momentum. Gambling, legalized in 1991, has produced less revenue than expected, and nothing like the boom that some promised. People have been leaving the state: From 1980, near the peak of oil prices, until 2004 Louisiana's population increased only 7%, far less than any other Southern state, less than any state except two in the Great Plains and the industrial triangle of Ohio, Pennsylvania and West Virginia. Louisiana has high rates of cancer, early death rates, a high incidence of AIDS. Louisiana has attracted few immigrants: its population is 32% black, the second highest of any state, but only 2% Hispanic and 1% Asian. It is a population with low incomes and work force participation and low levels of education. Income disparities here are greater than almost anywhere else in the United States. New Orleans's rich are notoriously unventuresome and tight-knit, determined to hold on to their wealth against the grasp of the impecunious and unlearned masses.

The most enduringly famous politician here, and by far the most talented, was Huey P. Long, who in less than a single term each as governor (1928–32) and senator (1932–35), left an imprint on the state's public life and imposed an organization to its politics that have faded into history only recently. Long's genius was not that he promised to tax the rich to help the poor—hundreds of idealists and demagogues in America have done that—but that, to an amazing extent, he actually delivered. He dominated the legislature so thoroughly that, as governor, he roamed the floors of both chambers at will, bringing to the podium bills he insisted be passed without changing a comma—and they were. He was ready to use bribery, intimidation and physical violence. He built a new skyscraper Capitol, a new Louisiana State University and more miles of roads than any state but rich New York and huge Texas. He also built a national following, and by 1935, he was planning to run for president on the platform of "Share the wealth, every man a king," when he was assassinated at age 42 in the hallway of the Capitol, where the bullet holes can still be seen in the marble walls.

For America, the Long threat may have moved Franklin D. Roosevelt to embrace the liberal programs—the Wagner Labor Act, social security, steeply graduated taxes—of the second New Deal. For Louisiana, Long delivered a political structure that revolved around him even after he was dead—and a class of political leaders who, lacking his talents, treated the state as Long's incompetent doctors had treated his fatal wound, leaving Louisiana without either a fully developed economy or a fully competent public sector. For 50 years, until Huey's son Senator Russell Long retired in 1986, Longs and Long protégés held high political office in Louisiana and elections were run along pro- and anti-Long lines. The Long experience has strengthened Louisiana's already strong predispositions—tolerance of corruption, disinterest in abstract reform and taste for colorful extremists regardless of their short-term means or long-term ends—in a way that helps explain the rise and fall of such unlikely politicians as the four-term Governor Edwin Edwards and the onetime Ku Klux Klan leader and state legislator David Duke, both of whom by 2003 were spending time in jail.

Louisiana has natural political divides. One divide is by religion: Catholic Cajun parishes (Louisiana has parishes rather than counties) cast about 30% of the state's vote, the New Orleans area casts around 25% or so, and about 45% are cast in Protestant parishes from Baton Rouge on north. White Protestants for years have wanted nothing to do with national Democrats, while Cajuns tend to mull it over. Another divide is by race: Blacks are overwhelmingly Democratic, whites split in seriously contested elections. A third divide is by income: Low- and high-income whites vote very differently and are much less influenced than voters in most other states by candidates' cultural values, marital status, lifestyles and the like. As a result, Louisiana politics since Huey P. Long's time has often been a struggle between reformist and conservative forces on one side and roguish populists on the other, a struggle waged in lavishly financed campaigns and with grandiloquent rhetoric.

For a quarter century, the lead role was played by Edwin Edwards as the roguish populist, with a number of rivals as reformist conservatives. Edwards was elected governor in 1971 and 1975 and was not eligible to run in 1979. In 1983 he beat incumbent Republican David Treen; in 1987 he lost to Buddy Roemer, a Democratic congressman who later switched parties. For much of this third term, Edwards faced corruption charges, until he was acquitted by a jury in 1986. In 1991 he ran again, and this time an even odder character surfaced. David Duke was an active Nazi sympathizer up through 1989, but he also had a knack for speaking to mainstream political issues in attractive political language. In 1989 he was narrowly elected to the state legislature from a district in suburban Jefferson Parish as a nominal Republican—a victory that got enormous national publicity. Then in 1991, Duke ran for governor, against Roemer and Edwards. Louisiana has a unique primary system, invented by Edwards: candidates of all parties run in a single primary; any candidate who gets 50% is elected; otherwise, the top two finishers, regardless of party, have a runoff. In late 2004 leaders of both parties talked of returning to the system of party primaries used in most other states, but the legislature did not act in 2005. Edwards received only 34% of the votes in that 1991 race, and Duke made the runoff by finishing second with 32%. All articulate opinion in Louisiana moved to Edwards's side, and Republicans from George H.W. Bush on down endorsed Edwards, who won 61%–39%.

In the first years of this century Louisiana has not set a clear political course. In 2000 the state, after voting twice for Bill Clinton, voted 53%–45% for George W. Bush. In 2002 Democratic Senator Mary Landrieu, elected by 5,788 votes in 1996, failed to win a majority in the November primary and faced a runoff with Republican Suzanne Haik Terrell. Shrewdly Landrieu cast this as a choice between an independent who would fight for Louisiana interests and a Republican who would vote in lockstep with Bush; she won 52%–48%. In 2003, when Republican Governor Mike Foster was ineligible for a third term, Republican Bobby Jindal led in the October primary with 33% of the vote to 18% for Democratic Lieutenant Governor Kathleen Babineaux Blanco. In the November runoff Jindal's youth, Indian ancestry and policy wonkishness didn't set well with voters in northern parishes who vote heavily Republican for president, and Blanco, a Catholic Cajun, was elected 52%–48%. In the 2004 Senate race, left open by the retirement of Democrat John Breaux, the balance fell the other way. Democrats had two serious candidates running, Congressman Chris John and state Treasurer John Kennedy. There was just one serious Republican, suburban New Orleans Congressman David Vitter and, as George W. Bush was carrying the state 57%–42% over John Kerry, Vitter surprised the pundits by winning outright with 51% of the vote. Vitter, who jousted with almost every other legislator when he served in Baton Rouge, fits the mold of the Republican reformer. Neither Landrieu nor Blanco falls in the Edwin Edwards mold; there is no evidence that either is corrupt, nor are they, by the standards of the Democratic party at least, particularly liberal. Nor is either one of them, any more than Vitter, assured of reelection based on their most recent electoral performance. Louisiana, having outgrown the Longs and Edwin Edwards, is embarked on a politics of uncertain direction.

The People		Race/Ethnic Origin			Military veterans: 392,486 (12.1%)	
Pop. 2004 (est):	4,515,770	2,794,391	62.5%	White	WWII: 19.5%	Korea: 12.7%
Pop. 2000:	4,468,976	1,443,390	32.3%	Black	Vietnam: 32.2%	Gulf War: 12.4%
Pop. 1990:	4,219,973	54,256	1.2%	Asian	**Most populous cities (2003):**	
Change 1990–2000:	Up 5.9%	24,129	0.5%	Native Am.	1. New Orleans	469,032
% of U.S. total:	1.6%	1,076	0.0%	Hawaiian	2. Baton Rouge	225,090
Pop. rank:	22d of 50	39,260	0.9%	Two+ races	3. Shreveport	198,364
Area size:	51,840 sq. mi.	4,736	0.1%	Other	4. Lafayette	111,667
State Native:	79.4%	107,738	2.4%	Hisp. Origin	5. Lake Charles	70,735
Non-citizen:	1.3%	**Ancestry**				
Language		French: 10.2%		USA: 8.4%	Urban population: 72.7%	
English: 85.9%	Other Eur.: 9.3%	German: 5.9%		Irish: 5.9%	Rural population: 27.3%	
Spanish: 3.5%		English: 4.4%				

Education		Work Sector			Legislature	
H.S. Grad:	74.8%	Private: 76.2%		Govt: 17.4%	Senate	24 D 15 R
College Grad:	18.7%	Self: 6.1%		Family: 0.3%	House	67 D 37 R 1 I
Industry		Unemployment: 7.3%			Legislative Term Limits: Yes	
Agri: 4.2%	Con: 7.9%	**Household Income**			**Registered Voters**	
Fin: 5.7%	Info: 2.0%	<15k: 24.1%		15-35k: 28.5%	D: 1,618,431	(55.4%)
Mfg: 15.5%	Prof: 29.3%	35-50k: 15.7%		50-100k: 24.2%	R: 700,691	(24.0%)
Public: 5.8%	Trade: 15.4%	100-150k: 4.8%		>150k: 2.6%	O: 604,273	(20.7%)
Other: 14.3%		Median: $32,566				
Occupation		Poverty status: 19.6%				
Blue collar: 25.8%	White collar: 56.6%	**Home Value**				
Gray collar: 17.5%		<50k: 28.3%	50-100k: 38.5%	100-200k: 25.4%	200-300k: 5.0%	
		300-500k: 2.0%	>500k: 0.9%	Median: $77,500		

Presidential politics   Louisiana's presidential politics is racially polarized. In 2004 the state voted 57%–42% for Bush; whites voted 75%–24% for him and blacks voted 90%–9% for John Kerry. Louisiana's black percentage is the second highest in the country, after Mississippi's, and rising: The state's white population increased by less than 1% in the 1990s and its black population increased 12%, as many whites left the state and some blacks in the North and West returned to their southern roots. But there is also religious polarization. In 2004 Louisiana Catholics, mostly but not all white, voted 68% for Bush, a big increase from 2000; Protestants, a large percentage of whom are black, voted 59% for him, the same as in 2000. Louisiana is one state with a solid anti-abortion majority. Governor Kathleen Babineaux Blanco, asked to explain why her candidate John Kerry lost the state, said, "His positions were too far to the left, especially on abortion."

Louisiana has never played a significant role in presidential primaries and caucuses,

2004 Presidential Vote

Bush (R)	1,102,169	(57%)
Kerry (D)	820,299	(42%)
Nader (BL)	7,032	(0%)
Other	13,606	(1%)

2004 Democratic Presidential Primary

Kerry (D)	112,639	(70%)
Edwards (D)	26,074	(16%)
Dean (D)	7,948	(5%)
Clark (D)	7,091	(4%)
McGaughey (D)	3,161	(2%)
Other	4,740	(3%)

2000 Presidential Vote

Bush (R)	927,871	(53%)
Gore (D)	792,344	(45%)
Nader (Green)	20,473	(1%)
Other	24,968	(1%)

with one odd exception. That was in 1996, when Republican allies of Phil Gramm set up a pre-Iowa-and-New-Hampshire February 6 caucus. The aim was to jump-start Gramm's campaign; instead the caucuses killed it. Pat Buchanan crisscrossed the bayous and upcountry parishes, meeting with voters, talking on cell-phones with any radio show that would have him. Only 20,000 Republicans showed up at 42 voting sites voted (as compared to 100,000 at 2,000 sites in Iowa), and Buchanan won more votes than Gramm and took 13 of the 21 delegates. Gramm's campaign in Iowa faltered, and he left the race before the vote in New Hampshire.

In December 1999, Governor Mike Foster got the state central committee to cancel the caucus and hold a March primary. He cited the low turnout in 1996 and the fact that only Orrin Hatch, Gary Bauer and Alan Keyes were competing in Louisiana. George W. Bush, Foster's candidate, won in March and Francis lost his seat on the party committee. In 2004 the primary was held March 9, when both party's nominations had already been clinched.

Congressional districting

109th Congress Lineup	
5 R	2 D
108th Congress Lineup	
4 R	3 D

Louisiana redistricted its congressional districts three times in the 1990s. The first two plans created two black-majority districts, one of them in each case highly irregular in shape; they were declared unconstitutional in federal court in December 1993 and July 1994. The first plan was used in the 1992 elections, the second in 1994. In January 1996 a federal court came up with a plan, adopted by the legislature, that cut through few parish boundaries and had much more regular lines, and had only one black-majority district, centered in New Orleans. It was upheld by the Supreme Court in June 1996.

In August 2001 six of the seven House incumbents (all except John Cooksey, who was running for the Senate) submitted to the legislature their own plan. Governor Mike Foster called a special session for redistricting in October, and the legislators made minor tweaks in the House incumbents' plan. It was opposed by the Black Legislative Caucus, which drew up a plan with a second black-majority district stretching from Lafayette and Baton Rouge along the Mississippi River to the Arkansas border. But that was rejected by solid margins. Foster signed the new plan in October; it certainly seemed likely to be upheld by the courts, since the Supreme Court had already approved an almost identical plan. It was submitted to the Justice Department in January 2002 and approved in April. Unexpectedly, the plan turned out to have an effect on the results. In the December 2002 runoff, Democrat Rodney Alexander won an upset victory for Cooksey's old seat. His margin of victory came from heavily black areas added to the district. But he switched to the Republican party in August 2004. In 2005 some Democrats urged the Democratic legislature to redistrict again, as Republicans in Texas had in 2003, to help their party gain a seat or two. But Democratic Governor Kathleen Babineaux Blanco seemed uninterested, and it was hard to see how Democrats could gain a seat without creating a grotesquely shaped district like the one the courts rejected in 1993 and 1994.

Governor

Kathleen Babineaux Blanco (D)

Elected 2003, term expires Jan. 2008, 1st term; b. Dec. 15, 1942, Coteau; home, Lafayette; U. of LA at Lafayette, B.A. 1964; Catholic; married (Raymond).

Elected Office: LA House of Reps., 1984–88; Public Service Comm., 1988–1995; Lt. Gov., 1996–2003.

Professional Career: H.S. teacher, 1964–65; District Mgr., US Census Bureau, 1979–80. Political Consultant, 1981–84.

Office: State Capitol, P.O. Box 94004, Baton Rouge, 70804, 225-342-0991; Fax: 225-342-7099; Web site: www.gov.state.la.us.

Election Results

2003 runoff	Kathleen Babineaux Blanco (D)	731,358	(52%)
	Bobby Jindal (R)	676,484	(48%)
2003 primary	Bobby Jindal (R)	443,389	(33%)
	Kathleen Babineaux Blanco (D)	250,136	(18%)
	Richard Ieyoub (D)	223,513	(16%)
	Claude Leach (R)	187,872	(14%)
	Randy Ewing (D)	123,936	(9%)
	Hunt Downer (R)	84,718	(6%)
	Other	48,960	(4%)
1999 primary	Mike Foster (R)	805,203	(62%)
	William Jefferson (D)	382,445	(30%)
	Other	107,557	(8%)

Kathleen Babineaux Blanco, a Democrat, was elected governor of Louisiana in November 2003. She was born in the Cajun village of Coteau, in the sugar cane-producing region south of Lafayette. Her father was an Electrolux vacuum salesman and ran a carpet-cleaning business. The family later moved south to New Iberia; they loaded their three-bedroom house onto a flatbed truck and took it with them. Blanco graduated from the University of Louisiana at Lafayette, taught high school in southwest Louisiana, got married and raised six children. With her husband, she ran a market research and political polling business. In 1971, together they managed then-state Senator J. Bennett Johnson's campaign for governor in the Acadiana region, no picnic in an election where Congressman Edwin Edwards was seeking to become the state's first Cajun governor. Edwards narrowly defeated Johnston in the December runoff.

Blanco began her own political career in 1984 with an upset victory in an open state House race; outspent by a wealthy opponent, this was the first in a series of low budget, winning campaigns. In 1988, she was elected to the Public Service Commission, where she became the first woman to serve as a commissioner; she chaired the commission, which regulates utilities and phone companies, in 1993 and 1994. In 1991, she entered the race for governor against incumbent Buddy Roemer, in a contest that also featured former Governor Edwards and former Ku Klux Klansman David Duke; she withdrew after failing to raise enough money to compete.

In 1995, Blanco won the first of two terms as lieutenant governor. The low-profile position has little responsibility but it offered one role that turned out to be consequential. As the chief of the state Department of Culture, Recreation and Tourism, Blanco had a platform that enabled her to travel to all 64 parishes to promote the state and, of course, herself. She claimed that under her leadership, tourism in Louisiana increased by 41 percent and led to the creation of 21,000 new tourism-related jobs.

Blanco joined in May 2003 what was already a very large field to succeed term-limited Republican Governor Mike Foster. In Louisiana, candidates of all parties compete in the October primary and then, if no one gets 50% of the vote, the top two finishers regardless of party compete in the November runoff. Blanco had two advantages that made her candidacy stand out in the primary—she was the only woman in the race and the only candidate from Acadiana. Her Democratic opponents included Attorney General Richard Ieyoub, former Congressman Buddy Leach, former state Senate President Randy Ewing; Republican candidates included state Senator Hunt Downer and Bobby Jindal, appointed by Foster at 24 as president of the Department of Health and Hospitals and later as head of the Louisiana state university system, and appointed by George W. Bush as HHS Assistant Secretary.

Blanco said she wanted to move beyond "the tired old politics of Louisiana" and stressed health care and education themes. She called for investing in pre-kindergarten programs for all 4-year-olds, laptops for 7th graders and increased teacher salaries. She opposed a processing tax on oil and gas and said her experience promoting Louisiana gave her greater economic development expertise than her opponents. For much of the primary campaign, Blanco remained atop the polls but insiders dismissed her candidacy, claiming she was too nice to win, lacked key interest group support or worse, that she was a lightweight. But in the October primary she finished second with 18% to Jindal's 33%, and ahead of Ieyoub, who had 16%, and Leach, who had 14%.

In the runoff against Jindal, Blanco focused on his youth, saying he was too immature to be governor. "The ship of state does not come with training wheels," she said. She promised to hold an emergency health care policy summit, chaired by Senator John Breaux and said she would not raise taxes unless education and health care spending was deeply threatened. Jindal signed a pledge not to raise taxes at all; he highlighted this as a key difference. Jindal often mentioned his connections to the Bush administration; Blanco ran radio ads that said the administration's negotiations in the Central American Free Trade Agreement would lead to lower tariffs on imported sugar, a volatile issue in sugar-producing Louisiana. Both candidates opposed abortion. In the final debate with Jindal, she was asked to name the "defining moment" in her life; she gave an emotional response, recalling the death of her 19-year-old son in an industrial accident in 1997.

She won 52%–48% to become the state's first female governor. Jindal carried the New Orleans, Baton Rouge, Shreveport and Monroe metro areas and won by wide margins in the fastest-growing parts of the state: St. Tammany Parish outside New Orleans, Livingston and Ascension Parishes outside Baton Rouge, Bossier Parish outside Shreveport. But Blanco carried her home area, the Cajun country, by a wide margin, and Jindal carried only one of the northern parishes which most Republicans have been carrying in other statewide races.

Her first year in office was cautious and did not feature an ambitious legislative agenda. She held summits on health care policy and poverty. In February 2004 she was one of 5 governors, the only Democrat, on a Defense Department-sponsored trip to Iraq. She focused on economic development, frequently traveling out of state, and pointed to her success in persuading Union Tank Car Co. to build a $100 million manufacturing facility in Alexandria rather than Texas; she failed to convince State Farm to keep its insurance claims-processing center in Monroe. She stood up to the owner of the football Saints on the issue of state stadium subsidies and got teacher salary increases that averaged $360. Blanco sought permanent renewal of the 2.8% tax on business utility bills and a 7-year phaseout of taxes on corporate debt and business equipment and machinery; she compromised and got a 5-year renewal of the business utilities tax, and 6-year phaseout of the sales tax on machinery and business equipment and the elimination of the tax on corporate debt, beginning in 2006. In March 2005 Blanco traveled on a trade mission to Cuba. She dined with President Fidel Castro, drawing criticism from Republicans and Cuban groups back home; she said the unplanned dinner was good for business and she stipulated that the group could not talk about politics. "If somebody had come to Louisiana and did $15 million worth of transactions and I asked them to meet with me and they turned me down, I'd probably dry up some of that [business]," she said.

Senior Senator

Mary Landrieu (D)

Elected 1996, seat up 2008, 2d term; b. Nov. 23, 1955, Arlington, VA; home, New Orleans; LA St. U., B.A. 1977; Catholic; married (Frank Snellings).

Elected Office: LA House of Reps., 1979–88; LA Treasurer, 1987–96.

DC Office: 724 HSOB, 20510, 202-224-5824; Fax: 202-224-9735; Web site: landrieu.senate.gov.

State Offices: Baton Rouge, 225-389-0395; Lake Charles, 337-436-6650; New Orleans, 504-589-2427; Shreveport, 318-676-3085.

Committees: *Appropriations*: Agriculture, Rural Development & Related Agencies; District of Columbia (RMM); Energy & Water; Labor, Health and Human Services, Education & Related Agencies; Military Construction & Veterans Affairs; State, Foreign Operations & Related Programs. *Energy & Natural Resources*: Energy; National Parks; Public Lands & Forests. *Small Business & Entrepreneurship*.

Group Ratings

	ADA	ACLU	AFS	LCV	ITIC	NTU	COC	ACU	NTLC	CHC
2004	85	56	100	67	83	11	71	32	18	16
2003	60	—	89	21	—	21	78	20	—	—

National Journal Ratings

	2003 LIB	—	2003 CONS	2004 LIB	—	2004 CONS
Economic	55%	—	44%	65%	—	31%
Social	59%	—	37%	54%	—	44%
Foreign	65%	—	32%	57%	—	42%

Key Votes of the 108th Congress

1. Ban Drilling in ANWR	N	5. Energy Bill	Y	9. Ban Same-Sex Marriage	N
2. Approve Bush Tax Cuts	N	6. Support Roe v. Wade	Y	10. Ban Bunker-Buster Bomb	Y
3. Medicare/Rx Bill	Y	7. Ban Partial-Birth Abortion	Y	11. Fund Iraq War	Y
4. Bar Overtime Pay Regs.	Y	8. Assault Weapons Ban	N	12. Restrict Missile Defense	N

Election Results

2002 runoff	Mary Landrieu (D)	638,654	(52%)	($7,384,554)
	Suzanne Haik Terrell (R)	596,642	(48%)	($2,760,276)
2002 primary	Mary Landrieu (D)	573,347	(46%)	
	Suzanne Haik Terrell (R)	339,506	(27%)	
	John Cooksey (R)	171,752	(14%)	
	Tony Perkins (R)	119,776	(10%)	
	Other	41,952	(3%)	
1996 runoff	Mary Landrieu (D)	852,945	(50%)	($2,504,815)
	Woody Jenkins (R)	847,157	(50%)	($1,878,242)

Mary Landrieu, a Democrat, was elected to the Senate in 1996 and reelected in 2002. Landrieu grew up in New Orleans, the oldest of nine children of Moon Landrieu (all with names starting with M), mayor of New Orleans in the 1970s. She was educated at Ursuline Academy and LSU and in 1979, at 23, became the youngest woman ever elected to the Louisiana state legislature, where she was sometimes the object of undue ridicule. In 1987 she was elected state treasurer; she was a sharp critic of Governor Edwin Edwards and opposed gambling as "political cancer." In 1995 she ran for governor, and in the September primary finished third, just 1% and 8,983 votes behind second-place finisher Congressman Cleo Fields. She immediately started running for the Senate seat held by Bennett Johnston, who was retiring 24 years after he was elected to the Senate after a narrow loss in a governor's race.

With a well-known name and a moderate platform—for a balanced budget amendment and capital gains tax cut, promising to make education a top priority—Landrieu shared a lead in the polls with Attorney General Richard Ieyoub, also a Democrat; under Louisiana law if they finished in the top two in the September primary, they would meet in a November runoff, and Democrats would be guaranteed a win no matter what. Woody Jenkins, a 25-year state legislator and strong abortion opponent, who had run twice unsuccessfully for the Senate as a Democrat, claimed the Republican endorsement; he surged in the polls, and led the September 21 primary with 26%, to 22% for Landrieu and 20% for Ieyoub; David Duke got 12%.

At this point Jenkins looked like the favorite; Republican candidates had won 55% of the total votes and Democrats only 44%. But he had little money left, and Landrieu, who ultimately outspent him, ran ads attacking him as an extremist.

The result was an exceedingly close election. The official results showed Landrieu ahead by 5,788 votes, 50.2%–49.8%. Jenkins filed a lawsuit claiming vote fraud, but withdrew it, and submitted his case to the Senate. At the behest of Majority Leader Trent Lott, the Senate seated Landrieu "without prejudice" to Jenkins's challenge. To the Senate Rules Committee Jenkins submitted evidence that more votes were counted in many New Orleans precincts than the number of voters who signed in, and that campaign operatives ferried in ineligible voters. But in June it was revealed that one of Jenkins's witnesses was a convicted felon, and several others retracted their testimony. Rules Chairman John Warner continued the hearings; Democrats protested, and Landrieu was bitter. Finally in October 1997 the committee voted unanimously to end the inquiry. While concluding that "isolated instances" of voter fraud did occur, Warner said there was no evidence to prove that there was a "widespread effort to illegally affect the outcome of this election," or that Landrieu had any involvement in the violation of election laws.

In the Senate, Landrieu has a generally moderate voting record. Her first bill was for a $5 million block grant for adoption services; her two children are adopted. She backs adoption tax credits and wants higher breaks for those who adopt special needs or foster children. She was the lead co-sponsor of the law providing for speedy citizenship for foreign-born children adopted by U.S. citizens; when it went into effect it created the largest number of new U.S. citizens ever on a single day. Landrieu was the only Democrat who has joined in co-sponsoring Sam Brownback's bills to prohibit human cloning for reproduction or research. In January 2001 Landrieu won a seat on the Appropriations Committee.

All the while she was running hard for reelection in 2002. She was an obvious Republican target, because of the closeness of her margin in 1996 and because George W. Bush carried Louisiana in 2000. In early 2001 the only active Republican candidate was 5th District Congressman John Cooksey, a north Louisiana ophthalmologist. But on September 18, 2001, a week after September 11, in a radio interview in Louisiana, he said, "If I see someone comes in that's got a diaper on his head and a fan belt wrapped around the diaper on his head, the guy needs to be pulled over." Cooksey spent $200,000 on radio ads defending his comments.

Cooksey's candidacy was undone by one word, "diaper." It was obvious that the Bush White House did not want to have the president portrayed as supporting a candidate whose remark would be an embarrassment to the United States in the Middle East. For such a candidate no flow of Republican money and no presidential visits would be forthcoming. The National Republican Senatorial Committee, headed by Bill Frist, started encouraging other Republicans to run. In May 2002 state Representative Tony Perkins, a sponsor of a school prayer bill, met with Frist and decided to run. Perkins telegraphed Frist's strategy. "Republicans' best shot is to get a multiple field of candidates in this race. If we can get Landrieu in a runoff, it will be like the Coverdell runoff [in Georgia] in 1992. This is our seat." Perkins also encouraged Elections Commissioner Suzanne Haik Terrell to run. "I would like to see Suzie Terrell in the race because she would draw votes from Mary in New Orleans." Terrell had been mentioned as a candidate for Senate, but during the spring seemed uninterested; she did not announce until July 9.

In July the NRSC started running what would eventually be $2 million of TV ads against Landrieu. "There's just something about Mary and higher taxes," said one. "Landrieu voted in favor of higher taxes over 120 times." Landrieu seemed further or imperiled in July when Cleo Fields said he was thinking about running and might spend $1 million of his own money. But Fields bowed out in early August. Playing defense, Landrieu ran ads saying she supported Bush 74% of the time and that only two Democrats, Georgia's Zell Miller and Louisiana's John Breaux, had voted more often with Bush. At the end of August Frist announced that the NRSC would support Terrell and spend the allowed $464,000 on her behalf. His strategy was obviously to hold Landrieu below 50% in November, and he evidently calculated, as Perkins had, that Terrell, a New Orleans Catholic, was better positioned than the two north Louisiana Protestants to take votes away from Landrieu in the New Orleans area. Other Republicans were angry. Governor Mike Foster, who had considered running himself up to the August 23 filing deadline, endorsed Cooksey. In mid-October Landrieu started running anti-Terrell ads, charging that taxes and spending went up in New Orleans when she was on the council. Perkins ran ads attacking Landrieu for living in a "Washington mansion"; she said she wanted to be close to her small children. The NRSC ran ads saying that Landrieu's voting record was similar to Hillary Rodham Clinton's. On November 5, as Republicans were gaining a majority in the Senate by picking up seats in Georgia, Minnesota and Missouri, Landrieu failed to clinch a victory. She won 46% of the vote, to 27% for Terrell, 14% for Cooksey and 10% for Perkins. The three Republicans together led Landrieu 51%–46%.

If Republicans had picked up only one seat in November and had lost one seat, as they did (in Arkansas), all eyes would have moved to Louisiana, for the race would have determined which party would have the majority in the Senate. Now it would just determine whether the Republican majority would be 51–49 or 52–48: important but not earth-shaking. On the Democratic side there was discontent among black leaders about Landrieu's ads proclaiming her 74%

support of Bush. In debates the two candidates tangled about abortion. After another debate, on leaving the TV studio Landrieu said to Terrell, "This is your last campaign." Terrell, taken aback, said "She threatened me." The candidates continued to argue about tax cuts, personnel rules for the Department of Homeland Security and privatizing government jobs. Then a Democratic opposition researcher made a propitious find—an article in the Mexican center-left newspaper *Reforma* reporting that the Bush administration had agreed with the Mexican government to double the amount of sugar that could be imported from Mexico. The Office of Special Trade Representative and the State Department denied that any such agreement had been made. But Landrieu trumpeted the claim in ads and promised to do everything she could to stop any such agreement. Sugar is a heavily protected crop, with U.S. prices kept at levels far above the world price; Louisiana is the prime cane sugar producing state. So it was a fine issue for Landrieu to document her claim that Terrell would be a "rubber stamp" for Bush, even though Terrell said she opposed any such deal as well. It turned out the *Reforma* story was wrong; Landrieu met with trade and State Department officials in January 2003 and reported that there was no deal. But it may have changed enough votes to give Landrieu her 52%–48% victory.

In her second term Landrieu from time to time made waves. As ranking Democrat on the District of Columbia Appropriations Subcommittee, she insisted on restrictions on D.C. school vouchers in September 2003. Voucher supporters ran an ad in the New Orleans newspaper saying, "My mom wants you to know that Sen. Mary Landrieu doesn't want me to go to the same school where her children go." In October 2003 she cast a crucial vote in blocking the class action bill; she insisted on changes and got some: cases in which two-thirds of plaintiffs were from one state could stay in state courts; lead plaintiffs could get larger shares of awards. She supported the Schumer amendment to the bankruptcy bill, which passed in 2003 and failed in 2005, making nondischargeable in bankruptcy debts arising from penalties for violence against abortion clinics. She has supported oil drilling in the Arctic National Wildlife Refuge and, when it passed in March 2005, was one of three Democrats voting for it (the others were the two senators from Hawaii). In 2004 she passed an amendment eliminating the reduction in veterans' widows pensions when they became eligible for Social Security. She supported an amendment to the bill criminalizing the killing of unborn children which would have funded domestic violence programs; she had a meeting with backers of the bill which she described as "contentious." In May 2004 she stalled the flood insurance bill because she opposed higher premiums for those making repetitive claims. She has sponsored an American Outdoors Act, to dedicate $1.6 billion in payments to state for offshore oil drilling to public works projects; this is similar to the CARA legislation which, after a fierce struggle, was defeated in 2000. In October 2004 she filibustered the corporate tax bill for three days in support of an amendment to give tax credits to employers who make up lost pay for Reservists and Guards troops called to active duty; she accepted a compromise limiting the tax credit to companies with 50 or fewer workers. In 2004 and 2005 she and George Allen, both representing Confederate states, sponsored a resolution apologizing for the Senate's refusal, from the 1890s to the 1940s, to pass anti-lynching legislation.

Landrieu voted for the Iraq war resolution in October 2002. But in October 2003 she wanted the Iraq reconstruction money in the supplemental appropriation to be a loan, not a grant. She made her case to George W. Bush at the White House. "He looked at me and said, 'It's not negotiable, and I don't want to debate it.'" She pronounced herself optimistic after a trip to Iraq shortly before the January 2005 election. In the fall 2004 campaign she endorsed neither of the two well-known Democrats running for John Breaux's seat, but campaigned extensively around the state against Republican David Vitter. "Don't send me a puppet to work with, send me a partner," she said over and over. On election night she had an abrupt conversation with Vitter, who against expectations won the seat with 51% of the vote; she told him the second-place finisher, Democrat Chris John, was not conceding and he evidently hung up. They pledged later to work together on Louisiana issues but already had two public disputes by early 2005. "In my mind, I'm going to continue to work with Senator Vitter on issues that we can work together on for our state, and we'll just hopefully move past this time of difficulty," she said.

Junior Senator

David Vitter (R)

Elected 2004, seat up 2010, 1st term; b. May 3, 1961, New Orleans; home, Metairie; Harvard U., A.B. 1983, Rhodes Scholar, Oxford U., B.A. 1985, Tulane Law Schl., J.D. 1988; Catholic; married (Wendy).

Elected Office: LA House of Reps., 1991–99; U.S. House of Reps., 1999–2004.

Professional Career: Practicing atty., 1988–99; Adjunct Law Prof., Tulane U. & Loyola U., 1995–98.

DC Office: 516 HSOB, 20510, 202-224-4623; Fax: 202-228-5061; Web site: vitter.senate.gov.

State Offices: Alexandria, 318-448-0169; Baton Rouge, 225-383-0331; Lafayette, 337-262-6898; Lake Charles, 337-436-0453; Metairie, 504-589-2753; Monroe, 318-325-8120; Shreveport, 318-861-0437.

Committees: *Commerce, Science & Transportation*: Consumer Affairs, Product Safety & Insurance; Disaster Prevention & Prediction; Fisheries & the Coast Guard; Global Climate Change & Impacts (Chmn.); National Ocean Policy Study; Surface Transportation & Merchant Marine; Trade, Tourism & Economic Development. *Environment & Public Works*: Clean Air, Climate Change & Nuclear Safety; Fisheries, Wildlife & Water. *Small Business & Entrepreneurship*.

Group Ratings (as Member of U.S. House of Representatives)

	ADA	ACLU	AFS	LCV	ITIC	NTU	COC	ACU	NTLC	CHC
2004	5	0	0	0	90	74	100	96	97	100
2003	10	—	0	0	—	62	97	92	—	—

National Journal Ratings (as Member of U.S. House of Representatives)

	2003 LIB	—	2003 CONS		2004 LIB	—	2004 CONS
Economic	0%	—	91%		12%	—	88%
Social	29%	—	70%		0%	—	91%
Foreign	0%	—	89%		7%	—	92%

Key Votes of the 108th Congress (as Member of U.S. House of Representatives)

1. Drilling in ANWR	Y	5. DC School Vouchers	Y	9. Ban Same-Sex Marriage	Y
2. Approve Bush Tax Cuts	Y	6. Ban Human Cloning	*	10. Fund Iraq War	Y
3. Medicare/Rx Bill	Y	7. Restrict Gun Liability	Y	11. Bar Cuba Embargo Funds	N
4. Bar Overtime Pay Regs.	N	8. Ban Partial-Birth Abortion	Y	12. Intelligence Reorg.	Y

Election Results

2004 primary	David Vitter (R)	943,014	(51%)	($7,206,714)
	Chris John (D)	542,150	(29%)	($4,868,165)
	John Kennedy (D)	275,821	(15%)	($1,919,874)
	Other	87,071	(5%)	
1998 primary	John Breaux (D)	620,502	(64%)	($3,858,472)
	Jim Donelon (R)	306,616	(32%)	($364,073)
	Other	42,047	(4%)	

Prior Winning Percentages: 2002 House (81%); 2000 House (80%); 1999 House (51%)

Louisiana's junior senator is David Vitter, a Republican elected in 2004. He grew up in the New Orleans area, the son of a Chevron petroleum engineer, graduated from Harvard and Tulane law school and was a Rhodes Scholar. He was a business attorney and taught law at Tulane and Loyola. Vitter was elected in 1991 to the state House, the successor to former Ku Klux Klansman and state legislator David Duke's seat. There he passed a term-limits bill through a reluctant state legislature. Slim and boyish-looking, he is noted for his ability to irritate other politicians; many were enraged by his crusade for term limits, and a popular sheriff sued him three times after Vitter criticized his ethics.

He ran for Congress and won in a May 1999 special election after the abrupt retirement of 1st District Congressman Bob Livingston. Livingston was the Appropriations Committee chairman until Newt Gingrich was forced to retire as speaker three days after the 1998 election; he quickly rounded up the votes and became Speaker-designate. Six weeks later, as the House was debating impeachment, Livingston confessed that he had had affairs and stunned everyone by announcing that he was resigning, even as he called on Bill Clinton to do so. Many Republicans jumped into the race, but the chief fear of Louisiana and national Republicans was that David Duke would run and make it into the runoff. The establishment choice was David Treen, 70, who won four terms in the House starting in 1972 and was elected governor in 1979. In contrast, Vitter said, "We need a younger congressman like me, so we can start building up the seniority we lost when Bob Livingston resigned." Treen, with 25%, and Vitter, with 22%, advanced to the runoff. Duke, unnervingly close to making the runoff, finished third with 19%. Low turnout was probably a factor in deciding this contest, as Vitter rallied his troops and won 51%–49%.

In the House, Vitter had the most conservative voting record in the delegation and one of the most conservative in the House. After enactment in 2000 of the bill to require more disclosure of political activity by Section 527 tax-exempt groups, Vitter sought to relax the new rules, arguing they were burdensome at the state and local level; a scaled back version was approved in 2002. He enacted easier access to prescription drug coverage for military retirees and advocated aggressive controls of HMOs. When the House debated the education bill in 2001, it passed his amendment to require secondary schools that take federal money to allow military recruiters to visit the schools. Vitter became a vigorous advocate of a national missile defense. Vitter twice won reelection in the heavily Republican, suburban New Orleans district with at least 80% of the vote. He considered running for governor in 2003, but decided not to.

In December 2003, Senator John Breaux, once the youngest member of Congress, announced he would not seek a fourth term. Two days later Vitter said he was running. Wooden in manner, a self-described loner and highly conservative, the suburban Vitter was the stylistic opposite of Breaux, a gregarious dealmaker and noted centrist from Cajun country who was a major force for reform of entitlements and health care. But the state party and national Republicans worked hard to clear the field for Vitter, viewing him as the strongest possible candidate thanks to his suburban political base and his habit of traveling the state to announce projects secured from his perch on Appropriations. He was also familiar in Cajun country after his well-publicized opposition to an Indian casino in southwestern Louisiana.

On the Democratic side, three serious candidates joined the race: Congressman Chris John, a native of Crowley, the town which produced not only Breaux but Congressman and later Governor Edwin Edwards; two-term state Treasurer John Kennedy; state Representative Arthur Morrell, an African-American from New Orleans. There was little doubt that Vitter would win the state's unique Election Day primary against a divided Democratic field; the real issue for Democrats was holding him below the 50%-plus-one threshold necessary to avoid a December runoff.

Vitter ran as a strong supporter of George W. Bush and called for making Bush's tax cuts permanent, new job creation and medical malpractice reform. He campaigned as a conservative who opposed abortion, gay marriage and gun ownership restrictions. He said he best represented "mainstream Louisiana values"; he painted John as an out-of-touch Washington liberal who was close to John Kerry. John, the Democratic frontrunner who had Breaux's endorsement, responded by referring to Vitter as a Republican Party puppet and strove to distance himself from Kerry's presidential campaign – a wise move in a state that Bush carried with 57% in November.

Sugar was an important issue, as it was during Senator Mary Landrieu's 2002 reelection campaign. Louisiana is the prime cane sugar producing state and worries about being undercut by cheap imports; Landrieu used to her advantage a report, later proved to be false, that the Bush administration had agreed with the Mexican government to double the amount of sugar that could be imported from Mexico. In 2004, Vitter broke with the Bush administration over the Central American Free Trade Agreement, opposing it because it did not exempt sugar imports from the deal.

Vitter ran some of the best and most creative television ads of the election cycle. He managed to make light of his public image as a stiff politician through the use of several humorous commercials, including one involving his daughter's home movies. John, meanwhile, failed to gain momentum and was caught in the crossfire between Vitter on the right and Kennedy and Morrell on the left.

With Vitter leading in the polls going into November, the Democratic candidates began scrambling to hold him below the all-important 50% threshold. The Democratic Senatorial Campaign Committee assisted their efforts by spending more than $1.5 million in attack ads criticizing Vitter's positions on prescription drug reimportation and Social Security. It wasn't enough. Vitter won the race outright with 51%; he became the first Republican in 121 years to represent Louisiana in the Senate. John was the leading Democratic vote-getter with 29 percent to 15% for Kennedy and 3% for Morrell. George W. Bush's strong performance helped Vitter, but Vitter ran strongly on his own, winning Mississippi River parishes that Bush lost, carrying nearly all of Louisiana north of Baton Rouge and posting large margins in the New Orleans suburbs. In populous St. Tammany Parish, which he represented in Congress, Vitter won by more than 5–1; his 60,000-vote margin there was more than enough to erase John's 25,000-vote advantage in New Orleans and Orleans Parish.

FIRST DISTRICT

Rep. Bobby Jindal (R)

Elected 2004, 1st term; b. June 10, 1971, Baton Rouge; home, Kenner; Brown U., B.A. 1991, Oxford U., M.Lit. 1994; Catholic; married (Supriya).

Professional Career: Secy., LA Dept. of Health and Hospitals, 1996–98; Exec. Dir., Natl. Bipartisan Comm. on the Future of Medicare, 1998–99; Pres., U. of LA System, 1999–2001; Asst. Sec., U.S. Dept. of HHS, 2001–03.

DC Office: 1205 LHOB, 20515, 202-225-3015; Fax: 202-226-0386; Web site: www.house.gov/jindal.

District Offices: Hammond, 985-340-2185; Mandeville, 985-893-9064; Metairie, 504-837-1259.

Committees: *Education & the Workforce* (23d of 27 R): Education Reform; Employer-Employee Relations. *Homeland Security* (16th of 19 R): Economic Security, Infrastructure Protection & Cybersecurity; Intelligence, Information Sharing & Terrorism Risk Assessment; Prevention of Nuclear & Biological Attack. *Resources* (24th of 27 R): Energy & Mineral Resources; Fisheries & Oceans.

Group Ratings and Key Votes: Newly Elected

Election Results

2004 primary	Bobby Jindal (R)	225,708	(78%)	($1,656,964)
	Roy Armstrong (D)	19,266	(7%)	
	M. V. Mendoza (D)	12,779	(4%)	
	Dan Zimmerman (D)	12,135	(4%)	
	Other	18,009	(6%)	
2002 primary	David Vitter (R)	147,117	(81%)	($1,703,084)
	Monica Monica (R)	20,268	(11%)	
	Robert Namer (R)	7,229	(4%)	
	Other	5,956	(3%)	

The People		Race/Ethnic Origin	Ancestry	
Area size:	2,840 sq. mi.	79.6% White	French: 13.3%	German: 10.9%
Urban population:	79.6%	12.8% Black	Irish: 9.4%	
Rural population:	20.4%	1.5% Asian	**2004 Presidential Vote**	
Pop. 2000:	638,355	0.3% Native Am.	Bush (R) 215,538	(71%)
Median income:	$40,948	0.0% Hawaiian	Kerry (D) 87,009	(28%)
Poverty status:	12.1%	1.0% Two+ races	Other 3,076	(1%)
Military veterans:	13.1%	0.1% Other	**2000 Presidential Vote**	
		4.7% Hispanic Origin	Bush (R) 179,196	(66%)
			Gore (D) 83,779	(31%)
			Other 6,650	(2%)
			Cook Partisan Voting Index: R +18	

Occupation	Blue collar: 20.2%	White collar: 65.3%	Gray collar: 14.5%

New Orleans, founded in 1718, the nation's fifth-largest city at the outbreak of the Civil War, is ancient for an American metropolis; yet it is still closely girded by the peculiar wilderness of the mushy Delta lands of the sluggish Mississippi River. Climb a levee overlooking the Mississippi and you will see an expanse of water with untidy clumps of trees and disorganized-looking, seemingly abandoned docks—what Mark Twain had in his mind's eye while writing *Life on the Mississippi* in the 1870s. Or drive just past the last block of a suburban subdivision, and you are in unreclaimed swamp, vegetation and wetness, thick with herons and alligators, flat as far as the eye can see. For years the river has funneled the products of half a continent down to a single port with an international heritage and flair; the New Orleans metropolitan area is still living off that geography and history, with an inward-looking elite preoccupied with who is in which Mardi Gras krewe and interested more in old families' genealogy than in Oil Patch geology. The old buildings of New Orleans are finely proportioned and its old neighborhoods charming, like those in France; and its early 20th century improvements, like Olmstead's City Park, are grand. But its middle and late 20th century streetscapes and subdivisions, like those of France, are without ornament or charm, utilitarian works of man made to master the below-sea-level environment.

The 1st Congressional District of Louisiana includes much of the newer part of the New Orleans metropolitan area, spread over the soggy lands of the lower Mississippi and Lake Pontchartrain. A bit less than half of its people live south of the lake in affluent white neighborhoods in New Orleans, in the Uptown area and west of City Park, in mostly white neighborhoods on the West Bank of the Mississippi opposite New Orleans and in the vast suburb of Metairie in Jefferson Parish, divided by slanting grids and elevated only where bridges jut out over the many canals. It also includes part of suburbanizing St. Charles Parish to the west. The boundaries have been drawn so that the next-door 2d District has a black majority; the black percentage in the 1st (13%) is the lowest of any Louisiana district. The 1st extends across the 26-mile Lake Pontchartrain Causeway to include St. Tammany Parish, with old towns lush with trees and clusters of new growth around giant intersections. This is the growth area of metropolitan New Orleans: the population of the city fell 7% between 1990 and 2004 and Jefferson Parish's increased only 1%, while St. Tammany Parish's population increased 40%. The district also includes, to the north and west, Washington and Tangipahoa Parishes, still mostly rural country. More than half of the district's population is north of Lake Pontchartrain. This is the most upscale, affluent, highly educated district in Louisiana, and by far the most Republican, supportive of political reformers and against economic redistribution. George W. Bush got 71% of the vote here in 2004.

The congressman from the 1st District is Bobby Jindal, a Republican first elected in 2004. He grew up in Baton Rouge, the son of immigrants from India; they came so his mother could do graduate work at LSU. He was born in the United States and named Piyush, but as a boy insisted on being called Bobby, after the youngest brother in "The Brady Bunch." As a teenager he converted from Hinduism to Catholicism. Jindal graduated from Brown University and was a Rhodes scholar; he worked briefly for the McKinsey consulting firm. His first political job was an internship with 4th District Congressman Jim McCrery and he quickly built a glittering resume.

He was appointed to head Louisiana's state Health and Hospitals Department at 24 after McCrery recommended him to Governor Mike Foster. He had little experience to suggest he could run a 13,000-employee agency that accounted for about 40% percent of the state budget. But Foster, at first a skeptic, was impressed by Jindal and hired him. Jindal erased a $400 million deficit within two years, then returned to Washington and, at 27, was executive director of the National Bipartisan Commission on the Future of Medicare, co-chaired by Senator John Breaux and Representative Bill Thomas. Next he served as president of the 80,000-student Louisiana state university system and was appointed by George W. Bush as Assistant Secretary for Planning and Evaluation at the Health and Human Services Department. In 2003 he ran for governor as a Republican, his first race for elective office, and narrowly lost a bid to become the nation's first Indian-American governor. He campaigned as a policy expert with ideas for restructuring state government and attracted national and international attention (his candidacy was front page news in India). In the October 2003 primary he ran first, with 33% of the vote, ahead of three Democrats, Lieutenant Governor Kathleen Blanco, with 18%, Attorney General Richard Ieyoub, with 16%, and former Congressman Buddy Leach, with 14%. In the November runoff he lost to Blanco 52%–48%. He carried the New Orleans, Baton Rouge, Shreveport and Monroe metro areas. But Blanco carried her home area, the Cajun country, by a wide margin, and Jindal carried only one of the northern parishes which most Republicans have been winning in other statewide races.

In 2004, he considered running for the seat of retiring Senator John Breaux, but deferred to Congressman David Vitter. Jindal then decided to run in Vitter's House district, where his wife's family lived and he won 68% in his campaign for governor. Republican state Representative Steve Scalise abandoned his campaign in August while trailing badly in fundraising and the polls, and Jindal was endorsed by state Republican leaders. He won 78% of the vote in November and was elected without a runoff. He is the first Asian Indian American elected to Congress since Dalip Saund won in the 29th District of California in 1956, 1958 and 1960. With help from McCrery, Jindal lobbied Republican leaders for assignment to the Energy and Commerce Committee. But no freshman has been assigned there for years. Instead Jindal got seats on Education and the Workforce, Homeland Security and Resources. He has the promise of a bright future in the House and influential mentors in Thomas and McCrery. He was elected president of the Republican freshman class and spoke out early for personal retirement accounts in Social Security. During President Bush's State of the Union address, he took the lead in dipping his finger in purple ink and raising it in solidarity with the Iraqis who had voted in their election three days before; he invited all members of the House to use the ink, but most who did were Republicans. Even before he took his House seat, some Republicans began talking about him as a challenger to Senator Mary Landrieu in 2008.

SECOND DISTRICT

Rep. William Jefferson (D)

Elected 1990, 8th term; b. Mar. 14, 1947, Lake Providence; home, New Orleans; Southern U., B.A. 1969, Harvard U., J.D. 1972, Georgetown U., LL.M. 1996; Baptist; married (Andrea).

Military Career: Army Reserves, 1969–78, Army Judge Advocate Corps, 1975.

Elected Office: LA Senate, 1979–90.

Professional Career: Law clerk, U.S. Dist. Judge Alvin Rubin, 1972–73; Legis. aide, U.S. Sen. Bennett Johnston, 1973–75; Practicing atty., 1975–90.

DC Office: 2113 RHOB, 20515, 202-225-6636; Fax: 202-225-1988; Web site: www.house.gov/jefferson.

District Office: New Orleans, 504-589-2274.

Committees: *Budget* (11th of 17 D). *Ways & Means* (9th of 17 D): Trade.

Group Ratings

	ADA	ACLU	AFS	LCV	ITIC	NTU	COC	ACU	NTLC	CHC
2004	80	63	75	91	90	11	57	17	3	33
2003	90	—	100	45	—	25	46	27	—	—

National Journal Ratings

	2003 LIB	—	2003 CONS	2004 LIB	—	2004 CONS
Economic	71%	—	27%	65%	—	34%
Social	67%	—	33%	66%	—	34%
Foreign	80%	—	20%	79%	—	21%

Key Votes of the 108th Congress

1. Drilling in ANWR	N	5. DC School Vouchers	N	9. Ban Same-Sex Marriage	Y
2. Approve Bush Tax Cuts	N	6. Ban Human Cloning	Y	10. Fund Iraq War	N
3. Medicare/Rx Bill	N	7. Restrict Gun Liability	N	11. Bar Cuba Embargo Funds	Y
4. Bar Overtime Pay Regs.	Y	8. Ban Partial-Birth Abortion	Y	12. Intelligence Reorg.	N

Election Results

2004 primary	William Jefferson (D)	173,510	(79%)	($960,790)
	Art Schwertz (R)	46,097	(21%)	($15,139)
2002 primary	William Jefferson (D)	90,310	(64%)	($1,049,231)
	Irma Dixon (D)	28,480	(20%)	
	Silky Sullivan (D)	15,440	(11%)	
	Other	7,926	(6%)	
2000 primary	William Jefferson (D)	unopposed		($563,238)

Prior Winning Percentages: 1998 (86%); 1996 (100%); 1994 (75%); 1992 (73%); 1990 (52%)

The People		Race/Ethnic Origin	Ancestry	
Area size:	444 sq. mi.	28.3% White	French: 6.3%	German: 4.3%
Urban population:	99.4%	63.7% Black	Irish: 3.6%	
Rural population:	0.6%	2.7% Asian	**2004 Presidential Vote**	
Pop. 2000:	638,562	0.3% Native Am.	Kerry (D) 183,928	(75%)
Median income:	$27,514	0.0% Hawaiian	Bush (R) 58,855	(24%)
Poverty status:	26.8%	1.0% Two+ races	Other 1,858	(1%)
Military veterans:	10.9%	0.2% Other	**2000 Presidential Vote**	
		3.8% Hispanic Origin	Gore (D) 165,587	(76%)
			Bush (R) 48,726	(22%)
			Other 4,457	(2%)
			Cook Partisan Voting Index: D +28	

Occupation	Blue collar: 21.4%	White collar: 56.2%	Gray collar: 22.4%

Founded by the French in 1718, ruled by the Spanish from 1763 to just days before the French took over to sell it to the United States in 1803, New Orleans was a Creole city—part French, a bit Spanish, more than a touch Caribbean—when the American flag was raised over what is now Jackson Square. The statue of Andrew Jackson still seems an alien intrusion in a square set off by a French Market, the Cabildo, the Presbytere, the Pontalba apartments and Cathedral St. Louis. New Orleans was the fifth largest American city from 1840 until the Civil War and the only sizable city in the South; yet even as it was sending southern cotton out to the mills of Lancashire, it was an alien cultural force in both the nation and region. Urbanized, yet poor and in many ways primitive, New Orleans had yellow fever epidemics late in the 19th century, even as it was installing electric lights; it had a riot in which Italian immigrants were massacred, even as it was laying streetcar tracks and telephone lines. This was one of the most corrupt American cities during Reconstruction and the Gilded Age, when its votes were regularly bid for and bought; like other Southern cities, it became rigidly segregated after 1890.

For a time during the 1970s oil boom, New Orleans seemed to be a fast-growing Sun Belt city; in the 1980s, it reverted to its rougher traditions and was beset by woes big and small. Its port lost business—oil to Houston, and Latin American trade to Miami—though it still ships large amounts of grain. In the 1990s, New Orleans took a turn for the better. Crime plummeted and no longer depressed tourism. Incomes went up and home ownership increased among blacks as well as whites. Mayor Ray Nagin campaigned to tackle corruption but he has been criticized by fellow African-Americans for not paying enough attention to community needs. Harrah's Casino opened in 1999, and it got the state to lower its minimum tax payment. But people come to New Orleans for things other than gambling. They want to see the gaudy bars of Bourbon Street and the restored houses there and in the Garden District. They want to see Mardi Gras and the krewes that parade for weeks before. And they want to dine in New Orleans's restaurants, with a cuisine all New Orleans's own, spicy and rich and unaffected by today's taste for low-fat food.

The 2d Congressional District of Louisiana includes almost all of the city of New Orleans, everything except a few affluent white neighborhoods, plus nearly half of Jefferson Parish, black neighborhoods in Metairie and Kenner, the West Bank towns of Harvey, Marrero and Westwego, between the levee and the swamp. Here is the French Quarter—the *Vieux Carre*—its 19th century homes still intact because the Americans who moved here after 1803 wanted to stay away from the snobbish Creoles and then built a new downtown across Canal Street, where streetcars now run for the first time since 1964. North of the Quarter is the site of Storyville, where prostitution was legal until 1918 and where jazz was probably first played; many old frame houses have long since been torn down and replaced by half-empty and crime-ridden housing projects. But many similar neighborhoods remain where preservation of old buildings has not been a priority; blacks and some working-class whites live in rickety frame houses that are not always strong enough to keep the rain out and never tight enough to protect against the summer humidity or the damp winter chill, along the vividly named streets—Elysian Fields, Spain, Desire, Arts—that go north from the river wharves. South of the quarter is the downtown flecked with skyscrapers and the ominous Superdome, and to the east is the old slum known as the Irish Channel—a reminder that New Orleans had more foreign immigrants than any other part of the South; a community of more than 10,000 Vietnamese refugees has grown, apparently comfortable in the hot and swampy environs. Up St. Charles Avenue is the Garden District. This was the home of rich early American settlers, and its antebellum homes are still covered with vines and Spanish moss. New Orleans, for many years a speckled black-and-white city, now has a 67% black majority, and the 2d District is overwhelmingly Democratic. John Kerry won 75% of the vote here; it is the only Louisiana district where he got more than 41%.

The congressman from the 2d District is Bill Jefferson, a Democrat first elected in 1990. Jefferson grew up in the northeast corner of Louisiana in Lake Providence. He graduated from Southern University and Harvard Law School, clerked for a federal judge, worked for Senator Bennett Johnston and settled in New Orleans to set up what became the largest black law firm in the South; he received an LL.M. from Georgetown while serving in Congress. Jefferson was elected to the state Senate in 1979; he twice ran for mayor and lost. In 1990, when Lindy Boggs retired, Jefferson won 25% in the primary to 22% for Marc Morial, whose father was New Orleans's first black mayor and who was later elected mayor himself. In the runoff, charges flew: Jefferson was dogged by reports of defaults on outstanding loans and mortgages, while Morial admitted he was the father of an eight-year-old girl living in the Ivory Coast. Jefferson won with 52% and became the first Louisiana black elected to Congress since Reconstruction.

In the House Jefferson has shown impressive political skills and has a moderate voting record among Democrats. From his seat on Ways and Means, Jefferson has opposed Social Security personal accounts and has questioned reliance on the payroll tax. He wants to expand the availability of Individual Retirement Accounts, and to repeal estate taxes. Jefferson co-sponsored the Africa free-trade law, and he bucked most Democrats on Ways and Means to join chairman Bill Thomas in support of trade promotion authority, which he said was vital to Louisiana's economy. He also worked with Thomas to reduce corporate taxes (in exchange for getting a tax break for shipping companies) and was one of the few Democrats on Ways and Means to speak positively about free trade with Central America. In September 2004, he sought unsuccessfully in the House to remove a rider to prevent engineering work on an additional runway at the New Orleans airport.

Jefferson has not had serious opposition for reelection. But he has eyed other offices, seeking to become the first black elected statewide since Reconstruction. In 1991, he filed to run for governor, but withdrew; in 1995, he began running for governor again, but withdrew in favor of Cleo Fields, and said he would run for Senate; in May 1996 he bowed out of that race. In January 1999, after Republican Mike Foster and other statewide officials met at the Governor's Mansion and promised not to oppose each other regardless of party, Jefferson was evidently peeved and ran for governor. He challenged Foster's claims of improving the state's economy and schools; he pledged to raise teacher pay, reduce class sizes, and push for tougher education standards. But voting ran pretty much along racial lines, and Foster won 62%–30%.

After the 2002 election, with support from the Congressional Black Caucus, Jefferson sought the chairmanship of the Democratic Congressional Campaign Committee. He cited his active fundraising for the committee plus his success in helping to elect Democrats in Louisiana; some union officials who were unhappy about his free trade views opposed him. Some black members were upset when Nancy Pelosi instead selected fellow Californian Bob Matsui, with whom she had a closer relationship.

THIRD DISTRICT

Rep. Charlie Melancon (D)

Elected 2004, 1st term; b. Oct. 3, 1947, Napoleonville; home, Napoleonville; U. of SW LA, B.S. 1971; Catholic; married (Peachy).

Elected Office: LA House, 1987–93.

Professional Career: Ex. Dir., South Central Planning and Dev. Comm., 1973–79; Owner, Melancon Insurance Agency, 1980–93; Baskin-Robbins franchise owner; Pres. & Gen. Mgr., American Sugar Cane League, 1993–2004.

DC Office: 404 CHOB, 20515, 202-225-4031; Fax: 202-226-3944; Web site: www.house.gov/melancon.

District Offices: Chalmette, 504-271-1707; Gonzales, 225-621-8490; Houma, 985-876-3033; New Iberia, 337-367-8231.

Committees: *Agriculture* (13th of 21 D): General Farm Commodities & Risk Management; Specialty Crops & Foreign Agriculture Programs. *Resources* (20th of 22 D): Energy & Mineral Resources; National Parks. *Science* (19th of 20 D): Research; Space & Aeronautics.

Group Ratings and Key Votes: Newly Elected

Election Results

2004 runoff	Charlie Melancon (D)	57,611	(50%)	($1,761,978)
	Billy Tauzin III (R)	57,042	(50%)	($1,924,780)
2004 primary	Billy Tauzin III (R)	84,680	(32%)	
	Charlie Melancon (D)	63,328	(24%)	
	Craig Romero (R)	61,132	(23%)	($1,033,107)
	Damon Baldone (D)	25,783	(10%)	($359,449)
	Charmaine Caccioppi (D)	19,347	(7%)	($247,253)
	Kevin Chiasson (R)	10,350	(4%)	($12,110)
2002 primary	Billy Tauzin (R)	130,323	(87%)	($1,566,897)
	William Beier (I)	12,964	(9%)	
	David Iwancio (I)	7,055	(5%)	

The People		Race/Ethnic Origin	Ancestry		
Area size:	12,675 sq. mi.	69.7% White	French: 17.4%	USA: 8.7%	
Urban population:	73.0%	24.6% Black	German: 5.9%		
Rural population:	27.0%	1.0% Asian	**2004 Presidential Vote**		
Pop. 2000:	638,322	1.6% Native Am.	Bush (R)	162,269	(58%)
Median income:	$34,463	0.0% Hawaiian	Kerry (D)	115,011	(41%)
Poverty status:	18.6%	1.0% Two+ races	Other	3,826	(1%)
Military veterans:	10.8%	0.1% Other	**2000 Presidential Vote**		
		2.1% Hispanic Origin	Bush (R)	133,749	(52%)
			Gore (D)	115,734	(45%)
			Other	7,967	(3%)
			Cook Partisan Voting Index: R + 5		

Occupation	Blue collar: 33.6%	White collar: 50.3%	Gray collar: 16.2%

Below sea level, veined with bayous and creeks and wide streams of water, crossed by only an occasional road or railroad, the wetlands of southern Louisiana are one of America's unique landscapes. Technically, most of this waterlogged land rests on islands in a broad river mouth, through which the waters of the Mississippi and its tributaries drain into the Gulf of Mexico. It is rich with animal life, herons and egrets, shrimp and crawfish, muskrats and alligators. Yet it supports more people than one might think, in surprisingly sturdy small towns, with shopping malls on high ground, and in cabins along the bayous and crossroad towns where Cajun French remains the first language and roadside diners feature crawfish etoufee. But the steep-roofed Cajun houses are not the only structures: Here and there, jutting out of the swampy land, are huge elaborate metal sculptures—petrochemical plants and refineries, processing the oil and natural gas trapped under these wetlands and the shallow continental shelf of the Gulf. In the 1960s and 1970s, the oil industry, by providing good jobs for young people here, helped preserve Cajun culture and built a Cajun pride that was seldom articulated a generation ago. Then oil payrolls plummeted and the wetlands were threatened by coastal erosion and battered by Hurricane Andrew in 1992. The erosion continues, as the wetlands get less water because the Mississippi is not permitted to flood, and the shrimp fishermen, who still sail out in Blessing of the Fleet (La Benediction des Bateaux) ceremonies in April or May, have found their catch declining and their profits threatened by competition from aquaculture-raised Asian and Latin American shrimp. But the petrochemical plants, oil refineries, aluminum smelters and sugar refineries still provide well-paying jobs in these parts, and most Cajuns have been able to remain in this land of good hunting and good food. The town of Vacherie on the Mississippi River is the most rooted place in the United States: 98% of people here were born in Louisiana and 80% in 2000 lived in the same house as in 1995.

The 3d Congressional District of Louisiana includes about half the Cajun country. It includes most of Louisiana's swamplands, covering Houma, where seven bayous converge; St. Bernard and Plaquemines Parishes, downriver from New Orleans; St. Charles, St. John the Baptist, St. James and Ascension Parishes on both sides of the Mississippi, once the greatest sugar producers in America, now studded with refineries and petrochemical plants; roughneck Morgan City, which services many offshore oil rigs; and Iberia Parish, the home of McIlhenny's Tabasco sauce. Behind the Mississippi's western levee, hunkered side by side in Vacherie, are twin reminders of the region's grandeur and pain: the stately Oak Alley plantation, whose stunning vista stood in for the home of a fictional, aristocratic governor in the 1998 movie *Primary Colors;* and the Laura Plantation, believed to be the original home of the famous Br'er Rabbit stories, and whose current owners are preserving and displaying the plantation's slave cabins to remind visitors of the facts many would prefer to forget. The ancestral language here is French (23% claim French or French Canadian ancestry), mainly Cajun but also Creole; the ancestral religion is Roman Catholic and the ancestral politics Democratic, though very conservative. There has been an influx of Mexicans and other immigrants from Central America, many of whom work on the oil rigs or at the chemical plants. George W. Bush won 52% of the vote here in 2000 and 58% in 2004.

The congressman from the 3d District is Charlie Melancon (pronounced, *meh-LAW-sawn*), a Democrat elected in 2004 in a contest that was decided in the December runoff. He grew up in Napoleonville, on a dead-end street called Hog-Pen Alley; his father was mayor. After graduating with a bachelor's in agribusiness from the University of Southwestern Louisiana, he worked on the 1971 campaign of Edwin Edwards for governor, and then on his transition team. He returned to Napoleonville, where he worked on the South Central Planning and Development Commission; later, he ran an insurance agency and owned several Baskin-Robbins franchises. He ran for the state House in 1975 and lost; he ran again in 1987 and was elected to the first of three terms. There he supported changes in education law and backed sugar cane interests. He co-sponsored the bill that resulted in creation of the state-backed Louisiana Workers Compensation Corporation. He resigned in 1993 to become president of the American Sugar Cane League.

Melancon was one of six candidates to replace Billy Tauzin, who was first elected in May 1980 as a Democrat, became a Republican in August 1995 and chaired the Energy and Commerce Committee from January 2001 to February 2004. In late 2003 rumors spread that Tauzin would resign to take a high-paying lobbying job; there was speculation there would be a special election to fill the seat. But Tauzin vigorously denied the rumors. Then in February he resigned the chairmanship and underwent surgery for cancer; in December 2004, he was named to head PhRMA, the giant pharmaceutical lobby. The early frontrunner for the seat was his son Billy Tauzin III, who learned politics at home from a master, left the Coast Guard Academy after less than three years and returned to Louisiana to work for BellSouth—at first, selling mobile phones and eventually becoming a lobbyist and regional manager. But Little Billy, as his detractors called him, did not clear the field. Craig Romero, an Iberia Parish cattle farmer and oil field supply salesman who had served in the state Senate as a Republican since 1996, criticized Tauzin's lack of experience in politics and in south Louisiana. He said that the senior Tauzin was seeking to "anoint" his successor, and criticized him for directing at least $200,000 to the state Republican party that was recycled to his son's campaign; Dad ran ads in October that thanked voters for their best wishes during his convalescence but did not make clear that he was retiring. Other Democrats ran, in addition to Melancon: state Representative Damon Baldone of Houma; Charmaine Caccioppi of Raceland, a longtime aide to former Senator Bennett Johnston. In the nonpartisan November primary, some Democrats feared that Tauzin and Romero would be the two frontrunners and there would be no Democrat in the runoff. But in the final weeks before the initial vote, Melancon benefited from several hundred thousand dollars in advertising by the Democratic Congressional Campaign Committee. That spending proved to be a wise move. In the November 2 vote, Tauzin won 32% of the vote and led in eight parishes, mostly in the Bayous. Melancon edged out Romero, 24%–23%; each ran very strongly in his base.

In the runoff, Romero expressed anger over Tauzin's late advertising that painted him as a liberal who voted to repeal Louisiana's ban on sodomy and he did not endorse either candidate. The candidates split over tax cuts for the wealthy, school vouchers, tort law and missile defense. Melancon voiced doubts about the war in Iraq, but said that he would not "second-guess" the decision. He said that he was pro-gun, anti-abortion and opposed to gay marriage (though he opposed amending the Constitution to ban same-sex marriage); he emphasized his experience, and said that he would protect sugar interests from the Central America Free Trade Agreement. Tauzin said that he was his own man, but he benefited from large contributions by interest groups that benefited from his father's blessings; Vice President Dick Cheney came in to speak on his behalf. When Tauzin talked about the benefits of youth in building seniority, local commentators compared unfavorably his background to that of Bobby Jindal, who won the neighboring 1st District. Democrats ran an ad depicting him as a young boy dressed up in adult clothing. Each national party spent close to $2 million in the runoff, mostly on negative ads. The final tally gave Melancon a win by 569 votes, 50.2%–49.8%. He carried six parishes in the northern and western parts of the district, including Romero's base of Iberia Parish. Tauzin won all of the parishes along the Gulf, but it wasn't enough. Melancon got seats on the Agriculture and Resources committees and he joined the Congressional Blue Dogs.

FOURTH DISTRICT

Rep. Jim McCrery (R)

Elected Apr. 1988, 9th full term; b. Sept. 18, 1949, Shreveport; home, Shreveport; LA Tech. U., B.A. 1971, LA St. U., J.D. 1975; Methodist; married (Johnette).

Professional Career: Practicing atty. 1975–78; Asst. Shreveport City Atty., 1979–80; Legis. Dir., U.S. Rep. Buddy Roemer, 1981–84; Regional Mgr., Georgia–Pacific Corp., 1984–88.

DC Office: 2104 RHOB, 20515, 202-225-2777; Fax: 202-225-8039; Web site: mccrery.house.gov.

District Offices: Leesville, 337-238-0178; Shreveport, 318-798-2254.

Committees: *Ways & Means* (5th of 24 R): Health; Human Resources; Social Security (Chmn.).

Group Ratings

	ADA	ACLU	AFS	LCV	ITIC	NTU	COC	ACU	NTLC	CHC
2004	5	0	0	0	100	63	100	96	75	81
2003	5	—	0	10	—	62	97	92	—	—

National Journal Ratings

	2003 LIB	—	2003 CONS		2004 LIB	—	2004 CONS
Economic	17%	—	81%		22%	—	78%
Social	23%	—	76%		23%	—	77%
Foreign	11%	—	80%		0%	—	96%

Key Votes of the 108th Congress

1. Drilling in ANWR	Y	5. DC School Vouchers	Y	9. Ban Same-Sex Marriage	Y
2. Approve Bush Tax Cuts	Y	6. Ban Human Cloning	*	10. Fund Iraq War	Y
3. Medicare/Rx Bill	Y	7. Restrict Gun Liability	Y	11. Bar Cuba Embargo Funds	N
4. Bar Overtime Pay Regs.	N	8. Ban Partial-Birth Abortion	Y	12. Intelligence Reorg.	Y

Election Results

2004 primary	Jim McCrery (R)	unopposed		($939,484)
2002 primary	Jim McCrery (R)	114,649	(72%)	($1,117,836)
	John Milkovich (D)	42,340	(26%)	
	Other	3,104	(2%)	
2000 primary	Jim McCrery (R)	122,678	(71%)	($574,127)
	Phillip R. Green (D)	43,600	(25%)	
	Other	7,689	(4%)	

Prior Winning Percentages: 1998 (100%); 1996 (71%); 1994 (80%); 1992 (63%); 1990 (55%); 1988 (68%); 1988 (51%)

The People		Race/Ethnic Origin	Ancestry	
Area size:	11,151 sq. mi.	62.0% White	USA: 10.2%	Irish: 6.9%
Urban population:	59.3%	33.3% Black	English: 5.6%	
Rural population:	40.7%	0.7% Asian	**2004 Presidential Vote**	
Pop. 2000:	638,466	0.8% Native Am.	Bush (R) 156,298	(59%)
Median income:	$31,085	0.1% Hawaiian	Kerry (D) 105,962	(40%)
Poverty status:	20.0%	1.1% Two+ races	Other 2,771	(1%)
Military veterans:	14.7%	0.1% Other	**2000 Presidential Vote**	
		2.0% Hispanic Origin	Bush (R) 129,908	(55%)
			Gore (D) 102,228	(43%)
			Other 5,466	(2%)
			Cook Partisan Voting Index: R + 7	

Occupation	Blue collar: 28.5%	White collar: 52.7%	Gray collar: 18.9%

Northwestern Louisiana, south of Arkansas and just east of Texas, is part of the Deep South. The overwhelming majority of people here are Protestants, not Catholics, often very tradition-minded, with names that are English or Scottish, not French. The tone is set not by wide-open New Orleans—which was not easily accessible by interstate until 1996, when the last chunk of I-49 was completed—but by the much smaller Shreveport, which could be just another East Texas oil town, albeit one which has its own, comparatively sedate, Mardi Gras. The countryside is agricultural, though there are few vestiges of large riverfront plantations and backward farm country. Roots go back here a long way. Natchitoches is the oldest town, founded by Louis Antoine Juchereay de St. Denis in 1714; since 1927 it has been running a Christmas Festival of Lights on the riverfront, with plenty of food and entertainment. Shreveport was founded when Captain Henry Miller Shreve, with the Army Corps of Engineers, in the 1830s dispatched a young deputy named Robert E. Lee to break up a 100-mile blockade of logs in the Red River, moving the region's epicenter upriver to a new town, which was named after him. Oil provided the basis for much of the economic growth of the 20th century. Defense facilities also helped, although the Fifth Infantry Division was moved from Louisiana's Fort Polk to Texas's Fort Hood in 1993; but Fort Polk is still operating and so is Barksdale Air Force Base near Shreveport, where George W. Bush landed on September 11, 2001 and spoke briefly to the nation. Some parts of this area remain isolated: the tiny town of Mink didn't get wire telephone service until January 2005. Politically, northern Louisiana voters, for more than 100 years, have been voting against cosmopolitan New Orleans and the Catholic Cajun south, sometimes for rip-roaring populists, and more often for market-oriented Republicans.

The 4th Congressional District of Louisiana consists of the northwest corner of the state. More than half the votes here are cast in Caddo and Bossier Parishes in the far corner around Shreveport, with the rest scattered around rural areas, like picturesque Natchitoches and strip-highway towns like Leesville near Fort Polk. This area seemed to be trending Republican in the 1980s, but in the middle 1990s it went the other way: Both Bill Clinton and Senator Mary Landrieu carried the district in 1996, a critical factor in her narrow 5,788-vote statewide margin. In 2000 George W. Bush carried the area by a comfortable 55% margin, but it voted for Landrieu again in the close 2002 Senate race and for Democratic Governor Kathleen Babineaux Blanco in 2003. In 2004, the district gave Bush 59%.

The congressman from the 4th District is Jim McCrery, a Republican first elected in April 1988. McCrery grew up in Leesville, graduated from Louisiana Tech in Ruston (next door to Grambling, site of the football-famous, historically black college) and LSU law school, and practiced law in Leesville and Shreveport. In 1981 he worked for Congressman Buddy Roemer, then a Democrat; in 1984 he went to work for Georgia Pacific. After Roemer was elected governor in 1987, McCrery ran as a Republican and won the special election 51%–49%. McCrery's toughest reelection race was in 1992, when the creation of the black-majority 4th District put him in the 5th District with 16-year incumbent Jerry Huckaby, a conservative Democrat. But the district, with few black voters, was heavily Republican and Huckaby had 88 overdrafts on the House bank. McCrery weathered some negative personal attacks, led in the October primary 44%–29% and won the November runoff 63%–37%.

McCrery has compiled a mostly conservative voting record and has worked on major legislation from his seat on the Ways and Means Committee. Armed with the intuition that made him one of only 72 House members to vote against the disastrous 1988 catastrophic health care bill, he advanced a Republican alternative to the Clinton health care plan in 1994. He worked on the Republicans' Medicare and prescription drug bills and on the party task force on HMO regulation. In 2003 he passed a bill making the Trade Adjustment Assistance tax credit usable for any health care insurance policy, without the previous restrictions. He sponsored a bill in 2004 to allow workers to transfer unused money from "use it or lose it" flexible savings accounts into health savings accounts; it passed in May. He favors a consumption tax, but has advanced no specific plan; in 2005 he sponsored a bill to make the 2003 dividend tax cut permanent. In the various energy bills he has sponsored tax credits for energy companies and green bond tax credits for projects that improve the environment; one intended beneficiary was a riverfront shopping center in Bossier City with a Hooters restaurant—the subject of some ridicule from Senator John McCain. McCrery was chairman of the Select Revenue Measures Subcommittee from 2001 to 2005 and has worked closely with Ways and Means Chairman Bill Thomas; his more diplomatic approach has enabled him to be an intermediary between Thomas and colleagues with whom he is not on speaking terms, like Small Business Chairman Don Manzullo in 2004. Those interested in learning Thomas's latest thinking often seek out McCrery.

In January 2005 McCrery was named chairman of the Social Security Subcommittee, over the more senior Wally Herger. He has long favored personal retirement accounts in Social Security, and on taking the chairmanship called them "an absolute necessity"; he said he was "not afraid" of using debt to finance the costs. He said Social Security was "one of the most successful programs ever" and that he was ready to listen to all ideas. Echoing Thomas's comments at the time, he said, "I want to think outside the box a bit, maybe combining tax reform with financing Social Security. I don't want to start off confined to the current miserable system." And he was thinking in similar terms to Thomas politically. "I just think we've got to go outside the Social Security box to get us a bill that some Democrats will feel comfortable with and Republicans will feel comfortable with and the president would sign." But in February 2005, after a meeting with White House economic counselor Al Hubbard, he said he favored Bush's approach of dealing more narrowly with Social Security. "I'm convinced the president's approach is worth pursuing in the legislative process. Frankly, I had not thought of the policy rationale they described yesterday." He debated the issue vigorously with the subcommittee's ranking Democrat, Sander Levin, in March. "The real question . . . should be whether we want to finally, at last, pre-fund part or all of our future obligations to the Social Security system."

Since 1994 McCrery has not faced serious competition at the polls. In early 2004 he talked about retiring, so he could be in Shreveport with his wife, who had a part-time job there, and his two young children. George W. Bush and Dick Cheney called him and failed to persuade him to run again. But then his wife called and said she had decided that the family should move to the Washington area and she should get a job there. "I went to bed Wednesday night and I cried and prayed," she said. "I knew he couldn't retire. It wouldn't be right. I woke up Thursday morning and came up with a solution." One thing that may have been on her mind is that he could become the chairman of Ways and Means. Bill Thomas reaches the end of House Republicans' six-year term limit in January 2007, and while he might obtain a waiver to continue that is not at all certain. McCrery ranks behind several committee Republicans in seniority: Clay Shaw, Nancy Johnson, Wally Herger. But he has raised enormous amounts of money for his leadership PAC—$569,000 in the 2002 cycle, $1.3 million in the 2004 cycle—and has made contributions to dozens of Republicans. "I don't think there is a member of Congress, outside of leadership or full committee chairman, who has raised more money than I have." McCrery is widely respected, and by some Democrats as well as Republicans, for his expertise and knowledge of health care and tax issues and lacks Thomas's acerbity. He has made no secret of his interest in the chairmanship; when asked in early 2005 whether he wanted it, he said, "Absolutely."

FIFTH DISTRICT

Rep. Rodney Alexander (R)

Elected 2002, 2d term; b. Dec. 5, 1946, Quitman; home, Quitman; attended LA Tech. U., 1965; Baptist; married (Nancy).

Military Career: Air Force Reserves, 1965–71.

Elected Office: Jackson Parish Police Jury, 1972–87; President, 1980–87; LA House of Reps., 1988–2002.

Professional Career: Insurance agent, 1990–93; contractor, 1993–present.

DC Office: 316 CHOB, 20515, 202-225-8490; Fax: 202-225-5639; Web site: www.house.gov/alexander.

District Offices: Alexandria, 318-445-0818; Monroe, 318-322-3500.

Committees: *Appropriations* (37th of 37 R): Agriculture, Rural Development, FDA & Related Agencies; Science, State, Justice, Commerce & Related Agencies.

Group Ratings

	ADA	ACLU	AFS	LCV	ITIC	NTU	COC	ACU	NTLC	CHC
2004	40	25	75	27	50	24	70	48	24	76
2003	60	—	75	20	—	25	67	52	—	—

National Journal Ratings

	2003 LIB	—	2003 CONS		2004 LIB	—	2004 CONS
Economic	55%	—	45%		50%	—	50%
Social	53%	—	46%		44%	—	55%
Foreign	53%	—	47%		51%	—	48%

Key Votes of the 108th Congress

1. Drilling in ANWR	N	5. DC School Vouchers	N	9. Ban Same-Sex Marriage	Y
2. Approve Bush Tax Cuts	Y	6. Ban Human Cloning	Y	10. Fund Iraq War	Y
3. Medicare/Rx Bill	Y	7. Restrict Gun Liability	Y	11. Bar Cuba Embargo Funds	N
4. Bar Overtime Pay Regs.	N	8. Ban Partial-Birth Abortion	Y	12. Intelligence Reorg.	Y

Election Results

2004 primary	Rodney Alexander (R)	141,495	(59%)	($1,344,520)
	Zelma Blakes (D)	58,591	(25%)	($20,303)
	Jock Scott (R)	37,971	(16%)	($149,557)
2002 runoff	Rodney Alexander (D)	86,718	(50%)	($831,088)
	Lee Fletcher (R)	85,744	(50%)	
2002 primary	Rodney Alexander (D)	52,952	(29%)	
	Lee Fletcher (R)	45,278	(25%)	
	Clyde Holloway (R)	42,573	(23%)	
	Robert Barham (R)	34,533	(19%)	
	Other	9,321	(5%)	

The People

Area size:	14,225 sq. mi.
Urban population:	52.9%
Rural population:	47.1%
Pop. 2000:	638,517
Median income:	$27,453
Poverty status:	23.6%
Military veterans:	12.0%

Race/Ethnic Origin

63.4% White
33.7% Black
0.5% Asian
0.4% Native Am.
0.0% Hawaiian
0.6% Two+ races
0.0% Other
1.3% Hispanic Origin

Ancestry

USA: 13.2%   Irish: 6.4%
French: 5.6%

2004 Presidential Vote

Bush (R)	168,484	(62%)
Kerry (D)	100,511	(37%)
Other	3,410	(1%)

2000 Presidential Vote

Bush (R)	143,628	(57%)
Gore (D)	100,287	(40%)
Other	7,706	(3%)

Cook Partisan Voting Index: R +10

Occupation   Blue collar: 26.9%   White collar: 53.5%   Gray collar: 19.5%

Northeast Louisiana is perhaps the least known part of the state. Along the Mississippi River and the Red River and their dozens of tributaries, it was plantation country before the Civil War, with black majorities still in many parishes. Away from the larger rivers, it is hill country, places where small farmers scratched out a living on land connected to parish courthouses by dusty lanes. Such was Winn Parish, where Huey P. Long, the pivotal figure in modern Louisiana politics, was born in 1893, and from which he began his meteoric political career—elected governor in 1928, senator in 1930, a national figure threatening both parties when he was assassinated in 1935 in the new high-rise Capitol he built in Baton Rouge.

The 5th Congressional District of Louisiana contains much of this country, from the river parishes to the hills of Winn Parish. The biggest urban areas here, with about 50,000 people each, are Monroe in the north and Alexandria in the south. Alexandria in Rapides Parish sits at the northernmost extension of Cajun, Catholic Louisiana, and is majority black; despite the generally poor economic climate, Union Tank Car plans a new plant there. Monroe in Ouachita Parish is heavily WASP and Baptist, and is home to one of the world's leading Bible collections, assembled by an heir to an early Coca-Cola bottler. Redistricting added some Cajun areas in Allen and Evangeline Parishes and heavily black precincts in Pointe Coupee and Iberville

Parishes, all Democratic areas. But George W. Bush increased his vote here from 57% in 2000 to 62% in 2004, his second-best showing in the state.

The congressman from the 5th District is Rodney Alexander, who was elected as a Democrat in December 2002 and switched to become a Republican in August 2004. Alexander graduated from Louisiana Tech and won election to the Jackson Parish police jury in 1972 at the age of 25. In 1988 he was elected to the state House, where he chaired the Health and Welfare Committee. He characterized himself as pro-guns, pro-life and pro-prayer. The 5th District seat opened in 2002 when Republican John Cooksey ran unsuccessfully for the Senate after serving three terms in the House. The primary turned out to be a regional contest. Alexander led with 29% of the vote, carrying three hill counties in his legislative district and five heavily black parishes along the Mississippi River. Republican Lee Fletcher, Cooksey's chief of staff for five years, was second with 25%, carrying Monroe's Ouachita Parish and three nearby parishes. Close behind, with 23%, was Republican Clyde Holloway, elected congressman by narrow margins in 1986, 1988 and 1990 from the old 8th District. Holloway, a tree farmer from Rapides Parish, carried seven parishes in the southern end of his district. After the primary, he was angry because he thought the House Republicans' campaign committee was steering contributors to Fletcher's campaign despite Holloway's prior service in the House; he called a press conference to denounce Fletcher as someone who "will do anything to win and he scares me." Alexander attacked Fletcher as a Washington insider and contrasted his "blue jeans" supporters with Fletcher's "blue blood" contributors. Alexander squeaked by with a 50.3%–49.7% victory, a margin of 974 votes. He carried two hill parishes, all the Mississippi River parishes and all but one of the parishes in the southern end of the district.

In the House, Alexander got seats on Agriculture and Armed Services, and had a voting record virtually in the center of the House. In November 2003, he showed independence from Democratic leaders when he voted for the Medicare/prescription drug bill. He voted to extend the tax cuts that Republicans enacted in 2001, and cosponsored legislation to prohibit desecration of the flag and bar gay marriages. Despite his occasional independence, Democratic leaders worked to keep Alexander happy and helped him to raise money for reelection. So they and many others were stunned when in the last hour before the election filing deadline Alexander switched parties. He explained his decision: "The Democratic Party has drifted to the left, and left us [conservative Democrats] in the open. I hate it . . . .I was a Democrat who was ashamed of some of the things the Democratic Party stood for." Another factor, he explained, was the candidacy of Democratic Zelma Blakes, an African American and political neophyte who he feared would draw votes from him and would leave him vulnerable to attacks from both the left and the right. Democrats were outraged and called him a liar. "Rodney is a confused politician who has placed loyalty at the very bottom of his priorities," said Senator John Breaux. "I've seen some cowardly things in my career, but this is the worst," added Senator Mary Landrieu. House Minority Whip Steny Hoyer said that he had never seen such "an act of perfidy."

National Republicans, who were not enthusiastic when Fletcher expressed interest in running again and had failed to attract a strong challenger for the district, quickly embraced Alexander. He explained that he came close to switching parties earlier in 2004, but that he held off because "I didn't want anyone thinking I changed because I couldn't win as a Democrat." Louisiana Democrats filed suit to reopen the qualifying period, but the state appeals court rejected their case. After he switched, Alexander said he would return contributions from Democratic colleagues; in October, after they complained about the delay, Alexander repaid them. But this election turned out to be an afterthought for both parties in Louisiana, where there were two hotly contested open seat House races and a serious contest for the Senate seat Breaux was vacating. Alexander won 59% of the vote, to 25% for Blakes and 16% for former state representative Jock Scott, a Republican. He carried all parishes except for two riverfront parishes near Baton Rouge, where Blakes led.

Although Alexander and House Republican leaders insisted that they had made no deal before his switch, he got a seat in January 2005 on the Appropriations Committee and its Agriculture Subcommittee. House Democrats hoped to find a credible challenger here in 2006, but it may be uphill going in a 62% Bush district.

SIXTH DISTRICT

Rep. Richard Baker (R)

Elected 1986, 10th term; b. May 22, 1948, New Orleans; home, Baton Rouge; LA St. U., B.A. 1971; United Methodist; married (Kay).

Elected Office: LA House of Reps., 1972–86.

Professional Career: Real estate developer, 1972–86.

DC Office: 341 CHOB, 20515, 202-225-3901; Fax: 202-225-7313; Web site: www.baker.house.gov.

District Office: Baton Rouge, 225-929-7711.

Committees: *Financial Services* (3d of 37 R): Capital Markets, Insurance & Government Sponsored Enterprises (Chmn.); Financial Institutions & Consumer Credit; Housing & Community Opportunity. *Transportation & Infrastructure* (13th of 41 R): Aviation; Highways, Transit & Pipelines; Water Resources & Environment. *Veterans' Affairs* (7th of 16 R): Economic Opportunity; Health.

Group Ratings

	ADA	ACLU	AFS	LCV	ITIC	NTU	COC	ACU	NTLC	CHC
2004	5	0	0	0	90	58	100	88	81	92
2003	5	—	0	10	—	65	100	92	—	—

National Journal Ratings

	2003 LIB	—	2003 CONS		2004 LIB	—	2004 CONS
Economic	17%	—	81%		28%	—	72%
Social	17%	—	79%		20%	—	80%
Foreign	0%	—	89%		17%	—	78%

Key Votes of the 108th Congress

1. Drilling in ANWR	Y	5. DC School Vouchers	Y	9. Ban Same-Sex Marriage	Y
2. Approve Bush Tax Cuts	Y	6. Ban Human Cloning	Y	10. Fund Iraq War	Y
3. Medicare/Rx Bill	Y	7. Restrict Gun Liability	Y	11. Bar Cuba Embargo Funds	N
4. Bar Overtime Pay Regs.	N	8. Ban Partial-Birth Abortion	Y	12. Intelligence Reorg.	Y

Election Results

2004 primary	Richard Baker (R)	189,106	(72%)	($1,090,347)
	Rufus Craig (D)	50,732	(19%)	($17,346)
	Edward Galmon (D)	22,031	(8%)	
2002 primary	Richard Baker (R)	146,932	(84%)	($790,953)
	Rick Moscatello (I)	27,898	(16%)	
2000 primary	Richard Baker (R)	165,637	(68%)	($916,205)
	Kathy J. Rogillio (D)	72,192	(30%)	
	Other	5,649	(2%)	

Prior Winning Percentages: 1998 (51%); 1996 (69%); 1994 (81%); 1992 (51%); 1990 (100%); 1988 (100%); 1986 (100%)

The People		Race/Ethnic Origin	Ancestry	
Area size:	3,210 sq. mi.	62.7% White	French: 10.3%	USA: 7.4%
Urban population:	75.5%	33.2% Black	Irish: 6.3%	
Rural population:	24.5%	1.4% Asian	**2004 Presidential Vote**	
Pop. 2000:	638,324	0.2% Native Am.	Bush (R) 172,080	(59%)
Median income:	$37,931	0.0% Hawaiian	Kerry (D) 117,255	(40%)
Poverty status:	16.6%	0.7% Two+ races	Other 2,524	(1%)
Military veterans:	11.2%	0.1% Other	**2000 Presidential Vote**	
		1.6% Hispanic Origin	Bush (R) 142,239	(55%)
			Gore (D) 111,602	(43%)
			Other 5,716	(2%)
			Cook Partisan Voting Index: R + 7	
Occupation	Blue collar: 23.6%	White collar: 61.5%	Gray collar: 15.0%	

Baton Rouge is the central node of Louisiana, on the boundary between the French-speaking, Catholic Cajun country and the heavily Baptist Deep South, its skyscraper Capitol and Exxon refinery sitting just beyond the levees that line the Mississippi River. Baton Rouge still bears the impress of the man who dominated Louisiana politics for much of the 20th century, Huey P. Long. Here Long became governor at 36 in the old (and still-standing) Gothic Capitol, when Baton Rouge had only 30,000 people, and was assassinated in 1935 in the hallway of the 34-story Art Deco Capitol he built, next door to the Governor's Mansion, which he also built. To the south are the buildings of Louisiana State University, much of which he built, in an amazingly short time. Today Baton Rouge is the center of a metro area of 728,000, almost all on the east bank of the Mississippi, and reaching far inland to Livingston Parish. This is one of the faster-growing parts of Louisiana: from 1990 to 2004, the population of East Baton Rouge Parish rose 9% and the populations of Livingston and Ascension Parishes increased 50%, the most of any parishes in the state. Baton Rouge tries to maintain all of Louisiana's traditions; according to James Carville, who comes from nearby Carville in Iberville Parish (where three generations of his family served as postmaster), it has "the best restaurants per capita of any city in the United States."

The 6th Congressional District of Louisiana includes just about all of metropolitan Baton Rouge, plus three small mostly rural parishes to the north. The city of Baton Rouge itself in 2000 had a 50% black majority; suburban East Baton Rouge Parish was 40% black and Livingston Parish 4% black. Overall the district is 33% black. Historically, all of this territory was Democratic. In the 1980s the Baton Rouge area moved toward the Republicans and in the 1990s it was fairly closely balanced. In 2004 East Baton Rouge Parish voted 54% for George W. Bush and Livingston Parish 77% for Bush; overall the 6th District voted 59% for Bush.

The congressman from the 6th District is Richard Baker, a Republican first elected in 1986. Baker has spent most of his adult life in public office. He came to Baton Rouge to attend LSU, then in 1972, at 23, was elected as a Democrat to the Louisiana House from a blue-collar district in Baton Rouge. He became a Republican in 1985, and in 1986, when Baton Rouge Republican Congressman Henson Moore ran for the Senate, Baker ran for the House and beat a Democratic state senator 51%–46%. In 1992 he was redistricted in the same district with Republican Congressman Clyde Holloway. The new district lines put Baker at a disadvantage, and he trailed 37%–33% in the September primary. But he won the November runoff 51%–49%.

Baker has had a conservative voting record and is chairman of the Capital Markets and Insurance Subcommittee of the Financial Services Committee. He worked on financial services deregulation, one of the most heavily lobbied issues in the 1990s; the issue was how, under what terms and conditions, to dismantle the wall separating banks and other institutions created by the Glass-Steagall Act of 1933. Baker generally favored deregulation, and served on the conference committee that finally reached agreement in November 1999.

Baker's greatest legislative enterprise has been to change the operation of the government-sponsored enterprises (GSEs) Fannie Mae and Freddie Mac, which purchase and securitize home mortgages. These are for-profit enterprises, yet the fact that they each have $2.25 billion lines of credit with the U.S. Treasury creates an impression in the marketplace that the government will bail them out if they become insolvent. Baker admitted that they were well-managed and not at risk, and argued that that was the best time for reform. In February 2000 Baker introduced legislation to create a new regulatory agency for the GSEs and terminate their line of credit, increase disclosure requirements, toughen capital mandates and give regulators more say in approving new activities. Fannie Mae and Freddie Mac vigorously opposed the bill and predicted it would never pass. In October they reached agreement. Fannie Mae and Freddie Mac agreed to increase their equity capital and subordinated debt to 4% of assets and to disclose more information to investors. By February 2001 Fannie Mae CEO Franklin Raines was praising Baker, but they still disagreed: Baker still wanted an independent regulator, while Raines was opposed. In summer 2001 Baker introduced a bipartisan bill to require Fannie Mae and Freddie Mac to register their stock with the SEC; they agreed to do so voluntarily, but did not issue SEC prospectuses for the securitized instruments they sell to investors—who are, they say, sophisticated enough to evaluate them. The GSEs seemed to have fended off a new regulator. But new developments weakened their position. In September 2004 OFHEO issued a report charging that Fannie Mae had manipulated earnings. After the OFHEO report was issued, Baker said, "The outrageous conduct outlined in OFHEO's report suggests that for too long Fannie Mae has acted as if it were somehow above the law while arrogantly flouting all accountability to the Congress, and that must come to an end." Fannie Mae increased its capital level and in December 2004 its CEO was forced to resign. In January 2005 Baker demanded that Fannie Mae executives return the huge bonuses they made which turned out to result from flawed accounting. "The arrogance of this is incredible to me. They got their enormous bonuses based on manipulated financial [statements]. It seems more egregious than even I thought." In April 2005, Baker introduced legislation calling for a new regulator, renaming OFHEO and moving it within the Treasury Department rather than HUD.

In 2000 Banking Chairman Jim Leach reached the end of House Republicans' six-year term limits, and Baker sought the chairmanship over the more senior Marge Roukema. But in the days after the November 2000 election, Baker presented a fallback position to the Republican leadership. An even bigger chairmanship struggle was going on in the Commerce Committee, between Louisiana's Billy Tauzin and Mike Oxley. Baker would support Oxley for the Banking Committee chairmanship, with Commerce's jurisdiction over securities and insurance transferred to Banking. Baker would keep his Financial Services subcommittee chair plus the securities jurisdiction; Roukema would get another subcommittee. And so it happened: Baker was in a position to continue his work on the GSEs, Oxley got a chairmanship and Roukema decided to retire in 2002. On two major bills in the next two years Baker and Oxley worked together. One was terrorism insurance, proposed after the September 11 attacks; after much negotiation, agreement was reached in November 2002.

The other big issue was auditor independence. Oxley and Baker avoided flamboyant hearings; they cancelled a hearing after former Enron Chairman Kenneth Lay said he would take the Fifth Amendment. In February 2002 they rolled out a bill which would create an accounting oversight board inside the SEC, require far more disclosure and would bar external auditing firms from doing certain financial systems consulting and internal auditing. Ranking Democrat John LaFalce criticized the bill for not completely separating accounting and consulting and for not placing the oversight board outside the SEC; he also called for CEOs to sign certified financial reports subject to criminal penalties. The committee approved the Oxley-Baker approach in April 2002 and the bill passed the House later that month. Meanwhile, in the Senate, Banking Committee Chairman Paul Sarbanes was preparing a bill with bipartisan support which went farther than Oxley and Baker but not as far as LaFalce. That bill was languishing when disclosure of the WorldCom accounting scandal in June propelled it forward. It passed the Senate by a wide margin and in conference, at the prodding of the Bush White House, Oxley and Baker yielded on most points of disagreement; the bill was passed and signed before the August recess. In the process, Baker proposed a Federal Account for Investor Restitution (FAIR) Fund, with money raised from monetary penalties levied against corporations and funds disgorged from executives guilty of fraud or malfeasance to be paid over to defrauded investors; this was included in what became the Sarbanes-Oxley Act. In July 2003 the committee approved a bill regulating corporate fraud, with limits on state enforcement actions, but in February 2004 it passed another without such limits and called for better communication between federal and state regulators.

In 2003 Baker supported legislation to require that mutual fund board chairmen be independent of managers, and in November the House passed a bill by 418–2 cracking down on certain mutual fund practices. In 2004 Baker opposed the trade-through rule imposed by SEC Chairman William Donaldson. "In the 21st century investors should be able to choose speed, anonymity and certainty over what is seen as an advertised but not a guaranteed best price. I do not believe that choice should be taken away from investors." He has taken an "incrementalist approach" to legislation imposing uniformity on regulation of insurance, which historically has been left to the states. In 2004 he got the House to pass a law delaying the FASB rule requiring expensing of stock options, but Senate Banking Chairman Richard Shelby opposed it and it did not become law. In 2007 Oxley will have reached House Republicans' six-year term limit; Baker is next in line in seniority to be chairman of the full committee.

With one major exception, Baker has not had difficulty winning reelection since 1992. That exception was in 1998, when he was challenged then by Democrat Marjorie McKeithen, the granddaughter of former Governor (1964–72) John McKeithen and daughter of Secretary of State Fox McKeithen, and won by only 50.7%–49.3%. Since then Baker has been reelected by wide margins.

SEVENTH DISTRICT

Rep. Charles Boustany (R)

Elected 2004, 1st term; b. Feb. 21, 1956, New Orleans; home, Lafayette; U. of SW LA, B.S. 1978, LA St. U., M.D. 1982; Episcopalian; married (Bridget).

Professional Career: Practicing surgeon, 1982–2004.

DC Office: 1117 LHOB, 20515, 202-225-2031; Fax: 202-225-5724; Web site: www.house.gov/boustany.

District Office: Lafayette, 337-235-6322.

Committees: *Agriculture* (19th of 25 R): Conservation, Credit, Rural Development & Research; General Farm Commodities & Risk Management. *Education & the Workforce* (24th of 27 R): 21st Century Competitiveness; Employer-Employee Relations. *Transportation & Infrastructure* (40th of 41 R): Coast Guard & Maritime Transportation; Water Resources & Environment.

Group Ratings and Key Votes: Newly Elected

Election Results

2004 runoff	Charles Boustany (R)	75,039	(55%)	($2,785,524)
	Willie Mount (D)	61,493	(45%)	($1,340,886)
2004 primary	Charles Boustany (R)	105,761	(39%)	
	Willie Mount (D)	69,079	(25%)	
	Don Cravins (D)	67,389	(25%)	($212,315)
	David Thibodaux (R)	26,526	(10%)	($118,238)
	Other	5,177	(2%)	
2002 primary	Chris John (D)	138,659	(87%)	($525,754)
	Roberto Valletta (I)	21,051	(13%)	

The People		Race/Ethnic Origin	Ancestry	
Area size:	7,294 sq. mi.	72.0% White	French: 14.1%	USA: 11.6%
Urban population:	68.9%	24.8% Black	Fr. Canadian: 6.6%	
Rural population:	31.1%	0.7% Asian	**2004 Presidential Vote**	
Pop. 2000:	638,430	0.2% Native Am.	Bush (R) 168,645	(60%)
Median income:	$31,453	0.0% Hawaiian	Kerry (D) 110,623	(39%)
Poverty status:	19.9%	0.7% Two+ races	Other 3,103	(1%)
Military veterans:	11.8%	0.1% Other	**2000 Presidential Vote**	
		1.4% Hispanic Origin	Bush (R) 141,378	(55%)
			Gore (D) 107,190	(42%)
			Other 7,357	(3%)
			Cook Partisan Voting Index: R + 7	

Occupation	Blue collar: 27.9%	White collar: 54.9%	Gray collar: 17.2%

More than 200 years ago, French-speaking settlers were forced to leave their land of Acadie, which the British had taken over and renamed Nova Scotia, and make their way to the wetlands of southern Louisiana. Here, without much notice, they built steep-roofed houses to slough off nonexistent snow and adapted French cuisine to the crawfish and muskrat they found in abundance in the pelican-tended swamps. The heart of the Cajun country is around Lafayette, just west of the Atchafalaya Basin, where Mississippi waters pour through bayous and canals, with only occasional bits of solid land visible on the 30-mile section of Interstate 10 built on elevated stilts. For half a century the Cajun country thrived, thanks to the oil and gas plentiful here and just off shore in the Gulf of Mexico; oil rigs are common, and every once in a while the swampy foliage parts to reveal a giant refinery or petrochemical plant. Cajun pride has experienced a resurgence: Cajun French is surviving decades of efforts to eliminate it; Cajun music—and its black-influenced variant, zydeco—are popular here and nationally; spicy Cajun cooking has become a tourist attraction here and, in watered-down form, familiar all over the United States. About 45% of the people in Acadiana speak French as a second language. Lafayette, with its Acadian Village and plethora of oil exploration firms, features its annual *Festivals Acadiens* to celebrate music, food and crafts. Unlike New Orleans, its Mardi Gras reveries do not require anti-discrimination statements; the result has been an all-white parade and an all-black parade.

The oil price crash of the middle 1980s hit the Cajun country hard. Rising expectations, and the giddy sense that the oil industry promised lasting prosperity, suddenly collapsed, leaving borrowers overextended and ordinary homeowners unable to maintain the standard of living they expected. Politically, the Cajun country seemed to move then toward national Democrats, whom it had shunned because their cultural liberalism seemed alien to the Cajun tradition of respecting the authority of Church and state while tolerating a certain amount of *laissez les bons temps rouler* spirit. The Cajun country voted for Bill Clinton in 1992 and 1996, as it had voted for Louisiana's foremost Cajun politician, Edwin Edwards, who was elected governor four times. It has given solid majorities to George W. Bush, but also favored Governor Kathleen Babineaux Blanco.

The 7th Congressional District of Louisiana covers much of the Cajun country, from Lafayette and the Atchafalaya west along I-10 to Lake Charles and the Texas border. Refineries and oil-field support industries provide many jobs, as do the rice and crawfish farming fields. Some 21% of the population claims either French or French Canadian ancestry.

The congressman from the 7th District is Charles Boustany, elected in 2004 and the first Republican elected from this area since 1884. Of Lebanese ancestry, he grew up in Lafayette, where his father was county coroner; he graduated from the University of Southwestern Louisiana and LSU Medical School. He worked as a heart surgeon and was active in civic and political affairs. His experience as a doctor had educated him about all sorts of public problems, he said. In 2004 7th District Democrat Chris John ran for the Senate, and Boustany was one of five candidates to run to succeed him. The other Republican candidate was David Thibodeaux of Lafayette, who had run unsuccessfully for this seat three times, most recently in 1996; but he raised little money, some party leaders viewed him as too conservative and Boustany quickly became the Republican favorite. The Democratic frontrunners were two state senators: Don Cravins of the Breaux Bridge area, who was seeking to become the first black to hold this seat, and state Senator Willie Mount of Lake Charles, who would have been the first woman elected here. Boustany raised plenty of money early and campaigned on his "prescription for prosperity"—expansion of health-savings accounts, high-speed Internet access for local small businesses, and opposition to the Central American Free Trade Agreement. He called for a Mississippi River Caucus to work to protect erosion of the state's coastline. The National Republican Congressional Committee ran ads attacking Mount's support for higher taxes in the Legislature, presumably because it saw Cravins as a weaker candidate in a runoff. Boustany led the November primary with 39% of the vote, to 25.2% for Mount, 24.6% for Cravins, and 10% for Thibodeaux. Boustany led in Lafayette Parish and two nearby parishes; Mount carried Lake Charles and two other parishes in the west; and Cravins led in two parishes in his home base north of Lafayette.

In the December 4 runoff, Cravins refused to endorse Mount because of his anger over the state Democratic Party's "unity ballot" sent to black voters, which included Mount's name and not his. "They should have put us both on the ballot or neither one," he said. Cravins's neutrality hurt Mount in the Lafayette area. Mount pointed to her legislative experience, while Boustany emphasized his "values" agenda. Boustany won 55%–45%. Mount won 60% in Lake Charles's Calcasieu Parish, which cast 32% of the vote. But Boustany trumped that with 70% in Lafayette Parish, which cast 30% of the vote. He got committee seats on Agriculture, Education and the

Workforce, and Transportation and Infrastructure. On the Education committee, he was an active proponent of legislation to permit small businesses to join together in associations to pay less for health insurance. In 2005, the Democratic Congressional Campaign Committee was actively recruiting Chris John, who lost in his Senate bid, to run for his old seat in 2006.

★ MAINE ★

Maine is a state with a distinctive personality—ornery, contrary-minded, almost bullheaded, rough-hewn. It is the state closest geographically to Europe, but it was not heavily settled until the mid-19th century, and then by people coming from the south and west—the opposite of America's usual pattern. In an urbanizing and rapidly changing country, Maine was famous for its pointed firs and steady habits, with a few dozen small factory and mill towns but nothing like a major metropolis. Maine grew in a rush and then mostly stopped: There were 600,000 people here in 1860 but its population did not top 1 million until the 1970s. Then the tremors of the New England high-tech booms of the 1980s and 1990s reverberated up I-95 and shook Maine. The simple, back-to-nature Yankee style came into vogue. The antique dockside buildings on Portland's waterfront were restored and an old-style Public Market was constructed; the Maine Mall expanded and saw office parks spring up nearby, a miniature edge city; real estate prices rose by hundreds of percents, not just in vacation coves, but in Portland and small towns that had never considered themselves picturesque. The L.L. Bean headquarters in Freeport, open 24 hours a day, 365 days a year, symbolized the boom: The two chaste initials and the Anglo-Saxon monosyllable suggesting the dry understatement of Down East Yankees; the 24-hour-a-day schedule recalling the hard work needed to eke out a living from the cold waters of the North Atlantic to the pine-covered north woods; the commercial success of the enterprise a prime example of Maine's unexpected boom. Something like the Maine slogan: "The way life should be."

Over these years, Maine's economy was transformed. It lost jobs in shoes, chicken processing, papermaking and timber, but gained in tourism, call centers and high-tech. Unemployment has been among the lowest in the nation, shoe factory jobs have been replaced by call center jobs. The Grand Banks have been overfished and fishing seasons shortened, but there's a new market among northern Europeans for Maine shrimp. The lobster industry has been thriving, with catches since 2000 near the all-time record, even as lumber mills close down. Scratching small Maine boiling potatoes out of the soil of Aroostook County has become harder; the nation's top potato producer 50 years ago, Maine fell to eighth place in the 1990s: small potatoes. But Loring Air Force Base, closed in 1994, has been developed and has generated jobs in food manufacturing, aircraft disassembly and storage, telemarketing and state government. Biotech has sprung up on southern Maine soil and Maine exports not just paper and lumber and seafood, but also computer parts, aircraft parts and in 2004, a $250 million oil exploration platform. Tourism continues to be the biggest business here, and Bath Iron Works, long the state's largest private employer, has a long-term contract to build 21 *Arleigh Burke* Class Naval destroyers, though the Maine delegation had their worst fears confirmed when Portsmouth Naval Shipyard, which repairs submarines, fell victim to the 2005 base-closing round. But it is the new economy that undergirds Maine's flannel-shirt lifestyle and its fierce pride.

Now in effect there are two Maines—booming coastal Maine and declining interior Maine. Growth is greatest in York County and along the coast from the New Hampshire line to the Penobscot River; population is declining or stable in the North Woods and the far northeast. Demographically, Maine is like Western Europe, with an aging population and the lowest birth rate in the United States; the U.S. as a whole grew by 18% from 1990 to 2004, but Maine grew by just 7%, as young people in their early 20s continue to leave the state. An aging population has its advantages (Maine was number 49 in the rate of violent crime in 2003) and disadvantages (health care costs are high and the percentage with employer-provided health insurance low). Maine has the highest high school graduation rate in the country, but its high schools and colleges have not been providing enough graduates to fill its job openings. There has been little

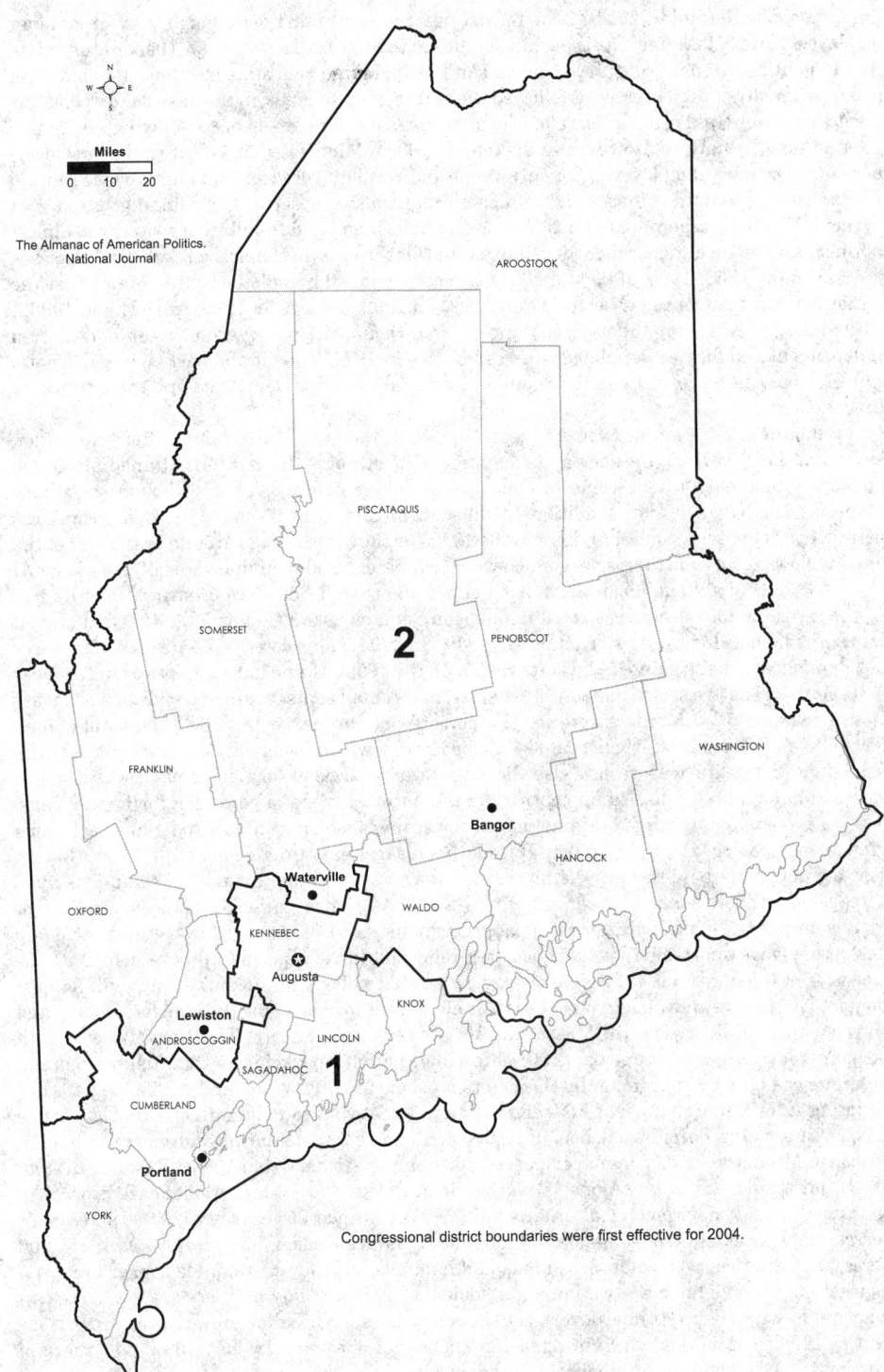

The Almanac of American Politics.
National Journal

Congressional district boundaries were first effective for 2004.

immigration here (and in 2004 Maine tourist businesses couldn't get enough visa for summer employees): in 2000 Maine was the whitest state in the nation, less than 1% Hispanic or Asian.

In politics, Maine is contrary-minded. Until 1958, Maine held state elections in September, a date originally chosen because it followed the state's early harvest; in the days before polls, the results here were taken as a gauge of national partisan movement—hence the saying, "As Maine goes, so goes the nation." However, in September 1936, Maine voted 56% for Republican Governor Lewis Barrows and in November only Maine and Vermont voted for Alf Landon over Franklin D. Roosevelt, prompting Roosevelt's campaign manager to observe, "As Maine goes, so goes Vermont." Maine's adherence to flinty Yankee Republicanism and Prohibition was echoed almost nowhere else in the nation. Since then, it has voted for the loser in the close presidential elections of 1948, 1960, 1968, 1976, 2000 and 2004—a record equaled by no other state. Maine cast the nation's highest percentages for Ross Perot, 30% in 1992 and 14% in 1996. In 1994 and 1998 it elected Angus King, an Independent and former Democrat, as governor, as it had elected Independent and former Republican James Longley in 1974. Thus in the past eight gubernatorial elections Maine voted twice for Republicans, three times for Democrats and three times for Independents.

If Maine's tradition-minded Yankees kept the state Republican long after the nation embraced the New Deal, the sons and daughters of its ethnics—Irish, French Canadian, Greek and Arab immigrants have come to equal the numbers of pure WASPs (though these new Mainers in many ways share traditional Yankee traits and values)—made the Democrats competitive, perhaps even dominant, here in the 1980s as they were losing ground in the rest of the nation. Now, ticket-splitting is very much the norm here. In 2000 Maine voted 49%–44% for Al Gore, 69%–31% for Republican Senator Olympia Snowe and 66%–32% Democratic in its two House races. In 2002 Maine reelected Republican Senator Susan Collins 58%–42% and elected Democrat John Baldacci as governor by 47%–41%. In 2004 Maine voted 54%–45% for John Kerry but Republicans made gains in the state House. In the 1990s Maine had more partisan turnover in its state legislative seats than any other state; in its small seats (average population of a state House seat is 8,724) Mainers vote for the person, not the party. In 2004 Protestants voted 55%–43% for Bush and Catholics 58%–40% for Kerry—which looks like Maine's politics of the past and is out of line with results elsewhere, and was good news for Democrats. But Bush also carried Mainers under 30—again contrary to the national trend, a good sign for Republicans.

As the economy changed, Maine moved toward a consensus on how to balance economic growth and preserve the environment. But there is disagreement raging about the North Woods. The big paper companies, long the biggest landowners in Maine, have been selling off huge acreage—7 million acres between 1998 and 2004. As Conservation Commissioner Patrick McGowan put it, "For generations the paper companies sort of managed everything for us up here. They gave sportsmen pretty much free rein, and in turn people up here helped out as stewards of the land. But with all of these new buyers, nobody quite knows what will happen now, and people are getting nervous." Local Mainers want to keep using the land for hunting and snowmobiling. But a Concord, Massachusetts group called Restore: The North Woods, with backing from Hollywood stars, wants to create a huge national park, bigger than Yellowstone and Yosemite combined. Environmental-minded rich people are buying up land with a view toward donating it for a national park; Roxanne Quimby, a beeswax lip balm millionaire who spends much of the year in Palm Beach, bought 50,000 acres and banned hunting and snowmobiling. In response Millinocket's city manager passes out bumper stickers that read, "Restore: Boston, Leave our Maine Way of Life Alone." Governor John Baldacci calls the national park proposal a "nonstarter," and has promoted alternatives—the West Branch Project with 329,000 acres, with recreational easements on some of the land, and a Nature Conservancy reserve with 185,000 acres, with eco-reserves, wilderness areas and land available for sustainable timber harvests. But not only people have a say. Maine has some 23,000 bears, and Mainers are not agreed on what to do with them. Animal lovers got the signatures for a ballot initiative banning bear-baiting, the usual method for hunting bears. The voters rejected it by just a 53%–47% margin; Portland voted 68% for it, Millinocket 73% against.

The People		**Race/Ethnic Origin**			**Military veterans:** 154,590 (15.9%)	
Pop. 2004 (est):	1,317,253	1,230,297	96.5%	White	WWII: 19.8%	Korea: 14.1%
Pop. 2000:	1,274,923	6,440	0.5%	Black	Vietnam: 33.1%	Gulf War: 8.2%
Pop. 1990:	1,227,928	9,014	0.7%	Asian	**Most populous cities (2003):**	
Change 1990–2000:	Up 3.8%	6,911	0.5%	Native Am.	1. Portland	63,635
% of U.S. total:	0.5%	334	0.0%	Hawaiian	2. Lewiston	35,922
Pop. rank:	40th of 50	11,731	0.9%	Two+ races	3. Bangor	31,550
Area size:	35,385 sq. mi.	836	0.1%	Other	4. South Portland	23,553
State Native:	67.3%	9,360	0.7%	Hisp. Origin	5. Auburn	23,313
Non-citizen:	1.3%	**Ancestry**				
Language		English: 16.0%		Irish: 11.2%	Urban population: 40.2%	
English: 87.9%	Other Eur.:10.0%	French: 10.6%		USA: 7.0%	Rural population: 59.8%	
Spanish: 1.3%		Fr. Canadian: 6.4%				

Education		**Work Sector**		**Legislature**	
H.S. Grad:	85.4%	Private: 75.9%	Govt: 14.5%	Senate	19 D 16 R
College Grad:	22.9%	Self: 9.3%	Family: 0.3%	House	76 D 73 R 2 I
Industry		Unemployment: 4.7%		Legislative Term Limits: Yes	
Agri: 2.6%	Con: 6.9%	**Household Income**		**Registered Voters**	
Fin: 6.2%	Info: 2.5%	<15k: 17.8%	15-35k: 29.0%	D: 297,831	(31.1%)
Mfg: 18.5%	Prof: 30.1%	35-50k: 18.3%	50-100k: 27.7%	R: 274,727	(28.7%)
Public: 4.5%	Trade: 17.0%	100-150k: 4.7%	>150k: 2.4%	O: 384,927	(40.2%)
Other: 11.8%		Median: $37,240			
Occupation		Poverty status: 10.9%			
Blue collar: 25.6%	White collar: 57.4%	**Home Value**			
Gray collar: 17.0%		<50k: 15.4%	50-100k: 39.6%	100-200k: 34.6%	200-300k: 6.5%
		300-500k: 2.7%	>500k: 1.2%	Median: $94,300	

Presidential politics   Maine has been a hard state to predict in recent presidential politics. It gave majorities to Republican George Bush in 1988 and Democrat Bill Clinton in 1996. In between, the 1992 race was very nearly a three-way tie, with Clinton in first place and Bush, who has spent nearly every summer of his life in Maine, in third place. In 2000, Al Gore won by a 49%–44% margin, with 6% for Ralph Nader. In 2004 Maine was a target state for both candidates. There were signs and stickers all over the state and turnout rose 14% in a state with population growth of 3% over the same period. But the result was more one-sided than expected earlier in the year: John Kerry won 54%–45%. Kerry's margin was larger than in two states

2004 Presidential Vote		
Kerry (D).....................	396,842	(54%)
Bush (R)	330,201	(45%)
Nader (BL).....................	8,069	(1%)
Other...........................	5,640	(1%)

2000 Presidential Vote		
Gore (D)......................	319,951	(49%)
Bush (R)	286,616	(44%)
Nader (Green)	37,127	(6%)
Other...........................	8,123	(1%)

that were on no one's target list, Delaware and Hawaii, and another, Washington, that had been conceded as safe for Kerry in August. The question arises whether Maine will be on anyone's target list in 2008.

Maine is one of two states (Nebraska is the other) which gives two electors to the statewide winner and one elector to the winner in each congressional district. In 2004, Kerry carried the 2d District by 20,762 votes, a 52%–46% margin.

Maine held its first-ever presidential primary on March 5, 1996, in an attempt to generate an early contest to which candidates would pay attention. But they didn't—at least not much. Maine abolished its presidential primary for 2004.

Congressional districting   The lines in Maine are drawn by a 15-member bipartisan Legislative Apportionment Committee; the legislature can amend the plan and must approve it by a two-thirds vote. The governor has a veto, though presumably that's academic since there would be a two-thirds majority to override it. Under state law the committee sends its plan to the legislature in spring 2003. This arguably violates the Constitution, since the 2002 elections were held within lines drawn on the basis of the 1990 Census. But no one has filed a lawsuit for the good reason that it makes no practical difference. There has been little change in the boundary between the two districts since Maine lost its third seat in the 1960 Census. In the 2003 session, however, the legislature failed to adopt a plan. On July 2, 2003, the state supreme court adopted a plan for the 2004 elections.

109th Congress Lineup
2 D
108th Congress Lineup
2 D

Governor

John Baldacci (D)

Elected 2002, term expires Jan. 2007, 1st term; b. Jan. 30, 1955, Bangor; home, Augusta; U. of ME, B.A. 1986; Catholic; married (Karen).

Elected Office: Bangor City Cncl., 1978–81; ME Senate, 1982–94; U.S. House of Reps., 1994–2002.

Professional Career: Restaurateur.

Office: 1 State House Station, Augusta, 04333, 207-287-3531; Fax: 207-287-1034; Web site: www.state.me.us/governor.

Election Results

2002 general	John Baldacci (D)	238,179	(47%)
	Peter Cianchette (R)	209,496	(41%)
	Jonathan Carter (Green)	46,903	(9%)
2002 primary	John Baldacci (D)	unopposed	
1998 general	Angus S. King Jr. (I)	246,772	(59%)
	James B. Longley Jr. (R)	79,716	(19%)
	Thomas J. Connolly (D)	50,506	(12%)
	Patricia H. Lamarche (I)	28,722	(7%)
	Other	15,293	(4%)

John Baldacci (pronounced *ball-DA-chee*) in 2002 became the first Democrat elected governor of Maine since 1986. Baldacci grew up in Bangor, then lived across the street from the house he grew up in and still attends the same church where he was christened. His family ran Momma Baldacci's, a restaurant started by his grandparents in 1933. He is of Italian and Lebanese descent, distantly related to former Senator George Mitchell, and the family restaurant used to get a daily delivery of rolls from former Senator William Cohen's father's bakery. Baldacci followed his father on the Bangor City Council in 1978, at 23; in 1982 he was elected to the state Senate, where he often dissented from Democrats and chaired the tax committee. When 2d District Congresswoman Olympia Snowe ran for the Senate in 1994, Baldacci ran for the House and campaigned by holding spaghetti dinners at $2 a head (children under 12 free). Maine's contrary-mindedness came out in the general election: Baldacci opposed the Clinton health care plan and pledged to oppose any new taxes; Republican nominee Richard Bennett was iffy about the Contract With America's defense spending increase. Baldacci won 46%–41%.

In the House, Baldacci had a mostly liberal voting record and chimed in on Maine issues. He was a leader in passing a law allowing drugs to be reimported from Canada and other foreign countries, which then-HHS Secretary Donna Shalala declined to implement. He was reelected three times with more than 70% of the vote.

Maine's congressional districts are good springboards to statewide office, for each one is within both the Portland and Bangor television markets; Baldacci's three immediate predecessors in the 2d District were all elected to the Senate. But Baldacci's goal was the governorship, and he had pledged to serve only eight years in the House. From the time Independent Angus King was elected to a second and last term in 1998, Baldacci was recognized as the frontrunner for 2002. Yet there was plenty of competition. The issues were framed by a *New York Times* story that said Maine was the most heavily taxed state, with 14% of incomes going to state and local government, and by the state's fiscal woes. Baldacci said he was against tax increases; to spur economic development, he wanted to increase state aid to public schools (to hold down property taxes), slow down the growth of state spending and eliminate the property tax on business equipment. He called for business tax breaks in distressed areas. He said a single-payer health care finance plan was unworkable and said he would set up an Office of Health Policy to coordinate changes in health care finance. Baldacci promised a "balanced economic strategy" with different approaches for rural and urban areas and reiterated his promise to limit spending increases to the rate of inflation. The leading Republican was former state Representative Peter Cianchette, who promised to cut the state tax burden by 20%; he said he would veto any tax increase and "any budget that grows faster than your paychecks." He called for a property tax cap, with no corresponding state aid. Independent candidate Jonathan Carter won the Green party nomination (there was actually a primary) and also qualified for the state's public financing system, which gave him $902,000 but limited his spending, almost as much as Baldacci's and Cianchette's $1.5 million. Carter called for single-payer health insurance and for a sales tax on professional services; like the others he was for eliminating the property tax on business equipment. Carter got the most attention when he ran an ad accusing Baldacci of supporting casino gambling despite his statements to the contrary; the ad featured ominous music and phrases from *The Sopranos*—ethnic stereotyping, many said.

On Election Day, Baldacci won a 47%–41% plurality over Cianchette; Carter got only 9%. Baldacci won absolute majorities only in the counties north and east of Bangor, and they accounted for 26,000 of his 29,000-vote plurality; interestingly, these same counties were the strongest area that same day for Republican Senator Susan Collins, who is from Aroostook County: Home town voting.

Facing a budget shortfall estimated at $1.2 billion, in 2003 Baldacci and the Democratic legislature managed to pass a balanced two-year budget without a tax increase. Baldacci also got enactment of his Pine Tree Opportunity Zones, to let economically ailing cities and towns offer business tax breaks. The legislature also passed Baldacci's ambitious Dirigo Health plan (*Dirigo*, the state motto, means "I lead"). Dirigo was designed to provide health insurance policies for low- and middle-income employees of small businesses and those with no employers, with state subsidies of individual premiums; it also authorized caps on medical expansion and fees for the state's 39 hospitals. In spring 2004 Baldacci sought bids from insurers; only one, Anthem Blue Cross Blue Shield, already Maine's largest health insurer, put in a bid. Anthem's DirigoChoice plan started taking enrollments in October 2004, but by spring 2005 enrollment was just over 5,000, representing about 1,200 self-employed people and 400 small businesses. Conservatives criticized the plan as not significantly cheaper than commercial alternatives. Anthem said that their target enrollment was only 10–15,000 by the end of 2005, considerably less than the 31,000 the state hoped to enroll.

In 2004 Baldacci addressed the tax issue, made more pressing by the fact that two ballot propositions were going before the voters—one in June which would require the state to pay 55% of education costs, up from 43%, and the other in November which would limit property taxes to 1% of valuation. The legislature did not act in its spring session, but it did increase state education spending by $340 million in the years 2006–10, but not immediately. In June, 55% of voters approved the education cost requirement, while 63% rejected the property tax limit in November. In December Baldacci presented a tax package: limiting property taxes to 6% of income by state loans, capping spending at all levels at rises in income and inflation and proposing a constitutional amendment to allow towns and cities to freeze property taxes at current levels. Not included were recommendations of Baldacci's economic development commission in January 2004: abolish the personal property tax on new business equipment and reducing the business tax burden to the New England average. In 2003 another commission recommended consolidation of schools; Baldacci proposed that in 2004, but it was rejected 76–53 by the state House. On gambling, Baldacci proposed allowing "racino" gambling at several sites; this was opposed by the owners of the one racetrack already operating slot machines.

Democrats lost ground in the November 2004 elections for state House, leaving their majority at 76–73, with one Green and one independent; they continued to have an 18–17 edge in the state Senate. Baldacci comes up for reelection in 2006. Possible Republican candidates include 2002 nominee Peter Cianchette, state Senate Minority Leader Paul Davis, 2002 congressional candidate Brian Hamel and state Senator Peter Mills.

Senior Senator

Olympia Snowe (R)

Elected 1994, seat up 2006, 2d term; b. Feb. 21, 1947, Augusta; home, Auburn; U. of ME, B.A. 1969; Greek Orthodox; married (John McKernan).

Elected Office: ME House of Reps., 1973–76; ME Senate, 1976–78; U.S. House of Reps., 1978–94.

Professional Career: Dir., Superior Concrete Co., 1969–78; Auburn Bd. of Voter Registration, 1971–73.

DC Office: 154 RSOB, 20510, 202-224-5344; Fax: 202-224-1946; Web site: snowe.senate.gov.

State Offices: Auburn, 207-786-2451; Augusta, 207-622-8292; Bangor, 207-945-0432; Biddeford, 207-282-4144; Portland, 207-874-0833; Presque Isle, 207-764-5124.

Committees: *Commerce, Science & Transportation:* Aviation; Fisheries & the Coast Guard (Chmn.); Global Climate Change & Impacts; National Ocean Policy Study; Surface Transportation & Merchant Marine. *Finance:* Health Care; International Trade; Taxation & IRS Oversight. *Intelligence (Select). Small Business & Entrepreneurship* (Chmn.).

Group Ratings

	ADA	ACLU	AFS	LCV	ITIC	NTU	COC	ACU	NTLC	CHC
2004	65	56	57	50	92	51	71	60	73	50
2003	55	—	44	74	—	52	65	35	—	—

National Journal Ratings

	2003 LIB	—	2003 CONS		2004 LIB	—	2004 CONS
Economic	49%	—	50%		48%	—	51%
Social	51%	—	46%		51%	—	48%
Foreign	48%	—	49%		52%	—	47%

Key Votes of the 108th Congress

1. Ban Drilling in ANWR	Y	5. Energy Bill	N	9. Ban Same-Sex Marriage	N
2. Approve Bush Tax Cuts	N	6. Support Roe v. Wade	Y	10. Ban Bunker-Buster Bomb	N
3. Medicare/Rx Bill	Y	7. Ban Partial-Birth Abortion	N	11. Fund Iraq War	Y
4. Bar Overtime Pay Regs.	Y	8. Assault Weapons Ban	Y	12. Restrict Missile Defense	Y

Election Results

2000 general	Olympia Snowe (R)	437,689	(69%)	($1,981,504)
	Mark Lawrence (D)	197,183	(31%)	($727,655)
2000 primary	Olympia Snowe (R)	unopposed		
1994 general	Olympia Snowe (R)	308,244	(60%)	($2,041,834)
	Tom Andrews (D)	186,042	(36%)	($1,482,060)
	Other	17,447	(3%)	

Prior Winning Percentages: 1992 House (49%); 1990 House (51%); 1988 House (66%); 1986 House (77%); 1984 House (76%); 1982 House (67%); 1980 House (79%); 1978 House (51%)

Olympia Snowe, Maine's senior senator, is a Republican first elected to the House in 1978 and to the Senate in 1994. Snowe grew up in Auburn and worked as a legislative staffer after college; in

1973, after her husband, state Representative Peter Snowe, died in an auto accident, she was elected to his seat. In 1978, when Congressman William Cohen ran for the Senate, she ran for the House in the northern 2d District, and won handily. She had a moderate record and won by large margins in the 1980s but more narrowly in the 1990s; in 1989 she married Governor John McKernan, her former House colleague. When Senator George Mitchell announced his retirement in March 1994, Snowe decided instantly to run. Immediately she went on the attack against her obvious Democratic opponent, 1st District Congressman Tom Andrews, whose winning margin two years before had been 107,000 votes, while hers was only 22,000. Snowe attacked him hard for voting for the bill that closed Loring Air Force Base in northern Maine and for opposing the balanced budget amendment. She won 60%–36%.

In the Senate, she was the least conservative of the 11 freshman Republicans elected in 1994. Her voting record has been around the middle of the Senate; she has voted with Democrats on some economic and many cultural issues and has been more conservative on defense and foreign policy. She sees herself as a centrist; in 2004 she said, looking ahead, "Maybe we can help to lessen the polarization, the partisanship. Obviously, the center is dwindling, and I think that's regrettable . . . We [shouldn't] just drive ideological wedges, but rather [see] how can we fashion the very best policy in the interests of the country."

In early 2001, with the Senate equally divided, Snowe played a pivotal role on some issues. She insisted successfully on limiting the size of the Bush tax cut. In May 2001 she led a group of Finance Committee members who insisted that the child care tax credit would be refundable, so that money would go to those with low incomes who pay no income tax. Many Republicans opposed this as a form of welfare; Snowe argued that these people needed tax relief. The provision went into the Senate bill and while the conference committee was pending Snowe sponsored a nonbinding resolution insisting on it that passed 94–4: so the refundable credit became law. She was one of two Republicans voting with Democrats in July 2001 for a $7.5 billion farm aid bill; that was stopped by George W. Bush's veto threat. She and Collins voted for the 2002 farm bill after insertion of the $2 billion dairy program. In November 2002, the pair threatened to vote against the homeland security bill because of provisions, added quietly in the House, limiting liability of vaccine makers for additives, permitting overseas companies to compete for contracts and targeting one project to Texas A&M University. Telephone lines buzzed with negotiations; Speaker Dennis Hastert was tracked down in Istanbul. Snowe and Collins agreed to vote for the bill after Majority Leader Trent Lott gave them a commitment that the three provisions would be revisited early in 2003; in January 2003, the new Majority Leader Bill Frist, honored that commitment.

In the 2004 budget negotiations Snowe played a key role. She insisted on applying the pay-as-you-go rule to tax cuts as well as to spending increases; with John McCain and Lincoln Chafee taking the same stand, it was made part of the Senate budget resolution. House Republicans would not accept that, and so there was no binding budget resolution that year. From her seat on the Finance Committee, Snowe inserted into the corporate tax bill provisions for tax deferral for military shipbuilding yards (Bath Iron Works is Maine's largest employer), income averaging for fishermen, favorable accounting provisions for reforestation and favorable treatment for energy plants that burn wood chips. On prescription drugs, she was one of the sponsors of the Tripartisan plan, developed in the Finance Committee in 2001 and which became the chief alternative to the Democrats' plan in summer 2002. She favors reimportation of prescription drugs and sponsored a bill in May 2004 to regulate wholesalers who reimport drugs and to forbid pharmaceutical companies from refusing to sell to Canadian companies that export drugs to the U.S.; it was considered more favorable to reimportation than a competing measure sponsored by her Maine colleague Susan Collins. With Collins, she sponsored a bill for $6 billion for child care and training for long-term employment for TANF recipients. With Hillary Rodham Clinton she sponsored a bill to provide kinship navigator programs and foster care funding for grandparents and other relatives taking care of children. Snowe has taken a lead role on many women's health care issues—more money for women's health research, more screening for osteoporosis, gender analysis in FDA clinical trials. She supports abortion rights and came out against George W. Bush's reinstatement of the Mexico City policy in 2001.

In January 2003 Snowe became chairman of the Small Business Committee and promised to work for more affordable health insurance, regulatory relief and access to foreign markets. She has called for less bundling of federal contracts so that small businesses can bid more easily for them. She has sponsored legislation to make Association Health Plans more attractive to small businesses and to raise from $5 million to $10 million the threshold above which businesses have to use accrual accounting. She and John Kerry successfully sponsored the reinstatement of the Women's Business Center Sustainability program at SBA. In reauthorizing the SBA in 2004, Snowe opposed removing the subsidy from 7(a) programs, which were suspended briefly for want of funding in January 2004. But under pressure from the Bush administration, she and House Chairman Don Manzullo agreed to an end to the subsidy and higher fees, in return for increases in the loan guarantee and maximum loan amount.

On the Finance Committee, Snowe joined Democrats in voting against the Australia Free Trade Agreement; she was opposed because it would increase dairy imports. She worked to extend the Milk Income Loss Compensation program. As chairman of the Oceans Subcommittee, she worked to reauthorize a lapsed 1996 fisheries law, but sought to drop the 10-year time frame for rebuilding fish stocks in return for limiting the catch on each stock according to scientific estimates. She opposed making fish quotas tradable. She urged the Bush administration to act on the September 2004 recommendations of the U.S. Commission on Ocean Policy, including a $4 billion trust fund for ocean initiatives funded by offshore oil and gas royalties. She worked for a compromise change in accounting methods to keep E-rate revenues going to connecting schools and libraries to the Internet. With other members of the Maine delegation, she worked to save the Portsmouth Naval Shipyard from closure in the 2005 base-closing round; she and Trent Lott unsuccessfully tried to postpone the round by two years. When the Pentagon's recommendations were released in May 2005, Maine faced close to a worst case scenario: the shipyard was slated for closure and Brunswick Naval Air Station was to have all of its aircraft and half its military personnel eliminated.

Snowe has enjoyed very high job ratings in Maine. She was reelected 69%–31% in 2000 and in early 2005 seemed unlikely to face strong opposition in 2006, but the latest round of base closing may complicate her reelection effort.

Junior Senator

Susan Collins (R)

Elected 1996, seat up 2008, 2d term; b. Dec. 7, 1952, Caribou; home, Bangor; St. Lawrence U., B.A. 1975; Catholic; single.

Professional Career: Legis. Aide, U.S. Sen. Bill Cohen, 1975–87, Staff Dir., Oversight of Gov. Mgmt. Subcmte., 1981–87; Professional & Financial Regulation Comm., 1987–92; New England Regional Dir., U.S. Small Business Admin., 1992; ME Dpty. Treas., 1993; Exec. Dir., Ctr. for Family Business, Husson Col., 1994–96.

DC Office: 461 DSOB, 20510, 202-224-2523; Fax: 202-224-2693; Web site: collins.senate.gov.

State Offices: Augusta, 207-622-8414; Bangor, 207-945-0417; Biddeford, 207-283-1101; Caribou, 207-493-7873; Lewiston, 207-784-6969; Portland, 207-780-3575.

Committees: *Aging (Special). Armed Services*: Emerging Threats & Capabilities; Personnel; Seapower. *Homeland Security & Governmental Affairs* (Chmn.).

Group Ratings

	ADA	ACLU	AFS	LCV	ITIC	NTU	COC	ACU	NTLC	CHC
2004	45	56	43	50	92	48	94	68	75	66
2003	45	—	11	68	—	64	78	45	—	—

National Journal Ratings

	2003 LIB	—	2003 CONS		2004 LIB	—	2004 CONS
Economic	48%	—	51%		47%	—	52%
Social	51%	—	46%		49%	—	49%
Foreign	51%	—	48%		43%	—	54%

Key Votes of the 108th Congress

1. Ban Drilling in ANWR	Y	5. Energy Bill	N	9. Ban Same-Sex Marriage	N
2. Approve Bush Tax Cuts	Y	6. Support Roe v. Wade	Y	10. Ban Bunker-Buster Bomb	N
3. Medicare/Rx Bill	Y	7. Ban Partial-Birth Abortion	N	11. Fund Iraq War	Y
4. Bar Overtime Pay Regs.	N	8. Assault Weapons Ban	Y	12. Restrict Missile Defense	N

Election Results

2002 general	Susan Collins (R)	295,041	(58%)	($3,961,167)
	Chellie Pingree (D)	209,858	(42%)	($3,806,798)
2002 primary	Susan Collins (R) .... unopposed			
1996 general	Susan Collins (R)	298,422	(49%)	($1,621,475)
	Joseph Brennan (D)	266,226	(44%)	($976,805)
	Other..	42,129	(7%)	

Susan Collins, Maine's junior Republican senator, was elected in 1996, the first time she won elective office. She grew up in Caribou, in potato-growing Aroostook County, about as far northeast as you can get in the United States, closer to the capitals of New Brunswick and Quebec than to the capital of Maine. Her family is in the lumber business, and also in politics: Her father was a state senator, her mother a mayor and her uncle a state Supreme Court justice. As a high school senior, she went to Washington on a Senate youth program, and Senator Margaret Chase Smith took her into her private office and talked to her for nearly two hours. Right after college, she got a job as an intern with William Cohen, then a congressman on the Judiciary Committee who voted to impeach Richard Nixon. She was a Cohen staffer for 12 years and served as the staff director for the Senate Governmental Affairs Subcommittee on Oversight of Government Management, which Cohen chaired from 1981–87. After Republicans lost their majority, Collins returned to Maine to work five years for Governor John McKernan as a financial regulation commissioner. In 1992 she was New England administrator of the Small Business Administration, and by 1994 she had announced her candidacy for governor. It was a disastrous campaign: She won the Republican nomination, but was overshadowed by independent Angus King, and ran third, with only 23% of the vote. She then became the executive director of the Husson College Center for Family Business.

Then in January 1996 Cohen surprised almost everybody by announcing he would retire from the Senate—almost as big a surprise as his selection as Defense Secretary by Bill Clinton a year later. But there was a precedent in Maine for a third-place gubernatorial finisher to be elected senator: George Mitchell was similarly humiliated in 1974, then, after being appointed senator in 1980, won smashing victories in 1982 and 1988. In the Republican primary Collins played up her resemblance to Olympia Snowe and Cohen and called for a balanced budget amendment, line-item veto and term limits (she pledged to serve no more than two terms). She won with 56% of the vote. In the general election she was opposed by former Congressman and Governor Joseph Brennan. Brennan attacked Collins on economic issues and gun control but Collins raised much more money and won 49%–44%.

Collins has compiled a middle-of-the-Senate voting record; she has joined Democrats on issues including the 1999 tax cut, campaign finance regulation and the partial-birth abortion ban. She was one of the Republicans who called for cutting the 2003 Bush tax cut in half; it ended up being cut, but by considerably less. She also was one of the Republicans who insisted that the pay-as-you-go rule applies to tax cuts as well as spending increases in the budget in 2004, as a result of which the House and Senate never agreed on a budget resolution. Her first great cause in the Senate was campaign finance regulation; she was beaten by a millionaire in 1994, faced two of them in the 1996 primary and had only meager finances herself. She said that limitations on self-financing candidates were a "cornerstone" of any reform for her. But these have not been included because they were held unconstitutional under *Buckley v. Valeo*. In March 2001 she sponsored with Ron Wyden the amendment requiring negative ads to include a picture of the candidate running them or otherwise be ineligible for the lowest discounted advertising rate.

As chairman of the Permanent Subcommittee on Investigations Collins probed into Medicare fraud, investment scams, unsafe food, Internet ripoffs and fraudulent telephone billing—slamming and cramming—day trading, direct mail sweepstakes, property flipping, lead paint; as ranking minority member she participated in Chairman Carl Levin's careful and apolitical investigation into fraudulent corporate accounting.

In January 2003 she became chairman of the full Governmental Affairs Committee, on whose staff she had once served. Her highest-profile issue there was intelligence reorganization. She responded favorably to the 9/11 Commission's recommendations. Working closely with Lieberman, she fashioned a bill that established a director of national intelligence and a new counterterrorism center. It was introduced in September 2004, and after a two-week debate in October was adopted by a 96–2 vote. With Lieberman's support, she beat back by 55–37 an amendment by Stevens that would have kept secret the total amount of intelligence spending and by 62–29 another by Robert Byrd which would have limited the ability of the national intelligence director to shift funds and personnel. But grudges remained: on several separate votes, majorities denied the Governmental Affairs Committee oversight jurisdiction of various homeland security functions, though the committee was renamed Homeland Security and Governmental Affairs. There remained the matter of reconciling the bill with the House version, which included several provisions on immigration and homeland security not in the Senate bill and gave less control to the national intelligence director. At one point Speaker Dennis Hastert refused to bring the bill to the floor because Republican committee chairmen opposed it. Collins insisted the White House get involved in negotiations and ended up reviewing the language with Dick Cheney. The House's extra provisions were deleted and the White House agreed to draft guidelines that would ensure that the military chain of command remained in place. The bill was finally approved in December—a major victory for Collins.

She was less successful on the committee's other major issue, Postal Service reorganization. Collins described it as in a "death spiral" of constantly increasing postage rates and decreasing mail volume. In June 2004 the committee approved Collins's bill, co-sponsored by Democrat Thomas Carper, by a unanimous vote. It was supported or not opposed by unions, large private mailers, consumer groups and competitors like UPS. It would give the Postal Service flexibility to compete on rates with FedEx and UPS and to enter into profitable agreements with large customers. It would set up a Postal Regulatory Commission and limit postage rate increases to inflation. The House committee passed a similar bill, also unanimously. But there were some differences between the committees and with the Bush administration, and no agreement was reached. As House sponsor John McHugh said after the November election, "The clock simply ran out." But the basis for action in the 109th Congress had been laid. On civil service issues, Collins has generally supported Bush administration proposals to change federal work rules, but has said that the administration should preserve employees' rights. She and Daniel Akaka got voice vote approval of a bill to allow dental and vision insurance to be added as options in the Federal Employees Health Benefit Program.

Collins supported the Medicare/prescription drug bill which passed in November 2003. In June 2004 she sponsored a bill to allow reimportation of prescription drugs which had tighter restrictions than a similar measure, which she said she would also vote for, supported by Olympia Snowe. Her concern was with the safety of online pharmacies.

In 2001 she got Snowe's seat on Armed Services, from which she looks after Bath Iron Works, Maine's biggest private employer; in 2004 she got a commitment that at least some work will be done of the first new DD(X) destroyer at Bath. She worked to bring back the 94th Military Police back from Iraq after an extended deployment. With the rest of the Maine delegation, she worked to save the Portsmouth Naval Shipyard from closing in the 2005 base-closing round. But when the Pentagon's recommendations were released in May 2005, Maine faced close to a worst case scenario: the shipyard was slated for closure and Brunswick Naval Air Station was to have all of its aircraft and half its military personnel eliminated. She has also worked on other local issues—she got fishermen included in Chapter 12 of the Bankruptcy Act, which covers farmers.

Maine is a border state, so Collins also tends to border issues. She sought a National Weather Service office for her hometown of Caribou, pointing out that since it is surrounded by Canada it does not receive weather warnings from adjacent Weather Service offices as most other American communities do.

When Collins came up for reelection in 2002, national Democrats were optimistic about their chances. Their candidate, former Maine Senate Majority Leader Chellie Pingree, was energetic and politically creative, and was the chief sponsor of the state law authorizing the state to negotiate with pharmaceutical companies purchases of prescription drugs for the uninsured. Pingree raised $1 million by January 2002, more than Collins did during that period; eventually both spent over $2 million. Not widely known in the state, she ran a series of ads in the first months of 2001—positive spots on herself and tough attacks on Collins. The Senate debate over prescription drugs in July helped Collins: She could say that her amendment to make prescription drugs less expensive had passed the Senate by a wide margin and that she had voted for a couple of different prescription drug benefit programs. Pingree ads insisted that Collins was "siding with the big drug companies." Collins ads replied that Pingree should "get her facts straight." George W. Bush came to Maine in August and said of Collins, "She's kind of an independent thinker, I might add. I don't do everything she says—and she doesn't do everything I say. But she's an ally, and I'm proud to call her friend." Collins won by a solid 58%–42% margin.

FIRST DISTRICT

Rep. Tom Allen (D)

Elected 1996, 5th term; b. Apr. 16, 1945, Portland; home, Portland; Bowdoin Col., B.A. 1967, Rhodes Scholar, Oxford U., B. Phil. 1970; Harvard J.D. 1974; Protestant; married (Diana).

Elected Office: Portland City Cncl., 1989–95; Portland Mayor, 1991.

Professional Career: Staffer, U.S. Sen. Edmund Muskie, 1970–71; Practicing atty., 1974–94; Chmn., ME Clinton–Gore Campaign, 1992; Public Policy Consultant, 1995.

DC Office: 1127 LHOB, 20515, 202-225-6116; Fax: 202-225-5590; Web site: www.tomallen.house.gov.

District Offices: Portland, 207-774-5019; Saco, 207-283-8054.

Committees: *Budget* (12th of 17 D). *Energy & Commerce* (19th of 26 D): Energy & Air Quality; Environment & Hazardous Materials; Health.

Group Ratings

	ADA	ACLU	AFS	LCV	ITIC	NTU	COC	ACU	NTLC	CHC
2004	100	89	100	91	50	11	38	8	0	15
2003	95	—	100	90	—	22	30	8	—	—

National Journal Ratings

	2003 LIB	—	2003 CONS		2004 LIB	—	2004 CONS
Economic	79%	—	20%		69%	—	31%
Social	92%	—	0%		73%	—	25%
Foreign	73%	—	25%		81%	—	18%

Key Votes of the 108th Congress

1. Drilling in ANWR	N	5. DC School Vouchers	N	9. Ban Same-Sex Marriage	N
2. Approve Bush Tax Cuts	N	6. Ban Human Cloning	N	10. Fund Iraq War	Y
3. Medicare/Rx Bill	N	7. Restrict Gun Liability	N	11. Bar Cuba Embargo Funds	Y
4. Bar Overtime Pay Regs.	Y	8. Ban Partial-Birth Abortion	N	12. Intelligence Reorg.	N

Election Results

2004 general	Tom Allen (D)	219,077	(60%)	($727,772)
	Charles Summers (R)	147,663	(40%)	($505,698)
2004 primary	Tom Allen (D)	unopposed		
2002 general	Tom Allen (D)	172,646	(64%)	($521,308)
	Steven Joyce (R)	97,931	(36%)	($172,350)

Prior Winning Percentages: 2000 (60%); 1998 (60%); 1996 (55%)

The People		Race/Ethnic Origin	Ancestry	
Area size:	5,400 sq. mi.	96.3% White	English: 16.2%	Irish: 12.1%
Urban population:	49.4%	0.6% Black	French: 9.5%	
Rural population:	50.6%	0.9% Asian	**2004 Presidential Vote**	
Pop. 2000:	637,450	0.3% Native Am.	Kerry (D) 211,703	(55%)
Median income:	$42,044	0.0% Hawaiian	Bush (R) 165,824	(43%)
Poverty status:	8.6%	0.9% Two+ races	Other 6,865	(2%)
Military veterans:	15.8%	0.1% Other	**2000 Presidential Vote**	
		0.8% Hispanic Origin	Gore (D) 168,266	(50%)
			Bush (R) 144,013	(43%)
			Other 22,926	(7%)
			Cook Partisan Voting Index: D + 6	

Occupation	Blue collar: 23.0%	White collar: 61.5%	Gray collar: 15.6%

The 1st District of Maine stretches from southernmost Kittery and nearby Kennebunkport to the craggy-shored ancestrally Republican counties to the east. The historic center is Portland, Maine's largest city, home to the yuppies and lawyers that have revived and renovated its downtown landmarks. Portland's antique charm, mostly booming economy and tolerant lifestyle have made it a haven for singles, for lesbians and gays: the 2000 Census reported that Portland has the nation's third-largest concentration of women living together and is tenth in men living together. L.L. Bean, open 24/7/365, is not far away in Freeport. Former farm towns have transformed into suburbia, and old mill towns like Biddeford and Sanford have seen commercial development. Most voters in the 1st District live within a couple hours drive of the Maine Mall—just off the Maine Turnpike and I-295 and near the airport—the state's heaviest concentration of retail and office space. Lobsters are not just a tradition here but an economic resource: Lobster fishing has been booming, even though fish stocks are down, and there's a new market in northern Europe for Maine shrimp. Politically, the 1st votes very much like the state as a whole, quirkily, often for independents, splitting tickets with abandon, a little more Democratic in presidential elections than the 2d. From 1968 to 1996 it elected three Democrats and three Republicans to the House, with each party holding the seat for 14 years.

The congressman from the 1st District is Tom Allen, a Democrat first elected in 1996. Allen grew up in Portland, where his grandfather and father served on the city council. He was class president in high school and college; at Bowdoin, he was captain of the football team and criticized fraternities because they wouldn't admit blacks. He was a Rhodes Scholar in Oxford the same years as Bill Clinton (who struck him as "one of the nicest, warmest people I ever knew"), Robert Reich and Strobe Talbott, and when he returned, he got a job on the staff of Senator Edmund Muskie. Then he dropped out of politics, went to law school, practiced in Portland, and worked on charities and community service. In 1989 he was elected to the Portland City Council, and in 1991 rotated into the position of mayor. In 1994 he ran for governor, finishing a distant second to former Governor Joseph Brennan in the Democratic primary. The 1st District race in 1996 was an obvious next step, and an attractive opportunity. Freshman Republican James Longley had a well-known name as son of the independent governor elected in 1974, and he had won the 1994 race 52%–48%. But Longley's moderate record was overshadowed by his support for the Contract with America and more than $1 million in ads run against him by the AFL-CIO. Allen, with heavy support from Portland, won a 52%–48% primary victory over state Senator Dale McCormick. In the general, the candidates disagreed on capital punishment, partial-birth abortion, term limits and the balanced budget amendment. Allen called for scaling back Republicans' $10 billion increase in defense spending. Longley pointed out that it included a Navy destroyer to be built at the Bath Iron Works; Allen backtracked and said he would of course support Maine defense contracts. Allen won 55%–45%.

Allen has a liberal voting record. His first major initiative was a bipartisan campaign finance bill, proposed with other freshmen. After Allen launched a discharge petition, Speaker Newt Gingrich allowed the freshman bill to come to the floor as the vehicle for campaign finance bills. When the more stringent Shays-Meehan bill passed the House later that year, he became an active proponent. When a revised version was later enacted, Common Cause lauded his leadership. On the Energy and Commerce Committee, he was an outspoken foe of the Republicans' Medicare prescription drug bill.

On other issues, Allen pushed to require coal-burning power plants and trash incinerators to cut mercury emissions 90%, and he feared the impact on fish in local lakes; he accused the Bush Administration of reneging on promises to do its own scientific analyses. He helped to secure $2.8 billion for three Aegis destroyers with construction work divided by Bath Iron Works in Maine and Ingalls Shipyard in Mississippi, plus funds for projects at Saco Defense, Brunswick Naval Air Station, and Portsmouth Naval Shipyard at Kittery. He worked to protect Brunswick and Portsmouth in the 2005 base-closing round but when the Pentagon's recommendations were released in May 2005, the shipyard was slated for closure and Brunswick was to have all of its aircraft and half its military personnel eliminated. Allen called the job losses "devastating."

He backed the Bush administration's plan to dismantle MX missiles, but voiced alarm that the planned reduction in shipbuilding would reduce the Navy's fleet to 240 ships. He voted against the use of force in Iraq because the resolution gave President Bush "a blank check," and later called the war "a major miscalculation." He launched a House Ocean Caucus and called for a presidential ocean policy adviser to focus on environmental, fishing and other topics that affect Maine's 3,500-mile shoreline. Without conservation of fishing stocks, he warned, quotas would become necessary.

Allen appears to have a secure hold on this once competitive district. Against a conservative who attacked him as "anti-defense," he won 64%–36% in 2002. Against an aide to Senator Olympia Snowe who criticized him for leaving Armed Services when base-closing rounds loomed, he won 60%–40% in 2004.

SECOND DISTRICT

Rep. Michael Michaud (D)

Elected 2002, 2d term; b. Jan. 18, 1955, Millinocket; home, East Millinocket; Schenck H.S., 1973; Catholic; single.

Elected Office: ME House, 1980–94; ME Senate, 1994–2001, Pres., 2001.

Professional Career: Mill worker, Great Northern Paper, 1973–2002.

DC Office: 437 CHOB, 20515, 202-225-6306; Fax: 202-225-2943; Web site: michaud.house.gov.

District Offices: Bangor, 207-942-6935; Lewiston, 207-782-3704; Presque Isle, 207-764-1036; Waterville, 207-873-5713.

Committees: *Small Business* (11th of 15 D): Rural Enterprises, Agriculture & Technology; Tax, Finance & Exports. *Transportation & Infrastructure* (28th of 34 D): Economic Development, Public Buildings & Emergency Management; Highways, Transit & Pipelines. *Veterans' Affairs* (6th of 12 D): Health (RMM).

Group Ratings

	ADA	ACLU	AFS	LCV	ITIC	NTU	COC	ACU	NTLC	CHC
2004	90	70	100	91	50	10	48	20	0	33
2003	95	—	100	85	—	24	40	36	—	—

National Journal Ratings

	2003 LIB	—	2003 CONS	2004 LIB	—	2004 CONS
Economic	70%	—	30%	63%	—	36%
Social	59%	—	41%	64%	—	35%
Foreign	75%	—	21%	68%	—	30%

Key Votes of the 108th Congress

1. Drilling in ANWR	N	5. DC School Vouchers	N	9. Ban Same-Sex Marriage	N
2. Approve Bush Tax Cuts	N	6. Ban Human Cloning	Y	10. Fund Iraq War	N
3. Medicare/Rx Bill	N	7. Restrict Gun Liability	Y	11. Bar Cuba Embargo Funds	Y
4. Bar Overtime Pay Regs.	Y	8. Ban Partial-Birth Abortion	Y	12. Intelligence Reorg.	Y

Election Results

2004 general	Michael Michaud (D) 199,303	(58%)	($1,309,195)
	Brian Hamel (R) 135,547	(39%)	($667,464)
	Other... 8,586	(3%)	
2004 primary	Michael Michaud (D) .... unopposed		
2002 general	Michael Michaud (D) 116,868	(52%)	($1,178,398)
	Kevin Raye (R) 107,849	(48%)	($1,128,820)

The People		Race/Ethnic Origin	Ancestry	
Area size:	29,985 sq. mi.	96.7% White	English: 15.8%	French: 11.7%
Urban population:	31.0%	0.4% Black	Irish: 10.3%	
Rural population:	69.0%	0.5% Asian	**2004 Presidential Vote**	
Pop. 2000:	637,473	0.8% Native Am.	Kerry (D) 185,139	(52%)
Median income:	$32,600	0.0% Hawaiian	Bush (R) 164,377	(46%)
Poverty status:	13.3%	0.9% Two+ races	Other 6,840	(2%)
Military veterans:	15.9%	0.1% Other	**2000 Presidential Vote**	
		0.7% Hispanic Origin	Gore (D) 151,685	(48%)
			Bush (R) 142,603	(45%)
			Other 21,705	(7%)
			Cook Partisan Voting Index: D + 4	

Occupation	Blue collar: 28.5%	White collar: 53.0%	Gray collar: 18.5%

The 2d District of Maine is heavily forested, rough-hewn and enormous. It covers the northern three-quarters of the state's acreage; it is the largest congressional district east of the Mississippi, larger than New Hampshire, Vermont and Massachusetts combined. The population is not evenly distributed, however: The district dips south to include the heavily Democratic mill town of Lewiston and east to Eastport, just across the bay and the Franklin D. Roosevelt Bridge from the Roosevelt Campobello International Park (Campobello is in New Brunswick, but is connected by bridge to the United States and not Canada). At Belfast on Penobscot Bay, art galleries and boutiques have replaced fish-processing plants. There are several different Maines here: The bays of coastal Maine, with their small fishing towns; the potato fields of far northern Aroostook County (at 6,543 square miles, Aroostook is so big that it covers an area greater than Rhode Island and Connecticut together); the mill towns on the fast-running streams of western Maine, penned in between mountains where there are more moose than people. This was one of America's frontiers in the 1850s, when Bangor on the Penobscot River was the lumber capital of the world; today tiny Bangor is the second-largest city in the district, planning a $184 million redevelopment of its industrial waterfront. This part of Maine has had its economic troubles, losing 22,000 jobs to neighboring Canada and other foreign markets after the 1993 passage of NAFTA, and further job losses in the shoe industry after that later. Potato production is only half what it was in 1980; a once-thriving sardine canning business is virtually gone; logging—long the largest business in Maine—has suffered job cutbacks as big paper companies sell off much acreage and a Massachusetts-based group seeks to create a North Maine Woods National Park. (Opponents' bumper stickers read: "If you don't like cutting trees, try using plastic toilet paper.") But there are also signs of life. Loring Air Force Base was closed in 1994, but new businesses from aircraft repair to telemarketing have replaced its civilian jobs and more. And some businesses persist: Washington County's sandy soil plains produce more than 90% of the nation's wild

blueberry crop. Politically, this is protest country: This was Ross Perot's strongest congressional district in the United States in 1992 and 1996. The 2d was carried narrowly by Al Gore in 2000 and by a little wider margin by John Kerry in 2004.

The congressman from the 2d District is Mike Michaud *(me-SHOO)*, a Democrat first elected in 2002 when John Baldacci gave up the seat and was elected governor. Michaud grew up in East Millinocket in the North Woods; he comes from a blue collar family and is one of the few members of Congress who did not attend college. For 28 years, he was a mill worker at the Great Northern Paper; unhappily, this dominant employer in this economically depressed area closed its plant a month after his election. "I know what it's like to work the day shift, the midnight shift. I've been on strike. I know what it's like to worry about whether you will have a job or not." In 1980 he was elected to the state House and in 1994 to the state Senate, where he chaired the Appropriations Committee and became Senate President. Michaud has an eclectic mix of political views, which would have been popular several decades ago among House Democrats but no longer now. He is staunchly pro-labor, but opposes abortion rights. He opposes drilling for oil in the Arctic National Wildlife Refuge, but strongly supports gun ownership rights.

In the six-way Democratic contest for Baldacci's seat, Michaud's chief opponent was state Senator Susan Longley of Lewiston, the daughter of former Independent Governor James Longley and sister of the 1st District's former Republican Congressman James Longley Jr. She emphasized her support for abortion rights in a district that had not elected a pro-life candidate since the *Roe v. Wade* decision in 1973. But with support from organized labor, Michaud got 31% to Longley's 28% and 20% for former state Senator Sean Faircloth. It was a regional contest: Michaud carried the five most rural counties, and won 66% of the vote in Aroostook; Longley carried six counties chiefly in the southern part of the district, and won 59% in trendy coastal Waldo County.

In the general, Michaud faced Kevin Raye, the veteran chief of staff to Senator Olympia Snowe. Michaud attempted to turn Raye's experience into a liability. His campaign slogan was, "I'm One of Us, Working for Us"—an attempt to contrast his blue collar background and union membership with Raye's white collar Washington experience. Michaud, perhaps to appeal to feminists despite his opposition to abortion, set out a 10-point "women's equity agenda," including family planning, increased child care aid, breast cancer research, and equal pay for equal work; Raye won the support of abortion rights groups. Michaud won 52%–48%. He ran better than most Democrats in rural areas, winning 53% in the seven northern counties, where unions conducted a voter turnout drive in the mill towns, while he and Raye split the four counties closest to Penobscot Bay.

In the House, Michaud's voting record was moderate for a Democrat and less liberal than that of Maine colleague Tom Allen. He proposed creation of the Northeast Regional Development Commission, for aid to economically distressed areas, such as northern Maine. He opposed the Bush administration's new overtime rules, and he worked to create a caucus to join workers and environmentalists on issues such as trade. In June 2004, he welcomed the reopening of the Great Northern paper mill under new ownership, but with significantly less employees. In 2004, Michaud faced Brian Hamel, a Republican with a record of job creation as the president of the Loring Development Authority. National Republicans took an early interest in the race; House Speaker Dennis Hastert and former New York City Mayor Rudy Giuliani campaigned for Hamel. But Hamel, who had never held elected office had trouble getting noticed in this sprawling district with a presidential election and two controversial referendums on the ballot. Michaud was reelected 58%–39%.

★ MARYLAND ★

Just south of the Mason-Dixon line and just north of the line between the Union and the Confederacy, the midpoint of the 13 colonies, Maryland has always been betwixt and between. It has a claim to be the typical American state, yet stands out for its particularities. This was the only one of the 13 colonies founded by Roman Catholics—the Calvert family—and its embrace of religious tolerance came less from abstract principle than from the Calverts' desire to protect their property from Protestant monarchs: A harbinger of Maryland's practical-mindedness. Similarly, although hot-blooded Baltimoreans wanted to secede in 1861 ("Maryland, My Maryland" condemns Abraham Lincoln's suppression of pro-Confederate rioters), practical heads prevailed.

The puritan impulse was never lively here: Prohibition was enforced only laxly in Baltimore, to the delight of its great journalist-cum-lexicographer H.L. Mencken, who called it Charm City; slot machines were legal in the rural counties of the Western Shore; horse-racing has thrived here, and seeks to escape its current problems by adding slots. An old state law guaranteeing blacks equal access to public accommodations specifically excluded the Eastern Shore. By not pursuing any one course rigorously, Maryland could be many things at once: Northern as well as Southern, moralistic as well as libertine, industrial as well as rural, leaving people to their own devices yet with a heavy government presence. Perhaps as a result, much of Maryland's political history reads like a chronicle of rogues.

Maryland's genial tolerance may have given it a little too savory a history, but this state cherishes its sense of uniqueness. The Chesapeake Bay, for example, is the nation's largest estuary, with water saltier than a river but fresher than the ocean and with unique watermen and shellfish. The terrapin and Chesapeake oyster are rare today; oystermen harvested 5.6 million bushels in 1900 but only 148,000 in 2002, 56,000 in 2003, 26,000 in 2004. Rockfish and Chesapeake Bay blue crabs are much scarcer too. Measures are being taken by the Maryland, Virginia and Pennsylvania state governments to limit runoff from farms and chicken operations, but still the decline goes on. A bipartisan poll in 2004 found that Bay pollution was rated the number two problem, after health care.

Maryland has some reason to be proud of the economy, or economies, it has built over the years. Half a century ago, half the state's population lived in the city of Baltimore and only one-fifth in the suburbs. Now the proportions are the other way around, and then some: 11% Baltimore, 75% in the suburbs. The Census Bureau classifies Washington-Baltimore as a single metropolitan area, the nation's fourth largest, with 8 million people. But Baltimore and Washington are not fraternal twins like Dallas and Fort Worth or Minneapolis and St. Paul; they are two quite separate cities, with different economic bases and different attitudes toward public life. Baltimore started off as a port and an industrial city, and has managed to stay diversified and successful as it spread out into the countryside from its new central core at the Inner Harbor and the solidly built edifices of its downtown grid streets. With its large suburban population, it ranks second in median household income, after similarly suburban New Jersey. It is home to the Orioles in their popular Oriole Park at Camden Yards, the first of the new-old ballparks of the 1990s, and to Johns Hopkins University, with its Georgian buildings along the affluent corridor that runs directly north from downtown all the way to the developing edge city of Hunt Valley.

Baltimore remains the focus of Maryland's public life, for 47% of Marylanders still live in its metropolitan area, and its influence is far greater than Washington's on the Eastern Shore and in the western counties. For years, most of Maryland's successful statewide politicians came from Baltimore; today, both senators live there and commute to Washington. Baltimore has a long Democratic tradition, and most voters in the metropolitan area are registered Democrats; their default mode is to vote Democratic. But in 2002 Maryland did something it hasn't done since 1966: It elected a Republican governor. Congressman Bob Ehrlich defeated Lieutenant Governor Kathleen Kennedy Townsend 52%–48%. This was very much a Baltimore victory: Ehrlich did not run any stronger in the Washington suburbs of Montgomery and Prince George's County than the Republican Ellen Sauerbrey did in her losing efforts against Democrat Parris Glendening in

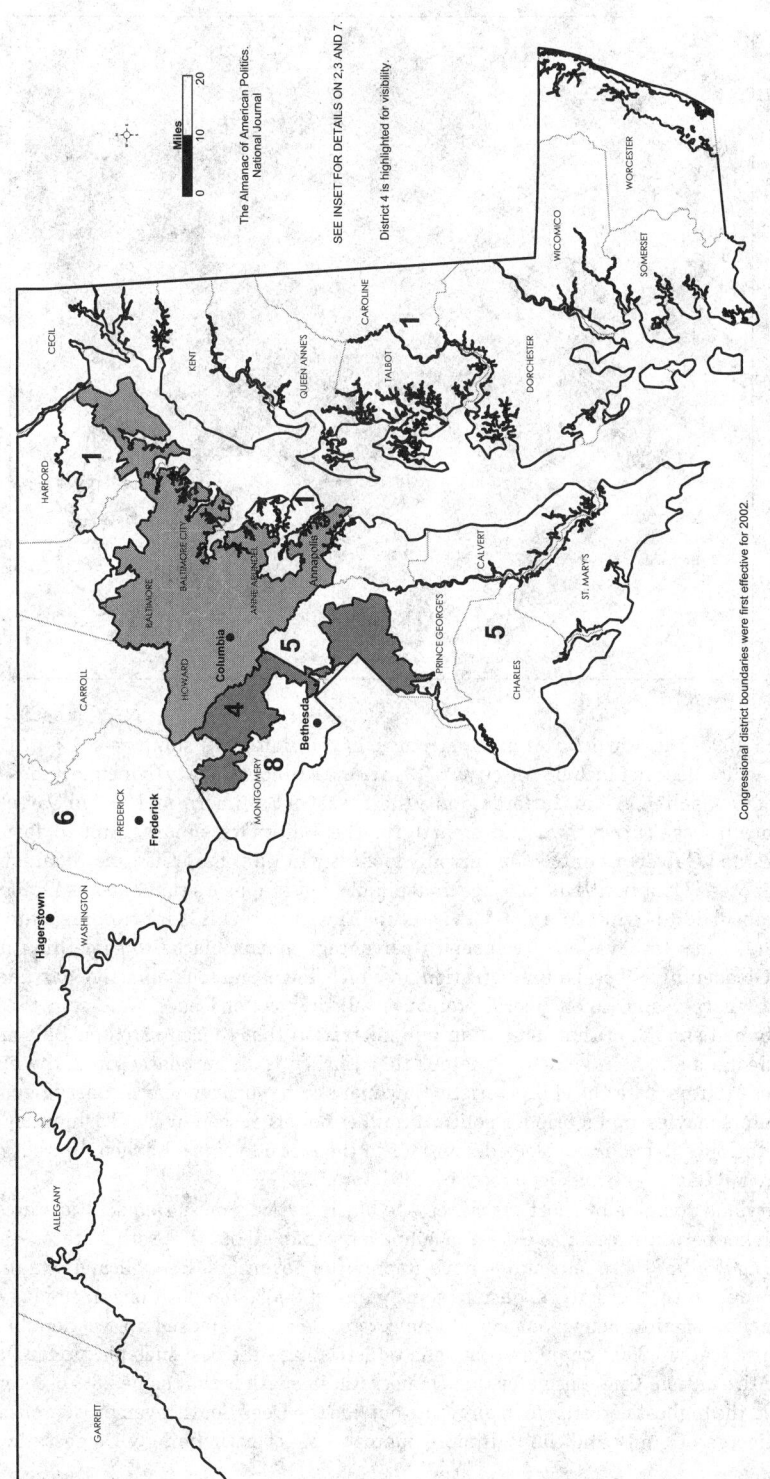

The Almanac of American Politics.
National Journal

SEE INSET FOR DETAILS ON 2,3 AND 7.

District 4 is highlighted for visibility.

Congressional district boundaries were first effective for 2002.

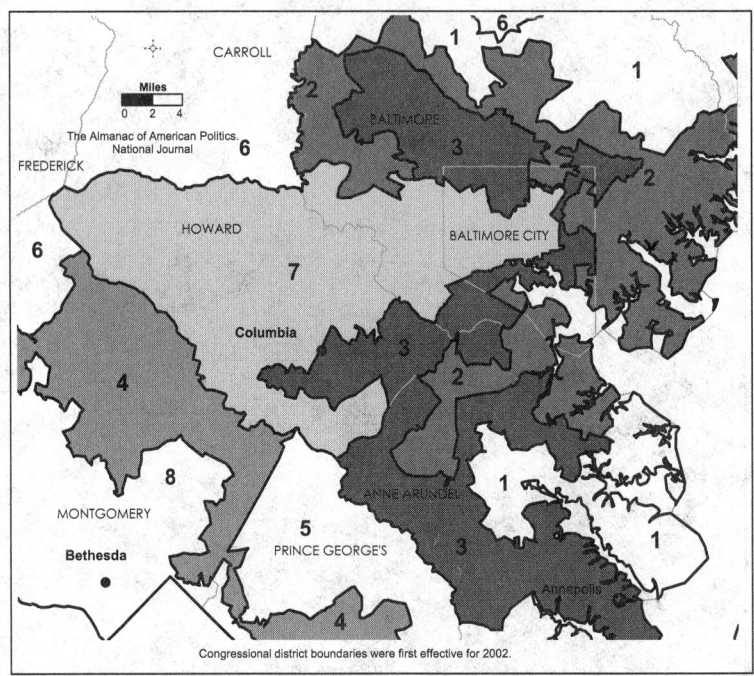

CARROLL

Miles
0   2   4

The Almanac of American Politics.
National Journal

FREDERICK

HOWARD

Columbia

MONTGOMERY

Bethesda

BALTIMORE

BALTIMORE CITY

ANNE ARUNDEL

PRINCE GEORGE'S

Annapolis

Congressional district boundaries were first effective for 2002.

1994 and 1998. But Ehrlich ran much stronger in the Baltimore suburbs—61% in Baltimore County (which does not include the city), 65% in Anne Arundel County (which includes the state capital of Annapolis), 74% in Harford County (northeast of Baltimore) and 79% in Carroll County to the northwest. Turnout was up smartly in the Baltimore suburbs and in fast-growing Frederick and Calvert Counties, but up only modestly in Baltimore City and Montgomery and Prince George's Counties. Exit polls are unavailable, but it appears that outside of Montgomery County, about 80% of white Marylanders voted for Ehrlich; with his black running mate, Michael Steele, he seems to have held Townsend's percentage among blacks to something not much higher. Glendening's liberal administration, in which Townsend took an active part, had raised spending sharply and taken liberal stands on all manner of issues. Voters in the suburbs evidently had enough of that, and of an administration that concentrated on Baltimore City, Prince George's and Montgomery. It helped that Ehrlich is an authentic son of the blue-collar suburb of Arbutus, with the characteristic Bawlmer accent you can hear in Barry Levinson and John Waters movies, and a brio for political conflict not often seen in the Washington suburbs. Indeed, the only Republicans elected governor in the last 60 years—Ehrlich, Spiro Agnew and Theodore McKeldin—all had deep roots in Baltimore.

Maryland remains by most measures one of the nation's most Democratic states. It produced higher percentages for Al Gore and John Kerry than all but three other states—although, interestingly, all of those four states have Republican governors. Republicans remain heavily outnumbered in the legislature, despite some gains in 2002. Top positions in the big counties' governments remain a near-monopoly of Democrats; Democrats picked up two Republican-held U.S. House seats in 2002, thanks to partisan redistricting—the best such pickup for Democrats in the entire nation. One reason for this Democratic strength is that some 28% of Marylanders are black, the highest percentage in any state outside the Deep South; even prosperous blacks in Prince George's County and the Baltimore suburbs vote overwhelmingly Democratic. Another overlapping reason is that this state and neighboring Virginia have by far the two highest percentages of federal and public employees, natural backers of the party of government. They help to keep the Washington suburbs solidly Democratic.

The People		Race/Ethnic Origin			Military veterans: 524,230 (13.3%)	
Pop. 2004 (est):	5,558,058	3,286,547	62.1%	White	WWII: 17.6%	Korea: 12.1%
Pop. 2000:	5,296,486	1,464,735	27.7%	Black	Vietnam: 32.1%	Gulf War: 12.3%
Pop. 1990:	4,781,468	209,738	4.0%	Asian	**Most populous cities (2003):**	
Change 1990–2000:	Up 10.8%	13,312	0.3%	Native Am.	1. Baltimore	628,670
% of U.S. total:	1.9%	1,913	0.0%	Hawaiian	2. Gaithersburg	57,365
Pop. rank:	19th of 50	82,946	1.6%	Two+ races	3. Frederick	56,128
Area size:	12,407 sq. mi.	9,379	0.2%	Other	4. Rockville	55,213
State Native:	49.3%	227,916	4.3%	Hisp. Origin	5. Bowie	53,660
Non-citizen:	5.4%	**Ancestry**				
Language		German: 12.5%		Irish: 9.3%	Urban population: 86.1%	
English: 85.2%	Other Eur.: 5.4%	English: 7.1%		USA: 4.6%	Rural population: 13.9%	
Spanish: 5.2%		Italian: 4.0%				

Education		Work Sector		General Assembly	
H.S. Grad:	83.8%	Private: 72.1%	Govt: 22.3%	Senate	33 D 14 R
College Grad:	31.4%	Self: 5.4%	Family: 0.2%	House of Del.	98 D 43 R
Industry		Unemployment: 4.7%			
Agri: 0.6%	Con: 6.9%	**Household Income**		Legislative Term Limits: No	
Fin: 7.1%	Info: 4.0%	<15k: 11.1%	15-35k: 20.2%	**Registered Voters**	
Mfg: 12.1%	Prof: 33.1%	35-50k: 15.4%	50-100k: 35.1%	D: 1,445,538	(54.6%)
Public: 10.5%	Trade: 13.3%	100-150k: 11.6%	>150k: 6.5%	R: 781,509	(29.5%)
Other: 12.4%		Median: $52,868		O: 419,592	(15.9%)
Occupation		Poverty status: 8.5%			
Blue collar: 18.1%	White collar: 67.7%	**Home Value**			
Gray collar: 14.2%		<50k: 5.2%	50-100k: 20.6%	100-200k: 47.9%	200-300k: 15.5%
		300-500k: 7.7%	>500k: 3.0%	Median: $143,300	

Presidential politics   With its large black population, concentrated in Baltimore City and Prince George's County, Maryland has become one of the most Democratic states in presidential elections. It was Bill Clinton's third-best state in 1992 and fifth-best in 1996, Al Gore's fourth-best in 2000 and John Kerry's fifth-best in 2004. In 2000 whites voted 51%–46% for George W. Bush, but blacks, casting one-quarter of the total, voted 92%–7% for Gore. In 2004 Bush did a little better with both groups, carrying whites 55%–44% and losing blacks 89%–11%.

Since 1992, Maryland has held its presidential primaries a week before Super Tuesday to try to get noticed, with limited success. The one notable result: In 1992, Paul Tsongas beat Clinton 41%–33%, with all his margin and more coming from suburban Baltimore and Montgomery County.

2004 Presidential Vote

Kerry (D)	1,334,493	(56%)
Bush (R)	1,024,703	(43%)
Nader (POP)	11,854	(0%)
Other	13,188	(1%)

2004 Democratic Presidential Primary

Kerry (D)	286,955	(60%)
Edwards (D)	123,006	(26%)
Sharpton (D)	21,810	(5%)
Dean (D)	12,461	(3%)
Kucinich (D)	8,693	(2%)
Other	28,551	(6%)

2000 Presidential Vote

Gore (D)	1,145,782	(57%)
Bush (R)	813,797	(40%)
Nader (Green)	53,768	(3%)
Other	12,133	(1%)

Congressional districting   Maryland was the scene of the Democrats'

109th Congress Lineup
    6 D   2 R

108th Congress Lineup
    6 D   2 R

most successful partisan gerrymandering in the 2002 cycle. Gerrymandering is not too harsh a word: The convoluted shapes of the districts in the Baltimore area would have made Elbridge Gerry blush. The goal of the plan was to protect all four of their incumbents and to draw districts that would be impossible to win for 2d District Republican Bob Ehrlich and 8th District Republican Connie Morella. The Bush 2000 percentage in the 2d fell from 55% to 41% and in the 8th from 36% to 31%. Ehrlich ran for governor and had his revenge. The 8th District attracted three Democratic challengers, each arguably a stronger candidate than any Morella had faced before, and she ended up losing narrowly to state Senator Chris Van Hollen. The four Democratic incumbents had no problems. The two other districts, the 1st, based in the Eastern Shore and the 6th, based in western Maryland, both snake into the Baltimore suburbs to take in heavily Republican precincts; they are safely Republican.

Governor

Robert Ehrlich (R)

Elected 2002, term expires Jan. 2007, 1st term; b. Nov. 25, 1957, Arbutus; home, Annapolis; Princeton U., B.A. 1979, Wake Forest U., J.D. 1982; Methodist; married (Kendel).

Elected Office: MD House of Delegates, 1986–94; U.S. House of Reps., 1994–2002.

Professional Career: Practicing atty., 1982–94.

Office: 100 State Circle, Annapolis, 21401, 410-974-3591; Fax: 410-974-2542; Web site: www.gov.state.md.us.

Election Results

2002 general	Robert Ehrlich (R)	879,592	(52%)
	Kathleen Kennedy Townsend (D)	813,422	(48%)
2002 primary	Robert Ehrlich (R)	229,927	(93%)
	James Sheridan (R)	9,181	(4%)
1998 general	Parris N. Glendening (D)	846,972	(55%)
	Ellen Sauerbrey (R)	688,357	(45%)

In 2002 Robert Ehrlich was elected to be the first Republican governor of Maryland since Spiro Agnew resigned in January 1969 to become Vice President of the United States. Ehrlich grew up in a rowhouse in the modest Baltimore suburb of Arbutus, the son of a car salesman. A six-footer at 13, he got a football scholarship to the elite Gilman School in Baltimore and then to Princeton, where he was a linebacker; he went to law school at Wake Forest, working part-time as assistant football coach, then practiced law in Baltimore. Ehrlich volunteered in Republican campaigns and in 1986, at 28, was elected to the Maryland House of Delegates. When 2d District Congresswoman Helen Delich Bentley ran for governor in 1994 (she lost the Republican primary to anti-tax legislator Ellen Sauerbrey), Ehrlich ran for the House. In the general election, he campaigned against the Democratic leadership and signed the Contract With America, though he opposed term limits. He was enthusiastic about tax cuts. He ran ads showing the rowhouse where he grew up and said the most important lessons he learned were around the dining room table. The result was a solid 63%–37% Ehrlich victory.

In the House, Ehrlich showed a willingness to cast tough votes, as when he opposed the minimum wage and argued that it would cost some workers their jobs. He broke with the Republican leadership on some issues, such as displaying the Ten Commandments in public schools. He voted against normal trade relations with China, siding with local unions. He was reelected easily in 1996, 1998 and 2000. He kept in touch with state politics and during 2001 was often mentioned as a candidate for governor. Speaker Dennis Hastert, fearful of losing the seat, urged him to run for reelection; many Maryland Republicans urged him to run for governor. But he did not commit himself until after he was faced with the redistricting plan announced by Governor Parris Glendening in February 2002. That plan reduced the Bush 2000 percentage in the 2d District from 55% to 41%, and it put Ehrlich's house barely outside the district, in the 1st

District represented by Wayne Gilchrest of the Eastern Shore. The new 2d was clearly designed for Democratic Baltimore County Executive Dutch Ruppersberger. A race for reelection would have been risky at best, so Ehrlich decided to run for governor—a risky race also, but one with greater rewards if he won—and announced in March 2002.

At that point, it seemed likely but not certain that his opponent would be Lieutenant Governor Kathleen Kennedy Townsend. Elected on the ticket with Glendening in 1994 and 1998, well known as the daughter of the late Senator Robert Kennedy, she had gained notice for her work on law enforcement issues. But her numbers in polls were not spectacular. Townsend started far ahead in money, with $4.4 million raised by January 2002, while Ehrlich had only $600,000 in his state campaign fund. But her association with Glendening was in many ways a liability. His Smart Growth anti-sprawl program got favorable attention (Ehrlich said he was for it), but his high spending policies and his frosty to nonexistent relationships with other Democratic politicians were problems. Townsend's own work on criminal justice was smirched by problems with boot camps that had been closed after a critical Baltimore *Sun* series in 1999. Glendening's divorce and marriage to a former staffer, followed by the birth of a child seven months later were not helpful; neither were his public attempts to get hired as chancellor of the University of Maryland at $375,000 a year nor the ads he ran in the primary for his friend John Willis against Comptroller William Donald Schaefer, his still very popular predecessor as governor (Schaefer easily won).

Townsend talked about government programs in education and health care; Ehrlich talked about holding down taxes and spending. To solve the state's fiscal woes, Ehrlich advocated legalizing slot machines at race tracks (they were already legal in next-door Delaware and now are in Pennsylvania as well) and Townsend talked about securitizing the state's future tobacco settlement payments. Gun control became a big issue. Ehrlich voted against many gun control proposals; Townsend strongly favored them. When Ehrlich said in September that he would review gun laws prohibiting certain handguns and using ballistic "fingerprinting" and consider repealing them if they were ineffective, Townsend attacked in shrill rhetoric underpinned by the belief that his positions would be anathema in the suburbs. In October, Republicans were worried that the Beltway sniper murders would spur a demand for new forms of gun control. In June 2002, Townsend picked as her running mate Charles Larson, a retired admiral who was a former superintendent at the Naval Academy—interpreted as an attempt to appeal to moderate whites. In July 2002, Ehrlich picked as his running mate state Republican Chairman Michael Steele, who is black—interpreted as an attempt to appeal to blacks.

Townsend's liberal policies and her attacks on Ehrlich as out of the mainstream because of his opposition to some gun control laws and his support for a partial-birth abortion ban may have had the desired effect among Washington area liberals in Montgomery County and blacks in Prince George's County and Baltimore City, but they were not well calculated to appeal to white voters in suburban Baltimore counties. As Townsend continued to stay under 50% in the polls— and even fall behind Ehrlich in some— Ehrlich's fundraising accelerated and exceeded hers. In the end, he raised $10.4 million to her $8.7 million. In November, Ehrlich won 52%–48%. Townsend carried the Democrats' "Big Three"—Baltimore City, Montgomery and Prince George's—by wide margins, but Ehrlich carried everything else, and in most cases by wide margins as well.

So Ehrlich returned to the State House in Annapolis, the oldest American capitol still in use; Republicans made gains in the legislature, with the help of court-ordered redistricting, but Democrats still had large majorities, and the two leaders, Speaker Michael Busch and Senate President Mike Miller maintained control of their chambers. Ehrlich's signature proposal, slot machines at race tracks, was favored by Miller but opposed by Busch and did not pass in 2003. In June 2003 he ordered agency heads to impound $650 million, 10% of funds in most cases, but over succeeding months made it available. But he did not waver on his promise not to allow an increase in income or sales taxes. In early 2004 he did back increases in education spending and in late 2004 he announced increases in spending on higher education. He continued to negotiate for slots, which he said would bring in $800 million. He said he would allow a state-run slot emporium in Baltimore and a ban on slots in Prince George's County if that would bring support.

But Busch and the House of Delegates held firm and in August he said the issue was dead until the 2006 election. He called for cabinet secretaries to prepare 12% spending cuts in the 2005 budget and for agencies not to release budget information until January 2005. And he predicted that without slots, the state's horse industry would die, horse farms would be sold off to developers and sprawl would result in more pollution of Chesapeake Bay.

Ehrlich and the legislators disagreed on many issues. Ehrlich argued for aid to faith-based initiatives; the legislature forbade funding to go to religious organizations; Ehrlich set up an Office of Community Initiatives to get around the ban. "The fringe left get all excited when you talk about faith-based institutions helping anybody," he said. He also sought changes in the legal rules regarding medical malpractice, but the legislature voted instead to impose a tax on HMOs to pay for reductions in physicians' malpractice insurance costs and passed it over Ehrlich's veto. Several HMOs in turn raised their rates.

In October 2004 the *Baltimore Sun* reported that Ehrlich had approved a deal for the state to buy an 836-acre parcel in St. Mary's County and then sell it at cost to a Baltimore real estate developer. In exchange, the developer would donate development rights (for which he would get a tax break) and give some of the land to schools. Democrats attacked the deal, which apparently was never consummated and environmental groups charged it violated Glendening's Smart Growth policy; the deal was abandoned. Ehrlich promised an open process of land sales, and said that this was in line with his policy to dispose of unneeded state property, citing sales of 300 vehicles, the state yacht and an airplane. In 2005, he supported a constitutional amendment that would require the legislature to approve the sale of public lands. In November he also prohibited appointees and state employees from talking with the *Sun* reporter who wrote the story and with a *Sun* columnist who wrote that Ehrlich's communications director was "struggling mightily to keep a straight face" at a meeting he had not attended. *Sun* editors sought a meeting with Ehrlich, but he refused until the *Sun* apologized for a 2002 editorial that said that Lieutenant Governor Michael Steele "brings little to the team but the color of his skin." The *Sun* refused to apologize and in December sued, on the ground that its First Amendment rights had been violated—a preposterous claim, since the *Sun* was left free to write anything it wanted. A federal judge dismissed the case in February.

Maryland legislators have four-year terms, and so there were no state election results in November 2004 by which to gauge Ehrlich's political standing. He took comfort from the fact that George W. Bush's percentage rose from 40% in 2000 to 43% in 2004, and said that "the era of the outer suburban, rural Democrat is on the wane in Maryland." Democrats took comfort from John Kerry's 56% win in the state. Ehrlich framed the race thusly: "For the Republican party, the issues are . . . appealing across racial lines, having more of an urban-friendly, African-American-friendly platform and outreach. For the Democrats, the issue is: Can a moderate emerge from the Democratic primary, given the prominence of very liberal special interest groups in Democratic primaries?" Two prominent Democrats who had considering challenging Kathleen Kennedy Townsend in 2002 seemed to be setting out to run for governor. Montgomery County Executive Douglas Duncan held fundraisers around the state, appeared in Prince George's County political events and church services and even ventured into Baltimore. Baltimore Mayor Martin O'Malley, reelected in 2004, traveled to Prince George's and other parts of the state, and raised over $1 million by March 2005 but did not officially announce he was running for governor.

Senior Senator

Paul Sarbanes (D)

Elected 1976, seat up 2006, 5th term; b. Feb. 3, 1933, Salisbury; home, Baltimore; Princeton, A.B. 1954, Rhodes Scholar, Oxford U., B.A. 1957, Harvard, LL.B. 1960; Greek Orthodox; married (Christine).

Elected Office: MD House of Delegates, 1966–70; U.S. House of Reps., 1970–76.

Professional Career: Law Clerk, Judge Morris A. Soper, U.S. 4th Circuit Crt. of Appeals, 1960–61; Practicing atty., 1961–62, 1965–70; A.A., Pres. Kennedy's Cncl. of Econ. Advisers, 1962–63; Exec. Dir., Baltimore Charter Revision Comm., 1963–64.

DC Office: 503 HSOB, 20510, 202-224-4654; Fax: 202-224-8858; Web site: mikulski.senate.gov.

State Offices: Baltimore, 410-962-4436; Bryans Road, 301-283-0947; Cumberland, 301-724-0695; Salisbury, 410-860-2131; Silver Spring, 301-589-0797.

Committees: *Banking, Housing & Urban Affairs* (RMM). *Budget. Foreign Relations*: African Affairs; European Affairs; International Economic Policy, Export & Trade Promotion (RMM); Near Eastern & South Asian Affairs. *Joint Economic Committee.*

Group Ratings

	ADA	ACLU	AFS	LCV	ITIC	NTU	COC	ACU	NTLC	CHC
2004	100	78	100	100	42	14	35	0	3	0
2003	100	—	100	84	—	17	27	10	—	—

National Journal Ratings

	2003 LIB	—	2003 CONS		2004 LIB	—	2004 CONS
Economic	93%	—	0%		93%	—	0%
Social	85%	—	0%		82%	—	0%
Foreign	90%	—	0%		86%	—	8%

Key Votes of the 108th Congress

1. Ban Drilling in ANWR	Y	5. Energy Bill	N	9. Ban Same-Sex Marriage	N
2. Approve Bush Tax Cuts	N	6. Support Roe v. Wade	Y	10. Ban Bunker-Buster Bomb	Y
3. Medicare/Rx Bill	N	7. Ban Partial-Birth Abortion	N	11. Fund Iraq War	N
4. Bar Overtime Pay Regs.	Y	8. Assault Weapons Ban	Y	12. Restrict Missile Defense	Y

Election Results

2000 general	Paul Sarbanes (D)	1,230,013	(63%)	($1,837,286)
	Paul H. Rappaport (R)	715,178	(37%)	($146,866)
2000 primary	Paul Sarbanes (D)	384,748	(83%)	
	George English (D)	45,984	(10%)	
	Sidney Altman (D)	31,502	(7%)	
1994 general	Paul Sarbanes (D)	809,125	(59%)	($2,767,187)
	William Brock (R)	559,908	(41%)	($3,201,650)

Prior Winning Percentages: 1988 (62%); 1982 (64%); 1976 (59%); 1974 House (84%); 1972 House (70%); 1970 House (70%)

Paul Sarbanes, the longest-serving Maryland senator in history, was first elected to the Senate in 1976. His liberalism is rooted in his experience growing up in Salisbury on the Eastern Shore, as the son of a Greek immigrant who owned the Mayflower Grill and taught himself enough on the side to discuss philosophy with his son's Princeton professors. Sarbanes was always interested in politics: As a Princeton student in 1952 he went up to Manhattan with a "Princeton for Adlai" sign and got into the candidate's hotel suite. As a big firm lawyer in Baltimore he worked on the city Charter Revision Commission. Working with small groups, organizing liberal supporters, he ran for office as an insurgent, and always won. He was first elected to the Maryland House of Delegates in 1966. In 1970, he challenged an incumbent in the primary and was elected to the U.S. House; another incumbent retired rather than run against him after redistricting in

1972. In 1976, he defeated former Senator Joseph Tydings in the Democratic primary and incumbent Senator Glenn Beall in the general by 59%–41%.

Since then, Sarbanes has been one of the most durable champions of liberal politics: On the Banking Committee, on which he has been ranking Democrat since 1995 and chairman from June 2001 to January 2003, on the Joint Economic Committee, which he chaired from 1991–95, and on Foreign Relations. He was one of just 21 senators who voted against the 1996 welfare act. In October 2001, he got the committee to pass a money laundering bill which was then attached to the anti-terrorism bill which sailed through the Senate with one dissenting vote; he later held oversight hearings and called for more aggressive enforcement when Riggs Bank's lack of disclosure on transfers of Saudi Arabian and Equatorial Guinean funds became known in 2004. He has been a leading critic of predatory mortgage lending and has called for disclosure of the high fees such lenders charge and questioned the need for requirements of high-cost single premium life insurance; he also has opposed preemption of tougher state laws on predatory lending. He has sought to base funding of Section 8 housing vouchers on accumulated costs rather than the 2004 omnibus bill's provision limiting it to 2003 costs plus inflation. He has sponsored a bill for disclosure of all the fees charged by firms that send immigrants' remittances back to their home countries. His own approach to investing is conservative: He purchased his first mutual fund in 2000 and since entering Congress has not owned stock.

Sarbanes's first moment in the national spotlight came in 1974 when he served on the House Judiciary Committee and sponsored articles of impeachment against Richard Nixon. Another came in July 2002, when the Senate passed and George W. Bush signed his bill regulating the accounting industry. The issue was raised by the collapse of Enron in late 2001 after the company's accountants approved statements that in retrospect were highly misleading. Sarbanes pursued the issue in his typical fashion. Without seeking publicity and with a minimum of partisan rhetoric, he held 10 hearings on the issue in March 2002, with many points of view represented; despite his liberal reputation, he was careful to listen to arguments made by the accounting industry and large corporations. He postponed a markup in May 2002, when ranking Republican and former Chairman Phil Gramm filed many amendments. But in June he did hold markup hearings, and gained the support on critical issues of Republican Mike Enzi of Wyoming, the only CPA in the Senate. Sarbanes's bill banned accounting firms from selling many, but not all, consulting services to firms for which they did audit work; it limited to five years the time an individual partner could work on one company's books and it set up an accounting regulatory board independent of the SEC. He did not go so far as to require companies to list stock options to executives and employees as expenses. Sarbanes's bill passed the committee 17–4 on June 18. Breaking news about the WorldCom scandal made the bill's prospects on the Senate floor far more favorable, and debate started July 2002. Sarbanes defended his bill and opposed Arizona Senator John McCain's amendment to require expensing of stock options. "Congress ought not to be legislating accounting standards," he has said. On July 15, the bill passed 97–0. It went to conference committee with a bill passed by the House in April which made lesser changes in the law. With George W. Bush pressing for a bill before the August recess, House Financial Services Chairman Michael Oxley yielded on most provisions, but did get the accounting regulatory board designated as being within the SEC, though independent of its commissioners. Senate Majority Leader Tom Daschle and Democratic campaign strategists probably would have preferred a protracted debate in which they could have portrayed Republicans as defenders of corrupt corporate executives. But Sarbanes preferred to make a law, and did; it was signed July 30. By 2004 there were complaints about the costs of compliance with Sarbanes-Oxley, especially from officers of small public companies.

Sarbanes is the second ranking Democrat on the Foreign Relations Committee, where he has tilted toward aid for Greece and away from Turkey; he has supported the resolution condemning the Turks for genocidal treatment of Armenians in World War I. He and his Maryland colleague Barbara Mikulski were two of the 15 senators who voted against normal trade relations in September 2000. Closer to home, Sarbanes sponsored the reauthorization of the Chesapeake Bay Restoration Act in 2000, which doubled federal spending to $40 million.

Sarbanes is not a senator who courts publicity; he sponsors few bills and sends out few press releases. He enjoys working on the mechanics of government, but returns every night to his home in Baltimore. When one lobbyist cracked that he had sponsored no major law and "the best he could have hoped for was having a Metro stop named after him," Sarbanes said, "Look, my name was on the first article of impeachment on the president of the United States. Having done that, I don't feel any great compulsion to throw out my name. I keep getting these assignments, you know. The Nixon impeachment. I got Iran-contra. I got Whitewater. I had a role in the Clinton impeachment when it was here." Publicity or no, he has been re-elected without great difficulty four times. His smallest margin was in the Republican year of 1994, when he beat former Tennessee Senator Bill Brock (who beat Albert Gore Sr. in 1970) by a solid 59%–41% margin. At one point, it looked like Sarbanes might face Republican Congressman Bob Ehrlich in 2000. But Ehrlich, after seeing how handily Governor Parris Glendening beat Republican Ellen Sauerbrey in 1998, decided not to run; instead he ran for governor in 2002 and won. Sarbanes won in 2000 by a 63%–37%, running 6% ahead of Al Gore's strong showing.

On March 11, 2005, Sarbanes announced he would not run for a sixth term in 2006. Former Congressman and NAACP president Kweisi Mfume was the first to announce his candidacy, then Congressmen Ben Cardin; as of mid-2005, Congressman Christopher Van Hollen was still exploring a run. On the Republican side, the strongest possible candidate was Lieutenant Governor Michael Steele, who was being recruited by the state and national parties.

Junior Senator

Barbara Mikulski (D)

Elected 1986, seat up 2010, 4th term; b. July 20, 1936, Baltimore; home, Baltimore; Mt. St. Agnes Col., B.A. 1958, U. of MD, M.S.W. 1965; Catholic; single.

Elected Office: Baltimore City Cncl., 1971–76; U.S. House of Reps., 1976–86.

Professional Career: Social worker, Baltimore Dept. of Social Svcs., 1965–70; Chmn., DNC Delegate Selection Comm., 1972; Adjunct prof., Loyola Col., 1972–76.

DC Office: 309 HSOB, 20510, 202-224-4524; Fax: 202-224-1651; Web site: sarbanes.senate.gov.

State Offices: Annapolis, 410-263-1805; Baltimore, 410-962-4510; Greenbelt, 301-345-5517; Hagerstown, 301-797-2826; Salisbury, 410-546-7711.

Committees: *Appropriations*: Commerce, Justice & Science (RMM); Defense; Homeland Security; Interior & Related Agencies; State, Foreign Operations & Related Programs; Transportation, Treasury, the Judiciary, HUD & Related Agencies. *Health, Education, Labor & Pensions*: Bioterrorism & Public Health Preparedness; Employment & Workplace Safety; Retirement Security & Aging (RMM). *Intelligence (Select)*.

Group Ratings

	ADA	ACLU	AFS	LCV	ITIC	NTU	COC	ACU	NTLC	CHC
2004	100	78	100	100	67	11	56	8	3	0
2003	90	—	100	79	—	13	39	15	—	—

National Journal Ratings

	2003 LIB	—	2003 CONS		2004 LIB	—	2004 CONS
Economic	75%	—	20%		74%	—	25%
Social	85%	—	0%		82%	—	0%
Foreign	86%	—	10%		75%	—	19%

Key Votes of the 108th Congress

1. Ban Drilling in ANWR	Y	5. Energy Bill	N	9. Ban Same-Sex Marriage	N
2. Approve Bush Tax Cuts	N	6. Support Roe v. Wade	Y	10. Ban Bunker-Buster Bomb	Y
3. Medicare/Rx Bill	N	7. Ban Partial-Birth Abortion	N	11. Fund Iraq War	Y
4. Bar Overtime Pay Regs.	Y	8. Assault Weapons Ban	Y	12. Restrict Missile Defense	Y

Election Results

2004 general	Barbara Mikulski (D)	1,504,691	(65%)	($5,997,093)
	E. J. Pipkin (R)	783,055	(34%)	($2,300,354)
	Other	33,989	(1%)	
2004 primary	Barbara Mikulski (D)	408,848	(90%)	
	Robert Kaufman (D)	32,127	(7%)	
	Other	13,901	(3%)	
1998 general	Barbara Mikulski (D)	1,062,810	(71%)	($3,014,312)
	Ross Z. Pierpont (R)	444,637	(30%)	($297,768)

Prior Winning Percentages: 1992 (71%); 1986 (61%); 1984 House (68%); 1982 House (74%); 1980 House (76%); 1978 House (100%); 1976 House (75%)

Barbara Mikulski, Maryland's junior senator, was first elected to the House in 1976 and to the Senate in 1986. She has with deep roots in immigrant, urban America and a fascination for the new technology and jobs growing in edge cities and beyond; she is a person who doesn't look anything like a traditional politician but who has become a savvy Senate insider. Her roots are in east Baltimore, where her Polish immigrant grandparents ran a bakery and her father a grocery store; she graduated from Mount St. Agnes College and got a social work degree at the University of Maryland. Mikulski got a job as a social worker and got her start in politics as organizing community groups to stop a highway from going through Highlandtown. She won, and in the process was elected to the Baltimore City Council in 1971. She ran for the Senate in 1974, and got a respectable 43% against incumbent Charles Mathias; when Paul Sarbanes ran for the other Senate seat in 1976, Mikulski ran for his 3d District House seat and won. Ten years later, she gave up that safe seat for what seemed like a chancy Senate race. She won handily, with 50% in the primary to 31% for Montgomery County Congressman Michael Barnes and 14% for Governor Harry Hughes. In the general, she beat Linda Chavez 61%–39%. She still lives in Baltimore and commutes to Washington; from her Baltimore office in Fells Point, the original port area, she can see where the highway she stopped would have gone through.

Mikulski is loud and brash, humorous and warm, brusque and aggressive when she feels it is necessary, curious and thoughtful when encountering another new part of the world. She was the first woman elected to the Senate whose husband or father did not serve in high office and every two years since 1992 she has held workshops for new women senators. In her first term, she won a seat on the Appropriations Committee; within two years, she was chairman of a subcommittee, handling housing, space and veterans' programs. Now she is ranking Democrat on the Commerce, Justice and Science Subcommittee.

Mikulski is the Senate's chief superintendent of the space program and an enthusiast for space exploration. She has paid close attention to the Goddard Space Center, the Wallops Flight Facility and Johns Hopkins's Applied Science Lab in Maryland, and secured them additional funding on occasion. She has vowed to continue to raise funds for a mission to Pluto, the only unexplored plant in the solar system, stating, "Pluto is a bargain at less than $500 million." She called the Hubble space telescope "the most successful NASA program since Apollo" and in January 2004 attacked NASA Administrator Sean O'Keefe for his decision to let the project die; in September 2004 she and Kay Bailey Hutchison moved to add $800 million to NASA's appropriation to repair the Space Shuttle fleet and service the Hubble space telescope.

On domestic policy, Mikulski is a liberal who insists that "where there are rights there are responsibilities" and has criticized fellow Democrats for being "angst-addicted." She has battled against the Federal Activities Inventory Reform Act, which encourages the contracting out of government work to private firms. She voted against higher CAFE standards—there are still auto assembly plants in Maryland—and, mindful of her Polish heritage, urged that Poles be allowed into the United States without visas. She has worked with other appropriators on projects in their states as well as her own. "When it comes to helping a senator who has an authentic need, I don't play politics. I solve problems." In 2004 she helped to fund over $1 billion of Maryland projects, including highways, HOPE VI mixed housing, homeland security at the Port of Baltimore, Chesapeake Bay cleanup, research on oyster bed reseeding and a crab hatchery at the University of Maryland. Former Republican Congresswoman Helen Delich

Bentley of Baltimore County has said, "Her presence on the Appropriations Committee in that capacity that she's in is extremely vital to the state of Maryland."

Mikulski is the senior woman in the Senate and has pushed many of what might be called women's issues—mammography clinic standards and homemaker IRAs, retaining a guaranteed benefit with inflation protection in Social Security reform. In the late 1980s she demanded that NIH include women in its medical protocols and in 1988 she succeeded in getting spousal impoverishment clauses into Medicaid. She was the chief Senate co-sponsor with John Chafee and his son and successor Lincoln Chafee of the 2000 breast cancer bill, which provided Medicaid financing of mammograms and Pap tests; she was denied a White House signing ceremony because the chief House sponsor was Rick Lazio, Hillary Rodham Clinton's opponent in the New York Senate race. Mikulski's skills are not just political. She coauthored *Capitol Offense* and *Capitol Venture*, mystery novels featuring freshman Senator Eleanor "Norie" Gorzack of Pennsylvania.

Mikulski's toughest Senate election was her first, which she won fairly easily against strong competition. In 1992 and 1998 she was re-elected with 71%, first against Alan Keyes, a former Reagan appointee who later ran for president twice and in 2004 ran for the Senate in Illinois, and then against Ross Pierpont, a genial 81-year-old physician who had run for office and lost 14 times. In 2004 she faced a more serious challenger in state Senator E. J. Pipkin, a Dundalk native who made millions as a bond trader on Wall Street and returned to live on the Eastern Shore. He opposed Governor Parris Glendening's plan to deposit dredge spoils in Chesapeake Bay and in 2002 spent $600,000 of his own money to beat a veteran state senator 62%–37%. In 2004 he put $1 million of his own money into his race against Mikulski. He argued that Mikulski's voting record was far to the left ("Who knew?" asked his spots) and that she had not done enough for Chesapeake Bay. Mikulski still outspent him 2–1 in Maryland's most expensive Senate race and won 65%–34%, somewhat less than her margins in 1992 and 1998. Pipkin carried his state Senate district (his term is four years and so he didn't have to give up the seat), two counties in western Maryland and two exurban Baltimore counties.

FIRST DISTRICT

Rep. Wayne Gilchrest (R)

Elected 1990, 8th term; b. Apr. 15, 1946, Rahway, NJ; home, Kennedyville; Wesley Col., A.A. 1971, DE St. Col., B.A. 1973, Loyola Col., 1984; Methodist; married (Barbara).

Military Career: Marine Corps, 1964–68 (Vietnam).

Professional Career: High schl. teacher, 1973–86; Natl. Forest Service worker, Bitterroot Natl. Forest, 1986.

DC Office: 2245 RHOB, 20515, 202-225-5311; Fax: 202-225-0254; Web site: www.gilchrest.house.gov.

District Offices: Bel Air, 410-838-2517; Chestertown, 410-778-9407; Salisbury, 410-749-3184.

Committees: *Resources* (6th of 27 R): Fisheries & Oceans (Chmn.); Forests & Forest Health. *Science* (12th of 24 R): Environment, Technology & Standards. *Transportation & Infrastructure* (6th of 41 R): Coast Guard & Maritime Transportation; Water Resources & Environment.

Group Ratings

	ADA	ACLU	AFS	LCV	ITIC	NTU	COC	ACU	NTLC	CHC
2004	35	25	0	45	78	54	95	56	68	53
2003	25	—	0	55	—	56	82	67	—	—

National Journal Ratings

	2003 LIB — 2003 CONS	2004 LIB — 2004 CONS
Economic	46% — 54%	47% — 52%
Social	51% — 48%	56% — 44%
Foreign	46% — 52%	45% — 54%

Key Votes of the 108th Congress

1. Drilling in ANWR	N	5. DC School Vouchers	Y	9. Ban Same-Sex Marriage	N
2. Approve Bush Tax Cuts	Y	6. Ban Human Cloning	N	10. Fund Iraq War	Y
3. Medicare/Rx Bill	Y	7. Restrict Gun Liability	Y	11. Bar Cuba Embargo Funds	N
4. Bar Overtime Pay Regs.	N	8. Ban Partial-Birth Abortion	Y	12. Intelligence Reorg.	Y

Election Results

2004 general	Wayne Gilchrest (R)	245,149	(76%)	($391,272)
	Kostas Alexakis (D)	77,872	(24%)	($113,435)
	Other	505	(0%)	
2004 primary	Wayne Gilchrest (R)	23,590	(62%)	
	Richard Colburn (R)	14,508	(38%)	
2002 general	Wayne Gilchrest (R)	192,004	(77%)	($440,605)
	Ann Tamlyn (D)	57,986	(23%)	($36,528)

Prior Winning Percentages: 2000 (64%); 1998 (69%); 1996 (62%); 1994 (68%); 1992 (52%); 1990 (57%)

The People		Race/Ethnic Origin	Ancestry	
Area size:	3,702 sq. mi.	84.7% White	German: 15.5%	Irish: 12.1%
Urban population:	64.2%	11.2% Black	English: 10.7%	
Rural population:	35.8%	1.4% Asian	**2004 Presidential Vote**	
Pop. 2000:	662,062	0.2% Native Am.	Bush (R) 213,144	(62%)
Median income:	$51,918	0.0% Hawaiian	Kerry (D) 124,163	(36%)
Poverty status:	7.3%	0.9% Two+ races	Other 3,828	(1%)
Military veterans:	15.2%	0.1% Other	**2000 Presidential Vote**	
		1.6% Hispanic Origin	Bush (R) 160,402	(57%)
			Gore (D) 111,807	(40%)
			Other 8,424	(3%)
			Cook Partisan Voting Index: R +10	

Occupation	Blue collar: 21.9%	White collar: 63.3%	Gray collar: 14.8%

Chesapeake Bay, technically not a bay but an estuary, was the central focus of the most thickly settled of the 13 colonies, and today remains a central focus for much of modern Maryland and a backwater where an older civilization lives on. The first British here were amazed at the Chesapeake's oysters and terrapin turtles and crabs and rockfish. But pollution, agricultural runoff and disease have vastly depleted their populations, and only a few watermen still make livings bringing them to shore. This was an estuary civilization in colonial days, with every little hamlet tied together by the highways of bays and creeks and inlets off the Chesapeake. The streets and docks of Chestertown, Oxford, St. Michaels and Cambridge still look something like what they did when George Washington slept there.

In post-colonial times, when most Americans were caught up in the romance of westward movement, these estuaries and peninsulas were mostly forgotten, off the main lines of railroads and highways, left behind by thousands moving west. In the 160 years between 1790 and 1950, the Eastern Shore counties of Maryland only doubled in population, perhaps the slowest growth rate on the Eastern Seaboard. Over the past half-century much of the Chesapeake has changed beyond recognition, as the Eastern Shore has grown vigorously, with second-home buyers and commuters across the Chesapeake Bay Bridge. This is a land of genteel estates fronting the water and of Frank Perdue's thriving chicken empire around Salisbury, of Easton's Waterfowl Festival and St. Michaels's Oysterfest, and the swarms of motorboats and sailing ships making their way up and down the inlets or under the twin spans of the Bay Bridge. People are attracted by its continuity with the past and closeness to nature. This growth has forced people along the Bay to address modern-day environmental and cultural problems.

The 1st Congressional District of Maryland includes all nine counties of the Eastern Shore. It extends across the Bay and grabs parts of Harford, Baltimore and Anne Arundel Counties, where the former countryside is speckled with suburban developments. The incredibly erose boundaries drawn by Democratic redistricters in 2002 bring into the 1st District the Timonium home of Governor Bob Ehrlich, who represented the adjacent 2d District. The Baltimore and Harford County suburbs north of Baltimore are as solidly Republican as any part of Maryland. In Anne Arundel, the 2d no longer includes the state capital in Annapolis, though it does include Arnold and Severna Park on the other side of the Severn River. Although it is hard to avoid thinking of this district as the Eastern Shore district, nearly half the votes are cast on the west side of the Bay. What the portions of the district west of the Bay have in common is that they are heavily Republican; this was one of only two districts in the state that voted for George W. Bush in 2000 and 2004.

The congressman from the 1st District is Wayne Gilchrest, first elected in 1990. He is a Republican with political views that stamp him as an independent thinker, both on national and local issues. Gilchrest served in the Marine Corps in the Dominican Republic and then in Vietnam, where he was wounded in the chest as a platoon leader and received the Purple Heart and Bronze Star; he returned to study rural poverty in Appalachia, taught history in high school for 13 years and painted houses in the summer. In 1988 he ran for Congress and lost to incumbent Democrat Roy Dyson 50.4%–49.6%; Dyson spent vastly more money but was embarrassed by a *Washington Post* story on his personnel practices. In 1990, Gilchrest was again vastly outspent, but this time defeated Dyson 57%–43%, drawing on his genuineness and *Mr. Smith Goes to Washington* demeanor. The 1992 redistricting placed him in the same district with Democratic incumbent Tom McMillen, a former star athlete at the University of Maryland, Rhodes Scholar and pro basketball player. McMillen raised far more money, but Gilchrest won 52%–48%. Since then, he has not faced a competitive Democratic challenger.

Gilchrest's voting record in recent years has been almost precisely at the midpoint of the House, making him a crucial vote on many issues. His specialty, helpful in a district centered on the Chesapeake Bay, is environmental protection, without sacrificing economic development. His committee assignments—Resources and Transportation, with the chairmanship of the Fisheries Conservation, Wildlife & Oceans Panel on Resources—give him some leverage on these issues. With little notice, he has helped to enact several pro-environment laws, including a measure to assist in conservation of marine turtles and another to expand the Blackwater National Wildlife Refuge in Cecil County. He encouraged a federal program to restore oysters in the Bay by expanding their protected areas, and he secured additional funding for farm conservation on the Shore to reduce agricultural runoff into the Bay. He worked to enforce international treaties to conserve migratory fish, plus tigers and African elephants. He led a bipartisan movement to create a single House committee with sole jurisdiction over oceans policy. He opposed the National Rifle Association in 1999 on its amendment to weaken restrictions on gun show sales—in a district where many are strongly opposed to gun control. He has made multiple visits to post-Saddam Iraq to assess conditions.

He has been a maverick to the point of being courageous—and occasionally effective—in taking on local economic and political powers. He attacked large poultry producers for running roughshod over local chicken growers. He opposed efforts backed by the Port of Baltimore to dredge the Chesapeake and Delaware Canal, which links the Chesapeake and Delaware Bays; his objections outraged powerful Marylanders, but the Army Corps of Engineers abandoned the plan. He opposed Governor Bob Ehrlich's plan to legalize slot machines. "Making it easier and encouraging people to be idle and mindless is not what the government is all about," he told a hearing in Annapolis.

Gilchrest does not accept PAC contributions, but he has won the endorsements of the Sierra Club and League of Conservation Voters. In the past two cycles, he has faced competitive primaries. In 2002, Baltimore County attorney and political unknown David Fischer loaned his campaign more than $300,000 and attracted support from the NRA and the Club for Growth. Fischer called Gilchrest out of step with the district's conservative views. "A safe Republican district deserves a congressman who actually votes like a Republican," said one of his newspaper ads, and he criticized Gilchrest for winning support from abortion rights and gay and lesbian groups. In the final two weeks before the September primary, the moderate Republican Main Street Partnership attacked Fischer's "distorted and negative campaign," which it called a violation of Ronald Reagan's 11th Commandment against attacking other Republicans. Gilchrest spent roughly $400,000 and won, 60%–36%. But he ran much better on the Eastern Shore (67%–30%) than in the suburbs (52%–44%). The challenge in 2004 came from conservative state Senator Richard Colburn, who ran unsuccessfully in the 1990 primary and was hoping to take advantage of a low turnout. Colburn ran billboards calling Gilchrest "the liberal incumbent." Gilchrest was backed by Speaker Dennis Hastert and the Main Street Partnership. He won more easily than expected, 62%–38%. His margins in the suburbs were bigger than in 2002 (60%–40%), and he narrowly lost two small counties on the Eastern Shore. In each case, he won the general with more than 75% of the vote.

SECOND DISTRICT

Rep. Dutch Ruppersberger (D)

Elected 2002, 2d term; b. Jan. 31, 1946, Baltimore; home, Cockeysville; U. of MD, 1963–67, U of Baltimore, J.D. 1970; Methodist; married (Kay).

Elected Office: Baltimore Cnty. Cncl. 1986–94; Baltimore Cnty. Exec., 1994–2002.

Professional Career: Prosecutor, Baltimore Cnty. State's Atty. Office, 1970–75.

DC Office: 1630 LHOB, 20515, 202-225-3061; Fax: 202-225-3094; Web site: dutch.house.gov.

District Office: Timonium, 410-628-2701.

Committees: *Government Reform* (15th of 17 D): Criminal Justice, Drug Policy & Human Resources; National Security, Emerging Threats & International Relations. *Permanent Select Committee on Intelligence* (8th of 9 D): Oversight; Technical & Tactical Intelligence; Terrorism, Human Intelligence, Analysis & Counterintelligence.

Group Ratings

	ADA	ACLU	AFS	LCV	ITIC	NTU	COC	ACU	NTLC	CHC
2004	90	60	86	91	50	12	55	12	6	33
2003	90	—	100	85	—	23	33	28	—	—

National Journal Ratings

	2003 LIB	—	2003 CONS		2004 LIB	—	2004 CONS
Economic	69%	—	31%		64%	—	35%
Social	64%	—	35%		66%	—	33%
Foreign	59%	—	39%		67%	—	33%

Key Votes of the 108th Congress

1. Drilling in ANWR	N	5. DC School Vouchers	N	9. Ban Same-Sex Marriage	N
2. Approve Bush Tax Cuts	N	6. Ban Human Cloning	N	10. Fund Iraq War	Y
3. Medicare/Rx Bill	N	7. Restrict Gun Liability	N	11. Bar Cuba Embargo Funds	Y
4. Bar Overtime Pay Regs.	Y	8. Ban Partial-Birth Abortion	Y	12. Intelligence Reorg.	Y

Election Results

2004 general	Dutch Ruppersberger (D)	164,751	(67%)	($648,488)
	Jane Brooks (R)	75,812	(31%)	($76,897)
	Other	6,732	(3%)	
2004 primary	Dutch Ruppersberger (D)	unopposed		
2002 general	Dutch Ruppersberger (D)	105,718	(54%)	($1,219,821)
	Helen Bentley (R)	88,954	(46%)	($1,071,333)

The People		Race/Ethnic Origin	Ancestry		
Area size:	359 sq. mi.	66.3% White	German: 15.6%		Irish: 10.4%
Urban population:	98.3%	27.1% Black	English: 5.9%		
Rural population:	1.7%	2.4% Asian	**2004 Presidential Vote**		
Pop. 2000:	662,060	0.3% Native Am.	Kerry (D)	144,090	(54%)
Median income:	$44,309	0.0% Hawaiian	Bush (R)	118,429	(45%)
Poverty status:	9.8%	1.5% Two+ races	Other	3,103	(1%)
Military veterans:	15.0%	0.2% Other	**2000 Presidential Vote**		
		2.2% Hispanic Origin	Gore (D)	127,510	(57%)
			Bush (R)	91,677	(41%)
			Other	5,285	(2%)
			Cook Partisan Voting Index: D + 8		

Occupation	Blue collar: 23.0%	White collar: 61.5%	Gray collar: 15.5%

The spokes of Baltimore's avenues spread out in all directions from the downtown centered on the Inner Harbor, connecting the central city with the suburbs where most residents of metropolitan Baltimore now live. The streets reach east to Dundalk and Essex, industrial suburbs where the tone of life was set for years by the giant Sparrows Point steel mill, long the biggest in the country. Northeastward, they extend to Havre de Grace and the oldest lighthouse in continuous use on the East Coast, plus modest working-class suburbs in Harford County. The locale of the Aberdeen Proving Grounds is now better known for its Ripken Stadium, the home of the Aberdeen Iron Birds, a Class A baseball team owned by hometown hero Cal Ripken, the Iron Man who set a baseball record by playing 2,632 consecutive games for the Baltimore Orioles. In an arc north of downtown are middle-income towns from Randallstown to White Marsh. A couple miles northwest of the county seat of Towson is Timonium, the annual site of the Maryland state fair.

The 2d Congressional District of Maryland is an irregularly shaped hodgepodge that includes much of this territory. Most of the district is not far from Chesapeake Bay, running south from Havre de Grace past the Aberdeen Proving Grounds and the bustling Port of Baltimore, with its container facilities and large warehouses plus space for more than 500,000 new cars and trucks that annually move through the port. To the south is the increasingly busy Baltimore-Washington International Airport, a major hub for low-cost airlines. The district juts inland to include some Baltimore County suburbs, residential neighborhoods in northeast Baltimore and an industrial pocket in far southeast Baltimore. At that point, the district crosses the Harbor Tunnel to capture the row homes of Brooklyn and Curtis Bay, whose residents are mainly descendants of German and East European immigrants who arrived there to work on the docks and in the factories along the Patapsco River and the harbor. The Democrats who drew the district lines obviously wanted to connect Democratic suburban and city neighborhoods while including as little Republican territory as possible. About 60% of its population is in Baltimore County, with the remainder divided roughly equally between Anne Arundel and Harford Counties and Baltimore City. The district's boundaries are very different from those of the old 2d District, and the inclusion of Baltimore neighborhoods helped raise the district's black percentage from 8% to 27% and lowered the Bush 2000 percentage from 55% to 41%—one of the biggest changes in the nation. Before the redistricting plan became public, 2d District Republican Congressman Bob Ehrlich, urged by many Maryland Republicans to run for governor and by Speaker Dennis Hastert to run for reelection, left both options open. But the plan helped Ehrlich make up his mind. In March 2002, he announced he was running for governor. That made it easier for the Democrats to achieve their goal of capturing the seat. But to their surprise, Ehrlich was elected governor by a 52%–48% margin over Democratic Lieutenant Governor Kathleen Kennedy Townsend (who had run unsuccessfully in the 2d District in 1986).

The congressman from the 2d District is Dutch Ruppersberger, a Democrat first elected in 2002, for whom this district was drawn. Ruppersberger grew up in Baltimore, attended the University of Maryland and graduated from the University of Baltimore Law School, and then served as Baltimore County assistant state's attorney. In 1986, he was elected to the Baltimore County Council; in 1994, he was elected Baltimore County executive, a position once held by a vice president of the United States, Spiro Agnew. Barred from seeking a third term in 2002, he claimed credit for the county government's high bond rating and for winning national acclaim for economic growth and sound management. He calls himself a pro-business Democrat and seriously considered running for governor in 2002, but decided not to challenge Townsend. When Democratic redistricters produced a favorable district, he announced he was running there. He faced some tough obstacles. In 2000, he had backed a property condemnation plan that would give him the power of eminent domain to redevelop large pieces of the county; the proposal was soundly rejected at the polls. In the 2002 Democratic primary, his little-known opponent, investment banker Osman "Oz" Bengur, spent more than $500,000 of his own money. But the state's Democratic establishment lined up behind Ruppersberger. He won 50%–36%.

The fall campaign was no easier. This open seat attracted former Congresswoman Helen Delich Bentley, who had won the 2d District seat in 1984 and held it until she ran, unsuccessfully, for governor in 1994. At 78, Bentley was by far the oldest candidate in a seriously contested House race in the 2002 cycle. But she was still feisty and energetic. She said that Republican leaders promised to restore her seat on Appropriations and that she would concentrate on national security and maritime issues. With a strong record of constituent service, cross-party popularity and a willingness to buck her own party, Bentley seemed to have a chance to overcome the new district's Democratic leanings. Both candidates supported additional dredging of shipping channels in the Bay plus increased port security. Ruppersberger won 54%–46%. His popular vote margin was more than 13,000 votes in the small part of the district in Baltimore City, which he carried 79%–21%, and only 3,000 votes in the rest of the district.

In the House Ruppersberger has had the least liberal voting record of Democrats from Maryland. Perhaps with the help of Baltimore native Nancy Pelosi, he became the first freshman appointed to the Intelligence Committee. He initiated Operation Hero Miles, to facilitate the use of frequent-flyer miles to assist U.S. troops in Iraq flying home on civilian airlines during the Christmas season, and made the program permanent by including it in the Defense Department spending bill. When General Motors announced in November 2004 that it was shutting down its Baltimore assembly plant, he assembled a team to assist laid-off workers and explore alternative use of the property.

In 2004 Ruppersberger did not have serious competition and won 67%–31%. The last two members who have held this seat, Bentley and Ehrlich, both ran for governor; Ruppersberger may be the next, but probably not until at least 2010.

THIRD DISTRICT

Rep. Ben Cardin (D)

Elected 1986, 10th term; b. Oct. 5, 1943, Baltimore; home, Baltimore; U. of Pittsburgh, B.A. 1964, U. of MD, LL.B., J.D. 1967; Jewish; married (Myrna).

Elected Office: MD House of Delegates, 1966–86, Speaker, 1979–86.

Professional Career: Practicing atty., 1967–86.

DC Office: 2207 RHOB, 20515, 202-225-4016; Fax: 202-225-9219; Web site: www.cardin.house.gov.

District Offices: Annapolis, 410-974-9703; Baltimore, 410-433-8886.

Committees: *Ways & Means* (4th of 17 D): Human Resources; Trade (RMM).

Group Ratings

	ADA	ACLU	AFS	LCV	ITIC	NTU	COC	ACU	NTLC	CHC
2004	95	79	100	100	60	13	43	0	0	23
2003	90	—	100	100	—	25	37	24	—	—

National Journal Ratings

	2003 LIB	—	2003 CONS		2004 LIB	—	2004 CONS
Economic	87%	—	9%		81%	—	18%
Social	73%	—	26%		73%	—	27%
Foreign	66%	—	32%		62%	—	38%

Key Votes of the 108th Congress

1. Drilling in ANWR	N	5. DC School Vouchers	N	9. Ban Same-Sex Marriage	N
2. Approve Bush Tax Cuts	N	6. Ban Human Cloning	N	10. Fund Iraq War	Y
3. Medicare/Rx Bill	N	7. Restrict Gun Liability	N	11. Bar Cuba Embargo Funds	N
4. Bar Overtime Pay Regs.	Y	8. Ban Partial-Birth Abortion	N	12. Intelligence Reorg.	Y

Election Results

2004 general	Ben Cardin (D)	182,066	(63%)	($1,011,951)
	Bob Duckworth (R)	97,008	(34%)	($140,972)
	Other	8,145	(3%)	
2004 primary	Ben Cardin (D)	54,398	(90%)	
	John Rea (D)	6,163	(10%)	
2002 general	Ben Cardin (D)	145,589	(66%)	($1,050,896)
	Scott Conwell (R)	75,721	(34%)	($27,859)

Prior Winning Percentages: 2000 (76%); 1998 (78%); 1996 (67%); 1994 (71%); 1992 (74%); 1990 (70%); 1988 (73%); 1986 (79%)

The People		Race/Ethnic Origin	Ancestry	
Area size:	293 sq. mi.	75.7% White	German: 14.3%	Irish: 11.1%
Urban population:	98.6%	16.2% Black	English: 7.7%	
Rural population:	1.4%	3.2% Asian	**2004 Presidential Vote**	
Pop. 2000:	662,062	0.3% Native Am.	Kerry (D) 163,088	(54%)
Median income:	$52,906	0.0% Hawaiian	Bush (R) 136,672	(45%)
Poverty status:	7.7%	1.5% Two+ races	Other 3,873	(1%)
Military veterans:	13.0%	0.2% Other	**2000 Presidential Vote**	
		2.9% Hispanic Origin	Gore (D) 143,685	(55%)
			Bush (R) 107,481	(41%)
			Other 8,456	(3%)
			Cook Partisan Voting Index: D + 7	
Occupation	Blue collar: 15.7%	White collar: 71.7%	Gray collar: 12.5%	

Baltimore, one of America's major cities since the Revolution, was transformed into one of America's star cities in recent years. Its Inner Harbor and new ballpark at Camden Yards became national models. Its cuisine—steamed crabs with Chesapeake spices and crab cakes—became known beyond the watershed of the Chesapeake Bay. The city "prefers diners and taverns tucked into venerable row houses to newer, trendier spots," wrote *The New York Times*. The central city of Baltimore has had terrible problems—high crime, abandoned neighborhoods, poor schools—but the greater Baltimore that has grown far beyond the city and county lines retains a distinctive character. This is a city built solidly on commerce, and one that has always known how to reap its pleasures. To the south, Annapolis was laid out as a capital in 1694, with one circle planned for the Statehouse and one for the Church; the marble-halled Statehouse, built in 1772, where the Continental Congress ratified the Treaty of Paris, is the oldest state capitol in continuous use. Annapolis is also the home of the United States Naval Academy and its waterfront, though gentrified, is a waterman's as well as a yachter's port.

The 3d Congressional District of Maryland consists of three oddly disjointed portions that extend from the locus of the Inner Harbor area. Its boundaries were designed by Democrats with politics in mind: The 3d envelops on three sides the majority-black 7th District and is itself enveloped on three sides by the 2d District, which redistricters made more Democratic than the 3d. One spoke extends northeast from black city neighborhoods into mostly white suburbs. Another extends north and west from the city to the Baltimore County seat of Towson and the heavily Jewish suburbs of Pikesville and Owings Mills, past the array of temples and synagogues on Park Heights Avenue in Baltimore city. The largest bloc of voters is in the crooked spoke that extends southwest, past the old rowhouse neighborhoods overlooking Fort McHenry and out past Governor Bob Ehrlich's birthplace in blue-collar Arbutus into Linthicum in Anne Arundel County, and continuing to Annapolis. Just over one-third of the district population resides in Anne Arundel County (including all of Annapolis); a quarter resides within Baltimore city itself, in neighborhoods like Roland Park, and among the restaurants and bars of Little Italy and Fells Point. A small portion of Howard County is also in the 3d, consisting of parts of Elkridge and Columbia in Howard County. Redistricting left the 3d District less Democratic than it had been; the Bush 2000 percentage vote increased from 34% to 41%.

The congressman from the 3d District is Ben Cardin, former Speaker of the Maryland House of Delegates and one of the many bright politicos produced by the Jewish neighborhoods of northwest Baltimore. He was elected to the House of Delegates in 1966, at 23, the first time he was eligible to run; after serving four years as Ways and Means chairman, he became speaker in 1979, at 35; he was easily elected to Congress in 1986 when Barbara Mikulski ran for the Senate. In the House, Cardin got a seat on Ways and Means in his second term and has been a productive and creative legislator. He supported NAFTA despite union opposition, backed a cap on medical malpractice damages despite trial lawyers' opposition, and voted for normal trade relations with China after securing for local consumption a rider designed to crack down on international dumping of subsidized steel in U.S. markets.

More than any Democrat at Ways and Means—and perhaps more than any Democrat in the House—he has worked skillfully on bipartisan legislation at a time when few were sufficiently clever or independent to pursue such initiatives. Few House members of either party "can match his stature as legislative architect and master of bipartisan lawmaking," the Baltimore *Sun* editorialized. Such has been his record, occasionally to the dismay of more partisan Democrats. He was co-sponsor with Ohio Republican Rob Portman of the 1998 IRS reform law, which shifted the burden of proof away from the taxpayer and toward the government, established greater oversight of the agency and encouraged electronic filing and updated technology. Again with Portman, he produced in 2000 bipartisan legislation to expand 401(k) savings and other retirement plans. In 2001, when Congress enacted the Bush tax cut, it included his and Portman's measure to increase the limits for maximum IRA and 401(k) contributions. In 2003, he and Portman teamed yet again on a plan to sponsor pension savings and rollovers for low and moderate-income workers. But they failed to enact the bill in the 108th Congress, when it became the ancillary victim of a walkout by committee Democrats and the directive by Chairman Bill Thomas for Capitol Police to evict them from an adjoining room. On Social Security, too, he has shown willingness to seek bipartisan reform with retirement accounts, but he was not receptive to George W. Bush's Social Security proposal; in March 2004 he told an audience of senior citizens to prepare for a benefit cut.

Cardin has been a workhorse on health care and welfare, but with less bipartisan success. He criticized the prescription drug coverage for Medicare beneficiaries that the House enacted in 2003 for failing to provide seniors what they needed, and he proposed an alternative to authorize HHS to negotiate lower drug prices. He wants more coverage for preventive care.

Cardin protested the new redistricting lines that removed more than one-third of his former district and added unfamiliar territory in Anne Arundel County, which now casts nearly 40% of the district's votes. Some thought he was facing retaliation from the chief map drawer, Governor Parris Glendening, for having considered running against him in 1998. In any case, Cardin has done just fine with the new lines. In 2004 he faced Republican Bob Duckworth, the circuit court clerk in Anne Arundel, who supported the war in Iraq and the constitutional amendment barring same-sex marriage. "I'm someone who's more in touch with the new voters in the new Third," he claimed. Cardin won Arundel by only 50%–48%, but his 2–1 or greater margins elsewhere gave him a 63%–34% victory. In April 2005, Cardin said he would run in 2006 for the Senate seat being vacated by Paul Sarbanes, who announced he would not seek a sixth term. Without Cardin running as the incumbent here, this district could be competitive in 2006.

FOURTH DISTRICT

Rep. Albert Wynn (D)

Elected 1992, 7th term; b. Sept. 10, 1951, Philadelphia, PA; home, Mitchellville; U. of Pittsburgh, B.S. 1973, Howard U., 1973–74, Georgetown U. Law Schl., J.D. 1977; Baptist; married (Gaines).

Elected Office: MD House of Delegates, 1982–87; MD Senate 1987–92.

Professional Career: Exec. Dir., Prince George's Cnty. Consumer Protection Comm., 1977–81; Chmn., Metro Wash. Cncl. of Consumer Agencies, 1980–81; Practicing atty., 1981–92.

DC Office: 434 CHOB, 20515, 202-225-8699; Fax: 202-225-8714; Web site: www.wynn.house.gov.

District Offices: Gaithersburg, 301-987-2054; Largo, 301-773-4094.

Committees: *Energy & Commerce* (13th of 26 D): Energy & Air Quality; Environment & Hazardous Materials; Telecommunications & the Internet.

Group Ratings

	ADA	ACLU	AFS	LCV	ITIC	NTU	COC	ACU	NTLC	CHC
2004	95	70	88	82	40	12	71	20	9	38
2003	90	—	100	90	—	20	43	16	—	—

National Journal Ratings

	2003 LIB	—	2003 CONS		2004 LIB	—	2004 CONS
Economic	64%	—	35%		58%	—	41%
Social	71%	—	29%		70%	—	29%
Foreign	92%	—	7%		81%	—	18%

Key Votes of the 108th Congress

1. Drilling in ANWR	N	5. DC School Vouchers	N	9. Ban Same-Sex Marriage	N
2. Approve Bush Tax Cuts	N	6. Ban Human Cloning	N	10. Fund Iraq War	N
3. Medicare/Rx Bill	N	7. Restrict Gun Liability	N	11. Bar Cuba Embargo Funds	Y
4. Bar Overtime Pay Regs.	Y	8. Ban Partial-Birth Abortion	N	12. Intelligence Reorg.	N

Election Results

2004 general	Albert Wynn (D)	196,809	(75%)	($722,207)
	John McKinnis (R)	52,907	(20%)	($91,985)
	Theresa Dudley (Green)	11,885	(5%)	($6,084)
	Other	259	(0%)	
2004 primary	Albert Wynn (D)	48,643	(84%)	
	George McDermott (D)	9,268	(16%)	
2002 general	Albert Wynn (D)	131,644	(79%)	($696,244)
	John Kimble (R)	34,890	(21%)	

Prior Winning Percentages: 2000 (87%); 1998 (86%); 1996 (85%); 1994 (75%); 1992 (75%)

The People		Race/Ethnic Origin	Ancestry	
Area size:	318 sq. mi.	27.6% White	German: 5.3%	Irish: 5.0%
Urban population:	97.9%	56.8% Black	English: 4.0%	
Rural population:	2.1%	5.6% Asian	**2004 Presidential Vote**	
Pop. 2000:	662,062	0.2% Native Am.	Kerry (D) 217,549	(78%)
Median income:	$57,727	0.0% Hawaiian	Bush (R) 58,170	(21%)
Poverty status:	7.3%	2.0% Two+ races	Other 1,843	(1%)
Military veterans:	12.2%	0.2% Other	**2000 Presidential Vote**	
		7.5% Hispanic Origin	Gore (D) 176,780	(77%)
			Bush (R) 49,202	(21%)
			Other 4,098	(2%)
			Cook Partisan Voting Index: D +30	

Occupation	Blue collar: 15.0%	White collar: 70.7%	Gray collar: 14.3%

In 1696, the proprietors of the colony of Maryland created a new county between the Potomac and Patuxent Rivers and named it after the husband of the heir to the throne, Prince George of Denmark. For 300 years Prince George's County has not often won national fame—maybe briefly when investigators chased the plotters of Abraham Lincoln's murder here—but it might now. Historically, Prince George's was tobacco country, rural and heavily settled, with blacks and Catholics and big property-owners who pretty much ran things. With its nearly two-thirds black population, Prince George's today is—or should be known as—the home of America's largest black middle class, a place that gives a hopeful glimpse of the future. Prince George's is affluent by national standards, with over 70% of women working, one of the highest percentages in the nation. With office and shopping mall growth, it has proved itself a far more commercially vibrant and culturally constructive community—including substantial home-schooling—than adjacent parts of the District of Columbia. New economic projects include the building of a 12-lane span across the Potomac to replace the crumbling Wilson Bridge and the huge National Harbor hotel and convention center going up at Oxon Hill near the bridge. Prince George's has always had many black residents, since the first tobacco crop was planted, but that population grew as middle-class blacks moved out of Washington into modest suburbs at the county's edge and affluent subdivisions far to the east. In the 1960s this was one of the nation's fastest-growing suburban counties. Its black percentage increased from 14% in 1970 to 37% in 1980 to 63% by 2000, while the total population kept rising. The county's median household income of more than $55,000 compares favorably with the national median of about $43,000 and doubles the national median for black households. But there are problems: Prince George's accounts for half of Maryland's car thefts and homicides doubled from 2000 to 2004.

The 4th Congressional District of Maryland includes most of Prince George's County inside the Capital Beltway. It also includes a large portion of Montgomery County that is mostly outside the Beltway—starting in Silver Spring, heading up Georgia Avenue and covering a sizable rural area all the way to Clarksburg at the Frederick County line. This Montgomery area is heavily Democratic, though not so much so as the district's portion of Prince George's, and overall this is the most Democratic district in Maryland. The biggest industry here is still government: It has the highest percentage of federal government employees of any congressional district in the nation; Suitland, inside the Beltway in Prince George's, is home of the Census Bureau.

The congressman from the 4th District is Albert Wynn, a Democrat effectively chosen in the 1992 primary. Wynn grew up in Prince George's County, attending all-black schools there until integration began in his sophomore year. He went to the University of Pittsburgh on a debate team scholarship and received a law degree from Georgetown University. After directing the county's consumer protection commission, he served a decade in the Maryland legislature, first as a member of the House of Delegates and later the Senate. When the new 4th District was created in 1992, 20 candidates—13 Democrats and seven Republicans—ran for the seat; Wynn was endorsed by the major local newspapers and won the Democratic primary with 28% of the vote. He hasn't had a close contest since then.

Although he is a loyal member of the Democratic Caucus, Wynn occasionally splits from the party line, especially in his work on the Energy and Commerce Committee. He worked with Republicans seeking to increase the profitability of electricity transmission systems, and was the only Maryland Democrat to support the energy bill in November 2003. When Democratic leaders strongly backed the Shays-Meehan bill, Wynn felt that its ban on soft money would make it much harder to conduct voter registration and turnout drives in black districts. He was the lead Democratic sponsor of an unsuccessful amendment to strip out the soft money ban. At home, he lobbied for a casino, convinced that gambling would bring jobs to Prince George's County. But a casino ran counter to Governor Bob Ehrlich's racetrack slots plan, and Wynn said he didn't want to put a "slot-barn" in the county. "If we can't have a high-end product with local control, then maybe we don't need gaming at all." He has been a steadfast ally of federal employees. On behalf of the American Federation of Government Employees, he took the lead in seeking to halt contracting out of federal jobs until Congress could improve its monitoring. After voting to authorize the use of force in Iraq, Wynn later voiced regret, especially when weapons of mass destruction could not be found. As a member of the Commerce committee, he has sought to ban automatic dialing systems that send recorded telephone messages; in his 2000 reelection campaign, his opponent had used such a tactic against him.

At home, he has become an independent force in county and state politics, sometimes to the dismay of other local Democrats. In the 2004 presidential primaries, he endorsed John Edwards and said that he had the best chance of galvanizing black voters. In 2004 he was reelected 75%–20% over a Republican who called him a local "dictator." Wynn had voiced interest in running for the Senate when a seat opened, but when Paul Sarbanes announced he would not seek a sixth term in 2006, Wynn declined to run.

FIFTH DISTRICT

Rep. Steny Hoyer (D)

Elected May 1981, 12th full term; b. June 14, 1939, New York, NY; home, Mechanicsville; U. of MD, B.S. 1963, Georgetown U., J.D. 1966; Baptist; widowed.

Elected Office: MD Senate, 1966–78, Pres., 1975–78.

Professional Career: Practicing atty., 1966–80; MD Bd. of Higher Educ., 1978–81.

DC Office: 1705 LHOB, 20515, 202-225-4131; Fax: 202-225-4300; Web site: www.hoyer.house.gov.

District Offices: Greenbelt, 301-474-0119; Waldorf, 301-843-1577.

Committees: *Minority Whip. Appropriations* (5th of 29 D): Labor, Health and Human Services, Education & Related Agencies; Transportation, Treasury, HUD, the Judiciary & District of Columbia.

Group Ratings

	ADA	ACLU	AFS	LCV	ITIC	NTU	COC	ACU	NTLC	CHC
2004	100	80	100	100	60	7	38	0	0	15
2003	90	—	100	85	—	22	40	24	—	—

National Journal Ratings

	2003 LIB	—	2003 CONS		2004 LIB	—	2004 CONS
Economic	73%	—	26%		80%	—	20%
Social	76%	—	23%		78%	—	19%
Foreign	57%	—	42%		71%	—	28%

Key Votes of the 108th Congress

1. Drilling in ANWR	N	5. DC School Vouchers	N	9. Ban Same-Sex Marriage	N
2. Approve Bush Tax Cuts	N	6. Ban Human Cloning	N	10. Fund Iraq War	Y
3. Medicare/Rx Bill	N	7. Restrict Gun Liability	N	11. Bar Cuba Embargo Funds	Y
4. Bar Overtime Pay Regs.	Y	8. Ban Partial-Birth Abortion	N	12. Intelligence Reorg.	Y

Election Results

2004 general	Steny Hoyer (D)	204,867	(69%)	($1,779,289)
	Brad Jewitt (R)	87,189	(29%)	($145,559)
	Other	6,279	(2%)	
2004 primary	Steny Hoyer (D)	unopposed		
2002 general	Steny Hoyer (D)	137,903	(69%)	($1,236,900)
	Joseph Crawford (R)	60,758	(31%)	

Prior Winning Percentages: 2000 (65%); 1998 (65%); 1996 (57%); 1994 (59%); 1992 (53%); 1990 (81%); 1988 (79%); 1986 (82%); 1984 (72%); 1982 (80%); 1981 (55%)

The People		Race/Ethnic Origin	Ancestry	
Area size:	1,509 sq. mi.	60.4% White	German: 10.5%	Irish: 9.9%
Urban population:	75.2%	30.0% Black	English: 8.1%	
Rural population:	24.8%	3.7% Asian	**2004 Presidential Vote**	
Pop. 2000:	662,060	0.4% Native Am.	Kerry (D) 177,035	(57%)
Median income:	$62,661	0.0% Hawaiian	Bush (R) 128,861	(42%)
Poverty status:	5.6%	1.9% Two+ races	Other 2,692	(1%)
Military veterans:	15.4%	0.2% Other	**2000 Presidential Vote**	
		3.5% Hispanic Origin	Gore (D) 139,068	(57%)
			Bush (R) 101,056	(41%)
			Other 5,871	(2%)
			Cook Partisan Voting Index: D + 9	

Occupation	Blue collar: 18.8%	White collar: 68.0%	Gray collar: 13.2%

Southern Maryland was first settled by Catholics, the Calvert family of the Lords Baltimore, who founded St. Mary's in 1634, not long after Jamestown and Plymouth Rock. Maryland became one of the two great Chesapeake tobacco colonies, and plantation houses were built on every inlet off the broad Potomac and Patuxent Rivers. For years, none of these towns grew much, and even today many people here are directly descended from the old families. This was never puritanical country: Liquor flowed even during Prohibition and slot machines were specifically allowed for years by Maryland law. But tobacco farming is nearing an end here, even if the area hasn't completely renounced its tobacco heritage: The highlight of the annual Charles County fair remains the crowning of Queen Nicotina. The area's economic base owes much to government installations like the Civil War Point Lookout prisoner-of-war camp and the Navy's Patuxent River complex, where many astronauts got their first training. And now metro Washington and Baltimore are spreading into southern Maryland, with rapid growth in the 1990s in Calvert County south of Annapolis—the fastest growing county in Maryland—and Charles County, south of Prince George's County; it is reaching even further south into St. Mary's County.

The 5th Congressional District of Maryland includes those three counties, plus a large slice of Prince George's—most of the county beyond the Capital Beltway. Its lines were drawn to assure a large black percentage in the adjacent 4th District, but there are also large numbers of blacks in the 5th—30% of the population in 2002—both new suburbanites and descendants of old southern Maryland families. Many of its people live north of Washington, in College Park, home of the University of Maryland, and in Hyattsville, Greenbelt, Beltsville, Laurel and Bowie. The 5th also includes southern Prince George's, from Clinton south, southern Anne Arundel County and all of St. Mary's, Calvert and Charles counties. Historically, this is a Democratic area, but southern Maryland voted heavily for Republican Governor Bob Ehrlich in 2002, and newcomers in fast-growing areas seem to be leaning Republican.

The congressman from the 5th District is Steny Hoyer, a veteran Democrat and minority whip, who was first elected to the House in 1981. Hoyer was elected to the Maryland Senate in 1966, at 27, just after graduating from law school. He was Senate president from 1975–78, the youngest in Maryland history; he made a misstep running for lieutenant governor on a losing ticket in 1978. But in 1981, after incumbent Gladys Spellman went into an irreversible coma, the 5th District, then entirely in Prince George's, was declared vacant. Hoyer won the special election by edging out Spellman's husband and several other Democrats in the primary and beating a well-financed, competent Republican candidate in the general.

Interestingly, Hoyer is of Danish descent, like the original Prince George; his first name, he says, was his parents' adaptation of the Danish name Steen, and the only other Steny he has encountered is a man from Milwaukee whose full first name is Stenerup. He has fine political instincts, works hard and can speak in an old-fashioned patriotic style that is genuinely moving. A fast riser in Maryland politics, he was also a fast riser in Congress. He excelled at constituency service and soon won a seat on the Appropriations Committee, where he became a key player for the whole D.C. metropolitan area. When Democrats had control, Hoyer chaired what used to be the Treasury, Postal Service and General Government Appropriations subcommittee, which oversaw several major components of the federal work force and the White House budget. He has worked for higher pay for federal workers and in 2004 argued that federal workers, with the additional burdens of homeland security, should get the same 3.5% pay raise as military personnel. In 2004 he hailed passage of the Federal Dental and Vision Benefits Enhancement Act.

Hoyer has pushed for funding for Chesapeake Bay cleanup and dredging the Bay for Baltimore harbor. He uses his Appropriations seat to fund programs and to see that local facilities are suited for them. Hoyer has worked indefatigably and shrewdly to maintain and increase jobs at the Goddard Space Flight Center in Greenbelt, at Pax River and the Naval Surface Warfare Center at Indian Head and to build the National Center for Weather and Climate Prediction in College Park. He secured funding for local military bases in anticipation of the next round of base closings scheduled for 2005. "There are significant pressures to reduce infrastructure. We must be vigilant." In March 2004, work began on a $21 million complex to test and develop the Joint Strike Fighter; in July, Hoyer helped deliver $40 million for the Presidential Helicopter Program. Citizens Against Government Waste rated him among the top 10 members in obtaining local projects, such as a $90,000 parking facility for La Plata and $50,000 for the Agricultural Research Service in Beltsville to study the health benefits of barley. When the Pentagon handed down base closing recommendations in May 2005, Hoyer's efforts paid off: Patuxent ended up gaining 87 jobs and Indian Head lost just 95 jobs out of 3,600.

Hoyer's voting record is fairly liberal, though less so than when he represented a near-black-majority district in the late 1980s. He broke with party lines by supporting the balanced budget amendment in 1995, but worked hard in 1996 to support Democratic stands on the minimum wage and health insurance portability; he backed NAFTA, GATT, fast track and normal trade relations with China. He was the chief House sponsor of the Americans with Disabilities Act of 1990; in January 2002, he criticized the Supreme Court for what he considered an overly narrow interpretation of it. In October 2002, he voted to authorize military action in Iraq. Later he said, "I think the execution of the policy has been bad. It alienated our allies." He argued that the administration didn't send enough troops to Iraq and that the United Nations "has shirked its own responsibility." He is a former chairman of the Helsinki commission and has been a champion of human rights around the world.

As ranking minority member on House Administration, he took the lead in October 2001 in hammering out bipartisan election reform legislation; it passed 362–63 in December 2001. Hoyer and Chairman Bob Ney have worked in a bipartisan manner on other issues as well and especially after September 11. On September 11, 2001, it was Hoyer's idea to have rank and file members stand behind the leadership in front of the Capitol in the evening, when members long-locked in partisan battle sang out together, "God Bless America." In a not very bipartisan House, Hoyer works closely with Republicans on Appropriations and has monthly lunches with Majority Whip Roy Blunt. Ney, with whom he has worked remarkably amicably, said, "Steny is well regarded by his colleagues as a fair-minded person. He's always held to his beliefs and party principles, but he's never injected unfair politics into his decisions."

In 1989, Hoyer was elected chairman of the Democratic Caucus, a term-limited position that he left in 1994. When he tried to move up in June 1991, he was beaten for majority whip by David Bonior, who had the support of liberals and committee chairmen, 160–109. He then became chairman of the Democratic Steering Committee and has been Parliamentarian at the 1992, 1996, 2000 and 2004 Democratic National Conventions. During much of 2000 he conducted a campaign for majority whip against Nancy Pelosi, all premised on the notion that Democrats would win control of the House. He ran as the candidate with the more moderate voting record, but that contest was mooted by the 2000 election. But in 2001 Bonior, faced with unfavorable redistricting, began running for governor of Michigan; Hoyer and Pelosi both sought to replace him as minority whip. Hoyer argued that he had greater experience in leadership positions and could do a better job of unifying the caucus; he cited his support from such different members as John Dingell, John Lewis and Charles Stenholm. Pelosi had more publicly committed votes going into the October 2001 caucus—100 versus 77—and she won 118–95 (both did less well than predicted, as often happens in secret ballot leadership races).

Looking ahead, it was plain to Hoyer that there might be another whip contest soon. If Democrats failed to win a majority in November 2002, Dick Gephardt might well resign as minority leader, which is what happened; if they succeeded in winning a majority, Gephardt would have been in line to be Speaker and Pelosi majority leader, leaving the majority whip position open. So Hoyer kept collecting commitments for a race that was likely but not certain to happen. In April 2002 he announced he had 141 pledges of public support from incumbent Democrats; in May he announced he had 19 more. After Gephardt announced his resignation as leader after the November election, Pelosi was easily elected to replace him; Hoyer was unanimously elected minority whip.

As minority whip, it is his job to be partisan, and he often has been. In June 2004, after 11 Democrats voted for the rule to consider the corporate tax bill, Hoyer sent a letter to all House Democrats admonishing them for supporting a procedure that prevented Democrats from offering amendments. This is standard procedure: both House Democrats and House Republicans when they have been in the majority have taken a dim view of members of their party who vote against the leadership's rule.

Since 1997 the two parties have had an ethics truce in which they have promised not to file politically inspired ethics complaints against the other parties' members and particularly leaders. But in early 2004 Hoyer called for consideration of complaints that Tom DeLay or other Republican leaders offered undue inducement to Nick Smith to vote for the Medicare/prescription drug bill in November 2003. Hoyer once again contributed to and campaigned indefatigably for Democratic House candidates in 2004 and issued his own denunciations of the Bush administration. "I think this is the most fiscally irresponsible administration in history. We have undermined our ability to invest in things that have a big payoff." He made it clear that he was willing to raise taxes to finance more government programs. "Unlike John Kerry, I am not prepared to make an absolute pledge" not to raise middle class taxes, he said.

After the 1992 redistricting added southern Maryland counties to his district and subtracted black precincts in Prince George's, Hoyer had some serious Republican competition; he won by only 53%–44% in 1992. But he increased his margins as the decade went on, and his district was the only one in Maryland substantially unchanged by the 2002 redistricting. He won easily in 2002 and 2004, although his margins in fast-growing Calvert County and southern Anne Arundel County were not overwhelming.

SIXTH DISTRICT

Rep. Roscoe Bartlett (R)

Elected 1992, 7th term; b. June 3, 1926, Moreland, KY; home, Frederick; Columbia Union Col., B.A. 1947, U. of MD, M.S. 1949, Ph.D. 1952; Seventh Day Adventist; married (Ellen).

Professional Career: Farmer; Prof., U. of MD, 1948–52; Asst. Prof., Loma Linda Schl. of Medicine, 1952–54; Asst. Prof., Howard U. Medical Schl., 1954–56; Research scientist, N.I.H., 1956–58; Research scientist, U.S. Naval Aerospace Medical Inst., 1958–62; Research scientist, Johns Hopkins U., 1962–67; Research Mgr., IBM, 1967–74; Pres., Roscoe Bartlett & Assoc., 1974–86.

DC Office: 2412 RHOB, 20515, 202-225-2721; Fax: 202-225-2193; Web site: www.bartlett.house.gov.

District Offices: Cumberland, 301-724-3105; Frederick, 301-694-3030; Hagerstown, 301-797-6043; Westminster, 410-857-1115.

Committees: *Armed Services* (7th of 34 R): Projection Forces (Chmn.); Tactical Air & Land Forces. *Science* (7th of 24 R): Energy; Space & Aeronautics. *Small Business* (2d of 18 R): Rural Enterprises, Agriculture & Technology; Workforce, Empowerment & Government Programs.

Group Ratings

	ADA	ACLU	AFS	LCV	ITIC	NTU	COC	ACU	NTLC	CHC
2004	10	15	13	0	70	80	90	92	94	100
2003	20	—	13	30	—	72	90	83	—	—

National Journal Ratings

	2003 LIB	—	2003 CONS		2004 LIB	—	2004 CONS
Economic	39%	—	60%		29%	—	70%
Social	24%	—	71%		39%	—	60%
Foreign	31%	—	65%		39%	—	59%

Key Votes of the 108th Congress

1. Drilling in ANWR	N	5. DC School Vouchers	Y	9. Ban Same-Sex Marriage	Y
2. Approve Bush Tax Cuts	Y	6. Ban Human Cloning	Y	10. Fund Iraq War	Y
3. Medicare/Rx Bill	Y	7. Restrict Gun Liability	Y	11. Bar Cuba Embargo Funds	N
4. Bar Overtime Pay Regs.	N	8. Ban Partial-Birth Abortion	Y	12. Intelligence Reorg.	Y

Election Results

2004 general	Roscoe Bartlett (R)	206,076	(67%)	($436,891)
	Kenneth Bosley (D)	90,108	(29%)	
	Other	9,673	(3%)	
2004 primary	Roscoe Bartlett (R)	31,867	(70%)	
	Scott Rolle (R)	13,481	(30%)	
2002 general	Roscoe Bartlett (R)	147,825	(66%)	($237,991)
	Donald DeArmon (D)	75,575	(34%)	($82,515)

Prior Winning Percentages: 2000 (61%); 1998 (63%); 1996 (57%); 1994 (66%); 1992 (54%)

The People		Race/Ethnic Origin	Ancestry	
Area size:	3,094 sq. mi.	91.5% White	German: 20.1%	Irish: 10.6%
Urban population:	60.5%	4.8% Black	English: 8.4%	
Rural population:	39.5%	1.0% Asian	**2004 Presidential Vote**	
Pop. 2000:	662,060	0.2% Native Am.	Bush (R) 209,764	(65%)
Median income:	$50,957	0.0% Hawaiian	Kerry (D) 110,821	(34%)
Poverty status:	6.7%	0.9% Two+ races	Other 3,635	(1%)
Military veterans:	14.0%	0.1% Other	**2000 Presidential Vote**	
		1.4% Hispanic Origin	Bush (R) 160,263	(61%)
			Gore (D) 95,282	(36%)
			Other 8,029	(3%)
			Cook Partisan Voting Index: R +13	
Occupation	Blue collar: 23.9%	White collar: 61.5%	Gray collar: 14.6%	

One of America's first frontiers was in western Maryland, where the Appalachian ridges that cross the state diagonally from northeast to southwest cut through the long green sloping fields. These wheat fields were settled first by Pennsylvania Dutch and Scots-Irish hill people, not Chesapeake Bay tobacco growers. Maryland is where the fall line comes closest to an ocean port, where the 19th century's great paths to the interior were staked out: The National Road, and then the nation's first railroad, the Baltimore & Ohio, crossed the wide valleys of bounteous farms and climbed over the Catoctin Mountains. Towns grew up on narrow streets lined with row houses that today are overhung with telephone and streetcar wires, overlooking long vistas of cornfields, pastureland and mountains of ancient stone rising above the plains. Across this placid land moved vast armies during the Civil War. In Frederick, city officials paid Confederates $200,000 not to burn down the town, and near Sharpsburg, blue and gray-clad soldiers fought the Battle of Antietam, on the bloodiest day in American military history. A century later, on the steps of City Hall in Cumberland—near the western edge of the district in the coal-laced hills of Appalachia—President Lyndon Johnson declared his War on Poverty. Poverty fell here in the 1970s, but local conditions worsened in the 1980s with the closure of several large factories. Today, there is a new rush of settlement into Carroll County, long part of metro Baltimore, and Frederick County, which is classified as part of metro Washington, both of which have been growing rapidly in recent years.

The 6th Congressional District includes all of western Maryland, runs east through all of Carroll County, takes in a small part of northern Montgomery County and cuts across the northern farmlands and hunt country of Baltimore and Harford Counties all the way to the Susquehanna River. The political tradition in most of this area, unlike the rest of Maryland, is Republican. This was Union country in the Civil War and has been mostly Republican ever since. The new rush of settlement—which made this the fastest growing district in Maryland in the 1990s—is mostly made up of young families of modest incomes seeking respite from metropolitan life, strengthening the area's already conservative leanings. Only eight of 24 counties in Maryland have more registered Republican voters than Democrats, and five of them are in this district.

The congressman from the 6th District is Roscoe Bartlett, a Republican "citizen legislator" first elected in 1992 who matches its current mood. He is an interesting character, a descendant of a signer of the Declaration of Independence and a Seventh Day Adventist with 10 children (he and his wife each have four children from previous marriages); he grew up in poverty in Pennsylvania, but his family would not take welfare. After getting a bachelor's degree in theology and biology, he earned a Ph.D. in physiology at the University of Maryland, where he also taught and wrote more than 100 scientific articles; over the years he has also operated a 145-acre dairy farm, where he still milks his goats. He was awarded 20 patents for inventing life-support equipment for pilots, astronauts and fire fighters, and ran his own business. In 1999, the Aeronautics and Astronautics Institute gave him an award for his career contributions to the advancement of medical knowledge and technologies. When Bartlett was elected to Congress in 1992, he was a 65-year-old retired University of Maryland professor who seemed to have no chance of winning. Democrat Beverly Byron had represented the district for 14 years and had a conservative voting record; when Bartlett challenged her in 1982, he lost 74%–26%. But in 1992 Byron was upset in the primary by a liberal who favored national health insurance and abortion rights. Bartlett's conservative views and his attacks on his opponent's perks in the state legislature won him a 54%–46% victory.

Bartlett has proved a surprisingly durable politician, though iconoclastic to the point of quirky. Profiled in *The Washington Post* as Maryland's Mr. Right, he described a visit to Iraq in 2004 when he visited the spider hole where Saddam Hussein was captured. "I was probably the only Congressman who laid down there. It's very interesting dirt—it doesn't collapse. The water table is at 17 feet throughout most of Iraq." Bartlett is the most conservative member of the state's congressional delegation and he has a consistently conservative voting record. He sometimes objects to Republican big spending, including George W. Bush's education act, but he voted for the 2003 Medicare/prescription drug bill He carries a copy of the Constitution and consults it frequently. He voted against normal trade relations with China and was one of 27 House Republicans to vote against trade promotion authority in 2002. As chairman of the Armed Services Projection Forces Subcommittee, he claimed credit for a study on increasing efficiency in the shipbuilding industry and steps to review potential changes in the Navy fleet. Earlier, Bartlett was gratified by enactment of his bill to end the Pentagon's practice of euthanizing military working dogs at the end of their useful career. His fiscal prudence was reflected in his opposition to expanded federal funds for the local Interstate highway.

Bartlett has been re-elected by solid margins. In 2004 he faced an unusual primary challenge from Frederick County State's Attorney Scott Rolle, who criticized Bartlett for not supporting the Bush administration strongly enough. Bartlett responded by calling out one of the big guns. Before more than 700 loyalists at a breakfast in Hagerstown four days before the vote, Vice President Cheney said, "In this time of testing, the president and I have been grateful to have Congressman Bartlett at our side." Bartlett won 70%–30% and carried Rolle's base of Frederick County 60%–40%.

SEVENTH DISTRICT

Rep. Elijah Cummings (D)

Elected April 1996, 5th full term; b. Jan. 18, 1951, Baltimore; home, Baltimore; Howard U., B.S. 1973, U. of MD, J.D. 1976; Baptist; divorced.

Elected Office: MD House of Delegates, 1982–96, Speaker Pro–Tem, 1995–96.

Professional Career: Practicing atty., 1976–96.

DC Office: 2235 RHOB, 20515, 202-225-4741; Fax: 202-225-3178; Web site: www.house.gov/cummings.

District Office: Baltimore, 410-685-9199.

Committees: *Government Reform* (7th of 17 D): Criminal Justice, Drug Policy & Human Resources (RMM); Federal Workforce & Agency Organization. *Transportation & Infrastructure* (13th of 34 D): Highways, Transit & Pipelines; Railroads. *Joint Economic Committee.*

Group Ratings

	ADA	ACLU	AFS	LCV	ITIC	NTU	COC	ACU	NTLC	CHC
2004	100	82	100	91	20	7	30	0	0	16
2003	90	—	100	90	—	20	25	14	—	—

National Journal Ratings

	2003 LIB	—	2003 CONS		2004 LIB	—	2004 CONS
Economic	77%	—	23%		93%	—	7%
Social	81%	—	19%		78%	—	19%
Foreign	87%	—	13%		90%	—	9%

Key Votes of the 108th Congress

1. Drilling in ANWR	N	5. DC School Vouchers	*	9. Ban Same-Sex Marriage	N
2. Approve Bush Tax Cuts	N	6. Ban Human Cloning	N	10. Fund Iraq War	N
3. Medicare/Rx Bill	N	7. Restrict Gun Liability	N	11. Bar Cuba Embargo Funds	Y
4. Bar Overtime Pay Regs.	Y	8. Ban Partial-Birth Abortion	N	12. Intelligence Reorg.	N

Election Results

2004 general	Elijah Cummings (D)	179,189	(73%)	($877,808)
	Tony Salazar (R)	60,102	(25%)	($109,426)
	Other	4,892	(2%)	
2004 primary	Elijah Cummings (D)	53,015	(91%)	
	Charles McPeek (D)	4,972	(9%)	
2002 general	Elijah Cummings (D)	137,047	(74%)	($466,160)
	Joseph Ward (R)	49,172	(26%)	

Prior Winning Percentages: 2000 (87%); 1998 (86%); 1996 (83%); 1996 (81%)

The People		Race/Ethnic Origin	Ancestry	
Area size:	296 sq. mi.	34.2% White	German: 7.9%	Irish: 6.0%
Urban population:	94.9%	58.8% Black	English: 4.6%	
Rural population:	5.1%	3.5% Asian	**2004 Presidential Vote**	
Pop. 2000:	662,060	0.2% Native Am.	Kerry (D)	192,081 (73%)
Median income:	$38,885	0.0% Hawaiian	Bush (R)	69,545 (26%)
Poverty status:	17.6%	1.3% Two+ races	Other	2,830 (1%)
Military veterans:	12.0%	0.2% Other	**2000 Presidential Vote**	
		1.7% Hispanic Origin	Gore (D)	166,410 (73%)
			Bush (R)	57,262 (25%)
			Other	5,766 (3%)
			Cook Partisan Voting Index: D +25	

Occupation	Blue collar: 16.2%	White collar: 66.7%	Gray collar: 17.1%

At the junction of North and South, terminus of America's first railroad and the East Coast port closest to the great West, Baltimore is one of the few American cities to have had large numbers of both blacks and European immigrants throughout its history. Its black community has a rich and notable history. The *Afro-American* newspaper has been published here for more than 100 years and there was once a black symphony orchestra. Eubie Blake, the famous black musician and one of the founders of ragtime music, grew up here and now has a museum in his honor on Charles Street. Jazz great Billie Holliday was born here; these were the stomping grounds of the great musician Cab Calloway and the great advocate Thurgood Marshall. Near downtown on the west side is the childhood home of Babe Ruth and the home of H.L. Mencken, two great white Baltimoreans. For years this side of town had a biracial, bipartisan politics in which Democrats like Governor Albert Ritchie and Republicans like Mayor and Governor Theodore McKeldin competed zestfully for black and white votes.

Baltimore has been a black majority city since the late 1970s, and most of its west side neighborhoods are heavily black. In the 1990s Baltimore had a terrible crime wave, with open drug markets on both the west and east sides. Mayor Martin O'Malley, elected in 1999, has taken a different approach as mayor, promising to build "a new Baltimore" with "zero tolerance" of crime; with his enthusiasm and photogenic family, plus encouragement from some party operatives, he quickly attracted national attention.

Maryland's 7th Congressional District includes most of Baltimore's black neighborhoods, reaches into the heavily black suburbs running west from the city, to Catonsville along the old Baltimore National Pike, and also extends west to include most of suburban Howard County. Democratic redistricters added Howard County in 2002 (and removed some black Baltimore neighborhoods) to strengthen Democrats' chances of capturing the mostly suburban 2d District (which they did). Redistricting reduced the black population of the district from 75% to 59%; essentially, Democratic redistricters decided to reduce the number of blacks and substitute the Baltimore suburbanites least inclined to resent an inner city voting record. About 40% of the district's votes are cast in Baltimore city's precincts, largely north of Pratt Street, in places like Druid Heights, Charles Village (home to Johns Hopkins University), Harlem Park and poverty-stricken Sandtown-Winchester. Howard County is quite a different area: It grew 32% in the 1990s and its largest community, Columbia, has been called a planned town, though it differs from most other Baltimore suburbs by attracting a culturally liberal population. It tends to vote Democratic, but not overwhelmingly, and in 2004 cast 37% of the district's votes. There is a sharp socioeconomic contrast between these two parts of the district: In Howard County, 32% of families earned more than $100,000 in 2000 and 4% of children under five were in poverty status; in Baltimore City, only 6% earned more than $100,000 and 32% of children were poor.

The congressman from the 7th District is Elijah Cummings, who won a 1996 special election after Kweisi Mfume resigned to become president of the NAACP. Cummings grew up in Baltimore, graduated from Howard University and the University of Maryland law school, practiced law in Baltimore, and in 1982, at 31, was elected to the Maryland House of Delegates. Two years later he was chairman of the Legislative Caucus, the youngest in its history, and he became known as a consensus builder. Cummings's main competition came from the Reverend Frank Reid III, stepbrother of Mayor Kurt Schmoke, who raised $255,000. Cummings had support from community development organizations and from businessmen and lobbyists. He raised $450,000, and won 37% of the vote to 24% for Reid. He has not been seriously challenged in a primary or general since then.

Cummings still lives in troubled west Baltimore, where urban realities have made him a crusader against drug abuse and a death-penalty foe; he favors strict gun control. His voting record is very liberal, usually the most liberal in the delegation; he was the only Marylander to oppose the 1996 welfare act. On the Government Reform Committee he has been ranking Democrat on the Criminal Justice subcommittee, where he also tends to the interests of his many federal employees.

Cummings was chairman of the Congressional Black Caucus in 2003 and 2004. He spoke out on issues ranging from a presidential succession crisis in Haiti to the ouster of Trent Lott as Senate majority leader and the appointment of federal judges. He endorsed Howard Dean in

December 2003; he later enthusiastically endorsed the Kerry-Edwards ticket. Redistricting contributed to a reduction in Cummings's winning percentage in 2002 and 2004 but he still won by landslide margins. In both years he carried Howard County only narrowly, but won more than 90% of the votes in Baltimore City.

EIGHTH DISTRICT

Rep. Chris Van Hollen (D)

Elected 2002, 2d term; b. Jan. 10, 1959, Karachi, Pakistan; home, Kensington; Swarthmore Col., B.A. 1982, Harvard U., M.P.P. 1985, Georgetown U., J.D. 1990; Protestant; married (Katherine).

Elected Office: MD House of Delegates, 1990–94; MD Senate, 1994–2002.

DC Office: 1419 LHOB, 20515, 202-225-5341; Fax: 202-225-0375; Web site: www.house.gov/vanhollen.

District Offices: Mount Rainier, 301-927-5223; Rockville, 301-424-3501.

Committees: *Education & the Workforce* (19th of 22 D): 21st Century Competitiveness; Select Education. *Government Reform* (13th of 17 D): Federal Workforce & Agency Organization; National Security, Emerging Threats & International Relations; Regulatory Affairs. *Judiciary* (17th of 17 D): Commercial & Administrative Law; The Constitution.

Group Ratings

	ADA	ACLU	AFS	LCV	ITIC	NTU	COC	ACU	NTLC	CHC
2004	100	85	100	100	60	11	38	4	3	8
2003	95	—	100	100	—	22	33	12	—	—

National Journal Ratings

	2003 LIB	—	2003 CONS		2004 LIB	—	2004 CONS
Economic	87%	—	9%		82%	—	17%
Social	90%	—	8%		84%	—	15%
Foreign	66%	—	32%		81%	—	18%

Key Votes of the 108th Congress

1. Drilling in ANWR	N	5. DC School Vouchers	N	9. Ban Same-Sex Marriage	N
2. Approve Bush Tax Cuts	N	6. Ban Human Cloning	N	10. Fund Iraq War	N
3. Medicare/Rx Bill	N	7. Restrict Gun Liability	N	11. Bar Cuba Embargo Funds	Y
4. Bar Overtime Pay Regs.	Y	8. Ban Partial-Birth Abortion	N	12. Intelligence Reorg.	N

Election Results

2004 general	Chris Van Hollen (D)	215,129	(75%)	($1,235,488)
	Chuck Floyd (R)	71,989	(25%)	($352,644)
	Other	562	(0%)	
2004 primary	Chris Van Hollen (D)	67,805	(91%)	
	Deborah Vollmer (D)	4,847	(7%)	
	Other	1,701	(2%)	
2002 general	Chris Van Hollen (D)	112,788	(52%)	($2,985,329)
	Constance Morella (R)	103,587	(47%)	($2,996,119)

The People		Race/Ethnic Origin	Ancestry		
Area size:	307 sq. mi.	56.1% White	German: 8.2% Irish: 7.9%		
Urban population:	98.8%	16.4% Black	English: 6.6%		
Rural population:	1.2%	10.9% Asian	**2004 Presidential Vote**		
Pop. 2000:	662,060	0.2% Native Am.	Kerry (D)	205,660	(69%)
Median income:	$68,306	0.0% Hawaiian	Bush (R)	90,108	(30%)
Poverty status:	6.2%	2.4% Two+ races	Other	3,196	(1%)
Military veterans:	9.6%	0.3% Other	**2000 Presidential Vote**		
		13.7% Hispanic Origin	Gore (D)	177,475	(66%)
			Bush (R)	84,088	(31%)
			Other	9,382	(3%)
			Cook Partisan Voting Index: D +20		

Occupation	Blue collar: 10.6%	White collar: 77.1%	Gray collar: 12.3%

Along an old road, down which colonial farmers rolled barrels of tobacco to the port of Georgetown 200 years ago, has grown one of America's most affluent and best-educated communities. The old road, now called Wisconsin Avenue and Rockville Pike, is the commercial spine of Montgomery County, Maryland. And this suburban jurisdiction just northwest of Washington, D.C., has for several decades ranked at or near the top counties in income and education. Today's Montgomery County is in large part a creation of the federal government, which has placed huge facilities there—Bethesda Naval Hospital, the National Institutes of Health, the Food and Drug Administration, the National Institute of Standards and Technology—and it has become the center of America's biotech industry, the home of firms like Celera and Human Genome Sciences which, in parallel with the Human Genome Project, are pioneering the study of the human gene. Some of the federal labs have gained high-security classification because of their research on bio-hazards and infectious diseases in the war on terrorism. Montgomery County has also become racially diverse: in 2000, it was 15% black, 12% Hispanic and 11% Asian.

Wisconsin Avenue and Rockville Pike have become strip highways, with 1950s commercial development and 1960s shopping centers like so many in the country. But the stores are upscale, some *very* upscale, and the new skyscrapers of downtown Bethesda are genuinely impressive. Author David Brooks mocked Bethesdans as "urban exiles" who frequent "anti-chain chain stores . . . that cater to people who consider themselves too refined and individualistic to shop at the mall or the mass-market big-box stores." Not all of Montgomery County is exclusively high-income: There are some modest neighborhoods in Silver Spring and Wheaton, and one of the nation's largest Asian populations—some, hard-working store owners; others, educated professionals with high incomes. Historically, the typical Montgomery County voter was a high-ranking civil servant. "A candidate knocking on doors in the 8th District can reasonably expect to be questioned about a government regulation by the person who wrote it," explained *The Washington Post*. As growing private-sector employment outpaces government work, the picture has changed. The growth here is in the private sector, and in the fastest-growing parts of the county, out the I-270 corridor past Rockville in Gaithersburg and Germantown.

The 8th Congressional District of Maryland includes most of the heavily populated parts of Montgomery County, which accounts for more than 90% of the population. Democratic redistricters in 2002 removed to the 4th District much of the eastern part of the county, and added a slice of heavily Democratic territory in Prince George's County. Perhaps its most unique precinct is Leisure World in Silver Spring, whose 6,000-plus senior citizens have one of Maryland's largest, most partisan and highest voter turnouts; Democratic candidates practically camp out there during primaries. Democrats drew these lines with the avowed purpose of defeating Republican Congresswoman Connie Morella, who was first elected in 1986.

The congressman from the 8th District is Chris Van Hollen, first elected in 2002 in one of the nation's most competitive congressional races. The son of a Foreign Service officer, Van Hollen was born in Pakistan, graduated from Swarthmore, got a master's from Harvard and a law degree from Georgetown University. He worked on the staff of the Senate Foreign Relations Committee in the late 1980s, and he co-authored a report on Iraq's use of chemical weapons. In

1990 he was elected to the House of Delegates and in 1994 to the state Senate, where he helped win the largest education funding increase for Montgomery County in its history. Wonky and telegenic, Van Hollen's legislative accomplishments earned him the moniker, "Mr. Fix-It" from the *Washington Post.*

The 2002 race attracted strong Democratic candidates: Van Hollen; Delegate Mark Shriver, a state representative and Kennedy cousin, who gained extensive labor support; and Ira Shapiro, a former Clinton administration trade official who stressed his familiarity with federal policy issues as a senior Senate aide. Bolstered by a crucial endorsement from the *Post*, Van Hollen defeated Shriver, 43%–41%, with 13% for Shapiro. Van Hollen had only eight weeks to take on Morella, who was widely viewed as hard working, cooperative with colleagues, congenial with constituents, and with a liberal voting record that was largely out of step with the Republican-controlled House. Morella once again proved her independence from her party by voting against military force in Iraq and by becoming the lead House sponsor of the amendment, opposed by the Bush administration, insisting on strict civil service protections for Department of Homeland Security employees. Van Hollen refrained from directly attacking Morella, but argued that her vote to organize the House with Republicans kept in power a conservative leadership out of line with the views of most district voters: She was an enabler of the Republican majority. Morella criticized Van Hollen's record in Annapolis, including his decision to quit a Senate subcommittee over proposed budget cuts. *The Washington Post* and the Baltimore *Sun* endorsed Morella, but it wasn't enough. In a race in which the two candidates together spent nearly $6 million, Van Hollen won 52%–47%. Nearly half of his popular vote margin came in the small sliver of the district in Prince George's (which is 55% black), which he carried 78%–21%. If the contest had been held in the old district, Morella clearly would have won, and probably by a wider margin than in 2000.

In the House, Van Hollen has been an activist liberal on most issues, though a bit less so on foreign policy. Although he had few opportunities for influence as a junior member of the minority party, Van Hollen scored an unexpected victory when he got the House—including 26 Republicans, some of them conservatives—to approve his amendment to limit a Republican plan to outsource more federal jobs. Despite that vote, the Bush Administration eventually got its way. With what *The New Republic* termed his "eager industriousness," Van Hollen has attacked the parliamentary restraints that Republicans impose on the minority party; his efforts have won him some favorable press notices, but minimal response from the majority.

In 2004 Van Hollen was reelected 75%–25% in what now is clearly a safe Democratic district. He is among the many Democrats in the Maryland delegation interested in running for a Senate seat when one comes open; that opportunity presented itself when Senator Paul Sarbanes announced in March 2005 that he would not run for a sixth term. Congressman Ben Cardin announced he was running in April but Van Hollen hedged his bets and by mid-2005 was still exploring a run.

★ MASSACHUSETTS ★

It would be a city on a hill, John Winthrop wrote of the Massachusetts Bay colony his Puritans were building, an example to the entire world. And Massachusetts, in the nearly four centuries since, has always assumed it has a lot to teach others. The New World Puritans' austere creed taught that only the select would be saved and that they must extirpate the forces of Satan—Indians, Papists, tolerationists. For 150 years, New England was partial to learning, but also insular, hostile to outsiders and economically stagnant. Then, after the American Revolution, the international war between royal Britain and revolutionary and Napoleonic France allowed New England ship owners to cross enemy lines to become the world's leading merchants. They made vast profits and invested the money in textile mills, then railroads, then coal mines and steel mills, providing much of the capital that made industrial America.

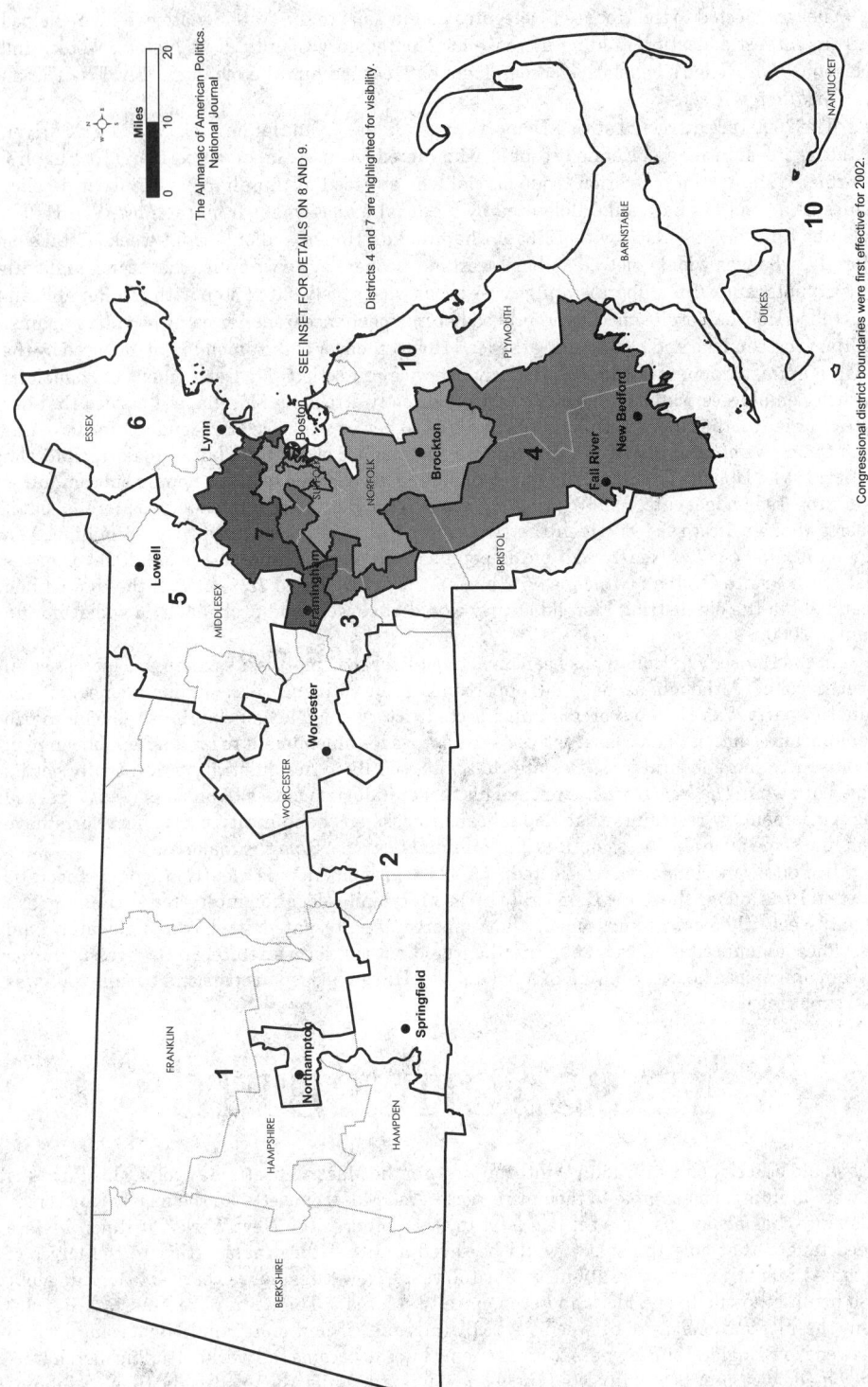

The Almanac of American Politics.
National Journal

SEE INSET FOR DETAILS ON 8 AND 9.

Districts 4 and 7 are highlighted for visibility.

Congressional district boundaries were first effective for 2002.

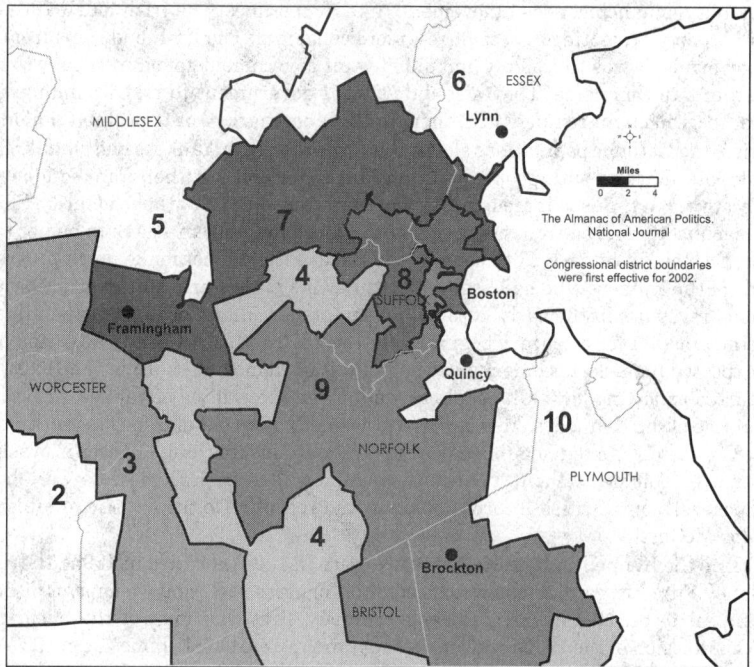

Massachusetts made a new America in other ways. Intellectually, New England flowered in the 19th century: Writers from Boston, Cambridge and Concord—Ralph Waldo Emerson, Henry Wadsworth Longfellow, Henry David Thoreau, John Greenleaf Whittier, Nathaniel Hawthorne—created an American literature and popularized an American philosophy, more than 200 years after Plymouth Rock. Demographically, New England Yankees surged across the continent: Long blocked from Upstate New York by mountains and the British-Iroquois alliance, they only reached Syracuse in the 1820s. By the 1850s, they were in Iowa and Kansas and Oregon's Willamette Valley, and by the 1870s, in Los Angeles. They helped start the Republican Party and did much to start—and win—the Civil War. They planted their economic system and their values, articulated in the *McGuffey Readers*, across the continent.

In the meantime, Massachusetts itself and Boston, the hub of the universe, were being remade. The potato famine of the 1840s and an economy that continued imploding for decades sent Irish immigrants across the Atlantic, and many came to Boston, looking for work in the mills, docks and factories. Yankee Protestants had seen Catholics as their great political and cultural enemy since the 17th century; they felt their commonwealth was under siege. As Catholics became a majority, first in Boston and then statewide, Protestants feared the Irish would use their political clout to ladle out government jobs and benefits to their own — and the Irish had a much better flair for politics than instinct for commerce. But they encountered such bigotry and rejection by the Yankees that even as successful an Irish Catholic as Joseph Kennedy felt obliged to move from Boston to New York in 1927. Politics in Massachusetts for years was a kind of culture war between Yankee Republicans and Irish Democrats, an argument not so much over the distribution of income or the provision of services as over whose vision of Massachusetts should be honored, and whose version of history should be taught—not unlike battles being fought between cultural liberals and conservatives today.

Sometimes, the stakes were concrete—control of patronage jobs, command of the Boston Police Department—but more often they were symbolic. Yankee Republicans tended to back activist government programs: Public works and protective tariffs to help business, the Civil War and Reconstruction to help suitably distant oppressed people like Southern blacks, uplifting (and productivity-enhancing) social movements like temperance. The Irish found 19th century Democrats—a party promoting *laissez-faire*—more congenial. The Irish had come from a place where the government was the enemy and didn't want government spending money to help the rich or to stimulate commerce. They also didn't want government to restrict immigration, to advance blacks (who might compete with them in the labor market) or to prohibit liquor.

The Irish and Catholic populations slowly rose over the years. Yankees had smaller families, moved west, intermarried with people of immigrant stock and lost their Yankee identity. The Irish mostly stayed put, raised large families and maintained their Catholic identity. Slowly but surely Massachusetts moved from being one of the most Republican states to one of the most Democratic. Economically, early 20th century Massachusetts did not make much progress. The descendants of the Yankees who had been so venturesome in the early 19th century became the most cautious investors in the early 20th, while the predominance of the textile mills in their home state meant that for a century beginning in the 1820s, Massachusetts imported low-skill labor and exported high-skill people. As textile mills started moving south in the 1920s, Massachusetts started exporting low-skill people as well. From the waning of Yankee authority until the national rise of the Kennedys, Massachusetts seemed to run out of things to teach the rest of the nation. The state's Yankee Republicans were backward looking, out of power in Washington, on the defensive at home, without a cause to champion. The Irish Democrats were hostile to Franklin Roosevelt's pro-British internationalism and receptive to the anti-Communism of the very Irish Joe McCarthy.

Then came the Kennedys. Rose Kennedy was born in 1890 (and died in 1995), the daughter of John "Honey Fitz" Fitzgerald, who was elected to Congress at 31 and was mayor of Boston in 1906–07 and 1910–14. Her husband Joseph Kennedy, first chairman of the Securities and Exchange Commission in the 1930s and ambassador to the Court of St. James from 1937–40, was perhaps the richest Catholic in the world and a shrewd and ruthless political operator. Their only residence in Massachusetts after 1927 was their summer home in Hyannis Port. In 1946 Joseph Kennedy moved his oldest surviving son, John, to Boston, and engineered his election to the House that year, to the Senate in 1952 and to the presidency in 1960. The Kennedys, with their elegant manners and great achievements, seemed like royalty to the Irish Catholics of Massachusetts, and John Kennedy's election in 1960 certified to U.S. Catholics, 78% of whom voted for him, that they too were Americans. Joseph and John Kennedy were, on many issues, conservative or skeptical. But Kennedy's administration was increasingly, even before his untimely death, identified as liberal, and his example and that of his brother, Edward, elected to the U.S. Senate in 1962, moved Massachusetts Catholics to the left. At the same time, Massachusetts Protestants were influenced by the leftward direction on the state's great campuses in the 1960s. The universities also provided the basis for a surging high-tech economy, to the point that Massachusetts started importing high-skill people even as it exported those with low skills.

In the 1970s and 1980s, Massachusetts, with one interval, had the most liberal governance and national politics of any state in the country. Massachusetts was the only state to vote for George McGovern in 1972 and, although it voted twice for Ronald Reagan, the son of an Irish Catholic, its Democratic percentage in presidential contests from 1968–88 was 53%, just 0.4% behind Rhode Island and well ahead of every other state. The state's senators included Edward Kennedy, liberal Republican Edward Brooke, and Democrats Paul Tsongas and John Kerry. Liberal governors such as Republican Francis Sargent and Democrat Michael Dukakis vastly increased spending and endorsed inexplicable policies that helped sink Dukakis's 1988 presidential campaign, notably the law that granted weekend furloughs to prisoners sentenced to life without parole. As historian David Hackett Fischer points out in *Albion's Seed*, the mindset of the original settlers remains strong even when the ethnic origin of current residents is far different, and the spirit of the Puritans, the faith that they had much to teach the rest of the world, is strong in Massachusetts liberals: In both the smug liberalism of Michael Dukakis, the hearty liberalism of Edward Kennedy and the combative liberalism of John Kerry.

Then, in the early 1990s, Massachusetts had a momentary political revolution. The 1980s "Massachusetts miracle" had turned into a nightmare, as the state's economy sagged badly, as the defense cutbacks long sought by Massachusetts politicians sent unemployment rising and high-tech firms like Wang and Digital withered and Cambridge-based Lotus's software was eclipsed by Redmond, Washington-based Microsoft's. The Northeast real estate bubble burst and Massachusetts banks foundered. The state government essentially went bankrupt. In 1990, as Dukakis retired, voters embraced big tax cuts and elected Republican William Weld in his place.

Republicans have held the governorship ever since. Weld favored a government that taxes and spends lightly, that is friendly to feminism and gay rights, that exerts some effort to protect the environment and that is tough on crime. Referenda limiting taxes and Weld's sharp spending cuts reduced the burden of government, and the state's private economy began recovering. Weld, who was reelected with 71% of the vote in 1994, has left the state, but his policies have prevailed under his successors—Paul Cellucci, who took office in 1997 when Weld resigned, Jane Swift, who took office in 2001 when Cellucci resigned, and Mitt Romney, who was elected in 2002.

Weld's cultural liberalism has also prevailed. Weld was one of America's first politicians to endorse gay rights, and he appointed Supreme Judicial Court Chief Justice Margaret Marshall, who pushed through the 4–3 decisions in November 2003 requiring the legislature to give equal marriage rights to gays and then, when the legislature declined, in May 2004 declaring that same-sex couples have the right to marry. Romney opposed the decision, and House Speaker Thomas Finneran pushed the legislature, acting in joint session in March 2004, to vote 105–92 to send to the voters a constitutional amendment banning same-sex marriage and endorsing civil unions. But under the Massachusetts Constitution, the legislature must act twice, and the ballot measures cannot come to the voters before 2006. There was an initial rush of same-sex couples to clerk's offices, though not out-of-state couples, barred from marrying in Massachusetts by a 1913 law; there were some 2,500 same-sex marriages the week after the court's decision and in the next six months only 1,700. (In heavily gay Provincetown and heavily lesbian Northampton same-sex marriages outnumbered opposite-sex marriages during that period.) In Democratic primaries and in the general election, opponents of same-sex marriage fared poorly, while Speaker Finneran was ousted by Salvatore DiMasi, a same-sex marriage backer from the once heavily Italian and now gentrified North End of Boston. By mid-2005 the legislature had not reaffirmed the amendments it passed in 2004. In June 2005, Romney announced he would support a proposed constitutional amendment in the form of a citizen's initiative, which would ban same-sex marriage without creating civil unions; the earliest it could end up on the ballot would be 2008. The issue should be decided with a "clean, straightforward, unambiguous amendment," he said.

In national politics Massachusetts has remained overwhelmingly Democratic. The state voted 62%–37% for its own John Kerry in 2004. George W. Bush topped 40% only in Plymouth County and Cape Cod, and the northeast Boston suburbs in Essex County. He lost by more than 2–1 in Boston, western Massachusetts north and west of Springfield and Martha's Vineyard. Massachusetts eliminated the last Republicans from its congressional delegation in 1996 and has voted for veto-proof Democratic majorities in the legislature ever since.

The People		Race/Ethnic Origin			Military veterans: 558,933 (11.5%)	
Pop. 2004 (est):	6,416,505	5,198,359	81.9%	White	WWII: 25.7%	Korea: 15.7%
Pop. 2000:	6,349,097	318,329	5.0%	Black	Vietnam: 28.4%	Gulf War: 6.6%
Pop. 1990:	6,016,425	236,786	3.7%	Asian	**Most populous cities (2003):**	
Change 1990–2000:	Up 5.5%	11,264	0.2%	Native Am.	1. Boston	581,616
% of U.S. total:	2.3%	1,706	0.0%	Hawaiian	2. Worcester	175,706
Pop. rank:	13th of 50	110,338	1.7%	Two+ races	3. Springfield	152,157
Area size:	10,555 sq. mi.	43,586	0.7%	Other	4. Lowell	104,351
State Native:	66.1%	428,729	6.8%	Hisp. Origin	5. Cambridge	101,587
Non-citizen:	6.9%	**Ancestry**				
Language		Irish: 16.8%		Italian: 10.1%	Urban population: 91.4%	
English: 78.8%	Other Eur.:11.4%	English: 8.5%		French: 6.0%	Rural population: 8.6%	
Spanish: 6.3%		German: 4.4%				

Education		Work Sector		General Court	
H.S. Grad:	84.8%	Private: 80.0%	Govt: 13.5%	Senate	34 D 6 R
College Grad:	33.2%	Self: 6.4%	Family: 0.2%	House	139 D 20 R 1 I
Industry		Unemployment: 4.6%		Legislative Term Limits: No	
Agri: 0.4%	Con: 5.5%	**Household Income**		**Registered Voters**	
Fin: 8.2%	Info: 3.7%	<15k: 14.4%	15-35k: 20.5%	D: 1,526,711	(37.3%)
Mfg: 17.0%	Prof: 35.3%	35-50k: 14.5%	50-100k: 32.9%	R: 532,319	(13.0%)
Public: 4.3%	Trade: 14.4%	100-150k: 10.9%	>150k: 6.8%	O: 2,039,604	(49.8%)
Other: 11.2%		Median: $50,502			
Occupation		Poverty status: 9.3%			
Blue collar: 18.7%	White collar: 67.0%	**Home Value**			
Gray collar: 14.3%		<50k: 1.5%	50-100k: 10.2%	100-200k: 45.1%	200-300k: 23.6%
		300-500k: 14.0%	>500k: 5.6%	Median: $182,800	

Presidential politics   Over the last ten presidential elections, Massachusetts has been the most Democratic state, giving Democratic nominees an average margin of 55%–38%. It was Bill Clinton's best state in 1996, Al Gore's second best in 2000 and, not surprisingly, John Kerry's best in 2004. What is also striking about Massachusetts is how many serious presidential candidates it has produced over the last quarter century: Edward Kennedy in 1980, Michael Dukakis in 1988, Paul Tsongas in 1992, John Kerry in 2004; another might be Mitt Romney in 2008. Only California and Texas have produced more serious candidates over the 1980–2004 period, but they are the number one and two states in population and Massachusetts is number 13. Some credit must be given to the fact that the first primary is in New Hampshire, just north of Massachusetts and most of it picking up Boston TV; but even more credit must go to the hyperpolitical culture of Boston. Only Chicago seems as preoccupied by its local political figures, but Boston also believes that they are capable of national leadership. Boston political hangers on and operatives were thick on the ground in New Hampshire in early 2004.

2004 Presidential Vote		
Kerry (D)	1,803,800	(62%)
Bush (R)	1,071,109	(37%)
Badnarik (Lib)	15,022	(1%)
Other	22,457	(1%)

2004 Democratic Presidential Primary		
Kerry (D)	440,964	(72%)
Edwards (D)	108,051	(18%)
Kucinich (D)	25,198	(4%)
Dean (D)	17,076	(3%)
Sharpton (D)	6,123	(1%)
Other	17,776	(3%)

2000 Presidential Vote		
Gore (D)	1,616,487	(60%)
Bush (R)	878,502	(33%)
Nader (Green)	173,564	(6%)
Other	32,389	(1%)

Massachusetts's presidential primary has long been held in early March and was once the scene of great commotion. It produced victories for native sons like Dukakis, Tsongas and Kerry (though at one point in late 2003 Kerry trailed Howard Dean in Massachusetts primary polls). In 2000, it voted solidly for Al Gore and John McCain, as many independents reregistered as Republicans. Candidates contesting New Hampshire always buy time on Boston TV stations, which reach much of the Granite State (most of the cost of which does not have to be charged against the low limit on spending in New Hampshire), and so their ads are widely seen in Massachusetts. But they don't usually bother campaigning here.

Congressional districting   Massachusetts's convoluted congressional district lines deserve their own biographer, someone with a sure political instinct and a touch of whimsy. This is, after all, the state whose Governor Elbridge Gerry gave name to the term "gerrymander" in the early 19th century. The state lost one seat in the 1980 and 1990 Censuses; it survived the 2000 Census without losing another. The redistricting process was a ruckus nonetheless.

109th Congress Lineup
10 D

108th Congress Lineup
10 D

Many legislators wanted simply to protect all 10 incumbents, but that was hard to do because the districts were already mind-bogglingly convoluted. In July 2001, House Speaker Thomas Finneran advanced a plan to smooth out the district lines and create a district that would unite southeastern Massachusetts—the congressmen who represent the area live in Boston and next-door Newton and Quincy and far off Worcester—and a Boston-based district with large percentages of blacks and Hispanics and to eliminate the district of Martin Meehan, who was contemplating running for governor. But other politicians complained loudly and Meehan opted out of the race for governor; state senators, helped by senior incumbent Edward Markey, came up with a plan to protect incumbents. Republican Governor Jane Swift came up with her own plan, which of course didn't pass in the heavily Democratic statehouse. In January 2002, both houses agreed on an incumbent protection plan and passed it over Swift's veto.

Governor

Mitt Romney (R)

Elected 2002, term expires Jan. 2007, 1st term; b. March 12, 1947, Detroit, MI; home, Belmont; Brigham Young U., B.A. 1971, Harvard U. M.B.A., J.D. 1975; Mormon; married (Ann).

Professional Career: V.P., Bain & Co., 1978–84, 1990–92; Founder, Bain Capital, 1984–90, 1992–99; CEO, Salt Lake Organizing Cmte. (2002 Winter Olympics), 1999–2002.

Office: State House, Rm. 360, Boston, 02133, 617-725-4005; Fax: 617-727-9725; Web site: www.mass.gov/gov.

Election Results

2002 general	Mitt Romney (R)	1,091,988	(50%)
	Shannon O'Brien (D)	985,981	(45%)
	Jill Stein (Green)	76,530	(4%)
	Other	38,379	(2%)
2002 primary	Mitt Romney (R)	unopposed	
1998 general	Paul Cellucci (R)	967,160	(51%)
	Scott Harshbarger (D)	901,843	(47%)
	Other	34,333	(2%)

Mitt Romney, elected governor of Massachusetts in 2002, is the son of George Romney, who was governor of Michigan from 1963 to 1969. The younger Romney grew up in Bloomfield Hills, Michigan, when his father was CEO of American Motors before he embarked on a political career. A devout Mormon, Mitt Romney graduated from Brigham Young University at a time when it was not beset by turmoil as so many other campuses were, and from Harvard Law School and Harvard Business School in 1975, where he overlapped with George W. Bush. Unlike Bush, who was eager to return to his home state, Romney stayed in the Boston area and became vice president of Bain & Company, a management consultant firm. In 1984, he founded Bain Capital, an investment company that provided crucial capital to Staples, Domino's Pizza and Brookstone; he had a considerable ownership stake in some of these companies. In 1990, he returned to Bain & Company as interim CEO and got it out of financial difficulties. In the process, he accumulated a considerable fortune and was active in civic and charitable affairs; for four years he was president of his stake in the Mormon Church—the rough equivalent of bishop. In 1994, he was the Republican nominee against Senator Edward Kennedy, and succeeded in giving him a good scare before losing 58%–41%—Kennedy's closest race since he was first elected in 1962. In February 1999, he was asked to head the Salt Lake City Winter Olympics Organizing Committee, which was in deficit and suffering from charges of misconduct. Romney erased a $379 million deficit, rallied 23,000 volunteers and ran an effective security operation at the February 2002

Winter Games; 87% of Utahns rated his performance positively. He recounted his experiences in his book *Turnaround: Crisis, Leadership and the Olympic Games*, published in August 2004, in time for the Republican National Convention.

After the Olympics, Romney immediately began talking about running for governor of Massachusetts. This was a dicey business: In fall 2001, he had said he wouldn't run, and in October 2001, Republican Governor Jane Swift announced she would. Swift had been elected lieutenant governor in 1998 and became governor in April 2001, when Paul Cellucci resigned to become ambassador to Canada. She took office at 36, pregnant with twins, and quickly aroused controversy. After budget struggles with the legislature, she had exceedingly low job ratings. On March 19, she abruptly left the governor's race; three hours later, Romney announced his candidacy. Financing was no problem: He ultimately spent $6.1 million of his own money and had fundraising help from the Bush White House. He ran as an outsider, a professional manager who wasn't part of the Beacon Hill crowd; in some public appearances he made PowerPoint presentations rather than standard speeches. He said he was against tax increases, but declined to rule them out. He supported aid to faith-based institutions. He worked at various jobs over the summer, riding a garbage truck and cleaning fish.

The Democratic nominee was state Treasurer Shannon O'Brien, who won the mid-September primary with 33% of the vote. O'Brien, with just six weeks for the general election campaign, argued that Romney was out of place in Massachusetts and was trying to "mask a very conservative set of belief systems." Although she said she wouldn't criticize his religion, she criticized him for making major contributions to Brigham Young, which bars expressions of homosexuality. Democrats circulated a news story that Romney, at a church meeting, had called homosexuality "perverse"; he denied using the word but said he opposed all extramarital sex. O'Brien herself came out in favor of same-sex marriage, though she added that she thought the legislature would never vote for it. O'Brien attacked Romney aggressively in debates, and when he referred to her style as "unbecoming," he was accused of being insensitive to women.

Such attitudes may be obligatory at gatherings of Democratic activists, but they evidently did not go over so well with voters in the broad swathes of suburban Massachusetts and in heavily Democratic central cities as well. Romney won 50%–45%, carrying the belt between Route 128 and Interstate 495 by wide margins and holding O'Brien to very small margins in working class towns like Quincy, Worcester, Lynn, Brockton and Lowell. O'Brien's core areas— Boston and the cities immediately adjacent, the New Bedford-Fall River area and the Pioneer Valley and the Berkshires in western Massachusetts—were not enough to produce a statewide majority.

In his first two years in office, facing an overwhelmingly Democratic legislature, Romney closed a budget gap and avoided a tax increase. He succeeded in eliminating the Metropolitan District Commission but not in merging the Turnpike Authority and the Highway Department; the legislature made the head of the Transportation Department the head of the Turnpike Authority. He reorganized the human services bureaucracy and fired University of Massachusetts President William Bulger. He proposed $8 billion in bonds to clear the school building project waiting list; the legislature applied sales tax funds to this and authorized $1 billion in bonds. Housing prices are high in Massachusetts, and Romney approved substantial funding to build thousands of new housing units, especially in downtown areas. Legislators were miffed when he insisted that all communications with appointees go through the governor's office and when Romney declined to give legislators permanent authority to create new committees with pay increases for chairmen. With his business background, Romney was less inclined than his predecessors to make deals with the legislature and seemed to relish conflict. "I ran on the platform of cleaning up the mess on Beacon Hill, [and] reform means changing the way things are. Legislatures by and large, despite the political titles, are conservative. They don't want to change the way things work. So of course it is going to be a battle."

Romney opposed the Supreme Judicial Court's November 2003 and May 2004 decisions mandating same-sex marriage. He said that he supported some kind of civil union arrangement and supported the constitutional amendment backed by the joint legislative session in March 2004. On other cultural issues, he supported capital punishment, favored stem-cell research (his wife was diagnosed with multiple sclerosis in 1998 and after treatment was in remission) and, though anti-abortion, said he would leave the status quo alone. He has pressed for a no-frills basic health insurance plan to reduce the number of uninsured, plus tightened standards for medical malpractice cases.

In heavily Democratic Massachusetts Romney has not hesitated to be a strong Republican partisan; Democratic legislators in response passed over Romney's veto a bill depriving governors of the power to fill a vacancy in the Senate. He campaigned against John Kerry, contrasting him with his colleague Edward Kennedy ("Senator Kennedy is a workhorse," he told *National Journal*) and arguing that Kerry would be "a most unfortunate person to have as president of the United States." Kerry, he said, "has interest groups that he is close to that have strong views on issues, sometimes differing views on issues, and he tries to blend a course between those differing, his own views, views of interest groups, that he's a very conflicted person." Romney actively recruited Republican candidates for seats in the legislature and financed radio and TV ads on issues like tuition for children of illegal immigrants. But these efforts proved a flop: Democrats picked up two seats in the state House and one in the state Senate.

Romney comes up for reelection in 2006. Likely Democratic candidates include Secretary of State William Galvin, Attorney General Thomas Reilly and former Assistant Attorney General Deval Patrick, who served in the Clinton administration. Another possible candidate is Chris Gabrieli, who ran for lieutenant governor in 2002. Romney has often been mentioned as a possible presidential candidate in 2008. He campaigned actively for George W. Bush in 2004 and is scheduled to become chairman of the National Governors Association in 2006. If he does run for president it will be exactly 40 years since his father did so.

Senior Senator

Edward Kennedy (D)

Elected 1962, seat up 2006, 7th full term; b. Feb. 22, 1932, Boston; home, Hyannis Port; Harvard U., B.A. 1956, The Hague Intl. Law Schl., 1958, U. of VA, LL.B. 1959; Catholic; married (Vicki).

Military Career: Army, 1951–53.

Professional Career: Western states coord., John F. Kennedy Pres. Campaign, 1960; Asst. Dist. Atty., Suffolk Cnty., 1961–62.

DC Office: 315 RSOB, 20510, 202-224-4543; Fax: 202-224-2417; Web site: kennedy.senate.gov.

State Office: Boston, 617-565-3170.

Committees: *Armed Services*: Emerging Threats & Capabilities; Personnel; Seapower (RMM). *Health, Education, Labor & Pensions* (RMM): Bioterrorism & Public Health Preparedness (RMM). *Judiciary*: Constitution, Civil Rights & Property Rights; Immigration, Border Security & Citizenship (RMM); Intellectual Property; Terrorism, Technology & Homeland Security. *Joint Economic Committee*.

Group Ratings

	ADA	ACLU	AFS	LCV	ITIC	NTU	COC	ACU	NTLC	CHC
2004	100	86	100	100	42	15	31	0	0	0
2003	95	—	100	89	—	17	26	10	—	—

National Journal Ratings

	2003 LIB	—	2003 CONS		2004 LIB	—	2004 CONS
Economic	75%	—	20%		88%	—	11%
Social	85%	—	0%		82%	—	0%
Foreign	90%	—	0%		93%	—	5%

Key Votes of the 108th Congress

1. Ban Drilling in ANWR	Y	5. Energy Bill	N	9. Ban Same-Sex Marriage	N
2. Approve Bush Tax Cuts	N	6. Support Roe v. Wade	Y	10. Ban Bunker-Buster Bomb	Y
3. Medicare/Rx Bill	N	7. Ban Partial-Birth Abortion	N	11. Fund Iraq War	N
4. Bar Overtime Pay Regs.	Y	8. Assault Weapons Ban	Y	12. Restrict Missile Defense	Y

Election Results

2000 general	Edward Kennedy (D)	1,889,494	(73%)	($3,662,652)
	Jack E. Robinson III (R)	334,341	(13%)	($150,430)
	Carla A. Howell (Lib)	308,860	(12%)	($1,055,186)
	Other	66,725	(3%)	
2000 primary	Edward Kennedy (D)	unopposed		
1994 general	Edward Kennedy (D)	1,265,997	(58%)	($11,493,735)
	Mitt Romney (R)	894,000	(41%)	($7,624,491)

Prior Winning Percentages: 1988 (65%); 1982 (61%); 1976 (69%); 1970 (62%); 1964 (74%); 1962 (55%)

Edward Kennedy has served more than 42 years in the Senate—longer than all but two other senators in American history—and he is still going strong. He has served with nine presidents of the United States and nine governors of Massachusetts, most of them Republicans; the only senators who have served longer are Strom Thurmond of South Carolina and Robert Byrd of West Virginia. Kennedy has had the highs and lows of his personal life followed by millions and criticized vitriolically by many. "I've made mistakes. Certainly there are things I'm not proud of," he admits. He has been a presidential candidate and, while still in his 30s, was widely assumed to be the next president. He is second in seniority in the Senate, behind Byrd. His reputation as an idealistic champion of the poor has been burnished by the praise of first-rate celebrators that no American political family has attracted before, and the nation has watched him cope impressively time and again with family tragedy, most recently when his nephew John Kennedy Jr. died in July 1999. To others, he is a symbol of personal immorality and unpunished criminal behavior, a man who has gotten away with things that would have ended the public career of almost anyone else. There is some basis for both views, but neither is an entirely fair picture of this politician, who was re-elected without much fuss in 2000 and seems likely to be again in 2006, and who, even after nearly a decade of Republican Senate majorities, has done much to set national policy.

In most of America and even in much of Massachusetts the luster of the Kennedys has worn off, and most Americans have no memory of the years when John Kennedy was president. But Edward Kennedy has remained a major political force. There was little in the early life of this youngest of the Kennedy siblings to suggest he would be a major politician, much less for so long. He grew up in Bronxville, New York, a rich suburb with many other rich Catholics, was thrown out of Harvard for cheating on a Spanish exam and served in the Army, returned to earn degrees at Harvard and Virginia Law School, and married a Bronxville girl who never developed a taste for politics. Then his brother was elected president of the United States at 43, and the 28-year-old Edward Kennedy was a national celebrity. His father insisted that he run for the Senate; a JFK college roommate was found to hold the seat until Kennedy reached the constitutional age of 30, in 1962. His family money and the enthusiasm among Massachusetts Catholics for this seeming royalty enabled him to beat strong candidates with good political names: Attorney General Edward McCormack, nephew of Speaker John McCormack, in the Democratic primary; George Cabot Lodge, son and great-grandson of senators, in the general. "He can do more for Massachusetts" was his slogan, as it had been John F. Kennedy's in his first Senate race 10 years before.

After his brothers' assassinations, Edward Kennedy was seen by many as their natural heir, and he could have been nominated for president in 1968, at 36, or in 1972, had he chosen to run. Instead, in the latter year, he gave the first of many stirring convention speeches promoting his trademark liberalism. In 1979, he did run for president, and began the race against incumbent Jimmy Carter far ahead in the polls. But he was unable to articulate his reasons for running, and his candidacy was greeted with adverse reaction to him personally as well as to his policies. It ended in a crushing defeat, relieved only by another stirring convention speech, after which he pointedly refused to raise Carter's hand on the podium. In retrospect, it is plain that Edward

Kennedy's presidential chances were ended in July 1969, with the accident at Chappaquiddick. But he has been re-elected with solid margins in Massachusetts, though he received spirited competition in 1994 from Mitt Romney, then a venture capitalist and now governor.

Kennedy has been a hardworking and practical politician who, after his brothers' deaths, took up liberal causes and attention to the poor, which had been the focus of Robert Kennedy in the last years of his life. He was elected Senate majority whip in 1967, but lost the post to Robert Byrd in 1971. He has worked hard for a quarter century without friendly support from a Democratic administration, until the election of Bill Clinton. As chairman of the Health, Education, Labor and Pensions Committee from 1987–94, Kennedy supported teachers' unions; on the Judiciary Committee, which he chaired back in 1979–80 (his chief aide was a young lawyer named Stephen Breyer, now on the U.S. Supreme Court), he supported abortion rights and feminist groups with energy and enthusiasm. He immediately pounced on Judge Robert Bork's nomination in 1987, but played a lesser role in the Clarence Thomas hearings, which came shortly after an incident in which his nephew William Kennedy Smith was arrested and charged with rape in Palm Beach, Florida.

In 1992, Kennedy supported Bill Clinton happily and basked as Clinton gave repeated homage to the Kennedy family. Legislatively, Kennedy was productive, though not as much as he wished. He worked to pass direct student loans, AmeriCorps, Goals 2000 and the School-to-Work Opportunity Act. He again sponsored the Family and Medical Leave Act which George H. W. Bush had vetoed; it was the first law Clinton signed. After Republicans won a Senate majority in 1994, Kennedy shifted his focus from expanding government to protecting it from downsizing. In 1996, he went on the offensive. He pushed the Kassebaum-Kennedy health care bill, an incremental measure to provide portability of health insurance and to limit exclusions for pre-existing conditions; he worked to keep Medical Savings Accounts out, and the bill passed. Kennedy has continued to press for increases in the minimum wage and in Pell grants.

Kennedy did not quit legislating even when George W. Bush took office in 2001. Kennedy goes back a long time with the family; sworn in in November 1962, he was technically a colleague of George W. Bush's grandfather Prescott Bush, whose last term ended in January 1963. He got on well with George H. W. Bush in 1989–93. George W. Bush started off his term by inviting Kennedy to the White House frequently and to view *Thirteen Days*, the film about the Cuban missile crisis. Kennedy played a major role in producing Bush's first major bipartisan achievement, the education bill passed by the Senate in June 2001 and signed in January 2002.

Kennedy also broke with Bush, after initial cooperation, on the Medicare/prescription drug bill passed in November 2003. Kennedy succeeded in getting a version to his liking through the Senate, but the House produced quite a different version that largely prevailed in the conference committee. But he pursued other bipartisan causes—automated exit and entry customs systems with biometric identifiers with Sam Brownback and Saxby Chambliss, strengthening defenses against biological warfare with Bill Frist, HMO regulation with John Edwards and John McCain, colon cancer screening with Jesse Helms, hate crimes legislation with Gordon Smith, FDA regulation of tobacco with Mike DeWine. Most of these bills did not become law, but no one doubts that Kennedy will persist. Even his partisan opponents admit that he has become a superb legislator. And he remains deeply involved in local issues. "Senator Kennedy is a workhorse," says Governor Mitt Romney, who ran against him in 1994. "Senator Kennedy works on any issue that's important to Massachusetts. He is on the phone with me or he's come to my office. I've gone to his office. He is a hard worker, and he cares about his state, and he cares about doing what's right for Massachusetts."

One issue on which Kennedy has taken a strong stand—and has strongly criticized George W. Bush—is Iraq. He voted against the Iraq war resolution, while his colleague John Kerry voted for it, and later called the case for the war "a fraud . . . cooked up in Texas." "Iraq is George Bush's Vietnam," he said in April 2004 at the sober Brookings Institution. "This is the pattern and the record of the Bush administration [on] Iraq, jobs, Medicare, schools, issue after issue—mislead, deceive, make up the needed facts, smear the character of any critics. Again and again we see this cynical, despicable strategy playing out." Kennedy played a key role in securing the 2004 Democratic National Convention for Boston—its first national convention ever—and campaigned heavily for Kerry in the Democratic primaries. When Kerry's campaign was foundering in fall 2003, Kennedy stepped in with advice and a key staffer—Kennedy has been known for his excellent staff since his first days in the Senate—Mary Beth Cahill was installed as Kerry's campaign manager. At the convention he conducted the Boston Pops playing "Stars and Stripes Forever" and delivered a rousing speech in the hall.

Kennedy was reelected with 73% of the vote in 2000. He indicated soon afterward that he intended to run for reelection in 2006, when he turns 74. There is little doubt that he will be reelected and if he serves out that term, he will have served 50 years in the Senate, more than anyone else in history, unless Robert Byrd reaches that milepost before him.

Junior Senator

John Kerry (D)

Elected 1984, seat up 2008, 4th term; b. Dec. 11, 1943, Denver, CO; home, Boston; Yale U., A.B. 1966, Boston Col., LL.B. 1976; Catholic; married (Teresa Heinz).

Military Career: Navy, 1966–70 (Vietnam), Naval Reserves, 1972–78.

Elected Office: MA Lt. Gov., 1982–84.

Professional Career: Organizer, Vietnam Veterans Against the War; Asst. Dist. Atty., Middlesex Cnty., 1976–81; Practicing atty., 1981–82.

DC Office: 304 RSOB, 20510, 202-224-2742; Fax: 202-224-8525; Web site: kerry.senate.gov.

State Offices: Boston, 617-565-8519; Fall River, 508-677-0522; Springfield, 413-785-4610; Worcester, 508-831-7380.

Committees: *Commerce, Science & Transportation*: Fisheries & the Coast Guard; Global Climate Change & Impacts; National Ocean Policy Study; Technology, Innovation & Competitiveness (RMM); Trade, Tourism & Economic Development. *Finance*: Health Care; Long-Term Growth & Debt Reduction (RMM); Social Security & Family Policy. *Foreign Relations*: East Asian & Pacific Affairs (RMM); International Economic Policy, Export & Trade Promotion; International Operations & Terrorism; Western Hemisphere, Peace Corps & Narcotics Affairs. *Small Business & Entrepreneurship* (RMM).

Group Ratings

	ADA	ACLU	AFS	LCV	ITIC	NTU	COC	ACU	NTLC	CHC
2004	25	100	100	17	0	0	0	0	0	0
2003	85	—	100	53	—	14	0	13	—	—

National Journal Ratings

	2003 LIB	—	2003 CONS		2004 LIB	—	2004 CONS
Economic	93%	—	0%		*	—	*
Social	*	—	*		*	—	*
Foreign	*	—	*		*	—	*

Key Votes of the 108th Congress

1. Ban Drilling in ANWR	Y	5. Energy Bill	*	9. Ban Same-Sex Marriage	*
2. Approve Bush Tax Cuts	N	6. Support Roe v. Wade	Y	10. Ban Bunker-Buster Bomb	*
3. Medicare/Rx Bill	*	7. Ban Partial-Birth Abortion	*	11. Fund Iraq War	N
4. Bar Overtime Pay Regs.	*	8. Assault Weapons Ban	Y	12. Restrict Missile Defense	*

Election Results

2002 general	John Kerry (D)	1,605,976	(80%)	($9,305,860)
	Michael Cloud (Lib)	369,807	(18%)	($207,684)
2002 primary	John Kerry (D)	unopposed		
1996 general	John Kerry (D)	1,334,135	(52%)	($12,619,152)
	William Weld (R)	1,143,120	(45%)	($8,002,123)
	Other	78,687	(3%)	

Prior Winning Percentages: 1990 (57%); 1984 (55%)

John Kerry, the Democratic nominee for president in 2004, has been a figure in national politics going back to 1971. The son of a Foreign Service officer, he grew up in many places and at one point attended boarding school in Switzerland. He graduated from Yale in 1966 and, after exploring alternatives, enlisted in the Navy. He served on a swift boat in Vietnam—hazardous duty—and was awarded a Silver Star and three Purple Hearts. He attended the Winter Soldier hearings in Detroit in April 1971 which veterans testified (some of them falsely, it turned out) about atrocities and became one of the leaders in Vietnam Veterans Against the War. He attracted much attention for his articulateness and for his background, unusual for a Vietnam veteran, when he testified before the Senate Foreign Relations Committee in April 1971. "How do you ask a man to be the last to die for a mistake?" he asked in congressional testimony—a good question, and one that also suggested his future political ambitions. He condemned "war crimes committed in Southeast Asia," which, he said, were "not isolated incidents, but crimes committed on a day-to-day basis with the full awareness of officers at all levels of command." Kerry became familiar enough to be featured in *Doonesbury* and plunged quickly into politics. He ran for Congress in 1972, after some widely observed district-shopping, and lost in a district carried by George McGovern. Chastened, he went to law school, worked as top aide to the Middlesex County district attorney, was elected lieutenant governor on a ticket with Michael Dukakis in 1982, and ran for senator in 1984. In both races, he upset a favored rival for the Democratic nomination; in the 1984 general election he beat Republican state chairman Raymond Shamie 55%–45%.

Kerry came to the Senate with a reputation as a strong liberal. He has had a similar voting record to fellow Senator Edward Kennedy, but there have been differences of nuance and interest: Kerry has been more respectful of economic free markets and more inclined in some cases to support an expansive U.S. foreign and military policy. In his first 20 years in the Senate Kerry was not a visibly active legislator—during the 2004 campaign factcheck.org said that only 11 of his bills became law—but was arguably more influential behind the scenes. One reason may have been his senior colleague: Edward Kennedy has been active on many legislative issues, as well as Massachusetts causes, and did not invite junior colleagues to play on his turf.

Kerry made his name more as an investigator, spending some time up blind alleys with klieg lights but also producing some important information. He used his Foreign Relations Western Hemisphere, Peace Corps, Narcotics and Terrorism Subcommittee chairmanship to investigate the infamous Bank of Credit & Commerce International scandal. Kerry's other great investigation was as chairman of the Select Committee on POW/MIA Affairs, on whether Americans were left behind in Vietnamese hands in 1973. Kerry and Republican Bob Smith of New Hampshire went to Vietnam and attempted to turn up new evidence. He concluded that there is evidence "that indicates the possibility of survival, at least for a small number," after 1973, but also said, "There is at this time no compelling evidence that any American remains alive in captivity in southeast Asia." By May 1995, Kerry and fellow Vietnam veteran Senator John McCain were convinced that Hanoi was fully cooperating and, aware they had standing on this issue that Bill Clinton conspicuously lacked, they convinced him to normalize relations with Vietnam. Kerry has remained close with McCain and other Vietnam veterans in the Senate. Like McCain, he spoke out strongly in favor of the bombing of Serbia in April 1999.

His toughest race came in 1996, when he was opposed by Republican Governor William Weld, who had been reelected in 1994 with 71% of the vote. Earlier, the two had worked together on some state problems and emphasized the similarity of their views, but the campaign inevitably produced disagreements and some gentlemanly acrimony. They held eight debates altogether, literate rounds of accusations and one-liners. They both spent liberally—Kerry, $12.6 million, the second highest of any Senate candidate that year; Weld, $8 million. It got more coverage than any other Senate race that year, but the outcome in retrospect was unsurprising: Democratic Massachusetts voted 52%–45% for its junior Democratic senator.

When Bill Clinton was president, Kerry took some interesting positions on issues that put him at odds with Democratic interest groups. He supported the balanced budget amendment and voted for the welfare act of 1996. In June 1998, he decried the "implosion" of public education and said it was caused not just by overcrowded classrooms but also by the "stifling bureaucracy" of school systems. His list of reforms, co-sponsored with Oregon Republican Gordon Smith, included some strongly opposed by the teachers' unions—important backers of the Democratic Party—ending teacher tenure, changing certification requirements to end the education school monopoly and allow lateral entry into teaching. He worked with Missouri Republican Christopher Bond to allow direct grants to charities, including faith-based organizations, for early childhood education of at-risk children. He favored normal trade relations with China and led the floor fight against the Thompson-Torricelli amendment, which would have required review of China's human rights practices.

After George W. Bush became president, Kerry spoke out little about education or faith-based charities and turned to sharp-edged opposition to administration policy. The Bush tax cut, he said, was "unfair, unaffordable and unquestionably ineffective in growing our economy." On the environment, he was one of the most outspoken opponents of oil drilling in the Arctic National Wildlife Refuge and threatened a filibuster on the issue. He criticized the administration for its rejection of the Kyoto Protocol, although he was one of 95 senators who voted in 1997 to reject Kyoto so long as it exempted developing nations like China and India—a main feature of the treaty then and now. On foreign policy, in June 2002 he said it was a "catastrophic mistake" not to press the Israelis to negotiate with the Palestinians; he said at the same time he would not negotiate with Yasir Arafat but would not support the calls that he be removed. He criticized the administration for letting Afghan troops take the lead in Tora Bora in late 2001 and said that may have allowed Al Qaeda and Taliban leaders to escape. Despite considerable criticism of administration policy on Iraq, he voted for the Iraq war resolution in October 2002 but said shortly afterward, "I'm going to keep asking tough questions to hold the President accountable for his promise to insist on arms inspections first, act multilaterally and only go to war as a last resort."

Many senators want to run for president; Kerry's peers have felt he had presidential ambitions since he was in prep school. He did not run in 1988, in his first term in the Senate. He did not run in 1992, presumably because he felt his vote against the Gulf war resolution in January 1991 would be a fatal liability. With Bill Clinton in office there was no opening in 1996. In February 1999, with Clinton obviously smoothing the way for his choice, Al Gore, Kerry announced he would not run in 2000. There were no such obstacles in his way to running in 2004. He had an additional advantage: money. His wife Teresa Heinz Kerry, inherited $600 million when her first husband, Pennsylvania Republican Senator John Heinz, died in a 1991 plane crash. Her net worth in 2004 was estimated at around $1 billion, making Kerry the richest member of Congress according to *Roll Call*. In 1996, when Kerry was hard-pressed by Weld and by his practice of not taking PAC contributions, he borrowed $1.9 million against his and his wife's joint assets. In December 2003, when he was trailing Howard Dean in the polls, Kerry borrowed $6.4 million against his share of their Beacon Hill townhouse (Heinz Kerry owns four other houses, in Georgetown, Nantucket, Sun Valley and the Pittsburgh suburb of Fox Chapel).

Kerry entered the presidential race in 2003 as the favorite to win the nomination. But by July 2003 he was trailing in the polls far behind Dean, whose outspoken opposition to the Iraq war attracted the left half of the Democratic electorate and whose innovative use of the Internet generated an unprecedented amount of small contributions. Kerry, who had voted for the war, began to criticize Bush's conduct of it, often in harsh terms. But at year's end he was still behind. Then, in mid-January, Dean's poll numbers in Iowa and New Hampshire started dropping. Kerry, well organized in Iowa and well known in New Hampshire, was the Democrat best positioned to fill the vacuum. His record in Vietnam, he suggested, would protect him against criticisms that he was too soft on foreign and military policy. "Bring it on!" he said at the end of his speeches. He won a solid though not overwhelming victory in the Iowa caucuses and, eight days later, an impressive victory in New Hampshire, the one state where primary turnout zoomed upward. Kerry won all the primaries but three (John Edwards won his native South Carolina, Howard Dean his adopted Vermont and Wesley Clark won in Oklahoma, where he made his last stand) and clinched the Democratic nomination on March 2, exactly seven months before the general election.

As early as May pollster John Zogby said the election was "Kerry's to lose." The Kerry campaign raised far more money than anyone expected; it was helped as well by billionaire-funded 527 organizations which spent more than $200 million to defeat Bush. Bush's job approval hovered under 50% and he trailed Kerry in polls for much of the seven-month campaign. Kerry performed well in debates, being judged the winner in snap polls in all three. Yet he lost. One reason may have been encapsulated by his March 16 defense of his November 2003 vote against the supplemental appropriation for Iraq: "I actually did vote for the $87 billion before I voted against it." The Bush campaign painted Kerry as a flip-flopper, and in fact he has a propensity, common in politicians, to try to please those on all sides of an issue. More important, he was trying to rally a Democratic party split between fiercely anti-war Bush haters on the one hand and, on the other, more moderate Democrats who hoped for the best in Iraq but preferred a Democrat to Bush on the issues.

Second, the credential which the Kerry campaign emphasized at the Democratic National Convention, his decorated service in Vietnam, was undermined by the ads and book sponsored by Swift Boat Veterans for Truth. Although old-line media declined at first to cover their charges, they were relayed over talk radio, Fox News Channel and conservative blogs; despite dismissals by the likes of *The New York Times* there was at least something to them. Kerry had claimed, in the *Boston Herald* in 1979, on the Senate floor in 1986 and to the Associated Press in 1992 to have served on secret missions in Cambodia in Christmas season 1968. But those claims were withdrawn by his campaign in August, and no one, including the boat mates who supported him, came forward to corroborate his claim to have served in Cambodia in later months.

Finally, Kerry was vulnerable to attack as a Massachusetts liberal. The Bush campaign highlighted his rating by *National Journal* as the number one liberal in the Senate in 2003—arguably unfairly, since he skipped most roll call votes that year while campaigning for president. But over his 20-year Senate career the *National Journal* rated him as the 11th most liberal senator—well to the left of midpoint. And the Massachusetts Supreme Judicial Court's legalization in May 2004 of same-sex marriage provided a vivid illustration of the difference between elite opinion in Massachusetts and majority opinion in the rest of the country. Democratic voter turnout efforts were successful; Kerry won 59 million votes, 16% more than Al Gore, and the second-highest total in American history. But Republican voter turnout efforts were even more successful; George W. Bush won 62 million votes, 23% more than he had four years before, and won the popular vote 51%–48%.

Kerry returned to Washington the week after the election and promised to be active legislatively and politically. Some Democrats criticized him when they learned that he ended the campaign with $15 million in his campaign treasury but he held the door open for another presidential race. "Sometimes God tests you. I'm a fighter, and I've come back before," he said at a post-election rally. When asked about running again in 2008, he noted: "What I've said is I'm not opening any doors, I'm not shutting any doors." But a post-election poll in Massachusetts showed 59% saying he should not run for president again and only 33% saying he should. His hold on his Senate seat surely remains solid. He was reelected in 2002 with 80% of the vote against a Libertarian and a nuclear freeze organizer unhappy with his vote on the Iraq war resolution. His seat comes up again in 2008; with Massachusetts's late primary and filing date, he probably could take his chances in the presidential primaries and, if unsuccessful, run for reelection to the Senate.

FIRST DISTRICT

Rep. John Olver (D)

Elected June 1991, 7th full term; b. Sept. 3, 1936, Honesdale, PA; home, Amherst; Rensselaer Polytechnic Inst., B.S. 1955, Tufts U., M.A. 1956, M.I.T., Ph.D. 1961; no religious affiliation; married (Rose).

Elected Office: MA House of Reps., 1968–72; MA Senate, 1972–91.

Professional Career: Chemistry Prof., U. of MA, Amherst, 1961–69.

DC Office: 1111 LHOB, 20515, 202-225-5335; Fax: 202-226-1224; Web site: www.house.gov/olver.

District Offices: Fitchburg, 978-342-8722; Holyoke, 413-532-7010; Pittsfield, 413-442-0946.

Committees: *Appropriations* (13th of 29 D): Interior, Environment & Related Agencies; Transportation, Treasury, HUD, the Judiciary & District of Columbia (RMM).

Group Ratings

	ADA	ACLU	AFS	LCV	ITIC	NTU	COC	ACU	NTLC	CHC
2004	100	95	100	100	40	10	19	0	0	7
2003	100	—	100	100	—	23	23	12	—	—

National Journal Ratings

	2003 LIB	—	2003 CONS		2004 LIB	—	2004 CONS
Economic	92%	—	0%		98%	—	0%
Social	92%	—	0%		88%	—	0%
Foreign	94%	—	0%		94%	—	4%

Key Votes of the 108th Congress

1. Drilling in ANWR	N	5. DC School Vouchers	N	9. Ban Same-Sex Marriage	N
2. Approve Bush Tax Cuts	N	6. Ban Human Cloning	N	10. Fund Iraq War	N
3. Medicare/Rx Bill	N	7. Restrict Gun Liability	N	11. Bar Cuba Embargo Funds	Y
4. Bar Overtime Pay Regs.	Y	8. Ban Partial-Birth Abortion	N	12. Intelligence Reorg.	N

Election Results

2004 general	John Olver (D)	unopposed		($460,462)
2004 primary	John Olver (D)	unopposed		
2002 general	John Olver (D)	137,841	(68%)	($635,460)
	Matthew Kinnaman (R)	66,061	(32%)	($192,969)

Prior Winning Percentages: 2000 (68%); 1998 (72%); 1996 (53%); 1994 (100%); 1992 (52%); 1991 (50%)

The People		Race/Ethnic Origin	Ancestry	
Area size:	3,192 sq. mi.	88.8% White	Irish: 13.5%	French: 10.7%
Urban population:	69.3%	1.6% Black	English: 9.0%	
Rural population:	30.7%	1.7% Asian	**2004 Presidential Vote**	
Pop. 2000:	634,479	0.2% Native Am.	Kerry (D) 185,377	(63%)
Median income:	$42,570	0.0% Hawaiian	Bush (R) 103,990	(35%)
Poverty status:	10.5%	1.2% Two+ races	Other 4,352	(1%)
Military veterans:	13.5%	0.1% Other	**2000 Presidential Vote**	
		6.3% Hispanic Origin	Gore (D) 150,418	(56%)
			Bush (R) 88,690	(33%)
			Other 27,700	(10%)
			Cook Partisan Voting Index: D +15	

Occupation	Blue collar: 23.9%	White collar: 59.8%	Gray collar: 16.4%

The stony hills and green-clad mountains of western Massachusetts, with more trees today than when Henry David Thoreau was writing in the 1840s, where stone wall fencing once bounded one working farm from another, probably do not look much different from 300 years ago. This was the frontier in the 17th century, where Puritan preachers founded new towns in the wilderness, farming the rocky soil and preaching against declension. This was also the site of the Indian uprising known as King Philip's War in 1676, and the Indian raid, supported by the French in Quebec, at Deerfield in 1704. This was Yankee New England's western frontier for nearly 200 years. In the 19th century, the area was the home of writers and artists: Emily Dickinson lived quietly in Amherst, Edith Wharton grandly on her estate in Lenox and Herman Melville struck a friendship with Nathaniel Hawthorne after purchasing a farm near Hawthorne's Pittsfield home, not far from where the Boston Symphony plays at the Tanglewood Festival each summer. There were mill towns here as well, jammed in mountain crevasses or along the wide Connecticut River; but as the 20th century went on, and trees grew up on stony land once farmed, western Massachusetts came to look less settled, except near giant factories like General Electric's now-closed electric transformer plant in Pittsfield and the Crane paper factory in nearby Dalton.

Western Massachusetts has also changed politically. For many years it was a heartland of the Republican Party—flinty, thrifty and chilly just like the area's most famous politician, Calvin Coolidge. But by the end of the 20th century, the area contained some of the most left-wing parts of America. Stockbridge attracted liberal artist Norman Rockwell and baby boom radical Arlo Guthrie, whose Alice's Restaurant was there. The concentration of colleges and universities in the Pioneer Valley, around Amherst, Northampton and South Hadley, brought together a critical mass of liberal scholars and an even more leftish graduate student proletariat. The results show up in the election returns: John Kerry carried Amherst, home of the University of Massachusetts, 85%–13% over George W. Bush. Western Massachusetts voted heavily for Democrat Shannon O'Brien for governor in 2002, even as she lost the rest of Massachusetts to Mitt Romney.

The 1st Congressional District covers most of western Massachusetts—all of Berkshire and Franklin Counties, most of Hampshire County (but not the college towns of Northampton and South Hadley), Holyoke and West Springfield on the Connecticut River, the more working-class areas of northern Worcester County and extends east to Pepperell in Middlesex County, about 40 miles from Boston. It is the state's largest congressional district (it borders four states) and covers about 40% of the land area of Massachusetts. Over time, the solidly Democratic voting base has shifted from low-income mill workers in places like Holyoke and Pittsfield to liberal and radical academics in the college towns.

The congressman from the 1st District is John Olver, a Democrat first chosen in a June 1991 special election after the death of longtime Republican Congressman Silvio Conte. Olver was educated at Tufts and MIT and came to UMass as a chemistry professor in 1961, at 25; his wife Rose is a professor of psychology and women's and gender studies at Amherst College. In 1968, he began a 22-year career in the legislature. In the special election to replace Conte, his Pioneer Valley base helped him win 31% in the fragmented Democratic primary. In the general, he faced Steven Pierce, former state House Republican leader and Governor William Weld's conservative opponent in the 1990 primary. With Massachusetts liberalism in grave disrepute, the contest was close; Weld scheduled it after students' summer vacation began. But Olver eked out a 50%–48% win, becoming the first Democrat to hold the seat since the Spanish-American War.

Olver has one of the most liberal voting records in the House. He has voted against the kind of international trade deals that decades ago would have added manufacturing jobs in the 1st District, and he favors Canadian-style single-payer health insurance. Olver has worked quietly to fund local projects on the Appropriations Committee. Olver is now ranking Democrat on the Transportation, Treasury and Independent Agencies Subcommittee, where he has sought expanded Amtrak service and subsidies in the Northeast Corridor. He also has advocated increased support for bicyclists, for both recreational and transportation options. With Wayne Gilchrest of Maryland, he formed the House's bipartisan Climate Change Caucus and filed legislation to cap greenhouse gas emissions starting in 2010. Olver does not seem a natural politico: He likes to rock climb, a solitary and meticulous business. In a delegation filled with natural-born politicos, Olver is notably shy. Some Massachusetts Democrats have said that as the state's only Appropriations member, he hasn't done much for their districts.

Olver has only had one close contest for reelection; in 1996 he beat Jane Swift, then a state representative and later governor, by 53%–47%. He has been reelected easily since, without opposition in 2004.

SECOND DISTRICT

Rep. Richard Neal (D)

Elected 1988, 9th term; b. Feb. 14, 1949, Springfield; home, Springfield; Amer. Intl. Col., B.A. 1972, U. of Hartford, M.A. 1976; Catholic; married (Maureen).

Elected Office: Springfield City Cncl., 1978–83; Springfield Mayor, 1984–88.

Professional Career: Staff Asst., Springfield Mayor William C. Sullivan, 1973–78; High Schl. & Col. teacher, 1978–83.

DC Office: 2266 RHOB, 20515, 202-225-5601; Fax: 202-225-8112; Web site: www.house.gov/neal.

District Offices: Milford, 508-634-8198; Springfield, 413-785-0325.

Committees: *Budget* (3d of 17 D). *Ways & Means* (7th of 17 D): Social Security.

Group Ratings

	ADA	ACLU	AFS	LCV	ITIC	NTU	COC	ACU	NTLC	CHC
2004	95	70	100	100	56	7	33	4	0	15
2003	95	—	100	95	—	21	33	20	—	—

National Journal Ratings

	2003 LIB	—	2003 CONS		2004 LIB	—	2004 CONS
Economic	82%	—	18%		97%	—	2%
Social	73%	—	26%		76%	—	23%
Foreign	75%	—	21%		83%	—	16%

Key Votes of the 108th Congress

1. Drilling in ANWR	N	5. DC School Vouchers	N	9. Ban Same-Sex Marriage	N
2. Approve Bush Tax Cuts	N	6. Ban Human Cloning	N	10. Fund Iraq War	Y
3. Medicare/Rx Bill	N	7. Restrict Gun Liability	N	11. Bar Cuba Embargo Funds	Y
4. Bar Overtime Pay Regs.	Y	8. Ban Partial-Birth Abortion	Y	12. Intelligence Reorg.	N

Election Results

2004 general	Richard Neal (D)	...............................unopposed	($427,864)
2004 primary	Richard Neal (D)	...............................unopposed	
2002 general	Richard Neal (D)	...............................unopposed	($441,767)

Prior Winning Percentages: 2000 (100%); 1998 (100%); 1996 (72%); 1994 (59%); 1992 (53%); 1990 (100%); 1988 (80%)

The People		Race/Ethnic Origin	Ancestry	
Area size:	952 sq. mi.	82.5% White	Irish: 13.4%	French: 10.8%
Urban population:	84.8%	5.5% Black	Italian: 8.9%	
Rural population:	15.2%	1.3% Asian	**2004 Presidential Vote**	
Pop. 2000:	634,444	0.2% Native Am.	Kerry (D) 169,460	(59%)
Median income:	$44,386	0.0% Hawaiian	Bush (R) 113,284	(40%)
Poverty status:	10.8%	1.2% Two+ races	Other 3,324	(1%)
Military veterans:	13.3%	0.1% Other	**2000 Presidential Vote**	
		9.2% Hispanic Origin	Gore (D) 150,148	(58%)
			Bush (R) 89,775	(35%)
			Other 19,588	(8%)
			Cook Partisan Voting Index: D +13	
Occupation	Blue collar: 24.1%	White collar: 60.6%	Gray collar: 15.4%	

As American as apple pie, the place where basketball was invented, the city where the Webster's unabridged dictionaries (2d and 3d editions) were edited and published, the site of the armory where M-1 rifles were manufactured during World War II: This is Springfield, Massachusetts. Springfield is the third largest city in the Bay State, but far from Boston. Historically overshadowed by Hartford as the center of the Connecticut River Valley, it is a medium-sized American city built by New England Yankees, where immigrants from a dozen different countries have worked their way up. Today, blacks and Hispanics make up nearly half its population. Like other New England cities, Springfield's downtown has emptied. Business leaders have tried to revive it, with the opening of the expanded Basketball Hall of Fame. But the once-powerful city was forced to submit to state control in 2004 in a financial bailout. Local companies, too, have been forced to adapt. The gun manufacturer Smith & Wesson in the 1990s embraced the marketing restrictions sought by gun control advocates, and then saw its sales sag, as gun control opponents—its natural market—shunned its products. Under new ownership, it abandoned that stance and sales rose again.

Springfield remains the largest city in the 2d Congressional District of Massachusetts, which stretches east from Springfield to a point 30 miles southwest of Boston. Its irregular boundaries stretch north to the college towns of South Hadley and Northampton (Hamp to oldsters; NoHo to the younger crowd), tourist destinations now with trendy restaurants. To the east it stretches across stony hills to the antique center of Brimfield and the factory towns of the Blackstone Valley just north of Woonsocket, Rhode Island. Historically, this was a Yankee Republican district for much of the 20th century, then a solidly Catholic Democratic district. Now it is more diverse culturally, and even more still solidly Democratic.

The congressman from the 2d District is Richard Neal, mayor of Springfield from 1984–88. Neal grew up in Springfield, went to work for the mayor in 1973, and was elected to the city council in 1978, while teaching high school and college history. As mayor, Neal worked to rehabilitate the downtown and revitalize neighborhoods. His predecessor, 36-year incumbent Edward Boland, a longtime friend of Tip O'Neill, essentially bequeathed him the House seat. In 1988, Boland announced his retirement just before the filing deadline, and after Neal had been making the rounds of the district for a year. Unopposed in the Democratic primary, Neal won 80% in the general.

Neal has a generally liberal voting record but has favored enough moderate initiatives to separate himself from more liberal Massachusetts colleagues. He voted for the final version of welfare reform, the partial-birth abortion ban and the Defense of Marriage Act; he refused to support Bill Clinton's health care plan. He serves on Ways and Means, where he voted for NAFTA and GATT and—after considerable hand wringing—for normal trade relations with China. But he opposed trade promotion authority in 2001 and 2002 and voted against the Iraq war resolution. When other Ways and Means Democrats cut a bipartisan deal to expand pensions and retirement incentives, he filed an alternative targeted more to blue-collar workers. Neal decries the complications of the tax code and has crusaded for repeal of the alternative minimum tax and its growing bite on middle-income taxpayers. He was first alerted to the problem by a local accountant; later he discovered that stock options had forced many workers at EMC Corporation, a Hopkinton-based software maker, into paying the AMT. So far, tax-writers have punted rather than raise the hundreds of billions of dollars that would be required to "fix" the AMT. But, as he warns, the problem is not going away.

Neal took the lead for House Democrats on a popular proposal to clamp down on companies that incorporate in Bermuda and other offshore havens to avoid U.S. taxes. He gave the initiative an additional bite when he directed its fire at companies that moved offshore after September 11, terming it "The Corporate Patriot Enforcement Act." Opponents said that such moves were not illegal, but when Democrats forced a late-night vote on adding Neal's proposal to the bill creating the Homeland Security Department, Republican leaders concluded they could not defeat it; 109 Republicans voted for Neal's proposal. After the November 2002 election, in conference committee, the provision was gutted by allowing the Department of Homeland Security to waive the provision when necessary to uphold national security or protect U.S. jobs. Neal raised the issue again in the 108th Congress, but Republicans managed to keep it from being passed. He showed a proclivity for making a point on behalf of futile causes when he called on House members to publicly reveal the details of pork-barrel projects that they have embedded in highway legislation.

Like many other Irish Catholic brethren over the years, Neal has encouraged American attempts at reconciliation in Northern Ireland. In 1980, when he was a city council member, he sponsored a plank at the Democratic National Convention for the unification of Ireland. In 1993, he started one-hour special orders sessions on Irish issues; a year later, he personally lobbied Clinton to grant a visa for Gerry Adams of Sinn Fein to visit the U.S.

Neal had serious primary challenges in 1990 and 1992, but won by satisfactory margins. Republicans have never mounted credible opposition; he has faced no opposition at all since 1996. With his secure local seat, he is free to wait to rise to the heights of seniority on Ways and Means.

THIRD DISTRICT

Rep. Jim McGovern (D)

Elected 1996, 5th term; b. Nov. 20, 1959, Worcester; home, Worcester; American U., B.A. 1981, M.P.A. 1984; Catholic; married (Lisa).

Professional Career: Aide, U.S. Sen. George McGovern, 1977–80; Sr. Aide, U.S. Rep. Joseph Moakley, 1982–96.

DC Office: 430 CHOB, 20515, 202-225-6101; Fax: 202-225-5759; Web site: www.house.gov/mcgovern.

District Offices: Attleboro, 508-431-8025; Fall River, 508-677-0140; Worcester, 508-831-7356.

Committees: *Rules* (2d of 4 D): Rules & Organization of the House (RMM).

Group Ratings

	ADA	ACLU	AFS	LCV	ITIC	NTU	COC	ACU	NTLC	CHC
2004	100	85	100	100	50	8	38	4	0	7
2003	100	—	100	100	—	23	23	8	—	—

National Journal Ratings

	2003 LIB	—	2003 CONS		2004 LIB	—	2004 CONS
Economic	92%	—	0%		89%	—	8%
Social	84%	—	13%		88%	—	0%
Foreign	89%	—	8%		94%	—	4%

Key Votes of the 108th Congress

1. Drilling in ANWR	N	5. DC School Vouchers	N	9. Ban Same-Sex Marriage	N
2. Approve Bush Tax Cuts	N	6. Ban Human Cloning	N	10. Fund Iraq War	N
3. Medicare/Rx Bill	N	7. Restrict Gun Liability	N	11. Bar Cuba Embargo Funds	Y
4. Bar Overtime Pay Regs.	Y	8. Ban Partial-Birth Abortion	N	12. Intelligence Reorg.	N

Election Results

2004 general	Jim McGovern (D)	192,036	(71%)	($1,184,239)
	Ron Crews (R)	80,197	(29%)	($152,853)
2004 primary	Jim McGovern (D)	unopposed		
2002 general	Jim McGovern (D)	unopposed		($628,444)

Prior Winning Percentages: 2000 (100%); 1998 (57%); 1996 (53%)

The People		Race/Ethnic Origin	Ancestry	
Area size:	612 sq. mi.	86.2% White	Irish: 16.1%	Italian: 9.5%
Urban population:	93.4%	2.6% Black	English: 8.5%	
Rural population:	6.6%	3.2% Asian	**2004 Presidential Vote**	
Pop. 2000:	634,585	0.2% Native Am.	Kerry (D) 167,402	(59%)
Median income:	$50,223	0.0% Hawaiian	Bush (R) 112,957	(40%)
Poverty status:	9.0%	1.5% Two+ races	Other 3,667	(1%)
Military veterans:	11.7%	0.3% Other	**2000 Presidential Vote**	
		6.0% Hispanic Origin	Gore (D) 153,044	(59%)
			Bush (R) 90,375	(35%)
			Other 17,711	(7%)
			Cook Partisan Voting Index: D +13	

Occupation	Blue collar: 20.6%	White collar: 65.5%	Gray collar: 13.8%

Worcester (its name still pronounced with a particularly pungent Massachusetts accent making it sound as if it had no *R*s), for more than 200 years has been one of the nation's centers of tinkering, contriving and inventing, even though it is one of the few active industrial cities not located on a river, lake or seacoast. In the mid-19th century, the city won renown as the valentine-making capital of the U.S. for its production of lavish valentines and greeting cards. Fifty years ago, Worcester's biggest industries were wire-making, textiles, grinding wheels and envelopes. It is where the birth control pill was invented and where Worcester native and Clark University professor Robert Goddard shot off experimental rockets before relieved locals saw him off to New Mexico.

In the 1970s and 1980s, electronics and computer firms sprouted along I-495—the circumferential highway 20 miles east of Worcester, as they had earlier around Route 128, closer to Boston. The high-tech boom brought prosperity, labor shortages, new residents and higher housing prices to central Massachusetts. Then, in the early 1990s, the minicomputer industry slumped, bringing recession and a collapse of real estate values. But Worcester's ingenious entrepreneurs and skilled labor force hustled, and local leaders set up a Biotechnology Research Institute to draw on the city's nine colleges and the University of Massachusetts medical center to place the city back on course. In 2004, the Environmental Protection Agency announced an environmental cleanup project designed to spur a downtown revitalization project

Just as the city's economy has changed, so has its face, with a 78% increase in Asians, 55% increase in blacks and a 61% increase in Hispanics (mainly Puerto Ricans) in the 1990s. Overall, population declined by 20% between 1950 and 1980, but rebounded to increase by almost 7% between 1980 and 2000.

The 3d Congressional District of Massachusetts has Worcester as its largest city, but not its geographic center. A little more than half its people live in Worcester and a cluster of adjacent towns. The other population cluster is 60 miles away, in and around the old textile mill town of Fall River, east of Rhode Island. The two are connected by a string of towns, in some places only a few miles wide, which reaches almost to Buzzards Bay. In national elections since 1992 this district has been solidly Democratic. In Massachusetts governor elections, however, the district is mixed. Worcester and Fall River (only a portion of which is in the district) voted by significant margins for Democrat Shannon O'Brien in 2002. But the Interstate 495 corridor and the towns northeast of Rhode Island gave even larger margins to Republican Mitt Romney.

The congressman from the 3d District is Jim McGovern, a Democrat first elected in 1996. McGovern grew up in Worcester, where his parents owned a package store. He went to American University in Washington, and while in graduate school worked in the office of former South Dakota Senator George McGovern (no relation). He ran McGovern's 1984 campaign in the Massachusetts presidential primary, where he finished third with 21% of the vote, and nominated him at the San Francisco convention. After that he got a job in Boston Congressman Joe Moakley's office and became chief of staff as Moakley became chairman of the Rules Committee. McGovern got into the spotlight himself, leading a 1989 investigation of the murders of six Jesuits and two lay women in El Salvador, which led to a cutoff of aid. In 1994, he ran for the House and lost in the Democratic primary 38%–30%. In 1996 he ran again, this time with no primary opposition. In the general election, two-term Republican Congressman Peter Blute stressed his "independence" from the House leadership and attacked McGovern for liberal stands on abortion and Cuba. The AFL-CIO targeted the district with TV ads, and McGovern ran a humorous spot that asked, "If you wouldn't vote for Newt, why would you ever vote for Blute?" McGovern won 53%–45%.

With deft maneuvers reflecting his Capitol Hill experience, McGovern has positioned himself to become a House power broker whenever the Democrats regain their majority in the House. In 2001, the dying Moakley made a personal request to Minority Leader Dick Gephardt that McGovern get a seat on Rules; the next seat went to Florida's Alcee Hastings, a member of the Congressional Black Caucus, but McGovern got a commitment for the next available Democratic seat, with seniority over Hastings. In 2002, he officially moved onto Rules, where he immediately showed familiarity with House procedures. Following the defeat of ranking member Martin Frost of Texas in 2004, McGovern became the number two Democrat behind 75-year-old Louise

Slaughter of New York. Democrats have not won a majority in the House since 1992, but they are currently only 15 seats short, and it's entirely possible that they will become the majority party again, in which case McGovern will be chairman or second-ranking member of Rules—positions of considerable leverage. But at the moment the minority party's impact is negligible on this leadership-chosen committee, and McGovern must be content with castigating the Republicans for heavy-handedness or mismanagement.

McGovern has continued to push openings to Cuba and has called for easing sanctions against Fidel Castro's totalitarian regime. He is a member of the Cuba Working Group, which has won bipartisan House votes to lift the travel ban to the island.

Although Republicans held this seat less than a decade ago, they have given up on it. McGovern was unopposed in 2000 and 2002 and won 71%–29% against a former Georgia state legislator in 2004.

FOURTH DISTRICT

Rep. Barney Frank (D)

Elected 1980, 13th term; b. Mar. 31, 1940, Bayonne, NJ; home, Newton; Harvard U., B.A. 1962, J.D. 1977; Jewish; single.

Elected Office: MA House of Reps., 1972–80.

Professional Career: Exec. Asst., Boston Mayor Kevin White, 1967–71; A.A., U.S. Rep. Michael Harrington, 1971–72; Teaching Fellow, Harvard JFK Schl. of Govt., 1978–80.

DC Office: 2252 RHOB, 20515, 202-225-5931; Fax: 202-225-0182; Web site: www.house.gov/frank.

District Offices: New Bedford, 508-999-6462; Newton, 617-332-3920; Taunton, 508-822-4796.

Committees: *Financial Services* (RMM of 32 D).

Group Ratings

	ADA	ACLU	AFS	LCV	ITIC	NTU	COC	ACU	NTLC	CHC
2004	100	95	100	100	30	12	20	4	3	7
2003	100	—	100	95	—	26	23	12	—	—

National Journal Ratings

	2003 LIB	—	2003 CONS	2004 LIB	—	2004 CONS
Economic	92%	—	0%	89%	—	11%
Social	90%	—	8%	88%	—	0%
Foreign	94%	—	0%	91%	—	7%

Key Votes of the 108th Congress

1. Drilling in ANWR	N	5. DC School Vouchers	N	9. Ban Same-Sex Marriage	N
2. Approve Bush Tax Cuts	N	6. Ban Human Cloning	N	10. Fund Iraq War	N
3. Medicare/Rx Bill	N	7. Restrict Gun Liability	N	11. Bar Cuba Embargo Funds	Y
4. Bar Overtime Pay Regs.	Y	8. Ban Partial-Birth Abortion	N	12. Intelligence Reorg.	N

Election Results

2004 general	Barney Frank (D)	219,260	(78%)	($1,290,341)
	Charles Morse (I)	62,293	(22%)	($21,985)
2004 primary	Barney Frank (D) .... unopposed			
2002 general	Barney Frank (D) .... unopposed			($476,688)

Prior Winning Percentages: 2000 (75%); 1998 (100%); 1996 (72%); 1994 (100%); 1992 (68%); 1990 (66%); 1988 (70%); 1986 (89%); 1984 (74%); 1982 (60%); 1980 (52%)

The People		Race/Ethnic Origin	Ancestry	
Area size:	844 sq. mi.	87.9% White	Irish: 13.5%	Portuguese: 13.4%
Urban population:	88.2%	2.0% Black	English: 9.0%	
Rural population:	11.8%	3.2% Asian	**2004 Presidential Vote**	
Pop. 2000:	634,624	0.2% Native Am.	Kerry (D) 194,914	(65%)
Median income:	$53,169	0.0% Hawaiian	Bush (R) 99,878	(33%)
Poverty status:	8.4%	1.9% Two+ races	Other 3,502	(1%)
Military veterans:	11.0%	1.6% Other	**2000 Presidential Vote**	
		3.3% Hispanic Origin	Gore (D) 178,354	(65%)
			Bush (R) 79,201	(29%)
			Other 18,067	(7%)
			Cook Partisan Voting Index: D +19	

Occupation	Blue collar: 19.2%	White collar: 67.6%	Gray collar: 13.2%

The political transformation of Massachusetts is nowhere better illustrated than in the Boston suburbs of Brookline and Newton. These were Yankee enclaves a century ago, with avenues built to resemble the sweep of Haussmann's Grand Boulevards in Paris, and villages of giant clap-board houses clustered within a few blocks of commuter railroad stations. Brookline was where The Country Club (the very first one) was established in 1882, and where Joseph Kennedy, an Irish Catholic 20-something banker seeking respectability, moved his family in 1914. Brookline and Newton then were solidly Republican in politics, the political base of leading politicians like Christian Herter, governor of Massachusetts and U.S. secretary of state in the 1950s; as late as 1960, Brookline and Newton and adjacent wards of Boston were electing a Republican congress-man. Then came the transformation, personified by the election in 1962 of Michael Dukakis at 29 to the Great and General Court (the legislature). As Massachusetts's university-educated classes became more liberal, as Brookline's and Newton's Jewish populations grew, and as young liberal-minded families refurbished the graceful old houses, these towns became Democratic bastions. Brookline and Newton, are the part of the liberal heart of Massachusetts: They voted 75%–20% for Bill Clinton in 1996, 73%–19% for Al Gore in 2000 and 77%–22% for John Kerry in 2004.

The 4th Congressional District of Massachusetts includes Brookline and Newton, which are the political home bases for its congressman, Barney Frank. Anchoring the hook-like northern tip of the district, they account for less than one-quarter of the district's votes. The shape results from successive redistrictings: In 1982, Frank's district was extended south to the old textile mill city of Fall River; in 1992, it lost much of Fall River and gained New Bedford, a great 19th century whaling port and still home to one of the largest fishing fleets in the United States, with the largest percentage of Portuguese-Americans in the nation; in 2002, it kept New Bedford and regained most of Fall River. Brookline and Newton are connected to the rest of the district by an attenuated series of towns—Wellesley, Dover, Sherborn, Millis, Norfolk, Sharon—and at some points the district is only a mile wide. This is a Democratic district in national politics, but not as Democratic or as uniformly culturally liberal as Brookline and Newton; in state politics it is more marginal: the suburban towns between Newton and Fall River voted for Republican Governor Mitt Romney in 2002. There is a bit of most kinds of America here: high-income WASPy Wellesley, French-Canadian mill-worker Fall River, Foxboro with its football stadium, Sharon with a middle-income Jewish population and countrified Dover.

Barney Frank, first elected to the House in 1980, is one of the intellectual and political leaders of the Democratic Party in the House—political theorist and pit bull all at the same time. In *Washingtonian*'s biennial polls of House staffers, he is consistently voted the brainiest and the funniest member of the House by wide margins. He grew up in Bayonne, New Jersey, and went to Harvard, where he got to know local politicians as well as political scientists. In 1967, he went to work for newly elected Boston Mayor Kevin White; in 1971, he went to Washington to work for Congressman Michael Harrington. In 1972, Frank was elected to the Massachusetts House from the Back Bay of Boston, then just starting to be a liberal singles neighborhood. In 1980, when Congressman Robert Drinan retired after Pope John Paul II commanded Jesuits to leave elective office, Frank moved to Brookline and ran in the 4th District. With a strong base in Brookline and Newton, he won. After redistricting threw him in with Republican incumbent Margaret Heckler in 1982, he beat her 60%–40%. He has been re-elected by wide margins since.

In the House, Frank quickly gained a reputation as one of the smartest talkers and best debaters in the chamber—maybe one of the best of all time. Frank listens to others' arguments and engages them in his inimitable rapid-fire delivery. While he stands at the left end of the American electoral spectrum, there is an element of solid small-c conservatism beneath him. More recently he said he is for "capitalism plus," that is, market capitalism with welfare state protections, and he has expressed unease at what he considers increasing isolationism in Congress, though in 2002 he opposed the Iraq war resolution.

Frank has worked hard, often behind the scenes, on many substantive issues. He has shaped immigration acts since 1986, working to expand legal immigration, to allow HIV-positive people to enter the country, to bar states from excluding children of illegal aliens from school and to change the 1996 law that required mandatory deportation of immigrants convicted of a crime carrying a one-year sentence even if the offense occurred many years ago; this had been hurting Azorean and Cape Verdean immigrants in New Bedford. With Banking Committee Republican Spencer Bachus he worked hard for debt relief for very poor countries.

After the 1998 election, Frank took the ranking position on Banking's Housing Subcommittee. In 2002, he worked cooperatively with Financial Services Chairman Michael Oxley on housing issues, including a program to help teachers, police officers and fire fighters make down payments on houses in the communities where they work. In January 2003 he became ranking Democrat on the full Banking Committee. Frank calls himself a "free market guy," but with limits. "That comes from looking at the world. You see the market works well at some things, but not others. ... Left to itself, the market will create more inequality than is necessary for efficiency or than is healthy. The job of the Democrats is to reduce inequality where it's not socially healthy." His own preference—to tax wealth "a fairly small percentage" and use the proceeds "to employ people on socially useful purposes"—he recognizes as politically unfeasible now, and so he went on to master parts of the Banking Committee's jurisdiction with which he was unfamiliar—securities, corporate governance, accounting issues, insurance, flood insurance. With Republican Paul Gillmor he sponsored a bill to prevent Wal-Mart from using industrial loan companies to get into the banking business. He has opposed preempting state laws on predatory lending and sought bipartisan support for protecting people against unscrupulous nonprofit credit counseling agencies. He worked with Republicans on flood insurance and check truncation and prepared to do so on identity theft.

Affordable housing has been a longtime Frank cause, and he called the practice of allowing Section 8 units and others to go out of the subsidized inventory "the worst failure of this administration." He seeks to produce more subsidized units. He sought to allow merged thrifts to maintain multiple memberships in Home Loan banks, to maintain their affordable housing accounts. In 2003 he put pressure on Fannie Mae and Freddie Mac to do more on manufactured housing loans and affordable housing. Long a supporter of Freddie and Fannie, he joined Oxley in June 2004 in supporting higher funding for their regulator OFHEO and in September joined Oxley in seeking power to subpoena top Fannie executives. But in November, after the HUD Inspector General raised questions about OFHEO's highly critical report on Fannie Mae's accounting, he dropped his support of additional OFHEO funding until the IG's issues were addressed. Still, this seems to be one of the House's more bipartisan committees. When Frank was concerned about Bank of America's elimination of jobs after it absorbed FleetBoston, Oxley agreed to conduct hearings on the effect of bank mergers on local economies.

For all his professional accomplishments, Frank's personal life once threatened to end his career. In May 1987, in a seemingly casual answer to a reporter's question, Frank disclosed that he is gay. Then in August 1989, the conservative *Washington Times* reported that Frank had employed as a personal aide a male prostitute and convicted drug possessor, Steve Gobie, and let him live in his apartment. When faced with a scandal that threatened to end his career, Frank told the truth. He admitted paying Gobie, but was careful never to use official or campaign funds; he denied that he tolerated prostitution in his apartment and said he had thrown the man out when he suspected it was going on. Frank called on the ethics committee to investigate. It did and dismissed all but two minor charges. The committee recommended a reprimand, but not censure; Frank agreed in a contrite appearance before the House in July 1990 and the House voted 287–141 against censure. The vote for reprimand was 408–18. "I think members will agree that I have always had a reputation for honesty, not always tact or tolerance," Frank said to the House. That reputation was one reason he survived and has thrived in the House; his brains, liberal stands, hard work and constituency service helped him not only survive, but become overwhelmingly popular in the 4th District. In 1998, as the House debated the impeachment of Bill Clinton, Frank acknowledged that Clinton lied in his deposition in the Paula Jones case, but ridiculed the case against him. Yet he was harshly critical of Bill Clinton's last minute pardons and in February 2001 proposed a constitutional amendment to prevent the president from using the pardoning power from a month before the presidential election until inauguration day.

Frank has been the House's leading legislator on gay rights issues. One was the issue, raised in the 1992 campaign by Bill Clinton and not by Frank or by gay advocacy groups, of gays in the military. To the disappointment of many in the gay community, Frank admitted that allowing open homosexuals to serve in the military would not be accepted by most in Congress or the Pentagon. In the years since, Frank has criticized the military when the number of service members discharged for homosexuality increased, and he helped persuade Al Gore to come out against "Don't ask, Don't tell" in 1999. Frank and Republican Christopher Shays have sponsored a bill to prohibit employment discrimination on account of sexuality, which gained a surprising degree of support in the Republican House. He spoke out against provisions of the faith-based charities act that would allow charities to discriminate against gay people in violation of state or local laws.

Frank hailed the Massachusetts Supreme Judicial Court's decision in November 2003 that led to the legalization of same-sex marriage. But he was critical of San Francisco Mayor Gavin Newsom's promotion of what turned out to be illegal same-sex marriages there. "I was against pretend marriage," he explained later. It was "political hoopla with no gain. We had [Governor Mitt Romney] at the time basically threatening not to follow the law [the Supreme Judicial Court decision]. Our response was, 'What are you, George Wallace? You can't do that. You can't have civil disobedience.' It totally undercut our argument to have Newsom also talking about not following the law." After George W. Bush's reelection victory and the passage of same-sex marriage bans in 11 states in November 2004, he reflected further, "The thing that agitated people were the mass weddings. It was a mistake in San Francisco, compounded by people in Oregon, New Mexico and New York. What it did was provoke a lot of fears. He created a sense there was chaos rather than give us a chance to show, as we have in Massachusetts, that this doesn't mean anything to anyone else." But he took satisfaction in the fact that the House fell far short in September 2004 of approving the Family Marriage Amendment. He was pleased that the Log Cabin Republicans declined to support Bush, and he noted that every Massachusetts legislator who supported same-sex marriage was reelected. He has often said "we would do better with fewer marches and rallies," and in December 2004 he said advocates of gay rights should pick fights sensibly. "You take risks for your gains, but you don't take risks for no gains."

Through all his work on national issues, Frank has not neglected the home front. He has worked especially hard on projects in Fall River and New Bedford. All of this seems to have paid off in the polls. In 2004 he was opposed by a former radio talk show host who claims that changes Frank made in the immigration laws in the 1980s allowed the legal entry of the 9/11 hijackers; Frank said that was nonsense and that they could and should have been barred under existing law. In the last weeks of the campaign Frank spent $350,000 on television—not because he was at risk of losing, but to give him more exposure should John Kerry be elected president and should he run for Kerry's Senate seat. Frank won his House race 78%–22%; he carried every city and town, including four towns which voted for George W. Bush.

FIFTH DISTRICT

Rep. Martin Meehan (D)

Elected 1992, 7th term; b. Dec. 30, 1956, Lowell; home, Lowell; U. of MA, B.S. 1978, Suffolk U., M.A. 1981, J.D. 1986; Catholic; married (Ellen Murphy).

Professional Career: Staff Asst., U.S. Rep. James Shannon, 1979–81; Research analyst, MA Legislature's Joint Cmte. on Elections, 1982–84; MA Dpty. Secy. of State for Securities & Corps., 1985–90; Middlesex Cnty. 1st Asst. Dist. Atty., 1990–92.

DC Office: 2229 RHOB, 20515, 202-225-3411; Fax: 202-226-0771; Web site: www.house.gov/meehan.

District Offices: Haverhill, 978-521-1845; Lawrence, 978-681-6200; Lowell, 978-459-0101.

Committees: *Armed Services* (7th of 28 D): Military Personnel; Terrorism, Unconventional Threats & Capabilities (RMM). *Judiciary* (10th of 17 D): Courts, the Internet & Intellectual Property; Crime, Terrorism & Homeland Security; Immigration, Border Security & Claims.

Group Ratings

	ADA	ACLU	AFS	LCV	ITIC	NTU	COC	ACU	NTLC	CHC
2004	100	85	100	100	56	11	22	4	0	7
2003	100	—	100	95	—	22	31	16	—	—

National Journal Ratings

	2003 LIB	—	2003 CONS		2004 LIB	—	2004 CONS
Economic	92%	—	0%		96%	—	3%
Social	84%	—	13%		86%	—	12%
Foreign	81%	—	17%		91%	—	9%

Key Votes of the 108th Congress

1. Drilling in ANWR	N	5. DC School Vouchers	N	9. Ban Same-Sex Marriage	N
2. Approve Bush Tax Cuts	N	6. Ban Human Cloning	N	10. Fund Iraq War	N
3. Medicare/Rx Bill	N	7. Restrict Gun Liability	N	11. Bar Cuba Embargo Funds	Y
4. Bar Overtime Pay Regs.	Y	8. Ban Partial-Birth Abortion	N	12. Intelligence Reorg.	N

Election Results

2004 general	Martin Meehan (D)	179,652	(67%)	($459,977)
	Thomas Tierney (R)	88,232	(33%)	($30,406)
2004 primary	Martin Meehan (D)	unopposed		
2002 general	Martin Meehan (D)	122,562	(60%)	($897,286)
	Charles McCarthy (R)	69,337	(34%)	($256,212)
	Ilana Freedman (Lib)	11,729	(6%)	($160,640)

Prior Winning Percentages: 2000 (100%); 1998 (71%); 1996 (100%); 1994 (70%); 1992 (52%)

The People

Area size:	582 sq. mi.
Urban population:	93.5%
Rural population:	6.5%
Pop. 2000:	635,326
Median income:	$56,217
Poverty status:	8.9%
Military veterans:	10.9%

Occupation Blue collar: 20.9%   White collar: 66.9%   Gray collar: 12.1%

Race/Ethnic Origin

79.7% White	
1.7% Black	
5.2% Asian	
0.1% Native Am.	
0.0% Hawaiian	
1.4% Two+ races	
0.2% Other	
11.6% Hispanic Origin	

Ancestry

Irish: 16.6%   Italian: 9.8%
English: 8.9%

2004 Presidential Vote

Kerry (D)	158,455	(57%)
Bush (R)	114,874	(41%)
Other	3,813	(1%)

2000 Presidential Vote

Gore (D)	145,277	(57%)
Bush (R)	93,406	(36%)
Other	18,433	(7%)

Cook Partisan Voting Index: D +11

The Merrimack River Valley at the northern edge of Massachusetts has had an erratic history: High-tech boom, bust, boom, bust, boom. When Massachusetts was a kind of maritime republic in the 19th century, with its farmers struggling to scratch out a living from the stony soil, a few clever Yankees used their profits from the sea trade to try to tame the rapidly flowing Merrimack and build cotton-spinning mills. Creating the cities of Lowell and Lawrence, they built model dormitories and recreation programs for their women workers. This was the center of America's textile industry for more than a century, long after the maritime industry faded. But in the 1920s, the price of labor rose and newly built mills in the Carolinas, much closer to the cotton supply, decimated the industry that Lawrence and Lowell built. Many residents—by then, rather elderly—waited forlornly for an upturn in the local economy.

It came eventually, largely due to an unexpected source. High-tech industry drove the growth, beginning in the 1960s around MIT, then moving out to the Route 128 ring road and then I-495, which passes through Lowell and Lawrence. Wang, headquartered in Lowell, grew spectacularly, and Senator Paul Tsongas spearheaded a national historic restoration of the old mill area. This was the Massachusetts miracle of the 1980s. Then came the bust: Wang's word processors and minicomputers slumped as businesses purchased personal computers and hooked them together in networks. But Lowell revived again. Its new immigrants—mostly from Cambodia and Puerto Rico—provide vitality and entrepreneurial creativity; the old Wang buildings are filled with health care, banking, telecommunications and Internet companies.

The 5th Congressional District of Massachusetts includes Lawrence and Lowell, which along with next-door towns account for about two-thirds of the district's population. The remainder of the district is the high-tech corridor south on circumferential Interstate 495. The district also includes tony suburbs like Concord, the mountains along the New Hampshire state line and the small towns west of Lowell that once hosted Fort Devens, which closed in 1996, though part of the base today survives as a training site for New England Army Reserve and National Guard soldiers. Except for Lowell and Lawrence, it is ancestrally Yankee Republican. It is culturally liberal and trended toward the Democrats in the early 1970s. Back then, the 5th produced two Democratic candidates who would later run for president: John Kerry, who lost the general election in 1972, and Paul Tsongas, who won the seat two years later. In the 1980s and 1990s, amid the high-tech boom, it went Republican in national and even statewide elections: A kind of Baja New Hampshire. In 1992, it gave Bill Clinton his lowest percentage in the state, while a big vote went to high-tech pioneer Ross Perot. But in the 1990s, its cultural liberalism moved it toward Democrats. Not as far as some Massachusetts districts: Al Gore carried the 5th District by 57%–36%, John Kerry by 57%–41%.

The congressman from the 5th District is Martin Meehan, a Democrat first elected in 1992. Meehan grew up in Lowell, one of seven children of a 43-year Lowell *Sun* typesetter. As a child, he memorized President Kennedy's speeches from long-playing records, kept a scrapbook on Robert Kennedy, and idolized Senator Edward Kennedy. He is a lifelong politico: He was an aide to Congressman James Shannon while working on his masters degree, worked in the Massachusetts secretary of state's office after law school, and was first assistant district attorney in Middlesex County from 1990 until he ran for Congress in 1992. He took on eight-year incumbent Democrat Chester Atkins, who had grown highly unpopular in the district, and beat him by the astonishing margin of 65%–35%. In the general, Meehan faced former Republican Congressman Paul Cronin, who beat Kerry in 1972 (the only open seat carried by George McGovern to also elect a Republican to the House), but lost to Tsongas in 1974. Meehan won 52%–38%.

Meehan combines a mostly liberal voting record with distinctive stands on issues. One of his crusades is against tobacco; his father, a smoker, had heart surgery when Marty was 11. He sponsored a bipartisan bill with a $1.50 a pack tax and a target of cutting youth smoking by 80%, and later proposed a ban on Internet sale of cigarettes to kids. His other great cause has been campaign finance reform. Starting in 1997, with Connecticut Rep. Christopher Shays and Senators Russ Feingold and John McCain, Meehan co-sponsored a series of campaign finance bills, and their proposal was finally enacted in 2002. It outlawed soft money, subjected non-candidate ads to disclosure and contribution limit requirements, strengthened FEC enforcement powers, required posting of forms on the Internet and created a commission to recommend more reforms. Despite the apprehensions of Democratic fundraisers, who were more dependent on soft money than Republicans, Meehan kept most Democrats and many Republicans aboard. With that success on the books, he moved to overhaul the Federal Election Commission.

Meehan serves on the Armed Services Committee and has generally moved to cut defense spending, but he boosts local Raytheon operations and its upgrades of the Patriot missile. Over the years, his voting record has drifted left: He voted for NAFTA in 1993 but against trade promotion authority in 1997 and 2001. He was one of three House Democrats from Massachusetts to vote to authorize George W. Bush to use force against Iraq.

When Meehan first ran for the House in 1992, he pledged to serve no more than four terms. In 1999, he said he would break his pledge. He roiled some Democrats when he voiced interest in the 2002 race for governor, but then changed his mind when threatened with the loss of his district through redistricting. Against nominal opposition in 2002, he was reelected to his House seat with only 60% of the vote. In 2004 he raised his vote share to 67%. In the run up to the 2004 election, Meehan led the unofficial race to raise funds with $4.5 million to run for the Senate should Kerry be elected president and his seat come open. But that became moot as the returns came in on November 2.

SIXTH DISTRICT

Rep. John Tierney (D)

Elected 1996, 5th term; b. Sept. 18, 1951, Salem; home, Salem; Salem St. U., B.A. 1973, Suffolk U., J.D. 1976; no religious affiliation; married (Patrice).

Professional Career: Practicing atty., 1976–96.

DC Office: 120 CHOB, 20515, 202-225-8020; Fax: 202-225-5915; Web site: www.house.gov/tierney.

District Offices: Lynn, 781-595-7375; Peabody, 978-531-1669.

Committees: *Education & the Workforce* (10th of 22 D): 21st Century Competitiveness; Employer-Employee Relations. *Permanent Select Committee on Intelligence* (9th of 9 D): Intelligence Policy; Oversight.

Group Ratings

	ADA	ACLU	AFS	LCV	ITIC	NTU	COC	ACU	NTLC	CHC
2004	100	95	100	100	30	7	19	0	0	9
2003	100	—	100	95	—	24	23	8	—	—

National Journal Ratings

	2003 LIB	—	2003 CONS		2004 LIB	—	2004 CONS
Economic	92%	—	0%		98%	—	0%
Social	89%	—	10%		88%	—	0%
Foreign	89%	—	8%		94%	—	4%

Key Votes of the 108th Congress

1. Drilling in ANWR	N	5. DC School Vouchers	N	9. Ban Same-Sex Marriage	N
2. Approve Bush Tax Cuts	N	6. Ban Human Cloning	N	10. Fund Iraq War	N
3. Medicare/Rx Bill	N	7. Restrict Gun Liability	N	11. Bar Cuba Embargo Funds	Y
4. Bar Overtime Pay Regs.	Y	8. Ban Partial-Birth Abortion	N	12. Intelligence Reorg.	N

Election Results

2004 general	John Tierney (D)	213,458	(70%)	($415,117)
	Stephen O'Malley (R)	91,597	(30%)	($48,633)
2004 primary	John Tierney (D)	unopposed		
2002 general	John Tierney (D)	162,900	(68%)	($515,113)
	Mark Smith (R)	75,462	(32%)	($30,078)

Prior Winning Percentages: 2000 (71%); 1998 (55%); 1996 (48%)

The People		Race/Ethnic Origin	Ancestry	
Area size:	805 sq. mi.	89.8% White	Irish: 18.6%	Italian: 13.1%
Urban population:	94.9%	1.9% Black	English: 10.6%	
Rural population:	5.1%	2.5% Asian	**2004 Presidential Vote**	
Pop. 2000:	636,554	0.1% Native Am.	Kerry (D) 185,264	(58%)
Median income:	$57,826	0.0% Hawaiian	Bush (R) 130,924	(41%)
Poverty status:	6.3%	1.1% Two+ races	Other 3,970	(1%)
Military veterans:	12.6%	0.2% Other	**2000 Presidential Vote**	
		4.4% Hispanic Origin	Gore (D) 172,840	(57%)
			Bush (R) 107,415	(36%)
			Other 20,760	(7%)
			Cook Partisan Voting Index: D +11	

Occupation	Blue collar: 17.2%	White collar: 69.7%	Gray collar: 13.1%

The North Shore of Massachusetts Bay has a number of times been at the leading edge of the nation's economy. In 1640, the Saugus Iron Works was built here—the beginning of American heavy industry. When Europe's great powers were convulsed in international war from 1792 to 1815, American ship owners suddenly became the richest in the world and traders from Boston and Salem accumulated the capital needed to build textile mills and railroads and to finance much of the American industrial revolution. From the small port of Salem, ships left for China, bringing back porcelain and artifacts, which helped change American styles forever. Salem, first settled in 1626, had the nation's first millionaire, Elias Hasket Derby; in 1900, it was the richest city per capita in the nation. But today the North Shore is a quiet place, from Boston Harbor north to the mouth of the Merrimack River, a collection of ethnic factory towns from Lynn on up through next-door Peabody (once one of the world's great leather producers with over 100 tanneries) to the former ship-building Newburyport, alternating with the high-income enclaves of Marblehead with its yachts and Beverly with its estates, and artsy Rockport. Moviegoers will recognize the fishing town of Gloucester as the homeport of the *Andrea Gail*, the 72-foot swordfishing boat whose tragic plight was dramatized in the novel and film *The Perfect Storm*. Although the ports were hard hit by overfishing of mackerel and herring in the 1970s and cod in the 1990s, pleasure boating surged in the past decade. Lynn is the district's largest city and its General Electric jet engine plant is the largest employer, though with far fewer jobs than the 13,000 at its peak in the late 1970s and with payrolls threatened by offset deals to produce some engines in the countries purchasing them.

The 6th Congressional District of Massachusetts includes the North Shore from Saugus and Lynn northward, plus towns and cities inland west to Burlington. Its high-income Yankee towns were historically liberal Republican, while Lynn, Salem, Peabody and the Merrimack mill towns are still Irish working-class Democratic. Gloucester fishermen struggle with depleted stocks and increased federal controls. The 6th has been a Democratic district on balance since the 1960s, but in the 1980s and in the early 1990s only marginally so. While this district is the site of the original gerrymander—named after Elbridge Gerry—the current 6th District boundaries are hardly grotesque by current national standards; it was barely changed by 2002 redistricting.

The congressman from the 6th District is John Tierney, a Democrat first elected in 1996. Tierney grew up in Salem in modest circumstances; he worked his way through Salem State College and Suffolk University Law School as a janitor on the night shift and clerk in a Boston law firm. For nearly 20 years, he practiced law in Salem. In 1994, he spied a political opening and ran for Congress. The incumbent, Peter Torkildsen, was a Republican elected in 1992 by beating veteran Democrat Nicholas Mavroules, who had been indicted for tax evasion and bribery. But in Republican 1994, Torkildsen won 51%–47%. In 1996, Tierney ran again. His ads, along with the AFL-CIO's, assailed Newt Gingrich and Republican Medicare "cuts." He called for greater educational opportunities, health care insurance for children, and aid to college students and criticized Torkildsen for not bringing enough defense dollars to the district. Torkildsen raised and spent $1.1 million, while keeping his promise to accept no PAC money. Tierney held his spending—$776,000 in total—mostly until the end. The result was one of the closest races in the country. After several recounts, which stretched into December, Tierney won by 371 votes.

In the House, Tierney has been a solid ally of the unions on Education and the Workforce Committee and a consistent liberal in his votes. He has been a leader among Democrats seeking to reduce prescription drug costs for senior citizens. With Governmental Affairs Committee chairman Tom Davis, Tierney sponsored the "gofeds" (Generating Opportunity by Forgiving Educational Debt for Service) proposal to eliminate taxes on money that federal agencies give to employees to pay off student loans. The ACLU praised his opposition to the Patriot Act. Tierney has pursued bipartisan efforts on behalf of local concerns. He joined with Massachusetts colleague Bill Delahunt and New Jersey Republican Jim Saxton to support a ban on big fishing trawlers from Georges Bank. He won inclusion in the 2004 omnibus appropriations bill of a provision for the town of Nahant to pay $2 million to purchase 12 Coast Guard cottages on three acres of prime real estate; residents feared that the land would be purchased by developers. The big spending bill also included $2 million for local public-transit facilities and $900,000 to restore historic properties in Essex County. And he worked with local officials fighting to keep the local Hanscom Air Force Base, with its 7,000 employees, from the base-closing list for 2005. Their efforts paid off: In May 2005, the Pentagon recommended a huge expansion of the base that will add 1,300 jobs to Hanscom by 2008.

Torkildsen challenged Tierney in a 1998 rubber match, but Tierney won 55%–42%. He has faced token opposition since then. He was reelected 70%–30% in 2004.

SEVENTH DISTRICT

Rep. Edward Markey (D)

Elected 1976, 15th full term; b. July 11, 1946, Malden; home, Malden; Boston Col., B.A. 1968, J.D. 1972; Catholic; married (Susan Blumenthal).

Military Career: Army Reserves, 1968–73.

Elected Office: MA House of Reps., 1973–76.

DC Office: 2108 RHOB, 20515, 202-225-2836; Fax: 202-226-0092; Web site: www.house.gov/markey.

District Offices: Framingham, 508-875-2900; Medford, 781-396-2900.

Committees: *Energy & Commerce* (3d of 26 D): Commerce, Trade & Consumer Protection; Energy & Air Quality; Telecommunications & the Internet (RMM). *Homeland Security* (3d of 15 D): Economic Security, Infrastructure Protection & Cybersecurity; Management, Integration & Oversight; Prevention of Nuclear & Biological Attack. *Resources* (3d of 22 D): Energy & Mineral Resources.

Group Ratings

	ADA	ACLU	AFS	LCV	ITIC	NTU	COC	ACU	NTLC	CHC
2004	100	90	100	100	30	12	10	0	0	7
2003	100	—	100	100	—	25	20	8	—	—

National Journal Ratings

	2003 LIB	—	2003 CONS		2004 LIB	—	2004 CONS
Economic	92%	—	0%		98%	—	0%
Social	90%	—	8%		88%	—	0%
Foreign	94%	—	0%		91%	—	7%

Key Votes of the 108th Congress

1. Drilling in ANWR	N	5. DC School Vouchers	N	9. Ban Same-Sex Marriage	N
2. Approve Bush Tax Cuts	N	6. Ban Human Cloning	N	10. Fund Iraq War	N
3. Medicare/Rx Bill	N	7. Restrict Gun Liability	N	11. Bar Cuba Embargo Funds	Y
4. Bar Overtime Pay Regs.	Y	8. Ban Partial-Birth Abortion	N	12. Intelligence Reorg.	N

Election Results

2004 general	Edward Markey (D)	 202,399	(74%)	($1,181,782)
	Ken Chase (R)	 60,334	(22%)	($62,022)
	James Hall (I)	 12,139	(4%)	
2004 primary	Edward Markey (D)	.... unopposed		
2002 general	Edward Markey (D)	.... unopposed		($705,775)

Prior Winning Percentages: 2000 (100%); 1998 (71%); 1996 (70%); 1994 (64%); 1992 (62%); 1990 (100%); 1988 (100%); 1986 (100%); 1984 (71%); 1982 (78%); 1980 (100%); 1978 (85%); 1976 (77%)

The People		Race/Ethnic Origin	Ancestry	
Area size:	188 sq. mi.	83.5% White	Irish: 18.5%	Italian: 16.9%
Urban population:	99.5%	3.3% Black	English: 7.5%	
Rural population:	0.5%	5.7% Asian	**2004 Presidential Vote**	
Pop. 2000:	634,287	0.1% Native Am.	Kerry (D) 192,133	(66%)
Median income:	$56,110	0.0% Hawaiian	Bush (R) 96,374	(33%)
Poverty status:	6.7%	1.9% Two+ races	Other 3,880	(1%)
Military veterans:	10.5%	0.5% Other	**2000 Presidential Vote**	
		4.8% Hispanic Origin	Gore (D) 181,417	(64%)
			Bush (R) 82,250	(29%)
			Other 20,891	(7%)
			Cook Partisan Voting Index: D +19	
Occupation	Blue collar: 14.3%	White collar: 72.9%	Gray collar: 12.8%	

The Yankee Protestants and Irish Catholics who settled Massachusetts arrived by boat, the Yankees to a cold stony land with a few Indians, the Irish to a crowded city with Yankees who seemed no more welcoming. The Yankees whose ancestors once farmed the soil had, by the early 20th century, founded suburbs filled with solid brick and white frame houses, furnished in Early American furniture. As the years went on, their local public schools were emptied as young people with children moved out, and attendance at Protestant churches went down. The Irish, for decades heavily concentrated in the crowded wards of Boston, started moving out into the Yankee suburbs 50 years ago. There were other ethnic groups here and there (Jews, Italians, French-Canadians) but the major conflict—fought out in neighborhood playgrounds, in school committee meetings and not least in political campaigns—was between Protestant Yankee Republicans and Catholic Irish Democrats.

The 7th Congressional District of Massachusetts is made up of Boston's northern and western suburbs, where vestiges of this conflict can still be seen. Geographically, it forms an arc around Boston, starting with the clapboard beach towns of Winthrop and Revere just beyond Logan Airport, going north as far as working-class Woburn (where Charles Goodyear developed the art of vulcanizing rubber) and west as far as modest-income Natick and Framingham. Framingham is home to many Brazilian immigrants who began arriving after World War II, when Boston-based mining companies began extracting mica from an area near the Brazilian city of Governador Valadares. The 7th also includes the university towns of Medford, home of Tufts University, and Waltham, home of Brandeis University, the patriot town of Lexington and high-income Lincoln and Weston. Many of these towns were Yankee Republican through the 1950s, but by the late 1960s they were solidly Democratic; the high-tech suburbs trended Republican again in the 1980s but swung against Republicans in the 1990s. The highest income areas seem to run across the grain of their ethnic experience: Weston, with many Catholics, often votes Republican (though it went 58%–41% for John Kerry in 2004), while WASPy Lincoln has been liberal Democratic since it voted for George McGovern in 1972. But in state politics, the suburbanites of the 7th District have been less liberal: This district was close in the gubernatorial election of 1998 and again in 2002, when Republican Mitt Romney won 51%–49%.

The congressman in the 7th District is Edward Markey, first elected in 1976 at age 30, and now dean of the Massachusetts House delegation. He grew up in Malden, where his father was a milkman; he went to Malden Catholic High, Boston College and Boston College law school, then immediately to the state House, at 26. In 1976, he ran for the House and won a 12-candidate primary with 22% of the vote; he had never been to Washington. Markey first made a name as a fierce opponent of nuclear power. In 1983, he was a leading political crusader for the nuclear freeze.

Seniority and events put Markey in position to be a serious legislator, and he has long since become one of the House's most legislatively productive and creative members. With help from Speaker Tip O'Neill, he got on the Commerce Committee; impressed by the high-tech boom around Route 128, he joined the old Communications Subcommittee early. Then, after only eight years in the House, he became chairman of the Energy Conservation and Power Subcommittee; after the 1986 election, with help from Chairman John Dingell, who liked aggressive and loyal younger Democrats, Markey became chairman of the Telecommunications Subcommittee. This is one of the plum positions in the House, with fabulous possibilities for campaign fundraising, and with subject matter that is intellectually more demanding (and, in lobbying terms, more fiercely contested) than almost anything else in Congress. In 2001 Markey passed up the ranking position on the Resources Committee to remain ranking member on the Telecommunications Subcommittee.

Markey has been a major shaper of public policy, often working with Republicans, often coming up with original initiatives, knowledgeable about the workings of these industries and inclined often toward deregulation, but also casting himself as the defender of consumers. He combined his penchant for regulation with political shrewdness to produce the 1992 cable TV re-regulation bill on which both houses overrode George H. W. Bush's veto—the only bill passed over his veto in his four-year term. Markey's influence was not greatly reduced when he became ranking minority member; bills in these areas are hard to pass without bipartisan consensus, and he was in a key position to create or withhold it. He was a major player in the passage of the landmark Telecommunications Act of 1996. Markey and then-Commerce Chairman Tom Bliley passed through the House a bill to de-monopolize the satellite communications industry, which became law in March 2000.

Markey was less successful in opposing the Tauzin-Dingell bill to revise the 1996 act by allowing the Bell phone companies—Verizon, SBC, BellSouth and Qwest—to offer broadband services without opening up their lines to competitors, including the CLECs which came into existence after the 1996 law and first soared and then thudded on the stock market. He and Republican ally Chris Cannon were defeated in a rare parliamentary vote in February 2002. Markey continued to press for digital television, seeking to force the FCC to require cable companies to carry digital TV before the required date of 2007. He also pressed for more auctions of currently government-owned spectrum, to allow the emergence of new wireless technologies that he says will boost the economy, with revenues to go into a trust fund to encourage digital TV and advanced wireless services. He sponsored a bill in 2003 to apply cable TV privacy provisions to satellite TV services and TiVo. In 2004, as the committee was increasing penalties for indecent broadcasting after Janet Jackson's appearance on the Super Bowl broadcast, Markey moved to scale FCC fines to percentages of profits or revenues.

Markey has waged an ongoing fight for tougher regulation of nuclear power plants. In October 2001, he got committee Republicans to go along with his proposal to require the Nuclear Regulatory Commission to force plant owners to come up with plans to defend their plants against terrorist attacks. In November 2001, he sponsored a bill to require that guards at nuclear plants be federal employees; in a March 2002 report, he pointed out that the NRC doesn't require plant guards to be U.S. citizens and limits its background criminal checks to the U.S. In another report, he pointed out that the number of security guards at nuclear facilities declined 40% between 1992 and 2001. Markey has a gift for memorable phrases. "We have a 'loose nuke' problem right here at home," he said in May 2002, because some 1,500 types of radioactive material had been lost in five years and only half traced down; he estimated that the loose material, put together, could create a "dirty bomb." In June 2002, he called for a permanent end to the testing of nuclear weapons. In August 2003 he criticized the Bush administration for abolishing a nuclear advisory panel established by the Clinton administration in 2000. From his seat on the Homeland Security Committee, Markey has worked hard on air cargo security issues; he points out that while passenger luggage is x-rayed, commercial cargo goes unscreened on passenger planes. In 2003, his amendment to require screening of all air cargo passed the House easily, but was opposed by the Bush administration and went nowhere in the Senate. A similar amendment was rejected by the House in 2004.

Other Markey causes include financial privacy—he and Republican Rep. Joe Barton got a provision into the financial services deregulation—and de-monopolizing the electric power industry. His moves to raise the miles per gallon standard for automobiles and SUVs were defeated by wide margins in committee and on the floor. He opposes drilling in the Arctic National Wildlife Reserve and sponsored a bill to designate the ANWR coastal area as wilderness.

Markey was one of three Massachusetts House members to vote for the Iraq war resolution in October 2002. By 2004 he said he regretted the vote. In June 2004 he sponsored a bill to bar the CIA from "extraordinary renditions"—turning terrorists to be interrogated by countries that use torture. Later in the year he opposed a bill by Republicans, one opposed by the Bush administration, to specifically authorize such practices. At home Markey has worked to keep open the Bedford VA facility and objected when Sprint installed a tower on St. Joseph's Hall in Watertown.

Markey's history with John Kerry goes back a long ways. In 1984 he was one of several Democrats who started running for the Senate seat being vacated by Paul Tsongas; Kerry was another. Kerry stayed in the race, and won the seat; Markey bowed out, and ran for the House again, after several other Democrats were off and running for the seat. But with help from his campaign manager, Mary Beth Cahill, he beat the one who stayed in, state legislator Sam Rotondi, by a 54%–41% margin—his closest call since he was first elected in 1976. Fast forward to fall 2003, when Kerry's presidential campaign was faltering. At the suggestion of Edward Kennedy, Kerry named Cahill as his campaign manager and Markey, who had already endorsed Kerry, went to work to persuade colleagues in the House not to endorse anyone, especially Howard Dean, until the voters in Iowa and New Hampshire had a chance to speak. Markey predicted, correctly, that Dean would fade and Kerry would rally to victory, and he was mostly successful in keeping House members off the Dean team. Markey supported Kerry actively in the winter primaries and in the fall.

He also made moves to run for the vacancy that would have been created had Kerry won. In October 2004 he spent $300,000 on ads in the Boston media market trumpeting his work against nuclear terrorism and, oddly, his support back in the days of the Cold War of the nuclear freeze. But the spending proved moot; no Senate vacancy looms in Massachusetts. Markey didn't need the money for his own race: he won 74%–22%.

EIGHTH DISTRICT

Rep. Michael Capuano (D)

Elected 1998, 4th term; b. Jan. 9, 1952, Somerville; home, Somerville; Dartmouth Col., B.A. 1973, Boston Col., J.D. 1977; Catholic; married (Barbara).

Elected Office: Somerville Alderman Ward 5, 1977–79; Somerville Alderman-At-Large, 1985–89; Somerville Mayor, 1989–98.

Professional Career: Chief Legal Cnsl., MA Legislature Taxation Cmte., 1978–84; Practicing atty., 1984–90.

DC Office: 1530 LHOB, 20515, 202-225-5111; Fax: 202-225-9322; Web site: www.house.gov/capuano.

District Office: Cambridge, 617-621-8628.

Committees: *Financial Services* (15th of 32 D): Capital Markets, Insurance & Government Sponsored Enterprises; Housing & Community Opportunity. *Transportation & Infrastructure* (24th of 34 D): Aviation; Highways, Transit & Pipelines.

Group Ratings

	ADA	ACLU	AFS	LCV	ITIC	NTU	COC	ACU	NTLC	CHC
2004	90	85	100	91	44	13	19	4	3	7
2003	100	—	100	90	—	25	20	12	—	—

National Journal Ratings

	2003 LIB	—	2003 CONS		2004 LIB	—	2004 CONS
Economic	85%	—	14%		89%	—	8%
Social	89%	—	10%		88%	—	0%
Foreign	81%	—	17%		83%	—	17%

Key Votes of the 108th Congress

1. Drilling in ANWR	N	5. DC School Vouchers	N	9. Ban Same-Sex Marriage	N
2. Approve Bush Tax Cuts	N	6. Ban Human Cloning	N	10. Fund Iraq War	N
3. Medicare/Rx Bill	N	7. Restrict Gun Liability	N	11. Bar Cuba Embargo Funds	Y
4. Bar Overtime Pay Regs.	Y	8. Ban Partial-Birth Abortion	N	12. Intelligence Reorg.	N

Election Results

2004 general	Michael Capuano (D)..........................unopposed		($953,342)
2004 primary	Michael Capuano (D)..........................unopposed		
2002 general	Michael Capuano (D)..........................unopposed		($448,944)

Prior Winning Percentages: 2000 (100%); 1998 (82%)

The People		Race/Ethnic Origin	Ancestry	
Area size:	92 sq. mi.	48.9% White	Irish: 9.9%	Italian: 7.3%
Urban population:	100.0%	21.9% Black	West Indian: 5.2%	
Rural population:	0.0%	8.1% Asian	**2004 Presidential Vote**	
Pop. 2000:	634,835	0.2% Native Am.	Kerry (D) 168,264	(79%)
Median income:	$39,300	0.1% Hawaiian	Bush (R) 40,885	(19%)
Poverty status:	19.9%	3.5% Two+ races	Other 3,683	(2%)
Military veterans:	5.5%	1.5% Other	**2000 Presidential Vote**	
		15.9% Hispanic Origin	Gore (D) 142,500	(73%)
			Bush (R) 28,903	(15%)
			Other 23,374	(12%)
			Cook Partisan Voting Index: D +33	
Occupation	Blue collar: 12.4%	White collar: 70.6%	Gray collar: 17.0%	

The "Hub of the Solar System" is what the elder Oliver Wendell Holmes called the Massachusetts State House in the 19th century, though over time, his statement has come to be remembered as referring to Boston as the "Hub of the Universe." Either way, this most political of cities often has been the focal point of essential moments in American history. These streets, originally laid out as 17th century cowpaths, are where Samuel Adams and Paul Revere plotted revolution, where the abolitionist movement helped ignite the Civil War and are the sites of rallies and headquarters of the various Kennedy campaigns. Today's Boston is a different city from the Boston of John Kennedy's time. Boston then was a gray city with no new buildings and dust on every windowsill; the sky was dark with pollution and the air was thick with ancient Yankee and Irish animosity. The old office buildings were full of Yankees seeking safe investments for their antique family fortunes; the State House and City Hall were full of Irishmen, scampering after good patronage jobs and regaling each other with political battle stories. Today that Boston is mostly gone. The new skyscrapers are full of well-educated venture capitalists, lawyers and management consultants, many working for high-tech companies radiating from Cambridge out into the countryside. Most of Boston's neighborhoods have changed. Minorities and young singles increasingly populate the central city. The city's population is down from 801,000 in 1950 to 589,000 in 2000; more than 80% of people in the metropolitan area live in the suburbs.

A long generation ago, students from suburbs across the country who were exploring Boston from their dormitories and campuses felt they were pawing through the living remnants of 1920s America, a quaint place where people called traffic circles "rotaries" and milk shakes "frappes." Massachusetts has since changed, and nowhere more than in Cambridge. As universities and high tech have become driving forces of economic growth, Cambridge has gone glitzy, with trendy restaurants and high-priced hotels, boutiques and upscale condominiums. Greater Boston may well have the heaviest concentration of graduate students and post-graduate hangers-on of any major city, and this graduate student proletariat's world is centered on Cambridge, with outposts in lower-income Somerville, Boston's Back Bay, and Allston and Brighton near the Harvard Business School. Although most unrelated activities seemed to shut down for the week, this new-fashioned city proudly paraded its wares during the 2004 Democratic National Convention, which nominated Beacon Hill's favorite son John Kerry.

These communities are part of Massachusetts's 8th Congressional District, a district with great historic sites, from the Paul Revere house in the North End to the frigate *U.S.S. Constitution* in the Charlestown docks. The district, with MIT and the software concentration in Cambridge's once downscale Lechmere Square, is one of the high-tech capitals of America. The 8th includes all of Cambridge, Somerville and Chelsea and many Boston neighborhoods—East Boston around Logan Airport, Brighton and the Back Bay, Fenway, Mattapan, Mission Hill, the South End. It shares Hyde Park, Roxbury, Dorchester and Jamaica Plain with the neighboring 9th District. For the first time in its history, whites are a minority of Boston's population. As they replace the Irish and Italians, Hispanics have caused a population boom in low-income Chelsea and in Dorchester, which annually celebrates one of the nation's largest Caribbean festivals. This is by far the most Democratic district in Massachusetts.

The congressman from the 8th District is Michael Capuano, the winner of a 10-candidate primary in 1998. It could be said that over the last 60-odd years this district has been represented alternately by townies and Kennedys: James Michael Curley, the scampish five-term mayor of Boston and one-term governor; followed by John F. Kennedy in 1946, then from 1952, Tip O'Neill, the most successful House speaker of this half-century; succeeded on his retirement in 1986 by Joe Kennedy; and now Capuano. He was born and raised in Somerville; his paternal grandfather emigrated from Italy, and his father was the first Italian-American elected official in Somerville; his mother is the granddaughter of Irish immigrants. Capuano graduated from Dartmouth and Boston College Law School. He returned to Somerville to raise his family, practice law and get into politics. By day, he worked for the legislature's Joint Committee on Taxation and practiced law; in off-hours, he served as alderman in the 5th Ward, like his father before him. He was elected alderman-at-large from 1985–89, then won election five times as the city's mayor. For decades an Irish and Italian town, Somerville now attracts many grad students and yuppies. Capuano seems to have been the right politician for this mix, with deep Somerville roots and a penchant for innovation and reform. So he had a solid base to run for the 8th District seat in 1998 when Joe Kennedy announced that he wouldn't seek re-election. In a 10-candidate field, Capuano led with 23%, with former Boston Mayor (1983–93) Ray Flynn the runner-up at 17%.

In the House, Capuano is well to the left on the national political spectrum, though relatively centrist within the Massachusetts delegation: For same-sex marriage, against the partial-birth abortion ban and opposed to the flag-burning amendment. He sponsored a proposal to expand federal terrorism risk insurance coverage to include group life insurance; the Financial Services Committee, on which Capuano serves, approved a modified version. On the Transportation Committee, he worried that headlines about tunnel leaks and other construction defects in the Big Dig would jeopardize support for new local highway projects, especially with lingering resentment over the cost of Tip O'Neill's legacy. "The last thing that I need while the highway bill is pending is a headline-grabbing investigation," he said after colleague Marty Meehan went public with criticism and backed a federal probe.

Capuano has not been shy about moving beyond local politics. When Catholic bishops across the nation said that they would deny communion to John Kerry because of his support for abortion, Capuano replied that all Catholics should vote their conscience. "It strikes me almost as un-Christian. Jesus himself never would have denied communion to anyone, even Mary Magdalene." He has evidently felt some frustration as a member of the minority in the House and talked about running for governor in 2006; in January 2005 he announced he would not run.

Since 1998 Capuano has not faced opposition in either primary or general elections. In 2004, local black ministers urged Charles Stith, who was Bill Clinton's ambassador to Tanzania, to run against Capuano as an independent. After Stith voiced some interest, other minority leaders backed Capuano and Stith changed his mind.

NINTH DISTRICT

Rep. Stephen Lynch (D)

Elected Oct. 2001, 2d full term; b. Mar. 31, 1955, Boston; home, South Boston; Wentworth Inst., B.S. 1988, Boston Col. Schl. of Law, J.D. 1991, Harvard U. JFK Schl. of Gov., M.A. 1998; Catholic; married (Margaret).

Elected Office: MA House of Reps., 1994–96; MA Senate, 1996–2001.

Professional Career: Structural ironworker, 1973–91; Practicing atty., 1991–2001.

DC Office: 319 CHOB, 20515, 202-225-8273; Fax: 202-225-3984; Web site: www.house.gov/lynch.

District Offices: Boston, 617-428-2000; Brockton, 508-586-5555.

Committees: *Financial Services* (24th of 32 D): Capital Markets, Insurance & Government Sponsored Enterprises; Housing & Community Opportunity; Oversight & Investigations. *Government Reform* (12th of 17 D): National Security, Emerging Threats & International Relations; Regulatory Affairs (RMM).

Group Ratings

	ADA	ACLU	AFS	LCV	ITIC	NTU	COC	ACU	NTLC	CHC
2004	85	55	100	100	40	13	43	28	3	46
2003	85	—	100	95	—	21	27	29	—	—

National Journal Ratings

	2003 LIB	—	2003 CONS		2004 LIB	—	2004 CONS
Economic	80%	—	19%		72%	—	28%
Social	61%	—	39%		66%	—	33%
Foreign	75%	—	25%		68%	—	30%

Key Votes of the 108th Congress

1. Drilling in ANWR	N	5. DC School Vouchers	N	9. Ban Same-Sex Marriage	N
2. Approve Bush Tax Cuts	N	6. Ban Human Cloning	Y	10. Fund Iraq War	Y
3. Medicare/Rx Bill	N	7. Restrict Gun Liability	N	11. Bar Cuba Embargo Funds	Y
4. Bar Overtime Pay Regs.	Y	8. Ban Partial-Birth Abortion	Y	12. Intelligence Reorg.	N

Election Results

2004 general	Stephen Lynch (D)	unopposed	($591,797)
2004 primary	Stephen Lynch (D)	unopposed	
2002 general	Stephen Lynch (D)	unopposed	($2,386,568)

Prior Winning Percentages: 2001 (66%)

The People		Race/Ethnic Origin	Ancestry	
Area size:	319 sq. mi.	79.3% White	Irish: 23.2%	Italian: 10.3%
Urban population:	98.4%	8.1% Black	English: 7.0%	
Rural population:	1.6%	3.7% Asian	**2004 Presidential Vote**	
Pop. 2000:	634,062	0.2% Native Am.	Kerry (D) 188,439 (63%)	
Median income:	$55,407	0.0% Hawaiian	Bush (R) 106,734 (36%)	
Poverty status:	7.5%	2.4% Two+ races	Other 3,378 (1%)	
Military veterans:	11.6%	1.8% Other	**2000 Presidential Vote**	
		4.6% Hispanic Origin	Gore (D) 167,059 (60%)	
			Bush (R) 93,529 (33%)	
			Other 19,051 (7%)	
			Cook Partisan Voting Index: D +15	

Occupation	Blue collar: 17.3%	White collar: 68.9%	Gray collar: 13.7%

The Irish remain the dominant political tribe in Boston and in Massachusetts, though even in South Boston, long the center of Irish Boston, vestiges of the old Irish neighborhoods are starting to gentrify. But Southie's influence endures in the memory of two Irish Democrats who represented the area for all but two years from the Great Depression to the start of the 21st century. The first was John McCormack, an old-style backroom dealmaker who served as House Speaker during the 1960s, when he arguably had passed his political prime; the second was Joe Moakley, a close pal of Tip O'Neill, who got his former seat on the Rules Committee and chaired the panel before Democrats lost their House majority in 1994. The 9th Congressional District, historically anchored in Boston, has followed the move of the Irish to the suburbs. Today, less than one-third of its residents are in Boston, mostly in still-Irish areas of South Boston, Hyde Park (shared with the 8th) and West Roxbury. Near-completion of the Big Dig highway construction, including a new tunnel under Boston Harbor, has spurred economic development along the waterfront, including office buildings, hotels, condominiums and a huge new convention center—all of which have boosted property values in South Boston. At long last, the ugly Central Artery, the North-South expressway that for five decades divided the city, has been moved underground and traffic moves far more efficiently, though with huge cost over-runs driving the Big Dig bill to $15 billion. In the traditionally Italian North End, the result has been likened to taking down the Berlin Wall, encouraging residents to walk the Freedom Trail to downtown. The 9th district also includes much of Beacon Hill, including the gold-domed State House facing Boston Common. From there, the 9th heads west to comfortable suburbs of Needham and Medfield and southeast to Braintree, ancestral home of the presidential Adamses, and Brockton, the old shoe manufacturing town. Ethnically, it is the nation's second-most heavily Irish congressional district (working-class Southie is home to an annual St. Patrick's Day parade, preceded by a political breakfast/roast that is a must-attend for state politicians). Only the neighboring 10th District has more residents of Irish ancestry—further evidence of the Irish move out of Boston to the far suburbs.

The congressman from the 9th District is Stephen Lynch, who won a special election in October 2001 to replace Joe Moakley, who had served since 1973 and was beloved by many House Democrats as a link between the party's old and new generations. Lynch grew up in Boston's housing projects and took pride in succeeding by the old ethnic codes of hard work, family loyalty and personal determination. After graduating from South Boston High School, he joined his father in working full-time as an ironworker while attending Wentworth Institute; eventually, he became the youngest president ever of the 2,000-member Local 7 of the Ironworkers union. After a fall on the job cut short his work on the iron, he graduated from Boston College law school and opened a legal practice representing working people. In 1994, he was elected to the state House. Fourteen months later, he won a special election for a seat in the state Senate.

Lynch built a political base in South Boston and had strong union ties, advantages that led him to seek the 9th District seat when Moakley announced in February 2001 that he would not seek reelection; Moakley died in May. Lynch was one of several Democrats who had expressed interest in the race. The most prominent was Max Kennedy, son of Robert and Ethel Kennedy, but his campaign never gathered any traction. When Kennedy bowed out in June, Lynch became the frontrunner. He stumbled following the *Boston Globe*'s revelations of his student loan defaults years earlier, plus a tax lien that was resolved in 1998; he also had been twice arrested two decades earlier, once for striking an anti-American student demonstrator and the other for smoking marijuana at a concert. Three other state senators opposed Lynch: Cheryl Jacques, Brian Joyce, and Marc Pacheco. The strongest foe was Jacques, who is openly gay and had support from EMILY's List and other national feminist groups, which criticized Lynch's anti-abortion views. But her switch to opposing capital punishment stirred controversy. Joyce, the most prolific fundraiser of the four, sought to rally suburban support. Pacheco vied with Jacques for the liberal vote, and was endorsed by teachers' unions. Citing her as "the most principled progressive in the race," the *Globe* endorsed Jacques. Moakley's two brothers, who probably wielded more influence, endorsed Lynch. Despite the Boston-based terror attacks on the September 11 primary day, Governor Jane Swift decided not to postpone balloting; Lynch won with 39%, to 29% for Jacques. In the anti-climactic general election five weeks later, he defeated another state senator, Jo Ann Sprague, 66%–33%.

In the House, Lynch votes roughly in the middle of the Democratic Caucus but has had the most conservative voting record in the Massachusetts delegation. "That's like being called the slowest of the Kenyans in the marathon," he quipped to the *Boston Herald*. Initially he turned his attention to security, both at the nation's airports and in the war on terrorism. He said that the nation was "grossly unprepared" for terror attacks on its rails and in its ports, and called for spending billions of dollars in accelerated responses. He was one of three Massachusetts House members to vote for the Iraq war resolution. Following his decision to give part of his own liver to an ailing brother-in-law during his 2001 campaign, Lynch filed a bill to streamline research on liver disease at the National Institutes of Health. He also showed unexpected support for gay-rights causes, developing a political alliance with Barney Frank to educate himself.

Lynch has been reelected without difficulty. The *Boston Phoenix* termed him "a man in a hurry." When John Kerry locked up the Democratic presidential nomination, Lynch was among the most aggressive prospective candidates for his Senate seat, emphasizing an appeal to working-class voters. "Those opportunities are so rare that I certainly would take a look at it, a serious look at it," he said.

TENTH DISTRICT

Rep. Bill Delahunt (D)

Elected 1996, 5th term; b. July 18, 1941, Quincy; home, Quincy; Middlebury Col., B.A. 1963, Boston Col., J.D. 1967; Catholic; divorced.

Military Career: Coast Guard, 1963; Coast Guard Reserves, 1963–71.

Elected Office: Quincy City Cncl., 1971; MA House of Reps., 1972–75.

Professional Career: Practicing atty., 1967–75; Asst. Clerk, Norfolk Superior Court, 1969–71; Norfolk Cnty. Dist. Atty., 1975–96.

DC Office: 2454 RHOB, 20515, 202-225-3111; Fax: 202-225-5658; Web site: www.house.gov/delahunt.

District Offices: Hyannis, 508-771-0666; Quincy, 617-770-3700.

Committees: *International Relations* (11th of 23 D): Oversight & Investigations (RMM); Western Hemisphere. *Judiciary* (11th of 17 D): Commercial & Administrative Law; Crime, Terrorism & Homeland Security.

Group Ratings

	ADA	ACLU	AFS	LCV	ITIC	NTU	COC	ACU	NTLC	CHC
2004	95	95	100	100	40	8	33	0	0	7
2003	95	—	100	90	—	24	14	8	—	—

National Journal Ratings

	2003 LIB	—	2003 CONS		2004 LIB	—	2004 CONS
Economic	92%	—	0%		93%	—	6%
Social	88%	—	11%		82%	—	17%
Foreign	94%	—	0%		96%	—	4%

Key Votes of the 108th Congress

1. Drilling in ANWR	*	5. DC School Vouchers	N	9. Ban Same-Sex Marriage	N
2. Approve Bush Tax Cuts	N	6. Ban Human Cloning	N	10. Fund Iraq War	N
3. Medicare/Rx Bill	N	7. Restrict Gun Liability	N	11. Bar Cuba Embargo Funds	Y
4. Bar Overtime Pay Regs.	Y	8. Ban Partial-Birth Abortion	N	12. Intelligence Reorg.	N

Election Results

2004 general	Bill Delahunt (D)	222,013	(66%)	($843,755)
	Michael Jones (R)	114,879	(34%)	($262,798)
2004 primary	Bill Delahunt (D)	unopposed		
2002 general	Bill Delahunt (D)	179,238	(69%)	($266,025)
	Luiz Gonzaga (R)	79,624	(31%)	($55,428)

Prior Winning Percentages: 2000 (74%); 1998 (70%); 1996 (54%)

The People		Race/Ethnic Origin	Ancestry	
Area size:	2,969 sq. mi.	92.2% White	Irish: 23.9%	English: 11.9%
Urban population:	92.2%	1.5% Black	Italian: 9.9%	
Rural population:	7.8%	2.7% Asian	**2004 Presidential Vote**	
Pop. 2000:	635,901	0.3% Native Am.	Kerry (D) 194,092	(56%)
Median income:	$51,928	0.0% Hawaiian	Bush (R) 151,209	(43%)
Poverty status:	5.9%	1.3% Two+ races	Other 3,910	(1%)
Military veterans:	15.1%	0.6% Other	**2000 Presidential Vote**	
		1.3% Hispanic Origin	Gore (D) 175,426	(54%)
			Bush (R) 124,956	(39%)
			Other 22,722	(7%)
			Cook Partisan Voting Index: D + 9	

Occupation   Blue collar: 18.1%   White collar: 66.7%   Gray collar: 15.2%

The South Shore of Massachusetts Bay, from Boston southward to Plymouth and then down Cape Cod (there is a lot of dispute about which way is up and down on the Cape), is Massachusetts's oldest-settled territory. The Pilgrims landed here at Plymouth Rock in 1620; this stony land was farmed by John Adams's father, who was anything but the aristocrat some later members of the Adams family would have had you believe. Daniel Webster lived in the South Shore town of Marshfield, today a high-income suburb of Boston far out on the usually clogged Southeast Expressway. Joseph P. Kennedy used to summer with his young family on Nantasket Beach in Hull, before moving out of Massachusetts when the Yankees wouldn't let them into their beach club in Cohasset in the 1920s; but the Kennedys continue to summer at their Hyannis Port compound on the Cape. Provincetown, at the tip of the Cape, is still a fishing port, one of the major gay vacation areas in the country, and increasingly a year-round mecca; the islands of Martha's Vineyard and Nantucket, rich whaling ports in the early 19th century, are now favored summer resorts for the trendy liberal rich of Boston, New York and Washington. Half the nation's cranberry growers are clustered among the bogs along Cape Cod Bay. But the Cape is also filled with retirees and, to the dismay of some, is the fastest-growing part of Massachusetts; the Cape's Barnstable County grew 19% in the 1990s.

The 10th Congressional District of Massachusetts follows the South Shore from Quincy (pronounced *quin*zee) to the Cape. It juts inland almost, but not quite to Brockton, and includes Martha's Vineyard and Nantucket, where the glitterati have generated a "not in my backyard" fury over a proposed windmill farm in the nearby channel waters. The South Shore and the Cape were once exclusively Protestant and Yankee, but in the Massachusetts way they have changed over the years, with Irish and Italian surnames as common as Yankee ones (this is the nation's most heavily Irish congressional district), and the descendants of Portuguese-Azorean fishermen have fanned out into the countryside. Liberal politics, well established on the Vineyard and Nantucket, have spread inland as well. The South Shore is generally Democratic territory, but in 2002 Republican Mitt Romney carried the area; in 2004 George W. Bush fell well short of John Kerry there.

The congressman from the 10th District is Bill Delahunt, a Democrat first elected in 1996. Delahunt is a lifelong resident of Quincy at the northern tip of the district; he graduated from Middlebury College and Boston College Law School and served in the Coast Guard. He practiced law and served on the Quincy Council. In 1972, he was elected to the state House; Governor Michael Dukakis in 1975 appointed him district attorney of Norfolk County, a job that Delahunt held for two decades. He ran for the House in 1996 when 24-year incumbent Gerry Studds retired and faced serious primary competition from former state Representative Philip Johnston and self-financed environmentalist Ian Bowles. The initial results showed 38% each for Delahunt and Johnston, with Johnston ahead by 266 votes; a recount declared Johnston still ahead by 175 votes. But Delahunt sued, and on October 4, a judge ruled that more than 900 punch card votes in Weymouth had not been properly tabulated. In shades of another election challenge four years later, the judge ordered a recount of every ballot with an indentation, dimple or other mark: Only in this district and in 14 counties in Texas had dimpled chads ever been counted as votes in the U.S. until the Broward, Palm Beach and Miami-Dade County canvassing boards started counting them in November 2000. On October 10, Delahunt was declared the winner by 108 votes, even as Johnston was being hailed at a Quincy rally by Ted Kennedy and Hillary Rodham Clinton. (Subsequently, Massachusetts eliminated punch card voting, and Delahunt voiced support for hand recounts of punch cards elsewhere). Johnston called the result a "travesty," and Delahunt had less than a month to campaign for the general against conservative state House Minority Leader Edward Teague. Both ran million-dollar campaigns, but Teague had been running ads against Johnston. Eight years earlier, George H. W. Bush carried this district over Michael Dukakis, but reaction here to the new Republican majority in the House was hostile; Delahunt won 54%–42%.

Delahunt has been an active legislator, and has kept a pledge to wear Cape Cod ties in the House and hand them out to colleagues of both parties. As the father of an adopted daughter who escaped Vietnam in the 1975 Operation Babylift, he has written laws to ease international adoptions. His positions on abortion are part of Massachusetts's move to the left: In 1974 as a state legislator he called *Roe v. Wade* "a tragic decision," but he switched to a pro-abortion rights position before running for the House and voted against the partial-birth abortion ban. His experience with contested elections made him an enthusiast for abolishing the Electoral College. On the Judiciary Committee during the Clinton impeachment, he was one of the few members who sat down in bipartisan breakfasts to discuss procedures. But he ended up siding completely with impeachment opponents. He took the lead in framing a Democratic motion to censure Bill Clinton and protested bitterly when Judiciary Chairman Henry Hyde would not allow it to be heard. With Illinois Republican Ray LaHood, he filed the Innocence Protection Act, which includes federal funding to the states for DNA testing of the accused; the House passed the measure, 393–14, in October 2004, and it became law. He also won enactment in 2004 of a pilot project to distribute commercial fishing gear, which would reduce expenses for fishermen plus the risk of injury to endangered whales. Delahunt also served on the four-member bipartisan ethics subcommittee that investigated claims by Republican Nick Smith of Michigan that efforts were made to bribe him to gain his support for Medicare reform in November 2003.

Delahunt has worked on local projects, including the Cape Cod land bank, the Salt Pond visitors' center at the National Seashore entry in Eastham, and conversion of the former Camp Edwards National Guard training site to a federal wildlife refuge.

Delahunt has easily won his re-election bids, with no need to count dimpled chads; he won 66%–34% in 2004. On Capitol Hill, he is the fourth tenant in a long-running apartment rental shared by Senators Chuck Schumer and Richard Durbin and Representative George Miller. He shares the living room with Schumer in conditions best described as ramshackle.

★ MICHIGAN ★

Is Michigan in economic trouble again? A quarter-century ago, it was one of the states hardest hit by the recession of the early 1980s, and seemed headed for disaster. But in the 1990s Michigan's economy rebounded. For most of a decade it led the nation in the number of new factories and factory expansions, and the quality of Michigan products was vastly better than a generation before. It was one of America's premier laboratories of innovation, busy expanding high-skill manufacturing while rethinking and downsizing government programs, just as it was once busy inventing the mass-production factory economy and then developing the giant industrial labor union and its version of the American welfare state. It was a manufacturing state that has transformed itself in line with the nation's movement from an industrial to a post-industrial economy, from domination by big units—big business, big labor, big government—to growth increasingly driven by small units—small businesses, individual workers, flexible government. Now that achievement suddenly seems threatened. From 1993 up through October 2000, Michigan's unemployment rate was lower than the nation's in almost every month. Then, with the national recession, unemployment shot up above the national average, as might be expected in a manufacturing state. But the national recovery that took hold in 2003 did not seem to take hold in Michigan. Unemployment averaged 5.3% in 2001 and 6.2% in 2002, about 0.5% above the national average—not alarming for a recessionary period. But Michigan's unemployment was 7.3% in 2003 and 6.8% in 2004—about 1.3% above the national average; Michigan was the only state to lose jobs in 2004. In December 2004 Michigan unemployment spiked to 7.3%, 1.9% above the national average and the third-highest in the nation—perhaps just a blip, but not a good sign. To explain this, the natural tendency is to fall back to looking at the problems of the Big Three auto companies. But Michigan's achievement in the 1990s seemed to be moving beyond dependence on just three big firms, toward a more diversified and dispersed economy. It would be unfortunate if that achievement proves ephemeral.

Michigan's roots go back to the Tocquevillian decade of the 1830s, when Alexis de Tocqueville visited Michigan and when it achieved statehood. These two peninsulas, explored and named by French explorers (which explains why Mackinac is pronounced with a silent final c and Michigan with a ch pronounced like sh), were settled in a rush by Yankee migrants from Upstate New York, who cut down trees and built farms and neat New Englandish towns complete with schools and colleges. Politically, Michigan was full of reformers who hated slavery, manned the Underground Railroad, promoted temperance and in 1855 gave Michigan a constitution that banned (as it does to this day) capital punishment. Michigan was one of the birthplaces of the Republican Party, which was founded in Jackson in 1854 (Ripon, Wisconsin, also stakes a claim as the party's birthplace) and swept the state in the elections later that year. Until 1929, Michigan was one of the most Republican states in the nation.

Michigan also developed an industrial economy. Its Lower Peninsula was mostly covered with trees, and lumber was the first boom industry on which Michigan overrelied; forests were clear-cut or swept by blazes like the 1881 fire that burned out half the Thumb. In the late 1800s, huge copper deposits were discovered on the Keweenaw Peninsula, which juts from the Upper Peninsula into icy Lake Superior; immigrants from Italy and Finland, Cornwall and Croatia came to work in the mines. Then came the auto industry. A combination of accident and shrewdness, of bankers willing to finance auto startups and the prickly genius of Henry Ford, ensured that America's fastest-growing industry for the first 30 years of the 20th century was centered in Michigan. Detroit became a boomtown—the nation's fastest-growing metropolitan area after Los Angeles—zooming from 426,000 in 1900 to 2.2 million in 1930 (it was 4.2 million in 2000). The auto industry drew labor from the Outstate Michigan, from southern Ontario and from the farms of Ohio and Indiana. During World War II and after, it brought whites from the Kentucky and Tennessee mountains and blacks from Alabama and Mississippi. It attracted Poles and Italians, Hungarians and Belgians, Greeks and Jews. This influx of a polyglot proletariat eventually changed Michigan's politics. The catalyst was the Great Depression of the 1930s and the company managers' desire to use machines efficiently, treating employees as

The Almanac of American Politics.
National Journal

Miles
0   20   40

SEE INSET FOR DETAIL ON 9, 11-14.

Congressional district boundaries were first effective for 2002.

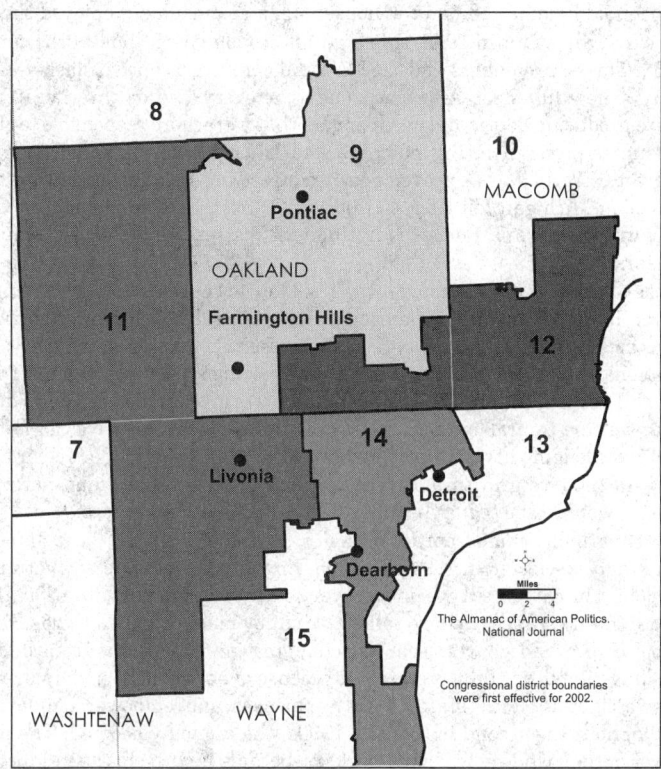

extensions of machines and with great distrust. The results were the 1937 sit-down strikes organized by the new United Auto Workers (UAW); management and labor fought, sometimes literally, for pieces of what both sides feared was a shrinking pie. The UAW won and organized most of the companies after Democratic Governor Frank Murphy refused to send in troops to break the illegal strikes. In the years that followed, autoworkers became a heavily Democratic voting bloc.

Michigan politics became a kind of class warfare, conducted with a bitterness that split families and neighbors. The union mostly won, because demographics benefited the Democrats: autoworkers and post-1900 immigrants produced more children than did Outstate Yankees or management. After Walter Reuther's election as UAW president in 1947, voters elected young, liberal G. Mennen Williams governor in 1948. By 1954, the Democrats, closely tied to the UAW, seemed to have become the natural majority in the state. As growth continued, economic issues became less bitter; by the early 1960s, the class-warfare atmosphere had dissipated. A Republican former auto executive, George Romney, was narrowly elected governor in 1962, and Henry Ford II joined Reuther in backing Lyndon B. Johnson in 1964. Romney and his successor, William Milliken, accepted the welfare-state policies endorsed by the UAW leadership and the Democrats. The state government was one of the nation's most generous, and not just to the poor and the unemployed: it supported one of the nation's most distinguished and extensive higher education systems, built state parks and recreation areas, and pioneered efforts to end racial discrimination.

This system, which had seemed eternal, came crashing down with the collapse of the domestic auto industry after the oil shock of 1973. Union-management relations had been static since 1941, and there had been no major technological changes in American autos since the automatic transmission in 1940. Michigan incomes had grown as Americans grew more affluent;

the one-car household became the two-car household, and consumers enjoyed the tail fins and chrome of new car styling. But in 1979, this big-unit economy went bust. It became startlingly clear that the Big Three automakers and the UAW did not have a captive market, Americans did not have to buy a new full-sized American-made car every two or three years, and foreign competitors were producing better and cheaper cars that were more responsive to changes in gas prices and consumer preference. Big business and labor, so well adapted for growth in the quarter century after World War II, proved poorly adapted for the quarter century that followed. Auto employment in Michigan fell from 437,000 in October 1978 to 289,000 in October 1982. Chrysler nearly went bankrupt, Ford was in financial distress, and General Motors posted its first losses in years.

The collapse of the big-unit economy after 1979 forced the state to experiment. The first to try was Governor James Blanchard, a Democrat elected in 1982 with a record of supporting big units. His major achievement in eight years in Congress was managing the Chrysler bailout in the House. Blanchard worked to build a small-unit economy; he was proud of his efforts to stimulate high-skill, capital-intensive, flexible manufacturing, and he used $750 million of state pension funds as venture capital for manufacturers of items from tape drives for microcomputers to fiberglass coffins. Dodging his traditional labor allies, Blanchard made it clear that Michigan must learn how to nurture growth and that workers, instead of seeking more vacation and earlier retirement, would have to hustle and work harder than ever before.

The second experiment came from John Engler, the Republican who beat Blanchard in 1990 and was resoundingly re-elected in 1994 and 1998. Engler believed in less government activism and industrial policy; he cut or held the line on every state program but education. In three terms he cut taxes more than 30 times; welfare rolls were cut by more than two-thirds. Engler pressed for public school choice and charter schools, changing state pensions from defined benefits (which produce huge liabilities for the state and a sense of entitlement in employees) to defined contributions (which reduce the state's future expenses and empower employees to act as investors). Throughout the second half of the 1990s, the economy boomed. The auto industry, once an employer of thousands of low-skill workers, became high-tech; the number of unionized auto workers fell to 250,000 in 2000, but jobs required much higher skills and auto workers' earnings averaged $60,000. With the auto companies requiring high standards and speedy turnaround from subcontractors, Michigan became the home of almost all the nation's auto parts engineering centers and of much of the nation's large-scale manufacturing experts. Michigan's population rose 7% in the 1990s after staying even in the 1980s; median household incomes rose 5% after inflation. Large parts of the state—the western and northern suburbs of Detroit, greater Grand Rapids, the northwest corner of the Upper Peninsula—were unmistakably booming. But there was one notable exception: the city of Detroit. Detroit's population fell to 951,000 in 2000, almost exactly half its 1,849,000 in 1950. Starting with the riot of 1967, crime rates in Detroit were enormously high for 25 years, and much of the city simply vanished—houses abandoned or burned down, commercial frontage with nearly 100% vacancy rates, the downtown a beleaguered fortress surrounded by blasted-out square miles. Detroit rebounded in the 1990s and after: crime and welfare rolls were down, new stadiums and a gambling casino were built downtown and old theaters refurbished.

The election results show how Michigan politics has changed. From the 1930s through the 1980s, politics divided Michigan between labor and management, and between the Detroit metro area and Outstate. In 1960, John Kennedy carried three-county metro Detroit 62%–38% and Richard Nixon carried Outstate 60%–39%, for a 51%–49% Kennedy victory. In 2004 John Kerry carried the three-county metro area 56%–43% while George W. Bush carried the rest of the state, which now casts 61% of the vote, by only 52%–47%, for a 51%–48% Kerry victory. Kerry's lead in the metro area came almost entirely from the city of Detroit, which cast only 7% of the state's votes but voted 94% for Kerry. In the industrial Michigan of 1960, economic status—and more specifically, union membership or non-membership—tended to drive party preference. In the post-industrial Michigan of 2004, economics played some role, but more often cultural attitudes drove voting behavior. Kerry carried affluent Oakland County, where many upscale voters moved toward the Democrats in the 1990s on cultural issues. Bush carried Macomb County, historically more blue collar and Democratic, though pretty affluent now, which in the 1970s and 1980s trended away from Democrats on cultural issues. The Grand Rapids area, with its large Dutch-American population and many Christian conservatives, voted heavily Republican. The industrial Flint, Saginaw and Bay City areas, where unions remain relatively strong, voted heavily Democratic, as did the areas around Lansing, the state capital, and Ann Arbor, home of the University of Michigan. The Upper Peninsula, historically Democratic, voted for Bush. In Detroit and heavily Democratic areas, turnout in 2004 increased relatively little over 2000; it increased most in the suburban ring around Detroit, but not enough for Bush to overtake Kerry. Overall the state is closely divided. If Democrats at the top of the ticket carried Michigan in 2000, 2002 and 2004, Republicans have retained majorities in the state legislature and, with help from a Republican districting plan, in the U.S. House delegation. Michigan remains one of the nation's prime political battlegrounds.

The People		Race/Ethnic Origin			Military veterans: 913,573 (12.4%)	
Pop. 2004 (est):	10,112,620	7,806,691	78.6%	White	WWII: 21.3%	Korea: 14.0%
Pop. 2000:	9,938,444	1,402,047	14.1%	Black	Vietnam: 31.4%	Gulf War: 8.4%
Pop. 1990:	9,295,297	175,311	1.8%	Asian	**Most populous cities (2003):**	
Change 1990–2000:	Up 6.9%	53,421	0.5%	Native Am.	1. Detroit	911,402
% of U.S. total:	3.5%	2,145	0.0%	Hawaiian	2. Grand Rapids	195,601
Pop. rank:	8th of 50	163,487	1.6%	Two+ races	3. Warren	136,016
Area size:	96,716 sq. mi.	11,465	0.1%	Other	4. Sterling Heights	126,182
State Native:	75.4%	323,877	3.3%	Hisp. Origin	5. Flint	120,292
Non-citizen:	2.9%	**Ancestry**				
Language		German: 14.9%		Irish: 7.9%	Urban population: 74.7%	
English: 89.2%	Other Eur.: 4.8%	English: 7.3%		Polish: 6.3%	Rural population: 25.3%	
Spanish: 3.5%		USA: 3.8%				

Education		Work Sector		Legislature	
H.S. Grad:	83.4%	Private: 83.1%	Govt: 11.4%	Senate	22 R 16 D
College Grad:	21.8%	Self: 5.2%	Family: 0.3%	House	58 R 52 D
Industry		Unemployment: 5.8%		Legislative Term Limits: Yes	
Agri: 1.1%	Con: 6.0%	**Household Income**		**Registered Voters**	
Fin: 5.3%	Info: 2.1%	<15k: 14.1%	15-35k: 24.8%	No party registration	
Mfg: 26.7%	Prof: 27.9%	35-50k: 16.5%	50-100k: 32.0%		
Public: 3.6%	Trade: 15.2%	100-150k: 8.6%	>150k: 4.1%		
Other: 12.2%		Median: $44,667			
Occupation		Poverty status: 10.5%			
Blue collar: 27.6%	White collar: 57.1%	**Home Value**			
Gray collar: 15.3%		<50k: 14.3%	50-100k: 30.3%	100-200k: 38.8%	200-300k: 10.6%
		300-500k: 4.4%	>500k: 1.5%	Median: $110,300	

Presidential politics   For three elections in a row—1984, 1988 and 1992—Michigan voted within 1% of the national average for all major presidential candidates. In the last three elections—1996, 2000 and 2004—Michigan voted 3% more Democratic than the nation as a whole. This despite the fact that Al Gore and John Kerry both backed higher gas mileage standards, opposed by both the Big Three auto companies and the United Auto Workers, and despite John Kerry's wobble on diversion of Great Lakes water ("It's a delicate balancing act. There are different ways of managing water rights with remunerations and the appropriate respect to states' rights"). Most of the difference can be accounted for by the move toward Demo-

2004 Presidential Vote
Kerry (D).....................2,479,183   (51%)
Bush (R) 2,313,746   (48%)
Nader (NPA)...................24,035   (0%)
Other..........................22,288   (0%)

2000 Presidential Vote
Gore (D).....................2,170,418   (51%)
Bush (R) 1,953,139   (46%)
Nader (Green) 84,165   (2%)
Other..........................24,779   (1%)

crats on cultural issues in the nation's largest metro areas, including Detroit. Republicans used to be able to count on big margins in affluent Oakland County, but it voted by narrow margins for Bill Clinton, Gore and Kerry. Macomb County, somewhat less affluent, heavily Democratic in the

1950s and 1960s, then trended Republican in the 1970s and 1980s, and is now closely divided, voting for Gore in 2000 and George W. Bush in 2004. Voters in union households voted 61%–37% for Kerry—a sign that union loyalty is not entirely a thing of the past—but they comprised just 37% of the electorate, down from around half in the 1970s. Michigan was a battleground state throughout the 2004 campaign, and both sides made great efforts to get out the vote. Both sides had their successes—Democratic turnout surged in Ann Arbor, Republican turnout surged in exurban Livingston County and northern Macomb County. But both had their disappointments as well. Turnout in Detroit, which voted 94% for Kerry, rose only 9%; the Republican margin in heavily Republican metro Grand Rapids declined, as the central city voted for Kerry. As in Ohio, the winning party's 2000 margin was reduced, but not enough for Kerry to carry Ohio or for Bush to carry Michigan.

Michigan has had problems getting influence in the presidential selection process. One reason is that it does not have party registration, which is required by Democratic party rules. So Michigan Democrats have to select their delegates through caucuses. In 2003, the Michigan Democratic party, led by Senator Carl Levin, attempted to challenge New Hampshire's first-in-the nation status by moving the 2004 Michigan Democratic caucuses to the same January date as the New Hampshire primary. Levin questioned why Iowa and New Hampshire should always vote first. "I see an absurdity in a system where candidates make dozens of visits to New Hampshire and understand their issues so thoroughly. We have a lot of issues that are important to us. We're a Great Lakes state, we have water issues, garbage being dumped in Michigan. . . . We're more diverse than New Hampshire." All good points, but national Democrats threatened not to recognize the Michigan delegation, and Michigan Democrats backed down. But Levin and Debbie Dingell, wife of Congressman John Dingell, did extract a promise of a new commission to reexamine the delegate selection process after the 2004 election. It was duly appointed and perhaps its first order of business should be to look in the Constitution for the provision that says Iowa and New Hampshire go first.

Michigan Democrats held their 2004 caucus on February 7, after the primaries that came one week after New Hampshire. Some 46,000 Democrats voted by Internet and 24,000 by mail, in addition to the 94,000 who managed to find the polling sites, which were different from and fewer than the precincts used in primary and general elections. John Kerry, supported by former Governor Jim Blanchard and Governor Jennifer Granholm's husband Dan Mulhern, won by a large margin.

Republicans, unhampered by party rules requiring party registration, can hold primaries in Michigan, though they didn't bother in 2004, when George W. Bush was unopposed. But the Republican primary in 2000, held February 22, did attract lots of attention. Governor John Engler hoped to deliver the state's delegates to Bush, whose candidacy he had backed early on. But John McCain, aroused after his defeat in South Carolina February 19, contested the state vigorously. In a stinging rebuke to Engler, McCain won 51%–43%. His admirers in the national press hailed this as a great breakthrough, but it turned out to be atypical and an augury of nothing. Turnout was a huge 1.3 million, far higher than the 524,000 of 1996 or the 437,000 of 1992; indeed, even Bush got more votes than were cast for all candidates in those primaries. But the VNS exit poll showed that 18% of the votes were cast by self-identified Democrats (almost double the percentage in any other primary that year) and only 47% by self-identified Republicans. Bush won solidly among Republicans, as he did everywhere except in a few Northeast states, but lost by 2–1 among self-identified Independents and 8–1 among Democrats. Nothing barred Democrats from voting; when Democrats held caucuses in March, only 22,000 bothered to vote or mail in ballots. In no other state would self-identified Democrats be such a large proportion of the electorate, and so Michigan's Republicans proved no more consequential in 2000 than the Democrats in 2004.

Congressional districting

Michigan has now lost four seats in the last three censuses—one after the 1980 Census, two after the 1990 Census, another one after the 2000 Census. In 2001, for the first time since the 1930s, redistricting was controlled by Republicans, with majorities in both houses of the legislature and with Governor John Engler determined to use the power to reverse the Democrats' 9–7 edge to a 9–6 Republican edge: He succeeded. There was no pretense of bipartisanship: bills were introduced in the House and Senate abruptly in June 2001 and passed on near party-line votes. The plan ended the 26-year congressional career of House Democratic Whip David Bonior, by removing just about every Macomb County precinct he carried heavily and adding the Thumb to the 10th District (it used to be numbered the 12th); he ran for governor and lost in the Democratic primary. It put two pairs of Democratic incumbents in the same districts; Jim Barcia of the 5th District decided to return to the state Senate, where he used to serve, while John Dingell, the dean of the House, slugged it out with liberal Lynn Rivers in the new 15th District. The 1st District, held by Democrat Bart Stupak, seems likely to go Republican if he is not running. A new Republican district was created in western Wayne and Oakland Counties, and shaky Republican incumbents Mike Rogers and Joe Knollenberg were strengthened. This was arguably the most successful partisan redistricting plan in the nation. In a state carried by Bill Clinton and Al Gore, only five of the 15 seats are now safely Democratic.

Governor

Jennifer Granholm (D)

Elected 2002, term expires Jan. 2007, 1st term; b. Feb. 5, 1959, Vancouver, BC; home, Northville; U. of CA, B.A. 1984, Harvard U., J.D. 1987; Catholic; married (Daniel Mulhern).

Elected Office: MI Atty. Gen., 1998–2002.

Professional Career: Prosecutor, U.S. Atty.'s Office, 1991–94; Corporation Cnsl., Wayne Cnty., 1994–98.

Office: P.O. Box 30013, Lansing, 48909, 517-373-3400; Fax: 517-335-6863; Web site: www.michigan.gov/gov.

Election Results

2002 general	Jennifer Granholm (D)	1,633,796	(51%)
	Dick Posthumus (R)	1,506,104	(47%)
	Other	37,665	(1%)
2002 primary	Jennifer Granholm (D)	499,129	(48%)
	David Bonior (D)	292,958	(28%)
	James Blanchard (D)	254,586	(24%)
1998 general	John M. Engler (R)	1,883,005	(62%)
	Geoffrey Fieger (D)	1,143,574	(38%)

Jennifer Granholm, a Democrat, was elected governor of Michigan in 2002. She was born in British Columbia, a Canadian citizen and so not eligible for the presidency—as many Democrats wish she was—and moved to California at age 4 when her father's work as a bank teller and branch manager took him there. She lived in Anaheim in the 1960s, where she could watch the fireworks over Disneyland, and then to San Jose and San Carlos, a middle-class suburb on the Peninsula south of San Francisco. She was a popular student in San Carlos High School and won the Miss San Carlos beauty/talent pageant. At 18 she became a U.S. citizen. That year she also moved to Los Angeles to try her luck as an actress even though her parents wanted her to be the first in the family to graduate from college. She graduated from the American Academy of Dramatic Arts with Nick Cassavetes but never got a part; she once was a contestant on *The*

Dating Game. She made her living as a tour guide at Universal Studios, took delivery complaints for the *Los Angeles Times* and was the first female tour guide at Marine World Africa USA in Redwood City, piloting boats with 25 tourists aboard. She returned to San Carlos and in 1980 won admission to the University of California at Berkeley. In 1984 she went off to Harvard Law School where she demonstrated in favor of disinvestment in South Africa and edited the Civil Rights and Civil Liberties Law Review. In Cambridge she met her husband, Dan Mulhern, from Inkster, Michigan, a working class suburb near Detroit's Metro Airport. After law school, they moved to Michigan. Thus was a star of Michigan politics born.

Granholm worked as a law clerk for federal appeals court Judge Damon Keith, then got a job in the U.S. Attorney's office in Detroit. In 1994 she got what turned out to be her great political break when she was appointed corporation counsel to Wayne County Executive Ed McNamara. McNamara, who obviously has an eye for political talent, has called Granholm a "child of destiny." In 1998 Frank Kelley, Michigan's attorney general since January 1962, announced that he was retiring (the "Eternal General," some called him). McNamara pushed Granholm forward to run for the office. She won the Democratic nomination at the state party convention in August 1998 and was elected in November—the only Democrat to win statewide, as Republican Governor John Engler and Secretary of State Candice Miller were reelected by wide margins. She might not have won except that conservatives at the Republican state convention nominated a little known candidate rather than Engler's choice, Scott Romney, son of former Governor George Romney and brother of Massachusetts Governor Mitt Romney.

Suddenly Granholm was the most visible Democrat in Michigan state government and an obvious candidate to succeed Engler in 2002, when he would be barred from running by term limits. What made her an attractive candidate was less her record than her persona. She is articulate, poised, always able to connect with her audience, enthusiastic, almost always striking a note of consensus rather than confrontation.

She was running to replace Engler, for more than a decade the dominant figure in Michigan state politics. Granholm had serious competition in the Democratic primary from former Governor Jim Blanchard and Congressman David Bonior. Blanchard had success as governor in reorienting Michigan's economy and was well-liked by Democrats; Bonior had a strong liberal record on union issues, foreign policy and the environment. Granholm campaigned as a consensus-minded centrist. Blanchard presented a detailed economic plan and called for repeal of the single business tax, then in the second year of a 22-year phase-out. Bonior campaigned as the champion of the working man and an opponent of big corporate interests. Granholm did not start off ahead in the polls, but her two opponents both targeted her for attacks. Much of the primary was a battle for endorsements. Bonior was endorsed by the state AFL-CIO and the United Auto Workers—endorsements that in the 1960s or 1970s would have cinched the nomination for him. But Granholm was endorsed in 2002 by the Teamsters and the Michigan Education Association—now at least as important factors in Democratic politics. In December 2001, Granholm was endorsed by EMILY's List, which had raised $1.4 million in bundled contributions for Senator Debbie Stabenow in 2000. The legislature passed a law that month limiting bundled contributions to $34,000, the limit for PACs. But it did not take effect until April 2002, by which time EMILY's List had raised more than $400,000 for Granholm. Blanchard and Bonior decided to take state matching funds and accept a spending limit of $2 million in the primary; Granholm rejected the matching funds and raised and spent $5.7 million.

By early 2002, Granholm was leading in polls both for the primary and the general election against the presumed Republican nominee Lieutenant Governor Dick Posthumus (who won 81%–19% over state Senator and now Congressman Joe Schwarz). Michigan does not have party registration, so voters can vote in either party's primary; in August 2002, 1.8 million voted, 58% of them in the Democratic primary, which was much more seriously contested. Granholm won 48% of the vote, Bonior 28% and Blanchard 24%.

Posthumus, Granholm's general election opponent, was not well known to voters. A farmer from Grand Rapids's Kent County with solid conservative credentials, he insisted he was a blue-collar candidate. He had a detailed program—a three-fifths requirement to raise taxes, more tax cuts and ending the single business tax, sparing school districts from spending cuts. He split with Engler to oppose slant oil drilling under the Great Lakes and opposed school vouchers, which had been beaten in a 2000 referendum. He attacked Granholm for saying she favored "tweaking" Proposal A—evidently allowing school districts to raise property taxes more than the measure allowed—and for opposing changes in welfare. But he concentrated much of his fire on her out-of-state origins. He portrayed himself as "raised in Michigan, went to Michigan public schools." "Let's just say I've got different values than come from Hollywood, Berkeley and Harvard." But most voters did not seem to care that Granholm grew up somewhere else; after all, she chose to live in Michigan.

Then on September 20 a reporter for Channel 50 exposed a memo from Detroit Mayor Kwame Kilpatrick in August. It promised Granholm that Kilpatrick would work to turn out 275,000 voters in Detroit if Granholm would agree that 20% of her appointees would be black, that all new state office buildings would be in Detroit, and that Detroiters would be named to head six state departments (including welfare, housing, corrections). Kilpatrick said he never sent the memo and Granholm said she never received it. But Posthumus pounced hard on it. "This memo hands over the ATM card to the state budget and says 'unlimited withdrawals.' It turns Michigan state government into a department store window at Christmas time. But this Christmas Santa will only be filling the stockings of Detroit and Wayne County." A few days later Engler brought up the issue of racial reparations. At a July 2002 NAACP meeting, all three Democratic gubernatorial candidates said they supported reparations; Granholm said, "I support reparations. I support the John Conyers bill," which would set up a commission to study reparations. She later said that reparations to her didn't mean money payments. Michigan and national Democrats said that bringing up the Kilpatrick memo and reparations was appealing to racism. Posthumus said they were legitimate issues and part of a pattern: "she has said one thing to the special interests and another to the voters."

Granholm won by a closer-than-expected 51%–47%. Only 220,000 Detroiters voted, but they cast more than 92% of their votes for Granholm and accounted for all of her popular vote margin and more. Granholm carried Oakland County and suburban Wayne County but lost Macomb County. She carried the Upper Peninsula, the Flint-Saginaw-Bay City corridor and the counties containing Lansing, Battle Creek and Kalamazoo; she lost Outstate by only 51%–47%—a good showing for a Democrat. Posthumus showed great strength only in the Grand Rapids area and the northern Lower Peninsula.

Granholm in any case did not seem interested in overturning most of Engler's achievements. Granholm delivered an optimistic State of the State speech calling for hard work and innovation and embarked on a series of town hall meetings where she sought citizens' ideas. Facing a $3 billion shortfall in a $39 billion budget, she set to work cutting spending; her first budget cut aid to universities and cities, sold 2,500 state cars, rescinded $220 million in contracts and adult education by 70% and arts spending 50%. More cuts followed in fall 2003 as revenues failed to meet expectations. She persuaded the legislature to delay by six months a scheduled rollback of income taxes in return for changes to the single business tax that would give employers relief for the portion they pay for employee health benefits. In 2004 she persuaded the legislature to raise the cigarette tax 75 cents but not to replace the expiring estate tax with an inheritance tax. The cigarette money went to preserve Medicaid; Granholm also joined other states to buy prescription drugs, and claimed to have saved senior and low-income people $130 million. She cut or froze revenue sharing grants to local governments by $523 million and got the legislature to increase the casino tax from 18% to 24%. After some balking from the state House, the legislature voted to allow local governments to collect property taxes five months earlier than scheduled. She proposed to cut per pupil school aid by $74 for the 18 highest-spending school districts, most of them in affluent suburbs, but demurred when the money was found by sale of state lands; she limited some state university spending to schools that did not raise their tuition by more than the rate of inflation. She signed tax cuts for startup and technology businesses. In October 2004 Granholm called for basic tax reforms, including review of the single business tax, in the lame duck session. "I think we're clearly in a state that is seeing declining tax revenues because the tax structure is based on an industrial 20th century economy when we have evolved in the 21st century." That was too much for legislators, but she advanced the issue again in early 2005, when Michigan was one of just three states facing a budget shortfall.

Granholm addressed Michigan's loss of more than 250,000 jobs in several ways. She got the legislature to approve $2 billion in bonds to attract high-tech businesses and started M-TEC training centers at community colleges. "The 20th century concept of one great job for life is over. Our challenge is to provide a high-skilled work force, and it's one of the biggest challenges we face." She welcomed new or expanded facilities by Hino Motors, Hyundai, Nissan, Suzuki, Aisin Seiki and Toyota. She promised tax concessions to keep Kmart's headquarters in Troy, but was frustrated when Illinois-based Sears took over Kmart in November 2004. She assigned Lieutenant Governor John Cherry to come up with ways to double the state's percentage of college graduates in a decade. In May 2003 she launched a "cool cities" initiative, to make Michigan more attractive to the highly educated young. In 2004 the first grants went out to local projects—the St. Aubin Marina in Detroit, the Riverside Arts Center in Ypsilanti (Hipsilanti, some called it), an arts center in an old pie factory in Saugatuck.

The Great Lakes hold one-fourth of the fresh water on earth, and all but one touches on Michigan. In January 2004 Granholm announced a water program, with a permitting process for large withdrawals, protections for small wetlands, tougher standards for septic systems and a ban on disposing of contaminated dredge spoils. It would prohibit new withdrawals of more than 2 million gallons a day. She joined with eight other Great Lakes states in July 2004 in a water compact requiring eight-state approval of withdrawals of 1 million gallons a day and a three-state veto of withdrawals over 5 million gallons a day; all this evidently to prevent shipping water to thirsty southwestern states.

Despite the state's economic and budget woes, Granholm's job ratings were very high in her first 18 months in office. By December 2004 they had fallen, but were still above 50%. She endorsed John Kerry for president in January 2004, and his victory in the state and Democrats' pickup of five state House seats in November 2004 were good signs for her chances in 2006. But that ballot will also include a measure banning state use of racial quotas and preferences. The University of Michigan's transparent use of racial preferences in admissions was upheld by the U.S. Supreme Court in a decision hailed by Granholm; but polling has shown most voters oppose racial quotas. In early 2005 two Republican legislators announced they were running for governor, state Senator Nancy Cassis and state Representative Jack Hoogendyk. In June, former Amway executive Dick DeVos, husband of former state Republican Chairman Betsy DeVos, also joined the Republican field.

Senior Senator

Carl Levin (D)

Elected 1978, seat up 2008, 5th term; b. June 28, 1934, Detroit; home, Detroit; Swarthmore Col., B.A. 1956, Harvard U., J.D. 1959; Jewish; married (Barbara).

Elected Office: Detroit City Cncl., 1969–77, Pres., 1973–77.

Professional Career: Practicing atty., 1959–64, 1971–73, 1978–79; MI Asst. Atty. Gen. & Gen. Cnsl., MI Civil Rights Comm., 1964–67; Detroit Chief Appellate Defender, 1967–69.

DC Office: 269 RSOB, 20510, 202-224-6221; Fax: 202-224-1388; Web site: levin.senate.gov.

State Offices: Detroit, 313-226-6020; Escanaba, 906-789-0052; Grand Rapids, 616-456-2531; Lansing, 517-377-1508; Saginaw, 989-754-2494; Traverse City, 231-947-9569; Warren, 586-573-9145.

Committees: *Armed Services* (RMM). *Homeland Security & Governmental Affairs*: Federal Financial Management, Govt. Information & International Security; Investigations (Permanent) (RMM); Oversight of Govt. Management, the Federal Workforce & the District of Columbia. *Intelligence (Select). Small Business & Entrepreneurship.*

Group Ratings

	ADA	ACLU	AFS	LCV	ITIC	NTU	COC	ACU	NTLC	CHC
2004	100	78	100	100	58	14	41	0	8	0
2003	100	—	100	84	—	18	39	25	—	—

National Journal Ratings

	2003 LIB	—	2003 CONS		2004 LIB	—	2004 CONS
Economic	90%	—	7%		93%	—	0%
Social	85%	—	0%		82%	—	0%
Foreign	79%	—	14%		75%	—	19%

Key Votes of the 108th Congress

1. Ban Drilling in ANWR	Y	5. Energy Bill	N	9. Ban Same-Sex Marriage	N
2. Approve Bush Tax Cuts	N	6. Support Roe v. Wade	Y	10. Ban Bunker-Buster Bomb	Y
3. Medicare/Rx Bill	N	7. Ban Partial-Birth Abortion	N	11. Fund Iraq War	Y
4. Bar Overtime Pay Regs.	Y	8. Assault Weapons Ban	Y	12. Restrict Missile Defense	Y

Election Results

2002 general	Carl Levin (D)	1,896,614	(61%)	($4,133,866)
	Andrew Raczkowski (R)	1,185,545	(38%)	($849,501)
2002 primary	Carl Levin (D)	unopposed		
1996 general	Carl Levin (D)	2,195,738	(58%)	($6,223,409)
	Ronna Romney (R)	1,500,106	(40%)	($3,208,968)
	Other	66,731	(2%)	

Prior Winning Percentages: 1990 (57%); 1984 (52%); 1978 (52%)

Carl Levin, first elected in 1978, is a durable and likable liberal Democrat, a member of one of Michigan's most respected political families. He is rumpled, unfashionable, speaks articulately but without apparent political artifice and takes unpopular stands on issues he cares about. He grew up in Detroit, graduated from Swarthmore and Harvard Law School, worked for the state Civil Rights Commission and the appellate public defender's office, and was elected to Detroit's city council in 1969 and 1973, with substantial support from both blacks and whites. In 1978 he ran for the Senate and was helped when incumbent Robert Griffin got out of the race and then back in; Levin won 52%–48%. In 1984 he won by a similar margin against a former astronaut who had given a public testimonial for his Japanese car; in 1990, 1996 and 2002 he was re-elected by wide margins. He is the longest serving senator from Michigan in history.

Levin was Armed Services Committee chairman from June 2001 to January 2003. He brought to the Senate the skepticism about defense spending and military involvements common among Democrats in the 1970s, and has built up an impressive expertise in military affairs. For a time he opposed the B-2 and he voted against the Gulf War resolution in 1991—on the advice of Colin Powell, he has said, and added that he was mistaken. On taking the chair, he said he would not concentrate on major weapons systems, but on military pay, health care and housing, plus purchasing systems; unlike his predecessor and successor, John Warner, he favored another round of base closings—one issue on which he agreed with Defense Secretary Donald Rumsfeld.

Where he disagreed most strongly with Rumsfeld was on missile defense, of which he has been the Senate's most persistent critic. He led a filibuster on the issue in September 1998, arguing that missile defense would undermine chances of Russian approval of the 1993 START II treaty. In June 2001, on becoming chairman, he said more testing was needed and a system was unlikely to be fielded until after the next presidential election. When Rumsfeld called the ABM Treaty "a Cold War construct," Levin replied, "I think it would be useful for you to at least attempt to understand" why some people fear abrogation could provoke Russia to boost ballistic missile capacity. On defense bills he worked to freeze any money that might conceivably conflict with ABM Treaty. On September 7, 2001, he got the committee to move $1.3 billion from missile defense to anti-terrorism programs. On September 16 John Warner said he was ready to file his own defense bill. On September 21 Levin backed down, saying he did not wish to "create dissent where we need unity." In December 2001 Levin was outflanked when George W. Bush invoked the clause in the ABM Treaty allowing him to abrogate it with six month's warning. Russian President Vladimir Putin responded nonchalantly. Still, in May 2002 he got the committee to approve a defense authorization bill that cut the Bush administration missile defense request by $812 million; in June, a Senate compromise was struck on the final version that gave Bush the authority to restore the cuts. In March 2004 Levin said he opposed $500 million in the defense authorization for missile defense and argued that the Pentagon would break a 1986 law if it spends certain monies before operational tests.

Levin was very skeptical about the need for military action in Iraq and argued fervently that any such action must be taken multilaterally. He welcomed Bush's announcement in a White House meeting in September 2002 that he would consult with Congress on military action. He argued that it was not necessary now because Saddam Hussein would be deterred from using weapons of mass destruction. He argued that the United States should not act without first receiving the approval of the United Nations. In October 2002 he offered an alternative resolution on military action in Iraq, calling on the administration to get the UN to vote a more vigorous weapons inspection program, but not authorizing military action until it was approved by the UN. It was defeated 75–24. In February 2003 he continued to argue that the United States should not take military action without another resolution from the United Nations, even if that meant that action could be stopped by a veto from France. In the May 2004 hearings on prison abuses in Iraq, Levin pressed Rumsfeld hard on the applicability of the Geneva Conventions. In September 2004 he called for investigation of the CIA's holding of 100 unidentified "ghost" detainees in Iraq. In October 2004 he issued a report charging that Pentagon official Douglas Feith deliberately exaggerated ties between Saddam Hussein's Iraq and Al Qaeda and ignored corrections requested by the CIA; Warner took "strong exception" to Levin's findings.

Levin joined Armed Services colleague John McCain in strongly questioning the Pentagon's leasing, rather than purchase, of KC-767 refueling tankers from Boeing. After emails obtained by McCain revealed improper negotiations between the Air Force and Boeing, Levin, McCain and Warner passed in November 2003 a proposal to lease only 20 of the aircraft and purchase 80 others, to keep the total cost down to $23.5 billion. In March 2004 Levin, McCain and Warner, disturbed by a Pentagon audit, imposed a hold on the project. Levin and McCain pressed for months for more disclosure of Pentagon documents, even as criminal charges were being brought against Darleen Druyun, a Pentagon negotiator on the contract who resigned in 2002 and took a $250,000 job at Boeing. After Druyun was convicted and sentenced to nine months in prison in October 2004, Levin, Warner and McCain demanded an investigation of everyone who participated in awarding the contract. Levin also expressed concern about the condition of the Army. In July 2004, after a *Detroit News* series on the frequency of truck accidents in training and exercises, he called for improved truck safety and new equipment. In November 2004, in hearings on the nominee for secretary of the Army, he said that the Army was stretched too thin, that there were not enough soldiers and protective gear in Iraq, that too many personnel were held in the service by stop loss orders and that the Army was not adequately replacing old equipment.

Levin has also weighed in on intelligence matters. He voted against confirmation of CIA Director Porter Goss in September 2004 on the grounds he was too partisan. He obtained passage of an amendment to the intelligence reorganization bill requiring the national intelligence director to be independent of the White House. "I don't want a more powerful 'yes man.' I don't want a more powerful person who will say intelligence is a slam dunk when it isn't." He got passage of another amendment barring the national intelligence director from shifting uniformed military personnel in defense intelligence agencies to agencies outside the Defense Department. In October 2004 he declined to sign the conference committee report on the grounds that the bill didn't contain enough safeguards against politicization of intelligence. He voted for the final bill in December though he said he was "mystified" that the Senate dropped language on the independence of the NID objected to by the White House.

Levin is the ranking minority member of the Permanent Investigations Subcommittee of Governmental Affairs. There he has worked over the years on money laundering. In June 2004 he returned to the subject in hearings on Washington's Riggs Bank, which concealed the assets of former Chilean dictator Augusto Pinochet and ignored improper payments to the thugs who run the government of Equatorial Guinea. In response he and Norm Coleman sponsored a bill requiring a one-year cooling off period before former federal bank examiners could work for the banks they supervised; the Senate passed it in October 2004. He and Coleman called for a 150% penalty for promoters of phony tax shelters, rather than the 50% the Bush administration proposed. With Susan Collins and Peter Fitzgerald, Levin sponsored a bill to outlaw certain mutual fund practices—soft dollar arrangements, revenue sharing, directed brokerage, market timing, distribution fees. In November 2004 the subcommittee started to investigate the UN Oil for Food program; Levin and Coleman sent a letter demanding documents from the UN. But when Coleman called in December for the resignation of Secretary General Kofi Annan, Levin said it was "unwarranted and unfair" to blame Annan when the U.S. let Jordan and Turkey import Iraqi oil.

Levin generally has one of the most liberal records in the Senate, with some Michigan accents. He opposed NAFTA and has complained about Japanese auto-parts and Korean car trade restrictions. When John Kerry and John McCain proposed raising CAFE auto mileage standards to 36 miles per gallon by 2015, Levin and Christopher Bond responded with an amendment requiring NHTSA to raise the standard for light trucks (including SUVs) within 15 months and for cars within two years; it passed 62–38. In August 2003 a Levin-Bond amendment passed which did not mandate an increase in fleet fuel economy. Levin argued that the CAFE fleet mileage regulation was "a system that has unfairly impacted American auto manufacturers since its inception" because U.S. automakers have fleets of large and small cars while most foreign makers make mostly small cars. Levin was angry when the Republican majority blocked votes on Michigan appointees to federal judgeships when Bill Clinton was president, and since George W. Bush became president, blocked all appeals court nominees for the 6th Circuit, which includes Michigan, Ohio, Kentucky and Tennessee; in June 2005, he relented and voted to confirm Richard Griffin and David McKeague.

Michigan touches on all but one of the Great Lakes, which have been threatened by invasive species; the zebra mussel has wiped out many native species and Asian carp are making their way up the Illinois River and threatening to enter the Great Lakes. In 2003 Levin and Susan Collins sponsored a bill to require ships entering U.S. ports to use ballast water exchange and he sponsored another to pay for electric barriers in the Illinois River. With Mike DeWine he sponsored a $6 billion Great Lakes trust fund, to pay for cleaning up the Lakes, restoring wetlands and repelling invasive species. Some 415 truckloads of Canadian trash are dumped in Michigan daily; Levin called for enforcement of a 1992 treaty requiring notice of such shipments and allowing the U.S. to stop them. Levin has also stepped forward to question why New Hampshire should always be the site of the first presidential primary. In March 2003 he proposed the Michigan Democrats caucus on the same day as the New Hampshire primary. He and other Michigan Democrats were persuaded not to, but national Democrats promised to appoint a commission after November 2004 to reconsider the caucus and primary schedule. A 40-member commission headed by Congressman David Price and former Labor Secretary Alexis Herman began its work in December 2004, with a one-year deadline.

Levin's reputation for candor and hard work, and his rumpled persona have given him great political strength in Michigan. Every six years his percentage has crept a little higher. In 2002, Levin won 61%–38% against Andrew "Rocky" Raczkowski, a term-limited state representative, who put "Rocky" on his bumper stickers but could not get it on the ballot though it is part of his legal name.

Junior Senator

Debbie Stabenow (D)

Elected 2000, seat up 2006, 1st term; b. Apr. 29, 1950, Gladwin; home, Lansing; MI St. U., B.A. 1972, M.S.W. 1975; United Methodist; married (Tom Athans).

Elected Office: Ingham Cnty. Comm., 1975–78, Chair, 1976–78; MI House of Reps., 1978–90; MI Senate, 1990–94; U.S. House of Reps 1996–00.

Professional Career: Consultant & Co–founder, MI Leadership Inst., 1995–96.

DC Office: 133 HSOB, 20510, 202-224-4822; Fax: 202-228-0325; Web site: stabenow.senate.gov.

State Offices: Detroit, 313-961-4330; East Lansing, 517-203-1760; Flint, 810-720-4172; Grand Rapids, 616-975-0052; Marquette, 906-228-8756; Traverse City, 231-929-1031.

Committees: *Democratic Conference Secretary. Agriculture, Nutrition & Forestry*: Marketing, Inspection & Product Promotion; Research, Nutrition & General Legislation. *Banking, Housing & Urban Affairs*: Financial Institutions; Housing & Transportation; Securities & Investment. *Budget*.

Group Ratings

	ADA	ACLU	AFS	LCV	ITIC	NTU	COC	ACU	NTLC	CHC
2004	100	78	100	100	92	18	65	8	15	0
2003	95	—	100	84	—	16	39	20	—	—

National Journal Ratings

	2003 LIB	—	2003 CONS		2004 LIB	—	2004 CONS
Economic	75%	—	20%		79%	—	13%
Social	85%	—	0%		82%	—	0%
Foreign	70%	—	28%		82%	—	16%

Key Votes of the 108th Congress

1. Ban Drilling in ANWR	Y	5. Energy Bill	N	9. Ban Same-Sex Marriage	N
2. Approve Bush Tax Cuts	N	6. Support Roe v. Wade	Y	10. Ban Bunker-Buster Bomb	Y
3. Medicare/Rx Bill	N	7. Ban Partial-Birth Abortion	N	11. Fund Iraq War	Y
4. Bar Overtime Pay Regs.	Y	8. Assault Weapons Ban	Y	12. Restrict Missile Defense	Y

Election Results

2000 general	Debbie Stabenow (D) 2,061,952	(49%)	($7,892,518)
	Spencer Abraham (R) 1,994,693	(48%)	($13,028,636)
	Other... 111,040	(3%)	
2000 primary	Debbie Stabenow (D) .... unopposed		

Prior Winning Percentages: 1998 House (57%); 1996 House (54%)

Michigan's junior senator is Debbie Stabenow, a Democrat elected in 2000. Stabenow grew up in the small Outstate town of Clare, where her father was an Oldsmobile dealer and her mother a nurse. She went to Michigan State, where she got a master's degree in social work and made money singing folk songs in coffeehouses. She marched in antiwar rallies and volunteered for George McGovern in 1972, when her then-husband ran an unsuccessful race for Ingham County Commissioner. Provoked when the commission closed a nursing home, she ran for the commission two years later and, at 24, beat an incumbent who referred to her as "that young broad." She was elected to the state House in 1978, at 28, and was elected to the state Senate in 1990. In 1994, while running for governor, she was at the storm center of state politics and policy. In response to Republican Governor John Engler's call for changes in education finance, she proposed to zero out the property tax and start over, apparently calculating that he would reject such a drastic tax cut. Instead he accepted her proposal and passed a plan reducing property taxes vastly and increasing the sales tax, which was approved by voters 70%–30% in March 1994. In the August 1994 primary for governor, the major forces in the Democratic Party opposed Stabenow: the Michigan Education Association, the UAW and AFL-CIO. She won 30% of the vote, ahead of

Larry Owen's 26% but behind former Congressman Howard Wolpe's 35%. Perhaps it is best she lost; she was chosen as Wolpe's running mate, but the ticket lost to Engler by a 61%–38% margin.

Undaunted, Stabenow almost immediately began running for Congress. The 8th District seat, which included Lansing's Democratic Ingham County and heavily Republican Livingston County to the east, was held by Republican Dick Chrysler. For the 1996 race, Stabenow raised more than $1 million in individual contributions, a tribute to her industriousness and the fundraising prowess of the feminist left; overall each spent $1.5 million. She won impressively, 54%–44%.

In the House, Stabenow had a fairly liberal voting record; she was sought out by the moderate Democratic Blue Dogs but did not join. She opposed trade promotion authority and the partial-birth abortion ban. In March 1999 she announced she was running against Senator Spencer Abraham in 2000; the same day Abraham ran full-page ads calling her a liberal.

This turned out to be one of the critical races in the 2000 Senate cycle. Abraham had been elected in 1994 by a 52%–43% margin over Congressman Bob Carr. The grandson of immigrants from Lebanon, his greatest achievement in the Senate was to squelch proposals to reduce the number of legal immigrants allowed in each year; in 2000 he secured near-unanimous approval for an increase in H1-B immigration visas for high-tech workers. The first barrage of ads in the race came not from either candidate or party, but from the Federation for American Immigration Reform, which in early 2000 spent $700,000 attacking Abraham for his stands on immigration and charging that his stands cost Michigan workers jobs. In 1999 Abraham's voting record became more moderate than before, and in July 2000 he called for a suspension of the federal gas tax until November, a move beaten in the Senate 59–40. In summer 2000 Abraham used his money advantage—he ultimately spent $13 million, to Stabenow's nearly $8 million—to run ads spotlighting his own program for prescription drugs for seniors and attacked Stabenow as a free-spending liberal favoring increased bureaucracy and opposing tax cuts, opposing welfare reform and supporting more lenient sentences for criminals. Stabenow resisted pressure and hoarded her money for an October ad buy.

This proved to be a good strategy: Stabenow was down by 17% in one mid-October poll but, after several weeks of equal advertising by each, wound up winning by 1%. Stabenow answered charges that she was a liberal by citing her votes for a balanced budget and ending the marriage penalty; she kept herself in the good graces of labor by voting against normal trade relations with China. Stabenow said Abraham was beholden to corporations and special interests and attacked his stands on prescription drug and HMO regulation. This race was light on debates— the candidates had just one televised debate—and heavy on ads by outside groups—the Sierra Club, Peace Action and EMILY's List for Stabenow, the Chamber of Commerce, Business Roundtable, Americans for Job Security, National Rifle Association and Michigan Right to Life for Abraham. This was the most expensive Senate race in Michigan history, and the first since 1942 in which neither candidate won a majority of the vote. Stabenow won 49%–48%. She carried only 13 of the state's 83 counties, but she ran essentially even in critical Oakland and Macomb Counties.

Senate Democrats made Stabenow head of the prescription drug task force, and she concentrated on the issue, organizing bus trips of seniors to Canada and pushing for a package of legislation that came to the floor in July 2002. The Senate, unlike the House, was unable to pass a prescription drug benefit. But it did pass a law withdrawing patent protection for pharmaceutical companies pending the outcome of suits brought by generic drug companies by 78–21. And it passed measures allowing reimportation of drugs from Canada—though both Clinton and Bush HHS secretaries found this to be unsafe and did not allow it—and to allow states to continue to negotiate prices with pharmaceutical companies on Medicaid drug purchases. But the House did not act on these. Stabenow continued to sponsor drug reimportation in 2003 and 2004; her bill included FDA inspection of foreign facilities. It generated considerable publicity but did not come to a vote.

Stabenow has sponsored measures affecting Michigan's environment. In January 2003 Toronto began shipping all its trash to a landfill southwest of Detroit: 180 truckloads a day, 1.1 million tons a year. By November 2004, 415 truckloads a day of Canadian trash was entering Michigan, most of it over the Blue Water Bridge in Port Huron. Stabenow opposed this and argued that it violated a 1992 treaty. In June 2003 she began an online campaign to amass signatures to demand that EPA enforce the treaty, which required notification of each shipment and allowed the U.S. to decline any shipment. In May 2004 she presented 165,000 signatures to EPA Administrator Mike Leavitt. Leavitt argued that only hazardous waste violated the treaty; Stabenow argued that all waste was covered. Leavitt said he would establish a pilot program to ask Canadian shippers for notification and promised he would fund the state's efforts to stop shipments that violate state standards; a law took effect in October 2004 requiring out-of-state shipments to meet state standards. But in late 2004 the shipments continued, and the fight on this issue did not seem to be over. In the meantime, Stabenow placed in the Senate transportation bill $204 million for Michigan border crossings, including a new plaza for the Blue Water Bridge and improvements on I-69 and I-94 segments feeding into the bridge. But the transportation bill was never passed. Stabenow also sponsored a bill to preserve Michigan's historic lighthouses, piers, museums and vessels. She sponsored an amendment to the corporate tax bill for $6.5 billion in accelerated tax relief for manufacturers; this act did pass. With Carl Levin, she sponsored a bill to end the Federal Prison Industries monopoly on federal office furniture; Michigan ranks number one not in autos but in office furniture.

Stabenow has proved to be an effective partisan. She blocked the approval of Engler aide Dennis Schornack to be the U.S. Chairman of the Joint International Commission, which handles U.S.-Canada border issues. With Levin, she blocked Bush appointments to the 6th Circuit Court of Appeals until June 2005. In November 2004, when Barbara Mikulski stepped down from the position of Secretary of the Democratic Caucus, Stabenow called Mikulski and asked for her support; they worked the phones and Stabenow got the job, the number three position in the leadership. It has not led to higher leadership posts in the recent past, but it does give her a seat and a voice at leadership meetings.

Stabenow comes up for reelection in 2006. A senator elected by a 49%–48% margin can expect serious competition, but by early 2005 two Republican House members, Candice Miller and Mike Rogers, indicated that they would not run. By June 2005 declared Republican candidates included engineer Bart Baron; former Detroit Councilman Keith Butler and Jerry Zandstra, a director at a religious think tank. Also mentioned as a candidate was Jane Abraham, Spencer Abraham's wife.

FIRST DISTRICT

Rep. Bart Stupak (D)

Elected 1992, 7th term; b. Feb. 29, 1952, Milwaukee, WI; home, Menominee; NW MI Comm. Col., A.A. 1972, Saginaw Valley St. Col., B.S. 1977, Thomas Cooley Law Schl., J.D. 1981; Catholic; married (Laurie).

Elected Office: MI House of Reps., 1988–90.

Professional Career: Escanaba Police Officer, 1972–73; MI St. Trooper, 1974–84; Practicing atty., 1981–92.

DC Office: 2352 RHOB, 20515, 202-225-4735; Fax: 202-225-4744; Web site: www.house.gov/stupak.

District Offices: Alpena, 989-356-0690; Crystal Falls, 906-875-3751; Escanaba, 906-786-4504; Houghton, 906-482-1371; Marquette, 906-228-3700; Petoskey, 231-348-0657; West Branch, 989-345-2258.

Committees: *Energy & Commerce* (11th of 26 D): Environment & Hazardous Materials; Oversight & Investigations (RMM); Telecommunications & the Internet.

Group Ratings

	ADA	ACLU	AFS	LCV	ITIC	NTU	COC	ACU	NTLC	CHC
2004	80	55	100	73	11	14	38	16	3	53
2003	85	—	100	55	—	25	29	38	—	—

National Journal Ratings

	2003 LIB	—	2003 CONS		2004 LIB	—	2004 CONS
Economic	68%	—	32%		70%	—	29%
Social	55%	—	44%		60%	—	39%
Foreign	70%	—	27%		77%	—	22%

Key Votes of the 108th Congress

1. Drilling in ANWR	N	5. DC School Vouchers	N	9. Ban Same-Sex Marriage	N
2. Approve Bush Tax Cuts	N	6. Ban Human Cloning	Y	10. Fund Iraq War	N
3. Medicare/Rx Bill	N	7. Restrict Gun Liability	Y	11. Bar Cuba Embargo Funds	Y
4. Bar Overtime Pay Regs.	Y	8. Ban Partial-Birth Abortion	Y	12. Intelligence Reorg.	N

Election Results

2004 general	Bart Stupak (D)	211,571	(66%)	($771,354)
	Don Hooper (R)	105,706	(33%)	($11,070)
	Other	5,397	(2%)	
2004 primary	Bart Stupak (D)	unopposed		
2002 general	Bart Stupak (D)	150,701	(68%)	($717,661)
	Don Hooper (R)	69,254	(31%)	($12,952)
	Other	2,732	(1%)	

Prior Winning Percentages: 2000 (58%); 1998 (59%); 1996 (71%); 1994 (57%); 1992 (54%)

The People		**Race/Ethnic Origin**	**Ancestry**	
Area size:	27,809 sq. mi.	93.8% White	German: 15.8%	English: 7.7%
Urban population:	33.4%	1.0% Black	Irish: 7.2%	
Rural population:	66.6%	0.4% Asian	**2004 Presidential Vote**	
Pop. 2000:	662,563	2.4% Native Am.	Bush (R) 177,315	(53%)
Median income:	$34,076	0.0% Hawaiian	Kerry (D) 151,450	(46%)
Poverty status:	11.2%	1.4% Two+ races	Other 3,623	(1%)
Military veterans:	16.9%	0.0% Other	**2000 Presidential Vote**	
		0.9% Hispanic Origin	Bush (R) 154,772	(52%)
			Gore (D) 135,503	(45%)
			Other 9,371	(3%)
			Cook Partisan Voting Index: R + 2	

Occupation	Blue collar: 28.8%	White collar: 50.7%	Gray collar: 20.5%

Michigan's Upper Peninsula, commonly known as the UP, is a land apart. Surrounded on three sides by frigid Lake Superior and Lake Michigan, it has its own flora, including the world's largest known living object, a giant fungus that lives under 37 acres of a forest floor and is 1,500 years old. Although the UP is no farther north than Montreal or Seattle, it has one of the coldest climates in settled parts of North America. "In October, usually, the first snow falls steady on the northland," writes Dixie Lee Franklin in *A Most Superior Land*, "whispering teasing promises of more to come"—for eight months more. Far away from any major city, with ground too frozen and stony and a growing season too short for most crops, the Upper Peninsula was explored by French voyagers more than 300 years ago but was never thickly settled until prospectors found rich veins of ore here. The mineral veins of the Keweenaw Peninsula produced 13.3 billion pounds of copper; the Marquette, Menominee and Gogebic iron ranges have produced more than one billion tons of iron ore. Starting in the 1880s, immigrants flocked here to work the mines: Irish, Italians, Swedes, Norwegians, miners' sons from Wales and Cornwall, and most prominently Finns, who must have found this cold land with its lakes and hills much like their home. By 1900, the UP was a northern industrial belt, with a few bosses and some absentee overlords and a work force disposed to radical ideas and union movements.

A major strike in 1913–14 and falling ore prices after World War I—events that would be long forgotten elsewhere—are remembered in the UP as the beginning of its decline: The UP's population peaked at 332,000 in 1920. The copper veins were mostly depleted by then, mining iron ore became less labor-intensive, and lumber and farming provided only a few thousand jobs. In the last half century, there has been great migration to Detroit, Chicago and the West Coast; the UP's population has hovered around 300,000, rising to 315,000 in 2004. But "Yoopers"—who some say have their own dialect, "Yoopanese"—remain devoted to their land. In 2004, the Legislature enacted a law permitting mines in Marquette County to start sulfide mining, a technique to find copper and nickel in rock formation. Later, the state reached a landmark deal to protect under a conservation easement 271,000 acres of forestlands and waterways in the UP.

The 1st Congressional District of Michigan includes the Upper Peninsula and 16 northern counties in the Lower Peninsula. Nearly half the people live in the UP; the remainder live south of the breathtaking Mackinac Bridge. This is a vast area, in sheer size the second-largest district east of the Mississippi (after Maine's 2d), and it has the most shoreline of any district; it is a 490-mile drive from Ironwood at the western end of the UP to the edge of Bay City on the southern tip of Saginaw Bay. The Lower Peninsula counties have two different personalities. On Lake Huron—the sunrise side—are smaller industrial towns and middle-class resorts. On Lake Michigan are affluent resort areas around Petoskey and Charlevoix, long summer places for people from Chicago (this is Ernest Hemingway's "up in Michigan"). Politically, the UP had long been Democratic, some parts more than others; but this is one part of Michigan that did not like national Democrats' environmental stands, and the UP twice voted for George W. Bush. The Lake Michigan shore of the Lower Peninsula is growing fast and heavily Republican, the sunrise side is growing more slowly and politically marginal. The 1st District voted solidly for Bush in 2000 and 2004 and narrowly for Republican governor candidate Dick Posthumus in 2002, even as both lost statewide.

The congressman from the 1st District is Bart Stupak, a Democrat and a "Yooper" from Menominee on the Wisconsin border. He was a police officer in Escanaba, then became a Michigan state trooper in 1974 and also earned a law degree; in 1984 he was injured in the line of duty and retired from the force. In 1988 he was elected to the Michigan House; in 1990 he lost a race for the state Senate. Stupak got into the 1992 House race when incumbent Republican Bob Davis, with 878 overdrafts in the House bank, decided to drop out. In the general he beat Republican Philip Ruppe, who had represented the district from 1966–78, by 54%–44%.

In the House, Stupak has paid great attention to local issues. He opposed slant drilling for oil and gas under the Great Lakes and worked on the successful bill to kill it in 2001. He worked with members from neighboring states on a multi-billion project to clean up the Great Lakes. Worried about the viability of the state's last two iron mines, both in Marquette County, he criticized George W. Bush's tariffs on steel imports because they were not high enough.

Stupak's voting record has been toward the center for House Democrats, though he is more conservative than most of them on cultural issues. He is strongly opposed to abortion, and spoke out against it at the 1996 Democratic National Convention; he used his speaking slot in 2000 to talk about his district. In 2004, Stupak attended John Kerry's convention in Boston, but he did not keep a high profile. In February 2003, the House passed the bill he co-sponsored to prohibit cloning, including for the production of embryos intended for research, but the bill stalled in the Senate.

All this has served him well in elections. Once in office, he had several competitive contests but none serious enough to jeopardize his seat. On Mother's Day 2000, Stupak suffered a personal tragedy, which for a time raised questions about his political future. His 17-year-old son B.J., a high school football player and class president, killed himself on the morning after his prom; more than 60 House members attended the funeral in Menominee. In coping with the tragedy, Stupak and his wife Laurie focused on their son's use of Accutane, a prescription-drug for acne treatment; the Food and Drug Administration had issued warnings about adverse psychological effects, including suicide attempts. In October, Stupak went public with his concerns and he later organized a House hearing about Accutane. He and his wife console other grieving families, and he devotes part of his Web site to Accutane. In December 2004, the FDA responded to calls by an advisory panel to tighten restriction on the drug, including creation of a mandatory registry for individuals who dispense or use it.

During the 2000 campaign, Stupak faced a vigorous challenge from Chuck Yob, a Republican national committeeman, who criticized Stupak for taking more than 80% of his campaign money from special interest groups; the NRA endorsed Yob. But Stupak argued that voters favored common-sense gun laws, and voters seemed to be in no mood for controversy after the family tragedy. Stupak won 58%–40%, losing only one county. Republicans hope to win the seat if Stupak does not run, but there is little chance as long as he does: he didn't break a sweat in his last two wins.

SECOND DISTRICT

Rep. Pete Hoekstra (R)

Elected 1992, 7th term; b. Oct. 30, 1953, Groningen, Netherlands; home, Holland; Hope Col., B.A. 1975, U. of MI, M.B.A. 1977; Christian Reformed; married (Diane).

Professional Career: Furniture Exec., Herman Miller Co., 1977–92.

DC Office: 2234 RHOB, 20515, 202-225-4401; Fax: 202-226-0779; Web site: www.hoekstra.house.gov.

District Offices: Cadillac, 231-775-0050; Holland, 616-395-0030; Muskegon, 231-722-8386.

Committees: *Permanent Select Committee on Intelligence* (Chmn. of 12 R). *Transportation & Infrastructure* (8th of 41 R): Coast Guard & Maritime Transportation; Highways, Transit & Pipelines.

Group Ratings

	ADA	ACLU	AFS	LCV	ITIC	NTU	COC	ACU	NTLC	CHC
2004	5	11	0	0	70	72	95	96	92	100
2003	10	—	0	10	—	63	88	82	—	—

National Journal Ratings

	2003 LIB	—	2003 CONS	2004 LIB	—	2004 CONS
Economic	0%	—	91%	17%	—	83%
Social	39%	—	61%	9%	—	85%
Foreign	30%	—	69%	16%	—	84%

Key Votes of the 108th Congress

1. Drilling in ANWR	Y	5. DC School Vouchers	*	9. Ban Same-Sex Marriage	Y
2. Approve Bush Tax Cuts	Y	6. Ban Human Cloning	Y	10. Fund Iraq War	Y
3. Medicare/Rx Bill	Y	7. Restrict Gun Liability	Y	11. Bar Cuba Embargo Funds	*
4. Bar Overtime Pay Regs.	N	8. Ban Partial-Birth Abortion	Y	12. Intelligence Reorg.	Y

Election Results

2004 general	Pete Hoekstra (R)	225,343	(69%)	($498,230)
	Kimon Kotos (D)	94,040	(29%)	($14,779)
	Other	5,622	(2%)	
2004 primary	Pete Hoekstra (R)	unopposed		
2002 general	Pete Hoekstra (R)	156,937	(70%)	($272,845)
	Jeffrey Wrisley (D)	61,749	(28%)	($23,316)
	Other	4,221	(2%)	

Prior Winning Percentages: 2000 (64%); 1998 (69%); 1996 (65%); 1994 (75%); 1992 (63%)

The People		Race/Ethnic Origin	Ancestry		
Area size:	5,508 sq. mi.	87.5% White	German: 15.3%	Dutch: 14.8%	
Urban population:	56.2%	4.5% Black	English: 7.1%		
Rural population:	43.8%	1.0% Asian	**2004 Presidential Vote**		
Pop. 2000:	662,563	0.6% Native Am.	Bush (R) 203,051	(60%)	
Median income:	$42,589	0.0% Hawaiian	Kerry (D) 131,552	(39%)	
Poverty status:	8.9%	1.2% Two+ races	Other 2,904	(1%)	
Military veterans:	13.2%	0.1% Other	**2000 Presidential Vote**		
		5.2% Hispanic Origin	Bush (R) 172,428	(59%)	
			Gore (D) 111,739	(38%)	
			Other 6,550	(2%)	
			Cook Partisan Voting Index: R + 9		

Occupation	Blue collar: 33.1%	White collar: 51.3%	Gray collar: 15.6%

Lining the eastern shoreline of Lake Michigan, where the lake winds temper the frigid Michigan winters, are some of the nation's longest and highest sand dunes. In the late 19th century, this shoreline was America's greatest lumber country; the ports on the small rivers were choked with logs and full of lumbermen from Norway and Sweden, Ireland and Scotland, Quebec and New England. During the timber boom, the shoreline just to the south was the locus of America's largest migration from the Netherlands and still has the nation's largest concentration of Dutch-Americans. Wooden shoes are now seen only in the Tulip Festival in Holland, but here conscientious Dutch work habits have produced some of the most highly skilled workers in America, and this has become a busy manufacturing area, with products ranging from baby food at Gerber in Fremont to self-dimming car mirrors at Gentex in Zeeland. With Herman Miller in Zeeland, Haworth in Holland and Steelcase in Grand Rapids, it is the center of the American office furniture industry.

The 2d Congressional District of Michigan occupies the Lake Michigan shoreline counties, plus a tier of counties inland including a small part of Grand Rapids's Kent County, from the lumber country around Manistee south to Holland and the resort town of Saugatuck. This district and the Grand Rapids metro area have the highest concentration of Dutch-Americans in the country. For years Dutch-American voters have been America's most Republican ethnically identifiable group (the only competitor: Cuban-Americans), and the 2d and 3d Districts centered on Grand Rapids are the two most Republican districts in Michigan. Holland and surrounding Ottawa County voted 72% for George W. Bush in 2004.

The congressman from the 2d District is Pete Hoekstra (pronounced *HOOK-stra*), first elected to the House in 1992. He emigrated from the Netherlands at 3, graduated from Hope College in Holland (with a semester in Washington during Watergate) and got an MBA at the University of Michigan. Hoekstra went to work at Herman Miller, where he helped develop the "Equa Chair" seat and became a vice president. In 1992, he decided to run what seemed an improbable campaign for Congress against Guy Vander Jagt, 26-year incumbent and chairman of the NRCC since 1975. Hoekstra saved up vacation time and took a county-by-county bicycle tour of the district. With an earnestness that rang true, Hoekstra called for citizen, not career, politicians; refused PAC money and supported abolishing PACs; advocated 12-year term limits; promised to uphold family values and to oppose abortion. Hoekstra spent only $55,600 to Vander Jagt's $725,000. But on primary day, he carried the heavily Dutch Ottawa and Allegan Counties, 53%–31%; they cast 59% of the primary vote, and so Hoekstra won 46%–40%. He won the general election easily and has not been threatened since.

Hoekstra brought to Washington a mistrust of government and a desire to apply the participatory management ideas he had developed at Herman Miller; he still works at a standup Herman Miller desk and sleeps on the office's black leather couch. In early 1994 he was asked by Newt Gingrich to plan how to manage a Republican House, something few others thought they would live to see. Only a few of his reforms were adopted: the House barred former members from lobbying on the floor, and it passed (though the Senate didn't) a ban on pensions to former members convicted of a felony.

In 1995, Hoekstra got the chair of the Oversight and Investigations Subcommittee of the Education and Workforce Committee. In summer 1997 he started on two major assignments from the leadership. The first was an investigation of labor law. Republican leaders hoped he would investigate the role of unions in the 1996 campaigns, but instead he conducted what he called the American Worker at a Crossroads project. Another assignment was investigating the Teamsters Union. The 1996 election of Teamsters president Ron Carey had to be set aside in 1997 and the union treasury was found depleted of $150 million. But the Teamsters were unforthcoming with evidence and subpoena problems delayed the probe until 1998 when the requirement of subcommittee approval for every deposition and subpoena was dropped. Hoekstra would not hold publicized hearings: "I don't want to grandstand. It's the wrong thing to do." In early 1999 the leadership took the issue away from Hoekstra and gave it to committee chairman Bill Goodling. In May 2001 he was one of 52 Republicans voting against the annual testing provisions in George W. Bush's education bill. He was the only Michigan member to vote against the bill in December 2001, when it passed overwhelmingly; he was unhappy that vouchers had been voted down.

In 1996 Hoekstra began a campaign to limit Federal Prison Industries, which employs prisoners at China-level prices to produce office furniture and auto components; for years it was the mandatory source for federal purchases of office furniture. Hoekstra and Michigan Senator Carl Levin argued that FPI aggressively marketed its products beyond its charters. Hoekstra stepped up his campaign after 2001, when office furniture manufacturers faced a slump; in June 2003 he charged that FPI was planning to build 11 new factories and increase employment 30% over five years. In November 2003 the House passed Hoekstra's bill phasing out the mandatory source requirement over five years; Levin, as chairman and ranking member of Armed Services, had already phased it out for the Defense Department and CIA. It eventually passed the Senate and became law in December 2004. On other issues with a local impact, Hoekstra hailed the end of the steel tariffs in December 2003 (office furniture manufacturers buy a lot of steel) and joined with Illinois Democrat Rahm Emanuel to co-sponsor the Great Lakes Financing Act, to authorize funding for combating invasive species and cleaning up the lakes which contain nearly one-fourth of the world's fresh water.

For several years Hoekstra was frustrated in his attempts to move up in the leadership, perhaps because of his less than perfect record of supporting leadership positions on issues like missile defense and normal trade relations with China; he has proposed a constitutional amendment to establish recall for members of Congress, nonbinding national referenda on issues and a "none of the above" choice in elections. In November 1998 he ran for vice chairman of the House Republican Conference but he was eliminated on the second ballot. After the 2000 election, he expressed interest in succeeding John Kasich as Budget chairman. But the position went to Jim Nussle instead. He sought the chairmanship of the Education and the Workforce Committee, but he lost to John Boehner in the Republican Steering Committee. Hoekstra unsuccessfully urged that the committee be divided into two parts with Hoekstra taking the education panel; party leaders were not keen on creating a new committee and may have known that Hoekstra didn't like Bush's testing proposal.

Hoekstra got a seat on the Intelligence Committee in 2001 and sponsored the bill to improve intelligence sharing between law enforcement and intelligence agencies that passed overwhelmingly in June 2002. He decried the limits on recruiting human intelligence agents imposed by CIA Director John Deutsch in 1996. In October 2003, when weapons inspector David Kay delivered his interim report, Hoekstra stressed Kay's finding that the Saddam Hussein regime had maintained weapons of mass destruction program capability. In August 2004, after Porter Goss was confirmed as CIA Director, Speaker Dennis Hastert and the Steering Committee had to select a new Intelligence chairman. Hoekstra was third in seniority but got the job. The most senior member, Ray LaHood, insisted on keeping his seat on Appropriations; that was evidently unacceptable to Hastert. Jim Gibbons, a rough-hewn Westerner, was apparently unacceptable too. So Hoekstra was named chairman. His appointment was hailed by ranking Democrat Jane Harman. When George W. Bush issued executive orders increasing the authority of the CIA director; Hoekstra and Harman issued a joint statement saying that they needed to be supported by legislation, and promised to advance it. When Bush ordered a 50% increase in clandestine operators and intelligence analysts, Hoekstra said he would be "prepared to triple the budget for intelligence" if needed. Hoekstra also supported intelligence reorganization along the lines recommended by the 9/11 Commission, although the House passed a somewhat different bill. He hailed final passage of the bill in December 2004 and said the committee would monitor "whether this person [the national intelligence director] is getting the support that's needed, whether there are elements elsewhere in the bureaucracy that are trying to undercut it."

In 1992, as term limits on state legislators passed in Michigan, Hoekstra pledged to serve only 12 years. By 2002 he had changed his mind and announced he would run again in an open letter to his constituents. He also communicates with his district by posting a daily travel diary from his foreign trips. He has been reelected without serious competition.

THIRD DISTRICT

Rep. Vernon Ehlers (R)

Elected Dec. 1993, 6th full term; b. Feb. 6, 1934, Pipestone, MN; home, Grand Rapids; Calvin Col., 1952–55; U. of CA at Berkeley, A.B. 1956, Ph.D. 1960, U. of Heidelberg, Germany, 1961–62; Christian Reformed; married (Johanna).

Elected Office: Kent Cnty. Comm., 1974–82, Chmn., 1978–81; MI House of Reps., 1982–86; MI Senate, 1986–93, Pres. Pro Tem, 1990–93.

Professional Career: Prof., Calvin Col., 1966–82.

DC Office: 1714 LHOB, 20515, 202-225-3831; Fax: 202-225-5144; Web site: www.house.gov/ehlers.

District Office: Grand Rapids, 616-451-8383.

Committees: *Education & the Workforce* (8th of 27 R): 21st Century Competitiveness; Education Reform. *House Administration* (2d of 6 R). *Science* (8th of 24 R): Energy; Environment, Technology & Standards (Chmn.). *Transportation & Infrastructure* (9th of 41 R): Aviation; Water Resources & Environment.

Group Ratings

	ADA	ACLU	AFS	LCV	ITIC	NTU	COC	ACU	NTLC	CHC
2004	20	25	0	45	100	56	100	67	60	84
2003	15	—	0	55	—	57	87	72	—	—

National Journal Ratings

	2003 LIB	—	2003 CONS		2004 LIB	—	2004 CONS
Economic	41%	—	59%		44%	—	56%
Social	44%	—	56%		49%	—	50%
Foreign	50%	—	49%		53%	—	46%

Key Votes of the 108th Congress

1. Drilling in ANWR	Y	5. DC School Vouchers	Y	9. Ban Same-Sex Marriage	Y
2. Approve Bush Tax Cuts	Y	6. Ban Human Cloning	Y	10. Fund Iraq War	Y
3. Medicare/Rx Bill	Y	7. Restrict Gun Liability	Y	11. Bar Cuba Embargo Funds	N
4. Bar Overtime Pay Regs.	N	8. Ban Partial-Birth Abortion	Y	12. Intelligence Reorg.	Y

Election Results

2004 general	Vernon Ehlers (R)	214,465	(67%)	($308,785)
	Peter Hickey (D)	101,395	(31%)	($1,054)
	Other	6,243	(2%)	
2004 primary	Vernon Ehlers (R)	unopposed		
2002 general	Vernon Ehlers (R)	153,131	(70%)	($371,513)
	Kathryn Lynnes (D)	61,987	(28%)	($8,290)
	Other	3,737	(2%)	

Prior Winning Percentages: 2000 (65%); 1998 (73%); 1996 (69%); 1994 (74%); 1993 (67%)

The People		Race/Ethnic Origin	Ancestry	
Area size:	1,897 sq. mi.	82.2% White	German: 14.6%	Dutch: 13.1%
Urban population:	77.1%	7.9% Black	Irish: 7.9%	
Rural population:	22.9%	1.6% Asian	**2004 Presidential Vote**	
Pop. 2000:	662,563	0.4% Native Am.	Bush (R) 197,493	(59%)
Median income:	$45,936	0.0% Hawaiian	Kerry (D) 133,460	(40%)
Poverty status:	8.6%	1.5% Two+ races	Other 1,964	(1%)
Military veterans:	11.4%	0.1% Other	**2000 Presidential Vote**	
		6.2% Hispanic Origin	Bush (R) 170,622	(60%)
			Gore (D) 110,121	(38%)
			Other 5,942	(2%)
			Cook Partisan Voting Index: R + 9	

Occupation	Blue collar: 29.5%	White collar: 56.7%	Gray collar: 13.8%

Grand Rapids is Michigan's second-largest city, the center of its most prosperous and confident metropolitan area. The city's roots are in trees: It grew as a center for processing and turning into furniture the hardwood forests of northern Michigan. By the early 20th century, Grand Rapids was the leading furniture manufacturer in the nation. The Depression of the 1930s knocked the bottom out of the residential furniture market, and many manufacturers moved to cheaper-labor North Carolina. So Grand Rapids had to reinvent itself, and did. It went into office furniture, and today, three of the nation's largest office furniture manufacturers (Steelcase, Haworth and Herman Miller) are located in or near here. It capitalized also on a knack for sales. Rich DeVos and Jay Van Andel started Amway, the direct sales empire, which now has half of its sales abroad, and Frederik and Hendrik Meijer started Meijer's Thrifty Acres, combining supermarkets with discount stores in a way that even Wal-Mart has not been able to equal. Grand Rapids is also the center of a machine tool empire, the home of Wolverine World Wide, maker of Hush Puppy shoes, and the headquarters of Bissell and its carpet sweepers. Fifty years ago Grand Rapids and its up-and-coming businesses were outshined by Detroit and the auto industry. Today, the Grand Rapids region has been growing rapidly and has been a major engine in Michigan's economy.

One ingredient in Grand Rapids's success is its unique ethnic mix. It was founded by New England Yankees, but much of its character was set by the Dutch immigrants who began arriving in western Michigan in the 1870s, and are still coming today; 13% of people here claim Dutch ancestry (probably no other American city has such a high proportion of "V" pages in the phone book). The Dutch brought with them a piety witnessed in their Reform and Christian Reform churches, and a culture of hard work and precision craftsmanship; their cultural conservatism and belief in market economics runs deep. Dutch tradition and entrepreneurial success have been the ingredients of a civic activism that has given Grand Rapids a host of creative civic institutions—and an Alexander Calder stabile—that are the match of any city in the country.

Politically, Grand Rapids has been the center of Michigan Republicanism for much of the last century. It has also produced national Republican leaders. Arthur Vandenberg, originally a newspaper editor, was U.S. senator from 1928–51; once an isolationist, he provided key support for the bipartisan internationalist foreign policies of Franklin D. Roosevelt and Harry Truman. Another was Gerald Ford, who rose to House Republican leader in 1965, vice president in 1973, and then president after Richard Nixon resigned in 1974. Nixon got a bit of a nudge from the Grand Rapids area when, in a February 1974 special election, it voted to replace Ford with a Democrat, a clear sign that the Republican heartland was turning on Nixon. Since then, however, the area became more Republican than ever; Grand Rapids and Kent County voted 59% for George W. Bush in 2000 and 2004.

The 3d Congressional District of Michigan includes Grand Rapids and almost all of Kent County, plus Ionia and Barry Counties to the east and south. It is one of the two most Republican districts in Michigan, indeed one of the most Republican in the Midwest.

The congressman from the 3d District is Vern Ehlers, first chosen in a December 1993 special election. Ehlers grew up in small-town Minnesota, the son of a Christian Reform minister, attended Calvin College in Grand Rapids, got a Ph.D. in physics at Berkeley and then returned to Calvin to teach for 17 years. In 1974, concerned about local waste management, he was elected Kent County commissioner; in 1982 he won a seat in the state House and in 1986 the state Senate. After Congressman Paul Henry died in July 1993, Ehlers ran to succeed him, as he had in both houses of the legislature. He won the November primary with 33% of the vote; a month later he whipped the Democrat 67%–23%.

Ehlers brought to House Republicans, then entering their 40th year in the minority, a majority mindset. That brought him to the attention of Newt Gingrich, who named him to his transition team after the 1994 election. He assigned Ehlers, the first research physicist in Congress, to lead efforts to revamp the House's computer system. In 1995 Ehlers responded with a system making available vote tallies, public hearing transcripts and texts of amendments and bills. His religious faith and scientific training have left Ehlers with a middle-of-the-House voting record. Ehlers often insists on the need for research to determine public needs. In February 2004 he passed an amendment to the transportation bill pegging future research at 1.08% of total spending. When controversy arose over the composition of National Academy of Science advisory panels, he said, "A single, guiding principle should be applied—select the most qualified person for the job." But he added that on presidential appointments, "It is important that the scientists be in tune with the philosophy of the appointing president."

As chairman of the Science Subcommittee overseeing EPA and NOAA, he has sponsored several laws that have won widespread backing. With Senator Carl Levin, he has sponsored measures to study invasive species, and in October 2004 he helped pass $9 million for an electric barrier in the Illinois River to prevent Asian carp from getting into the Great Lakes. The House also passed his bill to monitor and prevent algal blooms and hypoxia in the Great Lakes. He pressed with some success for more spending on Great Lakes problems; armed with a GAO report showing that there were 33 federal and 17 state programs impacting the Great Lakes, he sponsored a bill to consolidate some of them and pressed EPA Administrator Mike Leavitt to report on them in 2005. In 2004 his subcommittee passed a NOAA authorization bill, to codify the agency's powers and establish its structure; it had been established by executive order in 1970 and, as he put it, "Congress has passed a hodgepodge of issue-specific legislation for NOAA, resulting in a confusing collection of laws that are not coordinated by an overarching mission for the agency."

Ehlers has a penchant for compromise. As head of a three-member task force on Robert Dornan's challenge to his 984-vote defeat in 1996, Ehlers looked over the evidence and announced that it showed "a large amount" of vote fraud but not enough to vacate the seat. That may help explain why Speaker Dennis Hastert bypassed him and selected Bob Ney to chair the House Administration Committee after the 2000 election. Like most other Michigan Republicans, he opposed George W. Bush's steel tariffs, and he was one of the Republicans who voted to repeal the section of the Patriot Act allowing agents access to library records—a vote on which the leadership held open the roll call to round up a majority.

Ehlers refuses to take more than 30% of his campaign money from outside the district. He has been re-elected by very wide margins.

FOURTH DISTRICT

Rep. Dave Camp (R)

Elected 1990, 8th term; b. July 9, 1953, Midland; home, Midland; Albion Col., B.A. 1975, U. of San Diego Law Schl., J.D. 1978; Catholic; married (Nancy).

Elected Office: MI House of Reps., 1988–90.

Professional Career: Practicing atty., 1978–90; MI Special Asst. Atty. Gen., 1980–84; A.A., U.S. Rep. Bill Schuette, 1984–87.

DC Office: 137 CHOB, 20515, 202-225-3561; Fax: 202-225-9679; Web site: www.house.gov/camp.

District Offices: Midland, 989-631-2552; Traverse City, 231-929-4711.

Committees: *Ways & Means* (6th of 24 R): Health; Human Resources; Select Revenue Measures (Chmn.).

Group Ratings

	ADA	ACLU	AFS	LCV	ITIC	NTU	COC	ACU	NTLC	CHC
2004	10	5	13	0	100	55	100	88	78	92
2003	5	—	0	5	—	61	100	88	—	—

National Journal Ratings

	2003 LIB — 2003 CONS		2004 LIB — 2004 CONS	
Economic	26% —	73%	41% —	59%
Social	0% —	95%	9% —	85%
Foreign	36% —	63%	39% —	59%

Key Votes of the 108th Congress

1. Drilling in ANWR	Y	5. DC School Vouchers	Y	9. Ban Same-Sex Marriage	Y
2. Approve Bush Tax Cuts	Y	6. Ban Human Cloning	Y	10. Fund Iraq War	Y
3. Medicare/Rx Bill	Y	7. Restrict Gun Liability	Y	11. Bar Cuba Embargo Funds	N
4. Bar Overtime Pay Regs.	N	8. Ban Partial-Birth Abortion	Y	12. Intelligence Reorg.	Y

Election Results

2004 general	Dave Camp (R)	205,274	(64%)	($521,658)
	Mike Huckleberry (D)	110,885	(35%)	($83,217)
	Other	2,765	(1%)	
2004 primary	Dave Camp (R)	unopposed		
2002 general	Dave Camp (R)	149,090	(68%)	($697,237)
	Lawrence Hollenbeck (D)	65,950	(30%)	($10,172)
	Other	3,533	(2%)	

Prior Winning Percentages: 2000 (68%); 1998 (91%); 1996 (65%); 1994 (73%); 1992 (63%); 1990 (65%)

The People		Race/Ethnic Origin	Ancestry	
Area size:	8,053 sq. mi.	92.8% White	German: 19.5%	English: 8.9%
Urban population:	41.4%	2.1% Black	Irish: 8.2%	
Rural population:	58.6%	0.7% Asian	**2004 Presidential Vote**	
Pop. 2000:	662,563	0.8% Native Am.	Bush (R) 181,314	(55%)
Median income:	$39,020	0.0% Hawaiian	Kerry (D) 145,774	(44%)
Poverty status:	10.5%	1.1% Two+ races	Other 2,697	(1%)
Military veterans:	13.6%	0.1% Other	**2000 Presidential Vote**	
		2.4% Hispanic Origin	Bush (R) 154,539	(54%)
			Gore (D) 126,282	(44%)
			Other 7,468	(3%)
			Cook Partisan Voting Index: R + 4	

Occupation	Blue collar: 28.7%	White collar: 53.5%	Gray collar: 17.8%

Flat and treeless for miles, the central reaches of Michigan's Lower Peninsula are farm country, exposed to bitter winds and snow drifts in winter and shining sun for precious weeks in summer. Like the steppes of Eastern Europe, these are farmlands that produce hearty crops: potatoes, navy beans, sugar beets. The little cities here are often small factory towns, with neat tree-lined streets on a grid layout that suddenly end and turn to bare fields. Each city has some distinction. Midland in 1891 was a declining lumber town when Herbert Dow perfected an electrolytic process to extract chemicals from northern Michigan's extensive brine wells; that was the start of Dow Chemical, still headquartered in this now upscale town. Owosso in 1902 was the birthplace of Thomas E. Dewey, later New York governor and Republican nominee for president in 1944 and 1948. It was also the home of novelist James Oliver Curwood and his Curwood Castle writing studio; today it hosts the Curwood Festival, lovingly chronicled by Thomas Mallon in *Rockets and Rodeos*, and is the site of Mallon's novel *Dewey Defeats Truman*. Mount Pleasant, to the north, is the site of Central Michigan University.

The 4th Congressional District of Michigan includes much of this territory north of Lansing and Grand Rapids and west of Flint and Saginaw. It stretches north up the freeways, hemmed in between U.S. 131 to the west and I-75 to the east, both routes where thousands drive in fall to hunt and in winter to ski, into the rolling country around Houghton Lake, once lumber country and now a retirement and resort area, with trailers and condominiums between knotty-pine cottages clustered around icy green lakes. It has more farms than any other district in Michigan. Redistricting added the boom area around Traverse City, which has the world's largest concentration of red tart cherry orchards and is burgeoning with vacation homes, resorts and more than two dozen wineries: this district is the main reason Michigan leads the nation in production of tart cherries, blueberries and dry edible beans. Politically, it remains mostly Republican territory, though some counties vote Democratic on occasion; the most Republican areas are Midland and Traverse City. The district voted for George W. Bush in 2000 and 2004.

The congressman from the 4th District is Dave Camp, a Republican first elected in 1990. Camp grew up in Midland and returned there after school to practice law. In 1984 he managed the successful congressional campaign of his boyhood friend Bill Schuette; in 1990 Schuette unsuccessfully ran against Senator Carl Levin, and Camp ran for Congress after having served two years in the state House. His key victory was in the Republican primary, where he beat former legislator and Pat Robertson supporter Al Cropsey, 33%–30%. He has won since without difficulty.

Camp has a generally conservative voting record, especially on cultural issues, and is influential on the Ways and Means Committee, where he has been an ally of Chairman Bill Thomas. He played a key role in passing the welfare bill in 1996, helping to write the two bills vetoed by Bill Clinton. At the time, he and John Ensign circulated a letter signed by about 100 Republicans urging that they separate their welfare and Medicaid changes, which had been passed as one bill, and vote on welfare reform alone, daring Clinton to sign it and make history, or veto it and make it a campaign issue. Newt Gingrich and the Republican leadership decided to do this, essentially disengaging House Republicans from the flagging Bob Dole presidential campaign. The bill passed, Clinton signed it, and the incumbent president and incumbent congressional Republicans got credit in November. Camp has worked with Michigan Democrats to increase tax credits for gas-electric hybrids and other environmentally-friendly automobiles. In response to attacks from Democrats, he defended a provision that he added to the Medicare/prescription drug bill in 2003 permitting nursing homes to restart nurse aide training programs even if the facility has recently violated federal nursing home standards. Suspending the programs "exacerbates the nurse aide shortage," Camp said. Separately, he pushed legislation to assist patients with kidney disease. He has advocated changes in the federal Hope scholarships to direct more benefits to low-income students. In 2005, he became chairman of the Select Revenue Measures subcommittee at Ways and Means.

Camp has worked on other issues. In 2000, he helped win enactment of the International Adoption Act, which designates the State Department to help adoptive parents in dealing with officials in other nations. Since then, he has worked on the possible ratification by the Senate of a treaty on international adoption, which would remove additional obstacles. He authored the Organ Donor Card Insert Act, under which 70 million taxpayers received organ donor information with their income tax refunds. When House Republicans passed their prescription drug bill, they included an amendment by Camp to cover cholesterol screening for all beneficiaries. A grass-roots group in the district has protested Camp's support of international trade deals, which participants contend have caused the loss of local manufacturing jobs; Camp has sought expansion of trade-adjustment assistance for workers.

Camp has had minimal opposition in the 4th District. He keeps in close touch with the district by signing every constituent letter that leaves his office, often with a personal note—a total of roughly 30,000 each year.

FIFTH DISTRICT

Rep. Dale Kildee (D)

Elected 1976, 15th term; b. Sept. 16, 1929, Flint; home, Flint; Sacred Heart Seminary, B.A. 1952, U. of MI, M.A. 1961, Rotary Fellow, U. of Peshawar, Pakistan; Catholic; married (Gayle).

Elected Office: MI House of Reps., 1964–74; MI Senate, 1974–75.

Professional Career: H.S. teacher, 1954–64.

DC Office: 2107 RHOB, 20515, 202-225-3611; Fax: 202-225-6393; Web site: www.house.gov/kildee.

District Offices: Bay City, 989-891-0990; Flint, 810-239-1437; Saginaw, 989-755-8904.

Committees: *Education & the Workforce* (2d of 22 D): 21st Century Competitiveness (RMM); Employer-Employee Relations. *Resources* (4th of 22 D): Forests & Forest Health; National Parks.

Group Ratings

	ADA	ACLU	AFS	LCV	ITIC	NTU	COC	ACU	NTLC	CHC
2004	90	65	100	100	20	11	38	16	0	46
2003	90	—	100	90	—	23	27	28	—	—

National Journal Ratings

	2003 LIB	—	2003 CONS		2004 LIB	—	2004 CONS
Economic	73%	—	26%		77%	—	22%
Social	63%	—	36%		63%	—	36%
Foreign	66%	—	32%		68%	—	30%

Key Votes of the 108th Congress

1. Drilling in ANWR	N	5. DC School Vouchers	N	9. Ban Same-Sex Marriage	N
2. Approve Bush Tax Cuts	N	6. Ban Human Cloning	Y	10. Fund Iraq War	N
3. Medicare/Rx Bill	N	7. Restrict Gun Liability	N	11. Bar Cuba Embargo Funds	Y
4. Bar Overtime Pay Regs.	Y	8. Ban Partial-Birth Abortion	Y	12. Intelligence Reorg.	N

Election Results

2004 general	Dale Kildee (D)	208,163	(67%)	($608,283)
	Myrah Kirkwood (R)	96,934	(31%)	($281,615)
	Other	4,818	(2%)	
2004 primary	Dale Kildee (D)	unopposed		
2002 general	Dale Kildee (D)	158,709	(92%)	($416,089)
	Clint Foster (Lib)	9,344	(5%)	
	Other	5,286	(3%)	

Prior Winning Percentages: 2000 (61%); 1998 (56%); 1996 (59%); 1994 (51%); 1992 (54%); 1990 (68%); 1988 (76%); 1986 (80%); 1984 (93%); 1982 (75%); 1980 (93%); 1978 (77%); 1976 (70%)

The People		Race/Ethnic Origin	Ancestry	
Area size:	1,780 sq. mi.	75.0% White	German: 15.3%	Irish: 7.6%
Urban population:	79.4%	18.5% Black	English: 7.4%	
Rural population:	20.6%	0.7% Asian	**2004 Presidential Vote**	
Pop. 2000:	662,563	0.5% Native Am.	Kerry (D) 187,671	(59%)
Median income:	$39,675	0.0% Hawaiian	Bush (R) 129,457	(41%)
Poverty status:	13.7%	1.7% Two+ races	Other 1,889	(1%)
Military veterans:	13.2%	0.1% Other	**2000 Presidential Vote**	
		3.6% Hispanic Origin	Gore (D) 174,788	(61%)
			Bush (R) 106,445	(37%)
			Other 5,811	(2%)
			Cook Partisan Voting Index: D +12	

Occupation	Blue collar: 31.4%	White collar: 51.0%	Gray collar: 17.6%

The flat plains south of Saginaw Bay, the inlet of Lake Huron that separates Michigan's Thumb (people really call it that) from the mitten of the Lower Peninsula, is one of the nation's premier industrial areas. Some 130 years ago it was the nation's premier lumber country, with huge stands of virgin trees being cut down and 36 sawmills in Bay City, with logs piled high along both banks of the Saginaw River in the 15 miles between Bay City and Saginaw. When the land was clear, it was sown with beans—the navy beans that are the primary ingredient of Senate bean soup—and sugar beets. A century ago, industry followed. Flint, a small town on a minor branch of the Saginaw River, was the home base of W. C. Durant, the investor who merged several young auto firms and formed General Motors. GM put its Chevrolet and Buick factories in Flint and its power steering facility in Saginaw, chosen because it was already a center of precision machinery manufacturing. From 1910 through the 1960s, Flint grew lustily as it built Chevys and Buicks, attracting workers from the mountains of Kentucky and Tennessee and the Black Belt of Alabama; country music, blues and soul and Southern accents became common in an area originally settled by New England Yankees. There was turmoil, too. Flint was the scene in January 1937 of the great sit-down strike that, when Governor Frank Murphy refused to send the National Guard to enforce a court order, forced GM to recognize the United Auto Workers as the bargaining agent for all its workers. Yet in many ways the GM company towns built good lives for their citizens. The UAW-GM contracts produced the world's highest wages for industrial workers and lavish fringe benefits, including a generous health care plan.

Then disaster struck. Auto sales plummeted with the oil shock of 1979, and imports, especially from Japan, that were higher-quality and lower-price than American cars, took an increasing share of the market. GM managers and UAW leaders assumed that increased labor costs could be passed along to consumers, that buyers were indifferent to quality and eager for new models. Those assumptions proved vitally wrong: not even the cleverest advertising could persuade Americans to continue to buy a new American car every two years. In 1979 GM employed more than 70,000 workers in its Flint plants, a huge share of the labor force in a metro area of 430,000 people. Eventually, thousands left Flint as GM closed 12 of its 15 factories; by 2002 the GM payroll was down to less than 22,000. Flint's brave attempts to spruce up its downtown failed; its economic woes forced the state to take control of the city government. Michael Moore, the prolific and partisan filmmaker, has used his hometown of Flint as the locale for much of his work about deteriorating life in America. But there has been some upturn. American car manufacturers have grown more adaptable and resilient, and small high-skill manufacturing operations in the Saginaw area have grown up in old factory buildings once considered worthless; this is part of southern Michigan's industrial belt with the expertise to sustain just-in-time manufacturing. In December 2004, after the state announced jobs initiatives, GM said that it will invest $450 million to expand and refurbish engine and truck assembly operations in Flint.

The 5th Congressional District of Michigan includes Flint and surrounding Genesee County, Saginaw and eastern Saginaw County, Bay City and eastern Bay County and rural Tuscola County, which is part of the Thumb. Flint, evenly divided between the parties when the sit-down strikes divided the community in the 1930s, is now heavily Democratic; Saginaw and Bay City somewhat less so. Tuscola continues to vote Republican. Republican redistricters put together Flint, Saginaw and Bay City, and used the other parts of the old districts to make adjacent districts more Republican.

The congressman from the 5th District is Dale Kildee, a Democrat first elected in 1976. Kildee grew up in Flint, studied for the priesthood, taught at a Catholic high school in Detroit and at Flint Central. His door-to-door campaigning got him elected to a state legislative seat in 1964, at 35, and enabled him to beat a 26-year veteran of the state Senate in 1974. He won the House seat in 1976. Kildee has an intensity of conviction derived from the liberal tradition lively in the American Catholic church—a tradition with little regard for market economics, a strong sense of obligation to care for the needy and a cultural conservatism. He is always pro-union, opposes abortion, and is something of a stickler on ethics. He voted against authorization for U.S. military action against Saddam Hussein in 2002. On the Education and the Workforce Committee, he is a strong ally of teachers' unions, a backer of increased federal aid for education and an opponent of school choice.

On other issues, Kildee was the first House member to argue imported minivans should be subject not to the 2.5% tariff for cars but to the 25% tariff for trucks, which has been on the books since the early 1960s. The truck tariff has become a sticking point in U.S. negotiations with several countries, including Thailand, for bilateral trade agreements; he was a strong opponent of NAFTA. In the omnibus spending bill in 2004, he got $5 million to help contain the emerald ash borer, an exotic, bark-eating beetle that was discovered in Michigan in 2002, and replace some of the 6 million ash trees that the bug has destroyed. On the Resources Committee, he has concentrated on Indian issues; Kildee carries with his copy of the Constitution a copy of the 1832 Supreme Court decision that recognized Indian sovereignty.

Kildee was easily reelected until 1992, when the district was redrawn to include a large chunk of northern Oakland County, a mostly Republican area. Kildee was held below 55% in 1992 and 1994, but his margins later rebounded. In 2002, redistricting put Kildee in the same heavily Democratic district with Bay City Democrat Jim Barcia, one of the more conservative Democrats in the House and, like Kildee, an opponent of abortion. Barcia evidently found the prospect of taking on Kildee daunting, and ran successfully for the state Senate. Kildee has not faced serious competition in the redrawn district, though his Republican challenger in 2004 got some attention as a conservative black woman and former Detroit police officer. Republicans are not likely to pose a threat if the seat becomes open; one possible candidate is former Congressman Barcia.

SIXTH DISTRICT

Rep. Fred Upton (R)

Elected 1986, 10th term; b. Apr. 23, 1953, St. Joseph; home, St. Joseph; U. of MI, B.A. 1975; Protestant; married (Amey).

Professional Career: Project coord., U.S. Rep. David Stockman, 1975–80; Legis. Affairs, O.M.B., 1981–83, Dir., 1984–85.

DC Office: 2183 RHOB, 20515, 202-225-3761; Fax: 202-225-4986; Web site: www.house.gov/upton.

District Offices: Kalamazoo, 269-385-0039; St. Joseph, 269-982-1986.

Committees: *Energy & Commerce* (4th of 31 R): Commerce, Trade & Consumer Protection; Health; Telecommunications & the Internet (Chmn.).

Group Ratings

	ADA	ACLU	AFS	LCV	ITIC	NTU	COC	ACU	NTLC	CHC
2004	35	5	38	9	78	54	90	76	76	76
2003	10	—	13	30	—	58	93	80	—	—

National Journal Ratings

	2003 LIB — 2003 CONS		2004 LIB — 2004 CONS	
Economic	41% —	57%	49% —	51%
Social	40% —	58%	25% —	73%
Foreign	49% —	51%	45% —	54%

Key Votes of the 108th Congress

1. Drilling in ANWR	Y	5. DC School Vouchers	Y	9. Ban Same-Sex Marriage	Y
2. Approve Bush Tax Cuts	Y	6. Ban Human Cloning	Y	10. Fund Iraq War	Y
3. Medicare/Rx Bill	Y	7. Restrict Gun Liability	Y	11. Bar Cuba Embargo Funds	Y
4. Bar Overtime Pay Regs.	Y	8. Ban Partial-Birth Abortion	Y	12. Intelligence Reorg.	Y

Election Results

2004 general	Fred Upton (R)	197,425	(65%)	($678,684)
	Scott Elliott (D)	97,978	(32%)	($46,185)
	Other	6,755	(2%)	
2004 primary	Fred Upton (R)	unopposed		
2002 general	Fred Upton (R)	126,936	(69%)	($1,573,678)
	Gary Giguere (D)	53,793	(29%)	($18,028)
	Other	2,788	(2%)	

Prior Winning Percentages: 2000 (68%); 1998 (70%); 1996 (68%); 1994 (73%); 1992 (62%); 1990 (58%); 1988 (71%); 1986 (62%)

The People		Race/Ethnic Origin	Ancestry	
Area size:	3,420 sq. mi.	84.3% White	German: 17.2%	English: 8.3%
Urban population:	58.3%	8.8% Black	Irish: 8.3%	
Rural population:	41.7%	1.1% Asian	**2004 Presidential Vote**	
Pop. 2000:	662,563	0.5% Native Am.	Bush (R) 164,595	(53%)
Median income:	$40,943	0.0% Hawaiian	Kerry (D) 143,906	(46%)
Poverty status:	11.4%	1.6% Two+ races	Other 2,759	(1%)
Military veterans:	12.8%	0.1% Other	**2000 Presidential Vote**	
		3.6% Hispanic Origin	Bush (R) 138,658	(52%)
			Gore (D) 119,740	(45%)
			Other 7,413	(3%)
			Cook Partisan Voting Index: R + 2	
Occupation	Blue collar: 31.3%	White collar: 53.0%	Gray collar: 15.7%	

The southwest corner of Michigan is at the western end of the overland trail from Detroit, over which the state's two southern tiers of counties were settled by New England Yankees and Upstate New Yorkers in the 1830s and 1840s. They built small towns with schools and churches and colleges, supported temperance and opposed capital punishment, and in 1854 started the Republican party. There are towns in southwest Michigan that still recall proudly their past as termini of the Underground Railroad, and black families with ancestors who made their way north out of slavery to freedom. Later, big industries transformed some of the small towns into significant cities. Kalamazoo, started by Dutch-Americans who introduced celery to this country, became the home of Upjohn pharmaceuticals, now Pharmacia-Upjohn. Predominantly black and struggling Benton Harbor and predominantly white and prosperous St. Joseph, twin towns on Lake Michigan originally known for cherry and peach orchards, became the home of Whirlpool appliances. But those companies and other famous industrial names have moved out, along with their thousands of jobs. This southwest corner is where the influence of Michigan recedes: People here watch Chicago television and root for the Cubs or White Sox rather than the Tigers.

The 6th Congressional District of Michigan occupies this southwest corner of the state, with Kalamazoo and Benton Harbor-St. Joseph its two major urban areas, and three smaller counties and parts of two others besides. It was for many years arch-Republican territory, represented by a succession of congressmen who deplored federal spending and welfare state measures: New Deal opponent Clare Hoffman (1935–63), Nixon defender Edward Hutchinson (1963–77), and pork barrel critic and later Reagan Office of Management and Budget Director David Stockman (1977–81). In the 1990s, Kalamazoo trended toward the Democrats, and the 6th (with slightly different boundaries) cast small pluralities for Bill Clinton. George W. Bush lost Kalamazoo County in 2000 and 2004, but carried the district twice.

The congressman from the 6th District is Fred Upton, a Republican first elected in 1986. The grandson of one of the founders of Whirlpool, Upton grew up in St. Joseph, attended the University of Michigan and worked for David Stockman, first on his House staff, then from 1981–85 at OMB. He returned home and ran in the 1986 Republican primary against Congressman Mark Siljander, a conservative and evangelical Christian, and won 55%–45%. Upton is less like the congressional David Stockman, a scourge of federal spending, and more like the OMB Stockman, who rued the Reagan tax cuts.

Upton has a moderate voting record and he has often flaunted his independence in the Republican House. He has sought, with limited success, to use his leverage to reduce the size of tax cuts. He called for making Republican tax cuts in 1995 contingent on certification by the Clinton OMB that the budget was on a realistic path toward being balanced in 2002; as it turned out, the budget was balanced four years earlier than that target, at which point Upton based his tax-cutting caution on the need to pay down the national debt. He voted for the constitutional amendment to ban same-sex marriage in 2004. Between 1997 and October 2003, he did not miss a House vote.

Upton is now the 4th most senior Republican on the Energy and Commerce Committee. As chairman of the Oversight and Investigations Subcommittee in 1999 and 2000, he investigated the Salt Lake City Olympics scandal and defects in Firestone-Bridgestone tires; on that he worked to pass a package of safety reforms in 2000. In 2001, he became chairman of the Telecommunications Subcommittee, though he would have preferred the Health Subcommittee. He endorsed the Tauzin-Dingell bill to allow regional telephone companies to provide broadband service more easily. He criticized the recording industry for its inadequate parental advisory labels on music that contains sex, violence or strong language, but he took the view that the First Amendment bars Congress from such regulation. Bush signed his bill to create a "safe playground for kids" on the Internet—a ".kids" space free of pornography and other inappropriate materials. After the Janet Jackson "wardrobe malfunction" in a Super Bowl halftime show in February 2004, he helped to secure stiff increases in fines for broadcast indecency, from $27,500 to $500,000. "I am fed up with the smut and raw sex that has polluted the public airwaves," Upton complained. Also in 2004 he won House approval of the Junk Fax Prevention Act, which gave an opt-out notice to recipients. For the 109th Congress, he planned to tackle an array of telecommunications issues, including the universal service fund, Internet phone service, and a possible modernizing of the 1996 Telecommunications Act. Since the second-ranking Republican on Energy and Commerce, Michael Bilirakis, has announced he will retire from the House, Upton is in line for the full committee chairmanship in 2010, presuming Republicans retain their majority. In the meantime, Republican term-limit rules will make him switch subcommittee chairmanships in 2007.

Upton has been reelected by wide margins. In 2002 he faced a primary challenge from term-limited state Senator Dale Shugars, a conservative whose reelection Upton opposed in 1998. Upton spent more than $1 million on the primary and won 65%–32%.

SEVENTH DISTRICT

Rep. Joe Schwarz (R)

Elected 2004, 1st term; b. Nov. 15, 1937, Chicago, IL; home, Battle Creek; U. of MI, B.A. 1959; Wayne St. U., M.D. 1964; Catholic; divorced.

Military Career: Navy, 1965–67 (Vietnam).

Elected Office: Battle Creek city comm., 1979–87; mayor, 1985–87; MI Senate, 1986–2002; Senate pres. pro tempore, 1993–2002.

Professional Career: CIA officer, 1968–70; Practicing physician, 1964-present.

DC Office: 128 CHOB, 20515, 202-225-6276; Fax: 202-225-6281; Web site: www.schwarz.house.gov.

District Offices: Battle Creek, 269-965-9066; Jackson, 517-783-4486; Lansing, 517-323-6600.

Committees: *Agriculture* (20th of 25 R): Conservation, Credit, Rural Development & Research; Specialty Crops & Foreign Agriculture Programs. *Armed Services* (31st of 34 R): Readiness; Strategic Forces. *Science* (21st of 24 R): Energy; Environment, Technology & Standards.

Group Ratings and Key Votes: Newly Elected

Election Results

2004 general	Joe Schwarz (R)	176,053	(58%)	($750,290)
	Sharon Renier (D)	109,527	(36%)	($8,742)
	Other	16,062	(5%)	
2004 primary	Joe Schwarz (R)	20,440	(28%)	
	Brad Smith (R)	16,488	(22%)	
	Tim Walberg (R)	12,973	(18%)	
	Clark Bisbee (R)	10,301	(14%)	
	Gene DeRossett (R)	8,379	(11%)	
	Paul DeWeese (R)	4,886	(7%)	
2002 general	Nick Smith (R)	121,142	(60%)	($155,157)
	Mike Simpson (D)	78,412	(39%)	($48,905)
	Other	3,515	(2%)	

The People		Race/Ethnic Origin	Ancestry	
Area size:	4,365 sq. mi.	88.5% White	German: 17.4% English: 9.7%	
Urban population:	54.0%	5.6% Black	Irish: 8.3%	
Rural population:	46.0%	0.8% Asian	**2004 Presidential Vote**	
Pop. 2000:	662,563	0.4% Native Am.	Bush (R)	176,624 (54%)
Median income:	$45,181	0.0% Hawaiian	Kerry (D)	145,979 (45%)
Poverty status:	7.9%	1.4% Two+ races	Other	2,322 (1%)
Military veterans:	13.5%	0.1% Other	**2000 Presidential Vote**	
		3.2% Hispanic Origin	Bush (R)	141,647 (51%)
			Gore (D)	127,344 (46%)
			Other	6,682 (2%)
			Cook Partisan Voting Index: R + 2	

Occupation	Blue collar: 31.3%	White collar: 53.6%	Gray collar: 15.1%

The small cities and towns spotting the southern-tier farmland counties of Michigan have been incubators of innovation since they were settled by Yankees from New England 150 years ago. The state's public school system was established by two politicians from Marshall, whose hopes to make it the state capital were dashed. A few miles away, in Battle Creek, sanitarium operator W.K. Kellogg invented corn flakes as a health food; he and his one-time patient, C.W. Post, both established factories in the late 19th century and created the American breakfast cereal industry. Kellogg, a prospering firm that has increased jobs through corporate acquisitions, delivered its CEO, Carlos Gutierrez, to George W. Bush's second-term Cabinet. To the south is Hillsdale, where conservative Hillsdale College has been proudly admitting blacks and women since the 1850s and refusing all federal aid. Politically, this area has been Republican territory since 1854, when the party was founded in the manufacturing and prison town of Jackson as a kind of reformist institution out of the same activist impulse that produced local support for women's rights and Prohibition, and opposition to the death penalty. Southern Michigan mostly rejected New Deal tinkering and was hostile to the UAW, but the people here were receptive to moral claims made by later 20th century reformers challenging racial segregation, the Vietnam War and the Watergate cover-up.

The 7th Congressional District of Michigan covers all of five counties and parts of two others in Michigan's southern tiers. It typically votes Republican, but not always: Bill Clinton carried the district by small pluralities in 1992 and 1996, but it returned to the ancestral fold to vote for George W. Bush in 2000 and 2004.

The congressman from the 7th District is Joe Schwarz, first elected in 2004 at 66, is the oldest member of the new freshman class. Schwarz grew up in Battle Creek, got a history degree from the University of Michigan and then an M.D. from Wayne State University. He served in the Navy and as a Central Intelligence Agency attaché in Southeast Asia. He returned to Battle Creek, where he practiced medicine as an ear, nose and throat specialist, and was elected in 1979 to the Battle Creek City Commission. In 1986, he was elected to the state Senate, where for a decade he was president pro tempore. In 1992 he ran for the 7th District House seat, which was made much more Republican in redistricting. In the primary he faced state Senator Nick Smith, a county commissioner and an international lawyer who ran ads that claimed Schwarz shouted at and then backed his car into a hospital security officer who had written him a ticket. Smith, who supported a property tax freeze and opposed abortion, attacked Schwarz for raising PAC money in Washington and said he would take no PAC money himself. Smith won 43%–36%; Schwarz, in the middle of a four-year term, kept his state Senate seat. Schwarz was the Michigan chairman of John McCain's 2000 presidential campaign in Michigan, at a time when most Republican politicians followed Governor John Engler in supporting George W. Bush. Michigan was one of McCain's high-water marks: Michigan has no party registration, and 18% of the primary voters were self-identified Democrats and 35% self-identified Independents; they voted heavily for McCain and he beat Bush 51%–43%.

In December 2002, Smith announced he would not run for reelection in 2004, and in his last months aroused some controversy. He charged that Majority Leader Tom DeLay promised to raise $100,000 for his son Brad Smith's campaign to succeed him if Nick Smith would vote for the Medicare/prescription drug bill in November 2003. The House Ethics committee "admonished" DeLay but also "rebuked" Smith for making comments based on "speculation or exaggeration," and for failing to cooperate fully during the probe.

Brad Smith, a patent lawyer with no history in electoral office, was only one of five conservatives facing the relatively moderate Schwarz in the August 2004 Republican primary; others included term-limited state Representatives Clark Bisbee and Gene DeRossett and former state Representative Tim Walberg. The *Detroit Free Press* called Schwarz "an unconventional candidate who's as much at ease in the drawing room of the Detroit Opera House as in the union halls of Flint." But opponents questioned his party loyalty and criticized his opposition to a constitutional amendment banning same-sex marriage. He was also criticized as lacking commitment to gun ownership rights, for his support of abortion rights and as a supporter of higher taxes. Schwarz won with 28% of the vote to 22% for Smith and 18% for Walberg. Schwarz won more than half of the vote in his home base of Calhoun County and also carried adjacent Eaton County, while the other candidates splintered the vote in the five remaining counties.

This district, which Bill Clinton carried in 1996 and which Al Gore came reasonably close to winning in 2000—and which has suffered serious job losses since—was not seriously contested by Democrats. Schwarz won in November 2004 by 58%–36%. He won seats on the Armed Services Committee, Agriculture and Science Committees. He promised to seek more funding for research at Michigan universities. A physician, he disagreed with the Bush administration's stand on stem-cell research, but he supported medical malpractice law changes that would crack down on frivolous lawsuits.

EIGHTH DISTRICT

Rep. Mike Rogers (R)

Elected 2000, 3d term; b. June 2, 1963, Livingston Cnty.; home, Brighton; Adrian Col., B.A. 1985; Methodist; married (Diane).

Military Career: Army, 1985–88.

Elected Office: MI Senate, 1995–2000, Maj. Floor Ldr., 1999–2000.

Professional Career: Co-founder, E.B.I. Builders, 1985; FBI Spec. Agent, 1988–94.

DC Office: 133 CHOB, 20515, 202-225-4872; Fax: 202-225-5820; Web site: mikerogers.house.gov.

District Office: Lansing, 517-702-8000.

Committees: *Energy & Commerce* (25th of 31 R): Commerce, Trade & Consumer Protection; Energy & Air Quality; Environment & Hazardous Materials; Health. *Permanent Select Committee on Intelligence* (11th of 12 R): Intelligence Policy; Oversight.

Group Ratings

	ADA	ACLU	AFS	LCV	ITIC	NTU	COC	ACU	NTLC	CHC
2004	10	0	13	0	90	58	100	92	78	92
2003	5	—	0	5	—	63	100	88	—	—

National Journal Ratings

	2003 LIB	—	2003 CONS		2004 LIB	—	2004 CONS
Economic	9%	—	84%		37%	—	62%
Social	13%	—	86%		23%	—	77%
Foreign	11%	—	80%		10%	—	86%

Key Votes of the 108th Congress

1. Drilling in ANWR	Y	5. DC School Vouchers	Y	9. Ban Same-Sex Marriage	Y
2. Approve Bush Tax Cuts	Y	6. Ban Human Cloning	Y	10. Fund Iraq War	Y
3. Medicare/Rx Bill	Y	7. Restrict Gun Liability	Y	11. Bar Cuba Embargo Funds	N
4. Bar Overtime Pay Regs.	N	8. Ban Partial-Birth Abortion	Y	12. Intelligence Reorg.	Y

Election Results

2004 general	Mike Rogers (R)	207,925	(61%)	($797,146)
	Robert Alexander (D)	125,619	(37%)	($79,392)
	Other	6,879	(2%)	
2004 primary	Mike Rogers (R)	unopposed		
2002 general	Mike Rogers (R)	156,525	(68%)	($1,604,619)
	Frank McAlpine (D)	70,920	(31%)	($11,443)
	Other	3,152	(1%)	

Prior Winning Percentages: 2000 (49%)

The People		Race/Ethnic Origin	Ancestry	
Area size:	2,288 sq. mi.	87.7% White	German: 17.3%	English: 9.6%
Urban population:	70.0%	4.8% Black	Irish: 9.2%	
Rural population:	30.0%	1.9% Asian	**2004 Presidential Vote**	
Pop. 2000:	662,563	0.4% Native Am.	Bush (R) 191,287	(54%)
Median income:	$52,510	0.0% Hawaiian	Kerry (D) 161,282	(45%)
Poverty status:	8.4%	1.6% Two+ races	Other 2,668	(1%)
Military veterans:	11.0%	0.1% Other	**2000 Presidential Vote**	
		3.5% Hispanic Origin	Bush (R) 153,798	(51%)
			Gore (D) 141,770	(47%)
			Other 8,426	(3%)
			Cook Partisan Voting Index: R + 2	

Occupation	Blue collar: 23.0%	White collar: 62.6%	Gray collar: 14.4%

Lansing is Michigan's state capital, chosen in 1847 because of its geographic position halfway between Lake Huron and Lake Michigan and away from the border with Canada and the threat of invasion by British forces, but in ignorance of the fact that it has fewer days with sunshine than any place else in the state. But it is a tidy and pleasant city with more than its share of amenities. It has a beautifully restored Capitol and a fine state history museum and is neighbor to Michigan State University in East Lansing, started in 1855 as America's first land-grant college. Its Oldsmobile plant stimulated growth in the first half of the 20th century, and state government did the same in the second half. GM closed its Olds line in 2004, but two new highly efficient GM assembly plants have been constructed in the Lansing area and the Oldsmobile name remains alive at two local museums and at the baseball stadium where the Lansing Lugnuts play. Historically, the Lansing area voted Republican, up through the 1960s. But as public employee unions have grown in membership and strength, Lansing like some other state capitals has become heavily Democratic, as is university-influenced East Lansing.

Just east of Lansing's Ingham County is quite another part of Michigan, Livingston County (most of the counties in these parts were named for members of President Andrew Jackson's Cabinet; Livingston was secretary of state and Ingham secretary of the Treasury). Thirty years ago, Livingston County was mostly rural, known mainly for its many lakes. But in the years since then, thousands of Detroit area residents have driven out I-96 to Brighton and Howell and other Livingston townships, and subdivisions, schools and shopping malls have sprouted up. Most of these people are conservatives, happy to leave the problems of Detroit behind them, angry at high taxes and annoyed by government regulations and hewing to traditional religious faiths. They have made Livingston Michigan's fastest-growing county—its population rose 49% from 1990 to 2003—and one of its most Republican. In 1970 Livingston had 58,000 people to Ingham's 261,000; in 2004 Livingston had 178,000 to Ingham's 280,000. So as Ingham has grown more Democratic, Livingston has been casting bigger Republican margins to counterbalance Ingham's Democratic margins. In the close presidential election of 1968, 19,000 people voted in Livingston and gave Richard Nixon a 3,000-vote margin, while 90,000 voted in Ingham and gave Nixon a 9,000-vote margin (this was before East Lansing went Democratic). In the close presidential election of 2004, 93,000 people voted in Livingston and gave George W. Bush a 25,000-vote margin—up from 16,000 in 2000. By comparison, 133,000 voted in Ingham and gave John Kerry a 22,000 vote-margin, up from 21,000 in 2000.

The 8th Congressional District of Michigan includes all of Ingham and Livingston Counties, Shiawassee County south of Owosso, plus Clinton County directly north of Lansing and northern Oakland County. Its boundaries were determined by politics: After the 2000 Census Republicans controlled the redistricting process and in the 8th District they wanted to protect a freshman Republican elected by just 111 votes in 2000. So they removed Democratic-leaning Genesee County townships outside Flint and rural Washtenaw County townships that they felt might be infected by the adjacent liberal university town of Ann Arbor, and they added reliably Republican counties.

The congressman from the 8th District is Mike Rogers, a Republican first elected in 2000 (He is one of two Republican Mike Rogers in the House; the other hails from Alabama). He grew up in Brighton, in Livingston County, and graduated from Adrian College in southeastern Michigan. He was commissioned by the ROTC as commander of an Army rapid deployment unit. He graduated from the FBI Academy, and focused on public corruption cases as an FBI special agent in Chicago for six years. In 1994 he returned to Michigan, started a family home construction business and was elected to the state Senate, where in 1999 he became majority floor leader. In 2000, when Democrat Debbie Stabenow gave up the 8th District seat to run successfully for the Senate, Rogers and Democrat Dianne Byrum, a fellow state senator, both ran in the 8th. Political forecaster Charlie Cook predicted that this could be the closest race in the country, and it was. Each candidate raised about $2 million; neither faced primary opposition. It took six weeks to count the final tally, and Rogers won by 111 votes.

Rogers describes his political philosophy as consistent with Bush's "compassionate conservatism," with a bit more moderate record on cultural issues than on the economy. With his military, law-enforcement and legislative backgrounds, Rogers was well-positioned to advise colleagues on policies to respond to the September 11 attacks. He provided expertise on the high-tech tools used to track terrorists and on the use of wiretaps, sought federal aid to pay for National Guard troops at Michigan's borders with Canada, and urged that airport screeners have federal supervision. On the Energy and Commerce Committee, he sought more authority for Michigan to limit its flow of trash from other states and Canada. "Ontario sends every dirty diaper, every bottle, every broken hockey stick to Michigan," he complained. "Michigan cities should be able to decide if they want to be the receptacle of Canadian trash." He successfully led an effort to strip an amendment from the highway bill that would have approved new casinos in Romulus and Port Huron. He worked to find ways to confirm new federal appeals judges for Michigan after all nominations were blocked by the state's two Democratic senators.

His aggressive approach has made Rogers a rising star among House Republicans. With his significant fundraising skills, Republican leaders tapped him to be their campaign committee's finance chairman and chief fundraiser in their "Battleground 2004" program, which helped finance candidates in contested races. He could be positioning himself for a leadership bid within the House.

At home, Rogers has won reelection without problems. Political insiders in Michigan have speculated that he might make a strong statewide candidate, perhaps if Senator Carl Levin retires in 2008.

NINTH DISTRICT

Rep. Joe Knollenberg (R)

Elected 1992, 7th term; b. Nov. 28, 1933, Mattoon, IL; home, Bloomfield Township; E. IL U., B.S. 1955; Catholic; married (Sandie).

Military Career: Army, 1955–57.

Professional Career: Insurance agent, 1958–92.

DC Office: 2349 RHOB, 20515, 202-225-5802; Fax: 202-226-2356; Web site: www.house.gov/knollenberg.

District Offices: Farmington Hills, 248-851-1366; Troy, 248-619-0531.

Committees: *Appropriations* (12th of 37 R): Foreign Operations, Export Financing & Related Programs; Transportation, Treasury, HUD, the Judiciary & District of Columbia (Chmn.).

Group Ratings

	ADA	ACLU	AFS	LCV	ITIC	NTU	COC	ACU	NTLC	CHC
2004	5	5	13	9	100	50	100	84	67	84
2003	5	—	0	5	—	59	100	88	—	—

National Journal Ratings

	2003 LIB	—	2003 CONS	2004 LIB	—	2004 CONS
Economic	19%	—	81%	20%	—	79%
Social	5%	—	87%	39%	—	60%
Foreign	30%	—	69%	34%	—	63%

Key Votes of the 108th Congress

1. Drilling in ANWR	Y	5. DC School Vouchers	Y	9. Ban Same-Sex Marriage	N
2. Approve Bush Tax Cuts	Y	6. Ban Human Cloning	Y	10. Fund Iraq War	Y
3. Medicare/Rx Bill	Y	7. Restrict Gun Liability	Y	11. Bar Cuba Embargo Funds	N
4. Bar Overtime Pay Regs.	N	8. Ban Partial-Birth Abortion	Y	12. Intelligence Reorg.	Y

Election Results

2004 general	Joe Knollenberg (R)	199,210	(58%)	($1,412,320)
	Steven Reifman (D)	134,764	(40%)	($120,386)
	Other	6,825	(2%)	
2004 primary	Joe Knollenberg (R)	unopposed		
2002 general	Joe Knollenberg (R)	141,102	(58%)	($2,524,728)
	David Fink (D)	96,856	(40%)	($2,321,103)
	Other	4,922	(2%)	

Prior Winning Percentages: 2000 (56%); 1998 (64%); 1996 (61%); 1994 (68%); 1992 (58%)

The People		Race/Ethnic Origin	Ancestry	
Area size:	323 sq. mi.	81.4% White	German: 13.6%	Irish: 9.2%
Urban population:	99.3%	8.0% Black	English: 8.5%	
Rural population:	0.7%	5.6% Asian	**2004 Presidential Vote**	
Pop. 2000:	662,563	0.2% Native Am.	Bush (R) 180,073	(51%)
Median income:	$65,358	0.0% Hawaiian	Kerry (D) 174,078	(49%)
Poverty status:	5.4%	1.6% Two+ races	**2000 Presidential Vote**	
Military veterans:	10.6%	0.1% Other	Bush (R) 164,149	(51%)
		3.0% Hispanic Origin	Gore (D) 151,996	(47%)
			Other 5,987	(2%)
			Cook Partisan Voting Index: R + 0	

Occupation	Blue collar: 14.7%	White collar: 75.2%	Gray collar: 10.1%

Oakland County, Michigan, long considered just a suburban adjunct of Detroit, is now the center of a giant, spread-out, affluent urban area. It is only minutes on the Lodge or Chrysler Freeways from the empty, abandoned blocks of inner-city Detroit; but suddenly, north of the Eight Mile Road boundary, there are giant office buildings and multiplying small businesses, expensive houses on large lots and one shopping mall after another, high education levels and low crime rates. Even physically there is a distinction between the two areas: Detroit is on almost perfectly flat land, while much of Oakland County lies on a line of hills and lakes that marks the southernmost advance of an Ice Age glacier. Like most large suburban counties, Oakland is a mixture of communities, more diverse than the standard critique of suburbs suggest and, in this case, it is the heart of the metropolitan area. I-75 in eastern and northern Oakland County is now the nerve center of tier one and two auto company suppliers, many in the big office centers and near the upscale malls in Troy, others north into Auburn Hills, near Daimler Chrysler's North American headquarters. Near the center of Oakland is Bloomfield Hills, metro Detroit's wealthiest community; just to the north is the old factory town of Pontiac, with a black majority and a fair amount of poverty. Birmingham and Royal Oak, little suburbs set among farm fields half a century ago, are now upscale gentrified nodes amid a vast suburban expanse. Booming growth came in the 1990s to Rochester Hills, north of Troy, and West Bloomfield, west of Bloomfield Hills; the latter is increasingly the focus of metro Detroit's Jewish community and has a large number of Asians, many from India and Pakistan; others are Chaldeans, descended from Iraqi Catholics, numerous enough to have their own chamber of commerce. Oakland County has become the population center of metro Detroit. In 1950, the city of Detroit had 1,849,000 million people and Oakland County 396,000. In 2000, Detroit had 951,000 and Oakland 1,194,000.

The 9th Congressional District of Michigan includes a little more than half the population of Oakland County. It does not include Southfield, Oak Park, Ferndale, Hazel Park or Madison Heights in the southeast—all heavily Democratic and part of the 12th District. It does include almost all of Royal Oak, all of Birmingham and Bloomfield Hills, Rochester Hills and Auburn Hills, Farmington Hills (you begin to see the prestige value of hills to people who grew up in the flatlands of Detroit) and West Bloomfield, Pontiac and Waterford Township. It is Michigan's most affluent congressional district, and also one that trended toward the Democrats because of cultural issues during the 1990s. This has created problems for Republicans, for there is a strong Right to Life movement in Michigan, and as pro-life activists win Republican conventions and nominations, voters have moved toward Democrats. Republicans no longer win huge majorities in Birmingham and Bloomfield Township, and run no better in fast-growing Troy and Rochester

Hills. Royal Oak, Farmington Hills and West Bloomfield, once solidly Republican, now lean Democratic; while Waterford Township, with a more working class population, leans Republican. This is one part of Michigan where George W. Bush lost ground: he carried the 9th District 51%–47% in 2000 but by only 51%–49% in 2004.

The congressman from the 9th District is Joe Knollenberg, a Republican first elected in 1992. Knollenberg grew up the fifth child in a family of 13 on a farm in Downstate Illinois, went to college in Illinois and became an insurance agent. He moved to Oakland County in 1967 and became involved in civic affairs and Republican politics. When Republican William Broomfield retired in 1992 after 36 years in office—every one of them in the minority—Knollenberg ran to succeed him. With Broomfield's support and that of Michigan Right To Life, he was able to win the primary with 43% of the vote. He won the general election easily.

Knollenberg entered the House as a junior member of the minority. But in two years, with a change in control, he became a member of Appropriations advancing some cutting-edge ideas. He moved to zero out funding for the statistics required for CAFE standards and managed to zero out funding for implementation of the 1997 Kyoto treaty until the Senate ratifies it. Knollenberg has been a strong supporter of NAFTA, normal trade relations with China and trade promotion authority; Michigan is the sixth-largest exporter among states. He opposed George W. Bush's tariffs on steel imports in March 2002, as automakers and auto suppliers were faced with 20% to 50% price increases for steel; he hailed their repeal in December 2003. In July 2003 he got an assurance from Deputy Secretary of State Richard Armitage that the government would thenceforth use only U.S.-made vehicles in Iraq. He sponsored a bill to require counterfeiters of machinery to forfeit not only their earnings but the machinery they used to make fake goods after conviction; the auto parts industry estimates that counterfeits bring in more than $12 billion a year. He is the co-chairman of the Congressional Armenian Caucus, and pressed successfully for equal amounts of military aid for Armenia and Azerbaijan and to increase aid to Armenia from $62 million to $65 million plus $5 million for Artsakh (the Armenian enclave formerly known as Nagorno-Karabakh). "It's my job to make sure Armenia gets heard," he says.

In 2001 Knollenberg became chairman of the District of Columbia Subcommittee, and hence one of Appropriation's 13 "cardinals." In 2003 he became chairman of the Military Construction Subcommittee. His main goal was to raise the $850 million cap on privatized housing construction, supported by both Democrats and Republicans, to allow the Pentagon to hire private construction companies for military housing improvements. Knollenberg got the Appropriations Committee to increase the cap from $850 million to $1.35 billion, but did not persuade the Rules Committee to preclude its being scored as a spending increase, exceeding the subcommittee's $10 billion allocation of discretionary funds. The military construction appropriation is usually uncontroversial, but when the measure came to the floor in July 2004 the Republican leadership opposed the cap increase, and Jim Nussle raised a point of order against it; Nussle and the leadership prevailed after a long roll call 212–211. But Knollenberg and ranking Democrat Chet Edwards continued to argue that without the higher cap, 50,000 military families would have to wait for housing. The cap was lifted in the defense authorization passed in October 2004; Knollenberg and Edwards and their Senate counterparts were ready to raise it in the appropriation had that not happened.

In January 2005 the number of Appropriations subcommittees was reduced from 13 to 10 and Military Construction's jurisdiction was given to Defense. But Knollenberg came out a winner, because he was given the chairmanship of the Transportation Subcommittee, whose previous (and more senior) chairman, Ernest Istook, had antagonized the Republican leadership. Transportation handles much more money and many more politically sensitive—and locally important—projects than the subcommittees Knollenberg previously chaired.

Oakland County became more Democratic in the 1990s. Redistricting removed heavily Democratic Southfield and made the district slightly more Republican, but it also meant that nearly two-thirds of the district was new territory for Knollenberg. In 2002 he had vigorous and well-financed opposition from politically connected lawyer David Fink, who spent $1.2 million of his own money on his campaign. He said the race was "David versus Joe-liath" and that Knollenberg was beholden to the gun and pharmaceutical industries. Knollenberg replied that

Fink was a product of Wayne County Executive Ed McNamara's political machine and was a trial lawyer who defended big polluters. Knollenberg said that with his seniority and subcommittee chairmanship he could do more; Fink reminded him that he had promised in 1992 to retire in 2004. Knollenberg replied that he no longer believed in term limits. Knollenberg voted for the Iraq war resolution in October 2002; Fink said he would condition U.S. action on UN approval. This was a big-spending race in an affluent metropolitan district but Knollenberg won 58%–40%, an uptick from his 2000 showing. In 2004 against an indifferently financed challenger, Knollenberg won by the same 58%–40%.

TENTH DISTRICT

Rep. Candice Miller (R)

Elected 2002, 2d term; b. May 7, 1954, Detroit; home, Harrison Twnshp.; Macomb Cnty. Community Col., 1973–74, Northwood U.; Presbyterian; married (Donald).

Elected Office: Trustee, Harrison Twnshp. Bd., 1979–80; Harrison Twnshp. Supervisor, 1980–92; Macomb Cnty. Treasurer, 1992–94; MI Secy. of State, 1994–2002.

Professional Career: Secy.-Treas., D.B. Snider Inc. marina, 1972–79

DC Office: 228 CHOB, 20515, 202-225-2106; Fax: 202-226-1169; Web site: candicemiller.house.gov.

District Office: Shelby Twnshp., 586-997-5010.

Committees: *Armed Services* (26th of 34 R): Projection Forces; Readiness. *Government Reform* (13th of 23 R): Criminal Justice, Drug Policy & Human Resources; Regulatory Affairs (Chmn.). *House Administration* (6th of 6 R).

Group Ratings

	ADA	ACLU	AFS	LCV	ITIC	NTU	COC	ACU	NTLC	CHC
2004	10	0	25	9	90	47	100	84	72	91
2003	10	—	13	5	—	57	97	88	—	—

National Journal Ratings

	2003 LIB	—	2003 CONS		2004 LIB	—	2004 CONS
Economic	21%	—	75%		41%	—	59%
Social	24%	—	71%		9%	—	85%
Foreign	11%	—	80%		17%	—	78%

Key Votes of the 108th Congress

1. Drilling in ANWR	Y	5. DC School Vouchers	Y	9. Ban Same-Sex Marriage	Y
2. Approve Bush Tax Cuts	Y	6. Ban Human Cloning	Y	10. Fund Iraq War	Y
3. Medicare/Rx Bill	Y	7. Restrict Gun Liability	Y	11. Bar Cuba Embargo Funds	N
4. Bar Overtime Pay Regs.	N	8. Ban Partial-Birth Abortion	Y	12. Intelligence Reorg.	Y

Election Results

2004 general	Candice Miller (R)	227,720	(69%)	($442,297)
	Rob Casey (D)	98,029	(30%)	($16,585)
	Other	6,119	(2%)	
2004 primary	Candice Miller (R)	unopposed		
2002 general	Candice Miller (R)	137,339	(63%)	($1,421,613)
	Carl Marlinga (D)	77,053	(36%)	($970,409)
	Other	2,536	(1%)	

The People		Race/Ethnic Origin	Ancestry	
Area size:	3,663 sq. mi.	93.6% White	German: 19.1% Polish: 10.5%	
Urban population:	66.0%	1.5% Black	Irish: 8.2%	
Rural population:	34.0%	1.2% Asian	**2004 Presidential Vote**	
Pop. 2000:	662,562	0.3% Native Am.	Bush (R) 193,727	(57%)
Median income:	$52,690	0.0% Hawaiian	Kerry (D) 147,288	(43%)
Poverty status:	6.0%	1.2% Two+ races	Other 1,748	(1%)
Military veterans:	12.6%	0.1% Other	**2000 Presidential Vote**	
		2.1% Hispanic Origin	Bush (R) 152,780	(53%)
			Gore (D) 127,640	(45%)
			Other 6,242	(2%)
			Cook Partisan Voting Index: R + 4	

| **Occupation** | Blue collar: 31.5% | White collar: 55.2% | Gray collar: 13.4% |

Macomb County, Michigan, on the billiard-table-flat shore of Lake St. Clair just northeast of Detroit, has been one of the nation's most closely watched political battlegrounds, a place where it seemed the electoral fate of Michigan and even the entire country might be determined. It owes much of that to its reputation as blue collar suburbia, but that is no longer quite accurate: more people hold white-collar jobs than blue-collar these days and far fewer work in auto plants than in earlier generations. There are plenty of affluent subdivisions now, and boat ownership is close to the highest in the country. Macomb County is the product of the post-World War II boom: In 1940 it had 107,000 residents, many in the old sulphur-water spa town of Mount Clemens; Macomb passed the 400,000 mark in 1960 and 600,000 by 1970; in 2004, it reached 822,000. Many people came here from the east side of Detroit: These new suburbanites were heavily Catholic, often blue-collar, at least modestly affluent and ancestrally Democratic. They accepted the New Deal as part of their natural heritage but resented the efforts of Detroit politicians to tax them to pay for welfare, and they were fearful of the high crime rates in Detroit's black neighborhoods.

In 1960, Macomb County was the most Democratic major suburban county in the United States, voting 63% for America's first Catholic president, John F. Kennedy. For three decades afterwards Macomb moved away from the national Democrats—in 1962 because they would let Detroit tax suburbanites, in 1972 because they didn't vehemently oppose a metropolitan school busing plan. From 1976 through 1992, no Democratic presidential candidate got more than 40% of the vote here. In 1996, after great effort and with the advice of pollster Stan Greenberg, who has studied Macomb closely, Bill Clinton carried Macomb County by a 49%–39% margin; in 2000 Al Gore carried it by 50%–48%, nearly the national average. But the Democratic tide seems to have receded a little. In 2002 Macomb County voted 52%–47% for Republican governor candidate Dick Posthumus, even as he was losing statewide, and it elected more Republican state legislators than Democrats. In 2004 George W. Bush carried Macomb 50%–49%, even while losing more affluent Oakland County next door. Central and northern Macomb County have been filling up with expensive subdivisions not much different or less pricey than those in adjacent Oakland County; these areas have been growing rapidly—some by more than 40% in the 1990s—and are not as culturally liberal as affluent parts of Oakland County.

The 10th Congressional District of Michigan includes the northern two-thirds of Macomb County, with nearly half its voters. It also includes fast-growing Lapeer County, north of Macomb and Oakland and east of Flint; St. Clair County, with Port Huron and its Blue Water Bridge to Canada, and two rural counties in Michigan's Thumb (people really call it that). Northern Macomb has become increasingly Republican, Lapeer and St. Clair have long been pretty Republican and the Thumb has long been very Republican. Overall this is a comfortably Republican district—53% for George W. Bush in 2000 and 57% in 2004.

The congresswoman from the 10th District is Candice Miller, a Republican elected in 2002. Miller grew up in Macomb County. In 1979, at 25, she was elected Harrison Township trustee. A year later, she was elected as the youngest and first female supervisor in the township. In 1986 she ran against David Bonior and lost 66%–34%. In 1992, she won an upset bid to become

Macomb County treasurer. In 1994, she defeated 24-year incumbent Richard Austin and was elected Michigan secretary of state. In 1998 she carried all of Michigan's counties and set a state record for total votes. As secretary of state, she was credited with sharply increasing participation in the state's organ donation registry, creating fraud-proof driver's licenses and introducing technology into a hidebound agency. In its editorial endorsement, the *Detroit Free Press* called her performance in that job "innovative, progressive and popular."

Armed with huge name recognition as secretary of state, but prevented from running for reelection by term limits, Miller entered the House race as the favorite. Democrats hoped that Macomb County Prosecutor Carl Marlinga would be a strong candidate; he had held office 20 years and had been mentioned several times as a candidate for statewide office. But he could not keep pace with her fundraising and failed to do much to increase his name recognition north of Macomb. He called himself a "Hubert Humphrey Democrat"—not a big advantage in this district. Miller called herself a "George W. Bush Republican." She opposed abortion and supported NAFTA, trade promotion authority and favored making the Bush tax cuts permanent— all positions opposite to Marlinga. Both candidates supported gun rights. Citing the fact that her daughter is a member of the United Auto Workers, Miller reached out to unions, and was endorsed by the Teamsters (but not the AFL-CIO). Marlinga was hurt by allegations that he accepted campaign contributions from supporters of a convicted rapist who benefited from the prosecutor's handling of his case. Miller won by a huge 63%–36% margin; she carried Macomb County 61%–37%.

In the House, Miller had a moderate-to-conservative voting record. On the Armed Services Committee, she fought to protect the Selfridge Air National Guard Base, and sought additional Pentagon contracts for local firms, including the General Dynamics plant in Sterling Heights that manufactures the Army Stryker armored vehicle; in May 2005, the Pentagon recommended closing its Army garrison at Selfridge but the base was slated to gain new aircraft and 84 airmen. In January 2004, she joined the first congressional delegation to Libya, where she met Moammar Gadhafi and said that the trip reflected a Bush foreign policy success because Gadhafi "only has to look to Iraq to see what regime change can mean." At home, Miller supported a new casino for Port Huron, on behalf of the Chippewa tribe, but Michigan Representative Mike Rogers stripped the provision from the highway bill. She secured funds to study an early warning system and possible new equipment to prevent flooding along Lake St. Clair. She unexpectedly was admonished by the Ethics Committee in its review of charges against Majority Leader Tom DeLay dealing with efforts to influence the vote of Representative Nick Smith on the 2003 Medicare/ prescription drug bill. In response to the committee's claim that she intimidated Smith into voting for the bill, she referred to Smith's skills in martial arts when she told the *Detroit Free Press*, "If a black belt can be intimidated by an overweight, middle-age woman, that's too bad." Miller added that she accepted the committee's directive not to discuss on the House floor possible connections to political support for a family member.

In several comments, George W. Bush encouraged Miller to run in 2006 against Senator Debbie Stabenow; other Republicans said that she would be the strongest challenger. But Miller pulled the plug in January 2005, when she said, "At this time, I am happy where I am." That statement certainly appeared to leave the door open for a future bid.

ELEVENTH DISTRICT

Rep. Thaddeus McCotter (R)

Elected 2002, 2d term; b. Aug. 22, 1965, Detroit; home, Livonia; U. of Detroit, B.A. 1987, J.D. 1990; Catholic; married (Rita).

Elected Office: Schoolcraft Community Col. Trustees Bd., 1989–92; Wayne Cnty. Commission, 1992–98; MI Senate, 1998–2002.

DC Office: 1632 LHOB, 20515, 202-225-8171; Fax: 202-225-2667; Web site: www.house.gov/mccotter.

District Office: Livonia, 734-632-0314.

Committees: *Budget* (10th of 22 R). *International Relations* (19th of 27 R): Europe & Emerging Threats; Middle East & Central Asia. *Small Business* (11th of 18 R): Tax, Finance & Exports; Workforce, Empowerment & Government Programs. *Joint Economic Committee.*

Group Ratings

	ADA	ACLU	AFS	LCV	ITIC	NTU	COC	ACU	NTLC	CHC
2004	15	0	25	0	90	53	95	88	92	100
2003	5	—	13	5	—	62	100	92	—	—

National Journal Ratings

	2003 LIB	—	2003 CONS	2004 LIB	—	2004 CONS
Economic	21%	—	75%	43%	—	57%
Social	35%	—	64%	0%	—	91%
Foreign	31%	—	65%	17%	—	78%

Key Votes of the 108th Congress

1. Drilling in ANWR	Y	5. DC School Vouchers	Y	9. Ban Same-Sex Marriage	Y
2. Approve Bush Tax Cuts	Y	6. Ban Human Cloning	Y	10. Fund Iraq War	Y
3. Medicare/Rx Bill	Y	7. Restrict Gun Liability	Y	11. Bar Cuba Embargo Funds	N
4. Bar Overtime Pay Regs.	Y	8. Ban Partial-Birth Abortion	Y	12. Intelligence Reorg.	Y

Election Results

2004 general	Thaddeus McCotter (R)	186,431	(57%)	($735,845)
	Phillip Truran (D)	134,301	(41%)	($43,255)
	Other	6,484	(2%)	
2004 primary	Thaddeus McCotter (R)	unopposed		
2002 general	Thaddeus McCotter (R)	126,050	(57%)	($1,292,928)
	Kevin Kelley (D)	87,402	(40%)	($635,405)
	Other	6,953	(3%)	

The People		Race/Ethnic Origin	Ancestry	
Area size:	413 sq. mi.	89.5% White	German: 15.5%	Irish: 10.8%
Urban population:	97.0%	3.7% Black	Polish: 9.8%	
Rural population:	3.0%	3.0% Asian	**2004 Presidential Vote**	
Pop. 2000:	662,563	0.3% Native Am.	Bush (R) 183,835	(53%)
Median income:	$59,177	0.0% Hawaiian	Kerry (D) 164,037	(47%)
Poverty status:	4.3%	1.4% Two+ races	**2000 Presidential Vote**	
Military veterans:	12.1%	0.1% Other	Bush (R) 150,692	(51%)
		2.0% Hispanic Origin	Gore (D) 138,735	(47%)
			Other 6,022	(2%)
			Cook Partisan Voting Index: R + 1	
Occupation	Blue collar: 23.4%	White collar: 64.8%	Gray collar: 11.8%	

The inexorable pattern of growth and its consequences is a vivid tale in the western suburbs of Wayne County, 15 and 25 miles from downtown Detroit. Consider the case of Livonia, just west of Northwest Detroit. Half a century ago the 36 square miles of Livonia had 17,000 people; by 1960 there were 66,000 and by 2000 100,000. Similar growth occurred just to the south in Westland, named after a shopping center. To the west, around the old towns of Plymouth and Northville, affluent subdivisions sprang up; to the southwest, Canton Township grew 34% with more modest subdivisions. To the northwest Novi, in Oakland County, was the site of a new upscale shopping mall and emerged as one of the metro area's highest-income suburbs; Lyon Township just to the west looks to be the next boom area. Livonia is aging now—its school-age population was 38,000 in the 1970s and 17,000 in 2002—but these newer places are young, and all have been thriving while the central city of Detroit is terribly troubled. Tying these areas together was I-275, which runs along the western edge of Livonia and Westland and provides easy access to Metro Airport, the Northwest hub with nonstop flights to just about every big city in the country, as well as major European cities and Tokyo and Beijing. From affluent areas in Oakland County you have to budget an hour to drive to Metro; from I-275 it's more like 15 minutes.

Livonia was originally the political base of longtime Wayne County Executive Ed McNamara (1986–2002), who built the beautiful new midfield terminal at Metro (which is named after him). Livonia, originally settled by Detroiters, was long closely divided between the two parties, but the recent affluent influx into western Wayne County, plus Novi and other Oakland towns has made those areas more Republican. Racial minorities have become a majority in Wayne County; that's due partly to the rapid growth of Hispanics and Asian-Americans, many of them doing high-tech work in what local officials trumpet as the Automation Alley, the long miles of open road between Detroit and Ann Arbor.

The 11th Congressional District of Michigan covers much of this territory in western Wayne and Oakland Counties—Livonia and Redford Township just to the east, Westland and Canton Township, Northville and Plymouth, Novi and several fast-growing townships to the north and west. This was a new district, created in July 2001 by Republican redistricters, the residence of no incumbent at the time. The lines were carefully drawn to produce a district that voted 51% for George W. Bush in 2000 and with the clear intention of electing a Republican congressman.

The congressman from the 11th District is Thaddeus McCotter, a Republican first elected in 2002. He grew up in Livonia, where his mother Joan McCotter is city clerk. He graduated from Detroit's Catholic Central High School, where he was a first-team all-Catholic football player, and from the University of Detroit and its law school. He was elected to the Wayne County Commission in 1992, at 27, and became the driving force to change the county's charter to require a new tax to win approval of two-thirds of the commissioners and 60% of the voters in a referendum. In 1998, he was elected to the state Senate where, critically, he was vice-chairman of the Senate's reapportionment committee. He helped to design the new 11th District, which included his entire senate district, and became the early frontrunner in 2002. He received pre-primary endorsements and contributions from House Republican leaders Tom DeLay and Tom Davis and won the primary 69%–31%.

But McCotter did not win the seat without a contest. Democrat Kevin Kelley, Redford Township Supervisor and son of longtime Detroit Councilman Jack Kelley, entered the race late and was unopposed in the primary. Kelley called himself a "centrist Democrat"; both candidates supported the Bush tax cut, authorization of military force in Iraq and opposed individual investment accounts in Social Security. McCotter defined himself as a conservative who opposed abortion and gun control; Kelley supported abortion rights and restrictions on gun ownership. They drew sharp distinctions on trade policy. McCotter favored NAFTA, trade promotion authority and normal trade relations with China; Kelley opposed all three. Kelley hoped to benefit from governor candidate Jennifer Granholm's local popularity and hoped that his outgoing personality would be more appealing than McCotter's more reserved persona. But McCotter raised more money, much of it at a mid-October fundraiser with Bush. McCotter's 57%–40% margin was larger than expected.

In the House, McCotter had a moderate-to-conservative voting record. On the International Relations Committee, he called for fair and full representation for U.S. manufacturers in the rebuilding of Iraq. He urged the Bush administration to eliminate the steel tariffs imposed in March 2002. In response to reports of prank calls in Michigan and several other states, he filed a bill to make it a crime to spread false information about the death or injury of a member of the military. Less outgoing and more cerebral than many of his colleagues, he enjoys playing the guitar in his office. In 2004 against an underfinanced candidate he was reelected 57%–41%, almost exactly the same margin as two years before.

TWELFTH DISTRICT

Rep. Sander Levin (D)

Elected 1982, 12th term; b. Sept. 6, 1931, Detroit; home, Royal Oak; U. of Chicago, B.A. 1952, Columbia U., M.A. 1954, Harvard U., LL.B. 1957; Jewish; married (Vicki).

Elected Office: Oakland Bd. of Supervisors, 1961–64; MI Senate, 1964–70.

Professional Career: Practicing atty., 1957–64, 1970–76; Fellow, Harvard JFK Schl. of Govt., 1975; A.A., Agency for Intl. Devel., 1977–81.

DC Office: 2300 RHOB, 20515, 202-225-4961; Fax: 202-226-1033; Web site: www.house.gov/levin.

District Offices: Oak Park, 248-968-2025; Roseville, 586-498-7122.

Committees: *Ways & Means* (3d of 17 D): Social Security (RMM); Trade.

Group Ratings

	ADA	ACLU	AFS	LCV	ITIC	NTU	COC	ACU	NTLC	CHC
2004	100	75	100	100	50	9	38	0	3	15
2003	90	—	100	85	—	23	37	16	—	—

National Journal Ratings

	2003 LIB	—	2003 CONS		2004 LIB	—	2004 CONS
Economic	81%	—	18%		87%	—	13%
Social	78%	—	20%		76%	—	23%
Foreign	66%	—	32%		79%	—	20%

Key Votes of the 108th Congress

1. Drilling in ANWR	N	5. DC School Vouchers	N	9. Ban Same-Sex Marriage	N
2. Approve Bush Tax Cuts	N	6. Ban Human Cloning	N	10. Fund Iraq War	Y
3. Medicare/Rx Bill	N	7. Restrict Gun Liability	N	11. Bar Cuba Embargo Funds	Y
4. Bar Overtime Pay Regs.	Y	8. Ban Partial-Birth Abortion	N	12. Intelligence Reorg.	N

Election Results

2004 general	Sander Levin (D)	210,827	(69%)	($869,446)
	Randell Shafer (R)	88,256	(29%)	
	Other	5,051	(2%)	
2004 primary	Sander Levin (D)	unopposed		
2002 general	Sander Levin (D)	140,970	(68%)	($1,007,802)
	Harvey Dean (R)	61,502	(30%)	($43,323)
	Other	4,056	(2%)	

Prior Winning Percentages: 2000 (64%); 1998 (56%); 1996 (57%); 1994 (52%); 1992 (53%); 1990 (70%); 1988 (70%); 1986 (76%); 1984 (100%); 1982 (67%)

The People		Race/Ethnic Origin	Ancestry	
Area size:	160 sq. mi.	81.7% White	German: 14.1%	Polish: 11.4%
Urban population:	100.0%	12.0% Black	Irish: 8.0%	
Rural population:	0.0%	2.3% Asian	**2004 Presidential Vote**	
Pop. 2000:	662,563	0.3% Native Am.	Kerry (D) 193,894	(61%)
Median income:	$46,784	0.0% Hawaiian	Bush (R) 125,460	(39%)
Poverty status:	7.3%	2.1% Two+ races	**2000 Presidential Vote**	
Military veterans:	12.5%	0.2% Other	Gore (D) 175,524	(61%)
		1.5% Hispanic Origin	Bush (R) 106,628	(37%)
			Other 5,940	(2%)
			Cook Partisan Voting Index: D +13	

Occupation   Blue collar: 26.7%   White collar: 59.7%   Gray collar: 13.6%

The flat expanse of land just north of Eight Mile Road, Detroit's northern city limit, was mostly vacant in the years just after World War II. A string of suburbs in Oakland County ran along Woodward Avenue, Detroit's main street, where Henry Ford drove his first prototype in 1896, and which led to the Shrine of the Little Flower church in Royal Oak. There, in the 1930s, Father Charles Coughlin made his radio broadcasts backing and then opposing Franklin D. Roosevelt and denouncing bankers and Jews. In the 1950s and 1960s, Woodward was one of America's greatest cruising highways, where teenagers drove big Detroit cars up and down the eight lanes where the lights were timed at 42 miles per hour and zoomed into its drive-in restaurants—an era commemorated since 1994 with the Woodward Dream Cruise of old cars, a mega-celebration that annually draws more than 1 million for the one-day event. To the east in Macomb County was some industrial development along Van Dyke Road, but this was mostly empty land, too. Then Polish-Americans began marching out Van Dyke from Hamtramck to Warren; Italian-Americans headed out Gratiot from Detroit's east side to Roseville and Clinton Township; Belgian-Americans from the Mack corridor moved out farther to St. Clair Shores. Today, these areas are well-settled suburbs, long since built up, a few neighborhoods edging toward seediness, many others continually renovated and restored. Almost half of metro Detroit's population is now north of Eight Mile, in communities drawing on old traditions but crackling with economic creativity. Now Eight Mile, long known to Detroiters, is known to the world, thanks to *8 Mile*, the movie made by the rapper Eminem, telling the story of his emergence in Detroit's music scene during the 1990s.

The 12th Congressional District of Michigan is in this suburban territory, with two-thirds of its population in Macomb. On the Oakland County side are the southern part of Royal Oak and other Woodward Avenue suburbs, which have been economically revitalized and attract singles and gays as well as families; Oak Park, heavily Jewish in the 1950s and now perhaps the only small city in America with sizable numbers of Jews, Arabs and blacks; Hazel Park and Madison Heights, mostly peopled with descendants of the Appalachian migrants of a few decades ago; Southfield, Michigan's largest office space center (far ahead of Detroit), with a black middle class majority in 2000; and Ferndale, one of the original bedroom communities for autoworkers that has been revived with help from bonds to modernize downtown and is viewed as a model for how to rescue aging suburbs. On the Macomb County side are Warren and the southern part of Sterling Heights, site of the General Motors Technical Center, a big Chrysler plant and the now-privatized M-1 tank plant. Farther east are blue-collar communities of Macomb: Eastpointe (formerly known as East Detroit, it voted to change its name to make it sound less like Detroit and more like Grosse Pointe), Roseville, St. Clair Shores, Clinton Township and Mount Clemens. This district was drawn as heavily Democratic to protect the three Republicans in adjacent districts.

The congressman from the 12th District is Sander Levin, a Democrat first elected in 1982 and a member of one of Michigan's most respected political families; he is the older brother of Senator Carl Levin. Levin grew up in Detroit and got degrees from the University of Chicago, Columbia and Harvard Law School. He settled in the Woodward Avenue suburb of Berkley after school and was elected state senator in 1964; in 1970 and 1974 he ran for governor and lost narrowly each time to Republican William Milliken. In the Carter administration he was a top appointee at the Agency for International Development. In 1982, a House seat suddenly opened up in redistricting. Levin won a spirited primary and held the seat without difficulty. The 1992 redistricting moved him east, into Macomb County, and placed him in the same district with Democrat Dennis Hertel, who decided to retire; Levin easily won the nomination.

Levin is a hard worker, a details man, willing to spend endless hours with others working out solutions. On Ways and Means, he has played an important role on major issues. On welfare, Levin opposed the 1995 bills passed by Republicans but helped shape the bill passed in August 1996. Like most Democrats, he split with Republicans when the House sought to extend the welfare law, and he found little opportunity for bipartisanship on health issues after George W. Bush took office. After the death of Robert Matsui in January 2005, Levin became the ranking Democrat on the Social Security Subcommittee, which positioned him as a central player in that year's major debate. He said that Bush's initial warnings about the threats to the Social Security system were exaggerated, and he downplayed the need for Democrats to offer their own alternative.

Amid great controversy, Levin has been at the center of trade debates—seeking ways, as he often says, to shape globalization. He favored the Free Trade Agreement with Canada, which was designed in large part by auto manufacturers and the United Auto Workers. But he was wary of Japanese trade barriers and pushed unsuccessfully for stringent measures on Japanese minivans. He was a strong opponent of NAFTA in 1993, but supported GATT and normal trade relations with China, on which he played an instrumental role in crafting details with the Clinton administration. He opposed trade promotion authority in both the Clinton and Bush years. He also supported agreements that the Bush administration reached with Australia and Morocco, but he raised concerns over the impact on auto imports from a potential agreement with Thailand and he objected that Bush may have acted illegally when he lifted additional tariffs on steel. He wants trade agreements to contain provisions on workers' rights, fair ways of settling workers' disagreements and environmental provisions. Especially on China, his initiative made a major difference in public policy. In opposing the use of force in Iraq, he consulted extensively with his brother Carl, who was then chairman of the Senate Armed Services Committee. Each offered alternatives reflecting what they view as a more internationalist approach, but each was defeated.

After the 1992 redistricting, which removed much of metro Detroit's Jewish community from Levin's district and added unfamiliar territory in Macomb County, Levin had serious competition from Republican John Pappageorge, a retired Army colonel and M-1 tank executive. In the anti-incumbent atmosphere of 1992, Levin outspent Pappageorge by $1.18 million to $190,000 and won by just 53%–46%. In 1994, when Clinton was affirmatively unpopular and Republican Governor John Engler was running strong, Levin again greatly outspent Pappageorge and won by 52%–47%. But in the more pro-incumbent environment of 1996, Levin won by a larger 57%–41%. Since then Levin has won easily.

THIRTEENTH DISTRICT

Rep. Carolyn Cheeks Kilpatrick (D)

Elected 1996, 5th term; b. June 25, 1945, Detroit; home, Detroit; Ferris St. U., 1968–70, W. MI U., B.S. 1972, U. of MI, M.S. 1977; African Methodist Episcopal; divorced.

Elected Office: MI House of Reps., 1978–96.

Professional Career: Teacher, Detroit public schls., 1970–78.

DC Office: 1610 LHOB, 20515, 202-225-2261; Fax: 202-225-5730; Web site: www.house.gov/kilpatrick.

District Offices: Detroit, 313-965-9004; Wyandotte, 734-246-0780.

Committees: *Appropriations* (24th of 29 D): Foreign Operations, Export Financing & Related Programs; Transportation, Treasury, HUD, the Judiciary & District of Columbia.

Group Ratings

	ADA	ACLU	AFS	LCV	ITIC	NTU	COC	ACU	NTLC	CHC
2004	95	95	100	91	44	10	29	4	0	7
2003	100	—	100	80	—	23	24	12	—	—

National Journal Ratings

	2003 LIB	—	2003 CONS		2004 LIB	—	2004 CONS
Economic	87%	—	9%		96%	—	4%
Social	90%	—	10%		84%	—	15%
Foreign	84%	—	14%		88%	—	11%

Key Votes of the 108th Congress

1. Drilling in ANWR	N	5. DC School Vouchers	N	9. Ban Same-Sex Marriage	N
2. Approve Bush Tax Cuts	N	6. Ban Human Cloning	N	10. Fund Iraq War	N
3. Medicare/Rx Bill	N	7. Restrict Gun Liability	N	11. Bar Cuba Embargo Funds	Y
4. Bar Overtime Pay Regs.	Y	8. Ban Partial-Birth Abortion	N	12. Intelligence Reorg.	N

Election Results

2004 general	Carolyn Cheeks Kilpatrick (D)	173,246	(78%)	($591,551)
	Cynthia Cassell (R)	40,935	(18%)	
	Other	7,472	(3%)	
2004 primary	Carolyn Cheeks Kilpatrick (D)	unopposed		
2002 general	Carolyn Cheeks Kilpatrick (D)	120,869	(92%)	($343,173)
	Raymond Warner (Lib)	11,072	(8%)	

Prior Winning Percentages: 2000 (89%); 1998 (87%); 1996 (88%)

The People		**Race/Ethnic Origin**	**Ancestry**	
Area size:	108 sq. mi.	28.9% White	German: 5.4%	Polish: 4.2%
Urban population:	100.0%	60.5% Black	Irish: 4.2%	
Rural population:	0.0%	1.2% Asian	**2004 Presidential Vote**	
Pop. 2000:	662,563	0.3% Native Am.	Kerry (D) 188,555	(81%)
Median income:	$31,165	0.0% Hawaiian	Bush (R) 45,019	(19%)
Poverty status:	24.4%	1.8% Two+ races	**2000 Presidential Vote**	
Military veterans:	10.7%	0.2% Other	Gore (D) 167,830	(80%)
		7.2% Hispanic Origin	Bush (R) 39,024	(19%)
			Other 1,975	(1%)
			Cook Partisan Voting Index: D +32	

Occupation	Blue collar: 29.3%	White collar: 50.7%	Gray collar: 20.1%

Few central cities in America had as vibrant a 20th century history, and as sad a recent past, as Detroit. This was America's first automobile city, not just because it manufactured so many of the nation's cars but also because it was built to automobile scale. Detroit started the century as a second-rank city, no bigger than Milwaukee, with less than half a million people and extending no farther than four or five miles out from the site where the French built Fort Pontchartrain on the Detroit River in 1701. As the Motor City boomed, it grew outward along wide avenues and, starting in the 1950s, freeways; the auto companies put their factories and headquarters near the edge of urban settlement. As early as 1954, the nation's first big suburban shopping center, with parking for 10,000 cars, was drawing retail trade from downtown. Metro Detroit expanded to four million people, each generation moving out the roadways rapidly in many directions, leaving behind the previous generation's neighborhoods and civic institutions.

Today, that rapid movement has left large parts of Detroit literally empty. The central city had nearly 1.85 million people in 1950, but not even the help of a city bureaucracy detailed to round up uncounted residents could keep the total from falling below 1 million in 2000; in 2004 the population was estimated to be 911,000. The reason is obvious: crime. For 30 years Detroit had a murder rate drastically higher than in the suburbs, and naturally those who could afford to leave did so. Downtown, the giant Hudson's department store has been torn down and several skyscrapers are all but empty. There have been some positive developments. GM bought for $72 million the 70-story Renaissance Center, built in the 1970s for $350 million, and the company moved 10,000 employees there. Beyond downtown, some of the city's jewels have been maintained: the Detroit Institute of Arts, the hospital center, the old Fox Theater. New baseball and football stadiums have opened just north of downtown—the latter hosts the 2006 Super Bowl—and three gambling casinos have opened in nearby Greektown; residential and commercial projects have risen and more are planned on the long-neglected riverfront, with encouragement from a new shopping plaza and promenade at the Renaissance Center. But beyond these well-policed enclaves lie acres of vacant fields and half-empty blocks where there were once five-story apartments or brick houses; once vital neighborhoods are now home to pheasants. And the continuing job losses at the auto companies showed no sign of abating.

Detroit's fate is all the more tragic because it comes in a city where liberal reformers hoped to create model anti-poverty and anti-discrimination programs. Coleman Young, Detroit's mayor from 1973 to 1993, spent his energy on courting the Big Three; he bulldozed the viable Poletown neighborhood for a new Cadillac plant. Dennis Archer, who served the next eight years, took a more constructive and intelligent approach, and the city began to turn around, with lower crime, more jobs, new housing permits and a start at a growing private sector. In 2001, Kwame Kilpatrick, a former all-American football player who was elected to the state House, brought young blood when he was elected mayor, at age 32. He worked to inject a positive attitude in his youthful constituency, calling the city "a shining example in this world of revolutionary change," and he styled himself a national leader of urban America.

The 13th Congressional District of Michigan includes most of Detroit, plus a few adjacent suburbs, from the affluent Grosse Pointes with nearly 50,000 people looking out toward Lake St. Clair to the Downriver industrial towns of River Rouge, Ecorse, Lincoln Park and Wyandotte. It includes practically all of the east side of Detroit and the west side up to about five miles north of the Detroit River—the entire riverfront and downtown, the old General Motors and Fisher Buildings, most of Detroit's auto factories. At 108 square miles, this is the smallest district in the state, with the biggest problems: the state's highest rates of poverty, unemployment and percentages of residents on public assistance. Politically, the 13th is overwhelmingly Democratic, but voter turnout is low—222,000 in the House race in 2004, far below the 340,000 in the high-income 9th District. Redistricting reduced the district's black percentage from 70% to 61%, because more people had to be added to meet the population standard. But this remains one of the safest Democratic districts in the nation.

The congresswoman from the 13th District is Carolyn Cheeks Kilpatrick, a Democrat first elected in 1996. She was raised in Detroit, attended Ferris State and graduated from Western Michigan University and the University of Michigan. She taught business education in Detroit public schools and was elected to the state House in 1978. There, she got a seat on the Appropriations Committee and worked on local projects, notably the highly successful River Place hotel and office complex in the old Stroh Beer headquarters. Kilpatrick lost a race for the Detroit City Council, but won the 1996 Democratic primary for the congressional seat by a solid 51%–31% margin against her one-time political partner, incumbent Barbara-Rose Collins.

In her first term, Kilpatrick had one of the most liberal voting records in the House, but she has moderated slightly. She made a point of visiting the suburbs in her district, meeting local officials and assigning staffers to work with them—a contrast to Collins. On Appropriations since 1999, she has taken credit for funding Detroit-area projects for pre-college engineering and funding for buses and other transportation improvements in the Detroit area. She unveiled an agenda to encourage minority home ownership. She spurred the creation of the Detroit Area Regional Transportation Authority as an essential first step to increased national support for local funding. After visits to Africa, she has sought increased foreign aid for needy areas, including additional hundreds of millions of dollars to combat HIV/AIDS overseas.

Kilpatrick has had no problems winning reelection. In December 2004, the *Detroit Free Press* reported that her political action committee expenditures were chiefly for personal expenses of her family and friends; out of $27,000 in expenditures, just $200 went to a political candidate. She has been an active supporter of her son, the Detroit mayor, who faced a difficult reelection campaign in 2005. The city faced a budget crisis amid news reports about various scandals and the mayor's questionable use of a city-issued credit card; at a May rally for him, his mother gave an impassioned speech on his behalf. "Don't let nobody talk about y'all's boy! Too many people died for us! We're here to fight!"

FOURTEENTH DISTRICT

Rep. John Conyers (D)

Elected 1964, 21st term; b. May 16, 1929, Detroit; home, Detroit; Wayne St. U., B.A. 1957, LL.B. 1958; Baptist; married (Monica).

Military Career: National Guard, 1948–50; Army, 1950–54 (Korea), Army Reserves, 1954–57.

Professional Career: Legis. Asst., U.S. Rep. John Dingell, 1958–61; Practicing atty., 1959–61; Referee, MI Workmen's Comp. Dept., 1961–63.

DC Office: 2426 RHOB, 20515, 202-225-5126; Fax: 202-225-0072; Web site: www.house.gov/conyers.

District Offices: Detroit, 313-961-5670; Southgate, 734-285-5624.

Committees: *Judiciary* (RMM of 17 D): Courts, the Internet & Intellectual Property; The Constitution.

Group Ratings

	ADA	ACLU	AFS	LCV	ITIC	NTU	COC	ACU	NTLC	CHC
2004	90	100	100	82	33	10	11	0	0	8
2003	90	—	100	80	—	31	19	10	—	—

National Journal Ratings

	2003 LIB	—	2003 CONS	2004 LIB	—	2004 CONS
Economic	84%	—	16%	95%	—	5%
Social	92%	—	0%	88%	—	0%
Foreign	94%	—	0%	97%	—	3%

Key Votes of the 108th Congress

1. Drilling in ANWR	N	5. DC School Vouchers	N	9. Ban Same-Sex Marriage	N
2. Approve Bush Tax Cuts	N	6. Ban Human Cloning	N	10. Fund Iraq War	N
3. Medicare/Rx Bill	N	7. Restrict Gun Liability	N	11. Bar Cuba Embargo Funds	Y
4. Bar Overtime Pay Regs.	Y	8. Ban Partial-Birth Abortion	N	12. Intelligence Reorg.	N

Election Results

2004 general	John Conyers (D)	213,681	(84%)	($534,363)
	Veronica Pedraza (R)	35,089	(14%)	
	Other	5,809	(2%)	
2004 primary	John Conyers (D)	unopposed		
2002 general	John Conyers (D)	145,285	(83%)	($421,346)
	Dave Stone (R)	26,544	(15%)	

Prior Winning Percentages: 2000 (89%); 1998 (87%); 1996 (86%); 1994 (82%); 1992 (82%); 1990 (89%); 1988 (91%); 1986 (89%); 1984 (89%); 1982 (97%); 1980 (95%); 1978 (93%); 1976 (92%); 1974 (91%); 1972 (88%); 1970 (88%); 1968 (100%); 1966 (84%); 1964 (84%)

The People		Race/Ethnic Origin	Ancestry	
Area size:	123 sq. mi.	32.1% White	German: 5.0%	Polish: 4.8%
Urban population:	100.0%	61.1% Black	Arab: 4.7%	
Rural population:	0.0%	1.2% Asian	**2004 Presidential Vote**	
Pop. 2000:	662,563	0.3% Native Am.	Kerry (D) 219,075	(83%)
Median income:	$36,099	0.0% Hawaiian	Bush (R) 46,240	(17%)
Poverty status:	19.7%	3.3% Two+ races	**2000 Presidential Vote**	
Military veterans:	11.2%	0.2% Other	Gore (D) 198,687	(81%)
		1.8% Hispanic Origin	Bush (R) 44,345	(18%)
			Other 2,449	(1%)
			Cook Partisan Voting Index: D +33	
Occupation	Blue collar: 28.4%	White collar: 53.0%	Gray collar: 18.5%	

Detroit's early auto factories—Packard, Hudson, Ford Highland Park, Dodge Main, Briggs, Ford Rouge, Cadillac, Kelsey-Hayes, Chrysler, Plymouth, DeSoto—were built between 1905 and 1925 in an arc about five miles from the city's center, in green fields at what was then the edge of urban development. Almost instantly the flat farmlands all around were platted in grid streets and filled with wooden bungalows and brick prairie-style houses, often with a driveway at the side and a single elm in front. Commercial strips lined the mile-square and radial main streets, stretching straight as far as the eye could see. Detroit's neighborhoods filled up with factory workers and civil servants, professionals and maintenance men, corner store owners and management personnel, Catholics and Protestants and Jews: a middle-class melting pot. With one exception: Detroit in those days had few blacks; they did not begin their big migrations here from the South, especially Alabama, until around 1940, when defense plants began hiring in large numbers.

The history of black Detroit is one of conflict and uplift, inspiration and tragedy. The wartime mixture of Appalachian mountain whites and Deep South blacks proved volatile: there was a violent race riot in June 1943. During the war years, blacks were pent up in a few severely overcrowded neighborhoods like the Black Bottom, which is now the Chrysler Freeway. After 1945, when blacks began moving outward, real estate agents played on racial fears, and in the 1950s whole square miles of Detroit changed racial composition in months. In the 1960s there was hope that the civil rights movement, encouraged by Walter Reuther's UAW, and antipoverty programs would improve blacks' fortunes, and in fact many black Detroiters found good jobs and made good incomes, bought their own homes and built community institutions. Then came the riot of July 1967, followed by extensive white flight and terrible increases in crime. Detroit's first black mayor, Coleman Young, elected in 1973, responded with policies that may have seemed appropriate in the 1960s but had disastrous results in the 1970s and 1980s: He pressured major employers like the Big Three auto companies to build facilities in Detroit, raised taxes to support a vast army of city employees, and attributed city problems to white racism. Violent crime became a part of everyday life and arson became common.

Detroit took on a garrison atmosphere. Crime reduced the value of residential real estate to near zero, and the city's population dropped from 1.7 million in 1960 to 951,000 in 2000. In political dialogue, most black politicians called for, and most black voters seemed to support, an ever-increasing public sector. Yet the existing public sector, which took a larger share of residents' income than almost anywhere else in the country, served citizens very poorly. Turnaround came agonizingly late in the 1990s, as Mayor Dennis Archer, elected in 1993, worked to fight crime and encourage private-sector growth. Incomes rose and the median housing value doubled from $32,000 to $63,000.

The 14th Congressional District of Michigan consists of nearly half of Detroit (though not the downtown) and some disparate suburbs. Its part of Detroit is north and west of where the old auto plants were built and is mostly residential—square mile after square mile of grid streets, some always working class, some middle class, a few—Palmer Woods, Sherwood Forest, Rosedale Park—upscale. In most of them, abandoned houses and empty lots are commonplace where houses once stood, and yet in many neighborhoods, residents struggle to maintain their houses and patrol their streets. Commercial frontage on Detroit's straight-line avenues is still patchy and often vacant. Politically, this is one of the most Democratic districts in the United States.

The suburbs of the 14th are diverse. Highland Park is like much of Detroit; Hamtramck still retains the flavor of its original Polish immigrants (on Fat Tuesday, this is where to find the best paczki) who made it America's fastest-growing city in 1910–20; it had 56,000 people in 1930 but only 22,000 in 2000. Redistricting considerably altered the district, adding territory to the south from John Dingell's old 16th District. The 14th District now includes most of Dearborn, including the Ford headquarters, the Ford Rouge plant and Henry Ford's Greenfield Village. Dearborn was known from the 1940s to the 1970s as an adamantly all-white town under longtime Mayor Orville Hubbard. Today it still has few blacks, but it has America's largest Arab-American community with 30% claiming Arab ancestry; you can see signs in Arabic and can find mosques and Arab community centers. There was a parade in Dearborn when the statue of Saddam Hussein fell in April 2003 and Iraqis came there to vote in January 2005. From Dearborn, the district extends south, to take in working-class suburbs—Melvindale, Allen Park, Southgate,

Riverview, Trenton and Gibraltar. The last three are on the Detroit River, and the district also includes the island of Grosse Ile, a high-income community that works to keep some of its space open.

The congressman from the 14th District is John Conyers, the second most senior member of the House and one of its most liberal. First elected in 1964, he is a founder of the Congressional Black Caucus, and the ranking Democrat on the House Judiciary Committee. The son of a left-wing UAW operative, he grew up in Detroit. He played cornet in Northwestern and Cass Technical High Schools and, underage, watched jazz greats at Baker's Keyboard Lounge; in 1987 he passed a resolution declaring "the sense of Congress that jazz is [a] rare and valuable American national treasure." He served in the Army in Korea, practiced law and worked as a staffer for a young congressman named John Dingell. Conyers was one of six blacks in the House when first elected to Congress in 1964 and the only one to take a militant approach to politics; he won his primary, in which 60,000 votes were cast, by 108 votes. The civil rights heroine Rosa Parks, who had moved to Detroit, worked in his 1964 campaign and then worked in his Detroit office until her retirement in 1988. His response to the 1967 riots was to introduce the first bill for a guaranteed annual income. He first sponsored a Martin Luther King holiday bill days after the civil rights leader was murdered in 1968, and persevered until it passed in 1983. Since 1989 he has sponsored bills to establish a commission to examine slavery and its lingering effects, and for consideration of whether reparations should be paid to descendants of slaves. He opposed most controversial parts of the crime bills of the past three decades and welfare changes in the 1990s and calls for single-payer health plans and massive public works projects.

After September 11, Conyers worked together with the new Judiciary chairman, James Sensenbrenner, on terrorism legislation. In October 2001 they agreed that the government could detain immigrants suspected of terrorism without bringing charges, but only for seven days, and they introduced the antiterrorism bill together. Conyers also worked on tightening border security. In April 2002 Sensenbrenner got Conyers's support for splitting the INS into two agencies by agreeing to add counsel positions. Conyers has also weighed in on other legislation.

Conyers is the only member of the House ever to have served on two committees handling presidential impeachment, in 1974 and 1998. In May 1972, a month before the Watergate burglary, he called for impeaching Richard Nixon because of his conduct of the Vietnam War. As the hearings on Bill Clinton's impeachment opened in 1998, some Democrats were queasy about Conyers, sharing the judgment of Judiciary Committee Republican George Gekas that he was "predictably unpredictable." But Conyers, the ranking Democrat, performed ably. For all his criticisms of Clinton, Conyers rallied behind him; he managed to craft an alternative investigation resolution that Republicans wouldn't accept, the start of partisan divisions on the issue.

Conyers opposed the Iraq war resolution. He called for the resignation of Donald Rumsfeld after revelations of the Abu Ghraib prison abuses and voted against the resolution condemning them on the grounds it was not strong enough. He argued that Justice Department regulations required a special counsel to investigate the leaking of CIA operative Valerie Plame's name. He opposed the House version of the intelligence reorganization bill and called for an investigation of John Ashcroft's 32-city tour explaining the Patriot Act. He co-sponsored Charles Rangel's bill to reinstitute the military draft and then, along with Rangel, voted against it on the floor. He co-sponsored a constitutional amendment that would make immigrants eligible for the presidency 20 years after they became citizens; this would make Michigan Governor Jennifer Granholm eligible to run. He supported the city of Detroit's August 2004 referendum to legalize medical marijuana. In December 2004 he asked for an FBI investigation of election procedures into "inappropriate and likely illegal election tampering" in Hocking County, Ohio, and also asked television networks to turn over raw exit poll data. In January 2005 he said there were "massive and unprecedented voter irregularities in Ohio" and voted to challenge the Ohio electoral votes.

Over the years, Conyers has mostly been re-elected without difficulty. He made two runs for mayor of Detroit, in 1989 and 1993. But he ran a desultory campaign the first time and almost no campaign the second, and came in far behind. He had two serious primary opponents in 1994, but finished well ahead of both with 51% of the vote. He suffered some unfavorable publicity in 2003 and 2004. In November 2003 the *Detroit Free Press* after a two-month investigation reported that Conyers and his top staffers assigned congressional staff to work on political campaigns, including the city council campaign of former staffer JoAnn Watson and Conyers's wife's state Senate campaign. In May 2004 a former Conyers staffer was indicted for defrauding sponsors of a conference on the plight of black farmers, but prosecutors said Conyers was not involved. In 2003 he had one of the highest rates of absenteeism, 20%, in the House. In spring 2004 state Senator Samuel Thomas collected signatures to run in the Democratic primary, but in May he dropped out; if he had run that would have been Conyers's first serious challenge in 10 years.

FIFTEENTH DISTRICT

Rep. John Dingell (D)

Elected Dec. 1955, 25th full term; b. July 8, 1926, Colorado Springs, CO; home, Dearborn; Georgetown U., B.S. 1949, J.D. 1952; Catholic; married (Deborah).

Military Career: Army, 1944–46 (WWII).

Professional Career: Practicing atty., 1952–55; Wayne Cnty. Asst. Prosecuting Atty., 1953–55.

DC Office: 2328 RHOB, 20515, 202-225-4071; Fax: 202-226-0371; Web site: www.house.gov/dingell.

District Offices: Dearborn, 313-278-2936; Monroe, 734-243-1849; Ypsilanti, 734-481-1100.

Committees: *Energy & Commerce* (RMM of 26 D).

Group Ratings

	ADA	ACLU	AFS	LCV	ITIC	NTU	COC	ACU	NTLC	CHC
2004	95	84	100	100	40	8	33	4	0	38
2003	85	—	100	95	—	26	31	24	—	—

National Journal Ratings

	2003 LIB	—	2003 CONS		2004 LIB	—	2004 CONS
Economic	79%	—	20%		82%	—	17%
Social	64%	—	36%		69%	—	30%
Foreign	79%	—	20%		71%	—	28%

Key Votes of the 108th Congress

1. Drilling in ANWR	N	5. DC School Vouchers	N	9. Ban Same-Sex Marriage	N
2. Approve Bush Tax Cuts	N	6. Ban Human Cloning	Y	10. Fund Iraq War	N
3. Medicare/Rx Bill	N	7. Restrict Gun Liability	Y	11. Bar Cuba Embargo Funds	Y
4. Bar Overtime Pay Regs.	Y	8. Ban Partial-Birth Abortion	Y	12. Intelligence Reorg.	N

Election Results

2004 general	John Dingell (D)	218,409	(71%)	($1,127,151)
	Dawn Reamer (R)	81,828	(27%)	
	Other	7,726	(3%)	
2004 primary	John Dingell (D)	unopposed		
2002 general	John Dingell (D)	136,518	(72%)	($3,461,009)
	Martin Kaltenbach (R)	48,626	(26%)	
	Other	3,919	(2%)	

Prior Winning Percentages: 2000 (71%); 1998 (67%); 1996 (62%); 1994 (59%); 1992 (65%); 1990 (67%); 1988 (97%); 1986 (78%); 1984 (64%); 1982 (74%); 1980 (70%); 1978 (77%); 1976 (76%); 1974 (78%); 1972 (68%); 1970 (79%); 1968 (74%); 1966 (63%); 1964 (73%); 1962 (83%); 1960 (79%); 1958 (79%); 1956 (74%); 1955 (76%)

The People		Race/Ethnic Origin	Ancestry		
Area size:	981 sq. mi.	79.2% White	German: 15.0% Irish: 8.4%		
Urban population:	87.7%	11.7% Black	Polish: 6.7%		
Rural population:	12.3%	3.7% Asian	**2004 Presidential Vote**		
Pop. 2000:	662,563	0.4% Native Am.	Kerry (D) 191,091	(62%)	
Median income:	$48,963	0.0% Hawaiian	Bush (R) 118,217	(38%)	
Poverty status:	10.3%	2.0% Two+ races	Other 573	(0%)	
Military veterans:	11.1%	0.2% Other	**2000 Presidential Vote**		
		2.8% Hispanic Origin	Gore (D) 161,913	(60%)	
			Bush (R) 101,607	(38%)	
			Other 7,086	(3%)	
			Cook Partisan Voting Index: D +13		

Occupation   Blue collar: 26.2%   White collar: 59.0%   Gray collar: 14.7%

The southeast corner of Michigan is a part of the country most Americans don't think about much, and it doesn't look very interesting out the plane window as you approach Metro Airport. The flat marshlands along the shore of Lake Erie give way to flat farm lands, with rivers flowing lazily in summer and flashing with ice in winter. Here and there you see power plants with giant smokestacks and factories. Out on the horizon you can get a glimpse of the sprawl of metro Detroit, of the great auto and steel and chemical plants along the Detroit River; over on the other side is Ann Arbor, home of the University of Michigan.

The 15th Congressional District of Michigan includes much of this southeastern corner of the state. It owes its shape to Republican redistricters, who in July 2001 devised the nation's most successful partisan redistricting plan of the decennial cycle. The 15th was drawn to put two incumbent Democratic congressmen in the same district, John Dingell, the dean of the House, and Lynn Rivers, an Ann Arbor liberal first elected in 1994. Each had represented about half the new district. The district includes industrial parts of Wayne County, all of Monroe County and the Ann Arbor and Ypsilanti areas in Washtenaw County. In Wayne County, the 15th includes the western part of Dearborn and most of Dearborn Heights; the most heavily Arab-American parts of Dearborn were put in the 14th District, and these are more middle class, even affluent areas; the line cuts through Dearborn Heights and put one trailer park in two districts. To the south are working class suburbs: Taylor, Romulus (home of Metro Airport), and Woodhaven, site of a big Ford plant. Flat Rock is home to an automaking plant owned by both Ford and Mazda; in 2003 Ford announced it would move production of the Mustang muscle car here from its Dearborn Assembly Plant. Monroe was the birthplace of General George Armstrong Custer, and in his day agricultural; now it is more industrial, and the southern part is in many ways an extension of Toledo, Ohio. (Michigan and Ohio almost went to war over the Toledo land in the 1830s; Ohio got Toledo and Michigan got the Upper Peninsula as recompense) Ann Arbor is one of the nation's largest university towns, oriented to the university but also full of people, from auto executives to perennial graduate students, who like the atmosphere of a town with plenty of book stores, coffee houses and liberal neighbors; it voted 74% to legalize medical marijuana in November 2004. Ypsilanti, though it also has a university (Eastern Michigan), is less bookish and more industrial. All of these areas tend to vote Democratic, though Monroe is sometimes marginal, but they house very different kinds of Democrats. In Wayne County, union political operatives have dominated Democratic party politics for 50 years. In Ann Arbor, Democratic politics is dominated by leftist peace enthusiasts, environmentalists and, most of all, feminists.

The congressman from the 15th District is John Dingell, the senior member of the House of Representatives. His father, John Dingell, Sr., was elected to the House in 1932, from a district created as a result of the Detroit area's auto boom. The first Congressman Dingell was one of the most productive urban liberals of his day, a sponsor of Social Security and, starting in 1943, of national health insurance. John Dingell Jr. has been around Capitol Hill almost as long. He was a House page from 1938–43 and served in the Army in World War II; he graduated from Georgetown and its law school, paying his way by working as an elevator operator in the Capitol; he practiced law in Detroit and served as an assistant prosecutor in Wayne County. After his father died in September 1955, Dingell was elected to succeed him in December, at 29, from a district entirely within Detroit with large Polish, black and Jewish populations. He still uses his father's office furniture and every session continues to introduce as H.R. 15 (the number matches the district) the national health insurance bill his father co-sponsored in 1943. He is the only member of the House who served in the 1950s; indeed only two others served in the 1960s (John Conyers and David Obey); it is a measure of his seniority that the second most senior member of the House, Conyers, once served on his staff. He has an interesting personal life, raising his children after his divorce and marrying in 1981 a granddaughter of one of General Motors' Fisher brothers. Debbie Dingell is head of the General Motors Foundation and a Democratic national committeewoman, and an encourager of bipartisan amity as well; she headed the Michigan campaigns for Al Gore in 2000 and John Kerry in 2004, and helped each win 51% of the vote in this battleground state.

For 14 years, from 1981 to 1995, Dingell was chairman of the Energy and Commerce Committee and of its Investigative and Oversight Subcommittee, one of the most powerful and effective chairmen ever. It had wide jurisdiction, handled up to 40% of all House bills, and had the largest budget and staff of any House committee. As institutions will, the committee took on the character of its leader, widely known as "the truck": bright, aggressive, domineering, determined. Dingell and his committee superintended the breakup of AT&T and the sale of Conrail by public offering; Commerce's cable reregulation law of 1992 was the only bill on which Congress overrode George H.W. Bush's veto. After a decade of sparring over clean air legislation, Dingell worked together with Health Subcommittee Chairman Henry Waxman to produce the 1990 Clean Air Act.

On other issues, Dingell backed organized labor's agenda against NAFTA and trade promotion authority. An avid outdoorsman (he hunts deer, elk, caribou and moose), he long opposed gun control but voted for the 1994 crime bill and resigned from the National Rifle Association board. But in 1999 his amendment ended the push for more gun control legislation after the Columbine massacres. On the old Merchant Marine and Fisheries Committee, he was responsible for wildlife refuge legislation, and one of his proudest accomplishments is the creation in 2001 of the Detroit River International Wildlife Refuge, on both sides of the river from Zug Island in River Rouge south to Lake Erie. This is not publicly owned land; Dingell has worked to get donations of land or easements from private landowners, land preservation groups and the Army Corps of Engineers. In many ways, he is an old-fashioned Franklin D. Roosevelt Democrat, supporting big government and strenuous regulation, taking a conservative line on some cultural issues and backing an assertive foreign policy; he was the only Michigan Democrat to vote for the Gulf War resolution in January 1991, although he voted against the Iraq war resolution in October 2002.

When the Republican majority took over, many expected Dingell to sulk or to launch bitter attacks on the other side. But he did neither. As the senior House member, he swore in Newt Gingrich with good grace and proceeded to work with Republicans and produce legislation.

Dingell has been successful on occasion in forging Democratic positions that prevailed in the Republican House. He introduced a bill to regulate HMOs in February 1998 and then joined with Republican Greg Ganske. It lost 217–212 and a Republican alternative passed 216–210. The Senate never acted. In July 1999 Dingell came back, allied with Ganske and Republican Charlie Norwood, and in October 1999 the renamed Dingell-Norwood bill passed 275–151, with 68 Republicans voting yes. Again the Senate didn't act, and Dingell and Norwood tried again in 2001. In August 2001, Bush managed to convince Norwood to sign onto a bill with less regulation, which passed the House; but the Senate again didn't act. Dingell's goal remains national health insurance; asked what is a desirable system, he says, "Canada's, right across the river." He opposed the Republicans' Medicare/prescription drug bill in 2003 and went out on the road to criticize it in 2004; when Republicans admitted that Centers for Medicare & Medicaid Services head Thomas Scully concealed higher cost estimates for the bill, Dingell demanded access to all actuarial estimates. In June 2004, after an adverse Supreme Court decision, he said he would reintroduce his HMO regulation bill. "HMOs, foreign diplomats and the mentally insane are the only people in this country who are exempt from the consequences of their decisions." He also has worked to relieve the cost burden of health insurance plans from the auto companies.

In 2001 Dingell and Billy Tauzin pressed for their bill allowing regional Bell companies to provide broadband service. Despite opposition from the Judiciary Committee, this passed 273–157 in February 2002, but got no vote in the Senate. In 2004 Dingell and the new Energy and Commerce Chairman, Joe Barton, asked the FCC for an investigation of a la carte cable channels (customers would pay for only those channels they wanted). Dingell tended toward opposition.

Dingell has sprung into action when Michigan has been adversely affected. After the August 2003 blackout, which hit Michigan hard, he sponsored a stand-alone bill made up of the electricity provisions in the larger House and Senate versions of the energy bill. Dingell argued that there was consensus on the need for making the North American Electricity Reliability Council rules mandatory and for strengthening the regional transmission organizations, and that these measures should not be held hostage to Republicans' desire to pass more controversial measures. He amassed signatures on a discharge petition, but fell short of the needed 218 signatures in 2004. In January 2003 the city of Toronto started transporting all its trash—180 truckloads a day, 1.1 million tons a year—in a landfill in southwest Wayne County, in Dingell's district. Dingell had long complained of Canadian trash dumping, and he and Senator Debbie Stabenow insisted that EPA enforce a 1992 treaty which, they said, required that Canada give notice of each shipment and which allowed the U.S. to reject each one. EPA Administrator Mike Leavitt argued that only hazardous waste was covered by the treaty, but Dingell persisted and got a 12–4 subcommittee vote demanding enforcement. After voters in Romulus approved an Indian casino, Dingell put an amendment approving it on the transportation bill in March 2004, though it was later removed. Dingell has long opposed raising CAFE gas mileage standards, but has not followed the industry lead uncritically. In October 2003 the House accepted his amendment to require NHTSA to raise fuel economy standards enough to save 5 billion gallons of gasoline. He was also pushing an amendment with incentives for the auto companies to develop diesel engines with low sulfur emissions and to offer more diesel cars and trucks. "I'm giving the industry good counsel. One of my major jobs is to address environmental concerns. If I don't tell them where they have problems, I'm not being a good friend to the industry."

Since his first election in December 1955, Dingell has had only two serious challenges, both in Democratic primaries after being redistricted in with another incumbent. In 1964 he ran in a district mostly new to him against another incumbent who had followed his father to the House, John Lesinski of Dearborn, who was the only northern Democrat to vote against the Civil Rights Act of 1964. With strong support from the UAW, Dingell won 54%–46%. Then in July 2001 the Republican legislature put him in the same district with Lynn Rivers of Ann Arbor. Rivers was born in 1956, one year after Dingell was first elected to the House, and was first elected herself in 1994. Dingell was elected in the first of 40 consecutive years of Democratic majorities in the House; Rivers never served in a Democratic House. She had a leftish voting record and took no major role on legislation. After redistricting, some Democrats urged her to run in the 11th District, which included some of her old territory. But she decided to stay with Ann Arbor and run against Dingell in what she called a "David vs. Goliath match up."

It was that, and more. Their voting records were similar, though not identical, but their cultural backgrounds were as different as the working class suburbs of Wayne County and the university town of Ann Arbor. Rivers campaigned as a congresswoman who knew what the ordinary person went through and cast her votes accordingly. Dingell campaigned as a congressman who had gotten many things done and was in a position to do much more. On September 10, 2001, the day before the redistricting bill was to be signed, Nancy Pelosi, then running for minority whip, sent Rivers $10,000—"a minor annoyance," Dingell said, though he later refused to raise any money for the House Democrats' campaign committee. Rivers emphasized their differences on the partial-birth abortion ban, particular gun control proposals and environmental standards; Dingell voted for the first, opposed the second and tended to support the auto companies (and the UAW) on the third. Rivers said, "Clout is a wonderful thing, if you're using it for good. If you're using it to stop gun control legislation, that's not a good thing. If you're using it to limit women's choice, that's not a good thing." Dingell parried by pointing to the women's issues he had been instrumental on—breast and cervical cancer screening, minimum hospital stays after childbirth, children's health insurance.

This was Michigan's most expensive House primary ever. Dingell raised $2.5 million, from unions, the auto industry and regulated industries generally. Rivers, with major help from EMILY's List and its bundled contributions, raised $1.5 million, enough to make this a seriously contested race on television. For most of the months before the August 6 primary Dingell led in polls by about 10%. In June, Rivers started running spots in which she recounted her personal struggles. Her plainspoken, perky manner evidently got through: by late July, two polls showed the race even. Dingell fired back with a spot praising his effectiveness on prescription drugs, HMO regulation, children's health insurance and the Clean Air Act. In contrast, he said, "She's never authored a single piece of legislation that's been signed into law." On the stump, Dingell told reporters that he had had some difficult times in life as well. "I know what it is to sit up at night with sick kids and take care of kids and help with their homework. I know all of these things firsthand, because I've lived them. I got the kids in a terrible divorce because I had no choice. These things do not qualify me for office. They might qualify me for sympathy, but I'm Polish, and Poles don't ask for sympathy. I have the curious view that I should be judged on the basis of what I stand for, what I've done, my ability, my effectiveness, the kind of service I give my constituents, my legislative record, my personal integrity." For him the race came down to the question, "Are you going to replace one of the most effective members of the House of Representatives with one of the least effective members?" Dingell was endorsed by the *Ann Arbor News* as well as the *Detroit Free Press* and *Detroit News*. In the August primary Dingell won 59%–41%. He won 74%–26% in Wayne County, which cast 43% of the votes, even though part of it was in Rivers's old district, and 80%–20% in Monroe County, which cast 19% of the votes. Rivers won Washtenaw County 69%–31%.

The general election was anticlimactic; Dingell won easily in this Democratic district. In August 2004 he became the fourth longest-serving House member in history; in December 2005 he will have served 50 years; in February 2009, he will have been the longest-serving House member in history; in January 2013 he will have served longer in Congress than anyone else in history. Asked about his longevity in Congress, Dingell said, "I never expected to be in Congress this long," Dingell has said, and attributed his longevity to "hard work, good luck and a very tolerant, lovely wife." And despite his frustrations in a Republican House, he said, "What I've learned is that we are the most fortunate race in the history of mankind, with a government that is nearest to perfect as you can find on this planet."

★ MINNESOTA ★

Minnesota has long been a distinctive commonwealth, set far in America's frozen North, a state which in commerce, culture and politics has set one example after another for the rest of the nation. It is the node of transcontinental railroads that linked the winter wheat fields of the northern prairies to the greatest grain-milling center in the world and the great Pacific ports of Puget Sound. It is also the birthplace of Scotch tape, Betty Crocker, Target and the Mall of America, the home base of dyspeptic chroniclers of small town America from Sinclair Lewis to Garrison Keillor. Politically, Minnesota over the last half century provided the nation with some of its most articulate and honorable leaders—Harold Stassen, Hubert Humphrey, Eugene McCarthy, Walter Mondale—and with traditions of probity, civic-mindedness and innovation which are second to none. Yet while commercially and culturally Minnesota has never been stronger, its recent political history has been unusual. For more than a decade, two political parties, the Democratic-Farmer-Labor and the Republican—have been dominated by activists of left and right stubbornly out of touch with ordinary voters. At least partly in response, voters in 1998 elected a former professional wrestler and suburban mayor, Jesse "The Body" Ventura, as governor. What had been one of the nation's more heavily Democratic states became a polity very much up for grabs. In 2002 Republican Tim Pawlenty was elected governor and Republican

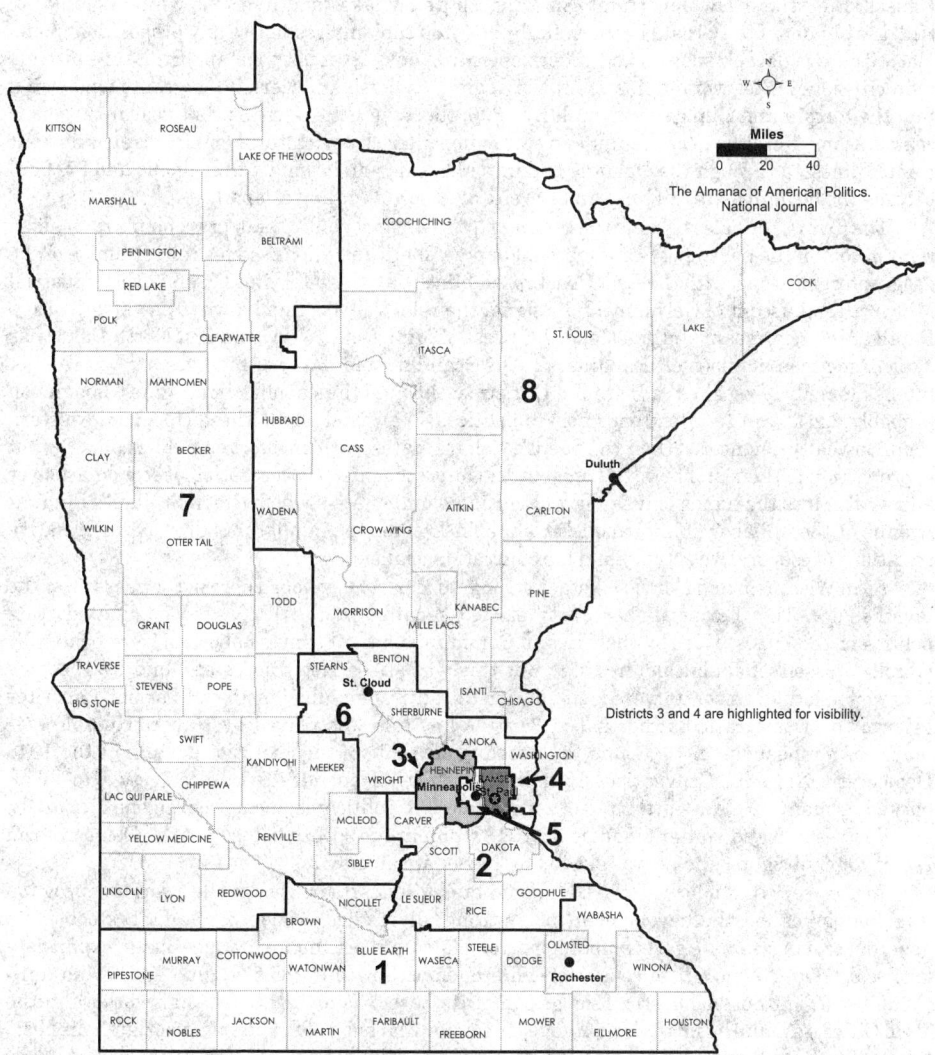

Norm Coleman was elected senator. In 2004 Minnesota moved toward the DFL. This battle-ground state was carried by John Kerry by a 51%–48% margin, and Republicans lost 13 seats and nearly lost their majority in the state House. Which way will Minnesota turn in 2006 and 2008? No one is sure.

Minnesota's distinctive traditions come from a distinctive history. The far northern states were ignored by most Yankee immigrants, who headed straight west into Iowa, Nebraska and Kansas. But others saw opportunity in Minnesota's icy lakes and ferocious winters. James J. Hill, the builder of the Great Northern Railroad ("You can't interest me in any proposition in any place where it doesn't snow"), and others operating out of Minneapolis and St. Paul—already twin cities by 1860—worked to attract Norwegian, Swedish and German migrants who would find the terrain and climate congenial. By 1890, the Twin Cities—rivals that year in a Census competition—were the nerve center of a sprawling and rich agricultural empire stretching west from Minnesota through the Dakotas and into Montana and beyond. Minneapolis and St. Paul became the termini of its rail lines and the site of its grain-milling companies.

The Twin Cities also became the center of a three-party politics and an economic radicalism reminiscent of the politics of Scandinavia. For our American regions seem a mirror image of the geography of Europe, with the East Coast resembling the British Isles and France, the industrial Midwest reminiscent of Germany and Poland, the relatively poor and always hawkish South a Baptist Mediterranean, and the Upper Midwest of Minnesota, Wisconsin and North Dakota as North American versions of Scandinavia. The Scandinavian flavor of life lives on: You can get lutefisk (smelly lye-soaked cod) around Christmastime in Minneapolis restaurants (though you probably don't want to). It extends also to politics. Like Scandinavia, these Upper Midwestern commonwealths pioneered their continent's welfare states, with an effect on public policy far out of proportion to their numbers. Alarmed by the unprecedented concentration of economic power and wealth into the hands of just a few identifiable millionaires who lived on St. Paul's Summit Avenue or the hill above Minneapolis's Hennepin Avenue, the immigrants drew on their native traditions of cooperative activity and bureaucratic socialism.

As in Wisconsin and North Dakota, a strong third party developed here in the years after the Populist era. This Farmer-Labor Party elected senators in the 1920s and dominated state politics in the 1930s. Hurt by their ties to Communists, the Farmer-Laborites were beaten by Harold Stassen's Republicans in 1938. But this was still a New Deal state, and by 1944 the bedraggled local Democrats were merged with the anti-Communist faction of Farmer-Laborites to form the Democratic-Farmer-Labor Party. A key role was played by Hubert Humphrey—mayor of Minneapolis in 1945, and the dazzling advocate of the civil rights plank at the 1948 Democratic National Convention. Humphrey's DFL—clean, idealistic, closely tied to labor, backed by many farmers—attracted dozens of talented politicians, including Eugene McCarthy, Orville Freeman and Walter Mondale. In 1948 Humphrey's speech helped put the Democrats on record for civil rights, and he was elected to the Senate at age 37.

In the years that followed, the DFL dominated Minnesota politics, while a series of progressive companies led the development of a strong, diversified economy. The DFL stood for a generous, compassionate government, for strong labor unions and high wages, for an expansionist fiscal policy to encourage consumer-led economic growth, for civil rights, and for an anti-Communist, but not bombastic, foreign policy. Its base was among blue-collar workers in the Twin Cities, in Duluth and the Iron Range, and among farmers of Scandinavian origin. Minnesota's business leaders were conservative politically and innovation-minded in their work. New entrepreneurs rose in the 1990s, and Minnesota's incomes rose to 11th in the nation; the slowdown after 2000 was less severe than in many other states. It is part of a long pattern: Minnesota's economy hums along, growing robustly in prosperous years and not falling behind in recessions, and squeaky-clean if sometimes eccentric Minnesota has levels of crime, divorce and aberrant behavior most states should envy. From 1990 to 2004, Minnesota's population grew by 17%, significantly more than any other Midwestern state.

Minnesota has more social connectedness than any other large state, Robert Putnam notes in *Bowling Alone*, and this spirit of civic participation is echoed in the party precinct caucuses and party conventions. The early DFLers were proud of this system, which allowed plenty of political participation and ended control by party bosses. But by the 1980s the conventions came to be dominated not by laborite Humphrey followers or the wives of management Republicans, but by left-wingers and counterculturites, right-wing abortion opponents and religious hardliners. The result was the nomination of left-wing and right-wing candidates usually rejected by the voters in primaries or general elections and in shrill, off-putting political rhetoric. All this left Minnesota open to the appeal of Jesse Ventura, candidate of the Independence party in 1998. Ventura was already known to Twin Cities television viewers—nearly three-quarters of the state's voters—and his clever ads tended to overshadow his more conventional rivals, Attorney General Skip Humphrey and DFL-turned-Republican St. Paul Mayor Norm Coleman. Ventura scored in the low teens in most polls, but he sparked a huge rise in turnout—Minnesota has Election Day registration—and won with 37% of the vote, to 34% for Coleman and only 28% for Humphrey—less than half the 60% his father won in his first electrifying election for senator exactly 50 years earlier.

Ventura pulled out a new electorate in Minneapolis-St. Paul media market beyond the Twin Cities core of Hennepin and Ramsey Counties. In 2002 this area went heavily Republican, voting 51%–30% for Pawlenty and 56%–41% for Coleman over former Vice President and Senator Walter Mondale, who had been nominated to run in Wellstone's place. In 2004 the Republican margin here was not as great, as George W. Bush carried the area 54%–45%. This was not enough to overcome the increased margins the DFL turned out in Hennepin and Ramsey Counties, nor to offset a trend against Bush and a reversion to DFL loyalties in Duluth and the Iron Range.

The People		Race/Ethnic Origin			Military veterans: 464,968 (12.8%)	
Pop. 2004 (est):	5,100,958	4,337,143	88.2%	White	WWII: 20.2%	Korea: 14.6%
Pop. 2000:	4,919,479	168,813	3.4%	Black	Vietnam: 32.8%	Gulf War: 7.6%
Pop. 1990:	4,375,099	141,083	2.9%	Asian	**Most populous cities (2003):**	
Change 1990–2000:	Up 12.4%	52,009	1.1%	Native Am.	1. Minneapolis	373,188
% of U.S. total:	1.8%	1,714	0.0%	Hawaiian	2. St. Paul	280,404
Pop. rank:	21st of 50	70,304	1.4%	Two+ races	3. Rochester	92,507
Area size:	86,939 sq. mi.	5,031	0.1%	Other	4. Duluth	85,734
State Native:	70.2%	143,382	2.9%	Hisp. Origin	5. Bloomington	83,080
Non-citizen:	3.3%	**Ancestry**				
Language		German: 25.2%		Norwegian: 11.8%	Urban population: 70.9%	
English: 89.6%	Other Eur.: 3.9%	Irish: 7.7%		Swedish: 6.8%	Rural population: 29.1%	
Spanish: 3.6%		English: 4.3%				

Education		Work Sector		Legislature	
H.S. Grad:	87.9%	Private: 80.4%	Govt: 12.4%	Senate	35 D 31 R 1 I
College Grad:	27.4%	Self: 6.9%	Family: 0.3%	House	68 R 66 D
Industry		Unemployment: 4.1%		Legislative Term Limits: No	
Agri: 2.6%	Con: 5.9%	**Household Income**		**Registered Voters**	
Fin: 7.2%	Info: 2.5%	<15k: 12.1%	15-35k: 23.8%	No party registration	
Mfg: 21.4%	Prof: 29.7%	35-50k: 17.0%	50-100k: 34.5%		
Public: 3.4%	Trade: 15.5%	100-150k: 8.3%	>150k: 4.4%		
Other: 11.8%		Median: $47,111			
Occupation		Poverty status: 7.9%			
Blue collar: 23.3%	White collar: 62.3%	**Home Value**			
Gray collar: 14.4%		<50k: 11.1% 50-100k: 27.6% 100-200k: 45.8% 200-300k: 10.1%			
		300-500k: 4.0% >500k: 1.3% Median: $118,100			

Presidential politics   Minnesota has the longest consecutive streak of voting Democratic for president of any state: the last time it voted Republican was in 1972, and even then it gave Richard Nixon his lowest percentage margin over George McGovern. But in 2000 and 2004 Minnesota was seriously contested, and gave Al Gore and John Kerry only 48%–46% and 51%–48% margins over George W. Bush. One might attribute the increasing Democratic margin to the decision of 2000 Ralph Nader voters to back John Kerry, but that was only part of the reason. Total turnout was up 15% in a state that allows new voters to register on Election Day, and the DFL seems to have turned out more new voters. Bush's popular vote margin increased by

2004 Presidential Vote		
Kerry (D)....................	1,445,014	(51%)
Bush (R)	1,346,695	(48%)
Nader (BL)....................	18,683	(1%)
Other..........................	17,995	(1%)
2000 Presidential Vote		
Gore (D)......................	1,168,266	(48%)
Bush (R)	1,109,659	(46%)
Nader (Green)	126,696	(5%)
Other..........................	34,064	(1%)

44,000 votes in the Twin Cities media market counties outside the metropolitan core. But in the core counties of Hennepin and Ramsey, John Kerry's popular vote margin was 71,000 votes more than Al Gore's. Whether Republicans can continue to increase their popular vote margin in fast-growing counties outside the metro core and whether the DFL can continue to increase their popular vote margin in the slow-growing Hennepin and Ramsey Counties core are both unclear.

Incidentally, one DFL elector cast his votes for both president and vice president for John Edwards. But neither reporters nor Secretary of State Mary Kiffmeyer could determine which elector had done so, and all 10 said they had voted for Kerry. Evidently it was just a mistake.

Minnesota has a tradition of selecting national convention delegates in caucuses. But caucus turnout has been low: In the 1998 DFL caucuses, an average of 4.4 voters showed up in each precinct, and in one-fourth of the precincts, no one showed up at all. DFL leaders, reeling from their party's third-place finish in 1998, tried to attract more voters to the March 2000 presidential precinct caucuses by moving them from Tuesday night to Saturday and by holding a presidential preference vote, with national convention delegates assigned proportionately. It made little difference: By the time Minnesotans caucused, the nomination was already clinched. Governor Tim Pawlenty sought in 2003 to move the caucus date to February 2004, but his effort failed. In 2004, Minnesota was one of 10 states holding contests on March 2. Kerry carried 51% of the 55,000 votes cast in the presidential preference vote, Edwards took 27% and Dennis Kucinich finished third with 17%.

Congressional districting   It never seemed likely that Minnesota's Republican House, DFL Senate and Independence party governor would agree on congressional redistricting, and they didn't—the new plan was drawn by a special panel of five judges appointed by Chief Justice Kathleen Blatz. The Republicans wanted to combine Minneapolis and St. Paul into one heavily Democratic district, in the hope of winning three or four of four suburban districts. Democrats designed a plan that would continue the longstanding practice of having predominantly rural districts anchored in each corner of the state; the result would be four rural districts, two dominated by Minneapolis and St. Paul and two in the suburbs. Governor Jesse Ventura submitted a plan with two urban, three suburban and three rural districts, with one of them stretching along the western side of the state from Iowa to Canada.

109th Congress Lineup
4 DFL   4 R
108th Congress Lineup
4 DFL   4 R

The special panel drew its own plan and, when Republicans, Democrats and Ventura couldn't agree by the March 19, 2002, deadline, it was publicly revealed and put into effect. Minneapolis and St. Paul would each continue to dominate a district. Three suburban and three rural districts were created, one running along the southern end of the state from Wisconsin to South Dakota. Republican and Democratic leaders and Ventura all said they were pleased with the plan: It is probably what they might have agreed to if someone had put a gun to their heads. The homes of two incumbents, DFLer Bill Luther and Republican Mark Kennedy were placed in the new 6th District. Luther, after pondering the decision for two months, decided to run in the new 2d District, much of which he had represented; he lost in November.

Governor

Tim Pawlenty (R)

Elected 2002, term expires Jan. 2007, 1st term; b. Nov. 27, 1960, St. Paul; home, Eagan; U. of MN, B.A. 1983, J.D. 1986; Protestant; married (Mary).

Elected Office: Eagan Planning Comm., 1988–89; Eagan City Cncl., 1990–92; MN House of Reps., 1992–2002, Maj. Ldr., 1999–2002.

Professional Career: Practicing atty., 1986–92.

Office: 130 State Capitol, 75 Rev. Dr. Martin Luther King Blvd., St. Paul, 55155, 651-296-3391; Fax: 651-296-2089; Web site: www.governor.state.mn.us.

Election Results

2002 general	Tim Pawlenty (R)	999,473	(44%)
	Roger Moe (DFL)	821,268	(36%)
	Tim Penny (I)	364,534	(16%)
	Other	67,198	(3%)
2002 primary	Tim Pawlenty (R)	172,927	(89%)
	Leslie Davis (R)	22,172	(11%)
1998 general	Jesse Ventura (Ref)	773,713	(37%)
	Norm Coleman (R)	717,350	(34%)
	Hubert Humphrey III (DFL)	587,528	(28%)
	Other	13,175	(1%)

Tim Pawlenty, a Republican, was elected governor of Minnesota in 2002, but his victory received none of the attention from the national press that greeted the victory of his predecessor, Jesse Ventura, in 1998. Pawlenty grew up in South St. Paul near the stockyards and a meatpacking plant; when he was 16 his mother died and his father lost his job at a trucking company. He worked his way through college and law school at the University of Minnesota, the first college graduate in his family. He first got involved in politics when interning for Senator David Durenberger. He practiced law and in 1992 was elected to the state House from Eagan in suburban Dakota County. Soon he became recognized as one of his party's leaders. Pawlenty started running for governor in 1998, but was persuaded to step aside for Norm Coleman, the mayor of St. Paul, who had switched parties and become a Republican. In 1999 Pawlenty was elected Majority Leader in the state House. In 2001 he set out to run against Senator Paul Wellstone, but White House political strategist Karl Rove thought Coleman would be a stronger candidate. Dick Cheney then called Pawlenty and said that it would be better if he got out of the Senate race and ran for governor. For the second time, Pawlenty deferred to Coleman.

Running for governor in 2002 was a formidable task. Brian Sullivan, a self-financing businessman, was already running for the Republican nomination and had a set of issue positions well tailored for the conservatives likely to dominate the Republican caucuses and convention. And the incumbent governor was Ventura, universally known and for his first three years highly popular. A former professional wrestler, talk radio host and suburban mayor, Ventura ran for governor in 1998 as the candidate of Ross Perot's Reform party.

Pawlenty set his own agenda and put forward his own persona. He talked constantly of his South St. Paul roots and said he wanted Republicans to be "the party of Sam's Club, not the country club." He promised never to raise taxes and took conservative stands on abortion and other cultural issues; he had voted for gay rights as a freshman legislator, but now said that was a mistake. Sullivan, with his earlier start, was in the lead; a straw poll of those attending the March 2002 precinct caucuses showed him leading Pawlenty 51%–37%. But Pawlenty's organizational work left him even when the state convention assembled in June. Almost every state House Republican showed up wearing a Pawlenty blue shirt, and he ended up winning 58%–42%.

The DFL nomination had already been settled. It was a three-way race between Roger Moe, the state Senate President since 1981, state Auditor Judi Dutcher, who was elected as a Republican in 1994 and 1998 and switched parties in January 2000, and state Senator Becky Lourey, who criticized Moe for stands on environmental issues and compromises with House Republicans. Moe, first elected to the legislature in 1970, had been poised to run for governor several times, but had always drawn back. Democrats chose him at their May convention after Lourey and Dutcher conceded. For the first time since 1978, no serious candidate challenged the candidate endorsed by either party's nominating convention.

The guiding assumption in both parties was that Ventura would run for another term. But on June 18 Ventura announced he wasn't running. Into that void stepped Tim Penny, a former Democratic congressman from a Republican-leaning district who was first elected in 1982 and retired in 1994 disgusted with the partisanship of Washington. Penny had returned to Minnesota, taught at colleges and the Humphrey Institute in Minneapolis; several of his former aides had been appointed to top jobs by Ventura. On June 26 Penny announced that he was switching to the Independence party and running for governor. He chose a Republican state senator as his running mate, and Ventura supported him.

Ventura had not cared about making friends in politics, but the three men running to succeed him had. Just about everyone in Minnesota politics agreed that Pawlenty, Moe and Penny were decent, likeable people: a Minnesota Nice campaign. Of course there were differences on issues. Pawlenty pledged no tax increase. "The last thing I want to do is raise your taxes," Moe said. But also: "You pay a high income tax because you have high incomes in this state and we enjoy a higher quality of life." Penny said he "would keep taxes on the table as a last resort," and suggested there would have to be tax increases and spending cuts, and that he was the only candidate leveling with the voters. Pawlenty favored restrictions on abortion; Moe and Penny opposed them. Pawlenty and Penny favored a concealed weapons law; Moe was against. Moe said that Pawlenty's regret at his gay rights vote showed that he had moved "incredibly far to the right." Penny said he represented "the sensible center."

For most of the campaign, polls showed the three in a three-way tie. Then in October it suddenly seemed that Pawlenty might be knocked out of the race. All three had accepted public financing of up to $400,000, which required them to limit spending to $2.2 million. The parties were allowed to spend money for their candidates, but not in "cooperation or concert." The Pawlenty campaign in the summer shot footage of the candidate talking about growing up in South St. Paul and making humorous comments and then sold the footage to the state Republican party. On October 9, the Campaign and Finance Disclosure Board ruled that this violated the law. Board Chairman Doug Kelley, a friend of Pawlenty, said that the cost of those ads had to be counted against Pawlenty's $2.2 million; initial estimates of that cost were $1 million, and Pawlenty had already spent $1 million. On October 12 Pawlenty appeared before cameras and said that while he disagreed with the ruling he would defer to the Board's "higher authority" and not appeal, but would negotiate with the Board on the amount of the fine. (Just before he spoke, a cell phone went off in the room. Pawlenty quipped, "It's not Cheney, is it?") On October 14 the Board fined the campaign $100,000 and charged it with $500,000 in ad spending; that left Pawlenty with about $600,000 to spend.

Pawlenty, who had raised more money than his competitors, remained even with them in polls and in late October pulled ahead. He won with 44% of the vote to 36% for Moe and 16% for Penny. After the election Penny speculated that the memorial service for Paul Wellstone moved undecided voters to Republicans.

Pawlenty may also have been helped by the fact that he was the only candidate committed to opposing a tax increase. For this was a Republican victory up and down the ballot. Walter Mondale failed to carry Minnesota for the first time in his long political career, and Norm Coleman was elected senator. Republicans Mary Kiffmeyer and Patricia Awada were elected, narrowly, secretary of state and auditor. The only statewide DFL winner was Attorney General

Mike Hatch, who handled the issue of replacing Paul Wellstone on the ballot calmly and fairly. Republicans increased their majority in the state House to 82–52 and narrowed the DFL margin in the state Senate to 35–31–1.

Pawlenty took office with a budget shortfall estimated at $4.2 billion. "It is massive, it is serious, and there is a possibility it could get worse," he warned at a joint public appearance with Senate Majority Leader John Hottinger and House Speaker Steve Sviggum. He began his first legislative session as governor with at least one advantage over his predecessor. Ventura "was the cherry on the sundae of surliness," said Hottinger; he once infuriated legislators by issuing more than 40 vetoes in one week and stamping them with a red ink pig stamp to signal them as pork. By contrast, Pawlenty had a close relationship with Sviggum and was on good terms with many Democratic legislators who appreciated his affability and "Boy Scout" demeanor. But much of that goodwill dissipated after an acrimonious budget battle. Pawlenty cut spending by more than $2 billion and held to his no-new-taxes pledge, explaining, "The days of a program for every problem and a state government that leads by blank check are over." There were small increases in health and human services, public education and criminal justice funding but overall state spending fell by .03% in from 2003 to 2004 and increased by just 2.3% in 2005, the lowest increase in a consecutive two-year period in more than 40 years. "We're transitioning from a classic liberal state to a swing or transition or center-right state," Pawlenty told the Minneapolis *Star Tribune*. "That's not to say we are going to become North Carolina, nor should we be. We want the traditions of Minnesota, the heritage of Minnesota, the priorities of Minnesota updated for the times. There's more than one way to better health care, more than one way to better schools."

Prominent University of Minnesota political historian Hy Berman ranked Pawlenty's first year in office as one of the more significant in state history. Among his accomplishments: a 24-hour waiting period for abortions, a conceal-carry gun law, repeal of the state's Profiles of Learning standards, establishment of tax-exempt zones in distressed rural areas, a bill requiring recitation of the Pledge of Allegiance in public schools. He flew to Bosnia to support Minnesota National Guard troops stationed there as peacekeepers, traveled on trade missions abroad and proposed an ambitious mail-order program to buy cheaper prescription drugs from Canada through a state-sponsored website. "There is a difference between paying a premium and being a chump."

Pawlenty was not as accomplished in 2004. The legislature could not agree on a plan to close the state's $160 million budget deficit; he balanced the budget largely by tapping a windfall of federal dollars that had been designated for the state's subsidized health insurance plan. Failed measures included Pawlenty's education initiatives, a bill for stricter penalties for sexual predators, a stadium bill, and Pawlenty's $740 million bonding bill, casualties of a partisan impasse over a proposed same-sex marriage constitutional amendment. The House had passed a measure to put the question on the November ballot; repeated attempts in the Senate failed to bring it to a vote. In October, Pawlenty sought $350 million in "revenue sharing" from Indian tribes in exchange for their continued state gambling monopoly. Democrats called the proposal "desperate" and the tribes called it a thinly veiled tax. Republicans aired ads calling for tribes to pay "their fair share."

The unproductive legislative session led to big Democratic gains in November. Democrats, campaigning on the theme of a "do nothing legislature," picked up 13 House seats, and narrowed the Republican majority from 81–53 to 68–66. It was the first time in 12 years that Democrats gained seats in the House. Republicans blamed the losses on the DFL-controlled Senate and claimed Senate leaders made a strategic calculation to refuse to pass the bonding bill for capital improvements, a risk-free gambit because Senate seats were not up for election until 2006. Looming in 2005 were two public safety priorities—tougher penalties for sex offenders and for methamphetamine crimes—the leftover bonding bill for building projects, same-sex marriage, another budget deficit and the longstanding debate over stadium projects (not just for the baseball Twins and football Vikings but also for the University of Minnesota Golden Gophers). Pawlenty also outlined education proposals that included financial incentives for school districts that create pay-for-performance plans for teachers.

Pawlenty still may face a competitive challenge in 2006—Attorney General Mike Hatch, Senate Majority Leader Dean Johnson and state Senator Steve Kelley were possible Democratic candidates in mid-2005—but that hasn't stopped speculation about his prospects for the national ticket in 2008. His anti-tax stance and tightfisted spending policy has attracted the notice of economic conservatives; his opposition to same-sex marriage makes him attractive to social conservatives. The easygoing manner, boyish handsomeness and a Minnesota Nice style compliment his knack for breaking down complex policy into articulate, easily digested sound bites. Pawlenty has downplayed talk about higher office. "What happens in 2008 isn't even on my radar screen," he told the *Star Tribune*. But he also said, "I can't rule it out because I'm not even considering it."

Senior Senator

Mark Dayton (DFL)

Elected 2000, seat up 2006, 1st term; b. Jan. 26, 1947, Minneapolis; home, Minneapolis; Yale U., B.A. 1969; Presbyterian; divorced.

Elected Office: MN Auditor, 1990–94.

Professional Career: Teacher, NYC public schools, 1969–71; Counselor & administrator, social service agency, Boston, MA, 1971–75; Legis. asst., U.S. Sen. Walter Mondale, 1975–76; Aide, MN Gov. Rudy Perpich, 1977–78; MN Comm. of Economic Development, 1978–82; MN Comm. of Energy & Economic Development, 1983–86; Founder & Pres., Vermillion Investment Co., 1987–90, 1995–97.

DC Office: 123 RSOB, 20510, 202-224-3244; Fax: 202-228-2186; Web site: dayton.senate.gov.

State Offices: Biwabik, 218-865-4480; E. Grand Forks, 218-773-1110; Fort Snelling, 612-727-5220; Renville, 320-905-3007.

Committees: *Agriculture, Nutrition & Forestry*: Forestry, Conservation & Rural Revitalization; Production & Price Competitiveness. *Armed Services*: Airland; Readiness & Management Support; Strategic Forces. *Homeland Security & Governmental Affairs*: Federal Financial Management, Govt. Information & International Security; Investigations (Permanent); Oversight of Govt. Management, the Federal Workforce & the District of Columbia. *Rules & Administration*.

Group Ratings

	ADA	ACLU	AFS	LCV	ITIC	NTU	COC	ACU	NTLC	CHC
2004	95	67	100	83	50	12	53	12	15	0
2003	75	—	100	79	—	17	35	20	—	—

National Journal Ratings

	2003 LIB	—	2003 CONS	2004 LIB	—	2004 CONS
Economic	75%	—	20%	69%	—	28%
Social	85%	—	0%	70%	—	26%
Foreign	90%	—	0%	86%	—	8%

Key Votes of the 108th Congress

1. Ban Drilling in ANWR	Y	5. Energy Bill	Y
2. Approve Bush Tax Cuts	N	6. Support Roe v. Wade	Y
3. Medicare/Rx Bill	N	7. Ban Partial-Birth Abortion	N
4. Bar Overtime Pay Regs.	Y	8. Assault Weapons Ban	Y

9. Ban Same-Sex Marriage	N
10. Ban Bunker-Buster Bomb	Y
11. Fund Iraq War	Y
12. Restrict Missile Defense	Y

Election Results

2000 general	Mark Dayton (DFL)	1,181,553	(49%)	($11,957,114)
	Rod Grams (R)	1,047,474	(43%)	($6,024,866)
	Jim Gibson (I)	140,583	(6%)	
	Other	49,910	(2%)	
2000 primary	Mark Dayton (DFL)	178,972	(41%)	
	Mike Ciresi (DFL)	96,874	(22%)	
	Jerry R. Janezich (DFL)	90,074	(21%)	
	Rebecca Yanisch (DFL)	63,289	(15%)	
	Other	4,190	(1%)	
1994 general	Rod Grams (IR)	869,653	(49%)	($2,439,798)
	Ann Wynia (DFL)	781,860	(44%)	($2,659,423)
	Dean M. Barkley (I)	95,400	(5%)	($24,266)

Mark Dayton, elected to the Senate in 2000, grew up in Minnesota, the son of Bruce Dayton, head of Dayton Hudson, one of the nation's major and most innovative retailers (it is now called Target Corporation, and in 2001 changed the name of Dayton's department stores to Marshall Field's). Mark Dayton graduated from Yale in the student-rebellion year of 1969 and taught 9th grade science in a New York public school in the Bowery for two years, then worked as a counselor and administrator for a Boston crisis center for teenage runaways. He was a conscientious objector and was active in the anti-Vietnam War movement and his name found its way—presumably because of his family and that of his then-wife, a Rockefeller—onto Richard Nixon's enemies list. In 1975 and 1976 he worked for then-Senator Walter Mondale; in 1977 he returned to Minnesota and worked for Governor Rudy Perpich. In 1979, after Perpich lost, Dayton funded with $400,000 a nonprofit agency to spur development in rural Minnesota.

In 1982 Dayton ran for the Senate, and spent the then enormous sum of $7 million of his own money. He beat former Senator Eugene McCarthy's quixotic campaign by 69%–24% in the DFL primary, but lost 53%–47% to Republican Senator David Durenberger. Between 1983 and 1986 he was Perpich's commissioner of Energy and Economic Development. In 1990 he was elected state auditor; in 1994 he decided not to run for reelection. In 1998 he ran in the Democratic primary for governor, but spent only $2 million of his own money, and finished fourth, far behind the winner, Skip Humphrey, with 18% of the vote.

In 2000 he stepped up to run against Senator Rod Grams. Grams was the most obviously vulnerable Republican senator up that year. Grams' very conservative voting record—as different from his colleague Wellstone's as those of any two senators from the same state have been for more than half a century—was out of line with Minnesota opinion on many issues, and he had no signal legislative accomplishments.

Grams attracted seven DFL opponents before Dayton entered the race; Dayton announced on April 3. He steered clear of the nominating convention, which chose state Senator Jerry Janezich, owner of a bar in the Iron Range. Instead, Dayton came up with innovative campaign ideas. He borrowed from a Senate candidate from Montana the idea of accompanying busloads of senior citizens to Canada to buy prescription drugs at lower prices than in the United States; this Rx Express got plenty of publicity. He set up a Healthcare Hotline for people having disputes with their HMOs, which are very common in Minnesota. He performed menial jobs across the state—the work days strategy pioneered by Iowa Senator Tom Harkin in 1974. He spent his own money liberally, but so did trial lawyer Mike Ciresi; Ciresi's firm received $427 million for working on Minnesota's $6.1 billion tobacco lawsuit and he spent some $5 million on the primary. In the September 12 primary, Dayton won 41%, to 22% for Ciresi, 21% for Janezich and 15% for construction executive Rebecca Yanisch.

The two major-party nominees presented the voters with a clear contrast on the issues. Dayton was for universal government-run health insurance (a position many of whose ardent backers are millionaires who self-financed their first campaigns: Dayton, Jon Corzine, Jay Rockefeller, Edward Kennedy), while Grams was for medical savings accounts. Dayton would have the government lower the price of prescription drugs; Grams' prescription drugs program would cover low-income seniors. Grams called for eliminating the estate tax and the marriage penalty and replacing the income tax with a flat tax; Dayton called for doubling the $500 per child tax credit (co-sponsored by Grams) and expanding the childcare dependent tax credit. But much of the campaign was dominated by negative charges and driven by Dayton's financial advantage. Dayton spent $11.9 million, almost all of it his own money, doubling the previous Minnesota record (set by himself in 1982); Grams spent only $6 million. Grams was hurt by publicity about two arrests of his 22-year-old son. Grams, who was divorced in 1996, was also dogged by rumors of an affair between him and his aide Christine Gunhus (they married the weekend after the election). In response Grams ran an ad showing his mother saying, "Have you ever had someone spend a million dollars a week telling lies about someone you love?" and dismissing Dayton with the Norwegian expression "Uff-da!" Given all this, Dayton won by only 49%–43%, with 6% for Independence party candidate Jim Gibson.

Dayton entered the Senate 100th in seniority. His major focus was on getting a prescription drug benefit for seniors; he donates his Senate salary to drug-buying trips to Canada. But that issue was put aside by September 11. The prime legislative achievement of Dayton's first two years was passage in May 2002 by a 61–38 vote of the Dayton-Craig amendment to the trade bill. It gave Congress the right to a separate vote on any provision in a trade agreement weakening U.S. dumping laws.

In 2003 the Senate version of the Medicare/prescription drug bill included his amendment, adopted by a grudging 93–3 vote, requiring that members of Congress get the same prescription drug benefit as Medicare recipients; it was dropped in conference. In September 2003 he placed a hold on all Mississippi nominations after Trent Lott secured a provision, sought by Northwest Airlines, to lessen noise abatement requirements at the Minneapolis airport. He continued to support the energy bill because it included requirements to use ethanol and biodiesel and inserted an $800 million loan guarantee for a Minnesota coal gasification plant. In November 2003 the Senate rejected his bill for $6.3 billion in farm disaster aid.

Dayton voted for the September 2001 resolution authorizing military action against Al Qaeda. After Bush sought a congressional vote on military action in Iraq, Dayton criticized "this rush to vote." He wrote that, "Gaining political advantage in a midterm election is a shameful reason to hurry decisions of this magnitude." He was undecided until three hours before the vote and decided to vote no. He voted for the $87 billion supplemental appropriation for Iraq in November 2003 but in the Armed Services Committee and on the floor harshly criticized the administration's course in Iraq. In May 2004 he accused Joint Chiefs Chairman Richard Myers of suppressing news of prisoner abuses in Iraq. At the Democratic National Convention he said, "I think the country was safer when George Bush was AWOL." He stayed up late there reading the 9/11 Commission report and charged in July that the FAA and NORAD covered up "catastrophic failures" that left the nation vulnerable on September 11; he pointed to discrepancies between NORAD's chronology issued in September 2001 and that they submitted later to the 9/11 Commission. In September he announced that he was boycotting Iraqi Prime Minister Ayad Allawi's speech to Congress. In December 2004 he said he was barred from an Armed Services trip to Iraq, but he did go there later and complained in January 2005 about inconsistencies in the numbers provided him of Iraqi security forces. "It's just disgraceful that they're intentionally and repeatedly misinforming members of Congress about the facts and the truth there."

In October 2004, after Congress had recessed for the election, Dayton attracted national attention when he announced that he was closing his Washington office because of security threats. No other member took such a position, and Dayton was attacked and ridiculed by Democrats as well as Republicans. Washington, D.C., Mayor Anthony Williams and D.C. Delegate Eleanor Holmes Norton were particularly scathing. The liberal *Minneapolis Star-Tribune*, often a Dayton defender, editorialized that many were "scratching their heads at Mark Dayton's preemptive shuttering of his Senate office." It went on, "In staking out this Cassandra position, Dayton has added considerably to unfortunate aspects of his reputation: loner, loose cannon, flake." Dayton stuck to his position. "I still believe in my soul I made the necessary and wise decision to protect my staff and constituents who might visit my office."

Dayton's action resulted in low poll showings and raised doubts about his ability to win reelection in 2006. Money was another problem. Back in July 2003 he said, "I'm telling people I can't afford to spend my own money next time." In January 2004 he said, "I'm going to raise money, and I'll keep raising money because I'm not going to walk into this final election barehanded and the other side ready to slit my throat. I wouldn't do that to myself. I wouldn't do that to the Democrats in Minnesota, and I wouldn't do that to the causes I believe in." In June 2004 he reported his net worth as between $5 million and $15 million—not enough to enable him to spend $12 million as he had in 2000 or perhaps even the $7 million he spent in 1982. He estimated that it would take $15 million to run but raised only $1.7 million in 2004. In November 2004 incoming NRSC Chairman Elizabeth Dole named Dayton as one of her top targets. So did Focus on the Family's Dr. James Dobson. Congressman Mark Kennedy, fresh from defeating a well-known and well-financed Democrat, made it no secret that he was running.

On February 9 Dayton announced he would not run and issued a brief statement. "Everything I've worked for, and everything I believe in, depends upon this Senate seat remaining in the Democratic Caucus in 2007. I do not believe I am the best candidate to lead the party to victory next year." The Republican nomination seemed to be determined early. On February 11, Kennedy announced he was running; he was soon supported by Senator Norm Coleman and 26 of the 31 Republican state senators. On March 4 Congressman Gil Gutknecht said he would not run; former Senator Rod Grams, who said he was running, had not picked up much support and dropped out in April. On the DFL side, many prominent possibilities quickly took themselves out of the race: Walter Mondale, Justice Alan Page, Buck Humphrey (grandson of the senator), Attorney General Mike Hatch, radio talk show host (and Minnesota native) Al Franken. Hennepin County Attorney Amy Klobuchar announced her candidacy in April; also making moves to run were 2000 candidate and trial lawyer Mike Ciresi, child safety advocate Patty Wetterling (who lost to Kennedy in 2004), real estate developer Kelly Doran and Minnesota Heart Institute Research Foundation president Ford Bell.

Junior Senator

Norm Coleman (R)

Elected 2002, seat up 2008, 1st term; b. Aug. 17, 1949, Brooklyn, NY; home, St. Paul; Hofstra U., B.A. 1971, U. of IA, J.D. 1976; Jewish; married (Laurie).

Elected Office: St. Paul Mayor, 1993–2001.

Professional Career: MN Atty. Gen.'s office, 1976–93.

DC Office: 320 HSOB, 20510, 202-224-5641; Fax: 202-224-1152; Web site: coleman.senate.gov.

State Offices: Mankato, 507-625-6800; St. Paul, 651-645-0323.

Committees: *Agriculture, Nutrition & Forestry*: Forestry, Conservation & Rural Revitalization; Production & Price Competitiveness. *Foreign Relations*: African Affairs; International Operations & Terrorism; Near Eastern & South Asian Affairs; Western Hemisphere, Peace Corps & Narcotics Affairs (Chmn.). *Homeland Security & Governmental Affairs*: Investigations (Permanent) (Chmn.); Oversight of Govt. Management, the Federal Workforce & the District of Columbia. *Small Business & Entrepreneurship*.

Group Ratings

	ADA	ACLU	AFS	LCV	ITIC	NTU	COC	ACU	NTLC	CHC
2004	30	11	14	0	100	60	100	84	88	100
2003	15	—	11	21	—	69	91	85	—	—

National Journal Ratings

	2003 LIB	—	2003 CONS		2004 LIB	—	2004 CONS
Economic	40%	—	58%		43%	—	55%
Social	0%	—	59%		34%	—	63%
Foreign	0%	—	78%		33%	—	61%

Key Votes of the 108th Congress

1. Ban Drilling in ANWR	Y	5. Energy Bill	Y	9. Ban Same-Sex Marriage	Y
2. Approve Bush Tax Cuts	Y	6. Support Roe v. Wade	N	10. Ban Bunker-Buster Bomb	N
3. Medicare/Rx Bill	Y	7. Ban Partial-Birth Abortion	Y	11. Fund Iraq War	Y
4. Bar Overtime Pay Regs.	N	8. Assault Weapons Ban	N	12. Restrict Missile Defense	N

Election Results

2002 general	Norm Coleman (R)	1,116,697	(50%)	($10,035,279)
	Walter Mondale (DFL)	1,067,246	(47%)	($1,833,029)
	Other...	70,696	(3%)	
2002 primary	Norm Coleman (R)	195,630	(94%)	
	Jack Shepard (R)	11,678	(6%)	
1996 general	Paul Wellstone (DFL)	1,098,493	(50%)	($7,459,878)
	Rudy Boschwitz (R)	901,282	(41%)	($4,385,982)
	Dean Barkley (Ref)	152,333	(7%)	($37,240)

Norm Coleman, a Republican, was elected to the Senate after a tumultuous and tragic campaign in 2002. Coleman grew up in a modest neighborhood in Brooklyn and graduated from James Madison High School, as did New York Senator Charles Schumer and Supreme Court Justice Ruth Bader Ginsburg. He graduated from Hofstra University on Long Island and the University of Iowa law school. In 1975 he went to work in the attorney general's office in St. Paul and became chief prosecutor and solicitor general, working closely with DFL Attorney General Skip Humphrey. In 1989 he ran for mayor of St. Paul but withdrew after losing the DFL endorsement. In 1993 he ran again and won by challenging the DFL endorsee in the primary. During his mayoral tenure, Coleman was credited with leading a downtown revitalization; he boasted of attracting 18,000 new jobs and not raising property taxes for his last seven years. Coleman's opposition to abortion and his bargaining stance toward public employee unions made him many enemies among the liberals who dominate DFL precinct caucuses, and in December 1996 he switched to the Republican party; he has the unusual distinction of having served as the 1996 state co-chairman for Bill Clinton and the 2000 state chairman for George W. Bush. In 1997 he ran for reelection and defeated the DFL candidate, and became the first Republican mayor of St. Paul since 1960. In 1998 he ran for governor. He won the Republican nomination but finished second, behind Reform Party nominee Jesse Ventura, by a 37%–34% margin; but he ran ahead of his old boss, DFL nominee Skip Humphrey, who won only 28% of the vote. Coleman did not run for reelection in 2001, and was considering running for governor again. But George W. Bush called and asked him to run for the Senate, and in February 2002 he announced he was running against Senator Paul Wellstone.

Wellstone was first elected in a major upset in 1990, when he was a Carleton College political science professor. He had probably the most liberal voting record of any senator and delivered stirring orations on many issues. In his first campaign Wellstone promised to accept no PAC money or contributions over $100 and to serve only two terms. In 1996 he dropped the $100 limit and in January 2001 he announced he would run for a third term. Wellstone's greatest political asset was his authenticity: You might not like the positions he took, but you knew he did so sincerely and without regard to political consequences. Going back on his two-term promise evidently made him seem insincere to some voters, and polls showed him under 50% of the vote and with no great advantage against Coleman.

Coleman's strategy was to portray Wellstone as an obstructionist and himself as someone who gets things done; an attempt to turn Wellstone's strength, his authenticity, into a weakness. Coleman took care to oppose Bush on some issues: he opposed oil drilling in the Arctic National Wildlife Refuge and favored an increase in the minimum wage. But he also called for making the 2001 tax cuts permanent, opposed Senate Democrats' union provisions in the homeland security bill and called for individual investment accounts for Social Security, though he ran an ad in October opposing "privatization." Wellstone, as always, campaigned as the tribune of the little guy, opposed to "Robin Hood in reverse" tax cuts. Using the fundraising system he had criticized in 1990, he raised more money than Coleman, though both campaigns were well-funded. After

Bush's speech to the United Nations September 12, Coleman came out in favor of authorizing military action in Iraq. Wellstone was opposed and favored action only with the approval of the UN. Polls showed the race exceedingly close.

On Friday, October 25, 11 days before the election, Wellstone, his wife and daughter and five others died in a plane crash in northern Minnesota. As the news became known about noon, Coleman suspended his campaign. Coleman after a meeting with supporters decided not to drop out of sight, as Missouri's John Ashcroft had done in October 2000 when his opponent died in a plane crash, but to participate publicly in the mourning process.

But behind the scenes, leaders of both parties were pondering what to do next. Minnesota has a law that allows parties to substitute a new nominee in these circumstances. On Saturday Wellstone's son David, his campaign treasurer Rick Kahn and his campaign manager met with Mondale and asked him to run. Mondale, though 74, was obviously the strongest candidate. He had been elected to the Senate by solid margins in 1966 and 1972 and after serving as Jimmy Carter's vice president had returned to Minnesota, run his 1984 presidential campaign from St. Paul and had been practicing law and serving on civic and charitable boards. Mondale declined to say he would run, and said he would not decide until after the funeral and memorial service, but let the Wellstone supporters tell reporters he was "highly likely to run."

Coleman and his advisers decided not to resume campaigning until after the memorial service, but to be ready to campaign vigorously beginning the morning after. Coleman would not attack Mondale, but speak respectfully of him, and campaign around the clock across the state as the candidate of 21st century ideas. In the meantime he would appear on TV and talk only about mourning. On Monday the Wellstones were buried after a private funeral. On Tuesday night, one week before the election, the memorial service was held at the Williams Arena at the University of Minnesota. It was broadcast statewide and across the country; most Minnesota voters were watching. Suddenly the memorial service turned into a campaign rally. Kahn spoke about Wellstone, then launched into campaigning. "We are begging you to help us win this election for Paul Wellstone," he thundered. Many in the crowd of more than 20,000 booed Republican senators who had come to show their respect. The next morning, Wellstone's campaign manager apologized for the tone of the memorial.

Coleman boarded a plane at 6:15 the next morning to campaign around the state, while the DFL met and nominated Mondale. Mondale and his staff were amazed when DFL pollster Paul Harstad reported that an overnight survey had shown 73% of voters agreeing that the memorial service went overboard, with 52% agreeing strongly. Mondale's Sunday night lead of 52%–39% had vanished and the race was suddenly at 43%–43%. Seldom if ever has political polling shown such an overnight shift. On Thursday, Coleman continued campaigning across the state while Mondale campaigned in Minneapolis. On Monday morning Mondale and Coleman appeared in their one televised debate. Coleman treated Mondale with great respect, always referring to him as Vice President, but argued that he was the candidate of the future. Mondale debated aggressively, referring to Coleman as Norman; he may have reflected the contempt DFL insiders have for Coleman as a party-switcher when he asked, "Who do you trust?" On the issues Mondale was clearly well-informed, but he sounded antique and abstract, while Coleman sounded contemporary and concrete. Afterwards, Coleman embarked on an 18-hour bus tour.

Coleman won 50%–47%, with a popular vote margin of 49,000; 11,000 absentee votes were counted for Wellstone. It was the first time Mondale had lost an election in Minnesota. This was a different Minnesota than the one that had reelected him to the Senate in 1972, 30 years before. In the Twin Cities core, Hennepin and Ramsey Counties, Mondale won 53%–44%. In the counties outside the Twin Cities media market, Mondale won 50%–46%; the city-based Coleman did not have as strong an appeal as George W. Bush had in 2000 in rural areas. But the difference was the Ventura Belt, the counties in the Twin Cities media market beyond the core. In 1972 they had cast 481,000 votes; in 2002 they cast 906,000, a rise of 88%. In 1972 Mondale had carried those counties 53%–47%. In 2002 Coleman carried them 56%–41%.

In the Senate Coleman generally voted with the Bush administration and achieved high visibility for a freshman. He chaired two important subcommittees, the Permanent Subcommittee on Investigations and the Foreign Relations subcommittee on Latin America. On the Investigations Subcommittee, he initiated hearings on the safety of Internet drugs, on tax loopholes, on the recording industry's crackdown on Internet piracy, on the Pentagon's purchases of first class and business class airline tickets, on credit counseling abuses. The recording industry hearings got attention from many who ordinarily pay no heed to politics. "I'm worried that the industry is using a shotgun approach," said Coleman, the father of two teenagers. "One of the problems with the 1998 DMCA [the Digital Millenium Copyright Act] is that it was created before the advent of KaZaA, Napster and the P2P technology that is used today to facilitate illegal downloading. This is what I mean when I say the law and technology are not in sync. It is a great challenge for Congress to adjust that balance because technology changes so much more quickly than the legislative process." In November 2004 he held hearings on corruption in the UN Oil for Food program; on December 1, in an opinion article in the *Wall Street Journal*, he called for the resignation of UN Secretary General Kofi Annan.

In addressing national issues, Coleman took care to look to Minnesota interests. After a trip to Brazil, he noted that ethanol was used widely there. He co-sponsored $3 billion in disaster relief for farmers and an extension of the Milk Income Loss Contract program. He supported energy bill provisions increasing the ethanol producer tax credit and providing a biodiesel tax credit and inserted into the energy bill $800 million in loan guarantees for a coal gasification plant in the Iron Range; he was present in October 2004 when Energy Secretary Spencer Abraham came to the Iron Range and announced a $36 million grant for the plant. He voted against ANWR oil drilling, but said he might vote for an energy bill that allowed it if it contained the above provisions. That was in line with his general approach: "What I tried to accomplish was to be part of a coalition that got things done. Working with the president, not against him. I try to find ways to get things done." He and Carl Levin sponsored an amendment, passed unanimously, requiring federal bank examiners to wait one year after retirement to work for banks they regulated. He also sponsored an amendment requiring the Pentagon to pay for servicemen's trips home on leave. His bill to extend Trade Adjustment Assistance to service workers got 54 votes, short of the 60 needed to survive a budget point of order. He introduced a bill with standards for Internet pharmacies; if that were passed, he said, he would support reimportation of prescription drugs, a measure strongly supported by his fellow Republican, Governor Tim Pawlenty. He secured grants for a runway extension for the Marshall airport, an I-94 interchange in Moorhead and $200,000 compensation for the sons of a National Guardsman who contracted AIDS in the 1980s while being treated for a service-related injury.

Coleman's one big disappointment came when he ran for the chairmanship of the NRSC in November 2004 and lost to Elizabeth Dole 28–27 on a secret ballot. Some speculated that he would run for a leadership position after the 2006 election. Coleman comes up for reelection in 2008, but in early 2005 most of the Senate race speculation in Minnesota revolved around the seat Mark Dayton was vacating. Al Franken, the Minnesota-raised comedian and talk show host, though he declined to run for the Dayton seat, said that he would decide by the end of 2005 whether to return to Minnesota and run against Coleman.

FIRST DISTRICT

Rep. Gil Gutknecht (R)

Elected 1994, 6th term; b. Mar. 20, 1951, Cedar Falls, IA; home, Rochester; U. of N. IA, B.A. 1973; Catholic; married (Mary).

Elected Office: MN House of Reps. 1982–94.

Professional Career: Sales Rep., Latta School Supply Co., 1973–82; Real Estate Auctioneer, 1979–94.

DC Office: 425 CHOB, 20515, 202-225-2472; Fax: 202-225-3246; Web site: www.gil.house.gov.

District Offices: Fairmont, 507-238-2835; Rochester, 507-252-9841.

Committees: *Agriculture* (8th of 25 R): Department Operations, Oversight, Nutrition & Forestry (Chmn.); Specialty Crops & Foreign Agriculture Programs. *Government Reform* (7th of 23 R): Criminal Justice, Drug Policy & Human Resources; Government Management, Finance & Accountability. *Science* (9th of 24 R): Environment, Technology & Standards; Research.

Group Ratings

	ADA	ACLU	AFS	LCV	ITIC	NTU	COC	ACU	NTLC	CHC
2004	5	0	0	0	89	79	90	92	97	100
2003	15	—	25	5	—	73	89	88	—	—

National Journal Ratings

	2003 LIB	—	2003 CONS	2004 LIB	—	2004 CONS
Economic	51%	—	49%	29%	—	70%
Social	24%	—	71%	0%	—	91%
Foreign	23%	—	77%	34%	—	63%

Key Votes of the 108th Congress

1. Drilling in ANWR	Y	5. DC School Vouchers	Y	9. Ban Same-Sex Marriage	Y
2. Approve Bush Tax Cuts	Y	6. Ban Human Cloning	Y	10. Fund Iraq War	Y
3. Medicare/Rx Bill	N	7. Restrict Gun Liability	Y	11. Bar Cuba Embargo Funds	N
4. Bar Overtime Pay Regs.	N	8. Ban Partial-Birth Abortion	Y	12. Intelligence Reorg.	Y

Election Results

2004 general	Gil Gutknecht (R)	193,132	(60%)	($666,410)
	Leigh Pomeroy (DFL)	115,088	(36%)	($58,826)
	Gregory Mikkelson (Ind)	15,569	(5%)	($7,472)
2004 primary	Gil Gutknecht (R)	unopposed		
2002 general	Gil Gutknecht (R)	163,570	(61%)	($770,201)
	Steve Andreasen (DFL)	92,165	(35%)	($123,060)
	Greg Mikkelson (Green)	9,964	(4%)	($16,761)

Prior Winning Percentages: 2000 (56%); 1998 (55%); 1996 (53%); 1994 (55%)

The People		Race/Ethnic Origin	Ancestry	
Area size:	13,521 sq. mi.	93.2% White	German: 31.7%	Norwegian: 14.3%
Urban population:	56.5%	1.0% Black	Irish: 7.1%	
Rural population:	43.5%	1.7% Asian	**2004 Presidential Vote**	
Pop. 2000:	614,935	0.2% Native Am.	Bush (R) 171,952	(51%)
Median income:	$40,941	0.0% Hawaiian	Kerry (D) 159,776	(47%)
Poverty status:	8.5%	0.8% Two+ races	Other 5,043	(2%)
Military veterans:	13.0%	0.1% Other	**2000 Presidential Vote**	
		3.0% Hispanic Origin	Bush (R) 146,212	(49%)
			Gore (D) 133,078	(45%)
			Other 17,501	(6%)
			Cook Partisan Voting Index: R + 1	

Occupation	Blue collar: 26.8%	White collar: 56.7%	Gray collar: 16.5%

The Mississippi River flows majestically southeast from Minneapolis and St. Paul, cutting through rolling hills and, where it widens, forming calm lakes lapping at the bottomlands: one of the finest river landscapes of North America, exemplified by the river towns of Wabasha and Winona, with their 19th century stone storefronts and mountain-like rock outcroppings above the river. This far north, the westward tide of Yankee migrants thinned out. After the Civil War, most settlers following the railroads on the flood plains west of the river were Germans and Scandinavians, bringing their families to this terrain so much like the Rhineland, and to the rolling uplands beyond, which resemble the northern European plain.

Southern Minnesota is a borderland between Yankee and German settlements. Along the Mississippi River, tourism spiked upward (from a nonexistent base) after the old St. Paul and Milwaukee Railroad was converted into a hiker-biker nature trail during the 1990s; "Historic Bluff Country" now draws enough visitors to support not one but two former jails that have been converted, with Minnesota practicality, into upscale bed-and-breakfasts. A little to the west is Rochester, home to the Mayo Clinic, founded in 1863 when English-born physician William Mayo set up a practice to examine inductees into the Union Army. Today, Rochester, with its large professional population, is prosperous and the growth center of southern Minnesota. Austin, a county away, is headquarters of the Hormel meatpacking firm that beat a bitter strike in the 1980s; its huge plant produces "miracle meat" Spam, Hormel chili, Dinty Moore stew and, say critics, too much ammonia-loaded waste. This is one place where class-conscious politics survives, though all sides are proud of their Spam Museum. The farther west you go, the more frequently you find communities with a German heritage, like New Ulm, where the "Hermann the German" monument guards the town and the Concord Singers—30 men decked out in lederhosen, red vests and white shirts—are described as one of the best male choruses in the nation. Further south is dairy country, with a sprinkling of small industry. In tiny Ormsby, North County Seed breeds soybeans to match the wishes of its international customers.

The 1st Congressional District of Minnesota includes the state's two southern tiers of counties, running along Interstate 90 just north of the Iowa border. It stretches 280 miles from the South Dakota border at Sioux Falls to the Wisconsin border at LaCrosse. Historically, this was a political borderland, with Civil War Republicans in the east and Farmer-Laborites more common in the west. Rochester has long been a Republican stronghold, though not by much in 2004; like many communities with large numbers of professionals, it has been trending toward Democrats. Austin with its working class tradition has long been solidly Democratic-Farmer-Labor. To the west, Mankato voted narrowly for John Kerry and the population-losing farm counties between Mankato and the South Dakota border voted solidly Republican.

The congressman from the 1st District is Gil Gutknecht, a Republican first elected in 1994. The name, he likes to explain, means "good hired hand," though "good indentured servant" might be closer to the mark. He grew up in Iowa, son of a union machinist, worked nine years as a school supply salesman, then became an auctioneer, eventually handling large real estate auctions. He was elected to the legislature in 1982 from Rochester and became Republican floor leader. Partisan, ebullient, he once told Iron Range DFLers that the state motto *L'etoile du Nord* did not mean "send the money north." When Democratic Congressman Tim Penny decided to retire, Gutknecht ran for the House. In the Republican primary, he argued that he was the more conservative candidate and beat former two-term Congressman Arlen Erdahl, 57%–36%. In the general against Mankato state Senator John Hottinger, Gutknecht called himself "the Minnesota equivalent of Newt Gingrich." Gutknecht won big in Rochester and in the river counties, for a 55%–45% victory.

Gutknecht was an enthusiastic member of the new Republican majority who proudly talked of listening to Gingrich's lecture tapes, and he has a mostly conservative voting record. But by the end of the Clinton era, he conceded that the Republican revolution was "greatly exaggerated" and that Gingrich had been "a disappointment to everybody" as speaker. He calls himself a "Teddy Roosevelt Republican," and has been an occasional maverick, especially on economic issues. With Rahm Emanuel, he led the cause to allow reimportation of prescription drugs from Canada and he opposed the Medicare/prescription drug bill when reimportation was not included. He supported trade promotion authority in order to increase farm exports. He sought to reduce the nation's dependence on foreign oil, and sought to require that 5% of the nation's fuel come from renewable sources by 2016; ethanol is a major local product. He soured on federal milk-support payments and the regional politics that it produced in Congress, even though thousands of Minnesota dairy farmers received benefits.

Gutknecht initially attracted active opposition in a district with a strong DFL base, but his occasional independence appears to play well. In 1998, state Senator Tracy Beckman, with Tim Penny as his campaign chairman, focused on Gutknecht's support for the Freedom to Farm Act together with the year's sharp drop in crop prices. Gutknecht wobbled a bit, voting against a Republican tax cut, and running ads saying he "listens to farmers," but he had a big money advantage, and won 55%–45%. Since redistricting, which slightly increased the district's Republican lean, he has not had a serious challenge. Even before Mark Dayton announced his retirement, Gutknecht said that he might run for the Senate in 2006. But when Dayton announced his retirement in February 2005, the 6th District's Mark Kennedy jumped in the race two days later and got the support of Senator Norm Coleman and 26 of the 31 Republican state senators. In March, Gutknecht announced he would run for reelection and not for the Senate.

SECOND DISTRICT

Rep. John Kline (R)

Elected 2002, 2d term; b. Sept. 6, 1947, Allentown, PA; home, Lakeville; Rice U., B.A. 1969, Shippensburg U., M.P.A. 1988; Christian; married (Vicky).

Military Career: Marine Corps, 1969–94 (Vietnam).

Professional Career: Vice-pres., Cntr. of the American Experiment, 2001–02.

DC Office: 1429 LHOB, 20515, 202-225-2271; Fax: 202-225-2595; Web site: www.house.gov/kline/.

District Office: Burnsville, 952-808-1213.

Committees: *Armed Services* (25th of 34 R): Military Personnel; Terrorism, Unconventional Threats & Capabilities. *Education & the Workforce* (16th of 27 R): Employer-Employee Relations; Workforce Protections.

Group Ratings

	ADA	ACLU	AFS	LCV	ITIC	NTU	COC	ACU	NTLC	CHC
2004	5	0	0	0	90	72	100	96	89	92
2003	5	—	0	5	—	62	100	88	—	—

National Journal Ratings

	2003 LIB	—	2003 CONS	2004 LIB	—	2004 CONS
Economic	9%	—	84%	13%	—	85%
Social	5%	—	87%	9%	—	85%
Foreign	11%	—	80%	10%	—	86%

Key Votes of the 108th Congress

1. Drilling in ANWR	Y	5. DC School Vouchers	Y	9. Ban Same-Sex Marriage	Y
2. Approve Bush Tax Cuts	Y	6. Ban Human Cloning	Y	10. Fund Iraq War	Y
3. Medicare/Rx Bill	Y	7. Restrict Gun Liability	Y	11. Bar Cuba Embargo Funds	N
4. Bar Overtime Pay Regs.	N	8. Ban Partial-Birth Abortion	Y	12. Intelligence Reorg.	Y

Election Results

2004 general	John Kline (R)	206,313	(56%)	($1,610,055)
	Teresa Daly (DFL)	147,527	(40%)	($1,182,465)
	Other	12,105	(3%)	
2004 primary	John Kline (R)	unopposed		
2002 general	John Kline (R)	152,970	(53%)	($1,534,873)
	Bill Luther (DFL)	121,121	(42%)	($2,263,619)
	Samuel Garst (NTX)	12,430	(4%)	

The People		Race/Ethnic Origin	Ancestry	
Area size:	3,154 sq. mi.	91.8% White	German: 28.4%	Norwegian: 11.3%
Urban population:	80.1%	1.6% Black	Irish: 9.2%	
Rural population:	19.9%	2.3% Asian	**2004 Presidential Vote**	
Pop. 2000:	614,934	0.4% Native Am.	Bush (R) 203,538	(54%)
Median income:	$61,344	0.0% Hawaiian	Kerry (D) 169,704	(45%)
Poverty status:	3.9%	1.1% Two+ races	Other 4,105	(1%)
Military veterans:	12.1%	0.1% Other	**2000 Presidential Vote**	
		2.6% Hispanic Origin	Bush (R) 150,366	(51%)
			Gore (D) 131,414	(44%)
			Other 14,526	(5%)
			Cook Partisan Voting Index: R + 3	

Occupation	Blue collar: 22.3%	White collar: 65.0%	Gray collar: 12.6%

Drive south from the Twin Cities and you will encounter new housing developments and big-box store parking lots inhabited by youngish families working in managerial, business and technical careers. Many come from elsewhere, attracted by Minnesota's strong economy and pleasant living (if you don't mind winter). They have turned such places as Eagan, Lakeville, Apple Valley, Mendota Heights and Burnsville in Dakota County into fast-growing, "mallified" suburbs. More upscale are the suburbs of Scott and Carver Counties; Scott County was the 12th fastest-growing county in the nation between 2000 and 2004 and the fastest growing Minnesota county, up 98%, between 1990 and 2004. Drive farther south on Interstate 35—a little farther every year—and suddenly you are surrounded by farm country, as well as modest towns such as Northfield, the idyllic home of Carleton College and its late professor-turned-Senator, Paul Wellstone. Northfield is only 40 miles from Minneapolis and St. Paul, and some people there commute to the Twin Cities core on I-35.

These places make up the 2d Congressional District of Minnesota. Historically, Dakota County, just south of St. Paul, which casts nearly half the votes in the district, was marginally Democratic, while the other counties were fairly heavily Republican. But in 1998 this was Jesse Ventura Country: in that three-way race he carried each of the counties in the district, with a sharply increased turnout. As the suburbs have continued growing, Ventura country has become more Republican. George W. Bush narrowly carried Dakota County in 2000 and 2004, and produced big margins for Republican Senator Norm Coleman and Governor Tim Pawlenty in 2002. The only remaining DFL stronghold here is Rice County, home of Northfield.

The congressman from the 2d District is John Kline, a Republican first elected in 2002 and one of only four challengers to defeat an incumbent that year: Kline's third try at beating DFL incumbent Bill Luther proved a charm. Kline grew up in Corpus Christi, Texas, where his father owned a small hometown newspaper and his mother managed the Corpus Christi Symphony Orchestra for more than 40 years. After graduating from Rice University he served 25 years in the Marine Corps. He served in Vietnam, commanded Marine aviation forces in Somalia and his headquarters duties included responsibility for the Corps's $50 billion program objective memorandum, a budget and planning analysis. He was assigned to the White House when Jimmy Carter was president and he carried the nuclear "football"—the package containing the launch codes—for Carter and for Ronald Reagan: he surely has had more face time with presidents than any other member of Congress. When he retired in 1994, he settled in Lakeville, in Dakota County, where he managed his wife's family farm.

In 1998, Kline challenged Luther, a Democrat who was first elected in 1994 who had a history of expensive and fierce campaigns in the old 6th. Kline favored tax cuts, more military spending and the resignation of Bill Clinton, and opposed abortion. He spent only $283,000; Luther, who raised $1.1 million in the cycle, spent only $412,000. That might have been a mistake: Luther won by only 50%–46%. Kline hardly stopped running; more experienced and better financed in 2000, he made the rematch one of the nation's high-profile House contests. The result was closer across the board, but Luther survived 50%–48%. Discouraged, Kline said he was unlikely to run again. Then the unexpected happened. The redistricting plan ordered into effect by the state supreme court in March 2002 placed Kline's home in a new 2d District that contained the home of no incumbent. Republican leaders in Minnesota and Washington urged Kline to run again, and a few days later he announced his candidacy. Luther, whose home was in the new 6th District, a dozen miles north of the 2d, waited two months before announcing which district he would run in, or whether he would retire. He didn't have a good choice: In contrast to his old 6th District, where George W. Bush got only 48% of the vote in 2000, majorities in both the new 2d and 6th Districts had voted for Bush.

Luther finally decided to run in the 2d and started with some advantages: 28 years of experience in elected office, $1.2 million in cash on hand. The acrimonious campaign resumed where it left off in 2000. Luther called Kline an extremist who held "Texas values." Luther's campaign manager encouraged Sam Garst, a Sierra Club activist and Luther supporter, to enter the race as a candidate of a new "No New Taxes" party—a purposefully deceptive banner designed to siphon votes from the Republican column. At first the Luther campaign denied all connection with Garst, but the facts came out: Luther had not discouraged the action. Even liberal local media harshly criticized the scheme as "un-Minnesotan" and characterized it as a cynical dirty trick in a hotly contested race where a few votes might make the difference. Kline got further mileage out of the issue by refusing to debate Luther unless Garst was included; Garst left town in the weeks before the election. What had twice been a close race turned out to be no contest in 2002. Kline won by a comfortable 53%–42%. Luther later said that the controversial memorial service for Paul Wellstone cost him independent and Republican support and conceded that he suffered from anger over the Garst candidacy.

In the House, Kline's voting record made him the most conservative member of the Minnesota delegation. Kline won a seat on Armed Services, plus the Education and Workforce Committee. He helped delay a plan by Defense Secretary Donald Rumsfeld to overhaul the officer management program; Kline worried that it would politicize the appointment of senior officers and hurt morale among young officers. He was among the House conservatives who criticized the intelligence reorganization bill because it might jeopardize the chain of command within the Pentagon, because the lines of authority were "too fuzzy." But when Armed Services Committee Chairman Duncan Hunter cut a deal with the White House, Kline went along.

Kline was reelected by a comfortable 56%–40%.

THIRD DISTRICT

Rep. Jim Ramstad (R)

Elected 1990, 8th term; b. May 6, 1946, Jamestown, ND; home, Minnetonka; U. of MN, B.A. 1968, George Washington U., J.D. 1973; Protestant; single.

Military Career: Army Reserves, 1968–74.

Elected Office: MN Senate, 1980–90.

Professional Career: Special Asst., U.S. Rep. Tom Kleppe, 1970; Practicing atty., 1973–80; Adjunct Prof., American U., 1975–78.

DC Office: 103 CHOB, 20515, 202-225-2871; Fax: 202-225-6351; Web site: www.house.gov/ramstad.

District Office: Minnetonka, 952-738-8200.

Committees: *Ways & Means* (7th of 24 R): Health; Oversight (Chmn.).

Group Ratings

	ADA	ACLU	AFS	LCV	ITIC	NTU	COC	ACU	NTLC	CHC
2004	25	10	0	36	100	67	100	76	86	69
2003	25	—	25	75	—	65	90	60	—	—

National Journal Ratings

	2003 LIB	—	2003 CONS		2004 LIB	—	2004 CONS
Economic	39%	—	60%		42%	—	58%
Social	55%	—	44%		39%	—	60%
Foreign	53%	—	46%		49%	—	50%

Key Votes of the 108th Congress

1. Drilling in ANWR	N	5. DC School Vouchers	N	9. Ban Same-Sex Marriage	Y
2. Approve Bush Tax Cuts	Y	6. Ban Human Cloning	N	10. Fund Iraq War	Y
3. Medicare/Rx Bill	Y	7. Restrict Gun Liability	Y	11. Bar Cuba Embargo Funds	Y
4. Bar Overtime Pay Regs.	N	8. Ban Partial-Birth Abortion	Y	12. Intelligence Reorg.	Y

Election Results

2004 general	Jim Ramstad (R)	231,871	(65%)	($921,476)
	Deborah Watts (DFL)	126,665	(35%)	($36,064)
2004 primary	Jim Ramstad (R)	19,232	(90%)	
	Burton Hanson (R)	2,159	(10%)	
2002 general	Jim Ramstad (R)	213,334	(72%)	($794,176)
	Darryl Stanton (DFL)	82,575	(28%)	

Prior Winning Percentages: 2000 (68%); 1998 (72%); 1996 (70%); 1994 (73%); 1992 (64%); 1990 (67%)

The People		Race/Ethnic Origin	Ancestry	
Area size:	513 sq. mi.	88.6% White	German: 22.8%	Norwegian: 11.3%
Urban population:	95.8%	3.8% Black	Irish: 8.6%	
Rural population:	4.2%	4.0% Asian	**2004 Presidential Vote**	
Pop. 2000:	614,935	0.3% Native Am.	Bush (R) 190,339	(51%)
Median income:	$63,816	0.0% Hawaiian	Kerry (D) 179,488	(48%)
Poverty status:	3.5%	1.4% Two+ races	Other 3,735	(1%)
Military veterans:	12.4%	0.1% Other	**2000 Presidential Vote**	
		1.8% Hispanic Origin	Bush (R) 161,999	(50%)
			Gore (D) 149,277	(46%)
			Other 13,483	(4%)
			Cook Partisan Voting Index: R + 1	

Occupation	Blue collar: 16.7%	White collar: 73.1%	Gray collar: 10.1%

Over the past half century, Minnesota's great twin metropolis has spread out from the neat streets inside the city limits of Minneapolis and St. Paul into the countryside all around. People have sorted themselves out geographically. In the lower lands along the Mississippi and Minnesota Rivers, where rail lines fan out from the Twin Cities heading toward the great farmlands of America, are the blue-collar suburbs, with modest houses on grid streets and warehouses and factories near the tracks. Inland, around the lakes Minnesota is so proud of, in subdivisions with curved streets hugging the hills, are the Twin Cities' more affluent neighborhoods, quiet and unflashy in the Minnesota way, but comfortable whether blanketed with snow or when the lake is glinting in the summer sun. In between are the freeway interchanges where some of the Twin Cities' great innovations can be seen—Southdale Shopping Center in Edina, the first enclosed mall and site of the first B. Dalton store, which begat the national book chains; huge indoor water parks; and the giant Mall of America, with its 4.2 million square feet, 525 stores, 50 restaurants, 14 theaters, 8 nightclubs and 13,000 employees; there are plans to add 5.7 million square feet on an additional 42 acres, including a 5,000 seat performing arts center and a rail connection to downtown Minneapolis. The mall, the nation's number one tourist attraction, is unmatched as a symbol of American consumerism; security was quickly heightened after the September 11 attacks.

The 3d Congressional District of Minnesota takes in Hennepin County suburbs north, south and west of Minneapolis. On the north side of the 3d is working-class Brooklyn Park, long a DFL stronghold but more famous now for its former mayor, later governor, Jesse Ventura; on the south is middle-income Bloomington, home of the Mall of America; to the west are Edina, Plymouth, Wayzata and other towns around Lake Minnetonka, traditionally Republican but marginal in the 2004 presidential election. This is the largest lake and these are the most affluent communities in the Twin Cities area. The area is home to the headquarters of such diverse companies as Cargill and Radisson Hotels, and large biotech facilities in Brooklyn Park and Maple Grove. This area trended Democratic in the 1990s, as Bill Clinton twice won pluralities here. The 3d may be the home of Minnesota's traditional Republican establishment, but it voted just 51% for George W. Bush in 2004.

The congressman from the 3d District is Jim Ramstad, a Republican first elected in 1990. He has been in politics since childhood: Raised in North Dakota, he used to go with his grandfather to visit Republican Senator Milton Young. He saw President Eisenhower in 1956 and met President Kennedy in 1963 at the same Rose Garden ceremony where a young Bill Clinton was photographed shaking Kennedy's hand (Ramstad is in the background of the now famous photo). He was an intern to Young and a staffer to Congressman Tom Kleppe while in his 20s. He moved to Minnesota and in 1980, at 34, he unseated a Democratic state senator (spending the then record-breaking sum of $77,932). In 1990, when Representative Bill Frenzel retired after 20 years, Ramstad ran for the House. The crucial contest was the Republican convention. Ramstad was pro-choice on abortion while most delegates were anti-abortion, but he had good endorsements, from Senator Rudy Boschwitz and Congressman Vin Weber, both anti-abortion, and won the party convention on the eighth ballot.

Ramstad's voting record has been slightly right of the middle of the House, a bit more conservative on economic issues. The House passed his Missing Children Tax Fairness Act, which allows families of abducted children to continue to claim a dependency exemption. On the Ways and Means Committee, he worked on the Taxpayer Bill of Rights, Medicare and hospital funding formulas and on saving the housing tax exemption for clergy members. He argues that the current tax system is too complex, too costly and too invasive. He has strongly supported free trade.

Ramstad has been a recovering alcoholic since 1981, when he awoke in jail after a night of drinking ended in a brawl, and he has backed measures for both discipline and therapy for substance abusers. He has counseled House colleagues with a drinking problem; with Patrick Kennedy, he organized a caucus to educate lawmakers on addiction and treatment. On other issues, Ramstad talked about his mother's Alzheimer's disease when he urged George W. Bush to support stem cell research. He has been an enthusiastic backer of Bush's faith-based initiative, plus tax cuts and the war in Iraq. He split with Republican leaders on campaign finance regulation, federalizing security agents at the airports and the Cuban trade embargo. He called the 2002 farm bill "a horrendous hit on taxpayers."

Ramstad has been easily reelected every two years in this high-turnout district. He has been listed among the best-dressed members of Congress. Near the end of the 2002 Senate contest, he unexpectedly became a player at the memorial service for Paul Wellstone. There Wellstone's campaign treasurer in a frenzied speech implored Ramstad to "help us win this race" in its closing days; Ramstad continued to back Norm Coleman, and many voters were repelled by the Democrats who turned a memorial service into a political rally. In Wellstone's memory, Ramstad pushed for equal coverage of mental and physical illness, but he said that Speaker Dennis Hastert blocked the bill. "I've spoken to him until I'm blue in the face," he told the *Associated Press*. In 2005, Ramstad gained the seniority to become chairman of the Oversight Subcommittee. He planned to focus on tax simplification and taxpayer rights.

FOURTH DISTRICT

Rep. Betty McCollum (DFL)

Elected 2000, 3d term; b. July 12, 1954, Minneapolis; home, St. Paul; Inver Hills Comm. Col., A.A. 1980, Col. of St. Catherine, B.A. 1987; Catholic; divorced.

Elected Office: N. St. Paul City Cncl., 1986–92; MN House of Reps., 1992–2000.

Professional Career: Teacher; Retail sales & management.

DC Office: 1029 LHOB, 20515, 202-225-6631; Fax: 202-225-1968; Web site: www.house.gov/mccollum.

District Office: St. Paul, 651-224-9191.

Committees: *Education & the Workforce* (16th of 22 D): 21st Century Competitiveness; Employer-Employee Relations. *International Relations* (21st of 23 D): Africa, Global Human Rights & International Operations; International Terrorism & Nonproliferation.

Group Ratings

	ADA	ACLU	AFS	LCV	ITIC	NTU	COC	ACU	NTLC	CHC
2004	100	90	100	100	40	8	24	0	0	7
2003	100	—	100	95	—	24	24	8	—	—

National Journal Ratings

	2003 LIB	—	2003 CONS		2004 LIB	—	2004 CONS
Economic	87%	—	9%		94%	—	5%
Social	92%	—	0%		76%	—	23%
Foreign	89%	—	8%		94%	—	4%

Key Votes of the 108th Congress

1. Drilling in ANWR	N	5. DC School Vouchers	N
2. Approve Bush Tax Cuts	N	6. Ban Human Cloning	N
3. Medicare/Rx Bill	N	7. Restrict Gun Liability	N
4. Bar Overtime Pay Regs.	Y	8. Ban Partial-Birth Abortion	N

9. Ban Same-Sex Marriage	N
10. Fund Iraq War	N
11. Bar Cuba Embargo Funds	Y
12. Intelligence Reorg.	N

Election Results

2004 general	Betty McCollum (DFL)	182,387	(57%)	($707,384)
	Patrice Bataglia (R)	105,467	(33%)	($194,717)
	Peter Vento (Ind)	29,099	(9%)	
2004 primary	Betty McCollum (DFL)	unopposed		
2002 general	Betty McCollum (DFL)	164,597	(62%)	($589,276)
	Clyde Billington (R)	89,705	(34%)	($93,250)
	Scott Raskiewicz (Green)	9,919	(4%)	

Prior Winning Percentages: 2000 (48%)

The People		Race/Ethnic Origin	Ancestry		
Area size:	220 sq. mi.	77.7% White	German: 22.0%	Irish: 9.5%	
Urban population:	99.9%	6.5% Black	Norwegian: 7.7%		
Rural population:	0.1%	7.5% Asian	**2004 Presidential Vote**		
Pop. 2000:	614,935	0.7% Native Am.	Kerry (D)	205,467	(62%)
Median income:	$46,811	0.0% Hawaiian	Bush (R)	123,313	(37%)
Poverty status:	9.6%	2.2% Two+ races	Other	4,341	(1%)
Military veterans:	11.8%	0.1% Other	**2000 Presidential Vote**		
		5.2% Hispanic Origin	Gore (D)	166,919	(57%)
			Bush (R)	109,670	(37%)
			Other	18,146	(6%)
			Cook Partisan Voting Index: D +13		

Occupation	Blue collar: 19.2%	White collar: 67.0%	Gray collar: 13.7%

Above the Mississippi River bluffs, forested when the first settlers arrived in the 1850s and one of America's great urban vistas today, stand the two great landmarks of St. Paul: the Minnesota Capitol and Archbishop Ireland's Cathedral. This is the older and smaller of the Twin Cities, settled mainly by Catholic Irish and German immigrants, while Minneapolis was attracting Protestant Swedes and Yankees. St. Paul became a major transportation hub, a railroad center and river port, while Minneapolis, farther up river at the Falls of St. Anthony, became the nation's largest grain milling center; both industries stoked the ire of farmers in the Dakotas who had no choice but to deal with them to make a living. Beneath the Capitol and the cathedral, the city's skywalk-linked downtown is home to the Ordway Music Theater, the headquarters of Minnesota Public Radio and an active pop music industry; the Winter Carnival is an annual highlight. Beyond the cathedral is Summit Avenue, on which capitalists like the Great Northern Railway's James J. Hill built grandiose Romanesque houses, and which, with Monument Avenue in Richmond and Meridian Street in Indianapolis, remains one of America's grand 19th century residential boulevards. The parallel Grand Avenue is home to a pleasant commercial strip with a walkable, urban feel; more modest neighborhoods elsewhere are notable for their grid streets lined with sturdy houses. Unexpectedly high ridership on a new light-rail line in Minneapolis raised support for expansion to St. Paul.

Minnesota's 4th Congressional District is made up of St. Paul, the Ramsey County suburbs to the north, and the southern suburbs of West St. Paul and South St. Paul. When a special panel of judges drew the new districts in 2002, they rejected a Republican proposal to combine Minneapolis and St. Paul into one district and made only modest changes in the boundaries. St. Paul was one of the most Democratic parts of Minnesota even before the Democratic-Farmer-Labor Party was formed in 1944, and it remained proudly DFL for a half-century; it did reelect Mayor Norm Coleman in 1997 after he switched to the Republican party, but he failed to carry a single precinct in the city when he ran successfully for the Senate in 2002. The area has become home to more than 24,000 Hmong immigrants, the largest concentration in any American city. The Hmong had been recruited by the CIA and U.S. Special Forces during the Vietnam War and resettled here after Laos fell to the Communists in 1975; another 5,000 refugees from Thailand were scheduled to arrive by 2005. The 4th District seat has been held by the DFL since it elected Eugene McCarthy in 1948, and remains the second-most Democratic district in the state.

The congresswoman from the 4th District is Betty McCollum, a Democrat first elected in 2000. The daughter of a military intelligence officer, she grew up in North St. Paul and graduated from the College of St. Catherine. For 11 years she taught high school social studies and then she was a retail sales manager for 14 years at Dayton's department store. After her daughter was hurt on the slide in a city park, McCollum ran and was elected in 1986 to the North St. Paul City Council. She served on the council until 1992, when she was elected to the state House of Representatives after defeating incumbents in both the primary and general.

The 4th District had been represented since 1976 by Bruce Vento, a Democrat with an almost perfectly liberal voting record. In February 2000 Vento announced he would not seek reelection and that he had malignant mesothelioma; he died on October 10, 2000. In the September primary, McCollum, who was endorsed by Minnesota's Democratic-Farmer-Labor Party and EMILY's List, faced three opponents. The primary at first appeared wide open, but in this race, unlike some statewide contests, the DFL convention endorsement counted for something, and McCollum won easily with 50% to 23% for state Senator Steve Novak. Republicans nominated state senator Linda Runbeck, a vigorously anti-abortion candidate. McCollum backed prescription drug coverage under Medicare and opposed large tax cuts before Congress paid down the debt. Runbeck, who opposed gun control and took conservative positions on health care and education, attacked McCollum and her Democratic allies for running "hateful, vicious attack ads" that distorted her positions on guns. This was a three-way race, thanks to the candidacy of former Ramsey County prosecutor Tom Foley, a long-time DFLer who ran on the ticket of Governor Jesse Ventura's Independence party. Once again, McCollum won unexpectedly easily, 48%–31%, with 21% for Foley. She was the first woman elected to the House from Minnesota since Coya Knutson was famously called home by her estranged husband in 1958 (see 7th District).

In the House, McCollum has a consistently liberal voting record. Although she worked on the No Child Left Behind Act as a member of the Education and Workforce Committee and backed the House version of the bill, she was one of six Democrats who voted against the final agreement and the only committee Democrat to do so. She made the national news when Fox News Channel showed footage of her leading the House in the Pledge of Allegiance and omitting the words "under God." She joined Senator Joe Lieberman in condemning excessive sex and violence in video games. McCollum cited faulty intelligence in strongly opposing the war in Iraq. Despite bitter divisions among local Hmongs, she called for normal trade relations with Laos, and the measure was enacted after the 2004 election. She quickly became an ally of Nancy Pelosi, whom she calls a mentor, and delivered the speech formally nominating her as party whip in October 2001. In return, McCollum has won some leadership assignments, including a seat on the steering committee.

McCollum was an early supporter of Wesley Clark in the 2004 presidential campaign. She has been reelected easily. In 2004, Peter Vento, son of the late congressman, ran as the Independent Party nominee, though he did not campaign much; he got 9% of the vote. McCollum was among the many Democrats mentioned as possible Senate candidates after Mark Dayton announced his retirement in February 2005, but in March she said she would not run.

FIFTH DISTRICT

Rep. Martin Olav Sabo (DFL)

Elected 1978, 14th term; b. Feb. 28, 1938, Crosby, ND; home, Minneapolis; Augsburg Col., B.A. 1959; Lutheran; married (Sylvia).

Elected Office: MN House of Reps., 1960–78, Min. Ldr., 1968–72, Speaker, 1972–78.

DC Office: 2336 RHOB, 20515, 202-225-4755; Fax: 202-225-4886; Web site: www.house.gov/sabo.

District Office: Minneapolis, 612-664-8000.

Committees: *Appropriations* (4th of 29 D): Defense; Homeland Security (RMM).

Group Ratings

	ADA	ACLU	AFS	LCV	ITIC	NTU	COC	ACU	NTLC	CHC
2004	100	95	100	100	20	7	24	0	3	15
2003	95	—	100	95	—	22	23	13	—	—

National Journal Ratings

	2003 LIB	—	2003 CONS		2004 LIB	—	2004 CONS
Economic	71%	—	27%		89%	—	8%
Social	92%	—	0%		83%	—	17%
Foreign	70%	—	27%		98%	—	0%

Key Votes of the 108th Congress

1. Drilling in ANWR	N	5. DC School Vouchers	N	9. Ban Same-Sex Marriage	N
2. Approve Bush Tax Cuts	N	6. Ban Human Cloning	N	10. Fund Iraq War	Y
3. Medicare/Rx Bill	N	7. Restrict Gun Liability	N	11. Bar Cuba Embargo Funds	Y
4. Bar Overtime Pay Regs.	Y	8. Ban Partial-Birth Abortion	N	12. Intelligence Reorg.	N

Election Results

2004 general	Martin Olav Sabo (DFL)	218,434	(70%)	($497,073)
	Daniel Nielsen Mathias (R)	76,600	(24%)	($11,504)
	Jay Pond (Green)	17,984	(6%)	
2004 primary	Martin Olav Sabo (DFL)	23,047	(91%)	
	Dick Franson (DFL)	2,264	(9%)	
2002 general	Martin Olav Sabo (DFL)	171,572	(67%)	($507,205)
	Daniel Nielsen Mathias (R)	66,271	(26%)	($9,589)
	Tim Davis (Green)	17,825	(7%)	

Prior Winning Percentages: 2000 (69%); 1998 (67%); 1996 (64%); 1994 (62%); 1992 (63%); 1990 (73%); 1988 (72%); 1986 (73%); 1984 (70%); 1982 (66%); 1980 (70%); 1978 (62%)

The People		Race/Ethnic Origin	Ancestry	
Area size:	130 sq. mi.	71.2% White	German: 17.6%	Norwegian: 9.3%
Urban population:	100.0%	12.8% Black	Irish: 7.6%	
Rural population:	0.0%	5.1% Asian	**2004 Presidential Vote**	
Pop. 2000:	614,935	1.5% Native Am.	Kerry (D) 237,418	(71%)
Median income:	$41,569	0.1% Hawaiian	Bush (R) 92,797	(28%)
Poverty status:	12.7%	3.0% Two+ races	Other 5,060	(2%)
Military veterans:	10.8%	0.2% Other	**2000 Presidential Vote**	
		6.0% Hispanic Origin	Gore (D) 185,874	(63%)
			Bush (R) 85,447	(29%)
			Other 24,577	(8%)
			Cook Partisan Voting Index: D +21	

Occupation   Blue collar: 17.9%   White collar: 67.2%   Gray collar: 14.9%

From almost nowhere in Minneapolis today can you see the geographic feature that put the city here—the Falls of St. Anthony, the head of navigation on the Mississippi River, where waters rush in rapids beneath low downtown bridges. In olden days, every riverboat had to stop here, and the waterpower generated by the falls was the energy source first for pioneers' grist mills and then for the giant grain mills that processed the wheat of the northern Great Plains into food for the United States and the world. By 1890 Minneapolis and St. Paul made up one of America's largest urban areas, living mainly off grain. Today, Minneapolis is a center of high-tech industry, banking and finance. It is a regional railroad center, home of Northwest Airlines, and the center of an economic region that extends almost 1,000 miles to the Rocky Mountains in Montana.

The city of Minneapolis, plus a few of its older, adjoining suburbs, comprise the 5th Congressional District. In the southwest corner are the affluent neighborhoods around Lake Calhoun and Lake Harriet—long built-up and proudly maintained, amidst trees that turn beautifully golden in early autumn. Not far away are Minneapolis's skywalk-laced downtown skyscrapers, the museum quarter up on the hill above Hennepin Avenue, and the Hubert H. Humphrey Metrodome, nicknamed (inaccurately, say some) the "Homerdome" but still unloved by baseball fans. Straddling the Mississippi River is the University of Minnesota, which has fostered the area's cutting-edge biotech research and medical innovations. Most of the 5th District, however, is lower on the income scale. Many of the working-class neighborhoods of small frame houses on grid streets with ample parks are now kept up by elderly homeowners, while new immigrants live in small communities of their own. Minneapolis does not have the endless stretches of abandoned blocks commonly seen in Chicago or Detroit, but all is not well, and crime rates are uncomfortably high.

For a place often thought of as monochromatically white and Scandinavian, the city is a place of surprising diversity. To the northeast, behind the railroad and warehouse district along the Mississippi, are many Hmongs from Laos. Hennepin County is now home to the largest number of African immigrants in the state, following a decade in which African immigrants to Minnesota jumped sevenfold. The Jewish community here has increased with immigrants from the former Soviet Union. Ticket machines on the new Hiawatha Avenue light-rail line, from downtown to the airport and Mall of America, do business in four languages—English, Spanish, Hmong and Somali.

The 5th is the most heavily Democratic district in the state. Minneapolis's political liberalism is drawn from the Yankee tradition of clean government, the Scandinavian tradition of cooperative enterprise and the industrial-labor tradition of economic redistribution. To this has been added in recent years, by feminists and the graduate student proletariat, a more antic cultural liberalism that is alien to both. George W. Bush got only 29% of the vote here in 2000, his worst performance in the state's eight districts. Al Gore and John Kerry carried this district by more than 2–1 margins.

The congressman from the 5th District is Martin Olav Sabo, born in North Dakota, the son of Norwegian immigrants, a DFL leader who has spent all his adult life in politics. He was elected to the Minnesota legislature in 1960 at age 22, was the minority leader at 30 and Speaker at 34. In 1978 he was elected to the House and in his first year got a seat on the Appropriations Committee. It began as a quiet career: Sabo can be articulate, even humorous, and certainly is knowledgeable and averse to the cheap shot. But he pursued his career with a certain Scandinavian reticence and aversion to national publicity that is unusual in Congress. Sabo also served on the Budget Committee, where he wrote the 1990 budget summit agreement's "firewalls" between defense and domestic spending, intended by liberals as an attempt to save domestic programs and by conservatives as a way of protecting the Pentagon. After Leon Panetta was appointed OMB director in 1993, Sabo defeated the more moderate John Spratt of South Carolina to become Budget Committee chairman. In that position it fell to Sabo to defend the first Clinton budget, which eventually passed by 218–216. Although that budget had untoward political consequences for many Democrats, he takes credit for passing "the largest deficit-reduction package in history."

In the minority, Sabo concentrated on Appropriations, where he is an ally of ranking Democrat David Obey. Sabo is senior Democrat on the Homeland Security Subcommittee, and has been active on transportation issues. He successfully pressured Homeland Security Department head Tom Ridge to abandon a plan to reduce the federal air marshal program, and he criticized flaws in the airline passenger screening program. With his penchant for mass transit, Sabo got more than $335 million to construct the local Hiawatha transit line.

On other issues, Sabo pursues goals both practical and visionary. He calls himself a "liberal decentrist," which means he supports liberal social causes but believes that the federal government should intervene only when local governments can't, or need help. He has a bill for public financing of House general election campaigns, and he wants to extend nationwide Minnesota's same-day voter registration. He opposed normal trade relations with China, despite the importunings of Minnesota's 3M, Honeywell and Cargill. Sabo filed an amendment to require additional safety inspections of trucks entering the United States from Mexico, which sparked major conflicts within Congress, with the Bush administration and with the Mexican government; the result was a compromise that delayed opening the border until there were systems in place to verify driver's licenses, train inspectors and install truck scales.

Continuing to practice old-fashioned political door-knocking that he began when he campaigned for Adlai Stevenson in 1956, Sabo has been reelected by wide margins of 2–1 or more. The locals concede that his Norwegian habits leave little conversation; it's simply good to be seen, he maintains. His daughter Julie was a state senator who ran unsuccessfully for lieutenant governor on the DFL ticket with Roger Moe in 2002.

SIXTH DISTRICT

Rep. Mark Kennedy (R)

Elected 2000, 3d term; b. Apr. 11, 1957, Benson; home, Watertown; St. John's U. (MN) B.A. 1979, U. of MI, M.B.A. 1983; Catholic; married (Debbie).

Professional Career: CPA, Arthur Anderson, 1978–81; Dir. of Finance, Pillsbury Co., 1983–87; Treas., Federated Dept. Stores, 1987–92; CFO, Shopko Stores, 1992–95; CFO Dept. 56, Inc., 1995–2000.

DC Office: 1415 LHOB, 20515, 202-225-2331; Fax: 202-225-6475; Web site: www.markkennedy.house.gov.

District Offices: Buffalo, 763-684-1600; Hugo, 651-653-5933; St. Cloud, 320-259-0099.

Committees: *Financial Services* (23d of 37 R): Capital Markets, Insurance & Government Sponsored Enterprises; Domestic and International Monetary Policy, Trade & Technology; Oversight & Investigations. *Transportation & Infrastructure* (24th of 41 R): Aviation; Highways, Transit & Pipelines.

Group Ratings

	ADA	ACLU	AFS	LCV	ITIC	NTU	COC	ACU	NTLC	CHC
2004	5	0	0	0	100	69	100	92	92	100
2003	5	—	0	25	—	63	93	84	—	—

National Journal Ratings

	2003 LIB	—	2003 CONS		2004 LIB	—	2004 CONS
Economic	9%	—	84%		23%	—	76%
Social	5%	—	87%		28%	—	70%
Foreign	0%	—	89%		17%	—	78%

Key Votes of the 108th Congress

1. Drilling in ANWR	Y	5. DC School Vouchers	Y	9. Ban Same-Sex Marriage	Y
2. Approve Bush Tax Cuts	Y	6. Ban Human Cloning	Y	10. Fund Iraq War	Y
3. Medicare/Rx Bill	Y	7. Restrict Gun Liability	Y	11. Bar Cuba Embargo Funds	N
4. Bar Overtime Pay Regs.	N	8. Ban Partial-Birth Abortion	Y	12. Intelligence Reorg.	Y

Election Results

2004 general	Mark Kennedy (R)	203,669	(54%)	($2,649,747)
	Patty Wetterling (DFL)	173,309	(46%)	($1,935,813)
2004 primary	Mark Kennedy (R)	unopposed		
2002 general	Mark Kennedy (R)	164,747	(57%)	($1,891,653)
	Janet Robert (DFL)	100,738	(35%)	($2,192,965)
	Dan Becker (I)	21,484	(7%)	($22,996)

Prior Winning Percentages: 2000 (48%)

The People		Race/Ethnic Origin	Ancestry	
Area size:	3,237 sq. mi.	94.9% White	German: 29.9%	Norwegian: 10.0%
Urban population:	63.8%	0.9% Black	Irish: 8.0%	
Rural population:	36.2%	1.4% Asian	**2004 Presidential Vote**	
Pop. 2000:	614,935	0.4% Native Am.	Bush (R) 216,574	(57%)
Median income:	$56,862	0.0% Hawaiian	Kerry (D) 161,601	(42%)
Poverty status:	4.7%	1.0% Two+ races	Other 4,576	(1%)
Military veterans:	12.4%	0.1% Other	**2000 Presidential Vote**	
		1.3% Hispanic Origin	Bush (R) 152,977	(52%)
			Gore (D) 123,247	(42%)
			Other 15,954	(5%)
			Cook Partisan Voting Index: R + 5	
Occupation	Blue collar: 26.9%	White collar: 60.3%	Gray collar: 12.8%	

The earliest settlers to the Twin Cities of Minneapolis and St. Paul came up the Mississippi River, or up the rail lines that were soon built on the bottomlands beside. They lived within walking distance of the mills and factories and railyards; as the first streetcars and then automobiles allowed them to live farther from work, they spread out in St. Paul and Minneapolis and then all around the lake-strewn countryside. The flatlands are bleak here when the winter sun struggles to shine through gray clouds. The lakes are often surrounded by, and sometimes indistinguishable from, swamps. Stillwater, an old lumber mill town built by pioneers on the hills above the St. Croix River, once nearly became Minnesota's capital, but later turned into an economic backwater, its Victorian structures ill-tended. Even so, the creativity and productivity of Minnesotans have turned this superficially grim countryside into some of the nation's most pleasant suburbs. Taking maximum advantage of their lakes, they refurbished old towns and farmhouses and built comfortable homes in new subdivisions.

The 6th Congressional District of Minnesota is a suburban and exurban district north of St. Paul and Minneapolis. It dips as far south and east as Stillwater, with new riverfront housing developments along the St. Croix. It spreads north over Washington and Anoka Counties, just north of the Twin Cities, with a mix of upscale and working class suburbs. To the northwest, along the Mississippi River, are Wright, Sherburne and Benton Counties, which have grown rapidly, from 140,000 in 1990 to 224,000 in 2003, up 59%. These were once rural areas, with here and there a small town and a small city as the county seat. Now this lake country is filling with new subdivisions and shopping centers, young voters usually from ancestrally DFL families who have become the key swing voters in the state. Farther to the northwest, the district also includes the eastern half of St. Cloud-based Stearns County, a heavily German Catholic area and a stronghold of anti-abortion sentiment. The 1990s saw an influx of Vietnamese, Chinese and Japanese people into St. Cloud, so that by 2000 there were more Asians than either blacks or Hispanics in the 6th District; since then, many Somalis have moved in. In 1998 the district, especially the fast-growing counties, was Jesse Ventura Country. At the same time, the newcomers tended to vote Republican for other office, and ever since. George W. Bush carried the district 52%–42% in 2000 and 57%–42% in 2004, the latter his best showing in any Minnesota district. In 2002 it produced big margins for Republican Senator Norm Coleman and Governor Tim Pawlenty.

The congressman from the 6th District is Mark Kennedy, a Republican first elected in 2000 in the old 2d District, which stretched to the state's southwest corner. He was born in Benson and grew up in Murdock and Pequot Lakes; his great-grandfather was a Swift County commissioner and his grandfather was mayor of Murdock. Kennedy graduated from St. John's University in 1978 and University of Michigan business school in 1983. He was a CPA with Arthur Andersen before becoming director of finance for Pillsbury. His path up the corporate ladder led him to Cincinnati as treasurer of Federated Department Stores, to Green Bay as chief financial officer of ShopKo, and finally back to Minneapolis as a senior vice president at Department 56, before he ran for Congress in 2000—his first bid for elected office. During those years he did political work for Senator Rudy Boschwitz and he served in 1998 as state Republican platform co-chairman.

In 2000, Kennedy challenged incumbent David Minge, a "common sense Democrat," as Minge put it. With his strong business background and the slogan "Mark Kennedy means business," Kennedy said that he could help the district market its farm products abroad and bring more businesses to its small towns. He campaigned on opening foreign markets to Minnesota's farm products, repealing the marriage penalty and the estate tax, and improving the district's roads. Minge remained in Washington for much of October while Kennedy was busy campaigning at home. Kennedy was one Republican who benefited from the coattails of George W. Bush, who carried the old district with 54% of the vote. Kennedy won by 155 votes.

In the House, Kennedy has a voting record that fits comfortably among House conservatives. In his first term, he took the advice of Republican leaders to build a large campaign war chest and prepare for the next campaign. The most important decision that he made then came after a panel of five judges issued the redistricting map on March 19, 2002. Kennedy's home was shifted inside the 6th District by 800 yards, but it included only Wright County from his old district, with just 14% of the old district's voters. The NRCC polled the new district and party leaders pledged to clear the primary field for him; Kennedy decided six days after the court decision to run in the new 6th. In July, Stillwater attorney Janet Robert announced her candidacy as a Democrat. She was anti-abortion and pro-gun, and had little political experience. But she had one attribute that endeared her to national Democrats: She was willing to spend lavishly on her own campaign. With her heavy advertising barrage, she attacked Kennedy for voting against corporate reforms, and she claimed that he misled shareholders when he was in the private sector. The *St. Paul Pioneer-Press* called her ads "among the dirtiest and most untruthful in the flood of negative ads this year." Robert spent $1.6 million of her own money, nearly the total of what Kennedy raised, but she had little to show for it. Kennedy won 57%–35%, a far bigger margin than expected.

Secure in his new district, Kennedy took advantage of the opportunity to make his mark on a variety of issues. He took several amendments to the House floor. On the highway bill, his proposal to repeal the permanent authority for tolls on existing highway lanes and replace that with tolls for new FAST (Freeing Alternatives for Speedy Transportation) lanes passed 231–193. In 2004 Kennedy lost, 162–259, in his attempt to replace a provision delaying the military base closing round from 2005 to 2007, but his view prevailed in the final version of the bill. When he sought to cut $425 million to a World Bank loan program that he said would help Iran develop nuclear weapons, he was defeated 133–288; opponents said that the proposal would have cut into other foreign aid.

At home, Kennedy had another competitive campaign in 2004. His Democratic challenger was Patty Wetterling, a former math teacher and soccer mom and a political newcomer who raised nearly $2 million based on her previous activity as a national advocate for missing children, including creation of the Wetterling Foundation; her 11-year-old son Jacob was abducted in 1989 and was never found. In the campaign, Wetterling emphasized her skills at listening to people; she conceded that she had a lot to learn, including on farm issues, and was something of a one-issue candidate on behalf of missing and exploited children. Kennedy emphasized local accomplishments and played to his party base, while Republican ads attacked Wetterling for campaign flip-flops and fundraising from national liberal groups. In the spirited contest, Kennedy prevailed, 54%–46%, with majorities in each of the seven counties; he ran strongest, 58%–42%, in his Wright County base. After the election, Kennedy made little secret of his interest in running against Senator Mark Dayton in 2006. Dayton announced his retirement on February 2005 and two days later Kennedy announced he was running for the seat. Kennedy was endorsed by Senator Norm Coleman and 26 of the 31 Republican state senators and seemed to have support from national Republicans; 1st District Republican Gil Gutknecht, who had expressed interest in the race, said in March 2005 he would not run for the Senate. A handful of local Republican officials showed interest in replacing Kennedy in the House, including state Senator Michele Bachmann, state Representatives Jim Knoblach and Phil Krinkie and former state Education Commissioner Cheri Pierson Yecke. On the Democratic side, former Transportation Commissioner Elwyn Tinklenberg announced he would run; Wetterling also was mentioned as a possible candidate, though in mid-2005 she seemed to be leaning toward the Senate seat.

SEVENTH DISTRICT

Rep. Collin Peterson (DFL)

Elected 1990, 8th term; b. June 29, 1944, Fargo, ND; home, Detroit Lakes; Moorhead St. U., B.A. 1966; Lutheran; divorced.

Military Career: Army Natl. Guard, 1963–69.

Elected Office: MN Senate, 1976–86.

Professional Career: Accountant, 1966–90.

DC Office: 2159 RHOB, 20515, 202-225-2165; Fax: 202-225-1593; Web site: collinpeterson.house.gov.

District Offices: Detroit Lakes, 218-847-5056; Marshall, 507-537-2299; Montevideo, 320-269-8888; Red Lake Falls, 218-253-4356; Redwood Falls, 507-637-2270; Willmar, 320-235-1061.

Committees: *Agriculture* (RMM of 21 D).

Group Ratings

	ADA	ACLU	AFS	LCV	ITIC	NTU	COC	ACU	NTLC	CHC
2004	55	30	75	18	60	27	76	52	25	58
2003	70	—	88	20	—	33	70	54	—	—

National Journal Ratings

	2003 LIB	—	2003 CONS		2004 LIB	—	2004 CONS
Economic	53%	—	47%		53%	—	47%
Social	55%	—	45%		50%	—	49%
Foreign	51%	—	48%		55%	—	44%

Key Votes of the 108th Congress

1. Drilling in ANWR	Y	5. DC School Vouchers	N	9. Ban Same-Sex Marriage	Y
2. Approve Bush Tax Cuts	N	6. Ban Human Cloning	*	10. Fund Iraq War	Y
3. Medicare/Rx Bill	Y	7. Restrict Gun Liability	Y	11. Bar Cuba Embargo Funds	Y
4. Bar Overtime Pay Regs.	Y	8. Ban Partial-Birth Abortion	Y	12. Intelligence Reorg.	Y

Election Results

2004 general	Collin Peterson (DFL)	207,628	(66%)	($523,484)
	David Sturrock (R)	106,349	(34%)	($127,271)
2004 primary	Collin Peterson (DFL)	unopposed		
2002 general	Collin Peterson (DFL)	170,234	(65%)	($535,214)
	Dan Stevens (R)	90,342	(35%)	($201,196)

Prior Winning Percentages: 2000 (69%); 1998 (72%); 1996 (68%); 1994 (51%); 1992 (51%); 1990 (54%)

The People		Race/Ethnic Origin	Ancestry	
Area size:	33,745 sq. mi.	93.1% White	German: 28.5%	Norwegian: 20.3%
Urban population:	34.0%	0.3% Black	Swedish: 7.0%	
Rural population:	66.0%	0.5% Asian	**2004 Presidential Vote**	
Pop. 2000:	614,935	2.4% Native Am.	Bush (R) 180,743	(55%)
Median income:	$36,453	0.0% Hawaiian	Kerry (D) 140,332	(43%)
Poverty status:	10.3%	0.9% Two+ races	Other 4,917	(2%)
Military veterans:	13.7%	0.0% Other	**2000 Presidential Vote**	
		2.6% Hispanic Origin	Bush (R) 155,794	(54%)
			Gore (D) 116,099	(40%)
			Other 18,706	(6%)
			Cook Partisan Voting Index: R + 6	

Occupation	Blue collar: 29.2%	White collar: 53.3%	Gray collar: 17.5%

Mark Twain's fabled Mississippi River begins so modestly in Minnesota's Itasca State Park, 2,552 miles from the Gulf of Mexico, that it can be crossed by foot on a series of stones. The lake-strewn country in which the river is born has made its own contributions to American literature: A century ago, Sinclair Lewis grew up in the town of Sauk Centre, which provided grist for his critical but affectionate portrayals of small-town America in *Main Street* and *Babbitt*. In those years, this seemingly placid country was seething with rage, as WASPy nationalists banned German from schools, renamed sauerkraut "liberty cabbage," and boycotted German-American businesses. This fed the bitter isolationism of the 1930s and 1940s, led by Charles Lindbergh, who grew up in Little Falls, just across the border in the 8th, as the son of an isolationist congressman who opposed declaring war on Germany in 1917. This part of Minnesota is probably also the home of Lake Wobegon; Garrison Keillor says he was inspired by small towns in Stearns County that were evenly divided between German Catholics and Norwegian Lutherans. Farther south, where the plains rise above the river-cut gorges, is great farming country, settled more than 100 years ago by Yankees, Germans and Scandinavians. Even today, farmers still toil against the elements to make a profitable living, so productively that their lands are slowly but surely depopulating; 100,000 acres of farmland in the Minnesota River watershed has been taken out of production by the Conservation Reserve Program. This area is the nation's leading producer of sugar beets and a leading producer of turkeys. On the shores of Plum Creek, near Walnut Grove, is where Laura Ingalls Wilder's family came on the way west to the "Little House on the Prairie" in South Dakota; after all their struggles, Laura's family left the farm for town as soon as they could. Their pain would be all too familiar to contemporary residents along the Red River of the North, which overflowed its banks in April 1997, inundating Grand Forks, North Dakota, and East Grand Forks, Minnesota, and dislocating 50,000 residents of the region—America's largest mass evacuation since the Civil War.

The 7th Congressional District of Minnesota covers almost all of the western part of the state. It takes in the wheat-farming plains adjoining North Dakota as well as the German Catholic areas strewn with farm villages named for saints. Many political traditions coexist here: some wheat counties are heavily DFL while heavily Norwegian Otter Tail County leans Republican. The 7th's political history reads like something out of *Lake Wobegon Days*. Back in 1958, DFL Congresswoman Coya Knutson was defeated for reelection when her husband Andy issued a plaintive statement urging her to come home and make his breakfast again; she was the only incumbent Democrat to lose in that heavily Democratic year. Other Scandinavian names followed, of varying partisan affiliations; for three decades this was one of America's prime marginal districts. In 2000 the unpopularity of Clinton administration environmental and gun control policies produced a 54%–40% margin for George W. Bush, his best showing in a Minnesota district. In 2004 ancestral Democratic loyalties resurfaced a bit, and Bush's margin 55%–43% margin here was smaller than in the fast-growing suburban 6th District.

The congressman from the 7th District is Collin Peterson, a Democrat who after four unsuccessful tries won the seat in 1990 and now seems safely entrenched even as the district has become more Republican. Peterson was born in Fargo, North Dakota, grew up across the Red River of the North on a farm in Baker, went to Moorhead State College, then started a CPA office in Detroit Lakes; all are within 50 miles of each other. In 1976 he was elected to the state Senate. He also started running for the House. He lost a DFL caucus in 1982; he lost to Republican Arlan Stangeland in 1984 and 1986 (by only 121 votes the second time; he declared victory and went to Washington to set up an office); he lost the DFL primary in 1988. But in 1990, when the *St. Cloud Times* reported that Stangeland made 341 credit card calls to a woman not his wife, Peterson won with a robust 54%. In office, he has been known as a free spirit, wearing cowboy boots and playing guitar in a country rock band called the Recess Renegades, acting as his own campaign consultant and pilot on flights within the district, and enjoying a cigar—often with Republicans—in the Speaker's Lobby off the House floor. He has a small staff, with community economic development professionals rather than Washington policy wonks. He opposes abortion and gun control; backs farm subsidies and labor unions; opposed Bill Clinton on his 1993 budget, NAFTA and normal trade relations with China. He pulled now-Congresswoman Katherine Harris out of a snow bank during an Aspen ski vacation in 1991; the two dated for a while and remain friends.

In the House Peterson has been something of a populist, with conservative leanings on social issues and definitely a maverick. His political fortune was bolstered by the Republican takeover in 1994, which made him a visibly different kind of Democrat. In 1995, while voting for parts of the Contract with America, he founded with Gary Condit the Blue Dog Democrats for "common sense legislation that embraces the ideas and values of mainstream America." With John Linder, he cosponsored "FairTax," a national sales tax that would replace all income, payroll, corporate and estate taxes. He sided with Republicans on HMO regulation and was one of 16 Democrats to vote for the Medicare/prescription drug bill in November 2003. When Minority Whip Steny Hoyer complained about his vote, Peterson said that the vote meant "life or death" for rural doctors and hospitals in his district. He was one of 10 House Democrats to vote for the Bush tax cut and he voted for the use of force in Iraq; but he opposed trade promotion authority, and said that his local farmers are furious about the Bush administration's trade deals. Peterson is the opposite of many middle-of-the-House Republicans, who favor heavy environmental restrictions; he takes the view of his constituents, who hunt and fish as a way of life and see environmentalists' policies as hindrances. He expressed reservations that the 1996 Freedom to Farm Act would cause low prices and joined the bipartisan majority on the committee in restoring market controls when the farm program was renewed in 2002.

When Charles Stenholm of Texas was defeated in 2004, Peterson was next in line to be ranking minority member on the Agriculture Committee. But his elevation was not automatic; the Democratic Caucus makes the decision and the Democratic leadership sought concessions before supporting him. Minority Leader Nancy Pelosi and other Democrats expressed unhappiness over his independence and demanded that he pay $70,000 in back dues to the Democratic Congressional Campaign Committee. "At the time they [first] asked me, I didn't have the money," Peterson explained to *The Hill.* "My money always comes in late." Democratic leaders had some leverage because Peterson clearly wanted the position; but he had leverage as well, since he could switch parties and almost surely still win reelection. Indeed, Democrats are unlikely to gain a majority until they win more districts like this. In any case, Peterson agreed to be more of a team player and to raise money for other Democrats and he became ranking member on the committee, in time to play an important role when the farm bill comes up for reauthorization in 2007.

Peterson's politics have been a smash hit with 7th District voters and an irritant to local DFL activists, while local Republicans have not produced well-financed opposition. He has not had a close contest since 1994; in 2004, he carried all 35 counties in the district against Marshall city councilor David Sturrock. Peterson laughed off campaign criticism that he supported the "ultra-liberal" Pelosi. Peterson has been mentioned as a possible appointee in the Bush administration, as he was in Jesse Ventura's. But he seems content with serving in the House.

EIGHTH DISTRICT

Rep. James Oberstar (DFL)

Elected 1974, 16th term; b. Sept. 10, 1934, Chisholm; home, Chisholm; St. Thomas Col., B.A. 1956, Col. of Europe, Bruges, Belgium, M.A. 1957; Catholic; married (Jean).

Professional Career: Navy civilian language teacher, Haiti, 1959–63; A.A., U.S. Rep. John Blatnik, 1963–74; A.A., U.S. House Public Works Cmte., 1971–74.

DC Office: 2365 RHOB, 20515, 202-225-6211; Fax: 202-225-0699; Web site: www.house.gov/oberstar.

District Offices: Brainerd, 218-828-4400; Chisholm, 218-254-5761; Duluth, 218-727-7474; North Branch, 651-277-1234.

Committees: *Transportation & Infrastructure* (RMM of 34 D).

Group Ratings

	ADA	ACLU	AFS	LCV	ITIC	NTU	COC	ACU	NTLC	CHC
2004	75	89	100	73	20	10	14	12	0	33
2003	85	—	100	65	—	26	24	40	—	—

National Journal Ratings

	2003 LIB	—	2003 CONS		2004 LIB	—	2004 CONS
Economic	74%	—	26%		82%	—	17%
Social	66%	—	33%		64%	—	36%
Foreign	86%	—	13%		97%	—	2%

Key Votes of the 108th Congress

1. Drilling in ANWR	N	5. DC School Vouchers	N	9. Ban Same-Sex Marriage	*
2. Approve Bush Tax Cuts	N	6. Ban Human Cloning	*	10. Fund Iraq War	N
3. Medicare/Rx Bill	N	7. Restrict Gun Liability	N	11. Bar Cuba Embargo Funds	Y
4. Bar Overtime Pay Regs.	Y	8. Ban Partial-Birth Abortion	Y	12. Intelligence Reorg.	N

Election Results

2004 general	James Oberstar (DFL)	228,586	(65%)	($972,916)
	Mark Groettum (R)	112,693	(32%)	($41,187)
	Other	9,204	(3%)	
2004 primary	James Oberstar (DFL)	37,353	(86%)	
	Michael Johnson (DFL)	6,314	(14%)	
2002 general	James Oberstar (DFL)	194,909	(69%)	($1,022,904)
	Bob Lemen (R)	88,673	(31%)	($17,584)

Prior Winning Percentages: 2000 (68%); 1998 (66%); 1996 (67%); 1994 (66%); 1992 (59%); 1990 (73%); 1988 (75%); 1986 (73%); 1984 (67%); 1982 (77%); 1980 (70%); 1978 (87%); 1976 (100%); 1974 (62%)

The People		Race/Ethnic Origin	Ancestry	
Area size:	32,419 sq. mi.	94.6% White	German: 20.2%	Norwegian: 10.8%
Urban population:	37.4%	0.5% Black	Swedish: 9.6%	
Rural population:	62.6%	0.4% Asian	**2004 Presidential Vote**	
Pop. 2000:	614,935	2.5% Native Am.	Kerry (D) 191,228	(53%)
Median income:	$37,911	0.0% Hawaiian	Bush (R) 167,439	(46%)
Poverty status:	10.4%	1.0% Two+ races	Other 4,890	(1%)
Military veterans:	16.2%	0.0% Other	**2000 Presidential Vote**	
		0.8% Hispanic Origin	Gore (D) 153,962	(49%)
			Bush (R) 136,884	(44%)
			Other 22,302	(7%)
			Cook Partisan Voting Index: D + 4	

Occupation	Blue collar: 28.9%	White collar: 52.9%	Gray collar: 18.2%

In the 1860s, prospectors in the Arrowhead region of the new state of Minnesota, northwest of Lake Superior in the low hills of the Mesabi Range, happened upon the nation's largest veins of iron ore; they moved on, looking for gold. But in the 1880s, Duluth banker George Stone and Philadelphia financier Charlemagne Tower started mining the Iron Range and created the northern end of the lifeline of American heavy industry. South from the Range run rail lines to the port of Duluth, nestled on dramatic bluffs over the always cold and, for long months every winter, frozen waters of Lake Superior—one of the most beautiful settings for a city in North America, and there is similar beauty on the North Shore of Lake Superior for the 150 miles from Duluth to the Canadian border. Duluth was a grain-shipping rival of Chicago and the premier iron ore port. Its city plan was drawn up by Daniel Burnham and its splendid turn-of-the-century buildings still celebrate the triumph of technology and civilization over wilderness and the elements. Millions of tons of ore have been dug out of the Range, loaded into rail cars for the ride to Duluth, and into Great Lakes freighters for shipment to Cleveland, Gary, Detroit, Chicago, Pittsburgh and Buffalo.

For most of the last century, in this land where the Arctic winds blow down over the Canadian Shield's thousands of inland lakes, about 100,000 people have lived on the Iron Range and another 100,000 in Duluth, most of them the products of America's 1880–1924 wave of immigration: Italians, Poles, Serbs and Croats, Jews, Swedes and Finns. In this punishing environment, they worked to the point of exhaustion, built solid houses with staunch central heating and wore layers of warm clothing to survive the winter: it got down to 54 below on the Range in January 2005. Life was rough: The work was hard, the hours long and the pay low. The churches, a separate one for each ethnic group, were the main community institutions. Living conditions improved vastly in the decades of great economic growth after World War II, but life remains rough-hewn today, and there is still economic distress. As iron mines and steel factories got more efficient they needed fewer workers; employment is well below its 1970s peak. As water fills abandoned open-pit mines and factories close and mines are shut down, the Iron Range looks bleaker. Duluth's population was down to 86,000 in 2003, and the Iron Range's was about the same. But all is not moribund. Northwest Airlines, with an $840 million investment from state government in 1993, has built a repair facility in Duluth and a reservations center in the Iron Range. The 2003 energy bill, never passed, included an $800 million loan guarantee for a proposed coal gasification plant in Hoyt Lakes. The port of Duluth still ships large quantities of grain, and in the late 1990s a new taconite and steelmaking factory was built—the first big new plant in more than 20 years. And up in Chisholm in the Range, Cleveland Cliffs, after settling a strike, announced a plant expansion in September 2004, the first one in these parts since the 1970s. There is a Greyhound Museum in Hibbing, where in 1914 an entrepreneur started transporting people in unsaleable open-air Hupmobiles, an enterprise that eventually became the Greyhound Bus Company. People here have made the best of the frozen climate: Nearby Eveleth boasts the world's longest hockey stick, 107 feet long, carved from aspen and aimed at a 700-pound puck; the severe winters of International Falls in Koochiching County have given rise to a cold weather testing industry—this is where automakers test a car's performance under extreme winter conditions.

The 8th Congressional District of Minnesota includes Duluth and the Iron Range, plus much of the north woods and lake country to the west and south; it moves all the way south to the boundaries of the Twin Cities metro area, to Isanti and Chisago Counties, where young families are building new homes near pleasant old lakeside towns. While the Iron Range grows only sluggishly, there has been vigorous population growth in the southern and western counties in the district, as young families move out farther from the Twin Cities core and older Minnesotans move farther north to enjoy life on the lakes. This district has been a bulwark of Minnesota's Democratic-Farmer-Labor Party since it was formed in 1944, and has been considered safely Democratic for years. But there are signs of change. In 2000, cultural issues like gun control and environmental restrictions here moved opinion toward the Republicans; George W. Bush lost the 8th District to Al Gore by only 49%–44%, a much smaller margin than his father's 60%–40% loss 12 years earlier. Bush campaigned on the Iron Range in July 2004 but the DFL came back some distance: John Kerry won here 53%–46%.

The congressman from the 8th District is Jim Oberstar, a Democrat first elected in 1974— "part scholar and part Iron Range street fighter, part pothole-filling ward healer and part workaholic," in the words of *St. Paul Pioneer Press*. Oberstar grew up in the Iron Range city of Chisholm, where his father was an iron miner and union official, who sent him off to St. Thomas College with $2,500 saved in quarters at the Slovenian National Benefit Society; Oberstar has been known to sing polka songs in Slovenian at a House Democratic retreat. He studied French in college and in Belgium; for four years he was a civilian employee of the U.S. Naval Mission to Haiti, teaching French and Creole to Marines, and French and English to Haitians (he also speaks Serbo-Croatian, Italian and Spanish). Then, in 1963, at 29, he landed a job as chief of staff to Congressman John Blatnik in Washington: he has been working for the 8th District for more than four decades. When Blatnik retired in 1974, Oberstar won a primary over Tony Perpich, brother of Governor Rudy Perpich. He won tough primaries in 1980 and 1984, the latter after briefly running for the Senate.

Oberstar's views are in the liberal Catholic tradition. He believes in an economically active government and has little faith in economic markets. He was long dubious about American military involvement abroad, especially in Central America, but favored the 1994 deployment in Haiti. He voted against the Iraq war resolution in October 2002. He is an opponent of abortion and a backer of adoption, sponsoring bills to insure family and medical leave and dependent deductions for families in the process of adopting; when he first proposed a $1,500 adoption tax deduction in the 1970s he was laughed out of Ways and Means, but now, thanks in large part to his effort, there is a $5,000 tax credit.

From this North Country district, Oberstar has been a supporter of local hunting and fishing activities and of the steel industry. When normal trade relations with China came before the House, he tried to get an amendment of the 1974 trade act that would treat steel slab imports as a direct threat to taconite miners; when the administration wasn't interested, he voted against the bill. He was disappointed by George W. Bush's steel tariffs in March 2002, because imported semi-finished slab steel, which competes with Minnesota's taconite, was not subject to the 30% top duty until imports reached 5.4 million tons, 77% of previous levels. But he seeks not just protection but expansion: in July 2003 he brought Minnesota taconite executives to see the new Chinese ambassador to sell taconite pellets to China.

Since October 1995, Oberstar has been ranking Democrat on Transportation and Infra-structure—a position of real power, even in a Republican Congress. This committee has a long tradition of bipartisanship, and of sponsoring members' roads (and, since 1994, other transpor-tation) projects; it has 75 members, the largest in the House. For six years Oberstar and Chairman Bud Shuster worked to make it more powerful than ever. Their great monument was the May 1998 TEA-21 transportation bill, with $217 billion in spending, including $10 billion in projects earmarked by members. Back when Oberstar's boss John Blatnik was chairman, the committee's power was threatened by an alliance of environmentalists and fiscal conservatives; by 1998 it was carrying all before it. Another reason: the 1991 ISTEA, of which 1998's TEA-21 was the reauthorization, included spending for mass transit, bicycle trails and pollution control research, at the option of states or House members. This has helped win the support of many liberals; Oberstar himself is a bicycling enthusiast, proud of logging 3,000 miles a year in Washington, Duluth, on the Range and in the Tour de Frog in St. Cloud. One special project is Safe Routes to School, grants for sidewalks, bike paths and safe crossings to encourage kids to walk to school; Oberstar has pushed for another $1 billion over six years and claims that the programs has stimulated states to raise spending on this from $20 million to $750 million. In April 2004 Oberstar and the new Transportation Chairman, Don Young, persuaded the House to pass a $275 billion, six year bill; the Senate in February 2004 passed a $318 billion bill. The White House insisted on capping spending at $256 billion, and the result was that no bill was passed in 2003 and 2004. Oberstar and Young were unfazed. In March 2005 the House passed a $284 billion bill by a vote of 417–9.

Oberstar once chaired Transportation's Aviation Subcommittee and remains involved in aviation issues. He worked hard for the state investment in Northwest Airlines, but criticized the company when it cut jobs in Duluth below the agreed on level in early 2004; by December most of the jobs were restored. He was one of the architects of the airline bailout bill in fall 2001 and strongly pushed for federal employees in airport security. When the bill to limit FAA regulation of private spaceflight until 2012 came forward on the last day of the lame duck session in 2004, Oberstar urged caution. But the bill passed 269–120 and passed the Senate a month later.

Oberstar's one political setback came in 1984, when he ran for the Senate but was denied endorsement by the liberal DFL convention. In the 8th District he has been re-elected by very wide margins; longtime DFL voters may be moving away from Democrats higher up on the ticket, but they remain faithful to Oberstar.

★ MISSISSIPPI ★

Mississippi bears the weight of a tragic history as it takes quickening steps toward the future. This green land was settled in a rush in Jacksonian America, mostly by small farmers heading west from Georgia and south from Tennessee—and also by a few big planters, who made and sometimes lost vast fortunes, built grand mansions and sent their sons to fight in the Civil War. For a century afterward, as industrial farmers drained the Delta lands, Missis-sippi with its racial segregation, subsistence farmers and sharecroppers and low wages, lived apart from most of America. Faulkner's Mississippi never knew the Homestead Act, the giant factories, the rushes of immigration, the rise of suburbs that were the indispensable backdrop of most of 20th century American life. Mississippi never developed great cities—its two commercial metropolises are just outside its borders, Memphis and New Orleans. But if it did not excel at commerce, it did produce great art. Mississippi gave us the music of the blues and Elvis Presley. It gave the world William Faulkner and Eudora Welty, Walker Percy and Shelby Foote. Their work was informed by a sense of the tragic missing or forgotten in most of America, where life is a triumphant sales pitch or a labor-saving invention.

Mississippi has made much progress in the last three decades, but the past still hangs heavy. For years no other state had such a painful contrast between image and reality, between an ideal sincerely strived for and the tawdry facts of everyday life. Magnolia trees on the lawns of

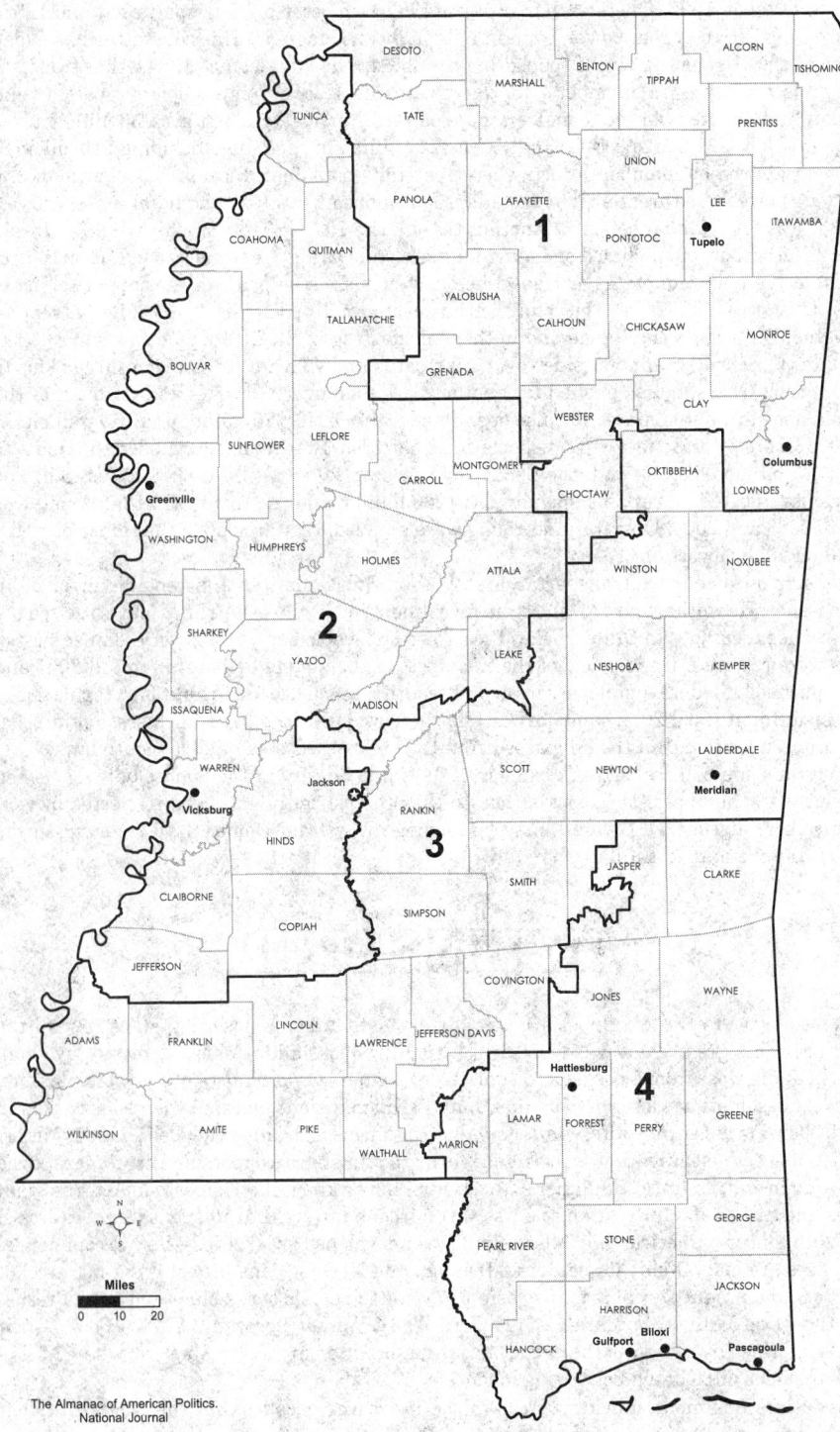

The Almanac of American Politics.
National Journal

Congressional district boundaries were first effective for 2002.

antebellum mansions, golden-haired young women in white dresses on the veranda, faithful black servants and retainers: This was once the ideal. And behind it stood loose-jointed frame houses and unpainted back-country stores, cabins without indoor plumbing and poor white crossroads clustered with askew advertising signs. This is a state, writes David Sansing, with "two souls, two hearts, two minds. We have the highest rate of illiteracy and the largest number of Pulitzer Prize winners in literature. We at one time have the scent of magnolias and the smell of burning crosses." Mississippi for years ranked 50th, often a very low 50th, among states in income, literacy, health and education levels, despite the best efforts of civic, political and business leaders. As Faulkner said of his state, "You don't love because: you love despite."

Today Mississippi still ranks 50th on many scales, but the gulf between Mississippi and the rest of America has narrowed enormously. In 1940, Mississippi had an economy based on low-wage, subsistence or sharecropper agriculture and a system of racial segregation enforced often by violence. If history is, as Sir Henry Maine wrote, the story of the progress from status to contract, then old Mississippi was still at the beginning, for status—race—meant just about everything. In the years since, Mississippi has moved, not always willingly, from status to contract, in its economy and in race relations. Per capita income in Mississippi was 36% of the national average in 1940; in 1990 it was 67% and in 2003 it was 74%, well below average but, given the lower cost of living here, a level recognizably American. In the 1990s incomes increased smartly and poverty declined. Most Mississippians of 50 years ago would be astonished by the physical comforts and mechanical marvels their grandchildren take for granted today: Nearly every classroom in the state is air-conditioned and is being wired to the Internet. They would be astonished as well by relations between blacks and whites. As *The Washington Post's* William Raspberry, a Mississippi native, wrote, "There is an easiness to relationships, a mutual respect and a willingness to move beyond race that, quite frankly, didn't exist during my years in the state. Mississippi is finally a good place to be." Forty years ago, blacks held no public offices in Mississippi; in 2005, the state had more black elected officials than any other, and 11 of 52 state senators and 36 of 122 state representatives were black. The Mississippi traditions of friendliness and courtesy seem to be trumping the historical tradition of racism: Mississippi may rank 50th in incomes, but it ranks number one in per capita charitable giving. Not everyone agrees that the state has moved forward: in 2003, after failing to defeat incumbent Republican Lieutenant Governor Amy Tuck, who is white, Democratic challenger Barbara Blackmon, an African-American state senator, said, "if my skin pigmentation were different, I would be the lieutenant governor of this state."

One way Mississippi has improved is in education. Governor William Winter, elected in 1979, finally made kindergarten mandatory and raised the dropout age to 14; Governor Ray Mabus, elected in 1987, also made major changes. But the uncomfortable fact is that most high taxpayers are white and most public school children are black, because many white children attend private academies. About 40% of state spending goes to education, but those who oppose higher spending or taxes can point to the fact that there is no demonstrated correlation between higher spending and improved test scores and learning. But test scores are rising and dropout rates are falling. Another way Mississippi has improved is by encouraging small businesses and service industry. The number of manufacturing jobs here has dropped since 1990, but the number of service jobs increased even more, and the new jobs tended to pay higher wages.

One big driver of growth has been gambling. Mississippi approved riverboat gambling in 1989, and Mississippi now has 29 casinos, 12 on the Gulf Coast and 9 in once-impoverished Tunica County, just south of Memphis, and the rest scattered along the Mississippi River with one inland. Mississippi is number three in gambling revenues, behind Nevada and New Jersey; gambling has produced 40,000 service jobs, at above-average wages. But this is not an unalloyed good. The original riverboats Mark Twain described in *Life on the Mississippi* were working vehicles, sooty and dangerous, taking chances on the treacherous river, but their captains showed how hard work could get people ahead. Mississippi's riverboat casinos are a form of entertainment, a diversion from gainful economic activity, which teaches the lesson that getting ahead depends on luck rather than talent and hard work.

But Mississippi has other sources of growth. It is home to the nation's second largest furniture industry, around Tupelo, and there has been rapid growth on the highway corridor from Tupelo northwest through Ole Miss's Oxford to the fast-growing suburbs of DeSoto County just south of Memphis. Growth has also been rapid around the $1.4 billion Nissan auto plant opened in May 2003 in Canton, just north of Jackson, attracted by $363 million in state aid and incentives, with 5,000 jobs and thousands more from nearby suppliers. I-55 heading north from Jackson in Madison County and Lakeland Drive heading east into Rankin County have become boom areas. And the Gulf Coast is prospering not only because of casinos but also because of the giant Northrop Grumman shipyard in Senator Trent Lott's hometown of Pascagoula.

Mississippi also seems to be casting aside the get-rich-quick mindset that was apparent so long in its courtrooms. By 2002 the state had become a trial lawyer's paradise, with seven product liability judgments of $100 million or more in six years; medical malpractice lawsuits raised insurance premiums so much that 73 doctors left the state, an obstetric clinic in the Delta closed down temporarily and there was only one neurosurgeon left on the Gulf Coast. Hundreds of cases were brought in tiny, impoverished Jefferson County where juries awarded huge judgments; there were more plaintiffs in court than the county had people. The U.S. Chamber of Commerce ran full-page ads in Mississippi newspapers calling for change, and Democratic Governor Ronnie Musgrove, though supported by trial lawyers, called a special session of the legislature in September 2002 which placed some limits on medical malpractice and product liability cases and on forum-shopping. In November 2002, a pro-plaintiff Supreme Court justice was ousted by the voters. In 2003 Republican Haley Barbour made tort law a major issue in his campaign against Musgrove and won 53%–46%. Barbour called a special session in May 2004 and in June signed a bill capping pain and suffering damages generally to $1 million and to $500,000 in medical malpractice cases, further limiting forum-shopping and protecting "innocent sellers" of faulty products. "I want to tell job creators across America that our scales of justice are now in balance," Barbour said. "It is time for them to come and take another look at Mississippi as a place to locate."

Politically, Mississippi is a conservative state, carried by Republicans in the last seven presidential elections. Republicans have held both U.S. Senate seats since John Stennis retired in 1988 and have generally done well in House elections. But Mississippi Democrats with good old boy personas can be competitive. Democrat Gene Taylor was elected to the heavily Republican Gulf Coast House seat in 1989 and has won by wide margins ever since. But conservative change came in 2003. Lieutenant Governor Amy Tuck, who presides over the Senate, switched to the Republican party in December 2002. Tim Ford, Speaker of the House for 16 years, retired. And Barbour, RNC chairman from 1993 to 1997 and a successful Washington lobbyist, returned home to Yazoo City and won a convincing victory for governor. There has been change too in Mississippi's attitude toward its past. In an April 2001 referendum voters chose by a 65%–35% margin to retain the Confederate battle cross in the state flag and rejected a new design produced by a commission headed by former Governor William Winter. But there was a different response when Winter sounded a call for justice in June 2004 in Neshoba County, where three civil rights workers were murdered in the summer of 1964. Haley Barbour attended and all agreed that an oral history of race relations in Neshoba County should be compiled and that justice still had to be done on the 1964 murders; in June 2005, one of the killers was convicted of manslaughter.

The People		Race/Ethnic Origin			Military veterans: 249,431 (12.0%)	
Pop. 2004 (est):	2,902,966	1,727,908	60.7%	White	WWII: 18.7%	Korea: 13.5%
Pop. 2000:	2,844,658	1,028,473	36.2%	Black	Vietnam: 31.0%	Gulf War: 13.1%
Pop. 1990:	2,573,216	18,349	0.6%	Asian	**Most populous cities (2003):**	
Change 1990–2000:	Up 10.5%	11,224	0.4%	Native Am.	1. Jackson	179,599
% of U.S. total:	1.0%	569	0.0%	Hawaiian	2. Gulfport	71,810
Pop. rank:	31st of 50	17,272	0.6%	Two+ races	3. Biloxi	48,972
Area size:	48,430 sq. mi.	1,294	0.0%	Other	4. Hattiesburg	46,664
State Native:	74.3%	39,569	1.4%	Hisp. Origin	5. Meridian	39,559
Non-citizen:	0.8%	**Ancestry**				
Language		USA: 12.7%		Irish: 6.1%	Urban population: 48.8%	
English: 94.4%	Spanish: 3.1%	English: 5.4%		German: 4.1%	Rural population: 51.2%	
Other Eur.: 1.6%		French: 2.1%				

Education		Work Sector			Legislature		
H.S. Grad:	72.9%	Private: 75.6%		Govt: 17.6%	Senate	28 D 24 R	
College Grad:	16.9%	Self: 6.4%		Family: 0.4%	House	75 D 47 R	
Industry		Unemployment: 7.3%			Legislative Term Limits: No		
Agri: 3.4%	Con: 7.6%	**Household Income**			**Registered Voters**		
Fin: 4.8%	Info: 1.8%	<15k: 24.9%		15-35k: 29.9%	No party registration		
Mfg: 23.7%	Prof: 25.3%	35-50k: 16.4%		50-100k: 22.8%			
Public: 5.1%	Trade: 15.2%	100-150k: 3.9%		>150k: 2.2%			
Other: 13.1%		Median: $31,330					
Occupation		Poverty status: 19.9%					
Blue collar: 31.6%	White collar: 52.3%	**Home Value**					
Gray collar: 16.1%		<50k: 36.4%	50-100k: 38.9%	100-200k: 19.1%	200-300k: 3.7%		
		300-500k: 1.3%	>500k: 0.7%	Median: $64,700			

Presidential politics

Mississippi voted 59%–40% for George W. Bush in 2004—almost the same as his 58%–41% margin four years before or his father's 60%–39% margin in 1988. There is no way of avoiding the conclusion that this is a racially polarized electorate: whites voted 85%–14% for Bush, blacks 90%–10% for John Kerry. White evangelical or born again Protestants made up 48% of the electorate and voted 88%–12% for Bush. Yet it should also be said that few Mississippi whites yearn for a return of racial segregation; they line up with Republicans on a whole raft of other issues—defense, crime, cultural attitudes, taxes—just as most blacks line up with Democrats on the same issues. And on some issues they are on the same page: whites voted 89% and blacks 77% for a constitutional amendment banning same-sex marriage in November 2004.

Mississippi holds a presidential primary on Southern Super Tuesday, which fell on March 9 in 2004, one week after the race for the Democratic nomination was over.

2004 Presidential Vote		
Bush (R)	684,981	(59%)
Kerry (D)	457,766	(40%)
Nader (Ref)	3,175	(0%)
Other	6,223	(1%)

2004 Democratic Presidential Primary		
Kerry (D)	59,815	(78%)
Edwards (D)	5,582	(7%)
Sharpton (D)	3,933	(5%)
Dean (D)	1,997	(3%)
Clark (D)	1,878	(2%)
Other	3,093	(4%)

2000 Presidential Vote		
Bush (R)	572,844	(58%)
Gore (D)	404,614	(41%)
Nader (Green)	8,122	(1%)
Other	8,604	(1%)

Congressional districting

Mississippi lost one of its five House districts in the 2000 Census; this is the first time Mississippi has had just four congressmen since the 1840s. In 2001 Democrats held the governorship and both houses of the legislature, and one might have expected that they would draw a plan ousting one of the state's two Republican congressmen. But the state House, led by Speaker Tim Ford, and the state Senate, led by Lieutenant

109th Congress Lineup	
2 D	2 R

108th Congress Lineup	
2 D	2 R

Governor Amy Tuck, could not agree on a plan. Ford wanted to draw a plan connecting northeast Mississippi, home of Republican incumbent Roger Wicker, and DeSoto County, just south of Memphis, with part of Rankin County, just east of Jackson and home of Republican incumbent Chip Pickering. Republicans called this the "tornado district" because it was shaped something like a funnel cloud. This plan would leave Pickering with the choice of running against Wicker in a primary where he would be at a great geographic disadvantage or running in a new 3d District against incumbent Democrat Ronnie Shows in a district that was 38% black. Tuck (who in December 2002 switched parties and became a Republican), Republicans and northeast Mississippians in the Senate favored a plan that would combine most of the old 3d and 4th Districts, represented by Pickering and Shows and would be 34% black. Governor Ronnie Musgrove called a special session in November 2001, and on the first day, the Senate and House passed versions of Ford's and Tuck's plans. Negotiations for a compromise went nowhere, and Ford moved to adjourn the session.

Action shifted to the courts. Democrats filed a lawsuit in state court and Republicans filed one in federal court. The Mississippi Supreme Court left the Democrats' case to Hinds County Chancery Judge Patricia Wise, elected from a heavily Democratic district. On December 21 she adopted a plan put forward by Democrats with a 38% black 3d District. On December 26 Attorney General Mike Moore forwarded it to the U.S. Justice Department for the preclearance required by the Voting Rights Act. On January 15, the three-judge federal court in the case brought by Republicans took the issue away from the Chancery Court on the ground that the Justice Department might not finish its review by Mississippi's March 1 filing deadline; the federal judges put forward a plan with a 30% black 3d District, similar to the state Senate's. On February 14 the Justice Department sent a five-page letter to Mississippi officials asking them to "explain the state's view of the legal basis for the Mississippi Supreme Court to vest a chancery court with jurisdiction to create and implement a statewide redistricting plan." Democrats complained that that was not an issue pertinent to the Voting Rights Act and that the three federal judges, all appointed by Republican presidents, were improperly trying to impose a plan favoring Pickering, who is the son of federal Judge Charles Pickering, whose nomination to a federal appeals court judgeship was rejected on party lines by the Senate Judiciary Committee in March 2002. On February 25 the federal court ordered its own plan into effect; Supreme Court Justice Antonin Scalia rejected an emergency appeal by Democrats.

Democrats were furious. They claimed that DOJ dragged its feet during the preclearance process and that Scalia, a friend of the Pickering family, should have recused himself from the case. But the districts in the federal court plan were about as compact as possible given the state's geography and the imperative, which everyone agreed on, of creating a black-majority 2d District. Democrats persisted in their appeal of the federal court decision even though it was obvious its lines would be in effect for the November 2002 election. On March 31, the Supreme Court ruled against their claim, holding that a federal court may impose a congressional redistricting plan when a state fails to properly enact its own plan.

Governor

Haley Barbour (R)

Elected 2003, term expires Jan. 2008, 1st term; b. Oct. 22, 1947, Yazoo City; home, Yazoo City; Attended U. of MS; U. of MS, J.D. 1973; Presbyterian; married (Marsha).

Professional Career: State Dir., US Census Bureau, 1969–70; RNC Committeeman, 1984–98; Dir., White House Office of Political Affairs, 1985–87; CEO, Founder, Barbour, Griffith & Rogers, 1991-present; Chmn., RNC, 1993–97.

Office: State Capitol, P.O. Box 139, Jackson, 39205, 601-359-3150; Fax: 601-359-3741; Web site: www.governor.state.ms.us.

Election Results

2003 general	Haley Barbour (R)	470,404	(53%)
	Ronnie Musgrove (D)	409,787	(46%)
	Other	14,296	(2%)
2003 primary	Haley Barbour (R)	158,284	(83%)
	Mitch Tyner (R)	31,762	(17%)
1999 general	Ronnie Musgrove (D)	379,034	(50%)
	Mike Parker (R)	370,691	(49%)
	Other	14,213	(2%)

Haley Barbour was elected governor in 2003, only the second Republican to win the office since Reconstruction. He was born and grew up in Yazoo City in the Mississippi Delta. His father was a local lawyer who died of a heart attack when Haley was 2 years old, leaving his 31-year-old mother to raise the three Barbour boys. A star athlete and class valedictorian, Barbour was voted Mr. Yazoo High School and won scholarship money to attend Ole Miss but he left his senior year before graduating to take a job on Richard Nixon's 1968 campaign. He returned to Ole Miss and graduated from its law school in 1973; then he ran Gerald Ford's 1976 campaign in the Southeast and worked on John Connally's campaign for president in 1980. In 1982 he was the Republican nominee for Senate against Senator John C. Stennis, then the senior member of the Senate, a chairman of Armed Services from 1969–81 and later chairman of the Appropriations Committee. Stennis had not faced a serious challenge since 1947, when he was elected to replace Theodore G. Bilbo, and some expected that the octogenarian would not seek reelection in 1982. But he did and Barbour approached the issue of Stennis' advanced age gingerly. He ran with the slogan, "A senator for the '80s," knowing that it would remind voters that he was running against a senator who was actually in his 80s. The strategy didn't work; Stennis won 64%–36%, carrying 80 of 82 counties despite being outspent by Barbour. But at age 35, Barbour showed a sophisticated understanding of the nexus between money and politics: in what was then the most expensive race in state history, he raised and spent more than $1 million at a time when that amount could buy a great deal of attention in Mississippi.

It also got him noticed in Washington, where he became Ronald Reagan's White House political director in 1985 and later an adviser to George H.W. Bush's presidential campaign. In 1991 he took advantage of his Republican connections and hung out his own shingle, founding Barbour, Griffith & Rogers, now one of D.C.'s powerhouse lobbying firms; then he served as Republican National Committee chairman from 1993–97. He chaired the party when it won a congressional majority for the first time in 40 years and he shared in the credit. When he left the RNC and returned to his lobbying firm, he was positioned as one of Washington's most powerful lobbyists, well-connected to key members of the House and Senate and much sought-after by big corporate clients with interests before the Republican Congress.

In all his time in Washington, Barbour had maintained his ties back home. He served as a Republican national committeeman from 1984 until 1998 and regularly commuted back to Yazoo

City where his wife and sons resided. He was approached in 2001 about running for governor and a year later announced he would challenge Governor Ronnie Musgrove in 2003.

Musgrove had been elected governor by the Mississippi House of Representatives in January 2000, after leading the popular vote in November 1999 by a 49.6%–48.5% margin. But winning the popular vote was not decisive under Mississippi law. The law said that if no candidate won a majority of the popular vote the winner would be determined by which candidate won the most state House districts. After the tedious tabulation, it appeared that 61 districts voted for Musgrove and 61 for Parker. Under the 1890 law, the decision then went to the state House of Representatives, where Democrats had a big margin. On January 4, 2000, Musgrove was finally elected by a margin of 86–36.

In his first legislative session, Musgrove achieved his biggest goal, a six-year, $338 million teacher pay raise, up to the Southeastern state average. And he was pleased to announce that Nissan was building a $930 million plant employing 4,000 in Canton, just north of Jackson. The issue of the Mississippi flag was kindled in May 2000, when the state Supreme Court ruled that the flag, which features the Confederate battle cross in the upper left corner, was not legally the state flag, because the 1894 law authorizing it was not included in the full codification in state laws in 1906. Musgrove appointed a commission to design a new flag which he and four other statewide officials endorsed, but legislators decided to send the issue to voters in a referendum in April 2001. Most blacks and many business leaders support the new design, but there was vocal opposition from many whites, and many feared—or hoped—that a large majority of white voters would choose that in the privacy of the voting booth. The new flag design was defeated by a resounding 65%–35%.

The big issue of 2002 was the civil justice system. Mississippi had become a trial lawyers' paradise, with huge verdicts awarded by juries in tiny impoverished counties. Musgrove was supported by and generally friendly to trial lawyers. In November 2002, as the legislature was conferring on the issue, a pro-trial lawyer state supreme court justice was defeated. Nonetheless, Musgrove vetoed a second time a bill opposed by trial lawyers capping damages from fraudulent lending. Meanwhile, there were newspaper reports that investigators were looking into allegations that two prominent trial lawyers Paul Minor and Richard Scruggs paid off debts owed by two judges and were looking into the pattern of Musgrove receiving big contributions from trial lawyers just before he made judicial appointments.

Musgrove's own survival was also in doubt. He was the last remaining Democratic governor in the Deep South after incumbents in Alabama, Georgia and South Carolina failed to win second terms in 2002. There was widespread speculation that he was seeking to be named president of Delta State University, rather than stand for reelection. Musgrove, though known for his hyperkinetic energy, seemed to lack a sense of urgency, raising money but not starting his campaign in earnest until a few months before the election. By that time, Barbour already had been touring the state for a year promising voters that he would use his Washington connections to help create jobs in Mississippi and had spent more than $2 million, much of it on television ads.

Musgrove won the August primary with 76% against four minor opponents; Barbour won 83%–17% against Mitch Tyner, a trial lawyer who pounded on him as a "fat cat" lobbyist and whose campaign created a website called WashingtonFatCat.com. Barbour ignored him; there was speculation that Tyner was a stalking horse for the trial lawyers lobby, which didn't like Barbour's calls for additional limits on civil lawsuits. Tyner denied it, but was revealed to be a donor to Musgrove's 1999 campaign.

Musgrove picked up where Tyner left off and both candidates sounded economic themes in the general election. "I've put Mississippi first. Haley Barbour has spent the last 20 years in Washington, D.C., putting special interests first," Musgrove said after winning the primary. He framed Barbour as an outsider who was closely tied to big tobacco and pharmaceutical companies. He called Barbour a "hired gun for Mexico" who lobbied for passage of NAFTA which, Musgrove said, cost Mississippi 41,000 jobs. Barbour denied lobbying for passage of NAFTA and said he didn't start lobbying for the Mexican government until 2000 or 2001, long after NAFTA had passed in 1993, and he focused only the issue of Mexican trucks entering the U.S.

In a September debate, Barbour claimed Musgrove mismanaged the state economy and wasn't serious enough about fixing the civil justice system. "We've got to hitch up our britches and get serious about tort reform," he said. Musgrove responded that Barbour was "running down Mississippi, talking about what we haven't done and what we couldn't do. Now that may be the way they do it in Washington, but that's not the way we do it here." Musgrove said Mississippi was faring better than most states despite a weak national economy; he pointed to the opening of the new Nissan auto plant in Madison County and took credit for creating 56,000 new jobs across the state. Attending the debate, in the front row of the Barbour section, was Melanie Musgrove, from whom the governor got divorced in 2001 after 24 years of marriage. She left afterwards without answering questions; Ronnie Musgrove said he hadn't noticed her in the audience.

Musgrove sought to keep his distance from the national Democratic party. His television ads referred to him as an "independent conservative" but Barbour sought to remind voters of Musgrove's endorsement of Al Gore in 2000 by airing a commercial with footage of Gore and Musgrove embracing. Musgrove was not helped by Senate Democrats' October 2003 filibuster of the nomination of Mississippi Judge Charles Pickering to the 5th Circuit Court of Appeals. Musgrove publicly backed Pickering's nomination, and sent senators a letter urging them to confirm Pickering, who was criticized for his record on civil rights issues. Barbour, also a strong Pickering supporter, was no bystander: His D.C. lobbying firm was heavily involved in the campaign supporting Pickering's nomination.

The Democratic nominee for lieutenant governor, trial lawyer and state Senator Barbara Blackmon, was no asset either. In October Blackmon drew widespread criticism for signing a sworn statement saying she had never had an abortion and then challenging Lieutenant Governor Amy Tuck to sign a similar affidavit. Barbour attacked the "liberal" Musgrove-Blackmon "ticket," though in Mississippi both offices are elected separately. The state Republican party sent mailers featuring photos of the two candidates inside a valentine heart. Some Democrats called that a thinly-veiled appeal to racism since Blackmon is African-American; they pointed also to Republican use of the state flag issue against Musgrove.

Money was not a problem for either candidate: Barbour raised $10.6 million to Musgrove's $8.5 million, in what was the most expensive race in state history. Barbour won 53%–46%. He carried 51 of 82 counties and won big margins amid heavy turnout in key Republican counties like fast-growing DeSoto County, just south of Memphis, and suburban Rankin County, just east of Jackson. That offset high black voter turnout, which Democrats had counted on because of the presence of two African-American statewide nominees, Blackmon and state treasurer candidate Gary Anderson. Both lost; Blackmon by a wide 61%–37% margin and Anderson by a narrower 52%–47%. Exit polls (the first live run conducted for the National Election Pool in preparation for 2004) showed a racially polarized electorate: black voters went 94% for Musgrove and white voters went 77% for Barbour.

Barbour took office facing Democratic majorities in the House and Senate and said job creation was his top priority. He unveiled a budget that called for $709 million in spending cuts over 2 years, threatened to veto any new tax increases and proposed a package of comprehensive changes to the civil justice system that included a lowering of the caps on pain-and-suffering damages. Barbour called a special session in May 2004 and in June signed a bill capping pain and suffering damages generally to $1 million and to $500,000 in medical malpractice cases, further limiting forum-shopping and protecting "innocent sellers" of faulty products. "I want to tell job creators across America that our scales of justice are now in balance," Barbour said. "It is time for them to come and take another look at Mississippi as a place to locate." He took credit for several economic development deals—a 500-job Textron Fastening Systems plant in Greenville and a 400-job FedEx Ground facility in Olive Branch. The legislature approved a nursing home bed tax increase to help fund the state's ailing Medicaid program but his attempt to cut rising costs by eliminating coverage for 50,000 recipients was stalled by a federal judge.

In 2005, he proposed cutting most agency budgets by 5%. The legislature failed to pass a budget in regular session but Barbour managed to address the state's Medicaid crisis by calling a special session in mid-March that restored the program to solvency by borrowing $240 million from the state's health care trust fund and instituting tighter restrictions on the number of prescriptions, emergency room visits and home health care visits. Barbour was not entirely forgotten in Washington. In November 2004, his office denied rumors he was under consideration for a Cabinet position under George W. Bush. And some Republicans listed him as a possible candidate for president in 2008.

Senior Senator

Thad Cochran (R)

Elected 1978, seat up 2008, 5th term; b. Dec. 7, 1937, Pontotoc; home, Jackson; U. of MS, B.A. 1959, J.D. 1965, Rotary Fellow, Trinity Col., Ireland, 1963–64; Baptist; married (Rose).

Military Career: Navy, 1959–61.

Elected Office: U.S. House of Reps., 1972–78.

Professional Career: Practicing atty., 1965–72.

DC Office: 113 DSOB, 20510, 202-224-5054; Fax: 202-224-9450; Web site: cochran.senate.gov.

State Offices: Gulfport, 228-867-9710; Jackson, 601-965-4459; Oxford, 662-236-1018.

Committees: *Agriculture, Nutrition & Forestry*: Forestry, Conservation & Rural Revitalization; Production & Price Competitiveness; Research, Nutrition & General Legislation. *Appropriations* (Chmn.): Agriculture, Rural Development & Related Agencies; Defense; Energy & Water; Homeland Security; Interior & Related Agencies; Labor, Health and Human Services, Education & Related Agencies; Legislative Branch. *Rules & Administration*.

Group Ratings

	ADA	ACLU	AFS	LCV	ITIC	NTU	COC	ACU	NTLC	CHC
2004	15	0	0	0	92	67	100	92	88	100
2003	5	—	11	0	—	72	100	85	—	—

National Journal Ratings

	2003 LIB	—	2003 CONS		2004 LIB	—	2004 CONS
Economic	0%	—	82%		18%	—	78%
Social	0%	—	59%		19%	—	71%
Foreign	0%	—	78%		0%	—	67%

Key Votes of the 108th Congress

1. Ban Drilling in ANWR	N	5. Energy Bill	Y
2. Approve Bush Tax Cuts	Y	6. Support Roe v. Wade	N
3. Medicare/Rx Bill	Y	7. Ban Partial-Birth Abortion	Y
4. Bar Overtime Pay Regs.	N	8. Assault Weapons Ban	N

9. Ban Same-Sex Marriage	Y
10. Ban Bunker-Buster Bomb	N
11. Fund Iraq War	Y
12. Restrict Missile Defense	N

Election Results

2002 general	Thad Cochran (R)	533,269	(85%)	($1,453,688)
	Shawn O'Hara (Ref)	97,226	(15%)	
2002 primary	Thad Cochran (R)	unopposed		
1996 general	Thad Cochran (R)	624,154	(71%)	($1,305,680)
	James W. Hunt (D)	240,647	(27%)	
	Other	13,861	(2%)	

Prior Winning Percentages: 1990 (100%); 1984 (61%); 1978 (45%); 1976 House (76%); 1974 House (70%); 1972 House (48%)

Thad Cochran was elected to the House in 1972 and the Senate in 1978, where he sits at Jefferson Davis's old desk. He grew up in small towns in northern Mississippi and near Jackson, the son of a principal and a teacher, graduated with high grades from Ole Miss (where he was a cheerleader, which was a very big deal) and its law school, served in the Navy, spent a year abroad and practiced law in Jackson. In 1972, as Richard Nixon was sweeping Mississippi, he was elected as a Republican to the House from the Jackson-area district with a plurality against a white Democrat and black independent. After three terms, he was ready to step down, when

Senator James Eastland retired; Cochran ran, and once again won with a plurality over a white Democrat and a black independent. In the House and in the Senate he has managed to amass a generally conservative record with little controversy or acrimony. His pleasant personal demeanor, his refusal to engage in racial politics and his Republican Party label, in a state where most whites have been voting Republican for president for three decades, have made him broadly acceptable to voters at home. His toughest race came in 1984, when he was opposed by popular former Governor William Winter. Winter could make a case for himself but not against Cochran; Cochran outraised him $2.7 million to $738,000, and won 61%–39%.

Cochran is now the chairman of the Appropriations Committee. He serves on the Defense Appropriations Subcommittee, where he has been a key proponent of missile defense. He has worked to fund projects big and small which are based in Mississippi—the DDG-51 Aegis destroyers, two of them to be built at Ingalls Shipyard in Pascagoula, the LHD-8 helicopter carrier, additional AN/APG-73 radars for the F-18 Hornet, Mississippi State University's research center where superfast computers do undersea modeling of Navy projects, the University of Mississippi computer labs receiving information from orbiting satellites. Timely amendments to appropriations that make major policy are a Cochran specialty. To the bill allowing reimportation of prescription medicines in July 2000 Cochran added an amendment to require the FDA to certify lack of risk to public health and safety; HHS Secretary Donna Shalala was unable to so certify, and the law became a dead letter. An October 2000 amendment delaying the imposition of regulations on the treatment of rats, mice and birds in research laboratories prevented a big increase in the cost of medical research. In 2003 and 2004 Cochran chaired the new Homeland Security Subcommittee, which sharply increased spending over what the agencies in the new department had spent before. He got additional screening technologies for the TSA, accelerated funding of the Coast Guard's Deepwater long-term recapitalization program and worked for funding of NOAA research vessels. With ranking minority member Robert Byrd he secured Senate passage of the New Shippers Review, to help Customs and Border Protection collect antidumping and countervailing duties on imports from countries evading payment.

In January 2005 Cochran succeeded Ted Stevens as chairman of the full committee. "We're not going to have runaway spending on the Appropriations Committee when I'm chairman," he said. "I won't tolerate it." Stevens noted that "he's less confrontational, perhaps, more deliberate." Cochran said he would not encourage earmarks. "If it's not agreed upon by all who are concerned, then it doesn't get included in the bill. I'm not going to engage in a practice of putting things in bills without consultation with other senators." And he sought to tamp down expectations that he would provide for Mississippi as Stevens had for Alaska. "I think Mississippi can be assured that our needs will be carefully considered, but it will be a tough budget year, and I don't want to enlarge expectations too much." And he warned that some Mississippi military bases could end up on the 2005 base closing list, which is in fact what happened. In May 2005, the Pentagon recommended closing Pascagoula Naval Station, shrinking Keesler Air Force Base and redistributing airplanes from the 186th Refueling Wing at Key Field in Meridian. Cochran said he wanted to avoid omnibus bills in which multiple subcommittees' bills are rolled into one huge piece of legislation. "It's my plan to have us stay on a schedule that will cause us to pass 13 individual appropriation bills." But that goal was endangered when the House Appropriations Committee reduced the number of its subcommittees from 13 to 10. That would have made subcommittees' jurisdictions incongruent, making it difficult to settle issues in conference committees. In response, the Senate committee abolished one of its 13 subcommittees and reshuffled jurisdictions.

On the Agriculture Committee Cochran played an important role in shaping the very different 1996 and 2002 farm bills. In 1996 he supported the move to phase out most crop subsidies over seven years, but insisted on maintaining the cotton marketing loan plan that he largely wrote in 1985. In 2002 he supported the strategy of reviving annual crop payments through the marketing loan program and the target price mechanism, which was abolished in 1996, and of vastly increasing the Conservation Reserve Program to provide money for producers of non-program crops, thus producing more support for the bill. The bill also required country-of-origin labeling for beef, pork, lamb and fish—the last being very important for Mississippi's big catfish farm industry; Cochran has worked hard to get the Senate to prevent a similar Vietnamese fish from being labeled catfish. After the bill passed Cochran argued that it was weaning farmers from subsidies. In January 2003 Cochran moved swiftly to fashion a $3.1 billion drought relief measure, about half the size of Tom Daschle's, which spread money not just to the drought-stricken Great Plains but to most of the South, with special aid for tobacco and catfish producers; he got it into the omnibus appropriation with a coalition of all Republicans and seven southern Democrats. He helped steer to passage the Healthy Forests Restoration Act in 2003. In 2004 he pushed through reauthorization of nutrition programs like WIC and the school lunch program, providing more access to the poor. In December 2004 he and ranking Democrat Tom Harkin got passage of a bill restoring $100 million which had been diverted for other purposes to the conservation program.

He helped create the Delta Health Alliance and introduced a bill to help close the health care gap between the races. Over the years he has built up a National Writing Program, to instruct teachers how to teach writing; for only $10 million it sends 100,000 teachers to summer programs on 167 campuses. He has fostered programs to improve arts education, foreign languages and civics and economics education.

Going into the 109th Congress, Cochran and Trent Lott have combined congressional service of 64 years; both were first elected to the House in 1972. Their relations have not always been harmonious. They clashed over judgeships and vied for White House favor in the 1980s and mixed it up in leadership fights in the 1990s. In 1990 Cochran challenged the more moderate John Chafee of Rhode Island for the chairmanship of the Senate Republican Conference, the number three leadership position, and won 22–21. When Lott challenged Alan Simpson for majority whip, the number two position, Cochran pointedly endorsed Simpson; Lott won anyway, with the support of junior conservatives, and thus leapfrogged Cochran. When Bob Dole announced in May 1996 that he would resign from the Senate in June, Cochran and Lott both entered the race for majority leader; Lott had the contest sewed up, but Cochran stayed in and lost 44–8. In January 2001, Cochran appeared by John McCain's side as a new co-sponsor of the latest version of the McCain-Feingold campaign finance bill; this had been strongly opposed by Lott, and Cochran's vote made the bill apparently filibuster-proof. It gave McCain leverage in his drive to get it early consideration. But Cochran spoke sympathetically about Lott after he relinquished the majority leadership in December 2002.

Cochran holds what seems to be one of the safest seats in the Senate. In 1990 he was unopposed and in 1996 he was re-elected 71%–27% over a Democrat who spent half of his $4,700 on gas for a borrowed car. In 2002 he beat a Reform party candidate 85%–15%. He comes up for reelection in 2008; in August 2004 he said, "I'll make that decision when the time comes, but I'm not making any promises either way to anyone at this point." He has a ways to go before he matches John Stennis's record as Mississippi's longest serving senator: that won't happen until March 2020.

Junior Senator

Trent Lott (R)

Elected 1988, seat up 2006, 3d term; b. Oct. 9, 1941, Grenada; home, Pascagoula; U. of MS, B.A. 1963, J.D. 1967; Baptist; married (Tricia).

Elected Office: U.S. House of Reps., 1972–88.

Professional Career: Practicing atty., 1967–68; A.A., U.S. Rep. William Colmer, 1968–72.

DC Office: 487 RSOB, 20510, 202-224-6253; Fax: 202-224-2262; Web site: lott.senate.gov.

State Offices: Gulfport, 228-863-1988; Jackson, 601-965-4644; Oxford, 662-234-3774; Pascagoula, 228-762-5400.

Committees: *Commerce, Science & Transportation*: Aviation; Fisheries & the Coast Guard; National Ocean Policy Study; Science & Space; Surface Transportation & Merchant Marine (Chmn.); Technology, Innovation & Competitiveness. *Finance*: International Trade; Social Security & Family Policy; Taxation & IRS Oversight. *Intelligence (Select)*. *Rules & Administration* (Chmn.). *Joint Committee on Taxation* (3d of 5 Sens.).

Group Ratings

	ADA	ACLU	AFS	LCV	ITIC	NTU	COC	ACU	NTLC	CHC
2004	5	22	14	33	100	74	100	96	90	100
2003	10	—	0	0	—	81	96	89	—	—

National Journal Ratings

	2003 LIB	—	2003 CONS		2004 LIB	—	2004 CONS
Economic	32%	—	67%		31%	—	65%
Social	0%	—	59%		0%	—	84%
Foreign	0%	—	78%		33%	—	61%

Key Votes of the 108th Congress

1. Ban Drilling in ANWR	N	5. Energy Bill	Y	9. Ban Same-Sex Marriage	Y
2. Approve Bush Tax Cuts	Y	6. Support Roe v. Wade	N	10. Ban Bunker-Buster Bomb	N
3. Medicare/Rx Bill	N	7. Ban Partial-Birth Abortion	Y	11. Fund Iraq War	Y
4. Bar Overtime Pay Regs.	N	8. Assault Weapons Ban	N	12. Restrict Missile Defense	N

Election Results

2000 general	Trent Lott (R)	654,941	(66%)	($3,663,052)
	Troy Brown (D)	314,090	(32%)	($40,349)
	Other	25,113	(3%)	
2000 primary	Trent Lott (R)	unopposed		
1994 general	Trent Lott (R)	418,333	(69%)	($2,516,189)
	Ken Harper (D)	189,752	(31%)	($345,379)

Prior Winning Percentages: 1988 (54%); 1986 House (82%); 1984 House (85%); 1982 House (79%); 1980 House (74%); 1978 House (100%); 1976 House (68%); 1974 House (73%); 1972 House (55%)

Trent Lott, Senate majority leader from June 1996 until June 2001, was first elected to the House in 1972 and to the Senate in 1988. He grew up in Pascagoula, the son of a shipyard worker and a teacher, went to Ole Miss (where he was a cheerleader, like his Mississippi colleague Thad Cochran) and worked his way through law school by running the Ole Miss alumni affairs office, accumulating good contacts along the way. After a year of law practice, he got a job with Democratic Gulf Coast Congressman William Colmer, chairman of the House Rules Committee. When Colmer retired in 1972, Lott ran for the House seat with Colmer's encouragement and endorsement—as a Republican. He was elected with 55% in what was the strongest Nixon district in the country that year. In 1974, Lott was the youngest member of the Judiciary Committee, loyally defending Richard Nixon in the impeachment hearings. In 1980, he was elected Republican whip, and he ran the Republican National Convention's platform committees in 1980 and 1984. In the House he was an ally of Jack Kemp and Newt Gingrich. He supported Kemp for president in 1988, and his decision to run for the Senate that year opened the way for Gingrich's rise: Lott was succeeded as whip by Dick Cheney; when Cheney became Defense secretary in March 1989, Gingrich was elected whip 87–85.

There is a discernible hard core of beliefs in Lott's career, and yet he is less the hard-edged ideologue that Washington insiders presume than he is an instinctive deal-maker, not much interested in quixotic gestures, an orderly and well-organized man who is dismayed by the dilatoriness of others. As one colleague put it in 2001, "After pork, Trent's default position is conservative—but he likes to compromise." His beliefs are reminiscent of the mostly unarticulated beliefs of the coalition of Southern conservative Democrats and small-town conservative Northerners which had controlled the House for most of the 35 years prior to when he arrived there: Against increased taxes, hostile to federal regulation of business and local government, for an assertive foreign policy and strong defense, for traditional rules of moral conduct. On one issue, civil rights, he has moved from Colmer's support for racial segregation to the small town Republicans' backing for equal rights—although doubts were raised about that by comments he made at Strom Thurmond's 100th birthday party in December 2002, comments that cost him the majority leadership. He can be sharp in debate, aggressively partisan and combative, but he is gregarious and personable, striving to keep on good terms with most other members and careful to cultivate those whose support he needs.

In the Senate, as in the House, Lott seemed less interested in committee work than in moving into a leadership position. After the 1992 election, he ran for Conference secretary, the number four leadership post, and won. In 1994, after he had been reelected 69%–31%, he challenged Republican Whip Al Simpson. Majority Leader Bob Dole and most Republican moderates backed Simpson, but Lott won most of the younger conservatives elected in 1992 and 1994 and won 27–26—the first Republican ever elected whip in both houses. In the process he leapfrogged over his Mississippi colleague Thad Cochran, who held the number three leadership position.

As whip for 17 months, Lott was careful not to usurp the prerogatives of Dole, who kept many decisions close to the chest. Then in May 1996 Dole surprised almost everyone when he announced he would resign from the Senate in June. Lott immediately began canvassing for votes for majority leader and found himself far ahead of Cochran, who ran anyway and lost 44–8. During the summer, Lott moved adroitly, pushing for a vote on welfare reform, disposing of the minimum wage issue, pushing for the compromise health care bill and the Safe Drinking Water Act. He gave Senate Republicans a solid record to run on—but left Dole with fewer issues on which to attack Clinton. He established a smooth working relationship with Democratic Leader Tom Daschle. After Dole lost and Gingrich faced ethics charges that threatened to topple him, Lott was suddenly the most visible Republican leader in Congress.

Then came impeachment, which tested both his influence among Republican senators and his close working relationship with Tom Daschle. In December 1998 after the House voted, Lott encouraged a plan to allow four days of argument in the impeachment trial, to be followed by a vote on whether the charges, if true, would justify impeachment; if that fell short of the two-thirds required for removal, as everyone assumed it would, the trial would be adjourned. House Judiciary Chairman Henry Hyde, the leader of the House managers, wrote an angry letter and Senate conservatives howled; Lott retreated. Democrats remained furious about the prospect of a lengthy, salacious trial, and raised the specter of partisanship which most senators, after the House debate and in line with Senate tradition, wanted to avoid. On January 7, Lott tagged along with Daschle for a scheduled press conference, and they agreed to an all-senators closed caucus the next day. In that extraordinary meeting, senators agreed to a suggestion by Phil Gramm and Edward Kennedy to postpone the issue of calling witnesses and go on with the trial. There was giddy delight at this demonstration of senatorial comity, though the House managers were furious and the Clinton defense team still wary. The trial proceeded in orderly fashion; the verdict went as expected, mostly along partisan lines, with Lott and most Republicans preventing a vote on censure until after the verdict, at which point Democrats weren't much interested.

In 1999 and 2000, Lott tried to bar non-germane amendments on appropriations bills, arguing that Democrats were using them to hurt Republicans in elections and that it was better procedure to have "clean votes" on issues. Democrats were immensely irritated, and in spring 2000 relations between Lott and Daschle turned very sour. In June 2000 Nebraska's Chuck Hagel said there could be changes in the leadership if Republicans lost seats in November; Hagel had contemplated running against Lott after the November 1998 elections, and ran unsuccessfully against campaign chairman Mitch McConnell instead. In July 2000 Lott steered estate tax repeal through, but at the cost of allowing votes on many Democratic amendments. In fall 2000 Lott followed a "no veto" strategy and tried to negotiate with the Clinton administration on appropriations; House Republican Whip Tom DeLay, who wanted to set clear conservative markers and get members out of town, opposed this. The result was relatively high spending, and a delay in many appropriations until after the November elections and, as seemed sensible, after the Florida recounts as well.

By late 2000, almost everyone seemed angry with Lott for one reason or another. But no one—not even Majority Whip Don Nickles, a frequent critic—moved to run against him. With the Senate divided 50–50, Democrats demanded equal numbers of members on each committee;

some Republican conservatives strongly opposed that, though some committee chairmen offered equal membership. On January 5, 2001, after negotiations with Daschle, Lott surprised many by agreeing to equal membership. There was a strong theoretical argument for that—committee membership should reflect the balance on the floor—but even stronger practical arguments. Lott wanted to make sure that no Democratic senator would challenge the Florida electoral votes on January 6, and thereby trigger debate on that issue. There was always the possibility that control could shift to the Democrats. Most observers pointed to 98-year-old Strom Thurmond as one senator who might leave office, but there were 45 senators with governors of a different party, 26 Democrats and 19 Republicans, whose departure could change the partisan balance. While there was some hope that Georgia's Zell Miller might cross the aisle and strengthen this fragile majority, it was not much suspected until May 2001 that James Jeffords would defect and unravel it. The visibly angry Lott called it a "coup of one."

Even as minority leader, Lott had sharp elbows. In July 2001 he decried "an anti-Mexican, anti-Hispanic, anti-NAFTA attitude among Democrats" when they sought to block Mexican trucks from entering the country. When it became clear in 2002 that Senate Democrats would pass no budget resolution, he said, "The Senate is becoming dysfunctional, the Daschle Democrat dysfunctional process." In the fall, things seemed to be going very much his way. In October 2002 Don Nickles announced he would not challenge Lott for the leadership, even though term limits would force him to leave his position as whip. Then, on election night, the returns revealed that the president's party for the first time in history went from a minority to a majority in the Senate in an off-year election. Lott would be majority leader again.

Then came Thurmond's 100th birthday party. Speaking from notes Lott said, "I want to say this about my state. When Strom Thurmond ran for president, we voted for him. We're proud of it. And if the rest of the country had followed our lead, we wouldn't have had all these problems over the years, either." There were audible gasps and silence, but Lott went on. Major media did not mention the comment over the next 24 hours. Asked about it, Lott's spokesman the next day said, "Senator Lott's remarks were intended to pay tribute to a remarkable man who led a remarkable life. To read anything more into these comments is wrong." But bloggers—people who write weblogs, commenting frequently on various topics—noticed. By Monday, December 9, conservative bloggers were writing about Lott's comments, and not favorably.

It was not surprising that liberals like Al Gore and Jesse Jackson called on Lott to resign the majority leadership, but it was noteworthy that demands for his resignation resounded over the conservative weblogs. On December 9 Lott, on vacation in Key West, Florida, three hours' drive from the nearest television studio, issued a statement saying, "A poor choice of words conveyed to some the impression that I embraced the discarded policies of the past. Nothing could be further from the truth, and I apologize to anyone who was offended by my statement." Tom Daschle downplayed the remarks and Lott's sometime adversaries—Jeffords and former Democratic Senator Paul Simon—came forward to testify that he was not a racist. But others poking through old clippings found similar comments. On Thursday, December 12, George W. Bush spoke to an inner city group in Philadelphia. "Any suggestion that the segregated past was acceptable or positive is offensive, and it is wrong. Recent comments by Senator Lott do not reflect the spirit of this country. He has apologized, and rightly so. Every day our nation was segregated was a day that America was unfaithful to our founding ideals."

On December 13 Lott held a press conference in Pascagoula and announced that he would appear on Black Entertainment Television the next week. "I apologize for opening old wounds and hurting many Americans who feel so deeply in this area. I take full responsibility for my remarks. . . . I only hope people will find it in their heart to forgive me for that grievous mistake on that occasion." Lott's hearty endorsement of affirmative action on BET December 16 dismayed some conservatives who opposed racial quotas and preferences precisely because they believe they violate the civil rights laws which Lott's old boss William Colmer strongly opposed. Lott had been elected majority leader at a November 14 Republican Conference meeting, and that could not be reconsidered until the next scheduled meeting January 6, unless five members called for a special meeting. Nickles was one such vote, and it quickly became clear that there would be others. On December 19 Bill Frist stepped forward and said he would accept the job of majority leader if his colleagues voted for him. On the morning of December 20 Lott stepped down. By the end of the day, Frist had the votes to become majority leader, and was elected by a Conference meeting held by conference call. Lott said later that he had no "vengeance in his heart" but noted a little tartly, "You can't just lay this at the door of the Democrats—some of the Republicans didn't do me any good either. I plan to look to the future, to be very sensitive to everything I say."

Some observers thought Lott would sulk in a corner or display bitterness at every turn, but he did neither. "I still think those comments were misinterpreted, but I made a mistake and I have no one else to blame but myself," he said. "I take a few licks now and then, but I get back up and keep fighting." He became chairman of the Rules Committee, which handles campaign finance and internal Senate matters, and started exploring changes in the filibuster rule and the presidential succession law. Freed from leadership responsibilities, he made some public criticisms of the Bush administration and of Bill Frist. In July 2003 he criticized Frist for taking up the Medicare/prescription drug bill, which he opposed, rather than the energy bill and for taking too much time for debate on judicial nominations. He also criticized the longer hours Frist imposed. In September he said the administration should provide more details on what was happening in Iraq. He opposed the administration on media ownership limits. His opposition to the Medicare/prescription drug bill, a priority for the administration and one on which Frist put his personal stamp, was strong. "What I have always wanted to see was a prescription program for the low-income elderly only," he said. It "will cost more than $400 billion minimum in the first 10 years. We put more furniture on the deck of a ship that's already listing, Medicare." But on November 24, two days after it was passed by the House, the Senate leadership was one vote short of the 60 required under the rules to bring it to the floor. Republican colleagues huddled around Lott, urging him to vote yes; he gestured angrily, then went forward, voted yes and stomped out of the chamber. That brought the bill forward and "the worst damn thing I have ever seen Republicans do" passed 54–44. Lott was still angry later. "I think that was a mistake. I regretted it then; I've regretted it terribly since then. I promised myself after that that I would not do that again. I'm not going to sacrifice my strong feelings on an issue because the leadership says, 'You gotta do that.'"

But even as he was criticizing the leadership, he was working behind the scenes with both Senate and House members to solve problems. He switched stands and supported Frist on expanding the TVA board, a local issue for both senators. But Lott pressed Frist and the White House to accept a deal with Frank Lautenberg on privatization of air traffic controller jobs to get the FAA authorization through. In March 2004 he switched and supported prescription drug reimportation from Canada and he was the only Republican to vote against the budget resolution (because it didn't have enough room for tax cuts). He refused to give money to the National Republican Senatorial Committee, chaired by George Allen, and gave it directly to candidates instead. In September 2004 he criticized Frist for concentrating on homeland security and appropriations and not breaking deadlocks on the energy, transportation and corporate tax bills (only the last one passed). He criticized the administration for not accepting a deal on nominations he concocted with Tom Daschle (Charles Pickering was on the list). But before the election he got the Rules Committee to eliminate the eight-year term limit on Intelligence Committee members and afterwards he got the Republican Conference, by a 27–26 vote, to give the majority leader power to choose half the new "A" committee members.

Lott was also active legislatively on several fronts. After Janet Jackson's "wardrobe malfunction" on the Super Bowl broadcast he sponsored a bill to increase the FCC's indecency fine from $27,500 to $275,000, with a maximum total of $3 million. In May 2004 his bill to postpone the 2005 round of base closings was beaten by only 49–47; he argued that the Pentagon should close bases abroad first. He warned Mississippians that Naval Station Pascagoula was in jeopardy because it had only interdiction missions; in May 2005, it appeared on the Defense Department's list of recommended closures. With Kay Bailey Hutchison and Conrad Burns, he sponsored a bill to provide Amtrak with $12 billion in guaranteed funding and $48 million in bonds—not the administration approach. He put a hold on a Commerce Department nomination to prevent money for a study of billfish—a matter of some interest in Pascagoula—from being sent to a firm in Brownsville, Texas. He pushed successfully to block a tax change that would have U.S.-based automakers paying less than Nissan, which has a big new plant in Canton, Mississippi. After Donald Rumsfeld made controversial statements in December, he said, "I'm not a fan of Secretary Rumsfeld. I don't think he listens enough to his uniformed officers. I would like to see a change in that slot in the next year or so." In January 2005 he criticized Mitch McConnell for allowing too much in committee spending. And he joined with John McCain in sponsoring legislation to subject 527 organizations to the same campaign finance regulations as PACs. As Senate Rules chairman, he presided over the inauguration ceremonies at the Capitol.

In September 2003 Lott said, "Look, I'm here. And I'm going to try to be helpful. Sometimes that will get me crossed up with the administration. I am sending the signal that they're going to have to deal with me, and they need to keep that in mind, because I can be a problem." His book *Master of the Game: Tales from a Republican Revolutionary*, was expected in summer 2005. Left unanswered was the question whether Lott would run for reelection in 2006. His standing in Mississippi still remained very high and his vote-winning record was solid. He gave up a safe House seat to run for the Senate in 1988, and was elected over Democratic Congressman Wayne Dowdy 54%–46%. In 1994 and 2000 Lott did not have serious competition and won easily. In 2003 and 2004 he raised $4 million for his leadership PAC, mostly from direct mail; he did not raise nearly as much for his campaign committee, but can presumably do so by renting his PAC's mailing list. Asked in December 2003 whether he would run again, he said, "I'll make that decision about a year in advance." In July 2004 he suggested that his decision might hinge on his chances to chair a major committee. "Odds are I'll end up being chairman of Finance or Commerce, depends on the years." There was talk in Mississippi that he might face former Attorney General Mike Moore or former Governor Ronnie Musgrove. If Lott does not run, the likeliest Republican candidate seemed to be Congressman and former Lott staffer Chip Pickering.

FIRST DISTRICT

Rep. Roger Wicker (R)

Elected 1994, 6th term; b. July 5, 1951, Pontotoc; home, Tupelo; U. of MS, B.A. 1973, J.D. 1975; Baptist; married (Gayle).

Military Career: Air Force, 1976–80; Air Force Reserve, 1980–present.

Elected Office: Tupelo City Judge Pro Tem, 1986–87; MS Senate, 1987–94.

Professional Career: Staff, U.S. House Rules Cmte., 1980–82; Practicing atty., 1982–94; Lee Cnty. Public Defender, 1984–87.

DC Office: 2455 RHOB, 20515, 202-225-4306; Fax: 202-225-3549; Web site: www.house.gov/wicker.

District Offices: Columbus, 662-327-0748; Grenada, 662-294-1321; Southaven, 662-342-3942; Tupelo, 662-844-5437.

Committees: *Appropriations* (15th of 37 R): Defense; Labor, Health and Human Services, Education & Related Agencies. *Budget* (5th of 22 R).

Group Ratings

	ADA	ACLU	AFS	LCV	ITIC	NTU	COC	ACU	NTLC	CHC
2004	0	0	13	9	90	48	100	87	73	100
2003	10	—	0	5	—	59	97	92	—	—

National Journal Ratings

	2003 LIB — 2003 CONS		2004 LIB — 2004 CONS	
Economic	33%	64%	22%	77%
Social	17%	79%	9%	85%
Foreign	11%	80%	24%	76%

Key Votes of the 108th Congress

1. Drilling in ANWR	N	5. DC School Vouchers	Y	9. Ban Same-Sex Marriage	Y
2. Approve Bush Tax Cuts	Y	6. Ban Human Cloning	Y	10. Fund Iraq War	Y
3. Medicare/Rx Bill	Y	7. Restrict Gun Liability	Y	11. Bar Cuba Embargo Funds	*
4. Bar Overtime Pay Regs.	N	8. Ban Partial-Birth Abortion	Y	12. Intelligence Reorg.	Y

Election Results

2004 general	Roger Wicker (R)	219,328	(79%)	($426,024)
	Barbara Washer (Ref)	58,256	(21%)	
2004 primary	Roger Wicker (R) .... unopposed			
2002 general	Roger Wicker (R)	95,404	(71%)	($395,163)
	Rex Weathers (D)................................	32,318	(24%)	
	Other................................	5,845	(5%)	

Prior Winning Percentages: 2000 (70%); 1998 (67%); 1996 (68%); 1994 (63%)

The People		Race/Ethnic Origin	Ancestry		
Area size:	11,647 sq. mi.	71.3% White	USA: 16.6%		Irish: 7.1%
Urban population:	38.5%	26.2% Black	English: 6.1%		
Rural population:	61.5%	0.4% Asian	**2004 Presidential Vote**		
Pop. 2000:	711,160	0.2% Native Am.	Bush (R)	187,979	(62%)
Median income:	$32,535	0.0% Hawaiian	Kerry (D)	111,509	(37%)
Poverty status:	16.4%	0.5% Two+ races	Other	2,439	(1%)
Military veterans:	11.4%	0.0% Other	**2000 Presidential Vote**		
		1.4% Hispanic Origin	Bush (R)	146,197	(59%)
			Gore (D)	98,350	(40%)
			Other	3,690	(1%)
			Cook Partisan Voting Index: R +10		

Occupation	Blue collar: 38.6%	White collar: 48.5%	Gray collar: 12.9%

The university town of Oxford, the "Jefferson" of William Faulkner's fictional Yoknapatawpha County, sits on a divide between the hill country of Mississippi and the flat farmlands of the Mississippi Delta. Named for Oxford, England, it is the home of the Center for the Study of Southern Culture and of Ole Miss, the University of Mississippi, which saw violence when James Meredith integrated the school in 1962, but now houses his papers in its library; Senator Thad Cochran was at the law school then and Senator Trent Lott a senior in college. To the west is the Delta, with a large black majority, and also DeSoto County, just south of Memphis, Tennessee, Mississippi's fastest-growing county and one of its most affluent and Republican ones. East of Oxford is the hill country, which stretches up to where the Tennessee River nicks the northeast corner of Tishomingo County. The Tennessee Valley Authority brought electricity here, the Tennessee-Tombigbee Waterway provided construction jobs for years and a new shipping canal when it was completed in 1985. This was traditional farming country, now more engaged in small manufacturing. The Golden Triangle in the Starkville area has become a center for aerospace research, including unmanned air vehicle designs. The biggest town here is Tupelo, a stronghold of private enterprise and traditional values. It is home to an upholstered furniture industry that is the largest manufacturing sector in the state and Donald Wildmon's American Family Association. Elvis Presley was born in Tupelo in 1935, in a two-room house that is open to visitors, as is the Elvis Presley Museum with a modest collection of memorabilia.

The 1st Congressional District of Mississippi includes Oxford, Tupelo, most of the hill country and DeSoto County. This is the descendant of the district represented by Jamie Whitten, the long-time chairman of the Appropriations Committee and the longest-serving House member in history, from his special election victory in November 1941 until January 1995: 53 years and 62 days. Historically this was hell-of-a-fellow Democratic territory; in an April 2001 referendum it voted overwhelmingly to keep the 1894 state flag with the Confederate battle cross. It voted solidly for Democratic Governor Ronnie Musgrove in 1999 but in 2003 favored his Republican successor Haley Barbour. In national politics it is solidly Republican, 59% for George W. Bush in 2000 and 62% in 2004.

The congressman from the 1st District is Roger Wicker, a Republican first elected in 1994. He grew up in Pontotoc, 20 miles west of Tupelo, the son of a state senator and circuit judge, attended public schools and was a House page in 1967: The first of the 1994 freshmen to get on the House floor. Wicker went to college and law school at Ole Miss, where he was student body president; he served in the Air Force and in 1980 became a staffer to Trent Lott on the House Rules Committee. In 1987, at 36, he was the first Republican elected to the state Senate from northern Mississippi since Reconstruction. When Whitten retired, he was one of six Republicans and three Democrats to run for the seat. Carrying his home base around Tupelo, Wicker led the primary 27%–19% over Grant Fox, a former aide to Thad Cochran. In the runoff, Wicker campaigned as a conservative, but Fox, just 27, hammered him for voting to override Governor Kirk Fordice's sales tax increase veto. Wicker won by 53%–47%. State Representative Bill Wheeler, the Democratic nominee, had support from blacks, unions and teachers—an advantage in the primary but not the general. The result wasn't close: A district held for 53 years by a Democratic titan voted 63%–37% Republican.

In the House, Wicker was elected president of the 73-member freshman class, one of the largest in the 20th century and has compiled a solidly conservative voting record. He also won Whitten's old seat on the Appropriations Committee and has moved up the seniority ladder so that he is close to a subcommittee chairmanship. He became part of "The Group," an informal network of Speaker Dennis Hastert's close legislative advisers. Yet despite his New South style, in some ways Wicker has acted like an old-style Democrat. He worked on local projects and supported funding of the Natchez Trace Parkway (started in the 1930s, but never completed) and Yalobusha River flood control. He sought to route a new Interstate highway through DeSoto County. He obtained a study of flame-retardant chemicals that blocked further regulation of upholstered furniture by the Consumer Product Safety Commission and claimed vindication when scientists for the National Research Council found little or no health risk from the chemicals. He passed a bill to establish academies for teachers and students of American history. In the old style, Wicker has used that focus to bring research dollars to Mississippi universities. He urged the Pentagon to spend in the United States its procurement funds to rebuild Iraq. In December 2004 he filed a resolution with 60 co-sponsors calling for Kofi Annan to resign as Secretary General of the United Nations because of fraud and mismanagement in the Oil for Food program in Saddam Hussein's Iraq.

Wicker has consistently been reelected by more than 2–1 margins and had no major-party opposition in 2004. Wicker could be a candidate for the Senate if Trent Lott or Thad Cochran should retire.

SECOND DISTRICT

Rep. Bennie Thompson (D)

Elected April 1993, 6th full term; b. Jan. 28, 1948, Bolton; home, Bolton; Tougaloo Col., B.A. 1968, Jackson St. U., M.S. 1972; Methodist; married (London).

Elected Office: Bolton Bd. of Aldermen, 1969–73; Bolton Mayor, 1973–79; Hinds Cnty. Supervisor, 1980–93.

DC Office: 2432 RHOB, 20515, 202-225-5876; Fax: 202-225-5898; Web site: www.house.gov/thompson.

District Offices: Bolton, 601-866-9003; Greenville, 662-335-9003; Greenwood, 662-455-9003; Jackson, 601-982-8582; Marks, 662-326-9003; Mound Bayou, 662-741-9003.

Committees: *Homeland Security* (RMM of 15 D).

Group Ratings

	ADA	ACLU	AFS	LCV	ITIC	NTU	COC	ACU	NTLC	CHC
2004	85	63	75	91	50	12	45	8	3	7
2003	90	—	100	65	—	22	43	16	—	—

National Journal Ratings

	2003 LIB	—	2003 CONS		2004 LIB	—	2004 CONS
Economic	71%	—	27%		67%	—	33%
Social	78%	—	20%		65%	—	34%
Foreign	93%	—	6%		80%	—	20%

Key Votes of the 108th Congress

1. Drilling in ANWR	N	5. DC School Vouchers	N	9. Ban Same-Sex Marriage	Y
2. Approve Bush Tax Cuts	N	6. Ban Human Cloning	N	10. Fund Iraq War	N
3. Medicare/Rx Bill	N	7. Restrict Gun Liability	N	11. Bar Cuba Embargo Funds	Y
4. Bar Overtime Pay Regs.	Y	8. Ban Partial-Birth Abortion	N	12. Intelligence Reorg.	Y

Election Results

2004 general	Bennie Thompson (D)	154,626	(58%)	($724,653)
	Clinton LeSueur (R)	107,647	(41%)	($331,464)
	Other	2,596	(1%)	
2004 primary	Bennie Thompson (D)	unopposed		
2002 general	Bennie Thompson (D)	89,913	(55%)	($647,649)
	Clinton LeSueur (R)	69,711	(43%)	($100,342)
	Other	3,426	(2%)	

Prior Winning Percentages: 2000 (65%); 1998 (71%); 1996 (60%); 1994 (54%); 1993 (55%)

The People		Race/Ethnic Origin	Ancestry	
Area size:	13,937 sq. mi.	34.5% White	USA: 6.8%	Irish: 3.7%
Urban population:	62.8%	63.2% Black	English: 3.3%	
Rural population:	37.2%	0.4% Asian	**2004 Presidential Vote**	
Pop. 2000:	711,164	0.2% Native Am.	Kerry (D) 153,786	(59%)
Median income:	$26,894	0.0% Hawaiian	Bush (R) 104,749	(40%)
Poverty status:	27.3%	0.5% Two+ races	Other 2,217	(1%)
Military veterans:	10.0%	0.0% Other	**2000 Presidential Vote**	
		1.2% Hispanic Origin	Gore (D) 134,513	(57%)
			Bush (R) 97,979	(41%)
			Other 4,464	(2%)
			Cook Partisan Voting Index: D +10	
Occupation	Blue collar: 28.8%	White collar: 52.2%	Gray collar: 19.0%	

"The Mississippi Delta," wrote Delta native David Cohn, "begins in the lobby of the Peabody Hotel in Memphis and ends on Catfish Row in Vicksburg." For centuries, the flooding Mississippi and Yazoo Rivers left their sediments here, producing a fertile dark soil. Ironically, what may well be America's richest agricultural land has been home for more than a century to many of its poorest people. The Delta, criss-crossed by rivers and famously disease-ridden, wasn't much settled until after the Civil War; the tradition here is not of paternal masters and gracious mansions, but of sharp, profit-seeking operators who used late 19th century technology to drain the land, line the river with levees and build railroads on tracks above the rise of the river. Black sharecroppers and field hands worked here in conditions almost of bondage. From this episode of industrial farming came both great misery and great art: Clarksdale in Coahoma County was the home of W.C. Handy and Muddy Waters, the real birthplace of blues music; Greenville on the Mississippi has produced writers of the caliber of Walker Percy and Shelby Foote; Yazoo City produced author Willie Morris and bluesman Skip James. Now Vicksburg's antebellum mansions, battlefield monuments and riverboat gambling bring in 1.5 million tourists annually.

Twentieth century technology changed life in the Delta. The mechanical cotton-picking machine, invented in 1944, came along just as northern factories were seeking low-wage workers; the great exodus to Chicago and Memphis began, and the Delta's population has been declining ever since. Income levels remain very low, poverty is over 50% in some areas and infant mortality is at Third World levels; the crime and drugs of urban Chicago have been brought back by Delta migrants returning home. Commercial development also has been stifled by the state's reputation as a haven for lawsuits and large jury awards. Yet, there are signs of hope: Soybeans have become a big dollar crop here; poultry farms have become a major enterprise, and the Delta produces a majority of the nation's catfish. Riverboat gambling operates in Tunica County, by some measures long the nation's poorest county, perhaps best known for its Sugar Ditch, the open sewer in the town of Tunica's black section. About 12 million people annually enter Tunica County's nine casinos (which have more square footage than Atlantic City's), and runways at the regional airport have been extended to accommodate Boeing 747s bearing even more tourists. The casinos have led to a local increase in per capita income and a decrease in welfare rolls, but there is still a gulf between the races, culturally and economically, and the Delta has been slow to develop a self-propelling market economy. At the edge of the Delta there are other economic stories. In 2003 Nissan opened a $1.4 billion, 5,000-job factory in Canton, historically a heavily black area but just north of fast-growing affluent suburbs of Jackson; one consequence was the tripling of land values, as thousands more jobs were created for suppliers, and property moved from agriculture to residential or commercial use. A few miles southwest in Clinton, just west of Jackson, is the former headquarters of WorldCom, which filed the largest bankruptcy in U.S. history in July 2002.

The 2d Congressional District of Mississippi includes the entire Delta, indeed the whole Mississippi riverfront from Tunica almost to Natchez. It includes most of heavily black and low-income Jackson and surrounding Hinds County except for the affluent Bellehaven neighborhood. This is Mississippi's one black-majority district, first created as such in 1984. The 2d includes a few counties in the east that are majority-white and vote Republican, but the political tone of the district is set by the black neighborhoods in Jackson and the black counties of the Delta. Before the Voting Rights Act of 1965, these were run politically by segregationists like Senator James Eastland, Judiciary Committee chairman from 1955 to 1979, and proud Delta landowner. In 1986, the district elected its first black congressman since Reconstruction, Mike Espy, whose grandfather and father built a chain of funeral homes and were among the biggest landowners in the state.

The congressman from the 2d District is Bennie Thompson, who grew up in Bolton, in Hinds County outside Jackson, graduated from Tougaloo College and Jackson State. He was elected alderman in Bolton in 1969, at 21, and mayor four years later; he was the first person in Mississippi to get a street named after Martin Luther King Jr. and he got the first fire engine for Bolton. In 1980 he became a Hinds County supervisor. A life-long grass-roots activist and labor organizer, he successfully encouraged other blacks to run for office. After Espy resigned in 1993 to become Secretary of Agriculture, Thompson ran for the House, and in an all-party primary, he ran ahead of Henry Espy, Mike Espy's brother and mayor of Clarksdale, by a 28%–20% margin. Republican Hayes Dent, an aide to Governor Kirk Fordice, led with 34%. Voting in the runoff was mostly along racial lines, and Thompson won 55%–45%, with his margin coming mostly from Hinds County.

Unlike Espy, Thompson has a solidly liberal voting record and initially made no particular attempt to win white votes, making almost as few concessions across the racial divide as had Eastland in his day. In time, he moderated his votes and reached out to the white community, including some large farmers.

Thompson complained that the Shays-Meehan campaign finance law hurt black politicians and demanded that the Democratic National Committee hire additional minority consultants. He criticized the recess appointment of Judge Charles Pickering to the federal appeals court despite Pickering's support from many blacks in his home area. He voted for the constitutional amendment to prohibit same-sex marriage; 77% of Mississippi blacks voted for a similar amendment in November 2004. Thompson said that Republican control of Washington has made it "tough for a Democrat to get legislation passed." In 2005, he became the ranking Democrat on the Homeland Security Committee. He called for more attention to the needs of first responders; but he caused turmoil inside the committee by firing some Democratic staffers, cutting the pay of others and hiring more minority aides.

In 2002, Thompson was reelected by a less than overwhelming 55%–43% margin against Republican challenger Clinton LeSueur, a former aide to the District of Columbia city council and consultant to the Yazoo Community Action Agency. LeSueur ran again in 2004, and spent three times the money he had in 2002. He emphasized personal responsibility and took culturally conservative views on abortion and gay rights. But LeSueur received little support from national Republicans and Thompson increased his majority to 58%–41%, almost identical to John Kerry's 59%–40% margin in the district. In spring 2005, there were reports that state Representative Chuck Espy, nephew to former Congressman Mike Espy, was planning a primary challenge to Thompson in 2006. According to a staff memo to Nancy Pelosi obtained by *Roll Call*, Thompson had requested assistance from the House minority leader in snuffing out Espy's potential candidacy because he did not want to end up like other black members who had "come under successful attack from 'younger' leaders."

THIRD DISTRICT

Rep. Chip Pickering (R)

Elected 1996, 5th term; b. Aug. 10, 1963, Laurel; home, Hebron; MS Col., 1981–82, U. of MS, B.A. 1986, Baylor U., M.B.A. 1988; Baptist; married (Leisha).

Professional Career: Baptist missionary, Budapest, Hungary, 1986–87; Spec. Asst. to the Admin. & Asst. Coord., East European & Soviet Secretariat, U.S. Dept. of Agriculture, 1989–90; Legis. Aide, U.S. Sen. Trent Lott, 1990–94.

DC Office: 229 CHOB, 20515, 202-225-5031; Fax: 202-225-5797; Web site: www.house.gov/pickering.

District Offices: Brookhaven, 601-823-3400; Meridian, 601-693-6681; Natchez, 601-442-2515; Pearl, 601-932-2410; Rankin, 601-932-2410; Starkville, 662-324-0007.

Committees: *Energy & Commerce* (Vice Chmn. of 31 R): Energy & Air Quality; Health; Oversight & Investigations; Telecommunications & the Internet.

Group Ratings

	ADA	ACLU	AFS	LCV	ITIC	NTU	COC	ACU	NTLC	CHC
2004	5	5	0	0	90	51	100	92	76	92
2003	5	—	0	0	—	60	97	87	—	—

National Journal Ratings

	2003 LIB	—	2003 CONS		2004 LIB	—	2004 CONS
Economic	9%	—	84%		26%	—	74%
Social	30%	—	65%		25%	—	73%
Foreign	38%	—	60%		25%	—	68%

Key Votes of the 108th Congress

1. Drilling in ANWR	Y	5. DC School Vouchers	Y	9. Ban Same-Sex Marriage	Y
2. Approve Bush Tax Cuts	Y	6. Ban Human Cloning	Y	10. Fund Iraq War	Y
3. Medicare/Rx Bill	Y	7. Restrict Gun Liability	Y	11. Bar Cuba Embargo Funds	N
4. Bar Overtime Pay Regs.	N	8. Ban Partial-Birth Abortion	Y	12. Intelligence Reorg.	Y

Election Results

2004 general	Chip Pickering (R)	234,874	(80%)	($832,981)
	Jim Giles (I)	40,426	(14%)	($300)
	Lamonica Magee (Ref)	18,068	(6%)	
2004 primary	Chip Pickering (R)	unopposed		
2002 general	Chip Pickering (R)	139,329	(64%)	($3,071,410)
	Ronnie Shows (D)	76,184	(35%)	($1,439,921)
	Other	3,638	(2%)	

Prior Winning Percentages: 2000 (73%); 1998 (85%); 1996 (61%)

The People		Race/Ethnic Origin	Ancestry	
Area size:	13,310 sq. mi.	63.7% White	USA: 13.5%	Irish: 6.1%
Urban population:	40.3%	33.1% Black	English: 6.0%	
Rural population:	59.7%	0.6% Asian	**2004 Presidential Vote**	
Pop. 2000:	711,115	0.9% Native Am.	Bush (R) 203,376	(65%)
Median income:	$31,907	0.0% Hawaiian	Kerry (D) 106,455	(34%)
Poverty status:	19.2%	0.5% Two+ races	Other 1,827	(1%)
Military veterans:	11.5%	0.0% Other	**2000 Presidential Vote**	
		1.2% Hispanic Origin	Bush (R) 173,434	(64%)
			Gore (D) 93,454	(35%)
			Other 2,752	(1%)
			Cook Partisan Voting Index: R +14	

Occupation	Blue collar: 28.9%	White collar: 56.7%	Gray collar: 14.5%

Mississippi, old and new: The old Mississippi is the Neshoba County fair, held every August since 1892 in the town of Philadelphia. This is traditionally the place where Mississippi politicians announce their candidacies, with the crowds watching to take their measure. When Ronald Reagan came here in 1980 and Michael Dukakis in 1988, neither mentioned what Philadelphia and Neshoba County are best known for nationally, nor is there any memorial except engraved stones at two black churches. It was here during the "Freedom Summer" of 1964 that three civil rights workers, two white and one black, were murdered for the crime of urging black American citizens to register and vote. In June 2005, a jury of nine whites and three blacks convicted Edgar Ray Killen, an 80-year old preacher and saw mill operator, of manslaughter in the murders; many local residents breathed a sigh of relief, though some wondered about taking action against such an old man. The new Mississippi is some 80 miles away, in Rankin and Madison Counties east and north of Jackson, where subdivisions, shopping centers and office complexes are sprouting up in the countryside, as well as the big new Nissan plant in Canton.

The 3d Congressional District of Mississippi includes the Rankin and south Madison County suburbs of Jackson, plus the affluent neighborhoods of northeast Jackson in Hinds County. It stretches north to Starkville, home of Mississippi State University, and south almost to Laurel. In the southwest it reaches over to include Natchez, where antebellum mansions sit on the bluffs overlooking the Mississippi River. In the middle are Neshoba County and Meridian, a small city that may go down in history as the site of departures of two White House chiefs of staff: Here Richard Nixon informed Bob Haldeman that he was out in April 1973 and here John Sununu penned his letter of resignation to George H. W. Bush in December 1991. The political tradition here was Southern Democratic, but the area's recent preference has been strongly Republican: Mississippi, old and new.

The congressman from the 3d District is Chip Pickering, a Republican first elected in 1996. He grew up in Laurel where he worked on the family dairy and catfish farm and attended public schools. His father, Judge Charles Pickering, was defeated for reelection as prosecutor in the 1968 after testifying against a Ku Klux Klan leader—something that took great courage in those days. The senior Pickering later was a state senator and state Republican chairman, and was nominated by George H. W. Bush to be a federal district judge and then confirmed without controversy by the Democratic-controlled Senate. When George W. Bush nominated him to be a federal appeals court judge, the Senate Judiciary Committee voted him down on party lines in March 2002; Chip Pickering said that Senator John Edwards had "distorted the facts." Bush renominated Charles Pickering again in 2003, and Chip Pickering worked hard to convince members of the Congressional Black Caucus to go along, but he was unsuccessful; in early 2004, Bush gave him a recess appointment, but Pickering had to step down at the end of the year.

Chip Pickering was more interested in football than politics at college; after that, he spent 17 months as a Southern Baptist missionary in then-Communist Hungary. He worked at the Agriculture Department in the administration of Bush the elder and worked on Senator Trent Lott's staff on telecommunications issues. In 1995, Congressman Sonny Montgomery, a Demo-crat who mostly voted with Republicans, announced that he would retire in 1996 after 30 years in the House. Chip Pickering returned to Mississippi and ran for the seat. Against nine Republicans and three Democrats, he made use of his party ties: His father's executive director at the state party had been Haley Barbour, Republican National Committee chairman from 1993 to 1997 and, since January 2004, governor. In the primary Pickering ran first in 13 of 19 counties, and won 27% of the vote; former state Representative Bill Crawford, with 24%, was second. Pickering won the runoff 56%–44% with big margins in the Jackson suburbs. Against 29-year-old John Arthur Eaves Jr., son of a well-known lawyer and Democratic politician, Pickering, age 33, spent more than $1 million in the general, twice what Eaves spent, and won 61%–36%.

In the House, Pickering has a conservative voting record, and his Capitol Hill contacts led to assignment on the Energy and Commerce Committee in his second term. As co-chairman of the Congressional Wireless Caucus, he sought increased focus on the industry's concerns: Competition, public safety, privacy and the spectrum. Although an opponent of the Tauzin-Dingell bill to enable the regional Bells to offer broadband service, he backed off when House passage became certain. On the Telecommunications and the Internet Subcommittee, Pickering sought to preempt state regulation of the growing Internet phone industry; after Congress failed to act, he praised the FCC when it asserted exclusive control in November 2004.

Redistricting placed Pickering in the same district with two-term Democrat Ronnie Shows in 2002. Democratic strategists hoped Shows could run as a populist, denouncing the executives of WorldCom, the bankrupt telecommunications giant that was headquartered just west of Jackson. He called for trade protections, attacked Republicans on Social Security, and distanced himself from national Democrats on gun control and abortion. But the new 3d District, though 33% black, had voted 64% for George W. Bush in 2000; 59% of its voters had been represented by Pickering and just 41% by Shows. Pickering raised twice as much money and ran the more skillful campaign. He voiced sympathy for WorldCom workers and brought in George W. Bush and Dick Cheney. He criticized Shows for taking a contribution from Hillary Rodham Clinton, and said that a vote for Shows was a vote for Dick Gephardt for Speaker. And Pickering wasn't shy about criticizing Shows for his lukewarm support for his father's nomination. In the end, it wasn't close. Pickering won 64%–35%. He won 71%–28% in his old territory and 53%–45% in Shows's.

Pickering's victory increased his prominence in the House and raised the possibility he might some day run for the Senate. In July 2003, Pickering revealed that he rejected a $1 million job offer to become president of the Cellular Telecommunications and Internet Association, saying that "public service is where I get a sense of mission." He remains a possible successor to either Lott or his colleague Thad Cochran. He would have many factors going for him, including resentment over the opposition to his father's nomination and his own proven campaign skills.

FOURTH DISTRICT

Rep. Gene Taylor (D)

Elected Oct. 1989, 8th full term; b. Sept. 17, 1953, New Orleans, LA; home, Bay St. Louis; Tulane U., B.A. 1974; Catholic; married (Margaret).

Military Career: Coast Guard Reserve, 1971–84.

Elected Office: Bay St. Louis City Cncl., 1981–83; MS Senate, 1983–89.

Professional Career: Sales rep., Stone Container Corp., 1977–89.

DC Office: 2311 RHOB, 20515, 202-225-5772; Fax: 202-225-7074; Web site: www.house.gov/genetaylor.

District Offices: Gulfport, 228-864-7670; Hattiesburg, 601-582-3246; Laurel, 601-425-3905; Ocean Springs, 228-872-7950.

Committees: *Armed Services* (5th of 28 D): Projection Forces (RMM); Readiness. *Transportation & Infrastructure* (11th of 34 D): Coast Guard & Maritime Transportation; Highways, Transit & Pipelines; Water Resources & Environment.

Group Ratings

	ADA	ACLU	AFS	LCV	ITIC	NTU	COC	ACU	NTLC	CHC
2004	60	15	75	55	40	30	52	54	38	76
2003	65	—	88	50	—	40	47	64	—	—

National Journal Ratings

	2003 LIB	—	2003 CONS	2004 LIB	—	2004 CONS
Economic	55%	—	45%	56%	—	44%
Social	44%	—	55%	23%	—	77%
Foreign	57%	—	42%	58%	—	41%

Key Votes of the 108th Congress

1. Drilling in ANWR	Y	5. DC School Vouchers	Y	9. Ban Same-Sex Marriage	Y
2. Approve Bush Tax Cuts	N	6. Ban Human Cloning	Y	10. Fund Iraq War	Y
3. Medicare/Rx Bill	N	7. Restrict Gun Liability	Y	11. Bar Cuba Embargo Funds	Y
4. Bar Overtime Pay Regs.	Y	8. Ban Partial-Birth Abortion	Y	12. Intelligence Reorg.	Y

Election Results

2004 general	Gene Taylor (D)	179,979	(64%)	($426,134)
	Michael Lott (R)	96,740	(35%)	($89,085)
	Other	3,663	(1%)	
2004 primary	Gene Taylor (D)	unopposed		
2002 general	Gene Taylor (D)	121,742	(75%)	($372,065)
	Karl Mertz (R)	34,373	(21%)	
	Other	5,753	(4%)	

Prior Winning Percentages: 2000 (79%); 1998 (78%); 1996 (58%); 1994 (60%); 1992 (63%); 1990 (81%); 1989 (65%)

The People		Race/Ethnic Origin	Ancestry	
Area size:	9,536 sq. mi.	73.5% White	USA: 13.4%	Irish: 7.3%
Urban population:	53.7%	22.1% Black	English: 6.3%	
Rural population:	46.3%	1.2% Asian	**2004 Presidential Vote**	
Pop. 2000:	711,219	0.3% Native Am.	Bush (R) 188,880	(68%)
Median income:	$33,023	0.0% Hawaiian	Kerry (D) 86,010	(31%)
Poverty status:	16.9%	0.9% Two+ races	Other 1,697	(1%)
Military veterans:	15.3%	0.1% Other	**2000 Presidential Vote**	
		1.8% Hispanic Origin	Bush (R) 154,997	(65%)
			Gore (D) 78,224	(33%)
			Other 4,152	(2%)
			Cook Partisan Voting Index: R +16	

Occupation   Blue collar: 29.7%   White collar: 51.9%   Gray collar: 18.4%

The strand where Mississippi faces the Gulf of Mexico has gone through several transformations. French explorers here founded Biloxi in 1699, before New Orleans or St. Louis, and made it the capital of an empire extending to what is now Yellowstone National Park. Two hundred years later, rich people from New Orleans came to this Gulf Coast in summer to get away from yellow fever and to rest on Victorian verandas; six American presidents have vacationed here. More recently the Gulf Coast, with the help of riverboat casinos since 1992, has grown more than any other major part of Mississippi; along much of the strand, new 1,000-room hotels rose as part of Mississippi's boom and about 50,000 jobs were created during the past decade. There is a military flavor to the Gulf Coast: Biloxi's Keesler Air Force Base is one of the four largest in the country. Pascagoula, once a small town, is now home of the more than 12,000 employees at Ingalls Shipyard, whose gray hangar-like buildings and skeletons of ships under construction loom over the flat landscape. The Pentagon's 2005 base closing recommendations hit hard here: Pascagoula Naval Station was slated for closure and Keesler was scheduled to shrink by about 400 jobs. To the west is the Stennis Space Center named for longtime (1947–89) Senator John Stennis, where Lockheed Martin has established an advanced propulsion center.

This is the heart of the 4th Congressional District of Mississippi. About half of its people live on the Gulf Coast; the rest are inland, in farm counties or around Hattiesburg and Laurel. This was mostly scrub land, not much good for plantations. With its low black percentage and mostly booming economy, the 4th District has become prime Republican territory. This district, in close to current form, gave Richard Nixon his highest percentage in all 435 districts in 1972, voted five times against fellow Southerners Jimmy Carter, Bill Clinton and Al Gore, and was represented for 16 years in the House by Lott until he was elected to the Senate in 1988.

The congressman from the 4th District is Gene Taylor, a Democrat chosen in a 1989 special election. Taylor graduated from Tulane and served in the Coast Guard Reserves as skipper of a search and rescue boat for 10 years. He was elected to the Bay St. Louis Council in 1981 and in 1983, at 30, was elected to the state Senate. In 1988, when Lott ran for the Senate, Taylor ran for his House seat, won the Democratic primary, but lost to Republican Larkin Smith 55%–45%. When Smith died in an August 1989 plane crash, Lott brushed aside Smith's widow and backed his own longtime aide Tom Anderson, who had spent little time in the district and proved to be an abrasive candidate. Taylor, combining a barely reined-in aggressiveness with a down-home manner, won the special 65%–35%.

In the House, Taylor has a conservative voting record and has bluntly criticized the leadership of both parties. When asked to vote for the 1998 budget, he characteristically remarked, "One of the people who is asking us to trust him is now being studied to see if he committed perjury. Another of the people who says trust us admitted lying to the ethics committee. That's not a very good place to start." Taylor is a peppery populist with a reasonably consistent view on issues. He is against abortion, gun control, free trade, foreign aid and federal deficits. He is strongly pro-defense and boasts of bringing defense contracts to the area. As a senior Democrat on the Armed Services Committee, he is a firm believer in improving pay and benefits. He was a leading proponent of the major expansion in 2000 of health benefits for military retirees. In 2004, he had the most conservative voting record of any House Democrat.

Feisty almost to the point of being belligerent, he opposes any U.S. military commitment that stops short of assured and total victory. He voted against the Gulf War resolution, lifting the arms embargo on Bosnia, and sending troops to Haiti, and won House passage of limits on forces in Colombia. But he seems to have become in recent years more willing to use military power. When faced with apparently ineffective American military involvement in Serbia in April 1999, he called for a declaration of war; in October 2002 he voted for the use of force in Iraq. He is a protectionist, loudly opposing NAFTA, GATT and normal trade relations with China. If anything holds his record together, it is boats. He promotes Ingalls and other shipyards, succeeded in widening and deepening the Gulfport shipping channel, champions the seafood industry, and wants to prohibit foreign-flag ships from conducting passenger "voyages to nowhere" from U.S. ports. He supports the federal shipbuilding program and revitalizing the Merchant Marine; he objects to waivers to the Jones Act, which requires coastal shipping to be conducted in U.S.-made ships. When American Classic Voyages went bankrupt while building a cruise ship in Pascagoula, Taylor sought to have the government finish construction and use the ship as a floating barracks. With Jo Ann Davis of Virginia, he organized the Shipbuilding Caucus to expand the Navy fleet. He vigorously opposed the 2005 base-closing round, arguing that Congress was surrendering its constitutional authority, that this was the wrong time because the nation is at war—and out of concern that facilities in his district may be on the closing list. But a House-Senate conference committee in October 2004 dropped a two-year delay that he helped insert in the House bill.

He is hardly ever a reliable Democratic vote. Taylor voted "present" for speaker in 1995, and he voted for John Murtha in 2001, 2003 and again in 2005, rather than Richard Gephardt or Nancy Pelosi. But Taylor has rebuffed all importunings to switch parties. "I personally would feel like a prostitute. I still believe the average working person's best interest is best served by the Democratic Party." Facing the possibility that the House would decide the 2000 presidential election, he said that he would vote for George W. Bush to reflect the views of his constituents.

Taylor seldom has much serious opposition, except in 1996, when Republican Dennis Dollar opposed him. Taylor won with a solid 58%–40%, even as Bob Dole was carrying the district by a similar margin. Since then, he has won overwhelmingly. In 2004, state representative Mike Lott (no relation to the Senator) sought to take advantage of George W. Bush's ample coattails in this area and complained that Taylor was too worried about the national deficit rather than the need for tax cuts. But Taylor won, 64%–35% in a district Bush was carrying 68%–31%. If the seat becomes open, Republicans would have an excellent chance to capture this seat. But Taylor shows no signs of accommodating them.

★ MISSOURI ★

When Meriwether Lewis and William Clark set out on their expedition across the Louisiana Purchase to the Pacific in May 1804, the place they embarked from was St. Louis. On high ground just below the point where the Missouri River swirls into the Mississippi, St. Louis was at the time the one well-established city in America's interior, with an aristocracy of French merchants, a brawling bourgeoisie of Yankee and Southern frontiersmen and fur traders and a proletariat of black slaves. Part of the Louisiana Purchase in 1803, St. Louis by 1821 was part of the new state of Missouri, and for decades St. Louis and Missouri were the gateways to the frontier. In Missouri Daniel Boone finally found elbow room. Here were the eastern termini of the Pony Express, in St. Joseph, and the Santa Fe Trail, in Westport, now part of Kansas City; here were railroads reaching across the continent, connecting the farmers of vast prairies with their markets. Here also were the Mississippi River steamboats, and the boyhood home of their great chronicler, Mark Twain.

For Missouri was not just the gateway to the frontier; it was also a focus of the furious battle over slavery. Missouri was the northernmost slave state in 1850; it was Missouri ruffians crossing the border and killing antislavery settlers in the Kansas Territory that led proximately to the Civil War, and Missouri had its own mini-civil war in the hilly counties along the Missouri River. Throughout the 19th century, both before and after the Civil War, Americans turned away from their oceans and headed inward to settle the great interior of the continent. They found Missouri at its heart, with farmland and mines, rivers and railroads, a major manufacturing state—and in the days before tractors, the nation's leading breeder and trader of mules. In 1874 the Eads Bridge opened, one of very few across the Mississippi, and St. Louis' Cupples Station was the largest rail hub in the world. At the turn of the 20th century, Missouri was the fifth largest state and St. Louis was the fourth largest city, site of the 1904 World's Fair, and one of the few cities with two major league baseball teams, the Cardinals and the Browns; Missouri after the 1900 Census had 16 congressional districts.

Today, Missouri does not loom as large in the national consciousness, yet it is in some ways still central. In the 20th century, Americans—like the Browns who moved to Baltimore in the 1950s and the football Cardinals who moved to Phoenix in the 1980s—increasingly headed toward the coasts, to the big cities of the East and West, and eventually to Florida and Texas. Missouri has had below average population growth since 1900, and today it is the 17th largest state, with just nine congressional districts. But Missouri was the geographic center of the nation's population in the 2000 Census: an imaginary, flat map of the United States population, if everyone weighed the same, would balance near Edgar Springs in Phelps County, Missouri. Missouri started perking up demographically in the 1990s, growing by 9% (its greatest decennial increase in a century); growth was particularly strong in the outer suburbs of St. Louis and Kansas City and in the Ozarks; dozens of rural counties that have been losing population for most of the 20th century started growing again. The state economy, long sluggish, was showing signs of solid growth. And Missouri has again captured Americans' imaginations: if Americans in 1904 flocked to St. Louis on the banks of the Mississippi, in the 1990s their vans and buses were jamming the two-lane road through the Ozarks to Branson, population 6,050, now one of America's top tourist destinations (with 7 million visitors a year), with country music stars and soft rock veterans.

Culturally, Missouri remains more conservative than most bigger states. Its relatively slow-growing metro areas have not overwhelmed the countryside; the biggest growth is at the far edges of the metro areas and in the Ozarks. This rural Missouri is a land of farms and small

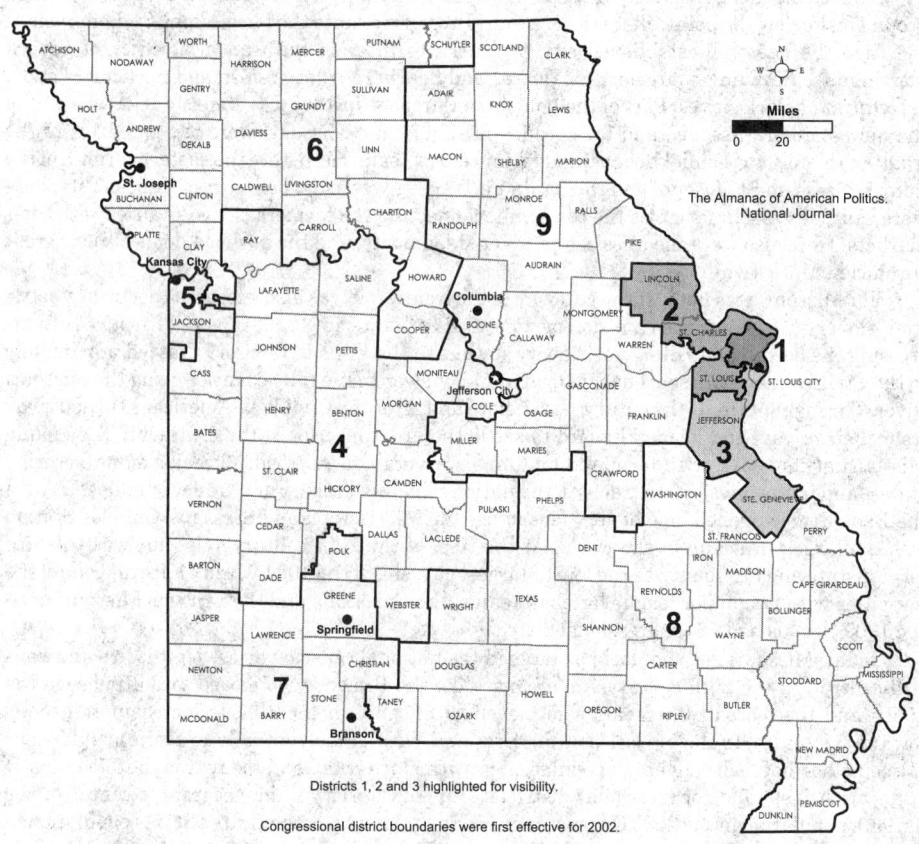

Districts 1, 2 and 3 highlighted for visibility.

Congressional district boundaries were first effective for 2002.

towns, thick with churches and free of glitzy shopping centers, laced with man-made lakes and boat launches, with only one town over 150,000 (Springfield) and 103 counties where life—and politics—seem not to have changed much over the past half-century.

For most of the 20th century, Missouri was one of America's political bellwethers: it has voted for every presidential winner but one (Eisenhower in 1956) since 1900. From the 1960s to the 1990s it mirrored national trends by moving its congressional politics from pretty solidly Democratic to leaning Republican. In the excruciatingly close presidential year of 2000, the results in Missouri were very close as well. George W. Bush carried the state by a 50%–47% margin. In 2004 the Republicans widened their lead. Bush carried the state 53%–46%, Republican Matt Blunt won the governorship 51%–48% and Senator Christopher Bond was reelected 56%–43%. Republicans won both houses of the legislature and the governorship for the first time since the 1920s.

The patterns of support in these 21st century elections were very different from what prevailed for most of the 20th century. Then Missouri's ancient Civil War political divisions still held: Little Dixie in the northeast, first settled by Virginians, and the northwest, settled by Southerners, voted Democratic; the Ozarks in the southwest, which was pro-Union, was unusually Republican; the southeast was split, like next-door Downstate Illinois. Now the real divide is between the state's two big metropolitan areas and the rural remainder of Missouri. The St. Louis metro area voted 54%–45% for John Kerry; metro Kansas City, about half as big, voted 52%–47% for Kerry. But the rest of Missouri, casting 43% of the votes, went 63%–36% for George W. Bush. Kerry carried St. Louis city, St. Louis County, Kansas City's Jackson County and just one of the 112 other counties in the state; Bush carried 111. Blunt carried 101 counties, Bond 112. Ancestrally Democratic rural counties have taken to electing Republican congressmen and legislators. Only one Democrat, Ike Skelton, represents a U.S. House district that is predominantly rural. It is probably too soon to say that Missouri has become a predominantly Republican state. But Democrats have a structural problem: positions insisted on by black politicians and voters in St. Louis and Kansas City are unpopular elsewhere in the state, and black politicians complain that they are overlooked by white Democrats after elections. But that means that Republicans, in Missouri as in Washington, have to grapple with the responsibilities of governing. This is the only state whose name is pronounced differently in different regions: in metro St. Louis they say Missouree, in the rest of the state Missouruh. Matt Blunt, before he was governor, tried to say Missouree but kept slipping back to Missouruh; and in recent elections Missouruh seems to be prevailing.

The People		Race/Ethnic Origin			Military veterans: 592,271 (14.2%)	
Pop. 2004 (est):	5,754,618	4,686,474	83.8%	White	WWII: 20.3%	Korea: 14.4%
Pop. 2000:	5,595,211	625,667	11.2%	Black	Vietnam: 31.6%	Gulf War: 9.2%
Pop. 1990:	5,117,073	61,041	1.1%	Asian	**Most populous cities (2003):**	
Change 1990–2000:	Up 9.3%	23,302	0.4%	Native Am.	1. Kansas City	442,768
% of U.S. total:	2.0%	2,939	0.1%	Hawaiian	2. St. Louis	332,223
Pop. rank:	17th of 50	71,905	1.3%	Two+ races	3. Springfield	150,867
Area size:	69,704 sq. mi.	5,291	0.1%	Other	4. Independence	112,079
State Native:	67.8%	118,592	2.1%	Hisp. Origin	5. Columbia	88,534
Non-citizen:	1.6%	**Ancestry**				
Language		German: 17.9%		Irish: 9.7%	Urban population: 69.4%	
English: 92.9%	Spanish: 3.1%	USA: 8.0%		English: 7.2%	Rural population: 30.6%	
Other Eur.: 2.8%		French: 2.7%				

Education		Work Sector		General Assembly	
H.S. Grad:	81.3%	Private: 80.0%	Govt: 12.8%	Senate	23 R 11 D
College Grad:	21.6%	Self: 6.9%	Family: 0.4%	House	97 R 66 D
Industry		Unemployment: 5.3%		Legislative Term Limits: Yes	
Agri: 2.2%	Con: 6.9%	**Household Income**		**Registered Voters**	
Fin: 6.7%	Info: 3.0%	<15k: 17.1%	15-35k: 28.9%	No party registration	
Mfg: 20.5%	Prof: 27.9%	35-50k: 17.5%	50-100k: 27.7%		
Public: 4.6%	Trade: 15.5%	100-150k: 5.7%	>150k: 3.0%		
Other: 12.8%		Median: $37,934			
Occupation		Poverty status: 11.7%			
Blue collar: 26.0%	White collar: 58.3%	**Home Value**			
Gray collar: 15.7%		<50k: 21.3%	50-100k: 38.6%	100-200k: 29.9%	200-300k: 6.3%
		300-500k: 2.6%	>500k: 1.2%	Median: $86,900	

Presidential politics　Missouri's peculiar balance of North and South, urban and rural, has helped to make it a presidential bellwether and explains its one deviation in the 20th century, in 1956 when it voted for Adlai Stevenson. He capitalized on farmer discontent and his lukewarmness on civil rights helped him carry traditional Southern Democrats. In the 1990s Missouri saw the two countervailing national trends—toward Democrats in major metropolitan areas, toward Republicans in rural areas—but in different proportions: the rural areas count for more here. Bill Clinton carried Missouri by 10% in 1992 and by 7% in 1996. In 2000 Al Gore could carry only a handful of counties outside Missouri's two big metropolitan areas, and lost by a 3% margin; John Kerry, despite big turnout in St. Louis, lost by 7%. Issues like gun control and abortion, which worked for him in the largest states, worked against him in Missouri. It did not help him that St. Louis's Archbishop Raymond Burke in June said that voting for Kerry would be a "grave" sin; George W. Bush carried Catholics 50%–49%. The Kerry campaign cut its ad budget by three-quarters in July and stopped advertising here altogether after the Republican National Convention. In November Democrats did widen their margin in metro St. Louis by 22,000 votes, but it was reduced by 23,000 in metro Kansas City and Bush's margin outside the two big metro areas increased by 116,000.

2004 Presidential Vote		
Bush (R)	1,455,713	(53%)
Kerry (D)	1,259,171	(46%)
Badnarik (Lib)	9,831	(0%)
Other	6,649	(0%)

2004 Democratic Presidential Primary		
Kerry (D)	211,745	(51%)
Edwards (D)	103,088	(25%)
Dean (D)	36,288	(9%)
Clark (D)	18,340	(4%)
Lieberman (D)	14,727	(4%)
Other	34,151	(8%)

2000 Presidential Vote		
Bush (R)	1,189,924	(50%)
Gore (D)	1,111,138	(47%)
Nader (Green)	38,515	(2%)
Other	20,315	(1%)

Missouri joined the Super Tuesday primary for 1988, then went back to multi-tiered caucuses to elect delegates in 1992 and 1996. In 2000 Missouri went back to the Super Tuesday primary. In 2000 Bush and Gore won easy victories, even though Gore's rival Bill Bradley grew up in Jefferson County, Missouri. In 2004 Missouri was not much contested, because it was assumed Missouri's Dick Gephardt would win there; but he dropped out before the February 3 primary. Kerry won with 51% of the vote; John Edwards, apparently unable to make a connection with Missouri's many southern-accented voters, won only 25%.

Congressional districting　Missouri did not lose any seats in the 2000 Census, and control of redistricting was split between the parties: Democrats held the governorship and had a majority in the state House; Republicans, by winning two special elections in January 2001, had an 18–16 margin in the state Senate. The main problem was how to adjust for the declining population of St. Louis. Back in 1950 the city of St. Louis had 856,000 people, enough for almost three

109th Congress Lineup	
5 R	4 D

108th Congress Lineup	
5 R	4 D

congressional districts; in 2000 it had 348,000 people, not enough for half a district. But it is heavily Democratic, and in early 2001 1st District Congressman William Lacy Clay was demanding more of the city, to keep the black percentage in his district well above 50%. That was resisted by 3d District Congressman Dick Gephardt, who didn't want his district moved farther out into Republican suburbs. Privately some Gephardt aides worried that Clay would persuade black House Democrats to make a deal with Republicans. But Gephardt, as House minority leader and as onetime boss of Governor Bob Holden, had leverage; Holden could be counted on to veto such a deal. On April 23 Gephardt and Clay met at the St. Louis Labor Central headquarters and made a deal; the city would be divided roughly along I-44. Some black legislators grumbled, but Clay assured them the new 1st District could be counted on to elect a black.

In early May, Democrats passed a plan in the House which protected all incumbents and pretty well followed the Gephardt-Clay deal. In Senate committee Republicans prepared a plan that would have given Gephardt a much more Republican district, but Democrats filibustered to keep it from the floor. A phalanx of Gephardt aides, "the machine," was busy lobbying through all this. On May 11, with "the machine" and representatives of all nine incumbents present, a deal was reached. Gephardt got the agreed on portion of St. Louis and the close-in, increasingly Democratic suburbs of Maplewood, Richmond Heights, Clayton and University City. Clay got the increasingly black northern suburbs of Florissant, Hazelwood, Bridgeton and St. Ann plus affluent Creve Coeur and Ladue. Republican Todd Akin of the 2d District lost all those areas and got Sunset Hills, Sappington and Concord from Gephardt's old district and new territory in suburban St. Charles and rural Lincoln Counties. Akin was the only incumbent who didn't like the plan, but said he wouldn't challenge it in court. It passed the House 117–37 and the Senate 28–5 in May and was signed by Holden June 1. Some Republicans complained that it did not make the 3d District more Republican. But otherwise it was a success for Republicans, especially considering that their sole leverage was an 18–16 margin in the state Senate. They have a 5–4 lead in the delegation, and it is generally agreed that the 4th District, safe for conservative Democrat Ike Skelton, will probably elect a Republican when he retires.

Governor

Matt Blunt (R)

Elected 2004, term expires Jan. 2009, 1st term; b. Nov. 20, 1970, Strafford; home, Springfield; U.S. Naval Acad., B.S. 1993; Baptist; married (Melanie).

Military Career: Navy, 1993–98; Naval Reserve, 1998-present.

Elected Office: MO House, 1998–2000; MO Secy. of State, 2000–04.

Professional Career: Naval officer, 1993–98.

Office: State Capitol Bldg., Rm. 216, Jefferson City, 65102, 573-751-3222; Fax: 573-751-1495; Web site: www.gov.state.mo.us.

Election Results

2004 general	Matt Blunt (R)	1,382,419	(51%)
	Claire McCaskill (D)	1,301,442	(48%)
	Other	35,738	(1%)
2004 primary	Matt Blunt (R)	534,393	(88%)
	Karen Lee Dee Skelton-Memhardt (R)	26,089	(4%)
	Other	44,275	(7%)
2000 general	Bob Holden (D)	1,152,752	(49%)
	Jim Talent (R)	1,131,307	(48%)
	Other	62,771	(3%)

Matt Blunt was elected governor of Missouri in 2004. He was born in the town of Strafford in southwest Missouri, the first child of House Majority Whip Roy Blunt; at the time, Roy Blunt was a high school teacher. After a decade as Greene County Clerk, Roy Blunt in 1984 was elected secretary of state and the family moved to Jefferson City, where Matt Blunt attended and graduated high school. Matt Blunt won an appointment to the Naval Academy in Annapolis, spent a summer interning in the office of Governor John Ashcroft, then went on active duty in the Navy for five years, serving as an engineering, administrative and navigation officer aboard various ships. One frigate he served on was assigned to the UN-authorized blockade of Haiti and conducted anti-drug missions off the South American coast.

When his tour ended, Blunt returned home to Missouri where he immediately he joined the family business by winning a state House seat in 1998. His grandfather, Leroy Blunt, had been elected to the Missouri House in 1978 (his opponent was Betty McCaskill, whose daughter Claire would one day figure prominently in his grandson's political career). Matt Blunt's father Roy was twice elected secretary of state, lost in the Republican primary for governor in 1992 and won election to the House in 1996, where he rose to become the third ranking Republican in the House. Matt Blunt served just one term in the state House.

In 2000, he was elected secretary of state at age 29. He appointed a bipartisan commission to investigate voting irregularities in that election and moved to improve enforcement of securities laws designed to protect investors. As a lieutenant commander in the Naval Reserves, he was called up for six months active duty in the United Kingdom after September 11. With the assistance of his deputy secretary of state, he performed some official duties from his overseas post; he even conducted a telephone interview with reporters, though he could not disclose his location.

It was clear even then that Matt Blunt had his eye on the governor's office; he met with Congressman Kenny Hulshof after the 2002 election and discussed their prospective 2004 candidacies for governor. Hulshof decided to run the day after the 2002 election, but his father died later that month, leaving his mother to run the family farm, and in January 2003 Hulshof announced he would not run for governor. That left Blunt, the one successful Republican statewide candidate on the 2000 ballot, as the likely nominee. He did not consider his age a problem; he pointed out that if elected in November 2004 he would be several months older than Senator Christopher Bond was when he was first elected governor in 1972 and that he would have had more experience in elective office. In the August primary, Blunt won 88% against five other Republican challengers.

On the Democratic side, there was a serious question as to whether incumbent Governor Bob Holden would be the nominee. Holden's administration started off on the wrong foot, holding a $1 million inaugural, the largest in state history, and then confessing that the committee was $417,000 in debt. In January 2001 he discovered he needed to cut state spending by $200 million and, thanks to Republican victories in special elections, he had to deal with a Republican state Senate, which killed his plan for a $500 million tax increase for roads. In the 2002 regular session the legislature resisted his proposal to dip into the rainy day fund and found enough revenue, but for the first time since 1997 did not provide full school funding. In November 2002 Republicans gained seats in the state Senate and had a 20–14 majority and gained control of the state House for the first time since 1948, with a 90–73 margin.

In early 2003 Holden's prospects for reelection in 2004 looked iffy. The *St. Louis Post-Dispatch* called him "a luckless politician who has encountered one problem after another since taking office." State Auditor Claire McCaskill, a Kansas City-area Democrat who was reelected 60%–37% in 2002, had in 2001 said, "I would never run against Bob Holden in a Democratic primary and I don't think anyone would be wise to do that." But she did and defeated Holden by 52%–45%.

Despite roots in the Ozarks, Holden was hurt in outstate Missouri by his 2003 veto of a concealed-carry gun law, his maneuvering to move a constitutional amendment to ban same-sex marriage to the August primary ballot (where it passed overwhelmingly 71%–29%) rather than the general election and by his handling of education spending. Holden, citing an unbalanced state budget, withheld in 2003 $210 million in funds appropriated for public schools. In April 2004, after financially-strapped school districts across the state were forced to cut budgets and approve property tax hikes and bond measures, Holden released the funds, saying that new budget developments made it fiscally possible to do so.

After his defeat, Holden said he had no regrets and attributed the loss to a tough state economic climate. He graciously conceded to McCaskill and the party and the state's major labor unions, which backed Holden, quickly united behind her. Blunt ran his first television ads after the primary and promised to make state government more accountable and efficient. He called for limiting awards in civil suits and restricting workers compensation insurance payments. He supported concealed-carry legislation and the constitutional amendment banning same sex marriage and opposed abortion. McCaskill supported abortion rights, though she opposed late term abortions, with an exception for the life of the mother; she opposed the concealed-carry gun law and the constitutional amendment banning same sex marriage. McCaskill, 51, a former state legislator and prosecutor, sought to take advantage of the 33-year-old Blunt's youth and relative inexperience in state government, noting that she would not need on-the-job training. In one debate, she congratulated Blunt and his wife, who were expecting their first child, then mentioned her 17-year-old son and said, "It's something we have in common. I was expecting my first child when I was 33 years old." In her closing statement she said, "I've learned an awful lot since I was 33 years old."

Blunt won 51%–48%, running 2% behind George W. Bush and 5% behind Senator Christopher Bond. Outstate Missouri proved pivotal, just as it did in the Democratic primary. McCaskill carried metro St. Louis 55%–44% and ran 5% ahead of John Kerry in metro Kansas City, winning there 57%–42%. But Blunt carried 90 of 97 counties in the rest of Missouri and won there 61%–38%. In his home area, in the counties of his father's congressional district, he led 67%–32%.

Blunt became governor as Missouri entered its fifth straight year of budget deficits. With a 23–11 Republican advantage in the Senate and a 97–66 margin in the House, it was the first time in eight decades that Republicans controlled all three branches of government. In his first proposed budget, Blunt called for cutting spending by $362 million, a reduction of more than 1,000 state jobs, and for deep cuts in Medicaid spending, saying that "Missourians can no longer afford the second most expensive Medicaid program in the United States."

Senior Senator

Christopher (Kit) Bond (R)

Elected 1986, seat up 2010, 4th term; b. Mar. 6, 1939, St. Louis; home, Mexico; Princeton U., B.A. 1960, U. of VA, LL.B. 1963; Presbyterian; divorced.

Elected Office: MO Auditor, 1970–72; MO Gov., 1972–76, 1980–84.

Professional Career: Practicing atty., 1964–69, 1977–80; MO Asst. Atty. Gen., 1969–70.

DC Office: 274 RSOB, 20510, 202-224-5721; Fax: 202-224-8149; Web site: bond.senate.gov.

State Offices: Cape Girardeau, 573-334-7044; Jefferson City, 573-634-2488; Kansas City, 816-471-7141; Springfield, 417-864-8258; St. Louis, 314-725-4484.

Committees: *Appropriations*: Agriculture, Rural Development & Related Agencies; Commerce, Justice & Science; Defense; Energy & Water; State, Foreign Operations & Related Programs; Transportation, Treasury, the Judiciary, HUD & Related Agencies (Chmn.). *Environment & Public Works*: Clean Air, Climate Change & Nuclear Safety; Superfund & Waste Management; Transportation & Infrastructure (Chmn.). *Intelligence (Select)*. *Small Business & Entrepreneurship*.

Group Ratings

	ADA	ACLU	AFS	LCV	ITIC	NTU	COC	ACU	NTLC	CHC
2004	20	0	29	0	100	62	100	96	85	100
2003	5	—	11	0	—	71	100	80	—	—

964 **Missouri** / *Senator*

National Journal Ratings

	2003 LIB	—	2003 CONS		2004 LIB	—	2004 CONS
Economic	24%	—	73%		31%	—	65%
Social	0%	—	59%		31%	—	66%
Foreign	0%	—	78%		0%	—	67%

Key Votes of the 108th Congress

1. Ban Drilling in ANWR	N	5. Energy Bill	Y	9. Ban Same-Sex Marriage	Y
2. Approve Bush Tax Cuts	Y	6. Support Roe v. Wade	N	10. Ban Bunker-Buster Bomb	N
3. Medicare/Rx Bill	Y	7. Ban Partial-Birth Abortion	Y	11. Fund Iraq War	Y
4. Bar Overtime Pay Regs.	N	8. Assault Weapons Ban	N	12. Restrict Missile Defense	N

Election Results

2004 general	Christopher (Kit) Bond (R)	1,518,089	(56%)	($7,848,506)
	Nancy Farmer (D)	1,158,261	(43%)	($3,548,116)
	Other	30,052	(1%)	
2004 primary	Christopher (Kit) Bond (R)	541,998	(88%)	
	Mike Steger (R)	73,354	(12%)	
1998 general	Christopher (Kit) Bond (R)	830,625	(53%)	($6,229,649)
	Jay Nixon (D)	690,208	(44%)	($2,568,879)
	Other	56,024	(4%)	

Prior Winning Percentages: 1992 (52%); 1986 (53%)

Christopher Bond was first elected to statewide office in 1970 and was first elected to the Senate in 1986. Bond grew up in the town of Mexico, Missouri, where his family were part owners of the largest business, A.P. Green, makers of heat-resistant bricks, which was sold to another firm in 1998. He graduated from Princeton and the University of Virginia law school, then clerked for Judge Elbert Tuttle, one of the great pioneers on civil rights in the Fifth Circuit in Atlanta. He returned to Missouri, practiced law and ran for Congress in 1968, at age 29, and narrowly lost. He was elected state auditor in 1970 and then elected governor at 33 in 1972, and became one of the youngest governors in the nation's history. He lost in an upset to Democrat Joseph Teasdale in 1976 and won a comeback victory against Teasdale in 1980. After two years in private life he ran for the Senate against Harriett Woods, who had come close to beating Bond's longtime ally, then-Senator John Danforth, in 1982. Woods ran a three-part ad showing a farmer breaking into tears as he and his wife told Woods about their foreclosure and named Bond as a board member of the insurance company that foreclosed; evidently this struck voters as either demagoguery or an invasion of privacy, and Woods fell in the polls. Bond won, 53%–47%.

Bond has a moderate voting record in the Senate. He has usually worked behind the scenes, trying to forge bipartisan consensus. He was the chief Republican sponsor of the Family and Medical Leave Act, vetoed by George H.W. Bush and signed by Bill Clinton. For years he was the lead Republican senator on housing issues, starting on the Banking Committee and then for years as chairman and ranking member of the VA-HUD Appropriations Subcommittee. There he has worked in bipartisan fashion with ranking Democrat Barbara Mikulski, funding the space program in which she takes an interest and projects affecting Missouri. Bond has sponsored many amendments aiding inner city organizations and encouraging small businesses in troubled urban areas and has worked cooperatively with many black community leaders in St. Louis and Kansas City, to the point that Kansas City's mayor declined to endorse his Democratic opponent in 1998. When Citizens Against Government Waste named Bond as a promoter of pork barrel projects, Bond replied in 1999, "If they think it's pork, it's an awfully healthy diet for the people of Missouri, and I'm proud to participate in it. Just tell 'em, 'In the next batch, I'll bring along my own barbecue sauce.'" He has opposed companies and European nations which have sought to ban genetically modified food, of which the chief producer is St. Louis-based Monsanto, and has sought tougher FDA regulation of compounded medicines in pharmacies.

On the Defense Appropriations Subcommittee, he has worked hard to keep in operation the F-15 production line at Boeing's (formerly McDonnell Douglas's) plant next to the St. Louis airport. In 2004 he got $120 million to build two more F-15s, keeping the production line open until 2008. He criticized the Air Force when an F-15 was bested in competition with a Russian-made SU-30 in tests in India; he said it sent a model without the most advanced radars and that the Air Force wanted to phase out F-15s in order to get more F-22s, made by Lockheed Martin. "I said they sent in the F-15 with one wing tied behind its back. You draw your own conclusions. . . . They're trying to push the F-22. They want to prevent the F-15 program from being [prolonged]. If there are continuing problems in the F-22 then there will be the option for the Air Force to get more of the F-15. I don't know why they are so resistant to keeping that option alive."

Other Missouri interests have prompted Bond initiatives. He was the co-sponsor with Carl Levin of the amendment, passed 62–38 in March 2002, that delayed any increase in CAFE auto mileage standards for two years; Missouri has auto assembly plants. In January 2003 he became chairman of the Environment and Public Works Subcommittee that has jurisdiction over reauthorization of highway and other transportation spending; he declined the chairmanship of the Small Business Committee to keep this one. He held hearings around Missouri on road issues in 2002 and pushed hard for a $318 billion transportation bill in 2003 and 2004 and he held out in the 2004 conference committee against a lower figure. In 2004 he inserted into the omnibus appropriation $1.7 billion for expansion of the locks used by barges on the Mississippi River, drawing strong opposition from environmental groups. When the Appropriations subcommittees were reorganized in February and March 2005 he did not oppose the breaking up of the VA-HUD Subcommittee; he ended up with the chairmanship of the Transportation, Treasury, the Judiciary, HUD, and Related Agencies Subcommittee. In March 2005 he said the Bush budget's $284 billion transportation bill "falls short of the investment that is needed to maintain and repair our nation's crumbling infrastructure, much less construct new roads to reduce the time spent in traffic and make much needed safety improvements in rural and urban roads."

In September 2003 Bond sponsored an amendment to bar states from imposing on small engines emission standards stricter than federal standards. At issue in his view were 1,750 jobs at two Briggs & Stratton lawn mower factories in Missouri which would be jeopardized by a strict California standard. It passed in November 2003 when Bond reduced the horsepower of affected engines from 175 to 50. But California Governor Arnold Schwarzenegger objected and began making calls around Capitol Hill. In conference committee Bond agreed to exempt California from the bill. "In the end, I was unable to guarantee protection of Californians from their fatally flawed rule, but at least Missouri and the rest of the nation is protected from safety hazards and job losses." Bond worked with Kansas City Mayor Kay Barnes to move 6,000 IRS employees to the main post office in Kansas; Democratic Congressman Dennis Moore, who represents Kansas City's Kansas suburbs, objected to the removal of jobs from his district but admitted he didn't have the clout to stop it.

Bond got his political start as part of a group of young reform-minded Republicans—his former Senate colleague John Danforth was another—working against the Democratic political establishment in Missouri, and he can be a strong partisan on occasion. On election night 2000 he was furious when St. Louis Democrats persuaded a state judge to order the polls opened three extra hours in the city; an appeals court overturned the order within 45 minutes, but Bond, who charged that Democrats tried to keep the St. Louis polls open till midnight to defeat him in 1972, said the election had been stolen, and indeed Republicans Jim Talent and John Ashcroft lost by narrow margins. In Washington Bond became heavily involved in the election procedures bill that was an obvious item of business after the 2000 Florida controversy. The centerpiece of the bill was its national standards for voting equipment coupled with $3.5 million in federal aid and statewide voter registries. Bond argued that the motor voter act had installed and kept on the rolls many names of those not entitled to vote, and insisted on a provision requiring mail-in registrants to vote in person the first time they vote and to present a driver's license or photo identification. He negotiated this with lead Democrat Christopher Dodd; "I've told him [Dodd] that I will agree with his concept that we need to make it easier to vote, if he agrees with my concept that we need to make it harder to cheat." The bill was eventually passed in October 2002.

Bond was reelected 52%–45% in 1992, a year in which Missouri Republicans lost every other major race. In 1998, against Attorney General Jay Nixon, he was reelected 53%–44%. Bond lost metro St. Louis by only 49%–48% and carried metro Kansas City (where he lived between his two terms as governor) 51%–45%; he carried rural Missouri 57%–39%. He may have lost some of his support among blacks when he joined John Ashcroft in 1999 in opposing the judicial nomination of Missouri Justice Ronnie White. Democrats hoped to target Bond in 2004, but its most prominent candidates did not run. Congressman Dick Gephardt was running for president, and Governor Bob Holden was running for reelection; Auditor Claire McCaskill was running against Holden in the Democratic primary. Attorney General Jay Nixon had already lost two Senate races, and Lieutenant Governor Joe Maxwell declined to run. But Treasurer Nancy Farmer stepped forward to run; DSCC Chairman Jon Corzine talked up her chances. But unlike Corzine, she was not capable of self-financing a campaign, and Bond outspent her $8.3 million to $3.5 million. Bond ran ads claiming that he had saved Missouri jobs and brought more in: 1,800 jobs at Briggs & Stratton and "thousands more" to Missouri suppliers, 5,000 at Boeing with "800 new jobs on the way." His ads claimed that as treasurer Farmer invested $1 billion out of state, "costing communities 10,000 lost Missouri jobs." Bond won only 14% of the black vote this time and lost metro St. Louis 52%–47%. But he carried usually Democratic metro Kansas City 51%–48% and carried the rest of the state 67%–33%, for a 56%–43% victory, his widest percentage margin ever in a Senate or governor's race.

Junior Senator

Jim Talent (R)

Elected 2002, seat up 2006, 1st term; b. Oct. 18, 1956, Des Peres; home, Chesterfield; Washington U., B.S. 1978, U. of Chicago Law Schl., J.D. 1981; Presbyterian; married (Brenda).

Elected Office: MO House of Reps., 1984–92, Min. Ldr., 1989–92; U.S. House of Reps., 1992–2000.

Professional Career: Practicing atty., 1981–92; Law Clerk, 7th Circuit Court of Appeals Judge Richard Posner, 1982–83.

DC Office: 493 RSOB, 20510, 202-224-6154; Fax: 202-228-1518; Web site: talent.senate.gov.

State Offices: Cape Girardeau, 573-651-0964; Jefferson City, 573-636-1070; Kansas City, 816-421-1639; Springfield, 417-831-2735; St. Louis, 314-432-5211.

Committees: *Aging (Special). Agriculture, Nutrition & Forestry:* Forestry, Conservation & Rural Revitalization; Marketing, Inspection & Product Promotion (Chmn.). *Armed Services:* Airland; Emerging Threats & Capabilities; Seapower (Chmn.). *Energy & Natural Resources:* Energy; Public Lands & Forests; Water & Power.

Group Ratings

	ADA	ACLU	AFS	LCV	ITIC	NTU	COC	ACU	NTLC	CHC
2004	20	11	29	0	100	64	100	96	88	100
2003	5	—	11	5	—	72	100	85	—	—

National Journal Ratings

	2003 LIB	—	2003 CONS		2004 LIB	—	2004 CONS
Economic	33%	—	62%		39%	—	58%
Social	0%	—	59%		0%	—	84%
Foreign	22%	—	68%		0%	—	67%

Key Votes of the 108th Congress

1. Ban Drilling in ANWR	N	5. Energy Bill	Y	9. Ban Same-Sex Marriage	Y
2. Approve Bush Tax Cuts	Y	6. Support Roe v. Wade	N	10. Ban Bunker-Buster Bomb	N
3. Medicare/Rx Bill	Y	7. Ban Partial-Birth Abortion	Y	11. Fund Iraq War	Y
4. Bar Overtime Pay Regs.	N	8. Assault Weapons Ban	N	12. Restrict Missile Defense	N

Election Results

2002 general				
	Jim Talent (R)	935,032	(50%)	($8,322,003)
	Jean Carnahan (D)	913,778	(49%)	($12,293,579)
	Other	28,810	(2%)	
2002 primary	Jim Talent (R)	395,994	(90%)	
	Joseph May (R)	18,525	(4%)	
	Other	27,552	(6%)	
2000 general	Mel Carnahan (D)	1,191,812	(51%)	($8,800,864)
	John Ashcroft (R)	1,142,852	(48%)	($9,378,581)
	Other	26,922	(1%)	

Prior Winning Percentages: 1998 House (70%); 1996 House (61%); 1994 House (67%); 1992 House (50%)

Jim Talent, a Republican, was elected Missouri's junior senator in 2002. He grew up in Des Peres and lives in Chesterfield, in western St. Louis County. He graduated from Washington University in St. Louis and the University of Chicago law school and clerked for Judge Richard Posner, the federal bench's most prolific writer of opinions and books. He returned to St. Louis and practiced business law. In 1984, at 28, he was elected to the state House. He served as House Minority Leader from 1989 to 1992. In 1992 he ran for the 2d District House seat in the St. Louis suburbs and in the primary beat George W. Bush's cousin George Herbert Walker 58%–32%. In the general Talent faced Democratic incumbent Joan Kelly Horn, who in 1990 defeated Republican Jack Buechner by a grand total of 54 votes. Redistricting had made the district more Republican, and Talent won 50%–48%.

In the House he had a solidly conservative record and became a leader on some conservative causes. On the Armed Services Committee he decried the Clinton defense budget cuts and managed to save the F-18, assembled by Boeing (formerly McDonnell Douglas) in St. Louis. In November 1998, when Speaker Newt Gingrich announced he would resign, Talent started running for speaker. But when Majority Whip Tom DeLay endorsed Bob Livingston, Talent withdrew from the race.

Talent was reelected by wide margins and could probably have held the House seat for many years. But in February 1999 he announced he was running for governor. He won the primary without serious competition and was locked in a close race with state Treasurer Bob Holden. The central figure in that contest was incumbent Governor Mel Carnahan, the Democratic nominee against Senator John Ashcroft. On October 16, 22 days before the election, Carnahan was killed in a plane crash. The campaigns were suspended; it was too late to change the ballots. A week later Governor Roger Wilson offered to appoint Jean Carnahan to the seat if her husband got more votes than Ashcroft; on October 30 she agreed and in effect became the candidate. On election night Democrats persuaded a judge to hold the polls in St. Louis open an extra 45 minutes. George W. Bush carried the state 50%–47%, but Mel Carnahan led Ashcroft 51%–48% and Bob Holden edged Talent 49%–48%, a margin of 21,000 votes. Ashcroft conceded, although some Republicans urged him to contest the result, and Wilson appointed Jean Carnahan to the vacancy in December. Under Missouri law, she would serve two years and an election for what would be the remaining four years of the term was held in November 2002.

In the Senate Carnahan was one of 42 Democrats to vote against the confirmation of Ashcroft to be attorney general. Talent, whose family has always remained in St. Louis County, got a fellowship at Washington University and worked part-time for a law firm in Washington. He seemed, with his nearly successful showing and his congressional experience, a likely candidate for the Senate. Carnahan declined to say whether she was running but in the first half of 2001 her campaign committee raised $2.3 million. Hovering over the race, as in November 2000, were the tragic circumstances in which Carnahan had come to office. Talent's approach was to stress his experience in office and in-depth knowledge of issues; after all, he had served in elective office for 16 years while Carnahan had never been elected to anything. Carnahan did have some political experience: for 40 years she kept a card catalogue of her husband's political acquaintances and wrote many of his speeches; she had an appealing personality and could speak articulately about issues. But in July 2002 *National Journal's* Charlie Cook wrote of "considerable anecdotal evidence from . . . both parties that Carnahan sometimes seems lost in the Senate."

Carnahan stressed that she had voted with George W. Bush 71% of the time, but also made standard Democratic arguments on issues like Social Security and prescription drugs. One Republican ad accused her of "undermining national unity" by opposing the administration stimulus package and she was attacked for opposing Bush's position on homeland security. Talent quoted the Bible readily; raised in a Jewish family, he became a Christian and as an adult had a profound religious experience while listening to evangelist Luis Palau on *Focus on the Family*. Carnahan led in polls up through the summer, as national Democratic groups and her campaign dominated the airwaves. But Talent seemed to pull ahead in September. In late October the race tightened again; the death of Minnesota Senator Paul Wellstone in a plane crash October 25 may have reminded many voters of Mel Carnahan's death in October 2000. George W. Bush came to Missouri to campaign for Talent no less than five times, including an appearance in St. Charles the day before the election. This may have made the difference. This was another close race: Talent won 50%–49%, with a 21,000-vote margin. He lost the St. Louis area 53%–46% and the Kansas City area 57%–41%, but carried rural Missouri 57%–42%.

Talent became a senator when the results were certified November 23. He said he would concentrate on reauthorization of the 1996 welfare act and on his bill to enable small businesses to buy health care plans through trade associations. He was not able to pass the latter, but with Democratic co-sponsors did pass two health bills: with Hillary Rodham Clinton, a bill for a tracking system to make sure active duty military and Reservists get health screenings; with Charles Schumer, a bill funding treatment of sickle cell disease, which mostly affects blacks. Talent and Schumer also joined to call for an investigation of the murder of black teenager Emmet Till in Mississippi in 1956, a crime for which no one has yet been punished. He sponsored the Bush administration's bill to reauthorize the 1996 welfare act. He sponsored a law that provided that small businesses certified at the federal level don't need to be recertified at the state and local levels.

On the Armed Services Committee Talent pressed, as he had in the 1990s, for increased defense spending. He argued that the Navy wouldn't be able to maintain superiority in seapower with current and projected spending. "Forward presence and surge capacity should not be an either-or proposition." He was pleased in June 2004 when Boeing won a $3.9 billion contract to produce in St. Louis the Multi-Mission Maritime Aircraft, a new anti-submarine plane. And he helped Boeing get $25 million in November 2004 for research at its St. Louis Phantom Works on the X-43C hypersonic plane; the X-43A had flown 7,000 miles per hour over the Pacific. On the transportation bill, Talent and Democrat Ron Wyden proposed a $30 billion bond issue to finance new transportation infrastructure; bondholders would receive income tax credits instead of interest. But his Missouri colleague Christopher Bond, head of the subcommittee handling the bill opposed it, and the Bush administration said it would veto a bill if it included the bonds. Talent formed a Biofuels Caucus with Norm Coleman, Tom Harkin and Blanche Lincoln. He and Bond introduced in March 2005 a bill to increase usage of renewable fuels from 4 billion gallons in 2006 to 8 billion gallons in 2012.

Talent comes up for reelection in 2006; it will be his third statewide election in six years. The first two were decided by very narrow margins, and Democrats in early 2005 hoped to field a strong candidate. But newly elected Congressman Russ Carnahan said he wasn't interested, as did his sister, Secretary of State Robin Carnahan. Lieutenant Governor Joe Maxwell said he would focus on his family and law practice. Auditor Claire McCaskill, who lost the 2004 governor's race 51%–48%, at first rejected the possibility of running against Talent but met with recruiters from the Democratic Senatorial Campaign Committee in May 2005. At the end of 2004 Talent's campaign treasury contained only $245,000, and he started fundraising in March 2005. But in the 2002 cycle he raised $8.9 million and he is likely capable of raising similar funds again.

FIRST DISTRICT

Rep. William Lacy Clay (D)

Elected 2000, 3d term; b. July 27, 1956, St. Louis; home, St. Louis; U. of MD, B.S. 1983; Catholic; married (Ivie).

Elected Office: MO House of Reps., 1983–90; MO Senate, 1991–2000.

Professional Career: Asst. Doorkeeper, U.S. House of Reps, 1976–83; Paralegal, 1982–2000; Real estate agent, 1986–2000.

DC Office: 131 CHOB, 20515, 202-225-2406; Fax: 202-225-1725; Web site: www.house.gov/clay.

District Offices: St. Louis, 314-367-1970; Vinita Park, 314-890-0349.

Committees: *Financial Services* (19th of 32 D): Capital Markets, Insurance & Government Sponsored Enterprises; Financial Institutions & Consumer Credit. *Government Reform* (10th of 17 D): Federalism & the Census (RMM); Regulatory Affairs.

Group Ratings

	ADA	ACLU	AFS	LCV	ITIC	NTU	COC	ACU	NTLC	CHC
2004	100	100	88	100	33	9	35	8	0	7
2003	95	—	100	85	—	25	32	17	—	—

National Journal Ratings

	2003 LIB — 2003 CONS		2004 LIB — 2004 CONS	
Economic	83%	— 17%	79%	— 20%
Social	92%	— 0%	88%	— 0%
Foreign	89%	— 11%	84%	— 15%

Key Votes of the 108th Congress

1. Drilling in ANWR	N	5. DC School Vouchers	N	9. Ban Same-Sex Marriage	N
2. Approve Bush Tax Cuts	N	6. Ban Human Cloning	N	10. Fund Iraq War	*
3. Medicare/Rx Bill	N	7. Restrict Gun Liability	N	11. Bar Cuba Embargo Funds	Y
4. Bar Overtime Pay Regs.	Y	8. Ban Partial-Birth Abortion	N	12. Intelligence Reorg.	Y

Election Results

2004 general	William Lacy Clay (D)	213,658	(75%)	($262,648)
	Leslie Farr (R)	64,791	(23%)	
	Other	5,322	(2%)	
2004 primary	William Lacy Clay (D)	unopposed		
2002 general	William Lacy Clay (D)	133,946	(70%)	($335,527)
	Richard Schwadron (R)	51,755	(27%)	($12,198)
	Other	5,454	(3%)	

Prior Winning Percentages: 2000 (75%)

The People		Race/Ethnic Origin	Ancestry	
Area size:	227 sq. mi.	45.8% White	German: 13.6%	Irish: 7.8%
Urban population:	99.2%	49.7% Black	English: 4.3%	
Rural population:	0.8%	1.5% Asian	**2004 Presidential Vote**	
Pop. 2000:	621,690	0.2% Native Am.	Kerry (D) 216,372	(75%)
Median income:	$36,314	0.0% Hawaiian	Bush (R) 71,367	(25%)
Poverty status:	15.8%	1.3% Two+ races	**2000 Presidential Vote**	
Military veterans:	13.6%	0.1% Other	Gore (D) 182,323	(72%)
		1.3% Hispanic Origin	Bush (R) 65,686	(26%)
			Other 5,022	(2%)
			Cook Partisan Voting Index: D +26	

Occupation	Blue collar: 20.7%	White collar: 61.9%	Gray collar: 17.4%

For a century or more, St. Louis seemed the center of America: the starting point for the Lewis and Clark expedition in 1804; the locus half a century later of the *Dred Scott* case, a Supreme

Court ruling that helped split the nation; the site of the 1904 World's Fair that introduced the hot dog and the ice cream cone and got 19 million people to *Meet Me in St. Louis*. Its 630-foot-high Gateway Arch is just below the point where the waters of the Missouri surge into the Mississippi, about halfway between New Orleans and Lake Superior, the Atlantic and the Pacific. This first major American city west of the Mississippi River was the final resting place of Daniel Boone and for many years was Chicago's rival as the transportation hub of America. In 1904 St. Louis already had the Eads Bridge, one of America's first suspension bridges; the Wainwright Building, one of Louis Sullivan's first skyscrapers; and Union Station, the world's largest passenger train station when it opened in 1894. Some 600,000 people lived then in densely packed brick houses on old street grids radiating outward from downtown. This was a heavily German city, with a Teutonic solidity and orderliness which distinguished it from the surrounding Southern-accented rural terrain; and from Mitteleuropa came the founders of St. Louis's great businesses—the Anheuser-Busch brewery, May Company department stores, Joseph Pulitzer's *St. Louis Post-Dispatch*—and its first great politician and a friend of Abraham Lincoln, Senator and Interior Secretary Carl Schurz. There is almost a European aura to Forest Park, the site of the 1904 fair, and the dozen mansion-lined private streets nearby, like Portland Place.

St. Louis is still one of the nation's 20 largest metro areas, but today it does not occupy as central a place in the national consciousness, and the central city itself has largely emptied out. The German order that made so many people comfortable living in close quarters and commuting by streetcar seems to have yielded to an American desire for Daniel Boone's wide open (suburban) spaces and the less restrictive automobile. St. Louis' population peaked at 856,000 in 1950; it was down to 343,000 in 2004, less than its 350,000 in 1880 and far less than the 1,009,000 now in suburban (and juridically separate) St. Louis County. Indeed, more blacks live in St. Louis County (193,000) than St. Louis City (178,000). Downtown St. Louis has been spruced up admirably: the Gateway Arch was finished in 1965; Union Station has been redeveloped; Laclede's Landing is stocked with shops. But most of St. Louis's old factories have closed and many of its once tight neighborhoods are only a memory.

Missouri's congressional districts have followed the people out of St. Louis, where the Democratic organization has been weakened by the loss of patronage and state approval of term limits. The 1st District of Missouri, historically based on the north side of the city, now has three-quarters of its residents in suburban St. Louis County. It includes St. Louis City north of I-64 and the northern and some central portions of St. Louis County. The district includes all the predominantly black suburbs to the north of the city, including Bellefontaine Neighbors, Ferguson, Spanish Lake and Black Jack. It also includes along I-70 working-class St. Ann and Bridgeton and, just west of the city, parts of the affluent suburbs of University City, Ladue and Creve Coeur. Before redistricting, the population of the district was 60% black; now it is 50% black. But blacks undoubtedly account for more than 50% of the votes in Democratic primaries that, in this heavily Democratic district, are the contests that matter.

The congressman from the 1st District is William Lacy Clay, a Democrat first elected in 2000 to the seat that his father Bill Clay had held for 32 years. Lacy Clay's whole life bears the imprint of his father's politics. Born in St. Louis, he moved to the Washington, D.C. area after his father's election in 1968 and grew up there as a congressman's son. He attended Silver Spring, Maryland, public schools and then the University of Maryland, studying by night for seven years while he worked as a House staffer by day. He had started law classes at Howard University when a special election for the state House in 1983 drew him back to St. Louis, and party leaders appointed him the Democratic nominee. Eight years later, Lacy Clay was again picked by party leaders to run in a special election for a safely Democratic state Senate seat, after the incumbent got a job with a congressional subcommittee.

In 1999 Bill Clay decided to retire after having helped to enact many labor and education laws. Lacy Clay had a serious contest. His most credible primary opposition was from St. Louis Councilman Charlie Dooley. Dooley raised nearly $400,000 and, though black, built up a base of support in the mostly white suburbs of St. Louis County. Dooley campaigned that the office should not be "inherited" and he attacked what he called Clay's old-style tactics of political threats and bossism. To make sure voters knew he was not challenging the incumbent, Dooley's billboards said, "Congressman Bill Clay is retiring this year." The St. Louis Labor Council and Missouri AFL-CIO, long allied to Bill Clay, declined to endorse his son, but he was endorsed by more than 30 locals. Many voters may have still have thought the two Clays were the same person; Lacy Clay played up his father's name and revved up the still reliable machine. He won the six-candidate primary 61%–28% over Dooley, winning St. Louis City 76%–12% and St. Louis County, where twice as many votes were cast, 49%–39%. The general election was no contest. Lacy Clay won 75%–22%, which was better than his father had done in recent elections.

In the House, Clay was president of the Democrats' freshman class and has had a liberal voting record. He sought to make the point that he was not entirely his father's son. "Call me 'Clay Lite'," he said as he discussed his softer image with the *St. Louis Post-Dispatch*. But the truth inevitably was more complex. He has worked to protect voting rights for blacks and the reliability of electronic voting equipment. On the reorganized Government Reform Committee, Clay became ranking Democrat on the Federalism and the Census Subcommittee, an important post for blacks concerned about maximizing their House seats following the next redistricting. On the Financial Services Committee, he complained that an investigation of Fannie Mae was a "political lynching of Franklin Raines," who eventually was forced out as CEO. After retired St. Louis Cardinal slugger Mark McGwire refused to tell House investigators whether he had used steroids, Clay demanded the removal of his name from a stretch of I-70 in St. Louis.

SECOND DISTRICT

Rep. Todd Akin (R)

Elected 2000, 3d term; b. July 5, 1947, New York, NY; home, Town and Country; Worcester Polytech Inst. (MA), B.S. 1971, Covenant Theological Seminary (MO), M. Div. 1985; Presbyterian; married (Lulli).

Military Career: Army Reserves 1972–80.

Elected Office: MO House of Reps., 1988–2000.

Professional Career: Marketing Mgr., IBM, 1974–78; Mgmt. Dir., Laclede Steel, 1977–80; Instructor, Maryville U.

DC Office: 117 CHOB, 20515, 202-225-2561; Fax: 202-225-2563; Web site: www.house.gov/akin.

District Offices: St. Charles, 636-949-6826; St. Louis, 314-590-0029.

Committees: *Armed Services* (18th of 34 R): Tactical Air & Land Forces; Terrorism, Unconventional Threats & Capabilities. *Science* (13th of 24 R): Energy; Research. *Small Business* (6th of 18 R): Regulatory Reform & Oversight (Chmn.).

Group Ratings

	ADA	ACLU	AFS	LCV	ITIC	NTU	COC	ACU	NTLC	CHC
2004	0	0	0	0	70	78	95	100	94	100
2003	5	—	13	10	—	76	90	92	—	—

National Journal Ratings

	2003 LIB	—	2003 CONS		2004 LIB	—	2004 CONS
Economic	31%	—	68%		0%	—	95%
Social	5%	—	87%		0%	—	91%
Foreign	23%	—	71%		4%	—	93%

Key Votes of the 108th Congress

1. Drilling in ANWR	N	5. DC School Vouchers	Y	9. Ban Same-Sex Marriage	Y
2. Approve Bush Tax Cuts	Y	6. Ban Human Cloning	Y	10. Fund Iraq War	Y
3. Medicare/Rx Bill	N	7. Restrict Gun Liability	Y	11. Bar Cuba Embargo Funds	N
4. Bar Overtime Pay Regs.	N	8. Ban Partial-Birth Abortion	Y	12. Intelligence Reorg.	Y

Election Results

2004 general	Todd Akin (R) 228,725	(65%)	($702,232)
	George Weber (D) 115,366	(33%)	
	Other 5,776	(2%)	
2004 primary	Todd Akin (R) .... unopposed		
2002 general	Todd Akin (R) 167,057	(67%)	($586,796)
	John Hogan (D) 77,223	(31%)	
	Other 4,548	(2%)	

Prior Winning Percentages: 2000 (55%)

The People		Race/Ethnic Origin	Ancestry	
Area size:	1,288 sq. mi.	93.2% White	German: 26.7% Irish: 12.7%	
Urban population:	91.7%	2.2% Black	English: 8.2%	
Rural population:	8.4%	2.0% Asian	**2004 Presidential Vote**	
Pop. 2000:	621,690	0.2% Native Am.	Bush (R) 215,123	(60%)
Median income:	$61,416	0.0% Hawaiian	Kerry (D) 142,824	(40%)
Poverty status:	3.6%	0.9% Two+ races	Other 155	(0%)
Military veterans:	13.5%	0.1% Other	**2000 Presidential Vote**	
		1.4% Hispanic Origin	Bush (R) 179,633	(59%)
			Gore (D) 119,907	(39%)
			Other 6,744	(2%)
			Cook Partisan Voting Index: R + 9	
Occupation Blue collar: 17.5% White collar: 71.3% Gray collar: 11.2%				

Just as the U.S. population's geographic center has moved west from the St. Louis area to rural Phelps County, so the center of metropolitan St. Louis area continues to move farther west from the Gateway Arch on the Mississippi River. The fulcrum point now is in St. Louis County, established in 1876 when the city, tired of paying for dusty back roads, separated itself from the sticks. There were then about 350,000 people in the city and 31,000 in the county. In 2004, the city had 343,000 and St. Louis County 1,009,000. By the 1960s, the center of office employment had moved from downtown across the county line to Clayton; now, the focus is fast moving out the Daniel Boone Expressway (U.S. 40) to Chesterfield, west of the I-270 ring road.

The 2d Congressional District of Missouri is made up of central and western St. Louis County, most of St. Charles County northwest across the Missouri River and rural Lincoln County to the north. In the center of St. Louis County, along the Daniel Boone Expressway, are the long-settled suburbs of Kirkwood, most of high-income Town and Country and Ladue, fast-growing Chesterfield and, to the south, Sunset Hills—all Republican areas, even more so in the newer family-oriented subdivisions than in the leafy precincts of the old rich. St. Charles County, where the supply of available land and affordable housing has become tight, now casts more votes than the city of St. Louis and is the most Republican suburban county in Missouri; the county council added a statement to its marriage licenses that the recipients are a man and a woman. This is a Republican district that voted 60% for George W. Bush in 2004.

The congressman from the 2d District is Todd Akin, a Republican first elected in 2000. He continues to live in his boyhood home, a 50-year-old farmhouse that rests in what has become an upscale neighborhood in Town and Country. He graduated from Worcester Polytechnic Institute and got a divinity degree at Covenant Seminary. After service as an Army combat engineer, he worked for IBM in the Boston area and then at Laclede Steel in Alton, Illinois, the same company where his father once worked. He was elected to the state House in 1988. During the next 12 years, as part of the Republican minority, he passed few bills. Undaunted, he took to the courts, filing one lawsuit to stop a tax increase for education improvements and another to stop riverboat gambling on barges moored in artificial ponds; the former case failed but the latter succeeded, forcing the gambling industry to spend millions on a referendum that changed the law in its favor. Akin is an avid student of American history and the Constitution, on which he lectures at various public and private institutions. While a state legislator, he sold standardized tests to parents who home school their children; he and his wife have home schooled their six children. State House reporters noted that he sometimes played gospel tunes on his guitar in the Capitol late at night.

When Congressman Jim Talent announced in early 1999 that he was running for governor, Akin ran for the House. He started off as the underdog to Gene McNary, the former Bush administration INS commissioner and well known from his 15 years as St. Louis County Executive, and as a three-time loser in statewide races between 1972 and 1984. A third candidate, former state Senate Minority Leader Franc Flotron, ran as a conservative. Akin called himself "a conservative with a soft edge," who tries to work as a team player. He emphasized that he had never voted to raise taxes, and he had strong support from religious conservatives; he may have benefited from staying above the personal attacks. In a low-turnout, rainy day Republican primary, Akin rallied his committed cadre to win the five-candidate contest by 56 votes. In the general election against state Senator Ted House, Akin focused on their differences on taxes. House depicted Akin as a narrow ideologue who was an ineffective legislator. House, whose TV ads did not identify himself as a Democrat, cited a report by a liberal activist group that Akin had written a supportive letter read at a militia rally in 1995 that focused on the right to bear arms; Akin responded that he had turned down an invitation to speak. Akin carried St. Louis County 57%–40% and won overall 55%–42%.

In the House, Akin has one of the most strongly conservative voting records. On the Armed Services Committee he emphasized what he said was the essential role played by special operation forces in fighting terrorism. With Dana Rohrabacher, he passed in the House a bill to promote development of the commercial human space flight industry, to encourage entrepreneurship especially in suborbital rockets. On the Republicans' education bill, he opposed mandatory school testing because he was concerned about excessive federal involvement. After a federal appeals court in California ruled that the reference to "one nation under God" in the Pledge of Allegiance was unconstitutional, Akin passed in the House a bill that would strip the lower courts of jurisdiction over challenges to the Pledge. He sponsored the Parents' Right to Know Act, which bars funding to family planning projects that provide contraceptive drugs and devices to minors before getting parental consent. He burned some bridges with Republican leaders when he voted against the Medicare/prescription drug bill; he worried that it would be a "budget buster" and would attract more illegal immigrants.

Back home, Akin was the only member of the delegation who did not support the redistricting plan even though the changes made what had been a competitive district a decade before significantly more Republican. Akin has been easily reelected.

THIRD DISTRICT

Rep. Russ Carnahan (D)

Elected 2004, 1st term; b. July 10, 1958, Columbia; home, St. Louis; U. of MO, B.S. 1979, J.D. 1983; Methodist; married (Debra).

Elected Office: MO House of Reps., 2000–04.

Professional Career: Practicing atty, 1988–96; Consultant, BJC HealthCare, 1996–2004.

DC Office: 1232 LHOB, 20515, 202-225-2671; Fax: 202-225-7452; Web site: www.house.gov/carnahan.

District Offices: Crystal City, 636-937-8039; St. Louis, 314-962-1523.

Committees: *Science* (11th of 20 D): Research. *Transportation & Infrastructure* (32d of 34 D): Aviation; Highways, Transit & Pipelines; Water Resources & Environment.

Group Ratings and Key Votes: Newly Elected

Election Results

2004 general				
	Russ Carnahan (D)	146,894	(53%)	($1,392,248)
	Bill Federer (R)	125,422	(45%)	($1,367,643)
	Other	5,600	(2%)	
2004 primary				
	Russ Carnahan (D)	24,507	(23%)	
	Jeff Smith (D)	22,783	(21%)	
	Steve Stoll (D)	19,372	(18%)	
	Joan Barry (D)	18,922	(18%)	
	Mariano Favazza (D)	9,647	(9%)	
	Mark Smith (D)	7,400	(7%)	
	Other	4,370	(4%)	
2002 general				
	Dick Gephardt (D)	122,181	(59%)	($3,389,306)
	Catherine Enz (R)	80,551	(39%)	($114,143)
	Other	4,146	(2%)	

The People		Race/Ethnic Origin	Ancestry	
Area size:	1,266 sq. mi.	85.7% White	German: 23.1% Irish: 11.6%	
Urban population:	86.7%	9.1% Black	English: 5.9%	
Rural population:	13.3%	1.6% Asian	**2004 Presidential Vote**	
Pop. 2000:	621,690	0.2% Native Am.	Kerry (D)	168,740 (57%)
Median income:	$41,091	0.0% Hawaiian	Bush (R)	127,668 (43%)
Poverty status:	10.1%	1.4% Two+ races	Other	657 (0%)
Military veterans:	13.2%	0.1% Other	**2000 Presidential Vote**	
		1.8% Hispanic Origin	Gore (D)	140,954 (54%)
			Bush (R)	112,460 (43%)
			Other	7,972 (3%)
			Cook Partisan Voting Index: D + 8	

Occupation	Blue collar: 24.2%	White collar: 60.4%	Gray collar: 15.4%

Middle America, it could be said, lies somewhere on the south side of metropolitan St. Louis. The geographical center of the country's population was here in 1980, just south of St. Louis in once rural and now mostly suburban Jefferson County; while that point has moved about 35 miles southwest, St. Louis is still the metro area nearest the demographic midpoint of a country most of whose people live in million-plus metro areas. Geographically, this is a node where some of the nation's main arteries come together. The Missouri River flows into the Mississippi a few miles north of St. Louis's Gateway Arch; the National Road and its successors, U.S. 40 and Interstate 70, cross the Mississippi just below the Arch. And the great tides of Southerners migrating west up the Mississippi and Germans migrating overland met here to create one of the nation's largest and most bustling cities out of a town founded by the French before the Revolutionary War. The south side of St. Louis is famous for its pleasant parks and tight-knit, neat neighborhoods, including "Little Bosnia" in the Bevo Mill neighborhood; its most famous symbols are the Anheuser-Busch brewery just south of downtown and Grant's Farm, where Ulysses S. Grant lived in the 1850s and where Anheuser-Busch now keeps the Budweiser Clydesdales. But many more people now live in the suburbs heading out all directions, well into Jefferson County to the south. In St. Louis County and south St. Louis, the Catholic Church has closed more than 20 parishes and eight schools since 1970, and the number of registered parishioners has dropped by half to about 115,000, while suburban parishes have been growing.

The 3d Congressional District of Missouri consists of the south side of St. Louis, part of suburban St. Louis County and, to the south, Jefferson County and rural Ste. Genevieve County, the site of Missouri's oldest permanent settlement, founded near a salt mine in 1730. Its St. Louis County portions are mostly suburbs close to the St. Louis City line—Clayton, Maplewood, Richmond Heights, Webster Groves, Affton, Lemay, Oakville. This is the descendant of districts dominated by St. Louis voters, but today the city casts less than 25% of its votes, fewer than in Jefferson County, where local Republicans have been making inroads; almost half are cast in St. Louis County. Ethnically, this has been a heavily German-American area since the mid-19th century. Politically, it has been Democratic since the New Deal of the 1930s. The district voted 57% for John Kerry in 2004; Ste. Genevieve was the only non-metropolitan Missouri county Kerry carried.

The congressman from the 3d District is Russ Carnahan, a Democrat elected in 2004. He succeeded Richard Gephardt, who retired after serving 28 years as a tireless party strategist, including nearly six years as majority leader and eight years as minority leader, and twice unsuccessfully sought the Democratic nomination for president. Carnahan is the son of the late governor Mel Carnahan and former Senator Jean Carnahan, who was appointed to the Senate seat that her husband won after he died in an airplane crash two weeks before the 2000 election. Russ Carnahan grew up in Rolla and graduated from the University of Missouri and its law school. He practiced law with his wife Debra until 1996, when he took a job as a lobbyist and consultant with BJC Health System, now BJC HealthCare, a non-profit that operates several nursing homes and hospitals. In 1990 he ran unsuccessfully against Republican Bill Emerson in the old 10th Congressional District in southeast Missouri. In 2000 he was elected to the state House and after the 2002 election became chairman of the House Democratic Caucus. In 2003 it was obvious that Gephardt was running for president and would not run for reelection, and Carnahan decided to run in the 3d District.

Carnahan was among four current or former state legislators running in the primary. Opponents ganged up on him, claiming he had a thin legislative record and was trading on his family name. His toughest opponent turned out to be Jeff Smith, a political science instructor at Washington University in St. Louis, who worked as a volunteer in Bill Bradley's presidential campaign in 2000 and Howard Dean's in 2004. He was endorsed by Dean and by the *St. Louis Post-Dispatch* and assembled a large corps of volunteers. Gephardt remained neutral, but many of his allies backed state Senator Steve Stoll, who supported gun rights and opposed abortion. This turned out to be a very close race. Carnahan won with 23% of the vote, Smith finished a close second with 21% and Stoll was not far behind with 18%. Smith led in St. Louis City and County; Stoll led by a wide margin in Jefferson and Ste. Genevieve Counties; Carnahan ran second or third in each—a sign that he greater name recognition but lacked a committed core of supporters. Smith took St. Louis County, which had the biggest turnout with 36% of the Democratic vote; he got 28% there to 27% for former state representative Joan Berry and 22% for Carnahan. In Jefferson County, which cast 30% of the vote, Stoll led Carnahan, 46%–22%.

In the general election Carnahan faced Republican author Bill Federer, who had lost twice to Gephardt. Federer spent heavily; he opposed all abortions and criticized Carnahan for supporting the national assault weapon ban, which expired September 13. Carnahan called for increased funding for education and said that he would "retarget" Bush's tax cuts to the middle class. Carnahan won 53%–45% on the same day his sister Robin Carnahan was elected Missouri's secretary of state. Federer led 50%–48% in Jefferson County, but Carnahan carried St. Louis County 52%–46%, and St. Louis City 61%–36%. Carnahan's margins in both primary and general were not so large as to preclude future opposition. Smith, who was a visiting professor at Dartmouth College in New Hampshire during the spring, left open the possibility that he might run again.

FOURTH DISTRICT

Rep. Ike Skelton (D)

Elected 1976, 15th term; b. Dec. 20, 1931, Lexington; home, Lexington; Wentworth Military Acad. Jr. Col., 1949–51, U. of MO, A.B. 1953, LL.B. 1956; Disciples of Christ; married (Susie).

Elected Office: MO Senate, 1970–76.

Professional Career: Lafayette Cnty. Prosecuting atty., 1957–60; MO Special Asst. Atty. Gen., 1961–63; Practicing atty., 1963–76.

DC Office: 2206 RHOB, 20515, 202-225-2876; Web site: www.house.gov/skelton.

District Offices: Blue Springs, 816-228-4242; Jefferson City, 573-635-3499; Lebanon, 417-532-7964; Sedalia, 660-826-2675.

Committees: *Armed Services* (RMM of 28 D): Tactical Air & Land Forces.

Group Ratings

	ADA	ACLU	AFS	LCV	ITIC	NTU	COC	ACU	NTLC	CHC
2004	65	30	88	64	70	13	60	48	20	61
2003	80	—	100	60	—	26	60	68	—	—

National Journal Ratings

	2003 LIB	—	2003 CONS		2004 LIB	—	2004 CONS
Economic	57%	—	43%		59%	—	41%
Social	51%	—	49%		51%	—	48%
Foreign	52%	—	47%		52%	—	47%

Key Votes of the 108th Congress

1. Drilling in ANWR	Y	5. DC School Vouchers	N	9. Ban Same-Sex Marriage	Y
2. Approve Bush Tax Cuts	N	6. Ban Human Cloning	Y	10. Fund Iraq War	Y
3. Medicare/Rx Bill	N	7. Restrict Gun Liability	Y	11. Bar Cuba Embargo Funds	N
4. Bar Overtime Pay Regs.	Y	8. Ban Partial-Birth Abortion	Y	12. Intelligence Reorg.	Y

Election Results

2004 general	Ike Skelton (D)	190,800	(66%)	($703,768)
	Jim Noland (R)	93,334	(32%)	
	Other	4,092	(1%)	
2004 primary	Ike Skelton (D)	unopposed		
2002 general	Ike Skelton (D)	142,204	(68%)	($596,705)
	Jim Noland (R)	64,451	(31%)	
	Other	3,583	(2%)	

Prior Winning Percentages: 2000 (67%); 1998 (71%); 1996 (64%); 1994 (68%); 1992 (70%); 1990 (62%); 1988 (72%); 1986 (100%); 1984 (67%); 1982 (55%); 1980 (68%); 1978 (73%); 1976 (56%)

The People		Race/Ethnic Origin	Ancestry	
Area size:	14,825 sq. mi.	92.4% White	German: 17.4%	USA: 11.0%
Urban population:	39.9%	3.2% Black	Irish: 8.6%	
Rural population:	60.1%	0.6% Asian	**2004 Presidential Vote**	
Pop. 2000:	621,690	0.5% Native Am.	Bush (R) 187,111	(64%)
Median income:	$34,541	0.1% Hawaiian	Kerry (D) 102,652	(35%)
Poverty status:	12.1%	1.3% Two+ races	Other 1,622	(1%)
Military veterans:	16.1%	0.1% Other	**2000 Presidential Vote**	
		1.9% Hispanic Origin	Bush (R) 147,694	(58%)
			Gore (D) 100,171	(39%)
			Other 6,024	(2%)
			Cook Partisan Voting Index: R +11	

Occupation   Blue collar: 31.9%   White collar: 51.4%   Gray collar: 16.7%

Missouri was the first state settled west of the Mississippi, and the folks who settled it were a picture of pioneer diversity. Virginians and other Southerners made their way to counties north of the Missouri River, while Germans settled around the still small capital city of Jefferson City. A taste of that diversity can be found in the Capitol, with its mural by Thomas Hart Benton, great-grandnephew and eponym of one of Missouri's first senators, who championed hard money and westward expansion for 30 years and lost his seat for opposing the expansion of slavery. The painting shows dance hall girls, black coal miners and a mother diapering an infant—all reminders that pioneer life was less homogeneous than many imagine.

The 4th Congressional District of Missouri occupies much of this early-settled part of central and western Missouri. It includes part of Blue Springs and Oak Grove in Jackson County east of Kansas City, but the overall atmosphere here is rural and small-town, with political traditions dating back to the community's early days. The rural counties around Kansas City were full of pro-slavery-expansion Bushwhackers who rode across the Kansas line to thwart the Yankee Jayhawks, and these areas today vote Democratic. The German area around Jefferson City was anti-slavery and remains among the most Republican parts of Missouri, and the new resort areas around Lake of the Ozarks are mixed. The southern portion of the district, near Springfield, was Union country during the Civil War but is Republican now. There are some big military bases here: Fort Leonard Wood in Pulaski County, where Marines, sailors and airmen train in joint exercises with Army troops, and Whiteman Air Force Base, near Knob Noster in Johnson County, from which B-2s took off and flew across the world to drop precision-targeted bombs in Afghanistan.

Much of this region is Truman country: Harry Truman was born in Barton County, at the southern end of the district, and lived in Independence, just a few miles from Blue Springs. He spent much of election night 1948, when just about everyone thought he would lose, in Excelsior Springs, on the border of Ray County, the district's one county north of the Missouri River. In his long life Truman spanned the gaps between country and city, South and North: his mother could remember her house being attacked by Yankee soldiers, and she remained pro-Confederate even when her son was in the White House; he got his political start in urban Independence and Kansas City and desegregated the military services. Truman Dam in Benton County forms one of the lakes of central Missouri and provides such good fishing that nearby Warsaw is known as Fishing Town U.S.A.

The congressman from the 4th District is Ike Skelton, who in many ways can be called a Truman Democrat; his father met Truman in 1928, when he was Lafayette County prosecutor and the future president was Jackson County judge, and they remained friends for life; his father supported Truman when he was nearly defeated in the 1940 Senate primary, and he took 17-year-old Ike to Washington for Truman's inaugural in 1949. In 1952 Skelton and a friend talked their way past the Secret Service in Jackson County and spoke with Truman himself. Skelton is from a military family: his father served in the Navy, he and his brothers went to military academies and he has sons in the Army and Navy; a teenage bout with polio made him ineligible for military service. He grew up in Lexington, of old Missouri stock; he is a distant cousin through the Boone family of New York Congresswoman Louise Slaughter. He remembers walking down the street 1944 watching C-47s droning overhead pulling gliders, training pilots for D-Day. Skelton graduated from the University of Missouri and its law school and returned to Lexington to practice law. He became county prosecutor in 1957, at 25, and was elected to the Missouri Senate in 1970. In 1976 he ran for Congress and won rather easily; Bess Truman, remembering the 1940 primary, endorsed him. Skelton looks and votes like an old-fashioned rural Missouri Democrat: his voting record puts him near the midpoint of this Republican House on economics and foreign issues, slightly to the right on cultural issues. He supports the same expansive, assertive foreign and defense policies the preponderance of Democrats supported in the days of Truman.

Skelton is the ranking Democrat on the Armed Services Committee where he has made great contributions to policy. He played a key role in passing the Goldwater-Nichols Act in 1986, which created the joint commands which have proved so successful in Iraq; and he has encouraged joint operations at Fort Leonard Wood. In 1987 and 1988 he chaired a panel on professional military education, which revamped the intermediate and senior officer schools; he has drawn up his own National Security List of 50 books on military history and analysis and has read them all. He has said that the first Bush administration and the Clinton administration both cut the military too much, and he has criticized the current Bush administration for not seeking higher force levels. In February 2005 he told Donald Rumsfeld that to prevent "a hollow army . . . a permanent addition to the force is needed. You're wearing 'em out, secretary, that's the bottom line." He has worked hard to improve housing and facilities for service members and their families and has proposed offering 18-month enlistments plus four years of Reserve duty to get more recruits. He warned the Clinton and Bush administrations that troops could be worn out by multiple deployments. He was reluctant to support sending troops to Bosnia in September 1995, and passed a resolution, 287–141, which called for strict neutrality in the peacekeeping effort. He supported the air war in the former Yugoslavia in March 1999.

In September 2002, after a meeting in the White House, he wrote George W. Bush a letter arguing that the occupation of Iraq would be difficult. With apparent reluctance he voted for the Iraq war resolution in October 2002. On the eve of military action, in March 2003, he wrote Bush another letter, saying that there was "great potential for a ragged ending to a war as we deal with the aftermath." In August 2004 he said that the Iraq war caused "a stretching and straining of the U.S. military like I have not seen before" and that the Pentagon was pushing Reservists "nearly to the breaking point." "I think we would be in the final phases of cleaning up Al Qaeda had we not gone into Iraq." He supported resolutions of inquiry to obtain the Joint Chiefs of Staff's "lessons learned" reports on pre-war Iraq intelligence. In December 2004 he urged the Pentagon to use M-113 armored personnel carriers in Iraq pending delivery of armored humvees.

Armed Services is one of the House's least partisan committees; most members are strong defense supporters and it usually reports bills with bipartisan support. Skelton is greatly respected by Republicans as well as Democrats on the committee. Skelton can be cautious about change. When Donald Rumsfeld proposed major changes in Pentagon procedures and personnel rules in 2003, Skelton said, "I went from shock and awe to disbelief." But he was not troubled by the intelligence reorganization bill that centralized spending control over intelligence in a national director of intelligence. "I'm convinced the military will not be shortchanged five cents." Looking ahead in January 2005, he said, "I am convinced that the straits of Taiwan are the most dangerous part of the world. The way to deter problems is to have a strong capability. We can't have signs that we're weakening." That would suggest support for sophisticated weaponry like the F-22. In March 2005 he called for maintaining a "firewall" between public affairs and information operations. The latter, he argued, "rightfully includes disinformation and misinformation designed to make our adversaries react in ways that benefit our commanders in the accomplishment of their assigned missions. . . . We must be aware that information that yields a tactical advantage may ultimately be to our strategic detriment as allies and the American people realize that we are releasing disinformation through the media."

Naturally Skelton looks out for the interests of Fort Leonard Wood and Whiteman Air Force Base which, as he points out, are both major bases with unique functions and thus were spared from the May 2005 base closing recommendations list. He encouraged joint operations at Leonard Wood and was instrumental in getting Whiteman, with its 12,400-foot runway, designated in 1987 as the home of the first wing of B-2s; the base had been used for the Minuteman II missile which was about to be phased out. As Knob Noster's city manager said, "I can tell you two words why the B-2s are here: Ike Skelton." His loyalty to Missouri only goes so far: in 1999, when other Missourians were trying to keep the F-15 line open in St. Louis County, Skelton said that he doubted any more F-15s would be built; he opposed ordering them in appropriations bills when they hadn't been authorized by Armed Services.

On non-military issues, Skelton tends to stick with other Democrats on taxes and economic issues, though he was one of only 20 Democrats who voted for trade promotion authority in 2001 and 2002: "For me it was the right thing to do. I represent a rural area. We have a lot of farms—a lot of soybeans, wheat and corn. And one-fourth of all that depends on foreign markets."

Skelton's toughest race came in 1982, when he was redistricted in with a Republican incumbent; he won 55%–45%. He has won by very large margins in recent years; in 1999 citizens in Lexington and Lafayette Counties began raising money to build the Ike Skelton Museum of the American Armed Forces. He regards his constituents warmly. "Wonderfully warm people.

Conservative. Religious. Hardworking. Patriotic." They seem to reciprocate. In 2004, when George W. Bush was carrying the district 64%–35%, Skelton was reelected 66%–32%—more ticket-splitting than just about anywhere in America. It is widely assumed that when he retires, the 4th District will elect a Republican to replace him.

FIFTH DISTRICT

Rep. Emanuel Cleaver (D)

Elected 2004, 1st term; b. Oct. 26, 1944, Waxahachie, TX; home, Kansas City; Prairie View A&M U., B.S. 1968, St. Paul Schl. of Theology, M.Div. 1974; Methodist; married (Dianne).

Elected Office: Kansas City Cncl., 1979–91; mayor, 1991–99.

Professional Career: Pastor, 1970-present; radio talk-show host, 2002–04.

DC Office: 1641 LHOB, 20515, 202-225-4535; Fax: 202-225-4403; Web site: www.house.gov/cleaver.

District Offices: Independence, 816-833-4545; Kansas City, 816-842-4545.

Committees: *Financial Services* (29th of 32 D): Housing & Community Opportunity; Oversight & Investigations.

Group Ratings and Key Votes: Newly Elected

Election Results

2004 general	Emanuel Cleaver (D)	161,727	(55%)	($1,521,741)
	Jeanne Patterson (R)	123,431	(42%)	($3,207,825)
	Other	7,867	(3%)	
2004 primary	Emanuel Cleaver (D)	72,810	(60%)	
	Jamie Metzl (D)	48,607	(40%)	
2002 general	Karen McCarthy (D)	122,645	(66%)	($445,602)
	Steve Gordon (R)	60,245	(32%)	($4,059)
	Other	3,277	(2%)	

The People		Race/Ethnic Origin	Ancestry	
Area size:	519 sq. mi.	66.3% White	German: 13.5% Irish: 8.8%	
Urban population:	96.1%	24.2% Black	English: 7.5%	
Rural population:	3.9%	1.3% Asian	**2004 Presidential Vote**	
Pop. 2000:	621,691	0.4% Native Am.	Kerry (D)	175,352	(59%)
Median income:	$38,311	0.2% Hawaiian	Bush (R)	118,915	(40%)
Poverty status:	12.4%	1.9% Two+ races	Other	714	(0%)
Military veterans:	14.0%	0.1% Other	**2000 Presidential Vote**	
		5.6% Hispanic Origin	Gore (D)	149,621	(60%)
			Bush (R)	91,626	(37%)
			Other	6,625	(3%)
			Cook Partisan Voting Index: D +12	

Occupation	Blue collar: 22.7%	White collar: 61.8%	Gray collar: 15.4%

Kansas City, named after a state it isn't in and a river it doesn't touch, is the center of one of America's large metro areas, the biggest on the central Great Plains. The first pioneers here started little towns on the bluffs above the Missouri River—Independence, Kansas City, Westport—that coalesced a few decades later. Here traders on the Santa Fe Trail set out to cross the Sand Hills of Kansas and reach Mexican territory; here Jayhawks and Bushwhackers set out to fight for control of Bleeding Kansas. Kansas City was a rail center and, in the 1920s, had one of the largest stockyards in the country, a major commercial center with lean skyscrapers and the Country Club Plaza, the first shopping center in America. It is famous for Harry Truman, who grew up on a farm now in the suburb of Grandview and who lived in his wife's family's house in

Independence, the old county seat just to the east. It is famous also for its black community, and jazz musicians like Scott Joplin, Charlie Parker and Count Basie, and for its much-praised barbecue.

The 5th Congressional District of Missouri includes most of Kansas City, the largest city in Missouri, plus Grandview and the bulk of Independence. The more suburban slices of Jackson County to the east in Blue Springs (which is shared with the 4th District) and Lee's Summit have been filled with new subdivisions and some clashes over development. It also includes fast-growing Belton and Raymore along U.S. 71 in Cass County just to the south. Most of the metro area's landmarks, including the Truman home, are here. Much of the metropolitan area growth is across the state line in Kansas, where there has been more resistance to tax increases; a proposed bistate tax for the region was defeated at the polls. One-quarter of the district's residents are black, the second highest percentage among Missouri districts. Politically, the seat has been solidly Democratic. John Kerry carried it 59%–40%.

The congressman from the 5th District is Emanuel Cleaver, a Democrat elected in 2004. He grew up in Waxahachie, Texas, in a three-room shack with no plumbing or electricity. He graduated from Prairie View A&M, moved to Kansas City and earned a divinity degree, then became pastor of St. James United Methodist Church. He was elected to the city council in 1979 and elected mayor in 1991. As mayor, Cleaver voiced support for the Clinton administration welfare reforms, which he described as "corrective surgery." He backed expansion of downtown's Bartle Hall Convention Center and supported the renovation of the deteriorating Liberty Memorial, the country's largest World War I memorial. In his second term he helped to create 300 jobs by luring a Harley Davidson factory to the city. After leaving office he hosted a radio talk show.

In December 2003, Democratic Congresswoman Karen McCarthy announced that she would not run for reelection, and Cleaver was widely expected to succeed her. Few expected just how tough Cleaver's road to Congress would be. In the primary he faced former National Security Council aide Jamie Metzl, who raised substantial funds, mostly from individuals. Metzl hammered Cleaver on ethics issues. He questioned the propriety of a loan that Cleaver took out to purchase a car wash business and criticized Cleaver for his failure to pay $36,000 in back taxes that he owed on the business. Cleaver managed to win the primary by 60%–40%. Metzl carried the district's portion of Cass County 59%–41% and ran 178 votes ahead in suburban Jackson County. But Cleaver led 68%–32% in Kansas City, where 57% of the votes were cast.

In the general election Cleaver faced Republican businesswoman Jeanne Patterson, who said she would spend whatever it took to make the race competitive. Patterson, whose husband is chief executive of Cerner, a Kansas City-based medical software provider, spent more than $3.2 million of her own money on the contest. Like Metzl, she made an issue of Cleaver's ethics. She talked about the bribery and fraud convictions of Cleaver's allies, though there was no evidence that he was involved in their crimes. Cleaver said that Patterson was politically inexperienced and was trying to buy the seat; he suggested that she was running to give Cerner influence on health care policy. He called himself a "hundred-aire" and criticized Patterson as a hypocrite for promising to create local jobs while her husband's company reportedly was outsourcing work to India. "Money does talk, and it is talking quite eloquently," he said in one debate. Cleaver won 55%–42%; Cleaver ran 4% behind John Kerry. Once again his Kansas City base came through: it cast 48% of the vote and went 71%–27% for Cleaver. Patterson carried suburban Jackson County 54%–43%.

Cleaver got a seat on the Financial Services Committee and said that he wanted to bring more civility to Congress. He continued preaching regularly at his church in Kansas City.

SIXTH DISTRICT

Rep. Sam Graves (R)

Elected 2000, 3d term; b. Nov. 7, 1963, Tarkio; home, Tarkio; U. of MO, B.S. 1986; Baptist; married (Lesley).

Elected Office: MO House of Reps., 1992–94; MO Senate 1994–2000.

Professional Career: Farmer.

DC Office: 1513 LHOB, 20515, 202-225-7041; Fax: 202-225-8221; Web site: www.house.gov/graves.

District Offices: Liberty, 816-792-3976; St. Joseph, 816-233-9818.

Committees: *Agriculture* (13th of 25 R): Conservation, Credit, Rural Development & Research; General Farm Commodities & Risk Management. *Small Business* (5th of 18 R): Rural Enterprises, Agriculture & Technology (Chmn.). *Transportation & Infrastructure* (23d of 41 R): Aviation; Highways, Transit & Pipelines; Railroads.

Group Ratings

	ADA	ACLU	AFS	LCV	ITIC	NTU	COC	ACU	NTLC	CHC
2004	10	6	0	0	90	61	100	92	92	91
2003	5	—	0	10	—	63	100	88	—	—

National Journal Ratings

	2003 LIB	—	2003 CONS		2004 LIB	—	2004 CONS
Economic	17%	—	81%		24%	—	75%
Social	36%	—	64%		24%	—	76%
Foreign	37%	—	62%		47%	—	51%

Key Votes of the 108th Congress

1. Drilling in ANWR	Y	5. DC School Vouchers	*	9. Ban Same-Sex Marriage	Y
2. Approve Bush Tax Cuts	Y	6. Ban Human Cloning	Y	10. Fund Iraq War	Y
3. Medicare/Rx Bill	Y	7. Restrict Gun Liability	Y	11. Bar Cuba Embargo Funds	Y
4. Bar Overtime Pay Regs.	N	8. Ban Partial-Birth Abortion	Y	12. Intelligence Reorg.	Y

Election Results

2004 general	Sam Graves (R)	196,516	(64%)	($1,741,133)
	Charlie Broomfield (D)	106,987	(35%)	($887,833)
	Other	4,352	(1%)	
2004 primary	Sam Graves (R)	unopposed		
2002 general	Sam Graves (R)	131,151	(63%)	($1,176,557)
	Cathy Rinehart (D)	73,202	(35%)	($240,835)
	Other	3,735	(2%)	

Prior Winning Percentages: 2000 (51%)

The People		Race/Ethnic Origin	Ancestry	
Area size:	13,124 sq. mi.	92.4% White	German: 17.1%	Irish: 9.8%
Urban population:	66.3%	2.8% Black	USA: 8.9%	
Rural population:	33.7%	0.8% Asian	**2004 Presidential Vote**	
Pop. 2000:	621,690	0.4% Native Am.	Bush (R) 178,669	(57%)
Median income:	$41,225	0.1% Hawaiian	Kerry (D) 132,007	(42%)
Poverty status:	8.7%	1.1% Two+ races	Other 2,001	(1%)
Military veterans:	14.5%	0.1% Other	**2000 Presidential Vote**	
		2.4% Hispanic Origin	Bush (R) 143,954	(53%)
			Gore (D) 119,861	(44%)
			Other 7,380	(3%)
			Cook Partisan Voting Index: R + 5	

Occupation	Blue collar: 25.9%	White collar: 58.6%	Gray collar: 15.5%

The rolling, surging fields along the Missouri River in northwest Missouri were settled in a rush in the late 19th century and they lost people for most of the 20th century. Fewer hands were needed on farms than half a century ago, far fewer than a century ago. In 1940, this area had one of the largest meatpacking operations in the world, but the meatpacking business for years generated no new jobs here. Barge traffic on the Missouri has all but disappeared, a victim of drought, low levels (because of recreational uses upstream) and court rulings in favor of environmentalists. The river town of St. Joseph, which was the starting point for the Pony Express to Sacramento, is the biggest town north of Kansas City, with 73,000 people in 2000; it recently spent more than $1 million for a port to service the barges, which has rarely been used. The counties of northwest Missouri, aside from those in the Kansas City metro area, had 508,000 people in 1900, 452,000 in 1940 and 318,000 in 1990. But in the 1990s, the local economy began to perk up a little, and the number climbed to 330,000; some counties that had been losing population since 1900 started to gain. Biopharming—the use of genetically modified crops, such as rice, to grow medications—has become a growth industry in some of these rural communities.

The 6th Congressional District of Missouri takes in all these counties plus part of metro Kansas City—Clay and Platte Counties and a small portion of Jackson County east of Independence. The Kansas City area casts about half the district's votes. The historic political tradition here was mostly Democratic, but it has been tempered by dislike for national Democrats' cultural liberalism. This was strong Perot country in 1992; Bill Clinton carried it with a plurality in 1992 and 1996. But the rural vote here, as across the nation has moved toward Republicans. George W. Bush carried the district with 53% in 2000 and 57% in 2004.

The congressman from the 6th District is Sam Graves, a Republican first elected in 2000. He is a lifelong resident of Tarkio in the northwest corner of the state. He graduated from the University of Missouri with a degree in agronomy, farmed with his father and brother, and joined the Farm Bureau. He ran for the state House in 1992 and beat a longtime Democratic incumbent; in 1994 he was elected to the state Senate. He attracted attention in 1998 with a five-hour filibuster against a school desegregation bill he said was slanted against rural areas; but the bill eventually passed. Graves got his opportunity to run for the U.S. House when Congresswoman Pat Danner, 22 minutes before the May withdrawal deadline and without a public announcement, delivered to the secretary of state her withdrawal from the race. Not by accident, the immediate favorite to succeed her was her son, state Senator Steve Danner. Graves quickly entered the race within the short window provided by state law and drew support from national Republicans. Teresa Loar, a moderate Republican on the Kansas City Council, who had already filed for office before Danner's retirement, attacked Graves as the darling of extremist and sexist party leaders. Graves beat her 68%–17%. Against three weak Democratic alternatives, Steve Danner was held to 56% in the Democratic primary—a bad omen for November. In the general, Danner called himself a conservative Democrat and the candidates agreed on some issues: the death penalty, repeal of the marriage penalty tax and trade relations with China. But they differed on education funding, abortion rights (Danner switched from pro-life to pro-choice), gun control and the performance of Bill Clinton. Graves called Danner a "tax and spend liberal" and said that when this acorn fell from the tree, "it rolled to the left." In an editorial endorsing Graves, the *Kansas City Star* said that Danner's campaign switch on abortion showed that he "engaged in raw opportunism at the slightest opportunity," and that his central principle was "me first." Graves won 51%–47%.

In the House, Graves showed some moderate instincts, especially on foreign policy, and has usually been a party loyalist. He supported 2002 the farm bill and tended mostly to local issues. He called for toughening the nationwide Amber Alert system to locate abducted children. In March 2005 the House passed his amendment to the transportation bill to preempt state laws on liability for damages involving rental cars, a measure of interest to St. Louis-based Enterprise Rent-A-Car.

In this previously competitive district, Graves has had no trouble with reelection; local Democrats and a few Republicans have complained about his hard-nosed political tactics. In 2004, national Democrats ran ads that attacked Graves for voting for the 2003 Medicare/ prescription drug bill and they talked up their nominee Charlie Broomfield, a former state representative who was well-financed; he criticized the Patriot Act and the Bush administration's handling of the war in Iraq. But Graves won 64%–35%, almost the same margin as in 2002, and he carried every county. Kansas City Mayor Kay Barnes has been mentioned as a possible challenger in 2006. Graves reportedly is interested in running for the Senate when a seat opens.

SEVENTH DISTRICT

Rep. Roy Blunt (R)

Elected 1996, 5th term; b. Jan. 10, 1950, Niangua; home, Strafford; SW Baptist U., B.A. 1970, SW MO St. U., M.A. 1972; Baptist; married (Abigail Perlman).

Elected Office: MO Secy. of State, 1984–93.

Professional Career: H.S. teacher, 1970–73; Greene Cnty. Clerk, 1973–85; Adjunct Instructor, Drury Col., 1976–82; Pres., SW Baptist U., 1993–96.

DC Office: 217 CHOB, 20515, 202-225-6536; Fax: 202-225-5604; Web site: www.blunt.house.gov.

District Offices: Joplin, 417-781-1041; Springfield, 417-889-1800.

Committees: *Majority Whip. Energy & Commerce (16th of 31 R).*

Group Ratings

	ADA	ACLU	AFS	LCV	ITIC	NTU	COC	ACU	NTLC	CHC
2004	0	0	0	0	100	67	100	96	81	92
2003	5	—	0	0	—	64	97	92	—	—

National Journal Ratings

	2003 LIB	—	2003 CONS		2004 LIB	—	2004 CONS
Economic	0%	—	91%		7%	—	92%
Social	5%	—	87%		36%	—	61%
Foreign	11%	—	80%		14%	—	86%

Key Votes of the 108th Congress

1. Drilling in ANWR	Y	5. DC School Vouchers	Y	9. Ban Same-Sex Marriage	Y
2. Approve Bush Tax Cuts	Y	6. Ban Human Cloning	Y	10. Fund Iraq War	Y
3. Medicare/Rx Bill	Y	7. Restrict Gun Liability	Y	11. Bar Cuba Embargo Funds	N
4. Bar Overtime Pay Regs.	N	8. Ban Partial-Birth Abortion	Y	12. Intelligence Reorg.	Y

Election Results

2004 general	Roy Blunt (R)	210,080	(70%)	($3,527,363)
	Jim Newberry (D)	84,356	(28%)	($214,240)
	Other	3,769	(1%)	
2004 primary	Roy Blunt (R)	unopposed		
2002 general	Roy Blunt (R)	149,519	(75%)	($1,331,576)
	Ron Lapham (D)	45,964	(23%)	
	Other	4,380	(2%)	

Prior Winning Percentages: 2000 (74%); 1998 (73%); 1996 (65%)

The People		Race/Ethnic Origin	Ancestry	
Area size:	5,555 sq. mi.	92.9% White	German: 13.5%	USA: 10.8%
Urban population:	59.1%	1.2% Black	Irish: 9.2%	
Rural population:	40.9%	0.7% Asian	**2004 Presidential Vote**	
Pop. 2000:	621,690	1.0% Native Am.	Bush (R) 202,486	(67%)
Median income:	$32,929	0.1% Hawaiian	Kerry (D) 97,557	(32%)
Poverty status:	13.0%	1.5% Two+ races	Other 1,705	(1%)
Military veterans:	14.4%	0.1% Other	**2000 Presidential Vote**	
		2.6% Hispanic Origin	Bush (R) 153,453	(62%)
			Gore (D) 87,663	(35%)
			Other 6,124	(2%)
			Cook Partisan Voting Index: R +14	

Occupation   Blue collar: 28.5%   White collar: 55.0%   Gray collar: 16.5%

One of the biggest tourist destinations in America today is Branson, Missouri—something almost no one predicted 25 years ago. Even today Branson has only 6,231 residents, is served by two-lane roads, is nowhere near a major airport; but it thrives, paralleling the surging popularity of country and western music. Branson was put on the map early in the century by Harold Bell Wright's novel, *The Shepherd of the Hills,* about the hardy people of the mountains, hills and meadows of southwest Missouri, just north of Arkansas. More tourists came in with completion of the Ozark Beach Dam that created Bull Shoals Lake in 1913, lured by the native bass and stocked trout. Then in the 1960s, new lakes were formed, a Shepherd of the Hills pageant and Silver Dollar City were started, and entertainers—the five Maybe brothers performing as "The Baldknobbers" and Box Car Willie from the Grand Ole Opry—started performing. Today Branson has 7 million visitors a year, 80% of whom have visited before, and more than two dozen theaters with 56,000 seats—more than Broadway. What do people like about Branson? The non-stop entertainment and fishing and boating; country music and family style entertainment; plenty of shopping and a safe atmosphere. Missourians like them enough to have rejected 56%–44% in August 2004 a ballot measure that would have allowed a gambling casino in Rockaway Beach a few miles away; they like things in Branson as they are. These are also the things that have made southwest Missouri the fastest growing part of the state in the last 20 years, generating new businesses and attracting retirees as well as vacationers. Workers come to Branson from as far away as Springfield, the biggest city in southwest Missouri. Springfield is the headquarters of such middle American institutions as the Mid-America Dairymen, the nation's largest milk producers' cooperative; the Bass Pro Shops Outdoor World, probably the nation's largest fishing equipment store; the Assemblies of God, one of the nation's and the world's largest and fastest-growing Protestant denominations; and two of the nation's three largest coachbuilders (stretch limousine manufacturers), Springfield Coach and DaBryan Coach Builders, with a third nearby in Seymour, Executive Coach, run by a Nigerian immigrant. Springfield and Greene County are home to 300 churches, one for every 826 people. Southwest Missouri is also dairy country and has a growing poultry industry; Latinos have been moving into McDonald County to work in chicken plants. The Ozarks, long considered a backwater, are on the cutting edge of many trends in today's America.

The 7th Congressional District of Missouri includes Branson and Springfield and most of southwest Missouri. Historically, this area has been Republican since it opposed secession in 1861: pro-Union Springfield changed hands several times as Missouri staged its own civil war. Its conservative response to the big-spending government of the 1960s and cultural liberalism of the 1970s reinforced its allegiance, and now this is the most Republican part of Missouri.

The congressman from the 7th District is Roy Blunt, a Republican first elected in 1996. Blunt grew up on a dairy farm near Springfield, in a political family; his father was a state representative. He graduated from Southwest Baptist University, 25 miles north of Springfield, and taught high school and college history and government. He got his start in politics by volunteering for John Ashcroft's unsuccessful campaign for Congress in 1972; the story goes that he showed up at campaign headquarters in his pickup truck, Ashcroft asked, "Have you got gas in this truck?" Blunt said yes and became his driver (another congressman, Democrat Earl Pomeroy of North Dakota, also started his political career driving around a future senator). In 1973, 33-year-old freshman Governor Christopher Bond, in his second appointment, named the 23-year-old Blunt to be Greene County clerk. In 1980 Senator John Danforth asked him to run for lieutenant governor; he did and lost. In 1984, at 34, Blunt was elected Missouri secretary of state, the first Republican to win that office in half a century; he was reelected with 60% of the vote in 1988. In 1992 he ran for governor and lost the Republican primary to William Webster, 44%–39%. Blunt became president of Southwest Baptist University. In 1996 Congressman Mel Hancock kept his pledge to serve only four terms and retired. In the primary Blunt faced Gary Nodler, businessman and one-time staffer to Congressman Gene Taylor, and won 56%–44%. In the general election Blunt won 65%–32%, running ahead of the Republican ticket and carrying every county with at least 62% of the vote. He has been reelected easily since.

Blunt has shown great political skills and is now majority whip. He wanted to run for freshman class president in 1997, but at then-Majority Whip Tom DeLay's suggestion ran for the freshman spot on the Republican Steering Committee, on which he worked to get good committee assignments for freshmen. RNC Chairman Ken Mehlman was working for freshman Kay Granger then and remembers Blunt, "He was the one person every single member of his class felt like they could go to solve a problem." In the process he got good committee assignments himself—Agriculture, International Relations, Transportation and Infrastructure. On International Relations, he supported the bill to penalize countries that practice or allow religious persecution—a concern of denominations like the Assemblies of God, which has more members abroad than in the United States.

Three weeks after the 1998 election Blunt won a seat on the Commerce Committee. Then in January 1999 Tom DeLay plucked him from the ranks of 48 deputy whips and appointed him Chief Deputy Whip, the position Dennis Hastert held until his astonishing elevation to speaker. Blunt has said that he never lobbied for the job and didn't even know he was being considered until he read it in a newspaper. On a number of issues Blunt was given the job of making more palatable to core Republicans measures that were going through in any case.

As chief deputy whip, Blunt spent much time meeting with lobbyists, organizing groups interested in different issues like trade, taxes and energy. He developed a reputation as a good listener and took care to pay attention to party moderates. David Rehr, a lobbyist close to the Republican leadership, describes him thus: "Roy is more of the velvet glove, almost a confessor figure. He's the kind of guy who is able to say, 'That's a really good idea, but maybe it's better to do it this way,' without being confrontational." Speaker Dennis Hastert assigned Blunt to mediate disputes between Republicans and to win over votes on critical issues. Blunt also weighed in on some local issues. After Democrat Rob Andrews complained that New Jersey-licensed limousines were not allowed into New York without paying a tax, Blunt, representing the number one stretch-limousine-producing district, sponsored a bill limiting local regulation of limousines that cross state lines. It was opposed by New York officials eager for revenue and Nevada limousine drivers, worried about competition from California drivers; but it passed by wide margins and was signed into law in November 2002.

In 2000 Blunt began keeping a list of members who would back him for a higher leadership position. In the 2002 cycle he headed the Battleground 2002 operation, which contributed $5.6 million to Republican House candidates. In December 2001 Majority Leader Dick Armey announced that he would retire in 2002. Immediately DeLay began to run for majority leader and Blunt said he would run for majority whip. Ray LaHood of Illinois, whose evenhanded presiding over important sessions has impressed members in both parties, announced he was running for whip too. But in February 2002 he said he would not run and was supporting Blunt; he found that Blunt had the support not only of most Republicans but of most moderates. In November 2002 both DeLay and Blunt were elected to their new positions without opposition; DeLay presented Blunt with a velvet-covered hammer.

As whip, Blunt made two decisions on his own which showed that he was not DeLay's puppet. One was his decision to name as his chief deputy whip Eric Cantor, who had served only one term and who is the only Jewish Republican in the House; Cantor was as astonished as everyone else. And he proposed to change House rules by repealing the eight-year term limit Newt Gingrich had imposed on speakers; that was agreed to by the whole House. Naturally there was speculation that Blunt might some day run for speaker, presumably against DeLay. Blunt was for the most part successful as whip, but stumbled a couple of times. In June 2003 the leadership had to pull a compensatory time bill from the floor when it became apparent there were not enough votes to pass it. *The Washington Post* soon after reported that Blunt had inserted into the homeland security bill in November 2002 a provision benefiting Philip Morris. But Blunt met his toughest challenge in 2003, passing the Medicare/prescription drug bill. In June he assembled a huge coalition and helped to produce a one-vote victory on the floor. The leadership's strategy was to get a bill through and then negotiate in conference with the Senate. As Blunt put it later, "Our strategy in conference has to be a starting point that doesn't worry about a filibuster. We don't need a bill that 75 or 90 senators will vote for. We just need a majority." In November on the vote on the conference report the leadership went to the floor without the needed 218 votes; the roll call started at 3 a.m. and lasted a record two hours and 53 minutes. Finally conservatives Trent Franks and Butch Otter were persuaded to switch their votes by the possibility that if the Republican bill failed the Democrats would get a vote on a bill with much more government involvement; they switched and the bill passed 220–215. Later Blunt reflected, "It was important that we win that vote on the floor. We passed legislation three times straight to add prescription drugs to Medicare. It is important for Medicare to catch up with medicine." In December 2004, after Republicans increased their majority from 229–206 to 232–203, Blunt worried that more Republicans would feel free to go off the reservation. "Members expect to get free votes. It will make a difference in how we approach issues on a day in and day out basis."

Blunt has been reelected by very wide margins. His son Matt Blunt was elected to the state House in 1998 and was elected to the statewide office of secretary of state in 2000—a sensitive position given the allegations of vote fraud in St. Louis in 2000. In January 2004, with his father at his side in the high school gym in Strafford in Greene County, Matt Blunt announced his candidacy for governor. But the two then parted their ways: Matt Blunt campaigned all over Missouri, while Roy Blunt did most of his campaigning for House Republicans across the nation. In November Matt Blunt was elected governor by a 51%–48% margin; he won 67%–32% in the counties in the 7th District. Roy Blunt was reelected by a 70%–28% margin.

Will Roy Blunt someday be speaker of the House? He stands below Tom DeLay on the leadership ladder, but DeLay is controversial and in early 2005 was attacked by Democrats and the news media on ethics issues; he might choose to stand aside, as he did when Newt Gingrich and Bob Livingston resigned in 1998. In any case, Speaker Dennis Hastert faces, thanks to Blunt's initiative, no limit in Republican rules from continuing to serve as speaker indefinitely and has shown no inclination to retire.

EIGHTH DISTRICT

Rep. Jo Ann Emerson (R)

Elected 1996, 5th full term; b. Sept. 16, 1950, Washington, D.C.; home, Cape Girardeau; Ohio Wesleyan U., B.A. 1972; Presbyterian; married (Ron Gladney).

Professional Career: Deputy Communications Dir., Natl. Repub. Cong. Cmte., 1984–91; Dir., State Relations & Grassroot Programs, Natl. Restaurant Assn., 1991–94; Sr. Vice Pres., Pub. Affairs, American Insurance Assn., 1994–96.

DC Office: 2440 RHOB, 20515, 202-225-4404; Fax: 202-226-0326; Web site: www.house.gov/emerson.

District Offices: Cape Girardeau, 573-335-0101; Farmington, 573-756-9755; Rolla, 573-364-2455.

Committees: *Appropriations* (22d of 37 R): Agriculture, Rural Development, FDA & Related Agencies; Energy & Water Development & Related Agencies; Homeland Security.

Group Ratings

	ADA	ACLU	AFS	LCV	ITIC	NTU	COC	ACU	NTLC	CHC
2004	20	0	43	9	78	42	86	76	78	90
2003	10	—	17	0	—	54	92	100	—	—

National Journal Ratings

	2003 LIB	—	2003 CONS		2004 LIB	—	2004 CONS
Economic	37%	—	63%		47%	—	52%
Social	39%	—	61%		25%	—	73%
Foreign	20%	—	79%		51%	—	48%

Key Votes of the 108th Congress

1. Drilling in ANWR	Y	5. DC School Vouchers	*	9. Ban Same-Sex Marriage	Y
2. Approve Bush Tax Cuts	*	6. Ban Human Cloning	Y	10. Fund Iraq War	Y
3. Medicare/Rx Bill	N	7. Restrict Gun Liability	Y	11. Bar Cuba Embargo Funds	Y
4. Bar Overtime Pay Regs.	Y	8. Ban Partial-Birth Abortion	Y	12. Intelligence Reorg.	Y

Election Results

2004 general	Jo Ann Emerson (R)	194,039	(72%)	($1,163,588)
	Dean Henderson (D)	71,543	(27%)	($17,801)
	Other	3,129	(1%)	
2004 primary	Jo Ann Emerson (R)	65,052	(89%)	
	Richard Allen Kline (R)	8,401	(11%)	
2002 general	Jo Ann Emerson (R)	135,144	(72%)	($777,711)
	Gene Curtis (D)	50,686	(27%)	
	Other	2,491	(1%)	

Prior Winning Percentages: 2000 (69%); 1998 (63%); 1996 (50%); 1996 (63%)

The People		Race/Ethnic Origin	Ancestry	
Area size:	18,818 sq. mi.	92.5% White	USA: 13.7%	German: 12.7%
Urban population:	39.6%	4.3% Black	Irish: 8.5%	
Rural population:	60.4%	0.4% Asian	**2004 Presidential Vote**	
Pop. 2000:	621,690	0.6% Native Am.	Bush (R) 173,378	(63%)
Median income:	$27,865	0.0% Hawaiian	Kerry (D) 97,778	(36%)
Poverty status:	18.2%	1.1% Two+ races	Other 1,886	(1%)
Military veterans:	15.1%	0.0% Other	**2000 Presidential Vote**	
		1.0% Hispanic Origin	Bush (R) 143,511	(59%)
			Gore (D) 93,244	(38%)
			Other 5,635	(2%)
			Cook Partisan Voting Index: R +11	

Occupation	Blue collar: 34.5%	White collar: 47.7%	Gray collar: 17.8%

Mark Twain might not recognize life on the Mississippi below St. Louis today, where the land flattens out and the river is hidden behind levees, which ordinarily, except during the terrible flood of 1993, screen small towns and river roads from the sight of rows of barges tethered together, full of coal and corn and soybeans. The Mississippi today is an industrial waterway. But it was never really all that romantic. Twain's steamboats, as he was at pains to point out, were dangerous, noisy contraptions, forever blowing up or getting embedded in roots and branches in the swirling river currents. This is one of the older settled parts of the U.S.: French settlers founded Missouri towns like Cape Girardeau in the late 1700s. The big influx started a few years after the 1811 earthquake centered on New Madrid; the spongy Mississippi valley land is seismically very active, and this was the site of one of the most devastating earthquakes in U.S. history.

The southeast quadrant of Missouri—the river valley and the hills to the west, with coal and lead mines with their miles of tunnels, plus the Bootheel that hangs down in the far southeast—has not seemed to change much in 50 years. For years there has been a population outflow from the Bootheel, as machines replaced low-wage farm workers and crops shifted from cotton to rice, corn and soybeans. Dairy cattle, pigs, apples, and berries—plus, some timber—are among the area's other products. St. Francois and Iron Counties produce about 80% of the nation's lead; EPA has ordered a cleanup of massive piles of lead waste. An aluminum smelting plant in New Madrid provides more than 1,000 jobs. The only big growth here has been around the retail and medical hub of Cape Girardeau and along I-44; the poverty rate in the Bootheel is the highest in the state. At a point 20 miles south of Rolla in Phelps County is Edgar Springs, the home to 190 residents and the population center of the nation, according to the 2000 Census; 10 years earlier, that designation was 35 miles to the northeast in Steelville.

The sprawling 8th Congressional District of Missouri covers this southeast corner of Missouri. The political heritage is mixed. The Bootheel was as solidly Democratic as the Mississippi Valley around Memphis once was, and some mining counties show traces of Democratic sentiment. Cape Girardeau is heavily Republican and an incubator of Republican talent: it is the home town of Rush Limbaugh, Lieutenant Governor Peter Kinder, and Jack Oliver, George W. Bush's chief fundraiser in 2004. For many years this district was safely Democratic, but since 1980, it has been represented by Republicans. This was one of the rural areas that trended to Republicans in the Clinton years, and George W. Bush won 59% of the vote here in 2000 and 63% in 2004.

The congresswoman from the 8th District is Jo Ann Emerson, first elected in 1996 to replace her late husband Bill Emerson, who died that June. Jo Ann Emerson grew up in Bethesda, Maryland, in a Republican family (her father was executive director of the Republican National Committee) but next door to Democrats Hale and Lindy Boggs, who served in Congress over a half-century. In 1975 she married Republican Bill Emerson, then a Washington lobbyist. In 1979, spotting the vulnerability of the Democratic incumbent in the Bootheel district, he went home to Missouri to run, and won with 55% of the vote. In 1995 he was diagnosed with cancer, but missed few votes during radiation therapy. After Bill's death, Jo Ann Emerson decided to run. She had worked for the American Insurance Association and National Restaurant Association and was a press aide at the National Republican Congressional Committee. Her views were conservative, and leading state and national Republicans quickly endorsed her. But Missouri law bars reopening the filing deadline if an incumbent dies less than 11 weeks before the primary, so she ran as an independent. Democrats nominated Emily Firebaugh, a timber company owner who attacked Emerson as a product of the Washington suburbs. Firebaugh spent $831,000, slightly more than Emerson. The Republican nominee Richard Kline was less trouble: In 1995 he had used pepper spray to try to place a Veterans Administration doctor under citizen's arrest. Bill Emerson's record, Jo Ann Emerson's conservative views, and the poignancy of the situation all worked toward an Emerson victory. She won 50%, with 37% for Firebaugh and 11% for Kline. In the same-day special election for the short term, she won with 63%.

In the House, Emerson has had a moderate-leaning voting record though sometimes conservative on cultural issues. On the Appropriations Committee and its Agriculture Subcommittee, her priority was addressing low prices for farm commodities. She worked with other members from farm districts to open agricultural trade with Cuba and made visits to Cuba to encourage deals; she pushed legislative steps to overturn Bush administration restrictions on the shipment of personal items to family members on the island. She demanded protection of U.S. food aid programs from international trade restrictions. After September 11 she bucked Attorney General—and former Missouri Senator—John Ashcroft by voting with House Democrats to federalize airport security.

Emerson cast the deciding vote in June 2003 on the House version of the Medicare/prescription drug bill. She opposed the measure but changed her vote in exchange for a promise from Speaker Dennis Hastert for a floor vote on reimportation of prescription drugs (she complained that her mother-in-law paid $11,000 a year for drug coverage) and assurance that Majority Whip Roy Blunt wouldn't whip Republicans to vote against it. She got the vote; Blunt did not do any whipping but former whip and now-Majority Leader Tom DeLay did. Emerson's side won, but the provision failed to become law. In November, she was one of 25 House Republicans who voted against the conference report on the Medicare/prescription drug bill. Her independence has not seemed to affect her influence among House Republicans, perhaps because she has been upfront with party leaders about her views.

Emerson has won reelection without difficulty. In 2002, she turned down the opportunity to run against Senator Jean Carnahan. Her stepdaughter served with the First Infantry Division in Iraq.

NINTH DISTRICT

Rep. Kenny Hulshof (R)

Elected 1996, 5th term; b. May 22, 1958, Sikeston; home, Columbia; U. of MO, B.S. 1980, U. of MS, J.D. 1983; Catholic; married (Renee).

Professional Career: Asst. Pub. Defender, 32d Judicial Circuit, 1983–86; Asst. Prosecuting Atty., Cape Girardeau, 1986–89; Spec. Prosecutor, MO Atty. Gen., 1989–96.

DC Office: 412 CHOB, 20515, 202-225-2956; Fax: 202-225-5712; Web site: www.house.gov/hulshof.

District Offices: Columbia, 573-449-5111; Hannibal, 573-221-1200; Washington, 636-239-4001.

Committees: *Budget* (6th of 22 R). *Ways & Means* (13th of 24 R): Health; Social Security.

Group Ratings

	ADA	ACLU	AFS	LCV	ITIC	NTU	COC	ACU	NTLC	CHC
2004	5	0	0	0	100	58	100	91	86	92
2003	5	—	0	5	—	62	100	92	—	—

National Journal Ratings

	2003 LIB	—	2003 CONS		2004 LIB	—	2004 CONS
Economic	17%	—	81%		28%	—	72%
Social	24%	—	71%		30%	—	70%
Foreign	40%	—	58%		10%	—	86%

Key Votes of the 108th Congress

1. Drilling in ANWR	Y	5. DC School Vouchers	Y	9. Ban Same-Sex Marriage	Y
2. Approve Bush Tax Cuts	Y	6. Ban Human Cloning	Y	10. Fund Iraq War	Y
3. Medicare/Rx Bill	Y	7. Restrict Gun Liability	Y	11. Bar Cuba Embargo Funds	N
4. Bar Overtime Pay Regs.	N	8. Ban Partial-Birth Abortion	Y	12. Intelligence Reorg.	Y

Election Results

2004 general	Kenny Hulshof (R)	193,429	(65%)	($1,017,285)
	Linda Jacobsen (D)	101,343	(34%)	($130,908)
	Other	4,675	(2%)	
2004 primary	Kenny Hulshof (R)	unopposed		
2002 general	Kenny Hulshof (R)	146,032	(68%)	($879,910)
	Donald Deichman (D)	61,126	(29%)	
	Other	6,967	(3%)	

Prior Winning Percentages: 2000 (59%); 1998 (62%); 1996 (49%)

The People		Race/Ethnic Origin	Ancestry	
Area size:	14,082 sq. mi.	92.6% White	German: 21.7% Irish: 9.3%	
Urban population:	45.8%	3.9% Black	USA: 9.2%	
Rural population:	54.2%	0.9% Asian	**2004 Presidential Vote**	
Pop. 2000:	621,690	0.3% Native Am.	Bush (R) 180,362	(59%)
Median income:	$36,693	0.0% Hawaiian	Kerry (D) 124,965	(41%)
Poverty status:	11.8%	1.1% Two+ races	Other 2,008	(1%)
Military veterans:	13.5%	0.1% Other	**2000 Presidential Vote**	
		1.1% Hispanic Origin	Bush (R) 145,604	(55%)
			Gore (D) 112,239	(42%)
			Other 7,093	(3%)
			Cook Partisan Voting Index: R + 7	

Occupation	Blue collar: 29.7%	White collar: 54.4%	Gray collar: 15.9%

Little Dixie, the swath of northeast Missouri along the Mississippi River, was settled by Southerners from Kentucky and Virginia. Its most famous native son is Mark Twain, born Sam Clemens in Hannibal, then as now a little town on bluffs overlooking the river. Hannibal was the thinly disguised St. Petersburg of Tom Sawyer and Huckleberry Finn, lovingly created years later complete with Pike County and other dialect by Twain, then living in New England. Little Dixie was pro-Confederate during the Civil War; Callaway County declared its independence from the Union. For many years faithfully Democratic, Little Dixie has reared some notable politicians as well. One was Champ Clark, speaker of the House from 1911 to 1919 and candidate for the Democratic presidential nomination in 1912; another was Clarence Cannon, author of the definitive text on the House's parliamentary procedures and chairman of the House Appropriations Committee from 1941 to 1964 except for four years of Republican control.

The 9th Congressional District of Missouri is the descendant of the Little Dixie districts that elected Clark and Cannon, but slow population growth has meant that it has had to be expanded far to the south and into the foothills of the Ozarks. It includes Columbia, home of the University of Missouri, and Fulton, home of Westminster College, where in 1946 Winston Churchill, accompanied by President Harry Truman, told the world that "from Stettin on the Baltic to Trieste on the Adriatic, an iron curtain has descended across the continent." The district includes the western edge of the St. Louis metro area, western St. Charles County and Franklin County south of the Missouri River. Despite its Democratic heritage, it votes mostly Republican now, 55% for George W. Bush in 2000 and 59% in 2004.

The congressman from the 9th District is Kenny Hulshof (pronounced *HULLZ-hoff*), a Republican first elected in 1996. He grew up on a farm in far southeast Missouri. After getting his bachelor degree in agriculture economics at the University of Missouri and his law degree from the University of Mississippi, he joined the public defender's office in Cape Girardeau. In 1989, he became a special prosecutor for the Missouri attorney general's office and traveled to 53 counties, obtaining 60 violent felony convictions and seven death sentences; he is certified as a specialist instructor in criminal law. In the midst of this, in 1994, he became the Republican nominee in the 9th District. This was a surprise: challenger Rick Hardy had held Democratic Congressman Harold Volkmer to a 48%–46% victory in 1992 and was running again; but after the filing deadline he withdrew from the race due to depression and exhaustion. Party leaders named Hulshof as Hardy's replacement. He was far outspent, but made a respectable showing, and lost 50%–45%.

In 1996 Hulshof ran again. Volkmer's combative temperament and irritation with the new Republican majority made him one of its most persistent antagonists. Hulshof narrowly won his primary; in the general election, Volkmer ran an ad showing Hulshof in a Porsche driven by Newt Gingrich and attacking him for signing away his independence in the Contract with America. Hulshof replied that his Porsche was a used car sitting in his yard, and he charged that Volkmer had voted to raise taxes 20 times in 20 years and had voted for 40% pay raises. The key moment came in October when Volkmer, in response to a question, said voters were not overtaxed and that he would not mind paying $1 million in taxes. Hulshof ran radio ads quoting Volkmer all over the district. Volkmer carried Little Dixie 53%–46%, but Hulshof led elsewhere for a 49%–47% win.

In the House, Hulshof had a voting record near the center of his party. He was elected president of the Republican freshman class and he decried "partisan bickering" 15 days after taking office. With Democratic freshman president Jim Davis, he supported the 1997 balanced budget agreement; he helped organize the civility retreats in Hershey and backed Shays-Meehan campaign finance regulation. The Republican leadership gave him a prized seat on Ways and Means as a freshman. He used the platform to back repeal of the estate tax, scaling back taxation of dividend and interest income, and favorable tax treatment of ethanol. He co-authored Bush's proposal to create education savings accounts, and he has been a leading advocate of making permanent the tax cuts of 2001. As a member of the Social Security Subcommittee, he praised Bush's reform initiative in 2005 but said that he was open to a variety of approaches. With a district crisscrossed by many long-distance rail lines, he proposed to cut the excise tax on rail fuel. On the ethics committee, he chaired the subcommittee that investigated allegations of undue pressure on members during the November 2003 vote on the Medicare/prescription drug bill and he joined the unanimous committee votes in October 2004 to admonish Majority Leader Tom DeLay on two counts; he praised its efforts as "the least partisan committee work I've ever been involved with." In early 2005, he was dropped from the panel and reportedly was miffed that he was given no explanation.

Hulshof has been reelected by wide margins. He was credited by some Missouri Republicans for gains the party made in legislative elections in his district that enabled them to gain majorities in both houses of the legislature in 2002.

★ MONTANA ★

Just a little more than 200 years ago, in April 1805, Meriwether Lewis and William Clark and their pirogues wended up the Missouri River just past the Yellowstone into what now is Montana. It was wild, open country, under a big sky—and most of it still is. To celebrate July 4, 1976, the late historian Stephen Ambrose took his family to Lemhi Pass at the other end of Montana, nearly 500 miles west, where Lewis was the first American to cross the Continental Divide—and noted that the land was little different from when Lewis and Clark passed through. Ambrose later retold the Lewis and Clark story in *Undaunted Courage* and he and his family settled in Montana; they are far from the only outsiders who have moved, part-time or full, into the Big Sky State in recent decades.

Yet American civilization has touched down only lightly on Montana. It is still a land of great empty vistas, with mountains in the west and vast expanses of plateaus and plains in the east—the 4th largest state in area and 44th in population. Almost nowhere in the state are wilderness and empty land out of sight. Montana sits atop America, spanning the Rockies so that on I-15 you can cross the Continental Divide three times. But since the time of Lewis and Clark, it has not been much of a crossroads. The first Americans here were itinerant trappers seeking fur and miners seeking gold, silver and copper, who built ramshackle towns where outlaws battled vigilantes—and, in a few cases gained sudden riches, which would make them kings not of this barren land but of the metropolises back East. Then came the workers who built and serviced the Northern Pacific and Great Northern railroads, followed by wheat farmers and ranchers.

Statehood came less than a century after the first white Americans, Lewis and Clark and their men, came here as agents of the government. The mining economy gave Montana a radical, class warfare political tradition. On one side was the Anaconda Mining Company, which until 1959 owned five of Montana's six daily newspapers, the Montana Power Company and many of its politicians. It had strong allies in the Stockmen's Association and the Farm Bureau. On the other side were progressives like Senators Thomas Walsh, who exposed the Teapot Dome

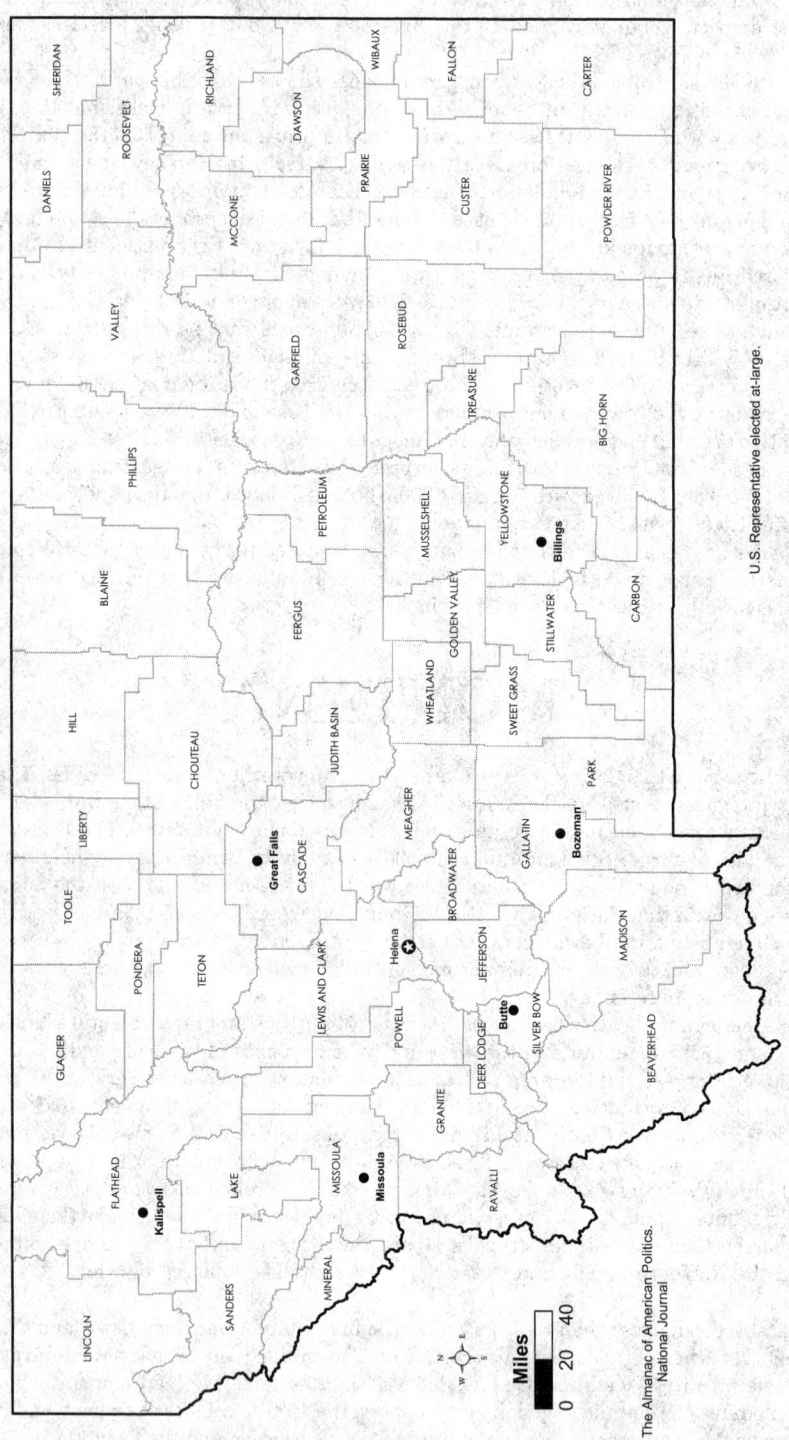

U.S. Representative elected at-large.

The Almanac of American Politics.
National Journal

Miles

0 20 40

scandal, and Burton Wheeler, a New Dealer who broke with Franklin D. Roosevelt over court packing and isolationism, the labor unions (Montana has no right-to-work law and is the most pro-union state in the Rockies), and pork barrel beneficiaries (for a while in the 1930s, Montana received more federal money per capita than almost any other state). The locus of all this was Butte, with its gold and copper mines on "The Richest Hill on Earth," with its gamblers and bootleggers, company goons and union thugs, IWW organizers and Socialist mayor, and millionaires who bought seats in the U.S. Senate. Today the mines are closed, the ore depleted, and the stone temples of commerce are grim; looming mineheads are being restored to a cleanliness they never enjoyed in the boom days.

Butte's population peaked in 1920, mines gradually closed all over the state, and agriculture—wheat growing and cattle grazing—became the mainstays of the economy. Class warfare died down. Other towns grew, though none is over 100,000 yet: Billings with its agricultural marketing in the east, the university town of Missoula, Great Falls just east of the Rockies, Kalispell near Flathead Lake, the university and resort town of Bozeman, and the state capital of Helena. The muscular tone of a land settled by ranch hands, miners and railroad workers, of cowboy hats, boots and blue jeans, of men who do hard physical work and relax hard afterwards, remains a link with Montanans going back to the mountain men, miners and cowboys who drove herds of Texas longhorns across the open range. And there is still the sense of space. Hunting and fishing are never far away; development in the small cities and resort areas has not been enough to drive the game away.

Over the past quarter-century, the Big Sky country attracted at first a trickle and then a flood of affluent Americans who purchased second homes here—high-visibility movie stars and billionaires like Ted Turner, but also just ordinary people buying small spreads near Big Sky or McLeod, near Bozeman, or around Flathead Lake or Big Timber or the Big Mountain ski resort in Whitefish. Many newcomers, from California and other urban states, set down roots here, as computers, modems and fax machines make it possible for small businessmen and entrepreneurs to work in Montana, far from their customers and clients, but in an environment they love—and not far from the coffee houses and gambling parlors you find on every highway. These new Montanans have added a spark of energy and inventiveness to a state much of which consisted of those left behind when others moved elsewhere. Montana's population grew 13% in the 1990s, despite losses in the eastern plains; its economy, fueled by construction, continued to grow during the national recession of 2001–02. Growth was especially vigorous around Bozeman and Big Sky, in Missoula and Ravalli County to the south and around Kalispell and Lake Flathead to the north.

Sometimes there are conflicts between newcomers' expectations and the hardiness of Montana life: Gallatin County issued a 20-page Code of the West, explaining to new residents that they shouldn't expect an immediate response from emergency services and they shouldn't plough their snow onto a county road. The DeLorme Montana Road Atlas gives advice on what you should do if you encounter a bear. There are lively political arguments over the grizzly bears and gray wolves reintroduced to Montana in the 1990s; the Bush administration has approved mining activities that environmentalists say will harm grizzlies and some Montanans want state, rather than federal, management so that ranchers can shoot more wolves.

There are two lively political traditions in Montana today. One draws on its heritage of class warfare politics, radical miners and angry labor unions, which made Montana for many years the most Democratic of the Rocky Mountain states. From 1952 to 1984 it elected only Democratic U.S. senators, and in 1992 it voted 38%–35% for Bill Clinton, with 26% for Ross Perot. The other, more recent tradition is in line with conservative activist Grover Norquist's "Leave-Us-Alone-Coalition"—a fierce opposition to higher taxes and federal government dictates. When a court ordered the legislature to set a speed limit, it was set at 75 miles per hour. Montana has not elected a Democrat to the U.S. House since 1994, though Democratic Senator Max Baucus was reelected in 1996 and 2002, and in 2000, Montana voted 58%–33% for George W. Bush, with 6% for Ralph Nader. In these races Democrats have carried only the old mining towns like Butte and Anaconda, Indian reservations (6% of Montanans are Indians), old railroad towns like Great Falls and Havre, university towns like Missoula and Bozeman, and the state capital of Helena.

In 2004 both traditions were apparent. Bush carried the state 59%–39% (evidently the Nader vote went for John Kerry) and Republican Congressman-at-Large Denny Rehberg was reelected with 64%. But Democrat Brian Schweitzer was elected governor and Democrats won a majority in the state Senate and a tie in the state House. This Democratic surge owed something to the unpopularity of Republican Governor Judy Martz, who in 2003 announced she would not seek a second term. But it was also the result of corporate malfeasance. In 1997 the legislature deregulated electricity rates and in 2000 Montana Power, the state's largest corporation, sold its power facilities for $2.1 billion and put all the money into a fiber optics firm. Bad timing: the fiber optics firm went bankrupt, and so did the buyer of the power facilities; the results were big local job losses, higher utility rates, big payouts to a few corporate executives and a rash of highly publicized lawsuits. Republican business-friendly policies were discredited and Schweitzer, a politically appealing rancher with longtime Montana roots who ran a strong race for U.S. Senate in 2000, argued convincingly for change.

The People		Race/Ethnic Origin			Military veterans: 108,476 (16.1%)	
Pop. 2004 (est):	926,865	807,823	89.5%	White	WWII: 19.7%	Korea: 13.4%
Pop. 2000:	902,195	2,534	0.3%	Black	Vietnam: 34.2%	Gulf War: 9.5%
Pop. 1990:	799,065	4,569	0.5%	Asian	**Most populous cities (2003):**	
Change 1990–2000:	Up 12.9%	54,426	6.0%	Native Am.	1. Billings	95,220
% of U.S. total:	0.3%	425	0.0%	Hawaiian	2. Missoula	60,722
Pop. rank:	44th of 50	13,768	1.5%	Two+ races	3. Great Falls	56,155
Area size:	147,042 sq. mi.	569	0.1%	Other	4. Butte	32,519
State Native:	56.1%	18,081	2.0%	Hisp. Origin	5. Bozeman	30,753
Non-citizen:	0.8%	**Ancestry**				
Language		German: 18.8%		Irish: 10.3%	Urban population: 54.0%	
English: 92.0%	Other Eur.: 3.3%	English: 8.8%		Norwegian: 7.4%	Rural population: 46.0%	
Spanish: 2.6%		USA: 3.6%				

Education		Work Sector		Legislature	
H.S. Grad:	87.2%	Private: 69.2%	Govt: 18.3%	Senate	27 D 23 R
College Grad:	24.4%	Self: 11.8%	Family: 0.7%	House	50 D 50 R
Industry		Unemployment: 6.3%		Legislative Term Limits: Yes	
Agri: 7.9%	Con: 7.4%	**Household Income**		**Registered Voters**	
Fin: 5.5%	Info: 2.2%	<15k: 20.2%	15-35k: 32.5%	No party registration	
Mfg: 11.4%	Prof: 28.2%	35-50k: 18.2%	50-100k: 23.5%		
Public: 5.9%	Trade: 15.8%	100-150k: 3.6%	>150k: 1.9%		
Other: 15.6%		Median: $33,024			
Occupation		Poverty status: 14.6%			
Blue collar: 22.0%	White collar: 58.6%	**Home Value**			
Gray collar: 19.4%		<50k: 19.4%	50-100k: 33.8%	100-200k: 34.5%	200-300k: 7.2%
		300-500k: 3.1%	>500k: 2.0%	Median: $95,800	

Presidential politics

Montana, with its 3 electoral votes, doesn't see much of 2004, presidential candidates. Its presidential primary is in early June, far too late to affect any results; in Dennis Kucinich campaigned here and finished second with 10% of the vote. But in 1992 and 1996, Montana was closely divided. Ross Perot won 26% in Montana in 1992 and 13.6% in 1996, which was his second-best showing that year. Almost all those votes seem to have gone for George W. Bush in 2000, as he carried the state by a wider margin than Ronald Reagan or Richard Nixon in 1984 and 1972. Ralph Nader won 6% in 2000, and those votes seem to have gone for John Kerry in 2004, who cut Bush's margin but still ran 20% behind.

2004 Presidential Vote		
Bush (R)	266,063	(59%)
Kerry (D)	173,710	(39%)
Nader (I)	6,168	(1%)
Other	4,493	(1%)

2004 Democratic Presidential Primary		
Kerry (D)	63,611	(68%)
Kucinich (D)	9,686	(10%)
Edwards (D)	8,516	(9%)
No Preference (D)	6,899	(7%)
Clark (D)	4,081	(4%)
Other	750	(1%)

2000 Presidential Vote		
Bush (R)	240,178	(58%)
Gore (D)	137,126	(33%)
Nader (Green)	24,437	(6%)
Other	9,245	(2%)

Governor

Brian Schweitzer (D)

Elected 2004, term expires Jan. 2009, 1st term; b. Sept. 4, 1955, Havre; home, Whitefish; CO St. U., B.S. 1978; MT St. U., M.S. 1980; Catholic; married (Nancy).

Professional Career: Farm developer, 1980–86; Farmer, rancher, 1986-present; Committee Member, Montana Farm Service Agency, 1993–99.

Office: State Capitol, Helena, 59620, 406-444-3111; Fax: 406-444-4151; Web site: www.state.mt.us/governor.

Election Results

2004 general	Brian Schweitzer (D)	225,016	(50%)
	Bob Brown (R)	205,313	(46%)
	Other	15,817	(4%)
2004 primary	Brian Schweitzer (D)	68,738	(73%)
	John Vincent (D)	26,057	(27%)
2000 general	Judy Martz (R)	209,135	(51%)
	Mark O'Keefe (D)	193,131	(47%)
	Other	7,926	(2%)

Brian Schweitzer, a Democrat elected governor of Montana in 2004, grew up on his family's ranch in the Judith Basin, east of Great Falls; his Irish grandparents had homesteaded in Hill County, near the Great Northern rail line. He graduated from Colorado State and Montana State with degrees in soil science and in the early 1980s went off to the Middle East. He developed a 15,000-acre farm in the Sahara in Libya and dairy, grain and vegetable farms in Saudi Arabia on irrigated cropland. In 1986 he returned to Montana and bought two farms. He raised cattle and exported bull semen and, innovation-minded, grew mint and dill. In 1993, when the Clinton administration took office, he was appointed to the three-member, part-time Farm Service Agency that helps distribute federal payments to farmers.

With that minimal experience, he embarked on a race against two-term Senator Conrad Burns in 2000. In fall 1999, he organized the first busload of seniors to Canada to buy prescription drugs at lower prices. With armed guards, he strode into the Capitol in Helena and poured out $47,000 in cash—the amount, he said, of contributions to Burns from tobacco PACs. Schweitzer charged that Montana had a third-world economy, exporting raw materials and educated young people. He attacked Burns for supporting a bill that would limit compensation to those with asbestos-related disease and shut down the giant asbestos tort cases. Burns, who had reneged on a 1988 promise to serve only two terms, outspent Schweitzer by 2–1 but won by only a 51%–47% margin.

The Senate race made Schweitzer a formidable political figure and an obvious candidate for governor in 2004. The incumbent, Republican Judy Martz, elected in 2000 by only a 51%–47% margin, had a rocky tenure. In August 2001 the state House majority leader was killed in the crash of a car driven by Martz's chief policy advisor, who was intoxicated; Martz took him from the hospital at 4 a.m. and washed his bloodstained clothes. She endured months of unfavorable publicity over a personal land purchase from a company involved in a lawsuit with the state until she was exonerated. Her job rating plunged in 2002 and in August 2003, one month after Republican Secretary of State Bob Brown entered the race, she announced she would not run for a second term. A big news story during her term was the collapse of Montana Power, the state's biggest corporation, which sold its power business in 2000 and invested the $2.1 billion proceeds in a fiber optics venture; the fiber optics business went bankrupt and so did the successor company operating the electric power business.

Schweitzer entered the race for governor as the clear frontrunner in the Democratic primary. He campaigned against one-party rule—Montana had had Republican governors since 1988—and championed small businesses against out-of-state corporations. He said Montana had a "salmon economy" ("all our young leave the state and then they come home to die") and that Republicans were to blame for high property taxes and for the state's low (number 50) wage levels. He made common cause with both environmental advocates and hunters and fishermen by championing hunting and fishing rights on private lands and opposing sale of public lands. He called for low-tuition technical colleges to provide training so young people can qualify for jobs in Montana and for a pharmacy purchasing pools to buy prescription drugs in Canada. He named Republican state Senator John Bohlinger as his lieutenant governor candidate and named him head of a Corps of Recovery (mimicking Lewis and Clark's Corps of Discovery) to come up with $60 million of spending cuts without cutting services. He won the June 2004 Democratic primary 73%–27%.

Republicans, long the dominant party, had a four-candidate primary. The winner, with 39% of the vote, was Bob Brown, a Helena veteran: he had been elected to the legislature in 1970, at 23, and served 26 years; for four years he was a lobbyist for USWest, Columbia Falls Aluminum Company and the state university system. His proudest accomplishment was the Lakeshore Protection Plan for Flathead Lake, Montana's largest, which relied on lakefront landowners to reduce pollution. Brown's three opponents were all more conservative and all from Yellowstone County (Billings); Brown, like Schweitzer, declined to take the Americans for Tax Reform pledge not to raise taxes. Brown favored limited oil and gas exploration on the Rocky Mountain Front and the ballot proposition to repeal the state's ban on cyanide mining; Schweitzer took the opposite stand on both issues.

Schweitzer raised more money than Brown, some of it from out-of-state contributors to his 2000 Senate race. With his flair for promoting new ideas and his invocation of his homesteader Montana roots, he seemed a more vibrant candidate than the reserved Brown. Like Brown, he backed the referendum banning same-sex marriage (it passed with 67% of the vote). The Republican Governors Association ran tough ads accusing Schweitzer of "unethical" business practices and Brown's wife charged that he hadn't been active in community affairs in their common hometown of Whitefish. But Schweitzer won by a 50%–46% margin, and Democrats swept to a 27–23 majority in the state Senate and a 50–50 tie in the state House (thus giving them control because state law requires that, in the case of a tie, the speaker must come from the governor's party). Schweitzer carried not only the usual Democratic areas (Butte, the Indian reservations, Missoula) but also Billings, the state's largest city, and Helena, the capital. Voters approved medical marijuana (62%) and the "right to hunt" (81%), rejected an extension of term limits (69%) and retained the ban on cyanide mining (58%)—an interesting set of views.

Senior Senator

Max Baucus (D)

Elected 1978, seat up 2008, 5th term; b. Dec. 11, 1941, Helena; home, Helena; Stanford U., B.A. 1964, LL.B. 1967; Protestant; married (Wanda).

Elected Office: MT House of Reps., 1973–74; U.S. House of Reps., 1974–78.

Professional Career: Staff atty., Civil Aeronautics Bd., 1967–69; Legal Asst., Securities & Exchange Comm., 1969–71; Practicing atty., 1971–74.

DC Office: 511 HSOB, 20510, 202-224-2651; Fax: 202-224-0515; Web site: baucus.senate.gov.

State Offices: Billings, 406-657-6790; Bozeman, 406-586-6104; Butte, 406-782-8700; Great Falls, 406-761-1574; Helena, 406-449-5480; Kalispell, 406-756-1150; Missoula, 406-329-3123.

Committees: *Agriculture, Nutrition & Forestry*: Marketing, Inspection & Product Promotion (RMM); Production & Price Competitiveness; Research, Nutrition & General Legislation. *Environment & Public Works*: Superfund & Waste Management; Transportation & Infrastructure. *Finance* (RMM): International Trade (RMM); Taxation & IRS Oversight. *Joint Committee on Taxation* (4th of 5 Sens.).

Group Ratings

	ADA	ACLU	AFS	LCV	ITIC	NTU	COC	ACU	NTLC	CHC
2004	85	78	86	83	100	30	71	29	41	0
2003	85	—	78	42	—	32	74	15	—	—

National Journal Ratings

	2003 LIB	—	2003 CONS		2004 LIB	—	2004 CONS
Economic	54%	—	45%		54%	—	45%
Social	79%	—	15%		56%	—	42%
Foreign	72%	—	26%		60%	—	39%

Key Votes of the 108th Congress

1. Ban Drilling in ANWR	Y	5. Energy Bill	Y	9. Ban Same-Sex Marriage	N
2. Approve Bush Tax Cuts	N	6. Support Roe v. Wade	Y	10. Ban Bunker-Buster Bomb	Y
3. Medicare/Rx Bill	Y	7. Ban Partial-Birth Abortion	N	11. Fund Iraq War	Y
4. Bar Overtime Pay Regs.	Y	8. Assault Weapons Ban	N	12. Restrict Missile Defense	Y

Election Results

2002 general	Max Baucus (D)	204,853	(63%)	($6,189,970)
	Mike Taylor (R)	103,611	(32%)	($1,839,020)
	Other	18,073	(5%)	
2002 primary	Max Baucus (D)	unopposed		
1996 general	Max Baucus (D)	201,935	(50%)	($4,280,747)
	Denny Rehberg (R)	182,111	(45%)	($1,358,165)
	Becky Shaw (Reform)	19,276	(5%)	

Prior Winning Percentages: 1990 (68%); 1984 (57%); 1978 (56%); 1976 House (66%); 1974 House (55%)

Max Baucus is from a well-known Montana ranching family; in 1897 his great-grandfather Henry Sieben started the huge Sieben Ranch, including the land in *A River Runs Through It*. Baucus grew up on a 125,000-acre (195 square miles) ranch near Helena, graduated from college and law school at Stanford, then worked four years at the now-abolished Civil Aeronautics Board and the Securities and Exchange Commission in Washington. He returned to Montana in 1971 and was executive director of the state constitutional convention in 1972. In 1973, he served in the state House. In 1974, at 32, he won the western House seat (Montana had two House seats until 1992) by walking 600 miles along highways through the district and beating three past or future holders of it (Democrats Pat Williams and Arnold Olsen in the primary and Republican Richard Shoup in the general). He won his Senate seat in 1978 by easily beating an appointed senator in the primary and a conservative Republican investment adviser in the general. Reelected easily in 2002, he became in March 2005 the longest-serving senator from Montana, though he has spent only four years of his adult life living full-time in the state.

Baucus is ranking minority member on the Senate Finance Committee and, from June 2001 to January 2003, was chairman. He is also the Democrat with the greatest seniority on the Environment and Public Works Committee, which he chaired in 1993–94. To these posts he has not brought the philosophic depth of Daniel Patrick Moynihan nor a reputation of loyalty to the Democratic leadership; he always remembers that he is a Democrat in a usually Republican state.

As ranking member and in his 18 months as chairman, Baucus has worked closely with Charles Grassley, chairman in early 2001 and again since January 2003. This is in line with Finance Committee tradition: Moynihan and William Roth did so in the 1990s and Russell Long and Bob Dole did so in the 1980s, regardless of which of them was chairman. In early 2001, when the incoming George W. Bush was pushing for a major tax cut, Baucus and Grassley worked together to produce a bipartisan package that could gain a committee majority. They unveiled their $1.3 trillion package in May; specific provisions were aimed at moderate Republicans Lincoln Chafee and Olympia Snowe and Democrats John Breaux and Bob Torricelli. The bill passed the committee 14–6 and the Senate 62–38 (with 12 Democrats, including Baucus). Key members of the coalition Grassley and Baucus assembled insisted they would not accept major changes from the Senate bill; so something very much like it came out of the conference committee. So, just as Jim Jeffords was in the process of leaving the Republican party, the first domestic priority of the Bush administration was passed into law.

Tom Daschle, who became majority leader in June 2001, was reportedly furious that Baucus refused to consult with the Democratic Caucus before markup; he presumably wanted the 50 Democrats to hold out for a much more Democratic tax cut that would have left the government with much more revenue in the out-years. Pressure from Daschle may have reined in Baucus in October 2001, when Baucus introduced a $70 billion stimulus package and Republicans urged him to negotiate a compromise with Grassley; Baucus instead called on Bush to step in; a smaller Baucus plan passed the committee 11–10 in November (with Jeffords as the swing vote). In effect, Daschle had forced Baucus to go along with his strategy for confrontation with Republicans on the floor rather than compromise in committee. Similarly, on welfare, Baucus was unable to come up with a united Democratic position; the 1996 law was not reauthorized in 2002, 2003 or 2004. Baucus was more successful on securing trade promotion authority for the president, for which there was a large majority in the Senate; after passage by an excruciatingly narrow margin in the House in December 2001, it was delayed some months by Daschle but became law in July 2002.

In September 2002, Baucus summoned all Finance members and told them that Daschle would allow no prescription drug bill to come out of committee and, according to some reports that Baucus denied, said that Daschle would strip him of his chairmanship if he marked one up; instead Daschle brought his own bill to the floor. That month Baucus also cancelled the markup on a small business tax cut after Daschle, the third-ranking Democrat on Finance, filed 78 amendments—one of four markups cancelled because Baucus could not assemble a majority. Baucus and Daschle fought over whether Baucus would brief the Democratic Caucus on the repeal of a tax law ruled by the WTO as an illegal export subsidy on which the European Union was threatening a $4 billion retaliatory tariff.

In the November 2002 elections, Republicans regained a majority in the Senate. That cost Baucus the Finance chairmanship, but it also gave him more freedom of action, and he began working closely again with Grassley on major legislation. Pressure to replace the export subsidy was strong as the European Union imposed $4 billion in retaliatory tariffs, and Grassley and Baucus came up with a corporate tax bill that passed the Senate 92–5 in May 2004. The export subsidies were repealed, $170 billion in tax cuts were granted to manufacturers (or businesses arguing successfully that they were manufacturers) and revenue losses were offset by increased penalties for corporate tax violations and crackdowns on tax shelters. "This is the biggest loophole-closing bill in my memory," Baucus said in May as the conference committee version was about to be approved. Baucus was one of six Democrats on the conference committee, a narrow majority, who acquiesced in the House's removal of FDA regulation of tobacco from the bill.

Baucus also worked with Grassley in drawing up in June 2003 a Medicare/prescription drug bill that won a majority in the Finance Committee and in the Senate. Baucus supported provisions sought mostly by Republicans for a larger role for private health insurance in Medicare but got Republicans to drop provisions that would allow greater prescription drug coverage in private plans than in Medicare. He and Grassley also got what they wanted on rural health care, including provisions to allow the government to step in areas where managed care or private insurance proved unavailable. This bill got its final shape in the conference committee dominated by House Ways and Means Chairman Bill Thomas, who allowed no House Democrats to participate; Baucus and John Breaux were the only Senate Democrats present. Thomas could argue that concessions to him were necessary in the House, where the conference bill was approved by one vote only after a three-hour roll call. But the final product was attacked bitterly by Edward Kennedy and other liberal Democrats who had been favorable to the concept when Baucus and Grassley were marking up their bill in Finance.

Trade issues had been Baucus's main concentration on Finance before he became ranking member and chairman. Although he, like other Democrats, voices support for insistence on labor conditions and environmental standards in trade agreements, he has generally been more favorable to lowering trade barriers than most congressional Democrats: Montana is an exporting state. He was a leading advocate of normal trade relations with China, a potentially huge market for Montana wheat. In 2000, he led the fight for approval of PNTR with China. When PNTR with China was approved, Baucus called for an end to the trade embargo on Cuba. After Japan banned U.S. beef in December 2003 Baucus negotiated directly with the Japanese to open up their market again; Japan announced in October 2004 that it would. Baucus endorsed the U.S.-Australia Free Trade Agreement, but was less enthusiastic about the Central American Free Trade Agreement, expressing concerns about lower environmental and labor standards in CAFTA nations.

Baucus could play a pivotal role on critical issues in 2005 and 2006. Two of George W. Bush's chief domestic priorities are personal retirement accounts in Social Security and major tax adjustments. Both must go through the Senate Finance Committee. In late 2004 Baucus seemed inclined to work on a bipartisan basis with Grassley, as he did on Medicare/prescription drugs and the tax bill in 2004; he joined a bipartisan group with Grassley and other moderates to discuss social security reform. With Tom Daschle defeated for reelection and a reduced number of Democratic senators, the Democratic leadership would seem to have less leverage to rein him in, as Daschle did in 2002. At the same time, the Democratic trend in Montana's state elections in 2004 would seem to leave him less vulnerable to electoral pressure at home. But in spring 2005 Baucus proved to be a trusted point man for Minority Leader Harry Reid by sticking to the party line and rejecting personal retirement accounts. "Privatization has to be off the table because it exacerbates or makes more difficult [achieving] Social Security solvency," he said.

When Baucus was first elected to the Senate in 1978, Montana had been represented there only by Democrats since 1952. But in the years since, Montana has trended Republican. Baucus was reelected in 1996 by only a 50%–45% margin, despite a huge money advantage, over Denny Rehberg, then lieutenant governor and since 2000, the state's congressman-at-large. The increasing conservatism of Montana voters and resentment at Clinton environmental policies put him in an uncomfortable position in the run up to the 2002 election. He supported the Clinton administration moratorium on mining in the Rocky Mountain Front north of Helena, but was neutral on the Clinton proposal to give national monument status to the 149-mile Missouri River Breaks area, which Republican Conrad Burns strongly opposed. He was the only Senate Democrat to oppose a resolution calling for gun control legislation by Memorial Day 2000.

But Baucus has worked hard to maintain a presence in Montana. In 1995–96 he walked 820 miles across the state and shook thousands of hands. He has a "day in the life" program of working a day a month at an ordinary job, building houses with Great Falls high school students, working at a high-tech aerospace firm in Helena, building a grandstand at the Glendive fairgrounds (for once a politician admits to grandstanding).

In early 2001, Baucus nonetheless seemed vulnerable. One Republican who could clearly beat him was Marc Racicot, who had high job ratings as governor from 1992 to 2000. But Racicot, having been the lowest-salaried governor in the nation, wanted to make money and refused to run, despite pleas from George W. Bush; in December 2001 Bush made him Republican National Committee chairman. That left the Republican nomination to state Senator Mike Taylor, sponsor of a law cutting the business equipment tax from 6% to 3% by 2003. Taylor had made millions in a hair salon and cosmetology school business and eventually spent $1 million of his own money on the campaign.

But Baucus had much more money. As chairman of the Senate Finance Committee, his fundraising capacity was enormous, and in all he spent over $6 million—almost four times as much as Taylor. Baucus ran ads showing how he helped Montana small businesses and showing George W. Bush thanking him at bill-signing ceremonies. Then, on October 10, Taylor announced he was dropping out of the race, because of an ad run by the Montana Democratic party that slyly suggested he was homosexual. The ad showed 1980s footage of Taylor, with open front shirt and gold chains, massaging a man's face applying facial cream; it stated that Taylor had failed to refund student loan money when students dropped out. Taylor claimed that his wife made paperwork errors and a Taylor aide said, "They're playing off the old stereotype of men who work in the hair-care profession." In any case, the race was already probably over. Taylor had only raised $658,000 from others and was unwilling or unable to put more of his own money in; he was still far behind Baucus in public polls, and national Republicans had decided this was not a priority race. In late October, Taylor resumed his campaign. It didn't matter. Baucus won 63%–32%, carrying all but two small counties.

Baucus, always fit and physically active, has had a few health problems. In November 2003 he took a bad fall in a 50-mile race in Maryland and two months later had surgery to relieve pressure on his brain. In June 2004 he had a pacemaker installed, and in July 2004 he suffered minor injuries in a motorcycle crash in Montana. But he still seems vigorous and is in a position to make a major impact on important national issues. He comes up for reelection in 2008.

Junior Senator

Conrad Burns (R)

Elected 1988, seat up 2006, 3d term; b. Jan. 25, 1935, Gallatin, MO; home, Billings; U. of MO, 1952–54; Lutheran; married (Phyllis).

Military Career: Marine Corps, 1955–57.

Elected Office: Yellowstone Cnty. Comm., 1986–88.

Professional Career: TWA and Ozark Airlines, 1958–61; Field rep., *Polled Hereford World*, 1962; Mgr., Billings Livestock Show, 1968; Radio & TV broadcaster, 1968–86.

DC Office: 187 DSOB, 20510, 202-224-2644; Fax: 202-224-8594; Web site: burns.senate.gov.

State Offices: Billings, 406-252-0550; Bozeman, 406-586-4450; Butte, 406-723-3277; Glendive, 406-365-2391; Great Falls, 406-452-9585; Helena, 406-449-5401; Kalispell, 406-257-3360; Missoula, 406-329-3528.

Committees: *Aging (Special)*. *Appropriations*: Agriculture, Rural Development & Related Agencies; Defense; Energy & Water; Interior & Related Agencies (Chmn.); Military Construction & Veterans Affairs; Transportation, Treasury, the Judiciary, HUD & Related Agencies. *Commerce, Science & Transportation*: Aviation (Chmn.); Consumer Affairs, Product Safety & Insurance; Science & Space; Surface Transportation & Merchant Marine; Technology, Innovation & Competitiveness; Trade, Tourism & Economic Development. *Energy & Natural Resources*: Energy; Public Lands & Forests (Vice Chmn.); Water & Power. *Small Business & Entrepreneurship*.

Group Ratings

	ADA	ACLU	AFS	LCV	ITIC	NTU	COC	ACU	NTLC	CHC
2004	5	0	0	0	100	73	100	100	93	100
2003	10	—	11	0	—	72	100	80	—	—

National Journal Ratings

	2003 LIB	—	2003 CONS		2004 LIB	—	2004 CONS
Economic	0%	—	82%		5%	—	91%
Social	0%	—	59%		0%	—	84%
Foreign	0%	—	78%		0%	—	67%

Key Votes of the 108th Congress

1. Ban Drilling in ANWR	N	5. Energy Bill	Y	9. Ban Same-Sex Marriage	Y
2. Approve Bush Tax Cuts	Y	6. Support Roe v. Wade	N	10. Ban Bunker-Buster Bomb	N
3. Medicare/Rx Bill	Y	7. Ban Partial-Birth Abortion	Y	11. Fund Iraq War	Y
4. Bar Overtime Pay Regs.	N	8. Assault Weapons Ban	N	12. Restrict Missile Defense	N

Election Results

2000 general	Conrad Burns (R)	208,082	(51%)	($4,337,961)
	Brian Schweitzer (D)	194,430	(47%)	($2,033,530)
	Other	9,089	(2%)	
2000 primary	Conrad Burns (R)	unopposed		
1994 general	Conrad Burns (R)	218,542	(62%)	($3,518,574)
	Jack Mudd (D)	131,845	(38%)	($1,107,591)

Prior Winning Percentages: 1988 (52%)

Conrad Burns makes weighty speeches on foreign policy and the future of the Internet even as he cuts the figure of a stereotypical Westerner, picking his teeth with a pocketknife, chewing tobacco, telling deadpan jokes. Burns grew up in northwest Missouri, joined the Marines after two years of college, worked for two airlines, then became a livestock fieldman and auctioneer and field representative of the *Polled Hereford World* and moved to Billings. When he was reassigned back east (to Des Moines), he quit so he could stay in Montana. He set up the Northern Ag Network, which grew from four radio stations in 1975 to 29 radio and six TV stations in 1988. Piqued at a local politician, Burns ran for Yellowstone County commissioner in 1986 and won; two years later, he ran against Democratic Senator John Melcher. Burns attacked him as "a liberal who is soft on drugs, soft on defense and very high on social programs." Melcher was hurt by public opposition to the "let-it-burn" policy that resulted in the Yellowstone fires of summer 1988. Burns, who ended every speech with a Western "You bet!" won 52%–48%. In 1994, he faced poorly-funded law professor Jack Mudd; Burns won 62%–38%, the first time Montana voters have ever re-elected a Republican senator.

Burns has a solidly conservative voting record in the Senate. In 1997, he became chairman of the Communications Subcommittee, one of the key regulatory posts in Congress. There, this former broadcaster has generally favored deregulation and encouragement of Internet commerce. He wrote Section 706 of the 1996 Telecommunications Act, which provided incentives for broadband data networks. His bill to provide for electronic authentication of online contracts and user identities became law in June 2000. With Ron Wyden, he has co-sponsored the extensions of the law exempting Internet transactions from taxation. Also with Wyden, he co-sponsored the 2003 CAN-SPAM law that bans fake originating addresses and harvesting of email addresses from webpages, requires a clear opportunity to opt out of further messages and labeling of pornography and directs the FTC to study a do-not-spam registry.

With Hillary Rodham Clinton, Burns sponsored a 2004 E-911 law that granted states money to upgrade technology to locate cellphone callers and provided penalties for states that misdirect the funds. He has worked on spectrum issues, including bills taking certain channels away from broadcasters and allocating them to law enforcement. On spectrum, he says, "I am the only person in the whole Congress who believes it is not a national resource. I think it's a technology." But he has supported spectrum auctions. Despite his deregulatory instincts, he opposed the 2003 FCC ruling allowing companies to own larger numbers of radio and TV stations. "We've all said we've seen a growth in the number of voices and a growth in outlets. We have seen that under existing rules. So my first reaction is, why change?" But Burns will be less of a voice on these issues, since Chairman Ted Stevens reshuffled the Commerce subcommittees and eliminated the Communications Subcommittee so that telecommunications issues can be heard at the full committee level. Burns became chairman of the Aviation Subcommittee instead.

On other issues, Burns was a strong advocate of allowing airline pilots to carry guns, and called for shifting airport security from the Transportation Department to Justice. He cast the lone vote against the election procedures bill passed in April 2002, on the grounds that it imposed too many mandates on state and local government.

On Montana issues, Burns is often critical of environmentalists. He opposed reintroduction of grey wolves into Yellowstone National Park, estimating the cost at $1.8 million per wolf. He has blocked Democrats' plans for a Montana wilderness bill and they have blocked his. He joined several Democrats in 2002 in seeking over $5 billion for drought relief for farmers, on the ground that they deserve it as much as victims of hurricanes and floods; this was opposed by George W. Bush, and Burns and others had to settle for $752 million coming out of farm programs. As chairman of the Appropriations Subcommittee on the Interior, he is well-positioned to steer money to Montana projects, like the ARS Northern Plains Research Lab, the Value-Added Ruminant Animal Consortium at Montana State, the U.S. 93 bypass project in Kalispell and the Marcus Daly mansion restoration in Hamilton.

Burns had a surprisingly hard time winning reelection in 2000 over Democrat Brian Schweitzer, who was elected governor in 2004. One reason was term limits: In February 1999, Burns announced he would break his pledge to serve only two terms. That same month, speaking before a Montana group, he referred to Arabs as "ragheads" and had to make a quick apology—his penchant for quips had gone too far. Schweitzer, a Whitefish rancher, turned out to be a tough opponent, with a penchant for original proposals and pithy phrases and, in his blue jeans and Dodge pickup, with a persona as down-home as Burns's. Schweitzer was the first candidate in the 1999–2000 cycle to call for a prescription drug benefit, and in fall 1999, he organized the first busload of seniors to Canada to buy drugs at lower prices. Burns responded ineptly and did not seem comfortable arguing that pharmaceutical companies set prices in order to fund pathbreaking research.

Burns was also thrown on the defensive on the asbestos issue. There was heavy publicity about the asbestos-related illnesses and deaths in the town of Libby, where children played in tailings from a closed vermiculite plant. In January 2000, a trial lawyer-financed group attacked Burns for supporting a bill that would limit compensation to those who had asbestos-related disease and shut down the giant asbestos tort cases; it showed a Libby resident accusing Burns of "standing up for the people who made me sick and killed my father." In March, Burns withdrew his support of the bill and pushed for $3.5 million for a Libby hospital and $8 million for local economic development. In addition, a group backed by the U.S. Chamber of Commerce and an asbestos company ran ads showing relatives of an asbestos victim blaming "asbestos lawyers" for clogging the courts and preventing them from getting compensation. Later, another group backed by pharmaceutical companies ran ads saying Schweitzer favored "Canadian-style government controls on prescription medicine."

Burns outspent Schweitzer by 2–1, and in ads talked about bringing $1 billion of federal money to Montana. He also linked Schweitzer to Al Gore. Polls in the closing weeks showed the race close, and Burns won by only 51%–47%. There is some speculation that Burns, who turns 71 in 2006, will not run for reelection when his seat comes up that year. But in 2003 he said there was never any doubt he would run. By mid-2005, two Democrats seemed likely to challenge him: state Senate President Jon Tester and state Auditor John Morrison.

Representative-At-Large
Denny Rehberg (R)

Elected 2000, 3d term; b. Oct. 5, 1955, Billings; home, Billings; WA St. U., B.A. 1977; Episcopalian; married (Jan).

Elected Office: MT House of Reps., 1984–90; MT Lt. Gov., 1991–96

Professional Career: Leg. Asst., U.S. Rep. Ron Marlenee, 1979–82; Rancher, 1982-present.

DC Office: 516 CHOB, 20515, 202-225-3211; Fax: 202-225-5687; Web site: www.house.gov/rehberg.

District Offices: Billings, 406-256-1019; Great Falls, 406-454-1066; Helena, 406-443-7878; Missoula, 406-543-9550.

Committees: *Appropriations* (35th of 37 R): Energy & Water Development & Related Agencies; Foreign Operations, Export Financing & Related Programs; Military Quality of Life & Veterans Affairs & Related Agencies.

Group Ratings

	ADA	ACLU	AFS	LCV	ITIC	NTU	COC	ACU	NTLC	CHC
2004	5	5	0	0	80	61	95	96	76	100
2003	10	—	0	0	—	62	93	88	—	—

National Journal Ratings

	2003 LIB — 2003 CONS		2004 LIB — 2004 CONS	
Economic	0%	— 91%	20%	— 80%
Social	37%	— 61%	9%	— 85%
Foreign	23%	— 71%	42%	— 57%

Key Votes of the 108th Congress

1. Drilling in ANWR	Y	5. DC School Vouchers	Y	9. Ban Same-Sex Marriage	Y
2. Approve Bush Tax Cuts	Y	6. Ban Human Cloning	Y	10. Fund Iraq War	Y
3. Medicare/Rx Bill	Y	7. Restrict Gun Liability	Y	11. Bar Cuba Embargo Funds	N
4. Bar Overtime Pay Regs.	N	8. Ban Partial-Birth Abortion	Y	12. Intelligence Reorg.	Y

Election Results

2004 general	Denny Rehberg (R)	286,076	(64%)	($608,199)
	Tracy Velazquez (D)	145,606	(33%)	($127,716)
	Other	12,548	(3%)	
2004 primary	Denny Rehberg (R)	unopposed		
2002 general	Denny Rehberg (R)	214,100	(65%)	($949,631)
	Steve Kelly (D)	108,233	(33%)	($18,757)
	Other	8,988	(3%)	

Prior Winning Percentages: 2000 (51%)

Dennis Rehberg, a Republican elected in 2000, is a rancher from Billings who raises cattle and cashmere goats on his family ranch and who has been involved in politics most of his adult life. After college, he worked in real estate and then on the Washington staff of Congressman Ron Marlenee. He returned to Montana in 1982 and was elected to the state House in 1984, at 29; he managed Marlenee's campaign in 1986 and Conrad Burns' first campaign for the Senate in 1988. He served as Burns' state director for two years, then was appointed lieutenant governor by Republican Stan Stephens, and was elected to that post on the ticket headed by Marc Racicot in 1992. In 1996, he ran against Senator Max Baucus. Rehberg backed term limits, promised to forego pay increases and attacked Baucus for backing the 1993 tax increase and the assault weapons ban. Baucus called Rehberg a "special interest" candidate backing billions in tax cuts for the rich and argued against Republican Medicare "cuts." Rehberg was outspent by $4.3 million to $1.4 million, but made it a close race: Baucus won 50%–45%.

Rehberg (pronounced *REE-berg*) returned to ranching. The opportunity to run for the House arose in September 1999 when incumbent Republican Rick Hill, reelected by only 53%–44% and facing vigorous opposition from Democratic Superintendent of Public Instruction Nancy Keenan, announced he would not run because of complications from eye surgery. Rehberg was unopposed for the Republican nomination. The general race against Keenan was a classic contest between a liberal Democrat and a conservative Republican. Both decried Montana's low-wage economy and how it made it difficult for young people to stay in the communities where they were raised. But it was not clear what either would do about it. Rehberg and Keenan also agreed on opposing gun control, repealing the marriage penalty and letting patients sue HMOs.

Naturally there was more discussion of their disagreements—on abortion rights, on inheritance taxes, a prescription drug benefit (Rehberg favored it for the needy, Keenan for all), and individual investment accounts in Social Security. The tone got testier, as outside groups—the AFL-CIO, the NEA, the Chamber of Commerce, the NFIB—spent over $100,000 each; something like $20 million was spent in this state with seriously contested races for Senate and House. Rehberg ran ads with strong endorsements from Governor Marc Racicot and often showing his family, especially his two-year-old daughter—an implicit contrast with Keenan, a former copper smelter worker and special education teacher who had never married. Rehberg won 51%–46%, almost precisely the same margin as in the races for governor and senator that year; all the Republicans were surely helped by George W. Bush's 58%–33% margin over Al Gore.

As a freshman, Rehberg concentrated on issues with impact in Montana. He worked with Senator Burns in 2002 to get $5 billion in drought relief for farmers in addition to the farm bill; they were frustrated by Bush's opposition, and had to settle for $752 million in farm bill funds. He sought repeal of the Clinton administration's restrictions on snowmobiling in Yellowstone National Park; after a hearing Rehberg organized, the Bush administration changed the policy.

In his second term Rehberg spent much time trying to preserve mandatory country of origin labeling of meat, a provision of the 2002 farm bill set to go into effect in September 2004. In 2003 he pressed for funding for it. In a law signed in January 2004 Congress delayed implementation by two years. In July 2004 the Agriculture Committee rejected a Rehberg amendment to leave mandatory country of origin labeling intact by 32–16 and, by voice vote, to make the labeling voluntary.

Rehberg has supported the Bush administration strongly on Iraq, but has disagreed on a few other issues. He favors reimportation of prescription drugs from Canada, backed the House's $318 billion transportation bill and opposed Bush's January 2004 proposals on immigration. He has harshly criticized the Endangered Species Act and says it leads farmers and ranchers to "shoot, shovel and shut up"—to kill animals that may be labeled endangered because of onerous enforcement.

Rehberg declined a repeat run against Senator Max Baucus in 2002, though polls suggested he would be competitive. He was reelected against unknown opponents by 65%–33% in 2002 and 64%–33% in 2004. He has been mentioned as a likely Senate candidate if Burns retires in 2006, but in late 2004 Burns seemed determined to run, and Rehberg won a seat on the Appropriations Committee—a sign he may be contemplating a long House career.

★ NEBRASKA ★

66 "The sea of Nebraska" is what the first settlers coming west called the Platte River—not actually a single river, but a braid of streams that weaves a silver chain around sandbars and islands, flooding the level floor of the great plain—a mile wide, as the saying goes, and six inches deep. Nebraska was formed in one rush of settlement in the 1880s, when its population increased from 452,000 to 1,062,000; it increased less than that, to 1,578,000, in the next 100 years. In the 1880s Omaha became a major railroad center, Lincoln the state capital, and farming and food products the main businesses. And for about 100 years, Nebraska remained pretty much that way. This is not what its founders intended: They hoped Nebraska would develop a diversified farming, industrial and commercial economy like Ohio, Illinois, Missouri or Minnesota. But while the 1880s were a time of plentiful rain here, the 1890s were a decade of drought, and Nebraska stopped growing. Many rural counties, and even Omaha, lost population and Nebraska exported people for 100 years: 48% of Nebraskans in 1890 were children; in 2000, only 26% were. For a long time the creative energies in the economy seem to have skipped over the Great Plains and moved far to the West.

The sudden boom of the 1880s and the bust of the 1890s produced the most colorful—and atypical—politics of Nebraska's history: The populist movement and William Jennings Bryan, the "silver tongued orator of the Platte." Bryan was only 36 when he delivered his Cross of Gold speech at the 1896 Democratic National Convention and was swept to the Democratic nomination. He was so radical that Democratic President Grover Cleveland wouldn't support him, but he still won 47% of the popular vote in the first of three attempts at the presidency. Since Bryan's time, Nebraska's most notable politician has been George Norris, who led the House rebellion against Speaker Joseph Cannon in 1911, and in the 1930s championed the state's unicameral legislature and pushed through the Norris-LaGuardia Anti-Injunction Act (the first federal pro-union legislation) and the Tennessee Valley Authority. But most Nebraskans were repelled by the New Deal, which seemed to threaten their way of life. Although it often elects Democratic governors and senators, Nebraska over the past half-century has been the second-most Republican state in presidential elections.

Since 1990, Nebraska has been growing robustly for the first time in decades. Its population grew 10%, to 1,747,000 between 1990 and 2004, less than the national average but more than Nebraska has grown since the 1910s. The growth has not been even. In 62 of its 93 counties population has declined. In tiny county seats stores are closing, across the plains farmhouses are shuttered up, small school buildings are half-empty. The acreage of irrigated land has been rising, but a state law passed in 2004 seems likely to reduce irrigation from wells; groundwater irrigation may have peaked out. At the same time metro Omaha and Lincoln grew smartly; so did the northeast corner of the state and the counties strung along the Platte River and I-80 from Omaha to North Platte. More than half the people in the state live in the Omaha and Lincoln metropolitan areas; only 6% of jobs in those areas are on farms. Omaha is the home base of the fast-growing ConAgra food combine, of the giant Peter Kiewit construction company and of mega-investor Warren Buffett, whose down-home wit complements his knack for picking winning stocks. The nearby Strategic Air Command base brought the world's most advanced phone system to the Omaha area 40-odd years ago; starting in the 1980s hotel chains, credit card companies and telemarketers set up operations, making this the world's leading telemarketing center. Nebraska ranks number one in combine manufacturing, with a big new plant in Grand Island; it is one of the leaders in meatpacking, with a big IBP plant across the Missouri River from Sioux City, Iowa; and there are 17 operational ethanol plants.

Nebraska's incomes and housing values shot up during the 1990s and its unemployment rate has been one of the lowest in the country. The number of jobs rose 18% when the population rose 8%. The problem is that Nebraska's aging population has not been producing enough young

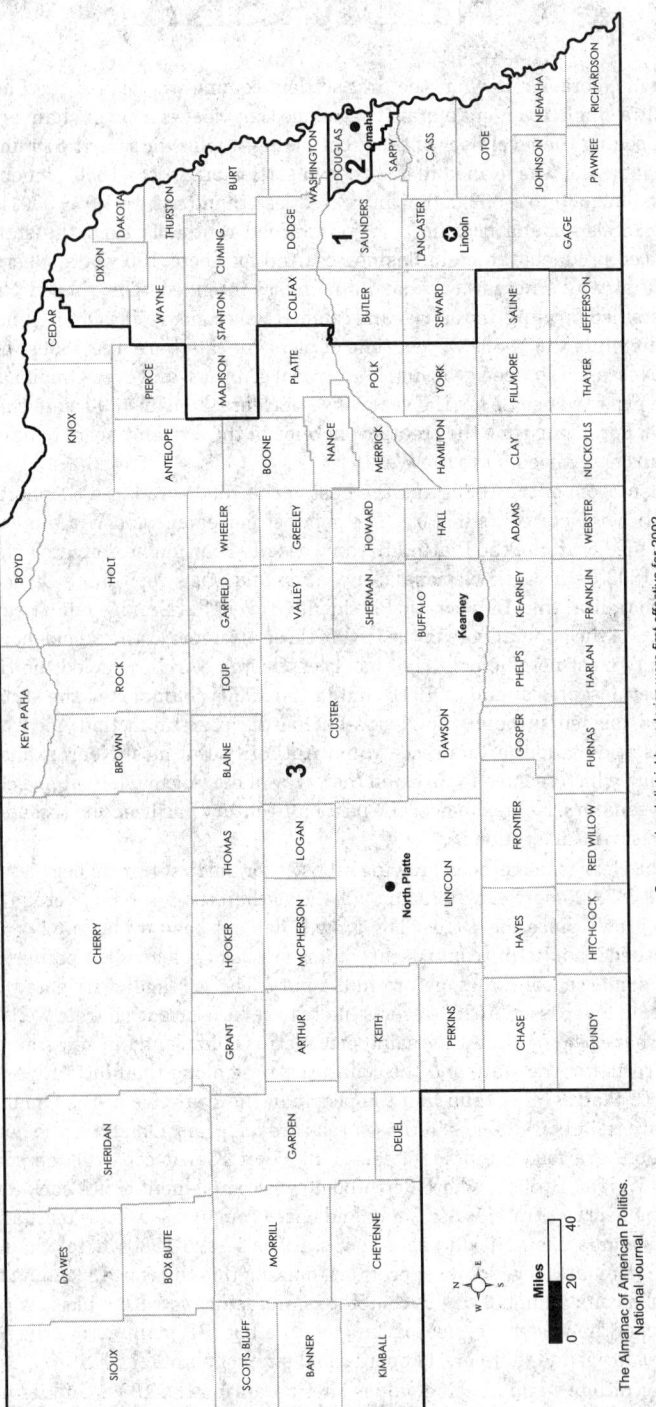

Congressional district boundaries were first effective for 2002.

The Almanac of American Politics.
National Journal

Miles
0   20   40

people to fill its jobs, but for the first time in a century there has been migration into the state. A hundred years ago Czechs, Germans and Danes came to work the farms on the plains—Willa Cather tells the story—and factories in Omaha. Now Latinos have been coming from Texas and Mexico to work in meatpacking factories: The Hispanic percentage rose from 2% to 6% in the 1990s, and in 2000, 8% of the state's children were Hispanic. Hispanic percentages are highest in the counties around Lexington (25%), South Sioux City (23%), Scottsbluff (17%) and Grand Island (14%). The state Department of Economic Development sent out 20,000 invitations to Nebraska graduates in Colorado to attend a Nebraska Alumni Celebration in Denver, where they are told how plentiful jobs are and how inexpensive housing is in their home state. Meanwhile, farm counties keep losing population; the drought of summer 2002 caused ranchers to cull their herds, as eastern Nebraska farmers sent hay to the dry counties in the west. Demographically, Nebraska increasingly looks like a Rocky Mountain state, with population concentrated in two cities and several smaller factory towns, with relatively few people spread out over farmlands. Every fall Saturday when the 'Huskers (Nebraskans don't say Cornhuskers) play in Lincoln, one out of every 25 Nebraskans is there.

Nebraska may be heavily Republican, but it is also a small enough community that attractive Democrats can win high office. The pattern has been this: A Republican governor raises taxes, a Democrat defeats him or her and then goes on to serve in the Senate. That is the template for the careers of Jim Exon, elected governor in 1970 and senator from 1978 to 1996; Bob Kerrey, elected governor in 1982 and senator from 1988 to 2000; and Ben Nelson, elected governor in 1990 and senator in 2000. But Republicans have grown stronger. Republican Chuck Hagel beat Nelson when Nelson first ran for the Senate in 1996. Governor Mike Johanns, elected in 1998, opposed tax increases; temporary increases in the sales, income and cigarette taxes were passed over his veto in 2002. In 2002 Hagel and Johanns were reelected by 83%–15% and 69%–28% margins—even greater than George W. Bush's 62%–33% 2000 margin here; now Hagel is being mentioned as a candidate for president and Johanns has been appointed Secretary of Agriculture. The last time a Democrat has won one of Nebraska's three congressional seats was in 1992. Self-identified Republicans hold 32 of the 49 seats in Nebraska's technically nonpartisan unicameral Senate and Republicans hold all five downballot statewide offices. In 2004 George W. Bush carried the state 66%–33%, carrying 92 of the state's 93 counties (the exception, Thurston County, is an Indian reservation); he ran under 60% in only five counties, two of them the counties containing Omaha and Lincoln. But Nebraska's Democrats are a game lot, and they include the country's richest man, investor Warren Buffett; in this mostly flat state, they have an awfully steep political hill to climb.

The People		Race/Ethnic Origin			Military veterans: 173,189 (13.7%)	
Pop. 2004 (est):	1,747,214	1,494,494	87.3%	White	WWII: 20.0%	Korea: 15.0%
Pop. 2000:	1,711,263	67,537	3.9%	Black	Vietnam: 32.3%	Gulf War: 10.8%
Pop. 1990:	1,578,385	21,677	1.3%	Asian	**Most populous cities (2003):**	
Change 1990–2000:	Up 8.4%	13,460	0.8%	Native Am.	1. Omaha	404,267
% of U.S. total:	0.6%	647	0.0%	Hawaiian	2. Lincoln	235,594
Pop. rank:	38th of 50	17,696	1.0%	Two+ races	3. Bellevue	46,734
Area size:	77,354 sq. mi.	1,327	0.1%	Other	4. Grand Island	43,771
State Native:	67.1%	94,425	5.5%	Hisp. Origin	5. Kearney	28,211
Non-citizen:	3.0%	**Ancestry**				
Language		German: 27.7%		Irish: 9.6%	Urban population: 69.7%	
English: 90.4%	Spanish: 5.4%	English: 6.9%		Swedish: 3.5%	Rural population: 30.3%	
Other Eur.: 2.9%		USA: 3.2%				

Education		Work Sector		Unicameral	
H.S. Grad:	86.6%	Private: 77.1%	Govt: 13.7%	Senate	49 I
College Grad:	23.7%	Self: 8.7%	Family: 0.5%	Legislative Term Limits: Yes	
Industry		Unemployment: 3.5%		**Registered Voters**	
Agri: 5.6%	Con: 6.5%	**Household Income**		D: 396,767	(34.2%)
Fin: 7.7%	Info: 2.5%	<15k: 14.9%	15-35k: 29.5%	R: 575,781	(49.6%)
Mfg: 18.4%	Prof: 28.0%	35-50k: 18.4%	50-100k: 29.2%	O: 187,651	(16.2%)
Public: 3.9%	Trade: 15.7%	100-150k: 5.5%	>150k: 2.6%		
Other: 11.9%		Median: $39,250			
Occupation		Poverty status: 9.7%			
Blue collar: 24.4%	White collar: 59.4%	**Home Value**			
Gray collar: 16.2%		<50k: 21.3%	50-100k: 40.2% 100-200k: 30.4% 200-300k: 5.3%		
		300-500k: 2.0% >500k: 0.7% Median: $86,900			

Presidential politics   Over the last 50 years, Nebraska has voted more Republican in presidential elections than all but one other state—61.1% to Utah's 61.6%. It was appropriate, perhaps, that this was the last state Bill Clinton visited as president, in December 2000. Greater Omaha usually goes Republican, while Lincoln is more closely divided; rural western counties are heavily Republican—Bush's 2004 percentages there ranged up to 90%. In the NEP exit poll, no statistically significant demographic group came close to voting for John Kerry. Nebraska law allows its electoral votes to be split, with one going to the winner of each congressional district and two to the statewide winner. But this has never made any difference. In spring 2004 Kerry backers hoped he would carry the 1st Congressional District; it voted 63%–36% for Bush.

Nebraska has a presidential primary in May that once attracted attention; the whole national press followed Robert Kennedy and Eugene McCarthy out here in 1968 and took note when Frank Church won in 1976. No more, though: Nominations are now sewn up long before May, and Nebraska votes as unnoticed then as in November.

2004 Presidential Vote
Bush (R)	512,814	(66%)
Kerry (D)	254,328	(33%)
Nader (I)	5,698	(1%)
Other	5,346	(1%)

2004 Democratic Presidential Primary
Kerry (D)	52,479	(73%)
Edwards (D)	10,031	(14%)
Dean (D)	5,400	(8%)
Kucinich (D)	1,490	(2%)
Sharpton (D)	1,367	(2%)
Other	805	(1%)

2000 Presidential Vote
Bush (R)	433,862	(62%)
Gore (D)	231,780	(33%)
Nader (Green)	24,540	(4%)
Other	6,837	(1%)

Congressional districting   Nebraska has had three congressional districts since the 1960 Census. Redistricting made only marginal changes for 2002; Democrats were angered when traditionally Democratic Saline County was moved from the 1st to the 3d District. No Democrat has been elected from a Nebraska district since 1992.

109th Congress Lineup
3 R

108th Congress Lineup
3 R

Governor

Dave Heineman (R)

Assumed office Jan. 2005, term expires Jan. 2007, 1st term; b. May 12, 1948, Falls City; home, Fremont; U.S. Military Acad., B.S. 1970; married (Sally).

Military Career: Army, 1970–75.

Elected Office: Fremont City Cncl., 1990–94; NE Treasurer, 1994–2001; NE Lt. Gov., 2001–05.

Professional Career: Ex. Dir., NE Republican party, 1979–81; Chief of Staff, U.S. Rep. Hal Daub, 1983–88.

Office: P.O. Box 94848, Lincoln, 68509, 402-471-2244; Fax: 402-471-6031; Web site: www.gov.state.ne.us.

Election Results

2002 general	Mike Johanns (R)	330,349	(69%)
	Stormy Dean (D)	132,348	(28%)
	Paul Rosberg (NEB)	18,294	(4%)
2002 primary	Mike Johanns (R)	128,277	(87%)
	Robert Wicht (R)	19,441	(13%)
1998 general	Mike Johanns (R)	293,910	(54%)
	Bill Hoppner (D)	250,678	(46%)

Dave Heineman became governor of Nebraska on January 21, 2005, when Mike Johanns resigned to become George W. Bush's Secretary of Agriculture. Heineman was born in Falls City (pop. 4,375) in the state's southeastern corner, 100 miles equidistant from Omaha and Lincoln. He grew up in a handful of small towns across the state, the son of an itinerant J.C. Penney's store manager, before graduating from Wahoo High School. He went east to attend the United States Military Academy at West Point and served five years in the Army, graduating from the Army's Airborne and Ranger schools and rising to the rank of captain. When his tour ended in 1975, he returned to Nebraska and immediately dove into politics as a volunteer for the Republican party in Omaha.

Heineman became the party's executive director in 1979, held the position for two years and for the rest of the decade worked in politics and government: campaign manager and aide to Congressman Hal Daub, political consultant to Governor Kay Orr's reelection campaign, local office manager for Congressman Doug Bereuter. In 1990, he won his first elective office, a seat on the Fremont City Council, and then was elected state Treasurer in 1994 and reelected in 1998. In 2001 he was chosen by Johanns to replace Lieutenant Governor David Maurstad, who resigned to become a regional director for the Federal Emergency Management Agency. He ran for lieutenant governor in 2002 on a ticket with Johanns; they won by 69%–28%.

As treasurer, Heineman modernized the state's money management system and its methods of returning unclaimed property to residents. As lieutenant governor, he served as the state's official lobbyist in Washington, its homeland security director and as chairman of Nebraska's Information Technology Commission, where he helped create a telecommunications backbone for state government, medical facilities and the University of Nebraska. All the while, he had his eye on the governorship. When Bereuter announced he would not seek reelection to Congress in 2004, Heineman declined to run for the open 1st District seat, saying he was focused on running for governor in 2006 when term limits would prevent Johanns from running again. "I would rather pursue my dream of becoming governor, even if that opportunity never materializes, than to pursue another office that I am not committed to." But he also said that if Congressman Tom Osborne, the former University of Nebraska football coach and the state's most popular politician, decided to run for governor, it was unlikely he would challenge him.

Johanns' next move seemed obvious: speculation that he would run against Senator Ben Nelson in 2006 began almost immediately after his 2002 reelection. According to some reports, Republicans tried to persuade Nelson to switch parties to stave off what was expected to be a tough challenge. Another option for Nelson: Ten days after the 2004 election, according to the *Omaha World-Herald*, White House strategist Karl Rove offered him the position of Secretary of Agriculture; the paper said Nelson considered it for five days before declining. If he had accepted, Johanns would have appointed his successor.

But Johanns' surprise Cabinet appointment reordered the 2006 political landscape. Nelson's reelection prospects suddenly grew brighter; the governor's race suddenly became a lot more complicated. If Heineman chose to run for a full term in 2006, potential Republican candidates, which included Osborne, Attorney General Jon Bruning and Omaha businessman David Nabity, would have to challenge a sitting governor in a primary, an unwelcome prospect for the party. By spring 2005, the picture became clearer. In March, Bruning announced he would not run for governor and would instead seek a second term as attorney general. On April 11, Heineman signaled his intention to run for governor by filing papers to form a campaign committee. "I enjoy this job. I like doing it. I want to continue doing it," he said. Senator Chuck Hagel endorsed Heineman's candidacy the same day. On April 30, Osborne said he would run for governor but only intended to serve a single term if elected.

Heineman began his first legislative session as governor on solid footing. Nebraska is the only state with a unicameral legislature, the Senate, often called the Unicam, and some of its 49 members were still angry over Johanns' heavy involvement in the 2004 campaign; Johanns had leveled tough criticisms of a 2003 tax increase that was passed over his veto. They welcomed a new face in the governor's office. After four lean years marked by contentious budget cuts and tax increases, the state's revenue outlook began to pick up. Johanns' final budget recommendations, crafted with Heineman's assistance, were released in January 2005 and called for a 5.6% increase in spending over the previous year and for a 6% increase in the 2006–07 budget. Johanns and Heineman agreed that none of the prior budget cuts should be restored and proposed increasing state aid to K-12 education by 9.9% in the first year of the two-year budget plan. The state would also pay off in a single lump sum the $146 million it owed to settle a lawsuit over Nebraska's failure to meet its commitment in an interstate compact to store low-level radioactive waste. Heineman praised Johanns in his first State of the State address in January and promised that four priorities would guide his decisions as governor: "education, economic vitality, efficiency in government and the protection of families."

Heineman's prospects for winning a full term in 2006 may have less to do with his accomplishments as governor than with the strength of his opposition: "Tom Osborne is on another plane than the rest of us," explained Attorney General Jon Bruning. After Osborne announced for governor, national party officials were hoping to convince Heineman to run against Ben Nelson, but Heineman told the *Lincoln Journal Star* in May that his interest in the Senate, on a scale of zero to 100, was "minus-1000 and dropping." Possible Democratic candidates for governor included Stormy Dean, the 2002 nominee for governor, University of Nebraska Regent Chuck Hassebrook, state Senators Chris Beutler, Pat Bourne and Matt Connealy, the unsuccessful 2004 nominee in the open 1st District.

Senior Senator

Chuck Hagel (R)

Elected 1996, seat up 2008, 2d term; b. Oct. 4, 1946, North Platte; home, Omaha; U. of NE, B.A. 1971; Episcopalian; married (Lilibet).

Military Career: Army, 1967–68 (Vietnam).

Professional Career: Newscaster & Talk Show Host, KBON & KLNG Radio, 1969–71; Admin. Asst., U.S. Rep. John Y. McCollister, 1971–77; Mgr., Govt. Affairs, Firestone Tire & Rubber Co., 1977–80; Dpty. Admin., Veterans' Admin., 1981; U.S. Dpty. Commissioner General, World's Fair, 1982; Pres., Collins, Hagel & Clarke Inc., 1983–84; Co–founder, Dir. & Exec. V.P.., Vanguard Cellular Systems Inc., 1984–87; Pres. & CEO, World USO, 1987–90; Pres. & CEO, Priv. Sector Cncl., 1990–92; Pres., McCarth & Co., 1992–95.

DC Office: 248 RSOB, 20510, 202-224-4224; Fax: 202-224-5213; Web site: hagel.senate.gov.

State Offices: Kearney, 308-236-7602; Lincoln, 402-476-1400; Omaha, 402-758-8981; Scottsbluff, 308-632-6032.

Committees: *Banking, Housing & Urban Affairs*: Financial Institutions; International Trade & Finance; Securities & Investment (Chmn.). *Foreign Relations*: East Asian & Pacific Affairs; European Affairs; International Economic Policy, Export & Trade Promotion (Chmn.); Near Eastern & South Asian Affairs. *Intelligence (Select)*. *Rules & Administration*.

Group Ratings

	ADA	ACLU	AFS	LCV	ITIC	NTU	COC	ACU	NTLC	CHC
2004	20	22	0	0	100	75	93	87	95	100
2003	15	—	29	0	—	78	87	100	—	—

National Journal Ratings

	2003 LIB	—	2003 CONS	2004 LIB	—	2004 CONS
Economic	33%	—	62%	37%	—	62%
Social	0%	—	59%	38%	—	60%
Foreign	22%	—	68%	47%	—	51%

Key Votes of the 108th Congress

1. Ban Drilling in ANWR	N	5. Energy Bill	Y	9. Ban Same-Sex Marriage	Y
2. Approve Bush Tax Cuts	Y	6. Support Roe v. Wade	N	10. Ban Bunker-Buster Bomb	N
3. Medicare/Rx Bill	N	7. Ban Partial-Birth Abortion	Y	11. Fund Iraq War	Y
4. Bar Overtime Pay Regs.	N	8. Assault Weapons Ban	N	12. Restrict Missile Defense	N

Election Results

2002 general	Chuck Hagel (R)	397,438	(83%)	($1,394,770)
	Charlie Matulka (D)	70,290	(15%)	
	Other	12,489	(3%)	
2002 primary	Chuck Hagel (R)	unopposed		
1996 general	Chuck Hagel (R)	379,933	(56%)	($3,564,316)
	Ben Nelson (D)	281,904	(42%)	($2,159,653)
	Other	14,952	(2%)	

Chuck Hagel, first elected in 1996, is Nebraska's senior senator. Hagel grew up in the Sand Hills and small towns of Nebraska; his father died when he was 16, and Chuck Hagel started supporting his family. He dropped out of college, worked as a radio DJ, then with his younger brother Tom volunteered for service in Vietnam. Promoted to sergeant because so many were dying, Chuck and Tom served together; in March 1968, when their armored personnel carrier hit a mine, Chuck, his body on fire, dragged Tom from the APC to safety. Chuck Hagel returned home, worked his way through the University of Nebraska in Omaha, then got a job in Omaha Congressman John McCollister's office. He rose to administrative assistant; after McCollister lost a Senate race in 1976, Hagel became a lobbyist for Firestone. He later got the number two position in the Reagan Veterans' Affairs Administration, but resigned after only one year. He was one of two main speakers at the 1982 groundbreaking of the Vietnam Veterans' Memorial. Then he made his great break, using all of his savings—$5,000—and starting Vanguard Cellular Systems, which became the second largest independent cell phone company in the nation; Hagel traveled on business to 60 countries and installed cell phone systems in Costa Rica, Saudi Arabia and Britain. Then he became head of World USO and then deputy director of the 1990 G-7 Summit. In 1992 he returned to Omaha, to work in investment banking; the McCarthy Group, of which he was a partner, owned a share of a company that is now known as Election Systems & Software, which manufactures nearly half of American voting machines. He was criticized later for naming in his disclosure forms the McCarthy Group, and not the firms in which it has an interest.

In 1995 he started running for the Senate, very much the underdog. His platform was solidly conservative, sometimes riskily so: He backed school choice, opposed racial quotas and preferences, backed the Freedom to Farm Act ("less government and more open markets"), opposed the estate tax. In the primary he called state Attorney General Don Stenberg a "career politician"; Stenberg hit him for living 20 years in Virginia and for contributing to Bob Kerrey's 1992 presidential campaign. Hagel won the May primary 62%–37% and in the general faced Governor Ben Nelson, who had won re-election in 1994 by a 73%–26% margin. Nelson had a record of tax-cutting; he supported the balanced budget amendment and other conservative causes. Nelson led consistently in polls, though by lower margins in the fall, and raised far more PAC money—$909,000, nearly half of his campaign funds—but Hagel spent $1 million of his own money and $3.5 million altogether. Hagel resisted advice from Republican campaign committee head Alfonse D'Amato to go negative; Nelson in the last weeks charged that Hagel had engaged in fraudulent franchising practices with Vanguard. Newspapers hit Nelson, and Hagel responded, "This is a guy who lies. This is a guy who cheats. This is a guy who will do anything." Hagel won 56%–42%, carrying 88 of 93 counties.

In the Senate, Hagel sought a seat on Foreign Relations and got it—because no one else wanted it. He quickly became, in columnist David Broder's words, "the freshman who probably has made the deepest impression on his colleagues of both parties." From a historically isolationist state, but one now heavily dependent on exports, Hagel has become a leading internationalist. His impulse is toward a bipartisan foreign policy when possible. Hagel called on his military experience in 1997 to support the treaty against land mines, which was opposed by the Clinton administration; he spoke for the chemical weapons treaty ratified by the Senate in 1997 over the objections of Foreign Relations Chairman Jesse Helms; he voted against the Comprehensive Test Ban Treaty in October 1999 but joined Democrats and the administration in trying to prevent the vote. In 1999 he questioned whether the U.S. should defend Taiwan against a Chinese attack. He supported the bombing of Serbia in spring 1999, but decried the Clinton policy of ruling out the use of ground troops. In George W. Bush's first full month as president, Hagel joined Christopher Dodd in sponsoring a resolution to open Cuba to all U.S. exports and to end all restrictions on travel and credit. "Our 40-year policy toward Cuba is senseless," he said. He was one of two senators to vote against extending trade sanctions on Iran and Libya.

After September 11, he has been one of the Republicans most cautious against taking action against states that sponsor terrorism. His experience traveling abroad on business and coordinating a G-7 summit may have led him to place a high value on reaching consensus with European nations. In February 2002 he was accusing the administration of a "cavalier approach" to the rest of the world and said that the axis of evil part of George W. Bush's first State of the Union speech was "name calling." Before Bush's September 12, 2002, speech to the United Nations, Hagel said he had "a completely open mind" on military action in Iraq. He backed Joseph Biden and Richard Lugar in their efforts to draft a resolution endorsing military action only after diplomatic efforts were exhausted in the United Nations; that was put aside after Bush got agreement on his draft from congressional Republican leaders and House Minority Leader Richard Gephardt. He voted for the Iraq war resolution, but insisted, "Actions in Iraq must come in the context of an American-led, multilateral approach to disarmament, not as the first case for a new American doctrine involving the preemptive use of force." In a *Foreign Affairs* article in July 2004, he wrote that U.S. policy should not be ruled by a sense of "divine mission," but should inspire allies to work with us on "making a better world." He argued for expanding free trade agreements, seeking long-term security through alliances, coalitions and international institutions like the United Nations and NATO and advancing democracy with an eye on realities in the Middle East, particularly anger toward the U.S. stance on Israel-Palestinian issues. "We're in deep trouble in Iraq," he told the press in September 2004. "It's beyond pitiful, it's beyond embarrassing. It is now in the zone of dangerous." Some of his comments were quoted by John Kerry in one of the presidential debates, and Hagel's comments on his fellow Vietnam veteran suggested he might be closer to him on Iraq than to Bush. "I like him," Hagel said. "He's smart, he's tough, he's capable. I don't agree with him on a lot of things [though] I am closer to him on foreign policy questions."

Hagel has a mostly conservative voting record in the Senate. He opposes abortion, favors school prayer, has taken stands in favor of vouchers. But he has been critical of his party's leaders on occasion. When in July 1999 Majority Leader Trent Lott and others put holds on the nomination of Richard Holbrooke to be U.N. ambassador, he said that was "an irresponsible way to govern." He spent much of his time that year and in early 2000 campaigning for John McCain for president. The two had often met with other senators who were Vietnam veterans and had developed a strong bond. He sharply criticized George W. Bush's campaign tactics in South Carolina, but he also was one of the few who would talk back to McCain. After McCain lost, Hagel was on Bush's short list of vice presidential prospects. Though he did not get that nomination, the McCain campaign, plus Hagel's own work on foreign policy, made him a national figure.

Hagel did not agree with McCain on campaign finance. He favored reducing soft money contributions but not limiting them; his amendment to do that was rejected 60–40 in March 2001. He supported oil drilling in the Arctic National Wildlife Refuge and opposed limits on drilling, logging and grazing in national forests. He voted against the 2001 education bill. He opposed the farm bill passed in 2002 and criticized its conservation sections for interfering with water rights under state law; he, Charles Grassley and Byron Dorgan did get the Senate to limit payments to $275,000. In late 2002 he led an uprising in the Republican Conference against riders added to the homeland security bill by House Majority Leader Dick Armey (he called that "dishonest, deceitful back room dealing") and got Trent Lott to make a commitment that those items would be revisited in the next Congress.

Hagel voted against the Medicare prescription drug bill in 2003, calling it "a sham and a ripoff for everybody . . . and actually it's going to make our problems worse." In January 2004 he sponsored an immigration bill with Tom Daschle to let illegal immigrants achieve "earned legalization" on demonstrating four years of work and mastery of the English language; willing workers would be matched with willing employers. Amid the election year hubbub about outsourcing of jobs, Hagel said, "Outsourcing cannot be understood as simply the number of jobs shipped overseas. As American companies outsource jobs, there are also potential benefits to American businesses and workers." With Tom Harkin, he sponsored a bill requiring the federal government to increased special education aid to states from the current 18% to the authorized maximum of 40% within six years; it got 56 votes, less than the 60 required to exceed budget limits. In September 2004 he proposed to waive the $1,200 enrollment fee for G.I. Bill of Rights benefits and to increase the death benefit for soldiers from $12,000 to $50,000; in January 2005 he raised that to $100,000. He sponsored the Vietnam Veterans Memorial education center that passed the Senate unanimously in July 2003. In March 2005 he introduced the first bill that session to change Social Security by adding voluntary personal retirement accounts.

In March 2003 Hagel and the entire Nebraska delegation sponsored a bill to double the use of ethanol in gasoline and to mandate five billion gallons of renewable fuels, mainly ethanol, by 2015. In October 2003 he voted against the McCain-Lieberman bill to impose limits on carbon dioxide emissions, but later promised his own bill on the subject in 2005. In March 2003, Hagel, Dorgan and Congressman Tom Osborne sponsored a Homestead Act, targeted at counties with a population decline of 10% over 20 years, with tax credits for expanding and incoming businesses, loan forgiveness of 50% of college loans for recent graduates, a $5,000 tax credit for home purchases and tax-free homestead savings accounts. He and Nebraska colleague Ben Nelson co-sponsored the $2.9 billion drought and hurricane relief package that passed the Senate in September 2004. When the White House made and then withdrew the nomination of Columbus,

Nebraska businessman Tony Raimondo as a "jobs czar," Hagel was furious that he had not been notified. Raimondo was a friend of Ben Nelson, Hagel's opponent in 1996, whose stands on the 2001 tax cuts, the 2002 farm bill and Department of Homeland Security labor regulations he had criticized in blunt terms. Asked if there was bad feeling between them, Hagel said, "We're not friends, we're colleagues. That's not unusual." They have nonetheless worked together on many Nebraska and some national issues.

In 2002 Hagel's Democratic opponent couldn't afford the $1,500 filing fee and filed as a pauper. Hagel raised $3.5 million, but spent only $2 million, and won 83%–15%, by a considerable margin the biggest percentage victory ever in a Nebraska Senate race. He won 78% or more in 91 of 93 Nebraska counties, and as much as 94% in one; the other two, in the northeast corner of the state, he carried with 68% and 74%. His Sandhills PAC gave $215,000 to House and Senate candidates, $30,000 to the Senate Republican campaign committee, $10,000 to the Nebraska Republican party and $5,000 to the Iowa Republican party in the 2004 cycle. Hagel has been mentioned as a possible presidential candidate in 2008. When asked the day after the 2004 election whether he would run, he said, "I've not reached that point yet; I don't need to reach that point yet. I'm going to continue to focus on my responsibilities in the Senate, and along the way on parallel tracks I'll assess my options for 2008." Some have speculated that he would not run against his friend McCain, but the two have had strikingly different positions on Iraq and the importance of respecting allies' wishes. Hagel's clear differences with George W. Bush on foreign policy may not be an advantage in Republican primaries, nor his position on taxes. "At some point somebody's going to ask you in a debate: 'Well, Senator, will you pledge that if you're elected never to raise taxes?' I couldn't take that pledge. It would be irresponsible. That may cost me the nomination."

Junior Senator

Ben Nelson (D)

Elected 2000, seat up 2006, 1st term; b. May 17, 1941, McCook; home, Omaha; U. of NE, B.A. 1963, M.A. 1965, LL.B. 1970; Methodist; married (Diane).

Elected Office: NE Gov., 1990–98.

Professional Career: Gen. Cnsl., Central Natl. Group Insurance, 1972–74, Pres. & CEO, 1977–81; NE Insurance Dir., 1975–76; Exec. V.P., Natl. Assn. of Insurance Commissioners, 1982–85; Practicing atty., 1985–90.

DC Office: 720 HSOB, 20510, 202-224-6551; Fax: 202-228-0012; Web site: bennelson.senate.gov.

State Offices: Chadron, 308-260-2278; Lincoln, 402-437-5246; Omaha, 402-391-3411.

Committees: *Agriculture, Nutrition & Forestry*: Forestry, Conservation & Rural Revitalization; Marketing, Inspection & Product Promotion; Research, Nutrition & General Legislation. *Armed Services*: Emerging Threats & Capabilities; Personnel (RMM); Readiness & Management Support; Strategic Forces. *Commerce, Science & Transportation*: Aviation; Disaster Prevention & Prediction (RMM); Science & Space; Surface Transportation & Merchant Marine; Technology, Innovation & Competitiveness; Trade, Tourism & Economic Development. *Rules & Administration*.

Group Ratings

	ADA	ACLU	AFS	LCV	ITIC	NTU	COC	ACU	NTLC	CHC
2004	65	33	86	67	100	34	81	52	43	83
2003	45	—	67	21	—	42	86	42	—	—

National Journal Ratings

	2003 LIB	—	2003 CONS		2004 LIB	—	2004 CONS
Economic	51%	—	48%		53%	—	46%
Social	46%	—	53%		45%	—	54%
Foreign	53%	—	46%		54%	—	45%

Key Votes of the 108th Congress

1. Ban Drilling in ANWR	Y	5. Energy Bill	Y	9. Ban Same-Sex Marriage	Y
2. Approve Bush Tax Cuts	Y	6. Support Roe v. Wade	N	10. Ban Bunker-Buster Bomb	N
3. Medicare/Rx Bill	Y	7. Ban Partial-Birth Abortion	Y	11. Fund Iraq War	Y
4. Bar Overtime Pay Regs.	Y	8. Assault Weapons Ban	N	12. Restrict Missile Defense	N

Election Results

2000 general	Ben Nelson (D)	353,093	(51%)	($2,794,887)
	Don Stenberg (R)	337,977	(49%)	($1,795,402)
2000 primary	Ben Nelson (D)	105,661	(92%)	
	Al Hamburg (D)	8,482	(7%)	
1994 general	Bob Kerrey (D)	317,297	(55%)	($5,009,792)
	Jan Stoney (R)	260,668	(45%)	($1,821,778)

Ben Nelson, two-term Democratic governor of Nebraska, was elected to the Senate in 2000 in his second try. Nelson grew up in McCook, the hometown of Senator George Norris and novelist Willa Cather; his high school principal, Ralph Brooks, a Democrat, was elected governor in 1958, by a 50.2%–49.8% margin. Nelson graduated from the University of Nebraska, practiced law, served as state insurance director and headed a major insurance company. He has collected several hundred clocks and is an avid hunter of turkeys and bears. In 1990 he ran for governor, taking on former Bob Kerrey staff aide Bill Hoppner in the primary, and won by all of 42 votes. In the general he beat Governor Kay Orr 50%–49%, because she raised taxes and her political consultants failed to place many of her paid-for TV spots in October. He cut spending increases by two-thirds and used his line-item veto to cut appropriations; in 1992, he got the Senate to pass and voters to approve a lottery, with proceeds to go to creative education and environmental projects. He built more prisons, trimmed workmen's comp and reorganized the human services department. He cut property taxes and reduced the income and sales taxes. His record won him high job ratings and re-election by a 73%–26% margin in the Republican year of 1994. When he ran for the Senate in 1996, he led in polls most of the way, but then fell behind in October and lost to Republican Chuck Hagel by a 56%–42% margin.

In 2000 Nebraska's other Senate seat came up. Everyone expected easy re-election for Senator Bob Kerrey, one of the Democratic Party's national stars. But in January 2000 he shocked Democrats and just about everyone else when he said that he would not run for reelection that fall. Nelson, a lawyer in Omaha with an interest in a public affairs firm in Washington, was obviously the strongest possible Democratic nominee and entered the race a month later. Six Republicans ran in the May primary. The winner was Attorney General Don Stenberg, with 50% of the vote.

Nelson and Stenberg agreed on some issues; both opposed abortion and backed tax cuts. But there were significant differences in style and a considerable history of partisan differences between the two in the 1990s. Nelson never mentioned his Democratic Party affiliation, unless asked directly about it. Stenberg ran as part of the "Bush-Hagel-Stenberg Team," sometimes bringing in Governor Mike Johanns as well. To which Nelson responded, "My opponent hasn't given us a single reason to vote for him apart from his party registration and the fact that he's associated with two people who are more popular than he is." Then there was style: Nelson is gregarious, has a good sense of humor, seems to enjoy campaigning; Stenberg was described as serious and studious—not a natural meeter-and-greeter. There were some serious differences on issues. Stenberg was for individual investment accounts as part of Social Security; Nelson was against. The two sparred over who was responsible for Nebraska's parlous position in a lawsuit brought by the four other states in a five-state compact to build a radioactive waste disposal site in Boyd County which Nebraska regulators blocked. Nelson led always in the polls and raised and spent more money; the big difference here was PAC contributions, of which the Democrat received three times as much as the Republican. Nelson was helped also by active campaigning by Bob Kerrey; George W. Bush, in a close national race, couldn't afford to spend time in locked-up (for him) Nebraska. Nelson's poll leads narrowed in October, to 12% in the *Omaha World-Herald*, and memories went back to 1996, when Nelson's poll leads vanished altogether. This time that didn't quite happen. Nelson won 51%–49%, carrying the Omaha area 54%–46%

and the Lincoln area 60%–39%; he lost the remaining half of the state 54%–46%. Nelson ran 16% ahead of Al Gore in the Omaha area, 18% in the Lincoln area and 19% ahead in the rest of the state—just enough to win.

Nelson turned out to be, after Zell Miller, the Senate Democrat most likely to support Bush and to differ from most Democrats. He was one of three Democrats to vote against the McCain-Feingold campaign finance bill and in May was one of five Democrats to vote for the Republican budget resolution (although in April he had voted against an earlier version). On the labor relations sections of the homeland security bill, he sought to stake out a middle position. But his version was unacceptable to the Bush administration, and the bill was not passed before the November 2002 election. A week after the election, Nelson was one of the senators who put together a compromise that would allow the president to cancel collective bargaining rights but allow that decision to be overturned by a future president and that allowed workers to appeal new rules or salary scales to a federal mediation board; they would be imposed after one month, but the unions could bring a case in court. His Democratic colleagues tolerated these apostasies; as one said, "He needs to do what he needs to do to keep his seat" in one of the most Republican states in the nation. In May 2003 Bush journeyed to Nebraska; Nelson said he was open to a tax cut over $350 billion, provided it included a cut in the dividend tax and $20 billion in aid to ailing states. Nelson supported Bush generally on Iraq; when the Abu Ghraib prison abuses were exposed, Nelson called for tearing down the prison. In August 2004 he said Bush would do well to appoint as CIA director one of two Nebraskans, Bob Kerrey or Chuck Hagel; he said nominee Porter Goss would face a "grueling confirmation process." He voted against the Family Marriage Amendment, arguing that same-sex marriage was a state issue after passage of the Defense of Marriage Act.

Many of Nelson's legislative initiatives have been aimed squarely at Nebraska problems. He got a white wheat initiative into the farm bill in April 2002; hard white wheat isn't produced in the U.S., but there's a big market for it in Asia. He voted for country of origin meat labeling. He voted for the farm bill in May 2002, saying that it provided $1.1 billion for Nebraska. When the Great Plains were hit by a drought in summer 2002, and Nelson argued that affected areas should get disaster relief, in the same way that places hit by hurricanes and floods do; the compensation would be for crops or livestock lost, rather than property destroyed. Twice in 2002 he got the Senate to pass disaster relief; both times it was rejected in the House. In January 2003, he started applying a name to each drought, as names are applied to hurricanes, and filed his bill again for relief from "Drought David." In September 2004, when a bill for hurricane relief came up, Nelson and Hagel attached $2.9 in drought relief; the House accepted that but only by reducing farm bill conservation spending as an offset. He co-sponsored a bill to double the use of ethanol; it was approved by the Senate in June 2003. He got into the 2003 Medicare prescription drug bill a pilot provision providing 100% reimbursement for Nebraska rural hospitals too small to qualify for higher reimbursement and too large to qualify for another provision requiring 100% reimbursement. He worked to get a fourth federal judge for Nebraska (dockets are bulging with drug cases) and to get a National Guard unit stationed at Offutt Air Force Base near Omaha. Nelson's relationship with colleague Chuck Hagel is not warm; he was angry when Hagel said that a Nelson staffer leaked the nomination of Columbus, Nebraska, businessman Tony Raimondo as manufacturing czar to the Kerry campaign. Raimondo later withdrew his name from consideration. "We're not friends, we're colleagues," Hagel said. Nelson responded, "He said we are not friends, we are colleagues. That's fine with me." Evidently there was bitterness left over from the 1996 campaign, when Nelson challenged Hagel's business ethics. Nelson said, "I've gotten over losing in 1996. I don't know if Senator Hagel has gotten over winning."

Republicans have tried to persuade Nelson to switch parties several times during his first four years and again after the November 2004 election. Ten days after the election, according to the *Omaha World-Herald*, White House strategist Karl Rove offered Nelson the position of secretary of agriculture; the paper said Nelson considered it for five days before declining. If he had accepted, Republican Governor Mike Johanns would have appointed his successor. On Bush's number one domestic issue, Social Security, Nelson said he was not opposed to personal retirement accounts "in principle," but added, "I don't know how the economics of that can work." He declined to sign the letter signed by 42 Democratic senators opposing personal retirement accounts.

Nelson comes up for reelection in 2006, a Democrat in a state George W. Bush carried with 66% of the vote. It was generally assumed that Johanns would run against him, but in December 2004 Bush announced he was appointing Johanns as U.S. secretary of agriculture. Soon after, Congressman Lee Terry said he would not run for the seat. Congressman Tom Osborne, the hugely popular former University of Nebraska football coach, also announced he would not run; in April 2005 Osborne said he would run for governor. This left the race for the Republican nomination wide open. National party officials were hoping to convince Governor Dave Heineman to run, but Heineman told the *Lincoln Journal Star* in May that his interest, on a scale of zero to 100, was "minus-1000 and dropping." Former Attorney General Don Stenberg, the Republican nominee in 2000, announced he would seek a rematch. Other interested candidates included Republican state Chairman David Kramer; Speaker of the Legislature Kermit Brashear (who ran second in the 1986 governor primary); Republican National Committeeman and health care administration businessman Kerry Winterer; and state Treasurer Ron Ross. Democratic party executive director Barry Rubin scoffed, "No matter who runs that person is Plan C for the Nebraska Republican party." Left open in mid-2005 was how strongly the Bush White House would back the Republican nominee against a Democrat who has often voted with the president.

FIRST DISTRICT

Rep. Jeff Fortenberry (R)

Elected 2004, 1st term; b. Dec. 27, 1960, Baton Rouge, LA; home, Lincoln; LA St. U., 1982, Franciscan U. of Steubenville, M.A. 1985, Georgetown U., M.P.P. 1986; Catholic; married (Celeste).

Elected Office: Lincoln City Cncl., 1997–2001.

Professional Career: Staffer, U.S. House Comm. on Ag., 1986; Research assoc., Gulf South Research Inst., 1987–89; Asst. Dir., Baton Rouge Downtown Dev. District, 1989–92; Sales rep., Sandhills Publishing, 1995–2004.

DC Office: 1517 LHOB, 20515, 202-225-4806; Fax: 202-225-5686; Web site: www.house.gov/fortenberry.

District Office: Lincoln, 402-438-1598.

Committees: *Agriculture* (24th of 25 R): Conservation, Credit, Rural Development & Research; Department Operations, Oversight, Nutrition & Forestry; General Farm Commodities & Risk Management. *International Relations* (25th of 27 R): Africa, Global Human Rights & International Operations; Middle East & Central Asia. *Small Business* (15th of 18 R): Rural Enterprises, Agriculture & Technology; Tax, Finance & Exports.

Group Ratings and Key Votes: Newly Elected

Election Results

2004 general	Jeff Fortenberry (R)	143,756	(54%)	($1,224,266)
	Matt Connealy (D)	113,971	(43%)	($989,884)
	Other	7,345	(3%)	
2004 primary	Jeff Fortenberry (R)	18,735	(39%)	
	Curt Bromm (R)	15,708	(33%)	
	Greg Ruehle (R)	10,077	(21%)	
	Other	3,236	(7%)	
2002 general	Doug Bereuter (R)	133,013	(85%)	($191,344)
	Robert Eckerson (Lib)	22,831	(15%)	

The People		Race/Ethnic Origin	Ancestry	
Area size:	12,034 sq. mi.	90.5% White	German: 30.8% Irish: 8.7%	
Urban population:	65.1%	1.4% Black	English: 6.8%	
Rural population:	34.9%	1.5% Asian	**2004 Presidential Vote**	
Pop. 2000:	570,325	1.2% Native Am.	Bush (R) 169,888	(63%)
Median income:	$40,021	0.0% Hawaiian	Kerry (D) 96,314	(36%)
Poverty status:	9.2%	1.1% Two+ races	Other 3,896	(1%)
Military veterans:	12.9%	0.1% Other	**2000 Presidential Vote**	
		4.2% Hispanic Origin	Bush (R) 138,799	(59%)
			Gore (D) 85,634	(36%)
			Other 12,242	(5%)
			Cook Partisan Voting Index: R +12	

Occupation   Blue collar: 26.2%   White collar: 57.7%   Gray collar: 16.1%

The eastern half of Nebraska, between the Missouri River and the 98th parallel, was laid out in relentless Midwestern mile-square grids and became some of America's prime farmland in the single decade of the 1880s. The land here has contours just regular enough and weather just favorable enough to make farming economically viable. The plains here have completed most of their gentle decline from the Rockies to sea level; above the river bottoms the land is open to the winds. This land was settled by Yankee-descended Midwestern farmers and immigrants from Germany and other countries. The immigrant heritage is not often remembered now, but traces of it can still be found. Many immigrants from Luxembourg, for example, settled along the Platte River in Butler County, where St. Mary's Presentation Parish still has a statue of Our Lady of Luxembourg. Not far away are villages with names that recall other immigrants' heritage—Prague (Czechs), Malmo (Swedes), Aloys (Germans). Now a new wave of immigrants is coming to eastern Nebraska, Latinos from Mexico and the southwest United States, to work in the meatpacking factories in the area. Wakefield (Dixon County) had the highest percentage increase in Hispanic population in the country in the 1990s, 8,700%—though that's a little less impressive when you realize that the Hispanic population went from 4 to 348. But there are larger numbers in other towns, and Nebraska's face is changing.

The 1st Congressional District of Nebraska is made up of 22 counties and parts of two others in the eastern part of the state; Omaha and most of its suburbs are in the 2d District. The 1st District's large city is Lincoln, the state capital and home of the University of Nebraska Cornhuskers. Lincoln, with the state government, the university and telemarketing, has been growing rapidly; it is affluent, with above-national-average incomes and unemployment that is among the lowest in the United States. In smaller towns there are significant farm equipment and meatpacking factories; population growth has been robust around Schuyler, Norfolk and Dakota City. Politically, Lincoln is fond of moderate Democrats but is still on balance Republican in national contests; the district voted 59% for George W. Bush in 2000 and 63% in 2004.

The congressman from the 1st District is Jeff Fortenberry, a Republican elected in 2004. Fortenberry grew up in Baton Rouge, Louisiana, the son of a life insurance salesman and a mother who worked as a 4-H extension agent. He graduated from Louisiana State University, got a master's degree in theology from Franciscan University of Steubenville, Ohio, and then another one in public policy from Georgetown. For a time, he studied for the priesthood. He worked as assistant director for the Baton Rouge Downtown Development District and in 1995 moved to Nebraska to take a public relations position with Sandhills Publishing, a publisher of trade magazines for the trucking, aircraft and computer industries. He then moved into publishing sales at the company, working on what he called a "truckers' eBay." His first foray into local politics came in 1997, two years after his arrival in Nebraska, when he won a seat on the Lincoln City Council. He served for four years, focusing on neighborhood concerns, and worked to increase the number of police officers.

In December 2003, Congressman Doug Bereuter, first elected in 1978, announced he would not run again and would resign September 1. Seven candidates ran for the Republican nomination, but only three mounted competitive campaigns: Fortenberry; Curt Bromm, the speaker of the state's unicameral legislature; and Greg Ruehle, a former executive vice president of the Nebraska Cattlemen's Association. Bromm, a moderate whom Bereuter endorsed, began as the front-runner. But he quickly lost momentum after a barrage of negative television ads financed by the Club for Growth, an anti-tax group that supported Ruehle. Fortenberry, a social conservative, drew criticism from his opponents as a single-issue candidate but his superior grass roots operation and surprising talent for fundraising carried him to victory in the primary. He won just seven of the 24 counties but in Lincoln's Lancaster County, which cast 43% of the votes, he got 52% to 29% for Bromm and 13% for Ruehle. The vote in the rest of the district was closer: 29% for Fortenberry, 36% for Bromm and 27% for Ruehle. Overall, Fortenberry won with 39% of the vote, to 33% for Bromm and 21% for Ruehle.

Some national Republicans worried that Fortenberry, a Louisiana native and relatively recent arrival in Nebraska who focused on family and cultural issues like abortion, would not be able to hold the seat in November. But Fortenberry made a point of talking about jobs, farming and health care, and emphasized that he was not a single-issue candidate. In the general, he faced state Senator Matt Connealy, who sought to become the first Democrat in nearly 40 years to represent the 1st. A farmer from Decatur, Connealy sought to exploit Republican divisions (Bromm refused to endorse Fortenberry after the primary) and characterized Fortenberry as a stranger to Nebraska farm issues, a potent charge in a state where one in four jobs is connected to agriculture. "If you want a guy in a slick suit with slick answers, I'm probably not your guy," he said. Fortenberry responded by promising to help families retain control of their farms by improving trade policies and by supporting ethanol development; he cited his 4-H participation as a youth, and his agriculture research performed during a brief stint as a Senate subcommittee special projects staffer. He also promised to stand up to trial lawyers. His main message, however, focused on socially conservative themes. He opposes abortion, favors capital punishment and supports a constitutional amendment defining marriage as between a man and a woman. He got campaign visits from national Republicans, including Vice President Dick Cheney and House Speaker Dennis Hastert, and tied himself to George W. Bush.

Connealy gained traction briefly by hammering Fortenberry's city council attendance record but his advance came to a halt when the Fortenberry campaign responded with an emotional ad explaining that the absences were connected to his infant daughter's open-heart surgery. Bromm, Fortenberry's primary opponent, criticized as "disingenuous and unfair" Republican ads that attacked Connealy's votes for raising taxes, but it wasn't enough to sink Fortenberry. He won 54%–43%, losing only two small Indian reservation counties along the river north of Omaha. In Lancaster County, which cast 46% of the votes, he won by only 49%–47%.

SECOND DISTRICT

Rep. Lee Terry (R)

Elected 1998, 4th term; b. Jan. 29, 1962, Omaha; home, Omaha; U. of NE at Lincoln, B.A. 1984; Creighton U., J.D. 1987; Methodist; married (Robyn).

Elected Office: Omaha City Cncl., 1991–98, Pres., 1995–96.

Professional Career: Practicing atty., 1988–98.

DC Office: 1524 LHOB, 20515, 202-225-4155; Fax: 202-226-5452; Web site: leeterry.house.gov.

District Office: Omaha, 402-397-9944.

Committees: *Energy & Commerce* (23d of 31 R): Commerce, Trade & Consumer Protection; Environment & Hazardous Materials; Telecommunications & the Internet.

Group Ratings

	ADA	ACLU	AFS	LCV	ITIC	NTU	COC	ACU	NTLC	CHC
2004	0	10	0	0	80	67	90	92	89	100
2003	5	—	0	10	—	68	97	80	—	—

National Journal Ratings

	2003 LIB	—	2003 CONS	2004 LIB	—	2004 CONS
Economic	45%	—	54%	29%	—	70%
Social	17%	—	79%	42%	—	58%
Foreign	23%	—	71%	34%	—	63%

Key Votes of the 108th Congress

1. Drilling in ANWR	Y	5. DC School Vouchers	Y	9. Ban Same-Sex Marriage	Y
2. Approve Bush Tax Cuts	Y	6. Ban Human Cloning	Y	10. Fund Iraq War	Y
3. Medicare/Rx Bill	Y	7. Restrict Gun Liability	Y	11. Bar Cuba Embargo Funds	N
4. Bar Overtime Pay Regs.	N	8. Ban Partial-Birth Abortion	Y	12. Intelligence Reorg.	Y

Election Results

2004 general	Lee Terry (R)	152,608	(61%)	($1,454,559)
	Nancy Thompson (D)	90,292	(36%)	($899,399)
	Other	6,864	(3%)	
2004 primary	Lee Terry (R)	unopposed		
2002 general	Lee Terry (R)	89,917	(63%)	($974,788)
	Jim Simon (D)	46,843	(33%)	($705,675)
	Other	5,254	(4%)	

Prior Winning Percentages: 2000 (66%); 1998 (66%)

The People

Area size:	421 sq. mi.
Urban population:	97.8%
Rural population:	2.2%
Pop. 2000:	570,421
Median income:	$45,235
Poverty status:	8.8%
Military veterans:	14.4%

Race/Ethnic Origin

79.6% White
10.2% Black
1.8% Asian
0.5% Native Am.
0.1% Hawaiian
1.5% Two+ races
0.1% Other
6.3% Hispanic Origin

Ancestry

German: 22.1%   Irish: 11.6%
English: 6.6%

2004 Presidential Vote

Bush (R)	153,041	(60%)
Kerry (D)	97,858	(38%)
Other	3,525	(1%)

2000 Presidential Vote

Bush (R)	125,973	(57%)
Gore (D)	85,853	(39%)
Other	10,183	(5%)

Cook Partisan Voting Index: R + 9

Occupation   Blue collar: 19.5%   White collar: 66.8%   Gray collar: 13.7%

Omaha, the commercial metropolis of Nebraska, the largest city on the Great Plains north of Kansas City and west of Minneapolis, got its start from government: Abraham Lincoln picked it as the eastern terminus of the Union Pacific railroad, from which emerged the stockyards and livestock exchange that made it a top livestock town. Over the years, Omaha filled up with cattle hands from the West and European immigrants, especially Germans and Czechs; it developed fine civic institutions from the Joslyn Art Museum to Boys Town, founded by Father Flanagan in 1917, the subject of a 1938 movie, and today gender-neutral as Boys and Girls Town but still innovative and thriving in its promotion of traditional values. Though a major city by the 1880s, Omaha has remained small enough (and famous on Wall Street as the place where Warren Buffett lives and works) to be readily comprehensible; you don't feel distant, physically or psychologically, from the other side of town, and you usually know people from a broader range of backgrounds than you would in a large homogeneous neighborhood within a big metropolitan area. The older, less affluent part of Omaha is near the river and Iowa. To the west, the city has been quietly booming, with affluent neighborhoods and new shopping malls. Downtown and the riverfront have been in a construction boom; the Tower at First National Center became the tallest structure between Minneapolis and Denver. Omaha's economy has been changing. It remains dependent on overseas trade of meat and has many processors of food products, like the hard-charging ConAgra company, Omaha Steaks and Nebraska Beef, but it also has the giant

Peter Kiewit construction firm. It has become the nation's telecommunications center, handling 20 million '800' and '900' calls a day and employs more than 30,000 people in over three dozen telemarketing centers. It is also ethnically diverse: 31% of students in the Omaha public schools are black and 17% Hispanic.

The 2d Congressional District of Nebraska includes most of metropolitan Omaha: Douglas County with Omaha and its western suburbs, and the eastern part of fast-growing Sarpy County with Bellevue and the old Strategic Air Command headquarters at Offutt Air Force Base. Politically, Omaha has long had competitive politics, with Democrats strong on the south side around the stockyards and the northeast and Republicans strong to the west. But as Omaha and Nebraska have boomed, they have become more Republican, and increasingly it is the Republican primary that decides elections here.

The congressman from the 2d District is Lee Terry, a Republican first elected in 1998. Terry grew up in Omaha, and became interested in politics at 14 when his father, TV anchor Lee Terry Sr., ran for the House in 1976; a conservative, he lost 55%–45% to 31-year-old Democrat John Cavanaugh. Terry Sr. remained a prominent local commentator on politics; Terry Jr. went off to college and law school, practiced law, and was elected to the Omaha Council from an affluent west side district in 1991, at 29. When Congressman Jon Christensen ran for governor, Terry announced for the House seat; his chief opponents were Brad Kuiper, owner of a pest control business in west Douglas County, and Steve Kupka, former chief of staff to Mayor Hal Daub and an official in Ronald Reagan's OMB. The contrast between the three was less on issues—all were for lower taxes and against abortion—than on style and approach. Kuiper, with less money than the other two, targeted religious conservatives and emphasized cultural issues. Kupka assembled Washington endorsements and, spending the most money, went on the attack. He criticized Terry for not opposing a 1991 garbage fee and said Terry had increased the city budget. Terry won 40% to 30% for Kupka and 26% for Kuiper. The general election was anticlimactic. Despite the fact that Democrats had won open seats here in 1976 and 1988, Terry won 66%–34% against Democrat Michael Scott. In April 1999, shortly after taking office, he reneged on his pledge to serve only three terms.

In Washington, Terry has had a moderate-to-conservative voting record. He attracted attention in 1999 when he purposely bundled Bill Clinton tax increases and user fees into one $19 billion bill and brought it to the floor; it lost 419–5. He became co-chairman of the Impact Aid Coalition to protect the interests of Offutt Air Force Base, and he reversed his previous opposition to mandatory trigger locks for guns "after a year of reflection." He got a seat on the Energy and Commerce Committee, where he became an advocate of pro-business legislation. He fought efforts to end the federal universal service fund for telecommunications services in rural areas, and he was one of eight House members who voted against "do not call" restrictions on telemarketers. The sales call is a "minor annoyance that puts bread on the tables of many people in my congressional district," he said. He advocated alternative energy sources, including hydrogen fuel cells. Separate from his committee work, he won unanimous House passage of a bill declaring that Veterans' Day should remain separate from other federal holidays; his proposal was in response to proposals to combine the holiday with the presidential election every four years, but local opponents later called his measure "symbolism." He sponsored a bill to expedite review of applications for offshore liquefied natural gas terminals. For the district, he claimed credit for $245 million in privatized housing at Offutt.

Terry has faced well-funded reelection opponents, but he has survived easily. In the 2000 general, he had surprisingly vigorous opposition from well-financed Democratic state Senator Shelley Kiel. But Terry got a favorable response with a 66%–31% victory. Two years later, Democrats initially hyped their challenger Jim Simon, an Internet millionaire and former Republican. Simon spent $230,000 of his own money, but failed to gain traction. Terry created a minor stir late in the campaign when he appeared in a TV ad for Pfizer, which offered lower costs for prescriptions. Simon suggested that it was a "disguised political ad," and Common Cause threatened to file an ethics complaint, but Terry supporters said that they were grasping at straws. Terry won 63%–33%. In 2004, state Senator Nancy Thompson ran an aggressive campaign with ads criticizing his support for budget deficits and failure to give adequate support to veterans. Democrats mocked him for contradicting his "decency" values when he held a Washington fundraiser at a Madonna concert; a spokesman for Terry called her a legitimate entertainer and said that he does not necessarily subscribe to her lyrics. Terry attacked Thompson for supporting higher taxes and having a poor legislative attendance record. Despite polls indicating a tight contest, Terry won 61%–36%. In December 2004 he said he would not be a candidate for Ben Nelson's Senate seat in 2006.

THIRD DISTRICT

Rep. Tom Osborne (R)

Elected 2000, 3d term; b. Feb. 23, 1937, Hastings; home, Lemoyne; Hastings Col., B.A. 1959, U. of NE, M.A. 1963, Ph.D. 1965; Methodist; married (Nancy).

Military Career: Army Natl. Guard, 1960–66.

Professional Career: Pro Football Player, Natl. Football League, 1959–62; Football Coach, U. of NE, 1962–97, Head Coach 1973–97.

DC Office: 507 CHOB, 20515, 202-225-6435; Fax: 202-226-1385; Web site: www.house.gov/osborne.

District Offices: Grand Island, 308-381-5555; Scottsbluff, 308-632-3333.

Committees: *Agriculture* (11th of 25 R): Conservation, Credit, Rural Development & Research (Vice Chmn.); Livestock & Horticulture. *Education & the Workforce* (13th of 27 R): 21st Century Competitiveness; Education Reform (Vice Chmn.). *Transportation & Infrastructure* (30th of 41 R): Highways, Transit & Pipelines; Railroads; Water Resources & Environment.

Group Ratings

	ADA	ACLU	AFS	LCV	ITIC	NTU	COC	ACU	NTLC	CHC
2004	10	10	13	9	80	47	95	84	73	92
2003	15	—	13	5	—	59	93	80	—	—

National Journal Ratings

	2003 LIB — 2003 CONS		2004 LIB — 2004 CONS	
Economic	9%	— 84%	35%	— 65%
Social	44%	— 56%	36%	— 61%
Foreign	40%	— 58%	49%	— 50%

Key Votes of the 108th Congress

1. Drilling in ANWR	Y	5. DC School Vouchers	N	9. Ban Same-Sex Marriage	Y
2. Approve Bush Tax Cuts	Y	6. Ban Human Cloning	Y	10. Fund Iraq War	Y
3. Medicare/Rx Bill	Y	7. Restrict Gun Liability	Y	11. Bar Cuba Embargo Funds	Y
4. Bar Overtime Pay Regs.	N	8. Ban Partial-Birth Abortion	Y	12. Intelligence Reorg.	Y

Election Results

2004 general	Tom Osborne (R)	218,751	(87%)	($63,654)
	Donna Anderson (D)	26,434	(11%)	($10,867)
	Other	4,951	(2%)	
2004 primary	Tom Osborne (R)	unopposed		
2002 general	Tom Osborne (R)	163,939	(93%)	($81,357)
	Jerry Hickman (Lib)	12,017	(7%)	

Prior Winning Percentages: 2000 (82%)

The People		Race/Ethnic Origin	Ancestry	
Area size:	64,899 sq. mi.	91.9% White	German: 30.3%	Irish: 8.5%
Urban population:	46.1%	0.3% Black	English: 7.2%	
Rural population:	53.9%	0.5% Asian	**2004 Presidential Vote**	
Pop. 2000:	570,517	0.7% Native Am.	Bush (R) 189,885	(75%)
Median income:	$33,866	0.0% Hawaiian	Kerry (D) 60,156	(24%)
Poverty status:	11.1%	0.6% Two+ races	Other 3,623	(1%)
Military veterans:	13.9%	0.0% Other	**2000 Presidential Vote**	
		6.0% Hispanic Origin	Bush (R) 169,090	(71%)
			Gore (D) 60,293	(25%)
			Other 8,952	(4%)
			Cook Partisan Voting Index: R +24	

Occupation   Blue collar: 27.6%   White collar: 53.5%   Gray collar: 18.8%

West of Grand Island, Nebraska is wheat and livestock country. For miles on end you can see nothing but rolling brown fields, sectioned off here and there by barbed wire fences, and in the distance a grain elevator towering over a tiny town and its miniature railroad depot. The winds, rain and tornadoes that come suddenly out of the sky remind you that the original settlers likened this part of the country to an ocean and thought themselves in their wooden wagons almost as helpless as passengers at sea in a rowboat. Settlers passed through here on the Oregon Trail in the 1840s, then set down roots in the 1880s, but the rain they hoped for fell too unreliably, and wheatlands gave way to pasture and open range. It is a beautiful but hard land, exacting much from its people, as the novels of western Nebraska's Willa Cather make poignantly clear. Dozens of small counties today have fewer people than they did in 1940 or 1900. Although soaking rains in 2004 were helpful, severe droughts in recent years have seemed a kind of endpoint, as ranchers sold off their herds that were thinning and sickening as the grasslands turned dry and brown, and reservoirs and aquifers were running dry. In North Platte, Bailey Yard is the world's largest railroad classification yard, covering 2,850 acres and handling 10,000 rail cars every 24 hours. Farther west on I-80 is the town of Sidney, home of Cabela's, the world's largest mail-order and Internet business for hunting, fishing and camping gear.

The 3d Congressional District of Nebraska has one-third of the state's people spread out over nearly 85% of its acreage. Except along the interstate and around Scottsbluff, the 3d has been losing population for decades and several of the western ranching counties are among the poorest in the nation; one such is Loup County, in the center of the state, which has the nation's lowest per capita income. The district includes 69 of Nebraska's 93 counties, and has moved so far east that it's on the outskirts of Lincoln. Still, it remains one of the nation's top-ranked ag districts, with more farms than all but one other congressional district and more cattle and calves than any other place in the nation. Geographically and politically, the 3d District is where the Midwest becomes the West. For years people here welcomed farm subsidies even as they angrily opposed federal interference. Politically, it is heavily Republican and sometimes ornery: In 1992 Ross Perot got more votes than Bill Clinton. It voted 71% for George W. Bush in 2000 and 75% in 2004.

The congressman from the 3d District is Tom Osborne, a Republican first elected in 2000, a man who had never run for office before but who was better known than most congressmen are after serving 20 years. He grew up in Hastings and excelled at basketball, football and track in high school and at Hastings College. He graduated in 1959 and played professional football for three years in Washington and San Francisco. Then he went to the University of Nebraska to work as a graduate assistant in the football program. He stayed for 36 years, working first under coach Bob Devaney, then becoming NU coach himself in 1973; he also got a master's degree and doctorate in educational psychology. He was head football coach for 25 years, at first compared unfavorably to Devaney, but over the whole period exceedingly successful. He won three national championships before retiring in 1998; he had perfect seasons in 1994, 1995 and 1997. His team was 87–11–1 in the 1990s and 60–3 over his last five years. After retiring he was inducted into the College Football Hall of Fame in 1999; the three-year waiting period was waived for only the second time.

Months after Congressman Bill Barrett announced that he was retiring, Osborne announced he was running. He had been urged to run for the Senate seat being vacated by Bob Kerrey, but declined; he said he did not want to commit to serve the six-year term. From the beginning, it was apparent that Osborne would win. Nevertheless, he campaigned hard. He traveled 60,000 miles and made more than 650 scheduled stops during the campaign; he often drove alone hundreds of miles to events to save the cost of paying a staffer to drive. At first he was uncomfortable shaking hands and asking for votes, but enjoyed talking to people in small groups; Nebraskans were delighted to meet him. He won the primary with 71% of the vote. His Democratic opponent, Rollie Reynolds, was a distant relative who called Osborne "my hero" and "everybody's hero." This was a positive campaign all around, with Osborne refusing to take PAC money; at 63, he won 82%–16%.

In the House, his voting record was in the middle of Republicans, though a bit dovish on defense issues. He tends to local issues with seats on the Agriculture, Education and Workforce, and Transportation and Infrastructure Committees. Although he voted for it, he was less than enthusiastic about the new farm bill, which he called too complicated but the best that could be done; he obtained additional ag research dollars for Nebraska. With Democrat Leonard Boswell, he sponsored a National Animal Identification System to safeguard the nation's beef supply; he urged caution in resuming cattle imports from Canada because of its problems with mad cow disease. To promote rural development, he encouraged a revival of pheasant hunting in Nebraska. Based on his coaching experience, he sponsored with Bart Gordon a bill to regulate "unscrupulous" sports agents by restricting when they may contact student-athletes; that bill passed in September 2004. Osborne filed a bill to require the attorney general to list steroid precursors and other performance-enhancing drugs as controlled substances, which would make over-the-counter sales illegal; in October 2004, Bush signed that bill. Osborne said that he was "pleasantly surprised" by his ability to pass legislation; but he confessed frustration with the slow pace of activity, the partisanship, and lack of discipline in the House, complaining that some things never seem to get done. His new crusade: Stop beer advertising during the broadcast of college sports events.

Osborne was reelected with 93% of the vote in 2002 and 87% in 2004. In December 2004, eight days after Governor Mike Johanns was nominated secretary of agriculture, Osborne said he would not run against Senator Ben Nelson in 2006. In April 2005, he announced he would run for governor instead, setting up a primary challenge in 2006 with Governor Dave Heineman, who succeeded to the office when Johanns resigned. Not long after Osborne's announcement, a crowded Republican field began to take shape in the 3d; Democrats are unlikely to be competitive in this open seat race.

★ NEVADA ★

A pyramid rising from the desert, New York skyscrapers across the street from the sphinx-like lion, a not-too-miniature Eiffel Tower and the gondolas of Venice, a flaming pirate ship next door to Roman ruins: this is what you see as the plane approaches the runway at Las Vegas. All these surrealistic monuments, and miles of spreading subdivisions, are set in one of North America's most forbidding landscapes, a bowl-shaped desert valley rimmed by barren peaks. Nature provided nothing here to encourage human settlement—Las Vegas is far from the lodes of gold and silver that attracted the first settlers of Nevada. Today's Nevada is wholly the creation of post-industrial, post-modern man. Its existence as a state is happenstance: The discovery of the Comstock Lode silver mine in 1859—$500 million worth was taken out in 20 years—brought settlers, and Abraham Lincoln's Republicans made it a state in 1864, even though Nevada did not meet the population requirement for statehood, because Republicans thought they needed an extra three electoral votes. But Nevada was not really a viable state; its population dropped by the early 20th century, and in the early 1930s there were only 91,000 Nevadans and the state government was about to go bankrupt. So Nevada decided to roll the

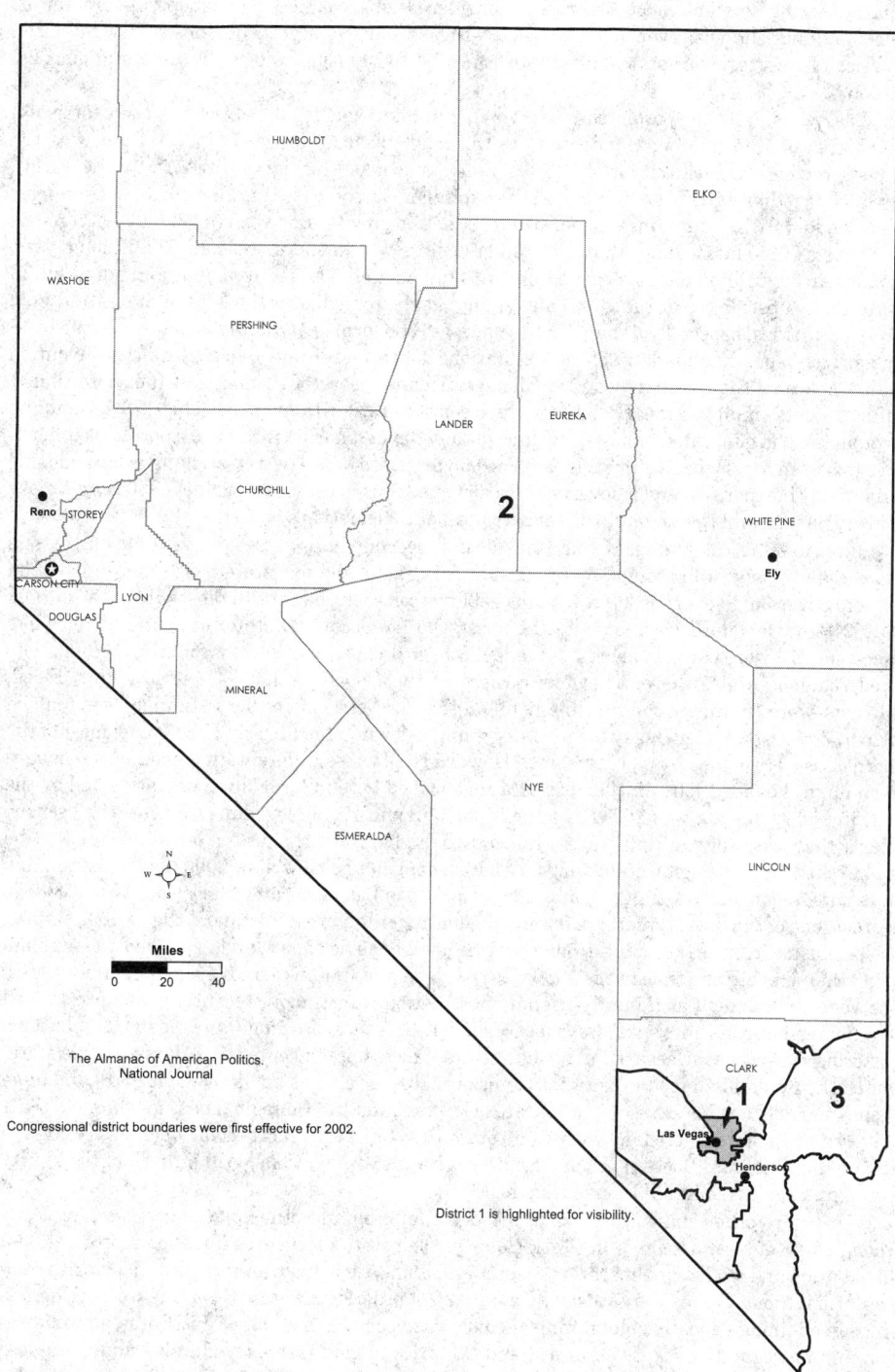

HUMBOLDT

ELKO

WASHOE

PERSHING

LANDER   EUREKA

2

CHURCHILL

WHITE PINE

Reno STOREY

Ely

CARSON CITY

LYON

DOUGLAS

MINERAL

NYE

ESMERALDA

LINCOLN

N
W E
S

Miles
0   20   40

The Almanac of American Politics.
National Journal

CLARK
1   **3**

Congressional district boundaries were first effective for 2002.

Las Vegas

Henderson

District 1 is highlighted for visibility.

dice. The state reduced its residency requirement for divorce to six weeks and legalized gambling. Catering to what most Americans considered sin—casinos, pawnshops, divorce mills, quick wedding chapels, even legal brothels—turned out to be good business. This has been America's fastest-growing state since 1960; from 1990 to 2004 it grew 94%, from 1.2 million to 2.3 million.

Las Vegas, a mere spot on the map when gambling was legalized, now is the center of a metro area of 1.65 million; Henderson, on the road southeast toward Hoover Dam, was the fastest-growing American city in the 1990s. Reno, known as "the biggest little city in the world," now has, together with Lake Tahoe and the capital of Carson City, another 482,000. Gaming—the Nevada word for gambling—generates most of this growth: Las Vegas's 132,000 hotel rooms (as of early 2005) house more than 37 million visitors who spend more than $33 billion a year, Reno's nearly 5 million tourists spend almost $4 billion, and not just in casinos and hotels but in increasingly upscale restaurants and malls. They come from all over the United States and from foreign countries, especially Japan. Though at least one form of gambling is now available in 48 states, Las Vegas has made itself a destination; it has more than twice as much convention exhibit space as the number two city, Chicago. This is a service economy: of the more than 1 million people employed, nearly 90% produce services rather than goods. The 6.75% gambling receipts tax has generated enough revenue so that Nevada has no income, corporate or inheritance tax; even in fiscal crisis in early 2003 no one proposed one. The cost of living is low, housing is relatively inexpensive and a newcomer doesn't stand out in the crowd. Some 5,000 people move in every month, and the unemployment rate is among the nation's lowest.

From mining to gaming, Nevada has been a second chance state, a place for outcasts to succeed and misfits to rebound. With Alaska, it is one of the few states with more men than women. Seven out of every 1,000 Nevadans get divorced each year, the highest rate in the nation. Only 21% of Nevadans were born in the state, the lowest of any state; in Stateline, on Lake Tahoe, just 5% were born in Nevada. Nevada has been an avenue of success for ethnic groups who faced roadblocks elsewhere. The four owners of the Comstock Lode—MacKay, Fair, Flood, O'Brien—were Irishmen; the first big hotel on the Las Vegas strip, the Flamingo, was built in 1946 by Jewish gangster Bugsy Siegel, later gunned down in his Beverly Hills home; most of the big casinos were owned by mobsters until Howard Hughes—a different kind of outcast—bought them up in the late 1960s. In the 1990s Latinos moved here in large numbers, attracted by the plentiful jobs; Nevada was 20% Hispanic in 2000. Some 4% of Nevadans told the 2000 census takers they were of multiple races, the fourth highest of any state. Nevadans tend to be unchurched and not highly educated: only 34% belonged to a church in 2000, lower than in any state but Oregon and Washington; only 17% of adults in Las Vegas and Clark County had college degrees, one of the lowest numbers for any big metropolitan area. For years, the casinos catered to older tastes in entertainment, from Frank Sinatra to girlie shows, and depended on gamblers for all their trade. For a time in the 1990s, as riverboat and Indian casinos opened in many states, Las Vegas billed itself as a family-friendly destination resort; more recently it has proclaimed that "what happens in Vegas stays in Vegas." Either way, its huge and flashy hotels have glittering attractions: Caesars Palace has an upscale shopping center with Roman-style storefronts, the pyramid-shaped Luxor that looms over this desert has an amusement park and huge obelisk inside, New York New York imitates Gotham, and the Bellagio has a museum-class art gallery and an eleven-acre lake with 1,000 fountains. Las Vegas has become decorous enough to attract the American Booksellers and Southern Baptist conventions. Will either political party ever dare to hold its national convention here?

There are other things in Nevada besides gambling and other places besides Las Vegas (though 70% of Nevadans live in Clark County). The state's low taxes have made it a regional distribution and credit card operations center and it has attracted warehouses and factories from California, though taxes were raised by a July 2004 order of the state Supreme Court. There is still some mining—mostly gold mining—which was booming in 2003, after Clinton administration mining regulations were scrapped and the price of gold rose. Nevada also mines the less glamorous diatomaceous earth, used for swimming pool filters and kitty litter. And a lot of older Californians cash out their expensive homes and come to low-tax Nevada to retire. A Wild West atmosphere remains in the "Cow Counties" beyond Las Vegas and Reno; half of the 37,000 wild horses that roam the American West can be found in Nevada.

For the past two decades, Nevada politics have been volatile. Historically, it was Democratic, sending politically shrewd Democrats to Washington and keeping them there to protect the interests of a state always heavily dependent on the federal government. The most powerful were Key Pittman, chairman of the Senate Foreign Relations Committee, who backed FDR's foreign policy only after Roosevelt agreed to buy absurdly large amounts of Nevada's silver, and Pat McCarran, author of the repressive McCarran Act, who shamelessly pushed aid for Reno and Las Vegas (the airport there is named for him) and became suddenly solicitous of civil liberties when mobsters and casino owners were called to testify before the Kefauver committee investigating racketeering. In the 1980s, Nevada trended sharply Republican, primarily because of newcomers.

In the 1990s, the dice have rolled both ways. Bill Clinton, to the surprise of managers on both sides, carried Nevada in 1992, by 37%–35%, and again in 1996, by 44%–43%. The key here was his promise to veto any bill that moves toward building the national nuclear waste repository in Yucca Mountain, some 90 miles north of Las Vegas. But that was not enough for Al Gore, who carried Clark County, but lost by wide margins in Reno and the Cow Counties; George W. Bush, without promising a veto on nuclear waste, carried the state 50%–46%. In 2004, despite Bush's approval of the repository in 2002, he once again lost Clark County and carried the state 50%–48%. From 1988 to 2000 Nevada had two Democratic senators, but Harry Reid, an able and experienced politician, beat Republican John Ensign by only 428 votes in 1998, and when Richard Bryan retired in 2000, Ensign won his seat by a solid 55%–40%. Republicans captured the governorship in 1998 and now hold all six statewide offices, the state Senate and two of the three U.S. House seats.

Nevada voters on balance seem to lean Republican, with a libertarian but sometimes culturally conservative streak. This is not the cultural liberalism of college-educated baby boomers. One reason that Gore and John Kerry lost the state is that they didn't win the margins here that they did in larger states among unmarried people without children, people who never attend church and people with graduate degrees. Another unique feature of Nevada politics: since 1975 voters can vote for "none of these candidates." "None" finished second in the 1998 Democratic primary for lieutenant governor and has occasionally finished first in races for minor offices, but the law is unfortunately toothless: even when there is a plurality for "none of the above," the top-running candidate wins.

Special issues are more important in Nevada than political parties. When Republican Kenny Guinn was elected in 1998 to succeed Democrat Bob Miller as governor, there was no major shift in policy: Both were supported strongly by the gaming industry. And the unions which have successfully organized Las Vegas casinos and hotels have no more been challenged by Guinn than they were by Miller.

The issue that preoccupies Nevada is the proposed Yucca Mountain nuclear waste repository. The federal government took responsibility for nuclear waste in 1982 and the Yucca Mountain site was singled out by chosen by Congress in 1987, when the Nevada delegation was unusually weak: Harry Reid was in his first year in the Senate and Republican Chic Hecht seemed to be facing sure defeat in 1988. The plan is to bury the waste deep within the mountain, 1,300 feet above the water table, in reinforced steel containers in a 1,400-acre maze with 100 miles of storage tunnels. Many in Nevada argue that rainwater will flush the radioactive material out of the depository and into the water table. More recently, Yucca Mountain opponents have charged that the site is geologically flawed and within an earthquake zone, and that transportation of nuclear waste across the country would be hazardous, especially after September 11. Bill Clinton promised to veto a temporary site—one reason he carried Nevada twice by narrow margins. Veto-proof majorities in the House voted for a temporary site in Nevada. Senators Bryan and Reid lobbied furiously to get enough votes to prevent a veto override in the Senate and succeeded in 1995, 1997 and 2000. In 2000, Bush pledged not to place a temporary storage site in Nevada. But he refrained from promising to veto a permanent repository, saying that his decision would be based on "sound science and not politics." In February 2002 Bush, on the recommendation of Energy Secretary Spencer Abraham, designated Yucca Mountain as the permanent site. The law provided for a veto by the governor, which could be overridden by majorities in both houses of Congress. In April 2002, with great ceremony, Governor Kenny Guinn issued his veto. In May 2002 the House cast a large majority for Yucca Mountain. In the Senate, Reid and Ensign lobbied furiously for votes, but in July 2002 the designation of Yucca Mountain was affirmed 60–39. Many Nevadans cheered when the D.C. Circuit Court of Appeals ruled in July 2004 that the EPA's health and safety standards were insufficient. But the court also upheld the selection of the site and the standards can be changed. The permanent site is not supposed to open until 2012, and could be delayed more by regulatory proceedings and lawsuits. Guinn and the Nevada delegation in Congress have vowed not to work for concessions on the building of the repository but to fight it every step of the way. But Nevada Republicans, as opposed to the site as Democrats, have started talking about seeking compensation from the federal government.

The People

Pop. 2004 (est):	2,334,771	**Race/Ethnic Origin**		**Military veterans:** 238,128 (16.0%)	
Pop. 2000:	1,998,257	1,303,001	65.2%	White	WWII: 16.0% — Korea: 13.9%
Pop. 1990:	1,201,833	131,509	6.6%	Black	Vietnam: 34.8% — Gulf War: 10.4%
Change 1990–2000:	Up 66.3%	88,593	4.4%	Asian	**Most populous cities (2003):**

The People

Pop. 2004 (est):	2,334,771
Pop. 2000:	1,998,257
Pop. 1990:	1,201,833
Change 1990–2000:	Up 66.3%
% of U.S. total:	0.7%
Pop. rank:	35th of 50
Area size:	110,561 sq. mi.
State Native:	21.3%
Non-citizen:	10.0%

Language

English: 76.0%	Spanish: 14.6%
Asian: 4.3%	

Race/Ethnic Origin

1,303,001	65.2%	White
131,509	6.6%	Black
88,593	4.4%	Asian
21,397	1.1%	Native Am.
7,769	0.4%	Hawaiian
49,231	2.5%	Two+ races
2,787	0.1%	Other
393,970	19.7%	Hisp. Origin

Ancestry

German: 10.9%	Irish: 8.5%
English: 7.8%	Italian: 5.1%
USA: 3.7%	

Military veterans: 238,128 (16.0%)

WWII: 16.0%	Korea: 13.9%
Vietnam: 34.8%	Gulf War: 10.4%

Most populous cities (2003):

1. Las Vegas	517,017
2. Henderson	214,852
3. Reno	193,882
4. North Las Vegas	144,502
5. Sparks	77,295

Urban population: 91.6%
Rural population: 8.4%

Education

H.S. Grad:	80.7%
College Grad:	18.2%

Industry

Agri: 1.6%	Con: 9.2%
Fin: 6.5%	Info: 2.2%
Mfg: 10.1%	Prof: 21.7%
Public: 4.5%	Trade: 14.0%
Other: 30.3%	

Occupation

Blue collar: 21.8%	White collar: 53.3%
Gray collar: 24.9%	

Work Sector

Private: 82.4%	Govt: 12.5%
Self: 4.9%	Family: 0.3%
Unemployment: 6.2%	

Household Income

<15k: 12.4%	15-35k: 25.4%
35-50k: 18.1%	50-100k: 32.8%
100-150k: 7.4%	>150k: 3.9%

Median: $44,581
Poverty status: 10.5%

Home Value

<50k: 7.7%	50-100k: 19.4%	100-200k: 55.0%	200-300k: 11.3%
300-500k: 4.5%	>500k: 2.1%	Median: $132,500	

Legislature

Senate	12 R 9 D
Assembly	26 D 16 R

Legislative Term Limits: Yes

Registered Voters

D: 429,808	(40.1%)
R: 434,239	(40.5%)
O: 207,054	(19.3%)

Presidential politics   In the 1940s, Nevada was a Democratic state; in the 1960s, it was divided much as the nation was, voting narrowly for John Kennedy in 1960 and Richard Nixon in 1968. In the 1980s, it was heavily Republican, voting more than 60% twice for Ronald Reagan and 59%–38% for George Bush in 1988. In the 1990s, it voted twice for Bill Clinton; critical to his margin was his pledge to veto bills moving nuclear waste to Yucca Mountain or temporary storage sites. But the basic Republican proclivity of the state produced a 50%–46% margin for George W. Bush in 2000, who promised only to block a temporary storage site and to make a decision on the permanent repository based on "sound science." In 2004 Nevada Democrats charged that Bush had broken his promise, a charge whose validity depends on how sound you think the science he relied on was. John Kerry came several times to the state and proclaimed,

2004 Presidential Vote

Bush (R)	418,690	(50%)
Kerry (D)	397,190	(48%)
Nader (I)	4,838	(1%)
Other	8,869	(1%)

2000 Presidential Vote

Bush (R)	301,575	(50%)
Gore (D)	279,978	(46%)
Nader (Green)	15,008	(2%)
Other	12,409	(2%)

"When John Kerry is president, there is going to be no nuclear waste at Yucca Mountain, period." He said he would appoint a blue ribbon panel to consider where to put the waste. But some doubt was cast on his resolve when Senator John Ensign highlighted seven pro-repository votes by Kerry and when Kerry selected as his running mate John Edwards, who voted for the permanent repository. Democrats made the obvious point that Kerry, not Edwards, would make the decision, and Senator Harry Reid said that the seven votes were on amendments he and Richard Bryan sponsored and which hardly anybody else voted for. But Bush said Kerry was using the issue as "a political poker chip" and the Bush campaign ran ads claiming Kerry had flip-flopped on the issue. Bush's narrow victory preserved Nevada's string of voting for the winners of the last seven presidential elections and indeed for every winner starting in 1912 except Jimmy Carter in 1976.

For many years Nevada saw little of presidents and presidential campaigning, but it saw plenty in 2004. Democrats ran strong organizational efforts in Las Vegas and Reno; they reduced Bush's margin in traditionally Republican Reno and Washoe County and produced a slight increase in their majority in Las Vegas and Clark County. But some of their efforts may have been misdirected. Union members cast 25% of Nevada's votes—the Las Vegas casinos are mostly unionized—but they gave Kerry only a 56%–42% margin. Latinos cast 10% of the votes, and voted only 60%–39% for Kerry. But the Bush campaign seems to have out-organized the Democrats in the Cow Counties. In these lightly populated places Bush's popular vote margin increased from 35,000 in 2000 to 41,000 in 2004. Some 40% of the voters thought Yucca Mountain was a very important issue, and 73% of them voted for Kerry. But 26% thought it was only somewhat important, and 56% of them voted for Bush.

Nevada's late March presidential primary attracted little attention for years; efforts to join a proposed Western states primary set for Friday, March 10, 2000, were defeated by Democrats in the Nevada House in June 1999. In 2004 some 9,000 Nevada Democrats caucused on February 14 and produced a majority for John Kerry; Republicans held a state convention in April.

Congressional districting

109th Congress Lineup	
2 R	1 D
108th Congress Lineup	
2 R	1 D

Nevada gained a second congressional district in the 1980 Census and a third congressional district in the 2000 Census. If growth continues at the present percentage rate, it will likely gain a fourth and may gain a fifth in the 2010 Census. Redistricting was easy in the 1980s and 1990s: the 1st District was the inner part of Clark County, politically marginal and won by both parties in the 1990s; the 2d District was the rest of the state, heavily Republican.

It was a little more difficult in 2001, with a third district and control of redistricting split between a Republican governor and state Senate and a Democratic Assembly. Clark County, with 69% of the Census population, was entitled to two of the seats and a small part of the third. For a time Republicans argued that two or all three of the districts should combine part of Clark County with part of the rest of the state. But that idea was dropped in the June 2001 special session. Eventually agreement was reached on a plan with an inner city Las Vegas 1st District, a 2d District including all the rest of the counties plus much of outer Clark County and a Y-shaped 3d District including much of the Las Vegas suburbs. The 1st District was safe for Democrat Shelley Berkley, the 2d safe for Republican Jim Gibbons and the 3d was drawn so that it was exactly even in party registration; it cast narrow pluralities for Al Gore in 2000 and George W. Bush in 2004.

Governor

Kenny Guinn (R)

Elected 1998, term expires Jan. 2007, 2d term; b. Aug. 24, 1936, Garland, AR; home, Las Vegas; Fresno St. U, B.A. 1957, M.A. 1958; Utah St. U., Ph.D. 1970; Non-denominational; married (Dema).

Professional Career: Planning Specialist, Clark Cnty. Schl. Dist., 1964–69; Superintendent, Clark Cnty. Schl. Dist., 1969–78; Nevada Savings & Loan, 1978–80; Pres. & COO, PriMerit Bank, 1980–85; CEO, 1985–87; Pres. & COO Southwest Gas Corp., 1987–93; Chairman & CEO 1988–93; Interim Pres., U.N.L.V., 1994–95.

Office: Capitol Bldg., Carson City, 89701, 775-684-5670; Fax: 775-684-5683; Web site: www.gov.state.nv.us.

Election Results

2002 general	Kenny Guinn (R)	344,001	(68%)
	Joe Neal (D)	110,935	(22%)
	Other	25,469	(5%)
	None of these candidates	23,674	(5%)
2002 primary	Kenny Guinn (R)	97,367	(83%)
	Shirley Cook (R)	7,717	(7%)
1998 general	Kenny Guinn (R)	223,892	(52%)
	Jan Laverty Jones (D)	182,281	(42%)
	Other	27,457	(6%)

Kenny Guinn was elected governor of Nevada in 1998 and reelected in 2002 in his only races for elective office. He grew up in the Central Valley of California, due west of Las Vegas but separated by Death Valley and Mount Whitney; he majored in physical education at Fresno State and got an education doctorate at Utah State. In 1964 he moved to Las Vegas to work for the Clark County School District; he became school superintendent in 1969. Later he went to work for the S&L that became PriMerit Bank and became chairman in 1987, then went to Southwest Gas Corporation and became chairman in 1993. In 1994 he spent a year as interim president of the University of Nevada at Las Vegas, then recovering from a basketball scandal. In the process he won much civic renown. In February 1996 he started running to replace term-limited Governor Bob Miller; immediately he picked up much of the support from the gaming industry Miller had, though he is a Republican and Miller a Democrat. He was christened "The Anointed One" by local political analyst Jon Ralston.

The Democratic nominee was Las Vegas Mayor Jan Laverty Jones. In 1994 she had run against Governor Bob Miller in the primary, and lost 63%–28%. Jones announced on filing day, only a few months after breast cancer surgery, and while still undergoing chemotherapy and radiation; she was open about this and showed great vigor. Guinn charged Jones with raising property taxes; Jones charged Guinn with raising gas rates. Guinn won 52%–42%.

Nevada's 63 citizen-legislators meet only four months every two years; they get $60 for postage and have no staff except secretaries. Nonetheless, the 1999 legislature proved productive. It passed Guinn's proposal for Millennium Scholarships, to allow B students in core subjects to go to college almost for free. Guinn succeeded in privatizing the state workmen's comp insurer and strengthening the ethics code. Guinn, like almost all Nevada politicians, has strongly opposed the proposed repository for nuclear waste at Yucca Mountain, 90 miles northwest of Las Vegas.

The other big issue in Nevada in 2002 was medical malpractice. Guinn called a special session of the legislature to revise Nevada's malpractice law. The legislature passed a law capping pain and suffering damages at $350,000, but provided exceptions for "gross malpractice" when proved by "clear and convincing evidence" or "exceptional circumstances." Trial lawyers predicted that without the exception, the courts would strike down the law. Doctors' organizations were not satisfied. They collected enough signatures to present their own version, without the exceptions, to the legislature in February 2003; the legislature had 40 days to enact it or it would go on the November 2004 ballot. It ended up on the ballot and passed with 59% in favor to 41%.

Guinn did not have strong competition in the 2002 election. In May it became apparent that the Democratic nominee would be Joe Neal, state senator for 30 years, and an advocate of raising the gross gambling tax. He often said that Yucca Mountain was inevitable. Guinn suspended his fundraising in May and contributed his money to other Republicans and local charities; he did little campaigning. He had the support of Las Vegas and teachers' unions and the result was what you might expect: Guinn won 68%–22%. Republicans swept all six statewide constitutional offices for the first time since 1890, held the state Senate and reduced Democrats' margin in the state House.

During the campaign Guinn boasted that he had not raised taxes. "We're running a state with 300,000 more people now than when I came in. And we have 1,000 fewer people on the state payroll." But even before the election, the Governor's Task Force on Tax Policy called for a $336 million tax increase. In December Guinn said he would seek $800 million in tax increases over two years, even though the Economic Forum, the state's official estimator, said that revenue would rise 5% in each of the next two years; the Nevada economy, hit fairly hard by September 11, had rebounded in 2002 and the state still led the nation in job growth and personal income increase.

Guinn said state government needed $234 million to cover costs of increased public school enrollment, $225 million for a program to reduce classroom size, $200 million for Medicaid and $80 million for increased university and community college enrollment. He also cited rising utility and workers compensation costs, health care costs for teachers and the need to replenish the state's rainy day fund. He introduced a $1 billion tax package for the 2003–05 biennial budget, which included a .25% gross receipts business tax designed to collect revenue from Nevada businesses with more than $450,000 in revenues. Under Guinn's plan, almost no one was spared: He called for tripling the annual $100 per employee business tax and the cigarette tax and almost doubling the alcohol tax. Even the casinos took a hit: the gross gaming tax would rise from 6.25 percent to 6.5 percent in 2005.

That the state would increase taxes by a significant amount was never in doubt; only the amount of the increase and the businesses affected were in question. The gambling industry and the state AFL-CIO backed Guinn's plan, but non-gambling businesses and the Chamber of Commerce, accustomed only to paying the employee business tax, opposed the gross receipts tax. Assembly Republicans attempted to draw the line on the tax hike at $700 million and preferred a proposal that would enact a payroll tax rather than a gross receipts tax. In Nevada, measures that raise taxes require a two-thirds majority in each chamber; the Assembly fell short of that threshold in two votes on a tax plan during the 2003 regular session. After two June special sessions failed to break the stalemate and approve a balanced budget that appropriated K-12 education funds (Nevada passes its budget in several parts), Guinn filed a lawsuit on July 1 asking the state supreme court to intervene and order the legislature to pass a budget.

On July 10, in a 6–1 ruling, the court handed down a remarkable decision. It instructed the legislature to temporarily disregard the constitutional provision requiring a two-thirds majority because it was a "procedural" requirement that must yield to the "fundamental" requirement to fund the schools. On July 21, an $836 million tax increase passed 17–2 in the Senate and 28–14 in the Assembly—two-thirds majorities anyway. The compromise measure rejected a gross receipts tax in favor of a payroll tax on the gross wages of workers; it increased alcohol taxes by 75%, cigarette taxes by 45 cents per pack and created a live entertainment tax ranging from 5% to 10%, depending on the size of the venue. The gambling receipts tax increased by .5%. Reaction to the court decision and tax increase was swift: a group announced a plan to recall Guinn and anti-tax Republicans predicted that the outcry would lead to the election of a Republican House majority in 2004. Neither occurred. The recall campaign failed to gather enough signatures to qualify for the ballot and Democrats picked up three House seats.

There was little turmoil in 2005, when the legislature next met. Strong sales tax revenues and a booming real estate market provided the state with a $326 million surplus. Guinn called for a $300 million vehicle registration rebate and proposed a $100 million bailout for his signature Millennium Scholarships and candidates began positioning for 2006, when Guinn is ineligible to run for a third term. Senate Minority Leader Dina Titus of Las Vegas and Assembly Speaker Richard Perkins of Henderson, both Democrats, were expected to run; longtime Senate Majority Leader Bill Raggio criticized both for paying attention to rural Nevada only once they set their sights on the governor's office. Congressman Jim Gibbons of Sparks, the 1994 Republican nominee for governor who lost to Bob Miller, was considered likely to make another run. Other possible Republican candidates included Lieutenant Governor Lorraine Hunt and state Senator Bob Beers.

Senior Senator

Harry Reid (D)

Elected 1986, seat up 2010, 4th term; b. Dec. 2, 1939, Searchlight; home, Searchlight; S. UT St. Col., A.S. 1959, UT St. U., B.S. 1961, George Washington U., J.D. 1964, U. of NV, 1969–70; Mormon; married (Landra).

Elected Office: NV Assembly, 1968–70; NV Lt. Gov., 1970–74; U.S. House of Reps., 1982–86.

Professional Career: Practicing atty., 1969–82; Henderson City Atty., 1964–66; Chmn., NV Gaming Comm., 1977–81.

DC Office: 528 HSOB, 20510, 202-224-3542; Fax: 202-224-7327; Web site: reid.senate.gov.

State Offices: Carson City, 775-882-7343; Las Vegas, 702-388-5020; Reno, 775-686-5750.

Committees: *Minority Leader. Appropriations*: Defense; Energy & Water (RMM); Homeland Security; Interior & Related Agencies; Labor, Health and Human Services, Education & Related Agencies; Transportation, Treasury, the Judiciary, HUD & Related Agencies.

Group Ratings

	ADA	ACLU	AFS	LCV	ITIC	NTU	COC	ACU	NTLC	CHC
2004	90	44	100	50	58	14	53	21	11	16
2003	70	—	100	84	—	17	35	21	—	—

National Journal Ratings

	2003 LIB	—	2003 CONS		2004 LIB	—	2004 CONS
Economic	82%	—	10%		64%	—	35%
Social	58%	—	41%		58%	—	41%
Foreign	86%	—	10%		86%	—	8%

Key Votes of the 108th Congress

1. Ban Drilling in ANWR	Y	5. Energy Bill	N	9. Ban Same-Sex Marriage	N
2. Approve Bush Tax Cuts	N	6. Support Roe v. Wade	N	10. Ban Bunker-Buster Bomb	Y
3. Medicare/Rx Bill	N	7. Ban Partial-Birth Abortion	Y	11. Fund Iraq War	Y
4. Bar Overtime Pay Regs.	Y	8. Assault Weapons Ban	N	12. Restrict Missile Defense	Y

Election Results

2004 general	Harry Reid (D)	494,805	(61%)	($7,040,588)
	Richard Ziser (R)	284,640	(35%)	($647,500)
	Other	30,623	(4%)	
2004 primary	Harry Reid (D)	unopposed		
1998 general	Harry Reid (D)	208,650	(48%)	($4,939,010)
	John Ensign (R)	208,222	(48%)	($3,490,256)
	Other	18,918	(4%)	

Prior Winning Percentages: 1992 (51%); 1986 (50%); 1984 House (56%); 1982 House (58%)

Harry Reid, a Democrat first elected to the House in 1982 and to the Senate in 1986, is the Senate minority leader. He grew up in Searchlight, Nevada, in the scorching desert south of Las Vegas, where his father was a hardrock miner and the family lived in a house without indoor plumbing. He hitchhiked 40 miles to high school in Henderson, where his civics teacher and boxing coach

Mike O'Callaghan became his political mentor. Henderson businessmen helped him pay for college, and he graduated from Southern Utah State (where he became a Mormon) and George Washington law school. He was an amateur boxer and at nights during law school he worked as a Capitol Police officer; he likes to say, "I would rather dance than fight, but I know how to fight." He returned to Henderson and practiced law. Reid was elected to the Assembly in 1968, at age 28; in 1970 O'Callaghan was elected governor and Reid, running separately, was elected lieutenant governor. In 1974 he came within 624 votes of beating Paul Laxalt in the race for senator, lost for mayor of Las Vegas in 1976, and then became head of the Gaming Commission from 1977 to 1981—as sensitive a post as any in Nevada. His life was threatened and mobsters put a bomb in his car. In 1982, when Nevada got two House seats for the first time and Congressman-at-Large Jim Santini ran for the Senate, Reid ran in the Las Vegas-based 1st District and won. Laxalt retired in 1986 and Reid ran for the Senate again; his opponent turned out to be Santini, who had switched parties at the last minute and was running as a Republican. Reid's ads depicted him as David to Santini's Goliath, and he won 50%–45%.

Reid has had a voting record more moderate than those of many Senate Democrats. He voted for the partial-birth abortion ban and against resolutions endorsing *Roe v. Wade*. He co-sponsored the constitutional amendment to allow the outlawing of flag burning. He was one of the few Democrats to vote for the Gulf War resolution in 1991 and voted for the Iraq war resolution in 2002. He has consistently and effectively opposed environmental groups on mining issues and blocked attempts by environmentalists and the Clinton administration to impose higher fees on hardrock miners. He has opposed most gun control measures. He pushed through a "source tax" amendment barring states from taxing the state pensions of retirees who move to another state, as many have to Nevada. He has steered counterterrorism money to Nevada and has worked to get the old Nevada nuclear test site, with its hundreds of underground tunnels, made into a $250 million center for training first responders how to cope with acts of terrorists. He has been a strong supporter of the gaming industry; when Bill Clinton proposed a 4% gaming tax, Reid promised, "I will become the most negative, the most irresponsible, the most obnoxious person of anyone in the Senate." He has worked to block the bill, backed by John McCain and others, to prohibit betting on college and amateur sports, which is legal only in Nevada; to block action he introduced many amendments, including one to ban gambling in all states but Nevada. In 2004 he blocked consideration of a bill limiting the state share of Indian gambling revenues and profits. He worked with Congressman Jim Gibbons on a Clark County Lands Act to declare some wilderness study areas as wilderness and open others to development; on another Clark County land transfer bill, he was criticized because his son and son-in-law worked for lobbying firms supporting the measure.

The key federal issue for Nevada during his years in the Senate has been the proposed nuclear waste repository in Yucca Mountain. The federal government assumed responsibility for nuclear waste in 1982 and a bill passed in 1987, Reid's first year in the Senate, named Yucca Mountain and one other contender as the only two sites; the other one was later ruled out. Reid has stubbornly and persistently opposed the repository with every parliamentary and political tool at his command but other senators with nuclear waste piling up in their states (and 39 states have it) and especially Larry Craig of Idaho, where the government established a temporary nuclear waste site, have pressed hard for designation of Yucca Mountain. Bill Clinton carried Nevada by narrow margins in 1992 and 1996 largely because he promised to veto even a temporary site in Yucca Mountain, and so during his presidency Reid's task was to assemble enough votes to prevent an override of his veto. He did so in 1997, then prevented a vote in 1998 and 1999, then kept 34 votes in line in April 2000—just barely enough. George W. Bush in 2000 pledged not to support a temporary site, but he also refrained from promising to veto a permanent site, saying that his decision would be based on "sound science and not politics." In February 2002 Bush, on the recommendation of Energy Secretary Spencer Abraham, designated Yucca Mountain as the permanent site. The law provided for a veto by the governor, which could be overridden by majorities in both houses of Congress. In April 2002, with great ceremony, Governor Kenny Guinn issued his veto. In May 2002 the House cast a large majority for Yucca

Mountain. Reid lobbied furiously for Democratic votes, while John Ensign, his 1998 opponent and now his Republican colleague, lobbied desperately for Republican votes.

Reid argued that the site was geologically flawed and that transporting nuclear waste to it would be hazardous, especially after September 11. He passionately when the issue was debated in July, enough so to convert Debbie Stabenow, who had voted for the Yucca Mountain site in the House. Altogether he got 35 Democrats and Jim Jeffords to vote his way. Ensign, opposed by the Bush administration, could get only two other Republicans, Lincoln Chafee and Ben Nighthorse Campbell. So the site was approved 60–39. But for Reid the fight was not over. Lawsuits had been filed against the plan, and the Energy Department must get approval from the Nuclear Regulatory Commission, which could take many years. Reid chaired the Appropriations subcommittee with jurisdiction over the Energy Department; in 2002 it cut $189 million from the Yucca Mountain budget. Reid fiercely opposed the Bush administration proposal to finance work at Yucca Mountain from a nuclear waste trust fund funded by utility industry fees, on the ground that this would remove it from congressional supervision; when that resulted in the non-funding of the work in November 2004, appropriators scrambled to find cuts in other programs to pay for the $577 million price tag. Reid threw in a provision allowing Nevada counties to use Energy Department funding to take part in NRC licensing procedures. Also in November 2004 Reid, elected to be the new minority leader, negotiated with the Bush administration over appointments; he agreed to approve 175 Bush nominees in return for the recess appointment of his aide Gregory Jaczko to the Nuclear Regulatory Commission, where he is likely to vote against the Yucca Mountain repository.

Reid had a close political call in his 1998 race against then-Congressman John Ensign, but he still spent much time seeking the votes of Democratic colleagues to replace Wendell Ford, who retired, as minority whip. After the election he got the job without opposition. For the next six years he was a constant presence on the floor, advancing the cause of his party and maintaining civil relations with Republican leaders. He played a key role in persuading Jim Jeffords to leave the Republican party in May 2001 and make the Democrats the majority party in the Senate again. For a month Daschle, Christopher Dodd and Reid talked with Jeffords and coaxed him to switch parties. Reid offered to decline the chairmanship of the Environment and Public Works Committee, to which he was entitled by seniority, and let Jeffords be chairman. That may have been the vital selling point, though Jeffords, Daschle and Reid deny that there was a quid pro quo.

He worked closely and cooperatively with Democratic Leader Tom Daschle, and in November 2002, when Daschle was considering running for president, he all but endorsed Reid to succeed him. "I honestly don't think he would be challenged if I were to run." But Daschle decided not to run for president. Reid's combativeness came out when Republicans ran all-night sessions in November 2003 to protest Democratic filibusters of nominees for appellate judgeships. Reid spoke for nine hours, reading from his book about his upbringing in Searchlight, Nevada. In 2004 Reid contributed generously to other Democrats; he gave $1 million to the Democrats' Senate campaign committee in September and in October, as Daschle's chances for winning reelection in South Dakota seemed to be waning, gave money to other colleagues as well.

After Daschle lost on November 2, Reid already had enough votes lined up to become Minority Leader; Christopher Dodd, who was interested in the post, declined to run. He was officially selected on November 16 and after some talk of working with Republicans seemed to indicate that he would be as tough a partisan as Daschle had been. "If they want to get something done, they have to work with us. They can't just run over us," he said of Republicans. Of George W. Bush's proposal for personal retirement accounts in Social Security he said, "For someone who wants to privatize Social Security, they're going to have to look for somebody to go to bed with other than me." He gave up his seat on the Environment Committee to accommodate other Democrats, said he would rely on ranking Democrats on committees for policy positions (Daschle sometimes blocked them from taking action) and donated another $500,000 to the Senate campaign committee in January 2005. In December 2004, looking ahead to battles over Supreme Court nominees, he said that Justice Antonin Scalia was "one smart guy" but that Justice Clarence Thomas was "an embarrassment to the Court." When Bush renominated several filibustered judicial appointees, he promised to filibuster them again and threatened to bring the business of the Senate to a halt if Republicans changed the rules by majority vote. In January 2005 he and House Minority Leader Nancy Pelosi gave a "prebuttal" of Bush's State of the Union speech two days before he delivered it; they also presented a Democratic response afterwards, in which Reid called for a Marshall Plan for America. In March 2005 he got 42 Democratic senators to sign a letter opposing personal retirement accounts in Social Security. "President Bush should forget about privatizing Social Security. It will not happen," he said. "They are trying to destroy Social Security by giving this money to the fat cats on Wall Street, and I think it's wrong." In February Reid prevented nongermane amendments from coming forward on the class action bill, which many Democrats and all Republicans supported. He was plainly irritated when the Republican National Committee shortly thereafter sent out an e-mail attacking him as "chief Democratic obstructionist," pointing out that his son and son-in-law were lobbyists (both had let their lobbyist registrations drop) and mentioning his $750,000 Washington condominium (Republicans had reminded South Dakotans that Daschle had bought a $1.7 million house in Washington). At a dinner at the White House that night Reid and Bush talked about the e-mail (neither disclosed what he said), and Reid told reporters afterwards, "When you have a real bad chafe—is that what they call it?—it's hard to get soothed."

Reid started off as minority leader politically strengthened because in November 2004 he won by a large margin in Nevada for the first time. He was elected in 1986 by 50%–45%. In the 1992 primary he won 53%–39% over Charles Woods, a businessman badly wounded and scarred in World War II; in the general, he beat rancher Demar Dahl 51%–40%. In 1998, against Congressman John Ensign, he was very hard pressed. Ensign's father Mike Ensign is head of the Mandalay Resort Group, one of the big Las Vegas casino operations, and Ensign raised plenty of money from the gaming industry, as did Reid: Reid spent $4.9 million and Ensign $3.5 million. Reid in his feisty way attacked Ensign harshly as an "extremist" who called environmentalists "socialists," and would gut Social Security. Reid carried Clark County, which casts two-thirds of the vote and is normally more Democratic than the rest of the state, by only 53%–44%; he may have won because he ran ahead of party lines in the usually Republican Reno area, where his work on local projects was appreciated, and lost there by only 48%–46%. The election night tally showed Reid ahead by 459 votes; Ensign called for a recount, and a hand count in Reno's Washoe County took weeks. Ensign finally conceded December 9, with Reid ahead by 428 votes. Two years later Ensign was elected by a wider margin to Nevada's other Senate seat after Reid's Democratic colleague Richard Bryan retired. Despite his strong partisanship and the bitterness and the closeness of the 1998 campaign, Reid and Ensign have become friendly colleagues who work together on many Nevada projects; like Oregon's Ron Wyden and Gordon Smith, they know that after one bitter race they will never run against each other again.

Going into the 2004 cycle Reid had a problem and found a solution. The problem was that there are so many newcomers to Nevada, most of them Republicans unfamiliar with his work in almost 40 years of public life. About 5,000 people have been moving to the Las Vegas area every month—which means nearly 300,000 Nevadans in 2004 were not in the state the last time Reid ran. Some 436,000 Nevadans voted in 1998, when Reid faced Ensign; 830,000 would vote in November 2004, which means that roughly half the voters (because some 1998 voters died or dropped out) never saw Reid's name on a November ballot before. The solution was to preclude serious opposition from 2d District Congressman Jim Gibbons or one of Nevada's several Republican statewide officeholders by showing strong support from Las Vegas big hitters. They are thoroughly bipartisan and have been the motivating force in Nevada state politics, smoothing the election of Democratic Governor Bob Miller in 1990 and 1994 and Republican Governor Kenny Guinn in 1998 and 2002. Reid got early support from Governor Guinn, former Reagan appointee Sig Rogich and gaming executives Terry Lanni and Mike Ensign. The Republican nominee turned out to be Richard Ziser, an evangelical Christian who led the drive to ban same-sex marriages on the 2000 and 2002 ballots. He got little financial support in Nevada or from national Republicans. Reid won with 61%, 10% more than he had won in any other Senate race, to 35% for Ziser. He carried Las Vegas's Clark County 65%–31% and Reno's Washoe County 58%–38%; he lost the usually Republican Cow Counties, which George W. Bush carried

65%–32%, by exactly 137 votes. He had the additional satisfaction of seeing his son Rory Reid elected chairman of the Clark County Commission.

Junior Senator

John Ensign (R)

Elected 2000, seat up 2006, 1st term; b. Mar. 25, 1958, Roseville, CA; home, Las Vegas; OR St. U., B.S. 1981, CO St. U., D.V.M. 1985; Christian; married (Darlene).

Elected Office: U.S. House of Reps. 1994–98.

Professional Career: Veterinarian, 1987–93; Gen. Mgr., Gold Strike Hotel, 1991–93.

DC Office: 356 RSOB, 20510, 202-224-6244; Fax: 202-228-2193; Web site: ensign.senate.gov.

State Offices: Carson City, 775-885-9111; Las Vegas, 702-388-6605; Reno, 775-686-5770.

Committees: *Armed Services*: Airland; Emerging Threats & Capabilities; Readiness & Management Support (Chmn.). *Budget. Commerce, Science & Transportation*: Aviation; Science & Space; Technology, Innovation & Competitiveness (Chmn.); Trade, Tourism & Economic Development. *Health, Education, Labor & Pensions*: Bioterrorism & Public Health Preparedness; Education & Early Childhood Development; Employment & Workplace Safety. *Veterans' Affairs*.

Group Ratings

	ADA	ACLU	AFS	LCV	ITIC	NTU	COC	ACU	NTLC	CHC
2004	15	11	14	17	100	89	75	92	98	100
2003	10	—	0	16	—	87	91	100	—	—

National Journal Ratings

	2003 LIB	—	2003 CONS		2004 LIB	—	2004 CONS
Economic	29%	—	68%		30%	—	69%
Social	0%	—	59%		19%	—	71%
Foreign	35%	—	62%		33%	—	61%

Key Votes of the 108th Congress

1. Ban Drilling in ANWR	N	5. Energy Bill	Y	9. Ban Same-Sex Marriage	Y
2. Approve Bush Tax Cuts	Y	6. Support Roe v. Wade	N	10. Ban Bunker-Buster Bomb	N
3. Medicare/Rx Bill	N	7. Ban Partial-Birth Abortion	Y	11. Fund Iraq War	Y
4. Bar Overtime Pay Regs.	N	8. Assault Weapons Ban	N	12. Restrict Missile Defense	N

Election Results

2000 general	John Ensign (R)	330,687	(55%)	($4,872,176)
	Ed Bernstein (D)	238,260	(40%)	($2,449,093)
	Other	31,303	(5%)	
2000 primary	John Ensign (R)	95,904	(88%)	
	Richard Hamzik (R)	6,202	(6%)	
	Other	6,833	(6%)	

Prior Winning Percentages: 1996 House (50%); 1994 House (48%)

John Ensign was elected to the Senate in 2000, in his second try for the office. Ensign grew up in northern Nevada and moved to Las Vegas at 16. For a time his mother was a change girl at a Reno casino, supporting three children with no help from her ex-husband. Then she married Mike Ensign, who became a top executive at Circus Circus and is now head of the Mandalay Resort Group. John Ensign graduated from Oregon State in 1981 and in 1985 graduated from veterinary school at Colorado State, where he became a born-again Christian. He built a successful veterinary practice in Las Vegas, with the first 24-hour clinic, and managed a family hotel, became involved in civic affairs and at his wife's suggestion became active in Promise Keepers. Disturbed at trends in national life, they decided he would run for the House in 1994, against 1st District incumbent James Bilbray. This was the more Democratic of Nevada's then two seats, and Bilbray was an eight-year incumbent. But 1994 was also a Republican year, and with the help of Ensign's stepfather's connections in the gaming industry he was able to raise substantial funds. On election night, Bilbray claimed victory, but when the votes came in Ensign had won by 1,436 votes. In the House, Ensign compiled a generally conservative voting record and got a seat on the Ways and Means Committee. In the summer of 1996 he and colleague David Camp persuaded Newt Gingrich to separate the welfare and Medicaid issues and present Bill Clinton with a welfare bill, which he signed 11 weeks before the election; Ensign can reasonably claim to be one of the fathers of the 1996 Welfare Act. He was re-elected in 1996 by 50%–44%.

Ensign decided to run against Senator Harry Reid in 1998. This was a hard-fought, high-spending race, targeted by both national parties and fought with intensity by the candidates; Reid spent $4.9 million and Ensign $3.5 million. Reid attacked Ensign harshly as an "extremist" who called environmentalists "socialists," and would gut Social Security. "You send Ensign to the Senate, you send nuclear waste to Nevada," he proclaimed. The election night tally showed Reid ahead by 459 votes; Ensign called for a recount, and it turned out that the Washoe County ballots had been misprinted, preventing some from being read by machines. The hand count there took weeks, and Ensign finally conceded December 9, with Reid ahead by 428 votes.

Then just two months later, in February 1999, Bryan announced that he would not run for re-election in 2000. Ensign, who had said he would not run against Bryan, announced his candidacy the next day. Democrats tried to enlist their strongest candidate, Bob Miller, who had just completed eight years as governor, but he preferred to remain in the private sector in Las Vegas. Then Attorney General Frankie Sue Del Papa launched her candidacy; an April poll showed Ensign with a narrow 45%–40% lead, but he was much farther ahead in money: $1.1 million to $250,000 by the end of June. In September Del Papa abruptly withdrew from the race, as she had withdrawn from the 1998 race for governor, citing difficulties in fundraising; her bad relations with Las Vegas unions did not help. Democratic efforts to recruit Brian Greenspun, owner of the *Las Vegas Sun*, failed. What appears to have happened is that the gaming industry, developers and other leading funders in Las Vegas, who had supported Miller and then Republican Kenny Guinn to succeed him, decided that Ensign was on the road to victory and that it might suit their interests to have in a Republican Senate one Democratic and one Republican senator.

That left the Democratic banner in the hands of Ed Bernstein, a personal injury lawyer who had run ads on Las Vegas TV for years. Bernstein put in $1.1 million of his own money; his main issues were prescription drugs for seniors and abortion. The candidates engaged in six debates; one highlight came when Ensign quizzed Bernstein about a water project in northern Nevada of which Bernstein obviously had never heard. Naturally both candidates promised to fight nuclear waste storage in Nevada; Ensign was careful to return a contribution from a Yucca Mountain contractor. Bernstein managed to tighten the race for a while, but Ensign ended up winning by a large 55%–40%. Ensign carried Las Vegas and Clark County 51%–45%, Reno and Washoe County 58%–35% and the Cow Counties 68%–27%.

Ensign and Reid, bitter rivals in 1998, quickly became cooperative colleagues. In December 2000 they announced that their first priority was blocking the move by John McCain and Sam Brownback to prohibit betting on college and amateur sports—they argue that sports books are well regulated by Nevada state authorities—and Ensign tried to gut the bill in the Commerce Committee in May 2001 but his amendment to do so failed 10–10. They co-sponsored a bill to make permanent the Social HMOs permitted in Nevada under Medicare.

As a freshman senator, Ensign has done much of his work by sponsoring amendments. To the election procedures bill, he added an amendment requiring paper documentation of votes so that they could be hand-counted if necessary, as in Washoe County in 1998; he was dismayed when Nevada Secretary of State Dean Heller said it didn't require paper documents. To the corporate accountability bill he added an amendment to discourage regulators from treating very small non-public accounting firms the same way as large CPAs. To the HMO regulation bill he sponsored amendments to prohibit genetic discrimination, to make sure its protections were available to union members and to protect doctors doing pro bono work in poor areas from lawsuits. He sponsored an amendment to ban interstate transportation of cockfighting paraphernalia and increase to two years the sentence for interstate transportation of cockfighting roosters; he failed to get it into the 2002 farm bill and it was stripped out of the forestry bill in November 2003. He sponsored another bill to outlaw the slaughter of horses in the U.S. for human consumption in other countries.

Ensign was the only member of Congress in Iraq when Saddam Hussein was captured in December 2003. He supported the Bush guest worker immigration proposal. "Without them [immigrants] the economy collapses, especially the economy of the state of Nevada. We've got to have those people. A lot of them are doing jobs Americans flat out wouldn't do." He announced in January 2004 he would support the filibuster of the energy bill because of its new subsidies for the nuclear power industry. He got Budget Chairman Don Nickles to delete from the 2004 budget resolution a proposal requiring casinos to withhold winnings from gamblers behind on child support payments. He called EPA's arsenic water standard an unfunded mandate; 140 community water systems in Nevada exceed the standard. As chairman of the Republican High Tech Task Force, he opposed the FASB's recommendation that stock options be expensed, but in April 2004 conceded, "We will unfortunately lose this battle." In May 2003 the Senate adopted his amendment allowing a one-time tax break for profits that were earned overseas if they are invested in the United States. With Lindsey Graham, he sponsored a bill to cut U.S. dues to the United Nations 10% unless the UN cooperates with American investigations of the Oil For Food program; in December 2004 he called for the resignation of UN Secretary General Kofi Annan.

One important federal issue for Nevada is the proposed nuclear waste repository in Yucca Mountain, 90 miles northwest of Las Vegas. The federal government assumed responsibility for nuclear waste in 1982 and a bill passed in 1987 named Yucca Mountain and one other contender as the only two sites; the other one was later ruled out. Ensign strongly opposed Yucca Mountain when he was in the House, but there the odds were very heavily against him. Creation of a temporary storage site in Yucca Mountain was prevented during the Clinton years by Clinton's promise to veto it—probably the reason he carried Republican-leaning Nevada twice by narrow margins—and by Harry Reid's success in getting at least 34 senators to oppose it, enough to prevent an override of Clinton's veto. George W. Bush in 2000 also pledged not to support a temporary site, but at the same time he refrained from promising to veto a permanent site, saying that his decision would be based on "sound science and not politics." In February 2002 Bush, on the recommendation of Energy Secretary Spencer Abraham, designated Yucca Mountain as the permanent site. The law provided for a veto by the governor, which could be overridden by majorities in both houses of Congress. In April 2002, Governor Kenny Guinn issued his veto. In May 2002, the House cast a large majority for Yucca Mountain. In the Senate Reid lobbied furiously for votes among Democrats, most of whom had stood with him before on the issue, while Ensign lobbied desperately for Republican votes. This was much more difficult because of the opposition of the Bush administration. Reid got 35 Democrats and Jim Jeffords to vote his way. Ensign could get only two other Republicans, Lincoln Chafee and Ben Nighthorse Campbell. So the site was approved 60–39. But the fight was not over. Lawsuits had been filed against the plan, and the Energy Department must get approval from the Nuclear Regulatory Commission, which could take many years. And Ensign has worked with Harry Reid to block funding of Yucca Mountain outside the congressional appropriations process.

Immediately after the November 2004 election, Ensign announced that he would seek a Republican leadership position after the 2006 election. Of course he could not seek such a position unless he is reelected that year, but in mid-2005 his prospects looked good. His support from Las Vegas gaming interests means that his campaign will be well funded and makes it likely that the campaign of any opponent will not. And his good working relations with Harry Reid suggest that the minority leader will look for new Democrats to be elected elsewhere than in this Republican-leaning state.

FIRST DISTRICT

Rep. Shelley Berkley (D)

Elected 1998, 4th term; b. Jan. 20, 1951, South Fallsburg, NY; home, Las Vegas; U.N.L.V., B.A. 1972; U. of San Diego Law Schl., J.D. 1976; Jewish; married (Larry Lehrner).

Elected Office: NV Assembly, 1982–84; Regent, U. Commun. Col. System of NV, 1990–98.

Professional Career: Cnsl., SW Gas Corp., 1977–82; VP, Sands Hotel, 1989–98; Chair, NV Hotel & Motel Assn., 1994.

DC Office: 439 CHOB, 20515, 202-225-5965; Fax: 202-225-3119; Web site: www.house.gov/berkley.

District Office: Las Vegas, 702-220-9823.

Committees: *International Relations* (16th of 23 D): Europe & Emerging Threats; Middle East & Central Asia. *Transportation & Infrastructure* (20th of 34 D): Aviation; Highways, Transit & Pipelines. *Veterans' Affairs* (11th of 12 D): Disability Assistance & Memorial Affairs (RMM).

Group Ratings

	ADA	ACLU	AFS	LCV	ITIC	NTU	COC	ACU	NTLC	CHC
2004	95	65	100	100	75	16	60	8	3	10
2003	85	—	100	65	—	24	36	23	—	—

National Journal Ratings

	2003 LIB — 2003 CONS	2004 LIB — 2004 CONS
Economic	69% — 31%	68% — 32%
Social	70% — 29%	78% — 19%
Foreign	69% — 30%	68% — 30%

Key Votes of the 108th Congress

1. Drilling in ANWR	N	5. DC School Vouchers	N	9. Ban Same-Sex Marriage	N
2. Approve Bush Tax Cuts	N	6. Ban Human Cloning	N	10. Fund Iraq War	Y
3. Medicare/Rx Bill	N	7. Restrict Gun Liability	N	11. Bar Cuba Embargo Funds	N
4. Bar Overtime Pay Regs.	Y	8. Ban Partial-Birth Abortion	N	12. Intelligence Reorg.	N

Election Results

2004 general	Shelley Berkley (D)	133,569	(66%)	($1,248,297)
	Russ Mickelson (R)	63,005	(31%)	($17,662)
	Other	5,862	(3%)	
2004 primary	Shelley Berkley (D)	27,765	(83%)	
	Ann Reynolds (D)	3,208	(10%)	
	Brian Kral (D)	2,412	(7%)	
2002 general	Shelley Berkley (D)	64,312	(54%)	($1,717,220)
	Lynette Boggs McDonald (R)	51,148	(43%)	($983,110)
	Other	4,254	(4%)	

Prior Winning Percentages: 2000 (52%); 1998 (49%)

The People		Race/Ethnic Origin	Ancestry	
Area size:	177 sq. mi.	51.5% White	German: 8.8%	Irish: 7.1%
Urban population:	99.9%	11.9% Black	English: 5.9%	
Rural population:	0.1%	4.6% Asian	**2004 Presidential Vote**	
Pop. 2000:	666,088	0.6% Native Am.	Kerry (D) 121,453	(57%)
Median income:	$39,480	0.4% Hawaiian	Bush (R) 89,800	(41%)
Poverty status:	13.9%	2.6% Two+ races	Other 3,457	(2%)
Military veterans:	14.4%	0.1% Other	**2000 Presidential Vote**	
		28.2% Hispanic Origin	Gore (D) 87,345	(56%)
			Bush (R) 63,163	(41%)
			Other 4,801	(3%)
			Cook Partisan Voting Index: D + 9	

Occupation	Blue collar: 23.0%	White collar: 47.8%	Gray collar: 29.2%

Las Vegas, a city whose garishness and sheer improbability is literally awesome, had a fittingly colorful beginning. It began as a Paiute Indian settlement that in the late 1700s served as a watering stop for Spanish priests making the 1,200-mile trek between New Mexico and California. By the 1800s, the Old Spanish Trail, as it came to be known, was used by horse and mule smugglers, by white explorers like John Fremont and by Mormon emigrants heading west. Las Vegas was still a small crossroads when Nevada, its mining industry a shambles, legalized gambling in the 1930s. The *WPA Guide* to Nevada, published in 1940, when the city had 10,000 people, describes a prim Las Vegas: "Relatively little emphasis is placed on the gambling clubs and divorce facilities—though they are attractions to many visitors—and much effort is being made to build up cultural attractions. No cheap and easily parodied slogans have been adopted to publicize the city, no attempt has been made to introduce pseudo-romantic architectural themes, or to give an artificial glamour or gaiety."

All that changed big-time after World War II, when gangster Bugsy Siegel built the Flamingo hotel on what became The Strip south of the city limits. Pseudo-romantic architectural themes became the order of the day (you find flamingoes in the waters of Florida, not in the deserts of Nevada) and one casino followed another. Organized crime provided much of the money and muscle for Las Vegas, and investment capital came from Teamsters pension funds. That changed in the late 1960s, when the eccentric billionaire Howard Hughes moved into the Desert Inn, bought most of the casinos and hired Mormons to run them. Then Hughes abruptly left town, most of his hotels eventually were torn down, and other operators built casinos like Caesars Palace and Circus Circus, the Mirage and Excalibur, the lavish Bellagio and Venetian. In the 1970s, the casinos were the haven of flashy high rollers, of Frank Sinatra and girl shows. Since the 1990s, diversification has been the buzz. Las Vegas produced more family-oriented entertainment, shopping, and even high art, with the Bellagio's museum-quality art collection on view, and Las Vegas built the biggest convention center in the country. But recent promotions have sounded a naughtier theme, "What happens in Vegas stays in Vegas." The scent of the underworld has not entirely disappeared; the flashy Oscar Goldman, a former Mob lawyer who was hired for his first job by Arlen Specter in the Philadelphia district attorney's office, was elected mayor and actively promoted the city. After September 11, 15,000 casino workers were laid off in the downturn but Vegas recovered smartly and remains one of the great leisure destinations in the world. Since the 1960s, it has grown faster than any other metropolitan area in the nation. After a monorail that runs parallel to the strip opened in July 2004, the "monofail" closed in September for major repairs, and reopened for Christmas.

The 1st Congressional District of Nevada consists of the inner core of Las Vegas that visitors are most likely to see. They cross into it as soon as they drive their rental cars out of the lot at McCarran International Airport and remain in the 1st as they cruise down Las Vegas Boulevard. On the three-mile Strip you can find 8 of the world's 10 largest hotels, each with thousands of rooms. North of Sahara Avenue, Las Vegas Boulevard enters the city of Las Vegas, the older and less glamorous part of town, although the city has moved to renovate downtown. The 1st continues north for another dozen miles through the housing developments and scrubland that follow the U.S. 95 and Interstate 15 diagonals, to include the sizable Hispanic and black communities of North Las Vegas. The 1st is home to the University of Nevada-Las Vegas and includes the Clark County Government Center, a circular sandstone complex whose beautiful Indian-inspired architecture is a testament to the power of the gambling dollar. The population of the 1st in 2000 was 12% black and 28% Hispanic, with a high percentage of union members; more than 80,000 Jews live in the area, supporting 18 synagogues and a Kosher supermarket. Overall, this is a safely Democratic district.

The congresswoman from the 1st District is Shelley Berkley, a Democrat first elected in 1998. Berkley was born on the Lower East Side of New York, and moved to Las Vegas as a child. "I am not a politician who happens to be Jewish. I am a Jew who happens to be in politics." Her parents emigrated from eastern Europe before World War II, and her father worked at the Sands and rose to maitre d'; she waited tables and was a keno runner as she made her way through the UNLV, where she was student body president, and the University of San Diego law school. She chaired the Nevada Hotel and Motel Association, was government and legal affairs vice president at the Sands and in-house counsel at Southwest Gas. She was elected to one term in the state House. In 1990, she was appointed to the University of Nevada Board of Regents and then was elected to two terms.

After the 1996 election, she decided to run in the 1st District. Incumbent Republican John Ensign, reelected by only 50%–44% after spending $1.9 million, decided to run against Senator Harry Reid, and Berkley—brassy, direct, effusive—seemed headed for victory. Republicans lacked a serious candidate until filing day in May 1998; 15 minutes before the deadline, Judge Donald Chairez resigned his post and filed for the seat. Then in June came a bombshell. The *Las Vegas Review-Journal* reported on tapes of Berkley's May 1997 telephone conversations to a friend and texts of a memo she sent the Sands's owner Sheldon Adelson when he was seeking approvals for his Venetian megahotel. They showed her advising him to make campaign contributions to local judges to curry favor and to grant concessions to Clark County commissioners to get their votes for approval. Adelson fired Berkley. She quickly apologized; the Clark County district attorney saw no cause for prosecution. But Chairez made his slogan, "Fairness, not favors!" With strong support from the gaming industry, Berkley outspent Chairez by $1.2 million to $554,000. She won narrowly, 49%–46%.

In the House, Berkley's voting record has been moderate. She keeps a close watch on the interests of the gaming industry. She led opposition in the House to a proposal by the National Collegiate Athletic Association to bar Nevada casinos from accepting bets on college sports. With the state's bipartisan delegation, she fought the plan to store nuclear waste at Yucca Mountain. Berkley forcefully backed George W. Bush on the use of force in Iraq, but later in July 2004 said that she was misled by phony intelligence and called for Defense Secretary Donald Rumsfeld's resignation. She fought for homeland security money for Las Vegas as a terrorist target.

Berkley has had tough re-election campaigns. In 2000, state Senator Jon Porter revived the 1998 controversy by attacking her for her conversations and notes to Adelson. Both candidates spent heavily, with Porter helped by pharmaceutical firms. Berkley won 52%–44%; in 2002 Porter ran and won in the new 3d District. That year Republicans nominated Las Vegas Councilwoman Lynette Boggs-McDonald, a former Miss Oregon and former Democrat, who hoped to become the first Republican black woman elected to the House. Boggs-McDonald was well-funded and had strong support from anti-abortion groups; she attacked Berkley for voting for spending bills that included money for the Yucca Mountain repository. But redistricting had removed many suburban precincts, and Berkley won 54%–43%. She was reelected easily in 2004.

SECOND DISTRICT

Rep. Jim Gibbons (R)

Elected 1996, 5th term; b. Dec. 16, 1944, Sparks; home, Reno; U. of NV, B.S. 1967, M.S. 1973; Southwestern U., J.D. 1979; Mormon; married (Dawn).

Military Career: Air Force, 1967–71 (Vietnam), NV Air Natl. Guard, 1975–96 (Persian Gulf).

Elected Office: NV Assembly, 1988–94.

Professional Career: Pilot, Western Airlines, 1979–87, Delta Airlines, 1987–96.

DC Office: 100 CHOB, 20515, 202-225-6155; Fax: 202-225-5679; Web site: www.house.gov/gibbons.

District Offices: Elko, 775-777-7920; Las Vegas, 702-255-1651; Reno, 775-686-5760.

Committees: *Armed Services* (13th of 34 R): Tactical Air & Land Forces; Terrorism, Unconventional Threats & Capabilities. *Homeland Security* (11th of 19 R): Intelligence, Information Sharing & Terrorism Risk Assessment; Prevention of Nuclear & Biological Attack. *Resources* (13th of 27 R): Energy & Mineral Resources (Chmn.).

Group Ratings

	ADA	ACLU	AFS	LCV	ITIC	NTU	COC	ACU	NTLC	CHC
2004	10	5	0	0	89	77	95	96	94	90
2003	5	—	0	5	—	67	97	84	—	—

National Journal Ratings

	2003 LIB — 2003 CONS		2004 LIB — 2004 CONS	
Economic	17%	— 81%	31%	— 69%
Social	30%	— 65%	27%	— 72%
Foreign	0%	— 89%	10%	— 86%

Key Votes of the 108th Congress

1. Drilling in ANWR	Y	5. DC School Vouchers	Y	9. Ban Same-Sex Marriage	N
2. Approve Bush Tax Cuts	Y	6. Ban Human Cloning	Y	10. Fund Iraq War	Y
3. Medicare/Rx Bill	Y	7. Restrict Gun Liability	Y	11. Bar Cuba Embargo Funds	N
4. Bar Overtime Pay Regs.	N	8. Ban Partial-Birth Abortion	Y	12. Intelligence Reorg.	Y

Election Results

2004 general	Jim Gibbons (R)	195,466	(67%)	($1,171,994)
	Angie Cochran (D)	79,978	(27%)	
	Janine Hansen (IAP)	10,638	(4%)	
	Other	4,997	(2%)	
2004 primary	Jim Gibbons (R)	unopposed		
2002 general	Jim Gibbons (R)	149,574	(74%)	($624,322)
	Travis Souza (D)	40,189	(20%)	($13,376)
	Janine Hansen (IAP)	7,240	(4%)	
	Other	4,197	(2%)	

Prior Winning Percentages: 2000 (65%); 1998 (81%); 1996 (59%)

The People		Race/Ethnic Origin	Ancestry	
Area size:	105,635 sq. mi.	74.8% White	German: 12.8%	Irish: 9.7%
Urban population:	78.5%	2.4% Black	English: 9.6%	
Rural population:	21.5%	2.8% Asian	**2004 Presidential Vote**	
Pop. 2000:	666,087	2.1% Native Am.	Bush (R) 172,422	(57%)
Median income:	$43,879	0.3% Hawaiian	Kerry (D) 123,490	(41%)
Poverty status:	10.1%	2.1% Two+ races	Other 5,641	(2%)
Military veterans:	17.1%	0.1% Other	**2000 Presidential Vote**	
		15.3% Hispanic Origin	Bush (R) 134,540	(57%)
			Gore (D) 87,705	(37%)
			Other 12,493	(5%)
			Cook Partisan Voting Index: R + 8	

Occupation	Blue collar: 24.3%	White collar: 54.9%	Gray collar: 20.9%

Outside of metro Las Vegas, huge, empty, and mountainous Nevada has only one sizable population cluster, located much further north near the border with California—the casino cities of Reno and Sparks; the small capital of Carson City; the restored Comstock Lode boomtown of Virginia City and the resort areas that surround (and endanger) the deep, impossibly blue waters of Lake Tahoe. Reno is so remote from Las Vegas that the only practical way to get there is by air; it takes more than nine hours to drive, eight of which are on two-lane highways that pass through just a handful of towns, none bigger than 7,000 people. Ghost towns that once bustled with miners dot the parched, sandswept deserts of Nevada; in some places, these lands remain distinctly rutted from the wagon trains that crossed them more than 100 years ago. Today these towns survive on mining, ranching and in some cases, servicing the human sins of greed and lust (it is in the small counties that you find Nevada's legal brothels). Immigrant Basque shepherds once tended their flocks in remote portions of northern Nevada and made carvings on aspen trees to pass the time; today, Basque festivals, social clubs and restaurants can be found in Winnemucca, Ely and Elko, while Reno is home to the national sheepherder's monument and the nation's only Basque Studies Department, at the University of Nevada-Reno.

The military has vast holdings in the Nevada interior: the Fallon Naval Air Station, home to the Navy Fighter Weapons ("Top Gun") School; the 3.1 million-acre Nellis Air Force Gunnery

Range; and the Energy Department's Nevada Test Site, where more than 800 underground tests of nuclear weapons were held, as well as 100 above-ground tests, all before July 1962. These explosions have left the Rhode Island-sized facility pockmarked with unstable "subsidence craters" as far as they eye can see. Many places in Nevada are dependent on other federal government programs: the Newlands Irrigation Project near Fallon was among the first projects of its kind, and Nevada's gold mining operations, booming since 2000, do not have to pay royalties to the federal government thanks to the Mining Act of 1872. Some 87% of the land in Nevada is owned by the federal government—a constant source of tension with local officials, ranchers, loggers and miners, whose pursuits, frequently solitary and often ornery, shaped Nevada's culture from its earliest days. On the desolate frontier, speculation runs wild: Until recently, Art Bell broadcast his popular radio show about the paranormal, aliens and other unexplained phenomena from tiny Pahrump, while the government's top-secret aviation experiments at places like Area 51 on the Nellis Gunnery Range have stoked UFO lore to the point that adjoining Route 375 was rededicated as the Extraterrestrial Highway in 1996. Anti-establishment views also flourish here in more mainstream ways. Nevada residents have long opposed a nuclear waste repository 1,000 feet beneath Yucca Mountain, 90 miles northwest of Las Vegas. Congress finally approved the project in 2002, with a scheduled opening of 2012, but stubborn opponents continued their battle.

The 2d Congressional District of Nevada takes in all of this and the vast majority of Nevada's land. Excluding single-member states, this is the largest congressional district in the nation. After the 2000 Census results came in, two districts were created entirely within Clark County, which had 69% of the state's population; the 2d consisted of all the other counties, plus small slices of Clark County. About one-half of the 2d's population is in Washoe County, which contains Reno and Sparks. Half a century ago, Reno was Nevada's largest city ("the Biggest Little City in the World," reads the neon sign across downtown Virginia Street). Local features include the National Automobile Museum and the National Bowling Stadium. It has grown vastly, but vastly less than Las Vegas, and is now overshadowed by it, and has become the state's third-largest city behind Henderson; its casinos were hit hard by Indian casinos in California. Its growth has been matched and more by growth around Lake Tahoe just to the west. People here are from all over: the Tahoe communities of Stateline, Zephyr Cove and Incline Village were three of the top eight American cities with the smallest percentage of residents born in the state. Historically, Reno has been Republican and Las Vegas Democratic. In the 1990s, when the federal government was widely viewed as unfriendly to mining, grazing and timber interests, the Cow Counties, as the counties outside Reno and Las Vegas are called, became even more Republican. All that has made the 2d District heavily Republican.

The congressman from the 2d District is Jim Gibbons, a Republican first elected in 1996. Gibbons grew up in Sparks, next door to Reno, went to the University of Nevada and served in the Air Force in Vietnam. He went to law school and has practiced law, but he also was a mining geologist, a hydrologist, a pilot for Delta and Western Airlines and vice commander of the Nevada Air National Guard. In 1988 he was elected to the Assembly; in 1990 he was called up to active duty in the Gulf War. While he was flying unarmed air reconnaissance missions of enemy targets in Kuwait, his wife took his place in the legislature. After his celebrated return, he proposed a ballot initiative to require a two-thirds supermajority to raise any state tax; it passed with more than 70% of the votes in 1994; this was suspended in July 2003 when the state Supreme Court required the legislature to pass Governor Kenny Guinn's tax increase by majority vote. In 1994, Gibbons ran for governor. He beat Secretary of State Cheryl Lau 52%–32% in the primary, but lost the general to Democratic incumbent Bob Miller, 53%–41%. In 1996, after Congresswoman Barbara Vucanovich retired, Gibbons ran in the 2d District. He had serious competition in the primary from Lau and Patty Cafferata, a former state treasurer (and Vucanovich's daughter). Gibbons carried the Reno area and Las Vegas suburbs to win with 42%, to 24% each for Lau and Cafferata. Gibbons won the general, 59%–35%.

Gibbons opposes federal intrusion on local rights. George W. Bush signed his bill to create the Sloan Canyon National Conservation Area south of Henderson and broaden local input in federal land policies. His independence often has left him voting against Republican dogma and placed him toward the center of the House on cultural issues. He strongly opposed the nuclear repository at Yucca Mountain and the proposed temporary storage at the Nevada Test Site. He bucked his party leadership by opposing normal trade relations with China, but he voted for trade promotion authority. He strongly backed the war in Iraq, but voiced reservations about the overhaul of intelligence agencies in 2004. "The worst thing we can do is rush headlong into this and stuff it into one big ugly bill." His independence was a factor when Speaker Dennis Hastert bypassed the disappointed Gibbons and selected Pete Hoekstra as Intelligence Committee chairman in August 2004.

Gibbons has been reelected easily. After the 2002 election, White House political strategist Karl Rove, like Gibbons a graduate of Sparks High School, tried to talk him into running against Senator Harry Reid in 2004. Gibbons decided against it, partly because he hoped to chair Intelligence. After he was passed over for that, he launched a campaign to replace term-limited Guinn as governor in 2006, and appeared to be the frontrunner. More controversial was the plan of his wife Dawn to replace her husband in Washington, raising objections that she would not be able to fulfill her duties as First Lady. Secretary of State Dean Heller also said that he would run for the seat and state Representative Sharron Angle was considering running. In November 2004, Gibbons sponsored an initiative to force funding of the education budget before any other part of Nevada government.

THIRD DISTRICT

Rep. Jon Porter (R)

Elected 2002, 2d term; b. May 16, 1955, Ft. Dodge, IA; home, Henderson; Attended Briar Cliff College, 1974–78.; Catholic; married (Laurie).

Elected Office: Boulder City Cncl., 1983–93; Boulder City Mayor, 1987–91; NV Senate, 1994–2002.

Professional Career: Indep. contractor, Farmers Insurance Group Corp., 1982–2000.

DC Office: 218 CHOB, 20515, 202-225-3252; Fax: 202-225-2185; Web site: www.house.gov/porter/.

District Office: Henderson, 702-387-4941.

Committees: *Education & the Workforce* (15th of 27 R): 21st Century Competitiveness; Select Education (Vice Chmn.). *Government Reform* (17th of 23 R): Federal Workforce & Agency Organization (Chmn.); National Security, Emerging Threats & International Relations. *Transportation & Infrastructure* (29th of 41 R): Aviation; Highways, Transit & Pipelines; Railroads.

Group Ratings

	ADA	ACLU	AFS	LCV	ITIC	NTU	COC	ACU	NTLC	CHC
2004	15	20	13	9	90	51	100	76	68	83
2003	5	—	0	10	—	61	100	92	—	—

National Journal Ratings

	2003 LIB	—	2003 CONS		2004 LIB	—	2004 CONS
Economic	9%	—	84%		31%	—	68%
Social	30%	—	65%		53%	—	47%
Foreign	23%	—	71%		34%	—	63%

Key Votes of the 108th Congress

1. Drilling in ANWR	Y	5. DC School Vouchers	Y	9. Ban Same-Sex Marriage	Y
2. Approve Bush Tax Cuts	Y	6. Ban Human Cloning	Y	10. Fund Iraq War	Y
3. Medicare/Rx Bill	Y	7. Restrict Gun Liability	Y	11. Bar Cuba Embargo Funds	N
4. Bar Overtime Pay Regs.	N	8. Ban Partial-Birth Abortion	Y	12. Intelligence Reorg.	Y

Election Results

2004 general	Jon Porter (R)	162,240 (54%)	($2,653,136)
	Tom Gallagher (D)	120,365 (40%)	($2,372,518)
	Other	15,313 (5%)	
2004 primary	Jon Porter (R)	unopposed	
2002 general	Jon Porter (R)	100,378 (56%)	($1,916,277)
	Dario Herrera (D)	66,659 (37%)	($1,809,383)
	Pete O'Neil (I)	6,842 (4%)	($11,560)
	Other	5,115 (3%)	

The People

Area size:	4,749 sq. mi.
Urban population:	96.3%
Rural population:	3.7%
Pop. 2000:	666,082
Median income:	$50,749
Poverty status:	7.5%
Military veterans:	16.4%

Race/Ethnic Origin

69.3% White
5.5% Black
5.9% Asian
0.5% Native Am.
0.4% Hawaiian
2.7% Two+ races
0.1% Other
15.6% Hispanic Origin

Ancestry

German: 11.1%   Irish: 8.7%
English: 7.7%

2004 Presidential Vote
Bush (R) 156,335 (50%)
Kerry (D) 152,150 (49%)
Other 4,608 (1%)

2000 Presidential Vote
Gore (D) 104,772 (49%)
Bush (R) 103,720 (48%)
Other 6,119 (3%)

Cook Partisan Voting Index: D + 1

Occupation   Blue collar: 18.4%   White collar: 56.8%   Gray collar: 24.8%

Las Vegas means The Meadows, and was the name of a place on the Old Spanish Trail from Santa Fe to California. In the early 20th century it was one of the terminuses of the Las Vegas & Tonopah Railroad, a link to Nevada's silver mines. Even at the end of the 1930s, when gambling was legalized in Nevada, Las Vegas was still a town of less than 10,000. Then came decades of amazing growth, as Las Vegas became America's greatest center of gambling and one of its greatest centers of entertainment; it grew to a metropolitan area of 1.6 million people by 2000. For the past 15 years, Las Vegas has been the fastest-growing metropolitan area in America—up 123% from 1990 to 2004—and Clark County in 2004 was the nation's 17th largest county. Although the real estate market remained hot, this is still frontier country, one of the few places in the nation with more men than women. Las Vegas has spread from the few blocks around Fremont Street that it occupied in the 1930s all across the bleak desert, in every direction. It is an exuberant, undisciplined and chaotic American city, within its pattern of grid-street mile roads, all manner of curved-street subdivisions and gated communities, an America uncontrolled by traditional elites.

The 3d Congressional District is a Y-shaped segment of Nevada's Clark County made up of most of the suburbs of Las Vegas. It includes the south end of the Las Vegas Strip and McCarran International Airport and spreads west, northeast and south. It includes active retiree communities, blue-collar towns such as Blue Diamond that still have a rural flavor and a variety of planned (and often gated) areas like Summerlin that cater to young families drawn by the job opportunities. Southeast of Las Vegas, the district takes in two additional population hubs: Henderson, the fastest-growing city in the United States in the 1990s, and Boulder City, originally built for federal workers at Hoover Dam. (Under an old agreement with the federal government, Boulder City is the only place in Nevada where gambling is prohibited). The 3d includes the Nevada halves of Lake Mead and Lake Mohave, on the Arizona border, and the state's southernmost tip including Searchlight (hometown of Senator Harry Reid) and Laughlin, right across the Colorado River from Bullhead City, Arizona. The 3d District is a creature of redistricting, drawn after the 2000 Census so that the new district would have almost a precisely equal number of registered Democrats and registered Republicans. Clark County historically was the most Democratic part of Nevada, but the newcomers attracted to the state in the 1990s have tilted toward Republicans; the result is this closely divided district, with small pluralities for Al Gore in 2000 and George W. Bush in 2004.

The congressman from the 3d District is Jon Porter, a Republican first elected in 2002. He grew up in Humboldt, Iowa, and attended Briar Cliff College in Sioux City. After moving to Nevada, he managed an office with more than 40 agents for the Farmers Insurance Group. He was elected mayor of Boulder City in 1987 and in 1994 was elected to the state Senate, where he earned a reputation as a consensus-building moderate. In 2000 he ran against Democrat Shelley Berkley in the 1st District, attacking her controversial memo to a hotel owner who was seeking approvals for another hotel; he lost 52%–44%.

When the new district lines were adopted, Porter ran in the new 3d District. National Democrats were enthusiastic about their political *wunderkind* candidate, 28-year-old Clark County Commissioner Dario Herrera, who seemed to have the political skills and savvy that could make him in time a major statewide politician.

But Herrera turned out to have serious problems. He spent much of the campaign defending himself against a spate of charges over alleged ethics violations—such as his winning a no-bid consulting deal and taking a questionable loan. In turn, he sought to discredit Porter on the grounds that as an insurance agent he was furthering his own interests in restricting recoveries for medical malpractice, a raging issue in Nevada. Though both candidates strongly opposed shipping the nation's nuclear waste to the nearby Yucca Mountain site, Herrera attacked Porter for accepting contributions from House Republicans who supported the Nevada nuclear waste repository. Herrera also criticized Porter for supporting "privatization" of Social Security. Porter had supported individual investment accounts in 2000, but retreated from that position and said that he would "always look at alternatives." It turned out to be no contest. Porter won 56%–37%, running far ahead of party lines—or perhaps it was Herrera running far behind party lines.

In the House, Porter carved out a voting record near the center of House Republicans, and his votes on social issues were especially moderate. He proposed creation of a new undersecretary for local government and tourism in the Homeland Security Department; the House approved the proposal as part of its intelligence reorganization bill. He argued that his experience on tax issues and the underrepresentation of Western states should warrant a seat on the Ways and Means Committee, but he didn't get one. Instead he became chairman of the Government Reform Subcommittee on Federal Workforce and Agency Organization, where he promised to devote attention to oversight of Energy Department contracts for the Yucca Mountain project.

Even with the failure of Herrera, House Democrats held out hope for a serious challenger in 2004. They eventually found Tom Gallagher, a former top executive of Park Place Entertainment who spent $940,000 of his own money on the campaign; Democratic party sources gave another $750,000. Democrats were embarrassed by the disclosure that Gallagher had contributed $2,000 to the Bush campaign in 2003. Gallagher called the 2003 Medicare prescription drug bill a "boondoggle" for the pharmaceutical companies, and he criticized Porter for "getting along with Tom DeLay and the House Republican leadership." Shelley Berkley criticized Porter for voting for the energy bill, on the ground that its subsidies for the nuclear industry would expedite the Yucca Mountain repository; Porter said that the issues were separate and criticized Gallagher because the nuclear industry was a client of his former law firm. Gallagher suffered from political inexperience and lack of local familiarity, and he lost 54%–40%.

★ NEW HAMPSHIRE ★

New Hampshire, in an odd corner of the country, with 44 hundredths of 1% of the nation's population, with unusual public policies, becomes every four years the epicenter of the political universe, the site where the contest for the presidency of the most powerful nation in the history of the world is temporarily centered, where every vote is avidly sought and where members of the political press vie for access to candidates and for tables at the latest cycle's most fashionable bars and restaurants. New Hampshire has done much to change the political world—not just the United States, but the entire world: It gave a huge boost to Dwight Eisenhower's candidacy in 1952, it prompted the retirement of Lyndon Johnson in 1968, it sent on his way to power first Jimmy Carter in 1976, then Ronald Reagan in 1980 and George H. W. Bush in 1988. The lever by which this small state moves the world is New Hampshire's first-in-the-nation presidential primary, first seriously contested in 1952, then sanctioned as the first-in-the-nation primary by Democratic rules writers in the 1970s, and exploited by Republicans in the 1980s. And New Hampshire did all this when its public policies were atypical of the nation and its political terrain unusual if not eccentric. This is one of the few states that over the last half century has had more registered Republicans than Democrats, and of all the states it was for many years arguably the one with the most antipathy to taxes. Yet in the last dozen years, New Hampshire has changed. The last two presidents have both lost the New Hampshire primary. By giving Patrick Buchanan 37% of the vote in 1992 and 27% in 1996, New Hampshire gave the impression that Buchanan was a serious candidate, but he never ran as well elsewhere and has disappeared from Republican politics. But New Hampshire did play a key role in nominating Al Gore in 2000 and John Kerry in 2004. That year New Hampshire was the only state that had a big increase in turnout in the Democratic primary—an increase that was a harbinger of its performance in November, when it was the only state that switched from George W. Bush in 2000 to John Kerry in 2004. Is New Hampshire still a trendsetter, or has it become an eccentricity? The answer is not clear, though the weight of the evidence points toward the latter.

New Hampshire's distinctiveness started early. In a country that prides itself on its feistiness and freedom from outside direction, it has always been even feistier and less fettered by authority. Before the Revolutionary War, New Hampshire was almost an outlaw colony, its great fortunes made by poachers in the king's forests and smugglers avoiding taxes. It was the first colony with an independent government and was fighting the British before the Minutemen stood at Lexington and Concord. In this environment, 19th century entrepreneurs built textile mills along fast-flowing rivers; the Amoskeag Mills in Manchester, lining the Merrimack River for a mile, were once the largest cotton mills on the globe, employing 17,000 people and producing enough cloth every two months to put a band around the world. Around the mills grew a city of red brick dormitories and three-family frame houses filled with immigrants from Quebec, Ireland, Poland and Greece, set down amid dirt-roaded villages of flinty Yankee farmers and mechanics. New Hampshire held to its traditions of local government and little external control, and for years its refusal to join most other states and enact an income or sales tax, or to provide statewide guidance of schools and social services, seemed to doom it to continued backwardness.

Instead low taxes proved to be New Hampshire's fortune. Starting in the 1960s, New Hampshire has had the fastest growth in the Northeast, attracting businesses from Massachusetts and other high-tax states. It became a location of choice for entrepreneurs and high-tech innovators, attracting an increasing number of people skeptical of government programs. From 1965–2000, Massachusetts grew from 5.5 million to 6.3 million, up 15%; New Hampshire grew from 676,000 to 1,236,000, up 83%. The bedraggled New Hampshire of 50 years ago, of poor Yankee farmers and French Canadian mill hands, has largely disappeared, and in its place one of the nation's most prosperous economic communities has arisen. The low taxes that spurred New Hampshire's growth would probably have been raised in the late 1960s or early 1970s, as they were in so many states at the time, but for the far from gentle advocacy of the Manchester *Union Leader* and its owner William Loeb. The *Union Leader* insisted that governors and legislators "take the pledge" to vote for no sales or income tax and, from 1970 to 1998, almost all did, and the

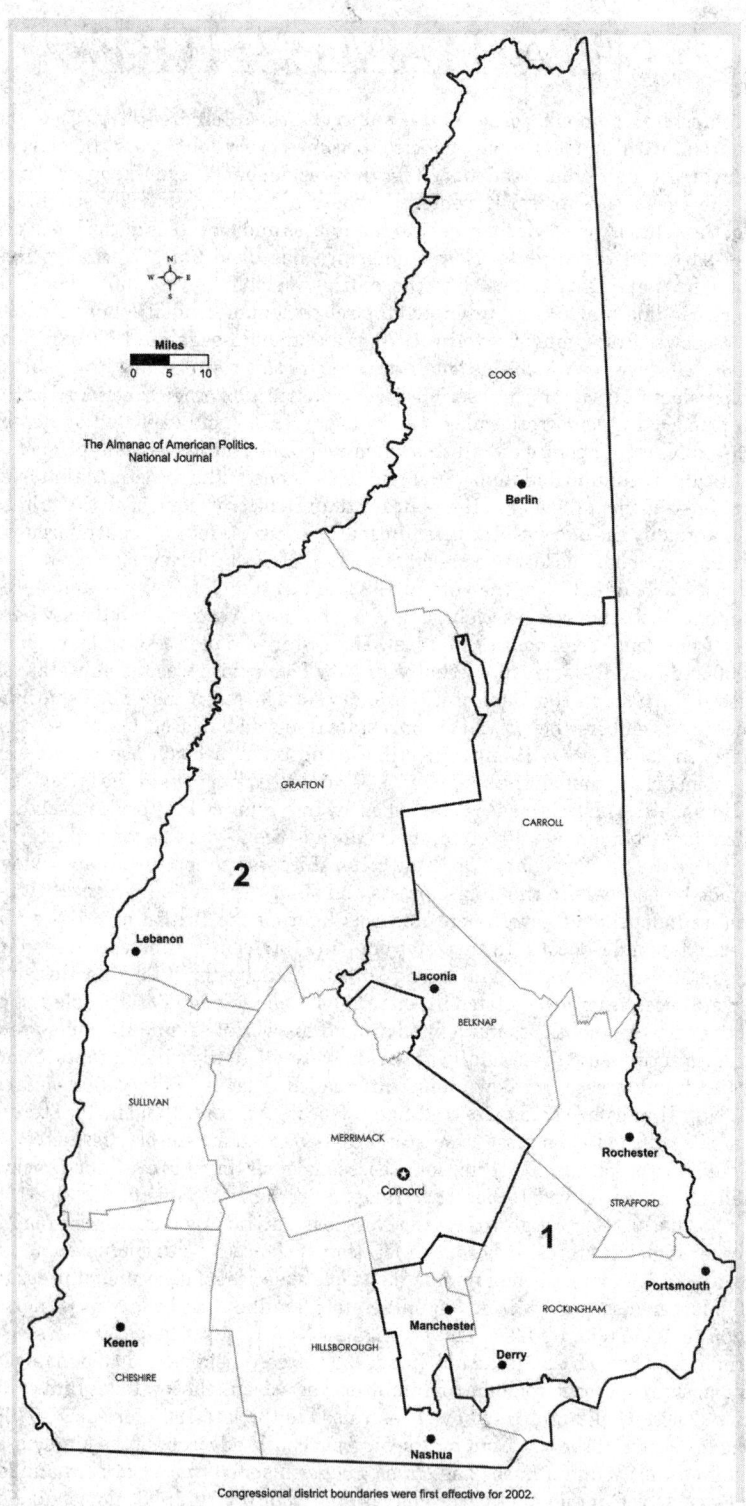

N
W—E
S

Miles
0   5   10

The Almanac of American Politics.
National Journal

COOS

Berlin

GRAFTON

CARROLL

2

Lebanon

Laconia

BELKNAP

SULLIVAN

MERRIMACK

Rochester

Concord

STRAFFORD

1

Portsmouth

Manchester

ROCKINGHAM

Keene

Derry

HILLSBOROUGH

CHESHIRE

Nashua

Congressional district boundaries were first effective for 2002.

two who didn't were defeated. That meant keeping education and welfare as local responsibilities and holding down spending. At the same time, New Hampshire boasted the highest SAT scores in the country and had the brainpower to participate fully in New England's high-tech boom. The old Amoskeag Mills were converted to offices, and once grimy Manchester is now a high-tech center.

This "Nouvelle Hampshire," to use *Washington Post* writer Henry Allen's term, has none of the architectural purity of Amoskeag. Its shopping centers and new subdivisions have a slap-dash, half-built look, as if there were no time for details in the hurry to build. But it is also a state that claims to have the highest proportion of high-tech jobs, 8% of the total, and the highest percentage of citizens with Internet access. It also is a big center for financial services, with giant mutual fund campuses stuck out in the woods. This New Hampshire has not been without its problems. The booming New Hampshire priced itself out of the growth market: Its giddily high real estate prices in the late 1980s kept out the new workers its businesses needed to continue expanding. The recession of the early 1990s was harsher here than anywhere else. Thousands of jobs disappeared; real estate prices crashed so that ordinary people lost not only short-term income but also long-term wealth. But by the mid-1990s growth returned again, and during the national recession of 2001–02 New Hampshire's unemployment stayed low, real estate prices were rising and incomes ranked seventh in the nation. It also has virtually no racial minorities; its population in 2000 was 1% black, 2% Hispanic and 1% Asian. This is not for lack of in-migration: in 2000, 50% of New Hampshire residents were born in another state and 4% in another country. Every few years, it seems, there is a new New Hampshire.

This helps to explain the state's political gyrations over the last dozen years. In 1992 in-migration had stopped and New Hampshire was reacting angrily to recession and rapidly declining house prices. It held George H.W. Bush to an unimpressive 53%–37% win over Patrick Buchanan in February and then voted for Bill Clinton over Bush in November. This turned out not to be a one-time fluke; like most states dominated by big metropolitan areas (most of New Hampshire gets Boston television) New Hampshire moved toward the Democrats in the 1990s, reassured by economic growth and comfortable with the Democrats' liberal stands on cultural issues. In 1996 New Hampshire voted 49%–39% for Clinton and elected Democrat Jeanne Shaheen as governor; Republican Senator Bob Smith came so close to losing that he was proclaimed the loser by the networks on election night.

But then New Hampshire's tax regime came under attack. The state Supreme Court in December 1997 ruled the state's school financing system unconstitutional because it leaves some districts with less taxable resources than others (the state provides only 10% of funding, far less than in the other 49 states) and gave the state an April 1999 deadline for coming up with a new system. The result was a statewide property tax—not anybody's first choice, but what the Democratic governor and Senate and the Republican House could agree on—and increases in business, cigarette and property sales taxes and a new tax on rental cars. In November 2002 voters had a clear choice: Republican Craig Benson took the pledge, while Democrat Mark Fernald supported an income tax. The verdict was clear: Benson won 59%–38%. But Benson fared less well in 2004, after quarreling with the Republican legislature and facing an opponent, businessman John Lynch, who did not favor a state income tax. Lynch won 51%–49%, even as Republicans maintained majorities in the legislature. A Democratic trend here was apparent in the presidential race as well: George W. Bush carried New Hampshire in 2000 by a 48%–47% margin and lost it in 2004 by 50%–49%. New Hampshire, a wintertime political battleground every four years, is also a fall political battleground every two.

The People		**Race/Ethnic Origin**			**Military veterans:** 139,038 (15.0%)	
Pop. 2004 (est):	1,299,500	1,175,252	95.1%	White	WWII: 18.4%	Korea: 13.6%
Pop. 2000:	1,235,786	8,354	0.7%	Black	Vietnam: 33.6%	Gulf War: 8.2%
Pop. 1990:	1,109,252	15,803	1.3%	Asian	**Most populous cities (2003):**	
Change 1990–2000:	Up 11.4%	2,698	0.2%	Native Am.	1. Manchester	108,871
% of U.S. total:	0.4%	330	0.0%	Hawaiian	2. Nashua	87,285
Pop. rank:	41st of 50	11,606	0.9%	Two+ races	3. Concord	41,823
Area size:	9,350 sq. mi.	1,254	0.1%	Other	4. Rochester	29,654
State Native:	43.3%	20,489	1.7%	Hisp. Origin	5. Dover	28,216
Non-citizen:	2.3%	**Ancestry**				
Language		Irish: 13.8%		English: 12.8%	Urban population: 59.2%	
English: 87.4%	Other Eur.: 9.0%	French: 10.4%		Fr.Canadian: 7.3%	Rural population: 40.8%	
Spanish: 2.3%		German: 6.1%				

Education		**Work Sector**		**General Court**	
H.S. Grad:	87.4%	Private: 79.4%	Govt: 12.8%	Senate	16 R 8 D
College Grad:	28.7%	Self: 7.6%	Family: 0.2%	House	253 R 147 D
Industry		Unemployment: 3.8%		Legislative Term Limits: No	
Agri: 0.9%	Con: 6.8%	**Household Income**		**Registered Voters**	
Fin: 6.3%	Info: 2.7%	<15k: 10.8%	15-35k: 22.4%	D: 228,395	(26.7%)
Mfg: 22.2%	Prof: 28.8%	35-50k: 17.2%	50-100k: 35.7%	R: 267,141	(31.2%)
Public: 3.8%	Trade: 17.3%	100-150k: 9.1%	>150k: 4.7%	O: 360,325	(42.1%)
Other: 11.2%		Median: $49,467			
Occupation		Poverty status: 6.5%			
Blue collar: 24.1%	White collar: 62.4%	**Home Value**			
Gray collar: 13.4%		<50k: 7.7%	50-100k: 24.8%	100-200k: 49.3%	200-300k: 12.2%
		300-500k: 4.5%	>500k: 1.4%	Median: $127,500	

Presidential politics Since 1920, New Hampshire has held the first-in-the-nation primary, and since 1952, when candidates' names were first put on the ballot, it has had extraordinary influence on the presidential selection process—a fact that will surely strike 23d century historians as bizarre. To be sure, there are arguments for having early contests in small states that provide a venue for "retail politics," in which candidates meet voters in person, listen and talk to them, exchange ideas and allow them to gauge their character. New Hampshire is small enough physically (unlike Iowa) that candidates can efficiently meet voters; everything except the lightly populated North Country is within an hour's drive of Manchester, and for all the state's abstract dislike of government, New Hampshire does an excellent job of keeping its roads clear of snow. New Hampshire's retail politics offers little-known candidates the ability to propel themselves into the national spotlight, though over the last 25 years none of those candidates has gone on to win his party's nomination. The last to do so were George McGovern and Jimmy Carter in the 1970s.

2004 Presidential Vote
Kerry (D)	340,511	(50%)
Bush (R)	331,237	(49%)
Nader (I)	4,479	(1%)
Other	1,435	(0%)

2004 Democratic Presidential Primary
Kerry (D)	84,377	(38%)
Dean (D)	57,761	(26%)
Clark (D)	27,314	(12%)
Edwards (D)	26,487	(12%)
Lieberman (D)	18,911	(9%)
Other	4,937	(2%)

2000 Presidential Vote
Bush (R)	273,559	(48%)
Gore (D)	266,348	(47%)
Nader (Green)	22,188	(4%)
Other	5,700	(1%)

In any case, New Hampshire retains its first-in-the-nation status not on its merits but because of threats. Democrats tried in the 1970s to confine primaries to a "window" period in which New Hampshire would have competition. But New Hampshire, with its outlaw tradition, insisted it would hold its primary before the window if necessary, confident that candidates and reporters would pay it heed even if its tiny delegation were threatened with not being seated at the national convention. Republicans made no such rules, but in 1996 let Iowa Governor Terry Branstad and New Hampshire Governor Steve Merrill, both Republicans, threaten voter retaliation against candidates who took part in caucuses or primaries held before their states' or even during the week afterwards. Democratic Governor Jeanne Shaheen continued the tradition in December 1998, demanding candidates take a pledge not to participate in such contests. In 2000 the Democrats imposed a *five-week* window of no contests after New Hampshire, which made Al Gore's 50%–46% victory here decisive; Bill Bradley's candidacy effectively died through inattention before he could reach Super Tuesday. Fortunately for George W. Bush, the *laissez faire* Republicans did not restrict other states as much as the rule-bound Democrats, and he could recover 19 days later in South Carolina. John McCain's smashing 49%–30% victory in New Hampshire knocked the wind out of the Bush campaign for about a week, but it turned out to be a template not for contests in other states, but for other contests in New England.

In 2003, the Michigan Democratic Party, led by Senator Carl Levin, attempted to challenge New Hampshire's first-in-the nation status by moving the 2004 Michigan Democratic caucuses to the same January date as New Hampshire's; after a noisy debate, Michigan backed down. But Levin got the national party to promise to convene another commission in 2005 to study the nomination process. New Hampshire Democrats predictably were threatening ostracism to any 2008 candidate who did not promise to campaign first in their state. This time New Hampshire may be in weaker position than before. Former Governor Jeanne Shaheen notes that if John Kerry had won, he would surely have kept New Hampshire first, out of gratitude; but he didn't, and other Democrats may not feel so warmly about the state. Neither, presumably, does Republican National Committee Chairman Ken Mehlman, formerly campaign manager for George W. Bush, who was beaten here in the 2000 primary and the 2004 general. New Hampshire may have to fight hard to stay first.

New Hampshire is still one of the few states with more registered Republicans than Democrats, but it effectively chose, or ratified Iowa caucusgoers' choice of, the Democratic nominee in both 2000 and 2004. Once upon a time New Hampshire's registered Democrats were mill workers in Manchester and other factory towns, ethnics who rejected the Yankee Republican consensus of the state. Those days are long gone. Democratic turnout is not concentrated in the two largest cities, Manchester and Nashua, which often vote Republican, but in the state capital of Concord and clusters of towns around universities—the area around Durham (the University of New Hampshire) and Dover in southeast New Hampshire, the area around Keene (Keene State College) in the southwest and the area around Hanover (Dartmouth University). Once upon a time the typical Democratic primary voter here was a textile mill worker; now she is more likely to be an assistant professor. In 2000 the upscale character of this electorate was already clear. Al Gore, with strong support from labor unions, had won a wide victory in Iowa. But in New Hampshire he was fortunate to squeeze out a 50%–46% victory against Bill Bradley, who ran to his right on some economic issues and to his left on cultural issues.

In the 2004 cycle, New Hampshire was the first venue in which Howard Dean raced to a lead, far ahead of New Hampshire's Massachusetts neighbor John Kerry. Some voters in the western part of the state were perhaps familiar with Dean's somewhat moderate record as governor of Vermont. But his real appeal—what kept volunteers buzzing at their computers in his crowded Manchester headquarters, earnest Democrats turning out at his public appearances and his poll numbers rising above 50% in a multicandidate field—came from his vitriolic denunciations of George W. Bush, especially on the war in Iraq. About half of Dean's support evaporated after his third-place showing in Iowa and his election night scream. But he had already set the tone of the campaign and stirred the enthusiasm of New Hampshire Democrats. Turnout was up a huge 42%, from 154,000 in 2000 to 219,000 in 2004. The mainstream media reported this as a huge outpouring of enthusiasm, as indeed it was, and continued to make similar comments on subsequent contests although, as it happened, none had a similar increase in Democratic turnout. Kerry argued, as he had in Iowa, that he was the Democrat best able to defeat Bush; New Hampshire gave him 38% of its votes, to 26% for Dean, 12.4% for Wesley Clark (who skipped Iowa), 12.1% for John Edwards (who had done much better in Iowa) and 9% for Joseph Lieberman (who skipped Iowa). In retrospect, New Hampshire nailed the nomination for Kerry: Lieberman soon dropped out and Dean did not long after; Clark was never able to make himself Kerry's chief rival; Edwards did, but never overtook him.

What do the New Hampshire primary electorates look like for 2008? The Democratic primary electorate seems likely to be leftish on cultural issues and not terrifically interested in economic issues. The larger Republican electorate seems likely to be moderate, perhaps even liberal on cultural issues, while conservative on economic issues; less fixated on tax cuts than in the 1970s and 1980s, more secular and with a much smaller segment of religious conservatives than Republican primary electorates in most other states.

Up through 1992 political reporters left New Hampshire the day after the primary and never returned in the fall; it was assumed that the state would go Republican in November. But Bill Clinton carried it twice, and in 2000 it was close again; Al Gore unaccountably visited the state just once in the general election campaign, but George W. Bush did, and carried it 48%–47%, with a popular vote margin of 7,211. In 2004 New Hampshire was a target state for both campaigns, and the enthusiasm evoked by the Dean campaign and transferred to Kerry in New Hampshire seems to have carried over into the fall: this was the only Bush 2000 state that went for Kerry. Again the margin was close, 50%–49%, with a popular vote margin of 9,274—without which it would not have mattered whether Bush carried Ohio. Interestingly Bush won majorities among both Protestants and Catholics—New Hampshire's old sectarian political divide was gone—but Kerry won 69% among those of no religion and 63% who never attended religious services, the latter comprising 24% of the electorate, outnumbering the 18% who attend services weekly in this relatively secular state. Total turnout was up 19% over 2000, not much more than the national average; Bush's popular vote total was up 21%, nearly his national average, but Kerry's was up 28% over Gore's, much more than his national average. The common myth about New Hampshire is that it has become more Democratic because of the people moving across the line from Massachusetts. The vote totals tell a different story. Bush carried Manchester and almost all the towns in Rockingham and Hillsborough Counties just over the Mass line, and he increased his percentage there from 2000 as well. People here are still voting against Taxachusetts. But Bush lost most of western New Hampshire and saw his percentage drop there, sometimes sharply, not just in college towns like Keene and Hanover, but in rural areas and mill towns; the same phenomenon was apparent around Concord (where the liberal *Concord Monitor* overshadows the conservative Manchester *Union Leader*) and around trendily restored Portsmouth. New Hampshire went Democratic not because it was becoming more like Massachusetts but because it was becoming more like Vermont.

Congressional districting

With only slight changes, New Hampshire's two congressional districts basically have had the same boundaries since 1881, neatly separating the Merrimack River mill towns of Manchester and Nashua, the state's largest cities. That was done originally to split the Catholic Democratic vote, but now both cities are high-tech Republican towns. If the split now gives Republicans an edge in both districts, it also gives Democrats a chance for upset victories in both. For 2002 the towns of Epsom and Pittsfield were moved from the 1st District to the 2d, an uncontroversial change which does not appreciably change the political balance in either district.

109th Congress Lineup
2 R
108th Congress Lineup
2 R

Governor

John Lynch (D)

Elected 2004, term expires Jan. 2007, 1st term; b. Nov. 25, 1952, Waltham, MA; home, Hopkinton; U of NH, B.A., 1974; Harvard U., M.B.A., 1979; Georgetown U., J.D., 1984; Catholic; married (Susan).

Professional Career: Ex. Dir., NH Dem. party, 1975–77; Dir. of Admissions, Harvard Bus. Schl., 1982–86; Partner, consulting firm, 1987–94; Pres. and CEO, Knoll Inc., 1994–2001, Pres., Lynch Group, 2001–04.

Office: State House Rm. 208, 107 N. Main St., Concord, 03301, 603-271-2121; Fax: 603-271-2130; Web site: www.state.nh.us/governor.

Election Results

2004 general	John Lynch (D)	339,925	(51%)
	Craig Benson (R)	325,614	(49%)
2004 primary	John Lynch (D)	43,798	(75%)
	Paul McEachern (D)	14,403	(25%)
2002 general	Craig Benson (R)	259,663	(59%)
	Mark Fernald (D)	169,277	(38%)
	Other	14,036	(3%)

John Lynch, a Democrat, was elected governor of New Hampshire in 2004 in his first run for political office. Lynch grew up in Waltham, Massachusetts, the fifth of six children; his father ran a local Boys Club and his mother was a schoolteacher. He graduated from the University of New Hampshire in 1974, got his MBA from Harvard Business School in 1979 and a law degree from Georgetown in 1984. He took an interest in politics in college, interned for Senator Tom McIntyre in 1975 and not long after became executive director of the Democratic state committee. He left state politics to attend business school and later became the school's admissions director; in 1994, he became president and CEO of Knoll, Inc., a Pennsylvania-based high-end office furniture maker. At Knoll, Lynch worked to transform a business with $50 million a year in losses into a streamlined enterprise with a profit of almost $240 million. All the while, he nurtured his New Hampshire connections. He commuted from Knoll's headquarters in East Greenville, Pennsylvania, to his home in Hopkinton and served as president of the University of New Hampshire alumni association. In the mid-1980s and 1990s he dabbled in state and local politics by working for the Merrimack County Democratic party, contributing to various campaigns and working to establish a New Hampshire chapter of the centrist Democratic Leadership Council. In 2001, he left Knoll and later opened his own management consulting firm on Elm Street in Manchester. In 2000 Governor Jeanne Shaheen appointed Lynch to the University System of New Hampshire's Board of Trustees, where he served as chairman from 2001 to 2004, when he resigned to run for governor.

Lynch was seeking to oust Craig Benson, a wealthy political outsider who won his first term in 2002 in the state's most expensive gubernatorial race ever. Benson, a high-tech entrepreneur, was one of three Republican former CEO's elected to New England governorships that year (Massachusetts' Mitt Romney and Rhode Island's Donald Carcieri were the others) and the only one with the advantage of a Republican-controlled legislature. But he had a tough time making the transition to the public sector. Benson preferred taking meetings at a chairless, waist-high desk designed in part to cut down on small talk; his brusque and heavy-handed style alienated legislators from both parties. In 2003, he vetoed a budget put together by the Republican majority, only to sign off on a budget two months later that was more expensive than the first, though it did give him authority to find $50 million more in budget savings. He broke with recent tradition by delivering his 2004 State of the State speech from the campus of Plymouth State University, rather than to a joint session in Representatives Hall at the State House.

Benson fared well in polls in his first year, as voters gave him high approval ratings for his hard-charging style and his call for a constitutional amendment to limit tax increases. One much-noted accomplishment seemed to epitomize his creative, businesslike approach: After getting stuck in a traffic jam caused by toll booths on Interstate 95, he moved to eliminate the $1 toll for southbound drivers at the Hampton toll plaza and doubled it for those heading north. But Benson's popularity began to fade after frequent missteps and controversies. Several of his appointees were forced to step down from office for ethical lapses; Benson and his state safety commissioner were accused of interfering with an investigation that eventually cleared Attorney General Peter Heed of allegations that he sexually harassed a woman. In October, the prosecutor cleared Benson and recommended that the safety commissioner be disciplined.

Lynch made the ethics issue a cornerstone of his campaign and promised in his campaign kickoff speech that he would "restore integrity, trust and a bipartisan spirit" to state government. He faced lawyer and former legislator Paul McEachern, a twice-unsuccessful gubernatorial nominee making his fourth run for governor, in the September primary. McEachern argued that he was the only real Democrat in the race and called for a low-rate income tax to address the state's chronic education funding problem. Lynch took the pledge not to support a sales or income tax and won 75%–25%.

The general election was dominated by two issues, taxes and ethics. Lynch highlighted his opposition to a sales or income tax but did back an increase in the cigarette tax; he said he would provide targeted aid to schools while phasing out the state property tax adopted in 1999. Benson hewed to a hard anti-tax position and insisted that Lynch's plan to repeal the statewide property tax would lead to a "back-door income tax." Lynch denied Benson's charges, insisting that existing revenues would enable him to pay for his spending priorities; he focused on the "culture of corruption" that he said marked the Benson administration and pointed out that Benson himself had been cited twice for having illegal landscaping in front of his beachfront home. "In two short years," he said, "Craig Benson and his administration have brought us scandal after scandal, like nothing we've seen in modern New Hampshire history."

The two candidates, both millionaires, largely self-financed their campaigns. Benson, after spending more than $9 million out of pocket in 2002, put up $3.3 million of his own money in 2004, out of a total of $4.1 million raised. Lynch raised $3 million, $2.1 million of it his own money. That was enough to keep him competitive through Election Day when he won 51%–49%. The governor's vote closely tracked presidential returns: John Kerry ran just 600 votes ahead of Lynch, winning the state by 50% to George W. Bush's 49%. Lynch and Kerry won the same six counties, both carrying western New Hampshire and Concord's Merrimack County and both losing in Manchester's Hillsborough County and Rockingham County. Benson became the first freshman governor in 78 years to be denied a second term; ever the outsider, he failed to give a concession speech or speak to campaign supporters on election night.

In Lynch's first act in office, he issued an executive order requiring everyone who works in the governor's office, regardless of title or pay grade, to file a financial disclosure form that details their sources of income, loans of $5,000 or more, the location of real estate other than homes worth $2,500 or more and businesses they or their spouses are involved in if the investment is 1% or more of the outstanding stock or securities issued by the business.

Senior Senator

Judd Gregg (R)

Elected 1992, seat up 2010, 3d term; b. Feb. 14, 1947, Nashua; home, Rye; Columbia U., A.B. 1969, Boston U., J.D. 1972, LL.M. 1975; Protestant; married (Kathleen).

Elected Office: NH Exec. Cncl., 1978–80; U.S. House of Reps., 1980–88; NH Gov., 1988–92.

Professional Career: Practicing atty., 1976–80.

DC Office: 393 RSOB, 20510, 202-224-3324; Fax: 202-224-4952; Web site: gregg.senate.gov.

State Offices: Berlin, 603-752-2604; Concord, 603-225-7115; Manchester, 603-622-7979; Portsmouth, 603-431-2171.

Committees: *Appropriations*: Commerce, Justice & Science; Defense; Homeland Security (Chmn.); Interior & Related Agencies; Labor, Health and Human Services, Education & Related Agencies; State, Foreign Operations & Related Programs. *Budget* (Chmn.). *Health, Education, Labor & Pensions*: Bioterrorism & Public Health Preparedness; Education & Early Childhood Development.

Group Ratings

	ADA	ACLU	AFS	LCV	ITIC	NTU	COC	ACU	NTLC	CHC
2004	15	12	0	17	83	83	88	88	93	100
2003	15	—	0	53	—	80	78	85	—	—

National Journal Ratings

	2003 LIB — 2003 CONS		2004 LIB — 2004 CONS	
Economic	47% —	52%	22% —	77%
Social	0% —	59%	41% —	58%
Foreign	0% —	78%	33% —	61%

Key Votes of the 108th Congress

1. Ban Drilling in ANWR	N	5. Energy Bill	N	9. Ban Same-Sex Marriage	Y
2. Approve Bush Tax Cuts	Y	6. Support Roe v. Wade	N	10. Ban Bunker-Buster Bomb	N
3. Medicare/Rx Bill	N	7. Ban Partial-Birth Abortion	Y	11. Fund Iraq War	Y
4. Bar Overtime Pay Regs.	N	8. Assault Weapons Ban	Y	12. Restrict Missile Defense	N

Election Results

2004 general	Judd Gregg (R)	435,846	(66%)	($1,897,466)
	Doris Haddock (D)	221,544	(34%)	($177,199)
2004 primary	Judd Gregg (R)	60,597	(92%)	
	Tom Alciere (R)	2,682	(4%)	
	Michael Tipa (R)	2,563	(4%)	
1998 general	Judd Gregg (R)	213,477	(68%)	($904,448)
	George Condodemetraky (D)	88,883	(28%)	($28,547)
	Other	12,596	(4%)	

Prior Winning Percentages: 1992 (48%); 1986 House (74%); 1984 House (76%); 1982 House (71%); 1980 House (64%)

Judd Gregg, a Republican, was first elected governor in 1988 and senator in 1992. He grew up in Nashua and was involved in politics early: in 1952, when he was 5, his father Hugh Gregg was elected governor. Hugh Gregg remained a power in presidential primary politics for many years and in 1988 provided crucial backing to George H.W. Bush; he died in September 2003. Judd Gregg was a student at Columbia during the student riots of 1968, but stayed true to New Hampshire Republicanism; he graduated from Boston University law school and returned to Nashua and practiced law. In 1978, at 31, he was elected to the Executive Council, which dates to the colonial era and approves state appointments and expenditures. In 1980 he was elected to the House, where he was an eager participant in the Reagan revolution. In 1988, he ran for governor and won handily; he was easily reelected in 1990.

In 1992, Gregg ran for the Senate when Warren Rudman retired, and in his taciturn way seemed sure he would win. But the New Hampshire economy had turned sour, and the race turned close. In the September primary he beat a construction company owner by only 50%–38%. In the general, he faced retired businessman John Rauh, who backed the line-item veto and balanced budget amendment and attacked Gregg for opposing abortion rights. He won by an unimpressive 48%–45% margin.

Gregg was chairman of the Health, Education, Labor and Pensions Committee for five months in 2001 and again from 2003 to 2005; he was the ranking minority member after Jim Jeffords left the Republican party in May 2001. In 2001 he was the lead Senate supporter of the Bush education bill. He worked with Edward Kennedy on the details; his amendment to allow private school choice in 10 cities was rejected in June 2002 by a 58–41 vote. In November 2001 he and Kennedy and House members John Boehner and George Miller reached a final compromise; it left in place the Bush proposal for annual testing in math and reading from grades three to eight and flexibility for states and school districts; it included allowing disadvantaged students to use federal funds for private tutoring and summer school. Gregg has opposed mandatory funding of special education, but has worked to increase discretionary funding up toward the 40% federal commitment. He points out that federal special education funding increased from $2.4 billion in 1996 to $10.5 billion in 2002. In January 2003 he moved to add $1.5 billion to the $2 billion in increases supported by the Bush administration in 2001 and 2002. In January 2003 he also pushed through an amendment increasing education spending by $5 billion and reducing other discretionary non-military spending by a corresponding amount.

Gregg worked on consensus health legislation with Democrats and other Republicans—a law requiring the FDA to test drugs' effects on children, a bill limiting pharmaceutical companies to one 30-month stay of an application to sell a generic drug. He got the Senate to approve FDA regulation of tobacco together with a buyout of tobacco quotas in the 2004 corporate tax bill, but the former was taken out in conference committee; Gregg voted against the overall bill on the grounds it cost too much. He has put together drug reimportation legislation which would allow imports first from Canada and later from the European Union, with licensing of Internet pharmacies; some Democrats opposed the bill as too restrictive. He got the Senate to pass speedily a bill cutting excess subsidies to college loan lenders, saving $270 million. He sponsored the Biodefense Act of 2005 and a bill setting down strict criteria for plaintiffs seeking punitive damages from health care providers or medical product manufacturers.

In November 2004 Gregg decided to leave the chairmanship of the HELP Committee to become chairman of the Budget Committee. He promised "very strong enforcement measures" and sought to "put the brakes on the growth of entitlements." He successfully supported reining in Medicaid spending and, as a former governor, sought to give the states more flexibility in the program. He sought to hold the cost of the Medicare prescription drug bill to the $400 billion over 10 years that was forecast when it was passed. Gregg passed up a chance to get on the Finance Committee to remain on Appropriations, where he has been somewhat more tightfisted than many of his colleagues. He has procured federal money to buy land to preserve Lake Tarleton, expand the Hubbard Brook Experimental Forest, and to purchase a conservation easement in the Ossipee Mountains. In 2003 he got $11.6 million to help the state government purchase easement rights on International Paper Company land in northern New Hampshire. On other environmental issues he has backed reform of the 1872 Mining Act and higher grazing fees. He was one of six Republicans to vote in January 2003 to delay the Bush administration's New Source Review rules. In 2005, when subcommittee jurisdictions were changed, he moved from chairing the Commerce-State-Justice Subcommittee to the new Homeland Security Subcommittee.

In 2003 Gregg and his New Hampshire colleague John Sununu voted against the energy bill because it banned the state of New Hampshire's lawsuit against the manufacturers of the fuel additive MTBE, which was found to be polluting. He called the energy bill "a gratuitous attack on the Northeast" and an "obscene attack on the American taxpayer." They effectively blocked the energy bill from passing.

Gregg has maintained a network of supporters in New Hampshire, but the Gregg organization that was so effective for George H.W. Bush in 1988 was unable to deliver a victory for George W. Bush in the 2000 primary. Gregg played Al Gore in candidate Bush's debate preparation;

whether he anticipated Gore's loud sighs in the first debate is not clear. Gregg's standing in New Hampshire seems strong. In 1998 he was opposed by a low-spending Democrat who called him a "draft dodger" and a "wimp" and who said at one rally that he would like to get Gregg between a dog and a fire hydrant. Gregg won 68%–28%. In 2003 he seemed to face opposition in the primary from former state Representative Tom Alciere and in the general election from state Senator Burt Cohen. But Alcicre, who had posted messages on the Internet condoning the killing of police officers, did not run. Cohen, who supported a state income tax in the legislature, had a campaign up and running for 18 months. But just before the filing date he discovered that his campaign manager and much of his campaign treasury was missing and he took himself out of the state. New Hampshire Democrats, eager for a nominee, found Doris "Granny D" Haddock, a 94-year-old longtime leftish activist who in 2000 walked 3,225 miles across America to support campaign finance regulation. Granite Staters may have admired her pluck, but not very many voted for her; Gregg won 66%–34% and became the first New Hampshire senator elected to a third term since Norris Cotton in 1968. A couple of footnotes about the flinty Yankees of the Gregg family. Hugh Gregg established, at least to the satisfaction of one encyclopedia, that the Republican party was founded not in Ripon, Wisconsin, or in Jackson, Michigan, in 1854, but at Blake's Hotel in Exeter, New Hampshire, on October 21, 1853. (But Exeter voted for John Kerry in 2004.) And Senator Gregg's wife Kathleen Gregg in October 2003 was accosted in their house by thieves armed with a knife; she coolly let them drive her to a local bank, cashed a check in a large amount and then escaped out a side door. They were apprehended two days later in New Jersey.

Junior Senator

John Sununu (R)

Elected 2002, seat up 2008, 1st term; b. Sept. 10, 1964, Boston, MA; home, Bedford; M.I.T., B.S. 1986, M.S. 1987, Harvard U., M.B.A. 1991; Catholic; married (Kitty).

Elected Office: U.S. House of Reps., 1996–2002.

Professional Career: Design Engineer, Remec Inc., 1987–89; Mgr. & Operations Specialist, Pittiglio, Rabin, Todd & McGrath, 1990–92; C.F.O. & Dir. of Operations, Teletrol Systems Inc., 1993–95; Consultant, JHS Associates, 1995–96.

DC Office: 111 RSOB, 20510, 202-224-2841; Fax: 202-228-4131; Web site: sununu.senate.gov.

State Offices: Berlin, 603-752-6074; Claremont, 603-542-6582; Manchester, 603-647-7500; Portsmouth, 603-430-9560.

Committees: *Banking, Housing & Urban Affairs*: Financial Institutions; International Trade & Finance; Securities & Investment. *Commerce, Science & Transportation*: Aviation; Fisheries & the Coast Guard; National Ocean Policy Study (Chmn.); Science & Space; Surface Transportation & Merchant Marine; Technology, Innovation & Competitiveness; Trade, Tourism & Economic Development. *Foreign Relations*: African Affairs; International Operations & Terrorism (Chmn.); Near Eastern & South Asian Affairs; Western Hemisphere, Peace Corps & Narcotics Affairs. *Joint Economic Committee*.

Group Ratings

	ADA	ACLU	AFS	LCV	ITIC	NTU	COC	ACU	NTLC	CHC
2004	10	38	0	17	91	82	93	100	95	100
2003	15	—	0	42	—	85	83	95	—	—

National Journal Ratings

	2003 LIB	—	2003 CONS		2004 LIB	—	2004 CONS
Economic	44%	—	55%		9%	—	90%
Social	41%	—	57%		31%	—	66%
Foreign	32%	—	65%		40%	—	58%

Key Votes of the 108th Congress

1. Ban Drilling in ANWR	N	5. Energy Bill	N	9. Ban Same-Sex Marriage	N
2. Approve Bush Tax Cuts	Y	6. Support Roe v. Wade	N	10. Ban Bunker-Buster Bomb	N
3. Medicare/Rx Bill	N	7. Ban Partial-Birth Abortion	Y	11. Fund Iraq War	Y
4. Bar Overtime Pay Regs.	N	8. Assault Weapons Ban	N	12. Restrict Missile Defense	N

Election Results

2002 general	John Sununu (R)	227,229	(51%)	($3,545,925)
	Jeanne Shaheen (D)	207,478	(47%)	($5,821,219)
	Other	12,428	(3%)	
2002 primary	John Sununu (R)	81,920	(53%)	
	Bob Smith (R)	68,608	(45%)	
	Other	2,694	(2%)	

Prior Winning Percentages: 2000 House (53%); 1998 House (67%); 1996 House (50%)

John E. Sununu, a Republican elected in 2002 when he defeated the state's senior senator and its governor, is the youngest member of the Senate. He grew up in Salem, on the Massachusetts border, one of eight children of John H. Sununu, who was elected to the first of three terms as governor in 1982 and served as White House chief of staff from 1989 to 1991. The younger Sununu graduated from M.I.T. and, like George W. Bush, got an M.B.A. at Harvard. He worked as an engineer for a microwave manufacturer, a high-tech consulting firm, the building automation manager Teletrol and as a consultant for JHS Associates. In April 1996, when Congressman Bill Zeliff announced for governor, Sununu and seven other Republicans got into the House race; Sununu won with 28% of the vote. In the general, Sununu faced Joe Keefe, former state Democratic chairman, who had run twice before in the district and who, with help from PACs, raised more money than Sununu. This was also a close race but Sununu won 50%–47%.

In the House, Sununu compiled a conservative voting record and climbed to important positions on the Appropriations and Budget Committees. In 2002, Republican incumbent Bob Smith was obviously vulnerable in the primary and seemed likely to lose the general election. How a New Hampshire Republican got himself into this predicament is an interesting tale. Smith, a fervent opponent of abortion, ran for the Senate in 1990 and won the general election 65%–32%. In 1996 Smith had well-financed competition from former Democratic Congressman Dick Swett. Smith won by only 49%–46%; he had a near-political-death experience on election night when the VNS exit poll declared him the loser (New Hampshire exit polls have leaned Democratic since 1988). Astonishingly, Smith proceeded to run for president. What prompted him to think he would make a plausible candidate is not clear: he had no executive experience in government and no major legislative achievement. His standing with New Hampshire voters was shaky and support from his colleagues was nonexistent. He spent much time on the road in 1997 and 1998 and became the first candidate to formally announce for the presidency in February 1999. Much of the buzz in New Hampshire was hostile, and many feared his presence would drive out other presidential contenders, and thus reduce the importance of New Hampshire's first-in-the-nation primary. In July 1999 Smith rose on the Senate floor and made a 50-minute speech announcing that he was leaving the Republican party and would run for president as an independent or third party candidate. Senate Republican leaders allowed him to keep his committee seats and seniority. Then in October 1999 Senator John Chafee died; he was chairman of the Environment and Public Works Committee and Smith held the next-ranking Republican seat. Four days later Smith abandoned his presidential candidacy, saying he could not raise enough money, and on November 1 he announced he was a Republican again. A day later he became chairman of the Environment Committee. Previously, his record on the committee had been solidly conservative, while his efforts as a subcommittee chairman to change the troubled Superfund program had gone nowhere. Now he took liberal stands on environmental issues, including opposing oil drilling in the Arctic National Wildlife Refuge.

By early 2001 New Hampshire polls showed Smith trailing Governor Jeanne Shaheen in the general election and Sununu in the primary; they also showed Sununu ahead of Shaheen. The Bush White House was officially on Smith's side: Dick Cheney assured him that the White House backed all incumbent Republican senators in March 2001. But Republican consultants believed that only a Sununu win in the primary could save the seat, and the White House appears to have made no attempt to persuade Sununu not to run. In October 2001 Sununu announced he was running for the Senate. Smith argued that with his seniority it would be a "serious matter" for Republicans to reject him. Sununu's argument was that he was the only one who could win. Smith's response: "The 1st District House seat is now in jeopardy. He's risking the president's agenda by running in this race. He's risking the Senate race because we have to spend money against each other and Shaheen is piling the money in the bank. So we could lose the House seat and the Senate seat. It wasn't me who did that." These arguments were undoubtedly dispositive for most primary voters, since the candidates disagreed on only a few issues—normal trade relations with China and ANWR oil drilling, both of which Smith opposed and Sununu favored.

It is highly unusual for leaders of both parties to refuse to support, much less oppose, one of their incumbents in a primary. But there were signs that even leaders officially on Smith's side were lukewarm in their support. Presidential adviser Karl Rove attended a Smith fundraiser, but White House Chief of Staff Andrew Card, who knew the Sununus for 30 years, endorsed Sununu. Majority Leader Trent Lott attended two Smith fundraisers but in April 2002 attended a Sununu fundraiser. Senate Republican campaign committee chairman Bill Frist said he supported Smith, but in October 2001 Smith upbraided him in the cloakroom for not supporting him strongly enough. Richard Shelby and Christopher Bond endorsed Sununu early on. Chuck Hagel sent $2,500 to both candidates. Judd Gregg, Smith's New Hampshire colleague for 10 years, said he was neutral. The House Republican leadership held a fundraiser for Sununu. The Manchester *Union Leader* endorsed Sununu. Despite all his support from leading Republicans, Sununu raised far less money than Smith, who raised much by direct mail; altogether Smith raised $3.8 million and Sununu $1.5 million.

A few differences on issues surfaced during the long campaign up to the September primary. One was policy in the Middle East. Sununu is of Lebanese descent, and was one of the few Republicans to vote against recognizing Jerusalem as the capital of Israel. The weekend before the primary, Smith ran an ad saying that Sununu voted to let terrorist suspects stay in the United States; Sununu replied that someone granted permanent residency status has rights under the Constitution. New Hampshire polls often produce conflicting results, as close observers of New Hampshire presidential primaries know. In the weeks before the September 10 primary, one New Hampshire poll showed the race even and one showed Sununu with a 22% lead. Both turned out to be wrong. Turnout was a record high and Sununu won 53%–45%. Sununu carried every county and even carried Smith's hometown. Smith made a gracious concession statement and endorsed Sununu.

Now, having beaten New Hampshire's senior senator, Sununu faced New Hampshire's governor, Jeanne Shaheen. The Senate Republican campaign committee had been running ads against Shaheen since the spring, focusing especially on education funding. This had been the central issue of her governorship. She was proud of extending kindergarten, regulating HMOs and joining the tri-state pool (with Maine and Vermont) to purchase prescription drugs at discount. But the real problem was how to respond to the state supreme court decision outlawing New Hampshire's local-based school financing. In 1999, when the legislature, with a Democratic state Senate for the first time in years, seemed on the verge of passing an income tax, she announced that she would veto it. Instead, the legislature passed a temporary statewide property tax, plus business tax increases. But this did not solve the problem permanently. In 2000 Shaheen declined to take the pledge to oppose income and sales taxes and was whipsawed on both sides. She won the Democratic primary by only 61%–38%, an unusually low primary showing for an incumbent governor, and in November beat state Senator (and former U.S. Senator) Gordon Humphrey by only 49%–44%.

Shaheen ran as a moderate on key issues. She said she supported the 2001 Bush tax cut and in October 2002 came out staunchly for the Iraq war resolution. She emphasized her support of abortion rights and with help from EMILY's List and other feminist groups and from likely presidential candidates she raised far more money than Sununu. She attacked Sununu for supporting "privatization" of Social Security. He responded with an articulate advocacy of voluntary individual investment accounts as part of Social Security—"modernization", as he put it.

In late September, supporters of Bob Smith launched a write-in campaign for him; eventually three different groups announced Smith write-in campaigns. In the end Smith got only 2,396 write-in votes and is now in the private sector; he mulled running for the Senate in 2004 in Florida.

The polls tightened in late October and national Democrats started to count this seat as a pickup. But the New Hampshire tax issue may have hurt Shaheen. She was on record in support of a sales tax and she was, necessarily, supporting gubernatorial nominee Mark Fernald, an outspoken advocate of an income tax. Fernald was defeated 59%–38% and Sununu defeated Shaheen 51%–47%. His margin was nearly 20,000 votes—eight times as great as the number of Smith write-ins.

In the Senate Sununu has a generally conservative voting record but has not supported the Bush administration all the time. In 2003 he voted against the Medicare/prescription drug bill as overexpensive and opposed the energy bill, partly because it barred a lawsuit by New Hampshire against the manufacturers of the gasoline additive MTBE, which caused environmental damage. He also criticized its "tax-and-spend provisions that cater to unique and narrowly defined business activities" and doubling of ethanol subsidies. With Congressman Paul Ryan he sponsored a version of voluntary personal retirement accounts as part of Social Security. Drawing on his own advocacy of that in the 2002 campaign, he said, "Every candidate that I know of that's been in a campaign where they have stood for the status quo . . . they've lost." On the Commerce committee he was active on telecom issues. The New Hampshire and Vermont senators sponsored a bill to change TV market definitions in small states so that satellite TV could carry more local stations. Sununu pushed for a bill providing federal and eliminating state regulation of Voice over Internet Protocol phone service. But in the July 2004 markup, Byron Dorgan and Conrad Burns amended it with provisions allowing states to enact universal service fees, requirements to carry 911 and taxes on providers. Sununu said, "This in effect guts the bill by turning back to state commissions all the powers they have over traditional phone service. This takes us 180 degrees in the wrong direction." He sponsored a similar bill in 2005. In December 2004 Sununu predicted that the Senate would pass a major telecom bill, and hoped it would create a framework to encourage Internet and voice data transmission. But he called for changes in the universal service formula.

Sununu surprised some cultural conservatives in July 2004 when he voted against the constitutional amendment to ban same-sex marriage (he said it should be a state issue unless courts overturn the Defense of Marriage Act) and in December 2004 when he opposed the House's uniform driver's license standards in the intelligence reorganization bill (he said there shouldn't be federal standards). With Larry Craig, he sponsored a bill to change some provisions of the Patriot Act, to require notification of sneak-and-peek search warrants within seven days, to require roving wiretaps to specify a specific suspect or location and to add sunsets to several provisions. With Chuck Hagel and Elizabeth Dole he sponsored a bill in January 2005 to create a tougher federal regulator for government sponsored enterprises Fannie Mae and Freddie Mac, with the power to shut down GSEs, to raise capital standards and to have approval rights over new programs and activities. He was one of three senators to vote against a resolution commending Israel's Prime Minister Ariel Sharon's proposed withdrawal from the Gaza strip; he said his ethnic background "has given me maybe a natural and personal interest in the region and in the peace process in particular."

FIRST DISTRICT

Rep. Jeb Bradley (R)

Elected 2002, 2d term; b. Oct. 20, 1952, Rumford, ME; home, Wolfeboro; Tufts U., B.A. 1974; Protestant; married (Barbara).

Elected Office: NH House of Reps., 1990–2002.

Professional Career: Owner, Evergrain Health Food store, 1981–97; Magician.

DC Office: 1218 LHOB, 20515, 202-225-5456; Fax: 202-225-5822; Web site: www.house.gov/bradley/.

District Offices: Dover, 603-743-4813; Manchester, 603-641-9536.

Committees: *Armed Services* (23d of 34 R): Readiness; Tactical Air & Land Forces. *Budget* (18th of 22 R). *Small Business* (9th of 18 R): Tax, Finance & Exports (Chmn.); Workforce, Empowerment & Government Programs. *Veterans' Affairs* (11th of 16 R): Disability Assistance & Memorial Affairs; Oversight & Investigations.

Group Ratings

	ADA	ACLU	AFS	LCV	ITIC	NTU	COC	ACU	NTLC	CHC
2004	30	5	13	27	70	54	90	76	72	83
2003	10	—	0	50	—	59	90	76	—	—

National Journal Ratings

	2003 LIB	—	2003 CONS		2004 LIB	—	2004 CONS
Economic	39%	—	60%		45%	—	55%
Social	45%	—	54%		40%	—	59%
Foreign	31%	—	65%		39%	—	59%

Key Votes of the 108th Congress

1. Drilling in ANWR	N	5. DC School Vouchers	Y	9. Ban Same-Sex Marriage	Y
2. Approve Bush Tax Cuts	Y	6. Ban Human Cloning	Y	10. Fund Iraq War	Y
3. Medicare/Rx Bill	Y	7. Restrict Gun Liability	Y	11. Bar Cuba Embargo Funds	N
4. Bar Overtime Pay Regs.	N	8. Ban Partial-Birth Abortion	Y	12. Intelligence Reorg.	Y

Election Results

2004 general	Jeb Bradley (R)	204,836	(63%)	($1,055,083)
	Justin Nadeau (D)	118,226	(37%)	($530,364)
2004 primary	Jeb Bradley (R)	27,285	(90%)	
	Bob Bevill (R)	3,076	(10%)	
2002 general	Jeb Bradley (R)	128,993	(58%)	($1,029,408)
	Martha Clark (D)	85,426	(39%)	($3,511,108)
	Other	7,568	(3%)	

The People		Race/Ethnic Origin	Ancestry	
Area size:	2,688 sq. mi.	95.1% White	Irish: 14.6%	English: 12.7%
Urban population:	66.6%	0.7% Black	French: 10.5%	
Rural population:	33.4%	1.2% Asian	**2004 Presidential Vote**	
Pop. 2000:	617,575	0.2% Native Am.	Bush (R) 171,013	(51%)
Median income:	$50,135	0.0% Hawaiian	Kerry (D) 163,191	(48%)
Poverty status:	6.7%	0.9% Two+ races	Other 2,749	(1%)
Military veterans:	15.0%	0.1% Other	**2000 Presidential Vote**	
		1.6% Hispanic Origin	Bush (R) 136,474	(49%)
			Gore (D) 128,278	(46%)
			Other 11,545	(4%)
			Cook Partisan Voting Index: R + 0	

Occupation	Blue collar: 23.6%	White collar: 62.7%	Gray collar: 13.7%

The greatest growth in New Hampshire over the past two decades has been in the southeast and south central parts of the state—the Seacoast and the Manchester area. Manchester was once famous for the Amoskeag Mills, the world's largest textile mill complex and in the first half of the 20th century was the quintessential mill town, with a few mansions for mill owners and managers and close packed neighborhoods of frame houses for mill workers, many of them immigrants—from Quebec, Ireland and Greece (Manchester has America's largest percentage of Greek Americans). By the beginning of the 21st century it was something quite different, a high-tech city, with big shopping malls at freeway interchanges, a spiffy new airport, spruced up neighborhoods and growth extending to the wooded suburbs all around. The Seacoast, within easy commuting distance of Massachusetts, is a collection of towns of ancient pedigree and high-tech growth. The biggest city on the coast is Portsmouth, the colonial capital of New Hampshire, with its busy Naval Shipyard and old seaport with well-preserved houses and a booming economy, including many galleries and bars. In the 2005 base closing round, the Pentagon recommended closing the shipyard. But Portsmouth did not immediately panic: The shipyard had been recommended for closure in two previous rounds and both times managed to get removed from the list during the hearing stage. There is a sign of hope nearby: The successful redevelopment of Pease Air Force Base after its 1991 closing and conversion to the Pease International Tradeport, with what developers termed high-end office buildings in an international trade environment (plus a convenient airport runway), has driven the Seacoast (sometimes called e-coast) economy with more than 160 businesses and several thousand jobs. Not far to the south is Exeter, home of Phillips Exeter Academy, on a campus most colleges would envy.

The 1st Congressional District of New Hampshire includes the Manchester area and the Seacoast from Manchester and next-door Bedford, its most affluent suburb, east to Portsmouth. It also extends north to Laconia and Lake Winnipesaukee, studded with summer resorts and Ossipee in Carroll County, which promotes rock and ice climbing. Politically, this is the more Republican of New Hampshire's two congressional districts: people came here from Massachusetts not to replicate its high-tax environment but to get away from it. Manchester, the largest city in the state, still has more registered Democrats than Republicans—a relic of its mill town days—but usually votes Republican in general elections. Portsmouth, with its trendy coffee shops, is Democratic, and so are Durham, home of the University of New Hampshire, and nearby Dover, once a mill town. But most of the smaller towns on the Seacoast and to the north are solidly Republican. George W. Bush carried the district 49%–46% in 2000 and 51%–48% in 2004.

The congressman from the 1st District is Jeb Bradley, a Republican first elected in 2002. He grew up in Wolfeboro on the shores of Lake Winnipesaukee and worked summers at his family's hardware store. He graduated from Tufts and met his wife—a native of Switzerland—in Nepal on a mountaineering adventure. He had a varied professional career, from running a health-food store to serving as a professional magician—arguably a useful background for his current job. In the often provincial world of New Hampshire politics, he was suspect because he switched parties in 1989, becoming a Republican one year before he ran for the state legislature, where he served for 12 years.

When 1st District Congressman John Sununu announced that he was running for the Senate, Bradley was one of eight Republicans in the primary to succeed him. There was no obvious frontrunner. Bradley characterized himself as a moderate in favor of abortion rights and a fiscal conservative who voted against both sales and income taxes. He supported gay adoption and environmental restrictions—positions too liberal for many Republicans. Meanwhile, businessman Sean Mahoney and assistant state Safety Commissioner John Stephen fought over who was the "true conservative" in the field; Stephen got the backing of some national conservative groups and the endorsement of the Manchester *Union Leader.* Bradley won the primary with 31%, as Stephen got 23% and Mahoney 19%. This race was ideological, but also regional. Stephen carried Manchester and most of the nearby towns. But Bradley edged him in Merrimack, Londonderry and Derry, and carried all but one of the towns north of Durham. In the general, Bradley faced Martha Fuller Clark, who had held Sununu to a 53%–45% margin in 2000 and never stopped campaigning after the election. She was one of the national Democratic party's favorite candidates and benefited from campaign support from potential presidential candidates. For 2002 she raised the phenomenal sum of $3.5 million (including $1.6 million of her own money), while Bradley spent $1 million. Bradley attacked Clark for her support of a state income tax—anathema to many New Hampshire voters. Clark pointed to Bradley's votes for business, inheritance and consumption taxes, and charged that he favored "privatization" of Social Security. In a radio interview he said that individual investment accounts should be a matter for discussion, but afterward said that his opposition to "privatization" was "crystal clear." This was still another district where the Social Security issue did not produce the magic Democrats expected. Instead, the income tax proved to be a millstone for Clark. Bradley won by a surprisingly large 58%–39%.

In the House, Bradley had a moderate voting record. In May 2005, he offered two amendments to the defense authorization bill, one to delay the base closing process and another to eliminate base closures; both failed. He filed bills to permit the reimportation of prescription drugs from Canada and to expand embryonic stem-cell research; he won House approval of his proposal to facilitate research on pancreatic islet cell transplantations, which some hope will provide a cure for diabetes. He dismissed criticism that his support of the ban on partial-birth abortions was a retreat from his earlier stance. He was reelected by a 63%–37% margin. He celebrated his reelection by climbing his last of New Hampshire's 48 mountains over 4,000 feet.

SECOND DISTRICT

Rep. Charles Bass (R)

Elected 1994, 6th term; b. Jan. 8, 1952, Boston, MA; home, Peterborough; Dartmouth Col., A.B. 1974; Episcopalian; married (Lisa).

Elected Office: NH House of Reps., 1982–88; NH Senate, 1988–92.

Professional Career: Field worker, U.S. Rep. William Cohen, 1974; Legis. Asst., U.S. Rep. David Emery, 1975–76, Chief of Staff, 1976–79; Vice Pres., High Standard Inc., 1980–93; Chmn., Columbia Architectural Products, 1980–93.

DC Office: 2421 RHOB, 20515, 202-225-5206; Fax: 202-225-2946; Web site: www.house.gov/bass.

District Offices: Concord, 603-226-0249; Keene, 603-358-4094; Littleton, 603-444-1271; Nashua, 603-889-8772.

Committees: *Energy & Commerce* (19th of 31 R): Commerce, Trade & Consumer Protection; Environment & Hazardous Materials; Oversight & Investigations; Telecommunications & the Internet.

Group Ratings

	ADA	ACLU	AFS	LCV	ITIC	NTU	COC	ACU	NTLC	CHC
2004	45	20	13	27	50	59	86	56	81	69
2003	20	—	0	45	—	59	87	68	—	—

National Journal Ratings

	2003 LIB — 2003 CONS		2004 LIB — 2004 CONS	
Economic	39% —	60%	46% —	53%
Social	48% —	52%	53% —	47%
Foreign	46% —	52%	47% —	51%

Key Votes of the 108th Congress

1. Drilling in ANWR	N	5. DC School Vouchers	Y	9. Ban Same-Sex Marriage	N
2. Approve Bush Tax Cuts	Y	6. Ban Human Cloning	N	10. Fund Iraq War	Y
3. Medicare/Rx Bill	Y	7. Restrict Gun Liability	Y	11. Bar Cuba Embargo Funds	N
4. Bar Overtime Pay Regs.	N	8. Ban Partial-Birth Abortion	Y	12. Intelligence Reorg.	Y

Election Results

2004 general	Charles Bass (R)	191,187	(58%)	($717,749)
	Paul Hodes (D)	124,275	(38%)	($625,062)
	Other	11,726	(4%)	
2004 primary	Charles Bass (R)	25,414	(71%)	
	Mark Brady (R)	10,167	(29%)	
2002 general	Charles Bass (R)	125,804	(57%)	($886,765)
	Katrina Swett (D)	90,479	(41%)	($1,457,913)
	Other	7,568	(2%)	

Prior Winning Percentages: 2000 (56%); 1998 (53%); 1996 (51%); 1994 (51%)

The People		Race/Ethnic Origin	Ancestry	
Area size:	6,662 sq. mi.	95.1% White	Irish: 13.0%	English: 12.9%
Urban population:	51.7%	0.6% Black	French: 10.3%	
Rural population:	48.3%	1.3% Asian	**2004 Presidential Vote**	
Pop. 2000:	618,211	0.2% Native Am.	Kerry (D) 177,320	(52%)
Median income:	$48,762	0.0% Hawaiian	Bush (R) 160,224	(47%)
Poverty status:	6.4%	0.9% Two+ races	Other 3,165	(1%)
Military veterans:	15.0%	0.1% Other	**2000 Presidential Vote**	
		1.7% Hispanic Origin	Gore (D) 134,343	(48%)
			Bush (R) 132,336	(47%)
			Other 12,801	(5%)
			Cook Partisan Voting Index: D + 3	
Occupation	Blue collar: 24.7%	White collar: 62.1%	Gray collar: 13.2%	

Political reporters covering New Hampshire's first-in-the-nation political primary usually stay in Manchester, the state's largest city and within an hour or so of driving time from the rest of the state except for the North Country. Yet there are other noteworthy cities and towns in New Hampshire. Concord, north of Manchester, is the state capital; on one side of Main Street is the handsome, small, granite Capitol, and on the other you can usually find the headquarters of the two political parties and many candidates: an entire state's politics within 100 yards. Nashua, south of Manchester and on the Massachusetts line, is the state's second largest city, a high-tech and financial services center that has been booming for two decades. To the east is Salem, the largest of the border suburbs, prosperous and growing. To the west of Nashua, past the pleasant country around Mount Monadnock, is Keene, the hub of southwest New Hampshire. To the north are the towns along the Connecticut River, some mill towns and others in vacation home territory; New Hampshire prosperity has spread to most of these, just across the river from Vermont. Hanover, home of Dartmouth College, is an unbearably picturesque tiny town amid the mountains. And every political reporter's itinerary has to include a trip, usually by plane, to the little lumber mill city of Berlin in the midst of the North Country and perhaps also to Dixville Notch, where the town's roughly two dozen voters cast their votes a minute past midnight and provide the first reported returns in every presidential election; Neil Tillotson, the town moderator in every election from 1960 to 2000, was unhappily not there in 2004; he died in 2002 at 102. (Hint for election analysts: if Dixville Notch doesn't go heavily Republican, the Republicans are in trouble.)

The 2d Congressional District of New Hampshire includes Concord, Nashua, Salem, Keene, the Connecticut River counties, Hanover, Berlin and Dixville Notch. It also includes Mount Washington, with its spectacularly violent weather, with winds measured up to 231 miles per hour, and the Bretton Woods resort where the world monetary system was established at a conference in 1944. Long-time residents grieved when the jagged, granite face of the Old Man of the Mountain eroded from Franconia Notch in 2003. Politically this is mixed country, but much of it has been trending Democratic. Nashua is more Democratic than Manchester, Salem more Republican. The area between Mount Monadnock and Keene and the territory running north along the Connecticut River to Hanover and Dartmouth has become very Democratic: much like Vermont across the river. Overall, this is the more Democratic of New Hampshire's two districts, and it got more so in 2004, after heavy campaigning for a year by backers of Howard Dean: it voted 48%–47% for Al Gore in 2000 and 52%–47% for John Kerry in 2004.

The congressman from the 2d District is Charles Bass, a Republican first elected in 1994. He has a long political pedigree: His grandfather Robert Bass was elected governor in 1910 and his father Perkins Bass served in the House from 1955 to 1963. Charles Bass, after graduating from Dartmouth, worked for Maine Congressmen William Cohen and David Emery, then returned to New Hampshire to run for Congress in 1980, at age 28; he finished third in the primary, with 22%, to 34% for now-Senator Judd Gregg and 25% for liberal Susan McLane. With his two brothers he ran a factory making architectural products and served in the state legislature for a decade. In 1994, he won the nomination to oppose two-term Congressman Dick Swett. Campaigning as pro-choice on abortion and as a fiscal conservative, a supporter of welfare cuts and tougher sentencing, Bass attacked Swett for voting with Bill Clinton 90% of the time and for raising most of his money out of state, much of it generated by his father-in-law, California Congressman Tom Lantos. Bass won 51%–46%.

In the House, Bass emphasized that he is an "independent voice" as he trended toward the center on many issues. He has focused on the environment, coming out early against the Bush administration plan for oil drilling in the Arctic National Wildlife Refuge and criticizing Bush for abandoning his one-sentence campaign promise to vastly reduce the level of carbon dioxide. He later joined several Democrats in filing an alternative to the administration's "clear skies" proposal, including tighter controls on power plant emissions. With Democrat Maurice Hinchey, he called for protection of the bison at Yellowstone National Park. He was an early supporter of the Shays-Meehan campaign finance bill. On the Energy and Commerce Committee, Bass has worked on high-tech issues and lower prescription-drug costs. In 2003, he quit Roy Blunt's whip team, after objecting to the leadership's handling of an education bill. In 2005, with a call for "pragmatic" policies, he joined Mark Kirk as co-leader of the moderate Republicans' Tuesday Group. Bass has pushed persistently, but with little impact, for biennial budgeting, which he said would add stability to government programs. At home, he has been a supporter of commuter rail service from Nashua into the Boston area.

Bass has regularly faced spirited opposition. In 2002, he faced his most lavishly funded challenger. Katrina Swett, wife of the incumbent whom Bass initially defeated and the daughter of California's Tom Lantos, received extensive national party support. Dick Gephardt showed up to open her campaign office. "I'll be here a lot," Lantos told New Hampshire reporters on a campaign visit. He helped her to raise $149,000 from congressional leadership PACs, plus money from California contributors such as Steven Spielberg and San Francisco financiers; altogether, she raised and spent $1.4 million. As in 1994, when he ran against her husband, Bass ran ads contending that his opponent's out-of-state and labor union contributions showed that she was out of touch with local voters. She attacked his contributions from big business and called Bass "the wealthy, privileged inheritor of an incredibly easy path." He spent $876,000, well over his former limit, but well below Swett's spending, and won by a solid 57%–41% margin. In 2004, against Concord attorney Paul Hodes, Bass won 58%–38%.

★ NEW JERSEY ★

" A valley of humility between two mountains of conceit": That is what Benjamin Franklin called New Jersey, which even in colonial days was overshadowed by the metropolises of New York and Philadelphia. New Jersey was named by King James II, then Duke of York, for the Channel Island on which he was sheltered during the English Civil War. New Jersey was plagued in its early years by rival claims from its neighbors and, still defensive, went to the Supreme Court in the 1980s to argue that it and not New York owns the Statue of Liberty and Ellis Island; New Jersey eventually got most of the islands' acreage, but New York got the immigrant museum and Great Hall which are built on fill land. But New Jersey has much to say for itself. It is "a sort of laboratory in which the best blood is prepared for other communities to thrive on," Woodrow Wilson said when he was governor, just a tad defensively.

Today, New Jersey is the nation's tenth most populous state: It boomed in the 1980s, suffered sharply in the early 1990s recession, came back strongly, and is now weathering the high-tech storms with mixed success. New Jersey was the home of Thomas Edison and of the old Bell Labs; its successors Lucent and AT&T were among its biggest employers in the 1990s, and later laid off many workers. Other big employers include several of the nation's biggest pharmaceutical firms—Merck, Johnson & Johnson, Bristol-Myers Squibb, Novartis, Schering-Plough. These industries give the state a high-income, high-education work force, and in 2000 New Jersey passed Connecticut and had the nation's highest median household income. But it still trailed in per capita income and wealth and has a lower percentage of college graduates than Colorado, Connecticut, Maryland, Massachusetts, Virginia, and the District of Columbia; this is the home not only of high-income Ph.D.'s, but also of *The Sopranos*. This is prosperous middle-income country, with more two-car than one-car families but fewer limousines than Manhattan, with an estimated 13,500 $1 million houses but not the multi-million dollar co-ops of Manhattan or mansions of Greenwich, Connecticut.

Within New Jersey's close boundaries is great diversity, geographically from beaches to mountains, demographically from old Quaker stock to new Hispanics, economically from inner city slums to hunt country mansions. Though New York writers are inclined to look on New Jersey as a land of 1940s diners and 1970s shopping malls, this state much more closely resembles the rest of America than does Manhattan, even if some of its traffic signals are arrayed horizontally rather than vertically and its accents can sometimes be incomprehensible to outsiders. The Jersey City row houses seen on emerging from the Holland Tunnel, many renovated by Wall Street commuters and Latin immigrants, give way within a few miles to the skyscrapers of Newark and its new Performing Arts Center. Farther out are comfortably packed middle-income suburbs and the horse country around Far Hills, the university town of Princeton, old industrial cities like Paterson and Trenton, and dozens of suburban towns and small factory cities where people work and raise families over generations. Among them are commuter towns like Middletown, whose commuter trails lead to Lower Manhattan, and which lost dozens of neighbors on September 11. A year later, only 37% of New Jersey citizens said their lives had returned to normal and 29% said they would never be the same; 43% said they thought about the attacks every day.

Whoever has legal title to Ellis Island, New Jersey has long been a magnet for immigrants, and it is again today. In 2000, 29% of its residents were born in another country or had a parent who was; only California and New York have larger percentages of foreign-born residents. Hudson County, the land along the ridge opposite Manhattan, was the home to hundreds of thousands of Irish, Italian, Polish and Jewish immigrants in the early 20th century; in 2003 it was 41% Hispanic, with Cubans, Puerto Ricans, Dominicans and Mexicans. Immigrants are plentiful in the little middle-American towns of Bergen County, Filipinos in Bergenfield, Guatemalans in Fairview, Koreans in Leonia, Indians in Lodi, Chinese in Palisades Park. The old central cities of Elizabeth and Paterson were half-Hispanic in 2000 and Camden, opposite

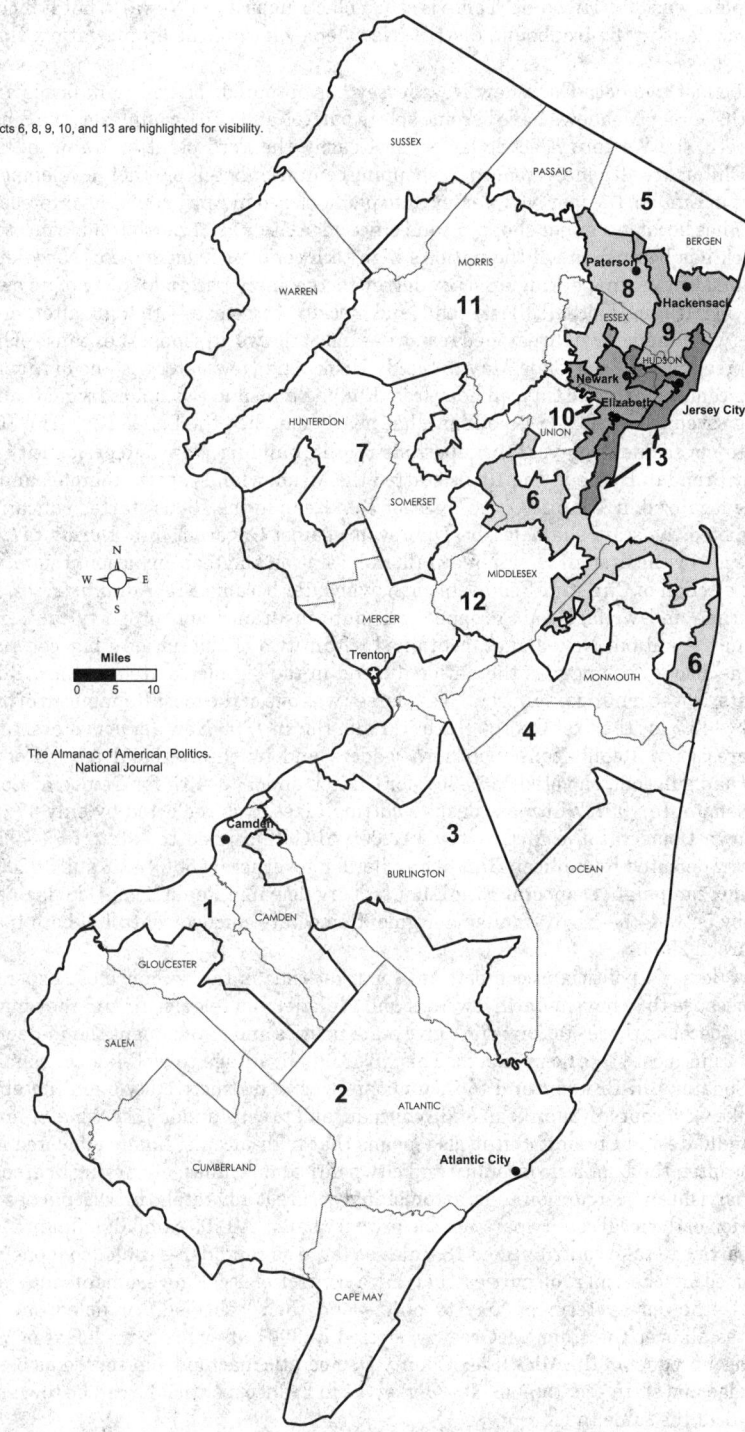

Districts 6, 8, 9, 10, and 13 are highlighted for visibility.

The Almanac of American Politics.
National Journal

Miles
0   5   10

Congressional district boundaries were first effective for 2002.

Philadelphia, was 39% Hispanic. There is still a black majority in Newark, but it includes many of the Brazilians in the Ironbound district. New Jersey has all the ethnic variety that America offers.

In the last two decades, a new New Jersey has sprouted. The oil tank farms and swamplands of the Jersey Meadows have become sports palaces and office complexes; the Singer factory in Elizabeth, the Western Electric factory in Kearny, the Ford plant in Mahwah, the Shulton plant in Clifton are all gone, replaced by shopping centers or hotels or other development, and the GM plant in Linden, the last New Jersey auto plant, closed in April 2005; the intersection of I-78 and I-287 has become a major shopping and office edge city; U.S. 1 north from Princeton to North Brunswick has become one of the nation's high-tech centers. Even some of New Jersey's long-ailing central cities are perking up. New Jersey increasingly has an identity of its own. It is the home of big league football, basketball and hockey franchises—though after nearly three decades, two of them have threatened to move—and of the world's longest expanse of boardwalks on the Jersey Shore from Cape May to Sandy Hook. And New Jersey is one of America's great gambling centers: Atlantic City, an hour from Philadelphia and two hours from Manhattan, had gambling revenues in 2004 ($4.8 billion) that nearly matched the Las Vegas strip ($5.3 billion).

State government played an important role in building New Jersey identity and pride. Governor Brendan Byrne in the 1970s started the Meadowlands sports complex and got casino gambling legalized in Atlantic City. Governor Tom Kean in the 1980s started education reforms and promoted the state shamelessly. The revolt against Governor Jim Florio's tax increase in 1990 was led by the first all-New Jersey talk radio station and took on national significance with the 1993 election of Christine Todd Whitman, who later became EPA Administrator. In the next decade crime and welfare rolls dropped, but auto insurance and property taxes remain the highest in the nation. New Jersey, contained within two of the nation's biggest metropolitan areas, was also a harbinger of the national trend in the big metro areas toward Bill Clinton's Democrats. Not so long ago, suburban New Jersey was one of the most Republican of big states: It voted 56%–42% for the first George Bush in 1988. But in 1996 New Jersey voters, turned off by the congressional Republicans' Southern leaders and by the national party's opposition to abortion and gun control, voted 54%–36% for Clinton and 53%–43% for Democrat Bob Torricelli for the Senate. In 1997 Whitman, despite cutting taxes, was reelected by only 47%–46% over little-known Democrat Jim McGreevey. In 2000 Al Gore carried the state 56%–40%. In 2001 McGreevey defeated Republican Bret Schundler for governor by 56%–42% and in 2002, after an unorthodox campaign, Democrat Frank Lautenberg defeated Republican Douglas Forrester for senator by 54%–44%—eerily similar margins. Democrats cinched control of both houses of the legislature in 2003.

New Jersey's politicians compete in a market that is the second most expensive in the nation, because they have to buy New York and Philadelphia television. And they have a special handicap, because those stations don't give state politics and government the in-depth coverage that voters in most states can expect. This gives an advantage to well-known candidates, like former Senator Bill Bradley, and to incumbents with a distinctive style and notable achievements, like Governors Byrne, Kean and Whitman, and to self-funders like Senator and gubernatorial candidate Jon Corzine. But it also means that high-income, highly educated New Jersey politics is often the business of county and city political machines, of varying degrees of competence, cronyism and corruption. It is, astonishingly, a great advantage in both parties to have the designation of the local county party on the primary ballot. A 1993 campaign finance law allowed county parties to take contributions 18 times as large as candidates could, so money is increasingly raised by chairmen of parties that have control of local government and can dole out contracts—the Jersey term is "pay to play"—and then "wheeled," or doled out, to favored candidates all over the state. McGreevey, elected in 2001 after his near-defeat of Whitman in 1997, was a product of the Middlesex County Democratic machine and served as both mayor of Woodbridge and state senator—in New Jersey, as in France, politicians can be town mayors and legislators at the same time.

McGreevey, after he shocked the state with his announcement that he would resign in November 2004, tried to change the rules to disempower the bosses. One reason he could do this is that New Jersey is notable for giving its governors more real power than any other state. They are the only statewide elected officials, they have great clout in the budget process and they appoint all judges and all 21 county prosecutors. Yet the governorship was in limbo after he resigned. McGreevey was succeeded by state Senate President Richard Codey, who under the state's 1947 constitution also remained in the state Senate; Codey later announced he would not run for a full term.

The People		Race/Ethnic Origin			Military veterans: 672,217 (10.6%)	
Pop. 2004 (est):	8,698,879	5,557,209	66.0%	White	WWII: 26.3%	Korea: 15.8%
Pop. 2000:	8,414,350	1,096,171	13.0%	Black	Vietnam: 28.1%	Gulf War: 6.2%
Pop. 1990:	7,730,188	477,012	5.7%	Asian	**Most populous cities (2003):**	
Change 1990–2000:	Up 8.6%	11,338	0.1%	Native Am.	1. Newark	277,911
% of U.S. total:	3.0%	2,175	0.0%	Hawaiian	2. Jersey City	239,097
Pop. rank:	9th of 50	133,689	1.6%	Two+ races	3. Paterson	150,782
Area size:	8,721 sq. mi.	19,565	0.2%	Other	4. Elizabeth	123,215
State Native:	53.4%	1,117,191	13.3%	Hisp. Origin	5. Trenton	85,314
Non-citizen:	9.4%	**Ancestry**				
Language		Italian: 13.8%		Irish: 12.2%	Urban population: 94.3%	
English: 73.0%	Spanish: 11.7%	German: 9.7%		Polish: 5.3%	Rural population: 5.7%	
Other Eur.: 10.4%		English: 4.8%				

Education		Work Sector		Legislature	
H.S. Grad:	82.1%	Private: 80.8%	Govt: 13.9%	Senate	22 D 18 R
College Grad:	29.8%	Self: 5.0%	Family: 0.2%	G. Assembly	47 D 33 R
Industry		Unemployment: 5.8%		Legislative Term Limits: No	
Agri: 0.3%	Con: 5.6%	**Household Income**		**Registered Voters**	
Fin: 8.9%	Info: 4.4%	<15k: 11.7%	15-35k: 19.4%	D: 1,163,224	(23.2%)
Mfg: 17.9%	Prof: 31.3%	35-50k: 14.3%	50-100k: 33.3%	R: 884,801	(17.7%)
Public: 4.5%	Trade: 15.7%	100-150k: 12.8%	>150k: 8.6%	O: 2,957,934	(59.1%)
Other: 11.3%		Median: $55,146			
Occupation		Poverty status: 8.5%			
Blue collar: 19.7%	White collar: 66.5%	**Home Value**			
Gray collar: 13.8%		<50k: 3.0% 50-100k: 14.4% 100-200k: 46.1% 200-300k: 20.4%			
		300-500k: 11.7% >500k: 4.4% Median: $167,900			

Presidential politics   For most of the 20th century New Jersey was a close state in close presidential elections, giving small margins to winners in 1960 and 1968 and to losers in 1948 and 1976, but no more. In the 1980s the vast suburban expanses of New Jersey leaned toward the Republicans; since 1995 they have leaned to the Democrats, though a little less so in 2004. This is a state with relatively few strong-belief Christians and with a high number of seculars and Jews; sophisticated and cynical, it reacted strongly against the Southern-accented Republicans of Newt Gingrich's revolution.

In 2004 Bush campaign strategists kept an eye on New Jersey polls to see if for some reason—the impact of September 11, for example—it might qualify for target status. A few public polls showed the race close or tied, but others showed John Kerry well ahead. The Bush campaign sent Laura Bush in September, and George W. Bush appeared in Burlington

2004 Presidential Vote
Kerry (D).................... 1,911,430   (53%)
Bush (R) 1,670,003   (46%)
Nader (I) 19,418   (1%)
Other.......................... 10,840   (0%)

2004 Democratic Presidential Primary
Kerry (D)...................... 198,213   (92%)
Kucinich (D) 9,251   (4%)
LaRouche (D) 4,514   (2%)
Ballard (D)...................... 2,826   (1%)

2000 Presidential Vote
Gore (D)...................... 1,788,850   (56%)
Bush (R) 1,284,173   (40%)
Nader (Green) 94,554   (3%)
Other.......................... 19,649   (1%)

County October 18. South Jersey saw all the spots aimed at target state Pennsylvania on Philadelphia TV; but they never bought time on the New York stations that reach 70% of the state. The Kerry campaign, shrewdly, did not flinch and spend much time or money in New

Jersey. Governor Jim McGreevey in early October refused to spend more than $25,000 of the state party's $2.5 million on voter turnout efforts; Senator Jon Corzine ponied up $250,000 of his own. Kerry carried the state 53%–46%, a solid margin but considerably smaller than Gore's, indeed smaller than Kerry's margin in the target state of Maine. The NEP exit poll showed interesting differences from 2000. Bush carried Catholics with 58%, up 7% from 2000; Archbishop John Myers of Newark said in May 2004 that any elected official who supports abortion rights was not worthy to receive communion. Bush won 24% among Jews (7% of the electorate, one of the highest figures in the nation), up 8% from 2000. The Bush campaign did much organizing work among Latinos, and they voted for Kerry by only 56%–43%; Bush's percentage among Latinos was much closer to his percentage among whites (54%) than among blacks (17%). And his percentages among blacks and Latinos were up 6% and 8% from 2000. New Jersey looks to be on the verge of being a competitive state in presidential elections again. Geographically, Bush's greatest gains over 2000 came in Monmouth County, many of whose residents died on 9/11, and in Ocean County, New Jersey's fastest-growing county, with many retirees from the metro New York area.

For years, New Jersey's June presidential primary was overshadowed by California's on the same day. In 1996 California voted in March, and New Jersey did not get to the polls until two months after the nominations were sewn up. In 1998 the state Senate refused to move the primary to March 7, and so it stayed in June—far, far too late to affect the outcome.

Congressional districting

New Jersey's population rose 9% between the 1990 and 2000 Censuses, and it did not lose a House seat in 2002 as it did in 1992. New Jersey has a 10-member congressional redistricting commission, equally divided between the parties, which is supposed to agree on new lines, with a previously selected arbiter available in case of ties, who can produce a compromise plan and see if it gets a majority of the commission; if not, the tie-breaker picks one of the two parties' plans. In 1991 the tiebreaker picked the Republican plan, with grotesquely shaped districts. But given New Jersey's post-1994 Democratic trend, by 2000 it yielded the Republicans only 6 of the state's 13 seats.

109th Congress Lineup	
7 D	6 R

108th Congress Lineup	
7 D	6 R

The redistricting commission first met in July 2001, two days after the 13 incumbents had agreed on a bipartisan congressional delegation plan. The biggest changes were in the 12th District, which Democrat Rush Holt had won three times by narrow margins, and by just 651 votes in 2000, and the 7th District, which freshman Republican Mike Ferguson had won by just 52%–46% in 2000. Furious attempts were made to change the plan by Republican Finn Caspersen Jr., who wanted to challenge Holt, and Democrat Susan Bass Levin, who had run unsuccessfully in the 3d in 2000 and wanted to have Cherry Hill, of which she is mayor, placed in the heavily Democratic 1st where she could run if incumbent Rob Andrews should retire. But Camden County Democratic Chairman George Norcross had other candidates in mind, and Ferguson was bound to resist the major changes needed to put Caspersen's very Republican hometown of Bedminster into the 12th. Anyway, tiebreaker Alan Rosenthal, a Rutgers political scientist, liked the idea of an incumbent-protection plan.

So in October 2001 the commission adopted the delegation plan with slight changes. The result is a map with very erose district lines and oddly shaped districts, drawn explicitly to protect incumbents and blessed by a political scientist. The partisan tilt is plain from the presidential election returns. Within these lines, George W. Bush carried only three of these districts in 2000, when he won 40% of the vote in New Jersey. But in 2004, when he won 46%, he carried all six of the districts represented by Republicans.

Governor

Richard Codey (D)

Assumed office Nov. 2004, term expires Jan. 2006, 1st term; b. Nov. 27, 1946, Orange, NJ; home, West Orange; Fairleigh Dickinson U., B.Ed. 1981; Catholic; married (Mary Jo).

Elected Office: NJ Assembly, 1973–1981; NJ Senate, 1981–present, Minority Ldr., 1998–2001, Democratic Pres., 2002–2003, President, 2004.

Professional Career: Insurance broker; funeral director.

Office: P.O. Box 001, Trenton, 08625, 609-292-6000; Fax: 609-292-3454; Web site: www.state.nj.us.

Election Results

2001 general	James McGreevey (D)	1,256,853	(56%)
	Bret Schundler (R)	928,174	(42%)
2001 primary	James McGreevey (D)	250,404	(96%)
	Elliot Greenspan (D)	11,682	(4%)
1997 general	Christine Todd Whitman (R)	1,133,394	(47%)
	James McGreevey (D)	1,107,968	(46%)
	Murray Sabrin (L)	114,172	(5%)
	Other	65,099	(2%)

Richard Codey, the acting governor of New Jersey from November 2004 to January 2006, has been a state legislator almost all his adult life and, under the New Jersey Constitution, remains one while also serving as chief executive. Codey grew up in Orange, in an apartment over his father's funeral home. Codey graduated from Oratory Prep and attended Fairleigh Dickinson University and worked as an insurance broker; he went back and got his degree while serving in the Senate. He got involved in local politics early, and became a member of the Essex County Democratic Committee at 21, then the voting age. In 1973 he was elected to the Assembly at age 26. There he chaired the State Government Committee for six years and sponsored the Casino Control Act of 1977 that legalized gambling in Atlantic City. In 1981 he was elected to the state Senate. There he chaired the Health, Institutions and Welfare Committee and helped pass a law requiring insurer to pay for 48-hour hospital stays for childbirth. In 1987 he heard that one-third of the employees at the Marlboro state mental hospital were ex-convicts. He assumed the identity of a dead ex-convict and got a job as an orderly, and then exposed the conditions there. Later he explained his interest in the issue. "Most people assume it's because of my wife's mental illness [depression]. But it's got nothing to do with that. I've always explained while I was a teenager working for Dad [a funeral home director], picking up bodies, I would go to Graystone [Park Psychiatric Hospital, near Parisippany] or wherever county psychiatric institution to pick up a body." What he saw, he said, "made *One Flew Over the Cuckoo's Nest* look like a picnic."

Codey worked on other issues in the state Senate and rose to leadership positions despite fights with influential Democrats. He worked on creating an Atlantic County regional development authority and an amendment allowing simulcasting of horseracing and betting in casino hotels; he used to own racehorses and his brother is the general manager of Freehold Raceway. He backed an assault weapons ban. In 1993, as assistant Senate minority leader, he unsuccessfully resisted when Camden County Democratic leader George Norcross and Middlesex County Democratic Chairman John Lynch—the most powerful state Democrats for a dozen years now—got two new assistant minority leaders appointed. In 1998 he was elected Senate minority leader despite clashes with Norcross and Lynch over leadership posts. In 2000 he was one of the few New Jersey Democratic politicians to back former New Jersey Senator Bill Bradley over Vice President Al Gore. After the 2001 state election, in which both parties won 20 seats in the state Senate, the leaders tried to depose him as party leader. But he survived and became co-president with Republican John Bennett. Both men also served briefly as acting governor.

Donald DiFrancesco, acting governor since Christine Todd Whitman resigned to become EPA administrator in January 2001, left the job when his term in the state Senate expired January 8, 2001; the newly elected governor did not take office until January 15. For 3 days, Bennett became acting governor and held several receptions in the governor's mansion, Drumthwacket. Codey began his 3 days as acting governor by having breakfast with inmates at Graystone Park Psychiatric Hospital and coached his son's junior high basketball team in a game that afternoon.

The elected governor to whom Codey turned over the job was Democrat Jim McGreevey. With fiscal problems looming, McGreevey increased the cigarette tax by 70 cents and also the corporate business tax. In June 2004 the legislature passed McGreevey's "millionaires tax," actually a tax on income over $500,000, to produce $800 million for property tax rebates. He got the legislature to pass the nation's first law requiring handguns to contain a device allowing only designated owners to fire them, but it could not be enforced until the technology is developed. He was embarrassed when two of his appointees, state police superintendent Joseph Santiago and homeland security adviser Golan Cipel, were forced to resign. He was embarrassed also when Amiri Baraka, whom he named as state poet laureate, published a poem in which he claimed that Jews were behind the World Trade Center bombing. McGreevey urged Baraka to resign but he refused; McGreevey then signed a bill eliminating the position.

In 2003 Democrats won a 22–18 majority in the state Senate, and Codey became the sole Senate President. The legislature passed and McGreevey signed a domestic partnership act, one of the nation's first. McGreevey's major accomplishments seemed to some to work to cross-purposes. One was the Highlands Water Protection and Planning Act, which put 395,000 acres near drinking water sources in North Jersey off limits to most development and set aside an adjoining 400,000 acres for low-density growth. The other was a "fast track" law, setting time limits for regulators to rule on development applications in areas classified as suitable for development. Hanging over all this were images of corruption. U.S. Attorney Christopher Christie obtained indictments of many local officials and of prominent McGreevey fundraisers Charles Kushner and David D'Amiano. Kushner was charged with trying to thwart a federal investigation by luring a grand jury witness into a tryst with a prostitute; D'Amiano's indictment said "State Official 1" would signal his agreement in an extortion scheme by using the word "Machiavelli," and there was testimony that McGreevey referred to Machiavelli in a meeting. Increasing publicity fell on the huge sums of money being raised by county party leaders, particularly George Norcross and John Lynch, also strong McGreevey supporters. Businesses with contracts with local government were pressed to contribute ("pay to play") by the county leaders, who then sent ("wheeled") the money to favored candidates in primaries and general election contests.

But the publicity here was nothing compared to the publicity given to McGreevey's announcement on August 12, 2004, that he would resign, effective November 15. "I am a gay American," McGreevey said, and hailed the nation's history of respecting minorities; he admitted to having an extramarital affair with a man. What he didn't mention was that the man was Golan Cipel, whom he had appointed to a $110,000 job at the Office of Homeland Security and then on his personal staff despite the man's lack of qualifications, and that Cipel was threatening to sue him for sexual harassment. New Jersey has no lieutenant governor, and Codey was in line to be McGreevey's successor.

But it was not clear just when he would become acting governor. If McGreevey resigned before September 3, a special election would be called on November 2. Norcross and Lynch had a ready candidate, Senator Jon Corzine, who had spent $63 million on his 2000 Senate campaign and had contributed millions to the county parties. And they had had continuing fights with Codey—in 2001 over who should be Speaker of the Assembly (the leaders' Albio Sires beat Codey's Joseph Doria), in early 2002 over who should head the New Jersey Sports and Exposition Authority (the leaders won), in late 2002 over who should be nominated for Essex County Executive (the leaders' Joseph DiVincenzo beat Codey's Tom Giblin), in 2003 whom should be nominated to run against a suddenly vulnerable John Bennett (Codey's candidate Ellen Karcher won the primary and in November). For the leaders, having Codey as governor for two months was highly preferable to having him governor for 14 months or, if he should win a full term in 2005, for five or nine years. But McGreevey resisted stubbornly and made some 200 lame duck appointments; he insisted on remaining governor for the whole 24 hours of November 15. In September 2004 McGreevey issued an executive order prohibiting contributions by companies that do business with state or local government. Leaders in the legislature, including Codey, worked to pass such a bill, though not successfully.

Codey announced he would continue to live in his house in West Orange and not move to the governor's mansion. "Where I come from, we were always trying to get out of public housing, not into it." He professed to be uninterested in pomp and ceremony. "Jim loved the roar of the crowd. It doesn't work for me. I don't need that approval. I've been in the legislature for 31 years." And he said he still had a passion to improve mental health treatment. "I think you've got to come up with a new system. The day before McGreevey resigned, I raided a boarding home for 71 mentally ill patients. I saw dead mice on the floor, cockroaches running all over, puddles of urine on the floor, which contains the kitchen or cafeteria. The heat in the rooms on an incredibly hot summer day exceeded 95. There was one bathroom in the place that totally worked. It was just an absolute disgrace. We've got to do away with those kinds of places."

Going into 2005, Codey seemed to have good will among legislators of both parties, but faced serious fiscal problems. A sales or income tax increase? "I'm not pledging. I'm saying it's the last thing I would want to do, clearly." Sports teams were threatening to leave the Meadowlands complex unless the state made major changes. The New Jersey Turnpike needed more lanes between Jamesburg and the Pennsylvania Turnpike Extension. Codey said he wanted to make adjustments in McGreevey's fast track law and he endorsed, and took credit for, McGreevey's stem cell research proposals. "That stem cell bill, that was all mine. My idea. Now I want to continue to make New Jersey one of the leaders in the country on stem cell research." He admitted that New Jersey couldn't match the $3 billion California voters agreed to spend, but said the state was well positioned, with all its pharmaceutical companies, to be a research center.

Looming over the first months of his governorship was the specter of Jon Corzine, clearly ambitious for the governorship and prepared to spend liberally from his perhaps $300 million in wealth to win it. At least one other Democrat was looking at running if Corzine didn't, or if Corzine and Codey both did, 1st District Congressman Rob Andrews, who lost narrowly to McGreevey in the 1997 primary. On December 2 Corzine announced he was running. He said his wealth insured that he would be "unbought and unbossed." "It's his right to run," Codey said. "He considers me a friend of his. So be it. It is what it is." Codey held a rally of Essex County Democrats on December 9 and he prepared meticulously for his State of the State speech January 11. But Corzine had far more support among party leaders—George Norcross and John Lynch, Congressmen Robert Menendez and Frank Pallone (both interested in the appointment to the Senate Corzine would make if elected governor), Speaker Albio Sires and many others whom Corzine had supported generously over the years. On January 31 Codey announced he was not running and backed Corzine. Codey noted that he would still remain Senate President throughout 2005 and after, assuming a Democratic majority; Corzine or a Republican governor would have to deal with him in 2006 and beyond.

In June 2005 Corzine won the primary with no serious opposition, and in a Democratic state seems to be the favorite. But George W. Bush's 46% in New Jersey in 2004 suggests the state is a little less Democratic than it used to be, and Corzine won the 2000 Senate race by only 50%–47% after spending $63 million.

Among the Republicans, Bret Schundler announced his candidacy in July 2004, when everyone thought McGreevey would be running for reelection. He promised to assemble an army of volunteers to circulate petitions calling on the state legislature to pass constitutional amendments limiting state and local spending increases to 1.3% times the inflation rate, with a view toward reducing property tax rates. He also joined state Senate Minority Leader Leonard Lance in a lawsuit challenging McGreevey's $1.9 billion of borrowing to balance the budget. And he said Corzine "lined up Democrat [sic] party bosses behind him by spreading around money and working New Jersey's corrupt pay-to-play system of politics with the gusto of a bond trader." Some Republican moderates disliked him because of his conservative stands, and some insiders because he challenged Acting Governor Donald DiFrancesco in 2001, but he did win the primary that year with 57% of the vote. Also declaring was Douglas Forrester, who was leading Senator Bob Torricelli in the 2002 Senate race and lost to his replacement, Frank Lautenberg, by only a 54%–44% margin when he spent $8 million of his own money. Forrester again spent freely, launching his campaign for governor with $1 million in TV and radio ads in November 2004. By early June he had spent $10 million of his own money, much of it on television and radio ads. Forrester, who held more moderate views than Schundler on abortion and gun rights, defeated him 36%–31%. Morris County Freeholder John Murphy finished third in the seven-candidate field with 11%.

Senior Senator

Jon Corzine (D)

Elected 2000, seat up 2006, 1st term; b. Jan. 1, 1947, Taylorville, IL; home, Summit; U. of IL (Urbana-Champaign), B.A. 1969; U. of Chicago, M.B.A. 1973; Christian; divorced.

Military Career: Marine Corps Reserves, 1969–75.

Professional Career: Officer, Continental IL Natl. Bank, 1970–73; Asst. V.P., BancOhio, 1973–75; Goldman Sachs, Bond Trader 1975–80, Partner 1980–99, Chmn. & CEO 1994–99.

DC Office: 502 HSOB, 20510, 202-224-4744; Fax: 202-228-2197; Web site: corzine.senate.gov.

State Offices: Barrington, 856-757-5353; Newark, 973-645-3030.

Committees: *Banking, Housing & Urban Affairs*: Housing & Transportation; International Trade & Finance; Securities & Investment. *Budget. Energy & Natural Resources*: Energy; National Parks; Water & Power. *Intelligence (Select)*.

Group Ratings

	ADA	ACLU	AFS	LCV	ITIC	NTU	COC	ACU	NTLC	CHC
2004	100	62	100	100	67	19	47	4	10	0
2003	90	—	100	84	—	17	27	15	—	—

National Journal Ratings

	2003 LIB	—	2003 CONS		2004 LIB	—	2004 CONS
Economic	70%	—	26%		79%	—	13%
Social	85%	—	0%		82%	—	0%
Foreign	86%	—	10%		93%	—	5%

Key Votes of the 108th Congress

1. Ban Drilling in ANWR	Y	5. Energy Bill	N	9. Ban Same-Sex Marriage	N
2. Approve Bush Tax Cuts	N	6. Support Roe v. Wade	Y	10. Ban Bunker-Buster Bomb	Y
3. Medicare/Rx Bill	N	7. Ban Partial-Birth Abortion	N	11. Fund Iraq War	Y
4. Bar Overtime Pay Regs.	Y	8. Assault Weapons Ban	Y	12. Restrict Missile Defense	Y

Election Results

2000 general	Jon Corzine (D)	1,511,237	(50%)	($63,209,506)
	Bob Franks (R)	1,420,267	(47%)	($6,389,936)
	Other	84,158	(3%)	
2000 primary	Jon Corzine (D)	251,216	(58%)	
	Jim Florio (D)	182,212	(42%)	
1994 general	Frank Lautenberg (D)	1,033,487	(50%)	($8,217,716)
	Garabed (Chuck) Haytaian (R)	966,244	(47%)	($5,110,378)
	Other	55,156	(3%)	

Jon Corzine, former chairman of Goldman Sachs, was elected senator from New Jersey in 2000 after waging the most expensive Senate campaign in American history. Corzine grew up on a family farm in Downstate Illinois, far from New Jersey; he went to college at the University of Illinois, business school at the University of Chicago and served six years in the Marine Corps

Reserve. In 1975 he joined Goldman Sachs in New York; his entry-level position included fetching coffee for his superiors. Corzine was a successful bond trader and a protégé of Robert Rubin, who became Treasury Secretary in the Clinton administration. In 1980 Corzine was made a general partner and in 1994 he became co-chairman and CEO. In May 1999 Goldman Sachs went public, and the $3.66 billion initial offering netted Corzine more than $300 million; he retired in 1999 after a management shakeup. Aside from contributing to Democratic (and some Republican) candidates, he was not involved in politics, indeed did not vote in primary elections from 1988 to 1998 or in the 1991, 1995 and 1998 general elections; in 1997 he co-chaired a presidential commission on increasing investment in technology, infrastructure and schools.

In early 1999, a Senate race was probably the farthest thing from Corzine's mind. Then, in February 1999, Senator Frank Lautenberg announced he would not run again in 2000 (Lautenberg later returned to win election to Senator Bob Torricelli's seat in 2002, and is now Corzine's junior colleague). Plunging immediately into the race was former Governor Jim Florio, still unpopular for the $2.8 billion tax increase he secured in 1990. In April Governor Christine Todd Whitman, presumably the strongest possible Republican candidate, announced she was running. Many Democratic insiders, including Torricelli, feared that Whitman would win the seat, and scurried around to find other contenders. They found Corzine, with $300 million and without a job. He started running, going around the state to meet leaders of the county Democratic organizations, who are considered vital in the primary, and, it was revealed much later, contributing generously to them and to community organizations. He quickly cornered organization support outside Florio's home area in South Jersey and, like most local Democratic insiders, endorsed Al Gore over New Jersey's Bill Bradley. Meanwhile, Corzine's great wealth and his willingness to spend it cleared the field; Whitman withdrew in September 1999. Corzine's money talked even while most New Jersey voters had never heard of him.

Still, Florio campaigned aggressively. He attacked Corzine's inexperience and spotty voting record. Even so, New Jersey Democratic leaders dreaded that Florio would lose to even the little-known candidates running for the Republican nomination. In March, three months before the primary, Corzine went up with TV ads in the New York and Philadelphia markets. He set forth his liberal stands on issues—for a universal health care system, for government payment of tuition to college or vocational or technical school for students with at least a B average, for gun control, for abortion rights. Corzine's investment—he spent $35 million up to the June primary—paid off. He won a 58%–42% victory.

After the primary, Corzine cut back on spending—for a while. The Republican primary, with a pathetically low turnout, was won by 7th District Congressman Bob Franks—amazingly, a member of the same church as Corzine. Corzine's ads talked about his big-government positions in appealing terms, but he made a political neophyte's mistakes and that got him bad publicity. In early September he told the Sierra Club he had voted for an open space referendum in 1998; but in 1998 he had not voted at all. Still stuck below 50% in the polls, he started running negative ads against Franks two weeks later. He had been refusing to make his income tax returns public, on the ground they violated a confidentiality agreement with Goldman Sachs. Then in mid-September he released records showing that in 1996–99 he made $145 million, paid $43 million in taxes and gave $25 million to charity. But when reporters started investigating which charities, they found that he had stepped up giving to New Jersey groups in 1999, and that he gave hundreds of thousands to groups whose leaders and sponsors later endorsed him. He gave $30,000 to a dinner honoring Lautenberg, who later endorsed him; he gave $50,000 to Operation Rainbow/PUSH, and Jesse Jackson endorsed him the night before the primary; he gave $25,000 to St. Matthew's A.M.E. Church in Orange and was endorsed by the Black Ministers Alliance of New Jersey. When he was asked whether he had contributed to any of the churches, he said no; it turned out his family foundation made the contribution.

Franks, like Florio, argued that Corzine was trying to buy a Senate seat and attacked him for failing to disclose the tax returns and for backing "universal" government programs that were unrealistic and too costly. When Corzine's numbers stalled because of his mistakes, Franks held onto his money and spent $2.5 million in the last two and a half weeks, when he also benefited from endorsements by *The New York Times* and *The Philadelphia Inquirer*. Corzine spent $7.4

million on turnout efforts including, embarrassingly, busing in residents of Philadelphia home-less shelters and halfway houses to work on his campaign. In the end Corzine spent more than $63 million, the all-time record. He won 50%–47%, with big margins in central cities—the turnout effort delivered. But that trailed the generic vote in increasingly Democratic New Jersey.

In the Senate Corzine has had a very liberal voting record; he has consistently argued that Democrats, having earned credibility on macroeconomic issues in the 1990s, should take forth-right liberal stands. He continued to support universal health care, called for a national morato-rium on the death penalty and a national ban of racial profiling; he voted against the Iraq war resolution in October 2002. He voted against the 2001 Bush tax cuts and in August 2002 said Congress should "rescind or freeze" them; in January 2003 he led Democrats in opposing that year's Bush tax cut, arguing that by siphoning off dividends it might reduce investment and called for a $300 rebate instead. On Social Security he was one of the Democrats' leading critics of individual investment accounts.

But he got the most attention on the issue of corporate accountability raised by the collapse of Enron in December 2001. Majority Leader Tom Daschle made a point of having Corzine at his side when speaking on the issue, and it is obviously a subject on which he has special expertise. Corzine argued that Enron and other scandals indicated the need for more regulation. On the Banking Committee, he worked with Chairman Paul Sarbanes on his corporate accountability bill, and bemoaned that it seemed stalled in June 2002. But then the WorldCom scandal came along, and the bill, slightly amended, became the Sarbanes-Oxley Act. He has argued that financial services regulation should be concentrated in the Federal Reserve and the SEC, not the Comptroller of the Currency or the Commodities Futures Trading Commission, and said that the current system provides no consolidated view of regulation of derivatives markets. In January 2004 he criticized the practices, exposed by New York Attorney General Eliot Spitzer, of mutual funds and proposed a study of whether they should be regulated.

Corzine has pushed for liberal legislation on many fronts, not always with success in a Republican Senate. He and colleague Frank Lautenberg voted against the Medicare/prescription drug bill in November 2003, though it was backed by some New Jersey pharmaceutical firms. He fought successfully in November 2003 to delay for a year the Education Department's reductions in deductions for state taxes when calculating Pell grants; this would hurt most in high-income states like New Jersey. He sponsored an amendment to the bill protecting gun manufacturers from lawsuits which would allow law enforcement officers to sue gun manufacturers and dealers. With Russ Feingold, he sponsored a ban on racial profiling, which would follow Justice Depart-ment guidelines and provide for civil enforcements and private lawsuits. He has worked for several years to raise the maximum penalty for willful work safety violations that result in an employee's death from six months to 10 years. He wants to increase the guaranty in VA home mortgage loans from $60,000 to $83,000, 25% of the Freddie Mac conforming limit; this would allow veterans to buy homes worth up to $333,000, which are pretty numerous in New Jersey. In July 2004 he and Sam Brownback sponsored a resolution declaring the Sudanese government's actions in Darfur a "genocide" and calling on other nations to join the United States and try to stop it.

September 11 hit New Jersey especially hard—Corzine noted that 10 people from Summit, his home town, died at the World Trade Center—and Corzine's major initiative in response was a chemical security bill that would require businesses that house chemicals to conduct vulnerabil-ity assessments and consider safer security technology. He sought to attach it to the homeland security bill in fall 2002, but others argued that it would put undue burdens on stores selling fertilizer and pesticide. In 2003 the Environment Committee passed an alternative requiring chemical companies to submit security plans to DHS for approval; chemical companies argued that Corzine's version would amount to government micromanagement. He was a co-sponsor of the Terrorism Risk Insurance Act, which became law in November 2002.

Corzine is a stronger partisan than many senators who have spent all their adult lives in politics, and from 1999 has thrown himself, and his money, into building the Democratic party in New Jersey and in the nation as a whole. In 2003 he liberally supported county Democratic organizations, which helped Democrats win majorities in both houses of the legislature.

Throughout the 2002 cycle he let it be known that he would like to become DSCC chairman after the election. He showed his skills at handling difficult political situations in the imbroglio over whether Bob Torricelli should drop out of the 2002 Senate race. He had backed Torricelli all along, but helped to negotiate Torricelli's departure and the selection of Frank Lautenberg to replace him. In December 2002 Tom Daschle chose Corzine to head the DSCC. Corzine did an excellent job of raising money in 2004, and during some periods the DSCC outraised its Republican counterpart, something few expected after the McCain-Feingold law outlawed soft money contributions. He helped to recruit candidates who could run far ahead of the party's presidential nominee in Alaska, Colorado and Oklahoma, and he recruited and discouraged primary competition for first class candidates in four of the five southern states where Democrats were retiring. "When you have primaries, you leave bloodied souls coming out of them." Through much of the spring and summer, Corzine said that Democrats had a better than 50% chance of gaining seats. Instead, they lost all five southern states and Daschle, despite late infusions of money, lost in South Dakota, for a net loss of four seats.

This must surely have been a disappointment to Corzine, but he had another political preoccupation: running for governor of New Jersey. Democrats in the state had become used to dropping candidates who seemed unable to win, as they had done to Torricelli in October 2004. In summer 2004, when McGreevey's job ratings were low, there was talk of replacing him with another candidate. When asked if he was interested, Corzine said, "Why would I work so hard to take back the majority in the Senate if I were leaving? It just doesn't actually fit with common sense." But he also said he missed being in an executive position. At the Democratic National Convention Corzine, not McGreevey, was head of the delegation. Then, on August 12, McGreevey announced that he had had an extramarital affair with a man and would resign effective November 15. Under New Jersey law, if he should resign before September 3 there would be a special election on November 2, and the rules would enable state party organizations to exercise significant influence in picking a favored candidate. Camden County Democratic Chairman George Norcross and Middlesex County Democratic Chairman John Lynch, both staunch supporters of McGreevey and Corzine (he had given $4 million to county organizations) and adversaries of state Senate President Richard Codey, who would become acting governor on McGreevey's resignation, urged McGreevey to resign before the deadline. They didn't want Codey to be governor for 14 months, as he would be if McGreevey resigned in November, and possibly for five or nine years, if he won the job in his own right. Corzine made it clear he would run for governor if McGreevey resigned before the deadline, and no one in either party seemed to have the name identification and the fundraising ability to beat him in November. On August 18 McGreevey and Corzine spoke on the phone and, as Corzine put it, "The governor made it clear in our conversation his absolute intent to serve until November 15, 2004. I accept that decision as final."

"If I really want to get things done, I need to be in the majority," Corzine has said. On election night 2004 it was clear he would not be in the majority in the Senate for at least two years and quite possibly much longer. The ability of a New Jersey governor to get things done is not in doubt: he or she is the strongest governor in the nation, the only statewide official who appoints all others, including the attorney general and the 21 county district attorneys. On November 4 Corzine held a meetings of political advisers and supporters—the beginning of his governor campaign, it seems. The one obstacle was Richard Codey. After he took office November 16 (McGreevey insisted on remaining governor for all 24 hours of November 15), Codey started to make appearances around the state and seemed to cast off his reluctance to run for the job in 2005. Meanwhile, 1st District Congressman Rob Andrews, who narrowly lost the 1997 gubernatorial primary to McGreevey, indicated that he might be interested in running for governor too; with his base in South Jersey, he looked like a formidable contender. On December 2, Corzine announced he was running. He said his wealth insured that he would be "unbought and unbossed." Codey made moves to demonstrate his own support but Corzine, Norcross and Lynch had lined up support from dozens of Democrats—Congressmen Robert Menendez and Frank Pallone (both interested in the appointment to the Senate Corzine would make if elected governor), Speaker Albio Sires and many others whom Corzine had supported generously over the years. All were aware that, if elected governor, Corzine would name his own successor as senator. On January 31 Codey announced he was not running and backed Corzine. Under New Jersey law, Codey as acting governor remained president of the Senate and would remain in the Senate, presumably as president, after the November 2005 election.

In June 2005 Corzine won the June primary with no serious opposition, and in a Democratic state would seem to be the favorite. But George W. Bush's 46% in New Jersey in 2004 suggests the state is a little less Democratic than it used to be, and Corzine won the 2000 Senate race by only 50%–47% after spending $63 million. The Republican nominee was Douglas Forrester, who lost to Lautenberg in the 2002 Senate race and spent $10 million out of pocket to win the party nomination for governor. He seemed likely to attack Corzine for his ties to Democratic bosses (Corzine donated to charity $88,000 he received from leading McGreevey fundraiser Charles Kushner after Kushner pleaded guilty to bribery) and to argue that he would raise taxes.

Who will be the new senator if Corzine becomes governor in January 2006? It will be his choice. In early 2005, those interested included six of the state's seven Democratic congressmen, in numeric order, Rob Andrews, Frank Pallone, Bill Pascrell, Steve Rothman, Rush Holt (whose father was elected senator from West Virginia at age 29 in 1934) and Bob Menendez. Another option for Corzine might be to appoint a "stop-gap" senator—who would not seek reelection and thus enable Corzine to avoid alienating the many interested candidates and their regional supporters. The Republican frontrunner in mid-2005 was state Senator Tom Kean Jr., whose father was elected governor in 1981 and 1985.

Junior Senator

Frank Lautenberg (D)

Elected 2002, seat up 2008, 1st term; b. Jan. 23, 1924, Paterson; home, Cliffside Park; Columbia U., B.S. 1949; Jewish; married (Bonnie).

Military Career: Army Signal Corps, 1942–46 (WWII).

Elected Office: U.S. Senate, 1982–2000.

Professional Career: Co–founder, Automatic Data Processing, 1952–82; NY & NJ Port Authority Comm., 1978–82.

DC Office: 324 HSOB, 20510, 202-224-3224; Fax: 202-228-4054; Web site: lautenberg.senate.gov.

State Offices: Camden, 856-338-8922; Newark, 973-639-8700.

Committees: *Commerce, Science & Transportation*: Aviation; Fisheries & the Coast Guard; Global Climate Change & Impacts (RMM); National Ocean Policy Study; Surface Transportation & Merchant Marine; Trade, Tourism & Economic Development. *Environment & Public Works*: Clean Air, Climate Change & Nuclear Safety; Fisheries, Wildlife & Water; Superfund & Waste Management. *Homeland Security & Governmental Affairs*: Federal Financial Management, Govt. Information & International Security; Investigations (Permanent); Oversight of Govt. Management, the Federal Workforce & the District of Columbia.

Group Ratings

	ADA	ACLU	AFS	LCV	ITIC	NTU	COC	ACU	NTLC	CHC
2004	100	67	100	100	55	15	38	0	5	0
2003	95	—	100	89	—	20	26	15	—	—

National Journal Ratings

	2003 LIB	—	2003 CONS		2004 LIB	—	2004 CONS
Economic	82%	—	10%		76%	—	21%
Social	85%	—	0%		82%	—	0%
Foreign	86%	—	10%		95%	—	1%

Key Votes of the 108th Congress

1. Ban Drilling in ANWR	Y	5. Energy Bill	N	9. Ban Same-Sex Marriage	N
2. Approve Bush Tax Cuts	N	6. Support Roe v. Wade	Y	10. Ban Bunker-Buster Bomb	Y
3. Medicare/Rx Bill	N	7. Ban Partial-Birth Abortion	N	11. Fund Iraq War	N
4. Bar Overtime Pay Regs.	Y	8. Assault Weapons Ban	Y	12. Restrict Missile Defense	Y

Election Results

2002 general	Frank Lautenberg (D).......................... 1,138,193	(54%)	($2,929,206)
	Douglas Forrester (R) 928,439	(44%)	($10,606,843)
	Other.. 45,972	(2%)	
1996 general	Robert G. Torricelli (D) 1,519,154	(53%)	($9,134,854)
	Dick Zimmer (R).............................. 1,227,351	(43%)	($8,238,181)
	Other... 136,961	(5%)	

Prior Winning Percentages: 1994 (50%); 1988 (54%); 1982 (51%)

Frank Lautenberg is, once again, New Jersey's junior senator. He was elected in 1982, 1988 and 1994 and retired in 2000, then returned to run again in October 2002 after Bob Torricelli withdrew from the race. With his personal wealth and name recognition, Lautenberg was an obvious choice to succeed Torricelli; New Jersey Democrats persuaded the state supreme court to let them put Lautenberg's name on the ballot. Lautenberg grew up in Paterson, the son of an immigrant silk worker. He served in the Army Signal Corps in World War II and says he never would have gone to college without the G.I. Bill of Rights. He graduated from Columbia and in 1952 started a company called Automatic Data Processing, which by the mid-1990s had almost 30,000 employees and processed the payroll for nearly 10% of private sector jobs in the United States—a brilliant success story. When ADP went public in 1961, Lautenberg's stock was worth $50,000; now his net worth is in the vicinity of $40 million. Lautenberg was a contributor to Democratic campaigns and got on Richard Nixon's enemies list when he contributed $90,000 to George McGovern in 1972.

But no one thought of him as a candidate until, not for the last time, scandal provided an opening: Democratic Senator Harrison Williams resigned in March 1982 as the Senate was considering his expulsion after his conviction in the Abscam case, and his appointed successor, Republican Nicholas Brady, made it clear he was not running for a full term (he became the first George Bush's Treasury Secretary). Lautenberg ran and spent $5 million of his own money and boasted of his high-tech experience. He beat several professional politicians in the primary and upset Republican Congresswoman Millicent Fenwick in the general 51%–48%. During the campaign he referred to the 72-year-old Fenwick, who was satirized in *Doonesbury*, as "eccentric" and a "national monument" and questioned her "fitness" and "ability to do the job."

Lautenberg believes government helped him and others work their way up, and in his first three terms had a solidly liberal voting record. He bucked the party only occasionally. As chairman and ranking Democrat on the Transportation Appropriations Subcommittee, he got Congress to ban smoking first on two-hour flights, then on all domestic flights. He is a strong backer of gun control and author of the 1996 law barring those convicted of domestic abuse from possessing firearms.

New Jersey is the second most expensive state to campaign in, because candidates must buy New York and Philadelphia TV, and Lautenberg's willingness to spend large amounts of his own money helped him win reelection over retired General Pete Dawkins in 1988 by 54%–46% and Assembly Speaker Chuck Haytaian in 1994 by 50%–47%. He can be an aggressive campaigner. In 1998 he seemed primed to run again, and no well-known Republican seemed eager to challenge him. But in February 1999 he announced that he would retire in 2000.

One thing he surely did not miss was dealing with his colleague Bob Torricelli. Relationships between senators of the same state and party are often frayed and acrimonious; but the relationship between Lautenberg and Torricelli was probably more hostile than any since 1859, when California Senator David Broderick was killed in a duel with his colleague William Gwin's best friend. In March 1999, as Torricelli, the chairman of the Senate Democrats' campaign committee, was briefing colleagues, Lautenberg accused him of being too friendly with Republican Governor Christine Todd Whitman; Torricelli was enraged and in full view after the meeting approached Lautenberg and, as *The New York Times* daintily put it, "made a vulgar threat on his manhood." So Lautenberg was one New Jersey Democrat who was not unhappy when Torricelli fell into disfavor with voters in his 2002 reelection campaign.

In most respects, Torricelli seemed a clear favorite to win. The three candidates in the June primary were mostly unknown—businessman Doug Forrester, South Jersey state Senators Susan Allen and John Matheussen. Money made the difference: Forrester, who started BeneCard, a manager of prescription drug benefits, was worth some $50 million and spent $3 million in the primary and beat Allen by a 45%–37% margin.

But scandal loomed over Torricelli. For three years the U.S. Attorney's office in Manhattan had been investigating charges that businessman David Chang had given lavish gifts and cash to Torricelli and that Torricelli had worked to advance Chang's business interests in Korea. Torricelli did give such assistance, but denied receiving gifts; he said he reimbursed Chang. In January 2002 U.S. Attorney Mary Jo White announced that Torricelli would not be prosecuted. But White had sent information about the charges to the Senate Ethics Committee; on July 30 the committee "severely admonished" Torricelli for violating the Senate rule against receiving gifts over $50 but did not release the evidence to the public.

Forrester made much of Torricelli's problems. In September, a federal judge in a lawsuit brought by news media ordered the unsealing of the memorandum on the case written by prosecutors in the U.S. Attorney's office. They found "credible" Chang's allegations that Torricelli had accepted "tens of thousands" of dollars in gifts and cash. As details poured out, Torricelli plummeted in the polls. On Saturday, September 28, a *Star-Ledger* poll showed Forrester ahead 47%–34%—a devastating result. On Sunday Governor Jim McGreevey, Senator Jon Corzine and other New Jersey Democratic leaders met in Trenton and patched in Majority Leader Tom Daschle over the phone: Obviously they were trying to get Torricelli to withdraw from the race. On Monday Torricelli's office announced he would hold a press conference at 11 a.m.; he finally appeared around 5 p.m. and, in a lugubrious speech, withdrew.

New Jersey Democrats were now in need of a well-known candidate to replace Torricelli. Congressman Bob Menendez, seeking a leadership position in the House, wasn't interested. Congressman Rob Andrews was presumably vetoed by McGreevey, who had narrowly beaten him in the 1997 gubernatorial primary. Congressman Frank Pallone, after giving it some thought, decided not to run. The risk of giving up a safe House seat to seek a nomination that might be rejected by a court may have seemed too great. Former Senator Bill Bradley let it be known he had no interest whatever. But Lautenberg, now evidently missing life in the Senate, said he would "seriously consider serving again if asked." It seems unlikely that Torricelli would have withdrawn if he had known that Lautenberg would get the nomination. But there was nothing he could do to stop him. Lautenberg was well known and capable of self-financing. McGreevey and the other Democrats quickly agreed on him.

New Jersey law does not contain a provision for substituting a new candidate so late in the campaign unless a candidate has died; ballots had already been printed with Torricelli's name. But the New Jersey Supreme Court is made up of judicial activists of both parties with a propensity to accommodate the insiders of both major parties. In October 2002 it quickly approved state Democrats' request to substitute Lautenberg for Torricelli and ordered the state Democratic party to pay the $800,000 needed to print new ballots. The Lautenberg campaign moved into the Torricelli headquarters and Lautenberg was again a candidate for the Senate, without having to spend months fundraising. The easiest source of funds proved unavailable: Torricelli would not send over a dime from his $5 million campaign treasury. Lautenberg spent $1.5 million of his own money, and those funds, plus $1.2 million from national and New Jersey Democrats, turned out to be enough in this Democratic state.

Now Forrester could no longer introduce himself as "the guy running against Bob Torricelli." He did run a cute ad on cable TV, showing a kid slamming his desk and saying, "I can't do this. I quit! If I fail this test, can I have Frank Lautenberg take it for me?" Forrester attacked Lautenberg as soft on defense and terrorism, citing his 1991 vote against the Gulf War resolution and he questioned whether Lautenberg at 78—six years older than Millicent Fenwick was when Lautenberg questioned her ability to do the job—was too old. Lautenberg attacked Forrester on

Social Security, prescription drugs, abortion and gun control: Forrester was against state-paid abortions and had written a 1992 column in the *West Windsor-Plainsboro Chronicle* on owning semiautomatic guns. "Liberty is all about the government allowing citizens to do weird things unless there is a compelling documented public purpose which should preclude them." On October 30 they appeared together for 30 minutes on News 12 New Jersey, a cable channel available to 55% of state households; Lautenberg seemed a little ragged, but was plainly still up to the job. Forrester spent $10 million altogether, $7.5 million of it his own money; the Senate Republican campaign committee did not make New Jersey a top priority. Unsurprisingly, Lautenberg won 54%–44%, a better showing than in 1994; but then New Jersey has become more Democratic than it was in 1994.

Lautenberg was disappointed when Senate Democrats did not give him credit for all his seniority; his previous service only entitled him to seniority over other freshmen. But he quickly directed his ire away from his fellow Democrats and toward the Bush administration. On the Commerce committee he maneuvered in June 2003 to overturn the FCC's changes in media concentration rules. He went on the warpath to stop privatization of the air traffic control system, holding up the FAA reauthorization in summer 2003 by demanding that the FAA refrain from even studying privatization. He got Trent Lott to agree to a one-year moratorium on privatizing any jobs, but that was unacceptable to the administration; passage of the bill waited until FAA Administrator Marion Blakey sent over a letter stating that no jobs "directly related to our air traffic control system" would be privatized during the fiscal year. Lautenberg voted against the Medicare/prescription drug bill, even though it was supported by many New Jersey pharmaceutical companies, and in 2004 tried to stop HHS from sending out letters explaining the new benefit. He spoke out stringently in November 2003 after George W. Bush signed the partial-birth abortion ban. On local issues, in 2003 Lautenberg tried to stop the state-authorized bear hunt on federal lands and in 2004 sponsored a bill with Jon Corzine and Congressman Rodney Frelinghuysen with $10 million to preserve land in the Jersey Highlands.

During 2004 Lautenberg kept up a drumbeat of criticism of the Pentagon for awarding sole-source contracts to Halliburton. He sponsored an amendment, aimed at Halliburton, to prevent foreign subsidies of U.S. corporations to do business with nations on the terrorist watch list; it was defeated in the Senate 50–49 in May 2004 when Max Baucus changed his vote. In October he tried to attach the amendment to a must pass bill and threatened a filibuster. In April 2004 he took to the floor of the Senate with an object he called a chicken hawk and made a thinly veiled attack on Dick Cheney. He called for Donald Rumsfeld's resignation in May 2004 after revelations of the Abu Ghraib abuses and in December 2004 called on George W. Bush to fire him after his remarks on armored vehicles. He requested a hearing after Disney refused to distribute director Michael Moore's film *Fahrenheit 9/11*. In June 2004 he urged Attorney General John Ashcroft to authorize a special counsel investigation of the Halliburton contract. That month he sponsored an amendment to allow the media to photograph coffins of servicemen at Dover Air Force Base and another for a $2,000 bonus for troops subject to stop loss orders. In September 2004 he called for a fixed five-year term for the new national intelligence director. When Bush made a campaign stop in New Jersey in October 2004, Lautenberg said, "President Bush, time and time again, has made decisions that made New Jersey more vulnerable to terrorism. He's here because of November 2, not 9/11." When asked why Lautenberg was more outspoken than in his first three Senate terms, his colleague Jon Corzine said, "He's less risk-averse. I think Frank couldn't care less." Lautenberg said, "I do feel unconstrained."

Lautenberg's seat comes up in 2008, when he turns 84, and in early 2005 few in New Jersey politics expected him to run again. But he regretted his decision to retire in 2000, and in December 2003 he said, "I like being back. If my health is good, I see no reason" not to run again.

FIRST DISTRICT

Rep. Robert Andrews (D)

Elected 1990, 8th full term; b. Aug. 4, 1957, Camden; home, Haddon Heights; Bucknell U., B.A. 1979, Cornell U., J.D. 1982; Episcopalian; married (Camille).

Elected Office: Camden Cnty. Bd. of Chosen Freeholders, 1987–90.

Professional Career: Practicing atty., 1982–90; Adjunct Prof., Rutgers Law Schl., 1985–86, 1989–90.

DC Office: 2439 RHOB, 20515, 202-225-6501; Fax: 202-225-6583; Web site: www.house.gov/andrews.

District Offices: Haddon Heights, 856-546-5100; Woodbury, 856-848-3900.

Committees: *Armed Services* (15th of 28 D): Military Personnel; Terrorism, Unconventional Threats & Capabilities. *Education & the Workforce* (5th of 22 D): Education Reform; Employer-Employee Relations (RMM).

Group Ratings

	ADA	ACLU	AFS	LCV	ITIC	NTU	COC	ACU	NTLC	CHC
2004	95	70	100	100	30	11	24	0	3	7
2003	75	—	100	100	—	25	38	20	—	—

National Journal Ratings

	2003 LIB	—	2003 CONS		2004 LIB	—	2004 CONS
Economic	75%	—	24%		85%	—	14%
Social	78%	—	20%		78%	—	22%
Foreign	66%	—	32%		62%	—	36%

Key Votes of the 108th Congress

1. Drilling in ANWR	N	5. DC School Vouchers	N	9. Ban Same-Sex Marriage	N
2. Approve Bush Tax Cuts	N	6. Ban Human Cloning	N	10. Fund Iraq War	Y
3. Medicare/Rx Bill	N	7. Restrict Gun Liability	N	11. Bar Cuba Embargo Funds	N
4. Bar Overtime Pay Regs.	Y	8. Ban Partial-Birth Abortion	N	12. Intelligence Reorg.	Y

Election Results

2004 general	Robert Andrews (D)	201,163	(75%)	($848,616)
	Daniel Hutchison (R)	66,109	(25%)	($176,791)
	Other	931	(0%)	
2004 primary	Robert Andrews (D)	unopposed		
2002 general	Robert Andrews (D)	121,846	(93%)	($643,964)
	Timothy Haas (I)	9,543	(7%)	

Prior Winning Percentages: 2000 (76%); 1998 (73%); 1996 (76%); 1994 (72%); 1992 (67%); 1990 (54%); 1990 (55%)

The People		Race/Ethnic Origin	Ancestry	
Area size:	352 sq. mi.	71.2% White	Irish: 16.8%	Italian: 14.8%
Urban population:	98.6%	16.3% Black	German: 13.0%	
Rural population:	1.4%	2.6% Asian	**2004 Presidential Vote**	
Pop. 2000:	647,258	0.2% Native Am.	Kerry (D) 170,786	(61%)
Median income:	$47,473	0.0% Hawaiian	Bush (R) 111,073	(39%)
Poverty status:	9.9%	1.3% Two+ races	**2000 Presidential Vote**	
Military veterans:	12.4%	0.1% Other	Gore (D) 144,226	(63%)
		8.2% Hispanic Origin	Bush (R) 77,367	(34%)
			Other 7,261	(3%)
			Cook Partisan Voting Index: D +14	

Occupation	Blue collar: 22.8%	White collar: 62.4%	Gray collar: 14.8%

The closely built streets of the little city of Camden, New Jersey, across the Delaware River from Philadelphia's skyline, have seen a fair amount of history. This was where the poet Walt

Whitman lived when he wrote some of the versions of his *Leaves of Grass*. It was an immigrant-jammed industrial city then, with tinkerers and inventors. In 1894, a Camden machinist named Eldridge Johnson produced the Victor Talking Machine—the birth of the company that became RCA Victor in 1929 and the beginning of the recorded music industry. In 1897, Camden was the site of the invention of condensed soup, and the Campbell Soup Company was founded soon afterwards. Camden remained for years afterward a major industrial locus on the Jersey side of the Delaware River, not the broadest and certainly not the most picturesque of our Atlantic estuaries, but probably the East Coast's premier industrial waterway, with a concentration of steel factories, chemical plants and oil tank farms equal to any in the country. The flat lands of South Jersey all around, mostly ignored in the 19th century, had easy access to cheap water transport and plenty of skilled labor from the Philadelphia area. For a quarter-century starting in the 1940s, they became one of the country's fastest-growing industrial areas.

In the 1980s and 1990s, Camden emptied out, many of its factories closed, its neighborhoods were beset by crime, its mostly minority residents were heavily dependent on public assistance, its local government was so incompetent that its mayor was convicted for doing favors for Philadelphia's organized crime leaders. The two largest businesses in Camden County now provide health services. The state pays for two-thirds of the budget for the nearly bankrupt city, which has been ranked the second-poorest in America; national crime data showed that Camden in 2004 was the nation's most dangerous city. But it also has a few attractions: A newly-developed riverfront park, the New Jersey Aquarium and the Sony Music/Pace amphitheater; an aerospace complex and a Campbell Soup office tower have gone up. The port of Camden has rebounded, spurred by Del Monte's largest fruit processing plant, plus large imports of foreign steel and exports of scrap metal.

The 1st Congressional District is, more or less, greater Camden, the Delaware riverfront from Riverton south to a point across from the Delaware state line, and suburbs running southeast to the flat vegetable fields of South Jersey. It is traversed by Black Horse Pike and White Horse Pike, two of the most heavily traveled roads in this densely populated part of South Jersey. Both routes dates back two centuries; today, they connect Philadelphia and its middle class South Jersey suburbs. Many of these boroughs and townships developed over the past half-century as a result of flight from Camden; a few, like Gloucester City, emerged on their own rather than as an outgrowth of the city. The PATCO High-Speed Line to Philadelphia is just a quick trip over the Delaware River from here, making for an easy commute from places such as prosperous Haddonfield. The district includes a growing number of Hispanics, primarily Puerto Ricans in Camden, though many Mexicans from Puebla, in central Mexico, have settled in the region. Politically, this is an area with a Democratic heritage.

The 1st District is represented by Rob Andrews, first elected in 1990. Andrews grew up in Bellmawr, the son of a shipyard worker, made a splendid record in college and law school, returned home and with then-Congressman Jim Florio's support was elected to the Camden County Board of Chosen Freeholders before he was 30. When Florio left Congress to become governor in January 1990, he postponed the special election to replace him until November; he supported Andrews, though Andrews was silent on Florio's controversial state tax increase. Andrews had other help. He had a Republican opponent who switched positions on abortion and claimed to have attended a college he hadn't. Even so, in the anti-Florio climate, Andrews won by only 54%–43%.

Andrews has a mostly moderate record on economics and foreign policy but is more liberal on cultural issues. After Democrats lost House control, Andrews remained a legislative activist, often by working with Republicans. He typically introduces more than 100 bills every two years, the most for any House member. As the ranking Democrat on the Employer-Employee Relations Subcommittee, he worked with committee Chairman John Boehner to expand its focus on pension and retirement issues; they agreed on the need to change private pension law and on legislation to permit employees to keep the same retirement account even when they changed jobs. As an ardent proponent of the use of force in Iraq, Andrews joined other House Democratic supporters in several meetings with George W. Bush. Even after conditions in Iraq worsened after the overthrow, Andrews remained convinced that conditions were "better than leaving Saddam Hussein in power."

After the 1996 election, he announced he was running for governor. Andrews was initially favored to win the primary in June 1997, but he ran into stiff competition from then-state Senator James McGreevey, who had the backing of more Democratic county organizations in North Jersey plus key elements of organized labor. Andrews swept South Jersey and carried Hudson County, but McGreevey's big margins in Middlesex, Essex and Union Counties gave him a 39%–37% win. Andrews declined to run for governor again in 2001, and after McGreevey was elected, McGreevey refused to support him as the successor to Senator Bob Torricelli. In early 2004 Andrews was already talking about challenging McGreevey in the 2005 primary; after McGreevey announced in August 2004 that he would resign, Andrews seemed even more interested in running and promised that his next campaign would focus more on policy changes than on the party activists and other insiders who dominated his 1997 campaign. But after Jon Corzine announced his candidacy in December 2004, and even before Acting Governor Richard Codey announced in January 2005 that he would not run, Andrews said he wasn't running and endorsed Corzine. Corzine, if elected governor in November 2005, would be able to appoint his successor in the Senate; Andrews is one of several New Jersey congressmen who would like that appointment.

Andrews has been re-elected to the House by overwhelming margins and he has continued to live in Haddon Heights, commuting by train to the Capitol and occasionally sleeping overnight in his office. Despite his on-and-off relations with Camden County Democratic Chairman George Norcross, his House seat seems safe as long as he wants it. Given his relative youth and the ferment among New Jersey Democrats, it seems likely that he will seek an opportunity to run statewide in the next few years. If that happens, it is likely that another Democrat would win the seat.

SECOND DISTRICT

Rep. Frank LoBiondo (R)

Elected 1994, 6th term; b. May 12, 1946, Bridgeton; home, Vineland; St. Joseph's U., B.A. 1968; Catholic; married (Tina).

Elected Office: Cumberland Cnty. Bd. of Chosen Freeholders, 1985–88; NJ Assembly, 1987–94.

Professional Career: Operations Mgr., LoBiondo Bros. Motor Express Inc., 1968–94.

DC Office: 225 CHOB, 20515, 202-225-6572; Fax: 202-225-3318; Web site: www.house.gov/lobiondo.

District Office: Mays Landing, 609-625-5008.

Committees: *Armed Services* (22d of 34 R): Tactical Air & Land Forces; Terrorism, Unconventional Threats & Capabilities. *Transportation & Infrastructure* (15th of 41 R): Aviation; Coast Guard & Maritime Transportation (Chmn.); Highways, Transit & Pipelines.

Group Ratings

	ADA	ACLU	AFS	LCV	ITIC	NTU	COC	ACU	NTLC	CHC
2004	30	5	38	73	70	48	76	60	70	92
2003	25	—	38	85	—	57	70	68	—	—

National Journal Ratings

	2003 LIB	—	2003 CONS		2004 LIB	—	2004 CONS
Economic	53%	—	47%		54%	—	46%
Social	47%	—	52%		42%	—	57%
Foreign	42%	—	57%		34%	—	63%

Key Votes of the 108th Congress

1. Drilling in ANWR	N	5. DC School Vouchers	N	9. Ban Same-Sex Marriage	Y
2. Approve Bush Tax Cuts	Y	6. Ban Human Cloning	Y	10. Fund Iraq War	Y
3. Medicare/Rx Bill	Y	7. Restrict Gun Liability	Y	11. Bar Cuba Embargo Funds	N
4. Bar Overtime Pay Regs.	Y	8. Ban Partial-Birth Abortion	Y	12. Intelligence Reorg.	Y

Election Results

2004 general	Frank LoBiondo (R)	172,779	(65%)	($872,384)
	Timothy Robb (D)	86,792	(33%)	($6,325)
	Other	5,871	(2%)	
2004 primary	Frank LoBiondo (R)	unopposed		
2002 general	Frank LoBiondo (R)	116,834	(69%)	($646,171)
	Steven Farkas (D)	47,735	(28%)	
	Other	4,230	(3%)	

Prior Winning Percentages: 2000 (66%); 1998 (66%); 1996 (60%); 1994 (65%)

The People		Race/Ethnic Origin	Ancestry	
Area size:	2,683 sq. mi.	71.7% White	Irish: 13.9%	Italian: 13.0%
Urban population:	79.0%	13.8% Black	German: 12.5%	
Rural population:	21.0%	2.4% Asian	**2004 Presidential Vote**	
Pop. 2000:	647,258	0.3% Native Am.	Bush (R) 141,123	(50%)
Median income:	$44,173	0.0% Hawaiian	Kerry (D) 138,797	(49%)
Poverty status:	10.3%	1.4% Two+ races	Other 2,578	(1%)
Military veterans:	13.0%	0.1% Other	**2000 Presidential Vote**	
		10.3% Hispanic Origin	Gore (D) 134,345	(54%)
			Bush (R) 105,630	(43%)
			Other 7,906	(3%)
			Cook Partisan Voting Index: D + 4	
Occupation	Blue collar: 23.0%	White collar: 53.6%	Gray collar: 23.4%	

The builders of the Camden & Atlantic Railroad in 1852 may not have known it, but when they extended their line to the little inlet town of Absecon, they were starting America's biggest beach resort, Atlantic City. Like all resorts, it was a product of developments elsewhere: Of industrialization and spreading affluence, of railroad technology and the conquest of diseases which used to make summer a time of terror for parents and doctors. In the years after the Civil War, first Atlantic City and then the whole Jersey Shore from Brigantine to Cape May became America's first seaside resort, and Atlantic City developed its characteristic features: The Boardwalk in 1870, the amusement pier in 1882, the rolling chair in 1884, salt water taffy in the 1890s, Miss America in 1921. By 1940, when 16 million Americans visited every summer, Atlantic City was a common man's resort of old traditions; it declined in the years after World War II as people could afford nicer vacations. By the early 1970s, Atlantic City was grim, with a bedraggled convention hall (site of the 1964 Democratic National Convention), empty hotels and bleak streets of rowhouses built in the ugliest Philadelphia style.

Then in 1977, New Jersey voters legalized casino gambling in Atlantic City and gleaming new hotels sprang up, big name entertainers came in and Atlantic City became more glamorous than it had been in 90 years. But not for all of its residents: casino and hotel jobs tend to be low-wage, and the slums begin just feet from the massive parking lots of the casinos. Atlantic City's gambling business has been thriving—its dozen casinos have net annual revenues of more than $4 billion, nearly as much as in Las Vegas—and huge new casinos were built on both Boardwalk and bayside. Atlantic City now has one of the nation's largest tourism economies and may be growing into what Las Vegas has become, not just a collection of gaudy casinos but also a gaggle of theme parks, with entertainment for the family as well as adults. Atlantic City no longer depends on the Miss America contest to extend its summer season; the casinos are more interested in legalizing sports gambling.

The Jersey Shore south of Atlantic City is a string of different resorts. There is the old Methodist town of Ocean City, where Gay Talese grew up the son of Italian immigrants, as he told movingly in *Unto the Sons*. There is Wildwood, with its refurbished 1950s motels and the

Doo Wop revival, and Cape May, with its beautifully preserved Victorian houses. Behind the Shore are swamp and flatland, the Pine Barrens and vegetable fields that gave New Jersey the name "Garden State." Growth has been slow in these small towns and gas station intersections, communities in whose eerie calmness in the summer you can hear mosquitoes whining. In the flatness, you can also find towns clustered around low-wage apparel factories or petrochemical plants on the Delaware estuary; the Northeast high-tech and service economy has not reached this far south in Jersey yet.

The 2d Congressional District covers this part of South Jersey. Politically, it has strong Democratic presences in the chemical industry towns along the Delaware River and in Vineland and a strong Republican presence in Cape May; Atlantic City often votes Democratic but has an antique Republican machine that goes back generations. Al Gore carried this district by a 54%–43% margin in 2000. But in 2004 it swung back toward the Republicans and George W. Bush carried it 50%–49%. This remains prime marginal territory, off the beaten track of Northeast politics.

The congressman from the 2d District is Frank LoBiondo, a Republican first elected in 1994. He grew up in Vineland, went to college in Philadelphia and worked for the family trucking firm, LoBiondo Brothers Motor Express, which originally carried produce from Jersey farms. In 1987 he was elected to the Assembly, where he stoutly opposed new taxes. LoBiondo also opposes gun control, and was backed by the National Rifle Association. In 1992 LoBiondo ran against veteran Congressman William Hughes, and lost 56%–41%. After Hughes decided to retire in 1994, LoBiondo ran again and in the primary faced state Senator William Gormley; LoBiondo attacked him as a taxer and NRA ads called him "a liberal in Republican clothing." LoBiondo won 54%–35%, an impressive margin. LoBiondo then easily won the 1994 general, 65%–35%. Since then, he has never fallen short of 60%.

In the House, LoBiondo has compiled a moderate voting record, especially on economic issues, that is in sync with his district but has made few ripples in Washington in recent years. He is a founder of the Congressional Gaming Caucus. He won House passage of the Honesty in Sweepstakes Act, to make clear that no purchase of merchandise is necessary to enter contests. He remains a friend of the NRA—one of two House members from New Jersey to vote for John Dingell's amendment that ended the push for gun control in 1999. He chairs the Coast Guard and Maritime Transportation Subcommittee, a useful assignment for New Jersey. He opposes oil drilling within 125 miles of the Jersey coast, and worked against the proposal by the Bush administration to reduce the federal contribution to beach replenishment. When Congress passed the intelligence reform bill, it included his provision to authorize Atlantic City's federal air marshal center to train foreign law enforcement officers serving on overseas air carriers serving the United States.

LoBiondo thought about running for the Senate in 2000 and 2002, but he did not get close to making either race. Contending that it was "unfair" to hold him to a promise that other members had broken, he announced that he would not keep his pledge to serve only 12 years and would run for reelection in 2006. Secure at home, he seems content to climb the seniority ladder at the Transportation and Infrastructure Committee.

THIRD DISTRICT

Rep. Jim Saxton (R)

Elected 1984, 11th full term; b. Jan. 22, 1943, Nicholson, PA; home, Mt. Holly; E. Stroudsburg St. Col., B.A. 1965, Temple U., 1967–68; United Methodist; divorced.

Elected Office: NJ Assembly, 1975–82; NJ Senate, 1982–84.

Professional Career: Jr. High schl. teacher, 1965–68; Real estate broker, 1968–84.

DC Office: 2217 RHOB, 20515, 202-225-4765; Fax: 202-225-0778; Web site: www.house.gov/saxton.

District Offices: Cherry Hill, 856-428-0520; Mt. Holly, 609-261-5800; Ocean County, 732-914-2020.

Committees: *Armed Services* (4th of 34 R): Military Personnel; Projection Forces; Terrorism, Unconventional Threats & Capabilities (Chmn.). *Resources* (3d of 27 R): Fisheries & Oceans; National Parks. *Joint Economic Committee* (Chmn.).

Group Ratings

	ADA	ACLU	AFS	LCV	ITIC	NTU	COC	ACU	NTLC	CHC
2004	35	5	38	73	90	48	81	64	65	100
2003	20	—	33	75	—	56	79	76	—	—

National Journal Ratings

	2003 LIB	—	2003 CONS		2004 LIB	—	2004 CONS
Economic	52%	—	48%		51%	—	48%
Social	44%	—	55%		44%	—	56%
Foreign	11%	—	80%		25%	—	68%

Key Votes of the 108th Congress

1. Drilling in ANWR	N	5. DC School Vouchers	N
2. Approve Bush Tax Cuts	Y	6. Ban Human Cloning	Y
3. Medicare/Rx Bill	Y	7. Restrict Gun Liability	Y
4. Bar Overtime Pay Regs.	Y	8. Ban Partial-Birth Abortion	Y

9. Ban Same-Sex Marriage	Y
10. Fund Iraq War	Y
11. Bar Cuba Embargo Funds	N
12. Intelligence Reorg.	Y

Election Results

2004 general	Jim Saxton (R)	195,938	(63%)	($919,338)
	Herb Conaway (D)	107,034	(35%)	($42,334)
	Other	5,890	(2%)	
2004 primary	Jim Saxton (R)	unopposed		
2002 general	Jim Saxton (R)	123,375	(65%)	($683,812)
	Richard Strada (D)	64,364	(34%)	
	Other	2,000	(1%)	

Prior Winning Percentages: 2000 (57%); 1998 (62%); 1996 (64%); 1994 (66%); 1992 (59%); 1990 (58%); 1988 (69%); 1986 (65%); 1984 (61%); 1984 (62%)

The People		Race/Ethnic Origin	Ancestry	
Area size:	1,180 sq. mi.	83.4% White	Irish: 15.8%	Italian: 15.0%
Urban population:	96.2%	8.5% Black	German: 13.5%	
Rural population:	3.8%	2.7% Asian	**2004 Presidential Vote**	
Pop. 2000:	647,257	0.1% Native Am.	Bush (R) 167,254	(51%)
Median income:	$55,282	0.0% Hawaiian	Kerry (D) 159,041	(49%)
Poverty status:	5.1%	1.3% Two+ races	**2000 Presidential Vote**	
Military veterans:	15.6%	0.1% Other	Gore (D) 141,964	(54%)
		3.8% Hispanic Origin	Bush (R) 114,621	(43%)
			Other 8,208	(3%)
			Cook Partisan Voting Index: D + 3	

Occupation   Blue collar: 18.6%   White collar: 67.6%   Gray collar: 13.7%

The Pine Barrens of New Jersey are one of the last vacant spots on the eastern seaboard; not quite *terra incognita*, but still not thickly populated. Encroached by the Philadelphia suburbs of South Jersey on the west and burgeoning retirement developments of the Jersey Shore on the east, they are crossed even today mostly by narrow two-lane roads; there are only a few small towns here, plus Fort Dix and McGuire Air Force Base. For years, the Barrens were seen as a barrier to civilization; only recently have environment-minded Jerseyites come to see them as a natural treasure.

The 3d Congressional District of New Jersey spans the Pine Barrens, and includes large parts of Burlington and Ocean Counties and Cherry Hill in Camden County. Most of its residents live in the South Jersey suburbs of Philadelphia, in spread-out Cherry Hill with its 1960s and 1970s shopping centers, or in the older towns along the Delaware River and newer ones inland toward McGuire. This is comfortable, but not hugely affluent, suburban country. Lockheed Martin is a big employer here, with its naval electronic and surveillance system plant in Moorestown. Politically it is marginal territory, with big Democratic margins in Willingboro and Cherry Hill. East of the Pine Barrens is Ocean County, including the barrier islands from Normandy Beach south to Little Egg Harbor, with older beachfront communities and larger clusters of new subdivisions and condominium complexes inland. Ocean County has been the fastest-growing part of New Jersey, a kind of Frost Belt Florida, with many retirees from New York and North Jersey eager to leave the urban areas' high crime and high taxes. The two big military bases have remained active, with Fort Dix especially busy after September 11 training troops for new assignments and sending war materials to their destination. Politically, Ocean County has been Republican, and seems to have become more so after September 11. This district voted 54%–43% for Al Gore in 2000, but in 2004 it was carried 51%–49% by George W. Bush.

The congressman from the 3d District is James Saxton, a Republican first elected in 1984. He grew up in South Jersey, worked as a teacher for three years, then became a real estate broker. In 1975 he was elected to the New Jersey Assembly. In 1984 he ran to fill a vacancy in the House caused by the death of a Republican incumbent, won the Republican primary 45%–41%, easily won the special election and had no serious challenge until 2000.

In the House, Saxton has compiled a moderate to conservative voting record, which leans to the right on foreign issues. When Republicans won the House, he became chairman of the Fisheries Conservation, Wildlife and Oceans Subcommittee. His environment-friendly record became an obstacle when he sought to become chairman of the Resources Committee in 2003. Although he was the most senior member seeking the position, most Western Republicans on the panel united against him. Saxton floated the idea of splitting the Resources panel so that he could chair a panel dealing with Merchant Marine issues, but Republican leaders had eliminated the Merchant Marine and Fisheries Committee in 1995 and weren't about to bring it back. Shortly before the leadership met and gave the chairmanship to Richard Pombo, Saxton withdrew from consideration with an unspoken understanding that he would get to chair a prime subcommittee at Armed Services—specifically, the newly-created Subcommittee on Terrorism, Unconventional Threats and Capabilities. He remained active on environmental issues, winning enactment in 2004 of his program to encourage volunteer programs in national wildlife refuges.

Saxton is now the fourth-ranking Republican on Armed Services and has been a consistent supporter of strong anti-terrorism efforts and aid to Israel. He chaired a task force to study the threat of terrorism, concluding that the nation needed prompt action to combat the risk of biological weapons. He filed a bill that would prevent French companies from receiving any U.S. funds spent rebuilding post-war Iraq; he sponsored another proposal that would prevent U.S. officials from participating in the annual Paris Air Show. He also worked to protect Dix and McGuire from base-closing review panels; both ended up gaining jobs under the Pentagon's May 2005 base closing recommendations. On the Joint Economic Committee, he pressured officials of the International Monetary Fund to open their operations to greater public view. He cited the "steeply progressive impact of the federal income tax" and defended the Bush administration plan to return most of the tax cut to higher-income taxpayers. But he was one of 22 House Republicans who opposed the Bush administration's proposed changes in overtime-pay rules. In

January 2005, he regained the JEC chairmanship, which rotates every two years between the House and Senate, and said that he would focus on continuation of economic expansion, plus additional reform of the IMF and World Bank; he has warned the Federal Reserve against undue increases in interest rates.

Democrats targeted Saxton early in the 2000 campaign with strong support for Cherry Hill Mayor Susan Bass Levin. Levin was well-funded; she depicted Saxton as too conservative and out of the mainstream locally. But he was helped by his endorsement from the local Sierra Club and New Jersey Environmental Federation and by staff resignations and other disarray in Levin's campaign. Levin carried her home area narrowly, but lost the rest of the district by solid margins; Saxton won 57%–41%. In 2004 Saxton won 63%–35%.

FOURTH DISTRICT

Rep. Chris Smith (R)

Elected 1980, 13th term; b. Mar. 4, 1953, Rahway; home, Hamilton; Trenton St. Col., B.S. 1975; Catholic; married (Marie).

Professional Career: Sales exec., family–owned sporting goods business, 1975–80; Exec. Dir., NJ Right to Life, 1976–78.

DC Office: 2373 RHOB, 20515, 202-225-3765; Fax: 202-225-7768; Web site: www.house.gov/chrissmith.

District Offices: Hamilton, 609-585-7878; Whiting, 732-350-2300.

Committees: *International Relations* (Vice Chmn. of 27 R): Africa, Global Human Rights & International Operations (Chmn.); Western Hemisphere.

Group Ratings

	ADA	ACLU	AFS	LCV	ITIC	NTU	COC	ACU	NTLC	CHC
2004	40	15	50	82	90	42	76	54	62	100
2003	30	—	25	85	—	56	69	75	—	—

National Journal Ratings

	2003 LIB	—	2003 CONS		2004 LIB	—	2004 CONS
Economic	52%	—	47%		56%	—	44%
Social	40%	—	58%		48%	—	51%
Foreign	40%	—	58%		42%	—	57%

Key Votes of the 108th Congress

1. Drilling in ANWR	N	5. DC School Vouchers	Y	9. Ban Same-Sex Marriage	Y
2. Approve Bush Tax Cuts	Y	6. Ban Human Cloning	Y	10. Fund Iraq War	Y
3. Medicare/Rx Bill	Y	7. Restrict Gun Liability	Y	11. Bar Cuba Embargo Funds	N
4. Bar Overtime Pay Regs.	Y	8. Ban Partial-Birth Abortion	Y	12. Intelligence Reorg.	Y

Election Results

2004 general	Chris Smith (R)	192,671	(67%)	($533,725)
	Amy Vasquez (D)	92,826	(32%)	($34,687)
	Other	2,056	(1%)	
2004 primary	Chris Smith (R)	unopposed		
2002 general	Chris Smith (R)	115,293	(66%)	($510,790)
	Mary Brennan (D)	55,967	(32%)	($73,386)
	Other	3,041	(2%)	

Prior Winning Percentages: 2000 (63%); 1998 (62%); 1996 (64%); 1994 (68%); 1992 (62%); 1990 (63%); 1988 (66%); 1986 (61%); 1984 (61%); 1982 (53%); 1980 (57%)

The People		Race/Ethnic Origin	Ancestry	
Area size:	762 sq. mi.	81.3% White	Italian: 15.9%	Irish: 15.2%
Urban population:	93.2%	7.5% Black	German: 11.8%	
Rural population:	6.8%	2.3% Asian	**2004 Presidential Vote**	
Pop. 2000:	647,258	0.1% Native Am.	Bush (R) 172,369	(56%)
Median income:	$54,073	0.0% Hawaiian	Kerry (D) 134,220	(44%)
Poverty status:	6.6%	1.1% Two+ races	**2000 Presidential Vote**	
Military veterans:	13.3%	0.1% Other	Gore (D) 123,764	(50%)
		7.6% Hispanic Origin	Bush (R)............. 114,309	(46%)
			Other 8,301	(3%)
			Cook Partisan Voting Index: R + 1	

Occupation	Blue collar: 20.1%	White collar: 65.3%	Gray collar: 14.5%

An invisible and not very well defined line lies across central New Jersey dividing North Jersey and South Jersey. North of the line people watch New York TV stations, eat hero sandwiches and root for the Yankees; south of the line they watch Philadelphia TV, eat hoagies and root for the Phillies. The state capital of Trenton lies south of the line, which passes east somewhere around Six Flags Great Adventure and Wild Safari in the Pine Barrens and heads southeast past Lakewood and Bricktown to the little village of Mantoloking on the Jersey Shore. But on both sides of the line there has also developed over the last two decades a stronger New Jersey identity. The big cities are, after all, far away, particularly when traffic is heavy, and the economy of central New Jersey has its own special character, with big pharmaceutical companies and Fort Dix and McGuire Air Force Base. New Jersey politics is also centered here: Trenton is the state capital and also the home of the first New Jersey-oriented talk radio station, started in 1989. Some parts of this area are old: Trenton has been a manufacturing center since the 19th century, with the Lenox and Boehm china factories, the old Roebling ironworks which produced parts for many of our great bridges (the reason for the sign you see across the Delaware River, "Trenton Makes, the World Takes"). But much of this area is also spanking new, with growing subdivisions just west of the Shore and office buildings stretching north from Princeton. Even Trenton has had some growth; preservationists are eyeing its antique buildings and, long the only state capital without a hotel, it now has the Marriott Lafayette Yard Conference Hotel near the War Memorial.

The 4th Congressional District of New Jersey covers much of the central part of the state and the invisible line separating North Jersey and South Jersey. It stretches from the eastern part of Trenton to Mantoloking, Point Pleasant, Sea Girt and Spring Lake on the Shore. It includes the old colonial town of Burlington on the Delaware River and the new spacious subdivisions of Colts Neck just west of the Shore. It includes the Lakehurst air terminal where the zeppelin *Hindenburg* exploded in 1937. This is one part of America where population movement has been eastward, away from the old neighborhoods of Trenton and its close-in suburbs and toward the new subdivisions of Ocean County and Wall Township. Politically, it is a mixed area. The Trenton area has long been solidly Democratic, but the Pine Barrens and Shore have leaned Republican. A Republican trend and increasing turnout in Ocean and Monmouth Counties carried this Gore 2000 district for George W. Bush in 2004.

The congressman from the 4th District is Christopher Smith, a youthful-looking Republican first elected in 1980. Smith grew up in the Trenton area, worked in his family's sporting goods business, and after graduating from college became executive director of the New Jersey Right to Life Committee in 1976. In 1980 he ran for the House in a more Trenton-centered 4th District and beat 26-year incumbent Frank Thompson, a convicted Abscam defendant. A fluke, it seemed, but Smith proceeded to beat several additional serious Democrats, winning more than 60% each time.

On abortion, Smith has worked to stop abortions in military hospitals. He has also worked to reinstate the Reagan-era restrictions that would deny federal funds to family planning organizations that promote abortions abroad. The ensuing struggle lasted more than two years, with Smith leveraging his opposition to the family planning money to prevent passage of the

Clinton administration's high-priority efforts to reorganize the State Department, pay U.S. dues to the United Nations and provide $18 billion for the International Monetary Fund. Smith finally was forced to yield in 1998 and 1999 omnibus spending bills, but he won in return White House agreement to restrict support for international abortion advocacy—which angered some Clinton loyalists. George W. Bush restored the family-planning restrictions in an executive order in his first full day in office. Smith also was a prime mover of legislation to ban partial-birth abortions; the House voted to override Clinton's vetoes, but Smith's side fell a few votes short of the two-thirds needed in the Senate.

Smith has fought not only Democrats but the House Republican leadership on the abortion issue. In July 2002 the bankruptcy bill, strongly backed by the leadership, came out of conference committee; the House had passed it 306–108 in March 2001. But it contained a provision, negotiated by Senator Charles Schumer and longtime abortion opponent Henry Hyde, providing that court judgments or fines could not be wiped out in bankruptcy: Schumer inserted this as a favor to abortion rights groups, after some abortion protesters declared bankruptcy to avoid paying fines. Smith and Joe Pitts led a group of abortion opponents and said they would vote against the bill unless the provision was removed. In November the leadership brought forward the rule to vote on the bill and Speaker Dennis Hastert took the unusual step of voting for it himself (the speaker usually does not vote). Smith and Pitts stood their ground despite furious efforts by Whip Tom DeLay, and the rule went down 243–172, with 87 Republicans voting against. It was only the second rule defeated during Hastert's first four years as speaker, and Hastert called Smith into his office to scold him in January 2003. Smith won a victory in 2004 when a provision stating that state and local governments could not force hospitals and care providers to perform abortions was put in the omnibus appropriation. But his Unborn Child Pain Awareness Act, requiring doctors to inform pregnant women that some experts say fetus can feel pain after 20 weeks, went nowhere.

His belief in a right to life has also led Smith to oppose both capital punishment and embryonic stem cell research. In 2002 he sponsored a bill providing $30 million for research into non-embryonic stem cells.

At a time when few lawmakers were focusing on events overseas, Smith worked on problems that bring him little reward at home. As chairman of the International Operations and Human Rights Subcommittee, Smith strongly criticized China for its forced sterilizations and abortions and its persecution of Christians and other religious minorities, and opposed normal trade relations with China. Smith has opposed China's one-child policy. "After 25 years of coercive central family planning, its disastrous effects are beginning to appear. The country's male-female ratio is now dangerously skewed." In July 2003, after a provision for $50 million for the United Nations Population Fund passed by one vote in committee, he led the fight against it and it was defeated on the floor 216–211.

Smith has condemned Russia for barring entry of foreign Catholic priests and Saudis for treating foreign servants as slaves. In 2000 he had the signal success of pushing to passage a bill combating sex trafficking around the world, including a provision opposed by the Clinton administration requiring yearly reports on each nation's record; Clinton signed it anyway. In 2003 he worked to extend it to 2005. Smith has also taken action on the subject: When he heard about Ukrainian girls being held against their will in brothels in Montenegro, he called the Montenegran prime minister, who ordered a raid on the operation. In 2003 he successfully sponsored a law providing $81 million for centers in the U.S. and abroad to counsel victims of torture. In July 2004 the House passed 323–45 his bill to bar increased aid to Vietnam unless the administration finds substantial progress toward releasing political prisoners and fostering religious freedom and democratic government. Smith's moral views have led him to take stands unusual for a Republican on domestic issues. In July 2003 he cast a critical vote in committee for Henry Waxman's resolution of approval for future global climate change agreements. In October 2004 he voted against James Sensenbrenner's amendment broadening the category of illegal immigrants subject to immediate deportation.

In January 2001 Smith became chairman of the Veterans Committee and there pushed for policies opposed by the Republican leadership—which resulted in his losing the chairmanship in

January 2005, two years short of the ordinary six-year limit. Over four years, Smith's veterans bills increased VA disability payments by $2.5 billion, increased G.I. Bill of Rights spending 46%, authorized $1 billion in aid to homeless veterans and added $100 million in health care benefits for surviving spouses of veterans. Smith's 2004 bill increased from 18 to 24 months the coverage of the Uniformed Services Employment and Reemployment Act, set up a pilot program for recruitment of nurses and authorized a new research center of veterans with multitrauma combat injuries.

By no means were all of these programs authorized by Smith's committee funded by the Appropriations Committee, and for three years Appropriations explicitly forbade spending on Smith's four research centers to develop responses to chemical, biological and radiological attacks. In early 2003 Smith called for making veterans benefits an entitlement—mandatory spending that would not have to go through Appropriations. This the leadership opposed and there were threats he'd lose the chair. In 2003 he voted for the Republican budget resolution that included a $1.8 billion increase in veterans spending, but in July 2003 appropriators did not include the money; Smith opposed that but disappointed Democrats by not voting against the rule sending the measure to the floor. In 2004 Smith voted against the Republican and for the Democratic budget resolution because the latter included more spending on veterans programs.

Over the last 30 years in both Republican and Democratic Houses the leadership of the majority party does not expect a committee chairman to vote against the party's budget resolution. It did not help that Smith ranked eighth lowest among House Republicans in party-line voting (though that was still 81%). It seems that Smith did not expect a challenge for the chair. But Steve Buyer, the fourth ranking Republican on the committee, asked for an interview with the Republican Steering Committee, and on January 5, 2005, it voted to make him chairman. That decision was ratified by the Republican Conference January 6; Smith was off the committee altogether. Smith was obviously disappointed. "I don't look at power as something to hold. I see the power of the gavel as a strategic opportunity to do good, to use it in every way to help veterans," he said in his speech to the Conference. New Jersey Republicans expressed dismay, and New Jersey Democrats and the leaders of just about every veterans group expressed outrage.

Smith tends to the needs of his district, which was particularly hard hit by the September 11 attacks: 57 4th District residents were killed, and later in September, the anthrax letters sent to New York and Washington passed through the post office sorting facility in Hamilton, just east of Trenton. The facility was closed and some 800,000 pieces of mail delayed. Smith introduced a bill to waive financial penalties for people whose mail was delayed; the banking industry agreed to do that voluntarily. He has worked to raise New Jersey Medicare reimbursement rates to New York City levels and to get funding for Project Polaris, a New York-New Jersey group combating sex trafficking. He voted to postpone the 2005 base closing round by two years and over 10 years worked to bring in $50 million for the Naval Air Engineering Station in Lakehurst; the station, which designs and builds aircraft carrier catapults and arresting gear, was spared when the Pentagon released its base closing recommendations in May 2005, though it was slated to lose 186 jobs.

Smith's devotion to principle and his reputation for tending to constituent problems have made him very popular in the 4th District. In 2004, Smith was reelected 67%–32%.

FIFTH DISTRICT

Rep. Scott Garrett (R)

Elected 2002, 2d term; b. July 9, 1959, Englewood; home, Wantage; Montclair St. U., B.A. 1981, Rutgers U., J.D. 1984; Protestant; married (Mary Ellen).

Elected Office: NJ Assembly, 1990–2002.

Professional Career: Practicing atty., 1984-present.

DC Office: 1318 LHOB, 20515, 202-225-4465; Fax: 202-225-9048; Web site: www.house.gov/garrett/.

District Offices: Newton, 973-300-2000; Paramus, 201-712-0330.

Committees: *Budget* (8th of 22 R). *Financial Services* (26th of 37 R): Financial Institutions & Consumer Credit; Oversight & Investigations.

Group Ratings

	ADA	ACLU	AFS	LCV	ITIC	NTU	COC	ACU	NTLC	CHC
2004	5	5	0	18	90	80	95	100	92	100
2003	15	—	13	10	—	76	93	100	—	—

National Journal Ratings

	2003 LIB	—	2003 CONS		2004 LIB	—	2004 CONS
Economic	33%	—	64%		24%	—	75%
Social	17%	—	79%		17%	—	81%
Foreign	11%	—	80%		4%	—	93%

Key Votes of the 108th Congress

1. Drilling in ANWR	N	5. DC School Vouchers	Y	9. Ban Same-Sex Marriage	Y
2. Approve Bush Tax Cuts	Y	6. Ban Human Cloning	Y	10. Fund Iraq War	Y
3. Medicare/Rx Bill	N	7. Restrict Gun Liability	Y	11. Bar Cuba Embargo Funds	N
4. Bar Overtime Pay Regs.	N	8. Ban Partial-Birth Abortion	Y	12. Intelligence Reorg.	Y

Election Results

2004 general	Scott Garrett (R)	171,220	(58%)	($1,268,289)
	Anne Wolfe (D)	122,259	(41%)	($475,949)
	Other	3,946	(1%)	
2004 primary	Scott Garrett (R)	unopposed		
2002 general	Scott Garrett (R)	118,881	(59%)	($1,342,264)
	Anne Sumers (D)	76,504	(38%)	($1,605,385)
	Other	4,466	(2%)	

The People		Race/Ethnic Origin	Ancestry	
Area size:	1,130 sq. mi.	86.3% White	Italian: 16.2%	Irish: 15.3%
Urban population:	82.7%	1.5% Black	German: 13.2%	
Rural population:	17.3%	6.6% Asian	**2004 Presidential Vote**	
Pop. 2000:	647,258	0.1% Native Am.	Bush (R) 184,530	(57%)
Median income:	$72,781	0.0% Hawaiian	Kerry (D) 137,019	(43%)
Poverty status:	3.6%	1.0% Two+ races	**2000 Presidential Vote**	
Military veterans:	11.6%	0.1% Other	Bush (R) 140,132	(52%)
		4.5% Hispanic Origin	Gore (D) 120,142	(45%)
			Other 9,431	(3%)
			Cook Partisan Voting Index: R + 4	

Occupation	Blue collar: 16.3%	White collar: 72.9%	Gray collar: 10.8%

The northern edge of New Jersey was first settled three centuries ago by the Dutch, for whom this plateau of land behind the Hudson River Palisades seemed a natural part of Nieuw Amsterdam. The Dutch influence is seen in old steep-roofed farmhouses and in many of the place names—Bergen County, Cresskill, Closter. But overall, northernmost New Jersey has the well-settled look of so many northeastern suburbs, with touches both of affluence and small-town hominess, criss-crossed at its edges with limited access highways lined with shopping centers. Not far away are Saddle River and Franklin Lakes, with million-dollar houses on multi-acre lots, and Park Ridge, with office buildings and condominiums. This area may look like WASP suburbia on the surface, but in fact it is home to successful people of all ethnic groups, many descended from those who first saw the Statue of Liberty from the steerage deck and passed through the inspection queues at Ellis Island.

The 5th Congressional District of New Jersey consists of most of northern Bergen County, plus a swath of North Jersey stretching west to the hill-enclosed upper reaches of the Delaware River, crossing one ridge of mountains after another, then running south to I-78. About 60% of its population is in Bergen County; to the west, little subdivisions set amid the lakes of western Passaic County are filling up with young families; farther west are once rural, now more or less suburban, Sussex and Warren Counties. Politically, this area has long been solidly Republican, although like all of New Jersey it moved toward Democrats in the 1990s. It was one of the state's three districts carried by George W. Bush in 2000 and one of six he carried in 2004.

The congressman from the 5th District is Scott Garrett, a Republican elected in 2002. Garrett graduated from Montclair State College and Rutgers law school and became a trial lawyer in Sussex County. In 1989, he was elected to the state House, where he quickly became one of the most conservative members. In 1998 and 2000, he challenged veteran Congresswoman Marge Roukema in the Republican primary. He attacked her for supporting abortion rights and gun control; she pointed to her conservative votes on economic issues and was supported by the Republican leadership. Each time, Garrett carried the western part of the district but Roukema ran strongly in her Bergen County base; she won by only 53%–47% in 1998 and 52%–48% in 2000. In November 2001, unhappy that she had been passed over for the chairmanship of the Financial Services Committee and frustrated by her party's move to the right, Roukema announced that she would not seek another term.

Garrett ran again in 2002. His challenge in the primary was to sell his views in Bergen County, where Sussex County is viewed as a distant province somewhere near Idaho. Garrett ran again as a supporter of tax cuts who wanted to streamline government and reduce bureaucracy and was opposed to abortion and gun control; the American Conservative Union and the Club for Growth endorsed him. Two well-known Republicans from Bergen entered the race: state Senator Gerald Cardinale and Assemblyman David Russo.They argued that nominating Garrett would put the seat at risk. Garrett won the primary with 41% to 26% for Russo and 25% for Cardinale. Garrett won a stunning 81% of the vote in Sussex, and 68% in Warren. But in Bergen County, Garrett won just 25%, raising Republican fears and Democratic hopes. The Democratic nominee was Anne Sumers, an ophthalmologist from Upper Saddle River in Bergen County, a former Republican who switched parties in early 2002 and stressed her agreement with Roukema on most issues. With help from the national party, Sumers attacked Garrett as an "extremist," pointing to his opposition to abortion and support for only limited federal aid to education. Roukema, recovering from surgery and chemotherapy, remained notably silent. Garrett pounced on Sumers's failure to vote in local school board elections and her musings on a liberal web site where she characterized American patriotism as "jingoistic." He said she was a vote for Dick Gephardt for Speaker. At the urging of the House Republicans' campaign committee, he soft-pedaled some of his more conservative views, including his support for school vouchers. Sumers outspent Garrett, $1.6 million to $1.3 million, including nearly $400,000 of her own money. But national Republicans spent heavily on issue ads on Garrett's behalf. This turned out to be less of a contest than many people thought; Garrett won 59%–38%. In Bergen County, which cast 64% of the total, he led 55%–43%.

In the House, Garrett quickly defined himself as the most conservative member of the New Jersey delegation and a tight-spender overall in the House. His vote against the Medicare/prescription drug bill showed his independence, but it also angered Republican leaders and limited Garrett's influence in the House. When the state delegation sent a letter to George W. Bush opposing oil exploration off the New Jersey shore, Garrett was the only member who did not sign on. He filed a bill to reduce the number of taxpayers subject to the alternative minimum tax. In December 2004, he joined four other House Republicans calling on Kofi Annan to step down as Secretary General following allegations of mismanagement at the United Nations. "To me, the question should not be whether Kofi Annan should remain in charge. The question is whether he should be in jail," he said.

In 2004, Garrett was reelected 58%–41%, winning 54%–45% in Bergen County.

SIXTH DISTRICT

Rep. Frank Pallone (D)

Elected 1988, 9th full term; b. Oct. 30, 1951, Long Branch; home, Long Branch; Middlebury Col., B.A. 1973, Fletcher Schl. of Law & Diplomacy, M.A. 1974, Rutgers U., J.D. 1978; Catholic; married (Sarah).

Elected Office: Long Branch City Cncl., 1982–88; NJ Senate, 1983–88.

Professional Career: Asst. prof., Rutgers U., 1979–80; Practicing atty., 1981–83; Instructor, Monmouth Col., 1984–86.

DC Office: 420 CHOB, 20515, 202-225-4671; Fax: 202-225-9665; Web site: www.house.gov/pallone.

District Offices: Hazlet, 732-264-9104; Long Branch, 732-571-1140; New Brunswick, 732-249-8892.

Committees: *Energy & Commerce* (6th of 26 D): Environment & Hazardous Materials; Health; Telecommunications & the Internet. *Resources* (9th of 22 D): Fisheries & Oceans (RMM).

Group Ratings

	ADA	ACLU	AFS	LCV	ITIC	NTU	COC	ACU	NTLC	CHC
2004	95	70	100	100	40	8	24	4	0	15
2003	95	—	100	100	—	22	30	16	—	—

National Journal Ratings

	2003 LIB	—	2003 CONS		2004 LIB	—	2004 CONS
Economic	81%	—	18%		89%	—	8%
Social	72%	—	27%		78%	—	19%
Foreign	75%	—	21%		74%	—	25%

Key Votes of the 108th Congress

1. Drilling in ANWR	N	5. DC School Vouchers	N	9. Ban Same-Sex Marriage	N
2. Approve Bush Tax Cuts	N	6. Ban Human Cloning	N	10. Fund Iraq War	N
3. Medicare/Rx Bill	N	7. Restrict Gun Liability	N	11. Bar Cuba Embargo Funds	N
4. Bar Overtime Pay Regs.	Y	8. Ban Partial-Birth Abortion	N	12. Intelligence Reorg.	N

Election Results

2004 general	Frank Pallone (D)	153,981	(67%)	($1,038,217)
	Sylvester Fernandez (R)	70,942	(31%)	($66,473)
	Other	5,228	(2%)	
2004 primary	Frank Pallone (D)	unopposed		
2002 general	Frank Pallone (D)	91,379	(66%)	($853,882)
	Ric Medrow (R)	42,479	(31%)	($28,970)
	Other	3,637	(3%)	

Prior Winning Percentages: 2000 (68%); 1998 (57%); 1996 (61%); 1994 (60%); 1992 (52%); 1990 (49%); 1988 (52%); 1988 (52%)

The People		Race/Ethnic Origin	Ancestry	
Area size:	388 sq. mi.	61.7% White	Italian: 12.7%	Irish: 12.6%
Urban population:	99.7%	16.1% Black	German: 8.1%	
Rural population:	0.3%	8.3% Asian	**2004 Presidential Vote**	
Pop. 2000:	647,257	0.1% Native Am.	Kerry (D) 144,105	(57%)
Median income:	$55,681	0.0% Hawaiian	Bush (R) 109,729	(43%)
Poverty status:	9.1%	1.7% Two+ races	**2000 Presidential Vote**	
Military veterans:	10.2%	0.3% Other	Gore (D) 132,583	(61%)
		11.7% Hispanic Origin	Bush (R) 74,828	(35%)
			Other 8,638	(4%)
			Cook Partisan Voting Index: D +12	

Occupation   Blue collar: 20.1%   White collar: 66.1%   Gray collar: 13.8%

For generations great transportation arteries have brought people out of the huge central cities of New York and Philadelphia and into the long-empty flatlands and hills of New Jersey—to vacation, to raise families and to work toward affluence and build communities. The railroads of the late 19th century created the towns of the Jersey Shore, from 1874, when the first train from New York City reached Long Branch, which quickly became the summer home of seven presidents from Grant to Wilson (Garfield, convalescing after he was shot, died there in 1881) and of New York racehorse owners and socialites. But the ambiance became honky-tonk, and the fishing pier plus much of the boardwalk went up in flames in 1987; only recently have developers sought to revive it. The great freight rail lines in the New York-Philadelphia corridor sparked big electrical and chemical industries here; they built on the inventions of Thomas Edison, many of them produced in his Menlo Park laboratory just off the rail lines. The same corridor was the site of America's first cloverleaf intersection, at the junction of U.S. 1 and U.S. 9, and the intersection of two of America's great post-World War II highways, the New Jersey Turnpike and the Garden State Parkway. The Turnpike, now 12 lanes wide, roars past oil tank farms and petrochemical plants, major rail lines, Newark Airport and the oily waters of Raritan Bay; the Parkway links leafy affluent suburbs a dozen miles west of the Hudson with the Jersey Shore.

The 6th Congressional District inelegantly ties together these great transportation nodes, and the upward mobility and economic progress that have taken place around them. The district is shaped something like an overturned capital F, with a long string of towns running from Piscataway to Sandy Hook, and two appendages running south: One along the Middlesex-Monmouth county line, the other along the Atlantic Ocean (Middlesex and Monmouth Counties account for 90% of the district's population). It includes the central core of Middlesex County: New Brunswick, Highland Park, Metuchen, Sayreville, parts of Edison Township and surrounding communities—a heavy industry area that also, since the time of Thomas Edison, has housed some of America's great research and development facilities, plus Rutgers, the state university of New Jersey. In recent years, Edison has seen an influx of immigrants from India, many of them engineers and doctors. The 6th also includes Monmouth County territory overlooking Lower New York Bay, with spacious estates on highlands above little port towns from Sandy Hook, home to the nation's oldest operating lighthouse (1764), south to the mile-long boardwalk of Belmar. Between them are Asbury Park, immortalized by a Bruce Springsteen album, and Ocean Grove, founded in 1869 as a Methodist resort "free from the dissipation and follies of fashionable watering places," still dry for teetotalers who throng to its 10,000-seat 1894 Great Hall. The Shore has remained a summer vacation area that attracts millions, but also hosts year-round communities, with their own upward-striving families.

The congressman from the 6th District is Frank Pallone, a moderate-to-liberal Democrat elected in 1988. Pallone is the son of a disabled Long Branch policeman; he has been an environmentalist since 1969, when as a college freshman in Vermont he worked for that state's first-in-the-nation bottle deposit law. He was elected to the Long Branch city council in 1982, at 31, and to the New Jersey Senate in 1983. When Representative Jim Howard, chairman of what was the Public Works and Transportation Committee, died in March 1988, Pallone ran for the House. The district leaned Republican, but residents were angry about untreated sludge, plastic containers and medical waste washing up on the beach. Pallone's bumper sticker, without mentioning party affiliation, said, "Stop Ocean Dumping." That, combined with conservative stands on taxes and crime, helped him to win 52% in both the special and general elections.

Pallone started as a political maverick but became more partisan after Democrats lost control of the House. He was an early supporter of Howard Dean's presidential campaign. With the district's many Indian-Americans (the most in the country, he says), he formed the Congressional Caucus for India and Indian-Americans; he is also a co-founder of the Congressional Armenian Caucus and helped to approve normal trade relations for Armenia. After the September 11 attacks, he said that U.S. defense relations with India had improved and he called for increased democracy in Pakistan and controls on its nuclear weapons technology. At home, Pallone's environmental focus turned to the ever-lively border war with New York, opposing offshore dumping near Sandy Hook of highly contaminated material dredged from New York harbor; the Army Corps of Engineers, he complained, failed to respond to New Jersey objections.

After the 1992 redistricting, his district became more safely Democratic. Since then, Pallone has been reelected with at least 60% of the vote except in 1998. That year he had a tough challenge from 28-year-old Republican Mike Ferguson, an education reformer close to former Governor Thomas Kean. An insurance group unhappy with Pallone's support for Clinton's HMO regulation plan spent nearly $2 million in an independent expenditure campaign, but in a pro-incumbent year, Pallone won 57%–40%. Two years later, Ferguson ran in the next-door 7th District and was elected.

Pallone's ambition for statewide office has run into obstacles. Rutgers political scientist Ross Baker told the *Asbury Park Press*, "His personal style is not one that commands respect. . . . It's hard for people to see him as a senator or governor. They see him as a representative." When Senator Frank Lautenberg announced his retirement in 1999, Pallone formed an exploratory committee but did not run. When Senator Bob Torricelli quit the 2002 Senate race on September 30, and Governor Jim McGreevey offered the nomination to Pallone, he reportedly agreed to run. But Pallone quickly withdrew, reportedly because his wife opposed the move. If so, she was shrewd: He would have given up a safe House seat for a candidacy that could have been abruptly ended by either state or federal judges. When Jon Corzine announced his campaign for governor in December 2004, Pallone endorsed him and said that he would like to fill Corzine's Senate seat. But he is not the only Democrat interested. He might have another chance to be elected to the Senate in 2008 if Lautenberg decides to retire at 84.

SEVENTH DISTRICT

Rep. Michael Ferguson (R)

Elected 2000, 3d term; b. July 22, 1970, Ridgewood; home, Warren; U. of Notre Dame, B.S. 1992, Georgetown U., M.P.P. 1994; Catholic; married (Maureen Malloy).

Professional Career: H.S. teacher, Mount St. Michael Acad., 1992–93; Exec. Dir., Better Schools Fndt., 1994; Dir., Save Our Schoolchildren, 1994; Exec. Dir., Catholic Campaign for America, 1995–97; Adjunct Prof., Brookdale Com. Col., 1997–2000; Founder & Pres., Strategic Educ. Initiatives, 1997-present.

DC Office: 214 CHOB, 20515, 202-225-5361; Fax: 202-225-9460; Web site: www.house.gov/ferguson.

District Office: Warren, 908-757-7835.

Committees: *Energy & Commerce* (24th of 31 R): Commerce, Trade & Consumer Protection; Health; Oversight & Investigations; Telecommunications & the Internet.

Group Ratings

	ADA	ACLU	AFS	LCV	ITIC	NTU	COC	ACU	NTLC	CHC
2004	30	5	25	45	89	48	95	67	78	100
2003	0	—	13	30	—	62	90	80	—	—

National Journal Ratings

	2003 LIB	—	2003 CONS	2004 LIB	—	2004 CONS
Economic	41%	—	59%	47%	—	53%
Social	36%	—	63%	44%	—	55%
Foreign	36%	—	64%	34%	—	63%

Key Votes of the 108th Congress

1. Drilling in ANWR	N	5. DC School Vouchers	Y	9. Ban Same-Sex Marriage	Y
2. Approve Bush Tax Cuts	Y	6. Ban Human Cloning	Y	10. Fund Iraq War	Y
3. Medicare/Rx Bill	Y	7. Restrict Gun Liability	Y	11. Bar Cuba Embargo Funds	N
4. Bar Overtime Pay Regs.	Y	8. Ban Partial-Birth Abortion	Y	12. Intelligence Reorg.	Y

Election Results

2004 general	Michael Ferguson (R)	162,597	(57%)	($2,847,822)
	Steve Brozak (D)	119,081	(42%)	($792,575)
	Other	4,169	(1%)	
2004 primary	Michael Ferguson (R)	unopposed		
2002 general	Michael Ferguson (R)	106,055	(58%)	($2,089,022)
	Tim Carden (D)	74,879	(41%)	($948,467)
	Other	2,068	(1%)	

Prior Winning Percentages: 2000 (52%)

The People		Race/Ethnic Origin	Ancestry	
Area size:	603 sq. mi.	79.0% White	Italian: 15.3%	Irish: 13.0%
Urban population:	90.4%	4.4% Black	German: 11.7%	
Rural population:	9.6%	8.2% Asian	**2004 Presidential Vote**	
Pop. 2000:	647,257	0.1% Native Am.	Bush (R) 164,176	(53%)
Median income:	$74,823	0.0% Hawaiian	Kerry (D) 144,767	(47%)
Poverty status:	3.4%	1.2% Two+ races	**2000 Presidential Vote**	
Military veterans:	10.6%	0.2% Other	Bush (R) 127,702	(49%)
		6.9% Hispanic Origin	Gore (D) 124,699	(48%)
			Other 9,099	(3%)
			Cook Partisan Voting Index: R + 1	

Occupation	Blue collar: 15.7%	White collar: 74.5%	Gray collar: 9.8%

The transportation arteries beneath the curve of the First Watchung Mountain are one of New Jersey's historic lines of development. The rail lines of the late 19th century opened up commuter suburbs; in the 1940s the four lanes of U.S. 22 created an automobile civilization; and finally I-78, completed in the mid-1980s, put Newark only an hour's distance from the Pennsylvania line. Interstate 78 stimulated the development of an Edge City called Bridgewater Commons— halfway between Philadelphia and Manhattan—where an enormous shopping mall and office developments that included the headquarters of AT&T rose up amid horse country around Far Hills and Bernardsville, where the likes of Malcolm Forbes and Charles Engelhard owned huge estates in horse country (New Jersey claims more horses per square mile than any other state). These are in Somerset County, the nation's number one county in per capita income.

The 7th Congressional District of New Jersey, with its contorted boundaries, covers these several generations of suburban development. It ranges across the breadth of the state, from the edge of Pennsylvania's Lehigh Valley in the west almost to Staten Island in the east. It is an agglomeration of places, some of affluence, not a district with a distinct character—the 7th includes parts of four counties, and parts of places such as Edison, Woodbridge, Bridgewater, Linden and Union. Its easternmost points are in Union County, just shy of Newark International Airport. It includes Summit, Scotch Plains and North and South Plainfield, but not heavily Democratic Plainfield. It follows I-78 and the Watchung Mountains far into the countryside; it includes western Somerset County and most of fast-growing Hunterdon County, where the county seat of Flemington was the site of the "trial of the century" for the kidnapping and murder of the 20-month-old son of Charles Lindbergh. There is, of course, a political imperative for the weird shape of the district: The 7th was designed as part of the bipartisan incumbents' plan to put heavily Democratic areas in the adjacent 12th, 6th and 10th Districts while moving Republican areas formerly in those districts, to this one. As a result, the Bush 2000 percentage in the 7th rose from 43% to 49%—the biggest partisan change in any New Jersey district.

The congressman from the 7th District is Michael Ferguson, a Republican first elected in 2000. He grew up in Ridgewood, in Bergen County; after graduating from Notre Dame, he taught history as an unpaid volunteer and coached basketball at Mount St. Michael Academy in the Bronx. He served as executive director of the Catholic Campaign for America and of the Better Schools Foundation in Washington; during that time, he focused on education issues while earning a master's degree in public policy from Georgetown. He returned to New Jersey to found Strategic Education Initiatives, an education consulting firm, and became an ally of Jersey City's Republican mayor Bret Schundler and a backer of school choice. In 1998, Ferguson challenged Frank Pallone in the 6th District, spending $1 million but losing 57%–40%.

When Bob Franks decided to give up the neighboring 7th District seat to run for the Senate in 2000, Ferguson moved to the district and entered the contest. He faced serious opposition in the primary. Ferguson raised the most money and focused on fiscal issues, but Tom Kean Jr., son of the popular former governor, had the highest name recognition and the most early endorsements; State Assemblyman Joel Weingarten suffered from votes to raise taxes. Ferguson focused on cutting taxes and won with 41% of the vote, to 28% for Kean and 23% for Weingarten. In the general, Ferguson faced Fanwood Mayor Maryanne Connelly, who in 1998 lost to Franks by 53%–44%. Ferguson barely mentioned his conservative views—for school prayer and a constitutional amendment banning abortion—but emphasized his centrist positions on the environment and health care. His centerpiece issue was education: He strongly backed school vouchers and urged increased accountability for public schools. Against the 55-year-old Connelly, a widow without children, Ferguson highlighted his youthfulness and two children. Ferguson won 52%–46%, running about even in the older suburbs and carrying the newer suburbs by wide margins. In 2003, the Federal Election Commission ordered him to pay a $210,000 fine for making an improper loan to himself from a trust created by his parents during the 2000 campaign.

In the House, Ferguson has been near the center on economic and cultural issues but more conservative on defense. He voted against oil drilling in the Arctic National Wildlife Refuge but voted for the Bush tax cuts, trade promotion authority, and authorization for war in Iraq. With a much-sought seat on the Energy and Commerce Committee, he appealed to constituent interests by supporting an overhaul of telecommunications laws. He was under greater pressure to show party loyalty, but he continued to display occasional independence, as with his procedural vote to bar the Bush administration from implementing new overtime pay regulations for workers.

Ferguson's voting record plus the redistricting changes strengthened him at home. But Democrats are reluctant to remove him from their top tier of targets. In 2002, against financier Tim Carden, who raised nearly $1 million, Ferguson raised more than twice that and won 58–41%. Two years later, his Democratic challenger Stephen Brozak also spent a bit short of $1 million; he ran on his service as an Iraq war veteran and sought to make the Bush administration's handling of the war his central issue. Ferguson emphasized tax cuts and support for the troops in Iraq. National Democrats sought to highlight Brozak's candidacy by giving him a speaking slot at the national convention in Boston. But the first-time candidate's campaign skills were disappointing and national Democrats lost enthusiasm. Ferguson won 57%–42%, almost the same as his 2002 margin. He lost Woodbridge, Edison and North Plainfield and carried almost all the other cities and towns in the district, winning 61% in Somerset County and 65% in Hunterdon County. Ferguson has been mentioned as a possible candidate for the Senate.

EIGHTH DISTRICT

Rep. Bill Pascrell (D)

Elected 1996, 5th term; b. Jan. 25, 1937, Paterson; home, Paterson; Fordham U., B.A. 1959, M.A. 1961; Catholic; married (Elsie).

Military Career: Army, 1961; Army Reserves, 1962–67.

Elected Office: Pres., Paterson Bd. of Ed., 1979–82; NJ Assembly, 1987–97, Minority Ldr. Pro-Tem; Paterson Mayor, 1990–97.

Professional Career: High Schl. teacher, 1960–74; Dir., Paterson Dept. of Public Works, 1974–77; Dir., Paterson Dept. of Policy, 1977–87.

DC Office: 2464 RHOB, 20515, 202-225-5751; Fax: 202-225-5782; Web site: www.pascrell.house.gov.

District Offices: Bloomfield, 973-680-1361; Passaic, 973-472-4510; Paterson, 973-523-5152.

Committees: *Homeland Security* (11th of 15 D): Economic Security, Infrastructure Protection & Cybersecurity; Emergency Preparedness, Science & Technology (RMM); Management, Integration & Oversight. *Transportation & Infrastructure* (16th of 34 D): Aviation; Highways, Transit & Pipelines; Water Resources & Environment.

Group Ratings

	ADA	ACLU	AFS	LCV	ITIC	NTU	COC	ACU	NTLC	CHC
2004	90	63	100	82	20	9	40	4	0	38
2003	80	—	100	90	—	20	33	20	—	—

National Journal Ratings

	2003 LIB	—	2003 CONS		2004 LIB	—	2004 CONS
Economic	79%	—	21%		88%	—	12%
Social	67%	—	33%		75%	—	24%
Foreign	61%	—	37%		68%	—	30%

Key Votes of the 108th Congress

1. Drilling in ANWR	N	5. DC School Vouchers	N	9. Ban Same-Sex Marriage	N
2. Approve Bush Tax Cuts	N	6. Ban Human Cloning	Y	10. Fund Iraq War	Y
3. Medicare/Rx Bill	N	7. Restrict Gun Liability	N	11. Bar Cuba Embargo Funds	N
4. Bar Overtime Pay Regs.	Y	8. Ban Partial-Birth Abortion	Y	12. Intelligence Reorg.	N

Election Results

2004 general	Bill Pascrell (D)	152,001	(69%)	($948,047)
	George Ajjan (R)	62,747	(29%)	($137,886)
	Other	4,072	(2%)	
2004 primary	Bill Pascrell (D)	unopposed		
2002 general	Bill Pascrell (D)	88,101	(67%)	($864,856)
	Jared Silverman (R)	40,318	(31%)	
	Other	3,400	(3%)	

Prior Winning Percentages: 2000 (67%); 1998 (62%); 1996 (51%)

The People		Race/Ethnic Origin	Ancestry	
Area size:	110 sq. mi.	53.7% White	Italian: 15.3%	Irish: 8.0%
Urban population:	100.0%	12.7% Black	German: 6.0%	
Rural population:	0.0%	5.3% Asian	**2004 Presidential Vote**	
Pop. 2000:	647,258	0.1% Native Am.	Kerry (D) 142,081	(59%)
Median income:	$51,954	0.0% Hawaiian	Bush (R) 99,239	(41%)
Poverty status:	10.7%	2.1% Two+ races	**2000 Presidential Vote**	
Military veterans:	8.3%	0.3% Other	Gore (D) 129,906	(60%)
		25.8% Hispanic Origin	Bush (R) 78,446	(36%)
			Other 6,784	(3%)
			Cook Partisan Voting Index: D +12	

Occupation	Blue collar: 22.4%	White collar: 64.1%	Gray collar: 13.5%

Paterson, New Jersey, is one of few American cities that have turned out pretty much as planned. The planner was Alexander Hamilton, who in the 1790s journeyed 20 miles from Manhattan into the interior of New Jersey to the Great Falls of the Passaic River. Watching the water surge down 72 feet—the highest falls along the East Coast—he predicted an industrial city would rise on this site. He formed the Society for Establishing Useful Manufactures, which opened a calico factory in 1794, and got Pierre L'Enfant, the designer of Washington, D.C., to design Paterson (named after then-Governor William Paterson). In 1836, Samuel Colt began manufacturing revolvers here; the first American locomotive, the Sandusky, was built here in 1837; a walkout of Paterson cotton workers in 1828 was America's first factory strike. Paterson ultimately became America's "Silk City," employing 25,000 silk mill workers before the great strike of 1913 led by the radical Industrial Workers of the World. Paterson kept producing locomotives and, after the silk mills started closing down following another unsuccessful strike in 1924, became a cloth-dying center. Throughout, it attracted immigrants from England, Ireland and, after 1890, Italy and Poland. And it continues to attract them today, even if its economy produces more service and fewer manufacturing jobs. In 2000 Paterson's population was 50% Hispanic (up 30% since 1990); downtown's "Little Palestine" reflects the city's sizable Arab community. Overall, this area lost population and reported an increase in poverty in the 1990s; in recent years, the population rebounded slightly.

The 8th Congressional District of New Jersey includes Paterson as its largest city and much suburban and industrial territory west and south of Paterson and north of Newark. More than half the population lives in Passaic County; the rest are in Essex County. It includes the mixed factory and middle-class towns south of Paterson on the Passaic River—Clifton, majority Hispanic and fast-growing Passaic, Nutley, Belleville, Bloomfield. In some of these towns you can see vestiges of the gritty Republicanism that prevailed in North Jersey in the 1940s and 1950s. On higher ground is affluent Montclair, with large populations of well-off blacks and Manhattan-oriented Boomers, the most Democratic part of the district except for Paterson. Over the Watchung Mountain are affluent West Orange and South Orange, both heavily Democratic, and the small Republican towns of Cedar Grove and Verona. In the 1980s the district leaned Republican, in the 1990s it became heavily Democratic and in 2004 it was still Democratic, but somewhat less so.

The congressman from the 8th District is Bill Pascrell, a Democrat elected in 1996. He grew up in Paterson, the grandson of Italian immigrants, graduated from Fordham, served in the Army, then taught high school for 14 years. From there he went into politics, as director of Paterson's department of public works, school board president, then in 1987 to the New Jersey Assembly. In 1990 he was elected mayor of Paterson, but continued to serve in the Assembly—a common practice in New Jersey (and also in France).

Meanwhile, he watched as the 8th District seat changed hands. After Public Works Committee chairman Robert Roe retired in 1992, liberal Democrat Herb Klein won, only to be replaced by Bill Martini in the Republican sweep in 1994. Pascrell ran against him in 1996 and attacked him as a tool of an "extremist" Republican leadership—one ad even showed Martini's face on a puppet operated by Speaker Newt Gingrich. Despite Martini's support from the Sierra Club and some labor unions, Pascrell rode the coattails of the Clinton-Gore campaign. In a district that went 58% for Clinton, Pascrell won 51%–48%. Since then, he has won at least 62% of the vote.

In the House, Pascrell has compiled a liberal record on economics, more moderate on cultural and foreign issues. He voted for the partial-birth abortion ban and for parental-notification requirements for abortions across state lines. He called it "my proudest day" in Congress when he won approval for expanded federal aid to local fire departments; since 2000, the program distributed more than $1 billion in local aid. But he said that the Pentagon "has blown it" in failing to protect the nation against the September 11 attacks. He voted in October 2002 to authorize the use of force in Iraq. In 2003, he made an unsuccessful bid for a seat on the Ways and Means Committee.

Like others in the House delegation, Pascrell has had ambitions for statewide office. He expressed interest in running for governor in 2001. But his support for Jim Florio in the 2000 Senate primary against Jon Corzine left him on the losing side of the New Jersey party establishment. In 2005 he supported Corzine for governor and said he would be interested in being appointed to the Senate to replace him. In the unlikely event that should happen, one possible replacement is his son, Passaic County Counsel Bill Pascrell III.

NINTH DISTRICT

Rep. Steven Rothman (D)

Elected 1996, 5th term; b. Oct. 14, 1952, Englewood; home, Fair Lawn; Syracuse U., B.A. 1974, Washington U., J.D. 1977; Jewish; divorced.

Elected Office: Englewood Mayor, 1983–89; Bergen Cnty. Surrogate Court Judge, 1993–96.

Professional Career: Practicing atty., 1977–93.

DC Office: 2303 RHOB, 20515, 202-225-5061; Fax: 202-225-5851; Web site: rothman.house.gov.

District Offices: Hackensack, 201-646-0808; Jersey City, 201-798-1366.

Committees: *Appropriations* (27th of 29 D): Foreign Operations, Export Financing & Related Programs; Transportation, Treasury, HUD, the Judiciary & District of Columbia.

Group Ratings

	ADA	ACLU	AFS	LCV	ITIC	NTU	COC	ACU	NTLC	CHC
2004	95	63	86	91	20	12	30	5	0	8
2003	80	—	100	95	—	22	38	16	—	—

National Journal Ratings

	2003 LIB	—	2003 CONS		2004 LIB	—	2004 CONS
Economic	66%	—	32%		72%	—	27%
Social	71%	—	28%		73%	—	25%
Foreign	64%	—	36%		67%	—	32%

Key Votes of the 108th Congress

1. Drilling in ANWR	N	5. DC School Vouchers	N	9. Ban Same-Sex Marriage	N
2. Approve Bush Tax Cuts	N	6. Ban Human Cloning	N	10. Fund Iraq War	Y
3. Medicare/Rx Bill	N	7. Restrict Gun Liability	N	11. Bar Cuba Embargo Funds	N
4. Bar Overtime Pay Regs.	Y	8. Ban Partial-Birth Abortion	*	12. Intelligence Reorg.	Y

Election Results

2004 general	Steven Rothman (D)	146,038	(68%)	($630,160)
	Edward Trawinski (R)	68,564	(32%)	($17,532)
	Other	1,649	(1%)	
2004 primary	Steven Rothman (D)	unopposed		
2002 general	Steven Rothman (D)	97,108	(70%)	($604,690)
	Joseph Glass (R)	42,088	(30%)	($5,476)

Prior Winning Percentages: 2000 (68%); 1998 (65%); 1996 (56%)

The People		Race/Ethnic Origin	Ancestry	
Area size:	100 sq. mi.	61.3% White	Italian: 16.2%	Irish: 9.0%
Urban population:	100.0%	6.6% Black	German: 6.6%	
Rural population:	0.0%	10.7% Asian	**2004 Presidential Vote**	
Pop. 2000:	647,257	0.1% Native Am.	Kerry (D) 144,723	(59%)
Median income:	$52,437	0.0% Hawaiian	Bush (R) 101,229	(41%)
Poverty status:	7.6%	2.1% Two+ races	**2000 Presidential Vote**	
Military veterans:	8.6%	0.3% Other	Gore (D) 135,406	(63%)
		18.8% Hispanic Origin	Bush (R) 72,695	(34%)
			Other 6,110	(3%)
			Cook Partisan Voting Index: D +13	

Occupation	Blue collar: 20.3%	White collar: 66.8%	Gray collar: 12.9%

The George Washington Bridge, one of several wondrous suspension bridges completed in America in the 1930s, strides the Hudson, its west tower almost up against the green cliff of New Jersey's Palisades. It is one of the glories of modern engineering, enabling people and goods to be transported through the irregular terrain of metropolitan New York—tidal rivers and cliffs and broad expanses of swamp. For a century the dramatic beauty of the Palisades contrasted with the ugly sprawl of the Hackensack River Valley and the Jersey Meadowlands not far to the west. This giant swamp was the image of New Jersey for many—a landscape of gas station signs, oil tank farms, truck terminals and 12 lanes of New Jersey Turnpike—a smelly, ugly place that meant you were still not where you wanted to go, full of garbage and pig farms, briefly famous when Secaucus tavern owner Henry Krajewski ran for president in 1956. But the Meadowlands—which survive as 8,400 acres of wetlands and home to thousands of species of animals and plants—were the largest hunk of empty real estate near such a huge city center, and eventually they were developed. In the 1970s, the state built in East Rutherford the Meadowlands Sports Complex—Giants Stadium (where the Giants and Jets play now), the Meadowlands Racetrack, the Brendan Byrne Arena (later Continental Airlines Arena, home of the Nets and Devils). Private development followed—hotels, warehouses, light industry, shopping centers (including a huge Wal-Mart)—in what became a small city. Now, a generation later, the state is planning to build a new $750 million stadium for the Giants at the Meadowlands.

The 9th Congressional District of New Jersey includes much of the Palisades and the Meadowlands. The scenery here is familiar to fans of the cable television series, *The Sopranos*: Jersey City, Kearny, North Arlington, Lodi (home to the fictitious Bada Bing; the actual strip club uses a different name). The 9th runs from the high-rise towers of Fort Lee, Cliffside Park and fast-growing Edgewater, where dwellers in luxury apartment houses brag about their views of New York City, west and north to the leafy suburbs of Englewood and Teaneck, and southwest to the high land overlooking the Meadowlands and the Passaic River in old small towns like Rutherford, with Polish-, German- and Italian-Americans. Blue-collar Palisades Park has become a center for Korean-Americans. Teaneck and Englewood are home to middle class blacks and young, Orthodox Jewish families. Fairview, Bergenfield and Hackensack, an old industrial town and the Bergen County seat, are home to growing numbers of Hispanics. This was a growth area in the 1950s and 1960s, as New Yorkers moved out of the City; it lost population in the 1970s and 1980s, as young people moved farther out and left empty nesters behind. Now the population in some towns is rising due to new immigrants. The conservative families, griping about taxes, who grew up in Bergen County are now being replaced by the heavily Democratic immigrants and "tower dwellers."

The congressman from the 9th District is Steve Rothman, a Democrat first elected in 1996. Rothman grew up in Englewood and Tenafly, went off to school at Syracuse University and Washington University law school in St. Louis, then practiced law. From 1983–89 he was mayor of Englewood; in 1993 he became a judge in the Bergen County Surrogate's Court. When 14-year Congressman Bob Torricelli ran for the Senate in 1996, Rothman resigned his judgeship and ran for the House. With the party endorsement, Rothman faced Republican Kathleen Donovan—Bergen County Clerk, former Assemblywoman, and chairman of the New York-New Jersey Port Authority, who was endorsed by the New Jersey Education Association and Cuban-American leader Jorge Mas Canosa. But this part of New Jersey swung sharply to the Democrats following the Republican takeover of the House. The 9th District voted overwhelmingly for Bill Clinton and 56%–42% for Rothman.

In the House, Rothman has been more liberal on economic issues than on defense. In 2001, he joined the Appropriations Committee. He voted for the Iraq war resolution. In 2004, he sought unsuccessfully to extend the assault weapons ban. On local issues, his most innovative work has been his call to limit further development and seek protection for the Meadowlands. After the Fish and Wildlife Service ruled that a local wildlife refuge was too expensive and a low priority, Rothman won approval in 2001 of $1.2 million for land acquisition as a small down payment for a plan to protect the open space. He later secured $1.4 million dollars more to help create an 8,400-acre state park in the one-third of the Meadowlands that had not been developed. He fought proposals to expand the Teterboro airport and to allow 737s to fly in there. In September 2003, the House approved his provision to ban 737s at Teterboro as part of the transportation appropriation.

Rothman has won reelection easily and by wide margins. He has been mentioned as a possible candidate to succeed Senator Jon Corzine if he is elected governor, but appears to be far down on the list of those to whom Corzine owes favors. Rothman also has said he will run for Senate in 2008, if Frank Lautenberg retires.

TENTH DISTRICT

Rep. Donald Payne (D)

Elected 1988, 9th term; b. July 16, 1934, Newark; home, Newark; Seton Hall, B.A. 1957; Baptist; widowed.

Elected Office: Essex Cnty. Bd. of Chosen Freeholders, 1972–78, Dir. 1977–78; Newark Municipal Cncl., 1982–89.

Professional Career: Elem. & High Schl. teacher, 1957–64; Exec., Prudential Insurance Co., 1964–72; Pres., YMCAs of the U.S., 1970; Vice Pres., Urban Data Systems Inc., 1975–88.

DC Office: 2209 RHOB, 20515, 202-225-3436; Fax: 202-225-4160; Web site: www.house.gov/payne.

District Offices: Elizabeth, 908-629-0222; Newark, 973-645-3213.

Committees: *Education & the Workforce* (4th of 22 D): 21st Century Competitiveness; Employer-Employee Relations. *International Relations* (5th of 23 D): Africa, Global Human Rights & International Operations (RMM); Western Hemisphere.

Group Ratings

	ADA	ACLU	AFS	LCV	ITIC	NTU	COC	ACU	NTLC	CHC
2004	95	100	100	100	20	14	5	0	0	9
2003	80	—	100	90	—	26	25	13	—	—

National Journal Ratings

	2003 LIB	—	2003 CONS	2004 LIB	—	2004 CONS
Economic	85%	—	15%	94%	—	5%
Social	92%	—	0%	88%	—	0%
Foreign	94%	—	0%	98%	—	0%

Key Votes of the 108th Congress

1. Drilling in ANWR	N	5. DC School Vouchers	N	9. Ban Same-Sex Marriage	N
2. Approve Bush Tax Cuts	N	6. Ban Human Cloning	*	10. Fund Iraq War	N
3. Medicare/Rx Bill	N	7. Restrict Gun Liability	N	11. Bar Cuba Embargo Funds	Y
4. Bar Overtime Pay Regs.	Y	8. Ban Partial-Birth Abortion	N	12. Intelligence Reorg.	N

Election Results

2004 general	Donald Payne (D)	155,697	(97%)	($483,000)
	Other	5,016	(3%)	
2004 primary	Donald Payne (D)	unopposed		
2002 general	Donald Payne (D)	86,433	(84%)	($355,909)
	Andrew Wirtz (R)	15,913	(16%)	

Prior Winning Percentages: 2000 (88%); 1998 (84%); 1996 (84%); 1994 (76%); 1992 (78%); 1990 (81%); 1988 (77%)

The People		Race/Ethnic Origin	Ancestry	
Area size:	69 sq. mi.	21.4% White	West Indian: 6.4% Italian: 4.2%	
Urban population:	100.0%	56.6% Black	Irish: 3.6%	
Rural population:	0.0%	3.6% Asian	**2004 Presidential Vote**	
Pop. 2000:	647,258	0.2% Native Am.	Kerry (D) 167,707	(82%)
Median income:	$38,177	0.0% Hawaiian	Bush (R) 36,660	(18%)
Poverty status:	17.5%	2.8% Two+ races	**2000 Presidential Vote**	
Military veterans:	8.1%	0.5% Other	Gore (D) 147,112	(83%)
		15.0% Hispanic Origin	Bush (R) 27,718	(16%)
			Other 3,004	(2%)
			Cook Partisan Voting Index: D +34	

Occupation   Blue collar: 23.6%   White collar: 58.0%   Gray collar: 18.4%

Newark has been the hollow core of New Jersey, the city to which main transportation arteries once led and whose corporate headquarters buildings were the tallest in the state. In 1930, 442,000 people lived here, one of every nine in New Jersey; in 2000, there were 273,000, one of every 30. Even so, Newark's core has recently been perking up; new office buildings have joined the Prudential and Public Service Electric & Gas headquarters, and the New Jersey Performing Arts Center has been a big hit. There has been industrial development around Newark Airport, and immigrant neighborhoods are showing new vitality. Port Newark-Elizabeth Marine Terminal is the largest container port on the East Coast and nationally ranks behind only Los Angeles and Long Beach; old warehouses there are being cleared for more growth. The glass and aluminum Newark Airport has been hugely expanded and is thriving as a hub for Continental, the most thriving of the legacy airlines. What hurt Newark for so many years was the plague of horrendous schools and high crime; large parts of the city were dominated by criminals and deserted by most law-abiding residents who could get out. Now crime rates have been declining, the state has taken over the schools and life is coming back to deserted streets. Now the question is whether crime will continue to fall and Newark can become once again the vital center of New Jersey.

The 10th Congressional District of New Jersey is centered in Essex County and is made up of most of Newark—the Central, South and West Wards—plus Irvington, most of the Oranges and part of Montclair to the west, and much of Elizabeth, Rahway, and Linden to the south. Its boundary lines wiggle around to include blacks in Jersey City, Montclair and Elizabeth, and leave Hispanics in the next-door 13th District. Overall the district is 57% black; it is by far the most Democratic district in New Jersey.

The congressman from the 10th District is Donald Payne, a Democrat first elected in 1988. He grew up in Newark, worked as a teacher and for Prudential, served on the Essex Board of Chosen Freeholders in the 1970s and was vice president of Urban Data Systems for 13 years. In 1980 and 1986, he ran against Congressman Peter Rodino, chairman of the House Judiciary Committee when it voted to impeach President Richard Nixon; Payne lost, even as an African-American in a district with a black majority. But when Rodino retired in 1988, Payne, at age 54, won 73% in the Democratic primary and easily won the general.

Payne has an impeccably liberal voting record. He served as chairman of the Congressional Black Caucus in 1995 and 1996, just as Republicans were defunding the caucuses. He rescued the Africa Subcommittee from abolition, and attacked cuts in aid to African countries. But he did not lionize all of Africa's leaders. He sponsored a resolution to cut off new investment in Sudan because of its practice of slavery—though he criticized as "unconscionable" the pullout from Sudan of international private-aid agencies. As the ranking Democrat on the Africa Subcommittee since 1999, roughly half the bills he has sponsored deal with Africa. He criticized foreign aid as insufficient to meet the needs of United Nations peacekeeping operations, and has pointed out that the more than 700 million people of Africa receive far less aid from the United States than do the six million of Israel. In 2001, he rallied support by Black Caucus members for passage of the Zimbabwe Democracy and Economic Recovery Act, which imposed sanctions against the regime of President Robert Mugabe; his goal, Payne said, was to ensure a secure, democratic and prosperous Zimbabwe. In 2003, George W. Bush named him as one of two members of Congress to serve as a delegate to the United Nations. But he was one of 22 House members who voted "present" on the March 2003 resolution of "unequivocal support" for the war in Iraq, calling the war "ill-conceived" and one that "could have been avoided through diplomacy." He criticized Secretary of State Colin Powell as not tough enough in stopping the war in Sudan; in July 2004, the House passed his resolution condemning the conflict and terming it "genocide." Payne also came to the defense of UN Secretary-General Kofi Annan in December 2004 when Republicans called for his resignation amid allegations concerning corruption in the Iraq oil-for-food program; with John Conyers, he sent a letter to House members saying, "To decide that the secretary-general must resign is an absolutely premature conclusion to draw when there is no evidence or even allegations that the secretary-general profited from the oil-for-food program."

Payne has been reelected by very wide margins. Alone among New Jersey Democratic congressmen, he has not been mentioned as a candidate to replace Senator Jon Corzine if he is elected governor in November 2005.

ELEVENTH DISTRICT

Rep. Rodney Frelinghuysen (R)

Elected 1994, 6th term; b. Apr. 29, 1946, New York City; home, Harding; Hobart Col., B.A. 1969; Episcopalian; married (Virginia).

Military Career: Army, 1969–71 (Vietnam).

Elected Office: Morris Cnty. Bd. of Freeholders, 1974–83; NJ Assembly, 1983–94.

Professional Career: Aide, Morris Cnty. Bd. of Freeholders, 1972–74.

DC Office: 2442 RHOB, 20515, 202-225-5034; Fax: 202-225-3186; Web site: www.house.gov/frelinghuysen.

District Office: Morristown, 973-984-0711.

Committees: *Appropriations* (14th of 37 R): Defense (Vice Chmn.); Energy & Water Development & Related Agencies.

Group Ratings

	ADA	ACLU	AFS	LCV	ITIC	NTU	COC	ACU	NTLC	CHC
2004	25	5	13	18	90	48	100	67	60	69
2003	10	—	13	55	—	59	93	68	—	—

National Journal Ratings

	2003 LIB	—	2003 CONS		2004 LIB	—	2004 CONS
Economic	44%	—	56%		37%	—	62%
Social	49%	—	51%		52%	—	48%
Foreign	31%	—	65%		34%	—	66%

Key Votes of the 108th Congress

1. Drilling in ANWR	N	5. DC School Vouchers	Y
2. Approve Bush Tax Cuts	Y	6. Ban Human Cloning	Y
3. Medicare/Rx Bill	Y	7. Restrict Gun Liability	Y
4. Bar Overtime Pay Regs.	N	8. Ban Partial-Birth Abortion	Y

9. Ban Same-Sex Marriage	N
10. Fund Iraq War	Y
11. Bar Cuba Embargo Funds	N
12. Intelligence Reorg.	Y

Election Results

2004 general	Rodney Frelinghuysen (R)	200,915	(68%)	($801,784)
	James Buell (D)	91,811	(31%)	($3,406)
	Other	3,276	(1%)	
2004 primary	Rodney Frelinghuysen (R)	unopposed		
2002 general	Rodney Frelinghuysen (R)	132,938	(72%)	($783,357)
	Vij Pawar (D)	48,477	(26%)	($15,793)
	Other	2,263	(1%)	

Prior Winning Percentages: 2000 (68%); 1998 (68%); 1996 (66%); 1994 (71%)

The People		Race/Ethnic Origin	Ancestry	
Area size:	628 sq. mi.	82.9% White	Italian: 16.8%	Irish: 14.4%
Urban population:	93.5%	2.6% Black	German: 11.8%	
Rural population:	6.5%	6.3% Asian	**2004 Presidential Vote**	
Pop. 2000:	647,258	0.1% Native Am.	Bush (R) 186,993	(58%)
Median income:	$79,009	0.0% Hawaiian	Kerry (D) 135,578	(42%)
Poverty status:	3.5%	1.0% Two+ races	Other 1,847	(1%)
Military veterans:	10.4%	0.1% Other	**2000 Presidential Vote**	
		6.8% Hispanic Origin	Bush (R) 151,617	(54%)
			Gore (D) 121,036	(43%)
			Other 9,763	(3%)
			Cook Partisan Voting Index: R + 6	

Occupation	Blue collar: 14.0%	White collar: 76.2%	Gray collar: 9.8%

New Jersey's Morris County, west of the Watchung Mountain ridges, was one of the first settled parts of the interior United States west of the seaboard. It has long been a place of comparative affluence, the home of skilled craftsmen during the Revolutionary War, with plenty of water mills and iron forges by the 19th century. But only in the late 20th century has it come into its own, as one of the most affluent parts of the United States. And it is not just a collection of country estates with huddled small towns for the servants to live in, but a well-rounded community with all the appurtenances of urbanity except high crime and poverty rates. The very rich have lived here for some time, connected to Manhattan by commuter rail lines. But starting in the 1970s, new residents rushed out the newly completed I-80 and I-280 or the ring road I-287. Prompted by court-required zoning changes, old farms and woods have been cleared to make way for new subdivisions, such as the North Caldwell gated community home of television's Tony Soprano. And this is not just a bedroom community. New office complexes and corporate headquarters have been rising, including Pfizer's expanded manufacturing and testing center; much of New Jersey's economic energy, entrepreneurial creativity and research expertise is out here. Large forested areas of state parkland remain, including the Wildcat Ridge Wildlife Management Area. After a hike through the area, Interior Secretary Gale Norton called Highlands preservations a national priority, including a habitat for hawks and more than 250 imperiled plant and animal species plus vital regional water supply.

The 11th Congressional District of New Jersey includes all of Morris County plus small slices of Sussex, Passaic, Essex and Somerset Counties. It is one of the most affluent districts in the country: It ranks second in the nation in median household income. It is family territory, with relatively few singles; not a strongly cultural conservative area, but not aggressively liberal either. It has few blacks but a larger share of Hispanics, and one of its biggest immigrant populations is of Indians, whose household incomes are double the national average. Politically, it is the most Republican district in New Jersey, and one of the most Republican in the Northeast. It was one of only three New Jersey districts to vote for George W. Bush in 2000, one of six in 2004.

The congressman from the 11th District is Rodney Frelinghuysen (pronounced *FREE-ling-high-zen*), a Republican and scion of one of New Jersey's most durable political families, which moved from Germany near the Dutch border in 1720 and settled in what is now the 11th District. Four Frelinghuysens served as senator from New Jersey, starting in 1793 and as recently as 1923; Theodore Frelinghuysen was the candidate for vice president in 1844 (leading to the memorable chant, "Hurrah! Hurrah! The country's risin'/ For Henry Clay and Frelinghuysen"); Frederick Frelinghuysen was Chester Arthur's secretary of state; Peter Frelinghuysen, Rodney's father, was elected to the House in 1952 and served until his retirement in 1974. History tends to repeat itself, and Frelinghuysens have been involved in every presidential impeachment: Rodney Frelinghuysen's great-great-grandfather Frederick voted to convict Andrew Johnson in 1868; his father Peter, after the revelations of July 1974, would have voted to impeach Richard Nixon if the president had not resigned; and this generation's Frelinghuysen voted to impeach Bill Clinton in December 1998. As a child, Rodney Frelinghuysen lived in the large brick house on Georgetown's N Street now owned by former *Washington Post* editor Ben Bradlee and his wife Sally Quinn; he attended St. Albans prep school with Al Gore. After college, the congressman's son was drafted and served in the Army in Vietnam, where he built roads in the Mekong Delta. In 1972 he was appointed an aide by then-Morris County Freeholder (and later 11th District Congressman) Dean Gallo; he served as a freeholder himself from 1974–83 and was elected to the Assembly in 1983.

Frelinghuysen ran for Congress in 1990 in what is now the 12th District, when its boundaries were different; he lost the primary to Dick Zimmer. In August 1994, after the primary, Gallo retired because of illness; he died two days before the election. Frelinghuysen was chosen to be the Republican nominee at a September party convention and was elected with 71% of the vote.

He showed his insider skills by winning a seat as a freshman on the Appropriations Committee, where he worked to cut spending on many programs, while maintaining a moderate voting record and concentrating on New Jersey projects for members of both parties. New Jersey has had no senator on Appropriations after 2000, and Frelinghuysen more than ever became the go-to guy for the entire delegation. He concentrated on big projects—construction of the Hudson-Bergen light rail, dredging of channels in the Port of New York and New Jersey, millions to slow erosion on the faraway Jersey Shore.

Frelinghuysen has taken moderate or even liberal stands on some issues, but is more conservative on defense. He has twice won House passage of his "Know Your Caller" bill, which bars telemarketers from interfering with caller-ID systems of customers seeking to avoid such solicitations. He has said that he has more Superfund sites in his district than any other congressman and "we need to continue the cleanup and the remediation." In 2004, he won enactment of legislation to protect the New Jersey Highlands. One of his favorite causes is Amber Alert, using emergency communications to track down child abductors, which now operates in many states and is credited with recovery of dozens of children. In Iraq, he said that it was vital for the United States to stay the course and he condemned European nations that have not sent troops there. After the 2002 election, he became one of the 13 "cardinals," as chairman of the Appropriations Subcommittee on the District of Columbia. He sought to avoid additional strings on local activities but was unable to remove restrictions that conservatives previously had added, including limits on abortion services and distribution of needles; he opposed voting representation in Congress for the District. But in 2005 incoming Appropriations Chairman Jerry Lewis reduced the number of subcommittees from 13 to 10, and Frelinghuysen did not get a chairmanship.

Frelinghuysen has not been seriously challenged for re-election. He has shown no interest in running statewide; this patrician evidently believes that his gritty work in the House is more important than taking a chance on gaining the glamour of serving in the Senate.

TWELFTH DISTRICT

Rep. Rush Holt (D)

Elected 1998, 4th term; b. Oct. 15, 1948, Weston, WV; home, Hopewell Township; Carleton Col., B.S. 1970, N.Y.U., PhD. 1981; Protestant; married (Margaret Lancefield).

Professional Career: Prof., Swarthmore Col., 1981–89; Asst. Dir., Princeton Plasma Physics Lab., 1989–98.

DC Office: 1019 LHOB, 20515, 202-225-5801; Fax: 202-225-6025; Web site: www.holt.house.gov.

District Office: West Windsor, 609-750-9365.

Committees: *Education & the Workforce* (14th of 22 D): 21st Century Competitiveness; Employer-Employee Relations. *Permanent Select Committee on Intelligence* (7th of 9 D): Intelligence Policy (RMM); Technical & Tactical Intelligence.

Group Ratings

	ADA	ACLU	AFS	LCV	ITIC	NTU	COC	ACU	NTLC	CHC
2004	95	90	100	100	40	9	19	4	0	7
2003	95	—	100	100	—	23	23	12	—	—

National Journal Ratings

	2003 LIB	—	2003 CONS		2004 LIB	—	2004 CONS
Economic	76%	—	24%		89%	—	8%
Social	90%	—	8%		88%	—	0%
Foreign	84%	—	14%		77%	—	23%

Key Votes of the 108th Congress

1. Drilling in ANWR	N	5. DC School Vouchers	N	9. Ban Same-Sex Marriage	N
2. Approve Bush Tax Cuts	N	6. Ban Human Cloning	N	10. Fund Iraq War	N
3. Medicare/Rx Bill	N	7. Restrict Gun Liability	N	11. Bar Cuba Embargo Funds	N
4. Bar Overtime Pay Regs.	Y	8. Ban Partial-Birth Abortion	N	12. Intelligence Reorg.	N

Election Results

2004 general	Rush Holt (D)	171,691	(59%)	($1,651,175)
	Bill Spadea (R)	115,014	(40%)	($341,354)
	Other	3,080	(1%)	
2004 primary	Rush Holt (D)	unopposed		
2002 general	Rush Holt (D)	104,806	(61%)	($1,787,764)
	DeForest Soaries (R)	62,938	(37%)	($624,112)
	Other	3,969	(2%)	

Prior Winning Percentages: 2000 (49%); 1998 (50%)

The People		Race/Ethnic Origin	Ancestry	
Area size:	642 sq. mi.	72.4% White	Italian: 13.7% Irish: 12.1%	
Urban population:	93.2%	11.4% Black	German: 9.3%	
Rural population:	6.8%	9.1% Asian	**2004 Presidential Vote**	
Pop. 2000:	647,258	0.1% Native Am.	Kerry (D) 165,776	(54%)
Median income:	$69,668	0.0% Hawaiian	Bush (R) 138,454	(46%)
Poverty status:	5.2%	1.4% Two+ races	**2000 Presidential Vote**	
Military veterans:	10.6%	0.2% Other	Gore (D) 141,568	(56%)
		5.5% Hispanic Origin	Bush (R) 101,145	(40%)
			Other 9,188	(4%)
			Cook Partisan Voting Index: D + 8	

Occupation	Blue collar: 13.8%	White collar: 75.7%	Gray collar: 10.4%

It was once the main East Coast arterial highway, carrying the nation's highest volume of truck traffic. Today it is crowded with cars taking high-salaried workers and clerical help to one of the East Coast's thickest concentrations of office buildings in one of the bigger edge cities spawned in the 1980s. This is U.S. 1, which once just connected the industrial cities of Trenton and New Brunswick on its way from Philadelphia to New York; now it is better thought of around here as connecting the university towns around Princeton and Rutgers, and is a locus of telecommunications and pharmaceutical research. This had been empty bucolic country, looked out on by F. Scott Fitzgerald's undergraduates from their Gothic Princeton towers; now it is filled with postmodern office campuses and hotels and restaurants clamoring for attention.

The 12th Congressional District of New Jersey meanders across the breadth of New Jersey, from the Delaware River in the west to the Atlantic Ocean. It extends several dozen miles on either side of U.S. 1 as it slices through Mercer and Middlesex Counties; it is home to both an Englishtown and a Frenchtown. To the west, it takes some of the rolling country of Hunterdon County. On the other side of U.S. 1, the 12th takes in Princeton and then some modest-income suburbs—Franklin in Somerset County, East Brunswick in Middlesex County—and some fast-growing Monmouth County areas such as Rumson, part of Middletown, and Holmdel; Monmouth, Marlboro and Manalapan have been rated among the best small towns on the East Coast. Redistricting made the 12th, represented for most of the 1990s by a Republican, more Democratic—virtually taking it off the table for effective competition.

The congressman from the 12th District is Rush Holt, a Democrat first elected in 1998. He has an impressive political pedigree that is, however, of no importance to this district. His father Rush D. Holt, a favorite of United Mine Workers leader John Lewis, was elected as the "boy senator" from West Virginia in 1934 when he was 29; he could not take his seat until June 1935 when he turned 30. But he clashed early and often with Franklin D. Roosevelt and lost the Democratic primary to Harley Kilgore in 1940. Former Senator Holt died when the young Rush Holt was 6, and he grew up in Washington, D.C., where his mother Helen, who had been West Virginia secretary of state, was an official in the Federal Housing Agency. He went off to Carleton College in Minnesota and to New York University, where he earned advanced degrees in physics, eventually becoming assistant director of the Princeton Plasma Physics Laboratory, which studies fusion. Holt—the only five-time *Jeopardy!* champion to serve in Congress—also was an arms-control expert for the State Department.

Holt entered politics in 1996, when Republican Congressman Dick Zimmer ran for the Senate against Bob Torricelli and lost. Holt finished third in the Democratic primary behind Lawrenceville Mayor David Del Vecchio and Princeton Town Committeeman Carl Mayer; cultural conservative Mike Pappas won the Republican primary, then the general election but by only 50%–47%. Pappas immediately became a top Democratic target in 1998. Holt decided early in the year that Bill Clinton's State of the Union message gave him an agenda to appeal to suburban voters. Mayer ran again, but national and local Democrats favored Holt, who won the endorsements of all five county Democratic organizations plus all of Mayer's former colleagues on the Princeton Town Committee; he won the primary 64%–36%. Then, in July, Pappas took to the House floor to recite a poem: "Twinkle, Twinkle Kenneth Starr, now we see how brave you are. We could not see which way to go, if you did not lead us so." New Jersey was pro-Clinton, anti-impeachment territory, and Pappas's ditty, replayed on network newscasts and incorporated into a Holt TV spot, proved a great liability. Holt emphasized gun control, abortion rights, the environment and preserving Social Security; he won in a 50%–47% upset.

Holt immediately became a Republican target, but he was undeterred. He compiled a solidly liberal voting record. As the second research physicist in the House, he worked with the other, Republican Vern Ehlers, to promote science education, trying to give science equal standing with reading and math in Title I. He sponsored an assortment of gun control measures, including one to require licensing and registration of all handguns (it attracted no co-sponsors). Based partly on his belief that his father's close defeat in West Virginia resulted from a faulty ballot count, Holt became a crusader for an improved paper trail for voting machines; his proposed Voter Confidence and Increased Accessibility Act had 157 co-sponsors. His amendments to prohibit recreational snowmobiling in Yellowstone Park were narrowly defeated in the House. In 2003, he won a seat on the House Intelligence Committee, and became an outspoken critic of the Bush Administration's failure to disclose sufficient information to Congress.

In 2000, the seat was fiercely contested. After flirting with another Senate bid, Zimmer declared for his old House seat; Pappas did too. Zimmer won the Republican primary 62%–38%. He immediately became the target of some $2 million of Democratic Congressional Campaign Committee negative ads. Zimmer acknowledged that the political terrain had changed. "There's a cultural divide between the Northeast and what's become the Republican base," he said during the primary. "The world looks different from suburban New Jersey than it does from Texas." This turned out to be one of the closest races in the nation. At one point on election night, Zimmer was declared the winner. But after all the votes were counted, Holt won by a bit more than 1,000 votes. In 2001, he focused heavily on redistricting. Holt was alone among the congressional delegation in his sharp opposition to the state redistricting commission's plan. But the new boundaries suited him fine. The proof came in 2002, when Holt's Republican opponent was former New Jersey Secretary of State DeForest "Buster" Soaries, a black minister with a 6,000-member Baptist church; unfortunately for him, many of the members of the congregation lived in New Brunswick, which was located in the 6th District. Soaries attracted little financial support from national Republicans; he was out-spent by more than 3–1. Holt won easily, 61%–37%. In December 2003, Holt endorsed Howard Dean for president. He was reelected 59%–40% in 2004.

THIRTEENTH DISTRICT

Rep. Robert Menendez (D)

Elected 1992, 7th term; b. Jan. 1, 1954, New York, NY; home, Union City; St. Peter's Col., B.A. 1976, Rutgers Law Schl., J.D. 1979; Catholic; married (Jane Jacobsen-Menendez).

Elected Office: Union City Board of Ed., 1974–82; Union City Mayor, 1986–92; NJ Assembly, 1987–91; NJ Senate, 1991–92.

Professional Career: Practicing atty., 1980–92.

DC Office: 2238 RHOB, 20515, 202-225-7919; Fax: 202-226-0792; Web site: menendez.house.gov.

District Offices: Bayonne, 201-823-2900; Jersey City, 201-222-2828; Perth Amboy, 732-324-6212; Union City, 201-558-0800.

Committees: *Democratic Caucus Chairman. International Relations* (6th of 23 D): International Terrorism & Nonproliferation; Western Hemisphere (RMM). *Transportation & Infrastructure* (7th of 34 D): Railroads; Water Resources & Environment.

Group Ratings

	ADA	ACLU	AFS	LCV	ITIC	NTU	COC	ACU	NTLC	CHC
2004	85	61	100	100	56	9	35	8	3	15
2003	90	—	100	95	—	24	37	24	—	—

National Journal Ratings

	2003 LIB	—	2003 CONS		2004 LIB	—	2004 CONS
Economic	76%	—	24%		77%	—	23%
Social	72%	—	27%		71%	—	28%
Foreign	66%	—	32%		68%	—	30%

Key Votes of the 108th Congress

1. Drilling in ANWR	N	5. DC School Vouchers	N
2. Approve Bush Tax Cuts	N	6. Ban Human Cloning	N
3. Medicare/Rx Bill	N	7. Restrict Gun Liability	N
4. Bar Overtime Pay Regs.	Y	8. Ban Partial-Birth Abortion	N

9. Ban Same-Sex Marriage	*
10. Fund Iraq War	N
11. Bar Cuba Embargo Funds	N
12. Intelligence Reorg.	N

Election Results

2004 general	Robert Menendez (D)	121,018	(76%)	($3,941,956)
	Richard Piatkowski (R)	35,288	(22%)	
	Other	3,235	(2%)	
2004 primary	Robert Menendez (D)	34,807	(87%)	
	Steven Fulop (D)	5,099	(13%)	
2002 general	Robert Menendez (D)	72,605	(78%)	($2,197,203)
	James Geron (R)	16,852	(18%)	
	Other	3,274	(4%)	

Prior Winning Percentages: 2000 (79%); 1998 (80%); 1996 (79%); 1994 (71%); 1992 (64%)

The People		Race/Ethnic Origin	Ancestry	
Area size:	74 sq. mi.	32.3% White	Italian: 7.3%	Irish: 5.3%
Urban population:	100.0%	11.3% Black	Polish: 3.8%	
Rural population:	0.0%	5.5% Asian	**2004 Presidential Vote**	
Pop. 2000:	647,258	0.1% Native Am.	Kerry (D) 127,168	(69%)
Median income:	$37,129	0.0% Hawaiian	Bush (R) 57,278	(31%)
Poverty status:	18.0%	2.4% Two+ races	**2000 Presidential Vote**	
Military veterans:	5.4%	0.6% Other	Gore (D) 114,586	(72%)
		47.6% Hispanic Origin	Bush (R) 39,554	(25%)
			Other 4,338	(3%)
			Cook Partisan Voting Index: D +23	

Occupation Blue collar: 28.4% White collar: 55.7% Gray collar: 15.9%

The Statue of Liberty, standing in New York Harbor since 1886, has been the great symbol of America welcoming immigrants to its shores. Actually, the statue is on the New Jersey side of the harbor, and so (as the Supreme Court ruled in 1998) is most of Ellis Island, where they were processed. The towns sitting on the granite and gneiss ridge of Hudson County, overlooking the harbor, have in particular been immigrant territory. When immigration was shut off in 1924, many children and grandchildren of the Irish and Italian immigrants stayed in Hudson County, living in the same neighborhoods, working on the same docks or factories and voting the dictates of the same political machine. Hudson County was the setting of one of America's classic political machines, undisciplined by any metropolitan elite. From 1917–49, the boss of Hudson County was Frank ("I am the law") Hague; his machine chose governors and U.S. senators, prosecutors and judges, and had influence in the White House of Franklin D. Roosevelt. Hague collected high taxes from industries clustered here—who then passed them on to consumers everywhere—and in return gave them an orderly city, free of most crime and vice, and a work force insulated against racketeers and militant unions. Hague's successor, John V. Kenny, was boss from 1949–71—continuous power for 54 years.

But Hudson County began changing again, in ways little noticed by either the local machine or Manhattan sophisticates. New immigrants were coming in—refugees from Castro's Cuba, other Latinos and Asians after the 1965 immigration act. Union City became predominantly Cuban, Jersey City neighborhoods became heavily Latino. Upscale young singles looking for lower rents moved into Hoboken's five-story Victorian apartments that sparkle with light off the Hudson, and were a quick commute through the PATH tubes to Wall Street or Greenwich Village. Starting in the 1980s, huge new condominium and office developments went up in Jersey City—Port Liberte, Newport, Liberty Place, Port Imperial South, a 45-story Goldman Sachs tower, back-office buildings for Chase Bank, Merrill Lynch, Paine Webber, U.S. Trust. In Hoboken, shopping and apartment complexes are going up on waterfront sites where Maxwell House Coffee and Lipton Tea had great factories (and where the movie classic, *On the Waterfront*, was filmed on location). Bayonne has become a cruise ship port. Aiding this private sector growth was reform of the public sector, notably by Jersey City's Republican mayor, Bret Schundler, a former Wall Streeter elected in 1992 after the incumbent went to jail, who was elected to full terms in 1993 and 1997. But old times seemed to return in November 2004 when electronic cartridges containing some 2,000 votes went missing in a close special election for mayor. Meanwhile, new immigrants continue to arrive. Union City is less Cuban today, as middle class Cubans move to Bergen County suburbs, and more Colombian, Ecuadoran, Peruvian and Dominican. The huge Art Deco New Deal-era Jersey City Medical Center in downtown Jersey City has been replaced by a new, privately run JCMS opened on the waterfront in June 2004. Hudson County, which seemed to be dying a generation ago, is now thriving with new life.

The 13th Congressional District of New Jersey includes most of Hudson County plus most of the immigrant entry ports along the water, from West New York and Weehawken, where Alexander Hamilton was killed in a duel with Vice President Aaron Burr in 1804, south past Jersey City and Bayonne (where you can still find bocce courts), past the Port of New York and New Jersey to the waterfront areas of Elizabeth, Linden, Carteret (with its Sikh community), Woodbridge and Perth Amboy. It also includes the Ironbound district of Newark, with Portuguese and Brazilian immigrants, crowded stores and $400,000 houses, Harrison and part of industrial Kearny. The district's population is 48% Hispanic; black neighborhoods in Jersey City were put into the majority-black, neighboring 10th District. The 13th is heavily Democratic.

The congressman from the 13th District is Robert Menendez, a Democrat first elected in 1992. He is of Cuban descent and grew up in Union City, America's most densely populated city (in 2000 it had 60,000 people in 1.3 square miles), and got into politics early. He was elected to the school board in 1974, at 20. He worked for Union City Mayor William Musto in the 1970s, but quit and testified against Musto in a corruption trial, and ran against him and lost in 1982. Menendez was elected mayor in 1986, to the Assembly in 1987 and Senate in 1991; he served both as mayor and legislator (a common practice in New Jersey) until his 1992 election to

Congress. He was the first New Jersey Latino in the legislature and Congress. When new district lines were created and incumbent Frank Guarini retired, Menendez won the 1992 primary 68%–32% and the general election 64%–31%.

In the House, Menendez serves on the International Relations Committee where he became ranking minority member on the Western Hemisphere Subcommittee in 2001. He has been a strong supporter of anti-Castro legislation—the 1992 Cuban Democracy Act, the 1996 Helms-Burton Act. But his concerns are not limited to Cuba. He supported the Caribbean Basin Initiative and the proposal to allow Central American and Haitian refugees long in this country to remain. He spoke out in support of Israel's military actions in May 2002 even though he said his district "has far more Arabs than Jews." He sponsored a bill in 2004 to put illegal immigrants on the path to permanent worker status and citizenship. In March 2004 he criticized the Bush administration for its inaction while President Jean-Bertrand Aristide was forced to leave Haiti. He sponsored a bill to authorize $500 million yearly for a Social Investment and Economic Development Fund for the Americas. He sponsored the Democratic substitute for reorganizing the intelligence community, which was defeated 213–203 in October 2004.

Noting the increasing importance of the financial services industry in Hudson County, he broke with many Democrats to support the bankruptcy bill and financial services deregulation; one Blue Dog Democrat called him "the pro-business member of the leadership." He was co-sponsor of a bill to double Alzheimer's research at NIH. In 2004 he sponsored a bill aimed at improving railroad security, with $5 billion for capital equipment and $800 million for operating expenses.

Menendez heads the Democratic party organization in Hudson County and is a major player in state politics. He has shown fine political skills—and, at times, sharp elbows— both at home and in Washington. He aggressively supported Loretta Sanchez against the election challenge brought by Robert Dornan, whom she ousted in November 1996; in November 1998, his party colleagues elected him vice chairman of the Democratic Caucus. When Senator Frank Lautenberg announced his retirement in February 1999, Menendez was widely expected to run for the Senate. But support was not forthcoming from New Jersey Senator Bob Torricelli, the DSCC Chairman, who wanted a deep-pockets candidate and found him in Jon Corzine, whom Menendez endorsed in November 1999. Menendez suffered some setbacks in Hudson County politics in the June 2003 primaries, in which several candidates he backed were beaten by candidates supported by Jersey City Mayor and state Senator Glenn Cunningham. But he came back strongly in 2004. When Cunningham died that year, Menendez and his allies blocked his wife from running for the state Senate. Menendez was opposed in the June Democratic primary by a candidate backed by Cunningham, but beat him 87%–13%. Some called him the political boss of Hudson County. "I bristle at the term," Menendez said. But he did admit to the existence of what some would call political bosses. "I think there are people with very significant influence in certain parts of the state."

One reason Menendez decided not to run for the Senate in 2000 is that Minority Leader Dick Gephardt urged him to stay in the House, arguing that as a leader of a Democratic majority he could be more important than a junior senator. Democratic caucus chairmen and vice-chairmen are limited to two two-year terms, so Menendez in 2001 began running for caucus chairman. He raised more than $1 million for House Democrats in the 2000 cycle and $3 million in the 2002 cycle and traveled around the country campaigning. His Hispanic background was an asset, and not just within the 20-member Hispanic Caucus. "There are 50 to 60 members who are not Hispanic but have significant Hispanic communities in their districts," he points out. "The Census was a real eye-opener. I have members asking me to travel with them to places I never thought I'd be invited." He issues a Latino Leadership Link every week in English and Spanish.

Menendez announced his candidacy for chairman of the Democratic Caucus in October 2001, just after the caucus picked Nancy Pelosi over Steny Hoyer to replace David Bonior as minority whip. Also running was Rosa DeLauro, who had been Assistant to Minority Leader Richard Gephardt. Leadership elections are decided by secret ballot, and are sometimes bitter; the total number of commitments announced by candidates usually exceeds the number of members of the caucus. Occasionally sour notes are sounded in public. In February 2002

Menendez charged that DeLauro backers were saying, wrongly, that he did not support abortion rights; he argued that the caucus, having chosen Pelosi for the number one post, would be better off with an Hispanic than another woman in the number three post. In an unusual turn, Pelosi openly endorsed DeLauro and Hoyer openly endorsed Menendez. Then, on September 30, came another opportunity to run for the Senate: Bob Torricelli dropped out of the race and Governor Jim McGreevey and other Democratic leaders sought another candidate. Menendez, with more than $2 million in his campaign treasury, probably could have had the nomination for the asking. He pondered the situation for a day, and then decided not to run; he said he was too committed to getting a Democratic majority in the House and becoming caucus chairman.

On November 5 he failed to achieve the first goal and on November 14, the day of the caucus election, he very nearly failed to achieve the second. The day before the caucus meeting, the 21 Blue Dogs met and pledged to vote as a bloc for their favorite candidate, which by a 16–5 vote was Menendez; it's not clear that all of them did. Menendez walked into the caucus with a list of 107 members who had agreed to openly support him. He won 104–103.

As caucus chairman, Menendez continued to show his fundraising prowess. He headed up a campaign committee group called Frontline Democrats with a view to raising $1 million. By June 2003 he had $2.8 million in his campaign fund, more than any other House member; over the 2003–04 cycle he raised $3.6 million. In December 2003 he ventured to Waterloo, Iowa, and endorsed Howard Dean for president.

In July 2004, when McGreevey's job rating was low, Menendez was one Democrat speculating about pushing him aside in favor of Senator Jon Corzine. Of Corzine, he said, "He's popular, and if people would think about where to turn outside of Governor McGreevey, he has the relationships, good will and good standing to attract support." On August 12 McGreevey announced that he had had an affair with a man and would resign, but not until November 15. Menendez, along with Camden County Democratic Chairman George Norcross and Middlesex County Chairman John Lynch, urged McGreevey to resign before September 3, which would trigger a November special election in which Corzine could run and which he would probably win, at which point he could appoint Menendez senator. But McGreevey refused and Senate President Richard Codey, a political adversary of Norcross's and Lynch's, became acting governor from November 15 until January 2006.

To be sure, Menendez continued to be active in the House. In October 2004 he announced he would be running for majority whip if Democrats regained a majority in the House. After the election he appointed a Democratic Task Force on Faith and Values in Politics. But he also clearly hankered to run for the Senate. In December 2004, after Corzine announced he would run for governor and before Acting Governor Richard Codey took himself out of the race, Menendez made it known that, if Corzine were elected, he would run for the Senate even if Corzine named someone else to the seat. It was noted that he had far more money for a campaign than Congressmen Rob Andrews and Frank Pallone, who also seemed interested in the Senate.

★ NEW MEXICO ★

America's oldest settlements and its newest technologies can be found, in surrealistic proximity, in New Mexico. For the oldest permanently inhabited city in the United States is not Plymouth, Massachusetts, or Jamestown, Virginia, or even St. Augustine, Florida, it is probably Acoma, New Mexico. Probably, because Acoma, inhabited by the Anasazi, "an agricultural, settled and architecturally sophisticated people," wrote historian Roger Kennedy in *Rediscovering America*, had perhaps 1,000 years of unrecorded history before Spanish conquistadors came upon them in 1540. Some 460 years later, much of what makes New Mexico distinctive derives from the people found here by the first European explorers—something true of no other state but Hawaii. While the Pilgrims built flimsy wood houses, the Indians in New Mexico were living in extensive dwellings hundreds of years old, made with the adobe that is still the characteristic building material here.

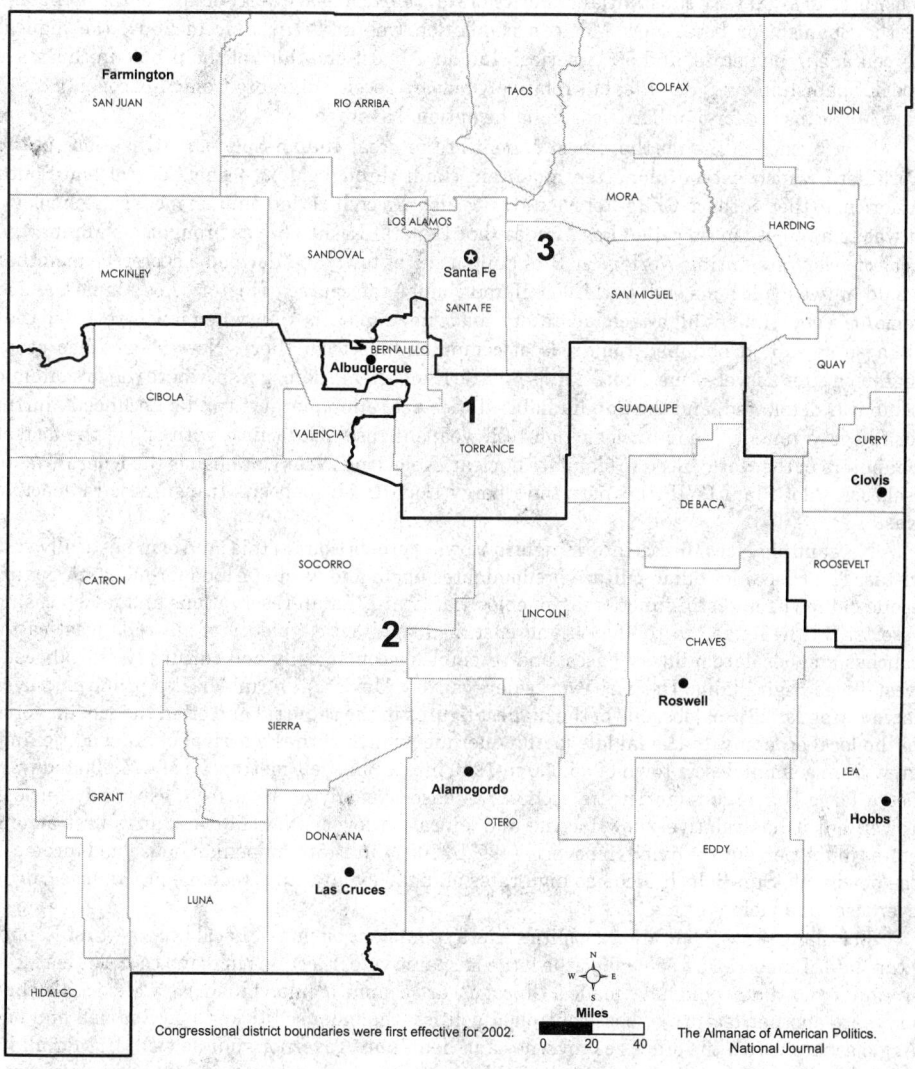

Congressional district boundaries were first effective for 2002.

Miles
0   20   40

The Almanac of American Politics.
National Journal

Other state cultures are generally based on what early white settlers brought to the land; natives have mostly disappeared or been killed off by diseases contracted from the first white settlers. Not in New Mexico. The English-speaking culture here is superimposed, at times rather lightly, on a society whose written history dates back to the Spanish settlement of Santa Fe in 1609, and to centuries long past when the Pueblo Indians set up stable agricultural societies on the sandy, rocky lands of northern New Mexico, using small pebbles as mulch to retain scarce moisture. Today, a very substantial minority of New Mexicans are descendants of these Indians or the Spanish, or both. New Mexico's population was 43% Hispanic in 2004, the highest percentage in any state, and 9% American Indian. Almost one-third of the people in this state speak Spanish in everyday life, but relatively few are recent migrants from Mexico: only 8% of New Mexicans are foreign-born, less than the national average.

New Mexico is the northernmost salient of the great Indian-Spanish civilizations of the Cordillera, which extend along the mountain chain through Mexico and Central and South America, to the southern Chile. Yet New Mexico also is a civilization built on modern technology. It was to a remote mesa called Los Alamos that General Leslie Groves brought his Manhattan Project scientists during World War II to build a secret town and develop a secret weapon that would in two explosions end World War II and change the course of history. Los Alamos, which remains a government high-tech laboratory, made news in early 1999 when it was revealed that Chinese spies had obtained hundreds of computer files from there. New Mexico has other high-tech sites as well—the White Sands Missile Range near Alamogordo, where the first atomic bomb was detonated, and the Sandia Laboratories near Albuquerque, run by Lockheed-Martin for the government, a non-nuclear high-tech weapons research facility, with one of the fastest computers in the world, used to simulate nuclear explosions. Near Carlsbad is the federal Waste Isolation Pilot Plant (WIPP), where the Energy Department deposits transuranic radioactive waste.

New and old New Mexico intermingle in varying proportions in this land of majestically vast vistas. The Hispanic-Indian culture predominates north and west of Albuquerque, with picturesque old towns and still-functioning pueblos, backward Indian reservations and lavish casino resorts. "Little Texas," in the south and east, has small cities, plenty of oil wells, vast cattle ranches and desolate military bases, and resembles, economically and culturally, the adjacent west Texas High Plains. Here, as everywhere in New Mexico, government is a prime employer (accounting for 23% of jobs, one of the highest figures in the country) and often the moving force in the local economy. In the middle is Albuquerque, which, with the arrival of air conditioning, grew from a small desert town of 35,000 in 1940 into a Sun Belt metropolis of 474,000 today; it has a large Hispanic minority. Its economy is based heavily on high tech, especially nuclear power, but it has relatively low income and education levels: New Mexico ranks first among states in the percentage living in poverty (18% in 2001) and 45th in median household income—the downscale Sun Belt. It also has high rates of highway fatalities, teenage pregnancies, drug overdoses and violent crime.

For many years, New Mexico politics was a somnolent business. Local bosses—first Republican, later Democratic—controlled the large Hispanic vote. Elections in many counties featured irregularities that would have made a Chicago ward committeeman blush. New Mexico also had for years another feature of boss-controlled politics: the balanced ticket, one Spanish and one Anglo senator, with the offices of governor and lieutenant governor split as well. But for all its distinctiveness, in national politics New Mexico was a bellwether, voting for every winning presidential candidate from 1912, when it became a state, until 1976, when it backed Gerald Ford. In the 1988 and 1996 elections it was just 1% off the national mark; in 2000, after some ragged vote counting, it reported a 365-vote margin for Al Gore. Currently, Democrats have a strong base in the north, from Hispanics and from liberal newcomers in Santa Fe and Taos. Albuquerque has been politically marginal; its migrants have been conservative culturally but liberal on economics. Southeast New Mexico is as conservative and Republican as west Texas. Southwest New Mexico, around Las Cruces and Silver City, is more Hispanic and marginally Democratic.

New Mexico politics also has its peculiarities. In the 1990s a Green Party formed, in protest against the practical-minded and sometimes corrupt politics of many Democratic wheelhorses; the Green candidate for governor won 10% of the vote in 1994, and Republican Gary Johnson might well have not been elected otherwise. Johnson was also a new political force—the first strongly conservative Republican to win major office in many years, and one of the few Republicans to come out for drug legalization. In 2002 Johnson was succeeded by Bill Richardson, former congressman, ambassador to the United Nations and Energy secretary, occasional negotiator with North Korea and some day perhaps the first Hispanic presidential nominee. The Green party was ruled off the ballot in 2001 after Ralph Nader failed to win 5%; but its gubernatorial candidate got 5% in 2002 and so it got back on, but its nominee got only 1,226 votes in 2004 as George W. Bush carried the state by 5,988.

The People		Race/Ethnic Origin			Military veterans: 190,718 (14.5%)	
Pop. 2004 (est):	1,903,289	813,495	44.7%	White	WWII: 18.0%	Korea: 13.2%
Pop. 2000:	1,819,046	30,654	1.7%	Black	Vietnam: 34.7%	Gulf War: 10.7%
Pop. 1990:	1,515,069	18,257	1.0%	Asian	**Most populous cities (2003):**	
Change 1990–2000:	Up 20.1%	161,460	8.9%	Native Am.	1. Albuquerque	471,856
% of U.S. total:	0.7%	992	0.1%	Hawaiian	2. Las Cruces	76,990
Pop. rank:	36th of 50	25,793	1.4%	Two+ races	3. Santa Fe	66,476
Area size:	121,589 sq. mi.	3,009	0.2%	Other	4. Rio Rancho	58,981
State Native:	51.5%	765,386	42.1%	Hisp. Origin	5. Roswell	44,228
Non-citizen:	5.4%	**Ancestry**				
Language		German: 8.2%		English: 6.3%	Urban population: 75.0%	
English: 58.2%	Spanish: 33.3%	Irish: 6.1%		USA: 4.2%	Rural population: 25.0%	
Other Eur.: 2.1%		Italian: 2.0%				

Education		Work Sector		Legislature	
H.S. Grad:	78.9%	Private: 68.5%	Govt: 22.7%	Senate	24 D 18 R
College Grad:	23.5%	Self: 8.4%	Family: 0.4%	House	42 D 28 R
Industry		Unemployment: 7.2%		Legislative Term Limits: No	
Agri: 4.0%	Con: 7.9%	**Household Income**		**Registered Voters**	
Fin: 5.5%	Info: 2.4%	<15k: 20.8%	15-35k: 30.2%	D: 550,519	(49.8%)
Mfg: 11.2%	Prof: 31.1%	35-50k: 17.0%	50-100k: 24.3%	R: 359,563	(32.5%)
Public: 8.0%	Trade: 14.9%	100-150k: 5.0%	>150k: 2.6%	O: 195,290	(17.7%)
Other: 14.9%		Median: $34,133			
Occupation		Poverty status: 18.4%			
Blue collar: 22.2%	White collar: 59.9%	**Home Value**			
Gray collar: 17.9%		<50k: 22.7%	50-100k: 31.1%	100-200k: 33.4%	200-300k: 7.7%
		300-500k: 3.6%	>500k: 1.6%	Median: $94,600	

Presidential politics   New Mexico's near-bellwether status seems more accidental than anything else; it's hard to think of a state more atypical of the nation, yet it keeps on voting at or near the national average. It voted Republican for president in the 1980s, Democratic in the 1990s. It gave Al Gore a 365-vote margin in 2000 when he did, after all, win the popular vote, and it gave George W. Bush a 5,988-vote margin in 2004. New Mexico was as closely contested as any state in 2004, with constant visits from the nominees and huge doses of advertising. It was also organized to the gills. During the campaign most of the coverage focused on Governor Bill Richardson's efforts to register new Democrats, and a plurality of new voters registered Demo-

2004 Presidential Vote		
Bush (R)	376,930	(50%)
Kerry (D)	370,942	(49%)
Nader (I)	4,053	(1%)
Other	4,379	(1%)

2000 Presidential Vote		
Gore (D)	286,783	(48%)
Bush (R)	286,418	(48%)
Nader (Green)	21,251	(4%)
Other	4,154	(1%)

cratic. The rolls may have swelled partly because the Democratic-dominated New Mexico Supreme Court ruled that people didn't need to show identification to register. But George W. Bush's volunteer-based organization quietly matched and perhaps exceeded their effort. Turnout was up 26% in a state where the population grew 5% in four years. Turnout was up 34% in Santa

Fe County, which grew 7% and voted 71% for John Kerry. But in Lea County in Little Texas, which grew only 1%, turnout was up 28% and the county voted 79% for Bush. Democrats increased their nominees' margins by 13,000 in Santa Fe and Taos Counties and 6,500 in Albuquerque's Bernalillo County. But in the 10 counties of Little Texas Bush's margin increased by 18,000 and in San Juan County, mining country around Farmington, it increased by another 5,000. In 2000 Bush's popularity among Texas Latinos didn't travel across the state border and he won only 32% of the Hispanic vote. In 2004 there were Viva Bush movements in all 33 counties and heavy emphasis on Bush's cultural conservatism, and he won 44% of the Hispanic vote. Bush led among white Anglos 56%–43%, and that was enough for a 50%–49% win. New Mexico had less trouble counting votes than in 2000, but it still took some time and in December the Green and Libertarian parties called for a recount. But they failed to put up the $1.4 million the state said it would cost.

New Mexico traditionally held its presidential primary in June, long after every major party nomination since 1984 has been settled. But in 2003 Governor Bill Richardson signed a bill allowing parties to hold caucuses in lieu of the presidential primary, and the Democrats held caucuses February 3.

Congressional districting   The boundaries of New Mexico's three congressional districts have been substantially the same since 1982, and seem likely to continue that way. Control of the redistricting process in 2001 was split between the Democratic legislature and Republican Governor Gary Johnson. In June 2001 the legislature passed a plan that would make the 1st District, held by Republican Heather Wilson, more Democratic. Johnson vetoed it. In September 2001 the legislature passed a plan that would make the 2d District, held by Republican Joe Skeen, more Democratic. Johnson vetoed it. Republicans had already taken the issue to court. A federal court decided to let the state court handle the issue. In January 2002, state District Judge Frank Allen, a Democrat, imposed his own plan. He said he was reluctant to make major changes and his plan shifted only 22,000 people into different districts. Democrats were disappointed; Republicans were pleased.

109th Congress Lineup
2 R   1 D
108th Congress Lineup
2 R   1 D

In February 2003 state Senate President Richard Romero, who lost to Wilson in 2002 and 2004, was pressing the legislature to redistrict the House seats once again; Democratic Governor Bill Richardson would surely sign a plan. But national Democrats urged caution and Richardson seemed uninterested, perhaps because a new plan might jeopardize his good relations with Senator Pete Domenici, who would be miffed if a new plan hurt Heather Wilson. So New Mexico is making do with the 2002 districts.

Governor

Bill Richardson (D)

Elected 2002, term expires Jan. 2007, 1st term; b. Nov. 15, 1947, Pasadena, CA; home, Santa Fe; Tufts U., B.A. 1970, Fletcher Schl. of Law and Diplomacy, M.A. 1971; Catholic; married (Barbara).

Elected Office: U.S. House of Reps., 1982–97.

Professional Career: Congressional rel., U.S. Dept. of State, 1973–75; Staff, Senate Foreign Relations Subcmte., 1975–78; Exec. Dir., NM Dem. Party, 1978; Pres., Richardson Trade Group, 1978–82; U.S. Ambassador to U.N., 1997–98; Secy., U.S. Dept. of Energy, 1998–2000.

Office: State Capitol, 4th Floor, Santa Fe, 87300, 505-476-2200; Fax: 505-576-2226; Web site: www.governor.state.nm.us.

Election Results

2002 general	Bill Richardson (D)	268,674	(55%)
	John Sanchez (R)	189,090	(39%)
	David Bacon (Green)	26,465	(5%)
2002 primary	Bill Richardson (D)	unopposed	
1998 general	Gary E. Johnson (R)	271,948	(55%)
	Martin Chavez (D)	226,755	(45%)

Bill Richardson, a Democrat, was elected governor of New Mexico in 2002, 20 years after he was first elected to Congress. Richardson is a unique politician—an Hispanic with an Anglo name, a newcomer when he was first elected in New Mexico where many families go back 300 years, an adept politician who has also been an international negotiator. He was born in California and grew up in Mexico City. His father was a banker from Boston and his mother Mexican; she now lives in Cuernavaca. He graduated from prep school in New England, where he met his wife. He was a good pitcher and in 1967 was drafted by the Kansas City Athletics. He graduated from Tufts's Fletcher School of Law and Diplomacy and got a master's there. That led to a job as a "sort of go-fer" at the State Department when Henry Kissinger was secretary of state and a job on Senator Hubert Humphrey's staff. Then in 1978 he moved to New Mexico to become executive director of the state Democratic party. He was fired after a month by Governor Bruce King and proceeded to run against 1st District Congressman Manuel Lujan. This was a Republican year and Lujan had deep roots in Albuquerque and had been in office since 1968. But Richardson held him to a 51%–49% victory. New Mexico got a third congressional district from the 1980 Census, and the legislature drew a new, heavily Hispanic 3d District in northern New Mexico. Richardson, based in Santa Fe, had already carried much of this territory in the 1980 race, and he ran and won in 1982. At age 35, after four years in New Mexico, he had a safe seat in the House.

In the House he had a somewhat moderate voting record and was not afraid to buck organized labor by lobbying hard for NAFTA in 1992 and 1993. After that he spent much time on foreign affairs. In July 1994 he traveled to Haiti and met with General Raoul Cedras and in a five-hour conversation tried to get him to cede power, unsuccessfully. In December 1994 he was traveling to North Korea when two U.S. helicopter pilots were gunned down for allegedly trespassing into North Korean airspace. He negotiated for the release of the surviving pilot but ended up returning with the remains of the one who died; the other pilot was soon released.

In January 1997 Richardson was nominated as ambassador to the United Nations. Here was an opportunity to be a major player in foreign policy, although Richardson was cabined in by the close supervision of his predecessor, Secretary of State Madeleine Albright. But he did negotiate agreements between the Taliban regime in Afghanistan and opposition forces and secured the release of Red Cross workers held hostage in Sudan, and the foreign policy experience he was gaining seemed likely to make him a plausible vice presidential candidate in 2000 or later. The only embarrassing thing about his service was the fact, later disclosed that, at the request of a White House staffer and without asking why, he offered a job to Monica Lewinsky; she rejected it as insufficiently grand. Then in June 1998 Energy Secretary Federico Pena resigned and Bill Clinton, eager to have at least one Hispanic in an official cabinet position, shifted Richardson to the post. This was not really a promotion: Energy is a department that is made up of several unrelated agencies, some of them with deep troubles. One of those was the Los Alamos National Laboratory, from which, it seemed, secret documents about the assembly of nuclear weapons made their way to China. The suspect was physicist Wen Ho Lee, and Richardson fired him in March 1999. Lee was indicted on 59 counts of transferring nuclear weapons data to unsecure computers, but the case against him was thoroughly botched; most charges were dropped and in September 2000 he pleaded guilty to one count of downloading sensitive material. Richardson was much criticized in Congress for his work on improving security in the national laboratories, and his connection to the case was a political liability. He was mentioned as a possible vice presidential candidate in 2000—the Democrats would have loved to run a Hispanic—but his name soon fell off the list.

After Al Gore's defeat, Richardson returned to Santa Fe; he did some work for Kissinger McClarty Associates and served on corporate boards, but it was obvious he was running for governor. He had considered running before, especially in 1994, but decided not to. The governor elected that year, Republican Gary Johnson, had been reelected in 1998 and was ineligible to run again.

Richardson announced his candidacy in January 2002 and pledged to shake 600 hands a day; on September 16 he broke Theodore Roosevelt's record of 8,513, set on New Year's Day 1908, by shaking 13,392 hands at the New Mexico State Fair and a tailgate party at the University of New Mexico (his campaign flew in a representative of the *Guinness Book of World Records* to document the feat). He had opposition from two Democrats, former state Representative Gary King, whose father Bruce King had served three non-consecutive terms as governor and state Land Commissioner Ray Powell. But at the state Democratic convention in March, he won 1,288 of 1,705 votes. King and Powell failed to get enough to qualify for the ballot. With his energy and his national contacts, Richardson raised and spent large sums, eventually $6.8 million, more than twice as much as both parties' candidates spent in 1998, and began running ads showing his vision for the state.

The Republican nominee was state Representative John Sanchez, a roofing contractor from Albuquerque's North Valley, who had won his seat in 2000 by defeating, by 206 votes, the 30-year Speaker of the New Mexico House Raymond Sanchez. In the general election Sanchez called for vouchers, merit pay for teachers and better testing; he ran a series of ads recounting his rise from poverty under the theme of "Dream Big." But Richardson had much more money and took many more specific stands on issues. He called for cutting the state income tax—New Mexico's 8.2% top rate is much higher than those of surrounding states—and eliminating the gross receipts tax. Amid news of drought and water conservation measures, he called for a statewide water policy and sketched one out in considerable detail. He opposed vouchers, but supported charter schools and tax credits for parochial schools. Like Sanchez he favored the death penalty and a concealed weapons law.

Richardson pledged he would not run any negative commercials unless first attacked. But in September he ran the first negative ads; his campaign defended the action saying, "we have been attacked with distortions, false and malicious statements." Sanchez then ran ads criticizing Richardson for serving on the board of Peregrine Systems, which misstated its earnings and whose CEO, Richardson's wife's brother-in-law, resigned. Richardson said he was only an outside director and had resigned that position in June 2002. Richardson ran ads criticizing Sanchez for absenteeism in the legislature and for doctoring his resume; Sanchez said he started his roofing business in 1980, but in the mid-1980s was also working as a flight attendant. "While Bill Richardson was cutting taxes for New Mexico, John Sanchez was serving orange juice at 30,000 feet." There was little suspense about the result: Richardson won 55%–39%. He ran not far behind in Little Texas, carried the Albuquerque area comfortably and won as much as 75% of the vote in Hispanic and Indian counties. He was the only one of four Clinton cabinet members running in 2002 who won. Inevitably, he was asked whether he had ambitions for national office. "I've always wanted to run for governor. I love this state, and I think the governor can make an enormous difference in people's lives—more so than any job I have held. I see this as a sort of culmination of my career. I am not interested in going back to Washington"—not even as vice president.

In office, he did not act like a governor whose horizon ended at the state line. He frequently traveled out of state—to Davos, Switzerland, for the 2003 World Economic Forum; to Chicago, to talk businesses into relocating to New Mexico; to Hollywood, to promote the state as a good location for shooting movies; to Mexico City, where he once lived, to meet with President Vicente Fox. Days after his swearing in, he met with a North Korean delegation in Santa Fe, with Secretary of State Colin Powell's permission, for three days of discussions about nuclear weapons; it became known as "green chile diplomacy". Other foreign dignitaries would follow: Spain's Foreign Minister Jose Maria Aznar, Saudi Arabian Ambassador Prince Bandar bin Sultan, Prince Andrew of Great Britain. He was a familiar face in the national media and in Times

Square too, where his picture appeared on a giant billboard advertising the virtues of New Mexico and its tax policy. In September 2003, he hosted the first party-sanctioned presidential debate in Albuquerque.

Richardson's first year in office was among the most productive and successful of all governors elected in his Class of 2002. "We will move so fast! You're not going to see us," he said in his address to the opening of the 2003 legislature. Move fast he did. He immediately started lobbying legislators of both parties for his tax cut. Unusually in New Mexico, they brought the issue up before the budget and on Valentine's Day 2003 Richardson signed a bill cutting the top income tax rate from 8.2% in steps to 4.9% and cutting the capital gains tax in half over five years. "I told you I'd act quickly," he said. He made sweeping replacements on boards and commissions and sought to make boards more accountable by asking his appointees to sign letters of resignation that he could invoke at will. He signed a bill to crack down on drunken drivers, an especially vexing problem in New Mexico, and signed an executive order that extended employee benefits to the domestic partners of gay and lesbian state workers. In September, voters approved two constitutional amendments strongly backed by Richardson: one to create a Cabinet-level education secretary appointed by the governor and another to permit the state to increase the annual payout from the state's Land Grant Permanent Fund for public schools.

Less successful was a fall special session where Richardson called for more fundamental changes in tax laws. There he supported a failed bill that offered further tax cuts but with a net increase of $135 million in state and local taxes and fees; among the proposed increases was a hike in alcohol taxes, already among the highest in the nation. Critics said it would hurt the tourism and hospitality industry. The session did produce a tougher sex offender law and a $1.6 billion transportation package; Richardson later said his grade for his first year was an A-minus that would have been an A but for mistakes he made in the special session.

The even-year, legislative "short session" in New Mexico is generally limited to budget issues, though the governor can add to the agenda; in 2004 Richardson pushed the limit. He got the food tax cut he wanted after threatening to call the legislature back into session, though the gross receipts tax on other goods and services increased and Republicans complained about his "bullying tactics". The legislature also passed tougher DWI penalties, a tougher truancy law and facilitated the school bureaucracy changes approved by voters in 2003.

Richardson played a highly visible role in state and national Democratic politics in 2004. At home, he used his $2 million PAC, Moving America Forward, to register new voters and influence state and local elections. He was the driving force in 2003 behind a bill allowing parties to hold caucuses in lieu of the presidential primary and state Democrats held their presidential nominating caucus in February 2004; New Mexico traditionally held its presidential primary in June, usually long after the party nomination had been settled. At the Democratic National Convention in Boston, he served as chairman. As chairman of the Western Governors Association, he pushed governors to agree to work toward establishing a single date for western presidential primary and caucuses in 2008 to give the region more clout in the nominating process and to focus attention on issues like water rights, energy, the environment and immigration.

All of this raised Richardson's already high national profile. During the 2004 campaign he said repeatedly he would not accept the vice-presidential nomination, but that did not dampen speculation. Richardson is often mentioned as a prospective candidate for president in 2008. In February 2005 the Associated Press reported that he told party leaders he was running. He denied saying that; AP stood by its story. He has said he will run for reelection in 2006 but beyond that, "I'm not ruling anything out," he told the Albuquerque *Journal*. "But I'm not focused on it, really."

Senior Senator

Pete Domenici (R)

Elected 1972, seat up 2008, 6th term; b. May 7, 1932, Albuquerque; home, Albuquerque; U. of NM, B.S. 1954, Denver U., LL.B. 1958; Catholic; married (Nancy).

Elected Office: Albuquerque City Comm., 1966–70, Mayor Ex–Officio, 1967–70.

Professional Career: Practicing atty., 1958–72.

DC Office: 703 HSOB, 20510, 202-224-5521; Fax: 202-224-2852; Web site: domenici.senate.gov.

State Offices: Albuquerque, 505-346-6791; Las Cruces, 505-526-5475; Roswell, 505-623-6170; Santa Fe, 505-988-6511.

Committees: *Appropriations*: Commerce, Justice & Science; Defense; Energy & Water (Chmn.); Homeland Security; Interior & Related Agencies; Transportation, Treasury, the Judiciary, HUD & Related Agencies. *Budget. Energy & Natural Resources* (Chmn.). *Homeland Security & Governmental Affairs*: Federal Financial Management, Govt. Information & International Security; Investigations (Permanent); Oversight of Govt. Management, the Federal Workforce & the District of Columbia. *Indian Affairs.*

Group Ratings

	ADA	ACLU	AFS	LCV	ITIC	NTU	COC	ACU	NTLC	CHC
2004	15	0	14	0	100	70	100	95	87	100
2003	5	—	11	0	—	71	100	85	—	—

National Journal Ratings

	2003 LIB	—	2003 CONS		2004 LIB	—	2004 CONS
Economic	27%	—	71%		16%	—	83%
Social	0%	—	59%		30%	—	69%
Foreign	0%	—	78%		0%	—	67%

Key Votes of the 108th Congress

1. Ban Drilling in ANWR	N	5. Energy Bill	Y	9. Ban Same-Sex Marriage	Y
2. Approve Bush Tax Cuts	Y	6. Support Roe v. Wade	N	10. Ban Bunker-Buster Bomb	N
3. Medicare/Rx Bill	Y	7. Ban Partial-Birth Abortion	Y	11. Fund Iraq War	Y
4. Bar Overtime Pay Regs.	N	8. Assault Weapons Ban	N	12. Restrict Missile Defense	N

Election Results

2002 general	Pete Domenici (R)	314,193	(65%)	($4,144,286)
	Gloria Tristani (D)	168,863	(35%)	($836,604)
2002 primary	Pete Domenici (R)	unopposed		
1996 general	Pete Domenici (R)	357,171	(65%)	($3,435,164)
	Art Trujillo (D)	164,356	(30%)	($155,213)
	Abraham J. Gutmann (Green)	24,230	(4%)	($12,025)

Prior Winning Percentages: 1990 (73%); 1984 (72%); 1978 (53%); 1972 (54%)

Pete Domenici, New Mexico's senior senator, was elected to his sixth term in 2002. He grew up in Albuquerque, the son of Italian immigrants who ran a grocery wholesale business. He played baseball for the Albuquerque Dukes, practiced law and was elected to the city commission in 1966. In 1970 he ran for governor and lost 51%–46% to Democrat Bruce King. In 1972, when a Senate seat opened up in a Republican year, he ran and won 54%–46%, beating a Democrat named Jack Daniels. Ever since he has been reelected by wide margins.

Domenici is now chairman of the Senate Energy and Natural Resources Committee, but for 22 years he was chairman or ranking minority member of the Budget Committee. He has also been a member of the Appropriations Committee and brought an appropriator's mindset to his work on the budget. He got a seat on the Budget Committee in 1973, his first year in the Senate, and after Republicans gained a majority in 1980 he became chairman in January 1981; he became ranking minority member in January 1987, chairman again in January 1995 and ranking minority member in June 2001. In 1990 he turned down the ranking minority position on Energy and Natural Resources, an important committee for New Mexico, to stay on the Budget. After supporting the 1981 Reagan tax cuts, Domenici was appalled at budget deficits and pushed for entitlement cuts and tax increases, but Democrats fought the first and Republicans the second. In May 1985, Domenici and Bob Dole got Republican senators to pass a freeze on Social Security cost-of-living adjustments; then Ronald Reagan dropped the COLA freeze in a compromise with House Speaker Tip O'Neill, and Senate Republicans, left exposed, lost their majority in 1986. After Republicans became the majority party Domenici's ideas—a consumption tax; more in spending on education and defense than tax cuts—were initially overruled by Speaker Newt Gingrich, but the tax increase he opposed in 1993 and the spending standstill in the budget eventually passed in early 1996 put the deficit on a downward trajectory. Domenici was the impresario in the negotiations that produced the May 1997 balanced budget agreement. He helped to shape the budget resolutions in 1999 and 2000, but as an appropriator helped work out the arrangements that resulted in exceeding the budget caps.

In February 2001 he worked to pass the $1.6 trillion Bush tax cut and charged that Democrats had "anti-tax cut fever." Shy one vote in the Senate, Republicans did not end up reaching Bush's goals on the budget resolution. But they came close, and would have ended up much further away if Domenici had been lukewarm about the Bush plan. In June 2001 Domenici lost the chairmanship, but the budget resolution had already passed and in 2002 the Democrats were not able to pass one. In November 2002 he decided, after finding new spots for some longtime staffers, to move to the chairmanship of the Energy Committee; under Senate Republican rules he was eligible for only two more years as Budget chairman.

Domenici took over the Energy chairmanship from his Democratic New Mexico colleague, Jeff Bingaman, who became ranking minority member; this was the first time in history senators from the same state held the top two positions on a committee. Among the reasons he did so were his continuing interest in New Mexico's Los Alamos and Sandia National Laboratories and in promoting the expansion of nuclear power. After the controversy over security lapses at Los Alamos, he sponsored the creation of a new Undersecretary of Energy for Nuclear Stewardship; this was approved 96–1. In 2001 he got the appropriation for the labs up to $5.8 billion, the highest ever and $500 million above the administration request. In 2003 he battled with House appropriator David Hobson who had cut funding for Sandia and Los Alamos. His knowledge of the labs' work made him interested in other programs. He favors development of new nuclear weapons and in 2003 prevailed over Dianne Feinstein in moving forward on bunker buster bombs. The labs also made him aware of homeland security problems before September 11; the Sandia Lab has one of the world's most comprehensive anthrax databases. In 2001 he called for bringing back the Price-Anderson Act, which protected the nuclear power industry from liability for catastrophic accidents. In 2005 he published a book, *A Brighter Tomorrow: Fulfilling the Promise of Nuclear Energy*. "It's time for a new seriousness," he told a reporter, "unless we really like Americans dying in foreign lands, energy prices driving entire sectors of the economy out of business and dirtier air and water."

As Energy chairman Domenici has worked to build support for a bill resembling the Bush energy proposals. He decided early on, in February 2003, not to include oil drilling in the Arctic National Wildlife Refuge, because Democrats were prepared to filibuster on that issue. He allowed votes on increasing CAFE auto mileage standards—that was rejected—and put in tax incentives for renewable energies, but not the requirement that utilities get 10% of their energy from such sources by 2020 that Bingaman favored. He put in plenty of provisions for nuclear power. In July 2003 the Senate passed the bill and most differences with the House seemed bridgeable. But several Northeastern Republican senators joined many Democrats in opposing a provision relieving oil companies from liability for MTBE, an additive that government fuel standards encouraged them to use. House Majority Leader Tom DeLay and Energy and Commerce Chairman Joe Barton both said they wouldn't accept a bill without the MTBE provision. In April 2004 the tax provisions of the energy bill were added to the corporate tax bill, and in May Domenici thought about putting the entire energy bill in that must-pass legislation. But Majority Leader Bill Frist said he wouldn't bring the energy bill to the floor unless Democrats agreed to limit debate to two or three days, and Minority Leader Tom Daschle said Democrats needed more time than that to propose amendments on climate change and fuel efficiency. In January 2005 Domenici reached out to Bingaman in order to produce a less contentious energy bill. At Domenici's suggestion ANWR drilling was put into the budget resolution and passed 51–49 in March 2005.

Domenici has been one of the leaders in the Senate to extend health insurance coverage for mental illness. He became interested in the issue after his daughter Clare, the fourth of his eight children, was diagnosed with atypical schizophrenia. He uses his Appropriations seat to help New Mexico projects. He opposed the Clinton administration arsenic standard in drinking water which, he said, would require New Mexico communities to spend $424 million to meet a standard "lacking a foundation of sound science" and when the Bush administration accepted it, he sought $5 billion to help communities across the nation reduce arsenic levels; he made sure fast-growing places like Rio Rancho north of Albuquerque were eligible. With Jeff Bingaman he sponsored a bill in 2003 for $975 million to improve border security and infrastructure. With Dianne Feinstein he sponsored a bill to allow Indian tribes to contract with the federal government to take care of forests on reservations. When New Mexico's Supreme Court—"partisan Democrats," Domenici said—were preparing to allow people to register to vote without identification in September 2004, Domenici sponsored a bill to require identification. Domenici and Bingaman got into the omnibus appropriation $10 million to the descendants of Hispanic homesteaders who had been paid only a few dollars an acre in the 1940s for land that became part of the Los Alamos Laboratory. When the U.S. Attorney for New Mexico said that the Pueblo Act of 1924 left certain pueblo areas "prosecution-free zones," Domenici and Bingaman in 2005 sponsored a bill to amend the 1924 law. They also worked together in 2004 and 2005 to secure provisions that would bar the Air Force from retiring 10 F-117s currently assigned to New Mexico's Holloman Air Force Base.

Domenici has not been successful in seeking Senate leadership positions. He lost the majority leadership to Bob Dole in 1984 and the post of Republican Policy Committee chairman to Don Nickles in November 1990. In December 2000 he made a last-minute race against Policy Committee Chairman Larry Craig; this was taken as a criticism of Majority Leader Trent Lott, although Domenici said it wasn't; in any case he lost 26–24.

Domenici has remained highly popular in New Mexico and has won reelection easily. In 2002 he was opposed by Gloria Tristani, granddaughter of longtime (1935–62) Senator Dennis Chavez and former state corporation commissioner and FCC member. He campaigned heavily across the state and was endorsed by 74 mayors, including dozens of Democrats. Some raised questions about his health; he has been stricken with acute pain in two fingers in his right hand since a touch football accident in 1999, but has reportedly reduced the pain by physical therapy and medication. On Election Day Domenici won 65%–35%; he lost only three counties, and those narrowly. He reached out immediately to Governor-elect Bill Richardson, of whom he had been critical in the past. In late 2004 Domenici seemed to be suffering much less from pain and was no longer getting around the Capitol in a motorized chair. When asked whether he would run again in 2008, he said in November 2004 "Some mornings I wake up feeling terrible. Some mornings I wake up feeling great. Now how's that going to affect my decision? Just let time tell."

Junior Senator

Jeff Bingaman (D)

Elected 1982, seat up 2006, 4th term; b. Oct. 3, 1943, El Paso, TX; home, Santa Fe; Harvard U., B.A. 1965, Stanford U., LL.B. 1968; United Methodist; married (Anne).

Military Career: Army Reserves, 1968–74.

Elected Office: NM Atty. Gen., 1978–82.

Professional Career: NM Asst. Atty. Gen., 1969; Practicing atty., 1970–78.

DC Office: 328 HSOB, 20510, 202-224-6621; Fax: 202-228-3261; Web site: bingaman.senate.gov.

State Offices: Albuquerque, 505-346-6601; Las Cruces, 505-523-6561; Las Vegas, 505-454-8824; Roswell, 505-622-7113; Santa Fe, 505-988-6647.

Committees: *Energy & Natural Resources* (RMM). *Finance*: Health Care; International Trade; Social Security & Family Policy. *Health, Education, Labor & Pensions*: Bioterrorism & Public Health Preparedness; Education & Early Childhood Development; Retirement Security & Aging. *Joint Economic Committee*.

Group Ratings

	ADA	ACLU	AFS	LCV	ITIC	NTU	COC	ACU	NTLC	CHC
2004	90	67	100	100	58	10	71	12	5	0
2003	95	—	100	79	—	19	48	10	—	—

National Journal Ratings

	2003 LIB	—	2003 CONS		2004 LIB	—	2004 CONS
Economic	70%	—	26%		79%	—	13%
Social	68%	—	26%		65%	—	34%
Foreign	65%	—	32%		84%	—	15%

Key Votes of the 108th Congress

1. Ban Drilling in ANWR	Y	5. Energy Bill	N	9. Ban Same-Sex Marriage	N
2. Approve Bush Tax Cuts	N	6. Support Roe v. Wade	Y	10. Ban Bunker-Buster Bomb	Y
3. Medicare/Rx Bill	N	7. Ban Partial-Birth Abortion	N	11. Fund Iraq War	Y
4. Bar Overtime Pay Regs.	Y	8. Assault Weapons Ban	Y	12. Restrict Missile Defense	Y

Election Results

2000 general	Jeff Bingaman (D)	363,744	(62%)	($2,568,649)
	Bill Redmond (R)	225,517	(38%)	($639,424)
2000 primary	Jeff Bingaman (D)	unopposed		
1994 general	Jeff Bingaman (D)	249,989	(54%)	($3,652,899)
	Colin R. McMillan (R)	213,025	(46%)	($1,537,563)

Prior Winning Percentages: 1988 (63%); 1982 (54%)

Jeff Bingaman, a Democrat first elected in 1982, is New Mexico's junior senator. He has a good political lineage: His father was a professor at Western New Mexico University in Silver City, and his uncle was campaign manager for longtime (1949–73) Senator Clinton Anderson. He graduated from Harvard and Stanford Law School, then returned to New Mexico. A year out of law school, Bingaman was counsel to the state constitutional convention; later he went into law practice in Santa Fe with former Governor Jack Campbell. Bingaman's wife, Anne, started a highly successful law practice of her own that helped finance his first campaigns; she was assistant attorney general for antitrust in the first Clinton term. In a small state, bright young people like Jeff Bingaman can rise fast. He ran for attorney general in 1978 and won; in 1982, he ran against Senator Harrison Schmitt, the former astronaut, also from Silver City, and won with 54%, partly because it was a recession year, but also because of Schmitt's misleading and negative ads.

Bingaman has followed a course in the Senate much like that of Clinton Anderson, who used his influence behind the scenes to great effect but shunned national publicity—so much so that

Roll Call called him "preternaturally reticent." He got seats on two committees of great importance to the state, Armed Services and Energy. From these seats Bingaman has had some say over New Mexico's Los Alamos and Sandia labs.

On the Energy committee, he became the top-ranking Democrat in 1999. Then, after Jim Jeffords switched parties, Bingaman became chairman in June 2001, with the responsibility of coming up with an energy bill in response to the Bush energy proposals. The House passed an energy bill in August, but Bingaman did not present his own version until September. It ignored the controversial proposal for oil drilling in the Arctic National Wildlife Refuge and left the issue of raising CAFE auto mileage standards to the Commerce committee. He wanted to encourage more nuclear energy and reauthorize the Price-Anderson Act, which shields plant operators from liability, to require reporting of emissions from so-called greenhouse gases and to give FERC authority over electricity transmission systems; he said the administration and House version had too much in the way of production incentives and too little on renewable energy and energy efficiency. But the administration approach, including ANWR drilling, seemed to have majority support on the committee and in October he withdrew his bill. Republicans, including New Mexico's Pete Domenici, were furious at this and at Bingaman and Tom Daschle's decision to bring the issue to the floor without committee consideration—a highly unusual tactic for such complex legislation.

Floor debate began in February 2002 and went on for six weeks. Bingaman was beaten by a 62–38 margin on his proposal to increase CAFE mileage standards in cars and SUVs to 35 miles per gallon but kept his proposal to require that 10% of electricity be produced by renewable energy sources by 2020. Bingaman accepted amendments on pipeline safety and maintained his provisions, opposed by environmental restriction groups, to increase the use of nuclear power and promote research in clean coal technology in New Mexico labs. He got in his provisions to encourage more oil and gas development on Indian reservations. The conference committee was delayed in June, as Bingaman claimed he should be conference chairman because the House side had chaired the conference on the Alaska Power Administration Sale Act in 1995; the House's Billy Tauzin argued that the last relevant conference was in 1992, when the Senate side got the chair, and that he should be chairman, and prevailed. The conferees met periodically, but never reached agreement; the bill died after the November election. Democrats lost their majority, and Domenici became chairman and Bingaman ranking minority member—the first time in history senators from the same state held the top two spots on a committee. This time Domenici put together an energy bill which, without ANWR drilling, passed the Senate in July 2003. When Domenici went into one-on-one negotiations with Tauzin before the conference committee met, Bingaman said his procedure was "deeply flawed." That fall the Senate and House remained in conflict over protecting oil companies for liability for the additive MTBE; the House insisted on it and the Senate wouldn't accept it. Domenici said Bingaman was to blame for the failure of the bill; Bingaman said it was Domenici's fault for keeping conference committee members out of negotiations. In April 2004 Bingaman wrote the White House with 13 suggestions for executive action to lower gasoline prices. In September Bingaman walked out of a committee markup to block approval of two bills sought by Lisa Murkowski, who was in a tight race for reelection.

Bingaman is a physical fitness buff, and with fellow runner Bill Frist sponsored a bill to combat obesity by providing grants for schools and communities to raise awareness of the importance of exercise and healthy diets. He sponsored a bill to bar the selection of New Mexico as a premium support site under the 2003 Medicare prescription drug act. Bingaman and Gordon Smith called in February 2005 for a commission to study Medicaid and opposed spending cuts. On the class action bill he offered an amendment in February 2005 to give federal judges guidance for certifying class action cases based on state consumer law; House leaders were insisting that the bill not be amended, and Bingaman's amendment was rejected 61–38. He voted against the confirmation of Attorney General Alberto Gonzales because, he said, Gonzales had tolerated or encouraged loosening the definition of torture.

Many of his bills have a New Mexico angle. He sought more funding for the U.S.-Mexico Border Health Commission and urged the U.S. to help investigate the murders of more than 300 women in Juarez, Mexico. With Pete Domenici he sponsored a bill in 2003 for $975 million to improve border security and infrastructure. Bingaman and Domenici got into the omnibus appropriation $10 million to the descendants of Hispanic homesteaders who had been paid only a few dollars an acre in the 1940s for land that became part of the Los Alamos Laboratory. When the U.S. Attorney for New Mexico said that the Pueblo Act of 1924 left certain pueblo areas "prosecution-free zones," Bingaman and Domenici in 2005 sponsored a bill to amend the 1924 law. They also worked together in 2004 and 2005 to secure provisions that would bar the Air Force from retiring 10 F-117s currently assigned to New Mexico's Holloman Air Force Base. Bingaman, Domenici and Tom Udall succeeded in making Santa Fe, Taos and Rio Arriba Counties a National Heritage Area, to provide funding for preservation of cultural sites, and in designating Manhattan Project sites as a National Historical Park.

Bingaman faced his most serious challenge in the Republican year of 1994, when Republican Colin McMillan, a rancher and former assistant Defense secretary, spent over $1 million of his own money and attacked Bingaman's vote for Clinton's 1993 tax increase and for what McMillan said was a vote to increase grazing fees. Bingaman ads boasted of his work on defense conversion, national education standards and education technology. Bingaman won 54%–46%. In 2000 he faced former Congressman Bill Redmond, who won the heavily Democratic 3d District in a 1997 special election and then lost to Tom Udall in 1998. Redmond called for tax cuts and charged that Bingaman should have worked for forest-thinning earlier. Bingaman talked about bringing high-wage jobs to the state, improving education and expanding access to health care. People heard more of what Bingaman was saying: he spent $2.56 million, Redmond only $639,000. Bingaman won 62%–38%; he lost only six counties and ran 14% ahead of Al Gore. In February 2005 Bingaman announced that he was running for a fifth term. Tom Benavides, a former Democrat who served in the state House and Senate and ran against Pete Domenici in 1990, immediately announced he would run. Santa Fe City Councilor David Pfeffer was also said to be interested in this race. Congressman Steve Pearce ruled out a race; Congresswoman Heather Wilson was said to be considering it. New Mexico Republicans said they would use Bingaman's vote against Gonzales against him.

FIRST DISTRICT

Rep. Heather Wilson (R)

Elected June 1998, 4th full term; b. Dec. 30, 1960, Keene, NH; home, Albuquerque; U.S. Air Force Acad., B.S. 1982, Rhodes Scholar, Oxford U., M.A. 1984, Ph.D. 1985; Methodist; married (Jay Hone).

Military Career: Air Force, 1978–89.

Professional Career: Dir., European Defense Policy & Arms Control, White House NSC, 1989–91; Pres. Keystone Intl. Inc., 1991–95; NM Secy. of Children, Youth & Families, 1995–98.

DC Office: 318 CHOB, 20515, 202-225-6316; Fax: 202-225-4975; Web site: wilson.house.gov.

District Office: Albuquerque, 505-346-6781.

Committees: *Energy & Commerce* (12th of 31 R): Energy & Air Quality; Environment & Hazardous Materials; Telecommunications & the Internet. *Permanent Select Committee on Intelligence* (6th of 12 R): Intelligence Policy; Oversight; Technical & Tactical Intelligence (Chmn.).

Group Ratings

	ADA	ACLU	AFS	LCV	ITIC	NTU	COC	ACU	NTLC	CHC
2004	25	15	38	27	80	46	95	84	70	76
2003	20	—	0	10	—	55	93	76	—	—

National Journal Ratings

	2003 LIB	—	2003 CONS		2004 LIB	—	2004 CONS
Economic	33%	—	64%		49%	—	50%
Social	42%	—	56%		49%	—	51%
Foreign	45%	—	55%		51%	—	48%

Key Votes of the 108th Congress

1. Drilling in ANWR	Y	5. DC School Vouchers	Y	9. Ban Same-Sex Marriage	Y
2. Approve Bush Tax Cuts	Y	6. Ban Human Cloning	Y	10. Fund Iraq War	Y
3. Medicare/Rx Bill	Y	7. Restrict Gun Liability	Y	11. Bar Cuba Embargo Funds	N
4. Bar Overtime Pay Regs.	N	8. Ban Partial-Birth Abortion	Y	12. Intelligence Reorg.	N

Election Results

2004 general	Heather Wilson (R)	147,372	(54%)	($3,401,887)
	Richard Romero (D)	123,339	(46%)	($2,106,588)
2004 primary	Heather Wilson (R)	unopposed		
2002 general	Heather Wilson (R)	95,711	(55%)	($2,728,165)
	Richard Romero (D)	77,234	(45%)	($1,206,962)

Prior Winning Percentages: 2000 (50%); 1998 (48%); 1998 (45%)

The People		Race/Ethnic Origin	Ancestry	
Area size:	4,720 sq. mi.	48.5% White	German: 9.6%	English: 7.0%
Urban population:	91.3%	2.3% Black	Irish: 6.9%	
Rural population:	8.7%	1.7% Asian	**2004 Presidential Vote**	
Pop. 2000:	606,400	2.9% Native Am.	Kerry (D) 139,820	(51%)
Median income:	$38,413	0.1% Hawaiian	Bush (R) 130,946	(48%)
Poverty status:	14.0%	1.6% Two+ races	Other 2,896	(1%)
Military veterans:	15.2%	0.2% Other	**2000 Presidential Vote**	
		42.6% Hispanic Origin	Gore (D) 106,572	(48%)
			Bush (R) 103,770	(47%)
			Other 10,385	(5%)
			Cook Partisan Voting Index: D + 2	

Occupation	Blue collar: 18.9%	White collar: 65.2%	Gray collar: 16.0%

The future and the past of New Mexico come together in its single metropolis, Albuquerque. Its Spanish and Indian past is memorialized in its name (for a 17th century Spanish grandee) and age (founded in 1706) and its quaint Old Town, but Albuquerque's future is decidedly high-tech. For decades, the Sandia National Laboratories, Kirtland Air Force Base and the University of New Mexico have attracted scientists and engineers to Albuquerque and promoted private sector technology growth. When rocket scientist Robert Goddard moved here in 1930 and nuclear scientist J. Robert Oppenheimer reconnoitered the site in 1940, Albuquerque was still a town of 35,000 sitting at the junction of the Rio Grande and the old U.S. 66 that paralleled the Santa Fe Railroad—"a dirty red sod-hut tortilla desert highway city," Tom Wolfe wrote. Now, metro Albuquerque, spreading out from Bernalillo County into Sandoval and Valencia Counties, has more people (765,000 in 2004) than all New Mexico did when the scientists first arrived. Here in 1975, Bill Gates founded a little company called Micro-Soft; although the software maker moved its 16 employees to Seattle in 1979, Intel now employs more than 5,000 people here in an advanced chip-making facility. Albuquerque's prosperous neighborhoods have climbed the gently rising heights to the east; poorer residents have spread north and south along the Rio Grande. Hemmed in by the Sandia mountains and by federal installations, growth is moving west and north, especially to the new town of Rio Rancho, home of the Intel plant and facilities for Sprint PCS and Victoria's Secret. Despite its cold winters, Albuquerque is counted as part of the Sun Belt. Its economy also differs from those of other Sun Belt cities; despite the tech base, it has lower income levels than Phoenix or Denver. While Albuquerque has seen some growth in tourism—it is home of the International Balloon Fiesta every October—it is heavily dependent on federal jobs.

The 1st Congressional District of New Mexico includes Albuquerque and some of its suburbs. It takes in most of Bernalillo County and stretches into the desert to include sparsely populated Torrance County. But the 1st does not include most of big-growth suburbs Corrales and Rio Rancho to the north in Sandoval County, and Isleta and Las Lunas to the south in Valencia County: this leaves it more Democratic than it would otherwise be. The 1st is 43% Hispanic. It voted 48%–47% for Al Gore in 2000 and 51%–48% for John Kerry in 2004.

The congresswoman from the 1st District is Heather Wilson, a Republican first elected in a June 1998 special election. She grew up in New Hampshire, graduated from the Air Force Academy, then became a Rhodes Scholar at Oxford. She served in the Air Force until 1989, and worked two years on the National Security Council in charge of NATO and European affairs. In 1991 she moved to New Mexico, to marry her former Air Force Academy law instructor; she started a consulting firm, and then Governor Gary Johnson appointed her secretary of the Children, Youth and Families Department.

In January 1998, Republican Congressman Steven Schiff announced he would not run again; he died two months later. Senator Pete Domenici backed Wilson strongly; she defeated a conservative state senator for the state central committee endorsement by winning 55 votes, the minimum required. The Democratic nomination was captured by Phil Maloof, a young state senator from a wealthy family that made its fortune through beer distribution, casinos, banking interests, hotels and sports franchises. Also running was Green Party candidate Bob Anderson. Wilson's first ad showed her two-year-old daughter running into her arms; she concluded speeches by talking about reading to her four-year-old son on the roof of their house. Maloof favored raising the minimum wage, opposed school vouchers and ran soft-focus ads playing on his family's 100-year history in New Mexico (next to Wilson's seven). Maloof spent $3.1 million, almost all of it his own. Wilson won 45% to 40% for Maloof and 15% for Anderson, though he spent less than $10,000. She thus became the second woman veteran and first woman service academy graduate to serve in Congress; the first woman veteran was Cathy Long who served in the Navy in the 1940s and represented the 8th District of Louisiana from 1985 to 1987. All three candidates ran again in November but the margin was similar: Wilson 48%, Maloof 42%, Anderson 10%.

In the House, Wilson's voting record has become more moderate. When she complained that Republicans planned to bring a bill to the House floor that would have moved the nuclear weapons program from the Energy Department to the Pentagon, party leaders made changes. Republican leaders tapped her as a leading advocate for George W. Bush's energy plan, and she sponsored the successful amendment to limit oil drilling in the Arctic National Wildlife Refuge to 2,000 acres. On the Energy and Commerce Committee, she blasted CBS executives for Janet Jackson's breast-baring during the 2004 Super Bowl halftime show, and supported the bills to increase penalties for broadcast indecency. With Gene Green, she won enactment of a bill to toughen anti-spam restrictions on commercial email. She worked to defend Kirtland in the base-closing procedure and sponsored additional criteria to the procedures; she also called for an increase in military troop levels. In 2005, she was forced to give up her seat on the Armed Services Committee in order to remain on Energy and Commerce. That move followed threats by Energy and Commerce Chairman Joe Barton to remove her from the committee after she joined Democrats in questioning the cost of the 2003 Medicare/prescription drug law. Perhaps not coincidentally, Wilson had criticized efforts by Majority Leader DeLay to change the rule that would force Republican leaders to step aside if they have been indicted. But she got a consolation prize, a seat on the Intelligence Committee, where she became chairman of the Technical and Tactical Intelligence Subcommittee. In February 2005, she was one of eight Republicans to vote against barring illegal immigrants from getting driver's licenses; she said it was a state matter.

Wilson has faced well-financed challengers. John Kelly, the former U.S. Attorney in New Mexico and a friend of Bill Clinton since both were undergraduates at Georgetown, ran in a 2000 campaign filled with controversial advertising by outside groups. Wilson won 50%–43%. In 2002, the challenger was Richard Romero, a state senator who was elected Senate president in 2001 in a coalition that ousted the Democratic incumbent. Romero had been rated a top-tier challenger by national Democrats, but he suffered from local Democratic divisions; one Democratic state senator called him Benedict Arnold. Wilson won with her largest majority, 55%–45%. In 2004, Romero ran again, and ran negative ads with side-by-side photos of Wilson and Osama bin Laden to highlight her vote against cargo screening on airline security legislation. The result was a nearly identical 54%–46% win for Wilson. During the campaign she said that House Democratic leaders had invited her to switch parties; Minority Leader Nancy Pelosi dismissed that. After the election, Attorney General Patricia Madrid, who is term-limited, said she might challenge Wilson in 2006.

SECOND DISTRICT

Rep. Steve Pearce (R)

Elected 2002, 2d term; b. Aug. 24, 1947, Lamesa, TX; home, Hobbs; NM St. U., B.B.A. 1970, E. NM U. M.B.A. 1991; Baptist; married (Cynthia).

Military Career: Air Force, 1970–76 (Vietnam).

Elected Office: NM House of Reps., 1996–2000.

Professional Career: Owner, Lea Fishing Tools.

DC Office: 1607 LHOB, 20515, 202-225-2365; Fax: 202-225-9599; Web site: www.house.gov/pearce.

District Offices: Hobbs, 505-392-8325; Las Cruces, 505-522-2219; Roswell, 505-622-0055; Socorro, 505-838-7516.

Committees: *Financial Services* (32d of 37 R): Financial Institutions & Consumer Credit; Housing & Community Opportunity. *Homeland Security* (14th of 19 R): Economic Security, Infrastructure Protection & Cybersecurity; Emergency Preparedness, Science & Technology; Intelligence, Information Sharing & Terrorism Risk Assessment. *Resources* (19th of 27 R): Energy & Mineral Resources; Water & Power.

Group Ratings

	ADA	ACLU	AFS	LCV	ITIC	NTU	COC	ACU	NTLC	CHC
2004	0	0	0	0	80	53	95	96	81	100
2003	5	—	0	5	—	61	97	92	—	—

National Journal Ratings

	2003 LIB	—	2003 CONS		2004 LIB	—	2004 CONS
Economic	9%	—	84%		13%	—	85%
Social	15%	—	85%		36%	—	61%
Foreign	11%	—	80%		25%	—	68%

Key Votes of the 108th Congress

1. Drilling in ANWR	Y	5. DC School Vouchers	Y	9. Ban Same-Sex Marriage	Y
2. Approve Bush Tax Cuts	Y	6. Ban Human Cloning	Y	10. Fund Iraq War	Y
3. Medicare/Rx Bill	Y	7. Restrict Gun Liability	Y	11. Bar Cuba Embargo Funds	N
4. Bar Overtime Pay Regs.	N	8. Ban Partial-Birth Abortion	Y	12. Intelligence Reorg.	Y

Election Results

2004 general	Steve Pearce (R)	130,498	(60%)	($1,997,549)
	Gary King (D)	86,292	(40%)	($1,143,705)
2004 primary	Steve Pearce (R)	unopposed		
2002 general	Steve Pearce (R)	79,631	(56%)	($1,573,911)
	John Smith (D)	61,916	(44%)	($826,735)

The People		Race/Ethnic Origin	Ancestry	
Area size:	69,598 sq. mi.	44.3% White	German: 7.4%	English: 5.9%
Urban population:	71.0%	1.6% Black	Irish: 5.7%	
Rural population:	29.0%	0.5% Asian	**2004 Presidential Vote**	
Pop. 2000:	606,406	4.8% Native Am.	Bush (R) 127,391 (58%)	
Median income:	$29,269	0.0% Hawaiian	Kerry (D) 91,073 (41%)	
Poverty status:	22.4%	1.2% Two+ races	Other 2,281 (1%)	
Military veterans:	14.9%	0.2% Other	**2000 Presidential Vote**	
		47.3% Hispanic Origin	Bush (R) 96,161 (54%)	
			Gore (D) 76,868 (43%)	
			Other 5,667 (3%)	
			Cook Partisan Voting Index: R + 6	
Occupation	Blue collar: 26.7%	White collar: 52.9%	Gray collar: 20.4%	

Southern and eastern New Mexico is a disparate landscape: endless sagebrush-strewn acreage and then, suddenly, 9,000-foot mountain peaks rising along the Continental Divide. The eastern part of this region—places like Clovis and Portales, Lovington and Hobbs—speaks with a Texas twang rather than a northern New Mexico lilt. In Little Texas, oil has long been the economic mainstay; cattle ranching is common and cotton is grown on irrigated land. One of the larger towns is Roswell, site of a supposed flying saucer landing in 1947 and now home of the International UFO Museum and Research Center. Further west is White Sands National Monument, with its immaculate gypsum dunes and animals with specially evolved white coloration that allows them to survive predators in the harsh environment; close by is Alamogordo, where the first atomic bomb was exploded at 5:29:45 a.m. Mountain War Time on July 16, 1945. Like many places on America's high plains, population here is thinning and old economic pillars are crumbling; Carlsbad, once reliant on potash mining, aggressively sought the Waste Isolation Pilot Plant, a nuclear waste repository. In central and western New Mexico, the scrub land shades into desert, and people are crammed into small cities, protected from summer's burning heat and winter's deathly cold. The Hatch Valley, in the desert adjoining Interstate 25, is home to perhaps the world's finest chili peppers—the traditional cornerstone of the Southwest's spicy cuisine. Places like Silver City and Bayard were built on mining, and occasional discord; the story of a strike by Mexican-American workers at a zinc mine here in 1950 and 1951 was told in *Salt of the Earth*, a movie with such a volatile message that it was blacklisted.

This is also an international frontier—the tiny town of Columbus was the site of a raid by Pancho Villa and his irregular band of soldiers in 1916. Las Cruces, now New Mexico's second largest city, has grown at rates well above the statewide average, thanks to migrants from Mexico coming up the Rio Grande. For decades, Anglo and Mexican ranchers across the border spoke "the common language of cattle"; communities frequently shared public services with their cross-border neighbors and left the gates open at night for stragglers stuck too late on the wrong side of the border. But rapid development due to NAFTA, a surge in illegal immigration and drug trafficking have brought enormous strains. Still, the New Mexico portion of the U.S.-Mexico border remains far sleepier than elsewhere: Whereas El Paso sees more than one million crossings a month, the three border posts that dot New Mexico's largely empty 150-mile frontier see less than 100,000.

The 2d Congressional District of New Mexico covers this southern part of the state, going as far north as the suburb of Las Lunas and the Isleta Pueblo south of Albuquerque and the Acoma Pueblo to the west. Demographically and politically, it is diverse. It includes most, but not all, of New Mexico's Little Texas—majority Anglo and solidly conservative, though with a Democratic heritage. It includes Las Cruces and the mining counties in the southwest corner of the state; Las Cruces is politically marginal and the mining counties Democratic. And it includes the Indian country around the pueblos, which is strongly Democratic. The district was 47% Hispanic in 2000, the highest of any New Mexico district, and 5% Indian. But more of the Hispanics are ineligible to vote here than in the 1st or 3d Districts.

The congressman from the 2d District is Steve Pearce, a Republican first elected in 2002. He grew up in Hobbs, near the Texas line, and graduated from New Mexico State in Las Cruces; he served in the Air Force and flew missions during the Vietnam War. He returned to Hobbs and started an oil-field service company. In 1996 he was elected to the state House. In 2000 he ran for the Senate, but lost the Republican primary to former Congressman Bill Redmond. In 2002, Republican Congressman Joe Skeen, stricken with Parkinson's disease, announced he would not run again. Pearce had two major competitors in the Republican primary: former state represen-tative Phelps Anderson of Roswell, the son of former Arco chairman Robert Anderson, and Ed Tinsley, the owner of the K-BOBS USA steakhouse chain, who got Skeen's endorsement. Pearce ran a deft primary campaign. Using youth volunteers, he maximized his vote in Little Texas. He built on his ties to Las Cruces, where he had gone to college, and carried its Dona Ana County with 38% of the vote. Tinsley carried ten counties, but with no geographic base won only 27% of the vote. Anderson, without much support outside his home county, won 24%.

In the general there did not seem to be much difference between Pearce and the Democratic nominee, state Senator John Arthur Smith of Deming. Smith was an opponent of abortion rights, a believer in Second Amendment rights, a conservative who had often split from liberal Demo-crats in the legislature. But he proved not to be as adroit a campaigner as Pearce. Smith boasted that he had never raised any money for his state Senate campaigns. This time he did raise some money, and was the beneficiary of national Democrats and independent spenders. But Pearce, with the help of two visits from George W. Bush, raised much more. Pearce piloted his own plane around the district; Smith drove his own car (this matters in a district that covers 69,598 square miles). Pearce issued a press release saying, "Pearce takes strong stand on Iraq, Smith weak on issue." Smith ended up supporting the Iraq war resolution, the only New Mexico House or Senate Democratic candidate for Congress to do so. Despite polls showing a close race, Pearce won by a solid 56%–44% margin. He won large percentages, from 58% to 77%, in Little Texas. Smith's margins in his home county and in the mining and Indian counties were not enough to offset this.

In the House, Pearce usually voted with conservatives. The House passed his bill to eradi-cate water-depleting tamarisks in Western states, including New Mexico. He also won House approval of his bill to revitalize potassium output on federal lands, a substantial source of jobs in New Mexico; most potash is used as fertilizer, and the decline in production during the past decade had raised costs for farmers. He encouraged the Bush administration to drill for natural gas in the large Otero Mesa desert grassland in his district, which Governor Bill Richardson strongly opposed. In 2004 New Mexico was a target state in the presidential election, and George W. Bush appeared often with Pearce. But Pearce ran a bit ahead of Bush, winning 60%–40%, against Gary King, a Clinton Energy Department official and son of former three-term Demo-cratic governor Bruce King. Pearce has said he wants to get Skeen's seat on Appropriations, but hasn't yet.

THIRD DISTRICT

Rep. Tom Udall (D)

Elected 1998, 4th term; b. May 18, 1948, Tucson, AZ; home, Santa Fe; Prescott Col., B.A. 1970; Cambridge U., B.L. 1975; U. of NM, J.D. 1977; Mormon; married (Jill Cooper).

Elected Office: NM Atty. Gen., 1990–98.

Professional Career: Law clerk, 10th Circuit Court of Appeals, 1977; Asst. U.S. Atty, 1978–81; Practicing atty., 1981–83, 1985–90; Chief Cnsl., NM Health & Environment Dept., 1983–84.

DC Office: 1414 LHOB, 20515, 202-225-6190; Fax: 202-226-1331; Web site: www.tomudall.house.gov.

District Offices: Clovis, 505-763-7616; Farmington, 505-324-1005; Gal-lup, 505-863-0582; Las Vegas, 505-454-4080; Rio Rancho, 505-994-0499; Santa Fe, 505-984-8950.

Committees: *Resources* (14th of 22 D): Forests & Forest Health (RMM); National Parks. *Small Business* (3d of 15 D): Rural Enterprises, Agriculture & Technology; Workforce, Empowerment & Government Programs. *Veterans' Affairs* (12th of 12 D): Disability Assistance & Memorial Affairs.

Group Ratings

	ADA	ACLU	AFS	LCV	ITIC	NTU	COC	ACU	NTLC	CHC
2004	100	90	100	100	40	13	29	8	6	15
2003	100	—	100	95	—	24	23	8	—	—

National Journal Ratings

	2003 LIB	—	2003 CONS	2004 LIB	—	2004 CONS
Economic	87%	—	9%	82%	—	17%
Social	88%	—	11%	70%	—	29%
Foreign	94%	—	0%	79%	—	20%

Key Votes of the 108th Congress

1. Drilling in ANWR	N	5. DC School Vouchers	N	9. Ban Same-Sex Marriage	N
2. Approve Bush Tax Cuts	N	6. Ban Human Cloning	N	10. Fund Iraq War	N
3. Medicare/Rx Bill	N	7. Restrict Gun Liability	N	11. Bar Cuba Embargo Funds	Y
4. Bar Overtime Pay Regs.	Y	8. Ban Partial-Birth Abortion	N	12. Intelligence Reorg.	N

Election Results

2004 general	Tom Udall (D)	175,269	(69%)	($452,489)
	Gregory Tucker (R)	79,935	(31%)	($56,051)
2004 primary	Tom Udall (D)	unopposed		
2002 general	Tom Udall (D)	unopposed		($290,534)

Prior Winning Percentages: 2000 (67%); 1998 (53%)

The People		Race/Ethnic Origin	Ancestry	
Area size:	47,271 sq. mi.	41.4% White	German: 7.4%	English: 6.0%
Urban population:	62.8%	1.1% Black	Irish: 5.6%	
Rural population:	37.2%	0.7% Asian	**2004 Presidential Vote**	
Pop. 2000:	606,240	18.9% Native Am.	Kerry (D) 139,336	(54%)
Median income:	$35,058	0.1% Hawaiian	Bush (R) 118,350	(45%)
Poverty status:	19.0%	1.4% Two+ races	Other 2,653	(1%)
Military veterans:	13.4%	0.1% Other	**2000 Presidential Vote**	
		36.3% Hispanic Origin	Gore (D) 102,809	(52%)
			Bush (R) 86,004	(43%)
			Other 9,676	(5%)
			Cook Partisan Voting Index: D + 6	

Occupation   Blue collar: 21.7%   White collar: 60.3%   Gray collar: 18.0%

"The dancing ground of the sun," the Pueblo Indians called the land of northern New Mexico, where the long vistas, dotted with low-lying scrub, are painted in pastel hues in the cold light and clear air. For 100 years, artists have been coming here, attracted by the scenery and by a unique civilization that is part Indian, part Anglo, part Spanish, and only a little Mexican (northern New Mexico was under Mexican control only from 1821–46). The region's long-surviving traditions, however, hide the instabilities of this blended civilization. The adobe pueblos, including some of the world's earliest apartment buildings, were built in spurts; the Spanish conquistadors and priests brought the Catholic religion, the baroque architectural accents and the Spanish language in a rush. Successive waves of American settlement have changed New Mexico in multiple ways. The Indian crafts that thrive today nearly died out in the 1880s, while the Palace of the Governors, built in Santa Fe in 1610, had its Victorian balustrade torn off in 1913 to restore its original appearance. Yet up the back roads in Rio Arriba or Taos Counties, one can find a religion that mixes Catholicism with adaptations of Indian festivals, buildings not that much different from the old pueblos and a standard of living reminiscent of the Indian past, sometimes punctuated by high rates of drug abuse—quite a contrast to the chi-chi ski lodges in the Taos Valley, the high security research facilities of Los Alamos or the affluent, bohemian activity in modern-day Santa Fe.

The 3d Congressional District of New Mexico contains most of the state's historic Spanish-speaking and Indian parts. The district's largest and dominant city is Santa Fe, where Georgia O'Keeffe was a major cultural force and local spas have encouraged the tourism boom. But the 3d also runs from the High Plains along the Texas border, past the haunting Sangre de Cristo Mountains, through the vast ridges and isolated buttes in the center, to the windy and dusty desert-like plains. Its Hispanic population is 36%, the lowest of the state's three districts, but in the central part of the district it ranges from almost half in Santa Fe County to more than 80% in Mora County. Another 19% of the district population is Indian, mostly in and around the Navajo Reservation in the west, which is hard hit by poverty and poor health. The politics of northern New Mexico is unique. For years, debate was conducted and votes bartered in Spanish, not by separatists, but by Republican and Democratic politicos, often cynically, sometimes corruptly; loyalties ran to families and communities more than to principles or parties. In the backcountry, you can still find more than just vestiges of the old communities and old politics—though no one is going to let you in on them, even if you speak good Spanish. Although the Little Texas counties, the Albuquerque suburb of Rio Rancho, the mining and ranching country around Farmington, and the nuclear scientists of Los Alamos tend to vote Republican, this is on the whole a Democratic district; both Hispanics and Indians are very Democratic, and in Santa Fe and Taos, the affluent and hippie migrants have produced such a strong leftist tilt that in 2003, Santa Fe's city council approved a minimum wage $3.35 over the federal level. Politically, this is a sharply divided district. Santa Fe, Taos and San Miguel Counties voted more than 70% for John Kerry in 2004. But Bush won 65% to 77% in the counties on the Texas border and 66% in Farmington's San Juan County. Overall the district, after voting 52%–43% for Al Gore in 2000, voted 54%–45% for Kerry in 2004. Bush's percentages were slightly down in Santa Fe, Taos and Los Alamos Counties and sharply up in the other counties.

The congressman from the 3d District is Tom Udall, a Democrat first elected in 1998, the son of Arizona Congressman (1955–61) and Interior Secretary (1961–69) Stewart Udall, nephew of Arizona Congressman (1961–91) Morris Udall, first cousin of Colorado Congressman Mark Udall, and distant cousin of Oregon Senator Gordon Smith, the only Republican in the bunch. Tom Udall grew up in Tucson and in McLean, Virginia, went to college in Arizona, got a degree at Cambridge University in England, and went to law school in New Mexico. He worked as a law clerk to a federal judge, then as a lawyer in New Mexico state government and went into private law practice. Politics was obviously on his mind. He ran for Congress in 1982 when the 3d District was newly created, and finished last among four candidates, with 13% of the vote; the winner was Bill Richardson, now governor. In 1988 he ran in the open Albuquerque-based 1st District, won the Democratic nomination but lost the general to Steven Schiff 51%–47%. In 1990 he was elected state attorney general.

In 1997, when Richardson resigned and the 3d District seat opened up, Udall did not run. Republican Bill Redmond, an independent Christian minister from Los Alamos, won in a shocking upset, assisted by a Green Party candidate nominee who won 17%. In 1998, Udall ran for the seat. He worked to consolidate the Democratic and leftist vote; drawing on lawyers, the arts community and friends of the Udall family, he raised daunting sums. The Sierra Club and the League of Conservation Voters criticized Redmond and ran waves of ads against him. As for the third party threat, Udall said, "I intend to make peace with the Greens." He was utterly successful. Udall won 53% of the vote, Redmond got the same 43% he had won 18 months before, while Green Party nominee Carole Miller saw her 17% evaporate to 4%.

In the House, Udall has a mostly liberal voting record. He has a seat on the Resources Committee, on which his father served and which his uncle chaired. He helped to enact a bill to explore establishment of a national historical park at Los Alamos. The House defeated his amendments for the Energy Department to enter cooperative agreements with domestic uranium miners, and to prohibit changes to the National Forest Management Act. As chairman of the Democrats' campaign finance task force, he was a vocal advocate of the Shays-Meehan campaign finance bill; he called for opening presidential debates to third party candidates—an odd stance for a Democrat in a seat Republicans won because of a Green candidacy. He voted against creation of the Homeland Security Department and he opposed the use of force in Iraq.

He proposed revisions in the Patriot Act, to limit authority to obtain search warrants and restore protections for libraries and bookstores; with Christopher Shays and Carolyn Maloney, he called for an independent agency to monitor civil liberties abuses in the war on terrorism. In May 2005, Udall and the rest of the New Mexico delegation protested the Pentagon's recommendation to close Cannon Air Force Base in Clovis; the proposed closure would mean the loss of 4,800 direct and indirect jobs generated by the base, roughly 20 percent of the local work force.

Udall has not been seriously challenged for reelection. In 2004 he was reelected 69%–31%, running far ahead of Kerry.

★ NEW YORK ★

It was a beautiful fall morning, the sunshine lighting a blue sky above the skyscrapers of Manhattan, commuters hurrying through the streets and subways to work, at 8:45 a.m. on September 11, 2001. Then, one minute later, the first plane hit the North Tower of the World Trade Center, and everything changed. When the second plane hit the South Tower 16 minutes later, it was clear that we were under attack, at war, even as office workers fled the burning buildings and New York fire fighters streamed in. The terrorists had chosen to attack Washington—the Pentagon and the building United Flight 93 was heading toward when heroes brought it down—and New York, the greatest city in the nation and the world, to inflict the greatest possible damage on our country. Yet the people of New York, like those at the Pentagon and on United 93, responded with the courage and determination, the devotion to duty and the willingness to take the initiative that made this city and this country great. Fire fighters and police officers and rescue workers risked death to help others. Strangers helped strangers. People who had no experience with disaster figured out how to cope and help others. Millions volunteered to give blood, send in money, or provide food and supplies. The *Wall Street Journal*, headquartered across the street from the World Trade Center, scrambled to put out a newspaper that was distributed at the regular time across the nation the next day. In less than a week the New York Stock Exchange was reopened. Mayor Rudolph Giuliani worked tirelessly to share with the nation the tragic news of deaths and to assert the determination to recover.

The bravery, the determination, the generosity that the world saw on that terrible day and the days after were some of the same qualities that had, over the centuries, made New York what it is—America's largest city, its financial capital, its center of arts and letters and media and its largest immigrant destination. New York's achievements were not inevitable. They happened because New Yorkers—and not least those people from elsewhere who opted to become New Yorkers—worked to make them happen. They did it in a city that has a certain enduring character that goes back to its birth as the 17th century Dutch colony of Nieuw Amsterdam. Simon Schama's *The Embarrassment of Riches* paints a picture of the old world Amsterdam: the richest city in the world; full of people who work hard all day and stay up late at night, smoke too much tobacco and drink too much coffee and gin, but are dazzlingly smart and shrewd; people who know their way around every corner of the globe and can make fine aesthetic discriminations, but are attached to their uncomfortable, crowded, bad-smelling city. They were merchants and manipulators with no aristocratic pedigree, welcoming any religious or ethnic group who can achieve and accumulate and show good taste, cherishing education and culture but indifferent to credentials. Probably fewer than 2% of today's New Yorkers are descended from the Dutch of Nieuw Amsterdam, but the character of the place endures in daily life and in the workings of its great institutions, and helps explain its miraculous growth. Combine Amsterdam and America: Dutch character with British-born political freedoms and American military strength and you have the opportunity to build a city-state that can lead the world—and be the natural target of terrorists who hate that civilization.

New York was not always the nation's leader. In 1776 it was only the seventh most populous colony. Only in the 19th century did the descendants of Dutch patroons, Huguenot refugees, British West Indies traders and Yankee farmers become the nation's most successful merchants

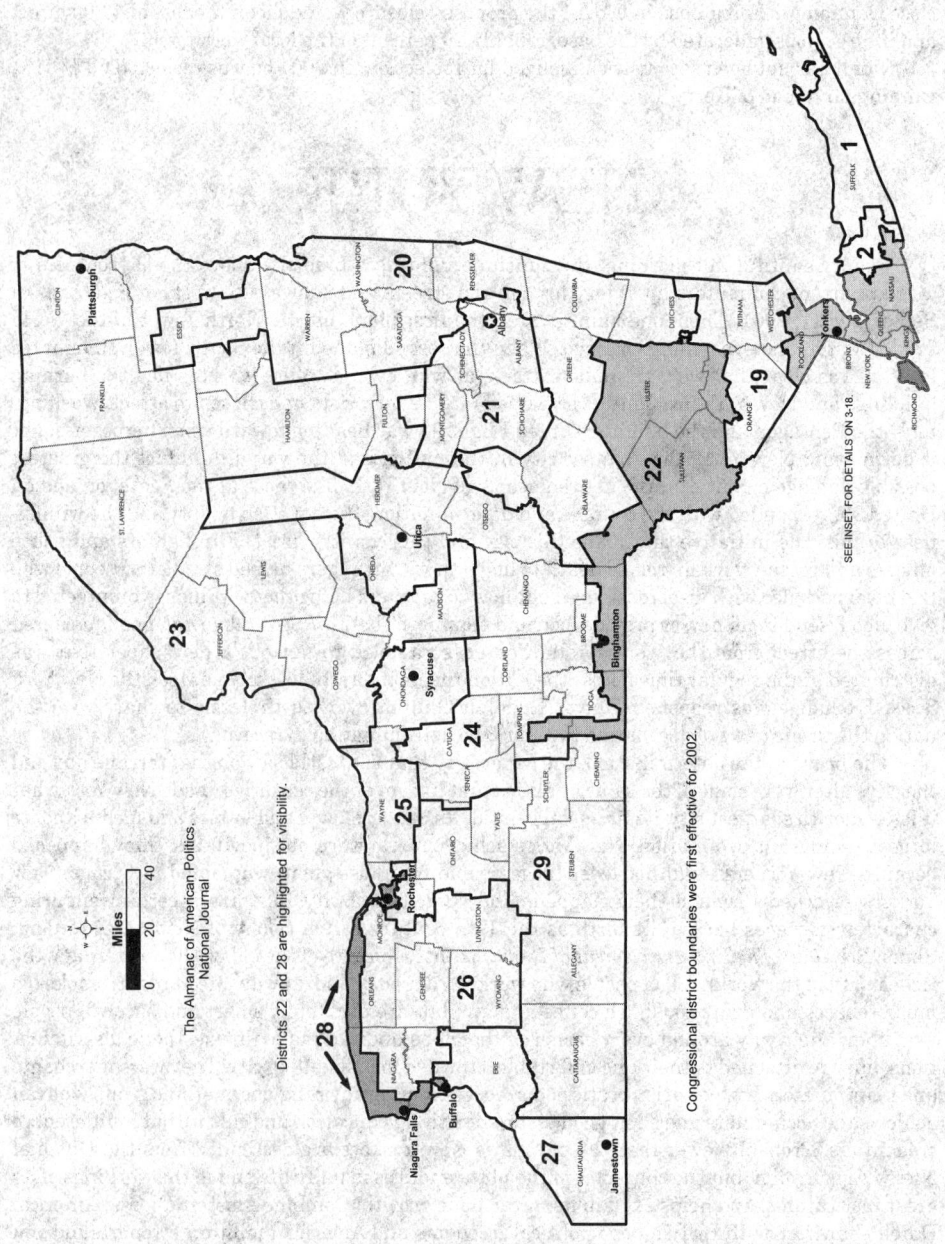

The Almanac of American Politics,
National Journal

Districts 22 and 28 are highlighted for visibility.

Congressional district boundaries were first effective for 2002.

SEE INSET FOR DETAILS ON 3-18.

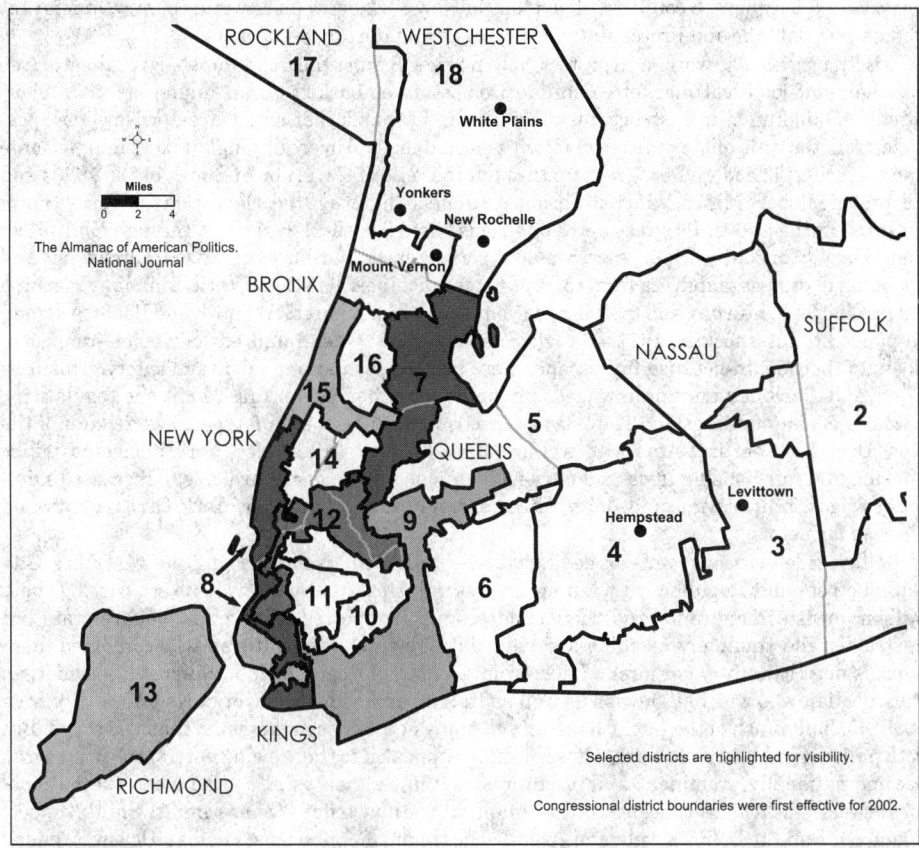

ROCKLAND
17

WESTCHESTER
18

White Plains

Yonkers

New Rochelle

Mount Vernon

The Almanac of American Politics.
National Journal

Miles
0   2   4

BRONX

NEW YORK

16
15
14
12
11
8
10
7
9
6
5
4
3
2
13

QUEENS

NASSAU

SUFFOLK

Levittown

Hempstead

KINGS

RICHMOND

Selected districts are highlighted for visibility.

Congressional district boundaries were first effective for 2002.

and capitalists, forging the first routes to the great American interior through the valleys of the Hudson and the Mohawk, and building grand brownstone mansions on broad midtown Manhattan avenues. That early diversity provides one clue to New York's success: if New York has been cynical, ready to cooperate with Loyalists and Revolutionaries, depending on who was ahead, it has also been tolerant, ready to accept anyone smart or rich enough to be counted a success. It has been propelled upward at each stage—forging ahead of London as a financial and manufacturing center by the first World War, and staying ahead of surging Chicago—by incorporating every wave of immigrants and consistently rewarding intelligence and hard work, with no concern about preserving hierarchies.

New York's success has been a product not only of market economics, but of government—and politics. The Iroquois, the most deeply-rooted and militarily strong Native Americans, kept in place for 100 years by an alliance with British troops, were driven out of most of Upstate New York after the Revolution. The Erie Canal, which connected western New York State with the Hudson River, was the project of Governor DeWitt Clinton's state government. And New York led the nation in political innovation: Martin Van Buren's Albany Regency was the first state political machine, an ally of New York City's Tammany Hall; Van Buren invented or institutionalized the Democratic party, the national convention and the inaugural parade. His adversaries, Thurlow Weed and William Seward, formed the Whig party and ultimately became Republicans; noting that Van Buren's Democrats were winning large margins from Irish Catholics and other immigrants, they too made bids for the newcomers' votes. Both parties served the function of mediating between the divergent interests of the New York City masses and Upstate New York's farmers and burghers, a conflict still evident in New York between city and country, immigrant and native, Catholic and Protestant, the Big Apple and the apple-knockers.

Both parties also worked to protect New Yorkers against the untrammeled workings of free economic and political markets. Old-line Democrats embarked on an unprecedented, labor-intensive building of infrastructure, of bridges and tunnels that made Greater New York possible, from the time of Mayor Abram Hewitt, elected in 1886 over the single-taxer Henry George and the young Theodore Roosevelt, up through the time of Governor Al Smith in the 1920s and his protégé Robert Moses, who built bridges, tunnels, highways, beaches and two World's Fairs up through the 1960s. Progressive Republicans, from Theodore Roosevelt through Elihu Root and Henry Stimson, worked to create civil service laws and bureaucratized purchasing and spending to protect taxpayers from corrupt party machines. The Democratic Tammany machine led by Charles F. Murphy and the talented young men he advanced, Al Smith and Robert Wagner, responded to the shocking 1911 Triangle Shirtwaist fire (when hundreds of women jumped 11 floors to their death because fire escapes were blocked) by passing labor and safety measures. The results included minimum wages, maximum work hours, working-conditions regulations, encouragement of unions and state-owned electric utilities—the prototype 20 years later of the New Deal and the first American welfare state. In years after, New York pioneered public housing and fair housing laws, industry-wide unions (in the garment trades), increased minimum wages, rent control and dairy price controls to help both New York City tenants and Upstate farmers.

Statewide elections were exceedingly close, with Democrats carrying the New York City Catholic vote and Republicans winning Protestants Upstate. Swing votes were cast by the 2 million Jewish immigrants and their children, who supported a generous welfare state but mistrusted the Tammany machine and valued civil rights. The politician who combined these appeals most cannily was Fiorello LaGuardia: a nominal Republican but almost a socialist, an Episcopalian who was half-Jewish as well as Italian, and who, as mayor of New York City from 1933–45, built much of the public housing and many of the civic monuments that still stand. But both parties produced politicians whose positions appealed to these swing voters, politicians who became nationally prominent and often presidential candidates at a time when the national media was much more concentrated in Manhattan than today: Democrats Al Smith, Robert Wagner, Franklin D. Roosevelt and Averell Harriman; Republicans Thomas Dewey, Wendell Willkie, Dwight Eisenhower (a New Yorker as president of Columbia University when he was elected president in 1952) and Nelson Rockefeller.

The polity that these men built was productive, generous, tolerant and closely regulated. In an America where people were becoming used to working in big units—employed by big corporations, represented by big unions, regulated by big government—this kind of New York was a natural leader. The financial dominance of Wall Street and the big banks was protected by federal regulation. The high-tech thrust of America in the mid-20th century was directed by big companies headquartered in New York's suburbs or Upstate: General Electric and IBM, Eastman Kodak and Xerox. This New York took for granted the productivity of its thousands of entrepreneurs and the high skills of its largely immigrant-born, public and Catholic school-educated work force. It was blasé about its own miraculous infrastructure—the bridges and subways, electronic cables and electric wires connecting it better than any place else with every corner of the world.

But in the last quarter of the 20th century New York's public strengths became weaknesses. The state that was clearly the national leader of a big-unit America lost the leadership of a country where growth now occurs in small economic units, where flexibility and adaptability are more important than centralized planning. The institutions, practices and infrastructure which helped produce its successes became ossified and brittle and in decline. Welfare-state benefits became too expensive, measures meant to protect against corruption stifled innovation, and both failed to achieve their objectives—ghettos throbbed with the pains of disorganization, and payoffs and rackets remained part of the everyday cost of doing business in New York as in no other place in the country. The noble aim of creating a public sector which would guarantee cheap rents, top-notch public schools and colleges, and public hospitals, instead guaranteed that none of these will be readily available: Rent control kept housing scarce, school bureaucracies stifled good teaching, public hospitals rationed care down. The attempt to create a fail-safe government produced a government that was sure to fail. The government that intended to aid growth seemed to be cutting it off—not completely, but enough to explain why New York state, which grew 32% in population from 1940 to 1965, grew only 2% from 1965 to 1997, while California was growing about 74% and Texas about 87%, making both larger now than New York.

People and businesses started voting with their feet, especially during the terms of Mayor John Lindsay, a liberal Republican who caved into municipal unions' demands and borrowed against next year's revenues to pay this year's bills. That brought the city to the brink of bankruptcy in 1975, two years after he left office. In the 1970s, the population of New York, city and state, dropped by 1 million—an unprecedented hemorrhage of talent and productivity. Retrenchment followed the mid-1970s bankruptcy crisis. Private financiers and the state government took control of city government, cut spending and negotiated cutbacks in jobs and salaries with public employees' unions. Wall Street boomed in the 1980s and Manhattan once again brimmed over with confidence. Some taxes were cut under Mayor (1978–90) Edward Koch and Governor (1983–95) Mario Cuomo, public employee unions were for a time reined in, rational management was installed. But institutional problems remained. New York's legislature remained unusually tightly controlled by the two chambers' leaders, the Democratic Assembly Speaker from New York City and the Republican state Senate President from Upstate, and these leaders engaged in classic political logrolling, lavishing taxpayers' dollars on each other's pet projects. Public employee unions reestablished their stranglehold. The mild recession of the early 1990s struck New York with great force: A private sector that had grown little if at all outside Wall Street could no longer finance the countercyclically growing demands of its oversized welfare state, while big companies Upstate—Xerox, Kodak, IBM—suffered serious reverses.

By the end of the 1990s New York seemed to have adapted and changed. Mayor Rudolph Giuliani, first elected in 1993, cut crime and welfare rolls in half and cut hard deals with the unions. Governor George Pataki, first elected in 1994, came into office and imposed huge tax and spending cuts in 1995. Wall Street and the financial services industry boomed in the late 1990s, to the point that the jobs lost in the 1990–94 recession were replaced. Then came September 11. Giuliani, under a cloud in his last months in office as his marriage collapsed publicly and he withdrew from the 2000 Senate race against Hillary Rodham Clinton, became a national hero. Americans who had heard about his successes in cutting crime and welfare dependency saw him in action and were impressed. Pataki also performed well in the national spotlight. But New York faced an economic downturn and a turn in the course of government. Despite heroic efforts at recovery, Manhattan and New York lost 200,000 jobs between 2001 and 2002. Downtown real estate values tumbled, as financial services firms decentralized and sought office space elsewhere. Giuliani was term-limited, and all the leading contestants were well to his left. Media billionaire Michael Bloomberg, long a Democrat, became a Republican and spent $70 million of his own money on the campaign, and beat Public Advocate Mark Green 45.1%–44.5%. Pataki, running for reelection in 2002, made a $1.8 billion deal with the hospital workers' union and insured that he would be reelected without serious opposition. Bloomberg, faced with a fiscal crunch in 2002, increased property taxes 18% and raised other taxes as well. In his third term as governor, Pataki tried to hold down spending, but big tax increases, supported by Assembly Democrats and Senate Republicans, were passed over his veto. The lessons of the 1970s, 1980s and 1990s seemed to have been forgotten.

New York does continue to grow, but sluggishly. New York City had more than 8 million people in the 2000 Census—8,008,000, more than the previous high, in 1950, of 7,984,000; that was up to 8,104,000 in the 2004 Census estimate. Some 36% of its residents in 2000 were born in other countries—almost as high as the 1910 peak of 41%. Immigrants have been streaming into outer borough neighborhoods, creating new businesses, churches and neighborhood institutions—Caribbean blacks in Flatbush, Chinese in Flushing and Borough Park, Colombians in Corona, Pakistanis in Jackson Heights, Greeks in Astoria, Russians in Brighton Beach. But as historian Fred Siegel points out, the outer boroughs are increasingly dependent on public sector jobs, with one-third of jobs in Brooklyn and half in the Bronx directly dependent on the city or state governments. Higher taxes will tend to squeeze out private sector jobs there even as the financial services industry is failing to provide the growth it did in the 1990s. An especially heavy burden is New York's Medicaid program, designed by Nelson Rockefeller in 1966 to be far more generous than any other state's and requiring local governments to spend money as mandated by the state. The good news is that this Medicaid spending provides a lot of jobs, including many for immigrants: hospitals are major employers in the outer boroughs. The bad news is that it tends to squeeze the life out of the private sector. The financial services industry was a huge cash cow for Medicaid in the 1990s. But the cash cow's milk production is not guaranteed and it can move across state lines, as financial services businesses have since September 11.

Upstate New York has serious problems as well. Burdened with a state tax system constructed to support New York City's welfare state, it has been at a substantial disadvantage with nearby Northeastern states, not to mention the Sun Belt, in attracting jobs. Up through the 1980s paternalistic big corporations like IBM, Kodak and Xerox were the bedrock of the Upstate economy. But in an increasingly competitive America, these corporations faltered and cut payrolls, while big steel plants in the Niagara Frontier area around Buffalo were closed. That pattern accelerated after September 11. Kodak, hard hit by competition from digital cameras, employed 60,000 people in the Rochester area in 1981; by 2005 that was down to 15,000. Xerox jobs in the area fell from 16,000 to 8,000. Steel jobs have been disappearing in Buffalo, to the point that the mayor proposed that the city be absorbed into Erie County. The Carrier air conditioning plant in Syracuse in 2004 was scheduled to be closed down. Schenectady, the birthplace of General Electric, was running out of cash as GE demanded that workers there increase their productivity. Between 1990 and 2004, 21 of Upstate New York's 50 counties lost population; only one, Saratoga County outside Albany, gained more than 10%. During that period Upstate's population grew only 1%, compared to 11% for New York City and 9% for its suburbs.

In the first half of the twentieth century, New York politics was a battle between the Democratic city, with more than half the state's population then, and Republican Upstate. As previously noted, Jewish voters, concentrated in the city and moored to neither party, provided critical swing votes. In the post-World War II period, the suburbs grew and tended to produce small Republican majorities. Today the picture is different. In national politics, George W. Bush, even with his improved 2004 showing here, lost New York City 75%–24% and trailed very narrowly in the suburbs (47%–51%) and Upstate (48.5%–49.5%). Large numbers of Jewish and black voters have turned Westchester from a Republican to a Democratic county; the Upstate counties containing Buffalo, Rochester, Syracuse, Albany and Binghamton produced Democratic margins to counterbalance Republican margins in smaller counties. Another pattern emerged in 2004, when Democratic Senator Charles Schumer was reelected against a lightly financed Republican with 71% of the vote; he got 86% in the city, 66% in the suburbs and 63% in Upstate. Two Democrats would like to emulate that pattern in 2006: Schumer's junior colleague Clinton and Attorney General Eliot Spitzer, who announced his candidacy for governor in February 2005. Whether they will depends on how strong their opposition is, particularly on whether Pataki runs for a fourth term, and whether they polarize the New York electorate so much that any opponent will get a large share of the vote, as may or may not be the case with Clinton.

The People		Race/Ethnic Origin			Military veterans: 1,361,164 (9.5%)	
Pop. 2004 (est):	19,227,088	11,760,981	62.0%	White	WWII: 25.4%	Korea: 15.5%
Pop. 2000:	18,976,457	2,812,623	14.8%	Black	Vietnam: 27.7%	Gulf War: 7.1%
Pop. 1990:	17,990,455	1,035,926	5.5%	Asian	Most populous cities (2003):	
Change 1990–2000:	Up 5.5%	52,499	0.3%	Native Am.	1. New York	8,085,742
% of U.S. total:	6.7%	5,230	0.0%	Hawaiian	2. Buffalo	285,018
Pop. rank:	3d of 50	366,116	1.9%	Two+ races	3. Rochester	215,093
Area size:	54,556 sq. mi.	75,499	0.4%	Other	4. Yonkers	197,388
State Native:	65.3%	2,867,583	15.1%	Hisp. Origin	5. Syracuse	144,001
Non-citizen:	11.0%	**Ancestry**				
Language		Italian: 11.4%		Irish: 10.2%	Urban population: 87.5%	
English: 70.4%	Spanish: 13.3%	German: 8.9%		English: 4.8%	Rural population: 12.5%	
Other Eur.: 11.4%		Polish: 4.1%				

Education		Work Sector		Legislature	
H.S. Grad:	79.1%	Private: 76.8%	Govt: 17.0%	Senate	35 R 27 D
College Grad:	27.4%	Self: 6.0%	Family: 0.2%	Assembly	104 D 46 R
Industry		Unemployment: 7.1%		Legislative Term Limits: No	
Agri: 0.6%	Con: 5.2%	**Household Income**		**Registered Voters**	
Fin: 8.8%	Info: 4.1%	<15k: 17.9%	15-35k: 23.1%	D: 5,534,574 (46.8%)	
Mfg: 15.5%	Prof: 34.5%	35-50k: 14.8%	50-100k: 29.0%	R: 3,209,082 (27.1%)	
Public: 5.2%	Trade: 13.8%	100-150k: 9.1%	>150k: 6.2%	O: 3,093,412 (26.1%)	
Other: 12.3%		Median: $43,393			
Occupation		Poverty status: 14.6%			
Blue collar: 19.3%	White collar: 63.8%	**Home Value**			
Gray collar: 16.9%		<50k: 9.1%	50-100k: 25.3%	100-200k: 32.0%	200-300k: 18.5%
		300-500k: 10.0%	>500k: 5.1%	Median: $147,600	

Presidential politics   In the first half of the 20th century, New York was the most pivotal—indeed, sometimes it seemed the dominant—state in presidential politics. It had the most electoral votes—45 from 1912–28, 47 from 1932–48, 45 from 1952–60—and of all the large states it was usually the most evenly divided between the two parties. But New York had just 33 electoral votes in 2000 and just 31 in 2004, and is among the largest states the most heavily Democratic. How has this come to pass? One reason is that Jewish voters, who did not identify strongly with either major party in the first half of the 20th century, became strong Democrats in the second. Increases in the percentage of black and Puerto Rican voters raised the Democratic percentage. White Catholic voters took conservative positions on cultural issues like crime and foreign policy in the 1970s and 1980s, which was one reason Senator James Buckley was elected on the Conservative party line in 1970, Ronald Reagan won New York's electoral votes narrowly in 1980 and 1984 and

2004 Presidential Vote		
Kerry (D-WF)	4,314,280	(58%)
Bush (R-C)	2,962,567	(40%)
Nader (I-PJ)	99,873	(1%)
Other	71,546	(1%)

2004 Democratic Presidential Primary		
Kerry (D)	437,754	(61%)
Edwards (D)	143,960	(20%)
Sharpton (D)	57,456	(8%)
Kucinich (D)	36,680	(5%)
Dean (D)	20,471	(3%)
Other	19,312	(3%)

2000 Presidential Vote		
Gore (D)	4,107,697	(60%)
Bush (R)	2,403,374	(35%)
Nader (Green)	244,030	(4%)
Other	66,898	(1%)

George H. W. Bush was beaten by only a 52%–48% margin in 1988. But these voters now, or their descendants were more likely to take liberal stands on cultural issues salient in the 1990s, gun control and abortion. So Bill Clinton carried New York by 50%–34% in 1992 and 61%–31% in 1996 and Al Gore by 60%–35% in 2000.

In 2004 George W. Bush ran better, losing the state 58%–40%. His percentage jumped 6% in the city and suburbs, and 4% Upstate. It jumped even more among some specific groups—11% among Catholics (he carried them 51%–48% over the Catholic John Kerry), 6% among Latinos, about the same percentage among Jews. Bush's percentage rose 11% in Staten Island, which probably has more police officers and fire fighters per capita than anywhere else in America; 10% in Rockland County, which has large Orthodox Jewish communities which vote unanimously for favored candidates; 9% in Brooklyn, which also has large Orthodox communities and 8% in Nassau County. In parts of metro New York with more seculars and Protestants, the Bush percentage rose very little—3% in Manhattan and Westchester County. In metro New York City, Bush's percentage rose 6%—a percentage exceeded in only two states (Hawaii, 8%; Rhode Island, 7%) and equaled in four others (nearby New Jersey and Connecticut and Jacksonian Tennessee and Alabama). The metro New York-New Jersey-Connecticut numbers seem to reflect a rallying to the president prompted by his leadership on and after September 11, big enough to make New Jersey and Connecticut, but not New York, conceivably competitive in national elections.

For years New York had boss politics, and it never had a presidential primary until 1968. Turnout is low. Democratic turnout was 1.1 million in 2000, well below the peak of 1.5 million in 1988, when Mayor Ed Koch's shrill support of Al Gore won him few votes as Michael Dukakis beat Jesse Jackson; on March 7, 2000, Gore beat Bill Bradley by a 2–1 margin. As for the Republican primary, the rules for qualifying for the ballot are so convoluted that no one but party insiders can master them; there were no contests here in the 1980s and Steve Forbes qualified in 1996 only after spending $1 million. In 2000 Republican state Chairman William Powers maneuvered to keep John McCain off the ballot, to give an uncontested victory to Bush, Governor George Pataki's candidate. But McCain went to court and got on the ballot. Voting was limited to registered Republicans, and McCain did not have the appeal here he showed in New England; he carried affluent parts of Manhattan and the suburbs, but Bush won just about everywhere else. Voters voted for delegates, not presidential candidates; Bush delegates got 50% of the vote, McCain delegates 44%. In 2004 New York's Democrats voted on March 2, the last day on which the race for the nomination was securely contested; John Kerry prevailed in every congressional district.

New York's minor parties no longer matter much. The Liberal Party and its predecessor, the American Labor Party, were founded to give Jewish garment workers a line on which to vote for Franklin D. Roosevelt and against local Tammany Hall candidates; the Liberal line was a help to Giuliani in the 1993 and 1997 mayoral elections. But in 2002 the Liberals endorsed Andrew Cuomo for governor, and he bowed out of the race a week before the Democratic primary. He got only 16,000 votes in November—far fewer than the 50,000 the Liberals needed to keep their position on the ballot. The Conservative Party was founded to withhold votes from liberal Republicans like Nelson Rockefeller and John Lindsay and encourage the Republican Party to nominate more conservative candidates. Lack of the Conservative line was a problem for Giuliani when he was running for senator, but the party did support the not-very-conservative Rick Lazio. It is quite comfortable with George Pataki, the first Conservative-backed governor, who got 177,000 votes on the Conservative line in 2002. The newest third party is the Working Families party, formed by the Communications Workers and United Auto Workers unions, which takes liberal views on economic issues and ignores cultural issues. It endorses Democratic candidates statewide but has had some distinctive local successes: its nominee was elected Albany County district attorney in 2004, and it determined the outcome of a couple of legislative races.

Congressional districting

When John Kennedy was elected president in 1960, New York elected 43 congressmen and California 30. In 2002, New York elected 29 congressmen and California 53. Reapportionment is carnage time for New York: the state lost five districts in the 1980 Census, another three in 1990 and two more in 2000. In 2002, as in 1992, New York produced the latest and most convoluted redistricting plan. New York has more than 200 state

109th Congress Lineup	
20 D	9 R
108th Congress Lineup	
19 D	10 R

legislators, but legislative decisions are made by three men, Governor George Pataki, Republican state Senate President Joseph Bruno and Democratic Assembly Speaker Sheldon Silver: party discipline is so strong that Bruno and Silver can always deliver majorities in their chambers, and Pataki has a veto. New York lost two seats in the 2000 Census, and before the

Census numbers came in, it was assumed that the final plan would cut one Democratic district in the City and one Republican district Upstate. But the Census figures showed that, for the first time in more than 50 years, most of the state's growth had come in New York City; its population was up 9%, the suburbs up 6% and Upstate up only 1%. So congressmen hired well-wired lobbyists and negotiations began.

Negotiators usually don't reach agreement until they have to; in this case, the deadline was in June 2002, when candidates have to start circulating their petitions. In January Republicans talked of targeting Republican Benjamin Gilman and Rochester Democrat Louise Slaughter, the oldest members of the delegation; Silver would have none of it. In April 2002 a three-judge court appointed Frederick Lacey, a former federal judge, as a special master with orders to draft a plan that could be adopted if the legislature failed to act. To that court Pataki in May submitted a plan that targeted Maurice Hinchey and Manhattan Democrat Carolyn Maloney: an obvious negotiating ploy, since Silver would never accept it. Senate Republicans prepared a plan putting two pairs of Democrats in the same districts; Assembly Democrats prepared a plan putting two pairs of Republicans in the same districts: more negotiating ploys. On May 13 Lacey presented a plan placing two pairs of Upstate members—Republican Sherwood Boehlert and Democrat Maurice Hinchey, Republican Jack Quinn and Democrat John LaFalce—in the same districts. On May 23, the court adopted the plan, but gave the legislature more time to act and said it would gladly accept its plan if it did so.

The pressure was on. Silver wanted to protect Hinchey and other Democrats discommoded by the plan. Bruno got a call from Dick Cheney urging him to deal, since the Lacey plan put some Republican seats at risk. Nita Lowey, chairman of the House Democrats' campaign committee, and Tom Reynolds, on the inside track to become chairman of the House Republicans' campaign committee, let it be known they wanted safer districts so they could concentrate on helping their parties across the country. The three decision-makers decided to target Slaughter and Gilman, though Slaughter said she would run in the primary against LaFalce and Gilman threatened to switch parties and run against Republican Sue Kelly. The last hitch was on Long Island. State Senate Republicans there didn't like the incumbent-protection plan agreed on by the Island's two Democratic and two Republican incumbents; they wanted a better shot at Democrat Carolyn McCarthy's district. But they were brought in line. The new plan was passed and signed June 5. Slaughter went into court and asked it to adopt the Lacey plan. On June 25 the court accepted the legislature's plan and the Justice Department gave it clearance under the Voting Rights Act. On June 26 LaFalce announced that he would not run against Slaughter. On July 2, Gilman, who was 79 and was serving his 30th year in the House, announced that he would retire. All the incumbents running were easily reelected, except for 1st District Republican Felix Grucci, who lost for reasons having nothing to do with redistricting.

In 2005, Democrats began talking about redrawing the congressional map before the next census. The party seemed likely to win the governorship in 2006 and some were hopeful it could pick up the four seats needed to control the state Senate. If that were to happen, a new map would be drawn in 2007, a payback of sorts for the mid-decade Republican redistricting in Texas. "In New York, we know how to hit back," Congressman Joseph Crowley told *National Journal* in June 2005.

Governor

George Pataki (R)

Elected 1994, term expires Jan. 2007, 3d term; b. June 24, 1945, Peekskill; home, Garrison; Yale U., B.A. 1967, Columbia U. Law Schl., J.D. 1970; Catholic; married (Libby).

Elected Office: Peekskill Mayor, 1982–84; NY Assembly, 1984–92; NY Senate, 1992–94.

Professional Career: Practicing atty., 1970–89.

Office: State Capitol, Albany, 12224, 518-474-8390; Web site: www.state.ny.us.

Election Results

2002 general	George Pataki (R-C)	2,262,255	(49%)
	Carl McCall (D-WF)	1,534,064	(34%)
	Thomas Golisano (Ind)	654,016	(14%)
	Other	128,743	(3%)
2002 primary	George Pataki (R)	unopposed	
1998 general	George Pataki (R-C)	2,571,991	(54%)
	Peter F. Vallone (D-WF)	1,570,317	(33%)
	Thomas Golisano (Ind)	364,056	(8%)
	Other	228,872	(5%)

Prior Winning Percentages: 1994 (49%)

George Pataki, the governor of New York who in 2005 was the nation's longest serving governor, was first elected in 1994. He grew up in Peekskill, a small industrial city on the Hudson in northern Westchester County, at the cusp of metropolitan New York City and Upstate New York. His father was the son of Hungarian immigrants, his mother is of Italian and Irish ancestry; his parents had a farm in Peekskill and built it into a business; those years are the primary subject of his autobiography *Pataki*. Pataki graduated from Yale and Columbia Law School, where he was an unabashed conservative in the late 1960s; he practiced law with a big Wall Street firm, then moved to a Westchester firm in 1974. In 1982, he was elected mayor of Peekskill; in 1984, he ran against an incumbent Democratic assemblyman and won. In 1992, after eight years as a member of a powerless minority, he challenged an incumbent Republican state senator and beat her by 558 votes. In the state Senate he chafed at the leadership of Nassau County's Ralph Marino and voted against the budget—an almost unheard of rebellion in lockstep-party-voting Albany. In all this he showed ambition, ruthlessness and a penchant for cutting government, but few were paying attention.

In 1993, the almost unknown Pataki began running for governor, taking on one of America's best-known politicians, Mario Cuomo. For all his national fame, and his feints at running for president in 1987 and 1991, Cuomo was in trouble in New York: he cut the top tax rates but also created other taxes and increased spending robustly; he claimed credit for a workfare program but tended to support the public employee unions. Pataki provided a clear contrast on the issues, and he also showed political skill. He got the support of Senator Alfonse D'Amato, fresh from re-election in 1992 and in control of the state Republican party apparatus. Pataki easily won the May 1994 convention and prevented a primary challenge and a Conservative Party candidacy. In the general election, Cuomo attacked Pataki for having raised taxes in Peekskill; Democrats charged that he was a puppet of D'Amato. Thomas Golisano, a Rochester businessman, was spending millions as an independent, advised by pro-Perot pollster Gordon Black; Perot endorsed him and polls showed him with 8%. But Golisano's share of the vote fell to 4%, and Cuomo got 45%, about where he was running in polls. Pataki won 49% of the vote, losing New York City 70%–28% but carrying the suburbs 54%–43% and Upstate 59%–32%.

As governor, Pataki showed determination and even ruthlessness in seeking his goals. After the election, he engineered a coup ousting Marino as Senate leader that was executed while the governor-elect was on vacation in Florida. Most legislation in New York is hammered out by three people: the governor, the Assembly speaker and the state Senate president. Other state legislators don't much matter. Party discipline is routinely followed; committees don't hold public hearings or markup sessions, and their chairmen can be fired by the leaders any time; most members can't offer amendments or get bills discharged from committees; legislation is typically written by the three leaders' staffers and then "jammed" through both houses without anyone reading it—and all this is enforced by the party leaders' control over expense and campaign funds. So Pataki moved suddenly from being a backbench legislator to being in the room for all the important negotiations with Democratic Assembly Speaker Sheldon Silver and Senate President Joseph Bruno. Pataki proposed cuts in taxes and a standstill in spending and, after bruising negotiations with Silver, got much of what he wanted. Pataki signed the death penalty into law in March.

He spent much effort on a $1.75 billion environmental bond issue, citing his longtime admiration for Theodore Roosevelt and gathering support from business, labor and environmental groups. In early 1997 Pataki unveiled his welfare plan, cutting benefits to recipients who do not find work by 45% over four years; he called for a three-year phase out of the estate and gift taxes, which sent many affluent New Yorkers to Florida. Pataki's budgets in 1997 and 1998 had above-economic-growth spending increases; he established who was in control, however, by line-item-vetoing $1.6 billion from the legislature's budget in April 1998. All this left Pataki in strong shape for reelection in 1998. The Democratic nomination was won by New York City Council Speaker Peter Vallone, a competent and constructive veteran widely admired in knowledgeable circles. But he was scarcely known outside New York City, and never had a chance against the well-financed Pataki. Pataki won 54%–33%, with 8% for Golisano, running a third-party candidacy.

Over many years now as governor, Pataki has tacked this way and that, emphasizing new issues and taking different stands that put him at different places on the political spectrum. His description of his political philosophy leaves him plenty of room: "I believe in limited government, low taxes, a tough approach to crime. But I also believe in activist government. I'm not one of those laissez faire types." During his second term he moved mostly to the left. Starting in 1999 he proposed changing the Rockefeller drug laws, with their mandatory minimum sentences; in 2004, the legislature finally acted and reduced the sentence for some low-level first-time drug offenders to 8 to 20 years in prison, down from 15 years to life. In 2001 Pataki pushed through an expansion of children's health insurance, which covered 543,000 children. He pushed through innovative gun-control laws in 2000, including requiring ballistic fingerprinting of every gun sold. He signed a hate-crimes law and set up a DNA review commission in 2000, plus laws for tougher sentences for sex offenders.

Most of all, he courted the public employee unions. He met one of the major demands by signing in July 2000 a cost of living adjustment for public employee retiree pensions. In January 2002 he met with Dennis Rivera, head of 1199, the state's largest union, and negotiated an agreement to increase the pay of hospital employees. He signed a law allowing unionization of employees of new Indian casinos. He supported higher pensions for police and fire fighters who work 30 years, which were much appreciated by the Policemen's Benevolent Association, the United Firefighters Association and the Corrections Officers Benevolent Association. His support of teachers' pay increases was appreciated by the NEA New York and his pressure on Mayor Michael Bloomberg for a $1 billion teacher pay settlement impressed the United Federation of Teachers.

But Pataki's greatest asset in 2002 was his performance on and in the days after September 11. He worked around the clock, often making public appearances with Mayor Rudolph Giuliani; they had had edgy relations in the past, but obviously bonded in the emergency. His job rating, already in the high 50s, soared much higher in fall 2001 and early 2002, and he established a closer connection with New York City, where he had won only 28% of the vote in 1994 and 33% in 1998. His call for a total of $54 billion of aid to the state—which included some Upstate projects—was off-putting to many in Washington, but was well-received by New York voters. Democratic strategist Howard Wolfson said Pataki's greatest asset in 2002 was the "Ground Zero" effect.

Nonetheless, two well-known Democrats ran for governor. One was Andrew Cuomo, son of the former governor and the HUD Secretary in the Clinton administration. The other was state Comptroller Carl McCall, a longtime insider in New York politics, who would be the first black major party nominee for governor. McCall stressed classic Democratic themes and highlighted his own rise from modest (though not impoverished, as he suggested) beginnings to high public office. McCall played an insider's game, Cuomo an outsider's game. McCall was endorsed by hundreds of Democratic politicians, including all four Democratic borough presidents, as well as NEA New York—though other big unions, courted by Pataki, stayed out of the Democratic primary. Cuomo campaigned with his wife, a daughter of Robert Kennedy, and had more celebrity; he led in polls in the spring. Cuomo avoided the Democratic state convention and instead got on the ballot by collecting petition signatures. But both candidates made serious mistakes in off-the-cuff comments. On a bus with reporters traveling from Buffalo to Utica, Cuomo in April 2002 denigrated Pataki's role on September 11. "He stood behind the leader. He held the leader's coat. He was a great assistant to the leader. But he was not a leader." McCall, speaking at a homeless youth shelter in New York in June, was asked about education aid to ex-convicts. "Just because you're an ex-offender, you should not be denied education aid. In fact, if you're an ex-offender, I think you ought to get preference." He tried to explain he had not meant what he said, but voters got the sense he was one of New York's far left Democrats.

Cuomo withdrew from the race on September 3, a week before the primary. McCall had passed him in the polls over the summer and, Cuomo said, the only way he could win was to wage a negative campaign that he didn't want to do. That left McCall with little money for the general election and Pataki quite a lot more—but Thomas Golisano had even more. He is the founder and CEO of Paychex, a payroll processing company; his fortune is estimated at $800 million. He had run in 1994 and 1998, winning 4% and 8% of the vote, much of it in and around his hometown of Rochester. Under New York's unique system, candidates can run for the nomination of more than one party, and Pataki ran for the Conservative and Independence party nominations as well as the Republican. Golisano was running for the Conservative nomination, which he was unlikely to win; he needed the Independence nomination to get on the ballot in November. Pataki operatives evidently encouraged people to re-register in the Independence party, to knock Golisano off the ballot on September 10. They nearly succeeded, but Golisano beat Pataki by a margin of only 9,572 to 9,026. Golisano, who had already spent $30 million, proceeded to spend $43 million more, most of it on ads savaging Pataki, calling him corrupt and saying that he had neglected the economy of Upstate New York. He succeeded in depressing Pataki's vote Upstate but Pataki ran better than he ever had in New York City, losing it to McCall by only a 53%–38% margin. Overall, Pataki won by a 49%–34% margin, with 14% for Golisano—not as sweeping a victory as in 1998.

Once reelected Pataki took a different tack on issues. He did press through the legislature in December a law banning discrimination against gays. But, with revenues slumping, he called for preserving previous tax cuts and said he opposed tax increases. In January 2003 he proposed a budget with cuts in spending on health care and education but suffered a stunning defeat in May when both the Democratic Assembly and Republican Senate overwhelmingly overrode his vetoes of their budget bills less than a day after he issued them; the legislature passed a budget which increased taxes and was $2 billion more than he proposed.

In January 2004, Pataki called for tougher anti-crime and terrorism laws and in February he joined five other governors on a surprise visit to Baghdad. He sought to cut taxes for manufacturers to help stem job losses, which were particularly acute in Upstate; one study reported that New York accounted for a higher rate of job loss in the recent economic downturn and accounted for one in 10 jobs lost in the nation. He saw one of the first bills he signed in 1995 to fulfill a campaign promise, a law to restore the death penalty, struck down by the state's highest court. After proposing a $90.8 billion budget in 2003, in 2004 he proposed a $99.8 billion budget that called for cutting back Medicaid spending by $800 million. For the 20th consecutive year the state missed its budget deadline as Pataki, Silver and Bruno, the only three that matter in New York's budget process, failed to come to agreement by the April 1 deadline. In July, a study by the Brennan Center for Justice confirmed what nearly everyone knew about the Albany culture: it ranked the state legislature as the least deliberative, most dysfunctional legislature in the nation, one of the most expensive to operate and one of the least productive. Responding to growing public criticism, the legislature passed a bill that lawmakers said would overhaul the budget process; Pataki vetoed it and the Senate decided not to override.

The Republican National Convention in New York City was a high point. Pataki took on a prominent role in the election campaign as a defender of George W. Bush's foreign policy and at the convention he had the slot to introduce Bush on the convention's final night. After the election, there were rumors that he might take a position in Bush's 2nd term Cabinet; he insisted he was not interested. "I don't want to go to Washington," he said. "I've never wanted to go to Washington. I would have gone to Washington four years ago if I wanted to go to Washington. I'm the governor and I hope to be governor for some time to come." But at home, he was the target of criticism from Republican Congressmen Peter King and John Sweeney who criticized the direction of the state party under Pataki's stewardship. The 2004 election was a dismal one for Republicans: they lost seats in the Assembly and Senate and were embarrassed by Senator Charles Schumer's landslide 71% reelection victory.

But Pataki won a victory in December 2004 when the state's highest court ruled that the governor has the sole authority to propose budgets and the legislature only has the power to delete or reduce expenditures or add spending subject to the governor's line-item veto; the ruling came in response to two lawsuits reaching back to the 1998 and 2001 budgets. He began 2005 by announcing an agreement with a Canadian paper manufacturer to protect from development more than 100,000 acres of forestland in the Sable Highlands area of the Adirondacks. He proposed a $105.5 billion budget, with $1 billion in Medicaid cuts to cover a projected budget deficit of $4.15 billion. This budget, for the first time in 21 years, was actually passed on time; it increased spending on education and transportation and raised taxes and fees on motor vehicles and mortgages.

Many in Albany believe Pataki will not run for reelection to a fourth term; there is speculation that after 10 years as governor he has ambitions for other office—perhaps a run for the Senate against Hillary Clinton, perhaps the vice presidency, maybe the presidency itself. In December 2004, he said he would not make any decisions about his future until after the next legislative session. Popular Attorney General Eliot Spitzer, the Democratic frontrunner who got great publicity from using investigative powers under a vaguely phrased state law to restructure the investment banking business, said he was running; he led Pataki, whose approval ratings were low in 2005, by a large margin in a head-to-head poll. But in June Nassau County Executive Tom Suozzi was said to be considering a challenge to Spitzer. On the Republican side, former Massachusetts Governor William Weld, a New York native who now works for a private equity firm in the city, said he was seriously considering running if Pataki and Rudy Giuliani did not.

Senior Senator

Charles Schumer (D)

Elected 1998, seat up 2010, 2d term; b. Nov. 23, 1950, Brooklyn; home, Brooklyn; Harvard U., B.A. 1971, J.D. 1974; Jewish; married (Iris).

Elected Office: NY Assembly, 1974–80; U.S. House of Reps., 1980–1998.

DC Office: 313 HSOB, 20510, 202-224-6542; Fax: 202-228-3027; Web site: schumer.senate.gov.

State Offices: Albany, 518-431-4070; Binghamton, 607-772-6792; Buffalo, 716-846-4111; Manhattan, 212-486-4430; Melville, 631-753-0978; Red Hook, 914-285-9741; Rochester, 585-263-5866; Syracuse, 315-423-5471.

Committees: *DSCC Chairman. Banking, Housing & Urban Affairs*: Economic Policy (RMM); Housing & Transportation; Securities & Investment. *Finance*: International Trade; Taxation & IRS Oversight. *Judiciary*: Administrative Oversight & the Courts (RMM); Antitrust, Competition Policy & Consumer Rights; Crime & Drugs; Immigration, Border Security & Citizenship. *Rules & Administration*.

Group Ratings

	ADA	ACLU	AFS	LCV	ITIC	NTU	COC	ACU	NTLC	CHC
2004	100	78	100	100	83	13	65	12	13	0
2003	100	—	100	95	—	19	39	10	—	—

National Journal Ratings

	2003 LIB	—	2003 CONS		2004 LIB	—	2004 CONS
Economic	82%	—	10%		58%	—	39%
Social	63%	—	35%		77%	—	19%
Foreign	72%	—	26%		75%	—	19%

Key Votes of the 108th Congress

1. Ban Drilling in ANWR	Y	5. Energy Bill	N	9. Ban Same-Sex Marriage	N
2. Approve Bush Tax Cuts	N	6. Support Roe v. Wade	Y	10. Ban Bunker-Buster Bomb	Y
3. Medicare/Rx Bill	N	7. Ban Partial-Birth Abortion	N	11. Fund Iraq War	Y
4. Bar Overtime Pay Regs.	Y	8. Assault Weapons Ban	Y	12. Restrict Missile Defense	Y

Election Results

2004 general	Charles Schumer (D-Ind-WF)	4,769,824	(71%)	($15,467,530)
	Howard Mills (R)	1,625,069	(24%)	($628,578)
	Other	307,982	(5%)	
2004 primary	Charles Schumer (D)	unopposed		
1998 general	Charles Schumer (D-Ind-L)	2,551,065	(55%)	($16,671,877)
	Al D'Amato (R-C-RTL)	2,058,988	(44%)	($24,195,287)
	Other	60,752	(1%)	

Prior Winning Percentages: 1996 House (75%); 1994 House (73%); 1992 House (89%); 1990 House (80%); 1988 House (78%); 1986 House (93%); 1984 House (72%); 1982 House (79%); 1980 House (77%)

Charles Schumer is New York's senior senator, first elected to the House in 1980 and to the Senate in 1998. Schumer grew up in Flatbush, Brooklyn, and graduated first in his class at James Madison High School, alma mater also of Justice Ruth Bader Ginsburg and Minnesota Senator Norm Coleman. He graduated from Harvard College and Law School and, with the latter diploma fresh in his hand in June 1974, immediately began running for an open Assembly seat. He won, at 23. In 1980 he was elected to the House from an open Brooklyn seat, just before he turned 30. Through energy, imagination, hard work, good humor and a certain amount of chutzpah, he became a skilled legislator, and one noted—and sometimes resented—for his knack for getting publicity: Bob Dole was one of the first to say that the most dangerous place in Washington was in between Schumer and a television camera.

From the unlikely venue of the Banking Committee, a panel that most talented members lobby to get off of, Schumer spotted the perverse incentives set up by the combination of deposit insurance and letting S&Ls make risky investments. On Judiciary and, eventually, as chairman of its Crime Subcommittee, he ranged far afield, contributing key provisions to immigration acts in 1986 and 1990, leading attacks on farm subsidies, and a nearly successful assault on sugar programs. Schumer sponsored the 1994 crime bill and got the House to pass the Brady bill, with its waiting period for handgun purchases, over strong opposition from the National Rifle Association.

The idea of running for statewide office was surely never far from his mind. In April 1997 Governor George Pataki's strong job rating, and especially his overwhelming strength Upstate, convinced Schumer to use his $5 million treasury to run for Alfonse D'Amato's Senate seat instead of the governorship. It was by no means obvious that Schumer would win. D'Amato was known for his assiduous constituent service and for his ability to win the tabloid wars that dominate campaigning in metropolitan New York. D'Amato was chairman of the Banking Committee and excelled at raising money; his early support did much to make Pataki governor. Schumer started off largely unknown outside his district and faced serious primary opposition from 1984 vice presidential nominee Geraldine Ferraro and Mark Green, New York City Public Advocate and D'Amato's opponent in 1986. By summer, Schumer was leading in polls and was much better financed, and in September he won the primary with 51% of the vote, to 26% for Ferraro and 19% for Green.

Schumer immediately launched an attack on D'Amato, saying he had told "too many lies for too long"; it echoed D'Amato's attacks on earlier opponents as "too liberal for too long." Schumer claimed he was tougher on crime, citing his support for longer sentences, limiting death row appeals, expanding capital punishment and broadening wiretap authority; he emphasized his support of abortion rights and gun control. D'Amato concentrated heavily on Schumer's missed votes while running for Senate, but the implication that Schumer was lazy was implausible. Still, by mid-October, Schumer's poll leads were mostly less than the statistical margin of error. But in a closed meeting before a Jewish group D'Amato called Schumer a "putzhead"; when that became public, he denied it, then backtracked unconvincingly after his own supporter, former Democratic Mayor Edward Koch, confirmed it. D'Amato lost confidence and momentum, and by early November was sagging in polls. Schumer, who announced in October that he would vote against impeachment though he believed Bill Clinton lied under oath, was the beneficiary of two visits from Clinton and no less than four from Hillary Rodham Clinton (the rousing receptions she got may have prompted her to run for the Senate in New York two years later). Though outspent, Schumer won 55%–44%, winning 74%–25% in a big turnout in New York City and losing the suburbs by only 51%–49%.

In the Senate, Schumer has had a solidly liberal voting record. He holds regular Sunday press conferences, to get in the Monday papers. He has made a practice of visiting all 62 counties each year, and regularly spends Mondays on Upstate swings that get him on Buffalo, Rochester, Syracuse and Albany television. He is one of three Americans in history who have cast two votes on the impeachment of the same president (the other two are Mike Crapo of Idaho and Jim Bunning of Kentucky, also congressmen elected to the Senate in 1998); Schumer voted against impeaching Clinton in the House in December 1998 and against conviction in the Senate in February 1999.

An ally of the securities industry on both the House and Senate Banking Committees, he has called for making electronic communications networks subject to the same regulations as stock exchanges and for making the New York Stock Exchange a profit-making corporation. He played a key role in the scuttling of the bankruptcy bill in 2002. He persuaded the Senate to pass an amendment that made fines and penalties for blocking access to or attacking abortion clinics not dischargeable in bankruptcy in May 2002; some abortion opponents had taken to declaring bankruptcy to avoid paying fines. But abortion opponents in the House, led by Chris Smith and Joe Pitts, refused to vote for the bill as long as it had Schumer's amendment. Leaders in both houses got Schumer and Henry Hyde, with whom he had long worked on the House Judiciary Committee, to negotiate a compromise amendment. But that too was unacceptable to the Smith-Pitts group, and when the House leadership introduced a rule to consider the bill in November 2002 it was defeated 243–172 and the bankruptcy bill died. Schumer tried again in

March 2005, but this time the abortion amendment was voted down, 53–46, in the Senate, and the bill was quickly passed, sent to the House and enacted. Schumer has also taken on the pharmaceutical companies by attempting to deny them extension of their patents beyond their original time when they challenge a generic drugmaker for patent infringement; he has called for requiring states to post prescription drug prices online. He has called for making it easier to switch cellphone companies, for disclosure of fees by money transfer companies, for a do-not-email registry to discourage spam, for more disclosure of interest rates by credit card companies. He disappointed some Democrats by agreeing to support the class action bill in return for some changes in 2004, but he persevered in opposing the energy bill despite claims by Upstate Congressman James Walsh that it included funding for a megamall in Syracuse. In January 2004 he and conservative commentator Paul Craig Roberts wrote an article arguing the "new developments," chiefly global competition, "call into question some of the key assumptions supporting the doctrine of free trade."

Schumer serves on Judiciary, where he has argued that senators should reject Bush appointees on "purely ideological grounds." Starting with the nomination of Miguel Estrada, he has led the opposition to at least 10 Bush judicial nominees whom he and various lobbying groups have said were out of the mainstream, and together with almost all other Democrats has been using the filibuster to prevent the confirmation of federal judges with majority support. He has taken strong exception to Senate Republicans who have advocated changing the rules to allow nominations to be considered by majority vote.

On September 11 Schumer was in Washington; his daughter was in school a few blocks from the World Trade Center. Amid the terrible news, Schumer and others in the New York delegation conferred and agreed to seek $20 billion in aid for New York. In the Oval Office on September 13 Schumer and Clinton met with George W. Bush. Bush asked how much New York needed. Schumer paused and said $20 billion. Bush's reaction: "You got it." The usually voluble Schumer's reaction? "My mouth dropped open." Of course there was more to it than that. The New Yorkers understood that some of the money would not be forthcoming immediately, since no one had decided how to reconstruct the World Trade Center site and its transportation facilities. Schumer worked to prevent OMB and House Republicans from putting off as much of the spending as they wanted and dealt with the backlash against Pataki's calling for $54 billion. The Bush administration turned to Schumer to get support for what became the USA Patriot Act, and Schumer and Clinton backed the proposal to let the FBI share information on terrorism with state and local police.

Channeling the flow of money into New York state and city has been part of Schumer's job. In 2004 he sought $7.1 billion in transit money over six years in the transportation bill. In 2005 he called for an additional $61 million for housing in New York City when inflation had increased costs. In 2004 he secured $21.8 million for job retraining from the Manufacturing Extension Partnership for an Albany area economic development commission. He announced $4.5 billion in disaster relief for the transit center linking PATH and New York City subway lines at the World Trade Center site—to the irritation of Governor George Pataki, who thought he was entitled to make the announcement. He secured grants for all manner of projects—$150,000 to refurbish the Natural History Museum of the Adirondacks in Tupper Lake, $68,000 to buy an ambulance for volunteer fire dept in Hermon in St Lawrence County, $720,000 for a center for the disabled in Schenectady, $125,000 for the Albany Institute of History and Art's online exhibits. He got funding for tritium cleanup at the Brookhaven National Laboratory and a federal takeover of the cleanup of a nuclear rods factory in Hicksville. Schumer does not have close ties to Governor George Pataki: he campaigned extensively for Democrat Carl McCall in 2002 and for much of 2004 was rumored to be interested in running for governor himself. He has gotten along much better with nominally Republican Mayor Michael Bloomberg. Schumer's wife Iris Weinshall is Bloomberg's Transportation Commissioner and in late October 2004 Bloomberg endorsed Schumer for reelection.

When Hillary Rodham Clinton was elected in November 2000, many thought there would be friction between the aggressive Schumer and the more famous Clinton. There mostly hasn't been, not in public anyway. Clinton was probably irritated after Schumer criticized Bill Clinton's

January 2001 pardon of Marc Rich. And they must have had some disagreements as they struggled to help New York after September 11: the more earthy Schumer seemed to get along better with Bush, the more disciplined Clinton seemed to get along better with some Republican senators. Relations between two senators of the same party from the same state are very often fractious, especially when both are seeking plenty of home state publicity; Schumer may be the senior senator, but Clinton is the better-known and the one regarded by many as her party's likeliest presidential nominee in 2008. As there is some lifestyle difference. While Clinton holds fundraisers in her $2.8 million house in Washington, Schumer shares a Capitol Hill townhouse with Senator Dick Durbin and Congressmen Bill Delahunt and George Miller.

Schumer has been a prodigious fundraiser since his early days in the House; he husbanded funds back then lest redistricting pit him against another Jewish Democratic incumbent in Brooklyn. Over the 2004 cycle Schumer raised $11.9 million. Speculation abounded that he was interested in running for governor in 2006; in the meantime his Senate race proved easy. Constant travels in Upstate New York made him as well known there as in New York City. The Republican nominee, Assemblyman Howard Mills, was little known and poorly financed; he was ignored by Schumer and hectored by Conservative nominee Marilyn O'Grady. No Democratic incumbent senator has been defeated in New York since direct election of senators began (although seven incumbent Republicans have lost). Schumer won 71%–24%, exceeding the 67%–31% record set by Daniel Patrick Moynihan in 1988; he won 66% of the vote in the suburbs, 63% Upstate and 86% in New York City. That only increased the rumors that Schumer would run for governor; some thought there was a game of chicken between him and highly publicized Attorney General Eliot Spitzer. Schumer protested that he wasn't running for governor. "If I was running for governor, I would have run a whole different race. The primary vote is 80% Downstate. I would have been Downstate all the time. I was Upstate." But the issue was settled in mid-November, when it was announced that Schumer would become chairman of the Democratic Senatorial Campaign Committee and that he would become a member of the Finance Committee. That committed Schumer to a continuing Senate career and left Spitzer free to run for governor. The work ahead, however, looked difficult. The lineup of Senate seats up in 2006 seemed to leave Republicans with more target seats than Democrats. On Finance he promised to work for pressuring China to revalue its currency and to pass provisions preventing American corporations from relocating overseas. Talk of possible major tax simplification left Schumer with the same primary goal as New York's representatives had during the debate over tax simplification in 1985 and 1986, preserving the deductibility on federal tax returns of (New York's very high) state and local taxes. In the meantime, his highest visibility battle was to prevent the confirmation of Bush judicial appointees opposed by most Democrats.

Junior Senator

Hillary Rodham Clinton (D)

Elected 2000, seat up 2006, 1st term; b. Oct. 26, 1947, Chicago, IL; home, Chappaqua; Wellesley Col., B.A. 1969; Yale U., J.D. 1973; Methodist; married (Bill).

Professional Career: Atty., Children's Defense Fund, 1973–74; Council, U.S. House of Reps. Judiciary Committee, 1974; Asst. professor, U. of AR School of Law, 1974–77, 1979–80; Practicing atty., 1977–92; Chair, Pres. Task Force on Health Care Reform, 1993.

DC Office: 476 RSOB, 20510, 202-224-4451; Fax: 202-228-0282; Web site: clinton.senate.gov.

State Offices: Albany, 518-431-0120; Buffalo, 716-854-9725; Hartsdale, 914-725-9294; Lowville, 315-376-6118; Melville, 631-249-2825; New York City, 212-688-6262; Rochester, 585-263-6250; Syracuse, 315-448-0470.

Committees: *Democratic Steering Committee Chairman. Aging (Special). Armed Services*: Airland; Emerging Threats & Capabilities; Readiness & Management Support. *Environment & Public Works*: Fisheries, Wildlife & Water (RMM); Transportation & Infrastructure. *Health, Education, Labor & Pensions*: Education & Early Childhood Development; Retirement Security & Aging.

Group Ratings

	ADA	ACLU	AFS	LCV	ITIC	NTU	COC	ACU	NTLC	CHC
2004	95	78	100	100	67	11	50	0	5	0
2003	95	—	100	89	—	21	35	10	—	—

National Journal Ratings

	2003 LIB	—	2003 CONS		2004 LIB	—	2004 CONS
Economic	90%	—	7%		63%	—	36%
Social	85%	—	0%		82%	—	0%
Foreign	79%	—	14%		58%	—	41%

Key Votes of the 108th Congress

1. Ban Drilling in ANWR	Y	5. Energy Bill	N	9. Ban Same-Sex Marriage	N
2. Approve Bush Tax Cuts	N	6. Support Roe v. Wade	Y	10. Ban Bunker-Buster Bomb	Y
3. Medicare/Rx Bill	N	7. Ban Partial-Birth Abortion	N	11. Fund Iraq War	Y
4. Bar Overtime Pay Regs.	Y	8. Assault Weapons Ban	Y	12. Restrict Missile Defense	N

Election Results

2000 general	Hillary Rodham Clinton (D-L-WF)	3,747,310	(55%)	($41,469,898)
	Rick Lazio (R-C)	2,915,730	(43%)	($40,576,273)
	Other	116,799	(2%)	
2000 primary	Hillary Rodham Clinton (D)	565,353	(82%)	
	Mark S. McMahon (D)	124,315	(18%)	
1994 general	Daniel Patrick Moynihan (D-L)	2,646,541	(55%)	($6,705,482)
	Bernadette Castro (R-C)	1,988,308	(42%)	($1,581,901)
	Other	155,487	(3%)	

Hillary Rodham Clinton, First Lady of the United States from 1993 to 2001, was elected junior senator from New York in November 2000. Clinton grew up in Park Ridge, Illinois; her father owned and ran a drape and curtain factory. She excelled at her studies and was elected to student government at Maine South High School. Park Ridge is a solidly Republican Chicago suburb, near O'Hare Airport, and the young Hillary Rodham was a Goldwater girl in 1964. She went to Wellesley College, where she became a Democrat in the turbulent election year of 1968: she wrote her senior thesis (kept under lock and key by the college since 1993) on applying the theories of radical Chicago organizer Saul Alinsky and argued that antipoverty programs did not give enough power to the poor. She was elected student government president, and pushed successfully for admission of more black students and admission of men to women's dorms. At the 1969 commencement she gave a speech that won notice in *Life* magazine. She went on to Yale Law School, where she worked with the attorney for Black Panthers accused of murder and clerked for a summer with Communist attorney Robert Treuhaft in Berkeley. At Yale she met Bill Clinton, and they became partners for life.

Bill Clinton was anything but reticent about his political ambitions in his native Arkansas. He showed her around the state and together they went to Austin in 1972 to run the McGovern campaign in Texas. After graduation in 1973, Bill Clinton moved to Fayetteville to teach law at the University of Arkansas. In 1974 Hillary Rodham moved to Washington to work for the House Judiciary Committee's special counsel John Doar on the impeachment of Richard Nixon. After Nixon resigned, she returned to Arkansas to teach law, and in October 1975 she and Clinton were married. In 1976 he was elected attorney general of Arkansas; she worked for Jimmy Carter's campaign. After that she worked for the Rose Law Firm in Little Rock and in 1977 was appointed part-time chairman of the Legal Services Corporation. Under her leadership, the Legal Services budget increased dramatically, including contributions to local political campaigns and conducting campaigns against ballot propositions. In 1978 Bill Clinton ran for governor, and after he won the Democratic nomination, tantamount to victory that year, Hillary Rodham invested $1,000 in commodities future and with the help of a friend who was general counsel of Tyson Foods, one of the state's biggest businesses, saw that turned into $100,000.

In 1980 Bill Clinton was defeated for re-election. He promptly took up a more moderate line and his wife began to call herself Hillary Clinton; in 1982 he beat the incumbent and became governor again. Hillary Clinton continued her law practice and service on the board of the

Children's Defense Fund and other organizations. She served on the boards of Wal-Mart, TCBY and in 1988 and 1991 was named by the *National Law Journal* as one of the 100 most influential lawyers in the country. It was in these years also that she and her husband invested in the Whitewater real estate project and that she performed legal work for the Morgan Guaranty Savings and Loan, which invested in the project and whose failure cost the federal government $73 million. Whitewater later became the subject of congressional hearings and an independent counsel investigation, both of which were impeded when Rose Law Firm billing records were subpoenaed in July 1994 but were not found until they turned up in the residential quarters of the White House in January 1996. Independent Counsel Robert Ray in September 2000 ended the investigation, saying he could not prove that the Clintons had been involved in criminal activity or that they concealed information from investigators or obstructed justice. In his final report in March 2002 Ray noted that Rose Law Firm records were found in the family quarters of the White House in January 1996 and that three witnesses told investigators they saw her "carrying records that had the appearance of the billing records in July 1995"; but he said that that evidence was insufficient to obtain and sustain a conviction beyond a reasonable doubt.

In 1991 Bill Clinton ran for president. It was widely rumored that he had had many extramarital affairs; at a Washington press breakfast the Clintons admitted that their marriage had not been without problems. After the election, Clinton announced that the leader of his task force on health care reform would be the first lady, Hillary Rodham Clinton—the first time her maiden name was featured. The task force under her direction and that of Ira Magaziner met secretly and without input from members of Congress; a complicated plan was finally produced after a couple of deadlines were not met. Clinton eventually did testify before Congress; there and in other public forums she was crisp, articulate, knowledgeable. But she was unable to persuade Congress to adopt her plan. It never came to the floor in either house, and was abandoned in September 1994. In the meantime, the first lady had problems with scandals. In May 1993 the members of the White House Travel Office were fired, and director Billy Ray Dale was later prosecuted—and acquitted by a jury within minutes. Clinton denied that she had any role in the firings, or in apparent plans to replace the charter service with one owned by Clinton friends and Hollywood producers Harry Thomason and Linda Bloodworth-Thomason. In June 2000 Independent Counsel Robert Ray concluded that Clinton had given "factually false" testimony in a sworn deposition, but declined to prosecute her.

Clinton persevered through the humiliations of the health care fiasco and the scandals with an aplomb that showed great discipline and determination. She wrote *It Takes a Village* and donated the proceeds to children's hospitals. In January 1998, when Bill Clinton denied the charge that he had had an affair with then-White House intern Monica Lewinsky, Hillary Rodham Clinton flew to New York to appear on the *Today* show and charge that the allegations were the product of "a vast right-wing conspiracy." She continued to support him, though with obvious frostiness, when he was forced to admit in August 1998 that the charges were true.

Meanwhile, she campaigned gamely for Democratic candidates in the 1998 elections, and was particularly moved by the warm applause she received in her four appearances in New York for Senate candidate Charles Schumer. Three days after the 1998 election, Senator Daniel Patrick Moynihan announced that he would not run for re-election in New York in 2000. Moynihan, the nation's best thinker among politicians since Lincoln and its best politician among thinkers since Jefferson, a man whose public career extended back into the 1950s and included many prescient warnings and original insights, who had served four terms in the Senate after serving in the cabinet or sub-cabinets of four successive presidents, obviously was not going to be replaced by a politician of similar magnitude; there aren't any. But there also weren't any obvious Democratic successors in New York. Moynihan, who passed away in March 2003, himself suggested state comptroller Carl McCall; Congresswoman Nita Lowey of Westchester County was interested in the race, though it was not clear that either had the stature to beat the likely Republican nominee, New York City Mayor Rudolph Giuliani. In early 1999 Bob Torricelli, the aggressive head of the Senate Democrats' campaign committee, called for Clinton to run. She said she was giving "careful thought" to it. She started making more trips to New York, and Lowey said she would be glad to step aside if Clinton ran. In July 1999 she appeared at Moynihans' Upstate farm and then began a "listening tour" across Upstate New York. Giuliani responded with an appearance in Arkansas.

Clinton's early campaign was not without troubles. There was widespread ridicule of the idea of someone with no previous connection with the state running for senator from New York. In August 1999 Bill Clinton granted clemency to four Puerto Rican terrorists who never expressed remorse for their violent crimes—an obvious pitch for the Puerto Rican vote. Embarrassed, she came out against the move, without giving a heads-up to Puerto Rican leaders. That same month the Clintons left their favorite vacation spot, fashionable Martha's Vineyard, for a sojourn in Skaneateles, a pleasant town in the Finger Lakes they would never have visited otherwise. In October the Clintons bought a house in woodsy Chappaqua in Westchester County and were then embarrassed because they borrowed most of the purchase price from Democratic fundraiser Terry McAuliffe; later they got more conventional financing. In November 1999 on a trip to Israel, Clinton embraced and kissed the wife of Yasir Arafat after a speech in which she lambasted the Israelis; Clinton explained later that she was acting in a diplomatic capacity, but her act brought back memories of her endorsement of an independent Palestinian state when that was not yet U.S. policy. In February 2000 she formally announced her candidacy, with her husband standing silently by, from a venue in Westchester. By that point her poll ratings had slipped, and she was running no better than even with Giuliani.

Carpetbagging is not necessarily a political crime in New York. Voters there in 1964 elected Robert Kennedy, though he lived in Virginia and had a technical residence in Massachusetts. Robert Kennedy won in 1964 not just because of Lyndon Johnson's coattails, but because he ran virtually even in usually Republican Upstate New York; national celebrities may be commonplace in New York City, but when they show up in Upstate towns and cities it is noted and appreciated. Hillary Rodham Clinton's strategy was similar. With her usual hard work, perseverance and intensity, she criss-crossed Upstate New York, listened to its voters' many complaints, learned about local issues and adopted appealing positions on them: the same slogging persistence she had shown in the dreary days in Arkansas and the tumultuous days after the failed health care initiative and scandal charges in Washington. In April Giuliani announced that he had prostate cancer; in May he announced that he was seeking a separation from his wife. Days later, in a dramatic press conference, he announced he was leaving the Senate race.

Within 24 hours the Republicans had another candidate, Long Island Congressman Rick Lazio. He had talked of running in summer 1999, until Governor George Pataki announced suddenly in August that he was backing his longtime rival Giuliani. Lazio had a moderate voting record in the House; like Giuliani he backed abortion rights. He raised plenty of money: Hillary haters from all over the country sent in contributions large and small, and he ended up spending $40 million. But his campaign was less than perfect. Lazio was vulnerable to attacks, made often by Clinton, that he had supported Newt Gingrich, a *bete noire* to most New York voters. And there were unforced errors. In the first debate on September 13, Lazio walked over to Clinton and presented her a paper with a pledge to eschew soft money ads. In a time when voters were eager for consensus, Lazio was providing them with confrontation, and this in-your-face behavior was especially repugnant to women. Nine days later they both agreed to not run ads financed by soft money, that is, contributions to parties; but this was unenforceable, since parties and others can spend what they want to, and the assumption that campaign finance was a vote-moving issue proved ill-founded. In the second debate, Lazio declined to say that he would vote for any Supreme Court nominee who opposed the key abortion rights decision of *Roe v. Wade*, a defensible position intellectually, but one difficult to sustain politically in New York; Clinton pounded him on it.

For a race that was close almost all the way in the polls, this Senate election—surpassing the 1998 New York Senate race as the most expensive in history not involving a self-financing candidate—was decided by a surprisingly wide margin. Clinton won 55%–43%, almost the same as Schumer's 55%–44% two years earlier. "Sixty-two counties, 16 months, three debates, two opponents and six black pantsuits later—here we are!" exulted Clinton on election night. She was helped, of course, by the fact that Al Gore was carrying New York 60%–35%. But she ran well on her own. She carried New York City by 74%–25%, the same margin as Schumer's in 1998. She trailed in the suburbs by only 53%–45%, despite Lazio's suburban provenance; he carried his Long Island base, but she carried her now native Westchester. And Lazio won Upstate by only 50%–47%; Clinton carried most of the large counties there, and her percentages in county after county, not usually 50% but seldom under 40%, are impressive evidence of her hard work in campaigning and mastering Upstate issues. Clinton carried the Jewish vote, according to the VNS exit poll, by only 53%–45%, which would usually mean disaster for a Democrat in New York, and she did far less well than Schumer and other Democrats among those with graduate degrees, a large percentage of whom are Jewish. But she carried Upstate women by 55%–43%, an excellent showing for a Democrat: the work paid off.

A few days after the election, Clinton took a victory lap around Upstate New York and had a harmonious meeting in Albany with Pataki. But her standing fell in the months after the election. In December 2000 she signed a book contract with Simon & Schuster for $8 million—$4.5 million more than the book contract for which Newt Gingrich was so roundly attacked in 1995. In departing the White House, the Clintons took $190,000 in gifts—far above the Senate's $50 limit—and many had to be returned when it was revealed that they included items donated to the White House, not the Clintons. Among the gifts were $7,375 worth of coffee tables and chairs donated by Denise Rich, former wife and advocate of Marc Rich, the fugitive financier pardoned by Bill Clinton on his last day in office, despite the opposition of New York U.S. Attorney Mary Jo White. Hillary Rodham Clinton said she had no opinion on the pardon. Nor, she said, did she have any role in the pardon of four Hasidic Jews from the Rockland County community of New Square who were convicted of fleecing the federal government of millions of dollars—a pardon White also opposed. But Clinton had visited New Square in August 2000, had won the community's vote by a margin of 1,400 to 12 and had been present at a White House Map Room meeting between their leaders and Bill Clinton on December 21, 2000, where they asked for the pardons. She said she had no knowledge as well that her brother Hugh Rodham had, while living at the White House, pushed for and obtained the pardon of two other felons for which he had been paid $400,000.

Many expected that Clinton would be greeted grudgingly and suspiciously by other senators because of her obvious presidential ambitions. In fact she has worked hard at the often tedious business of being a senator. She continued to travel around New York, especially Upstate: by June 2002 she had made 130 trips to Upstate New York. She worked on federal loans for the Mohawk Valley, a theater restoration in Gloversville, the arcana of dairy price supports. She turned down many opportunities for national appearances; only after September 11 did she appear again on *Meet the Press*, in December 2001. She worked hard in the Senate, attending just about every committee and subcommittee hearing, spending time on the floor, approaching Republican colleagues to ask if she could co-sponsor their bills. At Democratic caucus meetings, she would get coffee for other senators. Republicans found themselves sheepishly admitting they like her. At the same time, by all accounts she has taken a hard partisan line behind closed doors. She advised Tom Daschle that Senate Democrats should have a war room, as the Clinton campaign and White House did. She supported George W. Bush in the war on terrorism and voted for the Iraq war resolution, and told him in their meeting on September 13, 2001, that she was one of the few who understood the loneliness of the White House, but she advised down-the-line opposition to his domestic policies. Occasionally in public she sounded a partisan note. In May 2001 she cast the single vote against the Justice Department confirmation of Michael Chertoff, who had worked on the Whitewater independent counsel investigation. HILLPAC, her leadership PAC, raised $3.2 million in the 2002 cycle and contributed more than $1 million to Democrats across the country, including $21,000 in Iowa and $15,000 in New Hampshire; she put on fundraisers for fellow Democrats in her Washington house.

Clinton's propensity for bipartisanship and her partisanship were both on display at the opening of the 108th Congress in January 2003. In December she had gotten agreement with Don Nickles on a compromise proposal to extend unemployment benefits. It was the first item of business in the new Congress. But unexpectedly Clinton rose and offered an amendment to extend coverage to 1 million people whose benefits had expired. This triggered several hours of debate on parliamentary motions—a tough initiation for the new Majority Leader Bill Frist.

Eventually Clinton's amendment was rejected and a compromise was passed. In the new Congress, Clinton was elected head of the Democrats' Steering and Coordination Committee, a job that has never generated much publicity for its incumbent; but this gives her an institutional base for her behind-the-scenes partisan strategizing. She got a seat on the Armed Services Committee, on which no New York senator had served for years, and worked methodically on defense issues, seeking better pay and benefits for service members, visiting troops in Afghanistan, Iraq and elsewhere, arguing against base closings, as she did at Stewart Air National Guard Base. Lindsey Graham, who co-sponsored benefit increases with her, said, "People may think she has an antimilitary bias or is not strong on defense. But I find her to be very reasonable. I think she has been responsible in making sure the men and women in the military are well taken care of." Committee Chairman John Warner praised her as well: "She comports herself in a way consistent with the bipartisan reputation of the committee. I've not seen her try to grandstand." With Jim Talent, she passed a bill in 2004 providing a tracking system and regular health screening for military personnel, with a view toward preventing service-related illness like Gulf war syndrome. She pressed for hearings on insurance sales on military bases. She introduced a bill for federal aid for localities that lose first responders to National Guard and Reserve call-ups.

Clinton voted for the Iraq war resolution in October 2002 and did not flinch from supporting it later; she voted for the $87 billion supplemental in November 2003. "The fact is we're in Iraq and we're in Afghanistan, and we have no choice but to be successful," she said in December 2003. In spring 2004, when other Democratic senators were flocking to the premiere of Michael Moore's "Fahrenheit 9/11," she said Saddam Hussein was "a potential threat" who "was seeking weapons of mass destruction, whether or not he actually had them." She was critical of the conduct of operations, however. After a trip to Iraq in December 2003, she said, "Everybody told me we don't have enough intelligence, civil affairs, MPs, engineers." She said that the Bush administration wasn't "leveling with the American people about what it is we're up against, how long it's going to take, how much it's going to cost."

On domestic policy she described the administration as "radical," bent on dismantling the "central pillars of progress in our country during the 20th century" and seeking "to undo the New Deal." It was "making America less free, less fair, less strong and smart than it deserves to be in a dangerous world." But her specific proposals were more incremental and less confrontational. Worried about manufacturing job losses in Upstate New York, she called for a Manufacturing Research Agency in the Commerce Department. In April 2004 she sponsored a bill to spend $2.5 billion on making education universal, for girls as well as boys, around the world. In September 2004, with Nita Lowey, she sponsored a bill, backed by teachers unions, to increase spending on the 2002 education act. She spoke out forcefully against illegal immigration and said that George W. Bush has not "protected our borders."

On homeland security, Clinton got passed in September 2004 amendments providing $50 million for nonprofits and community organizations vulnerable to terrorist threats and $570 million to safeguard New York's trains and tunnels. Clinton had cast lone votes against Michael Chertoff, the onetime Whitewater investigator, for a Justice Department position and a judgeship, but when he was nominated for Homeland Security secretary in January 2005 she said coolly, "I look forward to meetings with Judge Chertoff in the very near future to discuss many important issues, including the specific homeland security needs of New York as well as the many homeland security challenges confronting our nation." She voted for his confirmation: working for homeland security for New York and the nation was evidently more important than any personal grudge. She returned to the White House for the unveiling of her and her husband's portraits in June 2004, just before Bill Clinton's *My Life* was released; gracious statements were made all round. At the July 2004 Democratic National Convention she spoke briefly but heartily in favor of John Kerry's candidacy, and stood aside gracefully to let him and John Edwards get most of the attention. Cynics opined that she wanted Kerry to lose, so she could run in 2008. But she campaigned in more than a dozen states for him.

But she made it plain after the November 2004 election that she took a different approach. When Kerry's defeat was blamed on values issues, she commented, "I don't think you can win an election or even run a successful campaign if you don't acknowledge what is important to people. We don't have to agree with them. But being ignored is a sign of such disrespect. And therefore I think we should talk about these issues." In January 2005, speaking to abortion rights supporters in Albany, she surprised many in the audience by saying, "Yes, we do have deeply held differences of opinion about the issue of abortion, and I, for one, respect those who believe with all their hearts and conscience that there are no circumstances under which any abortion should ever be available. There is an opportunity for people of good faith to find common ground in this debate. We should be able to agree that we want every child born in this country to be wanted, cherished and loved. We can all recognize that abortion in many ways represents a sad, even tragic choice to many, many women." She continued to support a partial-birth abortion ban only with an exception for the health of the mother and parental notification only with a judicial bypass. While many Democrats were skeptical of government aid to faith-based service providers, Clinton said, "There is no contradiction between support for faith-based initiatives and upholding our constitutional principles."

Clinton comes up for reelection in New York in 2006, and no one doubts that she can win; her poll ratings in 2004 were very high, and in every region of the state. Congressmen Vito Fossella and Peter King in late 2004 urged Colin Powell to return to the state and run against her, but he showed no sign of interest. The indictment in January 2005 of one of her 2000 campaign fundraisers for underreporting in-kind contributions to Hollywood fundraisers did not seem to have a major impact. In early 2005 there was word that her Republican opponent might be Manhattan lawyer Edward Cox, Richard Nixon's son-in-law, who seemed likely to be able to raise serious money and wage a serious campaign; another possible candidate was Jeanine Pirro, district attorney of Westchester County. Former Yonkers Mayor John Spencer said in June 2005 that he would run. But since the institution of popular election of senators, no Democratic senator from New York has been defeated for reelection.

In June 2003 her book *Living History* was released; she promoted it assiduously and it became a runaway bestseller. In early 2005 Hillary Rodham Clinton seemed to be the favorite for the Democratic presidential nomination in 2008. During her first four years in the Senate she eschewed presidential ambitions and said she was only interested in serving out her term. During the 2006 campaign she will undoubtedly be asked whether she will run in 2008, and undoubtedly she will have a stock response not ruling it out; New Yorkers have never shown much resentment when their officeholders run for president. Will Americans accept a woman, and a former First Lady, as president? Nations as diverse as Britain, India, Indonesia, the Philippines and Nicaragua have elected women as heads of government—in three cases women who were the daughters of former heads of government. In November 2004 she noted humorously that a woman was running for president in Afghanistan, "a feat that puts Afghanistan women ahead of American women." Clinton's firm stand on Iraq and her familiarity with military and defense issues from her seat on Armed Services could assure many that she is qualified to be commander-in-chief; she has gone some distance toward inoculating herself against the charge often made against Democrats, that she is soft on defense. Her statements on abortion and other values issues show her to be one Democrat determined not to repel cultural conservatives by condescension or contempt. She does tend to polarize the electorate and has a large core of detractors, but she also had a large core of those with strong positive feelings: the same that could be said of George W. Bush, and he won. The electorate was closely divided in 2004, and it would be unwise at this distance to write off the chances of any Democratic nominee in 2008, especially one this hard-working and determined.

FIRST DISTRICT

Rep. Tim Bishop (D)

Elected 2002, 2d term; b. June 1, 1950, Southampton; home, Southampton; Holy Cross Col., A.B. 1972; Long Island U., M.P.A. 1981; Catholic; married (Kathy).

Professional Career: Admin., Southampton College, 1973–02.

DC Office: 1133 LHOB, 20515, 202-225-3826; Fax: 202-225-3143; Web site: www.house.gov/timbishop/.

District Offices: Coram, 631-696-6500; Southampton, 631-259-8450.

Committees: *Education & the Workforce* (21st of 22 D): 21st Century Competitiveness; Workforce Protections. *Transportation & Infrastructure* (27th of 34 D): Highways, Transit & Pipelines; Water Resources & Environment.

Group Ratings

	ADA	ACLU	AFS	LCV	ITIC	NTU	COC	ACU	NTLC	CHC
2004	100	75	100	100	40	11	48	4	0	16
2003	90	—	100	100	—	19	30	12	—	—

National Journal Ratings

	2003 LIB	—	2003 CONS		2004 LIB	—	2004 CONS
Economic	77%	—	21%		73%	—	27%
Social	75%	—	24%		70%	—	29%
Foreign	75%	—	21%		62%	—	36%

Key Votes of the 108th Congress

1. Drilling in ANWR	N	5. DC School Vouchers	N	9. Ban Same-Sex Marriage	N
2. Approve Bush Tax Cuts	N	6. Ban Human Cloning	N	10. Fund Iraq War	Y
3. Medicare/Rx Bill	N	7. Restrict Gun Liability	N	11. Bar Cuba Embargo Funds	Y
4. Bar Overtime Pay Regs.	Y	8. Ban Partial-Birth Abortion	N	12. Intelligence Reorg.	Y

Election Results

2004 general	Tim Bishop (D-Ind-WF)	156,354	(56%)	($1,908,440)
	William Manger (R-C)	121,855	(44%)	($1,385,362)
2004 primary	Tim Bishop (D)	unopposed		
2002 general	Tim Bishop (D-WF)	84,276	(50%)	($972,095)
	Felix Grucci (R-C-Ind-RTL)	81,524	(49%)	($1,399,768)
	Other	1,991	(1%)	

The People		Race/Ethnic Origin	Ancestry
Area size:	1,944 sq. mi.	84.5% White	Italian: 21.1% Irish: 17.5%
Urban population:	94.0%	4.0% Black	German: 13.7%
Rural population:	6.0%	2.4% Asian	**2004 Presidential Vote**
Pop. 2000:	654,360	0.3% Native Am.	Bush (R) 154,249 (49%)
Median income:	$61,884	0.0% Hawaiian	Kerry (D) 152,165 (49%)
Poverty status:	6.0%	1.2% Two+ races	Other 5,991 (2%)
Military veterans:	12.1%	0.1% Other	**2000 Presidential Vote**
		7.5% Hispanic Origin	Gore (D) 139,490 (52%)
			Bush (R) 116,308 (44%)
			Other 10,705 (4%)
			Cook Partisan Voting Index: D + 3

Occupation	Blue collar: 20.3%	White collar: 64.4%	Gray collar: 15.3%

Long Island—"the Island" to most New Yorkers—is America's largest, most populous and in some ways most troubled island. Long Island stretches 103 miles, from the two-century-old Montauk Point lighthouse at its eastern extremity to Fort Hamilton at the foot of the Verrazano Narrows

Bridge. Between 12 and 20 miles wide, Long Island is ringed by gentle hills and cliffs above Long Island Sound and sandspit beaches that front the Atlantic Ocean. Including Brooklyn and Queens, some 7.5 million people live on Long Island, more than in all but 11 states. Brooklyn, at the western end of the island, is urban and thickly settled, while the Hamptons in the east are carefully manicured countryside, preserved as a playground by a style-conscious New York elite. Demographically, the Hamptons are only a small (though growing) part of Long Island. More important are the (slower growing) suburbs created in the post-World War II rush out of the city.

Developers looking for cheaper land for aircraft factories, shopping centers, subdivisions or office parks found them first in Nassau County, just east of Queens, and then further out in Suffolk County. Suffolk attracted young families, of Irish and Italian descent more often than Jewish or black, looking for more space and less crime than the city could offer. More recently Suffolk County has been attracting Latinos, Salvadorans as well as Puerto Ricans, in many of its lower income areas, increasingly so since 2000.

In the last two decades of the 20th century, life in Long Island turned sour, as defense plants were decimated by the end of the Cold War and cost overruns on nuclear plants led to electricity rate increases. But the Bush administration's defense buildup has resulted in more defense jobs here, and the Long Island Power Authority wants to build underwater cables to bring more energy from Connecticut across Long Island Sound.

Such upheavals, combined with partisan rivalries, have fed political turbulence. The 1st Congressional District of New York, consisting of the eastern end of Long Island, ousted its incumbent congressmen in both 2000 and 2002, the only district to do so. The 1st covers eastern Suffolk County, now more populous (1.47 million people) and faster growing (12% growth from 1990 to 2004) than Nassau County, its neighbor to the west. The district runs as far east as Smithtown on the North Shore and Patchogue on the South Shore. It also includes Shelter Island, located between the north and south fork of Long Island's "fishtail," and Plum Island, home to the U.S. Department of Agriculture's only animal infection research site. Some farmers continue to grow sweet corn and pumpkins. The 1st includes two areas frequented in the summer by urban sophisticates: all of the Hamptons, and most of Fire Island National Seashore, the only federal wilderness area in New York state, and a magnet for gay vacationers for decades. Politically, however, the more important areas are the Brookhaven National Laboratory and the defense plants in the center of the Island. Suffolk County was long one of the most conservative parts of New York, though not very conservative by today's national standards. Republican voter registration remains high, and Suffolk voted strongly for Governor George Pataki's reelection in 2002 and for county native Rick Lazio in the 2000 Senate race against Hillary Rodham Clinton. It voted solidly for Al Gore in 2000 but made a big swing toward George W. Bush in 2004, giving him a narrow winning margin.

The congressman from the 1st District is Tim Bishop, a Democrat first elected in 2002. He grew up in Southampton and graduated from Holy Cross College and Long Island University. He spent his entire professional career at Southampton College, where he began in 1973 as an admissions counselor and in 1986 became provost. He chaired the town of Southampton's board of ethics and was on the board of the Eastern Long Island Coastal Conservation Alliance. Few paid much attention when Bishop announced in March 2002 he would oppose Felix Grucci, the first-term Republican congressman, who had won the seat in a bizarre contest in 2000: Mike Forbes, a Republican elected in 1994 as part of the Gingrich revolution, switched parties in July 1999, then lost the low-turnout Democratic primary by 35 votes to Regina Seltzer, a 71-year-old retired librarian, and Grucci easily won the general, 56%–41%. In the House, Grucci had a moderate-to-conservative voting record typical for a New York Republican. Grucci seemed headed for reelection when, in late September, he ran an ad accusing Bishop of falsifying rape statistics at Southampton College and "turning his back on rape victims." This turned out to be untrue. The basis for the allegations had been several articles in the college newspaper; the articles turned out to be so riddled with inaccuracies that the editors of the student newspaper voluntarily retrieved every copy of the newspaper they could find. Grucci's campaign refused to repudiate the ad, on the ground that no correction had ever appeared in print. House Democrats' campaign committee quickly saw an opportunity to pick up a seat. Soon the airwaves became saturated with ads attacking Grucci both for the rape commercial and for his environmental voting record. In one spot, which began airing before the rape ad, the Grucci family's famed fireworks enterprise was linked to the chemical contamination of local drinking water. National Republican Congressional Committee operatives privately fumed that Grucci had failed to tell them about the college rape ad and that he had blundered in standing by his charges and failing to offer a positive message. This was one of the closest House races in the nation. The official result was delayed a week by a recount and Grucci did not concede until ten days after the election; Bishop won 50%–49%.

In the House, Bishop had a voting record near the center of the Democratic caucus. He opposed the war in Iraq and supported abortion rights and a rollback of the Bush tax cuts. Reflecting his professional background, he played a leading role on the Education and the Workforce Committee during the higher education reauthorization debate; he also opposed cutbacks in the Pell Grant program and co-sponsored a bill to prohibit the Department of Education from using updates to the Federal Needs Analysis Methodology to reduce federal grants for students.

Republicans quickly identified Bishop as one of their top targets for 2004. After several potentially strong candidates decided not to run, Bill Manger became the Republican nominee. Manger, who served four years as a village trustee in Southampton and was a top adviser to Rick Lazio in his Senate race, emphasized his independence from national Republicans and attacked Bishop for opposing tax cuts, including those for members of the military. He got campaign visits from Rudy Giuliani and Speaker Dennis Hastert but that wasn't nearly enough. Bishop won handily, 56%–44%. But this is a district that could be seriously contested again.

SECOND DISTRICT

Rep. Steve Israel (D)

Elected 2000, 3d term; b. May 30, 1958, Brooklyn; home, Dix Hills; George Wash. U., B.A. 1983; Jewish; married (Marlene Budd).

Elected Office: Huntington Town Bd., 1993–00, Maj. Ldr., 1997–00.

Professional Career: Legis. Asst., U.S. Rep. Richard Ottinger, 1980–83; Fundraising Dir., Touro Law Ctr., 1985–88; Pres., Steve Israel Assoc., Inc., 1992–98; Pres. & CEO, Inst. on Holocaust and Law, 1998–00.

DC Office: 432 CHOB, 20515, 202-225-3335; Fax: 202-225-4669; Web site: www.house.gov/israel.

District Office: Hauppauge, 631-951-2210.

Committees: *Armed Services* (18th of 28 D): Projection Forces; Tactical Air & Land Forces. *Financial Services* (20th of 32 D): Capital Markets, Insurance & Government Sponsored Enterprises; Financial Institutions & Consumer Credit.

Group Ratings

	ADA	ACLU	AFS	LCV	ITIC	NTU	COC	ACU	NTLC	CHC
2004	100	75	100	100	70	12	47	13	9	23
2003	90	—	100	100	—	18	47	24	—	—

National Journal Ratings

	2003 LIB	—	2003 CONS		2004 LIB	—	2004 CONS
Economic	62%	—	38%		72%	—	28%
Social	75%	—	24%		73%	—	25%
Foreign	59%	—	39%		61%	—	38%

Key Votes of the 108th Congress

1. Drilling in ANWR	N	5. DC School Vouchers	N	9. Ban Same-Sex Marriage	N
2. Approve Bush Tax Cuts	N	6. Ban Human Cloning	N	10. Fund Iraq War	Y
3. Medicare/Rx Bill		7. Restrict Gun Liability	N	11. Bar Cuba Embargo Funds	Y
4. Bar Overtime Pay Regs.	Y	8. Ban Partial-Birth Abortion	N	12. Intelligence Reorg.	Y

Election Results

2004 general	Steve Israel (D-Ind-WF)	161,593	(67%)	($1,077,719)
	Richard Hoffmann (R-C)	80,950	(33%)	($11,679)
2004 primary	Steve Israel (D)	unopposed		
2002 general	Steve Israel (D-Ind-WF)	85,451	(58%)	($1,416,138)
	Joseph Finley (R-C-RTL)	59,117	(40%)	
	Other	1,558	(1%)	

Prior Winning Percentages: 2000 (48%)

The People		Race/Ethnic Origin	Ancestry	
Area size:	330 sq. mi.	71.5% White	Italian: 18.8%	Irish: 14.1%
Urban population:	99.7%	9.8% Black	German: 10.3%	
Rural population:	0.3%	3.0% Asian	**2004 Presidential Vote**	
Pop. 2000:	654,360	0.2% Native Am.	Kerry (D) 148,625	(53%)
Median income:	$71,147	0.0% Hawaiian	Bush (R) 127,626	(45%)
Poverty status:	5.9%	1.4% Two+ races	Other 5,569	(2%)
Military veterans:	10.6%	0.2% Other	**2000 Presidential Vote**	
		13.9% Hispanic Origin	Gore (D) 146,723	(57%)
			Bush (R) 100,708	(39%)
			Other 8,165	(3%)
			Cook Partisan Voting Index: D + 8	

Occupation	Blue collar: 20.1%	White collar: 66.3%	Gray collar: 13.6%

Shortly after World War II, hundreds of thousands of New York City residents, many of them young veterans and their families, moved to detached suburban homes built on the former potato fields of central Long Island. Those in the first wave of postwar migration settled in Nassau County, and they included a cross-section of all but the poorest New Yorkers: roughly half Catholic, a quarter Protestant and a quarter Jewish. As Long Island developed its own employment base, another wave moved further east into Suffolk County. This group was more Catholic, less Jewish and more blue-collar than the first. Ancestrally Democratic, these voters were culturally conservative, and in the 1970s and 1980s, they tended to vote Republican. But in the 1990s, voters in Suffolk County joined the rest of the New York metro area in shunning a Republican party that was being run increasingly by politicians with southern accents.

The 2d Congressional District of New York includes most of western Suffolk County, part of the town of Islip and a small portion of Nassau County—Plainview, Woodbury and part of Jericho. For the most part, the 2d is the humbler part of Long Island: further east than most of the fashionable commuter suburbs, well south of the picturesque North Shore, not as far east as the ritzy Hamptons, and, aside from a handful of ferry-only resort towns on Fire Island, located inland from the southern shore. With some of the lowest-priced housing on the Island, this part of Long Island has been attracting young families and minorities. Brentwood, settled in 1851 as part of a free-love social experiment that lasted 13 years, is now more than half Hispanic; once a destination for Puerto Ricans, Brentwood is increasingly populated by Salvadorans, Guatemalans and Mexicans. For decades, it has been the state's largest Latino community after New York City and Yonkers. Illegal immigration has been a divisive issue in Suffolk County; in 2004, Democratic County Executive Steve Levy proposed getting police certified to enforce immigration law but the plan was later withdrawn. Though the 2d is historically Republican, it voted for Al Gore and John Kerry in 2000 and 2004. George W. Bush's performance spiked here in 2004, but not by enough to carry the district.

The congressman from the 2d District is Steve Israel, a Democrat first elected in 2000. He grew up in Wantagh and graduated from George Washington University in 1983. While in college, he worked full-time on Capitol Hill, first as a constituent correspondent for Robert Matsui of California, then as a legislative assistant for Richard Ottinger of New York. After college Israel returned to Long Island, where he was Suffolk director for the American Jewish Congress, fundraising director for Touro Law School and assistant for intergovernmental relations to Suffolk County Executive Patrick Halpin for three years. Then he started his own public relations and marketing firm and was president and CEO of the Institute on the Holocaust and the Law. In 1993 Israel was the only Democrat elected to the Huntington Town Council, where he made a reputation as a bipartisan leader who helped revive the town's finances.

Israel had not been planning to run until May 2000 when Rudolph Giuliani suddenly dropped out of the Senate race against Hillary Rodham Clinton and 2d District incumbent Rick Lazio announced he was running for the Senate. In the September primary, Israel squeaked out a 45%–41% victory. In the general, Republican Joan Johnson had an appealing story. A 66-year old Florida native who grew up in segregated areas and moved to New York to become a schoolteacher, she would have been the first black Republican woman elected to Congress. As the elected town clerk of Islip since 1991, she had the Suffolk County party's supposed organizational muscle behind her. But, despite help from Lazio, Johnson was a disappointing candidate. She pulled a TV ad attacking Israel for voting to raise taxes after Israel protested that he had opposed tax increases. Israel won by a surprisingly easy 48%–35%.

In the House, Israel's voting record is moderate but a tad more liberal on cultural issues. He showed an early sign of his connections and knowledge of House politics when he was elected as the freshman on the Democratic Steering Committee. Israel joined the Blue Dogs and was one of 28 House Democrats who voted for the House-Senate agreement on George W. Bush's tax cuts; he supported the use of force in Iraq, but opposed trade promotion authority. After irritating Democratic leaders by voting for the Republicans' prescription drug bill in 2002 because of a provision that increased annual Medicare payments to HMOs on Long Island, he partly redeemed himself with Democratic leaders by voting against the Medicare/prescription drug bill in 2003. But Israel also burned some bridges when he favored Steny Hoyer over Nancy Pelosi in their contest for minority whip. He said that national Democrats should study the success of centrist Democrats on Long Island. They prevailed locally, he said, by protecting national security, balanced budgets, and civil and human rights. The party icon, Israel added, should be former Senator Scoop Jackson of Washington, not Walter Mondale—a message not likely to be embraced by many of his House Democratic colleagues. In the spirit of Jackson, he called for requiring commercial airlines to be equipped with defenses against should-fired missiles. He filed another proposal to extend the filing period for Holocaust-era insurance claims and to reaffirm states' rights to demand information from insurers about their policies at the time.

When Lazio decided not to run again in March 2002, local Republicans grumbled about his delay in deciding, and quietly threw in the towel. Israel's opponent, a New York City firefighter who was off duty on September 11 but worked many days in the recovery search and suffered lung damage, was outspent 10–1, and Israel won 58%–40%. In 2004 Israel won 67%–33%.

THIRD DISTRICT

Rep. Peter King (R)

Elected 1992, 7th term; b. Apr. 5, 1944, Manhattan; home, Seaford; St. Francis Col., B.A. 1965, U. of Notre Dame, J.D. 1968; Catholic; married (Rosemary).

Military Career: Army Natl. Guard, 1968–73.

Elected Office: Hempstead Town Cncl., 1977–81; Nassau Cnty. Comptroller, 1981–92.

Professional Career: Practicing atty., 1968–72, 1978–81; Dep. Atty., Nassau Cnty., 1972–74; Exec. Asst., Nassau Cnty. Exec., 1974–76, Gen. Cnsl., 1977.

DC Office: 436 CHOB, 20515, 202-225-7896; Fax: 202-226-2279; Web site: www.house.gov/king.

District Office: Massapequa Park, 516-541-4225.

Committees: *Financial Services* (7th of 37 R): Capital Markets, Insurance & Government Sponsored Enterprises; Housing & Community Opportunity. *Homeland Security* (6th of 19 R): Emergency Preparedness, Science & Technology (Chmn.); Intelligence, Information Sharing & Terrorism Risk Assessment. *International Relations* (9th of 27 R): Europe & Emerging Threats (Vice Chmn.); International Terrorism & Nonproliferation.

Group Ratings

	ADA	ACLU	AFS	LCV	ITIC	NTU	COC	ACU	NTLC	CHC
2004	25	10	38	27	80	46	80	71	70	76
2003	15	—	13	10	—	59	83	76	—	—

National Journal Ratings

	2003 LIB	—	2003 CONS		2004 LIB	—	2004 CONS
Economic	47%	—	52%		47%	—	53%
Social	24%	—	71%		46%	—	53%
Foreign	31%	—	65%		8%	—	92%

Key Votes of the 108th Congress

1. Drilling in ANWR	Y	5. DC School Vouchers	Y	9. Ban Same-Sex Marriage	Y
2. Approve Bush Tax Cuts	Y	6. Ban Human Cloning	Y	10. Fund Iraq War	Y
3. Medicare/Rx Bill	Y	7. Restrict Gun Liability	Y	11. Bar Cuba Embargo Funds	N
4. Bar Overtime Pay Regs.	Y	8. Ban Partial-Birth Abortion	Y	12. Intelligence Reorg.	Y

Election Results

2004 general	Peter King (R-C-Ind)	171,259	(63%)	($536,345)
	Blair Mathies (D)	100,737	(37%)	($212,580)
2004 primary	Peter King (R)	8,110	(84%)	
	Robert Previdi (R)	1,564	(16%)	
2002 general	Peter King (R-C-Ind-RTL)	121,537	(72%)	($468,474)
	Stuart Finz (D)	46,022	(27%)	($137,472)
	Other	1,513	(1%)	

Prior Winning Percentages: 2000 (60%); 1998 (64%); 1996 (55%); 1994 (59%); 1992 (50%)

The People		Race/Ethnic Origin	Ancestry	
Area size:	393 sq. mi.	86.9% White	Italian: 23.1%	Irish: 17.7%
Urban population:	99.6%	2.1% Black	German: 12.0%	
Rural population:	0.4%	3.0% Asian	**2004 Presidential Vote**	
Pop. 2000:	654,361	0.1% Native Am.	Bush (R) 162,181	(52%)
Median income:	$70,561	0.0% Hawaiian	Kerry (D) 147,317	(47%)
Poverty status:	4.3%	1.0% Two+ races	Other 4,332	(1%)
Military veterans:	11.8%	0.1% Other	**2000 Presidential Vote**	
		6.9% Hispanic Origin	Gore (D) 150,165	(52%)
			Bush (R) 127,869	(44%)
			Other 10,251	(4%)
			Cook Partisan Voting Index: D + 2	

Occupation   Blue collar: 17.0%   White collar: 69.3%   Gray collar: 13.6%

September 1947 was a pivotal moment in American history—the month when 300 families moved into 750-square-foot houses that sold for $6,990, with no money down for veterans. This was Levittown—America's first mass-produced suburb, where delivery trucks dropped off piles of prefabricated materials 60 feet apart, so that roving teams of specialized workers could assemble them with power tools. By the time the final house was sold for $9,500 in November 1951, Levittown, a onetime potato field, had become synonymous with instant suburbanization. Southern State Parkway, the road that drew New York City's working- and middle-class families out to Long Island, was originally constructed in the 1920s by the legendary city-builder Robert Moses as a way of linking New Yorkers (at least those affluent enough to own a car) with the newly constructed Jones Beach State Park on Long Island. Three decades later, Moses widened the parkway to accommodate the growing ranks of long-distance commuters who populated Long Island's bedroom communities and worked in New York City. More than a half-century later, aging Nassau County is all but built out; it is sometimes referred to as the nation's "first mature suburb." Nassau County's population, 450,000 in 1940, zoomed to 1.3 million in 1960 and 1.4 million in 1970. In recent years it has stabilized at 1.3 million.

Nassau County created what may have been the nation's premier county Republican machine, established before the postwar population boom. The result was one of the highest-salaried, highest-spending local governments in America—one that thrived until the late 1990s, when fiscal laxity dropped the county's credit rating to near junk-bond status, despite tax rates that were among the highest in the country. Voters rebelled in November 1999, giving Democrats their first-ever majority in the county legislature, and in 2001 elected Democrat Thomas Suozzi as county executive. He has not only shaken up local government, but also criticized New York state government for its imposition of costly mandates and tax increases, agreed to by Assembly Democrats and Senate Republicans; he not only opposes Republican incumbents in general elections but Democrats in primaries.

The 3d Congressional District of New York includes roughly half of Nassau County. It covers much of the southern shoreline of Long Island, taking in the old railroad resort of Long Beach, plus Baldwin, Merrick and Massapequa in Nassau County and Amityville, Lindenhurst, most of Babylon, Bay Shore and Islip in Suffolk County. From there, the 3d runs north all the way to Long Island Sound, where old estates—including Sagamore Hill, the home Theodore Roosevelt built on Cold Spring Harbor in 1885—alternate with more modest homes built for servants and newer subdivision mansions. Most of the people in the district live in towns strung along either side of Sunrise Highway or just off the Southern or Northern State Parkways: Levittown, Hicksville, Syosset and Bethpage, home to a major Northrop Grumman facility. While few of greater New York's wealthiest live in the 3d, the overall level of affluence is high. September 11 likely had an effect on voting here in 2004: Al Gore carried this suburban district by 52%–44% in 2000, but it broke sharply toward George W. Bush in 2004, giving him a 52%–47% win.

The congressman from the 3d District is Peter King, a Republican first elected in 1992. King grew up in Sunnyside, Queens; his parents were Irish immigrants and Democrats, his father an NYPD detective. He went to St. Francis College and law school at Notre Dame, and clerked one summer at Richard Nixon's law firm with a Long Islander named Rudolph Giuliani. After school he followed the trek to the suburbs and became part of the Nassau County Republican machine. He started working as a lawyer and staffer in county government in 1972, at 28; in 1981 he became county comptroller. When 22-year Republican Congressman Norman Lent retired in 1992, King won the Republican primary 2–1. In the general, King ran as a political insider, fiscal conservative and abortion opponent; he won by just 50%–46%. He has not faced a close reelection since then.

King has a middle-of-the-House voting record, more conservative on foreign issues, but with distinctive interests and accents. He is against abortion, racial quotas and preferences, bilingual education, gun control and the National Endowment for the Arts. He is for English-only laws and against aid to illegal immigrants.

He came to the House as one of the nation's strongest supporters of the Irish Republican Army; within days of his election in 1992 he flew to Belfast to meet with leaders of Sinn Fein, the IRA's political arm. In the 1998 negotiations finale, King carried messages between the IRA and the Irish government. But in March 2005, after Sinn Fein/IRA's suspected involvement in a recent bank robbery and a highly-publicized murder, King called for the IRA to disband. He often seems more comfortable with Democrats and labor leaders—the kind of people he dealt with in Nassau County, than with southern or western Republicans. At home, he has been a big booster of the East Side Access project to connect the Long Island Rail Road to Grand Central Station in Manhattan.

King joined John McCain on a proposal to create a federal boxing commission to set safety standards and improve disclosure of finances and conflicts of interest. After the September 11 attacks, in which 160 of his constituents died, King became more of a party regular. He hailed Bush's $20 billion spending pledge for New York City and state, and attacked Democrats' criticism of how that was handled. He stuck with Bush in his opposition to labor protections at the new Homeland Security Department. King worked with New York City officials to increase federal reimbursement of protection of foreign officials. He said that the Vatican, because of the abuses of children by Catholic priests, had no right to criticize the United States for its abuses of Iraqi prisoners. "You wonder where the Vatican's moral compass is," he said. He added that domestic critics of the Bush administration's handling of post-Saddam Iraq had overstated the problems.

Over the years, King has been a provocative presence on broadcast chat shows. "France is no longer a world power, Belgium never was and Germany started two world wars," he said in a 2003 BBC interview. He also gained attention with two novels about politics and diplomacy in Northern Ireland; Bill Clinton wrote a flattering blurb for *Deliver Us from Evil*, in which a thinly-disguised Long Island congressman is the protagonist. His latest novel, *Vale of Tears,* focused on Muslim extremists and their control of many mosques in the United States; some Democrats condemned his comments as inflammatory. After the 2004 election, he decried the woes of the New York Republican Party, including its loss of local offices in Nassau County, and said that it had "no overwhelming vision or course." In January 2005, his chairmanship of the Financial Services Subcommittee on Domestic and International Monetary Policy was switched to Deborah Pryce, who rejoined the panel, and King was left to chair a new subcommittee on emergency preparedness, science and technology at Homeland Security.

FOURTH DISTRICT

Rep. Carolyn McCarthy (D)

Elected 1996, 5th term; b. Jan. 5, 1944, Brooklyn; home, Mineola; Glen Cove Nursing Schl., L.P.N. 1964; Catholic; widowed.

Professional Career: Nurse, 1964–93; Gun control activist, 1993–96.

DC Office: 106 CHOB, 20515, 202-225-5516; Fax: 202-225-5758; Web site: www.house.gov/carolynmccarthy.

District Office: Garden City, 516-739-3008.

Committees: *Education & the Workforce* (9th of 22 D): 21st Century Competitiveness; Employer-Employee Relations. *Financial Services* (21st of 32 D): Capital Markets, Insurance & Government Sponsored Enterprises; Financial Institutions & Consumer Credit.

Group Ratings

	ADA	ACLU	AFS	LCV	ITIC	NTU	COC	ACU	NTLC	CHC
2004	100	70	100	100	60	11	45	12	3	16
2003	85	—	100	95	—	22	40	28	—	—

National Journal Ratings

	2003 LIB	—	2003 CONS	2004 LIB	—	2004 CONS
Economic	64%	—	35%	73%	—	27%
Social	74%	—	25%	73%	—	25%
Foreign	75%	—	21%	59%	—	40%

Key Votes of the 108th Congress

1. Drilling in ANWR	N	5. DC School Vouchers	N	9. Ban Same-Sex Marriage	N
2. Approve Bush Tax Cuts	N	6. Ban Human Cloning	*	10. Fund Iraq War	Y
3. Medicare/Rx Bill	N	7. Restrict Gun Liability	N	11. Bar Cuba Embargo Funds	Y
4. Bar Overtime Pay Regs.	Y	8. Ban Partial-Birth Abortion	N	12. Intelligence Reorg.	Y

Election Results

2004 general	Carolyn McCarthy (D-Ind-WF)	159,969	(63%)	($1,688,005)
	James Garner (R-C)	94,141	(37%)	($304,521)
2004 primary	Carolyn McCarthy (D) .... unopposed			
2002 general	Carolyn McCarthy (D-L-Ind-WF).................	94,806	(56%)	($1,794,931)
	Marilyn O'Grady (R-C-RTL)	72,882	(43%)	($318,694)
	Other...	852	(1%)	

Prior Winning Percentages: 2000 (61%); 1998 (53%); 1996 (57%)

The People		Race/Ethnic Origin	Ancestry		
Area size:	103 sq. mi.	62.3% White	Italian: 17.5%	Irish: 12.4%	
Urban population:	100.0%	17.6% Black	German: 8.0%		
Rural population:	0.0%	4.5% Asian	**2004 Presidential Vote**		
Pop. 2000:	654,360	0.1% Native Am.	Kerry (D) 153,546	(55%)	
Median income:	$66,799	0.0% Hawaiian	Bush (R) 124,617	(44%)	
Poverty status:	6.4%	1.6% Two+ races	Other 3,178	(1%)	
Military veterans:	9.9%	0.3% Other	**2000 Presidential Vote**		
		13.6% Hispanic Origin	Gore (D) 156,276	(59%)	
			Bush (R) 99,263	(38%)	
			Other 8,612	(3%)	
			Cook Partisan Voting Index: D + 9		

Occupation   Blue collar: 16.6%   White collar: 67.9%   Gray collar: 15.5%

By the mid-20th century, Nassau County changed from almost entirely rural to almost entirely suburban. One of its first suburbs was Garden City, with its wide avenues and single-family homes, laid out more than a century ago by New York retailer A.T. Stewart at a time when reformers were urging that new communities retain the commercial vitality and social interaction of the city within a setting that preserved the healthful openness of the countryside. After World War II, freeways replaced strip highways and shopping centers sprang up at intersections, but many of the middle- and upper-income residents here continue to depend on the Long Island Railroad to get them to jobs in New York City. Garden City has maintained its high real estate prices and is now surrounded by some of Nassau County's key institutions: the county seat of Mineola; Hofstra University in Hempstead; Roosevelt Field, where Charles Lindbergh took off for Paris, now a shopping center; and the Nassau Coliseum.

The 4th Congressional District of New York includes Garden City and the towns all around. It has several suburbs just north of the Jericho Turnpike—New Hyde Park, Mineola, Westbury—as well as a large swath of southern Nassau County east of the Queens County line. This territory includes communities like Uniondale, Hempstead, Rockville Center and Valley Stream, as well as the "Five Towns"—the railway suburbs of Lawrence, Inwood, Cedarhurst, Hewlett and Woodmere. Nassau County has traditionally been Republican, and both Garden City and heavily Catholic East Meadow remain that way. But the Five Towns are heavily Democratic, and about one-third of the district's residents are black or Hispanic. Elmont, near the Queens line, once heavily white, now has a large Caribbean and Latin American population. The traditional Republican heritage in the 4th District is becoming a dim memory; the county legislature is now led by a Democratic majority.

The congresswoman from the 4th District is Carolyn McCarthy, a Democrat first elected in 1996. She was born in Brooklyn, trained as a nurse, married and raised a family on Long Island; originally, she was a Republican. In 1993 her husband was killed and her son seriously injured in the "Long Island Railroad Massacre," when a gunman opened fire on passengers as the train crossed the Nassau County line. McCarthy spoke movingly at the killer's trial and her strength in tragedy won many admirers. She began campaigning for gun control, and in 1995 lobbied her Congressman Daniel Frisa to vote against repeal of the assault weapons ban, unsuccessfully. McCarthy inquired about running against Frisa in the primary, but Nassau County Republicans discouraged this. But Democrats had been eyeing the seat for some time and recruited her. McCarthy initially knew little about politics. When told that Minority Leader Dick Gephardt wanted to meet her, she reportedly asked, "Who's Dick Gephardt?" But she learned quickly. As the Democratic nominee, she called for gun control and attacked Frisa as too close to Newt Gingrich. Frisa disappeared in the campaign's final week, did not show up at his election night party and never made a concession statement. McCarthy won 57%–41%.

In the House, McCarthy compiled a moderately liberal voting record and passionately sponsored gun control measures. She called for childproof locks on handguns, fines for parents if a child gets a handgun and shows it in public and jail terms if a crime is committed with a gun. With support from the NRA, the House approved her bill to assist states to gain more access to the federal background check system for gun buyers. The sniper spree in the Washington D.C. area gave her the opportunity to gain approval in the House of her bill—the Our Lady of Peace Act—to strengthen laws prohibiting the mentally ill from buying guns, again with NRA backing. In 2004, she led the unsuccessful effort to force a House vote on extending the assault weapon ban, which expired in September. Majority Leader Tom DeLay said that there were not enough votes to extend the ban and refused to schedule a vote; McCarthy criticized George W. Bush for "winking" at the NRA on the issue, but she also blamed Democrats for their lack of support. She continued her crusade with a call to ban .50 caliber sniper rifles. She worked with Nassau County school officials on a strategy to combat the growing problem of gangs and got a $500,000 appropriation to support local initiatives.

As she gained experience, McCarthy broadened her portfolio, using her experience as a mother and nurse to take an interest in education and health-care issues. She worked on HMO regulation with John Dingell, who had opposed her on some gun issues. She stood at Bush's side in 2002 when he signed her bill to give incentives to hospitals in hiring more nurses and remedy the acute shortages. She surprised people on some votes, opposing the partial-birth abortion ban and backing the use of force in Iraq.

At home, Republicans have thrashed around to line up opposition. She had a tough time in 2002, when she was challenged by ophthalmologist Marilyn O'Grady, who took a hard line on terrorism and immigration, opposed abortions, and ran ads that attacked McCarthy for taking a 1998 contribution from Barbra Streisand. Although O'Grady received little national attention or party support, McCarthy's margin shrunk to 56%–43%. In 2004, James Garner, the mayor of Hempstead and head of the U.S. Conference of Mayors, sought to rally support as a black Republican and called McCarthy a one-issue lawmaker. But Garner was criticized for local problems in Hempstead, and national Republicans showed no indication that they viewed this district as an opportunity. McCarthy scored her biggest win, 63%–37%.

FIFTH DISTRICT

Rep. Gary Ackerman (D)

Elected Mar. 1983, 11th full term; b. Nov. 19, 1942, Brooklyn; home, Jamaica Estates; Queens Col., B.A. 1965; Jewish; married (Rita).

Elected Office: NY Senate, 1978–83.

Professional Career: Jr. High schl. teacher, 1966–70; Editor & publisher, *Queens Tribune*, 1970–78; Pres., advertising agcy., 1972–78.

DC Office: 2243 RHOB, 20515, 202-225-2601; Fax: 202-225-1589; Web site: www.house.gov/ackerman.

District Office: Bayside, 718-423-2154.

Committees: *Financial Services* (8th of 32 D): Capital Markets, Insurance & Government Sponsored Enterprises; Financial Institutions & Consumer Credit. *International Relations* (3d of 23 D): Asia & the Pacific; Middle East & Central Asia (RMM).

Group Ratings

	ADA	ACLU	AFS	LCV	ITIC	NTU	COC	ACU	NTLC	CHC
2004	95	80	100	100	56	9	41	4	0	9
2003	95	—	100	90	—	21	26	13	—	—

National Journal Ratings

	2003 LIB	—	2003 CONS		2004 LIB	—	2004 CONS
Economic	91%	—	8%		83%	—	16%
Social	82%	—	18%		85%	—	14%
Foreign	59%	—	39%		71%	—	29%

Key Votes of the 108th Congress

1. Drilling in ANWR	N	5. DC School Vouchers	N	9. Ban Same-Sex Marriage	N
2. Approve Bush Tax Cuts	N	6. Ban Human Cloning	*	10. Fund Iraq War	Y
3. Medicare/Rx Bill	N	7. Restrict Gun Liability	N	11. Bar Cuba Embargo Funds	N
4. Bar Overtime Pay Regs.	Y	8. Ban Partial-Birth Abortion	N	12. Intelligence Reorg.	N

Election Results

2004 general	Gary Ackerman (D-Ind-WF)	119,726	(71%)	($675,631)
	Stephen Graves (R-C)	46,867	(28%)	
	Other	1,248	(1%)	
2004 primary	Gary Ackerman (D) .... unopposed			
2002 general	Gary Ackerman (D-L-Ind-WF)	68,773	(92%)	($630,086)
	Perry Reich (C)	5,718	(8%)	

Prior Winning Percentages: 2000 (68%); 1998 (65%); 1996 (64%); 1994 (55%); 1992 (52%); 1990 (100%); 1988 (100%); 1986 (77%); 1984 (69%); 1983 (49%)

The People		Race/Ethnic Origin	Ancestry	
Area size:	85 sq. mi.	44.2% White	Italian: 9.7%	Irish: 5.8%
Urban population:	100.0%	5.1% Black	German: 3.7%	
Rural population:	0.0%	24.5% Asian	**2004 Presidential Vote**	
Pop. 2000:	654,361	0.1% Native Am.	Kerry (D) 128,252	(63%)
Median income:	$51,156	0.0% Hawaiian	Bush (R) 74,635	(36%)
Poverty status:	12.1%	2.1% Two+ races	Other 1,834	(1%)
Military veterans:	6.7%	0.4% Other	**2000 Presidential Vote**	
		23.5% Hispanic Origin	Gore (D) 127,288	(67%)
			Bush (R) 56,027	(30%)
			Other 6,256	(3%)
			Cook Partisan Voting Index: D +18	

Occupation	Blue collar: 18.2%	White collar: 65.2%	Gray collar: 16.6%

Queens is to most Americans the mystery borough, little known though it contains both LaGuardia and Kennedy airports. Some of it is almost suburban: Bayside, Douglaston and Little Neck are upper-middle income neighborhoods far beyond the subway lines, with detached houses with driveways and views across the water. Other Queens neighborhoods are more modest, with crowded houses on side streets and apartment buildings on avenues. In the past two decades, Queens has become the number one immigrant destination in New York City and quite possibly the most diverse place in the world. Corona was once predominantly Italian and black (Louis Armstrong, Duke Ellington and Malcolm X lived here); today, there is a large Latin American community, with large numbers of Dominicans and also many Asians—a modern-day melting pot. Flushing, for many years a modest-income Jewish and white ethnic neighborhood is now the biggest Asian neighborhood in New York. West of 138th Street it is dominated by Taiwanese and ethnic Chinese from Malaysia, Vietnam and Thailand; shops there have a more urban, "Chinatown" feel. East of 138th Street is predominantly Korean, with development following a more suburban pattern. As Chinese businesses moved into Flushing's Main Street commercial strip, Korean storeowners moved east to Union Street, a major north-south artery, and Northern Boulevard. In 2004, Chinese businessman Jimmy Meng from Flushing defeated long-time machine incumbent Barry Grodenchik in a Democratic primary for the state Assembly, amid predictions that the political power of local Asians would rapidly increase. Just east of Flushing is Flushing Meadow, the huge drainage basin and former dumping ground that hosted two World's Fairs (1939 and 1964) and which now is home to the U.S. Open tennis tournament, and countless informal soccer games played among Queens' many immigrant groups.

Just a few miles but a world away is the North Shore of Long Island. For a century it has had an upper-crust ambiance—peninsulas jutting out into Long Island Sound, the vast green lawns, and the great capitalist mansions that inspired East Egg and West Egg in *The Great Gatsby*. In the 19th century, millionaires used steam yachts to commute from Manhattan to their estates here. During Prohibition, the richest people in business and entertainment spent their leisure time playing croquet while their servants unloaded bootleggers' shipments at private docks.

Inland, behind the expansive lawns, Long Island was still farm country, with little villages clustered at railroad stations, occasional colonial era houses, and acres of billboard-strewn wasteland along the highways to New York City. By the middle of the 20th century, the city grew out, and the Great Neck and Sands Point peninsulas became affluent, predominantly Jewish suburbs with thick hedges enveloping stately Tudor homes.

The 5th Congressional District of New York takes in this territory in Queens and suburban Nassau County. It includes most of Queens east of Flushing Meadow and north of Union Turnpike—Flushing, Bayside, Douglaston, Little Neck (but not the airports). And it includes the northwest corner of Nassau County—Great Neck, Sands Point, and Lake Success, Port Washington, and Kings Point, home of the U.S. Merchant Marine Academy. Both the Queens and Nassau County portions of the district have long voted heavily Democratic, but it's difficult to predict the future voting preferences of Asian and Hispanic residents, who are a combined one-half of the district population.

The congressman from the 5th District is Gary Ackerman, a Democrat first elected in 1983. Ackerman grew up in Flushing, taught junior high school, ran an advertising agency, started the weekly *Queens Tribune* in 1970 and sold it to publisher Jerry Finkelstein in 1978 (and then was part of an investment group that repurchased it in 2002). That same year he was elected to the New York Senate. He won his seat in the House in a special election from a district that was then centered in the heavily Jewish apartment complexes in central Queens. Ackerman is a colorful character, who always wears a white carnation and lives on a houseboat in Washington (the *Unsinkable II*, successor to the *Unsinkable I*, which sunk); he hosts an annual "Taste of New York" fundraiser, featuring pastrami sandwiches and stuffed cabbage, with waiters imported from New York. Acerbic but humorous, he is a pungent speaker, with a humor that makes even opponents smile.

Ackerman has a penchant for taking on worthy but neglected causes; his once solidly liberal voting record has moderated on foreign policy issues. Despite opposition from many constituents, including his wife, Ackerman defended his vote to authorize war in Iraq. He also backed the Bush administration's handling of the Israeli-Palestinian conflict; as ranking Democrat on the Middle East and Central Asia Subcommittee, he met frequently with leaders in the region. A long-time supporter of India, he urged Bush not to sell sophisticated weapons and F-16s to Pakistan. On domestic issues, he helped to pass the "Baby AIDS" bill requiring HIV testing of newborns and disclosure of the results to the mother; the bill also bars insurers from terminating coverage because of AIDS test results. Still, he occasionally stands out as a lonely liberal, as when he was one of only three members to vote against a House resolution criticizing a federal appeals court that ruled unconstitutional the phrase "under God" in the Pledge of Allegiance. Ackerman became knowledgeable on "mad cow" disease, and pushed for a ban on the commercial slaughter of downer cows. In July 2003, the House defeated his amendment to attach the proposal to an appropriation bill, 199–202; the White House later took regulatory action to adopt the ban. Following the former president's death, he filed the Ronald Reagan Memorial Stem Cell Research Act to increase federal funding.

Ackerman survived redistricting in 1992 when it moved him farther out on Long Island and into a district where two other incumbents also lived; both of them retired. Ackerman did better in the 2002 redistricting, even though the district could easily have been sliced up among its neighbors. The chief threat that he faces is a candidacy from immigrant communities.

SIXTH DISTRICT

Rep. Gregory Meeks (D)

Elected Feb. 1998, 4th full term; b. Sept. 25, 1953, Harlem; home, Far Rockaway; Adelphi U., B.A., 1975, Howard U., J.D., 1978; Baptist; married (Simone-Marie).

Elected Office: NY Assembly, 1992–98.

Professional Career: Asst. Dist. Atty., Queens Co., NY, 1978–84; NY St. Comm. of Investigations, 1984–85; Judge, NY St. Workers Compensation Bd., 1985–92.

DC Office: 1710 LHOB, 20515, 202-225-3461; Fax: 202-226-4169; Web site: www.house.gov/meeks.

District Offices: Far Rockaway, 718-327-9791; Richmond Hill, 718-738-4200; St. Albans, 718-949-5600.

Committees: *Financial Services* (12th of 32 D): Capital Markets, Insurance & Government Sponsored Enterprises; Financial Institutions & Consumer Credit. *International Relations* (12th of 23 D): Africa, Global Human Rights & International Operations; Western Hemisphere.

Group Ratings

	ADA	ACLU	AFS	LCV	ITIC	NTU	COC	ACU	NTLC	CHC
2004	75	83	100	91	80	12	55	9	3	7
2003	95	—	100	90	—	25	45	20	—	—

National Journal Ratings

	2003 LIB	—	2003 CONS		2004 LIB	—	2004 CONS
Economic	73%	—	26%		72%	—	28%
Social	90%	—	8%		81%	—	19%
Foreign	75%	—	21%		84%	—	16%

Key Votes of the 108th Congress

1. Drilling in ANWR	N	5. DC School Vouchers	N	9. Ban Same-Sex Marriage	*
2. Approve Bush Tax Cuts	N	6. Ban Human Cloning	N	10. Fund Iraq War	N
3. Medicare/Rx Bill	N	7. Restrict Gun Liability	N	11. Bar Cuba Embargo Funds	*
4. Bar Overtime Pay Regs.	Y	8. Ban Partial-Birth Abortion	N	12. Intelligence Reorg.	N

Election Results

2004 general	Gregory Meeks (D-WF) .... unopposed		($537,089)
2004 primary	Gregory Meeks (D) .... unopposed		
2002 general	Gregory Meeks (D-L-WF) 72,799	(97%)	($502,178)
	Other... 2,632	(3%)	

Prior Winning Percentages: 2000 (100%); 1998 (100%); 1998 (57%)

The People		Race/Ethnic Origin	Ancestry	
Area size:	46 sq. mi.	12.8% White	West Indian: 15.9% Italian: 3.4%	
Urban population:	100.0%	52.1% Black	USA: 3.0%	
Rural population:	0.0%	8.9% Asian	**2004 Presidential Vote**	
Pop. 2000:	654,361	0.5% Native Am.	Kerry (D) 154,468	(84%)
Median income:	$43,546	0.1% Hawaiian	Bush (R) 27,352	(15%)
Poverty status:	14.5%	6.1% Two+ races	Other 1,128	(1%)
Military veterans:	6.2%	2.6% Other	**2000 Presidential Vote**	
		16.9% Hispanic Origin	Gore (D) 145,684	(87%)
			Bush (R) 17,632	(10%)
			Other 4,874	(3%)
			Cook Partisan Voting Index: D +38	

Occupation	Blue collar: 20.5%	White collar: 57.4%	Gray collar: 22.1%

The eastern edge of Queens has been an important transportation hub for New York for almost 250 years. In the 1750s, the British laid out what is now Jamaica Avenue to help them defend Long Island. In the 1830s—nearly a century before most present-day commuters would have guessed—the Long Island Rail Road was built here. Today, this corner of Queens is sliced by the

Belt Parkway and the Van Wyck Expressway—two integral parts of Robert Moses' mid-century highway network—and is home to John F. Kennedy International Airport, one of the leading ports of entry for air travelers entering the United States. Jamaica is so well situated with transportation links that officials have worked mightily to improve its commercial vitality, and in 2003 local leaders announced the first large private office development in more than a decade. The old elevated subway line on Jamaica Avenue has been removed and buried underground, so that shoppers could have a less claustrophobic experience.

This part of Queens—rather than Harlem or Brooklyn—is home to New York City's largest collection of middle-class black homeowners. The neighborhoods of Springfield Gardens and Laurelton, St. Albans and Rosedale, Cambria Heights and Queens Village consist of block upon block of low-rise, frame and brick houses built mostly from the 1920s to the 1950s. There was a small black community in South Jamaica half a century ago, and since then many black families have bought houses and raised their families in neighborhoods that fan east from Jamaica. They fought to maintain the relatively spacious streets, relishing the light in their windows, the safe schools and the good neighborhood stores; these areas never experienced the kind of riots that damaged Harlem and parts of Brooklyn.

The 6th Congressional District of New York contains all of these southeast Queens neighborhoods, plus others less affluent and orderly, in southern Queens. It is bounded on the north, more or less, by the Jackie Robinson Parkway, on the east by the Nassau County line and on the west by Cross Bay Boulevard; to the south it includes part of the Rockaway Peninsula across Jamaica Bay from the rest of Queens. Richmond Hill and Ozone Park, previously white ethnic neighborhoods, now have sizable numbers of Latinos and South Asians. South Ozone Park is home to many immigrants from Guyana, Jamaica, Haiti, the Dominican Republic and Trinidad and Tobago. The Rockaway portions of the district, despite being just a few blocks from the beach, are a relatively undeveloped backwater, leveled by urban renewal in the late 1960s but never rebuilt, and now home to many of Queens' nursing homes; one area, called Almost Paradise, was a popular scuba diving spot until a developer moved in. As a whole, the 6th is 52% black, 17% Hispanic and 9% Asian; if there is a common denominator, it is the amount of time 6th District residents spend traveling to work. The district is ranked as the nation's worst for commuters—at 48 minutes of mean travel time to work. Politically, the district is overwhelmingly Democratic.

The congressman from the 6th District is Gregory Meeks, a Democrat first elected in 1998 to replace 11-year incumbent Floyd Flake, who resigned to devote more time to his church. Meeks grew up in Harlem, in public housing projects. After graduating from college and law school, he moved to Far Rockaway and pursued a public sector career. He became an assistant district attorney in 1978, a staffer for the Committee on Investigations in 1984, a workmen's comp judge in 1985; after losing a race for City Council in 1991, he was elected assemblyman in 1992. He became an ally of Flake, an extraordinary minister whose Allen A.M.E. Church congregation grew from 1,400 members in 1976 to 12,000 in 2000.

Flake supported Meeks to succeed him, though the party's initial favorite was state Senator Alton Waldon, who lost to Flake in the 1986 Democratic primary. At the January 1998 endorsement meetings Meeks won a bare majority of committeemen and thus became the Democratic nominee. Waldon ran on the Conservative and Independence lines, and spent $100,000; Assemblywoman Barbara Clark ran an independent candidacy and Republicans had a candidate as well. But Meeks had support from Flake, City Controller (now state Comptroller) Alan Hevesi, Congressman Charles Rangel, Al Sharpton and Jesse Jackson. He won with 57%, to 21% for Waldon, 13% for Clark, and 9% for Republican Celestine Miller.

Meeks got Flake's seat on the Financial Services Committee and has had a liberal voting record, though with some moderate ratings on economic issues. In 2000, Meeks emerged as a player. As one of the final undecideds on normal trade relations with China, both sides lobbied him furiously. Various factors finally convinced him to support the deal: vigorous advocacy by Rangel and Bill Clinton; support by United Parcel Service, a major employer at Kennedy airport; a White House-sponsored trip to China where he met with senior officials and saw first-hand the economic growth; and a last-minute agreement by the White House and Speaker Dennis Hastert to extend tax breaks and public investment to distressed urban and rural areas. He made many overseas trips—the most of any New York member, *Newsday* reported. One trip was to Venezuela, where he was a monitor in the referendum on whether to recall President Hugo Chavez.

Meeks has shown his ambition within the party. When several House Democratic leadership positions opened after the 2002 election, he campaigned to be vice-chairman of the Democratic Caucus. His initial approach was to claim a base among minority members, but he was forced to abandon that strategy when James Clyburn of South Carolina, the former chairman of the Congressional Black Caucus, entered the contest. Meeks then emphasized his youth and openness to a variety of viewpoints within the caucus. But on the first ballot, Clyburn won 95 votes to 56 for Meeks and 53 for Zoe Lofgren of California. Meeks could have forced a second ballot but decided not to. In early 2003, he was one of the first members of Congress to endorse John Kerry for president. Kerry rewarded Meeks by naming him a national co-chairman. Meeks spent considerable time with Kerry on his campaign, especially during the closing weeks, and advised him on relationships with minority groups across the nation. After the election, Meeks sought a leadership post at the Democratic National Committee, but he lost to California Congressman Mike Honda.

Locally, Meeks has sought to bring business deals to Queens by meeting with leaders of other nations, including India. He has been reelected each time without major party opposition. Some expect him to run some day for mayor, or perhaps for a Senate seat if there is an opening.

SEVENTH DISTRICT

Rep. Joseph Crowley (D)

Elected 1998, 4th term; b. Mar. 16, 1962, Elmhurst, NY; home, Elmhurst; C.U.N.Y. Queens College, B.A. 1985; Catholic; married (Kasey).

Elected Office: NY Assembly, 1986–98.

DC Office: 312 CHOB, 20515, 202-225-3965; Fax: 202-225-1909; Web site: www.crowley.house.gov.

District Offices: Bronx, 718-931-1400; Co-op City, 718-320-2390; Jackson Heights, 718-779-1400.

Committees: *Chief Deputy Minority Whip. Financial Services* (18th of 32 D): Capital Markets, Insurance & Government Sponsored Enterprises; Domestic and International Monetary Policy, Trade & Technology; Financial Institutions & Consumer Credit. *International Relations* (14th of 23 D): International Terrorism & Nonproliferation; Middle East & Central Asia.

Group Ratings

	ADA	ACLU	AFS	LCV	ITIC	NTU	COC	ACU	NTLC	CHC
2004	90	65	100	100	80	12	55	9	3	23
2003	95	—	100	90	—	21	37	24	—	—

National Journal Ratings

	2003 LIB	—	2003 CONS		2004 LIB	—	2004 CONS
Economic	66%	—	32%		70%	—	30%
Social	71%	—	29%		76%	—	24%
Foreign	66%	—	32%		73%	—	27%

Key Votes of the 108th Congress

1. Drilling in ANWR	N	5. DC School Vouchers	N	9. Ban Same-Sex Marriage	N
2. Approve Bush Tax Cuts	N	6. Ban Human Cloning	N	10. Fund Iraq War	N
3. Medicare/Rx Bill	N	7. Restrict Gun Liability	N	11. Bar Cuba Embargo Funds	Y
4. Bar Overtime Pay Regs.	Y	8. Ban Partial-Birth Abortion	Y	12. Intelligence Reorg.	N

Election Results

2004 general	Joseph Crowley (D-WF)	104,275	(81%)	($1,160,532)
	Joseph Cinquemain (R-C)	24,548	(19%)	($26,337)
2004 primary	Joseph Crowley (D)	15,738	(63%)	
	Dennis Coleman (D)	4,716	(19%)	
	Aniello Grimaldi (D)	2,280	(9%)	
	Curtis Brooks (D)	2,102	(9%)	
2002 general	Joseph Crowley (D-WF)	50,967	(73%)	($837,900)
	Kevin Brawley (R-C)	18,572	(27%)	

Prior Winning Percentages: 2000 (72%); 1998 (69%)

The People		Race/Ethnic Origin	Ancestry	
Area size:	42 sq. mi.	27.6% White	Italian: 9.6%	Irish: 5.0%
Urban population:	100.0%	16.5% Black	West Indian: 3.6%	
Rural population:	0.0%	12.8% Asian	**2004 Presidential Vote**	
Pop. 2000:	654,360	0.2% Native Am.	Kerry (D) 129,909	(74%)
Median income:	$36,990	0.0% Hawaiian	Bush (R) 44,607	(25%)
Poverty status:	17.7%	2.7% Two+ races	Other 1,367	(1%)
Military veterans:	6.4%	0.6% Other	**2000 Presidential Vote**	
		39.5% Hispanic Origin	Gore (D) 114,365	(75%)
			Bush (R) 31,682	(21%)
			Other 6,236	(4%)
			Cook Partisan Voting Index: D +28	

Occupation   Blue collar: 21.1%   White collar: 57.4%   Gray collar: 21.6%

Over the last two decades, hundreds of thousands of immigrants have been moving into many of New York City's modest neighborhoods—neighborhoods that had been emptying out as the children of the immigrants who came to New York between 1890 and 1924 died or moved to the suburbs or Florida. These are places which affluent New Yorkers and traveling journalists seldom see as they whiz by on freeways to destinations in Manhattan—rather, these are the neighborhoods pop star Jennifer Lopez sings about. Most of the housing here was built in the decades after 1910, when the subways first started connecting these neighborhoods with job sites in Manhattan. You can find many of these neighborhoods in the East Bronx, off the Bruckner Expressway and near the cluster of highways north of the Bronx-Whitestone Bridge—places like Bruckner, Morris Park, Schuylerville, and Throgs Neck, which is named after Dutchman John Throgmorton, who settled the area and farmed the land. The district includes the Hunts Point meat and produce markets, where some of the nation's toniest restaurants handpick their daily provisions. Increasingly these neighborhoods are full of Latinos, many from Puerto Rico, but many also from the Dominican Republic and other Caribbean and Latin countries. Lopez hails from Castle Hill; her *On the 6* album is a reference to the Number 6 train that whisked her to Manhattan auditions. Here are two massive apartment projects: Parkchester, built just after World War II by Metropolitan Life Insurance in the center of the Bronx, and Co-op City—35 buildings and more than 15,000 apartments that were built in the late 1960s by a consortium of labor unions on marshy land near Eastchester Bay. Out past the bay is City Island, a Cape Cod-like resort area with boatmakers and plenty of fish restaurants; it is hard to believe here that you are in New York City.

Across the bridges in Queens are Jackson Heights, home to Little India and a sizable Latino community; Elmhurst, a place so diverse that one local high school counts students from 100 different countries who speak 57 different languages; and Woodside, a long-settled Irish enclave with residents from 49 nations who speak 34 languages. These are the places serviced by the Number 7 elevated line—you can find Pakistanis and Peruvians, Koreans and Dominicans, Indians and Filipinos, Mexicans and Bangladeshis.

These Bronx and Queens neighborhoods are all in the 7th Congressional District of New York. The district is polyglot indeed: its population in 2000 was 17% black, 40% Hispanic and 13% Asian. Politically, the 7th District votes heavily Democratic in presidential and congressional elections. But more important for its political future may be those who don't vote at all. In 2004 only 129,000 people voted in this district of 654,000, not much more than half the 254,000 who voted in the nearby suburban 4th District.

The congressman from the 7th District is Joseph Crowley, a Democrat first elected in 1998 and effectively chosen by one man, his predecessor Tom Manton, who remained the boss of the efficient Queens County Democratic Party. Crowley grew up in Woodside, where his family was involved in politics; his uncle Walter Crowley was elected to succeed Manton on the City Council in 1984. When Walter Crowley died in 1985, Crowley wanted to succeed him, though he was only 23; Manton chose his chief of staff, Walter McCaffrey, instead. In 1986 Assemblyman Ralph Goldstein from Elmhurst died; fresh from Queens College, Crowley ran and won at 24, with support from Manton. Crowley was interested in Irish affairs and sponsored the law that requires public school students to be taught about the Irish potato famine. He played guitar and sang tenor with the Budget Blues Boys, a group of assemblymen who performed on cold Albany nights.

Crowley's elevation to Congress came suddenly. In 1998, Manton filed for re-election by the July 16 filing deadline. Then at 11:00 a.m. on July 21, he convened a meeting of Queens Democratic committeemen, announced he was retiring and got them to vote in Crowley as the Democratic nominee. Other potential candidates were not notified ahead of time and were naturally miffed, but quickly accepted the reality. Manton argued that Crowley, at 36, was in a good position to accumulate seniority and power in Washington. Crowley was plainly delighted. "What you're hearing is not so much about the process, but sour grapes. What happened here is simply that I was offered an ice cream cone, and I took it." His Republican opponent had no money and no chance. Crowley won in November 69%–26%.

Once elected, Crowley voted with moderate Democrats and he demonstrated his legislative experience and leadership ambition. He served six months as the freshman Democrats' class president. Despite his opposition to abortion, he cited his experience in witnessing crude abortion practices in Malawi as he fought for $50 million in annual family planning funds for the United Nations. The House defeated his amendment to the highway bill to create a pilot program for buses fueled by natural gas at the nation's busiest airports. The September 11 attacks struck a grievous blow to Crowley's community, with the loss of many local firefighters, including his first cousin, who was a battalion chief; he passed in the House an amendment to issue the Public Safety Officers Medal of Valor to 414 who died on September 11. He fought to change funding formulas for homeland security, which he said shortchanged New York. On the Financial Services Committee, he advocated Wall Street interests and encouraged bipartisanship. He responded to constituent interests by urging the State Department to permit India to buy Patriot missile systems from the Army, and he urged steps to make India a permanent member of the United Nations Security Council. He worked with Majority Whip Roy Blunt as a leader on behalf of business interests in gaining approval of the free-trade agreement with Australia; Blunt praised his efforts to secure a majority of Democratic votes.

Still bitter about how Crowley was elected in 1998, several Queens Democrats threatened to challenge him in the 2000 primary. But City Councilman Walter McCaffrey, the only one to actually file, withdrew in July at the prompting of party leaders after disclosures that he had spent campaign money for personal expenses. Crowley again defeated a token Republican opponent. Redistricting radically reshaped his constituency. In the old district, Queens cast 74% of the votes and the Bronx only 26%. In the new district in 2002, the Bronx cast 62% and Queens 38%. But Crowley has been reelected easily. He also has worked to help Democrats win more House seats. In 2002, he made an effort to help elect Tim Bishop in Suffolk County; in 2004, he was like a big brother in providing money and connections to Brian Higgins in the hard-fought and successful campaign to take the open Buffalo area seat.

After the 2004 election, Crowley sought to chair the Democratic Congressional Campaign Committee, highlighting his fundraising connections to New York's financial community. But he suffered from having been an active supporter of Minority Whip Steny Hoyer, who had named Crowley one of eight chief deputy whips, and the post went to Rahm Emanuel. Crowley also failed to convince Minority Leader Nancy Pelosi in his bid for a Ways and Means Committee vacancy. But he was named to lead the DCCC's Business Council, a key fundraising post, and he expressed again his interest in a leadership position. His enthusiasm and ambition, plus his relative youth, should give him plenty of opportunity to be a player in the House.

EIGHTH DISTRICT

Rep. Jerrold Nadler (D)

Elected 1992, 7th full term; b. June 13, 1947, Brooklyn; home, Manhattan; Columbia U., B.A. 1970, Fordham U., J.D. 1978; Jewish; married (Joyce Miller).

Elected Office: NY Assembly, 1976–92.

Professional Career: Legis. Asst., NY Assembly, 1972; Law Clerk, 1976.

DC Office: 2334 RHOB, 20515, 202-225-5635; Fax: 202-225-6923; Web site: www.house.gov/nadler.

District Offices: Brooklyn, 718-373-3198; Manhattan, 212-367-7350.

Committees: *Judiciary* (4th of 17 D): Commercial & Administrative Law; The Constitution (RMM). *Transportation & Infrastructure* (6th of 34 D): Highways, Transit & Pipelines; Railroads.

Group Ratings

	ADA	ACLU	AFS	LCV	ITIC	NTU	COC	ACU	NTLC	CHC
2004	100	100	100	100	30	9	29	0	0	15
2003	100	—	100	95	—	21	21	8	—	—

National Journal Ratings

	2003 LIB	—	2003 CONS		2004 LIB	—	2004 CONS
Economic	92%	—	0%		94%	—	5%
Social	92%	—	0%		88%	—	0%
Foreign	94%	—	0%		94%	—	4%

Key Votes of the 108th Congress

1. Drilling in ANWR	N	5. DC School Vouchers	N	9. Ban Same-Sex Marriage	N
2. Approve Bush Tax Cuts	N	6. Ban Human Cloning	N	10. Fund Iraq War	N
3. Medicare/Rx Bill	N	7. Restrict Gun Liability	N	11. Bar Cuba Embargo Funds	Y
4. Bar Overtime Pay Regs.	Y	8. Ban Partial-Birth Abortion	N	12. Intelligence Reorg.	N

Election Results

2004 general	Jerrold Nadler (D-WF)	162,082	(81%)	($867,427)
	Peter Hort (R-Ind-C)	39,240	(19%)	($142,401)
2004 primary	Jerrold Nadler (D)	unopposed		
2002 general	Jerrold Nadler (D-L-WF)	81,002	(76%)	($684,568)
	Jim Farrin (R-Ind)	19,674	(18%)	($64,595)
	Other	5,805	(5%)	

Prior Winning Percentages: 2000 (81%); 1998 (86%); 1996 (82%); 1994 (82%); 1992 (81%); 1992 (100%)

The People		Race/Ethnic Origin	Ancestry	
Area size:	28 sq. mi.	68.7% White	Italian: 8.7%	Russian: 7.2%
Urban population:	100.0%	5.4% Black	Irish: 5.7%	
Rural population:	0.0%	11.0% Asian	**2004 Presidential Vote**	
Pop. 2000:	654,360	0.1% Native Am.	Kerry (D) 180,080	(72%)
Median income:	$47,061	0.0% Hawaiian	Bush (R) 66,948	(27%)
Poverty status:	18.7%	2.5% Two+ races	Other 2,723	(1%)
Military veterans:	5.1%	0.5% Other	**2000 Presidential Vote**	
		11.7% Hispanic Origin	Gore (D) 162,240	(74%)
			Bush (R) 39,280	(18%)
			Other 18,448	(8%)
			Cook Partisan Voting Index: D +28	

Occupation   Blue collar: 10.1%   White collar: 79.2%   Gray collar: 10.7%

Over the course of the 20th century, New York City spread so far beyond its origins in lower Manhattan that, for a while, it became easy to forget how pivotal the southern end of the island had been in making the city what it is today. That all changed in an instant, on the morning of September 11, 2001, when Al Qaeda terrorists flew two hijacked jets into the twin towers of the World Trade Center, killing approximately 2,800 people, and laying waste to at least 13 blocks. The target was chosen deliberately: The terrorists struck the tallest buildings in America's biggest city, toppling a complex whose name embodied the reach of American capitalism. Lower Manhattan has long been home to Wall Street and the Financial District, but over the years it has embodied America's striving spirit in other ways as well. The Brooklyn Bridge, begun in 1867 just a few blocks east of the Twin Towers site and completed in 1883, was half again as long as any bridge then standing, and seven times higher than any buildings in the adjoining boroughs. The Holland Tunnel, built in 1927, was the first underwater vehicular tunnel built anywhere in the world. Just offshore stand Ellis Island, where members of the great immigration wave first set foot on American soil, and the Statue of Liberty, the symbol of freedom they saw as they sailed in.

The 8th Congressional District of New York includes all of these places. From the Battery, at the very southern tip of Manhattan Island, the 8th spreads out in two directions, north and south. As the 8th District moves up the west side of Manhattan, it takes in the Financial District; Battery Park City, the attractive modern apartments built on infill west of the now-torn down West Side Highway; the artist lofts of TriBeCa and SoHo, in former warehouses and factories; Greenwich Village and Chelsea, New York's leading gay areas and strong voting blocs; Clinton, the new, economically diverse incarnation of the old slum Hell's Kitchen; the Theater District and the cleaned-up Times Square; the huge Port Authority bus terminal; and long stretches of the Upper West Side, including Lincoln Center and the American Museum of Natural History, as far north as West 89th Street. Mayor Michael Bloomberg wanted to build a new $2 billion stadium near the Javits Convention Center to house the NFL Jets but in June 2005 the state Public Authorities Control Board rejected the plan. South from the Battery, the 8th crosses into Brooklyn, running along the Brooklyn waterfront before taking in the inland neighborhood of Borough Park and the waterside enclaves of Sea Gate, Brighton Beach and Coney Island, once known as the world's largest playground.

In both halves of the 8th District, there is a strong Jewish heritage. The city's Dutch founders came from the European country then most tolerant of Jews. German Jews came to New York in large numbers in the 19th century, with many considering themselves more German than Jewish; a few founded merchant banking, retail and clothing empires. Around 1890, Ashkenazi Jews from Eastern Europe began arriving from Poland, Lithuania, Belarus, Ukraine, Hungary and Romania. In the years after World War I, as many as 400,000 Jews a year debarked at Ellis Island until a 1924 law virtually shut down immigration. Had a malapportioned, rural-dominated, nativist Congress not done that, perhaps two million of the six million who perished in the Holocaust would instead have become Americans. Ashkenazi Jews initially lived on the Lower East Side but moved out to Brooklyn and the Bronx almost as soon as the subways were built. Their children moved up faster than any new group in memory, despite widespread prejudice in the professions and in educational institutions. They invented new businesses, from the rag trade to show biz: second-caste people from third-rate countries almost immediately becoming elite in the world's foremost country. Their descendants live all over the country, but New York has the largest Jewish population of any city in the world.

One big voting area of the 8th is the Upper West Side: the venerable apartments along Central Park West, West End Avenue and Riverside Drive, and the brownstones on the cross streets which house some of America's most idealistic and dedicated liberals (and radicals). These professional people—lovingly satirized on *Seinfeld,* the long-running sitcom that reso-nated far beyond Manhattan—include a mix of the wealthy and less-affluent intellectuals. In the 1950s, West Siders took up the reform banner and eviscerated the old Tammany Hall Democratic machine; in the 1960s, they fought the Vietnam War and helped oust a Democratic administra-tion. Another big voting area is Greenwich Village, which in the 1910s was America's original Bohemia, now with a mix of expensive apartments and cheaper dwellings. Politically, the Village has long had a taste for what it regards as radical, though some of its ideas are now mainstream, such as the historic-preservation and urbanist policies developed in the Village's successful fight against a proposed lower Manhattan expressway, led by *The Death and Life of Great American Cities* author Jane Jacobs.

The Brooklyn part of the district is probably more Jewish than the Manhattan part. Brighton Beach and Coney Island house the largest concentration of recent Russian Jewish immigrants in New York. Here you can see Cyrillic as well as Roman letters on store signs; Borough Park has one of the nation's largest Orthodox communities, with Yiddish-language ATM's, plus saunas and massages in Russian bathhouses. The eight-block shopping district along Brighton Beach Avenue hosts a handful of furriers catering to the decided preference among Russian women for fur coats. The political attitudes in these neighborhoods are quite different from those of most American Jews, who are liberal on both cultural and economic issues. The Russians, many of whom live close to poverty, favor free enterprise and are anti-socialist. The Hasidic Jews of Borough Park are conservative, hostile to racial preferences and favor tough police treatment of crime. Still, voters in these areas tend to register as Democrats and vote Democratic in most elections. The district voted 74%–18% for Al Gore in 2000, but gave John Kerry a smaller 72%–27% margin in 2004; this resulted from a sharp increase for Bush in Brooklyn and especially in Borough Park, where Bush won 66%.

The congressman from the 8th District is Jerrold Nadler, a West Side liberal Democrat first elected in 1992. He was born in Brooklyn and moved around; his father was a chicken farmer in New Jersey, ran a gas station on Long Island and owned a traveling auto parts store. At Columbia he campaigned for Eugene McCarthy with his roommate Dick Morris and was there during the 1968 campus riots. He worked as a legislative staffer and ran for the Assembly in 1976, at 29; in the primary he beat Ruth Messinger (the Democratic nominee for mayor in 1997) by 73 votes. In 1992 he was suddenly presented with the opportunity to run for Congress. Two incumbents were based in the new 8th District. Stephen Solarz of Brooklyn, a lead backer of the Gulf War resolution, shied away from running in leftish Manhattan, and ran and lost in the Hispanic-majority 12th District. That left the 8th to Manhattan's Ted Weiss, long an Upper West Side icon. But he died the day before the September primary, which he won anyway. The nomination was decided by a convention of almost 1,000 county Democratic committee members, many of them involved in acerbic ideological and personal squabbles for decades. The key vote was procedural, for a system of weighted voting under which Nadler won 62% of the votes and Councilwoman Ronnie Eldridge 21%; opponents decried this system, after they lost. Nadler became the Democratic nominee and thus congressman. He has not been seriously challenged since.

Nadler's voting record has been among the most liberal in the House, with a strong civil libertarian bent. As ranking Democrat on the Constitution Subcommittee, he opposed Republican constitutional amendments to overturn court rulings. He also has been a leading foe of abortion restrictions, including legislation designed to give legal standing to the fetus. With Senator Hillary Rodham Clinton, he filed a proposal to protect confidential medical records from being used in court. He led the fight in the House against the proposed Federal Marriage Amendment, and he proposed to give same-sex domestic partners the same immigration rights and benefits as heterosexual spouses. He fought the bankruptcy bill, saying its tighter restrictions were "a wish list of every big money special interest group." Although his district includes Wall Street, he strongly opposes individual investment accounts in Social Security.

On local issues, he successfully fought developer Donald Trump's attempts to alter the West Side Highway to accommodate his luxury housing project on old rail yards between 59th and 72d Streets. (In a book, Trump termed Nadler "one of the most egregious hacks in contemporary politics.") He fought to get more rail competition east of the Hudson, and worked to save Amtrak. His greatest project is a rail-freight tunnel under the Hudson, from the 65th Street rail yard in Bay Ridge to little-used rail yards in either Bayonne, New Jersey or Staten Island. Lack of a rail-freight line means that New York gets only about 3% of its freight by rail, compared to 30% in the average large city; cheaper freight could lower consumer prices, help rebuild small manufacturing in New York and could revive the Brooklyn docks, which Governor Nelson Rockefeller abandoned in the 1960s when vessels began the switch to container cargo. The cost would be huge—more than $2 billion—but it could provide a way upward for the city's economy and its hundreds of thousands of new immigrants. Nadler's proposal was ridiculed for years, but he persisted and got $12 million for a two-year design and environmental study of the tunnel. Mayor Rudolph Giuliani endorsed it, and others have come to appreciate it as well. If it is built, it would be an impressive monument for a career.

As the representative of Ground Zero, Nadler found that his work life became both sad and frenetic. When the second airplane struck the tower, he rushed to catch a 10 a.m. train from Washington to Manhattan; after delays en route, he finally arrived at 6 p.m. to view a scene of emptiness that he later called "surrealistic." He worked with city, state and federal officials and local business leaders to identify immediate needs and then to secure $20 billion for the clean-up and eventual rebuilding. He spearheaded numerous actions on behalf of affected families, local communities and small business. As a member of the Judiciary Committee, he vigorously opposed the USA Patriot Act. He opposed the Iraq war resolution.

Proving that he still has good connections in Albany, he managed to survive redistricting with the Manhattan-Brooklyn district largely intact. In 2003, Nadler had a second round of stomach-reduction surgery to force a severe reduction in his appetite; he lost more than 100 pounds and gained renewed energy.

NINTH DISTRICT

Rep. Anthony Weiner (D)

Elected 1998, 4th term; b. Sept. 4, 1964, Brooklyn; home, Brooklyn; S.U.N.Y. Plattsburgh, B.A. 1985; Jewish; single.

Elected Office: NY City Cncl., 1991–98.

Professional Career: Aide, U.S. Rep. Charles Schumer, 1985–91.

DC Office: 1122 LHOB, 20515, 202-225-6616; Fax: 202-226-7253; Web site: www.house.gov/weiner.

District Offices: Brooklyn, 718-743-0441; Kew Gardens, 718-520-9001; Rockaway, 718-318-9255.

Committees: *Judiciary* (13th of 17 D): Courts, the Internet & Intellectual Property; Crime, Terrorism & Homeland Security. *Transportation & Infrastructure* (25th of 34 D): Aviation; Coast Guard & Maritime Transportation; Highways, Transit & Pipelines.

Group Ratings

	ADA	ACLU	AFS	LCV	ITIC	NTU	COC	ACU	NTLC	CHC
2004	100	80	100	100	60	12	38	4	0	8
2003	100	—	100	95	—	22	30	21	—	—

National Journal Ratings

	2003 LIB — 2003 CONS	2004 LIB — 2004 CONS
Economic	91% — 8%	81% — 19%
Social	78% — 20%	85% — 14%
Foreign	79% — 21%	76% — 24%

Key Votes of the 108th Congress

1. Drilling in ANWR	N	5. DC School Vouchers	N	9. Ban Same-Sex Marriage	N
2. Approve Bush Tax Cuts	N	6. Ban Human Cloning	N	10. Fund Iraq War	N
3. Medicare/Rx Bill	N	7. Restrict Gun Liability	N	11. Bar Cuba Embargo Funds	Y
4. Bar Overtime Pay Regs.	Y	8. Ban Partial-Birth Abortion	N	12. Intelligence Reorg.	N

Election Results

2004 general	Anthony Weiner (D-WF) 113,025	(71%)	($1,329,530)
	Gerard Cronin (R-Ind-C) 45,451	(29%)	($8,093)
2004 primary	Anthony Weiner (D) .... unopposed		
2002 general	Anthony Weiner (D-L-WF) 60,737	(66%)	($263,994)
	Alfred Donohue (R-C) 31,698	(34%)	

Prior Winning Percentages: 2000 (68%); 1998 (66%)

The People		Race/Ethnic Origin	Ancestry	
Area size:	103 sq. mi.	64.0% White	Italian: 12.3%	Irish: 7.5%
Urban population:	100.0%	4.0% Black	Russian: 7.2%	
Rural population:	0.0%	14.5% Asian	**2004 Presidential Vote**	
Pop. 2000:	654,360	0.1% Native Am.	Kerry (D) 111,850	(56%)
Median income:	$45,426	0.0% Hawaiian	Bush (R) 87,449	(44%)
Poverty status:	12.2%	3.0% Two+ races	Other 1,658	(1%)
Military veterans:	7.1%	0.7% Other	**2000 Presidential Vote**	
		13.6% Hispanic Origin	Gore (D) 123,763	(67%)
			Bush (R) 54,699	(30%)
			Other 6,649	(4%)
			Cook Partisan Voting Index: D +14	

Occupation   Blue collar: 17.6%   White collar: 68.4%   Gray collar: 14.0%

Forty years ago, most of the neighborhoods in New York's outer boroughs were almost all-white. A few were WASPy and high-income—Forest Hills in Queens, with its famous tennis stadium and large Tudor houses on winding lanes within view of massive high-rises, is a notable example, but most of them were filled by descendants of the great mass of immigrants who came over from eastern and southern Europe between 1890 and 1924 and from northern Europe earlier—Irish and Italians, Jews and Hungarians, Poles and Czechs and Greeks. The great pitched battles of city politics in the 1960s were between John Lindsay, a liberal Manhattan Republican, and his mostly outer borough opponents. Lindsay won big margins in Manhattan from Harlem blacks, Upper East Side Republicans, Upper West Side and Greenwich Village liberal Democrats, but he lost the other four boroughs collectively both times he ran, and was elected each time with only a plurality of the votes. Lindsay's attitudes and policies—soft on law enforcement, high on taxes, contempt for middle class taxpayers who wanted low taxes and safe neighborhoods—fueled an exodus of middle class New Yorkers, and the city lost 1 million people in the 1970s. Some of this neighborhood change would have happened anyway: neighborhoods settled by immigrants in the 1920s were full of old people, and the increasing number of blacks were bound to move out of the old ghettoes anyway; unnoticed, increasing numbers of immigrants started coming to the United States after the 1965 changes in immigration law, and eventually large numbers came to New York.

But there are still white upper-middle and lower-middle class neighborhoods in the outer boroughs, though they are ethnically more diverse than those of 40 years ago. Many of these neighborhoods are gathered in the convoluted boundaries of the 9th Congressional District, which includes parts of Queens and Brooklyn. Its population is only 4% black and 14% Hispanic, and some of its neighborhoods, like Howard Beach on Jamaica Bay, have remained remarkably insular and seemingly unaffected by the changes swirling elsewhere. The 9th begins in Queens near Fresh Meadows, just inside Nassau County; it then runs west through Pomonok and the old rail suburbs of Kew Gardens and Forest Hills, built to resemble English cottage neighborhoods. The district continues west to Rego Park, with its 1950s high-rise apartments, Middle Village, the old German (and now more Eastern European) neighborhood of Glendale, and part of Maspeth. From there, the 9th heads south, taking in Woodhaven, Lindenwood and Howard Beach. It then crosses over open parkland to include the shoreline areas of Bergen Beach, Mill Basin, Mill Island, Marine Park and Sheepshead Bay. It also takes in Broad Channel, the only inhabited island in Jamaica Bay's Gateway National Recreation Area, where many descendants of the original fishing families still live. On the Rockaway Peninsula, the 9th includes the neighborhoods of Seaside, Rockaway Park, Belle Harbor, Roxbury; and the tight-knit, well-secured enclave of Breezy Point, once referred to as the "Irish Riviera." Like nearby Gerritsen Beach, Breezy Point is a clannish, white ethnic middle class enclave where the bungalows and brick homes often change hands by word of mouth alone. The 9th has a large and diverse Jewish population, with politically conservative Orthodox neighborhoods and liberal voters. This is a Democratic district, but more a conservative Democratic district: it voted 67%–30% for Al Gore in 2000 but in 2004, after George W. Bush's response to September 11, it gave John Kerry only a 56%–44% margin. The 25-percentage point erosion in the Democratic margin of victory marked the greatest swing of any congressional district in the nation.

The congressman from the 9th District is Anthony Weiner, a Democrat first elected in 1998. Weiner grew up in Brooklyn, went Upstate to SUNY-Plattsburgh, then returned to work in the House for the energetic Charles Schumer. In 1991 Weiner was elected to the City Council, at 27, the youngest member ever. In 1997, as Schumer prepared to run for the Senate, Weiner began running for the House. Assemblywoman Melinda Katz, based in Forest Hills, ran with the support of the Queens Democratic organization and the Robert F. Kennedy Democratic Club. Assemblyman Daniel Feldman, based in Sheepshead Bay, had the endorsement of the Brooklyn Democratic organization and Congressman Jerrold Nadler. Councilman Noach Dear, based in Borough Park, ran with the endorsement of Orthodox leaders and was sharply more conservative. This was mainly a battle of organizations and endorsements. In the final weeks, Schumer endorsed Weiner. The September 15 primary was so close that the results weren't certified for two weeks. In a turnout of 45,000, Weiner won with 28.1%, to 27.5% for Katz, and 22% each for Dear and Feldman. Weiner won the general election easily.

In the House, Weiner usually votes with the liberals but styles himself a moderate on issues dealing with business and crime. Except for his eagerness to appear on cable talk shows—as befits a Schumer protégé—Weiner had few moments in the legislative spotlight and he worked mostly as a backbencher on local issues. He sought to protect local pharmacies from the invasion of chain drug stores by permitting them to negotiate collectively with insurance and drug companies, and he filed a bill to require disclosure to customers by retail chain stores that charged exorbitant interest rates on their credit cards. In July 2004, the House passed his amendment, on a 217–191 vote, to prohibit U.S. foreign aid to Saudi Arabia; he cited Saudi support of terrorists, including within their own nation. On a distinctly non-local issue, he took steps designed to prevent a space object from colliding with terra firma, when he filed the SPACE (Studying and Preventing Asteroid Collisions with Earth) Act.

In 2000, Dear challenged Weiner in the Democratic primary. Some thought the race would be close, but Weiner won 74%–26%. Dear was on the Republican and Conservative lines in November; this time Weiner beat him 68%–32%. Redistricting moved the 9th more into Queens and left Weiner with 30% new territory, but the basic character of the district remained the same and he has been easily reelected. The Federal Election Commission fined him for excessive contributions in 1998 that he received from his parents. In early 2005, Weiner set out to run for the Democratic nomination for mayor; other candidates included former Bronx borough president Fernando Ferrer, Manhattan borough president Virginia Fields, and city council Speaker Gifford Miller. Weiner featured his trademark self-deprecating humor and sought to build an outer borough base that focused on the needs of working people and he called for a new football stadium in Queens instead of Manhattan. Previous New York mayors who have served on Capitol Hill include Ed Koch, John Lindsay and Fiorello LaGuardia.

TENTH DISTRICT

Rep. Edolphus Towns (D)

Elected 1982, 12th term; b. July 21, 1934, Chadbourn, NC; home, Brooklyn; NC A&T, B.S. 1956, Adelphi U., M.S.W. 1973; Baptist; married (Gwendolyn).

Military Career: Army, 1956–58.

Professional Career: Baptist Minister; Social Worker; Prof., Medgar Evers Col.; NY public schl. teacher; Dpty. Hospital Admin., 1965–71; Brooklyn Dpty. Borough Pres., 1976–82.

DC Office: 2232 RHOB, 20515, 202-225-5936; Fax: 202-225-1018; Web site: www.house.gov/towns.

District Offices: Brooklyn, 718-855-8018; Brooklyn, 718-272-1175; Brooklyn, 718-774-5682; Brooklyn, 718-434-7931.

Committees: *Energy & Commerce* (5th of 26 D): Commerce, Trade & Consumer Protection; Health; Telecommunications & the Internet. *Government Reform* (4th of 17 D): Government Management, Finance & Accountability (RMM).

Group Ratings

	ADA	ACLU	AFS	LCV	ITIC	NTU	COC	ACU	NTLC	CHC
2004	90	85	100	82	44	6	33	0	0	8
2003	80	—	100	65	—	27	33	14	—	—

National Journal Ratings

	2003 LIB	—	2003 CONS		2004 LIB	—	2004 CONS
Economic	70%	—	29%		81%	—	19%
Social	83%	—	16%		81%	—	18%
Foreign	94%	—	0%		91%	—	9%

Key Votes of the 108th Congress

1. Drilling in ANWR	Y	5. DC School Vouchers	*	9. Ban Same-Sex Marriage	N
2. Approve Bush Tax Cuts	N	6. Ban Human Cloning	N	10. Fund Iraq War	N
3. Medicare/Rx Bill	N	7. Restrict Gun Liability	N	11. Bar Cuba Embargo Funds	Y
4. Bar Overtime Pay Regs.	Y	8. Ban Partial-Birth Abortion	N	12. Intelligence Reorg.	*

Election Results

2004 general	Edolphus Towns (D-WF)	136,113	(91%)	($757,121)
	Harvey Clarke (R)	11,099	(7%)	
	Other	1,554	(1%)	
2004 primary	Edolphus Towns (D)	unopposed		
2002 general	Edolphus Towns (D-L)	73,859	(98%)	($741,570)
	Other	1,639	(2%)	

Prior Winning Percentages: 2000 (90%); 1998 (92%); 1996 (91%); 1994 (89%); 1992 (96%); 1990 (93%); 1988 (89%); 1986 (89%); 1984 (85%); 1982 (84%)

The People		Race/Ethnic Origin	Ancestry	
Area size:	18 sq. mi.	16.2% White	West Indian: 14.8%	USA: 3.9%
Urban population:	100.0%	60.2% Black	Subsaharan: 2.5%	
Rural population:	0.0%	2.7% Asian	**2004 Presidential Vote**	
Pop. 2000:	654,361	0.2% Native Am.	Kerry (D) 166,840	(86%)
Median income:	$30,212	0.0% Hawaiian	Bush (R) 25,359	(13%)
Poverty status:	29.0%	2.6% Two+ races	Other 1,195	(1%)
Military veterans:	5.3%	0.9% Other	**2000 Presidential Vote**	
		17.2% Hispanic Origin	Gore (D) 149,018	(88%)
			Bush (R) 13,058	(8%)
			Other 8,029	(5%)
			Cook Partisan Voting Index: D +41	

Occupation	Blue collar: 17.5%	White collar: 60.4%	Gray collar: 22.1%

Bedford, a century ago one of Brooklyn's fashionable neighborhoods, has given its name to half of what is Brooklyn's best known black neighborhood, Bedford-Stuyvesant. African-Americans began settling here in the 1930s, with the opening of the new subway line that was celebrated in Duke Ellington and Billy Strayhorn's "Take the A Train." After World War II, the pace accelerated, as crime and crowding in Harlem—as well as a large migration of blacks from the South—drove black New Yorkers to the aging but solid brownstones of "Bed-Stuy." When job growth slowed, Bed-Stuy, like New York's other black neighborhoods, faced more than its share of poverty and crime. But after a 1966 visit by Robert F. Kennedy and Jacob Javits, New York's two senators, Bed-Stuy won a Model Cities designation, which brought federal development funds and the establishment of the Bedford-Stuyvesant Restoration Corporation, the first such community development organization in the United States. Even as the black community expanded far and wide across Brooklyn, Bed-Stuy grew to become almost as powerful a symbol of black New York as Harlem. As an NYU film student in 1983, Brooklyn native Spike Lee made *Joe's Bed-Stuy Barbershop: We Cut Heads*, about a tonsorial parlor that fronts for the numbers racket; five years later, he shot *Do the Right Thing* on Stuyvesant Avenue between Lexington Avenue and Quincy Street, a film that succinctly captured the racial tensions then brewing in the old neighborhood.

By the end of the 1990s, Bed-Stuy was in better shape than many other areas of Brooklyn. The neighborhood's stately, Hopperesque architecture largely avoided the wrecking ball, and community vigilance has kept the streets maintained. The revitalized residential area has developed a Caribbean flavor which, combined with the modest prices for handsome brownstones, has led to a noticeable wave of gentrification.

The 10th Congressional District of New York takes the shape of a sideways "V" as it zigzags across Brooklyn. It takes in several neighborhoods near, but not on, the East River, including part of affluent Brooklyn Heights; downtown Brooklyn, with Borough Hall and the $500 million courthouse complex; the rising arts area of Fort Greene; and part of Williamsburg (shared with the 12th), inhabited by Hasidic families with large numbers of children. From there, it runs southeasterly through Bed-Stuy, Clinton Hill and East New York, until it hits the Queens border and turns to the southwest to take in three communities along Jamaica Bay: Spring Creek, Starrett City, and Canarsie, the site of Jonathan Rieder's classic sociological study of Jewish and Italian flight from increasingly black neighborhoods. In the 1990s, Canarsie again experienced significant demographic change—the most dramatic of any neighborhood in New York City—as the neighborhood's black population grew from 10% to 60%, mainly due to an influx of Caribbean immigrants who prize the backyards and single-family homes. The 10th also includes Remsen Village, Flatlands and part of East Flatbush. The recent boom and sharp drop in crime rates helped improve even the borough's most hopeless areas, such as East New York, as gutted blocks were torn down and in many cases rebuilt. The district is 60% black—the highest of any New York district—and 17% Hispanic. Politically, it is overwhelmingly Democratic, one of the most Democratic districts in the nation.

The congressman from the 10th District is Edolphus Towns, first elected in 1982, when retirements and redistricting created two open seats in Brooklyn. He is a Democrat from East New York who is as experienced in government as in politics. He was born in North Carolina, the son of a tobacco sharecropper, graduated from North Carolina A&T, served two years in the Army and soon moved to Brooklyn, where he taught in the public schools and at Medgar Evers College. He became a social worker and hospital administrator, and was active in community affairs. In 1976, he became Brooklyn's deputy borough president, a position he held for six years.

In the House, Towns's voting record has lost some of its liberal edge, especially on economic issues. Starting out he worked on the Student Athlete Right-to-Know Act, which requires colleges to report the graduation rates of student athletes, and on strengthening the National Health Service Corps and the Minority Health Initiative. Responding to a local tragedy, he sought to ban the sale of toy guns that resemble real guns and convinced local stores to end sales of certain models. He worked on local projects, notably the new federal courthouse complex for Brooklyn.

Towns often took a community, rather than national, perspective. In 2001, as the senior Democrat on the Commerce, Trade and Consumer Protection Subcommittee, he attacked a report by the Federal Trade Commission that criticized marketing of what the agency called violent entertainment by the recording industry that targeted children. "It is simply wrong for the government to suggest that this music and its message are not suitable for America's teens because it contains, in some cases, explicit content," he said, referring to the mostly rap and hip-hop music. With Energy and Commerce Committee Chairman Joe Barton and the support of several large auto parts suppliers, he introduced the Right to Repair Act, to require automakers to give more information about their vehicles to repair shops. With Mary Bono, he cosponsored the bill to crack down on "spyware" that secretly monitors Internet transmissions.

For years Towns was re-elected without difficulty. In 1997 he endorsed Rudolph Giuliani for mayor; this took some courage, or showed bad judgment, since Giuliani got only 15% of the vote in two Bedford-Stuyvesant assembly districts. In 1998 Kings County Democratic Chairman Clarence Norman recruited a primary opponent in Barry Ford, a Harvard-educated Wall Street lawyer. Towns' critics concentrated on the tobacco issue. He opposed anti-tobacco legislation on the ground it would hurt farmers: "Tobacco is bad. So is starvation. Both will kill you." The Campaign for Tobacco-Free Kids put up billboards reading, "Representative Towns: Big Tobacco or Kids?" Others called him "the Marlboro man" and attacked him for accepting $54,000 from tobacco interests over 10 years. Towns beat Ford, but by only 52%–36%. Emboldened by that result, Ford barely stopped campaigning for the next two years. This time, Ford was better known and he appeared to have a real prospect of ousting Towns. But the incumbent campaigned much harder. Towns defended his support for Giuliani by pointing to the mayor's support for commercial development. He decided not to take campaign contributions from tobacco companies. Towns won this time, 57%–43%.

Since then, Democratic leaders in Brooklyn have been beset by infighting and indictments, and Towns has faced token opposition. There has been speculation that he would like to pass the district to his son, Assemblyman Darryl Towns, when he retires. Towns turns 72 in 2006.

ELEVENTH DISTRICT

Rep. Major Owens (D)

Elected 1982, 12th term; b. June 28, 1936, Memphis, TN; home, Brooklyn; Morehouse Col., B.A. 1956, Atlanta U., M.L.S. 1957; Baptist; married (Maria).

Elected Office: NY Senate, 1974–82.

Professional Career: Librarian; Brooklyn Public Library, 1958–65; Community Coord., 1964–65; V.P., Metro. Cncl. of Housing, 1964; Chmn., Brooklyn Congress on Racial Equality; Exec. Dir., Brownsville Community Cncl., 1966–68; NYC Community Devel. Agency, Comm., 1968–73; Dpty. Admin., 1972–74; Dir., Community Media Library Program, Columbia U., 1973–74.

DC Office: 2309 RHOB, 20515, 202-225-6231; Fax: 202-226-0112; Web site: www.house.gov/owens.

District Office: Brooklyn, 718-773-3100.

Committees: *Education & the Workforce* (3d of 22 D): 21st Century Competitiveness; Workforce Protections (RMM). *Government Reform* (3d of 17 D): Criminal Justice, Drug Policy & Human Resources; Federal Workforce & Agency Organization; Government Management, Finance & Accountability.

Group Ratings

	ADA	ACLU	AFS	LCV	ITIC	NTU	COC	ACU	NTLC	CHC
2004	100	95	100	100	30	13	15	0	0	18
2003	100	—	100	100	—	24	21	8	—	—

National Journal Ratings

	2003 LIB — 2003 CONS	2004 LIB — 2004 CONS
Economic	85% — 14%	88% — 11%
Social	82% — 17%	83% — 16%
Foreign	94% — 0%	97% — 2%

Key Votes of the 108th Congress

1. Drilling in ANWR	N	5. DC School Vouchers	N	9. Ban Same-Sex Marriage	N
2. Approve Bush Tax Cuts	N	6. Ban Human Cloning	N	10. Fund Iraq War	N
3. Medicare/Rx Bill	N	7. Restrict Gun Liability	N	11. Bar Cuba Embargo Funds	Y
4. Bar Overtime Pay Regs.	Y	8. Ban Partial-Birth Abortion	N	12. Intelligence Reorg.	N

Election Results

2004 general	Major Owens (D-WF)	144,999	(94%)	($474,168)
	Other	9,199	(6%)	
2004 primary	Major Owens (D)	14,718	(45%)	
	Yvette Clarke (D)	9,371	(29%)	
	Tracy Boyland (D)	7,119	(22%)	
	Gabriel Pearse (D)	1,179	(4%)	
2002 general	Major Owens (D-WF)	76,917	(87%)	($317,477)
	Susan Cleary (R-Ind)	11,149	(13%)	($10,580)
	Other	798	(1%)	

Prior Winning Percentages: 2000 (87%); 1998 (90%); 1996 (92%); 1994 (89%); 1992 (94%); 1990 (95%); 1988 (93%); 1986 (91%); 1984 (91%); 1982 (91%)

The People		Race/Ethnic Origin	Ancestry	
Area size:	12 sq. mi.	21.4% White	West Indian: 23.2% USA: 4.1%	
Urban population:	100.0%	58.5% Black	Italian: 2.8%	
Rural population:	0.0%	4.1% Asian	**2004 Presidential Vote**	
Pop. 2000:	654,361	0.2% Native Am.	Kerry (D)	172,654 (86%)
Median income:	$34,082	0.0% Hawaiian	Bush (R)	26,172 (13%)
Poverty status:	23.2%	3.0% Two+ races	Other	1,616 (1%)
Military veterans:	4.1%	0.6% Other	**2000 Presidential Vote**	
		12.1% Hispanic Origin	Gore (D)	149,740 (83%)
			Bush (R)	15,652 (9%)
			Other	15,828 (9%)
			Cook Partisan Voting Index: D +40	

Occupation   Blue collar: 15.7%   White collar: 61.2%   Gray collar: 23.1%

Brooklyn. The single word used to arouse laughter in a comedian's monologue, applause when someone said that's where they were from. It evoked an accent that twisted the English language almost to non-recognition, a raucous and brusque confrontational style, a sense of humor with an edge, the chip-on-the-shoulder assertiveness of those sure they will always be in second place. Brooklyn would never be more important than Manhattan; the Dodgers would always lose the World Series to the Yankees or the pennant to the Giants, and when they finally did win, in 1955, they moved to Los Angeles two years later. Brooklyn, as its Dutch name testifies, was a separate community from the 17th century on, one of the largest cities in the country in the 19th century, with its own celebrities (Henry Ward Beecher, Walt Whitman, John Roebling). By 1898, when the five boroughs were welded into Greater New York, one million people lived in Brooklyn, but the Brooklyn of the comedians really came into being as the subways were built in the early 20th century. In 1913, a transit agreement was struck to interlink the city's then-independent lines and triple the track to 619 miles; this agreement helped Brooklyn expand well beyond its established neighborhoods near the Brooklyn Bridge and into then-rural southwestern Brooklyn.

Suddenly, Manhattan factory workers no longer had to live in the Lower East Side tenements that social reformer Jacob Riis had exposed in the 1890s; they moved in droves into neighborhoods of three- to five-story apartments and four-family houses. Brooklyn grew from 1.1 million in 1900 to 1.6 million in 1910 to 2 million in 1920 and 2.6 million in 1930. The old

Brooklynites were mostly Protestant—Dutch, Yankee, German—plus some Catholic Irish. The new Brooklynites were heavily Italian and Jewish, and peopled the sports and entertainment businesses for a long generation, making their hometown nationally famous. In 1940, Brooklyn had 2.7 million people: one of every 49 Americans lived in Brooklyn. But in 2000, Brooklyn had 2.47 million people—one of every 119 Americans—and it is no longer a staple of national comedy. Some of its old neighborhoods have been ravaged by crime, but there is also great vitality among upwardly mobile Hispanic, Asian, Caribbean and Russian immigrants, among the hard-working black middle class, and among new generations of Italians and Jews.

The heart of the old Brooklyn was Ebbets Field, where the Dodgers played. Around the time Jackie Robinson suited up for the Brooklyn Dodgers in 1947 as the first black player in Major League Baseball, Brooklyn was experiencing an influx of blacks into Brownsville and Crown Heights near Ebbets Field. Just as rapid was the flight of ethnic whites, driven away by "blockbusting," in which hard-nosed real estate brokers stoked white fears, then bought their homes cheaply and re-sold high. After "Dem Bums" left for Los Angeles in 1958 and Ebbets Field was knocked down to be replaced by an apartment complex, Brooklyn's black neighborhoods continued to grow. Many of New York's black families came from the American South, but large numbers, particularly in Flatbush and Crown Heights, come from "the Islands"—Jamaica, Haiti, the Dominican Republic, Barbados, Trinidad and Tobago. Speaking deeply accented English, French, Spanish or various forms of Creole, they bring aromatic cooking (jerk chicken, spiced bread, peanut punch and Matouk's Special Hot Calypso Sauce) and reggae and calypso music—as well as strong families and an entrepreneurial spirit. The annual Labor Day West Indian Carnival reflects this strong local Caribbean presence. In a controversial step designed to promote community development, the owner of the New Jersey Nets basketball team announced plans in 2004 to build a new arena in Brooklyn for his team as part of a large office and residential complex.

The 11th Congressional District of New York begins at the edge of downtown Brooklyn and includes some of the borough's jewels—the Grand Army Plaza, the Parisian-style Eastern Parkway (the world's first six-lane parkway), and Prospect Park, home to the Brooklyn Library, the Brooklyn Museum and the Brooklyn Botanic Garden, with its Japanese landscaping and placid duck ponds. Park Slope, on Prospect Park's west side, has become increasingly affluent, filling up with professionals who appreciate the easy commute to downtown Manhattan. On the east side of Prospect Park is Crown Heights, with its mix of modest apartment buildings and nicely restored row houses; it was the scene of violent clashes between blacks and Hasidic Jews in 1991 (the Lubavitch Hasids, the largest Hasidic sect in the world, has its headquarters in Crown Heights). Prospect Park South, also adjoining the park, is another affluent neighborhood whose suburban feel, once enforced by restrictive covenants, contrasts sharply with the vibrant Caribbean street life just around the corner on Flatbush's Church Avenue and with struggling, depopulated Brownsville to the east. Most of these neighborhoods are places of great ethnic diversity: One minute you are in "La Saline," nicknamed for the slum district of Port-au-Prince, a center of the Haitian community in the East Flatbush-Crown Heights area; the next, you are in "Little Pakistan" in Midwood, home to the largest concentration of Pakistanis living in America. From the 1920s to the 1960s the area defined by the 11th District had the largest concentration of Jews in America but today the population is 59% black and 12% Hispanic. Politically, the district is overwhelmingly Democratic, but the borough's party organization has been weakened by allegations of corruption.

The congressman from the 11th District is Major Owens, a Democrat first elected in 1982, who claims to be the first librarian elected to Congress. Owens grew up in Memphis, went to Morehouse College and Atlanta University, and became a librarian. He worked in the Brownsville Community Council and with the Congress of Racial Equality, and served as commissioner of the city's Community Development Agency under Mayor John Lindsay. In 1974, he was elected to the New York Senate. When Congresswoman Shirley Chisholm, the daughter of an immigrant from Barbados and presidential candidate in 1972, announced her retirement in 1982, Owens entered the primary to succeed her and beat Chisholm's choice. Until 2000, Owens had no serious electoral competition.

Owens has one of the most liberal voting records in the House. He often makes long, vigorous floor speeches after the House has finished work for the day—speaking passionately of the need to support libraries, vital institutions in immigrant communities of New York's outer boroughs. On occasion, he engages in "rap" during these late-night talks, such as this *Message to the Republican Mob*: "Before you merely mauled welfare mothers, But now you're messing with the Great American Middle Class; We'll kick your rear! Grandfathers are full of fear, New anger after every tear, Our pensions down the drain, No shelter from age old rain ... " In 2004, he went a step further by writing a rap play titled, "The Viagra Monologues", which deals with issues surrounding male sexuality and monogamy; an official with the local chapter of the National Organization for Women called it "offensive." He advocated enhanced U.S. trade with Caribbean Basin nations, but criticized as a "coup" the replacement of Jean-Bertrand Aristide as president of Haiti.

Owens had opposition in the 2000 Democratic primary from City Councilwoman Una Clarke, his Jamaican-born former protégé. Although they had long been close friends and he had helped her win the council seat, their relationship became rancorous, and she accused Owens of being ineffective and anti-immigrant. Owens accused Clarke, whose council seat was term-limited, of betraying their friendship. Despite Clarke's strong showing in the Caribbean precincts, Owens won 54%–46%. After running without opposition in 2002, Owens had another tough primary in 2004. By announcing in advance that this will be his last term, he gave would-be successors an opportunity to get an early start. Their incentive to run was all the greater because of the prospect that his son Chris Owens, his campaign manager and an HMO administrator, would seek to replace him. The two main challengers were both city councilwomen in their 30s: Tracy Boyland, whose father and brother served in the state Assembly, and Yvette Clarke, the daughter of Una Clarke. Owens, who was slow to raise money, defended his record and experience and highlighted the connections of Boyland and Clarke family members to influential Republicans, including Governor George Pataki and former Mayor Rudolph Giuliani. He won the low-turnout primary with 45% to 29% for Clarke and 22% for Boyland. In all likelihood there will be a multicandidate primary challenge for this very Democratic seat in 2006. When City Councilman David Yassky, who is white, said he would run for the seat, Owens called him a "colonizer" for running in a district originally designed to elect a minority to Congress.

TWELFTH DISTRICT

Rep. Nydia Velazquez (D)

Elected 1992, 7th term; b. Mar. 28, 1953, Yabucoa, PR; home, Brooklyn; U. of PR, B.A. 1974, N.Y.U., M.A. 1976; Catholic; married (Paul Bader).

Elected Office: NY City Cncl., 1984–86.

Professional Career: Instructor, U. of PR, 1976–81; Adjunct prof., Hunter Col., 1981–83; Special Asst., U.S. Rep. Edolphus Towns, 1983; Migration Dir., PR Dept. of Labor & Human Resources, 1986–89; Secy., PR Dept. of Community Affairs in the U.S., 1989–92.

DC Office: 2241 RHOB, 20515, 202-225-2361; Fax: 202-226-0327; Web site: www.house.gov/velazquez.

District Offices: Brooklyn, 718-599-3658; Brooklyn, 718-222-5819; Manhattan, 212-673-3997.

Committees: *Financial Services* (6th of 32 D): Capital Markets, Insurance & Government Sponsored Enterprises; Housing & Community Opportunity. *Small Business* (RMM of 15 D).

Group Ratings

	ADA	ACLU	AFS	LCV	ITIC	NTU	COC	ACU	NTLC	CHC
2004	100	94	88	100	40	14	32	8	3	8
2003	90	—	100	95	—	25	25	9	—	—

National Journal Ratings

	2003 LIB	—	2003 CONS		2004 LIB	—	2004 CONS
Economic	82%	—	17%		84%	—	15%
Social	92%	—	0%		88%	—	0%
Foreign	84%	—	16%		98%	—	0%

Key Votes of the 108th Congress

1. Drilling in ANWR	N	5. DC School Vouchers	*	9. Ban Same-Sex Marriage	N
2. Approve Bush Tax Cuts	N	6. Ban Human Cloning	N	10. Fund Iraq War	N
3. Medicare/Rx Bill	N	7. Restrict Gun Liability	N	11. Bar Cuba Embargo Funds	Y
4. Bar Overtime Pay Regs.	Y	8. Ban Partial-Birth Abortion	N	12. Intelligence Reorg.	N

Election Results

2004 general	Nydia Velazquez (D-WF)	107,796	(86%)	($551,994)
	Paul Rodriguez (R-C)	17,166	(14%)	
2004 primary	Nydia Velazquez (D) .... unopposed			
2002 general	Nydia Velazquez (D-WF)	48,408	(96%)	($563,174)
	Cesar Estevez (C)	2,119	(4%)	

Prior Winning Percentages: 2000 (87%); 1998 (84%); 1996 (85%); 1994 (92%); 1992 (77%)

The People		Race/Ethnic Origin	Ancestry	
Area size:	20 sq. mi.	23.3% White	Italian: 4.7%	Polish: 4.4%
Urban population:	100.0%	8.8% Black	Irish: 3.4%	
Rural population:	0.0%	15.9% Asian	**2004 Presidential Vote**	
Pop. 2000:	654,360	0.2% Native Am.	Kerry (D) 130,019	(80%)
Median income:	$29,195	0.0% Hawaiian	Bush (R) 29,942	(19%)
Poverty status:	28.3%	2.5% Two+ races	Other 1,750	(1%)
Military veterans:	4.0%	0.7% Other	**2000 Presidential Vote**	
		48.5% Hispanic Origin	Gore (D) 102,465	(77%)
			Bush (R) 19,604	(15%)
			Other 11,268	(8%)
			Cook Partisan Voting Index: D +34	

Occupation	Blue collar: 27.5%	White collar: 50.9%	Gray collar: 21.5%

In 1957, amid a vast wave of migration that seemed destined to make Puerto Ricans the majority in New York, Leonard Bernstein wrote his musical, *West Side Story*, with Romeo as an Italian-American and Juliet as a Manhattan Puerto Rican. But New York never became majority Puerto Rican. Before World War II, there were 60,000 Puerto Ricans in New York City; three decades later, there were 800,000. But they were among the first immigrants to arrive in a city whose industrial base was stagnant. With cheap airfares and no need to go through passport control, the inflow and outflow of Puerto Ricans balanced out by the early 1960s, and in the late 1990s the number of Puerto Ricans in New York was declining, as young New Yorkers of Puerto Rican descent increasingly moved to Puerto Rico. But by then, New York City was experiencing a vast influx of Latinos from places not under the U.S. flag, and today most New York Hispanics come not from Puerto Rico but from the Dominican Republic, Colombia, Mexico, Panama and Peru.

The 12th Congressional District of New York was designed to stitch many of these diverse people together. More than two-thirds of the people here live in Brooklyn, and most of the rest in Queens, with the rest in Manhattan. In Brooklyn the district hugs the waterfront and dips inward to include areas with large Hispanic populations—but this is New York, so it gets many others as well. Overall the district in 2000 was 49% Hispanic, 16% Asian and 9% black. The 12th includes the upscale Brooklyn Heights waterfront, with its stunning but, after September 11, haunting views of Lower Manhattan, and nearby Carroll Gardens with young professionals intermingled with Italian immigrants. To the south is Sunset Park, once the home of Irish, Polish and Norwegian immigrants, now filled with Chinese, Puerto Ricans, Colombians and Ecuadorans. North of Brooklyn Heights is DUMBO (Down Under the Manhattan Bridge Over-pass), with artists in old industrial lofts, and just above it Vinegar Hill. North of the Brooklyn Navy Yard, a major base for the Navy until it was shuttered in 1966, and now an industrial park, is Williamsburg, with Orthodox Jews and recent Latino arrivals and some hip young people as well. Inland is Bushwick, with low-income Latinos and a lot of new housing thanks to longtime Assemblyman Vito Lopez. Just a few streets away, across the Brooklyn-Queens border, is Ridgewood, once mostly Irish, then Polish, now filled with new arrivals from Poland, Romania, Albania, Serbia and Bosnia. Nearby is industrial Maspeth. In Manhattan, the 12th District includes parts of the Lower East Side, Chinatown and Little Italy. In 1910, 373,000 people lived there, mostly Jewish and Italian immigrants. Today there are only a few Jews and virtually no Italians (only Italian restaurants remain); its population of 91,000 is mostly Chinese, with some Latinos and some young professionals renting newly converted apartments. Politically, the 12th District is heavily Democratic.

The congresswoman from the 12th District is Nydia Velazquez, chosen by a narrow margin in the 1992 Democratic primary and reelected ever since. She grew up in Puerto Rico, taught at the University of Puerto Rico in the 1970s and at Hunter College in the 1980s, worked for Congressman Ed Towns in 1983 and served on the New York city council in 1984. Then she worked for Puerto Rico's government offices in New York. She was one of three major contenders when the district was created in 1992. The others were liberal Elisabeth Colon and incumbent Stephen Solarz; he decided to run here rather than in the Manhattan-dominated 8th or in the 9th District in which Charles Schumer had a heavy advantage. Velazquez got the endorsements of then-Mayor David Dinkins and of Jesse Jackson, and in a light turnout beat Solarz 34%–28%, with 26% for Colon. After the primary, confidential hospital records were leaked to a New York tabloid showing that in September 1991, Velazquez had attempted suicide, was hospitalized and later underwent counseling. Evidently, that was of little concern to voters: she won in November with 77%.

In the House she has a solidly liberal voting record. Since 1998, Velazquez has been ranking Democrat on the Small Business Committee. Citing the 2 million minority-owned and 9 million woman-owned businesses, she spoke out for repeal of the estate tax in June 2000 and voted for it. But when Bill Clinton vetoed the bill, she voted to uphold his veto after a phone call from him. In 2001 she called for repeal of the 1996 welfare law, and wants no time limits on welfare and benefits for legal immigrants. After September 11, she and Jerrold Nadler got $550 million in Community Development Block Grant aid for businesses impacted by the attacks; in 2003 she called for a GAO investigation on why more than half the New York small businesses applying for disaster loans after September 11 did not receive them. She called for tests of the effects of the dreadfully polluted air that blew over Brooklyn after the attacks. She hailed the $5 million Army Corps of Engineers study of how to clean up the Gowanus Canal (at one time, it was a Mafia dumping ground) and said she envisaged a time when it was filled with gondolas and lined with restaurants. When funding for the SBA's 7(a) loan program lapsed in January 2004, she joined Small Business Chairman Don Manzullo demanding reinstatement of the program; the SBA had previously guaranteed lenders 75% if the borrower defaulted on loans up to $750,000. But the Bush administration insisted on abolishing the SBA subsidy and funding the program with higher fees to borrowers and lenders. In June 2004 Manzullo and Velazquez got the House, 281–137, to add $79 million to the SBA budget but the funds would not go straight to 7(a). The SBA reauthorization foundered on this issue, but in November 2004 Manzullo and Senate Chairman Olympia Snowe got the administration to agree on increased fees, with increases in the amounts of loans; Manzullo was agreeable since 7(a) lending remained strong after the authorization expired on October 1. With Senator Jim Talent and several House members she co-sponsored a bill to help small businesses get association health plans which passed the House 252–162 in May 2004.

Velazquez has been a major voice on issues relating to Puerto Rico. She used to favor independence, a cause favored by less than 5% of voters in Puerto Rico; by 1997 she favored continuation of the current commonwealth status (more accurately described in the Spanish term, *estado liberado asociado*, free associated state). She attacked the March 1998 bill setting the terms for a referendum on status as "a one-sided bill that is biased in favor of Puerto Rican statehood" that shows "a lack of respect for the people of Puerto Rico." She said its definition of commonwealth was biased, because it did not guarantee U.S. citizenship to future generations of Puerto Ricans (citizenship is now based not on the Fourteenth Amendment, but on a law passed by Congress in 1917, which could be repealed). Velazquez strongly advocated clemency for members of the FALN terrorist group—which was responsible for the deaths of six people—who had been imprisoned for 19 years after being convicted on seditious conspiracy and weapons charges and who had not expressed regret. When Bill Clinton granted clemency in August 1999 conditioned on a renunciation of violence, she said that the clemency should have been unconditional; she was dismayed when the House condemned the clemency by a 311–41 vote.

Velazquez has been one of many combatants in New York City's political wars but she has won reelection easily. In February 2004 she called for a federal investigation of Assemblyman Vito Lopez's selection of an organization his girlfriend ran to repair dilapidated houses. In March 2004 she asked Mayor Michael Bloomberg to use homeland security money to reopen six Brooklyn firehouses. In May 2004 she said Martha Stewart should be sentenced to community service in a training center in Bushwick.

THIRTEENTH DISTRICT

Rep. Vito Fossella (R)

Elected Nov. 1997, 4th full term; b. Mar. 9, 1965, Staten Island; home, Staten Island; U. of PA., B.S. 1993, Fordham U., J.D. 1994; Catholic; married (Mary Pat).

Elected Office: NY City Cncl., 1994–97.

Professional Career: Practicing atty., 1994.

DC Office: 1239 LHOB, 20515, 202-225-3371; Fax: 202-226-1272; Web site: www.house.gov/fossella.

District Offices: Brooklyn, 718-630-5277; Staten Island, 718-356-8400.

Committees: *Energy & Commerce* (15th of 31 R): Energy & Air Quality; Environment & Hazardous Materials; Telecommunications & the Internet. *Financial Services* (20th of 37 R): Capital Markets, Insurance & Government Sponsored Enterprises; Financial Institutions & Consumer Credit.

Group Ratings

	ADA	ACLU	AFS	LCV	ITIC	NTU	COC	ACU	NTLC	CHC
2004	20	6	14	27	90	61	90	78	84	81
2003	15	—	0	10	—	66	96	86	—	—

National Journal Ratings

	2003 LIB	—	2003 CONS		2004 LIB	—	2004 CONS
Economic	30%	—	69%		45%	—	55%
Social	42%	—	58%		43%	—	57%
Foreign	35%	—	65%		8%	—	92%

Key Votes of the 108th Congress

1. Drilling in ANWR	Y	5. DC School Vouchers	*	9. Ban Same-Sex Marriage	Y
2. Approve Bush Tax Cuts	Y	6. Ban Human Cloning	Y	10. Fund Iraq War	Y
3. Medicare/Rx Bill	Y	7. Restrict Gun Liability	Y	11. Bar Cuba Embargo Funds	N
4. Bar Overtime Pay Regs.	N	8. Ban Partial-Birth Abortion	Y	12. Intelligence Reorg.	Y

Election Results

2004 general	Vito Fossella (R-C)	112,934	(59%)	($1,134,213)
	Frank Barbaro (D-Ind-WF)	78,500	(41%)	($423,793)
2004 primary	Vito Fossella (R)	unopposed		
2002 general	Vito Fossella (R-C-RTL)	72,204	(70%)	($893,650)
	Arne Mattsson (D-L-WF)	29,366	(28%)	($6,757)
	Other	2,123	(2%)	

Prior Winning Percentages: 2000 (65%); 1998 (65%); 1997 (61%)

The People		Race/Ethnic Origin	Ancestry	
Area size:	113 sq. mi.	70.9% White	Italian: 29.5% Irish: 11.5%	
Urban population:	100.0%	6.3% Black	German: 4.3%	
Rural population:	0.0%	9.1% Asian	**2004 Presidential Vote**	
Pop. 2000:	654,361	0.1% Native Am.	Bush (R) 118,370	(55%)
Median income:	$50,092	0.0% Hawaiian	Kerry (D) 96,474	(45%)
Poverty status:	11.9%	2.3% Two+ races	Other 1,916	(1%)
Military veterans:	9.0%	0.2% Other	**2000 Presidential Vote**	
		11.0% Hispanic Origin	Gore (D) 101,079	(52%)
			Bush (R) 85,119	(44%)
			Other 6,538	(3%)
			Cook Partisan Voting Index: D + 1	

Occupation	Blue collar: 18.3%	White collar: 65.0%	Gray collar: 16.7%

Staten Island is part of New York City, yet a land apart, closer geographically to New Jersey than to Brooklyn. Its inclusion in Greater New York as part of the great 1898 consolidation was something of an afterthought, and for two-thirds of a century it was connected to the rest of the City only by ferry or through Bayonne, New Jersey, until the Verrazano Narrows Bridge—one of Robert Moses's last and most impressive infrastructure achievements—opened to traffic in 1965. Hilly Staten Island (or Richmond County) is the state's southernmost county, one-tenth as densely populated as Manhattan—and that's after it grew 22% between 1990 and 2004, the fastest growth rate of any county in New York state. Ethnically, Staten Island is the most heavily Italian part of the United States; the 13th District has the highest percentage of residents of Italian ancestry in the nation; the signs on coffee shops here read *Caffe* and on delicatessens *Salumeria*. The Staten Island Ferry docks at St. George, the government hub and home of the Staten Island Yankees' new ballpark. The north and south shores that spread out from there are notable for their pleasant Victorian homes, while the island's west shore is industrial marshland, with new development on the now-closed Fresh Kills dump. Staten Island's interior consists of blocks of suburbia alternating with scrubland that's rapidly being turned into suburbia; this growth, plus a relative shortage of mass transit, has brought significant traffic congestion to this spacious island. Developers want to build a NASCAR racetrack on the island.

Culturally, Staten Islanders are deeply conservative—more so than in most of New York's suburbs, and quite a contrast from Manhattanites who live a 20-minute ferry ride away. Taking a cue from Fresh Kills, their motto is apt: "Don't dump on us." Not many people here read the *New York Times*; the local paper is the *Staten Island Advance* (emphasis on the first syllable, please), the foundation of the Newhouse publishing empire. Fed up with New York City's high income taxes and social programs, Staten Island residents voted in November 1993 for secession, but the legislature never acted. That same year, Staten Islanders provided the margin of victory for Mayor Rudolph Giuliani, whose agenda of cutting crime and welfare rolls soothed the secessionist fervor. The Giuliani years produced an economic boom, with a new ferry terminal, additional shops and hundreds of new homes near cleaned-up beaches. The biggest victory was the closing of Fresh Kills in March 2001, though it was opened again temporarily to help in the cleanup of the World Trade Center site. The September 11 terrorist attacks killed nearly 250 Staten Islanders—nearly 10% of the dead, including nearly one-quarter of all the fire fighters who died.

The 13th Congressional District of New York is made up of Staten Island plus a few adjacent neighborhoods with similar demographics over the Verrazano Narrows Bridge in Brooklyn. These include heavily Catholic and Italian Bay Ridge and Bensonhurst—middle-class enclaves with large single-family houses and small apartment buildings. The entertainment industry has found in these two neighborhoods some of its most memorable characters: The Three Stooges (Moe, Curly and Shemp) actually grew up in Bensonhurst; it was also home to the fictional Ralph Kramden of *The Honeymooners*. And it was on the streets of Bensonhurst and Bay Ridge that John Travolta danced to fame in *Saturday Night Fever*. The district also includes Fort Hamilton, the only active-duty military base in New York City and one of the oldest military posts still in operation in the United States. The 13th is seeing a rising number of immigrants—a few white ethnic neighborhoods near St. George have experienced an influx of newcomers from West Africa, Mexico, South America, Southeast Asia, and Russia—but Staten Island remains New York's whitest borough; the 13th is only 6% black and 11% Hispanic. Voters here solidly backed Republicans George Pataki for governor and Rick Lazio for senator, and Staten Island provided Republican mayoral candidate Michael Bloomberg with his winning margin in 2001. The 13th District voted 52%–44% for Al Gore in 2000. But—September 11 may have been the reason—it snapped back and voted 55%–45% for George W. Bush in 2004, one of the biggest increases in Bush percentage in the country.

The congressman from the 13th District is Vito Fossella, a Republican who won a November 1997 special election. Fossella comes from a political, and Democratic, Staten Island family: his great-grandfather, James O'Leary, was a New Deal congressman from 1935–44, elected from Staten Island and the Wall Street tip of Manhattan; his father, Vito Fossella Sr., chaired the city's Board of Standards under Mayor Edward Koch; his uncle, Frank Fossella, was elected to the city council in 1981 and was beaten in 1985 by Republican Susan Molinari, Vito Fossella Jr.'s predecessor in Congress. Despite the party difference, the families became close. Vito Fossella graduated from Penn and Fordham law school and became a Republican in 1990, at 25, because of his conservative philosophy; he switched from pro-choice to pro-life in 1995, after the birth of his son. He worked on the campaigns of Susan Molinari, who succeeded her father, Guy Molinari, in the House. In 1994, Fossella, less than a year after finishing law school, was elected to the city council to fill a vacancy, with the help of the Molinaris.

Fossella was elected to Congress after Susan Molinari's surprise resignation, in what turned out to be a high visibility contest. Democrats picked Eric Vitaliano, a 15-year assemblyman from the conservative mid-Island district, an abortion opponent and sponsor of New York's death penalty. Vitaliano criticized Fossella as inexperienced and constantly tried to link Fossella with House Speaker Newt Gingrich. Fossella hit Vitaliano for supporting needle exchanges and for not taking Americans for Tax Reform's anti-tax-raise pledge. Two other factors helped Fossella. One was $750,000 in independent expenditures by the national Republican Party, attacking Vitaliano for supporting tax increases, and a group called Victory 97, which paid for posters depicting Vitaliano's allegedly silly spending programs: snow-making equipment in Ulster County, a state Museum of Cheese. The other was the re-election campaign of Giuliani, in a district where few local Democratic officeholders would admit they supported their liberal nominee Ruth Messinger. On Election Day, Giuliani carried the district 3–1 and Fossella won 61%–39%.

In the House, Fossella has one of the most conservative voting records in the New York delegation. He serves on the Energy and Commerce, and Financial Services committees, both locally useful slots. He worked on interstate waste issues, pushed for rerouting Newark Airport flights away from Staten Island, and got $20 million to dredge the Arthur Kill as part of a revitalization project. He sponsored the law that designates September 11 as Patriot Day, a day of reflection, and he helped to organize the ceremonial session of Congress in Lower Manhattan to observe the first anniversary of the attacks. On the highway bill, he said that he would block funding for the Second Avenue subway line unless Democrats in Albany approved spending for reconstruction of the Staten Island ferry terminal.

Fossella did not face a serious challenge until 2004, when 76-year-old former Assemblyman Frank Barbaro ran an aggressive campaign with help from allies in organized labor. With substantial funding, Barbaro attacked Fossella as anti-union and too conservative even for this district. Fossella defended his record of helping to rebuild lower Manhattan after the September 11 attacks and his support for tax cuts. He won 59%–41%, with 63% in Staten Island; Barbaro got 53% of the vote in Brooklyn, his home, which cast only 24% of the total. In local politics, Fossella has criticized Mayor Michael Bloomberg for not aiding the Republican party and, after the November 2004 elections, urged Colin Powell to come back to New York and run against Senator Hillary Rodham Clinton in 2006.

FOURTEENTH DISTRICT

Rep. Carolyn Maloney (D)

Elected 1992, 7th term; b. Feb. 19, 1948, Greensboro, NC; home, Manhattan; Greensboro Col, A.B. 1968; Presbyterian; married (Clifton).

Elected Office: NY City Cncl., 1982–92.

Professional Career: NYC Bd. of Ed., 1970–77; Legis. aide, NY Assembly & NY Senate, 1977–82.

DC Office: 2331 RHOB, 20515, 202-225-7944; Fax: 202-225-4709; Web site: www.house.gov/maloney.

District Offices: Manhattan, 212-860-0606; Queens, 718-932-1804.

Committees: *Financial Services* (4th of 32 D): Domestic and International Monetary Policy, Trade & Technology (RMM); Financial Institutions & Consumer Credit; Oversight & Investigations. *Government Reform* (6th of 17 D): Federalism & the Census; Government Management, Finance & Accountability; National Security, Emerging Threats & International Relations. *Joint Economic Committee* (7th of 10 Reps.).

Group Ratings

	ADA	ACLU	AFS	LCV	ITIC	NTU	COC	ACU	NTLC	CHC
2004	100	85	100	100	60	10	45	4	0	7
2003	95	—	100	100	—	20	33	12	—	—

National Journal Ratings

	2003 LIB	—	2003 CONS	2004 LIB	—	2004 CONS
Economic	83%	—	16%	84%	—	15%
Social	90%	—	8%	86%	—	12%
Foreign	75%	—	21%	87%	—	12%

Key Votes of the 108th Congress

1. Drilling in ANWR	N	5. DC School Vouchers	N	9. Ban Same-Sex Marriage	N
2. Approve Bush Tax Cuts	N	6. Ban Human Cloning	N	10. Fund Iraq War	Y
3. Medicare/Rx Bill	N	7. Restrict Gun Liability	N	11. Bar Cuba Embargo Funds	Y
4. Bar Overtime Pay Regs.	Y	8. Ban Partial-Birth Abortion	N	12. Intelligence Reorg.	N

Election Results

2004 general	Carolyn Maloney (D-Ind-WF)	186,688	(81%)	($918,162)
	Anton Srdanovic (R-C)	43,623	(19%)	($23,217)
2004 primary	Carolyn Maloney (D)	unopposed		
2002 general	Carolyn Maloney (D-L-Ind-WF)	95,931	(75%)	($916,773)
	Anton Srdanovic (R-C)	31,548	(25%)	($44,255)

Prior Winning Percentages: 2000 (74%); 1998 (77%); 1996 (72%); 1994 (64%); 1992 (50%)

The People		Race/Ethnic Origin	Ancestry	
Area size:	15 sq. mi.	65.9% White	Irish: 8.1%	Italian: 7.7%
Urban population:	100.0%	4.8% Black	German: 6.1%	
Rural population:	0.0%	11.4% Asian	**2004 Presidential Vote**	
Pop. 2000:	654,361	0.1% Native Am.	Kerry (D) 201,782	(74%)
Median income:	$57,152	0.0% Hawaiian	Bush (R) 66,494	(24%)
Poverty status:	12.4%	3.1% Two+ races	Other 3,160	(1%)
Military veterans:	6.0%	0.6% Other	**2000 Presidential Vote**	
		14.0% Hispanic Origin	Gore (D) 168,842	(70%)
			Bush (R) 56,055	(23%)
			Other 16,908	(7%)
			Cook Partisan Voting Index: D +26	

Occupation   Blue collar: 7.8%   White collar: 82.1%   Gray collar: 10.2%

The Upper East Side of Manhattan, the home today of people with more accumulated wealth than anywhere else in the world, began as much of New York City did—as farmland. Its eastern border was established at Fifth Avenue when work began on Central Park in 1857, but most of the area was still farmland when the park was completed in 1873. During the 1880s, the avenues—Fifth, Madison, Park, Lexington, Third, Second, First—were paved, and rich New Yorkers and many who had made their money elsewhere—Pittsburgh steel baron Andrew Carnegie, Montana mining magnate William Clark—built mansions on Fifth Avenue. Third Avenue, with its elevated train line, was lined with walkups for working class commuters, while the side streets off Fifth Avenue were lined with massive brownstone houses shielded from the industrial haze along the East River. The Upper East Side began taking on its present character in 1913, when Grand Central Terminal was opened and the New York Central rail line was buried under Park Avenue: what had been a filthy railroad cut became a broad boulevard lined with grand apartment buildings. The federal income tax, passed the same year, had the unintended consequence of encouraging New York's rich to dispense with grand mansions and live, quietly and out of sight, in apartment buildings where doormen protected their privacy.

The emergence of the modern Upper East Side represented yet another iteration of the pattern noticed by the mid-19th century New York diarists Philip Hone and George Templeton Strong: On such a compact island, it took only a generation or so before buildings were torn down and rebuilt. Even today, New York is being transformed by gleaming postmodern skyscrapers and high-priced storefronts, though its most enduring landmarks were products of the first half of the 20th century: the Flatiron Building in 1901; the Woolworth Building and Grand Central in 1913; the Chrysler Building, Empire State Building and Rockefeller Center in the 1920s and 1930s; and the United Nations headquarters, the world's first glass-fronted skyscraper, after World War II. This area also holds the more humble distinction as the site of the first public housing project in America—the First Houses, built in lower Manhattan in 1935 by Mayor Fiorello LaGuardia.

The 14th Congressional District of New York includes within its irregular borders the Upper East Side and nearly all of these buildings. The district begins at East 96th Street, the historic dividing line between Manhattan's wealthiest and poorest neighborhoods, near where the railroad emerges from its tunnel and comes out in the middle of Park Avenue, and runs all the way down to East 9th Street in the East Village. It includes all of Central Park; much of the midtown corporate district; Murray Hill and Gramercy Park, and also parts of the East Village and the Lower East Side. Midtown Manhattan's skyscrapers and the Garment District are also here. The 14th also takes in Roosevelt Island, a 147-acre expanse in the East River that was transformed in the early 1970s from a hospital-and-prison complex to an ethnically diverse residential neighborhood (and stripped of its old name, Welfare Island). The 14th also includes part of Queens across the East River: Long Island City, Steinway, part of historically Irish Sunnyside and all of the vibrantly Greek Astoria, now with a growing number of Asians, Latinos and Arabs. The institutions of the 14th are famous and powerful—from the United Nations to the New York Public Library to St. Patrick's Cathedral—and its stores of culture are among the world's finest: the Metropolitan Museum of Art, the Guggenheim, the Whitney and the Frick, but also a rising arts cluster in Long Island City with the contemporary art gallery P.S. 1 and the American Museum of the Moving Image adjoining the old Astoria movie studios, where most movies were made before the industry moved to sunnier Hollywood.

The 14th District is the latest version of the Upper East Side-based Silk Stocking district, originally created in 1918. The Silk Stocking district has always been dominated by its affluent and highly educated voters, leaders in securities, publishing, advertising, entertainment, broadcasting and communications. Historically, the Silk Stocking creed was confidence in its duty to lead the nation and mistrust of the city's (usually Democratic) immigrant masses—the politics of Theodore Roosevelt, the old *New York Herald Tribune* and Henry Luce's *Time* magazine. While it did not trust union leaders and Democratic Party politicians, it accepted much of the New Deal. This district believed the nation should be led by the well-educated Protestant gentlemen one saw strolling down Madison Avenue to their clubs, who held high government posts from Theodore Roosevelt's day and past Franklin's. But the attitude of the Manhattan elite was transformed from liberal Republican to leftish Democratic in a way personified by the Silk Stocking district's most famous congressman, John Lindsay. He was elected in 1958 as a liberal Republican, an advocate of civil liberties full of mistrust of machine Democrats and unions, and in 1965 he was elected mayor of New York. While mayor, he ran up huge debts that led the city to the brink of bankruptcy in 1975, while neighborhoods deteriorated and the city lost 1 million people in the 1970s. He was succeeded as congressman and ultimately as mayor by Edward Koch, whose political travels were the reverse: Koch started as a liberal reform Democrat and became more conservative, and in the process lost the support of elite Manhattan by backing capital punishment, opposing racial quotas and questioning poverty programs. Attitudes have changed again: the troubled mayoralty of David Dinkins led Manhattanites to back Rudolph Giuliani, and they applauded his successes in cutting crime and welfare and taxes. But Giuliani and his successor Michael Bloomberg, who lives in his town house on East 79th Street, are firm cultural liberals on abortion, gay rights and gun control. To the national Republican party of Newt Gingrich in the 1990s and now George W. Bush, who brought the Republican Convention of 2004 to a less than enthralled Manhattan, the Upper East Side is unremittingly hostile: these are people that seem to come from another country. The Upper East Side reacted with similar disdain to Barry Goldwater in 1964, and voted for Lyndon Johnson by a wide margin, as did the entire country; but, when the rest of the country narrowly favored George W. Bush over Al Gore and then John Kerry, the Upper East Side voted for the Democrats by wider margins than it had voted for Johnson. In American politics today, cultural issues trump economics: the affluent Upper East Side votes heavily Democratic (the 10021 zip code was the nation's top zip code for Democratic campaign contributions in the 2004 election cycle) while low-income Mississippi and Montana vote heavily Republican.

The congresswoman from the 14th District is Carolyn Maloney, a Democrat first elected in 1992. Born and educated in North Carolina, she visited New York in 1970 at the age of 22, loved it and "just stayed." She worked on welfare education programs during the 1970s, and from 1977 to 1982 she was a legislative staffer in Albany. She was elected to the New York City Council in 1982. For 1992, redistricting made the Silk Stocking district more Democratic and Maloney ran against incumbent Bill Green, a thoughtful liberal Republican who shared Manhattan's cultural liberalism but could not compete with the enthusiasm of a Democratic Party dominated by the feminist left. And he was poorly positioned to appeal to voters in the outer borough neighborhoods that were for the first time added to the district, who liked Republicans conservative on cultural issues but liberal on economics. Maloney lost the Manhattan part of the district 50%–44%, but carried Queens heavily and won 50%–48% overall.

Maloney started off in the House with a certain naiveté but stayed to make serious contributions on important issues and has had a liberal voting record. On the Financial Services Committee, she worked to keep banks from controlling other businesses, sought more oversight of the Federal Reserve, added some privacy provisions to the Gramm-Leach-Bliley financial modernization law, and in 2002 added language to the corporate accountability bill that requires a company to disclose publicly whenever its board votes to violate its own ethics code. With an eye to Astoria, she helped found the Congressional Caucus on Hellenic Issues; with an eye to the corporate suites, she voted for normal trade relations with China. A leader of the Women's Caucus, she demanded that the FDA permit over-the-counter sales of morning-after birth control pills, and opposed separating men and women in basic training. In 2001, she delivered a speech on the House floor dressed in a blue burkha to highlight the Taliban's cruel treatment of women.

With part of her district in Lower Manhattan and close to Ground Zero, the aftermath of the September 11 attacks kept her busy. She was among the most outspoken House Democrats urging George W. Bush to quickly send New York the $20 billion that Congress approved for cleanup and recovery and she urged him to appoint a coordinator to work with the city. Her proposal to give a $1,000 tax credit to visitors to the city went nowhere. In 2004, she teamed with Republican Christopher Shays to push for House action on the intelligence-reform proposals urged by the commission created to investigate the causes of the September 11 attacks and backed reluctantly by George W. Bush and most Republicans. With Shays, she also sponsored in

March 2004 a Remember 9/11 Health bill to provide federal insurance coverage to individuals who were injured or suffered poor health because of the terror attacks.

Any doubts that Maloney had a firm lock on the district were dispelled in the Republican year of 1994. Manhattan Councilman Charles Millard spent almost $1 million against her; but the 14th District was voting 78% for Mario Cuomo (who lost his bid that year for a fourth term as governor) and Maloney won 64%–35%. Aside from the perils of redistricting, she has not had to worry about reelection since then.

FIFTEENTH DISTRICT

Rep. Charles Rangel (D)

Elected 1970, 18th term; b. June 11, 1930, New York City; home, Harlem; N.Y.U., B.S. 1957, St. John's U., LL.B. 1960; Catholic; married (Alma).

Military Career: Army, 1948–52 (Korea).

Elected Office: NY Assembly, 1966–70.

Professional Career: Asst. U.S. Atty., S. Dist. of NY, 1959–64; Legal Cnsl., NYC Housing & Redevel. Bd., Neighborhood Conservation Bureau, 1963–68; Gen. Cnsl., Natl. Advisory Comm. on Selective Svc., 1966.

DC Office: 2354 RHOB, 20515, 202-225-4365; Fax: 202-225-0816; Web site: www.house.gov/rangel.

District Office: Manhattan, 212-663-3900.

Committees: *Ways & Means* (RMM of 17 D): Oversight. *Joint Committee on Taxation* (4th of 5 Reps.).

Group Ratings

	ADA	ACLU	AFS	LCV	ITIC	NTU	COC	ACU	NTLC	CHC
2004	95	94	100	91	67	9	30	0	3	8
2003	85	—	100	90	—	24	25	14	—	—

National Journal Ratings

	2003 LIB	—	2003 CONS	2004 LIB	—	2004 CONS
Economic	92%	—	0%	77%	—	22%
Social	92%	—	0%	82%	—	17%
Foreign	79%	—	21%	93%	—	7%

Key Votes of the 108th Congress

1. Drilling in ANWR	N	5. DC School Vouchers	*	9. Ban Same-Sex Marriage	*
2. Approve Bush Tax Cuts	N	6. Ban Human Cloning	N	10. Fund Iraq War	N
3. Medicare/Rx Bill	N	7. Restrict Gun Liability	*	11. Bar Cuba Embargo Funds	Y
4. Bar Overtime Pay Regs.	Y	8. Ban Partial-Birth Abortion	N	12. Intelligence Reorg.	N

Election Results

2004 general	Charles Rangel (D-WF)	161,351	(91%)	($1,728,867)
	Kenneth Jefferson (R)	12,355	(7%)	
	Other	3,345	(2%)	
2004 primary	Charles Rangel (D)	19,087	(76%)	
	Ruben Vargas (D)	3,254	(13%)	
	Geoffrey Johnson (D)	2,779	(11%)	
2002 general	Charles Rangel (D-WF)	84,367	(88%)	($1,749,972)
	Jessie Fields (R-Ind)	11,008	(12%)	($34,001)

Prior Winning Percentages: 2000 (92%); 1998 (93%); 1996 (91%); 1994 (97%); 1992 (95%); 1990 (97%); 1988 (97%); 1986 (96%); 1984 (97%); 1982 (97%); 1980 (96%); 1978 (96%); 1976 (97%); 1974 (97%); 1972 (96%); 1970 (87%)

The People		Race/Ethnic Origin	Ancestry		
Area size:	16 sq. mi.	16.4% White	West Indian: 2.8% German: 2.0%		
Urban population:	100.0%	30.5% Black	Irish: 2.0%		
Rural population:	0.0%	2.8% Asian	**2004 Presidential Vote**		
Pop. 2000:	654,361	0.2% Native Am.	Kerry (D) 194,186	(90%)	
Median income:	$27,934	0.0% Hawaiian	Bush (R) 20,049	(9%)	
Poverty status:	30.5%	1.8% Two+ races	Other 2,255	(1%)	
Military veterans:	4.6%	0.4% Other	**2000 Presidential Vote**		
		47.9% Hispanic Origin	Gore (D) 165,002	(87%)	
			Bush (R) 12,430	(7%)	
			Other 13,292	(7%)	
			Cook Partisan Voting Index: D +43		

Occupation   Blue collar: 14.8%   White collar: 63.8%   Gray collar: 21.4%

Harlem, for many years America's most famous black ghetto, is now rebounding from decades of grim times. Harlem's development came relatively late in New York City's history. When Alexander Hamilton and Roger Morris built mansions in northern Manhattan, they were far out in the countryside. Early critics of Central Park questioned the necessity of setting aside open land when picnickers could always go to Harlem. By the late 19th entury, Harlem had become a commuter neighborhood for Germans and then Jews and Italians. After the turn of the century, real-estate speculators began constructing blocks of impressive brownstones, hoping to capitalize on the impending arrival of the subway. But overbuilding led to high vacancy rates, and some landlords, in desperation, agreed to rent to African-Americans as long as they were willing to pay a premium. After generations of being shunted from one neighborhood to the next as the city developed, enough black residents were willing to do so that the neighborhood soon turned into the locus of New York City's African-American community. Harlem expanded from its nucleus around Lenox Avenue and 125th Street, while the Italian neighborhood to the east later known as Spanish Harlem grew outward from 116th Street and Pleasant Avenue. In northwest Harlem's Sugar Hill lived many of the greatest black Americans—W.E.B. DuBois, Thurgood Marshall, Ralph Ellison, Joe Louis.

For a long moment Harlem was a wondrous place, a center of writers and professionals and entertainers; the rosters of the Apollo Theater on 125th Street in the 1920s and 1930s were filled with the names of great artists still remembered today. Back then, the *WPA Guide* described Harlem as "the spiritual capital of Black America." But starting with the summer 1964 riot, Harlem faced decades of deterioration. Hundreds of brownstones were abandoned or pulled down. As successful black families moved outward—to Springfield Gardens in Queens or Williamsbridge in the Bronx or to the Westchester or New Jersey suburbs—Harlem was increasingly left with welfare mothers and criminal gangs, and its population dropped by one-third between 1970 and 1990.

But in the 1990s things started turning better. The federal government gave $300 million in investment capital, and the huge drop in crime under Mayor Rudolph Giuliani made Harlem real estate valuable again. Brownstones were renovated, vacant city buildings sold off; neighborhood schools upgraded; commercial frontage repaired; arts spaces opened. Harlem was made an Enterprise Zone, with favorable federal and state tax treatment, and the Metropolitan Economic Revitalization Fund, run by New York Secretary of State Randy Daniels, pumped money into new developments, as did Calvin Butts's Abyssinian Baptist Church. Younger African-Americans are returning, while visitors from overseas, especially Japan and Europe, flock to the area for historical tours, prompting a boomlet in niche hotels and guest houses. Supermarkets have opened, there is a big shopping center on 125th Street, with the same stores found in suburban malls, chain drug stores have opened numerous branches. And in July 2001, Bill Clinton opened his post-presidential office at 55 West 125th Street.

Politically, Harlem has been heavily Democratic ever since the 1930s, when black voters switched from the Republican party of Abraham Lincoln to the Democratic party of Franklin Roosevelt. Oddly, Harlem did not get its own congressional district until 1944; the lines, previously drawn in 1918, were based on the 1910 Census, when Harlem had far fewer people. The new congressman was Adam Clayton Powell Jr., minister at the Abyssinian Baptist Church and a brilliant orator who became the most famous (and infamous) black politician of his time: chairman of the Education and Labor Committee when it passed the Great Society programs in 1965, then excluded from Congress in 1967 (illegally, the Supreme Court ruled) for refusing to honor a New York decree in a libel case brought by a plaintiff he called a "bag woman."

Today, the 15th Congressional District of New York includes not just Harlem but all of northern Manhattan, down to 89th Street on the west side and 96th Street on the east side. On the west side, the district's southern reaches include portions of the white-liberal Upper West Side as well as the Morningside Heights precincts around Columbia University. On the east side, 96th Street is where the railroad comes out of the tunnel that runs under Park Avenue to Grand Central Station and the Upper East Side gives way to Harlem. Spanish Harlem, just to the north, was once Italian (it was Fiorello LaGuardia's political base and Al Pacino was born there), and later heavily Puerto Rican; today, "El Barrio" has fewer Puerto Ricans and more Latinos with roots in other Latin countries. Still further north, the district includes Washington Heights, once mainly Jewish, and Inwood, once heavily Italian. Now both are heavily Latino, the center of Dominican life in New York as Dominicans replace Puerto Ricans as New York's most numerous Latino group. Washington Heights was hit especially hard by the crack epidemic in the late 1980s and early 1990s, but now it too is recovering thanks to reduced crime and immigrant vitality. Governor George Pataki in 2002 made a point of coming to shop on Dyckman Street, the boundary between Washington Heights and Inwood, and speaking to passers-by in his recently acquired Spanish. The district also includes imposing parts of New York's infrastructure—the huge Con Edison plant on the East River, Wards Island, home to the Triborough Bridge, and the city prison on Rikers Island: but there are no voters here. Overall, the district is 31% black and 48% Hispanic—figures that testify to decades of black flight from Harlem and the continuing in-rush of immigrants from the Western Hemisphere. In 2004 this was the most heavily Democratic congressional district in the nation, 90% for John Kerry and 9% for George W. Bush.

The congressman from the 15th District is Charles Rangel, first elected to the House in 1970. Rangel is now the senior member of the New York delegation and ranking Democrat on Ways and Means. He grew up in Harlem and served in the Army in Korea, where he rescued 40 men from behind the lines in Kunu-ri and was awarded the Bronze Star. He graduated from New York University and St. John's University law school, served as legal counsel in several government agencies and was elected to the Assembly in 1966; he was part of a group of young black politicians, with state Senator Basil Paterson, Carl McCall and Assemblyman Percy Sutton, who for many years dominated Harlem and greatly influenced New York politics. In 1970 Rangel challenged Powell in the Democratic primary and narrowly won. Like most Harlem politicians, he has long argued that government aid and racial preferences are needed to solve Harlem's problems. Yet much in his own career suggests otherwise.

Rangel's main emphasis for a decade was denunciation of the drug trade. From 1983 until it was abolished in 1993 with the other House select committees, Rangel chaired the Select Committee on Narcotics Abuse and Control, and seldom missed a chance to relate other problems to drugs; after all, he has seen how they can destroy a community. On Ways and Means Rangel worked, with success, to protect state and local income tax deductibility in the 1986 tax reform and is an author of the Federal Empowerment Zone demonstration, the Low Income Housing tax credit and the Targeted Jobs tax credit. All those are aimed at turning around places like Harlem.

Rangel combines political shrewdness with a winning personality, but when Republicans took control of the House he indulged in some extravagant rhetoric. When a bipartisan majority voted to end racial preferences in broadcasting in 1995, Rangel lashed out in a letter to Ways and Means Chairman Bill Archer: "Mr. Chairman, in America we cannot afford to be colorblind. Just like under Hitler, people say they don't mean to blame any particular individuals and groups, but in the U.S. those groups always turn out to be minorities and immigrants." Archer refused to speak to Rangel except in public committee meetings and refused to meet with him in private until June 1999, when Archer and Rangel were working on Social Security. Rangel defended Bill

Clinton against impeachment with great vigor, but he did not always get along with Clinton. He resented it when the administration negotiated directly with Republicans, leaving congressional Democrats out of the loop.

Since January 1997 Rangel has been ranking Democrat on Ways and Means; if Democrats win back a majority in 2006, he would be its first New York City chairman since Fernando Wood in 1877–81. Rangel remembered how he had been beaten for House whip in 1986 by Tony Coelho, a champion Democratic fundraiser, and decided for the first time to become a major fundraiser himself: of course it helped that with only a few more Democratic seats he would chair Ways and Means. In 1999 he raised $2.3 million for Democratic candidates, more than anyone else except Minority Leader Dick Gephardt and DCCC Chairman Patrick Kennedy; he raised another $4 million in 2000 but only $1.1 million in the 2004 cycle.

Amid all this politicking, Rangel still found time for legislating. He worked hard for a bill to cut tariffs on apparel and other imports from sub-Saharan Africa, and also from the Caribbean and Central America. His chief partners in this were Republicans Ed Royce and Tom DeLay; it was opposed by unions and textile interests, and also by Jesse Jackson Jr. and other members of the Congressional Black Caucus. Jackson said it would help only multinational corporations and "African elites," but it passed the House 309–110 in May 2000. Rangel favors eliminating all sanctions on trade with Cuba; he favors allowing Haitian and Dominican immigrants into the United States on the same basis as refugees from Cuba. During 2004 Rangel did not take a position on the Central American Free Trade Agreement. But in March 2004 he did praise the administration for including the Dominican Republic in the agreement, and in October 2004 criticized it for threatening to exclude the Dominican Republic if it didn't repeal its tax on soft drinks with high-fructose corn syrup; Rangel said that issue should be taken to the WTO. In early 2005 he was heavily lobbied to support CAFTA.

Rangel voted against the Iraq war resolution in October 2002 and in November 2003 called for the resignation of Donald Rumsfeld. In March 2004, he had discussions with Haiti's ousted President Jean-Bertrand Aristide; he relayed Aristide's claim that "the so-called resignation was dictated to him over the phone by representatives of the United States embassy," but added, "I'm not in a position to contradict Secretary Powell. But this information about Aristide asking to leave the country, or that his life was in danger, was never shared with us." He was arrested after protesting outside the Sudanese Embassy in 2004, as he had been outside the South African Embassy in 1984. On the last day of 2002 he called for a revival of the military draft, contending that "a disproportionate number of the poor and members of minority groups make up the enlisted ranks of the military, while the most privileged Americans are underrepresented or absent." He introduced a bill in 2003 to require some form of national service, military or civilian, from Americans from 18 to 26, and found 13 co-sponsors. When House Republican leaders brought it to a vote in October 2004, he called it a "political maneuver to kill rumors of the president's intention to reinstate the draft after the November election," and voted against it, saying it had had no committee hearings; it was voted down 402–2.

Ways and Means Chairman Bill Archer was crisp and to the point; Bill Thomas, who succeeded him in 2001, is acerbic and uncollegial, and has made few moves to bipartisanship. Rangel's frustration came out when he was asked in October 2002 about a Thomas tax proposal. "It's almost accepted now that all Thomas has to do is to talk to DeLay and Armey, and then his bills come to the floor. I am embarrassed that I would hear about [the tax proposal] from you, [but] it is not unusual." But Rangel has not been an easy man to be bipartisan with. Of the fall 2001 stimulus package he said, "This isn't an economic stimulus bill. This is a corporate welfare bill." In 2003 he joined with Republican Philip Crane to back a five-year phased-in reduction of the corporate income tax from 35% to 31.5%, with the full reduction to go to manufacturers with all their operations in the United States. But the House rejected that in favor of Thomas's approach.

At times, the mistrust between Rangel and other Democrats and Thomas has been disruptive. In July 2003, a Ways and Means markup of pension legislation ended in chaos after Democrats walked out in protest; they charged that they hadn't had enough time to review a substitute amendment that the committee had met to mark up. Thomas called on Capitol Police to remove them from the library where they had gathered; in their absence, Republicans approved the bill by voice vote. Rangel later offered a resolution to nullify the markup and chastise Thomas but dropped it after Thomas took to the House floor and gave an emotional apology for his actions.

Rangel also protested when he was excluded by Thomas from the conference committee on the 2003 Medicare prescription drug bill; at one point in October he, Stephanie Tubbs Jones and Marion Berry showed up at the room where the conference was meeting. But the only Democrats Thomas allowed to participate were Senators Max Baucus and John Breaux. In January 2005 Rangel said that on any broad tax bill he would insist on retaining the deductions for state and local taxes and for home mortgages, as he had on the tax bill being considered in 1985 and 1986.

In April 2004 he called on Attorney General John Ashcroft to investigate the 1955 murder of Emmet Till in Mississippi, a crime for which the perpetrators have never been held responsible. He introduced a bill to allow the mother and other relatives of Amadou Diallo, killed in a tragic mistake by New York police, to remain in the United States.

Rangel has long been a major player in New York city and state politics. He strongly backed his old friend Carl McCall for governor, and in December 2001 said he would vote for George Pataki if the nomination went to McCall's rival, Andrew Cuomo. In October 2002 Rangel attacked the DNC for not backing McCall strongly enough; the DNC had put $240,000 and the RNC $1.5 million into New York.

Rangel himself has been easily reelected. In 1994 he faced primary opposition from the son of his predecessor, the Puerto Rican-raised Councilman Adam Clayton Powell IV (Adam Clayton Powell III, another son, is a respected media expert). Rangel spent $1.4 million and won 61%–33%. In March 2004 Powell, elected to the Assembly in 2000, formed an exploratory committee and said, "I have had my eye on that seat for a long time." He is not the only one. As Assemblyman Keith Wright said, "Everyone is interested in that seat. In fact, if you're in politics in Harlem and you're not interested in looking at that congressional seat, something is wrong." But he added that no one but Powell would run against Rangel, and in 2004 Powell didn't. Rangel, excluded from so much Ways and Means business by Bill Thomas, has said serving in Congress is "not as exciting" as it once was. But when asked in March 2004 when he might retire, he said, "I haven't come to any decisions. I haven't even discussed it with my wife."

SIXTEENTH DISTRICT

Rep. Jose Serrano (D)

Elected Mar. 1990, 8th full term; b. Oct. 24, 1943, Mayaguez, PR; home, Bronx; Lehman Col.; Catholic; married (Mary).

Military Career: Army Medical Corps, 1964–66.

Elected Office: Dist. 7 Schl. Bd., 1969–74; NY Assembly, 1974–90.

Professional Career: Banker, 1961–69.

DC Office: 2227 RHOB, 20515, 202-225-4361; Fax: 202-225-6001; Web site: www.house.gov/serrano.

District Office: Bronx, 718-620-0084.

Committees: *Appropriations* (10th of 29 D): Homeland Security; Science, State, Justice, Commerce & Related Agencies.

Group Ratings

	ADA	ACLU	AFS	LCV	ITIC	NTU	COC	ACU	NTLC	CHC
2004	100	94	100	100	30	9	30	0	0	18
2003	90	—	100	95	—	20	21	18	—	—

National Journal Ratings

	2003 LIB	—	2003 CONS	2004 LIB	—	2004 CONS
Economic	91%	—	9%	93%	—	7%
Social	92%	—	0%	88%	—	0%
Foreign	89%	—	11%	97%	—	2%

Key Votes of the 108th Congress

1. Drilling in ANWR	N	5. DC School Vouchers	*	9. Ban Same-Sex Marriage	N
2. Approve Bush Tax Cuts	N	6. Ban Human Cloning	*	10. Fund Iraq War	N
3. Medicare/Rx Bill	N	7. Restrict Gun Liability	N	11. Bar Cuba Embargo Funds	Y
4. Bar Overtime Pay Regs.	Y	8. Ban Partial-Birth Abortion	N	12. Intelligence Reorg.	N

Election Results

2004 general	Jose Serrano (D-WF)	111,638	(95%)	($351,845)
	Ali Mohamed (R-C)	5,610	(5%)	
2004 primary	Jose Serrano (D)	unopposed		
2002 general	Jose Serrano (D-WF)	50,716	(92%)	($214,152)
	Frank Dellavalle (R-C)	4,366	(8%)	

Prior Winning Percentages: 2000 (96%); 1998 (95%); 1996 (96%); 1994 (96%); 1992 (91%); 1990 (93%); 1990 (92%)

The People		Race/Ethnic Origin	Ancestry	
Area size:	13 sq. mi.	2.9% White	West Indian: 3.9% Subsaharan: 3.1%	
Urban population:	100.0%	30.3% Black	USA: 2.3%	
Rural population:	0.0%	1.6% Asian	**2004 Presidential Vote**	
Pop. 2000:	654,360	0.3% Native Am.	Kerry (D) 130,109	(89%)
Median income:	$19,311	0.0% Hawaiian	Bush (R) 14,766	(10%)
Poverty status:	42.2%	1.6% Two+ races	Other 799	(1%)
Military veterans:	3.9%	0.5% Other	**2000 Presidential Vote**	
		62.8% Hispanic Origin	Gore (D) 112,786	(92%)
			Bush (R) 6,634	(5%)
			Other 2,630	(2%)
			Cook Partisan Voting Index: D +43	

Occupation	Blue collar: 23.6%	White collar: 46.4%	Gray collar: 30.0%

It may not quite be "the beautiful Bronx," as borough historian Lloyd Utlan calls it, but The Bronx seems to have rebounded from rock bottom. The beautiful days were in the 1930s and 1940s, when Presidents Roosevelt and Truman rode down 138th Street, when Babe Ruth, Lou Gehrig and Joe DiMaggio knocked home runs out of Yankee Stadium, when Art Deco apartment buildings were built along the Grand Concourse, when shoppers thronged Tremont Avenue stores, and when Bronx County Democratic Chairman Ed Flynn was chairman of the Democratic National Committee. As early as the 1880s, the Bronx (then known as the Northside and only recently annexed from Westchester County) was linked to the level eastern half of Manhattan by elevated steam locomotives. The borough really took off in 1906 with the arrival of the first subway, which allowed the children of immigrants to move from grim Lower East Side tenements to spacious walkup apartments flooded with light. The Bronx's population grew from 200,000 in 1900 to 430,000 in 1910—enough, had the borough been independent, to rank as America's sixth largest city—and 1.2 million in 1930. The Bronx's population peaked at nearly 1.5 million in 1950. But after a quarter-century of deterioration, the population shrunk to 1.2 million by 1990. Now it's up again, to 1.3 million, as new immigrants revive neighborhoods that had been given up for dead.

The downfall began in the mid-1960s. Rent control, insisted upon by tenants, guaranteed that owners of low-rent property wouldn't maintain it; once empty, many buildings were torched for the insurance money, sometimes as many as four blocks a week. At the same time, a drop in low-income, low-skill jobs in Manhattan and the Bronx—abetted by high, union-enforced wages and organized crime—led to a rise in welfare dependency and crime, with empty building shells becoming the perfect venue for drug dealing. And the 13-year, $250 million effort to build the Cross-Bronx Expressway—a brainchild of Robert Moses that crossed 113 streets and avenues, hundreds of utility mains and ten mass-transit lines—made things worse. As workers plowed through acres of tough bedrock, the project shredded entire neighborhoods, forcing 40,000 people to move from their homes and forever changing the landscape. In the upheaval, longtime residents fled in droves—whites to the suburbs or the Sun Belt, Puerto Ricans to their homeland, African Americans to the South or other cities—and the rapid turnover strained PTAs and other civic institutions. A vicious cycle emerged: Crime drove away jobs, which drove away fathers, which produced more crime. When Tom Wolfe imagined the "wrong turn" that sunk a high-flying Wall Street career in *Bonfire of the Vanities*, he set it in the South Bronx; the movie version filmed the scene under the Bruckner Expressway.

Presidents and presidential candidates came in—Jimmy Carter in 1977, Ronald Reagan in 1980—promising help. Ironically, the South Bronx was never the worst slum in New York; it just looked the worst. The borough's saviors were churches and creative community groups that, without much centralized planning, built single-family pastel bungalows and small-scale apartment projects for the elderly, single-parent families and former homeless. With their help, the South Bronx has turned a corner; local enthusiasts want to move beyond its reputation by renaming the area Downtown Bronx. A building spree has created the Bronx's first new wave of housing starts since the 1950s, and the first new cluster of private residences since the 1930s. This remains a low-income area, with many still on public assistance, but low-income families in the Bronx are now finding it possible to work their way up. As immigrants from Ecuador, Ghana and Bangladesh settled in, the population once again rose; a few corners of the South Bronx have even seen yuppies and artists colonizing old industrial space. Charlotte Street, which Carter and Reagan visited as the worst of the slums, is now Charlotte Gardens, with owner-occupied houses worth $180,000. As with other parts of New York City, the main obstacle now for the South Bronx is its weak commercial sector—a legacy of redlining and the reality of the area's low disposable incomes. Here, bank branches are still far outnumbered by check-cashing outlets, and theaters and restaurants are virtually nonexistent.

The 16th Congressional District of New York includes most of the South Bronx. It is bounded by the Harlem River on the west, the East River on the south, the Bronx River and Bronx Park (home of the Bronx Zoo) on the east, and goes just past Fordham Road on the north. It includes the Parisian-style Grand Concourse, where single-family homes for the wealthy were replaced in the 1930s by stylish Art Deco apartment buildings; this was one of America's biggest Jewish neighborhoods up through the 1960s. It also includes Belmont, a Bronx "Little Italy" and site of an old-fashioned food market on Arthur Avenue. The 16th also includes the low-rent commercial strips of Westchester Avenue, Boston Road and the Hub, and the industrial flatlands of Bruckner Boulevard, Mott Haven and Hunts Point (though not the meat and produce markets). The 16th is 30% black, 63% Hispanic—the latter the highest percentage in any New York district. This has long been New York's largest concentration of Puerto Ricans, but an increasing proportion of Hispanics here now are from other parts of Latin America. Measured by median income and percentage of families below poverty status, it ranks as the most impoverished congressional district in the nation. This was the most heavily Democratic district in the nation in 2000 (92%–5% for Al Gore) and the second most heavily Democratic in 2004 (89%–10% for John Kerry).

The congressman from the 16th District is Jose Serrano, first chosen in a 1990 special election. A native of Mayaguez, Puerto Rico, who grew up in the Millbrook project in the South Bronx, Serrano moved up while other Bronx politicians fell by the wayside because of corruption. He was elected to the New York Assembly in 1974 and chaired its Education Committee. In 1985, he ran for Bronx borough president, bucking the Democratic organization, and nearly won. Then in January 1990 South Bronx Congressman Robert Garcia was convicted for accepting money from the minority contractor Wedtech; his conviction was later reversed, but his resignation led to Serrano's election to the House.

Serrano has one of the most liberal voting records in the House. He has used his position on the Appropriations Committee to address past injustices by the FBI and to monitor law enforcement excesses after September 11. In 1997, Dick Gephardt passed over him for the less senior Robert Menendez of New Jersey—a better fundraiser, with his Cuban-American connections—to be chief deputy whip. In 1998 Serrano ran for Democratic Caucus vice-chairman as "the candidate who refuses to raise money to buy your vote for leadership." But he withdrew in favor of Menendez, and supported him when he later became caucus chairman. By contrast, Serrano is known as Fidel Castro's greatest champion in the House. He says he admires Castro and has sought repeal of economic sanctions and the Helms-Burton Act. The Appropriations Committee reorganization in February 2005 stripped Serrano of his ranking Democratic subcommittee post.

The pro-statehood Serrano has devoted much time to the cause of Puerto Rico, which he calls an American "colony." Serrano strongly defended Bill Clinton's clemency for Puerto Ricans members of the FALN terrorist group as an example of reconciliation. In 2000, he was arrested for blocking passage at the White House to protest the Navy's bombing range at Vieques, Puerto Rico. Serrano wants to ensure that the Census form permits Hispanics to list their own racial identity. In 2004, Serrano tried to distance himself from a Puerto Rican cultural heritage group run by political allies; local news reports noted that he had secured $1 million in federal funds for the group, but after three years the group had produced little more than an Internet web site.

In New York politics, Serrano backed former Bronx Borough President Fernando Ferrer for mayor in 2001 and 2005; he backed Al Sharpton for president in 2004. His son Jose, a former city councilman, ousted an incumbent in 2004 to win a state Senate seat. Serrano the elder remains secure in his district: in 2004, he won 95%.

SEVENTEENTH DISTRICT

Rep. Eliot Engel (D)

Elected 1988, 9th term; b. Feb. 18, 1947, Bronx; home, Bronx; Hunter-Lehman Col., B.A. 1969, C.U.N.Y., Lehman Col., M.A. 1973, NY Law Schl., J.D. 1987; Jewish; married (Patricia).

Elected Office: NY Assembly, 1977–88.

Professional Career: Teacher, guidance counselor, NYC public schl., 1969–77.

DC Office: 2161 RHOB, 20515, 202-225-2464; Fax: 202-225-5513; Web site: www.house.gov/engel.

District Offices: Bronx, 718-796-9700; Mt. Vernon, 914-699-4100; West Nyack, 845-735-1000.

Committees: *Energy & Commerce* (12th of 26 D): Energy & Air Quality; Telecommunications & the Internet. *International Relations* (10th of 23 D): Europe & Emerging Threats; Middle East & Central Asia.

Group Ratings

	ADA	ACLU	AFS	LCV	ITIC	NTU	COC	ACU	NTLC	CHC
2004	90	75	100	100	50	12	35	4	0	15
2003	95	—	100	100	—	19	30	16	—	—

National Journal Ratings

	2003 LIB	—	2003 CONS		2004 LIB	—	2004 CONS
Economic	92%	—	0%		80%	—	20%
Social	84%	—	13%		77%	—	22%
Foreign	61%	—	37%		64%	—	35%

Key Votes of the 108th Congress

1. Drilling in ANWR	N	5. DC School Vouchers	N	9. Ban Same-Sex Marriage	N
2. Approve Bush Tax Cuts	N	6. Ban Human Cloning	N	10. Fund Iraq War	Y
3. Medicare/Rx Bill	N	7. Restrict Gun Liability	N	11. Bar Cuba Embargo Funds	N
4. Bar Overtime Pay Regs.	Y	8. Ban Partial-Birth Abortion	N	12. Intelligence Reorg.	N

Election Results

2004 general	Eliot Engel (D-WF) 140,530	(76%)	($961,863)
	Matt Brennan (R) 40,524	(22%)	
	Other 3,482	(2%)	
2004 primary	Eliot Engel (D) 18,854	(59%)	
	Kevin McAdams (D) 6,416	(20%)	
	Other 3,543	(11%)	
	Jessica Flagg (D) 3,225	(10%)	
2002 general	Eliot Engel (D-L-WF) 77,535	(63%)	($1,009,681)
	C. Scott Vanderhoef (R-C-Ind) 42,634	(34%)	($196,664)
	Other 3,674	(3%)	

Prior Winning Percentages: 2000 (90%); 1998 (88%); 1996 (85%); 1994 (78%); 1992 (80%); 1990 (61%); 1988 (56%)

The People		Race/Ethnic Origin	Ancestry	
Area size:	146 sq. mi.	41.3% White	West Indian: 10.1% Irish: 8.7%	
Urban population:	99.9%	30.4% Black	Italian: 8.4%	
Rural population:	0.1%	4.5% Asian	**2004 Presidential Vote**	
Pop. 2000:	654,360	0.2% Native Am.	Kerry (D) 149,727	(67%)
Median income:	$44,868	0.0% Hawaiian	Bush (R) 73,896	(33%)
Poverty status:	16.0%	2.6% Two+ races	Other 584	(0%)
Military veterans:	7.7%	0.5% Other	**2000 Presidential Vote**	
		20.4% Hispanic Origin	Gore (D) 141,525	(69%)
			Bush (R) 54,362	(27%)
			Other 8,438	(4%)
			Cook Partisan Voting Index: D +21	

Occupation   Blue collar: 16.0%   White collar: 64.9%   Gray collar: 19.1%

The Bronx, settled mostly in the early 20th century, was originally a collection of middle-class neighborhoods clustered around subway stops, places where the children of immigrants left behind Manhattan's gloomy tenements and walkups and basked in the sunlight, wide avenues and hilly vistas. Different ethnic groups collected here and there: Irish in Kingsbridge, in the valley between Riverdale and the Grand Concourse; well-to-do WASPs and Jews in Riverdale, on the palisades above the Hudson River; middle-class blacks in Williamsbridge in the north central part of the borough. When neighboring areas in the South Bronx began to deteriorate, many of these residents fled, most often to Westchester County or the Sun Belt. Some moved to the southern cities of Westchester County on the Bronx border, some of which have taken on a central city character: Yonkers has been plagued by financial troubles and a landmark housing discrimination case; Mount Vernon has a black majority and economic problems that contrast sharply with much of Westchester. Others drove over the Tappan Zee Bridge to the pleasant suburbs of Rockland County, just north of Bergen County, New Jersey.

The 17th Congressional District of New York includes the bulk of these Bronx neighborhoods, plus Baychester, Eastchester and Spuyten Duyvil, and the century-old Van Cortlandt Park—at 1,146 acres, New York City's third-largest. It also includes leafy Woodlawn, still a magnet for Irish immigrants and more like neighboring Westchester County than the Bronx. But the district skips around Marble Hill, an African-American and Latino enclave on the Bronx mainland that, eccentrically, was kept as part of Manhattan after engineers diverted the Harlem River around it in 1895, hoping to improve shipping flow. In addition to the Bronx, the 17th reaches deep into the suburbs. It takes in Mount Vernon and Yonkers—which is Dutch for "young squire," in honor of its founder in the mid-1600s—and a narrow strip of land running north from Yonkers along the Hudson River. Across the Tappan Zee, the district includes the southern half of Rockland County, including Nyack, Orangetown, Suffern, Ramapo and part of Clarkstown. Rockland casts 40% of the vote, the Bronx casts 37% and Westchester 23%. Redistricting reduced the district's black percentage from 44% to 30% and its Hispanic percentage from 36% to 20%, and made the district less heavily Democratic.

The congressman from the 17th District is Eliot Engel, a son of the Bronx who now lives in Riverdale, a political junkie who memorized the names of all 100 senators when he was a boy, who was first elected to the House in 1988. He was a New York City teacher and guidance counselor who replaced incumbents struck by scandal. He was elected to the New York Assembly in a 1977 special election, at 30, to replace a convicted incumbent, and to the House in 1988 to replace Democrat Mario Biaggi after he was convicted in two tawdry bribery cases.

Engel's once strongly liberal voting record has become more moderate, especially on foreign policy. On the International Relations Committee, he made his name as the backer of one ethnic cause after another; members of just about any ethnic group can be found in the Bronx. He has been a prime sponsor of the resolution to recognize Jerusalem as the capital of Israel and criticized proposals to dismantle West Bank settlements. He keeps an eye on Albanian rights in the Former Yugoslav Republic of Macedonia. He called for investigation of the internment of Italian nationals and other harsh restrictions during World War II and sponsored a bill to create a clearinghouse at the Federal Communications Commission to empower Italian-Americans to monitor bias in entertainment. Engel is not a 1970s-style dove: He supported the Gulf War resolution, the bombing of Serbia to get a settlement in Bosnia, and the use of force in Iraq, though he criticized George W. Bush's handling of that conflict following the ouster of Saddam Hussein. In collaboration of Tom DeLay, Engel passed in 2003 a bill holding Syria accountable for the security problems it has created in the Middle East, including the spread of terrorism, and allowing the United States to impose economic sanctions.

On the Energy and Commerce Committee, he worked with New Yorkers and Californians to permit refiners to produce reformulated gasoline rather than more expensive ethanol. An Engel tradition: Since 1989 he has staked out an aisle seat hours before each State of the Union speech, so that he can shake the president's hand or give an occasional hug. At home, Engel is a relentless constituency service congressman.

When his district was mostly in the Bronx and almost 80% black and Hispanic, he faced constant primary challenges. In the 2000 primary, Assemblyman Larry Seabrook, with support from Bronx Democratic Chairman Roberto Ramirez, argued that the district needed "real leadership" and attacked Engel for living in suburban Maryland. Seabrook had a meeting with Congressional Black Caucus members, which brought angry comments from other Jewish members who argued that all Democrats should support their incumbent colleagues. When Seabrook produced a campaign button that said, "Vote First African-American Congressman," Engel objected to the use of race in the campaign. Engel won 50%–41%. Now that redistricting made his district more suburban, Engel is unlikely to be threatened by a black or Hispanic primary challenger. Instead, he had vigorous competition in the 2002 general election from Rockland County Executive Scott Vanderhoef, who criticized Engel's record of voting against tax cuts and defense spending. Vanderhoef carried Rockland County by 53%–45%. But Engel won 66%–31% in Westchester and 83%–13% in the Bronx, for an overall victory margin of 63%–34%—far from marginal. In 2004, New York City firefighter Kevin McAdams challenged Engel in the primary for his support of the war in Iraq and for not spending more time in his district. Engel demanded that McAdams denounce the firefighters association for endorsing Bush. He won more easily than expected: 59%–20%. This incumbent who looked like an endangered species for much of the last decade now looks stronger than ever.

EIGHTEENTH DISTRICT

Rep. Nita Lowey (D)

Elected 1988, 9th term; b. July 5, 1937, Bronx; home, Harrison; Mt. Holyoke Col., B.A. 1959; Jewish; married (Stephen).

Professional Career: Asst. for Econ. Devel. & Neighborhood Preservation, NY Secy. of State; Dep. Dir., Division of Econ. Opportunity, 1975–85; NY Asst. Secy. of St., 1985–87.

DC Office: 2329 RHOB, 20515, 202-225-6506; Fax: 202-225-0546; Web site: www.house.gov/lowey.

District Offices: Rockland, 845-639-3485; White Plains, 914-428-1707; Yonkers, 914-779-9766.

Committees: *Appropriations* (9th of 29 D): Foreign Operations, Export Financing & Related Programs (RMM); Labor, Health and Human Services, Education & Related Agencies. *Homeland Security* (7th of 15 D): Emergency Preparedness, Science & Technology; Intelligence, Information Sharing & Terrorism Risk Assessment.

Group Ratings

	ADA	ACLU	AFS	LCV	ITIC	NTU	COC	ACU	NTLC	CHC
2004	100	79	100	100	60	10	47	4	3	23
2003	95	—	100	95	—	20	33	20	—	—

National Journal Ratings

	2003 LIB	—	2003 CONS		2004 LIB	—	2004 CONS
Economic	77%	—	21%		77%	—	23%
Social	84%	—	13%		78%	—	22%
Foreign	59%	—	39%		61%	—	39%

Key Votes of the 108th Congress

1. Drilling in ANWR	N	5. DC School Vouchers	N	9. Ban Same-Sex Marriage	N
2. Approve Bush Tax Cuts	N	6. Ban Human Cloning	N	10. Fund Iraq War	Y
3. Medicare/Rx Bill	N	7. Restrict Gun Liability	N	11. Bar Cuba Embargo Funds	Y
4. Bar Overtime Pay Regs.	Y	8. Ban Partial-Birth Abortion	N	12. Intelligence Reorg.	Y

Election Results

2004 general	Nita Lowey (D-Ind-WF)	170,715	(70%)	($1,742,423)
	Richard Hoffman (R)	73,975	(30%)	($96,662)
2004 primary	Nita Lowey (D)	unopposed		
2002 general	Nita Lowey (D-WF)	98,957	(92%)	($1,646,414)
	Michael Reynolds (RTL)	8,558	(8%)	

Prior Winning Percentages: 2000 (67%); 1998 (83%); 1996 (64%); 1994 (57%); 1992 (56%); 1990 (63%); 1988 (50%)

The People		Race/Ethnic Origin	Ancestry	
Area size:	270 sq. mi.	67.1% White	Italian: 17.2% Irish: 11.0%	
Urban population:	99.3%	9.5% Black	German: 6.2%	
Rural population:	0.7%	5.2% Asian	**2004 Presidential Vote**	
Pop. 2000:	654,360	0.1% Native Am.	Kerry (D)	164,342 (58%)
Median income:	$68,887	0.0% Hawaiian	Bush (R)	119,981 (42%)
Poverty status:	7.8%	1.6% Two+ races	**2000 Presidential Vote**	
Military veterans:	9.2%	0.3% Other	Gore (D)	155,700 (58%)
		16.2% Hispanic Origin	Bush (R)	103,248 (38%)
			Other	9,268 (3%)
			Cook Partisan Voting Index: D +10	
Occupation	Blue collar: 12.8%	White collar: 73.2% Gray collar: 13.9%		

The great granite ridges that form the spine of Manhattan and the Bronx move north into lower Westchester County, the thin peninsula of land between Long Island Sound and the Hudson

River. This was active territory from early on. Washington Irving, the first fully professional writer in America, has his headless horseman chase schoolmaster Ichabod Crane through Sleepy Hollow, a fictionalized version of Tarrytown, on the east bank of the Hudson. Revolutionary War battles were fought here, and figures like John Peter Zenger, Alexander Hamilton and John Jay lived here. Blessed with some of America's loveliest scenery, and easily accessible from Manhattan by train since the mid-19th century, this became some of America's first suburban terrain, with grand estates built by great millionaires—Jay Gould's Gothic revival Lyndhurst and John D. Rockefeller's spectacular Kykuit, with villages for retainers clustered around the railroad stations. Today, Westchester still looks suburban, perhaps more than ever now that it has a nice patina of age. It has little commuter railroad stations across from faux Tudor drugstores, soda fountains and cobblestone post offices; it also has shopping malls and galleries and plenty of corporate headquarters, from IBM and Texaco to PepsiCo and Reader's Digest (as well as corporate watchdogs: *Consumer Reports* magazine is based in Yonkers). Intensive development slows down north of White Plains, for just to the north Westchester is crossed by the first of several mountain ridges—the closest the Appalachians come to the ocean. The county does have its share of homeless people and racial ghettos, and it has some seedy neighborhoods.

The 18th Congressional District of New York contains the heart of suburban Westchester County and also crosses over the Hudson River into Rockland County. It includes a host of affluent suburbs, many within easy reach of Grand Central via the Metro North rail lines—Bronxville, Tuckahoe, Eastchester, New Rochelle, Scarsdale, White Plains, Larchmont, Mamaroneck, Rye, Harrison, Armonk and Chappaqua, where Bill and Hillary Rodham Clinton bought a house. It also includes most of the Hudson River towns of Hastings-on-Hudson, Dobbs Ferry, Irvington and Tarrytown to the east, plus Haverstraw across the Hudson in Rockland County. Historically, Westchester was a Republican county, with a successful Republican political machine and an electorate made up of affluent professionals who naturally preferred the party opposed to big city political bosses and labor union leaders. But Westchester today is mostly Democratic, after a heavy influx of Jews who broke down many legal restrictions and other barriers to residence after World War II. One reason for Westchester's political transition is that Jewish voters, long Democratic, became even more so thanks to the visibility of Christian conservatives in the Republican party. Another reason is that on the cultural issues of greatest import, gun control and abortion, affluent suburbanites in America's biggest metropolitan area have been strongly on the liberal side. In addition, Westchester is by no means all-white: the 18th District is 10% black, 16% Hispanic and 5% Asian. George Pataki, who began his political career as mayor of Peekskill in northern Westchester, carried the county by handsome margins in 1998 and 2002. But the county gave strong support to Al Gore and John Kerry in 2000 and 2004 and, unlike the Long Island suburbs, voted for Hillary Rodham Clinton in 2000.

The congresswoman from the 18th District is Nita Lowey, a Democrat first elected in 1988. She was born in the Bronx, raised her family in Queens, and now lives in upper-crust Harrison in Westchester. She went to work for Mario Cuomo in 1975, after he was appointed secretary of state, and later became assistant secretary of state. In the 1988 Democratic primary, she faced Hamilton Fish III, son and grandson of Republican Hudson River congressmen, but as a former publisher of *The Nation* considerably to the left of Lowey; she won 44%–36%. Her opponent in the general was Joseph DioGuardi, a two-term incumbent who trumpeted his experience as a CPA but was dogged by charges of illicit contributions; she won 50%–47%. Each spent over $1 million, with Lowey spending $657,000 of her own money.

In the House, Lowey's voting record leans left, though she is a moderate on foreign policy. She was a Clinton loyalist when it was tough to be so, voting for the 1993 budget and tax package in this high-income district, splitting with most New York Democrats and organized labor to support both NAFTA and normal trade relations with China. When Clinton proposed to change the health care finance system, she organized 72 members who demanded that it cover abortions. Much of Lowey's legislative work has been done on Appropriations. Pursuing her interest in feminist issues, she backed funds for international family planning, and led the unsuccessful opposition to George W. Bush's reversal of the policy when he took office. As the senior Democrat on the Foreign Operations Subcommittee of Appropriations, she has been a strong advocate of aid to Israel. She voted for the Iraq war resolution and against trade promotion authority. With Hillary Rodham Clinton, she proposed a $2.5 billion global education fund to steer poor youth away from terrorist breeding groups.

Lowey has actively supported the National Endowment for the Arts. When Republicans threatened to eliminate funding for the Public Broadcasting System, she scored points with an appearance by muppets Bert and Ernie to make their case at a congressional hearing. She called on the Nuclear Regulatory Commission to deploy federal security teams to replace private guards at every nuclear power plant. With neighboring Representative Sue Kelly, she passed in the House a proposal to require better security training for all airplane crew members, but Republicans defeated a plan to set federal standards. She has argued that Social Security will be jeopardized by creation of personal retirement accounts.

Since Lowey first won, the boundaries of her district have been twice sharply changed by redistricting, but she has been reelected by wide margins. Her party loyalty and avid fundraising led Minority Leader Dick Gephardt to appoint her chairman of the Democratic Congressional Campaign Committee in 2001. House Democrats had been dispirited after failing to win control, and Lowey faced a difficult task. She advised candidates to cooperate closely with Democratic interest groups—environmental, abortion rights, civil rights—in addition to organized labor. In early 2002 she sounded optimistic and said that Democrats' recruiting efforts, their fundraising, their apparent success in preventing Republican gains in redistricting, and their attacks on Republicans for "privatizing" Social Security would enable the party to recapture the House. By the fall prospects were not so rosy. Ultimately, Democrats defeated only three Republican incumbents, while losing five of their own. House Republicans' six-seat gain was an acute disappointment to Lowey, who quietly bowed out of the chairmanship: like other DCCC chairmen, she had failed to deliver a majority that seemed in close reach.

NINETEENTH DISTRICT

Rep. Sue Kelly (R)

Elected 1994, 6th term; b. Sept. 26, 1936, Lima, OH; home, Katonah; Denison U., B.A. 1958, Sarah Lawrence Col., M.A. 1985; Presbyterian; married (Edward).

Professional Career: Owner/Mgr., Kelly & Assoc. bldg. rehab.; Researcher, Harvard U., 1958–60; Owner/Mgr., Kelly Florist, 1980–83; Prof., Sarah Lawrence Col., 1988–91.

DC Office: 2182 RHOB, 20515, 202-225-5441; Fax: 202-225-3289; Web site: www.house.gov/suekelly.

District Offices: Fishkill, 845-897-5200; Goshen, 845-291-4100; Yorktown Heights, 914-962-0761.

Committees: *Financial Services* (Vice Chmn. of 37 R): Capital Markets, Insurance & Government Sponsored Enterprises; Financial Institutions & Consumer Credit; Oversight & Investigations (Chmn.). *Small Business* (3d of 18 R): Regulatory Reform & Oversight; Tax, Finance & Exports. *Transportation & Infrastructure* (12th of 41 R): Aviation; Highways, Transit & Pipelines; Water Resources & Environment.

Group Ratings

	ADA	ACLU	AFS	LCV	ITIC	NTU	COC	ACU	NTLC	CHC
2004	40	10	25	64	100	52	86	56	76	69
2003	15	—	25	70	—	57	77	64	—	—

National Journal Ratings

	2003 LIB	—	2003 CONS		2004 LIB	—	2004 CONS
Economic	50%	—	50%		52%	—	48%
Social	49%	—	50%		45%	—	54%
Foreign	42%	—	58%		25%	—	68%

Key Votes of the 108th Congress

1. Drilling in ANWR	Y	5. DC School Vouchers	Y	9. Ban Same-Sex Marriage	Y
2. Approve Bush Tax Cuts	Y	6. Ban Human Cloning	Y	10. Fund Iraq War	Y
3. Medicare/Rx Bill	Y	7. Restrict Gun Liability	Y	11. Bar Cuba Embargo Funds	N
4. Bar Overtime Pay Regs.	Y	8. Ban Partial-Birth Abortion	Y	12. Intelligence Reorg.	Y

Election Results

2004 general	Sue Kelly (R-Ind-C)	175,401	(67%)	($1,250,053)
	Michael Jaliman (D)	87,429	(33%)	($67,453)
2004 primary	Sue Kelly (R)................................	unopposed		
2002 general	Sue Kelly (R-Ind-C)	121,129	(70%)	($968,982)
	Janine Selendy (D)	44,967	(26%)	($13,153)
	Other...	7,016	(4%)	

Prior Winning Percentages: 2000 (61%); 1998 (62%); 1996 (46%); 1994 (52%)

The People		Race/Ethnic Origin	Ancestry	
Area size:	1,470 sq. mi.	83.5% White	Italian: 17.6% Irish: 16.5%	
Urban population:	78.7%	5.0% Black	German: 10.6%	
Rural population:	21.3%	2.2% Asian	**2004 Presidential Vote**	
Pop. 2000:	654,361	0.2% Native Am.	Bush (R)............. 162,960	(54%)
Median income:	$64,337	0.0% Hawaiian	Kerry (D) 137,432	(45%)
Poverty status:	6.4%	1.2% Two+ races	Other 2,097	(1%)
Military veterans:	11.8%	0.2% Other	**2000 Presidential Vote**	
		7.7% Hispanic Origin	Bush (R)............. 133,157	(49%)
			Gore (D) 126,785	(47%)
			Other 11,698	(4%)
			Cook Partisan Voting Index: R + 1	
Occupation	Blue collar: 18.5%	White collar: 67.2%	Gray collar: 14.3%	

The great interior of America can be said to begin where the Hudson River squeezes through the series of Appalachian ridges at the Hudson Highlands. This choke point was the barrier to British military power during the Revolutionary War, when American forces built a chain across the river to keep the British from sailing north. It was over control of this part of the Hudson that Benedict Arnold betrayed his country, and it was here that the new nation built its Military Academy high on the cliffs at West Point. The Hudson was the impetus for the builders of the Erie Canal and the water-level New York Central Railroad, the great projects that made New York City the port of the American interior, as well as for the builders of the Croton Aqueduct not far away, which provided the water without which New York could not grow—and which provided a way for the first cockroaches to reach the city. Some distant day the great aqueduct may crumble, but the cockroaches will remain.

The 19th Congressional District of New York covers much of the lower Hudson Valley, sprawling across parts of five counties. West of the Hudson, the district takes in much of Orange County, New York's second-fastest growing county from 1990 to 2004, where old farming villages like Warwick adjoin mountains, farms and new, middle-income subdivisions on the nation's biggest deposit of muck soil outside the Everglades. The district includes Kiryas Joel, a politically controversial Satmar Hasidic settlement that became embroiled in a long-running battle over whether it could establish a government-funded but religiously run school district for disabled children. While it excludes two of Orange County's biggest population centers, Middletown and Newburgh, it takes in portions of northern Rockland County, including Stony Point, the home of James A. Farley, Franklin D. Roosevelt's campaign manager in 1932 and 1936. The district crosses the Hudson where the rebels' chain lay, near West Point. East of the river, the district begins in northern Westchester County, including Peekskill, where George Pataki was mayor before becoming governor; Croton-on-Hudson; Yorktown; and Mt. Kisco. Farther north, the 19th takes in all of Putnam County and part of Dutchess County, including the suburbs (but not the center city) of Poughkeepsie, and Wappingers Falls; Putnam has become popular for first-time homebuyers who take the 80-minute commute to Grand Central Station. The region has proved attractive to middle- and higher-income public and corporate employees seeking reasonably priced housing in safe areas, a trend that has led to robust growth at a time when other areas of New York state are losing population; immigrants from Ecuador who have settled here find the mountains and farm land similar to home. Politically, this area moved toward Democrats in the 1990s, but voted for George W. Bush in 2004.

The congresswoman from the 19th District is Sue Kelly, a Republican first elected in 1994. Kelly is not a Hudson Valley aristocrat but the daughter of an Ohio doctor. She met her husband while she was a botany researcher at Harvard; they raised their family in Katonah, where she volunteered in many organizations. She had a business renovating buildings and owned a florist shop. She also had political experience as campaign manager for Assemblyman Jon Fossel in the 1970s. When Congressman Hamilton Fish, a Hudson County aristocrat, decided to retire, Kelly decided to use the $150,000 she had saved to buy a new business to help finance a campaign for Congress instead. It was a crowded field, in which Kelly emerged as the only candidate who supported lower taxes, "huge" budget cuts and abortion rights. Her chief opponent in the primary was Joseph DioGuardi, twice elected in the Westchester district to the south and twice defeated there by Nita Lowey. Kelly won the primary with 23% to DioGuardi's 20%, with two other candidates at 19% and 18%. The Democratic nominee was Hamilton Fish III, son of the retiring congressman but as publisher of the leftish *The Nation*, with quite different politics. This was expected to be a close race. But with solid margins in the northern counties Kelly beat Fish 52%–37%, with 10% for DioGuardi on the Conservative and Right-to-Life lines.

Kelly, with her middle-of-the-House voting record, has been whipsawed by criticism from right and left. She supported the Contract with America, which earned her howls from the left. On abortion, Kelly irritated many conservatives by being one of the few Republicans to vote against the partial-birth abortion ban in 1996, but she switched and voted for it in 2003. And in 1998 she joined other Republican women to ask why feminist Democrats were not outraged about the charges brought against Bill Clinton; she voted for two of the four impeachment counts. So when she was chosen as the Republican co-chair of the Congressional Caucus for Women's Issues, feminists complained loudly. Kelly stood her ground—in February 2000 calling Hillary Rodham Clinton, her new constituent (though, post-redistricting, Chappaqua is now in the 18th), "a carpetbagger" who did not know New York or have the background to represent the state. The First Lady's spokesman responded by calling Kelly's comments "not very neighborly."

On the House Small Business Committee, she has passed bills to increase small business access to capital and repeal an archaic ban on banks paying interest on checking accounts used by small firms. She was unsuccessful when she sought to circumvent seniority and seek the committee chairmanship in 2001. But she is well-positioned to take the post in 2007. In 2002, she showed some partisan spirit, as chairman of the Oversight and Investigation Subcommittee of Financial Services, when she criticized Senate Democrats for failing to move the terrorism insurance bill, which businesses and real estate developers insisted was essential after September 11. She supported the war in Iraq and has chaired numerous hearings on terrorist financing, both at home and abroad. In 2004, the House passed her amendment to provide new law enforcement tools and increase funding for the Treasury Department to combat terrorist financing and prevent money laundering. At home, Kelly strongly opposed a proposal to close a veterans' hospital in Rockland County and she got the Veterans Department to agree to continue some inpatient services. She got funds to implement E-Z pass at the congested Woodbury toll plaza on I-87, and has taken various steps to expand Stewart Airport.

In elections, she has been challenged on all sides. Not even a plea from Speaker Newt Gingrich's office could keep DioGuardi from challenging Kelly again in the 1996 Republican primary. Kelly won the primary, but by a narrow 53%–42%. In the general, Kelly beat the Democrat by only 46%–39%, with 12% for DioGuardi. Her later victories were more convincing. Her 2000 opponent was Larry Otis Graham, author of best-selling *Our Kind of People: Inside America's Black Upper Class*. Graham, who boasted of campaign advice from his Chappaqua neighbor Bill Clinton, criticized Kelly as out of touch with her constituents; he lost, 61%–36%. Redistricting made this district more secure.

TWENTIETH DISTRICT

Rep. John Sweeney (R)

Elected 1998, 4th term; b. Aug. 9, 1955, Troy; home, Clifton Park; Russell Sage Col., B.A. 1981, W. New England Law Schl., J.D. 1990; Catholic; married (Gayle Ford).

Professional Career: Practicing atty., 1990–92; Exec. Dir. & Chief Cnsl., NY State Repub. Cmte., 1992–95; NY Comm. of Labor, 1995–97; Dpty. Secy., Gov. George Pataki, 1997–98.

DC Office: 416 CHOB, 20515, 202-225-5614; Fax: 202-225-6234; Web site: www.house.gov/sweeney.

District Offices: Clifton Park, 518-371-8839; Delhi, 607-746-9700; Glens Falls, 518-792-3031; Redhook, 845-758-1222.

Committees: *Appropriations* (28th of 37 R): Foreign Operations, Export Financing & Related Programs; Homeland Security; Transportation, Treasury, HUD, the Judiciary & District of Columbia (Vice Chmn.).

Group Ratings

	ADA	ACLU	AFS	LCV	ITIC	NTU	COC	ACU	NTLC	CHC
2004	25	5	38	18	80	48	81	72	65	69
2003	20	—	25	15	—	55	79	76	—	—

National Journal Ratings

	2003 LIB	—	2003 CONS	2004 LIB	—	2004 CONS
Economic	46%	—	53%	47%	—	52%
Social	5%	—	87%	42%	—	58%
Foreign	48%	—	52%	25%	—	68%

Key Votes of the 108th Congress

1. Drilling in ANWR	Y	5. DC School Vouchers	Y	9. Ban Same-Sex Marriage	N
2. Approve Bush Tax Cuts	Y	6. Ban Human Cloning	Y	10. Fund Iraq War	Y
3. Medicare/Rx Bill	Y	7. Restrict Gun Liability	Y	11. Bar Cuba Embargo Funds	N
4. Bar Overtime Pay Regs.	Y	8. Ban Partial-Birth Abortion	Y	12. Intelligence Reorg.	Y

Election Results

2004 general	John Sweeney (R-Ind-C)	188,753	(66%)	($1,392,817)
	Doris Kelly (D)	96,630	(34%)	($22,823)
	Other	1,353	(0%)	
2004 primary	John Sweeney (R)	unopposed		
2002 general	John Sweeney (R-C)	140,238	(73%)	($808,955)
	Frank Stoppenbach (D)	45,878	(24%)	($18,451)
	Other	5,162	(3%)	

Prior Winning Percentages: 2000 (68%); 1998 (55%)

The People		Race/Ethnic Origin	Ancestry	
Area size:	7,200 sq. mi.	93.4% White	Irish: 15.1%	German: 11.8%
Urban population:	44.9%	2.4% Black	Italian: 9.8%	
Rural population:	55.1%	0.8% Asian	**2004 Presidential Vote**	
Pop. 2000:	654,360	0.2% Native Am.	Bush (R) 170,307	(54%)
Median income:	$44,239	0.0% Hawaiian	Kerry (D) 145,289	(46%)
Poverty status:	7.9%	0.9% Two+ races	Other 2,635	(1%)
Military veterans:	14.3%	0.1% Other	**2000 Presidential Vote**	
		2.2% Hispanic Origin	Bush (R) 146,792	(51%)
			Gore (D) 127,419	(44%)
			Other 15,232	(5%)
			Cook Partisan Voting Index: R + 3	

Occupation	Blue collar: 22.7%	White collar: 61.1%	Gray collar: 16.2%

The Hudson River, an avenue of commerce in colonial days, an inspiration to artists in the federal republic, is still one of America's great sights, though it is no longer central, as it was not so long ago, to the nation's consciousness and politics. The classic mansions overlooking the river, like Clermont, whose builder Robert Livingston financed Robert Fulton's first steamboat, and Montgomery Place, built by Janet Livingston Montgomery, widow of the general who attacked Quebec in 1775, are reminders of the cool serenity of the 18th century mind and the daring nature of its spirit. Robert Livingston (whose descendants include Eleanor Roosevelt, former Governor Thomas Kean of New Jersey and former Congressman Bob Livingston of Louisiana) administered the first oath of office to George Washington in 1789 and helped negotiate the Louisiana Purchase in 1803. It was on a visit to his lands in the 1790s that James Madison and Aaron Burr welded the Virginia-New York alliance that set the course of American political history. The Hudson was also a center of America during the Romantic Era: From Frederick Church's Moorish mansion, Olana, you can see the still unspoiled river landscape that inspired his art and that of others of the Hudson River school of painters. Later, the photographer Alfred Stieglitz and his wife, the painter Georgia O'Keeffe, drew inspiration from the mountains and placid waters in Lake George, where they had a summer home.

The Hudson gave birth to America's passionate party politics. Nearby is Kinderhook, home of Martin Van Buren, the innkeeper's son who in alliance with Andrew Jackson invented the torchlight parade, the national party convention and, some argue, the Democratic party itself. Later in the 19th century, the Hudson was lined with the palaces of the nation's first great millionaires and the comfortable country homes of New York's gentry. One of the latter, Springwood in Hyde Park, was the birthplace and home of Franklin D. Roosevelt; this politician, who expanded government at home and was the victorious commander-in-chief of American military forces throughout the world, was most comfortable looking out over his sloping lawn down to the river on which he remembered iceboating during the winters of the 1880s.

The sprawling 20th Congressional District of New York clamps around the Albany metro area and includes much of the Hudson Valley—the grand river south of Albany and the smaller river, freshly fed by the Adirondacks, to the north. It includes four full counties (Warren, Washington, Columbia and Greene), most of Saratoga County, and parts of five others (Dutchess, Essex, Rensselaer, Delaware and Otsego). The northern extreme of the 20th extends right up to Lake Placid in the Adirondacks, site of the 1980 Winter Olympics, while the southern extreme in Dutchess County is close enough for commuters from New York to travel back and forth regularly. The district extends west just short of Cooperstown, home of the National Baseball Hall of Fame, and includes Oneonta, home of the less well-known National Soccer Hall of Fame; it includes Saratoga Springs with its grand race track and the nearby battlefield where the British were decisively stopped in 1777. Despite Van Buren and Roosevelt, this has been a Republican area since the birth of the Republican Party; indeed, Roosevelt never carried his home territory except when he ran for state Senate in 1910. The 20th was one of only six New York districts to vote for George W. Bush in 2000 and one of nine to vote for him in 2004.

The congressman from the 20th District is John Sweeney, a Republican first elected in 1998. Sweeney grew up in Troy, the son of a shirt factory worker active in the Amalgamated Shirt Cutters Union; he lived for a time in a housing project. He worked his way through college, then worked for the Rensselaer County government, heading a DWI project. He went to law school part time, graduated and practiced law. He caught the eye of Republican State Chairman William Powers, who made Sweeney executive director of the party in 1992. After George Pataki was elected governor in 1994, he appointed Sweeney as Labor commissioner, then in 1997 as deputy secretary to the state Executive Chamber, one of his top aides.

In April 1998, Gerald Solomon announced he was retiring. In this heavily Republican district there was naturally a contest for the party's nomination. But it was effectively settled in a few days in May. Assemblyman John Faso, probably the best-known prospect, declined to run because he had been elected minority leader in March. Solomon backed Roy McDonald, a township supervisor in Saratoga County, the district's largest; of the nine candidates running, he said that only Sweeney was unacceptable. Facing pressure from Powers, Saratoga County Republican Chairman Jasper Nolan announced he was not supporting McDonald, who, suddenly with no chance in the endorsement convention, withdrew from the race. Powers's message, though not public, was obvious: Pataki wanted Sweeney. Sweeney had yet to officially announce, but as Solomon said, "John Sweeney is going to be the candidate." Sweeney refused to join debates but won the September primary with 52%. Sweeney easily won the general.

In the House, Sweeney has been conservative on foreign issues and more centrist on others. He impressed Republican leaders with his fundraising and got an Appropriations Committee seat. He used that post to press the White House to deliver more rapidly on its commitment of $20 billion to New York for post-September 11 recovery. Even after that agreement, he bucked other New York House Republicans and continued to work with Nita Lowey on Appropriations to secure more money for the state. He won House approval of a bill to issue Freedom Bonds for the first time since World War II, but the Treasury Department was cool to the idea because it feared the bonds would discourage spending and slow down the economy. Sweeney lobbied for Southwest Airlines service to Albany, where the airport has grown rapidly. He initially objected to the plan announced by EPA in the closing days of the Clinton administration requiring General Electric to spend $490 million to clean up the PCBs in the Hudson, mostly by dredging the sediment along 40 miles of the river. When the Bush White House sustained the earlier decision, he applauded the added performance standards that EPA set in its final order. Sweeney has shown an occasional populist touch. He fought to bar federal contracts to MCI for a year when the telecom giant's predecessor corporation went bankrupt. "Bad behavior is just frankly not something that the federal government should sanction." Following revelations of steroid abuse by athletes, he said that performance-enhancing substances should require a prescription. He broke with conservatives by opposing the constitutional ban on same-sex marriages.

Sweeney's star has been on the rise: the *New York Times* describes his style as "alternating between street fighter and smooth political operator to get his way." He is connected both in Albany and Washington. He has been known as the member of the delegation closest to Pataki and is on friendly terms with the Bush White House: his former chief of staff Brad Card is the brother of Bush's chief of staff Andrew Card.

He has turned down opportunities to run statewide, and appears to be settling in for a lengthy House career. He has not had a serious reelection challenge.

TWENTY-FIRST DISTRICT

Rep. Michael McNulty (D)

Elected 1988, 9th term; b. Sept. 16, 1947, Troy; home, Green Island; Holy Cross Col., B.A. 1969; Catholic; married (Nancy Ann).

Elected Office: Green Island Town Supervisor, 1969–77; Green Island Mayor, 1977–82; NY Assembly, 1982–88.

DC Office: 2210 RHOB, 20515, 202-225-5076; Fax: 202-225-5077; Web site: www.house.gov/mcnulty.

District Offices: Albany, 518-465-0700; Amsterdam, 518-843-3400; Johnstown, 518-762-3568; Schenectady, 518-374-4547; Troy, 518-271-0822.

Committees: *Ways & Means* (8th of 17 D): Oversight; Select Revenue Measures (RMM).

Group Ratings

	ADA	ACLU	AFS	LCV	ITIC	NTU	COC	ACU	NTLC	CHC
2004	90	60	100	100	20	10	33	16	9	46
2003	90	—	100	100	—	16	24	24	—	—

National Journal Ratings

	2003 LIB	—	2003 CONS		2004 LIB	—	2004 CONS
Economic	91%	—	8%		82%	—	17%
Social	63%	—	36%		60%	—	40%
Foreign	63%	—	36%		65%	—	34%

Key Votes of the 108th Congress

1. Drilling in ANWR	N	5. DC School Vouchers	N	9. Ban Same-Sex Marriage	N
2. Approve Bush Tax Cuts	N	6. Ban Human Cloning	Y	10. Fund Iraq War	Y
3. Medicare/Rx Bill	N	7. Restrict Gun Liability	N	11. Bar Cuba Embargo Funds	Y
4. Bar Overtime Pay Regs.	Y	8. Ban Partial-Birth Abortion	Y	12. Intelligence Reorg.	N

Election Results

2004 general	Michael McNulty (D-Ind-C-WF)	194,033	(71%)	($442,149)
	Warren Redlich (R)	80,121	(29%)	($41,497)
2004 primary	Michael McNulty (D)	unopposed		
2002 general	Michael McNulty (D-C-Ind-WF)	161,329	(75%)	($421,837)
	Charles Rosenstein (R)	53,525	(25%)	($20,786)

Prior Winning Percentages: 2000 (74%); 1998 (74%); 1996 (66%); 1994 (67%); 1992 (63%); 1990 (64%); 1988 (62%)

The People		Race/Ethnic Origin	Ancestry	
Area size:	1,962 sq. mi.	85.5% White	Irish: 15.0%	Italian: 12.4%
Urban population:	84.3%	7.5% Black	German: 11.8%	
Rural population:	15.7%	2.1% Asian	**2004 Presidential Vote**	
Pop. 2000:	654,361	0.2% Native Am.	Kerry (D) 169,693	(55%)
Median income:	$40,254	0.0% Hawaiian	Bush (R) 133,016	(43%)
Poverty status:	11.2%	1.3% Two+ races	Other 5,182	(2%)
Military veterans:	13.1%	0.2% Other	**2000 Presidential Vote**	
		3.2% Hispanic Origin	Gore (D) 165,003	(56%)
			Bush (R) 114,979	(39%)
			Other 15,101	(5%)
			Cook Partisan Voting Index: D + 9	
Occupation	Blue collar: 18.9%	White collar: 66.0%	Gray collar: 15.0%	

Albany, as readers of its novelist laureate William Kennedy know, is within living memory an antique city. Its solid rowhouses show its 19th century prosperity; its once teeming lumberyards and railroad car shops, old restaurants and hotels, have the patina of age and the accumulated grime of decades of coal smoke burned during six-month-long winters. Its history goes back to 1624, when the Dutch built Fort Orange on the banks of the Hudson so seagoing ships could dock at the edge of the great gloomy forests near the confluence of the Hudson and the Mohawk—the natural crossroads of Upstate New York even before the building of the Erie Canal and the New York Central Railroad. This was one of America's early industrial centers. Troy, a few miles upriver, was a steel town rivaling Pittsburgh in the 1840s, and later the leading producer of detachable collars; Cohoes, at the junction of the Hudson and the Mohawk, became a leading textile producer; Schenectady, a few miles up the Mohawk, was the site of Charles Steinmetz's fabled General Electric laboratories and long remained a GE town. Albany was one of America's biggest lumber towns as well as the state capital.

Albany, with a state capitol completed in 1899 after 32 years, for the then-staggering sum of $25 million, has one of the nation's most famed Democratic political machines, dating back to 1921, when Daniel O'Connell and his brothers and local aristocrat Edwin Corning took control of City Hall. They never really relinquished it: O'Connell died in 1977 at age 91, still boss after 56 years, and his early partner's son, Erastus Corning II, was mayor from 1942 until his death in 1983. The machine was sustained by legions of city and county employees, by a certain creativity when it came to counting votes, and by the raffish atmosphere that was found in the speakeasies of so many cities during Prohibition and lingered in Albany for decades after: read Kennedy and you are there. Curiously, the machine made possible the transformation of antique Albany into the shinier metropolis it is today. Mayor Corning and Nelson Rockefeller collaborated on a smorgasbord of civic-improvement projects: the monumental South Mall, the distinctive, ovoid performing arts center known as the Egg, expressways, and a renovated Union Station. Yuppies began buying and renovating old townhouses.

The 21st Congressional District of New York includes most of the Albany metro area: all of Albany County, Schenectady County (including Schenectady, where the industrial base has faded and many houses are empty), Montgomery County (including Amsterdam, a carpet-making town until the mills moved south in 1955), and rural Schoharie County; parts of Rensselaer (including the gentrified Troy, with its bustling antique shops), Fulton and Saratoga Counties. Times have not been great here: Albany lost 5% of its population during the 1990s, Schenectady 6% and Troy 9%. While the outer counties lean modestly Republican, the Democratic machine vote in Albany makes this a comfortably Democratic district. Even Democrat Carl McCall, who lost every other county in the state outside New York City, beat incumbent Governor George Pataki in Albany County in 2002.

The congressman from the 21st District is Michael McNulty, a Democrat first elected in 1988. McNulty's roots in Albany politics go back to his grandfather, who served as Albany County sheriff; his father was mayor of the industrial suburb of Green Island for 30 years (not consecutively) until he retired in 2002, when he was succeeded by Michael's sister, Ellen McNulty-Ryan. Michael McNulty was first elected to office in 1969, at 22, and served 13 years as town supervisor and mayor in Green Island; while also serving as an insurance broker, he was elected to the Assembly in 1982, at 35. The opening in Congress came without much warning. In 1988, four days after the July filing deadline and on the last day for withdrawal, 30-year incumbent Democrat Samuel Stratton announced he was retiring for health reasons, giving the Democratic machine a chance to name a replacement, who turned out to be McNulty. He won the general by 62%–38% against a venture capital specialist who attacked him for having been chosen by party bosses. Since then, he has had no trouble in general elections.

McNulty's voting record is like that of an old-style ethnic Democrat: liberal on economics, less so on foreign and cultural issues. He is one of the few New York Democrats endorsed by the Conservative Party. He opposes abortion and voted for the amendment allowing penalties for flag desecration. But he supported campaign finance regulation, even though some abortion foes opposed it. He strongly opposed the welfare law and wants to increase payments to unemployed adults, legal immigrants and families with high shelter costs. On Ways and Means, he usually has operated independently of both parties.

On local issues, McNulty criticized the Army when it cut the number of jobs at the Watervliet Arsenal, and wondered whether further cuts would require closure and dependence on foreign producers; the facility was revived by a Navy contract for new cannons, and the Army in 2002 turned over management to a civilian firm to attract private businesses. Its base mission will sustain the arsenal, McNulty said. "But the Army presence there has continued to decrease because of the nation's own decreased need for a large Army cannon."

McNulty in 1998 brought Hillary Rodham Clinton to Troy to commemorate Kate Mullaney, who organized the all-female Collar Laundry Union in 1864. In 2004, his proposal to make a national museum of her home was enacted. With Senator Clinton, he proposed giving homeland security block grants to local communities for emergency response and public safety. He strongly backed George W. Bush on Iraq.

In 1996 he had primary opposition on the left from Lee Wasserman, head of Environmental Advocates, a statewide lobbying firm, and won by only 57%–43%. Since then, McNulty seems to have solidified his base, and he remains secure. But he has suffered from post-polio syndrome, and his declining energy level and his perennially low profile have spurred retirement rumors.

TWENTY-SECOND DISTRICT
Rep. Maurice Hinchey (D)

Elected 1992, 7th term; b. Oct. 27, 1938, New York, NY; home, Saugerties; S.U.N.Y. New Paltz, B.S. 1968, M.A. 1969; Catholic; married (Ilene).

Military Career: Navy, 1956–59.

Elected Office: NY Assembly, 1974–92.

Professional Career: Cement plant worker, 1959–64; NY St. Thruway toll collector, 1959–68; Analyst, NY St. Dept. of Educ., 1971–74.

DC Office: 2431 RHOB, 20515, 202-225-6335; Fax: 202-226-0774; Web site: www.house.gov/hinchey.

District Offices: Binghamton, 607-773-2768; Ithaca, 607-273-1388; Kingston, 845-331-4466.

Committees: *Appropriations* (20th of 29 D): Agriculture, Rural Development, FDA & Related Agencies; Interior, Environment & Related Agencies. *Joint Economic Committee* (8th of 10 Reps.).

Group Ratings

	ADA	ACLU	AFS	LCV	ITIC	NTU	COC	ACU	NTLC	CHC
2004	95	94	100	100	20	9	25	0	0	7
2003	95	—	100	95	—	25	28	8	—	—

National Journal Ratings

	2003 LIB	—	2003 CONS		2004 LIB	—	2004 CONS
Economic	92%	—	0%		93%	—	7%
Social	84%	—	13%		88%	—	0%
Foreign	94%	—	0%		93%	—	6%

Key Votes of the 108th Congress

1. Drilling in ANWR	N	5. DC School Vouchers	N	9. Ban Same-Sex Marriage	N
2. Approve Bush Tax Cuts	N	6. Ban Human Cloning	N	10. Fund Iraq War	N
3. Medicare/Rx Bill	N	7. Restrict Gun Liability	N	11. Bar Cuba Embargo Funds	Y
4. Bar Overtime Pay Regs.	Y	8. Ban Partial-Birth Abortion	N	12. Intelligence Reorg.	N

Election Results

2004 general	Maurice Hinchey (D-Ind-WF)	167,489	(67%)	($631,944)
	William Brenner (R)	81,881	(33%)	($6,497)
2004 primary	Maurice Hinchey (D) .... unopposed			
2002 general	Maurice Hinchey (D-L-Ind-WF)	113,280	(64%)	($652,929)
	Eric Hall (R-C)	58,008	(33%)	($39,499)
	Other	5,196	(3%)	

Prior Winning Percentages: 2000 (62%); 1998 (62%); 1996 (55%); 1994 (49%); 1992 (50%)

The People		Race/Ethnic Origin	Ancestry	
Area size:	3,334 sq. mi.	79.9% White	Irish: 13.2%	German: 11.8%
Urban population:	67.8%	7.7% Black	Italian: 11.1%	
Rural population:	32.2%	2.5% Asian	**2004 Presidential Vote**	
Pop. 2000:	654,361	0.2% Native Am.	Kerry (D) 151,890	(54%)
Median income:	$38,586	0.0% Hawaiian	Bush (R) 127,253	(45%)
Poverty status:	14.3%	1.7% Two+ races	Other 3,629	(1%)
Military veterans:	12.3%	0.2% Other	**2000 Presidential Vote**	
		7.8% Hispanic Origin	Gore (D) 131,421	(51%)
			Bush (R) 108,460	(42%)
			Other 17,578	(7%)
			Cook Partisan Voting Index: D + 6	

Occupation	Blue collar: 21.4%	White collar: 60.8%	Gray collar: 17.8%

In colonial days, the Catskills looming over the mid-Hudson River Valley were a great barrier—a mysterious place where Rip Van Winkle was said to have fallen asleep for 20 years after drinking with nine pipe-playing dwarfs, and where Indians lurked in the days of James Fenimore Cooper.

Eventually, the area became part of a great pathway west, along the Erie Lackawanna and Delaware & Hudson Railroad lines, with engines steaming over giant viaducts and along narrow river valleys through the hills and mountains. Later in the 19th century, huge kosher hotels were built in Sullivan County in the Catskills—the Jewish resort area popularly known as the Borscht Belt. These thrived when Jews were excluded from other resorts, but fell on hard times in the late 20th century, as discrimination ended; some still exist to cater to nearby Russian Jewish immigrants and a kosher clientele. Today, the Catskills are no longer on great transportation lines; there is little passenger train service and the area is bypassed by major airlines. Traffic on Route 17, the gateway to the Catskills from New York City (known locally as the "Quickway"), has become clogged on weekends, however, and figures to get worse with the opening of five new Indian casinos in Sullivan and Ulster counties approved by Governor George Pataki, with the first scheduled to open in 2007.

The sprawling 22d Congressional District of New York includes all of Sullivan and Ulster Counties and most of the Catskills area; it also covers part of the Hudson Valley and part of the Southern Tier counties along the New York-Pennsylvania border. Its two population centers are on its east and west ends. On the east are Newburgh, Poughkeepsie and Kingston, old towns in the Hudson Valley. Poughkeepsie is the home of Vassar College and Kingston, in Ulster County, was the political base of long-time Governor and two-term Vice President George Clinton. This area has been growing relatively rapidly, with new residents from metro New York. In the west, connected to the rest of the district by a narrow corridor of Southern Tier townships, is the technology-dependent town of Binghamton and the university town of Ithaca, where Cornell University sits high above the Cayuga's waters and is by far the largest employer in Tompkins County. The Binghamton area has been losing population, like much of Upstate New York. In between are the Catskills, including Bethel, site of the misnamed 1969 Woodstock music festival. Most of this territory voted Republican for many years, though Sullivan County, with the only large rural Jewish population in the U.S., has long been Democratic. Today most of the area is Democratic, especially the university towns of Ithaca, Poughkeepsie and New Paltz in Ulster County and the actual Woodstock (not where the festival was held), a favorite country house place for liberal New Yorkers.

The congressman from the 22d is Maurice Hinchey, a Democrat first elected in 1992. Hinchey grew up in a humble background, enlisted in the Navy at 18, labored in a cement factory for five years, then worked his way through college as a New York State Thruway toll collector. He was an analyst for the state education department; then in the Democratic year of 1974, at 36, he was elected from Ulster County to the Assembly and served for nine terms. When he ran for Congress, Hinchey called for national health insurance, a repeal of Reagan-Bush tax cuts for the rich and corporations, and "reindustrializing America." His Republican opponent Bob Moppert, a Binghamton moving company owner, called for less government spending and bureaucracy. In a contest that was not only partisan but geographic, Hinchey beat Moppert 50%–47%.

Hinchey has one of the most liberal voting records in the House. One issue that caused Hinchey discomfort is gun control. He backed the Brady Bill on handguns. But in 1994, as he faced a tough reelection campaign in a non-metropolitan district, he agonized over the assault weapons ban, deciding at the last minute to vote against it, despite a call from Bill Clinton. As part of the House minority, he has mostly taken on lost causes. But with the election of George W. Bush, Hinchey sought partisan opportunities. He sparked a House debate with his proposal to prohibit the private donation of food and beverages for official events at the Vice President's residence; his amendment was defeated, with 54 Democrats opposed. After the September 11 attacks, he criticized the White House for spending disaster relief money on national security. Hinchey was a vocal opponent of the war in Iraq, and condemned the "deplorable" humanitarian conditions that the United States had created there. He showed his increasingly iconoclastic side in September 2004 when he was one of 16 House members voting against a resolution of sympathy for the victims of September 11; he objected to the Republicans' inclusion of "political" language on the "destruction of two terrorist regimes" in Afghanistan and Iraq, and called the measure "back-slapping, self-congratulatory." With Dana Rohrabacher, he backed state laws that authorize the use of medical marijuana. He has traveled frequently: According to

PoliticalMoneyLine, between 2000 and 2005 he took more than 20 privately-funded foreign trips to places such as Prague, Rome, Havana, Shanghai, Grand Cayman Island and Morocco, ranking him as one of the top members of Congress who received travel gifts and leading the *New York Post* to call him a "junket junkie." When *The Ithaca Journal* suggested his trips constituted a conflict of interest, Hinchey responded that it was "a result of the paper falling victim to Republican spin."

At home, he directed several appropriations grants to the revitalization of downtown Poughkeepsie. In February 2005 he advanced the theory, for which he admitted he had no evidence, that White House strategist Karl Rove had created the forged documents on which Dan Rather based his September 2004 broadcast on George W. Bush's National Guard service. In March 2005 he appeared at a rally protesting the Iraq war in New Paltz sponsored by ANSWER, a group that publicizes its support of Stalin's regime in the Soviet Union and the current North Korean government; another speaker was Lynne Stewart, the lawyer convicted not long before of conspiracy with the terrorist who engineered the 1993 bombing of the World Trade Center.

Hinchey remained a Republican target but built impressive strength in the district. Moppert tried again in 1994, embracing the Contract with America while trying to tie Hinchey to Clinton. He vastly outspent the challenger but the result was one of the nation's closest races; he won 49%–48%, with the outcome uncertain until almost two weeks after the election. In 1998, the favored Republican candidate, radio station owner William (Bud) Walker, was overshadowed by Randall Terry, the Binghamton talk radio host who founded Operation Rescue in 1987 and staged anti-abortion rallies. Terry spent $1.2 million, most of it from abortion opponents across the country. Walker won the Republican primary by an unimpressive 53%–35%. In the general, Hinchey won 62%–31%, with 7% for Terry as the Right-to-Life candidate. His district became more secure after Hinchey survived redistricting with flying colors. Although Pataki presented a plan that would have sliced up Hinchey's district among its neighbors, Assembly Speaker Sheldon Silver would have none of it; he was a friend of Hinchey's from their time in the Assembly, and in early 2002 Hinchey hired as his redistricting lobbyist Patricia Lynch, Silver's chief of staff until 2001. The new 22d District, thanks to Silver, was tailor-made for Hinchey.

TWENTY-THIRD DISTRICT

Rep. John McHugh (R)

Elected 1992, 7th term; b. Sept. 29, 1948, Watertown; home, Pierrepont Manor; Utica Col., B.A. 1970, S.U.N.Y. Albany, M.P.A. 1977; Catholic; divorced.

Elected Office: NY Senate, 1984–92.

Professional Career: Confidential Asst., Watertown City Mgr., 1971–76; Research & Liaison Chief, NY Sen. Douglas Barclay, 1976–84.

DC Office: 2333 RHOB, 20515, 202-225-4611; Fax: 202-226-0621; Web site: www.mchugh.house.gov.

District Offices: Canastota, 315-697-2063; Mayfield, 518-661-6486; Plattsburgh, 518-563-1406; Watertown, 315-782-3150.

Committees: *Armed Services* (5th of 34 R): Military Personnel (Chmn.); Readiness. *Government Reform* (5th of 23 R): Energy & Resources; National Security, Emerging Threats & International Relations. *Permanent Select Committee on Intelligence* (9th of 12 R): Intelligence Policy; Technical & Tactical Intelligence; Terrorism, Human Intelligence, Analysis & Counterintelligence.

Group Ratings

	ADA	ACLU	AFS	LCV	ITIC	NTU	COC	ACU	NTLC	CHC
2004	20	5	29	9	67	47	90	64	73	91
2003	35	—	50	15	—	48	68	71	—	—

National Journal Ratings

	2003 LIB	—	2003 CONS		2004 LIB	—	2004 CONS
Economic	49%	—	50%		44%	—	56%
Social	44%	—	56%		36%	—	61%
Foreign	46%	—	54%		41%	—	59%

Key Votes of the 108th Congress

1. Drilling in ANWR	Y	5. DC School Vouchers	N	9. Ban Same-Sex Marriage	Y
2. Approve Bush Tax Cuts	Y	6. Ban Human Cloning	Y	10. Fund Iraq War	Y
3. Medicare/Rx Bill	Y	7. Restrict Gun Liability	Y	11. Bar Cuba Embargo Funds	N
4. Bar Overtime Pay Regs.	Y	8. Ban Partial-Birth Abortion	Y	12. Intelligence Reorg.	Y

Election Results

2004 general	John McHugh (R-Ind-C)	160,079	(71%)	($471,790)
	Robert Johnson (D)	66,448	(29%)	($21,141)
2004 primary	John McHugh (R)	unopposed		
2002 general	John McHugh (R-C)	unopposed		($289,089)

Prior Winning Percentages: 2000 (74%); 1998 (79%); 1996 (71%); 1994 (79%); 1992 (61%)

The People		Race/Ethnic Origin	Ancestry	
Area size:	14,739 sq. mi.	92.9% White	Irish: 12.0%	German: 9.9%
Urban population:	34.7%	2.6% Black	French: 9.9%	
Rural population:	65.3%	0.6% Asian	**2004 Presidential Vote**	
Pop. 2000:	654,361	0.9% Native Am.	Bush (R) 134,174	(51%)
Median income:	$35,434	0.0% Hawaiian	Kerry (D) 123,216	(47%)
Poverty status:	13.5%	0.8% Two+ races	Other 4,810	(2%)
Military veterans:	14.3%	0.1% Other	**2000 Presidential Vote**	
		2.1% Hispanic Origin	Bush (R) 119,472	(49%)
			Gore (D) 115,611	(47%)
			Other 10,520	(4%)
			Cook Partisan Voting Index: R + 0	
Occupation	Blue collar: 27.4%	White collar: 52.4%	Gray collar: 20.2%	

Some early 19th century visionaries believed that the North Country of Upstate New York—a battleground in both the Revolutionary War and the War of 1812—was the land of the future. Financier Gouverneur Morris, French slave trader James Leray, and Dutch silver speculator David Parish bought up thousands of acres between the Adirondacks and the St. Lawrence River and tried to unload them on farmers unaware of the shortness of the growing season and the unnavigability of the river. These developers left behind grand mansions, but their hopes for huge profits were frustrated when the Erie Canal turned the stream of settlement westward, and Canadians built their new capital of Ottawa far north of the river (Queen Victoria picked the site, and put it as far from the U.S. border as possible). But northern New York was not without its business successes: It was in Watertown in 1878 that 26-year-old Frank Woolworth put a sign over a table of odds and ends that read "Any Article 5 Cents," starting America's first retail chain and inventing the concept of discount stores.

More recently, the North Country has looked to government for help. The St. Lawrence Seaway proved too small for most oceangoing freighters and remains frozen three months of the year; the locks are slow and icebreakers would wreck the shoreline. The state government has built prisons in Ogdensburg and Cape Vincent and Malone. North Country and Vermont members of Congress tried to get Lake Champlain declared one of the Great Lakes, to qualify for funding for various programs; the gambit failed as Michigan members bellowed in protest. The biggest initiative has been the enlargement of Fort Drum, near Watertown and adjacent to Lake Bonaparte, where despite the Army's preference for warm weather training sites, a 10,000-person light infantry division, the 10th Mountain Division, has been stationed since 1985; the 10th Mountain performed valiantly in Afghanistan and Iraq. Private developers have built big malls in Watertown and Massena (attracting Canadians, as even New York has lower taxes than Ontario). Communities in the Adirondack park have experienced big growths in values on the 40 per cent of the property that is privately owned.

The 23d Congressional District of New York covers most of the North Country, starting at Lake Champlain, running westward along the St. Lawrence Seaway and over the Adirondacks Forest Preserve to Lake Ontario. It also includes Madison County to the south. The district has only a few population centers, including Plattsburgh on Lake Champlain and Watertown and Oswego on Lake Ontario. Geographically it is the largest district in New York state, and one of the largest in the East. Politically, it is mostly ancestral Republican country; it gave George W. Bush a small plurality in 2000 and a small majority in 2004.

The congressman from the 23d District is John McHugh, a Republican first elected in 1992. McHugh has long been in government. He worked for the Watertown city manager in 1971; for eight years, he was a staffer for state Senator Douglas Barclay. In 1984, he was elected to succeed Barclay in Albany. McHugh specialized in dairy issues (New York has long price-fixed dairy products to help farmers) and military bases—both part of the North Country's economic life-blood. When incumbent David Martin announced his retirement, McHugh ran, with plenty of financing plus Martin's endorsement. He won the Republican primary with 70%, then won the general 61%–24%.

McHugh combines a relatively moderate voting record with a concern about local economic needs. In 1993 he got a seat on Armed Services and hired none other than Martin to monitor the Defense Base Closure and Realignment Commission. But that yielded little return. In that year's base closure round, the commission voted to close Plattsburgh Air Force Base, a major employer in McHugh's district, plus Griffiss Air Force Base, in Sherwood Boehlert's district to the south.

After Republicans won control of the House, McHugh chaired the Government Reform subcommittee with jurisdiction over the Postal Service, a somewhat dubious honor since it gave him responsibility for one of Congress's perennial headaches. He has worked on what would have been the biggest reform of Postal Service law since the 1970s. His version passed his subcommittee in 1998 but moved no further. With help from chairman Tom Davis, McHugh made another try in 2004 with a bipartisan plan that won unanimous support in the committee. The proposal would have created a new corporate structure and given the Postal Service greater flexibility to set rates and reduce its costs, and included provisions to assure that it does not abuse its monopoly status in dealing with private competitors carrying first-class mail. Without major reform, McHugh warned, the alternatives are steep increases in postal rates or a taxpayer bailout. But despite optimistic predictions in the spring of 2004, Republican leaders did not move the bill to the House floor; among their reservations was the Bush administration's insistence that the Postal Service absorb $27 billion in disputed pension costs for postal retirees who have had military service. McHugh was more successful in enacting his Semipostal Authorization Act, which allows the Postal Service to issue added-value stamps to advance causes—such as health or safety—that it considers in the public interest, with a maximum 25% surcharge made available for the cause.

McHugh has been moving up in seniority on the Armed Services Committee. As chairman of the Military Personnel Subcommittee, he has jurisdiction over a broad range of issues dealing with benefits and the demands placed on military officers. He sought a permanent increase of nearly 40,000 Army and Marine troops, but the Pentagon preferred to keep the changes temporary. Preserving Fort Drum in the 2005 base-closing round has been a high priority; with $500 million of recent improvements that he has encouraged, McHugh calls it the nation's "most modern military installation." In 2005, the base was spared from any cuts under the Pentagon's base closing recommendations. He takes a parochial view on trade issues. He opposed trade promotion authority because of fear that the dairy industry would not be adequately protected. In September 2003, he was one of 11 Republicans who broke with their party in opposing a plan for school vouchers for children in Washington, D.C.

McHugh has been reelected against token opposition since 1992.

TWENTY-FOURTH DISTRICT

Rep. Sherwood Boehlert (R)

Elected 1982, 12th term; b. Sept. 28, 1936, Utica; home, New Hartford; Utica Col., B.A. 1961; Catholic; married (Marianne).

Military Career: Army, 1956–58.

Elected Office: Oneida Cnty. Exec., 1978–82.

Professional Career: P.R. Mgr., Wyandotte Chemicals Corp., 1961–64; A.A., U.S. Rep. Alexander Pirnie, 1964–72; A.A., U.S. Rep. Donald Mitchell, 1973–79.

DC Office: 2246 RHOB, 20515, 202-225-3665; Fax: 202-225-1891; Web site: www.house.gov/boehlert.

District Offices: Auburn, 315-255-0649; Cortland, 607-758-3918; Utica, 315-793-8146.

Committees: *Science* (Chmn. of 24 R). *Transportation & Infrastructure* (3d of 41 R): Highways, Transit & Pipelines; Railroads; Water Resources & Environment.

Group Ratings

	ADA	ACLU	AFS	LCV	ITIC	NTU	COC	ACU	NTLC	CHC
2004	40	29	25	55	100	56	84	50	75	53
2003	25	—	38	65	—	49	80	52	—	—

National Journal Ratings

	2003 LIB	—	2003 CONS		2004 LIB	—	2004 CONS
Economic	52%	—	47%		51%	—	49%
Social	53%	—	47%		55%	—	45%
Foreign	49%	—	51%		47%	—	53%

Key Votes of the 108th Congress

1. Drilling in ANWR	N	5. DC School Vouchers	N	9. Ban Same-Sex Marriage	*
2. Approve Bush Tax Cuts	Y	6. Ban Human Cloning	N	10. Fund Iraq War	Y
3. Medicare/Rx Bill	Y	7. Restrict Gun Liability	Y	11. Bar Cuba Embargo Funds	N
4. Bar Overtime Pay Regs.	Y	8. Ban Partial-Birth Abortion	Y	12. Intelligence Reorg.	*

Election Results

2004 general	Sherwood Boehlert (R-Ind)	143,000	(57%)	($1,524,703)
	Jeffrey Miller (D)	85,140	(34%)	($32,965)
	David Walrath (C)	23,228	(9%)	($234,640)
2004 primary	Sherwood Boehlert (R)	22,908	(59%)	
	David Walrath (R)	15,394	(40%)	
	Other	588	(2%)	
2002 general	Sherwood Boehlert (R)	108,017	(71%)	($1,063,823)
	David Walrath (C)	32,991	(22%)	($104,975)
	Mark Dunau (Green)	6,660	(4%)	
	Other	5,109	(3%)	

Prior Winning Percentages: 2000 (61%); 1998 (81%); 1996 (64%); 1994 (71%); 1992 (64%); 1990 (84%); 1988 (100%); 1986 (69%); 1984 (73%); 1982 (56%)

The People		Race/Ethnic Origin	Ancestry	
Area size:	6,356 sq. mi.	92.2% White	Irish: 12.3%	German: 11.9%
Urban population:	50.5%	3.3% Black	Italian: 10.9%	
Rural population:	49.5%	0.9% Asian	**2004 Presidential Vote**	
Pop. 2000:	654,361	0.2% Native Am.	Bush (R) 147,509	(53%)
Median income:	$36,082	0.0% Hawaiian	Kerry (D) 130,568	(47%)
Poverty status:	12.6%	1.1% Two+ races	Other 2,367	(1%)
Military veterans:	14.2%	0.1% Other	**2000 Presidential Vote**	
		2.3% Hispanic Origin	Bush (R) 129,050	(48%)
			Gore (D) 126,021	(47%)
			Other 12,639	(5%)
			Cook Partisan Voting Index: R + 1	

Occupation   Blue collar: 24.4%   White collar: 57.3%   Gray collar: 18.3%

One of the first American frontiers was the Mohawk River Valley of Upstate New York—a frontier that remained static for 150 years. From the establishment of Fort Orange in 1624 in what now is Albany until the Revolutionary War, white settlers did not dare move west along the Mohawk. The British used their Iroquois allies as a buffer against the French and in return kept New England Yankees from moving westward. Only after the French were driven from the colonies in 1759 did the pressures for westward settlement prevail; the British tried to keep their word to the Indians, but once the Revolutionary War started, the Iroquois dominion ended.

This is the background of *Drums Along the Mohawk* and of James Fenimore Cooper's *Leatherstocking Tales*. But there is little in these rolling hills today to evoke the bloody violence whose conclusion made possible the digging of the Erie Canal and the building of the New York Central Railroad. The canal was a staggering engineering feat. In 1811, it cost more to ship goods 30 miles inland from New York City than it cost to send them to England. But after eight years of work by 9,000 men, the canal opened in 1825, ahead of schedule and on budget, effectively tying together the nation and cementing the importance of New York City to America's future. Then the New York Central built its water-line route, and the Mohawk Valley became one of the nation's early industrial centers. The little Oneida County hamlets of Utica and Rome, where the canal builders had to dig through the route's highest ground, became sizable factory towns. Even the utopian Oneida Community, with its believers in plural marriage and communal ownership, operated a stainless steel factory. First settled by New England Yankees, these towns attracted a new wave of immigration from the Atlantic coast in the early 20th century, including many Italian- and Polish-Americans.

The 24th Congressional District of New York sprawls through parts of 11 counties in central New York, few of them heavily populated. The biggest centers are Utica and Rome in Oneida County and Auburn in Cayuga County, which sits amidst the narrow Finger Lakes and was the home of Governor, Senator and Secretary of State William Seward. Nearby Seneca Falls was the birthplace of the women's movement in 1848, when Boston transplant Elizabeth Cady Stanton and Lucretia Mott produced a Declaration of Sentiments that initiated the push for women's suffrage. Abolition and temperance were also popular here. Today, this is a part of Upstate New York that feels itself bypassed by more recent economic growth and in need of government assistance. Oneida County's population fell 6% between 1990 and 2004, and in the latter year the county lost jobs at Rome Cable, Remington Arms, Oneida Ltd. and Union Tools. Six of the district's other 10 counties lost people as well; the booming business here is the Oneida Indians' Turning Stone Casino. At the south end of Otsego Lake is Cooperstown, where baseball was supposedly invented in 1839 and which is the home of the Baseball Hall of Fame. Like much of New York, the 24th District is historically Republican, but trended to Democrats in the 1990s. George W. Bush carried it only narrowly in 2000 and by a wider margin in 2004.

The congressman from the 24th is Sherwood Boehlert, a Republican first elected in 1982, now chairman of the Science Committee. Boehlert grew up and went to college in Utica, served in the Army, worked briefly for Wyandotte Chemical. Working as a waiter when he was a student at Utica College, he became friendly with Congressman Alexander Pirnie. In 1964, at 28, he got a job on Pirnie's staff; soon he was Pirnie's chief of staff and, after Pirnie retired in 1972, was chief of staff for his successor, Donald Mitchell, until 1978. Then he went back to Utica and was elected Oneida County Executive. When Mitchell retired in 1982, Boehlert won the seat. For many years Boehlert has had one of the most liberal voting records of any Republican House member—number three in both 1999 and 2000 *National Journal* ratings and sixth in 2004—and has taken a lead role in defeating what he considers extreme party positions, while maintaining party loyalty on many other matters and trying to forge bipartisan consensus on some issues. He sided with labor in March 2001 as one of 13 Republicans to oppose the repeal of the ergonomics rule, has voted for increased minimum wages, has voted against the partial-birth abortion ban and has supported the National Endowment for the Arts.

Boehlert has played a particularly critical role on environmental issues. His convictions here are strong. After Republicans took control in 1995 he took the lead in opposing environmental policy riders on EPA and other appropriations. In 1995 Speaker Newt Gingrich—to whom he gave crucial support when Gingrich won the whip's post by 2 votes in 1989—named him co-head, with conservative Richard Pombo, of a task force on environmental issues. This produced some results: Republicans agreed on the bipartisan Safe Drinking Water Act of 1996 and the environmental provisions of the 1996 farm bill. But in mid-1997 the intra-party truce broke down; after Boehlert rallied votes to water down an attempt by Western Republicans to exempt flood control projects from the Endangered Species Act, they complained bitterly. In January 2001, he urged caution about overturning last-minute Clinton administration environmental regulations and orders, but he supported the Bush administration on reconsidering 2006 levels of arsenic in drinking water. On the Water Resources and Environment Subcommittee he chaired from 1995 until 2001, Boehlert tried to reach bipartisan agreement on Superfund reform, but without success.

As Science Committee Chairman since 2001, Boehlert has been involved in some important issues. The September 11 attacks prompted action on cyberterrorism; in February 2002 the House passed Boehlert's bill for $880 million in grants to the National Science Foundation for research on cyberterrorism. He sponsored the bill signed into law in December 2003 authorizing $3.7 billion for nanotechnology research over four years.

In 2001 Boehlert supported the space program and opposed administration proposals to cut back the space station to allow just three astronauts to work there. After the loss of the space shuttle Columbia in February 2003, he and Senate Commerce Committee Chairman John McCain held joint hearings on the entire space program. In July 2003 Boehlert went ahead with the markup of a bill to allow NASA to offer higher bonuses and salaries up to $198,600 to recruit scientists and engineers, despite Democrats' desire to wait for the Columbia accident report; the bill was signed in January 2004. After China launched a manned space vehicle, Boehlert in October 2003 cautioned against a crash program to match it. "Our vision can't be based on some dreamy, ahistorical view that we can recreate the Apollo era." That month Boehlert and ranking Democrat (he became a Republican in January 2004) Ralph Hall called on NASA Administrator Sean O'Keefe to postpone work on the Orbital Space Plane. "Before any work is done, and especially before any money is spent, NASA needs to have a clearer idea of what the next vehicle for human space flight will be required to do." Boehlert was elated by the success of the Mars land rover in January 2004, but said, "Any decisions on the future of manned space flight must be made in the context of budget realities [and] the continuing need for reforms called for by the Columbia Accident Investigation Board." He endorsed George W. Bush's call for missions to the moon and eventually to Mars, but said, "I'm for people in space but on a limited basis, on an as-needed basis." Boehlert steered to passage the reauthorization of indemnification of contractors for liability in the space program, and supported the bill to keep the FAA from immediately regulating space tourism. "This industry is at the stage where it is the preserve of visionaries and adventurers and daredevils. These are people who will fly at their own risk."

Boehlert served on the Intelligence and Homeland Security Committees, but said the latter should not have sole jurisdiction on its issues. "Homeland security is too diffuse and too important . . . to leave with one committee." He is the third ranking Republican on the Transportation. Republican term limits will cost Boehlert the Science chairmanship after the 2006 election, but he may compete with Transportation's second ranking Republican, Tom Petri, and others for the chair of that committee.

Some of Boehlert's votes have a local angle: he supports dairy subsidies and helped get the Northeast Dairy Compact into the House farm bill (the 24th is part of New York City's milkshed); he sponsored Pledge of Allegiance Day (the Pledge was written by Francis Bellamy in Rome in 1892). He sponsored reauthorization of the Manufacturing Extension Partnership and helped get a $25 million facility for the Rome Air Force Research Laboratory. He put into the energy bill an amendment with $300 million to overhaul diesel school buses, but voted against the energy bill because it included oil drilling in the Arctic National Wildlife Refuge. As a baseball buff, Boehlert was relieved when redistricters kept Cooperstown in his district. The foyer of his Rayburn Building office is lined with pictures of local baseball heroes—William Hulbert of Burlington Flats, the founder of the National League, Bud Fowler of Fort Plain, the first black to play professional baseball, Ben Egan of Augusta, the first catcher for Babe Ruth. Boehlert was a minority owner of Utica Blue Sox until February 2002, when the team was sold to Cal Ripken Jr. and moved to Aberdeen, Maryland. He remains chairman of the Minor League Baseball Caucus and, as an aide said, "He considers anyone ever inducted into the Hall of Fame to be his constituent."

The 24th District is a solidly Republican constituency; Boehlert has won general elections easily. But he has had serious competition in the Republican primary. In 2000 David Vickers, a high school Spanish teacher, held him to a 57%–43% margin, although the challenger spent only $27,000. Boehlert was hurt in Oneida County by his opposition to congressional ratification of old Indian treaties which would extinguish the Oneida Indians' land claims; he backed government payments in out-of-court settlements. Boehlert won the general election with 61% of the vote, but Vickers got 21% as the nominee of the Conservative and Right-to-Life parties. In June 2002 redistricting removed Madison County and added all or parts of five new counties. Vickers did not run again, but at the last minute David Walrath, a physician and Cayuga County legislator, ran. He said he was a "real Republican" and Boehlert a "big-spending liberal"; like Vickers he called for congressional action to extinguish Indian land claims, which were being asserted by the Cayuga Indians in the new parts of the district. He wrested the Conservative nomination from Boehlert and got a court to take Boehlert off the Independence party line, which meant that unless Boehlert won the Republican primary he would not be on the general election ballot. Boehlert spent $1 million over the course of the campaign and Walrath only $99,000. Outside spending also favored Boehlert. The moderate Main Street Partnership spent $10,000 on a phone bank to support Boehlert, while the conservative Club for Growth, which was spending $150,000 on a Maryland primary held the same day in which its candidate lost by a wide margin, contributed only $1,000 for Walrath. Even so the result was very close. Boehlert won by only 53%–47%. He carried the parts of the district he had been representing since 1992 by 58%–42%. But in the new counties in the district, Walrath won 59%–41%. Boehlert had no Democratic opponent in November and won 71% of the vote.

In 2004 Walrath ran again. The White House and the House leadership left no doubt where it stood: Karl Rove spoke at a Boehlert rally in October 2003 and Tom DeLay sent a check. Former Speaker Newt Gingrich asked the Club for Growth not to support Walrath and came in to speak for Boehlert four days before the primary. Boehlert raised and spent $1.4 million, Walrath only $156,000, most of that early on. Walrath's campaign was plagued with problems: in February a warrant was issued to him for payment of $3,600 in back taxes; in May he demoted an aide who sent three letters to the editor and signed them with a Boehlert supporter's name. "My opponent has been attacking me to deflect attention from a record he can't defend," said Walrath. "I am at the peak of my influence in a town where experience and seniority really count," Boehlert proclaimed. "My opponent is ineffective and doesn't vote like a Republican," Walrath replied. Boehlert bragged that he had voted for every tax cut since Ronald Reagan was president and noted that he voted for the partial-birth abortion ban and against the ban on snowmobiles in national parks. Walrath continued to oppose the Cayuga Indian land claim; Boehlert said it should be settled locally. Boehlert won the September 15 primary 59%–40%, his best showing in three successive primaries; he lost only Cayuga County.

On September 28 Boehlert had heart bypass surgery and did no more active campaigning. He won the general election with 57% of the vote; Walrath as the Conservative nominee got 9%. After the election Boehlert said he planned to continue in office "as long as I'm productive, enjoying it and in good health." As for primary challenges, he said, "I just hope finally they'll go away."

TWENTY-FIFTH DISTRICT

Rep. James Walsh (R)

Elected 1988, 9th term; b. June 19, 1947, Syracuse; home, Syracuse; St. Bonaventure U., B.A. 1970; Catholic; married (Dede).

Elected Office: Syracuse Common Cncl., 1978–88, Pres. 1986–88.

Professional Career: Peace Corps, Nepal, 1970–72; Social worker, Onondaga Cnty. Social Svcs. Dept., 1972–74; Marketing exec., NYNEX, 1974–88.

DC Office: 2369 RHOB, 20515, 202-225-3701; Fax: 202-225-4042; Web site: www.house.gov/walsh.

District Offices: Palmyra, 315-597-6138; Syracuse, 315-423-5657.

Committees: *Appropriations* (7th of 37 R): Labor, Health and Human Services, Education & Related Agencies; Military Quality of Life & Veterans Affairs & Related Agencies (Chmn.).

Group Ratings

	ADA	ACLU	AFS	LCV	ITIC	NTU	COC	ACU	NTLC	CHC
2004	20	10	25	36	100	49	90	67	65	92
2003	5	—	14	30	—	60	93	79	—	—

National Journal Ratings

	2003 LIB	—	2003 CONS	2004 LIB	—	2004 CONS
Economic	31%	—	68%	49%	—	50%
Social	30%	—	65%	49%	—	51%
Foreign	23%	—	71%	43%	—	56%

Key Votes of the 108th Congress

1. Drilling in ANWR	N	5. DC School Vouchers	Y	9. Ban Same-Sex Marriage	Y
2. Approve Bush Tax Cuts	Y	6. Ban Human Cloning	Y	10. Fund Iraq War	Y
3. Medicare/Rx Bill	Y	7. Restrict Gun Liability	Y	11. Bar Cuba Embargo Funds	N
4. Bar Overtime Pay Regs.	N	8. Ban Partial-Birth Abortion	Y	12. Intelligence Reorg.	Y

Election Results

2004 general	James Walsh (R-Ind-C)	189,063	(90%)	($656,874)
	Howie Hawkins (PJ)	20,106	(10%)	
2004 primary	James Walsh (R)	unopposed		
2002 general	James Walsh (R-Ind-C)	144,610	(72%)	($939,783)
	Stephanie Aldersley (D)	53,290	(27%)	($39,999)
	Other	2,131	(1%)	

Prior Winning Percentages: 2000 (69%); 1998 (69%); 1996 (55%); 1994 (58%); 1992 (56%); 1990 (63%); 1988 (57%)

The People		Race/Ethnic Origin	Ancestry	
Area size:	2,561 sq. mi.	86.6% White	German: 13.9%	Irish: 13.9%
Urban population:	79.0%	7.1% Black	Italian: 12.4%	
Rural population:	21.0%	1.8% Asian	**2004 Presidential Vote**	
Pop. 2000:	654,361	0.6% Native Am.	Kerry (D) 158,063	(50%)
Median income:	$43,188	0.0% Hawaiian	Bush (R) 150,098	(48%)
Poverty status:	10.4%	1.5% Two+ races	Other 5,935	(2%)
Military veterans:	12.7%	0.1% Other	**2000 Presidential Vote**	
		2.3% Hispanic Origin	Gore (D) 148,623	(51%)
			Bush (R) 132,126	(45%)
			Other 12,619	(4%)
			Cook Partisan Voting Index: D + 3	

Occupation	Blue collar: 20.8%	White collar: 65.0%	Gray collar: 14.2%

Syracuse is a middle American city in the middle of Upstate New York, halfway between Albany and Buffalo on the Erie Canal and the old New York Central Railroad, which were for years the nation's major east-west transportation routes. Built on a swamp that was a salt spring, Syracuse is the home of many practical-minded inventions—the dental chair, Stickley mission furniture, the drive-in bank teller, the foot measuring devices used in shoe stores—and was an early manufacturer of typewriters. It is the site of the New York State Fair, which attracts 1 million visitors annually, and of Syracuse University, which plays basketball inside the Carrier Dome, the only domed stadium in the northeastern U.S. The agricultural hinterland is rich with specialty crops like wine grapes, and its industrial jobs are mostly high-skill. But Onondaga County lost 2% of its population between 1990 and 2004, with a big loss in the 20–35 age group. Manufacturing jobs are being lost, and the Carrier air conditioner factory is being shut down, but there are job gains in business services, education and health care, and unemployment has run below the national average. To attract young workers, Syracuse's Metropolitan Development Association held a 40 Below Summit of young professionals and artists in November 2004.

The 25th Congressional District of New York includes all of Syracuse and Onondaga County. West of Syracuse it includes territory just south of Lake Ontario, northern Cayuga County and Wayne County, where in the village of Palmyra Joseph Smith had his vision of the angel Moroni and saw the golden tablets that led him to found the Mormon Church. The district's western end is in the suburbs of Rochester in Monroe County, which in the June 2002 redistricting plan was split up between four districts. Historically, Syracuse and Rochester have been heavily Republican, partly out of antipathy to New York City. But in the 1990s, economically ailing Upstate New York trended sharply toward national Democrats (to bring in federal dollars) even as it voted for Republican Governor George Pataki (to hold down taxes). This district voted 51% for Al Gore in 2000 and 50% for John Kerry in 2004.

The congressman from the 25th District is James Walsh, a Republican first elected in 1988. He grew up in Syracuse, the son of Syracuse mayor and Congressman (1973–79) William Walsh. He came to the House as almost a professional civic activist: He was a volunteer in the Peace Corps in Nepal, a social worker, then worked for New York Telephone and NYNEX, which detailed him to a local university. He was elected five times to the Syracuse common council, then ran for Congress in 1988 when a Republican incumbent nearly beaten two years earlier decided to retire. He won by a solid 57%–42%. Like other Republicans from economically sluggish Upstate areas, he is open to government intervention in the economy.

Walsh has a seat on the Appropriations Committee, and has now been chairman of four subcommittees—part of the "college of cardinals." In 1995 and 1996 he chaired the District of Columbia Subcommittee, just as Marion Barry was returned to the mayor's office after serving time in prison. In 1997 and 1998 Walsh chaired the Legislative Branch Subcommittee, which sets Congress's own budget. He suffered the embarrassment in spring 1997 of seeing his appropriation defeated because of defections by 11 Republicans, who were determined to uphold promises to cut Congress's budget.

From 1999 to 2004 Walsh was chairman of the VA-HUD-Independent Agencies Subcommittee. In his first two years he battled with HUD Secretary Andrew Cuomo, attacking Cuomo for using anti-drug money to fund a gun buy-back program, and said at one point that HUD employees could be arrested. Walsh has not been shy about supporting what some call pork barrel projects, many for the Syracuse area. "Our economy's in tough shape right now, so we're not bashful at all in helping our own state." In 2004 he obtained $115 million for local projects, including $53.9 million for the Syracuse veterans hospital and $6 million for research at Cornell University on wine grapes.

In November 2001 Walsh and Democrat Nita Lowey pushed for $11 billion in aid to New York in the defense supplemental. This was opposed by the Bush administration, and Dick Cheney brought Walsh to the White House to ask him to defer the money until later. Walsh refused. Although Walsh and Upstater John Sweeney crossed party lines, their amendment, reduced to $9.7 billion, was defeated by two votes in committee. Walsh continued fighting and threatened to vote against the rule unless it allowed a vote on his amendment. But in a meeting with OMB Director Mitch Daniels and Deputy Whip Roy Blunt, he gave way, and agreed to accept $1.75 billion. Sweeney and New York Democrats were furious, but Walsh said, "I was concerned that we could lose everything if we just went right at the president and drew a veto." In 2002 Walsh resisted an amendment by Sweeney that would make New York schools eligible for aid for fear of the precedent it would create. Walsh complained to Dennis Hastert in August about the level of spending allowed, but worked doggedly and in October 2002 the subcommittee approved a $90.9 billion appropriation, under both the Senate level and the president's request, though funding for some programs, like AmeriCorps, were eliminated, which Walsh said would probably be added in conference. In 2003 the subcommittee's appropriation was held to $90.8 billion; in 2004 it was $92.9 billion. This was above the Bush budget, to which Walsh's response was, "It looks to me as if the president's budget is very, very tight for what I do." He resisted Bush's cut in the Section 8 housing programs and instead increased it by $1.5 billion; veterans health spending was raised, but NASA, AmeriCorps and other HUD spending were cut. In 2003 Walsh added to the energy bill a provision authorizing "green bonds," which would reduce the cost of financing the proposed Destiny USA mall near Syracuse by $100 million. He complained when Senator Charles Schumer opposed the energy bill on other grounds. "If New York's senators support jobs and opportunity for Upstate, they'll work to push for the passage of this legislation, not play politics to hinder it." But Schumer attached the green bonds provision to the corporate tax bill, which passed in late 2004.

In November 2002 House Republicans changed their rules to make Appropriations subcommittee chairmen, previously chosen by the full committee chairmen, subject to veto by the Steering Committee—clipping the cardinals' wings. In October 2004 Walsh asked Speaker Dennis Hastert for a waiver from the six-year Republican term limit on Appropriations subcommittee chairmanships. Incoming Appropriations Chairman Jerry Lewis decided to reduce the number of subcommittees from 13 to 10. Walsh ended up with the chairmanship of the Military Quality of Life Subcommittee, which means he retains jurisdiction over veterans programs and gains military construction, but loses HUD and NASA.

Walsh is co-chairman of the congressional Friends of Ireland and a strong supporter of the Easter peace accords signed in 1998. That year he sponsored the "Walsh Visas" to allow 4,000 unemployed young people a year from Northern Ireland and adjacent counties in the Irish Republic to live and work in Pittsburgh, Boston, Washington, Colorado Springs and, yes, Syracuse. In March 2004 he hosted Sinn Fein's Gerry Adams at Syracuse's St. Patrick's Day Parade. In March 2005, when Adams was shunned by George W. Bush, Edward Kennedy and others who had received him in the past because of IRA/Sinn Fein participation in a bank robbery and the murder of Robert McCartney, Walsh met with him anyway. Walsh also met with McCartney's five sisters, who were demanding justice for their brother's murderers.

Walsh has mostly won re-election without difficulty. After he sponsored school vouchers in Washington, D.C., the AFL-CIO targeted Walsh's district, ran an estimated $500,000 in TV ads against Walsh and a vigorous organizing campaign in 1996. With a late-spending and organizational surge, Walsh won 55%–45%. Since then, he has been reelected by overwhelming margins. He had no Democratic opponent in 2004.

TWENTY-SIXTH DISTRICT

Rep. Tom Reynolds (R)

Elected 1998, 4th term; b. Sept. 3, 1950, Belfonte, PA; home, East Amherst; Springville-Griffith Inst., Kent St. U.; Presbyterian; married (Donna).

Military Career: NY Air Natl. Guard, 1970–76.

Elected Office: Concord Town Bd., 1974–82; Erie Cnty. Legislature, 1982–88; NY Assembly, 1988–98, Min. Ldr., 1995–98.

Professional Career: Real estate & insurance broker; Erie Cty. Repub. Chmn., 1990–96.

DC Office: 332 CHOB, 20515, 202-225-5265; Fax: 202-225-5910; Web site: www.house.gov/reynolds.

District Offices: Rochester, 585-663-5570; Williamsville, 716-634-2324.

Committees: *NRCC Chairman. House Administration* (5th of 6 R). *Ways & Means* (17th of 24 R): Select Revenue Measures; Trade.

Group Ratings

	ADA	ACLU	AFS	LCV	ITIC	NTU	COC	ACU	NTLC	CHC
2004	5	0	0	0	100	60	100	92	86	92
2003	5	—	0	10	—	61	100	84	—	—

National Journal Ratings

	2003 LIB	—	2003 CONS		2004 LIB	—	2004 CONS
Economic	25%	—	74%		26%	—	73%
Social	30%	—	65%		31%	—	67%
Foreign	0%	—	89%		14%	—	85%

Key Votes of the 108th Congress

1. Drilling in ANWR	Y	5. DC School Vouchers	Y	9. Ban Same-Sex Marriage	Y
2. Approve Bush Tax Cuts	Y	6. Ban Human Cloning	Y	10. Fund Iraq War	Y
3. Medicare/Rx Bill	Y	7. Restrict Gun Liability	Y	11. Bar Cuba Embargo Funds	N
4. Bar Overtime Pay Regs.	N	8. Ban Partial-Birth Abortion	Y	12. Intelligence Reorg.	Y

Election Results

2004 general	Tom Reynolds (R-Ind-C)	157,466	(56%)	($2,522,713)
	Jack Davis (D-WF)	125,613	(44%)	($1,356,713)
2004 primary	Tom Reynolds (R)	unopposed		
2002 general	Tom Reynolds (R-Ind-C)	135,089	(74%)	($642,641)
	Ayesha Nariman (D)	41,140	(22%)	($8,377)
	Other	7,230	(4%)	

Prior Winning Percentages: 2000 (69%); 1998 (57%)

The People		Race/Ethnic Origin	Ancestry		
Area size:	2,749 sq. mi.	92.3% White	German: 20.6%	Irish: 12.3%	
Urban population:	71.2%	3.0% Black	Italian: 11.9%		
Rural population:	28.8%	1.5% Asian	**2004 Presidential Vote**		
Pop. 2000:	654,361	0.3% Native Am.	Bush (R)	176,235	(55%)
Median income:	$46,653	0.0% Hawaiian	Kerry (D)	137,543	(43%)
Poverty status:	6.9%	0.8% Two+ races	Other	4,384	(1%)
Military veterans:	12.9%	0.1% Other	**2000 Presidential Vote**		
		1.9% Hispanic Origin	Bush (R)	144,516	(51%)
			Gore (D)	126,693	(44%)
			Other	14,188	(5%)
			Cook Partisan Voting Index: R + 3		

Occupation   Blue collar: 23.4%   White collar: 61.7%   Gray collar: 14.8%

The destination of the Erie Canal, the great state engineering project that made New York the Empire State—is Lake Erie, and for its last hundred miles the canal passed through the rolling countryside of western New York. This was land scarcely settled, except by Indians, when the canal was begun in 1817, and in many ways it is part of the Midwest: water here flows not into the Atlantic but into the Great Lakes; people speak not in the pungent accents of New York City but in a flat Midwestern tone. The economy, based originally on farming fertile land, by the late 19th century became dominated by heavy industry. This land was settled mostly by New England Yankees, with cultural folkways quite different from those of New York City; later they were joined by Irish, Italian and Polish immigrants who came to work in the factories of Buffalo and Rochester. For most of its history, western New York had an economy more prosperous than that of the rest of the country, as you can still see in the solid houses and schools, stores and factories built to weather the Upstate winter. But economic growth here in the past quarter century has lagged behind the rest of the nation. Many of Buffalo's factories have closed and Rochester's premier industries, Kodak and Xerox, fell on hard times and laid off thousands.

The 26th Congressional District of New York covers much of western New York. About half its people are in the suburbs of Buffalo in Erie and Niagara Counties, though none in the city of Buffalo itself. It extends from the city limits of Buffalo to the city limits of Rochester and includes that city's northwestern suburbs. In between is rural and small town territory, with many towns bearing the classical names sprinkled by state commissioners across Upstate New York. One such is Attica, scene of the terrible prison riot in 1970. Politically, this is ancestrally Republican territory. For a long time this was due to Upstaters' distrust of Democratic New York City. But as economic growth has lagged, Upstate New York has moved toward the Democratic party. Not enough to make the 26th District Democratic, however: it is one of six New York districts that voted for George W. Bush in both 2000 and 2004.

The congressman from the 26th District is Tom Reynolds, a Republican first elected in 1998. Reynolds grew up in Springville, in southern Erie County, and became an insurance and real estate broker there. He got into politics early: in 1973 he was aide to an assemblyman and that same year, at 23, he was elected to the Concord town council. In 1982 he was named to a vacant seat in the Erie County Legislature. In 1988 he was elected to the Assembly and also helped run the congressional campaign of Bill Paxon, who was elected to succeed Jack Kemp in Congress from the Buffalo suburbs. From 1990 to 1996 he was Erie County Republican chairman, from 1995 to 1998 the Assembly minority leader. In early 1998 what is now the 26th District seat suddenly fell open when Paxon announced he would not run for reelection. At his side when he made his announcement in Erie County was his long-time friend and ally Reynolds, who announced the next morning he was running for the House. No serious Republican opposition appeared; Democrats nominated a professor at SUNY-Geneseo. It was not a suspenseful or eventful campaign. Reynolds won 57%–43%.

In the House, Reynolds has had the most conservative voting record in the New York delegation. With help from Paxon, he quickly won the favor of the Republican leadership and became only the second Republican freshman in a century to win a seat on the Rules Committee. That assignment gave him quick entry into the House's leadership circles and the Capitol's back rooms. Like Paxon, Reynolds proved a skillful fundraiser, gaining appointment to chair the National Republican Congressional Committee's Battleground 2000 program, which raised $21 million from House members. In 2001 Speaker Dennis Hastert gave Reynolds a slot on the leadership-friendly House Administration Committee, which has responsibility for campaign finance legislation. As a further sign of the leadership's gratitude to Reynolds for his campaign service and a mark of his growing influence, Hastert also got him a seat on the Ways and Means Committee; technically he did not join the committee until four years later, after the retirement of Ways and Means Upstate neighbor Amo Houghton. In the meantime, Reynolds became active as a legislative strategist. When the House took up the campaign finance regulation, he said that the Shays-Meehan bill had a loophole allowing Democrats to use their $40 million soft money building fund for hard money purposes; the language was fixed.

After September 11, some Democrats criticized Reynolds as more interested in the priorities of the White House than the needs of New York, but Reynolds responded that he played an essential role as honest broker in getting money to his home state; many champions of New York City agreed. Senator Hillary Rodham Clinton also worked with him on issues dealing with western New York. "We respect each other," she told a Buffalo audience. "And he makes me laugh. He's got a great personality." Clinton also helped to build early cooperation between Reynolds and Rahm Emanuel of Illinois, who had been an aide at the Clinton White House; the two House members cosponsored a bill to clean up the Great Lakes.

In November 2002, both Reynolds and Jerry Weller ran vigorous campaigns to chair the NRCC. Weller's district is adjacent to that of Speaker Dennis Hastert, who said he was neutral; other leadership members, notably Tom DeLay, backed Reynolds. He won 123–91. As NRCC chairman, Reynolds became an active spokesman for House Republicans. He worked on close terms with Hastert, with whom he shared many qualities: beefy, former state legislators with an earthy style, who gained influence by their backroom skills rather than their public personality; the two of them frequently could be seen in private conversations. Hastert called Reynolds "hardworking and tenacious." He was an active fundraiser for George W. Bush's campaign and built close relationships with top officials of the Bush administration, including Dick Cheney and Karl Rove; he played a prominent role at the 2004 convention in New York. Throughout the cycle Reynolds insisted that relatively few seats were in play and that incumbent Republicans would do fine; he concentrated on holding some open Republican seats and looking for attractive targets in Democratic districts. He suffered setbacks in February and June 2004 when Democrats captured two previously Republican-held seats in special elections in Kentucky and South Dakota. But in November 2004 Republicans gained a net three seats and saw only two incumbents lose—which increased Reynolds's already considerable influence in Republican ranks, and some mentioned him as a possible future leader. His rapid rise in House influence is "not bad for a kid from Springville," he often says.

In 2002 redistricting posed a challenge for Reynolds. Sluggish population growth meant that Upstate New York would lose a seat, and Reynolds's elongated district was in perfect geographical position to be carved up among its neighbors. On May 23, 2002, a three-judge federal court placed Democrat John LaFalce and Republican Jack Quinn in the same Buffalo-Niagara Falls district, which would have left Reynolds in a district without much of a Republican edge. But the court gave the legislature more time to act. The legislature in this case meant Democratic Assembly Speaker Sheldon Silver, Republican state Senate President Joseph Bruno and Governor George Pataki. Reynolds worked with Democrat Nita Lowey, then head of her party's House campaign committee, to convince the trio that they should agree on a plan that would give the two of them safe districts so that they could campaign for their parties across the country. Dick Cheney phoned Bruno to put on the pressure. On June 5, the legislature passed its plan, which left Reynolds with a relatively safe 26th District. In November 2002, he won by a 74%–22% margin. In 2004 he was opposed by Jack Davis, a businessman and former Republican who spent $1.25 million of his own money on his campaign. He ran ads depicting Reynolds as a free trader who outsourced American jobs—an effective line of attack in Upstate New York, where manufacturing job losses have been steep—but received little help or attention from national Democrats. Reynolds won by a surprisingly close 56%–44%. He carried each of the seven counties except Niagara, where Davis got 51%. After the election, Davis promised to remain politically active.

TWENTY-SEVENTH DISTRICT

Rep. Brian Higgins (D)

Elected 2004, 1st term; b. Oct. 6, 1959, Buffalo; home, Buffalo; S.U.N.Y. Buffalo, B.A. 1984, M.A. 1985, Harvard U. M.P.A. 1996; Catholic; married (Mary Jane).

Elected Office: Buffalo City Cncl., 1987–93; NY Assembly, 1998–2004.

DC Office: 431 CHOB, 20515, 202-225-3306; Fax: 202-226-0347; Web site: house.gov/higgins.

District Offices: Buffalo, 716-852-3501; Jamestown, 716-484-0729.

Committees: *Government Reform* (16th of 17 D): Energy & Resources; National Security, Emerging Threats & International Relations. *Transportation & Infrastructure* (31st of 34 D): Coast Guard & Maritime Transportation; Highways, Transit & Pipelines; Water Resources & Environment.

Group Ratings and Key Votes: Newly Elected

Election Results

2004 general	Brian Higgins (D-Ind-WF)	143,332	(51%)	($1,372,162)
	Nancy Naples (R-C)	139,558	(49%)	($1,581,433)
2004 primary	Brian Higgins (D)	18,790	(44%)	
	Paul Clark (D)	11,150	(26%)	
	Michael Collesano (D)	5,042	(12%)	
	Mark Thomas (D)	3,961	(9%)	
	Other	3,363	(8%)	
2002 general	Jack Quinn (R-C)	120,117	(69%)	($772,921)
	Peter Crotty (D-WF)	47,811	(27%)	($38,359)
	Other	5,991	(4%)	

The People		Race/Ethnic Origin	Ancestry	
Area size:	2,444 sq. mi.	88.8% White	German: 19.2%	Polish: 14.7%
Urban population:	81.5%	4.0% Black	Irish: 12.5%	
Rural population:	18.5%	0.7% Asian	**2004 Presidential Vote**	
Pop. 2000:	654,361	0.8% Native Am.	Kerry (D) 158,433	(53%)
Median income:	$36,884	0.0% Hawaiian	Bush (R) 132,416	(45%)
Poverty status:	12.0%	1.0% Two+ races	Other 6,709	(2%)
Military veterans:	14.0%	0.1% Other	**2000 Presidential Vote**	
		4.6% Hispanic Origin	Gore (D) 149,840	(53%)
			Bush (R) 114,859	(41%)
			Other 16,090	(6%)
			Cook Partisan Voting Index: D + 7	

Occupation	Blue collar: 25.3%	White collar: 57.9%	Gray collar: 16.8%

Buffalo, with its massive 1920s skyscraper City Hall overlooking the Niagara River and Lake Erie, has gone through rough times. The butt of many jokes about the snow that piles up at the eastern end of Lake Erie and that supposedly keeps it immobilized half the year, Buffalo also should be credited with building a heavy industrial base in the late 19th and early 20th centuries, as America's number one grain milling center and as a major steel producer. Today, the Lackawanna steel mills are cold, and grain milling waned after the St. Lawrence Seaway opened in the 1950s. Buffalo is eclipsed economically by the bigger Great Lakes industrial cities of Cleveland, Detroit and Chicago, and its architecturally bold downtown skyscrapers are far overshadowed by the high-rise horizon of Toronto, not many miles away. Buffalo was the nation's 15th largest city in 1950 when it had a population of 580,000; in 2003 it was number 60, with a population down to 285,000, less than it had in 1900. Surrounding Erie County, once well over 1 million, was down to 936,000 in 2004. The downward spiral of what some call the Incredible

Shrinking City intensified in the 1980s when the Bethlehem Steel plants were shuttered. Mayor Anthony Masiello even suggested that the city be absorbed into Erie County. Buffalo still has considerable assets: a high-skill labor force and inexpensive real estate, including a gentrified and handsome waterfront on a now-cleaner Lake Erie and some impressive cultural institutions. Local boosters contend that the city retains untapped potential as a tourist mecca, and they criticize powerbrokers in Albany for focusing excessive attention on New York City as the state's economic engine. Right across Buffalo's Peace Bridge is the richest part of Canada, the golden horseshoe from Niagara Falls through Hamilton to Toronto. But Buffalo's hopes of becoming Toronto's back office have faded, as the Canadian dollar has weakened, and New York taxes are still high enough to leave Buffalo at a serious disadvantage.

The 27th Congressional District of New York consists of the eastern and southern two-thirds of Buffalo, plus most of the Erie County suburbs east and south of the city—from working-class Cheektowaga and Lackawanna to higher-income Hamburg and Orchard Park. The 27th also includes Chautauqua County, the famed birthplace of a movement to promote high-minded discourse. It was there that a training camp for Methodist Sunday school teachers was founded in 1874, attracting some 25,000 people to educational talks and inspirational lectures from the likes of Ralph Waldo Emerson and William Jennings Bryan; rounds of lectures continue every summer. Although some of the Buffalo suburbs are Republican, this district overall is solidly Democratic. But as Buffalo struggled, it became politically volatile. In 1992 Buffalo gave Ross Perot 28% of the vote, his best showing in a central city anywhere; in 1994 Mario Cuomo, who had always run well in Buffalo, lost Erie County to George Pataki, who carried Erie County again in 1998 and 2002. But in contests for president and senator, Buffalo and Erie County have remained solidly Democratic.

The congressman from the 27th District is Brian Higgins, a Democrat elected in 2004 in the last contest to determine a winner that year. Higgins grew up in Buffalo and graduated from Buffalo State College, and got master's degrees more than a decade later at both his alma mater and Harvard. His father was prominent in local politics; he served on the city council and as commissioner of the New York State Workers Compensation Board during the administration of Governor Hugh Carey. The younger Higgins was a political junkie, securing staff jobs in the Erie County sheriff's office, the State Assembly, and the county Legislature. In 1993, after six years on the Buffalo city council, he ran for county comptroller and lost to Republican Nancy Naples. In 1998, he was elected to the New York Assembly and served three terms. In a district crowded with unionized workers, Higgins often reminded voters that his father and uncle were bricklayers and he stressed his Irish immigrant heritage.

In April 2004 Jack Quinn, a Republican who was first elected in 1992 and who was reelected with support from local unions, announced his retirement from the House. His move stunned both parties—including Tom Reynolds, who represents the adjacent district and chairs the National Republican Campaign Committee. That immediately made the 27th District one of the country's most hotly contested races. Naples, a former Merrill Lynch executive in Manhattan and a popular local figure with strong name recognition, quickly wrapped up the Republican nomination, while five Democrats battled for their party's nomination. Higgins was the favorite of local and national Democratic leaders, organized labor and the *Buffalo News,* which called him "an unusually productive member of a largely dysfunctional legislative body" in Albany. Higgins viewed the primary as a done deal and focused his criticisms on Naples and George W. Bush. West Seneca supervisor and certified public accountant Paul Clark, who appealed to the large base of Polish voters in the district, emerged as his chief opponent; he criticized Higgins as a career politician who had failed to solve problems. Higgins won the September primary with 44% to 26% for Clark; Chautauqua County Executive Mark Thomas got more than two-thirds of the vote in that county, but it cast only 12% of the total vote, and he got only 9% overall.

The general election evoked memories of the bitter 1993 county comptroller contest between Higgins and Naples. Higgins reminded voters that Naples supported many of George W. Bush's policies, including his handling of national security. He criticized Republicans for shifting the tax burden from the rich to the middle class and promised that he would make health care more available and protect Social Security. His television ads publicized his efforts to develop the

Buffalo waterfront, but Republicans forced local stations to drop a spurious Democratic ad that claimed that Naples supported county tax increases. Naples criticized Higgins for his record in Albany, including support for tax increases, and she emphasized her own performance in local government. She had strong support from NRCC Chairman Tom Reynolds of the next-door 26th District. Higgins won 51%–49%; Naples took 57% of the vote in Chautauqua County, which cast 20% of the district's votes; Higgins won 53% in Erie County. It took 16 days of recounts and a court challenge before Naples conceded the more than 3,000-vote victory. Higgins already had participated in freshman orientation in Washington.

Reynolds seems likely to try to defeat Higgins in 2006. Possible candidates include Erie County Sheriff Patrick Gallivan and Assemblyman Jack Quinn III, the son of the former congressman.

TWENTY-EIGHTH DISTRICT

Rep. Louise Slaughter (D)

Elected 1986, 10th term; b. Aug. 14, 1929, Harlan Cnty., KY; home, Fairport; U. of KY, B.S. 1951, M.S. 1953; Episcopalian; married (Robert).

Elected Office: Monroe Cnty. Legislature, 1976–79; NY Assembly, 1982–86.

Professional Career: Regional Coord., Lt. Gov. Mario Cuomo, 1976–79.

DC Office: 2469 RHOB, 20515, 202-225-3615; Fax: 202-225-7822; Web site: www.louise.house.gov.

District Offices: Buffalo, 716-853-5813; Niagara Falls, 716-282-1274; Rochester, 585-232-4850.

Committees: *Rules* (RMM of 4 D): Legislative & Budget Process.

Group Ratings

	ADA	ACLU	AFS	LCV	ITIC	NTU	COC	ACU	NTLC	CHC
2004	95	87	100	100	22	8	44	0	0	16
2003	100	—	100	95	—	21	27	8	—	—

National Journal Ratings

	2003 LIB	—	2003 CONS		2004 LIB	—	2004 CONS
Economic	92%	—	0%		86%	—	14%
Social	83%	—	16%		75%	—	25%
Foreign	87%	—	13%		80%	—	19%

Key Votes of the 108th Congress

1. Drilling in ANWR	N	5. DC School Vouchers	N	9. Ban Same-Sex Marriage	N
2. Approve Bush Tax Cuts	N	6. Ban Human Cloning	N	10. Fund Iraq War	N
3. Medicare/Rx Bill	N	7. Restrict Gun Liability	N	11. Bar Cuba Embargo Funds	Y
4. Bar Overtime Pay Regs.	Y	8. Ban Partial-Birth Abortion	N	12. Intelligence Reorg.	*

Election Results

2004 general	Louise Slaughter (D-WF)	159,655	(73%)	($353,874)
	Michael Laba (R-C)	54,543	(25%)	($14,725)
	Other	5,678	(3%)	
2004 primary	Louise Slaughter (D)	19,966	(79%)	
	Francina Cartonia (D)	3,202	(13%)	
	Other	2,149	(9%)	
2002 general	Louise Slaughter (D-WF)	99,057	(62%)	($982,355)
	Henry Wojtaszek (R-Ind-C)	59,547	(38%)	($215,720)

Prior Winning Percentages: 2000 (66%); 1998 (65%); 1996 (57%); 1994 (57%); 1992 (55%); 1990 (59%); 1988 (57%); 1986 (51%)

The People		Race/Ethnic Origin	Ancestry	
Area size:	2,282 sq. mi.	62.0% White	German: 13.4% Italian: 11.0%	
Urban population:	93.5%	28.7% Black	Irish: 9.7%	
Rural population:	6.5%	1.4% Asian	**2004 Presidential Vote**	
Pop. 2000:	654,360	0.5% Native Am.	Kerry (D) 162,319	(63%)
Median income:	$31,751	0.0% Hawaiian	Bush (R) 92,627	(36%)
Poverty status:	18.7%	1.7% Two+ races	Other 4,581	(2%)
Military veterans:	12.2%	0.1% Other	**2000 Presidential Vote**	
		5.5% Hispanic Origin	Gore (D) 151,402	(60%)
			Bush (R) 88,461	(35%)
			Other 14,160	(6%)
			Cook Partisan Voting Index: D +15	

Occupation	Blue collar: 23.2%	White collar: 58.3%	Gray collar: 18.5%

Rochester, with a metro area of just over one million, is one of the major cities of Upstate New York. Located where the Erie Canal, the backbone of Upstate, crosses the Genesee River, Rochester became a major industrial city—the "Flour City" in the 1830s, as it milled the wheat produced by western New York farmers; then, a high-tech city, after a bank clerk named George Eastman began making photographic dry plates and marketed the first still camera and film for Thomas Edison's motion picture camera. Later, Bausch & Lomb developed its lens business here. Rochester, the home of Susan B. Anthony and Frederick Douglass, has lived on high-tech versions of the eye. Its great industries—Bausch & Lomb, Eastman Kodak, and Xerox (which started here as Haloid)—have thrived on technical innovation, precision workmanship, high reliability and customer service, lending Rochester an affluent and well-educated population as well as fine civic institutions, including the George Eastman House, one of the world's leading repositories of photographic and motion-picture history. This was the city that in 1918 invented the Community Chest and at one time had the nation's highest United Way contributions. Unhappily, Rochester's big employers have fallen on hard times, and young professionals have been leaving the area. Kodak, hard hit by competition from digital cameras, employed 60,000 people in the Rochester area in 1981; by 2005 that was down to 15,000. Xerox jobs in the area fell from 16,000 to 8,000.

Not far west of Rochester is a very different part of Upstate New York, the Niagara Frontier—the local name for the Buffalo-Niagara Falls area. The Niagara Frontier was once an armed frontier, between the United States and British-held Upper Canada, where American troops crossed the raging Niagara River during in the War of 1812 to fight the Battle of Lundys Lane. Later in the 19th century Niagara Falls became a prime vacation spot—a must-see sight for European tourists and American honeymooners. Few tourists today notice the huge water intakes farther up the river or the hydroelectric power lines strung out on giant pylons fanning out in every direction, providing cheap public power for the chemical and steel factories that made the Niagara Frontier one of the heavy industry capitals of America. But the city of Niagara Falls has suffered hard times. Tourists tend to stay on the Canadian side, which has better views of the Falls. Niagara Falls has lost 70% of its manufacturing since the 1960s and had the nation's third-lowest rate of job growth in the late 1990s; it has suffered double-digit unemployment and population losses. The downtown, leveled by urban renewal, remains troubled but there is hope: the Seneca Nation of Indians is expanding its casino in the city's faded convention center, one of three Indian casinos planned for the Niagara Frontier.

The 28th Congressional District of New York was created by redistricting in 2002. It includes Rochester, Niagara Falls and part of Buffalo, all connected by a thin strip of land along Lake Ontario and the Niagara River. Most of Rochester's suburbs are in three other districts, but the 28th includes Grand Island, Tonawanda and the northeast quadrant of Buffalo, where it includes much of the city's downtown and its fine cultural institutions. This is mainly a central city district, and 29% of its residents are black, by far the highest percentage in any Upstate district. Politically, this is a solidly Democratic district.

The congresswoman from the 28th District is Louise Slaughter, a Democrat first elected in 1986. A coal miner's daughter and a descendant of Daniel Boone (which makes her a cousin of

Missouri Democrat Ike Skelton), she grew up in Kentucky and still speaks with the accent and pungent phraseology of the mountains. Slaughter worked as a local staffer for Mario Cuomo when he was lieutenant governor in the 1970s and she won a seat on the Monroe County Legislature in 1976; she was elected to the New York Assembly in 1982. In 1986 she beat a one-term conservative Republican congressman 51%–49%, after charging that he did nothing to free *Associated Press* reporter Terry Anderson, a Rochester native held hostage in Lebanon. She secured what had been a marginal seat by tending carefully to local problems, by winning the support of area businessmen and the local *Democrat & Chronicle* newspaper—ironically, the flagship of Gannett, a chain founded by a diehard Upstate Republican.

Slaughter became a member of the Rules Committee, a proponent of her party's changes in House procedures (and a disparager of the Republicans'). She has regularly scored a liberal voting record, including opposition to NAFTA and trade promotion authority. Slaughter is a prime supporter of the National Endowment for the Arts and has sponsored bills for free broadcast time for candidates. A microbiologist by training, and consistent with the Rochester-area research mindset, Slaughter opposed proposals to ban human cloning. With Bob Ney, she pushed for House action in 2004 on a Senate-passed bill to prevent employers and insurers from testing for genetic markers that suggest potential debilitating ailments, but Republican leaders refused to schedule the measure.

It took Slaughter many years to gain a higher position. In December 1994 she lost the race for vice chairman of the Democratic Caucus, and in 1996 she failed to become ranking Democrat on the Budget Committee. In 2005, she finally got a senior post after Martin Frost lost in Texas and she became the ranking Democrat on the Rules Committee. As a loyal lieutenant of Minority Leader Nancy Pelosi, Slaughter became an outspoken critic of Republican policies and their management of the House. In March, she released a 147-page report that highlighted what Democrats said was "profound abuse" of House rules by Republicans in the 108th Congress.

Slaughter backs feminist causes and is active on health issues. In 1991 she was one of the seven women House members who marched on the Senate to protest its treatment of Anita Hill. The Lewinsky scandal and impeachment left Slaughter uncomfortable. In March 1998 she said defensively, "I have not changed a bit from my days with Anita Hill. Sexual harassment in the workplace is a terrible thing and should not be tolerated." She said she was ready to call for Bill Clinton's resignation in August, but backed away when she saw the videotape of his testimony in which she thought his rights were abridged. As chairwoman of the bipartisan Congressional Caucus for Women's Issues, she issued a broad agenda of steps to combat violence against women.

Redistricting was a perils-of-Pauline nightmare for Slaughter. Sluggish population growth meant that Upstate New York had to lose one congressional district, and there was much political maneuvering to determine which it would be. In May 2002, a three-judge federal court adopted a plan by a special master that would have left Slaughter with a safe Rochester-area seat. But the court gave the legislature time to adopt a plan of its own. On June 5 the legislative leaders reached agreement on a plan that connected Rochester and Democratic parts of Monroe County in this earmuff-shaped district with Niagara Falls and part of Buffalo. It placed Slaughter in the same district as Democrat John LaFalce, the party's ranking member on the Banking Committee, whose campaign would undoubtedly be well financed. Slaughter had represented only 43% of the new district; LaFalce had represented 39% and was much better known in the remaining 18% in the Buffalo area. Slaughter called the decision to carve up Monroe County between four districts "appalling" and said that the needs of Rochester and Buffalo were different and sometimes competing. LaFalce sent clear signals that he would run against Slaughter, but three weeks later he announced his retirement. Slaughter still faced the possibility of primary opposition from a Buffalo-area Democrat. But none stepped forward. In the general election Slaughter campaigned in much new territory, but most of it was Democratic. She lost in the thin strip of land connecting Rochester and Niagara Falls, but she won 73% of the vote in Monroe County and 60% in Erie County, for a 62%–38% victory against an inexperienced Republican challenger. In 2004, she won easily in both the primary and general elections. In this solidly Democratic district, Slaughter's chief threat is a primary challenge.

TWENTY-NINTH DISTRICT

Rep. Randy Kuhl (R)

Elected 2004, 1st term; b. April 19, 1943, Bath; home, Hammondsport; Union College, B.S. 1966, Syracuse U., J.D. 1969; Episcopalian; divorced.

Elected Office: NY Assembly, 1980–86; NY Senate, 1986–2004.

Professional Career: Practicing atty., 1970-2005.

DC Office: 1505 LHOB, 20515, 202-225-3161; Fax: 202-226-6599; Web site: www.kuhl.house.gov.

District Office: Corning, 607-937-3333.

Committees: *Agriculture* (21st of 25 R): Livestock & Horticulture. *Education & the Workforce* (27th of 27 R): 21st Century Competitiveness; Education Reform. *Transportation & Infrastructure* (37th of 41 R): Aviation; Economic Development, Public Buildings & Emergency Management.

Group Ratings and Key Votes: Newly Elected

Election Results

2004 general	Randy Kuhl (R)	136,883	(51%)	($937,340)
	Samara Barend (D-WF)	110,241	(41%)	($612,443)
	Mark Assini (C)	17,272	(6%)	($267,016)
	Other	5,819	(2%)	
2004 primary	Randy Kuhl (R)	25,552	(64%)	
	Mark Assini (R)	13,303	(33%)	
	Other	1,074	(3%)	
2002 general	Amo Houghton (R-C)	127,657	(73%)	($970,302)
	Kisun Peters (D)	37,128	(21%)	
	Other	9,846	(6%)	

The People		Race/Ethnic Origin	Ancestry	
Area size:	5,761 sq. mi.	92.5% White	German: 16.3%	Irish: 12.2%
Urban population:	58.4%	2.7% Black	English: 11.1%	
Rural population:	41.6%	1.8% Asian	**2004 Presidential Vote**	
Pop. 2000:	654,361	0.5% Native Am.	Bush (R) 171,317	(56%)
Median income:	$41,875	0.0% Hawaiian	Kerry (D) 127,481	(42%)
Poverty status:	9.9%	1.0% Two+ races	Other 4,660	(2%)
Military veterans:	14.2%	0.1% Other	**2000 Presidential Vote**	
		1.4% Hispanic Origin	Bush (R) 152,004	(53%)
			Gore (D) 121,596	(43%)
			Other 11,318	(4%)
			Cook Partisan Voting Index: R + 5	

Occupation   Blue collar: 23.0%   White collar: 61.3%   Gray collar: 15.7%

The Southern Tier of New York is one of the nation's forgotten stretches of territory, yet it has an interesting and distinctive history. Elmira was the hometown of Mark Twain's beloved wife, Olivia, and is where Twain is buried. Corning is the headquarters of Corning Glass Works, a company successful over the years not only in manufacturing but in its artistic distinction, which is showcased at a well-visited glass museum. This area has an Indian presence—some small reservations as well as the Seneca-Iroquois National Museum—plus miles and miles of dairy farms and much of New York's wine country. Sheltered by hills, the lands at the edge of Upstate's deep lakes constitute the nation's largest grape-growing area outside California, the leader in Concord grapes, with headquarters of prime New York State wineries and a major Welch's grape juice plant. But this country is isolated, and ill-served by air travel or Interstate highways. Cattaraugus County, slightly inland from Lake Erie, is actually 110 miles closer to Washington, D.C., than it is to New York City, though getting to either destination requires considerable patience. The cruelest cut, however, was the Internet bust. Corning's prospects grew dramatically when fiber optics and other high-tech components were being installed at a feverish pace, but the reduction in orders following the bust forced the company to lay off more than 1,000 of its local workers, in a town of only 11,000 people.

The 29th Congressional District of New York includes much of the state's Southern Tier, from Elmira to Cattaraugus County; to the north it also includes the westernmost of the Finger Lakes and the southern suburbs of Rochester. Politically, this has been Republican country since the party's founding. The towns and countryside are no longer homogeneously Protestant, but they remain solidly Republican in most elections. Despite the trend in Upstate New York toward national Democrats, the 29th remains solidly Republican. This was George W. Bush's best congressional district in New York in both 2000 and 2004.

The congressman from the 29th District is John "Randy" Kuhl, a Republican elected in 2004. He grew up in western New York and graduated from Union College and Syracuse University law school. He worked ten years as a lawyer before winning election to the state Assembly in 1980; in 1986, he was elected to the state Senate. In April 2004 Amo Houghton, former CEO of Corning and one of the richest members of Congress, announced he was retiring after 18 years in the House after being assured that the district would not be sacrificed in redistricting. Kuhl quickly became the frontrunner to succeed him. Even with the endorsement of Houghton, who wanted a successor from the Southern Tier, he endured two tough campaigns before winning the seat. Kuhl kicked off his campaign in April with an attempt to inoculate himself against attack by apologizing for a 1997 drunk driving conviction, but that issue turned out to be the least of his worries. He drew heavy criticism for his service in Albany, in a legislature that is widely regarded as the most dysfunctional legislative body in the nation. Then, shortly before the September 14 Republican primary, Kuhl's conservative opponent, Monroe County legislator Mark Assini, turned up the heat by releasing a radio ad that accused Kuhl of being a bigot. The attack, based on an 11-year-old comment about groups with "genetic traits", does not seem to have been effective. Assini carried his base in the Rochester suburbs of Monroe County with 69% of the vote, but only 19% of the votes were cast there. Kuhl won just about everywhere else in the district and beat Assini by 64%–33%. The general election was expected to be anticlimactic in this solidly Republican district. Kuhl called for lowering taxes to attract more investment to western New York and said that he would work to ensure that the local agricultural sector remained competitive. The Democratic nominee, Samara Barend, 27, had never held elected office; she had served briefly as an aide to former Senator Daniel Patrick Moynihan and had worked on Senator Hillary Rodham Clinton's 2000 campaign. Kuhl, with his extensive political experience, was endorsed by the national and state AFL-CIO as "a strong advocate for working men and women and their families." But Kuhl's campaign was rocked in late October by the unauthorized release of his sealed divorce records, which included charges of excessive drinking and womanizing and an accusation that Kuhl had pulled out two shotguns at a dinner party and threatened to shoot his wife. Both Kuhl and his ex-wife denounced the release of the records, which had been obtained by Barend's campaign manager after a staffer got them from a county clerk's office; apparently the documents were inadvertently released. Barend initially denied any role in the incident and refused demands to fire her campaign manager. But Kuhl's campaign said that she was lying. As damaging as the documents appeared to be, they weren't enough to overcome widespread distaste for the manner in which they were made public. Kuhl's win was narrower than had been expected, 51%–41%, with 6% to Assini on the Conservative Party line. In Monroe County, which cast 36% of the total vote, Barend led 48%–39%. Kuhl carried the other counties, including 67% in Corning-based Steuben County.

Kuhl got seats on three committees: Agriculture, Education and the Workforce, and Transportation and Infrastructure. He said that he wanted to follow Houghton on Ways and Means, but freshmen are seldom assigned to that panel, and Tom Reynolds of the next-door 26th District already had a seat on the committee. Kuhl promised to hold a town meeting annually in each of the 143 towns in the district.

★ NORTH CAROLINA ★

North Carolina, in its third century as a state, has become one of the leading-edge parts of the nation, a state whose growing economy, booming demography and vibrant culture are in many ways typical of the way the nation is going—or would like to go. This was mostly unanticipated. Few people 30 years ago picked North Carolina as a state that would chart a path to the future. It had no great central city, no Atlanta primed to become another Chicago or Los Angeles, but rather a series of small metropolitan areas spaced out over thickly settled countryside. It did not have what seemed to be cutting-edge industries: the biggest employer was textiles, typically an underdeveloped nation's first industry, and the other two were stolid furniture and soon-to-be-disfavored tobacco. Geographically, it seemed to be off the nation's main lines of commerce—too steamy to be businesslike in the summer, too cold to be a resort in the winter. It did not seem socially advanced, with a population made up almost entirely of native-born Anglo-Saxons and African-Americans and with an attachment to traditional and sometimes fundamentalist religion.

Yet North Carolina has emerged as one of America's leading growth states. Its population grew by 45% from 1980 to 2004, from 5.9 million to 8.4 million; it ranks just behind also-fast-growing Georgia as the 11th largest state and is likely to pass New Jersey soon and become number 10. Its economy has diversified and grown steadily. The number of textile and tobacco jobs is down, but Research Triangle Park, between Raleigh, Durham and Chapel Hill, has become one of the world's leading pharmaceutical and high-tech research centers: semiconductors, photonics, nanotechnology and security technology. GlaxoSmithKline has headquarters here, and Cisco, IBM, Nortel, and Sony Ericsson have big facilities. And the Triangle's success has been echoed by the Centennial Campus at Raleigh's North Carolina State University and the Piedmont Research Triad in Winston-Salem, which attracted a 2,000-job Dell facility in 2004. North Carolina has become one of the nation's leading banking centers, the headquarters of Bank of America (formerly NationsBank and NCNB) and Wachovia, both of which have been buying up other banks; Winston-Salem's Wachovia merged with Charlotte's First Union in 2003. North Carolina even has a film industry: *Dirty Dancing*, *Evil Dead 2* and *Teenage Mutant Ninja Turtles* were shot here, as well as the TV show *Dawson's Creek*. Charlotte and Raleigh-Durham accounted for half the state's population growth from 1990 to 2003, and they are now not just regional centers but major metro areas, with national sports franchises and huge hub airports. Nearly half the state's population—and more than half its affluent population—are in the Charlotte, Raleigh-Durham and Greensboro-Winston-Salem metro areas which have spread out into formerly rural counties. North Carolina is not just Mayberry any more.

Not all of North Carolina is upscale. The state is the nation's number two hog producer; some people are worried about the state's decline in manufacturing jobs, as low-wage factories close and work moves to lower-wage factories in less affluent states or abroad. The furniture industry is pressed by competition from China. The October 2004 tobacco buyout, ending tobacco allotments, is spurring farmers to shift to other crops like blueberries and pumpkins, even sheep and goats; some, free to compete in the market, are shifting from flue leaf to burley leaf, but the old tobacco economy will never be the same. North Carolina, number one in the percentage of workers in manufacturing jobs in 1993, was number five in 2002. But manufacturing job losses have been overwhelmed by the rise in service jobs, and the unemployment rate is low enough that thousands of Latinos moved into North Carolina seeking jobs in construction and meat and chicken factories. The state's Hispanic population rose from 77,000 to 379,000 in a decade, the biggest percentage rise in any state. Yet for all its metropolitan growth, life in North Carolina has not lost its rural tone. This has always been thickly settled rural land, and if one is never out of sight of others there is also plenty of green space and reminders of rural roots, from barbecue stands to country Baptist churches to stock car tracks.

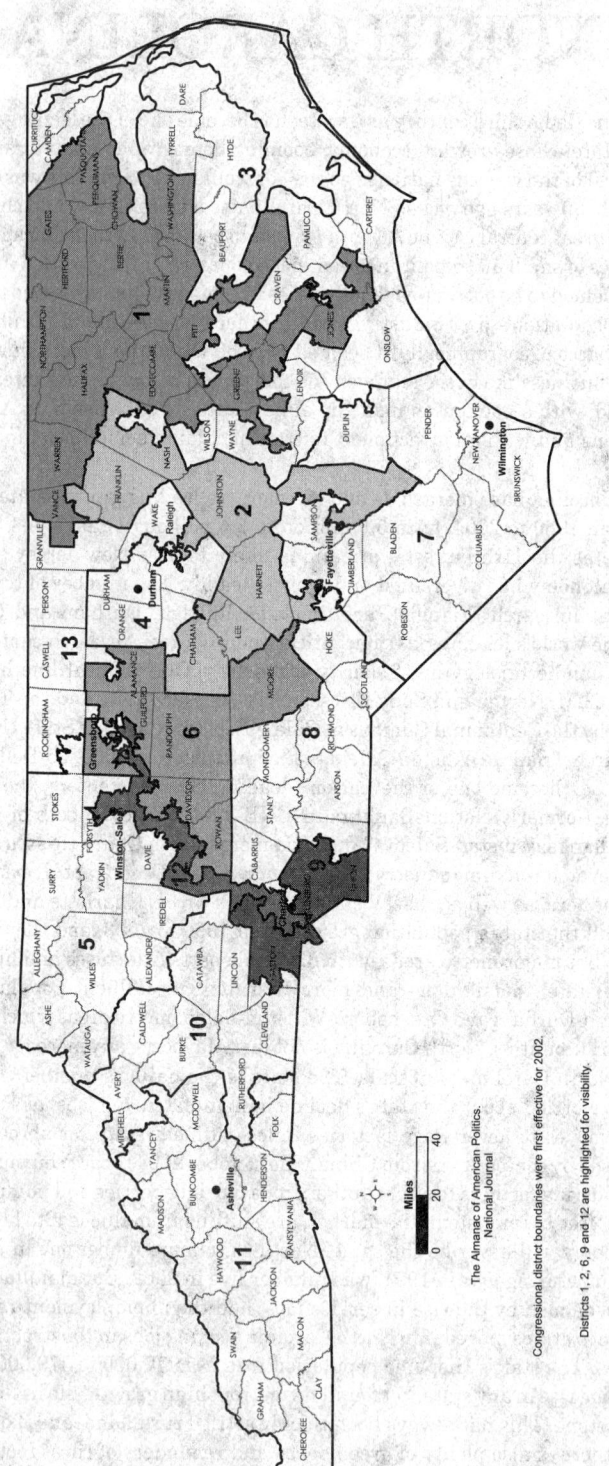

The Almanac of American Politics,
National Journal

Congressional district boundaries were first effective for 2002.

Districts 1, 2, 6, 9 and 12 are highlighted for visibility.

Change has not been directed from any single establishment; the forces that have produced it are diverse and sometimes hostile. North Carolina historically had a small and articulate elite, which looked for guidance from the University of North Carolina at Chapel Hill and the liberal editors of the state's newspapers, most prominently the Raleigh *News & Observer* and the *Charlotte Observer*. Quite different attitudes are nurtured by tradition-minded churches in a state where churchgoing is deeply ingrained, endorsed for years through Sunday blue laws and strengthened periodically by religious revivals. When North Carolina was an economically backward state, infant mortality was common, indoor plumbing was not, and religion was a fountain of hope and a source of discipline; it is still, perhaps even more, in this now bustling air-conditioned, cable- and computer-wired commonwealth.

North Carolina has grown with the aid of both its progressive and tradition-minded citizens, and in spite of—sometimes because of—the polarized politics that has developed between the two sides. North Carolina's professionals tend to share progressive values; its businessmen and conservative Protestants tend to share tradition-minded values. Both groups have contributed to the state's economic dynamism and cultural energy. Liberal progressivism has provided an impetus toward building good schools and universities and highways and amenities like the nation's first state-funded symphony and state high schools for science and mathematics and the arts.

From these two strands of North Carolina tradition developed a polarized, increasingly party-line politics that is pretty evenly balanced, waged partly on economic issues but even more on cultural attitudes. It is a politics in which Democrats and Republicans have been distinctive, sometimes bitter in their rivalries, for years not overlapping in their ideas but by the mid-1990s converging on at least some issues. This politics was built on historic partisan patterns. Coastal North Carolina settlers tended to be British Anglicans who became Methodists, slaveholders who supported the Confederacy and voted Democratic; Piedmont settlers tended to be Scots-Irish Presbyterians with a scattering of German sects, Union men in 1861 and Republicans ever after. The most effective paladins of both traditions for the last quarter century, Republican Senator Jesse Helms and Democratic Governor Jim Hunt, were each elected to statewide office five times over 25 years, and in 1984 waged what was then the most expensive Senate race in U.S. history; once bitter rivals, they later reconciled, and worked together on some issues. Now they have both retired from office.

Most elections here have been decided by relatively narrow margins. Since 2000, election results have fallen into a pattern: Democrats tend to win state contests, Republicans tend to win federal elections. George W. Bush carried the state 56%–43% in 2000 and by a nearly identical 56%–44% in 2004, when North Carolina's John Edwards was on the Democratic ticket. Democrat Mike Easley from East Carolina—traditionally Democratic country where Jesse Helms ran well—won the governorship in 2000 by 52%–46% and 56%–43% in 2004. Democrats have held the state Senate through his governorship, won the state House in 2000, ended up with a 60–60 tie there after the 2002 election, then won a majority in 2004. North Carolina's two U.S. senators are now Republicans. Elizabeth Dole won her seat in 2002 over Clinton White House Chief of Staff Erskine Bowles by a 54%–45% margin. In 2004 Congressman Richard Burr beat Bowles for the seat vacated by Edwards by a 52%–47% margin. Republicans hold just seven of North Carolina's 13 House seats, because of a districting plan drawn by Democrats and because two moderate Democrats win in areas easily carried by Bush; in 2004 he carried 9 of the 13 current districts.

North Carolina's electorate breaks along cultural, not economic lines. In the 2004 exit poll blacks, 21% of the voters according to the NEP exit poll—quite possibly an oversampling—voted 85%–14% for John Kerry. But conservative white Protestants, 24% of the electorate, voted 95%–5% for George W. Bush. Bush carried voters with incomes of $30,000 on up (only 28% had lower incomes). Geographically, the Piedmont urban counties, filling up with professionals and with significant black populations, have trended Democratic; the counties farther out, filling up with middle-income families working in decentralized businesses, have been producing large Republican majorities. Coastal east Carolina, once overwhelmingly Democratic, is now mixed, mostly for Bush; smaller counties in and near the western mountains are heavily Republican.

The result is a close balance between two cultural and political blocs which have contributed to North Carolina's unanticipated growth—though neither is inclined to give the other much credit.

The People		Race/Ethnic Origin			Military veterans: 792,646 (13.0%)	
Pop. 2004 (est):	8,541,221	5,647,155	70.2%	White	WWII: 17.3%	Korea: 12.5%
Pop. 2000:	8,049,313	1,723,301	21.4%	Black	Vietnam: 32.3%	Gulf War: 13.3%
Pop. 1990:	6,628,637	112,416	1.4%	Asian	**Most populous cities (2003):**	
Change 1990–2000:	Up 21.4%	95,333	1.2%	Native Am.	1. Charlotte	584,658
% of U.S. total:	2.9%	3,165	0.0%	Hawaiian	2. Raleigh	316,802
Pop. rank:	11th of 50	79,965	1.0%	Two+ races	3. Greensboro	229,110
Area size:	53,819 sq. mi.	9,015	0.1%	Other	4. Durham	198,376
State Native:	63.0%	378,963	4.7%	Hisp. Origin	5. Winston-Salem	190,299
Non-citizen:	3.9%	**Ancestry**				
Language		USA: 11.7%		English: 8.1%	Urban population: 60.2%	
English: 90.7%	Spanish: 5.4%	German: 8.0%		Irish: 6.3%	Rural population: 39.8%	
Other Eur.: 2.4%		Scotch-Irish: 2.7%				

Education		Work Sector		General Assembly	
H.S. Grad:	78.1%	Private: 78.8%	Govt: 14.5%	Senate	29 D 21 R
College Grad:	22.5%	Self: 6.4%	Family: 0.3%	House	63 D 57 R
Industry		Unemployment: 5.2%		Legislative Term Limits: No	
Agri: 1.6%	Con: 8.2%	**Household Income**		**Registered Voters**	
Fin: 6.0%	Info: 2.3%	<15k: 16.9%	15-35k: 27.7%	D: 2,582,462 (46.8%)	
Mfg: 24.4%	Prof: 26.9%	35-50k: 17.7%	50-100k: 28.3%	R: 1,903,119 (34.5%)	
Public: 4.1%	Trade: 14.9%	100-150k: 6.0%	>150k: 3.4%	O: 1,034,411 (18.7%)	
Other: 11.6%		Median: $39,184			
Occupation		Poverty status: 12.3%			
Blue collar: 29.7%	White collar: 56.0%	**Home Value**			
Gray collar: 14.3%		<50k: 18.0% 50-100k: 35.1%	100-200k: 33.7% 200-300k: 8.2%		
		300-500k: 3.6% >500k: 1.5%	Median: $95,800		

Presidential politics   North Carolina was not a competitive state in the 2000 and 2004 campaigns, despite the presence of North Carolina Democratic Senator John Edwards on the Democratic ticket in 2004. He was the first North Carolinian on a major party national ticket since William A. Graham was nominated by the Whigs in 1852. The Kerry-Edwards campaign gamely ran ads in the state in July, but took them off the air in August when polls showed the state out of reach. Edwards came back in October to vote early, but otherwise was not much of a presence in his home state. Did Edwards help the Democratic ticket? Probably a little. In 2004 Bush won the same 56% of the vote he had in 2000, in an electorate 20% larger.

2004 Presidential Vote		
Bush (R)	1,961,166	(56%)
Kerry (D)	1,525,849	(44%)
Badnarik (Lib)	11,731	(0%)
Other	2,261	(0%)

2000 Presidential Vote		
Bush (R)	1,631,163	(56%)
Gore (D)	1,257,692	(43%)
Other	26,135	(1%)

In contrast, Bush's percentage went up in 2004 in Virginia, South Carolina and Georgia. The Kerry-Edwards ticket won higher percentages in the metropolitan counties containing (in order of increase) Durham, Chapel Hill, Asheville, Charlotte, Raleigh, Winston-Salem and Greensboro. But Bush made larger gains in East Carolina counties, including those with large black percentages, and especially those around Fort Bragg and Camp Lejeune.

North Carolina's presidential primary has been crucial only once, in 1976, when after five straight losses, Ronald Reagan started denouncing the Panama Canal Treaty and won his first victory over Gerald Ford. It has been part of the Super Tuesday primary since 1988, but has been overshadowed by the even larger states that vote that day.

Congressional districting North Carolina won a 12th House seat in the 1990 Census and, quite unexpectedly, a 13th seat in the 2000 Census. It beat out Utah for the latter by just 856 people, and because its apportionment population includes some 18,000 U.S. troops and diplomats who claim North Carolina as their home, Utah filed a lawsuit arguing that its apportionment population should be credited with Mormon missionaries overseas who claim Utah as

109th Congress Lineup
7 R   6 D
108th Congress Lineup
7 R   6 D

their home. But in April 2001 a three-judge federal panel ruled unanimously against Utah and in November 2001 the Supreme Court affirmed that decision without opinion.

In the 1990s, North Carolina was the epicenter of race-based redistricting litigation, home to a legal controversy that went to the U.S. Supreme Court four times. Democratic legislators created their plans for 2002 with this litigation in mind. The state House and Senate passed the same plan in November 2001; in North Carolina the governor does not have a veto on redistricting bills. The plan created a new 13th District seat in the northern Piedmont which leaned Democratic in state elections, though it was even in the 2000 presidential race; the district ended up electing Democrat Brad Miller, not coincidentally the chairman of the Senate redistricting committee. The plan significantly weakened 8th District Republican Congressman Robin Hayes. It marginally improved the Republican-leaning 2d and 7th Districts seats held by Democrats Bob Etheridge and Mike McIntyre. It created six heavily Republican districts and three solidly Democratic districts, with the other four districts tailored to the needs of local Democrats. Republicans filed suit even before the plans were passed. But while their arguments about the Democratic plans for redistricting state legislative seats prevailed in the state Supreme Court, their case against the congressional district lines was dropped after the Justice Department approved the maps and the U.S. Supreme Court refused to intervene. Litigation over two different sets of legislative maps delayed North Carolina's usual May state primary election until September in 2002 and July in 2004.

Governor

Michael Easley (D)

Elected 2000, term expires Jan. 2009, 2d term; b. Mar. 23, 1950, Nash County; home, Southport; U. of N.C. (Chapel Hill), B.A. 1972; N.C. Central U., J.D. 1975; Catholic; married (Mary).

Elected Office: NC Atty. Gen., 1992–2000.

Professional Career: Asst. D.A., N.C. 13th Dist., 1976–78, 1979–82; N.C. Dist. Atty., 1982–90; private practice, 1978–79, 1990–92.

Office: State Capitol, Raleigh, 27603, 919-733-4240; Fax: 919-733-5166; Web site: www.state.nc.us.

Election Results

2004 general	Michael Easley (D)	1,939,154	(56%)
	Patrick Ballantine (R)	1,495,021	(43%)
	Other	52,513	(2%)
2004 primary	Michael Easley (D)	379,498	(85%)
	Rickey Kipfer (D)	65,061	(15%)
2000 general	Michael Easley (D)	1,530,324	(52%)
	Richard Vinroot (R)	1,360,960	(46%)
	Other	50,778	(2%)

Mike Easley, a Democrat, was elected governor of North Carolina in 2000, the first time either party won a third consecutive term since 1968. Easley grew up on a tobacco farm near Rocky Mount, 50 miles east of Raleigh, and graduated from the University of North Carolina and North

Carolina Central University Law School. He has spent his whole adult life in government. He served as an assistant district attorney and in 1982, at 31, became district attorney in three southeast counties. In 1992 he took a big step upward by winning election statewide as attorney general. He backed the death penalty and supported gun rights. He appeared in $1 million worth of public service ads, many warning about predatory lending to old people; his constant appearances irritated Republicans, who pushed through a law banning such appearances in election years.

Reelected in 1996, Easley started running for governor in 1999, obviously a strong candidate but by no means the favorite. His main Democratic primary opponent, Lieutenant Governor Dennis Wicker, was endorsed by teachers' unions, feminist groups and black leaders. But Easley won the May primary by 59%–36%. Meanwhile, the Republican nomination went to former Charlotte Mayor Richard Vinroot. Easley called for prescription drugs for seniors and HMO regulation, improvements in public schools and a lottery to fund education. He avoided the national Democratic Party and didn't attend the convention in Los Angeles. Vinroot opposed the lottery but said he would allow a referendum; he pledged not to raise taxes and called for school vouchers for low-income children in failing schools.

For most of the campaign, Easley ran about 10% ahead in polls. Then, when the presidential candidates debated at Wake Forest University in Winston-Salem on October 11, Vinroot tied Easley to Al Gore. One ad called Easley an "Al Gore liberal." Easley attacked Vinroot for his support of vouchers and opposition to a lottery. Easley had more money, and in the last week ran an ad with an endorsement from North Carolina's Andy Griffith. That helped portray him as a down-home, rural Carolinian, running against a city slicker. Even as George W. Bush was carrying North Carolina, Easley won 52%–46%.

Easley came to the governorship at a time when voters were used to an expanding economy and used to the leadership talents of Jim Hunt, elected in 1976 and 1980 and again in 1992 and 1996, and at a time when North Carolina's booming economy was slowing down. As the first North Carolina governor never to have been a legislator in nearly 50 years, he lacked the horsetrading skills that are useful in dealing with a legislature and did not spend much time negotiating with legislative leaders. He attracted more attention dealing with emergencies—three ice storms and seven hurricanes in his first term—and when he slammed into the speedway wall at 120 m.p.h. at Lowes's Motor Speedway in Concord in 2003. "It was fun for about four or five laps, but the last part wasn't too good. I was pushing and the car was running tight and it got loose on me and I wrecked." In his first years Easley had some success. In September 2001 he persuaded the legislature to pass his budget with money for his More at Four academic preschool program and smaller class sizes for grades K-3; he proposed a 1% increase in the sales tax and the legislature passed that and an income tax increase as well. He passed programs for HMO regulation and prescription drugs for seniors, character enhancement and school accountability report cards. But as time went on he faced severe fiscal problems. In February 2002 he used executive power to take money from trust funds and withhold money from local governments to stanch a $1.2 billion shortfall. In May 2002 he presented a budget which cut overall spending and depended on receipts from an as yet unapproved lottery, but provided money for More at Four and more teachers in early grades and cut aid to local governments; they could increase their sales taxes by a half-percent if they liked. In June 2002 the state Senate rejected his education spending increases; in July 2002 the House, with Republicans solidly against, blocked his plan to cut local aid. In response Easley cut 2,600 state jobs. In September the House rejected putting the lottery on the ballot 69–50. But a budget agreement was reached that month protecting Easley's More at Four and class size proposals and gave state agency heads greater flexibility in making cuts.

In November 2002 Republicans gained seven seats in the state Senate and emerged with a 61–59 majority in the House (though a January 2003 party switch left the House evenly divided). The next day Easley astonished legislators by vetoing his first bill. The Founding Fathers of North Carolina, suspicious of executive tyranny, had written a state constitution in which the governor had no veto; only in 1996 did the voters grant the governor a limited veto. Hunt had never used it; Easley did, on a bill designating appointments to boards and commissions. The legislature, summoned to the required special session to consider override, let it stand: The first veto by a governor of North Carolina since Josiah Martin vetoed a bill in 1774. Faced with another budget shortfall, Easley got the legislature to extend the 2001 tax increase, but later called for a small cut in the corporate tax rate. In 2004, as revenues started coming in more generously, Easley got $60 million for More for Four and reducing K-3 class sizes. He claims that North Carolina fourth graders lead the nation in math scores and rank above average in reading and near the top in writing, and that North Carolina leads the nation in high school graduates going on to college. Easley also pushed through $3 billion in bonds for university and community college facilities and $700 million in bonds for transportation and infrastructure. He pushed a One North Carolina Agenda which he claims has brought in 12,000 jobs and $1 billion in investment since 2001 and Job Development Investment Grants which he claims has brought in 8,600 jobs and $1.3 billion investment since 2003. In November 2004 he persuaded the legislature to pass $242 million in incentives to get Dell to build a plant with 2,000 jobs in Winston-Salem.

Easley entered the 2004 campaign year with good but not stellar job ratings and there was a serious contest for the Republican nomination. The favorite was Richard Vinroot, running in his third straight gubernatorial race; he directed most of his fire at Easley. "I told you this fellow would raise taxes." Former one-term Congressman Bill Cobey ran with the endorsement of former Senator Jesse Helms; he and Vinroot represented the two wings of the party that had clashed in many primaries before. But the nomination went to the third candidate, state Senator Patrick Ballantine, who resigned in April and campaigned as a strong conservative. The primary was delayed from May until July because of a pending lawsuit over legislative districting. Ballantine won, with 30.4% of the votes to 30.0% for Vinroot—much lower than his 2000 showing—and 27% for Cobey. When the results were announced, Vinroot declined to ask for the runoff he was entitled to under state law since no candidate got 40%.

Ballantine tried to break into Easley's area of strength in east Carolina and campaigned in all 100 counties. "Mike Easley is a big tax-and-spender," he said. "First he blamed Jim Hunt, then it was George W. Bush, then it was 9/11, then it was the legislature, then it was the drought and then it was the rain." And he said he was in favor of teacher salary increases and literacy programs. Easley came scorching back in debate. "If Patrick Ballantine is a champion of education, then Saddam Hussein is a champion of civil rights." Easley ran on his record. "Every other state said, 'We've got to cut. We've got to cut everything, including education.' We all got together, and we said, 'We've got to cut, but we're not going to cut education.'" He raised $9 million to Ballantine's $4.5 million, and his campaign ran many negative ads, suggesting Ballantine was way off to the right. Easley conspicuously declined to attend the Democratic National Convention (though he had campaigned for John Edwards in North Carolina) and supported a constitutional amendment to ban same-sex marriage. He ran ads with Andy Griffith and boasted of his endorsement by the National Rifle Association.

Easley won 56%–43%. He won the votes of 43% of whites and 87% of blacks; he won at least 44% among every income group and 51% among college graduates and 19% of Republicans. He won 21% among white conservative Protestants and 34% of evangelicals and born-again Christians. The negative ads helped: he won only 51% of those who said they were voting for a candidate but 73% among those who said they were voting primarily against his opponent. Easley carried all of east Carolina except for three counties on the coast and Johnston County outside Raleigh; he carried all the big metropolitan counties but lost in the Piedmont textile counties and in several mountain counties.

Going into his second term, Easley continued to press for a lottery; all the surrounding states have them now. "We're the only state in America that plays the lottery and gives away the proceeds. We are building new schools in South Carolina, Virginia, Georgia and Tennessee while we're packing our kids in trailers here at home." And he said he would press the legislature to pass a Learn and Earn program which would let high school students take classes at community colleges and worked toward an associate's or bachelor's degree as well as a high school diploma. Democrats made gains in legislative elections and again had majorities in both houses.

National Democrats, noting that the only presidents their party has elected in the last 40 years were Southern governors, began casting an eye on Easley (who, with Mark Warner of Virginia, Phil Bredesen of Tennessee and Kathleen Babineaux Blanco of Louisiana are the only Democratic governors in the 11 Confederate states). But he seems unlikely to be a candidate. When his wife was asked about his political future in October 2004, she said, "What else would he run for? He's happy being in North Carolina." When asked about his legacy, Easley has quipped that he wants to be forgotten, to have no portrait made and no jails named after him. He has not been active in the Democratic Governors Association or in other national Democratic groups. And it seems unlikely that he would run against fellow Tar Heel John Edwards, who certainly might run again in 2008.

Senior Senator

Elizabeth Dole (R)

Elected 2002, seat up 2008, 1st term; b. July 29, 1936, Salisbury; home, Salisbury; Duke U., B.A. 1958, Harvard U., M.A. 1960, J.D. 1965; Methodist; married (Robert).

Professional Career: Deputy Asst., U.S. Consumer Affairs, 1969–73; Fed. Trade Commission, 1973–79; Public liason, U.S. Pres. Ronald Reagan, 1981–83; Secy., U.S. Dept. of Trans., 1983–87; Secy., Dept. of Labor, 1989–90; Pres., Amer. Red Cross, 1991–95, 1997–99.

DC Office: 555 DSOB, 20510, 202-224-6342; Fax: 202-224-1100; Web site: dole.senate.gov.

State Offices: Greenville, 252-329-1093; Hendersonville, 828-698-3747; Raleigh, 919-856-4630; Salisbury, 704-633-5011.

Committees: *Aging (Special)*. *Armed Services*: Airland; Emerging Threats & Capabilities; Personnel. *Banking, Housing & Urban Affairs*: Housing & Transportation; International Trade & Finance; Securities & Investment.

Group Ratings

	ADA	ACLU	AFS	LCV	ITIC	NTU	COC	ACU	NTLC	CHC
2004	25	11	33	0	92	64	100	92	88	100
2003	15	—	11	11	—	72	91	80	—	—

National Journal Ratings

	2003 LIB	—	2003 CONS		2004 LIB	—	2004 CONS
Economic	29%	—	68%		39%	—	58%
Social	0%	—	59%		16%	—	81%
Foreign	32%	—	65%		0%	—	67%

Key Votes of the 108th Congress

1. Ban Drilling in ANWR	N	5. Energy Bill	Y	9. Ban Same-Sex Marriage	Y
2. Approve Bush Tax Cuts	Y	6. Support Roe v. Wade	N	10. Ban Bunker-Buster Bomb	N
3. Medicare/Rx Bill	Y	7. Ban Partial-Birth Abortion	Y	11. Fund Iraq War	Y
4. Bar Overtime Pay Regs.	N	8. Assault Weapons Ban	N	12. Restrict Missile Defense	N

Election Results

2002 general	Elizabeth Dole (R)	1,248,664	(54%)	($13,735,220)
	Erskine Bowles (D)	1,047,983	(45%)	($13,306,317)
	Other	34,534	(1%)	
2002 primary	Elizabeth Dole (R)	342,631	(80%)	
	Jim Snyder (R)	60,477	(14%)	
	Other	22,998	(5%)	
1996 general	Jesse Helms (R)	1,345,833	(53%)	($14,589,266)
	Harvey B. Gantt (D)	1,173,875	(46%)	($7,992,980)

Elizabeth Dole, former Secretary of Transportation and Secretary of Labor, former president of the American Red Cross and candidate for president, was elected senator from North Carolina in 2002. She grew up in Salisbury, in the Piedmont textile country between Charlotte and Greensboro; her father was a wholesale florist and her mother had the pleasure of attending, at 101, her daughter's election night celebration. Elizabeth Hanford, as she then was, graduated from Duke, got a master's in education at Harvard and taught school in Boston. She spent the summer of 1960 working in the office of North Carolina Senator B. Everett Jordan; in the fall, she worked on Lyndon Johnson's campaign train through the South. In 1962 she went to Harvard Law School, one of 29 women in a class of 550; her classmates included future Congresswomen Patricia Schroeder and Elizabeth Holtzman. In summers she worked at the Peace Corps headquarters, the United Nations and Oxford University. After graduation she practiced law briefly in Washington. With help from Democratic Governor Terry Sanford she got a job at HEW, then at the White House Office of Consumer Affairs. She stayed on after the change in administrations in 1969 and changed her registration from Democratic to Independent; she worked on projects like freshness dating on food products and a conference on hunger in America. In 1973 she was nominated to a six-year term on the Federal Trade Commission. In 1975 she married Senator Bob Dole and campaigned with him when he was nominated for vice president in 1976.

In all these jobs she was a hard-working perfectionist with no sharp ideological edge. She always maintained her gracious Southern manners and showed an enthusiasm and friendliness that was off-putting to some but which served her well in a series of positions that few or no women had held. In 1981 she headed Ronald Reagan's Public Liaison office and in 1983 she was appointed Secretary of Transportation; in that capacity, she likes to point out, she was the first woman to head a branch of the armed services, the Coast Guard. In 1989 George H. W. Bush appointed her Secretary of Labor. In 1991 she became head of the American Red Cross, which had grave organizational problems and whose blood bank program was in trouble. She restructured the organization and put in place new blood bank procedures. She took a leave of absence to work on her husband's presidential campaign from November 1995 to January 1997; many will remember her speech about her husband at the San Diego convention, in which she walked about and spoke fluently and fervently. In 1999 she resigned from the Red Cross to run for president. She placed third in the August 1999 Iowa straw poll, but dropped out of the race in October. She did not endorse George W. Bush at that point and did not take a job in the Bush administration.

In early 2001 it was not clear whether North Carolina Senator Jesse Helms would run for reelection. White House political strategists were already looking at Dole as a possible candidate; in August 2001 Helms announced his retirement. Dole moved back to her mother's house in Salisbury and registered to vote. She started out with very high ratings from the public. But some Republican insiders worried that Dole would be a brittle candidate. Her perfectionism and insistence on tight control of every public event would keep her distant to the voters, they feared, and a campaign based on her Washington resume would seem out of touch with North Carolina voters.

Dole did not make these mistakes. Instead she made two very shrewd decisions. One was to conduct a tour of all of North Carolina's 100 counties. Everywhere she drew crowds, not just in the big metro areas but also in small towns—175 in Hendersonville, 120 in Mars Hill, 200 in Asheville. People mobbed her, asked for autographs, and clicked photos of her. Sometimes they also noticed Bob Dole, traveling with her over back roads. She said that she had a religious renewal in the early 1980s and that her religious faith was the center of her life and that she hoped that September 11 would cause a "spiritual renewal." In November 2001, former Charlotte Mayor Richard Vinroot dropped out of the race; her other primary competitors were little-known and attracted little attention or support. When they questioned her conservatism, she said, "Just to set the record straight, in case there is any misunderstanding, I am pro-life and I am a strong supporter of the Second Amendment of the Constitution, protecting the constitutional rights of law-abiding citizens." In February 2002 Helms endorsed her. Their connections went back a long way: Helms had been a friend of her mother since his first campaign in 1972; Bob Dole had asked for Helms to vouch for him with her when he was wooing her daughter.

Dole's other wise decision was to develop a set of specific stands on issues and distribute them as the "Dole Plan." She set out a detailed plan for individual investment accounts in Social Security. On taxes she called for higher depreciation, more flexibility for Medical Savings Accounts and permanent repeal of the estate tax. On gun control she switched her positions from her 1999 campaign, this time opposing background checks on individuals' sales of guns at gun shows and a ban on assault weapons. Tobacco and textiles have long been political issues in North Carolina: Dole presented a plan for buying out tobacco quotas and called for electronic labeling of U.S.-manufactured cloth to enable duties to be laid on imports of cloth falsely labeled Made in U.S.A.

But she favored trade promotion authority, which was opposed by all the other three Republicans and six Democrats running for the seat. It was widely believed that North Carolina had lost many textile jobs since NAFTA went into effect in 1995. Secretary of State Elaine Marshall, the first candidate in the race, strongly criticized NAFTA and opposed trade promotion authority. So did state Representative Dan Blue, who had been the first black Speaker of North Carolina's House. And so did former White House Chief of Staff Erskine Bowles. Though he had supported NAFTA and had lobbied Congress to give Bill Clinton trade promotion authority, he opposed it now.

Bowles was an investment banker from a prominent family. His father, Hargrove "Skipper" Bowles was the Democratic nominee for governor in 1972 who lost in a Republican year but was still remembered fondly. His wife, Crandall Close, was CEO of Springs Industries, a large textile firm started by her family. Bowles, as Clinton's chief of staff, negotiated the 1997 budget package that led to a balanced budget; he had been trusted by Republican leaders when they seethed with mistrust of Clinton. But it didn't help Bowles that Blue and Marshall continued to hammer him on trade and that, because of a lawsuit against the Democratic legislature's state legislative redistricting plans, the primary was delayed from May to September 10.

Dole won the Republican primary with 80% of the vote; Bowles won the Democratic primary with 43% of the vote, to 29% for Blue and 15% for Marshall. This was a heavy-spending race. Dole raised and spent $13.7 million, Bowles spent nearly as much; he put in $2.9 million of his money before October 15 and then another $3.6 million. Some of the ads got personal. A Dole ad criticized Bowles's wife for laying off workers in North Carolina and creating new jobs in Mexico and China; Bowles responded in an angry face-on ad and ran an ad showing racecar driver Junior Johnson saying he wouldn't let the Republicans "run Erskine Bowles into the wall." One debate was videotaped behind locked doors in accordance with the candidates' demands. Bowles attacked Dole on trade and Social Security. She stood her ground on both issues, arguing for free trade and promoting her Dole plan for Social Security: she would hold up papers with her plan written out and then say she would show Bowles's plan—and hold up a blank sheet of paper. Bowles attacked Dole for opposing Clinton's family leave law when she was Secretary of Labor and for opposing a 1990 civil rights law; she replied that she thought the family leave measure had worked out all right and the civil rights bill was a quota bill. Dole ads often mentioned Bill and Hillary Rodham Clinton; Bowles's ads avoided mentions of the Clintons. The late surge of Bowles's spending enabled him to close the gap in the polls, but this seems mostly to have been a matter of the coalescence of the usual party constituencies.

Dole won 54%–45%, just shy of Bush's 56%–43% lead in 2000. She carried two of the three big metro areas by wide margins—Charlotte (57%–42%) and Greensboro-Winston Salem—and finished just behind Bowles in Raleigh-Durham (49%–50%), where the Democratic margins in Durham and Chapel Hill are balanced by the Republican margins in much faster-growing areas in Wake County like Cary. In the other half of the state, Dole led 54%–46%. West of Raleigh-Durham, Dole carried all but a few mountain and sand hill counties. She carried the central part of eastern North Carolina but lost in heavily black counties to the north and south.

Dole started off quietly in the Senate, as Hillary Rodham Clinton had two years before; she turned down requests to appear on television shows and instead traveled around North Carolina to places like Flat Rock (pop. 1,690) and Winterville (4,791). "I think being the new senator from North Carolina, it's important to put North Carolina first for a while." She accepted Barbara Mikulski's gracious offer to give up her desk, which had been Bob Dole's. She got seats on Armed Services, Banking and Agriculture: "I chose the committees that would be most beneficial to North Carolina." Her first bill was to give full federal recognition to the Lumbee Indians, recognized as a tribe by the state in 1885 and by Congress in 1956, but denied tribal benefits. This was opposed by those who feared the Lumbees would build a casino off Interstate 95—Republican Congressman Walter Jones, the North Carolina Family Council, the Eastern Band of Cherokees who have their own casino in East Tennessee. Dole's bill passed the Indian Affairs Committee, but was kept off the floor by parliamentary maneuvers. Dole's maiden speech, in June 2003, was on hunger in America; she called for a public-private partnership to encourage gleaning, with tax deductions to farmers and businesses that donate food; she held up North Carolina's Society of St. Andrews as an example.

On broader national issues, she had a conservative voting record and generally supported the Bush administration. She was the only woman senator to vote against a resolution declaring *Roe v. Wade* "appropriate." She did disagree with the administration on media ownership rules, the Singapore Free Trade Agreement and on whether to conduct an inventory of oil and gas reserves off the Outer Banks. With Chuck Hagel and John Sununu, she sponsored a bill to set up a new regulatory authority for the Government Sponsored Enterprises Fannie Mae and Freddie Mac. Unlike the current Office of Federal Housing Enterprise Oversight, it would have authority to determine the GSEs' missions and to close down failing GSEs; it could raise capital standards and regulate the type and amount of non-mission assets; the new agency would be funded by assessments on the GSEs rather than appropriations. This measure did not go to the floor, but the subject became more prominent when OFHEO in September 2004 issued a report concluding that Fannie Mae overstated risk-based capital by $20 billion and minimum capital by $3 billion. Fannie Mae CEO Franklin Raines was forced to resign in December. In early 2005 the questions seemed to be whether a new regulatory commission would be established, as Dole's bill provided, or whether the GSEs should be privatized altogether.

Dole's other big issue was one more prominent in North Carolina: the tobacco buyout. In 2003 she cosponsored a bill to end the 1938 tobacco quota system and to spend $10.1 billion over 10 years to buy out quota-holders and tobacco farmers. She argued that tobacco quotas were being reduced sharply and stood to be reduced even more, and that the cost of renting quotas (many quota holders treat them as an investment) raised the U.S. price of tobacco above the world price. It was widely believed that the buyout could succeed only if it was tied to giving the FDA regulatory power over tobacco, a position taken by the largest tobacco company, Altria, but opposed by the others. Dole tried to put the buyout without FDA regulation on the November 2003 omnibus, but failed. Political pressure built as Democrats seemed more favorable to the buyout than Republicans: John Kerry endorsed the buyout while George W. Bush in May 2004 said there should be no changes in tobacco law; Erskine Bowles, running for the Senate again, attacked his opponent Congressman Richard Burr for not doing enough to get a buyout. In October the buyout, without FDA regulation, was attached to the corporate tax bill; House Ways and Means Chairman Bill Thomas saw it as a way to attract 13 southern Democrats. In the Senate Dole overcame opposition from those who sought FDA regulation, and the buyout was included in the corporate tax bill signed by Bush.

On other North Carolina issues, Dole weighed in against EPA approval of a wood treatment which, she said, would cost North Carolina jobs (though Bob Dole was lobbying for the other side) and hailed the International Trade Commission decision in December 2004 to uphold tariffs on government-subsidized furniture from China. She got funding for textile tracers, detection devices to prevent illegal textile imports. She got Armed Services Chairman John Warner to co-sign a letter urging the Navy to determine where F-18A Hornets should be based—the competing bases were in North Carolina and Warner's Virginia—without regard to political considerations.

Despite her quiet start in the Senate, Dole called Secretary of State Colin Powell and offered to go to Iran on a humanitarian mission after the Bam earthquake in December 2003. The Iranians rejected the offer in January. And Dole put her fundraising skills to work for her fellow Republicans, working with NRSC Chairman George Allen to raise $2,000 maximum contributions. She traveled extensively for Republican candidates in fall 2004 and that year her leadership PAC raised $686,000. In November she ran against Norm Coleman to be the new NRSC chairman. Coleman argued that there were too many southerners in the leadership and cited his own extensive campaigning efforts. Allen supported Dole; both claimed a majority of the votes. Dole won 28–27.

Junior Senator

Richard Burr (R)

Elected 2004, seat up 2010, 1st term; b. Nov. 30, 1955, Charlottesville, VA; home, Winston-Salem; Wake Forest U., B.A. 1978; Methodist; married (Brooke).

Elected Office: U.S. House of Reps., 1994–2004.

Professional Career: Natl. Sales Mgr., Carswell Distributing, 1978–94.

DC Office: 217 RSOB, 20510, 202-224-3154; Fax: 202-228-2981; Web site: burr.senate.gov.

State Offices: Asheville, 828-350-2437; Gastonia, 704-833-0854; Rocky Mount, 252-977-9522; Winston-Salem, 336-631-5125.

Committees: *Energy & Natural Resources*: Energy; National Parks; Water & Power. *Health, Education, Labor & Pensions*: Bioterrorism & Public Health Preparedness (Chmn.); Education & Early Childhood Development; Employment & Workplace Safety. *Indian Affairs. Veterans' Affairs.*

Group Ratings (as Member of U.S. House of Representatives)

	ADA	ACLU	AFS	LCV	ITIC	NTU	COC	ACU	NTLC	CHC
2004	10	10	13	0	100	55	94	87	81	84
2003	15	—	25	10	—	63	93	88	—	—

National Journal Ratings (as Member of U.S. House of Representatives)

	2003 LIB	—	2003 CONS	2004 LIB	—	2004 CONS
Economic	38%	—	61%	42%	—	58%
Social	45%	—	54%	40%	—	60%
Foreign	0%	—	89%	37%	—	62%

Key Votes of the 108th Congress (as Member of U.S. House of Representatives)

1. Drilling in ANWR	Y	5. DC School Vouchers	N	9. Ban Same-Sex Marriage	Y
2. Approve Bush Tax Cuts	Y	6. Ban Human Cloning	Y	10. Fund Iraq War	Y
3. Medicare/Rx Bill	Y	7. Restrict Gun Liability	Y	11. Bar Cuba Embargo Funds	N
4. Bar Overtime Pay Regs.	N	8. Ban Partial-Birth Abortion	Y	12. Intelligence Reorg.	Y

Election Results

2004 general	Richard Burr (R)	1,791,450	(52%)	($12,853,110)
	Erskine Bowles (D)	1,632,527	(47%)	($13,359,764)
	Other	48,105	(1%)	
2004 primary	Richard Burr (R)	302,319	(88%)	
	John Hendrix (R)	25,971	(8%)	
	Albert Wiley (R)	15,585	(5%)	
1998 general	John Edwards (D)	1,029,237	(51%)	($8,331,382)
	Lauch Faircloth (R)	945,943	(47%)	($9,375,771)
	Other	36,963	(2%)	

Prior Winning Percentages: 2002 House (70%); 2000 House (93%); 1998 House (68%); 1996 House (62%); 1994 House (57%)

North Carolina's junior senator is Richard Burr, first elected to the House in 1994 and to the Senate in 2004. Burr grew up in Winston-Salem, was a star football player at Reynolds High and Wake Forest, then worked in sales for a wholesaling firm. In 1992 Burr ran against Congressman Steve Neal, a Democrat first elected in 1974; Burr was outspent 3–1 and lost 53%–46%. Neal retired in 1994 and Burr ran again. His Democrat opponent was state Senator Sandy Sands, a rural trial lawyer who attacked Burr for using Jerry Falwell's Liberty University studio to produce his 1992 ads. Burr supported the Contract with America, promised to make defense of tobacco his number one issue and worked hard to tie Sands to the Clinton administration. Burr won a solid 57% of the vote and did not have a serious challenge in the next four House elections.

In the House Burr had a mostly conservative voting record, though far from the most conservative in the North Carolina delegation. On the Commerce committee, his early cause became streamlining the FDA drug and medical device approval process, which he claimed kept life-saving products from patients. At first Burr took a radical approach that aroused much opposition, but then for over two years worked with the agency, doctors, patients, consumer groups and the pharmaceutical industry to come up with a consensus. With broad bipartisan support his FDA Modernization Act became law in 1997. He helped to set up the National Institute for Biomedical Imaging and Bioengineering in NIH. After September 11 he sponsored amendments incorporated into law to improve defenses against bioterrorism and to compensate people injured by smallpox vaccination. He inserted into the 2003 energy bill a provision allowing two firms that supply 60% of the world's isotopes for medical diagnoses to continue receiving U.S. bomb grade uranium. He strongly opposed FDA regulation of tobacco and when Bill Clinton called for the Justice Department to sue the tobacco companies, Burr said, "This is an administration whose policy is to drive the industry out." With others from North Carolina, he later called for an optional buyout of tobacco quotas. He sought a crackdown on illegal textile imports, routed by China through other countries to evade quotas, and he opposed normal trade relations with China. But he backed George W. Bush's call for trade promotion authority after securing what he said were promises that the local textile industry would have a seat at the table; this was not an easy vote, he said, but it gave U.S. textile companies an opportunity to become more competitive internationally. To help furniture manufacturers threatened by imports, he called for accelerated depreciation of their equipment.

By 1999 Burr made no secret of his interest in running for the Senate. He had promised to serve only five terms in the House, and it looked like there would be opportunities in 2002, when Jesse Helms would turn 80, and in 2004, when Democrat John Edwards's seat would come up. In 1999 he passed on invitations to run for governor because he didn't have "the fire in my belly." He was interested in running for Helms's seat in 2002, but deferred to Elizabeth Dole when it became apparent that the Bush White House was pushing her and that her standing with voters was very high. In early 2003, he moved toward running for Edwards's seat even before Edwards, running for president, made it clear in September 2003 that he wouldn't run for reelection; he had $2 million in his campaign account and got encouragement from White House political strategist Karl Rove.

Unlike the 2002 Senate race, there were no seriously contested primaries: Burr won 88% of the Republican vote and Erskine Bowles, the 2002 nominee, was unopposed in the Democratic primary. Bowles was an investment banker from a prominent family. His father, Hargrove "Skipper" Bowles was the Democratic nominee for governor in 1972 who lost in a Republican year; his wife, Crandall Close, was CEO of Springs Industries, a large textile firm started by her family. Bowles, as Bill Clinton's chief of staff, negotiated the 1997 budget package that led to a balanced budget; he had been trusted by Republican leaders when they seethed with mistrust of Clinton. Bowles, well known from the 2002 campaign, led by about 10% in most polls up through September. He started running ads six months before the election and had the resources to continue doing so; in 2002 he had spent $6.5 million of his own money, more than half of it in October on a late burst of ads. Burr decided to hold back on spending and didn't run ads until September, presumably hoping to match whatever Bowles could spend in the last week. In the end they both spent about the same, Burr $12.7 million and Bowles $13.2 million; this was the third-most expensive Senate campaign in 2004. But Burr's spending was concentrated in the last eight weeks.

Bowles presented a 10-point economic program and, pointing to recent losses of furniture and textile jobs, said he was "the only candidate with a real jobs plan." He called for expanding health insurance for children and providing tax credits for health insurance for small businesses. He said that he had shown the ability when in government to work with both parties. He depicted Burr as a fighter for special interests, especially pharmaceutical and tobacco companies; one ad called Burr the king of the special interests, and indeed Burr raised $2.8 million from corporate PACs, more than any other Senate candidate in 2004. One major issue was the tobacco buyout. The issue was before Congress, and the entire North Carolina delegation favored ending the tobacco quota system in place since 1938; tobacco quotas had been cut back in recent years and seemed likely to be again. At issue was whether the buyout should be coupled with FDA regulation of tobacco. The Senate passed its corporate tax bill—must-pass legislation, because it was needed to avoid European trade sanctions—with both the buyout and FDA regulation. In the House Burr voted for the buyout without FDA regulation. "I'm not opposed to new regulation for the industry. But the FDA's the wrong agency, if you truly want to do it right," he said. He argued that the toxicity of cigarettes should be regulated by the CDC and packages and labeling by the FTC. Bowles charged that Burr had voted against a $13 billion buyout with FDA regulation and for only a $10 billion buyout without because Winston-Salem-based R.J. Reynolds opposed FDA regulation; Altria, the biggest cigarette manufacturer, favored it. In the fall he interrupted his campaign to fly to Washington and lobby for the buyout; he claimed he persuaded Senate Democrats not to filibuster.

Bowles may have been lobbying, but Burr was appointed by House Republican leaders to the conference committee on the corporate tax bill. The House side held out for the buyout without FDA regulation, and the Senate yielded. The bill passed the Senate nonetheless on October 11. Republicans made much of Burr's role. Senate Majority Leader Bill Frist (a past advocate of FDA regulation) came to North Carolina and proclaimed, "It took monumental leadership, and without Richard Burr providing that monumental leadership, this bill would not have occurred." This may have been the turning point of the campaign. Burr had pulled even with Bowles in polls by late September, and Burr's ads were running in volume. They linked Bowles to Bill Clinton and to his policies on tax increases, welfare for immigrants, trade with China and trade policy generally; one, dubiously, called Bowles Clinton's "chief negotiator" on NAFTA. Both candidates skittered back from previous free trade positions; the vote on NAFTA was in 1993, before Burr was in Congress. A Burr ad said Bowles "doesn't have the courage to stand up for traditional marriage"; Bowles called that a "last resort."

George W. Bush carried North Carolina 56%–44%; Burr beat Bowles 52%–47%. Burr ran 4% behind Bush in the state's three big metropolitan areas, which cast just over half the votes; he ran 5% behind Bush in the rest of the state. The support for each candidate followed the contours in other recent federal elections. Bowles won big majorities in rural black-majority counties and in the counties containing Durham and Chapel Hill. Bowles carried the largest metropolitan counties, but Burr carried almost every rural county in the Piedmont and the mountains.

In the Senate, Burr got seats on the Energy, Health, Veterans Affairs and Indian Affairs committees. At the top of his agenda, he said, was changing NIH as he had worked to change the FDA in the 1990s. "Given the sheer volume of research money we're running through NIH, I think it makes sense to look at NIH from top to bottom to see if it's structured right. You've had a ramp-up of 100% in research dollars. Given that that's supposed to be chasing the best potential research items, is the NIH structured in a way to do that?" Unlike George W. Bush, he supported using frozen embryos in fertility clinics in stem-cell research. Burr does not come up for reelection until 2010, and is a Republican in a Republican-leaning state. But there seems to be a jinx on this seat: since Sam Ervin retired in 1974, none of its holders has won a second term: Democrat Robert Morgan lost in 1980, Republican James Broyhill lost in 1986, Democrat Terry Sanford lost in 1992, Republican Lauch Faircloth lost in 1998 and Democrat John Edwards, running for president, did not seek reelection in 2004.

FIRST DISTRICT

Rep. G.K. Butterfield (D)

Elected July 2004, 1st full term; b. April 27, 1947, Wilson; home, Wilson; NC Central U., B.A. 1971, J.D. 1974; Baptist; divorced.

Military Career: Army, 1968–70.

Elected Office: NC Superior Ct., 1988–2001, 2002–04; NC Sup. Ct., 2001–02.

Professional Career: Practicing atty., 1974–88.

DC Office: 413 CHOB, 20515, 202-225-3101; Fax: 202-225-3354; Web site: www.house.gov/butterfield.

District Offices: Tarboro, 252-823-0236; Weldon, 252-538-4123; Williamston, 252-789-4939; Wilson, 252-237-9816.

Committees: *Agriculture* (11th of 21 D): Conservation, Credit, Rural Development & Research; Department Operations, Oversight, Nutrition & Forestry; General Farm Commodities & Risk Management. *Armed Services* (26th of 28 D): Readiness; Tactical Air & Land Forces.

Group Ratings (Only Served Partial Term)

	ADA	ACLU	AFS	LCV	ITIC	NTU	COC	ACU	NTLC	CHC
2004	35	75	100	—	100	—	57	0	—	—
2003	—	—	—	—	—	—	—	—	—	—

National Journal Ratings (Only Served Partial Term)

	2003 LIB	—	2003 CONS		2004 LIB	—	2004 CONS
Economic	*	—	*		*	—	*
Social	*	—	*		*	—	*
Foreign	*	—	*		*	—	*

Key Votes of the 108th Congress (Only Served Partial Term)

1. Drilling in ANWR	*	5. DC School Vouchers	*	9. Ban Same-Sex Marriage	N
2. Approve Bush Tax Cuts	*	6. Ban Human Cloning	*	10. Fund Iraq War	*
3. Medicare/Rx Bill	*	7. Restrict Gun Liability	*	11. Bar Cuba Embargo Funds	Y
4. Bar Overtime Pay Regs.	Y	8. Ban Partial-Birth Abortion	*	12. Intelligence Reorg.	Y

Election Results

2004 general	G.K. Butterfield (D)	137,667	(64%)	($403,957)
	Greg Dority (R)	77,508	(36%)	($39,130)
2004 primary	G.K. Butterfield (D)	43,257	(71%)	
	Samuel Davis (D)	7,577	(13%)	
	Christine Fitch (D)	4,301	(7%)	
	Donald Davis (D)	3,296	(5%)	
	Other	2,111	(3%)	
2004 special	G.K. Butterfield (D)	48,567	(71%)	
	Greg Dority (R)	18,491	(27%)	
	Other	1,201	(2%)	
2002 general	Frank Ballance (D)	93,157	(64%)	($706,687)
	Greg Dority (R)	50,907	(35%)	($12,355)
	Other	2,093	(1%)	

The People		Race/Ethnic Origin	Ancestry	
Area size:	7,664 sq. mi.	44.4% White	USA: 10.7%	English: 6.1%
Urban population:	47.7%	50.5% Black	Irish: 3.6%	
Rural population:	52.3%	0.5% Asian	**2004 Presidential Vote**	
Pop. 2000:	619,178	0.7% Native Am.	Kerry (D) 128,129	(57%)
Median income:	$28,410	0.0% Hawaiian	Bush (R) 94,738	(42%)
Poverty status:	21.1%	0.8% Two+ races	Other 554	(0%)
Military veterans:	12.3%	0.1% Other	**2000 Presidential Vote**	
		3.1% Hispanic Origin	Gore (D) 111,558	(57%)
			Bush (R) 82,204	(42%)
			Cook Partisan Voting Index: D + 9	

Occupation	Blue collar: 34.8%	White collar: 45.5%	Gray collar: 19.7%

Eastern North Carolina in colonial days was a smaller version of the Chesapeake Bay colonies of Virginia and Maryland—a fertile land laced by dozens of rivers and inlets, with tobacco plantations and farms with docks on the water accessible to the ocean and so to London. North Carolina was settled later than the Chesapeake colonies, and was poorer, with smaller landholdings. But vestiges of its 18th century past can still be seen in New Bern with its Tryon Palace, the governor's house when this was the capital, and the tiny, well-preserved town of Edenton on Albemarle Sound, where 51 Edenton women in 1774 protested the taxing of tea and cloth—an act considered the first women's political protest on these shores. The historic Albemarle tour features more than 30 sites, including Confederate ironclads.

Today, east Carolina is still tobacco country, and is still largely inhabited by the descendants of the original white settlers and black slaves of 250 years ago. They live in small towns and cities and in some of the most thickly settled rural land in the United States. Tobacco is a labor-intensive crop that for many years produced yields of $4,000 an acre; a family lucky enough to have a tobacco quota could make a living off 40 acres. But anti-smoking campaigns have cut cigarette sales, and tobacco quotas have been cut. In 2004 Congress voted a $10 billion buyout of quota holders, and many old east Carolina tobacco fields are now planted with cucumbers, sweet potatoes, blueberries, and especially cotton. Some fields have gone back to woods; Halifax County is North Carolina's number one deer hunting county. There have been socioeconomic troubles in this region: several of the rural counties have had high HIV infection rates. Several inland counties in northeast North Carolina lost population from 1990 to 2003; Perdue closed a chicken-processing plant, and even fast-food giant Hardee's, founded here in Rocky Mount, decamped to St. Louis.

The 1st Congressional District of North Carolina covers much of the old tobacco country of east Carolina. It touches Albemarle and Pamlico Sounds in the east and juts inland to reach black neighborhoods in Greenville and Goldsboro. Together, the 1st and the 3d blanket the eastern quarter of the state, with intricately drawn boundaries whose fingers reach deep into each other's territory, like hands in a tight embrace. There is a political reason. The 1st is 51% percent black, the highest percentage of any district in the state, and solidly though not over-whelmingly Democratic. The 3d is only 17% black and, with retirees and new residents in fast-growing coastal counties, votes heavily Republican. The 1st is also notable for its unique and curious gender ratio: There are 57,000 more female voters here than male voters—a far greater disparity than in any other congressional district in the state.

The congressman from the 1st District is G.K. (George Kenneth) Butterfield, who won a special election in July 2004 to replace incumbent Frank Ballance, who had announced his retirement after less than one term and then resigned in June 2004; Ballance cited medical problems, but he pleaded guilty five months later to federal fraud charges in the operation of his anti-drug foundation. Butterfield grew up in Wilson County and got his bachelor and law degrees from North Carolina Central University. He handled thousands of civil and criminal cases during 12 years as a superior court judge until February 2001, when Governor Mike Easley appointed him to the state Supreme Court. After Butterfield lost election in 2002 to a full term, Easley appointed him as a special superior court judge. He stepped down from that position in May 2004 to run in the 1st District. But Ballance's resignation accelerated that schedule and forced Butterfield to win two House elections within four months.

In the July special election to fill the remainder of Ballance's term, which was held on the same date as the primary, party caucuses selected the nominees, and the six-week contest in this safe Democratic district received little local or national attention. Butterfield said that his priorities would be strengthening the rural economy and halting U.S. job losses. He won 71%–27%, and got Ballance's seats on Agriculture and Small Business, logical assignments for this rural district. In the House, he urged the Federal Communications Commission to move slowly to all-digital cable television. "In poor rural places like eastern North Carolina, this could leave a lot of people in the dark when it comes to watching television," he said. Butterfield also called for an investigation of plans by the Navy to build a landing strip in Washington County for the new F/A-18 Super Hornet jets. In November Butterfield's margin was reduced to a still comfortable 64%–36%; he carried all but one county.

SECOND DISTRICT

Rep. Bob Etheridge (D)

Elected 1996, 5th term; b. Aug. 7, 1941, Turkey; home, Lillington; Campbell U., B.S. 1965; Presbyterian; married (Faye).

Military Career: Army, 1965–67.

Elected Office: Harnett Cnty. Comm., 1973–76, Chmn., 1975–76; NC House of Reps., 1978–88; NC Superintendent of Public Instruction, 1988–96.

Professional Career: Farmer, 1965–present; V.P. Sales, Sorensen Industries, 1968–87; Owner, Layton Hardware, 1973–90; Co–owner, WLLN Radio, 1979–91.

DC Office: 1533 LHOB, 20515, 202-225-4531; Fax: 202-225-5662; Web site: www.house.gov/etheridge.

District Offices: Lillington, 910-814-0335; Raleigh, 919-829-9122.

Committees: *Agriculture* (4th of 21 D): Conservation, Credit, Rural Development & Research; General Farm Commodities & Risk Management (RMM). *Homeland Security* (13th of 15 D): Emergency Preparedness, Science & Technology; Intelligence, Information Sharing & Terrorism Risk Assessment.

Group Ratings

	ADA	ACLU	AFS	LCV	ITIC	NTU	COC	ACU	NTLC	CHC
2004	85	50	88	91	90	13	52	20	3	30
2003	90	—	100	80	—	26	47	28	—	—

National Journal Ratings

	2003 LIB	—	2003 CONS	2004 LIB	—	2004 CONS
Economic	74%	—	25%	63%	—	36%
Social	62%	—	37%	62%	—	37%
Foreign	61%	—	37%	53%	—	46%

Key Votes of the 108th Congress

1. Drilling in ANWR	N	5. DC School Vouchers	N	9. Ban Same-Sex Marriage	Y
2. Approve Bush Tax Cuts	N	6. Ban Human Cloning	N	10. Fund Iraq War	Y
3. Medicare/Rx Bill	N	7. Restrict Gun Liability	Y	11. Bar Cuba Embargo Funds	N
4. Bar Overtime Pay Regs.	Y	8. Ban Partial-Birth Abortion	Y	12. Intelligence Reorg.	Y

Election Results

2004 general	Bob Etheridge (D)	145,079	(62%)	($989,599)
	Billy Creech (R)	87,811	(38%)	($137,820)
2004 primary	Bob Etheridge (D)	unopposed		
2002 general	Bob Etheridge (D)	100,121	(65%)	($652,178)
	Joseph Ellen (R)	50,965	(33%)	($7,423)
	Other	2,098	(1%)	

Prior Winning Percentages: 2000 (58%); 1998 (57%); 1996 (53%)

The People		Race/Ethnic Origin	Ancestry	
Area size:	3,979 sq. mi.	59.1% White	USA: 12.3%	English: 6.7%
Urban population:	49.5%	30.1% Black	German: 5.7%	
Rural population:	50.5%	0.9% Asian	**2004 Presidential Vote**	
Pop. 2000:	619,178	0.6% Native Am.	Bush (R) 128,220	(54%)
Median income:	$36,510	0.1% Hawaiian	Kerry (D) 107,912	(46%)
Poverty status:	14.3%	1.2% Two+ races	Other 777	(0%)
Military veterans:	13.1%	0.1% Other	**2000 Presidential Vote**	
		7.9% Hispanic Origin	Bush (R) 98,607	(53%)
			Gore (D) 85,552	(46%)
			Other 1,378	(1%)
			Cook Partisan Voting Index: R + 3	

Occupation	Blue collar: 32.6%	White collar: 52.1%	Gray collar: 15.3%

The coastal plain of North Carolina was long bypassed by history. It was settled after Virginia and South Carolina, and only filled in with English settlers as Scots-Irish families were streaming down the valley of Virginia to the western Piedmont. This has always been tobacco country, a high-yield crop that for many years could support a family on 40 acres. Tobacco, an important colonial crop, became even more so after James B. Duke created Bull Durham tobacco and Lucky Strike cigarettes. But this was long a backward area. Its small farms and little cities were homes mainly to tenant farmers and mill hands, people raising families in thin-walled frame houses, often with no electricity or running water.

In many ways, life here has improved, in large part because this region adjoins one of the nation's fastest-growing metropolitan areas, Raleigh-Durham. The population of Wake County, which includes Raleigh, grew 70% from 1990 to 2004; there has been similar growth in surrounding Franklin (43%), Johnston (68%), Harnett (47%) and Chatham (43%) Counties. The dynamic local economy has generated tens of thousands of jobs, with subdivisions and retirement communities sprouting up all around. While counties to the east have seen denim mills close and tobacco plots replaced with less lucrative crops, other parts of the region have boomed. Raleigh combines North Carolina State University and glitzy new cultural institutions with country-cured hams and collard greens at such culinary destinations as Big Ed's City Market Restaurant.

The 2d Congressional District of North Carolina consists of an irregular loop south of Raleigh, taking in parts of nine counties, including Wake County, which is split between three congressional districts. It dips south to include parts of hog-producing Sampson County and Cumberland County, including parts of the Army's Fort Bragg and Pope Air Force Base. The district has an 8% Hispanic population, the highest of any in North Carolina; Latinos have been coming to work in meat and chicken processing factories. This is by and large the blue collar, country music part of the booming Raleigh-Durham metro area, a place where most voters have a Democratic heritage but many have gotten into the habit of voting Republican for major offices. In 2000 it voted for George W. Bush and for Democratic Governor Mike Easley. In 2002 it voted for Republican Senator Elizabeth Dole. Despite the presence of John Edwards on the Democratic ticket, the 2d voted for Bush again in 2004.

The congressman from the 2d District is Bob Etheridge, a Democrat first elected in 1996. His biography seems tailored to the district: He was born in the hamlet of Turkey in Sampson County, grew up in Johnston County, went to Campbell University in Harnett County, where he was a basketball star, and he owned a hardware store in Lillington, the county seat. He is a tobacco farmer; he served four years on the Harnett County Commission in the 1970s, was elected to the North Carolina House in 1978 and served 10 years, eventually chairing the Appropriations Committee. In 1988 and 1992 he was elected state superintendent of public instruction. In the mid-1990s, Governor Jim Hunt called for abolishing the superintendent post and transferred 300 employees to the state Board of Education. Etheridge, spying an opportunity, decided to run for the House in 1996 against freshman David Funderburk, a longtime ally of Jesse Helms. Funderburk tried to tie Etheridge to FDA Commissioner David Kessler's announcement that tobacco could be regulated as a drug. Etheridge responded by citing his own tobacco credentials: "I own tobacco allotments and have for years. I'd like to know how many days Mr. Funderburk spent priming tobacco, setting tobacco, and how many days he spent under the hot sun in the tobacco fields." Etheridge won 53%–46%.

In the House, Etheridge has compiled a moderate voting record, a bit to the left of center. Etheridge bellowed his opposition to all attempts to regulate tobacco: He voted against the 1997 budget because it included a cigarette tax increase; he opposed eliminating crop insurance for tobacco farmers; he led the fight for a $125 million bailout for tobacco farmers whose surplus did not sell on the open market, including a few thousand dollars for his own farm. After China agreed to drop its ban on imported tobacco products, he voted for normal trade relations. He worked for years on the tobacco buyout bill, which finally was enacted in 2004 and reportedly paid him and his wife $31,000. Utilizing his previous work, he won a provision in the Higher Education Reauthorization Act to teach values in public schools, and sought federal funds to research and implement "character education" programs. He supported the flag burning amendment and partial-birth abortion ban, and voted to override Bill Clinton's veto of estate tax repeal.

He split with his party in 2001 when he was among 21 House Democrats—and the only one from North Carolina—voting for trade promotion authority; North Carolina high-tech and farm interests supported the measure. The state has suffered setbacks from expanded trade, he said, but "we've been a net winner." Etheridge also split with most House Democrats to support the use of force in Iraq. He won enactment of his bill to assist weather forecasters to improve hurricane warnings for inland areas; his district was devastated by Hurricane Floyd in 1999. In 2003, he won enactment of his "hometown heroes" bill to extend benefits to public safety officers who die of heart attacks and strokes while on duty.

The Democratic legislature's redistricting plan, by adding a part of Raleigh, made the district more Democratic. Etheridge has won easily since then. In each of the past two cycles, Etheridge's opportunities to run for open Senate seats were pre-empted by the self-financing Erskine Bowles. Etheridge seems safe, but in an open seat contest this district could be competitive.

THIRD DISTRICT

Rep. Walter Jones (R)

Elected 1994, 6th term; b. Feb. 10, 1943, Farmville; home, Farmville; NC St. U., 1962–65, Atlantic Christian Col., B.A. 1967; Catholic; married (Joe Anne).

Military Career: NC Natl. Guard, 1967–71.

Elected Office: NC House of Reps., 1982–92.

Professional Career: Mgr., Walter B. Jones Office Supply Co., 1967–73; Salesman, Dunn Assoc., 1973–82; Pres., Benefit Reserves Inc., 1989–94; Pres., Judson Co., 1990–94.

DC Office: 422 CHOB, 20515, 202-225-3415; Fax: 202-225-3286; Web site: www.jones.house.gov.

District Office: Greenville, 252-931-1003.

Committees: *Armed Services* (11th of 34 R): Military Personnel; Readiness; Tactical Air & Land Forces. *Financial Services* (17th of 37 R): Financial Institutions & Consumer Credit (Vice Chmn.); Housing & Community Opportunity. *Resources* (10th of 27 R): Fisheries & Oceans; National Parks.

Group Ratings

	ADA	ACLU	AFS	LCV	ITIC	NTU	COC	ACU	NTLC	CHC
2004	30	0	38	18	44	71	70	79	94	100
2003	25	—	25	5	—	76	70	88	—	—

National Journal Ratings

	2003 LIB	—	2003 CONS		2004 LIB	—	2004 CONS
Economic	50%	—	50%		52%	—	48%
Social	24%	—	71%		0%	—	91%
Foreign	49%	—	50%		34%	—	66%

Key Votes of the 108th Congress

1. Drilling in ANWR	Y	5. DC School Vouchers	Y	9. Ban Same-Sex Marriage	Y
2. Approve Bush Tax Cuts	Y	6. Ban Human Cloning	Y	10. Fund Iraq War	Y
3. Medicare/Rx Bill	N	7. Restrict Gun Liability	Y	11. Bar Cuba Embargo Funds	N
4. Bar Overtime Pay Regs.	Y	8. Ban Partial-Birth Abortion	Y	12. Intelligence Reorg.	*

Election Results

2004 general	Walter Jones (R)	171,863	(71%)	($586,012)
	Roger Eaton (D)	71,227	(29%)	($15,265)
2004 primary	Walter Jones (R)	unopposed		
2002 general	Walter Jones (R)	131,448	(91%)	($462,499)
	Gary Goodson (Lib)	13,486	(9%)	

Prior Winning Percentages: 2000 (61%); 1998 (62%); 1996 (63%); 1994 (53%)

The People		Race/Ethnic Origin	Ancestry	
Area size:	10,048 sq. mi.	76.3% White	USA: 12.9%	English: 9.9%
Urban population:	53.2%	16.6% Black	German: 7.6%	
Rural population:	46.8%	0.9% Asian	**2004 Presidential Vote**	
Pop. 2000:	619,178	0.4% Native Am.	Bush (R) 169,674	(68%)
Median income:	$37,510	0.1% Hawaiian	Kerry (D) 79,936	(32%)
Poverty status:	12.4%	1.2% Two+ races	Other 839	(0%)
Military veterans:	15.7%	0.1% Other	**2000 Presidential Vote**	
		4.4% Hispanic Origin	Bush (R) 134,471	(64%)
			Gore (D) 73,035	(35%)
			Other 1,589	(1%)
			Cook Partisan Voting Index: R +15	
Occupation	Blue collar: 27.3%	White collar: 55.9%	Gray collar: 16.8%	

Nearly 500 years ago, Giovanni da Verrazano sailed past the Gulf Stream and landed on a sand spit island he thought was the outer edge of China. He was wrong: It was the Outer Banks of North Carolina. These are probably America's most unstable barrier islands, constantly changing shape and cut by new inlets as they are battered by the ocean currents and storm winds, as recently as 2003 when 30-foot waves from Hurricane Isabel pounded the beaches. They were settled early by Europeans: Sir Walter Raleigh's Roanoke colony was founded here in 1587, then vanished shortly thereafter; Edward Teach—Blackbeard—and other pirates lurked in Pamlico and Albemarle Sounds behind the islets. History is still very much alive on the Outer Banks. An antique form of English is spoken on Ocracoke Island, reachable only by ferry; the 208-foot lighthouse on Cape Hatteras, America's tallest, looks out on some of the most treacherous currents in the Atlantic; the sands along Kitty Hawk, with their constant winds, are where the Wright Brothers made mankind's first heavier-than-air flight in December 1903. Today, the Outer Banks have become vacation and retirement country, with affluent beachfront communities around Kitty Hawk, Nags Head and Duck and, much farther south, around Beaufort (BOWfort, not BEWfort as in South Carolina) and Morehead City. Inland, amid swamps, is the Marine Corps' Camp Lejeune, home base of one-fifth of the Marine Corps, many of whom have served in Iraq. The flat lands of east Carolina have long been tobacco and peanut-growing country, and are now also hog-raising land.

The 3d Congressional District of North Carolina covers the Outer Banks and much of the coastal plain of North Carolina, though the northeastern tier—from the desolate Great Dismal Swamp to the affluent oceanside resort communities—move more in the orbit of Virginia's Hampton Roads than North Carolina's Research Triangle. The 3d exists in balance with the 1st, with which it shares most of eastern North Carolina. Fingers of the 3d go deep inland to include mostly white portions of Goldsboro and Greenville, where tobacco farms are fading and a pharmaceutical company is the largest industrial employer. The 3d is predominantly white and Republican, compared to the 1st, which is half-black and heavily Democratic. This is one of the parts of the country where party registration here is misleading, an artifact of the past. There are nearly 50,000 more registered Democrats than Republicans but the district voted for George W. Bush by 68%–32 in 2004.

The congressman from the 3d District is Walter Jones, a Republican first elected in 1994. He grew up in eastern North Carolina, attended North Carolina State and Atlantic Christian College, and served in the National Guard. His father, Walter Jones Sr., was a Democratic congressman from the old 1st District; he served a quarter-century and chaired the Merchant Marine and Fisheries Committee. The younger Jones was elected in 1982 to the state House, where he voted to oust the Democratic speaker and often broke with Democratic leaders. In 1992 he ran as a Democrat in the new black-majority 1st District after his father decided to retire, led the primary with 38%, but lost the runoff to Eva Clayton 55%–45%. In April 1993, he switched to the Republican Party, and later announced he was running for Congress in the 3d District. This pitted Jones against four-term Congressman Martin Lancaster, a Democrat who had worked hard on local projects. But Lancaster voted for the Clinton budget and tax package in 1993 and the crime bill in 1994, and failed to persuade the Clintons to drop the cigarette tax from their health care package. Jones ran an ad showing Lancaster jogging with Bill Clinton: "How'd Martin Lancaster get so out of touch? Well, look who he's running around with in Washington." Jones won 53%–47%.

In the House, Jones got seats on Armed Services and on Resources, which absorbed his father's Merchant Marine panel. His voting record began as consistently conservative but has moderated some on non-cultural issues. His occasional independence has rankled party leaders, as when he opposed the Medicare prescription drug bill in 2003. In June 2005, he attracted media attention when, with some of the most liberal members of the House, he cosponsored a resolution calling for the Bush administration to publish a timetable for withdrawing troops from Iraq. At the same time, Jones expressed regret over his 2003 effort to rename House cafeteria French fries "Freedom fries." The British newspaper, the London *Guardian*, ran the headline, "French fries protester regrets war jibe."

But Jones favors more defense spending, and he passed a bill for a $500 tax credit for military personnel on food stamps. He opposed normal trade relations with China which, he said, "steals technology and sells it to our enemies, steals our nuclear secrets and tries to influence our election process." Following crashes of the Osprey helicopter, including one near Camp Lejeune, Jones—who has taken a demonstration flight in the aircraft—defended it as "the fighting machine that the Marines say they need." To give Marines more influence in the Pentagon, he wants a renamed Department of the Navy and Marine Corps. Jones, who posted the Ten Commandments in his Capitol Hill office, supported politically active churches with his proposal to permit them to endorse candidates without losing their tax-exempt status. The bill generated lots of traffic on the Internet, but the House defeated it 178–239 in 2002.

In North Carolina, Jones has generated controversy by intervening in conflicts outside his district. He prompted federal review of a conflict at the University of North Carolina when a student was accused of criticizing homosexuals, called for the state school superintendent to remove from an elementary school in Wilmington a book about two gay princes who got married, and opposed full recognition to the Lumbee Indians for fear that they would build a big casino on Interstate 95. Democrats criticized his effort to rename a lake near Raleigh for former Senator Helms. Jones also has pursued environmental issues of local import. He opposes oil drilling on the North Carolina coast and won victory of a sort when Conoco gave up its federal leases for drilling off the Outer Banks. He opposed a Bush administration proposal to shift to local governments a greater share of the cost for beach restoration.

Jones has easily won re-election.

FOURTH DISTRICT

Rep. David Price (D)

Elected 1996, 5th term; b. Aug. 17, 1940, Irwin, TN; home, Chapel Hill; U. of NC, B.A. 1961, Yale U., B.D. 1964, Ph.D. 1969; Baptist; married (Lisa).

Elected Office: U.S. House of Reps., 1986–94.

Professional Career: Legis. Aide, U.S. Sen. Bartlett, 1963–67; Prof., Yale U., 1969–73, Duke U., 1973–present; Exec. Dir., NC Dem. Party, 1979–80, Chmn., 1983–84; Staff Dir., DNC Comm. on Pres. Nominations, 1981–82.

DC Office: 2162 RHOB, 20515, 202-225-1784; Fax: 202-225-2014; Web site: www.house.gov/price.

District Offices: Chapel Hill, 919-967-7924; Durham, 919-688-3004; Raleigh, 919-859-5999.

Committees: *Appropriations* (15th of 29 D): Homeland Security; Military Quality of Life & Veterans Affairs & Related Agencies.

Group Ratings

	ADA	ACLU	AFS	LCV	ITIC	NTU	COC	ACU	NTLC	CHC
2004	95	75	88	100	90	13	52	12	6	15
2003	90	—	100	95	—	21	43	20	—	—

National Journal Ratings

	2003 LIB	—	2003 CONS	2004 LIB	—	2004 CONS
Economic	73%	—	26%	66%	—	34%
Social	75%	—	24%	78%	—	19%
Foreign	64%	—	35%	65%	—	34%

Key Votes of the 108th Congress

1. Drilling in ANWR	N	5. DC School Vouchers	N	9. Ban Same-Sex Marriage	N
2. Approve Bush Tax Cuts	N	6. Ban Human Cloning	N	10. Fund Iraq War	Y
3. Medicare/Rx Bill	N	7. Restrict Gun Liability	N	11. Bar Cuba Embargo Funds	Y
4. Bar Overtime Pay Regs.	Y	8. Ban Partial-Birth Abortion	N	12. Intelligence Reorg.	Y

Election Results

2004 general	David Price (D)	217,441	(64%)	($1,192,561)
	Todd Batchelor (R)	121,717	(36%)	($49,474)
2004 primary	David Price (D) .... unopposed			
2002 general	David Price (D)	132,185	(61%)	($702,372)
	Tuan Nguyen (R)	78,095	(36%)	($7,869)
	Other..	5,766	(3%)	

Prior Winning Percentages: 2000 (62%); 1998 (57%); 1996 (54%); 1992 (65%); 1990 (58%); 1988 (58%); 1986 (56%)

The People		Race/Ethnic Origin	Ancestry	
Area size:	1,298 sq. mi.	68.8% White	English: 10.2%	German: 9.8%
Urban population:	83.2%	20.6% Black	Irish: 7.7%	
Rural population:	16.8%	3.9% Asian	**2004 Presidential Vote**	
Pop. 2000:	619,178	0.3% Native Am.	Kerry (D) 193,126	(55%)
Median income:	$53,847	0.0% Hawaiian	Bush (R) 154,743	(44%)
Poverty status:	9.2%	1.3% Two+ races	Other 1,833	(1%)
Military veterans:	10.3%	0.2% Other	**2000 Presidential Vote**	
		5.0% Hispanic Origin	Gore (D) 131,532	(53%)
			Bush (R) 112,885	(46%)
			Other 3,180	(1%)
			Cook Partisan Voting Index: D + 6	
Occupation	Blue collar: 14.3%	White collar: 74.8%	Gray collar: 10.9%	

Back in the 1950s, few people would have predicted that the countryside around Raleigh and Durham, North Carolina, would become one of America's high-tech boom areas. But Governor Luther Hodges did, when he started the 6,900-acre Research Triangle Park as an R&D industrial park between the musty state capital of Raleigh, the Lucky Strike-manufacturing city of Durham and the small university town of Chapel Hill. With the drawing power of three universities—North Carolina State in Raleigh, Duke in Durham and the University of North Carolina in Chapel Hill—Research Triangle Park slowly began attracting top-tier R&D organizations, which in turn spawned a dynamic entrepreneurial sector. Today, GlaxoSmithKline, IBM, Nortel Networks and Cisco Systems are among the park's largest tenants; the facility's 38,000 full-time employees earn an average salary of $56,000. A sleepy metro area which once trailed the nation in income is now a fast-growing, vibrant, affluent metropolis—the prime engine of North Carolina's growth. The Raleigh-Durham airport, which had four gates in the 1970s, now has 49.

Three decades of vibrant economic growth have made the Triangle affluent, but it still prides itself on its homier touches, from slow-cooked pit barbecue to a minor-league baseball stadium in Durham that features a smoke-snorting replica of a bull, a prop made famous by the movie *Bull Durham*. This combination of upscale and down-home has proved to be a popular draw. From 1990 to 2003, the Raleigh-Durham metro area grew by 51%, from 855,000 to 1.3

million: The fastest metropolitan growth north and east of Atlanta. Hispanics and Asians flocked into Durham, upscale liberals who like university towns flocked into Chapel Hill and Raleigh's Wake County boomed with new suburbs. Local civic leaders worked to spruce up the Triangle's old city cores, including renovation of old tobacco and industrial warehouses in Durham. A commuter rail system under construction will connect Raleigh, Durham and Research Triangle Park.

The 4th Congressional District of North Carolina covers much of the fast-growing Research Triangle area. It includes Durham County and Chapel Hill's Orange County, part of Chatham County to the south and a little less than half of Wake County. Politics here revolves around cultural issues. The Democratic base here is made up of two parts, the black community, with 21% of the district's population, and whites with post-graduate degrees. This part of the Triangle has one of the highest concentrations of Ph.D.s in the nation, and their livelihoods—in academia, in the sciences, in the social services—tend to depend on government. Durham and Orange Counties are heavily Democratic, the strongest areas in North Carolina for Erskine Bowles and against Elizabeth Dole and Richard Burr in the past two Senate elections except for a few rural counties with large black percentages. The burgeoning suburbs of Wake County are pretty heavily Republican, like so many fast-growing areas at the edge of metropolitan development across the nation, and provide some counterbalance. On balance, though, this is a district that votes for Democrats, not only local moderates but also for Al Gore and John Kerry.

The congressman from the 4th District is David Price, a Democrat first elected in 1986; he lost his seat in 1994 and regained it in 1996. Price grew up in east Tennessee, the son of a school principal and an English teacher. He is an interesting blend of political scientist, practical politician, and a lay Baptist preacher. He came to Chapel Hill to go to college, worked as a young aide on Capitol Hill, earned a degree in divinity and a Ph.D. in political science at Yale and taught there for four years, then became a political science professor at Duke in 1973. He was executive director of the North Carolina Democratic Party in the 1980 election cycle and chairman from 1983–84—both, in effect, appointments of Governor Jim Hunt; he helped develop North Carolina's robust straight-ticket politics. He worked for Hunt when he headed a commission on revising the Democratic party's nominating rules. In 1986 he ran for the House and beat Republican Bill Cobey, who won in the 1984 sweep. In 1994 Price lost 50.4%–49.6% to Fred Heineman, a former New York City cop and Raleigh police chief in the 1970s. In 1996 Heineman made unforced errors and was outspent by Price, who regained the seat 54%–44%. Price has written several books, including *The Congressional Experience*, about his observations on Congress.

In the House, his voting record typically places him near the center of House Democrats. During his first years, Price helped pass laws increasing the percentage of a home's value the FHA can insure and aiding technical education at community colleges. When he returned, Price rejoined the Appropriations Committee on which, had he not lost in 1994, he would have had enough seniority to be ranking minority member of a subcommittee. His Education Affordability Act, "my personal centerpiece," on which he had been working for a dozen years, was folded into the 1997 Balanced Budget Act; it made interest on student loans tax deductible and allowed penalty-free withdrawals from IRAs for education expenses. In 2004, the House passed large parts of his bill to encourage bright students to become teachers. After disclosure of Iraqi prisoner abuses, he called for coverage under military law of contractors who commit federal offenses or war crimes while supporting the Defense Department overseas.

In the appropriations process, Price has nurtured local projects such as $272 million for a new EPA complex in Research Triangle Park, more than $60 million for the Triangle Transit Authority to develop a regional rail line and $4 million for hog waste research by North Carolina State University. With Republican Steve Horn, a fellow political scientist in the House, Price sponsored the "stand by your ad" requirement for candidates to appear in the full frame of TV ads reading their disclaimers on the air, so they would more likely be held responsible for negative ads. This became part of the campaign-reform law in 2002; he wants a similar requirement for Internet ads. The political scientist in Price has expressed concern about the breakdown of congressional civility and the need for Congress to defend its prerogatives against the president. After the 2004 election, the divinity scholar said that Democrats need to do a better job in articulating "moral values."

Chastened by his defeat in 1994, he has spent more time working the grass roots. Price won reelection in 1998 by 57%–42% and has won with more than 60% since. In 2005, he was named co-chairman of the Democratic National Committee's Nominating Calendar Commission, to review the presidential primary schedule—a task very much like the one he worked on with Jim Hunt a quarter-century before.

FIFTH DISTRICT

Rep. Virginia Foxx (R)

Elected 2004, 1st term; b. June 29, 1943, Bronx, NY; home, Banner Elk; U. of NC, A.B. 1968, M.A.C.T. 1972, U. of NC-Greensboro, Ed.D. 1985; Catholic; married (Thomas).

Elected Office: Watauga Bd. of Ed., 1976–88; NC Senate, 1994–2004.

Professional Career: Owner, Grandfather Mountain Nursery; Asst. Dean of General College, Appalachian St. U.; Pres. Mayland CC, 1987–1994.

DC Office: 503 CHOB, 20515, 202-225-2071; Fax: 202-225-2995; Web site: www.house.gov/foxx.

District Office: Clemmons, 336-778-0173.

Committees: *Agriculture* (22d of 25 R): Department Operations, Oversight, Nutrition & Forestry; Livestock & Horticulture; Specialty Crops & Foreign Agriculture Programs. *Education & the Workforce* (25th of 27 R): 21st Century Competitiveness; Employer-Employee Relations. *Government Reform* (22d of 23 R): Criminal Justice, Drug Policy & Human Resources; Federalism & the Census; Government Management, Finance & Accountability (Vice Chmn.).

Group Ratings and Key Votes: Newly Elected

Election Results

2004 general	Virginia Foxx (R)	167,546	(59%)	($1,182,132)
	Jim Harrell (D)	117,271	(41%)	($383,579)
2004 runoff	Virginia Foxx (R)	23,092	(55%)	
	Vernon Robinson (R)	19,201	(45%)	
2004 primary	Vernon Robinson (R)	13,824	(24%)	
	Virginia Foxx (R)	13,119	(22%)	
	Ed Broyhill (R)	12,608	(22%)	
	Jay Helvey (R)	8,517	(15%)	
	Nathan Tabor (R)	7,660	(13%)	
	Other	2,899	(5%)	
2002 general	Richard Burr (R)	137,879	(70%)	($420,600)
	David Crawford (D)	58,558	(30%)	($12,311)

The People		Race/Ethnic Origin	Ancestry	
Area size:	4,424 sq. mi.	87.9% White	USA: 15.7%	English: 9.9%
Urban population:	42.9%	6.7% Black	German: 9.5%	
Rural population:	57.1%	0.8% Asian	**2004 Presidential Vote**	
Pop. 2000:	619,178	0.2% Native Am.	Bush (R) 191,034	(66%)
Median income:	$39,710	0.0% Hawaiian	Kerry (D) 95,811	(33%)
Poverty status:	9.5%	0.7% Two+ races	Other 1,140	(0%)
Military veterans:	12.3%	0.1% Other	**2000 Presidential Vote**	
		3.6% Hispanic Origin	Bush (R) 163,705	(66%)
			Gore (D) 81,704	(33%)
			Other 2,147	(1%)
			Cook Partisan Voting Index: R +15	

Occupation	Blue collar: 33.2%	White collar: 54.1%	Gray collar: 12.7%

From the Atlantic Ocean, the terrain of North Carolina rises slowly through the Piedmont—a transitional land of modest hills that lies between the coastal plain and the Blue Ridge mountains. The Blue Ridge, named for the mysterious blue haze that blankets it, provides the headwaters of the New River, which cuts majestic crevasses—alternately lush and mined-out—as it flows north to West Virginia. The lower Piedmont lands of North Carolina were first settled by independent-minded Scots-Irish farmers and by followers of British and German sects like the Moravians. This was hardscrabble farm country at the time of the Civil War, with few slaves. By the late 19th century, it was becoming industrialized, with textile mills alongside streams, furniture factories not far from hardwood forests and R. J. Reynolds's cigarette factories in Winston-Salem. The Piedmont economy was hailed as the basis of a progressive New South, although textile mills paid low wages and tobacco employed fewer workers. Now, as both of those industries continue to shut down jobs and the rural counties lose population, lots of complaints are heard, even though North Carolina has been attracting new and growing businesses.

North Carolina's present-day affluence owes more to pharmaceuticals, banking and high-skill Piedmont factories. Lowe's, the $31 billion home improvement giant, is based in little Wilkesboro, population 3,000. Dell plans to build a computer-assembly plant in the area. The 2001 merger of banking giants Wachovia and First Union proved bittersweet for Winston-Salem, Wachovia's home base since 1879: First Union, the larger of the two entities, let the new company keep Wachovia's name but shifted its headquarters to First Union's building in Charlotte. Yet for all the economic progress here, large swaths of the region remain rural, from chicken-raising Wilkes County to Appalachian State University in Boone, a key center for resurgent pride in the culture of Appalachia, a region toward which the rest of America has so often displayed condescension. This was one of the birthplaces of stock car racing, but the old track at North Wilkesboro no longer has major NASCAR events.

All these places lie within the boundaries of the 5th Congressional District. The 5th begins in the heart of the Piedmont: The suburbs of Winston-Salem (though not the city, which is in the 12th). From there, it drops south just short of the outer fringes of metropolitan Charlotte; then heads west and north to the Tennessee line, taking in mountain communities like Boone. When legislators drew a new 13th District along the state's northern tier, they pushed today's 5th much farther west than it had reached during the 1990s. Still, the core of its population base remains much the same: The Winston-Salem suburbs in Forsyth County, plus small industrial cities in Stokes and Surry Counties, including Mount Airy, the model for Mayberry in *The Andy Griffith Show*. The district is solidly Republican.

The congresswoman from the 5th District is Virginia Foxx, a Republican who won a fiercely contested Republican primary in 2004 and replaced Richard Burr, who was elected to the Senate. She graduated from the University of North Carolina and had a diverse professional and political background before winning election to Congress at age 61. She owned a nursery and landscape company and taught sociology and was assistant dean of the General College at Appalachian State University; later, she became president of Mayland Community College. She served 12 years on the Board of Education of Watauga County, on the western edge of the district (nearly as close to Knoxville as to Winston-Salem), and in 1994 was elected to the state Senate. In the legislature she sponsored a constitutional amendment to ban same-sex marriage and a bill to deny Social Security to illegal aliens. She actively supported gun rights and home schools, and opposed abortion rights.

Foxx was one of eight candidates in the Republican primary, five of whom ran serious campaigns; collectively they spent more than $6 million. Ed Broyhill, the son of former 10th District Congressman and Senator James Broyhill, started off as the early front-runner and spent $1.2 million of his own money. Broyhill was endorsed by his father's onetime colleague Jesse Helms, but was hurt by stories about business reverses. Aggressively on the attack was Winston-Salem Councilman Vernon Robinson, a retired Air Force officer, who campaigned as a staunch conservative, "the black Jesse Helms," as he put it. He was supported by Jack Kemp and raised impressive sums on the Internet from all over the country. Robinson finished first in the July primary, with 24% of the vote. Foxx unexpectedly finished second, with 22%, just 511 votes ahead of Broyhill. Foxx had big leads in three mountain counties in her home area; Robinson carried Forsyth County, where 35% of the votes were cast, and one adjacent county; Broyhill carried counties adjacent to his father's old House seat.

The four-week campaign for the August runoff was heatedly contested. Robinson said that Foxx was "fighting the cultural war on the wrong side." Robinson aired several controversial ads targeting his tougher position on illegal aliens (which cost him Kemp's support); Foxx said she supported stricter immigration laws. Foxx warned voters that Robinson's aggressive style would make him a weak general election candidate who could lose, although that seemed unlikely in a district that voted 66% for George W. Bush in 2000. Foxx won 55%–45%, with between 73% and 82% in her home area in the three mountain counties. Robinson carried Forsyth County, which cast 40% of the vote, but by only 38 votes; he also carried Stokes and Rockingham Counties north of Winston-Salem and Alexander and Iredell Counties to the southwest. Mountain Republicans evidently rejected Robinson not because he was black but because of a long coolness toward Jesse Helms's brand of Republicanism.

Some Democrats argued that the general election would be close because of the local appeal of vice presidential nominee John Edwards. But the Kerry-Edwards ticket won none of the counties in the district, and Foxx won 59%–41%. In the House, her committee assignments seemed a good fit for her district and personal background: Agriculture, Government Reform, Education and the Workforce.

SIXTH DISTRICT

Rep. Howard Coble (R)

Elected 1984, 11th term; b. Mar. 18, 1931, Greensboro; home, Greensboro; Appalachian St. U., 1949–50, Guilford Col., B.A. 1958, U. of NC, J.D. 1962; Presbyterian; single.

Military Career: Coast Guard, 1952–56, 1977–78, Coast Guard Reserves, 1960–81.

Elected Office: NC House of Reps., 1968–70, 1978–84.

Professional Career: Asst. U.S. Atty., NC Middle Dist., 1969–73; Secy., NC Dept. of Revenue, 1973–77; Practicing atty., 1979–83.

DC Office: 2468 RHOB, 20515, 202-225-3065; Fax: 202-225-8611; Web site: www.house.gov/coble.

District Offices: Asheboro, 336-626-3060; Graham, 336-229-0159; Greensboro, 336-333-5005; High Point, 336-886-5106; Salisbury, 704-645-8082.

Committees: *Judiciary* (3d of 23 R): Commercial & Administrative Law; Crime, Terrorism & Homeland Security (Chmn.). *Transportation & Infrastructure* (4th of 41 R): Aviation; Coast Guard & Maritime Transportation; Highways, Transit & Pipelines.

Group Ratings

	ADA	ACLU	AFS	LCV	ITIC	NTU	COC	ACU	NTLC	CHC
2004	5	0	13	9	70	73	95	88	92	91
2003	5	—	0	0	—	66	86	84	—	—

National Journal Ratings

	2003 LIB	—	2003 CONS		2004 LIB	—	2004 CONS
Economic	41%	—	57%		33%	—	65%
Social	5%	—	87%		0%	—	91%
Foreign	42%	—	57%		41%	—	58%

Key Votes of the 108th Congress

1. Drilling in ANWR	Y	5. DC School Vouchers	Y	9. Ban Same-Sex Marriage	Y
2. Approve Bush Tax Cuts	Y	6. Ban Human Cloning	Y	10. Fund Iraq War	Y
3. Medicare/Rx Bill	Y	7. Restrict Gun Liability	Y	11. Bar Cuba Embargo Funds	N
4. Bar Overtime Pay Regs.	N	8. Ban Partial-Birth Abortion	Y	12. Intelligence Reorg.	Y

Election Results

2004 general	Howard Coble (R)	207,470	(73%)	($400,493)
	William Jordan (D)	76,153	(27%)	($12,223)
2004 primary	Howard Coble (R)	unopposed		
2002 general	Howard Coble (R)	151,430	(90%)	($316,561)
	Tara Grubb (Lib)	16,067	(10%)	

Prior Winning Percentages: 2000 (91%); 1998 (89%); 1996 (73%); 1994 (100%); 1992 (71%); 1990 (67%); 1988 (62%); 1986 (50%); 1984 (51%)

The People		Race/Ethnic Origin	Ancestry	
Area size:	2,989 sq. mi.	85.3% White	USA: 15.3%	German: 10.1%
Urban population:	51.6%	8.6% Black	English: 8.9%	
Rural population:	48.4%	1.0% Asian	**2004 Presidential Vote**	
Pop. 2000:	619,178	0.4% Native Am.	Bush (R) 200,942	(69%)
Median income:	$43,503	0.0% Hawaiian	Kerry (D) 87,295	(30%)
Poverty status:	8.2%	0.7% Two+ races	Other 1,202	(0%)
Military veterans:	13.8%	0.1% Other	**2000 Presidential Vote**	
		3.9% Hispanic Origin	Bush (R) 160,141	(67%)
			Gore (D) 76,315	(32%)
			Other 1,727	(1%)
			Cook Partisan Voting Index: R +17	

Occupation	Blue collar: 32.3%	White collar: 55.8%	Gray collar: 11.9%

For more than half a century, furniture store managers and owners from all over the country twice a year have converged on the huge Furniture Mart in High Point, the center of the U.S. furniture business, for the giant trade show put on by manufacturers; it now attracts about 70,000 visitors. High Point sits amidst rolling farmland originally settled by Quakers; it was the site of the Battle of Guilford Courthouse in the Revolutionary War. The furniture business grew here early in the 20th century because of the hardwoods in the mountains not far west and the abundance of low-wage labor in the flatlands not far east. For many years the furniture business has proven more resilient than textiles and tobacco, but in the past five years it has faced serious competition from China and many furniture jobs have been lost. The Triad area—Greensboro, High Point, and Winston-Salem—has been forced to scramble for new engines of economic growth to keep pace with booming Raleigh-Durham and Charlotte. Some seem to be coming. The Triad won the competition for a new Dell installation, with 2,000 jobs, with the help of state tax breaks; Federal Express is planning a new hub at Piedmont Triad airport, between Winston-Salem and Greensboro, with some 1,500 workers. At the same time, the region's Hispanic population is growing. The town of Robbins in Moore County—the childhood home of former Senator John Edwards—is now 48% Hispanic, as Latinos moved in to seek jobs in chicken processing and furniture making.

The 6th Congressional District of North Carolina is centered on greater Greensboro and High Point, which collectively cast about one-third of the votes. The Furniture Mart itself is not physically located within the 6th, but the district takes in other parts of High Point, which calls itself "North Carolina's International City," plus Quaker-settled Randolph County, golf-course-sprinkled Moore County to the south, parts of furniture-manufacturing Davidson County, most of textile-making Alamance County, much of populous Guilford County (though not central Greensboro) and the eastern half of Rowan County. Many of these areas are historically Republican, and others have become heavily Republican in the last generation; this is one of North Carolina's most Republican districts.

The congressman from the 6th District is Howard Coble, a Republican first elected in 1984. He grew up in Guilford County, went to Guilford College, then after wrecking his father's car joined the Coast Guard, in which he started off collecting garbage and served for five years. He was an insurance claims representative, went to law school and became an assistant U.S. attorney, state revenue commissioner and served in the state House for eight years. Coble was elected to Congress in what was then a swing district; it was the third time the 6th had changed parties in three elections. Coble won reelection in 1986 by just 79 votes—in a contest that

Democrats complained was decided by the Guilford County election board's refusal to hold a recount. But his personal popularity and subsequent redistricting made this a safe seat.

Coble is a friendly man who asks visitors if they mind if he smokes his cheap cigars; he likes bluegrass music and eats pork brains and eggs for breakfast. He is solidly conservative, with interesting twists. He is tightfisted, and since his first term he has tried to pass legislation to abolish pensions or health coverage for congressional retirees; he hasn't found many co-sponsors, but he has refused to back down on his pledge to boycott the program himself. Like many of his constituents, he is leery of free trade. He opposed fast track for NAFTA, but finally voted for it in 1993 (without visiting the White House or selling his vote, he said); but he opposed GATT and normal trade relations with China. He was one of three House Republicans from North Carolina to oppose trade promotion authority in 2001 and 2002. With Democratic colleague Mel Watt, he launched a House caucus to inform members of job losses in the furniture industry.

"I see my role more as one of keeping bad legislation off the books," Coble once said. But as a subcommittee chairman he became legislatively productive. In 1997 he became chairman of the Courts and Intellectual Property Subcommittee of Judiciary. Arguing that copyright industries produce more GDP than manufacturing and that patent protection is essential to technological progress, Coble supported greater protection for intellectual property. When the Bush administration sought budget cuts from the Patent and Trademark Office, Coble told the appropriators to "keep their grubby paws out of the PTO's coffers." In 2002, he shepherded the enactment of additional changes in the patent law, including the development of an electronic system for the filing and processing of patent and trademark applications. In January 2004, the Judiciary Committee approved his bill to protect commercial databases from piracy.

Despite his own limitations in operating a computer, Coble says that has not been an obstacle to dealing with the digital revolution and that he has come to appreciate the developers of the Internet. In the 106th Congress, Coble became the center of added controversy after he slipped a four-line amendment to the copyright law into an unrelated bill on home satellites; his "work for hire" provision, which recording companies requested, extended their control of recorded music to 35 years after its release; Coble said that he thought he was merely formalizing what already was common practice. After strong objections from prominent musicians such as rock star Don Henley (who wrote a song complaining about the unfairness) and bluegrass banjoer Earl Scruggs—and, not incidentally, from subcommittee member Mary Bono, widow of Sonny Bono—Coble agreed with ranking Democrat Howard Berman to repeal the earlier measure. In 2003, after the defeat of George Gekas, Coble moved up to the number-three Republican spot on the Judiciary Committee and became chairman of the Crime, Terrorism and Homeland Security Subcommittee. He expressed interest in chairing the new Homeland Security Committee, but that position went to Christopher Cox. In February 2003, Coble stirred controversy after a radio interview in which he said that Japanese internment camps of World War II were "appropriate at the time." He later explained, "I was just stating historical fact. . . . If those comments were offensive to anyone, I apologize for that. I did not intend to be insensitive or uncaring."

In 2004, Coble faced his first Democratic opponent since 1996 and won 73%–27%. He is in line to chair the Judiciary Committee in 2007, when he will be age 75. Take notice: He has cosponsored a constitutional amendment that would permit Congress to reverse Supreme Court decisions by two-thirds votes in the House and Senate.

SEVENTH DISTRICT

Rep. Mike McIntyre (D)

Elected 1996, 5th term; b. Aug. 6, 1956, Lumberton; home, Lumberton; U. of NC, B.A. 1978, J.D. 1981; Presbyterian; married (Dee).

Professional Career: Practicing atty., 1981–96.

DC Office: 2437 RHOB, 20515, 202-225-2731; Fax: 202-225-5773; Web site: www.house.gov/mcintyre.

District Offices: Fayetteville, 910-323-0260; Lumberton, 910-671-6223; Wilmington, 910-815-4959.

Committees: *Agriculture* (3d of 21 D): Conservation, Credit, Rural Development & Research; Specialty Crops & Foreign Agriculture Programs (RMM). *Armed Services* (12th of 28 D): Tactical Air & Land Forces; Terrorism, Unconventional Threats & Capabilities.

Group Ratings

	ADA	ACLU	AFS	LCV	ITIC	NTU	COC	ACU	NTLC	CHC
2004	60	20	63	73	50	17	60	60	17	75
2003	70	—	100	65	—	27	52	52	—	—

National Journal Ratings

	2003 LIB	—	2003 CONS		2004 LIB	—	2004 CONS
Economic	60%	—	40%		63%	—	37%
Social	51%	—	49%		44%	—	55%
Foreign	56%	—	44%		47%	—	51%

Key Votes of the 108th Congress

1. Drilling in ANWR	N	5. DC School Vouchers	N	9. Ban Same-Sex Marriage Y
2. Approve Bush Tax Cuts	N	6. Ban Human Cloning	*	10. Fund Iraq War Y
3. Medicare/Rx Bill	N	7. Restrict Gun Liability	Y	11. Bar Cuba Embargo Funds N
4. Bar Overtime Pay Regs.	Y	8. Ban Partial-Birth Abortion	Y	12. Intelligence Reorg. Y

Election Results

2004 general	Mike McIntyre (D)................................ 180,382	(73%)	($758,418)
	Ken Plonk (R)...................................... 66,084	(27%)	
2004 primary	Mike McIntyre (D)............................ unopposed		
2002 general	Mike McIntyre (D)................................ 118,543	(71%)	($555,393)
	James Adams (R) 45,537	(27%)	
	Other... 2,574	(2%)	

Prior Winning Percentages: 2000 (70%); 1998 (91%); 1996 (53%)

The People		Race/Ethnic Origin	Ancestry	
Area size:	6,510 sq. mi.	63.0% White	USA: 11.1%	English: 7.7%
Urban population:	45.1%	23.1% Black	German: 6.1%	
Rural population:	54.9%	0.5% Asian	**2004 Presidential Vote**	
Pop. 2000:	619,178	8.5% Native Am.	Bush (R) 141,459	(56%)
Median income:	$33,998	0.0% Hawaiian	Kerry (D) 110,589	(44%)
Poverty status:	16.7%	0.9% Two+ races	Other 858	(0%)
Military veterans:	14.1%	0.1% Other	**2000 Presidential Vote**	
		3.9% Hispanic Origin	Bush (R)............. 108,091	(52%)
			Gore (D) 100,025	(48%)
			Other 1,420	(1%)
			Cook Partisan Voting Index: R + 3	

Occupation	Blue collar: 32.4%	White collar: 50.5%	Gray collar: 17.2%

Southernmost North Carolina was long a somnolent part of America. Its one port, Wilmington, was far overshadowed by Charleston and Norfolk; its miles of beaches seemed too hot in the summer and too cold in the winter to attract many tourists; its farmlands inland were mainly planted in tobacco. Tobacco was America's first export crop, and one that can be cultivated profitably in only a few places in the world; it is labor-intensive, requiring close tending and serial picking (one leaf on a stalk matures before the one above it). Under the tobacco quota system established in 1938, however, tobacco farmers could make a living off small plots; it produced more voters per federally assisted acre than any other crop. But tobacco has become disfavored in recent decades, as smoking has declined and tobacco companies have been hit by lawsuits; tobacco quotas were cut back in the years after 2000, and in 2004 North Carolina politicians managed to pass a $10 billion buyout and in the process abolish the quota system. So tobacco farmers are diversifying; some have switched to blueberries.

Despite all these trends, the coastal counties of southernmost North Carolina and some inland counties have become one of the fastest-growing parts of North Carolina in the last dozen years. One reason is the military. Wilmington is home of the World War II battleship U.S.S. *North Carolina*, and a little further south the Army runs the 16,000-acre Military Ocean Terminal at Sunny Point—the largest ammunition port in the U.S., and the Army's main deep-water port on the east coast, built securely amidst enormous sand berms. Condominiums have sprouted along and near the beaches north and south of Wilmington, and tourism has boomed. This area also has perhaps the busiest American movie and television-production facilities outside of Los Angeles; the film industry accounted for 11% of the Wilmington area's economy. Inland, in Sampson and Duplin Counties, the growth industry is hog farming— vertically integrated factory farming, loved by the industry for its robotic efficiency, criticized by environmentalists for its enormous output of hog waste, which is directed into high-tech waste- treatment pools known as lagoons; the waste from 1,000 hogs produces enough energy to run a natural gas engine for 12 years. One Smithfield Foods facility has a slaughter limit of 8.48 million animals a year and is believed to be the largest slaughterhouse in the world; the state legislature in 1997 imposed a ban on new or expanded hog farms.

The 7th Congressional District of North Carolina covers much of this territory. The district consists of three main areas: the Wilmington region, with affluent condo-dwellers along the beach and retiree subdivisions reclaimed from timbered-out pinelands further inland; the out- skirts of Fayetteville, heavily dependent on Fort Bragg and Pope Air Force Base, even when the servicemen have been shipped overseas; and economically disadvantaged Robeson County, the home of the Lumbee Indians, whose origins have been lost to antiquity but who were treated by state segregation laws as a race distinct from whites and blacks and were recognized as a tribe by the state in 1885. For many years, this was a solidly Democratic district. Robeson County—with 20% of the district's population, and where whites, blacks and Lumbees each comprise about a third of the population—remains heavily Democratic in both national and state elections. But the Wilmington area and the hog-farming counties are now pretty heavily Republican, voting for George W. Bush and Senator Richard Burr in 2004. The Fayetteville area and the old tobacco counties are politically marginal. The result is a district Republican in national contests but still Democratic in some state races; it voted strongly for former area district attorney Mike Easley for governor in 2000 and 2004.

The congressman from the 7th District is Mike McIntyre, a Democrat first elected in 1996. McIntyre grew up in Lumberton, in Robeson County, graduated from college and law school at Chapel Hill and practiced law in Lumberton, where his family has been prominent for 200 years. When he was an intern in the office of Congressman Charlie Rose, where he watched the Watergate hearings and President Nixon's resignation speech, he whispered to his father that he would like one day to run for Rose's seat. McIntyre was active in civic affairs and in his church and was often asked to run for office. In 1995, four months before Rose announced his retirement, McIntyre decided to run. When Rose chose not to run, seven Democrats and four Republicans filed. McIntyre's chief opposition in the primary was Rose Marie Lowry-Townsend, a Lumbee and a liberal, who had support from the National Education Association, labor PACs and national women's groups. Lowry-Townsend led McIntyre 30%–23% in the primary. In the runoff McIntyre called for smaller government and cited his close ties to the district and involvement in commu- nity activities and won 52%–48%. McIntyre's platform was almost as conservative as Republican

Bill Caster's—on some things, more so. He was moved by state labor leaders to withdraw his support for a national right-to-work law, but continued to favor right-to-work in North Carolina. Caster ridiculed McIntyre's emphasis on his community ties: "While it's all well and good to coach Little League, that doesn't mean you're ready to go to Congress." McIntyre won 53%–46%.

McIntyre joined the conservative Blue Dog Democrats and got seats on Armed Services and Agriculture. His voting record—conservative among Democrats, especially on cultural issues— stands slightly left of the middle of the House. He voted for the anti-flag burning amendment, the partial-birth abortion ban, and constitutional ban on same-sex marriage, and he placed the Ten Commandments in his office. But he supported racial quotas and preferences and opposed school vouchers.

McIntyre proposed buyout legislation for tobacco farmers, which finally was enacted in 2004 without FDA regulation of cigarettes. He co-chaired the Rural Health Care Coalition, where he secured Medicaid funding relief, and he co-chaired caucuses on fatherhood and Special Operations Forces. He opposed normal trade relations with China and trade promotion authority, and he sought to impose a higher tariff on new imports of Caribbean Basin footwear; Converse's plant west of Lumberton was once the country's largest shoe factory. He proposed additional subsistence payments and job-training assistance for workers who have lost their jobs because of NAFTA; he estimated the loss at nearly 10,000 jobs in Robeson and Columbus Counties. With support from Senators Elizabeth Dole and Richard Burr, McIntyre hopes for progress in the century-old battle for federal recognition of the Lumbees; the Eastern Band of Cherokees have blocked the proposal, apparently out of fear the Lumbees would build a casino competing against theirs in the southwest corner of the state. As many of the troops based in the district headed to the Persian Gulf, McIntyre voted to authorize the use of force in Iraq, but he later criticized the Bush administration for its post-Saddam planning.

McIntyre has won endorsements from the U.S. Chamber of Commerce, Gary Bauer's Campaign for Working Families and the VFW; Republicans have not seriously challenged him. McIntyre says that he is not been interested in switching parties, having been active in the Democratic Party since high school. He has been reelected without serious opposition.

EIGHTH DISTRICT

Rep. Robin Hayes (R)

Elected 1998, 4th term; b. Aug. 14, 1945, Concord; home, Concord; Duke U., B.A. 1967; Presbyterian; married (Barbara).

Elected Office: Concord Bd. of Aldermen, 1978–81; NC House of Reps., 1992–96, Maj. Whip, 1995–96.

Professional Career: Businessman, 1967-present; Owner, Mt. Pleasant Hosiery Mill, 1988-present.

DC Office: 130 CHOB, 20515, 202-225-3715; Fax: 202-225-4036; Web site: www.hayes.house.gov.

District Offices: Concord, 704-786-1612; Rockingham, 910-997-2070.

Committees: *Agriculture* (9th of 25 R): Livestock & Horticulture (Chmn.); Specialty Crops & Foreign Agriculture Programs. *Armed Services* (14th of 34 R): Military Personnel; Readiness; Terrorism, Unconventional Threats & Capabilities. *Transportation & Infrastructure* (18th of 41 R): Aviation; Highways, Transit & Pipelines.

Group Ratings

	ADA	ACLU	AFS	LCV	ITIC	NTU	COC	ACU	NTLC	CHC
2004	5	0	25	9	60	49	95	88	84	100
2003	5	—	0	5	—	61	93	88	—	—

National Journal Ratings

	2003 LIB	—	2003 CONS		2004 LIB	—	2004 CONS
Economic	21%	—	75%		37%	—	62%
Social	0%	—	95%		0%	—	91%
Foreign	23%	—	71%		34%	—	66%

Key Votes of the 108th Congress

1. Drilling in ANWR	Y	5. DC School Vouchers	Y	9. Ban Same-Sex Marriage	Y
2. Approve Bush Tax Cuts	Y	6. Ban Human Cloning	Y	10. Fund Iraq War	Y
3. Medicare/Rx Bill	Y	7. Restrict Gun Liability	Y	11. Bar Cuba Embargo Funds	N
4. Bar Overtime Pay Regs.	N	8. Ban Partial-Birth Abortion	Y	12. Intelligence Reorg.	Y

Election Results

2004 general	Robin Hayes (R)	125,070	(56%)	($1,611,679)
	Beth Troutman (D)	100,101	(44%)	($225,675)
2004 primary	Robin Hayes (R) .... unopposed			
2002 general	Robin Hayes (R)	80,298	(54%)	($2,287,339)
	Chris Kouri (D)	66,819	(45%)	($673,171)
	Other	2,619	(2%)	

Prior Winning Percentages: 2000 (55%); 1998 (51%)

The People		Race/Ethnic Origin	Ancestry	
Area size:	3,318 sq. mi.	61.8% White	USA: 10.8%	German: 7.6%
Urban population:	69.4%	26.6% Black	English: 5.9%	
Rural population:	30.6%	1.7% Asian	**2004 Presidential Vote**	
Pop. 2000:	619,178	1.7% Native Am.	Bush (R) 126,041	(54%)
Median income:	$38,390	0.1% Hawaiian	Kerry (D) 105,248	(45%)
Poverty status:	12.4%	1.4% Two+ races	Other 815	(0%)
Military veterans:	14.0%	0.2% Other	**2000 Presidential Vote**	
		6.6% Hispanic Origin	Bush (R) 105,484	(54%)
			Gore (D) 89,672	(46%)
			Other 1,568	(1%)
			Cook Partisan Voting Index: R + 3	
Occupation	Blue collar: 31.8%	White collar: 53.3%	Gray collar: 14.9%	

In the Carolina Piedmont, ranging from Atlanta to Durham along Interstate 85, lies the thickest concentration of America's once-mighty textile industry. Within North Carolina, I-85 brushes past Concord and Kannapolis, the latter named for its founding company, Cannon Mills. While eastern Carolina was settled by Englishmen from the coast, this Piedmont land was settled mainly by Scots and diverse groups like Quakers and Moravian sects, coming down the Blue Ridge from Pennsylvania through Virginia. These migratory patterns were reflected in Civil War divisions and continue in current voting habits. The coastal counties all the way up through the Sand Hills were Confederate and are now Democratic. The textile mill towns along I-85 were anti-secession and are now Republican.

Parts of both these areas are in the 8th Congressional District. The most populous county in the district is Cabarrus County, which includes the southern end of the textile corridor around Kannapolis and Concord. In recent years, Cabarrus, fed by migration from Charlotte, has moved beyond its textile and small town roots and become an exurban county, growing by 48% from 1990 to 2004; it now casts one-fourth of the district's votes. The bankruptcy of Pillowtex (once known as Cannon Mills) in July 2003 eliminated some 4,800 jobs in Cabarrus and Rowan Counties; it was a major setback to the old way of life. The 8th extends east to include part of Fayetteville's Cumberland County, which casts 19% of the vote, but stops short of including the heavily military neighborhoods just outside the gates of Fort Bragg. The irregular boundaries of the district have a political explanation. Democratic redistricters included as much of the Democratic Sand Hills as they could, but removed most of Union County, a fast-growing and heavily Republican area just east of Charlotte. And they added central city precincts in Charlotte and Mecklenburg County with some blacks and some affluent white liberals. So this is a split personality district, with very different political leanings in the textile country, the Sand Hills and Charlotte. It has usually been carried by Republican presidential candidates and by North Carolina Democrats in close statewide contests. It has long been targeted by both Democrats and Republicans as a marginal district and has often been seriously contested, though over the past three decades it has only changed political hands twice, in 1974 and 1998.

The congressman from the 8th District is Robin Hayes, a Republican elected in 1998. He grew up in Concord, the grandson of Cannon Mills founder Charles Cannon, a legendary figure in textile country, once the dominant economic and political force in this part of North Carolina. Hayes graduated from Duke and returned to Concord, where he ran several businesses—selling Mack trucks, building highways, running the Mount Pleasant Hosiery Mills. He coached football at a local college and worked in the Prison Fellowship movement. He was elected a Concord alderman and in 1991 he switched to the Republican Party. In 1992 Hayes was elected to the North Carolina House, and became majority whip. In 1996 he ran for governor, won the Republican primary, but lost the general to Jim Hunt 56%–43%.

In November 1997 Hayes announced he was running against 8th District Democratic Congressman Bill Hefner; two months later, Hefner surprised just about everyone by announcing that he would retire. After several better-known Democrats decided not to run, Mike Taylor, a Stanly County lawyer with an attractive biography but little name recognition, emerged as the nominee. Hayes campaigned on a standard conservative platform, stressing the issues he had pushed in the legislature and calling for "top-to-bottom comprehensive tax reform." Taylor's military record helped him win the endorsement of the VFW, but Hayes outspent Taylor by 3–1, and Taylor was a non-presence in the Charlotte media market. Hayes won 51%–48%.

In the 2000 general, Taylor never stopped running, and national Democrats raised more money. But Hayes fought back. Hayes traveled the campaign trail with a four-foot-wide reusable blank check signed "Uncle Sam." At each stop he took a felt-tip pen and wrote in the federal money he had brought in: $650,000 to extend water lines to a school in Stanly County, $258,000 for a pilot housing program in Troy, $4 million for two airports. The vote again broke down on historic lines, with Hayes winning 2-to-1 in the textile country and Taylor taking the Sand Hills counties, 3-to-2. Overall Hayes ran about as well as George W. Bush and won 55%–44%.

In the House, Hayes has compiled a conservative voting record, devoting much of his energy to getting federal money for the folks back home. In December 2001, he became the focal point in the dramatic House vote on trade promotion authority. The Republican leadership took the issue to the floor without having a majority of votes in hand and held the vote open until they could squeeze them out. Hayes delayed casting his electronic vote past the usual 15-minute deadline and, with the outcome still in doubt, he found himself surrounded by Republican leaders pleading for his vote. After his "aye" vote produced a 215–214 victory for Bush, Hayes broke down in tears in the House chamber after what he called "a very intense experience." Later, he said that he got no projects for his district in exchange for the vote, but that George W. Bush had assured him that he would treat the textile industry fairly in future trade agreements, and that textiles imported from the Caribbean would have to be finished and dyed in the United States. When the final House-Senate agreement came for a vote in July 2002, Hayes voted against it because it permitted additional textile and apparel imports; others provided the majority this time. Republicans embraced him as a hero for putting his career on the line, and Democrats vowed that Hayes would pay the price in the next election.

Democrats targeted Hayes again in 2002. The Democratic nominee was 32-year-old attorney Chris Kouri, a political newcomer who was best known for having won all-Ivy League football honors as a running back at Yale before getting drafted by the Miami Dolphins. He failed to make the team and eventually became a lawyer in Charlotte. Although Democrats rhetorically rallied around Kouri after his primary win, their financial and political commitment faded. Kouri, while attacking Hayes for his trade vote, lacked sufficient funds to convey his message. Hayes spent heavily and called his opponent "a liberal trial lawyer from Charlotte." Hayes won 54%–45%. In 2004, Democrats appeared to fumble an opportunity to take advantage of the area's economic woes. After Richardson and Kouri decided not to run, their nominee was Beth Troutman, the 27-year-old daughter of a local businessman, a Chapel Hill graduate and a former beauty queen whose most recent job had been in Hollywood as an assistant to the executive producer of *The West Wing*. She brought in several cast members to campaign for her; Hayes's response: "Hollywood vs. North Carolina: I like the odds in that race." Negative reaction to the Pillowtex closing, the largest mass job loss in state history, was a threat to Hayes; against an underfunded opponent, he won by only 56%–44%.

NINTH DISTRICT

Rep. Sue Myrick (R)

Elected 1994, 6th term; b. Aug. 1, 1941, Tiffin, OH; home, Charlotte; Heidelberg Col., 1959–60; Methodist; married (Ed).

Elected Office: Charlotte City Cncl., 1983–85; Charlotte Mayor, 1987–91.

Professional Career: Pres. & CEO, Myrick Advertising, 1985–94; Pres. & CEO, Myrick Enterprises, 1992–94.

DC Office: 230 CHOB, 20515, 202-225-1976; Fax: 202-225-3389; Web site: myrick.house.gov.

District Offices: Charlotte, 704-362-1060; Gastonia, 704-861-1976.

Committees: *Energy & Commerce* (27th of 31 R): Commerce, Trade & Consumer Protection; Environment & Hazardous Materials; Health.

Group Ratings

	ADA	ACLU	AFS	LCV	ITIC	NTU	COC	ACU	NTLC	CHC
2004	0	0	0	0	100	80	95	100	97	92
2003	10	—	0	5	—	66	96	92	—	—

National Journal Ratings

	2003 LIB	—	2003 CONS		2004 LIB	—	2004 CONS
Economic	0%	—	91%		7%	—	93%
Social	17%	—	79%		0%	—	91%
Foreign	0%	—	89%		10%	—	86%

Key Votes of the 108th Congress

1. Drilling in ANWR	Y	5. DC School Vouchers	Y	9. Ban Same-Sex Marriage	Y
2. Approve Bush Tax Cuts	Y	6. Ban Human Cloning	Y	10. Fund Iraq War	Y
3. Medicare/Rx Bill	Y	7. Restrict Gun Liability	Y	11. Bar Cuba Embargo Funds	N
4. Bar Overtime Pay Regs.	N	8. Ban Partial-Birth Abortion	Y	12. Intelligence Reorg.	Y

Election Results

2004 general	Sue Myrick (R)	210,783	(70%)	($991,241)
	Jack Flynn (D)	89,318	(30%)	($36,080)
2004 primary	Sue Myrick (R)	unopposed		
2002 general	Sue Myrick (R)	140,095	(72%)	($916,659)
	Ed McGuire (D)	49,974	(26%)	
	Other	3,374	(2%)	

Prior Winning Percentages: 2000 (69%); 1998 (69%); 1996 (63%); 1994 (65%)

The People		Race/Ethnic Origin	Ancestry		
Area size:	1,018 sq. mi.	82.9% White	German: 11.2%	USA: 9.5%	
Urban population:	84.2%	10.3% Black	English: 9.0%		
Rural population:	15.8%	2.0% Asian	**2004 Presidential Vote**		
Pop. 2000:	619,178	0.3% Native Am.	Bush (R) 193,419	(63%)	
Median income:	$55,059	0.0% Hawaiian	Kerry (D) 110,769	(36%)	
Poverty status:	6.2%	0.8% Two+ races	Other 1,134	(%)	
Military veterans:	12.4%	0.1% Other	**2000 Presidential Vote**		
		3.5% Hispanic Origin	Bush (R) 157,734	(63%)	
			Gore (D) 91,353	(36%)	
			Other 2,066	(1%)	
			Cook Partisan Voting Index: R +12		

Occupation	Blue collar: 20.4%	White collar: 69.5%	Gray collar: 10.2%

"An agreeable village but in a damn rebellious country," recorded General Cornwallis when, before the unpleasantness at Yorktown, he visited Charlotte, North Carolina. "A veritable nest of hornets." This town, settled by Scots-Irish and German colonists who came down the Blue Ridge from Pennsylvania, is now a metropolitan area of 1.4 million people. Before the California gold rush, Charlotte was the gold mining capital of the country; in 1837, the U.S. Mint established a branch here. Now, Charlotte is headquarters to two of the nation's biggest banks: Bank of America, formed from the 1998 merger of Charlotte-based NationsBank and San Francisco's Bank of America; and Wachovia, created by the 2001 merger of Charlotte's First Union and Winston-Salem's Wachovia. All told, $1.5 trillion in banking resources are headquartered in Charlotte—more than in any American city except New York. Charlotte is also home to eight companies in the Fortune 500, including Duke Energy, Sonic Automotive, B.F. Goodrich and Nucor; it is the center of the nation's biggest textile manufacturing region, and serves as an airline hub for troubled USAirways.

The past two decades have brought Charlotte cultural growth worthy of its growing business stature. It now boasts a $50 million performing arts center across from the 60-story Bank of America tower, and is home to the NFL Panthers and the new NBA Bobcats franchise owned by Black Entertainment Television founder Robert Johnson. The rebelliousness Cornwallis noted can be seen in this region's passion for the booming stock-car circuit: One of the nation's biggest auto-racing tracks is here, and just up the road is Mooresville, home of the sport's giant, the late Dale Earnhardt and his family. Charlotte has built a boosterish pride in its capacity for accommodation. It is proud that it responded amicably to a busing order approved in a landmark Supreme Court case in 1971; that it twice elected Harvey Gantt, who is black, then replaced him with Sue Myrick, a Republican whose grievance wasn't race but traffic. Charlotte's metro area is projected to equal Atlanta's current size by 2030, and environmental critics said it had the worst sprawl of the 15 fast-growing metro areas. A 11-mile light-rail project from downtown south to the I-485 outerbelt is behind schedule and way over budget. But businesses and people are voting for Charlotte with their money and their feet.

The 9th Congressional District of North Carolina includes about half of Mecklenburg County; it extends west to include most of Gaston County, long a textile center, and south to take in upscale bedroom communities in Union County, North Carolina's fastest-growing county from 1990 to 2004 (population up 82%), where one-seventh of the population is employed in construction. Democratic redistricters happily made this district more Republican, in order to keep Republican precincts out of the 8th and 12th Districts. Mecklenburg County as a whole is politically marginal, with a large black minority and some neighborhoods of affluent white liberals, but the 9th District is overwhelmingly Republican.

The congresswoman from the 9th District is Sue Myrick, a Republican first elected in 1994. Myrick grew up and went to college in Ohio, raised her family in Charlotte, owned an advertising agency and Amway distributorship. In 1981 she ran for the Charlotte city council and lost. She ran again and won in 1983, ran for mayor and lost in 1985, then beat Harvey Gantt in 1987. Despite nasty personal charges, she was reelected in 1989; she is proud of making infrastructure improvements and preventing property tax increases for four years. Myrick ran for the Senate in 1992, but was beaten by Lauch Faircloth in the primary 48%–30%; had she won John Edwards might never have been elected in 1998 and in that case would not have been a presidential candidate and vice presidential nominee in 2004. In 1994 Charlotte Congressman Alex McMillan, passed over for the ranking position on the House Budget Committee, retired. In the first round of the primary, against State House Minority Leader David Balmer, Myrick led by just 34%–28%. But before the runoff three weeks later, it was revealed that Balmer had falsely claimed on his resume to have graduated in the top 20% of his law school class and to have played varsity soccer. Myrick won 68%–32%, then easily won the general.

Myrick was a leader of the 1994 Republican freshman class. She served on Newt Gingrich's transition team and was freshman liaison to the leadership. But she communicated with leaders of the unsuccessful coup against Gingrich in July 1997, and later that month lost the post of Conference secretary by 110–65 to Deborah Pryce, whom Gingrich backed.

Myrick, a conservative, has taken a lead role on many Republican initiatives. Representing a prosperous and growing district, she turned down the Transportation Committee's offer of $15 million for Charlotte's outerbelt because she felt the transportation bill would bust the budget: "I said when I ran for this job, 'If you want somebody to bring home the bacon, don't send me.'" With relatively few textile workers in her district, she voted for trade promotion authority, contending that critics were "standing outside, throwing stones." After apparent congressional leaks of post-September 11 intelligence data, Myrick proposed that members of Congress undergo the same background checks as non-elected security officials. Not surprisingly, the bill was not passed; an expert at congressional procedure said that criminal penalties exist for any such leak, but that the law is difficult to enforce because a prosecutor must prove intent.

Myrick had surgery for breast cancer in 1999 and underwent three months of chemotherapy and another six weeks of radiation treatment. After that, she sponsored the law to provide Medicaid coverage for low-income women for mammograms and pap smears. Myrick became co-chairman of the Cancer Caucus, and co-sponsored with Nita Lowey a bill to require the National Institutes of Health to explore the connection between the environment and cancer. Myrick was declared cancer-free and has continued to win reelection easily.

After the 2002 election, Myrick filed a change in the rules of the House Republican Conference to require that each of the then 13 (now 10) Appropriations subcommittee chairmen secure party approval; Speaker Dennis Hastert modified the proposal to give the review power to the leadership's Steering Committee, and it was approved. In 2003, she became chairman of the Republican Study Committee, activist conservatives who have urged spending restraint. She said that she felt "betrayed" by Senate Republicans for halving President Bush's proposed tax cuts, and that Republicans needed to "get a handle on the deficit." Accusing Bush's trade policies of being "out of touch" with her constituents, she warned in August 2003, "If he doesn't care about us, we won't care about him come election time." Myrick considered, but quickly decided against, Senate bids in 2002 and 2004. In January 2005, after eight years on the leadership-controlled Rules Committee, she switched to Energy and Commerce, where she planned to focus on health issues.

TENTH DISTRICT

Rep. Patrick McHenry (R)

Elected 2004, 1st term; b. Oct. 22, 1975, Charlotte; home, Cherryville; Attended NC St. U., Belmont Abbey Col., B.A. 1999; Catholic; single.

Elected Office: NC House of Reps., 2002–04.

Professional Career: Real estate broker, 2000–02.

DC Office: 224 CHOB, 20515, 202-225-2576; Fax: 202-225-0316; Web site: www.house.gov/mchenry.

District Offices: Hickory, 828-327-6100; Shelby, 704-481-0578; Spruce Pine, 828-765-2701.

Committees: *Budget* (19th of 22 R). *Financial Services* (37th of 37 R): Domestic and International Monetary Policy, Trade & Technology; Financial Institutions & Consumer Credit; Oversight & Investigations. *Government Reform* (20th of 23 R): Criminal Justice, Drug Policy & Human Resources (Vice Chmn.); Energy & Resources; Federal Workforce & Agency Organization.

Group Ratings and Key Votes: Newly Elected

Election Results

2004 general	Patrick McHenry (R)	157,884	(64%)	($936,071)
	Anne Fischer (D)	88,233	(36%)	($10,710)
2004 runoff	Patrick McHenry (R)	15,015	(50%)	
	David Huffman (R)	14,930	(50%)	
2004 primary	David Huffman (R)	14,280	(35%)	
	Patrick McHenry (R)	10,760	(26%)	
	Sandy Lyons (R)	8,000	(20%)	
	George Moretz (R)	7,821	(19%)	
2002 general	Cass Ballenger (R)	102,768	(59%)	($640,420)
	Ron Daugherty (D)	65,587	(38%)	($295,383)
	Other	4,937	(3%)	

The People		Race/Ethnic Origin	Ancestry	
Area size:	3,362 sq. mi.	84.9% White	USA: 16.5%	German: 10.4%
Urban population:	49.9%	9.2% Black	English: 6.9%	
Rural population:	50.1%	1.5% Asian	**2004 Presidential Vote**	
Pop. 2000:	619,178	0.2% Native Am.	Bush (R) 169,484	(67%)
Median income:	$37,649	0.0% Hawaiian	Kerry (D) 82,965	(33%)
Poverty status:	10.6%	0.7% Two+ races	Other 1,043	(0%)
Military veterans:	12.8%	0.1% Other	**2000 Presidential Vote**	
		3.5% Hispanic Origin	Bush (R) 143,124	(65%)
			Gore (D) 75,592	(34%)
			Other 1,693	(1%)
			Cook Partisan Voting Index: R +15	

Occupation	Blue collar: 41.9%	White collar: 45.4%	Gray collar: 12.6%

Steeped in the hues that gave them the name "Blue Ridge," the heavily wooded mountains of North Carolina seem placid and ancient. Geologically, they are some of the oldest ranges in the world; economically, the region is blue collar and oriented towards manufacturing, though there is some cotton farming, too. During the 1990s, residents here benefited from investment in fiber-optic factories, which, along with the general economic boom, helped reduce the local unemployment rate to near-record lows. But the Internet bust hurt the fiber optic business; textiles and furniture were also troubled, and the local unemployment rate rose. At the same time, this corner of North Carolina is adapting—as are so many other rural areas in the U.S.—to growing diversity. County seats like Morganton in Burke County are now home not just to Hispanics but to newcomers from Laos; the influx of recent arrivals have occasionally prompted anti-immigrant backlash in this previously insular region, including the occasional rejection of school bond proposals on the grounds that they could help immigrants disproportionately. Ironically, this part of North Carolina desperately needs more education: The region around Hickory, in Catawba County, ranked dead last among the state's 11 metropolitan areas in education rates. The Catawba Valley has produced about one-third of the nation's hosiery, and is at risk of major job losses due to international competition, especially from China. According to the most recent Census, almost a third of adults in this district lacked a high-school degree.

The 10th Congressional District of North Carolina stretches from Tennessee, where the mountains are high enough to support a modest ski industry, all the way south to the South Carolina border. It is a district comprised mostly of small towns; it is still predominantly white, ranges throughout 10 counties, and is bisected by Interstate 40, which runs the length of North Carolina from Wilmington in the east to Asheville in the west. The largest population center in the 10th is Hickory in Catawba County, which accounts for just over 20% of the district's population. This remains a very Republican area—home to a rough-hewn, hill variety of Republicanism that is unsympathetic to government regulators, from factory inspectors to revenuers on the lookout for illegal stills. Despite job losses and worries about international competition, it remains one of North Carolina's most Republican districts, and George W. Bush increased his percentage here in 2004 to 67%.

The congressman from the 10th District is Patrick McHenry, a Republican elected in 2004 at age 29, the youngest member of the 109th Congress. He grew up in Cherryville, graduated from Belmont Abbey College and served as president of the state College Republicans. After college, he became a real estate broker. In 1997, after Bill Clinton was accused of rewarding big contributors with nights in the Lincoln bedroom and then made a trip to North Carolina, McHenry stood in the motorcade dressed in a Abraham Lincoln costume with a sign reading, "Who's been sleeping in my bed?" In 2000 he ran a web site, www.notHillary.com, opposing Hillary Rodham Clinton's Senate candidacy in New York. At the start of the Bush administration, he was appointed to a job in the Labor Department. In 2002 he was elected to the state House. In December 2003, 10th District Congressman Cass Ballenger announced he would retire after serving 18 years and McHenry was one of four Republicans running to succeed him. In this solidly Republican district, his toughest battle was in the primary. In a district ranking first among 435 in percentage of manufacturing and blue-collar jobs, trade policy and job creation issues seemed likely to dominate the debate. But the two candidates who made conservative "Christian values" their focal point—McHenry and Catawba County Sheriff David Huffman—were the leading vote-getters in the July primary. Huffman finished first, with 35%, but failed to reach the 40% threshold required to avoid a runoff; McHenry was second with 26%. Huffman won 43% in his base of Catawba, which cast one-third of the total vote, but McHenry as the only non-Catawba candidate won five of the other nine counties. Retired cable television executive Sandy Lyons, a self-financing millionaire who was endorsed by Ballenger, ran an unexpectedly poor third, with 20%.

In the four-week runoff, the campaign took a negative turn. Huffman questioned McHenry's record as a businessman and accused him of having noisy all-night parties at his house, which also served as his campaign headquarters and residence for some of his campaign staffers; six of McHenry's neighbors later insisted Huffman's claim was untrue. McHenry accused Huffman of campaign finance irregularities and called him a friend of Bill Clinton. McHenry was an energetic grassroots campaigner and said he and his campaign knocked on more than 60,000 doors and made 100,000 phone calls. In television ads, he billed himself as a "pro-life, pro-gun, anti-gay-marriage," Christian conservative. He was endorsed by the Wall Street-based Club for Growth. McHenry won the runoff by 85 votes, after a recount. Huffman carried Catawba County 59%–41%. But McHenry rolled up huge majorities in the counties south of I-40 and close to his Gaston County home. He easily won the general against Anne Fischer, who lost her home to foreclosure during the campaign and described herself as a part-time stress release facilitator.

In the House, McHenry was assigned to the Financial Services and Government Reform committees. He said that he hopes to define how a conservative should vote, and cited former Senator Jesse Helms as his role model. His top legislative priorities were medical malpractice reform and allowing small business owners to form pools to purchase health insurance. In this strongly Republican district, he should have plenty of time to learn the ropes.

ELEVENTH DISTRICT

Rep. Charles Taylor (R)

Elected 1990, 8th term; b. Jan. 23, 1941, Brevard; home, Brevard; Wake Forest U., B.A. 1963, J.D. 1966; Baptist; married (Elizabeth).

Elected Office: NC House of Reps., 1966–72, Min. Ldr., 1968–72; NC Senate, 1972–74, Min. Ldr., 1972–74.

Professional Career: Tree farmer.

DC Office: 339 CHOB, 20515, 202-225-6401; Fax: 202-226-6422; Web site: www.house.gov/charlestaylor.

District Offices: Asheville, 828-251-1988; Hendersonville, 828-697-8539; Murphy, 828-837-3249; Rutherfordton, 828-286-8750; Waynesville, 828-456-7559.

Committees: *Appropriations* (8th of 37 R): Interior, Environment & Related Agencies (Chmn.); Science, State, Justice, Commerce & Related Agencies.

Group Ratings

	ADA	ACLU	AFS	LCV	ITIC	NTU	COC	ACU	NTLC	CHC
2004	5	0	25	9	60	56	95	88	81	92
2003	15	—	0	0	—	66	90	80	—	—

National Journal Ratings

	2003 LIB	—	2003 CONS		2004 LIB	—	2004 CONS
Economic	32%	—	67%		31%	—	68%
Social	13%	—	87%		9%	—	85%
Foreign	23%	—	71%		42%	—	57%

Key Votes of the 108th Congress

1. Drilling in ANWR	Y	5. DC School Vouchers	Y	9. Ban Same-Sex Marriage	Y
2. Approve Bush Tax Cuts	Y	6. Ban Human Cloning	Y	10. Fund Iraq War	Y
3. Medicare/Rx Bill	Y	7. Restrict Gun Liability	Y	11. Bar Cuba Embargo Funds	N
4. Bar Overtime Pay Regs.	N	8. Ban Partial-Birth Abortion	Y	12. Intelligence Reorg.	Y

Election Results

2004 general	Charles Taylor (R)	159,709	(55%)	($2,083,993)
	Patsy Keever (D)	131,188	(45%)	($1,224,306)
2004 primary	Charles Taylor (R)	unopposed		
2002 general	Charles Taylor (R)	112,335	(56%)	($1,416,941)
	Sam Neill (D)	86,664	(43%)	($586,033)
	Other	3,261	(2%)	

Prior Winning Percentages: 2000 (55%); 1998 (57%); 1996 (58%); 1994 (60%); 1992 (55%); 1990 (51%)

The People		Race/Ethnic Origin	Ancestry	
Area size:	6,088 sq. mi.	89.8% White	USA: 13.2%	English: 9.8%
Urban population:	43.9%	4.6% Black	German: 8.7%	
Rural population:	56.1%	0.5% Asian	**2004 Presidential Vote**	
Pop. 2000:	619,177	1.5% Native Am.	Bush (R) 169,872	(57%)
Median income:	$34,720	0.0% Hawaiian	Kerry (D) 126,979	(43%)
Poverty status:	12.0%	0.9% Two+ races	Other 1,747	(1%)
Military veterans:	15.6%	0.1% Other	**2000 Presidential Vote**	
		2.6% Hispanic Origin	Bush (R) 150,004	(58%)
			Gore (D) 102,321	(40%)
			Other 4,514	(2%)
			Cook Partisan Voting Index: R + 7	

Occupation   Blue collar: 31.5%   White collar: 51.9%   Gray collar: 16.6%

Western North Carolina, the protrusion of the Tar Heel state deep into the eastern United States' highest and oldest mountains, is a land of long and ornery traditions. First settled by whites not long after the Revolutionary War, it still has Indian communities and hollows where people are descended from the first white settlers. Its biggest city, Asheville, memorialized in Thomas Wolfe's novels, was a retreat for lung patients; the boardinghouse in which he grew up was restored in 2004 and reopened as a bed-and-breakfast. Asheville was also the home of the brilliant eccentric George Vanderbilt, who built the chateau-like Biltmore mansion amidst vast forests on which he pioneered scientific forestry. A dozen miles east was Black Mountain College, frequented by such innovators as Buckminster Fuller and minimalist composer John Cage. Asheville's historic structures, from Gothic Revival to Art Deco, remain well preserved and are a magnet for tourists, who in turn support some of the few coffeehouses, microbreweries and artsy cinemas within hours of here. Not far to the west is the Eastern Band of Cherokee's gambling casino, which has given the tribe a yearly budget of $130 million and considerable political influence. Over a ridge is the Great Smoky Mountains National Park, the nation's most heavily visited, 20 degrees cooler in the summer than the lowland towns an hour or so away. The climate and the forested, green, fog-wisped mountains have attracted millions of tourists to this area—so many that, every summer, the park's one transverse road becomes hopelessly clogged with traffic. And many Americans bring a little bit of western North Carolina home with them each winter: the Fraser fir trees that grow on private land in the mountains are America's favorite Christmas trees ("incomparable needle retention", boosters say), and North Carolina is the number two state in the business.

The 11th District of North Carolina includes the western end of the state, including Asheville's Buncombe County, which accounts for one-third of the votes. Only 5% of the voters in the district are black, the lowest percentage in any district in North Carolina; 1.5% are Indians. The orneriness of the mountain country has been manifest in its politics. This part of the state was reluctant to secede in the Civil War. There were few slaves and many small farmers loyal to the Union, and those who took up the Confederate cause did so out of loyalty to Governor Zebulon Vance, an Asheville native and reluctant secessionist. For a long time, the partisan balance here was close, and for a dozen years the 11th was one of the nation's most closely contested districts, throwing out incumbents in five of six elections between 1980 and 1990. But in the last dozen years, coinciding with an influx of retirees in the mountains south of Asheville, it has tilted Republican. In 2004, however, it was one North Carolina district which gave George W. Bush a slightly lower percentage than it did in 2000.

The congressman from the 11th District is Charles Taylor, a Republican elected first in 1990. He grew up in Brevard, where he has been a tree farmer and one of the biggest private landholders in the area; the *Associated Press* estimated his net worth in 2004 at between $55 and $72 million. He served in the legislature from 1966–74, and ran for Congress in 1988 and narrowly lost. In 1990 he ran again and won. Taylor has a very conservative voting record and has spent much energy on district projects. He voted against NAFTA, normal trade relations with China, GATT "and all the horses they rode in on"; he was one of the 34 Republicans to vote against the Bush education bill.

Taylor has served on the Appropriations Committee since 1993. In 1997 he became chairman of the District of Columbia Subcommittee, one of the then 13 "cardinals," who tend to aid each other on local projects. In January 2003 he became chairman of the Interior Subcommittee, with jurisdiction over the national parks and historic sites. This has sometimes led to local controversy. The Hendersonville newspaper criticized him when he wouldn't back expansion of the Carl Sandburg National Historic Site in nearby Flat Rock, but he later changed his mind. Swain County officials were nonplussed when he obtained funding for a road built into the national park that was cut off by the waters that backed up behind Fontana Dam in the 1940s; the county preferred a $52 settlement with the federal government. But overall the post has brought Taylor opportunities to bring money into the district.

Despite all this Taylor has faced spirited challenges from Democrats in 2000, 2002 and 2004. In May and August 2000, two counties threatened to garnish Taylor's congressional pay for unpaid property taxes; his lawyer said the dispute arose because Taylor claimed a forestry tax break the counties denied. North Carolina newspapers reported that a federal grand jury was investigating $1 million in loans from a bank controlled by Taylor to a supporter that were never repaid and that Taylor had extended high-interest loans to a former KGB officer for construction of apartments and commercial buildings in Russia. Taylor had articulate opposition from lawyer Sam Neill, former head of the University of North Carolina governing board, who said that Taylor "cheats on his local taxes." After the Sierra Club ran ads against him, Taylor accused them of favoring using taxpayer money to take private property, banning hunting, raising gasoline taxes and using "your tax dollars for involuntary forced abortions in China." But Taylor also made a case for himself. In September, Taylor obtained $4 million funding to help the Foothills Conservancy protect land around Lake James. In October 2000, he got $2.5 million for the Asheville Regional Airport and funding to extend the "road to nowhere" north of Lake James to provide access to a cemetery blocked since the TVA flooded the area when it built Fontana Dam in 1943. Also in October Bill Cosby laid the groundwork for a Deliver the Dream retreat for families of seriously ill children, on 200 acres donated by Taylor and his family. Taylor won 55%–42%, carrying all but one county.

In 2002 Neill ran again, but the campaign was quite different. Taylor's legal problems were mostly clarified. The president of the Taylor bank pleaded guilty to fraud and a bank lawyer was indicted, but federal prosecutors never questioned Taylor, and there seemed to be no evidence he was involved. Taylor appealed his tax cases to state boards and lost; he paid the taxes. North Carolina's primary was put off until September because of court redistricting suits, and Neill didn't spend much money or do much campaigning this time; most of his campaign funds came from his own money. The result was much the same as in 2000: Taylor won 56%–43%.

In 2004 Taylor's opponent was Buncombe County (Asheville) Commissioner and retired teacher Patsy Keever. She said she would campaign not on the old charges against Taylor (though an Asheville photographer attracted attention with a website highlighting the charges) but on the economy and what she said were 5,000 manufacturing jobs lost since 2003. She criticized Taylor for proposing a 23% sales tax to replace the income tax. She did not run any ads until September, instead campaigning on themed tours—change coming around the mountain, a kitchen table tour. But she excelled at raising small contributions and national Democrats, spotting an opportunity, helped her raise as much in PAC contributions as Taylor did; she outraised him nearly 3–1 from June to September 2004, and Taylor equaled her spending only by shelling out $308,000 of his own money. In September Keever went on the air, with ads spotlighting job losses, decrying Taylor's votes on education and air pollution bills, and charging Taylor with "leaving our soldiers behind," based on votes to deny bonuses to soldiers serving in Iraq and against health insurance subsidies to families of guardsmen and reservists ordered to active duty. Taylor replied that he had voted to increase military pay, to reduce service members' housing expenses and to increase funding for veterans programs; he pointed out that he had a son serving in Iraq. He argued that Keever was too liberal for western North Carolina and that he was in a position to help the district. "Western North Carolina has never before had an appropriations chairman from either party and that's important to us. A lot of people in the state [government] think North Carolina stops at Hickory." He pointed out that the other two North Carolina mountain districts would have freshmen congressmen (because Richard Burr of the 5th District was running for the Senate and Cass Ballenger of the 10th was retiring) and said the area couldn't afford to be represented by three freshmen. "While politicians promise and bicker, Congressman Charles Taylor delivers. He wrote the Smoky Mountains Clean Air Act. Chairman of the Interior Subcommittee, he's devoted millions to improving our environment and our national parks and forests," said one ad. And he boasted that he founded the "Pisgah Forest Institute, to bring our teachers a science-based understanding of our environment." Taylor endured a little more negative publicity, in March 2004 when an ethics group called for an investigation of how a top Taylor staffer arranged a job with a regional economic development corporation Taylor had helped, and in July 2004 when the heirs of two employees of Taylor's bank slain in a holdup sued the bank and him personally for not protecting them; the suit was settled in September.

In October both an academic and a Democratic poll showed Keever within 2% of Taylor; Taylor said his own poll showed him 18% ahead. In November Taylor won by what now seemed the customary margin of 55%–45%. He ran just a little behind George W. Bush and just a little ahead of Senate candidate Richard Burr in most counties. Keever carried Buncombe County, but Taylor carried all the rest except for Jackson County, which he lost by 49 votes.

TWELFTH DISTRICT

Rep. Melvin Watt (D)

Elected 1992, 7th term; b. Aug. 26, 1945, Mecklenburg; home, Charlotte; U. of NC at Chapel Hill, B.S. 1967, Yale U., J.D. 1970; Presbyterian; married (Eulada).

Elected Office: NC Senate, 1984–86.

Professional Career: Practicing atty., 1971–92; Co–owner, East Town Manor nursing home, 1989–present; Campaign Mgr., Harvey Gantt Senate Campaign, 1990.

DC Office: 2236 RHOB, 20515, 202-225-1510; Fax: 202-225-1512; Web site: www.house.gov/watt.

District Offices: Charlotte, 704-344-9950; Greensboro, 336-275-9950.

Committees: *Financial Services* (7th of 32 D): Capital Markets, Insurance & Government Sponsored Enterprises; Domestic and International Monetary Policy, Trade & Technology; Financial Institutions & Consumer Credit. *Judiciary* (6th of 17 D): Commercial & Administrative Law (RMM); The Constitution.

Group Ratings

	ADA	ACLU	AFS	LCV	ITIC	NTU	COC	ACU	NTLC	CHC
2004	95	100	88	100	60	14	29	0	3	7
2003	100	—	100	100	—	25	21	8	—	—

National Journal Ratings

	2003 LIB	—	2003 CONS		2004 LIB	—	2004 CONS
Economic	92%	—	0%		84%	—	16%
Social	92%	—	0%		88%	—	0%
Foreign	89%	—	8%		91%	—	7%

Key Votes of the 108th Congress

1. Drilling in ANWR	N	5. DC School Vouchers	N	9. Ban Same-Sex Marriage	N
2. Approve Bush Tax Cuts	N	6. Ban Human Cloning	N	10. Fund Iraq War	N
3. Medicare/Rx Bill	N	7. Restrict Gun Liability	N	11. Bar Cuba Embargo Funds	Y
4. Bar Overtime Pay Regs.	Y	8. Ban Partial-Birth Abortion	N	12. Intelligence Reorg.	N

Election Results

2004 general	Melvin Watt (D)	154,908	(67%)	($519,881)
	Ada Fisher (R)	76,898	(33%)	($104,667)
2004 primary	Melvin Watt (D)	24,374	(85%)	
	Kimberly Holley (D)	4,241	(15%)	
2002 general	Melvin Watt (D)	98,821	(65%)	($358,869)
	Jeff Kish (R)	49,588	(33%)	($3,604)
	Other	2,830	(2%)	

Prior Winning Percentages: 2000 (65%); 1998 (56%); 1996 (71%); 1994 (66%); 1992 (70%)

The People		Race/Ethnic Origin	Ancestry	
Area size:	827 sq. mi.	44.6% White	USA: 8.0%	German: 6.5%
Urban population:	88.5%	44.6% Black	English: 4.6%	
Rural population:	11.5%	2.1% Asian	**2004 Presidential Vote**	
Pop. 2000:	619,178	0.4% Native Am.	Kerry (D) 149,940 (63%)	
Median income:	$35,775	0.0% Hawaiian	Bush (R) 88,955 (37%)	
Poverty status:	15.9%	1.1% Two+ races	Other 871 (0%)	
Military veterans:	11.3%	0.1% Other	**2000 Presidential Vote**	
		7.1% Hispanic Origin	Gore (D) 115,445 (57%)	
			Bush (R) 85,950 (42%)	
			Other 1,495 (1%)	
			Cook Partisan Voting Index: D +11	

Occupation	Blue collar: 32.1%	White collar: 51.9%	Gray collar: 16.0%

"This is perhaps the Negro's temporary farewell to Congress," said George White, a Tarboro, North Carolina lawyer and Republican, in his last days in the House of Representatives in 1901. Segregation was being imposed by law, and blacks informally but effectively were being stricken from the voting rolls in the rural South. It was 28 years until another black candidate was elected to Congress (from Chicago), and 72 years until another African American won in the South (in Atlanta). When George White said farewell, most North Carolina blacks lived on farms or in tiny towns. As the 20th century went on, few moved to the textile towns, where most mills hired only whites, but some blacks did move to each of North Carolina's larger cities. In the years after the Voting Rights Act of 1965, these blacks were numerous enough to elect members of state legislatures, and some black candidates managed to appeal to enough whites to win in white-majority constituencies, notably Charlotte Mayor Harvey Gantt. But North Carolina blacks were not concentrated in high enough numbers either in the rural areas or in the cities to constitute geographically regularly shaped black-majority constituencies, and no North Carolina black followed George White to Congress until the Democratic legislature after the 1990 Census drew two irregularly shaped black-majority districts. That resulted in the election in 1992 of Eva Clayton in the mostly rural and small-town 1st District—and Mel Watt in the 12th District, whose original boundaries connected blacks in such far-flung cities as Charlotte, Winston-Salem, Greensboro and Durham.

This 12th Congressional District of North Carolina was the most litigated district in the country during the 1990s, and was the focus of no less than four Supreme Court cases. Its original shape—a series of scattered black precincts connected in some places by nothing wider than the lanes of Interstate 85—stretched 160 miles from Gastonia, west of Charlotte, through Winston-Salem and Greensboro all the way to Durham. In the current version, drawn in 2001, the 12th remains a 100-mile-long, snake-like agglomeration that roughly parallels I-85 and includes black voters in and near Charlotte, Winston-Salem, Greensboro, Lexington, Salisbury and High Point, the international furniture center. A near-majority, 45%, of its residents are black. The Charlotte-area precincts account for a bit more than one-third of the district population, the Greensboro area is slightly more than 20%, while the Winston-Salem portion accounts for a little under 20%. This is North Carolina's most urban district, and includes the nation's second-largest banking center in downtown Charlotte; politically it is reliably though not overwhelmingly Democratic.

The congressman from the 12th District is Mel Watt, a Democrat first elected in 1992. Watt grew up in a place called Dixie outside Charlotte, now overgrown with woods, in a tin-roofed house with no electricity or running water. His dream was to attend the University of North Carolina, and he was one of the first black students there; he made a fine academic record, went on to Yale Law School, and then to a civil rights law practice in Charlotte. He served one term in the state Senate, then decided not to seek office again until his sons completed high school. He managed Harvey Gantt's campaigns for city council and mayor in the 1980s and for the U.S. Senate in 1990.

In 1992 Watt decided to run in the 12th District. The contest turned out to be the kind of friends-and-neighbors Democratic primary common in the old segregated South. Watt won 47% of all votes in a four-way race, well over the 40% necessary for victory without a runoff in North Carolina; his base in Charlotte was bigger than those of his rivals, and he made inroads in other counties as well. He won the general election easily.

In the House, Watt has compiled a liberal voting record, among the most liberal of southern Democrats. He voted against crime bills because of death penalty provisions, against gun bans in urban housing projects, against increased prison sentences for crimes against children because he said that would interfere with the U.S. Sentencing Commission's autonomy, and against the constitutional amendment to prohibit desecration of the flag. He vehemently opposed the 1996 Welfare Reform Act; and he cast the only vote in the House against Megan's Law requiring registration of convicted sex offenders because, he said, individuals ought to be able to get on with their lives once they have paid their debt to society. When the Judiciary Committee debated George W. Bush's plan to assist faith-based social services, Watt said that he was made nauseous by a resolution that Patrick Kennedy offered to honor George Washington for his letter to a Rhode Island synagogue in support of religious tolerance. "For us to be applauding the statements discussing bigotry that were written by a person who owned slaves is a little bit more than I can, without a churning stomach, be able to tolerate," Watt told the committee. When the bill reached the House floor, Watt tried unsuccessfully to remove provisions that permit religious groups to receive federal funds to hire people only of their own faith. He opposed the relaxation of media-ownership rules by the Federal Communications Commission because he feared, "fewer and fewer large corporations will control more and more of our media, and I believe we could expect lower standards." In 2004, he helped to preserve funding for the Hope VI housing program to revitalize severely distressed public housing.

Even with the many twists and turns in the 12th District since he was first elected, like many incumbents before him, Watt has shown the ability to entrench himself with voters regardless of their race. His toughest reelection contest came in 1998, when the black share of the population had shrunk to 36%. Republican nominee Scott Keadle, a Rowan County dentist and property developer, called for major tax cuts, attacked Watt as an "extreme liberal," and concentrated on his vote against Megan's Law. In their final debate, Watt defended his vote by saying, "Would the next step be to register everyone who commits a murder?" But later he conceded that his vote had been wrong and he voted funds for state compliance with the law. Watt won 56%–42%, with support from the district's many white liberals. After the 2000 Census some Democrats grumbled that Watt should have agreed to shift more of his black voters to either the 6th or 8th District in the interest of eventually defeating a Republican incumbent.

In January 2005, Watt became chairman of the Congressional Black Caucus. He quickly showed his independence when he voted against a formal challenge by several Black Caucus members to the November 2004 presidential vote count in Ohio. He led the CBC members to a meeting with George W. Bush, where they gave him a copy of the Caucus agenda and voiced hope that this would be "the first of many" discussions; Bush included what appeared to be a couple of the CBC's proposals in his State of the Union address.

THIRTEENTH DISTRICT

Rep. Brad Miller (D)

Elected 2002, 2d term; b. May 19, 1953, Fayetteville; home, Raleigh; U. of NC, B.A. 1975, London Schl. of Economics, M.S.C. 1978, Columbia U., J.D. 1979; Episcopalian; married (Esther Hall).

Elected Office: NC House of Reps., 1992–94; NC Senate, 1996–2002.

Professional Career: Clerk, Judge J. Dickson Phillips Jr., U.S. Fourth Circuit Ct. of Appeals, Durham, 1979–80; Practicing atty., 1980–2002.

DC Office: 1722 LHOB, 20515, 202-225-3032; Fax: 202-225-0181; Web site: www.house.gov/bradmiller.

District Offices: Greensboro, 336-574-2909; Raleigh, 919-781-9101.

Committees: *Financial Services* (25th of 32 D): Capital Markets, Insurance & Government Sponsored Enterprises; Housing & Community Opportunity. *Science* (9th of 20 D): Environment, Technology & Standards; Space & Aeronautics.

Group Ratings

	ADA	ACLU	AFS	LCV	ITIC	NTU	COC	ACU	NTLC	CHC
2004	90	70	88	100	70	14	43	8	3	15
2003	95	—	100	95	—	22	34	8	—	—

National Journal Ratings

	2003 LIB	—	2003 CONS		2004 LIB	—	2004 CONS
Economic	81%	—	18%		66%	—	34%
Social	73%	—	26%		68%	—	31%
Foreign	68%	—	31%		59%	—	40%

Key Votes of the 108th Congress

1. Drilling in ANWR	N	5. DC School Vouchers	N	9. Ban Same-Sex Marriage	N
2. Approve Bush Tax Cuts	N	6. Ban Human Cloning	N	10. Fund Iraq War	Y
3. Medicare/Rx Bill	N	7. Restrict Gun Liability	N	11. Bar Cuba Embargo Funds	N
4. Bar Overtime Pay Regs.	Y	8. Ban Partial-Birth Abortion	N	12. Intelligence Reorg.	Y

Election Results

2004 general	Brad Miller (D)	160,896	(59%)	($1,181,327)
	Virginia Johnson (R)	112,788	(41%)	($350,395)
2004 primary	Brad Miller (D)	unopposed		
2002 general	Brad Miller (D)	100,287	(55%)	($989,529)
	Carolyn Grant (R)	77,688	(42%)	($416,344)
	Other	5,295	(3%)	

The People		Race/Ethnic Origin	Ancestry	
Area size:	2,294 sq. mi.	63.3% White	USA: 10.0%	English: 8.7%
Urban population:	73.7%	26.9% Black	German: 6.8%	
Rural population:	26.3%	2.0% Asian	**2004 Presidential Vote**	
Pop. 2000:	619,178	0.3% Native Am.	Kerry (D) 147,144 (52%)	
Median income:	$41,060	0.0% Hawaiian	Bush (R) 132,581 (47%)	
Poverty status:	11.6%	1.2% Two+ races	Other 1,180 (0%)	
Military veterans:	11.3%	0.2% Other	**2000 Presidential Vote**	
		6.0% Hispanic Origin	Bush (R) 113,600 (50%)	
			Gore (D) 112,953 (49%)	
			Other 2,429 (1%)	
			Cook Partisan Voting Index: D + 2	

Occupation	Blue collar: 25.7%	White collar: 60.5%	Gray collar: 13.8%

In the last two decades, metropolitan growth has come to some of the long humble countryside of North Carolina. A generation ago, Raleigh, Durham, Burlington and Greensboro were a string of small cities connected by I-85 across the central Piedmont, moderately prosperous, with textile, tobacco and furniture factories, but not very big: just a few miles from the center of town, farm fields started, dotted by country towns with barbecue restaurants and churches. The counties to the north were almost purely rural, with a few factory towns. Today, many of the old tobacco fields are used for growing other crops. The booming metropolitan areas of North Carolina have spread far beyond the old city limits and county lines into the adjacent counties. Wake County, which includes Raleigh, grew 70% between 1990 and 2004, and the surrounding counties also grew between 38% and 74%. Rural roads are now clogged in the morning with commuters headed for jobs in the new office parks, and income levels have risen far above what they once were.

Much of this territory now makes up the 13th Congressional District of North Carolina, a district created after the state, to the surprise of just about everybody, gained a new House seat from the 2000 Census. Almost half, 47%, of the residents in the 13th live in Wake County. It includes the center of Raleigh, a tangent going off to North Carolina State University and much of the northern part of the county, but includes relatively few of the affluent new subdivisions that are mostly in the 4th District. Another 18% of its residents live in Guilford County, where it includes black neighborhoods and the University of North Carolina's Greensboro campus. The rest of the district includes all or most of four counties up to the Virginia border—Granville, Person, Caswell, Rockingham—historically rural and Democratic, with fairly large black percentages. The district lines were drawn by the Democratic legislature to produce a new Democratic district, one of the few created in the South in recent decades which does not have a majority or near-majority of blacks; only 27% of its residents are black. But the rural counties have a historical Democratic heritage, and university neighborhoods are heavily Democratic. The district was very closely divided in the 2000 and 2004 presidential races, with George W. Bush winning narrowly in 2000 and John Kerry winning by a slight margin in 2004.

The congressman from the 13th District is Brad Miller, a Democrat first elected in 2002. Born and raised in Fayetteville by his widowed mother, a school bookkeeper, Miller graduated from the University of North Carolina and got a master's degree at the London School of Economics and a law degree from Columbia. After clerking for a federal appeals court judge, he began practicing law in Raleigh. In 1992, he was elected to the state House, where he authored a safe gun storage law. But he was swept away after one term in the 1994 Republican landslide. He was elected in 1996 to the state Senate where, like many members of the House, he had a hand in drawing his own district as chairman of the Senate's redistricting committee.

Miller drew a district very much in his political interest, but he couldn't be sure that he could run in the seat he had drawn for himself. Utah brought a lawsuit against the Census Bureau, arguing that because the census counted servicemen with legal residence in a state but serving overseas as part of the state's apportionment population, it should also count Mormon missionaries domiciled in a state but serving overseas. North Carolina has a lot of servicemen, but Utah has many Mormon missionaries, and such a count would have increased Utah's population enough that it, rather than North Carolina, would have gotten the 435th district under the formula dictated by a 1928 law. Utah lost in federal court and appealed; in June 2002 the U.S. Supreme Court unanimously affirmed and North Carolina kept its 13th District. With the Court's ruling, four experienced Democrats launched an 11-week sprint to the September primary, which seemed likely to determine the winner in November. Miller raised the most money and got early endorsements from labor unions, teachers' unions and the League of Conservation Voters; he also had a geographic advantage because he is from Wake County. In the primary, Miller led with 40% (enough to avoid a runoff in North Carolina) to 24% for former Congressman Robin Britt. Britt won the four western counties, where his name was familiar. But Wake County cast 49% of the vote, and Miller won 58% of the vote there to only 10% for Britt.

In the general, Miller faced Carolyn Grant, a commercial real-estate broker and former head of the Raleigh Chamber of Commerce. Grant, who ran unsuccessfully for Raleigh mayor as a Democrat in 1999 and then switched parties, called Miller a tax-and-spend Democrat, referring to his support for $1 billion in new taxes in the recent legislative session, but also criticizing him for voting to cut prescription drug assistance for the elderly. Miller said that North Carolina had the second-best record of any state in cutting taxes during the prior six years and that he supported elimination of the sales tax on food. When he pointed out that Grant had contributed to his campaign in 1998, she responded that she did not know "how liberal" he was. Grant got little help from national Republicans and Miller won 55%–42%.

In the House, after David Price, Miller had the most liberal record of the state's white Democrats. He focused on job training and efforts to create new manufacturing jobs. He filed a bill to prohibit anti-predatory lending practices, which he modeled on a similar North Carolina law. He was challenged for reelection by a Republican House staffer who criticized his votes against the partial-birth abortion ban and the medical malpractice bill. Miller said she had lived in Washington for the past eight years and criticized her support for the war in Iraq. Miller increased his majority to 59%–41%, and appeared to entrench himself, at least until the next redistricting.

★ NORTH DAKOTA ★

Two hundred years ago, in late 1804, the Lewis and Clark expedition paddled up the Missouri River and reached what is now North Dakota. There they bivouacked for the winter across the river from what is now the state capital of Bismarck. Lewis and Clark, North Dakota proudly proclaims, spent more nights in North Dakota, 146, than in any other state. And here you can still see on the Lewis and Clark Trail much of the pristine land that the expeditioners saw. North Dakota has long been the state least visited by other Americans, and North Dakotans hope the Lewis and Clark bicentennial and an official commemoration that will last until 2007 will change that. The state passed a 1% lodging tax to double its tourism budget to $2.9 million and the Three Affiliated Tribes—Mandan, Arikara, Hidatsa—are selling pottery, basketry, quill and bead work and the traditionally crafted leather pouches commissioned by the U.S. Mint to hold the commemorative Lewis and Clark Westward Journey nickels.

What Lewis and Clark and later venturers into this territory—George Armstrong Custer, Theodore Roosevelt—saw was Indian country, a vast unfenced land where the Indians built a civilization based on the buffalo and, a Spanish import, the horse. The history of North Dakota is short: Roosevelt did not arrive until nearly 80 years after Lewis and Clark, and bicentennial tourists came just a little more than 120 years after Roosevelt. There are still a few North Dakotans alive today who knew the men and women that settled this land and saw the state enter the Union in 1889. As children, they walked in the ruts left by the early settlers' wagon trains; they saw the Indians, recently defeated, herded onto reservations. This was some of the best wheat land in the world, empty by then of buffalo, connected to markets by rail, ready to become a cog in the industrial world.

And so, in a sudden rush of settlement during the 20 years before World War I, North Dakota filled up to pretty much its present population. There were 632,000 people here in 1920 and in counts since, the number has fluctuated between 617,000 and 680,000. In the 2000 Census it was 642,000—when it was the state with the lowest growth rate since 1950—and the Census estimate for 2004 is 634,000. Wheat is not the only crop here, there are also pinto beans and soybeans and sunflowers, and as the plains become more arid in the west, ranching and livestock grazing—along with strip mining and oil and natural gas production—are important; hardy root crops like potatoes and sugar beets grow as well. But wheat is still number one. Typically the state produces about one-tenth of the U.S. crop, and a fair percentage of the world's; its durum wheat is the main ingredient of American pasta.

Its dependence on agriculture shaped North Dakota's politics. Farmers, as much as they like to extol their way of life, are seldom content with the workings of the market. When prices are high, it is often because of low production; when they are low, farmers seek protection. The boosterish optimism of the first settlers was soon followed by cries reverberating with varying intensity for government protection against market forces. Since commodity prices tend to fall during periods of economic growth, there has been a countercyclical element in North Dakota politics, a tendency to vote against the national trends, and a radical strain going back to the 1910s and still lively in recent years. That radical strain also owes much to the immigrant origins

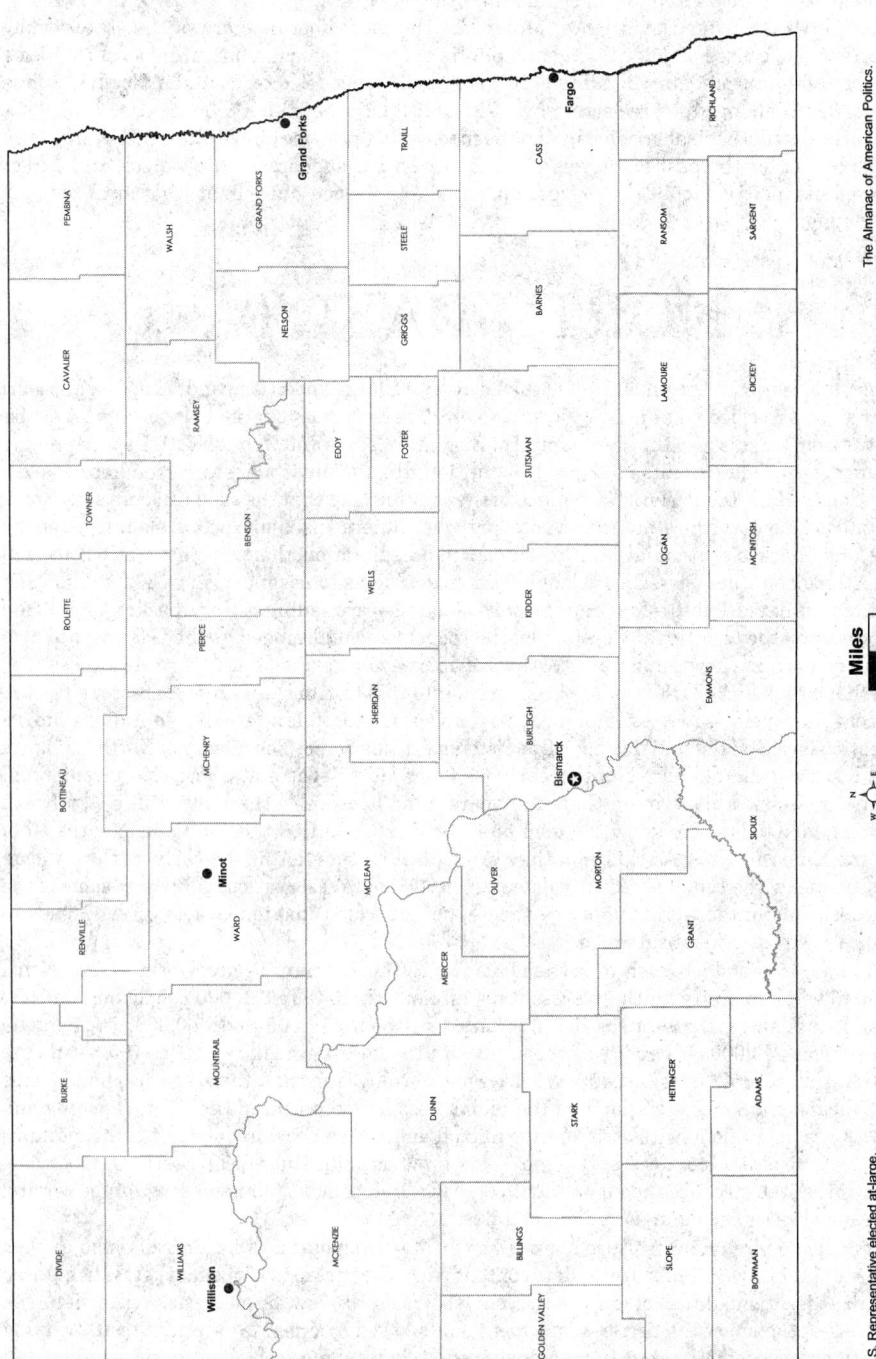

The Almanac of American Politics.
National Journal

Miles
0 10 20

N
W   E
S

U.S. Representative elected at-large.

of so many of North Dakota's early settlers: Norwegians in the eastern part of the state, Canadians along the northern border, colonies of Poles and Czechs and Icelanders, and Germans throughout the state.

These immigrants produced orderly small towns and grain and other cooperatives; they also provided support for the Non-Partisan League, which flourished from its founding in 1915 to its alliance with the Democratic Party around 1960. It appealed to marginal farmers, cut off in many cases from the wider American culture by language barriers and seemingly at the mercy of the grain millers in Minneapolis, the railroads of St. Paul, the banks of New York and the commodity traders of Chicago. The NPL's program was socialist—government ownership of railroads and grain elevators—and, like most North Dakota ethnics, it opposed going to war with Germany. The NPL often determined the outcome of the usually decisive Republican primary and sometimes swung its support to the otherwise heavily outnumbered Democrats, instituting reforms and creating a state-owned bank. By 1960, the NPL had more or less merged into the Democratic Party, a merger symbolized by the election of the late Democratic Senator Quentin Burdick, whose father, Usher Burdick, served 20 years in the House as an NPL-endorsed Republican. North Dakota's leading Democrats of recent decades, Senators Kent Conrad and Byron Dorgan, have championed a politics clearly of NPL lineage: For government farm programs, wary if not hostile to American military involvement abroad, and cheerfully championing the little guy from North Dakota against out-of-state corporations.

This is a place where everyone knows everyone else; for years there has been no voter registration because people obviously spot anyone not eligible. People have been around practically forever: the 2000 Census reported that North Dakota had the highest proportion of any state, and tiny McIntosh County the highest proportion of any county, of residents 85 and older. This communal closeness has produced an innate conservatism in North Dakota. Divorce is as uncommon here as anywhere in the United States, the two-parent family is still very much the norm and abortions are available in only one clinic in the state. Politics is personal, too, in a state where every politician is known to many voters. North Dakota is one of only three states with an all-Democratic congressional delegation (Massachusetts and Hawaii are the others: the three don't have much else in common). The two senators and congressman are all allies who have worked together for years.

Yet there are signs of change even in this settled commonwealth. The land, it seems, is emptying out. Increasing agricultural productivity has meant fewer farmers living directly off the land, and more people living in towns and off other industries. In hundreds of small towns, local city halls are padlocked, banks are open just three hours a week, and bars have closed. Yet at the same time, North Dakota's small cities have grown. Back in 1955 North Dakota-born sociologist Carl Kraenzel predicted in *The Great Plains in Transition* that sutland communities (places on transportation lines) would grow and yonland communities (places away from transportation lines) wane; and so it has happened. North Dakota's four biggest counties, containing Fargo, Grand Forks, Bismarck and Minot, grew from 134,000 in 1930 to 317,000 in 2000, while the state's other 49 counties dropped from 546,000 to 325,000; in 2000, these four counties cast half the state's votes. In effect, North Dakota is developing the demographics of the Rocky Mountain states, with population concentrated in a few cities and towns. And these are the engines of its economic growth. Microsoft bought Great Plains Software in 2000 for $1.1 billion and is now the state's third largest employer; U.S. Bancorp is the second largest. Alien Technology has a plant in Fargo that produces the tiny radio frequency tags used by Wal-Mart and the military. In 2004 North Dakota's unemployment rate was the lowest in the nation; its wages and incomes were rising more than the national average, with per capita income rising from 81% of the nation's in 1997 to 91% in 2003; its farm incomes were the highest ever; its state government faced the problem of dealing with a surplus.

North Dakota may even be solving the problem it has agonized about for years: how to retain its young people. It spends more per capita on state colleges than any other states, only to see graduates go off to Minneapolis and Denver, Chicago and California. But the outflow may have been stanched. The Census Bureau estimates that the state's population rose between 2003 and 2004, for the first time in years, and the percentage of native North Dakota State University graduates rose to over two-thirds. In 2003, for the first time in 10 years, North Dakota was not at the top of Allied Van Lines's list of outbound moves. Fargo and Bismarck, Grand Forks and Minot still have the coldest winters of American cities, but they are also spouting hip restaurants and Starbucks, industrial parks and office buildings.

On balance, these developments tend to undermine the state's radical tradition. If the typical elderly North Dakotan is a hard-working retired farmer, with fond memories of NPL agitation and a belief in government programs (those over 60 voted only 52% for George W. Bush in 2004), the typical young North Dakotan is a family person with a college education more trusting of markets and the private sector (those under 45 voted 69% for Bush). Democrats Byron Dorgan and Earl Pomeroy were reelected by large margins in 2004, but George W. Bush carried the state 63%–35% and Republican Governor John Hoeven was reelected 71%–27%. Democrats used to win many of the downballot races in North Dakota, but in 2004 they won only one, with 50.3% of the vote, and Republicans won better than 2–1 majorities in the legislature. It's too soon to say that North Dakota has moved away from its radical political roots, but a conservative strain in its heritage is asserting itself.

The People		Race/Ethnic Origin			Military veterans: 61,365 (12.7%)	
Pop. 2004 (est):	634,366	589,149	91.7%	White	WWII: 19.8%	Korea: 14.1%
Pop. 2000:	642,200	3,761	0.6%	Black	Vietnam: 32.7%	Gulf War: 11.3%
Pop. 1990:	638,800	3,566	0.6%	Asian	**Most populous cities (2003):**	
Change 1990–2000:	Up 0.5%	30,772	4.8%	Native Am.	1. Fargo	91,484
% of U.S. total:	0.2%	218	0.0%	Hawaiian	2. Bismarck	56,344
Pop. rank:	47th of 50	6,666	1.0%	Two+ races	3. Grand Forks	48,618
Area size:	70,700 sq. mi.	282	0.0%	Other	4. Minot	35,424
State Native:	72.5%	7,786	1.2%	Hisp. Origin	5. Mandan	16,781
Non-citizen:	1.1%	**Ancestry**				
Language		German: 30.6%		Norwegian: 20.9%	Urban population: 55.8%	
English: 90.1%	Other Eur.: 6.5%	Irish: 5.4%		Swedish: 3.5%	Rural population: 44.2%	
Spanish: 2.1%		English: 3.4%				

Education		Work Sector		Legislative Assembly	
H.S. Grad:	83.9%	Private: 72.2%	Govt: 16.5%	Senate	32 R 15 D
College Grad:	22.0%	Self: 10.7%	Family: 0.6%	House	67 R 27 D
Industry		Unemployment: 4.5%		Legislative Term Limits: No	
Agri: 8.2%	Con: 6.2%	**Household Income**		**Registered Voters**	
Fin: 5.9%	Info: 2.3%	<15k: 19.0%	15-35k: 31.5%	No state voter registration	
Mfg: 12.8%	Prof: 30.2%	35-50k: 18.6%	50-100k: 25.2%		
Public: 4.8%	Trade: 16.4%	100-150k: 3.8%	>150k: 1.9%		
Other: 13.1%		Median: $34,604			
Occupation		Poverty status: 11.9%			
Blue collar: 22.2%	White collar: 59.4%	**Home Value**			
Gray collar: 18.4%		<50k: 34.5%	50-100k: 41.2%	100-200k: 20.8%	200-300k: 2.4%
		300-500k: 0.8%	>500k: 0.3%	Median: $68,300	

Presidential politics   Massachusetts and Hawaii, the other states with all-Democratic congressional delegations, are heavily Democratic in presidential elections; North Dakota is heavily Republican. In olden days, North Dakota veered toward Democrats when farm prices fell; in 2000, though prices were low, it voted heavily 61%–33% for George W. Bush. In 2004, when farm prices were high, Bush won 63%–35%. John Kerry carried four counties, three of them with Indian reservations.

North Dakota chooses its national convention delegates in party caucuses. With a tiny number of delegates, an out-of-the-way location and frigid weather in the early primary season, they attract little attention.

2004 Presidential Vote		
Bush (R)	196,651	(63%)
Kerry (D)	111,052	(35%)
Nader (I)	3,756	(1%)
Other	1,374	(0%)

2000 Presidential Vote		
Bush (R)	174,852	(61%)
Gore (D)	95,284	(33%)
Nader (Green)	9,486	(3%)
Other	8,634	(3%)

Governor

John Hoeven (R)

Elected 2000, term expires Dec. 2008, 2d term; b. March 13, 1957, Bismarck; home, Bismarck; Dartmouth, B.A. 1979; Northwestern U., Kellogg Grad. Schl., M.B.A. 1981; Catholic; married (Mikey).

Professional Career: Exec. V.P., First Western Bank, 1986–93; Pres. & CEO, Bank of ND, 1993–00.

Office: State Capitol, 600 E. Boulevard, Bismarck, 58505, 701-328-2200; Fax: 701-328-2205; Web site: www.governor.state.nd.us.

Election Results

2004 general	John Hoeven (R)	220,803	(71%)
	Joseph Satrom (D)	84,877	(27%)
	Other	4,193	(1%)
2004 primary	John Hoeven (R)	unopposed	
2000 general	John Hoeven (R)	159,255	(55%)
	Heidi Heitkamp (D)	130,144	(45%)

John Hoeven, the governor of North Dakota, is a Republican first elected in 2000. He was born in Bismarck and grew up in Minot; he graduated from Dartmouth College and received an MBA from Northwestern. In 1981, he entered the family business, First Western Bank in Minot and became executive vice president. He was active in many civic endeavors. In 1993 he was chosen to be head of the state-owned Bank of North Dakota—a Non-Partisan League creation—by a board that included his predecessor as governor, Republican Ed Schafer, and his 2000 Democratic opponent, Attorney General Heidi Heitkamp. Under Hoeven's stewardship, the bank's worth rose from $990 million to $1.6 billion and its loan portfolio increased from $200 million to $1 billion; it returns $50 million into the state's biannual budget. Hoeven was not always a Republican; in 1996, he thought out loud about running as a Democrat against Schafer. He gave serious consideration to running in 2000 only when Schafer announced in October 1999 he would not run again. In November Hoeven, who had never won elective office, announced his candidacy.

This was a generally civil campaign, between two candidates who knew each other well. Bismarck is a small town, where officeholders can scarcely avoid each other, and North Dakotans are a civil people. Hoeven cited his work in attracting jobs by founding Minot's Magic Fund, a city sales tax used for business development, and by organizing to keep Minot Air Force Base off the base-closure list, as well as his work at the Bank of North Dakota. He called for economic development with high-paying jobs in technology and said that education was crucial in preparing future workers; he pledged more money for teacher training and salaries. Heitkamp, who grew up in the town of Mantador (population 77), was elected tax commissioner in 1984 and 1988 and attorney general in 1992 and 1996. She said she would try to keep young people in the state through a recruitment and mentoring program, by reinstating a living wage for employees of companies receiving financial assistance and by giving tax incentives to companies guaranteeing high-wage jobs. But in September 2000 Heitkamp announced that she had breast cancer. She underwent a mastectomy September 25, and Hoeven suspended his ads for two days. Quickly she returned to the campaign trail. For several weeks, she led in polls, but the momentum went back to Hoeven, and he won 55%–45%. Voters over the age of 60 backed the Democrat, voters under 60 the Republican: A familiar North Dakota pattern. At the same time, Republicans won seven of nine of the statewide offices and increased their majorities in the legislature. North Dakota's skyscraper Capitol, towering over neatly-kept Bismarck and the rolling plains beyond, now contained more Republicans in high office than at any time since the NPL allied with the Democrats around 1960.

As governor, Hoeven began Phase 2 of the North Dakota Telecommunications Network and combined several state agencies—tourism, economic development, finance, job training—into a Department of Commerce. In December 2002, Hoeven presented a budget that drew $50 million from two trust funds and borrowed $20 million to complete the Telecommunications Network and which provided for teacher salary increases and $10 million for a Devils Lake outlet. Legislators resisted earmarking teacher salary increases; Hoeven vetoed their budget and, in a three-day special session, got 70% of education funds earmarked for salary increases. Altogether teacher got $75 million in salary increases in his first term. Hoeven called for $3.8 million in ethanol subsidies; the legislature voted $1.2 million. In 2004 Hoeven promoted GoE! ethanol fuel and required its use in state vehicles; the North Dakota Corn Growers Association pushed for a requirement that 10% of regular gas be ethanol. In June 2004 Hoeven presented an accountability plan, suggested by Democrats, for businesses having contracts with the state. He proposed a Centers of Excellence program, borrowing $50 million to generate $150 million in economic development centered on the state's universities and sent Lieutenant Governor Jack Dalrymple, scion of a bonanza farm family and founding chairman of Dakota Growers Pasta Company, on trade missions to Taiwan and Japan. He brought suit to roll back the Burlington Northern Santa Fe Railroad's rate increases and eliminated the sales tax on used farm machinery and parts.

Water is a controversial issue in river-crossed North Dakota. For years there was concern about the rising water level in land-locked Devils Lake, which was submerging farmland, and houses and after heavy rains threatened local roads. North Dakotans in Congress tried to get the federal government to act, but Hoeven stepped in and construction began in October 2003 on a channel to divert the water through the Sheyenne River which drains into the northward-flowing Red River of the North. This generated protests from Minnesota and Manitoba officials, worried about water quality, and Manitoba threatened a lawsuit; North Dakota retaliated by suing Manitoba over high roads that act as dikes on the Red River. North Dakota and Manitoba were also involved in disputes over the Northwest Area Water Supply Project, begun in 2002 to bring Missouri River water to Minot. Drought has brought Missouri River levels down in recent years, in November 2003 cutting off the water supply of Fort Yates and Cannon Ball; Hoeven pressed for maintaining higher levels above the Dakota dams, to help hunting, fishing and recreational businesses. The Army Corps of Engineers said it would raise levels in 2005.

In 2004 Hoeven was opposed by former state Senator Joseph Satrom, who had low name identification and little money. Hoeven pointed to the state's economic growth and indications that the state was finally gaining population and not losing young people. It didn't help Satrom that he opposed the constitutional amendment banning same-sex marriage, which was approved by 73% of the voters. Hoeven won 71%–27%, the biggest percentage victory since C. Norman Brunsdale was reelected in 1952. Democratic Agriculture Commissioner Roger Johnson held on to his job with 50.3% of the votes, but Republicans swept other partisan offices with percentages ranging up to 73% and increased their majorities in the legislature. In December 2004, Hoeven submitted a $5.5 billion budget with spending increases on education (more teacher salary increases) and corrections, a $15 increase in the motor vehicle registration fee, $5 million in bonuses to North Dakota soldiers and $900,000 for the railroad lawsuit; he projected a $200 million surplus.

Hoeven has been mentioned as a candidate against Senator Kent Conrad in 2006. The state's Republican leanings, his own popularity and that of George W. Bush might work for him. But Conrad also has had high job ratings, and it is not always possible for a candidate to turn his popularity as governor into a lead in a race for the Senate. If Hoeven runs and wins, he would be succeeded by Lieutenant Governor Jack Dalrymple, who ran against Conrad in 1992 and lost 63%–34%.

Senior Senator

Kent Conrad (D)

Elected 1986, seat up 2006, 2d full term; b. Mar. 12, 1948, Bismarck; home, Bismarck; Stanford U., B.A. 1971, George Washington U., M.B.A. 1975; Unitarian; married (Lucy Calautti).

Elected Office: ND Tax Commissioner, 1981–86.

Professional Career: Asst., ND Tax Commissioner, 1974–80; Dir., Mgmt. Planning & Personnel, ND Tax Dept., 1980.

DC Office: 530 HSOB, 20510, 202-224-2043; Fax: 202-224-7776; Web site: conrad.senate.gov.

State Offices: Bismarck, 701-258-4648; Fargo, 701-232-8030; Grand Forks, 701-775-9601; Minot, 701-852-0703.

Committees: *Agriculture, Nutrition & Forestry*: Marketing, Inspection & Product Promotion; Production & Price Competitiveness (RMM). *Budget* (RMM). *Finance*: International Trade; Social Security & Family Policy (RMM); Taxation & IRS Oversight. *Indian Affairs*.

Group Ratings

	ADA	ACLU	AFS	LCV	ITIC	NTU	COC	ACU	NTLC	CHC
2004	90	44	86	83	58	23	53	20	10	16
2003	80	—	89	53	—	16	70	15	—	—

National Journal Ratings

	2003 LIB	—	2003 CONS		2004 LIB	—	2004 CONS
Economic	61%	—	38%		61%	—	38%
Social	57%	—	42%		64%	—	35%
Foreign	60%	—	35%		71%	—	26%

Key Votes of the 108th Congress

1. Ban Drilling in ANWR	Y	5. Energy Bill	Y	9. Ban Same-Sex Marriage	N
2. Approve Bush Tax Cuts	N	6. Support Roe v. Wade	Y	10. Ban Bunker-Buster Bomb	Y
3. Medicare/Rx Bill	Y	7. Ban Partial-Birth Abortion	Y	11. Fund Iraq War	Y
4. Bar Overtime Pay Regs.	Y	8. Assault Weapons Ban	Y	12. Restrict Missile Defense	Y

Election Results

2000 general	Kent Conrad (D)	176,470	(62%)	($2,312,543)
	Duane Sand (R)	110,420	(38%)	($399,584)
2000 primary	Kent Conrad (D)	unopposed		
1994 general	Kent Conrad (D)	137,157	(58%)	($1,927,866)
	Ben Clayburgh (R)	99,390	(42%)	($941,192)

Prior Winning Percentages: 1992 (63%); 1986 (50%)

Kent Conrad, North Dakota's senior senator, was first elected to the Senate in 1986. He grew up in North Dakota; his parents were killed in an auto accident when he was five, and he was raised by his grandparents. One grandfather owned a bi-weekly newspaper in Bismarck and had been North Dakota chairman for Progressive Robert LaFollette in 1924; another was the physician for longtime Governor and Senator William Langer: it was a family full of connections in the small world of North Dakota politics. Conrad's first political effort was to lead, in 1968, a campaign to grant voting rights to 19-year-olds. He graduated from Stanford, and then returned in 1974 to work on Byron Dorgan's unsuccessful House campaign. When Dorgan ran for Congress again in 1980, Conrad ran for tax commissioner and won; when Dorgan declined to run against Senator Mark Andrews in 1986, Conrad ran and won 50%–49%. In 1986 Conrad earnestly promised not to run again unless "the federal deficit, the trade deficit and real interest rates will be brought under control." By 1992 the latter two arguably were, and he could argue that he had worked to cut the budget deficit. Early 1992 polls showed Conrad well ahead, but in April 1992, after ruminating on the issue and after his wife had been mugged and dragged down the street near their Capitol Hill home, Conrad announced he was retiring because he had not kept his pledge, and Dorgan ran for his seat.

Then, in September 1992, the elderly Senator Quentin Burdick, no ally of Dorgan and Conrad, died. State law said a special election had to be held after November but before January, so Conrad ran for this seat while serving his last month in the other. He was nominated unanimously at the Democratic state convention. His Republican opponent Jack Dalrymple, now Lieutenant Governor, called for an absurdly expensive $5 per bushel wheat program, and an anti-abortion independent lambasted Conrad; Conrad had far more money and won easily, 63%–34%. For a few hours in December 1992, Conrad technically held both Senate seats: he was sworn in December 14 to fill Burdick's term, and a few hours later Dorgan was sworn in to fill his. In 1994 Conrad's new Senate seat came up again. Republican Ben Clayburgh, 70-year-old former head of the state medical association, accused Conrad of voting most of the time with Bill Clinton; Conrad responded with an ad saying he voted with Bob Dole more than 50% of the time. Dole endorsed Clayburgh, but in a Republican year Conrad won by a reduced margin of 58%–42%.

Conrad became ranking minority member on the Budget Committee in January 2001 and chairman in June 2001. Throughout his career he has always called for balanced budgets and decried budget deficits, and he had the pain of watching as chairman while the surplus turned to deficit. From the 1930s to the 1970s, Republicans were the great critics of deficits; since the 1980s Democrats have increasingly taken that stand, Conrad foremost among them. One reason may be that surpluses leave more room for spending, while deficits create pressure against it; as conservative Paul Gigot wrote of Conrad in *The Wall Street Journal*, "Nobody is better at using the rhetoric of fiscal conservatism to disguise demands for larger government." In spring 2001 Conrad worked to get in the budget resolution $73 billion for farm programs over the next 10 years: This left room for the farm bill passed in 2002. But he also called for a continued surplus. Once chairman, he started lambasting the Bush administration and, using his trademark charts (he is known as "the chart man" on Capitol Hill), argued that the tax cut passed in May 2001 and lower than expected revenue would lead to deficits. But he did not seek to undo the tax cut. In March 2002 Conrad presented a $2.1 trillion dollar budget with a $90 billion deficit; it would pay off more of the national debt than the Bush budget. His plan passed in committee but in the 51–49 Senate there were not enough senators willing to constrain appropriators and Conrad's resolution never came to a vote. For the first time since the Budget Committees were set up in 1974, no budget resolution passed Congress. The Republicans won back a Senate majority in November 2002 and in January 2003 Conrad became ranking minority member again. As ranking member, he supported the pay-as-you-go rules for tax cuts as well as spending, which prevented agreement between the Senate and House on a budget resolution in 2004.

On the Finance Committee, Conrad voted against the Bush tax cuts in 2001 and 2003 and against repeal of the estate tax. He was one of 11 Democratic senators to vote for the 2003 Medicare prescription drug bill—not perfect, in his view, but a step forward in providing help for many North Dakota seniors. He sponsored bills that in his view would improve it, one with Blanche Lincoln to allow federal negotiation of prices with pharmaceutical companies, reimportation of subsidies, removal of incentives for private Medicare insurers; another to limit to three the number of discount cards in any region. Conrad could turn out to be a pivotal vote on Social Security. He praises the system, but concedes that there are problems.

The Finance Committee has jurisdiction over trade issues, which are increasingly intertwined with agriculture issues. One interest Conrad seeks to protect is North Dakota's beet sugar farmers and processors. His objections helped insure that sugar was not included in the Australia Free Trade Agreement. Even so, in June 2004, he passed an amendment in committee by 11–10 giving the House and Senate committees a veto over waiver of limits on Australian beef imports; this was unconstitutional, said the Bush administration and the Congressional Research Service, and the FTA was approved without it. In March 2004 Special Trade Representative Robert Zoellick included limited imports from the Dominican Republican in the Caribbean Free Trade Agreement. Some sugar lobbyists were unperturbed, but Conrad spoke out strongly against any increases in sugar imports, lest they lead to more. "This is about whether we have sugar in our future. This is whether we have 30,000 jobs in the valley. This is about whether we have a strong and vibrant economy in the Red River Valley of North Dakota and Minnesota."

However surprising it may be to some that North Dakota is a sugar producer, it is not in any way a cotton producer. Yet Conrad reacted sharply when the WTO in May 2004 ruled, in a case brought by Brazil, that the cotton program in the 1996 and 2002 farm bills was an illegal subsidy with effect on world markets. As he noted, that threatened the treatment of other crops, including those produced in North Dakota. Conrad called for an appeal of the ruling and said, "What's happened in the last year has confirmed that world trade is moving in the direction of scaling back programs that don't fit squarely in the [European Union's] 'green box.' " He predicted that sugar programs would have to be cut in the next farm bill and treatment of other crops changed, and called for more efforts to open markets in middle-income countries.

This would represent a change in what Conrad has worked for over many years. In 2001 and 2002 he worked on putting together a farm bill which abandoned the 1996 Freedom to Farm Act's promise of getting rid of subsidies, a promise undermined by Congress when, starting in 1997, it passed disaster relief for farmers every year. With $73 billion in the budget resolution to spend over 10 years, the Senate Agriculture Committee was able to sharply increase the wheat subsidy at the price of increasing cotton and rice subsidies as well. He was one of four Senate conferees and helped insure that the bill required country of origin labeling for meat and better treatment of pulses—peas, lentils and other crops planted in rotation on wheat fields. In May 2004 he called for Agriculture Secretary Ann Veneman's resignation when the Agriculture Department allowed beef imports from Canada despite the ban prompted by mad cow disease (the Department said the imports were safe); he protested when the Risk Management Agency decreased its support for the federal crop insurance program, which he said could reduce the number of companies offering crop insurance.

North Dakota sits astride North America's longest river, the Missouri, and Conrad has spent much time on water issues. He worked to maintain high summer levels in Lake Sakakawea against Missouri senators who want drawdowns to keep barges afloat in their state, but received a setback in 2004 when a federal appeals court rules that the applicable 1944 law gave navigation priority over fish, wildlife and recreational considerations. He argued that the latter produced much more economic benefit, and that the Army Corps of Engineers's program of building a replacement wildlife habitat downriver was unduly expensive. To enhance security on the Canadian border, Conrad inserted into the 2004 intelligence bill an amendment authorizing a project that would put baseball-sized balls with infrared motion sensors all along the border; they would have nanoblock integrated circuits developed by North Dakota State University and would be run by a computer program developed by the University of North Dakota. Conrad has also sponsored the Lewis & Clark Legacy Trails program, to spend $1.58 million to develop trails along the Missouri River and Lake Sakakawea, so that Americans today can see pristine lands where Lewis and Clark went upriver. Conrad's penchant for spotting details was proved in November 2004, when he took to the floor to announce that a staffer had found in the omnibus appropriations bill a provision allowing the chairmen of the two Appropriations Committee to authorize staffers to look at individual income tax returns in IRS offices. It turned out to have been inserted by a House staffer concerned that the IRS was blocking all access to regional offices on the grounds that individual returns might be visible; but it was universally agreed that it must go, and the House and Senate quickly repudiated it.

Conrad was reelected in 2000 against Duane Sand, an Annapolis graduate and 15-year Navy veteran who returned to North Dakota and campaigned door-to-door in every city and town with a post office. Conrad spent far more money, $2.3 million, and national Republicans didn't target this race. Conrad ran 29% ahead of Al Gore and won 62%–38%, carrying every demographic group. In early 2005, there was speculation that the Bush White House was encouraging Governor John Hoeven, just reelected by a 71%–27% margin, to run against Conrad in 2006. Whether national Republicans target this race may depend on what Conrad does on Social Security and other issues. Conrad has shown impressive strength and is a familiar figure after 20 years in the Senate. But the defeat of Tom Daschle, who had similar strengths, in South Dakota in 2004 suggests that this might be a seriously contested seat.

Junior Senator

Byron Dorgan (D)

Elected 1992, seat up 2010, 3d term; b. May 14, 1942, Dickinson; home, Bismarck; U. of ND, B.S. 1965, U. of Denver, M.B.A. 1966; Lutheran; married (Kimberly).

Elected Office: ND Tax Commissioner, 1969–80; U.S. House of Reps., 1980–92.

Professional Career: Martin–Marietta Exec. Develop. Prog., 1966–68; ND Dpty. Tax Commissioner, 1968–69.

DC Office: 322 HSOB, 20510, 202-224-2551; Fax: 202-224-1193; Web site: dorgan.senate.gov.

State Offices: Bismarck, 701-250-4618; Fargo, 701-239-5389; Grand Forks, 701-746-8972; Minot, 701-852-0703.

Committees: *Democratic Policy Committee Chairman. Appropriations:* Agriculture, Rural Development & Related Agencies; Commerce, Justice & Science; Defense; Energy & Water; Interior & Related Agencies (Chmn.); Transportation, Treasury, the Judiciary, HUD & Related Agencies. *Commerce, Science & Transportation:* Aviation; Science & Space; Surface Transportation & Merchant Marine; Technology, Innovation & Competitiveness; Trade, Tourism & Economic Development (RMM). *Energy & Natural Resources:* Energy (RMM); Public Lands & Forests; Water & Power. *Indian Affairs* (RMM).

Group Ratings

	ADA	ACLU	AFS	LCV	ITIC	NTU	COC	ACU	NTLC	CHC
2004	95	56	100	83	36	13	50	20	5	16
2003	80	—	89	47	—	11	61	10	—	—

National Journal Ratings

	2003 LIB	—	2003 CONS		2004 LIB	—	2004 CONS
Economic	63%	—	36%		76%	—	21%
Social	59%	—	37%		59%	—	40%
Foreign	74%	—	22%		75%	—	19%

Key Votes of the 108th Congress

1. Ban Drilling in ANWR	Y	5. Energy Bill	Y	9. Ban Same-Sex Marriage	N
2. Approve Bush Tax Cuts	N	6. Support Roe v. Wade	Y	10. Ban Bunker-Buster Bomb	Y
3. Medicare/Rx Bill	Y	7. Ban Partial-Birth Abortion	Y	11. Fund Iraq War	Y
4. Bar Overtime Pay Regs.	Y	8. Assault Weapons Ban	Y	12. Restrict Missile Defense	Y

Election Results

2004 general	Byron Dorgan (D)	211,843	(68%)	($2,676,756)
	Mike Liffrig (R)	98,553	(32%)	($381,125)
2004 primary	Byron Dorgan (D)	unopposed		
1998 general	Byron Dorgan (D)	134,747	(63%)	($1,681,842)
	Donna Nalewaja (R)	75,013	(35%)	($152,183)
	Other	3,598	(2%)	

Prior Winning Percentages: 1992 (59%); 1990 House (65%); 1988 House (71%); 1986 House (76%); 1984 House (79%); 1982 House (72%); 1980 House (57%)

Byron Dorgan, North Dakota's junior senator, was first elected to the House in 1980 and to the Senate in 1992. Dorgan grew up in Regent, North Dakota (population 268), where his family had a farm equipment and petroleum business and raised cattle and horses; he was one of nine students in his high school graduating class. After college and business school he worked for a Denver aerospace firm, then in 1969, at 26, was appointed state tax commissioner. His politics are very much out of the Non-Partisan League tradition: He has a strong mistrust of economic markets, a deep belief that government should intervene to protect the family farmer and small businessman, and a capacity to frame issues in a popular and unthreatening way. His first big issue, as tax commissioner, was taxing out-of-state corporations, which struck a chord in a state always hostile to big out-of-state money. To his work Dorgan brought the zest and cornball good humor that New Deal enthusiasts liked to summon up when liberals thought they represented the ordinary, inarticulate little guy, in contrast to the conservatives seen as old stuffed shirts.

Dorgan ran for the House in 1974, and lost to Republican Mark Andrews. In 1980, when Andrews ran for the Senate, Dorgan was elected to the House. His lowest reelection percentage in a House race was 65%, in 1990 against Ed Schafer, who was elected governor in 1992 and 1996. Dorgan declined to challenge Andrews for the Senate in 1986, a race his successor as tax commissioner, Kent Conrad won, and he declined to take on 80-year-old fellow-Democrat Quentin Burdick in 1988. Only with Conrad's surprise decision not to run for re-election in 1992 did Dorgan finally run for the Senate. He and his Republican opponent both backed normal trade relations with China (a major buyer of North Dakota wheat), but remained wary of free trade otherwise. Dorgan won by a solid 59%–39% margin.

In the Senate, Dorgan's voting record has been very much the same as Conrad's; this is one case where senators of the same party from the same state have worked harmoniously together. They call themselves and Congressman Earl Pomeroy "Team North Dakota." Dorgan strongly backed fellow Dakotan Tom Daschle for Senate Democratic leader in 1994, and became an assistant floor leader; he considered running for whip against Harry Reid four years later, but withdrew. In December 1998 he became co-chairman of the Democratic Policy Committee. In 2004, when Daschle was defeated and it quickly became apparent that Whip Harry Reid had the votes to succeed him as minority leader, Dorgan started running for whip, but quickly dropped out when it was clear Richard Durbin had the votes. "It seemed to me that a number of our members felt that, for our two top spots, at least one should be from a blue state," he said. Reid suggested that he might run for Democratic National Chairman, but he soon decided not to.

Dorgan continues to be a champion of family farms, even as their numbers decline. He backed the big crop insurance and disaster relief packages starting in 1997. On the 2002 farm bill, he and Charles Grassley led the move to limit farm subsidies. He argued that too much would go to a few rich farmers and feared that such payments would build opposition to the farm bill as a whole; anyway, not many North Dakota or Iowa farmers qualify for huge payments. It failed in committee, opposed by senators from states with big cotton and rice farms, but in February 2002, the Senate passed by voice vote a limit of $275,000 per farmer.

Throughout Dorgan's record one sees a traditional North Dakota distrust of economic markets. During the 1990s he often criticized Alan Greenspan for backing high interest rates and he was one of four senators to vote against his reconfirmation as Federal Reserve chairman in February 2000. He wants a more vigorous antitrust policy; he called for an 18-month moratorium on agribusiness mergers in 1999 and a two-year moratorium on airline mergers in 2001. He opposes individual investment accounts for Social Security and opposed full repeal of the estate tax. With Olympia Snowe, he sponsored the successful repeal of the FCC's media concentration rules which would allow companies to own more stations. In the Commerce Committee he succeeded in amending John Sununu's bill to exempt VOIP communications from state regulations for three years with amendments upholding state universal service fund fees and requiring payment of access charges to local telephone companies.

Dorgan has been a prime mover in scaling back the embargo on Cuba. In 2004 he attacked the Bush administration proposal to require Cuban purchasers to make payments before goods were shipped. Dorgan has worked closely with Conrad on water issues: They worked to limit the drawdown on Lake Sakakawea in the Missouri River and fought Missouri's senators who wanted more water let out to keep the barges floating on the river in their state. In 2004 he sponsored a bill to allow the import of Canadian pesticides and herbicides even if not approved by EPA. Dorgan has been a backer of wind energy projects, in which North Dakota leads the nation. He has worked for several years to create a Red River Valley Research Corridor, to link North Dakota colleges and businesses with federal research contracts. He claims to have provided $100 million in research contracts and hailed in 2002 the groundbreaking of the Alien Technology plant in Fargo, near North Dakota State University. Into the November 2004 omnibus appropriation he inserted $3 million for a hydrogen fuel cell research center at the University of North Dakota. In the March 2004 budget resolution he got some $2.2 billion for a New Homestead Act—venture capital investments in startups and expanding businesses in rural counties with more than 10% population loss over 20 years. With Ron Wyden, he passed the law banning butane lighters on airliners.

Dorgan was easily re-elected in 1998 and 2004. In 1998 he beat state Senator Donna Nalewaja 63%–35%, carrying every county but one in which the vote was tied. After the 2002 election, national Republicans tried to recruit former Governor Ed Schafer, but he declined to run. The Republican nominee, rancher Mike Liffrig, attracted some attention in September with two ads, one attacking Dorgan for supporting human cloning (he altered a bill he sponsored in response), the other portraying couples at the altar and then showing two men in black ties about to kiss each other and pairs of men and women getting married. "You can kiss our North Dakota values goodbye or you can kiss Senator Dorgan goodbye," the voiceover said. Dorgan, who voted for the Defense of Marriage Act in 1996 and against the Family Marriage Amendment in 2004, was not badly hurt; he ran ads featuring condemnation of the Liffrig ads by the Fargo *Forum* and *Grand Forks Herald*. With far more money and 32 years of winning statewide races, Dorgan won 68%–32%. This time he carried every county.

Representative-At-Large

Earl Pomeroy (D)

Elected 1992, 7th term; b. Sept. 2, 1952, Valley City; home, Valley City; U. of ND, B.A. 1974, J.D., 1979; Presbyterian; married (Laurie Kirby).

Elected Office: ND House of Reps., 1980–84; ND Insurance Commissioner, 1984–92.

Professional Career: Practicing atty., 1979–84; Natl. Assn. of Insurance Commissioners., Vice Pres. 1989, Pres. 1990.

DC Office: 1501 LHOB, 20515, 202-225-2611; Fax: 202-226-0893; Web site: www.house.gov/pomeroy.

District Offices: Bismarck, 701-224-0355; Fargo, 701-235-9760.

Committees: *Agriculture* (17th of 21 D): General Farm Commodities & Risk Management; Livestock & Horticulture. *Ways & Means* (13th of 17 D): Oversight; Social Security.

Group Ratings

	ADA	ACLU	AFS	LCV	ITIC	NTU	COC	ACU	NTLC	CHC
2004	85	55	100	82	50	12	67	28	9	38
2003	65	—	88	50	—	16	57	40	—	—

National Journal Ratings

	2003 LIB	—	2003 CONS		2004 LIB	—	2004 CONS
Economic	56%	—	44%		56%	—	43%
Social	53%	—	46%		62%	—	37%
Foreign	59%	—	39%		58%	—	42%

Key Votes of the 108th Congress

1. Drilling in ANWR	N	5. DC School Vouchers	N	9. Ban Same-Sex Marriage	N
2. Approve Bush Tax Cuts	N	6. Ban Human Cloning	Y	10. Fund Iraq War	Y
3. Medicare/Rx Bill	Y	7. Restrict Gun Liability	Y	11. Bar Cuba Embargo Funds	Y
4. Bar Overtime Pay Regs.	Y	8. Ban Partial-Birth Abortion	Y	12. Intelligence Reorg.	Y

Election Results

2004 general	Earl Pomeroy (D)	185,130	(60%)	($1,809,046)
	Duane Sand (R)	125,684	(40%)	($1,007,576)
2004 primary	Earl Pomeroy (D)	unopposed		
2002 general	Earl Pomeroy (D)	121,073	(52%)	($1,761,813)
	Rick Clayburgh (R)	109,957	(48%)	($1,089,336)

Prior Winning Percentages: 2000 (53%); 1998 (56%); 1996 (55%); 1994 (52%); 1992 (57%)

Earl Pomeroy, North Dakota's lone House member, is a Democrat first elected in 1992. Pomeroy grew up in Valley City and after college served as Byron Dorgan's driver during the 1974 campaign, then went to law school and practiced law in Valley City. In 1980, when Dorgan and

Kent Conrad won statewide elections, Pomeroy at 28 won a seat in the legislature; in 1984 and 1988 he was elected insurance commissioner. In 1992, he was planning to retire from politics and serve in the Peace Corps in Russia; then Dorgan ran for Conrad's seat in the Senate and Pomeroy decided to run for Dorgan's seat in the House. Articulate, cheerful and sincere, a critic of insurance companies yet unabrasive, he was the obvious choice for the House seat and was nominated unanimously by the Democratic convention. He won the general 57%–39%, almost exactly Dorgan's margin in the Senate race.

Pomeroy has compiled a moderate to liberal voting record, defending North Dakota interests and working with Republicans as well as Democrats on some issues. In the Republican Congress, he strongly supported the adoption tax credit and brought his two-year-old daughter, adopted from Korea, onto the floor for the vote. He strongly supported normal trade relations with China and has pushed for more exports of North Dakota wheat there. Pomeroy voted against repeal of the estate tax. When Republican leaders brought up a bill to make it permanent in June 2002, Pomeroy offered an amendment to raise the $1 million exemption to $3 million; it was rejected 231–197. In 2003 Pomeroy supported the Medicare prescription drug bill, which among other things increased the Medicare reimbursement rate for rural and small city hospitals; this brought in $48 million to Bismarck hospitals alone and $183 million statewide. He has urged more audits of corporate taxpayers and called for Congress to change the requirement that corporations use the 30-year Treasury bond rate in calculating the reserves needed for defined benefit pension plans. In an anticipatory mode he sponsored in 2004 a bill to extend the ethanol tax credit from its current expiration date in 2007 to 2010. In 2004 he sponsored a bill to overrule an IRS ruling that made retired farmers' income from the Conservation Reserve Program subject to self-employment tax.

In 2003 Pomeroy got a seat on the Agriculture Committee, a gift from the Democratic leadership since it is unusual for a Ways and Means member to serve on another committee. He opposed the 1996 Freedom to Farm Act, supported the crop insurance and disaster relief bills that have provided the rough equivalent of the old subsidies that the Freedom to Farm Act tried to phase out; he backed the 2002 farm act that vastly altered its terms and expanded the Conservation Reserve Program, in which North Dakota is the third largest participant, with 3.3 million acres. In that bill he pressed successfully for country-of-origin meat labeling; in 2004 he opposed the postponement of the effective date for that from 2004 to 2006. The 2002 farm act does not expire until 2007; in the meantime, the biggest agricultural issues are related to trade, over which Ways and Means has jurisdiction. Pomeroy hailed Special Trade Representative Robert Zoellick's WTO suit against alleged subsidies by the Canadian Wheat Board; he was cheered when the WTO ruled in April that Canada unfairly excluded foreign wheat from its distribution arrangements and was unhappy when in August 2004 the WTO ruled that the Canadian system does not violate WTO rules. In future negotiations, he said, "We don't think it should involve concessions on our part for something that we think is illegal." When Zoellick negotiated an allowance of sugar imports from the Dominican Republic as part of the Central American Free Trade Agreement in March 2004, he protested vigorously and said that the only way to settle sugar issues should be through worldwide WTO negotiations, not regional free trade agreements. North Dakota has a thriving sugar beet industry; Pomeroy said, "Granting subsidized foreign sugar access to our markets in an incremental fashion amounts to 'death by a thousand cuts' for our sugar industry." He voted against the Australian Free Trade Agreement in July 2004, arguing that the Australian Wheat Board provided subsidies; it passed anyway.

During the devastating Grand Forks flooding in April 1997, Pomeroy helped man the dikes and slept in a nearby Air Force shelter in order to help residents deal with the disaster; later he worked and got nearly $500 million in flood relief, and has worked for a $300 million system of levees and walls to prevent future floods. He worked to get federal funding for an emergency outlet for Devils Lake, which has no natural outlet and whose water has risen to record levels and flooded more than 100,000 acres. But he was foiled by the Republican leadership, and in 2003 work was begun by the state government on a channel connecting Devils Lake with the Sheyenne River and through it the Red River of the North. In June 2004, as rains lifted the lake level to its highest point in recorded history, he asked the Risk Management Agency to streamline landowners' claims for reimbursement. Pomeroy opposed having a military base-closing round in 2005, unsuccessfully; he has worked since to keep open Grand Forks Air Force Base, one of three major bases of refueling tankers.

Pomeroy has had serious challenges every two years. In 2002 he faced Tax Commissioner Rick Clayburgh in his toughest race so far. Clayburgh argued that North Dakota would do better with a Republican congressman. He repeatedly attacked Pomeroy for leaving the Agriculture Committee just before it was going to consider the farm bill in order to take the seat on Ways and Means. Republicans hit Pomeroy for voting against estate tax repeal and trade promotion authority. And they attacked him as well for backing "privatization" of Social Security, by which they meant the Clinton plan of having the government invest payroll taxes in the stock market. In October Pomeroy ran an ad showing him near George W. Bush at the signing of a bill of which he was one of 39 co-sponsors continuing a tax exemption for clergy housing expenses. "President Bush signed Pomeroy's bill to stop a $2 billion tax on our rural churches," the announcer intoned. Clayburgh ran an ad assailing the "Earl Pomeroy hustle," voting for liberal measures in Washington while sounding conservative in North Dakota. Pomeroy won 52%–48%; he carried Fargo, Minot and Grand Forks, Clayburgh's hometown; Clayburgh carried Bismarck.

In 2004 Pomeroy was opposed by Duane Sand, a 15-year Navy officer who returned to North Dakota and in 2000 lost to Senator Kent Conrad by a 62%–38% margin. Sand argued that as a member of the minority party Pomeroy was "looking through the keyhole in the door" when decisions were made. He was reinforced by a late October appearance by Speaker Dennis Hastert, who said, "When we're talking about water policy, when we talk about farm policy, there's really nobody there to represent North Dakota." Pomeroy's campaign replied that he had delivered on Medicare reimbursement, disaster relief legislation and agricultural policy. The result was Pomeroy's widest victory margin yet, 60%–40%, even as George W. Bush was carrying the state 63%–35%.

★ OHIO ★

Ohio was the first entirely American state, and one which ever since has seemed an epitome of American normalcy. The original 13 states started as British colonies, and the next three, Vermont, Kentucky and Tennessee, were spun off from them. But Ohio sprung Athena-like from the head of Congress, as the first state formed from the Northwest Territory. The Northwest Ordinance of 1787 established 6-by-6 mile square townships, which imposed geometric order on diverse American landscapes west to the Pacific; it set aside one square mile per township for public schools, and the landscape was soon peppered with schoolhouses and small colleges, the foundation stones of a literate republic. The Ordinance prohibited slavery, opening the way for free labor to clear fields, raise crops, build mills and factories, and in less than half a century, make this wilderness one of the most productive parts of western civilization. Ohio in the years after the Civil War became one of the great industrial states, the original headquarters of John D. Rockefeller's Standard Oil, the site of major steel mills along the narrow and languidly flowing Cuyahoga and Mahoning Rivers, and home of the biggest soap companies, machine tool makers, tire manufacturers and producers of safety glass. Dayton was the home of the Wright brothers, of James Ritty and James Patterson, the inventor and manufacturer of the cash register, of Charles Kettering, who invented the automobile starter and many other things. Akron was the home of Harvey Firestone, B. F. Goodrich and F. A. Seiberling, founder of Goodyear—the great tire manufacturers. They invented their devices and built their factories in a state that was culturally split, settled by New Englanders in the northeast in the Western Reserve and by Virginians in the south, split between the Southern-accented counties south of the National Road and U.S. 40 and the Northern-accented cities and towns to the north; between Butternut and Copperhead territory that didn't want to fight the Civil War and Yankee territory that fiercely prosecuted the War and Reconstruction afterwards.

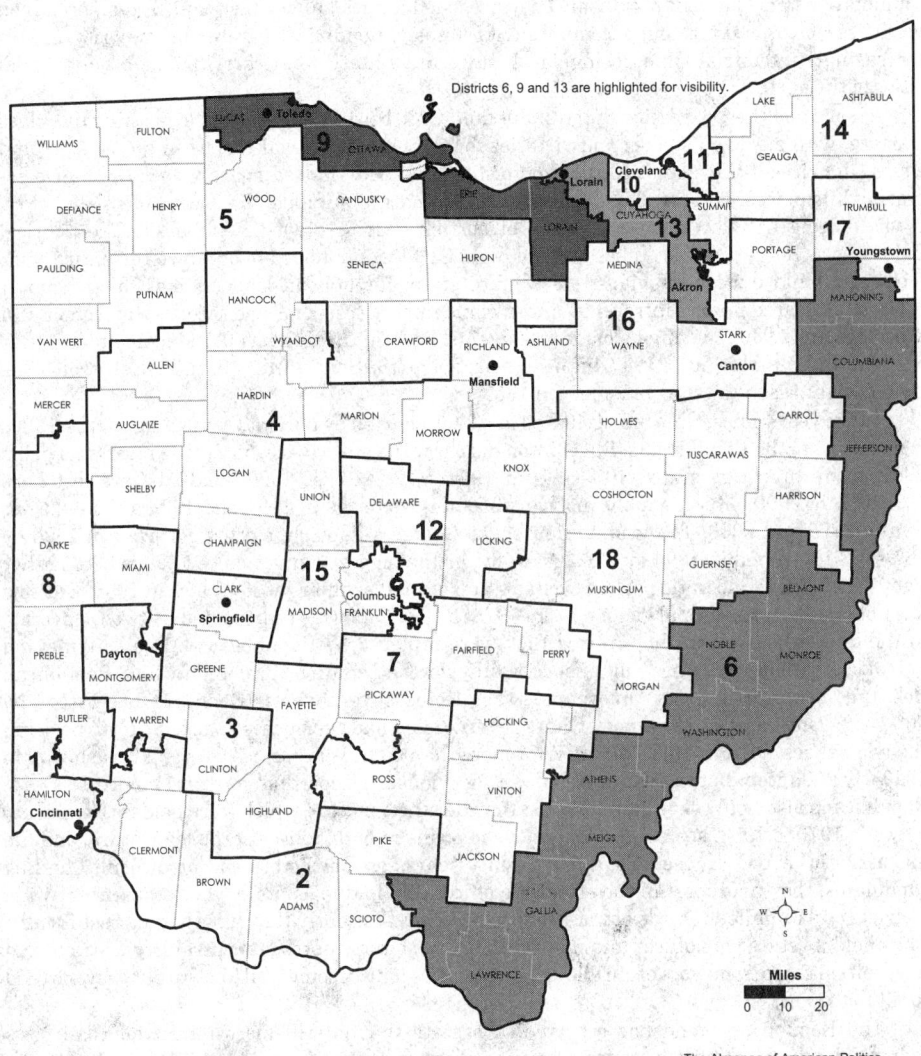

Districts 6, 9 and 13 are highlighted for visibility.

Congressional district boundaries were first effective for 2002.

The Almanac of American Politics.
National Journal

This split heritage made Ohio politically a closely divided state—and a nationally pivotal one. A little more than a century ago Ohio produced the candidate and campaign manager—Governor and former Ways and Means Chairman William McKinley and iron and coal industrialist Mark Hanna; McKinley won the presidency in 1896 and 1900 and inaugurated a 34-year period of Republican national majorities. McKinley's Republicans were for high tariffs and hard money, had a friendly regard for workers and even some unions, but no patience with large union combinations and nascent socialism. They preached a nationalist Americanism tempered by a wariness about making major commitments abroad. Republicans were the majority in this increasingly industrial Ohio, losing rural Butternut counties but carrying the big industrial cities of the north.

Then came the Depression of the 1930s, and Ohio became the scene of something like class warfare, with sit-down strikes and victories for the CIO industrial unions in autos, steel and tires. CIO cities—Cleveland, Akron, Youngstown, Toledo—moved sharply toward the Democrats, while places with few CIO members—Cincinnati, Columbus, the dozens of small factory towns dotting the flat limestone plains of northern Ohio—stayed Republican. The political fighting was fierce and the stakes seemed high. CIO leaders hoped to organize the entire work force and build a Scandinavian-style welfare state; Republican leaders like Ohio's Senator Robert Taft feared union control of business would imperil freedoms and throttle the economy. In the 1930s and 1940s the unions made great gains. But Taft held them off, reducing union power with the Taft-Hartley Act of 1947, his own reelection to the Senate in 1950, and the election of his rival Dwight Eisenhower as president in 1952.

In the years since, Ohio has oscillated and been courted by national campaigns. In the 1990s Ohio swung to the Republicans. Bill Clinton did carry the state twice, but by the narrowest of his margins in any large state—40%–38% in 1992, 47%–41% in 1996—and Al Gore lost here 50%–46% in 2000. Ohio Republicans won smashing victories in 1994 and 1998 and held their own in 1996 and 2000. The leading figure was George Voinovich, elected governor in 1990 by 56%–44%, reelected in 1994 by 72%–25%—by far the biggest margin since 1826, when neither Republican nor Democratic parties existed—and elected senator by 56%–44% in 1998. But this has not just been a personal victory. From 1976 to 1994 Ohio was represented by two Democrats in the Senate, but when they retired they were replaced by Republicans: Mike DeWine and Voinovich, both of whom had run unsuccessfully for the Senate before. And in 1998 Republican Bob Taft, bearer of a great Ohio name, was elected governor over Democrat Lee Fisher by 50%–45%. Until Taft's 1998 victory, Ohio's governorship had been passed back and forth between the two parties, with neither holding it for more than eight years, since George K. Nash won in 1899. By 2006 Republicans will have held it for a longer period than any party since 1856–74. Republicans also hold every downballot statewide office, most of which were held by Democrats between 1970 to 1994, seemingly impervious margins in both houses of the legislature, and the majority of the U.S. House delegation. Twenty years ago Democrats had no difficulty finding candidates; they held most of the statewide offices and had legislators who represented swing districts and compiled records attractive to most voters. Recently they have had more difficulty. They hold no statewide offices and most of their legislators represent central city districts and have leftish records; mayors of shrinking central cities may become well known, but they too tend to tilt to the left.

The Republican trend has occurred in a state that is still more industrial than post-industrial, a state changed by the immigration of the early 20th century but little touched by the immigration of the late 20th century, a state where cultural liberalism has a far smaller constituency than it does on the East or West Coasts or even in nearby Illinois and Michigan. It used to be said that Ohio was a typical state, a great test market, for in income levels, urban-rural balance, and ethnic mix, as well as presidential percentages, it is not very far from the national average. But economically and culturally, it is different, a template perhaps for Indiana and Missouri but not for Oregon and Arizona. Ohio trails only California, three times as large, in manufacturing jobs, yet it has 400,000 fewer of them than it did in the peak year, 1969, and its population and income have been increasing at less than the national average; from 2000 to 2004 it had a lower rate of population growth than any state but West Virginia and North Dakota. The

Ohio economy seems stuck in the 2001–02 recession. Employment peaked at 5,586,000 in April 2001, fell to 5,490,000 in September 2002 and by March 2005 had risen to only 5,548,000—below the level of four years before. The unemployment rate rose from 3.9% in April 2001 to 5.5% in January 2003 and was 6.3% in March 2005. This is much lower than during some past recessions and unemployment has been highest not in the big metro areas but in rural counties in the eastern, southern and western parts of the state. But pretty much gone is the old tradition of heading straight from high school and perhaps military service to a high-wage factory job.

Politically, there are two distinct parts of Ohio. One, call it Northeast Ohio, is the part where the CIO unions organized the big factories, the heavy industry area along Lake Erie and reaching south to the coal-mining counties across the Ohio River from West Virginia. In Northeast Ohio giant steel mills closed in Cleveland and the Mahoning Valley around Youngstown in the 1980s, and population declined as young people moved out. Politically, the Democratic voting habits instilled by the CIO unions are still evident, though there was no movement toward Democrats on cultural issues in the 1990s here, as there was in larger metro areas. George W. Bush lost the area 55%–41% in 2000; Bob Taft carried it by only 49%–48% in 2002; Bush lost it by a 54%–46% margin in 2004. The rest of the state, call it Southwest Ohio, is a more diversified industrial area, never so dependent on big industries like steel, tires and autos. It did not lose so many jobs or suffer such population loss in the early 1980s as Northeast Ohio. Instead it began building a new, more supple and adaptable manufacturing economy, with smaller factories, less rigid management and fewer union members, an economy which did reasonably well in the 1990s but has had only spotty growth since 2000. In this part of Ohio the cultural atmosphere in small towns and even its big cities become culturally much more liberal, with the possible exception of Columbus, Ohio's fastest-growing metro area, with something of a post-industrial, information-based economy. Politically, this area was and is heavily Republican; the old Butternut Democratic tradition in southern Ohio has largely disappeared. George W. Bush carried this part of the state 56%–40% in 2000 and 60%–40% in 2004 and Bob Taft carried it 65%–31% in 2002. Moreover, this part of the state is becoming more important politically. Between 1980 and 2000 turnout in Northeast Ohio rose only 3%, while it rose 16% in Southwest Ohio; in 2004 the Democrats' heroic efforts increased turnout in Northeast Ohio 18% over 2000, but the Bush campaign's efforts helped increase turnout in Southwest Ohio 21%.

So where does Ohio stand in history? Is it New Deal Ohio, with ethnic factory workers arranged against small town businessmen, ethnic Catholics versus rural Protestants, all engaged in a contest to see how far and in what ways government should be enlarged? Or is it McKinley's Ohio, with mechanical tinkerers and can-do manufacturers, adaptive businessmen and employees, striving to work hard, raise families and serve communities that feel little class conflict or economic envy? The results of recent elections, the continuing though sometimes narrow Republican victories here, suggest that it is, despite highly publicized manufacturing losses, more McKinley's Ohio. But in 2006 the governorship will be open after a record 16 years of Republican dominance, and Ohio's Democrats will have a chance to advance an alternative vision of Ohio.

The People		Race/Ethnic Origin			Military veterans: 1,144,007 (13.5%)	
Pop. 2004 (est):	11,459,011	9,538,111	84.0%	White	WWII: 21.7%	Korea: 13.7%
Pop. 2000:	11,353,140	1,290,662	11.4%	Black	Vietnam: 30.7%	Gulf War: 8.8%
Pop. 1990:	10,847,115	131,670	1.2%	Asian	**Most populous cities (2003):**	
Change 1990–2000:	Up 4.7%	21,985	0.2%	Native Am.	1. Columbus	728,432
% of U.S. total:	4.0%	2,336	0.0%	Hawaiian	2. Cleveland	461,324
Pop. rank:	7th of 50	137,770	1.2%	Two+ races	3. Cincinnati	317,361
Area size:	44,825 sq. mi.	13,483	0.1%	Other	4. Toledo	308,973
State Native:	74.7%	217,123	1.9%	Hisp. Origin	5. Akron	212,215
Non-citizen:	1.5%	**Ancestry**				
Language		German: 18.8%		Irish: 9.5%	Urban population: 77.3%	
English: 91.4%	Other Eur.: 4.1%	English: 6.9%		USA: 6.5%	Rural population: 22.7%	
Spanish: 3.0%		Italian: 4.4%				

Education		Work Sector		General Assembly	
H.S. Grad:	83.0%	Private: 82.0%	Govt: 12.2%	Senate	22 R 11 D
College Grad:	21.1%	Self: 5.5%	Family: 0.3%	House	60 R 39 D
Industry		Unemployment: 5.0%		Legislative Term Limits: Yes	
Agri: 1.1%	Con: 6.0%	**Household Income**		**Registered Voters**	
Fin: 6.3%	Info: 2.4%	<15k: 15.6%	15-35k: 26.9%	No party registration	
Mfg: 25.0%	Prof: 27.8%	35-50k: 17.3%	50-100k: 30.4%		
Public: 4.1%	Trade: 15.5%	100-150k: 6.5%	>150k: 3.3%		
Other: 12.0%		Median: $40,956			
Occupation		Poverty status: 10.6%			
Blue collar: 27.8%	White collar: 57.3%	**Home Value**			
Gray collar: 14.9%		<50k: 12.2% 50-100k: 37.5% 100-200k: 38.6% 200-300k: 7.8%			
		300-500k: 2.9% >500k: 1.0% Median: $100,500			

Presidential politics   With 20 electoral votes and a tradition of close partisan competition, Ohio is a crucial state in presidential politics. Of the large industrial states—Pennsylvania, Ohio, Michigan, Illinois—Ohio has been consistently the most Republican for 50 years, with the single exception of 1976, when Jimmy Carter ran well in the Southern-accented counties below U.S. 40 and carried the state by 11,000 votes. Ohio matched the national average in 1984 and 1988, came close to doing so in 1996 and was only 2% points off in 2000. In 2004 George W. Bush matched his national percentage here and John Kerry ran 1% ahead of his. No Republican has ever been elected president without carrying Ohio; no Democrat, in today's electoral vote arithmetic, can be sure of winning without it. On election night 2004, after it became clear that Bush had won Florida, all eyes were on Ohio: if Bush's lead held up here, he would be president again; if not, John Kerry would be elected even though trailing in the popular vote by 3 million.

2004 Presidential Vote
Bush (R) 2,859,764   (51%)
Kerry (D)..................... 2,741,165   (49%)
Badnarik (Lib)................ 14,676   (0%)
Other........................... 12,298   (0%)

2004 Democratic Presidential Primary
Kerry (D)...................... 632,590   (52%)
Edwards (D) 416,104   (34%)
Kucinich (D) 110,066   (9%)
Dean (D) 30,983   (3%)
Lieberman (D) 14,676   (1%)
Other........................... 16,595   (1%)

2000 Presidential Vote
Bush (R) 2,350,363   (50%)
Gore (D)....................... 2,183,628   (46%)
Nader (Green) 117,799   (3%)
Other........................... 50,208   (1%)

The dynamics of the presidential race in Ohio were quite different in 2000 and 2004. In 2000 Bush, despite holding narrow leads in polls, made Ohio a priority state from start to finish, while the Gore campaign, looking to opportunities elsewhere, pulled out much of its advertising in mid-October—perhaps its greatest strategic mistake. Bush carried Ohio by only 50%–46%. In 2004 both campaigns recognized that Ohio was a major, perhaps the major, target state. Job losses, especially manufacturing job losses, seemed to make the atmosphere especially favorable to Democrats on economic issues. The 527 organizations spent $9.7 million on ads in Ohio markets, more than in any other state, and the top five media markets in ad exposures included Toledo, Dayton, Columbus and Cleveland. Democrats and anti-Bush 527 organizations ran a classic industrial era registration and turnout drive aimed especially at black neighborhoods in central cities and at university communities. By all measures it was spectacularly successful. The Democratic popular vote margin was increased by 60,000 votes in Cleveland's Cuyahoga County, and Democratic margins were increased as well in the counties containing Columbus, Cincinnati, Akron, Toledo, Lorain, Youngstown and Warren and in a five-county cluster centered on the university town of Athens. Overall, in the 18 counties where the Democratic margin was increased or the Republican margin reduced (or in the case of Canton's Stark County, which had a 6% job loss, a Bush margin was converted to a Kerry margin), the Democratic margin increased by 183,000. If the Bush margin in the remaining 70 counties had remained static, Kerry would have erased Bush's 2000 margin of 165,000 votes and carried the state by some 17,000.

But the Bush margin did not remain static. The Bush campaign ran a post-industrial registration and turnout organization, with some 65,000 volunteers, networking with evangelical and Catholic churches, farmers, doctors and community organizations. It made 3.9 million phone calls to voters, 1.8 million in the last five days. Not all of these were obvious targets. In a tier of seven counties on the western edge of the state which had no population growth or population decline from 2000 to 2004, the Bush margin went up by 13,000 in those four years. In Cincinnati's population-losing Hamilton County, the Bush margin declined by 19,000 votes, but in the three population-gaining counties surrounding it the Bush margin increased by 37,000. The Bush campaign converted a Gore margin into a Bush margin in Springfield's Clark County, transatlantically famous as the target of a letter-writing campaign by readers of Britain's left-wing *Guardian* newspaper.

Job losses and economic issues were not the primary movers of votes. Bush carried 10 of the 12 counties, most of them small, with the largest percentage of job losses. A 43%–38% plurality preferred Bush over Kerry on the issue of economic recovery, and he held larger leads on moral values and the war on terrorism. Members of union households, one-third of voters, preferred Kerry 58%–42%, while those in other households favored Bush by a similar margin. But there was a starker difference along the lines of religion. Bush won 56% among Protestants and 55% among Catholics, the latter a 5% gain from 2000. Those attending religious services weekly preferred Bush 65%–35%, with no appreciable difference between Protestants and Catholics, while occasional attenders favored Kerry 57%–43% and the 14% who never attend religious services preferred Kerry 63%–35%. In states like New York and California, voters with graduate school degrees vote overwhelmingly Democratic, but in Ohio they were evenly split between the two candidates. Cultural liberalism has not made the inroads among the highly educated and those with high incomes here in the heartland that it has made on the coasts.

The initial count showed Bush 136,000 votes ahead of Kerry—many times the margin that any candidate has ever successfully challenged. There was some controversy over the provisional ballots. Secretary of State Kenneth Blackwell, a Republican and Bush backer, had been backed up by the courts in his ruling that provisional ballots had to be cast in the voter's precinct, not just anywhere in the same county as the Democrats wanted. When the 155,000 provisional ballots were counted, the Bush margin was reduced to 119,000. Still there were cries of vote fraud and charges that lines were longer in Democratic areas and that the voting machines had been programmed to produce overly Republican results. The Green and Libertarian parties sued to get a recount, and Jesse Jackson alleged that 130,000 votes were switched from Kerry to Bush. But no substantial evidence was brought forward to substantiate these charges, and Ohio's electoral votes were cast a second time for George W. Bush.

In 1996 Ohio switched its presidential primary from May to March 19, and voted on the same day as Illinois, Michigan and Wisconsin. But even then, just four weeks after New Hampshire, the race was already over. In May 1999 the state legislature voted to move the date to March 7, and Ohio was seriously contested. George W. Bush and Al Gore, with serious organizational support, won overwhelming victories as they clinched their parties' nominations. In 2004 Ohio held its primary on March 2, with seven other states; John Kerry won easily here and elsewhere and clinched the Democratic nomination exactly nine months before the general election, which was held, appropriately for Ohio, on the birthday of Warren G. Harding, Ohio's most recent president.

Congressional districting

Ohio lost one House seat in the 2000 Census and now has a House delegation of 18 members, its smallest since the 1820s. Republicans had majorities in the legislature and held the governorship, and so had control of the process for the first time since 1960. It was clear that the Republicans could eliminate the seat of 13th District Democrat Sherrod Brown and imperil the chances of 6th District Democrat Ted Strickland. But Strickland threatened to run against 18th District Republican Bob Ney and Brown made it clear that if his seat was eliminated he would run for governor. Governor Bob Taft, even though he had ousted

109th Congress Lineup		
11 R	6 D	1 V

108th Congress Lineup	
12 R	6 D

Brown as secretary of state in 1990, did not want to face a well-financed and politically adept challenger, and asked Republican legislators not to target him. The legislature did not act in 2001.

Then, in January 2002, the Republicans effectively lost control. Ohio's filing deadline for the May primary was February 21, and under the Ohio Constitution, a law passed in 2002 could take immediate effect only if it had a two-thirds vote in both houses. This meant the Republicans had to get the votes of at least one Democrat in the Senate and seven in the House. In the circumstances, the Republicans constructed a pretty ingenious plan, which they unveiled January 16. All 11 Republican incumbents got districts very similar to their current ones. So did the two Cleveland Democrats. Every other Democrat got a significantly different district. The incumbent put into the most parlous position was the 17th District's Jim Traficant. But he was facing trial on bribery charges (he was convicted in April and expelled from the House in July), and had been voting with Republicans on many issues; if one Democrat had to go, Democrats obviously preferred to sacrifice him. The 3d District was made significantly more Republican, but incumbent Tony Hall had long run far ahead of party lines; so long as he continued to run the seat seemed safe Democratic. The 14th District's Tom Sawyer had been given much of Traficant's old territory, but he had cast some free trade votes and organized labor didn't care if he was discomfited. Ted Strickland, given a seat stretching 325 miles along the Ohio River and up to Youngstown, was happy, even though he might have to face Traficant in a primary; the seat was much more Democratic than his previous district. Brown, given a safe Democratic seat, was pleased too. So on January 17 Democrats made a deal: they would provide the votes to give the plan immediate effect and avoid having to reschedule the congressional primary for August or September at a cost to taxpayers of $7 million. The plan passed on January 22.

Then on January 26 Tony Hall said he might give up his seat for a humanitarian job and George W. Bush offered him the ambassadorship to the Food and Agriculture Organization in Rome. Republican Dayton Mayor Mike Turner had already announced he would run for the seat; Hall did not file for reelection and resigned when he was confirmed by the Senate, and Turner easily won the seat. The upshot was that the legislature's plan, and Hall's well-timed appointment, increased the Republican edge in the delegation from 11–8 to 12–6. In 2003 longtime Republican state Chairman Robert Bennett, noting that his party controlled the legislature and the governorship, suggested that Ohio might want to redistrict once again, as Texas did in 2003 and Georgia would in 2005. But Republicans evidently concluded that they had little to gain and that the current district lines suited them just fine.

The Republican edge may not be as large after the 2010 Census, even if Republicans retain control of the process. For the first four years of the decade Ohio had the second lowest population growth of any state, after West Virginia (North Dakota lost population), and if that continues demographers estimate that Ohio will lose another two seats. That might cost Democrats one of their Northeast Ohio seats, but it will take some pretty adept redistricting to prevent Republicans from losing one as well.

Governor

Bob Taft (R)

Elected 1998, term expires Jan. 2007, 2d term; b. Jan. 8, 1942, Boston, MA; home, Cincinnati; Yale U., B.A. 1963, Princeton U., M.A. 1967, U. of Cincinnati, J.D. 1976; Protestant; married (Hope).

Elected Office: OH House of Reps., 1976–81; Hamilton Cnty. Commissioner, 1981–90; OH Secy. of State, 1991–98.

Professional Career: Peace Corps, East Africa, 1963–65; State Dept., Vietnam, 1967–69; Budget Officer & Asst. Dir., IL Budget Bureau, 1969–73.

Office: Office of the Governor, 77 S. High St., 30th Fl., 43215, 614-466-3555; Fax: 614-644-0951; Web site: www.state.oh.us/gov.

Election Results

2002 general	Bob Taft (R)	1,865,007	(58%)
	Timothy Hagan (D)	1,236,924	(38%)
	John Eastman (I)	126,686	(4%)
2002 primary	Bob Taft (R)	unopposed	
1998 general	Bob Taft (R)	1,678,721	(50%)
	Lee Fisher (D)	1,498,956	(45%)
	Other	176,536	(5%)

Bob Taft, elected governor in 1998 and 2002, is from a famed Ohio family. His great-grandfather William Howard Taft was elected president in 1908 and appointed chief justice of the United States in 1921. His grandfather, Robert A. Taft, was elected senator in 1938, 1944 and 1950; a strong and principled conservative known as "Mr. Republican," he ran for president and lost the Republican nomination in 1940 and 1952, and was Senate majority leader when he died in 1953. His father, Robert Taft Jr., was elected to the House in 1962, 1966 and 1968 and to the Senate in 1970, then lost to Howard Metzenbaum in 1976. The increasing informality of American politics can be gauged by the style of the Tafts' names: President Taft used three full names, the first Senator Taft an initial, the second Senator Taft a Jr. and this latest Taft calls himself simply Bob—and didn't make reference to his illustrious family in his campaign ads. He grew up in Cincinnati, graduated from Yale, served two years in the Peace Corps in East Africa, got a masters degree at Princeton and worked four years as a budget officer in Illinois state government. Then he returned to Cincinnati, graduated from the University of Cincinnati law school and was elected to the state House in 1976. In 1981 he was elected Hamilton County commissioner. In 1990 he started to run for governor, then was persuaded by Republican National Chairman Lee Atwater in one of his last political acts to step aside for George Voinovich and run for secretary of state instead; he beat incumbent Democrat (and now Congressman) Sherrod Brown for that office, critical for redistricting the state legislature, in November.

The common expectation was that Taft would run for governor in 1998, when Voinovich would be ineligible for a third term. Taft had strong Democratic opposition: Lee Fisher, elected attorney general in 1990, defeated by a narrow margin in heavily Republican 1994. On primary day, voters rejected Issue 2, a one-cent sales tax for schools and property tax relief, written in response to a 1997 state Supreme Court decision requiring more school funding. Both Taft and Fisher supported it, and had to scramble to come up with new ways to address the number one issue, education, without a tax increase. Fisher promised to cut property taxes by 15% over two years; Taft proposed much smaller tax cuts, a homestead exemption and a $2,500 college tuition deduction for families with incomes under $50,000. Taft won 50%–45%.

In his first year in office Taft fulfilled many of his campaign promises. Working with the Republican legislature, he required students to take reading tests in the fourth grade to be academically promoted, and created the college tuition deduction, a homestead tax cut, tougher penalties for juvenile criminals and cheats who exploit the elderly. He reduced the inheritance tax and made other state tax cuts, and got voter approval of a $400 million environmental bond issue. But in early 2001 Taft faced more difficulties. Because of term limits, the legislature included many new members and some new leaders. Tax revenues, which had increased at a spritely pace in 2000, increased very little in 2001. The state Supreme Court had set a June 15 deadline for a new school finance program, and Medicaid costs were skyrocketing. The legislature responded by cutting higher education spending, and Taft issued 49 line-item vetoes in June. Taft successfully opposed conservative initiatives on abortion, a concealed-weapons law and video lottery slots at race tracks. The cigarette tax was raised and the rainy day fund drained. A Golden Buckeye discount card for prescription drugs was passed. In February 2002 Taft announced his $1.6 billion, 10-year Third Frontier Project, to use tobacco settlement money and bonds (which voters were asked to approve in November 2003) to fund biomedical research, scientific research centers and support industries and high-tech products with growth potential—high-tech as a substitute for manufacturing.

Taft went into the 2002 election cycle a strong favorite and raised huge sums, eventually $12 million. This deterred some opponents, and the Democratic nomination went to former Cuyahoga County Commissioner Tim Hagan, a spirited liberal who in the cynical cauldron of Cleveland politics had paid some price for adherence to principle. Hagan did not trim his liberal principles in this campaign, but opposed Taft on abortion, taxes and spending, prescription drugs, capital punishment, the video lottery and medical malpractice. Hagan had trouble raising money, eventually netting $1 million and tapping friends of his wife, actress Kate Mulgrew. Taft angered some conservatives when he named as his lieutenant governor candidate Columbus Councilwoman Jennette Bradley, a supporter of abortion rights. Taft won 58%–38%.

A month after the election the state supreme court issued its third decision ruling the state school finance system unconstitutional and ordered the legislature to change it. But it didn't retain jurisdiction, set no deadline and appointed no lower court monitor. Lieutenant Governor Maureen O'Connor in November had been elected to replace a justice who favored the decision and seemed likely to produce a 4–3 majority against it, and so Taft and the legislature ignored the decision. They had fiscal problems aplenty without it. Projections showed a $720 million shortfall in the current budget and a $4 billion deficit in 2003–05. In February 2003 Taft proposed a budget with a 10% spending increase, $3.1 billion in new taxes and a wage freeze. Conservative legislators argued that spending had increased too much—more than doubling in the 1990s—and that Taft had refused to challenge public employee unions. Eventually the legislature, led by Speaker Larry Householder, passed a 1-cent sales tax increase, to last until June 2005. That was sharply opposed by Secretary of State Kenneth Blackwell, but his threat to put the issue on the ballot was foiled by public employee unions. Taft did not fare better at the ballot: In November 2003 voters turned down his $500 million in Third Frontier bonds by a 51%–49% margin; the measure passed in Democratic counties but was rejected in Republican areas. On other issues Taft jousted with Republican legislators. He rejected one bill reorganizing treatment of the mentally retarded because it didn't give him flexibility to close facilities and accepted another which reduced the review times. He had resisted for several years bills to allow citizens to carry concealed weapons. But in January 2004 he accepted a measure that required background checks and training and allowed the news media (but not the general public) to see who was granted permits, some 45,000 of which were issued by the end of the year. In February 2004 Taft signed a bill rejecting same-sex marriages and refusing to recognize those contracted in other states and barring domestic partner benefits for unmarried state employees. That did not satisfy some. Cultural conservatives got signatures on a constitutional amendment barring same-sex marriage, civil unions and domestic partner benefits on the November ballot. Taft and Attorney General Jim Petro opposed it, as did Senators Mike DeWine and George Voinovich and virtually all major state newspapers; they argued that it would drive businesses granting domestic partner benefits out of the state. Nonetheless it passed 62%–38%, losing only in university-dominated Athens County.

Republicans seem not to have been hurt much by their tax increases and by charges of illegal fundraising made against Householder and some of his top aides. In November 2004 they lost two seats in the state House and held steady in the state Senate. But they faced continuing fiscal problems. In January 2005 Taft proposed a continued freeze in local government funding, with cuts in 2006 and 2007. His job ratings remained low. County campaign funds, which Republicans used to funnel anonymous contributions in large amounts to statewide candidates, were shut down in April 2005.

Meanwhile attention focused on the 2006 race for governor; Taft is ineligible for a third term. Probably the best known Republican running was Secretary of State Kenneth Blackwell, a former Cincinnati councilman and mayor and a strong fiscal and cultural conservative. He has criticized Taft and Republican legislative leaders often for raising taxes and overspending. His major platform plank was repeal of the sales tax increase and a constitutional amendment limiting the growth of state spending. He seemed likely to be supported by religious conservatives. Attorney General Jim Petro, from the Cleveland suburbs, elected in 2002, took a different approach. He had opposed the amendment to ban same-sex marriage, among other moderate stands. But he chose as his running mate Cincinnati Councilman Phil Heimlich, a staunch conservative. A third likely candidate was Auditor Betty Montgomery, from the Toledo suburbs, who also took moderate stands and promised to ferret out waste, fraud and abuse. Blackwell hoped to win a three-way race with his strong conservative support.

Ohio Democrats are well positioned to argue that Ohio Republicans have been in office too long: the only party controlling the governorship longer was Thomas Jefferson's Democratic Republicans, who held it from 1803 to 1822, and no one has a living memory of that now that Jim Rhodes is gone. The first Democrat out on the trail was Michael Coleman, elected mayor of Columbus in 1999, the first Democrat to win there in 28 years, and reelected with 95% of the vote in 2003. He announced in February 2005 and embarked on a listening tour in a bus in Toledo and in heavily Republican northwest Ohio in March. In May, 6th District Congressman Ted Strickland said he would run. Other possible candidates were state Senator and former Congressman Eric Fingerhut and former Congressman Dennis Eckart. Another name, more well known nationally, was mentioned: talk show host Jerry Springer. His candidacy would not be as implausible as one tuning in on his program might think. He has an attractive story: his parents were Holocaust survivors and as he likes to say, "I love this country because I know it worked for me. It gave my family life." He served as a Cincinnati councilman in the 1970s and, after resigning after he was caught frequenting a prostitute in Northern Kentucky, was reelected by a solid margin and served as mayor. He ran for governor in 1982 and finished a respectable third in the Democratic primary. He is an articulate and fervent liberal with a good sense of humor and the ability to self-finance a campaign; he contributed some $250,000 to Ohio Democrats, who made him a delegate-at-large to the Democratic National Convention. Of course the character of his program must be counted as a serious liability. As he has said, "There are pluses and minuses. The plus is that I'm known by everybody. The minus is that I'm known by everybody." But he may have the raw political talent to turn that liability into an asset.

A footnote for history. If either Kenneth Blackwell or Michael Coleman wins, he will be the second black elected governor in American history; the first was Douglas Wilder of Virginia, elected in 1989.

Senior Senator

Mike DeWine (R)

Elected 1994, seat up 2006, 2d term; b. Jan. 5. 1947, Springfield; home, Cedarville; Miami U. of OH, B.S. 1969, OH Northern U., J.D. 1972; Catholic; married (Fran).

Elected Office: Greene Cnty. Prosecuting atty., 1977–81; OH Senate, 1980–82; U.S. House of Reps., 1982–90; OH Lt. Gov., 1990–94.

Professional Career: Practicing atty; Greene Cnty. Asst. Prosecuting atty., 1973–75.

DC Office: 140 RSOB, 20510, 202-224-2315; Fax: 202-224-6519; Web site: dewine.senate.gov.

State Offices: Cincinnati, 513-763-8260; Cleveland, 216-522-7272; Columbus, 614-469-5186; Marietta, 740-373-2317; Toledo, 419-259-7536; Xenia, 937-376-3080.

Committees: *Appropriations*: District of Columbia; Labor, Health and Human Services, Education & Related Agencies; Legislative Branch; Military Construction & Veterans Affairs; State, Foreign Operations & Related Programs; Transportation, Treasury, the Judiciary, HUD & Related Agencies. *Health, Education, Labor & Pensions*: Bioterrorism & Public Health Preparedness; Education & Early Childhood Development; Retirement Security & Aging (Chmn.). *Intelligence (Select)*. *Judiciary*: Antitrust, Competition Policy & Consumer Rights (Chmn.); Crime & Drugs; Immigration, Border Security & Citizenship; Intellectual Property; Terrorism, Technology & Homeland Security.

Group Ratings

	ADA	ACLU	AFS	LCV	ITIC	NTU	COC	ACU	NTLC	CHC
2004	35	22	29	0	92	57	88	68	83	100
2003	15	—	11	16	—	69	96	85	—	—

National Journal Ratings

	2003 LIB	—	2003 CONS		2004 LIB	—	2004 CONS
Economic	38%	—	61%		46%	—	53%
Social	0%	—	59%		49%	—	49%
Foreign	22%	—	68%		47%	—	51%

Key Votes of the 108th Congress

1. Ban Drilling in ANWR	Y	5. Energy Bill	Y	9. Ban Same-Sex Marriage	Y
2. Approve Bush Tax Cuts	Y	6. Support Roe v. Wade	N	10. Ban Bunker-Buster Bomb	N
3. Medicare/Rx Bill	Y	7. Ban Partial-Birth Abortion	Y	11. Fund Iraq War	Y
4. Bar Overtime Pay Regs.	N	8. Assault Weapons Ban	Y	12. Restrict Missile Defense	N

Election Results

2000 general	Mike DeWine (R)	2,665,512	(60%)	($5,699,889)
	Ted Celeste (D)	1,595,066	(36%)	($477,176)
	Other	188,223	(4%)	
2000 primary	Mike DeWine (R)	1,029,860	(80%)	
	Ronald Dickson (R)	161,185	(12%)	
	Frank Cremeans (R)	104,219	(8%)	
1994 general	Mike DeWine (R)	1,836,556	(53%)	($6,084,663)
	Joel Hyatt (D)	1,348,213	(39%)	($4,921,223)
	Joseph J. Slovenec (I)	252,031	(7%)	($192,867)

Prior Winning Percentages: 1988 House (74%); 1986 House (100%); 1984 House (74%); 1982 House (56%)

Michael DeWine, Ohio's senior senator, is a Republican first elected to the House in 1982 and to the Senate in 1994. DeWine grew up in Yellow Springs, the home of liberal Antioch College, where his family owned a successful seed business. He graduated from Miami of Ohio and Northern Ohio University law school and settled in Cedarville, in a part of the state with rolling hills, winding creeks and covered bridges, where he and his wife have long hosted an annual ice cream social. There DeWine was elected Greene County prosecutor in 1976, at 29, where he resisted plea bargaining; in order to nail a drug dealer, once put up the collateral to get $50,000 cash to stage a buy. In 1980, at 33, he was elected to the Ohio Senate. In 1982, when incumbent

Clarence Brown ran for governor, DeWine won a six-candidate Republican primary with 69% and was elected to a U.S. House seat. Elected lieutenant governor in 1990, two years later DeWine ran against Senator John Glenn. It was a hard-hitting campaign: He attacked Glenn for his part in the Keating Five case. In September 1992 Glenn was below 50% in the polls. But Democrats brought up DeWine's 31 overdrafts on the House bank and the time he fell asleep at the Iran-Contra hearings. Glenn won 51%–42%, his closest general election margin ever.

In 1994 DeWine decided to run for the Senate again. This time the incumbent, Howard Metzenbaum, was retiring, and hoped to be succeeded by his son-in-law, Joel Hyatt, founder of the storefront Hyatt Legal Services chain. But in the May primary, Hyatt defeated Cuyahoga County Commissioner Mary Boyle by only 47%–43%, while DeWine won by 53%–32% over Bernadine Healy, former director of the National Institutes of Health. From then on, DeWine had solid leads in most polls. DeWine won statewide 53%–39%.

The common motif that runs through DeWine's career is a concern for children and the championing of legislation often prompted by tragedy striking a particular child, including his own: his daughter Becky died in an auto accident in 1993, at 22, and he and his wife decided to donate her organs; DeWine spends much effort on organ donor programs and awareness. With Jay Rockefeller, he sponsored a law to change the family preservation emphasis in social work, and helped pass a law requiring the best interest of the child as paramount in custody cases involving abusive or drug-problem parents. In the recesses of the Senate's impeachment trial, he made calls to try to get medical benefits for a Middletown five-year-old with xeroderma pigmentosum, a disease so rare it was not on the Social Security Administration's list of covered treatments. He took over the chairmanship of the District of Columbia Appropriations Subcommittee—generally regarded as a thankless task—with a determination to reform the District's child welfare system, which he described as "wrought with dysfunction, chaos and tragedy." He continued to monitor D.C. childcare and in April 2004 he called on the District to shut down the Oak Hill Youth Center. He has looked after unborn children as well: he was chief sponsor of the bill, approved by the Senate 61–38 in March 2004, to make it a crime to injure or kill a fetus in the course of a violent federal crime. With Republican Gordon Smith and Democrats Christopher Dodd and Jack Reed, he sponsored a bill to provide $82 million over three years for prevention of teen suicides, with funding for screening and mental health treatment; it became law in 2004.

DeWine has often worked with Democrats on a bipartisan basis. "I've done it deliberately. Not to be too philosophical about it, but when you go to the Senate, you don't know how long you'll be there. So you want to use your time wisely." He co-sponsored a bill authorizing FDA regulation of tobacco with Edward Kennedy (it was dropped from the corporate tax bill in conference in fall 2004), a bill providing for health screening of newborns with Christopher Dodd and a bill requiring pharmaceutical companies to test drugs on children with Hillary Rodham Clinton. He and Democrat Herb Kohl have run the Antitrust Subcommittee on a bipartisan basis in both the Clinton and Bush years. In June 2003 they held hearings on media concentration that led to the congressional overturning of the FCC ruling increasing the percentage of an area's broadcast stations a single company could own. In June 2003 DeWine and Kohl called for FCC scrutiny of News Corporation's proposed takeover of DirecTV, and in September they asked for concessions before it was approved. In February 2004 they said Comcast's proposed takeover of Disney "may well pose a risk to competition in the marketplace of ideas and the diversity of news, information and entertainment available to the American public." In April 2004 the Senate passed their bill increasing the penalties for antitrust crimes, encouraging criminal prosecutions, authorizing the courts to engage in substantive review of Justice Department settlements, limiting the liability of corporations that take part in corporate leniency programs and abolishing treble damages for standard development organizations that set industry product and safety standards. In February 2003 they held hearings on gasoline prices and sponsored a bill to make oil-producing and –exporting cartels illegal. In October 2004 they sponsored a bill to authorize regulation of the sale of medical products to hospitals. In February 2005 they sponsored a bill authorizing Justice Department wiretaps of antitrust law violators.

DeWine has split from Republicans on several high visibility issues; he voted for the hate crimes bill in 2000 and 2001 and opposed oil drilling in the Arctic National Wildlife Refuge in

2002 and 2003. Although he does not serve on Foreign Relations, DeWine has taken an interest in Latin American issues. He has made many trips there—15 to Haiti and 6 to Colombia and others to Mexico, Panama, Chile and Peru. He has pushed for tougher interdiction of drugs, supports Plan Colombia and praises Colombia's President Alvaro Uribe. He has worked for more money for AIDS treatment in Haiti. DeWine serves on the Intelligence Committee and has called for more central control of intelligence.

DeWine has worked on an assortment of Ohio issues; Ohio's two senators are the only state's who have a joint office handling constituency services. He has used his seat on the Military Construction Appropriations Subcommittee to look after the interests of Wright-Patterson Air Force Base near Dayton.

DeWine came up for reelection in 2000. Democrats thought he might be vulnerable, but well-known Democrats declined to run, and DeWine spent much of late 1999 and early 2000 campaigning for John McCain in Ohio and elsewhere; he was one of only four senators who endorsed McCain (the others were Jon Kyl, Chuck Hagel and Fred Thompson). DeWine's Democratic opponent turned out to be Ted Celeste, former Ohio State Board of Trustees chairman, and brother of former Governor Richard Celeste. DeWine spent $5.7 million, much of it on television. Celeste spent $477,000, and put up one ad on the Internet which focused on prescription drug prices. DeWine won 60%–36%, the first Ohio Republican senator to be reelected since John Bricker in 1952. He won 23% of the votes of blacks and 24% of Democrats and lost union members by only 55%–44%, and non-high school graduates by 52%–43% and carried all other demographic groups. He won 83 of 88 counties, losing only the two Mahoning Valley steel counties, two eastern Ohio coal counties and usually Republican Madison County, where there was local opposition to his proposal to create a Little Darby Creek National Wildlife Refuge.

In November 2002 DeWine announced that he would run for reelection in 2006; some had thought he might run for governor, and in December 2004, in a speech in Cleveland, he sounded as if he might. "Are we heading in the wrong direction? The answer is clearly yes. ... We need to accept the fact that our economic base has eroded and that we need to pivot to a new economy and educate our work force for new jobs." But he made no move to run for governor and in mid-2005 seemed committed to the Senate race. Most well-known Ohio Democrats seemed to be concentrating on the open-seat race for governor. In the meantime, DeWine was supporting his son, Hamilton County Commissioner Pat DeWine, in his race for the 2d District House seat vacated by Trade Representative Rob Portman. In May, Mike DeWine's role in brokering a Senate compromise over judicial nominees was thought to have seriously hurt his son's campaign; Pat DeWine, once the frontrunner for the seat, finished a distant fourth.

Junior Senator

George Voinovich (R)

Elected 1998, seat up 2010, 2d term; b. July 15, 1936, Cleveland; home, Cleveland; Ohio U., B.A. 1958, Ohio St. U., J.D. 1961; Catholic; married (Janet).

Elected Office: OH House of Reps., 1966–71; Cuyahoga Cnty. Auditor, 1971–76; Cuyahoga Cnty. Commissioner, 1977–78; OH Lt. Gov., 1979; Cleveland Mayor, 1979–89; OH Gov., 1990–98.

Professional Career: OH Asst. Atty. Gen., 1963–64.

DC Office: 524 HSOB, 20510, 202-224-3353; Fax: 202-228-1382; Web site: voinovich.senate.gov.

State Offices: Cincinnati, 513-684-3265; Cleveland, 216-522-7095; Columbus, 614-469-6697; Toledo, 419-259-3895.

Committees: *Environment & Public Works*: Clean Air, Climate Change & Nuclear Safety (Chmn.); Transportation & Infrastructure. *Ethics (Select)* (Chmn.). *Foreign Relations*: European Affairs; International Economic Policy, Export & Trade Promotion; International Operations & Terrorism; Near Eastern & South Asian Affairs. *Homeland Security & Governmental Affairs*: Federal Financial Management, Govt. Information & International Security; Oversight of Govt. Management, the Federal Workforce & the District of Columbia (Chmn.).

Group Ratings

	ADA	ACLU	AFS	LCV	ITIC	NTU	COC	ACU	NTLC	CHC
2004	30	33	29	0	83	60	94	76	82	100
2003	15	—	22	11	—	69	100	83	—	—

National Journal Ratings

	2003 LIB	—	2003 CONS		2004 LIB	—	2004 CONS
Economic	33%	—	62%		38%	—	61%
Social	0%	—	59%		46%	—	53%
Foreign	32%	—	65%		42%	—	57%

Key Votes of the 108th Congress

1. Ban Drilling in ANWR	N	5. Energy Bill	Y	9. Ban Same-Sex Marriage	Y
2. Approve Bush Tax Cuts	Y	6. Support Roe v. Wade	N	10. Ban Bunker-Buster Bomb	N
3. Medicare/Rx Bill	Y	7. Ban Partial-Birth Abortion	Y	11. Fund Iraq War	Y
4. Bar Overtime Pay Regs.	N	8. Assault Weapons Ban	Y	12. Restrict Missile Defense	N

Election Results

2004 general	George Voinovich (R)	3,464,356	(64%)	($8,956,380)
	Eric Fingerhut (D)	1,961,171	(36%)	($1,166,538)
2004 primary	George Voinovich (R)	640,082	(77%)	
	John Mitchel (R)	195,476	(23%)	
1998 general	George Voinovich (R)	1,922,087	(56%)	($6,756,712)
	Mary O. Boyle (D)	1,482,054	(44%)	($2,236,137)

George Voinovich, a Republican, was elected to the Senate in 1998 after a long career in public life. He is of Serbian and Slovenian descent and grew up in heavily ethnic Cleveland. He graduated from Ohio State and its law school, then practiced law in Cleveland. He was elected to the state House in 1966, at 30. He was elected Cuyahoga County auditor in 1971 and county commissioner in 1977. In 1978 he was selected by 69-year-old Governor James Rhodes to be lieutenant governor. In 1979, after Mayor Dennis Kucinich bankrupted Cleveland, Voinovich ran for mayor. It was a strenuous campaign, running as a Republican in a heavily Democratic city, and one touched by tragedy: his daughter was killed in an auto accident at the time. In 10 years in office, he fixed the budget and sparked the city's renaissance. His one defeat came in 1988, when he lost 57%–43% to Senator Howard Metzenbaum. In 1990 Voinovich ran for governor and beat Attorney General Anthony Celebrezze Jr., 56%–44%; in 1994 he was re-elected by the spectacular margin of 72%–25%. Voinovich got the state government's fiscal house in order, with the help of a tax increase in 1992.

In February 1997 Senator John Glenn announced he would retire in 1998, and Voinovich, not eligible to run for reelection as governor, was the obvious favorite; he led in polls for nearly two years. His Democratic opponent was another Clevelander (as a boy Voinovich delivered newspapers to her family's house), Cuyahoga County Commissioner Mary Boyle, who lost the 1994 Senate primary but this time had no competition for the nomination. Boyle campaigned on education, blaming Voinovich for allowing Ohio schools to decline; she called for HMO regulation and a minimum wage increase. Voinovich mostly ignored her attacks and outspent her by almost 3–1, running ads that highlighted his record as governor. In November his margin over Boyle was a decisive but not overwhelming 56%–44%.

Voinovich came to the Senate, after 32 years in public office, as a big government Republican, willing to back tax increases as he did in 1992 but dubious about cutting them, as he was in 1999 and 2000. In his previous positions he had been required to balance budgets, and he seemed viscerally repelled by deficits. In 1999 he voted against the Republicans' $792 billion tax cut, against the smaller Democratic tax cut, and against the bipartisan moderates' compromise tax cut. In April 2000 he was one of two Republicans to vote against the Republican budget. In July 2000 he was one of four Republicans to vote against estate tax repeal and the only Republican to vote against marriage penalty relief. He did support the Bush tax cuts in May 2001, when it looked as if the surplus would be permanent. In October 2001 he worked to scale back the tax cuts in House Republicans' stimulus package. In February 2003 he came out against the $700 billion Bush tax cut and in April he and Olympia Snowe insisted they would back no cut higher than $350 billion. That led Finance Chairman Charles Grassley and Majority Leader Bill Frist to say they would insist on that figure from conference, to the rage of the House Republican leadership. When George W. Bush came to Ohio in April 2003, Voinovich was cordial but refused to budge. In 2004 Voinovich declined to back the "paygo" amendment, requiring all tax cuts and spending increases to be offset by tax increases or spending cuts elsewhere, but enough other Senate Republicans did, and the Senate and House did not agree on a budget resolution. In March 2005 he did back a paygo amendment, along with Lincoln Chafee and John McCain, but they did not have enough votes to prevail in the Senate and agreement on a budget resolution was reached. Voinovich lamented the administration's refusal to include adjustments for reducing the alternative minimum tax in the budget.

Voinovich is interested not only in maintaining government's revenue flow, but in how government works. As chairman of the Government Reform subcommittee on Government Management, Restructuring and the District of Columbia, he found that agencies could not say how much they spend on training. In October 2001 he introduced a bill that he hoped would lead to the first major change in civil service laws since 1978. It provided for chief human capital officers at each agency; hiring from a wider pool of applicants rated either basically qualified, highly qualified or superior (current practice is to choose among those rated, often arbitrarily, the top three); greater leeway for demonstration projects; allowing agencies to buy out workers for $25,000 to reshape their work forces. In June 2002 Voinovich made some changes, pursuant to comments by government employee unions and others, and got the support of subcommittee Chairman Daniel Akaka. In July 2002 Voinovich and Akaka got a version of this bill inserted as the personnel section in the homeland security bill. There it became law in December 2002. This was a major achievement: the new department has 173,000 employees and, together with Defense, which has been seeking its own civil service changes, accounts for most federal government employees. Voinovich, now subcommittee chairman again, submitted another version of his bill to cover the rest in January 2003.

As an Environment and Public Works subcommittee chairman, he steered to passage in September 2000 a giant energy and water authorization, which included the $1.1 billion Everglades restoration project estimated to eventually cost $7.8 billion. But a month later he voted against a water and power appropriation, which included many Ohio projects, arguing that it spent too much money: authorizing committee members like to keep appropriators on a short leash. In January 2003 Energy Committee Chairman Jim Inhofe asked him to manage George W. Bush's Clear Skies Initiative providing a cap-and-trade system to limit emissions of sulfur dioxide, nitrogen oxide and mercury. In June he rejected calls for carbon dioxide controls. "Regulation of carbon is not going to happen." In November 2003 Voinovich and Inhofe increased the first year mercury emissions, bringing target dates closer and providing for one-year extensions if needed to maintain a reliable supply of electricity. But this did not satisfy committee Democrats and Republican Lincoln Chafee. In March 2005 he floated a compromise, with a voluntary carbon dioxide emissions program. It was rejected in committee 9–9 because of Chafee's opposition. "Chafee thinks this is the biggest problem facing the world, and the chairman [Inhofe] has a sign in his office saying this is a hoax," Voinovich said. "There is a limited window here."

Voinovich has sometimes surprised colleagues by his stands on foreign issues. He is the only Serbian-American in the Senate, and as a college freshman wrote a paper on how the United States sold out Yugoslavia at the February 1945 Yalta conference; in 1991 his Serbian relatives were forced out of their homes in the newly independent Croatia. In March and April 1999 he strongly opposed the bombing of Serbia, but he called Slobodan Milosevic a "war criminal" and tried to convince the State Department to support forces to depose him. In July 2004 he opposed the Australian Free Trade Agreement and complained that the administration hadn't done enough to enforce trade laws and to stop China from manipulating its currency. In April 2005, after not attending earlier hearings on the subject, held up the confirmation of John Bolton as ambassador to the United Nations; in May 2005 he spoke out strongly against Bolton in committee but voted with other Republicans to send the nomination to the floor without recommendation.

Voinovich came up for reelection in 2004. In early 2003 he had $2.5 million in his campaign treasury and was getting high job ratings. In March 2003 state Senator Eric Fingerhut, who was elected to one term in the House in 1992 and defeated in 1994, announced he was running. For several months the Democrat getting the most attention was Jerry Springer, the successful host of a talk show aimed at unsuccessful people, who had a successful political career in the 1970s and 1980s as councilman and mayor in Cincinnati; at one point he resigned after it was revealed he had paid for a prostitute with a credit card, but he was later returned to office. But in August 2003, with some apparent reluctance, he took himself out of the race. That left Fingerhut as the only serious Democratic candidate. In 2004 he embarked on a hike across Ohio. But Voinovich outspent him by $9.9 million to $1.1 million and won the election 64%–36%, just shy of beating John Glenn's record percentage in a Senate race set in 1974. Voinovich carried all 88 counties. In 2005 he continued what he called his "crusade" to save Ohio families from the ravages of casino gambling.

FIRST DISTRICT

Rep. Steve Chabot (R)

Elected 1994, 6th term; b. Jan. 22, 1953, Cincinnati; home, Cincinnati; William & Mary Col., B.A. 1975, N. KY U., J.D. 1978; Catholic; married (Donna).

Elected Office: Cincinnati City Cncl., 1985–90; Hamilton Cnty. Comm., 1990–94.

Professional Career: Elem. Schl. teacher, 1975–76; Practicing atty., 1978–94.

DC Office: 129 CHOB, 20515, 202-225-2216; Fax: 202-225-3012; Web site: www.house.gov/chabot.

District Office: Cincinnati, 513-684-2723.

Committees: *International Relations* (10th of 27 R): Asia & the Pacific; Middle East & Central Asia (Vice Chmn.). *Judiciary* (7th of 23 R): Commercial & Administrative Law; Crime, Terrorism & Homeland Security; The Constitution (Chmn.). *Small Business* (4th of 18 R): Tax, Finance & Exports.

Group Ratings

	ADA	ACLU	AFS	LCV	ITIC	NTU	COC	ACU	NTLC	CHC
2004	10	0	0	18	90	78	95	96	97	92
2003	10	—	13	15	—	76	90	100	—	—

National Journal Ratings

	2003 LIB	—	2003 CONS	2004 LIB	—	2004 CONS
Economic	27%	—	71%	33%	—	65%
Social	24%	—	71%	9%	—	85%
Foreign	40%	—	58%	17%	—	78%

Key Votes of the 108th Congress

1. Drilling in ANWR	Y	5. DC School Vouchers	Y	9. Ban Same-Sex Marriage	Y
2. Approve Bush Tax Cuts	Y	6. Ban Human Cloning	Y	10. Fund Iraq War	Y
3. Medicare/Rx Bill	N	7. Restrict Gun Liability	Y	11. Bar Cuba Embargo Funds	N
4. Bar Overtime Pay Regs.	N	8. Ban Partial-Birth Abortion	Y	12. Intelligence Reorg.	Y

Election Results

2004 general	Steve Chabot (R)	173,430	(60%)	($479,225)
	Greg Harris (D)	116,235	(40%)	($86,663)
2004 primary	Steve Chabot (R)	unopposed		
2002 general	Steve Chabot (R)	110,760	(65%)	($490,317)
	Greg Harris (D)	60,168	(35%)	($23,388)

Prior Winning Percentages: 2000 (53%); 1998 (53%); 1996 (54%); 1994 (56%)

The People		Race/Ethnic Origin	Ancestry		
Area size:	420 sq. mi.	68.6% White	German: 23.6%		Irish: 9.8%
Urban population:	94.8%	27.4% Black	English: 5.4%		
Rural population:	5.2%	1.3% Asian	**2004 Presidential Vote**		
Pop. 2000:	630,730	0.2% Native Am.	Bush (R) 152,441		(51%)
Median income:	$37,414	0.0% Hawaiian	Kerry (D) 149,180		(49%)
Poverty status:	13.9%	1.2% Two+ races	**2000 Presidential Vote**		
Military veterans:	12.5%	0.2% Other	Bush (R) 136,372		(51%)
		1.1% Hispanic Origin	Gore (D) 120,927		(46%)
			Other 8,463		(3%)
			Cook Partisan Voting Index: R + 1		

Occupation	Blue collar: 23.1%	White collar: 60.5%	Gray collar: 16.5%

From its seven hills, Cincinnati, dubbed the Queen City of the West in the 19th century, looks down on the curves of the Ohio River. Ohio's first major metropolis and a heavily German beehive of riverboats and sausage factories, known in the 1850s as Porkopolis, this was the nation's fourth-largest city and a chief destination for slaves on the Underground Railroad at the outbreak of the Civil War, which has been memorialized at the new Freedom Center along the riverfront. Cincinnati has long given off an air of the recent past; Mark Twain said he'd like to be there for the apocalypse because everything in Cincinnati is 10 years behind. Growing slowly over many decades, Cincinnati has long-settled good looks and urbanity somehow consistent with its natural terrain: the bottomlands along the river, the hills and rolling terrain above. In the middle of Cincinnati is Mill Creek, lined with factories; on the hills to the west, above the restored Union Terminal with the children's, historic, and natural history museums, are the modest streetcar suburbs of the 19th century and the early years of the 20th. On Mount Adams and toward the northeast are set a string of affluent neighborhoods, with stately mansions like the William Howard Taft house, and the comfortable Tudors and colonials of the 20th century bourgeoisie—Reform Jewish as well as WASP and German. Families have lived for generations in the same neighborhoods, though typically not ethnic enclaves.

Cincinnati was the site of great innovations: the first iron suspension bridge, in 1867, connecting Cincinnati to northern Kentucky and designed by John Roebling, who later built the Brooklyn Bridge; the first baseball team, the Red Stockings, in 1869; the country's leading Reform Jewish seminary, Hebrew Union College, in 1875. Cincinnati has not had the growth spurts of cities like Cleveland or Houston; it spawned not flashy but solid industries, America's biggest concentration of machine tool makers (now a fraction of its once-robust size), plus the Procter & Gamble soap business, with its twin-towered headquarters at the edge of downtown and its Ivorydale manufacturing facility, which has made soap since the 1880s. Downtown Cincinnati's spruced-up Fountain Square shows off well-maintained skyscrapers of the past plus a revival of museums and arts institutions; its first-class restaurants still attract a dressy clientele. Old ethnic neighborhoods on the west side, crowded with brick row houses on steep hills, keep their thick local accents and special local foods, from German sauerbraten to Cincinnati chili in Price Hill and Camp Washington. Baseball's career hitting (and betting) leader Pete Rose grew up here, and many Catholic schools remain. Yet Cincinnati is not facing altogether good times. Crime has raged and there has been a flight to the suburbs; in the low-income Over-the-Rhine community (originally named because its residents crossed the canal that ran through downtown), riots broke out after a white police officer shot an unarmed young black man in 2001. The city's population declined 13% between 1990 and 2004.

The 1st Congressional District of Ohio includes almost all of Cincinnati, except for parts of its affluent eastern edge, plus most of the middle-class suburbs that cling to the woody hills west of I-71 and south of I-275. It covers the southwest quarter of Butler County plus the western parts of Hamilton County all the way to the Indiana border, including North Bend, the home of President William Henry Harrison. Ancestrally Republican, Cincinnati was a German anti-slavery island in a Southern-stock pro-Confederate sea. City elections here were for years competitive between old-line Republicans and a combination of Democrats and Charterites (the latter started by Charles Taft, liberal brother of Senator Robert Taft Sr. and great-uncle of Governor Bob Taft). But with the recent population decline Cincinnati has become noticeably more Democratic, while the suburbs, which now cast more votes than the city, remain pretty heavily Republican. This leaves the 1st a closely divided district, one which George W. Bush carried with just 51% of the vote in 2000 and 2004.

The congressman from the 1st District is Steve Chabot (pronounced *SHAB-butt*), a Republican first elected in 1994. Like so many of the local congressmen here over the decades, he grew up in Cincinnati and served on the city council; until recently, his home was around the corner from his mother's. He graduated from William and Mary, taught elementary school for a year, then graduated from Northern Kentucky law school and started a family law practice. In 1985, at 32, he was elected to the council, and in 1990 he was elected to the Hamilton County Commission. Chabot ran for Congress in odd circumstances. In 1992, first term Democrat Charles Luken (son of longtime incumbent Tom Luken) retired suddenly after the June primary; he later became mayor of Cincinnati. In the special primary to replace him, moderate Democratic Councilman David Mann defeated liberal state Senator William Bowen, by 416 votes, and won the general 51%–43%. In the House, Mann voted against the Clinton tax package and for NAFTA, which infuriated local unions; Bowen ran in the primary again in 1994 and this time Mann won by 667 votes. In the fall, Chabot backed the balanced budget amendment, strongly opposed abortion, and attacked Mann's support of Bill Clinton. Chabot won comfortably, 56%–44%.

Chabot has a generally conservative voting record in the House, but he has been a maverick willing to split from his party and willing to take political risks for principle. He voted against the Appalachian Regional Commission, a $2 million study of light rail in the Cincinnati area and a bill containing $6 million for the National Underground Railroad Freedom Center in Cincinnati; he argued that the city should solve problems with local resources and not depend on Washington. Despite a 5 a.m. phone call from George W. Bush, he was the only Ohio Republican to oppose the Medicare/prescription drug bill in November 2003.

Most of his committee work has been on Judiciary. As chairman of the Constitution Subcommittee, perennially a forum for bitter ideological debate but little legislative action, he has been a House leader for a constitutional amendment to protect the rights of crime victims. In 2003 he helped to enact the partial-birth abortion ban by specifying its policy findings and narrowing its terms in an attempt to comply with Supreme Court decisions. He pushed measures to impose restrictions on minors who cross state lines to get an abortion and to make violence against an unborn child a crime. Chabot opposed the proposed constitutional amendment by Brian Baird to permit governors to fill House vacancies in the event of a national disaster. On the International Relations Committee, he is a founder of the Taiwan Caucus and he criticized the International Court of Justice advisory opinion on the legality of the Israeli security fence.

In his first years in the House Chabot was a prime Democratic campaign target. In 1996 the AFL-CIO spent over $1 million, running nearly 2,000 television ads against him, but Chabot won 54%–43%. In 1998 Chabot was opposed by Cincinnati Mayor Roxanne Qualls. This was one of the hardest fought races in the country, and one of the most expensive. Qualls argued that Chabot's views were too conservative for the district; they disagreed on the partial-birth abortion ban and school vouchers. Chabot won 53%–47%. Redistricting made the district safer, and he won with 65% of the vote in 2002 and 60% in 2004.

SECOND DISTRICT
Vacant

Election Results

2005 special general	Jean Schmidt (R)			
	Paul Hackett (D)			
2005 special primary	Jean Schmidt (R)	14,331	(31%)	
	Bob McEwen (R)	11,663	(26%)	
	Tom Brinkman (R)	9,320	(20%)	
	Pat DeWine (R)	5,467	(12%)	
	Eric Minameyer (R)	2,113	(5%)	
	Other (R)	2,788	(6%)	
2005 special primary	Paul Hackett (D)	7,935	(57%)	
	Victoria Wells Wulsin (D)	3,800	(27%)	
	Charles Sanders (D)	1,215	(9%)	
	James John Parker (D)	663	(5%)	
	Other (D)	280	(2%)	
2004 general	Rob Portman (R)	227,102	(72%)	($559,338)
	Charles Sanders (D)	89,598	(28%)	($20,152)

The People		Race/Ethnic Origin	Ancestry	
Area size:	2,630 sq. mi.	91.7% White	German: 21.3%	Irish: 11.1%
Urban population:	73.0%	4.7% Black	USA: 8.6%	
Rural population:	27.0%	1.3% Asian	**2004 Presidential Vote**	
Pop. 2000:	630,730	0.2% Native Am.	Bush (R) 211,489	(64%)
Median income:	$46,813	0.0% Hawaiian	Kerry (D) 119,139	(36%)
Poverty status:	8.4%	0.9% Two+ races	Other 476	(0%)
Military veterans:	13.0%	0.1% Other	**2000 Presidential Vote**	
		1.0% Hispanic Origin	Bush (R) 175,382	(63%)
			Gore (D) 96,027	(34%)
			Other 8,187	(3%)
			Cook Partisan Voting Index: R +13	

Occupation   Blue collar: 23.2%   White collar: 63.7%   Gray collar: 13.1%

The most Republican major metro area in the nation over the longest time span has been Cincinnati. Back in the 1850s, when Harriet Beecher Stowe wrote *Uncle Tom's Cabin* here, Cincinnati was an island of German, pro-Union, Republican sentiment in a Southern, Democratic, pro-slavery sea. Later Cincinnati attracted fewer southern and eastern European immigrants than Great Lakes industrial cities like Cleveland, Detroit and Chicago; its ethnic character (like its physical appearance) and its political preference have remained pretty well fixed. Even many of the Appalachians here are Republicans, from Civil War Republican counties in the hills. Democratic constituencies here never got very large: economically, it was never a strong CIO town; culturally, it is home to a strong anti-pornography movement that was the site of obscenity charges filed against *Hustler* publisher Larry Flynt. The local Republican record remains intact: It was the only million-plus metro area that George H.W. Bush and Bob Dole carried by more than 50% in 1992 and 1996, and George W. Bush twice won it handily.

For 140 years after 1852, Cincinnati and surrounding Hamilton County were divided by a north-south line into two congressional districts. But by 1990 Hamilton County no longer had enough people for two full districts, and today both the Cincinnati-based districts include territory in other counties. Ohio's 2d Congressional District includes the eastern edge of Cincinnati and the boutiques of Hyde Park Square, a more transient area than the west side neighborhoods; the mostly affluent suburbs of eastern Hamilton County; and the fast-growing suburbs of Clermont County and southern Warren County. In Clermont, Miami Township has become a bedroom community and a center of commercial development along the I-275 loop. The district also includes counties farther east on the Ohio River, all the way to the old industrial city of Portsmouth and the hills of rural Pike County, the site of a former nuclear weapons facility that the Energy Department is converting to a long-term storage facility for the waste. These are very different areas. The metropolitan parts of the district, with 77% of its people, are mostly affluent and politically very Republican. The counties farther east are less well off, though there was some growth here in the 1990s. Portsmouth, however, has a depressed economy and an Appalachian frame of mind. They are close to marginal in most elections, and Pike County has an historical Democratic tradition, though Bush won each of these counties in his reelection. Overall, this is a very Republican district, 64% for Bush in 2004.

The seat from the 2d District was temporarily vacant following the April 2005 resignation of Rob Portman, a Republican who became the United States Trade Representative and a member of President Bush's Cabinet. An aide in the first Bush White House, Portman was elected in May 1993 and had been one of the most important legislators in the House, with a seat on Ways and Means and work on taxpayer rights, tax incentives for savers, and lower taxes on dividend and interest income. He turned down opportunities to seek House leadership offices, notably in 2002 when Tom DeLay and Roy Blunt moved up the ladder without opposition, but he retained his broader ambitions. So, it was not a complete surprise that he left Congress, though the USTR post previously has not opened political doors for its occupants.

The contest to replace Portman in the House almost certainly was decided by the June 14 Republican primary. The early favorite was Pat DeWine, the son of the state's senior senator. He had the highest name identification and the most lavish financing, with the help of his father plus the Cincinnati corporate establishment. But his election the previous November as Hamilton County commissioner led many to believe that he was too eager to move up the political ladder; he had three small children and recently divorced his wife after acknowledging an affair with a local business lobbyist. Another problem erupted in late May after Senator DeWine angered local conservatives by joining the bipartisan group of 14 Senators who sought middle ground over whether to end Senate filibusters of judicial nominees. The other leading contenders were former Representative Bob McEwen, who became a Washington-based lobbyist after he was defeated in 1992; state Representative Tom Brinkman; and anti-abortion activist and former state Representative Jean Schmidt, who narrowly lost a state Senate primary in 2004. The contest demonstrated the perils of negative campaigning. As DeWine's support dropped, he made a heavy ad buy against McEwen. The Club for Growth ran ads against Schmidt for her backing of tax hikes proposed by Governor Bob Taft. Conservatives ended up dividing their votes between McEwen, Brinkman and Schmidt. Benefiting from her strong base in Clermont County, Schmidt was the surprise winner with 31% to 26% for McEwen and 20% for Brinkman; DeWine was a distant fourth with 12%. Democrats nominated Iraq war veteran Paul Hackett, but the August 2 general election in this heavily Republican district was expected to be a mere formality.

THIRD DISTRICT

Rep. Mike Turner (R)

Elected 2002, 2d term; b. Jan. 11, 1960, Dayton; home, Dayton; OH N. U., B.A. 1982, Case Western Reserve U., J.D. 1985, U. of Dayton, M.B.A. 1992; Protestant; married (Lori).

Elected Office: Dayton Mayor, 1994–2001.

Professional Career: Practicing atty.

DC Office: 1740 LHOB, 20515, 202-225-6465; Fax: 202-225-6754; Web site: www.house.gov/miketurner.

District Offices: Dayton, 937-225-2843; Wilmington, 937-383-8931.

Committees: *Armed Services* (24th of 34 R): Strategic Forces; Tactical Air & Land Forces. *Government Reform* (14th of 23 R): Federalism & the Census (Chmn.); National Security, Emerging Threats & International Relations; Regulatory Affairs. *Veterans' Affairs* (13th of 16 R): Health.

Group Ratings

	ADA	ACLU	AFS	LCV	ITIC	NTU	COC	ACU	NTLC	CHC
2004	5	0	13	0	90	57	100	88	73	100
2003	5	—	0	0	—	59	100	92	—	—

National Journal Ratings

	2003 LIB	—	2003 CONS		2004 LIB	—	2004 CONS
Economic	21%	—	75%		33%	—	65%
Social	29%	—	70%		34%	—	65%
Foreign	11%	—	80%		25%	—	68%

Key Votes of the 108th Congress

1. Drilling in ANWR	Y	5. DC School Vouchers	Y	9. Ban Same-Sex Marriage	Y
2. Approve Bush Tax Cuts	Y	6. Ban Human Cloning	Y	10. Fund Iraq War	Y
3. Medicare/Rx Bill	Y	7. Restrict Gun Liability	Y	11. Bar Cuba Embargo Funds	N
4. Bar Overtime Pay Regs.	N	8. Ban Partial-Birth Abortion	Y	12. Intelligence Reorg.	Y

Election Results

2004 general	Mike Turner (R)	197,290	(62%)	($1,019,127)
	Jane Mitakides (D)	119,448	(38%)	($565,435)
2004 primary	Mike Turner (R) .... unopposed			
2002 general	Mike Turner (R)	111,630	(59%)	($1,045,016)
	Richard Carne (D)	78,307	(41%)	($567,746)

The People		Race/Ethnic Origin	Ancestry		
Area size:	1,610 sq. mi.	79.5% White	German: 17.9%	Irish: 9.1%	
Urban population:	84.7%	16.9% Black	USA: 8.5%		
Rural population:	15.3%	1.1% Asian	**2004 Presidential Vote**		
Pop. 2000:	630,730	0.2% Native Am.	Bush (R) 178,323	(54%)	
Median income:	$41,591	0.0% Hawaiian	Kerry (D) 148,978	(45%)	
Poverty status:	10.2%	1.2% Two+ races	Other 134	(0%)	
Military veterans:	14.3%	0.1% Other	**2000 Presidential Vote**		
		1.1% Hispanic Origin	Bush (R) 130,446	(52%)	
			Gore (D) 112,102	(45%)	
			Other 6,874	(3%)	
			Cook Partisan Voting Index: R + 3		
Occupation	Blue collar: 26.0%	White collar: 59.7%	Gray collar: 14.3%		

Dayton, a medium-sized city once known as the home of the typical American voter, became the name of the international peace agreement reached in November 1995 that stopped the slaughter in the former Yugoslavia. The 21 days of negotiating took place at nearby Wright-Patterson Air Force Base, and the people of Dayton played a role. "From the time we landed at the airport," wrote U.S. negotiator Richard Holbrooke, "until the time we left, we felt that we were in a community that was literally praying for us. People were lighting candles in their windows, there were signs all over the airport and on the byways. That would never have happened in New York or in Washington. And it made a tremendous impression on people."

Dayton has made a difference in people's lives in America and around the world for many years. Here, just south of the old National Road that spans the Midwest, was the home of James Ritty, who in 1879 invented the cash register—that indispensable instrument of mass retail trade—and of John Henry Patterson, who bought it from Ritty for $6,500 in 1884 and established the National Cash Register company (NCR). It was the home of a former Patterson employee, Tom Watson Sr., who feuded with him and went off to found IBM. It was in Dayton in the 1890s that Wilbur and Orville Wright, tinkering in their bicycle shop and observing the horseless carriages driven through Dayton's streets, experimented with kites and gliders and constructed the first wind tunnel in the world and the first heavier-than-air flying machine, which they took to ever-windy Kitty Hawk, North Carolina, to fly in December 1903. A few years later, Dayton's Charles Kettering invented the automatic starter for cars. In the 1970s and 1980s, Dayton's economy seemed to be sputtering. General Motors, the area's largest employer, was in trouble; NCR was taken over in a merger. But the local economy has turned around. DHL has invested

$350 million in its local hub at the Wilmington Air Park in Clinton County, which has more than 100 nightly flights. There are more scientists, engineers, computer specialists and technicians here than GM workers. The area's small manufacturers and suppliers have shown that Dayton's spirit of tinkering and innovation, practical organization and mechanical dreaming continue to thrive, as much as its neighborliness and compassion. The spiritual has its place, too: In Monroe, a 62-foot styrofoam and fiberglass sculpture of Christ welcomes parishioners at Solid Rock, a nondenominational mega-church; it is believed to be the largest such sculpture in the world. Politically, the area has been known as a bellwether since Richard Scammon and Ben Wattenberg's *The Real Majority* of 1970 profiled the Dayton housewife. Since then, the area has mostly voted for statewide and national winners, leaning a bit more Democratic than Ohio as a whole; Dayton's Montgomery County is the fourth-largest county in Ohio and politically the most evenly divided politically of its big counties.

The 3d Congressional District of Ohio includes most of Dayton and all but the northeast corner of Montgomery County. The 2002 redistricting added the northern half of fast-growing suburban Warren County to the southeast, and mostly rural and small town Clinton and Highland Counties. Those changes made the district distinctly more Republican; George W. Bush won 54% here in 2004.

The congressman from the 3d District is Mike Turner, a Republican first elected in 2002. Turner grew up in Dayton and graduated from Ohio Northern University, Case Western law school and the University of Dayton business school and became a corporate lawyer. In 1993, at age 33, he narrowly defeated a scandal-touched Democratic incumbent to win the first of two terms as mayor of Dayton. Although he narrowly lost for reelection in 2001, Ohio and national Republican leaders considered him a prime challenger in the 3d District, which had been marginal in national contests but which since 1978 had been routinely electing and reelecting Democratic Congressman Tony Hall. On January 24, 2002, Turner announced he was running for Congress, the same day the Ohio legislature passed the redistricting plan that made the district more Republican. A week later, Bush nominated Hall as ambassador to the Food and Agriculture Organization in Rome. Hall had a long and fervent interest in anti-hunger programs at home and abroad, and the Bush administration long before had been sounding him out for the job: here was a chance to appoint a liberal Democrat to a position where his strongly held views were congruent with administration policy and at the same time pick up a House seat that had long been safely Democratic.

In the Republican primary Turner had fierce opposition from newspaper publisher Roy Brown, grandson and son of Congressmen Clarence Brown and Clarence Brown Jr., who represented the neighboring 7th District from 1938 to 1982. Brown spent $1.3 million of his own money in the primary, largely on ads attacking Turner's record on taxes and crime and lambasting him as not a true conservative. Brown owned more than 50 newspapers, 10 in the 3d District; Turner contended that Brown's campaign guided his newspapers' coverage of the race. He filed a complaint with the Federal Election Commission alleging that the coverage amount to an illegal corporate contribution. The Montgomery County Republican party censured Brown as "unfit to hold public office" for allegedly misleading voters. A few days before the primary, the Ohio Election Commission ruled by a 5–2 vote that Brown violated state law with false statements in a televised ad. Voters evidently took the same view. Turner beat Brown 80%–14%; Brown spent more than $160 for each vote that he received. In Montgomery County Turner's margin was 87%–8%. NRCC chairman Tom Davis, who supported Turner in the primary, said that Brown should have sued his consultants for malpractice. The general election was comparatively sedate. The Democratic nominee was Rick Carne, Hall's chief of staff. He had little support from the national party but he raised nearly $600,000, with help from a local appearance by Dayton native Martin Sheen, President Bartlet on *West Wing*. Turner spent about the same amount. Turner won 59%–41%.

In the House, Turner's voting record placed him toward the center of his party. He got a seat on Armed Services and pledged to work to keep Wright-Pat off the base-closing list; the base did not appear on the Pentagon's May 2005 recommendation list. On Government Reform, he took over as chairman of the Federalism and the Census Subcommittee, where he held hearings on urban issues such as polluted "brownfield" sites plus planning for the 2010 Census. As chairman of Speaker Dennis Hastert's Saving America's Cities working group, Turner promoted the kind of public-private partnerships that he used for economic development in Dayton and worked with the likes of former HUD Secretary Jack Kemp, Chicago Mayor Richard M. Daley, Washington Mayor Anthony Williams and former New Orleans Mayor Marc Morial. Against a well-financed Democratic challenger in 2004, Turner was reelected 62%–38%, with a convincing 59% of the vote in Montgomery County.

FOURTH DISTRICT

Rep. Michael Oxley (R)

Elected June 1981, 12th full term; b. Feb. 11, 1944, Findlay; home, Findlay; Miami U. (OH), B.A. 1966, OH St. U., J.D. 1969; Lutheran; married (Patricia).

Elected Office: OH House of Reps., 1972–81.

Professional Career: FBI Spec. Agent, 1969–71; Practicing atty., 1972–1981.

DC Office: 2308 RHOB, 20515, 202-225-2676; Web site: oxley.house.gov.

District Offices: Findlay, 419-423-3210; Lima, 419-999-6455; Mansfield, 419-522-5757.

Committees: *Financial Services* (Chmn. of 37 R).

Group Ratings

	ADA	ACLU	AFS	LCV	ITIC	NTU	COC	ACU	NTLC	CHC
2004	0	5	0	0	100	58	100	96	81	76
2003	0	—	0	5	—	63	97	84	—	—

National Journal Ratings

	2003 LIB	—	2003 CONS		2004 LIB	—	2004 CONS
Economic	21%	—	75%		9%	—	88%
Social	36%	—	64%		36%	—	61%
Foreign	30%	—	70%		14%	—	86%

Key Votes of the 108th Congress

1. Drilling in ANWR	N	5. DC School Vouchers	Y	9. Ban Same-Sex Marriage	Y
2. Approve Bush Tax Cuts	Y	6. Ban Human Cloning	Y	10. Fund Iraq War	Y
3. Medicare/Rx Bill	Y	7. Restrict Gun Liability	Y	11. Bar Cuba Embargo Funds	N
4. Bar Overtime Pay Regs.	N	8. Ban Partial-Birth Abortion	Y	12. Intelligence Reorg.	Y

Election Results

2004 general	Michael Oxley (R)	167,807	(59%)	($1,909,844)
	Ben Konop (D)	118,538	(41%)	($178,197)
2004 primary	Michael Oxley (R)	unopposed		
2002 general	Michael Oxley (R)	120,001	(68%)	($1,140,989)
	Jim Clark (D)	57,726	(32%)	($6,916)

Prior Winning Percentages: 2000 (67%); 1998 (64%); 1996 (65%); 1994 (100%); 1992 (61%); 1990 (62%); 1988 (100%); 1986 (75%); 1984 (78%); 1982 (65%); 1981 (50%)

The People		Race/Ethnic Origin	Ancestry		
Area size:	4,642 sq. mi.	91.7% White	German: 23.4%	USA: 9.7%	
Urban population:	58.6%	5.2% Black	Irish: 8.1%		
Rural population:	41.4%	0.6% Asian	**2004 Presidential Vote**		
Pop. 2000:	630,730	0.2% Native Am.	Bush (R) 193,875	(65%)	
Median income:	$40,100	0.0% Hawaiian	Kerry (D) 102,332	(34%)	
Poverty status:	9.4%	1.0% Two+ races	Other 1,384	(0%)	
Military veterans:	14.0%	0.1% Other	**2000 Presidential Vote**		
		1.2% Hispanic Origin	Bush (R) 158,862	(62%)	
			Gore (D) 88,760	(35%)	
			Other 8,244	(3%)	
			Cook Partisan Voting Index: R +14		

Occupation	Blue collar: 37.5%	White collar: 47.1%	Gray collar: 15.5%

Central Ohio looks mostly like farmland to the traveler. Yet this is manufacturing country, indeed one of America's premier manufacturing areas, where the economy is based on factories in small towns and on rural highways. These places seem far from anywhere important, yet are on one of the great east-west routes—the old rail lines and newer highways—that cross the country. They seem old-fashioned and rooted in an older technological time, yet here is Wapakoneta, a typically Ohioan-Indian name, the hometown of Neil Armstrong, first man on the moon and home of the Neil Armstrong Air and Space Museum. A county away is Bellefontaine, site of the first concrete street in America. Politically, this crossroads on the flat limestone plains of northern Ohio is one of the Republican heartlands of the United States. On the B&O tracks from Dayton to Toledo that intersect the east-west rail lines used by Richard Nixon in 1968, Ronald Reagan in 1984, George Bush in 1992 and Bill Clinton in 1996 to make whistle-stop campaign tours, one can summon up memories of past campaign styles and loyalties.

Much of central Ohio makes up the 4th Congressional District. It includes Lima, whose name was pulled from a hat; Findlay, where a museum holds the captain's bathtub from the *U.S.S. Maine*, sunk in the Havana harbor in 1898; Marion, where young Socialist-to-be Norman Thomas delivered newspapers edited by President-to-be Warren Harding; and Mansfield, home of John Sherman, one of Ohio's great 19th century Republican statesmen, and his brother General William Tecumseh Sherman, who marched his troops through Georgia for the Union and refused to be considered for president. This has been a Republican stronghold since the Civil War, industrial since the late 19th century, quietly prosperous most of the years since World War II, though shaken by the collapse of the auto-steel-coal industries after the oil shock of 1979 and troubled by recent manufacturing job losses. George W. Bush carried the district 62%–35% in 2000 and 65%–34% in 2004; he increased his popular vote margin over four years by 21,000 in a district that has had little population growth in that time—one of the reasons he carried Ohio, and the presidency, a second time.

The congressman from the 4th District is Michael Oxley, a Republican first elected in June 1981, now chairman of the Financial Services Committee. Oxley grew up in Findlay. He graduated from Miami of Ohio and Ohio State law school, then worked three years for the FBI and returned home to practice law. He worked for his Republican congressman and in 1972, at 28, was elected to the state House. In 1981, after the incumbent died, Oxley ran for the House and won the special election during the heyday of Reagan popularity by the surprisingly narrow margin of 378 votes.

In 1983 Oxley got a seat on the Energy and Commerce Committee, which under Chairman John Dingell had a broad and expanding jurisdiction over complex regulatory issues. Although in the minority for 14 years, Oxley played a significant role in major legislation, able to unite his own Republicans and work with Democrats across the aisle. He was a major player on the 1990 Clean Air Act, working with Ohioans of both parties to protect that state's high-sulfur power plants and big factories from being saddled with high costs. He played a major role in the 1996 Telecommunications Act.

In late 1996 Oxley fought with Louisiana's Billy Tauzin for the chairmanship of the Telecommunications and Finance Subcommittee. Speaker Newt Gingrich had promised the spot to

Tauzin when he switched parties in August 1995 and Tauzin, who was first elected in May 1980, has 13 months' more seniority in the House. The solution was to split the subcommittee, whose jurisdiction was perhaps greater than that of any other in Congress. Tauzin got first choice and took Telecommunications, Trade and Consumer Protection; Oxley got Finance and Hazardous Materials. He played an important role in the landmark financial services deregulation passed in November 1999, which broke down the walls between banks, securities firms and insurance companies. Although regarded as pro-business, and although he has raised vast sums from regulated industries, Oxley has often taken stands they have vigorously opposed. He and Democrat Edward Markey pushed successfully for stock exchanges to list prices in dollars and cents rather than eighths of a dollar; their bill prompted the exchanges to do this over broker opposition.

In January 2001 Oxley became chairman of Financial Services. After September 11, he and ranking Democrat John LaFalce sponsored a money-laundering bill, to attempt to cut off money from terrorists; it was passed in October. In October and November he and Richard Baker pressed for terrorism insurance, but wanted it in the form of loans, not grants, and not on the first dollar lost—not exactly what the industry wanted. They produced a bipartisan bill out of committee, but the leadership added a provision limiting insurers' liability to lawsuits and it passed pretty much along party lines.

After the bankruptcy of Enron in December 2001, Oxley took up the issue of corporate accounting. His bill prevailed over a Democratic alternative in committee 49–12 and on the floor 334–90. It barred accounting firms hired as external auditors from doing certain consulting and inside auditing, created an accounting board within the SEC and required disclosure of off-balance-sheet deals like those at Enron. The House bill passed in April, and the Senate did not act until June, after the WorldCom collapse made the issue hot again. Senate Banking Chairman Paul Sarbanes and Republican Mike Enzi, the only accountant in the Senate, produced a bill with restrictions more stringent than Oxley's, and it passed unanimously in June. Many House Republicans, notably Tauzin, wanted the House to simply pass the Senate bill, to get on record against corporate misdeeds before the August recess. But in July Oxley persuaded Speaker Dennis Hastert to let him take the issue to conference. In the circumstances Sarbanes had the upper hand. The Senate acceded to some changes: CEOs and CFOs but not board chairmen would have to sign the certification on company reports under criminal penalties, and they could be held liable only for knowing and willful but not reckless conduct. Oxley suggested the law be called the Sarbanes Act; Sarbanes said it should be the Sarbanes-Oxley Act. George W. Bush signed it before the end of July.

Oxley, like other House Republican committee chairmen, has raised prodigious sums for other Republicans and has stayed close to the lobbying community, an essential (though not sole) source of information on complex regulatory issues. In 2003 and 2004 Oxley worked closely with the new ranking Democrat, Barney Frank, on several issues. Jointly they backed the SEC rule requiring independent board chairmen at most mutual funds. They also successfully pushed through the House in September 2004 an amendment allowing banks to use the *matricula consular* documents provided by Mexican consulates, as identification; on this Oxley was opposed by most Republicans and supported by most Democrats. On the regulation of the government-sponsored enterprises Fannie Mae and Freddie Mac, Oxley took a less stringent view than subcommittee chairman Richard Baker. He did not support the limits on investment suggested by Federal Reserve Chairman Alan Greenspan in March 2004 and in early 2005 did not support limiting Freddie's and Fannie's ability to invest in their own mortgage-based securities. Instead Oxley said, "What we need . . . is a strong, credible regulator." In March 2004 Oxley delivered to an insurance group his "road map" for federal legislation on the insurance industry, which has been regulated solely by the states under the McCarran-Ferguson Act of 1945. He opposed optional federal chartering of insurance companies, sought by life insurers and big property-casualty companies, and rejected dual state-federal regulation. Instead he called for a federal-state advisory council, with a federal official endorsing or refusing to endorse its recommendations; he strongly opposed state price controls on auto and other insurance and said there had to be ways for life insurers to get new products on the market as fast as financial institutions have been able to after passage of the 1999 financial services deregulation act.

For many years Oxley has been reelected by wide margins; in 2002 he won with 68% of the vote. In 2004 he was opposed by a 28-year-old Ben Konop, a former aide to Toledo Democrat Marcy Kaptur, who left his Washington law firm and rented an apartment near Ohio Northern University and proceeded to campaign by walking around the district. Oxley spent $1.9 million, including a $500,000 advertising campaign in the last days of the campaign and argued that he paid close attention to district matters and delivered solutions on local problems. Konop charged that he did nothing to prevent local job losses or the closing of the Lima Correctional Institution and spent too much time on national issues. Oxley was reelected by the reduced margin of 59%–41%. Konop actually carried Lima's Allen County, which hasn't voted Democratic for president since 1936. Oxley will reach the end of House Republicans' six-year term limit on committee chairmen at the end of this term, and does not seem positioned to claim the chairmanship of Energy and Commerce, which passed to Texas's Joe Barton on Tauzin's resignation in February 2004. In these circumstances he might decide to retire from the House in 2006.

FIFTH DISTRICT

Rep. Paul Gillmor (R)

Elected 1988, 9th term; b. Feb. 1, 1939, Old Fort; home, Old Fort; Ohio Wesleyan U., B.A. 1961, U. of MI, J.D. 1964; Methodist; married (Karen).

Military Career: Air Force, 1965–66.

Elected Office: OH Senate, 1966–88.

Professional Career: Practicing atty., 1965–88.

DC Office: 1203 LHOB, 20515, 202-225-6405; Fax: 202-225-1985; Web site: www.gillmor.house.gov.

District Offices: Defiance, 419-782-1996; Norwalk, 419-668-0206; Tiffin, 419-448-9016.

Committees: *Energy & Commerce* (6th of 31 R): Environment & Hazardous Materials (Chmn.); Health; Telecommunications & the Internet. *Financial Services* (13th of 37 R): Capital Markets, Insurance & Government Sponsored Enterprises; Financial Institutions & Consumer Credit.

Group Ratings

	ADA	ACLU	AFS	LCV	ITIC	NTU	COC	ACU	NTLC	CHC
2004	5	0	0	9	67	59	100	84	73	84
2003	5	—	0	15	—	57	93	76	—	—

National Journal Ratings

	2003 LIB	—	2003 CONS	2004 LIB	—	2004 CONS
Economic	29%	—	70%	35%	—	64%
Social	5%	—	87%	25%	—	73%
Foreign	23%	—	71%	25%	—	68%

Key Votes of the 108th Congress

1. Drilling in ANWR	Y	5. DC School Vouchers	Y	9. Ban Same-Sex Marriage	Y
2. Approve Bush Tax Cuts	Y	6. Ban Human Cloning	Y	10. Fund Iraq War	Y
3. Medicare/Rx Bill	Y	7. Restrict Gun Liability	Y	11. Bar Cuba Embargo Funds	N
4. Bar Overtime Pay Regs.	N	8. Ban Partial-Birth Abortion	Y	12. Intelligence Reorg.	Y

Election Results

2004 general	Paul Gillmor (R)	196,649	(67%)	($440,891)
	Robin Weirauch (D)	96,656	(33%)	($77,145)
2004 primary	Paul Gillmor (R)	unopposed		
2002 general	Paul Gillmor (R)	126,286	(67%)	($666,804)
	Roger Anderson (D)	51,872	(28%)	($21,544)
	John Green (Lib)	10,096	(5%)	

Prior Winning Percentages: 2000 (70%); 1998 (67%); 1996 (61%); 1994 (73%); 1992 (100%); 1990 (68%); 1988 (61%)

The People		Race/Ethnic Origin	Ancestry		
Area size:	6,158 sq. mi.	93.7% White	German: 29.9%	Irish: 7.5%	
Urban population:	48.9%	1.1% Black	USA: 7.3%		
Rural population:	51.1%	0.4% Asian	**2004 Presidential Vote**		
Pop. 2000:	630,730	0.2% Native Am.	Bush (R) 188,935	(61%)	
Median income:	$41,701	0.0% Hawaiian	Kerry (D) 119,308	(39%)	
Poverty status:	7.6%	0.7% Two+ races	Other 1,558	(1%)	
Military veterans:	12.8%	0.1% Other	**2000 Presidential Vote**		
		3.8% Hispanic Origin	Bush (R) 158,037	(59%)	
			Gore (D) 99,818	(37%)	
			Other 9,383	(4%)	
			Cook Partisan Voting Index: R +10		

Occupation   Blue collar: 39.8%   White collar: 46.0%   Gray collar: 14.2%

Undergirded by limestone, as flat and fertile as any place in America, northwest Ohio sits astride the land routes in parts of the country that were economically the most productive in the years they were settled. Here were the "Firelands," reserved for Connecticut Yankees whose farms were burned in the Revolution, and the neat and substantial small towns built by German Protestants in the mid-19th century. Northwest Ohio is the beginning of the great corn and hog belt that stretches through Indiana and Illinois into Iowa, and has long been a Republican heartland. Fremont, settled by abstemious Yankees, was the home of President Rutherford B. Hayes, whose wife Lucy served only lemonade in the White House; nearby Sandusky, settled by Germans who built big wineries and breweries, has its own Merry-Go-Round Museum.

This is also prime industrial country: its limestone, rail connections and location near the Great Lakes have spurred the growth of a factory economy that financially is far more important than agriculture. After the first settlement, northwest Ohio grew steadily for many decades, surging ahead in the 1950s and 1960s as its small factories supplied the big auto plants in Detroit and Ohio. Growth lagged noticeably in the 1980s, when the domestic auto industry collapsed, but returned in the 1990s as small firms sold not only to the Big Three but to foreign customers. That gave this area the highest percentage of blue-collar workers in the state.

The 5th Congressional District of Ohio sweeps across northwest Ohio, from northern Ashland County, almost within the ambit of metro Cleveland, across the limestone plains through Sandusky County and Fremont, past the university town of Bowling Green and the Toledo suburb of Perrysburg, to the towns of Defiance and Napoleon and on to the northwest corner where Ohio borders Michigan and Indiana. Its factories include the Heinz ketchup plant in Fremont—the world's largest—and the largest Whirlpool washing machine plant in Clyde, both in Sandusky County. In Seneca County is the Arm and Hammer Baking Soda plant—which is, of course, the world's largest. It does not include Toledo and the Lake Erie shoreline directly east. Historically, this has been a solidly Republican district from the Civil War through the New Deal and up through today; as part of his big push in western Ohio, George W. Bush increased his lead here from 59%–37% in 2000 to 61%–39% in 2004.

The congressman from the 5th District is Paul Gillmor, a Republican first elected in 1988. He grew up in northern Ohio, graduated from Ohio Wesleyan and Michigan law school, practiced law and was elected, at 27, to the state Senate in 1966, where he later became Senate president. For years Gillmor eyed this House seat and waited for incumbent Delbert Latta to retire; he even passed a state law blocking the party from designating Latta's son as nominee if Latta resigned. In the 1988 primary Gillmor beat the junior Latta by exactly 27 votes out of 63,000 cast. He has not been seriously challenged since then.

Gillmor has a relatively moderate voting record. He focused on internal reform in his first years in the House, working to freeze committee funding. He is comfortable with Republican moderates on cultural and foreign issues and has been both a member of the Tuesday Group and a deputy on Roy Blunt's whip team. On Energy and Commerce, he has chaired the Subcommittee on Environment and Hazardous Materials, where he sought to resolve long-deadlocked Superfund legislation, in part by giving more authority to the states. In describing his low-profile congressional career, the Cleveland *Plain Dealer* profiled Gillmor as digging into his work, unwilling to engage in publicity stunts and not especially interested in leadership politics: "a workmanlike lawmaker, chewing on unlit cigars as he pondered public policy." In 2003, he drafted a section of the energy bill that would permit greater flexibility in use of the $2 billion trust fund for cleaning up leaking underground gasoline storage tanks. Also that year he enacted the Fair and Accurate Credit Transactions (FACT) Act, requiring credit agencies to disclose when inquiries on a consumer's report are considered adversely. With Mike Ross, whose Arkansas district includes Bill Clinton's birthplace, he co-sponsored the Presidential Sites Improvement Act to maintain landmarks such as the Rutherford Hayes library. With Earl Pomeroy, he has pushed for a national data base for sex offenders; that has been a harder sell because, as he described, the Justice Department has been "lukewarm at best."

In 2002, Gillmor had a rare primary contest with term-limited state Representative Rex Damschroder, who finished third in the 1988 primary. He criticized Gillmor for living in the Columbus area and not spending enough time in the district. Gillmor defended his record with a blast of advertising, including an endorsement from Dick Cheney, and won the primary 69%–31%. Damschroder won his home base of Sandusky County 54%–46%, but he did not come close in any other county. Gillmor won easily in November 2002 and was reelected without difficulty in 2004.

SIXTH DISTRICT

Rep. Ted Strickland (D)

Elected 1996, 5th term; b. Aug. 4, 1941, Lucasville; home, Lisbon; Asbury Col., B.A. 1963, M.A., 1967, U. of KY, Ph.D. 1980; Methodist; married (Frances).

Elected Office: U.S. House of Reps., 1992–94.

Professional Career: Assoc. Minister, Trinity Methodist Church, 1967–68; Dir. of Soc. Svcs., KY Methodist Home, 1968–70; Consulting psychologist, Southern OH Correctional Facility, 1985–92, 1995–96; Prof., Shawnee St. U., 1988–92, 1995–96.

DC Office: 336 CHOB, 20515, 202-225-5705; Fax: 202-225-5907; Web site: www.house.gov/strickland.

District Offices: Boardman, 330-965-4220; Marrieta, 740-376-0868; Martins Ferry, 740-633-2275; Wheelersburg, 740-574-2676.

Committees: *Energy & Commerce* (15th of 26 D): Commerce, Trade & Consumer Protection; Energy & Air Quality; Health. *Veterans' Affairs* (8th of 12 D): Oversight & Investigations (RMM).

Group Ratings

	ADA	ACLU	AFS	LCV	ITIC	NTU	COC	ACU	NTLC	CHC
2004	95	75	100	100	10	14	38	8	3	23
2003	95	—	100	85	—	25	33	24	—	—

National Journal Ratings

	2003 LIB	—	2003 CONS		2004 LIB	—	2004 CONS
Economic	65%	—	34%		75%	—	24%
Social	66%	—	34%		70%	—	29%
Foreign	81%	—	17%		85%	—	15%

Key Votes of the 108th Congress

1. Drilling in ANWR	N	5. DC School Vouchers	N	9. Ban Same-Sex Marriage	N
2. Approve Bush Tax Cuts	N	6. Ban Human Cloning	N	10. Fund Iraq War	N
3. Medicare/Rx Bill	N	7. Restrict Gun Liability	Y	11. Bar Cuba Embargo Funds	Y
4. Bar Overtime Pay Regs.	Y	8. Ban Partial-Birth Abortion	Y	12. Intelligence Reorg.	N

Election Results

2004 general	Ted Strickland (D) .... unopposed		($215,879)
2004 primary	Ted Strickland (D) 73,405	(83%)	
	Diane DiCarlo Murphy (D) 15,054	(17%)	
2002 general	Ted Strickland (D) 113,972	(59%)	($862,112)
	Mike Halleck (R) 77,643	(41%)	($180,074)

Prior Winning Percentages: 2000 (58%); 1998 (57%); 1996 (51%); 1992 (51%)

The People		Race/Ethnic Origin	Ancestry	
Area size:	5,236 sq. mi.	95.2% White	German: 15.2% Irish: 9.9%	
Urban population:	50.0%	2.4% Black	USA: 8.4%	
Rural population:	50.0%	0.5% Asian	**2004 Presidential Vote**	
Pop. 2000:	630,730	0.2% Native Am.	Bush (R) 153,983	(51%)
Median income:	$32,888	0.0% Hawaiian	Kerry (D) 149,080	(49%)
Poverty status:	14.0%	0.8% Two+ races	Other 938	(0%)
Military veterans:	14.5%	0.1% Other	**2000 Presidential Vote**	
		0.8% Hispanic Origin	Bush (R) 129,689	(49%)
			Gore (D) 125,292	(47%)
			Other 11,969	(4%)
			Cook Partisan Voting Index: D + 0	

Occupation   Blue collar: 31.3%   White collar: 51.7%   Gray collar: 17.0%

In the years after the American Revolution, the Ohio River was one of the great highways west. From Pittsburgh, where the Allegheny and Monongahela meet and form the Ohio, the river led south and west toward the Mississippi and the great port of New Orleans. Shipping goods downriver by raft was cheaper than sending them over the Appalachian chains, and so the Ohio became a great highway of commerce. For hundreds of miles, the Ohio twisted this way and that through rounded-off mountains and rolling hills, land that marked the boundary between post-Revolutionary Virginia and the Northwest Territory, between slaveholding territory and soil that the Confederation Congress decided in 1787 should be free. Across this boundary settlers made their way in those years—Yankees in 1788 to Marietta, Ohio's first town, and, in larger numbers, Virginians from those parts of Virginia that became Kentucky in 1792 and West Virginia in 1863. By the late 19th century the Ohio was an industrial river; coal was nearby, barge transportation was available and railroads were built in the narrow valleys between the hills, steel mills went up on the riverfront. This produced prosperity for a while, but it also produced pollution—Steubenville on the Ohio River once had the nation's dirtiest air—and after the old-line steel industry fell on hard times, the Ohio River was lined with some of the least prosperous parts of America. Even with mandates from the Clean Air Act, the pollution in much of this area from coal-fired power plants remains so bad that many residents have considered moving. In 2002 American Electric Power paid $20 million to buy out the village of Cheshire in Gallia County, and it mostly vanished.

The 6th Congressional District of Ohio is made up of a string of counties running 325 miles along the Ohio River plus part of the Mahoning Valley, named after a narrow tributary of the Ohio. In the north it includes the Youngstown suburbs of Boardman, Canfield and part of Poland in Mahoning County, and East Liverpool and Steubenville on the Ohio. It curves along the lightly populated stretch of the river south from Marietta, the old industrial town of Ironton and it extends to the city limits of Portsmouth, not quite in the Cincinnati metropolitan area, where the Scioto River empties into the Ohio. Much of this area is part of poverty-ridden Appalachia. Historically, the northern part of the district was Republican and the southern part Democratic, but that was a long time ago. The steel and coal areas in the north became Democratic during the 1930s and the southern counties started trending Republican in the 1960s. This district was designed by incumbent-protection-minded redistricters to reelect a Democratic congressman, but the cultural conservatism of this region, much like that of West Virginia and eastern Kentucky across the river, put it narrowly in George W. Bush's column, by 49%–47% in 2000 and 51%–49% in 2004.

The congressman from the 6th District is Ted Strickland, a Democrat first elected to the House in 1992. He grew up in Lucasville, just north of Portsmouth, site of a state prison; he was the son of a steelworker and eighth of nine children. He graduated from Asbury College and got a Ph.D. from the University of Kentucky. He was a Methodist minister, director of a children's home and then a prison psychologist and psychology professor at Shawnee State College. He and his wife both made their way up as counseling professionals. He ran for the House unsuccessfully in 1976, 1978 and 1980, and then ran again in 1992 when redistricting placed two Republican incumbents in the district. One lost in the primary 50.2%–49.8% and Strickland defeated the other 51%–49%. In his first term Strickland voted for the Clinton budget and tax package, but against the 1994 crime bill because of its gun control provisions and against NAFTA. As the 1994 election neared, Strickland suggested there might be a need for tax increases to pay for health care programs; Republican challenger Frank Cremeans seized on this and won 51%–49%. In a 1996 rematch, Strickland attacked Cremeans for Medicare "cuts" and scaling down the Earned Income Tax Credit, which he called a tax increase on the poor. Strickland won 51%–49%.

Back on Capitol Hill, Strickland's voting record has been generally moderate but a bit more liberal on foreign policy. He voted against the authorization of force in Iraq. He got a seat on the Energy and Commerce Committee; he complained in 2001 when the Nuclear Regulatory Commission failed to challenge the closing of the USEC uranium enrichment plant in Piketon, which eliminated more than 1,700 local jobs and left the nation only one other such facility, in Paducah, Kentucky. In the energy bill that year, he won a provision—opposed by the Bush administration—to authorize the Energy Department to spend $170 million to keep the plant on standby. In response the Clean Air Trust subsequently named Strickland its "villain of the month." In February 2003, he was one of seven House members who voted against a bill to restrict residential calls by telemarketers; his district has at least three call centers. Later, as a disincentive to outsourcing, he introduced a bill to require that workers in a call center identify their location during the telephone call. With Senator Mike DeWine, he enacted a bill in 2004 to give $100 million to states and localities to treat mentally ill people who have been arrested or sent to prison.

In 1998, Strickland faced Lieutenant Governor Nancy Hollister and won by what was then the huge (for this district) margin of 57%–43%—the first time a 6th District incumbent was reelected since 1990. In 2001 Ohio Republicans had control of redistricting, and Strickland threatened to run against Republican Bob Ney in the neighboring 18th District if his own district was eliminated. The result was this skinny riverfront district, at one end of which was Strickland's home in Lucasville and at the other the home in Poland of incumbent Democrat Jim Traficant, then under indictment for bribery. But Traficant in 2002 chose to run as an Independent in the new 17th District; he was convicted in court and defeated in the election. Strickland was elected easily, even though 59% of the voters were new to him. In 2004, he had no Republican opponent.

After the 2004 election, Strickland was mentioned as a possible candidate for governor or senator; in January he appeared to rule out a run for governor. But in May, after Columbus Mayor Michael Coleman, the leading Democratic candidate, seemed to falter, Strickland changed his mind and said he would run for governor. His decision makes it likely there will be a highly competitive contest for this seat in 2006.

SEVENTH DISTRICT

Rep. David Hobson (R)

Elected 1990, 8th term; b. Oct. 17, 1936, Cincinnati; home, Springfield; OH Wesleyan U., B.A. 1958, OH St. U., J.D. 1963; Methodist; married (Carolyn).

Military Career: OH Air Natl. Guard, 1958–63.

Elected Office: OH Senate, 1982–90, Majority Whip, 1986–88, Pres. Pro-Tem, 1988–90.

Professional Career: Real estate agent, 1969–90; Restaurant owner, 1977–93.

DC Office: 2346 RHOB, 20515, 202-225-4324; Fax: 202-225-1984; Web site: www.house.gov/hobson.

District Offices: Lancaster, 740-654-5149; Springfield, 937-325-0474.

Committees: *Appropriations* (9th of 37 R): Defense; Energy & Water Development & Related Agencies (Chmn.).

Group Ratings

	ADA	ACLU	AFS	LCV	ITIC	NTU	COC	ACU	NTLC	CHC
2004	5	5	13	9	90	49	100	88	68	76
2003	5	—	0	0	—	59	100	92	—	—

National Journal Ratings

	2003 LIB	—	2003 CONS		2004 LIB	—	2004 CONS
Economic	21%	—	75%		17%	—	80%
Social	37%	—	61%		42%	—	57%
Foreign	38%	—	60%		32%	—	67%

Key Votes of the 108th Congress

1. Drilling in ANWR	Y	5. DC School Vouchers	Y	9. Ban Same-Sex Marriage	N
2. Approve Bush Tax Cuts	Y	6. Ban Human Cloning	Y	10. Fund Iraq War	Y
3. Medicare/Rx Bill	Y	7. Restrict Gun Liability	Y	11. Bar Cuba Embargo Funds	N
4. Bar Overtime Pay Regs.	N	8. Ban Partial-Birth Abortion	Y	12. Intelligence Reorg.	Y

Election Results

2004 general	David Hobson (R)	186,534	(65%)	($1,049,259)
	Kara Anastasio (D)	100,617	(35%)	($25,807)
2004 primary	David Hobson (R)	unopposed		
2002 general	David Hobson (R)	113,252	(68%)	($730,531)
	Kara Anastasio (D)	45,568	(27%)	($14,707)
	Frank Doden (I)	8,812	(5%)	($4,475)

Prior Winning Percentages: 2000 (68%); 1998 (67%); 1996 (68%); 1994 (100%); 1992 (71%); 1990 (62%)

The People		Race/Ethnic Origin	Ancestry	
Area size:	2,866 sq. mi.	88.7% White	German: 17.6%	USA: 10.1%
Urban population:	71.3%	7.5% Black	Irish: 9.3%	
Rural population:	28.7%	1.0% Asian	**2004 Presidential Vote**	
Pop. 2000:	630,730	0.3% Native Am.	Bush (R) 176,365	(57%)
Median income:	$43,248	0.0% Hawaiian	Kerry (D) 132,124	(43%)
Poverty status:	8.8%	1.3% Two+ races	Other 1,306	(0%)
Military veterans:	15.3%	0.1% Other	**2000 Presidential Vote**	
		1.1% Hispanic Origin	Bush (R) 137,548	(55%)
			Gore (D) 102,846	(41%)
			Other 7,644	(3%)
			Cook Partisan Voting Index: R + 6	

Occupation Blue collar: 28.1% White collar: 57.1% Gray collar: 14.8%

The hills and plains of central Ohio are dotted with towns and small cities that have been manufacturing centers almost since they were settled in the early 19th century, when the dominant technologies were the waterwheel and the open forge. In the decades since, they have been replaced by one new technology after another—the automobile and the airplane—and the local manufacturing economy, sometimes with uncomfortable fits and starts, has adjusted and advanced. This has been the story of Springfield, oft studied as a typical American city. In the early 1980s, International Harvester, the city's largest employer, went bankrupt, downsized dramatically and was renamed Navistar. In 1996, the company cut 3,000 jobs from its Springfield plant, and after more cuts, the workforce was pared down to 2,800 in 2000, though it remained Clark County's largest employer. More recently, there have been smaller job losses at other manufacturing facilities, as the Vining Broom plant was moved out of town. But amid these highly publicized and visible examples of capitalism's creative destruction there have been less noticed examples of its creativity. Small manufacturing businesses have grown up in empty factory space, diesel-electric hybrid truck engines are being produced in the old Navistar plant and service employment has grown. Politically Springfield and Clark County became quite a battleground in the 2004 election. Al Gore carried the county in 2000, and Democrats hoped that local job losses would increase their margin. So did the editors of the British left-wing newspaper the *Guardian*, which obtained the addresses of 14,000 Clark County voters and urged its readers to write personal letters to them urging them to throw out the iniquitous George W. Bush. But the letters aroused fierce resentment, and while Democrats concentrated their turnout efforts on Springfield's black precincts, Bush campaign volunteers scoured the whole county and turned a 324-vote Gore plurality into a 1,406-vote Bush majority.

The 7th Congressional District of Ohio is made up of a portion of south central part of Ohio, southwest, south and southeast of Columbus. It includes Springfield and Clark County and, just to the south, the Greene County suburbs of Dayton around Wright-Patterson Air Force Base, whose name recalls the fathers of the airplane and the cash register, both from Dayton. The other population centers are in Fairfield County, southeast of Columbus, and a southeastern part of Columbus's Franklin County, added in the 2002 redistricting, including part of the east side of Columbus, Whitehall, Blacklick Estates, Canal Winchester and Lockbourne. The district has always been Republican territory. It backed the policies of Ohio Republican President William McKinley—tariff protection, railroad regulation, antitrust suits against monopolies, discouragement of labor unions—and of Governor James Rhodes—low taxes, promotion of new businesses and jobs. It is culturally conservative and economically mostly satisfied with free markets. It has given good margins to recent Republican presidential contenders.

The congressman from the 7th District is Dave Hobson, a Republican first elected in 1990. He grew up in Springfield, graduated from Ohio Wesleyan and Ohio State law school and worked in commercial real estate in Springfield. In 1982 he was elected to the state Senate and in 1990, when Congressman Mike DeWine ran for lieutenant governor, he was elected to the House. He is a practical-minded politician who in his second term got a seat on Appropriations and has a moderate to conservative voting record. Hobson's steady demeanor and backroom skills continue to make him a resource for House Republican leaders; he worked on health issues with Dennis Hastert long before he became Speaker. But Hobson does not seek the spotlight on Capitol Hill: When leadership meetings break up and many head for the ever-present microphones and television cameras, Hobson typically passes them by. For the most part he has supported the Republican leadership. But not always; in November 2003 he threatened to vote against the Medicare/prescription drug bill because it allowed competitive bidding for home health care equipment. "I have tried to be a team player. I am a team player. But there comes a time when you've got to do what you've got to do." He is loyal to his neighbors: in November 2004 he filed an ethics complaint against Jim McDermott based on an October 2004 court judgment requiring McDermott to pay Ohio Republican John Boehner $60,000 and attorney's fees.

In 1999 Hobson became chairman of the Military Construction Appropriations Subcommittee, a body that usually does its legislating on a bipartisan basis and with due regard to members' local concerns. He said that his top priority was to ensure that military families have the quality housing and secure work facilities they deserve. He has traveled indefatigably to inspect military facilities, not just to Germany and Italy, but Korea and to Bosnia and Kosovo over Thanksgiving. He has looked after the interests of Wright-Pat. When its 445th Airlift Wing's C-141s were about to be phased out, he met with Air Force Chief of Staff John Jumper in May 2002 and got assurances that they would be assigned C-5As (although he would have preferred the newer C-17) and that if they didn't work out another mission would be found. The 2002 redistricting added Defense Supply Center Columbus and Rickenbacker Air National Guard Base in Franklin County to the district, but Hobson, who served there after college, was already working for a $10 million Reserve unit facility and a $6 million fire station for Rickenbacker.

In January 2003 Hobson became chairman of the Energy and Water Appropriations Subcommittee. There he worked on projects for his district and those of many other members, and he also set national policy. He pressed for funding the Yucca Mountain nuclear waste repository, and in 2003 his bill provided $765 million for it, $174 million than the Bush administration requested. In conference he was sharply opposed by Nevada's Harry Reid, ranking member of the Senate subcommittee and a strong opponent of Yucca Mountain. Still Hobson ended up with $580 million, $155 million more than the Senate bill. He also worked to slow down development of new nuclear weapons. "We have too much of a Cold War arsenal." In 2003 he scaled back spending on the bunker buster weapon from $15 million to $5 million and settled for $7.5 million in conference; in 2004 he scaled it back from $15 million to $5 million and, in May 2005, zeroed out funds for the bunker buster. He said the development of the bunker buster and other weapons were "very provocative and overly aggressive policies that undermine our moral authority to argue that other nations should forgo nuclear weapons." Once again he went up against a powerful adversary in the Senate, appropriator Pete Domenici, who was enraged when Hobson cut funding for the Sandia and Los Alamos Laboratories in New Mexico.

Hobson has worked to make eight counties in southwest Ohio a national aviation heritage area. He has obtained $21.5 million for expansion of the Rickenbacker Intermodal Facility, $500,000 for a conference center at Ohio University's Lancaster campus, and $4.3 million to lengthen Wright-Pat runways so they can accommodate C-5s.

Hobson was irritated by the 2002 redistricting, which stretched the district west to include Perry County, home of Ohio House Speaker Larry Householder; Hobson reportedly thought that would make it harder for state Senator Steve Austria of Greene County to succeed him. In the general election Hobson won only 53% in the new parts of the district, Perry and Franklin Counties. But he won 70% in the rest, for a 68%–27% victory. In 2004, as George W. Bush carried the district 57%–43%, Hobson won 65%–35%.

EIGHTH DISTRICT

Rep. John Boehner (R)

Elected 1990, 8th term; b. Nov. 17, 1949, Cincinnati; home, West Chester; Xavier U., B.S. 1977; Catholic; married (Debbie).

Military Career: Navy, 1969.

Elected Office: Union Township Bd. of Trustees, 1981–85, Pres., 1984; OH House of Reps., 1984–90.

Professional Career: Pres., Nucite Sales Inc., 1976–90.

DC Office: 1011 LHOB, 20515, 202-225-6205; Fax: 202-225-0704; Web site: www.johnboehner.house.gov.

District Offices: Troy, 937-339-1524; West Chester, 513-779-5400.

Committees: *Agriculture* (Vice Chmn. of 25 R): General Farm Commodities & Risk Management; Livestock & Horticulture. *Education & the Workforce* (Chmn. of 27 R): 21st Century Competitiveness; Employer-Employee Relations.

Group Ratings

	ADA	ACLU	AFS	LCV	ITIC	NTU	COC	ACU	NTLC	CHC
2004	0	0	0	0	100	70	100	100	83	91
2003	5	—	0	5	—	63	100	88	—	—

National Journal Ratings

	2003 LIB	—	2003 CONS	2004 LIB	—	2004 CONS
Economic	0%	—	91%	8%	—	92%
Social	17%	—	79%	33%	—	66%
Foreign	11%	—	80%	0%	—	96%

Key Votes of the 108th Congress

1. Drilling in ANWR	Y	5. DC School Vouchers	Y	9. Ban Same-Sex Marriage	Y
2. Approve Bush Tax Cuts	*	6. Ban Human Cloning	Y	10. Fund Iraq War	Y
3. Medicare/Rx Bill	Y	7. Restrict Gun Liability	Y	11. Bar Cuba Embargo Funds	N
4. Bar Overtime Pay Regs.	N	8. Ban Partial-Birth Abortion	Y	12. Intelligence Reorg.	Y

Election Results

2004 general	John Boehner (R)	201,675	(69%)	($1,407,907)
	Jeff Hardenbrook (D)	90,574	(31%)	($41,184)
2004 primary	John Boehner (R)	unopposed		
2002 general	John Boehner (R)	119,947	(71%)	($1,226,866)
	Jeff Hardenbrook (D)	49,444	(29%)	($18,186)

Prior Winning Percentages: 2000 (71%); 1998 (71%); 1996 (70%); 1994 (100%); 1992 (74%); 1990 (61%)

The People		Race/Ethnic Origin	Ancestry	
Area size:	2,031 sq. mi.	91.8% White	German: 22.0% USA: 9.8%	
Urban population:	78.1%	4.4% Black	Irish: 8.9%	
Rural population:	21.9%	1.2% Asian	**2004 Presidential Vote**	
Pop. 2000:	630,730	0.2% Native Am.	Bush (R)	199,265 (64%)
Median income:	$43,753	0.0% Hawaiian	Kerry (D)	109,374 (35%)
Poverty status:	8.8%	1.1% Two+ races	Other	439 (0%)
Military veterans:	13.8%	0.1% Other	**2000 Presidential Vote**	
		1.3% Hispanic Origin	Bush (R)	155,132 (61%)
			Gore (D)	91,744 (36%)
			Other	7,371 (3%)
			Cook Partisan Voting Index: R +12	
Occupation	Blue collar: 29.9%	White collar: 56.0%	Gray collar: 14.0%	

The far west end of Ohio—where U.S. 40, the old National Road, heads straight as an arrow in its last miles across Ohio to Indiana, and the rail lines crisscross the land from Cincinnati to Dayton—has since the early 20th century housed some of the nation's prime industrial country. Here the Great and Little Miami rivers drain south into the Ohio; U.S. 40 jogs southward twice to go over the Miami and Stillwater River dams, built after the great flood of 1913 that killed 361 people in Dayton and caused $1 billion in damage. Around Dayton and Cincinnati, in large factory towns like Middletown and Hamilton and smaller factory towns like Troy and Piqua, Ohioans, after the recession of the early 1980s, adapted to new conditions and began to produce exports to Europe, Latin America and Asia as well as for the American market. At the same time people leaving the central cities of Dayton and Cincinnati moved into new subdivisions amid new shopping malls and office parks in Butler County, between those two cities. Hamilton, the Butler County seat founded in 1791 and named after the Treasury Secretary then, lost jobs when International Paper shut down a plant, but many more were created all around it. Hamilton has tried to rally; in the 1950s it refused to let I-75 through town, but recently it got the state to build Route 129 to link it with I-75 and the growth it has brought.

The 8th Congressional District of Ohio covers much of this territory. It includes all of Butler County (except four lightly populated townships), two counties to the north on the Indiana line and part of a third. It also includes Miami County north of Dayton and, added in redistricting in 2002, the northeastern corner of Montgomery County, including part of Dayton, all of Huber Heights and part of Wright-Patterson Air Force Base. Politically, this is very Republican territory; the district voted 61% for George W. Bush in 2000 and 64% in 2004. In September 2004 Bush appeared at a rally here that attracted 50,000 people; some called it the largest political rally in Ohio history.

The congressman from the 8th District is John Boehner (pronounced *BAY-ner*), a Republican first elected in 1990 and now chairman of the Committee on Education and the Workforce. Boehner grew up in Cincinnati, one of 12 children, and graduated from Xavier University, the only college graduate in his family. He moved to Butler County and started a plastics packaging company, served on the Union Township Board of Trustees, and in 1984, at 34, was elected to the Ohio House. He won the congressional seat in the 1990 primary, by beating not one but two of his predecessors—incumbent Buz Lukens, who inexplicably ran after he was convicted of having sex with a 16-year-old girl, and Tom Kindness, who gave up the seat to run against Senator John Glenn in 1986 and then, as Boehner put it, deserted the district to become a Washington lobbyist. Boehner won 49%, to 32% for Kindness and 17% for Lukens. Boehner has since been reelected without difficulty.

In the House, Boehner joined the Gang of Seven, young freshman Republicans who insisted on revealing the names of all 355 members who had overdrafts at the House bank, and then went on to assail Democratic leaders and Republican go-alongers on the pay raise and the House Post Office scandal. Boehner's Gang of Seven infuriated House veterans, but they struck a chord around the nation. In the process Boehner became a top lieutenant of Minority Whip Newt Gingrich, raising money for Republican candidates and managing Gingrich's campaign for Republican leader. He was a major player in drafting and championing the 10-point Contract With America. After the 1994 election, he ran for chairman of the Republican Conference and, with Gingrich's backing, beat California's Duncan Hunter 122–102.

That made Boehner number four in the Republican leadership, and he worked hard to prepare the party message and to enforce discipline on issues from repealing the assault weapons ban to fielding ethics charges against Gingrich. Boehner also pushed for the Freedom to Farm bill in 1996, which purported to phase out most subsidies. But starting in 1998 Congress started voting disaster relief for farmers; Boehner led the fight against the House's 2002 farm bill, which restored subsidies.

The Gingrich years were a turbulent time for Boehner. The ethics investigation on Gingrich placed Boehner in the middle of a legal altercation after a Florida couple taped Boehner's cell phone conversation with Republican leaders while he was driving through the state. The couple, Democratic activists, presented the tape to their congresswoman, Karen Thurman, who suggested they turn it over to Jim McDermott of Washington, senior Democrat on the House ethics committee, who then made the contents available to *The New York Times*. In 1998 Boehner sued McDermott in federal court for invasion of privacy; the trial judge ruled that the suit would infringe First Amendment rights, but the D.C. Circuit Court of Appeals reversed the decision. McDermott appealed to the Supreme Court, which decided another case instead and sent this one back to the D.C. Circuit, which sent it to District Court. McDermott attempted to settle the case, but the two could not agree on terms. In October 2004 the judge ruled that McDermott must pay Boehner $60,000 plus attorney's fees; the next month the 7th District's Dave Hobson filed an ethics committee complaint against McDermott.

After Republicans lost five seats in the 1998 election, Boehner was challenged for the conference chairmanship by J.C. Watts. Some Republicans believed that Boehner had been part of the July 1997 coup against Newt Gingrich, and Boehner's fate was probably sealed when Dick Armey held the majority leadership even though he had misled members about his role in the coup. Someone had to go, and it was Boehner, who lost 121–93. After such a loss many members withdraw from legislative work. But Boehner plunged into action as chairman of the Employer-Employee Relations Subcommittee. By June 1999 the subcommittee passed eight bills restructuring managed care and health insurance; Speaker Dennis Hastert, pleased by Boehner's initiative and dismayed that other committees had not acted, adopted these as the Republican health care agenda.

After the 2000 election Boehner sought the chairmanship of the Education and the Workforce Committee. Incumbent William Goodling was retiring; also seeking the job were second ranking Republican Tom Petri and the less senior Pete Hoekstra. Boehner got Armey's support and Hastert told him, "If I were you, I'd go ahead." He helped Ralph Regula oust Bud Shuster from his post on the Steering Committee, which in turn chose him. Boehner, like many others, had long considered the committee a "partisan pit." Since 1960 Democrats had assigned only union loyalists to the committee and most Republican members took stands on employment issues opposed by industrial unions and stands on education opposed by teachers' unions. The basic education bill was up for reauthorization in 1999, but the committee was unable to produce a bill. Boehner knew that that would be the committee's first order of business and that George W. Bush's education proposals were one of his top priorities. So he tried to encourage a sense of bipartisanship. When Bush aides failed to invite the committee's ranking Democrat, George Miller, to a December 21 meeting in Austin on education, Boehner got him on the guest list and Senator Judd Gregg switched place cards at the lunch tables so that Miller sat next to Bush. In the past committee Democrats had concentrated on pumping more money into schools and opposing anything the unions disliked. But Miller had been teaching school dropouts and believed that current programs weren't teaching disadvantaged children what they should, and he became convinced that Bush and Boehner shared his concern.

So Boehner and Miller worked together on the House bill. Boehner knew he could not pass it with Republicans alone, because some were opposed to nationally required tests, a central feature of Bush's program. Committee Republicans wanted to push their Straight A's concept, replacing categorical programs with block grants. Miller said this would be anathema to committee Democrats, and Boehner agreed to drop it. Instead he backed a provision by Democrat Tim Roemer to give school districts more flexibility. Jim DeMint offered Straight A's as an amendment, but Bush talked him out of it; he had gotten Edward Kennedy to agree to greater flexibility in funding in the Senate version and didn't want to drive away Democrats in the House. The bill did include Bush's principles of annual testing and accountability. It passed committee with six Republicans and one Democrat opposed and passed on the floor 384–45 in May 2001. The Democratic takeover of the Senate in June actually helped the bill's chances. Jim Jeffords as committee chairman was fixated on getting huge funding increases for special education and had to be worked around, while Kennedy, the new chairman, was committed to compromise and accepted amendments that gave school districts flexibility and provided, in place of vouchers, private tutoring for disadvantaged students in failing schools.

Negotiations continued during summer and fall between Boehner, Miller, Kennedy and ranking Senate Republican Judd Gregg. Annual testing for grades 3–8 stayed in, but tests other than the NAEP were allowed. Some flexibility stayed in: except for Title I funds, districts could reallocate 50% of funding to suit their needs, and seven states and 150 school districts would get demonstration projects with more flexibility. The number of education programs was reduced from 55 to 45, as opposed to 70 in the Senate bill. The final agreements came in November, and in December the House passed the bill 381–41, with most of the nays from Republicans, and the Senate 87–10. Bush came to Hamilton High School to sign the bill in January 2002. After working on the bill, Boehner seemed to be increasingly concerned about children in central city schools. In May 2004 he shocked an audience of Dayton city leaders when he said, "I don't see the commitment in the Dayton area to fixing the Dayton public schools. Giving those kids on the West Side a chance is the right thing to do."

In 2003 and 2004 Boehner worked on reauthorization of IDEA, the special education act. This again was a bipartisan undertaking. Teacher's unions were seeking a relaxation of IDEA's requirement that administrators take special ed students' disabilities into account when disciplining them and that Individualized Education Programs be submitted annually for each special ed student. The House version, passed 251–171 in April 2003, relaxed the discipline requirement; the Senate version, passed 95–3 in May 2004, didn't. The differences were ironed out in conference committee after the November 2004 election. The final bill retained the requirement that disabilities be taken into account on discipline, provided stronger certification requirements and provided for withholding of state funds if local districts fail to comply with the act. Waivers were authorized for 15 states on paperwork requirements and on allowing Individualized Education Programs to be required every three years rather than every year. To complaints that Congress has funded only 19% of special ed costs, rather than the 40% authorized by the first IDEA in 1975, Boehner agreed to discretionary targets to increase the percentage up through 2011.

Another issue covered by the committee is pensions. In October 2003 Boehner steered to passage by 397–2 a bill requiring employers to use a blend of corporate bond rates when calculating payments funding their pension plans. As bankrupt airlines handed over their pension obligations to the Pension Benefit Guaranty Corporation, Boehner in January 2005 said, "We have a huge pension underfunding problem," and called for bipartisan action. But when the AFL-CIO encouraged unions to keep pension funds away from financial service firms that backed the Bush Social Security changes, Boehner charged the unions would be making illegal investment decisions based on politics. On student loans, Boehner has backed the status quo in which government direct loans compete with private lenders. In October 2004 he got the House to pass unanimously a bill to end the guaranteed return of 9.5% to private lenders, though not retroactively as some Democrats wanted; it also provided for $17,500 in loan forgiveness for math, science and special ed teachers. In early 2005 Boehner set out to reauthorize the Higher Education Act, on a budget-neutral basis. But he and Miller showed little interest in George W. Bush's proposal to extend the No Child Left Behind approach to high schools.

The addition of part of Montgomery County to the district required some political adjustment; Boehner carried the area with only 56% of the vote in 2002 while winning districtwide with 71%. In 2004 he was reelected 69%–31%, with 54% in Montgomery County. He lost some campaign money along the way: his campaign treasurer pleaded guilty in October 2003 to embezzling $618,000 because of a gambling habit. When Tom DeLay was under attack for supposed ethics violations in early 2005 and some supposed that he might step down as majority leader, there was talk that Boehner might fill that position. But for the moment he remained a busy committee chairman.

NINTH DISTRICT

Rep. Marcy Kaptur (D)

Elected 1982, 12th term; b. June 17, 1946, Toledo; home, Toledo; U. of WI, B.A. 1968, U. of MI, M.A. 1974, M.I.T., 1981–82; Catholic; single.

Professional Career: Urban planner, Lucas Cnty. Planning Comm., 1969–75; Urban planning consultant, 1975–77; White House Asst. Dir. for Urban Affairs, 1977–80; Dpty. Secy., Natl. Consumer Coop. Bank, 1980–81; Author.

DC Office: 2366 RHOB, 20515, 202-225-4146; Fax: 202-225-7711; Web site: www.house.gov/kaptur.

District Office: Toledo, 419-259-7500.

Committees: *Appropriations* (7th of 29 D): Agriculture, Rural Development, FDA & Related Agencies; Defense.

Group Ratings

	ADA	ACLU	AFS	LCV	ITIC	NTU	COC	ACU	NTLC	CHC
2004	95	61	100	100	20	9	33	8	0	38
2003	95	—	100	95	—	21	24	24	—	—

National Journal Ratings

	2003 LIB	—	2003 CONS	2004 LIB	—	2004 CONS
Economic	83%	—	17%	85%	—	14%
Social	63%	—	36%	65%	—	34%
Foreign	80%	—	20%	80%	—	20%

Key Votes of the 108th Congress

1. Drilling in ANWR	N	5. DC School Vouchers	N	9. Ban Same-Sex Marriage	N
2. Approve Bush Tax Cuts	N	6. Ban Human Cloning	N	10. Fund Iraq War	N
3. Medicare/Rx Bill	N	7. Restrict Gun Liability	Y	11. Bar Cuba Embargo Funds	Y
4. Bar Overtime Pay Regs.	Y	8. Ban Partial-Birth Abortion	Y	12. Intelligence Reorg.	*

Election Results

2004 general	Marcy Kaptur (D)	205,149	(68%)	($615,506)
	Larry Kaczala (R)	95,983	(32%)	($255,894)
2004 primary	Marcy Kaptur (D)	unopposed		
2002 general	Marcy Kaptur (D)	132,236	(74%)	($344,261)
	Ed Emery (R)	46,481	(26%)	

Prior Winning Percentages: 2000 (75%); 1998 (81%); 1996 (77%); 1994 (75%); 1992 (74%); 1990 (78%); 1988 (81%); 1986 (78%); 1984 (55%); 1982 (58%)

The People		Race/Ethnic Origin	Ancestry	
Area size:	1,244 sq. mi.	79.6% White	German: 21.3%	Irish: 8.9%
Urban population:	86.0%	13.6% Black	Polish: 6.4%	
Rural population:	14.0%	1.0% Asian	**2004 Presidential Vote**	
Pop. 2000:	630,730	0.2% Native Am.	Kerry (D) 181,889	(58%)
Median income:	$40,265	0.0% Hawaiian	Bush (R) 129,825	(42%)
Poverty status:	12.0%	1.5% Two+ races	Other 133	(0%)
Military veterans:	13.6%	0.1% Other	**2000 Presidential Vote**	
		4.0% Hispanic Origin	Gore (D) 134,907	(55%)
			Bush (R) 100,704	(41%)
			Other 7,894	(3%)
			Cook Partisan Voting Index: D + 9	

Occupation	Blue collar: 29.2%	White collar: 54.9%	Gray collar: 15.8%

Toledo was one of America's boomtowns in the 1920s, "a decade of fabulous figures," as historian Harlan Hatcher wrote. The Willys-Overland plant employed 25,000 workers and turned out an automobile every 30 seconds; the Libbey-Owens-Ford merger made Toledo, with local supplies of natural gas and sand, the nation's largest glass manufacturer; the city built $20 million coal and iron ore docks and a transcontinental airport. Toledo had long been well-situated, where the Maumee River empties into Lake Erie, where two dozen rail lines connected it with the East Coast, Chicago, and the coal fields of Kentucky and West Virginia. It was also well positioned to be a center of the brash auto industry, a national leader when it first produced the Jeep in the 1940s. But by the early 1980s auto company management had allowed the unions to bid wages and benefits too high while watching quality decline. Subsidies, beyond the temporary Chrysler loan and a few small trade barriers, were not forthcoming, so Toledo and other auto-dependent cities went through tough times. But revival was on the way. Toledo's small manufacturers in search of markets showed energy and ingenuity. They produced one of America's hottest vehicles, the Jeep Cherokee; the old plant was set to close, but the city offered Chrysler $300 million in incentives to stay, and a new plant was built along I-75. Since then, DaimlerChrysler has built the Jeep Liberty here and is building a new Jeep Wrangler facility; facilities for additional parts and services are likely. Other auto companies are developing the Toledo-to-Ann Arbor corridor as a major auto research area.

The 9th Congressional District of Ohio is centered on Toledo, spreading east through the flatlands of Ottawa and Erie Counties on the Lake Erie shore and inland to southern Lorain County southwest of Cleveland, including Oberlin, home of Oberlin College, founded in 1833 and the first American college to admit women as well as men and blacks as well as whites. Port Clinton, on Lake Erie, bills itself as the "Walleye Capital of the World" and drops a walleye on New Year's Eve to rival Times Square. Sandusky is home of the giant Cedar Point amusement park. Not far away is Milan, birthplace of the great inventor and capitalist Thomas Edison. Politically, Toledo has been heavily Democratic since CIO unions organized the plants in the late 1930s; the collapse of the auto industry so unnerved the district that in 1980 it voted for Ronald Reagan and elected a Republican congressman, but it switched back to the Democrats in 1982 and stayed with them in almost all elections ever since. But the suburbs and the countryside around are mostly Republican, and one survey showed that the Toledo media market had more campaign ads than anywhere else in the nation in 2004.

The congresswoman from the 9th District is Marcy Kaptur, a Democrat first elected in 1982. She is now the senior female House Democrat and has pushed for more portraits and statues of women in the Capitol. Kaptur is fervent and dedicated to sometimes old-fashioned principles, always a loyal daughter of Toledo. She grew up there in a blue-collar neighborhood, her parents worked at local auto plants and the family operated a small grocery store. She has spent almost her entire career in public service. "The unfailingly polite, plain-spoken hometown girl," wrote the *Cleveland Plain Dealer*; she and her brother Steve live in the house where they grew up. She graduated from the University of Wisconsin, the first in her family to attend college, got a master's degree from the University of Michigan and then spent eight years as an urban planner in Toledo. She worked in the Carter White House and was shrewd enough to return home in 1980. That year Republican Ed Weber defeated 26-year incumbent Thomas Ashley. In 1982, when no other Democrat would run against Weber, she did and won 58%–39% despite being outspent 3–1.

Kaptur's great cause is trade. She has long been convinced that Toledo and places like it have lost jobs and industry because of unfair trade practices and low wage competition in countries like Mexico and China. She pressured the Japanese to buy more American auto parts, but has been leery of Japanese investment in the United States. Kaptur was probably Congress's most vocal and dedicated opponent of NAFTA. She became something of a national figure in August 1995, when she appeared before Ross Perot's United We Stand and made a rousing speech, mostly on trade, that had delegates cheering. Perot praised her and offered his vice presidential nomination a year later; she turned it down. She argued that 100,000 jobs had been transferred from Ohio to Mexico, and criticized Bill Clinton for doing nothing for sagging U.S. industries and for ignoring Democrats opposed to NAFTA. She was a vocal opponent of normal trade relations with China and trade promotion authority, and predicted that the Central American Free Trade Agreement would destroy jobs in Ohio. She co-chairs the Congressional Ukrainian Caucus and was an enthusiastic supporter of Viktor Yushchenko and his Orange Revolution. Despite her liberal persona, her iconoclasm sometimes veers her voting record toward the middle. Kaptur opposed funding for abortion and favored the partial-birth abortion ban. She sponsored the legislation that authorized the World War II Memorial, which opened in 2004 on the Washington Mall. On the Appropriations Agriculture Subcommittee, where she was the ranking Democrat until she gave up her position to serve on the Appropriations Defense Subcommittee, she sought to limit farm payments, which led Republicans in 2002 to threaten her favorite projects; she backed off, saying, "I may be blockheaded sometimes, but I'm not stupid." She strongly opposed the war in Iraq. In 2005, she and Kay Granger became the first women to serve on the Defense Appropriations Subcommittee. She has published a book on women in Congress, has hosted a weekly radio show on nearly 100 stations. After the 2002 election she ran a quixotic one-day campaign for minority leader against Nancy Pelosi.

Kaptur is exceedingly popular in Toledo and has not been seriously challenged in two decades. In 2004 her Republican opponent was Lucas County Auditor Larry Kaczala, who criticized Kaptur for comparing Osama bin Laden to American revolutionaries. But Kaptur won 68%–32%. She has declined opportunities to run for statewide office.

TENTH DISTRICT

Rep. Dennis Kucinich (D)

Elected 1996, 5th term; b. Oct. 6, 1946, Cleveland; home, Cleveland; Cleveland St. U., 1967–70, Case Western Reserve U., B.A., M.A., 1973; Catholic; divorced.

Elected Office: Cleveland City Cncl., 1970–75, 1983–85; Cleveland Mayor, 1977–79; OH Senate, 1994–96.

Professional Career: Clerk, Municipal Courts, 1976–77; Radio Talk Show Host, 1979, 1989; Lecturer, 1980–83; Consultant, 1986–94; TV Reporter, Channel 8, 1989–92.

DC Office: 1730 LHOB, 20515, 202-225-5871; Fax: 202-225-5745; Web site: www.house.gov/kucinich.

District Offices: Lakewood, 216-228-8850; Parma, 440-845-2707.

Committees: *Education & the Workforce* (12th of 22 D): Education Reform; Workforce Protections. *Government Reform* (8th of 17 D): Energy & Resources; National Security, Emerging Threats & International Relations (RMM).

Group Ratings

	ADA	ACLU	AFS	LCV	ITIC	NTU	COC	ACU	NTLC	CHC
2004	90	93	100	100	11	23	6	0	0	25
2003	90	—	100	85	—	29	15	19	—	—

National Journal Ratings

	2003 LIB	—	2003 CONS	2004 LIB	—	2004 CONS
Economic	85%	—	15%	87%	—	13%
Social	70%	—	30%	88%	—	0%
Foreign	86%	—	14%	96%	—	3%

Key Votes of the 108th Congress

1. Drilling in ANWR	N	5. DC School Vouchers	*	9. Ban Same-Sex Marriage	N
2. Approve Bush Tax Cuts	N	6. Ban Human Cloning	Y	10. Fund Iraq War	N
3. Medicare/Rx Bill	N	7. Restrict Gun Liability	N	11. Bar Cuba Embargo Funds	Y
4. Bar Overtime Pay Regs.	Y	8. Ban Partial-Birth Abortion	N	12. Intelligence Reorg.	N

Election Results

2004 general	Dennis Kucinich (D)	172,406	(60%)	($406,033)
	Edward Herman (R)	96,463	(34%)	($298,082)
	Barbara Ferris (NP)	18,343	(6%)	
2004 primary	Dennis Kucinich (D)	74,692	(86%)	
	George Pulling (D)	12,639	(14%)	
2002 general	Dennis Kucinich (D)	129,997	(74%)	($518,620)
	Jon Heben (R)	41,778	(24%)	
	Other	3,761	(2%)	

Prior Winning Percentages: 2000 (75%); 1998 (67%); 1996 (49%)

The People		Race/Ethnic Origin	Ancestry	
Area size:	196 sq. mi.	87.2% White	German: 16.6%	Irish: 12.8%
Urban population:	99.4%	4.2% Black	Polish: 8.6%	
Rural population:	0.6%	1.7% Asian	**2004 Presidential Vote**	
Pop. 2000:	630,730	0.2% Native Am.	Kerry (D) 175,149	(58%)
Median income:	$41,841	0.0% Hawaiian	Bush (R) 125,102	(41%)
Poverty status:	9.1%	1.5% Two+ races	Other 1,363	(0%)
Military veterans:	13.2%	0.1% Other	**2000 Presidential Vote**	
		5.0% Hispanic Origin	Gore (D) 122,219	(53%)
			Bush (R) 96,623	(42%)
			Other 11,540	(5%)
			Cook Partisan Voting Index: D + 8	

Occupation	Blue collar: 23.3%	White collar: 62.5%	Gray collar: 14.1%

Cleveland, one of America's great cities at the beginning of the 20th century, faced some hardships in the latter half of the century, but may be on its way back in the new century. It grew as a center of heavy industry: This was the original base of John D. Rockefeller's Standard Oil; the city's twisting and deep Cuyahoga River was the site of several of the nation's largest steel mills; great industrial fortunes here built civic institutions like the museums in Wade Park, Case Western University and the Cleveland Symphony, and financed the campaigns of northeast Ohio Republican Presidents James Garfield and William McKinley. On the old Public Square, designed like a New England town green by the Yankees who settled this Western Reserve (the northeast corner of Ohio) in the early 19th century, the two eccentric Van Sweringen brothers, trolley magnates of the early 20th century, built the Terminal Tower, for many years the highest skyscraper in interior America. This yeasty, ethnic city, with more than 40 nationalities— Hungarians, Czechs, Serbs, Croatians, Poles, Italians, Germans (the Hapsburg Empire and more)—and many distinct ethnic neighborhoods, produced a robust two-party politics. In the 1930s, after CIO unions organized steel factories and auto assembly plants, Cleveland became solidly Democratic, though with some affluent Republican suburbs.

Disgruntled by local taxes, Rockefeller and his corporate operations moved to New York, and Cleveland never led the nation as it hoped: America's fourth largest city in 1910, it was overtaken in size first by Detroit, eventually by the likes of Houston and Dallas; today, it's the center of the nation's 16th largest metropolitan area. The central city declined from 914,000 in 1950 to 461,000 in 2003, as the children who grew up in the tightly packed neighborhoods made more money and moved to the close-in suburbs and then outer suburban counties. The 1970s were a bad decade for Cleveland, which became an object of ridicule by national sophisticates. Its heavy industries were fast declining, Lake Erie and the Cuyahoga River were badly polluted (the river caught fire in June 1969) and the city faced bankruptcy under the youthful Mayor Dennis Kucinich. The city government was rescued by George Voinovich, elected mayor in 1979 and later governor and senator. Downtown Cleveland revived, with the theater district center at Playhouse Square, the Jacobs Field baseball stadium, Gund Arena, and the Rock and Roll Hall of Fame. People swim in a clean Lake Erie; restaurants and pleasure boat docks line the Cuyahoga where diners can sip Burning River pale ale. Although many corporate headquarters have departed and LTV shut down its steel plant, Cleveland remains home to several of the nation's largest law firms, and some businesses, like iron ore giant Cleveland-Cliffs, have sharply revived; the city's number one employer is health services, and the Cleveland Clinic is internationally renowned. Although the "Comeback City" has not yet earned the title, its population declined only 5% in the 1990s, while the metropolitan area grew.

The 10th Congressional District of Ohio includes most of the west side of Cleveland and the western and southern suburbs in Cuyahoga County. Excluded is one salient of mostly black Cleveland precincts attached to the 11th District across the river. Suburbs in the 10th include Lakewood, well-established by the 1920s and still comfortable middle-class territory, plus Rocky River and Bay Village, growing more affluent westward along the lake. Inland is Parma, a creation of the 1950s, when second- and third-generation ethnics moved out to subdivision houses set amid what was once America's densest concentration of bowling alleys. The district extends east of Cleveland on the southern edge of the county in Cuyahoga Valley suburbs. The political tradition in the 10th is primarily Democratic, though Voinovich has carried the area; George W. Bush got only 41% of the vote here in 2004.

The congressman from the 10th District is Dennis Kucinich, first elected in 1996, still unrepentant that he plunged the city into default and a persistent presidential candidate in 2004. Kucinich grew up as the oldest of seven children whose father was a truck driver; the family moved 21 times to various parts of Cleveland. Kucinich was a political prodigy who was elected to the city council in 1969, at 23; he saw himself as the champion of the working man, eager for confrontations with Cleveland's business establishment. He was elected mayor in 1977 when the city government was in terrible financial straits. Kucinich was unwilling or unable to balance the budget and meet obligations; when bankers demanded he sell city-owned properties, he refused and they called in their loans. The public verdict was negative: after surviving a recall petition by 236 votes of 120,000 cast, Kucinich was defeated in 1979. He argues that his primary goal was to preserve the city-owned Muni Light electric system, that he succeeded in that and has saved residents millions of dollars on their electric bills. He taught at Cleveland State and Case Western Reserve, hosted a radio talk show and was a TV reporter. In 1994 Kucinich staged a political comeback and was elected to the state Senate. In 1996 he ran for the House. The Republican incumbent Martin Hoke was elected twice against Democrats with ethical problems. Kucinich campaigned against NAFTA and GATT and defended his ties with labor unions. Democrats, many of them former Kucinich critics, rallied around him: The Cleveland city council named a public power plant for him on the same day Bill Clinton campaigned for him in Parma. Kucinich won, but by only 49%–46%.

Kucinich has a mostly liberal voting record, but has been centrist on social issues. He has been a vocal foe of international trade agreements and bars his staff from parking foreign cars in congressional lots. A vegan since before he was elected to Congress, Kucinich attacked companies that produce genetically modified foods. He continues to emphasize his local roots, with a website dedicated to polka, bowling and Kielbasa. He has co-chaired the Progressive Caucus with Barbara Lee, Democrats who believe their party should move to the left.

In early 2003, Kucinich decided to run for president. His motivating force was his opposition to American military action in Iraq and elsewhere. He voted to authorize the use of force in Afghanistan after the September 11 attacks, but after the defeat of the Taliban he focused on nonviolent responses and called for the creation of a Department of Peace. He joined five other House Democrats who filed a lawsuit to prevent George W. Bush from invading Iraq without an explicit declaration of war. In seeking the 2004 Democratic presidential nomination, he called himself an "FDR Democrat" who wanted to "return the Democratic Party to its roots," including strong ties to organized labor, and he promised "a dramatic choice for Democrats," especially those who are antiwar. "Miracles occur," he claimed when he announced his candidacy. He spoke to enthusiastic audiences of peace activists on both coasts. On one issue on which he had been out of line with most leftish Democrats, he switched during the campaign: Long an opponent of abortion, he voted present on two anti-abortion bills in 2002. After he launched his presidential campaign, he changed his position completely: "I want to state clearly that no one will be appointed to the U.S. Supreme Court if they don't commit to supporting *Roe v. Wade* and a woman's right to choose." Even though few people took his campaign seriously and he did not come close to winning a single state as he trailed Howard Dean in seeking the affection of party leftists, Kucinich remained buoyant and enjoyed the attention. Long after John Kerry had clinched the nomination, he continued his campaign. At the Democratic convention in Boston, the 67 Kucinich delegates were a rump group for "peace and justice," and for shifting the party to the left.

At home, former Cuyahoga County Elections Board Chairman Tom Coyne considered running against him in the 2004 primary and said, "I don't think his views are consistent with the people of the district any more." But he decided against it, and Kucinich was renominated easily. Against an Army veteran who was an interrogator in Afghanistan, he won the general election 60%–34%. Back in the House, he resumed his post as ranking Democrat at the wide-ranging platform of the Government Reform Subcommittee on National Security, Emerging Threats and International Relations.

ELEVENTH DISTRICT

Rep. Stephanie Tubbs Jones (D)

Elected 1998, 4th term; b. Sept. 10, 1949, Cleveland; home, Cleveland; Case Western Reserve U., B.A. 1971, J.D. 1974.; Baptist; widowed.

Elected Office: Cleveland Municipal Court Judge, 1981–83; Cuyahoga Cnty. Court of Common Pleas Judge, 1983–91; Cuyahoga Cnty. Prosecutor, 1991–98.

Professional Career: Asst. Gen. Cnsl. & EEO Admin., NE OH Regional Sewer Dist., 1974–76; Asst. Cuyahoga Cnty. Prosecutor, 1976–79; Equal Employment Opportunity Comm., 1979–81.

DC Office: 1009 LHOB, 20515, 202-225-7032; Fax: 202-225-1339; Web site: http://www.house.gov/tubbsjones.

District Office: Shaker Heights, 216-522-4900.

Committees: *Standards of Official Conduct* (2d of 5 D). *Ways & Means* (14th of 17 D): Select Revenue Measures; Social Security.

Group Ratings

	ADA	ACLU	AFS	LCV	ITIC	NTU	COC	ACU	NTLC	CHC
2004	85	100	100	82	40	13	38	5	3	8
2003	90	—	100	80	—	21	22	12	—	—

National Journal Ratings

	2003 LIB	—	2003 CONS		2004 LIB	—	2004 CONS
Economic	87%	—	9%		79%	—	21%
Social	87%	—	12%		88%	—	0%
Foreign	92%	—	8%		76%	—	23%

Key Votes of the 108th Congress

1. Drilling in ANWR	N	5. DC School Vouchers	N	9. Ban Same-Sex Marriage	N
2. Approve Bush Tax Cuts	N	6. Ban Human Cloning	N	10. Fund Iraq War	*
3. Medicare/Rx Bill	N	7. Restrict Gun Liability	N	11. Bar Cuba Embargo Funds	Y
4. Bar Overtime Pay Regs.	Y	8. Ban Partial-Birth Abortion	*	12. Intelligence Reorg.	N

Election Results

2004 general	Stephanie Tubbs Jones (D)	.... unopposed		($501,711)
2004 primary	Stephanie Tubbs Jones (D)	.... unopposed		
2002 general	Stephanie Tubbs Jones (D)	 116,590	(76%)	($422,417)
	Patrick Pappano (R)	 36,146	(24%)	($61,671)

Prior Winning Percentages: 2000 (85%); 1998 (80%)

The People		Race/Ethnic Origin	Ancestry	
Area size:	135 sq. mi.	38.8% White	German: 6.5%	Irish: 5.2%
Urban population:	100.0%	55.5% Black	Italian: 4.9%	
Rural population:	0.0%	1.6% Asian	**2004 Presidential Vote**	
Pop. 2000:	630,730	0.1% Native Am.	Kerry (D) 237,469	(81%)
Median income:	$31,998	0.0% Hawaiian	Bush (R) 52,372	(18%)
Poverty status:	19.5%	1.4% Two+ races	Other 1,943	(1%)
Military veterans:	11.9%	0.2% Other	**2000 Presidential Vote**	
		2.3% Hispanic Origin	Gore (D) 172,146	(79%)
			Bush (R) 38,382	(18%)
			Other 6,706	(3%)
			Cook Partisan Voting Index: D +33	

Occupation	Blue collar: 21.3%	White collar: 61.4%	Gray collar: 17.3%

Like most great American cities, Cleveland grew in great bursts of migration, when capitalists' investments suddenly were paying off beyond their wildest dreams and low-wage workers were attracted from ready corners of the country and the world. Cleveland's greatest surge of growth started in the 1890s and lasted through the 1920s, as tens of thousands of immigrants from central and southern Europe arrived here, looking for jobs in steel, auto and other factories. Bohemians came to the tightly packed neighborhoods along Broadway, Hungarians a bit to the northeast, Jews north of University Circle along East 105th Street, and Italians ran produce markets in Little Italy along Mayfield Road. As the nation's heavy industries geared up for World War II and enjoyed years of prosperous growth afterward, a second surge of immigrants came, this time blacks from the American South. From Cleveland's old ghetto, south of Carnegie Avenue downtown to East 105th, the rapidly increasing number of blacks covered most of the east side by the middle 1960s, with only a few Bohemian and Italian enclaves remaining east of the Cuyahoga. Migration stopped around 1965, but blacks continued to move beyond the city limits to the east side suburbs. These bursts of migration led to political changes. A string of ethnic mayors—Frank Lausche, Anthony Celebrezze, Ralph Locher—was followed by the election in 1967 of Carl Stokes, the nation's first black big-city mayor, and Cleveland had racially polarized politics for much of the 1970s. Even so, the west side stayed mostly white and Cleveland did not have a black majority until the 2000 Census, when its population was 51% black. But civic pride was battered when the Census Bureau announced in 2004 that Cleveland is the poorest of the nation's 68 big cities; nearly half of all children lived in poverty.

The 11th Congressional District of Ohio includes most of the east side of Cleveland, plus the suburbs just to the east, which together have about as many people as the city now. Some of these—East Cleveland, Warrensville Heights—are mostly black; some, notably Shaker Heights, have stable black percentages in carefully maintained neighborhoods where racial integration has succeeded. Near the campus of Case Western Reserve University on the east side, Severance Hall is one of the nation's grand symphony orchestra homes. Other suburbs are the destination of blacks seeking low-crime neighborhoods and middle-class schools not often found among Cleveland's impressive museums and medical centers. Still others—Mayfield Heights and South Euclid—have been the destination of Cleveland's relatively few new immigrants, most of them from eastern Europe. Overall, 56% of the people in the 11th District are black. Politically, this is by far the most Democratic district in Ohio.

The congresswoman from the 11th District is Stephanie Tubbs Jones, first elected in 1998. She grew up in Cleveland, the daughter of a Hopkins Airport skycap, graduated from college and law school at Case Western and worked as a local government lawyer. She served eight years as judge on the Court of Common Pleas of Cuyahoga County and in 1990 narrowly lost as a Democratic nominee for Ohio Supreme Court. In 1991 she was appointed by the county's Democratic Party as the first woman and first black prosecutor in Cuyahoga County; she easily won election with 79%. When Louis Stokes announced his retirement after 30 years in the House, she decided to run for the seat. Her chief opponents in the primary were state Senator Jeffrey Johnson and Reverend Marvin McMickle, minister of the Antioch Baptist Church, one of the city's largest black congregations. Tubbs Jones, the early favorite, campaigned in both black and white neighborhoods, unlike her opponents. Stokes was officially neutral, but helped her raise money in Washington. She won 51% of the vote, with 20% each to Johnson and McMickle. The general election was a formality in this district.

In the House, Tubbs Jones has a solidly liberal voting record. She showed her political skills by winning appointment as the freshman on the Democratic steering committee, which makes committee assignments. Later, she became president of the Democratic sophomore class. She wisely sought ways to cooperate with influential Republicans in the Ohio delegation. She worked with Steve LaTourette to require Medicare HMO insurers to maintain service and benefits for at least three years. She offended the sizable bloc of Jewish voters in her district when she voted present in 2002 on a resolution to support Israel in the fight against terrorism. In 2003 she was one of 11 House Democrats who voted against the resolution supporting the troops and George W. Bush at the start of the Iraq war. As the first African-American woman to serve on the Ways and Means Committee, she spoke out strongly against personal retirement accounts in Social Security.

At the urging of Democratic leaders, she considered running for governor in 2002 but decided not to. She had no opposition in the primary or general election in 2004, which enabled her to campaign actively for John Kerry. She protested, both before and after the November election, alleged voting irregularities. During the Electoral College count in January 2005, she lodged the formal complaint that resulted in a two-hour debate challenging the Ohio result, the first such debate of a state vote since 1969; the House sustained the result, 267–31, with four of Ohio's six Democrats voting in favor.

TWELFTH DISTRICT

Rep. Pat Tiberi (R)

Elected 2000, 3d term; b. Oct. 21, 1962, Columbus; home, Columbus; OH St. U., B.A. 1985; Catholic; married (Denice).

Elected Office: OH House of Reps., 1992–2000, Maj. Ldr., 1999–2000.

Professional Career: Staff asst., U.S. Rep. John Kasich, 1984–92; Realtor, ReMax Achievers, 1995–2000.

DC Office: 113 CHOB, 20515, 202-225-5355; Fax: 202-226-4523; Web site: www.house.gov/tiberi.

District Office: Columbus, 614-523-2555.

Committees: *Education & the Workforce* (11th of 27 R): 21st Century Competitiveness; Employer-Employee Relations; Select Education (Chmn.). *Financial Services* (22d of 37 R): Capital Markets, Insurance & Government Sponsored Enterprises; Financial Institutions & Consumer Credit; Housing & Community Opportunity.

Group Ratings

	ADA	ACLU	AFS	LCV	ITIC	NTU	COC	ACU	NTLC	CHC
2004	10	5	0	9	90	57	100	96	78	76
2003	5	—	0	5	—	63	100	88	—	—

National Journal Ratings

	2003 LIB	—	2003 CONS		2004 LIB	—	2004 CONS
Economic	0%	—	91%		27%	—	72%
Social	36%	—	64%		31%	—	67%
Foreign	38%	—	60%		42%	—	57%

Key Votes of the 108th Congress

1. Drilling in ANWR	Y	5. DC School Vouchers	Y	9. Ban Same-Sex Marriage	Y
2. Approve Bush Tax Cuts	Y	6. Ban Human Cloning	Y	10. Fund Iraq War	Y
3. Medicare/Rx Bill	Y	7. Restrict Gun Liability	Y	11. Bar Cuba Embargo Funds	Y
4. Bar Overtime Pay Regs.	N	8. Ban Partial-Birth Abortion	Y	12. Intelligence Reorg.	Y

Election Results

2004 general	Pat Tiberi (R) 198,112	(62%)	($853,384)
	Edward Brown (D) 122,109	(38%)	($29,540)
2004 primary	Pat Tiberi (R) .... unopposed		
2002 general	Pat Tiberi (R) 116,982	(64%)	($777,343)
	Edward Brown (D) 64,707	(36%)	($41,214)

Prior Winning Percentages: 2000 (53%)

The People		Race/Ethnic Origin	Ancestry	
Area size:	1,031 sq. mi.	72.1% White	German: 16.8%	Irish: 9.3%
Urban population:	88.1%	21.7% Black	English: 7.5%	
Rural population:	11.9%	2.1% Asian	**2004 Presidential Vote**	
Pop. 2000:	630,730	0.2% Native Am.	Bush (R) 178,080	(51%)
Median income:	$47,289	0.0% Hawaiian	Kerry (D) 171,881	(49%)
Poverty status:	10.0%	1.9% Two+ races	Other 263	(0%)
Military veterans:	12.5%	0.2% Other	**2000 Presidential Vote**	
		1.7% Hispanic Origin	Bush (R) 129,840	(51%)
			Gore (D) 115,083	(46%)
			Other 7,340	(3%)
			Cook Partisan Voting Index: R + 1	
Occupation	Blue collar: 18.0%	White collar: 68.4%	Gray collar: 13.6%	

Columbus is on the verge of becoming a major metropolis. With city limits stretching toward farmland at each point of the compass, the central city of Columbus had 728,000 people in 2003, far more than Cleveland (461,000) or Cincinnati (317,000). The metropolitan area, though less populous than Cleveland and a bit smaller than Cincinnati, is growing much more rapidly; Columbus's Franklin County passed the 1 million mark in the 1990s. Columbus is centrally located, not only in the center of Ohio, but a one-day truck drive from more than one-half of the nation's population. With its growing jobs base, Columbus was the only one of the 15 largest cities in Ohio to gain population in the 1990s. It has the advantages of being a state capital, the home of Ohio State University, and a major white-collar employment town: It is the home of Nationwide Insurance, and AEP; The Limited is based at the Easton Town Center, a huge mall that was built in the 1990s on farmland. Columbus likes to brag that its airfreight operations at Port Columbus, the airport, make it the largest in the country dedicated to cargo. This economic base and civic infrastructure has attracted the kind of upscale, enterprising people who have produced much of America's growth in recent years. It has also attracted more new immigrants than other Ohio cities—Latinos, Asians, Somalis, Ethiopians and Russian Jews. The politics of Columbus have traditionally been Republican. It had few of the eastern European immigrants and CIO unions that made Cleveland so Democratic. But in 1999 Columbus elected African-American Democrat Michael Coleman as mayor, and in 2000 Franklin County was carried, though just barely, by Al Gore. In 2004 thanks to outmigration by whites and a vigorous registration and turnout drive by Democrats, John Kerry carried the county 54%–45%.

The 12th Congressional District of Ohio is one of two districts dominated by Columbus and Franklin County. It includes 39% of the city, including most of the east side, plus the affluent suburb of Bexley, home of the Governor's Mansion, and the northeastern suburbs in Franklin County. It also includes Delaware County directly north of Columbus, Ohio's fastest-growing county (up 113% from 1990 to 2004), and most of Licking County east of Columbus, including the small industrial town of Newark and the lovely college town of Granville. With a big margins in Delaware and Licking Counties, George W. Bush won here 51%–49% in 2004.

The congressman from the 12th District is Pat Tiberi, a Republican first elected in 2000. The son of Italian immigrants, he grew up in Columbus and graduated from Ohio State. He worked as a real estate agent and was for eight years an assistant to Congressman John Kasich, who helped Tiberi win in 1992, at age 30, a seat in the state House. He became majority leader and supported business-friendly legislation and changes in tort law. In 1999 Kasich announced his retirement, after a brief run for the presidency and six years as chairman of the Budget Committee. Tiberi won support to replace his mentor from most of the Republican establishment plus the U.S. Chamber of Commerce. He faced a noisy but not very effective primary challenge from state Senator Gene Watts, who sought to rally the conservative base. Tiberi won 73%–21%. The resounding victory gave him a big boost heading into the general election against Maryellen O'Shaughnessy, a Columbus city council member. She told her personal story as the single mother of a 10-year-old son and set out differences with Tiberi on prescription drug benefits, campaign finance, taxes and Social Security. Tiberi played up his Columbus roots and his membership in the Ohio State marching band, and attacked O'Shaughnessy for the negative Democratic party ads that labeled him as the defender of insurance companies on prescription drugs. This was one of the most-watched House races in the nation; with campaign help from Kasich, who retained his local popularity, Tiberi won 53%–44%.

In the House, Tiberi's record has been conservative on economic and cultural issues but more centrist on foreign and defense policy. He called for scrapping the income tax code and creating a national commission to craft a new tax system. He called for lifting the embargo of Cuba. With other fiscal conservatives, he criticized the Appropriations Committee, and sought unsuccessfully to change House Republican rules to make it easier for the speaker to remove appropriators who signed a discharge petition. As chairman of the Select Education Subcommittee on Education and the Workforce, he planned to focus on early childhood education. On the Financial Services Committee, he has focused on housing and home ownership issues, including a bill to require an increase in zero-down-payment mortgages for first-time homebuyers, which he said would help 150,000 purchasers. When Rob Portman resigned from the House, Tiberi was the Ohio delegation's choice to fill his seat on the Ways and Means Committee; after a bruising fight, the seat went to Devin Nunes of California. Although he has been far more low-key than Kasich, Tiberi is positioned to emerge from the shadows of the influential Ohio delegation.

Despite the district's narrow partisan balance, Tiberi has not been seriously challenged for reelection. In 2004 he won with 62% of the vote and carried Franklin County with 54%.

THIRTEENTH DISTRICT

Rep. Sherrod Brown (D)

Elected 1992, 7th term; b. Nov. 9, 1952, Mansfield; home, Lorain; Yale U., B.A. 1974, OH St. U., M.A. 1979, M.A. 1981; Lutheran; married (Connie Schultz).

Elected Office: OH House of Reps. 1974–82; OH Secy. of State, 1982–90.

Professional Career: Prof., OH St. U. at Mansfield, 1979–81.

DC Office: 2332 RHOB, 20515, 202-225-3401; Fax: 202-225-2266; Web site: www.house.gov/sherrodbrown.

District Offices: Akron, 330-865-8450; Lorain, 440-245-5350.

Committees: *Energy & Commerce* (7th of 26 D): Commerce, Trade & Consumer Protection; Health (RMM); Telecommunications & the Internet. *International Relations* (7th of 23 D): Asia & the Pacific.

Group Ratings

	ADA	ACLU	AFS	LCV	ITIC	NTU	COC	ACU	NTLC	CHC
2004	95	84	100	91	10	11	24	4	0	23
2003	100	—	100	95	—	27	25	12	—	—

National Journal Ratings

	2003 LIB	—	2003 CONS		2004 LIB	—	2004 CONS
Economic	87%	—	9%		89%	—	8%
Social	81%	—	19%		85%	—	15%
Foreign	94%	—	0%		81%	—	18%

Key Votes of the 108th Congress

1. Drilling in ANWR	N	5. DC School Vouchers	N	9. Ban Same-Sex Marriage	N
2. Approve Bush Tax Cuts	N	6. Ban Human Cloning	N	10. Fund Iraq War	N
3. Medicare/Rx Bill	N	7. Restrict Gun Liability	N	11. Bar Cuba Embargo Funds	Y
4. Bar Overtime Pay Regs.	Y	8. Ban Partial-Birth Abortion	N	12. Intelligence Reorg.	N

Election Results

2004 general	Sherrod Brown (D)	201,004	(67%)	($601,435)
	Robert Lucas (R)	97,090	(33%)	($7,518)
2004 primary	Sherrod Brown (D)	unopposed		
2002 general	Sherrod Brown (D)	123,025	(69%)	($606,396)
	Ed Oliveros (R)	55,357	(31%)	

Prior Winning Percentages: 2000 (65%); 1998 (62%); 1996 (60%); 1994 (49%); 1992 (53%)

The People		Race/Ethnic Origin	Ancestry	
Area size:	537 sq. mi.	81.5% White	German: 17.3% Irish: 10.1%	
Urban population:	92.7%	12.1% Black	English: 6.7%	
Rural population:	7.3%	1.2% Asian	**2004 Presidential Vote**	
Pop. 2000:	630,730	0.2% Native Am.	Kerry (D)	177,472 (56%)
Median income:	$44,524	0.0% Hawaiian	Bush (R)	140,908 (44%)
Poverty status:	9.4%	1.3% Two+ races	Other	230 (0%)
Military veterans:	14.0%	0.1% Other	**2000 Presidential Vote**	
		3.5% Hispanic Origin	Gore (D)	133,458 (53%)
			Bush (R)	110,812 (44%)
			Other	9,559 (4%)
			Cook Partisan Voting Index: D + 6	

Occupation	Blue collar: 26.3%	White collar: 59.2%	Gray collar: 14.4%

Fifty years ago most of the people of metro Cleveland were clustered in the city itself, in tightly packed blocks of houses on the limestone plains above the Cuyahoga River valley with its giant steel mills. Around the city there were some comfortable suburbs, then as you drove past them you found yourself amid miles of farm fields before you got to the nearby industrial cities— Akron, the "Rubber Capital" with its Firestone, B.F. Goodrich and Goodyear tire factories, or Lorain, a sort of mini-Cleveland, on Lake Erie with steel mills lining the narrow Black River. In the half-century since, the population of Cleveland has fallen by half and the metro area has spread out over the northern Ohio countryside. The suburbs have spread from Cleveland to Akron without interval; the shoreline from Cleveland to Lorain has been filled in. Medina County, between Lorain and Akron, has been transformed from farmland to suburbia; only the Cuyahoga River valley between Cleveland and Akron has been off limits to development, protected by the creation of the Cuyahoga Valley National Park. The economy has changed as well. In 1950 Cleveland depended on heavy manufacturing, especially steel, and Akron on tires. Today most of the steel mills have gone cold or been torn down, the old tire factories have mostly been converted to other uses, and Ford announced the closing of its assembly plant in Lorain. Akron has memorialized the past in the National Inventors Hall of Fame and has developed itself as the "Polymer Center of America," with 80% of the nation's polymer research and a first-class polymer engineering program at the University of Akron. Downtown Akron has been revived by entertainment areas, the University of Akron, and some upscale housing.

The 13th Congressional District of Ohio is made up of much of this area in metro Cleveland, but none of the city itself. It includes the west side of Akron and its western suburbs; the lines separating it from the 14th and 17th Districts in Akron's Summit County are absurdly convoluted. It includes the northern and eastern parts of Lorain County, including Lorain and Elyria just to the south; the southern tier of suburban townships in Cleveland's Cuyahoga County—Strongsville, North Royalton, Broadview Heights; and the northern tier of suburban townships in Medina County, including Brunswick. Fifty years ago this would have been a Republican area, with Democratic precincts in Akron and Lorain. Today, as Clevelanders have spread far and wide, the area is Democratic, though not overwhelmingly so: George W. Bush twice got 44% of the vote here.

The congressman from the 13th District is Sherrod Brown, first elected in 1992. He grew up in Mansfield, the son of a doctor, graduated from Yale in 1974, won a seat in the state House later that year (another House member, mistaking him for an intern, gave him a dollar to get her a cup of coffee), and later got master's degrees in education and public administration from Ohio State. He has never stopped running. In 1982 he was elected secretary of state at 29 and worked hard to increase voter registration and turnout. In 1990 he lost that office to Bob Taft, who is now governor. In 1992 Brown ran for the open 13th District House seat. With solid labor support, he campaigned loud and hard against NAFTA and championed universal health care. He won 53%–35%.

In the House, Brown has a consistently liberal voting record and has been a politically adept member of the Energy and Commerce Committee. On trade he has been one of the most voluble pro-labor and "fair-trade" members from the Great Lakes area attacking NAFTA, GATT, normal trade relations with China and trade promotion authority. In 2004, he added an amendment to an appropriation bill clarifying that fast-food workers are not part of the nation's manufacturing sector. As ranking Democrat on the Health Subcommittee, his influence has been spotty because Republicans have written their health care proposals mostly in party task forces. He has sponsored bus trips to Canada for consumers to buy prescription drugs. But Brown has had some legislative successes. He helped to enact the Children's Health Act, which created a new Pediatric Research Institute. In 2003, he helped to secure an increase in Medicaid funding. To prevent the transmission of antibiotic-resistant bacteria in food, he has urged a ban on the use of antibiotics on farm animals, including penicillin and tetracycline. He called for enforcement of laws against importing goods made with slave labor in China and helped to increase funding for international programs to fight tuberculosis. He authored *Congress from the Inside*, a book that reviews why House Democrats lost their majority in 1994, including his conclusion "we were blamed for everything the voters did not like." Later, he authored *Myths of Free Trade*.

Brown had a serious Republican challenge in 1994 from Lorain County Prosecutor Gregory White, but he survived by 49%–46%. Since then he has won easily. After the 2000 election Brown seemed threatened by redistricting. After he let it be known that he would run for governor if his district was eliminated, Taft asked legislators not to eliminate Brown, though he had defeated Brown years earlier and had good ratings in the polls. In the resulting 13th District, the bad news for Brown was that he had not represented 56% of his constituents. The good news for him was that they were much more Democratic than the constituents he lost, and he quickly became secure. His quiet accumulation of seniority likely would make him a significant player in the House if and when Democrats regain control. But he continued to be mentioned as a candidate for statewide office; in May 2005 he announced he would not run for governor in 2006.

FOURTEENTH DISTRICT

Rep. Steven LaTourette (R)

Elected 1994, 6th term; b. July 22, 1954, Cleveland; home, Madison; U. of MI, B.A. 1976, Cleveland St. U., J.D. 1979; Methodist; married (Jennifer Laptook).

Elected Office: Lake Cnty. Prosecuting atty., 1988–94.

Professional Career: Lake Cnty. Asst. Public Defender, 1980–83; Practicing atty., 1983–88.

DC Office: 2453 RHOB, 20515, 202-225-5731; Fax: 202-225-3307; Web site: www.house.gov/latourette.

District Office: Painesville, 440-352-3939.

Committees: *Financial Services* (15th of 37 R): Domestic and International Monetary Policy, Trade & Technology; Financial Institutions & Consumer Credit; Oversight & Investigations. *Government Reform* (9th of 23 R): Criminal Justice, Drug Policy & Human Resources; National Security, Emerging Threats & International Relations. *Transportation & Infrastructure* (11th of 41 R): Highways, Transit & Pipelines; Railroads (Chmn.); Water Resources & Environment.

Group Ratings

	ADA	ACLU	AFS	LCV	ITIC	NTU	COC	ACU	NTLC	CHC
2004	15	20	38	9	89	45	86	71	65	84
2003	25	—	25	10	—	56	87	76	—	—

National Journal Ratings

	2003 LIB	—	2003 CONS		2004 LIB	—	2004 CONS
Economic	46%	—	53%		48%	—	51%
Social	48%	—	51%		45%	—	54%
Foreign	40%	—	58%		25%	—	68%

Key Votes of the 108th Congress

1. Drilling in ANWR	Y	5. DC School Vouchers	Y	9. Ban Same-Sex Marriage	Y
2. Approve Bush Tax Cuts	Y	6. Ban Human Cloning	Y	10. Fund Iraq War	N
3. Medicare/Rx Bill	Y	7. Restrict Gun Liability	Y	11. Bar Cuba Embargo Funds	N
4. Bar Overtime Pay Regs.	Y	8. Ban Partial-Birth Abortion	Y	12. Intelligence Reorg.	Y

Election Results

2004 general	Steven LaTourette (R)	201,652	(63%)	($2,430,424)
	Capri Cafaro (D)	119,714	(37%)	($1,991,894)
2004 primary	Steven LaTourette (R)	unopposed		
2002 general	Steven LaTourette (R)	134,413	(72%)	($532,692)
	Dale Blanchard (D)	51,846	(28%)	

Prior Winning Percentages: 2000 (69%); 1998 (66%); 1996 (55%); 1994 (48%)

The People		Race/Ethnic Origin	Ancestry	
Area size:	1,820 sq. mi.	94.0% White	German: 16.9% Irish: 11.2%	
Urban population:	74.1%	2.5% Black	Italian: 9.0%	
Rural population:	25.9%	1.1% Asian	**2004 Presidential Vote**	
Pop. 2000:	630,730	0.1% Native Am.	Bush (R)	178,510 (53%)
Median income:	$51,304	0.0% Hawaiian	Kerry (D)	159,929 (47%)
Poverty status:	5.7%	0.8% Two+ races	Other	1,190 (0%)
Military veterans:	13.6%	0.1% Other	**2000 Presidential Vote**	
		1.3% Hispanic Origin	Bush (R)	147,148 (52%)
			Gore (D)	124,582 (44%)
			Other	11,360 (4%)
			Cook Partisan Voting Index: R + 2	

Occupation   Blue collar: 25.1%   White collar: 62.0%   Gray collar: 12.9%

The imprint of the westward track of New England Yankee migration is still apparent today on the shores of Lake Erie in northern Ohio. The Yankees, cooped up in New England for 200 years, shot across the country through upstate New York, west across Ohio and Michigan to Chicago, and on to Kansas and southern California in just two or three generations, providing inspiration, manpower and technical might for the Union victory in the Civil War, and leaving their imprint along the way. One place they stopped was the Western Reserve, the northeast corner of Ohio, created for the excess population of Connecticut; its towns, colleges and cultural institutions were established by Yankees. This area produced some of the strongest opposition to slavery and support of the Union armies and Republican party in the nation. Its thrifty, hard-working, well-educated citizens built communities with fine schools and, with their accumulated savings, invested in what became some of the nation's leading industries. A century ago, that brought great masses of immigrants to Cleveland and the other cities of northeast Ohio. After the Great Depression and the bloody CIO organizing drives of the late 1930s, the Western Reserve was Democratic during Ohio's class-warfare politics. Now, like Connecticut and Massachusetts, it may be moving toward a post-industrial economy. Factory employment has dropped, but total jobs are rising again; small, adaptive business units with highly skilled workers are the growth sectors.

The 14th Congressional District of Ohio takes in parts or all of seven counties of northeast Ohio and the old Western Reserve. It includes Lake County, northeast of Cleveland, with abandoned industrial sites (including the former Diamond Shamrock factory that became known as Hiroshima because of its nasty wasteland) and middling-to-affluent suburbs; and Geauga County, directly east of Cleveland, with prosperous suburbs amid Western Reserve villages that still participate in a maple syrup festival even though the loss of farmland has cut production. On the east end of the state are Ashtabula and the northern part of Trumbull County: industrial country. It includes the affluent suburbs at the eastern edge of Cleveland's Cuyahoga County, comfortable suburbs in northern Summit County and the northern tier of townships in Portage County to the east. In the 19th century the Western Reserve was heavily Republican; the congressman from this area from 1863 to 1880 was James Garfield, also a general in the Civil War, who was elected with some of the highest Republican percentages in the nation; in 1880 he was elected president and in 1881 was assassinated. In the 1930s this grew politically competitive, as Cleveland became heavily Democratic, and it has been in most years since. But this district was designed, in an incumbent-protection redistricting plan, to gather together Republican territory in the Western Reserve, and the district voted 52%–44% for George W. Bush in 2000 and 53%–47% in 2004.

The congressman from the 14th District is Steve LaTourette, a Republican first elected in 1994. LaTourette grew up in the Cleveland area and went to law school at Cleveland State University; in the 1980s he worked as a public defender and in private practice in Lake County, and became Lake County district attorney in 1988, at 34. Well-known and well-liked, in 1994 he won a three-candidate Republican primary with 54%. In the general he faced Congressman Eric Fingerhut, a 35-year-old political prodigy who in 1992 was elected to replace two retiring Democratic incumbents. LaTourette attacked Fingerhut for backing the Clinton budget and tax increase, for being soft on crime and for hypocritically using his franking privileges. He won 48%–43%; Fingerhut now holds a solidly Democratic district in the Ohio Senate and lost 64%–36% to Senator George Voinovich in 2004.

In the House, LaTourette has the most moderate voting record of Ohio's Republican members and he shows more irreverence than one might expect from a former prosecutor. He invited humorist Dave Barry to spend several days on his press staff, with predictably funny results. He backs up his independence with action. When the House passed a bill to increase savings incentives, he made a seemingly minor change to calculate construction workers' pension benefits based on a worker's three highest years of earnings, instead of the three highest consecutive years; that makes a big difference for workers in carpentry and plumbing, where annual income can vary widely. He broke with many House Republicans to oppose normal trade relations with China. He is chairman of the Railroads Subcommittee of Transportation and Infrastructure, which also gave him a seat at the table for the transportation bill. His high-priority projects include improvements of Ohio Routes 82 and 8. He also used his subcommittee to pass legislation to add Ashtabula, Mahoning and Trumbull Counties to the Appalachian Regional Commission. In 2004, he joined the unanimous committee votes to admonish Majority Leader Tom DeLay on three charges. When Speaker Dennis Hastert without explanation removed LaTourette from the committee in 2005, he was privately unhappy but remained a loyal party soldier.

In contrast to many members of the Class of 1994, LaTourette quickly secured his former Democratic seat without a competitive challenger. In 2004, he was pressed by Democratic challenger Capri Cafaro, a 26-year-old shopping center heiress who spent nearly $2 million of her own funds; her father had been granted immunity in exchange for his cooperation in the prosecution of Congressman Jim Traficant and was sentenced to probation. Cafaro struggled with the issues and in convincing voters of her maturity. "When LaTourette talks to her, he seems almost scolding, like a teacher addressing a student," according to a campaign profile in *Cleveland Scene*. He won 63%–37%, with more than 60% everywhere but Ashtabula County. During the contest LaTourette acknowledged an affair with his former chief aide who had become a lobbyist; Democrats had asked for a Justice Department investigation of possible violation of lobbying laws after photos showed LaTourette leaving her home in suburban Virginia early in the morning. His former wife endorsed Cafaro and complained, "Washington corrupts people."

FIFTEENTH DISTRICT

Rep. Deborah Pryce (R)

Elected 1992, 7th term; b. July 29, 1951, Warren; home, Columbus; OH St. U., B.A. 1973, Capital U. Law Schl., J.D. 1976; Presbyterian; divorced.

Elected Office: Franklin Cnty. Municipal Court Judge, 1985–92.

Professional Career: Admin. Law Judge, OH Dept. of Insurance, 1976; Columbus City Asst. Prosecutor & Asst. City Atty., 1978–85; Practicing atty., 1992.

DC Office: 204 CHOB, 20515, 202-225-2015; Web site: www.house.gov/pryce.

District Office: Columbus, 614-469-5614.

Committees: *Republican Conference Chairman. Financial Services* (4th of 37 R): Domestic and International Monetary Policy, Trade & Technology (Chmn.).

Group Ratings

	ADA	ACLU	AFS	LCV	ITIC	NTU	COC	ACU	NTLC	CHC
2004	15	5	0	9	100	55	100	83	70	61
2003	0	—	0	15	—	59	100	76	—	—

National Journal Ratings

	2003 LIB	—	2003 CONS		2004 LIB	—	2004 CONS
Economic	9%	—	84%		27%	—	72%
Social	49%	—	51%		51%	—	48%
Foreign	31%	—	65%		23%	—	76%

Key Votes of the 108th Congress

1. Drilling in ANWR	Y	5. DC School Vouchers	Y	9. Ban Same-Sex Marriage	N
2. Approve Bush Tax Cuts	Y	6. Ban Human Cloning	N	10. Fund Iraq War	Y
3. Medicare/Rx Bill	Y	7. Restrict Gun Liability	Y	11. Bar Cuba Embargo Funds	N
4. Bar Overtime Pay Regs.	N	8. Ban Partial-Birth Abortion	Y	12. Intelligence Reorg.	Y

Election Results

2004 general	Deborah Pryce (R) 166,520	(60%)	($1,008,306)
	Mark Brown (D) 110,915	(40%)	
2004 primary	Deborah Pryce (R) 36,860	(84%)	
	Charlie Morrison (R) 7,254	(16%)	
2002 general	Deborah Pryce (R) 108,193	(67%)	($872,928)
	Mark Brown (D) 54,286	(33%)	

Prior Winning Percentages: 2000 (68%); 1998 (66%); 1996 (71%); 1994 (71%); 1992 (44%)

The People		Race/Ethnic Origin	Ancestry	
Area size:	1,182 sq. mi.	85.2% White	German: 18.5%	Irish: 10.4%
Urban population:	91.3%	7.2% Black	English: 8.0%	
Rural population:	8.8%	3.3% Asian	**2004 Presidential Vote**	
Pop. 2000:	630,730	0.2% Native Am.	Bush (R) 154,105	(50%)
Median income:	$43,885	0.0% Hawaiian	Kerry (D) 151,869	(50%)
Poverty status:	10.8%	1.7% Two+ races	Other 174	(0%)
Military veterans:	11.6%	0.2% Other	**2000 Presidential Vote**	
		2.3% Hispanic Origin	Bush (R) 117,175	(52%)
			Gore (D) 98,204	(44%)
			Other 8,931	(4%)
			Cook Partisan Voting Index: R + 1	

Occupation   Blue collar: 19.8%   White collar: 66.3%   Gray collar: 13.9%

Columbus, smack in the center of Ohio, was founded in 1812 to be the state capital. Its flat-domed Capitol at Broad and High, with the statue of William McKinley out front, is surrounded by high-rises, public and private, while the city has been growing in all directions into the countryside, and now is on the verge of becoming a large metropolis. It is the headquarters of state government and Ohio State, one of the nation's largest universities. It is the headquarters of the Batelle Memorial Institute, the think tank that helped invent compact discs, office copy machines and the universal product code; a major industry here is data retrieval. Columbus, which has kept annexing suburbs, is now Ohio's largest central city by far, with 728,000 people in 2000; Franklin County topped 1 million in 2000 and the metro area extends into formerly rural counties. Columbus is rapidly building civic landmarks—the Center of Science and Industry on the riverfront, the Jerome Schottenstein Center for sports and concerts at OSU, a hockey stadium for the Columbus Blue Jackets and the nation's first stadium built for a professional soccer team, the Columbus Crew. And there is residential building downtown in thriving entertainment districts. With the nation's highest proportion of residents age 25 to 34, Columbus has been attracting young professionals and immigrants more than any other Ohio city and continues to be a prime test market for products of all kinds.

The 15th Congressional District of Ohio includes all of Columbus except the east side, plus southern and western Franklin County and once-rural Madison and Union Counties directly to the west. Union County is where Honda built a motorcycle plant in 1979 and an auto assembly plant in 1982; Honda has spent $6 billion there and in 2004 announced a new $123 million paint facility. The 15th includes white working class areas on the south side of the city and in nearby Grove City, and the Ohio State University campus. Politically, these Democratic areas have long been more than balanced by the heavily Republican suburb of Upper Arlington, across the Olentangy River from Ohio State, and by Republican subdivisions sprouting up in rural land between the old villages. But Columbus was the scene of a highly successful registration and turnout drive by Democrats in 2004, and Columbus and Franklin County went Democrat. The 15th District as a whole, 52% for George W. Bush in 2000, gave him only a 50.3% majority in 2004.

The congresswoman from the 15th District is Deborah Pryce, a Republican first elected in 1992. Pryce grew up in Warren, graduated from Ohio State and Capital University law school, worked in state government and as a city prosecutor, and was elected municipal court judge in 1985. In 1992, when incumbent Chalmers Wylie retired after 26 years, Pryce ran for the House. She was unopposed in the primary but had tough competition in the general from Democrat

Richard Cordray and from anti-abortion independent Linda Reidelbach. Pryce talked much about congressional reform—term limits, rotating chairmanships, line-item veto—and called for limiting annual spending increases to 3%. She won with 44% of the vote to Cordray's 38% and Reidelbach's 18%.

In the House, Pryce has a voting record that is mostly conservative on economic and foreign issues, more moderate on cultural issues. In her first term she was elected interim president of her Republican class and helped to write the Contract with America. Pryce has been particularly interested in issues relating to children, adoption and cancer. Her adoptive daughter developed cancer in September 1998 and died at age nine in September 1999; she adopted a newborn in 2002. Pryce started Hope Street Kids, an organization to raise funds for cancer research, using funds donated in memory of her daughter. She is co-chairwoman of the House Cancer Working Group and sponsored a bill in 2001 to require private insurers to provide coverage of routine patient costs of cancer patients who qualify to participate in a clinical trial. She sponsored grants to help pediatric palliative care programs and to give parents of children with cancer access to both curative and palliative care; this was included in the 2003 Medicare/prescription drug act.

Pryce is chairman of the Republican Conference, the number four position in the Republican leadership, tasked with disseminating House Republicans' message. She was elected conference secretary in July 1997 and in November 2000 she was elected conference vice chair without opposition. In November 2002, after Conference Chairman J.C. Watts retired, she was elected to his post, with 133 votes to 61 for J.D. Hayworth and 28 for Jim Ryun. Although in charge of the party's message, Pryce has not often been seen on national television or quoted in national print media. "Controversy is part of politics, but not the part I like to participate in. Do I like being behind the scenes better than out in front? Yes. I work better. I'm more effective that way. I'm way more comfortable." She plays more of an inside role, keeping Republicans, especially moderates, together; Pryce argues for maintaining party unity and accepting bills with conservative provisions, to keep the process moving, knowing that the Senate or the administration may modify things. She complained when there were no women members standing behind George W. Bush when he signed the partial-birth abortion bill in November 2003. In March 2004 she accepted the assignment of leading attacks by House Republicans on John Kerry.

As a member of the Rules Committee, Pryce did not have much occasion to shepherd legislation to passage. In 2000 she inserted into an appropriation $235 million for graduate medical programs at children's hospitals; Children's Hospital of Columbus stood to get $5 million. She got in the corporate tax bill a provision ending the double taxation of attorney's fees, which had been taxable for both the client and the lawyer.

In January 2005 Pryce left the Rules Committee and returned to the Financial Services Committee; one reason she did was that Speaker Dennis Hastert decreed that House Republicans' six-year term limit did not apply to Rules Chairman David Dreier. Pryce was credited for her former service and became fourth ranking Republican in seniority and became chairman of the Domestic and International Monetary Policy Subcommittee. She has been mentioned as a possible successor to Financial Services Chairman Mike Oxley, who reaches the end of his six years in January 2007; but she would have to prevail against the claims of Louisiana's Richard Baker, who has more seniority.

Pryce has won reelection easily. In 2004 she ran well ahead of George W. Bush and won 60%–40%.

SIXTEENTH DISTRICT

Rep. Ralph Regula (R)

Elected 1972, 17th term; b. Dec. 3, 1924, Beach City; home, Navarre; Mt. Union Col., B.A. 1948, William McKinley Law Schl., LL.B. 1952; Episcopalian; married (Mary).

Military Career: Navy, 1944–46 (WWII).

Elected Office: OH House of Reps., 1964–66; OH Senate, 1966–72.

Professional Career: Teacher & schl. principal, 1948–52; Practicing atty., 1952–73; OH Bd. of Educ., 1960–64.

DC Office: 2306 RHOB, 20515, 202-225-3876; Fax: 202-225-3059; Web site: www.house.gov/regula.

District Offices: Canton, 330-489-4414; Medina, 330-722-3793.

Committees: *Appropriations* (Vice Chmn. of 37 R): Labor, Health and Human Services, Education & Related Agencies (Chmn.); Transportation, Treasury, HUD, the Judiciary & District of Columbia.

Group Ratings

	ADA	ACLU	AFS	LCV	ITIC	NTU	COC	ACU	NTLC	CHC
2004	0	0	13	9	90	48	100	88	68	84
2003	5	—	0	0	—	59	97	92	—	—

National Journal Ratings

	2003 LIB	—	2003 CONS		2004 LIB	—	2004 CONS
Economic	21%	—	75%		17%	—	80%
Social	30%	—	65%		31%	—	67%
Foreign	23%	—	71%		25%	—	68%

Key Votes of the 108th Congress

1. Drilling in ANWR	Y	5. DC School Vouchers	Y	9. Ban Same-Sex Marriage	Y
2. Approve Bush Tax Cuts	Y	6. Ban Human Cloning	Y	10. Fund Iraq War	Y
3. Medicare/Rx Bill	Y	7. Restrict Gun Liability	Y	11. Bar Cuba Embargo Funds	N
4. Bar Overtime Pay Regs.	N	8. Ban Partial-Birth Abortion	Y	12. Intelligence Reorg.	Y

Election Results

2004 general	Ralph Regula (R)	202,544	(67%)	($606,430)
	Jeff Seemann (D)	101,817	(33%)	($59,667)
2004 primary	Ralph Regula (R)	unopposed		
2002 general	Ralph Regula (R)	129,734	(69%)	($252,109)
	Jim Rice (D)	58,644	(31%)	

Prior Winning Percentages: 2000 (69%); 1998 (64%); 1996 (69%); 1994 (75%); 1992 (64%); 1990 (59%); 1988 (79%); 1986 (76%); 1984 (72%); 1982 (66%); 1980 (79%); 1978 (78%); 1976 (67%); 1974 (66%); 1972 (57%).

The People		Race/Ethnic Origin	Ancestry	
Area size:	1,741 sq. mi.	92.4% White	German: 21.9%	Irish: 9.5%
Urban population:	73.6%	4.8% Black	English: 7.3%	
Rural population:	26.4%	0.6% Asian	**2004 Presidential Vote**	
Pop. 2000:	630,730	0.2% Native Am.	Bush (R)	171,561 (54%)
Median income:	$41,801	0.0% Hawaiian	Kerry (D)	146,066 (46%)
Poverty status:	8.3%	1.1% Two+ races	Other	1,085 (0%)
Military veterans:	13.6%	0.1% Other	**2000 Presidential Vote**	
		0.9% Hispanic Origin	Bush (R)	141,311 (53%)
			Gore (D)	112,270 (42%)
			Other	10,908 (4%)
			Cook Partisan Voting Index: R + 4	

Occupation	Blue collar: 30.5%	White collar: 54.7%	Gray collar: 14.8%

A little more than a century ago, Canton, Ohio, was at the center of American politics. Canton was already an industrial city then, though not with the huge steel factories built in Youngstown or Cleveland. Its high-skill workers were fashioning new kinds of plows and reapers, making watches and, beginning in 1899, roller bearings. Canton did not attract masses of immigrants. Its factories did not run on harsh stopwatch discipline; there were not the class warfare politics here that would be seen later in other northern Ohio industrial cities. Instead Canton was united in admiring its first citizen, William McKinley, who rose to the rank of major at 22 in the Civil War, was elected congressman and governor, and chaired the House Ways and Means Committee. As Republican nominee for president in 1896, McKinley campaigned from his front porch in Canton, meeting with delegations brought in by train from all over the country. This spectacle, with its display of technological virtuosity and personal modesty, sounds an appealing and reverberating note in American politics, as does the McKinley platform—the "full dinner pail," the gold standard, the enforcement of law and order in labor relations—which has long been viewed as antiquated but still provides useful instruction. A century later Canton is a community still based on manufacturing, but one troubled by manufacturing job losses. Its largest employer, locally owned Timken, announced in May 2004 it would lay off 1,300 of its 4,800 workers over the next two years. Hoover won concessions from its union, then in June 2004 cut about 500 jobs. Less widely reported were new jobs in smaller factories, like an Alliance casting plant reopened to make rail car parts with 420 jobs. Canton may be suffering a net loss of jobs. But this is nothing like the closure of steel plants in the Mahoning Valley in the late 1970s and early 1980s.

The 16th Congressional District of Ohio includes all of Canton and Stark County, plus Wayne County to the west and most of Ashland and Medina Counties. Wayne County is the site of the College of Wooster and the headquarters of Rubbermaid and Smuckers, which has acquired new brands from other food companies (Jif peanut butter, Hungry Jack pancakes, etc.) and doubled its sales and profits in recent years. In the southern part of the county (and in Holmes and Tuscarawas Counties to the south) is the largest Amish settlement in the world, where people drive horse-drawn tractors, eschew automobiles and electricity, quit school after the eighth grade and refuse to recognize daylight savings time. Ashland is a smaller, non-metropolitan county; Johnny Appleseed once lived on what is now the campus of Ashland University, known for its Ashbrook Center for Public Affairs. Medina County, north of Wayne, is part of the Cleveland metropolitan area, as young families buy houses in new subdivisions off I-71; its most heavily suburbanized northern townships, however, are in the 13th District. Politically, this area is generally Republican, though not always by wide margins. Stark County was something like ground zero in the 2004 presidential campaign, and was the only Ohio county which George W. Bush carried in 2000 but lost in 2004, both times by narrow margins. But the other counties kept the district in the Republican column and Bush carried it 53%–42% in 2000 and 54%–46% in 2004.

The congressman from the 16th District is Ralph Regula, a Republican first elected in 1972 and the dean of the Ohio delegation. He grew up in outer Stark County, the son of a farmer and coal mine operator; he served in the Navy in World War II, worked his way through the William McKinley School of Law while teaching elementary school, and was elected to the Ohio legislature in 1964, just before turning 40. He still has a cattle farm near Canton. When incumbent Frank Bow, first elected in 1950, retired in 1972, Regula ran for the House and was easily elected.

Regula is now the senior Republican member, but not the chairman, of the Appropriations Committee. From 1995 to 2001 he chaired the Interior Subcommittee. On the Interior Subcommittee, Regula was a counterweight to the Resources Committee and its chairman, Don Young of Alaska, who added riders to Regula's appropriations strongly opposed by environmental groups and the Clinton administration. Regula resisted these, and often gave them up in end-of-session conference committees when Clinton threatened a veto. Young and Regula also got into a fight over Mount McKinley. Young introduced a bill to rename the mountain Denali, an Alaska Native name; Regula, McKinley's successor in the House, replied heatedly that that controversy had already been settled in 1980, when the McKinley name stayed on the mountain but the park was renamed Denali National Park. In his last year as Interior chairman, Regula increased the appropriation by 26%, added a ban on the Interior Department moving callers into voice mail between 7:30 a.m. and 4:30 p.m. and designated the Cuyahoga Valley National Recreation Area a national park, but not subject to national park air standards. He has continued to nurture the

Cuyahoga Valley National Park, with $2.5 million in the 2004 omnibus. He also created the Ohio & Erie National Heritage Corridor in 1996 along the old Ohio & Erie Canal and funded it with $7 million since 1997. In 1996 he established visitors' fees at recreation areas run by the Forest Service, the Bureau of Land Management, the Fish and Wildlife Service and the National Park Service. These have sparked resentment in the West, but in the November 2004 omnibus appropriation he extended them for 10 years.

In January 2001 Regula took over the Labor-HHS-Education Subcommittee, whose appropriation is second in size only to Defense. There he worked harmoniously with ranking Democrat David Obey and produced a $123 billion appropriation approved in October 2001. In summer 2002, Speaker Dennis Hastert was under pressure from conservative Republican Study Committee members to bring forward the Labor-HHS bill before any other appropriations; they wanted to hold it to the president's $129.9 billion level, while the Senate had voted $136.4 billion and Regula struggled to reconcile the demands of education and health constituencies. Regula argued that an appropriation under the Bush limit couldn't win a majority on the floor, and as a result all appropriations except Defense and Military Construction were postponed until after the election. In February 2003, when the appropriations were finally passed, Regula's bill provided increases for Title I and special education $500 million under the Bush figure. In February 2004 Regula said he was looking to see where programs weren't serving their purpose, but he did not impose major cuts. His appropriations included language encouraging NIH to consider making its research more affordable.

Regula is one of two cardinals (the term for Appropriations subcommittee chairmen) from Ohio; the other is Dave Hobson, and they both look after the interests of the state. In the 2001 defense bill he got a provision requiring the Defense Department to buy American-made gloves; the Ansell Perry plant in Massillon, the only surgical glove manufacturer in the United States, had shut down, but there were potential buyers and this would guarantee business. Regula has been chairman of the Congressional Steel Caucus and has often weighed in on trade issues.

In November 2002 the Republican Conference chose to give the Steering Committee a veto over the selection of Appropriations subcommittee chairmen; this tended to make cardinals more amenable to the demands of the Republican leadership and more assiduous in raising funds for other Republicans. Appropriations Chairman Bill Young would reach the end of his six-year term limit in January 2005, and Regula, first in line in seniority, competed hard for the position. His CARE PAC gave $553,000 to 87 Republican candidates, $15,000 to the House Republican campaign committee and $91,000 to 18 state Republican parties. He said that he would consider changing earmarks for Democrats and revamping the committee staff, a target of criticism by fiscally conservative Republicans. "Funding efforts have to reflect the goals of the leadership. This is what my promise is: I would push hard within the culture of the Appropriations Committee to provide good management." But all of this proved in vain. In January 2005, 26 of the 34 votes on the Republican Steering Committee were cast for Jerry Lewis of California. Regula, like the other competitor, Hal Rogers of Kentucky, was a good sport. "That is the way of elections. You win some, you lose some and you move on." This was a blow to both Regula and the Ohio delegation and Lewis named him vice chairman of the full committee; Speaker Dennis Hastert named him to the NATO Parliamentary Assembly and the Smithsonian Board of Regents.

In 2004 Regula ran 13% ahead of George W. Bush and was reelected 67%–33%. When asked whether he will run again in 2006, when he will be 81, he said, "You never want to predict the future, but I still enjoy what I'm doing. I still have two years as chair of the labor, health, education and welfare . . . We do a lot of good for a lot of people." Local politicians say that he hopes his son, Stark County Commissioner Richard Regula will succeed him.

SEVENTEENTH DISTRICT

Rep. Tim Ryan (D)

Elected 2002, 2d term; b. July 16, 1973, Niles; home, Niles; Bowling Green St. U., B.A. 1995, Franklin Pierce Law Ctr., J.D. 2000; Catholic; married (Julie).

Elected Office: OH Senate, 2000–02

Professional Career: Aide, U.S. Rep. Jim Traficant, 1995–97.

DC Office: 222 CHOB, 20515, 202-225-5261; Fax: 202-225-3719; Web site: timryan.house.gov.

District Offices: Akron, 330-630-7311; Warren, 330-373-0074; Youngstown, 330-740-0193.

Committees: *Armed Services* (24th of 28 D): Readiness; Tactical Air & Land Forces. *Education & the Workforce* (20th of 22 D): 21st Century Competitiveness; Select Education.

Group Ratings

	ADA	ACLU	AFS	LCV	ITIC	NTU	COC	ACU	NTLC	CHC
2004	80	70	100	100	20	11	35	17	0	25
2003	95	—	100	100	—	23	30	28	—	—

National Journal Ratings

	2003 LIB	—	2003 CONS		2004 LIB	—	2004 CONS
Economic	77%	—	21%		83%	—	16%
Social	63%	—	36%		58%	—	41%
Foreign	93%	—	6%		83%	—	16%

Key Votes of the 108th Congress

1. Drilling in ANWR	N	5. DC School Vouchers	N	9. Ban Same-Sex Marriage	N
2. Approve Bush Tax Cuts	N	6. Ban Human Cloning	Y	10. Fund Iraq War	N
3. Medicare/Rx Bill	N	7. Restrict Gun Liability	Y	11. Bar Cuba Embargo Funds	Y
4. Bar Overtime Pay Regs.	*	8. Ban Partial-Birth Abortion	Y	12. Intelligence Reorg.	N

Election Results

2004 general	Tim Ryan (D)	212,800	(77%)	($495,122)
	Frank Cusimano (R)	62,871	(23%)	($9,700)
2004 primary	Tim Ryan (D)	unopposed		
2002 general	Tim Ryan (D)	94,441	(51%)	($596,646)
	Ann Womer Benjamin (R)	62,188	(34%)	($293,316)
	James Traficant (I)	28,045	(15%)	($150,129)

The People		Race/Ethnic Origin	Ancestry		
Area size:	1,033 sq. mi.	84.5% White	German: 15.5% Irish: 10.3%		
Urban population:	84.3%	11.6% Black	Italian: 9.2%		
Rural population:	15.7%	0.7% Asian	**2004 Presidential Vote**		
Pop. 2000:	630,730	0.2% Native Am.	Kerry (D)	188,531	(63%)
Median income:	$36,705	0.0% Hawaiian	Bush (R)	111,663	(37%)
Poverty status:	12.3%	1.2% Two+ races	**2000 Presidential Vote**		
Military veterans:	14.6%	0.1% Other	Gore (D)	150,748	(60%)
		1.6% Hispanic Origin	Bush (R)	88,184	(35%)
			Other	10,767	(4%)
			Cook Partisan Voting Index: D +14		

Occupation	Blue collar: 31.8%	White collar: 51.6%	Gray collar: 16.6%

For nearly a century, the Mahoning Valley, between the Lake Erie docks that unload iron ore from Great Lakes freighters and the coalfields of western Pennsylvania and West Virginia, was one of the steel capitals of the United States. The first coal mine here opened in 1826, canals followed, and in 1892 the first steel mill was built in Youngstown. The valley soon filled up with mills, converters, and furnaces. Now the steel mills stand empty, smokeless and silent—except those that have been dynamited or torn down. Big steel management allowed foreign producers to gain a technological edge in the 1950s and 1960s; worldwide overcapacity in steel grew as almost every developing country decided it needed its own steel mill, while cooperation between the United Steelworkers and management after the 119-day strike in 1959 boosted wages and fringe benefits to price domestic steel out of the market. Import restrictions kept the furnaces hot for a while, but the oil shock of 1979 produced sharply higher energy prices and a collapse in the U.S. auto and steel markets. Every plant in the Mahoning Valley closed, and in the early 1980s metro Youngstown had one of the nation's highest unemployment rates; from 1990 to 2004 the population of Youngstown's Mahoning County has declined by 6% and next-door Trumbull County's by 3%. Steel has since revived, but not here: in decentralized mini-mills around the country or in huge new rolling plants in northern Indiana. The high-wage living standard vanished, though not all work: several aluminum plants recently opened in nearby Warren; young people looking for opportunities routinely leave. Youngstown's population declined 14% in the 1990s to 82,000, about half of its size in the 1930s. Organized crime, it seems, has deeply infiltrated local government; a federal investigation has led to more than 70 convictions, including a prosecutor, a sheriff and a congressman. And there have been other failures in industrial Northeastern economy: the massive Northeast power blackout in August 2003 resulted from preventable control room failures at the FirstEnergy plant in nearby Akron.

The 17th Congressional District of Ohio includes most of the Mahoning Valley industrial area—Youngstown, but not its southern Mahoning County suburbs, Warren and almost all of Trumbull County. In addition, it includes nearly all of Portage County to the west and part of eastern Summit County and Akron. It contains two loci of 1970s protest—Kent State University, where four war-protesting students were killed by National Guardsmen in 1970, and Lordstown, site of the General Motors plant where workers purposely built shoddy cars to protest the tedium of the assembly line. The division of Akron and Summit County among three districts in the 2002 redistricting was a matter of some local controversy, but was essential to a compromise between Republican and Democratic legislators. This is a Democratic district, 63% for John Kerry in 2004, his second best district in Ohio, even though the Democratic mayor of Youngstown endorsed George W. Bush, who held a rally at the Youngstown-Warren Airport in late October.

The congressman from the 17th District is Tim Ryan, a Democrat first elected in 2002 when he beat two incumbents, one in the Democratic primary and one in the general election. Ryan grew up in Niles and graduated from Bowling Green State University. His first job was with 17th District Congressman James Traficant. In 2000, after graduating from Franklin Pierce Law Center, Ryan was elected to the state Senate. His opening to run for Congress came from Traficant's downfall. For years Traficant was a colorful figure in the House, whose ranting orations and retro haircut ("I do my hair with a weed whacker," he said; it turned out to be a wig) entertained C-SPAN viewers. The Democratic leadership scorned him and he voted for Dennis Hastert for speaker; Democrats stripped him of his committee assignments. In May 2001 Traficant was indicted on bribery charges.

After Traficant did not file for reelection, most insiders thought the 17th District would be won by Akron-based incumbent Tom Sawyer, first elected in 1986. But Ryan noted that in the new district the Mahoning Valley had more people than metro Akron. Traficant, who defended himself in court, was convicted on 10 counts of bribery in April 2002. Ryan's opponents seized on his two years on Traficant's staff and accused him of everything short of wearing his denim suits. After one exchange Ryan exclaimed, "Would you guys let it go about Jim Traficant?" By standard measures, Sawyer should have won easily. He outspent Ryan by nearly 6–1 and had the backing, as incumbents almost always do, of the Democratic Congressional Campaign Committee. But his record on issues gave Ryan an opening. After much public agonizing Sawyer had voted for NAFTA in 1993, and he was one of the few Rust Belt Democrats to vote for normal trade relations for China in 1999 after Bill Clinton visited Akron a few days before the vote. Ryan hammered on these votes in the Mahoning Valley, where it is gospel writ that free trade exported its high-paying jobs abroad. Ryan also got the endorsement of the National Rifle Association in a district with more blue-collar hunters than upscale suburban women who abhor guns. In Summit and Portage Counties, Sawyer led Ryan 62%–16%. But that produced a margin of only 6,846 votes. In

Mahoning and Trumbull Counties, where Sawyer had never run before, Ryan led 48%–18%. That produced a popular vote margin of 16,521. Overall Ryan beat Sawyer 41%–27%.

Republicans had some hopes of winning the district, particularly after Traficant announced he was running as an Independent. The Republican nominee was state Representative Ann Womer Benjamin. Ryan slammed Womer Benjamin and the Ohio Republican legislature for votes that led to higher tuitions at state universities. Republicans fired back with ads highlighting several disorderly conduct charges lodged against Ryan while he attended college. It remained an open question how strong Traficant's appeal remained in the Mahoning Valley. But in July he was expelled from the House by a 420–1 vote, and in August he was sentenced and taken off to federal prison. In the end the district's Democratic leanings and Ryan's labor support proved decisive. He won 51% of the vote to 34% for Womer Benjamin and 15% for Traficant.

Ryan cast liberal votes on economic and foreign policy, while his splits with Democrats on abortion and guns placed him in the center on social issues. Under local pressure to keep the Youngstown Air Reserve Station, with its C-130 Hercules aircraft and 2,000 employees and reservists, off the base-closing list, he joined the Armed Services Committee and co-chaired the Domestic Industrial Base Congressional Caucus; the station was a net gainer under the Pentagon's May 2005 recommendations. The House passed his bill to study the feasibility of establishing the Western Reserve Heritage Area. Worried about the loss of local call center jobs, he was one of seven members who voted against the national do-not-call list. With Armed Services Committee chairman Duncan Hunter in April 2005, he sponsored the Chinese Currency Act addressing China's alleged manipulation and undervaluation of its currency. As the youngest Democrat in the 108th Congress, Ryan worked loyally on party initiatives and often discussed issues on the House floor with Kendrick Meek, who shared his youthful perspective. In 2004, he ran unopposed in the primary and won the general by the smashing margin of 77%–23%. In December 2004, the Federal Election Commission fined him $6,000 for an illegal loan in the 2002 primary.

EIGHTEENTH DISTRICT

Rep. Bob Ney (R)

Elected 1994, 6th term; b. July 5, 1954, Wheeling, WV; home, St. Clairsville; OH St. U., B.S. 1976; Catholic; married (Elizabeth).

Elected Office: OH House of Reps., 1980–82; OH Senate, 1984–94.

Professional Career: Teacher, Iran, 1978; Program Mgr., OH Office of Appalachia, 1979; Bellaire Safety Dir., 1980.

DC Office: 2438 RHOB, 20515, 202-225-6265; Fax: 202-225-3394; Web site: www.house.gov/ney.

District Offices: Chillicothe, 740-779-1634; Jackson, 740-288-1430; New Philadelphia, 330-364-6380; St. Clairsville, 740-699-2704; Zanesville, 740-452-7023.

Committees: *Financial Services* (10th of 37 R): Capital Markets, Insurance & Government Sponsored Enterprises; Housing & Community Opportunity (Chmn.). *House Administration* (Chmn. of 6 R). *Transportation & Infrastructure* (14th of 41 R): Aviation; Highways, Transit & Pipelines; Water Resources & Environment.

Group Ratings

	ADA	ACLU	AFS	LCV	ITIC	NTU	COC	ACU	NTLC	CHC
2004	10	15	13	0	90	52	100	92	81	83
2003	10	—	13	5	—	59	100	84	—	—

National Journal Ratings

	2003 LIB	—	2003 CONS		2004 LIB	—	2004 CONS
Economic	33%	—	64%		36%	—	63%
Social	46%	—	54%		39%	—	60%
Foreign	23%	—	71%		39%	—	59%

Key Votes of the 108th Congress

1. Drilling in ANWR	Y	5. DC School Vouchers	N	9. Ban Same-Sex Marriage	Y
2. Approve Bush Tax Cuts	Y	6. Ban Human Cloning	*	10. Fund Iraq War	Y
3. Medicare/Rx Bill	Y	7. Restrict Gun Liability	Y	11. Bar Cuba Embargo Funds	N
4. Bar Overtime Pay Regs.	N	8. Ban Partial-Birth Abortion	Y	12. Intelligence Reorg.	Y

Election Results

2004 general	Bob Ney (R)	177,600	(66%)	($1,484,643)
	Brian Thomas (D)	90,820	(34%)	($18,417)
2004 primary	Bob Ney (R)	unopposed		
2002 general	Bob Ney (R)	unopposed		($713,837)

Prior Winning Percentages: 2000 (64%); 1998 (60%); 1996 (50%); 1994 (54%)

The People		Race/Ethnic Origin	Ancestry	
Area size:	6,876 sq. mi.	95.9% White	German: 16.7%	USA: 10.2%
Urban population:	43.3%	1.9% Black	Irish: 8.7%	
Rural population:	56.7%	0.3% Asian	**2004 Presidential Vote**	
Pop. 2000:	630,730	0.2% Native Am.	Bush (R) 163,121	(57%)
Median income:	$34,462	0.0% Hawaiian	Kerry (D) 121,495	(43%)
Poverty status:	12.6%	1.0% Two+ races	Other 1,216	(0%)
Military veterans:	14.3%	0.1% Other	**2000 Presidential Vote**	
		0.6% Hispanic Origin	Bush (R) 132,709	(55%)
			Gore (D) 98,328	(41%)
			Other 9,810	(4%)
			Cook Partisan Voting Index: R + 6	

Occupation	Blue collar: 37.5%	White collar: 45.8%	Gray collar: 16.7%

The hills of eastern Ohio are one of those obscure parts of America, seen by most Americans, if they are at all, from speeding cars on the Interstates or U.S. highways on their way to some place else. They were settled early on in our history, in the 1790s, mostly by Virginians (there was no West Virginia until 1863), and for the most part sparsely: this was hard land to clear and hard land to farm, better suited for dairy cattle than the plains that lay beyond. In some places near the Ohio River there was industrial development early on. The local clay was used to make pottery, the coal that lies near the surface was dug up, a green vitriol works was built, and a nail factory went into operation, all before 1814, and in time the area became dotted with small factory towns and some coal mines. Farther south there was little industrial development and the landscape has a timeless feel today. This is a part of America little affected by the flow of immigrants from Europe in 1880–1924, southern blacks in 1940–65 or Latino and Asian immigrants since 1970. Some counties have seen sharp job losses, as coal mines and factories shut down; others have benefited from local economic development and construction of a gasoline pipeline from the Ohio River to Columbus. This passes over scenic country, much of it forest lands opened up to hunters by MeadWestvaco. The most distinctive people here are the Amish, driving their horses and buggies over covered bridges in Holmes, Tuscarawas and Wayne Counties, the largest concentration of Amish in the world; they run shops now as well as farm and no longer eschew all farm machinery.

The 18th Congressional District of Ohio covers much of this hill country, from Holmes and Tuscarawas Counties in the north to Ross and Jackson Counties in the south. It includes such cities as New Rumley, the birthplace of General George Custer; Zanesville, the birthplace of writer Zane Grey and architect Cass Gilbert and home of a famous Y-shaped bridge; and Chillicothe, the first capital of Ohio, on the Scioto River, beneath Mount Logan, which is stamped on the Great Seal of the state of Ohio. Politically, much of this area was ancestrally Democratic, but in the last two decades it has become more Republican. George W. Bush won 55% of the vote here in 2000 and 57% in 2004.

The congressman from the 18th District is Bob Ney, a Republican first elected in 1994. Ney grew up in Bellaire, in Belmont County just across the Ohio River from Wheeling, West Virginia, and worked as a teacher and as safety director for the city of Bellaire. He worked as a teacher in Iran in 1978 and is the only House member who speaks fluent Farsi; he has called for dialogue with the self-styled reformers in the Iranian government. In 1979 Governor James Rhodes appointed him head of his Office of Appalachia. In 1980 he was elected to the state House, at 26, in quite an upset, beating Wayne Hays, the longtime congressman and chairman of the House Administration Committee who quit this seat in 1976 amid scandal and won a state House seat two years later. Ney lost that seat in the Democratic year of 1982 and spent some time teaching English in Saudi Arabia. In 1984 he was appointed to the state Senate and was elected later that year. When Democrat Douglas Applegate announced his retirement from the U.S. House in 1994, Ney gave up his Finance Committee chairmanship in Columbus to run. Democrats nominated state Representative Greg DiDonato. Most unions backed DiDonato, except for teachers' unions, who backed ex-teacher Ney. His Belmont County home base turned out to be the key; while it gave only 35% to Republican Senate candidate Mike DeWine that year, it voted 67% for Ney, enough to clinch a 54%–46% victory.

In his first years in the House, Ney opposed the Republican leadership on several issues. He removed language eliminating provisions of the Coal Industry Retiree Health Benefits Act that make former employers pay for retirees' health care. He helped organized labor by protecting the bargaining rights of unionized bus drivers, and he opposed Republican leaders' anti-union bills. He was a leader among House Republicans opposed to normal trade relations with China. With other Steel Belt members, he backed quotas on foreign steel.

In January 2001 Ney became chairman of the House Administration Committee, the very panel where Wayne Hays created his power base as "Mayor of Capitol Hill." Ney was the only 1994 freshman who asked to be on the committee, and wanted even then to be chairman. Hastert passed over the more senior Vern Ehlers, who had voted against the leadership on rules votes, to pick Ney, who dissented on substantive issues important to his district but supported the leadership on rules. In 2001 he started off by moving to give Democrats one-third of committee staff funding—something they had been asking for in vain since Republicans took over. House Administration had been a partisan battleground since Democrats resolved the Indiana 8th District election contest in their own favor in 1985 though Indiana state officials said the Republican won. Now Ney and ranking minority member Steny Hoyer cooperated to the point of consulting each other's staffs; together they worked efficiently after September 11.

House Administration has jurisdiction over election law, and that put Ney in the center of two fights in 2001 and 2002. The first was over campaign finance regulation. He opposed the Shays-Meehan bill and produced his own alternative, co-sponsored by Albert Wynn, a member of the Congressional Black Caucus. Hastert hoped that Ney-Wynn could prevail over Shays-Meehan, but after the rule to consider them was voted down in July 2001, both bills were pulled from the floor. In January 2002 Shays-Meehan backers got 218 signatures on a petition to discharge their bill from the Rules Committee; Ney-Wynn had become irrelevant and Shays-Meehan was passed in March. The other issue was how to change election laws after the Florida fiasco. On this Ney reached bipartisan agreement with Hoyer in November 2001. Their bill set minimum national standards but not mandates for state laws; provided $400 million to buy out punch card voting machines and upgrade others and $2.25 billion for new machines and voter education; had procedures for absentee ballots and handicapped voters; and set up an Election Assistance Commission with a Standards Board. In December it was passed 326–63. The Senate took longer to act, and the conference committee took time handling difficult points, but a law similar to Ney-Hoyer was enacted in April 2002.

Hoyer became minority whip in January 2003, though he sometimes worked with Ney on election issues; the new ranking Democrats were John Larson in 2003 and Juanita Millender-McDonald in 2005. After France blocked a Security Council resolution authorizing military force in Iraq, Ney had the House restaurant rename French fries "freedom fries" and French toast "freedom toast." Ney and Millender-McDonald agreed that, after a two-year experiment in which all Congressional Research Service reports were posted on its website, that posting would no longer be automatic but instead at the discretion of the members requesting the studies. In March 2004, when Sheila Jackson Lee demanded that the fourth floor of the Rayburn Building be roped off between 8 a.m. and 4 p.m. for an afternoon visit by singer and accused child molester Michael Jackson, Ney, whose office is on that floor, reopened the hall and said that Jackson was to be treated like any other well-known guest. In January 2005 Ney decided that the House would no longer pay the $227,000 bill for members' Blackberries; they could put the cost on their own office accounts instead. In 2004 Ney and the Republican leadership were attacked for blocking Democrat Rush Holt's bill to require a paper trail for all ballots. Ney pointed out that Hoyer and Senators Christopher Dodd and Mitch McConnell had joined him in March expressing concerns and that hearings in July showed opposition from disabilities groups. "Paper-based systems have a very long and documented history of failure and inaccuracy, with demonstrated error rates that exceed more modern electronic systems." In February 2005 he passed in committee the bill requiring elections of House members within 45 days (later changed to 49) if large numbers of members are killed or rendered incompetent by catastrophic attack.

On other issues, Ney has continued to back trade restrictions and sponsored a bill to preempt state predatory lending laws and impose federal limits. He showed the power of the House Admin chairman after the White House allowed him to bring only one guest into a 2002 Christmas party (his daughter went and his wife returned to her hotel room, rather than the houseboat he lives on in Washington); soon after, Cabinet officials lost 40 of their 44 House parking spaces. With Senator George Voinovich, he successfully resisted cuts in the Appalachian Regional Commission.

After the November 2004 election, *Roll Call* ran a story on Ney's relations with lobbyist Jack Abramoff. In 2002 Abramoff told clients in a Indian tribe that Ney and Dodd would add an amendment to an elections bill reopening their casino in Texas which had been closed by a federal judge. A tribal official said Ney requested that the tribe pay for a trip to Scotland; Ney went on the trip, which included conferences on military issues and golf course outings, and was told that it was financed, as is allowed under House rules, by a foundation connected with Abramoff. Ney met later with Abramoff and tribal officials. Ney said that Abramoff assured him that Dodd favored the provision, but when he asked Dodd, the Connecticut senator said he had never heard of it. In any case the provision was not in the bill that went to the floor in October 2002. In March 2005 Ney said he would be happy to discuss the matter with members of the ethics committee.

Ney was elected in a district represented by Democrats for 46 years and had serious challenges in 1996 and 1998. In 2002 the legislature removed the Ohio River counties from his district and added five new counties in the south and two in the north. That raised the Bush 2000 percentage in the district from 51% to 55%. Ney was unopposed in the primary and general election. In November 2004 he won 66%–34%. Ney reaches the end of House Republicans' six-year term limit on chairmen in January 2007; he might seek a waiver of the term limit. By some accounts he is interested in a position in the Republican leadership should it open up.

★ OKLAHOMA ★

Oklahoma, our fifth-newest state, is approaching its centennial in 2007 proud of its history of rising from humble beginnings, but not sure whether it is keeping pace with the growth and growing sophistication of the American economy. The fact that it is one of only five states admitted to the Union in the 20th century may come as a surprise to most Americans, but not to Oklahomans; the Capitol dome, left unconstructed when the Capitol was opened in 1917, was finally finished in 2002. But all of Oklahoma's history has been a story of stops and sudden starts. Oklahoma was settled in a rush, first by the Five Civilized Tribes driven west by Andrew Jackson's troops over the Cherokees' Trail of Tears in the 1830s. Then came white settlers one morning in April 1889 when, in the great land rush memorialized in an Edna Ferber novel, the Rodgers and Hammerstein musical and half a dozen Hollywood movies, thousands of would-be homesteaders drove their wagons across the territorial line at the sound of a gunshot, the most adventurous or unscrupulous of them literally jumping the gun—the Sooners.

The heritage of these rushes remains. Oklahoma has the second-largest Indian population in the country, after California—273,000 in the 2000 Census—though there is just one reservation and the status of many other tribal entities is often disputed. Some Indian tribes here have unsuccessfully sought a return of native lands and face high unemployment rates. But there has been much intermarriage over the years, and many Oklahomans—and not a few of its politicians—proudly claim Indian blood. Assimilation into everyday life, plus commemoration of historic traditions and efforts to keep the Cherokee, Choctaw, Chickasaw and Seminole languages from dying out—you can see street signs in the Cherokee alphabet in Tahlequah—seem to have provided a better life for most Native Americans here than other approaches have elsewhere. The counties with a large Indian heritage in the eastern part of the state have been growing smartly, even as the Great Plains farm and oil counties west of Oklahoma City and Tulsa have lost population.

Statehood came to Oklahoma late, in 1907, at which point it filled up with farmers, rising from 1.5 million people in 1907 to 2.4 million in 1930. Oil helped: The first well was drilled here in 1897 and by 1920, Tulsa was an oil boom town. Then in the 1930s came a decade of bust—or dust—as soil loosened by erosion was whipped into giant swirling clouds: The Dust Bowl. "On a single day, I heard, 50 million tons of soil were blown away," John Gunther reported later. "People sat in Oklahoma City, with the sky invisible for three days in a row, holding dust masks over their faces and wet towels to protect their mouths at night, while the farms blew by." Okies headed in droves west on U.S. 66 to the green land of California, and Oklahoma's population sank to 2.3 million in 1940 and 2.2 million in 1950, not to reach its 1930 level again until 1970.

Then oil brought another boom: As the oil shocks of 1973 and 1979 sent oil prices up, Oklahoma's population rose from 2.5 million in 1970 to 3 million in 1980 and 3.3 million in 1983. Then, with the collapse of oil prices and of Oklahoma's farm economy as well, it was bust again. A giddy rise was followed by a giddier fall: The rig count fell from 882 in January 1982 to 232 in February 1983 and was just 153 in April 2005. Just as the dust cloud symbolized Oklahoma's 1930s bust, so the auction of oil drilling equipment was a symbol of the 1980s calamity. The 1990 Census reported just 3.1 million Oklahomans, after more than a decade of population increases. But in the 1990s, Oklahoma began building a more diversified economy, with high-tech employers as well as oil and gas firms. Population rose 10% in the decade, to 3.45 million in 2000, and another 2% to 3.52 million in 2004. But incomes have not risen much, and Oklahoma continues to have above-average rates of divorce, teenage pregnancy and crime, and a low rate of college graduates. Oklahoma knows it has risen far, but still has some distance to go.

In federal elections, Oklahoma is a safely Republican state—George W. Bush carried all 77 counties in 2004—but in state politics there is vigorous two-party competition and Democrats still have an edge in party registration. But they are conservative Democrats: the NEP exit poll showed Republicans leading Democrats by only 43%–40% in party identification, but conservatives outnumbered liberals 43%–13%. The state's House delegation was transformed from 4–2

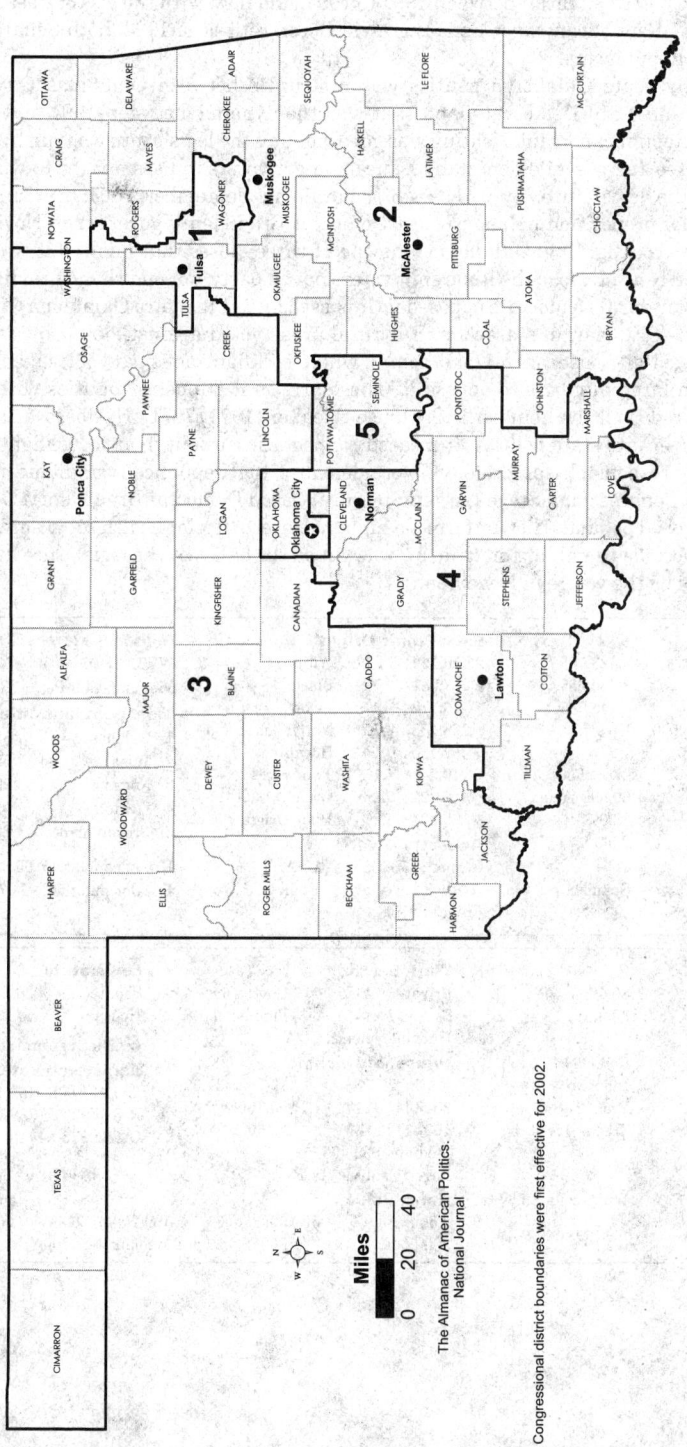

The Almanac of American Politics.
National Journal

Congressional district boundaries were first effective for 2002.

Democratic to 6–0 Republican between 1991 to 1994, and now, with the loss of a seat in the 2000 Census, is 4–1 Republican; since Senator David Boren retired in 1994, both Senate seats have been held by Republicans.

For many years Oklahoma politics was a struggle between Oklahoma City and Tulsa Republicans and rural Democrats, and that was the dynamic between 1994 and 2002, when Tulsa-based Republican Frank Keating was governor and the legislature was run by rural-based Democrats. Keating prevailed on many issues and got voters to pass a right-to-work law, long opposed by the legislature, by a 54%–46% margin in September 2001. But another, quite different ballot proposition helped to elect Democrat Brad Henry governor in November 2002. The issue was cockfighting: Oklahoma was one of three states that allowed it (the others are Louisiana and New Mexico); the issue split voters not on party, but on urban/rural lines. Keating favored the ban; rural Democrats opposed it. It passed by 2–1 in metro Oklahoma City and Tulsa and by a 56%–44% margin statewide. But rural areas voted against, 55%–45%, and in Little Dixie (southeast and east central Oklahoma), where cockfighting is part of local culture, voters turned out in large numbers to oppose it. These are, as it happens, counties with an historic Democratic tradition, the home of U.S. House Speaker (1971–76) Carl Albert, a tradition that still carries over into state politics. Increased Democratic turnout in anti-cockfighting counties was probably responsible for the 6,866-vote defeat of the Republican candidate for governor, former Tulsa Congressman Steve Largent, by rural-based Democrat Brad Henry. Once in office, Henry has proved popular. His platform—a higher cigarette tax for health programs, a lottery for education, racetrack gambling machines—was put on the ballot by the legislature in spring 2004 and approved by the voters in November.

The People		**Race/Ethnic Origin**			**Military veterans:** 376,062 (14.7%)	
Pop. 2004 (est):	3,523,553	2,556,368	74.1%	White	WWII: 18.6%	Korea: 13.2%
Pop. 2000:	3,450,654	257,981	7.5%	Black	Vietnam: 34.6%	Gulf War: 11.5%
Pop. 1990:	3,145,585	46,172	1.3%	Asian	**Most populous cities (2003):**	
Change 1990–2000:	Up 9.7%	266,158	7.7%	Native Am.	1. Oklahoma	523,303
% of U.S. total:	1.2%	2,100	0.1%	Hawaiian	2. Tulsa	387,807
Pop. rank:	27th of 50	140,249	4.1%	Two+ races	3. Norman	99,197
Area size:	69,898 sq. mi.	2,322	0.1%	Other	4. Lawton	91,730
State Native:	62.6%	179,304	5.2%	Hisp. Origin	5. Broken Arrow	83,607
Non-citizen:	2.5%	**Ancestry**				
Language		German: 10.1%		USA: 9.1%	Urban population: 65.3%	
English: 90.8%	Spanish: 5.0%	Irish: 8.2%		English: 6.7%	Rural population: 34.7%	
Other Eur.: 1.8%		French: 1.8%				

Education		**Work Sector**			**Legislature**	
H.S. Grad:	80.6%	Private: 74.6%		Govt: 16.8%	Senate	26 D 22 R
College Grad:	20.3%	Self: 8.2%		Family: 0.5%	House	57 R 44 D
Industry		Unemployment: 5.2%			Legislative Term Limits: Yes	
Agri: 4.1%	Con: 6.9%	**Household Income**			**Registered Voters**	
Fin: 6.0%	Info: 2.7%	<15k: 20.7%		15-35k: 31.3%	D: 1,101,072	(51.4%)
Mfg: 18.1%	Prof: 27.8%	35-50k: 17.1%		50-100k: 24.3%	R: 816,933	(38.1%)
Public: 5.9%	Trade: 15.4%	100-150k: 4.3%		>150k: 2.3%	O: 225,973	(10.5%)
Other: 13.0%		Median: $33,400				
Occupation		Poverty status: 14.7%				
Blue collar: 26.7%	White collar: 56.9%	**Home Value**				
Gray collar: 16.4%		<50k: 33.9%	50-100k: 40.6%	100-200k: 20.3%	200-300k: 3.3%	
		300-500k: 1.3%	>500k: 0.6%	Median: $67,700		

Presidential politics   Oklahoma has been a solidly Republican state in presidential elections since the 1950s. There are no large blocs of voters here who back national Democrats and most Oklahomans find national Republicans acceptable. It has been a long time since Oklahoma has been on anyone's list of target states, and seems unlikely ever to be. Interestingly, even as Democrats were winning state elections because of their strength in rural areas, George W. Bush's percentages increased sharply more in rural counties than in the state's two big metro areas; for the first time in memory the Republican percentage was identical, at 66%, in the two big metro areas and in the rest of Oklahoma.

2004 Presidential Vote		
Bush (R)	959,792	(66%)
Kerry (D)	503,966	(34%)

2004 Democratic Presidential Primary		
Clark (D)	90,526	(30%)
Edwards (D)	89,310	(30%)
Kerry (D)	81,073	(27%)
Lieberman (D)	19,680	(7%)
Dean (D)	12,734	(4%)
Other	9,062	(3%)

2000 Presidential Vote		
Bush (R)	744,337	(60%)
Gore (D)	474,276	(38%)
Other	15,616	(1%)

Nor has Oklahoma's presidential primary attracted much attention. For years it was held in March, as one of many Super Tuesday primaries, and was ignored. In 2001 one Democratic legislator tried to abolish the primary; instead the legislature rescheduled it for February 3, 2004, a week after New Hampshire. As one of two primaries in a southern-accented state that day (the other was South Carolina), Oklahoma was targeted by John Edwards and Wesley Clark, desperate for a win after John Kerry's triumphs in Iowa and New Hampshire. Clark won—his first and only electoral victory—but with just 29.9%, to 29.5% for Edwards and 27% for John Kerry. Kerry carried the counties including Oklahoma City, Tulsa and Norman (home of the University of Oklahoma), and not much else; Clark got big pluralities in the counties around Fort Sill and Altus Air Force Base, and not much else; Edwards carried most suburban and rural counties, but seldom by big pluralities. Edwards's failure to win Oklahoma the same day he won South Carolina may have hurt him; in any case he won no more contests. Clark's failure to win big may have hurt him too. Kerry's third-place finish proved no problem for him, as he won nearly all the other Democratic contests. But his anemic percentage here was a harbinger of his Oklahoma performance in November.

Congressional districting   Oklahoma lost one of its six House seats in the 2000 Census, and for months there was a deadlock over redistricting between Republican Governor Frank Keating and the Democratic legislature. Keating wanted to keep a Tulsa-centered district, especially before the December 2001 special election in which his wife Cathy Keating ran for the Tulsa-centered 1st District seat vacated by Steve Largent. But she lost the Republican nomination. In 2002, the solution appeared after 3d District Congressman Wes Watkins announced he was retiring. Watkins was a Republican (although he used to be a Democrat) and the 3d District was centered in Little Dixie; the seat was safe for Watkins, but Democrats carry the area in state elections and would have a good chance to win an open seat contest. The issue went to court, and in May 2002, a county judge ordered the adoption of a plan that eliminated Watkins's district and gave the other incumbents safe seats; it also had the virtue of creating an Oklahoma City-centered district rather than splitting the city between several districts as it had been since 1981. Democrats, happy that Democratic incumbent Brad Carson got a safe seat, let the matter drop.

109th Congress Lineup	
4 R	1 D

108th Congress Lineup	
4 R	1 D

Governor

Brad Henry (D)

Elected 2002, term expires Jan. 2007, 1st term; b. July 7, 1963, Shawnee; home, Shawnee; U. of OK, B.S. 1985, J.D. 1988; Baptist; married (Kim).

Elected Office: OK Senate, 1992–2002.

Professional Career: Practicing atty., 1989–2002; Atty., City of Shawnee, 1990–2002.

Office: 212 State Capitol Bldg., Oklahoma City, 73105, 405-521-2342; Fax: 405-521-3353; Web site: www.governor.state.ok.us.

Election Results

2002 general	Brad Henry (D)	448,143	(43%)
	Steve Largent (R)	441,277	(43%)
	Gary Richardson (I)	146,200	(14%)
2002 runoff	Brad Henry (D)	135,336	(52%)
	Vince Orza (D)	122,855	(48%)
2002 primary	Vince Orza (D)	154,263	(44%)
	Brad Henry (D)	99,883	(29%)
	Kelly Haney (D)	59,044	(17%)
	Jim Dunegan (D)	28,130	(8%)
1998 general	Frank Keating (R)	505,498	(58%)
	Laura Boyd (D)	357,552	(41%)
	Other	10,535	(1%)

Brad Henry, a Democrat, was elected governor of Oklahoma in an upset in 2002. Henry grew up in Shawnee, one county east of Oklahoma City; he was the kind of boy who built a tree house with multiple floors and 20 rooms and whose Future Farmers of America project was to borrow $10,500 from a bank to buy 15 crossbred cow-calf pairs. He graduated from the University of Oklahoma and its law school and returned home to practice law. In 1992, at 29, he was elected to the state Senate. There he achieved little statewide notice. He opposed right-to-work, but voted to put the issue on the ballot; when his committee bottled up Governor Frank Keating's covenant marriage bill, Keating called him "anti-family." At the beginning of the 2002 race for governor, Henry was not on anyone's political radar screen. The candidate considered most likely to win was Republican Congressman Steve Largent, a football star at the University of Tulsa and with the Seattle Seahawks, who resigned from the House in February 2002 to make the race; the favorite for the Democratic nomination was Oklahoma City area restaurateur Vince Orza, a former Republican who lost the 1990 Republican runoff for governor by a 51%–49% margin. Henry was not sure whether to run; he did not announce until the breathtakingly late date of June 24.

But he had a good campaign plan. He had one big issue (a lottery to fund education), one big vehicle (an RV in which he traveled around the state) and one big endorser (former University of Oklahoma and Dallas Cowboys football coach Barry Switzer). Voters may not be much interested in meeting politicians, but Oklahoma voters are very interested in meeting football coaches. Henry's folksy, aw-shucks manner appealed to rural voters when the other major figures in gubernatorial politics—Keating, Largent, Orza—were from Oklahoma's two major cities. In the Democratic primary August 27, two months and three days after Henry announced, Orza led with 44% of the vote, short of the 50% needed to avoid a runoff, and Henry finished second with 29%; he carried only five counties. Orza called for ending reliance on the state income tax, which presumably meant a higher sales tax; Henry backed the lottery, plus an income tax exemption on seniors' retirement income. Henry had the support of third-place finisher state Senator Kelly Haney, a full-blooded Seminole-Creek; he took care to meet with tribal chiefs, who were conducting a big voter registration drive. Henry won the September 17 runoff by 52%–48%; he lost Oklahoma and Tulsa Counties, but carried their metropolitan areas and won 53%–47% in the rest of Oklahoma as well.

Against Largent in the general, there were clear contrasts. Largent opposed the lottery, called for moving from the income tax to consumption taxes over the next 10 years, and eliminating the sales tax on food. Henry was for across-the-board teacher salary increases and against merit pay—the teachers' union positions—while Largent took the other side on both. Largent, as Keating did, called for cutting administrative costs in schools; some rural Oklahomans feared that meant consolidating small school districts. And there was another issue that didn't qualify for the ballot until August 20: whether to ban cockfighting. In urban Oklahoma this was a popular stand; Keating endorsed it and so did Largent. But it was highly unpopular in Little Dixie in southeastern Oklahoma, where cockfighting is part of local culture. Henry came out against the cockfighting ban.

Another factor was the independent candidacy of businessman Gary Richardson, who spent $2 million of his own money on his campaign. Richardson called for the elimination of tolls on Oklahoma's turnpikes; both Henry and Largent were against. Richardson also called for eliminating a whole raft of taxes—the personal and corporate income taxes, the sales tax on groceries, the capital gains tax, the business franchise tax, the estate tax—and for replacing them with a tax on the gross revenues of all business operations. Polls showed Richardson with double-digit support, but his issue positions were less important than his ads attacking Largent. On September 11, 2001, though Congress was planning on going into session, Largent was bowhunting in Idaho and out of touch with his staff; he didn't hear about the attacks until two days later. In the meantime, his staff issued a statement from him, for which he had to apologize. Richardson's ads showed one of the World Trade Center towers collapsing and then asked about Largent's whereabouts, then showed Largent answering a reporter's aggressive question about the issue with an expletive. While all these things were working against Largent, Henry ran ads showing his young family and showcasing his folksy style. October polls showed the race closing. In November, Henry won by less than 7,000 votes of more than 1 million cast, 43.3%–42.6%, with 14% for Richardson. Largent led 46%–40% in the Oklahoma City area and 45%–39% in the Tulsa area—far less than the usual Republican leads there—while Henry carried the rest of Oklahoma, which cast 44% of the vote, 48%–39%. This, in many ways, was a victory for rural Oklahoma over urban Oklahoma.

Like many incoming governors in 2003, Henry faced budget shortfalls; he and the legislature avoided tax increases, cut projected spending and drew down the rainy day allowance to zero. In February 2004 Henry rolled out his program—a cigarette tax increase to pay for health care, the lottery for education, increased gambling at racetracks, plus a permanent cut in the top income tax rate from 7% to 6.65%, tax exemptions for retirees and zero capital gains tax on the sale of Oklahoma property. In March 2004 he accepted the legislature's main budget bills. In May 2004 he achieved major victories on his platform; most legislators may have been unwilling to vote for them outright, but they voted to put them on the November ballot. All passed, most by handsome margins. One was expansion of tribal casinos and racetrack gambling, with proceeds for education, mostly for K-12 and college tuitions, but also with money for school consolidation and the teachers' retirement fund. Another was a lottery to provide insurance premiums for teachers and to raise their salaries to the average levels of surrounding states. A third was the cigarette tax increase, with proceeds for health care—more coverage for the uninsured, financing a cancer research center and strengthening the state trauma system (which nearly fell apart when Oklahoma University's trauma center was downgraded). Also there was an income tax exemption for retirees, the cut in the top income tax rate and elimination of capital gains taxes on sales of Oklahoma property (including stock in Oklahoma-chartered corporations).

Republicans complained that the legislature did nothing about workmen's comp and argued that the tort law bill Henry signed fell far short of his promise of changes like those made in Texas and to eliminate "junk science" in courtrooms. Henry replied, "That's part of the equation, but it's not the equation. I think it comes down to education. That's why I'm working so hard to invest in education. What we're figuring out—and the evidence is crystal clear in that Dell competition—is workforce development is absolutely the key to our economic development efforts." Oklahoma had indeed won a competition for a Dell facility, but after a report said that 12% of adult Oklahomans were "essentially illiterate", Henry responded with a "Read, y'all" marketing campaign.

On other issues Henry seemed in line with Oklahoma values. He made Oklahoma one of only a few states to agree to having local police cooperate to enforce federal immigration laws. He opposed a federal constitutional amendment banning same-sex marriages, but firmly backed the current ban in Oklahoma law and signed a bill banning adoption by same-sex couples. He stood by as the state Senate rejected a bill for county-option cockfighting. He appointed the first black justice to the Oklahoma Supreme Court.

Henry attended the Democratic National Convention, his first, and firmly endorsed John Kerry for president. But he said again and again that he wanted "to bring a more bipartisan atmosphere to the Capitol" and he decried the negative campaigning against Democrat Brad Carson in the Senate race financed by $1.5 million donated by two Oklahomans to a 527 organization. His success in the 2004 referendums was balanced by his party's bad showing the same day in legislative elections. Many state House Democrats were forced to retire by term limits, and Republicans converted a 48–53 minority in the state House to a 57–44 majority; they also gained two seats in the state Senate and reduced Democrats' majority to 26–22, with term limits looming there in 2006. With a high job rating and success in the 2004 referendums, Henry in early 2005 seemed to be in good shape for reelection in 2006. But his narrow margin in 2002 and the Republicans' strength in other contests suggests he could have serious competition. Possible Republican challengers include former Senate Minority Leader Jim Williamson, former Congressman J.C. Watts, Lieutenant Governor Mary Fallin, House Speaker Todd Hiett and Robert Sullivan, a Tulsa oil company executive.

Senior Senator

James Inhofe (R)

Elected 1994, seat up 2008, 2d full term; b. Nov. 17, 1934, Des Moines, IA; home, Tulsa; U. of Tulsa, B.A. 1973; Presbyterian; married (Kay).

Military Career: Army, 1957–58.

Elected Office: OK House of Reps., 1966–69; OK Senate, 1969–77, Repub. Ldr., 1975–77; Repub. gubernatorial nominee, 1974; Tulsa Mayor, 1978–84; U.S. House of Reps., 1986–94.

Professional Career: Businessman, land developer, 1962–86.

DC Office: 453 RSOB, 20510, 202-224-4721; Fax: 202-228-0380; Web site: inhofe.senate.gov.

Committees: *Armed Services*: Airland; Readiness & Management Support; Strategic Forces. *Environment & Public Works* (Chmn.).

Group Ratings

	ADA	ACLU	AFS	LCV	ITIC	NTU	COC	ACU	NTLC	CHC
2004	10	12	14	0	100	76	100	100	93	100
2003	5	—	0	5	—	76	100	84	—	—

National Journal Ratings

	2003 LIB	—	2003 CONS		2004 LIB	—	2004 CONS
Economic	27%	—	71%		17%	—	82%
Social	0%	—	59%		0%	—	84%
Foreign	22%	—	68%		0%	—	67%

Key Votes of the 108th Congress

1. Ban Drilling in ANWR	N	5. Energy Bill	Y	9. Ban Same-Sex Marriage	Y
2. Approve Bush Tax Cuts	Y	6. Support Roe v. Wade	N	10. Ban Bunker-Buster Bomb	N
3. Medicare/Rx Bill	Y	7. Ban Partial-Birth Abortion	Y	11. Fund Iraq War	Y
4. Bar Overtime Pay Regs.	N	8. Assault Weapons Ban	N	12. Restrict Missile Defense	N

Election Results

2002 general	James Inhofe (R)	583,579	(57%)	($3,040,220)
	David Walters (D)	369,789	(36%)	($2,072,137)
	James Germalic (I)	65,056	(6%)	
2002 primary	James Inhofe (R)	unopposed		
1996 general	James Inhofe (R)	670,610	(57%)	($2,510,946)
	James Boren (D)	474,162	(40%)	($301,621)
	Other	38,378	(3%)	

Prior Winning Percentages: 1994 (55%); 1992 House (53%); 1990 House (56%); 1988 House (53%); 1986 House (55%)

James Inhofe (pronounced *IN-hoff*), Oklahoma's senior senator, was first elected to the Senate in 1994. He grew up in Tulsa, served in the Army, and worked in real estate, insurance and aviation. He has for years regularly flown planes and is one of Congress's few certified commercial pilots; he flew around the world following Wiley Post's route and on short notice flew into Texas military bases to check on readiness. He was elected to the Oklahoma House in 1966, at 31, and to the Oklahoma Senate in 1969; he ran for governor in 1974 and lost to David Boren, 64%–36%. In 1976, Inhofe ran for the U.S. House against Jim Jones and lost; from 1979–84, he was mayor of Tulsa. He won the heavily Republican 1st District House seat in 1986, but held it with uninspiring margins. He was hurt by negative publicity about a family business lawsuit (he eventually was awarded $3.6 million) and charges of campaign finance irregularities, leveled often by the liberal-leaning *Tulsa World*. Inhofe's great achievement in the House was reforming the arcane discharge petition rule. For years, House rules kept secret the names of signers of petitions to discharge bills stuck in committees; members could say they had worked to bring legislation to the floor when they had done just the opposite. That was changed September 28, 1993, and one of the first bills to benefit from the new rules was the aviation liability reform bill, co-sponsored by Inhofe, which limited the liability of small airplane manufacturers in lawsuits resulting from crashes.

Inhofe jumped into the 1994 Senate race when his onetime opponent David Boren, a conservative Democrat who carried not only every county but every precinct in 1990, announced he was retiring to become president of the University of Oklahoma. The Democratic nominee was moderate Dave McCurdy, congressman since 1980 from southwest Oklahoma. But in Oklahoma in 1994, the Clinton burden was too heavy for even McCurdy to carry. McCurdy had voted for the 1993 Clinton budget and tax package with its original Btu tax and for the 1994 crime bill with its assault weapons ban. Inhofe won by a solid 55%–40%. In the Senate, Inhofe was president of the conservative 11-member freshman class. He was elected to a full six-year term in 1996 over James Boren, David Boren's cousin, by 57%–40%.

Inhofe has a very conservative voting record and is blunt and even acerbic in expressing his views. "I'm not afraid of controversy. I'm not afraid to say what's on my mind and what's on a lot of people's minds," he said after one controversy. "Philosophically, I'm very, very rigid in the things I believe in," he said after another. As a junior member of the Senate he spoke his mind in pungent terms. He compared Clinton EPA administrator Carol Browner to Tokyo Rose and said her agency used "Gestapo tactics." In a 2003 speech he said that the theory that man-made emissions have caused global warming was "the greatest hoax ever perpetrated on the American people." Citing scientists' conclusions and climate statistics, he repeated the same claim, despite protesters' posters attacking him, in an international meeting in Milan in January 2004. During the Armed Services Committee's hearings on the prison abuses in Abu Ghraib in May 2004—abuses he like other committee members condemned—he added, "I'm probably not the only one up at this table that is more outraged about the outrage than we are by the treatment" of Iraqi prisoners. He was outraged that "so many humanitarian do-gooders" were "crawling all over these prisons looking for human rights violations while our troops, our heroes, are fighting and dying." There were howls of outrage from *bien pensant* opinionmakers, but Inhofe reported that 70% of the calls and emails he received were positive — and he said that he wouldn't have held hearings on the issue at all.

In January 2003 Inhofe became chairman of the Environment and Public Works Committee. For much of his time on the committee he had bucked environmental restriction groups, opposing the Clinton administration EPA and favoring oil drilling in the Arctic National Wildlife Refuge and more oil and gas drilling exploration in the United States generally. As for the Endangered Species Act, "America has adopted an attitude that places more value on the life of a critter than on a human being. We want to protect the Arkansas River shiner, a bait fish in Oklahoma, yet we will allow unborn babies to have their brains sucked out in a partial-birth abortion." He supported the Bush administration's Clear Skies initiative, but in August 2003 said he would drop the cause unless the administration spoke out more strongly for it. He successfully resisted Hillary Rodham Clinton's demand for hearings on administration responses to health hazards in Lower Manhattan after the September 11 attacks. He introduced the Bush administration's Chemical Facilities Security bill.

Yet much of Inhofe's first two years as chairman were devoted to an issue on which he was opposed by the Bush administration and by his own Oklahoma colleague Don Nickles. This was the reauthorization of the transportation act, generally (though not entirely accurately) known as the highway bill, one of the main institutional responsibilities of the committee. By early 2004 Inhofe had hammered out agreement in the Senate on a $318 billion transportation bill; House Transportation Committee Chairman Don Young was seeking a $375 billion bill, while the Bush administration wanted to cap spending at $256 billion. Inhofe argued that funds were needed to maintain the highway system and would be funded entirely by user fees (primarily the gas tax); Nickles, as chairman of the Budget Committee, maintained that that level of spending would increase the deficit. It was a rare instance of disagreement between the two, with Nickles, who did not seek reelection in 2004, being the free market purist: Nickles had opposed and Inhofe supported federal terrorism insurance in 2002 and maintaining the travel ban on Cuba in 2003 (but on a 2004 trip to Cuba, Inhofe refused to meet or have his picture taken with Fidel Castro). On the transportation bill, Inhofe was nettled when eight conservative Republicans, including Nickles, signed a letter calling for delay. With bipartisan support he got the Senate to pass the $318 billion bill (which would have increased Oklahoma spending by 42%) in February 2004 by 76–21, but the White House renewed its veto threat, and the House bill was failing to get out of committee. In March Bill Frist and Tom Daschle agreed that both parties would support the Senate bill, and in April Young got the House, cowed by the veto threat and pressured by Speaker Dennis Hastert, to pass a $275 billion bill.

Inhofe was the chairman of the conference committee, and his goal was to get a bill passed in 2004. He did not succeed. In July 2004, with House Ways and Means Chairman Bill Thomas unaccountably taking the lead, the House offered a $299 billion bill, with $284 billion guaranteed to be spent over its six-year life—and the veto threat withdrawn. Inhofe said, "I was not happy with that number." Later that month Inhofe proposed $301 billion, with $289 billion guaranteed. The numbers sound close together, but the political differences were significant: one goal of Inhofe's bill was to guarantee that every state got 95% of its gas tax money back, but when the total spending was decreased that meant that other states would lose projects. In September Inhofe announced a deal with Thomas for $299 billion, but Senate Democrats balked. James Jeffords, the nominally Independent senator from Vermont who was ranking minority member of the committee, said, "I have not seen a shred of evidence that you can draft a bill at $299 billion in contract authority and $284 billion in guaranteed funding that does not pit state against state and region against region." Senate Democrats and one, two or three Republicans prevented agreement in conference, and behind Inhofe's back other members sought an eight-month extension of the old transportation authorization, to kick the issue into the 109th Congress. By the end of September it was apparent that no bill would pass in 2004; this would remain Inhofe's chief task in 2005.

Inhofe is now the third ranking Republican on the Armed Services Committee, after Chairman John Warner and John McCain. There he has been a strong supporter of missile defense and one of the leaders of the successful fight in October 1999 to deny ratification to the Comprehensive Test Ban Treaty. He supported the Bush administration on Iraq and argued that the administration had not aggressively enough made the case that there were connections between

Saddam Hussein and al Qaeda before September 11 and that some weapons of mass destruction—enough to kill 47 million people, Inhofe said—were found in Iraq after major military operations. He was one of two senators to vote against the intelligence reorganization in December 2004—a not atypically lonely position, for he had also cast lonely votes against Richard Holbrooke for UN Ambassador, against the May 1997 budget deal and the October 1998 omnibus budget, and against the bipartisan Everglades bill in 2000.

As Environment Committee chairman, Inhofe has not been averse to sponsoring Oklahoma projects, like the Corps of Engineers projects at Arcadia Lake and Waurika Lake and the completion of the channel to the Port of Catoosa near Tulsa. But he has been unafraid to weigh into local controversy. One such is over the 40 square mile Superfund site at Tar Creek, in northeast Oklahoma, where lead and zinc mines were shut down in the 1960s. In 2003 Inhofe came forward with a $45 million proposed cleanup, but refused to support relocation of people in the towns of Picker and Cardin, where high lead levels were found in the blood of children. Democratic Congressman Brad Carson was sponsoring a voluntary buyout, but Inhofe insisted, "The residents are all on my side . . . not on Brad Carson's side. They want to clean up their community. They don't want this thing where they have two communities destroyed. We are going to win this." Governor Brad Henry in February 2003 threatened to sue the federal government, but hesitated before backing a voluntary buyout in January 2004. Inhofe said local legislators were against a buyout, though not all were, and kept insisting, "There will never be a buyout. I promise you that." In April 2004, Inhofe met with local residents, many of them his harsh critics, and they emerged saying that he genuinely wanted to solve their problems; in June 2004 the legislature passed Henry's bill for a $5 million voluntary buyout. More than half the families eventually agreed to the buyout.

Inhofe was reelected most recently in 2002. His Democratic opponent was former Governor David Walters, who in October 1993 pleaded guilty to a misdemeanor count of violating campaign finance laws in his 1990 campaign; the prosecution dropped eight felony counts. Oklahoma voters seem to have a fixed view of Inhofe: the result was almost identical to those in 1994 and 1996. He won statewide 57%–36%, winning big margins in metro Oklahoma City (62%–31%) and metro Tulsa (60%–34%) and winning more narrowly (52%–41%) in the rest of the state. He continues to keep a weather eye on Oklahoma politics: he called for Oklahoma prosecutors to investigate as violations of state fraud laws Moveon.org and National Resources Defense Council advertisements in April 2004 which he said inaccurately charged that Bush administration policies would weaken controls on mercury emissions, and he predicted accurately that Republicans would win a majority of seats in the Oklahoma House in November 2004. His seat is up in 2008.

Junior Senator

Tom Coburn (R)

Elected 2004, seat up 2010, 1st term; b. Mar. 14, 1948, Casper, WY; home, Muskogee; OK St. U., B.S. 1970, OK U., M.D. 1983; Southern Baptist; married (Carolyn).

Elected Office: U.S. House of Reps., 1994–2000.

Professional Career: Mgr., Coburn Optical Industries, 1970–78; Practicing physician, 1983–present.

DC Office: 172 RSOB, 20510, 202-224-5754; Fax: 202-224-6008; Web site: coburn.senate.gov.

State Offices: Lawton, 580-357-9878; Oklahoma City, 405-231-4941; Tulsa, 918-581-7651.

Committees: *Homeland Security & Governmental Affairs*: Federal Financial Management, Govt. Information & International Security (Chmn.); Investigations (Permanent); Oversight of Govt. Management, the Federal Workforce & the District of Columbia. *Indian Affairs*. *Judiciary*: Constitution, Civil Rights & Property Rights; Corrections & Rehabilitation (Chmn.); Crime & Drugs; Immigration, Border Security & Citizenship; Intellectual Property.

Group Ratings and Key Votes: Newly Elected

Election Results

2004 general	Tom Coburn (R)	763,433	(53%)	($5,078,647)
	Brad Carson (D)	596,750	(41%)	($6,172,076)
	Sheila Bilyeu (I)	86,663	(6%)	
2004 primary	Tom Coburn (R)	145,974	(61%)	
	Kirk Humphreys (R)	59,877	(25%)	
	Bob Anthony (R)	29,596	(12%)	
	Other	2,944	(1%)	
1998 general	Don Nickles (R)	570,682	(66%)	($2,415,565)
	Don E. Carroll (D)	268,898	(31%)	($8,618)
	Other	20,133	(2%)	

Prior Winning Percentages: 1998 House (58%); 1996 House (55%); 1994 House (52%)

Tom Coburn, a Republican who previously served six years in the House, was elected Oklahoma's junior senator in 2004. Coburn grew up in Muskogee, where his father started a company, Coburn Optical Services, which became the town's biggest employer. Coburn graduated from Oklahoma State, and while there married his childhood sweetheart, who was Miss Oklahoma 1967. His father moved his business to Virginia, and Tom Coburn joined him and worked there. These were years of campus and youth rebellions, but not for the Coburns. "I was focused on business, kind of driven. I was sort of aloof to the counterculture. I never even heard of marijuana." Coburn took over the lens division and raised sales from $100,000 to $40 million. In 1975 the company was sold to Revlon and Coburn, after being stricken with melanoma, decided to go to the University of Oklahoma Medical School. After graduating, at 35, he moved to Muskogee and opened Maternal and Family Practice Associates; he has delivered some 4,000 babies and went on medical missions to Haiti and Iraq. In 1994 he read that 2d District Congressman Mike Synar was talking about nationalizing health care, and decided to run against him. "I had a deep sense that things were not right in our country. I saw Washington as a city dominated by self-serving career politicians who were more concerned with protecting their positions than responding to the needs of the country." Synar was beaten by a 71-year-old retired teacher in the Democratic runoff, and Coburn won the general election, in a district that leaned toward Democrats in state elections, 52%–48%.

Coburn was one of 73 House Republican freshmen who arrived in Washington in 1995 determined to make changes. A strong opponent of abortion, he passed amendments requiring AIDS counseling for pregnant women and labels on condoms disclosing that they don't prevent infections which lead to cervical cancer. He passed a bill requiring HIV testing of infants if their mothers had not been tested. He sought more money for veterans' health care. He regularly conducted slide shows for members and staffers on the effects of sexually transmitted diseases. Some of the 1994 freshmen accommodated to Washington; Coburn didn't. He was one of the leaders of the attempted coup against Speaker Newt Gingrich in July 1997. He angered appropriators by opposing their bills and offering amendments. He got the ethics committee to reverse itself in March 1998 and rule that he could continue to practice medicine and he delivered nearly 400 babies while in office. In 1994 he had promised to serve only three terms; in 2000 he kept his promise and did not run for reelection, but returned to his medical practice in Muskogee. And he wrote a book, *Breach of Trust: How Washington Turns Outsiders into Insiders,* in which he called members of Congress "Pharisees" and attacked Republican leaders by name.

In October 2003 Senator Don Nickles announced that he would not run for a fifth term in 2004. Several politicians soon entered the race—Oklahoma City Mayor Kirk Humphreys and state Corporation Commissioner Bob Anthony, both Republicans, and Democrat Brad Carson, who had been elected to Coburn's seat in 2000. Coburn was urged by many to run, but declined; he was treated for colon cancer in 2003. In February 2004 he told his former colleague Steve Largent that he had prepared a press release announcing he would not run. But his mother told him, "If you're supposed to be a U.S. senator, you will. Put it in the Lord's hands and leave it there." After sleeping on it, he had "an impression in my spiritual life that I was supposed to do this." He called his mother and said he changed his mind and announced his candidacy publicly.

He admitted the downsides. "Financially, it's terrible. For my family, it's terrible. And politically, it's stupid to get into a race six to nine months after everyone's already into it. But it's kind of been one of those things that's marked my life. I learned to be obedient to that still inner voice."

Leading Republicans had already lined up for Humphreys. He had been endorsed by Senators Nickles and Jim Inhofe (Coburn told them they should keep their commitments) and Congressmen John Sullivan and Tom Cole. Some 13 Republican senators had contributed $60,000 to Humphreys's campaign. Polls showed a close race, usually with Coburn just a bit ahead of Humphreys. Negative campaigning may have helped Coburn. Anthony accused Humphreys of "shady" business and land deals. Humphreys attacked Coburn for attending a Las Vegas fundraiser (Coburn returned contributions from gambling figures) and ran an ad attacking Coburn for voting against intelligence and airport spending bills. The Club for Growth, supporting Coburn, replied with ads claiming the bills were loaded with pork. A week before the primary, Coburn was endorsed by Congressman Ernest Istook; a day later, Nickles weighed in with a warning against negative campaigning. Coburn's cultural and fiscal conservatism, his opposition to Washington insiders and his keeping of his term-limits promise made him many fans across the state, and he ended up winning the primary with 61% of the vote, to 25% for Humphreys and 12% for Anthony. Coburn carried 76 of 77 counties, losing one county with few registered Republicans by the margin of 19–13. In the counties of his old House district he won with between 73% and, in Muskogee County, 91% of the vote.

The winner of the Democratic nomination, with 79% of the primary vote, was Congressman Brad Carson. Part Cherokee, Southern Baptist, Carson had a sterling resume. He was an honors graduate at Baylor, a Rhodes Scholar at Oxford; he went to law school at Oklahoma rather than Yale, was a White House Fellow, then practiced with a big firm in Oklahoma City and returned to eastern Oklahoma. Coburn's retirement led to the first open seat race in the 2d District in 26 years; Carson defeated a longtime legislator and former state Democratic chairman in the primary and a well-known car dealer in the general election. He had one of the most moderate voting records of any House Democrat and favored gun rights, the death penalty and the war in Iraq. When Nickles announced his retirement, Carson ran. National Democrats, happy to have such a politically adept candidate with a chance in a heavily Republican state, eagerly supported him; he raised more money than Coburn.

There was an obvious contrast between the two candidates' views on representation. Coburn described himself as a part-time lawmaker, determined to uphold principle and willing to take on his own party's leadership. Carson described himself as a practical-minded lawmaker, committed to a political career, "fight[ing] for Oklahoma" and eager for bipartisanship. Carson attacked Coburn for turning down $15 million in transportation spending for his district. Coburn responded, "I've put every project in the bill that the Oklahoma Department of Transportation asked me to put in the bill. I was then offered a bribe by the committee to vote for the bill. I could have $15 million to spend wherever I wanted to. I don't believe that's the kind of government we want."

Carson was aided by Coburn's penchant for impolitic statements. "I favor the death penalty for abortionists," he said in July 2004, explaining later that he meant only if abortion should become illegal. "The battle for our culture is a battle between good and evil." And, in Altus in August 2004, "You have a bunch of crapheads in Oklahoma City [state legislators] that have killed the vision of anyone wanting to invest in Oklahoma." Also, at Altus, on Indians: "Listen, I know the tribal issues; I was a congressman where most of the Indians are in this state. The problem is, most of them are not Indians." He told an audience in Hugo that a campaign worker had told him "lesbianism is so rampant in some of the schools in southeast Oklahoma that they'll only let one girl go to the bathroom. Now think about it. Think about that issue. How is it that that's happened to us?" Naturally, hostile editorialists and others jumped on these. Carson said, "We've got someone running for Congress, for the U.S. Senate right now in Tom Coburn, who's already made us a laughingstock all across not only the country but the whole globe." State Democratic Chairman Jay Parmley called Coburn "just flat crazy" and an "extremist." September polls showed the race tight and some showed Carson ahead.

Coburn brought in celebrities to campaign for him—Senator Elizabeth Dole, Focus on the Family's Dr. James Dobson, George H. W. Bush. Carson did not want national Democrats in, though he did say he supported John Kerry. Coburn made the point, "Brad Carson is a vote for Ted Kennedy and Hillary Clinton to run the Senate." One Coburn ad showed illegal immigrants: "Brad Carson voted to make it easier for illegal immigrants to cross our borders and take our jobs. And Carson voted to allow immigrants to get on welfare." Carson counterattacked: "Tom has opposed key bills that help our state. The road bill—Tom is opposed to it. The farm bill—Tom is opposed to it. The prescription drug benefit for seniors—Tom is opposed to it. The Patriot Act—Tom is opposed to it." The most incendiary issue was raised in September, when news broke of a lawsuit, long since settled, by a woman who claimed Coburn in 1990 sterilized her without her consent when operating on her ectopic pregnancy and then filed a false Medicaid claim; Coburn said she gave oral consent and never sought reimbursement for the sterilization. Coburn "sterilized an underage girl without her consent," a Carson ad said, then committed Medicaid fraud "to get paid for the illegal procedure." Don Nickles called the ad "slanderous" and "a blatant attempt at character assassination." Coburn charged that Democrats had connived with reporters to raise the issue.

Though Coburn was outspent by Carson he was aided by ads run by the Club for Growth and a 527 organization that received $1 million from two Oklahoma City oilmen. Coburn's standing in the polls rose in October and on November 2 he won by a solid 53%–41% margin. Carson carried all but two of the counties in his congressional district and won in some other rural, historically Democratic counties as well. But Coburn won 56%–37% in the Oklahoma City area and 55%–41% in the Tulsa area, and more narrowly, 49%–45%, in the rest of the state. In an increasingly straight ticket era, the Kerry candidacy was obviously a heavy weight on Carson's fortunes: he ran 7% ahead of Kerry and Coburn 13% behind George W. Bush. For most Oklahomans, Carson wrote in a post-2004 election article in the *New Republic*, "transcendent cultural concerns are more important than universal healthcare or raising the minimum wage or preserving farm subsidies. Pace Thomas Frank, the voters aren't deluded or uneducated. They simply reject the notion that material concerns are more real than spiritual or cultural ones." One might add: they don't care if a frank expression of their views makes them the laughingstock of the world. Interestingly, the NEP exit poll showed that more voters considered Carson too extreme than Coburn.

Interestingly, also, Coburn took a cautious approach as he prepared to enter the Senate. He took no part in the effort to deny Arlen Specter the chairmanship of the Judiciary Committee. "I have a reputation in Washington that's not necessarily accurate and I don't want to inflame that any more before people get to know me and know my heart," he said. "My goal in the Senate is I need to get done what I need to get done. And initially that means no confrontation." But maybe not forever. Senate rules give any one senator the ability to obstruct proceedings far more than Coburn was ever able to in the House. "I'll be sleeping every night" with the 1,500-page *Riddick's Senate Procedure*, he said. "My goal is to learn the rules as well as Robert Byrd." In the meantime he sought to challenge the Senate rule that bars senators from earning money practicing medicine.

FIRST DISTRICT

Rep. John Sullivan (R)

Elected Jan. 2002, 2d full term; b. Jan. 1, 1965, Tulsa; home, Tulsa; Northeastern St. U., B.B.A., 1992; Catholic; married (Judy).

Elected Office: OK House of Reps., 1994–2001.

Professional Career: Trucking salesman, 1988–92; Gas and Fleet sales rep., 1991–98; Realtor, 1997–2002.

DC Office: 114 CHOB, 20515, 202-225-2211; Fax: 202-225-9187; Web site: sullivan.house.gov.

District Offices: Bartlesville, 918-336-6500; Tulsa, 918-749-0014.

Committees: *Energy & Commerce* (28th of 31 R): Energy & Air Quality; Environment & Hazardous Materials; Telecommunications & the Internet.

Group Ratings

	ADA	ACLU	AFS	LCV	ITIC	NTU	COC	ACU	NTLC	CHC
2004	0	0	0	0	100	73	100	100	92	100
2003	0	—	0	5	—	62	100	92	—	—

National Journal Ratings

	2003 LIB	—	2003 CONS		2004 LIB	—	2004 CONS
Economic	0%	—	91%		0%	—	95%
Social	23%	—	77%		19%	—	80%
Foreign	0%	—	89%		10%	—	86%

Key Votes of the 108th Congress

1. Drilling in ANWR	Y	5. DC School Vouchers	Y	9. Ban Same-Sex Marriage	Y
2. Approve Bush Tax Cuts	Y	6. Ban Human Cloning	Y	10. Fund Iraq War	Y
3. Medicare/Rx Bill	Y	7. Restrict Gun Liability	Y	11. Bar Cuba Embargo Funds	N
4. Bar Overtime Pay Regs.	N	8. Ban Partial-Birth Abortion	Y	12. Intelligence Reorg.	Y

Election Results

2004 general	John Sullivan (R)	187,145	(60%)	($1,019,758)
	Doug Dodd (D)	116,731	(38%)	($325,976)
	Other	7,058	(2%)	
2004 primary	John Sullivan (R)	44,082	(70%)	
	Bill Wortman (R)	15,778	(25%)	
	Evelyn Rogers (R)	2,779	(4%)	
2002 general	John Sullivan (R)	119,566	(56%)	($1,470,177)
	Doug Dodd (D)	90,649	(42%)	($546,083)
	Other	4,740	(2%)	

Prior Winning Percentages: 2002 (54%)

The People		Race/Ethnic Origin	Ancestry	
Area size:	1,790 sq. mi.	73.8% White	German: 11.1%	Irish: 8.7%
Urban population:	89.6%	9.4% Black	English: 7.9%	
Rural population:	10.4%	1.4% Asian	**2004 Presidential Vote**	
Pop. 2000:	690,131	5.8% Native Am.	Bush (R) 206,744	(65%)
Median income:	$38,610	0.0% Hawaiian	Kerry (D) 109,486	(35%)
Poverty status:	11.3%	4.2% Two+ races	**2000 Presidential Vote**	
Military veterans:	14.1%	0.1% Other	Bush (R) 165,759	(62%)
		5.3% Hispanic Origin	Gore (D) 99,283	(37%)
			Other 3,566	(1%)
			Cook Partisan Voting Index: R +13	

Occupation   Blue collar: 23.2%   White collar: 62.9%   Gray collar: 14.0%

Tulsa was one of America's oil boomtowns in the early 20th century, settled not just by people from the immediate hinterland but by Midwesterners and New Englanders of Yankee stock. In the 1920s, as its skyscrapers rose in downtown on heights above the Arkansas River, it was a raw town, intent on culture. It was optimistic and ready to seek economic change, yet culturally and politically conservative, with a Yankee elite and an Indian heritage recalled today in the Gilcrease Museum—left by one-eighth Creek Indian oil millionaire Thomas Gilcrease—and an ethnic variety suggested by the Gershon & Rebecca Fenster Museum of Jewish Art. In the decades since, Tulsa has boomed and occasionally busted. It has remained cosmopolitan and conservative. Ordinary people here do not resent the oil companies or the new rich; they identify with them. As voters showed with their approval of the Vision 2025 economic development referendum, Tulsa is working to diversify from being solely one of America's leading petroleum centers. After Citgo Petroleum announced that it was moving its corporate headquarters to Houston, Tulsa persuaded American Airlines to move its maintenance and engineering center to Tulsa from Kansas City. *Forbes* ranked Tulsa third in the nation for its low cost of doing business. The city also is the headquarters of Oral Roberts University and its 60-story City of Faith hospital, and nearby is Catoosa, which was made a seaport by the federally-financed McClellan-Kerr Waterway.

The 1st Congressional District of Oklahoma includes Wagoner and Washington Counties and parts of Rogers and Creek Counties: just about all of the Tulsa metropolitan area. The political tradition here is heavily Republican, strengthened in recent decades by national Democrats' cultural liberalism. Even during the collapse of oil prices in the 1980s, Tulsa remained full of a contagious enthusiasm for new business enterprises and innovations. People here see not class conflict, but a coincidence of economic interests.

The congressman from the 1st District is John Sullivan, a Republican first elected in a January 2002 special election to replace Steve Largent, who resigned to run (unsuccessfully) for governor. Sullivan grew up in Tulsa and graduated from Northeastern Oklahoma State University. In Tulsa he worked in the transportation, oil and gas, and real estate industries. In 1994, at 29, he was elected to the state House, where he served as Republican whip.

He was not the frontrunner in the special primary election in December 2001. The best-known candidate was Cathy Keating, wife of Governor Frank Keating, who enthusiastically backed her campaign. She had a big fundraising advantage, but stumbled in the brief five-week campaign. Sullivan accused her of being too moderate for a conservative district; she had no legislative record to dispute his claims. Sullivan, meanwhile, built a strong grass-roots network among conservative activists. He led the first round of balloting, 46%–30%. Under state law, Sullivan's failure to win 50% entitled Keating to a runoff. But his unexpectedly large lead, plus the unlikelihood that four weeks of campaigning during the Christmas and New Year seasons would capture voter attention, convinced her to drop her candidacy. So on January 8, Sullivan faced the Democratic nominee, Doug Dodd, a Tulsa attorney and former school board member. Dodd ran a spirited campaign and raised some money from labor PACs. Even though this is a district George W. Bush carried with more than 60% of the vote in 2000 and 2004, Sullivan only won 54%–44%. National Democrats may have regretted they did not target this race.

In January 2004 Sullivan won a seat on the Energy and Commerce Committee, where oil and gas issues often are front and center. He pledged to work to break the deadlock on energy legislation. He fought for Tulsa's fair share of highway and transit funds; he had help from Senator Jim Inhofe, who managed the highway bill across the Capitol. He got the Environmental Protection Agency to expedite its review of the threat to a local watershed. In July 2003, as a passenger in a car driven by one of his aides, he was injured in a collision with a security barrier in front of the Capitol. Overseas, he joined House delegations in visits to Israel and Iraq, where he backed Administration policies. But he opposed creation of a national intelligence czar as "a dangerous centralization of power."

In two campaign rematches, Sullivan increased his majority against Dodd. In 2002, Dodd criticized him for missing a vote on increased subsidies for farmers, and noted that he misrepresented his arrest record on an application to coach youth soccer; still, Sullivan raised his margin to 56%–42%. In August 2004, he faced a primary challenge from Bill Wortman, who attacked

Sullivan's veracity on several issues and was backed by two disgruntled ex-consultants who complained that Sullivan had failed to pay for earlier services (Sullivan later reached agreement with the Federal Election Commission on a settlement). Sullivan won 70%–25%. In the fall campaign Dodd focused on the high cost of the "mess" in Iraq and the loss of U.S. jobs to outsourcing, but Sullivan ran as an insider and cited the accomplishments of Bush and the Republican congressional majorities. He won 60%–38%.

SECOND DISTRICT

Rep. Dan Boren (D)

Elected 2004, 1st term; b. Aug. 2, 1973, Shawnee; home, Paden; TX Christian U., B.S. 1997, U. of OK, M.B.A. 2000; Methodist; single.

Elected Office: OK House of Reps., 2002–04.

Professional Career: Aide, OK Corp. Comm., 1997–98; Loan processor, Danc First Corp., 1999–2000; Staffer, U.S. Rep. Wes Watkins 2000–01.

DC Office: 216 CHOB, 20515, 202-225-2701; Fax: 202-225-3038; Web site: www.house.gov/boren.

District Offices: Claremore, 918-341-9336; McAlester, 918-423-5951; Muskogee, 918-687-2533.

Committees: *Armed Services* (28th of 28 D): Projection Forces; Tactical Air & Land Forces. *Resources* (21st of 22 D): Energy & Mineral Resources; Forests & Forest Health.

Group Ratings and Key Votes: Newly Elected

Election Results

2004 general	Dan Boren (D)	179,579	(66%)	($2,018,285)
	Wayland Smalley (R)	92,963	(34%)	($46,832)
2004 primary	Dan Boren (D)	73,421	(58%)	
	Kalyn Free (D)...................................	46,061	(36%)	
	Bryan Bigby (D)	5,328	(4%)	
	Other..	2,497	(2%)	
2002 general	Brad Carson (D)	146,748	(74%)	($1,021,705)
	Kent Pharaoh (R)................................	51,234	(26%)	($304,887)

The People		Race/Ethnic Origin	Ancestry	
Area size:	21,225 sq. mi.	70.2% White	USA: 10.2%	Irish: 7.8%
Urban population:	35.6%	4.0% Black	German: 7.2%	
Rural population:	64.4%	0.3% Asian	**2004 Presidential Vote**	
Pop. 2000:	690,130	16.8% Native Am.	Bush (R)............. 166,826	(59%)
Median income:	$27,885	0.0% Hawaiian	Kerry (D) 114,113	(41%)
Poverty status:	18.5%	6.2% Two+ races	**2000 Presidential Vote**	
Military veterans:	15.4%	0.0% Other	Bush (R)............. 123,952	(52%)
		2.4% Hispanic Origin	Gore (D) 110,791	(47%)
			Other 3,438	(1%)
			Cook Partisan Voting Index: R + 5	

Occupation	Blue collar: 33.2%	White collar: 48.3%	Gray collar: 18.5%

The land that is now northeast Oklahoma a century ago was the Indian Territory, the place where in the 1830s the Five Civilized Tribes were driven from Georgia and Alabama over the Trail of Tears. Almost one in four people here report their race as American Indian, and in some counties one-third or more claim they are at least partly of Native American descent. The Indian percentage is highest in the hilly counties just west of the Ozarks of Arkansas, where county names—Cherokee, Osage, Sequoyah—recall the Civilized Tribes; the street signs in Tahlequah, once the Cherokee capital, are written in the Cherokee script as well as English. This pleasant land of gentle hills and man-made lakes recently has grown at a healthy pace, from overspill from Tulsa and also from retirees and young families moving into the land that became the home of the Civilized Tribes more than 150 years ago.

South of this Indian country is Oklahoma's Little Dixie, settled between 1889 and 1907 by white Southerners, most of them poor. Some of the county names—LeFlore, Pontotoc—are straight from Mississippi. Today, Interstate highways and turnpikes connect people to jobs in more vibrant metropolitan areas, while dam-made lakes have spurred the creation of resort and retirement communities. Still, traditional cultural attitudes and folkways remain strong. Oklahoma voted in November 2002 on a proposition to outlaw cockfighting, which won by 2–1 margins in metro Oklahoma City and Tulsa. But cockfighting is part of local culture in many towns in Little Dixie, and voters there turned out in large numbers and voted to keep cockfighting by similar margins—as much as 78% in some counties.

The 2d Congressional District includes most of the eastern third of Oklahoma, except for metropolitan Tulsa. It includes Muskogee, subject of Merle Haggard's song, "Okie from Muskogee," Will Rogers's hometown of Claremore in Rogers County and the late Speaker of the House Carl Albert's home in McAlester in Pittsburg County in Little Dixie. McAlester is also the site of a massive army ammunition plant that manufactures non-nuclear bombs ranging in size from 500 to 5,000 pounds (during the war in Iraq, it was forced to add a night shift). This area was ancestrally Democratic, but in the 1980s and early 1990s it trended Republican on cultural issues. In the late 1990s it moved back toward the Democrats, or at least Oklahoma Democrats; Al Gore and John Kerry ran better here than in Oklahoma's other districts, but still lost the 2d to George W. Bush. Democrat Brad Henry carried every county here in the 2002 race for governor and Democrat Brad Carson carried all but two in the 2004 race for the Senate.

The new congressman from the 2d District is Dan Boren, who hails from one of Oklahoma's most prominent political families. His grandfather, Lyle Boren, represented southeastern Oklahoma in Congress from 1937 to 1947. His father, David Boren, was elected governor in 1974 and senator in 1978; he became chairman of the Senate Intelligence Committee before he resigned in 1994 to become president of the University of Oklahoma (Boren was breakfasting with CIA director and former Boren staffer George Tenet on September 11, 2001). Dan Boren grew up in Shawnee and in Longview, Texas, where he lived with his mother and stepfather. He graduated from Texas Christian University and the University of Oklahoma Business School; he worked as a college fundraiser, a staffer on the state Corporation Commission and a district aide to Republican Congressman Wes Watkins, who represented Little Dixie until he retired in 2002. Based in rural Okfuskee County, Boren ran for the state House in 2002, raised $200,000 and unseated a Republican who had switched from the Democratic party. He quickly became chairman of the Democratic Caucus. Then, just a year into his term, 2d District Congressman Brad Carson announced that he was running for the Senate, and Boren announced he would run for the House seat. The four-way, July 27 Democratic primary narrowed to a contest between Boren and former district prosecutor Kalyn Free. Boren, who had the backing of business and industry, was the more conservative of the two candidates. At times during their campaign, Boren sounded like a Republican: He claimed that Free would vote like Ted Kennedy if elected to Congress. While Boren supported abortion rights, he opposed partial-birth abortion and favored requiring parental consent for minors wishing to have abortions. He also backed a federal constitutional amendment to ban same-sex marriage. Unlike many other Democrats, Boren opposed repeal of the Bush tax cuts. And Boren said he "more than likely would have" voted to authorize the use of U.S. military force in Iraq. Boren's positions aroused significant opposition from left-leaning interest groups. Free was endorsed by several labor unions, environmental groups, plus MoveOn.org. EMILY's List poured more than $500,000 into her campaign, but that wasn't enough. Boren won the Democratic primary 58%–36%, easily avoiding a runoff. He led in all 25 counties, and ran especially well with 71% in Pittsburg County, home of Carl Albert. In a district that has been solidly Democratic in non-presidential elections, Boren won 66%–34% over Republican horse breeder Wayland Smalley.

Over the past 30 years, this has been a district that has sent young and little-experienced candidates to Washington—Democrat Mike Synar at age 28 in 1978, Republican Tom Coburn after a career in obstetrics in 1994, Democrat Brad Carson at 33 in 2000. Boren, at 31 and after only two years in the legislature, is in that tradition. Although he labels himself a "very conservative Democrat," he has opposed major changes in Social Security, favors the reimportation of prescription drugs from Canada and wants to penalize companies that ship jobs overseas. He appears to have a safe House seat, but it seems possible that he may run some day for governor, as his father did, or for senator, as his two predecessors in this seat did in 2004.

THIRD DISTRICT

Rep. Frank Lucas (R)

Elected May 1994, 6th full term; b. Jan. 6, 1960, Cheyenne; home, Cheyenne; OK St. U., B.S. 1982; Baptist; married (Lynda).

Elected Office: OK House of Reps., 1988–94.

Professional Career: Farmer & rancher.

DC Office: 2342 RHOB, 20515, 202-225-5565; Fax: 202-225-8698; Web site: www.house.gov/lucas.

District Offices: Stillwater, 405-624-6407; Woodward, 580-256-5752; Yukon, 405-373-1958.

Committees: *Agriculture* (5th of 25 R): Conservation, Credit, Rural Development & Research (Chmn.); General Farm Commodities & Risk Management. *Financial Services* (9th of 37 R): Capital Markets, Insurance & Government Sponsored Enterprises; Domestic and International Monetary Policy, Trade & Technology; Financial Institutions & Consumer Credit. *Science* (10th of 24 R): Research; Space & Aeronautics.

Group Ratings

	ADA	ACLU	AFS	LCV	ITIC	NTU	COC	ACU	NTLC	CHC
2004	0	0	0	0	78	53	95	96	81	92
2003	10	—	13	5	—	58	97	88	—	—

National Journal Ratings

	2003 LIB — 2003 CONS		2004 LIB — 2004 CONS	
Economic	9% —	84%	22% —	78%
Social	39% —	60%	23% —	76%
Foreign	11% —	80%	25% —	68%

Key Votes of the 108th Congress

1. Drilling in ANWR	Y	5. DC School Vouchers	Y	9. Ban Same-Sex Marriage	Y
2. Approve Bush Tax Cuts	Y	6. Ban Human Cloning	Y	10. Fund Iraq War	Y
3. Medicare/Rx Bill	Y	7. Restrict Gun Liability	*	11. Bar Cuba Embargo Funds	N
4. Bar Overtime Pay Regs.	*	8. Ban Partial-Birth Abortion	Y	12. Intelligence Reorg.	Y

Election Results

2004 general	Frank Lucas (R)	215,510	(82%)	($371,139)
	Gregory Wilson (I)	46,621	(18%)	
2004 primary	Frank Lucas (R)	unopposed		
2002 general	Frank Lucas (R)	148,206	(76%)	($458,929)
	Robert Murphy (I)	47,884	(24%)	

Prior Winning Percentages: 2000 (59%); 1998 (65%); 1996 (64%); 1994 (70%); 1994 (54%)

The People		Race/Ethnic Origin	Ancestry	
Area size:	34,384 sq. mi.	81.0% White	German: 12.4% USA: 10.0%	
Urban population:	50.7%	3.8% Black	Irish: 8.2%	
Rural population:	49.3%	0.8% Asian	**2004 Presidential Vote**	
Pop. 2000:	690,131	6.0% Native Am.	Bush (R) 209,598	(72%)
Median income:	$32,098	0.1% Hawaiian	Kerry (D) 82,670	(28%)
Poverty status:	15.0%	3.0% Two+ races	**2000 Presidential Vote**	
Military veterans:	14.0%	0.1% Other	Bush (R) 163,302	(65%)
		5.2% Hispanic Origin	Gore (D) 84,691	(34%)
			Other 2,805	(1%)
			Cook Partisan Voting Index: R +18	

Occupation	Blue collar: 28.2%	White collar: 54.1%	Gray collar: 17.7%

First settled just a century ago, western Oklahoma is a fertile land forever at the mercy of the elements. The western plains are scorching hot under the summer sun and snow-blown in winter; this is one of the windiest parts of America. Visitors to the Tallgrass Prairie Preserve, maintained by the Nature Conservancy near Pawhuska, can experience what settlers of untilled land found when they arrived here: a swaying ocean of 10-foot-high grasses filled with insects emitting a dull, incessant roar. Many rural counties here are not much more populous than they were during the virgin sod era. Far fewer people live here than did before the Dust Bowl hit in the 1930s, and fewer than during the Anadarko Basin oil and natural gas boom of the 1970s. But you can still see what the old towns looked like. In 1910, three years after statehood, Oklahoma moved its capital south 25 miles from Guthrie to Oklahoma City, leaving behind what has become one of the nation's largest historic preservation districts, including the Oklahoma Frontier Pharmacy Museum with racks of glass patent medicine bottles and a working soda fountain.

The 3d Congressional District includes Oklahoma's western plains, from the panhandle—an outlaw no man's land that did not officially join the Indian Territory until 1890—to the northern fringes of Oklahoma City. The 3d extends to north central Oklahoma, including Ponca City, the university town of Stillwater and Osage County, site of the state's one Indian reservation just west of Tulsa. A few of the southern counties, settled by farmers crossing the Red River from Texas, are ancestrally Democratic. But farmers coming south from Kansas settled most of these plains, and they have always been heavily Republican. In Kingfisher County, which harvests more rye than any other in the nation, George W. Bush won by more than 3-to-1 margins in both 2000 and 2004. Those divisions have been as permanent as if Oklahoma had been split down the middle during the Civil War. There are few blacks in this part of Oklahoma, but an increasing number of Hispanics are moving here, as in other parts of the Great Plains, to work in hog farms and meatpacking plants.

The congressman from the 3d District is Frank Lucas, a Republican chosen in a 1994 special election, which was a precursor to the party's takeover of the House later that year. Lucas's roots in western Oklahoma extend more than 100 years; he owns a farm and cattle ranch in Roger Mills County and was elected to the Oklahoma House in 1988, at 28. He got his chance to run for Congress in 1994 when Glenn English, a 19-year conservative Democrat, resigned to head the National Rural Electric Cooperative Association. Lucas had serious competition in both the primary and general elections. In the primary, he trailed state Senator Brooks Douglass 36%–34%, who campaigned from his Oklahoma City base with a Western accent. In the runoff, Lucas ridiculed "some Johnny-come-lately dressed up like a drugstore cowboy" and carried all the rural areas to win 56%–44%. In the general, he faced Dan Webber, 27-year-old press secretary to outgoing Senator David Boren. Lucas ran an ad showing the U.S. Capitol ("this is where Dan Webber has worked his entire adult life") and Oklahoma farmland ("this is where Frank Lucas has worked his entire adult life"); he won 54%–46%. Since then, Lucas has been re-elected by wide margins.

Lucas at times has had one of the most conservative voting records in the House, but he has a practical bent. As the representative (before the 2002 redistricting) of the site of the Oklahoma

City bombing, he introduced the resolution condemning it, the bill for relief spending and the bill to authorize the bombing monument and make it part of the national parks system. He supported the 1995 antiterrorism bill and, after the Oklahoma City trial was moved to Denver, sponsored the amendments to allow closed circuit broadcasting of out-of-town trials and to allow bombing victims, survivors and relatives to watch the trial and still testify in the sentencing hearing. On the 2002 farm bill, as a subcommittee chairman, he helped to unravel the 1996 Freedom to Farm Act that he had once embraced. He helped write the conservation incentives to control erosion, aid farmers suffering drought, and protect air and water quality, and he said that the package would be good for agriculture-dependent Oklahoma. He joined other House conservatives in opposing the final deal on the 2004 intelligence bill because of its "super-concentration of power" in a single czar.

Back home, Lucas's main challenge is the physical size of the district: From his home in Cheyenne, it extends 80 miles south, 240 miles west to the Panhandle, and 270 miles east to Tulsa's outskirts — more than 34,000 square miles in total. Since redistricting, he has not had major party opposition. Indeed, the only trouble Lucas encounters seems to be on his ranch: he broke his nose years ago when a cow slammed a gate on him and lost a tooth in 2003 while trying to attach an identification tag to a 250-pound heifer. After the 2004 election, he was briefly mentioned as a possible nominee for Agriculture Secretary; he has said he wants to stay in Congress long enough to become chairman of the Agriculture Committee.

FOURTH DISTRICT

Rep. Tom Cole (R)

Elected 2002, 2d term; b. April 28, 1949, Shreveport, LA; home, Moore; Grinnell Col., B.A. 1971, Yale U., M.A. 1974, U. of OK, Ph.D. 1984; Methodist; married (Ellen).

Elected Office: OK Senate, 1988–91.

Professional Career: OK Repub. Party chmn, 1985–89; Exec. Dir. NRCC, 1991–95, OK Secy. of State, 1995–99; Pol. consultant, 2000-present.

DC Office: 236 CHOB, 20515, 202-225-6165; Fax: 202-225-3512; Web site: www.house.gov/cole/.

District Offices: Ada, 580-436-5375; Lawton, 580-357-2131; Norman, 405-329-6500.

Committees: *Rules* (7th of 9 R): Rules & Organization of the House. *Standards of Official Conduct* (5th of 5 R).

Group Ratings

	ADA	ACLU	AFS	LCV	ITIC	NTU	COC	ACU	NTLC	CHC
2004	0	0	0	0	78	68	100	96	83	100
2003	5	—	0	5	—	60	100	88	—	—

National Journal Ratings

	2003 LIB	—	2003 CONS		2004 LIB	—	2004 CONS
Economic	0%	—	91%		9%	—	88%
Social	17%	—	79%		30%	—	70%
Foreign	11%	—	80%		25%	—	68%

Key Votes of the 108th Congress

1. Drilling in ANWR	Y	5. DC School Vouchers	Y	9. Ban Same-Sex Marriage	Y
2. Approve Bush Tax Cuts	Y	6. Ban Human Cloning	Y	10. Fund Iraq War	Y
3. Medicare/Rx Bill	Y	7. Restrict Gun Liability	Y	11. Bar Cuba Embargo Funds	N
4. Bar Overtime Pay Regs.	N	8. Ban Partial-Birth Abortion	Y	12. Intelligence Reorg.	Y

Election Results

2004 general	Tom Cole (R)	198,985	(78%)	($750,550)
	Charlene Bradshaw (I)	56,869	(22%)	
2004 primary	Tom Cole (R)	unopposed		
2002 general	Tom Cole (R)	106,452	(54%)	($1,261,547)
	Darryl Roberts (D)	91,322	(46%)	($563,729)

The People		Race/Ethnic Origin	Ancestry	
Area size:	10,409 sq. mi.	77.6% White	USA: 10.0%	German: 9.9%
Urban population:	63.3%	6.6% Black	Irish: 8.6%	
Rural population:	36.7%	1.7% Asian	**2004 Presidential Vote**	
Pop. 2000:	690,131	5.5% Native Am.	Bush (R) 194,977	(67%)
Median income:	$35,510	0.1% Hawaiian	Kerry (D) 96,100	(33%)
Poverty status:	13.1%	3.6% Two+ races	**2000 Presidential Vote**	
Military veterans:	15.8%	0.1% Other	Bush (R) 144,568	(61%)
		4.8% Hispanic Origin	Gore (D) 91,078	(38%)
			Other 2,497	(1%)
			Cook Partisan Voting Index: R +13	

Occupation	Blue collar: 26.4%	White collar: 57.2%	Gray collar: 16.5%

In the years just after 1900, the brown hills west of Oklahoma City and north of the Red River suddenly filled up with farmers riding north from Texas, past the well-watered green lands of the east toward the bare pasture lands of the west. These were young people with large families, and in the years since, this land has emptied out, as children have grown up and moved elsewhere and fewer hands are needed for farming. The first settlers here arrived just as the buffalo were dying out: from an estimated 60 million animals to no more than 1,000. So in 1901, President William McKinley established the nation's first wildlife preserve in the Wichita Mountains, 25 miles northwest of Lawton. Fifteen bison were donated by the New York Zoological Society and arrived at the preserve via rail in 1907—a major factor in the survival of the species. Government has played a role in the survival of people, too, in this part of Oklahoma. Population in southwest Oklahoma clusters around major government institutions: The state capital in Oklahoma City; the University of Oklahoma in Norman; the Army Field Artillery Center at Fort Sill, in Lawton; the giant repair depot at Tinker Air Force Base, in southern Oklahoma City.

The 4th Congressional District of Oklahoma begins a few miles from the oil-derrick-surrounded state Capitol in Oklahoma City, smack dab in the middle of the state, and proceeds south and west to cover half of Oklahoma's Red River Valley. Demographically, this district is becoming more suburban, but the cultural tone remains country. That is true even in the Oklahoma City suburbs, which stretch out over the mile-grid roads, where in new subdivisions dust may still get tracked indoors and people still prefer chicken-fried steak to stir-fried chicken (though they eat both). At the same time there is technical sophistication here, at OU and at Fort Sill. But there was dismay when Defense Secretary Donald Rumsfeld cancelled the Crusader, a computerized cannon being developed at Fort Sill. Ancestrally, this is Democratic country, but Norman, Lawton and the Oklahoma City fringe have voted pretty solidly Republican over the past decade.

The congressman from the 4th District is Tom Cole, a Republican first elected in 2002. Cole grew up in Moore, just south of Oklahoma City and north of Norman. He is a fifth-generation Oklahoman, and his mother was a state representative and senator (and a member of the Chickasaw Nation hall of fame); his father served in the Air Force and later worked at Tinker. Cole graduated from Grinnell College, took a masters degree at Yale, and got a Ph.D. in British history at the University of Oklahoma, studying for a year at the University of London. From 1985 to 1989, he was the state Republican chairman in Oklahoma. In 1988, he was elected to the state Senate. He moved to Washington in 1991 as executive director of the National Republican Congressional Committee, then returned to Oklahoma and was appointed Secretary of State—the first Republican to hold that office. He went back to Washington to serve as chief of staff at the Republican National Committee in the 2000 campaign. During much of this period he was one of the partners in a polling and political consulting firm in Oklahoma City, whose clients have included three Republican presidents, Governor Frank Keating and J.C. Watts.

In July 2002 J. C. Watts, former college and professional football player, chairman of the House Republican Conference, 4th District Congressman since 1994, announced that he would not seek reelection. Cole moved quickly to run. Despite his party connections, he still faced formidable opposition. Watts endorsed Cole, but that failed to dissuade attorney Marc Nuttle from running. The two had much in common—their positions on most issues, their party connections. Nuttle had been Cole's predecessor at the NRCC, and then worked on Pat Robertson's 1988 campaign; Nuttle and Cole worked together to pass a right-to-work law in a September 2001 referendum. In the showdown between the strategists, Nuttle called himself a "grass-roots" activist and Cole a "party" activist who raised half his campaign funds from outside the state, much of it from other consultants. But Cole proved to be the stronger candidate. He won 60% of the vote in the August primary, in which two-thirds of the votes were cast in metro Oklahoma City (which includes Norman).

Cole also had tough competition in the general election, from former state senate Majority Leader Darryl Roberts, who defeated Watts's 1998 opponent 48%–34% in the Democratic primary. Amid talk of war in Iraq, Roberts argued that his service of more than 30 years in the Marine Corps, including a stint in Vietnam, taught him about duty and honor; he was appealing to the "yellow dog" Democratic tradition that is particularly strong in the Red River counties. Cole countered by citing the Democratic presidential nominees Roberts had supported, and described him as "pro-tax," "pro-abortion," and "pro-lawsuit." Roberts had only limited national party support; Cole had much more and won 54%–46%.

In the House, Speaker Dennis Hastert delivered on his promise to Cole of a seat on the Armed Services Committee, of obvious importance to the district. But Cole took a leave from the panel in early 2005 when he was appointed to the Rules Committee. In February 2005, Hastert appointed him to the Ethics committee. In February 2004, Democrats harshly criticized Cole's comment to a county convention that "if George Bush loses the election, Osama bin Laden wins the election;" Cole refused to apologize. The remark had no effect on his rapid ascent: Roy Blunt named Cole as one of his deputy whips and in May 2005 Cole said he would seek the NRCC chairmanship for the 2008 election cycle.

FIFTH DISTRICT

Rep. Ernest Istook (R)

Elected 1992, 7th term; b. Feb. 11, 1950, Ft. Worth, TX; home, Warr Acres; Baylor U., B.A. 1971, OK City U. Law Schl., J.D. 1976; Mormon; married (Judy).

Elected Office: OK House of Reps., 1986–92.

Professional Career: Political reporter, Oklahoma City KOMA Radio, 1972–73, WKY Radio, 1973–76; Dir., OK Alcohol Beverage Control Bd., 1977; Practicing atty., 1977–92.

DC Office: 2404 RHOB, 20515, 202-225-2132; Fax: 202-226-1463; Web site: www.house.gov/istook.

District Offices: Oklahoma City, 405-234-9900; Seminole, 405-303-2868; Shawnee, 405-237-6202.

Committees: *Appropriations* (10th of 37 R): Homeland Security (Vice Chmn.); Interior, Environment & Related Agencies; Labor, Health and Human Services, Education & Related Agencies.

Group Ratings

	ADA	ACLU	AFS	LCV	ITIC	NTU	COC	ACU	NTLC	CHC
2004	0	0	13	9	88	63	94	92	72	92
2003	10	—	0	0	—	65	90	88	—	—

National Journal Ratings

	2003 LIB	—	2003 CONS		2004 LIB	—	2004 CONS
Economic	27%	—	73%		16%	—	84%
Social	17%	—	79%		0%	—	91%
Foreign	21%	—	77%		7%	—	93%

Key Votes of the 108th Congress

1. Drilling in ANWR	Y	5. DC School Vouchers	Y	9. Ban Same-Sex Marriage	Y
2. Approve Bush Tax Cuts	Y	6. Ban Human Cloning	Y	10. Fund Iraq War	Y
3. Medicare/Rx Bill	Y	7. Restrict Gun Liability	Y	11. Bar Cuba Embargo Funds	N
4. Bar Overtime Pay Regs.	N	8. Ban Partial-Birth Abortion	Y	12. Intelligence Reorg.	Y

Election Results

2004 general	Ernest Istook (R)	180,430	(66%)	($1,371,961)
	Bert Smith (D)	92,719	(34%)	($11,292)
2004 primary	Ernest Istook (R) .... unopposed			
2002 general	Ernest Istook (R)	121,374	(62%)	($794,780)
	Lou Barlow (D)	63,208	(32%)	($232,697)
	Donna Davis (I)	10,469	(5%)	

Prior Winning Percentages: 2000 (68%); 1998 (68%); 1996 (70%); 1994 (78%); 1992 (53%)

The People		Race/Ethnic Origin	Ancestry	
Area size:	2,089 sq. mi.	67.7% White	German: 9.7%	Irish: 7.7%
Urban population:	87.5%	13.6% Black	USA: 7.6%	
Rural population:	12.5%	2.5% Asian	**2004 Presidential Vote**	
Pop. 2000:	690,131	4.4% Native Am.	Bush (R) 181,644	(64%)
Median income:	$33,893	0.1% Hawaiian	Kerry (D) 101,595	(36%)
Poverty status:	15.8%	3.3% Two+ races	**2000 Presidential Vote**	
Military veterans:	14.2%	0.1% Other	Bush (R) 135,761	(62%)
		8.3% Hispanic Origin	Gore (D) 82,584	(38%)
			Other 1,338	(1%)
			Cook Partisan Voting Index: R +12	

Occupation	Blue collar: 23.6%	White collar: 60.6%	Gray collar: 15.8%

Oklahoma City, like many state capitals, was not the spontaneous creation of commerce but the deliberate creation of government, sited in the geographic center of the state, on what turned out to be oil lands. Oil rigs were pumping crude on the grounds of the then-domeless Capitol until 1989; a derrick still stands sentinel outside the governor's window. The land here is browner and more eroded by creeks than the greener, rolling Oklahoma farmland farther east. From its center Oklahoma City has grown far out into the countryside, followed, as in so many southwestern cities, by expanding city limits so that it extends into four counties and three congressional districts and covers 621 square miles. Oklahoma City became the center of the nation's attention in April 1995, when a bomb destroyed the Alfred P. Murrah Federal Building, killing 168 and injuring more than 500. The profound grief has persisted here, but was channeled into the construction of the Oklahoma City National Memorial on the site of the blast, movingly dedicated exactly five years later in April 2000.

The 5th Congressional District includes most of Oklahoma County and Oklahoma City, all except a small section of the county including Midwest City and Tinker Air Force Base. Also included are Pottawatomie and Seminole Counties to the east. These two counties partake of the ancestral Democratic leanings of most of Oklahoma. But Oklahoma City is solidly Republican in state as well as national politics and Oklahoma County casts 88% of the district's votes.

The congressman from the 5th District is Ernest Istook, first elected in 1992, in his views and attitudes a forerunner of the Republican freshmen of 1994. With heavy turnover, he became in just two terms the most senior of the state's House delegation. Istook is the grandson of Hungarian immigrants; after graduating from Baylor, he was a radio reporter in Oklahoma City and went to law school at night. He practiced law and was elected to the Oklahoma House in 1986. In 1992, he ran for the House, taking on 16-year incumbent Republican Mickey Edwards, who had 386 overdrafts on the House bank. Edwards finished third in the primary, with 26% to

32% for Istook and 37% for 1990 gubernatorial nominee Bill Price, who harshly criticized Edwards. Istook ran on conservative issues and won the runoff 56%–44%. He won the general election by only 53%–47% over oil and gas lawyer Laurie Williams, who attacked Istook for his anti-abortion stance. He has been easily reelected since.

Istook has a very conservative voting record. "Oklahoma has the kind of values that the rest of the nation needs to have," he says. He has used his seat on Appropriations to press for various controversial amendments. One was his 1995 effort to ban organizations that receive federal funds from using more than 5% of their money for lobbying. This was fought vociferously by nonprofits; both houses passed different forms of the Istook amendment, but no limit was passed. Istook was the chief sponsor of the Religious Freedom amendment, which came to a vote in a revised form in June 1998; it got 224 votes, well short of the required two-thirds. He opposed the Medicare prescription drug bill in June 2003 but at the request of the leadership agreed to pair his vote with the absent Bill Young of Florida.

Young was then chairman of the Appropriations Committee, and Istook is the only Oklahoman in either house on Appropriations. In 1999, after only six years in Congress, he became chairman of the D.C. Appropriations Subcommittee, and thus a member of the "College of Cardinals." In 2001, he became chairman of the Treasury-Postal Appropriations subcommittee, which supervises the White House budget. In March 2002, he criticized the Bush administration for not providing enough information on homeland security and threatened to withhold the $329 million appropriation for the Executive Office of the President unless Homeland Security chief Tom Ridge testified before Congress.

In 2003 he became chairman of the Transportation Subcommittee. This has jurisdiction over the highway projects many members covet. In his early years on the committee, Istook declined to use his seat to bring home pork; his attitude seems to have changed. In August 2003 he was earmarking $2 million for an I-44 interchange in Tulsa, $5 million for a Tulsa Airport taxiway and $30 million for the relocation of I-40 in the heart of Oklahoma City. He boasted that Oklahoma was receiving more transportation appropriated funds per capita than any other state. He used the transportation appropriation to make the Oklahoma City National Memorial an affiliate, not a property, of the National Park Services so that local people could control it and helped head the effort to raise privately an $18 million endowment for it. But he told Oklahoma City officials that a light rail line would be "hugely expensive" and would not make sense; at the same time he held up $500 million for a light rail line from downtown Seattle to Sea-Tac airport for lack of planning.

Istook is not a fan of Amtrak either. In 2004 the administration sought $900 million for Amtrak while 21 House Republicans signed a letter urging $1.8 billion. Istook wrote them in February and warned, "Any request for Amtrak funding, even if submitted in a separate document, must and will be weighed against your other requests, and I will consider it as a project request for your district." He pointed out that the Heartland Flyer which runs from Oklahoma City to Dallas, has revenues of $883,000 from passengers and $5.2 million from the state of Oklahoma and still doesn't make a profit. In his 2004 appropriation Amtrak got $1.22 billion, and without further notice Istook cut transportation projects from the 21 letter signers' districts. Two of the signers, James Gerlach and Rob Simmons, were from marginal districts; another, John McHugh, almost came to blows with Istook. Speaker Dennis Hastert was angry with this treatment of fellow Republicans, and in December 2004 Istook sent the 21 a letter apologizing for not communicating better.

Istook was also embarrassed in November 2004 by the disclosure that his appropriation contained a provision allowing the Appropriations chairman and designated staff to inspect individual income tax returns. Democrats bellowed with horror, and so did many Republicans. Istook at first said the provision was prepared by the IRS and that "nobody's privacy was ever jeopardized." It turned out that it was drafted by a staffer who wanted members to be able to visit IRS offices as part of agency oversight; the IRS resisted this on the grounds that individual returns might be visible on computer screens. The Senate passed a resolution saying the provision had no effect, and the House quickly followed.

After this and the flap with the 21 letter signers (two of them, McHugh and Curt Weldon, served on the Steering Committee, which nominates Appropriations subcommittee chairmen), there was talk that Istook might lose his cardinalship; when the number of subcommittees was reduced from 13 to 10 in 2005, it came as no surprise when he lost his chair.

Istook was easily reelected from 1994 to 2000 in a district that included only part of the Oklahoma City area and jutted northward to include other heavily Republican areas. But the 2000 Census cost Oklahoma a House seat, and the Democratic legislature wanted to eliminate one of the state's Republican-held districts. This put Istook in potential jeopardy. But the solution presented itself when 3d District Republican Wes Watkins announced his retirement and a state court judge in May 2002 approved a plan that would protect the five remaining incumbents. Istook was easily reelected in 2002 and 2004. But not before he made a stab at running for the Senate seat being vacated by Don Nickles. He planned to announce his candidacy on October 11, 2003. But Senator Jim Inhofe told him that he planned to endorse Oklahoma City Mayor Kirk Humphreys the day before, even though Humphreys was not yet a declared candidate. Inhofe did just that, and Istook, who had been raising large amounts of money far more useful in a seriously contested Senate race than in a shoo-in reelection race, announced he was not running for the Senate. In the process he attacked "party leaders" who would "anoint" a candidate; he ultimately got something in the nature of revenge. A week before the July 2004 primary he endorsed his former House colleague Tom Coburn over Humphreys and had the satisfaction of seeing his candidate defeat Inhofe's a week later by a 61%–25% margin.

★ OREGON ★

Oregon is an experimental commonwealth and laboratory of reform on the Pacific Rim, a maker of national trends. It is far removed from where most Americans live, but closer in touch with the rest of America than sometimes appears: Within minutes after a tree branch brushed a power line in Oregon in August 1996, the entire western power grid shut down all the way from the Canadian border to San Diego, where the Republican National Convention was opening two days later. Oregon has led the nation with bike trails and Nike sneakers, light rail trams and Pendleton shirts, with assisted suicide and mail-in ballots. Oregon is an affluent high-tech civilization where one can still see much the same land and water—and rain—that Lewis and Clark saw in 1805 when they came down the Columbia River gorge, past what is now Portland, to the vast Pacific Ocean.

This Oregon was settled by Americans when John Jacob Astor set up his fur trading post at Astoria in 1811 and when New England Yankees in the 1840s rode the Oregon Trail and floated down the Columbia to the well-watered Willamette Valley. In this remote land, nearly 2,000 miles from the Mississippi River frontier and 700 miles from the small Mexican settlements in California, they built an orderly, productive society—a kind of western New England. It grew steadily over the years, with a few booms—when timber, always its first industry, surged in 1900–10, during the war and after in the 1940s, and in the 1970s when home building skyrocketed and Oregon's natural environment began to be widely appreciated.

Newcomers find a state that has a distinctive culture. Founded by New England Yankees accustomed to town meeting government, Oregonians nearly a century ago pioneered in bringing the people closer to government: This was the first state to pass initiative and referendum, recall of elected officials, and election of U.S. senators by popular vote. It was also the first state to institute Labor Day, workmen's compensation and the eight-hour workday for women. In recent decades Oregon, founded by New England churchmen, has become America's most unchurched state, with the lowest rate of church membership, with large numbers of believers in astrology, New Age spiritualism and the like; in the 2004 exit poll 28% of voters said they had no religion. To the innovations of this cultural left, the public voices of Oregon's big institutions, like those of New England, have been friendly. Oregon over the last two generations produced the first

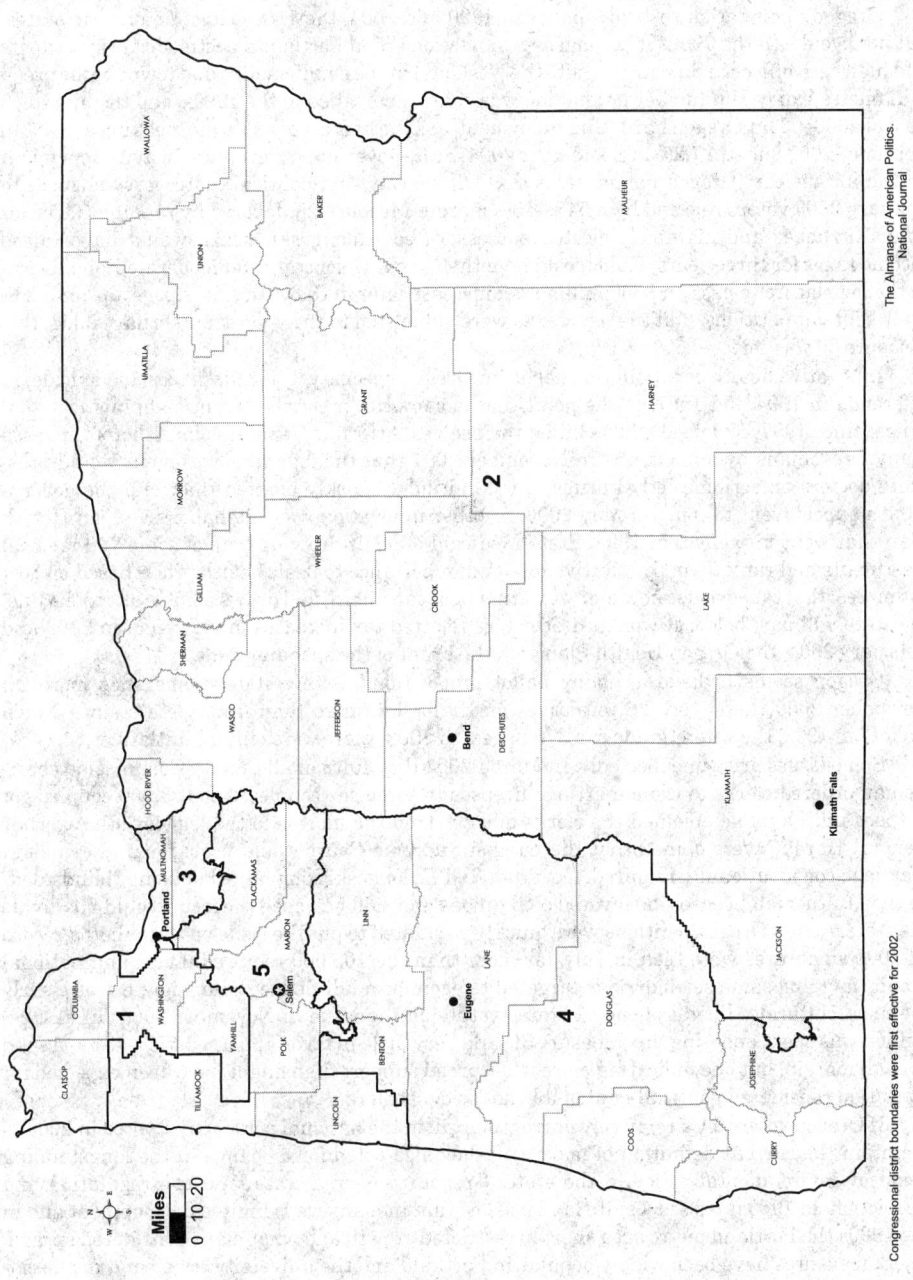

Congressional district boundaries were first effective for 2002.

bottle-deposit law, decriminalized medical marijuana, legalized most abortions before *Roe v. Wade*, and backed limits on development and use of property. It is one of two states that ban self-service gas (the other is New Jersey).

Oregon's population rose 26% between 1990 and 2004, the 11th fastest among the states, but not evenly. In the 1990s it thronged with newcomers in Portland's postmodern skyscrapers and high-tech offices in Silicon Forest to the west, and in the smaller cities and towns of the green Willamette Valley. But lumber production was sharply curtailed in the 1990s, and the high-tech bust of 2000–03 hit Oregon hard. Unemployment was the highest of any state, peaking at 8.1% in February 2002 but still 7.2% in September 2004. State government revenues, heavily dependent on the income tax (Oregon has no sales tax) fell sharply, and political controversy ensued. In January 2003 voters rejected by a 54%–46% margin Measure 28, favored by retiring Governor John Kitzhaber and his newly elected successor Ted Kulongoski, which would have raised income taxes for three years. Kulongoski nonetheless got Democrats and moderate Republicans in the legislature to pass an $800 million tax increase later in the year. Anti-tax groups immediately sent out petitions, and the new taxes were submitted to the voters in February 2004; this Measure 30 was rejected 59%–41%.

Innovative health care policy has been an Oregon specialty. It legalized assisted suicide, in referenda in 1994 and 1997, to the point that doctors can prescribe but not administer lethal drugs; since 1997, 129 people have killed themselves. Attorney General John Ashcroft angered many Oregonians by announcing in November 2001 that the federal government would prosecute doctors prescribing lethal drugs; a federal judge quickly blocked that, and the government's appeal went to court in May 2003. Another innovation was Kitzhaber's Oregon Health Plan that went into effect in 1994. State Medicaid officials draw up lists of some 700 medical treatments and rank them by effectiveness and importance to basic health. Then based on cost estimates, the state decides how many treatments it can afford, and draws a line—above the line, the state will pay; below, it won't. After voters rejected tax increases in referenda in 2003 and February 2004, the Oregon Health Plan took the brunt of the spending cuts.

Oregon seems to have as many ballot propositions as any state—sometimes more. In November 2000 there were 26 initiatives on the ballot, more than in any state since North Dakota in 1932; the voters' guide ran 376 pages. In 2002, there were only 12 initiatives.

Some issues arise unexpectedly. In March 2004 the Multnomah County Commission chairwoman ordered clerks to issue marriage licenses to same-sex couples. About 3,000 couples got licenses until a judge enjoined the clerks and referred the matter to the legislature. Attorney General Hardy Myers opined that the Oregon Supreme Court would probably find same-sex marriage constitutionally required. Governor Ted Kulongoski complained of being "blindsided" by the Multnomah licenses; he favored civil unions and said he hoped the issue would not divide the state. Across Oregon petitions were quickly circulated to put the issue on the ballot; a record 244,000 signatures were filed in July, far more than the 108,000 required. Local and national groups favoring same-sex marriage targeted Oregon for a full-fledged campaign; it was clearly the most culturally liberal of the 11 states voting on the issue in November 2004. In all $2.9 million was spent opposing this Measure 36, and very little in favor. It passed 57%–43%—a solid enough margin, but one indicating more widespread support than might have been expected for a position considered politically untenable not so long before.

If Oregon voters, by a relatively narrow margin in the national perspective, voted in 2004 to maintain the current definition of marriage, they also voted for a change in the longstanding trend of environmental policy in the state. Oregon pioneered state land use regulation and restriction; in 1973 it passed a state land use law that in many ways limited development and in the 1990s the Portland metro area sharply restricted growth and what many considered sprawl. These measures have been widely popular in Portland and the university towns and to a lesser extent in the suburbs. But environmental restrictions have raised hackles in non-metropolitan Oregon. Logging in the Pacific Northwest was largely wiped out because of restrictions imposed to protect the threatened spotted owl (parks officials have been known to fake evidence of owl habitation). This provoked sharp protests, and moves toward Republicans, in timber country. In 2001 the Interior Department cut off water to 1,000 farmers in the Klamath Basin, to protect the endangered and in any case unhappily named sucker fish. This became a major issue in the local media and helps explain why parched eastern Oregon, which once elected the Democratic chairman of the Ways and Means Committee, has become as heavily Republican as Portland is Democratic. In 2004 the discontent seemed to run statewide. State land use law prevents landowners from building houses on land without farming it, even if the land is unsuitable for farming. An aggrieved landowner sparked a petition drive that put on the November ballot Measure 37, requiring state and local governments to excuse property owners from rules enacted after they bought the land or compensate them for complying. In something of a surprise it passed 61%–39%, carrying even Portland's Multnomah County. It seems likely to make many land use restrictions nugatory, since state and local governments are not likely to be able to afford compensation for loss of value they have been happy to inflict on landowners.

Is there some common thread in Oregonians' votes on ballot issues? One common thread seems to be a regard for personal autonomy and a readiness to discard traditional rules and ways of doing things; who would have thought that 43% would vote to allow same-sex marriage? Another seems to be a desire for putting some limits on the ability of officeholders to spend public money and to impose costs on citizens. Voting on most of these measures has followed similar patterns, with Portland and the university towns of Eugene and Corvallis taking liberal positions and counties east of the Cascades and outside the metro area taking more conservative stands.

These cultural and regional differences have been reflected increasingly in Oregon's partisan politics. In the 1980s and 1990s, the gulf between liberal Portland and Multnomah County and conservative eastern and southern Oregon widened and since 2000 it has been a chasm—and has left the state as a whole fairly close to evenly divided. In 2004 John Kerry carried Multnomah County 72%–27% and George W. Bush carried the counties east of the Cascades 63%–36%. The balance has generally tilted toward the Democrats, but not always. Oregon voted for Michael Dukakis in 1988 and for Bill Clinton twice. But Clinton's margin was smaller in 1996 than 1992, and in 2000 Al Gore won here by only 47.0%–46.5%; one reason was that Ralph Nader won 4% here in 1996 and 5% in 2000. In 2004 Nader was not on the ballot, and his votes seem to have gone to Kerry, who carried the state 51%–47%. Starting in 1986, Oregon has elected only Democratic governors, though only once by a wide margin; starting in 1994, it has elected Republican legislatures, except in 2002 and 2004 when it produced first an evenly split and then a Democratic state Senate.

In 1998 Oregonians voted by referendum to hold all elections by mail. So there are no polls open on Election Day; voters have until that night to get their ballots to the election clerk. Unfortunately, Oregon has no statewide registry, so people can cast votes in multiple counties. Proponents of mail-in ballots argue that they increase the percentage of eligibles who vote, which has always been high in Oregon anyway, and they give voters time to read over and think about the numerous ballot initiatives. Opponents fear they increase the possibility of fraud.

The People		Race/Ethnic Origin			Military veterans: 388,990 (15.1%)	
Pop. 2004 (est):	3,594,586	2,857,616	83.5%	White	WWII: 20.6%	Korea: 13.0%
Pop. 2000:	3,421,399	53,325	1.6%	Black	Vietnam: 33.9%	Gulf War: 8.5%
Pop. 1990:	2,842,321	100,333	2.9%	Asian	Most populous cities (2003):	
Change 1990–2000:	Up 20.4%	40,130	1.2%	Native Am.	1. Portland	538,544
% of U.S. total:	1.2%	7,398	0.2%	Hawaiian	2. Salem	142,914
Pop. rank:	28th of 50	82,733	2.4%	Two+ races	3. Eugene	142,185
Area size:	98,381 sq. mi.	4,550	0.1%	Other	4. Gresham	95,816
State Native:	45.3%	275,314	8.0%	Hisp. Origin	5. Beaverton	80,520
Non-citizen:	5.6%	Ancestry				
Language		German: 14.8%		English: 9.5%	Urban population: 78.7%	
English: 86.7%	Spanish: 6.7%	Irish: 8.6%		USA: 4.6%	Rural population: 21.3%	
Other Eur.: 3.5%		Norwegian: 3.1%				

Education		Work Sector		Legislature	
H.S. Grad:	85.1%	Private: 76.3%	Govt: 14.4%	Senate	18 D 12 R
College Grad:	25.1%	Self: 8.9%	Family: 0.4%	House	33 R 27 D
Industry		Unemployment: 6.5%		Legislative Term Limits: No	
Agri: 3.2%	Con: 6.9%	**Household Income**		**Registered Voters**	
Fin: 6.1%	Info: 2.4%	<15k: 15.1%	15-35k: 27.3%	D: 829,197	(38.7%)
Mfg: 19.1%	Prof: 28.1%	35-50k: 17.7%	50-100k: 29.9%	R: 761,717	(35.6%)
Public: 4.4%	Trade: 16.5%	100-150k: 6.5%	>150k: 3.5%	O: 550,335	(25.7%)
Other: 13.2%		Median: $40,916			
Occupation		Poverty status: 11.6%			
Blue collar: 23.9%	White collar: 59.1%	**Home Value**			
Gray collar: 17.0%		<50k: 7.8% 50-100k: 16.5% 100-200k: 49.9% 200-300k: 16.2%			
		300-500k: 7.2% >500k: 2.4% Median: $145,800			

Presidential politics   Oregon was once the most Republican state in the West, voting for Thomas Dewey over Harry Truman in 1948; in the 1980s and early 1990s it was one of the most Democratic. Now it seems more evenly balanced, much less Democratic than California, much less Republican than the Rocky Mountain states. Oregon was the closest West Coast state in 2000, when it backed Al Gore by only a 47.0%–46.5% margin. It remained a target state throughout the 2004 race, although ad volume started going down after mid-October when voters started mailing their ballots in. It got plenty of campaign appearances; on August 13 both George W. Bush and John Kerry held rallies in Portland.

2004 Presidential Vote

Kerry (D)	943,163	(51%)
Bush (R)	866,831	(47%)
Badnarik (Lib)	7,260	(0%)
Other	19,528	(1%)

2004 Democratic Presidential Primary

Kerry (D)	289,804	(79%)
Kucinich (D)	60,019	(16%)
Miscellaneous	10,150	(3%)
LaRouche (D)	8,571	(2%)

2000 Presidential Vote

Gore (D)	720,342	(47%)
Bush (R)	713,577	(47%)
Nader (Green)	77,357	(5%)
Other	22,692	(1%)

Oregon once had an important presidential primary, scheduled in May. In 1948 Oregon ended Harold Stassen's serious presidential prospects, when he lost 52%–48% to Dewey; in 1968 Oregon gave Robert Kennedy his only defeat when it voted 44%–38% for Eugene McCarthy. Oregon in those days was part of a West Coast campaign swing, just before the California primary; at a time when campaigners were not used to flying all over the country they, like National Football League teams in the 1950s, scheduled West Coast contests together to minimize travel time. For 1992 and 1996, Oregon scheduled its primary for Super Tuesday in March, but it was overshadowed by bigger contests in the South. In 2000 and 2004 the primary was held again in May. That, of course, was well after the parties' nominees were determined. But in 2004 Ohio Congressman Dennis Kucinich spent four weeks campaigning in Oregon, hoping to inspire a New Age, Department of Peace, single payer health system constituency. Kerry won nonetheless by a 79%–16% margin.

Congressional districting   Oregon's new congressional map looks a lot like the one it replaced. This was not what the Republican-controlled legislature originally set out to do. Republican redistricters intended to alter the boundaries of the marginal 1st District by shifting solidly Democratic western Multnomah County (1st District Congressman David Wu's political base) from the 1st to the 3d District—an attempt to pack Democratic voters into the 3d while making the 1st more competitive for a Republican challenger. But in June 2001 Democratic Governor John Kitzhaber vetoed the Republican plan. In the inevitable lawsuit, a Multnomah County judge in October chose the Democratic alternative, saying it was less

109th Congress Lineup
4 D   1 R

108th Congress Lineup
4 D   1 R

disruptive and that it better preserved communities of interest: judicial incumbent protection. The decision left the old map largely in place with the exception of a few Multnomah County neighborhoods that were added to the 5th District.

Governor

Ted Kulongoski (D)

Elected 2002, term expires Jan. 2007, 1st term; b. Nov. 5, 1940, Missouri; home, Portland; U. of MO, B.A. 1967, J.D. 1970; Catholic; married (Mary).

Military Career: Marine Corps, 1959–63.

Elected Office: OR House of Reps., 1974–78; OR Senate, 1978–82; OR Atty. Gen., 1992–96; OR Sup. Ct., 1996–01.

Professional Career: Practicing atty., 1971–87; OR Insurance Commissioner, 1982–92.

Office: 160 State Capitol, 900 Court St., Salem, 97301, 503-378-3111; Fax: 503-378-6827; Web site: www.governor.state.or.us.

Election Results

2002 general	Ted Kulongoski (D)	618,004	(49%)
	Kevin Mannix (R)	581,785	(46%)
	Tom Cox (Lib)	57,760	(5%)
2002 primary	Ted Kulongoski (D)	170,799	(49%)
	Jim Hill (D)	92,294	(26%)
	Bev Stein (D)	76,517	(22%)
1998 general	John Kitzhaber (D)	717,061	(64%)
	Bill Sizemore (R)	334,001	(30%)
	Other	62,036	(6%)

Ted Kulongoski (pronounced *koo-lun-GAW-ski*), elected governor of Oregon in 2002, comes from as humble a background as any governor. He was born in rural Missouri; after his father died he was raised by nuns in a Catholic boys' home from age 4 to 14. He joined the Marine Corps after high school and later saved enough money working in a steel mill and as a truck driver to attend the University of Missouri; he graduated from college and law school there at 26 and 29. He moved to Eugene, Oregon, and practiced labor law, representing mostly labor unions; as a legislative staffer he helped write a law giving public employee unions collective bargaining rights. He was elected to the Oregon House in 1974 and the Oregon Senate in 1978; he was regarded as a champion of labor unions. In 1980 he ran against Senator Bob Packwood and held him to a 52%–44% victory in a Republican year. In 1982 he ran against Governor Victor Atiyeh and lost by the humiliating margin of 61%–36%—the last time a Republican was elected governor here. He moved to Portland and practiced law. In 1987 he was appointed Insurance Commissioner by Governor Neil Goldschmidt and helped broker his workmen's compensation changes in 1990, which earned him resentment from some unions. In 1992, after a tough Democratic primary, he was elected attorney general; in 1996 he was elected to the Oregon Supreme Court. In 2001 he resigned to run for governor.

The overriding issue facing state government at the time was the budget shortfall. The great achievement of Governor John Kitzhaber, a physician elected in 1994 and 1998, was the Oregon Health Plan, which expanded Medicaid by rationing treatments. But as revenue flows weakened, the number of treatments it provided had to be reduced, and by November 2001 the budget shortfall was estimated at $720 million in a $16 billion budget. Oregon's revenue stream is especially volatile, because the state has no sales tax and relies heavily on the income tax; in addition, Measure 5, passed in 1990, limits property tax increases, so the state provides 80% of school funding. Budget problems kept making the news during the 2002 campaign cycle; altogether there were five special sessions of the legislature and constant news about shortfalls and cuts.

Of the six major candidates, three Democrats and three Republicans, Kulongoski was the best known: He had appeared on the statewide ballot four times in the preceding 22 years and had served in the legislative, executive and judicial branches of state government. He argued that he had the experience to solve the state's major problems—unemployment, the budget, school financing, the state employees' pension fund. Kitzhaber and the preceding two Democratic governors, Barbara Roberts and Goldschmidt, quickly endorsed him. Against former state Treasurer Jim Hill and former Multnomah County Commission Chairman Bev Stein, Kulongoski depicted himself as the more moderate candidate and pitched his message to older voters and moderates. With late contributions from public employees unions, he outspent the others and won the May 2002 primary with 49% of the vote, to 26% for Hill and 22% for Stein.

The winner of the Republican primary was Kevin Mannix, a Democratic state representative from 1988 to 1996 and Democratic candidate for attorney general in 1996. He switched parties in 1997 and was elected to the state Senate as a Republican in 1998 and came close to winning as the Republican candidate for attorney general in 2000. Mannix was a prolific drafter of legislation—135 of his bills became law in 10 years—and a sponsor of ballot initiatives—his parental consent for abortion lost in 1992 but three tough on crime measures won in 1996. He ran as a "populist Republican," pledged to oppose new taxes and solidly opposed to abortion. Mannix was endorsed by Oregon Right to Life and his campaign kept alive by $81,000 in loans from individuals during the last two weeks; he won with 35% of the vote.

After the primaries, Kulongoski called Mannix "divisive" and criticized him for using the abortion issue in the primary. Mannix replied that he wouldn't focus on cultural issues as governor. The campaign focused more on fiscal issues. In September the legislature made more cuts in planned spending and authorized a January 2003 special referendum, on a three-year increase in the top income tax from 9% to 9.8%. Kulongoski supported the proposal, reluctantly he said; Mannix opposed it, and said he could make enough cuts to make it unnecessary. This Measure 28 was rejected 54%–46%. Kulongoski called for doubling car registration fees to $30 (which would still be the lowest in the nation) to pay for repairing bridges, and he said that localities should pay a greater share for education and that he would try to develop a consensus for a permanent, stable funding base for them, with everything on the table including a sales tax—long verboten in Oregon. He called for all children to be covered by the Oregon Health Plan and added that that would mean removing some adults now covered. He opposed the Bush forest plan, favored Vermont-style civil unions, and criticized Mannix for voting for a cigarette tax increase as part of a budget package. Mannix campaigned with gusto and good humor and seemed more articulate in debate; the tax issue was one that could unite Republicans and brought large contributions in the last weeks.

By all measures—party label, experience and familiarity, the positions on abortion—Kulongoski seemed to be an easy winner. But on election night Mannix was ahead in the count. In Oregon voters cast their votes by mail or at election clerks' offices, and have up to Election Day to get them to the clerks. It takes time to process and count the votes cast on Election Day, and the clerks' offices in big counties took time to count them. The big counties, especially Multnomah (Portland) and Lane (Eugene), took several days, and it was not until Wednesday evening that it was clear that Kulongoski was well ahead and Mannix conceded. When all the votes were in, Kulongoski won 49%–46%. Kulongoski carried only eight of 36 counties—Multnomah, the counties containing the state's two big universities, three on the Pacific coast and two on the Columbia River on either side of Portland.

Kulongoski had a stormy first two years in office. After the rejection of Measure 28, spending had to be cut near the end of the two-year budget cycle, and some public schools had to shorten their school year. In May 2003 Multnomah County, putting its money where its mouth was, voted an income tax of its own, the first local income tax in the state. In August 2003 Kulongoski persuaded a majority of the divided legislature—Republicans had a majority in the House, the Senate was 15–15—to vote for a tax increase. Anti-tax increase groups quickly got out petitions and put Measure 30 on the ballot in February 2004. Kulongoski favored the increase but avoided full-throated support. This time the tax increase was rejected 59%–41%; even Multnomah County voters, apparently feeling taxed enough, voted against. Kulongoski let the scheduled $545 million cuts, phased in this time over the remaining 17 months of the budget cycle, go into effect; the Oregon Health Plan was particularly hard hit.

On other issues, in July 2003 Kulongoski got the legislature to pass a 10-year bill to borrow $2.5 billion to repair and replace bridges and roads; by December 2004 the state found that half the bridges were in good shape and the money could be used on road projects. In July 2003 he signed a law requiring the state pension plan to invest $100 million in Oregon venture capital projects and another levying a 1% lodging tax to pay for tourism promotion. He sent letters to hundreds of California small businesses urging them to move to Oregon and even ventured to Sonoma, California, to Amy's Kitchen, an organic frozen food producer, which opened a 200-employee plant in Medford.

Kulongoski's political career was intertwined with that of Neil Goldschmidt, elected mayor of Portland in 1972 at 32, then Jimmy Carter's Transportation Secretary; he was elected governor in 1986 and appointed Kulongoski, his political career then in limbo, to a top post and relied on him heavily on his key issue, workmen's compensation. Goldschmidt, prominent in Portland civic life in the 1990s, supported Kulongoski in his 1992, 1996 and 2002 campaigns and suggested one of his 2002 proposals, a perpetual college scholarship fund. In November 2003 Kulongoski appointed Goldschmidt head of the state Board of Higher Education and called on him to rejuvenate Oregon's state universities, hit by stagnant enrollment and tuition increases. It soon became a controversial appointment. It was disclosed that SAIF, the state-owned workmen's comp insurer, had paid Goldschmidt $1 million in lobbying fees and failed to report that. Also, Goldschmidt had agreed to head the board of PGE, the Portland utility, on completion of its acquisition by Texas Pacific. Then, on April 26, 2004, Goldschmidt abruptly resigned. The reason soon appeared. On May 6, after *Willamette Week* put the story on its website, Goldschmidt admitted to the Portland *Oregonian* that he had had an affair with a 14-year-old girl in 1975 and 1976 when he was mayor of Portland. This was a felony, though the statute of limitations had long ago passed. Kulongoski said he "had no knowledge" of the charge, but a Goldschmidt aide said he had told Kulongoski several times about it in the 1990s. Kulongoski said that the aide had only said that Goldschmidt had fathered an illegitimate child and said he felt that Goldschmidt had "betrayed" him. The story did not end there. Goldschmidt's wife Diana Goldschmidt, as a member of the Oregon Investment Council, had in October 2003 approved investing $300 million in state funds in Texas Pacific's acquisition of PGE. She said that she voted before Goldschmidt was approached by Texas Pacific to become involved in the deal, but in September 2004 Kulongoski demanded she resign and, when she refused, he fired her.

Kulongoski's major environmental initiative, announced on a two-day boat ride in April 2004, was a Willamette River cleanup. He sought no new restrictions, but asked for state and federal funds. In July 2004 he announced a Willamette River Cleanup Authority and in September announced that G.I. Joe's and Columbia Sportswear would sponsor the 34-mile Willamette River Trail. He called for a mixture of logging and conservation in the Tillamook and Clatsop State Forests, with logging money to go perhaps to college scholarships; a ballot initiative to dedicate half of the forests to wildlife was rejected 62%–38% in November 2004. He was the only area governor to join a 2004 lawsuit by environmental and Indian groups to stop a federally approved increase of water flows over Columbia River dams lest it hurt salmon. After voters in November 2004 passed Measure 37, requiring state and local governments to excuse property owners from rules adopted after they bought their land or to compensate them, Kulongoski said governments should compensate rather than waive their rules and mobilized state government to respond comprehensively.

As attorney general, Kulongoski had been wary of gambling. But as governor he supported the Confederated Tribes of Warm Springs's proposal to build a casino on nontribal land in Cascade Locks, 40 miles east of Portland, and in December 2004 abandoned his opposition to existing video poker and called for electronic slots (line games) to be allowed, with proceeds to pay for state police patrols.

Democrats made gains in both houses of the legislature in November 2004, but Republicans still had a majority in the House. In December Kulongoski presented an $11.9 billion biennial budget with a doubling of scholarships but also an increase in college tuition. "There is not going to be a general tax increase coming out of this legislature," he conceded. He is expected to seek a second term in 2006. Several Democrats, including Lane County Commissioner Peter Sorensen and state Senator Vicki Walker, seemed interested in challenging him in the primary. Possible Republican candidates included 2002 nominee and state Republican Chairman Kevin Mannix; attorney Ron Saxton, who lost to Mannix in the 2002 primary; and state Senator Jason Atkinson of southern Oregon.

Senior Senator

Ron Wyden (D)

Elected Jan. 1996, seat up 2010, 2d full term; b. May 3, 1949, Wichita, KS; home, Portland; Stanford U., B.A. 1971, U. of OR, J.D. 1974; Jewish; divorced.

Elected Office: U.S. House of Reps., 1980–96.

Professional Career: Co–Dir. & Co–Founder, OR Gray Panthers, 1974–80; Dir., OR Legal Svcs. for the Elderly, 1977–79; Prof. of Gerontology, U. of OR, 1976, Portland St. U., 1979, U. of Portland, 1980.

DC Office: 230 DSOB, 20510, 202-224-5244; Fax: 202-228-2717; Web site: wyden.senate.gov.

State Offices: Bend, 541-330-9142; Eugene, 541-431-0229; LaGrande, 541-962-7691; Medford, 541-858-5122; Portland, 503-326-7525; Salem, 503-589-4555.

Committees: *Aging (Special). Budget. Energy & Natural Resources*: National Parks; Public Lands & Forests (RMM); Water & Power. *Finance*: Health Care; International Trade. *Intelligence (Select)*.

Group Ratings

	ADA	ACLU	AFS	LCV	ITIC	NTU	COC	ACU	NTLC	CHC
2004	100	78	100	100	75	18	59	4	13	0
2003	90	—	89	89	—	15	43	15	—	—

National Journal Ratings

	2003 LIB — 2003 CONS		2004 LIB — 2004 CONS	
Economic	64%	— 35%	65%	— 31%
Social	85%	— 0%	82%	— 0%
Foreign	90%	— 0%	75%	— 19%

Key Votes of the 108th Congress

1. Ban Drilling in ANWR	Y	5. Energy Bill	N	9. Ban Same-Sex Marriage	N
2. Approve Bush Tax Cuts	N	6. Support Roe v. Wade	Y	10. Ban Bunker-Buster Bomb	Y
3. Medicare/Rx Bill	Y	7. Ban Partial-Birth Abortion	N	11. Fund Iraq War	Y
4. Bar Overtime Pay Regs.	Y	8. Assault Weapons Ban	Y	12. Restrict Missile Defense	Y

Election Results

2004 general	Ron Wyden (D)	1,128,728	(63%)	($2,817,706)
	Al King (R)	565,254	(32%)	($32,930)
	Other	86,568	(5%)	
2004 primary	Ron Wyden (D)	unopposed		
1998 general	Ron Wyden (D)	682,425	(61%)	($2,866,368)
	John Lim (R)	377,739	(34%)	($413,187)
	Other	57,583	(5%)	

Prior Winning Percentages: 1996 (48%); 1994 House (73%); 1992 House (77%); 1990 House (81%); 1988 House (99%); 1986 House (86%); 1984 House (72%); 1982 House (78%); 1980 House (72%)

Ron Wyden, Oregon's senior senator, was first elected to the House in 1980 and to the Senate in January 1996. Wyden grew up in California, graduated from Stanford, and came to Oregon to attend the University of Oregon Law School. After graduating in 1974 he founded the Gray Panthers, an advocacy group for the elderly; his first foray into electoral politics was sponsoring a successful referendum reducing the price of dentures. In 1980, at 31, he challenged an incumbent in the heavily Democratic 3d District, which covers most of Portland, and won the primary 60%–40%. Wyden has a genius for coming up with sensible-sounding ideas no one else has thought of and a knack for making the counter-intuitive political alliances that proved helpful in passing unfamiliar measures through the House.

Wyden's way to the Senate was opened by the Senate Ethics Committee's recommendation in September 1995 that Oregon Senator Bob Packwood be expelled. Wyden, who had long been eyeing the seat, decided to run in the January 1996 special election to replace him—the first election Oregon conducted by mail-in ballot. With his home base in Portland, whose TV stations cover most of the state, he had greater name identification than any competitor. But he had spirited opposition in the primary from Eugene-based Congressman Peter DeFazio, who carried his own district overwhelmingly, holding Wyden to a 50%–44% win. The Republican nomination was won by state Senate President Gordon Smith, a frozen vegetable tycoon from eastern Oregon who ultimately spent $2 million of his own money. Most polls had the race in a dead heat and there were many negative ads; toward the end, Wyden said he would pull his negative spots. Wyden picked up strength the week before the January 30 deadline and won 48%–47%.

In the Senate, Wyden continued some of his crusades from the House. In April 1997 he and Republican Charles Grassley called for disclosure of the names of senators who place "holds" on legislation—a cause Wyden started working on in 1992 when a bill he backed was killed in the Senate by anonymous holds. Wyden and Grassley persevered, and in March 1999 Trent Lott and Tom Daschle unveiled a new procedure: A senator putting a hold on a bill must inform the sponsor, the committee chairman and the two party leaders.

Another Wyden cause was the Internet. He and California Congressman Christopher Cox sponsored the three-year ban on Internet taxation that passed in October 1998. In 2001 they sought to extend it permanently, but also to set up a procedure to allow states to tax Internet sales if they adopt uniform sales tax rules, with one sales tax rate per state, and provide a means to file and remit sales taxes electronically; the ban was extended until 2005. In 2003 he worked with George Allen to extend it further; in 2004, the Senate passed a four-year extension that grandfathered in pre-1998 taxes and permitted states to apply telephone taxes to voice over Internet protocol (VOIP) services. The bill was signed in December 2004. Wyden has also worked on Internet privacy issues and on anti-spam ("Can-Spam") legislation which passed in 2003; as spam purveyors evolved, he moved to restrict spam messages over text-messaging systems and cell phones and to require notification and permission by distributors of spyware and adware. In 2001 and 2002 he was chairman of the Science, Technology and Space Subcommittee. He has sought to require federal agencies to systematically develop checklists to fight cyberterrorism and encouraged the development of a volunteer force of programmers and engineers to reconstruct networks damaged by emergencies like September 11. In November 2002 he became co-chairman with Bill Frist of the Congressional Forum on Technology and Innovation, which conducts frequent briefing sessions for members and staffers. He has called for changes in the 1996 telecom act. "With the old media, everything would conveniently fit into boxes. The FCC did this. The Commerce Department did that. Now with the convergence of technologies, you're trying to come up with a new set of policies." He was a sponsor of the campaign finance law provision requiring candidates to appear in their television ads, and has sought to extend that requirement to print, Internet and phone message ads.

On health care, Wyden voted against Oregon's assisted suicide law, but has defended it, threatening to filibuster against Don Nickles's attempts in 1999 and 2000 to repeal it and attacking Attorney General John Ashcroft's decision in 2001 to prosecute doctors who prescribe lethal drugs for terminally ill patients. He also worked hard to get a waiver for the Oregon Health Plan and to bring the abortifacient RU-486 to the United States. He was one of 11 Senate Democrats to vote for the 2003 Medicare/prescription drug law, in the face of criticism from many Democrats and former allies. "It was clearly the toughest call I've ever had to make. It wasn't a bill I would have written. But I thought it was the right thing to do to get started." He got amendments creating his national commission to look at health care and to extend a managed care option for rural Oregon; he later worked to prevent Portland from becoming one of the markets selected for competition between Medicare and managed care and, with Snowe, sponsored a bill to allow HHS to negotiate prices with pharmaceutical companies.

Wyden voted against the Iraq war resolution. In July 2003 he criticized the Bush administration for using "any snippet of information to justify the decision they had made." That same month he criticized a Pentagon program using futures trading to gauge the likelihood of terrorist attacks; the program was quickly dropped. In April 2004 he called for release of six years of documents on Osama bin Laden and al Qaeda. In August he demanded an investigation of why Oregon National Guardsmen were ordered to leave a detention area where they intervened to prevent Iraqi guards from attacking handcuffed prisoners. He serves on the Intelligence Committee and in December 2004 was criticized for revealing allegedly classified information when he publicly referred to a "major acquisition program" that was "too necessary" and "unnecessary." A day later, *The Washington Post* said the program was a $9.5 billion spy satellite system; Wyden said his words were authorized by committee Chairman Pat Roberts.

Ten months after Wyden was elected, his opponent Gordon Smith won the state's other Senate seat: The first time two senators were elected who had run against each other in the same year. With the departure of Packwood and Mark Hatfield, Oregon had lost 56 years of Senate seniority and had gained two senators who everyone expected would be bitter enemies. But instead they became friends and collaborators. They have held dozens of town meetings together across Oregon and have met for lunch every Thursday with their chiefs of staff. After losing a bet with Smith, Wyden answered phones for him: "Senator Smith's office; this is Ron Wyden."

As chairman of the Forestry and Public Lands Subcommittee in 2001 and 2002, he was thrust into national and local controversies. With ranking minority member Larry Craig, he developed a bill to permanently protect timber stands older than 120 years, allowing the lumber industry more access to timber west of the Cascades and setting up a system to speed up tree thinning east of the Cascades. After the huge forest fires in the summer of 2002, he worked with Dianne Feinstein on a compromise national forest thinning plan. This resulted in passage of the Healthy Forests Restoration Act in 2003. Oregon Republican Congressman Greg Walden's similar bill passed the House in May 2003, and Wyden and Feinstein agreed to continuing limits on clear-cutting, limiting judicial review to those who participated in the initial process, reviewing injunctions after 45 days and requiring judicial decisions within 100 days. He added $760 million for thinning forests. Some environmental groups were unhappy, but this was popular in rural Oregon. In April 2004 he proposed breaking up the Biscuit fire zone into areas, so logging could be done quickly where there was no controversy. In July 2004 he proposed doubling the wilderness area in the Mount Hood National Forest.

His stands on many issues seem related to Oregon interests. He supported permanent repeal of the estate tax, pointing out the problems it caused for family businesses that own large stands of timber. In 2003 he worked to block welfare act reauthorization because it didn't extend the 1996 waiver for Oregon's welfare-to-work program which counts mental health treatment and drug treatment toward working hours. In August 2003 he questioned why EPA was investigating Portland's $1 billion sewer building project 10 years after it had been begun and when Portland already had the second highest sewer fees of any big city. In November 2003 he filibustered the energy bill, because he said it did little to protect Oregon and Washington consumers from the double-digit increases in electricity rates seen in 2000 and 2001. When gas prices in Oregon shot up to $2.25 per gallon, he protested the FTC's approval, in both Clinton and Bush years, of oil company mergers; in July 2004 he used a maneuver that antagonized Commerce Chairman John McCain to block the nomination of Deborah Majoras to be head of the FTC because she did not share his views.

Wyden portrays himself as a bipartisan problem solver. "Look at my record. My record is based on the proposition that if you want to get anything done, it's got to be bipartisan. But sometimes you have to stand alone." He continues to hold open meetings in all 36 counties every year—a bit daring for a Democrat, perhaps, in a state where in 2004 George W. Bush carried 28 of them, with percentages ranging up to 79%. All this has paid off at election time. In November 1998 Wyden was elected to a full term by a 61%–34% margin. In 2002, when Smith was up for reelection, Wyden did some campaigning for Democrat Bill Bradbury, but let it be known early on that he would have nothing to do with attacks on Smith. For his 2004 campaign Wyden raised $5 million but spent only $3.1 million of it; he donated $500,000 to other Democratic Senate campaigns. His Republican opponent was a Klamath County rancher who, while websurfing at a friend's house the day before the filing deadline, noticed that no well-known names had filed to run against Wyden and mouse-clicked his name in together with the filing fee; he won the six-candidate primary with 35% of the vote. Wyden won 63%–32%, carrying 33 of 36 counties; the three counties he lost have 26% of Oregon's land area but cast only 1% of its votes. Since he was elected to the Senate, Wyden had fought for a seat on the Finance Committee; in January 2005 he finally got it. Gordon Smith also serves on the committee, only the third time in history two senators from the same state have served on Finance; ranking Democrat Max Baucus said Wyden's relationship with Smith would be "helpful." But the Social Security issue looming in 2005 could be an interesting test of his bipartisanship.

Junior Senator

Gordon Smith (R)

Elected 1996, seat up 2008, 2d term; b. May 25, 1952, Pendleton; home, Pendleton; Brigham Young U., B.A. 1976, Southwestern U., J.D. 1979; Mormon; married (Sharon).

Elected Office: OR Senate, 1992–96, Pres., 1994–96.

Professional Career: Law Clerk, NM Supreme Court, 1979–80; Practicing atty., 1980–81; Pres., Smith Frozen Foods, 1980–96.

DC Office: 404 RSOB, 20510, 202-224-3753; Fax: 202-228-3997; Web site: gsmith.senate.gov.

State Offices: Bend, 541-318-1298; Eugene, 541-465-6750; Medford, 541-608-9102; Pendleton, 541-278-1129; Portland, 503-326-3386.

Committees: *Aging (Special)* (Chmn.). *Commerce, Science & Transportation*: Aviation; Disaster Prevention & Prediction; Fisheries & the Coast Guard; National Ocean Policy Study; Surface Transportation & Merchant Marine; Trade, Tourism & Economic Development (Chmn.). *Energy & Natural Resources*: National Parks; Public Lands & Forests; Water & Power. *Finance*: International Trade; Long-Term Growth & Debt Reduction (Chmn.); Social Security & Family Policy. *Indian Affairs*.

Group Ratings

	ADA	ACLU	AFS	LCV	ITIC	NTU	COC	ACU	NTLC	CHC
2004	40	0	29	17	100	61	100	76	85	83
2003	20	—	13	32	—	69	86	78	—	—

National Journal Ratings

	2003 LIB	—	2003 CONS		2004 LIB	—	2004 CONS
Economic	39%	—	60%		45%	—	54%
Social	41%	—	57%		42%	—	56%
Foreign	35%	—	62%		0%	—	67%

Key Votes of the 108th Congress

1. Ban Drilling in ANWR	Y	5. Energy Bill	Y	9. Ban Same-Sex Marriage	Y
2. Approve Bush Tax Cuts	Y	6. Support Roe v. Wade	N	10. Ban Bunker-Buster Bomb	N
3. Medicare/Rx Bill	Y	7. Ban Partial-Birth Abortion	Y	11. Fund Iraq War	Y
4. Bar Overtime Pay Regs.	N	8. Assault Weapons Ban	Y	12. Restrict Missile Defense	N

Election Results

2002 general	Gordon Smith (R)	712,287	(56%)	($5,651,098)
	Bill Bradbury (D)	501,898	(40%)	($2,104,194)
2002 primary	Gordon Smith (R)	unopposed		
1996 general	Gordon Smith (R)	677,336	(50%)	($3,527,252)
	Tom Bruggere (D)	624,370	(46%)	($3,301,736)
	Other	58,524	(4%)	

Gordon Smith, Oregon's junior senator, was first elected to the Senate in 1996. Smith was born in Pendleton and grew up, after his father sold his food processing business to serve as an aide to Eisenhower Agriculture Secretary Ezra Taft Benson, in the Washington suburbs. He is a cousin of former Congressmen Morris and Stewart Udall and of their sons, Congressmen Mark Udall and Tom Udall. Smith served two years as a Mormon missionary in New Zealand, then graduated from Brigham Young and from law school in Los Angeles, was a law clerk in New Mexico and practiced law in Arizona. Then he bought the family frozen vegetable processing company in Pendleton, and guided it out of debt to profitability; Smith Frozen Foods is now one of largest private label packers of frozen vegetables in the country. In 1992 he was elected to the state Senate and in 1995 became Senate president, a fast rise. In 1995 and 1996 he ran for the Senate seat from which Bob Packwood resigned. He lost, after a battle of negative ads, to Ron Wyden 48%–47% in January 1996. The month before, Mark Hatfield had announced his retirement after 30 years in the Senate. At first Smith was reluctant to run again—indeed, he is the only American in history to run in two Senate races in the same year—but Republicans urged him to do so. Attacked during the Wyden race for being endorsed by the conservative Oregon Citizens' Alliance, Smith positioned himself closer to the center and turned down the OCA endorsement this time; when OCA head Lon Mabon ran against him in the primary, Smith beat him 78%–8%. Smith's opponent in the general was Tom Bruggere, another self-made millionaire who, like Smith, owned a Ferrari. In an ad shot in soft focus, Smith said he continued to oppose abortion, but promised not to back a constitutional amendment banning it and at the end of the campaign said he would vote for Medicaid to cover abortions in cases of rape, incest or threat to life of the mother; he promised to work for a balance of environmental protection, economic development and job creation. Smith won 50%–46%.

Against some expectations, Smith has compiled one of the more moderate voting records of Senate Republicans. He voted for mandatory background checks and for child safety locks on guns—both reversals of previous stands. He continued to oppose abortion, but in 2000 backed the use of embryonic stem cells in medical research; the cells are used in research to combat Parkinson's disease, which has stricken several of his relatives. He did not change his position on assisted suicide, however. While his Oregon colleague Wyden repeatedly threatened to filibuster Don Nickles's bill which would have overturned the assisted suicide law Oregon voters approved in 1994 and 1997 referenda, Smith voted for it. "For me, it's an issue of principle on which I'm prepared to stake my political career," he said later. He called on the Bush administration not to prosecute physicians for prescribing lethal drugs, but in November 2001 Attorney General John Ashcroft signaled he would do so; he was blocked from acting by a federal judge and appealed the decision to the Supreme Court. In the meantime Smith opposed congressional action.

Smith strongly supported the 2000 prescription drug bill sponsored by Wyden and Olympia Snowe in 2000 and in summer 2002 wrote his own bill with Bob Graham that at one point seemed the compromise most likely to pass the Senate. Since 1999 he has been Edward Kennedy's chief co-sponsor of the hate crimes bill that adds penalties for crimes committed because of the victim's gender, sexual orientation or disability. He disappointed some of his admirers in gay rights groups by sponsoring his own version of a constitutional amendment banning same-sex marriage; he said he favors letting states decide whether to recognize civil unions. He voted against the McCain-Feingold campaign finance regulation bill when it passed with 59 votes in April 2001, but when it came back from conference committee in February 2002 he indicated he would provide a 60th vote against a filibuster, and thus assured its passage. He was one of the few Republicans to vote for the Comprehensive Test Ban Treaty in October 1999. He supported the Iraq war resolution in October 2002. He offered amendments to the 2003 Medicare/prescription drug bill to insure that health clinics serving the poor get reimbursement and to require cost-based reimbursement for both screening and diagnostic mammography.

Smith has tended to oppose measures sought by environmental restriction groups as undue limits on economic activity. He very strongly opposed breaching dams on the Snake River. He championed the cause of the Klamath Basin farmers who were denied irrigation water because it was said to be needed to protect the endangered sucker fish—a heavily publicized case in Oregon. He parted with most of his fellow Republicans to vote against oil drilling in the Arctic National Wildlife Refuge and to vote for higher CAFE auto gas mileage standards. He questioned Wyden's

2004 proposal to double the wilderness area in the Mount Hood National Forest, and threatened to sponsor an amendment to end all legal challenges to salvage logging in the area affected by the 2002 Biscuit fire.

The election of Wyden in January 1996 and Smith in November 1996 was the first time two senators were elected who had run against each other in the same year. Surprisingly, considering the negative character of their campaign, they became friends. They have held dozens of joint town meetings across Oregon and have issued dozens of joint press releases; they lunch together every Thursday. They have worked together when bills have special impact on Oregon.

Smith got a seat on the Finance Committee in January 2003. Wyden got a seat there two years later, only the third time in history that a state has had both its senators on the Finance Committee. Smith was a lead sponsor of the main provision in the 2004 corporate tax bill which reduced the tax on foreign profits brought back to the United States from 35% to 5.25%; this resulted in a major repatriation of capital for many firms abroad, including some firms with big operations in Oregon, like Nike, Intel and Hewlett-Packard. In December 2004 he sponsored a bill with Kent Conrad to shield from income taxes half of annuity incomes for retirees up to $20,000. In September 2003 Smith's 21-year-old son, afflicted with bipolar disease, killed himself. Smith announced this on the Senate floor in March 2004 and said he would sponsor a bill to train childcare professionals and to develop screening for mental health and behavioral conditions. He presented his bill, authorizing $60 million in grants to states and tribes and $22 million to colleges and universities, in July, and in September, as Smith spoke tearfully on the floor, it was passed by both houses on the same day.

Smith came up for reelection in 2002. It was generally agreed that the strongest potential opponent was Governor John Kitzhaber but he declined to run. That left Secretary of State Bill Bradbury, who announced in October 2001. Bradbury attacked Smith's votes on environmental issues, abortion, tax cuts, education spending and assisted suicide. He had revealed to voters some time before that he has multiple sclerosis, which made it difficult for him to walk long distances; he carried a director's chair so he wouldn't have to stand for long periods.

Smith had two strong assets. One was his work with Wyden. Wyden endorsed Bradbury and conducted fundraisers for him, but he also pledged not to attack Smith in any way and they continued to send out joint press releases. The other asset was money. By April 2002 Smith had raised $4 million—nearly twice as much as Bradbury would during the whole campaign. And, although Smith had spent none of his own money on his November 1996 campaign, Democrats knew that he could always get out his checkbook and match whatever they raised for Bradbury. In the spring, the DSCC ran some ads attacking Smith. But for most of the spring and summer and into October Smith had a monopoly on airtime. He ran ads on his accomplishments, stressing in the Portland media market his support of expanded health care benefits for women and children and his opposition to oil drilling in ANWR. In the Medford media market, he stressed his opposition to the cutoff of irrigation water to Klamath Basin farmers. On radio ads in rural areas, he called Bradbury an "environmental extremist." In September, he ran in the Portland market an ad featuring Judy Shepard, mother of murdered student Matthew Shepard, praising him for his support of including gays in the hate crimes bill—the first pro-gay rights TV ad run by any candidate, the Human Rights Campaign said. Lon Mabon, running as a third party candidate, said, "If you vote for Gordon Smith, you're voting for homosexuality." Bradbury went up with TV ads in October, attacking Smith for opposing assisted suicide and accusing Smith of preferring his own views to those of voters. But he couldn't come close to matching Smith, who ultimately spent $5.6 million to his $2.1 million. Smith won 56%–40%, carrying every county in the state but one, Multnomah (Portland).

FIRST DISTRICT

Rep. David Wu (D)

Elected 1998, 4th term; b. Apr. 8, 1955, Hsinchu, Taiwan; home, Portland; Stanford U., B.S. 1977; Harvard Med. Schl., 1978; Yale Law Schl., J.D. 1982; Presbyterian; married (Michelle).

Professional Career: Law clerk, 9th Circuit Court of Appeals, 1982–83; Campaign staff, Gary Hart for President, 1984; Practicing atty., 1984–98.

DC Office: 1023 LHOB, 20515, 202-225-0855; Fax: 202-225-9497; Web site: www.house.gov/wu.

District Office: Portland, 503-326-2901.

Committees: *Education & the Workforce* (13th of 22 D): 21st Century Competitiveness; Employer-Employee Relations. *Science* (7th of 20 D): Environment, Technology & Standards (RMM); Space & Aeronautics.

Group Ratings

	ADA	ACLU	AFS	LCV	ITIC	NTU	COC	ACU	NTLC	CHC
2004	90	65	88	100	70	16	55	12	9	23
2003	90	—	88	85	—	18	37	20	—	—

National Journal Ratings

	2003 LIB	—	2003 CONS		2004 LIB	—	2004 CONS
Economic	69%	—	31%		67%	—	32%
Social	64%	—	35%		68%	—	31%
Foreign	73%	—	25%		55%	—	44%

Key Votes of the 108th Congress

1. Drilling in ANWR	N	5. DC School Vouchers	N	9. Ban Same-Sex Marriage	N
2. Approve Bush Tax Cuts	N	6. Ban Human Cloning	Y	10. Fund Iraq War	N
3. Medicare/Rx Bill	Y	7. Restrict Gun Liability	N	11. Bar Cuba Embargo Funds	N
4. Bar Overtime Pay Regs.	Y	8. Ban Partial-Birth Abortion	N	12. Intelligence Reorg.	Y

Election Results

2004 general	David Wu (D)	203,771	(58%)	($2,752,272)
	Goli Ameri (R)	135,164	(38%)	($2,327,527)
	Dean Wolf (CNP)	13,882	(4%)	
	Other	1,521	(0%)	
2004 primary	David Wu (D)	unopposed		
2002 general	David Wu (D)	149,215	(63%)	($1,050,961)
	Jim Greenfield (R)	80,917	(34%)	
	Other	7,904	(3%)	

Prior Winning Percentages: 2000 (58%); 1998 (50%)

The People		Race/Ethnic Origin	Ancestry	
Area size:	3,236 sq. mi.	81.1% White	German: 15.0% English: 9.5%	
Urban population:	86.7%	1.1% Black	Irish: 8.4%	
Rural population:	13.3%	5.0% Asian	**2004 Presidential Vote**	
Pop. 2000:	684,280	0.7% Native Am.	Kerry (D)	200,489 (55%)
Median income:	$48,464	0.2% Hawaiian	Bush (R)	161,738 (44%)
Poverty status:	8.7%	2.3% Two+ races	Other	4,507 (1%)
Military veterans:	13.4%	0.1% Other	**2000 Presidential Vote**	
		9.4% Hispanic Origin	Gore (D)	150,768 (50%)
			Bush (R)	131,808 (44%)
			Other	17,057 (6%)
			Cook Partisan Voting Index: D + 6	

Occupation   Blue collar: 20.6%   White collar: 65.3%   Gray collar: 14.1%

Postmodern skyscrapers rising above the riverfront and below a range of hills: This is downtown Portland. The city—which would have been named Boston if a coin toss had gone the other way—started here, along the Willamette River just before it flows into the Columbia, and downtown was built on the narrow margin of land west of the river and below the hills, not on the flat expanse that stretches east towards the snow-capped peak of Mount Hood. Downtown Portland was once a dowdy place, proper in a New Englandish way, with a few formal buildings above the warehouses and factories. But in the last 20 years there has been an explosion of creativity here, symbolized by handsome high-rises—the pyramid-crested brick KOIN Tower, the wedge-shaped Justice Center—restored Victorian storefronts, a downtown transit trolley and a light rail line known as MAX (Metropolitan Area Express), and just across the river the new Oregon Museum of Science and Industry. The affluent neighborhoods in the hills overlooking downtown are full of old lumber barons' mansions with splendid views.

Just over the hills are the valleys and interstices between green mountains of suburban Washington County. This was once farm country, with 39,000 people in 1940; now it has 488,000 and is an integral part of metro Portland. This is an affluent area, which grew 57% between 1990 and 2004, with clusters of towns and protected forest areas that feature a high-tech, healthy-lifestyle aura; major employers here are Tektronix, Intel, Sequent Computer Systems, Columbia Sportswear and Adidas. Beaverton has the world headquarters of Nike, housed in 16 buildings over a 175-acre spread. Like Silicon Valley, the Silicon Forest has an environment—at the foot of mountains, woodsy and even rustic, but outfitted with all the comforts and services of modern civilization—that appeals to a highly skilled work force. As they say locally, wood chips have been replaced by computer chips, though after the high-tech bust of 2000, this area was buffeted by cutbacks and layoffs.

The 1st Congressional District of Oregon includes downtown Portland and its western hills, and all of suburban Washington County. The 1st also proceeds nearly 100 miles northwest from Portland along the Columbia River to the rain-swept port of Astoria on the Pacific Coast where Lewis and Clark spent the winter of 1805–06 at what is now the Fort Clatsop National Memorial, and southwest to Yamhill County, a prime site for turkey farms during the 1960s but where metro growth has been spreading. Like Oregon, the 1st District is historically New England Republican, electing only Republican congressmen from 1892 to 1972; like New England, it then trended sharply left on cultural issues, even as its high-tech economy brought new affluence, and starting in 1974 it has elected nothing but Democrats. But the political balance has been close: no House candidate won more than 52% of the vote in the District in the 1990s.

The congressman from the 1st District is David Wu, a Democrat first elected in 1998, the first Chinese-American to have served in the House. He was born in Taiwan in 1955 and came to the U.S. with his family to join his father, studying at Rensselaer Polytechnic Institute, in 1961. He grew up mostly in Orange County, California, graduated from Stanford, started medical school at Harvard (where he shared an apartment with Bill Frist), then switched to law school at Yale. He clerked for a federal judge in Portland and settled there; he worked on Jimmy Carter's campaign in 1980 and Gary Hart's in 1984. He started his own law firm in 1988 and served on the Portland Planning Commission.

In 1997, Congresswoman Elizabeth Furse, a liberal Democrat and supporter of term limits, announced she would not run again, and Wu ran. The Democratic frontrunner was Linda Peters, who was well known as Washington County Board chairwoman and had the backing of EMILY's List. Wu left his law practice and spent $100,000 of his own money. He attacked Peters in ads for taking a personal loan from a developer and for misspending tax dollars while traveling on county business. Furse, the League of Women Voters and state party leaders criticized Wu's attacks, but he won the primary 52%–43%. The Republican nominee, 29-year-old Molly Bordonaro, the daughter of a prominent real estate man in Portland, came out of the primary with more money than Wu, a more united party behind her and was running even in the polls. Yet Wu won. One reason was that, with help from national Democrats and labor unions, he caught up in fundraising. Another was that Wu established himself early as a moderate. He used his own life story to extol America's system of education and to call for more spending on Head Start (his wife was a Head Start teacher) and aid to college students. Wu won 50%–47%.

In the House, Wu joined the centrist New Democrat Coalition but was also an early ally of Nancy Pelosi in her leadership races; he has had a voting pattern close to that of suburban Portland's other House Democrat, Darlene Hooley. On education, health care, abortion and gun control, he was a reliable Democratic vote. He voted against normal trade relations with China because of "our commitment to American values and the sacrifices of countless families like mine," and he opposed trade promotion authority. To assist unemployed high-tech workers, he filed a proposal to train individuals for jobs in advanced manufacturing industries. In November 2003 he was one of 16 Democrats who voted for the Republican leadership's Medicare/prescription drug bill. On the extended three-hour roll call he sat stoically and silently on the House floor among acutely displeased Democrats, looking as though he preferred to be anywhere else in the world that night. He decided that the bill was good for his constituents, but he had promised party leaders that he would not cast his "yea" vote until a majority of House members had gone on record in support; he was the only member who had not cast a vote for much of that time, and he became the final and largely irrelevant supporter in the 220–215 passage of the bill. After the vote, he conceded that he needed to do fence-mending with Democrats on Capitol Hill and at home who feared that passage of the bill would strengthen George W. Bush.

In the 2004 election Wu faced spirited competition from Goli Ameri, an Iranian-born communications consultant who was new to politics but showed a good grasp of local economic issues and raised lots of money. Ameri supported Bush on Iraq and tax cuts, but she differed on reimportation of prescription drugs, stem-cell research and oil drilling in the Arctic National Wildlife Refuge. In mid-October the Portland *Oregonian* published a lengthy article on which reporters had worked for many months, which set out in great detail charges that Wu had engaged in sexual harassment and a physical attack on a former girlfriend when they both were Stanford undergraduates. He was not arrested and no criminal charges were filed, but the university disciplined him and he privately apologized. Wu refused to cooperate with the newspaper's investigation, and his campaign manager referred to its "unsubstantiated allegations." After the story was published, Wu issued a statement taking responsibility and admitting to "inexcusable behavior." Some Wu supporters questioned the newspaper's decision to publish the story so close to the election, just a few days after it had endorsed Ameri in an editorial. "We believe candidates who ask the public for support should expect their past to be scrutinized," explained the *Oregonian*. "We have carefully considered the political context and community expectations for political leaders in making this [publishing] decision, and we have discussed at great length the ethical questions involved." In a debate three days later, Ameri brought up the matter. "I cannot in good conscience stand here and pretend that violating the most fundamental human right, a woman's safety, is merely a wrongdoing." Wu replied that Ameri's attack was "unfortunate." She ran campaign ads on the incident, but the news story and extensive coverage appeared to cause little political harm for Wu. He won 58%–38%; he carried Washington County, which cast 63% of the vote, by a 55%–41% margin.

SECOND DISTRICT

Rep. Greg Walden (R)

Elected 1998, 4th term; b. Jan. 10, 1957, The Dalles; home, Hood River; U. of OR, B.S. 1981; Episcopalian; married (Mylene).

Elected Office: OR House of Reps., 1988–94, Majority Ldr., 1991–93; OR Senate, 1994–96.

Professional Career: Press secy., U.S. Rep. Denny Smith, 1981–84, Chief of staff, 1984–86; Owner, Columbia Gorge Broadcasters Inc., 1986-present.

DC Office: 1210 LHOB, 20515, 202-225-6730; Fax: 202-225-5774; Web site: walden.house.gov.

District Offices: Bend, 541-389-4408; Medford, 541-776-4646.

Committees: *Energy & Commerce* (22d of 31 R): Energy & Air Quality; Oversight & Investigations; Tele-communications & the Internet. *Resources* (14th of 27 R): Forests & Forest Health (Chmn.); Water & Power.

Group Ratings

	ADA	ACLU	AFS	LCV	ITIC	NTU	COC	ACU	NTLC	CHC
2004	15	0	25	9	100	53	100	80	72	69
2003	15	—	0	10	—	60	96	80	—	—

National Journal Ratings

	2003 LIB	—	2003 CONS		2004 LIB	—	2004 CONS
Economic	19%	—	80%		29%	—	70%
Social	45%	—	54%		36%	—	61%
Foreign	48%	—	51%		34%	—	63%

Key Votes of the 108th Congress

1. Drilling in ANWR	Y	5. DC School Vouchers	Y	9. Ban Same-Sex Marriage	Y
2. Approve Bush Tax Cuts	Y	6. Ban Human Cloning	Y	10. Fund Iraq War	Y
3. Medicare/Rx Bill	Y	7. Restrict Gun Liability	Y	11. Bar Cuba Embargo Funds	N
4. Bar Overtime Pay Regs.	N	8. Ban Partial-Birth Abortion	Y	12. Intelligence Reorg.	Y

Election Results

2004 general	Greg Walden (R)	248,461	(72%)	($1,009,266)
	John McColgan (D)	88,914	(26%)	($30,874)
	Other	9,490	(3%)	
2004 primary	Greg Walden (R)	unopposed		
2002 general	Greg Walden (R)	181,295	(72%)	($842,862)
	Peter Buckley (D)	64,991	(26%)	($68,530)
	Other	5,998	(2%)	

Prior Winning Percentages: 2000 (74%); 1998 (61%)

The People		Race/Ethnic Origin	Ancestry	
Area size:	70,227 sq. mi.	86.1% White	German: 13.6%	English: 9.9%
Urban population:	64.2%	0.4% Black	Irish: 8.7%	
Rural population:	35.8%	0.8% Asian	**2004 Presidential Vote**	
Pop. 2000:	684,280	1.9% Native Am.	Bush (R)	218,288 (61%)
Median income:	$35,600	0.1% Hawaiian	Kerry (D)	135,560 (38%)
Poverty status:	13.0%	1.8% Two+ races	Other	4,895 (1%)
Military veterans:	17.3%	0.1% Other	**2000 Presidential Vote**	
		8.8% Hispanic Origin	Bush (R)	182,924 (60%)
			Gore (D)	105,971 (35%)
			Other	18,078 (6%)
			Cook Partisan Voting Index: R +11	

Occupation	Blue collar: 26.3%	White collar: 54.0%	Gray collar: 19.7%

The Cascade Mountains that wall eastern Oregon off from the rest of the state are a magnificent chain of once (and quite possibly still) active volcanic mountains that drain almost every drop of moisture out of the air coming in from the Pacific. They separate green, wet western Oregon from the brown, parched east. Eastern Oregon has 70% of the state's land, but only 477,000 of its 3.59 million people, most of whom still make their living off the land: Beef and dairy cattle, timber and lumber, fish from the Columbia River and wheat from the irrigated plains. The effect of the Cascades can be felt in the one place they are breached—by the Columbia River Gorge. There, surrounded by brown hills on both sides, funneled winds pound in steadily from the west, making the confluence of the Columbia and Hood rivers the best windsurfing site in the United States. The world's largest wind farm opened here in 2002; it features 400 windmills capable of generating electricity for 60,000 homes.

The 2d Congressional District of Oregon covers all of the state east of the Cascades and the southernmost valley between the Cascades and the Coast Range. Much of this land is empty: Harney County, with a land area larger than that of nine states, has a population of 7,132. Population concentrations here are far apart: Pendleton, a genuine rodeo town amid the north-eastern wheat fields; La Grande in the rich Grande Ronde Valley; The Dalles, where the

Columbia River Gorge begins, and wheat and dairy farmers face new overseas competition; the town of Bend, the fastest-growing part of eastern Oregon, where saw mills have closed and the wilderness and high desert plateau have brought tourism; and nearby Crook County, which has seen an invasion of real estate developers. Until it voted for George H. W. Bush in 1992 Crook County was a bellwether, the only county in the country to have voted for the winning presidential candidate in every election in the 20th century; by 2004, with the local reaction against Democrats, it voted 68% for George W. Bush. In the district's southwestern corner west of the Cascades, near the once huge volcano whose blown-off cone is now the 1,932-foot deep Crater Lake (the deepest in the nation), is the lumber and pear orchard country around Medford, Ashland, Klamath Falls and Grants Pass.

Politically, the 2d District has grown very suspicious of the federal government and very Republican. The cultural liberalism of Portland isn't welcome here: This is part of the leave-us-alone Rocky Mountain basin, not the culturally hip West Coast. The federal government owns three-quarters of the district's land, and under the Clinton administration and court decrees much of it has been fenced off from local use. Court decisions protecting the spotted owl eviscerated the logging industry here, and the cutoff of water in 2001 from the Klamath Basin to protect the endangered sucker fish threatened to destroy the livelihoods of 1,400 local farmers. Logging still is endangered, but the flow of water has been restored.

The congressman from the 2d District is Greg Walden, a Republican elected in 1998. He grew up on a cherry orchard near The Dalles in the Columbia gorge; his father served in the state House. Walden served as press secretary and chief of staff to Congressman Denny Smith from 1981–87, then returned to Hood River as a radio station owner. In 1988 he was elected to the state House, and in his second term became majority leader. He is conservative on economic issues but more moderate on cultural issues; he supports abortion rights but opposes federal funding of abortions.

When 2d District Congressman Bob Smith retired in 1998, after serving one term as chairman of the Agriculture Committee, Walden ran and faced substantial primary opposition. His opponents grumbled about outside interference, as Walden was backed by $130,000 in ads by Americans for Limited Terms and $50,000 in ads by Gary Bauer's Family Research Council. Walden's wide support and the $500,000 he raised enabled him to win with 55% of the vote to 33% for religious broadcaster Perry Atkinson. The general election was anticlimactic. Against a Democrat who ran as a conservative, Walden won 61%–35%.

In the House Walden has been an active legislator. Roy Blunt named him a deputy whip—recognition that he usually is a party loyalist on major issues. On the Energy and Commerce Committee, he criticized regulators from the Food and Drug Administration for removing from prescriptions strong warning labels that might alarm users and their families; after a lengthy series in the Portland *Oregonian,* he urged the FDA to encourage development of cold remedies that cannot be converted to methamphetamines.

Walden serves on the Resources Committee and in March 2004 became chairman of the Forests and Forest Health Subcommittee. On the committee Walden successfully sponsored measures to sell the Bend Pine Nursery, establish a forest research center in Prineville and promote Oregon's famous pears. He successfully sought to reopen the flow of water to farmers in the Klamath Basin; a hearing in Klamath Falls drew 4,000 spectators and protesters. He played a central role in assembling bipartisan support for the Healthy Forests Restoration Act. This was a response to the wildfires that have raged in the West, including the Biscuit fire in Oregon in 2002, caused by unlogged dry timber. Walden's bill passed the House in May 2003, and Walden worked with Senator Ron Wyden who was working on a similar measure that passed the Senate. The final result continues limits on clear-cutting, but also places strict time limits on judicial actions. Walden has said he will work in the 109th Congress to change the Endangered Species Act by encouraging a greater role for peer-reviewed science.

Walden now has won re-election three times with more than 70% of the vote. He declined to run for governor in 2002, but may have other opportunities to run statewide.

THIRD DISTRICT

Rep. Earl Blumenauer (D)

Elected May 1996, 5th full term; b. Aug. 16, 1948, Portland; home, Portland; Lewis & Clark Col., B.A. 1970, J.D. 1976; no religious affiliation; married (Margaret).

Elected Office: OR House of Reps., 1972–78; Multnomah Cnty. Comm., 1978–86; Portland City Cncl., 1986–96.

Professional Career: Asst. to Pres., Portland St. U., 1970–77.

DC Office: 2446 RHOB, 20515, 202-225-4811; Fax: 202-225-8941; Web site: www.house.gov/blumenauer.

District Office: Portland, 503-231-2300.

Committees: *International Relations* (15th of 23 D): Asia & the Pacific; Oversight & Investigations. *Transportation & Infrastructure* (14th of 34 D): Highways, Transit & Pipelines; Railroads; Water Resources & Environment.

Group Ratings

	ADA	ACLU	AFS	LCV	ITIC	NTU	COC	ACU	NTLC	CHC
2004	95	89	100	100	70	11	26	9	0	8
2003	100	—	100	85	—	30	27	12	—	—

National Journal Ratings

	2003 LIB	—	2003 CONS		2004 LIB	—	2004 CONS
Economic	79%	—	20%		79%	—	21%
Social	84%	—	13%		88%	—	0%
Foreign	84%	—	14%		93%	—	7%

Key Votes of the 108th Congress

1. Drilling in ANWR	N	5. DC School Vouchers	N	9. Ban Same-Sex Marriage	N
2. Approve Bush Tax Cuts	N	6. Ban Human Cloning	N	10. Fund Iraq War	N
3. Medicare/Rx Bill	N	7. Restrict Gun Liability	N	11. Bar Cuba Embargo Funds	Y
4. Bar Overtime Pay Regs.	Y	8. Ban Partial-Birth Abortion	N	12. Intelligence Reorg.	N

Election Results

2004 general	Earl Blumenauer (D)	245,559	(71%)	($701,713)
	Tami Mars (R)	82,045	(24%)	
	Other	18,956	(5%)	
2004 primary	Earl Blumenauer (D)	76,811	(89%)	
	John Sweeney (D)	9,207	(11%)	
2002 general	Earl Blumenauer (D)	156,851	(67%)	($353,543)
	Sarah Seale (R)	62,821	(27%)	
	Other	15,305	(7%)	

Prior Winning Percentages: 2000 (67%); 1998 (84%); 1996 (67%); 1996 (68%)

The People		Race/Ethnic Origin	Ancestry		
Area size:	1,054 sq. mi.	77.2% White	German: 14.5%	Irish: 8.7%	
Urban population:	93.1%	5.2% Black	English: 8.4%		
Rural population:	6.9%	5.4% Asian	**2004 Presidential Vote**		
Pop. 2000:	684,279	0.9% Native Am.	Kerry (D)	242,075	(67%)
Median income:	$42,063	0.3% Hawaiian	Bush (R)	118,442	(33%)
Poverty status:	11.7%	3.3% Two+ races	Other	568	(0%)
Military veterans:	13.1%	0.2% Other	**2000 Presidential Vote**		
		7.6% Hispanic Origin	Gore (D)	176,831	(61%)
			Bush (R)	93,213	(32%)
			Other	20,264	(7%)
			Cook Partisan Voting Index: D +18		

Occupation   Blue collar: 24.6%   White collar: 59.4%   Gray collar: 16.0%

Portland, the Rose City set between Mount Hood to the east and the Tualatin Mountains to the west, spanning the Willamette River with its airport and industrial back to the Columbia, is still one of America's least known major cities—and one of its most distinctive. For most of its history Portland was a prosaic city in a magic setting; it was in many ways a muscular, blue-collar town, which piled Oregon lumber and Oregon pears into freight cars, or unloaded machines from back East or autos from Japan on its docks. But in the past three decades Portland has been transformed. Out on the Pacific Rim, it increasingly makes its living on foreign trade, seeing East Asians as customers more than competitors. It has become a home of high-tech industries, particularly in the Washington County suburbs to the west—Silicon Forest. Government has also produced change. Oregon's land-use act, passed in 1973, required local governments to set geographic limits on growth; Metro, the regional government established in 1979 just as growth was accelerating, has created something of a counterweight against the endless spread outward of population into former farmland. With its first light-rail service, Portland encouraged the development of high-density commercial space and housing around transit stops; bicycle paths wind throughout the metropolitan area, and downtown, west of the Willamette River, boasts proud postmodern structures amid classic masonry buildings. In May 2003, Multnomah County voters approved a referendum for a local income tax to pay for schools and services.

In the process, the central city of Portland, like San Francisco and Seattle, has attracted political and cultural liberals. And, like those two cities, Portland has its share of traffic congestion and high home prices. This "livable community" was rated the best city to live in by *Money* magazine in 2000 and its long-term approach to transportation, creating mixed-use neighborhoods and increasing development density, may ultimately pay off. But its national ranking has declined, with more than 50,000 lost jobs in the Portland area and, for a time, one of the nation's highest unemployment rates for a metropolitan region, due partly to the dot-com bust and perhaps exacerbated by excessive controls on growth.

The 3d Congressional District of Oregon includes the part of Portland and Multnomah County east of the Willamette River and part of suburban Clackamas County to the south. It extends over suburban plains and hills to the splendid scenery of Mount Hood high in the Cascades and the Bonneville Dam in the Columbia River Gorge. Politically, it remains dominated by a cultural liberalism, which sets Portland apart even from its suburbs and the rest of Oregon. In 2000 Multnomah County voted 64%–28% for Al Gore with 7% for Ralph Nader; in 2004, with turnout up 22%, it voted 72%–27% for John Kerry.

The congressman from the 3d District is Earl Blumenauer, who won a special election in May 1996 to replace Ron Wyden after he was elected to the Senate. Blumenauer grew up in Portland, graduated from Lewis and Clark College and its Northwestern Law School. He was inspired by the civil rights and anti-Vietnam war movements while in his teens; in 1969, in college, he headed a statewide campaign to lower Oregon's voting age. He has held public office almost all his adult life. In 1972, at 23, he was elected to the Oregon House; in 1978 he was elected to the Multnomah County Board of Commissioners; in 1986 he was elected to the Portland City Council. In these offices he has championed many of the policies that have made Portland distinctive—regional light rail transit, curbside recycling, land use planning. He encouraged bike riding and Regional Rail Summits, which try to bring neighborhood residents into the planning for higher densities at transit nodes. Blumenauer has had some setbacks, notably when he lost the 1992 mayoral race. But after Wyden won the Senate race, he was the obvious successor. He won the special election 68%–25%. His campaign slogan: "Vote Earl, Vote Often."

In the House, Blumenauer has a liberal voting record and a distinctive agenda. He rides his bicycle everywhere from his Capitol Hill apartment, and formed a Bicycle Caucus with more than 100 members; he fought for showers for bike commuters on Capitol Hill and boasts that he has never driven a car in Washington. He was astonished to find that the House subsidized parking for employees, but not mass transit; now, employees can get subsidized transit fares. He is interested in what seem like quixotic projects now, but may not be in a few years: An interstate highway system for bicycle paths, development of "livable communities" on the sites of Denver's closed Stapleton Airport and closed military bases, less dependence on driving as a tool to improve public health. On the big energy bill in 2003, the House approved his amendment for a bicycling pilot program in the Transportation Department, including the feasibility of converting auto trips to bicycle trips. He demands that the Army Corps of Engineers show greater concern for the environment. Blumenauer has actively promoted trade across the Pacific—a key element of Portland's economy. He supported normal trade relations with China but he joined the 90% of House Democrats who opposed trade promotion authority in 2002.

Blumenauer proudly terms Portland a model for the future of the city. And he has taken his gospel of livability and civic values elsewhere, through his Livable Cities Task Force (more than 50 members) and his own political action committee. Lately, he has stepped up his political activity. He seriously considered running for mayor of Portland in 2004, but surprised some local Democrats when he decided instead that the city needs "strong, effective leadership" in Congress. In the 2004 presidential campaign, he endorsed John Kerry before the Iowa caucuses and worked actively for him. On Capitol Hill, he became a vigorous national Democratic fundraiser. In his safe seat, Blumenauer has won reelection handily.

FOURTH DISTRICT

Rep. Peter DeFazio (D)

Elected 1986, 10th term; b. May 27, 1947, Needham, MA; home, Springfield; Tufts U., B.A. 1969, U. of OR, M.S. 1977; Catholic; married (Myrnie).

Military Career: Air Force, 1967–71.

Elected Office: Lane Cnty. Bd. of Commissioners, 1982–86.

Professional Career: Dist. Dir., U.S. Rep. James Weaver, 1977–82.

DC Office: 2134 RHOB, 20515, 202-225-6416; Fax: 202-225-0032; Web site: www.defazio.house.gov.

District Offices: Coos Bay, 541-269-2609; Eugene, 541-465-6732; Roseburg, 541-440-3523.

Committees: *Homeland Security* (6th of 15 D): Economic Security, Infrastructure Protection & Cybersecurity. *Resources* (5th of 22 D): Forests & Forest Health. *Transportation & Infrastructure* (3d of 34 D): Aviation; Highways, Transit & Pipelines (RMM); Railroads.

Group Ratings

	ADA	ACLU	AFS	LCV	ITIC	NTU	COC	ACU	NTLC	CHC
2004	95	75	100	100	20	13	43	16	11	16
2003	100	—	100	85	—	29	14	21	—	—

National Journal Ratings

	2003 LIB	—	2003 CONS		2004 LIB	—	2004 CONS
Economic	92%	—	0%		75%	—	24%
Social	69%	—	31%		62%	—	38%
Foreign	89%	—	8%		65%	—	35%

Key Votes of the 108th Congress

1. Drilling in ANWR	N	5. DC School Vouchers	N	9. Ban Same-Sex Marriage	N
2. Approve Bush Tax Cuts	N	6. Ban Human Cloning	*	10. Fund Iraq War	N
3. Medicare/Rx Bill	N	7. Restrict Gun Liability	Y	11. Bar Cuba Embargo Funds	Y
4. Bar Overtime Pay Regs.	Y	8. Ban Partial-Birth Abortion	N	12. Intelligence Reorg.	Y

Election Results

2004 general	Peter DeFazio (D)	228,611	(61%)	($909,241)
	Jim Feldkamp (R)	140,882	(38%)	($591,318)
	Other	5,416	(1%)	
2004 primary	Peter DeFazio (D)	unopposed		
2002 general	Peter DeFazio (D)	168,150	(64%)	($286,417)
	Liz VanLeeuwen (R)	90,523	(34%)	($150,482)
	Other	4,808	(2%)	

Prior Winning Percentages: 2000 (68%); 1998 (70%); 1996 (66%); 1994 (67%); 1992 (71%); 1990 (86%); 1988 (72%); 1986 (54%)

The People		Race/Ethnic Origin	Ancestry		
Area size:	18,034 sq. mi.	89.7% White	German: 14.7%	English: 10.1%	
Urban population:	69.2%	0.5% Black	Irish: 8.8%		
Rural population:	30.8%	1.5% Asian	**2004 Presidential Vote**		
Pop. 2000:	684,280	1.2% Native Am.	Kerry (D) 188,479	(49%)	
Median income:	$35,796	0.1% Hawaiian	Bush (R) 187,292	(49%)	
Poverty status:	13.7%	2.5% Two+ races	Other 5,801	(2%)	
Military veterans:	16.9%	0.1% Other	**2000 Presidential Vote**		
		4.2% Hispanic Origin	Bush (R) 156,362	(49%)	
			Gore (D) 142,123	(44%)	
			Other 22,601	(7%)	
			Cook Partisan Voting Index: D + 0		

Occupation	Blue collar: 26.3%	White collar: 55.2%	Gray collar: 18.5%

Eugene is nestled in the southernmost bit of lowland at the end of Oregon's Willamette Valley, surrounded by mountains on three sides. It is a farming center, a lumber metropolis and, most notably, a leafy university town. Settlers first arrived here in 1846, farming in the valley and cutting timber in the hills. In 1876, the University of Oregon was established, a symbol of Oregon's strong Yankee cultural ethic and sparse settlement; its first graduating class had just five students. Thousands of miles from most Americans, Eugene and next-door Springfield, once a lumber town and now with computer chip factories, have grown into comfortable middle-sized towns. Eugene has bicycle paths along the riverbanks and on main streets and likes to bill itself as the Running Capital of the Universe; it is where Phil Knight and his former University of Oregon track coach, Bill Bowerman, started Nike—the first soles formed on a waffle iron. Now the third-largest city in Oregon (behind Portland and Salem) and one of the most livable in the nation, it offers the ambience of a small town and the counter-culture without the isolation, and its liberal voters have been vital to Democrats statewide.

Beyond Eugene and Springfield, southwestern Oregon is surrounded by green-clad mountains and for years cut more timber than any other place in the country. But demand for wood is volatile, dependent on the vagaries of interest rates; East Asia increasingly wants unprocessed logs rather than milled lumber, which means fewer jobs for Oregon. The 1980s were tough on this region: recession reduced the demand for housing, and cutting of old-growth forests was banned to protect the spotted owl. Fears grew that federal restrictions on logging would destroy the area's economy. But even as the lumber industry languished, a robust local economy and active job retraining resulted in local job gains in the 1990s. Recent development has been diverse, including health care, tourism and retirement communities for California transplants. But Timber Country, including forest product businesses, continues to struggle.

The 4th Congressional District of Oregon includes Eugene and Springfield and surrounding Lane County; it goes south on Interstate 5 to include Roseburg in Douglas County, once one of the premier logging counties in the United States. It extends north to Albany and includes most of Corvallis, but not Oregon State University. It includes the entire southern half of Oregon's stunning Pacific coastline; the decline of commercial fishing has hit this area hard. Eugene is now heavily Democratic. Roseburg and Albany and their surrounding counties vote heavily Republican, leaving a clash of left and right in the district. The travails of the logging industry moved the area to the right: the 4th District (with only slightly different boundaries) voted 54%–44% against George H. W. Bush in 1988, but in 2000 it voted 49%–44% for George W. Bush. In 2004, however, the 4th narrowly went for John Kerry, one of just two districts in the nation to flip from Bush to Kerry.

The congressman from the 4th District is Peter DeFazio (pronounced *da-FAH-zee-oh*), a Democrat first elected in 1986. He grew up in Massachusetts, came to Oregon for graduate school, and went to work for 4th District Congressman Jim Weaver. In 1982 he moved to Springfield and won a seat on the county commission. When Weaver retired in 1986, DeFazio

4th District / **Oregon**   1405

won the House seat in a tight race. He beat Bill Bradbury (the 2002 Democratic nominee for senator) by a 34%–33% margin and won the general election 54%–46%. DeFazio has compiled a record that seems to satisfy both Eugene and the rest of the district—liberal on most issues, moderate or even conservative on some social issues. An original founder of the loose-knit Progressive Caucus, he made the case that millions of Americans were suffering during the Clinton administration's booming prosperity. He opposed NAFTA, GATT and trade promotion authority. A leader of the fight against normal trade relations with China, he said that supporters were "a lot of well-intentioned people . . . who think it means their salvation, and actually what it means is their destruction." Since the election of George W. Bush, DeFazio's populist criticism has grown more outspoken, and is sometimes directed at his own party.

DeFazio often takes idiosyncratic views. He has been a harsh critic of airlines and their broken promises to consumers; a pet cause has been his advocacy of poor treatment of dogs and cats during flights. Unlike most Democrats, he has offered a specific proposal to fix Social Security: Remove the payroll deduction limitation that benefits the top wage earners. He took the lead in the House with his amendment to permit airline pilots to carry guns in the cockpit. The Bush administration opposed this, and the Senate had avoided the issue. But DeFazio won by an astonishing 250–175; the Senate a few weeks later followed suit and Bush went along. After the catastrophic wildfires in summer 2002, DeFazio teamed with Republican colleague Greg Walden to seek a middle ground to speed the thinning of brush in the forests. DeFazio's environmental allies denounced him as a turncoat. The bipartisan effort collapsed in committee in 2002, but produced legislation that passed the House in May 2003 and ultimately became law. As the senior Democrat on the Aviation Subcommittee of Transportation and Infrastructure in 2003, he criticized poor oversight by the Federal Aviation Administration and he called for a more active role by Congress to stabilize the industry. In 2005, DeFazio moved up to the ranking Democrat on the Highways Subcommittee, where he is positioned to play a major part in the transportation reauthorization the 108th Congress failed to pass. He voted against the authorization of force in Iraq and criticized the Bush administration's lack of a strategy after the overthrow of Saddam Hussein.

DeFazio has won re-election by impressive margins in a district which before 1986 was often marginal. After Senator Bob Packwood resigned in 1995, DeFazio ran to succeed him. He had far less money than Portland Congressman Ron Wyden, whom he attacked for receiving money from Packwood contributors. His opposition to gun control, NAFTA and GATT provided clear contrasts with Wyden. But Wyden won a 50%–44% victory in the primary, and went on to win the seat. Since then, DeFazio has called for public financing of campaigns. In the 2002 cycle, DeFazio considered running for the Senate against Gordon Smith. But he said he would run only with the "strongest possible support" from Democratic leaders. The DSCC sent a message: No big money until DeFazio raised lots himself and rose in the polls. So he decided to remain in the House. In 2004, DeFazio beat former FBI agent Jim Feldkamp 61%–38%, his smallest margin since he was first elected, but still an impressive majority in a district only narrowly carried by John Kerry. Feldkamp said that he would run again. Should DeFazio not run, this might well be a seriously contested seat.

FIFTH DISTRICT

Rep. Darlene Hooley (D)

Elected 1996, 5th term; b. Apr. 4, 1939, Williston, ND; home, West Linn; OR St. U., B.S. 1961; Lutheran; divorced.

Elected Office: West Linn City Cncl., 1977–80; OR House of Reps., 1980–86; Clackamas Cnty. Comm., 1987–96.

Professional Career: Teacher, 1961–75.

DC Office: 2430 RHOB, 20515, 202-225-5711; Fax: 202-225-5699; Web site: www.house.gov/hooley.

District Offices: Salem, 503-588-9100; West Linn, 503-557-1324.

Committees: *Financial Services* (9th of 32 D): Capital Markets, Insurance & Government Sponsored Enterprises; Financial Institutions & Consumer Credit. *Science* (5th of 20 D): Research (RMM). *Veterans' Affairs* (9th of 12 D): Economic Opportunity.

Group Ratings

	ADA	ACLU	AFS	LCV	ITIC	NTU	COC	ACU	NTLC	CHC
2004	95	75	88	100	78	18	60	16	11	25
2003	95	—	100	90	—	28	38	21	—	—

National Journal Ratings

	2003 LIB	—	2003 CONS		2004 LIB	—	2004 CONS
Economic	64%	—	35%		61%	—	38%
Social	67%	—	31%		68%	—	31%
Foreign	70%	—	27%		57%	—	42%

Key Votes of the 108th Congress

1. Drilling in ANWR	N	5. DC School Vouchers	N	9. Ban Same-Sex Marriage	N
2. Approve Bush Tax Cuts	N	6. Ban Human Cloning	N	10. Fund Iraq War	Y
3. Medicare/Rx Bill	N	7. Restrict Gun Liability	N	11. Bar Cuba Embargo Funds	Y
4. Bar Overtime Pay Regs.	Y	8. Ban Partial-Birth Abortion	N	12. Intelligence Reorg.	Y

Election Results

2004 general	Darlene Hooley (D)	184,833	(53%)	($2,054,417)
	Jim Zupancic (R)	154,993	(44%)	($1,291,211)
	Other	9,808	(3%)	
2004 primary	Darlene Hooley (D)	59,407	(86%)	
	Andrew Kaza (D)	10,027	(14%)	
2002 general	Darlene Hooley (D)	137,713	(55%)	($622,126)
	Brian Boquist (R)	113,441	(45%)	($158,065)

Prior Winning Percentages: 2000 (57%); 1998 (55%); 1996 (51%)

The People

Area size:	5,829 sq. mi.			
Urban population:	80.4%			
Rural population:	19.6%			
Pop. 2000:	684,280			
Median income:	$44,409			
Poverty status:	10.9%			
Military veterans:	14.8%			

Race/Ethnic Origin
83.6% White
0.6% Black
1.9% Asian
1.1% Native Am.
0.2% Hawaiian
2.2% Two+ races
0.1% Other
10.3% Hispanic Origin

Ancestry
German: 16.0%   English: 9.7%
Irish: 8.1%

2004 Presidential Vote

Bush (R)	181,070	(50%)
Kerry (D)	176,558	(49%)
Other	4,058	(1%)

2000 Presidential Vote

Bush (R)	149,276	(48%)
Gore (D)	144,657	(47%)
Other	17,047	(5%)

Cook Partisan Voting Index: D + 1

Occupation   Blue collar: 22.1%   White collar: 60.6%   Gray collar: 17.4%

The Willamette Valley was the great Promised Land at the end of the Oregon Trail, shielded by the Coast Range from the cold storms of the Pacific but squeezing most of the moisture out of the clouds in the form of rain, fog and persistent mist. Here, New England Yankees planted small towns they called Salem and Oregon City, founded schools and colleges, built high-spired churches and eventually Salem's cylindrical-domed Art Deco state Capitol. This was one of the few valleys in the West that settlers found readily suitable for agriculture. The Willamette Valley's soil is fertile, the plain created by the waters of the Willamette sweeping down from the mountains is broad, and the rains everyone hears about in Oregon are dependable. Into this land metro Portland has spread, with young people leapfrogging over the lands protected from development and into Clackamas and Marion Counties to the south. In 2003, rapidly growing Salem passed Eugene as the second-largest city in Oregon.

The 5th Congressional District of Oregon includes much of the northern Willamette Valley. Near Portland it has the old pioneer town of Oregon City, and spreads south to the state capital of Salem (where the two bridges crossing the Willamette have become jammed at rush hour) and includes part of Corvallis (home of Oregon State University). Then the district hops over the Coast Range to take in Lincoln and Tillamook Counties, fishing and logging and cheese-making communities; it also includes all of rural Polk County. Although the area remains one of the nation's chief producers of processed vegetables, its longtime crops of beans and berries have dropped significantly; nurseries have become a new growth industry. Historically, the Willamette Valley was Republican, like New England whence most of its settlers came, but, also like New England, it has been trending Democratic, and now is prime marginal territory. The Corvallis area is heavily Democratic, the Salem area more likely to be Republican while Clackamas County is competitive territory, more Republican than the more affluent Washington County west of Portland. This is a district that was nearly evenly divided in the 2000 and 2004 presidential elections.

The congresswoman from the 5th District is Darlene Hooley, a Democrat first elected in 1996. Born in North Dakota, Hooley moved with her family to Salem at age 8. She worked as a reading and physical education teacher in rural Woodburn Gervais and raised her family in West Linn, on the Willamette north of Oregon City. Angry when council members wouldn't replace the rugged asphalt after her son fell off a playground swing and cut his head, she served on the park district board and then was elected to the city council in 1976, at 37. In 1980 she was elected to the Oregon House; in 1987 she was appointed to the Clackamas County Board of Supervisors.

In 1996, Hooley decided to run for Congress. Republican Jim Bunn, elected 50%–47% in 1994, combined religious conservatism with a moderate record on issues and support of the Oregon Health Plan and Portland light rail. Hooley had two Democratic primary opponents, but with big fundraising help from EMILY's List, she won the primary with 51%. She attacked Bunn for supporting Newt Gingrich and Medicare "cuts." Ultimately, she spent $1.1 million, twice as much as the incumbent. Working most strongly against Bunn was his divorce and subsequent marriage to his 31-year-old chief of staff, whom he was paying $97,500—more than any other staffer in Oregon's House delegation. Hooley won 51%–46%.

In the House, Hooley has a mostly liberal record, though she has been somewhat centrist on economic issues. She failed repeatedly to get a seat on Appropriations and serves on the Financial Services Committee. On that panel, she led a bipartisan group that passed legislation designed to reduce identity theft by permitting consumers a free annual credit report and requiring banks and credit agencies to keep an eye on fraud. It became law in December 2003; Hooley called it the strongest consumer measure enacted in years, though some liberal activists disagreed. She led the fight to preserve Oregon's assisted suicide law and argued for it on states' rights grounds. She joined the moderate New Democrats, contending that she wanted to work with business in a district dependent on trade; in contrast to David Wu in the adjacent suburban district, she voted for normal trade relations with China. But Hooley joined the other House Democrats from Oregon in opposing trade promotion authority in 2002. She voted against the use of military force in Iraq, but later supported funds for the military and reconstruction.

In this marginal seat, which was represented by two Republicans and two Democrats during the 1990s, Hooley has had a series of competitive contests. In 2004, the election was hard-fought. Jim Zupancic, an entrepreneur in the voice-mail business and former school board chairman in Lake Oswego, won a spirited May primary, 56%–44%, against state Sen. Jackie Winters, who voted for an income tax increase rejected by voters in February 2004. In the general, both candidates were well-funded. Zupancic called for changes in medical malpractice, attacked Hooley's "extreme liberal" record and said she did not support job-creation. Hooley kept her distance from John Kerry and emphasized constituent services and her focus on consumer issues. Hooley won, 53%–44%. She carried all seven counties, though her home base of Clackamas, which cast one-third of the vote, was the closest: 51%–46%.

★ PENNSYLVANIA ★

Pennsylvania started off as the center of America: Philadelphia was the 13 colonies' largest city when it hosted the Continental Congress in 1776 and the Constitutional Convention in 1787. This was one of the newer colonies, founded 52 years after Massachusetts and 75 years after Virginia. Under the benevolent rule of the early Penns and with its Quaker traditions, Pennsylvania soon became the major settlement in the Middle Colonies: Its tolerance attracted Englishmen of all religious sects and thousands of Germans as well. Bordermen from Scotland, Yorkshire and Northern Ireland crossed the corduroy-like ridges of the Appalachians and settled the mountainous interior where General Braddock had been beaten by the French and Indians not long before, and where a decade later George Washington would again lead troops when the Whiskey Rebellion flared up. On the banks of the wide Delaware estuary, with its thriving commerce and rich hinterland, Philadelphia was, after London and Dublin, the largest Georgian city in the late 18th century. It seemed destined to be the London of America, the metropolis of government and commerce and culture.

But Philadelphia—and Pennsylvania—failed to hold the central position the Founders had expected. The nation's capital was put on the Potomac rather than the Delaware as part of a political deal, and the Erie Canal and the water-level railroad from the Hudson to Lake Erie channeled trade away from Philadelphia to New York. Philadelphia lost its chance to be the nation's financial capital when Andrew Jackson in righteous rage vetoed the rechartering of the Second Bank of the United States. Philadelphia's Quaker tradition, tolerant of diversity and indifferent to others' behavior, was overshadowed in intellectual life by New England's Puritan tradition, angrily intolerant and ready to use the state to impose cultural values from abolition to prohibition.

Instead, Pennsylvania became America's energy and heavy industry capital. The key was coal. Northeast Pennsylvania was the nation's primary source of anthracite, the hard coal used for home heating, and western Pennsylvania was laced with bituminous coal, the soft coal used in steel production. Connected with Philadelphia by the Pennsylvania Railroad, Pittsburgh, where the Allegheny and Monongahela Rivers join to become the Ohio, was the center of the nation's steel industry by 1890. Immigrants poured in from Europe and from the surrounding hills to work in western Pennsylvania's mines and factories. Pittsburgh became synonymous with industrial prosperity, the inspiration behind the civic pride that celebrated huffing smokestacks. In 1900, Pennsylvania was the nation's second largest state and growing rapidly. But the boom ended conclusively with the Depression of the 1930s, and in parts of Pennsylvania it has never returned. After World War II, both home heating and industry switched away from coal. John L. Lewis's United Mine Workers traded higher pay and benefits for payroll cuts. Even when coal prices boomed in the 1970s, strip mining created relatively few new jobs. Similarly, Pennsylvania steel began its decline three decades ago, when management decided not to keep up with new technology and agreed to big wage and benefit increases with the mistaken confidence they could pass the costs along. Big steel got import quotas in 1969—Pennsylvania has been the nation's most protectionist state since the first Bessemer converter furnaces were lit—but they

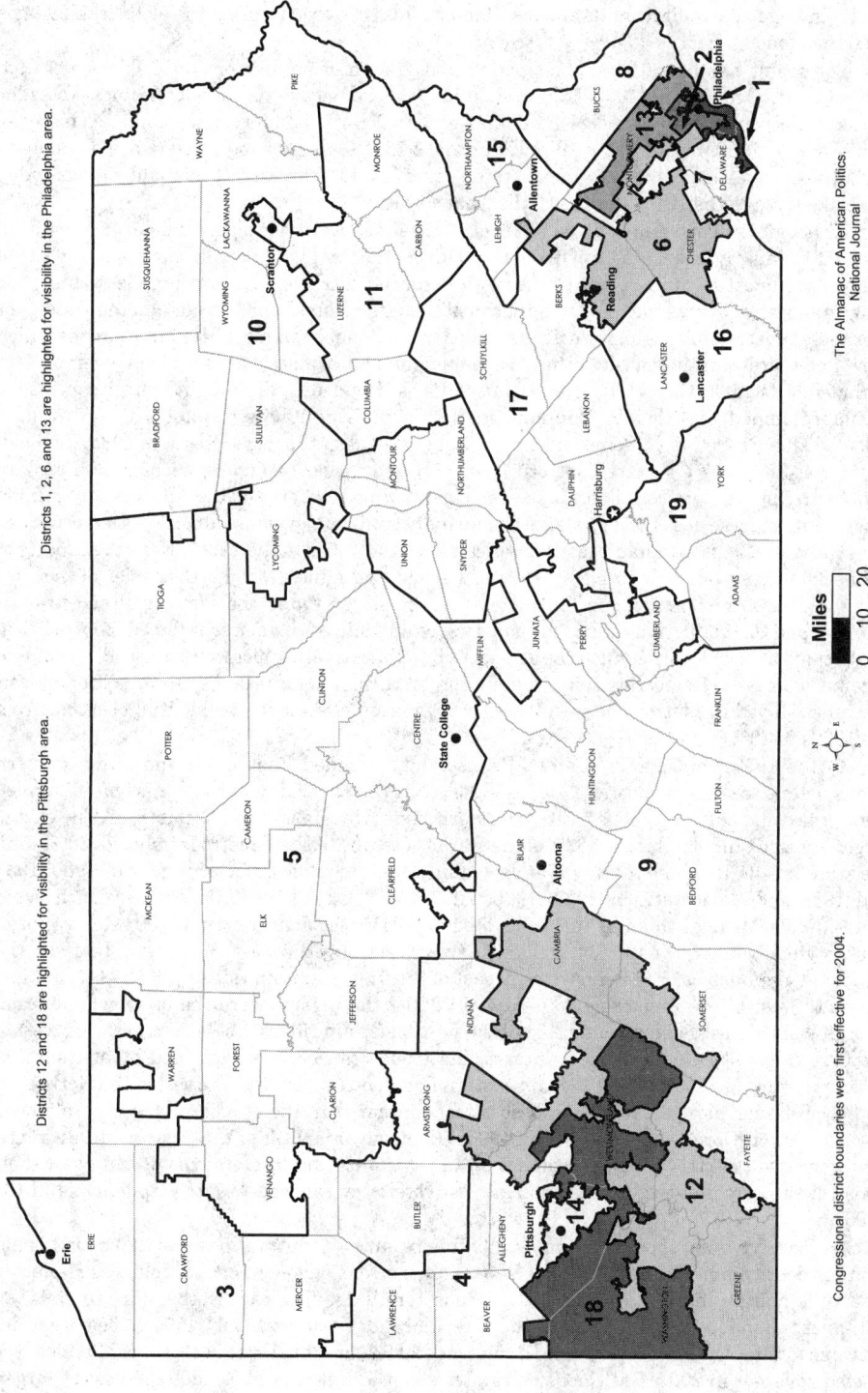

Districts 1, 2, 6 and 13 are highlighted for visibility in the Philadelphia area.

Districts 12 and 18 are highlighted for visibility in the Pittsburgh area.

The Almanac of American Politics.
National Journal

Congressional district boundaries were first effective for 2004.

didn't create jobs. By the time quotas lapsed in the 1990s, the industry had modernized, but mostly in huge new Indiana mills and small mini-mills scattered far from the factories that once lined the Monongahela.

The result has been the slowest population growth of any major state: There were 9.5 million Pennsylvanians in 1930, 12.4 million in 2004. Pennsylvania cast 36 electoral votes for Franklin Roosevelt in 1940 and 21 for John Kerry in 2004; it had 30 congressman, as many as California, in 1960, but now has 19 to California's 53. People growing up here are as likely to leave the state as stay, and few out-of-staters move in. Pennsylvania looks and sounds today more like it did in the 1940s than any other major state.

Although Pennsylvania started off as our center of government, government has not been central to Pennsylvania for most of its history. During the Civil War, Pennsylvania was the site of the northernmost advance of the Confederate Army, at Carlisle, just north of Gettysburg; for generations after, it was the most Republican of the large states—for Lincoln and the Union, for the steel industry and the high tariff. Its malodorous Republican machines built parties which were not representative of one ethnic segment but had a place for just about everyone: in Philadelphia's huge City Hall, a knockoff of Paris' Hotel de Ville; in Pittsburgh's massive, Roman-columned City-County Building; in Harrisburg's grandiose Capitol with its rotunda modeled after St. Peter's in Rome and staircase modeled after the Paris Opera. In 1932, Pennsylvania was the only big state that stuck with Herbert Hoover and voted against Franklin Roosevelt. But the New Deal, John L. Lewis's United Mine Workers and the CIO industrial union movement, and a series of bloody strikes made industrial Pennsylvania almost as Democratic in the 1930s and 1940s as it had been Republican from the 1860s to the 1920s. Even then, parts of Pennsylvania not heavy with big steel factories and coal mines—the northern tier of counties along the New York border, the central part of the state around the Welsh railroad town of Altoona, and the Pennsylvania Dutch country around Lancaster, an area referred to by political consultants as the "T"—remained the strongest Republican voting bloc in the East. Philadelphia became a heavily Democratic city, but in the suburban counties, the antique Republican machines stayed in control. The result was a key marginal state in presidential elections from the 1950s to the 1990s.

In the 1980s, prosperous eastern Pennsylvania trended Republican and ailing western Pennsylvania trended Democratic. In the 1990s, culturally liberal eastern Pennsylvania trended Democratic and culturally conservative western Pennsylvania trended Republican. The east is larger—metro Philadelphia cast 33% of the state's votes in 2004 and metro Pittsburgh 20%—and the state has mostly gone its way: Pennsylvania voted Republican for president in 1980, 1984 and 1988 and Democratic in 1992, 1996, 2000 and 2004. Metro Philadelphia, which voted 50%–49% for Michael Dukakis in 1988, voted 59%–41% for John Kerry in 2004. Metro Pittsburgh, which voted 59%–40% for Dukakis, gave Kerry only a 52%–48% margin. In 1988, the senior George Bush carried Pennsylvania east of the first mountain ridge by 53%–46%, but lost the state west of the first ridge 48%–51%. In 2004, the regions were the other way around. George W. Bush lost Pennsylvania east of the first mountain ridge 44%–56% but carried west of the first ridge 53%–46%. These countervailing trends can best be explained by attitudes on cultural issues. Metro Philadelphia and eastern Pennsylvania are like the rest of the Northeast, liberal on issues like gun control and abortion; content with the economy, voters here moved toward Clinton-Gore Democrats in the 1990s. Pennsylvania west of the first mountain ridge, however, is full of strong-belief Catholics and Protestants and hunters who do not want their guns taken away. Relieved of economic stress, voters here moved toward Republicans in the 1990s.

In Pennsylvania, there is an unusually fine balance on cultural positions. Abortion is not political death here: The late Governor Bob Casey, a strong opponent of abortion, was re-elected by a wide margin in 1990. And when Governor Tom Ridge first ran for the office in 1994, an anti-abortion independent got 13% of the vote, and Ridge won with only 45%. To be sure, Gore was able to carry the state in 2000 and Democrat and former Philadelphia Mayor Ed Rendell was elected governor in 2002. But Gore's margin was just 51%–46% and Rendell's not much larger, 53%–44%. Republicans have done very well otherwise. They hold both of the state's U.S. Senate seats and, thanks in part to a partisan districting plan, have a 12–7 edge in the House delegation. In 2002, they held the offices of attorney general and treasurer, held their margin in the state Senate and increased it in the state House: Rendell had no coattails. Rendell's victory in 2002 and John Kerry's 51%–48% victory here in 2004 were largely regional: they piled up big majorities in the Philadelphia media market and ran unimpressively elsewhere. Compared to 2000, the Democratic margin in metro Philadelphia increased by 96,000 votes, but George W. Bush increased his margin by 34,000 in metro Pittsburgh and 122,000 in the rest of the state—including many coal and manufacturing counties. Pennsylvania seems likely to be closely contested again in 2006.

The People		Race/Ethnic Origin			Military veterans: 1,280,788 (13.7%)	
Pop. 2004 (est):	12,406,292	10,322,455	84.1%	White	WWII: 25.7%	Korea: 15.2%
Pop. 2000:	12,281,054	1,202,437	9.8%	Black	Vietnam: 28.7%	Gulf War: 6.8%
Pop. 1990:	11,881,643	218,296	1.8%	Asian	**Most populous cities (2003):**	
Change 1990–2000:	Up 3.4%	14,904	0.1%	Native Am.	1. Philadelphia	1,479,339
% of U.S. total:	4.4%	2,691	0.0%	Hawaiian	2. Pittsburgh	325,337
Pop. rank:	6th of 50	113,097	0.9%	Two+ races	3. Allentown	105,958
Area size:	46,055 sq. mi.	13,086	0.1%	Other	4. Erie	101,373
State Native:	77.7%	394,088	3.2%	Hisp. Origin	5. Reading	80,305
Non-citizen:	2.0%	**Ancestry**				
Language		German: 18.6%		Irish: 11.8%	Urban population: 77.0%	
English: 89.2%	Other Eur.: 5.4%	Italian: 8.5%		English: 5.8%	Rural population: 23.0%	
Spanish: 3.7%		Polish: 4.9%				

Education		Work Sector		General Assembly	
H.S. Grad:	81.9%	Private: 82.4%	Govt: 11.3%	Senate	30 R 20 D
College Grad:	22.4%	Self: 6.0%	Family: 0.3%	House	110 R 93 D
Industry		Unemployment: 5.7%		Legislative Term Limits: No	
Agri: 1.3%	Con: 6.0%	**Household Income**		**Registered Voters**	
Fin: 6.6%	Info: 2.6%	<15k: 16.7%	15-35k: 27.0%	D: 3,985,486 (47.6%)	
Mfg: 21.4%	Prof: 30.4%	35-50k: 16.9%	50-100k: 29.0%	R: 3,405,278 (40.7%)	
Public: 4.2%	Trade: 15.7%	100-150k: 6.6%	>150k: 3.7%	O: 975,899 (11.7%)	
Other: 11.9%		Median: $40,106			
Occupation		Poverty status: 11.0%			
Blue collar: 25.2%	White collar: 59.5%	**Home Value**			
Gray collar: 15.3%		<50k: 17.9%	50-100k: 36.0%	100-200k: 34.4%	200-300k: 7.4%
		300-500k: 3.1%	>500k: 1.2%	Median: $94,800	

Presidential politics   For the last 70 years Pennsylvania has been a swing state in every close presidential election and even in some that were not close. Yet it is not typical of the country. With its older, deeply-rooted population, it tends to be culturally more conservative than the rest of the country; with its long-dying blue-collar communities, it tends to be economically more liberal—though both tendencies are being muted with time. But it does present a problem for political strategists of both parties: Combinations of issue positions which work for Democrats on the East and West Coasts or for Republicans in the South and the Heartland do not work well here. This was a state that was targeted by strategists for both parties in both 2000 and 2004; in his first term George W. Bush visited the state more than 30 times, more than any other state but Texas. During the campaign period, John Kerry visited just as often this state that is still the legal residence of his wife Teresa Heinz Kerry. Both parties made yeoman

2004 Presidential Vote
Kerry (D)..................... 2,938,095   (51%)
Bush (R) 2,793,847   (48%)
Badnarik (Lib)................. 21,185   (0%)
Other........................... 12,637   (0%)

2004 Democratic Presidential Primary
Kerry (D)....................... 585,683   (74%)
Dean (D) 79,799   (10%)
Edwards (D) 76,762   (10%)
Kucinich (D) 30,110   (4%)
Other........................... 17,528   (2%)

2000 Presidential Vote
Gore (D)..................... 2,485,967   (51%)
Bush (R) 2,281,127   (46%)
Nader (Green) 103,392   (2%)
Other........................... 41,699   (1%)

efforts to register and turn out voters, and with considerable success: turnout was up 23% in Philadelphia, despite declining population, and it was up as well in rural counties which are losing population. There are echoes, but rather faint ones, of the economically polarized politics of the past: the NEP exit poll showed John Kerry carrying large majorities of those with incomes under $30,000 and George W. Bush carrying large majorities of those with incomes over $150,000. But with the vast majority with incomes in between, 69% of the voters, the race was pretty much even. Voters in union households, 30% of the total favored Kerry 62%–37%; but these are less likely to be steelworkers and more likely to be teachers today than a generation ago. But there is a balancing here: 46% of Pennsylvania voters were gun owners, and they voted 62%–38% for Bush. There is relatively little evidence in the exit poll of traditional religious polarities. Protestants voted 55%–45% for Bush, Catholics only 51%–49% for Kerry, with Catholics attending mass weekly voting for Bush; those with other religions or none voted 71%–27% for Kerry.

Pennsylvania's April presidential primary has not been crucial since 1976, when Jimmy Carter clinched the Democratic nomination here by beating Henry Jackson and Morris Udall. In 1999 the legislature moved the primary date from April 25 to April 4, but it made little difference; both parties' nominations had already been cinched by then. In December 2004 Governor Ed Rendell started pushing for a primary in January or February.

Congressional districting

Pennsylvania has 19 House members, the fewest since the 12th Congress assembled in 1811, when it had 18. It lost two seats in the reapportionment following the 2000 Census, just as it had after the seven preceding Censuses.

109th Congress Lineup
12 R   7 D

108th Congress Lineup
12 R   7 D

In 2001 and 2002 Republicans, with the governorship, a 29–21 majority in the state Senate and a 104–99 majority in the state House, were in firm control of redistricting and were determined to redraw the lines so as to transform an 11–10 margin in the House delegation to 13–6. Demographics suggested eliminating one district each from Philadelphia and the Pittsburgh area.

In December 2001, state Senate Republicans unveiled their plan. Involved in drawing it were Senator Rick Santorum and Congresswoman Melissa Hart. Both had won Pittsburgh area House seats previously held by Democrats—Santorum in 1990 and Hart in 2000—and both wanted to eliminate one Democratic and create one Republican district in the Pittsburgh area. Hart insisted she wanted to keep Democratic Beaver County in her 4th District. The Senate plan put three pairs of Democratic incumbents into the same districts: Tim Holden and Paul Kanjorski, John Murtha and Frank Mascara, and Joe Hoeffel and Robert Borski. It created new Republican-leaning districts with no incumbents in metro Philadelphia and Pittsburgh. It seemed likely to raise the Republican edge to 13–6. The Senate passed it December 11, 27–22, basically along party lines.

But House Majority Leader John Perzel of Philadelphia had a different idea. Perzel is from Northeast Philadelphia, and had been reelected by only 92 votes in 2000, after Democrats put together a registration and voter turnout drive; he was eager to get even. He also cultivated a good relationship with Bob Brady, 1st District congressman and Philadelphia Democratic chairman. Perzel and Brady wanted to preserve three Philadelphia seats, which meant putting more Philadelphia than suburban Democrats in the new district pairing Philadelphian Bob Borski and suburbanite Joe Hoeffel. Perzel's House plan protected Murtha, the second-ranking Democrat on the House Appropriations Committee, and did not create a new Republican-leaning suburban Pittsburgh district.

In the days that followed, Perzel got phone calls from NRCC Chairman Tom Davis and White House political strategist Karl Rove. Georgia Democrats had just passed a redistricting plan that seemed likely to cost Republicans seats they had counted on, and they asked Perzel to accept the Senate plan. He said there weren't enough votes to pass it in the House. But by early January 2002, House and Senate Republicans reached agreement. Their new plan made adjustments in western Pennsylvania to please Murtha; Mascara's house was placed across the street in the new Republican-leaning district in suburban Pittsburgh. Instead of pairing Democrats Holden and Kanjorski, it put Holden and Republican George Gekas in the same district. Overall it eliminated four Democratic seats and created two Republican-leaning seats.

Lawsuits were filed in both federal and state courts. Democrats argued that the plan was unconstitutional as an obvious partisan gerrymander. But the U.S. Supreme Court in racial redistricting cases in the 1990s had said that, while it was unconstitutional to draw contorted boundaries for racial reasons, it was permissible to do so for partisan reasons. The state Supreme Court rejected the Democrats' arguments. But on April 8, the three-judge federal court ruled that the plan was unconstitutional because there was a difference of 19 between the districts' population, and that the difference should have been 1; this was based on a 1980s U.S. Supreme Court case overturning a much larger population discrepancy. The court invited the legislature to amend its plan and said the election could be put off from May 21 to July 16. The legislature passed a new plan April 15 with a population discrepancy of only 1 and with minor changes, which transferred 0.6% of the state's population into different districts. But the primary season was already on; the filing deadline was March 12. Republicans asked the court to allow 2002 elections to take place under the first plan and some Democrats, afraid that their gubernatorial candidates Ed Rendell and Bob Casey Jr. would exhaust their funds in their primary fight while Republican Mike Fisher was unopposed, joined them. The court acceded.

The plan achieved some but not all of its partisan aims. Republicans took the new suburban districts, but won only narrowly in the new 6th District. Mascara decided to run against Murtha in the primary; Murtha won handily. Borski decided to retire from the House. Democrat Holden beat Republican Gekas in the new Republican-leaning 17th District. The result was a 12–7 Republican delegation. But the results indicate that Republicans' hold on several districts is shaky and suggest they may change partisan hands some time between 2004 and 2010. In January 2003 a three-judge federal court approved the legislature's April 15 plan. In April 2004 the Supreme Court upheld the plan by a 5–4 vote. The plurality opinion, by Justice Antonin Scalia, held that the Constitution doesn't provide "a judicially enforceable limit on the political considerations that the states and Congress may take into account when districting." In other words, there is no way for a court to say when a political plan that meets the equal population standard is too political. Justice Anthony Kennedy, casting the swing vote, upheld the Pennsylvania plan but said that there still might be some role for judges in policing political gerrymanders. But Kennedy set forth no clear standard, and it seems unlikely that the courts will ever encounter a more plainly political plan than Pennsylvania's.

Governor

Ed Rendell (D)

Elected 2002, term expires Jan. 2007, 1st term; b. Jan. 5, 1944, New York, NY; home, Harrisburg; U. of PA, B.A. 1965, Villanova U., J.D. 1968; Jewish; married (Marjorie).

Military Career: Army Reserve, 1968–74.

Elected Office: District Atty., City of Philadelphia, 1977–85; Philadelphia Mayor, 1991–99.

Office: 225 Capitol Bldg., Harrisburg, 17120, 717-787-2500; Fax: 717-772-8284; Web site: www.governor.state.pa.us.

Election Results

2002 general	Ed Rendell (D)	1,913,235	(53%)
	Mike Fisher (R)	1,589,408	(44%)
	Other	79,917	(2%)
2002 primary	Ed Rendell (D)	702,442	(57%)
	Bob Casey Jr. (D)	539,794	(43%)
1998 general	Tom Ridge (R)	1,736,844	(57%)
	Ivan Itkin (D)	938,745	(31%)
	Peg Luksik (Const)	315,761	(10%)
	Other	33,802	(1%)

Ed Rendell, a Democrat, was elected governor of Pennsylvania in 2002, the first Philadelphian elected to that position since 1914. He grew up in Manhattan, in an apartment overlooking the Hudson on Riverside Drive; his father was a middleman in the women's clothing business and an ardent New Dealer and his mother's family owned a big women's clothing manufacturer that clashed often with unions. That Rendell became a Democrat who, as mayor, clashed with unions is not perhaps a coincidence. After his father died when he was 14, he acted up and was thrown out of Riverdale Country School for a year. He graduated from the University of Pennsylvania and from the Villanova University law school, and never left Philadelphia. He got a job in Philadelphia District Attorney Arlen Specter's office prosecuting homicides. In 1977, at 33, he was elected district attorney himself, and reelected in 1981. The district attorney is a prominent figure not just in Philadelphia but also in the entire Philadelphia media market, where some 40% of Pennsylvania voters live; prominent enough that former Philadelphia district attorneys are now Pennsylvania's governor and senior U.S. senator. In 1985 he did not run for reelection but started running for governor; Pennsylvania law requires mayors and district attorneys to resign if they run for statewide office. Since 1955 the two major parties have alternated in the governor's office every eight years; Republican Governor Richard Thornburgh was ineligible to run in 1986, and it seemed the Democrats' turn. In the Democratic primary he faced former Auditor General Bob Casey, who had lost in gubernatorial primaries in 1966, 1970 and 1978. This time Casey won, 51%–40%. Rendell carried the Philadelphia market, but in the rest of the state he seemed perhaps too young, too brash, too Philadelphian.

In 1987 Rendell ran unsuccessfully in the Democratic primary against Philadelphia's first black mayor, Wilson Goode. At 43, Rendell seemed to be through politically. But in 1991 he ran for mayor again. With Goode ineligible to run again and the city's finances in dreadful shape, Rendell, campaigning with his usual energy and ebullience, won the Democratic primary 49%–27%. In the general election he faced former Mayor Frank Rizzo, but Rizzo died of a heart attack in July 1991 and Rendell won easily in November, 64%–30%. Brash, energetic, cheerful, rumpled and a big sports fan, Rendell became a popular public figure in Philadelphia; he continues to serves as a cable television commentator for an Eagles football post-game show, a gig that began in 1998. In 2000 Rendell was named Democratic National Chairman. He campaigned for Al Gore, who had called him "America's mayor," but during the Florida controversy Rendell was readier to concede than Gore and his top advisers.

Immediately after the 2000 election Rendell set out to run for governor in 2002. Tom Ridge, the Republican governor elected in 1994 and 1998, was ineligible to run and became George W. Bush's homeland security adviser in October 2001; he was succeeded by Lieutenant Governor Mark Schweiker, who had previously announced he wanted to spend more time with his family and would not run for governor. In the 2002 Democratic primary, Rendell faced Auditor General Bob Casey Jr., whose father had defeated him 16 years earlier.

Early polls showed a close race in the Democratic primary, and many thought that this year, as in 1986, Rendell would be too Philadelphian for the rest of the state. There was a clear contrast between the candidates on issues. Casey, like his father, opposed abortion and said he would sign a ban on abortion if *Roe v. Wade* were reversed. He opposed gun control. Rendell favored abortion rights and gun control. There was a clear difference on economic issues as well. Rendell had an economic development initiative for parts of the state that missed the 1990s boom. Casey concentrated on extending government benefits; he advocated low-cost health insurance for unemployed workers and a $1 rise in the minimum wage. There was also a contrast in demeanor. Rendell embarked on a bus caravan traveling all over the state and campaigned with his usual brio; Casey was tightly scripted, polite and earnest.

Pennsylvania allows unlimited contributions to state campaigns, and this was a big money race: the two candidates spent more than $25 million on the primary. Rendell, a tremendous fundraiser, raised huge amounts from his Philadelphia and national contacts. Casey raised over $5 million from unions, including public employee unions still bitterly opposed to Rendell. Casey ran largely negative ads, calling Rendell's Philadelphia story a half-truth and blaming him for the conditions of the city's public schools, which had just been taken over by the state. Some of the Casey ads were scorching; a Philadelphia police officer was shown saying about Rendell, "He lies. Cops deal with liars all the time, and we have no respect for anybody who lies." The Democratic state committee endorsed Casey, and he counted on local endorsements, from influential state Senator Vince Fumo and union leaders, to dent Rendell's margin in Philadelphia.

Rendell spent $740,000 on Election Day activities, including $450,000 cash to be handed out in the city's 66 wards. But his popularity in the suburbs was even more decisive. Rendell won 79% of the vote in Philadelphia and even more in the suburbs. Altogether he carried the eight counties in the Philadelphia media market 79%–21%. Overall Rendell won 57%–43%, though he carried only two of the 59 counties outside the Philadelphia market (Lancaster and the county containing Penn State). Analysts agreed that Casey had run too negative a campaign and had not given voters enough reason to vote for him. In contrast, Rendell ran a mostly positive campaign and presented detailed policies.

After the primary Rendell led conservative Attorney General Mike Fisher in the polls, but not by much. Pennsylvania's pattern of alternating parties in the governorship every eight years goes back to the 1954 election, but it is not a law of nature. Ridge and Schweiker had high job ratings. Pennsylvania elects judges in off-years, the auditor and treasurer in presidential years, and so there is a statewide partisan race every year, and Republicans had been winning almost all of them since 1990. Republicans held majorities in both houses of the legislature. Fisher had more experience in state government: he had been elected to the state House in 1974 and the state Senate in 1980 and as attorney general in 1996 and 2000; he had been the unsuccessful nominee for lieutenant governor in 1986 and an unsuccessful candidate in the 1994 primary for governor. His opposition to abortion was by no means a political liability in Pennsylvania. Nor was his platform—cutting the corporate income tax from 9.9% to 7%, expanding the state's prescription drug program with slots money, increased research and development tax credits, requiring school districts to give voters a choice between the property tax and an earned income tax. After the primary, Rendell was almost out of money; he had $1 million to Fisher's $5 million.

Rendell started off on a positive note, saying that Fisher had been a good attorney general and a good state senator. Fisher started more negatively, calling Rendell a "tax-and-spend liberal" and said his success as mayor was greatly exaggerated. Fisher got some bad publicity over the proposed sale of Hershey Foods by the trust that owns the company, when it was revealed that a Fisher aide had told trustees the sale, unpopular in central Pennsylvania, was a good idea. But Fisher fought the sale in court and got a judge to halt it, turning a minus into a plus. George W. Bush raised nearly $2 million for Fisher, who eventually raised $13.8 million. But Rendell vastly outraised him, with $42 million for the entire campaign, more than any other candidate in 2002 except California Governor Gray Davis, Texas Governor Rick Perry and New York Governor George Pataki. In the end, what elected Rendell was his popularity in the Philadelphia media market. In Pennsylvania, outside the two big media markets, Fisher led 58%–39%. But in the Philadelphia media market Rendell won a smashing 68%–30% victory. He won 84% of the vote in Philadelphia, but he also won huge margins in the suburbs where Republicans have a huge registration advantage and which they usually carry in statewide races. Turnout was again higher in the Philadelphia media market, which cast 41% of the state's votes.

Once in office, Rendell set about paring the state budget, with help from the unlikely quarter of AFSCME, when sent in a proposal to save $259 million by reducing the state work force and restricting overtime. He had problems with the Republican-controlled General Assembly, a far more partisan and far less malleable body than the overwhelmingly Democratic city council he had been accustomed to in Philadelphia. He proposed a 33% increase in the state income tax to help pay for early childhood education, but legislators scaled it down to just 10% and gave him less money than he wanted. His ambitious plan for slot machines to pay for property tax relief failed. The state got stuck in a bitter, nine-month budget stalemate after Rendell vetoed the $4 billion education appropriation.

But in his second year in office, Rendell won a victory on the most important piece of his agenda—slot machines. The fractious issue of legalizing gambling to pay for property tax relief created divisions within both parties; aside from those who opposed the idea on moral grounds, there were questions about how to regulate it, whether to allow gaming rights to two Indian tribes, how the revenue would be shared, whether the machines should be purchased from state manufacturers. Rendell traveled the state in support of his legalized gambling plan and promised Republicans who supported his tax package, which included the slots proposal, he would not campaign against them; he said an expansion of gambling would staunch the flow of dollars to bordering states such as Delaware, New Jersey and West Virginia, all of which permit slots and other forms of wagering. The plan passed in July. The final deal authorized as many as 61,000 slot machines at 14 locations—more slots than any state other than Nevada. The 14 licenses would go to existing horse racing tracks, resorts and tracks and casinos that will be built later and were expected to bring in $1 billion per year in revenues to help the state reduce property taxes by an average of 20% statewide and pay for economic development.

Rendell had other successes in 2004. The legislature passed several items on his environmental agenda, including a bill requiring that 18% of the state's electricity come from renewable sources within 15 years and one that provided funding for rebuilding and repairing sewer and water systems. In November, Rendell won a Pittsburgh bailout package that gave the city new taxing authority. But he failed to secure a permanent funding solution for troubled transit systems in Philadelphia and Pittsburgh, caught between urban mass transit needs and those of rural areas seeking dollars for aging highways and bridges. His relations with the legislature remained stormy. State newspapers reported that in November, near the end of the two-year session, Senate President Pro Tem Robert Jubelirer marched into his office with other Republican leaders and angrily confronted Rendell using very salty language. Republicans contended that Rendell had double-crossed them by indicating that he would back a pay raise for lawmakers if they passed several priority items on his agenda; after they complied, according to Republican accounts, he insisted on more. Rendell declined to comment publicly on the encounter.

When asked to assess his own performance after two years, Rendell used sports metaphors to give himself high marks. He said his achievements were an example of "winning ugly" and joked that he was "having a better year than Peyton Manning," the record-setting Indianapolis Colts quarterback. Ever the sports fan, he postponed the annual budget address in 2005 "in consideration of potential scheduling difficulties for those traveling out of state during the days immediately preceding Feb. 8." (Translation: The Eagles were in the Super Bowl and he was planning to attend).

But in May 2005, Rendell suffered a blow that threatened to kill his signature achievement. A companion bill to the legalized gambling legislation, known as Act 72, allowed school districts to opt in to the property tax relief system; districts that took that option would then receive a share of the gambling revenues in exchange for lowering property tax rates. A decision was required by May 30. The vast majority of the state's 501 school districts, it turned out, voted against participating in the distribution scheme, in part because opting in would make it more difficult for them to increase property taxes in the future. Rendell said he was disappointed, but would find another way to accomplish property tax relief.

The inability to enact property tax relief hurt Rendell's standing in polls in 2005, but he remains popular and in a solid position for reelection. Possible Republican challengers in June 2005 included Senate Majority Leader Jeff Piccola of Dauphin County, former Lieutenant Governor Bill Scranton, the son of the former Pennsylvania governor and the unsuccessful nominee for governor in 1986 against Bob Casey, and former Pittsburgh Steelers wide receiver Lynn Swann, a football television commentator who was a prominent supporter of George W. Bush in 2004.

Senior Senator

Arlen Specter (R)

Elected 1980, seat up 2010, 5th term; b. Feb. 12, 1930, Wichita, KS; home, Philadelphia; U. of PA, B.A. 1951, Yale U., LL.B. 1956; Jewish; married (Joan).

Military Career: Air Force, 1951–53.

Elected Office: Philadelphia Dist. Atty., 1965–73.

Professional Career: Practicing atty., 1955–56, 1974–80; Asst. Cnsl., Warren Comm., 1964; PA Asst. Atty. Gen., 1964–65.

DC Office: 711 HSOB, 20510, 202-224-4254; Fax: 202-228-1229; Web site: www.senate.gov/~specter.

State Offices: Allentown, 610-434-1444; Erie, 814-453-3010; Harrisburg, 717-782-3951; Philadelphia, 215-597-7200; Pittsburgh, 412-644-3400; Scranton, 570-346-2006; Wilkes-Barre, 570-826-6265.

Committees: *Appropriations*: Agriculture, Rural Development & Related Agencies; Defense; Homeland Security; Labor, Health and Human Services, Education & Related Agencies (Chmn.); State, Foreign Operations & Related Programs; Transportation, Treasury, the Judiciary, HUD & Related Agencies. *Judiciary* (Chmn.): Administrative Oversight & the Courts; Antitrust, Competition Policy & Consumer Rights; Constitution, Civil Rights & Property Rights; Corrections & Rehabilitation. *Veterans' Affairs*.

Group Ratings

	ADA	ACLU	AFS	LCV	ITIC	NTU	COC	ACU	NTLC	CHC
2004	45	22	50	17	91	50	87	75	83	83
2003	25	—	33	32	—	65	87	65	—	—

National Journal Ratings

	2003 LIB	—	2003 CONS		2004 LIB	—	2004 CONS
Economic	46%	—	53%		49%	—	48%
Social	49%	—	49%		42%	—	56%
Foreign	52%	—	47%		51%	—	48%

Key Votes of the 108th Congress

1. Ban Drilling in ANWR	N	5. Energy Bill	Y	9. Ban Same-Sex Marriage	Y
2. Approve Bush Tax Cuts	Y	6. Support Roe v. Wade	Y	10. Ban Bunker-Buster Bomb	N
3. Medicare/Rx Bill	Y	7. Ban Partial-Birth Abortion	Y	11. Fund Iraq War	Y
4. Bar Overtime Pay Regs.	Y	8. Assault Weapons Ban	N	12. Restrict Missile Defense	N

Election Results

2004 general	Arlen Specter (R)	2,925,080	(53%)	($20,307,099)
	Joe Hoeffel (D)	2,334,126	(42%)	($4,540,209)
	James Clymer (CNP)	220,056	(4%)	($212,896)
	Other	79,843	(1%)	
2004 primary	Arlen Specter (R)	530,839	(51%)	
	Pat Toomey (R)	513,693	(49%)	
1998 general	Arlen Specter (R)	1,814,180	(61%)	($4,535,887)
	Bill Lloyd (D)	1,028,839	(35%)	($187,157)
	Other	114,753	(4%)	

Prior Winning Percentages: 1992 (49%); 1986 (56%); 1980 (50%)

Arlen Specter, one of the nation's most durable career politicians, has held public office and has been an important national figure off and on for more than four decades. Specter grew up in Russell, Kansas, also the hometown of Bob Dole; his father was an immigrant who worked as a tailor, owned a junkyard and sent four children through college. Specter came to Philadelphia at 17 to attend the University of Pennsylvania. After college he served in the Air Force, went to Yale

Law School and practiced law in Philadelphia. In 1964 he was a top staffer for the Warren Commission investigating the Kennedy assassination and helped develop the single-bullet theory; at one point, he held Oswald's weapon and aimed it out the Texas Schoolbook Depository window toward Dealey Plaza. After the Warren Commission, he returned to his law practice, switched to the Republican Party, and was elected district attorney in Democratic Philadelphia in 1965 and again in 1969. As D.A. he gave his first job to a Penn law graduate from New York named Ed Rendell, who is now governor of Pennsylvania. Specter lost the race for D.A. in 1973, and was beaten in Republican primaries for senator in 1976 and governor in 1978. In 1980 he ran for the Senate again. He narrowly (36%–33%) edged a former state Republican chairman in the primary and beat a low-spending Democrat 50%–48% in the general. In 1986, he won reelection by a 56%–43% margin; in 1992 he was reelected 49%–46% after he became a target of feminists for his questioning of Anita Hill during the confirmation hearings of Clarence Thomas. He ran for president in 1995, but withdrew before the first caucus or primary.

Throughout this career of narrow victories and numerous defeats, Specter's assets have been brains and hard work. He is respected by colleagues and constituents, though not always well-liked. He sides with conservatives on some divisive issues, with liberals on others, building up no permanent credit with either. He is aggressive and prosecutorial, well-prepared and persuasive once he takes a stand. These traits are both his strengths and weaknesses; they explain why he was vulnerable in 1992, and why he won; why he ran for president, and why his campaign went nowhere. His voting record is almost precisely at the midpoint of the Senate, and he has played key roles on a variety of issues. Though he switched and voted to override Bill Clinton's partial-birth abortion veto, he is generally pro-choice on abortion—an issue he featured in his presidential campaign, infuriating many Republican activists. He pushes tough penalties for crime and supports capital punishment. On a closely divided and rancorous Judiciary Committee, he played a key role on several Supreme Court nominations. More than anyone else, he defeated Robert Bork in 1987 and, more than anyone but John Danforth, he secured the confirmation of Clarence Thomas in 1991.

He opposed George W. Bush's $250,000 limit on pain and suffering damages in medical malpractice cases, arguing that there should be no limit for egregious cases of severe bodily impairment, disfigurement or death; his son Shanin Specter is a Philadelphia malpractice lawyer who won a $49 million settlement in 2000. In 2003 he hired a former federal appeals judge to draw up specifications for a trust fund to handle asbestos claims.

On many issues, Specter has been one of the few Republicans voting with Senate Democrats—on the Republican tax cut in August 1999, the Comprehensive Test Ban Treaty in October 1999, the minimum wage in November 1999, on the federal tobacco lawsuit in July 2000, HMO regulation in July 2000, on overtime regulations in September 2003 and March 2005. He voted against school choice in the District of Columbia.

To foreign policy he often brings a legalistic approach. His May 1999 amendment to the defense authorization bill, invoking the War Powers Act to prevent the deployment of ground troops in the former Yugoslavia, failed 52–48. In July 2002 he called for a congressional vote on military action in Iraq. "We have a responsibility institutionally under the Constitution to declare war, and we have a responsibility to acquaint the American people as to what is involved." In debate on the resolution in October, he expressed doubts about whether Congress can delegate authority to president, but he voted for the resolution. In January 2003 he said it was not necessary for the United States to go back to the UN Security Council before taking action, but "realistically we should." He favors the International Criminal Court opposed by the Bush administration.

Specter has played a major role in encouraging medical research. In 2002 he sponsored one of the two major competing bills on stem cell research. Specter's bill would allow embryonic stem cell research but ban cloning for reproductive purposes; his chief co-sponsors were Tom Harkin and Orrin Hatch. For most of the year he skirmished with Sam Brownback, sponsor of a bill that would ban embryonic stem cell research. In September 2002 Specter claimed he had 60 votes for his bill, but it was not brought to the floor.

Specter is not shy about using his place on the committee to funnel money into Pennsylvania, from the Philadelphia Navy Yard to Lake Erie; he has traveled indefatigably to all over Pennsylvania's 67 counties and promoted projects in most or all of them. He pressed the Defense Department to declare Philadelphia a strategic military seaport, which it did in February 2004, and worked to get $40 million in federal funding for a Philadelphia terminal for high-speed cargo ships; he has worked, against objections from New Jersey's Rob Andrews, for dredging of the Delaware River. When Citizens Against Government Waste listed him in its "Pig Book," he said, "If they left me out, I'd be worried."

After Jim Jeffords left the Republican party in May 2001, Specter was given a position in the leadership as a representative of Republican moderates. Specter also is known as one of Capitol Hill's sternest taskmasters; a *PoliticsPA.com* poll of opinion leaders rated him the hardest politician to work for and a *Washingtonian* poll of Capitol Hill staffers rated him the third "meanest" senator. *The Washington Post* reported Specter is notorious for his demands on overseas trips, which include daily squash matches at 5:00 p.m., English-speaking drivers, "customs expeditors", and planned excursions for his wife.

Specter has always had opposition in Republican primaries, but his most serious challenge came in 2004 from Lehigh Valley Congressman Pat Toomey. In 1986 he was renominated 76%–24% over a social studies teacher who said he had entered the race at God's urging; in 1992 he won 65%–35% over a state representative who opposed abortion; in 1998 he won with 67% against two candidates who won 18% and 15%. In February 2003 Toomey, who promised to serve only three terms when he was first elected in the House in 1998, announced he was running as an advocate of tax cuts and an opponent of abortion. White House political strategist Karl Rove made it clear to Toomey that George W. Bush would support Specter; White House Chief of Staff Andrew Card in February 2003 attended a fundraiser for Specter in Toomey's district. On Toomey's side was *National Review* (which called Specter "the worst Republican senator"), former Judge Robert Bork and former Attorney General Edwin Meese, former presidential candidate Steve Forbes and longtime conservative strategist Paul Weyrich. The Club for Growth raised $1 million for Toomey and spent $1 million of soft money on advocacy ads. But Specter had much more: in March 2003 he had $7 million in his campaign treasury and he spent $15 million up through the April 2004 primary.

Specter campaigned on his seniority and his seat on the Appropriations Committee; his campaign slogan was "Courage. Clout. Convictions." "I would say it's an election to see if there's going to be any place in the Republican party for a big tent," he said. "It's more than the soul of the Republican party; it's to have some balance within the party and within the two-party system." Toomey's framing of the issues was directed at conservative Republicans. "Today we have complete control. And the question that I'm posing to Republican primary voters all across Pennsylvania is a simple one: Are we going to seize this opportunity to govern with a common sense conservative agenda, or are we going to let it slip away by reelecting a liberal who will fight our agenda?" Toomey's message was undercut by frequent appearances for Specter by his conservative colleague Rick Santorum and by Dick Cheney and George W. Bush. Specter had not backed Santorum in his 1994 primary, but had provided him critical help in the general election that year; the Bush White House has made it clear that it supports all incumbent Republicans and hopes that moderate incumbents will keep that in mind when casting key votes on priority issues. Toomey started off little known outside his own congressional district, but spent enough money to get his message across, and nearly won. After 24 years in the Senate Specter won the primary by only 51%–49%. He carried metro Philadelphia 57%–43%, but Toomey carried metro Pittsburgh 58%–42%. Toomey won 2–1 in his 15th District and carried Lancaster and York Counties in the Pennsylvania Dutch territory and several industrial counties in the ring around Pittsburgh. Perhaps decisive were Specter's large majorities in most of the state's small counties. "They know my footprint all over the northern tier," he said. "I have a very strong bond with the people of Pennsylvania. It comes from having visited every one of the counties." And certainly he would not have won without the vigorous support of Bush, Cheney and Santorum.

Even so, immediately after the primary Specter trumpeted his differences with the Bush administration on issues like overtime pay, vouchers and stem-cell research. The Democratic nominee, suburban Philadelphia Congressman Joe Hoeffel, protested, "He's been meek, a supporter of the Bush program, which has alarmed a lot of moderates, with the budget deficits growing and the deceptions in Iraq and all the rest." He claimed that Specter had voted 89% for positions taken by Bush which have "taken the country down the wrong course." But Specter had much more money to deliver his message of clout and convictions. Overall Specter spent $21.6 million to Hoeffel's $4.6 million; in the last three weeks of the campaign Specter outspent Hoeffel by $1.2 million to $450,000. National Democrats were reluctant to pour money into an iffy race in a large and expensive state. In September Specter was endorsed by the Philadelphia Black Clergy and the state AFL-CIO. In debates Specter relished taking the center position between Hoeffel, who had a very liberal voting record, and Constitution Party nominee James Clymer, who attacked him from the right and ended up winning 4% of the vote. In 1998, against a very low spending opponent, Specter won 61%–35%. In 2004 Specter won 53%–42%, trailing 53%–47% in metro Philadelphia and leading 51%–49% in metro Pittsburgh. Specter won 25% among blacks, 48% in union households, and 23% among liberals. But his overall percentage of 53% was not much above Bush's 48%; though he ran 6% ahead of Bush in metro Philadelphia and more than that in the counties containing Scranton and Erie, he ran behind Bush in most of Pennsylvania west of Harrisburg except for the sparsely-populated northern tier.

Two days after the election Specter enraged many cultural conservatives when he warned Bush not to nominate judges who would try to overturn *Roe v. Wade*. Senate Republicans impose six-year term limits on their committee chairmen and committee members elect them by secret ballot. The term limit meant that Orrin Hatch would no longer chair the Judiciary Committee and seniority put Specter next in line. Suddenly the Concerned Women of America, the Family Research Council and Dr. James Dobson were demanding that Republican senators deny Specter the chairmanship. Specter immediately sought to clarify his statement. "I did not warn the president about anything and was very respectful of his constitutional authority," he said. "I voted for every one of President Bush's nominees in committee and on the floor, every last one of them." Two days later White House chief strategist Karl Rove said, "Senator Specter's a man of his word. We'll take him at his word." But Majority Leader Bill Frist pointedly declined to endorse Specter for the chairmanship and said he would have to make his case to Republican senators. With his usual assiduousness, he did. On November 18 all the Republicans on the Judiciary Committee appeared with Specter and endorsed him. Specter read out a statement, "I have not and would not use a litmus test to deny confirmation to pro-life nominees. I have no reason to believe I will be unable to support any individual President Bush finds worthy of nomination." He met with leaders of cultural conservative organizations and said that there were "relevant recent precedents" to require only 51 votes to end the Democratic filibusters of judicial nominees.

In early 2005 leaders of conservative groups were still grumbling at Specter's staff appointments and the fact that he called for delay in the renomination of judicial appointees whose confirmations had been denied by filibusters. And business groups were worried about Specter's stand on the asbestos trust fund. But he did shepherd to passage the class action bill in February 2005. And he did commit himself to bring all Bush judicial nominees to the floor and not to oppose a rules change to stop filibusters, though he seemed less than eager to see such a move.

A bit of history: Specter is the first Pennsylvania senator to be popularly elected to five terms and in November 2005 will break the record tenure for a Pennsylvania senator, set by Boies Penrose, who served from 1897 to 1921.

Junior Senator

Rick Santorum (R)

Elected 1994, seat up 2006, 2d term; b. May 10, 1958, Winchester, VA; home, Penn Hills; PA St. U., B.A. 1980, U. of Pittsburgh, M.B.A. 1981, Dickinson Law Schl., J.D. 1986; Catholic; married (Karen).

Elected Office: U.S. House of Reps., 1990–94.

Professional Career: A.A., PA Sen. J. Doyle 1981–86; Exec. Dir., PA Senate Local Govt. Cmte., 1981–84; Exec. Dir., PA Senate Transportation Cmte., 1984–86; Practicing atty., 1986–90.

DC Office: 511 DSOB, 20510, 202-224-6324; Fax: 202-228-0604; Web site: santorum.senate.gov.

State Offices: Allentown, 610-770-0142; Altoona, 814-946-7023; Erie, 814-454-7114; Harrisburg, 717-231-7540; Philadelphia, 215-864-6900; Pittsburgh, 412-562-0533; Scranton, 570-344-8799.

Committees: *Republican Conference Chairman. Aging (Special). Agriculture, Nutrition & Forestry*: Production & Price Competitiveness; Research, Nutrition & General Legislation (Chmn.). *Banking, Housing & Urban Affairs*: Financial Institutions; Housing & Transportation; Securities & Investment. *Finance*: Health Care; Social Security & Family Policy (Chmn.); Taxation & IRS Oversight. *Rules & Administration.*

Group Ratings

	ADA	ACLU	AFS	LCV	ITIC	NTU	COC	ACU	NTLC	CHC
2004	15	11	14	0	100	83	94	96	95	100
2003	10	—	0	0	—	81	100	90	—	—

National Journal Ratings

	2003 LIB	—	2003 CONS	2004 LIB	—	2004 CONS
Economic	0%	—	82%	24%	—	75%
Social	0%	—	59%	19%	—	71%
Foreign	0%	—	78%	39%	—	60%

Key Votes of the 108th Congress

1. Ban Drilling in ANWR	N	5. Energy Bill	Y	9. Ban Same-Sex Marriage	Y
2. Approve Bush Tax Cuts	Y	6. Support Roe v. Wade	N	10. Ban Bunker-Buster Bomb	N
3. Medicare/Rx Bill	Y	7. Ban Partial-Birth Abortion	Y	11. Fund Iraq War	Y
4. Bar Overtime Pay Regs.	N	8. Assault Weapons Ban	N	12. Restrict Missile Defense	N

Election Results

2000 general	Rick Santorum (R)	2,481,962	(52%)	($10,616,262)
	Ron Klink (D)	2,154,908	(46%)	($3,641,167)
	Other	98,246	(2%)	
2000 primary	Rick Santorum (R)	unopposed		
1994 general	Rick Santorum (R)	1,735,691	(49%)	($6,732,849)
	Harris Wofford (D)	1,648,481	(47%)	($6,300,560)
	Other	129,189	(4%)	

Prior Winning Percentages: 1992 House (61%); 1990 House (51%)

Rick Santorum, Pennsylvania's junior Senator, was first elected to the House in 1990 and to the Senate in 1994. Santorum is the son of an Italian immigrant who was a clinical psychologist for the Veterans' Administration; he was born in Virginia and moved to Butler, Pennsylvania, at age 7. He started in politics working for John Heinz's first Senate campaign in 1976; he graduated from Penn State and the University of Pittsburgh business school and worked his way through Dickinson law school as a staffer for state Senate Republicans in Harrisburg; he worked for a blue chip law firm in Pittsburgh for four years. In 1990, at 32, he challenged seven-term incumbent Congressman Doug Walgren, who outspent him $717,000 to $251,000. Santorum knocked on 25,000 doors, amassed an army of volunteers including many right-to-lifers, attacked Walgren for voting for a pay raise seven times and for living in the Washington suburbs. Santorum opposed the congressional pay raise, backed the line-item veto and came out for limits on PAC contributions. He won 51%–49%.

In the House he had a solid conservative voting record and was one of the "Gang of Seven" freshman Republicans who helped expose the House bank scandal. Redistricting gave him a seat shorn of many Republican suburbs and centered on the industrial Monongahela Valley, historically very Democratic. Santorum beat a state senator 61%–38%—an astonishing victory. Brash and confident, Santorum immediately started running for the Senate. His opponent was Harris Wofford, appointed in May 1991 to replace John Heinz after his death in a plane crash, and subsequently elected in a November 1991 special election upset win over former Governor Dick Thornburgh 55%–45%. Wofford won the special election by emphasizing health care; he was politically hurt when the Clinton health care bill failed to pass. This was a race of sharp contrasts in issues and style: Santorum, brashly eager to chop government, backing medical savings accounts and opposing gun control; Wofford, a former civil rights activist, earnestly working for government health care financing, backing the 1994 crime bill and gun control. Wofford appealed to a long liberal tradition; Santorum scoffed at him for championing 1960s ideas in the 1990s. Santorum won 49%–47%.

Santorum was not cowed by the traditions of the Senate. In his first full month there he argued about the balanced budget amendment with Robert Byrd, who was first elected to the Senate the year Santorum was born. Then, when senior Republican Mark Hatfield cast a decisive vote against the amendment, Santorum called on Hatfield to be removed as Appropriations chairman. Senior senators and Washington insiders tut-tutted. Hatfield wasn't removed, but Senate Republicans changed the rules, limiting chairmen to six years and calling for secret ballot elections of chairmen starting in 1997. Later in 1995 Santorum took to the floor a dozen times with a "Where's Bill?" sign, asking where the Bill Clinton's balanced budget was; Democrats were furious.

Santorum's voting record remains one of the most conservative in the Senate, but he is not quite so brash anymore. After the 2000 election he was elected chairman of the Republican Conference, the number three position in the leadership, in charge of communicating Senate Republicans' message. He has taken the lead on important legislation, and on occasion at some political risk. Santorum floor-managed the welfare bill to passage three times in 1995 and 1996; the first two times it was vetoed by Clinton, but in August 1996, 13 weeks before the election, Clinton signed it. Santorum has also taken the lead on the partial birth abortion ban. It was vetoed twice by Clinton; in March 2003, Santorum introduced the measure one again and it passed the Senate 64–33; it passed the House and was signed into law. This was not just a theoretical issue for him: In 1996 he and his wife had to decide what to do when their unborn child had a fatal defect; the baby was born in October 1996 and died two hours later.

The 1996 welfare bill contained a provision allowing more leeway for faith-based organizations to get government money to provide social services. Some use of this was made by the Clinton administration, and George W. Bush mentioned faith-based services frequently in his 2000 campaign. As president, Bush issued an executive order allowing more grants to faith-based organizations and called for Congress to pass legislation providing tax deductions and credits to strengthen such groups. This proved to be a rocky process, in which Santorum and Joe Lieberman took the lead role in the Senate. The House passed a bill in July 2001 with expanded block grants, tax breaks and a provision exempting faith-based organizations from state anti-discrimination laws, similar to that in the 1996 welfare act; some organizations want to hire members of their own faith and some refuse to hire homosexuals. In February 2002 Santorum and Lieberman introduced their bill, expanded block grants to states for child care and family welfare, providing a charitable deduction of $800 to couples who take the standard deduction, tax breaks for corporations who give money to charities, and tax deductions to banks which match individual development accounts set by low-income people for their education or starting a business. The Finance Committee passed a pared-down version in June 2002, without the corporate tax breaks. But Santorum was unable to get the measure to the floor, and in 2003 objections to the anti-discrimination clause prevented the legislation from going forward in the form he wanted.

As Republican Conference chairman, Santorum has worked aggressively to develop a unified voice for the party and to get Republican senators in touch with constituencies they have previously not had much to do with. One project has been to increase the number of Republicans hired to run business lobbies. Since the days of the New Deal, most Washington lobbyists have been Democrats, a natural development given that the Democrats held the White House from 1932 to 1952 and for most of the years from 1960 to 1980 and had majorities in the House and, except for six years, in the Senate from 1954 to 1994.

In December 2002 Santorum was one of the staunchest defenders, in public and in private, of Majority Leader Trent Lott after his comments at Strom Thurmond's 100th birthday party December 5. But support for Lott crumbled and it was clear that the required five senators would call for a meeting of the Republican Conference when Congress convened on January 6; on December 20, Lott bowed out. Santorum began calling senators seeking support for the position himself and got a public endorsement from Arlen Specter. But by the end of the afternoon it was clear that Bill Frist had the votes. Santorum convened a Conference meeting by phone call on December 23, and Frist was chosen without opposition. Before the Lott affair, Santorum was in line to become chairman of the Rules Committee and was making plans for the job. But in January he stepped aside to allow Lott to become chairman.

Santorum has taken some stands with a view to local interests and out of personal beliefs. He backed minimum wage increases in the House and Senate, and supported the steel import quota bill that died in June 1999. He backed George W. Bush's steel import quotas in March 2002 and worked to try to link oil drilling in the Arctic National Wildlife Refuge with the proposal for the government legacy payments—payments of health insurance costs for steelworkers whose companies have gone bankrupt. He opposed George W. Bush's proposal for a $250,000 cap on pain and suffering damages in medical malpractice cases, objecting to the amount of the cap; in 1999 his wife sued a chiropractor for $500,000 for back injuries and was awarded $175,000. In 2004 he and Specter called for lifting the import duties for electron guns used in cathode ray tubes, LCD panels and flat screen TVs; this was to prevent Sony from moving jobs from its Westmoreland County plant to Mexico.

Santorum's strong religious views have influenced his views on public policy. "What I'm concerned about is we have some in our society today who say you can come to the public square influenced by anything other than faith. If you are influenced by faith, somehow that is illegiti-mate and your faith can only be private. I think that is a very dangerous thing because it leaves the public square with sort of a secular world." His five children are home-schooled; there was some controversy in 2004 when the Penn Hills school district reversed its approval of his school-age children's enrollment in the Pennsylvania Cyber Charter School. He has said that *Griswold v. Connecticut*, the 1965 Supreme Court case that first recognized a "right of privacy" was a "massive usurpation of power by the judiciary." After the Supreme Court ruled in April 2003 that laws against sodomy were unconstitutional, Santorum aroused controversy by saying, "If the Supreme Court says that you have the right to consensual [homosexual] sex within your home, then you have the right to bigamy, you have the right to polygamy, you have the right to incest, you have the right to adultery. You have the right to anything." To critics he said, "I have no problem with homosexuality. I have a problem with homosexual acts." When a school district in York County sought to teach the theory of intelligent design as a possible alternative to evolution, Santorum stopped short of calling for the teaching of creationism, but cited scientists skeptical of evolution theory and said he encouraged "careful examination of the evidence for Darwinian theory."

Santorum is the first Republican generally classified as conservative to have been elected senator in Pennsylvania since 1952, and some thought he would be in trouble in 2000. But he ended up winning convincingly. His Democratic opponent was Congressman Ron Klink, a former Pittsburgh TV anchor, who in the primary advertised heavily on Pittsburgh TV and won with 41% of the vote over two candidates from eastern Pennsylvania, state Senator (now Congress-woman) Allyson Schwartz and former state Labor Secretary Tom Foley. Klink, like Santorum, opposed abortion and gun control; he attacked Santorum for proposing personal retirement accounts as part of Social Security. On paper, Klink's candidacy seemed well suited to Pennsyl-vania. But after the April primary he was far behind in money—Santorum had $3.7 million cash on hand while Klink had $119,000 plus debts of $446,000—and Klink had difficulty raising more, because his views on abortion and gun control were out of line with the Democratic contributor base. Santorum ran positive ads about his record, campaigning as a "compassionate conservative," emphasizing his ability to work with Democrats like Joe Lieberman and then-Philadelphia (now Governor) Mayor Ed Rendell. The first Klink ads did not go up until September; he went negative against Santorum, and voters never really heard a positive case for Klink. Santorum won 52%–46%. He ran behind in metro Philadelphia 53%–45%, but this 8% margin was far less than Al Gore's 25% margin over George W. Bush there. Santorum ran slightly behind his 1994 showing in metro Pittsburgh, which Klink carried 52%–46%. But in the rest of the state, which cast 46% of the votes, Santorum won a whopping 60%–37% margin, a big improvement over 1994.

After 2000 Santorum began taking a role in other elections. He played a key role in Pennsylvania redistricting: Republicans went into the 2002 election with an 11–10 edge in the delegation and emerged ahead 12–7. In the 2004 Senate race Santorum staunchly backed his colleague Arlen Specter against the challenge from Congressman Pat Toomey, whose voting record was much closer to Santorum's than Specter's was. Specter won 51%–49%; as Specter admitted, if he had not had Santorum's support he probably would have been defeated. Some religious conservatives criticized Santorum sharply, and a few even promised to work against him when his term came up in 2006. When Specter's election to be chairman of the Judiciary Committee was in doubt after the November 2004 election, Santorum declined to endorse him and said it was a matter for Judiciary Committee Republicans to decide. He also said that Toomey would be a good OMB director. Meanwhile, Santorum prepared to take a lead role on Social Security personal retirement accounts, as chairman of the Social Security Subcommittee and as head of Senate Republicans' Social Security Communications Working Group.

Santorum comes up for reelection in 2006, and this could be one of the most seriously contested races in the nation. His high-profile cultural conservatism makes him an attractive target for Democratic contributors not only in Pennsylvania but nationally. Immediately after the 2004 election, Governor Ed Rendell seemed to be leaning toward backing outgoing state Treasurer Barbara Hafer, who had been elected to that post twice and as state auditor twice as a Republican and became a Democrat in 2003; as a pro-choice Republican she had lost to pro-life Democratic Governor Bob Casey in 1990 by a 68%–32% margin. But Rendell changed his mind and backed incoming state Treasurer and former two-term state Auditor Bob Casey, Jr., son of the late governor who lost the Democratic primary to Rendell 57%–43% in April 2002. In November 2004 Casey, an opponent of abortion and gun control, was elected treasurer by a 61%–37% margin, winning 3.3 million votes, more than anyone else had ever won for any office in Pennsylvania. DSCC Chairman Charles Schumer and Senate Minority Leader Harry Reid encouraged Casey to run for the Senate and in March he announced his candidacy. Rendell persuaded Hafer to withdraw two days later. One public poll showed Casey leading Santorum 49%–42%; another showed him ahead just 44%–43%. Casey's issue profile was similar to Klink's, but he entered the race with much greater name identification, a proven record of winning votes statewide and, presumably, access to funding, whatever the views of Democratic contributors on abortion and guns, through Rendell and Schumer. Santorum also had strengths: he has won two Senate elections and his race looked like the number one priority for the Bush White House in 2006; presumably he will be able to call on Specter for help as well.

FIRST DISTRICT

Rep. Robert Brady (D)

Elected May 1998, 4th full term; b. April 7, 1945, Philadelphia; home, Philadelphia; St. Thomas More H. S.; Catholic; married (Debra).

Elected Office: 34th Ward Dem. Exec. Cmte. Mbr., 1967–present, Ward Ldr., 1980.

Professional Career: Carpenter; Real estate salesman; Philadelphia Dpty. Mayor for Labor, 1984–87; Chmn., Philadelphia Dem. Party, 1986; Legis. Rep., Metro. Regional Cncl. of Carpenters & Joiners, 1987–98; Lecturer, U. of PA, 1997-present.

DC Office: 206 CHOB, 20515, 202-225-4731; Fax: 202-225-0088; Web site: www.house.gov/robertbrady.

District Offices: Chester, 610-874-7094; Philadelphia, 215-389-4627.

Committees: *Armed Services* (14th of 28 D): Readiness; Tactical Air & Land Forces. *House Administration* (2d of 3 D).

Group Ratings

	ADA	ACLU	AFS	LCV	ITIC	NTU	COC	ACU	NTLC	CHC
2004	95	80	100	100	20	6	19	4	0	23
2003	100	—	100	50	—	20	31	17	—	—

National Journal Ratings

	2003 LIB	—	2003 CONS		2004 LIB	—	2004 CONS
Economic	69%	—	30%		98%	—	0%
Social	84%	—	13%		86%	—	12%
Foreign	88%	—	11%		77%	—	22%

Key Votes of the 108th Congress

1. Drilling in ANWR	Y	5. DC School Vouchers	N	9. Ban Same-Sex Marriage	N
2. Approve Bush Tax Cuts	N	6. Ban Human Cloning	N	10. Fund Iraq War	N
3. Medicare/Rx Bill	N	7. Restrict Gun Liability	N	11. Bar Cuba Embargo Funds	Y
4. Bar Overtime Pay Regs.	Y	8. Ban Partial-Birth Abortion	N	12. Intelligence Reorg.	N

Election Results

2004 general	Robert Brady (D)	214,462	(86%)	($361,532)
	Deborah Williams (R)	33,266	(13%)	
	Other	857	(0%)	
2004 primary	Robert Brady (D)	unopposed		
2002 general	Robert Brady (D)	121,076	(86%)	($355,578)
	Marie Delaney (R)	17,444	(12%)	
	Other	1,570	(1%)	

Prior Winning Percentages: 2000 (88%); 1998 (81%); 1998 (74%)

The People		Race/Ethnic Origin	Ancestry	
Area size:	68 sq. mi.	33.0% White	Irish: 8.9%	Italian: 7.8%
Urban population:	100.0%	44.9% Black	German: 5.0%	
Rural population:	0.0%	4.8% Asian	**2004 Presidential Vote**	
Pop. 2000:	646,357	0.2% Native Am.	Kerry (D)	227,327 (84%)
Median income:	$28,261	0.0% Hawaiian	Bush (R)	41,509 (15%)
Poverty status:	26.9%	1.8% Two+ races	Other	531 (0%)
Military veterans:	10.2%	0.2% Other	**2000 Presidential Vote**	
		15.0% Hispanic Origin	Gore (D)	181,274 (84%)
			Bush (R)	31,722 (15%)
			Other	2,679 (1%)
			Cook Partisan Voting Index: D +36	
Occupation	Blue collar: 21.2%	White collar: 56.9%	Gray collar: 21.9%	

In Center City Philadelphia, the 1680s look out on the 1780s, 1880s, 1980s and beyond. The statue of William Penn, who founded the city in 1682, stands 37 feet high atop the 548-foot tower of the 1880s Second Empire-style City Hall at Market and Broad. To the east is Independence Hall, where Americans in the 1780s drew up the nation's Constitution; to the west is the tower of One Liberty Place, with its "romantic modernist" spire, the 1980s building that broke tradition to rise above City Hall. Philadelphia is built on a certain order. Other American colonies were settled by practical men, out to make money or replicate a farm settlement back home. But Penn was a Quaker, a member of one of those rationalizing sects of the 17th century, who intended to impose order on his new environment, and did: no cowpath street patterns here, like those in Boston or Charleston, but a grid of numbered and named streets, with precisely spaced open squares. Penn's city of brotherly love has turned out to be a commercial and industrial metropolis that grew steadily over the years, spreading out over the countryside. Yet there are still places in which you can see the distant past: in the restored townhouses of Society Hill and the tree-shaded public buildings around Independence Hall and, on the way to the ornate City Hall, the Federal and Greek Revival buildings and the temples of commerce, built when Philadelphia was the nation's largest city. Interspersed are I.M. Pei's modernist Society Hill Towers (though the rich in Philadelphia, unlike New York or Chicago, don't much like apartments) and the 1920s masonry-faced skyscrapers and 1990s glass-and-steel towers built around City Hall and in Center City farther west.

For all the grandeur of City Hall, Philadelphia has seldom had a city government of which to be proud. "Corrupt beyond redemption" is how Lincoln Steffens described the city more than a century ago. Corruption and incompetence have reigned here off and on since then. While the city's private economy grew robustly in the 1980s, the city government lurched unknowingly toward bankruptcy under Mayor Wilson Goode. Then in 1991 Democrat Ed Rendell was elected mayor—and did well enough to become in 2002 the first former Philadelphia mayor to be elected governor since 1906. Unfortunately, Rendell's push for reform stalled in the mid-1990s. Philadelphia still has an inordinately expensive city government and neighborhoods ravaged by crime that have emptied out over the years. But there are signs of hope. Philadelphia has some of the nation's most vibrant and charitably active churches; its economy attracts some Latino and Asian immigrants, though many fewer than New York or Chicago; and its Center City is still attractive. The Philadelphia metropolitan area is still the sixth largest in the country, but most people there live outside the city.

The 1st Congressional District of Pennsylvania contains much of Philadelphia east of Broad Street; City Hall is on the district line. The 1st includes all of 18th century Philadelphia—Independence Hall, the U.S. Mint, and Elfreth's Alley (the oldest continually occupied residential block in the country)—as well as Chinatown, Society Hill, Overbrook, Northern Liberties and Penn's Landing. It includes Philadelphia's four-square-block, 1.3 million-square-foot convention center, opened in 1993. North of Center City, the 1st takes in much of heavily black North Philadelphia, a couple of wards of Northeast Philadelphia (connected to the rest by irregular boundaries), Kensington and its closely packed 19th century homes, where descendants of Irish and Italian immigrants lived for years in tiny frame houses; now the neighborhood (as well as nearby Fairhill) is increasingly Hispanic. South of Center City, the 1st includes heavily Italian South Philadelphia, where Italian families and their grocery stores and restaurants have been pressed tightly into narrow streets under a tangle of overhead wires; this is the neighborhood where the various *Rockys* were filmed and the original Philadelphia cheesesteaks are sold. Near there, the district takes in the city's stadium and arena complex, where the 2000 Republican convention was held, as well as the adjoining Navy Yard, established in 1762 and closed in 1996. From there, the 1st includes the Delaware River shore southwest into Delaware County to impoverished Chester. The district also includes three wards in heavily black West Philadelphia and a few small adjacent suburbs. The population of the district in 2000 was 45% black, less than the 61% black 2d District, and 15% Hispanic (mainly Puerto Rican), the highest of any Pennsylvania district. This is a heavily Democratic district.

The congressman from the 1st District is Bob Brady, a Democrat elected first in May 1998, who is the personification of Philadelphia's old-fashioned urban politics. He grew up in Overbrook Park in West Philadelphia, with an Irish father who was a policeman and an Italian mother; he depicts himself as a roll-up-your-sleeves guy who represents working class voters.

After high school he went to work as a carpenter and quickly rose up the ranks of the carpenters' union leadership. He entered politics in 1967, at 22, when the local ward leader wouldn't replace a burnt-out streetlight. Brady was elected to the 34th Ward Democratic Executive Committee, and in 1980 he was elected ward leader. In 1975 he became assistant sergeant-at-arms of the city council; he was a consultant to the state Senate and member of the Pennsylvania Turnpike Commission and on the board of the city's Redevelopment Authority. In 1986 he became chairman of the Philadelphia Democratic Party, where he has been a close ally of local powerbrokers like the late state Senator Buddy Cianfrani and state Senator Vincent Fumo. Brady is proud to be the boss of what he calls the nation's largest big city machine—or, as he defines it, an "organization" that mostly operates below the public's radar screen, and dispenses "street money" to workers on Election Day to make sure that its candidates win. Brady is known for making "arrangements" with others—"they're always arrangements, never deals," he insists— and that has enabled him to remain chairman for the better part of two decades.

In November 1997, Thomas Foglietta, a veteran of South Philly politics, resigned after being confirmed as ambassador to Italy, and Brady ran for the seat. In other cities, this might have led to a primary fight with black politicians; in Philadelphia, ward leaders in the district determined the Democratic nomination for the special election. That gave Brady a great advantage; former 2d District Congressman Lucien Blackwell, probably his strongest opponent, dropped out of the race even before Brady officially declared. With the endorsement of many black leaders and a strong Election Day organization, he won the special election with 74% of the vote. He is among the last of a dying breed—the white ethnic politician who represents an urban, primarily minority district.

Even after he was elected to the House, Brady's attention focused back home. He mediated the local teachers' strike in 2000, and he sought common ground between the mayor and city council on a deal for two new stadiums. His ties to City Hall and to local unions gave him credibility with both sides. As Mayor John Street won reelection in 2003, even as the feds were investigating city contracts, Brady worked to resolve local intra-party conflicts. According to the *Philadelphia Daily News,* he chewed out feuding city council Democrats at one memorable private meeting. "You are a [friggin'] embarrassment. You're embarrassing me, embarrassing yourselves. You're like a bunch of 10-year-old children. If you're not careful, you're not going to be here next year," he said, banging the table. "I've got 30 ward leaders who don't want to support you and 30 more who want to run against you."

In the House, where he has a liberal voting record, his positions on national issues are not always set in stone; he decided that he was in favor of abortion rights after asking his mother. For "the most powerful man in Philadelphia," *Philadelphia* magazine wrote, "Washington gas-bagging is not his thing." His initiatives reflect his local orientation. His loyalty to unions led him to buck environmentalists and most Democrats, and vote to allow oil drilling in the Arctic National Wildlife Refuge. But these national issues and the aura of the Capitol are not what motivate Brady; his most important job remains running the party's city committee. "Ninety-five percent of my day is not Congress," he said in 2002. He did get three bills passed that year: each named a local post office. That was three more bills than he passed during the next two years.

Even with his patented disdain for Washington, Brady has shown his impact on national politics in one very important way: He delivers votes in a battleground presidential state. The fact that Philadelphia gave John Kerry a 412,000-vote margin in the 2004 presidential election was a big factor in keeping Pennsylvania in the Democratic column. And the fact that Brady keeps the party organization in line back home was a major reason why that happened.

SECOND DISTRICT

Rep. Chaka Fattah (D)

Elected 1994, 6th term; b. Nov. 21, 1956, Philadelphia; home, Philadelphia; Community Col. of Philadelphia, U. of PA, M.A. 1986, Harvard U. Kennedy Schl. of Gov., 1984; Baptist; married (Renee Chenault).

Elected Office: PA House of Reps., 1982–88; PA Senate, 1988–94.

Professional Career: Asst. Dir., House of Umoja, 1977–79; City of Philadelphia, Spec. Asst. to Dir. of Housing & Community Dev., 1980, Spec. Asst. to Managing Director, 1981.

DC Office: 2301 RHOB, 20515, 202-225-4001; Fax: 202-225-5392; Web site: www.house.gov/fattah.

District Offices: Philadelphia, 215-848-9386; Philadelphia, 215-387-6404.

Committees: *Appropriations* (26th of 29 D): Foreign Operations, Export Financing & Related Programs; Science, State, Justice, Commerce & Related Agencies.

Group Ratings

	ADA	ACLU	AFS	LCV	ITIC	NTU	COC	ACU	NTLC	CHC
2004	85	95	100	100	20	7	22	0	0	23
2003	95	—	100	80	—	19	21	16	—	—

National Journal Ratings

	2003 LIB	—	2003 CONS		2004 LIB	—	2004 CONS
Economic	91%	—	9%		98%	—	0%
Social	88%	—	12%		88%	—	0%
Foreign	89%	—	8%		86%	—	13%

Key Votes of the 108th Congress

1. Drilling in ANWR	N	5. DC School Vouchers	N	9. Ban Same-Sex Marriage	N
2. Approve Bush Tax Cuts	N	6. Ban Human Cloning	N	10. Fund Iraq War	N
3. Medicare/Rx Bill	N	7. Restrict Gun Liability	N	11. Bar Cuba Embargo Funds	Y
4. Bar Overtime Pay Regs.	Y	8. Ban Partial-Birth Abortion	N	12. Intelligence Reorg.	N

Election Results

2004 general	Chaka Fattah (D)	253,226	(88%)	($384,313)
	Stewart Bolno (R)	34,411	(12%)	($16,973)
2004 primary	Chaka Fattah (D)	unopposed		
2002 general	Chaka Fattah (D)	150,623	(88%)	($287,182)
	Thomas Dougherty (R)	20,988	(12%)	

Prior Winning Percentages: 2000 (98%); 1998 (87%); 1996 (88%); 1994 (86%)

The People		Race/Ethnic Origin	Ancestry	
Area size:	60 sq. mi.	29.9% White	Irish: 6.8%	Italian: 5.4%
Urban population:	100.0%	60.7% Black	German: 4.7%	
Rural population:	0.0%	4.3% Asian	**2004 Presidential Vote**	
Pop. 2000:	646,355	0.2% Native Am.	Kerry (D) 266,174	(87%)
Median income:	$30,646	0.0% Hawaiian	Bush (R) 37,811	(12%)
Poverty status:	23.8%	1.7% Two+ races	Other 759	(0%)
Military veterans:	10.6%	0.2% Other	**2000 Presidential Vote**	
		3.0% Hispanic Origin	Gore (D) 221,517	(87%)
			Bush (R) 29,458	(12%)
			Other 3,529	(1%)
			Cook Partisan Voting Index: D +39	

Occupation	Blue collar: 14.6%	White collar: 65.8%	Gray collar: 19.5%

Looking out over the Schuylkill River north of Center City Philadelphia, you can still see the landscape painted 100 years ago by Philadelphia artist Thomas Eakins—the tightly-packed but formidable rowhouses, the old fieldstone houses of Germantown, the gray-blue water flowing past boat houses below the small Greek temples of the Water Works and the larger temple of the

Philadelphia Museum of Art. On both sides of this romantic scene are some of Philadelphia's long-established black neighborhoods: West Philadelphia, across the Schuylkill on either side of Market Street; North Philadelphia, on either side of Broad Street; Germantown to the northwest, off the narrow diagonal of Germantown Avenue that ran through open fields in Benjamin Franklin's time. Many of these neighborhoods continue to suffer from poverty and blight, and the city has 600,000 fewer people today than in 1950. But the city has launched a plan to reconnect the communities on the Schuylkill by energizing business and residential communities and boosting tourism, including modifications of several downtown bridges over the river and improved links to the river park. Another innovative step has been the city's plan to make inexpensive wireless Internet access a municipal service that is available to all residents, starting in 2006. Although free-marketeers object that this will turn broadband into a public utility, Mayor John Street said that the city's plan will include corporate and foundation financing, with private companies assisting its operation: Shades of Ben Franklin.

The 2d Congressional District of Pennsylvania takes in much of the city of Philadelphia west of Broad Street, plus Cheltenham Township in suburban Montgomery County. It doesn't include the key colonial landmarks—they're in the neighboring 1st—but it does include most of the skyscrapers of Center City and well-heeled Rittenhouse Square, the Philadelphia Zoo (America's first), the University of Pennsylvania, Drexel University, and lush Fairmount Park, the largest landscaped urban park in the world, which climaxes at the grand Philadelphia Museum of Art, where a *Rocky*-like run up the steps became *de rigueur* for tourists. The 2d includes West Oak Lane, Strawberry Mansion and, further west, the distinguished old neighborhoods of Mount Airy, Chestnut Hill and East Falls, mostly pleasant these days but dotted with some grittier precincts. The 2d also covers Roxborough and the old mill area of Manayunk, recently renovated. This is Pennsylvania's one black-majority district: 61% of its population in 2000 was black. Pennsylvania never had slavery—thanks to William Penn and his Quaker legacy—and Philadelphia has been home to a large black community since before the Civil War. That heritage is reflected in places like the John Coltrane House on North 33d Street, designated a national historic landmark in celebration of the jazz innovator's early years here. Suburban Cheltenham Township includes old, comfortable communities like Cheltenham, Melrose Park, Elkins Park and Glenside. The 2d was George W. Bush's 3d-worst performing district in the nation—he won just 12 percent here in 2004, the same as in 2000.

The congressman from the 2d District is Chaka Fattah (pronounced *SHOCK-ah Fa-TAH*), first elected in 1994. Fattah grew up in Philadelphia, and in 1982, at 25, was elected to the state House—the youngest member ever. In 1988 he was elected to the state Senate, where he worked to fend off bankruptcy for Philadelphia. In 1991, much to everyone's surprise, 2d District Congressman William Gray resigned to become head of the United Negro College Fund. In the election to succeed him, local Democratic ward leaders nominated Councilman Lucien Blackwell, a former longshoreman, boxer and labor union stalwart. Fattah ran under the Consumer Party label while state Welfare Secretary John White ran as an independent. Blackwell won the November 1991 special election with 39% to 28% for Fattah and 27% for White. In 1994 Fattah ran again, in the Democratic primary. Blackwell relied mostly on ward politicians; Fattah was endorsed by the Black Clergy of Philadelphia and Vicinity and by state Senator Hardy Williams. This time Fattah won, 58%–42%.

Fattah's voting record has been among the most liberal in the House. Much of his focus has been on education issues. He talked up his proposal for a study to eliminate the federal tax code and replace all individual and corporate taxes with a system that would tax all individual transactions; this generated some interest among Republicans. But most Democrats were leery of something that looked like a consumption tax and were not much interested in broad tax changes so long as they remained in the minority. Unlike locally oriented Bob Brady, the city's other congressman, Fattah's focus is more as a national Democrat. "My number one political priority is to elect a Democratic majority in Congress," he says.

In 2001, with the help of senior Pennsylvania Democrat John Murtha, Fattah won a seat on the Appropriations Committee, a useful slot for a member who seemed intent on a long House career; he said that he would use the position to push for more money for education. In 2003, he suffered an unexpected setback. He hoped to become the ranking minority member on the House Administration Committee. But Minority Leader Nancy Pelosi decided to enforce the rule barring a second committee assignment for members on Appropriations, and Fattah got bumped off House Administration altogether.

Since entering the House, Fattah has had no serious primary or general election challenge. After the 2004 election, he expressed interest in running for mayor of Philadelphia in 2007, a sign of the restlessness among talented Democrats who have little prospect for influence in the Republican House. This prompted grumbling among other local Democrats already planning to run for mayor, and even some threats that Fattah could face a primary challenge in 2006.

THIRD DISTRICT

Rep. Phil English (R)

Elected 1994, 6th term; b. June 20, 1956, Erie; home, Erie; U. of PA., B.A. 1978; Catholic; married (Christiane).

Elected Office: Erie City Controller, 1985–89.

Professional Career: Staff aide, PA Senate; 1980–84; Chief of Staff, PA Sen. Melissa Hart 1990–92; Exec. Dir., PA Senate Finance Cmte., 1990–94.

DC Office: 1410 LHOB, 20515, 202-225-5406; Fax: 202-225-3103; Web site: www.house.gov/english.

District Offices: Butler, 724-285-7005; Erie, 814-456-2038; Hermitage, 724-342-6132; Meadville, 814-724-8414; Warren, 814-723-7282.

Committees: *Ways & Means* (10th of 24 R): Health; Human Resources; Trade. *Joint Economic Committee.*

Group Ratings

	ADA	ACLU	AFS	LCV	ITIC	NTU	COC	ACU	NTLC	CHC
2004	25	10	38	27	80	59	90	68	65	84
2003	20	—	13	15	—	60	93	72	—	—

National Journal Ratings

	2003 LIB	—	2003 CONS		2004 LIB	—	2004 CONS
Economic	44%	—	56%		47%	—	52%
Social	46%	—	53%		47%	—	52%
Foreign	11%	—	80%		39%	—	59%

Key Votes of the 108th Congress

1. Drilling in ANWR	Y	5. DC School Vouchers	N	9. Ban Same-Sex Marriage	Y
2. Approve Bush Tax Cuts	Y	6. Ban Human Cloning	Y	10. Fund Iraq War	Y
3. Medicare/Rx Bill	Y	7. Restrict Gun Liability	Y	11. Bar Cuba Embargo Funds	N
4. Bar Overtime Pay Regs.	Y	8. Ban Partial-Birth Abortion	Y	12. Intelligence Reorg.	Y

Election Results

2004 general	Phil English (R)	166,580	(60%)	($1,595,195)
	Steven Porter (D)	110,684	(40%)	($224,002)
2004 primary	Phil English (R)	unopposed		
2002 general	Phil English (R)	116,763	(78%)	($778,773)
	AnnDrea Benson (Green)	33,554	(22%)	($19,353)

Prior Winning Percentages: 2000 (61%); 1998 (63%); 1996 (51%); 1994 (49%)

The People		Race/Ethnic Origin	Ancestry		
Area size:	4,777 sq. mi.	93.7% White	German: 20.8%	Irish: 10.5%	
Urban population:	58.4%	3.5% Black	Italian: 7.1%		
Rural population:	41.6%	0.5% Asian	**2004 Presidential Vote**		
Pop. 2000:	646,311	0.1% Native Am.	Bush (R) 152,473	(53%)	
Median income:	$35,884	0.0% Hawaiian	Kerry (D) 133,764	(47%)	
Poverty status:	11.6%	0.8% Two+ races	Other 861	(0%)	
Military veterans:	14.6%	0.1% Other	**2000 Presidential Vote**		
		1.3% Hispanic Origin	Bush (R) 127,598	(51%)	
			Gore (D) 116,118	(46%)	
			Other 6,233	(2%)	
			Cook Partisan Voting Index: R + 2		

Occupation	Blue collar: 30.7%	White collar: 52.3%	Gray collar: 17.0%

The best natural harbor on Lake Erie is in a state with the second-shortest Great Lakes shoreline. It is Erie, Pennsylvania, protected by the Presque Isle ("almost an island") peninsula—a cowlick-shaped, seven-mile-long sand spit blanketed by mature forest. Erie is in Pennsylvania's far northwest corner, only about 100 miles from Cleveland but 428 miles from Center City Philadelphia. There is farmland here, and even some woods, but this land between the Great Lakes and the basin of the Ohio River has been prime territory for heavy industry for more than a century. In the 1990s, under Governor Tom Ridge, an Erie native, the state invested $100 million in Erie's waterfront—a cruise ship terminal, a convention center, a ballpark for the single-A Erie SeaWolves baseball team, and restorations to the Warner Theatre—in an attempt to boost tourism. The effort spruced up a dying downtown, but it didn't buffer Erie from the recent economic downturn, as companies like General Electric, the area's largest employer, International Paper and Gunite/EMI laid off employees and closed plants.

The 3d Congressional District of Pennsylvania occupies this northwest corner of the state—all of Erie County, most of Mercer, Crawford and Butler Counties and about half of Warren, Venango, and Armstrong Counties. Erie County has 43% of the district's population, and had modest population gains from 1990 to 2003. Growth has been greater in Butler County, the northern edge of the Pittsburgh metropolitan area, while other parts of the district have lost population. Politically, the mix of industrial and rural voters makes for closely balanced territory. Erie and Mercer Counties vote Democratic in most national elections, but they have also voted for Republicans with working class appeal, like Ridge, from a Catholic working class family in Erie, Senator Rick Santorum and 2002 governor candidate Mike Fisher, whose running mate was Erie state Senator Jane Earll. The other counties are culturally conservative and solidly Republican. This is a district that voted 51% for George W. Bush in 2000 and 53% in 2004, 5% more than in the state as a whole.

The congressman from the 3d District is Phil English, a Republican first elected in 1994. English grew up in Erie and has worked at little else but politics and government. At 20, he was an alternate to the 1976 Republican National Convention, and he worked during the early 1980s as a Republican staffer in Harrisburg. In 1985 he became Erie controller; in 1988, he was the unsuccessful Republican nominee for state treasurer. In 1990 he helped produce Rick Santorum's upset win in the suburban Pittsburgh 18th District, the first step on Santorum's path to the Senate; he went on to become chief of staff to state Senator Melissa Hart, who was elected to the House in the adjacent 4th District in 2000. In 1994, when Ridge ran for governor, English ran for the House and won 66% in the Republican primary. In the general, English promised to reform welfare, cut wasteful spending and create jobs for northwestern Pennsylvania with an 18-point plan for revitalizing small business and manufacturing. Key to the outcome was Erie, English's home—and probably more important, Ridge's—which supported the Republican ticket, giving English a 49%–47% victory.

In the House, the obviously vulnerable English became one of the first freshman Republicans since George H. W. Bush in 1967 to win a seat on Ways and Means, an excellent spot from which to both legislate and raise money. Early on, English made a record on local issues, working to stop Korea's dumping of steel pipe and tubing (the Shenango Valley in Mercer County is the leading U.S. producer), preserving spending on low income home heating and protecting Erie Forge & Steel from the IRS. While he supports the Republican leadership on most votes, he has a moderate record on economic and foreign issues and has dissented prominently on occasion. He has been one of the House Republicans most willing to support a minimum wage increase and was an early proponent of limiting the tax deduction for pay to corporate chief executives.

English worries about the collapse of manufacturing across the nation, including northwest Pennsylvania. "We need to move quickly and directly to save the manufacturing base." He would impose tariffs on imports from China to respond to Beijing's alleged currency manipulation. In October 2003, he got House passage, on a 411–1 vote, of his resolution calling on China to let market forces set its exchange rate. "I think we have attracted the attention of the Chinese and Bush administration," he said. He also called for higher tariffs on imports from Vietnam. English supports major tax changes to replace individual and corporate income taxes with a consumption tax to promote savings and level the playing field for U.S. businesses and workers. He wants to repeal the alternative minimum tax on corporations, which he called a job-killer. He voted for normal trade relations with China and trade promotion authority.

As chairman of the Steel Caucus, English welcomed George W. Bush's March 2002 decision to impose quotas on steel imports. He helped pass a resolution opposing any changes to U.S. anti-dumping laws in the Doha trade negotiations and a bill to cover health insurance costs of retired steelworkers whose companies went bankrupt. After the World Trade Organization ruled against Bush's efforts to protect the U.S. steel industry, English urged him to hold firm, especially against European threats. But when Bush agreed in December 2003 to go along with the ruling, English was conciliatory; the President had kept his promises, and the steel industry was "on stronger footing."

English had a tough reelection challenge in 1996 from Democrat Ron DiNicola, who returned home from law practice in Los Angeles to run in Erie. "California office. California driver's license. And a great tan," English's campaign proclaimed. English won 51%–49%. He has had no serious challenge since then. In May 2005, he announced his candidacy for the chairmanship of the National Republican Congressional Committee when Tom Reynolds's term ends after the 109th Congress. English is now one of three House Republicans from traditionally Democratic western Pennsylvania, a tribute to skillful redistricting, a cautious centrism and hard work by local Republicans, including Santorum, Hart, the 18th District's Tim Murphy, Ridge and English. Democrats wondering why they are in the House minority ought to look here.

FOURTH DISTRICT

Rep. Melissa Hart (R)

Elected 2000, 3d term; b. Apr. 4, 1962, Pittsburgh; home, Bradford Woods; Washington & Jefferson Col., B.A. 1984, U. of Pittsburgh, J.D. 1987; Catholic; single.

Elected Office: PA Senate, 1991–2000.

Professional Career: Praticing atty., 1987–2001.

DC Office: 1024 LHOB, 20515, 202-225-2565; Fax: 202-226-2274; Web site: hart.house.gov.

District Offices: Allison Park, 412-492-0161; Ellwood City, 724-752-0490.

Committees: *Standards of Official Conduct* (4th of 5 R). *Ways & Means* (22d of 24 R): Human Resources; Select Revenue Measures.

Group Ratings

	ADA	ACLU	AFS	LCV	ITIC	NTU	COC	ACU	NTLC	CHC
2004	10	0	0	9	100	68	100	92	81	92
2003	5	—	0	0	—	63	100	84	—	—

National Journal Ratings

	2003 LIB	—	2003 CONS		2004 LIB	—	2004 CONS
Economic	9%	—	84%		30%	—	70%
Social	40%	—	58%		36%	—	61%
Foreign	11%	—	80%		0%	—	96%

Key Votes of the 108th Congress

1. Drilling in ANWR	Y	5. DC School Vouchers	Y	9. Ban Same-Sex Marriage	Y
2. Approve Bush Tax Cuts	Y	6. Ban Human Cloning	Y	10. Fund Iraq War	Y
3. Medicare/Rx Bill	Y	7. Restrict Gun Liability	Y	11. Bar Cuba Embargo Funds	*
4. Bar Overtime Pay Regs.	N	8. Ban Partial-Birth Abortion	Y	12. Intelligence Reorg.	Y

Election Results

2004 general	Melissa Hart (R)	204,329	(63%)	($1,368,946)
	Stevan Drobac (D)	116,303	(36%)	($14,082)
	Other	3,285	(1%)	
2004 primary	Melissa Hart (R)	unopposed		
2002 general	Melissa Hart (R)	130,534	(65%)	($1,167,856)
	Stevan Drobac (D)	71,674	(35%)	($76,980)

Prior Winning Percentages: 2000 (59%)

The People		Race/Ethnic Origin	Ancestry	
Area size:	1,318 sq. mi.	94.3% White	German: 20.7%	Irish: 12.4%
Urban population:	78.5%	3.4% Black	Italian: 11.7%	
Rural population:	21.5%	0.9% Asian	**2004 Presidential Vote**	
Pop. 2000:	646,609	0.1% Native Am.	Bush (R) 179,855	(54%)
Median income:	$43,547	0.0% Hawaiian	Kerry (D) 149,070	(45%)
Poverty status:	7.5%	0.7% Two+ races	Other 1,255	(0%)
Military veterans:	14.7%	0.1% Other	**2000 Presidential Vote**	
		0.6% Hispanic Origin	Bush (R) 152,313	(52%)
			Gore (D) 134,688	(46%)
			Other 6,167	(2%)
			Cook Partisan Voting Index: R + 3	
Occupation	Blue collar: 22.4%	White collar: 63.7%	Gray collar: 13.9%	

For a century, one of America's great industrial zones was near the intersection of the Beaver and Ohio Rivers in western Pennsylvania. This was steel country, with mills rising black and brooding from the bottomlands and filling the narrow river valleys with smoke. Immigrant families lived in small frame houses on hillsides, looking down on riverscapes lined with piles of iron ore, limestone and coal, and littered with cranes, stocks and furnaces. This was not an environmentalist's idea of perfection, but it was a land of opportunity for thousands whose lives were far worse before moving to steel country. One grandchild of a Hungarian immigrant steelworker in Beaver Falls grew up to be Joe Namath—just one of the great quarterbacks to hail from southwestern Pennsylvania (fellow Hall of Famers Jim Kelly, Joe Montana and Dan Marino are a few of the others). For a few heady years, high union wages and early retirement plans seemed to make working in the mills the way to affluence. But the industry crashed after the oil shock of 1979, when mills were closed and jobs vanished. Today, thousands of workers who long ago exhausted their unemployment benefits have given up and left the Beaver and Ohio valleys.

The 4th Congressional District of Pennsylvania includes much of this steel country, plus a large swath of suburban Pittsburgh. The 4th begins around Farrell in Mercer County, located as close to Erie as to Pittsburgh, then travels south along Route 60 through steel-mill country in Lawrence and Beaver Counties; Aliquippa, a typically distressed former steel-mill city, was where composer Henry Mancini and football icon Mike Ditka grew up but then left for brighter futures elsewhere, like many others. It then turns to the east, taking in a fast-growing tier of suburban southern Butler County and the longer-established Allegheny County suburbs north of Pittsburgh: old-money Sewickley and Fox Chapel; affluent McCandless and middle-class Ross in the North Hills. It also takes in a tiny portion of Westmoreland County. The steel mill areas tend to be Democratic, with unions still capable of flexing some muscle. The suburbs of Butler County are tax-averse and strongly Republican, with strong growth in Cranberry and Seven Fields near the Turnpike. The older suburbs in Allegheny County are politically marginal—more Democratic than Butler, but much more Republican than the city of Pittsburgh. Overall the district's heritage is Democratic but it has been trending modestly toward the Republicans. George W. Bush carried this district with 52% of the vote in 2000 and 54% in 2004.

The congresswoman from the 4th District is Melissa Hart, a Republican first elected in 2000. She grew up in the Pittsburgh area, graduated from Washington and Jefferson College and the University of Pittsburgh law school. After law school, she worked as a real estate lawyer for a Pittsburgh firm. She was elected to the state Senate in 1990 by defeating an incumbent Democrat; she was an early protégé of Rick Santorum, who was elected to the House that year. When Democrat Ron Klink decided to challenge Senator Santorum in 2000, Hart ran unopposed for the Republican nomination in this seat, which had not elected a Republican in 18 years.

In the Democratic primary, state Representative Terry Van Horne unexpectedly led the eight-candidate field, with 24% of the vote. A key event in the campaign came the morning after the primary when the National Republican Congressional Committee eagerly drew attention to a racial slur Van Horne had used in reference to a black state representative in 1994. Van Horne, who had apologized on the floor of the state House after making the comment, said it had been taken out of context, and the target of the slur accepted Van Horne's apology long ago. But Jesse Jackson Jr. and other members of the Congressional Black Caucus expressed their concern when they learned of the comment. Van Horne and Hart clashed over prescription drug plans for seniors and campaign finance. She touted her labor roots and hoped that her anti-tax, anti-abortion, pro-gun views would play well. With a big fundraising advantage, she won by a surprisingly large 59%–41%, carrying every county.

In the House, she has had a mostly conservative voting record. Republican leaders quickly spotlighted this hard-charging newcomer, tapping her to give the party response to Bill Clinton on the Saturday after her election. Speaker Dennis Hastert designated her to serve as a liaison for members' concerns. George W. Bush signed her Born-Alive Infants Protection Act, which made it a crime to kill a baby during a botched abortion. Later, she sponsored the Unborn Victims of Violence Act, also known as the Laci and Conner Peterson Act, which made it a separate crime if a fetus is injured or killed as the result of violence against its mother. After objections from Appropriations Labor-HHS Subcommittee Chairman Ralph Regula, she reluctantly agreed not to offer her amendment to bar funds for school-based health clinics that distribute "morning after" pills. Despite pressure from the steel industry, she voted for trade promotion authority. In 2003, she helped to write part of an anti-spam law that authorized the Federal Trade Commission to shut down several companies that were peddling access to sexually explicit materials without required labels.

After the 2002 election, Hart ran for vice-chairman of the Republican Conference against Jack Kingston of Georgia. But Kingston had served longer and won 159–56. Two years later, she won a seat on the Ways and Means Committee. This was unusual, since Phil English of the next-door 3d District already was already on the committee; interestingly, English was chief of staff to Hart when she served in the state Senate. She promised to work to strengthen Social Security and Medicare, reform taxes, and reduce the debt. At the 2004 Republican national convention, Hart co-chaired the Platform Committee.

In redistricting, her willingness to keep Beaver County—the most heavily Democratic part of the district—and add the North Hills in Allegheny County, which had been in her old state Senate district, enabled Republicans to come up with a plan that created a second Republican-leaning district in the Pittsburgh suburbs, the new 18th District south of the city. She has not been seriously challenged for reelection. During the 2004 campaign, Chris Heinz, son of the late Senator John Heinz and the stepson of Senator John Kerry, talked about running against Hart in

2006. Although his mother Teresa Heinz Kerry has a 90-acre estate in Fox Chapel, he has been a resident of New York for several years; in April 2005, he said he would not challenge Hart.

FIFTH DISTRICT

Rep. John Peterson (R)

Elected 1996, 5th term; b. Dec. 25, 1938, Titusville; home, Pleasantville; PA St. U., 1974–76; Methodist; married (Sandy).

Military Career: Army, 1958–64.

Elected Office: Pleasantville Borough Cncl., 1969–77; PA House of Reps., 1977–84; PA Senate, 1984–96.

Professional Career: Owner, Peterson's Golden Dawn Food Market, 1958–84.

DC Office: 123 CHOB, 20515, 202-225-5121; Fax: 202-225-5796; Web site: www.house.gov/johnpeterson.

District Offices: State College, 814-238-1776; Titusville, 814-827-3985.

Committees: *Appropriations* (24th of 37 R): Interior, Environment & Related Agencies; Labor, Health and Human Services, Education & Related Agencies. *Resources* (12th of 27 R): Energy & Mineral Resources; Forests & Forest Health.

Group Ratings

	ADA	ACLU	AFS	LCV	ITIC	NTU	COC	ACU	NTLC	CHC
2004	15	5	25	9	90	52	100	83	75	92
2003	10	—	0	5	—	59	90	88	—	—

National Journal Ratings

	2003 LIB	—	2003 CONS		2004 LIB	—	2004 CONS
Economic	21%	—	75%		38%	—	61%
Social	14%	—	85%		28%	—	70%
Foreign	23%	—	71%		47%	—	53%

Key Votes of the 108th Congress

1. Drilling in ANWR	Y	5. DC School Vouchers	Y	9. Ban Same-Sex Marriage	Y
2. Approve Bush Tax Cuts	Y	6. Ban Human Cloning	Y	10. Fund Iraq War	Y
3. Medicare/Rx Bill	Y	7. Restrict Gun Liability	Y	11. Bar Cuba Embargo Funds	Y
4. Bar Overtime Pay Regs.	N	8. Ban Partial-Birth Abortion	Y	12. Intelligence Reorg.	Y

Election Results

2004 general	John Peterson (R)	192,852	(88%)	($511,015)
	Thomas Martin (Lib)	26,239	(12%)	
2004 primary	John Peterson (R)	47,216	(78%)	
	Bob Perry (R)	13,501	(22%)	
2002 general	John Peterson (R)	124,942	(87%)	($456,607)
	Thomas Martin (Lib)	18,078	(13%)	

Prior Winning Percentages: 2000 (83%); 1998 (85%); 1996 (60%)

The People		Race/Ethnic Origin	Ancestry	
Area size:	11,108 sq. mi.	96.0% White	German: 21.3%	Irish: 9.1%
Urban population:	46.0%	1.3% Black	English: 6.7%	
Rural population:	54.0%	1.1% Asian	**2004 Presidential Vote**	
Pop. 2000:	646,397	0.1% Native Am.	Bush (R) 165,343	(61%)
Median income:	$33,254	0.0% Hawaiian	Kerry (D) 105,295	(39%)
Poverty status:	13.5%	0.6% Two+ races	Other 1,031	(%)
Military veterans:	14.4%	0.1% Other	**2000 Presidential Vote**	
		0.8% Hispanic Origin	Bush (R) 137,837	(59%)
			Gore (D) 89,180	(38%)
			Other 6,197	(3%)
			Cook Partisan Voting Index: R +10	
Occupation	Blue collar: 32.5%	White collar: 51.1%	Gray collar: 16.4%	

North central Pennsylvania—isolated from the rest of the country by chains of mountains, and off the main east-west rail and highway lines until the 1970s—is one of those empty spaces that make even the northeastern states seem lightly populated compared to the densely packed terrain of Western Europe or East Asia. Here you can find Forest and Cameron Counties, with fewer than 6,000 people each, dependent on tourism; Forest County has the highest percentage of second homes or cottages or any county in the nation. Pressed tightly by narrow valleys and fast-flowing rivers, roads here are often forced to switch back as they wind their way precariously over the mountains; Tioga County is home to Pine Creek Gorge, known as "Pennsylvania's Grand Canyon." This part of the state is a prime area for hunting (in 2004, 218 black bears were shot in Clinton County), fishing, all-terrain vehicles and snowmobiles, in wide-open spaces like the Allegheny National Forest, which sprawls across four counties and is a popular recreational area. To the west are Titusville, where Colonel Edwin Drake sank the first successful oil well in 1859, and Oil City, headquarters of Quaker State Oil from 1931 until it left for Texas in 1995; the last oil and natural gas wells were capped here in 1964. DuBois in Clearfield County is home to glass production and a powdered metal industry; timbering also remains important here. Elk County and the Elk State Forest feature a free-roaming herd of elk, of course, but also is home to a new trout hatchery that also cleans polluted water.

Punxsutawney in Jefferson County is home of the legendary groundhog Phil, who predicts the arrival of spring every year based on whether he sees his shadow on Gobbler's Knob on Feb. 2; the 1993 movie *Groundhog Day* sparked a tourism boomlet in this town of 6,000, even though the movie was filmed in Woodstock, Illinois. To the southeast is the Nittany Valley, home of State College and Pennsylvania State University. Penn State has long been known for its powerful football teams coached by Joe Paterno ("JoePa," locally); the university's cutting-edge facilities, combined with the city's gridded downtown, have spawned a high-skills job market. Tiny Coudersport in Potter County is the home of the cable giant Adelphia Communications, the company that self-destructed in 2002 amid allegations of massive embezzlement by the founding Rigas family. Yet there is something solid and grounded in this part of America. The sturdily built courthouses and banks in the center of each county seat testify to the long history of hard work and thrift in this part of the country. Interstate 80 runs through this part of Pennsylvania, making it accessible to big markets, and there has been some modest population growth since 1990.

The 5th Congressional District of Pennsylvania is the state's largest in area, taking in an enormous swath of north central Pennsylvania. Politically, this area became Republican in the 1850s when the party was founded, and it has remained heavily Republican ever since. It is the state's most rural district; George W. Bush won 59% of the vote here in 2000 and 61% in 2004.

The congressman from the 5th District is John Peterson, a Republican first elected in 1996. Peterson grew up in Titusville, the son of a steelworker; he served in the Army as a cook, then opened a grocery store that eventually became Peterson's Golden Dawn Supermarket chain. He served on the Pleasantville Borough Council for eight years, then in 1977, at 39, was elected to the state House in a special election. In 1984 he was elected to the state Senate, where he chaired the Public Health and Welfare Committee. In 1996 Bill Clinger announced his retirement after 18 years in the House; Peterson was an obvious candidate. Three other Republicans ran. The one who attracted the most attention was Bob Shuster, the brother of current 9th District Congressman Bill Shuster and son of Bud Shuster, who then was the influential chairman of the Transportation and Infrastructure Committee. But Shuster grew up outside the district and Peterson's chief competition was Daniel Gordeuk, a Centre County surgeon with strong local roots. Peterson won with 38%, to 28% for Gordeuk, and 18% for Shuster. In the general, Peterson attacked the Democratic nominee as "an old-fashioned liberal" and won 60%–40%.

In the House, Peterson has been a Republican loyalist. He has been a critic of environmental restriction advocates, complaining about their "push for world government" in the Kyoto treaty and their lawsuits to prevent logging in national forests. Curiously for an easterner, he has been a leader of the Western Caucus; he shares many of their concerns on private property rights and access to public lands. In the 171 counties where the federal government is landlord to at least half of the local land (none are in Pennsylvania), he advocated a "no net gain" rule when the government purchases land for national parks and wilderness areas. On local issues, he passed a bill to establish the Oil Region National Heritage Area to promote the history of Titusville and Oil Creek Valley, and preserve the Drake well. He demanded that the Commerce Department take action against Chinese factories that were counterfeiting the Zippo lighter, which originally was manufactured in Bradford. With a seat on the Appropriations Committee, he passed an amendment to block a cost-sharing requirement for the Essential Air Service program that would have forced many rural airports to pay tens of thousands of dollars in new fees. With Democrat Allen Boyd of Florida, Peterson co-chaired the Rural Caucus, to promote the interests of rural areas in national debates. In the 2003 Medicare/prescription drug bill, they got changes in payments to rural health care providers plus a multi-billion dollar package for health services in rural areas. At a Capitol Hill press conference on Groundhog Day 2005 with a groundhog alleged to be Punxsutawney Phil, Peterson defended $100,000 for the Punxsutawney Weather Discovery Center; critics of government waste were not amused.

Peterson has not had a Democratic opponent since he was first elected.

SIXTH DISTRICT

Rep. Jim Gerlach (R)

Elected 2002, 2d term; b. Feb. 25, 1955, Ellwood City; home, Upper Uwchlan Township; Dickinson Col., B.A. 1977, J.D. 1980; Presbyterian; divorced.

Elected Office: PA House of Reps., 1990–94; PA Senate, 1994–2002.

Professional Career: Practicing atty., 1980–2002.

DC Office: 308 CHOB, 20515, 202-225-4315; Fax: 202-225-8440; Web site: www.house.gov/gerlach/.

District Offices: Exton, 610-594-1415; Trappe, 610-409-2780; Wyomissing, 610-376-7630.

Committees: *Financial Services* (31st of 37 R): Capital Markets, Insurance & Government Sponsored Enterprises; Domestic and International Monetary Policy, Trade & Technology. *Transportation & Infrastructure* (27th of 41 R): Aviation; Economic Development, Public Buildings & Emergency Management; Water Resources & Environment.

Group Ratings

	ADA	ACLU	AFS	LCV	ITIC	NTU	COC	ACU	NTLC	CHC
2004	20	20	14	55	90	46	100	68	68	83
2003	5	—	0	50	—	58	97	76	—	—

National Journal Ratings

	2003 LIB	—	2003 CONS		2004 LIB	—	2004 CONS
Economic	44%	—	56%		44%	—	55%
Social	47%	—	52%		50%	—	50%
Foreign	31%	—	65%		25%	—	68%

Key Votes of the 108th Congress

1. Drilling in ANWR	N	5. DC School Vouchers	Y	9. Ban Same-Sex Marriage	N
2. Approve Bush Tax Cuts	Y	6. Ban Human Cloning	Y	10. Fund Iraq War	Y
3. Medicare/Rx Bill	Y	7. Restrict Gun Liability	Y	11. Bar Cuba Embargo Funds	N
4. Bar Overtime Pay Regs.	N	8. Ban Partial-Birth Abortion	Y	12. Intelligence Reorg.	Y

Election Results

2004 general	Jim Gerlach (R)	160,348	(51%)	($2,231,609)
	Lois Murphy (D)	153,977	(49%)	($1,910,539)
2004 primary	Jim Gerlach (R)	unopposed		
2002 general	Jim Gerlach (R)	103,648	(51%)	($1,261,590)
	Dan Wofford (D)	98,128	(49%)	($1,386,721)

The People		Race/Ethnic Origin	Ancestry	
Area size:	819 sq. mi.	86.3% White	German: 18.9% Irish: 12.6%	
Urban population:	85.8%	6.7% Black	Italian: 9.8%	
Rural population:	14.2%	2.0% Asian	**2004 Presidential Vote**	
Pop. 2000:	646,221	0.1% Native Am.	Kerry (D) 167,431	(51%)
Median income:	$55,611	0.0% Hawaiian	Bush (R) 156,634	(48%)
Poverty status:	6.1%	1.0% Two+ races	Other 1,064	(0%)
Military veterans:	12.6%	0.1% Other	**2000 Presidential Vote**	
		3.7% Hispanic Origin	Gore (D) 130,472	(49%)
			Bush (R) 129,318	(49%)
			Other 5,589	(2%)
			Cook Partisan Voting Index: D + 2	
Occupation	Blue collar: 20.0%	White collar: 68.1%	Gray collar: 11.9%	

The gentle hills of southeastern Pennsylvania, settled in the 18th century by Quaker townsmen, Welsh farmers, German peasants, and members of pietistic sects who became known as the Pennsylvania Dutch, were America's first polyglot interior. Before and after independence, a diverse lot looking for tolerance in the area above Philadelphia and the Delaware River and below the first chains of the Appalachians found a land that yielded riches, first in crops, then in ironworking and other industry. Here are places like Valley Forge, where General George Washington and his men spent the terrible winter and spring of 1777–78, while the British luxuriated in Philadelphia 20 miles away. In Revolutionary times, this area was countryside, a long day's ride from the markets and docks of Philadelphia. In the years after, the great rail lines were built from Philadelphia: the Main Line of the Pennsylvania Railroad headed west to industrial Pittsburgh and the Midwest, and the Reading Railroad headed northwest to Reading and the anthracite coalfields beyond. Factories were built in some of the towns here, and many farms continued to thrive, but by the late 19th century some of this land had become commuter territory. The most lavish Philadelphia suburbs were built on the Main Line, where in mansions shaded by huge trees Philadelphia's captains of commerce could get respite from the rowhouses and narrow streets of the city. By the late 20th century highways spread over the area and giant shopping centers sprung up: this was affluent suburbia for the masses, or a large part of them. Prosperity even came to some of the factory towns. Reading, the decaying industrial town described in John Updike's *Rabbit* novels, in the 1970s was the site of the first factory outlet store, when a company called Vanity Fair began selling seconds and overruns of stockings and lingerie at wholesale prices in what had been the Berkshire Knitting Mills; it grew to more than 300 outlets there selling deeply-discounted goods on the polished wood floors of converted brick mills. But by 2004, most of the original shops were boarded up, and Vanity Fair had opened a smaller outlet center a couple of miles away. With hundreds of such outlets now spread across the countryside, the original had become a victim of its own success.

The 6th Congressional District of Pennsylvania includes parts of this countryside in Chester, Berks and Montgomery Counties. Chester County has the highest median income levels in Pennsylvania and is the fastest growing major county in the state; Lower Merion Township in Montgomery County is the home of some of Philadelphia's wealthiest people, like philanthropist Leonore Annenberg. The boundaries of the 6th District are irregular. Geographically, the main body of the district is northern Chester County, including Coatesville, Downingtown and Phoenixville, and southern Berks County. The district also includes a salient that runs northward in eastern Berks County. There is another salient, much more heavily populated, reaching south into Montgomery County from Pottstown to Lower Merion Township. The district includes Valley Forge and most of the Main Line suburbs—Ardmore, Bryn Mawr, part of Paoli—and it includes a part but not all of Reading. Until the 1990s this area had been heavily Republican. But in the 1990s the suburbs of Philadelphia, like those in the nation's other very large metropolitan areas, trended to the Democrats, and the trend has continued since 2000. Al Gore won the district 49.2%–48.7% in 2000, Democratic Governor Ed Rendell carried it 2–1 in 2002 and John Kerry carried it 51%–48% in 2004.

The congressman from the 6th District is Jim Gerlach, a Republican first elected in 2002. He grew up in Ellwood City, Pennsylvania, midway between Pittsburgh and Youngstown, Ohio. He graduated from Dickinson College and its law school, just west of Harrisburg. He continued moving east, settled in Chester County and practiced law. He was elected to the state House in 1990 and to the state Senate in 1994. When Republicans in 2002 created a new district in suburban Philadelphia, Gerlach was the obvious intended beneficiary. He had spirited competition from Democrat Dan Wofford, executive director of the Philadelphia Education Fund's College Access Program and a former adviser to Governor Bob Casey. Wofford had not previously run for office, but his name was well known; his father Harris Wofford was elected to the Senate in a 1991. Gerlach centered his campaign on his legislative accomplishments, including votes to expand Pennsylvania's prescription drug program for low-income seniors. Wofford attacked Gerlach as a career politician; they disagreed on abortion and Medicare. Polls showed the race close and national Republicans spent more than $1.5 million on ads for Gerlach. The outcome was not clear until the early morning hours; Gerlach won 51%–49%.

In the House, Gerlach's voting record was mostly moderate though more conservative on foreign policy. He was a strong supporter of middle-class tax cuts and eliminating the marriage penalty. George W. Bush signed his bill to create a new veterans cemetery in the Philadelphia area. Gerlach introduced a bill to improve the water quality of the nation's estuaries, including the Delaware River estuary. He also supported legislation to save forests in the Pennsylvania Highlands. Following the beheading by Iraqi insurgents of Chester County businessman Nick Berg, Gerlach raised questions about how U.S. authorities handled events leading to his detention.

In 2004, Gerlach was a prime Democratic target. After Dan Wofford decided not to run again, local Democrats settled on attorney Lois Murphy, who managed Rendell's 2002 campaign in Montgomery County. A former staffer in both Washington and Pennsylvania for NARAL ProChoice America, she received strong support from EMILY's List and criticized Gerlach for his lack of leadership in Congress, especially on fiscal issues; she attacked him for being supported by Majority Leader Tom DeLay. Gerlach defended his support for the Republican agenda as consistent with the views of his constituents. Despite her initial low name identification, the well-financed Murphy made this an unexpectedly close contest but, like Wofford, she fell just short. Gerlach won 51%–49% again, with 56% of the vote in Chester County, 52% in Berks County and 43% in Murphy's Montgomery County base. This district looks like to be seriously contested again in 2006; Murphy has said she may run again.

SEVENTH DISTRICT

Rep. Curt Weldon (R)

Elected 1986, 10th term; b. July 22, 1947, Marcus Hook; home, Aston; West Chester St. Col., B.A. 1969; Protestant; married (Mary).

Elected Office: Marcus Hook Mayor, 1977–82; Delaware Cnty. Cncl., 1982–86, Chmn. 1985–86.

Professional Career: Elem. schl. teacher & Vice Principal, 1969–76; Dir., Training & Manpower Devel., CIGNA Corp., 1976–81.

DC Office: 2466 RHOB, 20515, 202-225-2011; Fax: 202-225-8137; Web site: curtweldon.house.gov.

District Offices: Bridgeport, 610-270-1486; Upper Darby, 610-259-0700.

Committees: *Armed Services* (Vice Chmn. of 34 R): Projection Forces; Tactical Air & Land Forces (Chmn.). *Homeland Security* (4th of 19 R): Emergency Preparedness, Science & Technology; Intelligence, Information Sharing & Terrorism Risk Assessment. *Science* (4th of 24 R): Energy; Research.

Group Ratings

	ADA	ACLU	AFS	LCV	ITIC	NTU	COC	ACU	NTLC	CHC
2004	15	20	13	27	89	50	100	79	73	100
2003	5	—	0	35	—	56	96	75	—	—

National Journal Ratings

	2003 LIB	—	2003 CONS		2004 LIB	—	2004 CONS
Economic	45%	—	55%		45%	—	54%
Social	46%	—	54%		46%	—	54%
Foreign	36%	—	63%		47%	—	53%

Key Votes of the 108th Congress

1. Drilling in ANWR	Y	5. DC School Vouchers	Y	9. Ban Same-Sex Marriage	Y
2. Approve Bush Tax Cuts	Y	6. Ban Human Cloning	Y	10. Fund Iraq War	Y
3. Medicare/Rx Bill	Y	7. Restrict Gun Liability	Y	11. Bar Cuba Embargo Funds	N
4. Bar Overtime Pay Regs.	N	8. Ban Partial-Birth Abortion	Y	12. Intelligence Reorg.	Y

Election Results

2004 general	Curt Weldon (R)	196,556	(59%)	($678,444)
	Paul Scoles (D)	134,932	(40%)	($23,763)
	Other	3,039	(1%)	
2004 primary	Curt Weldon (R)	unopposed		
2002 general	Curt Weldon (R)	146,296	(66%)	($619,156)
	Peter Lennon (D)	75,055	(34%)	

Prior Winning Percentages: 2000 (65%); 1998 (72%); 1996 (67%); 1994 (70%); 1992 (66%); 1990 (65%); 1988 (68%); 1986 (61%)

The People		Race/Ethnic Origin	Ancestry	
Area size:	294 sq. mi.	88.4% White	Irish: 21.8%	Italian: 14.3%
Urban population:	98.6%	5.4% Black	German: 13.3%	
Rural population:	1.4%	3.7% Asian	**2004 Presidential Vote**	
Pop. 2000:	646,522	0.1% Native Am.	Kerry (D) 184,392	(53%)
Median income:	$56,126	0.0% Hawaiian	Bush (R) 163,095	(47%)
Poverty status:	5.4%	0.9% Two+ races	Other 233	(0%)
Military veterans:	12.9%	0.1% Other	**2000 Presidential Vote**	
		1.3% Hispanic Origin	Gore (D) 150,805	(51%)
			Bush (R) 140,862	(47%)
			Other 6,945	(2%)
			Cook Partisan Voting Index: D + 4	

Occupation	Blue collar: 16.1%	White collar: 72.6%	Gray collar: 11.3%

The close-in suburbs of the great eastern cities were home to some of the most curious and long-lasting political machines in America. They were Republican; they conducted business in the accents of ordinary people, ethnic as well as WASP; they had a tolerance for patronage, and for what city reform liberals would call corruption, that was sharply at odds with their embodiment of middle-class morality; they were old, going back to the days when political machines were as much a part of the urban landscape as trolley lines or overhead electrical wires. One such machine was the War Board of Pennsylvania's Delaware County, a ruthlessly effective Republican organization that continues to influence local politics even in its current and greatly diminished form. But while party registration in Delaware County runs 2–1 Republican, in national races voters here recently have voted for Democrats. Delaware County voted for Bill Clinton, Al Gore and John Kerry by increasing margins, and it voted 2–1 for Democrat Ed Rendell for governor in 2002. The reasons are partly demographic—in recent decades many Democrats have moved out to the suburbs from Philadelphia—and partly ideological. Republicans of the Newt Gingrich stripe are unfamiliar here, and Sun Belt Republicanism is not popular.

The 7th Congressional District of Pennsylvania includes almost all of Delaware County, except for a few towns with large black populations that are appended to Philadelphia's 1st District. The 7th extends north to include a few Montgomery County suburbs, such as modest

Conshohocken, an old Schuylkill River factory town, affluent Upper Merion Township and King of Prussia, an edge city where the Schuylkill Expressway intersects the Pennsylvania Turnpike. The 7th takes in southeastern Chester County, including the commercial hub of West Chester and a few further-out suburbs such as Malvern and part of Paoli. The 7th includes the elite small colleges of Haverford and Swarthmore, and the refined farm country of Chadds Ford, home to generations of Wyeths who used wheat-brown tones to limn the region's seasonal moods on canvas. Its housing is aging but well maintained; its population is above average in income but distinct from the inhabitants of more affluent commuter towns. People here have deep roots in greater Philadelphia, but many rarely venture into Center City.

The congressman from the 7th District is Curt Weldon, a Republican originally backed by the War Board and first elected in 1986. He grew up in Delaware County, graduated from West Chester State College and worked as a teacher and personnel trainer. He first came to public attention in 1977 as mayor of gritty Marcus Hook, the southernmost Pennsylvania town on the Delaware River, the home of oil tank farms and a rusty-looking steel mill. In 1982 he was elected to the Delaware County Council. In 1984 he ran against liberal Democratic Congressman Bob Edgar (who got to Congress when the War Board split 10 years earlier), lost by 412 votes, then ran successfully in 1986 when Edgar ran unsuccessfully for the Senate.

Weldon started off as a local congressman but has become a major force on international issues of the greatest import. Weldon is usually a partisan Republican but not always a free-market enthusiast; like Pennsylvania Republicans of yore, he supports trade restrictions and voted against NAFTA and trade promotion authority. Although he has supported unions on some issues, including family-leave legislation, he favors repeal of the Davis-Bacon Act and voted for the flextime plan to permit workers to take compensatory time off rather than overtime pay. He strongly backs the partial-birth abortion ban.

Weldon is now the second ranking Republican on the Armed Services Committee and chairman of the Tactical Air and Land Forces Subcommittee. After he spotlighted the discovery of the Soviet radar at Krasnoyarsk in the 1980s, a violation of the ABM treaty, he has been for more than a decade a strong advocate of missile defense. His warnings were vindicated by the July 1998 Rumsfeld report revealing that missile threats could come from rogue states without notice. He helped to write the 1998 law which committed a reluctant Clinton administration and, later, the much more eager Bush administration to full development of missile defense. From 1995 to 2001 Weldon chaired the Research and Development Subcommittee; from 1999 to 2001 he attempted to create a "data fusion center" which he called the National Operations Analysis Hub, to collate intelligence information for all sources; he protested in July 2004 when the 9/11 Commission report failed to mention his efforts.

In 2003 Weldon became chairman of the Strategic Forces Tactical Land and Air Subcommittee. He has been the House's strongest advocate of the Marine Corps's V-22 Osprey, one of whose prime contractors, the Boeing helicopter division, is located in Ridley Park in Delaware County. The tilted-rotor aircraft takes off and lands like a helicopter and flies like a plane. But the Osprey has had serious troubles. It was cancelled by Defense Secretary Dick Cheney in 1989, but reinstated by Congress soon after. Since then, Weldon has assembled an Osprey coalition that has kept it alive despite crashes in 1991, 1992 and 2000. In 2002 the House voted for 12 Ospreys, the Senate for nine. In the meantime, Weldon bristled in December 2001 when Boeing announced layoffs of 1,500 employees at Ridley Park. In February 2004, as committee Chairman Duncan Hunter lined up votes to resist cuts in the Bush defense budget, Weldon warned that other major programs could be cancelled as the Comanche fighting vehicle was; he mentioned specifically the F-22. In May 2004 he proposed a $75 million fund to pay defense contractors to avoid outsourcing of U.S. jobs. In January 2005 he worked to revive the Robust Nuclear Earth Penetrator bunker-busting bomb, rejected by Congress in 2004.

Weldon has made no secret of his ambition to become Armed Services chairman. In 2000 Floyd Spence was about to leave the chairmanship because of House Republicans' term limits, and next in seniority was the elderly and quiet Bob Stump. Weldon, then seventh-ranking Republican in seniority, ran for chairman, with a detailed program for action and proposals to involve junior members more in decision-making and to encourage members to reach out to labor unions and other constituencies favoring defense spending. Duncan Hunter, the next in seniority after Stump, supported Stump but said he would be a candidate for the chairmanship if the Republican Steering Committee rejected Stump. Weldon lost by 1 vote and charged that Republican leaders had reneged on promises not to support Stump. But the chairmanship of the Military Procurement Subcommittee somewhat assuaged him. In April 2002 Stump announced that he would not run for reelection. Hunter promptly said he would seek the chairmanship; Weldon did not raise a fuss. In May Weldon announced he would support Hunter, with whom he had worked closely on many issues.

Weldon's accomplishments have not been limited to committee work. He has taken a special interest in Russia. He was a Russian studies major in college and is fluent in Russian; he has made more than 30 trips to Russia. He presented the Bush administration with a 41-page outline of how to foster partnerships between the U.S. and Russia in preparation for George W. Bush's 2001 meeting with Vladimir Putin in Crawford, Texas. In May 2004 he called for expanding technical cooperation with Russia on missile defense and praised the Russian-American Observation Satellite program established by the George H.W. Bush administration. In February 2004 the *Los Angeles Times* wrote that Weldon had "gone to bat" for two Russian firms and for two Serbian businessmen who had paid his daughter's public relations firm a total of $1 million. Weldon replied that his relations with the two Serbs had gone back to the 1990s and said that his urging the Navy to look at the drone produced by one Russian firm and lobbying a trade agency to approve a grant to a Russian energy firm to develop a gas field in Siberia were entirely proper. "The stuff I've done with these companies is documented, and it is substantive. I don't have anything to apologize for." He submitted documents to the ethics committee in April 2004 and by June 2005 the ethics committee had made no statement about the case.

Weldon supports high defense spending but also sees great merit in negotiating with potential adversaries. In May and June 2003, after having great difficulty getting a government plane, Weldon led a congressional delegation on a three-day trip to North Korea, the first codel there in five years, "to open a channel of communication." He sketched out a 10-point plan which included a one-year nonaggression pact, to be made permanent if other conditions were met, a North Korean renunciation of nuclear weapons and a return to the Nuclear Non-Proliferation Treaty, diplomatic recognition of North Korea and some $40 billion in aid over 10 years. This was not accepted by the Bush administration, and it stopped Weldon from leading another delegation there in October 2003. Weldon and other members journeyed to Pyongyang again in January 2005 and returned saying North Korea would return to six-party talks if the U.S. stopped acting in a "belligerent manner." Weldon lamented that Bush had named North Korea as part of the "axis of evil" in January 2002 and in January 2005 wrote him and asked that he not make provocative statements in his next State of the Union address. "The key thing is not to make inflammatory statements. We don't need to punch our chest and say how great we are and talk about the negative aspects of other societies."

In January 2004 Weldon led the first congressional delegation to visit Libya since 1979. He set it up after communicating with the Libyans through Ukraine President Leonid Kuchma and at a dinner with Muammar el-Qaddafi's son Saif Islam at the Four Seasons in London. He congratulated Muammar el-Qaddafi on renouncing nuclear weapons and said, "We're here to say thank you and to acknowledge that and to see some of the evidence." Here his statements seem to have been more in line with administration policy and he said, "My goal is to let them know that the president sets our foreign policy with the secretary of state and that we're not there to speak on behalf of the country."

Weldon has drawn on his experience as a former volunteer firefighter and as founder of the Congressional Fire Services Caucus and put into the 2002 and 2004 defense authorizations provisions for the transfer of military technology to firefighters and other first responders, our "domestic defenders" as he calls them, and he called for speedily transferring spectrum from non-digital television to first responders. He was skeptical of Tom Ridge's ability to adequately coordinate homeland security without budget authority and supported creation of the Department of Homeland Security. In September 2002, before the homeland security bill passed, he said the House should see that it reported to only one authorizing committee and one appropriations subcommittee, instead of to the 88 committees and subcommittees currently with jurisdiction over its activities. He proposed a resolution to that effect at the Republican Conference meeting after the November election, and no one rose in opposition. The House adopted his proposals. Speaker Dennis Hastert created a new Select Committee on Homeland Security, on which Weldon serves; Appropriations Committee chairman Bill Young reorganized his committee and created a Homeland Security Subcommittee. In December 2004 he urged Hastert to set up a task force on oceans policy, with a view toward having a select committee on the oceans.

Weldon has been reelected every two years, usually by robust margins. In 2002, he was reelected with 66% of the vote. In 2004, as John Kerry was carrying the district, and despite weak opposition—the first Democratic nominee dropped out when he was ordered to serve in Iraq and the second spent little money—Weldon was reelected with 59%—a solid win, but a significant dropoff in an area that seems to be getting more Democratic.

EIGHTH DISTRICT

Rep. Mike Fitzpatrick (R)

Elected 2004, 1st term; b. June 28, 1963, Philadelphia; home, Levittown; St. Thomas U., B.A. 1985, Dickinson Schl. of Law, J.D. 1988; Catholic; married (Kathleen).

Elected Office: Bucks Co. Comm., 1994–2004.

Professional Career: Practicing atty., 1994–2004.

DC Office: 1516 LHOB, 20515, 202-225-4276; Fax: 202-225-9511; Web site: www.house.gov/fitzpatrick.

District Offices: Doylestown, 215-348-7511; Langhorne, 215-752-7711.

Committees: *Financial Services* (35th of 37 R): Capital Markets, Insurance & Government Sponsored Enterprises; Housing & Community Opportunity; Oversight & Investigations. *Small Business* (16th of 18 R): Tax, Finance & Exports; Workforce, Empowerment & Government Programs.

Group Ratings and Key Votes: Newly Elected

Election Results

2004 general	Mike Fitzpatrick (R)............................ 183,229	(55%)	($1,046,153)
	Virginia Schrader (D) 143,427	(43%)	($613,850)
	Other... 4,608	(1%)	
2004 primary	Jim Greenwood (R) 38,279	(69%)	
	Joseph V. Montone (R) 17,098	(31%)	
2002 general	Jim Greenwood (R) 127,475	(63%)	($889,736)
	Timothy Reece (D)................................ 76,178	(37%)	

The People		Race/Ethnic Origin	Ancestry	
Area size:	634 sq. mi.	90.8% White	German: 18.5%	Irish: 18.1%
Urban population:	90.8%	3.4% Black	Italian: 10.6%	
Rural population:	9.2%	2.4% Asian	**2004 Presidential Vote**	
Pop. 2000:	645,403	0.1% Native Am.	Kerry (D) 177,008	(51%)
Median income:	$59,207	0.0% Hawaiian	Bush (R) 165,239	(48%)
Poverty status:	4.5%	0.9% Two+ races	Other 1,997	(1%)
Military veterans:	12.9%	0.1% Other	**2000 Presidential Vote**	
		2.3% Hispanic Origin	Gore (D) 144,878	(51%)
			Bush (R) 130,500	(46%)
			Other 9,050	(3%)
			Cook Partisan Voting Index: D + 3	

Occupation	Blue collar: 20.9%	White collar: 68.0%	Gray collar: 11.1%

Bucks County was one of William Penn's three original settlements and the launching point for George Washington's crossing of the frigid Delaware River to surprise English and Hessian forces on Christmas Day 1776. But it had a split personality from the start. Upper Bucks County was at once a paradise of bucolic hills and creeks running into the Delaware River and, after Penn's secretary James Logan built the Durham Furnace iron works in 1727, one of the nation's major industrial sites. In the 1920s, Bucks County's well-settled farmland, old fieldstone houses and covered bridges in its northern parts captured the imagination of writers and artists, attracting the New York theatrical crowd—Oscar Hammerstein, Moss Hart, Dorothy Parker, S. J. Perelman. After World War II, its location between Philadelphia and Trenton, New Jersey, brought industrial Lower Bucks County to the forefront. The ocean-navigable Delaware River and several rail lines resulted in huge new developments: U.S. Steel's Fairless Works, one of the few big postwar steel plants, down by the river, and the Levitt organization's second Levittown, in what had been farmland and swamp between U.S. 13 and U.S. 1. But most of the steel mill closed in 1991, and Bucks County's economy depends more on more modern technologies.

Bucks County's political tradition was heavily Republican and protectionist; more recently it has been marginally Republican and environmentalist. This was the home of Senator Joseph Grundy, longtime head of the Pennsylvania Manufacturers Association, who opposed the 1930 Smoot-Hawley tariff as insufficiently protectionist. Development in Bucks came after the New Deal, unlike other suburban Philadelphia counties where most blue-collar immigration occurred years earlier, when county political organizations were ready to enroll new residents in their party. So Lower Bucks around the Fairless Works and Levittown, with its tightly-packed homes filled with blue collar workers, became Democratic. In Upper Bucks, faster-growing and still attracting trendy New Yorkers, green space programs have kept large areas away from developers.

The 8th Congressional District of Pennsylvania includes all of Bucks County, a tiny finger of Montgomery County around Willow Grove and parts of two wards in Northeast Philadelphia. Bucks has the third highest income of any county in the state and the district as a whole has the highest percentage of married persons. Bucks County's population has been just slightly less than that of a full congressional district for several decades, and the 8th District has been virtually unchanged during the last three redistricting cycles. The 8th was marginal in elections during the 1980s; since then, it has moved like other Philadelphia suburbs toward national Democrats and voted for Democratic presidential candidates since 1992. It also joined the rest of southeastern Pennsylvania in voting decisively for Democrat Ed Rendell for governor in 2002.

The congressman from the 8th District is Mike Fitzpatrick, a Republican elected in 2004. This seat opened unexpectedly when six-term incumbent Jim Greenwood announced in July 2004 that he would retire at the end of his term and become the head in Washington of the Biotechnology Industry Organization, which has many members from Bucks County. Fitzpatrick was well-known locally as a Bucks County commissioner for 10 years. But he was not Greenwood's first choice, chiefly because Fitzpatrick had disagreed with Greenwood's strong backing of abortion rights and federal funding for stem-cell research. Greenwood said his polling revealed that an abortion opponent would have trouble winning the district. Because the primary had been held in April, the local Republican Party organization selected the new nominee on August 12. Three other Republicans, including Greenwood's candidate, state Senator Joe Conti, made perfunctory challenges of the party machine, but Fitzpatrick was selected. Greenwood endorsed Fitzpatrick in September after he indicated he did not oppose abortion in cases of rape or incest, or when the life of the pregnant woman is at stake. Fitzpatrick, whose wife had been a research biologist, also said that he did not necessarily oppose federal funding for stem-cell research—positions that irritated some local anti-abortion groups.

The Democratic nominee, chosen in the April primary when it was assumed that the unbeatable Greenwood would be the Republican candidate, was Virginia Schrader, a lawyer, abortion-rights supporter and political neophyte. The Democratic Congressional Campaign Committee explored the possibility of replacing her with a better-known Democratic officeholder, but Governor Ed Rendell stood by her and Schrader was unwilling to step aside. She tried to portray Fitzpatrick as an extremist ideologically out of sync with the culturally moderate district. But he was difficult to pigeonhole as an ideologue after his decade-long stint on the Bucks County Commission, where he was recognized for his work on land preservation. Schrader continued to be viewed as a long shot and suffered from a huge fundraising disadvantage. In the campaign's homestretch, Schrader closed the polling gap on Fitzpatrick and Democrats hoped that she would benefit from the coattails of John Kerry. The National Republican Congressional Committee gave Fitzpatrick considerable financial support and ran TV ads in the expensive Philadelphia media market. One ad pointed out that Hezbollah had paid to air Michael Moore's "Fahrenheit 9/11," which Schrader's campaign screened to raise money; Schrader was so angry at this that she walked out of a debate after Fitzpatrick refused to disavow the ad. Fitzpatrick won 55%–43%, even as John Kerry carried the district 51%–48%.

Assuming he pays due diligence to his district, it likely would take an experienced challenger and a Democratic tide to unseat him.

NINTH DISTRICT

Rep. Bill Shuster (R)

Elected May 2001, 2d full term; b. Jan. 10, 1961, McKeesport; home, Hollidaysburg; Dickinson Col., B.A. 1983; American U., M.B.A. 1987; Lutheran; married (Rebecca).

Professional Career: Mgr., Goodyear Tire & Rubber Co., 1983–87; District Mgr., Bandag Inc., 1987–90; Gen. Mgr., Shuster Chrysler, 1990–01.

DC Office: 1108 LHOB, 20515, 202-225-2431; Fax: 202-225-2486; Web site: www.house.gov/shuster.

District Offices: Chambersburg, 717-264-8308; Hollidaysburg, 814-696-6318; Indiana, 724-463-0516; Somerset, 814-443-3918.

Committees: *Armed Services* (29th of 34 R): Tactical Air & Land Forces; Terrorism, Unconventional Threats & Capabilities. *Small Business* (7th of 18 R): Workforce, Empowerment & Government Programs. *Transportation & Infrastructure* (25th of 41 R): Economic Development, Public Buildings & Emergency Management (Chmn.); Highways, Transit & Pipelines; Water Resources & Environment.

Group Ratings

	ADA	ACLU	AFS	LCV	ITIC	NTU	COC	ACU	NTLC	CHC
2004	5	0	0	0	90	64	100	96	84	100
2003	10	—	13	5	—	59	93	92	—	—

National Journal Ratings

	2003 LIB	—	2003 CONS		2004 LIB	—	2004 CONS
Economic	29%	—	70%		25%	—	75%
Social	37%	—	61%		0%	—	91%
Foreign	21%	—	77%		17%	—	78%

Key Votes of the 108th Congress

1. Drilling in ANWR	Y	5. DC School Vouchers	Y	9. Ban Same-Sex Marriage	Y
2. Approve Bush Tax Cuts	Y	6. Ban Human Cloning	Y	10. Fund Iraq War	Y
3. Medicare/Rx Bill	Y	7. Restrict Gun Liability	Y	11. Bar Cuba Embargo Funds	N
4. Bar Overtime Pay Regs.	*	8. Ban Partial-Birth Abortion	Y	12. Intelligence Reorg.	Y

Election Results

2004 general	Bill Shuster (R)	184,320	(69%)	($1,217,650)
	Paul Politis (D)	80,787	(30%)	($15,810)
2004 primary	Bill Shuster (R)	43,097	(51%)	
	Michael DelGrosso (R)	40,845	(49%)	
2002 general	Bill Shuster (R)	124,184	(71%)	($1,099,169)
	John Henry (D)	50,559	(29%)	($8,723)

Prior Winning Percentages: 2001 (52%)

The People		Race/Ethnic Origin	Ancestry	
Area size:	7,199 sq. mi.	96.4% White	German: 24.3% Irish: 9.0%	
Urban population:	40.5%	1.6% Black	USA: 7.5%	
Rural population:	59.5%	0.4% Asian	**2004 Presidential Vote**	
Pop. 2000:	646,628	0.1% Native Am.	Bush (R) 183,717	(67%)
Median income:	$34,910	0.0% Hawaiian	Kerry (D) 89,208	(33%)
Poverty status:	11.1%	0.6% Two+ races	Other 646	(0%)
Military veterans:	14.6%	0.0% Other	**2000 Presidential Vote**	
		0.9% Hispanic Origin	Bush (R) 149,393	(64%)
			Gore (D) 80,008	(34%)
			Other 4,079	(2%)
			Cook Partisan Voting Index: R +15	

Occupation	Blue collar: 34.2%	White collar: 48.9%	Gray collar: 16.9%

Today, the old towns of south central Pennsylvania look much as they did 60 years ago: farm-houses and red barns set amidst rolling hills in the shadow of mountain ridges, seemingly isolated from the pulsing rhythms of 21st century America. But this tranquility was shattered on September 11, 2001, when United Airlines Flight 93, crashed into an empty former coalfield near Shanksville in Somerset County, killing all 40 passengers and crew on board. To Americans, the crash site became a symbol of both sadness and pride at the passengers' effort to wrest back control of the plane, initiated by the now-famous cry of "Let's roll!" The plane was headed to Washington; the bravery of the passengers prevented its reaching the hijackers' target, probably the Capitol or perhaps the White House. Just as Shanksville's 245 residents were grappling with the aftermath of Flight 93—the influx of visitors, the fears of commercialization—Somerset County was struck by another bolt of lightning, less than a year later and only 13 miles away. Nine miners at the Quecreek coal mine were trapped by rising waters 240 feet underground, and as a breathless nation looked on, rescuers strained to dig rescue shafts. After 77 hours in confinement, the miners were lifted one by one to safety—a joyous counterpoint to the heart-break just 10 months earlier.

The area's usual placidity owes much to the Appalachian mountains, which run like a series of vertebrae up and down central Pennsylvania, long posing a formidable barrier. Up close, the mountains look tantalizingly low: you imagine that you could hike over them in an hour or so. But they are much more daunting than they seem. During the 18th century, the mountains provided Quaker Pennsylvania with a rampart against Indian attacks and allowed the common-wealth to become the richest and most populous of the colonies. But the colonials and British regulars led by General Braddock to defeat near Pittsburgh in 1754 found the mountains hard going, despite guidance from George Washington; 19th century pioneers in Conestoga wagons found it not much easier, for there are few gaps in the ridges. In the 19th century, when businessmen were ready to trade throughout the vast interior, the mountains proved to be a barrier, and people flocked to the easier routes through New York: the Erie Canal and the New York Central Railroad. It took the aggressive capitalists who built the Pennsylvania Railroad to get trains over these ridges. Conquering the mountains near Altoona required the work of several hundred Irish laborers, equipped with hand tools, gunpowder and pack animals, to build Horseshoe Curve between 1851 and 1854—one of the finest examples of railroad engineering anywhere, and today a National Historic Landmark that is celebrated by "railfans" who come from all over the world to visit it and a nearby railroaders museum; the local AA baseball team is called the Altoona Curve. Altoona also is the site of Leap the Dips, the oldest operating roller coaster in the world, which began in 1902 and reopened in 1999 after a 14-year retirement.

Though Pennsylvania's rail links remained important—the Nazis considered them key sabotage targets during World War II—the war-bound nation in 1940 opened the road of the future here: the Pennsylvania Turnpike, the first highway in America that was able to move vehicles dependably at high speeds over long distances. "The Pennsylvania Turnpike is a tri-umph of engineering," writes Tom Lewis in *Divided Highways*, a recent study of the Interstate highway system. "The road tunnels under the Allegheny Mountains and cuts about five hours off the journey between the cities. It is like no other road in America: a maximum rise at any point of just three feet in every 100; a minimum sight distance of 600 feet; bridges and underpasses that do away with cross traffic; and wide, banked curves that eliminate the need to slow down." Federal officials set a seemingly impossible 20-month deadline for construction, but the road was completed only three months late after 30,000 workers—five times the number that built the Hoover Dam—converged on western Pennsylvania during the project's final months.

Pennsylvania's 9th Congressional District takes in a wide swath of south and central Pennsylvania, including six full counties and parts of eight others. Most of the 9th is not coal country and was thus spared the boom-bust cycles of northeastern Pennsylvania and West Virginia. But this is a slow-growth, low-income area today. The largest city is Altoona, which withered from 82,000 people in 1930 to 48,000 in 2004 as the once-prosperous Pennsylvania Railroad succumbed to competition from truck traffic and became the bankrupt Penn Central and now privatized Conrail. Since the 1940s, Hollidaysburg near Altoona has been home to the small and scrupulously independent company that manufactures the Slinky, the inexpensive wire-coil toy invented accidentally by Navy engineer Richard James. Politically, this part of Pennsylvania has been solidly Republican since 1860, when Mercersburg native James Buchanan left the White House, and has not come close to electing a Democrat to Congress for decades. George W. Bush won 64% of the vote here in 2000 and 67% in 2004, both times his best performance in the state.

The congressman from the 9th District is Bill Shuster, a Republican first elected in a May 2001 special election. His father Bud Shuster, for six years the powerful chairman of the Transportation and Infrastructure Committee, announced his resignation in January 2001, after he failed to get an exemption from the Republicans' six-year term limit on chairmanships. As Transportation chairman, Bud Shuster was a generous local benefactor: his work can be seen in the Bud Shuster Highway (as Interstate 99 in Bedford and Blair Counties is known). Bill Shuster grew up in the Pittsburgh area, where his father started a successful business. After graduating from Dickinson College and American University's business school, he moved to Blair County, where he owned the family's car dealership, Shuster Chrysler in East Freedom, near Altoona. Although he was a newcomer to politics, he had plenty of experience observing his father.

The contest for the House seat was for all practical purposes decided at a district-wide Republican convention. Facing nine other contenders, Shuster—with back-room help from his father—ran an insider campaign that took advantage of the family's years of service. Although there was some local grumbling about a Shuster dynasty, opponents failed to coalesce behind a single candidate. In a key move, Shuster's allies obtained a state court injunction forcing a vote on a new slate of delegates for Blair County after claiming that the original slate supporting his opponent had been seated in violation of the rules. Shuster won 69 of the 133 votes, 2 more than the required majority. National Democrats ignored the race, which seemed to them hopeless; Governor Tom Ridge and Speaker Dennis Hastert came in for Shuster and George W. Bush cut a radio spot. But Democrat H. Scott Conklin campaigned vigorously as an opponent of abortion and gun control, Shuster won by a closer than expected 52%–44%. National Republicans attributed the narrow margin to residual intra-party ill will over his nomination; national Democrats said the district was just too Republican for a Democrat to win.

In the House, Bill Shuster has a voting record a bit more conservative than his father's. He won his father's former seat on the Transportation Committee, although of course he was at the bottom of the committee in seniority. He claimed credit for new local water and sewer projects that his father had earlier written into law; local officials call them "Shuster grants."

Shuster has been easily reelected. But he had an unusually strong challenge in the April 2004 primary from Michael DelGrosso, a management consultant whose family owns a Blair County tomato sauce company; he said that the district needed a new economic approach. DelGrosso carried Blair County and three nearby counties in the northern part of the district, but Shuster ran strongly enough elsewhere to squeeze out a 51%–49% win. Hanging over the campaign were allegations that Shuster ordered a staffer to spy on DelGrosso; after the primary, the House Ethics Committee criticized Shuster for improper handling of payroll records of a

House aide but said the aide's activities were not done on official time. In 2005, Shuster got a seat on the Armed Services Committee; he was thrilled in May when the Letterkenny Army Depot in Franklin County, the smallest maintenance depot in the Army but one of the largest employers in the county, was slated to gain jobs under the Pentagon's recommendations for base closing and realignment.

TENTH DISTRICT

Rep. Don Sherwood (R)

Elected 1998, 4th term; b. Mar. 5, 1941, Nicholson; home, Tunkhannock; Dartmouth Col., B.A. 1963; Methodist; married (Carol).

Military Career: Army, 1964–66.

Elected Office: Tunkhannock Area Schl. Bd., 1975–98, Pres., 1992–98.

Professional Career: Businessman; Auto dealer, 1967-present.

DC Office: 1131 LHOB, 20515, 202-225-3731; Fax: 202-225-9594; Web site: www.house.gov/sherwood.

District Offices: Clarks Summit, 570-585-8190; Sunbury, 570-286-1723; Williamsport, 570-327-8161.

Committees: *Appropriations* (29th of 37 R): Foreign Operations, Export Financing & Related Programs (Vice Chmn.); Interior, Environment & Related Agencies; Labor, Health and Human Services, Education & Related Agencies.

Group Ratings

	ADA	ACLU	AFS	LCV	ITIC	NTU	COC	ACU	NTLC	CHC
2004	0	5	13	9	90	48	100	88	73	84
2003	10	—	0	5	—	61	93	88	—	—

National Journal Ratings

	2003 LIB	—	2003 CONS		2004 LIB	—	2004 CONS
Economic	20%	—	79%		21%	—	78%
Social	30%	—	65%		33%	—	66%
Foreign	11%	—	80%		37%	—	62%

Key Votes of the 108th Congress

1. Drilling in ANWR	Y	5. DC School Vouchers	Y	9. Ban Same-Sex Marriage	Y
2. Approve Bush Tax Cuts	Y	6. Ban Human Cloning	Y	10. Fund Iraq War	Y
3. Medicare/Rx Bill	Y	7. Restrict Gun Liability	Y	11. Bar Cuba Embargo Funds	N
4. Bar Overtime Pay Regs.	N	8. Ban Partial-Birth Abortion	Y	12. Intelligence Reorg.	Y

Election Results

2004 general	Don Sherwood (R)	191,967	(93%)	($904,949)
	Veronica Hannevig (CNP)	14,805	(7%)	
2004 primary	Don Sherwood (R) .... unopposed			
2002 general	Don Sherwood (R)	152,017	(93%)	($1,001,321)
	Kurt Shotko (Green)	11,613	(7%)	

Prior Winning Percentages: 2000 (53%); 1998 (49%)

The People		Race/Ethnic Origin	Ancestry		
Area size:	6,663 sq. mi.	95.5% White	German: 18.5% Irish: 11.0%		
Urban population:	44.6%	1.9% Black	Italian: 7.4%		
Rural population:	55.4%	0.5% Asian	**2004 Presidential Vote**		
Pop. 2000:	646,534	0.1% Native Am.	Bush (R) 170,880	(60%)	
Median income:	$35,996	0.0% Hawaiian	Kerry (D) 112,923	(40%)	
Poverty status:	10.3%	0.6% Two+ races	Other 1,196	(0%)	
Military veterans:	15.3%	0.1% Other	**2000 Presidential Vote**		
		1.4% Hispanic Origin	Bush (R) 140,387	(56%)	
			Gore (D) 100,754	(40%)	
			Other 7,887	(3%)	
			Cook Partisan Voting Index: R + 8		
Occupation	Blue collar: 31.1%	White collar: 52.6%	Gray collar: 16.4%		

The northeast corner of Pennsylvania is a land of crevassed valleys and rugged mountains, criss-crossed by giant viaducts built for the railroads linking the East Coast with the Great Lakes and mines to the big cities that heated their houses with the region's anthracite coal. Except for a row of anthracite coal cities from Scranton to Wilkes-Barre, this part of Pennsylvania still has a wild look to it: the superstructure of railroads and Interstate 80 pass through an area that seems otherwise little touched by recent prosperity. This is a land of numerous long-established small towns, with solidly built courthouses and banks and elderly citizens—a part of the Northeast that seems worlds away from the region's huge central cities and growing suburbs. The biggest towns here are Lewisburg, home of Bucknell University and a major federal penitentiary, and Williamsport, home of the Little League World Series. Only at the eastern edge is there significant growth. Pike County on the Delaware River grew 94% from 1990 to 2004, attracting many tired of paying high taxes in New Jersey and New York. The local Pocono mountains also are a destination for weekenders and, for a few days each November, for bear hunters.

The 10th Congressional District of Pennsylvania includes all of northeast Pennsylvania except for Scranton, Wilkes-Barre and fast-growing Monroe County, which are in the 11th District. The area's most consequential congressman was probably David Wilmot who in the 1840s introduced the Wilmot Proviso barring slavery from the New Mexico and California Territories acquired in the Mexican War; this raised the issue of slavery in the territories which led proximately to the Civil War. Wilmot was a founder of the Republican party and was elected to the Senate; most people in this part of Pennsylvania have been Republicans ever since. In 2002 Republican redistricters put Scranton and Wilkes-Barre together in the 11th District, leaving the 10th a solidly Republican constituency.

The congressman from the 10th District is Don Sherwood, a Republican first elected in 1998. He has deep roots in Tunkhannock in Wyoming County, 40 winding miles northwest of Scranton. After graduating from Dartmouth and serving in the Army, Sherwood became a Chevrolet dealer in 1967—at age 26, the youngest Chevy dealer in the East. He served 24 years on the Tunkhannock school board. He raises and grooms Belgian horses, which he shows throughout the state. When Joseph McDade, a Scranton Republican who had showered projects on Scranton from his seat on the Appropriations Committee, announced that he would not run again in 1998, Sherwood ran for the seat, assembling a grass-roots organization of 1,800 volunteers and announcing an agenda that combined small business goals to cut taxes and to "eliminate the IRS as we know it" with calls for a minimum wage increase and HMO regulation. With a personable style and an open wallet—he ultimately spent $795,000 of his own money on the campaign—he won 43% in the eight-candidate Republican primary, well ahead of the 23% for Scranton Mayor James Connors. In the general election he faced Pat Casey, son of former Governor Robert Casey, a Scranton native and strong opponent of abortion. Casey argued that by entering Congress at a young age he would put money in the district for years to come, and said that Sherwood's ideas on Social Security and education are "walking in lockstep with Dick Armey and Newt Gingrich." Sherwood argued that he was "a proven job creator" and that his support of a higher minimum wage showed he was alert to the district's needs. Sherwood got a big boost in the closing days when Speaker Newt Gingrich came in and pledged to assign him to fill McDade's seat on Appropriations; when Gingrich resigned after the election, the offer was not honored and the seat was given to John Peterson. This was one of the closest races in the nation: Sherwood won by just 515 votes, 49%–48%.

In the House, Sherwood has compiled a mostly conservative voting record. He supported a bipartisan plan for a $1 increase in the minimum wage. But he opposed organized labor with his votes for normal trade relations with China and trade promotion authority. He sponsored an amendment of the Death on the High Seas Act to allow damage claims for airline crashes at sea; the victims of the TWA 800 crash off Long Island in 1996 included 21 students and chaperones from the local Montoursville High School, most of whose families had been unable to file claims because of maritime law. To protect local dairymen, Sherwood got 199 co-sponsors on his bill to impose tariffs on milk-protein concentrates.

Democrats again nominated Casey to oppose Sherwood in 2000, and both again spent heavily. Sherwood won by a larger margin this time, 53%–47%. After the election, Republican leaders gave him the Appropriations seat that he had been denied two years earlier.

Redistricting transformed what had been one of the most closely divided districts in the nation in 1998 to an utterly safe Republican seat; no Democrat has filed to run against Sherwood since then. In 2005, the National Republican Congressional Committee named him chairman of incumbent retention but his own seat suddenly seemed in jeopardy after the Wilkes-Barre *Times Leader* reported in April 2005 that D.C. police had been called to Sherwood's Capitol Hill apartment in September 2004 by a 29-year-old woman who accused him of punching and choking her. Sherwood said he was giving her a back rub. Sherwood's accuser later said she had a five-year affair with the married congressman. He described her as a "casual acquaintance", but issued an apology "for the pain and embarrassment I have caused my family and my supporters." In June 2005, the woman filed suit against Sherwood, seeking $5.5 million in damages.

ELEVENTH DISTRICT

Rep. Paul Kanjorski (D)

Elected 1984, 11th term; b. Apr. 2, 1937, Nanticoke; home, Nanticoke; Temple U., 1957–61, Dickinson Law Schl., 1962–65; Catholic; married (Nancy).

Military Career: Army Reserves, 1960–61.

Professional Career: Practicing atty., 1966–85; Nanticoke City Solicitor, 1969–81; Admin. Law Judge, 1971–80.

DC Office: 2188 RHOB, 20515, 202-225-6511; Fax: 202-225-0764; Web site: kanjorski.house.gov.

District Offices: Mount Pocono, 570-895-4176; Scranton, 570-496-1011; Wilkes-Barre, 570-825-2200.

Committees: *Financial Services* (2d of 32 D): Capital Markets, Insurance & Government Sponsored Enterprises (RMM); Domestic and International Monetary Policy, Trade & Technology; Financial Institutions & Consumer Credit. *Government Reform* (5th of 17 D): Federalism & the Census; Government Management, Finance & Accountability.

Group Ratings

	ADA	ACLU	AFS	LCV	ITIC	NTU	COC	ACU	NTLC	CHC
2004	80	60	100	82	10	10	30	21	12	46
2003	85	—	100	60	—	23	27	32	—	—

National Journal Ratings

	2003 LIB	—	2003 CONS		2004 LIB	—	2004 CONS
Economic	65%	—	35%		73%	—	27%
Social	55%	—	44%		63%	—	37%
Foreign	70%	—	27%		77%	—	22%

Key Votes of the 108th Congress

1. Drilling in ANWR	Y	5. DC School Vouchers	N	9. Ban Same-Sex Marriage	N
2. Approve Bush Tax Cuts	N	6. Ban Human Cloning	Y	10. Fund Iraq War	N
3. Medicare/Rx Bill	N	7. Restrict Gun Liability	Y	11. Bar Cuba Embargo Funds	Y
4. Bar Overtime Pay Regs.	*	8. Ban Partial-Birth Abortion	Y	12. Intelligence Reorg.	N

Election Results

2004 general	Paul Kanjorski (D)	171,147	(94%)	($378,979)
	Kenneth Brenneman (CNP)	10,105	(6%)	
2004 primary	Paul Kanjorski (D)	unopposed		
2002 general	Paul Kanjorski (D)	93,758	(56%)	($1,179,632)
	Louis Barletta (R)	71,543	(42%)	($566,407)
	Other	3,304	(2%)	

Prior Winning Percentages: 2000 (66%); 1998 (67%); 1996 (68%); 1994 (67%); 1992 (67%); 1990 (100%); 1988 (100%); 1986 (71%); 1984 (59%)

The People		Race/Ethnic Origin	Ancestry	
Area size:	2,249 sq. mi.	93.3% White	German: 14.5%	Irish: 13.2%
Urban population:	72.6%	2.5% Black	Italian: 12.0%	
Rural population:	27.4%	0.7% Asian	**2004 Presidential Vote**	
Pop. 2000:	646,209	0.1% Native Am.	Kerry (D) 143,205	(53%)
Median income:	$34,979	0.0% Hawaiian	Bush (R) 127,866	(47%)
Poverty status:	11.3%	0.7% Two+ races	Other 843	(0%)
Military veterans:	15.3%	0.1% Other	**2000 Presidential Vote**	
		2.5% Hispanic Origin	Gore (D) 127,140	(54%)
			Bush (R) 101,629	(43%)
			Other 6,983	(3%)
			Cook Partisan Voting Index: D + 5	

Occupation   Blue collar: 29.8%   White collar: 54.0%   Gray collar: 16.1%

"Coal is the theme song of this city in the hills," the *WPA Guide* said of Scranton in 1940, but even as those words were written, the anthracite kingdom around Scranton and Wilkes-Barre was crumbling. In the 19th century anthracite had become America's main home heating fuel and the valley along the East Branch of the Susquehanna River and the creek that extends north was America's number one source of anthracite. Thousands of immigrants flocked to this valley, settling in a chain of little cities north and south of Wilkes-Barre (named for two backers of the American revolution) and Scranton (named for the leading founding family). There, they took honest jobs with long hours, modest pay, poor working conditions and high death rates—facts of life that made the violently pro-union Molly Maguires popular here, and which spawned periodic clashes between them and the Pinkerton security forces hired by the industrial moguls. While the supply of coal was endless—the area produced 40% of the world's hard coal—demand proved fleeting. Anthracite production peaked in 1917, with long strikes in 1922 and 1925 quickening the conversion to oil and gas. Demand for anthracite began to fall in the 1920s and plummeted in the 1940s; the counties containing Wilkes-Barre and Scranton, Luzerne and Lackawanna, had 755,000 people in 1930 and 523,000 in 2003. As the area's 50 collieries shut down, the once-ubiquitous coal dust vanished; the local ethnic mix—Irish and Polish, Ukrainian and Welsh—grew less distinctive; and former boomtowns full of young families became time-worn communities of senior citizens. Visitors can see how suddenly growth stopped here: at the edge of town streets with houses obviously built in the 1910s and 1920s suddenly end, with only open space beyond. In the 1960s and 1970s, textile and apparel mills brought low-wage, non-union jobs to a formerly high-wage, unionized area. But the anthracite kingdom, created by unbridled (and often exploitative) free enterprise, increasingly looked to the government for sustenance.

Two longtime Appropriations Committee members, Democrat Daniel Flood of Luzerne (1945–47, 1949–53, 1955–80) and Republican Joseph McDade of Lackawanna (1963–99) specialized in funneling money and projects into the area, of which the most visible today is Scranton's $66 million Steamtown train historic site.

The 11th Congressional District of Pennsylvania is the anthracite district. It includes almost all of Luzerne County, where downtown Wilkes-Barre is being revitalized, plus Scranton and surrounding towns in Lackawanna County. It also includes Columbia County west of Luzerne, Carbon County south of Luzerne and Monroe County to the east. Monroe is a different sort of place: it contains most of the Pocono resort area and the often congested Interstate 80 bridge to New Jersey; New Yorkers and New Jerseyites looking for lower taxes and pleasant scenery have moved here in large numbers and the county's population rose 66% from 1990 to 2004. More typical of the district are small towns like Centralia, site of a massive underground fire that has burned unchecked since 1962 and might burn for another 100 years, forcing out all but a dozen stubborn residents who want to mine the coal, and Jim Thorpe, created in 1953 from the unification of neighboring (and rival) Mauch Chunk and East Mauch Chunk. The cities changed their name after offering to provide a gravesite for the great football, baseball and Olympic track star when Thorpe's widow was shopping his remains to whichever town agreed to build him a suitable memorial. Downtown, however, is lively today, with hilly streets, high-ceilinged craft shops and homey restaurants that the Molly Maguires would have recoiled from—and they are here largely because of tourists drawn by Thorpe, the Oklahoma Indian who never came to Carbon County until his death. Since the 1930s, the miners have always been a large Democratic voting bloc, and this is a solidly Democratic district. But these Democrats tend to be cultural conservatives, pro-gun and anti-abortion. In 2004, John Kerry held his first rally in Scranton after the Democratic convention. Kerry, George W. Bush and their running mates made 10 campaign appearances in the area. Bush closed the gap, but Kerry still won the district 53%–47%.

The congressman from the 11th District is Paul Kanjorski, a Democrat first elected in 1984. Kanjorski grew up in Nanticoke, near Wilkes-Barre. As a 16-year-old page in the House of Representatives in 1954, he was on the floor when Puerto Rican terrorists started shooting from the gallery and wounded five congressmen; sprayed by dust from the gunfire, Kanjorski helped to bring stretchers into the chamber. He attended, but did not graduate from, college and law school, then passed the bar exam and returned home to practice law; he was a workmen's compensation administrative law judge for nine years and Nanticoke city solicitor for 12. He ran for Congress and won the Democratic primary by pointing out the incumbent was in Central America while flood-soaked Wilkes-Barre area residents had to boil tap water because of contamination.

In the House, Kanjorski's voting record has been liberal on economics and moderate on cultural issues. He opposes abortion rights but has voted for international family planning aid. He is a tough partisan. While chairing a subcommittee with jurisdiction over White House operations, he sharply attacked the first Bush White House for lavish spending; Bush once apologized at a breakfast meeting for the skimpy meal, blaming Kanjorski's investigations. But with Bill Clinton in the White House, Kanjorski vociferously attacked fellow Pennsylvanian Bill Clinger's investigation of the White House travel office firings and delayed issuance of the report. On the Financial Services Committee, where he is the number-two Democrat, Kanjorski helped to write the post-Enron bill to crack down on corporate fraud and he pushed a "subprime lending" bill to protect consumers from predatory practices. With Republican Ken Calvert, he wants to keep banks out of the real estate business. He voted to authorize force in Iraq, but he later voiced regret and criticized the military for diverting funds from fighting al Qaeda.

Most important to Kanjorski is helping his economically ailing district. He obtained more than $100 million for Wilkes-Barre redevelopment. The *New York Times* called him "a master of earmarking" for getting millions of dollars for the Earth Conservancy Applied Research Center, a public-private project for developing new technologies to reclaim mine-ravaged northeastern Pennsylvania. When Clinton called for 10 more National Historic Rivers, Kanjorski's intervention led Clinton to expand the list to 14—including the Susquehanna, which supplies more than half of the fresh water to the Chesapeake Bay and occasionally causes severe floods. But his eagerness to deliver money to the district got him into trouble in 2002. A federal probe prompted by local union and civic leaders revealed that Kanjorski had obtained $7.5 million in federal grants for Cornerstone Technologies, a high-tech research and development company partly owned by his nephew and other family members. Kanjorski insisted there was no wrongdoing and that he had not violated House rules or profited personally. No charges were filed against him. Kanjorski accused Senator Rick Santorum of instigating the FBI investigation.

Republicans targeted Kanjorski in 2002. Their candidate was Hazleton Mayor Lou Barletta, who hammered Kanjorski on the newspaper allegations. National Republicans ran ads asking, "And who does Paul Kanjorski create jobs for? Not average Pennsylvania families. But his own family. Like his nephews." Kanjorski conceded that he had been investigated, but said that his partisan opponents manufactured the allegations to damage him politically. This was Kanjorski's closest contest since he was first elected, but he won decisively, 56%–42%. Barletta decided not to run again in 2004, and Kanjorski had no Republican challenger.

TWELFTH DISTRICT

Rep. John Murtha (D)

Elected Feb. 1974, 16th full term; b. June 17, 1932, New Martinsville, WV; home, Johnstown; U. of Pittsburgh, B.A. 1962, Indiana U. of PA, 1963–64; Catholic; married (Joyce).

Military Career: Marine Corps, 1952–55, 1966–67 (Vietnam); Marine Corps Reserves, 1955–66, 1967–90.

Elected Office: PA House of Reps., 1969–74.

Professional Career: Owner, Johnstown Minute Car Wash.

DC Office: 2423 RHOB, 20515, 202-225-2065; Fax: 202-225-5709; Web site: www.house.gov/murtha.

District Office: Johnstown, 814-535-2642.

Committees: *Appropriations* (2d of 29 D): Defense (RMM).

Group Ratings

	ADA	ACLU	AFS	LCV	ITIC	NTU	COC	ACU	NTLC	CHC
2004	50	44	100	73	30	13	48	30	17	53
2003	85	—	100	45	—	26	43	52	—	—

National Journal Ratings

	2003 LIB	—	2003 CONS	2004 LIB	—	2004 CONS
Economic	56%	—	44%	64%	—	35%
Social	55%	—	44%	60%	—	40%
Foreign	53%	—	46%	66%	—	33%

Key Votes of the 108th Congress

1. Drilling in ANWR	Y	5. DC School Vouchers	N	9. Ban Same-Sex Marriage	*
2. Approve Bush Tax Cuts	N	6. Ban Human Cloning	Y	10. Fund Iraq War	Y
3. Medicare/Rx Bill	N	7. Restrict Gun Liability	Y	11. Bar Cuba Embargo Funds	N
4. Bar Overtime Pay Regs.	Y	8. Ban Partial-Birth Abortion	Y	12. Intelligence Reorg.	N

Election Results

2004 general	John Murtha (D) .... unopposed			($1,559,185)
2004 primary	John Murtha (D) .... unopposed			
2002 general	John Murtha (D) 124,201	(73%)		($2,386,861)
	Bill Choby (R)...................................... 44,818	(27%)		($17,584)

Prior Winning Percentages: 2000 (71%); 1998 (68%); 1996 (70%); 1994 (69%); 1992 (100%); 1990 (62%); 1988 (100%); 1986 (67%); 1984 (69%); 1982 (61%); 1980 (59%); 1978 (69%); 1976 (68%); 1974 (58%); 1974 (50%).

The People		Race/Ethnic Origin	Ancestry		
Area size:	2,781 sq. mi.	95.0% White	German: 17.3%	Irish: 9.8%	
Urban population:	62.5%	3.3% Black	Italian: 9.2%		
Rural population:	37.5%	0.3% Asian	**2004 Presidential Vote**		
Pop. 2000:	646,249	0.1% Native Am.	Kerry (D) 141,046	(51%)	
Median income:	$30,612	0.0% Hawaiian	Bush (R) 133,088	(49%)	
Poverty status:	13.6%	0.7% Two+ races	Other 119	(0%)	
Military veterans:	15.3%	0.1% Other	**2000 Presidential Vote**		
		0.6% Hispanic Origin	Gore (D) 131,960	(55%)	
			Bush (R) 105,451	(44%)	
			Other 3,595	(1%)	
			Cook Partisan Voting Index: D + 5		

Occupation	Blue collar: 30.5%	White collar: 51.4%	Gray collar: 18.1%

The mountains and valleys within a 100-mile radius of Pittsburgh comprise one of America's most beautiful—and economically troubled—regions. This has been tough, hard-working country ever since Scots-Irish farmers settled here in the 1790s. Their first big product was whiskey—this was the site of the Whiskey Rebellion of 1794—but historically the most important product was bituminous coal. Discovered in the 19th century, it was the basic energy source for the production of iron and steel. The offspring of the original settlers were joined by immigrants from Italy, Poland and Czechoslovakia, living in little frame houses packed into the towns on interstices between hills and rivers, within walking distance of steel factories, foundries and coal mine shafts. It is an industrial landscape and yet there are spots of natural beauty, like the swirling waters of the Youghiogheny River, now much enjoyed by rafters. But the water coming down from the mountains can be dangerous. Its best known community is Johnstown, where on May 31, 1889, floodwater from the ruptured South Fork Dam, gaining speed during an 18-mile trip down steep-walled valleys, poured into the little industrial city with a force equal to Niagara Falls. During 10 awful minutes buildings crumpled like paper, the tumbling hearths and gaslights ignited the wreckage, a flaming pile of debris converged on a 30-acre expanse, and 2,209 people died. This was the worst single-day civilian loss of life in American history until September 11, 2001, when airliners crashed into the World Trade Center and the Pentagon and came down in a field just 50 miles southwest of Johnstown near Shanksville. The 1889 flood and its class overtones (the dam, built at a rural retreat owned by western Pennsylvania's richest families, had been negligently maintained) are documented thoughtfully by the Johnstown Flood Museum in the old Carnegie Library. The museum provides an offset to the economic woes of Johnstown, whose population fell from 67,000 in 1920 to 24,000 in 2004—a decline similar to that of many communities in this region. Life was never easy here; after some prosperous years in the 1960s and 1970s, the "Cradle of the American Steel Industry" was hit hard by the recession that followed the 1979 oil shock. Young people have been leaving the area for years, downtown has been deserted and this district now has the highest elderly percentage in the state. In towns like Windber, the hospital has replaced the coal company as the largest employer. On the western side of the district, the town of Washington has plans for downtown revitalization.

The 12th Congressional District of Pennsylvania, with highly irregular boundaries, contains much of this coal and steel country. It includes all of Greene County and parts of Fayette, Somerset, Cambria, Indiana, Armstrong, Washington and Westmoreland Counties. The boundaries were drawn by Republican legislators who wanted to create a new Republican-leaning 18th District in the southern suburbs of Pittsburgh while also accommodating Democratic Congressman John Murtha, second ranking minority member on the Appropriations Committee, who has worked assiduously to help Pennsylvania. The district includes Murtha's home base of Johnstown and Democratic territory in the southwestern corner of the state.

Politically, this was one of the most Republican parts of America from the Civil War up to the 1930s. Republican policies, including high tariffs and hostility to labor unions, were seen as protecting jobs and increasing growth in the steel economy centered on Pittsburgh. With the coming of the New Deal, and success of the United Mine Workers and the United Steelworkers, the area began voting mostly Democratic. Since 1945, on the Monday before primary and general elections, Democratic pols from across southwestern Pennsylvania have attended the "rally in the valley" held at the Slovak Home in the mill town of Monessen. But it has not followed the national Democratic Party on all issues. Voters here have strongly favored trade restrictions on steel imports, even when most other Democrats were free traders in the 1960s and 1970s; more recently most House Democrats have been opposing free trade measures. Voters here also tend to take conservative stands on cultural issues and foreign policy. This carefully carved district voted 55%–44% for Al Gore in 2000. But after George W. Bush imposed import quotas on steel and boosted clean coal technology, the district voted only 51%–49% for John Kerry.

The congressman from the 12th District is John Murtha, a Democrat first elected in a February 1974 special election that signaled the political weakness of Richard Nixon. Murtha grew up in this area, served in the Marine Corps, then graduated from the University of Pittsburgh and re-enlisted in the Marines in 1966, at 34; he was the first Vietnam veteran to serve in Congress. For his service there he was awarded the Bronze Star, two Purple Hearts and the Vietnamese Cross for Gallantry. Murtha is a member of the Appropriations Committee and the ranking Democrat on the Defense Subcommittee, his party's key man on the defense budget. His voting record—hawkish on foreign policy, interventionist on economics and usually tradition-minded on cultural issues—seems perfectly suited to the steel and coal country. Murtha is also one of those old-time politicians who operate best in secret, holding court in the back corner of the House chamber where he trades gossip and votes to colleagues who crowd around him as if they were kissing his ring (since 2001, Gene Taylor has voted for him as Speaker). He speaks for attribution to few national or local reporters, hardly ever appears on television, and rarely speaks in the House chamber except for the annual defense spending bill, which often passes with little debate. He wields power not only on his committee work but also on many back-room issues dear to his colleagues, including pay raises, committee assignments and, after the trial and acquittal of Pennsylvania Republican Joseph McDade, a provision requiring the Justice Department to reimburse members of Congress who are indicted but acquitted. With John Dingell, he has opposed some gun control proposals.

On foreign issues, Murtha voted for the Gulf War resolution in 1991 and the use of force in Iraq in 2002, but opposed intervention in Bosnia and deployment in Somalia, arguing that UN officials lacked the know-how to command U.S. troops. He complained loudly that troops in Iraq were poorly equipped, with both personal gear and machines, and he questioned the civilian decision-making. In October 2004, he was one of two House members who voted to reinstate the military draft. He is caught sometimes between Democratic demands for lower defense spending to make more money available for domestic programs and Republican desires to spend even more on defense, but he seeks to come up with appropriations that a broad cross-section of the House will sustain. He opposed normal trade relations with China because of its threat to use force against Taiwan; as a stalwart of organized labor, he opposed trade promotion authority. Inside the Democratic Caucus, he gained added respect and influence as the campaign manager for Nancy Pelosi in her 2001 contest against Steny Hoyer for Democratic whip, adding his old-style influence to her new-age style. In January 2005, with encouragement from the University of Pittsburgh Medical Center, he called for a war against diabetes.

After a close 1990 primary, Murtha spent more time traveling around the district and developed a more secure electoral base. He has used the defense bill to direct tens of millions of dollars to his district, often for health facilities and other projects that had nothing to do with the military; he has also delivered large sums for the lock and dam replacement project on the Monongahela River. His tending to local concerns paid off handsomely in 2002, when Republicans consulted Murtha during the redistricting process and made adjustments to the boundaries to suit him; one was to put the house of four-term Democrat Frank Mascara in the new Republican-leaning 18th District. A month later, Mascara finally decided that his chances in the general election in the 18th were poor and that he would run against Murtha. Each had represented about half of the new 12th District. Mascara's campaign was poorly financed and organized. Murtha campaigned actively around the new district, emphasizing his "record of getting things done." Mascara attacked Murtha for ducking debates, and for being "the David

Copperfield of politics . . . handing out checks and then disappearing from his district." Murtha won 64%–36%. In the general, Murtha won 73%–27%.

Murtha has continued to reign from his fiefdom at the Capitol: protecting the Pentagon and the troops, cutting deals wherever he could, and receiving visitors from his throne in the Pennsylvania corner of the House.

THIRTEENTH DISTRICT

Rep. Allyson Schwartz (D)

Elected 2004, 1st term; b. Oct. 3, 1948, Queens, NY; home, Jenkintown; Simmons Col., B.A. 1970, Bryn Mawr Col., M.S.W. 1972; Jewish; married (David).

Elected Office: PA Senate, 1990–2004.

Professional Career: Exec. Dir., Elizabeth Blackwell Center, 1975–88; Dep. Comm., Philadelphia Human Rights Dept., 1988–90.

DC Office: 423 CHOB, 20515, 202-225-6111; Fax: 202-226-0611; Web site: www.house.gov/schwartz.

District Offices: Jenkintown, 215-517-6572; Philadelphia, 215-335-3355.

Committees: *Budget* (17th of 17 D). *Transportation & Infrastructure* (33d of 34 D): Highways, Transit & Pipelines; Water Resources & Environment.

Group Ratings and Key Votes: Newly Elected

Election Results

2004 general	Allyson Schwartz (D)	171,763	(56%)	($4,572,500)
	Melissa Brown (R)	127,205	(41%)	($1,927,499)
	Other	9,156	(3%)	
2004 primary	Allyson Schwartz (D)	24,309	(52%)	
	Joe Torsella (D)	22,232	(48%)	
2002 general	Joe Hoeffel (D)	107,948	(51%)	($1,554,821)
	Melissa Brown (R)	100,295	(47%)	($1,827,440)
	Other	3,627	(2%)	

The People		Race/Ethnic Origin	Ancestry	
Area size:	258 sq. mi.	85.7% White	Irish: 19.5%	German: 15.6%
Urban population:	98.5%	5.9% Black	Italian: 10.4%	
Rural population:	1.5%	4.0% Asian	**2004 Presidential Vote**	
Pop. 2000:	647,435	0.1% Native Am.	Kerry (D) 182,552	(56%)
Median income:	$49,319	0.0% Hawaiian	Bush (R) 140,900	(43%)
Poverty status:	7.1%	1.0% Two+ races	Other 1,345	(0%)
Military veterans:	12.8%	0.1% Other	**2000 Presidential Vote**	
		3.1% Hispanic Origin	Gore (D) 155,903	(56%)
			Bush (R) 117,773	(42%)
			Other 5,972	(2%)
			Cook Partisan Voting Index: D + 8	

Occupation	Blue collar: 19.3%	White collar: 68.1%	Gray collar: 12.6%

Montgomery County, Pennsylvania, is the proximate hinterland of Philadelphia: rolling hills cut on one side by the Schuylkill River and at intervals by the Pennsylvania and Reading Railroad lines radiating outward from Center City. Older suburbs, both rich and modest, grew up around rail stations, with comfortable houses within walking distance for commuters. Further out are 18th and 19th century villages, once surrounded by farm fields, now encroached by subdivisions where people depend on cars, not rail lines, to get to work. Montgomery County has its shopping malls and office parks, but there are not many freeways here; most of the traffic here is along roads on the area's diagonal grid or along the old pikes laid out when Pennsylvania was a colony.

It is the most populous and second most affluent county in metropolitan Philadelphia, with solid job growth prospects.

Quite a different place, though adjacent to southern Montgomery County, is Northeast Philadelphia. This is relatively new urban territory, with more than half its houses built after 1950. When the alley-wide streets of North and South Philadelphia and the river wards were already teeming and the Main Line suburbs were already well-settled, the workers of Philadelphia's docks, factories and Center City offices were just starting to fill up vacant land here. They settled in neighborhoods like Bustleton, Somerton and Torresdale. Many of Philadelphia's Hispanics live in the industrial river wards along the Delaware River, but the other wards of Northeast Philadelphia are still mostly white and ethnic, the kind of places where city cops and firefighters live and the kind that gave big margins to Mayor Frank Rizzo in the 1970s and 1980s. Construction of federal Section 8 housing for low-income tenants caused a local furor. More recently, outside investors and Hasidic Jews from New York have bid up residential prices.

The 13th Congressional District of Pennsylvania includes much of southeastern and central Montgomery County and most of Northeast Philadelphia. Historically Montgomery was quintessentially Republican, with a style of politics set for years by Ivy-educated Republican men, and with Republicans of more modest and sometimes ethnic backgrounds manning the precincts and staffing local offices. But Montgomery County, like other affluent suburbs in the Boston-Washington corridor, swung toward the Democratic Party in national politics in the 1990s, with abortion and other cultural issues usually trumping economic interests. The same county that voted by large margins for Ronald Reagan and George H.W. Bush in the 1980s has voted strictly for Democratic presidential candidates since then. In 2002 Montgomery County backed Democrat and former Philadelphia Mayor Ed Rendell for governor by a 2–1 margin, though Republicans in 2004 regained control of the county commission. Northeast Philadelphia has a different political heritage. Operating in a city where Democrats hold most local offices, Northeast Philadelphia's feisty Republican organization has won some elections and shown facility in making deals to get its share of patronage. In 2004, 59% of the district's votes were cast in Montgomery County, 41% in Northeast Philadelphia.

The congressman from the 13th District is Allyson Schwartz, a Democrat elected in 2004. Her mother fled Vienna as a teenager in 1938 after the Germans annexed Austria and traveled alone to America, where she settled at a Jewish foster home in Philadelphia. Her father was a dentist in Flushing, Queens, where she grew up. A graduate of Simmons with a master's in social work from Bryn Mawr, Schwartz started a women's health center in 1975 and worked on health care issues as first deputy commissioner for the Philadelphia Department of Human Services; her husband is a cardiologist. In 1990 she was elected to the state Senate, where she received some criticism for too eagerly seeking publicity. In 2000 she ran for the U. S. Senate and finished second in the Democratic primary, with 27% of the vote, behind Congressman Ron Klink, who had 41%.

In 2004 13th District incumbent Joe Hoeffel ran, unsuccessfully, against Senator Arlen Specter. Schwartz ran for the 13th District seat, and Schwartz faced serious competition in both the primary and the general election. In the primary she faced Joe Torsella, an aide to Governor Ed Rendell when Rendell was mayor of Philadelphia, and more recently head of the National Constitution Center in Philly. She was backed by EMILY's List which made a $170,000 independent expenditure on Schwartz's behalf in March and April, and raised other funds, phoned voters and sent out mailings that even a Torsella strategist said were the best he had ever seen. Torsella won 57% of the vote in Northeast Philadelphia, which had a larger turnout, but Schwartz carried the affluent suburbs of Montgomery County with 62%, for an overall win of 2,000 votes, 52%–48%. On the Republican side, Melissa Brown, an ophthalmologist who supports abortion rights, was nominated with 39% of the vote in a three-way primary; Brown ran a strong race against Hoeffel in 2002, but lost 51%–47%.

In the general election, "the two opponents proved that women can sling mud as capably as any men," the *Philadelphia Inquirer* wrote. Schwartz called herself a "new Democrat," not a liberal; Brown called her a radical. Schwartz called the Republican "sleazy" because of her links to a bankrupt HMO and a lawsuit that the state insurance department filed against her. Both candidates emphasized health care. Schwartz emphasized her sponsorship of the state Children's Health Insurance Program, which provides health insurance for 133,000 children from low-income families. Brown, a physician with an M.B.A, called for changes in tort law, arguing that it would keep doctors' liability insurance down and lower the cost of health care. Schwartz gained the upper hand in the contest because of her lengthy tenure in the state Senate and her considerable fundraising advantage; she raised $3.7 million, with $500,000 after the primary from EMILY's List. Schwartz won 56%–41%, a bigger majority than Hoeffel had when he was an incumbent; she won 60% of the vote in Northeast Philadelphia and 53% in Montgomery County.

FOURTEENTH DISTRICT

Rep. Mike Doyle (D)

Elected 1994, 6th term; b. Aug. 5, 1953, Pittsburgh; home, Swissvale; PA St. U., B.S. 1975; Catholic; married (Susan).

Elected Office: Swissvale Borough Cncl., 1977–81.

Professional Career: Insurance agent, 1975–77; Exec. Dir., Turtle Creek Valley Citizens Union, 1977–79; Chief of Staff, PA Sen. Frank Pecora, 1978–94; Co–Founder/Owner, Eastgate Insurance Agency, 1983–present.

DC Office: 401 CHOB, 20515, 202-225-2135; Fax: 202-225-3084; Web site: www.house.gov/doyle.

District Offices: McKeesport, 412-664-4049; Penn Hills, 412-241-6055; Pittsburgh, 412-261-5091.

Committees: *Energy & Commerce* (18th of 26 D): Energy & Air Quality; Environment & Hazardous Materials; Telecommunications & the Internet. *Standards of Official Conduct* (5th of 5 D).

Group Ratings

	ADA	ACLU	AFS	LCV	ITIC	NTU	COC	ACU	NTLC	CHC
2004	80	65	100	82	40	6	48	12	3	53
2003	85	—	100	70	—	21	34	38	—	—

National Journal Ratings

	2003 LIB — 2003 CONS		2004 LIB — 2004 CONS	
Economic	61%	39%	77%	22%
Social	62%	37%	63%	36%
Foreign	79%	20%	74%	25%

Key Votes of the 108th Congress

1. Drilling in ANWR	N	5. DC School Vouchers	N	9. Ban Same-Sex Marriage	N
2. Approve Bush Tax Cuts	N	6. Ban Human Cloning	Y	10. Fund Iraq War	N
3. Medicare/Rx Bill	N	7. Restrict Gun Liability	N	11. Bar Cuba Embargo Funds	Y
4. Bar Overtime Pay Regs.	Y	8. Ban Partial-Birth Abortion	Y	12. Intelligence Reorg.	N

Election Results

2004 general	Mike Doyle (D).............................. unopposed	($745,788)
2004 primary	Mike Doyle (D).............................. unopposed	
2002 general	Mike Doyle (D).............................. unopposed	($648,209)

Prior Winning Percentages: 2000 (69%); 1998 (68%); 1996 (56%); 1994 (55%)

The People		Race/Ethnic Origin	Ancestry		
Area size:	170 sq. mi.	72.9% White	German: 15.5%	Irish: 12.1%	
Urban population:	99.8%	22.5% Black	Italian: 9.8%		
Rural population:	0.2%	1.7% Asian	**2004 Presidential Vote**		
Pop. 2000:	646,013	0.2% Native Am.	Kerry (D) 205,636	(69%)	
Median income:	$30,139	0.0% Hawaiian	Bush (R) 88,316	(30%)	
Poverty status:	17.1%	1.4% Two+ races	Other 2,325	(1%)	
Military veterans:	14.1%	0.3% Other	**2000 Presidential Vote**		
		1.1% Hispanic Origin	Gore (D) 183,640	(70%)	
			Bush (R) 74,085	(28%)	
			Other 6,007	(2%)	
			Cook Partisan Voting Index: D +22		

Occupation	Blue collar: 18.6%	White collar: 61.7%	Gray collar: 19.7%

The Golden Triangle is the inevitable focus of Pittsburgh, the tip of land where the Allegheny and Monongahela Rivers come together to form the Ohio. It has been a strategic site for more than 200 years. It was there, to Fort Duquesne during the French and Indian War, that Braddock's army was heading (with George Washington helping lead the way) when it was ambushed and defeated in 1754. A few years later, the first American city west of the Appalachian chain was carved out of the wilderness here and named after the English statesman William Pitt. Pittsburgh grew rapidly in the days when most of the nation's commerce moved over water. When railroads became ascendant, Pittsburgh still did nicely, since rail lines tend to run along the riverside rather than scaling the mountains. Then came Andrew Carnegie, a Scottish immigrant working as a telegrapher for the Pennsylvania Railroad who foresaw that steel would replace iron for railroad bridges; he built a steel factory in Pittsburgh, then not much more than a rail junction but blessed with ready deposits of coal and access to iron ore from the Great Lakes. With associates like Henry Clay Frick and Henry Phipps, Carnegie built his capacity to the point that when he sold out in 1901, the resulting U.S. Steel Corporation held a near-monopoly.

The Pittsburgh that Carnegie and his steel men built is one of giant mills in the bottomlands along the rivers and massive buildings downtown, such as H.H. Richardson's classic stone City-County Building. There were once 12 cable cars going up the Duquesne Incline and other routes, connecting mills with the neighborhoods above. Back then, the smog—a word used here before it was in Los Angeles—was so bad that street lights had to stay on all day downtown; a famous 1947 photograph shows a midnight-like darkness at nine in the morning. But then an alliance of local elected officials and corporate titans (including the leaders of such local Fortune 500 companies as USX, Heinz, Alcoa, and PPG) pushed through a series of forceful and visionary projects designed to improve the city's quality of life. Early on, this model produced tremendous successes: In the 1950s, Mayor David Lawrence and financier Richard King Mellon led efforts to cut air pollution, control river flooding, and construct an advanced network of highways and tunnels. They also turned a derelict industrial zone at the three-rivers confluence into Point State Park—a triangular gem that remains popular with office workers.

Pittsburgh is not just a downtown; it is a city of neighborhoods, built on or beneath vertiginous hills; neighborhoods that look right next to each other on the map are in fact quite separate and distinct. There is the uptown neighborhood around Carnegie-Mellon University and the University of Pittsburgh with its neo-Gothic "cathedral of learning"; they have helped to spur robust high-tech and medical sectors that have replaced many of the manufacturing jobs lost in previous decades. Among and atop the hills are neighborhoods as different as the predominantly black Hill District, where the famed Pittsburgh Crawfords of baseball's Negro Leagues once played, and WASPy Shady Side and Jewish Squirrel Hill, with fine mansions and fashionable shops. Artist Andy Warhol grew up in the Soho neighborhood, and the Andy Warhol museum is located on the north side. Along the Monongahela River in Pittsburgh and southeast are small industrial neighborhoods and towns, like Clairton (where the classic movie *The Deer Hunter* was set and filmed) with less than half as many residents as a half-century ago. Local officials boast of more bridges than any other city in the world except Venice.

The 14th Congressional District of Pennsylvania includes all of Pittsburgh and mostly working class suburbs to the east, south and west. There is some verdant suburbia here, but much of the district is in the Monongahela (or Mon) Valley, where the old steel mills stand or once stood, and the hills above. More affluent suburbs to the north and south are in the Republican held 4th and 18th Districts. This is a heavily Democratic district.

The congressman from the 14th is Mike Doyle, a Democrat first elected in 1994. Of Irish and Italian descent, Doyle grew up in the Mon Valley town of Swissvale, worked in steel mills during summers off from Penn State, worked as an insurance agent, for a nonprofit agency and was elected to the Swissvale Borough Council in 1977, at 24. In 1978 he became chief of staff to state Senator Frank Pecora, who was then a Republican. Pecora switched parties in 1992 and briefly gave Democrats control of the state Senate—the Jim Jeffords of the Mon Valley. In 1994 Doyle, who had just switched to the Democratic Party, ran for the 18th District seat held then by Rick Santorum, who was running for the Senate; Doyle was one of seven Democrats and four Republicans to seek the open seat. Doyle was assisted by endorsements from unions and community leaders and won with 20% of the vote; the next finisher had 18%. In the general, he faced John McCarty, an aide to the late Senator John Heinz; McCarty was pro-choice and Doyle anti-abortion. Doyle campaigned for sweeping health care changes, against the new General Agreement on Tariffs and Trade, and for rebuilding the Mon Valley's industrial base. In a Republican year, he won 55%–45%.

In the House, Doyle has a mixed voting record, toward the right on cultural issues, toward the left on economics. Doyle rarely seeks attention, nor does he cause much ruckus. In late October 2004, he criticized national White House security adviser Condoleeza Rice for "transparently political appearances" on behalf of George W. Bush. As a Steel Caucus member, he worked to reduce foreign imports and pushed a bill to create a national historic site at the former U.S. Steel facilities along the Mon River as part of the local Rivers of Steel program. He lives on Capitol Hill with his "family" of bipartisan House colleagues and is one of the dwindling number of members who drive home after each week's final vote.

Republicans controlled redistricting after the 2000 Census, and state Senate Republicans had not forgotten Doyle's role in Pecora's party switch. But in August 2001, 14th District Democrat Bill Coyne announced he would retire. Republicans concentrated on creating a new Republican-leaning 18th District in Pittsburgh's southern suburbs; they attached Doyle's Mon Valley base to the 14th District. Doyle had reason to worry that a city-based Democrat might run for the seat, but in 2002 and again in 2004 Doyle was renominated and reelected without opposition. In the House, he settled in to build seniority on the Energy and Commerce Committee.

FIFTEENTH DISTRICT

Rep. Charlie Dent (R)

Elected 2004, 1st term; b. May 24, 1960, Allentown; home, Allentown; PA St. U., B.A. 1982, Lehigh U., M.P.A. 1993; Presbyterian; married (Pamela).

Elected Office: PA House of Reps., 1990–98; PA Senate, 1998–2004.

Professional Career: Development officer, Lehigh U., 1986–90.

DC Office: 502 CHOB, 20515, 202-225-6411; Fax: 202-226-0078; Web site: www.dent.house.gov.

District Office: Bethlehem, 610-861-9734.

Committees: *Government Reform* (21st of 23 R): Federalism & the Census (Vice Chmn.); National Security, Emerging Threats & International Relations. *Homeland Security* (19th of 19 R): Emergency Preparedness, Science & Technology; Intelligence, Information Sharing & Terrorism Risk Assessment; Management, Integration & Oversight. *Transportation & Infrastructure* (33d of 41 R): Aviation; Economic Development; Public Buildings & Emergency Management.

Group Ratings and Key Votes: Newly Elected

Election Results

2004 general	Charlie Dent (R)	170,634	(59%)	($1,971,131)
	Joe Driscoll (D)	114,646	(39%)	($2,295,656)
	Other	5,854	(2%)	
2004 primary	Charlie Dent (R)	25,376	(51%)	
	Joe Pascuzzo (R)	16,152	(33%)	
	Brian O'Neill (R)	7,749	(16%)	
2002 general	Pat Toomey (R)	98,493	(57%)	($1,029,593)
	Ed O'Brien (D)	73,179	(43%)	($824,636)

The People

Area size:	851 sq. mi.
Urban population:	87.2%
Rural population:	12.8%
Pop. 2000:	646,300
Median income:	$45,330
Poverty status:	8.2%
Military veterans:	13.5%

Race/Ethnic Origin

86.4% White
2.8% Black
1.7% Asian
0.1% Native Am.
0.0% Hawaiian
1.0% Two+ races
0.1% Other
7.9% Hispanic Origin

Ancestry

German: 21.9%   Irish: 9.0%
Italian: 8.1%

2004 Presidential Vote

Kerry (D)	150,939	(50%)
Bush (R)	150,213	(50%)
Other	1,404	(0%)

2000 Presidential Vote

Gore (D)	119,393	(49%)
Bush (R)	116,817	(48%)
Other	8,865	(4%)

Cook Partisan Voting Index: D + 2

Occupation   Blue collar: 26.5%   White collar: 59.4%   Gray collar: 14.1%

Allentown, Pennsylvania, has long been derided by show-biz songwriters, from "42nd Street" back in 1933, in which it was scorned as nowhere, the polar opposite of Broadway, to Billy Joel's "Allentown" in 1982, with its grim picture of closed factories and unemployment. Though both contain nuggets of truth, neither is an entirely fair portrait of Pennsylvania's Lehigh Valley today: Allentown and next-door Bethlehem did suffer when big employers—Mack Truck in Allentown and Bethlehem Steel in Bethlehem—closed down big plants in the 1980s. But the Lehigh Valley around Allentown and Bethlehem in recent years had solid growth and low unemployment rates, thanks to a mix of regional health care networks, telephone call-centers for insurance companies (Aetna) and banks (Wachovia), long-surviving industries (such as Air Products and Chemicals, energy utility PPL and the remnants of Mack Truck's local operations), and small startups that don't earn the visibility of the big closedowns but which together have created more new jobs than have been lost. In the Lehigh Valley, 43% of employees work for companies with 100 or fewer workers, and 10% for companies with 10 or fewer. Some 8% of the population here is Hispanic, higher than in any other Pennsylvania metro area—a sure sign that the area is generating new jobs. The redevelopment plan of Bethlehem includes industrial parks, a convention center, hotel complex and National Museum of Industrial History housed in part of the old steel plant; the first working facility to move onto the site is a large refrigerated warehouse. If the Lehigh Valley is off the main lines of traffic, it does at least have several features that make it attractive to people from the big city. Commuters are connected by I-78 to New York and by the Turnpike Extension to Philadelphia; it has lower taxes and living costs than New Jersey or Philadelphia; it has a cluster of colleges (Lehigh, Muhlenberg, Moravian) and a strong regional newspaper (the Allentown *Morning Call*); and it has both Dorney Park, one of the nation's oldest amusement parks, and the Crayola Crayon factory in Easton. Easton's old industrial buildings, just across the Delaware River from New Jersey, have become something of a magnet for artists seeking inexpensive loft and warehouse space.

The 15th Congressional District of Pennsylvania consists of the Lehigh Valley plus a small adjoining slice of northern Montgomery County. Politically, this has long been a classic swing area, located at the intersection of heavily Democratic industrial precincts and the Republican farmlands of the Pennsylvania Dutch Country. The valley backed Ronald Reagan twice, the elder George Bush in 1988 and Bill Clinton twice; it voted for Al Gore and John Kerry by miniscule margins. In the past five governors' races, it voted for the winner each time: twice for Democrat Robert Casey, twice for Republican Tom Ridge and for Democrat Ed Rendell in 2002.

The congressman from the 15th District is Charlie Dent, a Republican elected in 2004. Dent grew up in Allentown, graduated from Penn State and got a graduate degree at Lehigh, where he later worked as a development officer. In 1990 he was elected to the state House and in 1998 to the state Senate, where he chaired the Urban Affairs and Housing Committee. He enacted a bill to make assaults on gays a hate crime. In 2003, when 15th District Republican Pat Toomey announced that he would keep his 1998 promise to serve only three terms and would run against Senator Arlen Specter in the 2004 Republican primary, Dent immediately became the front-runner to succeed him. His lifelong residence in the Lehigh Valley was in sharp contrast to the background of the Democratic nominee, businessman Joe Driscoll. Driscoll grew up in Massachusetts, where he went sailing with the Kennedys and made enough money to spend $2 million on this race. But he lived for years in posh Lower Merion Township in Montgomery County, just outside Philadelphia. In 2003 he considered running against incumbent Republican Jim Gerlach in the 6th District but after Lehigh Valley Democrats failed to recruit a local candidate in January 2004 Driscoll announced he would run in the 15th; he bought a townhouse in Upper Macungie Township in September though his wife and children continued living outside the district. In the April primary, Driscoll was opposed by a perennial candidate who had run for office nine times without success and who sued to have Driscoll removed from the ballot for allegedly lying about his residence. The judge ruled that Driscoll could run here but that he must list his home in Lower Merion Township. He won, but by only 56%–44%. On the Republican side, Dent's two opponents charged he was too liberal but he won with 51% to 33% for Joe Pascuzzo and 16% for Brian O'Neill.

Dent framed the campaign as a contest between a native son and a carpetbagging outsider. Aside from his college years and a stint in Washington, he had spent his entire life in the Lehigh Valley. He portrayed Driscoll as a Philadelphia outsider whom Democrats recruited because of his ability to self-finance his race. Dent said that Driscoll considered the Lehigh Valley "a speed bump on his way to Congress." Driscoll said that he would continue to live there, even if he lost the election. He sought to deflect the residency issue with aggressive criticism of the Bush administration; he claimed that a vote for Dent was an endorsement of Bush's policies. He blamed rising health care costs on Republicans, while Dent called for reform of medical malpractice insurance costs. When Driscoll criticized him for taking a $10,000 contribution from Majority Leader Tom DeLay's PAC, Dent responded, "99% of my opponent's campaign money comes from outside the 15th District." Dent's moderate record, which included support for abortion rights, made it difficult to tie him to Bush; he insisted he would be an independent voice in Washington. Dent won 59%–39%, a wider margin than Toomey had won in his three races. A few weeks after the election, Driscoll's real estate agent said that he put his townhouse here up for sale and moved back to Lower Merion Township.

SIXTEENTH DISTRICT

Rep. Joe Pitts (R)

Elected 1996, 5th term; b. Oct. 10, 1939, Lexington, KY; home, Kennett Square; Asbury Col., B.A. 1961, West Chester U., M.Ed. 1972; Protestant; married (Virginia).

Military Career: Air Force, 1963–69 (Vietnam).

Professional Career: High schl. teacher, 1969–72; PA House of Reps., 1972–96; Owner, Landscape & Nursery Co., 1974–90.

DC Office: 221 CHOB, 20515, 202-225-2411; Fax: 202-225-2013; Web site: www.house.gov/pitts.

District Offices: Lancaster, 717-393-0667; Unionville, 610-444-4581.

Committees: *Energy & Commerce* (20th of 31 R): Commerce, Trade & Consumer Protection; Environment & Hazardous Materials; Health.

Group Ratings

	ADA	ACLU	AFS	LCV	ITIC	NTU	COC	ACU	NTLC	CHC
2004	5	0	0	9	100	75	95	100	97	100
2003	5	—	0	5	—	71	100	92	—	—

National Journal Ratings

	2003 LIB	—	2003 CONS		2004 LIB	—	2004 CONS
Economic	25%	—	74%		9%	—	88%
Social	0%	—	95%		0%	—	91%
Foreign	11%	—	80%		4%	—	93%

Key Votes of the 108th Congress

1. Drilling in ANWR	Y	5. DC School Vouchers	Y	9. Ban Same-Sex Marriage	Y
2. Approve Bush Tax Cuts	Y	6. Ban Human Cloning	Y	10. Fund Iraq War	Y
3. Medicare/Rx Bill	Y	7. Restrict Gun Liability	Y	11. Bar Cuba Embargo Funds	N
4. Bar Overtime Pay Regs.	N	8. Ban Partial-Birth Abortion	Y	12. Intelligence Reorg.	Y

Election Results

2004 general	Joe Pitts (R)	183,620	(64%)	($429,653)
	Lois Herr (D)	98,410	(34%)	($83,737)
	Other	3,269	(1%)	
2004 primary	Joe Pitts (R)	unopposed		
2002 general	Joe Pitts (R)	119,046	(88%)	($432,695)
	Will Todd (Green)	8,720	(6%)	
	Kenneth Brenneman (CNP)	6,766	(5%)	

Prior Winning Percentages: 2000 (67%); 1998 (71%); 1996 (59%)

The People		Race/Ethnic Origin	Ancestry	
Area size:	1,326 sq. mi.	84.5% White	German: 25.3%	Irish: 8.8%
Urban population:	76.0%	4.0% Black	English: 6.1%	
Rural population:	24.0%	1.4% Asian	**2004 Presidential Vote**	
Pop. 2000:	646,328	0.1% Native Am.	Bush (R) 182,856	(61%)
Median income:	$45,934	0.0% Hawaiian	Kerry (D) 113,193	(38%)
Poverty status:	9.4%	0.9% Two+ races	Other 1,472	(0%)
Military veterans:	11.6%	0.1% Other	**2000 Presidential Vote**	
		9.0% Hispanic Origin	Bush (R) 144,862	(62%)
			Gore (D) 82,729	(35%)
			Other 5,713	(2%)
			Cook Partisan Voting Index: R +11	

Occupation	Blue collar: 29.7%	White collar: 54.5%	Gray collar: 15.8%

The Pennsylvania Dutch Country, settled by Germans in the 18th century when it was Pennsylvania's frontier, remains a distinctive part of America. These Germans were Amish and Mennonite, pietistic sects seeking religious liberty and determined to farm rich lands in the same intensive way they had in Germany. Today, many of their descendants—the Eisenhower family is the most famous example—have blended into mainstream America, but in the Dutch area around Lancaster, many "Plain People" still live in the old way. Though larger communities exist in Ohio and Indiana, tourists can still see families of Plain People clad in black, clattering over the back roads in horse-drawn carriages, with scrupulously tended farms set amid rolling hills and barns decorated with hex signs (the scene was captured memorably in the 1983 film *Witness*). Beneath the surface, Amish communities are facing the strains of modernity: In recent years, Amish teens have attracted public attention for using drugs and alcohol while participating in the "rumschpringes"—a period when adolescents are freed from their community's rigid rules and mores, before being given the choice of returning to the fold as an adult. Still, the community remains robust, and tourism, much of it linked to interest in the Amish, brings in more than five million people annually. Agriculture is the other pillar of the local economy: Farmers here produce some of the highest per-acre yields on earth. Within an easy drive from Philadelphia, Baltimore and Washington, this area has also become home to outlet malls.

Lancaster County and Chester County each grew by double-digit rates in the 1990s—partly from religious families, partly from newcomers moving in—making this the heart of one of Pennsylvania's fastest-growing regions.

The 16th Congressional District of Pennsylvania includes all of Lancaster County, plus parts of southwestern Chester County that adjoin the Maryland and Delaware borders, as well as a small slice of Berks County that reaches as far as Reading. Outside the regional hub of Lancaster, the 16th is mostly small-town territory, with numerous quaint and quirkily named, if somewhat touristy, villages, such as Bird-in-Hand, Blue Ball and Intercourse (the first two named for the posted logos of old pubs, the third for reasons that are obscure, but almost certainly non-sexual). Closer to Philadelphia, the district takes in the metropolis' spreading suburbs, including West Chester, Kennett Square, fragrant with the manure that makes it America's leading mushroom-growing center as well as the glorious perfumes of the flowers at Longwood Gardens, and the fringe of the Wyeth country west of Chadds Ford. During the 1990s, Reading and Berks County attracted a large number of Hispanics, who found jobs in a growing if not terribly affluent economy. But their inclusion in this district—now the second-most Hispanic in the state, at 9%—has not altered the political equation. This is one of the most Republican districts in Pennsylvania and, for that matter, in the whole Northeast. It has favored the party of Lincoln ever since it abandoned the party of Pennsylvania's only president, Lancaster resident James Buchanan, on the eve of the Civil War. Lancaster County was the only county within an hour's drive of Philadelphia to back Republican Mike Fisher over Democrat Ed Rendell in the 2002 gubernatorial race, and by more than a 2–1 margin. In 2004, Karl Rove said a big vote in the county was key to a statewide win, and George W. Bush added 30,000 votes to his total in 2000.

The congressman from the 16th District is Joe Pitts, a Republican first elected in 1996. Pitts was born in Kentucky, spent time in the Philippines with his parents where they served as religious missionaries, joined the Air Force after college, served three tours of duty and flew 116 B-52 combat missions in Vietnam. He returned to become a math and science teacher in Malvern, in Chester County, and later owned a nursery near Kennett Square. He and his daughter have exhibited their artwork, everything from painting to sculpture, at local galleries. In 1972, at 33, he was elected to the Pennsylvania House. In 1989 he became chairman of the Appropriations Committee; he oversaw the restoration of the glorious Pennsylvania Capitol. When Congressman Bob Walker, one of the conservative reformers close to Newt Gingrich who helped revolutionize the House, cited the "Pennsylvania Dutch tradition" of not serving over 20 years and said he was retiring, Pitts plunged into the primary. He spoke favorably of home-schooling and unfavorably of gambling, and ran as a "true conservative." He raised the most money and won with 45% to 26% for the runner-up, a moderate. In the general, Pitts easily defeated newspaper publisher James Blaine, a descendant of James G. Blaine, the "Plumed Knight" and Republican presidential nominee in 1884.

In the House, Pitts has a firmly conservative record. He was an early advocate of repeal of the estate and gift tax, which was a core component of the first Bush tax cut. He led the Pro-Life Caucus and headed the Republicans' "values action team" that worked with the Christian Coalition and other family groups to promote a pro-family agenda. He founded two diverse groups: the Religious Prisoners' Congressional Task Force, to plead for human rights around the world, and the Electronic Warfare Working Group, to encourage more congressional support for military technology. On the Energy and Commerce Committee he advocated privacy protections for individual cell phone numbers after the industry discussed a directory assistance data base; the Health Subcommittee had a hearing on his bill for research into depression suffered by women who have had an abortion. In February 2004, he objected to plans by the UPN television network for "Amish in the City," a reality series about Amish teenagers; the program was dropped.

Pitts played a key role in killing the bankruptcy bill in 2002. He joined Chris Smith of New Jersey in objecting to a provision, added by Senator Charles Schumer, which would make fines and criminal penalties for abortion protesters non-dischargeable under bankruptcy. Pitts and Smith rallied anti-abortion Republicans and said they would vote against the bill if the provision was not removed. Despite a determined effort by Tom DeLay to revive the bill, Pitts and Smith held their ground. The rule failed 243–172, with 87 Republicans voting against it. But in March 2005 the Senate rejected the Schumer amendment and passed the bankruptcy bill, and the issue is unlikely to arise again in the House.

Pitts has been reelected easily. In November 2002, several days before the election, he announced he was reneging on his 1996 pledge to serve only 10 years. "It was a political type of decision," he told the Lancaster *Intelligencer Journal*, explaining his initial support for term limits. "I felt like, as the only politician who had been in the legislature at that point, that that was what I should have done." No adverse reaction was evident.

SEVENTEENTH DISTRICT

Rep. Tim Holden (D)

Elected 1992, 7th term; b. Mar. 5, 1957, Pottsville; home, St. Clair; U. of Richmond, 1976–78, Bloomsburg St. U., B.A. 1980; Catholic; married (Gwen).

Elected Office: Schuylkill Cnty. Sheriff, 1985–92.

Professional Career: Real estate agent; Insurance broker, Holden Insurance Agency, 1980–85; Probation Officer, 1980–85.

DC Office: 2417 RHOB, 20515, 202-225-5546; Fax: 202-226-0996; Web site: www.holden.house.gov.

District Offices: Harrisburg, 717-234-5904; Lebanon, 717-270-1395; Pottsville, 570-622-4212; Temple, 610-921-3502.

Committees: *Agriculture* (2d of 21 D): Conservation, Credit, Rural Development & Research (RMM); Department Operations, Oversight, Nutrition & Forestry. *Transportation & Infrastructure* (18th of 34 D): Aviation; Highways, Transit & Pipelines.

Group Ratings

	ADA	ACLU	AFS	LCV	ITIC	NTU	COC	ACU	NTLC	CHC
2004	70	30	100	73	50	14	67	48	14	69
2003	70	—	100	70	—	23	40	56	—	—

National Journal Ratings

	2003 LIB	—	2003 CONS		2004 LIB	—	2004 CONS
Economic	57%	—	42%		63%	—	36%
Social	52%	—	48%		49%	—	50%
Foreign	59%	—	39%		53%	—	47%

Key Votes of the 108th Congress

1. Drilling in ANWR	N	5. DC School Vouchers	N	9. Ban Same-Sex Marriage	Y
2. Approve Bush Tax Cuts	N	6. Ban Human Cloning	Y	10. Fund Iraq War	Y
3. Medicare/Rx Bill	N	7. Restrict Gun Liability	Y	11. Bar Cuba Embargo Funds	N
4. Bar Overtime Pay Regs.	Y	8. Ban Partial-Birth Abortion	Y	12. Intelligence Reorg.	Y

Election Results

2004 general	Tim Holden (D)	172,412	(59%)	($1,608,093)
	Scott Paterno (R)	113,592	(39%)	($1,057,940)
	Other	5,782	(2%)	
2004 primary	Tim Holden (D)	unopposed		
2002 general	Tim Holden (D)	103,483	(51%)	($1,714,892)
	George Gekas (R)	97,802	(49%)	($1,427,486)

Prior Winning Percentages: 2000 (66%); 1998 (61%); 1996 (59%); 1994 (57%); 1992 (52%)

The People		Race/Ethnic Origin	Ancestry		
Area size:	2,378 sq. mi.	87.3% White	German: 26.0%	Irish: 8.7%	
Urban population:	68.6%	7.3% Black	Italian: 5.1%		
Rural population:	31.4%	1.1% Asian	**2004 Presidential Vote**		
Pop. 2000:	646,420	0.1% Native Am.	Bush (R)	172,343	(58%)
Median income:	$40,473	0.0% Hawaiian	Kerry (D)	124,141	(42%)
Poverty status:	8.4%	0.9% Two+ races	Other	1,768	(1%)
Military veterans:	14.8%	0.1% Other	**2000 Presidential Vote**		
		3.2% Hispanic Origin	Bush (R)	139,932	(56%)
			Gore (D)	103,603	(41%)
			Other	6,994	(3%)
			Cook Partisan Voting Index: R + 7		

Occupation   Blue collar: 30.2%   White collar: 55.1%   Gray collar: 14.8%

Through the center of Pennsylvania flows the Susquehanna, the longest river in the East if you include the Chesapeake Bay, which is actually the flooded lower Susquehanna Valley. Starting in Cooperstown, New York, emptying into the Chesapeake next to the antique town of Havre de Grace, Maryland, the Susquehanna is the one river strong enough to break through the Appalachian chains of central Pennsylvania. But few songs are written to celebrate the Susquehanna—it has not given a name to a fever (Potomac), a school of painting (Hudson) or economics (Charles), or to a state (Delaware, Connecticut, Ohio, Mississippi, Alabama, Illinois, Missouri, Colorado, Tennessee)—and its dams are silting up and threaten environmental havoc on the tenuously recovering Chesapeake, unless the unwieldy grouping of states through which the Susquehanna runs can find a solution; already, millions of fish and fish eggs are killed each year by power plants.

The 17th Congressional District of Pennsylvania includes two distinct areas: the agricultural lands adjoining the Susquehanna River, and the industrial areas of Schuylkill and Berks Counties. The first is centered on the state capital of Harrisburg; it includes Dauphin County, part of Perry County just across the river and Lebanon County to the east. Harrisburg features a string of mansions-turned-lobbying headquarters gracefully lining the banks of the Susquehanna and boasts Pennsylvania's marvelously restored Capitol building—its dome is modeled after St. Peter's in Rome, its stairway on the Paris Opera. Nearby is Hershey, the town erected by chocolate magnate Milton S. Hershey as a carefully planned, almost utopian village for his factory workers and their families. The surrounding area, fed by a steady flow of tourists to Hersheypark, has attracted top-flight hospitals and cultivated a prosperous air; the U.S. House of Representatives held "civility retreats" here during the 1990s. Directly south of Hershey is Middletown, whose leafy, gridded streets and handsome homes give no hint that it is the location of the Three Mile Island nuclear plant, site in 1979 of the worst nuclear accident in American history.

The eastern half of the district has a grittier heritage. In Berks and Schuylkill Counties the farmers were rough-hewn and more violence-prone, and the towns existed solely to mine rich veins of anthracite coal, the primary energy source of late 19th and early 20th century America; although the big companies abandoned the mines long ago, some local entrepreneurs still go deep underground to blast their way into the anthracite. These mountain towns were less orderly, filled with tough-talking miners and factory workers who stayed menacingly in the background unless a character stumbled into the wrong roadhouse at night or the wrong diner at dawn—the Pennsylvania that John O'Hara grew up in and wrote about in the 1930s and 1940s. Pottsville, nestled amid mountains and the home of Yuengling lager (known locally as "Vitamin Y"), produced the Maroons, the team that may have won the 1925 National Football League championship (the league disputed the claim, to Pottsville's eternal chagrin) and whose ties to coal country are emblematic of the game's hardscrabble roots. Pottsville and its neighbors have never rebounded from the switch from anthracite coal to oil and natural gas for home heating: With a disproportionately aging population, Schuylkill County had 228,000 people in 1940 and 147,000 in 2004.

Politically, the 17th leans Republican. Harrisburg has been a Republican town from the days when the party seemed to conquer all in Pennsylvania; Republicans held the governorship for all but eight years from 1860 to 1934 and filled the ornate halls of the Capitol with Republican patronage hacks. Lebanon County is even more solidly Republican. Schuylkill County, in contrast, has a Democratic heritage from its mining days, though its Democrats tend to take conservative stands on cultural issues like abortion and guns. Berks County is somewhat more Republican. Overall, the district voted 56% for George W. Bush in 2000 and 58% in 2004.

The congressman from the 17th District is Tim Holden, a Democrat first elected from the old 6th District in 1992 and the winner of a 2002 battle between incumbents thrown together by redistricting. Holden comes from a political family from the coal mining hamlet of St. Clair; his great-grandfather was a coal miner who founded the forerunner to the United Mine Workers, and his father served four terms as Schuylkill County commissioner. Holden gained fame as a local football player, although tuberculosis cut short his college career. In 1985, at age 28, after selling insurance and real estate in the family business for five years, he was elected Schuylkill County sheriff. Holden's opponent in the 1992 race for an open seat was the better-financed John Jones III, a lawyer, but Holden's regular guy appeal played well in culturally conservative but economically polarized Schuylkill County; he won 52%–48%.

Holden has a moderate voting record, though a bit more conservative on cultural issues: He is one of the centrist Blue Dog Democrats and has consistently been near the center of the House. "The problems our country is facing need to be solved in a bipartisan manner," he says. "There's about 70 liberals and 70 ultraconservatives still in the House. They need to be left behind." After voting to override Bill Clinton's veto of the marriage penalty tax repeal and for cutting back the estate tax, he voted against the Bush tax cut a year later. He is anti-abortion and opposed the FDA's approval of the RU-486 drug. On the Agriculture Committee, where he is the number-two Democrat, Holden looks after dairy programs. He also has gained influence as the senior Pennsylvanian on the Transportation and Infrastructure Committee. Most of all, he has worked hard at home, talking issues and solving constituents' problems. As the Pottsville *Republican & Evening Herald* wrote, "It would be hard to imagine a legislator more precisely in tune with his county on virtually any and every issue that has come before Congress." He appears to relish his low profile and avoids the usual Capitol Hill partisanship.

That experience proved vital to Holden after redistricting in 2002. The new 17th District combined Holden's Schuylkill County base with the Harrisburg base of Republican incumbent George Gekas. A senior member of the Judiciary Committee, Gekas had not been seriously tested since he was first elected in 1982. At age 72, he was slow to learn modern campaign techniques and was showing his age; nor did he seek to influence redistricting. The Republican edge in the district favored Gekas and each was well-funded by additional expenditures by their party and interest groups. The candidates agreed on abortion and gun control; both voted to authorize the use of force in Iraq. But they had plenty of differences. Gekas usually supported business and favored more trade overseas; Holden is pro-union and has opposed new trade deals. Holden spent many hours knocking on doors in Dauphin and Lebanon County emphasizing his independence, while Gekas was less organized and slower to introduce himself to voters in Schuylkill County. Supporters of Gekas hoped that his partisan appeal, with a late appearance by George W. Bush, would turn the tide. It didn't. Holden won 51%–49%. In Dauphin County, which had the largest turnout, Gekas won 56%–44%; in Lebanon, the other part of his base, Gekas won 61%–39%. But Holden was far stronger in his base, winning Schuylkill 72%–28%.

After this setback, Republicans said Holden was a prime target for 2004. But well-known Republican officials declined to run. The Republican primary featured six candidates, including former professional football player Ron Hostetler, accounting consultant Frank Ryan and Scott Paterno, a lawyer and the son of longtime Penn State football coach Joe Paterno. None had significant political experience, nor did any break out of the pack. Paterno won the primary with 27%; his positive name identification probably was the biggest factor. Against Holden, Republicans again ran a less than stellar campaign, in which Paterno lacked a base in the district or the skills to undercut the incumbent's popularity. Paterno also suffered because House Republicans were focused on three more competitive races in the Philadelphia area and the close presidential contest in the state. Holden won 59%–39%, with 74% of the vote in Schuylkill County and an impressive 58% in Dauphin County.

EIGHTEENTH DISTRICT

Rep. Tim Murphy (R)

Elected 2002, 2d term; b. Sept. 11, 1952, Cleveland, OH; home, Upper St. Clair; Wheeling Jesuit U., B.S. 1974, Cleveland St. U., M.S. 1976, U. of Pittsburgh, Ph.D. 1979; Catholic; married (Nan Missig).

Elected Office: PA Senate, 1996–2002

Professional Career: Practicing psychologist, 1976–2002; author.

DC Office: 322 CHOB, 20515, 202-225-2301; Fax: 202-225-1844; Web site: murphy.house.gov.

District Offices: Greensburg, 724-850-7312; Pittsburgh, 412-344-5583.

Committees: *Energy & Commerce* (29th of 31 R): Commerce, Trade & Consumer Protection; Energy & Air Quality; Environment & Hazardous Materials.

Group Ratings

	ADA	ACLU	AFS	LCV	ITIC	NTU	COC	ACU	NTLC	CHC
2004	20	0	25	9	90	59	95	92	81	100
2003	10	—	13	0	—	61	97	92	—	—

National Journal Ratings

	2003 LIB	—	2003 CONS		2004 LIB	—	2004 CONS
Economic	9%	—	84%		40%	—	59%
Social	24%	—	71%		25%	—	73%
Foreign	11%	—	80%		0%	—	96%

Key Votes of the 108th Congress

1. Drilling in ANWR	Y	5. DC School Vouchers	Y	9. Ban Same-Sex Marriage	Y
2. Approve Bush Tax Cuts	Y	6. Ban Human Cloning	Y	10. Fund Iraq War	Y
3. Medicare/Rx Bill	Y	7. Restrict Gun Liability	Y	11. Bar Cuba Embargo Funds	*
4. Bar Overtime Pay Regs.	Y	8. Ban Partial-Birth Abortion	Y	12. Intelligence Reorg.	Y

Election Results

2004 general	Tim Murphy (R)	197,894	(63%)	($1,103,313)
	Mark Boles (D)	117,420	(37%)	($149,356)
2004 primary	Tim Murphy (R)	unopposed		
2002 general	Tim Murphy (R)	119,885	(60%)	($893,568)
	Jack Machek (D)	79,451	(40%)	($126,488)

The People		Race/Ethnic Origin	Ancestry	
Area size:	1,437 sq. mi.	95.4% White	German: 19.4% Irish: 12.3%	
Urban population:	84.1%	2.0% Black	Italian: 11.8%	
Rural population:	15.9%	1.3% Asian	**2004 Presidential Vote**	
Pop. 2000:	646,374	0.1% Native Am.	Bush (R) 183,210	(54%)
Median income:	$44,938	0.0% Hawaiian	Kerry (D) 154,079	(46%)
Poverty status:	6.3%	0.6% Two+ races	Other 1,275	(0%)
Military veterans:	14.9%	0.1% Other	**2000 Presidential Vote**	
		0.6% Hispanic Origin	Bush (R) 154,252	(52%)
			Gore (D) 139,346	(47%)
			Other 5,240	(2%)
			Cook Partisan Voting Index: R + 2	

Occupation	Blue collar: 13.7%	White collar: 20.0%	Gray collar: 63.3%

Pittsburgh was built on the unlikeliest terrain of any of our major cities. Just about the only level places in the city and its suburbs are the bottomlands along the rivers. Everything else is hills that approach the magnitude of mountains. Only a propitious location, where the Allegheny and Monongahela rivers join to form the Ohio, and the confluence of economically valuable natural resources, coal from the mountains and iron ore from the Great Lakes, can explain the fact that a vast metropolitan area has been built on such land. The great cities of California were built around and over mountains; but they are vast expanses of contiguous communities, most of them little distinguishable from the next. The cities and towns of greater Pittsburgh, in contrast, are discontinuous, separated from each other not just by miles but by altitude. So the region's high-income suburbs and its gritty factory towns are not concentrated in one quarter, but are scattered all around. This is long-settled country, with many more old towns than sparkling new suburbs.

The 18th Congressional District of Pennsylvania covers an irregularly shaped swath of the southern part of the Pittsburgh metropolitan area and was designed by Republican redistricters in Harrisburg to maximize the Republican vote. It includes most of southern Allegheny County, most of Westmoreland County to the east and most of Washington County to the west; it stretches from the Pittsburgh city limit to the West Virginia border. It contains the well-run Pittsburgh International Airport in Moon Township, where the financial troubles of USAirways cost thousands of jobs and reduced operations, but created opportunity by opening the gates to low-fare carriers. To the east are Monroeville, Greensburg and Ligonier, where a fort was an important frontier outpost in the French and Indian War, but the area is now green with prosperity and dotted with the vast estates of Mellons and other scions of Pittsburgh's industrial elite; to the west is Canonsburg, which has unveiled a "singing sculpture" of its most famous son, the crooner Perry Como. The district's backbone is comprised of middle- to upper-middle-class bedroom suburbs, like Mount Lebanon and Upper St. Clair in Allegheny County and Penn Township and Greensburg in Westmoreland County. These areas lean Republican, but not overwhelmingly so. Democrats grumble that the Republican trend in Westmoreland reflects the local influence of the *Tribune-Review*, the Greensburg-based newspaper owned by conservative Richard Mellon Scaife, named by Clintonite conspiracy theorists as the mastermind of the vast right wing conspiracy. Although John Kerry spent some time at his wife Teresa Heinz Kerry's estate in Fox Chapel, the Democratic ticket did not do well here in 2004. George W. Bush carried the district with 52% of the vote in 2000 and 54% in 2004.

The congressman from the 18th District is Tim Murphy, a Republican first elected in 2002. He grew up in Cleveland in a family of 11 children. He graduated from Wheeling Jesuit University, got a Ph.D. from the University of Pittsburgh and became a child psychologist. He worked in several Pittsburgh area hospitals and was an adjunct faculty member in public health and pediatrics at the University of Pittsburgh. He became a public figure while offering medical advice as "Dr. Tim" in television appearances and on radio talk shows; he co-authored *The Angry Child: Regaining Control When Your Child is Out of Control.* In 1996 Murphy was elected to the state Senate.

Redistricters drew the 18th with Murphy in mind. But they also included in the district the house of Democratic Congressman Frank Mascara, so that he would not be in the same district with 12th District Democrat John Murtha. Mascara ran against Murtha anyway and lost by a wide margin. Mascara's decision not to run here was an acknowledgement of Murphy's strength. Murphy was unopposed in the Republican primary. He presented himself as an experienced and accomplished legislator who opposed abortion and supported gun rights. Murphy had extensive support from Pennsylvania and national Republicans and outspent Democratic nominee Jack Machek, an school district administrator, $894,000 to Machek's $126,000. Murphy's support of the Republican plan for prescription drugs for seniors was evidently not a handicap in a district that has a high percentage of elderly residents. Murphy won 60%–40%—an impressive showing in an open seat race.

In the House, Murphy had a mostly conservative voting record, especially on foreign-policy issues. He discovered that his new job was a big step from Harrisburg. "What hit me with a broadside was that, as a congressman, you don't have to convince people across the state, but people across the country," he told the *Tribune-Review.* He sponsored a resolution encouraging Americans to invest in Iraqi schools and hospitals. In January 2005, he made a giant step by winning a seat on the Energy and Commerce Committee. That gives him an opportunity to focus on health care issues, including medical malpractice reform, Medicaid restructuring and new medical technologies. He co-chaired with Patrick Kennedy the 21st Century Health Care Caucus, and he also co-chaired the Mental Health Caucus, where he focused in particular on veterans with mental illness.

He won reelection 63%–37% against pediatrician Mark Boles, a former professional acquaintance and a political neophyte.

NINETEENTH DISTRICT

Rep. Todd Platts (R)

Elected 2000, 3d term; b. Mar. 5, 1962, York; home, York; Shippensburg U., B.S. 1984, Pepperdine U., J.D. 1991; Episcopalian; married (Leslie).

Elected Office: PA House of Reps., 1992–2000.

Professional Career: Practicing atty., 1991–93.

DC Office: 1032 LHOB, 20515, 202-225-5836; Fax: 202-226-1000; Web site: www.house.gov/platts.

District Offices: Carlisle, 717-249-0190; Gettysburg, 717-338-1919; York, 717-600-1919.

Committees: *Education & the Workforce* (10th of 27 R): Education Reform; Employer-Employee Relations. *Government Reform* (10th of 23 R): Government Management, Finance & Accountability (Chmn.); National Security, Emerging Threats & International Relations. *Transportation & Infrastructure* (22d of 41 R): Highways, Transit & Pipelines; Railroads.

Group Ratings

	ADA	ACLU	AFS	LCV	ITIC	NTU	COC	ACU	NTLC	CHC
2004	20	5	13	9	60	52	95	84	73	76
2003	20	—	25	25	—	56	90	80	—	—

National Journal Ratings

	2003 LIB	—	2003 CONS		2004 LIB	—	2004 CONS
Economic	45%	—	55%		46%	—	53%
Social	44%	—	55%		34%	—	65%
Foreign	36%	—	63%		17%	—	78%

Key Votes of the 108th Congress

1. Drilling in ANWR	Y	5. DC School Vouchers	N	9. Ban Same-Sex Marriage	Y
2. Approve Bush Tax Cuts	Y	6. Ban Human Cloning	Y	10. Fund Iraq War	Y
3. Medicare/Rx Bill	Y	7. Restrict Gun Liability	Y	11. Bar Cuba Embargo Funds	N
4. Bar Overtime Pay Regs.	N	8. Ban Partial-Birth Abortion	Y	12. Intelligence Reorg.	Y

Election Results

2004 general	Todd Platts (R)	224,274	(91%)	($171,605)
	Charles Steel (Green)	8,890	(4%)	
	Other	11,930	(5%)	
2004 primary	Todd Platts (R)	unopposed		
2002 general	Todd Platts (R)	143,097	(91%)	($224,480)
	Ben Price (Green)	7,900	(5%)	
	Michael Paoletta (Lib)	6,008	(4%)	

Prior Winning Percentages: 2000 (73%)

The People		Race/Ethnic Origin	Ancestry	
Area size:	1,666 sq. mi.	92.2% White	German: 28.1%	Irish: 9.0%
Urban population:	71.4%	2.9% Black	USA: 6.7%	
Rural population:	28.6%	1.1% Asian	**2004 Presidential Vote**	
Pop. 2000:	646,389	0.1% Native Am.	Bush (R) 198,192 (64%)	
Median income:	$45,345	0.0% Hawaiian	Kerry (D) 110,274 (36%)	
Poverty status:	6.8%	0.9% Two+ races	Other 1,515 (0%)	
Military veterans:	14.3%	0.1% Other	**2000 Presidential Vote**	
		2.7% Hispanic Origin	Bush (R) 153,892 (61%)	
			Gore (D) 90,125 (36%)	
			Other 6,766 (3%)	
			Cook Partisan Voting Index: R +12	

Occupation	Blue collar: 29.3%	White collar: 57.1%	Gray collar: 13.6%

The Mason-Dixon Line, the historic boundary between Maryland and Pennsylvania, runs through some of the country's most pleasant rolling farmlands, west of the Susquehanna River up through the first of the Appalachian chains. This area was home to the westernmost capital of the United States during the Revolutionary War: the small city of York, capital from September 1777 to June 1778. York is where the Continental Congress passed the Articles of Confederation, received word from Benjamin Franklin in Paris that the French would help the colonies with money and ships and issued the first proclamation calling for a national day of thanksgiving. A little more than four score years later, Robert E. Lee's Confederate troops crossed over this invisible line and were repulsed in the Battle of Gettysburg in July 1863. Not much today suggests that this region was either a frontier or the object of bloody struggle: The green farmland seems peaceful, prosperous and mostly undisturbed by the current era's commercial trappings and stylistic excesses; this is where Dwight D. Eisenhower, a man of Pennsylvania Dutch stock, chose to quietly spend his retirement years.

For more than 50 miles, the Mason-Dixon Line forms the southern boundary of the 19th Congressional District of Pennsylvania, which includes all of Adams and York Counties and part of Cumberland County to the north—relatively fast-growing areas in slow-growing Pennsylvania. The 19th takes in the fruit belt of Adams County, the Harrisburg suburbs across the Susquehanna and part of the old town of Carlisle, with Dickinson College, the Carlisle Barracks, and the U.S. Army War College, where George W. Bush in May 2004 described his plans for Iraq and where free-wheeling discussions of military operations sometimes create consternation elsewhere. Hanover, in York County, is one of the world's snack headquarters—home to Snyder's of Hanover, which makes one of every four pretzels sold in the U.S. (people in this area take their pretzels seriously), as well as potato-chip giant Utz Quality Foods. The district's biggest city is York, the site of Harley-Davidson's largest manufacturing plant and the USA Weightlifting Hall of Fame at the York Barbell Company. York is a place where many residents commute less than an hour to work in Baltimore and where the Orioles, not the more distant Phillies, are the baseball team of choice; a few hardy souls who like the inexpensive housing commute from here to jobs in Washington. The city also hosts a rapidly growing Hispanic population, mainly Puerto Rican, but with increasing numbers of Mexicans; in Gettysburg, many Hispanics work the abundant orchards. Politically, the 19th is heavily Republican. George W. Bush won 61% of the vote here in 2000 and 64% in 2004.

The congressman from the 19th District is Todd Platts, a Republican first elected in 2000. Platts grew up in York, graduated from Shippensburg University and Pepperdine University School of Law. In 1992, at age 30, after practicing law in Lancaster, he was elected to the state House of Representatives, where he served four terms.

In 2000, Platts was the first to announce his candidacy after longtime Congressman Bill Goodling, chairman of the Education and the Workforce Committee, announced his retirement. Platts's chief primary opponents were state Representative Al Masland, attorney and Goodling-endorsed Dick Stewart and Charlie Gerow, head of the state Citizens Against Government Waste. The campaign motto for Platts, who refused contributions from political action committees and was outspent by his chief Republican rivals, was "Putting People First" (his conservative supporters apparently weren't bothered by the fact that the phrase had been the title of a book by Bill Clinton). Platts won with 33% to 29% for Masland and 19% for Stewart, rolling up huge margins in his home base of York County. In the general, Platts won 73%–26%, after spending about one-third the amount of the average House freshman that year.

In the House, Platts has a comparatively moderate voting record. He has taken a special interest in oversight of federal agencies: He pushed legislation to require review of all government programs at least once every five years to evaluate their performance, and he chaired hearings where he demanded that the Homeland Security Department improve its accounting practices. He sponsored legislation to overturn a federal court ruling that he said created loopholes in the Whistleblower Protection Act. On the highway bill, Platts pushed for a new transit center and road improvements in Gettysburg. He has gained seniority on the Education and the Workforce, and Transportation and Infrastructure committees, and now chairs the Government Management, Finance and Accountability Subcommittee on the Government Reform Committee. Inside Congress, he risked the opprobrium of many colleagues by proposing with Democrat Marty Meehan a smoking ban on the House side of the Capitol.

Other than a perfunctory primary challenge in 2002, Platts has twice been reelected without major party opposition.

★ RHODE ISLAND ★

The tiny city-state with a mouthful of an official name, Rhode Island and Providence Plantations, has as turbulent a political history as any state in the Union. A successful trading community since the 1600s, a leader in manufacturing since Samuel Slater replicated from memory an English water-powered cotton textile mill in Pawtucket in 1791, Rhode Island also had its beginning as an upstart community, a refuge for religious dissenters, "the sewer of New England," as the orthodox Cotton Mather put it. Rhode Island profited from slavery (two-thirds of America's slaves arrived on ships owned by Rhode Islanders) and war (the state boomed during the Civil War), and carried its tradition of tolerating just about anything into its politics. Rhode Island refused to pay its share for the Revolutionary War, declined to send delegates to the 1787 Constitutional Convention and delayed joining the Union until the other 12 states had, prompting George Washington to say, "Rhode Island still perseveres in that impolitic, unjust— and one might add without much impropriety—scandalous conduct, which seems to have marked all her public counsels of late." The new nation's first bank failure occurred here in 1809, when a bank capitalized at $45 issued $800,000 in bank notes. In the 1840s, conflict between hard money merchants and soft money farmers resulted in two state governments and a conflict known as Dorr's War, with the outcome determined when merchant Dorr's two ancient cannons failed to fire.

Then, in the 1930s, Rhode Island had something resembling a political revolution. Thousands of immigrants from French Canada, Ireland and Italy came to Rhode Island to work in the textile mills and this colony of dissident Protestants became the most heavily Catholic state in the nation. Yankee Republicans tried to appeal to Catholics by running French Canadians for office. But national events—Al Smith's candidacy in 1928, when he carried Rhode Island, and Franklin Roosevelt's New Deal—moved the Catholics toward the Democrats. Then came the revolution: in 1935, the Democrats under Governor Theodore Green, although they had won only 20 of the 42 state Senate seats, refused to seat two Republicans. With the lieutenant governor's tie-breaker, they voted Democrats into the seats, and proceeded in 14 minutes to declare the state Supreme Court seats vacant, abolish state boards that controlled Democratic cities, strengthen the power of the governor and reorganize state government to purge Republicans. This ended the direct political control of Rhode Island's "Five Families"—the Browns, Metcalfs, Goddards, Lippitts and Chafees—who owned or ran many of the textile mills, the Rhode Island Hospital Trust (long the largest bank), the Providence *Journal-Bulletin*, Brown University, the Rhode Island School of Design and the state Republican Party. The Democrats have won

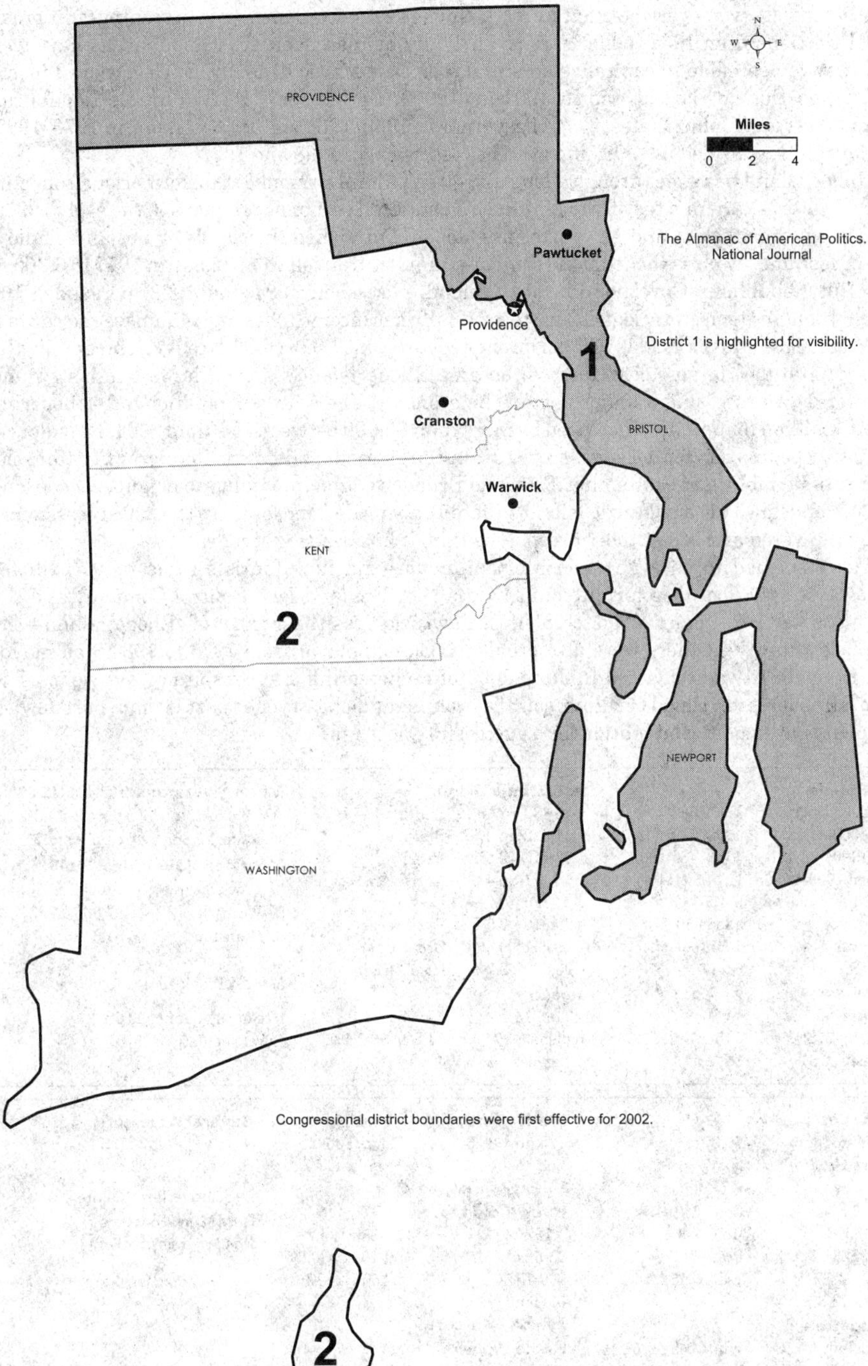

PROVIDENCE

N
W ⊕ E
S

Miles
0   2   4

PAWTUCKET

The Almanac of American Politics.
National Journal

Providence

District 1 is highlighted for visibility.

1

Cranston

BRISTOL

Warwick

KENT

2

NEWPORT

WASHINGTON

Congressional district boundaries were first effective for 2002.

2

most elections with the lion's share of votes from Rhode Island's Catholic majority, starting with Green's election in 1936, at age 69, to the first of his four terms as U.S. senator. From 1940 to 1980, Democrats won every election for U.S. House seats; its Democratic percentages in presidential elections from 1968 to 2004 are rivaled only by Massachusetts. Republicans have won when they've been able to capitalize on scandal or Democratic disarray, as Governors Lincoln Almond and Donald Carcieri did in 1994 and 2002. But the only really durable Republican politician has been John Chafee, elected governor in 1962, 1964 and 1966, senator in 1976, 1982, 1988 and 1994, who died in 1999; and even he lost twice, in 1968 and 1972.

Rhode Island has gone through a long and often painful economic transformation, from blue collar to white collar, from textiles to high-tech. It suffered economic problems in the early 1990s, as the submarine factory and Navy base at Quonset Point shed thousands of jobs and employment in costume jewelry, Rhode Island's major manufacturer, fell from 32,500 in 1977 to 6,300 in 2000. But Republican Governor Lincoln Almond, elected in 1994 and 1998, persuaded the overwhelmingly Democratic legislature to gradually cut income taxes and eliminate the car tax, and Providence Mayor Buddy Cianci promoted brilliantly successful redevelopment in the state's capital and largest city. Tourism became Rhode Island's second largest industry, and computer data processing a major part of the economy. The state's population, after hovering around 1 million for decades, increased by more than 80,000 between 1990 and 2004. Providence, after losing population for decades, grew 10% in that period, and Latino immigrants—from the Dominican Republic and Guatemala, Peru and Ecuador—brought vitality to neighborhoods long given up for dead. This new Rhode Island suffered only modest job losses in the 2001 recession; it quickly recovered and is now more prosperous than it has been for decades.

There seemed to be a new sense of optimism—and fun. Tourists came to see Nibbles Woodaway, the 58-foot-long termite built by the New England Pest Control Company and the state marketed Mr. Potato Head, created in Pawtucket, as the symbol of "Rhode Island—the birthplace of fun." Yet there were also problems. Cianci, mayor from 1975 to 1984, and mayor again from 1991, was convicted in June 2002 of racketeering and conspiracy and went off to prison. His successor, David Cicilline, son of a prominent mob lawyer, is part Italian, part Jewish and openly gay: a new combination for a successful politician.

The People		Race/Ethnic Origin			Military veterans: 102,494 (12.8%)	
Pop. 2004 (est):	1,080,632	858,433	81.9%	White	WWII: 25.4%	Korea: 14.9%
Pop. 2000:	1,048,319	41,922	4.0%	Black	Vietnam: 29.6%	Gulf War: 7.0%
Pop. 1990:	1,003,464	23,416	2.2%	Asian	**Most populous cities (2003):**	
Change 1990–2000:	Up 4.5%	4,181	0.4%	Native Am.	1. Providence	176,365
% of U.S. total:	0.4%	320	0.0%	Hawaiian	2. Warwick	87,365
Pop. rank:	43d of 50	20,816	2.0%	Two+ races	3. Cranston	81,679
Area size:	1,545 sq. mi.	8,411	0.8%	Other	4. Pawtucket	74,330
State Native:	61.4%	90,820	8.7%	Hisp. Origin	5. East Providence	49,906
Non-citizen:	6.0%	**Ancestry**				
Language		Italian: 14.1%		Irish: 13.7%	Urban population: 90.9%	
English: 77.2%	Other Eur.:12.8%	English: 8.9%		French: 8.1%	Rural population: 9.1%	
Spanish: 7.5%		Portuguese: 6.5%				

Education		Work Sector		General Assembly	
H.S. Grad:	78.0%	Private: 80.6%	Govt: 13.8%	Senate	33 D 5 R
College Grad:	25.6%	Self: 5.4%	Family: 0.2%	House	59 D 16 R
Industry		Unemployment: 5.6%		Legislative Term Limits: No	
Agri: 0.5%	Con: 5.4%	**Household Income**		**Registered Voters**	
Fin: 6.9%	Info: 2.3%	<15k: 17.7%	15-35k: 24.2%	No party registration	
Mfg: 20.3%	Prof: 31.3%	35-50k: 15.7%	50-100k: 30.8%		
Public: 4.5%	Trade: 15.5%	100-150k: 7.6%	>150k: 3.9%		
Other: 13.3%		Median: $42,090			
Occupation		Poverty status: 11.9%			
Blue collar: 22.9%	White collar: 61.1%	**Home Value**			
Gray collar: 16.0%		<50k: 2.0%	50-100k: 21.0%	100-200k: 59.6%	200-300k: 11.1%
		300-500k: 4.5%	>500k: 1.8%	Median: $130,500	

Presidential politics   Rhode Island is almost always one of the most Democratic states in presidential elections—over the last generation, the most Democratic, though just a little bit less so lately. It voted 61%–32% for Al Gore in 2000—his best state in the country—but gave its neighbor John Kerry a somewhat smaller margin of 59%–39% in 2004, less than his margin in Massachusetts. Turnout in 2004 was 437,000, beating the record of 432,000 in 1980. Protestants, once the Republican base here, gave George W. Bush only a 52%–47% majority; Catholics, who made up 57% of the voters, went 59%–40% for Kerry. Rhode Island's Catholic majority is heavily Democratic and, interestingly, pro-choice on abortion: In states where Catholics are beleaguered minorities they may stand together and strongly oppose abortion; here, where they're the strong majority and where the mostly Mediterranean Catholics traditionally didn't pay strict attention to the mostly Irish priests, they come out against the church position.

2004 Presidential Vote		
Kerry (D)	259,760	(59%)
Bush (R)	169,046	(39%)
Nader (Ref)	4,651	(1%)
Other	3,677	(1%)

2004 Democratic Presidential Primary		
Kerry (D)	25,466	(71%)
Edwards (D)	6,635	(19%)
Dean (D)	1,425	(4%)
Kucinich (D)	1,054	(3%)
Uncommitted	415	(1%)
Other	764	(2%)

2000 Presidential Vote		
Gore (D)	249,508	(61%)
Bush (R)	130,555	(32%)
Nader (Green)	25,052	(6%)
Other	3,668	(1%)

Rhode Island holds a presidential primary the same day as Massachusetts, usually with the lowest turnout rate in the nation. It has not won much attention. In 2000, when the primary was held on March 7 and the outcomes were not entirely clear, 83,000 voted. Al Gore beat Bill Bradley 57%–41%—one of Bradley's better performances—and John McCain beat George W. Bush 60%–36%. In 2004, when the primary was held March 2 and the outcomes reasonably clear, 38,000 voted. The results mirrored those next-door: Kerry beat John Edwards 71%–19% here and 72%–18% in Massachusetts.

Congressional districting   Rhode Island legislators had a heck of a time redrawing the boundaries of their own districts in 2001 and 2002; voters in 1994 adopted a constitutional amendment reducing the size of the state House after the 2000 Census from 100 to 75 seats and the state Senate from 50 to 38. Redistricting the state's two congressional districts was much easier. Rhode Island's two congressional districts have remained pretty much the same since 1842, except for the period from 1912 to 1932 when the state had three districts. Providence is split and both districts are overwhelmingly Democratic. For 2002, 14,000 people needed to be moved from the 2d District to the 1st. Incumbents Patrick Kennedy and James Langevin agreed on a change in Providence that gave Kennedy his old state legislative district near Providence College.

109th Congress Lineup
2 D

108th Congress Lineup
2 D

Governor

Donald Carcieri (R)

Elected 2002, term expires Jan. 2007, 1st term; b. Dec. 16, 1942, East Greenwich; home, East Greenwich; Brown U., B.A. 1965; Catholic; married (Suzanne).

Professional Career: High schl. teacher, 1965–71; Banker, Old Stone Bank, 1971–81; Director, Catholic Relief Services, Jamaica, 1981–83; CEO, Cookson America, 1983–97.

Office: The State House, Room 115, Providence, 02903, 401-222-2080; Fax: 401-861-5894; Web site: www.governor.state.ri.us.

Election Results

2002 general	Donald Carcieri (R)	181,687	(55%)
	Myrth York (D)	150,147	(45%)
2002 primary	Donald Carcieri (R)	17,227	(67%)
	James Bennett (R)	8,518	(33%)
1998 general	Lincoln Almond (R)	156,180	(51%)
	Myrth York (D)	129,105	(42%)
	Robert J. Healey (Cool Moose)	19,250	(6%)
	Other	1,910	(1%)

Donald Carcieri, elected governor of Rhode Island in 2002, grew up in East Greenwich, on Narragansett Bay, where his father was a teacher and coach at the town high school and a quahogger in the summer. East Greenwich today is one of Rhode Island's most affluent suburbs; in the 1950s, Carcieri says, it was a modest town of fishermen and farmers. Carcieri was class president and a top athlete in high school and attended Brown on scholarship and played varsity football and baseball. He taught high school math in Newport and then in Concord, Massachusetts. Then he went to work for Old Stone Bank and in 10 years became executive vice president. In 1981 he moved to Kingston, Jamaica, to be head of the Catholic Relief Service's West Indies operation. In 1983 he returned to Rhode Island and went to work for Cookson America, the U.S. branch of a London conglomerate that owns dozens of manufacturing, electronic and precious metals companies around the world. He rose to become CEO of Cookson America and a joint managing director of Cookson Group Worldwide. He moved Cookson America's headquarters to the former Providence train station, overlooking Burnside Park and the State House. He retired in 1997 and in 2002 started running for governor.

The incumbent, Republican Lincoln Almond, was ineligible to run for a third term. Three Democrats and two Republicans ran to succeed Almond; Carcieri was the only one with no experience in public office, though he did serve as the Bush chairman in Rhode Island in 2000. His primary opponent was James Bennett, former chairman of the Convention Center Authority and owner of Mitkem, an environmental testing laboratory. Carcieri and Bennett mostly agreed on priorities—rein in the legislature, cut spending increases, promote economic development. Both avoided Rhode Island's matching fund public financing and spent their own money on their campaigns—$600,000 for Carcieri and $275,000 for Bennett. Bennett spent much of his money on fierce negative ads against Carcieri, charging that under his leadership Cookson's debt rose, layoffs increased, and Carcieri was given a $2.6 million golden handshake. But Carcieri won the September primary 67%–33%.

Running again as the Democratic nominee was Myrth York, who lost to Almond in 1994 and 1998, with a liberal message. She had a new team of consultants and ran ads showing her family. Her father started a chemical equipment company, and she manages her family's money; she spent $2 million of her own money before the primary.

The *Providence Journal* post-primary poll showed York ahead 49%–35%, but she had led in early polls in 1994 and 1998 as well. Their differing stances were apparent in a September debate. York said, "I have a knowledge of government and a knowledge of how to get things done in government. Government is there to provide opportunity for folks." Carcieri said, "I believe if real change is going to happen in the state, it's going to have to come from somebody who owes nothing to the system, somebody from outside." Carcieri pledged not to raise taxes in his first year; York said she didn't want to but wouldn't make a pledge. York called for new prescription drug and education programs; Carcieri said economic development was his goal. The *Providence Journal's* M. Charles Bakst said that York sounded scripted and Carcieri likeable.

In mid-October York started running a series of negative ads about Cookson. One said the company brokered a "tin mining deal" that ravaged an Amazon rain forest, another that it owned a plant in Philadelphia that released hazardous lead into the neighborhood, a third with neighbors of the plant denouncing Carcieri. A radio ad talked about an accident in which 15 Amazon miners were killed. Carcieri's pollster said that his polls showed Carcieri behind after the primary, drawing even in mid-October and gaining rapidly as York's negative spots were airing. The *Journal's* polls and the election result suggest this was accurate. Carcieri won 55%–45%. York won big in Providence but in the rest of the state carried only East Providence and the tiny textile mill town of Central Falls. Altogether York spent $3.8 million of her own money, Carcieri $1.5 million of his.

Carcieri faced an overwhelmingly Democratic legislature (32–6 in the Senate, 63–11–1 in the House) but posted early achievements. In January 2003 he won praise for scheduling monthly office hours for average citizens to meet the governor for a 10-minute private visit; he said he got the idea from former New Mexico Governor Gary Johnson. He was tested in February 2003, when a nightclub fire in West Warwick killed 100 people and injured many others. In a state with only one million residents, nearly everyone knew someone affected by the tragedy. At a Warwick church memorial service several days afterwards, Carcieri stood in the back of the church greeting mourners; his empathy, decisiveness and calm resolve in the days after the fire won him much acclaim. In July, he signed the Comprehensive Fire Safety Act, requiring most nightclubs to install sprinklers, banning pyrotechnics from all but the largest venues, and eliminating a grandfather clause that exempted buildings constructed before the state fire code was written. State officials called the new fire regulations the toughest in the nation.

He held a weekly deli lunch with legislators and got them to agree to send to the voters a measure strengthening the governor's appointment authority on commissions and boards. For more than three centuries dating back to the original colonial charter, the General Assembly has had wide-ranging powers, including the authority to appoint members to, and have legislators serve on, hundreds of boards and commissions that make state policy and control billions in state assets. Critics claim this has encouraged political patronage, cronyism and a culture of behind-the-scenes dealmaking; voters thought so too after a decade of assorted scandals that brought down a state supreme court justice, and sent former Governor Edward DiPrete and Providence Mayor Buddy Cianci to prison. In a referendum in 2004, the "separation of powers" measure passed 78%–22%.

But, like his predecessor Lincoln Almond, Carcieri ran into resistance when it came time to limit spending. Almond had lost control of spending because of the Democrats' huge majorities in the legislature; Carcieri, also facing huge majorities, vetoed the budget in July 2003 but was overridden. In 2004, Carcieri proposed cutting $7.9 million from public schools and shifting some money to charter and alternative high schools but the legislature nixed his proposals and kept funding at the same levels. He vetoed the $5.9 billion budget, calling it "seriously flawed" and saying there was "too much spending, too much taxing and too many special interests", and again the legislature overrode his veto, approving tax increases on hotel rooms, cell phone usage and on cigarettes, raising the price of cigarettes to the highest in the nation.

Even before the tax hike, the price of cigarettes was already high enough to attract smokers from Rhode Island and surrounding states to a tax-free smoke shop run by the Narragansett Indian Tribe. The tribe had opened the shop in Charlestown in 2003 after Carcieri and the legislature refused to place on the ballot a referendum on a Foxwoods-style Indian casino. Carcieri said that the tribe was flouting state law by not charging taxes; he claimed the tribe was blackmailing the state when it made closure contingent on his support for a casino. After a state judge issued a warrant, Carcieri ordered a state police raid in July 2003. Tribe members physically resisted the move to close down the shop and a donnybrook ensued. Scenes of Indians wrestling and battling with cops were televised across the country; Chief Sachem Matthew Thomas and seven other tribe members were arrested. This was a black eye for the administration. It forced the governor to create an independent review panel that concluded that both sides were at fault, the police for their strategy and the tribe for actively resisting. "I think there is ample blame to go around," Carcieri said.

Carcieri has said he will seek reelection in 2006. Lieutenant Governor Charles Fogarty is a likely challenger.

Senior Senator

Jack Reed (D)

Elected 1996, seat up 2008, 2d term; b. Nov. 12, 1949, Providence; home, Cranston; U.S. Military Acad., West Point, B.S. 1971, Harvard U., M.P.P. 1973, J.D. 1982; Catholic; married (Julia Hart).

Military Career: Army, 1967–79; Army Reserves, 1979–91.

Elected Office: RI Senate, 1984–90; U.S. House of Reps., 1990–96.

Professional Career: Assoc. Prof., U.S. Military Acad. at West Point, 1978–79; Practicing atty., 1982–90.

DC Office: 728 HSOB, 20510, 202-224-4642; Fax: 202-224-4680; Web site: reed.senate.gov.

State Offices: Cranston, 401-943-3100; Providence, 401-528-5200.

Committees: *Armed Services*: Airland; Emerging Threats & Capabilities (RMM); Seapower; Strategic Forces. *Banking, Housing & Urban Affairs*: Financial Institutions; Housing & Transportation (RMM); Securities & Investment. *Health, Education, Labor & Pensions*: Bioterrorism & Public Health Preparedness; Education & Early Childhood Development. *Joint Economic Committee*.

Group Ratings

	ADA	ACLU	AFS	LCV	ITIC	NTU	COC	ACU	NTLC	CHC
2004	100	78	100	100	42	17	35	0	8	0
2003	100	—	100	95	—	23	26	20	—	—

National Journal Ratings

	2003 LIB	—	2003 CONS		2004 LIB	—	2004 CONS
Economic	93%	—	0%		79%	—	13%
Social	85%	—	0%		82%	—	0%
Foreign	90%	—	0%		95%	—	1%

Key Votes of the 108th Congress

1. Ban Drilling in ANWR	Y	5. Energy Bill	N	9. Ban Same-Sex Marriage	N
2. Approve Bush Tax Cuts	N	6. Support Roe v. Wade	Y	10. Ban Bunker-Buster Bomb	Y
3. Medicare/Rx Bill	N	7. Ban Partial-Birth Abortion	N	11. Fund Iraq War	Y
4. Bar Overtime Pay Regs.	Y	8. Assault Weapons Ban	Y	12. Restrict Missile Defense	Y

Election Results

2002 general	Jack Reed (D)	253,773	(78%)	($1,767,967)
	Robert Tingle (R)	69,808	(22%)	
2002 primary	Jack Reed (D)	unopposed		
1996 general	Jack Reed (D)	230,676	(63%)	($2,732,011)
	Nancy J. Mayer (R)	127,368	(35%)	($773,789)

Prior Winning Percentages: 1994 House (68%); 1992 House (71%); 1990 House (59%)

Jack Reed, Rhode Island's senior senator, was elected to the House in 1990 and the Senate in 1996. He grew up in working-class Cranston, the son of a school custodian; he graduated from West Point, served in the 82d Airborne, got a degree at Harvard's Kennedy School, then taught at West Point. In 1979 he retired from the Army and went to Harvard Law School. He practiced law briefly in Washington and then in Providence. In 1984, at 35, he beat an incumbent in the primary for state Senate, where he served for six years, was close to the party leadership and built a good reputation. When Republican Claudine Schneider left the House to run against Senator Claiborne Pell in 1990, Reed ran for the House seat, overcoming several better-known candidates in the primary, and winning with 59% over Save the Bay Executive Director Trudy Coxe in the general.

Reed compiled a substantially, though not quite totally, liberal record in the House. On the Education and the Workforce Committee he worked for the Goals 2000 Act and on reauthorization of the Elementary and Secondary Education Act.

In 1995, when Pell announced his retirement after 36 years in the Senate, Reed almost immediately started running. Reed was easily nominated and faced state Treasurer Nancy Mayer in the general. National Republicans spent nearly $1 million on ads attacking Reed as a liberal for opposing workfare and for supporting labor unions; in liberal, heavily unionized Rhode Island these did not hurt him and may have helped. Mayer's campaign was overshadowed by Reed's: She spent $773,000 and he spent $2.7 million. His biography was his message: Reed launched his campaign in a school conference room named after his late father, stressed how he came up from humble beginnings by hard work and called for education spending to help others rise as he had. That message, and his pleasant, unassuming demeanor evidently touched a chord. He won 63%–35%, an impressive first Senate victory.

In the Senate, Reed has a liberal voting record. He serves on the HELP Committee and has sought to amend major bills. When the Bush administration called for cuts in Low-Income Home Energy Assistance in 2002, he called for increases. He has worked on the national project to eliminate lead poisoning in children by 2010, and criticized the administration for not spending more.

Reed is one of the few senators of his generation with military experience. He was appointed to the governing board of West Point in 1998 and got a seat on the Armed Services Committee in January 1999. He wants to consolidate the Naval War College and the Naval Undersea Warfare Center, two of the remaining Rhode Island military facilities; defense jobs in the state declined from 44,000 in 1970 to 8,000 in 1999. He supported Bill Clinton's bombing strikes in Afghanistan and Sudan in 1998, and in October 2002 voted against the Iraq war resolution. In December 2002 he led the successful fight in committee to cut $15 million off research into a bunker buster nuclear weapon and $812 million off the missile defense budget. "Every billion dollars spent on missile defense is a billion not spent on counterterrorism efforts." He has sought to increase permanently the size of the Army. In October 2003 the Senate voted 52–45 for his amendment to increase the Army by 10,000 troops; it was dropped in conference. In March 2004 he and Chuck Hagel called for a permanent increase of 30,000, rather than the 30,000 increase for only four years announced by Defense Secretary Donald Rumsfeld. In June the Senate voted for an increase of 20,000; Reed sought to have the increase registered in the base budget, not in the supplemental appropriation.

Reed was critical of the U.S. performance in Iraq after the initial military victory. In March 2004 he argued that the United Nations must approve a resolution to create an interim government. In May 2004 he said military intelligence officers in the Abu Ghraib prison "seemed to think there was authority" to violate international treaties. In September 2004 he found the reports of Army General George Fay and former Defense Secretary James Schlesinger incomplete on the subject of prison abuses. He opposed the nomination of Francis Harvey to be secretary of the Army. In 2005, on his fifth trip to Iraq, he summarized his approach: "My job is to be critical about what's going on and what needs to be improved. I think my criticism has been accurate, certainly in the operations in this region, in that we didn't organize ourselves for the appropriate occupation and stabilization" after the overthrow of Saddam Hussein. He was one of 12 Democrats who voted against the confirmation of Condoleezza Rice as secretary of state.

In July 2001, after Democrats got their majority in the Senate, Reed got a seat on Appropriations. But when Democrats lost their majority in the 2002 election, he was rotated off the committee and did not get back on in 2005.

In Rhode Island politics, Reed has always been his own man, unentangled with the various machine politicians who come and go. In 2002, against a pit manager at Foxwoods Resort Casino, he was reelected 78%–22%. This is a Senate seat whose members have had long tenures. Theodore Green, elected at 69, served 24 years; Claiborne Pell, elected at 41, served 36 years. Reed, elected just before turning 47, has the prospect of long service before him.

Junior Senator

Lincoln Chafee (R)

Appointed Nov. 1999, seat up 2006, 1st full term; b. Mar. 26, 1953, Warwick; home, Warwick; Brown U., B.A., 1975; Episcopalian; married (Stephanie).

Elected Office: Warwick city council, 1986–92; Warwick mayor, 1992–99.

Professional Career: Farrier, 1976–83; Cranston Print Works, 1984–85; Rhode Island Forging Steel, 1985–86; Planner, General Dynamics, 1986–90; Exec. dir., Northeast Corridor Initiative, 1990–92.

DC Office: 141-A RSOB, 20510, 202-224-2921; Fax: 202-228-2853; Web site: chafee.senate.gov.

State Offices: Newport, 401-845-0700; Providence, 401-453-5294.

Committees: *Environment & Public Works*: Fisheries, Wildlife & Water (Chmn.); Transportation & Infrastructure. *Foreign Relations*: East Asian & Pacific Affairs; European Affairs; Near Eastern & South Asian Affairs (Chmn.); Western Hemisphere, Peace Corps & Narcotics Affairs. *Homeland Security & Governmental Affairs*: Federal Financial Management, Govt. Information & International Security; Investigations (Permanent); Oversight of Govt. Management, the Federal Workforce & the District of Columbia.

Group Ratings

	ADA	ACLU	AFS	LCV	ITIC	NTU	COC	ACU	NTLC	CHC
2004	55	67	57	50	100	49	82	40	63	50
2003	65	—	44	79	—	46	57	35	—	—

National Journal Ratings

	2003 LIB	—	2003 CONS		2004 LIB	—	2004 CONS
Economic	52%	—	47%		52%	—	47%
Social	51%	—	46%		60%	—	39%
Foreign	54%	—	44%		43%	—	54%

Key Votes of the 108th Congress

1. Ban Drilling in ANWR	Y	5. Energy Bill	N	9. Ban Same-Sex Marriage	N
2. Approve Bush Tax Cuts	N	6. Support Roe v. Wade	Y	10. Ban Bunker-Buster Bomb	Y
3. Medicare/Rx Bill	N	7. Ban Partial-Birth Abortion	N	11. Fund Iraq War	Y
4. Bar Overtime Pay Regs.	Y	8. Assault Weapons Ban	Y	12. Restrict Missile Defense	N

Election Results

2000 general	Lincoln Chafee (R)	222,588	(57%)	($2,265,221)
	Robert A. Weygand (D)	161,023	(41%)	($2,297,885)
	Other	7,742	(2%)	
2000 primary	Lincoln Chafee (R)	unopposed		
1994 general	John H. Chafee (R)	222,856	(65%)	($2,086,236)
	Linda J. Kushner (D)	122,532	(35%)	($805,867)

Lincoln Chafee, the junior senator from Rhode Island, was appointed to the office in November 1999, a week after the death of his father, Senator John Chafee. Lincoln Chafee grew up in Warwick, Rhode Island, on a 20-acre estate; there he developed his love of horses. His father was elected governor when he was eight, and he remembers going to the 1964 Republican National Convention, at 11, and the hostility of the Goldwater supporters there for Rockefeller Republicans. In 1969 John Chafee became Secretary of the Navy; Lincoln Chafee was at Andover, where one of his schoolmates was Jeb Bush. In 1976 John Chafee was elected to the Senate; the year before, Lincoln Chafee graduated from Brown, where he was captain of the wrestling team, and went off to horseshoeing school at Montana State University. For seven years he worked as a farrier at racetracks in the United States and Canada. In 1984 he returned to Rhode Island. In

1985 he was elected to the Rhode Island Constitutional Convention and in 1986 was elected to the city council in Warwick, the state's second largest city. In 1992 he was elected mayor of Warwick, by 335 votes, the first Republican in 32 years. He was reelected three times. In March 1999, John Chafee announced that he would not seek re-election in 2000; the next day Lincoln Chafee announced he would run for the seat. The older Chafee was a productive legislator who was greatly beloved in Rhode Island, respected as a member of one of Rhode Island's "Five Families," who had volunteered for the Marine Corps and served in combat in World War II and Korea.

John Chafee died in October 1999. After a week of mourning, Governor Lincoln Almond appointed Lincoln Chafee to the Senate; he was only the second son appointed to the Senate to succeed his father, the other being Harry Byrd, Jr., in 1965. Chafee had not been running strong in the polls against possible Democratic opponents, and some thought he was hurt when in August 1999 he admitted he had used cocaine. In the Senate, he promised to continue in his father's tradition and pursued many of his interests. On one of his first votes he was one of four Republicans to vote against the party's minimum wage bill. In 2000 he voted with Democrats on the estate tax and HMO regulation. But he said he would not switch parties—"I'm named after Abraham Lincoln"—and said that Senate Republican leaders "have been very understanding of my votes." Obviously they understood that only a Republican who often voted with Democrats, and probably only a Chafee, could hold this seat in what was in 2000 the nation's most Democratic state.

Certainly he could expect Democratic competition. Senate seats don't come up often in Rhode Island: John Chafee held his for 23 years, Claiborne Pell for 36, John Pastore for 26, Theodore Green for 24—they and the two incumbents were the state's only senators between 1950 and 1999. The first Democrat to announce was 2d District Congressman Robert Weygand, who was not on good terms with machine Democrats. Weygand won a bruising September primary by a 57%–43% margin. In the meantime, the Republican Senate campaign committee was running ads praising Chafee for his independence and citing his votes against Republican positions on HMO regulation and prescription drugs. Democrats made much of a $6,000 fund Chafee used as mayor to buy presents for children of city employees and contribute to charity. Chafee actually spent less than Weygand. Chafee won 57%–41%, running 25% ahead of George W. Bush in Rhode Island.

After the election Chafee said he liked the tone of the Bush campaign, but he did not like many of the early Bush policies. Chafee was the first Senate Republican to oppose the Bush tax cut in 2001. In the spring, Democratic Whip Harry Reid approached Chafee and asked if he wanted to switch parties. Chafee said no. But he didn't discourage Jim Jeffords from switching in May. Again and again he broke ranks with Republicans—on the budget and tax cut in May 2001, on HMO regulation in June, on a letter urging Tom Daschle to bring up the defense appropriation first in March 2002, on the Department of Homeland Security in September. He said in June 2001 he would consider switching parties if Republicans won back a majority in the Senate. But when they gained two seats in and a 51–49 majority in November 2002, he said, "No. I've always said that's an extreme step." Of course a switch in those circumstances would not give the Democrats a majority.

On the Environment committee his father once chaired, he was chairman of the Superfund Subcommittee. His vote helped to defeat the energy bill in November 2003. When the bill came up in committee in February 2005, he said that he might not insist on mandatory carbon dioxide emission caps, but voted against the bill, which prevented it from coming to the floor. Chafee played a key role on the Medicare/prescription drug bill. He voted for the Senate version in June 2003, but said that he was worried about the cost and he opposed the conference committee version. In November he voted against cutting off a filibuster by Edward Kennedy. But the filibuster was cut off and, hours later, he cast a key vote to waive the budget rules. That enabled the legislation to come forward, at which point he voted against it. In December 2004 he looked askance at George W. Bush's call for personal retirement accounts in Social Security. "It's the wrong time, and I regret that we're looking at this in the context of huge deficits." In January 2005 he and Dianne Feinstein sponsored a constitutional amendment to abolish the Electoral College.

In January 2003 Chafee became chairman of the Near Eastern and South Asian Affairs Subcommittee of Foreign Relations; he was third in seniority because more senior members were denied waivers to stay or get back on the committee. He has generally opposed Bush administration policy in the region. He was the only Senate Republican to vote against the Iraq war resolution in October 2002 and fervently opposed military action in Iraq up through March 2003. Although he was pleased by progress he saw on a trip to Iraq in October 2003, in April 2004 he said, "The entire Bush administration seems to have missed the lessons of Vietnam, and now we find ourselves mired in a country in which we don't share the ethnicity, the religion or the language of the people." In July 2004 he said America was less secure because of its involvement in Iraq, and after a trip there in December 2004 said conditions were deteriorating. He was one of four senators to vote against the Syria Accountability Act in November 2003. Chafee has consistently called for the United States to put more pressure on Israel to make concessions to the Palestinians and said that it was unrealistic to wait for suicide attacks to end to begin negotiations; he has lamented that the Bush administration has been "disengaged" from the peace process. In January 2005 he was one of three senators to meet with Venezuela's President Hugo Chavez.

In 2003 Chafee said it was "inconceivable" that he would leave the Republican party and he endorsed George W. Bush for reelection. But he declined to be co-chairman of the Bush campaign in Rhode Island and in 2004 withdrew his endorsement. When asked as the Republicans assembled in New York whom he would vote for, he said repeatedly, "I'm a Republican." On Election Day he told reporters he had cast a "symbolic protest" vote for George H. W. Bush and refused to rule out leaving the Republican party. But after Republicans increased their majority in the Senate and Senate Republican leaders assured him he was welcome, he said he would stay in the party, though not necessarily "forever." In December 2004 he said, "You tend to be supportive [of the party] as you come into the [election] cycle. If I need their help occasionally, I'm going to have to help them. But I'm not going to sacrifice my principles either." Conservative leaders did not seem willing to challenge him. In 2004 Stephen Moore of the Club for Growth said it would not support a primary challenger; Americans for Tax Reform's Grover Norquist said, "A Republican from Rhode Island is a gift from the gods and is not to be looked at askance." In early 2005 there was talk that Cranston Mayor Stephen Laffey might oppose him in the primary.

Chafee's cooperative attitude toward other Republicans may have been strengthened by the fact that Rhode Island and national Democrats seemed to be targeting him. His ratings in the polls were not high and one poll showed him trailing 2d District Congressman Jim Langevin. In December 2004, 1st District Congressman Patrick Kennedy said he wouldn't run and urged Langevin to do so. In February 2005 Secretary of State Matt Brown, formerly head of City Year Rhode Island, announced he was running; within a month he had raised $500,000, mostly at out-of-state fundraisers. In March 2005 Langevin said he was not running and said that he was confident that either Kennedy or former Attorney General Sheldon Whitehouse would be the Democratic nominee. Brown, he said, "does not have the experience to be a United States senator" and "I would certainly encourage Matt to get out of the race." At this point Kennedy considered running but decided not to. State AFL-CIO Chairman Frank Montanaro also called on Whitehouse to run, but said his organization might not endorse anyone in the general election because Chafee "has given us some good votes." In April Whitehouse, who spent $500,000 of his own money on his unsuccessful 2002 gubernatorial campaign, announced he was running. He was promptly endorsed by Langevin and Kennedy. Interestingly, Chafee's and Whitehouse's fathers were roommates at Yale in the 1940s.

FIRST DISTRICT

Rep. Patrick Kennedy (D)

Elected 1994, 6th term; b. July 14, 1967, Brighton, MA; home, Portsmouth; Providence Col., B.A. 1991; Catholic; single.

Elected Office: RI House of Reps., 1988–94.

DC Office: 407 CHOB, 20515, 202-225-4911; Fax: 202-225-3290; Web site: www.house.gov/patrickkennedy.

District Office: Pawtucket, 401-729-5600.

Committees: *Appropriations* (18th of 29 D): Labor, Health and Human Services, Education & Related Agencies; Science, State, Justice, Commerce & Related Agencies.

Group Ratings

	ADA	ACLU	AFS	LCV	ITIC	NTU	COC	ACU	NTLC	CHC
2004	95	70	100	100	50	11	40	8	0	15
2003	95	—	100	95	—	23	27	21	—	—

National Journal Ratings

	2003 LIB	—	2003 CONS		2004 LIB	—	2004 CONS
Economic	80%	—	19%		82%	—	17%
Social	81%	—	18%		73%	—	25%
Foreign	75%	—	21%		58%	—	41%

Key Votes of the 108th Congress

1. Drilling in ANWR	N	5. DC School Vouchers	N	9. Ban Same-Sex Marriage	N
2. Approve Bush Tax Cuts	N	6. Ban Human Cloning	N	10. Fund Iraq War	Y
3. Medicare/Rx Bill	N	7. Restrict Gun Liability	N	11. Bar Cuba Embargo Funds	N
4. Bar Overtime Pay Regs.	Y	8. Ban Partial-Birth Abortion	Y	12. Intelligence Reorg.	Y

Election Results

2004 general	Patrick Kennedy (D)	124,923	(64%)	($1,958,492)
	David Rogers (R)	69,819	(36%)	($2,133,062)
2004 primary	Patrick Kennedy (D)	unopposed		
2002 general	Patrick Kennedy (D)	95,233	(60%)	($2,935,810)
	David Rogers (R)	59,316	(37%)	($1,972,236)
	Other	4,314	(3%)	

Prior Winning Percentages: 2000 (67%); 1998 (67%); 1996 (69%); 1994 (54%)

The People		Race/Ethnic Origin	Ancestry	
Area size:	565 sq. mi.	82.6% White	Irish: 12.9%	Italian: 11.4%
Urban population:	95.5%	4.1% Black	Portuguese: 9.3%	
Rural population:	4.5%	1.9% Asian	**2004 Presidential Vote**	
Pop. 2000:	524,157	0.3% Native Am.	Kerry (D) 131,245	(62%)
Median income:	$40,616	0.0% Hawaiian	Bush (R) 77,480	(36%)
Poverty status:	11.9%	2.3% Two+ races	Other 3,900	(2%)
Military veterans:	12.5%	1.3% Other	**2000 Presidential Vote**	
		7.5% Hispanic Origin	Gore (D) 125,174	(63%)
			Bush (R) 61,396	(31%)
			Other 12,705	(6%)
			Cook Partisan Voting Index: D +16	

Occupation	Blue collar: 23.2%	White collar: 61.3%	Gray collar: 15.5%

The 1st Congressional District is the eastern half of Rhode Island, east of Narragansett Bay, a line that cuts through Providence and then proceeds west and north to the Massachusetts-Connecticut-Rhode Island border. It includes much of Providence (including elite East Side and College Hill around Brown University) and all of next-door Pawtucket whose Slater Mill is known as the birthplace of the American Industrial Revolution. The onetime textile mill towns of the Blackstone Valley, Woonsocket and Central Falls are also in the 1st, along with high-income Barrington and Bristol and, south on the ocean, the old city of Newport, with its restored 18th century houses and the summer "cottages" that are really palaces. Newport was once home to the America's Cup races and now hosts a famous jazz festival; it is also the site of the oldest synagogue in North America, to whose congregation George Washington declared that the United States gives "to bigotry no sanction, to persecution no assistance." Ethnically, this district is the more French-Canadian and the less Italian of the two Rhode Island districts; politically, it is strongly Democratic.

The congressman from the 1st District is Patrick Kennedy, a Democrat first elected in 1994. Patrick Kennedy was born in 1967, his father Edward Kennedy's fifth year in the Senate; a week after his second birthday came the terrible accident at Chappaquiddick. He grew up in McLean, Virginia, and had a somewhat troubled youth, spending time in a drug rehabilitation clinic in 1986 before enrolling at Providence College, at 20, in 1987. Almost immediately, in 1988, he ran for a seat in the state House and beat the longtime incumbent John Skeffington as the tiny (population 9,800) district was inundated with visits by Kennedy family members and funds raised by the Kennedy national fundraising network. He became chairman of the Rules Committee in 1992, a year after spending the now-infamous Easter weekend in Palm Beach with his father and cousin William Kennedy Smith. In 1994, when the 1st District's Republican Congressman Ron Machtley ran for governor, Kennedy decided to run for Congress. Kennedy had an attractive and energetic Republican opponent, Kevin Vigilante, a doctor who worked with handicapped orphans in Romania and with female prison inmates infected with HIV. But Kennedy had the advantages of money and his family name, and won 54%–46% in a Republican year.

In the House Kennedy has a mostly liberal voting record and has proven an excitable if not always eloquent debater. He started off by avoiding national media and working on local issues, from the Naval Undersea Warfare Center in Newport to visas for Portuguese immigrants. He has been strongly opposed to Fidel Castro, whom he blames for the death of his uncle John F. Kennedy; he voted for the Helms-Burton Act, backed the 2000 bill that would have made Elian Gonzalez a U.S. citizen and for keeping the travel ban on Cuba in 2003. He has strongly supported gun control—another issue with family reverberations. He supported reauthorization of the assault weapons ban and in 2003 criticized presidential candidate Howard Dean for his statements that new gun control laws should be left to the states.

After winning re-election by 69%–28% in 1996, he took on a more combative role and seemed to be eyeing a race for the Senate seat held by John Chafee. He criticized Chafee sharply for several votes but Chafee fought back gamely, returning often to the state, working hard on local projects, and his standing in the polls, never weak, slowly rose. Meanwhile, the harshness of Kennedy's attacks evidently grated; his job approval fell from 62% to 44% during the year. In 1998 Kennedy's career took another turn. In April he said he wanted a seat on Appropriations—not a likely goal if he intended to seek only one more term in the House. He struck up a friendship with Minority Leader Dick Gephardt; Kennedy let it be known that he would support Gephardt for president against Al Gore. When Gephardt decided not to run for president, but to concentrate on helping Democrats win a House majority, he enlisted Kennedy as a key ally. In November 1998, after Kennedy easily won reelection, Gephardt named him chairman of the DCCC. A few days later Kennedy announced what was already pretty plain, that he would not run for the Senate.

As DCCC chairman, Kennedy excelled not as a strategist but as a fundraiser. He traveled indefatigably around the country to fundraisers, and made yeoman efforts to raise soft money, even while calling for campaign finance legislation that would outlaw it. As a result, the DCCC in 1999 and 2000 raised nearly $50 million in soft money, reaching parity with the Republicans'

NRCC; the NRCC raised more hard money, but Kennedy vastly reduced the disadvantage his party labored under in the 1996 and 1998 cycles. But Democrats were unsuccessful in their efforts for a net gain of six seats to regain a majority in the House.

Instead he seemed to be moving from national politics to concentration on Rhode Island, where he had spent only 40 days in 1999 and 2000, and where his standing was in decline because of a series of imbroglios. In March 2000, he shoved an airport security guard in Los Angeles, sending her backward and jostling the metal detector archway. A police complaint was filed, but the Los Angeles city attorney decided against prosecution. In an informal hearing in May 2000, Kennedy apologized to the woman. But she sued him in March 2001, and Kennedy said his insurance company would handle the suit. The insurance company, it appeared, had already been busy settling multiple damage claims against Kennedy by owners of sailboats he had chartered. None of this hurt him in the 2000 election. Against a Republican who spent $9,000, he won 67%–33%. But his job approval in the district fell from 63% in February 2000 to 42% in September 2001.

In January 2001 Kennedy took back the seat on Appropriations to which he had been named in 1998, but from which he had taken a leave of absence to chair the DCCC. He worked on some other legislation, co-sponsoring the mental health parity bill which passed in the Senate but did not come to a vote in the House, but he mostly concentrated on getting federal money, especially defense dollars, for Rhode Island. Much of that was for hospitals, schools and bridges—musical instruments in East Providence, youth programs for the Cumberland police, mentors at the Meeting Street school—but he also worked to bring in money for Rhode Island's military bases and defense industries. In the 2002 campaign Kennedy claimed he had brought $90 million to the district, more per capita, he boasted, than his father's colleague and erstwhile rival Robert Byrd. In the 2004 campaign he claimed that he had brought in $162 million in four years. His involvement on these military issues may help to explain his differences with his father on the B-1 bomber and the Iraq war resolution, both of which Patrick Kennedy supported. As the insurgency against U.S. forces grew, Kennedy criticized the administration's policies and in 2004 said that the administration had deceived him by its statements on weapons of mass destruction.

Kennedy has taken distinctive stands on some other issues. One is parity for mental health treatments in insurance. In 2000 he appeared with Tipper Gore in Rhode Island and disclosed that he had been receiving treatment and therapy for manic depression. In 2004 he co-sponsored with his father and Republicans Pete Domenici and Jim Ramstad a bill extending Paul Wellstone's 1996 parity law by eliminating unequal limits on numbers of inpatient days and outpatient days in insurance policies. On another health care issue, he teamed up with former Speaker Newt Gingrich in 2004 to urge more extensive use of information technology in health care. He has voted several times for the partial-birth abortion ban. In the 1990s he supported the death penalty, but in 2000 changed his mind because he thought there was disparate impact on blacks and because people sentenced to death had been exonerated by DNA evidence. He has strongly supported Indian gambling and in 2001 and 2002 was the House's top recipient of donations from Indian tribes; he said it was because the tribes respected his family. He got some bad publicity in June 2003 when at a Democratic fundraiser he said, "I have never worked a [expletive] day in my life"; his point was that the Bush tax cut benefited rich people like his family members who didn't need the money.

In 2001 and 2002 Rhode Island Republicans noticed falling job ratings and thought he was vulnerable. The 2002 nominee, conservative David Rogers, a Portsmouth technical analyst and former Navy Seal, raised $2 million, mostly by direct mail (not so hard when you're running against a Kennedy) and ran ads saying that some of Kennedy's acts were "arrogant, unstable and embarrassing." Kennedy won by the solid margin of 60%–37%. In 2003 Kennedy supported Dick Gephardt for president and campaigned extensively for him in the Iowa caucuses, even as his father was stumping for John Kerry. In 2004 Rogers ran again, and this time Kennedy won by the increased margin of 64%–36%.

After the election many urged Kennedy to run against Republican Senator Lincoln Chafee. Early in his career a Senate seat seemed his obvious goal; but he passed up the chance to run in 2000 to help his party in House races, and in December 2004 he said he wouldn't run because he wanted to keep working in the House and on the Appropriations Committee. He urged his 2d District colleague Jim Langevin to run. But in March 2005 Langevin said he wouldn't, and added that either Kennedy or former Attorney General Sheldon Whitehouse should be the party's candidate. Kennedy gave some consideration to running for the Senate, but on March 30 said he would not; in April, he and Langevin endorsed Whitehouse.

SECOND DISTRICT

Rep. Jim Langevin (D)

Elected 2000, 3d term; b. Apr. 22, 1964, Warwick; home, Warwick; RI Col., B.A. 1990, Harvard U., M.P.A. 1994; Catholic; single.

Elected Office: RI House of Reps., 1988–94; RI Sec. of State, 1994–2000.

DC Office: 109 CHOB, 20515, 202-225-2735; Fax: 202-225-5976; Web site: www.house.gov/langevin.

District Office: Warwick, 401-732-9400.

Committees: *Armed Services* (17th of 28 D): Projection Forces; Terrorism, Unconventional Threats & Capabilities. *Homeland Security* (14th of 15 D): Economic Security, Infrastructure Protection & Cybersecurity; Intelligence, Information Sharing & Terrorism Risk Assessment; Prevention of Nuclear & Biological Attack (RMM).

Group Ratings

	ADA	ACLU	AFS	LCV	ITIC	NTU	COC	ACU	NTLC	CHC
2004	85	53	100	100	44	15	45	25	6	46
2003	85	—	100	100	—	22	27	20	—	—

National Journal Ratings

	2003 LIB	—	2003 CONS	2004 LIB	—	2004 CONS
Economic	81%	—	18%	74%	—	26%
Social	61%	—	38%	59%	—	40%
Foreign	81%	—	17%	65%	—	34%

Key Votes of the 108th Congress

1. Drilling in ANWR	N	5. DC School Vouchers	N	9. Ban Same-Sex Marriage	N
2. Approve Bush Tax Cuts	N	6. Ban Human Cloning	Y	10. Fund Iraq War	Y
3. Medicare/Rx Bill	N	7. Restrict Gun Liability	N	11. Bar Cuba Embargo Funds	Y
4. Bar Overtime Pay Regs.	Y	8. Ban Partial-Birth Abortion	Y	12. Intelligence Reorg.	Y

Election Results

2004 general	Jim Langevin (D)	154,392	(75%)	($727,295)
	Chuck Barton (R)	43,139	(21%)	($49,633)
	Other	9,634	(5%)	
2004 primary	Jim Langevin (D)	unopposed		
2002 general	Jim Langevin (D)	129,312	(76%)	($774,848)
	John Matson (R)	37,740	(22%)	($5,964)
	Other	2,323	(1%)	

Prior Winning Percentages: 2000 (62%)

The People		Race/Ethnic Origin	Ancestry	
Area size:	980 sq. mi.	81.2% White	Italian: 16.7% Irish: 14.4%	
Urban population:	86.3%	3.9% Black	English: 9.8%	
Rural population:	13.7%	2.6% Asian	**2004 Presidential Vote**	
Pop. 2000:	524,162	0.5% Native Am.	Kerry (D) 128,515	(57%)
Median income:	$44,129	0.0% Hawaiian	Bush (R) 91,566	(41%)
Poverty status:	11.9%	1.6% Two+ races	Other 4,428	(2%)
Military veterans:	13.1%	0.3% Other	**2000 Presidential Vote**	
		9.8% Hispanic Origin	Gore (D) 124,314	(60%)
			Bush (R) 69,076	(33%)
			Other 14,366	(7%)
			Cook Partisan Voting Index: D +13	

Occupation	Blue collar: 22.6%	White collar: 60.8%	Gray collar: 16.6%

The 2d Congressional District is the western half of Rhode Island. While the 1st includes many mill towns, the 2d has most of its population in towns like working-class Cranston and more upscale Warwick which, despite their British names, are inhabited mostly by people with Irish, Italian, French and Portuguese surnames. The 2d also includes the fastest-growing part of the state: South County, which is not an official place but the common name for Rhode Island south of East Greenwich, including the affluent suburbs and beachfront communities to the south along Narragansett Bay, the Kingston home of the University of Rhode Island, and the area around Westerly, where many residents work at the Electric Boat shipyards in Groton, Connecticut. It includes Rhode Island's rolling farm land, though there is not that much acreage, and the communities along the Bay and the Ocean, where many people still make their living building boats and catching fish. Although this remains a heavily Democratic district, George W. Bush cut the Democratic margin from 60%–33% in 2000 to 57%–41% in 2004.

The congressman from the 2d District is Jim Langevin, a Democrat first elected in 2000. Langevin grew up in Warwick, and as a boy hoped to become an FBI agent. But in 1980, at age 16, when he was a police cadet in the Boy Scout Explorer program, he was shot by a police officer when a gun accidentally discharged. The bullet went through his upper back and throat and damaged the upper part of his spinal column; ever since, he has been a quadriplegic, getting around in a wheelchair, the first to serve in Congress. He received $2.2 million in a settlement with the city of Warwick and currently hires a home health care aide; it takes him two and a half hours to get dressed each morning. This tragic accident focused attention on him, at first unwanted, but he says it made him determined to make something of his life. He worked as an intern in the State House and for Senator Claiborne Pell. In 1988, while he was a student at Rhode Island College, he was elected to the state House of Representatives, where he styled himself as a reformer; his 1st District colleague Patrick Kennedy was also elected that year to the state House as a college student. While in the state House Langevin graduated from college and received a master's degree from the Kennedy School at Harvard. In 1994 Langevin was elected Rhode Island's secretary of state.

When Congressman Bob Weygand ran for the Senate in 2000, Langevin decided to run for his House seat. It was a four-way race in the Democratic primary, and Langevin's most strenuous opposition came from Kate Coyne-McCoy, executive director of the Rhode Island Association of Social Workers. Langevin had support from many Democratic Party leaders and some unions, and won the party endorsement at the April convention, from which Coyne-McCoy angrily withdrew. But she waged an aggressive campaign, financed by unions, health care workers and EMILY's List. "There's no such thing as being too liberal," Coyne-McCoy said. Langevin called her positions "unrealistic and extreme." He favored less stringent forms of gun control and said, "No one has to tell me how dangerous weapons can be." Coyne-McCoy attacked Langevin for opposing abortion rights. He said, "because of what happened to me, I became aware of how precious life is . . . I'm pro-life." He spoke often of the accident that paralyzed him: "Certainly, being disabled is part of who I am, but it doesn't define me." In the primary, he led Coyne-McCoy

47%–29%. In the general, his chief opposition came from Rodney Driver, nominee of the Conscience for Congress Party, a retired mathematics professor who spent $300,000 of his retirement savings. Langevin won 62%–21%.

In the House, Langevin has been liberal on economic issues and more centrist on cultural and foreign issues: an apt representative of his district's ethnic communities. The House chamber was made wheelchair-accessible for Langevin, with two of the fixed seats in the front of the chamber removed to give him space to maneuver and talk to colleagues. Because he has only limited use of his hands, Langevin was unable to cast a secret ballot until Rhode Island purchased special voting machines. Despite the opposition of anti-abortion groups, he urged George W. Bush to support embryonic stem-cell research, arguing that it might alleviate suffering from certain diseases and injuries, and assist infertile couples to have children; he voted against the bill to permit therapeutic cloning. He sponsored several gun control bills. On the Armed Services and Homeland Security committees, he focused on internal threats and getting more resources to first responders. Langevin called universal health care coverage his overriding priority, and sponsored a bill to mandate the federal government to provide all Americans the health care choices available to federal employees to be financed by an increase in the payroll tax. In March 2005 he was one of two House Democrats from New England who supported federal judicial review in the Terri Schiavo case. He has won reelection easily.

In early 2005, a statewide poll showed Langevin ahead of Republican Senator Lincoln Chafee. In December 2004 1st District Democrat Patrick Kennedy said he would not run against Chafee and urged Langevin to do so. Other Rhode Island and national Democrats weighed in, as did DSCC Chairman Charles Schumer. But abortion rights groups objected to an anti-abortion candidate in Rhode Island. In March 2005 Langevin surprised many Democrats when he said he would not run for the Senate; he said he had important work to do in the House and did not rule out a later run for statewide office. As for Secretary of State Matt Brown, who announced in February that he was running for the seat, Langevin said he "does not have the experience to be a United States senator" and "I would certainly encourage Matt to get out of the race." In April 2005, Brown University political scientist Jennifer Lawless, a Rhode Island resident for two years, said she would run against Langevin the 2006 Democratic primary because of his anti-abortion position and his unwillingness to take a political risk by challenging Chafee.

★ SOUTH CAROLINA ★

South Carolina, at times beleaguered and under attack, stands proud but not untroubled, a state that has made much progress but still feels it has some distance to go. Within living memory, this state looked like an underdeveloped country. Beneath a thin veneer of rich people, it was among the poorest of states, with income levels less than half the national average and with high levels of illiteracy and disease. South Carolina was founded by planters from Barbados and even today there are reminders of the West Indies—the semitropical climate, the lush foliage and trademark palmettos, and the billions in damage from hurricanes. But economically and culturally, South Carolina is now clearly part of the booming South Atlantic region from Maryland to Florida, filling up with new retirement condominiums, time shares (it ranks number two in the country), factories and office buildings, giant shopping centers, growing robustly in the 1990s.

South Carolina started off with a plantation economy built on the swampy Low Country below the Fall Line, where the great 18th and 19th century planters built rice paddies and cultivated exotic crops like indigo in the days before cotton was king. The great wealth of these Low Country planters was destroyed by the Civil War which they, more than any other Southerners, provoked. But their pride and way of life continued as did that of former slaves. As late as 1940, 43% of South Carolinians were black, most living in conditions inconceivable today. South Carolina's economic growth started only in the 1920s, with that lowest-wage of industries, textiles. Mills were built in the Up Country above Columbia, hiring poor whites (never blacks)

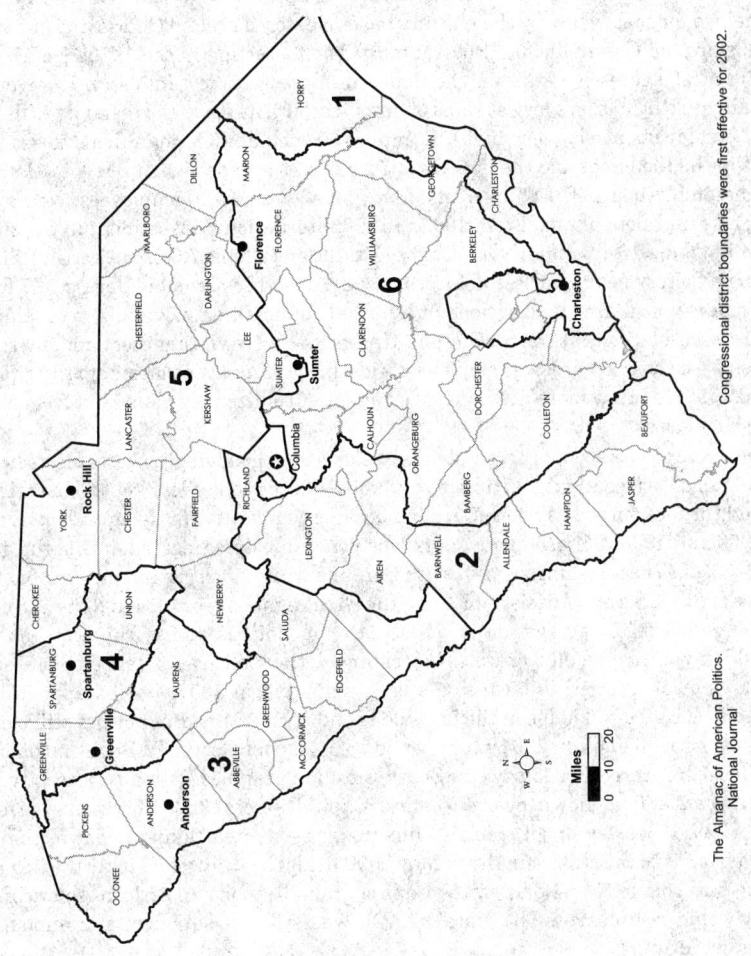

The Almanac of American Politics.
National Journal

Congressional district boundaries were first effective for 2002.

from the hardscrabble farms in the area. Politics remained a rough business, with harsh appeals to racial fear and economic envy, and with limited participation: in 1940, just 99,000 South Carolinians voted for president, 96% of them Democratic—the highest Democratic percentage in the nation. In the 1946 Democratic primary, the year Strom Thurmond was elected governor, only 271,000 people voted in a state of more than 2 million.

Now this once underdeveloped country has joined the First World. Personal incomes rose 40% in the 1990s, up toward national levels, and factory productivity rose 59%. Poverty fell sharply; health standards are as good as those in the rest of the nation. Educational achievement still lags, though not nearly so much as before, with 80% of white and 65% of black adults classified as high school graduates; homeownership is above the national average. South Carolina was helped for some years by the military bases clustered around Charleston and by the big textile mills around Greenville and Spartanburg. Then, starting in the 1970s, South Carolina became the most aggressive state in the South in attracting new industry. It advertised its business climate (the nation's lowest rates of unionization), its taxes (low) and its willingness to meet local employers' needs (very high). It enticed French and German firms to set up major operations in the Piedmont and the Low Country, a process capped when BMW in 1992 built its first U.S. assembly plant off I-85 in Spartanburg, now with 4,700 employees. Nearby are big Michelin and Fuji Photo plants. From 1960 to 1990 international investment in the state grew from $80 million to $16.4 trillion. Now Vought Aircraft and Alenia Aeronautica, an Italian firm, are building a factory near Charleston International Airport to assemble Boeing 7E7 fuselages. But even more typical are the decisions of hundreds of small employers to open plants, rent offices and create jobs in what has become one of America's more vibrant economic environments: 95% of businesses have 50 or fewer employees. South Carolina keeps losing textile and apparel jobs, but has gained many more not from government-subsidized big plants but from expansion of existing businesses.

As South Carolina's economy grew, it slowly, sometimes grudgingly, overcame its heritage of slavery and racial segregation. Starting in the 1950s, fewer people were kept from voting by the poll tax, and turnout surged as South Carolina became competitive in the presidential elections of 1952, 1956 and 1960. Clemson University was peaceably desegregated during the governorship (1959–62) of Ernest Hollings; most South Carolina whites opposed integration, but not with the violence of Alabama and Mississippi. Then the Civil Rights Act of 1964 and the Voting Rights Act of 1965 ended legal segregation of public accommodations and workplaces and brought blacks suddenly into the electorate. This changed the political balance. Senator Strom Thurmond, who set a record filibustering a civil rights bill in 1957, started appointing black staffers and a black federal judge in the late 1960s and early 1970s. But politics still cleaves the electorate along racial lines: In 2004 whites voted 78%–22% for George W. Bush and blacks voted 85%–15% for John Kerry. For four years South Carolina grappled with a controversy over the Confederate battle flag, flown over the state Capitol since 1962. Successive governors— Republican David Beasley and Democrat Jim Hodges—favored taking it down; the NAACP organized a boycott of the state. Finally in May 2000 the legislature voted to fly the flag not from the Capitol, but from a 30-foot pole on the Capitol grounds, while an African-American history monument would rise nearby. The state NAACP was still not satisfied, and announced the boycott would continue.

Until the 1960s, South Carolina was an inward-looking state, with few people except military personnel moving in. That has changed as the economy has grown. Most of the newcomers are white, with conservative attitudes but less feeling for the state's ancient traditions; there have been only a few immigrants. The fastest growth in the 1990s came in coastal resort areas around Hilton Head and Myrtle Beach and in suburban counties outside Columbia and just south of Charlotte, North Carolina. This growth has reduced the state's black percentage to 30% in 2000, well above the national average of 12% but far below the near-majority of the 1940s. Politically, this change has helped move South Carolina toward the Republicans. But that change might not have occurred without the efforts of two individuals. One was Strom

Thurmond, who had voted for Franklin D. Roosevelt at the 1932 Democratic National Convention, but who switched to the Republican party in September 1964 and provided critical votes to nominate Richard Nixon at the 1968 Republican National Convention. South Carolina voted for Barry Goldwater in 1964 and Nixon in 1968 and has only once voted for a Democrat since, Jimmy Carter in 1976 by a narrow margin. The other individual was Carroll Campbell, elected governor in 1986 and 1990, who with the aid of Lee Atwater built a Republican party capable of electing statewide officials and majorities in the legislature. In 1988 Campbell and Atwater, by then George H. W. Bush's campaign manager, set up the early Republican primary, on the Saturday before Super Tuesday, which enabled George H. W. Bush to clinch the Republican nomination that year; it did the same for Bob Dole in 1996 and, against John McCain's strong challenge, for George W. Bush in 2000. In 1989 Campbell and Atwater seemed to be Thurmond's heirs. But Atwater died of a brain tumor at 39 in 1991. In 1994 Campbell helped his protégé David Beasley win the governorship. It was widely assumed that Campbell, making good money as a Washington lobbyist, would be appointed to fill Thurmond's seat if it should become vacant. But Beasley was defeated for reelection in 1998 and in 2001 Campbell announced that, at 61, he was battling Alzheimer's disease. Thurmond served out his eighth term as he had the other seven and as a United States senator celebrated his 100th birthday in December 2002.

South Carolina's other senator for years, Democrat Ernest Hollings, retired in 2004 after 38 years, 36 of them as a junior senator—a record. South Carolina politics now belongs to a new generation. The state continues to be heavily Republican, though Democrats have been competitive and cannot be counted out. But in 2002 the Republican trend continued. Republicans had a fierce primary and runoff for governor, and the surprise winner, former Congressman Mark Sanford, who moved to the state as an adult, beat Hodges 53%–47%. In the race to succeed Thurmond, Congressman Lindsey Graham won 54%–44%. In 2004 George W. Bush carried the state 58%–41%, Republican Congressman Jim DeMint beat Democrat Inez Tenenbaum for Hollings's Senate seat by the same margin as Graham had won in 2002, 54%–44%, and Republicans increased their majorities in the state Senate and in the state House.

The People		Race/Ethnic Origin			Military veterans: 420,971 (14.0%)	
Pop. 2004 (est):	4,198,068	2,652,291	66.1%	White	WWII: 16.1%	Korea: 12.0%
Pop. 2000:	4,012,012	1,178,486	29.4%	Black	Vietnam: 34.1%	Gulf War: 13.1%
Pop. 1990:	3,486,703	35,568	0.9%	Asian	**Most populous cities (2003):**	
Change 1990–2000:	Up 15.1%	12,765	0.3%	Native Am.	1. Columbia	117,357
% of U.S. total:	1.4%	1,270	0.0%	Hawaiian	2. Charleston	101,024
Pop. rank:	26th of 50	33,290	0.8%	Two+ races	3. North Charleston	81,577
Area size:	32,020 sq. mi.	3,266	0.1%	Other	4. Rock Hill	56,114
State Native:	64.0%	95,076	2.4%	Hisp. Origin	5. Greenville	55,926
Non-citizen:	1.8%	**Ancestry**				
Language		USA: 11.9%		German: 7.2%	Urban population: 60.5%	
English: 92.6%	Spanish: 4.0%	English: 7.0%		Irish: 6.8%	Rural population: 39.5%	
Other Eur.: 2.5%		Scotch-Irish: 2.5%				

Education		Work Sector		General Assembly	
H.S. Grad:	76.3%	Private: 78.1%	Govt: 15.9%	Senate	27 R 19 D
College Grad:	20.4%	Self: 5.7%	Family: 0.3%	House	74 R 50 D
Industry		Unemployment: 5.7%		Legislative Term Limits: No	
Agri: 1.1%	Con: 8.3%	**Household Income**		**Registered Voters**	
Fin: 5.6%	Info: 2.1%	<15k: 18.8%	15-35k: 28.3%	No party registration	
Mfg: 24.4%	Prof: 25.5%	35-50k: 17.6%	50-100k: 27.3%		
Public: 4.7%	Trade: 15.2%	100-150k: 5.3%	>150k: 2.8%		
Other: 13.0%		Median: $37,082			
Occupation		Poverty status: 14.1%			
Blue collar: 30.4%	White collar: 54.2%	**Home Value**			
Gray collar: 15.3%		<50k: 24.3%	50-100k: 38.3%	100-200k: 26.9%	200-300k: 6.1%
		300-500k: 3.0%	>500k: 1.5%	Median: $83,100	

Presidential politics   In presidential general elections South Carolina is reliably Republican. It was the only Deep South state to vote for Richard Nixon over George Wallace in 1968 and since then has voted Democratic only once, for Jimmy Carter in 1976. It was one of the top three Republican states in 1988 and 1992. In 2004 Democratic vice presidential candidate John Edwards did return to his Seneca, South Carolina, boyhood home, but did not linger long.

South Carolina does not set one day for presidential primaries or caucuses; each of its two major parties selects a date and decides whether it will be a primary or caucus. In 1987 Lee Atwater purposefully scheduled the Republican primary here for the Saturday before Super Tuesday, and in 1988 George H.W. Bush won a 49%–21%–19% victory over Bob Dole and Pat Robertson, forecasting the Southern sweep that clinched his nomination four days later. Democrats chose their delegates by caucus; a Democratic primary would have had an electorate about 50% black and would surely have pro-

2004 Presidential Vote		
Bush (R)	937,974	(58%)
Kerry (D)	661,699	(41%)
Nader (I)	5,520	(0%)
Other	14,705	(1%)

2004 Democratic Presidential Primary		
Edwards (D)	132,660	(45%)
Kerry (D)	87,620	(30%)
Sharpton (D)	28,495	(10%)
Clark (D)	21,218	(7%)
Dean (D)	13,984	(5%)
Other	9,866	(3%)

2000 Presidential Vote		
Bush (R)	786,892	(57%)
Gore (D)	566,039	(41%)
Nader (Green)	20,279	(1%)
Other	10,832	(1%)

duced a victory for South Carolina native Jesse Jackson, which would not have been helpful to the party in state elections. In 1992 Bush beat Pat Buchanan 67%–26%, squashing Buchanan's claims to Southern support. Democrats held a primary the same day, which Bill Clinton won with 63% of the vote. In 1996 former Governor Carroll Campbell and Governor David Beasley led a grass-roots campaign that gave Bob Dole, after his disappointing showings elsewhere, an impressive 45%–29% victory over Buchanan: turnout was 276,000. And in 2000 Campbell and Beasley, both now ex-governors, supported George W. Bush, as he beat John McCain 53%–42%: turnout was 573,000. Democrats chose their delegates by caucus in 1996 and 2000.

In 2004 Democrats held a primary on February 2, a week after New Hampshire, and attracted 292,000 voters, only about half of what Republicans attracted in 2000. Native son John Edwards won 45% of the vote, more than John Kerry's 30%, but perhaps not the landslide he wanted. Kerry had the endorsement of Congressman Jim Clyburn, South Carolina's most popular black politician, after Clyburn's early favorite, Dick Gephardt, dropped out. Al Sharpton hoped that a black-majority turnout would make him a contender; most voters appear to have been black, but Sharpton got only 10% of the vote. Edwards campaigned hard in South Carolina and spent little time in Oklahoma, which voted the same day; there he lost to Wesley Clark by 1,300 votes. That kept Clark in the race and gave Edwards a Southern rival who probably cost him some votes.

Congressional districting   Control of the South Carolina redistricting process was split between Democratic Governor Jim Hodges and the Republican-controlled legislature. The legislature, after toying with proposals for major changes, passed in September 2001 a plan with no major changes. It expanded the black-majority 6th District, which extends from Columbia to Charleston and includes much of the Low Country and Pee Dee area, and increased its black percentage from 61% to 63%. Hodges vetoed the plan and Republicans failed to override. A three-judge federal court took over, and in March 2002 decided on a plan that smoothed out the lines considerably and reduced the black percentage in the 6th District to 57%.

109th Congress Lineup	
4 R	2 D

108th Congress Lineup	
4 R	2 D

Governor

Mark Sanford (R)

Elected 2002, term expires Jan. 2007, 1st term; b. May 28, 1960, Ft. Lauderdale, FL; home, Charleston; Furman U., B.A. 1983; U. of VA, M.B.A. 1988; Episcopalian; married (Jenny).

Elected Office: U.S. House of Reps., 1994–2000.

Professional Career: Real estate investor, 1988–92; Owner, Norton & Sanford real estate investment firm, 1992–2002.

Office: P.O. Box 12267, Columbia, 29211, 803-734-2100; Fax: 803-734-5167; Web site: www.state.sc.us/governor.

Election Results

2002 general	Mark Sanford (R)	585,422	(53%)
	Jim Hodges (D)	521,140	(47%)
2002 runoff	Mark Sanford (R)	183,820	(60%)
	Bob Peeler (R)	121,881	(40%)
2002 primary	Mark Sanford (R)	122,143	(39%)
	Bob Peeler (R)	119,026	(38%)
	Charlie Condon (R)	49,469	(16%)
	Ken Wingate (R)	12,366	(4%)
1998 general	Jim Hodges (D)	574,035	(53%)
	David Beasley (R)	486,342	(45%)
	Other	16,758	(2%)

Mark Sanford, a Republican and something of a maverick, was elected governor of South Carolina in 2002. He grew up in Fort Lauderdale, the son of a heart surgeon; the family spent summers and vacations on 3,000-acre farm in Beaufort County, once known as Coosaw Plantation, and moved there permanently when Mark was 18. He graduated from high school in South Carolina and from Furman University in Greenville and the University of Virginia business school. He worked in real estate investment in New York where he met his wife, a Midwesterner; in 1992 he started a real estate investment firm in Charleston. He lives in the suburb of Sullivans Island and is perpetually tanned from windsurfing in the ocean. In 1994, 1st District incumbent Arthur Ravenel ran for governor, and Sanford, with no political experience, ran for the House. It was a family campaign, managed by his wife and financed by $100,000 of his own money. Sanford campaigned as an outsider: he pledged to serve only three terms, to take no PAC money, to vote for no tax increases and to refuse any salary increase until the budget was balanced. He finished second in the primary and then won the runoff 52%–48%. He carried the general election with 66%.

In the House Sanford voted more often than almost any other member against spending increases. He was one of the few members voting against measures passed by nearly unanimous votes and he opposed what he considered pork barrel spending, including projects in South Carolina. He spent much of late 1999 and early 2000 campaigning for John McCain across the state, as did Lindsey Graham, even though most state Republican insiders backed George W. Bush.

Back in South Carolina full-time in 2001 Sanford started running for governor. Well known and well liked in Charleston and the coast, he was unknown in the rest of the state, and he set about getting better acquainted. He was not the only Republican running. Lieutenant Governor Bob Peeler, originally from Cherokee County east of Greenville-Spartanburg, was traveling around the state in his trademark red pickup truck; he had backed George W. Bush in 2000 and was supported by most of the state Republican establishment, although former Governor Carroll Campbell endorsed Sanford. Attorney General Charlie Condon, who had won much publicity from his conservative stands on hot-button issues, had been running for the Senate, but switched abruptly to the governor race.

Their ultimate target was Governor Jim Hodges, the Democrat who had upset Republican incumbent David Beasley in 1998. Hodges was an obscure legislator whose main accomplishment was an all-day kindergarten bill. His chief plank was a lottery to pay for college scholarships, similar to Zell Miller's HOPE scholarships in Georgia, and for school construction and all-day kindergarten. Hodges played a major role in getting the legislature to vote in May 2000 to take the Confederate flag off the dome and put it up on the Capitol grounds; he also got the legislature to pass a Martin Luther King Holiday, plus a Confederate Memorial Day in May. Hodges's biggest success came when voters approved the lottery in November 2000 and it was passed by the legislature in June 2001. In his first three years Hodges raised teacher pay and increased school construction, while tests scores improved. Despite his achievements, Hodges's job ratings were not particularly high, and Republicans were confident they could beat "the accidental governor," as some called him, in this basically Republican state.

The three Republicans called for major changes in taxes and spending. Sanford liked to say, "People pay a wealth premium to live in South Carolina" and pointed out that the 7% top income tax rate kicked in at $12,000. He proposed phasing out the income tax over 18 years and making up for fluctuations in revenues with a transition fund established by a sales tax on gas. He also called for school vouchers. Sanford, capitalizing on his ties in the business world and from the McCain campaign, raised more money and ran more ads than the other two. Peeler led in polls in the run up to the June 11 primary, and many expected that Condon would cut into Sanford's Low Country base. Instead, Sanford finished first with 39% of the vote, just ahead of Peeler's 38%; Condon was far behind with 16%. Sanford had huge strength in metro Charleston and the coast, where he beat Peeler 59%–16%, with 19% for Condon.

Still, Sanford carried only 11 of 46 counties, and standard analysis would suggest that more of the culturally conservative Condon's votes would go to Peeler in the June 25 runoff. But the race was not defined ideologically. Peeler's strategists felt this "looks like more of a Bush-McCain thing" and that he would win if he could argue that Sanford was not a real conservative. Peeler criticized Sanford for votes on the breast cancer stamp, military housing and supporting military action; Sanford said these issues were taken out of context and were "negative." Congressman Lindsey Graham, nominated unopposed for senator on June 11, cut a spot endorsing Sanford; Sanford won 60%–40%.

Hodges approached the general election campaign much as Peeler had the runoff. The day after the runoff negative ads started running, spotlighting Sanford's votes in the House. Hodges played up his modest background and recalled working in a textile mill for $2.10 an hour, and called Sanford a wealthy Charleston plantation owner from south Florida. But Hodges had embarrassments of his own. One of his ads attacked Sanford for having voted "against programs for disabled kids." But then it was revealed that Hodges had transferred $300,000 from the Continuum of Care for Emotionally Disturbed Children fund to the operating account for the governor's office. Hodges had also been embarrassed by his failure to keep an oft-repeated promise to block the shipment of spent plutonium to the Savannah River Site for reprocessing. Energy Secretary Spencer Abraham promised that the reprocessed fuel would be shipped out of state, but Hodges wanted a commitment in writing and in April 2002 brought a suit in federal court. This backfired: in June 2002, a week before the runoff, a federal judge ordered Hodges not to block the shipment; Hodges backed down on his promise to stand in the road in front of the convoy.

Hodges had more money, but Sanford seemed to attract more attention. Dressed usually in khakis and a plaid shirt, he talked about his plans for change and getting away from politics as usual. In November Sanford won 53%–47%. Metro Charleston and the coast, which had voted for Hodges in 1998, this time went 55%–45% for Sanford. So did metro Columbia-Aiken. The Greenville area gave Sanford a 60%–40% margin. Hodges carried the rest of the state by only 55%–45%.

As governor, Sanford continued to defy convention. He instituted an "open door at four" policy: citizens could line up to get five-minute audiences with the governor (they sometimes went longer). After the departure of his chief of staff, he brought in his wife Jenny, a former investment banker who ran her husband's campaigns, to temporarily fill the void though both denied she would be chief of staff. Sanford wondered out loud whether he should quit the Air Force Reserve, which he joined in 2002 just prior to running for governor, lest he be called to active duty; he decided to stay in and arranged that Lieutenant Governor Andre Bauer, 33, should become acting governor. He was not called up but did spend two weeks in the spring in training. In 2005, he spent two weeks in Texas training as a medical evacuation officer and missed the opening of the legislative session. He was later transferred to another unit, the Air Force's National Security Emergency Preparedness Agency.

From the legislature he asked some pretty major changes: abolishing the elective offices of secretary of state, treasurer, comptroller, adjutant general, superintendent of education and agriculture commissioner, and putting their functions under the governor; putting the state universities, accustomed to lobbying for themselves, under a single board of regents; enacting school vouchers ("education passports") for children in failing schools. Sanford managed to lower the DUI blood alcohol threshold to .08, win campaign finance changes that added more transparency and bring the Division of Motor Vehicles directly under the governor's office, but he failed to enact any of his major initiatives in his first year.

That was the beginning of a strained relationship with the Republican-controlled legislature. South Carolina's governorship is constitutionally weak and the legislature relatively strong; Sanford struggled to work within these confines. He frequently pointed out that he was the first governor in 50 years not to have come out of the legislature or state government, an observation that was obvious from his approach. After the failure of his plan in 2003 to swap a phase out of the income tax for an increase in the cigarette tax, Sanford promised to visit districts of lawmakers from both parties who did not support the plan and vetoed local issue bills that were routinely signed in the past. He angered legislators by commissioning a poll to measure his personal popularity against theirs. In 2004, Sanford again pursued an ambitious agenda, advocating tax credits for families who send their children to private schools, transfer them to another public school or home-school them. He called for worker's compensation reform, government restructuring, increasing the number of charter schools, containing health insurance costs and for a capital access program that would encourage financial institutions lend to small businesses. His tax plan drew the most attention; he proposed a 15 percent reduction in income taxes, offset by a 5-cent sales tax on lottery tickets and a 61-cent tax increase on a pack of cigarettes.

The General Assembly, primarily the Senate, again balked at his proposals. Sanford did little to placate recalcitrant legislators. He issued 106 budget vetoes to cut spending and the House overrode 105 of them. He also vetoed an economic development bill that began as the Life Sciences Act, offering tax incentives to biotech and medical research companies. Though he once supported the economic development initiative, he objected to various projects that legislators tacked onto the final bill; the legislature overwhelmingly overrode his veto. He angered legislators in the final week of the five-month legislative session by sneaking two piglets into the State House to symbolize the legislative appetite for pork. The pigs defecated on the carpet; the public, it turned out, loved the stunt. Another veto came in December, aimed at a property tax bill that would have capped valuation increases. Sanford cited the bill's unintended consequences and was applauded by the state Chamber of Commerce and the state School Boards Association.

Sanford's penchant for showmanship again surfaced in March 2005 when he brought a horse and buggy to the State House entrance to draw attention to his efforts to restructure government. "We have a system of government in this state that to a large extent is still stuck in 1895," he said. In May, he launched another round of vetoes, issuing 163 budget vetoes this time.

Sanford is up for reelection in 2006. In spring 2005, his poll ratings remained high; there was mention of him as a possible presidential candidate in 2008. Possible Democratic challengers in 2006 included state Senator Tommy Moore, Florence Mayor Frank Willis and Michael Hollings, son of former Senator Ernest Hollings.

Senior Senator

Lindsey Graham (R)

Elected 2002, seat up 2008, 1st term; b. July 9, 1955, Central; home, Seneca; U. of SC, B.A. 1977, J.D. 1981; Baptist; single.

Military Career: Air Force, 1982–88; SC Air Natl. Guard, 1989–94 (Operation Desert Storm); Air Force Reserves, 1995–present.

Elected Office: SC House of Reps., 1992–94; U.S. House of Reps., 1994–2002.

Professional Career: U.S. Air Forces Europe Circuit Trial Counsel, 1984–88; Asst. Oconee Cnty. Atty., 1988–92; Practicing atty., 1988–94; Judge Advocate, McEntire Air Natl. Guard Base, 1989–94; Central SC City Atty., 1990–94.

DC Office: 290 RSOB, 20510, 202-224-5972; Fax: 202-224-3808; Web site: lgraham.senate.gov.

State Offices: Columbia, 803-933-0112; Florence, 843-669-1505; Greenville, 864-250-1417; Mt. Pleasant, 843-849-3887; Rock Hill, 803-366-2828; Seneca, 864-888-3330.

Committees: *Armed Services*: Airland; Emerging Threats & Capabilities; Personnel (Chmn.); Strategic Forces. *Budget. Judiciary*: Antitrust, Competition Policy & Consumer Rights; Constitution, Civil Rights & Property Rights; Crime & Drugs (Chmn.); Intellectual Property; Terrorism, Technology & Homeland Security. *Veterans' Affairs.*

Group Ratings

	ADA	ACLU	AFS	LCV	ITIC	NTU	COC	ACU	NTLC	CHC
2004	25	11	14	17	83	73	88	92	88	100
2003	15	—	0	5	—	81	83	90	—	—

National Journal Ratings

	2003 LIB	—	2003 CONS		2004 LIB	—	2004 CONS
Economic	33%	—	62%		39%	—	58%
Social	0%	—	59%		0%	—	84%
Foreign	46%	—	52%		43%	—	54%

Key Votes of the 108th Congress

1. Ban Drilling in ANWR	N	5. Energy Bill	Y	9. Ban Same-Sex Marriage	Y
2. Approve Bush Tax Cuts	Y	6. Support Roe v. Wade	N	10. Ban Bunker-Buster Bomb	N
3. Medicare/Rx Bill	N	7. Ban Partial-Birth Abortion	Y	11. Fund Iraq War	Y
4. Bar Overtime Pay Regs.	N	8. Assault Weapons Ban	N	12. Restrict Missile Defense	N

Election Results

2002 general	Lindsey Graham (R)	600,010	(54%)	($6,213,563)
	Alex Sanders (D)	487,359	(44%)	($4,211,812)
2002 primary	Lindsey Graham (R)	unopposed		
1996 general	Strom Thurmond (R)	619,739	(53%)	($2,632,682)
	Elliott Close (D)	510,810	(44%)	($1,913,574)
	Other	30,419	(3%)	

Prior Winning Percentages: 2000 House (68%); 1998 House (100%); 1996 House (60%); 1994 House (60%)

Lindsey Graham, first elected to the House in 1994 and the Senate in 2002, is South Carolina's senior senator; Graham reached in two years a position it took his former colleague Ernest Hollings 36 years to reach. Graham grew up in Pickens County, where his parents owned a beer joint. His parents died after he went to college at the University of South Carolina; he became his younger sister's legal guardian. He was the first in his family to graduate from college, then received a master's and a law degree from the University of South Carolina, and then served in the Air Force as a prosecutor in Germany, Crete and other distant locales. In 1988 he returned home and practiced law in Seneca, the same town where former Senator John Edwards grew up; they were born in the same hospital two years apart. Graham also served as a judge advocate at

McEntire Air National Guard Base. He was called up to active duty and served stateside during the Gulf War. In 1992 he was elected to the state House.

In 1994, with the retirement of 20-year Congressman Butler Derrick, Graham ran for the House. Both parties had contested primaries, but the Republican contest attracted more votes—41,000 versus 35,000—and Graham won without a runoff with 52% of the vote. In the general he faced state Senator Jim Bryan. Graham called for term limits, supported more defense spending and opposed gays in the military. His attitude toward the Clinton administration and the Democratic leadership was unequivocal: "I'm one less vote for an agenda that makes you want to throw up." Graham won 60%–40%—a smashing victory in a district represented only by Democrats since Reconstruction.

In the House Graham had a solidly conservative voting record but did not always support the Republican leadership. In July 1997 he helped organize the fight to overthrow Speaker Newt Gingrich. This coup soon foundered, and in a Republican Conference meeting, when Dick Armey said no member of the leadership was involved, Graham lunged to the microphone to contradict him.

As a member of the Judiciary Committee, Graham played a major role in the impeachment of Bill Clinton. When Clinton defenders quibbled about the meaning of words and insisted that Clinton's deposition testimony was "legally accurate," Graham exploded in opposition. He was especially upset at the way Clinton used the official powers of the White House to discredit Monica Lewinsky. Yet he voted against impeaching Clinton for lying in the Paula Jones deposition, on the ground that it was later ruled immaterial by the judge. In the Senate trial Graham's folksy manner and clear description of Clinton's offenses—"Where I come from, a man who calls someone up at 2:30 in the morning is up to no good"—made him one of the most effective managers. He defied most South Carolina Republican leaders and supported John McCain in 2000 and was a tireless and highly visible supporter all over South Carolina.

Senator Strom Thurmond, reelected to his eighth term in 1996 one month before he turned 94, promised not to run again in 2002. It is not often that a Senate seat comes open in South Carolina; the last one before this was in 1941 (Thurmond and Ernest Hollings both won their seats by beating incumbent senators appointed to fill vacancies). Yet in this now heavily Republican state Graham had no opposition in the Republican primary: his work on impeachment and in the McCain campaign made him well known and well liked statewide. He was endorsed by three former governors and Bob Dole; Strom Thurmond added his endorsement in November 2001. Democrats portrayed him as lacking in substance, and state Democratic Chairman Dick Harpootlian said on the day Graham announced in February 2001 that he was "light in the loafers"; Graham accused him of slander since the phrase is sometimes used as a pejorative reference to homosexuality. Harpootlian denied any such imputation. But for all their bravado, state and national Democrats had a hard time coming up with a candidate. Finally they found a candidate, and an attractive one at that, Alex Sanders, president of the College of Charleston, with a colorful resume. Sanders ran off as a teenager and joined the circus, and was briefly a juggler and fire eater; in 1966 he was elected to the state House, in 1974 he lost a race for lieutenant governor, in 1976 he was elected to the state Senate, in 1985 he was appointed to the state Court of Appeals and in 1992 he was named college president. Sanders was also a folksy raconteur, gifted at telling hundreds of old stories, charming and well connected around the state.

Sanders was an active and energetic candidate. He dialed assiduously for dollars, even as he complained about being handed a script, and raised eventually $4.2 million, below Graham's $5.8 million, but a considerable achievement for a candidate who was always behind in the polls. He supported the Bush tax cuts (though he said he was for more tax cuts only to create jobs) and military action in Iraq. But he opposed the death penalty, on religious grounds. And he opposed a constitutional amendment to allow criminalization of flag burning. Graham hammered him on the death penalty and the flag amendment but most of all on his party. He said Sanders would advance the liberal agenda of Tom Daschle, Hillary Rodham Clinton and Edward Kennedy, and pointed to his contributions from Democratic celebrities. "Barbra Streisand, great singer, very liberal. My opponent is a nice guy, but he's getting Democratic support out the ying-yang."

Democratic ads hit Graham for supporting individual investment accounts in Social Security. Graham stood his ground and argued that the system would be broke by 2040, when many of today's voters would be about to retire. In one of their four debates Sanders, perhaps weary of being attacked for associating with glamorous liberals, said of Graham's endorsement by Rudolph Giuliani, "He's an ultraliberal. His wife kicked him out and he moved in with two gay men and a Shih Tzu. Is that South Carolina values? I don't think so." But Sanders was put on the defensive by his own comment that South Carolinians could prove they were not racists by voting for him. Trying to explain, he said, "When I said I would show America that we are not ignorant, racist, redneck Dixiecrats, I was referring to the false stereotype many people in the North have of us in South Carolina. None of these terms are applicable to Senator Thurmond, and I most certainly was not referring to him."

Graham won 54%–44%, about the margin one might have projected from the polls. So Graham took the place of a senator first elected in the year before he was born. He has had a mostly conservative voting record but has disagreed with the Bush administration on important issues. He voted against the Medicare/prescription drug bill in June and November 2003 and in March 2005 called for annual ceilings on the program's costs. He called the medical malpractice bill "one of the worst pieces of legislation I have ever seen." He voted against it in July 2003 and February 2004 when Republicans tried to limit debate and failed. "I believe my vote not to let the federal government take over the South Carolina legal system was the right thing to do for the state as a whole." He and Richard Durbin sponsored a bill to ban punitive damages on doctors participating in Medicare and Medicaid. But he supported the class action bill that passed in February 2005 and co-sponsored a bill requiring that the losing party pays the other side's legal fees in lawsuits between parties from different states. In March 2005 he proposed a federal law shielding reporters from having to disclose their sources in court.

Graham has not always been a party loyalist. Dismayed by federal deficits, he said in December 2003, "Are we the party of fiscal responsibility that we advertise ourselves to be? No. We're using the war as an excuse, overly, I think." With Hillary Rodham Clinton he co-sponsored a bill to expand health care provision for Reservists and National Guard troops. With Tom Daschle he cosponsored a bill to provide ordinary health insurance to reservists. Graham has called for quotas on clothing imports from China and called for more aggressive trade policies toward countries that dump textiles. He co-sponsored a bill in 2003 to impose a 27.5% tariff on goods from China if it does not delink its currency from the dollar.

Graham voted for the Iraq war resolution and generally backed the war. But in November 2003 he said that half of the $20 billion for reconstruction there should be loans, not grants. And, drawing on his experience as a military lawyer and the fact that he was the only senator serving in the Guard or Reserves, he aggressively investigated the Abu Ghraib abuses and sought to learn if higher officers shared responsibility.

In the House Graham and Mark Sanford sponsored a bill allowing workers to divert two-thirds of their payroll tax to personal retirement accounts. He talked about Social Security's impending fiscal problems and called for changes in his 2002 campaign. In November 2003 he unveiled his own plan: 4% of the payroll tax could go to personal retirement accounts, up to $1,300, with transition costs to come from cuts in government spending. At the Heritage Foundation in December 2004 he said any change in Social Security would require "some sacrifice." He again proposed 4% personal retirement accounts, with higher taxes for workers who do not choose them; he would also raise the income limit subject to the payroll tax. This was sharply criticized by some conservatives, but Graham persisted. He participated in private meetings with both Democratic and Republican senators, and he insisted that raising the payroll tax limit was necessary if a plan was to get Democratic support. In February 2005 he said he would hold off introducing a bill until there was a "solution mix."

On local issues, in August 2003 Graham withdrew his support for a second Catawba tribe bingo hall off I-95 after Governor Mark Sanford opposed it. In June 2004 he put into the defense authorization a provision allowing the Savannah River Site to reclassify nuclear waste; he said this would allow the waste to be disposed of more quickly and cheaply. It survived Maria Cantwell's attempt to delete it by a 48–48 vote. In February 2005, after a fatal railroad accident in South Carolina, he sponsored a rail safety bill to increase fines, require a one-year review of all rail lines and a review of all 250,000 rail crossings, with rankings of the 10,000 most in need of improvement.

Graham does not come up for reelection until 2008 and seems to be in good political shape at home. "In my state we change senators about every 50 years. So if I don't screw up too badly, I'm probably going to be around for a while. And I can take the long view of things."

In February 2005 Dick Harpootlian, impressed by Graham's independence, sent him a $2,000 contribution. "It means a lot to me that people think I'm trying to be fair and represent everyone in South Carolina," Graham said. "As to the check, there's no way I'm cashing that baby. I'm framing it."

Junior Senator

Jim DeMint (R)

Elected 2004, seat up 2010, 1st term; b. Sept. 2, 1951, Greenville; home, Greenville; U. of TN, B.S. 1973, Clemson U., M.B.A. 1981; Presbyterian; married (Debbie).

Elected Office: U.S. House of Reps., 1998–2004.

Professional Career: Sales Rep., Scott Paper, 1973–75; Acct. Rep., Henderson Advertising, 1975–81; V.P., Leslie Advertising, 1981–84; Pres., DeMint Marketing, 1983–98.

DC Office: 340 RSOB, 20510, 202-224-6121; Fax: 202-228-5143; Web site: demint.senate.gov.

State Offices: Charleston, 843-727-4525; Columbia, 803-771-6112; Greenville, 864-233-5366.

Committees: *Aging (Special). Commerce, Science & Transportation:* Aviation; Consumer Affairs, Product Safety & Insurance; Disaster Prevention & Prediction (Chmn.); National Ocean Policy Study; Technology, Innovation & Competitiveness; Trade, Tourism & Economic Development. *Environment & Public Works:* Clean Air, Climate Change & Nuclear Safety; Fisheries, Wildlife & Water. *Joint Economic Committee.*

Group Ratings (as Member of U.S. House of Representatives)

	ADA	ACLU	AFS	LCV	ITIC	NTU	COC	ACU	NTLC	CHC
2004	0	5	0	0	88	75	92	100	84	100
2003	20	—	13	5	—	78	93	96	—	—

National Journal Ratings (as Member of U.S. House of Representatives)

	2003 LIB	—	2003 CONS		2004 LIB	—	2004 CONS
Economic	39%	—	61%		0%	—	95%
Social	0%	—	95%		0%	—	91%
Foreign	29%	—	70%		17%	—	83%

Key Votes of the 108th Congress (as Member of U.S. House of Representatives)

1. Drilling in ANWR	Y	5. DC School Vouchers	Y	9. Ban Same-Sex Marriage	Y
2. Approve Bush Tax Cuts	Y	6. Ban Human Cloning	Y	10. Fund Iraq War	Y
3. Medicare/Rx Bill	N	7. Restrict Gun Liability	Y	11. Bar Cuba Embargo Funds	N
4. Bar Overtime Pay Regs.	N	8. Ban Partial-Birth Abortion	Y	12. Intelligence Reorg.	Y

Election Results

2004 general	Jim DeMint (R)	857,167	(54%)	($9,036,086)
	Inez Tenenbaum (D)	704,384	(44%)	($6,265,786)
	Other	35,670	(2%)	
2004 runoff	Jim DeMint (R)	154,644	(59%)	
	David Beasley (R)	106,480	(41%)	
2004 primary	David Beasley (R)	107,847	(37%)	
	Jim DeMint (R)	77,567	(26%)	
	Thomas Ravenel (R)	73,167	(25%)	
	Charlie Condon (R)	27,694	(9%)	
	Other	8,394	(3%)	
1998 general	Ernest Hollings (D)	563,296	(53%)	($4,968,456)
	Bob Inglis (R)	488,217	(46%)	($2,143,278)
	Other	17,444	(2%)	

Prior Winning Percentages: 2002 House (69%); 2000 House (80%); 1998 House (58%)

South Carolina's junior senator is Jim DeMint, a Republican elected in 2004. DeMint was born in Greenville where his father was stationed in the Air Force; when his parents divorced, his mother earned money by turning their home into a dancing school, The DeMint Academy of Dance and Decorum. He graduated from the University of Tennessee and Clemson business school, and returned to Greenville to work as a paper salesman and in his father-in-law's advertising business. In 1983 he founded DeMint Marketing, a research firm with businesses, schools, colleges and hospitals as clients. In 1992 he went to work for 33-year-old lawyer Bob Inglis's House campaign, honing the Inglis message using focus groups and advertising expertise. Inglis upset an incumbent Democrat by 50%–48%, and kept his promise to serve only three terms. In 1998 when Inglis ran for the Senate, DeMint ran in the 4th District. Like Inglis, he pledged to serve only three terms and take no PAC money. He called for a national sales tax or flat tax, for individual retirement accounts in Social Security, and for the right-to-life amendment. The favorite was state Senator Mike Fair, a former University of South Carolina quarterback. In the primary Fair led with 32%; DeMint came in second with 23%. In the runoff two weeks later, Fair bragged about his experience, but DeMint called him a "career politician." The result was a 53%–47% upset win for DeMint. He won the general election 58%–40%.

In the House, DeMint was elected president of the freshman class and joined other junior Republicans seeking to rein in spending by the appropriators. He resisted local pressures and was the only South Carolina House member to vote for permanent normal trade relations with China, arguing that the best way to remedy human-rights abuses was "to export our products and principles." The libertarian Cato Institute ranked DeMint in the top 1% of "free traders" in the House.

When George W. Bush in 2001 proposed his $1.6 trillion tax-cut package, DeMint was among a small group who immediately pushed for more; he was a leading advocate of the expanded adoption tax credits in the final package. He sponsored an amendment to Bush's education bill to create a state-based block-grant program; to preserve his bipartisan coalition, Education and the Workforce Chairman John Boehner tried to discourage DeMint. Bush, in a meeting in the Oval Office, got DeMint to back down. Social Security was another legislative interest. He worked to advance individual investment accounts in Social Security by getting 117 House members to sign a letter of support for the Social Security Commission and introduced legislation in 2003 that allowed people under age 55 to set aside 3% to 8% of their monthly Social Security contributions in personal investment accounts.

DeMint's votes on trade provoked serious opposition in his textile-producing district. In 2002, Public Service Commissioner and former state Representative Phil Bradley challenged him in the primary. Bradley had the support of textile titan Roger Milliken, long a financer of conservative and protectionist candidates. DeMint defended his support for free trade as beneficial for international investment in the district, and said that he also sought to protect domestic workers. DeMint won 62%–38%.

After the election, DeMint said that he would keep his promise to serve only three terms in the House and that he would run for Democrat Ernest Hollings's Senate seat in 2004. DeMint couldn't be more different than the man he sought to replace. DeMint was from South Carolina's Up Country while Hollings was a Charleston native with a Low Country political base. Hollings was one of the Senate's leading protectionists; DeMint an unwavering free trader. Where Hollings served in a variety of elected offices over a political career that spanned more than a half-century, DeMint's public service began in 1998, when he won his first House term. DeMint soon gained the backing of White House political strategist Karl Rove; in August 2003, Hollings announced he would not seek reelection. Commenting on South Carolina's increasingly Republican electorate, Hollings said, "It wouldn't be easy for anybody who's a Democrat in this state to get elected," he said.

There were three competitive challengers to DeMint in the June 8 Republican primary: former Governor David Beasley, who lost for reelection in 1998, former Attorney General Charlie Condon of Sullivan's Island, and Thomas Ravenel, a millionaire Charleston developer and son of former Congressman Arthur Ravenel.

South Carolina has lost nearly 70,000 manufacturing jobs since 1999. Trade policy is a consequential issue here. DeMint and Ravenel ran as free traders; Beasley and Condon took protectionist positions. DeMint got money from the Club for Growth. Beasley's biggest contributor was textile magnate Roger Milliken and he received contributions from many textile executives and political action committees. Beasley ran ads featuring an empty textile plant and talked about how unfair trade practices sent jobs to China; he claimed DeMint advocated trade policies that had cost the state more than 50,000 jobs. A Condon ad singled out DeMint's vote to allow China into the World Trade Organization and showed Red Army soldiers. DeMint responded with ads showing the BMW manufacturing plant near Greer and pointed to increased U.S. exports to China.

Beasley was ahead in polls for much of the primary campaign, but he was not close to the 50% percent threshold required to win the nomination outright; the real battle was for second place, which would assure a spot against Beasley in the runoff two weeks later. As expected, Beasley led the primary with 37%; DeMint came in second with 26%, 4,400 votes ahead of Ravenel, who had 25%. Condon finished fourth with 9%. In the June 22 runoff, DeMint picked up endorsements from Ravenel and Condon and won support from Republican voters still unhappy over Beasley's switches while governor on the Confederate battle flag and lottery issues; he won 59%–41% percent.

DeMint's general election opponent was State Superintendent of Education Inez Tenenbaum, a popular Democrat who had twice won statewide election. Tenenbaum ran on her record in education, and said she had secured more than $750 million for school construction and renovation and worked to increase teacher pay. South Carolina high school students, she said, were improving their SAT scores at the fastest rate in the nation. Her signature outfits were red dresses and suits and she campaigned around the state aboard the Red Dress Express, a recreational vehicle with an image of her on its sides.

She picked up where the Republican primary and runoff campaign left off, arguing that DeMint's House votes cost the state tens of thousands of jobs. She opposed the Central American Free Trade Agreement, which DeMint supported, and she was funded by textile interests. But it was taxes that gave traction to Tenenbaum. DeMint had co-sponsored a bill to replace all federal taxes with a 23% national sales tax, explaining that trade and tax policy were the paths to creating an attractive business environment in South Carolina and the nation; he repeatedly described how Daimler-Chrysler might be Chrysler-Daimler were U.S. taxes more hospitable than German ones. Tenenbaum said DeMint's advocacy for a national sales tax would result in a tax hike on 95 percent of all South Carolina residents and hammered him on the issue in ads and in staged events; his standing in the polls began to drop in the fall and he ran radio and television ads accusing Democrats of misrepresenting his position. The Democratic Senatorial Campaign Committee spent $2.5 million through September for Tenenbaum; in October, the National Republican Senatorial Committee ran a $1.3 million ad campaign to shore up DeMint.

DeMint's campaign was also sidetracked by controversy over comments he made in the first debate. He said during the debate "folks teaching in schools need to represent our values"; afterwards he said he would not require teachers to admit whether they were gay but if they were, "I do not think they should be teaching at public schools." Two days later, he suggested that unwed pregnant women also should not teach in the public schools. "I just think moral decisions are different with a teacher." On October 17, the two nominees appeared together on NBC's *Meet the Press*, where host Tim Russert grilled DeMint about his comments and pressed Tenenbaum, a former abortion rights group lobbyist, on her position on abortion.

Overall, DeMint spent $9 million to Tenenbaum's $6.2 million. He won 54%–44%, the same as Lindsey Graham in 2002. DeMint narrowly lost Charleston County by 100 votes, but won big margins in his Up Country home turf. He won 63%–35% in Greenville County and 59%–38% in Spartanburg County. South Carolina now two Republican senators for the first time since 1873. As recently as 2002 South Carolina's senior and junior senators, Strom Thurmond and Ernest Hollings, had 86 years of seniority between. In 2005, Graham and Jim DeMint had less than three years between them.

FIRST DISTRICT

Rep. Henry Brown (R)

Elected 2000, 3d term; b. Dec. 20, 1935, Bishopville; home, Hanahan; The Citadel; Baptist Col.; Baptist; married (Billye).

Military Career: SC Natl. Guard, 1953–62.

Elected Office: Hanahan City Council, 1981–85; SC House of Reps., 1985–00.

Professional Career: V.P., Piggly Wiggly Carolina Co., 1958–85.

DC Office: 1124 LHOB, 20515, 202-225-3176; Fax: 202-225-3407; Web site: www.house.gov/henrybrown.

District Offices: Myrtle Beach, 843-445-6459; N. Charleston, 843-747-4175.

Committees: *Resources* (20th of 27 R): Forests & Forest Health; National Parks. *Transportation & Infrastructure* (20th of 41 R): Aviation; Highways, Transit & Pipelines; Water Resources & Environment. *Veterans' Affairs* (8th of 16 R): Health (Chmn.).

Group Ratings

	ADA	ACLU	AFS	LCV	ITIC	NTU	COC	ACU	NTLC	CHC
2004	0	0	0	0	100	55	100	96	75	92
2003	10	—	0	10	—	59	97	92	—	—

National Journal Ratings

	2003 LIB	—	2003 CONS		2004 LIB	—	2004 CONS
Economic	21%	—	75%		17%	—	80%
Social	5%	—	87%		17%	—	81%
Foreign	0%	—	89%		10%	—	86%

Key Votes of the 108th Congress

1. Drilling in ANWR	Y	5. DC School Vouchers	Y	9. Ban Same-Sex Marriage	Y
2. Approve Bush Tax Cuts	Y	6. Ban Human Cloning	Y	10. Fund Iraq War	Y
3. Medicare/Rx Bill	Y	7. Restrict Gun Liability	Y	11. Bar Cuba Embargo Funds	N
4. Bar Overtime Pay Regs.	N	8. Ban Partial-Birth Abortion	Y	12. Intelligence Reorg.	Y

Election Results

2004 general	Henry Brown (R)	186,448	(88%)	($205,460)
	James Dunn (Green)	25,674	(12%)	
2004 primary	Henry Brown (R)	47,066	(83%)	
	Bob Batchelder (R)	9,326	(17%)	
2002 general	Henry Brown (R)	127,562	(89%)	($189,806)
	James Dunn (UCIT)	9,841	(7%)	
	Other	5,022	(4%)	

Prior Winning Percentages: 2000 (60%)

The People		Race/Ethnic Origin	Ancestry	
Area size:	3,419 sq. mi.	73.7% White	German: 9.6% USA: 9.3%	
Urban population:	78.4%	20.9% Black	English: 8.9%	
Rural population:	21.6%	1.2% Asian	**2004 Presidential Vote**	
Pop. 2000:	668,668	0.4% Native Am.	Bush (R) 172,836	(61%)
Median income:	$40,713	0.1% Hawaiian	Kerry (D) 109,790	(39%)
Poverty status:	11.5%	1.1% Two+ races	Other 1,353	(0%)
Military veterans:	17.2%	0.1% Other	**2000 Presidential Vote**	
		2.5% Hispanic Origin	Bush (R) 139,758	(59%)
			Gore (D) 91,510	(38%)
			Other 6,849	(3%)
			Cook Partisan Voting Index: R +10	

Occupation	Blue collar: 23.0%	White collar: 59.7%	Gray collar: 17.3%

Looking out across the harbor to Fort Sumter are the glorious mansions of the Battery, gazing on the same view that the hot-blooded young swells of Charleston saw in April 1861 when they fired the shots that began the Civil War. Today there are few more beautiful urban scenes in America than the pastel "single houses" of Charleston, built flush with the sidewalk, turning their shoulders to the streets, with open piazzas inside their iron gateways facing south to catch the breeze. Charleston, founded in 1670, was blessed with one of the finest harbors on the Atlantic, at the point where, Charlestonians say, the Ashley and Cooper Rivers meet to form the Atlantic Ocean. It was one of the South's two leading cities through the Civil War; across its docks went cargoes of rice, indigo, cotton and slaves, enriching the white planters and merchants who dominated the state's economic and political life. After the Civil War, Charleston became an economic backwater, enabling the old buildings to survive; more recently, prosperity and insurance payouts after Hurricane Hugo in 1989 have funded loving restorations, making the center city look better than ever—and able to attract an annual $5.7 billion in tourism revenue.

This old society, descended from Barbados planters and French Huguenots, Sephardic Jews and the second sons of English gentry, was once a leading force in American political life. The hotheads in the gallery disrupted the 1860 Democratic National Convention here so boisterously that it was adjourned and reconvened in Baltimore, while Southern Democrats split off and nominated their own candidate, enabling Abraham Lincoln to win with 38% of the popular vote. The local accent seems to outsiders to have a touch of New Jersey and can be incomprehensible when rapidly spoken. The history of black South Carolinians, memorialized in George Gershwin's *Porgy and Bess*, is long and noteworthy, but the tale of slavery, once hidden under a blanket of politeness, is only now emerging, as many, though not all, plantations near Charleston add programs on the history of slavery to tours once dominated by romantic tales of the old South.

Some 25 years ago, Navy and Air Force bases accounted for 20% of payrolls in metropolitan Charleston. Many of these bases are now closed, but a vibrant private economy with lots of small companies has emerged, most notably at the 1,600-acre Charleston Naval Base, which, thanks to concerted efforts by regional officials, has created thousands of new jobs since it closed in 1996. Now Vought Aircraft and Alenia Aeronautica are building an aircraft factory near the Charleston airport. Ninety miles northeast, Myrtle Beach has also bounced back impressively from the loss of an air force base in 1991; after years in which the site sat dormant, a mix of commercial and residential development has sparked a boom in retirees and vacationers. Although far from an Interstate, Myrtle Beach and the Grand Strand, the miles of beachfront and 123 golf courses, attract 14 million tourists annually and the population of Horry County population has more than doubled since 1980. Myrtle Beach has taken steps to rein in its visual clutter, hoping to join the rest of the Low Country as one of the most gracefully growing regions of the United States.

The 1st Congressional District of South Carolina stretches along the coast from south of Charleston to north of Myrtle Beach, including Murrells Inlet, Pawleys Island and Litchfield Beach. It includes the heavily white Battery and the area west of the Ashley River but not the heavily black areas to the north and in North Charleston; still, the 1st District's population is

21% black. It also includes the burgeoning suburbs in Berkeley and Dorchester Counties. This is solidly Republican country, 61% for George W. Bush in 2004. But the conservatism of the Low Country district is more economic and less cultural than the conservatism of Up Country South Carolina; many voters here favor environmental restrictions and efforts to curb sprawl. This area was strong for John McCain in the 2000 presidential primary and nearly unanimous for Mark Sanford, the former 1st District congressman, in the 2002 nomination for governor.

The congressman from the 1st District is Henry Brown, a Republican first elected in 2000. Brown grew up on a small farm in Cordesville in Berkeley County, worked at the Charleston Naval Shipyard as his father had, and then spent almost 30 years working for the Piggly Wiggly grocery chain, where he eventually became a vice president. In 1981, at age 45, Brown was elected to the city council in Hanahan, north of North Charleston. In 1985 he was elected to the state House in a special election; after the 1994 election he became chairman of the Ways and Means Committee. When Sanford, first elected to the House in 1994, made clear he would keep his promise to serve only three terms in the House, Brown and other Republicans started running for the seat after the 1998 election. Brown stressed issues of concern to the district's many senior citizens—property tax relief and shoring up Social Security. To boost his name recognition, he distributed 20,000 "Oh! Henry" chocolate bars. His chief opponent, Buck Limehouse, was best known as head of the state's Transportation Commission. Brown won endorsements from many legislators and from Christian conservatives. Limehouse, a Charleston developer, spent $790,000 to Brown's $315,000 and had the support of most party leaders. In the six-candidate primary Brown led 44%–34%. In the runoff two weeks later, Brown won 55%–45%. In the anticlimactic general election, Brown won 60%–36%.

In the House, Brown has usually had a conservative voting record. Responding to court decisions, he sponsored a constitutional amendment to ban child pornography, and the House passed his resolution expressing support for public schools that display "God Bless America." In March 2004, he fueled a local controversy when brush that he was burning on his property, with a permit, jumped to adjacent federal lands and burned 20 acres. When the Forest Service told him that he would be fined, Brown threatened to retaliate with congressional action; after the regulators agreed to clarify a regulation, he agreed to pay a $250 fine. In 2005 he lost a bid for Appropriations. Instead, he added Resources to his previous seats on Transportation and Veterans Affairs. Brown had no Democratic opponent in 2002 or 2004.

SECOND DISTRICT

Rep. Joe Wilson (R)

Elected Dec. 2001, 2d full term; b. July 31, 1947, Charleston; home, Springdale; Washington & Lee U., B.A., 1969, U. of S.C., J.D., 1972; Presbyterian; married (Roxanne).

Military Career: Army Reserves, 1972–75; SC Natl. Guard, 1975–2001.

Elected Office: SC Senate, 1985–2001.

Professional Career: Practicing atty., 1972–2001.

DC Office: 212 CHOB, 20515, 202-225-2452; Fax: 202-225-2455; Web site: joewilson.house.gov.

District Offices: Beaufort, 843-521-2530; West Columbia, 803-939-0041.

Committees: *Armed Services* (21st of 34 R): Tactical Air & Land Forces; Terrorism, Unconventional Threats & Capabilities. *Education & the Workforce* (14th of 27 R): Education Reform; Employer-Employee Relations. *International Relations* (21st of 27 R): Asia & the Pacific; Oversight & Investigations.

Group Ratings

	ADA	ACLU	AFS	LCV	ITIC	NTU	COC	ACU	NTLC	CHC
2004	0	0	0	0	70	75	100	96	97	92
2003	5	—	0	0	—	67	93	88	—	—

National Journal Ratings

	2003 LIB	—	2003 CONS		2004 LIB	—	2004 CONS
Economic	0%	—	91%		0%	—	95%
Social	15%	—	84%		20%	—	77%
Foreign	36%	—	63%		32%	—	68%

Key Votes of the 108th Congress

1. Drilling in ANWR	Y	5. DC School Vouchers	Y	9. Ban Same-Sex Marriage	Y
2. Approve Bush Tax Cuts	Y	6. Ban Human Cloning	Y	10. Fund Iraq War	Y
3. Medicare/Rx Bill	Y	7. Restrict Gun Liability	Y	11. Bar Cuba Embargo Funds	N
4. Bar Overtime Pay Regs.	N	8. Ban Partial-Birth Abortion	Y	12. Intelligence Reorg.	Y

Election Results

2004 general	Joe Wilson (R) 181,862	(65%)	($944,659)
	Michael Ellisor (D) 93,249	(33%)	($12,990)
	Other... 4,447	(2%)	
2004 primary	Joe Wilson (R) .... unopposed		
2002 general	Joe Wilson (R) 144,149	(84%)	($1,305,481)
	Mark Whittington (UCIT) 17,189	(10%)	($8,178)
	James Legg (Lib) 9,650	(6%)	

Prior Winning Percentages: 2001 (73%)

The People		Race/Ethnic Origin	Ancestry	
Area size:	5,237 sq. mi.	68.0% White	German: 10.0% USA: 9.9%	
Urban population:	66.0%	26.2% Black	English: 7.9%	
Rural population:	34.0%	1.1% Asian	**2004 Presidential Vote**	
Pop. 2000:	668,668	0.3% Native Am.	Bush (R)............. 174,340	(60%)
Median income:	$42,915	0.0% Hawaiian	Kerry (D)........... 114,253	(39%)
Poverty status:	11.0%	0.9% Two+ races	Other 1,604	(1%)
Military veterans:	15.1%	0.1% Other	**2000 Presidential Vote**	
		3.3% Hispanic Origin	Bush (R)............. 145,953	(58%)
			Gore (D).............. 97,985	(39%)
			Other 6,374	(3%)
			Cook Partisan Voting Index: R + 9	

Occupation   Blue collar: 22.6%   White collar: 63.1%   Gray collar: 14.3%

In 1786, soon after the Revolutionary War, the South Carolina legislature decided to move the state's capital away from the Charleston aristocracy and into the Up Country interior, away from a city named after a king to a new city named after a discoverer of America: so began Columbia. The State House was built on high ground above the Congaree River in a town of one-and-a-half story houses with first floor porticoes, dormers and raised brick basements—"Columbia cottages." In 1865, General William Tecumseh Sherman's army burned almost everything here but the State House. Columbia recovered, but grew slowly, with state government and the university, the Army's Fort Jackson and local insurance companies providing steady employment. Manufacturing boomed in the 1970s, making Columbia a confident city, not just a village-capital. For a time, Columbia's politics was personified by Jimmy Byrnes, the Democrat who returned from top posts in Franklin D. Roosevelt's Washington to serve as governor and lament the *Brown v. Board of Education* decision in 1954. Since then, upwardly mobile South Carolinians, transplanted from underdeveloped rural areas to comfortable two-car-garage subdivisions, turned Republican, first in national and then in state and local elections. Metro Columbia area has been mostly Republican: the increasing black percentage in Columbia's Richland County has helped Democrats carry it, but faster-growing Lexington County across the river has remained heavily Republican.

The 2d Congressional District of South Carolina includes most of metro Columbia, except for black neighborhoods in northern and western Columbia and the southern and eastern parts of Richland County that are in the black-majority 6th District. It contains the city's affluent white neighborhoods and the spread-out towns of Richland and Lexington Counties, with their shopping centers, churches and the Army's huge training center, Fort Jackson. The district extends south, taking in Barnwell County, which includes half of the Savannah River Site, one of the nation's nuclear weapons manufacturing complexes; it takes in horse farm country around Aiken and several lightly populated, low-income, black-majority rural counties. The 2d also includes fast-growing Beaufort County on the coast, with the old county seat of Beaufort, the carefully manicured developments of Hilton Head Island and the Marine Corps's Parris Island training base. This part of the district distinctively blends old and new: Beaufort's wonderful mansions and evocative Spanish moss provided the backdrop for the prose of Pat Conroy and the 1983 movie *The Big Chill*, while the posh condominium developments and golfing resorts around Hilton Head and the Sun City Hilton Head development started in 1993 helped drive up Beaufort County's population by 57% from 1990 to 2004—the state's highest growth rate. Local officials complain of a "capacity crunch" and some people in Hilton Head want it to secede from the county. On nearby St. Helena Island slaveowners, hating the heat and mosquitoes, ran largely absentee operations, thus allowing Gullah culture—a fusion of English and African elements—to thrive. The current lines of the 2d make the district 26% black—enough to whittle down but not jeopardize its Republican margins. George W. Bush won 60% of the vote here in 2004.

The congressman from the 2d District is Joe Wilson, a Republican first chosen in a December 2001 special election. Wilson grew up in Charleston and graduated from Washington and Lee and the University of South Carolina law school. He worked as aide to 2d District Congressman Floyd Spence and Senator Strom Thurmond and was deputy general counsel at the Energy Department in the Reagan administration. He practiced law in West Columbia for 25 years and worked on many campaigns, including Spence's; in 1984, he was elected to the state Senate, where he chaired the Transportation Committee. He retired as a lawyer in the Army National Guard and one of his sons has been an intelligence officer in Iraq. In 2001, when Spence died after more than 30 years in the House and just after serving six years as chairman of the Armed Services Committee, Wilson immediately became the frontrunner to replace his longtime ally and pledged to continue his focus on national defense. He won the Republican primary with 76% of the vote and in December defeated his Democratic opponent 73%–25%.

In the House, Wilson followed Spence to Armed Services and has had a mostly conservative voting record, though he has been a bit more to the center on foreign policy. He advocated a closer military relationship with India in the war on terrorism and he became co-chairman of the Caucus on India and Indian Americans. He joined most other Carolina Republicans in opposing trade promotion authority, but was an early supporter of the Bush proposal to eliminate double taxation of dividends. On the Education and the Workforce Committee, he got the House to pass a bill to expand college loan forgiveness for math, science and special education teachers who work in impoverished areas.

Wilson has not faced a serious challenge for reelection. When he demanded in April 2004 that John Kerry apologize for criticizing soldiers in Vietnam in 1971, former Senator Max Cleland said that Wilson was part of the "chicken hawks" who never went to war. Wilson attacked the name-calling and Kerry's accusation that the military was "complicit in war crimes."

THIRD DISTRICT

Rep. Gresham Barrett (R)

Elected 2002, 2d term; b. Feb. 14, 1961, Westminster; home, Westminster; The Citadel, B.S. 1983; Baptist; married (Natalie).

Military Career: Army, 1983–87.

Elected Office: SC House of Reps., 1996–2002.

Professional Career: Furniture store owner, 1987–96.

DC Office: 1523 LHOB, 20515, 202-225-5301; Fax: 202-225-3216; Web site: www.house.gov/barrett.

District Offices: Aiken, 803-649-5571; Anderson, 864-224-7401; Greenwood, 864-223-8251.

Committees: *Budget* (9th of 22 R). *Financial Services* (28th of 37 R): Capital Markets, Insurance & Government Sponsored Enterprises; Financial Institutions & Consumer Credit; Oversight & Investigations. *International Relations* (23d of 27 R): Europe & Emerging Threats; International Terrorism & Nonproliferation.

Group Ratings

	ADA	ACLU	AFS	LCV	ITIC	NTU	COC	ACU	NTLC	CHC
2004	0	0	0	0	70	80	100	100	100	100
2003	10	—	13	5	—	76	87	96	—	—

National Journal Ratings

	2003 LIB	—	2003 CONS		2004 LIB	—	2004 CONS
Economic	29%	—	70%		0%	—	95%
Social	5%	—	87%		0%	—	91%
Foreign	36%	—	63%		10%	—	86%

Key Votes of the 108th Congress

1. Drilling in ANWR	Y	5. DC School Vouchers	Y	9. Ban Same-Sex Marriage	Y
2. Approve Bush Tax Cuts	Y	6. Ban Human Cloning	Y	10. Fund Iraq War	Y
3. Medicare/Rx Bill	N	7. Restrict Gun Liability	Y	11. Bar Cuba Embargo Funds	N
4. Bar Overtime Pay Regs.	N	8. Ban Partial-Birth Abortion	Y	12. Intelligence Reorg.	Y

Election Results

2004 general	Gresham Barrett (R) .... unopposed			($647,828)
2004 primary	Gresham Barrett (R) .... unopposed			
2002 general	Gresham Barrett (R) 119,644	(67%)		($960,402)
	George Brightharp (D) 55,743	(31%)		($64,187)
	Other... 2,808	(2%)		

The People		Race/Ethnic Origin	Ancestry	
Area size:	5,568 sq. mi.	76.0% White	USA: 15.0%	Irish: 8.0%
Urban population:	50.3%	20.5% Black	English: 7.3%	
Rural population:	49.7%	0.6% Asian	**2004 Presidential Vote**	
Pop. 2000:	668,669	0.2% Native Am.	Bush (R) 169,283	(66%)
Median income:	$36,092	0.0% Hawaiian	Kerry (D) 86,947	(34%)
Poverty status:	13.3%	0.7% Two+ races	Other 1,986	(1%)
Military veterans:	13.5%	0.1% Other	**2000 Presidential Vote**	
		1.9% Hispanic Origin	Bush (R) 142,414	(63%)
			Gore (D) 77,694	(34%)
			Other 5,185	(2%)
			Cook Partisan Voting Index: R +14	

Occupation	Blue collar: 36.8%	White collar: 48.7%	Gray collar: 14.5%

The South Carolina Up Country, many days' travel by wagon from the Low Country plantations, was first settled by Scots-Irish farmers, including the family of John C. Calhoun around the time of the Revolutionary War. The pioneers wanted to make big plantations of these forests, but the land was too hilly for the labor-intensive rice crops grown in the Low Country and sometimes too cold for cotton. So relatively few slaves were brought here, and the land became mostly small farms owned by whites. Today, the racial and cultural tone of Up Country South Carolina shows traces of these roots. This is a mostly white part of the South, with a hell-of-a-fella tone to daily life and a tradition-minded slice of Middle America. Yet even this area has been touched by change. Aiken, with its horsey trappings, has long attracted affluent transplants. The nearby Savannah River Site—a 310-square-mile federal weapons plant complex that for four decades produced tritium and plutonium that fueled America's nuclear arsenal—employed generations of highly trained engineers (and produced nuclear waste), but more than 10,000 were laid off in the past decade; some local leaders want to build a nuclear power plant there. Today, Interstate 85—once the Main Street of America's textile belt—sits amidst a booming southeastern corridor that runs from Raleigh-Durham to Atlanta. Clemson University, founded here by Calhoun's son-in-law and one of state's two land-grant institutions, has helped attract European companies seeking sites for big plants to this area.

The 3d Congressional District of South Carolina follows the Georgia border north from the Savannah River Site through the tree-harvesting country around McCormick County to mountains along the North Carolina border. The southern part of the 3d has a few heavily black areas, like Edgefield County, where Strom Thurmond grew up and first won public office in the 1930s; Edgefield County grew significantly in the 1990s as it became part of the metropolitan area around Aiken and Augusta, Georgia. This part of South Carolina, ancestrally Democratic, began trending Republican in the 1950s, first in Yankified Aiken, then in the Up Country as cultural issues became more important in this fervently religious area. The 3d has consistently voted Republican even when Democrats have won statewide elections. In 2004 George W. Bush won 66% of the vote here, his best showing in a South Carolina district.

The congressman from the 3d District is Gresham Barrett, a Republican first elected in 2002. Barrett grew up in Westminster in Oconee County and graduated from The Citadel in Charleston. After serving as an artillery captain in the First Cavalry Division at Fort Hood, he returned home to run his family's furniture store. In 1996 he was elected to the state House. In 2001 when Lindsey Graham, the first Republican to hold this seat since Reconstruction, started running for the Senate, Barrett quickly became the frontrunner to succeed him. He opposed abortion, defended gun owner rights, called for a national missile defense system and new weapons technology as part of the effort to "hunt down scum like Osama bin Laden and wipe their kind from the face of the Earth." He told voters that government should operate more like a business—his business, specifically. Government should work "like Barrett's Furniture, where you get service, you get simplicity and people are there to help you." With a superior grass roots organization, he got 43% of the vote in the six-candidate June primary. In the two-week runoff campaign, second-place-finisher state Representative Jim Klauber argued that Barrett wasn't tough enough in cracking down on illegal immigrants; Barrett insisted that military issues were paramount. He raised more money, won more endorsements and won the runoff 65%–35%. Barrett won the general election 67%–31%.

In the House, Barrett hoped for a seat on Armed Services but instead got Budget and Financial Services. Ever the Citadel graduate (his father, brother and two nephews are also grads), he drew attention for his crisp, military bearing. "With his pressed suits and posture as perfect as the Washington Monument's, Gresham Barrett is perhaps Congress' most starched member," wrote *The State* newspaper. He joined the Republican Study Committee and had a conservative voting record with occasional maverick tendencies; he was one of the 15 House Republicans who voted against both the Medicare deal and the omnibus appropriations bill in late 2003. The House passed his amendment for the Energy Department to study the feasibility of commercial nuclear energy production at Savannah River. He sponsored a bill to stop immigration into the United States from any "known terrorist state." Barrett was unopposed in 2004.

FOURTH DISTRICT

Rep. Bob Inglis (R)

Elected 2004, 1st term; b. Oct. 11, 1959, Bluffton; home, Travelers Rest; Duke U., B.A. 1981, U. of VA Law Schl., J.D. 1984; Presbyterian; married (Mary Anne).

Elected Office: U.S. House of Reps., 1992–98.

Professional Career: Practicing atty., 1984–92.

DC Office: 330 CHOB, 20515, 202-225-6030; Fax: 202-226-1177; Web site: www.house.gov/inglis.

District Offices: Greenville, 864-232-1141; Spartanburg, 864-582-6422.

Committees: *Education & the Workforce* (18th of 27 R): 21st Century Competitiveness; Select Education. *Judiciary* (12th of 23 R): Courts, the Internet & Intellectual Property; Immigration, Border Security & Claims. *Science* (18th of 24 R): Energy; Research (Chmn.).

Group Ratings and Key Votes: Newly Elected

Election Results

2004 general	Bob Inglis (R)	188,795	(70%)	($511,913)
	Brandon Brown (D)	78,376	(29%)	($15,778)
	Other	3,273	(1%)	
2004 primary	Bob Inglis (R)	52,125	(84%)	
	Carole Wells (R)	7,140	(12%)	
	Jack Adams (R)	2,628	(4%)	
2002 general	Jim DeMint (R)	122,422	(69%)	($458,695)
	Peter Ashy (D)	51,462	(29%)	
	Other	3,533	(2%)	

Prior Winning Percentages: 1996 (71%); 1994 (73%); 1992 (50%)

The People		Race/Ethnic Origin	Ancestry	
Area size:	2,165 sq. mi.	74.6% White	USA: 13.7%	English: 8.0%
Urban population:	73.5%	19.7% Black	Irish: 7.5%	
Rural population:	26.5%	1.3% Asian	**2004 Presidential Vote**	
Pop. 2000:	668,669	0.2% Native Am.	Bush (R) 181,255	(65%)
Median income:	$39,417	0.0% Hawaiian	Kerry (D) 94,760	(34%)
Poverty status:	11.4%	0.8% Two+ races	Other 3,232	(1%)
Military veterans:	12.8%	0.1% Other	**2000 Presidential Vote**	
		3.2% Hispanic Origin	Bush (R) 151,975	(64%)
			Gore (D) 78,449	(33%)
			Other 5,843	(2%)
			Cook Partisan Voting Index: R +15	

Occupation   Blue collar: 30.8%   White collar: 56.0%   Gray collar: 13.2%

A century ago, Northern investors seeking sites for textile mills looked at the Up Country of South Carolina and found what was described then as "mild climate, abundant water power, proximity to the cotton fields and plenty of native [white] labor already accustomed to a low standard of living." As mills fled New England, textile factories settled along the Southern Railway and Seaboard Coast Line tracks between Charlotte and Atlanta, especially in the Piedmont of South Carolina. The textile country might look bucolic, but Greenville, Spartanburg and the dozens of mill towns thick in the surrounding countryside became as industrial as Lancashire or the Ruhr, with mills rising up on what were once twisting woodland paths. In the days before child labor laws, factory work sometimes began at age six, condemning workers to a life of illiteracy; escapes to a brighter future, such as the brilliant but brief baseball career of West Greenville's Shoeless Joe Jackson, were rare.

Today, this same stretch of land along Interstate 85, which parallels the Southern Railway, remains one of the largest textile-producing areas in the United States, even though many mills have shut down and others are not likely to survive. But there is much more to the local economy than textiles. Although more than 20,000 textile and apparel jobs have been lost since 2000, with closings accelerated by the end of the Multifiber Agreement in January 2005, many of those workers have taken jobs with the new companies that have moved in. So many other jobs have been created that the South Carolina Textile Manufacturers Alliance dropped "Textiles" from its name. Financial sweeteners, tax incentives, the absence of unions and solid infrastructure—airports, interstate highways, and the busy port of Charleston—have attracted an enormous BMW plant, the American headquarters of Michelin and a big Fuji Photo factory, among many others. Greenville's revitalized downtown now boasts fancy hotels and restaurants, including Korean, Thai and Vietnamese cuisine—each catering to the new corporate manager class.

The 4th Congressional District of South Carolina includes all of Greenville and Spartanburg Counties, plus much smaller Union County and a sliver of Laurens County. Culturally, the 4th ranges from conservative to very conservative, with strong influence from Greenville's many evangelical and fundamentalist churches. Bob Jones University is here; it has dropped its longtime ban on interracial dating but students are still prohibited from smoking, drinking, dancing and wearing jeans or shorts to class. Large new subdivisions continue to sprout between Greenville and Spartanburg. Newcomers to the area have brought religious diversity. Greenville has growing populations not only of Catholics and Jews, but also Muslims, Buddhists, Hindus, Baha'is, and the only gay-oriented church within 60 miles. Still, this is a heavily Republican district, with the smallest black percentage in the state, and George W. Bush won 65% of the vote here in 2004. Here the real political divide is between religious and economic conservatives.

The congressman from the 4th District once again is Bob Inglis, who was elected in 2004 after having served from 1993 to 1999. He grew up in the Low Country, excelled at Duke and the University of Virginia law school and moved to Greenville to practice commercial law. He ran for the House against a Democratic incumbent in 1992 and pledged to serve only three terms, to take no money from political action committees and to oppose pork barrel projects even in South Carolina; he won 50%–48%. In the House, Inglis kept his promises. His calls for change went mostly unheeded in his first term, but when Republicans won the House they voted to apply all laws to Congress, cut staff and passed a gift ban. He resisted joining the Washington culture and slept in his office on an air mattress. In 1998 he ran against Senator Ernest Hollings and lost 53%–46%.

In 2004, Inglis traded places with Jim DeMint, his House successor, who honored his own term-limits pledge and was elected to the Senate as Hollings retired. Inglis again ran as the citizen-politician. He was "reinvigorated" by his time in private life, which he spent practicing law. But this time he refused to make another term limits pledge, which he said would be "unilateral disarmament" for local interests. He suggested that the Capitol Hill culture had changed, so that the same strategies that made sense after Republicans captured the House majority in 1994 no longer were required. Ever the budget hawk, Inglis enlisted his wife as his top campaign aide, eschewed political consultants, ran his race out of his home and refused PAC contributions. By getting an early start and raising large amounts of money, he scared off any serious competition. He won 84% of the vote in the Republican primary. In November, he defeated funeral home executive Brandon Brown, 70%–29%. He was reassigned to the Judiciary Committee, with his accrued seniority, and also joined the Education and the Workforce and Science Committees as the most senior freshman. With two junior Republicans holding Senate seats, he may be settled in for a long career in the House. This time, he pledged, no more "sanctimony."

FIFTH DISTRICT

Rep. John Spratt (D)

Elected 1982, 12th term; b. Nov. 1, 1942, Charlotte, NC; home, York; Davidson Col., A.B. 1964, Oxford U., M.A. 1966, Yale U., LL.B. 1969; Presbyterian; married (Jane Stacy).

Military Career: Army Operations, U.S. Dept. of Defense, 1969–71.

Professional Career: Practicing atty., 1971–82; Pres., Bank of Ft. Mill, 1973–82; Pres., Spratt Insurance Agcy., 1973–82.

DC Office: 1401 LHOB, 20008, 202-225-5501; Fax: 202-225-0464; Web site: www.house.gov/spratt.

District Offices: Darlington, 843-393-3998; Rock Hill, 803-327-1114; Sumter, 803-773-3362.

Committees: *Armed Services* (2d of 28 D): Strategic Forces; Tactical Air & Land Forces. *Budget* (RMM of 17 D).

Group Ratings

	ADA	ACLU	AFS	LCV	ITIC	NTU	COC	ACU	NTLC	CHC
2004	80	50	88	100	40	10	48	20	6	23
2003	95	—	100	90	—	20	32	29	—	—

National Journal Ratings

	2003 LIB	—	2003 CONS		2004 LIB	—	2004 CONS
Economic	70%	—	30%		63%	—	36%
Social	65%	—	35%		62%	—	37%
Foreign	75%	—	25%		59%	—	40%

Key Votes of the 108th Congress

1. Drilling in ANWR	N	5. DC School Vouchers	N	9. Ban Same-Sex Marriage	Y
2. Approve Bush Tax Cuts	N	6. Ban Human Cloning	N	10. Fund Iraq War	Y
3. Medicare/Rx Bill	N	7. Restrict Gun Liability	Y	11. Bar Cuba Embargo Funds	N
4. Bar Overtime Pay Regs.	Y	8. Ban Partial-Birth Abortion	Y	12. Intelligence Reorg.	Y

Election Results

2004 general	John Spratt (D)	152,867	(63%)	($757,151)
	Albert Spencer (R)	89,568	(37%)	($1,215)
2004 primary	John Spratt (D) .... unopposed			
2002 general	John Spratt (D)	121,912	(86%)	($406,711)
	Doug Kendall (Lib)	11,013	(8%)	
	Steve Lefemine (CNP)...........................	8,930	(6%)	

Prior Winning Percentages: 2000 (59%); 1998 (58%); 1996 (54%); 1994 (52%); 1992 (61%); 1990 (100%); 1988 (70%); 1986 (100%); 1984 (92%); 1982 (68%)

The People		Race/Ethnic Origin	Ancestry		
Area size:	7,141 sq. mi.	64.1% White	USA: 14.8%	Irish: 5.6%	
Urban population:	46.7%	32.2% Black	English: 5.6%		
Rural population:	53.3%	0.5% Asian	**2004 Presidential Vote**		
Pop. 2000:	668,668	0.6% Native Am.	Bush (R)	143,001	(57%)
Median income:	$35,416	0.0% Hawaiian	Kerry (D)	104,850	(42%)
Poverty status:	15.2%	0.7% Two+ races	Other	2,471	(1%)
Military veterans:	13.0%	0.1% Other	**2000 Presidential Vote**		
		1.8% Hispanic Origin	Bush (R)	119,052	(55%)
			Gore (D)	93,637	(43%)
			Other	3,979	(2%)
			Cook Partisan Voting Index: R + 6		
Occupation	Blue collar: 37.5%	White collar: 48.5%	Gray collar: 14.1%		

Some of the fiercest battles of the Revolutionary War were fought in South Carolina's Up Country, on hilly lands just being settled by Scots-Irish farmers moving up from the Low Countryor down the Virginia Piedmont valley. This was a country of violent passions and unclear lines; Carolinians have long argued over which side of the North and South Carolina boundary Andrew Jackson was born in 1767. Ever since, the fighting spirit and Calvinist faith of Up Country Carolinians have never wavered. This "Olde English District" remains intensely religious and pro-military. But it is no longer impoverished. For many years, the dominant industry here was textiles, traditionally the first factory enterprise of industrializing countries, with low pay and poor working conditions. But in the 1980s and 1990s the number of textile jobs declined, and small business prosperity more recently has been barreling out the interstates from Greenville-Spartanburg and Columbia and Charlotte, to transform counties once dependent on tobacco fields and textile mills.

The 5th Congressional District of South Carolina consists of all or part of 14 counties, mostly in the Up Country. It includes fast-growing (up 40% from 1990 to 2004) York County, part of the Charlotte, North Carolina, metro area; growth accelerated here after settlement of the Catawba Indians' land claims in 1993. Just to the east is Lancaster County, where Del Webb's Sun City Carolina Lakes has plans for 12,000 new homes, more than half the county's total. Further east, the 5th includes Dillon County, site of the pink, orange and turquoise South of the Border tourist attraction heralded on 250 billboards on I-95, and Darlington, site of the Southern 500 stock car race every Labor Day. It also includes lowland tobacco country, including Marlboro and Chesterfield Counties. Politically, this homeland of Andrew Jackson is ancestrally Democratic. But Republicans are now competitive if not dominant here: the tobacco counties are heavily Democratic but York County is trending Republican. George W. Bush won 55% of the districtwide vote in 2000 and 57% in 2004; in 2002 the 5th was carried by Democratic Governor Jim Hodges, who lives in the district, and by Republican Senator Lindsey Graham.

The congressman from the 5th District is John Spratt, ranking minority member on the House Budget Committee and assistant to the minority leader, a Democrat first elected in 1982. He comes from a prominent York County family and graduated from Davidson College, Oxford University and Yale Law School. He served two years in the Army, in the Operations Analysis Group in the office of the Pentagon comptroller. He first got involved in politics in Charles Ravenel's unsuccessful 1974 campaign for governor. In 1982 the 5th District incumbent announced his retirement a week before the filing deadline; Spratt put a campaign together fast and won 38% in the primary, 55% in the runoff against a high-spending candidate, and 68% in the general. And so a campaign quickly put together has given Spratt a seat in the House for more than 20 years and a key role in shaping national legislation.

Spratt is the second-ranking Democrat on the Armed Services Committee. In the 1980s, he worked with Chairman Les Aspin and, in his thick Carolina accent and with impressive knowledge of details, stitched together compromises on the MX missile, binary nerve gas weapons, the Strategic Defense Initiative, and the Savannah River Site and other nuclear plants—keeping military projects flowing through the House, many of whose members were constantly looking to cut military spending. In the late 1990s Spratt was the House Democrats' lead man on missile defense; his amendment on the subject prevailed in February 1995 by 218–212, the first significant defeat of a Contract with America promise in the Republican House. Later he called for development of missile defense, but warned against hasty departure from the ABM treaty. After George W. Bush abrogated the treaty, Spratt moved in May 2004 to shift money from ballistic missile defense to theater defenses against tactical missiles, like the Navy's Area Missile Defense system and the Patriot missiles; that was defeated.

On the Iraq war resolution, Spratt played a key role for House Democrats. In September 2002, after Bush's speech at the United Nations, Minority Leader Dick Gephardt turned to Spratt and Ike Skelton, ranking Democrat on Armed Services, for help in drafting an alternative to the broad White House resolution authorizing the use of force. Spratt sought another round of weapons inspections and wanted Bush to ask for U.N. approval and suggested removing a phrase authorizing any action to ensure peace and security in the region; the administration agreed to delete it. He sought advice from Anthony Zinni, Joseph Hoar and other retired generals with experience in the region, and found that they were wary of military action against Iraq. When Gephardt went to the White House and agreed on a resolution, Spratt continued to prepare a Democratic alternative, working with Minority Whip Nancy Pelosi. He saw "no need to invoke preemptive intervention or to draw a tenuous connection between Iraq and Al Qaeda." His resolution authorized military action if the U.N. approved and left room for the administration to seek another resolution from Congress if the U.N. did not approve. "Iraq's defiance of Security Council resolutions is enough to warrant force, particularly if it does not comply with a new, tougher round of arms inspections," Spratt said, but he also argued that it was worth getting approval from others. He offered his resolution as an amendment and it was defeated 270–155; Democrats favored it 147–60 but Republicans opposed it 210–8. Spratt joined the majority and voted for the resolution sponsored by the administration and Gephardt, which passed 296–133. After the 2002 election, Gephardt stepped down and Pelosi was elected minority leader; one of her first acts was to appoint Spratt assistant to the leader and name him her designee on budget issues—a sign, it appeared, that she would be paying attention to moderates in the Democratic Caucus.

In 1991 Spratt got a seat on the Budget Committee. His moderate voting record made him a natural point of contact between the parties, but Democrats did not see him as their leader: In their November 1992 caucus, he was beaten for Budget chairman by the more liberal Martin Sabo by 149–112. He rotated off the committee in 1992, then ran for the ranking Democrat position on Budget again in December 1996. Democrats, now in the minority, were more ready for his leadership; he beat the more liberal Louise Slaughter by 106–83. He played a major role in putting together the May 1997 agreement to reach a balanced budget.

The bipartisanship of that period has not continued, and Spratt has been given the role of offering Democratic alternatives which are beaten on party lines. In early 2001 he urged Bush to approach the budget as Bill Clinton did in 1997, with negotiations between leaders of both parties. But the new Budget chairman, Jim Nussle, instead offered a budget resolution based on Bush's program, with a $1.6 trillion tax cut over 10 years and a 4% increase in non-defense spending. Spratt's alternative offered a smaller tax cut, with one-third of the surplus going to tax cuts, one-third to increased spending and one-third to a "strategic reserve fund." He decried the size of the Republican tax cuts. After September 11, he issued a report predicting that the budget surplus would disappear in 2002 and quite possibly for several years. In 2002 he called for negotiations like those that produced the 1997 budget agreement or the 1990 budget summit in which Bush's father agreed to break his promise and raise taxes. "He can take a page from his father's experience and hope it doesn't cost him what it cost his dad. But his dad did the right thing." In 2002 Republicans once again passed a budget resolution along party lines; surveying the deficits ahead, Spratt blamed them on the 2001 Bush tax cuts, but said that he would not urge their repeal. In July 2003, in response to another monopartisan budget resolution, Spratt said, "Republican claims that spending discipline and economic growth are the solution to our budget problem are not supportable." In September 2003 he presented forecasts that operations in Iraq could cost $418 billion over 10 years. In 2004 Nussle joined Spratt in expressing concern about the administration's practice of omitting from budget projections expenses for Iraq and Afghanistan provided for in supplemental appropriations. In January 2005, as Republicans continued their monopartisan approach, he complained that CBO forecasts of the deficit were unduly optimistic because they did not include all Iraq and Afghanistan costs.

On other issues, Spratt has a moderate record, a bit to the left of the middle of the House. He voted for NAFTA in 1993, but in 2003 said he would oppose the Central America Free Trade Agreement. He fought Senator Lindsey Graham's bill to reclassify nuclear wastes at the Savannah River Site so they could be destroyed there, but Graham prevailed. In February 2005 he criticized the Bush approach to Social Security. In 2004, *Washingtonian*'s poll of congressional staffers rated him number two in the House in the workhorse category, behind Bill Thomas, chairman of Ways and Means, and tied with David Obey, ranking Democrat on Appropriations. His response was cautious. "I think it's positive. It's better than being called a show horse, I guess."

Spratt had two tough races, in 1994 and 1996, when he won by margins of 52%–48% and 54%–45%. Since then he has been reelected easily; he had no Republican opponent in 2002 and won with 63% of the vote in 2004.

SIXTH DISTRICT

Rep. James Clyburn (D)

Elected 1992, 7th term; b. July 21, 1940, Sumter; home, Columbia; SC St. U., B.A. 1962; African Methodist Episcopal; married (Emily).

Professional Career: Teacher, 1962–66; Dir., Charleston Neighborhood Youth Corps, 1966–68; Exec. Dir., SC Comm. for Farm Workers, 1968–71; Asst., SC Gov. West, 1971–74; SC Human Affairs Comm., 1974–92.

DC Office: 2135 RHOB, 20515, 202-225-3315; Fax: 202-225-2313; Web site: www.house.gov/clyburn.

District Offices: Columbia, 803-799-1100; Florence, 843-622-1212; Santee, 803-854-4700.

Committees: *Democratic Caucus Vice Chairman. Appropriations* (19th of 29 D): Energy & Water Development & Related Agencies; Transportation, Treasury, HUD, the Judiciary & District of Columbia.

Group Ratings

	ADA	ACLU	AFS	LCV	ITIC	NTU	COC	ACU	NTLC	CHC
2004	90	65	71	100	40	10	45	13	3	8
2003	90	—	100	85	—	21	39	21	—	—

National Journal Ratings

	2003 LIB	—	2003 CONS		2004 LIB	—	2004 CONS
Economic	76%	—	23%		71%	—	29%
Social	74%	—	25%		66%	—	33%
Foreign	93%	—	6%		74%	—	25%

Key Votes of the 108th Congress

1. Drilling in ANWR	N	5. DC School Vouchers	N	9. Ban Same-Sex Marriage	N
2. Approve Bush Tax Cuts	N	6. Ban Human Cloning	N	10. Fund Iraq War	N
3. Medicare/Rx Bill	N	7. Restrict Gun Liability	N	11. Bar Cuba Embargo Funds	Y
4. Bar Overtime Pay Regs.	*	8. Ban Partial-Birth Abortion	N	12. Intelligence Reorg.	Y

Election Results

2004 general	James Clyburn (D)	161,987	(67%)	($725,832)
	Gary McLeod (R)	75,443	(31%)	($3,927)
	Other	4,157	(2%)	
2004 primary	James Clyburn (D)	unopposed		
2002 general	James Clyburn (D)	116,586	(67%)	($398,652)
	Gary McLeod (R)	55,760	(32%)	($10,616)

Prior Winning Percentages: 2000 (72%); 1998 (73%); 1996 (69%); 1994 (64%); 1992 (65%)

The People		Race/Ethnic Origin	Ancestry	
Area size:	8,490 sq. mi.	40.3% White	USA: 9.0%	English: 4.1%
Urban population:	48.0%	56.7% Black	German: 3.7%	
Rural population:	52.0%	0.5% Asian	**2004 Presidential Vote**	
Pop. 2000:	668,670	0.3% Native Am.	Kerry (D) 151,061	(61%)
Median income:	$28,967	0.0% Hawaiian	Bush (R) 97,248	(39%)
Poverty status:	22.4%	0.7% Two+ races	Other 482	(0%)
Military veterans:	12.4%	0.1% Other	**2000 Presidential Vote**	
		1.5% Hispanic Origin	Gore (D) 126,287	(58%)
			Bush (R) 87,252	(40%)
			Other 2,991	(1%)
			Cook Partisan Voting Index: D +11	

Occupation   Blue collar: 33.0%   White collar: 48.1%   Gray collar: 18.9%

South Carolina was first settled by planters from Barbados, bringing with them a tropical plantation economy, which they transferred to the not-quite-tropical climate of the Carolina coastal lowlands. Here the flat Low Country and many islands are laced with sluggish-flowing rivers and swamps, and here the planters brought thousands of slaves directly from Africa. Colonial South Carolina was one of the richest parts of North America, with dazzling Georgian architecture in Charleston and classic plantation gardens; the planters built great irrigation systems and grew rice and cotton and the dye-plant indigo, all heavily in demand in Britain and elsewhere. All this wealth, of course, was built on the slave labor of countless African Americans. In colonial times, a majority of South Carolinians were slaves, as were a majority of lowlands residents when Fort Sumter was fired upon (although there were also many free blacks in Charleston, a few of whom owned slaves themselves). South Carolina's black heritage has left a lasting imprint on American culture, and the African-influenced Gullah language still can be heard here. The poverty that was the almost universal lot of lowland blacks after the Civil War has eased only in the last generation, as development came to the coast and long cultural isolation dissipated. But many blacks decided not to wait, abandoning South Carolina for opportunities in the North. Today, heavily black rural counties are suffering steeper losses in manufacturing jobs than urban areas are.

The 6th Congressional District of South Carolina, created in 1992 as a black-majority district, includes only a bit of the South Carolina coast, which is increasingly lined with affluent retirement and recreational communities. The district's boundaries, less jagged since the 2002 redistricting, take in the black central city neighborhoods of Charleston, North Charleston and Columbia but leave their affluent white areas, both urban and suburban, in the adjacent 1st and 2d Districts. The 6th includes Orangeburg, home of the historically black South Carolina State University, and Florence, at the center of the Pee Dee tobacco-growing country in eastern South Carolina. The 6th's population in 2000 was 57% black, and in 2004 it gave George W. Bush only 39% of the vote—the only South Carolina district he failed to carry.

The congressman from the 6th District is James Clyburn, a Democrat first elected in 1992. Clyburn grew up in Sumter, the son of a minister. In 1960 he was one of seven young people who organized the state's first sit-ins, at a five-and-dime store in the Orangeburg town square; in February 2001, Governor Jim Hodges apologized for the massacre that took place there in 1968, when highway patrolmen killed three protesters and wounded 27 others. Clyburn worked as a teacher, in government antipoverty programs and on the staff of Governor John West. In 1974 he became state Human Affairs commissioner, serving 18 years under Republican and Democratic governors. Twice he ran for secretary of state, losing narrowly. Then the new, black-majority 6th District was created. The white incumbent, Democrat Robin Tallon, at the last minute decided not to run. Clyburn did, and in the Democratic primary won 56% of the vote against four black opponents, all with serious claims for the nomination. Clyburn, well known statewide, ran first or second in every part of the district and piled up 88% of the vote in his home county of Sumter.

Clyburn, the only black to represent South Carolina in Congress since 1897, has a moderate-to-liberal voting record. He has good working relationships with leading businessmen and Republicans and—like many South Carolinians before him—has focused on local priorities first. He supported the balanced budget amendment and joined the moderate New Democrat Coalition at its inception in 1997, the only black House member to do so. When cigarette tax increases were proposed, he urged safeguards for tobacco farmers. In September 2004 and March 2005, the House passed his bill to create a Gullah/Geechee Heritage Corridor from northern Florida to North Carolina.

On the Appropriations Committee, he has focused on local projects. As chairman of the Congressional Black Caucus in 1999, he urged the Democratic National Committee to become more responsive to blacks; he also sought to create a Policy and Leadership Institute for the Black Caucus to develop new liberal positions and protect black lawmakers in redistricting. After the 2002 election he won a three-candidate contest to become vice-chairman of the Democratic Caucus with 95 votes to 56 for Gregory Meeks and 53 for Zoe Lofgren. He said the leadership needed to reflect the party's diversity and not "just white men." In 2003, he demanded an apology after Tom DeLay said that minority Democrats in Texas were "more Democrat than they are minority" if they turn down his offer for additional minority districts from redistricting. "We have long and sordid experiences with policies and practices that are acted upon purportedly on our behalf without our inclusion in the process," he said. Clyburn is poised to move higher on the leadership ladder. In 2006 Bob Menendez is ineligible for a third term as Democratic Caucus Chairman (and may be running for the Senate), and in early 2005 Clyburn seemed the frontrunner to succeed him.

Back home Clyburn has not faced serious opposition for reelection. He has relished his role as a major player and potential kingmaker in the state's often pivotal Democratic presidential primary. Blacks cast about half the votes in the primary, and Clyburn is the most prominent black politician in the state. He first backed Dick Gephardt in December 2003, with whom he had worked in the House. But Gephardt withdrew after the Iowa caucuses, and Clyburn endorsed frontrunner John Kerry rather than South Carolina native John Edwards.

★ SOUTH DAKOTA ★

When the Census Bureau proclaimed the closing of the American frontier in 1890, one of the last places where it had closed was the southern part of the Dakota Territory, just admitted to the Union in 1889 as the state of South Dakota. For years this land had been the home of the Oglala Sioux, one of the largest Native American tribes, who had built a buffalo hunting civilization by becoming masters of the horses the Spaniards had imported to North America 350 years earlier. It was the Sioux warrior chief Sitting Bull, now buried on a bluff above the Missouri River, who destroyed Custer at Little Big Horn in 1876; it was Oglala Sioux who were the victims at the massacre of Wounded Knee in 1890. After half a century of horrifying disease and a decade of defeat, the Sioux were a traumatized people, and still are today, living on reservations with proud traditions but in terrible poverty. They are isolated far from the main-stream economic marketplace, beset by high rates of crime, alcoholism and suicide, with life expectancy and disease rates like those of sub-Saharan Africa; on the Pine Ridge Reservation in Shannon County unemployment is 70% and incomes average $3,500 a year. But infant mortality has been reduced and the American Indian population has been growing—by 23% in the 1990s. In 2004, 98 buffalo were rounded up on California's Catalina Island, the descendants of animals brought there to film a Western in the 1920s, and returned to the Lakota Reservation. Indians are in the process of getting a great monument, the late Korczak Ziolkowski's Crazy Horse sculpture, which—when and if finished—will dwarf Mount Rushmore (which was left unfinished itself at the start of World War II).

Less tragic and more successful, though not without its moments of violence, was the whites' settlement of South Dakota. It was a rapid process: the first gold strikes in the Black Hills came in 1876, and soon the mountains swarmed with settlers. Deadwood became a city of 20,000 where Calamity Jane ruled the saloons and Wild Bill Hickok was shot in the back while holding two pair—aces and eights. Ranchers, knowing that the buffalo could not be contained by barbed wire fences, massacred them so thoroughly that when Teddy Roosevelt got to the Dakota Territory in 1884, he had a hard time finding one to shoot. It was not long before the railroad came through, and then settlers, many of them German and Scandinavian immigrants recruited by the railroads, had built sodhouses, broken the land and set down enough roots to justify making both the two Dakota states.

Geographically, South Dakota has never entirely filled up. In the 25 years between state-hood and World War I, the eastern third of the state, sectioned off Midwestern style into 640-acre square miles, was settled by farmers. But moving westward, before a traveler reaches the Missouri River in the middle of the state, green turns to brown, cultivation grows sparse and then stops; the West River plains are open grazing land, scarcely touched by the white men who were so eager to establish dominion over them a century ago. The land is punctuated, not by roads meeting every mile at precise angles, but by buttes, gullies and grasslands sweeping to the horizon with no sign of human habitation except the occasional missile silos that once pointed toward the Soviet Union.

South Dakota's political patterns were fairly well set by the early 1900s. Its early settlers were mostly Midwesterners who brought their Republicanism with them. Voters here never had much use for the Non-Partisan League, which caught on in the more Scandinavian soil of North Dakota, and there was never anything here comparable to the Farmer-Labor Party of Minne-sota. But the nature of the farm economy—its dependence on the great railroads and milling companies, and on the vagaries of international markets—meant that South Dakota was subject to periodic farm revolts. It voted for Populists and William Jennings Bryan in the 1890s; it supported the early New Deal; it revolted against the Eisenhower Administration in the 1950s by electing a young congressman named George McGovern, then a professor at Dakota Wesleyan University in Mitchell, home also of the Corn Palace, built in 1892 and decorated every year with 13 murals using 275,000 ears of corn. South Dakota also shared the isolationist impulse of much of the Great Plains; McGovern's opposition to the Vietnam War in the late 1960s was not a liability here. In the early 1970s, Democrats seemed on the verge of becoming the majority party.

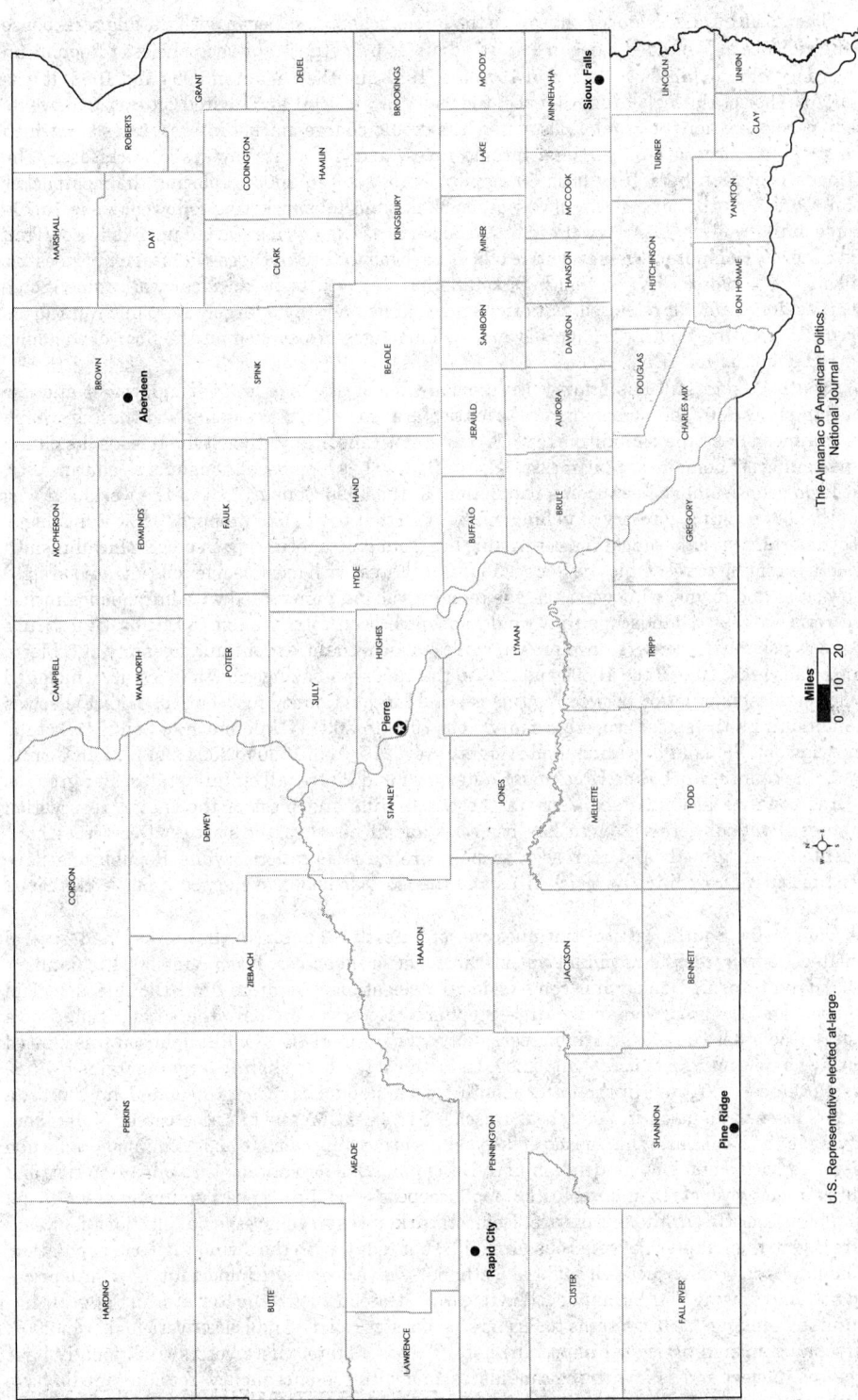

The Almanac of American Politics.
National Journal

U.S. Representative elected at-large.

Miles
0 10 20

Then South Dakota moved sharply to the Republicans. This began with the angry response to the violence at Wounded Knee in 1975. And it was perpetuated by the policies of Republican Governor William Janklow, elected in 1978 and 1982 and then again in 1994 and 1998. It was Janklow who got the legislature to repeal the usury law in 1981 and invited Citicorp to move its credit card operations to Sioux Falls, where they could charge market interest rates and which had no state corporate or personal income taxes, and a literate low-wage work force. The Citibank operation here grew from 50 employees to 3,200 in 2003, replacing the meatpacker John Morrell as the biggest employer; other banks and telemarketing followed; some 15,700 people in the Sioux Falls area work in financial services. New firms started up, like NordicTrak and Gateway Computer (their executive offices have moved to San Diego but most employees are still in North Sioux City) as South Dakotans have proved to be an ideal work force. Some meatpacking plants have closed, but others are manned now by a largely Hispanic work force, recruited from the Southwest and beyond; 40 languages are spoken on the floor of the John Morrell plant in Sioux City.

South Dakota still has a low-wage economy, but it also has low unemployment and low housing prices (10% of houses in rural counties are vacant); its residents and those in North Dakota spend less time commuting to work than Americans in any other state. It leads the nation in percentage of home-based businesses. South Dakota has long been thought of as a farm state, but farm counties have been losing population; in the 1990 Census, 11% of the workforce was employed in farming, forestry or fishing but by 2000 that figure had dropped to 8%. Ranching is also important, and there is still some mining here, but it is tapering off. Demographically, South Dakota is coming to resemble the Rocky Mountain states, with most people concentrated around a few cities and towns, while vast acreage remains vacant, punctuated with infrequent ranches and resort areas—a landscape that would not have been totally alien to Sitting Bull. South Dakota's population centers have grown, while its farm counties continue to empty out. Metro Sioux Falls grew 10% in the 1980s and 22% in the 1990s—amazing growth in a state which had sometimes lost population between censuses—and Lincoln County, just south of Sioux Falls, was the nation's ninth fastest-growing county from 2000 to 2004. While much of South Dakota is emptying out, Sioux Falls's Minnehaha County grew 27% from 1990 to 2004 and Lincoln County 104%; the counties including Brookings, Watertown and Pierre, all on Interstates, also grew, as did the counties around Rapid City in the Black Hills and most of the Indian reservation counties. Politically, this growth has been a standoff between the parties: Democrats have benefited from growth and increased turnout on the reservations, while Republicans have benefited from growth in the Black Hills and the two parties have slugged it out in the Sioux Falls area.

Politically, South Dakota continues to vote mostly Republican, but it has had several talented Democrats who have had considerable electoral success. From June 2004 to January 2005 it had an all-Democratic congressional delegation—Senators Tom Daschle and Tim Johnson and Congresswoman-at-Large Stephanie Herseth—for only the second time in its history (the other time was during a period of five days in 1936–37). But Johnson was elected only by narrow margins in 1996 and 2002, Herseth won by only slightly larger margins in June and November 2004 and in the latter month former Republican Congressman John Thune, a narrow loser to Johnson in 2002, beat Daschle 51%–49%. Meanwhile, the career of Janklow, serving in the House after his second eight-year governorship, came to an ignominious end when he was convicted of felony manslaughter in December 2003 for running through a stop sign and killing a motorcyclist. In state politics Republicans have held the governorship since 1978 and have big majorities in the legislature. Democrats' chances in congressional elections for years were tied to their support of generous farm bills, but today, with the dwindling farm population, their stands on other issues—drought aid, ethanol—have been more important. Low farm prices did nothing to swing South Dakota voters toward Al Gore in 2000—the Republican Congress has continued sending out large sums to farmers as disaster relief—and prices were higher in 2004. Personal campaigning is still important here. This is a state where voters traditionally have expected to meet and talk with the candidates, and with some frequency. Yet other media have become important. Republicans have charged that the Sioux Falls *Argus-Leader*, the state's leading newspaper, has through selective reporting tilted some close contests toward the Democrats. Democrats charged that pro-Republican weblogs, a couple of them paid by the Thune campaign, tilted the 2004 Senate race toward the Republicans.

The People		Race/Ethnic Origin			Military veterans: 79,370 (14.4%)	
Pop. 2004 (est):	770,883	664,585	88.0%	White	WWII: 19.3%	Korea: 16.1%
Pop. 2000:	754,844	4,563	0.6%	Black	Vietnam: 31.3%	Gulf War: 11.0%
Pop. 1990:	696,004	4,316	0.6%	Asian	Most populous cities (2003):	
Change 1990–2000:	Up 8.5%	60,988	8.1%	Native Am.	1. Sioux Falls	133,834
% of U.S. total:	0.3%	219	0.0%	Hawaiian	2. Rapid City	60,876
Pop. rank:	46th of 50	8,960	1.2%	Two+ races	3. Aberdeen	24,086
Area size:	77,116 sq. mi.	310	0.0%	Other	4. Watertown	20,191
State Native:	68.1%	10,903	1.4%	Hisp. Origin	5. Brookings	18,464
Non-citizen:	1.1%	**Ancestry**				
Language		German: 29.1%		Norwegian: 10.9%	Urban population: 51.9%	
English: 91.0%	Other Eur.: 3.8%	Irish: 7.4%		English: 5.0%	Rural population: 48.1%	
Spanish: 2.2%		Dutch: 3.4%				

Education		Work Sector			Legislature	
H.S. Grad:	84.6%	Private: 72.9%		Govt: 15.3%	Senate	25 R 10 D
College Grad:	21.5%	Self: 11.0%		Family: 0.8%	House	51 R 19 D
Industry		Unemployment: 4.4%			Legislative Term Limits: Yes	
Agri: 8.1%	Con: 6.3%	**Household Income**			**Registered Voters**	
Fin: 7.4%	Info: 2.1%	<15k: 18.4%		15-35k: 31.2%	D: 191,523	(38.1%)
Mfg: 15.7%	Prof: 27.0%	35-50k: 19.0%		50-100k: 25.5%	R: 238,580	(47.5%)
Public: 4.8%	Trade: 15.3%	100-150k: 3.8%		>150k: 2.1%	O: 72,158	(14.4%)
Other: 13.3%		Median: $35,282				
Occupation		Poverty status: 13.2%				
Blue collar: 23.3%	White collar: 59.1%	**Home Value**				
Gray collar: 17.6%		<50k: 31.1%	50-100k: 39.4%	100-200k: 23.6%	200-300k: 3.7%	
		300-500k: 1.4%	>500k: 0.7%	Median: $74,300		

Presidential politics   South Dakota has voted Democratic for president just four times since statehood, in 1896, 1932, 1936 and 1964. But it was fairly close in five of the seven elections between 1972, when South Dakota's George McGovern was the Democratic nominee, and 1996, when Bill Clinton came within 3% of winning. In 2000 the cultural liberalism and environmental policies of Al Gore were far from popular here, and George W. Bush carried the state 60%–38%. Gore carried only Indians, a rising but small percentage of the electorate, and ran even among the elderly, but the percentage of voters who remember Franklin D. Roosevelt is on the wane. In 2004 Bush once again carried the state 60%–38%; he carried every county except those containing Indian reservations and the University of South Dakota. Bush's share of the vote declined by 0.4%, making South Dakota the only other state besides Vermont where his percentage fell. Bush's share

2004 Presidential Vote		
Bush (R)	232,584	(60%)
Kerry (D)	149,244	(38%)
Nader (I)	4,320	(1%)
Other	2,067	(1%)

2004 Democratic Presidential Primary		
Kerry (D)	69,473	(82%)
Uncommitted (D)	5,105	(6%)
Dean (D)	4,838	(6%)
LaRouche (D)	2,943	(3%)
Kucinich (D)	2,046	(2%)

2000 Presidential Vote		
Bush (R)	190,700	(60%)
Gore (D)	118,804	(38%)
Other	6,765	(2%)

of the vote increased in the Sioux Falls area and most of eastern South Dakota, but fell in West River, where outrage against Clinton-Gore environmentalism had cooled. His biggest drops were in Indian reservation counties, where Democratic registration drives vastly increased turnout in 2002 and 2004. He lost Shannon County in the Pine Ridge Reservation by 1,415 votes in 2000 and 3,040 votes in 2004.

In 1988 South Dakota switched its presidential primary from the traditional June date to February, just one week after New Hampshire. It proved to be a booster of Great Plains candidates who did not fare well elsewhere: Bob Dole in 1988 and 1996, Dick Gephardt in 1988, Bob Kerrey and Tom Harkin in 1992. In 2000 the primary was moved back to June and has attracted little notice.

Governor

Mike Rounds (R)

Elected 2002, term expires Jan. 2007, 1st term; b. Oct. 24, 1954, Huron; home, Pierre; SD St. U., B.S. 1977; Catholic; married (Jean).

Elected Office: SD Senate, 1990–2000; Maj. Ldr. 1994–2000.

Professional Career: Practicing atty., 1979-2002.

Office: 505 E. Capitol Ave., Pierre, 57501, 605-773-3212; Fax: 605-773-5844; Web site: www.state.sd.us/governor.

Election Results

2002 general	Mike Rounds (R)	189,920	(57%)
	Jim Abbott (D)	140,263	(42%)
	Other	4,376	(1%)
2002 primary	Mike Rounds (R)	49,331	(44%)
	Mark Barnett (R)	32,868	(30%)
	Steve Kirby (R)	29,065	(26%)
1998 general	Bill Janklow (R)	166,621	(64%)
	Bernie Hunhoff (D)	85,473	(33%)
	Other	8,093	(3%)

Mike Rounds, a Republican, was elected governor of South Dakota in 2002. He grew up in a family of 11 children in Pierre, the state's tiny capital; his father was director of the Office of Highway Safety and worked as a lobbyist for the petroleum industry. Rounds graduated from South Dakota State University, the first governor to do so. He worked as a partner in an insurance and real estate agency in Pierre and participated, as you would expect, in many civic activities. In 1990 he was elected to the state senate and in 1996 he became senate majority leader. He was prevented by term limits from running for reelection in 2000. In December 2001 he announced he was running for governor.

Rounds sought to replace the governor who had dominated state government for the past quarter-century, Bill Janklow. Janklow was elected attorney general in 1974; in 1978 and 1982 he was elected governor. Term-limited, he ran for the Senate and lost in 1986; in 1994, he returned and defeated Governor Walter Dale Miller in the Republican primary. He won the general election 55%–41%. He was reelected 64%–33% in 1998. In his second two terms, Janklow cut the state payroll and cut property taxes by 30%; the inheritance tax was abolished by voters. As voters considered outlawing video lotteries, which have been legal since 1989 and bring $100 million annually to the state, he said the video games were a "lousy" way to raise money but warned that outlawing them would require the biggest tax increase in state history; voters came out for the games 54%–46%. For most of the 1990s, sales tax revenues increased 5% to 7% a year, but in 2001–02 they increased by only 1%, and by November 2001 it was apparent that South Dakota, whose main source of general revenues is the sales tax, faced a budget shortfall.

In the Republican primary Rounds faced two much more well-financed opponents, former Lieutenant Governor Steve Kirby and Attorney General Mark Barnett. Rounds ran on property tax relief and opposition to an income tax and abortion. "No gimmicks, no grandstanding, just good government," read his fliers. He was willing to tell people what they didn't want to hear. He told a truckers' group that he was responsible for applying the sales tax to transportation services and said he might favor a higher gas tax if it would bring in much more federal money. He was the only candidate in either party to oppose mandated use of ethanol fuel, despite the state's many ethanol plants and corn growers. He told the South Dakota Education Association that there were "very limited funds" for education spending increases. He refused to pledge to oppose all tax increases.

At candidate forums and then in their ads and direct mail, Kirby and Barnett bitterly attacked each other, on economic development and on other substantive and character issues. They had plenty of money to launch these attacks: Kirby spent over $2.5 million and Barnett $1.75 million. Rounds spent just $147,000. But he had a strategy. In April 2002 he spelled it out. "For the time being, I haven't minded being considered by the other two candidates as this fly buzzing away over in the corner. I've heard several people say just stay out of the negative, there's enough of that. I'd like to run my spots right between Kirby and Barnett. Hopefully, people will see some differences."

Evidently they did. South Dakota is a small state in which voters expect to see candidates in person; candidate forums held in small towns can make some difference here. While Kirby and Barnett attacked each other, Rounds always seemed to be smiling. In the June primary Rounds won 44% of the vote, to 30% for Barnett and 26% for Kirby. It was a classic illustration of the rule that it is not wise to launch a negative campaign in a multi-candidate race.

The Democratic nominee was Jim Abbott, a businessman who served in the legislature, lost races for lieutenant governor in 1994 and the House in 1996 and was on leave as president of the University of South Dakota. This was a gentlemanly race between old friends; after the primary Abbott said, "Mike Rounds is just a good guy. I really think the people of South Dakota like the idea of a positive message for the future, and this contest offers interesting options." Abbott called for state-sponsored research for economic development and for higher education to work with the private sector to create jobs. While negative ads were hitting the air in the Senate race, the dialogue in the governor race was positive. Rounds led in polls from the primary on and in November won 57%–42%. Abbott carried Indian reservations and the area around the University of South Dakota in Vermillion.

After the election Rounds went to work on the state budget problems. In December Janklow presented figures showing spending requests $54 million higher than projected revenue, with $90 million in the state reserve. One problem was the state's structural deficit, exacerbated by the repeal of the state inheritance tax in 2000. In 2003 Rounds angered conservatives by proposing tax increases on cigarettes and alcoholic beverages and making more interstate phone calls subject to the sales tax. Though the legislature failed to pass his proposed tax on alcohol, it ended up passing 19 of the 22 bills requested by Rounds. Even without revenues from the tax measures he requested, he successfully cut the cost of prescription drugs for senior citizens and managed to increase state aid to school districts by $15.1 million. He also got a 2% pay raise for state workers, though it was 1% less than what he sought. But the big news story that year was Janklow. In August, Janklow, well known for his aggressive driving, blew through a stop sign in his car and killed a motorcyclist. In December, a jury in his hometown of Flandreau convicted him of felony manslaughter; he announced his resignation from Congress the same day, effective in January 2004. Rounds decided against calling a quick special election to replace Janklow. He preferred to save the state $400,000 by scheduling the election in June, to coincide with regularly scheduled primary elections.

With the state entering its fifth year of drought in 2004, Rounds issued a proclamation calling for a day of prayer for rain in South Dakota. He also sought mammon: Citing extreme temperatures, drought, infestations and severe storms, he requested federal drought aid from the Department of Agriculture for 30 mostly West River counties.

In 2004, Rounds signed a $2.9 billion state budget that gave state employees the 3% across-the-board salary increase that he sought the year before, with an extra 2.5 percent going to those below the midpoint of their salary ranges. A restrictive abortion bill attracted national attention. The legislation, which passed both the House and Senate, would have banned almost all abortions in the state; the only exception was to save the life of the mother. The bill's sponsor acknowledged that the measure would be challenged in court but had hoped for it to eventually reach the U.S. Supreme Court, where it might be used to overturn the *Roe v. Wade* decision. Abortion rights advocates, as expected, harshly criticized the bill. But many abortion opponents also opposed it, convinced that it could not survive legal scrutiny and might have the unintended effect of spurring a decision that strengthened abortion rights. Rounds said he supported overturning *Roe* but he issued a "form veto", which suggests changes and clarification of some of the bill's provisions. He issued the technical veto to ensure that existing abortion regulations remained in place during what state officials expected would be a lengthy court challenge; the Senate rejected the revisions and the bill died.

Rounds has spent much time on economic development issues. He has sought tax breaks for the building and operation of two new coal-fired power plants. And as part of an effort to confront the state's ongoing depopulation and the outmigration of young South Dakotans, he has focused on improving the state's quality of life, attracting more tourist spending, job creation and research and technology development through his signature program, the 2010 Initiative. The plan lays out a series of economic growth goals by the year 2010, including increasing the gross state product by $10 billion and doubling visitor spending to $1.2 billion. One of his ideas, the creation of a premium beef marketing initiative, was passed by the legislature in 2005. Under the South Dakota Certified Beef Program, cattle raised, closely monitored, butchered and packed in South Dakota would qualify for an official state seal of approval; the program would also create a tracking system to enable verification of the age of the beef. It would be financed by licensing fees paid by farmers and ranchers who voluntarily enroll in the program.

Rounds has said he plans to seek re-election. The first Democrat to announce a challenge was Huron city commissioner Ron Volesky, a former state legislator who finished a distant second in the 2002 primary for governor and then became the party nominee for attorney general that same year; he lost that race too.

Senior Senator

Tim Johnson (D)

Elected 1996, seat up 2008, 2d term; b. Dec. 28, 1946, Canton; home, Vermillion; U. of SD, B.A. 1969, M.A. 1970, J.D. 1975, MI St. U., 1970–71; Lutheran; married (Barbara).

Military Career: Army, 1969.

Elected Office: SD House of Reps., 1978–82; SD Senate, 1982–86; U.S. House of Reps., 1986–96.

Professional Career: Budget Analyst, MI Senate, 1971–72; Practicing atty., 1975–85; Clay Cnty. Dpty. Atty., 1985.

DC Office: 136 HSOB, 20510, 202-224-5842; Fax: 202-228-5765; Web site: johnson.senate.gov.

State Office: Aberdeen, 605-226-3440.

Committees: *Appropriations*: Agriculture, Rural Development & Related Agencies; Energy & Water; Legislative Branch; Military Construction & Veterans Affairs; State, Foreign Operations & Related Programs. *Banking, Housing & Urban Affairs*: Financial Institutions (RMM); International Trade & Finance; Securities & Investment. *Budget. Energy & Natural Resources*: Energy; Public Lands & Forests; Water & Power (RMM). *Ethics (Select)* (RMM). *Indian Affairs.*

Group Ratings

	ADA	ACLU	AFS	LCV	ITIC	NTU	COC	ACU	NTLC	CHC
2004	85	67	100	33	36	16	59	11	6	16
2003	80	—	100	58	—	16	39	15	—	—

National Journal Ratings

	2003 LIB	—	2003 CONS		2004 LIB	—	2004 CONS
Economic	75%	—	20%		72%	—	27%
Social	68%	—	26%		63%	—	36%
Foreign	90%	—	0%		86%	—	8%

Key Votes of the 108th Congress

1. Ban Drilling in ANWR	Y	5. Energy Bill	Y	9. Ban Same-Sex Marriage	N
2. Approve Bush Tax Cuts	N	6. Support Roe v. Wade	Y	10. Ban Bunker-Buster Bomb	Y
3. Medicare/Rx Bill	N	7. Ban Partial-Birth Abortion	Y	11. Fund Iraq War	Y
4. Bar Overtime Pay Regs.	Y	8. Assault Weapons Ban	*	12. Restrict Missile Defense	Y

Election Results

2002 general	Tim Johnson (D)	167,481	(50%)	($6,152,991)
	John Thune (R)	166,957	(50%)	($5,989,043)
2002 primary	Tim Johnson (D)	65,438	(95%)	
	Herman Eilers (D)	3,558	(5%)	
1996 general	Tim Johnson (D)	166,533	(51%)	($2,990,554)
	Larry Pressler (R)	157,954	(49%)	($5,138,298)

Prior Winning Percentages: 1994 House (60%); 1992 House (69%); 1990 House (68%); 1988 House (72%); 1986 House (59%)

Tim Johnson, a Democrat, was first elected to the Senate in 1996. He grew up in Canton, Flandreau and Vermillion in southeast South Dakota, graduated from the University of South Dakota and served briefly in the Army (he was discharged because of a hearing problem). He graduated from Michigan State University business school and worked for the state Senate. Then he graduated from the University of South Dakota law school and started a law practice in Vermillion. He was elected to the state House in 1978, at 31, and reelected in 1980; in 1982 and 1984 he was elected to the state Senate. When Congressman Tom Daschle ran for the Senate in 1986, Johnson ran for the House. He beat state Senator Jim Burg in the primary 48%–45%. He won the general by 59%–41%, and was reelected with larger percentages every two years thereafter.

In the House, Johnson compiled a generally liberal voting record, though he voted for the balanced budget amendment and was the only Democrat to switch his vote to support lifting the Bosnia arms embargo. In 1996 Johnson ran against Republican Senator Larry Pressler, then chairman of the Commerce committee. This was a high-spending, high-stakes race: Pressler spent $5.1 million, with over $1.7 million from PACs; Johnson spent almost $3 million, with $850,000 from PACs. TV ads began in August 1995, when the race was about even, and it stayed that way for 15 months. Since South Dakota TV is cheap, that meant one barrage of ads after another—plus seven debates. Pressler attacked Johnson as too liberal, going back to a 1981 vote in the legislature against workfare. Johnson attacked Pressler as a Newt-oid Medicare cutter and charged that he switched from opposition to support of maritime subsidies after receiving $29,000 from maritime PACs. Pressler spent much time in 1995 and 1996 on the telecommunications bill, the most-lobbied and arguably most complex bill before the 104th Congress. He succeeded in passing the bill, but back home Johnson was charging that phone and cable rates were going up. The final result was a 51%–49% Johnson victory, narrower than the final month's polls suggested.

In the Senate, Johnson's voting record has been generally liberal, except on some cultural issues; he supported the partial-birth abortion ban. He has co-sponsored bills prohibiting meatpackers from owning, feeding or keeping livestock.

By early 2001 it was apparent that Johnson would face a tough challenge in 2002. He had been elected with 51% of the vote in a state that voted 60%–38% for George W. Bush. In spring 2001 Bush talked popular Republican Congressman John Thune into running for the Senate. Tom Daschle, majority leader starting in June 2001, said the race was "the most important political effort for me" in 2002. Daschle helped Johnson by getting him a seat on the Appropriations Committee, from which he could funnel money into South Dakota. And Johnson was careful to cast some moderate votes on important issues.

Thune announced in October 2001. He argued that the state would have been better off with a bipartisan Senate delegation. Of course, there was a caveat: a Thune victory could give the Republicans a Senate majority and make Daschle minority leader again. The two candidates spent record amounts for South Dakota—Johnson $6.1 million, Thune $6.0 million—and the national parties and independent expenditure groups on both sides spent much more. A week of

TV ads costs only about $80,000 in South Dakota, as compared to about $1.5 million in Los Angeles. The ads started running in late 2001 and by November 2002 the average voter had seen more than 1,000 of them.

Thune was the more outgoing of the two, a candidate who loved shaking hands and seldom forgot a face. Johnson, more reserved, was nevertheless tenacious and moderate in demeanor. Of all the seriously contested Democratic senators in 2002, Johnson ran the most conservative-sounding campaign. "Tim Johnson has strongly supported President Bush, the war against terrorism, his tax cut and his education reform," one ad said. Thune nonetheless attacked him for voting against making the tax cut permanent. Johnson replied that he supported eliminating the estate tax for family farmers and ranchers and family-owned businesses and to increase the exemption to $4 million for individuals. Thune attacked Johnson for favoring "privatization" of Social Security and called for no changes in the program; he was referring to Johnson's positive statements in the 1990s about a proposal advanced by Bill Clinton for the federal government to invest part of Social Security revenues in the stock market. Johnson replied that he now backed nothing of the sort. Thune also said that Johnson "voted seven times to raise $300 billion from Social Security;" this was a reference to votes on the entire budget, and used national Democrats' device of claiming that such spending robs Social Security.

Both local and international issues got some airing during the campaign. The biggest local issue was the drought that hit western South Dakota for most of 2002. Ranchers were selling off their herds for low prices; business losses were estimated at $1.8 billion. Daschle and Johnson responded by sponsoring $5 billion in disaster aid for farmers and ranchers, arguing that if floods and tornadoes triggered disaster relief, then droughts should too. But this was opposed by the Bush administration, which wanted any aid to come out of the federal dollars approved for farm spending. On August 15 George W. Bush came to South Dakota amid speculation that he would offer more. But, to the disappointment of the Thune campaign, he didn't. By this time, there seemed to be some improvement in Johnson's showing in the polls, though almost no polls throughout the campaign showed a margin for either candidate outside the statistical margin of error. In mid-September Agriculture Secretary Ann Veneman announced $750 million in aid for 30 states. Democrats grumbled that $750 million was a pittance, but Daschle's $5 billion, now raised to $6 billion, was stalled in the Senate.

Defense was another issue often stressed. Thune attacked Johnson for voting against the Gulf War resolution in January 1991 and for joining the group of Democratic members of Congress who sued George H.W. Bush challenging his conduct of the war. Johnson pointed out that his son, Brooks Johnson, served in the 101st Airborne Division in Afghanistan from December 2001 to June 2002 and could be sent to Iraq (which he later was) if the United States went in. While Daschle was still publicly undecided, Johnson announced that he would vote for the Iraq war resolution. On the floor of the Senate he said, "There is a strong possibility that I may be voting to send my own son into combat, and that gives me special empathy for the families of other American servicemen and women whose own sons and daughters may also be sent to Iraq. Nevertheless, I am willing to cast this vote—one of the most important in my career both as a senator and certainly as a father—because I recognize the threat that Saddam Hussein represents to world peace." Republicans continued to attack Johnson on defense issues and his support of the Democratic position on homeland security.

There was one more issue blazing in October: fraudulent Indian voter registrations. The state Democratic party set up offices on each of the state's Indian reservations and paid bonuses to contractors who brought in signed voter registration cards. One such contractor was fired in October and charged with submitting scores of illegally filled out registration cards, including one purportedly signed by a woman who had died two weeks before, and many more with mismatched birth dates and nonexistent addresses. On October 22, a consultant for the Sioux Tribes Voter Education and Registration Committee was indicted on five counts of forgery of voter registration cards. Attorney General Mark Barnett and the U.S. attorney launched investigations. All this made headlines in a state with a tradition of squeaky-clean voting and a memory of the violent Indian movement of the 1970s. Johnson said that the voter registration operation was run by the state Democratic party and that his campaign had nothing to do with it.

At one debate Johnson challenged Thune to stop his negative ads. Thune said he would do so as soon as Johnson held a news conference to explain what he knew about this vote fraud.

This election turned out to be the closest in the nation. During most of election night and into the morning Thune led in the counting. Then the last two precincts came in, from Shannon County, which includes most of the Pine Ridge Indian Reservation. Those two precincts put Johnson over the top, by a margin of 524 votes—in percentage terms, 50.1%–49.9%. In Shannon County, 3,118 votes were cast, as compared to 1,953 in the 2000 presidential election. The county voted 92%–8% for Johnson. In the six main reservation counties, turnout was 11,275, up from 7,500 in 2000 and 7,000 in 1994. These six counties voted 78%–21% for Johnson. In 43 of the other 60 counties, including the 10 largest, Johnson's percentage declined from 1996, when he won 51% statewide. Many Republicans urged Thune to contest the election. But on November 13, he announced he would not. Johnson had won two full terms in the Senate by the smallest combined popular vote margin, 9,103, of any senator since George Malone of Nevada, elected by a combined margin of 7,970 in 1946 and 1952.

In his second term Johnson, back in the minority again, worked hard on several South Dakota issues. He had backed country of origin meat labeling as long ago as 1992 and helped put it in the 2002 farm bill. Congress later postponed it until September 2006 and the House Agriculture Committee in 2004 voted to make it voluntary. Some members tried to put such a provision in the omnibus appropriation in November 2004. Johnson worked against that, and it was left out. When two cases of mad cow disease were discovered in Canada within two weeks in January 2005, Johnson said that was an even stronger reason for country of origin labeling. He and Republican Mike Enzi sponsored a bill to bar the import of live cattle from Canada until country of origin labeling takes effect. In March Johnson hailed a federal court decision barring an Agriculture Department order permitting such imports.

Johnson sponsored a bill in 2003 to provide more incentives and funding for housing on Indian reservations. In 2004 he proposed a series of tax credits for businesses on reservations and the building of wind-powered electricity plants there; this was included in the JOBS bill in May 2004. In 2004 and 2005 he co-sponsored with Craig Thomas bills to pay for cleanup of hazardous waste at busted meth labs. Water projects are important to South Dakota, and over the years Johnson shepherded the Mid-Dakota Project to bring water to the Huron area; its final tranche of $17 million was voted in 2004. That year Johnson helped obtain $18.75 million for the Lewis and Clark Rural Water System, to bring Missouri River water to northwest Iowa, southwest Minnesota and southeast South Dakota; in 2005 he sought $35 million for this, arguing that money should be available because the Mid-Dakota project was finished. The November 2004 omnibus appropriation also included $2.25 million for the Perkins County water project, $4 million to replace the Meridian Bridge in Yankton and funding to keep 150 technical jobs at the EROS Data Center near Sioux Falls. In 2004 Johnson asked Veterans Secretary Anthony Principi to lift the moratorium on VA health care for non-disabled veterans with incomes over $33,000 in the Sioux Falls area; in 2005 he sponsored a bill to make veterans health care an entitlement, not subject to annual appropriations. He promised to seek $50 million for Sioux Falls to clear a rail yard so that it can build a downtown arena on the Zip Feed mill site.

Johnson was obviously saddened by his colleague Tom Daschle's narrow loss to John Thune in November 2004. Nevertheless he quickly convened a meeting of the new delegation—himself, Thune and Democratic Congresswoman Stephanie Herseth—and said they would work together on South Dakota projects.

Junior Senator

John Thune (R)

Elected 2004, seat up 2010, 1st term; b. Jan. 7, 1961, Pierre; home, Sioux Falls; Biola U., B.A. 1983, U. of SD, M.B.A. 1984; Baptist; married (Kimberley).

Elected Office: U.S. House of Reps., 1996–2002.

Professional Career: Legis. Asst., U.S. Sen. James Abdnor, 1985–87; Special Asst., U.S. Small Business Admin., 1987–89; Exec. Dir., SD Republican Party, 1989–91; SD Railroad Dir., 1991–93; Exec. Dir., SD Municipal League, 1993–96.

DC Office: 383 RSOB, 20510, 202-224-2321; Fax: 202-228-5429; Web site: thune.senate.gov.

State Offices: Aberdeen, 605-225-8823; Rapid City, 605-348-7551; Sioux Falls, 605-334-9596.

Committees: *Armed Services*: Emerging Threats & Capabilities; Readiness & Management Support; Strategic Forces. *Environment & Public Works*: Superfund & Waste Management (Chmn.); Transportation & Infrastructure. *Small Business & Entrepreneurship. Veterans' Affairs.*

Group Ratings and Key Votes: Newly Elected

Election Results

2004 general	John Thune (R)	197,848	(51%)	($14,666,225)
	Tom Daschle (D)	193,340	(49%)	($19,991,369)
2004 primary	John Thune (R)	unopposed		
1998 general	Tom Daschle (D)	162,884	(62%)	($4,861,541)
	Ron Schmidt (R)	95,431	(36%)	($492,854)
	Other	3,796	(1%)	

Prior Winning Percentages: 2000 House (73%); 1998 House (75%); 1996 House (58%)

The junior senator from South Dakota is John Thune, a Republican elected in the most important of the 34 Senate elections held in 2004. He grew up in Murdo, on the dusty plains west of the Missouri River, where his father was a teacher and the family was Democratic; he went to college and business school at the University of South Dakota. As a high school freshman he met then-Congressman Jim Abdnor, when Abdnor spotted him at a grocery checkout counter and recalled that he had missed one of six free throws in the basketball game the previous night. They kept in touch and Thune got a job on by-then Senator Abdnor's staff in Washington in 1985; he stayed with Abdnor after he lost to Tom Daschle and was appointed to the Small Business Administration. He returned to South Dakota in 1989, at 28, to become executive director of the state Republican Party. In 1991 he became state railroad director under Governor George Mickelson and in 1993 director of the state Municipal League.

Thune nevertheless entered the 1996 race for the House as very much an underdog. The favorite in the Republican primary was Lieutenant Governor Carole Hillard, but Thune attracted the support of religious conservatives and presidential campaign leaders, fresh from organizing for the presidential primary. He won 59%–41%. The Democratic nominee was Rick Weiland, a former state director for Senator Daschle. Thune was against all tax increases (and against Bob Dole's tax cut, pending a balanced budget) and pledged to refuse the congressional pension; he promised to serve only three terms. Weiland attacked Newt Gingrich and Medicare "cuts" and called for an "impact fee" on big hog producers to build a loan fund for small hog producers. Thune won 58%–37%.

In the House, Thune had a conservative voting record and served on the Agriculture and Transportation committees; he was chosen the freshman class representative to the Republican leadership. In May 1997 he criticized the House leadership for attaching other issues to the bill for relief of floods that had devastated much of North Dakota and Minnesota and damaged much of South Dakota that spring. As farm prices started plunging in 1998, Thune proposed to increase price supports; after meeting resistance, he proposed a bill to allow farmers to receive the present value of Freedom to Farm Act transition payments due up to 2002. He said he was pleased with the ultimate $6 billion emergency aid package, which allowed farmers to claim 1999 payments early.

On Transportation and Infrastructure, Thune worked on the May 1998 transportation bill, which raised South Dakota's payments from roughly $120 million to $180 million, and for funding of other South Dakota water projects. He backed country-of-origin meat labeling for animals born, raised and slaughtered in the United States. He won reelection 75%–28% in 1998 and in 2000 he won 73%–25%, with the largest vote margin ever for a statewide candidate.

After winning reelection in 2000, Thune did not flinch from keeping his promise to run for no more than three House terms. Instead the question was whether he would run to replace Governor William Janklow or against Senator Tim Johnson. National Republicans hoped he would run for the Senate. Johnson had been elected by only 51%–49% in 1996, and Thune led him in Republican polls by 48%–41% in March 2001. But Thune's wife and daughters, after trying life in metropolitan Washington, had chosen to live in Sioux Falls, and Thune seemed to be opting for a run for governor. In December 2000 he set up an exploratory committee for the governor race but on his trip to South Dakota in March 2001 and in a White House dinner in April, George W. Bush urged Thune to run for the Senate; in December 2000 Thune had $483,000 in his House campaign treasury, which he could use for a Senate run.

Tom Daschle, majority leader starting in June 2001, said the race was "the most important political effort for me" in 2002. Daschle helped Johnson by getting him a seat on the Appropriations Committee, from which he could funnel money into South Dakota. But Thune argued that the state would have been better off with a bipartisan Senate delegation. Of course, there was a caveat: a Thune victory could give the Republicans a Senate majority and make Daschle minority leader again. Johnson argued that he and Daschle made a uniquely powerful team. The two candidates spent record amounts for South Dakota—Johnson $6.1 million, Thune $6.0 million—and the national parties and independent expenditure groups on both sides spent much more.

The biggest local issue was the drought that hit western South Dakota for most of 2002. Daschle and Johnson responded by sponsoring $5 billion in disaster aid for farmers and ranchers, arguing that if floods and tornadoes triggered disaster relief, then droughts should too. But this was opposed by the Bush administration, which wanted any aid to come out of the $190 billion approved for farm spending. On August 15 George W. Bush came to South Dakota amid speculation that he would offer more. But, to the disappointment of the Thune campaign, he didn't.

Defense was also a central issue. Thune attacked Johnson for voting against the Gulf War resolution in January 1991 and for joining the group of Democratic members of Congress who sued George H.W. Bush challenging his conduct of the war. Johnson pointed out that his son served in the 101st Airborne Division in Afghanistan from December 2001 to June 2002 and could be sent to Iraq (which he later was) if the United States went in; Johnson announced that he would vote for the Iraq war resolution.

There was one more issue blazing in October: fraudulent Indian voter registrations. The state Democratic party set up offices on each of the state's Indian reservations and paid bonuses to contractors who brought in signed voter registration cards. In October, a consultant for the Sioux Tribes Voter Education and Registration Committee was indicted on five counts of forgery of voter registration cards; Attorney General Mark Barnett and the U.S. attorney launched investigations. All this made headlines in a state with a tradition of squeaky-clean voting and a memory of the violent Indian movement of the 1970s. Johnson said that the voter registration operation was run by the state Democratic party and that his campaign had nothing to do with it.

This election turned out to be the closest in the nation. During most of election night and into the morning Thune led in the counting. Then the last two precincts came in, from Shannon County, which includes most of the Pine Ridge Indian Reservation. Those two precincts put Johnson over the top, by a margin of 524 votes—in percentage terms, 50.1%–49.9%. In Shannon County, 3,118 votes were cast; the vote was 92%–8% for Johnson. In the six main reservation counties, turnout was 11,275, up from 7,500 in 2000. These six counties voted 78%–21% for Johnson. Many Republicans urged Thune to contest the election. But on November 13, he announced he would not. "The people of South Dakota have been subjected to one of the longest and most expensive campaigns in South Dakota history. I choose not to subject them to more."

After the 2002 election, Thune opened up his own lobbying firm and was a consultant to a D.C. law firm. But it wasn't long before he began thinking about seeking public office again. In December 2003, his successor in the House, former Governor William Janklow, announced he would resign in January; Thune was mentioned as a possible candidate. The other possibility was a challenge to Senator Tom Daschle.

Daschle had been reelected by wide margins in 1992 and 1998 against lightly funded opponents. In 2001 and 2002 he was one of several national Democrats considering running for president; in January 2003 he announced he would not run for president. But even as he was committing himself to the Senate, it seemed clear he would have trouble winning reelection. Thune's favorable ratings remained high after his defeat, and Republican polls in November 2002 and March 2003 showed Thune 1% to 2% ahead of Daschle—the same kind of dead heat in almost every poll taken during the Johnson-Thune race. Thune figured to have the advantage of all-out support from the Bush White House and fundraising prowess as great as Daschle's, assets that none of Daschle's previous opponents had. And George W. Bush, who carried South Dakota 60%–38% in 2000, would be at the top of the ballot.

Daschle was Senate majority leader from June 2001 to January 2003 (and for 17 days in January 2001) and minority leader from January 1995 to June 2001, and then again from January 2003 going forward. The emergence of a 50–50 Senate and the election of George W. Bush made him one of the pivotal figures in American politics.

In December 2001 Dick Cheney said Daschle "unfortunately has decided . . . to be more of an obstructionist." In January 2002 Daschle delivered a speech arguing that the Bush tax cut "probably made the recession worse" and set the stage for "the most dramatic fiscal deterioration in our nation's history." Increasingly Republicans attacked Daschle for obstructionism and Democrats rallied to his defense. Ads ran in South Dakota attacking and backing him.

In June 2002 Bush called for a new Department of Homeland Security, something previously championed mostly by Democrats. But Bush said that the labor relations provisions of the Senate Democrats' bill were unacceptable. "The Senate is more interested in special interests in Washington and not interested in the security of the American people," said Bush at a September 23 campaign appearance in New Jersey. Two days later Daschle rose in the Senate and spoke with evident anger, saying that Bush was "politicizing" the debate. This came two weeks after Bush's speech to the United Nations and his announcement that he would ask for congressional authorization of military action in Iraq. The Senate voted on the resolution October 11; Daschle and Tim Johnson were two of 29 Democrats to vote in favor. But the homeland security bill was the subject of continued debate, and no version passed the Senate before the election.

Daschle's insistence on solidarity with federal employees' unions on homeland security helped to undermine Democrats' credibility on national security. On Election Day Democrats picked up one seat in Arkansas but lost three in Georgia, Minnesota and Missouri; Tim Johnson held on by 524 votes. The next day Daschle's face was etched with disappointment. But, perhaps heeding some Democrats who argued that their party had not opposed Bush vociferously enough, he seemed determined to carry on, from the minority, much as before. Senate Democrats embarked on a filibuster of a lower court nomination—the first in history. On March 17, 2003, as Bush was to address the nation that evening announcing a final 48-hour ultimatum to Saddam Hussein, Daschle said, "I'm saddened, saddened that this president failed so miserably at diplomacy that we're now forced to war. Saddened that we have to give up one life because this president couldn't create the kind of diplomatic effort that was so critical for our country." Republicans chastised him for criticizing the president at an inappropriate time.

In January 2004, Thune made it official: he would run against Daschle. "I had people encouraging me to run for House. But the House isn't where the problem is. The House is going to be just fine. I don't know of a place more in need of leadership than the U.S. Senate," he said. "We need to put aside partisanship and the politics of obstruction and give the leadership that is right for the country."

With that statement, Thune was laying out the lead theme in his campaign—that Daschle was the chief obstructionist in the Senate, the leader of the Democratic forces that stood stubbornly in the way of the Bush administration agenda. To underscore this idea, in May Majority Leader Bill Frist broke with Senate tradition and traveled to South Dakota to campaign against Daschle.

Daschle began running ads in the summer of 2003. His campaign revolved around the same theme used by Tim Johnson against Thune–Daschle's clout as a national party leader. He argued that a freshman senator could not hope to match his influence in Washington and he highlighted the various pork projects he delivered to South Dakota – in the last fiscal year alone, according to his campaign, he brought home more than $269 million for more than 90 projects.

This was the most expensive election of the year, as both national parties and numerous third-party interest groups poured millions of dollars into South Dakota; through mid-October, the two candidates raised a combined $33 million. By the end, they had spent $35 million. Much of that money paid for television advertising; almost nothing was off-limits. The state Republican party sent a mailer attacking the lobbying practices of Daschle's wife Linda, a former FAA official who later became an aviation industry lobbyist. The Club for Growth ran an ad called "Tom's House" that featured Daschle's $2 million house in a tony D.C. neighborhood; another showed Daschle as a bobble-head doll, nodding in unison with Ted Kennedy and Hillary Clinton bobble-head dolls. Daschle's campaign criticized Thune for continuing his lobbying work even as he was running for office; Thune said candidates were entitled to make a living and that his work was for South Dakota clients. Daschle aired an ad that featured footage of him embracing Bush; this infuriated Republicans who frequently referred to Daschle as "the obstructionist-in-chief" to the Bush agenda. Thune boasted of his friendship and ability to work with the president. He said Daschle was out of touch with South Dakota values and priorities and contended that the majority leader put the interests of the national party over the needs of the state. "He's not the same guy who put his suitcase in his station wagon and drove the family to Congress in 1978," Thune told *National Journal*. "He now is an inside-Washington, D.C., guy who lives in a multimillion-dollar mansion. The broader question is, who is more in touch with South Dakota?"

Having Bush at the top of the ticket was a help to Thune: Bush won 60% in South Dakota. But South Dakota Republicans also orchestrated a highly effective, Internet-based campaign against Daschle, and the newspaper they viewed as his mouthpiece, the Sioux Falls *Argus Leader*. The paper is the state's largest and its primary news source; GOP activists, some of whom were paid by Thune's campaign committee for research consulting, attacked the newspaper's coverage of Daschle and questioned its writers' objectivity on web logs, or blogs, and a quasi-news Web site.

This was a closely fought race which brought out a huge turnout, up 23% from 2000 in a state with only modest growth. Thune won 51%–49%, marking the first defeat for a Senate party leader since Ernest McFarland lost to Barry Goldwater in 1952. The popular vote margin was 4,508—small, but more than eight times as large as the 524-vote margin by which he lost to Tim Johnson in 2002. The contours of the vote were very much the same. Thune narrowly lost Sioux Falls's Minnehaha County, but won fast-growing Lincoln County next door by a bigger popular vote margin. He carried the counties including Mitchell, North Sioux City, Pierre and, by wide margins, Rapid City's Pennington County and the Black Hills counties around it. Daschle won most of the counties in eastern South Dakota, where he started his congressional career by winning his 1978 House race by 139 votes. As compared to 2002, Thune's percentage rose in most eastern South Dakota counties and fell in most West River counties, but he increased his share of the vote significantly in the Pine Ridge and Rosebud Reservations (Shannon and Todd Counties): his refusal to question the reservation vote in November 2002 may have helped him.

Thune returned to Washington a conquering hero, celebrated by Republicans as a giant-killer. Senator George Allen, chairman of the National Republican Senatorial Committee, put it this way during the campaign: "When John Thune wins in South Dakota, that's like picking up three seats in itself." But in May he suffered a setback when the military base closings recommended by the Defense Department included Ellsworth Air Force Base. He had said during the 2004 campaign that a Republican senator with good relations with the Bush administration could better look out for Ellsworth's interests; when the base appeared on the closure list, the Democratic Senatorial Campaign Committee immediately used the opportunity to attack him.

Representative-At-Large

Stephanie Herseth (D)

Elected June 2004, 1st full term; b. Dec. 3, 1970, Aberdeen; home, Brookings; Georgetown U., B.A. 1993, M.A. 1996, J.D. 1997; Lutheran; Single.

Professional Career: Clerk, U.S. District Court, Judge Charles Kornmann 1998–99; Clerk, Judge Diana Gribbon Motz, U.S. Court of Appeals, 1999–2000; Practicing atty., 2000–01; Ex. Dir., SD Farmers Union Foundation, 2003; Legal cnsl., South Dakota Made Store, 2003.

DC Office: 331 CHOB, 20515, 202-225-2801; Fax: 202-225-5823; Web site: http://www.house.gov/herseth/.

Committees: *Agriculture* (10th of 21 D): Conservation, Credit, Rural Development & Research; General Farm Commodities & Risk Management; Livestock & Horticulture. *Resources* (22d of 22 D): Forests & Forest Health. *Veterans' Affairs* (7th of 12 D): Economic Opportunity (RMM).

Group Ratings (Only Served Partial Term)

	ADA	ACLU	AFS	LCV	ITIC	NTU	COC	ACU	NTLC	CHC
2004	55	40	75	56	75	13	50	31	31	—
2003	—	—	—	—	—	—	—	—	—	—

National Journal Ratings (Only Served Partial Term)

	2003 LIB	—	2003 CONS		2004 LIB	—	2004 CONS
Economic	*	—	*		60%	—	40%
Social	*	—	*		55%	—	45%
Foreign	*	—	*		60%	—	39%

Key Votes of the 108th Congress (Only Served Partial Term)

1. Drilling in ANWR	*	5. DC School Vouchers	*	9. Ban Same-Sex Marriage	Y
2. Approve Bush Tax Cuts	*	6. Ban Human Cloning	*	10. Fund Iraq War	*
3. Medicare/Rx Bill	*	7. Restrict Gun Liability	*	11. Bar Cuba Embargo Funds	Y
4. Bar Overtime Pay Regs.	Y	8. Ban Partial-Birth Abortion	*	12. Intelligence Reorg.	Y

Election Results

2004 general	Stephanie Herseth (D)	207,837	(53%)	($4,026,661)
	Larry Diedrich (R)	178,823	(46%)	($2,526,515)
	Other	2,808	(1%)	
2004 special	Stephanie Herseth (D)	132,420	(51%)	
	Larry Diedrich (R)	129,415	(49%)	
2002 general	Bill Janklow (R)	180,023	(53%)	($1,314,087)
	Stephanie Herseth (D)	153,656	(46%)	($1,511,189)
	Other	3,128	(1%)	

South Dakota's lone member of the House is Stephanie Herseth, a Democrat first chosen in a June 2004 special election. Herseth grew up on a farm near Brookings in northeastern South Dakota, in a family with a fine political pedigree. Her grandfather Ralph Herseth was governor from 1958 to 1960. Her grandmother Lorna Herseth was secretary of state from 1972 to 1978. Her father Lars Herseth served in the legislature from 1974 to 1986 and 1988 to 1996; in 1986 he ran for governor and lost by only 52%–48%. In a state where voters expect to meet candidates the

Herseths were well liked and well respected. Herseth graduated from Georgetown University and its law school, interned with Senator Tim Johnson (a college classmate of her father), clerked for federal judges in South Dakota and Maryland, taught at Georgetown law school and worked for big law firm in Washington. She turned down invitations to run against Attorney General Mark Barnett in 1998. In 2002 she decided to run for the House.

The seat was open because Republican incumbent John Thune, first elected in 1996, was running against Democratic Senator Tim Johnson; he lost that race narrowly, then beat Senator Tom Daschle in 2004. In the House race the clear favorite was Republican former Governor Bill Janklow. Blunt, plain-spoken and often tactless, Janklow announced for the House in March 2002 pledging to be a "sledgehammer." In the June primary he beat former Senator Larry Pressler 55%–27%, while Herseth beat the 1996 Democratic House nominee, Rick Weiland, by a 58%–32% margin. She was in her own right a dynamic candidate, articulate and eager to meet people. She also proved to be a great fundraiser: with help from EMILY's List, she raised $1.5 million, more than Janklow's $1.3 million.

Herseth, who started running when she was only 30, argued that South Dakota had "a tradition of sending young passionate leaders to Congress," and cited Democrats Tom Daschle and Tim Johnson and Republicans Larry Pressler and John Thune, all first elected in their 30s. She avoided phrases that might be construed as "liberal," saying "that's not a term that's respected here." When asked about abortion, she would typically say she wanted to make it "as rare as possible." When asked about gun control she noted that she grew up on a farm in pheasant hunting country and said she saw no need for new restrictions on guns. For her part, Herseth was respectful of Janklow. "When I made the decision to seek office, I never thought I would be running against Bill Janklow. He is larger than life, especially for people of my generation." She noted that, while she was still in high school, then-Governor Janklow took time from his schedule to answer questions from her for a report she was writing.

The two candidates agreed on many local issues but they differed in their approaches to Iraq. In September 2002 Janklow said, "I'd love to have the support of our allies, but it's the American World Trade Center they flew the planes into. I'd love to have the support of our allies, but if we can't get the support of these people, then in this war they're not our allies, and we may have to go it alone." Herseth said, "We are looking at putting our men and women in urban warfare, hand-to-hand combat on the streets of Baghdad. I view it as a sliding scale. To the extent that we have little support from allies, the need goes way up for congressional approval. With more allied support, the bar goes down a little for congressional approval."

By September the polls suggested that this was an even race. Herseth was an attractive and energetic candidate, while some South Dakotans thought that Janklow had just run to block Pressler and was not really interested in the job. Janklow stepped up his campaign pace and the NRCC bought up a block of TV time for the six weeks before the election. But in contrast to the Senate race, the ads in this contest were all positive. When the NRCC ran a spot attacking Herseth as a carpetbagger, Janklow insisted it be pulled. Janklow evidently pulled ahead in October, as the nation contemplated military action in Iraq, and on Election Day he won 53%–46%. But Janklow's House career was cut short. In August 2003 he sped through a stop sign in his Cadillac and killed a motorcyclist. He was indicted, tried and, in December 2003, convicted of felony manslaughter, and immediately announced that he would resign. Governor Mike Rounds declared that the vacancy would be filled in a special election held in June 2004, the same day as South Dakota's primary. The two parties would nominate candidates.

After the 2002 election Herseth taught at South Dakota State University and headed the South Dakota Farmers Union Foundation. She was the obvious choice for the House race for the Democrats, and was unanimously chosen in March 2004. The Republican nominee was state Senator Larry Diedrich, a corn, hog and soybean farmer who had headed the South Dakota and American Soybean Associations and served eight years in the legislature. Herseth campaigned as a "fiscally conservative and ideologically moderate" candidate; she called for changes in the 2003 Medicare/prescription drug act and a ban on meatpacker ownership of livestock. She supported abortion rights; he opposed abortion and criticized her for refusing to promise to vote for a constitutional amendment banning same-sex marriage. He also criticized her opposition to making some tax cuts permanent and focused attention on her lack of life experience. Herseth, who was single, said, "A lot of people today know women, or even have women in their family, who have postponed marriage and family-raising for professional reasons. Some of the stereotypes that were once out there are not so strong any more." Herseth started off far ahead in the polls. But Diedrich campaigned hard and caught up by late May. The result on June 1 was almost even: Herseth won 51%–49%, with a popular vote margin of just 3,005. Turnout in the heavily Republican Black Hills area was low; Herseth carried the Indian reservations by wide margins.

House Minority Leader Nancy Pelosi and Democratic campaign committee Chairman Robert Matsui hailed Herseth's victory, as well as that of Ben Chandler in the Kentucky 6th in February, as proof that Democrats could win in districts carried by George W. Bush in 2000. Sometimes special elections are harbingers of results in November, sometimes not. These turned out not to be, but Pelosi gave Herseth committee assignments that positioned her well for November: Agriculture, Veterans' Affairs, Resources. Diedrich was the Republican nominee and, after recovering from heart surgery in June, kept on running. As in the special election contest, the candidates debated frequently and civilly; Herseth even gave Diedrich credit for lobbying an Appropriations subcommittee chairman for the Lewis and Clark Water Project. But negative notes were also struck. Ads run by Diedrich and national Republicans attacked Herseth for roll call votes—against making the marriage penalty ban, the child tax credit and the deductibility of state sales taxes permanent; against EPA authority to waive state laws requiring low-pollution gasoline blends. National Democrats ran ads criticizing Diedrich's votes as a legislator to increase taxes on gasoline, cell phones and hospitals and opposing abolition of the inheritance tax. Herseth said, "My litmus test is simple: what makes sense for South Dakota? That philosophy has often put me at odds with my party, but I ran for Congress not to vote in lockstep with my party, but to represent our state." At one debate Herseth was asked how she would vote if the presidential election went to the House. "I represent South Dakota. And I'm going to put South Dakota first," she said. When Diedrich pressed her to say whom she would vote for, she said, "I guess Larry is parsing my words. I would vote for George Bush for president." When Diedrich criticized her for calling liberal Manhattan Democrat Jerrold Nadler her mentor, Herseth said, "You know, my parents raised me to be polite and courteous. I have to work with people outside of our region to support policies that are right for rural America."

This race was overshadowed by the hot and even closer race between John Thune and Tom Daschle, in a state that everyone knew would vote for George W. Bush. But while Daschle lost, Herseth managed to widen her margin to 53%–46%. In her first full term she argued against reopening the border to imports of Canadian cattle and pushed for increasing by $226 million the payments to two South Dakota Indian tribes for land lost when flooded by Missouri River dams. She called for making veterans benefits an entitlement, not subject to annual appropriations. Many Democrats see her as a future national star; she could run for Tim Johnson's Senate seat if he retires in 2008, or for the governorship or against John Thune in 2010. Looking ahead in January 2005, she said, "Let's just say that while I haven't mapped out any long-term strategy, I'm not ruling anything out."

★ TENNESSEE ★

Tennessee is a battleground state, with a fighting temperament since it was settled 200 years ago by the likes of Andrew Jackson and went on to produce so many soldiers it came to be known as the Volunteer State. This was a frontier battleground in the 1790s, from which Jackson launched his wars on the Indians and the British. It was a military battleground in the 1860s, when Yankee troops swept down the Tennessee and Cumberland Rivers on their way to Mississippi and through Chattanooga's Lookout Mountain on their way to Atlanta and the sea. It has been a cultural battleground for much of the 20th century. On one side were the Fugitives, writers like John Crowe Ransom and Allen Tate, who contributed to "I'll Take My Stand," a manifesto calling for retaining the South's rural economy and heritage. On the other side have been business leaders and politicians who have made Tennessee the fastest-growing state of the interior South: Tennessee has given birth to the first supermarket (a Piggly Wiggly), the Holiday Inn, Federal Express and Goo-Goo Clusters.

This state has also been a marshaling ground for the music traditions that have a large place in Americans' lives. East Tennessee is one of the homes of bluegrass music and mountain fiddling, with string bands and vocal harmony; Knoxville's *Tennessee Barn Dance* has been broadcast since 1942. Gospel music has long been centered in Nashville, which is also the nation's leading center of religious publishing. Country music got its commercial start in Nashville, with broadcasts of the Grand Ole Opry from Ryman Auditorium starting in 1925; Nashville remains indisputably the capital of country music. The Mississippi lowlands around Memphis, economically and culturally the metropolis of the Mississippi Delta, gave birth to the blues in the years from the 1890s to 1920; and the blues were in turn the inspiration for the jazz musicians of Beale Street in the 1920s and Elvis Presley, whose Graceland mansion is now a major tourist destination, in the 1950s and 1960s.

Tennessee is and has long been a political battleground. Its political divisions have their roots in the Civil War, and many counties today still vote their 1860s loyalties: The Union counties, mainly in the east but with a scattering to the west, vote solidly Republican, while the Confederate counties in middle and west Tennessee long voted heavily Democratic. Within the limits of these enduring party loyalties, political entrepreneurs have set the tone for the state. From the 1920s to 1948, Edward Crump, longtime mayor of Memphis, used his total control of Democratic primary votes there to elect governors and senators. The Tennessee Valley Authority and the cheap electric power it generated provided an institutional base for reform liberal Democrats Estes Kefauver and Albert Gore Sr., elected to the Senate in 1948 and 1952. They were soon national figures, with reliable enough backing from Tennessee's yellow-dog Democratic majority to vote for civil rights bills and to refuse to sign the segregationist Southern Manifesto. Kefauver died in 1963 and Gore was defeated in 1970, but lived on to see his son twice elected vice president, before dying in December 1998. Tennessee has never had a large black population—16% in 2000, half of whom live in and around Memphis—and the state was not riven by the racial animosity that seared so much of the South in the 1950s and 1960s, thanks in large part to the actions of its leading politicians, but also to the continuing hold of ancestral partisan preferences.

Today the political balance has changed, and Tennessee has become a mostly Republican state. Democrats' cultural liberalism has moved rural voters in west and middle Tennessee away from their ancestral loyalties, and the surging growth in the ring of counties around Nashville in the 1990s has created a new voting bloc that is conservative on both economic and cultural issues. The first movement toward the Republicans occurred in the 1960s and 1970s, symbolized by the elections of Republican Senators Howard Baker and Bill Brock in 1966 and 1970, and Republican Governor Lamar Alexander in 1978. Then, as Jimmy Carter changed the image of the Democratic Party, Democrats rallied; Democrats Jim Sasser and Al Gore were elected to the Senate in 1976 and 1984, and Democrat Ned Ray McWherter was elected governor in 1986.

This movement was still strong enough for the Clinton-Gore ticket to carry Tennessee 47%–42% in 1992. But the narrowness of the margin was a warning of what was ahead. In 1994

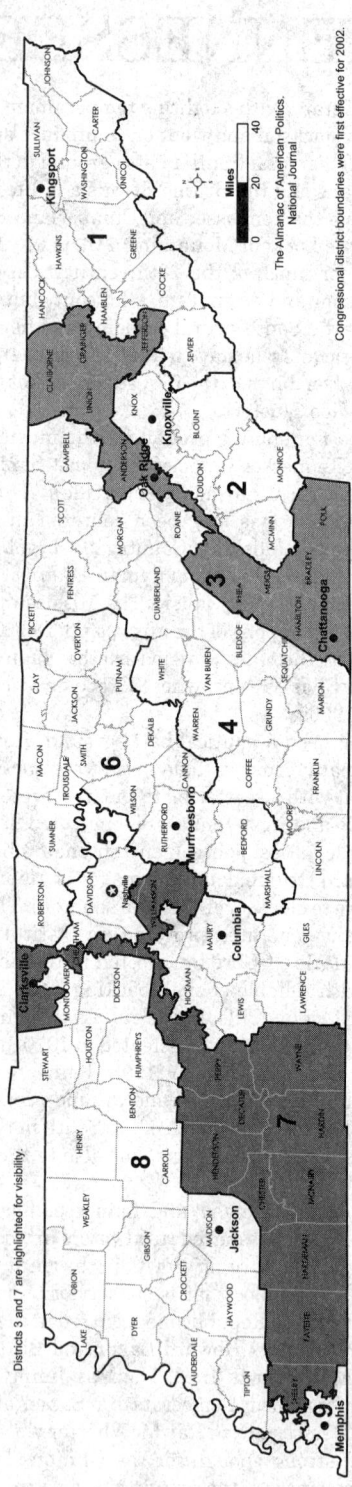

Districts 3 and 7 are highlighted for visibility.

The Almanac of American Politics.
National Journal

Congressional district boundaries were first effective for 2002.

Tennessee turned against the Clinton administration and produced a kind of political revolution. Republican Fred Thompson, famous as a Watergate investigator and movie actor, won the remainder of Gore's Senate term by a landslide, surgeon Bill Frist beat Sasser, and Republican Don Sundquist was elected governor. Republicans won a majority of the vote for the U.S. House, gaining two seats and coming close in a third. The Republican trend was strong enough in 1996 that only after extraordinary efforts—Gore made 16 appearances here and the campaign pumped in money for late ads—was the Clinton-Gore ticket able to win by a narrow 48%–46% margin.

In 2000 the tide was even stronger. George W. Bush targeted the state early and worked it energetically; the Gore campaign, though headquartered in Nashville, seemed to assume it would come around in the end, and only campaigned hard here in the last few days. Bush carried the state 51%–47% and Gore became only the fourth major party nominee to lose his home state in 85 years (the others were South Dakota's George McGovern in 1972, Kansas' Alf Landon in 1936 and New Jersey's Woodrow Wilson in 1916). In his gracious concession speech, Gore noted that he had some fence-mending to do in Tennessee, but the problem was not that he was personally unpopular; the problem was that the issue positions and cultural tone of the Clinton-Gore administration was alien and grating in rural Tennessee and in the suburban subdivisions expanding from Nashville and other cities out into the countryside. The 2002 election saw some move back to Tennessee Democrats: Former Nashville Mayor Phil Bredesen won the governorship by 51%–48%. Tennessee has now alternated the parties in the governor's office at eight-year intervals for a quarter-century. Democrats, aided by partisan redistricting, also picked up one congressional district and maintained control of the legislature. But Republican Lamar Alexander, 20 years after he won his second election as governor, was elected to the U.S. Senate by a 54%–44% margin. In 2004 Bush carried Tennessee by a solid 57%–43% margin and Republicans won the popular vote for the House and, for the first time since Reconstruction, elected a majority of state senators.

This is a Tennessee that is expanding economically but is not abandoning its cultural roots. If its economy lagged behind the nation's through much of the 20th century, its respect for hard work and its open climate for entrepreneurism have enabled it to grow mightily in its last decades and in the first years of the 21st. The expansion started in the early 1980s, when Alexander helped bring big auto plants to middle Tennessee. The lack of strong unions and of bitter racial divisions—Tennessee was mostly untouched by the racial strife of the 1930s and the civil rights strife of the 1960s—attracted Japanese companies here, which in turn attracted General Motors.

When the country music business boomed, so did tourism. Nashville is also a health care center. The Nashville establishment traditionally supported Democrats in Tennessee politics, but now Nashville money has become heavily Republican: metro Nashville gave $9.3 million, mostly to Republicans, in the 2004 cycle, with $4.6 million coming from just three zip codes—37205, 37215 and 37027.

Despite all that growth, Tennessee state politics has become, well, a battleground. Tennessee grew more rapidly than most of its neighboring states in the 1990s in part because of its low taxes. It has no income tax (the state Supreme Court ruled in 1931 that the state Constitution didn't list the income tax as one the legislature could impose, and so it couldn't) and it ranks low on the list of state and local taxes as a percentage of per capita income. But since Governor Ned Ray McWherter created the TennCare program in 1994, spending has accelerated—from $2.5 billion in 1995 to $8 billion in 2004 on TennCare alone. For three straight years beginning in 1999, Republican Governor Don Sundquist, elected on a no-income-tax platform in 1994, called for and failed to get an income tax. In July 2002 the legislature compromised and raised the sales tax from 6% to 7%. Democratic Governor Phil Bredesen, elected on a no-tax-increase pledge in 2002, kept his word. He got the budget balanced in 2003 and in December 2004, after public interest lawyers challenged the TennCare cuts he persuaded the legislature to enact, scaled back the program considerably.

The People

Pop. 2004 (est):	5,900,962	
Pop. 2000:	5,689,283	
Pop. 1990:	4,877,185	
Change 1990–2000:	Up 16.7%	
% of U.S. total:	2.0%	
Pop. rank:	16th of 50	
Area size:	42,143 sq. mi.	
State Native:	64.7%	
Non-citizen:	1.9%	

Language

English: 93.5%	Spanish: 3.3%
Other Eur.: 2.0%	

Race/Ethnic Origin

4,505,930	79.2%	White
928,204	16.3%	Black
56,077	1.0%	Asian
13,820	0.2%	Native Am.
1,810	0.0%	Hawaiian
54,824	1.0%	Two+ races
4,780	0.1%	Other
123,838	2.2%	Hisp. Origin

Ancestry

USA: 14.7%	Irish: 7.8%
English: 7.6%	German: 7.0%
Scotch-Irish: 2.2%	

Military veterans: 560,141 (13.1%)

WWII: 17.3%	Korea: 12.8%
Vietnam: 33.9%	Gulf War: 11.0%

Most populous cities (2003):

1. Memphis	645,978
2. Nashville	544,765
3. Knoxville	173,278
4. Chattanooga	154,887
5. Clarksville	107,953

Urban population: 63.6%
Rural population: 36.4%

Education

H.S. Grad:	75.9%
College Grad:	19.6%

Industry

Agri: 1.4%	Con: 7.3%	
Fin: 5.8%	Info: 2.4%	
Mfg: 25.2%	Prof: 26.0%	
Public: 4.0%	Trade: 15.6%	
Other: 12.3%		

Occupation

Blue collar: 30.2%	White collar: 55.6%
Gray collar: 14.2%	

Work Sector

Private: 78.4%	Govt: 13.9%
Self: 7.3%	Family: 0.3%
Unemployment: 5.4%	

Household Income

<15k: 19.2%	15-35k: 28.9%
35-50k: 17.4%	50-100k: 26.2%
100-150k: 5.2%	>150k: 3.1%
Median: $36,360	
Poverty status: 13.5%	

Home Value

<50k: 19.0%	50-100k: 40.1%	100-200k: 29.9%	200-300k: 6.8%
300-500k: 2.9%	>500k: 1.3%	Median: $88,300	

General Assembly

Senate	17 R 16 D
House	53 D 46 R

Legislative Term Limits: No

Registered Voters
No party registration

Presidential politics   Tennessee has been about evenly divided in presidential politics at several different points in the last half-century, even as its basic political leanings have switched from Democratic to Republican. It was close in the Eisenhower-Stevenson races in the 1950s, in the Carter-Reagan race of 1980 and again in 1992, 1996 and 2000. But the fact that native son Al Gore was unable to win here as the representative of the incumbent party in a time of peace and prosperity suggests that Tennessee is likely to be out of reach for presidential Democrats in the near future. Tennessee was not a battleground state in the 2004 presidential election, and George W. Bush carried it 57%–43%. John Kerry carried the counties including Memphis and Nashville, but lost heavily in the suburban ring around Nashville and otherwise carried only 15 ancestrally Democratic rural counties; Bush carried 81 of 99 counties altogether.

For several cycles Tennessee held its presidential primary on Super Tuesday (though Tennessee holds its state primaries on Thursdays, the only state to do so). But it was far from the biggest state to vote that day, and so received little attention. In 2004 it voted earlier, on February 10, just two weeks after New Hampshire; the only other primary that day was in Virginia. This was just a week after John Edwards had won in South Carolina and Wesley Clark had led Edwards and Kerry in a virtual three-way tie in Oklahoma. Edwards's and Clark's home states were both contiguous to Tennessee, and as southerners and, in Clark's case, as a general, they would seem to have special appeal in the state. But Kerry won the primary with 41% of the vote to 27% for Edwards and 23% for Clark. Kerry had big pluralities in the largest counties but

2004 Presidential Vote

Bush (R)	1,384,375	(57%)
Kerry (D)	1,036,477	(43%)
Nader (I)	8,992	(0%)
Other	7,475	(0%)

2004 Democratic Presidential Primary

Kerry (D)	151,527	(41%)
Edwards (D)	97,914	(27%)
Clark (D)	85,315	(23%)
Dean (D)	16,128	(4%)
Sharpton (D)	6,107	(2%)
Other	12,394	(3%)

2000 Presidential Vote

Bush (R)	1,061,949	(51%)
Gore (D)	981,720	(47%)
Nader (Green)	19,781	(1%)
Other	12,731	(1%)

carried most small counties as well. Turnout was 369,000—far lower than the record Democratic primary turnout in 1988 of 576,000, when Al Gore was running.

Congressional districting

Tennessee's Democratic legislature controlled redistricting after the 2000 Census; Republican Governor Don Sundquist's veto could be overridden by majority votes in both houses. But in January 2002 the Democrats, with help from 6th District Democrat Bart Gordon, drew lines which were agreed to by most Republicans. The congressional district plan cut across party lines far more often than ever before in Tennessee. It took six Democratic-leaning counties out of Republican Zach Wamp's 3d District and placed them in the 4th District, whose incumbent Republican Van Hilleary was running for governor. That enabled Democratic state Senator Lincoln Davis to win the 4th: He led by only 2,000 votes in the counties formerly in the district, but by nearly 8,000 in the counties added, and would surely have trailed in the Republican East Tennessee counties that were subtracted. Heavily Republican Williamson County south of Nashville was taken out of Gordon's 6th and split between the 4th and the heavily Republican 7th District.

109th Congress Lineup
5 D   4 R
108th Congress Lineup
5 D   4 R

Governor

Phil Bredesen (D)

Elected 2002, term expires Jan. 2007, 1st term; b. Nov. 21, 1943, Oceanport, NJ; home, Nashville; Harvard U., B.S. 1967; Catholic; married (Andrea Conte).

Elected Office: Lexington, MA, City Cncl., 1972–73; Nashville Mayor, 1991–99.

Professional Career: Founder, HealthAmerica Corp., 1975–86.

Office: State Capitol, Nashville, 37243, 615-741-2001; Fax: 615-532-9711; Web site: www.state.tn.us/governor.

Election Results

2002 general	Phil Bredesen (D)	837,284	(51%)
	Van Hilleary (R)	786,803	(48%)
2002 primary	Phil Bredesen (D)	426,418	(79%)
	Randy Nichols (D)	38,322	(7%)
	Charles Smith (D)	34,547	(6%)
1998 general	Don Sundquist (R)	669,973	(69%)
	John Jay Hooker (D)	287,750	(29%)
	Other	18,513	(2%)

Phil Bredesen is a Democrat who was elected governor of Tennessee in 2002, on his second try. Bredesen grew up far from Nashville, in Shortsville, New York, 30 miles southeast of Rochester; his parents were divorced and his mother worked as a bank teller; his grandmother lived with him and took in sewing for a living. He got a scholarship at Harvard and graduated with a degree in physics, and in 1967 he moved to Lexington, Massachusetts, and went to work for Itek; it was classified work and he got a draft deferment for it. He caught the political bug early. In 1968 he volunteered for Eugene McCarthy in New Hampshire and then for Robert Kennedy and for John Lindsay for mayor in New York in 1969. In 1970 he ran for the Massachusetts state Senate and lost to a longtime incumbent. In 1972 he won a seat on the Lexington Town Meeting. He went to work for Searle, a pharmaceutical firm, and moved to London, where he met his wife. She was recruited by Hospital Corporation of America; he quit his job to follow her to Nashville in 1975. There he got a job with Hospital Affiliates International, negotiating management contracts with hospitals. He wanted to start his own business and in 1980, with $50,000 cash and $250,000 in backing from local venture capitalists, operating from a computer in his den, he started HealthAmerica, which began acquiring and operating HMOs across the country. When it went public in 1983, it ran 20 HMOs with 400,000 members. His backers decided to sell the firm in 1986, and got $400 million from MaxiCare; Bredesen pocketed $47 million, while MaxiCare, under other management, later went bankrupt.

The political bug bit again. This time his goal was not the Lexington Town Meeting, but the mayoralty of Nashville, a particularly powerful position since the city includes all of Davidson County and the mayor has broad powers. Bredesen spent $2 million on his 1987 mayoral campaign but lost in the runoff to Congressman Bill Boner. Bredesen ran again in the January 1988 special election to succeed Boner, but lost the primary 40%–36% to former gubernatorial candidate Bob Clement. In 1991 Bredesen ran for mayor again and won with 71%. As mayor, Bredesen had some spectacular successes. He lined up financing for a hockey arena and, later, a football stadium and brought the NHL Predators and NFL Tennessee Titans to Nashville. He got voters to approve $100 million to build schools. He enticed Dell to locate a facility in Nashville. Nashville boomed in the 1990s and he took credit for 106,000 new jobs. Once a regional center, Nashville now seemed to be a major national metro area.

Nashville is Tennessee's largest media market, covering almost all of Middle Tennessee, and a successful Nashville mayor is a natural candidate for statewide office. In 1994 Bredesen spent $6 million on running for governor and won the Democratic nomination with 53% of the vote in a 10-candidate field. He did not campaign heavily in East and West Tennessee and lost to Republican Don Sundquist by a 54%–45% margin. But in the years that followed, Bredesen had a more successful record than Sundquist. The state government's problem is that it had an increasingly expensive health care program, TennCare, and one of the nation's lowest revenue bases, with no state income tax. TennCare, established in 1994 with federal waivers, covered not only those eligible for Medicaid but others with relatively low incomes or who were uninsured; enrollment zoomed and costs increased higher than average. In his second term, Sundquist went back on a campaign promise and sought an income tax. Most Republicans opposed him, arguing that Tennessee's low taxes helped account for the fact that the state had had much more economic growth than most neighboring states. The legislature, barraged at critical points by honking motorists and slogan-chanting anti-tax crusaders mobilized by radio talk show hosts, refused to pass one.

Against this background Bredesen, who had not run for reelection as mayor in 1999, decided to run for governor again. He said that he opposed an income tax and argued that his experience managing health care systems would enable him to straighten out TennCare. He won the Democratic primary easily, but the favorite was Republican Congressman Van Hilleary, who based his campaign on opposition to an income tax. Hilleary charged that Bredesen was a rich northerner who didn't really understand Tennessee. Bredesen undercut that by sitting down with folks over coffee and telling how he had grown up poor in a small town. Unusual for a Democrat, he appeared on conservative talk radio shows and made a favorable impression.

Much of Hilleary's campaign was based on the premise that Bredesen didn't really oppose an income tax. In September Hilleary ran an ad saying that "Phil BredeSundquist" had raised property taxes three times in Nashville (as indeed Bredesen had). Bredesen responded the next day with an on-camera ad: "Well, Mr. Hilleary, I'll say it again as clearly as I know how. I do not support an income tax." Bredesen focused more on fixing TennCare. "Everybody in the state of Tennessee knows somebody on TennCare they don't think should be on TennCare. It needs to be the bronze package, not the platinum package," he said. Hilleary, who said TennCare was "not my passion," said he would cut $300 to $400 million from TennCare. On other issues, there was agreement: Both candidates opposed gun control, supported scheduled teacher pay raises, called for children to learn to read by the third grade, wanted more spending on higher education, more spending to promote tourism and expansion of the Tennessee Industrial Infrastructure Program.

Bredesen spent $3 million of his own money on his campaign, to counter, he said, money raised for Hilleary by George W. Bush. This turned out to be the closest Tennessee governor's race since 1896; Bredesen won 51%–48%. This time he had campaigned across the state, raising money in small fundraisers, holding chili suppers is rural counties. He broke into the Republican base in East Tennessee, carrying Knoxville's Knox County—and holding Hilleary to a narrow lead in his own region. Bredesen carried Nashville solidly and carried or held Hilleary to narrow margins in all but one of the Republican-trending counties around Nashville. Bredesen had a big lead in Memphis and carried rural West Tennessee, often a swing area in Tennessee elections.

Facing a predicted $800 million budget shortfall, Bredesen got the legislature to cut state spending 9% across the board in 2003 and to vote in a lottery to pay for college scholarships; it had a record $10.8 million in sales on its first day in January 2004. He supported changes in workmen's comp supported by businesses and opposed by trial lawyers. He got the legislature to limit driver's licenses to citizens and aliens with permanent resident status; others could get certificates of driving which would not be valid identification.

In 2004 he proposed selective increases in spending, restoring $16 million of $18 million in cuts for conservation land purchases, restoring the $36 million in cuts in subsidies to local governments over two years; he refused to restore $65 million in cuts to the state roadbuilding fund. He pushed through a $174 million education increase, raising teacher pay above the Southeastern average and starting voluntary pre-kindergarten. He got $8 million for industrial infrastructure, $11 million for job training connected to Nissan and Toyota and a $10 million Memphis biotech initiative; $95 million was added to the rainy day fund. When a tax study commission came in with a recommendation for an income tax in December 2004, he said, "I don't feel bound by its recommendations to do anything."

The big elephant remained in the room: TennCare. By early 2004 it consumed nearly one-third of the state budget and its 2005 cost was estimated to be $650 million over what was budgeted. In May 2004 the legislature approved Bredesen's changes: recipients were limited to 10 doctor visits a year and six prescription medicines (the average for TennCare was 30); medical necessity was to be determined by the medical contractor, not the patient's doctor; only the least expensive adequate care would be covered. One reason TennCare had so many benefits and cost so much was that self-styled public interest groups, notably the Tennessee Justice Center, kept going to court to enforce old consent decrees. In June 2004 the Tennessee Justice Center went to court again. In September Bredesen asked the Centers for Medicare and Medicaid Services for approval of all his changes. But the lawsuits went on, and on November 10 Bredesen announced that he was ready to abolish TennCare and move back to standard Medicaid, which would eliminate coverage for 430,000 people, one-third of beneficiaries.

Twice in the next weeks Bredesen met with the head of the Tennessee Justice Center to get concessions. But they would make none. On January 10, 2005, he announced that all non-Medicaid-eligible adults would be removed from TennCare and that strict limits would be imposed on prescription drugs and doctor visits, with no appeals; the cost increase was reduced from $650 million to $75 million.

Bredesen's ratings in the polls suggested that he was very well positioned to win reelection in 2006. On many of his programs he had been receiving support from most Republicans in the legislature, which left him needing only a few Democrats to prevail. Back in 2002 he had given $750,000 to the state Democratic party for local races; he gave less in 2004, though he did campaign extensively for Democrats. When Republicans won a majority in the state Senate and gained a seat in the state House, he said he didn't think he would have much difficulty dealing with them, though some were threatening to bring up for the required second passage a constitutional amendment banning same-sex marriage.

Meanwhile, some national Democrats, given pause by their defeats in November 2004, began to give Bredesen a lookover. *The New Republic* ran a laudatory cover story on him in January 2005. University of Tennessee law professor Glenn Reynolds, proprietor of the influential Instapundit.com, wrote an admiring article for *The Wall Street Journal*. In January Bredesen was the keynote speaker at the Democratic National Committee Council meeting in Atlanta. Was this the kind of Democrat who could be elected president? Bredesen seemed not totally uninterested, but told *The New Republic*, "The people who have the opportunities are the ones who put their heads down and do the best job they can at the job at hand, and that produces the kind of opportunities that people who put their heads up don't have." He had been governor, after all, for only two years, and he would have to face Tennessee voters again in 2006. But his story seems to be of interest not only in Tennessee.

Senior Senator

Bill Frist (R)

Elected 1994, seat up 2006, 2d term; b. Feb. 22, 1952, Nashville; home, Nashville; Princeton U., A.B. 1974, Harvard Med. Schl., M.D. 1978; Presbyterian; married (Karyn).

Professional Career: Practicing surgeon, 1978–94; Dir., Vanderbilt Medical Ctr. Heart–Lung Transplant Program, 1986–93.

DC Office: 509 HSOB, 20510, 202-224-3344; Fax: 202-228-1264; Web site: frist.senate.gov.

State Offices: Chattanooga, 423-756-2757; Jackson, 731-424-9655; Kingsport, 423-323-1252; Knoxville, 865-637-4180; Memphis, 901-683-1910; Nashville, 615-352-9411.

Committees: *Majority Leader. Finance:* Health Care; International Trade; Social Security & Family Policy. *Health, Education, Labor & Pensions:* Bioterrorism & Public Health Preparedness. *Rules & Administration.*

Group Ratings

	ADA	ACLU	AFS	LCV	ITIC	NTU	COC	ACU	NTLC	CHC
2004	20	0	14	0	100	66	100	92	88	100
2003	10	—	11	11	—	72	96	90	—	—

National Journal Ratings

	2003 LIB	—	2003 CONS		2004 LIB	—	2004 CONS
Economic	0%	—	82%		18%	—	78%
Social	0%	—	59%		31%	—	66%
Foreign	0%	—	78%		0%	—	67%

Key Votes of the 108th Congress

1. Ban Drilling in ANWR	N	5. Energy Bill	Y	9. Ban Same-Sex Marriage	Y
2. Approve Bush Tax Cuts	Y	6. Support Roe v. Wade	N	10. Ban Bunker-Buster Bomb	N
3. Medicare/Rx Bill	Y	7. Ban Partial-Birth Abortion	Y	11. Fund Iraq War	Y
4. Bar Overtime Pay Regs.	N	8. Assault Weapons Ban	N	12. Restrict Missile Defense	N

Election Results

2000 general	Bill Frist (R)	1,255,444	(65%)	($4,664,737)
	Jeff Clark (D)	621,152	(32%)	($173,406)
	Other	52,017	(3%)	
2000 primary	Bill Frist (R)	unopposed		
1994 general	Bill Frist (R)	834,226	(56%)	($7,017,424)
	Jim Sasser (D)	623,164	(42%)	($5,020,515)
	Other	23,001	(2%)	

Bill Frist, first elected to the Senate in 1994, is now the 20th Senate majority leader (the title goes back only to 1925). Frist grew up in Nashville, in a well-known Tennessee family: His father practiced medicine for 55 years and was the physician for seven Tennessee governors. Both his brothers are doctors, too. Frist grew up in Nashville and was class president, football quarterback and yearbook editor at Nashville's Montgomery Bell Academy. He graduated from Princeton and Harvard Medical School, studied at Massachusetts General Hospital, in England and at Stanford, and became a heart and lung transplant surgeon, setting up the transplant program at Vanderbilt. He performed 250 transplants and in 1989 wrote a book, *Transplant,* on the social and ethical issues of these surgeries; he has written more than 100 peer-reviewed articles. In 1968 his father and brother, Thomas Frist Jr., set up HCA (which through a 1994 merger became Columbia/ HCA), the world's largest hospital company; the Frists lost control of the firm in the late 1980s. After it was hit with charges of Medicare violations in 1997, Thomas Frist Jr. came back from semi-retirement to run it. Bill Frist piloted his first plane at 16, and flew small planes to pick up donated organs; he runs marathons (two within 13 days in 1999). He still practices some medicine, at clinics in Washington, and on five trips to Africa, where he has tended patients in war zones in Sudan and in Uganda. He resuscitated a constituent in the Dirksen Building in September 1995, treated the wounded in the Capitol shooting in July 1998, tended Strom Thurmond when he collapsed on the Senate floor in October 2001, and treated accident victims on Florida's Alligator Alley on New Year's Day 2003.

Frist is a man of intensity and focus, and for years that focus was medicine, not politics; he never voted until he was 36, after he moved back to Nashville. He decided to switch careers and run in 1994 as a Republican against Democratic Senator Jim Sasser. Frist seemed unlikely to win: Sasser was chairman of the Budget Committee and running for majority leader, and he had won his previous race in 1988 with 65% of the vote. And Frist had tough primary opposition from east Tennessee businessman Bob Corker, who attacked him for not voting and for obtaining cats from animal shelters for experiments as a medical student (which he mentioned in *Transplant*). But Frist, spending liberally, beat Corker 44%–32%. In the general, Frist backed welfare reform, federal spending cuts, school prayer and term limits; he followed Howard Baker in calling for citizen-politicians and pledged to serve just two terms. Sasser emphasized school prayer, the balanced budget amendment and cracking down on illegal immigrants; he portrayed Frist as a bored, rich surgeon. Frist outspent Sasser, spending $3.7 million of his own money. Sasser led in polls up through October, but in November Frist won 56%–42%.

Frist is the first practicing physician to serve in the Senate since Royal Copeland of New York died in June 1938. Naturally he got involved in health issues—the Senate ethics committee ruled that he is not prohibited from voting on any "legislation of general applicability to the health care industry," and his HCA stock was put into a blind trust. He played a key role on the 1996 health care bill on portability and pre-existing conditions, working to include Medical Savings Accounts.

On some health issues, Frist has worked with Democrats. In 2000, Frist and Ted Kennedy steered through a $919 million authorization for public health laws, including $540 million for research on bioterrorism and $180 million to refurbish Centers for Disease Control labs.

On HMO regulation and prescription drugs, Frist took the lead in forging Republican positions. In June 2000 he sponsored a Medicare bill with commission chairman John Breaux, which would have private insurers competing to provide coverage to Medicare beneficiaries, overseen by a new government agency that would approve the content of plans, and would include prescription drug coverage with subsidies for all seniors and a progressive sliding scale of subsidies depending on income. The Breaux-Frist proposal went nowhere in 1999 because of opposition from the Clinton administration. But George W. Bush campaigned on the issue in 2000 and in early 2003 made it one of his priorities. Republicans had campaigned on the issue of prescription drugs for seniors in 2002 and House Republicans passed their version of a free-standing benefit. But Frist has argued all along that it makes better sense to make a prescription drug benefit part of a larger Medicare revision, and in 2003 he gained his chance to bring it forward. With support from Kennedy, a bipartisan bill passed the Senate in June 2003. The House passed a bill with significant differences, and Kennedy and some other Democrats attacked the result that came back from the conference committee. But Frist persisted, and in November the bill passed the Senate after, as Frist put it, "six years of empty promises, stalled negotiations and partisan gridlock." Frist has also been a leader on stem-cell research. In July 2001 he set out ten "essential components" of policy, including funding adult stem-cell research, banning human cloning and using excess embryos from in vitro fertilization procedures which otherwise would be discarded.

Frist became a member of the Africa Subcommittee in 1997, which led to his medical trips to Africa. After treating AIDS patients, he showed Jesse Helms pictures of them and got him to co-sponsor $500 million for a global AIDS fund. He backed down to the Bush administration and agreed to seek only $200 million, and was much criticized by Democrats, but he got Bush in 2003 to commit to spending $15 billion over several years. In August 2004, on a trip to the Darfur region of Sudan, he said that people in the region were undergoing genocide.

After letters with anthrax were sent to Majority Leader Tom Daschle's office, Frist stepped forward and used his expertise to provide information and reassurance. He emphasized anthrax's sensitivity to antibiotics and encouraged anyone who might be exposed to take drugs; mistakenly, as he admitted, he underestimated the danger from anthrax in envelopes. In November 2001 he and Kennedy sponsored a bioterrorism preparedness bill, with $3 billion to expand the nation's supply of vaccines, expand the Centers for Disease Control and Prevention, beef up state public health laboratories and provide training for response to a bioterrorism attack. It became law in June 2002. In March 2002, his book, *When Every Moment Counts: What You Need to Know About Bioterrorism from the Senate's Only Doctor,* was published in English and Spanish, with royalties going to the Tennessee Public Health Association. In 2002 he wrote a bill restricting lawsuits against pharmaceutical companies that used the mercury-based preservative thimerosal as a preservative; his approach was that parents claiming that thimerosal caused autism in their children should go through the vaccination compensation process established by Congress in the 1980s. This provision was put into the homeland security bill by House Majority Leader Dick Armey in November 2002, and was attacked as a special interest provision to help Eli Lilly, which had contributed to Republicans. Frist continued to argue it was good public policy, but after he was elected majority leader agreed to honor Trent Lott's commitment to several Republican senators to allow the issue to be revisited in 2003, and said he would argue for the bill on its merits.

Frist got his start as a national Republican leader when he was chosen to deliver the response to Bill Clinton's State of the Union address in January 2000. He chaired the Platform Committee at the Republican National Conventions in 2000 and 2004. In December 2000, this surgeon who had no experience in politics a few years before was elected chairman of the National Republican Senatorial Committee, with the assignment of regaining a Senate majority in 2002 when 20 Republican and 14 Democratic Senate seats were up. He did it. He excelled in fundraising—the NRSC outspent its Democratic counterpart by $66 million—and in political strategy. He kept in close touch with White House political strategist Karl Rove but also made decisions on his own, as when he ran ads showing Bush in March 2002 in five states where Democratic incumbents seemed vulnerable; Republicans picked up seats in two of the states. In November 2002 Republicans gained two seats, enough for a 51-vote majority. Never since popular election of senators came in had a president's party regained a Senate majority in an off-year election. Frist was suddenly a party hero and, interested in concentrating on health care issues, declined a second term at the NRSC three days after the election. Then Majority Leader Trent Lott made his now famous but then little-noticed statement at Thurmond's 100th birthday party December 5. As the furor began, Frist told a reporter December 10, "The statement was unfortunate, and it was off the cuff and casual. I know Trent Lott and he's not a racist. It's important people understand the Republican party leads on issues of equity and fairness and nondiscrimination. Any implication otherwise would be a disappointment to me." On December 15 Don Nickles called for a Republican Conference meeting January 6 to reconsider Lott's leadership. Frist, who had voted for Lott for whip in December 1994, when Lott won by one vote, started making calls by December 19 seeking support should Lott step down. On the morning of December 20 Lott bowed out. By the end of the day it was clear that Frist would be the new majority leader. He was officially chosen in a conference call December 23.

Frist was elevated after only eight years in the Senate (Lyndon Johnson had only six years in the Senate when he was elected majority leader in 1954) and to a position that confers less power than many people assume. The majority leader has the right of recognition, which means he can offer amendments and speak before any other senator. But Senate rules require supermajorities and unanimous consent for many procedures; the majority leader is less often the tamer of lions than the herder of cats. Frist generally but not always deferred to committee chairmen; he worked closely but not slavishly with the Bush White House; he seems to have created a sense of common good feeling among his Republican colleagues. In 2003 he led the Republicans to many victories. The third round of Bush tax cuts were quickly approved. The

Medicare prescription drug bill, after a long process and with some of the Medicare competition and medical savings accounts Frist has long favored, was passed. The partial-birth abortion ban was passed and signed into law. He also pushed through the corporate tax bill with a tobacco buyout.

On some things he was less successful. Democrats filibustered successfully against 10 Bush judicial appointees—the first filibusters against appeals court nominees in Senate history. In November 2003 Frist held the Senate in session for 30 hours in a sort of protest; but to no avail. His most embarrassing setback came on the bill to limit class action lawsuits. In early 2004 there seemed to be 62 votes in favor, enough to defeat any filibuster or delaying tactic. Frist delayed action until July, at which point Minority Leader Tom Daschle wanted to add a minimum wage increase and reauthorization of the assault weapons ban to the bill. Frist decided to pull the bill instead. Nor was he successful on the asbestos liability bill or medical malpractice. He angered Senate Democrats when in May 2004 he traveled to South Dakota and campaigned against Daschle. He also angered Democrats when he agreed to House Ways and Means Chairman Bill Thomas's demand that House Democrats and all Senate Democrats except Max Baucus and John Breaux be excluded from the conference committee on the Medicare/prescription drug bill. He failed to gain agreement with the House on a budget resolution, and none passed; similarly, the transportation bill failed when both houses insisted on more spending than was acceptable to the Bush White House. He did shepherd the intelligence bill to passage, but did not resist when its chief Senate sponsor, Susan Collins, saw her Governmental Affairs Committee lose jurisdiction over several homeland security functions to established committees.

Republicans gained four Senate seats in the November 2004 elections, which put Frist in a stronger position. Nine days later, he signaled that he would change the rules—presumably by getting the vice president to rule that filibusters were not in order and then upholding that with 50 votes—in a speech to the Federalist Society. "The minority seeks nothing less than to realign the relationship between our three branches of government. ... One way or another, the filibuster of judicial nominees must end." Just after the election Arlen Specter said that it would be hard to confirm a Supreme Court appointee who opposed *Roe v. Wade*; conservatives threatened to deprive Specter of the chairmanship of the Judiciary Committee. Frist pointedly did not back Specter. That forced Specter to make commitments to move nominations forward promptly, which he might not otherwise have made. A few days later Republican senators, by a 27–26 vote, gave Frist the right to choose senators to fill half the vacancies on committees, instead of having them all chosen by seniority; this gave him leverage over colleagues inclined to differ with party positions.

Frist was reelected in 2000 against weak opposition by a 65%–32% margin, with the highest number of votes cast for a senator in Tennessee history. He has stayed involved in Tennessee matters, publicizing the new Medicare/prescription drug discount charges and supporting the TennCare changes of Democratic Governor Phil Bredesen. But he has given every indication that he will stick to his promise not to run in 2006. Tennessee politicians have taken him at his word. In October 2004, his 1994 primary opponent, Bob Corker, now mayor of Chattanooga, announced he was running for the seat, and raised $2 million by December. Other Republicans also said they were running, including former Congressman Ed Bryant, who lost to Lamar Alexander in the 2002 Senate primary; state Representative Beth Harwell; and former Congressman Van Hilleary. In November 2004 Democratic state Senator Rosalind Kurita announced her candidacy. And in May 2005 Democratic Congressman Harold Ford said he was running too.

In January 2007 Frist will be 54 and will have risen to the top of two professions and then moved on. In Washington political circles there was little doubt in early 2005 that he would run for president. Out of office, he could spend all his time campaigning; he could easily raise money. But Frist has taken pains to say his plans are uncertain. In August 2004 he said, "Whatever [my future] is, it will be in some kind of public service, but public service to me is working in delivering health care to people who wouldn't otherwise get it, or it could be in government. I just don't know." But his Tennessee colleague Lamar Alexander, who ran for president twice himself, seemed to have fewer doubts. In September 2004 he said, "He's got the pole position in practical, tactical terms, which means: Can you raise the money, are you right on the issues, do you have that slightly irrational sense of purpose, good temperament, tough enough persistence?"

Junior Senator

Lamar Alexander (R)

Elected 2002, seat up 2008, 1st term; b. July 3, 1940, Maryville; home, Nashville; Vanderbilt U., B.A. 1962, N.Y.U., J.D. 1965; Presbyterian; married (Honey).

Elected Office: TN Governor, 1978–86.

Professional Career: Pres., Univ. of TN, 1988–91; U.S. Edu. Sect., 1991–93; Co-director, Empower America, 1994–95; Prof., Harvard U. JFK Schl. of Govt., 2001–02.

DC Office: 302 HSOB, 20510, 202-224-4944; Fax: 202-228-3398; Web site: alexander.senate.gov.

State Offices: Chattanooga, 423-752-5337; Jackson, 731-423-9344; Knoxville, 865-545-4253; Memphis, 901-544-4224; Nashville, 615-736-5129; Tri-Cities, 423-325-6240.

Committees: *Aging (Special)*. *Budget. Energy & Natural Resources:* Energy (Chmn.); National Parks; Public Lands & Forests. *Foreign Relations:* African Affairs; East Asian & Pacific Affairs; International Economic Policy, Export & Trade Promotion; International Operations & Terrorism. *Health, Education, Labor & Pensions:* Bioterrorism & Public Health Preparedness; Education & Early Childhood Development (Chmn.); Employment & Workplace Safety.

Group Ratings

	ADA	ACLU	AFS	LCV	ITIC	NTU	COC	ACU	NTLC	CHC
2004	15	22	0	0	92	75	94	92	92	100
2003	10	—	11	5	—	73	100	85	—	—

National Journal Ratings

	2003 LIB	—	2003 CONS		2004 LIB	—	2004 CONS
Economic	18%	—	77%		5%	—	91%
Social	0%	—	59%		19%	—	71%
Foreign	0%	—	78%		40%	—	58%

Key Votes of the 108th Congress

1. Ban Drilling in ANWR	N	5. Energy Bill	Y	9. Ban Same-Sex Marriage	Y
2. Approve Bush Tax Cuts	Y	6. Support Roe v. Wade	N	10. Ban Bunker-Buster Bomb	N
3. Medicare/Rx Bill	Y	7. Ban Partial-Birth Abortion	Y	11. Fund Iraq War	*
4. Bar Overtime Pay Regs.	N	8. Assault Weapons Ban	N	12. Restrict Missile Defense	N

Election Results

2002 general	Lamar Alexander (R)	891,420	(54%)	($3,761,804)
	Bob Clement (D)	728,295	(44%)	($2,832,990)
2002 primary	Lamar Alexander (R)	295,052	(54%)	
	Ed Bryant (R)	233,678	(43%)	
	Other	19,752	(3%)	
1996 general	Fred D. Thompson (R)	1,091,554	(61%)	($3,469,369)
	Houston Gordon (D)	654,937	(37%)	($795,969)
	Other	32,173	(2%)	

Lamar Alexander, former governor of Tennessee and Secretary of Education, was elected Tennessee's junior senator in 2002. Alexander grew up Maryville, in East Tennessee between Knoxville and the Smoky Mountains, the son of a principal and a teacher; he started piano lessons at 4 and still plays. Like Bill Clinton, he was elected governor of Boys State. He graduated from Vanderbilt, where he wrote editorials in the *Hustler* urging integration, and New York University law school; he clerked for Judge John Minor Wisdom of the Fifth Circuit federal appeals court. Alexander was always a Republican, and in 1966 he wrote Howard Baker, then the Republican candidate for Senate, and volunteered for his Senate campaign against Frank

Clement; Baker gave him a job—the critical connection in Alexander's career. In 1967 he served on Baker's staff in Washington; briefly he lived in a group house with a Democratic congressional staffer named Trent Lott. In 1969, on Baker's recommendation, Alexander got a job working for Bryce Harlow in Richard Nixon's White House. On a trip back to Tennessee to scout the possibilities of running against Senator Albert Gore Sr. in 1970, he met Memphis dentist Winfield Dunn, who was running for governor; Alexander agreed to manage his campaign and Dunn became the first Republican elected governor in 50 years. He decided that next time he would be the candidate, so in 1974, at 34, he ran for governor. He ran a conventional campaign and in that Watergate year lost 55%–44% to Democratic Congressman Ray Blanton.

He ran again in 1978, but differently this time: Wearing a red plaid shirt, he walked 1,000 miles across Tennessee. This time he won 56%–44%. After the election Blanton started issuing many pardons of criminals: It turned out that he was taking bribes. To stop him, the U.S. attorney, a Democrat, urged that Alexander be sworn in three days early; Democratic legislative leaders and the state's chief justice agreed. In a hurried ceremony, Alexander took the oath and announced that he was naming Fred Thompson, famous from his work as Baker's chief counsel in the Senate Watergate hearings, as a special prosecutor. As governor, Alexander got Nissan to build its first American plant in Rutherford County, and General Motors to build its Saturn plant in Williamson County; they became the sparkplugs of rapid growth in the counties around Nashville. He was reelected 60%–40% in 1982. In 1988 he became president of the University of Tennessee and in 1991 he became George H.W. Bush's education secretary. In these years he also reaped big profits from small investments: An option to buy the *Knoxville Journal* was sold to Gannett and yielded $620,000; an option given for his consultant work at Whittle Communications became $330,000. Alexander started a company called Corporate Child Care and is still part-owner.

In 1993 he went to work at the Nashville office of Baker's law firm. The next year turned out to be a good Republican year in Tennessee: Fred Thompson and Bill Frist were elected to the Senate and Don Sundquist was elected governor. Alexander probably could have won either office. But he was after bigger things: He was running for president. His 1996 campaign was keyed to the mood of 1994: He campaigned as an outsider, wore his red plaid shirt and called, as Baker often had, for citizen-politicians. Of members of Congress, he said, "Cut their pay and bring them home!" His bumper stickers said, "Lamar!" But he also had a sophisticated message, based on the idea that the nation needed more decentralized government; he had a superb fundraising organization that made Nashville one of the leading Republican money sources in the nation. He hired top notch political consultants and brilliant organizers in Iowa and New Hampshire. Alexander finished third in the Iowa caucuses, behind Bob Dole and Pat Buchanan and ahead of Steve Forbes. New Hampshire was his best chance for a breakthrough. Dole, the favorite, had been concentrating his fire on Buchanan. But five days before the primary Dole began running ads attacking Alexander. This was shrewd strategy: Buchanan was likely to do well in New Hampshire but obviously could never be nominated; the candidate who finished second in New Hampshire would likely be his chief rival and would easily win the nomination. So it turned out. But the second-place finisher in New Hampshire nearly wasn't Dole. Buchanan did win, with 27% of the vote, to 26% for Dole and 23% for Alexander.

In 1999 Alexander started running for president again. But the plaid shirt and the 1994-style themes failed to resonate. George W. Bush, with his celebrity and his fundraising, dominated the race and Forbes's extensive, expensive campaigning in Iowa left little room for Alexander. His fundraising faltered and after his disappointing sixth-place finish in the August 1999 Ames, Iowa, straw poll, he dropped out within days and endorsed Bush. He didn't go to the 2000 Republican National Convention, though, he revealed later, he was interviewed by Dick Cheney as a possible vice presidential nominee; he said he had run his last race for public office.

Then, on Friday, March 8, 2002, just 27 days before the filing deadline, Senator Fred Thompson announced that he would not run for reelection. He gave Alexander a heads-up on his decision, and on Monday, March 11, Alexander announced.

Alexander's candidacy was welcome to the Bush White House and to Bill Frist, chairman of the Republicans' Senate campaign committee; a 2001 poll by Alexander's pollster Whit Ayres showed that 93% of voters could identify him, though he had not campaigned in Tennessee in 20 years, and that 66% of voters had favorable feelings toward him and only 16% unfavorable. Nashville's Democratic Congressman Bob Clement, son of three-term Governor Frank Clement, also made it clear he was interested. When suburban Memphis Congressman Ed Bryant said he might run, some Republicans tried to talk him out of it; it was clear he would start out behind in a four-month race. But on April 1 he announced.

Bryant's campaign theme was that he was the real conservative in the race. But Alexander campaigned as a conservative, backing individual investment accounts in Social Security, permanent tax cuts, school vouchers (a "G.I. Bill for kids") and a two-year federal budget cycle. On talk radio shows, whose listeners are very likely to be Republican primary voters, he ran a series of "plain talk" ads taking conservative stands on taxes, campaign finance, the Pledge of Allegiance, Judge Charles Pickering, charter schools and oil drilling in the Arctic National Wildlife Refuge. Bryant's ads called him "the one without the plaid shirt" and urged, "Don't be plaid. Be solid for Bryant." Alexander was endorsed on March 12 by Governor Don Sundquist, unpopular with many of his fellow Republicans for his advocacy of a state income tax. Bryant charged that Alexander had favored an income tax when he was governor. Alexander replied that he had considered an income tax as one of several alternatives and "rejected it." Bryant noted that he did increase the sales and gasoline taxes. Alexander won 54%–43%.

Alexander began running ads immediately after the primary and did not stop until November; Clement didn't put ads up until mid-September. But Clement started with good name identification: He had been elected congressman from Nashville, the center of the state's largest media market, starting in January 1988. He like Alexander was a university president (Cumberland University). Clement had a relatively moderate voting record: He voted for the Bush tax cuts and in October 2002 for the Iraq war resolution. They differed on Social Security, prescription drugs, and campaign finance regulation. But much of the campaign dialogue concerned their business investments. Clement said Alexander was a political insider who became wealthy through political connections. Alexander charged that Clement, while Public Service Commissioner in the 1970s, served on the board of one of the banks of Jake Butcher—Alexander's 1978 opponent, whose banks imploded in scandal in the 1980s. Clement at first denied that he'd served on the board, then said it was just an advisory board, and that he had served a decade before the scandal. Alexander said that Clement had voted 143 times to raise taxes and attacked him for backing Senate Democrats' stand on homeland security; he said Clement would be part of "that crowd" voting against George W. Bush.

Alexander led in polls all along, though the lead narrowed as partisan lines strengthened: He won 54%–44%. He won 63% in his native (and ancestrally Republican) East Tennessee, which cast nearly 40% of the votes. Clement carried Nashville's Davidson County and rural counties in Middle Tennessee, but Alexander carried the fast-growing ring of suburban counties around Nashville and held Clement to 53% in his home area. In West Tennessee, Alexander made some inroads among Memphis blacks and carried the rural counties, for 50% in this (ancestrally Democratic) region. Memphis Mayor Willie Herenton introduced him at his victory party.

And so a politician who ran for governor at 34 became a senator at 62. On his office wall he mounted not the usual array of framed photographs but a 27-foot authentic barn wall, with 40 antique items (a guitar made of matches, a banjo made from a fruitcake tin) on loan of the Museum of Appalachia in Norris, Tennessee. As a former governor and cabinet secretary, he got a little seniority over other freshmen, and he joined his Tennessee colleague, Majority Leader Bill Frist, on the Health, Education, Labor, and Pensions Committee. There he worked on small bills, sponsoring three that became law in 2003 and 2004—to help states ensure special education teachers meet federal standards, to permit parents more choice in special education services for small children, to create summer academies for teachers and students to study American history and civics. He mostly supported the Bush administration. But he differed on air pollution. He joined Democrat Tom Carper's bill that would limit emissions not only of sulphur dioxide, nitrous oxide and mercury (as in the Bush bill), but also carbon dioxide, with a Kyoto-style cap and emissions trading. Air pollution has been high in the Knoxville and Smoky Mountains area, threatening the tourism industry; Alexander said Bush's bill "does not go far enough, fast enough in my back yard." He hailed TVA for restarting its nuclear reactors in East Tennessee and Alabama and called for more nuclear power and coal gasification. Alexander also opposed the bill by George Allen and Ron Wyden to extend the moratorium on Internet taxes. That bill would have extended the moratorium to state taxes on DSL lines instituted before the first moratorium was passed in 1998. Alexander, the former governor, urged state and local governments to get involved and said the Allen-Wyden bill would cost them revenue. After a six-month impasse, the Senate passed a four-year extension with Alexander's grandfathering in of pre-1998 taxes and also did not prohibit states from applying telephone taxes to voice over Internet protocol (VOIP) services. That approach prevailed in conference committee, and the bill was signed in December 2004. But Alexander said it was only a temporary solution.

FIRST DISTRICT

Rep. Bill Jenkins (R)

Elected 1996, 5th term; b. Nov. 29, 1936, Detroit, MI; home, Rogersville; TN Tech., B.B.A. 1957, U. of TN, J.D. 1961; Baptist; married (Kathryn).

Military Career: Army, 1960–62.

Elected Office: TN Assembly, 1962–71, Speaker, 1969–71; TN Circuit Court Judge, 1990–96.

Professional Career: Farmer, 1961–present; Practicing atty., 1961–90; Commissioner, TN Dept. of Conservation, 1971–72; Dir., TN Valley Authority, 1971–78.

DC Office: 1207 LHOB, 20515, 202-225-6356; Fax: 202-225-5714; Web site: www.house.gov/jenkins.

District Office: Kingsport, 423-247-8161.

Committees: *Agriculture* (7th of 25 R): General Farm Commodities & Risk Management; Specialty Crops & Foreign Agriculture Programs (Chmn.). *Judiciary* (9th of 23 R): Courts, the Internet & Intellectual Property; The Constitution.

Group Ratings

	ADA	ACLU	AFS	LCV	ITIC	NTU	COC	ACU	NTLC	CHC
2004	0	0	0	0	90	62	95	91	81	92
2003	10	—	13	5	—	62	89	88	—	—

National Journal Ratings

	2003 LIB	—	2003 CONS		2004 LIB	—	2004 CONS
Economic	43%	—	56%		39%	—	60%
Social	30%	—	65%		20%	—	77%
Foreign	21%	—	77%		9%	—	91%

Key Votes of the 108th Congress

1. Drilling in ANWR	Y	5. DC School Vouchers	Y	9. Ban Same-Sex Marriage	Y
2. Approve Bush Tax Cuts	Y	6. Ban Human Cloning	Y	10. Fund Iraq War	Y
3. Medicare/Rx Bill	Y	7. Restrict Gun Liability	Y	11. Bar Cuba Embargo Funds	N
4. Bar Overtime Pay Regs.	N	8. Ban Partial-Birth Abortion	Y	12. Intelligence Reorg.	Y

Election Results

2004 general	Bill Jenkins (R)	172,543	(74%)	($160,643)
	Graham Leonard (D)	56,361	(24%)	($27,775)
	Other	4,656	(2%)	
2004 primary	Bill Jenkins (R)	32,726	(90%)	
	David Smith (R)	3,747	(10%)	
2002 general	Bill Jenkins (R)	unopposed		($107,482)

Prior Winning Percentages: 2000 (100%); 1998 (69%); 1996 (65%)

The People		Race/Ethnic Origin	Ancestry	
Area size:	4,174 sq. mi.	95.0% White	USA: 18.9%	English: 8.2%
Urban population:	55.4%	2.1% Black	Irish: 7.8%	
Rural population:	44.6%	0.4% Asian	**2004 Presidential Vote**	
Pop. 2000:	632,143	0.2% Native Am.	Bush (R) 172,079	(68%)
Median income:	$31,228	0.0% Hawaiian	Kerry (D) 79,507	(31%)
Poverty status:	14.8%	0.7% Two+ races	Other 1,800	(1%)
Military veterans:	14.2%	0.1% Other	**2000 Presidential Vote**	
		1.5% Hispanic Origin	Bush (R) 132,304	(61%)
			Gore (D) 81,335	(37%)
			Other 3,441	(2%)
			Cook Partisan Voting Index: R +14	

Occupation	Blue collar: 34.4%	White collar: 50.0%	Gray collar: 15.6%

Between the corduroy-like ridges of the Appalachian chains, as they bend west and then south, the valley of Virginia extends far into northeastern Tennessee. The communities of this region—a hilly patchwork of industrial centers, small farms and federal land—were largely shaped by the building of railroads in the 1850s. The land rush immediately after the Revolutionary War populated the area; here in tiny Jonesborough the early settlers established the free state of Franklin in 1784, and many pioneer cabins, federal mansions and Greek Revival churches are lovingly preserved. It was the railroads, however, that determined the winners and losers. Other Appalachian areas were cut off from the rest of America, with tracks running only to the coal mines, but the small industrial cities that had grown up here—Johnson City, Kingsport, Bristol—were on the main lines of national commerce even before the Civil War. As President, Abraham Lincoln talked about building a 150-mile railroad through these hills, partly as a political gesture to Union supporters; the route, now known as "the Rathole" because of its topography, was not completed until after the Civil War. The War had a different political effect here than in most of the South: Northeast Tennessee, the home of wartime Governor and then Vice President Andrew Johnson, had few slaves and with its connection to northern industry was Union territory. It remains heavily Republican to this day.

The political continuity may be surprising because this area has had continuous economic growth and has developed the sort of industrial economy that produced unions and Democrats in the North. Its growth has been helped by modest wage levels, a skilled and hard-working labor force, low electric power rates because of the Tennessee Valley Authority and good transportation routes (rail lines and now Interstate 81). Its small cities boast major paper and printing plants, and have the look of comfortable, clean, 1920s factory towns. They continue to grow, and growth has been rapid in Sevier County near Knoxville, where Gatlinburg and Pigeon Forge (home of Dolly Parton's Dollywood theme park) have more than 14,000 hotel rooms at the entry point to the Great Smoky Mountains National Park, the nation's most-visited national park. The area surrounding the park suffers from heavy acid rain and ozone pollution from nearby power plants and factories.

The 1st Congressional District takes in the far northeastern end of Tennessee, a district so heavily Republican that it has not elected a Democrat to the House for more than 100 years. Nonetheless, it has had turbulent politics on occasion. For almost 40 years (1921–61, with one four-year and one two-year hiatus), the seat was held by B. Carroll Reece, a fierce mountain politician who was Republican national chairman from 1946–48. After Reece died in 1961, and his widow was elected to fill out his term, there was a hotly contested primary in 1962. The winner, Jimmy Quillen, a bread-and-butter politician, homebuilder and former owner of the *Johnson City Times*, represented the 1st for the next 34 years, a record tenure for the Tennessee delegation.

The congressman from the 1st District is Bill Jenkins, first elected in 1996. Jenkins is a lawyer from Rogersville in Hawkins County, and a farmer who raises beef cattle and grows burley tobacco. He was elected to the state House in 1962, at 25. In 1969 the state House was evenly split between Democrats and Republicans; Jenkins was elected Speaker, the only Republican to hold that position in the 20th century. In 1971 he was named to the TVA Board of Directors; in 1990 he was elected circuit court judge. When Quillen announced his retirement, Jenkins resigned his judgeship to run for Congress. He was one of 11 Republicans—the Quillen 11—who filed to run in the primary. Tennessee has no runoff, and this was what political scientist V.O. Key called a "friends and neighbors" primary: There were few perceptible differences on issues, and candidates struggled to get enough votes out in their home areas to win. Jenkins won with just 18% of the votes, including 74% in Hawkins County. In second, just 331 votes behind, was state Senator Jim Holcomb, who had conservative Christian activist support. Jenkins won in November 65%–32%.

In the House, Jenkins has a conservative voting record and avoids the spotlight. He has been a longtime advocate of restoring the deductibility of state sales taxes in states like Tennessee without an income tax; that change was approved in 2004, with a strong push from the Texas delegation. He defended TVA against advocates of competition, contending that other utilities would not necessarily have lower fuel or labor costs.

Jenkins has not had much serious opposition. In 2003, Jenkins moved from the back benches to become chairman of the Agriculture Specialty Crops and Foreign Agriculture Programs Subcommittee. From that post, he was a leading advocate of the tobacco buyout program that was enacted in 2004; three acres of his tobacco fields were eligible.

SECOND DISTRICT

Rep. John Duncan (R)

Elected 1988, 9th full term; b. July 21, 1947, Lebanon; home, Knoxville; U. of TN, B.S. 1969, George Washington U., J.D. 1973; Presbyterian; married (Lynn).

Military Career: Army Natl. Guard & Army Reserves, 1970–87.

Professional Career: Practicing atty., 1973–81; Knox Cnty. judge, 1981–88.

DC Office: 2267 RHOB, 20515, 202-225-5435; Fax: 202-225-6440; Web site: www.house.gov/duncan.

District Offices: Athens, 423-745-4671; Knoxville, 865-523-3772; Maryville, 865-984-5464.

Committees: *Government Reform* (12th of 23 R): Government Management, Finance & Accountability; National Security, Emerging Threats & International Relations. *Resources* (5th of 27 R): Forests & Forest Health; National Parks. *Transportation & Infrastructure* (5th of 41 R): Aviation; Highways, Transit & Pipelines; Water Resources & Environment (Chmn.).

Group Ratings

	ADA	ACLU	AFS	LCV	ITIC	NTU	COC	ACU	NTLC	CHC
2004	5	5	13	9	70	75	90	88	97	84
2003	15	—	13	10	—	72	83	76	—	—

National Journal Ratings

	2003 LIB	—	2003 CONS	2004 LIB	—	2004 CONS
Economic	41%	—	57%	43%	—	56%
Social	30%	—	65%	31%	—	67%
Foreign	53%	—	46%	39%	—	59%

Key Votes of the 108th Congress

1. Drilling in ANWR	N	5. DC School Vouchers	Y	9. Ban Same-Sex Marriage	Y
2. Approve Bush Tax Cuts	Y	6. Ban Human Cloning	Y	10. Fund Iraq War	N
3. Medicare/Rx Bill	Y	7. Restrict Gun Liability	Y	11. Bar Cuba Embargo Funds	N
4. Bar Overtime Pay Regs.	N	8. Ban Partial-Birth Abortion	Y	12. Intelligence Reorg.	N

Election Results

2004 general	John Duncan (R)	215,795	(79%)	($418,308)
	John Greene (D)	52,155	(19%)	
	Other	4,978	(2%)	
2004 primary	John Duncan (R)	41,362	(91%)	
	Dibbie Howard (R)	3,861	(9%)	
2002 general	John Duncan (R)	146,887	(79%)	($362,876)
	John Greene (D)	37,035	(20%)	
	Other	2,059	(1%)	

Prior Winning Percentages: 2000 (89%); 1998 (89%); 1996 (71%); 1994 (90%); 1992 (72%); 1990 (81%); 1988 (57%); 1988 (56%)

The People		Race/Ethnic Origin	Ancestry	
Area size:	2,492 sq. mi.	90.1% White	USA: 14.0%	English: 8.9%
Urban population:	71.4%	6.2% Black	German: 8.9%	
Rural population:	28.6%	1.0% Asian	**2004 Presidential Vote**	
Pop. 2000:	632,144	0.3% Native Am.	Bush (R) 185,450	(64%)
Median income:	$36,796	0.0% Hawaiian	Kerry (D) 100,032	(35%)
Poverty status:	12.2%	1.0% Two+ races	Other 2,377	(1%)
Military veterans:	13.5%	0.1% Other	**2000 Presidential Vote**	
		1.3% Hispanic Origin	Bush (R) 144,412	(59%)
			Gore (D) 95,100	(39%)
			Other 4,246	(2%)
			Cook Partisan Voting Index: R +11	
Occupation	Blue collar: 25.9%	White collar: 59.6%	Gray collar: 14.5%	

Knoxville, the largest city in East Tennessee, is nestled between mountain ridges where the Holston and French Broad Rivers join to form the Tennessee River. It was established not long after the first wave of pioneers came through the gaps and down between the mountains of the Appalachian chain. During the Civil War it was Union territory, and it has remained Republican in allegiance and progressive on civil rights ever since: The ancestral tug of Tennessee politics. But its Republican heritage is tempered by another tradition, that of the Tennessee Valley Authority. A venturesome program when created in the 1930s, it is now part of the fabric of life in East Tennessee, sometimes criticized as its cheap hydroelectric power capacity was filled and more of its production came from expensive and sometimes poorly functioning nuclear plants.

Both TVA and the region have undergone turbulent changes in recent years. TVA has cut its payroll sharply and held down rates; in a competitive electricity market, and laboring under billions of dollars in debt mostly incurred in building its nuclear plants, its director proposed spinning off navigation and flood control functions to state or federal agencies. A worrisome sign for area jobs and the low cost of living: Heavy ozone pollution in Knoxville led the Environmental Protection Agency to impose growth limits, which have discouraged industrial expansion. Although TVA is spending several billion dollars to reduce pollution at its coal-fired power plants, North Carolina planned legal action because it hasn't moved fast enough. Delay in construction of a national nuclear-waste repository at Yucca Mountain in Nevada has forced TVA to spend tens of millions of dollars for new storage pools. But Knoxville has overcome setbacks and grown robustly without much notice in the national press. Education entrepreneur Christopher Whittle's downtown campus is now a federal courthouse complex; the 1982 World's Fair site is the home of the Women's Basketball Hall of Fame. And the University of Tennessee's football stadium on fall Saturdays contains one of the nation's largest crowds—it qualifies as the state's 5th largest city during games—cheering the Vols. The city is also the home base of Instapundit.com, the weblog of University of Tennessee law professor Glenn Reynolds. One man with a laptop and WiFi in Knoxville can in our networking age be a player in national politics.

The 2d Congressional District of Tennessee includes Knoxville and Knox County, plus four mountainous counties and part of one other to the south. It is heavily Republican and has not elected a Democratic congressman since the Civil War. Knox County surprised many by giving a narrow plurality to Democratic Governor Phil Bredesen in 2002, but Republican Van Hilleary carried the rest of the district by a wider margin.

The congressman from the 2d District is John "Jimmy" Duncan, a Republican first elected in 1988; his father, who was senior Republican on the House Ways and Means Committee, represented the 2d from 1964 until his death in May 1988. Jimmy Duncan studied in Knoxville and Washington, practiced law and was a trial judge in the 1980s. When his father died, he won the seat despite a spirited challenge from Democrat Dudley Taylor, a scion of another prominent East Tennessee political family. Taylor attacked Duncan for signing up with the National Guard in 1970 and for his ties to scandal-tarred banker and Democratic politician Jake Butcher. But Duncan won with 56% in the special election and 57% in November. He has not been seriously challenged since then.

Duncan has been a frequent maverick on economic and foreign policy issues. He opposed normal trade relations with China, trade promotion authority and he was one of 10 Republicans to vote against the new Homeland Security Department. In October 2002, he was one of six Republicans—and the only Tennessean—who voted against the use of force in Iraq. He said that this was his most difficult vote in 14 years in the House and argued that there was not sufficient proof that Saddam Hussein had weapons of mass destruction. A year later, he opposed the $87 billion spending package for Iraq. "It's the most massive foreign aid program in history," he said in January 2004, after a trip to Iraq. "They've got a country over there with their own oil wells." Citing privacy concerns, he was the only Tennessee Republican to oppose continued authority for federal investigation of library records. For six years, he chaired the Aviation Subcommittee on Transportation and Infrastructure, but in 2001 he switched and became chairman of the Water Resources Subcommittee, a pork-dispensing panel of great interest to many members. He was a team player in helping to negotiate the final deal on the airline security bill after the September 11 attacks. But his independence had its price. He was a candidate for the chairmanship of the Resources Committee in 2003 but Speaker Dennis Hastert's Steering Committee passed over Duncan and five other senior members and gave the post to Richard Pombo. Perhaps mindful of that setback, and aware that he will have other opportunities for a committee chairmanship, he voted for the Medicare/prescription drug bill in November 2003.

Duncan sometimes takes his thrifty approach to unusual extremes. He questioned excessive bonuses and pensions for TVA executives, won enactment of his bill to have TVA's inspector general appointed by the President rather than the TVA board, and said that $6.5 million in annual hospitality expenses "seems ridiculously expensive to me." But he hasn't been shy about seeking funding for local projects, from resurfacing the Foothills Parkway in the Great Smoky Mountains National Park to a rail and trolley system for downtown Knoxville. In 2004 he authored a land swap between the Great Smoky Mountains National Park and an adjacent Alcoa aluminum plant. Under the terms, FERC would renew Alcoa's hydroelectric dam operating license and Alcoa would give the park 100 dry acres in exchange for 180 flooded acres; Alcoa also granted a permanent easement on several thousand acres to the Tennessee Nature Conservancy.

In Knoxville, Duncan's annual barbecue dinner draws as many as 10,000 people, and reinforces his local popularity.

THIRD DISTRICT

Rep. Zach Wamp (R)

Elected 1994, 6th term; b. Oct. 28, 1957, Fort Benning, GA; home, Chattanooga; U. of NC, 1976–77, 1979–80, U. of TN, 1978–79; Baptist; married (Kim).

Professional Career: Regional Sales Super., 1981–82, Partner, Wamp Alliance Architectural Devel. Co., 1983–89; Real Estate broker, 1989–94.

DC Office: 1436 LHOB, 20515, 202-225-3271; Fax: 202-225-3494; Web site: www.house.gov/wamp.

District Offices: Chattanooga, 423-756-2342; Oak Ridge, 865-576-1976.

Committees: *Appropriations* (18th of 37 R): Energy & Water Development & Related Agencies; Homeland Security; Interior, Environment & Related Agencies.

Group Ratings

	ADA	ACLU	AFS	LCV	ITIC	NTU	COC	ACU	NTLC	CHC
2004	0	0	13	9	89	54	100	88	81	100
2003	15	—	13	5	—	62	90	96	—	—

National Journal Ratings

	2003 LIB	—	2003 CONS		2004 LIB	—	2004 CONS
Economic	45%	—	54%		23%	—	76%
Social	5%	—	87%		9%	—	85%
Foreign	23%	—	71%		39%	—	59%

Key Votes of the 108th Congress

1. Drilling in ANWR	Y	5. DC School Vouchers	Y	9. Ban Same-Sex Marriage	Y
2. Approve Bush Tax Cuts	Y	6. Ban Human Cloning	Y	10. Fund Iraq War	Y
3. Medicare/Rx Bill	N	7. Restrict Gun Liability	Y	11. Bar Cuba Embargo Funds	N
4. Bar Overtime Pay Regs.	N	8. Ban Partial-Birth Abortion	Y	12. Intelligence Reorg.	N

Election Results

2004 general	Zach Wamp (R)	166,154	(65%)	($1,003,532)
	John Wolfe (D)	84,295	(33%)	($92,074)
	Other	6,187	(2%)	
2004 primary	Zach Wamp (R)	30,183	(90%)	
	Timothy Sevier (R)	3,334	(10%)	
2002 general	Zach Wamp (R)	112,254	(65%)	($644,166)
	John Wolfe (D)	58,824	(34%)	($35,550)
	Other	2,843	(2%)	

Prior Winning Percentages: 2000 (64%); 1998 (66%); 1996 (56%); 1994 (52%)

The People		Race/Ethnic Origin	Ancestry	
Area size:	3,597 sq. mi.	85.2% White	USA: 16.4%	Irish: 8.0%
Urban population:	64.2%	11.1% Black	English: 7.9%	
Rural population:	35.8%	0.9% Asian	**2004 Presidential Vote**	
Pop. 2000:	632,143	0.3% Native Am.	Bush (R) 163,612	(61%)
Median income:	$35,434	0.0% Hawaiian	Kerry (D) 102,390	(38%)
Poverty status:	13.4%	1.0% Two+ races	Other 2,063	(1%)
Military veterans:	13.6%	0.1% Other	**2000 Presidential Vote**	
		1.6% Hispanic Origin	Bush (R) 132,792	(57%)
			Gore (D) 96,441	(41%)
			Other 3,843	(2%)
			Cook Partisan Voting Index: R + 8	

Occupation	Blue collar: 31.7%	White collar: 54.3%	Gray collar: 14.0%

Through some of the most vivid scenery of the Appalachian chain, etching its way through the serrated ridges of East Tennessee, is the river that gave Tennessee its name. From Knoxville, the river cuts through a ridge and then plunges down a long valley to the city of Chattanooga at the Georgia line. There it switches course again, winding around the tabletop Lookout Mountain and then moving into northern Alabama. At the base of the mountain, Chattanooga was just a village when it was a Civil War battlefield; it then became the industrial "Dynamo of Dixie." Four decades ago it was labeled America's most polluted city. But regional political leaders, prodded by influential and civic-minded remnants of its Industrial Age aristocracy, used creative measures, such as a locally built electric shuttle bus, to reduce pollution and spruce up the city's scenic river banks. With big job cuts at the Tennessee Valley Authority, the region has pinned its hopes for growth more on the private sector, including a large food-service industry. Chattanooga is the proud home of the 12-story-high Tennessee Aquarium, the world's largest fresh water aquarium, with an exhibit in which you can follow the course of a drop of rain from the headwaters of the Tennessee until it flows out the Mississippi River into the Gulf. At Lookout Mountain, the popular century-old Incline Railway climbs at a 72.7 per cent grade; nearby are the 145-foot waterfall of Ruby Falls, as well as the rock formations and native gardens at Rock City. Riverfront redevelopment has been completed with a new pier and Chattanooga Green open space.

The 3d Congressional District of Tennessee includes Chattanooga and runs northeasterly from the Tennessee-Georgia border to the Virginia border, making this one of three Tennessee districts that span the state from north to south. Most of the population is in Chattanooga and the counties around it. Its thin strip of land to the north includes Dayton, the "buckle of the Bible Belt" where John Scopes was tried for teaching evolution in 1925 and was defended by Clarence Darrow and prosecuted by William Jennings Bryan. Farther north is Oak Ridge, which was secretly constructed in virgin Appalachian forest during World War II to house the nuclear facility that made uranium isotopes for the Hiroshima bomb and is now the Oak Ridge National Laboratory; for years, it did not appear on maps. After Libya ended its nuclear program, tons of equipment were flown here in January 2004 and inspected. A new neutron source is being built here to provide the world's most intense exploration of atomic structures. Politically, this area was split historically, with Chattanooga Democratic and the mountain counties Republican; today, however, it is a solidly Republican area, with none of its counties voting less than 57% for George W. Bush in 2004.

The congressman from the 3d District is Zach Wamp, a Republican first elected in 1994. Wamp left college before graduating to become a salesman for a local film company and a real estate developer in Chattanooga, selling $22 million in real estate in five years. Years later, he spoke about his heavy cocaine use during this period, including weeks in drug rehabilitation. In 1992 he ran for Congress against 20-year Democratic incumbent Marilyn Lloyd. She won by just 49%–47%, the closest margin of her career, and retired in 1994. Wamp ran again as a strong conservative; one of his proposals was to pay members of Congress the same as a lieutenant colonel and billet them in officer housing. Democrat Randy Button won a close primary and attacked Wamp's character. Wamp accused Button of flip-flopping on issues and, like many Republicans, ran an ad showing his opponent's face morphing into Bill Clinton's. Wamp won 52%–46%.

In the House, Wamp got a seat on the Appropriations Committee. He has a moderate-to-conservative record laced with locally appealing stands. He called himself "a heat-seeking missile on behalf of Tennessee and my district." He won Bill Clinton's approval of additional benefits for employees with work-related illnesses at Oak Ridge, a city with a tongue-in-cheek reputation for people who "glow in the dark."

Wamp has taken some maverick stances. His support for TVA, including opposition to Rodney Frelinghuysen's attempt to sell off its non-hydro power plants, annoyed many conservatives. He is co-chairman of the House Renewable Energy and Efficiency Caucus, which he uses to cite Chattanooga's successes in this area. He vocally supported the McCain-Feingold campaign finance bill, a stance that irritated the Republican leadership and prompted the National Right to Life Committee to run radio ads against him, even though he is opposed to abortion; the committee feared that the new law would prevent it from running issue-advocacy ads at campaign time. When the bill was enacted, he offered an amendment helpful for Republicans, to double the maximum individual contribution to $2,000 per candidate. Later, he reversed his policy against taking PAC contributions, which he said was no longer practical following the elimination of "soft money." In November 2003, he opposed the new prescription drug benefit under Medicare because it lacked sufficient cost-control steps. "I just feel like the pharmaceutical industry is actually going to benefit more in this legislation," he said. He tacked toward social conservatives in sponsoring a bill to permit local governments to post the Ten Commandments in public buildings, and he sought to restrict Internet access to pornography for children. He tried unsuccessfully after the 2000 election to repeal the House Republicans' three-term limit on chairmanships. He rented a home on Capitol Hill with three other House Republicans and three Democrats. "My attitude toward the Congress has changed," Wamp told *The New York Times Magazine*. "We must realize public service is a great way of life. I came in with the attitude there were a bunch of thieves here. That's not true." An avid user of the House gym, he founded the Congressional Fitness Caucus.

In 1996 he faced a spirited challenge from the second-place finisher in the 1994 Democratic primary. With Marilyn Lloyd's endorsement, Wamp won 56%–43%. Since then, he has won easily, including two contests against Chattanooga radio talk show host John Wolfe. In 1994 Wamp said he would serve only 12 years in the House and Bill Frist, running for the Senate, said he would only serve two terms. Frist seemed bent on keeping his promise, and in 2004 Wamp spent months traveling across the state, presumably with a view to running for the Senate. But Chattanooga Mayor Bob Corker said he was running for the Senate and within two months raised $2 million; Wamp said he would remain in the House, where he is positioned to wield influence on the Appropriations Committee for many years. Wamp hasn't officially renounced his term limits pledge but said he's leaning toward running for reelection in 2006. He also voiced interest in a leadership post. After the election, he criticized as a "PR disaster" the short-lived House Republican rules change designed to protect Majority Leader Tom DeLay if he had been indicted.

FOURTH DISTRICT

Rep. Lincoln Davis (D)

Elected 2002, 2d term; b. Sept. 13, 1943, Pall Mall; home, Pall Mall; TN Tech. U., B.S. 1966; Baptist; married (Lynda).

Elected Office: Byrdstown Mayor, 1978–82; TN House of Reps, 1980–84; TN Senate, 1996–2002.

Professional Career: Owner, Diversified Construction Co.

DC Office: 410 CHOB, 20515, 202-225-6831; Fax: 202-226-5172; Web site: www.house.gov/lincolndavis.

District Offices: Columbia, 931-490-8699; Jamestown, 931-879-2361; McMinnville, 931-473-7251; Rockwood, 865-354-3323.

Committees: *Agriculture* (20th of 21 D): Conservation, Credit, Rural Development & Research. *Science* (10th of 20 D): Energy; Environment, Technology & Standards. *Transportation & Infrastructure* (29th of 34 D): Economic Development, Public Buildings & Emergency Management; Highways, Transit & Pipelines.

Group Ratings

	ADA	ACLU	AFS	LCV	ITIC	NTU	COC	ACU	NTLC	CHC
2004	60	22	63	55	89	24	86	56	28	72
2003	75	—	88	60	—	27	70	65	—	—

National Journal Ratings

	2003 LIB	—	2003 CONS	2004 LIB	—	2004 CONS
Economic	56%	—	44%	55%	—	45%
Social	50%	—	49%	46%	—	53%
Foreign	56%	—	44%	53%	—	46%

Key Votes of the 108th Congress

1. Drilling in ANWR	N	5. DC School Vouchers	N	9. Ban Same-Sex Marriage	Y
2. Approve Bush Tax Cuts	N	6. Ban Human Cloning	Y	10. Fund Iraq War	Y
3. Medicare/Rx Bill	Y	7. Restrict Gun Liability	Y	11. Bar Cuba Embargo Funds	Y
4. Bar Overtime Pay Regs.	Y	8. Ban Partial-Birth Abortion	Y	12. Intelligence Reorg.	Y

Election Results

2004 general	Lincoln Davis (D)	138,459	(55%)	($1,145,419)
	Janice Bowling (R)	109,993	(44%)	($322,815)
	Other	4,194	(2%)	
2004 primary	Lincoln Davis (D)	36,462	(91%)	
	Harvey Howard (D)	3,435	(9%)	
2002 general	Lincoln Davis (D)	95,989	(52%)	($1,280,211)
	Janice Bowling (R)	85,680	(46%)	($556,643)
	Other	2,631	(1%)	

The People

		Race/Ethnic Origin	Ancestry	
Area size:	10,155 sq. mi.	92.6% White	USA: 20.0%	Irish: 8.1%
Urban population:	32.1%	4.4% Black	English: 7.2%	
Rural population:	67.9%	0.3% Asian	**2004 Presidential Vote**	
Pop. 2000:	632,143	0.3% Native Am.	Bush (R)	154,457 (58%)
Median income:	$31,645	0.0% Hawaiian	Kerry (D)	109,802 (41%)
Poverty status:	15.2%	0.8% Two+ races	Other	1,935 (1%)
Military veterans:	13.2%	0.0% Other	**2000 Presidential Vote**	
		1.6% Hispanic Origin	Bush (R)	111,639 (50%)
			Gore (D)	109,559 (49%)
			Other	3,507 (2%)
			Cook Partisan Voting Index: R + 3	

Occupation   Blue collar: 40.4%   White collar: 45.1%   Gray collar: 14.4%

The invisible line between Civil War Republican and Civil War Democratic territory runs along the Cumberland Plateau, the westernmost upswelling of the Appalachians, west of the valley where the Tennessee River runs south from Knoxville to Chattanooga. This is cave country: under its green hills Tennessee has 8,500 caves, more than any other state, with 13 species of bats. This invisible line separates the Tennessee Valley, which had few slaves and whose economic ties were with the North, from the rolling farmlands of middle Tennessee, first settled by Andrew Jackson in the 1790s and resolutely Democratic from the time he became the first president to call himself a Democrat in 1829. Here are places like Sewanee, the pleasant home of the University of the South; Bledsoe County, the pumpkin capital of the world; Columbia, home of President James K. Polk and the site of Maury County's Mule Day celebration every April, where a Saturn plant has accelerated growth; and Lynchburg in dry Moore County, where Jack Daniel's sour-mash whiskey—the nation's number-two spirit in overseas sales, behind Johnny Walker Red Label Scotch—has been distilled for generations and which is every bit the idealized small town that the distillery's folksy, black-and-white advertisements make it out to be. In Campbell County, the construction of the Tennessee Valley Authority's Norris Dam in 1933 forced the resettlement of 3,000 families and left some of the lowest standards of living in the state, but the area has since become a retirement and tourist haven. Near the Alabama line, Decherd is a manufacturing center for Nissan. Cattle are the district's number-one commodity.

The 4th Congressional District of Tennessee runs across this line and crosses the state for some 200 miles. It reaches almost to Virginia in the northeast and almost to Mississippi in the southwest and ranks as the fourth most rural district in the nation.

The congressman from the 4th District is Lincoln Davis, a Democrat first elected in 2002. Davis grew up in Fentress County on his family farm, which was purchased from World War I hero Sergeant Alvin York, a great celebrity in the 1920s and 1930s who was played by Gary Cooper in an Oscar-winning performance in the 1941 movie *Sergeant York*. Davis started his own construction company, which builds homes and businesses, and develops land. He also has been a soil scientist, and farms cattle and tobacco. He began his political career in 1978 as mayor of Byrdstown near the Kentucky border and was elected to the state House in 1980. In 1984, when Al Gore left the House to run for the Senate, Davis ran for the House but lost the Democratic primary to Bart Gordon 28%–22%. He lost the 4th District House primary 31%–27% in 1994, for the seat won by Republican Van Hilleary. After he returned to office as a state senator, the third time proved a charm.

In 2002 Hilleary ran for governor, and the newly drawn 4th District was open. Davis was the early favorite to win; he won support in the Democratic primary from national and local party leaders, organized labor, anti-abortion groups, and the National Rifle Association. But he had a difficult time against Democratic newcomer Fran Marcum. A wealthy businesswoman with EMILY's List backing, she spent $1.6 million of her own money. Her ads depicted Davis as a political retread, and tied him to the legislature's unpopular handling of budget problems. Davis won, 57%–43%. In the general, Janice Bowling, a Tullahoma alderwoman and self-described "pistol-packing Mama," attempted to seize on Gore's endorsement of Davis in the primary by asking voters to vote against Gore one more time. As part of her folksy message, she campaigned in a white chenille dress, red boots and an American flag scarf, and was a strong backer of George W. Bush's defense policy. She was significantly outspent by Davis, and complained that Republican financial backing came too late. Davis promised not to let any opponent "out-gun me, out-pray me, or out-family me." In the words of *The Tennessean,* Davis combined a "folksy, slap-on-the-back attitude with the oratorical punch of a revival preacher." He won 52%–46%. Redistricting made the difference. Davis carried the counties added to the district in 2002 by nearly 8,000 votes—almost all of his 10,000-vote margin. Bowling would probably have carried the Republican counties removed by redistricting by more than the remaining 2,000-vote margin.

In the House, Davis fit near the center and toward the conservative end of the Democratic Caucus. He appeared to keep his pledge to stay in close touch with the grass roots and keep his distance from most national Democrats on cultural issues. He joined the Blue Dogs, and criticized "the new philosophy of deficit spending." He was one of 16 House Democrats to vote for the 2003 Medicare/prescription drug bill, citing the need to reduce the high local cost of prescription drugs. He sought funds to clean up abandoned coal mines on the Cumberland Plateau. On Iraq, he largely supported George W. Bush. Davis endorsed Wesley Clark for president and then avoided mention of presidential politics after John Kerry won the Democratic nomination.

In 2004, Bowling again was the Republican nominee but again received little party support. She criticized Davis for opposing tax cuts and said that he had not been tough enough on illegal aliens. Davis emphasized his independence and willingness to listen to constituents. With endorsements from the Chamber of Commerce, National Right to Life and the NRA, he increased his victory margin to 55%–44%. Bowling carried five counties, running best in her home area, the southern part of the district.

FIFTH DISTRICT

Rep. Jim Cooper (D)

Elected 2002, 2d term; b. June 19, 1954, Nashville; home, Nashville; U. of NC, B.A. 1975, Oxford U., B.A./M.A. 1977, Harvard U., J.D. 1980; Episcopalian; married (Martha).

Elected Office: U.S. House of Reps., 1982–94.

Professional Career: Practicing atty., 1980–82; Investment banker, 1995–99; Founder and partner, investment bank, 1999–2002.

DC Office: 1536 LHOB, 20515, 202-225-4311; Fax: 202-226-1035; Web site: www.cooper.house.gov.

District Offices: Mt. Juliet, 615-773-2305; Nashville, 615-736-5295.

Committees: *Armed Services* (20th of 28 D): Strategic Forces; Tactical Air & Land Forces; Terrorism, Unconventional Threats & Capabilities. *Budget* (9th of 17 D).

Group Ratings

	ADA	ACLU	AFS	LCV	ITIC	NTU	COC	ACU	NTLC	CHC
2004	85	55	63	100	100	15	57	13	9	25
2003	80	—	100	100	—	28	53	32	—	—

National Journal Ratings

	2003 LIB	—	2003 CONS		2004 LIB	—	2004 CONS
Economic	63%	—	36%		60%	—	40%
Social	64%	—	35%		60%	—	39%
Foreign	57%	—	42%		70%	—	29%

Key Votes of the 108th Congress

1. Drilling in ANWR	N	5. DC School Vouchers	N	9. Ban Same-Sex Marriage	Y
2. Approve Bush Tax Cuts	N	6. Ban Human Cloning	N	10. Fund Iraq War	Y
3. Medicare/Rx Bill	N	7. Restrict Gun Liability	Y	11. Bar Cuba Embargo Funds	Y
4. Bar Overtime Pay Regs.	Y	8. Ban Partial-Birth Abortion	Y	12. Intelligence Reorg.	N

Election Results

2004 general	Jim Cooper (D)	168,970	(69%)	($1,169,268)
	Scott Knapp (R)	74,978	(31%)	
2004 primary	Jim Cooper (D)	unopposed		
2002 general	Jim Cooper (D)	108,903	(64%)	($1,888,568)
	Robert Duvall (R)	56,825	(33%)	($17,615)
	Other	5,158	(3%)	

Prior Winning Percentages: 1992 (66%); 1990 (69%); 1988 (100%); 1986 (100%); 1984 (75%); 1982 (66%)

The People		Race/Ethnic Origin	Ancestry	
Area size:	932 sq. mi.	68.2% White	USA: 10.8%	Irish: 7.6%
Urban population:	88.7%	23.4% Black	English: 7.6%	
Rural population:	11.3%	2.0% Asian	**2004 Presidential Vote**	
Pop. 2000:	632,143	0.3% Native Am.	Kerry (D) 140,874	(52%)
Median income:	$40,419	0.1% Hawaiian	Bush (R) 129,455	(48%)
Poverty status:	12.2%	1.6% Two+ races	Other 1,994	(1%)
Military veterans:	11.7%	0.2% Other	**2000 Presidential Vote**	
		4.2% Hispanic Origin	Gore (D) 130,111	(57%)
			Bush (R) 95,309	(42%)
			Other 4,015	(2%)
			Cook Partisan Voting Index: D + 6	

Occupation   Blue collar: 21.9%   White collar: 64.2%   Gray collar: 13.8%

Nashville is the home of country music and is in almost every way the heart of Tennessee. This was one of the first American cities established west of the Appalachians; Andrew Jackson built his Hermitage nearby above the banks of the Cumberland River, and his political home base has remained Democratic ever since. It was the capital of Tennessee early on, just as it was, and still is, the center of the state's political life and discourse, the so-called "Athens of the South": home to *The Tennessean,* a classically partisan Democratic paper, and the state's biggest television market. Nashville is proud of its universities and of its columned Capitol and its Parthenon; this is perhaps the greatest center of Greek Revival architecture in America. Nashville is firmly established as the religious publishing center of the country, producing more bibles than any other city in the world. Country music, an art form that emerged from the hardscrabble, mountainous counties of East Tennessee, is a more than $2 billion-a-year business and is one of the nation's dominant radio formats. The industry, run from a series of deceptively modest homes-turned-offices on what's called Music Row, congregated in Nashville because local radio station WSM had a clear channel from which to beam its weekly "barn dances" throughout the South in the 1920s; these later became known as the Grand Ole Opry, the longest continuously running radio show. An expanded Country Music Hall of Fame and Museum opened in the downtown revitalization project.

For years, both the city's Parthenon-building elite and its religious leaders resented the growing local influence of country music; the former looked down on the music's uneducated practitioners, while the latter cringed at the musicians' unwholesome travails and occasional indecorous deaths. But all three groups made their peace in the 1970s, and since then Nashville has become one of the South's boom cities—the fastest growing metropolitan area between Atlanta and Dallas-Fort Worth. New-generation industry moved in; a large local employer is the Corrections Corporation of America, the world's largest operator of private prisons. An agreeable quality of life, plenty of medium-wage, high-skill labor, a central location, and absence of urban strife and militant unions have all helped make Nashville the largest metropolitan area in the state. The rapid growth has caused local concern, with Mayor Bill Purcell lamenting that he doesn't want his city "to become like Atlanta." But it is, with suburban growth in all directions, despite delay in constructing Route 840 north of Nashville. The dominant cultural tone remains conservative, and fast-growing surrounding counties have become increasingly Republican, but Nashville and Davidson County remain Democratic bulwarks of Republican-trending Tennessee.

The 5th Congressional District of Tennessee includes most of Nashville-Davidson County, plus the bulk of suburban Wilson County to the east and Cheatham County to the west. The 5th is reliably Democratic in statewide elections; to Congress it has elected rather liberal Democrats—this is, after all, the home of the first Democratic president. It was the home of Al Gore when he was a divinity student at Vanderbilt and reporter for *The Tennessean,* and was the site of his 2000 presidential campaign headquarters; in June 2002, he and Tipper bought a house in the elegant Belle Meade neighborhood.

The congressman from the 5th District is Jim Cooper, a Democrat elected in 2002; he served in the very different 4th District from 1982 to 1994, when he ran unsuccessfully for the Senate. His father, Prentice Cooper, was governor for six years. Jim Cooper, educated at the University of North Carolina, Oxford and Harvard Law School, won the 4th District seat in 1982 by beating the bearer of another famous name, Cissy Baker, the daughter of then-Senate Majority Leader Howard Baker. When he first took office at age 28, he was the youngest member of the House. Notable for his frankness, he spoke out against tobacco use and opposed the National Rifle Association. He participated actively in the "group of nine" Democrats on the Energy and Commerce that helped to produce a compromise between John Dingell and Henry Waxman on the Clean Air Act of 1990. In 1994, he ran against Fred Thompson for the Senate seat Gore vacated when he was elected vice president. Ads captured a personal contrast between the two candidates: Thompson appeared in workshirts, speaking confidently to the camera while walking up porch stairs; the much shorter and youthful-looking Cooper appeared before a church in starched white shirt and tie. Thompson won 60%–39%.

Cooper then went to work as an investment banker in Nashville and as a teacher in Vanderbilt's business school. In 2002, when local Congressman Bob Clement jumped into the open Senate race, Cooper joined a flurry of Democratic candidates. His toughest opponent was Davidson County Sheriff Gayle Ray, the first woman sheriff in Tennessee, who had support from

EMILY's List. Ray attacked Cooper's voting record on health care, particularly on women's health issues. Cooper, an abortion-rights supporter, recalled his actions as a key player on health care initiatives and said that Ray's charges were inaccurate. He ran an ad showing his children describing what he does well (banjo playing, helping with homework, getting health care for senior citizens) and what he doesn't do well (cooking, playing basketball). The AFL-CIO and *The Tennessean* endorsed Ray; Cooper had support from the Sierra Club and several smaller newspapers. Cooper raised twice as much money as Ray and spent $700,000 of his own money. He won the primary with 47%, Ray faded at the end and got 23%, while state Representative John Arriola won 24% in the seven-candidate field. In the general, Cooper easily defeated Nashville businessman Robert Duvall 64%–33%.

Cooper returned to the House with more seniority than other freshmen because of his previous House service. But he was not able to get back his old seat on the Commerce committee, where 6th District colleague Bart Gordon is now a member. Instead, he joined the Armed Services, Budget, and Government Reform committees; in January 2005 he dropped off Government Reform. His voting record was near the center of Democrats from Tennessee. He won passage in the House of resolutions honoring the life of Johnny Cash and recognizing the benefits and importance of school-based music education. He advocated federal grants to encourage adoption, and he voiced alarm about the growing cost of Medicare. After the 2004 election, he replaced Charlie Stenholm of Texas as policy co-chairman for the Blue Dogs. At home, he urged the Army Corps of Engineers to approve a new amusement theme park near Percy Priest Lake.

Cooper was reelected easily. He has not been mentioned as a likely candidate for Bill Frist's Senate seat in 2006.

SIXTH DISTRICT

Rep. Bart Gordon (D)

Elected 1984, 11th term; b. Jan. 24, 1949, Murfreesboro; home, Murfreesboro; Middle TN St. U., B.S. 1971, U. of TN, J.D. 1973; United Methodist; married (Leslie).

Military Career: Army Reserves, 1971–72.

Professional Career: Practicing atty., 1974–84; Chmn., TN Dem. Party, 1981–83.

DC Office: 2304 RHOB, 20515, 202-225-4231; Fax: 202-225-6887; Web site: www.house.gov/gordon.

District Offices: Cookeville, 931-528-5907; Gallatin, 615-451-5174; Murfreesboro, 615-896-1986.

Committees: *Energy & Commerce* (8th of 26 D): Health; Telecommunications & the Internet. *Science* (RMM of 20 D).

Group Ratings

	ADA	ACLU	AFS	LCV	ITIC	NTU	COC	ACU	NTLC	CHC
2004	75	35	71	73	78	21	75	42	15	46
2003	75	—	100	80	—	25	53	48	—	—

National Journal Ratings

	2003 LIB	—	2003 CONS		2004 LIB	—	2004 CONS
Economic	57%	—	42%		57%	—	43%
Social	57%	—	43%		54%	—	46%
Foreign	68%	—	31%		64%	—	35%

Key Votes of the 108th Congress

1. Drilling in ANWR	N	5. DC School Vouchers	N	9. Ban Same-Sex Marriage	Y
2. Approve Bush Tax Cuts	N	6. Ban Human Cloning	Y	10. Fund Iraq War	Y
3. Medicare/Rx Bill	N	7. Restrict Gun Liability	Y	11. Bar Cuba Embargo Funds	Y
4. Bar Overtime Pay Regs.	Y	8. Ban Partial-Birth Abortion	Y	12. Intelligence Reorg.	Y

Election Results

2004 general	Bart Gordon (D) 167,448	(64%)	($852,690)
	Nick Demas (R) 87,523	(34%)	($37,399)
	Other 5,671	(2%)	
2004 primary	Bart Gordon (D) 28,524	(93%)	
	Robert Hall (D) 2,066	(7%)	
2002 general	Bart Gordon (D) 117,034	(66%)	($595,537)
	Robert Garrison (R) 57,401	(32%)	
	Other 3,112	(2%)	

Prior Winning Percentages: 2000 (62%); 1998 (55%); 1996 (54%); 1994 (51%); 1992 (57%); 1990 (67%); 1988 (76%); 1986 (77%); 1984 (63%)

The People		Race/Ethnic Origin	Ancestry	
Area size:	5,576 sq. mi.	89.0% White	USA: 19.0%	English: 8.1%
Urban population:	53.2%	6.3% Black	Irish: 8.1%	
Rural population:	46.8%	0.9% Asian	**2004 Presidential Vote**	
Pop. 2000:	632,143	0.3% Native Am.	Bush (R) 167,372	(60%)
Median income:	$39,721	0.0% Hawaiian	Kerry (D) 111,203	(40%)
Poverty status:	11.1%	0.8% Two+ races	Other 1,721	(1%)
Military veterans:	12.3%	0.1% Other	**2000 Presidential Vote**	
		2.6% Hispanic Origin	Bush (R) 112,096	(49%)
			Gore (D) 111,872	(49%)
			Other 3,729	(2%)
			Cook Partisan Voting Index: R + 4	
Occupation	Blue collar: 33.9%	White collar: 52.9%	Gray collar: 13.1%	

The rolling countryside of Middle Tennessee, west of the Cumberland Plateau and the last chain of Appalachians, has been called "the dimple of the universe." This is hilly and fertile land, cut by deep rivers ambling along in S-curves. The terrain here was never much suited for plantation crops; this has long been a land of small farmers and small county seat towns, nestled amid what people here regard as some of the loveliest scenery on earth. Middle Tennessee has also been one of the heartlands of the Democratic Party. It was the political home base of Andrew Jackson and supported him nearly unanimously; during the Civil War, though it had very few slaves, it resisted the invading Union armies. For 140 years after Jackson, it voted solidly Democratic and elected as its congressmen some of the luminaries of the national Democratic Party: James K. Polk (1825–39), speaker of the House and later president; Cordell Hull (1907–21, 1923–31), later senator and secretary of State; Albert Gore Sr., (1939–53), later senator; and Albert Gore Jr., (1977–85), later senator and vice president.

The 6th Congressional District includes 14 Middle Tennessee counties north, east and south of Nashville, plus the eastern half of Wilson County just east of Nashville. The heritage here is old and rural, but economic growth has fanned out into the farmland from Nashville, evident in thousands of jobs created by Japanese companies and American startups, firms fleeing the North and entrepreneurs fleeing taxes. Nissan's Smyrna plant, 20 miles southeast of Nashville, has the largest automobile production capacity in the nation. This was the fastest growing district in Tennessee from 1990 to 2003. Many new voters here are Republican but Democrats who controlled redistricting in 2002 were determined to stop the Republican advance by removing rapidly growing Republican suburbs from this district. They added Robertson County north of Nashville, which is significantly less Republican than the portions of Wilson and Williamson Counties that were removed. That reduced the Bush 2000 margin in the new 6th to a mere 224 votes. But it may not have been enough to halt Republican advances. Without the presence of its former representative, Al Gore, on the Democratic ticket, Bush carried the 6th by 60%–40% in 2004, representing a 20-point swing in Bush's margin of victory between 2000 and 2004.

The congressman from the 6th District is Bart Gordon, a Democrat first elected in 1984 when Gore gave up his House seat to run for the Senate. Gordon grew up in Murfreesboro in Rutherford County and graduated from Middle Tennessee State University and the University of Tennessee law school. He practiced law and became Tennessee Democratic chairman in 1981:

Politics has been most of his life. In 1984, he ran a computerized fund-raising operation and voter contact system—then a novelty in this district where a personal handshake from a candidate was the norm. He won a multi-candidate primary with 28% of the vote (the 4th District's Congressman Lincoln Davis was second with 22%) and won the general 63%–37%.

In the House, Gordon has built a moderate record and used his insider skills to pass legislation and build a close relationship with Democratic leaders. Gordon, who lost his seat on the Rules Committee and moved to Commerce when Republicans took control of the House, has worked to protect the Tennessee Valley Authority from proponents of electricity deregulation. He has voted with Republicans to make permanent the repeal of the marriage penalty and the estate tax, but he also seeks to repeal tax breaks for companies that send jobs overseas. He opposed trade promotion authority and voted to authorize the use of force in Iraq, but voted to make reconstruction funds a loan rather than a grant. He won enactment of his proposal for Federal Trade Commission oversight of the practices of sports agents representing student athletes. He made progress in gaining federal support for activities to prevent teen suicide. The House defeated his proposal to increase funds for the Manufacturing Extension Partnership program, a nationwide network of non-profit centers that assists small and medium-sized manufacturers; the Bush administration phased out the program's grants. He assisted Nissan in securing an exemption from a change in fuel economy regulations that would have cost hundreds of local jobs. On the Science Committee, where he became ranking Democrat in January 2004, he welcomed George W. Bush's support for human space flight to Mars and a return to the Moon, but he said that the specific NASA request raised more questions than it answered about its financial impact on other space programs.

When Gordon first won the seat it seemed safely Democratic. But in the mid-1990s, with the population surge in metro Nashville and the unpopularity of the Clinton administration, it suddenly became marginal, and Gordon's close ties to the Democratic leadership were no longer an asset. In 1994 he was challenged by Steve Gill, a lawyer from heavily Republican Williamson County. Gordon spent $1.4 million with $608,000 of it from PACs—more than Gill spent altogether. Gordon carried the smaller rural counties 58%–42%, for a slim overall margin of 51%–49%. In a rematch in 1996 he won 54%–42% and, against another candidate, he won 55%–45% in 1998. Gordon was Tennessee House Democrats' point man in redistricting, and the changes in the district lines seem to have made him invulnerable; in the newly drawn district he has won 66% and 64% of the vote. A notable accomplishment in the increasingly fit House: Gordon has won Congress's 5K race an impressive 16 times.

SEVENTH DISTRICT

Rep. Marsha Blackburn (R)

Elected 2002, 2d term; b. June 6, 1952, Laurel, MS; home, Brentwood; MS St. U., B.S. 1973; Presbyterian; married (Chuck).

Elected Office: TN Senate, 1998–2002.

Professional Career: Retail marketing consultant, 1973–98.

DC Office: 509 CHOB, 20515, 202-225-2811; Fax: 202-225-3004; Web site: www.house.gov/blackburn.

District Offices: Clarksville, 931-503-0391; Franklin, 615-591-5161; Memphis, 901-382-5811.

Committees: *Energy & Commerce* (31st of 31 R): Commerce, Trade & Consumer Protection; Oversight & Investigations; Telecommunications & the Internet.

Group Ratings

	ADA	ACLU	AFS	LCV	ITIC	NTU	COC	ACU	NTLC	CHC
2004	0	0	0	0	90	75	100	100	97	100
2003	5	—	0	0	—	71	97	92	—	—

National Journal Ratings

	2003 LIB	—	2003 CONS	2004 LIB	—	2004 CONS
Economic	9%	—	84%	25%	—	75%
Social	0%	—	95%	0%	—	91%
Foreign	0%	—	89%	10%	—	86%

Key Votes of the 108th Congress

1. Drilling in ANWR	Y	5. DC School Vouchers	Y	9. Ban Same-Sex Marriage	Y
2. Approve Bush Tax Cuts	Y	6. Ban Human Cloning	Y	10. Fund Iraq War	Y
3. Medicare/Rx Bill	Y	7. Restrict Gun Liability	Y	11. Bar Cuba Embargo Funds	N
4. Bar Overtime Pay Regs.	N	8. Ban Partial-Birth Abortion	Y	12. Intelligence Reorg.	Y

Election Results

2004 general	Marsha Blackburn (R) ....unopposed		($575,587)
2004 primary	Marsha Blackburn (R) ....unopposed		
2002 general	Marsha Blackburn (R) 138,314	(71%)	($552,213)
	Tim Barron (D) 51,790	(26%)	($18,969)
	Other.. 5,454	(3%)	

The People		Race/Ethnic Origin	Ancestry	
Area size:	6,349 sq. mi.	83.5% White	USA: 12.3%	English: 9.1%
Urban population:	61.0%	11.4% Black	Irish: 9.1%	
Rural population:	39.0%	1.5% Asian	**2004 Presidential Vote**	
Pop. 2000:	632,139	0.2% Native Am.	Bush (R) 206,410	(66%)
Median income:	$50,090	0.1% Hawaiian	Kerry (D) 104,792	(33%)
Poverty status:	8.0%	1.1% Two+ races	Other 2,216	(1%)
Military veterans:	14.2%	0.1% Other	**2000 Presidential Vote**	
		2.2% Hispanic Origin	Bush (R) 146,213	(59%)
			Gore (D) 99,423	(40%)
			Other 3,098	(1%)
			Cook Partisan Voting Index: R +12	

Occupation	Blue collar: 24.0%	White collar: 64.0%	Gray collar: 12.0%

Rural Tennessee north of Mississippi is one of the most sparsely settled areas in the state. Along each side of the Tennessee River, as it flows north and widens out into Kentucky Lake amid heavy forests, are small rural communities; many go back to pre-Civil War days and some have not grown much since. One of those towns is Waynesboro, where Davy Crockett delivered campaign speeches from the base of a huge natural stone double bridge overlooking the Buffalo River. Farther west is McNairy County, where Sheriff Buford Pusser of *Walking Tall* fame carried his big stick until his untimely death in 1974; here, the land is flatter and more open, a northward extension economically and demographically of the northern Mississippi farmlands. This mostly empty land is bounded on two sides by large metropolitan areas, Nashville to the east and Memphis to the west, with Nashville now the largest in Tennessee. South of Nashville is booming Williamson County, with its bedroom communities of Franklin and Brentwood; this is the most affluent, highly educated and fastest-growing county in Tennessee. To the north, along the Cumberland River, is fast-growing Clarksville, with many well-restored 19th century homes and the sprawling Fort Campbell army base, which has more than 20,000 military personnel just across the Kentucky border.

The 7th Congressional District of Tennessee spans this territory, packing Republican voters from Montgomery County's seat of Clarksville, south through the western half of Cheatham County and most of Williamson County plus a bite of Nashville-Davidson, then rambling west across the Tennessee River and south to the Mississippi border and finally to the white neighborhoods on the east side of Memphis and Shelby County. On the map, this looks like a rural district. Demographically, it's mostly suburban. Almost 40% of its votes are cast in metro Memphis and

30% in metro Nashville, mostly in Williamson County; another 11% are in Montgomery County and only 21% in the smaller rural counties. Redistricting added Republican Williamson County making the 7th nearly as solidly Republican as the 1st District in faraway East Tennessee. In 2004, when John Kerry won Nashville by about 25,000 votes (55%–45%), George W. Bush carried the four rapidly growing counties in the southern and eastern suburbs of Nashville by 91,000 votes (66%–33%).

The congresswoman from the 7th District is Marsha Blackburn, a Republican first elected in 2002. She grew up in a Farm Bureau family in Laurel, Mississippi, where her father sold oil-field production equipment. Her interest in gardening and canning won her a 4-H college scholarship at Mississippi State University, where she majored in merchandising and clothing. After that, she sold books and became a sales manager with Southwestern Company, which sells educational materials, and moved to Williamson County. (Her hilltop home is known as "Up Yonder," named by its former owner, Grand Ole Opry star Minnie Pearl). Blackburn became director of retail fashion for a Nashville department store and was appointed by Governor Don Sundquist as executive director of the Tennessee Film, Entertainment and Music Commission. In 1992, she was the Republican nominee against Bart Gordon in the 6th District and attacked his spending record and the congressional pay raise; she lost 57%–41%. She was elected in 1998 to the Tennessee Senate, where she became an outspoken opponent of Sundquist's proposed income tax. She was well known there for her appearances on conservative radio talk shows and for organizing rallies opposed to the income tax.

In March 2002, after Congressman Ed Bryant decided to run for the Senate, Blackburn decided to run in the 7th District. Seven candidates ran in the Republican primary; three were well known in the Memphis area. Blackburn was the only well-known candidate from the Nashville area. An opponent called her "an uncomplicated obstructionist," and a *Tennessean* columnist said her career was "marked by unblemished negativism." But she benefited from $100,000 in advertising and another $90,000 in contributions by the anti-tax Club for Growth, and from attacks by the Shelby County candidates on one another. She ran as pro-life, pro-gun and pro-military. The Memphis area cast 50% of the votes in the primary and the Nashville area only 25%. But Blackburn won with 40% of the total to 20% for the runner-up. She won 78% in the Nashville area, and was competitive in the Memphis area, with 24%. Blackburn won the general election, 71%–26%.

In the House, Blackburn continued her low-tax message and her voting record was among the most conservative in the House. She urged renewal of the federal ban on Internet access taxes, and urged across-the-board cuts for non-defense discretionary spending. She cosponsored the bill to make sales taxes deductible in states that have no income tax; it was passed as part of the corporate tax bill. On the Judiciary Committee, she worked on intellectual property tax issues important to the music industry. A survey of Capitol Hill staff by *Washingtonian* magazine rated her the top newcomer among House Republicans.

Blackburn was reelected without opposition in 2004. In late 2004 Blackburn was being mentioned both as a candidate to succeed Bill Frist in the Senate and as a challenger to Democratic Governor Phil Bredesen in 2006. In January 2005, she won a seat on the Energy and Commerce Committee, which would help her fundraising in a Senate race but also increased her incentive to remain in the House. A month later, she announced she would not run for the Senate in 2006 but left the door open for a future run.

EIGHTH DISTRICT

Rep. John Tanner (D)

Elected 1988, 9th term; b. Sept. 22, 1944, Halls; home, Union City; U. of TN, B.S. 1966, J.D. 1968; Disciples of Christ; married (Betty Ann).

Military Career: Navy, 1968–72; TN Natl. Guard, 1974–2000.

Elected Office: TN House of Reps., 1976–88.

Professional Career: Practicing atty., 1973–88.

DC Office: 1226 LHOB, 20515, 202-225-4714; Fax: 202-225-1765; Web site: www.house.gov/tanner.

District Offices: Jackson, 731-423-4848; Millington, 901-873-5690; Union City, 731-885-7070.

Committees: *Chief Deputy Minority Whip. Ways & Means* (10th of 17 D): Oversight; Trade.

Group Ratings

	ADA	ACLU	AFS	LCV	ITIC	NTU	COC	ACU	NTLC	CHC
2004	60	45	86	55	90	29	56	43	30	46
2003	90	—	100	45	—	37	70	44	—	—

National Journal Ratings

	2003 LIB	—	2003 CONS		2004 LIB	—	2004 CONS
Economic	60%	—	39%		55%	—	45%
Social	57%	—	42%		54%	—	46%
Foreign	63%	—	36%		58%	—	41%

Key Votes of the 108th Congress

1. Drilling in ANWR	Y	5. DC School Vouchers	N	9. Ban Same-Sex Marriage	Y
2. Approve Bush Tax Cuts	N	6. Ban Human Cloning	Y	10. Fund Iraq War	Y
3. Medicare/Rx Bill	N	7. Restrict Gun Liability	Y	11. Bar Cuba Embargo Funds	Y
4. Bar Overtime Pay Regs.	Y	8. Ban Partial-Birth Abortion	Y	12. Intelligence Reorg.	N

Election Results

2004 general	John Tanner (D)	173,623	(74%)	($614,785)
	James Hart (R)	59,853	(26%)	($47,892)
2004 primary	John Tanner (D)	unopposed		
2002 general	John Tanner (D)	117,811	(70%)	($553,863)
	Mat McClain (R)	45,853	(27%)	
	Other	4,306	(3%)	

Prior Winning Percentages: 2000 (72%); 1998 (100%); 1996 (67%); 1994 (64%); 1992 (84%); 1990 (100%); 1988 (62%)

The People		Race/Ethnic Origin	Ancestry	
Area size:	8,528 sq. mi.	74.4% White	USA: 15.8%	Irish: 7.6%
Urban population:	47.0%	22.3% Black	English: 6.3%	
Rural population:	53.0%	0.4% Asian	**2004 Presidential Vote**	
Pop. 2000:	632,142	0.3% Native Am.	Bush (R) 131,524	(53%)
Median income:	$33,001	0.0% Hawaiian	Kerry (D) 116,327	(47%)
Poverty status:	15.0%	0.8% Two+ races	Other 1,423	(1%)
Military veterans:	13.5%	0.1% Other	**2000 Presidential Vote**	
		1.6% Hispanic Origin	Gore (D) 109,221	(51%)
			Bush (R) 102,998	(48%)
			Other 2,633	(1%)
			Cook Partisan Voting Index: D + 0	

Occupation	Blue collar: 37.0%	White collar: 47.7%	Gray collar: 15.3%

West of Nashville and the lakes along the Tennessee River and north of Memphis, the rivers roll lazily through flat or gently rolling land that almost could be the northern end of Mississippi. Cotton and soybeans are the main crops, and they often are abundant; more blacks remain in rural areas here than in any other part of Tennessee, a reminder of its old plantation economy. The towns here are small, edged in by farm fields; the river bottoms, often flooded, are heavily forested. Duck hunters along the Obion River want a levee to trap water, but critics say that would be environmentally destructive. Here is Henning, the hometown of Alex Haley, where he used to sit on his porch and listen to his aunts tell him stories about slave ships and the Civil War that became *Roots*.

The 8th Congressional District of Tennessee includes much of this West Tennessee farmland, from the lakes west to the Mississippi. Its largest city is Jackson, which has a Toyota plant; it also includes the northern fringes of Memphis. Historically, this is Democratic country; Republicans haven't represented most of the counties that make up the 8th since the end of Reconstruction. The region trended Republican in national races in the 1960s and 1970s, then turned back toward the Democrats with the help of some smart local politicians. One of them was Ned Ray McWherter, House speaker from 1973–86, then governor for eight years. In the 1990s, movement was back toward the Republican party. Rural Carroll County is something of a bellwether in Tennessee politics, voting 50%–49% for George W. Bush in 2000 and 56%–43% in 2004. Overall, the district voted 51%–48% for Al Gore in 2000 but switched to Bush 53%–47% in 2004.

The congressman from the 8th District is John Tanner, a Democrat first elected in 1988. Tanner, who is a cousin of McWherter, grew up in Obion County, went to college and law school at the University of Tennessee, served four years in the Navy, then practiced law in Union City; he served in the Army National Guard, and retired as a colonel. In 1976, at 32, he successfully ran for the Tennessee House, where he served 12 years. In 1988, when the incumbent retired, Tanner ran for Congress and won with a whopping 66% in a four-candidate primary and 62% in the general.

Tanner's voting record put him solidly in the middle of the Democratic House and slightly to the left of midpoint after Republicans took control. He has a seat on Ways and Means; his 8th District predecessor Jere Cooper served there from 1932 to 1957, the last three years as chairman. He has worked on tax issues, including elimination of estate taxes on family-owned farms and small businesses. In 1999 he joined Republican Jennifer Dunn in sponsoring legislation to eliminate the estate tax. The bill passed but was vetoed by Bill Clinton. George W. Bush made it a centerpiece in the tax cuts that were part of his first legislative initiative; but Tanner voted against that bill because of its overall size. He supported trade promotion authority when sought by both Clinton and Bush, and normal trade relations with China in 2000. His advocacy of those measures at Ways and Means angered many Democrats and their interest-group allies. They have been more supportive of his call for expanded travel and trade with Cuba.

In 1992 Tanner could have been a senator for the asking. McWherter was ready to appoint him to succeed Al Gore, but Tanner chose to stay in the House. If he had moved up, he would have had to defend the seat against Fred Thompson in what turned out to be the very Republican year of 1994. Instead, Tanner became a major force in the House. He was a founder of a group of moderate-to-conservative Democrats called the Blue Dogs. Tanner co-sponsored their welfare proposal, which he claims was "the genesis for the broad welfare reform plan that Clinton signed" in 1996. His modifications helped win the support of half the House's Democrats; that bipartisanship, as well as Tanner's support, disappeared in 2003 and 2004 when House Republicans sought to extend the law with tougher requirements for eligibility. He has become a harsh critic of Republican deficit policies, and has offered alternatives to make their tax cuts revenue-neutral. He has sponsored a resolution would require a three-fifths vote in the House to pass any bill that would increase the federal deficit.

In the 8th District, Tanner has been re-elected by wide margins. In 2000, the United Steelworkers backed his Democratic primary opponent because of Tanner's free trade votes; Tanner won the primary 87%–13%. He regularly has won in November with more than 70% of the vote. In 2004, the Republican was a eugenicist who called for reducing birth rates among racial minorities; Republican leaders publicly denounced him and his views. Tanner won 74%–26%. In 2005, Steny Hoyer named Tanner a chief deputy whip.

NINTH DISTRICT

Rep. Harold Ford (D)

Elected 1996, 5th term; b. May 11, 1970, Memphis; home, Memphis; U. of PA, B.A. 1992, U. of MI, J.D. 1996; Baptist; single.

Professional Career: Staff Aide, U.S. Senate Budget Cmte., 1992; Spec. Asst., Clinton/Gore Transition Team, 1992; Spec. Asst., DNC Chairs Ron Brown & Alexis Herman, 1993; Spec. Asst., U.S. Dept. of Commerce, 1993.

DC Office: 325 CHOB, 20515, 202-225-3265; Fax: 202-225-5663; Web site: www.house.gov/ford.

District Offices: East Memphis, 901-766-8121; Memphis, 901-544-4131.

Committees: *Budget* (6th of 17 D). *Financial Services* (16th of 32 D): Capital Markets, Insurance & Government Sponsored Enterprises; Financial Institutions & Consumer Credit.

Group Ratings

	ADA	ACLU	AFS	LCV	ITIC	NTU	COC	ACU	NTLC	CHC
2004	75	47	86	91	89	14	55	21	7	33
2003	80	—	100	90	—	23	48	35	—	—

National Journal Ratings

	2003 LIB	—	2003 CONS		2004 LIB	—	2004 CONS
Economic	68%	—	31%		62%	—	38%
Social	65%	—	35%		62%	—	38%
Foreign	65%	—	34%		70%	—	30%

Key Votes of the 108th Congress

1. Drilling in ANWR	*	5. DC School Vouchers	*	9. Ban Same-Sex Marriage	Y
2. Approve Bush Tax Cuts	N	6. Ban Human Cloning	*	10. Fund Iraq War	Y
3. Medicare/Rx Bill	N	7. Restrict Gun Liability	Y	11. Bar Cuba Embargo Funds	Y
4. Bar Overtime Pay Regs.	Y	8. Ban Partial-Birth Abortion	Y	12. Intelligence Reorg.	N

Election Results

2004 general	Harold Ford (D)	190,648	(82%)	($1,225,931)
	Ruben Fort (R)	41,578	(18%)	
2004 primary	Harold Ford (D)	unopposed		
2002 general	Harold Ford (D)	120,904	(84%)	($863,754)
	Tony Rush (I)	23,208	(16%)	

Prior Winning Percentages: 2000 (100%); 1998 (79%); 1996 (61%)

The People		Race/Ethnic Origin	Ancestry	
Area size:	340 sq. mi.	34.9% White	English: 4.9% Irish: 4.7%	
Urban population:	99.6%	59.5% Black	USA: 4.5%	
Rural population:	0.4%	1.5% Asian	**2004 Presidential Vote**	
Pop. 2000:	632,143	0.2% Native Am.	Kerry (D)	171,547 (70%)
Median income:	$33,806	0.0% Hawaiian	Bush (R)	74,020 (30%)
Poverty status:	19.4%	0.9% Two+ races	Other	899 (0%)
Military veterans:	11.2%	0.1% Other	**2000 Presidential Vote**	
		3.0% Hispanic Origin	Gore (D)	147,898 (63%)
			Bush (R)	83,531 (36%)
			Other	2,758 (1%)
			Cook Partisan Voting Index: D +18	
Occupation	Blue collar: 24.0%	White collar: 60.4% Gray collar: 15.6%		

Memphis, the largest city in Tennessee though its metropolitan area is second to Nashville, is in the state's far southwestern corner, 500 miles from the Appalachian border with Virginia but only 20 miles from Mississippi's cotton fields and riverboat casinos. Metropolitan Memphis has one of the highest percentages of blacks in the country—evidence of the city's economic heritage as a capital of the Cotton Kingdom. Big Mississippi planters used to come north to sell their crop in the courtyard of the Peabody Hotel where the ducks march each day, then make financial arrangements for the next growing season.

Such facts have shaped the city's most celebrated tradition, the blues—a musical form worlds apart from Nashville's country music, which emerged from mountainous, mainly white Middle and East Tennessee. The Memphis sound originated from the self-taught musical stylings of poor, rural blacks in the Mississippi Delta. Throughout the first half of the 20th century, the most talented black musicians migrated north to Memphis and congregated downtown on Beale Street. The blues sound was later adapted by Elvis Presley, a poor white from rural Mississippi, in pivotal sessions in July 1954 at Sam Phillips' Sun Studio in Memphis—the birth of rock 'n' roll, and the beginnings of an Elvis cult that long outlived the man. In the early 1960s Memphis once again became the crucible of a new sound, soul music, which emerged as a counterpoint to rock, its increasingly white-dominated cousin. For some years Memphis tried to live down this musical heritage; much of Beale Street was razed and set on a misguided path toward urban renewal. But the city has come to recognize its history as an asset. Graceland, Presley's garishly decorated mansion, attracts hordes of musical pilgrims from all over the world, and a Museum of American Soul Music opened in 2003 on the site of the Stax studio, demolished in 1989, where Otis Redding, Isaac Hayes, the Staple Singers and Sam & Dave once made their records.

Music is not the city's only asset. Geographically central, Memphis is the home of the first supermarket chain (the Piggly Wiggly, founded in 1916; its symbol, Mr. Pig, has slimmed down) and the first Holiday Inn. Home of the world's busiest cargo airport, Memphis calls itself "America's distribution center": by far its biggest employer, and still growing, is FedEx, which ships its domestic packages in and out of Memphis Airport every night. For some years racial discord has scarred the political life of Memphis. It is the city where Martin Luther King Jr. was assassinated in 1968; the site of the murder, the Lorraine Motel, was converted into a civil rights museum. Even today, resurgent Beale Street is one of the few racially integrated spaces in the city, a division that holds equally true in voting. Blacks vote almost unanimously Democratic; whites vote Republican by margins almost as great. Blacks now outnumber whites in Shelby County; many have moved into the middle class, although Memphis continues to have the highest poverty rate in Tennessee.

The 9th Congressional District of Tennessee consists of most of the city of Memphis, some of its suburban fringe and about 30 precincts in east Shelby County. Redistricting in 2002 reduced the black percentage from 66% to 60%, but the 9th remains the strongest Democratic district in the state. In 2004, Bush bettered his 2000 performance in every Tennessee district except this one, where he ran much worse.

The congressman from the 9th District is Harold Ford Jr., a Democrat first elected in 1996 at age 26; his father, Harold Ford Sr., had been elected in 1974 at 29 and served for 22 years. Harold Ford Jr. grew up in Memphis until 1979, when the family moved to Washington. He graduated from St. Albans School, a classmate of Jesse Jackson's son Yusef and a friend of John Kerry's step-sons, and from the University of Pennsylvania in 1992. He worked on the Clinton transition team and at the Economic Development Administration (and thus technically worked for Commerce Secretary Ron Brown, whom he has praised as a "profound influence"). Months before his election, he graduated from University of Michigan law school.

The Fords are a large family—Harold Ford Sr. has 11 siblings and Harold Ford Jr. has 75 first cousins—from a humble background. Ford Sr. grew up in a house with no plumbing, but the family built a successful funeral home business. There's been a Ford on the Memphis Council since 1971; other Fords have served on the county commission and in the state Senate. Ford Sr. became a lobbyist after retiring from Congress in favor of his son, who had cut an ad for him at age 4, calling for "lower cookie prices." Ford won the primary 60%–34%. In the general, "Jr."—as his campaign buttons read—won 61%–37%, slightly better than the 58% his father had won during his last three elections.

In the House, Harold Ford Jr. has been notably more moderate on issues than his father and most members of the Black Caucus, although he has the most liberal voting record in the

Tennessee delegation. He talks regularly with his father, but they often disagree on issues. A member of the New Democrat Coalition, he voted against needle exchanges, for prayer in school and anti-flag burning constitutional amendments, for the balanced budget amendment, the capital gains tax cut, repeal of the estate tax, normal trade relations with China, aid to tobacco farmers, and the use of force in Iraq. He has backed the concept of private accounts in Social Security, and has sided with conservatives on national education testing and trade promotion authority, but he has taken liberal stands on affirmative action and against cutting tax rates. He worked with Majority Whip Roy Blunt to gain overwhelming passage in the House of a bill to expand charitable contributions to faith-based institutions; Senate Democrats stymied enactment in 2004. With bipartisan support, he has proposed creation of KIDS savings accounts to give every American a $500 savings account, at birth.

After the 2002 election, Ford shook up the Democratic Caucus for a few days when he quixotically challenged Nancy Pelosi for minority leader. Pledging a "clean break" in the party's strategy, he made a flood of media appearances in the six days before the caucus vote. He said Pelosi was too far to the left. On November 14, Pelosi won 177–29. At Newt Gingrich's suggestion, he was tapped for a Pentagon advisory group on force transformation.

At home in Memphis, Ford's appeal has crossed racial lines. He was reelected with 82% in 2004, against his first Republican opponent since 1998. In the summer of 1999 he crisscrossed Tennessee testing the ground for a run against Senator Bill Frist. He promised he would decide whether to run by Labor Day, but the deadline passed and, while campaigning less, he did not announce he was not running until February 2000; some Democrats groused that he had left the party without a serious candidate. In March 2002, when Senator Fred Thompson announced that he would not run for reelection, Ford resumed his exploratory tour. In Knoxville he told National Rifle Association members that the debate over guns had become too polarized and that he would join their organization. When it became clear that most of the party establishment was backing Congressman Bob Clement, Ford said he would not run.

Frist has consistently said he will not run for reelection in 2006, and in May 2005 Ford said he would run for the open Senate seat. Though Tennessee has been trending Republican, his moderate record and his appeal across racial boundaries could make him a strong candidate. Running as a Democrat in Tennessee is more of a challenge than is the issue of race, he has said. But there is another obstacle, what former Senator Jim Sasser called the "uncle problem." Ford's uncle, state Senator John Ford, has attracted a considerable amount of unflattering publicity over the years for a wide range of personal and ethical troubles; in May, the day after Harold Ford filed paperwork to run for the Senate, his uncle was indicted on federal corruption charges.

His temporary setbacks have not quelled Ford's ambitions, or clouded his prospects for higher office. He was the keynote speaker at the 2000 Democratic National Convention. In 2001, *People* magazine listed him among the "50 most beautiful people in the world." If he is elected to the Senate he could easily become a prominent national figure and in the years ahead, he could be a plausible national candidate.

★ TEXAS ★

Texas is a nation-sized state, one of four to have been an independent republic (the others are California, Vermont and Hawaii) and the one that stuck to it the longest. It is a state with an international image and international impact. The nation has voted for president 11 times since 1960: four times it has elected Californians and four times Texans. These two largest states have put their stamp on national politics in our times, just as New York did up from 1900 to 1960, when it was the residence of five of the winners and eight of the losers in 15 elections. Texas has been the second-largest state in area since Alaska was admitted to the Union in 1959; it became the second largest in population in 1994, when it passed New York. The key to Texas's history is that this is a society with no aristocratic past, a state not formed by plantation owners or plutocrats but by dirt farmers. Texas was founded by Southerners, mainly Tennesseans, who

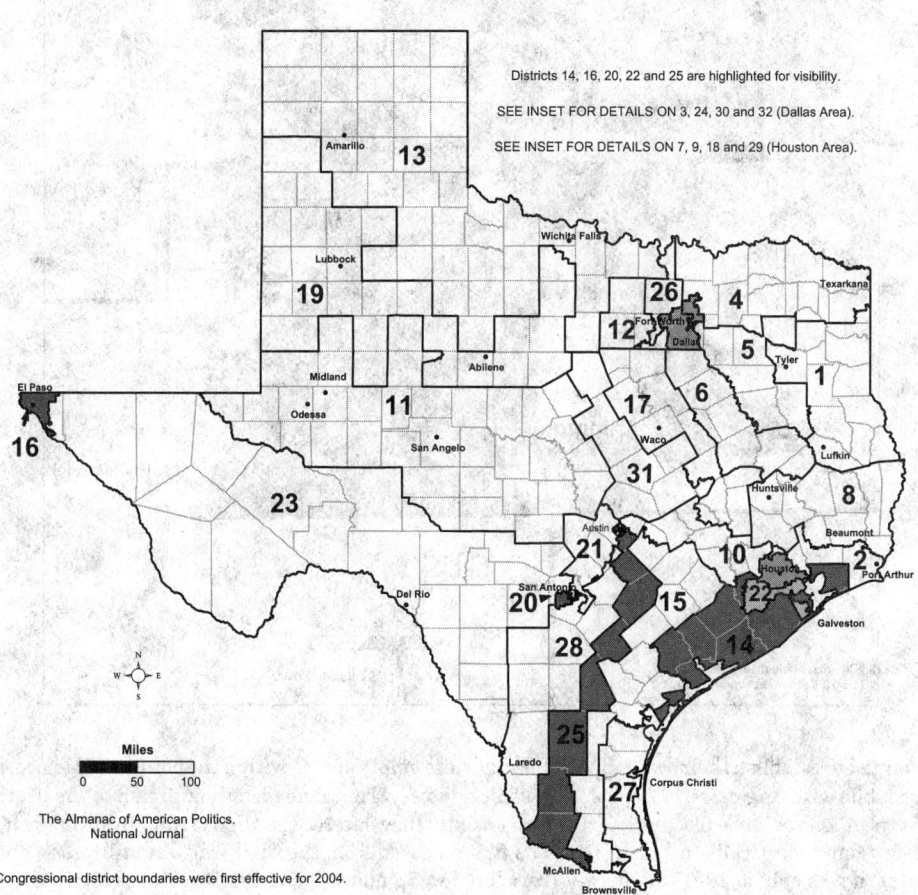

Districts 14, 16, 20, 22 and 25 are highlighted for visibility.

SEE INSET FOR DETAILS ON 3, 24, 30 and 32 (Dallas Area).

SEE INSET FOR DETAILS ON 7, 9, 18 and 29 (Houston Area).

The Almanac of American Politics.
National Journal

Congressional district boundaries were first effective for 2004.

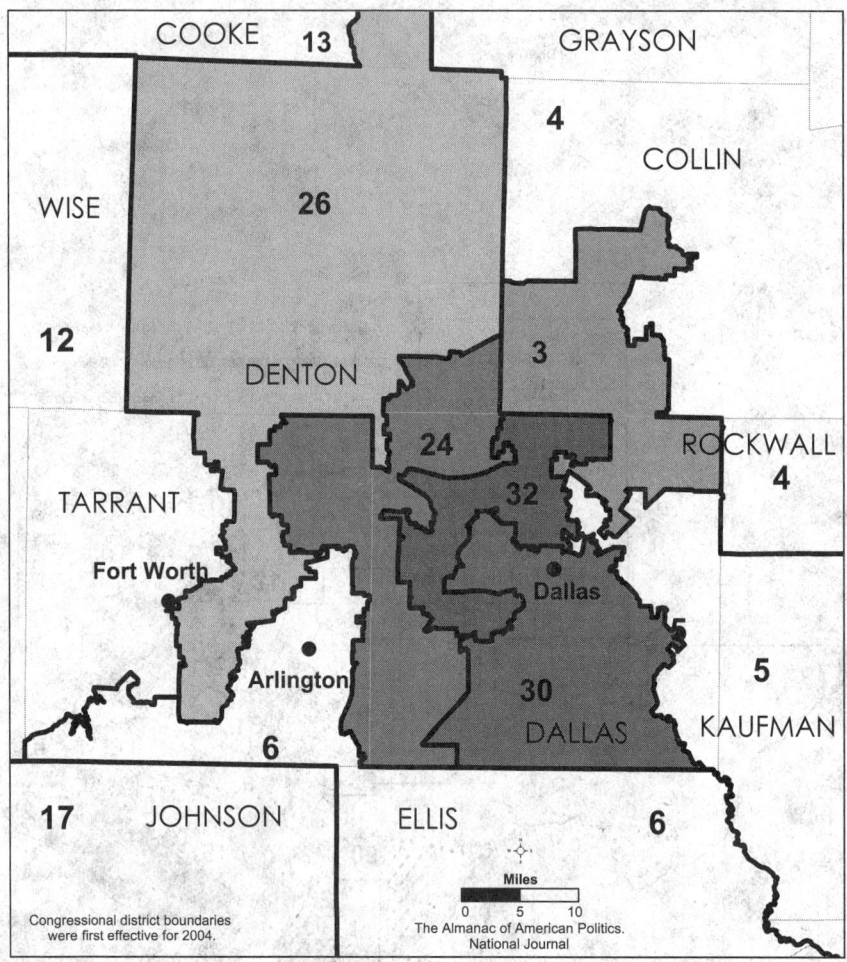

COOKE 13

GRAYSON

4

COLLIN

WISE

26

12

DENTON

3

24

ROCKWALL

4

32

TARRANT

Fort Worth

Dallas

Arlington

5

30

KAUFMAN

6

DALLAS

17   JOHNSON

ELLIS   6

Congressional district boundaries
were first effective for 2004.

Miles
0   5   10

The Almanac of American Politics.
National Journal

wanted to establish their own republic in what were empty spaces within the borders of Mexico, a republic with Anglo-Saxon freedoms and black slavery. They defended their dream to the death at the Alamo and to a bloody victory at San Jacinto; they entered the Union willingly in 1845 and left it enthusiastically in 1861. The Texas that emerged from the Civil War was still young and poor; it was only in 1901 that oil was discovered at Spindletop, and the Texas wildcatters made their first fortunes.

Without the underpinnings and burdens of tradition, 20th century Texas produced fabulous wealth, generously rewarding success while being unforgiving of failure. It has respect for learning and style—think of its great universities, or Neiman Marcus—and it revels in rough manners and western wear. Texans are prone to wild swings in fortune—think of Sam Houston, or the great wildcatters, or Lyndon B. Johnson. And as the 20th century ended, Texans, for all their history of slavery and segregation, have proved open to immigrants and friendly with their neighbors in Mexico. NAFTA, the opening up of the border and the coming together of these two countries which are at such different economic levels and have such different cultures, is a project mainly of Texans of both political parties, of President George H. W. Bush and Treasury Secretary Lloyd Bentsen, Governors Ann Richards and George W. Bush. At the same time, Texas has become a high-tech powerhouse, a country with some of the nation's most creative busi-

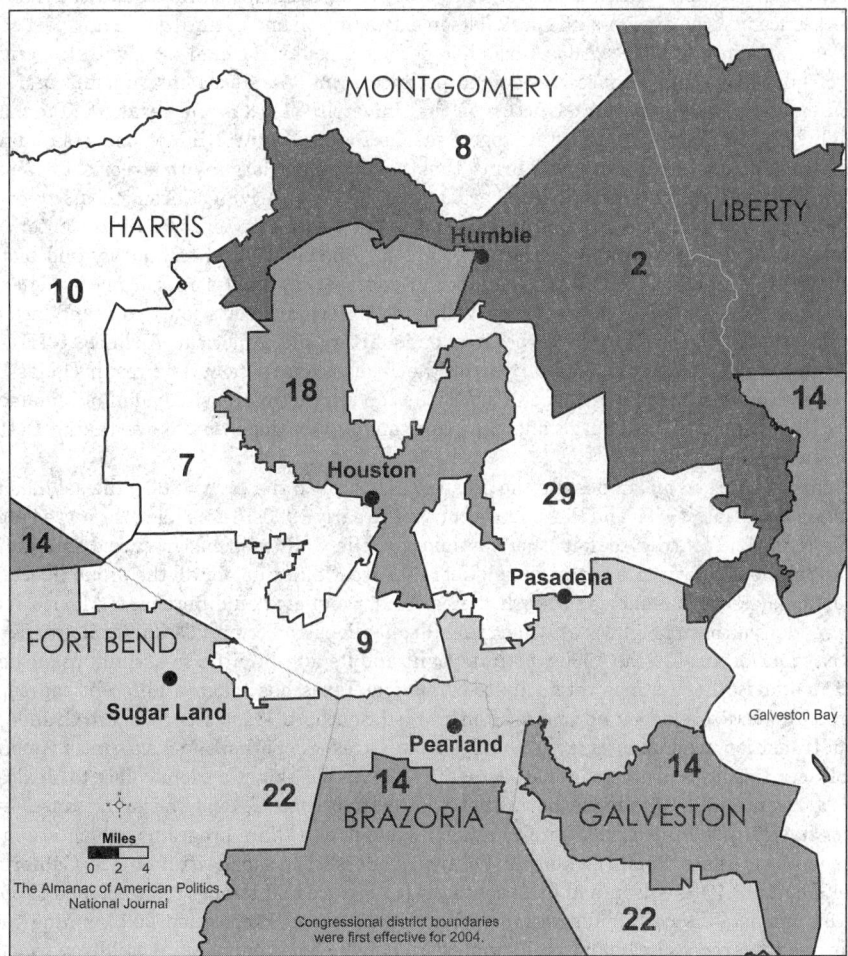

MONTGOMERY

8

HARRIS

LIBERTY

10

Humble

2

18

14

7

Houston

29

14

Pasadena

FORT BEND

9

Sugar Land

Galveston Bay

Pearland

14

22

14

14

BRAZORIA

GALVESTON

Miles
0 2 4

The Almanac of American Politics.
National Journal

Congressional district boundaries
were first effective for 2004.

22

nesses. But its success is not just economic. There are large elements of heroism—some mythical, some genuine—in the Texas history that every grade and high school student here learns.

Texas started off as a marchland on the border of the Third World, with an economy based on commodities, mainly cotton, whose prices were in long-term decline. Its farmers felt like part of a colonial economy controlled by bankers and Wall Street financiers. After Spindletop, Texas became the nation's—and for a time the world's—leading producer of oil. But oil prices, too, fell in free markets, and were propped up by politicians—the 1936 "hot oil" act that Sam Rayburn, as chairman of the House Commerce Committee, pushed through and the oil depletion allowance maintained for years by Rayburn when he was speaker, Senate Majority Leader Johnson, Senate Finance Committee Chairman Bentsen and others. These politicians also got subsidies for cotton growers and contracts for defense plants and space facilities in World War II and through the long years of the Cold War. Most Texas voters stayed Democratic up to 1970 because of Confederate memories, New Deal affections and the clout and competence of Texas's Democratic politicians.

But as Texas's economy became complex and creative, Texas's politics changed from a mostly Democratic effort to prop up the price of commodities to an increasingly Republican push to open up markets. By the 1970s Texas's economy was no longer dependent on raw commodities.

The "awl bidness" here is less a matter of extracting oil from Texas; instead, Texas has the greatest concentration of high-skill specialists in extracting oil and natural gas in any part of the world. Also, beginning in the 1960s Texas has become a center for high tech, with the critical mass of knowledge and finances needed to produce firms like Texas Instruments and Dell Computer, and a university infrastructure in the University of Texas and Texas A&M to match the highway system that ties the state together. The Dallas-Fort Worth Metroplex is rich with defense contractors and with small firms that have become large with exports to Mexico. Houston is home to firms like Schlumberger and the once-thriving Enron, to many of the high-tech spinoffs from the space program, and to the enormous Texas Medical Center. San Antonio, with the Air Force's prime hospital, has significant medical technology and biotech industries. Austin, as UT doubled its number of engineering professors, became a high-tech center vying for second place after Silicon Valley in California. Texas's low taxes (and lack of a state income tax) helped attract corporate headquarters like American Airlines, GTE, J.C. Penney and Exxon. Oil is just a small part of the Texas economy now. As a result Dallas-Fort Worth and Houston have moved on the list of the top ten metro areas ahead of old industrial centers like Cleveland, Pittsburgh and St. Louis, and are on their way to overtaking Detroit, Boston and Philadelphia.

Texas has surged ahead despite the crash of oil prices in the early 1980s, the savings and loan crisis in the late 1980s and the defense cuts of the early 1990s. Texas has also surged ahead because it, in vivid contrast to that other onetime republic, California, has nurtured and profited from its relationship with its southern neighbor, Mexico. California, for all the proud liberalism of its articulate elite, has shown its scorn, disgust and, worst of all, indifference to Mexico; it has portrayed its southern neighbor as generating illegal aliens and criminals California taxpayers must pay for; for most of the 1990s, both its right and its left did little to assimilate Mexican-Americans and other Latinos into a united America. Texas has taken a different course. Its border with Mexico is longer, and more often crossed; southern Texas along the Rio Grande is a kind of transition zone. Monterrey, 140 miles from Laredo, is perhaps Mexico's most America-friendly city. Despite a history of racial segregation, Texas has shown a friendly face to Mexicans, while Mexican immigrants have shown they wanted to become Texans and Americans. Fewer Latinos have crossed the border here to take advantage of welfare programs, which are much less generous in Texas than in California. Political leadership has made a difference. California's former Governor Pete Wilson had little contact with Mexico and strongly championed Proposition 187 against services for illegal immigrants in 1994 and Proposition 209 banning racial quotas and preferences in 1996; a chilly tone was set, which has only been partially warmed by Wilson's successors Gray Davis and Arnold Schwarzenegger. George W. Bush, like Governor Ann Richards before him, journeyed often to Mexico and invited Mexican leaders to Texas, emphasizing the positive in public and leaving any negative details to private negotiations. Governor Rick Perry, who prepared for his office by taking Spanish lessons, has followed Richards's and Bush's lead. So, increasingly, has the Texas economy. Nearly half of U.S. merchandise exports to Mexico are from Texas, significantly more than California; 70% of U.S. exports to Mexico go through Texas. The NAFTA secretariat of labor is in Dallas, the North American Development Bank is headquartered in San Antonio, the Border Environmental Cooperation Commission is in Juarez, across the Rio Grande from El Paso, and the busiest truck crossing between the countries is the new World Trade Bridge near Laredo and Nuevo Laredo. The only thing marring the relationship was a recently-settled dispute over the distribution of Rio Grande water.

Texas stands as a model for the American future, a model admired by many and disparaged by others. Quite explicitly in the 2000 campaign George W. Bush constantly cited his Texas record; Al Gore highlighted the state's shortcomings. Texas is an open society, unpretentious, delivered from its heritage of racial and ethnic discrimination. But it also has vast income disparities, between struggling and population-losing rural counties and the surging cities, and between the gleaming affluent neighborhoods spreading out into the countryside and the poor and crime-ridden neighborhoods of rickety frame houses not far from the urban cores. Texas presents a contrast with and a challenge to the traditions of other megastates—New York which pioneered the American welfare state, California which used high taxes to build highways and schools, the Great Lakes industrial states with their big labor unions. For Texas has some of the lowest taxes in the country and some of the lowest welfare levels; it has few union members and a relatively small public sector; it has resisted court-ordered moves to equalize spending among school districts; it continues to be a violent state, with a high crime rate and the highest number of executions. For years, out-of-state elites and liberals in Texas have called on the state to become more like New York or California or Michigan. But most Texans prefer their own model. Indeed, in important respects New York and California and Michigan are choosing to become more like Texas. Low taxes and high tech, few barriers to opportunity but a less elaborate safety net, moving away from reliance on agriculture and oil, bypassing the era of big factories and big unions of the Great Lakes and eschewing the liberal cultural values of the two coasts. In 1845, when the Republic of Texas was annexed by the United States, New Englander Edward Everett Hale wrote a pamphlet entitled "How to Conquer Texas Before It Conquers Us," calling for emigration from the North to dilute "an unprincipled population of adventurers." But the newcomers joining ancestral Texans—think of the Bushes—have put the stamp of Texas on the whole United States.

Politically, Texas is now an indisputably Republican state: George W. Bush carried it 59%–38% in 2000 and 61%–38% in 2004. It was not always so: both George Bushes and Senator Kay Bailey Hutchison and former Senator Phil Gramm each lost an election before they started winning. One-party Democratic dominance ended in the 1960s, and for two decades Democratic victories were largely the product of Lloyd Bentsen, when he was on the ballot in 1970, 1976, 1982 and 1988 and when he exerted his influence for Ann Richards for governor in 1990. Metro Dallas-Fort Worth and Houston were the first parts of Texas to go Republican, and Bentsen relied on Democratic strength in the Texas countryside to win. But that is a thing of the past. George W. Bush carried 230 of 254 counties in 2000 and 236 in 2004; he carried rural Texas, outside the four big metro areas and the Rio Grande border country 65%–33% in 2000 and 69%–30% in 2004. At the same time, Republicans have retained a strong hold on the big metro areas: in 2004 the Dallas-Fort Worth Metroplex voted 62%–38% for Bush and metro Houston 58%–41%. Bush also carried metro San Antonio 59%–40% and, despite increased anti-Bush voting in the university precincts of Austin, he carried metro Austin 49.4%–48.9%. The border counties, heavily Hispanic, voted 58%–40% against Bush in 2000. He reduced that margin to 55%–45% in 2004.

Republicans now hold all 29 statewide elective offices, including all seats on the state Supreme Court. They turned a 72–78 deficit in the state House into an 88–62 majority and elected Tom Craddick the first Republican Speaker since 1871. Craddick is from Midland, the Permian Basin town in the west Texas desert which is also the home town of George W. Bush, Laura Bush and, former Commerce Secretary Donald Evans and General Tommy Franks. Who in the late 1950s and early 1960s, when they were all in Midland public schools, imagined that this one small town (there were 25,000 people in Midland County in 1950 and 67,000 in 1960) would produce so many leaders?

There are two threats to this Republican dominance. The first is the inevitable increase in the number of Latino voters. In 2000, 32% of Texas residents were Hispanic; more than half of Texas's population increase in the 1990s was accounted for by the increase in the number of Hispanics. To be sure, very many of these people are not U.S. citizens, and many who are citizens do not vote. White House political strategist Karl Rove has long been aware that Republicans must win a large share of the Latino vote if they are to remain dominant in the state. George W. Bush has cultivated Latino voters, starting in 1994 when he had little chance of reducing Ann Richards's margins among them; in 1998 the two exit polls showed him winning 49% and 39% of Hispanic votes. In 2000 against Al Gore he did not do as well: the VNS exit poll showed Gore carrying Texas Hispanics 54%–42%. But in 2004 the NEP exit poll showed Bush winning 49% of Hispanic votes, just behind John Kerry's 50%. Bush carried heavily Hispanic Cameron County on the Mexican border; he carried the heavily Hispanic 15th, 27th and 28th congressional districts. West Texas rural counties where Hispanics are 30% to 50% of the population voted 2–1 and 3–1 for Bush, but it's not clear how many Hispanics there voted. Not all Republicans will do as well with Hispanics as Bush. But it seems unlikely that they will be an overwhelmingly Democratic bloc as Texas blacks have been—and in 2004 Bush increased his share of votes among Texas blacks according to NEP from 5% to 17%.

The other threat to Republican dominance is the very fact that Republicans are plainly in control, in a position to be held responsible for any failures in public policy. In October 2003, U.S. House Majority Leader Tom DeLay, Texas Speaker Tom Craddick and Lieutenant Governor David Dewhurst slammed through a bill redrawing Texas's 32 congressional districts that was as partisan a gerrymander as the Democrats' 1991 plan. As a result, Texas's House delegation, which was 17–15 Democratic after the 2002 election, is now 21–11 Republican. That produced negative feedback in the form of indictments by Austin District Attorney Ronnie Earle of three of DeLay's allies on campaign finance charges; Republicans replied that Earle, a liberal Democrat, had also indicted Senator Kay Bailey Hutchison in 1993 on what turned out to be baseless charges, quickly dismissed in court. On substantive issues, Governor Rick Perry and the now solidly Republican legislature faced difficult choices in early 2005 on the budget, school finance and state water policy. And Republicans faced intraparty fights. In the 1960s and 1970s divisive fights between conservative and liberal Democrats gave Republicans openings to capture state-wide office, as Senator John Tower did in 1961 and Governor Bill Clements in 1978. Now divisive fights between more or less conservative Republicans may give Democrats similar openings. Texas politics is played for keeps, but it doesn't stand still.

The People		Race/Ethnic Origin			Military veterans: 1,754,809 (11.7%)	
Pop. 2004 (est):	22,490,022	10,933,313	52.4%	White	WWII: 17.1%	Korea: 11.7%
Pop. 2000:	20,851,820	2,364,255	11.3%	Black	Vietnam: 34.6%	Gulf War: 13.3%
Pop. 1990:	16,986,510	554,445	2.7%	Asian	**Most populous cities (2003):**	
Change 1990–2000:	Up 22.8%	68,859	0.3%	Native Am.	1. Houston	2,009,690
% of U.S. total:	7.4%	10,757	0.1%	Hawaiian	2. San Antonio	1,214,725
Pop. rank:	2d of 50	230,567	1.1%	Two+ races	3. Dallas	1,208,318
Area size:	268,581 sq. mi.	19,958	0.1%	Other	4. Austin	672,011
State Native:	62.2%	6,669,666	32.0%	Hisp. Origin	5. Fort Worth	585,122
Non-citizen:	9.5%	**Ancestry**				
Language		German: 8.4%		USA: 6.3%	Urban population: 82.5%	
English: 68.6%	Spanish: 25.9%	Irish: 6.1%		English: 6.0%	Rural population: 17.5%	
Other Eur.: 2.8%		French: 1.9%				

Education		Work Sector			Legislature	
H.S. Grad:	75.7%	Private: 78.0%		Govt: 14.6%	Senate	19 R 12 D
College Grad:	23.2%	Self: 7.1%		Family: 0.3%	House	87 R 63 D
Industry		Unemployment: 6.0%			Legislative Term Limits: No	
Agri: 2.7%	Con: 8.1%	**Household Income**			**Registered Voters**	
Fin: 6.8%	Info: 3.1%	<15k: 17.0%		15-35k: 27.0%	No party registration	
Mfg: 17.6%	Prof: 28.8%	35-50k: 16.5%		50-100k: 27.9%		
Public: 4.5%	Trade: 15.9%	100-150k: 7.2%		>150k: 4.3%		
Other: 12.5%		Median: $39,927				
Occupation		Poverty status: 15.4%				
Blue collar: 24.1%	White collar: 60.6%	**Home Value**				
Gray collar: 15.3%		<50k: 27.6%	50-100k: 38.4%	100-200k: 24.6%	200-300k: 5.5%	
		300-500k: 2.6%	>500k: 1.3%	Median: $77,800		

Presidential politics Texas is now solidly Republican in presidential politics and a massive counterweight to the state it replaced in 1994 as the second largest, New York. The contrast can be seen in the results of the 2000 and 2004 elections. In 2000 New York cast 33 electoral votes for Al Gore and Texas cast 32 for George W. Bush; Gore's 1.5 million popular vote margin in New York overshadowed Bush's 1.36 million vote margin in Texas. In 2004 it was the other way around. Texas cast 34 electoral votes for Bush and New York 31 for John Kerry; Bush's 1.7 million popular vote margin in Bush overshadowed Kerry's 1.35 million margin in New York. Texas seems at least as far out of reach for Democrats as New York does for Republicans. The best the Democratic ticket has done here in recent years was 43% in 1988, when Lloyd Bentsen was on the ticket, and 44% in 1996, as Ross Perot split the opposition to Bill Clinton and Bob Dole carried the state anyway with 49%.

2004 Presidential Vote		
Bush (R)	4,526,917	(61%)
Kerry (D)....................	2,832,704	(38%)
Badnarik (Lib).................	38,787	(1%)
Other........................	12,341	(0%)

2004 Democratic Presidential Primary		
Kerry (D).....................	563,237	(67%)
Edwards (D)	120,413	(14%)
Dean (D)	40,035	(5%)
Sharpton (D)..................	31,020	(4%)
Lieberman (D)	25,245	(3%)
Other........................	59,281	(7%)

2000 Presidential Vote		
Bush (R)	3,799,639	(59%)
Gore (D).....................	2,433,746	(38%)
Nader (Green)	137,994	(2%)
Other........................	36,258	(1%)

Texas's presidential primary, originally in May, was moved to March for Super Tuesday in 1988. The Republican primary electorate is heavily conservative; the Democratic primary electorate is increasingly liberal—and shrinking. Texas does not have party registration, and so turnout in each party's primaries is a fair index of party preference. In 1988, 1.7 million Texans voted in the Democratic primary; Michael Dukakis led with 33% of the vote and Jesse Jackson got 25%, ahead of Al Gore, running as a southern moderate, with 20%. In 1992, nearly 1.5 million voted in the Democratic primary, 66% of them for Bill Clinton. In 1996, 2000 and 2004, when the Democratic nomination was uncontested by the time Texas voted, although there were still live contests for state office, turnout continued to fall—921,000 in 1996, 786,000 in 2000 and 839,000 in 2004.

Congressional districting Before 2001, redistricting in Texas had always been the prerogative of Democrats. For many years it was not particularly partisan; there weren't enough Republicans to matter. By the 1990s there were, and in 1991 the Democrats produced their masterpiece. Modified slightly by a 1996 court ruling, it clumped heavily Republican areas into hugely Republican districts, then carved out with incredibly convoluted lines three new districts for Democrats. Starting in 1994, Republicans outpolled Democrats in House races and Anglo Democrats found themselves increasingly imperiled. Still, Democrats held a 17–13 majority in the delegation after the 2000 election.

109th Congress Lineup
21 R   11 D

108th Congress Lineup
17 D   15 R

Texas gained two new seats after the 2000 Census, and Republicans like House Majority Whip Tom DeLay predicted that their party would pick up six to eight seats. It didn't happen. The legislature was unable to agree on a map in 2001; a three-judge federal court in Tyler, with two Democratic- and one Republican-appointed judges, later took control and on November 14 came up with its own plan.

The plan protected all incumbents and created two new Republican districts. But in effect, the partisan Democratic plan of 1991 was given new life, with the Republicans given two new seats as a consolation prize. The result was, predictably, a 17–15 Democratic delegation. The statewide popular vote for the House in 2002 was 53% Republican and 44% Democratic.

In 2002 Republicans won big majorities in the legislature—88–62 in the House and 19–12 in the Senate. In early 2003 Tom DeLay, now House Majority Leader, urged the legislature to pass a new plan; Senate Republicans were reluctant. DeLay continued to press new House Speaker Tom Craddick, a longtime ally. As the legislative session neared adjournment, the House Redistricting Committee approved a new map on May 6. The disciplined Republican majority ignored Democrat protests. On the eve of the House's scheduled May 12 debate, 51 Democrats fled the state and secretly settled in a Holiday Inn in Ardmore, Oklahoma, to prevent the Republicans from getting the two-thirds required for a quorum. This spectacle attracted national attention; the state police—possibly with the assistance of the new federal Homeland Security Department personnel—were dispatched to track down the self-styled "Killer D's." Once their location was revealed, the Democrats insisted they would not return to Austin until after May 15, the final day the House could take up the bill in its regular session. The maneuver worked, temporarily. Governor Rick Perry convened a special session on June 30 and in late July the House approved the redistricting plan and sent it to the Senate. Then 11 Senate Democrats skedaddled.

When enough Democrats showed up to make a quorum, Republicans started arguing about the plan. Craddick insisted on a district in which his hometown of Midland would be the largest city; Midland candidates (including George W. Bush) have lost in the past to candidates from Lubbock or from districts that sprawled to San Antonio. DeLay insisted on splitting Austin's Democratic Travis County among three districts, two of them Republican. Republicans in Williamson County, just north of Austin, insisted that their county dominate a district. Finally all the arguments were resolved and details of the final plan were unveiled on October 9. Passage was perfunctory.

The plan was obviously intended to benefit Republicans: 22 of the 32 districts had voted Republican in statewide races, and two others came close to doing so. Republicans could argue that this was not much different from the plan used in 2002, 21 of whose 32 districts voted for George W. Bush in 2000. But the 2003 plan also shuffled around counties, so that Democrats who had been representing districts carried by Bush suddenly found themselves running in unfamiliar territory.

The plan attempted to comply with the Voting Rights Act by drawing safe districts for Texas's two black and five Hispanic incumbent Democrats. The previous plan had two districts that were more than 40% black; so did the new plan, but it added a 38% black district in Houston (which elected a black Democrat in 2004), while the next highest black percentage in the old plan was 23%. The old plan had seven districts with Hispanic majorities; the new plan had eight. What the plan did was make what Texans called WD-40s—white Democrats over 40—an endangered species. There were 15 of them in the Texas delegation elected in 1992, 11 in 2000, 10 in 2002 and only three in 2004.

Democrats quickly went into federal court and drew a panel with two Republican-appointed and one Democratic-appointed judges. On December 19 the Justice Department ruled the plan was in compliance with the Voting Rights Act; the court ruled that it was permissible to redistrict more than once in the 10 years between censuses. On January 2, 2004, Congressman Ralph Hall, the oldest member of the House, a Democrat elected from a heavily Republican district, announced that he was switching parties. On January 6 the court approved the plan 2–1. That same day 2d District Democrat Jim Turner announced his retirement. In September three DeLay associates who pushed the redistricting plan were indicted by Austin District Attorney Ronnie Earle on campaign finance charges related to the 2002 state House elections; Earle had been criticized by Republicans when an indictment he brought in 1993 against Senator Kay Bailey Hutchison was summarily dismissed. In October 2004 the U.S. Supreme Court ordered the three-judge court to reconsider the case in light of its decision in a redistricting case arising in Pennsylvania, in which the Supreme Court upheld a Republican plan as egregiously partisan as this one. In June 2005, the federal court again rejected the legal challenge.

But by then the election had already been held and the new House had taken office. George W. Bush carried Texas 61%–38%; in the 32 House races Republicans won 58% of the votes to Democrats' 39%. Five WD-40s were defeated; only three survived, Chet Edwards of Waco and two others, Lloyd Doggett and Gene Green, in majority-Hispanic districts. The Texas delegation, 17–15 Democratic before Hall's party switch, was 21–11 Republican in January 2005. Overall, Republicans gained three seats in the House, with the help of Texas, to bring their total to 232, the most won by Republicans in any biennial election since 1946; if Texas had not redistricted and Hall had not switched parties, there would have been only 226. Texas now has the House's largest Republican delegation, with 21 members, ahead of California's 20 and Florida's 18.

Governor

Rick Perry (R)

Assumed office Dec. 2000, term expires Jan. 2007, 1st full term; b. Mar. 4, 1950, Paint Creek; home, Austin; Texas A&M U., B.S. 1972; United Methodist; married (Anita).

Military Career: Air Force, 1972–77.

Elected Office: TX House of Reps., 1984–90; Comm., TX Dept. of Agriculture, 1990–98; Lt. Gov., 1998–2000.

Professional Career: Farmer & rancher.

Office: State Capitol, P.O. Box 12428, Austin, 78711, 512-463-2000; Fax: 512-463-1849; Web site: www.governor.state.tx.us.

Election Results

2002 general	Rick Perry (R)	2,632,541	(58%)
	Tony Sanchez (D)	1,819,843	(40%)
	Other	101,598	(2%)
2002 primary	Rick Perry (R)	unopposed	
1998 general	George W. Bush (R)	2,550,821	(68%)
	Garry Mauro (D)	1,165,592	(31%)
	Other	21,665	(1%)

Rick Perry succeeded George W. Bush as governor of Texas on December 21, 2000 and was elected to a four-year term on November 5, 2002. Perry grew up on his family's farm in Paint Creek, in Haskell County, near where his great-great grandfather settled after fighting in the Civil War, and was elected to the Texas House in the 1890s. His family owns a 10,000-acre ranch, and his father served 28 years as a county commissioner, as a Democrat. Rick Perry was an Eagle Scout and went to Texas A&M to study to be a veterinarian; that didn't pan out, though he did receive a degree in animal science. There, he became a yell leader—cheerleader on lesser campuses, and a coveted position at A&M. These were the years of great student rebellions, but apparently not at College Station; Perry says he never saw a war protest. After college he served five years in the Air Force, piloting C-130 transports. In 1977 he returned to work on the family ranch. In 1984 he was elected to the state House, as a Democrat; this part of West Texas was for a very long time strong Democratic territory. In 1989 he was passed over for a leadership position and switched to the Republican Party. In 1990 he ran for agriculture commissioner against the picaresque incumbent Jim Hightower. Perry, with the help of Karl Rove, got the support of the Farm Bureau and won an upset victory. In an increasingly Republican Texas, Perry was easily reelected in 1994.

Then in 1998, when storied Democratic incumbent Bob Bullock retired, Perry ran for lieutenant governor. This is an important position in Texas, more powerful than the governorship, some say; the lieutenant governor not only presides over the state Senate but controls its proceedings and appoints its committee members and chairmen. Governors and lieutenant governors are elected separately in Texas, and Bush and Perry ran separate campaigns; Karl Rove worked for Perry in 1990 and 1994 but not in 1998. Perry, interestingly, had no Republican primary opposition for a post that obviously could lead directly to the governorship. Perry and his Democratic opponent, state Comptroller John Sharp, managed to raise $15 million for the campaign. Sharp was a new Democrat who had done some interesting work on government reform, and served as student body president at A&M when Perry was yell leader. Perry's 50%–48% victory opened the way to the governor's office for him.

For five weeks after the 2000 presidential election it was not clear whether he would become governor, but he was obviously preparing. On December 21 he was sworn in—the first Aggie governor of Texas. In 2002, Democrats believed that Perry was vulnerable and gamely tried to put together a winning ticket. The chief organizer was John Sharp, who decided to run for lieutenant governor again, not governor, and worked to get a gubernatorial candidate who could swell Democratic turnout among Latinos. His dream candidate was Tony Sanchez, chief share-holder of International Bank of Commerce and Sanchez Oil & Gas in Laredo, who was said to have a net worth of $600 million. Sanchez was no political naif: in the early 1970s, he had worked for Lieutenant Governor Ben Barnes, one of Texas's canniest politicians and still a major lobbyist today. Sanchez returned to Laredo and with his father developed a huge pool of natural gas on the Mexican border near Laredo and started International Bank of Commerce and Tesoro Savings & Loan; the latter went under in the Texas S&L crisis in 1989, but overall this was a classic Texas business success story. Sharp and former San Antonio Mayor Henry Cisneros persuaded Sanchez to run for governor; they helped to push aside former UT quarterback Marty Akins, who in September 2001 announced he would run for comptroller instead.

Sanchez seemed to be sweeping toward an easy victory in the March 2002 primary. Then in January 2002 former Attorney General Dan Morales filed for governor. Morales hinted that taxes might have to be raised, but otherwise campaigned as the more moderate candidate. Sanchez spent $18 million on ads, most of them positive, and won the primary 61%–33%. But the primary fight was an offputting spectacle to many Anglo voters. They were willing enough to vote for Latinos—Morales was elected statewide twice as a Democrat and Republican Tony Garza was elected to the Railroad Commission (it regulates oil) in 1998—but the spectacle of Sanchez outflanking Morales on the left on ethnic issues was not appealing, and Sanchez entered the general election campaign with about one-quarter of voters having unfavorable feelings toward him. Meanwhile, in the April 2002 runoff, Democrats nominated for senator the black and business-friendly former mayor of Dallas, Ron Kirk. Sharp had got his "dream team," which he hoped would drive Latino and black turnout up even while he maintained greater appeal to Anglo voters than either of the two at the top of the ticket.

Perry and Sanchez agreed on many issues: they favored a moment of silence in schools, for example, and both ruled out higher taxes. But much of the campaign consisted of vitriolic negative ads. Sanchez's general theme was that Perry was beholden to campaign contributors and did their bidding. Perry hit Sanchez for not voting in some elections and for his business practices. In the fall he ran a number of hard-hitting ads linking Sanchez to drug kingpins' money laundering. It was undisputed that some $25 million was laundered through Tesoro Savings & Loan in the early 1980s; Sanchez claimed that the S&L followed regulations and that he did not know of the transactions and that no one in the S&L was charged with a crime. Nevertheless Perry ads linked the money laundering to the murder in 1985 of a Drug Enforce-ment Administration agent in Mexico. In one Perry ad another DEA agent said, "We investigated the murder. The same drug dealers who killed Kiki laundered millions in drug money through Tony Sanchez's bank." Sanchez was outraged. He said that Perry was "by far the most disgusting human being I have ever known. This is an absolute bald-faced lie and he knows it. Going into this race, I thought he was a man of no substance. I didn't realize just how bad he really is. He is a disgusting human being."

Election night was a nightmare for the "dream team." Perry beat Sanchez 58%–40%, although Sanchez spent $67 million to Perry's $28 million, and Republicans won up and down the line. And Ron Kirk and John Sharp, who led the Democratic ticket, both lost. The high Latino turnout that Democrats had hoped for did materialize, but only in the Rio Grande Valley. Elsewhere in the state, turnout in Latino neighborhoods in Houston, Dallas and San Antonio was not up much; the big increases were in heavily Republican counties at the edge of metro areas. Democrats spent three times as much as before on turnout operations, but Republicans registered 420,000 new voters, many in the fast-growing suburban counties, and that proved much more productive. Republicans won big margins in the legislature—19–12 in the state Senate and 88–62 in the state House. The new leaders of the legislature were Lieutenant Governor David Dewhurst in the Senate and Speaker Tom Craddick in the House—the first Republican speaker since 1871.

Perry called his victory a mandate for restricting tort lawsuits, providing rate relief on homeowner insurance and changes in medical malpractice law; he also sought a school vouchers program. Facing forecasts that state revenues would fall $10 billion short of the cost of maintaining current levels of spending, he ordered 7% cuts for the rest of the fiscal year in all programs except education, Medicaid and children's health in January 2003. The state Senate voted for disclosure of homeowners insurance rates to regulators in February 2003. In January 2003 the federal government and Mexico reached an agreement obliging Mexico to release 350,000 acre-feet of water into the Rio Grande, where it could be used by south Texas farmers. But this was far short of the 1.4 million acre-feet Mexico owes under a 1944 treaty and Perry called it "unacceptable."

Redistricting dominated the Texas political landscape in 2003. In early 2003 House Majority Leader Tom DeLay urged the legislature to pass a new plan; Senate Republicans and Dewhurst, the presiding officer, were reluctant. DeLay continued to press Craddick, a longtime ally. As the legislative session neared adjournment, the House Redistricting Committee approved a new map on May 6. It would have added five to seven new Republican seats and jeopardized each of the delegation's 10 Anglo Democrats, though it protected the five incumbent Latino Democrats and two African-Americans; it appeared to create two additional open seats designed for Latinos and one for a black candidate. On the eve of the House's scheduled May 12 debate, 51 Democrats fled the state and secretly settled in a Holiday Inn in Ardmore, Oklahoma, to prevent the Republicans from getting the two-thirds required for a quorum. This spectacle attracted national attention; the state police were dispatched to track down the self-styled "Killer D's." Once their location was revealed, the Democrats insisted they would not return to Austin until after May 15, the final day the House could take up the bill in its regular session. The maneuver worked, temporarily. Perry then convened a special session on June 30; after House Republicans passed their plan, that 30-day session deadlocked when Senators abided by their traditional rule for two-thirds approval to debate legislation. But Perry called a second 30-day session. When Republicans threatened to take action this time with a simple majority, 11 Senate Democrats fled to Albuquerque to prevent a quorum for legislative action or apprehension by state law-enforcement officers. With cheers from Democrats nationwide and growing anger from Republicans, they remained there for the month of August. When Perry indicated in early September that he would call a third special session, Democratic state senator John Whitmire effectively broke the deadlock by returning to Houston and to his legislative duties.

When enough Democrats showed up to make a quorum, Republicans started arguing about the plan; on October 9, all the arguments were resolved and details of the final plan were formally posted. Passage was perfunctory. Perry's view: "For too long millions of Texans have lived in gerrymandered districts that were drawn to protect incumbents rather than the public interest. Starting today, the voters of Texas can know that their power to choose their congressman or congresswoman will not be hampered by an incumbent protection scheme."

The hardnosed political maneuvering came at a high personal cost for Perry. In early 2004, the Capitol buzzed with rumors about his marriage and suggesting he would soon resign, fanned by widely-circulated e-mails and Democratic-oriented websites; at a February political rally, state Democratic chairman Charles Soechting insinuated Perry was gay. Perry at first refused to address the speculation. But by March he was forced to publicly address the issue, denying the rumors and calling them "uncorroborated filth." He called it part of "an obvious, orchestrated effort" by his political opponents. He told the *Austin American-Statesman,* Soechting "crosses the line of everything decent . . . .He took it to a new level, I would suggest to you, knowing there were TV cameras and knowing there was a reporter from a mainstream newspaper there." Soechting responded with a statement saying, "What is truly indecent is the state of children's health care, public schools and insurance rates under Perry's regime."

In April 2004, Perry unveiled a plan to use sin taxes—increasing levies on cigarettes, adding a $5 tax on admission to adult entertainment venues and adding video gambling machines to pari-mutuel tracks—to help address the state's long-running school finance problems. The proposed package was designed to pay for property tax reduction, to raise more money for schools and put an end to the "Robin Hood" school finance plan that distributes property tax money from high-property-value school districts to less wealthy ones. But one of Perry's most persistent critics on the plan was from his own party. Comptroller Carole Keeton Strayhorn, former mayor of Austin and mother to White House Press Secretary Scott McClellan and Medicare chief Dr. Mark McClellan, was thinking about challenging Perry in the 2006 primary; she questioned the numbers behind the proposal and said that most school districts would gain little or no money. Perry, whose plan also called for increasing cigarette taxes by $1 dollar per pack, said that it was part of effort to hike taxes on legal but unhealthy behavior. The feud escalated, with Strayhorn accusing the governor of conducting a political "witch hunt" against her by having her agency scrutinized by the state auditor's office (a spokesman for the governor, denying the claim, noted that the governor's office itself had been audited seven times through 2002); the governor's allies noted that a considerable portion of Strayhorn's campaign contributions came from trial lawyers and that an even larger portion came from donors connected to John Sharp, the Democrat who Perry defeated in the 1998 lieutenant governor's race and who helped put together the ticket to defeat Perry in 2002.

Against this backdrop, Perry failed to pass his plan, just as his predecessors George W. Bush and Ann Richards failed in their efforts to fix the state's chronic education funding problem. Then, in September 2004, a state district court judge ruled that the school finance system was unconstitutional and gave the legislature a year to come up with a solution; the state appealed directly to the Texas Supreme Court, which had previously issued several orders on education funding. In 2005, Perry declared school financing a "legislative emergency." But the House and Senate were unable to come to agreement, this time coming close to a deal but failing in the final hours of the session.

Without a school funding solution, Perry's standing in the polls suffered; a May 2005 Texas Poll found that his job approval rating had dropped to 45%, a precarious position for an incumbent. Senator Kay Bailey Hutchison gave long thought to challenging Perry in the March 2006 primary, but on June 17 she announced she would not run. The next day, Strayhorn made it clear she would. "I am not a weak leadin', ethics ignorin', pointin' the finger at everyone blamin', special session callin', public school slashin', slush fund spendin', toll road buildin', special interest panderin', rainy day fund raidin', fee increasin', no property tax cuttin', promise breakin', do-nothin' Rick Perry phony conservative."

Senior Senator

Kay Bailey Hutchison (R)

Elected June 1993, seat up 2006, 2d full term; b. July 22, 1943, Galveston; home, Dallas; U. of TX, B.A. 1962, J.D. 1967; Episcopalian; married (Ray).

Elected Office: TX House of Reps., 1972–76; TX Treasurer, 1990–93.

Professional Career: Political & legal corresp., KPRC–TV, 1967–70; Vice Chmn., Natl. Transp. Safety Bd., 1976–78; V.P. & Gen. Cnsl., RepublicBank Corp., 1978–82; Owner, McCraw Candies, 1984–88.

DC Office: 284 RSOB, 20510, 202-224-5922; Fax: 202-224-0776; Web site: hutchison.senate.gov.

State Offices: Abilene, 325-676-2839; Austin, 512-916-5834; Dallas, 214-361-3500; Harlingen, 955-425-2253; Houston, 713-653-3456; San Antonio, 210-340-2885.

Committees: *Republican Conference Vice Chair. Appropriations*: Commerce, Justice & Science; Defense; Energy & Water; Labor, Health and Human Services, Education & Related Agencies; Military Construction & Veterans Affairs (Chmn.); Transportation, Treasury, the Judiciary, HUD & Related Agencies. *Commerce, Science & Transportation*: Aviation; National Ocean Policy Study; Science & Space (Chmn.); Surface Transportation & Merchant Marine; Technology, Innovation & Competitiveness. *Rules & Administration. Veterans' Affairs.*

Group Ratings

	ADA	ACLU	AFS	LCV	ITIC	NTU	COC	ACU	NTLC	CHC
2004	25	22	14	17	92	73	94	84	93	100
2003	10	—	11	5	—	74	100	75	—	—

National Journal Ratings

	2003 LIB	—	2003 CONS		2004 LIB	—	2004 CONS
Economic	33%	—	62%		26%	—	73%
Social	43%	—	56%		38%	—	60%
Foreign	22%	—	68%		0%	—	67%

Key Votes of the 108th Congress

1. Ban Drilling in ANWR	N	5. Energy Bill	Y	9. Ban Same-Sex Marriage	Y
2. Approve Bush Tax Cuts	Y	6. Support Roe v. Wade	Y	10. Ban Bunker-Buster Bomb	N
3. Medicare/Rx Bill	Y	7. Ban Partial-Birth Abortion	Y	11. Fund Iraq War	Y
4. Bar Overtime Pay Regs.	N	8. Assault Weapons Ban	N	12. Restrict Missile Defense	N

Election Results

2000 general	Kay Bailey Hutchison (R)	4,082,091	(65%)	($3,518,862)
	Gene Kelly (D)	2,030,315	(32%)	($4,602)
	Other	164,246	(3%)	
2000 primary	Kay Bailey Hutchison (R)	unopposed		
1994 general	Kay Bailey Hutchison (R)	2,604,218	(61%)	($6,114,755)
	Richard Fisher (D)	1,639,615	(38%)	($3,360,850)

Prior Winning Percentages: 1993 (67%)

Kay Bailey Hutchison, senior senator from Texas, is a Republican who first won her seat in a June 1993 special election. She is of old Texas stock, the great-great-granddaughter of Charles S. Taylor, a signer of the Texas Declaration of Independence, who was a friend and business partner of Senator Thomas Jefferson Rusk, the first man to hold this seat; Hutchison is the first woman. She grew up in LaMarque, near the refinery town of Texas City, a prom queen who went to college and then law school at the University of Texas; unable to get a law job in 1967, she worked for a Houston TV station as a reporter. In 1972, she won a seat in the legislature, its first Republican woman. In 1976 she went to Washington to fill the number two position at the National Transportation Safety Board. She married her former colleague Ray Hutchison, moved to Dallas and went into banking and became a small business owner in 1978. In 1982, she lost a House race to Steve Bartlett, later mayor of Dallas. But she stayed active in Republican politics and in 1990 was elected state treasurer, a breakthrough race for state Republicans. Hutchison began her political career when it was no advantage to be a woman and has been mocked by liberals for her tight-lipped good manners and by Washington conservatives as a "Texas pompom girl." Her response: "This is what I have faced all my life—the trivialization of me—which I have not ever let bother me. I have always been able to rise above the expectations." Indeed: She is a senator from the nation's second-largest state, one of four senators in history (Barbara Boxer, Dianne Feinstein and Daniel Patrick Moynihan are the others) to have been elected with 4 million votes or more.

Her big break came in January 1993 when Lloyd Bentsen resigned his Senate seat after 22 years to become Secretary of the Treasury. To replace him, Governor Ann Richards appointed Bob Krueger, a two-term congressman in the 1970s who was elected railroad commissioner (actually, oil regulator) in 1990. Running against him in the May 1993 all-party primary were three Republicans, Hutchison and Congressmen Joe Barton and Jack Fields. Krueger opposed the Clinton budget and tax plan, but Democrats were so unpopular in Texas then—Bill Clinton had a 73% negative job rating—that Krueger won only 29% of the total vote, just behind Hutchison, also with 29%; Barton and Fields won 14% each. Hutchison kept the focus on Clinton and won the June runoff by an astonishing 67%–33%. Three serious Democrats were running as she entered the race for the full term in 1994. The potentially strongest candidate, moderate Houston Congressman Mike Andrews, was eliminated in the March primary. In the April runoff, former Attorney General Jim Mattox lost 54%–46% to Richard Fisher, a free-spending moderate who campaigned extensively in the Border counties in Spanish. Hutchison cruised to a solid 61%–38% victory.

Hutchison has a mostly conservative voting record. She is opposed to outlawing abortion and favors embryonic stem cell research, but voted for the partial-birth abortion ban. She has supported the Bush energy bills, including oil drilling in the Arctic National Wildlife Refuge. Hutchison has long sought to repeal the marriage penalty; in 1997 she sponsored a bill to do so that was vetoed by Bill Clinton. She supported it as part of the 2001 Bush tax cut and advanced her own version with relief for homemakers. In January 2003 she co-sponsored with Evan Bayh a bill to repeal it immediately and permanently. She also co-sponsored with two Democrats a bill to allow IRA holders over 59 to withdraw money for charitable donations without paying tax. On the Aviation Subcommittee she sponsored a 2000 law strengthening airport security that was being put into effect on September 11. After that tragedy she worked with Chairman Jay Rockefeller and strongly supported federalization of airport security. That position prevailed unanimously in the Senate; in conference committee she worked out a compromise with the House, which had voted for private security personnel, which seems likely to effectively federalize the program. Hutchison had hoped to be chairman of the Aviation Subcommittee, but in January 2003 Trent Lott returned to the committee and with greater seniority, claimed the post; she became chairman of the Surface Transportation Subcommittee instead. She has been a longtime supporter of the Amtrak system and of Amtrak lines in Texas, but has argued that Amtrak should get tougher on its unions. In 2005, when Bush's budget cut Amtrak funding, she disagreed. "We need to either commit to a national railroad or abandon the pretense of one. National or nothing. The budget represents an inadequate middle ground." Hutchison is also a strong supporter of the manned space program; she grew up near what is now the Johnson Space Center. Before the February 2003 Columbia disaster she warned of underfunding, and afterwards she expressed confidence in the program and called for more funding.

Hutchison is vice-chairman of the Senate Republican Conference. During the Clinton years, Hutchison was critical of administration foreign policy; she was wary of U.S. involvement in the former Yugoslavia, called for an eventual pullout from Bosnia, and decried Clinton administration policy in Kosovo. She has supported the foreign policy of the Bush administration. She serves on the Appropriations Committee and over the years has shepherded the Military Housing Privatization Initiative, in which the government hires private firms to build military housing; in February 2004 she helped get $1.37 billion for housing at San Antonio's Fort Sam Houston. In July 2002 she sponsored an amendment to change the base closing ranking and evaluation systems, which she says have produced mistakes in previous base closing rounds. In her appropriating work, she has come into conflict with House Majority Leader Tom DeLay. In 2001 she earmarked $25 million for Houston Metro, for either a study of expanding its rail line or for improvements in the Katy Freeway; Tom DeLay on the House Appropriations Committee put in a provision barring federal funds for Houston Metro rail. Later she got into disputes with DeLay and South Texas Democrat Solomon Ortiz over whether to give priority to the Corpus Christi Packery Channel, Brownsville' Brazos Island Harbor dredging or its West rail project. She has worked to put pressure on Mexico to deliver the 734,000 acre-feet of water it owes the United States under a 1944 treaty. She has sponsored a Weather Modification Act to fund cloud seeding for parched areas like West Texas.

Hutchison was reelected in 2000 by a 65%–32% margin; she carried 237 of 254 counties. After the election she showed some interest in running for governor in 2002, but that would have meant a primary against Governor Rick Perry and in March 2001 she announced she would not do so. But in the 2003 legislative session Perry ran into conflicts with Republican legislators, Lieutenant Governor David Dewhurst and Comptroller Carole Keeton Strayhorn (or "one mean grandma" as she likes to call herself). Looking ahead to the 2005 session, difficult issues of school finance and transportation seemed unresolved. Hutchison, busy in Washington and traveling around the state, remained above the fray during the regular session and the bitter controversy over redistricting. She had said before that she only expected to serve two terms in the Senate and she let Republicans know she might run for governor and asked for their support. She criticized Perry for missing out on $104 million of CHIP children's health money. Into the November 2004 omnibus appropriation she, or someone, inserted a provision allowing money raised for federal campaigns to be spent in state campaigns; at the end of 2004 she had $6.7 million, less than Perry's $7.9 million but more than Strayhorn's $5.7 million. Her favorable ratings in polls in late 2004 and early 2005 were higher than Perry's or Strayhorn's and her unfavorable ratings much lower than Perry's. At the beginning of 1990, neither Hutchison nor Perry held statewide office, indeed no Republican held statewide office except the state's governor and senators. Fifteen years later they seemed to be approaching a costly battle of the titans in the 2006 Republican primary, with little prospect of a strong Democratic candidate.

But on June 17, 2005, Hutchison announced she would not run for governor and would instead run for reelection in 2006. The next day, Strayhorn announced that she would challenge Perry in the March primary.

Junior Senator

John Cornyn (R)

Elected 2002, seat up 2008, 1st term; b. Feb. 2, 1952, Houston; home, San Antonio; Trinity U., B.A. 1973, St. Mary's Law Schl., J.D. 1977, U. of VA, L.L.M. 1995; Church of Christ; married (Sandy).

Elected Office: San Antonio Dist. Ct. judge, 1984–90; TX Sup. Ct., 1990–97; TX Atty. Gen., 1998–02.

Professional Career: Practicing atty., 1977–84.

DC Office: 517 HSOB, 20510, 202-224-2934; Fax: 202-228-2856; Web site: cornyn.senate.gov.

State Offices: Austin, 512-469-6034; Dallas, 972-239-1310; Harlingen, 956-423-0162; Houston, 713-572-3337; Lubbock, 806-472-7533; San Antonio, 210-224-7485; Tyler, 903-593-0902.

Committees: *Armed Services:* Emerging Threats & Capabilities (Chmn.); Readiness & Management Support; Strategic Forces. *Budget. Judiciary:* Constitution, Civil Rights & Property Rights; Corrections & Rehabilitation; Immigration, Border Security & Citizenship (Chmn.); Intellectual Property; Terrorism, Technology & Homeland Security. *Small Business & Entrepreneurship. Joint Economic Committee.*

Group Ratings

	ADA	ACLU	AFS	LCV	ITIC	NTU	COC	ACU	NTLC	CHC
2004	5	11	0	17	100	74	100	100	95	100
2003	10	—	11	0	—	79	100	85	—	—

National Journal Ratings

	2003 LIB	—	2003 CONS		2004 LIB	—	2004 CONS
Economic	0%	—	82%		5%	—	91%
Social	0%	—	59%		0%	—	84%
Foreign	0%	—	78%		33%	—	61%

Key Votes of the 108th Congress

1. Ban Drilling in ANWR	N	5. Energy Bill	Y	9. Ban Same-Sex Marriage	Y
2. Approve Bush Tax Cuts	Y	6. Support Roe v. Wade	N	10. Ban Bunker-Buster Bomb	N
3. Medicare/Rx Bill	Y	7. Ban Partial-Birth Abortion	Y	11. Fund Iraq War	Y
4. Bar Overtime Pay Regs.	N	8. Assault Weapons Ban	N	12. Restrict Missile Defense	N

Election Results

2002 general	John Cornyn (R)	2,496,243	(55%)	($9,769,780)
	Ron Kirk (D)	1,955,758	(43%)	($9,426,763)
	Other	62,011	(1%)	
2002 primary	John Cornyn (R)	478,825	(77%)	
	Bruce Lang (R)	46,907	(8%)	
	Douglas Deffenbaugh (R)	43,611	(7%)	
	Dudley Mooney (R)	32,262	(5%)	
	Other	17,757	(3%)	
1996 general	Phil Gramm (R)	3,027,680	(55%)	($14,078,131)
	Victor M. Morales (D)	2,428,776	(44%)	($978,862)

John Cornyn, a Republican, was elected to the Senate in 2002. He was born in Houston and grew up in San Antonio. He graduated from high school in Japan; his father was an oral pathologist in the Air Force stationed there and after retiring from the service settled in San Antonio and taught at the University of Texas Health Science Center. John Cornyn graduated from Trinity University and St. Mary's University law school, both in San Antonio, in the 1970s. He practiced law for five years with a firm that defended doctors and insurance companies in medical malpractice cases. In 1984 he ran for district court judge on the Republican ticket in Bexar County and upset a strong favorite in the race.

In 1990 he was elected to the state supreme court as a Republican. Cornyn generally ruled for defendants in tort cases, but not always; he dissented in 1995 from a decision that stripped juries of the right to determine the credibility of expert witnesses. The same year he wrote a 5–4 decision upholding the "Robin Hood" school finance system in which property-wealthy school districts had to send money to property-poor districts. In 1997 he resigned from the court to run for attorney general. In the March 1998 Republican primary and runoff he defeated two better-known opponents. In the general election he faced a grizzled veteran of Texas politics, Jim Mattox, a populist-sounding Democrat, congressman from Dallas from 1976 to 1982, attorney general from 1982 to 1990, second place finisher to Ann Richards in the 1990 primary and runoff for governor. Cornyn won 54%–44%.

Cornyn was the first Republican attorney general since Reconstruction. He argued two cases before the U. S. Supreme Court, including the Santa Fe Independent School District's defense of reading the Lord's Prayer at football games (the Court nixed it).

Cornyn had been planning to run for reelection in 2002. But on September 4, 2001, Senator Phil Gramm announced that he would not run for reelection. Cornyn immediately set out to run for the Senate and seemed to have the support of George W. Bush. Cornyn announced September 21 and said he hoped to raise $6 million for the March primary, he had no serious opposition there and didn't raise that much until later. National Democrats found a Texas candidate they liked: Dallas Mayor Ron Kirk. Kirk had an interesting life story: he is black, the son of the first black mailman in Austin and a teacher; he graduated from the University of Texas and its law school and was an aide to Senator Lloyd Bentsen. In 1995 he was elected mayor of Dallas and in 1999 he was reelected by a wide margin. In 2001 he announced he was resigning as mayor and in January 2002 he announced he was running for the Senate.

Kirk was not the only Democrat who ran. Another was Congressman Ken Bentsen of metro Houston, nephew of Senator and Treasury Secretary Lloyd Bentsen. But neither Kirk nor Bentsen ran first in the March primary. That place went to Victor Morales, a geography teacher and track coach from the Dallas suburb of Crandall, who raised $7,000 for his campaign. Morales had won the nomination to run against Gramm in 1996 with 36% of the vote against two former congressmen; his main assets were his Hispanic identity and the fact that he had the same last name as Attorney General Dan Morales. (This scenario may recur as more Hispanics enter politics. There are many fewer surnames among American Hispanics than among American Anglos.) In 2002 Morales won 33.2% of the vote in the primary, to 33.1% for Kirk and 27% for Bentsen. In the four weeks before the runoff, Kirk was endorsed by Bentsen and Houston Mayor Lee Brown. In the lower-turnout runoff, Kirk won 60%–40%.

In the general election Cornyn ran as a supporter of George W. Bush, and of making the 2001 tax cuts permanent, extending the research and development tax credit and raising Texas's share of gas tax funds from 90.5 cents to 95 cents per dollar of gas tax revenues. He supported school vouchers, individual investment accounts as part of Social Security and colorblind standards nationally in college and university admissions. Kirk took an opposite stand on all these issues, but portrayed himself as a moderate Democrat who would often support Bush. Cornyn favored Bush-level spending on missile defense; Kirk did not. On Iraq, Kirk equivocated, taking different stands at different times.

Kirk was a favorite of Democratic contributors and spent much time—50 days, Cornyn's spokesman charged—outside Texas schmoozing with Democratic contributors in Washington, on the Upper East Side of Manhattan, in Beverly Hills and similar venues. Republicans ran ads linking him to Hillary Rodham Clinton and liberal out-of-state moneygivers. Eventually he spent $8.9 million—almost as much as Cornyn's $9.5 million, most of it raised in Texas. Kirk was helped here by his sense of humor and a considerable charm, making fun of his bald pate and answering—mindful of Texas mores—when asked whether he owned a gun, "I have a wife and two little girls. You figure it out." But in the course of the campaign Kirk made some mistakes. He opposed the nomination to a federal judgeship of Texas Supreme Court Justice Priscilla Owen—something Republicans seized on in ads. He refused to disclose his income tax returns, except for allowing reporters one peek at his 2001 return. When Cornyn came out for a bill in the legislature requiring district attorneys to seek the death penalty for killers of law enforcement officials (the Austin district attorney had not sought the death penalty for the killer of a Travis County sheriff's deputy), Kirk said Cornyn was acting like he was running for district attorney—and then had to apologize abjectly to a convention of law enforcement officials a few days later, while Cornyn met with the deputy's widow. In San Antonio on September 12 he said that Cornyn might not support military action in Iraq if our military forces were not "disproportionately ethnic [and] disproportionately minority." He said he supported military action only if it met with international approval. Four days later he apologized and then said he backed Bush's position; he endorsed the Iraq war resolution in October.

Texas Democrats called their ticket of Kirk for senator and Tony Sanchez for governor the "dream team." They hoped it would draw a large turnout of blacks and Hispanics. Democrats at one point they said they would register 500,000 new Hispanics, though they later scaled that back and concentrated on Election Day get-out-the-vote. Meanwhile Republicans quietly registered thousands of new voters in the heavily Republican fast-growing suburban counties around Dallas-Fort Worth, Houston, San Antonio and Austin. Polls showed the race close in the spring, with Cornyn well under 50%; one nonpartisan firm and Kirk's pollster showed Kirk ahead or leading in the summer and fall. Democrats operated on the assumption that Kirk had to win 85% of blacks, 65% of Hispanics and 35% of whites to win. He clearly achieved the first and probably achieved the second of those goals, but failed by a solid margin to achieve the third. Cornyn won 55%–43%—almost the same numbers as in his race for attorney general in 1998, and a fair reflection of basic party identification in Texas in recent years. Kirk carried historically Republican Dallas County 50%–49%. But Cornyn carried the entire Dallas-Fort Worth Metroplex 58%–41%. Cornyn carried metro Houston 55%–43% and the combined San Antonio and Austin metro areas 51%–47%. The Border went 69%–29% for Kirk, a 148,000-vote margin. But rural Texas, much larger, went 62%–37% for Cornyn, a 346,000-vote margin. Kirk may have increased black turnout in Dallas, and Sanchez clearly increased Hispanic turnout in Laredo, but otherwise black and Hispanic turnout does not seem to have risen much above that in 1994, the last big-turnout off-year election. In contrast, turnout was up from 25% to 52% in fast-growing counties around Dallas-Fort Worth, Houston, San Antonio and Austin. Cornyn holds the seat once held by Sam Houston, Lyndon B. Johnson and John Tower and is the first Texas senator to come from San Antonio, which in the state's first decades was its largest city and which he argues is the most representative.

In the Senate Cornyn has been an active member of the Judiciary Committee. In 2003 and 2004 he chaired the Constitution Subcommittee and held hearings on continuity of government, hostility to religious expression in the public square and same-sex marriage. He proposed a constitutional amendment to give each house of Congress the authority to decide how vacancies would be filled if one-quarter or more of its members were killed or incapacitated. He was a lead sponsor of the amendment, which got less than 50 votes, to ban same-sex marriage. He insisted that he was acting not out of ill will but because of "the traditional institution of marriage and its importance as a stabilizing influence on our society." He also supported amendments to expand the rights of crime victims and to overturn the Ninth Circuit decision banning the phrase "one nation under God" in the Pledge of Allegiance. He co-sponsored the class action and bankruptcy bills opposed by trial lawyers but passed by the Senate and signed by Bush in 2005. He sought to amend the bankruptcy bill to require companies to file for bankruptcy in the state where their primary business or assets are located; this was a response to Enron's filing in New York, and Edward Kennedy, miffed that Massachusetts's Polaroid filed out of state, joined him. But Joseph Biden and Tom Carper of Delaware, legal home of 500,000 corporations, threatened to kill the bankruptcy bill, and Cornyn withdrew the amendment. Cornyn took a lead role in seeking to confirm Bush appellate judgeship appointees and urged colleagues to change the Senate rules to stop the Democrats' filibusters. He opposed demands for disclosure of documents after the Abu Ghraib abuses were discovered. He moved to strengthen the Freedom of Information Act with a bill that would penalize federal agencies and employees that fail to respond to requests in a timely manner; agencies would be deemed to waive any exemptions, except national security, personal privacy and proprietary business information, and would be required to discipline employees who fail to comply. It would require agencies to give requesters individualized tracking numbers and credible status reports.

Cornyn's hometown of San Antonio is only 150 miles from Mexico, and he has taken an interest in immigration and citizenship issues; in January 2005 he became chairman of the Immigration Subcommittee. (Its ranking Democrat, Edward Kennedy, floor managed his first bill, on immigration, in 1965.) One of Cornyn's first successful bills reduced from three years to one the waiting period for citizenship for legal aliens serving in the armed forces. He sponsored a bill to increase the time Mexicans with border crossing cards can remain in the United States from 72 hours to six months, the same time allowed for Canadians. And he proposed guest worker legislation, to allow workers with willing employers to get either seasonal visas (primarily farm workers) or nonseasonal visas for 12 months which could be extended to 36 months; some of their wages would be taken by the government and placed in bank accounts in their home countries, for their use when they return. This proposal was criticized by some who want to put guest workers on the path to citizenship and by others who argue that we should deport illegal aliens and not let guest workers in. Cornyn argues that it is unrealistic to expect that we will deport the estimated 8 to 10 million illegal aliens in the country and that people who want to work should be encouraged. He opposes military patrol of the border or building a fence along most of its length—these would disrupt life in South Texas, he argues—but backed the measure passed by the House in February 2005 that would allow completion of the 14-mile fence in San Diego despite the objections of the California Coastal Commission and that would bar driver's licenses for illegal aliens being recognized by airport screeners or federal building security agents. Cornyn argued that these security measures should be treated as part of a larger immigration bill, despite the contrary arguments of House Judiciary Chairman James Sensenbrenner. But it is not clear whether he will be able to develop a consensus in the Senate on an issue on which tempers sometimes run hot and on which there are wide differences of opinion.

FIRST DISTRICT

Rep. Louie Gohmert (R)

Elected 2004, 1st term; b. Aug. 18, 1953, Pittsburg; home, Tyler; TX A&M U., B.A. 1975, Baylor U. Law Schl., J.D. 1977; Baptist; married (Kathy).

Military Career: Army, 1978–82.

Elected Office: Smith Cnty. Dist. Ct. judge, 1992–2002.

Professional Career: Practicing atty., 1982–92; Chief Justice, TX 12th Ct. of Appeals, 2002–03.

DC Office: 508 CHOB, 20515, 202-225-3035; Fax: 202-225-5866; Web site: www.gohmert.house.gov.

District Offices: Longview, 903-236-8597; Marshall, 866-535-6302; Tyler, 903-561-6349.

Committees: *Judiciary* (23d of 23 R): Commercial & Administrative Law; Crime, Terrorism & Homeland Security; Immigration, Border Security & Claims. *Resources* (25th of 27 R): Energy & Mineral Resources; Water & Power. *Small Business* (18th of 18 R): Regulatory Reform & Oversight.

Group Ratings and Key Votes: Newly Elected

Election Results

2004 general	Louie Gohmert (R)	157,068	(61%)	($1,829,275)
	Max Sandlin (D)	96,281	(38%)	($1,690,816)
	Other	2,158	(1%)	
2004 runoff	Louie Gohmert (R)	16,841	(57%)	
	John Graves (R)	12,618	(43%)	
2004 primary	Louie Gohmert (R)	19,421	(42%)	
	John Graves (R)	13,933	(30%)	
	Wayne Christian (R)	6,854	(15%)	
	Lyle Thorstenson (R)	4,604	(10%)	
	Other	1,723	(4%)	
2002 general	Max Sandlin (D)	86,384	(56%)	($1,070,933)
	John Lawrence (R)	66,654	(44%)	($81,432)

The People		Race/Ethnic Origin	Ancestry	
Area size:	8,916 sq. mi.	70.6% White	USA: 12.1%	Irish: 7.4%
Urban population:	50.9%	18.3% Black	English: 6.8%	
Rural population:	49.1%	0.5% Asian	**2004 Presidential Vote**	
Pop. 2000:	651,619	0.3% Native Am.	Bush (R) 178,409	(69%)
Median income:	$33,461	0.0% Hawaiian	Kerry (D) 78,609	(31%)
Poverty status:	16.0%	0.9% Two+ races	**2000 Presidential Vote**	
Military veterans:	13.3%	0.0% Other	Bush (R) 152,963	(68%)
		9.3% Hispanic Origin	Gore (D) 73,596	(32%)
			Cook Partisan Voting Index: R +17	

Occupation	Blue collar: 30.3%	White collar: 53.3%	Gray collar: 16.4%

The gently rolling land of East Texas, cut by rivers headed south to the Gulf of Mexico, has been part of the United States for 160 years. Settled early on by farmers from Tennessee, it has been part of Scots-Irish America, a land of people of fighting faith, given to graceful courtesy but unwilling to endure a slight without recompense. One hundred years ago this was one of the poorest parts of America, a place where farmers scratched a living off the land and hoped for good prices in the marketplace and good weather for its crops. When a peach blight in the early 20th century wiped out much of the local fruit industry, many farmers turned to growing roses, which proved ideally suited to the climate and soil of area around Tyler, one of the larger East Texas towns. By the 1940s, more than half the nation's supply of rose bushes was grown within 10 miles of Tyler, which has become known for its annual Texas Rose Festival and the East Texas State Fair. Longview, which in the 1870s was the western terminus of the Southern Pacific Railroad, became a trading center for wagon trains and local cotton growers and timber cutters; then, in

1943, the Big Inch pipeline began sending millions of barrels of crude oil from Longview to the East for refining. Since then, the Longview area has become an industrial center for earth-moving equipment and chemicals and home to the Stroh Brewery, the largest in Texas. Marshall, the hometown of Lady Bird Johnson, participates in the Holiday Trail of Lights, a Christmas festival that stretches from towns in Louisiana to Texas. It was in the fields and woodlands of Nacogdoches and other nearby counties that the debris, including human remains, fell when Space Shuttle *Columbia* was lost in February 2003; more than a year later, when NASA already had reached its conclusion over the cause of the failure and the pieces had little investigative value, local farmers and hunters were still retrieving small particles of tile, or metal or plastic debris.

The 1st Congressional District of Texas includes the heart of East Texas; it's a rectangular collection of 12 counties, of which the most populous are Tyler's Smith County, Longview's Gregg County and Lufkin's Angelina County in the south. Also included is the southeast corner of Cass County east of Route 59, which is primarily the McLeod school district. East Texas is ancestrally Democratic, a region that nodded to the rhetoric of William Jennings Bryan and Franklin D. Roosevelt. But Tyler and Longview moved toward the Republican party as long ago as the 1950s, and the rest of East Texas followed, seemingly convinced that the party of Andrew Jackson and Sam Houston had abandoned bellicose alertness for emollient conciliation and celebration of ordinary people's values for elitist disdain. When George H. W. Bush ran for the Senate against Lloyd Bentsen in 1970 East Texas was solidly Democratic; by the time George W. Bush ran for reelection as governor in 1998, it was solidly Republican. Until 2004 East Texas was represented by Democrats in the House. But the 2003 Republican redistricting changed that by reshaping the old 1st District, removing now Republican counties which had become used to voting for the Democratic incumbent and adding heavily Republican Smith and Gregg Counties. In 2004, George W. Bush carried 69% of the district vote.

The congressman from the 1st District is Louie Gohmert, a Republican elected in 2004 when he defeated four-term Democrat Max Sandlin. Gohmert grew up in Mount Pleasant, got an Army scholarship at Texas A&M, where he was class president, and then attended Baylor law school. After law school he served as a captain in the Army, then practiced law in Tyler and spent a decade as a district court judge before Governor Rick Perry in July 2002 named him chief justice of the local appeals court. While on the bench, he earned a reputation as a tough law-and-order judge with a knack for attracting attention. In 1996 he ordered an HIV-positive convicted car thief, as a condition of probation, to notify future sexual partners of his HIV status and to obtain written consent from each before engaging in sexual activity. After the 2003 redistricting, Gohmert was one of six Republicans who filed in the primary to challenge Sandlin, who had a moderate voting record and was politically close to Minority Leader Nancy Pelosi. The best-known candidates were Gohmert and lawyer John Graves, the unsuccessful Republican nominee in 2002 against then-Democratic Congressman Ralph Hall in the old 4th District. Gohmert led in the primary with 42% of the vote to 30% for Graves. In the month-long runoff campaign, few differences separated the two conservatives. Both opposed abortion, supported a constitutional amendment banning gay marriage, and wanted to make the Bush tax cuts permanent. Gohmert voiced reservations about the privacy threats posed by new law enforcement tools in the Patriot Act. Graves carried 9 of the 13 counties, but Gohmert prevailed by winning an overwhelming 77% in his Smith County, the district's most populous, which cast 47% of the total vote; overall he won 57%–43%.

In the general, Gohmert continually linked Sandlin to the national Democratic party and its presidential nominee, John Kerry. In one debate, Gohmert repeatedly asked Sandlin about his choice for president; Sandlin sidestepped the question. Sandlin also kept his distance from House Democrats, but he cited his work on the Ways and Means Committee to expand health care services in rural areas. Gohmert frequently mentioned his strong support for Bush and, unlike Sandlin, attended his party's national convention. He ran a TV spot that claimed that Sandlin's campaign ads "had more holes in them than a CBS story by Dan Rather"—a reference to the discredited CBS report about Bush's National Guard service. Sandlin criticized Gohmert for being supported by Majority Leader Tom DeLay. The result wasn't close: Gohmert won

61%–38%, with 79% in Smith County and 64% in Gregg County. Sandlin led in only two small rural counties plus the sliver of Cass in the new district.

SECOND DISTRICT

Rep. Ted Poe (R)

Elected 2004, 1st term; b. Sept. 10, 1948, Temple; home, Humble; Abilene Christian U., B.A. 1970, U. of Houston, J.D. 1973; Church of Christ; married (Carol).

Military Career: Air Force Reserve, 1970–76.

Elected Office: Harris Cnty. Judge, 1981–2003.

Professional Career: Asst. dist. atty., 1973–81.

DC Office: 1605 LHOB, 20515, 202-225-2401; Fax: 202-225-5547; Web site: www.house.gov/poe.

District Offices: Beaumont, 409-212-1997; Humble, 281-446-0242.

Committees: *International Relations* (27th of 27 R): Europe & Emerging Threats; International Terrorism & Nonproliferation. *Small Business* (13th of 18 R): Regulatory Reform & Oversight; Tax, Finance & Exports. *Transportation & Infrastructure* (34th of 41 R): Aviation; Water Resources & Environment.

Group Ratings and Key Votes: Newly Elected

Election Results

2004 general	Ted Poe (R)	139,951	(56%)	($1,522,863)
	Nick Lampson (D)	108,156	(43%)	($2,405,430)
	Other	3,931	(2%)	
2004 primary	Ted Poe (R)	14,932	(61%)	
	George Fastuca (R)	3,668	(15%)	
	Clint Moore (R)	2,868	(12%)	
	Mark Henry (R)	2,423	(10%)	
	Other	531	(2%)	

The People		Race/Ethnic Origin	Ancestry		
Area size:	2,180 sq. mi.	64.2% White	German: 8.8%		Irish: 7.4%
Urban population:	89.5%	19.0% Black	USA: 6.8%		
Rural population:	10.5%	2.6% Asian	**2004 Presidential Vote**		
Pop. 2000:	651,620	0.3% Native Am.	Bush (R)	160,365	(63%)
Median income:	$47,029	0.0% Hawaiian	Kerry (D)	92,842	(37%)
Poverty status:	11.4%	1.1% Two+ races	**2000 Presidential Vote**		
Military veterans:	12.9%	0.1% Other	Bush (R)	140,442	(63%)
		12.6% Hispanic Origin	Gore (D)	83,347	(37%)
			Cook Partisan Voting Index: R +12		
Occupation	Blue collar: 23.4%	White collar: 62.9%	Gray collar: 13.7%		

The spongy land of the Texas Gulf Coast, where the French explorer LaSalle and the Spanish colonizer Galvez dreamed of thriving settlements, remained mostly unsettled until well into the 19th century. When oil was found at the Spindletop field near Beaumont in 1901, the area all around boomed. First oil exploration, then petroleum refining, then petrochemicals: The straight-edged metal of oil rigs and the intricate curving metalwork of refineries shine through the swampy landscape of southeast Texas. The rig workers and mechanical engineers they brought here have given a kind of permanent roughneck air to the region. In the early days of Spindletop, the town was so overrun by boomers who drained the local water supply that some doctors advised people to drink whiskey instead of water. The Women's Christian Temperance Union jumped in to create a counterforce.

The 2d Congressional District of Texas occupies much of this territory. Nearly 40% of its people live in and around Beaumont and Port Arthur, still very much oil country, an active industrial area with some of the country's largest oil refineries and chemical plants and dense pollution. It is among the few places in Texas where labor unions have had any strength. Beaumont is the home of several trial lawyers who have become billionaires through asbestos and tobacco cases; local juries are known for their willingness to bring in large verdicts against big corporations. Port Arthur was the home of 1960s blue and rock singer Janis Joplin, who is memorialized with a bust in the city library. But the majority of the people in the district live in Harris County, in suburbs north and east of Houston, where oil is an important part of the economy but hardly all of it. The Humble oil field was once the largest in Texas and the local Humble Oil and Refining Company is now known as Exxon; the community now serves as a retail and shipping center for the nearby George Bush Intercontinental Airport. In the 2003 redistricting, the new 2d was created by adding parts of the old 8th District in Harris County and the old 9th District in Jefferson County. Only a sliver was taken from the old 2d District, which was carved into six separate pieces; 2d District Democrat Jim Turner, who had been ranking Democrat on the Homeland Security Committee, announced his retirement the day the redistricting plan was upheld by a federal court.

The congressman from the 2d District is Ted Poe, a Republican elected in 2004. A former prosecutor who served 22 years as a Houston-area district court judge, Poe became a publicity magnet and a judicial celebrity for meting out humiliating punishments to criminals: he required murderers to hang pictures of their victims in their prison cells and car thieves to give their vehicles to victims. He ordered drunken drivers and shoplifters to stand at the entrances to stores and taverns carrying signs publicizing their offenses; this became known as "shame sentencing." He also gained national recognition as a regular legal commentator since 1999 on cable television channels such as Fox, MSNBC and CNN. He appeared on *Dateline NBC* and *60 Minutes*.

In 2003, Poe stepped down as judge to run for Congress. In the six-way Republican primary, Poe's opponents couldn't buy that kind of attention, although some tried. Former Enron executive George Fastuca spent $390,000 of his own money. Mark Henry, the owner of a charter airline service, poured in $380,000 in personal funds. Poe, on the other hand, didn't put up a penny of his own money in the primary. Thanks to his name recognition and bench experience, Poe won 61% of the vote in the March 2004 primary.

In the general, Poe faced incumbent Democrat Nick Lampson, first elected in 1996 in the old 9th District. Lampson had a moderate voting record, a low-key style and was a big booster of NASA. At first it was not clear whether Poe would be able to capitalize on the favorable redistricting. National Republicans fretted about his fundraising and his seemingly complacent campaign. His positions were in tension with George W. Bush's: he was skeptical about the federal role in education, he opposed Bush's proposal to grant temporary work permits to immigrants and he supported a national sales tax to replace the income tax. Lampson, who briefly thought about running instead against Tom DeLay in the 22d District, outspent Poe nearly 2-to-1 and worked feverishly to make inroads in the Republican Harris County suburbs. But on Election Day, the district's solid Republican bent and its geography were too much to overcome. Lampson led 68%–31% in Jefferson County, where 36% of votes were cast. But Poe won 70%–28% in Harris County, where 58% of the votes were cast. Overall Poe won 56%–43%.

Poe became the Houston-area Republican on the Transportation and Infrastructure Committee, where he worked to restore funding to maintain and dredge the Sabine-Neches Ship Channel. He was among the congressional observers of the historic elections in Iraq in January 2005.

THIRD DISTRICT

Rep. Sam Johnson (R)

Elected May 1991, 7th full term; b. Oct. 11, 1930, San Antonio; home, Dallas; S. Methodist U., B.B.A. 1951, George Washington U., M.S. 1974; Methodist; married (Shirley).

Military Career: Air Force, 1950–79 (Korea & Vietnam).

Elected Office: TX House of Reps., 1984–91.

Professional Career: Home builder.

DC Office: 1211 LHOB, 20515, 202-225-4201; Fax: 202-225-1485; Web site: www.samjohnson.house.gov.

District Office: Richardson, 972-470-0892.

Committees: *Education & the Workforce* (5th of 27 R): 21st Century Competitiveness; Employer-Employee Relations (Chmn.). *Ways & Means* (9th of 24 R): Health; Oversight; Social Security.

Group Ratings

	ADA	ACLU	AFS	LCV	ITIC	NTU	COC	ACU	NTLC	CHC
2004	0	0	0	0	90	77	100	100	95	100
2003	5	—	0	0	—	71	100	92	—	—

National Journal Ratings

	2003 LIB	—	2003 CONS		2004 LIB	—	2004 CONS
Economic	9%	—	84%		28%	—	72%
Social	0%	—	95%		15%	—	84%
Foreign	0%	—	89%		15%	—	84%

Key Votes of the 108th Congress

1. Drilling in ANWR	Y	5. DC School Vouchers	Y	9. Ban Same-Sex Marriage	Y
2. Approve Bush Tax Cuts	Y	6. Ban Human Cloning	Y	10. Fund Iraq War	Y
3. Medicare/Rx Bill	Y	7. Restrict Gun Liability	Y	11. Bar Cuba Embargo Funds	N
4. Bar Overtime Pay Regs.	*	8. Ban Partial-Birth Abortion	Y	12. Intelligence Reorg.	Y

Election Results

2004 general	Sam Johnson (R)	180,099	(86%)	($771,636)
	Paul Jenkins (I)	16,966	(8%)	($9,017)
	James Vessels (Lib)..............................	13,287	(6%)	
2004 primary	Sam Johnson (R)	12,429	(84%)	
	Brian Rubarts (R)	2,357	(16%)	
2002 general	Sam Johnson (R)	113,974	(74%)	($921,485)
	Manny Molera (D)	37,503	(24%)	($78,120)
	Other...	2,656	(2%)	

Prior Winning Percentages: 2000 (72%); 1998 (91%); 1996 (73%); 1994 (91%); 1992 (86%); 1991 (53%)

The People		Race/Ethnic Origin	Ancestry	
Area size:	266 sq. mi.	63.3% White	German: 10.7%	English: 7.9%
Urban population:	99.0%	9.2% Black	Irish: 7.6%	
Rural population:	1.0%	8.3% Asian	**2004 Presidential Vote**	
Pop. 2000:	651,619	0.4% Native Am.	Bush (R) 174,711	(67%)
Median income:	$60,878	0.0% Hawaiian	Kerry (D) 86,718	(33%)
Poverty status:	7.0%	1.6% Two+ races	**2000 Presidential Vote**	
Military veterans:	9.5%	0.1% Other	Bush (R) 139,717	(70%)
		16.9% Hispanic Origin	Gore (D) 60,386	(30%)
			Cook Partisan Voting Index: R +17	

Occupation	Blue collar: 15.2%	White collar: 74.7%	Gray collar: 10.1%

North Dallas: the subject of a trashy novel in the 1970s, the putative location of the 1980s TV program "Dallas," conjures up a certain image: of sudden affluence and insolent disdain for those who do not partake in it, of shady dealings and immoral trysts in an environment in which all visible expressions endorse traditional values, of a ruthless drive for money and power overriding all human sympathy. But all this is caricature. Dallas was named, improbably, for the stuffy and otherwise forgotten Philadelphia lawyer who was James K. Polk's vice president. It got its start as a railroad junction and cotton-shipping center. In the 1960s Dallas was at the cutting edge of high-tech, the home of Texas Instruments and Ross Perot's EDS and of many defense contractors. The high-tech and defense businesses are not as robust as they were in the 1980s but the Dallas-Fort Worth Metroplex thrived in the 1990s, with growth from corporate headquarters relocated from less business-friendly precincts, from small businesses growing quickly in an entrepreneur-friendly climate with no state income tax and from companies making money trading with Mexico; Dallas has been the nation's greatest beneficiary of NAFTA. The Metroplex, one way or the other, continues to thrive.

Dallas's growth has extended far into the countryside. The home of the city's elite may still be in the mansion-lined streets of Highland Park, only a few miles north of downtown. But the center of Dallas's entrepreneurial economy has moved north to the LBJ Freeway and edge cities beyond, and the residential center of Dallas's business and professional classes has moved ever farther north in Dallas County, to the rolling, scrub-covered hills, as they recently were, of Collin County to the north. Back in 1960 it was mostly rural, still part of the country congressional district that sent Speaker Sam Rayburn to the House. It had 41,000 people then and actually lost population in the 1950s. Then the Dallas-Fort Worth Metroplex moved in, with a force that can be discerned in the numbers: 66,000 in 1970, 144,000 in 1980, 264,000 in 1990, 491,000 in 2000, 627,000 in 2004. The biggest city here now is Plano, with 241,000 people, a former farming community that became a corporate headquarters and edge city with DART light-rail service, site of mega-mansion subdivisions, the state's ninth-largest city and the new face of successful Texas. Plano is 10% Asian, many of Chinese ancestry, and they slightly outnumber Latinos: a new face of Texas. Today Plano is mostly built up, and the fastest growth is in the old county seat of McKinney. Politically, Collin County is very Republican, indeed more Republican than Dallas County ever was: it cast more votes in 2004 than all but five other Texas counties, and gave 71% of them to George W. Bush.

The 3d Congressional District of Texas includes most of Collin County and centers on Plano; it also covers the northeastern corner of Dallas County, beyond the LBJ Freeway, including much of Garland and Rowlett. This was the fastest-growing district in Texas in the 1990s and is solidly Republican, casting 67% of its votes for George W. Bush in 2004. Of the Dallas-area districts, this remained the most intact during the 2003 redistricting.

The congressman from the 3d District is Sam Johnson, a Republican first elected in 1991. Johnson grew up in Dallas, graduated from SMU and George Washington University. He was an Air Force fighter pilot who flew 87 combat missions in the Korean and Vietnamese wars. After his F-4 was shot down over North Vietnam during his 25th mission there, he was imprisoned from 1966 to 1973 in the "Hanoi Hilton", where he spent 42 months in solitary confinement; he was left with a slight stoop in his walk and a disfigured hand. On his return, Johnson started a homebuilding company and was elected to the Texas House in 1984. He was elected to the U.S. House in a 1991 special election after incumbent Steve Bartlett was elected mayor of Dallas. Johnson ran second in the primary, behind former Peace Corps director Tom Pauken. In the runoff he emphasized his war record and, although he was less familiar with legislative issues in debate, won 53%–47% over Pauken, who as Texas Republican chairman later was a sharp critic of Governor George W. Bush.

In the House, Johnson typically has been among members with the most conservative voting record, opposing pork barrel projects of all kinds, voting for more IRAs and against extending unemployment benefits. He was a founder and chair of the Conservative Action Team (now known as the Republican Study Committee), which pressed Republican leaders to stick with goals ranging from budget targets to shutting down the National Endowment for the Arts. Every Congress he offers a constitutional amendment to repeal the 16th Amendment, which authorized the federal income tax. On the Ways and Means Committee, he sponsored the successful repeal in 2000 of the earnings limit for Social Security recipients. He was a leading advocate of expanding tax-free savings accounts. In 2003, he helped to enact the Military Family

Tax Relief Act, which doubled the death benefit and reduced taxes on families that suffer death by an active member of the military. On the Education and the Workforce Committee, he chairs the Subcommittee on Employer-Employee Relations; he won House passage of his bill to encourage small businesses to join forces to purchase health insurance at lower costs. With Mac Thornberry, he introduced legislation to make the voting process easier for military personnel. Johnson has been a defender of the F-22 fighter jet, partly produced at the Lockheed Martin plant in Fort Worth.

Even though he was a POW with John McCain for a year and a half, Johnson strongly backed George W. Bush in the 2000 primaries; McCain "cannot hold a candle to George Bush," he said. He was an outspoken critic in the 2004 campaign of John Kerry and his military record in Vietnam, which Johnson said was "nothing short of aiding and abetting the enemy." On the House floor he called Kerry "Hanoi John."

This is one of the safest Republican seats in the country. Johnson originally pledged to serve only 12 years, but changed his mind. In 2004, he did not face major-party opposition in the general election.

FOURTH DISTRICT

Rep. Ralph Hall (R)

Elected 1980, 13th term; b. May 3, 1923, Fate; home, Rockwall; U. of TX, TX Christian U., S. Methodist U., LL.B. 1951; United Methodist; married (Mary Ellen).

Military Career: Navy, 1942–45 (WWII).

Elected Office: Rockwall Cnty. Judge, 1950–62; TX Senate, 1962–72.

Professional Career: Practicing atty., 1951–80; Pres. & CEO, TX Aluminum Corp., 1967–68; Spec. Cnsl., Howmet Corp., 1970–74.

DC Office: 2405 RHOB, 20515, 202-225-6673; Fax: 202-225-3332; Web site: www.house.gov/ralphhall.

District Offices: McKinney, 214-726-9949; New Boston, 903-628-8309; Rockwall, 972-771-9118; Sherman, 903-892-1112; Sulphur Springs, 903-885-9370; Texarkana, 903-794-4445.

Committees: *Energy & Commerce* (2d of 31 R): Energy & Air Quality (Chmn.); Environment & Hazardous Materials; Health. *Science* (2d of 24 R): Energy; Space & Aeronautics.

Group Ratings

	ADA	ACLU	AFS	LCV	ITIC	NTU	COC	ACU	NTLC	CHC
2004	5	5	13	9	89	51	100	84	70	92
2003	15	—	25	15	—	42	93	76	—	—

National Journal Ratings

	2003 LIB — 2003 CONS		2004 LIB — 2004 CONS	
Economic	50%	— 49%	38%	— 61%
Social	42%	— 56%	30%	— 70%
Foreign	46%	— 52%	39%	— 59%

Key Votes of the 108th Congress

1. Drilling in ANWR	N	5. DC School Vouchers	Y	9. Ban Same-Sex Marriage	Y
2. Approve Bush Tax Cuts	Y	6. Ban Human Cloning	Y	10. Fund Iraq War	Y
3. Medicare/Rx Bill	Y	7. Restrict Gun Liability	Y	11. Bar Cuba Embargo Funds	N
4. Bar Overtime Pay Regs.	N	8. Ban Partial-Birth Abortion	Y	12. Intelligence Reorg.	Y

Election Results

2004 general	Ralph Hall (R)	182,866	(68%)	($1,152,827)
	Jim Nickerson (D)	81,585	(30%)	($199,803)
	Other..	3,491	(1%)	
2004 primary	Ralph Hall (R)	22,484	(77%)	
	Mike Murphy (R)	3,524	(12%)	
	Mike Mosher (R).................................	3,122	(11%)	
2002 general	Ralph Hall (D)	97,304	(58%)	($635,633)
	John Graves (R)	67,939	(40%)	($160,820)
	Other..	3,042	(2%)	

Prior Winning Percentages: 2000 (60%); 1998 (58%); 1996 (64%); 1994 (59%); 1992 (58%); 1990 (100%); 1988 (66%); 1986 (72%); 1984 (58%); 1982 (74%); 1980 (52%)

The People		Race/Ethnic Origin	Ancestry	
Area size:	9,839 sq. mi.	79.2% White	USA: 12.7%	Irish: 8.3%
Urban population:	49.6%	10.4% Black	German: 7.5%	
Rural population:	50.4%	0.6% Asian	**2004 Presidential Vote**	
Pop. 2000:	651,619	0.7% Native Am.	Bush (R) 192,926	(70%)
Median income:	$38,276	0.0% Hawaiian	Kerry (D) 81,269	(30%)
Poverty status:	12.8%	1.1% Two+ races	**2000 Presidential Vote**	
Military veterans:	14.4%	0.0% Other	Bush (R) 146,416	(66%)
		7.9% Hispanic Origin	Gore (D) 74,476	(34%)
			Cook Partisan Voting Index: R +17	

Occupation   Blue collar: 28.3%   White collar: 56.4%   Gray collar: 15.3%

The Red River Valley is just one of the hearts of Texas. This is hardscrabble farm country along an unnavigable river. First settled in the 1830s, in the days of the Texas Republic, many counties here reached their population peak around 1900, when a large extended farm family worked every 160 acres. It included towns like Denison, which was the birthplace of Dwight Eisenhower, and Sherman, which was the site of a major race riot in 1930 when a black farm worker accused of rape was trapped in the courthouse after an angry white mob set it on fire. To the east is Texarkana, noteworthy because its neat grid streets cross the Texas-Arkansas state line, which is straddled by the downtown post office; this small city and its hinterland produced two presidential candidates in the 1990s: Ross Perot grew up in Texarkana, Texas, while Bill Clinton's boyhood home of Hope, Arkansas, is only 30 miles east. This was the part of Texas that sent Sam Rayburn to Congress in 1912; he served as speaker from 1940 until his death in 1961, except for two terms when Republicans had the majority. The Red River Valley then was one of the strongest Democratic parts of the country, with a sentimental regard for Confederate veterans and a seething hatred of Wall Street bankers. This was Rayburn's politics, and he arguably was the most skillful lawmaker of the 20th century: He helped write the securities laws that have for 70 years provided the basis for confidence in American securities markets and other regulatory measures that have fared less well. Today Rayburn's politics has almost completely vanished from the area. The cause of the Confederacy has been left behind, populist suspicion of Wall Street has been replaced by active brokerage accounts and allegiance to the Democratic Party is a thing of the distant past.

The 4th Congressional District of Texas is the lineal descendant of the seat that Rayburn held, and still includes his hometown of Bonham in Fannin County, which houses a Rayburn museum. But it is quite a different district. In Rayburn's time it was a farm district, separate and distinct from citified Dallas. Today it still has its farm counties, but they are only a short Interstate ride away from the Dallas-Fort Worth Metroplex, and nearly half the district's people live in the Metroplex itself. The counties at the edge of the Metroplex, Collin (only part of which is in the district) and Rockwall, are among the fastest-growing in the country. They are home now to upwardly mobile families, far more trusting of free markets than of government regulation, and more than 2–1 Republican. In 1940, when Rayburn first became speaker, his district voted 90% for Franklin D. Roosevelt. In 2004, the 4th District voted 70% for George W. Bush.

The congressman from the 4th District is Ralph Hall, who was first elected in 1980, currently the oldest member of the House. Hall grew up in Rockwall County and had a 30-year career in local politics and business; he was a county judge as long ago as 1950 and from 1962 to 1972 served in the Texas Senate. In 1980 he was elected to the House as a Democrat. His evolution to the Republican Party was a long time in gestation. He supported just about everything in the Contract with America in 1995 and was one of five House Democrats who voted to impeach Bill Clinton. He voted with Bush on key tax, trade and foreign policy votes. During the 2002 campaign he promised to vote for Republican Speaker Dennis Hastert if his vote decided which party would control the House. In January 2003 he voted "present" rather than vote for Nancy Pelosi, because "she just don't think like we do." But Hall is not a pure free marketeer: He voted against NAFTA. On the Energy and Commerce Committee, he backed limits on the FCC's authority to regulate religious broadcasters but was skeptical about allowing the regional Bells into long distance and favored cable reregulation.

Republicans restlessly waited for years for Hall to join them. When he failed to switch after the 2001 redistricting, local and national Republicans expressed interest in a serious challenge to Hall; Tyler Mayor Kevin Eltife made plans to run. But they backed off after Hall met with Bush at the White House and said that the president strongly opposed a challenge. In March 2003, Hall was the only Democrat to vote for the Republican budget, which barely passed. Bush called to thank him. "I didn't want him to have a setback in Washington, D.C., when he's working his heart out two oceans away to win a war," Hall said. The 2003 redistricting finally convinced Hall that it was time to switch. With Republican candidates lined up to run against him, he switched parties on January 2, 2004 the final day for filing because, he said, his Democratic affiliation was limiting his ability to get appropriations for his district. And so he moved from being the most conservative Democrat in the House to a relatively centrist Republican who seemed more comfortable with his new team and being part of the majority. When he joined their side, Republicans rewarded him with the chairmanship of the Energy and Air Quality Subcommittee, an attractive perk for a Texan, where he joined the push to enact an energy bill.

Party-switching played well at home. With support from Bush and Speaker Dennis Hastert, he won 77% against two opponents in the Republican primary; in the general, he won 68%–30%, his largest margin in more than a decade. The landslide win apparently left him in good spirits for in 2005 Hall held a debt retirement fundraiser for his Democratic opponent Jim Nickerson, who ran a "clean race" against him. The *Dallas Morning News* was less forgiving: the newspaper urged Hall to retire in 2006. If he does, it would be no surprise if his son, Rockwall County District Judge Brett Hall, a Republican, runs for this seat.

FIFTH DISTRICT

Rep. Jeb Hensarling (R)

Elected 2002, 2d term; b. May 29, 1957, Stephenville; home, Dallas; TX A&M U., B.A. 1979, U. of TX, J.D. 1982; Christian; married (Melissa).

Professional Career: Practicing atty., 1982–84; TX Dir., U.S. Sen. Phil Gramm, 1985–89; Exec. Dir., NRSC, 1991–93; Communications Exec., 1993–02.

DC Office: 132 CHOB, 20515, 202-225-3484; Fax: 202-226-4888; Web site: www.house.gov/hensarling/.

District Offices: Athens, 903-675-8288; Dallas, 214-349-9966.

Committees: *Budget* (12th of 22 R). *Financial Services* (25th of 37 R): Capital Markets, Insurance & Government Sponsored Enterprises; Financial Institutions & Consumer Credit.

Group Ratings

	ADA	ACLU	AFS	LCV	ITIC	NTU	COC	ACU	NTLC	CHC
2004	0	0	0	0	100	83	95	100	95	91
2003	5	—	0	5	—	73	90	92	—	—

National Journal Ratings

	2003 LIB	—	2003 CONS		2004 LIB	—	2004 CONS
Economic	9%	—	84%		0%	—	95%
Social	29%	—	71%		28%	—	70%
Foreign	0%	—	89%		0%	—	96%

Key Votes of the 108th Congress

1. Drilling in ANWR	Y	5. DC School Vouchers	Y	9. Ban Same-Sex Marriage	Y
2. Approve Bush Tax Cuts	Y	6. Ban Human Cloning	Y	10. Fund Iraq War	Y
3. Medicare/Rx Bill	Y	7. Restrict Gun Liability	Y	11. Bar Cuba Embargo Funds	*
4. Bar Overtime Pay Regs.	N	8. Ban Partial-Birth Abortion	Y	12. Intelligence Reorg.	Y

Election Results

2004 general	Jeb Hensarling (R)	148,816	(64%)	($1,043,478)
	Bill Bernstein (D)	75,911	(33%)	($18,538)
	Other	6,118	(3%)	
2004 primary	Jeb Hensarling (R)	unopposed		
2002 general	Jeb Hensarling (R)	81,439	(58%)	($2,040,082)
	Ron Chapman (D)	56,330	(40%)	($914,592)
	Other	2,139	(2%)	

The People		Race/Ethnic Origin	Ancestry	
Area size:	5,609 sq. mi.	71.5% White	USA: 11.3%	Irish: 7.7%
Urban population:	67.7%	12.4% Black	German: 7.6%	
Rural population:	32.3%	1.5% Asian	**2004 Presidential Vote**	
Pop. 2000:	651,619	0.4% Native Am.	Bush (R) 160,240	(67%)
Median income:	$41,007	0.0% Hawaiian	Kerry (D) 77,952	(33%)
Poverty status:	11.0%	1.2% Two+ races	**2000 Presidential Vote**	
Military veterans:	13.2%	0.1% Other	Bush (R) 137,553	(66%)
		12.9% Hispanic Origin	Gore (D) 69,894	(34%)
			Cook Partisan Voting Index: R +16	

Occupation	Blue collar: 26.0%	White collar: 59.6%	Gray collar: 14.4%

Not all of Dallas is glitz and postmodern marble. East of downtown on one of the three street grids that run skew to each other is an older Dallas, with neighborhoods of high-ceilinged old mansions, modest bungalows and shotgun houses running out toward the old airport at Love Field or the State Fair Grounds and the Cotton Bowl in east Dallas. Some of this older Dallas is being renovated and rebuilt, with chic cafes and trendy stores serving those who make their livings catering to the rich farther north. Other once middle-class neighborhoods are filling up with immigrants from Mexico and other parts of Latin America, once again noisy with children as they were in the 1950s when people moved here not from Mexico or Central America but from the almost all-Anglo counties of north and central Texas. The 2000 Census showed that 30% of the population in Dallas County is Hispanic.

The 5th Congressional District includes much of east and southeast Dallas County, including many such neighborhoods in Dallas and suburban Mesquite, with more than 2,000 local businesses and a weekly rodeo from April until September. It also covers a more upscale slice of Dallas inside the Freeway, including parts of Lakewood and White Rock Lake. Nearly half of the population is in Dallas County. The 5th District also contains six counties in East Texas, the largest of which are Henderson and Kaufman, where Oscar-award winner Jamie Foxx grew up in Terrell. As rural areas have swung away from the Democrats, the district switched from being a battleground in the early 1990s to safely Republican. In 2004, George W. Bush won 67% of the vote here.

The congressman from the 5th District is Jeb Hensarling, a Republican first elected in 2002. After the 2003 redistricting, Pete Sessions, who had represented the 5th District for the previous six years, decided to run in the new and more compact 32d District on the north side of Dallas, even though the new 5th included 74% of his old district while the 32d included only 16%. Hensarling grew up in Morris County in East Texas and Lubbock County in West Texas. He worked on his father's poultry farm near College Station as a teenager and decided that he did not want to be a farmer. In high school, he started a Republican club and began organizing political events. He graduated from Texas A&M and the University of Texas law school and practiced law for two years in San Antonio. Then he got a job on the staff of Senator Phil Gramm. He managed Gramm's 1990 campaign and was executive director of the National Republican Senatorial Committee when Gramm was chairman. He returned to Texas to become vice president of communications for Green Mountain Energy, a local utility, and he was co-founder of Family Support Assurance, a firm that has tried to modernize child support collections.

After Sessions announced he would not run again in the 5th District, Hensarling announced and became the frontrunner for the Republican nomination. Like his mentor, he listed cutting taxes as his top priority. Against four opponents, he won the nomination with 54% of the vote in the 2002 primary. Democrats nominated Ron Chapman, a former Dallas County appellate judge who had been on the Dallas County ballot since 1978 and shared the name of a popular Dallas radio disc jockey. Actively backed by Texas Democratic delegation leader Martin Frost, Chapman described himself as a loyal Democrat who could work with Republicans. By fall, Hensarling referred to his opponent as "Judge Softie" for twice allowing a man charged with attempted murder to go free from his courtroom. The folksy Chapman emphasized his public service, fiscal conservatism and deep local roots. He tried to paint Hensarling as too extreme for the district, but his message failed to take hold as a parade of Republican luminaries paraded into the district on his behalf, including George W. Bush, Dick Cheney, Bush adviser Karen Hughes and, of course, Phil Gramm. Perhaps the most significant endorsement came when Ron Chapman the disc jockey backed Hensarling at a press conference and sought to make clear that he was not the Democrat running for Congress. Hensarling won 58%–40%.

In the House, Hensarling had a solidly conservative voting record. He styled himself as a fiscal conservative in the mold of Gramm and was not afraid to push Republican leaders to take more conservative positions, though he usually voted with them in the end when they didn't. With fellow freshmen Republicans Mario Diaz-Balart and Tom Feeney of Florida, he created "Washington Waste Watchers" to root out waste, fraud and abuse in the federal bureaucracy. On the Republican Study Committee, he took the lead in working with other conservatives on budget legislation designed to increase spending discipline; his efforts did not endear him to Republican appropriators. In the majority, his challenge was to influence Republican policy and strategy without abandoning his own beliefs or stirring the pot too much. That dilemma was apparent when he struggled over whether to support the Medicare/prescription drug bill, which many conservatives criticized for creating a costly and complicated new government entitlement but which was strongly supported by Bush and DeLay. Even though he claimed credit for a cost-containment provision of limited impact, he waited until the final hours before deciding to vote for the bill. If this bill failed, he concluded, a more expensive one might be passed. In 2005 he continued to push for spending discipline in the congressional budget process, while balancing his interest in being a team player.

SIXTH DISTRICT

Rep. Joe Barton (R)

Elected 1984, 11th term; b. Sept. 15, 1949, Waco; home, Ennis; Texas A&M U., B.S. 1972, Purdue U., M.S. 1973; United Methodist; married (Terri).

Professional Career: Asst. to V.P., Ennis Business Forms, 1973–81; White House Fellow, U.S. Dept. of Energy, 1981–82; Consultant, Atlantic Richfield Co., 1982–84.

DC Office: 2109 RHOB, 20515, 202-225-2002; Fax: 202-225-3052; Web site: joebarton.house.gov.

District Offices: Arlington, 817-543-1000; Ennis, 817-543-1000.

Committees: *Energy & Commerce* (Chmn. of 31 R).

Group Ratings

	ADA	ACLU	AFS	LCV	ITIC	NTU	COC	ACU	NTLC	CHC
2004	0	0	0	0	90	69	100	96	94	91
2003	5	—	0	0	—	67	97	92	—	—

National Journal Ratings

	2003 LIB	—	2003 CONS		2004 LIB	—	2004 CONS
Economic	21%	—	75%		15%	—	84%
Social	14%	—	85%		31%	—	67%
Foreign	0%	—	89%		15%	—	84%

Key Votes of the 108th Congress

1. Drilling in ANWR	Y	5. DC School Vouchers	Y	9. Ban Same-Sex Marriage	Y
2. Approve Bush Tax Cuts	Y	6. Ban Human Cloning	*	10. Fund Iraq War	Y
3. Medicare/Rx Bill	Y	7. Restrict Gun Liability	Y	11. Bar Cuba Embargo Funds	N
4. Bar Overtime Pay Regs.	N	8. Ban Partial-Birth Abortion	Y	12. Intelligence Reorg.	Y

Election Results

2004 general	Joe Barton (R)	168,767	(66%)	($1,883,891)
	Morris Meyer (D)	83,609	(33%)	($101,080)
	Other	3,251	(1%)	
2004 primary	Joe Barton (R)	unopposed		
2002 general	Joe Barton (R)	115,396	(70%)	($1,324,767)
	Felix Alvarado (D)	45,404	(28%)	($13,367)
	Other	3,237	(2%)	

Prior Winning Percentages: 2000 (88%); 1998 (73%); 1996 (77%); 1994 (76%); 1992 (72%); 1990 (66%); 1988 (68%); 1986 (56%); 1984 (57%)

The People		Race/Ethnic Origin	Ancestry	
Area size:	6,336 sq. mi.	65.8% White	German: 8.7%	USA: 8.6%
Urban population:	80.0%	12.8% Black	Irish: 7.3%	
Rural population:	20.0%	3.4% Asian	**2004 Presidential Vote**	
Pop. 2000:	651,619	0.4% Native Am.	Bush (R) 173,476	(66%)
Median income:	$45,857	0.1% Hawaiian	Kerry (D) 87,454	(34%)
Poverty status:	10.4%	1.5% Two+ races	**2000 Presidential Vote**	
Military veterans:	12.4%	0.1% Other	Bush (R) 140,140	(66%)
		15.9% Hispanic Origin	Gore (D) 71,283	(34%)
			Cook Partisan Voting Index: R +15	

Occupation	Blue collar: 24.1%	White collar: 62.4%	Gray collar: 13.5%

The Dallas-Fort Worth Metroplex—yes, the name is part of everyday speech there—has spread outward from its historic nodes in downtown Dallas and Fort Worth. Although Dallas is the larger population center, much of the development has moved west, across the dusty plains where one crosses the barely perceptible Balcones Escarpment, the geologist's boundary between green and grassy East Texas and the brown and barren West. This was empty territory a few decades ago; now it has mostly been filled in, with subdivisions and shopping centers that leave some feeling of the shape of this land under the enormous Texas sky. The biggest city here is Arlington, once seemingly all suburban, with all-American attractions like Six Flags over Texas, Wet 'n' Wild and the Ballpark in Arlington, commissioned by the former part owner of the Texas Rangers, George W. Bush. But this is not just white bread suburbia any more. Arlington's population in 2000 was 18% Hispanic, 14% black and 6% Asian; just a couple miles south of Six Flags is a mixed Latino-Vietnamese area with Mexican restaurants and Asian delis, and the Arlington police gives extra pay to officers who can speak Spanish or Vietnamese. Arlington today is mostly grown; the big growth now comes south of Fort Worth and Arlington, in Crowley and Mansfield, where the Big League Dreams sports complex is about to be joined by a residential/retail town center. Growth has been so robust that Tarrant County, the third largest county in Texas, was in 2004 the 18th largest county in the country, just ahead of New York County, New York (Manhattan), and just behind Clark County, Nevada (Las Vegas).

The 6th Congressional District of Texas includes all of Arlington and the southern fringe of Fort Worth to the west. Two-thirds of its people live in Arlington and Tarrant County. The largest number of the rest are in Ellis County, directly south of Dallas County, which also has been growing rapidly. The district also includes all or part of six counties running to the southeast, most of the way to Houston. Politically, this territory was ancestrally Democratic for many years; all of it voted for John F. Kennedy over Richard Nixon in 1960. But those days are gone. In 2004, the 6th District voted 66% for George W. Bush.

The congressman from the 6th District is Joe Barton, a Republican first elected in 1984. Barton grew up in Ennis, in then rural Ellis County just south of Dallas. He graduated from Texas A&M and Purdue, worked as an oil company engineer and was a White House Fellow. When Phil Gramm ran for the Senate in 1984, Barton ran for his 6th District House seat, and won the Republican runoff by only 10 votes and the general with 57% of the vote. At first, Barton had two great causes, one defunct, the other successful—in a way. The first was the superconductor Supercollider, an enormous scientific laboratory that was to have been built in Waxahachie, in Ellis County. In retrospect this was a Texas project, alive only so long as George H.W. Bush was president; despite Barton's efforts, the House voted 282–143 to zero it out in 1993. His other cause has been sponsorship of a constitutional amendment requiring a two-thirds vote to raise taxes. When the House took up the issue in early 1995, leadership whispered there was no way the tax limitation measure could win the needed 290 votes. In fact it got 253. Barton claimed progress across the country, where many states have approved tax-limitation plans. But the budget surpluses starting in 1998 changed the conversation, and the amendment has been mostly forgotten.

In 1995 Barton became chairman of the Energy and Commerce Oversight and Investigation Subcommittee and conducted extensive hearings on food and drug laws. These resulted in enactment, with bipartisan support, of significant FDA modernization, encouraging the agency to more quickly review innovative drugs and medical devices. In 1999 Barton became chairman of the Energy and Power Subcommittee. Barton's subcommittee had jurisdiction over part of the Bush energy plan, which Barton generally supported. He surprised some by supporting higher fuel economy standards and reaching agreement with Michigan Democrat John Dingell on the issue. His bill, passed in subcommittee in July 2001, required a cut of 5 billion gallons in light truck gas consumption by 2010.

All the while Barton pressed for action on electricity regulation. In December 2001, despite the implosion of Enron, heretofore the nation's largest electricity trader, he was pressing for subcommittee action and seeking agreement with Democrat Rick Boucher, though their positions continued to differ. In February 2002 the subcommittee held markup hearings but Barton suspended them, at Tauzin's request, to assess the Enron collapse more fully. In July, he circulated another draft, which differed considerably from the version that passed the Senate. Barton retreated from requiring utilities to join regional transmission organizations and sought to encourage them to do so, to produce an easy basis for exchanges of traded electricity. His version repealed the 1930s Public Utility Holding Company Act and repealed also the 1978

Public Utility Regulatory Policies Act except to the extent it was maintained in the Senate bill. Interestingly, this was an issue on which a Republican like Barton was trying to increase federal regulatory power while Democrats like John Dingell and Henry Waxman were trying to maintain state primacy. In September Tauzin took the issue before the full committee and, amid an onslaught of Democratic amendments, pushed it through. Later in September a House-Senate conference committee took it up but it went no farther. Tauzin reintroduced the bill in the 108th Congress; it passed the House again in April 2003.

In February 2004 Tauzin announced he would retire from Congress, and Barton was selected to succeed him as Energy and Commerce chairman. He said he wanted to focus on investigations, as John Dingell had when he was chairman from 1981 to 1995. He appointed Texan Ralph Hall, who had just switched to the Republican party, to his old subcommittee chairmanship. He aroused partisan feelings sometimes, as when in September 2004 he blocked committee Democrats' demand for information on Dick Cheney's 2001 energy task force. But he also worked successfully to win Democratic votes in some issues and to defend and expand the committee's jurisdiction. Not all his efforts were successful. In November 2004 he said he would no longer grant committee members waivers to serve on other committees; several, including some who had seats on Financial Services to follow their issues when the committee jurisdictions were altered in 2001, protested, and Barton said he would issue waivers on a case-by-case basis. He sought a waiver himself to serve as chairman of the Oversight and Investigations Subcommittee, as Dingell had; it was not granted. He got Michael Bilirakis, who had announced he would retire in 2006, removed as chairman of the Health Subcommittee, but did not get his initial choices on some other subcommittees. He said he wanted to bump Heather Wilson off the committee after she voted with Democrats to seek internal administration cost estimates of the Medicare prescription drug bill; she is still on.

Conflicts with other committees are inevitable on Energy and Commerce. Barton clashed with Judiciary Chairman James Sensenbrenner on database privacy; Barton pushed a bill seeking consumers' access to information, while Sensenbrenner backed one allowing less access backed by content providers. Barton supported a bill to amend the Digital Millennium Copyright Act to allow individuals to make backup copies of copyrighted material; Judiciary was opposed. Barton held a hearing in May 2004 on Medicare physician payments after Ways and Means Chairman Bill Thomas publicly urged the Bush administration to revise them. Barton got Energy and Commerce to approve 45–5 a computer spyware bill that cracked down on these programs; Bob Goodlatte and Judiciary backed a more cautious approach. Barton sought to maintain the committee's jurisdiction over cybersecurity and prevailed in a closed Republican caucus which backed him 65–59 over Homeland Security Chairman Christopher Cox.

Telecommunications issues are a major responsibility of Energy and Commerce. After CBS's Dan Rather broadcast charges against George W. Bush based on phony documents, Barton said he might call a hearing on the subject after the election, but rejected any pre-election hearing; in the end no hearing was held. In October 2004 Barton and Chip Pickering asked the FCC to assert jurisdiction over VoIP Internet phoning. After Janet Jackson's "wardrobe malfunction" during the 2004 Super Bowl broadcast, the committee voted to increase the fines on broadcast indecency. In October 2004 Barton tried to put the bill raising the maximum fine for one incident from $32,500 to $500,000 in the defense authorization. That failed, but the House passed the bill in February 2005; in March Barton said he supported similar restrictions on satellite and cable service. In early 2005 there was pressure to pass a revision of the 1996 telecommunications act. But in February Barton called for a stand-alone bill to require broadcasters to return the analog spectrum to the government by the end of 2006; current law allows them to delay until 85% of households have digital TV. Much of the focus of any telecom changes will be on the universal service fund, dearly beloved by Senate Commerce Chairman Ted Stevens; Barton seemed to be setting out a marker when he said, "We could just repeal it. That's one way to deal with it. Do we have a universal service fund for newspapers? . . . No, because the market can allocate that."

On the energy bill, Barton insisted on retaining provisions barring liability of the manufacturers of MTBE, the fuel additive which federal regulations encouraged oil companies to put in gasoline; that provision prevented passage in the Senate in 2003 and 2004. In April 2004 he said he was open to exempting the Defense Department from the Clean Air Act, RCRA and the Superfund; but he opposed it in September and had a turf fight with Armed Services's Joel Hefley on the subject. In December 2004 he seemed to despair of a comprehensive energy bill. "I would just as soon split the bill up, move what you can move, do it by bits and pieces, and if we can get good things passed that way, I'm all for it." But the Bush administration and Senate Energy Chairman Pete Domenici kept pressing. Barton still seemed wary of provisions that might kill the bill in the Senate. He called for keeping oil drilling in the Arctic National Wildlife Refuge out of the bill and in February 2005 considered capping spending on coastal restoration, electricity reliability, ultradeep drilling research and energy-savings performance contracts to $500 million over 10 years. In April 2005, a bill with most of these was voted in committee 39–16 and passed on the floor 249–183, in both cases with many Democratic votes.

Energy and Commerce is a great platform for generating contributions, and Barton has raised much more money than he is ever likely to need to spend in his district. In June 2004 he hosted a fundraiser for Billy Tauzin III, who was running for his father's seat, as Tauzin had hosted a fundraiser for Barton's son when he ran for Congress (both sons lost). When Texas Democrat Chris Bell charged that Tom DeLay put a provision favoring Westar into the energy bill in 2002 in return for a political contribution, Barton said that he had put the provision in some time before. At home he was criticized by Democrats for seeking in 2003 and 2004 to keep Ellis County outside EPA's Dallas region for purposes of the Clean Air Act; Ellis County is home to three cement producers and other companies whose PACs or executives contributed to Barton's campaigns, and the county produces 40% of the industrial emissions in North Texas. Barton said there was no connection between the contributions and his action and argued that there was no scientific basis for Ellis County's inclusion. But in April 2004, the EPA decided otherwise, and that Ellis County must work to reduce air pollution.

Barton has also had some political disappointments. He ran for the Senate in 1993 after Lloyd Bentsen resigned to be Treasury secretary but finished third with just 14% of the vote in the May all-party primary. In September 2001, when Phil Gramm announced his retirement from the Senate, Barton considered running for his seat. But in early October, busy with electricity and energy legislation and amid talk that the Bush White House favored Attorney General John Cornyn, he announced he would not run. He has been reelected easily in the 6th District.

SEVENTH DISTRICT

Rep. John Culberson (R)

Elected 2000, 3d term; b. Aug. 24, 1956, Houston; home, Houston; Southern Methodist U., B.A. 1981, S. TX Col. of Law, J.D. 1988; Methodist; married (Belinda).

Elected Office: TX House of Reps., 1986–2000, Maj. Whip, 1999–2000.

Professional Career: Jim Culberson Advertising, 1981–85; Practicing atty., 1988–2000.

DC Office: 1728 LHOB, 20515, 202-225-2571; Fax: 202-225-4381; Web site: www.culberson.house.gov.

District Office: Houston, 713-682-8828.

Committees: *Appropriations* (32d of 37 R): Science, State, Justice, Commerce & Related Agencies; Transportation, Treasury, HUD, the Judiciary & District of Columbia.

Group Ratings

	ADA	ACLU	AFS	LCV	ITIC	NTU	COC	ACU	NTLC	CHC
2004	0	0	17	9	90	59	100	96	81	92
2003	15	—	13	5	—	69	93	100	—	—

National Journal Ratings

	2003 LIB	—	2003 CONS	2004 LIB	—	2004 CONS
Economic	41%	—	57%	9%	—	91%
Social	30%	—	65%	0%	—	91%
Foreign	0%	—	89%	0%	—	96%

Key Votes of the 108th Congress

1. Drilling in ANWR	Y	5. DC School Vouchers	Y	9. Ban Same-Sex Marriage	Y
2. Approve Bush Tax Cuts	Y	6. Ban Human Cloning	Y	10. Fund Iraq War	Y
3. Medicare/Rx Bill	N	7. Restrict Gun Liability	Y	11. Bar Cuba Embargo Funds	N
4. Bar Overtime Pay Regs.	N	8. Ban Partial-Birth Abortion	Y	12. Intelligence Reorg.	Y

Election Results

2004 general	John Culberson (R)	175,440	(64%)	($617,860)
	John Martinez (D)	91,126	(33%)	($26,993)
	Other	7,085	(3%)	
2004 primary	John Culberson (R)	26,561	(92%)	
	Sam Texas (R)	2,245	(8%)	
2002 general	John Culberson (R)	96,795	(89%)	($472,911)
	Drew Parks (Lib)	11,674	(11%)	

Prior Winning Percentages: 2000 (74%)

The People		Race/Ethnic Origin	Ancestry	
Area size:	198 sq. mi.	67.5% White	German: 11.3%	English: 9.3%
Urban population:	99.7%	5.6% Black	Irish: 7.4%	
Rural population:	0.3%	6.9% Asian	**2004 Presidential Vote**	
Pop. 2000:	651,620	0.2% Native Am.	Bush (R) 179,456	(64%)
Median income:	$57,846	0.0% Hawaiian	Kerry (D) 99,422	(36%)
Poverty status:	7.4%	1.6% Two+ races	**2000 Presidential Vote**	
Military veterans:	9.9%	0.2% Other	Bush (R) 172,336	(69%)
		18.0% Hispanic Origin	Gore (D) 76,046	(31%)
			Cook Partisan Voting Index: R +16	

Occupation   Blue collar: 11.2%   White collar: 79.4%   Gray collar: 9.3%

When George H. W. Bush moved from Midland in West Texas to Houston in 1960, he bought a house in Briarwood, in what was then the western edge of the fast-growing city, beyond Memorial Park and Loop 610, before the Galleria and high-rises went up around the intersection of Post Oak and Westheimer. Bush returned to Houston in 1993 and built a new house a mile from his old one, just west of lush Memorial Park. Bush's favorite shopping mall is nearby on Sage and San Felipe and his favorite barbecue joint a mile east on Memorial; his office is atop the Park Laureate building at 10000 Memorial. Today these landmarks are no longer at the edge of the vastly bigger and economically vibrant Houston metropolitan area, but near its epicenter, certainly its retail center and not far from its commercial center, though the industrial center of gravity remains far to the east, near the Ship Channel. Downtown has survived the Enron collapse and is sprouting residential apartments. Near the lavish Galleria, business leaders have made this area more than a shopping center. With extensive landscaping and art, they have sought to give it a unique and inviting image, and they have made improvements on the 610 to increase mobility for commuters and shoppers.

The 7th Congressional District of Texas is the lineal descendant of the district that elected George H.W. Bush as its first member of the House in 1966 and the first Republican to represent Houston. It occupied far more territory then, half of Harris County. In successive redistrictings, its boundaries have been pared back and new districts created out of the old, as the population of the west side of Houston has skyrocketed. Today more than 1.5 million people live in the area where 350,000 lived when Bush was first elected. The 7th District today touches the western edge of downtown Houston and includes most of the land between the Katy Freeway and Westheimer running straight west to Highway 1960. To the south it includes the affluent neighborhoods southwest of downtown Houston, Rice University and the Texas Medical Center, Belleaire and a swatch of Houston southwest of 610. It extends north to include much territory along the Sam Houston Freeway and Highway 1960 to the radial Route 249. Within its boundaries live most of Houston's business and professional elite, the partners of the big law firms and the people you read about on the society page. Back in the 1980s the 7th District was one of the most Republican districts in the country, sometimes the most Republican, and it still is heavily Republican. But like many precincts of the very elite, from Greenwich, Connecticut, to Bloomfield Hills, Michigan, and Hillsborough, California, it—or at least a significant minority of longtime Republicans living here—has not taken a liking to George W. Bush's brand of Republicanism. Within these boundaries he won 69% of the vote in 2000 but dropped to 64% in 2004, a lower percentage than he won in 14 other Texas districts. The younger Bush now runs much stronger in the modest-income counties of West Texas than he does in the high-income precincts of Houston where his parents live and where he spent some of what he admits now were his misspent years.

The congressman from the 7th District is John Culberson, a Republican first elected in 2000 and only the second man to hold the seat after the senior Bush. Culberson grew up in Houston and graduated from Southern Methodist University, then worked for his father's advertising agency. He graduated from South Texas College of Law and worked as a civil defense attorney. In 1986, at 29, Culberson won a seat in the Texas House, where he served for 14 years. In 2000 Bill Archer, Bush's successor in the House, retired after serving six years as chairman of the Ways and Means Committee. Naturally there was a seriously contested primary in this safe Republican seat. The frontrunners were Culberson and Peter Wareing, a Houston merchant banker and son-in-law of Texas oilman Jack Blanton. Culberson led Wareing in the first round 38%–27%. Wareing spent nearly $4 million to Culberson's $650,000. But Culberson had an extensive grassroots campaign and won the runoff four weeks later 60%–40%. The general election was no contest.

Culberson calls himself a "Jeffersonian Republican" and is passionate about transferring power from the federal to local governments; he has had a firmly conservative voting record. He opposes racial quotas and preferences, gun control, and abortion (except in cases of rape, incest, or to save the life of the mother). In the Archer tradition, he says his goal is to junk the current tax system and replace it with a national sales tax. On the Transportation and Infrastructure Committee in his first term he proposed a "trusted traveler" card for those who pass background checks to assist frequent flyers to avoid standard airport screening. He battled with Houston officials who wanted to increase spending for light rail, and insisted on expanded highway capacity, including the Katy Freeway, as part of the plan to relieve gridlock. "We shouldn't shoehorn people into a transportation design based on what Washington think tanks believe." In November 2003, he complained that the transit authority had not adequately described its spending plans and opposed the ballot referendum in Houston to authorize $640 million in revenue bonds for 22 additional miles of light rail transit; the proposal passed narrowly.

In the House, Culberson has often gone his own way. He ruffled feathers as one of only two Texas Republicans to oppose the 2003 Medicare/prescription drug bill. Also in the face of White House opposition, he passed an appropriations rider to prohibit funding of a regulation to permit banks to accept Mexican *matricula consular* documents as identification; in September 2004, the House defeated his proposal, 222–177. He was outraged when immigration officials in Houston promised a group of Latinos that their agents would not perform random workplace raids. "If they expected to get funded, they must enforce the immigration laws." Though the district lines have changed twice since he was first elected, he did not face serious competition in either 2002 or 2004.

EIGHTH DISTRICT

Rep. Kevin Brady (R)

Elected 1996, 5th term; b. Apr. 11, 1955, Vermillion, SD; home, The Woodlands, TX; U. of SD, B.S. 1990; Catholic; married (Cathy).

Elected Office: TX House of Reps., 1990–96.

Professional Career: Exec., Woodlands Chamber of Commerce, 1978–96.

DC Office: 428 CHOB, 20515, 202-225-4901; Fax: 202-225-5524; Web site: www.house.gov/brady.

District Offices: Conroe, 936-441-5700; Huntsville, 936-439-9542; Orange, 409-883-4197.

Committees: *Ways & Means* (16th of 24 R): Social Security; Trade. *Joint Economic Committee.*

Group Ratings

	ADA	ACLU	AFS	LCV	ITIC	NTU	COC	ACU	NTLC	CHC
2004	0	6	0	0	100	76	100	100	96	92
2003	10	—	0	5	—	64	97	88	—	—

National Journal Ratings

	2003 LIB	—	2003 CONS		2004 LIB	—	2004 CONS
Economic	0%	—	91%		0%	—	95%
Social	22%	—	77%		17%	—	83%
Foreign	23%	—	71%		10%	—	86%

Key Votes of the 108th Congress

1. Drilling in ANWR	Y	5. DC School Vouchers	Y	9. Ban Same-Sex Marriage	Y
2. Approve Bush Tax Cuts	Y	6. Ban Human Cloning	Y	10. Fund Iraq War	Y
3. Medicare/Rx Bill	Y	7. Restrict Gun Liability	Y	11. Bar Cuba Embargo Funds	N
4. Bar Overtime Pay Regs.	N	8. Ban Partial-Birth Abortion	Y	12. Intelligence Reorg.	Y

Election Results

2004 general	Kevin Brady (R)	179,599	(69%)	($670,875)
	James Wright (D)	77,324	(30%)	
	Other	3,705	(1%)	
2004 primary	Kevin Brady (R)	unopposed		
2002 general	Kevin Brady (R)	140,575	(93%)	($222,082)
	Gil Guillory (Lib)	10,351	(7%)	

Prior Winning Percentages: 2000 (92%); 1998 (93%); 1996 (59%)

The People		Race/Ethnic Origin	Ancestry	
Area size:	8,415 sq. mi.	80.1% White	USA: 10.8%	German: 9.1%
Urban population:	49.6%	8.7% Black	Irish: 8.4%	
Rural population:	50.4%	0.7% Asian	**2004 Presidential Vote**	
Pop. 2000:	651,620	0.5% Native Am.	Bush (R) 194,696	(72%)
Median income:	$40,459	0.0% Hawaiian	Kerry (D) 73,946	(28%)
Poverty status:	12.6%	0.9% Two+ races	**2000 Presidential Vote**	
Military veterans:	13.8%	0.1% Other	Bush (R) 155,003	(69%)
		9.0% Hispanic Origin	Gore (D) 68,522	(31%)
			Cook Partisan Voting Index: R +20	

Occupation   Blue collar: 28.7%   White collar: 55.7%   Gray collar: 15.6%

When Houston Intercontinental Airport opened in 1969, it was located 25 miles away from downtown Houston or from just about any other concentration of population, at the northern edge of Harris County and just south of the Montgomery County line. What is known now as George Bush Intercontinental is still a jaunt from downtown Houston. But rapid expansion and growth of commercial office space and upscale residential subdivisions have continued even farther to the north in once rural Montgomery County, rising on land that once held roadside stands and barbecues and unpainted farmhouses with water pooling on low swampy fields. The arrival of railroads in the late 19th century made timber a production a major local industry, but much of the land was stripped by the 1920s and it was turned over to livestock. Fortunes rose again in 1931 when wildcattter George Strake struck oil near Conroe. Thousands of other wildcatters and roughnecks quickly joined in the boom; this became one of the richest oil producing areas in the nation, and active production continues. In 1972, construction began on a planned community called The Woodlands; development of this new city has barely slowed since then. Greater Houston has spread far out into this countryside, past the now mislabeled Farm-Market Route 1960, out past The Woodlands and Conroe. Montgomery County had just 49,000 people in 1970, just after the airport opened. Since then its population has risen to 128,000 in 1980, 182,000 in 1990, 293,000 in 2000 and 362,000 in 2004.

The 8th Congressional District includes all of Montgomery County, which contains about half its people. Before the 2003 redistricting 60% of its population was in Harris County; now none is, and it extends east to the Sabine River on the Louisiana border, including all of eight counties and parts of two others. It covers the Big Thicket National Preserve, a primeval swamp described as "America's Ark" because of its vast array of animals and plants; defenders fear encroachment by residential growth and off-road vehicles. It includes the town of Huntsville, with one of Texas's oldest prisons, and the oil refinery town of Orange on the Sabine River. The redistricting changes have made the district less affluent and metropolitan, and a little less Republican. The old 8th District voted 78% for George W. Bush in 2000, his highest figure in the nation. Within the new 8th District in 2004 he won a comparatively modest 72%.

The congressman from the 8th District is Kevin Brady, a Republican first elected in 1996. Brady grew up and went to college in South Dakota, moved to Montgomery County in 1978 and headed The Woodlands Chamber of Commerce for 18 years. In 1990 he was elected to the Texas House. When Congressman Jack Fields announced in 1995 he was retiring, Brady decided to run. His main opponent in the decisive Republican primary was Eugene Fontenot, a physician who wanted "to restore America to its Christian heritage." Brady was the choice of party regulars; Fontenot was endorsed by religious conservatives. Fontenot attacked Brady for being one of two Republicans to vote against the concealed weapons law. Brady had opposed most gun control bills, but not this one; when he was 12, his father was shot and killed while trying a case in a South Dakota courtroom. Brady and Fontenot ran against each other four separate times in that one year. After Fontenot led Brady in the March primary, Brady won the April runoff 53%–47%. After the U.S. Supreme Court in June ordered a redrawing of 13 districts, Brady led Fontenot 41%–39% in an all-party primary in November. Finally, in the December runoff, turnout was sharply down and party regular Brady won 59%–41%.

In the House, Brady has compiled a conservative voting record, though a bit less so on foreign issues. He gained a reputation as more of a pragmatist than other Texas Republicans. With the murder of his father always a fresh memory, he has been an advocate of victims' rights and the death penalty. In January 2001 he took Bill Archer's seat on Ways and Means; he is an advocate of abolishing the IRS and moving toward a consumption tax. But while waiting until that day arrives, Brady has tinkered successfully with the status quo. He strongly backed the Bush tax cuts and helped to win House passage of a scaled-back version of Bush's plan to give tax breaks for contributions to faith-based groups. He has been leading supporter of the Central America Free Trade Agreement; Texas would benefit, he argues, because it has become the nation's largest export state, with especially rapid growth in trade with Central America. Brady was a central figure in the successful effort in 2004 to make state and local sales taxes deductible in the seven states, including Texas, that have no personal income tax. In addition to his energetic work on Ways and Means, Brady has been a deputy whip to Roy Blunt. He has strongly defended Tom DeLay on ethics charges.

Since his four contests in 1996, Brady has had no problem winning reelection. In his radically redrawn district in 2004, he won 69%–30%.

NINTH DISTRICT

Rep. Al Green (D)

Elected 2004, 1st term; b. Sept. 1, 1947, New Orleans, LA; home, Houston; TX Southern U., J.D. 1973; Baptist; single.

Elected Office: Harris Cnty. justice of the peace, 1977–2004.

Professional Career: Practicing atty., 1973–77; Pres., Houston NAACP, 1986–95.

DC Office: 1529 LHOB, 20515, 202-225-7508; Fax: 202-225-2947; Web site: www.house.gov/algreen.

District Office: Houston, 713-383-9234.

Committees: *Financial Services* (28th of 32 D): Financial Institutions & Consumer Credit; Housing & Community Opportunity. *Science* (18th of 20 D): Energy; Space & Aeronautics.

Group Ratings and Key Votes: Newly Elected

Election Results

2004 general	Al Green (D)	114,462	(72%)	($838,834)
	Arlette Molina (R)	42,132	(27%)	($133,372)
	Other	1,972	(1%)	
2004 primary	Al Green (D)	18,034	(66%)	
	Chris Bell (D)	8,492	(31%)	
	Other	607	(2%)	
2002 general (TX 25)	Chris Bell (D)	63,590	(55%)	($1,107,790)
	Tom Reiser (R)	50,041	(43%)	($4,538,270)
	Other	2,495	(2%)	

The People		Race/Ethnic Origin	Ancestry	
Area size:	154 sq. mi.	17.4% White	SubSaharan: 3.1% German: 3.1%	
Urban population:	99.8%	37.0% Black	USA: 2.5%	
Rural population:	0.2%	10.7% Asian	**2004 Presidential Vote**	
Pop. 2000:	651,619	0.1% Native Am.	Kerry (D)	112,065 (70%)
Median income:	$34,870	0.0% Hawaiian	Bush (R)	48,052 (30%)
Poverty status:	18.4%	1.7% Two+ races	**2000 Presidential Vote**	
Military veterans:	7.1%	0.2% Other	Gore (D)	99,394 (69%)
		32.8% Hispanic Origin	Bush (R)	45,579 (31%)
			Cook Partisan Voting Index: D +21	
Occupation	Blue collar: 22.7%	White collar: 58.0% Gray collar: 19.2%		

Spreading out in all directions from its historic center at Allen's Landing on Buffalo Bayou, Houston has become one of the great metropolises of North America. A half-century ago, the steaming flatlands south of Houston running down to the Gulf of Mexico did not seem a likely site for one of the world's most advanced civilizations. But they are today. It was Houston where most of the scientific work was done that put the first man on the moon—the first word spoken on the moon was "Houston." Houston is the undisputed center of expertise in the oil business, where the greatest concentration of experts in the world is within a few miles of each other. Houston has also become one of the great medical centers of the world, with the giant Texas Medical Center looming as impressively massive as any great office skyscraper complex. And Houston became one of the great surprise growth cities of the 1990s, creating thousands of small businesses, with special growth among immigrants. All this success and sophistication are testimony to human—and Texan—creativity, and to the triumph of air conditioning. For who supposed that all these people would move here if they had to sweat through Houston's steamy five-month summer?

The 9th Congressional District of Texas slices across the southern part of metro Houston on the streets and freeways and waterways spreading out from the center of the city. It occupies much of the territory that was in the 25th District before the 2003 redistricting; it was redrawn to include more blacks and Asians. The new 9th begins just southwest of where I-45 crosses the I-610 Loop; it continues west with a slight intrusion inside 610 at the Reliant Astrodome and then heads past Meadows Place and Mission Bend outside Beltway 8 toward the western end of Harris County. It includes two wedges of Fort Bend County, which form a crescent around Tom DeLay's 22d District. The district includes many heavily black neighborhoods, low-income and middle-income, in Harris and Fort Bend Counties; its population is 37% black, the third highest in any Texas district. It also includes many Asians, who form 11% of the total, the highest percentage in Texas, and one of the highest in any district east of California or west of New York. Along Belleaire Boulevard is a Chinese-American community, with signs in Chinese characters over the stores and banks. In the Alief neighborhood of southwest Houston, Vietnamese boat people settled, created quality schools and an Asian-oriented shopping mall; in 2004, the Vietnamese Democratic challenger from Alief narrowly ousted a long-time Anglo Republican stalwart in the state House. Nearby, a Pakistani Muslim was elected to the Houston city council. And of course there are many Hispanics in the district, 33% of the total population, though many are not citizens or not voters. Although many of the Asians pride themselves on their economic conservatism, overall this is a heavily Democratic district, which voted 70% for John Kerry in 2004. Why did the Republican redistricters create such a district? One reason was to remove Fort Bend County blacks from DeLay's district. Another was to attract black support in the legislature. Only two of Texas's 32 districts were represented by blacks, the 18th in Houston and the 30th in Dallas, both with about 40% black and 30% Hispanic populations under both the old and new plans. But under the old plan, the district with the next highest black percentage, the 25th, was only 23% black—not enough to elect a black congressman in a racially polarized contest. The new 9th could elect a black congressman in such a contest—and did.

The congressman from the 9th District is Al Green, a Democrat first elected in 2004 when he was the surprise winner of a bitter Democratic primary. Green grew up in New Orleans, attended college at Florida A&M and graduated from Texas Southern law school. From 1986 to 1995 he was president of the Houston chapter of the NAACP and in 1977 he was elected justice of the peace and served 27 years. The legislature created the new district boundaries in October 2003, but Democrats challenged them in federal court where they were not approved until January 2004. At that point, Green saw an obvious opening and resigned to run for Congress. The congressman from the old 25th District was Chris Bell, a Democrat first elected in 2002. That year, he ran with liberal support and beat a more conservative black candidate. The race in the March 2004 Democratic primary against Green was a different matter. Green said that he wanted to fight racial profiling and discrimination in law enforcement, frequently used subtle racial references on the campaign trail (including his promise to bring "a mountain of soul" to the new district) and amassed an impressive roster of endorsements from prominent local and national black leaders. Bell responded by asking voters "not to focus on the color of my skin, but on the size of my heart." He spent more than $1 million on the primary, while Green spent less than half as much. Green downplayed partisanship and emphasized his ability to study all sides of an issue. But Bell, who was endorsed by the AFL-CIO, Texas teachers, abortion-rights groups and Minority Leader Nancy Pelosi, struggled as a white candidate running in a district where minorities constituted two-thirds of the electorate and where slightly more than half of the district was new to him in a two-month campaign.

As the primary neared, the racially charged atmosphere intensified. When state Democratic chairman Charles Soechting endorsed Bell, Green said that it reminded him of "the double standards when African-Americans had to ride on the back of the bus and drink from colored-only water fountains." Bell said Green accepted money from a former Republican official who worked against black interests; Green claimed that Bell wrongly informed voters that the NAACP endorsed him. The Congressional Black Caucus was drawn into the campaign after California's Maxine Waters hand-delivered a $5,000 check to Green from the caucus's political action committee; she announced that nearly a dozen CBC members backed Green over Bell. Bell said that Black Caucus Chairman Elijah Cummings had earlier promised to support him. Although the caucus itself never made a formal endorsement, its role in the primary angered other Democratic members, who argued that House members should be supportive of all incumbents, rather than their challengers. In the end, it may not have mattered. Green won the primary in a landslide, 66%–31%. "It's been a divisive race and in some ways a rather ugly race," Bell said in conceding. Other Democratic incumbents expressed anger over the outcome. The general election was a foregone conclusion. After his primary defeat, Bell filed ethics charges against Tom DeLay; some Republicans made the absurd argument that Bell was not entitled to file charges because he was a lame duck, though in all other respects he remained a full member of Congress until January 3, 2005. Bell has said that he is considering running for statewide office in 2006.

In the House Green got a seat on the Financial Services Committee. In an example of how "the enemy of my enemy can be my friend," DeLay developed a personal bond with Green and worked with him on local issues.

TENTH DISTRICT

Rep. Michael McCaul (R)

Elected 2004, 1st term; b. Jan. 14, 1962, Dallas; home, Austin; Trinity U., B.A. 1984, St. Mary's U., J.D. 1987; Catholic; married (Linda).

Professional Career: Fed. prosecutor, 1990–99; Dep. Atty. Gen., 1999–2003; Chief, Western Div. of TX., U.S. Attys. Office, 2003–04.

DC Office: 415 CHOB, 20515, 202-225-2401; Fax: 202-225-5955; Web site: www.house.gov/mccaul.

District Offices: Austin, 512-473-2357; Brenham, 979-830-8497; Katy, 281-398-1247; Tomball, 281-255-8372.

Committees: *Homeland Security* (18th of 19 R): Emergency Preparedness, Science & Technology; Management, Integration & Oversight; Prevention of Nuclear & Biological Attack. *International Relations* (26th of 27 R): International Terrorism & Nonproliferation; Western Hemisphere. *Science* (22d of 24 R): Research; Space & Aeronautics.

Group Ratings and Key Votes: Newly Elected

Election Results

2004 general	Michael McCaul (R)	182,113	(79%)	($2,988,391)
	Robert Fritsche (Lib)	35,569	(15%)	
	Lorenzo Sadun (WI)	13,961	(6%)	($40,613)
2004 runoff	Michael McCaul (R)	15,084	(63%)	
	Ben Streusand (R)	8,803	(37%)	
2004 primary	Ben Streusand (R)	9,364	(28%)	
	Michael McCaul (R)	7,953	(24%)	
	John Devine (R)	7,096	(21%)	
	Dave Phillips (R)	4,460	(13%)	
	Teresa Doggett Taylor (R)	1,494	(4%)	
	Pat Elliott (R)	1,245	(4%)	
	Other	1,647	(5%)	

The People		Race/Ethnic Origin	Ancestry		
Area size:	3,846 sq. mi.	66.5% White	German: 13.9%	English: 7.6%	
Urban population:	80.8%	9.1% Black	Irish: 7.6%		
Rural population:	19.2%	3.9% Asian	**2004 Presidential Vote**		
Pop. 2000:	651,620	0.3% Native Am.	Bush (R)	177,555	(62%)
Median income:	$52,465	0.0% Hawaiian	Kerry (D)	109,287	(38%)
Poverty status:	8.2%	1.3% Two+ races	**2000 Presidential Vote**		
Military veterans:	10.9%	0.1% Other	Bush (R)	152,201	(67%)
		18.7% Hispanic Origin	Gore (D)	76,643	(33%)
			Cook Partisan Voting Index: R +13		

Occupation   Blue collar: 18.6%   White collar: 69.9%   Gray collar: 11.5%

Two of Texas's major cities are named for pioneer leaders of the Texas Republic, Sam Houston and Stephen Austin. They are not entirely attractive characters today: Houston had episodes of alcoholic depression, Austin was a slaveholder who argued that Mexico infringed Texas's liberty when it freed its slaves. But they were also men of courage and determination, with a passion for liberty and a willingness to fight for it, who built a distinctively American culture in what was then the northeast of Mexico. Today the two metropolises named for them have quite different characters. Houston is about commerce, the world capital of the "awl bidness," an entrepreneurial paradise spread out over the swampy, humid plains just north of the Gulf of Mexico. Austin is the creature of government, of the state government headquartered in the grand Capitol and of the University of Texas, with a huge endowment of land in West Texas that turned out to be underlaid with oil. But Austin in recent years has taken on some of Houston's character. North of the Capitol and the University, in land that was vacant when Lyndon Johnson celebrated his 87-vote victory in the 1948 primary in the Driskill Hotel, there has grown up an entrepreneurial Austin, high-tech and free-market, spreading out over the hills and into adjacent Williamson County. The historic Austin is a liberal enclave in the heart of a conservative state; this new Austin is more in lines with the mores and manners of most of Texas. Curiously, there is no superhighway between Austin and Houston. To get from one to the other you travel over roads through rural counties with monuments and plaques recalling the days of the Texas Republic. Only in recent years has metropolitan growth spread to these historic places.

The 10th Congressional District of Texas connects the western edge of Houston with the new northern precincts of Austin through a corridor of still mostly rural counties. It is split into three roughly equal parts. The largest of these is in Austin and Travis County, where the district includes the northern third of Austin, with one tentacle reaching southwest beyond the city limits and another dropping south to Austin State Hospital, where one city block near Guadalupe and 38th Streets is shared by three congressional districts: the 10th, the 21st and the 25th. The second largest is the western edge of Houston's Harris County, "21st century suburban America in its most common and oft-replicated form," sniffed the *Austin American-Statesman*. This is a fast-growing area, with lots of young families, new subdivisions and sparkling megachurches. In between are the six lightly populated rural counties, some of which (Austin and Washington) surprisingly enough have historic Republican voting traditions. Overall this is a very heavily Republican district—62% for George W. Bush in 2004. When Lloyd Doggett, the liberal Democratic congressman from the old Austin-based 10th District, saw the boundaries of the new 10th in the October 2003 redistricting, he decided to run in the Hispanic-majority 25th District which stretches from the Latino west side of Austin to the Rio Grande.

The congressman from the 10th District is Michael McCaul, a Republican first elected in 2004. He grew up in Dallas, studied business and history at Trinity University and went to law school at St. Mary's University, both in San Antonio. He worked as a federal prosecutor then became a deputy attorney general in Austin in 1999. In 2002, he joined the U.S. Attorney's office and was chief of the Terrorism and National Security Section for Western Texas. McCaul was one of eight candidates to run in the Republican primary; no Democrat even bothered to file to run in this district. The top contenders were McCaul, mortgage company owner Ben Streusand and former Judge John Devine. McCaul, who is from Austin and whose father-in-law is Clear Channel Communications CEO Lowry Mays, focused on his anti-terrorism work in the U.S. Attorney's office. "I'm the only candidate that's had a top-secret security clearance," he said. "I won't have a learning curve." Streusand, based in Harris County, called for less government regulation and opposed the Bush administration's immigration proposals. Devine, who had refused to remove a Ten Commandments display from his Harris County courtroom, had the support of Christian conservatives and called for a crackdown on illegal immigration. In the March 9 primary, Streusand carried 7 of the 8 counties to finish with 28% of the vote, to 24% for McCaul and 21% for Devine, who led in Harris County and ran behind everywhere else. McCaul won the runoff spot over Devine by just 857 votes.

The runoff came on April 13. McCaul and Streusand agreed on most issues. Both supported the Bush tax cuts and favored replacing the federal income tax with either a flat tax or a sales tax. In the absence of clear distinctions, the pair traded accusations about each other's background. McCaul criticized Streusand's past donations to Democratic candidates; Streusand, who was supported by Gary Bauer but few in the Republican establishment, questioned why McCaul served in the Clinton administration Justice Department. Streusand spent $3.6 million, nearly all of it his own money. McCaul spent $2.9 million, of which $1.9 million was his own; he ended up with the second-largest campaign debt of all freshman members. But he sounded more thoughtful and had more endorsements, from former President George H.W. Bush, Governor Rick Perry and Senators Kay Bailey Hutchison and John Cornyn. McCaul won 63%–37% in a contest in which only 24,000 votes were cast. He carried every county except one, which he lost by 7 votes of 255 cast; he won 73% of the vote in Travis County and 52% in Harris County, which between them cast 72% of the votes.

With no Democratic opponent in November, McCaul spent the fall helping Republican challengers against Democratic incumbents in other Texas districts. He said that a top priority was the permanent extension of the Bush tax cuts. Freshman Republicans chose him as their liaison to the House leadership. He was assigned to Homeland Security, International Relations, and Science Committees; he had hoped for a seat on Judiciary.

ELEVENTH DISTRICT

Rep. Mike Conaway (R)

Elected 2004, 1st term; b. June 11, 1948, Borger; home, Midland; E. TX St. U., B.B.A. 1970; Baptist; married (Suzanne).

Military Career: Army, 1970–72.

Elected Office: Midland Schl. Bd., 1985–88.

Professional Career: Tax mgr., Price Waterhouse & Co., 1972–80; CFO, Keith G. Grohm & Lantern Petroleum Comp., 1980–81; CFO, Arbusto Energy, Inc./Bush Exploration, 1982–84; CFO, Spectrum 7 Energy Corp., 1984–86; CFO, United Bank, 1987–90; Supt., TX Comm. Bank, 1990–92; TX Bd. of Pub. Accountancy, 1995–2002; Owner, K. Michael Conaway, CPA, 1993–2004.

DC Office: 511 CHOB, 20515, 202-225-3605; Fax: 202-225-1783; Web site: www.conaway.house.gov.

District Offices: Brownwood, 866-882-3811; Llano, 325-247-2826; Midland, 432-687-2390; Odessa, 866-882-3811; San Angelo, 325-659-4010.

Committees: *Agriculture* (23d of 25 R): General Farm Commodities & Risk Management; Livestock & Horticulture. *Armed Services* (33d of 34 R): Military Personnel; Tactical Air & Land Forces. *Budget* (21st of 22 R).

Group Ratings and Key Votes: Newly Elected

Election Results

2004 general	Mike Conaway (R)	177,291	(77%)	($1,573,274)
	Wayne Raasch (D)	50,339	(22%)	
	Other	3,347	(1%)	
2004 primary	Mike Conaway (R)	38,792	(75%)	
	Bill Lester (R)	13,255	(25%)	

The People		Race/Ethnic Origin	Ancestry		
Area size:	35,185 sq. mi.	64.6% White	German: 9.5%		USA: 8.6%
Urban population:	70.8%	4.0% Black	English: 6.9%		
Rural population:	29.2%	0.5% Asian	**2004 Presidential Vote**		
Pop. 2000:	651,620	0.4% Native Am.	Bush (R)	188,929	(78%)
Median income:	$32,711	0.0% Hawaiian	Kerry (D)	52,174	(22%)
Poverty status:	15.8%	0.8% Two+ races	**2000 Presidential Vote**		
Military veterans:	13.5%	0.0% Other	Bush (R)	163,488	(75%)
		29.6% Hispanic Origin	Gore (D)	55,244	(25%)
			Cook Partisan Voting Index: R +25		
Occupation	Blue collar: 26.8%	White collar: 54.8%	Gray collar: 18.4%		

More than 400 years ago, in the 1540s, the conquistador Francisco Coronado and his men rode their horses over the plains of the land they called the Llano Estacado, land that is now the plains of west Texas. What they saw was a vast empty land, gradually and imperceptibly rising in elevation to the west, with only scrub vegetation and small bands of Comanche Indians. What they did not see, lying far beneath the surface, was oil, discovered in the 1940s in large amounts in the Permian Basin. When oil was found, two tiny county seats 25 miles apart suddenly became small cities—Odessa, home of the roughneck oil well workers, and Midland, the more upscale town where oil entrepreneurs lived and started their own Petroleum Club. The Permian Basin boomed in the years just after World War II: in 1940, Ector and Midland Counties had a population of 26,000, in 1950 it was 67,000 and in 1960, 159,000. Since then growth has slowed, as new discoveries have grown fewer and oil prices, after shooting upward in the 1970s, fell; in 2000, Ector and Midland Counties had 237,000 people. It was to the Permian Basin in 1948 that George and Barbara Bush moved, in search of oil wealth and to raise a growing family. They moved around a lot, to three rented houses in Odessa (two since torn down and the third pretty grim) and then, after a year in Bakersfield, California, to three larger but by no means grand houses in Midland (typical 1950s ranches, one now a museum). Those houses, the Bushes' previous houses in New Haven and Houston and the Adams farmhouse in Braintree, Massachusetts, are the only houses in the United States where one president of the United States has raised another.

Midland in the 1950s was an affluent town by west Texas standards, but hardly a luxurious town to today's tastes; air conditioning had not yet become standard in homes or schools, and there were no mansions at the edge of town, just barren desert and oil derricks. There was a lively civic culture, with lots of volunteer organizations and new churches; today Midland has its own cultural institutions such as the Museum of the Southwest and the Petroleum Museum (the largest such museum in the world). And this small city in the 1950s was producing more than its share of the leaders of America today. Passing through the Midland public schools were George W. Bush, Laura Bush, former Commerce Secretary Donald Evans and General Tommy Franks. Odessa, too, has gained its place in the modern culture. The popular movie *Friday Night Lights*, based on a non-fiction best seller, depicted the passion of its high school football though perhaps not to local liking.

The 11th Congressional District of Texas covers much of West Texas; Ector and Midland are its two biggest counties. The district sweeps 400 miles across much of the state, from the hills of fast-growing Burnet County just north of Austin and the Texas German country of Gillespie County, on the eastern edge of which you can find the LBJ Ranch, west across wide open space past San Angelo, Midland and Odessa to the New Mexico line at Loving County, which with 52 people in 2004 is the smallest county in Texas and, for that matter, the United States. There are 36 counties here; geographically the district is larger than 12 states; 54% of the population is in Midland, Ector and Tom Green (San Angelo) Counties; none of the other counties has more than 39,000 people. Politically, west Texas in the 1940s was, like every place in Texas except a few Texas German counties, almost totally Democratic. That began to change in the 1950s as Midland moved toward Republicans; newcomers like the Bushes were an important part of this trend. In 1962 a Republican was also elected to the U.S. House in a district then made up of the Permian Basin and El Paso, but that was mostly because the incumbent was ensnared in the Billie Sol Estes scandal, and he was defeated in 1964. That same year Midland elected a Republican to the state House, where he was outnumbered by Democrats by 149–1. He was replaced in 1968 by another Republican, Tom Craddick, who has remained in the legislature ever since and in January 2003 was elected Speaker; by this time Republicans outnumbered Democrats 88–62. The current 11th District was created in the October 2003 redistricting, and it was the first Texas district in which Midland and Odessa were dominant: Craddick insisted on that. It is also overwhelmingly Republican. When George W. Bush ran for the House in 1978, from a district that included Midland and Lubbock, he lost to Democrat Kent Hance: rural West Texas was still voting Democratic. That is no longer the case today. In 2004 the 11th District cast 78.3% of its votes for Bush: his highest percentage in the nation.

The congressman from the 11th District is Mike Conaway, a Republican elected in 2004. Conaway grew up in Odessa and graduated from East Texas State University, before it became known as Texas A&M-Commerce. He worked as a certified public accountant for, among others, George W. Bush and was Bush's business partner in Arbusto/Bush Exploration during the 1980s; Governor Bush named him to the state Board of Public Accountancy, and he later chaired the National Association of State Boards of Accountancy. In May 2003, he finished second in the all-party special primary election in the old 19th District, which included nearly half of the new 11th. In June, he lost by less than 600 votes in a hard-fought runoff with Randy Neugebauer of Lubbock. After the new redistricting plan was passed in October, he was the obvious frontrunner for this seat. Democrat Charles Stenholm, who represented much of this area in the old 17th District, decided to run against Neugebauer in the new 19th District. Conaway's Republican primary opponent Bill Lester was a political science professor who campaigned against Bush's proposed guest worker program. The plan called for allowing documented foreigners to work in the United States for a period of three years, so long as those jobs would have gone unfilled by Americans. Lester called for militarization of the border, with helicopter patrols. Conaway, a supporter of the Bush proposal, said that increased documentation would strengthen national security by separating "those who are seeking economic opportunity" from "those who would do us harm." Conaway won 75%- 25%. He carried 33 of the 36 counties, losing only in the eastern part of the district. In the general election he won 77%–22% over Wayne Raasch and carried every county.

Conaway scored well on committee assignments, with seats on Agriculture, Armed Services and Budget. He hasn't been shy about his personal connections. "I believe I will be more effective if the president knows my first name than if he didn't," he told his hometown newspaper.

TWELFTH DISTRICT

Rep. Kay Granger (R)

Elected 1996, 5th term; b. Jan. 18, 1943, Greenville; home, Ft. Worth; TX Wesleyan Col., B.S. 1965; Methodist; divorced.

Elected Office: Ft. Worth City Cncl., 1989–91; Ft. Worth Mayor, 1991–96.

Professional Career: Teacher, 1965–78; Life Insurance Agent, 1978–85; Chmn., Ft. Worth Zoning Comm., 1981–88; Founder & Pres., Kay Granger Insurance Co., Inc., 1985–present.

DC Office: 440 CHOB, 20515, 202-225-5071; Fax: 202-225-5683; Web site: kaygranger.house.gov.

District Office: Ft. Worth, 817-338-0909.

Committees: *Appropriations* (23d of 37 R): Defense; Labor, Health and Human Services, Education & Related Agencies.

Group Ratings

	ADA	ACLU	AFS	LCV	ITIC	NTU	COC	ACU	NTLC	CHC
2004	0	0	0	0	100	54	100	91	78	84
2003	5	—	0	10	—	60	100	84	—	—

National Journal Ratings

	2003 LIB	—	2003 CONS		2004 LIB	—	2004 CONS
Economic	27%	—	71%		28%	—	71%
Social	24%	—	71%		34%	—	65%
Foreign	31%	—	65%		32%	—	67%

Key Votes of the 108th Congress

1. Drilling in ANWR	Y	5. DC School Vouchers	Y	9. Ban Same-Sex Marriage	Y
2. Approve Bush Tax Cuts	Y	6. Ban Human Cloning	Y	10. Fund Iraq War	Y
3. Medicare/Rx Bill	Y	7. Restrict Gun Liability	Y	11. Bar Cuba Embargo Funds	N
4. Bar Overtime Pay Regs.	N	8. Ban Partial-Birth Abortion	Y	12. Intelligence Reorg.	Y

Election Results

2004 general	Kay Granger (R)	173,222	(72%)	($895,146)
	Felix Alvarado (D)	66,316	(28%)	($15,948)
2004 primary	Kay Granger (R)	unopposed		
2002 general	Kay Granger (R)	121,208	(92%)	($989,881)
	Edward Hanson (Lib)	10,723	(8%)	

Prior Winning Percentages: 2000 (63%); 1998 (62%); 1996 (58%)

The People		Race/Ethnic Origin	Ancestry	
Area size:	2,217 sq. mi.	66.5% White	USA: 9.0%	German: 8.3%
Urban population:	82.8%	5.6% Black	Irish: 7.4%	
Rural population:	17.2%	2.3% Asian	**2004 Presidential Vote**	
Pop. 2000:	651,619	0.5% Native Am.	Bush (R)	162,192	(67%)
Median income:	$41,735	0.0% Hawaiian	Kerry (D)	79,862	(33%)
Poverty status:	11.3%	1.2% Two+ races	**2000 Presidential Vote**	
Military veterans:	13.0%	0.1% Other	Bush (R)	128,635	(64%)
		23.7% Hispanic Origin	Gore (D)	72,219	(36%)
			Cook Partisan Voting Index: R +14	
Occupation	Blue collar: 28.0%	White collar: 58.0%	Gray collar: 14.0%	

Fort Worth, Texas, has a fair claim to being the quintessential mid-American city: halfway across the continent, just west of the Balcones Escarpment that divides the dry treeless grazing lands of West Texas from the humid green croplands of East Texas, "where the blue sky begins," as its 19th century boosters proclaimed. It is Southern in heritage and Northern in its advanced post-industrial economy. It has the nation's longest row of Western wear shops and one of the nation's richest families, the Basses, whose steel-sheen skyscrapers, outlined at night by lights, dominate the skyline. This is where the West begins, Fort Worth boosters say, adding, as Will Rogers said, that Dallas is "where the East peters out."

But Cowtown, as the city is sometimes called, is not the primitive West. Fort Worth has a high-tech economy, though one hard hit by defense cuts. The big Lockheed Martin (formerly General Dynamics) plant has produced the B-24, B-36, B-52, F-111, F-16 and F-22 bombers and fighters; since Lockheed Martin won the contract for the Joint Strike Fighter in October 2002, it is likely to stay in production well beyond 2010. Next door is Carswell Air Force Base, the home of B-52s for years, slated for closure in 1993 but turned into a Joint Reserve Base. The assembly lines at Bell Helicopter Textron's nearby plant were kept going only when the Texas delegation and others overruled the cancellation of the accident-prone V-22 Osprey. Fort Worth also has some of the nation's premier small museums, the Amon Carter Museum of Western Art designed by Philip Johnson, the Kimbell Museum designed by Louis Kahn and the Museum of Modern Art opened in December 2002. And it has Texas-sized watering holes and eateries, like Billy Bob's Texas, the world's largest honky-tonk in the Stockyards, and nearby Joe T. Garcia's. Now local leaders are talking about damming the Trinity River and creating an elongated lake between the Stockyards and the antique Tarrant County Courthouse at the north edge of downtown. *The New York Times* got it right when it wrote that Forth Worth is "an irresistible combination of cowboys and culture." Other cities have their claims, but the visitor from abroad who wants to see what is quintessentially American would be well advised to fly to Dallas/Forth Worth International Airport and head west.

The 12th Congressional District of Texas includes two-thirds of Fort Worth and western suburban Tarrant County, plus all of Parker and Wise Counties to the west and northwest. It includes the northern and western neighborhoods of the city and the affluent southwest quarter beyond Texas Christian University; downtown and the Stockyards; the heavily black areas on the east side are in the 26th District. Parker County to the west was once rural, windswept open land around the courthouse town of Weatherford; now it is sprouting new subdivisions and growing rapidly. The historical heritage here is Democratic: Fort Worth stayed Democratic in the 1950s when Dallas went Republican; Speaker Jim Wright grew up in Weatherford and was first elected to the House from Tarrant County in 1954. But in the past 20 years Fort Worth and

Tarrant County have trended Republican. Their heavily Democratic areas are mostly in other districts, and the 12th, represented by the Democratic Speaker of the House as recently as 1989, is now solidly Republican—67% for George W. Bush in 2004.

The congresswoman from the 12th District is Kay Granger, a Republican first elected in 1996. Granger grew up in Fort Worth, graduated from Texas Wesleyan College, worked as a teacher in North Richland Hills, raised three children and started her own insurance agency. In 1989 she was elected to the Fort Worth Council, and two years later was elected as the nonpartisan mayor. In 1995 Congressman Pete Geren, a conservative Democrat elected to replace Wright in 1989, announced his retirement; both Republican and Democratic leaders tried to recruit Granger. She said she was a Republican and ran in the Republican primary. Attacked as a liberal, partly for her pro-choice stand on abortion, she won 69% in a three-candidate race. Granger's Democratic opponent was Hugh Parmer, a former Fort Worth mayor and the Democratic nominee against Senator Phil Gramm in 1990. That turned out to be a liability: it was revealed that he had large unpaid debts left over from that campaign. Parmer attacked Republican Medicare plans and Newt Gingrich. Granger called for a balanced budget and tax cuts for business and ran on her record as mayor. Granger won 58%–41%, a stunning victory in Jim Wright's old district, and an important one for maintaining the Republican majority.

In the House, Granger's voting record has tended to be moderate on cultural issues and more conservative on economics. She became a favorite of Republican leaders, winning enactment of tax-free savings accounts for higher education expenses and serving as the only freshman on Dennis Hastert's health care task force. She split with most Republicans in applauding the FDA's approval of the RU-486 abortion pill. One setback was the Republican leadership's indifference toward legislation that diluted the Wright Amendment's protection of Dallas/Fort Worth International Airport from competition by Dallas's Love Field; after that, Granger worked to create a local regional airport authority to encourage cooperation between the DFW and Love. Granger had served on the DFW board, and when DFW had difficulty in meeting security deadlines in summer 2002, she sponsored a bill to give flexibility to the 40 largest airports; a compromise version made its way into the homeland security bill in November 2002, covering all airports and requiring TSA monitoring and reports. In 2004 Tennessee Republican Marsha Blackburn, concerned that the Wright Amendment prevented low-cost Southwest from offering service from Nashville to Dallas, sponsored a bill to repeal the Wright Amendment. Granger and the other three Republicans representing Tarrant County fought it and in 2005 apparently convinced Blackburn to drop the idea.

In 1999 Granger became the third Texas Republican on the Appropriations Committee, where her seat on the Military Construction Subcommittee allowed her to keep a close eye on local Pentagon spending; in 2005 she got a seat on the Defense Subcommittee. She has worked to maintain production of the F-16, the F-22, the F-35, the V-22 and the Joint Strike Fighter. In February 2005 the Pentagon announced that production of the F-22 would cease in 2008, with only 179 of the 381 planes the Air Force wanted. "That drastic cutback is not in our national interest," Granger said. "You're talking about a drastic difference in what the Air Force says they need and what's been proposed by the administration." She went to the Pentagon in February 2005 to urge Donald Rumsfeld to continue production to 2011. Granger has come forward with some original initiatives. After September 11, Granger came up with the idea of auctioning off for eBay a flag that has flown over the Capitol with matting signed by every member of the 107th Congress to raise money for victims of the attacks. In mid-November the bids had only gone to $17,000, much less than she expected, so she went on the *Today* show, and the flag and matting sold for $80,100. In 2002 she proposed a $256 million program to fight obesity; to promote it she brought the Duchess of York to Cowtown. In 2003 she and Sander Levin proposed a national gynecological cancer detection program. In 2004 she backed the $360 million project to dam the Trinity River and create an elongated lake between downtown and the Stockyards. In January 2005 she journeyed to Iraq, and she and Ellen Tauscher conducted a training session for women candidates in the January 30 election.

Granger has an eye for political talent; from 1996 to 1999 her chief of staff was Ken Mehlman, Bush-Cheney '04 campaign manager and Republican National Chairman in 2005.

She was reelected in 1998 and 2000 by wide margins. The 2001 and 2003 redistricting plans treated her kindly; she got some new territory, but it was solidly Republican. In 2002 she had no Democratic opponent in Jim Wright's old district; in 2004 she won 72%–28%.

THIRTEENTH DISTRICT

Rep. Mac Thornberry (R)

Elected 1994, 6th term; b. July 15, 1958, Clarendon; home, Clarendon; TX Tech. U., B.A. 1980, U. of TX Law Schl., J.D. 1983; Presbyterian; married (Sally).

Professional Career: Legis. Cnsl., U.S. Rep. Tom Loeffler, 1983–85; Chief of Staff, U.S. Rep. Larry Combest, 1985–88; Dpty. Asst. Secy. of State for Legis. Affairs, 1988–89; Practicing atty., 1989–94; Rancher 1989–94.

DC Office: 2457 RHOB, 20515, 202-225-3706; Fax: 202-225-3486; Web site: www.house.gov/thornberry.

District Offices: Amarillo, 806-371-8844; Wichita Falls, 940-692-1700.

Committees: *Armed Services* (9th of 34 R): Strategic Forces; Terrorism, Unconventional Threats & Capabilities. *Permanent Select Committee on Intelligence* (8th of 12 R): Oversight (Chmn.); Technical & Tactical Intelligence.

Group Ratings

	ADA	ACLU	AFS	LCV	ITIC	NTU	COC	ACU	NTLC	CHC
2004	0	0	0	0	100	74	100	100	92	100
2003	10	—	0	5	—	59	97	92	—	—

National Journal Ratings

	2003 LIB	—	2003 CONS	2004 LIB	—	2004 CONS
Economic	0%	—	91%	0%	—	95%
Social	0%	—	95%	20%	—	77%
Foreign	11%	—	80%	25%	—	68%

Key Votes of the 108th Congress

1. Drilling in ANWR	Y	5. DC School Vouchers	Y	9. Ban Same-Sex Marriage	Y
2. Approve Bush Tax Cuts	Y	6. Ban Human Cloning	Y	10. Fund Iraq War	Y
3. Medicare/Rx Bill	Y	7. Restrict Gun Liability	Y	11. Bar Cuba Embargo Funds	N
4. Bar Overtime Pay Regs.	N	8. Ban Partial-Birth Abortion	Y	12. Intelligence Reorg.	Y

Election Results

2004 general	Mac Thornberry (R)	189,448	(92%)	($383,724)
	M. J. Smith (Lib)	15,793	(8%)	
2004 primary	Mac Thornberry (R)	unopposed		
2002 general	Mac Thornberry (R)	119,401	(79%)	($441,738)
	Zane Reese (D)	31,218	(21%)	

Prior Winning Percentages: 2000 (68%); 1998 (68%); 1996 (67%); 1994 (55%)

The People		Race/Ethnic Origin	Ancestry	
Area size:	40,403 sq. mi.	73.7% White	USA: 10.8%	German: 9.3%
Urban population:	69.9%	5.7% Black	Irish: 7.6%	
Rural population:	30.1%	1.1% Asian	**2004 Presidential Vote**	
Pop. 2000:	651,620	0.6% Native Am.	Bush (R) 183,375	(78%)
Median income:	$33,501	0.0% Hawaiian	Kerry (D) 52,431	(22%)
Poverty status:	14.0%	1.2% Two+ races	**2000 Presidential Vote**	
Military veterans:	13.6%	0.1% Other	Bush (R) 158,529	(74%)
		17.6% Hispanic Origin	Gore (D) 56,229	(26%)
			Cook Partisan Voting Index: R +25	

Occupation	Blue collar: 27.1%	White collar: 53.3%	Gray collar: 19.7%

Heading west in Texas, the population thins out, the land becomes browner until you can travel through whole counties containing only a few hundred people each—plus quite a few more head of cattle. And then the land rises nearly 1,000 feet in elevation, up steep hillsides from the gullies that surround the rivers that for most of the year are just tiny trickles, to the tilted tableland that is the High Plains of West Texas. The winds here sweep down from the Rockies, the land is barren except where irrigated, often with the now dangerously depleted waters of the Ogallala Aquifer; and so one passes through grazing land to cotton fields and then grazing land again. But here and there in this demanding environment—sticky-hot in the summer, swept by north winds from Canada in winter, always threatened in "Tornado Alley"—comfortable cities have been built to house the people and businesses that bring forth some of the nation's most abundant oil, natural gas, helium and other elements from the earth.

The 13th Congressional District of Texas covers about 40,000 square miles; it extends from the New Mexico border to just north of Dallas and includes all of 42 counties and parts of two others. Population declined here in the 1980s, in some rural counties by as much as 30%, with only small gains in and around two of the three biggest cities, Wichita Falls and Amarillo. In the 1990s, the district's population increased 5%, but that was the smallest gain in any Texas district, with population increasing in the larger cities but declining in most rural counties. Around Wichita Falls, in the eastern part of the district, is the agricultural land of the Red River Valley, dusty land with empty skylines, with Sheppard Air Force Base and one of Bell Helicopter's V-22 Osprey plants. The area claims to produce more cotton than any other congressional district, produces much of the world's milo (a variety of sorghum) and is home to one of the nation's oldest and largest cattle auctions. This was long white Anglo Texas: few blacks got this far west and there were not many Latinos either. But Latinos lately have been moving here in large numbers, to work in the fields or in crop processing. Today, the district is 6% black and 18% Hispanic. Much of the High Plains economy is based on natural resources. The largest city here is Amarillo, once the helium capital of North America (before Congress shut down production), now the center of the largest natural gas development in the world, and still—not Chicago—the windiest city in the United States. Just outside town is the Pantex plant that secretly assembled the nation's thousands of nuclear warheads and was the epicenter of American defense in the Cold War; its 16,000 acres have been used to dismantle some disarmed weapons and now maintains the remainder of the arsenal.

The Red River Valley, settled by Confederate veterans, was heavily Democratic up through the 1970s. The High Plains, settled overland from Kansas wheatlands, was for years more Republican. Both parts are now solidly Republican. Redistricting in 2003 shifted only a few counties around. The 78% that George W. Bush won here in 2004 was his third-best performance in the nation; sparsely populated Ochiltree County, on the Oklahoma border, gave Bush 92%, his highest percentage of any county in the nation.

The congressman from the 13th District is Mac Thornberry, a Republican first elected in 1994. His great-great-grandfather Amos Thornberry, a Union Army veteran and staunch Republican, moved to Clay County, just east of Wichita Falls, in the 1880s; a year after Amos died in 1925, his son bought the cattle ranch that Mac Thornberry, his brothers and father now run. From the window of his ranch house, writes *The Texas Techsan*, "as far as the eye can see is the Golden Spread of Texas for which this part of the state is named. There are no buildings, no roadways, no signs of life. Gaze out long enough and you begin to think you can actually see the curvature of the earth." After college and law school in Texas, Thornberry worked for Congressmen Tom Loeffler and Larry Combest and at the State Department in Washington. He returned to practice law in West Texas. In 1994, he took on three-term Democratic Congressman Bill Sarpalius, whom he attacked for voting for the Clinton budget and tax package. He profited from news stories about how Sarpalius did not pay a moving company that shipped his furniture to Washington, then accepted a fee for speaking at the company's convention in Las Vegas. Thornberry won 55%–45%.

In the House, Thornberry has compiled a conservative voting record, though hardly the most ideological in the Texas delegation. His hard work on defense and homeland security issues has earned him a reputation as one of the brainiest and most accessible lawmakers on those issues. In March 2001 he took the recommendations of a commission chaired by former Senators Gary Hart and Warren Rudman and sponsored the first bill to create a homeland security agency; in 2002, with Joseph Lieberman, he played a key role in the bipartisan effort to create the new department. As chairman of the Cybersecurity Subcommittee on Homeland Security, he criticized the new Homeland Security Department for delays in integrating its computer networks and intelligence analysis, and said that Congress must establish ways to measure how spending is deterring terrorists. With California's Zoe Lofgren, he sponsored a bill defining cybersecurity and designating a high-level official to coordinate Administration work on this policy. On the Armed Services Committee he has enthusiastically championed missile defense and has called for better coordination of military space programs. He called for a renewal of bipartisanship in articulating a national security strategy. In September 2004, he gained a seat on the Intelligence Committee and became chairman of its oversight subcommittee, but was forced to leave the Homeland Security Committee.

On domestic issues, Thornberry has pressed hard for estate tax repeal and tax credits to encourage production in marginal wells. Thornberry has been reelected easily every two years, and in 2004 had no major party opposition for the first time.

FOURTEENTH DISTRICT

Rep. Ron Paul (R)

Elected 1996, 5th term; b. Aug. 20, 1935, Pittsburgh, PA; home, Surfside; Gettysburg Col., B.A. 1957, Duke U., M.D. 1961; Protestant; married (Carol).

Military Career: Flight Surgeon, Air Force, 1963–68.

Elected Office: U.S. House of Reps., 1976, 1978–84.

Professional Career: Practicing physician, 1968–96.

DC Office: 203 CHOB, 20515, 202-225-2831; Web site: www.house.gov/paul.

District Offices: Lake Jackson, 979-285-0231; Victoria, 361-576-1231.

Committees: *Financial Services* (12th of 37 R): Domestic and International Monetary Policy, Trade & Technology; Financial Institutions & Consumer Credit; Oversight & Investigations (Vice Chmn.). *International Relations* (12th of 27 R): Asia & the Pacific; Western Hemisphere. *Joint Economic Committee.*

Group Ratings

	ADA	ACLU	AFS	LCV	ITIC	NTU	COC	ACU	NTLC	CHC
2004	50	64	25	27	44	90	56	78	92	76
2003	60	—	50	5	—	89	46	71	—	—

National Journal Ratings

	2003 LIB	—	2003 CONS		2004 LIB	—	2004 CONS
Economic	53%	—	47%		47%	—	53%
Social	53%	—	47%		46%	—	54%
Foreign	73%	—	25%		80%	—	20%

Key Votes of the 108th Congress

1. Drilling in ANWR	*	5. DC School Vouchers	N	9. Ban Same-Sex Marriage	N
2. Approve Bush Tax Cuts	Y	6. Ban Human Cloning	N	10. Fund Iraq War	N
3. Medicare/Rx Bill	N	7. Restrict Gun Liability	N	11. Bar Cuba Embargo Funds	Y
4. Bar Overtime Pay Regs.	N	8. Ban Partial-Birth Abortion	Y	12. Intelligence Reorg.	*

Election Results

2004 general	Ron Paul (R) .... unopposed			($744,969)
2004 primary	Ron Paul (R) .... unopposed			
2002 general	Ron Paul (R) 102,905	(68%)		($1,309,118)
	Corby Windham (D) 48,224	(32%)		($40,410)

Prior Winning Percentages: 2000 (60%); 1998 (55%); 1996 (51%); 1982 (99%); 1980 (51%); 1978 (51%); 1976 (56%)

The People		Race/Ethnic Origin	Ancestry	
Area size:	9,369 sq. mi.	62.1% White	German: 10.7%	Irish: 7.0%
Urban population:	71.1%	9.8% Black	USA: 6.4%	
Rural population:	28.9%	1.7% Asian	**2004 Presidential Vote**	
Pop. 2000:	651,619	0.3% Native Am.	Bush (R) 169,480	(67%)
Median income:	$41,335	0.0% Hawaiian	Kerry (D) 82,792	(33%)
Poverty status:	13.3%	1.0% Two+ races	**2000 Presidential Vote**	
Military veterans:	13.5%	0.1% Other	Bush (R) 140,826	(64%)
		24.9% Hispanic Origin	Gore (D) 78,634	(36%)
			Cook Partisan Voting Index: R +14	

Occupation	Blue collar: 27.8%	White collar: 56.2%	Gray collar: 16.1%

Retreating east from the Alamo, the ragtag army led by Sam Houston passed over what would become, after their bloody and conclusive victory at San Jacinto, some of the prime cropland in the Republic and later the state of Texas. The hilly and river-crossed land between Houston and Austin, named after Texas' first two leaders, was settled early. The first capital of the Republic of Texas was in Brazoria County. The flat coastal plains, steamy and humid so much of the year, were settled later when the railroads came in. The Gulf of Mexico coastline, though it has plenty of inlets, never had any important ports in the stretch between Houston and Corpus Christi until the discovery of oil here made it worthwhile to build channels to ship the oil out.

This is the land of the 14th Congressional District of Texas. With rural countrysides and the cities of Victoria and El Campo, it runs along the Gulf Coast between Corpus Christ and Port Arthur. Victoria is a rail hub that serves Gulf ports; it also includes large industrial plants, including DuPont, Union Carbide, Alcoa and BP Chemicals. Redistricting in 2003 removed parts of the old Texas German country and added most of hurricane-prone Galveston, on a barrier island on the Gulf. It was an immigrant port known as the Ellis Island of the West until a 1900 hurricane devastated the area and killed thousands; the city is now guarded by a 17-foot seawall and connected to the mainland by a hurricane-resistant bridge. This is a district that is mostly small-city Texas, but much of it now surrounds the suburban fringes of metropolitan Houston. This country is ancestrally Democratic but it has trended Republican since the 1980s, and voted 67% for George W. Bush in 2004. Despite the shift in redistricting of more than half of its population, the partisan mix was barely affected.

The congressman from the 14th District is Ron Paul, a Republican first elected as long ago as 1976, and also once a Libertarian candidate for president. Paul grew up in Pennsylvania, graduated from Duke Medical School, served as an Air Force flight surgeon, then moved to Texas to practice obstetrics and gynecology in Brazoria County, southwest of Houston. Paul was dismayed when Richard Nixon cut the connection between the dollar and gold in 1971 and became interested in politics. He was elected to the House in 1976 and served four terms, then ran for the Senate in 1984 and lost the Republican primary to Phil Gramm 73%–16%. His House seat was won by a young legislator and exterminating firm owner, Tom DeLay. In 1988, as the Libertarian candidate for president, Paul ran third with 432,000 votes, 0.47% of the total. In his first stint in the House, Paul advanced some ideas that in the mid-1990s had almost become mainstream—term limits and abolition of the income tax. Other Paul ideas remain outside the political pale: endorsing a group that wants to end all government funding of education, cutting $150 billion from the defense budget and returning to the gold standard. Paul practices what he preaches. He will not accept payment by Medicare or Medicaid, he wouldn't let his children accept federal student loans and he refuses his congressional pension.

Paul reentered electoral politics after Congressman Greg Laughlin switched parties and became a Republican in June 1995. Laughlin had a moderate voting record, by no means the most conservative of Texas Democrats. Republicans offered him a seat on Ways and Means if he switched, and he did. Paul decided to run again in 1996, raising money from his nationwide network of Libertarians, gold bugs and subscribers to the *Ron Paul Political Report*. Laughlin led in the primary with 43% of the vote, but Paul won the runoff 54%–46%. Democrats ran Charles "Lefty" Morris, a former president of the state trial lawyers' association. Morris ("Lefty is right") hit Paul for favoring abolition of the minimum wage, repealing federal anti-drug laws and anti-prostitution laws. Paul ran 1% ahead of Bob Dole and won 51%–48%.

With his libertarian views, Paul's voting record is anything but rock solid Republican; *National Journal* ratings place him near the middle of the House. Frequently, his insistence on limited government made Paul the House's lonely dissenter—against bills to require states to report on their progress in improving student achievement, to award Congressional Gold Medals to Rosa Parks and Pope John Paul II, to pass the Patriot Act after September 11. He favors relaxation of restrictions on illegal drugs, and he filed a lawsuit challenging the McCain-Feingold campaign finance act as a violation of the First Amendment. Unsurprisingly, he voted against the Medicare/prescription drug bill in 2003. His isolationist views on foreign policy have made his voting record on those issues indistinct from many liberal Democrats. He was the only Republican to vote "present" on the resolution expressing support for the military forces at the start of the war with Iraq. He supports virtually no role for the U.S. government overseas—from military defense to international trade; he calls himself a "non-interventionist," not an isolationist. In a July 2003 speech in the House, which he called "Neo-Conned!", he harshly attacked the Bush administration and its supporters. "The so-called conservative revolution of the past two decades has given us massive growth in government size, spending and regulation." His iconoclasm has reached the point that he is probably the least dependable and persuadable Republican in the House—even though his district is next door to Tom DeLay's. Interestingly, many liberals have begun to praise him. And he does offer alternatives. In 2003 and 2004 he was among the most prolific legislators, sponsoring 68 bills and eight amendments. None passed.

For a while, Paul appeared on House Democrats' target lists, but he easily survived. Amazingly, he ran without any opposition in 2004. Democrats do not really have a chance in this district; more regular Republicans may have their eyes on it, but have not yet seriously challenged Paul in the Republican primary. It's unlikely that the Republican leadership will ever let him have a chairmanship. But it may be unwise to underestimate someone who, however offbeat, has managed to be elected to the House nine times, at least once in each of four decades.

FIFTEENTH DISTRICT

Rep. Ruben Hinojosa (D)

Elected 1996, 5th term; b. Aug. 20, 1940, Mercedes; home, Mercedes; U. of TX, B.B.A. 1962, M.B.A. 1980; Catholic; married (Marty).

Elected Office: TX Bd. of Educ., 1974–84.

Professional Career: Pres. & CEO, H&H Foods Inc., 1962–present.

DC Office: 2463 RHOB, 20515, 202-225-2531; Fax: 202-225-5688; Web site: www.house.gov/hinojosa.

District Offices: Beeville, 361-358-8400; Edinburg, 956-682-5545.

Committees: *Education & the Workforce* (8th of 22 D): Education Reform; Select Education (RMM). *Financial Services* (17th of 32 D): Capital Markets, Insurance & Government Sponsored Enterprises; Financial Institutions & Consumer Credit.

Group Ratings

	ADA	ACLU	AFS	LCV	ITIC	NTU	COC	ACU	NTLC	CHC
2004	90	69	100	73	78	11	63	13	3	25
2003	80	—	100	65	—	22	53	40	—	—

National Journal Ratings

	2003 LIB	—	2003 CONS		2004 LIB	—	2004 CONS
Economic	62%	—	38%		61%	—	39%
Social	65%	—	34%		67%	—	32%
Foreign	65%	—	34%		70%	—	30%

Key Votes of the 108th Congress

1. Drilling in ANWR	Y	5. DC School Vouchers	N	9. Ban Same-Sex Marriage	N
2. Approve Bush Tax Cuts	N	6. Ban Human Cloning	*	10. Fund Iraq War	Y
3. Medicare/Rx Bill	N	7. Restrict Gun Liability	Y	11. Bar Cuba Embargo Funds	Y
4. Bar Overtime Pay Regs.	Y	8. Ban Partial-Birth Abortion	Y	12. Intelligence Reorg.	*

Election Results

2004 general	Ruben Hinojosa (D)	96,089	(58%)	($818,826)
	Michael Thamm (R)	67,917	(41%)	($49,898)
	Other	2,352	(1%)	
2004 primary	Ruben Hinojosa (D)	unopposed		
2002 general	Ruben Hinojosa (D)	unopposed		($271,632)

Prior Winning Percentages: 2000 (88%); 1998 (58%); 1996 (62%)

The People		Race/Ethnic Origin	Ancestry	
Area size:	10,804 sq. mi.	27.2% White	German: 7.2%	USA: 3.1%
Urban population:	74.8%	2.7% Black	English: 2.9%	
Rural population:	25.2%	0.5% Asian	**2004 Presidential Vote**	
Pop. 2000:	651,619	0.1% Native Am.	Bush (R)	95,086 (55%)
Median income:	$28,061	0.0% Hawaiian	Kerry (D)	77,998 (45%)
Poverty status:	28.7%	0.4% Two+ races	**2000 Presidential Vote**	
Military veterans:	10.0%	0.0% Other	Bush (R)	76,689 (50%)
		69.0% Hispanic Origin	Gore (D)	75,580 (50%)
			Cook Partisan Voting Index: R + 1	

Occupation   Blue collar: 27.7%   White collar: 51.3%   Gray collar: 21.0%

The Lower Rio Grande Valley of south Texas is one of America's 20th century frontiers. A century ago, there was little here but desert wilderness. Only a handful of people lived anywhere near the shallow, sluggish Rio Grande; there was no Border Patrol because in this desert land very few people bothered to cross it. Then came pioneers like Lloyd Bentsen Sr., father of the former senator and Treasury secretary, who arrived after World War I with $5 in his pocket and became one of the biggest Valley landowners. Bentsen and others cleared the land and dug canals, hired Mexican and Mexican-American workers, and with irrigated water from the Rio Grande planted citrus groves, cornfields and palm windbreaks, ran cattle and drilled for oil and gas. Along U.S. 83 north of the Rio Grande these pioneers built a string of towns with Anglo names and storefronts. But most of the people here were Latino in culture and language. Wage levels higher than in Mexico (though low by U.S. standards) brought more Mexicans over the border. But if wages are low, so is the cost of living—which makes this a haven for low-income "winter Texan" retirees coming from the North in their RVs. The days are past when ranchers and oilmen wielded absolute political power here. There is instead a robust, mostly Hispanic, politics.

The 15th Congressional District of Texas is one of four districts dividing up the Lower Rio Grande Valley. Some 63% of its residents live just north of the river in Hidalgo and Cameron Counties, in or near the string of towns from McAllen to Harlingen. This is a fast growing area: Hidalgo and Cameron Counties' population rose 60% from 1990 to 2004, from 644,000 to 1,030,000; the local infrastructure has barely kept up. The 15th then stretches north through a narrow corridor of land between Corpus Christi and San Antonio and extends 350 miles to Bastrop County on the outskirts of Austin. In the northern end of the district, much of which is Texas German country, the population drops below 20% Hispanic. These northern counties were added in the 2003 redistricting as a result of the decision by redistricters to add a new "*fajita* district", the 25th, extending from Austin to the border. The changes increased the number of counties in the 15th from 8 to 13 and reduced its Hispanic percentage to 69%. One might expect a district with such a large Hispanic population to be heavily Democratic. But in state contests it has given Democrats only small majorities, and it has given majorities of its votes to George W. Bush, 50% in 2000 and 55% in 2004.

The congressman from the 15th District is Ruben Hinojosa, a Democrat first elected in 1996. His background is not in politics but in business and civic affairs. He grew up in Mercedes, where his family owns H&H Foods, which produces Mexican foods and beef patties and is one of the largest employers in the Valley. Hinojosa graduated from the University of Texas, then went into the family business and was active in civic affairs, primarily in education and regional development. He served on the state Board of Education and led an effort to create three regional magnet schools. After former House Agriculture Committee Chairman Kika de la Garza announced he would not seek reelection in 1996, Hinojosa ran. In the Democratic primary he led Anglo lawyer Jim Selman 34%–33%. Selman questioned Hinojosa's Democratic credentials and said he profited from government contracts. Hinojosa emphasized his interest in improving educational opportunities in the Lower Rio Grande Valley and extending I-69 to the Valley. Not the kind of liberal who leads most national and Texas Hispanic organizations, he called for reducing the capital gains tax and giving investment tax credits to those making capital improvements. Hinojosa won the runoff 52%–48% and easily won the general.

Hinojosa has had a moderate-to-conservative voting record among House Democrats. He has sought to protect benefits for legal immigrants, to promote NAFTA and to demand that Mexico deliver on its agreement for water to south Texas farmers. He has a proclivity for holding out on votes to make last minute legislative deals. With Democrat Gregory Meeks, he was one of only two undecided congressmen who took up Bill Clinton's offer of a visit to China to assess whether to approve normal trade relations; Hinojosa got assurances of funding for the Cross-Border Institute for Regional Development before voting for it. He again was one of the final members to decide on George W. Bush's proposal for trade promotion authority. This time, he shook hands with Tom DeLay on the House floor in a deal for earmarked funding for a job training project that Hinojosa wanted. He had support in 2003 from the Texas delegation for a Democratic opening on Ways and Means, but it went to Max Sandlin, and Hinojosa became ranking Democrat on the Select Education Subcommittee, which has jurisdiction over historically black and Hispanic colleges. He supported additional incentives for teachers of English as a second language and more grants to develop graduate degree programs at institutions that serve Hispanics.

After breezing through reelection in 2000 and 2002, Hinojosa faced serious opposition in 2004, largely because of redistricting. Republican Michael Thamm, a plumbing contractor and former mayor of Cuero in DeWitt County, one of the counties added to the district, received little national attention or party support. He sounded standard Republican themes and spent only $50,000; Hinojosa spent $819,000 and devoted more time than in the past to reminding voters that he favored school prayer and opposed abortion. Thamm won the six most northern counties 60%–38%. But in Hidalgo County, which cast 37% of the vote (though it has 50% of the population), Hinojosa won 70%–29%. He won 58%–41% overall. Since redistricting, he has spent much time traveling around the northern end of the district and meeting with constituents, who before 2003 had no reason to know anything about him; at his first meeting in Bastrop County, which is closer to the residences of 29 other congressmen's than to Hinojosa's, he was introduced as "Congressman Hiroshima." But he impressed local officials, even Republicans, with his hard work and moderate voting record. In 2005 he switched and voted for the Republicans' class action bill. "I got so many calls from south and central Texas that they would prefer I vote for it. Some of my colleagues said, 'Ruben, you are not being consistent,' but it is a different congressional district." In early 2005, he announced that he was running for vice-chairman of the Democratic Caucus, whenever James Clyburn moved up to replace Bob Menendez as caucus chairman. But his short-lived candidacy was abandoned within two weeks, a sign that Hinojosa's politics are not a perfect fit in the Democratic Caucus.

SIXTEENTH DISTRICT

Rep. Silvestre Reyes (D)

Elected 1996, 5th term; b. Nov. 10, 1944, Canutillo; home, El Paso; El Paso Commun. Col., A.A. 1977; Catholic; married (Carolina).

Military Career: Army, 1966–68 (Vietnam).

Elected Office: Canutillo Schl. Board, 1968–70.

Professional Career: Border Patrol Agent, 1969–95.

DC Office: 2433 RHOB, 20515, 202-225-4831; Fax: 202-225-2016; Web site: www.house.gov/reyes.

District Office: El Paso, 915-534-4400.

Committees: *Armed Services* (8th of 28 D): Readiness; Strategic Forces (RMM). *Permanent Select Committee on Intelligence* (3d of 9 D): Oversight; Terrorism, Human Intelligence, Analysis & Counterintelligence. *Veterans' Affairs* (10th of 12 D): Oversight & Investigations.

Group Ratings

	ADA	ACLU	AFS	LCV	ITIC	NTU	COC	ACU	NTLC	CHC
2004	70	58	100	45	70	14	62	26	8	30
2003	80	—	100	55	—	21	50	40	—	—

National Journal Ratings

	2003 LIB	—	2003 CONS		2004 LIB	—	2004 CONS
Economic	64%	—	36%		59%	—	40%
Social	60%	—	39%		67%	—	33%
Foreign	63%	—	36%		65%	—	34%

Key Votes of the 108th Congress

1. Drilling in ANWR	Y	5. DC School Vouchers	N	9. Ban Same-Sex Marriage	*
2. Approve Bush Tax Cuts	N	6. Ban Human Cloning	Y	10. Fund Iraq War	Y
3. Medicare/Rx Bill	N	7. Restrict Gun Liability	Y	11. Bar Cuba Embargo Funds	Y
4. Bar Overtime Pay Regs.	Y	8. Ban Partial-Birth Abortion	Y	12. Intelligence Reorg.	N

Election Results

2004 general	Silvestre Reyes (D)	108,577	(68%)	($618,785)
	David Brigham (R)	49,972	(31%)	($27,985)
	Other	2,224	(1%)	
2004 primary	Silvestre Reyes (D)	unopposed		
2002 general	Silvestre Reyes (D)	unopposed		($413,161)

Prior Winning Percentages: 2000 (68%); 1998 (88%); 1996 (71%)

The People		Race/Ethnic Origin	Ancestry	
Area size:	582 sq. mi.	17.4% White	German: 3.9%	Irish: 2.6%
Urban population:	98.3%	2.9% Black	USA: 2.4%	
Rural population:	1.7%	0.9% Asian	**2004 Presidential Vote**	
Pop. 2000:	651,619	0.3% Native Am.	Kerry (D) 92,792	(56%)
Median income:	$31,245	0.1% Hawaiian	Bush (R) 71,454	(44%)
Poverty status:	23.6%	0.7% Two+ races	**2000 Presidential Vote**	
Military veterans:	11.6%	0.1% Other	Gore (D) 81,874	(59%)
		77.7% Hispanic Origin	Bush (R) 56,283	(41%)
			Cook Partisan Voting Index: D + 9	

Occupation	Blue collar: 24.7%	White collar: 58.1%	Gray collar: 17.2%

El Paso, Texas, and Juarez, Mexico, face each other across the narrow Rio Grande, their tree-shaded streets spread out below the rough brown face of Comanche Peak. The two border cities are surrounded by hundreds of miles of some of North America's most rugged and desolate landscape, 600 miles from Dallas-Fort Worth. There is much history here: Texas claims the first

Thanksgiving took place in San Elizario near El Paso in 1598, and there were Spanish conquistadors coming through the pass of the north, *El Paso del Norte*, on their way to Santa Fe years before that. In the 1950s, El Paso and Juarez each had a population of 140,000; in 2000 U.S. Census counted 679,000 in El Paso County (78% of them counted as Hispanic) and the Mexican census counted 1.2 million in metro Juarez. This is a bilingual, bicultural pair of cities, where most people have a Mexican heritage; the thrust of growth comes from the fertile union of a Spanish-speaking people and an English-speaking economy. El Paso is one of the lowest-wage and lowest-education cities in the U.S.; Juarez is one of the highest-wage in Mexico. Cotton is the predominant local crop, and the city is known as a boot-making center. *Maquiladora* plants pioneered a cross-border economy and NAFTA strengthened it, and it is not all low-skill either; south of the border, there is a big General Motors technical center.

The 16th Congressional District of Texas is made up of 96% of El Paso County—the city itself, the suburban fringe and giant Fort Bliss to the north and the colonias, most without electricity and running water, spread out to the east and south. El Paso feels distant from the rest of Texas—it's closer to Los Angeles than to Beaumont, and El Paso is in a different time zone from the rest of the state. As governor, George W. Bush paid close attention to El Paso, and in his 1998 reelection he carried El Paso County 50%–49%—a considerable achievement given the overwhelmingly Latino electorate. As presidential candidate, Bush got 41% against Al Gore and 44% against John Kerry in this district. This was the only district that was not changed by redistricting in 2003; with the county isolated by geography, 78% Hispanic, and firmly Democratic, Republicans had little to gain by changing the borders.

The congressman from the 16th District is Silvestre Reyes, a Democrat first elected in 1996. He grew up on a farm in Canutillo, five miles north of El Paso, the oldest of 10 children; he went to college in El Paso and Austin. He served in the Army in Vietnam, then "took as many civil service tests as I could, and the Border Patrol called" in 1969. He worked for the Immigration and Naturalization Service in four cities in Texas and Glynco, Georgia, and returned to El Paso in 1993 as chief patrol agent. When he got there he found that "people could basically cross the border at any time, wherever they wanted to." More than 40 boatmen ran "what were essentially international ferries" with 8,000 illegals crossing the border every day. Reyes started Operation Hold the Line, positioning 400 officers on the border instead of trying to intercept illegals after they had already crossed into El Paso (amazingly enough, that had been firmly-rooted INS policy). Mexico complained about threats to its sovereignty, merchants worried about loss of sales, homeowners fretted about finding domestic help, border agents feared losing credit for apprehending aliens. But Reyes reduced the flow of illegals here by more than half; the move was almost universally popular north of the border and has been accepted to the south.

By November 1995 Reyes's name recognition was 65%, higher than most elected officials; he resigned from the INS and ran for Congress. Reyes talked of the need for integrity and common sense. His target was Ron Coleman, a Democrat first elected in 1982, around whom scandals swirled: he had 673 overdrafts at the House bank and he was accused by Texas Attorney General Dan Morales of trying to block prosecution of a local developer. In December 1995, Coleman announced he was retiring, and he and labor unions backed Jose Luis Sanchez, his legislative assistant. Sanchez harshly attacked Reyes as a crypto-Republican and for backing a capital gains tax cut. Reyes hewed to his moderate platform, including water conservation research, more high-tech jobs, more highways and border crossings. After Reyes led the primary 42%–28%, Sanchez and the unions pressed hard in the runoff, but Reyes won 51%–49% and easily won the general.

In the House, Reyes' voting record has been moderate-to-conservative among Democrats. He said that the permanent solution for the border is economic stabilization for Mexico and spoke out against decertification of Mexico for its drug enforcement record, saying it would upset the Mexican economy. He backed retraining for workers displaced by NAFTA, which he said has been a great success overall, and he praised President Bush for calling for a guest-worker program. From the Armed Services Committee, where he is ranking Democrat on the Strategic Forces Subcommittee, Reyes has been a supporter of the missile-defense program; he worked to protect Fort Bliss from possible base closing (it ended up a net gainer under the Pentagon's May

2005 recommendations), and in early 2004 he claimed credit when 3,800 additional soldiers were stationed there. He opposed the use of force in Iraq, and later criticized the intelligence failures in Iraq in the months before the war. He called the embedding of reporters with military units a bad idea because "it provides the enemy with propaganda." With California's David Dreier, Reyes proposed in January 2005 to require a digitized Social Security identification card for all immigrants seeking a job in the United States.

As chairman of the all-Democratic Hispanic Caucus since 2001, Reyes set as a major priority the expansion of its membership by recruiting and providing financial help to prospective candidates; he set a goal of electing an additional six to 10 Hispanics to Congress in the 2002 election. But redistricting did not result in many new Hispanic-majority seats as Anglo and black Democrats concentrated on protecting incumbents in California, Texas and Florida, and only two new Hispanic Democrats were elected, in California and Arizona. Reyes urged the four Hispanic Republicans—three Cuban-Americans from Miami-Dade County and Henry Bonilla from San Antonio—to return to the Hispanic Caucus, but they demanded that the caucus support free elections in Cuba; the deep divisions on Fidel Castro among Hispanic Democrats made that a non-starter.

SEVENTEENTH DISTRICT

Rep. Chet Edwards (D)

Elected 1990, 8th term; b. Nov. 24, 1951, Corpus Christi; home, Waco; TX A&M U., B.A. 1974, Harvard U., M.B.A. 1981; Methodist; married (Lea Ann).

Elected Office: TX Senate, 1982–90.

Professional Career: Legis. & Dist. Dir., U.S. Rep. Olin Teague, 1975–77; Marketing Rep., Trammell Crow Co., 1981–85; Pres., Edwards Communications, 1985–90.

DC Office: 2264 RHOB, 20515, 202-225-6105; Fax: 202-225-0350; Web site: www.house.gov/edwards.

District Offices: Cleburne, 817-645-4743; College Station, 979-691-8797; Waco, 254-752-9600.

Committees: *Appropriations* (16th of 29 D): Energy & Water Development & Related Agencies; Homeland Security; Military Quality of Life & Veterans Affairs & Related Agencies (RMM). *Budget* (5th of 17 D).

Group Ratings

	ADA	ACLU	AFS	LCV	ITIC	NTU	COC	ACU	NTLC	CHC
2004	65	35	75	45	89	16	81	48	14	23
2003	80	—	100	30	—	26	64	44	—	—

National Journal Ratings

	2003 LIB	—	2003 CONS		2004 LIB	—	2004 CONS
Economic	56%	—	43%		55%	—	44%
Social	61%	—	39%		53%	—	46%
Foreign	61%	—	37%		57%	—	42%

Key Votes of the 108th Congress

1. Drilling in ANWR	Y	5. DC School Vouchers	N	9. Ban Same-Sex Marriage	Y
2. Approve Bush Tax Cuts	N	6. Ban Human Cloning	N	10. Fund Iraq War	Y
3. Medicare/Rx Bill	N	7. Restrict Gun Liability	Y	11. Bar Cuba Embargo Funds	Y
4. Bar Overtime Pay Regs.	Y	8. Ban Partial-Birth Abortion	N	12. Intelligence Reorg.	Y

Election Results

2004 general	Chet Edwards (D) 125,309	(51%)	($2,664,661)
	Arlene Wohlgemuth (R) 116,049	(47%)	($2,562,877)
	Other... 3,390	(1%)	
2004 primary	Chet Edwards (D) .... unopposed		
2002 general (TX 11)	Chet Edwards (D) 74,678	(52%)	($1,566,761)
	Ramsey Farley (R)............................... 68,236	(47%)	($614,493)
	Other... 1,943	(1%)	

Prior Winning Percentages: 2000 (55%); 1998 (82%); 1996 (57%); 1994 (59%); 1992 (67%); 1990 (53%)

The People		Race/Ethnic Origin	Ancestry	
Area size:	7,808 sq. mi.	71.4% White	German: 10.6%	USA: 8.2%
Urban population:	64.2%	10.3% Black	Irish: 7.4%	
Rural population:	35.8%	1.4% Asian	**2004 Presidential Vote**	
Pop. 2000:	651,620	0.4% Native Am.	Bush (R) 172,355	(70%)
Median income:	$35,253	0.1% Hawaiian	Kerry (D) 74,358	(30%)
Poverty status:	17.0%	1.0% Two+ races	**2000 Presidential Vote**	
Military veterans:	12.6%	0.1% Other	Bush (R) 140,611	(68%)
		15.4% Hispanic Origin	Gore (D) 66,307	(32%)
			Cook Partisan Voting Index: R +18	

Occupation	Blue collar: 26.5%	White collar: 57.2%	Gray collar: 16.3%

Waco, at the intersection of lines from Dallas to Austin and Houston to Amarillo, is arguably the geographic and cultural heart of Texas. The city was named after Indians the Mexicans called Huecos; by the late 19th century it was one of the largest cotton markets in the world, a rip-roaring town with legalized prostitution and with a graceful ox-cart-wide suspension bridge across the Brazos which, when it opened in 1870, was the longest single-span suspension bridge in the United States and the second longest in the world. Waco was the home of atheist William Cowper Brann, author and publisher of *The Iconoclast* magazine, who was shot down in the streets but managed to kill his attacker. Waco is remembered now as the site of the tragedy of February 1993, when agents of the Bureau of Alcohol, Tobacco and Firearms moved in on David Koresh's Branch Davidian compound, Ranch Apocalypse, near Waco, and Koresh and his followers were burned to death in the ensuing fire. But Waco should be famous for other things as well. It is the home of Baylor University, the oldest college in Texas and the largest Baptist university in the world. In Waco's McLennan County, is the tiny town of Crawford, with its Rainey Creek, which traverses George W. Bush's 1,583-acre Prairie Chapel Ranch. Waco is only a little more than an hour away from the gallerias of the Dallas-Fort Worth Metroplex, but it is still in touch with Texas's rural roots, with the days when cotton was the basis of Texas's economy.

The 17th Congressional District of Texas includes all of nine counties and parts of three more but is centered on Waco and two other population centers. To the north is Johnson County, directly south of Fort Worth's Tarrant County, a fast-growing (population rose 36% between 1990 and 2004) part of the Dallas-Fort Worth Metroplex. Once almost entirely rural, with odd settlements like the Mennonites in Grandview, it is now becoming suburban, or at least exurban. The other population center is Brazos County, whose largest city, College Station, is home to Texas A&M University. Its agricultural and military tradition sets it apart from the University of Texas; it has a more conservative atmosphere and is the site of the George H.W. Bush Presidential Library. It is a world-class university, with 44,000 students; its president is former CIA Director Robert Gates and it has opened a campus in Qatar. The political tradition in central Texas for over a century was Democratic, heavily so. This area voted for Democrat Hubert Humphrey in 1968, when most of the rural South went for George Wallace and Richard Nixon; it voted Democratic when Texas first elected a Republican governor in 1978 and voted for Democrat Ann Richards, a Waco native, in 1990. But it seems to have followed most of Texas and become Republican. George W. Bush carried the area when running for governor in 1994 and 1998; the district voted 68% for him for president in 2000 and 70% in 2004. This was in effect a new district created by the Republican redistricters in October 2003. Only 7% of its residents lived in the old 17th District, which stretched far to the west; it includes parts of six old districts. The incumbent here was Chet Edwards, a Democrat from Waco, who had proved able to win reelections in the heavily Republican 11th District. But only 35% of the residents of the new 17th District lived in his old district; he lost Fort Hood, and Johnson and Brazos Counties were new territory for him. The redistricters obviously intended to beat Edwards, but at least in 2004 they did not succeed.

The congressman from the 17th District is Chet Edwards, a Democrat first elected in 1990, and only the third congressman from the Waco-centered district since 1937. Edwards is one of those highly skilled and motivated Democrats who has made politics his life—and who kept the Texas legislature and the U.S. House Democratic for so many years. He grew up in Corpus Christi, was a junior golf champion and graduated from Texas A&M, where he studied economics under Phil Gramm, then a conservative Democrat. He got the attention of 6th District Congressman Olin Teague when he invited Ralph Nader to a campus event: Teague berated Edwards at first, but was impressed enough to hire him as his district director when he graduated from A&M. In 1978, Teague retired and Edwards, at 26, ran for the seat. In the Democratic primary, Edwards wound up in third place, just 115 votes behind Phil Gramm, who went on to win the seat; if Edwards had won just 116 more votes, a lot of Texas and national political history would be different. Edwards went off to Harvard to get an M.B.A., returned and moved to Duncanville in southwest Dallas County, and at age 31 ran for the state Senate in 1982 and won.

In 1990 when 11th District Democrat Marvin Leath retired, Edwards moved his residence to Waco, and ran for the 11th District seat unopposed in the Democratic primary. With a promise of an Armed Services Committee slot from Speaker Thomas Foley and strong support from Leath, Edwards won a 53%–47% victory. In the House, Edwards worked for Fort Hood and eventually won a seat on Appropriations, where he claims credit for $700 million in construction there. When Democrats were in the majority Edwards took conservative stands on some but by no means all issues. He worked successfully to stop the designation of 33 Texas counties as a critical habitat for the allegedly endangered golden-cheeked warbler and supported the Private Property Owners Bill of Rights. He voted against the Brady bill but for the assault weapons ban and the 1994 crime bill.

After Democrats lost their majority in 1994, Minority Leader Dick Gephardt asked Edwards to serve as one of four chief deputy whips. Edwards accepted, but promptly voted for the Contract with America's balanced budget amendment and line-item veto. In 1998 and 1999 he led opposition to the school-prayer constitutional amendment and opposed a resolution for a national day of prayer and fasting after the Columbine shootings in 1999. Later that year, he sponsored an amendment to ban government funds for "pervasively sectarian" groups. He has been critical of George W. Bush's proposals to fund services provided by faith-based organizations; he also opposed the partial-birth abortion ban.

On several measures, he has worked with the Democratic leadership, supporting a waiting period for sales at gun shows and opposing repeal of the estate tax. He has not been shy about using his seat on Appropriations to fund local projects.

In the years running up to the 2003 redistricting, Edwards won reelection in an increasingly Republican district by narrowing margins. In 2000, against retired Texaco executive Ramsey Farley, who raised over $500,000 and attacked him on education, taxes and abortion, he won 55%–44%. In 2002 Farley ran again and national Republicans ran ads against Edwards arguing that he had the voting record of a Northeastern liberal. Edwards argued that he supported Bush on terrorism, education, welfare, energy and the Iraq war resolution. Edwards gleefully pointed out that Farley had said he "very vehemently" opposed Bush's education bill. Edwards spent $1.6 million to Farley's $614,000. Yet he won by only a 52%–47% margin.

In January 2003 Edwards resigned his position as chief deputy whip to spend more time on district affairs. When the new district lines were announced in October 2003 it was obvious he would face a serious challenge. The Republicans had a spirited three-way primary. Waco school board president Dot Snyder spent $200,000 of her own money and started off well known in the district's largest population center. Retired Army Colonel Dave McIntyre spent only $61,000 but had a local base in College Station. The most controversial candidate was state Representative Arlene Wohlgemuth from Johnson County. She made a name in the legislature for the "Memorial Day massacre" in 1997, when in retaliation for the defeat of a parental consent bill she made a point of order that killed 52 bills, many sponsored by Republicans; the parental consent law was passed in 1999. In 2003, when Republicans finally won a majority in the state House, she shepherded through a reorganization of the state's health and human services department which, among other things, reduced enrollment in the CHIP children's health program. Wohlgemuth was supported by many religious conservatives and by the economic conservatives of the Club for Growth, which raised $374,000 for her. In the March 9 primary Wohlgemuth led with 41% of the vote; she won 68% in Johnson County. In second place was Snyder, with 31%; but she led Wohlgemuth in Waco's McLennan County by only 44%–35%. In third place was McIntyre, with 28%; he won 60% in Brazos County. In the five-week runoff campaign Wohlgemuth launched some sharp attacks on Snyder and argued that she was the stronger conservative. Wohlgemuth won with 55%; almost all of her margin came from Johnson County, where she won 68% of the vote.

Now Edwards was facing an experienced and aggressive challenger in a district sure to vote for its local president by more than a 2–1 margin. "I am proud that I will be receiving the vote of President George W. Bush," Wohlgemuth frequently proclaimed. In the race for speaker, she said, she would not vote for "Nancy Pelosi of San Francisco." Her ads showed her with George W. Bush at the top of the stairs to Air Force One. She attacked Edwards for voting against the partial-birth abortion ban. "This is a Republican district. It deserves to have a conservative Republican representing it." Edwards responded aggressively. He attacked her as overly partisan. "While Mrs. Wohlgemuth is focusing on partisanship on every breath in this campaign, I find voters feel strongly, including Republicans, that we need less partisanship in Washington, not more." And he repeatedly charged that her health and human services bill had removed 147,000 children from the CHIP program; she said the real number was 26,000. He argued that his seniority and his seat on the Appropriations Committee made him much better positioned to help the district, and he cited the projects he had funded; he pledged to fight to keep the threatened Waco VA hospital open. "I respect President Bush, and I have strongly supported him in his war on terror and his energy and education bills. But my philosophy has never changed. When I think an administration is doing right for district and country, I will support them. When it is not, I respectfully disagree."

It seemed obvious that both candidates would carry their home bases and so they campaigned heavily elsewhere, with frequent debates—two in one day in October. Brazos County was a key battleground. Edwards signed off in his ads for the Bryan-College Station TV market by saying, "I'm Chet Edwards, Class of '74, and I approved this message." Wohlgemuth reminded locals that her two daughters had graduated from A&M and that therefore she was an "Aggie mom." Both candidates stayed off expensive Dallas-Fort Worth TV for most of the time, but advertised elsewhere. Edwards spent $2.7 million to her $2.6 million. Wohlgemuth raised money from local and national conservatives and was the beneficiary of $325,000 in national Republican ads. Edwards raised large sums from the unions and trial lawyers who had been his allies since his days in the Texas Senate.

Edwards was one of five white male Democratic incumbents in Texas seriously threatened by the 2003 redistricting (another one retired), and he was the only one to win, by a 51%–47% margin. In McLennan and Bosque Counties, the only two counties in his old 11th District, he led 63%–36%, a big improvement over his 2002 showing there, and an impressive 30% ahead of John Kerry. In Johnson County and the two adjacent counties in the DFW media market, Wohlgemuth led 61%–37%, running 13% behind Bush. Edwards ran ahead of Wohlgemuth by 268 votes in Brazos County and carried all but one of the smaller counties, running ahead 55%–44%.

After the election Edwards continued to talk about the need for bipartisanship and approached DeLay on the House floor and urged that they cooperate on Texas issues. He said he would continue to look after Fort Hood on the Military Construction Subcommittee though it is no longer in his district.

EIGHTEENTH DISTRICT

Rep. Sheila Jackson Lee (D)

Elected 1994, 6th term; b. Jan. 12, 1950, Queens, NY; home, Houston; Yale U., B.A. 1972, U. of VA Law Schl., J.D. 1975; Seventh Day Adventist; married (Elwyn).

Elected Office: Houston City Cncl., 1990–94.

Professional Career: Practicing atty., 1975–77, 1978–87; Staff Cnsl., U.S. House Select Assassinations Cmte., 1977–78; Houston Assoc. Municipal Judge, 1987–90.

DC Office: 2435 RHOB, 20515, 202-225-3816; Fax: 202-225-3317; Web site: jacksonlee.house.gov.

District Offices: Houston, 713-691-4882; Houston, 713-861-4070; Houston, 713-655-0050.

Committees: *Homeland Security* (10th of 15 D): Economic Security, Infrastructure Protection & Cybersecurity; Intelligence, Information Sharing & Terrorism Risk Assessment; Management, Integration & Oversight. *Judiciary* (8th of 17 D): Crime, Terrorism & Homeland Security; Immigration, Border Security & Claims (RMM). *Science* (13th of 20 D): Energy; Space & Aeronautics.

Group Ratings

	ADA	ACLU	AFS	LCV	ITIC	NTU	COC	ACU	NTLC	CHC
2004	95	95	88	82	20	10	53	4	0	7
2003	95	—	100	85	—	20	31	8	—	—

National Journal Ratings

	2003 LIB	—	2003 CONS		2004 LIB	—	2004 CONS
Economic	73%	—	27%		71%	—	29%
Social	88%	—	12%		82%	—	18%
Foreign	88%	—	11%		85%	—	14%

Key Votes of the 108th Congress

1. Drilling in ANWR	N	5. DC School Vouchers	N	9. Ban Same-Sex Marriage	N
2. Approve Bush Tax Cuts	N	6. Ban Human Cloning	N	10. Fund Iraq War	N
3. Medicare/Rx Bill	N	7. Restrict Gun Liability	N	11. Bar Cuba Embargo Funds	Y
4. Bar Overtime Pay Regs.	Y	8. Ban Partial-Birth Abortion	N	12. Intelligence Reorg.	N

Election Results

2004 general	Sheila Jackson Lee (D)	136,018	(89%)	($370,856)
	Tom Bazan (I)	9,787	(6%)	($10,666)
	Brent Sullivan (Lib)	7,183	(5%)	
2004 primary	Sheila Jackson Lee (D)	unopposed		
2002 general	Sheila Jackson Lee (D)	99,161	(77%)	($395,662)
	Phillip Abbott (R)	27,980	(22%)	($21,455)
	Other	1,785	(1%)	

Prior Winning Percentages: 2000 (76%); 1998 (90%); 1996 (77%); 1994 (73%)

The People		Race/Ethnic Origin	Ancestry	
Area size:	228 sq. mi.	19.7% White	German: 3.7%	USA: 2.6%
Urban population:	99.9%	40.1% Black	Irish: 2.6%	
Rural population:	0.1%	3.3% Asian	**2004 Presidential Vote**	
Pop. 2000:	651,619	0.2% Native Am.	Kerry (D)	125,155 (72%)
Median income:	$31,291	0.0% Hawaiian	Bush (R)	48,753 (28%)
Poverty status:	23.3%	1.0% Two+ races	**2000 Presidential Vote**	
Military veterans:	8.3%	0.1% Other	Gore (D)	118,488 (72%)
		35.6% Hispanic Origin	Bush (R)	45,151 (28%)
			Cook Partisan Voting Index: D +23	
Occupation	Blue collar: 30.0%	White collar: 52.1%	Gray collar: 17.8%	

Houston contains, within its vast bounds, disparities of income and wealth as striking as any city in the United States. This is what one must expect in an expanding city with dynamic economic growth, vast immigration, absence of centralized planning and openness to cultural diversity. The contrast is most glaringly apparent at the edge of Houston's gleaming downtown with its keynote Pennzoil, Heritage Plaza and Bank of America buildings, plus Minute Maid Park (formerly Enron Field) for baseball's Astros and the Toyota Center for indoor sports, and newly renovated housing in what was once the city's warehouse district. Only a few blocks away are slums where blacks and Mexican-Americans live in unpainted frame houses full of cracks wide enough to let in Houston's humid, smoggy air. But the contrasts are less obvious as one moves out from Houston's historic center. Half a century ago, when Houston pioneers like Jesse Jones, millionaire cotton broker and newspaper publisher, started building downtown skyscrapers, they were operating in a town with a Third World economy, a low-skill producer of basic commodities, where a few got rich and many lived near subsistence level. Since then, Houston has had a high-tech advanced economy offering a myriad of opportunities and wide range of economic outcomes. As Houston's blacks and Hispanics have moved outward from the city, increasingly they are living in comfortable middle-class neighborhoods. Highway congestion has increased the demand for additional mass transit. In recent years, the area suffered from a series of man-made and natural disasters. The biggest headlines came in late 2001 with the collapse and bankruptcy of Enron, the local energy and energy trading company whose executives cooked the books to conceal huge debt. Its collapse cost thousands of Houstonians their jobs, as did the merger of Compaq into Hewlett-Packard.

The 18th Congressional District of Texas contains central Houston and many of these outlying neighborhoods. The district includes Houston's downtown and the black and Latino neighborhoods immediately south toward Loop 610. On the north it has two spokes running out from Loop 610 and beyond: northeast between the Eastex Freeway and Beaumont Highway and extending to near Jacinto City and Galena Park, and northwest between the Northwest Freeway and Hempstead and then heading east to include George Bush International Airport. The 2003 redistricting reduced the black percentage from 42% black to 40%, with about 60,000 blacks south of Loop 610 added to the new 9th District; nearly as many blacks were added from the old 29th District north of downtown. The Hispanic population increased from 33% to 36%. Politically, this and the 30th District in Dallas are the two most heavily Democratic districts in Texas.

The congresswoman from the 18th District is Sheila Jackson Lee, a Democrat first elected in 1994. A native of Queens, New York, she was educated at Yale and Virginia law school, worked on Capitol Hill and practiced law in Houston, served as a local judge and won two terms in an at-large seat on the Houston city council. After a local term limits law took effect in 1994, she ran for Congress. The incumbent was Craig Washington, a talented but storm-tossed legislator, an iconoclast who voted against the space station and NAFTA, both of which are big pluses for the Houston area economy. Jackson Lee supported NAFTA and raised lots of money from business interests who favored it—including Kenneth Lay, then a rising star at Enron. She won the Democratic primary unambiguously, 63%–37%, and has been re-elected easily since.

In the House, Jackson Lee has a liberal voting record, though she has been leaning toward the center on economic issues. She has been prolific in proposing bills and offering amendments on the floor. Several of those that passed required studies, added small amounts to spending bills, or were non-controversial, such as prohibiting the use of children as soldiers in Afghanistan. But in the Republican House her more substantive proposals—for example, in favor of NASA funding and abortion—have usually been defeated. In 2003–2004, she forced a House vote on 12 of her amendments; each was defeated. She emerged into national prominence as an outspoken and contentious defender of President Clinton during impeachment; she has modeled herself on Barbara Jordan, the first black representative elected by the 18th District and an eloquent advocate of the impeachment of Richard Nixon in the Judiciary Committee. But Jackson Lee was embarrassed when the conservative *Weekly Standard* wrote that she violated House ethics rules by having an aide drive her one block to and from her Capitol Hill apartment every day. After she joined five other House Democrats who filed a lawsuit in February 2003 to prevent George W. Bush from invading Iraq without action by Congress, she was raucously jeered at a "Rally for America" held in her district by a local talk radio station.

As ranking Democrat on the Immigration, Border Security and Claims Subcommittee, Jackson Lee faces conflicting desires among her constituents: Latinos tend to favor greater immigration and more generous treatment of immigrants, but some African-Americans and union leaders see immigrants as dangerous competition for jobs. Frequently, but not always, she has taken the pro-immigrant side. She has an opportunity to play a key role on this difficult issue.

Although she has not faced serious opposition to her reelection, she revealed a partisan instinct during a pep talk to the Texas delegation at the 2004 Democratic convention in Boston. Recounting the litany of great Democrats from Texas, she rose to the occasion: "It would be a disgrace if we do not pay tribute and honor to them by getting every single vote out . . . .Mark my words, if we got to get 'em out of the graveyard, we're going to get 'em.'" Just joking, she said later.

NINETEENTH DISTRICT

Rep. Randy Neugebauer (R)

Elected June 2003, 1st full term; b. Dec. 24, 1949, Lubbock; home, Lubbock; TX Tech. U., B.B.A. 1972.; Baptist; married (Dana).

Elected Office: Lubbock City Cncl., 1992–98; Mayor Pro Tempore, Lubbock, 1994–96.

Professional Career: Mgr., Sentry Property Mngt., 1972–75; Instructor, South Plains College, 1975–78; V.P., First National Bank, 1975–82; Pres., Prestige Homes, 1983–87; Pres., Lubbock Land Co., 1987-present.

DC Office: 429 CHOB, 20515, 202-225-4005; Fax: 202-225-9615; Web site: www.house.gov/neugebauer.

District Offices: Abilene, 325-675-9779; Big Spring, 432-264-7592; Lubbock, 806-763-1611.

Committees: *Agriculture* (18th of 25 R): General Farm Commodities & Risk Management; Livestock & Horticulture; Specialty Crops & Foreign Agriculture Programs. *Financial Services* (33d of 37 R): Domestic and International Monetary Policy, Trade & Technology; Financial Institutions & Consumer Credit; Housing & Community Opportunity.

Group Ratings (Only Served Partial Term)

	ADA	ACLU	AFS	LCV	ITIC	NTU	COC	ACU	NTLC	CHC
2004	5	0	0	0	100	73	100	96	100	100
2003	10	—	0	9	—	57	95	89	—	—

National Journal Ratings (Only Served Partial Term)

	2003 LIB	—	2003 CONS	2004 LIB	—	2004 CONS
Economic	*	—	*	23%	—	76%
Social	*	—	*	9%	—	85%
Foreign	29%	—	71%	25%	—	68%

Key Votes of the 108th Congress (Only Served Partial Term)

1. Drilling in ANWR	*	5. DC School Vouchers	Y	9. Ban Same-Sex Marriage	Y
2. Approve Bush Tax Cuts	*	6. Ban Human Cloning	*	10. Fund Iraq War	Y
3. Medicare/Rx Bill	Y	7. Restrict Gun Liability	*	11. Bar Cuba Embargo Funds	N
4. Bar Overtime Pay Regs.	N	8. Ban Partial-Birth Abortion	*	12. Intelligence Reorg.	Y

Election Results

2004 general	Randy Neugebauer (R)	136,459	(58%)	($3,245,173)
	Charlie Stenholm (D)	93,531	(40%)	($2,479,274)
	Other	3,524	(2%)	
2004 primary	Randy Neugebauer (R)	unopposed		
2003 spec. runoff	Randy Neugebauer (R)	28,546	(51%)	
	Mike Conaway (R)	27,959	(49%)	
2003 spec. primary	Randy Neugebauer (R)	13,091	(22%)	
	Mike Conaway (R)	12,270	(21%)	
	Carl Isett (R)	11,015	(19%)	
	David Langston (R)	8,053	(14%)	
	Stace Williams (R)	2,609	(4%)	
	Other	11,331	(19%)	

The People		Race/Ethnic Origin	Ancestry	
Area size:	25,356 sq. mi.	63.6% White	USA: 9.9%	German: 7.7%
Urban population:	74.0%	5.3% Black	English: 6.7%	
Rural population:	26.0%	0.8% Asian	**2004 Presidential Vote**	
Pop. 2000:	651,619	0.4% Native Am.	Bush (R) 181,516	(77%)
Median income:	$31,575	0.0% Hawaiian	Kerry (D) 52,800	(23%)
Poverty status:	17.5%	0.9% Two+ races	**2000 Presidential Vote**	
Military veterans:	11.6%	0.1% Other	Bush (R) 152,237	(75%)
		29.0% Hispanic Origin	Gore (D) 51,302	(25%)
			Cook Partisan Voting Index: R +25	

Occupation	Blue collar: 23.8%	White collar: 56.8%	Gray collar: 19.4%

Until water was discovered in the giant Ogallala Aquifer that lies under the area around Lubbock, this was Indian country, then a land of Army forts and cattle ranches. When the water was tapped, well into the 20th century, what had been grazing land suddenly became cotton fields, with green crops grown in circles where sprinklers reached, separated by parched land. Lubbock became a regional center, the home of Texas Tech, and grew rapidly at mid-century: Lubbock County's population increased from 51,000 in 1940 to 101,000 in 1950 and 156,000 in 1960—lots of people in sparsely settled west Texas. Since then the regional economy has grown more slowly, as the Aquifer seemed to be going dry; in 2000, Lubbock County's population reached 242,000, and populations of the neighboring, much smaller, counties declined. Cotton growers struggled with international competitors and trade rulings, plus pressure to reduce agricultural subsidies, which the growers contend are a small fraction of the overall economic return. Lubbock has also made a great and outsized contribution to American popular culture. This one small city and nearby counties have produced a slew of fine musicians: Buddy Holly, Tanya Tucker, Jimmy Dean, Waylon Jennings, Mac Davis, Joe Ely, Roy Orbison, Don Williams. A discordant note came from Lubbock's Natalie Maines of the Dixie Chicks, who told a London audience in March 2003 that she was ashamed that George W. Bush came from Texas; the Dixie Chicks quickly disappeared from the playlists of some country stations. As a local congressman once noted in his website, people around here are "fiercely independent as Texans, steeped in patriotism when it comes to Flag and Country."

Lubbock is separated from the great metropolises of Texas by hundreds of miles of mostly, but not entirely, empty land. Nearly 200 miles southeast of Lubbock, over gully-ridden territory, are Abilene and the surrounding cattle country, with ranches specializing in Angora goats and sheep and exotic animals like ostriches, emus and aoudad sheep; there also are cotton fields and pecan trees and mesquite, and many oil wells. At Dyess Air Force Base near Abilene are stationed some of the nation's B-1 bombers. The communities here maintain their traditions and keep close to nature: Sweetwater in Nolan County has an annual Rattlesnake Roundup; Olney in Young County stages a One-Armed Dove Hunt; Archer City, the boyhood and current home of novelist Larry McMurtry, and chronicled in *The Last Picture Show* and *Texasville*.

The 19th Congressional District of Texas connects these two wide-open regions. The population in Lubbock and its surrounding area is about twice as large as the Abilene area. The district, a product of the 2003 redistricting, was designed to safeguard the just-elected Republican incumbent from Lubbock against the likely challenge from a savvy and veteran Democrat from Abilene, and to allow the creation to the south of a new solidly Republican district dominated by Midland and Odessa, which had been in the old 19th District. Both goals were achieved. As recently as 1978, these parts of West Texas were Democratic enough that in an open seat election they rejected the candidacy of an attractive young Midland oilman named George W. Bush in favor of Lubbock Democrat Kent Hance. Today they are heavily Republican, so much so that Bush received 77% of the votes for president in this district in 2004.

The congressman from the 19th District is Randy Neugebauer (pronounced *NAW-ga-bauer*), a Republican who won the seat in a June 2003 special election. Once again, a Lubbock native prevailed in the final showdown with a Midland contender. That was Neugebauer, who graduated from Texas Tech, became a banker and then ran his own land-development company. From 1992 to 1998, he was a Lubbock city councilman. The contest was prompted by the unexpected resignation, announced a week after the November 2002 election, of Larry Combest. In the primary, there were four leading contenders in the all-party 17-candidate contest to succeed Combest, all Republican. They were Mike Conaway, a Midland accountant, plus three from Lubbock: Neugebauer, state representative Carl Isett, and former Mayor David Langston. The question appeared to be which Lubbock candidate would face Conaway in the runoff. Neugebauer was the biggest spender and in his advertising emphasized homeland defense and the need for secure borders. He also focused on his business connections to oil and farming. Neugebauer was helped because Isett—the only active office-holder—was tied down by legislative business in Austin. Langston, who previously won election as a Democrat, pitched himself as a Bush-like "compassionate conservative." Neugebauer surprisingly finished first, with 821 more votes than Conaway. In third place, Isett trailed Conaway by 1,255 votes; Langston finished farther back. In Lubbock County, which cast nearly half of the total vote, Neugebauer won 30% to 28% for Isett and 21% for Langston. Conaway swept the Midland and Odessa areas. The runoff featured few differences on the issues. Not surprisingly, both supported Combest's farm bill and Bush's national-security policy. Each sought to maximize the vote in his geographic base and to steal some votes from his opponent's turf. Regional patterns again held firm. In the combined vote from Midland and Odessa areas, Conaway won 85% of the vote, but in Lubbock County, which cast 47% of the vote, Neugebauer led 71%–29%. Overall, Neugebauer won 51%–49%.

In the House, Neugebauer naturally got a seat on the Agriculture Committee and later was appointed to Financial Services. He was a reliable conservative. The House passed his amendment to add $3 billion for drought assistance to farmers, which was offset by a reduction in payments from a farm conservation program; it was part of the disaster-aid bill, chiefly for hurricane victims, that Bush signed in October 2004. But he barely had a chance to get settled before the Texas legislature redrew the district lines in October 2003. The new lines placed the home of Democrat Charlie Stenholm, Congressman from the old 17th District since 1978 in the new 13th District; but that district was almost entirely unfamiliar territory for him, and heavily Republican to boot, and he decided to run in the 19th. Stenholm was arguably the last conservative Democrat from Texas in the House. He and Phil Gramm were leaders of the "Boll Weevils," backing the 1981 Reagan budget and tax cuts. He was one of five Democrats who voted to impeach Bill Clinton. But he stood with Democrats on tax issues. Stenholm also sponsored bills to add individual investment accounts to Social Security. But as the years went by, Republican leaders decided that Stenholm talked a good game but rarely delivered, though as ranking Democrat on the Agriculture Committee he did work closely with Combest in fashioning the 2002 farm bill. At home, his reelection margins in recent years had grown closer as the Republican tilt in his district grew even more pronounced.

This was one of two Texas contests between incumbents in 2004; the other was in the 32d District between Pete Sessions and Martin Frost. Most of the advantages—the district's partisan tilt, the fact that Neugebauer had represented 58% of its residents and Stenholm only 31%—favored the Republican. Both candidates promised to protect farm subsidies. Neugebauer called for cuts in other spending programs, such as food stamps; Stenholm was open to tax increases.

Stenholm emphasized his social conservatism, his dedication to West Texas constituent services, and his independence as a Democrat; he criticized Neugebauer ads suggesting that Stenholm was not pro-life on abortion, and sought to link Neugebauer with Tom DeLay. Although Neugebauer ran as a loyal White House ally, his support for drug reimportation from Canada showed his willingness to go his own way; he sought to link Stenholm with John Kerry. The Texas Farm Bureau, which earlier honored Stenholm as "one of the giants of Texas agriculture," endorsed Neugebauer. Neugebauer won 58%–40%. In Lubbock County, where Stenholm hoped to win 40% of the vote, he trailed 65%–33%; the county cast 40% of the total vote. In his own base of Abilene, which cast half as many votes as Lubbock, Stenholm led 50%–48%. Neugebauer carried 22 of the 27 counties.

After the election, Stenholm sold his home in Abilene and settled in Washington as a lobbyist and agricultural policy consultant. He dismissed suggestions that he might run for Texas agriculture commissioner. "Until something changes, anybody with a 'D' after their name is going to have a difficult time being elected to any statewide office. That time will come, but possibly not in my lifetime." About the only thing that could jeopardize Neugebauer's tenure is a radically different redistricting plan.

TWENTIETH DISTRICT

Rep. Charles Gonzalez (D)

Elected 1998, 4th term; b. May 5, 1945, San Antonio; home, San Antonio; U. of TX, B. A. 1969; St. Mary's Law Schl., J.D. 1972.; Catholic; divorced.

Military Career: TX Air Natl. Guard, 1969–75.

Elected Office: Judge, San Antonio Municipal Court; Judge, Bexar Cnty. Court at Law, 1983–87; Judge, 57th State Judicial Dist. Court, 1988–97.

Professional Career: Elem. schl. teacher, 1969–71; Practicing atty., 1972–82.

DC Office: 327 CHOB, 20515, 202-225-3236; Fax: 202-225-1915; Web site: www.house.gov/gonzalez.

District Office: San Antonio, 210-472-6195.

Committees: *Energy & Commerce* (23d of 26 D): Commerce, Trade & Consumer Protection; Energy & Air Quality; Environment & Hazardous Materials; Telecommunications & the Internet.

Group Ratings

	ADA	ACLU	AFS	LCV	ITIC	NTU	COC	ACU	NTLC	CHC
2004	95	75	88	82	80	14	62	20	0	7
2003	95	—	100	75	—	23	50	16	—	—

National Journal Ratings

	2003 LIB	—	2003 CONS		2004 LIB	—	2004 CONS
Economic	62%	—	37%		61%	—	38%
Social	78%	—	20%		78%	—	19%
Foreign	70%	—	27%		70%	—	29%

Key Votes of the 108th Congress

1. Drilling in ANWR	N	5. DC School Vouchers	N	9. Ban Same-Sex Marriage	N
2. Approve Bush Tax Cuts	N	6. Ban Human Cloning	N	10. Fund Iraq War	Y
3. Medicare/Rx Bill	N	7. Restrict Gun Liability	N	11. Bar Cuba Embargo Funds	Y
4. Bar Overtime Pay Regs.	Y	8. Ban Partial-Birth Abortion	N	12. Intelligence Reorg.	N

Election Results

2004 general	Charles Gonzalez (D)	112,480	(65%)	($757,300)
	Roger Scott (R)	54,976	(32%)	($13,447)
	Other	4,348	(3%)	
2004 primary	Charles Gonzalez (D)	unopposed		
2002 general	Charles Gonzalez (D)	unopposed		($633,493)

Prior Winning Percentages: 2000 (88%); 1998 (63%)

The People		Race/Ethnic Origin	Ancestry	
Area size:	184 sq. mi.	23.4% White	German: 6.0%	Irish: 3.5%
Urban population:	99.8%	6.6% Black	English: 2.9%	
Rural population:	0.2%	1.4% Asian	**2004 Presidential Vote**	
Pop. 2000:	651,619	0.2% Native Am.	Kerry (D) 96,539	(55%)
Median income:	$31,937	0.1% Hawaiian	Bush (R) 78,757	(45%)
Poverty status:	19.9%	1.1% Two+ races	**2000 Presidential Vote**	
Military veterans:	14.2%	0.1% Other	Gore (D) 90,541	(58%)
		67.1% Hispanic Origin	Bush (R) 64,927	(42%)
			Cook Partisan Voting Index: D + 8	

Occupation	Blue collar: 24.0%	White collar: 56.6%	Gray collar: 19.4%

San Antonio, with its antique past and theme-park future, its Hispanic heritage, its military superstructure and its high-tech hopes, is unlike any other city in the United States. Here on a plaza is the Alamo, preserved by the Daughters of the Republic of Texas, where Davy Crockett, Jim Bowie and 184 others were wiped out in 1836 (Crockett was a Tennessee congressman for three terms; if he had not lost his reelection in 1834, he presumably would not have left Tennessee for Texas). The Spanish architecture recalls San Antonio's days as the most important town in Texas, when the state was part of Mexico, and contrasts with the 31-story Tower Life Building, which contrasts with the armadillo-like Alamodome; the stark terrain contrasts with the lushness of the Paseo, the 1970s-redeveloped Riverwalk along the tiny San Antonio River. The city includes old neighborhoods redolent of the Texas Germans who were its chief Anglo citizens for many years.

For most of the 20th century, San Antonio's economy was built on the military. What the locals call "Military City, U.S.A." remains the home of three Air Force bases, Fort Sam Houston and two military hospitals. In 1995 Bill Clinton bent the rules of the base closing process to keep in San Antonio the thousands of depot jobs at Kelly Air Force Base, a move so resented that Congress blocked new rounds of base closings until 2005. Kelly was finally closed in 2001. In its May 2005 recommendations, the Pentagon again proposed closing a local facility—Brooks City Base—but Fort Sam Houston was a big winner. Fort Sam's renowned Brooke Army Medical Center was slated for transformation into a regional military medical center, accompanied by a gain of 9,300 jobs. The local health industry, which includes the Texas Health Science Center, was already thriving prior to the announcement; the industry is the largest local employer. San Antonio also has many military retirees and it has become a tourist center. The city also is the home of telecom-giant SBC Communications, which has battled to move into the cable-TV business and announced its takeover of AT&T. In 2004, San Antonio surpassed Dallas as Texas's second largest city and the eighth largest in the country, though its metro area of 1.7 million is only about one-third the size of metro Houston or the Dallas-Fort Worth Metroplex. Its low education and income levels are affected by the proximity of the Mexican border, which has become a source of major commercial growth. Yet it has mostly avoided polarized politics and ethnic anger as it has made progress as a low-wage, high-tech center, with some linkage to nearby Austin. There have been local complaints that the four-year term limits for the mayor and council members make it difficult for local officials to get things done.

The 20th Congressional District of Texas includes most of central San Antonio and its west side. The district is wholly contained within Bexar County; affluent Anglo neighborhoods are set off and placed in the 21st or 23d Districts. On the west it extends beyond Lackland Air Force Base toward the county line. Redistricting in 2003 swapped some precincts with the 28th District, but had little impact on the partisan or ethnic compositions, now 67% Hispanic. This is one of the state's eight Hispanic-majority districts, and it was the first to elect a Hispanic congressman, in 1961. It is Democratic, but not overwhelmingly so: George W. Bush won 45% of the vote here in 2004.

The congressman from the 20th District is Charles Gonzalez, a Democrat first elected in 1998. He is one of eight children of Henry B. Gonzalez, who held the seat for 37 years after winning a 1961 special election. Charles Gonzalez grew up in San Antonio, graduated from the

University of Texas and St. Mary's University School of Law, and served in the Texas Air National Guard. He was an elementary school teacher, practiced law and served as a judge from 1982 to 1997. In late 1997, at 81 and in poor health, his father announced his retirement. Charles Gonzalez was the frontrunner for the seat, but the contest was more competitive than many had expected. Gonzalez campaigned as a consensus-builder, emphasizing his background in negotiation and compromise. Symbolizing the economic transformation of San Antonio, he said he would work for the entire district, not simply the low-income groups. Taking a more feisty tone was Maria Berriozabal, a former city council member, who called for more outspoken leadership. She displayed a picture of Henry Gonzalez in her campaign literature and claimed that she was more his model than was Charles. Just before the March primary, his father issued a brief statement endorsing his son. Gonzalez led Berriozabal in the primary 44%–22%. In the April runoff, Gonzalez benefited from a fundraising advantage of more than 2–1 and mostly ignored his opponent. He won 62%–38% and easily won the general election.

In the House, Gonzalez has a relatively moderate voting record, especially on economic issues. After taking his father's seat on the now renamed Financial Services Committee, he moved to Energy and Commerce after Ralph Hall switched parties in January 2004 and created a Democratic vacancy; when Nancy Pelosi turned down his bid for a seat on that committee a year earlier, some thought that Gonzalez suffered because he had backed other candidates when she ran for minority whip and minority leader. On Energy and Commerce, he backed a proposal to force satellite television operators to end a practice that forced users to have two satellite dishes to receive Spanish language channels. He demanded that the Federal Railroad Administration enforce safety requirements after the Union Pacific Railroad, which had several serious accidents in the area, sought to avoid U.S. inspections on its trains crossing the border from Mexico. For both the Democratic Caucus and the Hispanic Caucus—which his father had refused to join—Gonzalez has been a leading proponent of census sampling. But he opposed Latino activists who wanted to create an additional Hispanic-majority district for Texas in the 2001 redistricting; because of low voter turnout among Hispanics, he said, such a step would reduce the Democratic majorities in other districts, an argument corroborated by the Republicans' 2003 redistricting.

In 2004, Gonzalez faced his first reelection challenge since he took office. Initially his ex-wife Becky Whetstone, a marriage and family therapist, said that she would run so that voters would have a choice and he would be "held accountable." But she failed to get the 500 signatures required to get on the ballot as an Independent. Gonzalez beat Republican Roger Scott 65%–32%.

TWENTY-FIRST DISTRICT

Rep. Lamar Smith (R)

Elected 1986, 10th term; b. Nov. 19, 1947, San Antonio; home, San Antonio; Yale U., B.A. 1969, S. Methodist U., J.D. 1975; Christian Scientist; married (Beth).

Elected Office: TX House of Reps., 1981–82; Bexar Cnty. Comm., 1982–85.

Professional Career: U.S. Small Business Admin., 1969–70; Business writer, *Christian Science Monitor*, 1970–72; Practicing atty., 1975–76.

DC Office: 2184 RHOB, 20515, 202-225-4236; Fax: 202-225-8628; Web site: lamarsmith.house.gov.

District Offices: Austin, 512-402-9743; San Antonio, 210-821-5024.

Committees: *Homeland Security* (3d of 19 R): Economic Security, Infrastructure Protection & Cybersecurity; Emergency Preparedness, Science & Technology. *Judiciary* (4th of 23 R): Courts, the Internet & Intellectual Property (Chmn.); Immigration, Border Security & Claims. *Science* (3d of 24 R): Research; Space & Aeronautics. *Standards of Official Conduct* (3d of 5 R).

Group Ratings

	ADA	ACLU	AFS	LCV	ITIC	NTU	COC	ACU	NTLC	CHC
2004	0	0	13	9	100	57	100	92	78	92
2003	5	—	0	0	—	59	100	92	—	—

National Journal Ratings

	2003 LIB	—	2003 CONS		2004 LIB	—	2004 CONS
Economic	9%	—	84%		9%	—	88%
Social	5%	—	87%		9%	—	85%
Foreign	0%	—	89%		17%	—	78%

Key Votes of the 108th Congress

1. Drilling in ANWR	Y	5. DC School Vouchers	Y	9. Ban Same-Sex Marriage	Y
2. Approve Bush Tax Cuts	Y	6. Ban Human Cloning	Y	10. Fund Iraq War	Y
3. Medicare/Rx Bill	Y	7. Restrict Gun Liability	Y	11. Bar Cuba Embargo Funds	N
4. Bar Overtime Pay Regs.	N	8. Ban Partial-Birth Abortion	Y	12. Intelligence Reorg.	Y

Election Results

2004 general	Lamar Smith (R)	209,774	(61%)	($606,121)
	Rhett Smith (D)	121,129	(36%)	
	Other	10,216	(3%)	
2004 primary	Lamar Smith (R)	unopposed		
2002 general	Lamar Smith (R)	161,836	(73%)	($798,990)
	John Courage (D)	56,206	(25%)	($167,000)
	Other	4,051	(2%)	

Prior Winning Percentages: 2000 (76%); 1998 (91%); 1996 (76%); 1994 (90%); 1992 (72%); 1990 (75%); 1988 (93%); 1986 (61%)

The People

		Race/Ethnic Origin	**Ancestry**
Area size:	2,630 sq. mi.	73.1% White	German: 15.2% English: 9.7%
Urban population:	82.0%	3.8% Black	Irish: 8.6%
Rural population:	18.0%	3.0% Asian	**2004 Presidential Vote**
Pop. 2000:	651,619	0.3% Native Am.	Bush (R) 210,121 (61%)
Median income:	$55,609	0.1% Hawaiian	Kerry (D) 137,096 (39%)
Poverty status:	7.0%	1.4% Two+ races	**2000 Presidential Vote**
Military veterans:	15.4%	0.1% Other	Bush (R) 182,723 (67%)
		18.1% Hispanic Origin	Gore (D) 88,996 (33%)
			Cook Partisan Voting Index: R +13

Occupation   Blue collar: 13.4%   White collar: 75.7%   Gray collar: 10.9%

The Balcones Escarpment is the invisible line, or rather the physiographic break, that separates the flat lands of coastal Texas from the stony hills to the north and west. It is a boundary between cropland and grazing land, between acres rich with greenery and acres whose rolling brown hills blaze out in color when the wildflowers bloom in Texas's early spring, between places where the sky is hemmed in by trees and buildings and places where the sky seems all around you, to the horizon far in the distance. The Balcones Escarpment separates Dallas and Fort Worth; it runs through Austin and the western edge of San Antonio. But it is less familiar to Texans today than the highway that runs pretty much along the same line: Interstate 35. I-35 splits into I-35E and I-35W in the Dallas-Fort Worth Metroplex, with one running through each city. To the south it is one of the most heavily traveled and congested Interstates in America, thick with truck traffic in the populated stretches between the Metroplex and Austin and San Antonio and also in the lightly populated near-desert between San Antonio and Laredo on the Mexican border. For this is one of the great routes of commerce in America, or rather between the United States and Mexico, and Laredo is the greatest freight crossing on America's southern border.

I-35 connects Austin and San Antonio, two Texan cities with very different beginnings and different characters now. Austin is the creation of state government, with the pink marble Capitol and the sprawling University of Texas. It has become one of America's leading high tech centers—the fourth largest by one count—but still has an economy heavily dependent on state government. San Antonio was the creation of Texas's Mexican settlers, a town with a Spanish accent and a heavily Latino population. It is proud of the Alamo (which strikes most visitors as tinier than expected) and the Riverwalk but it also has its corporate headquarters—SBC Communications is a big employer—and an array of military bases: three Air Force bases, Fort Sam Houston and two military medical centers. In between Austin and San Antonio, on I-35, are fast-growing Hays and Comal Counties, both settled initially by Texas Germans. Here you find San Marcos, where Lyndon Johnson went to college, and New Braunfels, founded in 1845 by German settlers. The Texas German country has always been a set of orderly communities in rip-roaring Texas, economically prosperous in a state that considered itself poor until it struck oil. It was anti-slavery and politically Republican in a state whose enthusiasm for the Democratic Party had roots in Confederate loyalties and populist rebellions. These counties have been growing rapidly, and seem as thronged with new subdivisions and shopping centers as I-35 is with trucks heading to the border. The lands around Canyon Lake and Dripping Springs are being populated with young families with high incomes seeking homesites in spacious new subdivisions spread out over the hills.

The 21st Congressional District of Texas includes much of this territory; it could be called the I-35 district. About 40% of its people are in Austin's Travis County—many in the hilly western part of the county beyond Loop 360, but it also includes downtown Austin, the Capitol and the University of Texas campus: at one point nearby three districts meet, one connected to San Antonio, one to Houston and one to the Lower Rio Grande Valley. Travis County overall has been a liberal Democratic county, trending more to Republicans with high-tech growth in the 1990s, but reacting negatively to its former resident George W. Bush in 2004. The 21st District's portion of Travis County is mixed: the older neighborhoods of Austin are Democratic and usually outvote the Republican precincts in the hills. Another 40% or so of the 21st's residents are in San Antonio's Bexar County, including Fort Sam Houston and Randolph Air Force Base, older affluent areas on the north side of San Antonio and suburban land north and east of the city. This is mostly Anglo San Antonio, though 24% of the Bexar County residents in the district are Hispanic. The rest of the people are in Hays and Comal Counties and, just 9,100 of them, in Blanco County, where Lyndon B. Johnson grew up in Johnson City and which was his legal residence when he was first elected to the House in 1937 (the LBJ Ranch is farther west, in Gillespie County which is Texas German country). The 2003 redistricting removed nine hill counties from the district and added much of the portion in Travis County.

The political heritage of the district is mixed. While Travis County was always Democratic and the Texas German country Republican, San Antonio, with a significant German heritage, was mixed. In 1931 the death of Bexar County's Republican Congressman Harry Wurzbach gave Democrats a majority in the House and enabled them to elect John Nance Garner of Uvalde as Speaker, while Wurzbach's replacement in the House, Democrat Richard Kleberg (of the King Ranch family) gave the then 23-year-old Johnson his first Washington job. Today the Travis County portion of the district leans Democratic, but the rest is heavily Republican; it voted 67% for George W. Bush in 2000 and, after Democratic anti-Bush turnout increased in Austin, 61% in 2004.

The congressman from the 21st District is Lamar Smith, a Republican first elected in 1986. Smith is from an old San Antonio and south Texas ranching family; their Jim Wells County ranch has been in the family for four generations. He graduated from Yale and SMU law school, worked as a reporter for the *Christian Science Monitor* and a lawyer in San Antonio, was elected to the Texas House in 1980 and the Bexar County Commission in 1982. In 1986, when Congressman Tom Loeffler ran for governor, Smith ran for the House. At that time the 21st District ranged far west and had more acreage than Ohio; Smith decided to run after a Midland oilman named George W. Bush decided not to. Smith won by beating two other San Antonio-based candidates in the primary and then winning the runoff 54%–46% against a religious conservative; his campaign was run by then little-known Texas political consultant Karl Rove.

Smith compiled a conservative voting record and pursued original initiatives when Democrats held the majority. One bill added 100,000 acres to Big Bend National Park along the Rio Grande; another sponsored the first Bush administration's government-wide ethics act. In the majority, Smith chaired the Immigration Subcommittee of Judiciary from 1995 to 2001. He's long been a believer in stronger action to stop illegal immigration and to reduce legal immigration; he opposed Bill Clinton's proposal for, and George W. Bush's suggestion of legalization of, illegal immigrants living in the United States for many years. But he has supported some liberalizing immigration provisions. His bill to split the INS into two agencies, one concentrating on law enforcement, the other on aid to immigrants, was passed as part of the homeland security bill in November 2002. He opposed the Bush guest worker program in 2004 and charged that it "opens up every job in America" to low-wage competition; he called for enforcement of the law prohibiting employers from hiring illegal aliens.

In 2001, having served the six years permitted by House Republican rules as chairman of the Immigration Subcommittee, Smith became chairman of what was then the Crime Subcommittee. There he focused on cybercrime and high-tech issues. He strongly supported the Patriot Act, which passed in October 2001, and produced the provisions allowing extended wiretaps.

In 2003 Smith became chairman of the Courts, the Internet and Intellectual Property Subcommittee. He co-sponsored with John Conyers and Howard Berman a bill to create new judgeships to determine copyright royalty rates and distribution of royalties and to remedy defects in Copyright Arbitration Royalty Panels. It passed the House unanimously in March 2004, the Senate in October and was signed into law in December. In 2003 Smith, Berman and Conyers sponsored a bill providing for criminal penalties of mass downloaders of music and requiring file-sharing software to contain warnings of security risk. In July 2004 Smith passed a bill allowing firms to sell software that could delete offensive passages from movie DVDs; it became law in April 2005 as part the Family Entertainment and Copyright Act. He also sponsored a bill to ban eight particular words from radio and television. In 2004 Smith also passed a Patent and Trademark Office Fee Act that devoted fees paid by those registering copyrights and trademarks to the operation of the office. He sponsored a bill to deny recognition to trademarks registered by the Castro regime in Cuba.

Smith is second in seniority among Republicans on the Science Committee. Most Texans have been strongly supportive of the manned space program. But after the loss of space shuttle Columbia in February 2003, Smith expressed some skepticism. "I think we need to revisit the question of whether manned missions are absolutely necessary. That's not to say we ought to exclusively do one or the other. Maybe we should undertake fewer manned missions." From January 1999 to January 2001, Smith chaired the ethics committee but the practice of bringing ethics complaints for partisan reasons had been discontinued, and Smith had few cases to contend with. In January 2005 he accepted an assignment to serve on the ethics committee again, but not as chairman.

Smith has been easily reelected by wide margins. After the 2003 redistricting added much of Travis County to the district, his margin went down, to 61%–36% in 2004. He still carried Bexar County 70%–28% but in Democratic-leaning Travis County he won by only 50%–46%.

TWENTY-SECOND DISTRICT

Rep. Tom DeLay (R)

Elected 1984, 11th term; b. Apr. 8, 1947, Laredo; home, Sugar Land; U. of Houston, B.S. 1970; Baptist; married (Christine).

Elected Office: TX House of Reps., 1978–84.

Professional Career: Owner, Albo Pest Control, 1973–84.

DC Office: 242 CHOB, 20515, 202-225-5951; Fax: 202-225-5241; Web site: tomdelay.house.gov.

District Offices: Stafford, 281-240-3700; Webster, 281-557-8855.

Committees: *Majority Leader.*

Group Ratings

	ADA	ACLU	AFS	LCV	ITIC	NTU	COC	ACU	NTLC	CHC
2004	0	0	0	0	100	63	100	100	86	92
2003	5	—	0	0	—	64	100	92	—	—

National Journal Ratings

	2003 LIB	—	2003 CONS		2004 LIB	—	2004 CONS
Economic	0%	—	91%		5%	—	93%
Social	5%	—	87%		9%	—	85%
Foreign	0%	—	89%		0%	—	96%

Key Votes of the 108th Congress

1. Drilling in ANWR	Y	5. DC School Vouchers	Y
2. Approve Bush Tax Cuts	Y	6. Ban Human Cloning	Y
3. Medicare/Rx Bill	Y	7. Restrict Gun Liability	Y
4. Bar Overtime Pay Regs.	N	8. Ban Partial-Birth Abortion	Y

9. Ban Same-Sex Marriage	Y
10. Fund Iraq War	Y
11. Bar Cuba Embargo Funds	N
12. Intelligence Reorg.	Y

Election Results

2004 general	Tom DeLay (R)....................................	150,386	(55%)	($3,143,559)
	Richard Morrison (D)	112,034	(41%)	($685,935)
	Other..	10,200	(4%)	
2004 primary	Tom DeLay (R).............................	unopposed		
2002 general	Tom DeLay (R)...................................	100,499	(63%)	($1,274,921)
	Tim Riley (D)	55,716	(35%)	($192,709)
	Other..	2,869	(2%)	

Prior Winning Percentages: 2000 (60%); 1998 (65%); 1996 (68%); 1994 (74%); 1992 (69%); 1990 (71%); 1988 (67%); 1986 (72%); 1984 (65%)

The People		Race/Ethnic Origin	Ancestry
Area size:	1,002 sq. mi.	60.6% White	German: 10.6% Irish: 7.1%
Urban population:	94.6%	9.3% Black	English: 7.0%
Rural population:	5.4%	8.0% Asian	**2004 Presidential Vote**
Pop. 2000:	651,619	0.3% Native Am.	Bush (R)............ 177,378 (64%)
Median income:	$57,932	0.0% Hawaiian	Kerry (D) 98,180 (36%)
Poverty status:	7.3%	1.4% Two+ races	**2000 Presidential Vote**
Military veterans:	11.1%	0.1% Other	Bush (R)............ 151,311 (67%)
		20.3% Hispanic Origin	Gore (D) 73,845 (33%)
			Cook Partisan Voting Index: R +15

Occupation	Blue collar: 19.8%	White collar: 69.1%	Gray collar: 11.0%

Those seeking the story of Houston's booming growth over the last dozen years would be well advised to go out the Southwest Freeway 45 minutes or so (if the traffic is not too bad) to Sugar Land. There has been a big change from the locale of *The Sugarland Express,* a B-movie in the 1970s about a fugitive convict—or, the sugar plantations that flourished here before the Civil War. Here in once rural Fort Bend County, on the site of the old Imperial Sugar Mill, is a privately planned city of 70,000, with privatized water and other services, immaculately clean and fast-growing (there were 33,000 people here in 1990). The entrepreneurial spirit is alive and well, with thousands of new and growing businesses, and so is a communitarian spirit, with dozens of churches and civic associations buzzing with activity. People welcome the new freeways and toll roads being built, to link them with Houston's airports and other business nodes. The image of suburbia has long been one of an all-white haven, but Sugar Land and Fort Bend County are welcoming to immigrants and minorities. Some 20% of the county population is black, and 77% of its blacks own their own homes; another 21% are Hispanic and 11% are Asian, the highest of any county in Texas. A reporter from the *San Francisco Chronicle* came to Sugar Land to see "the anti-San Francisco" and seemed charmed by a community that "welcomes immigrants, shopping centers and jogging paths." Sugar Land has elected Daniel Wong, from Macao, to the city council and Dinesh Shah, from India, to the board of the Chamber of Commerce. People came from around the world to construct and consecrate the huge new Hindu temple. "Sugar Landers consider themselves thoroughly diverse. There are Chinese Republicans and Indian Republicans. Palestinian Catholics run the town's popular Brookstreet Barbeque. Muslims have a bagpipe band. Hindus are building a temple." This is 21st century America.

The 22d Congressional District of Texas includes more than two-thirds of Fort Bend County, including Sugar Land; in the 2003 redistricting, small pieces along the border with Harris County were moved to the new 9th District, and helped to elect the new black Democrat. It also includes one-quarter of Brazoria County, centering on fast-growing Pearland, just south of Houston, plus parts of Galveston County including Santa Fe, La Marque and Hitchcock. Nearly one-half of its residents are in Harris County: working class Deer Park, Pasadena and LaPorte south of the Houston Ship Channel; and the more upscale Webster, Clear Lake and Taylor Lake Village surrounding the Johnson Space Center. Overall the district's population is 61% Anglo, 9% black, 20% Hispanic and 8% Asian. Politically, the 22d District remains Republican, but not quite so heavily as before the 2003 redistricting. George W. Bush won here 67%–33% in 2000, but his majority fell to 64%–36% in 2004—still comfortable but Bush won a higher share of the vote in 16 of the 32 Texas districts.

The congressman from the 22d District is Tom DeLay, of Sugar Land, a Republican first elected in 1984 and House Majority Leader since 2003. He was born in Laredo, on the border. His father was in the oil business, and between ages 9 and 14 he lived in Venezuela; he claims to have come close to being killed in one of its revolutionary upheavals. He attended Baylor University for two years and was asked to leave, and graduated from the University of Houston. Then he settled in Sugar Land and started a pest control business—he is our only political leader who is a former exterminator. In his business he developed a hatred for the Environmental Protection Agency, which he has called "the Gestapo of government." In 1978 he was elected to the state House, the first Republican legislator from Fort Bend County in the 20th century. When 22d District Congressman Ron Paul (now congressman from the 14th District) ran for the Senate in 1984, DeLay ran for the House. He won a five-candidate primary with 53% of the vote and won the general election 65%–35%.

DeLay's voting record in the House has been very conservative; he has combined a strong ideological motivation and a knack for practical politics. The motivation comes at least partly from a profound religious experience he had in 1985—at about the same time and about the same point in his life as George W. Bush. In his second term he got a seat on the Appropriations Committee, where he opposed a $1.2 billion monorail and has opposed extension of Houston's light rail line into Fort Bend County without approval of the voters. He has been a big booster of NASA and the 15,000 employees at the Johnson Space Center. A self-described "space nut," DeLay pressed hard, and successfully, to give NASA its full $16.2 billion budget in 2004, when most other domestic agencies were being trimmed. He was firm that the spending bill that includes the agency would not be scheduled for House action until "NASA was taken care of."

DeLay showed early on an interest in leadership positions and prowess as a vote-counter. In March 1989 he managed the campaign of moderate Edward Madigan to replace Dick Cheney as minority whip; but Madigan lost 87–85 to Newt Gingrich—a result that made a revolutionary change in the House and a lasting adversary for DeLay. Madigan's loss didn't stop DeLay from running in December 1992 against incumbent Bill Gradison for the post of Republican Conference Secretary; DeLay won 95–71. It was clear that Robert Michel would retire as minority leader in 1994, and that Gingrich would run to succeed him. DeLay started running for whip, presumed to be the second highest leadership post at a time when almost no one thought Republicans would win a majority in the 1994 elections; that meant that DeLay was trying to leapfrog Dick Armey on the leadership ladder. After the Republicans won their majority in 1994, Gingrich was easily elected speaker and Armey majority leader and DeLay kept running for whip. He had serious opposition from Robert Walker, Gingrich's best friend in the House, and Bill McCollum. But DeLay had done much more to prepare, campaigning in 25 states and contributing $2 million to Republican candidates. DeLay showed his vote-counting acumen by proclaiming that he was not interested in the second-ballot votes he would need if no one had a majority. He won with 119 votes to 80 for Walker and 28 for McCollum.

So DeLay came to the whip position as an independent operator, capable of amassing a majority of Republican members. As whip, his job was to assemble majorities on the House floor, and he proved himself a master of that. Over his eight years as whip he built a massive and loyal organization of as many as 67 deputy whips. Through them he could keep in close touch with Republican members of all stripes. He became known as "the Hammer," for his ability to hammer out majorities on the floor of the House over eight years when there were never more than 236 Republican members and at one time as few as 221—just three more than the majority of 218. He kept Republicans together not just by hammering them, but by serving their needs. His first floor office—invaded by a gun-wielding maniac in July 1998 who killed two Capitol policemen—was always stocked with food during late night sessions; his staff was happy to make travel arrangements for members. As one Republican member said, "His whip operation is a cross between the concierge at the Plaza and the mafia. They can get you anything you want, but it will cost you." Like Democratic whips before him, he expected members to support the leadership on procedural votes, especially the rules limiting debate voted by the Rules Committee, and, with others in the leadership, made committee assignments in light of such votes. Moderate Republican members were unhappy, but he insists that he supported them in campaigns. His vote-counting ability enabled him to make the minimum substantive concessions to amass a majority; no need for more concessions to get votes that aren't needed. And on occasion he brought measures to the floor without a majority in hand and, while Speaker Dennis Hastert kept the roll call running, squeezed out the critical votes on the floor, as he did on the Medicare/prescription drug bill in November 2003.

In all these respects DeLay followed the pattern of Democratic whips before him, except that he seemed to have been better at corralling majorities than they mostly were. But he has also tried to change the culture of Washington. In his first years as whip, he focused on regulatory commissions through riders on environmental issues, demanding cost-benefit analyses or placing a moratorium on new regulations. On these he was mostly frustrated by Clinton vetoes and by moderate Republican dissenters. He also sought to change the culture of K Street—the shorthand term for Washington's lobbying community. He worked closely with sympathetic lobbyists, bringing them in on the drafting of legislation, and has also raised money from them in very large amounts. K Street from New Deal days until 1994 had been overwhelmingly Democratic. DeLay insisted that trade associations and big corporations must hire Republicans as lobbyists. That brought him bad publicity and a private rebuke from the ethics committee when in October 1998 he attacked the Electronics Industries Alliance for hiring as its president former Democratic Congressman Dave McCurdy. But as Republicans kept winning House elections, it became clear to K Street denizens that they must hire Republicans if they wanted to be effective, and they have hired more and more, including many former members of DeLay's staff. DeLay has also had great success raising money, from K Street and elsewhere.

DeLay's relationship with Gingrich was tense; he supported him when his reelection as speaker was uncertain in January 1997, but he met with leaders of the coup against Gingrich in July 1997, telling them the leadership would support a floor vote to oust him. But the coup failed, and at a Republican Conference meeting a few days later, DeLay stepped dramatically forward and admitted his participation in the coup attempt, while Dick Armey seemed to deny his. From that point forward, it was clear DeLay had much more support in the conference than Armey. In November 1998, when Gingrich quit after the disappointing results of the election, DeLay supported Bob Livingston for speaker. But on the morning of the Clinton impeachment vote, Livingston shocked everyone by announcing that he would resign. Members began hovering around DeLay at the back of the chamber. Armey clearly did not have the support to win the speakership; DeLay, aware that he was "too nuclear," made no move to run. Instead he turned to the man he had named Chief Deputy Whip, Dennis Hastert, little known outside the House but respected by Republican members as a hard worker, consensus builder and party loyalist. "And so I pulled Denny aside and told him that he had to run for speaker. And he turned white as a sheet." Within hours it would be clear that Hastert would be the next speaker. Many assumed that Hastert would be DeLay's puppet, but Hastert and DeLay often disagreed on basic strategy, and Hastert usually prevailed.

For the most part, Hastert, Armey and DeLay delivered for the new administration; Bush, unlike his father, could count on a favorable vote in the House and then could negotiate with the

Senate. The danger for House Republicans has been that that they would be left hanging out there with an unpopular issue while Bush and the Democratic (from June 2001 to January 2003) Senate would get the credit. This didn't happen often. The most notable example was on airline security, in which DeLay squeezed out a 218–214 vote in November 2001 against federalizing employees. But the Senate voted 100–0 for federal security employees, and Bush didn't fight it hard.

In December 2001 Dick Armey announced that he would not run for reelection in 2002, and hours later DeLay quietly began running for the post. Ray LaHood, often a critic of the leadership, said he wanted to run; some Republicans pressed John Boehner, voted out of the leadership in 1998 and fresh from his success managing the education bill, to run. But Tom Reynolds announced that DeLay had 140 votes, far more than a majority, and Boehner showed no interest. So instead of a long and divisive leadership battle, the succession passed quietly and smoothly. DeLay became majority leader without opposition and his chief deputy whip Roy Blunt was elected whip. Reynolds was elected chairman of the campaign committee.

As majority leader, DeLay spent less time arm-twisting for votes and more time working on the agenda for House action. On Capitol Hill, he polished his public image and took pains to portray himself as a disciplined, measured leader who was responsive to all types of House Republicans. "I spend more time on planning, strategies, developing agendas, and making the trains run on time," he said. DeLay met regularly with committee chairmen to define priorities. He was far more hands-on than Armey in seeking to influence legislative details, on issues from dealing with the balky Senate on the size of tax cuts and working out details of Medicare reform to adding sexual-abstinence programs to Bush's AIDS fighting initiative for Africa. A new feature was his weekly "pen and pad" sessions with reporters in which he talked for 30 minutes about the legislative agenda, and other topics on his mind. He felt the pressure of increased public expectations in the all-Republican government. "You can't go home and explain that there is only a one-vote margin in the Senate . . . .All they know is that there is a Republican Senate, a Republican House, and a Republican president, and you ought to be able to get something done." As much as any elected Republican in Washington, he thought seriously about the party's long-term agenda, including his interest in tax reform, regulatory reform, and reorganizing Congress.

One issue on which DeLay has surprised his detractors has been foster care. In 1994, his wife Christine DeLay became a trained court appointed special advocate and the DeLays became foster parents to several children. DeLay was infuriated in 2000 at the violent death of two-year-old Brianna Blackmond, supposedly under the care of the District of Columbia foster care agency, after she was returned to the custody of her biological mother by a judge who heard nothing from the agency or the lawyer appointed to represent the girl. DeLay angrily confronted District officials. He sought action in the House to change the D.C. system; D.C. Delegate Eleanor Holmes Norton, usually opposed to congressional interference in District affairs, said, "His commitment is sincere, and it's deep, and he has special credibility because he and his wife have had foster children." Back in Texas, a DeLay charity raised money for a $5 million foster home, The Oaks at Rio Bend, to serve 250 abandoned and abused children, with sports facilities, a chapel, counseling—and no government money.

He has often been outspoken on foreign policy. He called the return of Elian Gonzalez to totalitarian Cuba "the lowest point of the Clinton administration's tenure, a statement I make with full knowledge of its considerable excesses and transgressions." In June 2000 he sponsored a bill to bar the U.S. from cooperating with the International Criminal Court established in the 1998 Rome treaty unless and until the Senate ratified it, which the House approved a year later; the Bush administration did not oppose it. In 2002 he emerged as the House's loudest voice in support of Israel. In April, when the Bush administration was still talking about encouraging talks between Israel and Palestinians and was ambiguous on the role of Yasir Arafat, DeLay went to Westminster College in Fulton, Missouri, where Winston Churchill had named the Iron Curtain in 1946, and delivered a speech linking Yasir Arafat with terrorism. It was a prod to Bush, who had said he would not negotiate with terrorists, and a jab at State Department Arabists, who argued that Arafat was the only person to negotiate with. "The defense of freedom demands more of us than value-neutral brokerage. It is time for us to stand squarely against the terrorist organizations which systematically attack Israel." In the House DeLay co-sponsored with Democrat Tom Lantos, Congress's only Holocaust survivor, a resolution supporting Israel and denouncing Arafat. With minor changes in wording, it passed 352–21, with 29 voting present; almost all of the nays and abstentions came from Democrats. DeLay was an outspoken defender of the war in Iraq and he attacked Democratic critics. "The blame-America-first hate speech of the American Left has infected the Democratic Party's national leadership to a dangerous degree."

His heightened visibility increased the Democrats' attacks on him. Many of them believed that DeLay, with his outspoken and blunt conservatism, would be a target Democrats could run against, as they had run against Newt Gingrich. But DeLay had been much less known to the public than Gingrich was, and as a member of the House leadership of the president's party he is not likely to be a prominent agenda-setter. To be sure, DeLay is a conviction politician willing to take unpopular stands in the glare of the public spotlight, as he did during the impeachment of Bill Clinton; Clinton would probably not have been impeached without him. The partisan enmity increased exponentially when DeLay pushed ahead in 2003 with his controversial redistricting plan in Texas. In that acrimonious battle, DeLay was the ringleader who, with his aides, coordinated the overall strategy and was unwilling to back down. He was convinced that the existing districting plan, a product of Democrats, was unfair, and that it was long past time to give Republicans a fair chance in his home state; Republicans had been winning a majority of the popular votes but only a minority of seats. The fact that Republicans might gain a half-dozen seats in the narrowly divided House was an obvious benefit, of course. "DeLay's success shows a reckless kind of strength," said archenemy Martin Frost.

But once DeLay achieved his redistricting plan and Republicans moved to pick up their half-dozen seats, the battle had only begun. Houston's Chris Bell, a freshman Democrat who lost his seat in the March 2004 primary, filed in June an ethics complaint against DeLay, whom he called "the most corrupt politician in the United States today." His charges included allegations that DeLay misused federal agencies in an attempt to locate Democratic legislators who had fled from Austin rather than provide a quorum for the redistricting bill. The House ethics committee ruled that DeLay had violated no rules of the House but issued "admonishments"—the mildest possible reprimand—for three offenses: asking the FAA to search for the Texas Democrats; appearing to link a fundraising event by an energy company with that firm's interest in energy legislation, and his efforts to secure the vote of Michigan Republican Nick Smith on the Medicare prescription drug bill. Minority Leader Nancy Pelosi chastised DeLay's "abuse of power." But most Republicans echoed DeLay's response that the charges against him were politically motivated and that he had become the Democrats' "whipping boy," as House Republican campaign chairman Tom Reynolds said. But John Kerry never raised the issue, and there was no evidence that the issue affected a single House campaign result in November.

Meanwhile, DeLay also was distracted by Austin District Attorney Ronnie Earle, a liberal Democrat, who back in 1994 had indicted Senator Kay Bailey Hutchison on flimsy charges he was forced to drop the first day the case came to court. Earle indicted three DeLay political associates and eight corporations for violating Texas's campaign finance law. Even though there was scant indication that Earle would indict DeLay, allies of the majority leader after the election moved to revise a House Republican rule (House Democrats had no such rule) that requires a party leader to step aside if indicted for a felony. Several House Republicans objected, both publicly and privately, and in January the proposal was dropped. In succeeding months DeLay was the subject of headline stories in *The Washington Post* and *The New York Times* that alleged that he had taken trips financed by lobbyists and that he had put his wife and daughter on his campaign payroll. But the trips appeared to be legal under House rules and no rule or law prohibits putting relatives on campaign payrolls; many members of both parties do so. Democrats and DeLay's critics in the press sought to sully him as corrupt and make him the kind of widely known bete noire that Gingrich was in his time. Earle appeared at a Democratic fundraiser in May 2005 and compared DeLay to a bully. DeLay insisted that he wanted the ethics committee to look into the charges against him; Democrats, in protest of rules changes that

House Republicans pushed through requiring a bipartisan agreement to go ahead on ethics investigations, boycotted the committee and prevented it from meeting.

Perhaps the most ominous sign for DeLay came in the 2004 election results. He has regularly been reelected by wide margins. But the increasing minority populations in the district have led some Democrats to think he might be vulnerable, and his winning percentage dropped from 65% in 1998 to 60% in 2000. The 2003 redistricting did little to alter the partisan balance of the district but 30% of the voters were new to DeLay, and he unexpectedly had serious competition. Democrat Richard Morrison, an attorney and political neophyte, received virtually no help from House Democrats, but he raised more than $600,000, some with help from Howard Dean and waged a vigorous campaign against DeLay. The *Houston Chronicle,* a long-time adversary of DeLay, endorsed Morrison for his "promises to place the district's interests above grasping for partisan power in Washington." DeLay won 55%–41%, and was held to 53% in his home county of Fort Bend, which cast 40% of the vote. DeLay did better in the Harris County suburbs, 59%–38%, where the turnout was nearly equal to Ford Bend County. Morrison won Galveston County 56%–41%, but it cast only 8% of the vote. Senior House members usually run ahead of their parties' presidential candidates in their districts; DeLay ran 9% behind Bush, and must expect serious competition from Democrats at home in 2006.

TWENTY-THIRD DISTRICT

Rep. Henry Bonilla (R)

Elected 1992, 7th term; b. Jan. 2, 1954, San Antonio; home, San Antonio; U. of TX, B.A. 1976; Baptist; married (Sheryl Shelby).

Professional Career: TV Reporter, 1976–80; Asst. Press Secy., PA Gov. Thornburgh, 1981; Writer/producer, WABC, New York, 1982–85; Asst. News Dir., WATF–TV, Philadelphia, 1985–86; KENS–TV, San Antonio, Exec. News Producer, 1986–89, Public Affairs, 1989–92.

DC Office: 2458 RHOB, 20515, 202-225-4511; Fax: 202-225-2237; Web site: www.house.gov/bonilla.

District Offices: Alpine, 915-837-1313; Del Rio, 830-774-6547; Laredo, 956-726-4682; San Antonio, 210-697-9055.

Committees: *Appropriations* (11th of 37 R): Agriculture, Rural Development, FDA & Related Agencies (Chmn.); Defense.

Group Ratings

	ADA	ACLU	AFS	LCV	ITIC	NTU	COC	ACU	NTLC	CHC
2004	0	0	13	9	100	48	100	92	65	76
2003	5	—	0	0	—	61	100	92	—	—

National Journal Ratings

	2003 LIB	—	2003 CONS		2004 LIB	—	2004 CONS
Economic	29%	—	70%		29%	—	70%
Social	14%	—	85%		25%	—	73%
Foreign	30%	—	69%		10%	—	86%

Key Votes of the 108th Congress

1. Drilling in ANWR	Y	5. DC School Vouchers	Y	9. Ban Same-Sex Marriage	Y
2. Approve Bush Tax Cuts	*	6. Ban Human Cloning	Y	10. Fund Iraq War	Y
3. Medicare/Rx Bill	Y	7. Restrict Gun Liability	Y	11. Bar Cuba Embargo Funds	N
4. Bar Overtime Pay Regs.	N	8. Ban Partial-Birth Abortion	Y	12. Intelligence Reorg.	Y

Election Results

2004 general	Henry Bonilla (R)	170,716	(69%)	($1,211,717)
	Joe Sullivan (D)	72,480	(29%)	($9,335)
	Other	3,307	(1%)	
2004 primary	Henry Bonilla (R)	unopposed		
2002 general	Henry Bonilla (R)	77,573	(52%)	($2,413,172)
	Henry Cuellar (D)	71,067	(47%)	($1,055,342)
	Other	1,912	(1%)	

Prior Winning Percentages: 2000 (59%); 1998 (64%); 1996 (62%); 1994 (63%); 1992 (59%)

The People		Race/Ethnic Origin	Ancestry	
Area size:	52,735 sq. mi.	41.0% White	German: 9.4%	English: 5.7%
Urban population:	74.4%	1.6% Black	Irish: 5.1%	
Rural population:	25.6%	1.1% Asian	**2004 Presidential Vote**	
Pop. 2000:	651,620	0.3% Native Am.	Bush (R)	163,389 (65%)
Median income:	$38,081	0.0% Hawaiian	Kerry (D)	89,874 (35%)
Poverty status:	18.4%	0.8% Two+ races	**2000 Presidential Vote**	
Military veterans:	12.9%	0.1% Other	Bush (R)	131,962 (64%)
		55.1% Hispanic Origin	Gore (D)	75,363 (36%)
			Cook Partisan Voting Index: R +13	

Occupation   Blue collar: 20.1%   White collar: 63.3%   Gray collar: 16.6%

The Census Bureau declared in 1890 that the American frontier was closed, but there still is a frontier of sorts in Texas. You can see it just northwest of San Antonio, where the Balcones Escarpment rises, a stony ridge that separates flat coastal Texas from the hills and plains of the west. From the top of the ridge you can see most of San Antonio spread out before you on gently rolling turf, the downtown skyscrapers near the Alamo in the distance. Metro San Antonio has now spread up on the ridge and past, with attendant controversy; proposals to build a Wal-Mart Supercenter stirred fears about depletion of the Edwards Aquifer Recharge Zone. To the north and west is the Texas Hill Country. This is the site of some of the oldest Texas German communities, established by immigrants who fled after the failure of the democratic revolutions of 1848. The Texas German country has always been a set of orderly communities in rip-roaring Texas, economically prosperous in a state that considered itself poor until it struck oil. It was anti-slavery and politically Republican in a state whose enthusiasm for the Democratic Party had roots in Confederate loyalties and populist rebellions. Today the Hill Country has new settlers, young families with high incomes seeking homesites in spacious new subdivisions and older retirees who revel in the Hill Country's scenery and its moderate weather; when it's suffocatingly hot in San Antonio it's pleasantly warm in the hills.

Fifty or so miles west of San Antonio, the hills flatten out and become the parched uplands of West Texas. This is a borderland, just north of Mexico, where people are concentrated in tiny hamlets amid the empty ranchlands and most residents are Latino. Once Indians were the threat on this frontier; now the challenge is assimilation and the threat is lack of water. The aquifers of West Texas are being drained; state law allows landowners to pump out as much water as they want. The Rio Grande, dried out by a dam in New Mexico, gets most of its water from the Rio Conchos in the Mexican state of Chihuahua; Mexico owes the United States hundreds of thousands of acre-feet under a 1944 treaty. Big cities have sprung up on the border. But in the hundreds of miles between El Paso and Juarez, Chihuahua (which between them have about 2 million people), and Laredo and Nuevo Laredo, Tamaulipas (which between them have about 800,000), there are only a few border crossings and much wilderness. The mountains of Big Bend National Park rise above the Rio Grande, where in the clean air you can find dozens of species of birds and can see for 180 miles; eccentrics have built an art colony in Marfa and stage a chili cookoff in Terlingua. El Paso/Juarez and Laredo/Nuevo Laredo are engines of commerce. Juarez has the largest concentration of *maquiladoras* in Mexico, and Laredo is the biggest freight crossing point on the U.S.-Mexico border, with $160 billion in goods crossing the crowded bridge downtown or the new higher bridge built several miles upriver. Laredo has more warehouse space than San Antonio and Austin combined; its downtown streets and shopping malls are crowded with Mexicans coming over to buy goods at low prices. Some fear that this part of the United States will become Mexicanized. In the late 1970s young Latinos organized the La Raza Unida party and took over local government in Dimmit County. But separatism had a short shelf life. Mexico in the last dozen years has been struggling to become more like the United States, and Texas Latinos have joined the mainstream of American politics. Texas's frontier in many ways is thriving. But all this activity makes people thirsty. Private companies are buying ranchland so they can pump water out to Texas's growing cities, and some Texans are even talking about building a pipeline from Hoover Dam in Nevada.

The 23d Congressional District of Texas is geographically the largest in the state, larger than almost any state east of the Mississippi. It stretches from San Antonio to the outskirts of El Paso, from Laredo to the New Mexico border. It includes the northwest suburbs of San Antonio and part of the city, most of the Hill Country centered on Kerrville, the northern and western half of Laredo, the eastern edge of El Paso County and all the mostly empty and parched land in between. Most of the population is clustered in a few areas—30% in San Antonio's Bexar County, 14% in Laredo, 7% each are in and around the border towns Del Rio and Eagle Pass. Politically, there are wide differences within the district. Most of the border counties are Democratic; the Bexar County portion of the district is affluent and heavily Republican, as are the ranching counties with low Hispanic populations are also Republican. The 2003 redistricting removed half of Laredo and added Hill Country counties. The result was that this 55% Hispanic district voted 64% for George W. Bush in 2000 and 65% in 2004.

The congressman from the 23d District is Henry Bonilla, a Republican first elected in 1992. He was raised in a Latino neighborhood on the south side of San Antonio. His grandmother worked as a maid, and his father held down two jobs. Bonilla graduated from the University of Texas and then worked as a TV reporter, producer and executive in San Antonio, New York, Philadelphia and, starting in 1986, San Antonio again. In 1991, Bexar County Republican leaders recruited Bonilla to run for Congress against incumbent Democrat Albert Bustamante; he reportedly was being investigated by the FBI, had 30 overdrafts on the House bank and, after the election, was convicted of two counts of misuse of office for racketeering and bribery. Bonilla backed standard conservative planks but developed his own issues as well. Bustamante called Bonilla "a eunuch for the plantation owners" for opposing a minimum wage bill, but Bonilla won 59%–38%.

In 1993 Republicans gave Bonilla a seat on Appropriations, the first time a freshman had won one in 25 years. There he has displayed a talent for placing deregulatory riders on appropriations bills—to eliminate funding for enforcing a rule on cardboard balers and to block the Labor Department from developing ergonomic standards. Bonilla voted enthusiastically for NAFTA and against gun control. He and Solomon Ortiz of the 27th District have been co-chairmen of the Border Caucus since 1997, and have worked successfully to get Mexico to abandon deposits on cars brought from the U.S., to withdraw tax proposals which would affect U.S. companies operating *maquiladoras*; they have sought equality in duty-free rules and reversal of a decision not to allow commuter students to attend U.S. colleges and universities. Bonilla has refused to join the all-Democratic Hispanic Caucus, lamenting that it lacks a bipartisan agenda and was a founder of the all-Republican Congressional Hispanic Caucus. He criticized a National Council of La Raza survey report. "All too often Hispanics are portrayed as victims, cowering in the neighborhoods, waiting for the federal government to rescue them. This is simply not the case," he wrote in July 2001. "There is a booming Hispanic middle class, with good prospects for future growth. Average Latino income has almost doubled in the past decade, and the amount of Latinos with a college education has risen almost 50%. . . . I don't know about the people who represent these 'professional minority' groups, but when I look in the mirror every morning I first see an American. I'm proud of my culture, but more proud and grateful to say I live in this country."

In January 2001 he became chairman of the Agriculture Appropriations Subcommittee, one of the "college of cardinals." As an appropriator, Bonilla was hostile to the Republican leadership's attempt to confine the committee to the administration's total for discretionary spending. He has earmarked money for district projects and he made sure to keep in money for a rail spur from San Antonio to the site of the newly announced Toyota plant. He serves on the Defense Appropriations Subcommittee and announced in September 2002 that San Antonio's Fort Sam Houston was chosen as the new home of the U.S. Army South. In March 2003 he announced a $16 million Colonias Gateway Initiative, a nonprofit entity to coordinate aid to colonias. In June 2003 he sponsored the successful amendment to delay country of origin meat labeling until 2006; in 2004 he tried unsuccessfully to make country of origin labeling voluntary.

Redistricting in November 2001 did not change the district much, and he seemed to be on the way to easy reelection. Instead he had tough competition from Henry Cuellar, a state representative from Laredo from 1986 to 2000, who was appointed secretary of state by Governor Rick Perry in December 2000 and resigned in January 2002. Bonilla said that he didn't need Laredo to win; he had never won more than 49% of the vote in Laredo's Webb County. That didn't go over well with outgoing Webb County Republican Chairman Gene Belmares, who in January 2002 endorsed Cuellar. "If Henry Bonilla has said publicly that he does not need Laredo to win, and if he does not want to include us as Republicans, fine. I will support Henry Cuellar." It was clear that Laredo businessman Tony Sanchez's $60 million campaign for governor would produce a big increase in voter turnout in Webb County, and Democrats hoped that would make Cuellar competitive. Cuellar attacked Bonilla for his votes against funding the CHIP program, passage of the Family and Medical Leave Act, funding Pell grants, student loans, work study and classroom construction. And he accused him of being insufficiently Hispanic. "He said he 'doesn't wake up in the morning thinking he's Hispanic.' I don't know what he means by that."

Bonilla had the money advantage, with $2.4 million to Cuellar's $1 million. For most of the campaign, this race was not on either national party's radar screen. Bonilla had, after all, never won less than 59% of the vote. But despite miscues—he ended up hiring three campaign managers—Cuellar came up with an effective strategy given his comparative lack of funds. He started off by flying around to all the small communities in the district. Then he conducted an extensive blockwalking campaign in San Antonio and elsewhere; by August he claimed that he and his teams had walked every street in the district except in Laredo. He spent much of the last two months concentrating on turning out the vote in Webb County and only in the last month ran television ads. In Laredo he was helped by the great local enthusiasm for Tony Sanchez; Cuellar carried the county 84%–15%. On election night, that seemed to make the difference. Cuellar's 26,000-vote margin in Webb County gave him a 15,000-vote lead as the evening went on. But in San Antonio Bexar County officials were having trouble with their vote scanning machines. The final Bexar County totals were not reported until Wednesday night, and Bonilla's 75%–24% lead there erased Cuellar's lead and showed a 6,000-vote, 52%–47% victory for Bonilla. Cuellar acknowledged the loss, but seemed as if he were interested in a rematch.

Bonilla supported Tom DeLay's drive to redistrict Texas's congressional seats in 2003, and was one of its beneficiaries. The redistricting plan removed half of troublesome Webb County from the district, added heavily Republican Hill Country counties and made the Bexar County part of the district more Republican. Cuellar decided to run in the 28th District and beat incumbent Ciro Rodriguez in the March 2004 primary. In the 23d District Bonilla won 69%–29%. He carried Bexar County 71%–28% and, in a huge turnaround from 2002, the Webb County portion of the district 58%–41%. He lost Zavala County and the district's portion of El Paso County but carried all the other counties, some of them 85% to 95% Hispanic. When House Republicans gathered after the election, he moved to change party rules so that members who were indicted were not required to relinquish leadership positions. This was obviously to help DeLay: three of his aides had been indicted on campaign finance charges by Austin District Attorney Ronnie Earle. Many Republicans believed that Earle, a liberal Democrat, was politically motivated; his indictment of Senator Kay Bailey Hutchison a decade before had been peremptorily dismissed on the first day in court. "This takes the power away from any partisan crackpot district attorney who may want to indict" party leaders, Bonilla said. Bonilla ended the year with $1.2 million in his campaign account and in early 2005 made moves to run for the Senate when it looked as if Hutchison would run for governor. In February 2005 he said, "If she makes the decision on her own to move on, then I am in that race, no ifs, ands or buts." But Hutchison announced in June that she would seek reelection to the Senate.

TWENTY-FOURTH DISTRICT

Rep. Kenny Marchant (R)

Elected 2004, 1st term; b. Feb. 23, 1951, Bonham; home, Coppell; Southern Nazarene U., B.A. 1973, attended Nazarene Theol. Sem. 1975–76; Nazarene; married (Donna).

Elected Office: Carrollton City Cncl., 1980–84; mayor, 1984–86; TX House of Reps., 1986–2004.

Professional Career: Homebuilder, developer, 1975–2004.

DC Office: 501 CHOB, 20515, 202-225-6605; Fax: 202-225-0074; Web site: marchant.house.gov.

District Office: Irving, 972-556-0162.

Committees: *Education & the Workforce* (20th of 27 R): Employer-Employee Relations; Workforce Protections. *Government Reform* (18th of 23 R): Energy & Resources; Federal Workforce & Agency Organization; National Security, Emerging Threats & International Relations (Vice Chmn.). *Transportation & Infrastructure* (31st of 41 R): Economic Development, Public Buildings & Emergency Management; Highways, Transit & Pipelines.

Group Ratings and Key Votes: Newly Elected

Election Results

2004 general	Kenny Marchant (R)	154,435	(64%)	($781,923)
	Gary Page (D)	82,599	(34%)	($15,255)
	Other	4,340	(2%)	
2004 primary	Kenny Marchant (R)	9,073	(73%)	
	Cynthia Newman (R)	1,103	(9%)	
	Bill Dunn (R)	1,096	(9%)	
	Terry Waldrum (R)	1,074	(9%)	
2002 general	Martin Frost (D)	73,002	(65%)	($1,566,087)
	Mike Rivera Ortega (R)	38,332	(34%)	($39,910)
	Other	1,560	(1%)	

The People		Race/Ethnic Origin	Ancestry	
Area size:	354 sq. mi.	63.9% White	German: 10.5%	English: 8.0%
Urban population:	99.2%	9.6% Black	Irish: 8.0%	
Rural population:	0.8%	6.2% Asian	**2004 Presidential Vote**	
Pop. 2000:	651,620	0.4% Native Am.	Bush (R) 161,864	(65%)
Median income:	$56,098	0.2% Hawaiian	Kerry (D) 86,786	(35%)
Poverty status:	6.3%	1.5% Two+ races	**2000 Presidential Vote**	
Military veterans:	10.9%	0.1% Other	Bush (R) 142,930	(68%)
		17.9% Hispanic Origin	Gore (D) 66,587	(32%)
			Cook Partisan Voting Index: R +15	

Occupation	Blue collar: 17.0%	White collar: 72.9%	Gray collar: 10.0%

The gigantic (larger than Manhattan Island) Dallas-Fort Worth International Airport bisects the Metroplex and its two adjacent counties with its large terminals and the Texas-sized highway network that feeds them. DFW, as nearly everyone calls it, also has been a focal point for the huge local development in both Dallas and Tarrant Counties. "DFW is no longer solely an airport. DFW is our home," the *Fort Worth Star-Telegram* wrote. Whole new Dallases and Fort Worths, with as many people as the central cities had in the 1950s—Grand Prairie and Irving—grew up around the airport during the next two decades in these once impoverished lands and became central to one of America's richest and most productive metropolitan areas. North of DFW are newer and more upscale suburbs: Grapevine and Southlake, with its huge shopping malls, in northeast Tarrant County; Coppell, Farmers Branch and Carrollton across the International Parkway in northwest Dallas County. To the north are the fast-growing suburbs and exurbs of Denton County. DFW and its supporters fiercely oppose efforts to repeal the Wright Amendment, which limits the number of cities that can be reached from flights at the old Love Field in Dallas.

The 24th Congressional District of Texas contains much of this area. The district includes three large spokes that reach out from DFW. The largest extends northeast through Dallas County and into Denton County, up to Route 121, including one-third of Irving and almost all of Farmers Branch, Coppell and Carrollton. To the west, another spoke reaches into Tarrant County out to Precinct Line Road, including Grapevine, Bedford, Colleyville and Southlake. South of the airport it includes almost all of Grand Prairie, part of Irving, Cedar Hill and part of Duncanville. About half of the population is in Dallas County, a third is in Tarrant County and a sixth is in Denton County. The district was transformed by the October 2003 redistricting. Before that it included heavily Democratic areas like the Oak Cliff neighborhood in Dallas and the black neighborhoods in eastern Fort Worth. That plan was designed by 24th District Democrat Martin Frost in 1991 and was largely carried over by the court which set the district lines in 2001. Frost, ranking Democrat on the Rules Committee, was one of his party's most effective and durable partisans, and was one of the chief targets of Majority Leader Tom DeLay, who pressed hard for the 2003 redistricting. The plan left Frost with no good choices. The new 24th District had voted 68% for George W. Bush in 2000. If he had followed his black constituents in Fort Worth, he would have to run in the 26th District, which had voted 62% for Bush. In something of a surprise, he decided to run in the new 32d District in Dallas County, which had voted 64% for Bush. That left the new 24th without an incumbent.

The congressman from the 24th District is Kenny Marchant, a Republican elected in 2004. A local homebuilder and successful developer, Marchant served a quarter-century in elected offices: on the Carrollton City Council and then as mayor, then in the state House. He also has been active in private humanitarian projects around the world; the Ken Marchant Foundation funds church loans, mission projects and scholarships. In contrast to other upwardly mobile Republicans in Austin, he enjoyed a reputation on both sides of the aisle as a levelheaded peacemaker. Despite serving in some of the Legislature's most partisan posts, the mild-mannered and deeply religious Marchant managed to maintain a cool demeanor, even as his colleagues descended into acrimonious conflict. As *Texas Monthly* wrote: "His role was that of the genial, kindly sheriff in a western who allows the cowboys to gamble, drink and fight—but when they show up at the jail, rope in hand, he stands on the steps and says, 'Boys, just go on home and cool off.' "

Marchant had been chairman and floor leader of the Texas House Republican caucus and served on the House Redistricting Committee during the state's bitter 2003 redistricting battle. Unsurprisingly, the redistricting plan couldn't have been more favorable to him. In their effort to draw a Dallas-area seat that Martin Frost could not win, Republicans designed a district where Marchant could not lose. He denied that the new 24th was created specifically for him, but it incorporated nearly all of his state legislative district and was heavily Republican. Marchant did not draw serious opposition in either the primary or the general. This was a welcome change from 2002, when he set out to run in the new 32d District only to withdraw when 5th District incumbent Republican Pete Sessions unexpectedly decided to run there.

Marchant campaigned as "a proven leader for George W. Bush," a reference to his close legislative relationship with the former governor. A social and fiscal conservative, he opposes abortion and restrictions on gun ownership, and he favors a federal constitutional amendment banning gay marriage. His legislative priorities are more localized. He called for more funding for transportation, including DFW. His top highway priority was funding for the huge "Grapevine funnel" project north of DFW. In the primary, Marchant defeated three other candidates with 73% of the vote. In November Marchant won 64%–34%. At 54, he settled comfortably into what could be a productive new career. In the House, he got meat and potatoes assignments to the Transportation, Government Reform, and Education and Workforce committees.

TWENTY-FIFTH DISTRICT

Rep. Lloyd Doggett (D)

Elected 1994, 6th term; b. Oct. 6, 1946, Austin; home, Austin; U. of TX, B.B.A. 1967, J.D. 1970; Methodist; married (Libby).

Elected Office: TX Senate, 1972–1984; TX Supreme Ct. Justice, 1989–94.

Professional Career: Practicing atty., 1970–89; Adjunct Prof., U. of TX Law Schl., 1989–94.

DC Office: 201 CHOB, 20515, 202-225-4865; Fax: 202-225-3073; Web site: www.house.gov/doggett.

District Offices: Austin, 512-916-5921; McAllen, 956-687-5921.

Committees: *Ways & Means* (12th of 17 D): Health; Select Revenue Measures.

Group Ratings

	ADA	ACLU	AFS	LCV	ITIC	NTU	COC	ACU	NTLC	CHC
2004	95	79	100	100	56	15	39	4	15	15
2003	90	—	100	100	—	28	30	8	—	—

National Journal Ratings

	2003 LIB	—	2003 CONS	2004 LIB	—	2004 CONS
Economic	86%	—	13%	79%	—	20%
Social	78%	—	20%	77%	—	23%
Foreign	89%	—	8%	80%	—	19%

Key Votes of the 108th Congress

1. Drilling in ANWR	N	5. DC School Vouchers	N	9. Ban Same-Sex Marriage	N
2. Approve Bush Tax Cuts	N	6. Ban Human Cloning	N	10. Fund Iraq War	N
3. Medicare/Rx Bill	N	7. Restrict Gun Liability	N	11. Bar Cuba Embargo Funds	Y
4. Bar Overtime Pay Regs.	Y	8. Ban Partial-Birth Abortion	N	12. Intelligence Reorg.	N

Election Results

2004 general	Lloyd Doggett (D)	108,309	(68%)	($1,969,528)
	Rebecca Armendariz Klein (R)	49,252	(31%)	($804,160)
	Other	2,656	(2%)	
2004 primary	Lloyd Doggett (D)	40,306	(64%)	
	Leticia Hinojosa (D)	22,305	(36%)	
2002 general (TX 10)	Lloyd Doggett (D)	114,428	(84%)	($190,484)
	Michele Messina (Lib)	21,196	(16%)	

Prior Winning Percentages: 2000 (85%); 1998 (85%); 1996 (56%); 1994 (56%)

The People		Race/Ethnic Origin	Ancestry	
Area size:	8,079 sq. mi.	21.9% White	German: 4.9%	Irish: 3.1%
Urban population:	87.1%	7.3% Black	English: 2.7%	
Rural population:	12.9%	1.1% Asian	**2004 Presidential Vote**	
Pop. 2000:	651,619	0.2% Native Am.	Kerry (D)	101,989 (63%)
Median income:	$28,348	0.0% Hawaiian	Bush (R)	59,814 (37%)
Poverty status:	28.8%	0.7% Two+ races	**2000 Presidential Vote**	
Military veterans:	8.0%	0.1% Other	Gore (D)	85,145 (62%)
		68.6% Hispanic Origin	Bush (R)	52,458 (38%)
			Cook Partisan Voting Index: D +14	

Occupation	Blue collar: 27.7%	White collar: 52.2%	Gray collar: 20.2%

Austin, the capital of the second largest state in the U.S. and site of its largest Capitol building, is also the southernmost capital in the continental 48 states. It is one of many capitals with a first-rate university, but one of the few (Nashville is the other) with its own musical tradition. Not long ago, Austin seemed as laid-back and countrified as there had never been much commerce here, and for much of the year the Capitol basked in a sun that seemed to ban gainful employment. Its skies were untainted with the smoke of industry, its ground unpocked with pumping oil rigs, its downtown streets lined not with business offices but with buildings holding a few lobbyists and the antique Driskill Hotel. Its biggest industry was the University of Texas—with 50,000 students and endowed with thousands of west Texas acres that turned out to sit on top of oil. The university has long had a distinguished faculty and some of the world's great scholarly collections; it houses the LBJ Presidential Library with its 35 million documents, has spawned a community of liberal intellectuals since the 1940s and helped spark Austin's high-tech boom in the 1980s and 1990s. Half a century ago, in Lyndon B. Johnson's time, Austin had a metropolitan population of 132,000. The compact Austin that was Johnson's headquarters in 1948 when the Duval County returns came in and gave him the 87-vote victory that made his national career is a very different Austin from the metropolitan center of 1.2 million that waited up in the rain, alternatively enthused and downcast, hoping to celebrate the election of George W. Bush in 2000.

Growth has also brought political change. For many years Austin was the central focus of Texas's hardy but almost always outnumbered liberals, based in the university, state government and the *Texas Observer*. Confident that the future was theirs, that Texas would follow America into the New Deal and the welfare state, they mocked the conservative business lobbyists who called the shots when the "lege" was in session and celebrated Texas zaniness with the verve of a Sixth Street band. Adding to the cultural scene is the mania surrounding Lance Armstrong, the champion international cyclist who has adopted Austin as his hometown. But history—or at least Austin—has not moved in the direction Texas liberals expected. As the Austin area grew, it became more conservative; as its private sector has led the local economy, the techies who settled in the Silicon Hills going from Austin's Travis County to once-rural Williamson County have tended to vote Republican. The city core and the University area are still Democratic, Texas liberals still are potent in the media, and 31% of the population is Latino— with 10% black and 5% Asian. But this is a state capital, in which George W. Bush could feel more at home than he would have 30 years before (when his application for admission was rejected by the UT law school). Bush lost Austin and Travis County 59%–41% when he first ran for governor in 1994, but he carried Travis 60%–38% in 1998 for re-election and 47%–42% in 2000 for president (with 10% for Ralph Nader). But in 2004 Austin's liberal community rallied and registered large numbers of new voters, and Bush lost Travis County 56%–42%, even as he increased his margin statewide; Kerry got 57% more votes in the county than Al Gore had.

The 25th Congressional District of Texas, a new seat created by the 2003 redistricting, includes most of the east side of Austin and Travis County, including most of the city's heavily black and Latino neighborhoods. The Capitol and the UT campus are just outside, in the 21st District, while the 10th District includes most of the Republican northern part of the city and county. It was part of Tom DeLay's redistricting strategy to split Travis County among three districts, two of them safely Republican and the other a new heavily Hispanic district. This was accomplished by extending the 25th District south to the Mexican border on the Rio Grande. As a result, the district's two main population centers are some 300 miles apart: the Travis County portion, 49% Hispanic, and the Hidalgo County portion, 89% Hispanic, each account for just under 40% of the district's residents. The district includes one-third of Austin and three-quarters of McAllen, just north of the Rio Grande. This is the slowest-growing part of Austin, but McAllen and other towns in the Lower Rio Grande Valley have been growing rapidly, spurred by NAFTA, though pockets of deep poverty remain. "Where once there were orange groves, now there are new homes and schools," wrote the *San Antonio Express-News*. The seven rural counties in the thin 300-mile *fajita* strip between Travis and Hidalgo are rural and lightly populated. They include Starr County, the poorest in Texas and home of many blatant and wealthy drug smugglers, and Duval County, sometimes the most Democratic county in the United States, whose boss George Parr provided the key votes Lyndon Johnson needed for his 87-vote victory in the 1948 Democratic Senate runoff (conveniently, many people voted in alphabetical order). The district is 69% Hispanic and strongly Democratic. John Kerry defeated Bush here 63%–37%, his best showing in Texas outside of the three urban districts with black pluralities. But with only 39% of the district now in Travis County (and 38% in Hidalgo), many Austin liberals feared that they would lose their seat in Congress to the Hispanics on the border. Republican redistricters contended that they were merely seeking to assure a safely Democratic district. Both groups underestimated the resilience of a veteran Democratic incumbent.

The congressman from the 25th District is Lloyd Doggett, first elected in 1994 in the old 10th. He is a liberal Democrat with a dream resume and a political career with some notable twists. Doggett grew up in Austin, finished first in his class and was president of UT's student body in 1967. In 1972, he was elected to the state Senate at 26, and as part of a surprisingly large liberal bloc in the 1970s, he pushed laws against job discrimination and cop-killer bullets and for generic drugs; he has always been a close ally of trial lawyers, the one strong institutional force supporting liberal Democrats in Texas. In the "lege," he was one of the "killer bees" who hid out to prevent a quorum on changing the rules in the Democratic primary and filibustered—wearing sneakers—against what he called anti-consumer bills. In 1984 he ran for the U.S. Senate, narrowly edging two congressmen to win the Democratic nomination. Then, despite the campaign help of James Carville and Paul Begala, Doggett lost the general 59%–41% to party-switching Congressman Phil Gramm. Doggett came back and, with strong support from trial lawyers, was elected to the Texas Supreme Court in 1988. When Jake Pickle retired after 31 years, Doggett ran for Congress after his judgeship had expired. He won the Democratic primary with token opposition, and in the general won by the solid, but not quite overwhelming, margin of 56%–40%.

In the House, Doggett's voting record has placed him among the most liberal Texans, and he has never served in the majority. He was a vocal critic of Newt Gingrich, and a close ally of Minority Whip David Bonior and Nancy Pelosi, and backed her against Texan Martin Frost in her race for minority leader. In 1999, he became the first Texas Democrat assigned to the Ways and Means Committee since Pickle retired. Along with other Ways and Means Democrats, he sought to restrict the use of offshore tax havens. He has voted against most of George W. Bush's major proposals. Three days after September 11, his parliamentary objections stymied late night action on a $15 billion airline aid bill and forced a more thorough debate. He was a leader in opposing the resolution authorizing the use of force in Iraq; even Doggett was surprised that 126 House Democrats voted to oppose it. Still, he is not everyone's cup of tea. Rich Oppel, editor of the *Austin American-Statesman,* said that while he often agrees with Doggett, he has gained "a reputation for rhetoric with the subtlety of a stevedore's punch."

When gleeful Republicans hoped that redistricting would put a stake through his heart, Doggett took up the challenge. As some other dislocated Texas Democrats took their fight to the courts, Doggett took his case to the voters of his new district. He started by working hard to get the support of elected officials and party activists along the border. "I chose to spend not a few hours here in the Valley in the month of December [2003], but a few weeks, to resume old friendship," he said in introducing supporters in McAllen. Meanwhile, the best-known Hispanic challengers for a Democratic primary were outmaneuvered. State representative Kino Flores of Mission cited a lack of money when he withdrew six weeks after declaring his candidacy. Veteran state Senator Gonzalo Barrientos, a long-time Doggett rival, made bold claims but never declared his candidacy. Instead, Barrientos endorsed Leticia Hinojosa, a former district court judge from McAllen who worked for Legal Aid before becoming the first female judge in the Valley. She called herself a "pragmatist," in contrast to the outspoken Doggett, and she claimed a closer identification with voters. "I'm Leticia Hinojosa, and I grew up poor in the Valley," she said in her radio ad. But Doggett's strong local base and relentless pursuit of new voters prevailed. He campaigned less against Hinojosa than against the redistricters. If he lost, Doggett told voters, "Tom DeLay will have won." He won the primary, 64%–36%. He led 88%–12% in Travis County, which cast 33% of the primary vote and where 49% of the county's population in the 25th was Hispanic. Of his 18,000 vote margin, almost 16,000 came from Travis. Just as impressively, Doggett held Hinojosa to a standoff in Hidalgo County. She carried only two of the other seven counties.

Although the primary effectively sealed his reelection, Doggett faced a spirited challenge in the general from Becky Armendariz Klein. She called herself a conservative "new voice with new ideas," and cited her experience working at the Pentagon, as policy director for then-Governor George W. Bush and, most recently, as chairwoman of the Texas Public Utility Commission.

Klein raised more than $800,000 and jabbed repeatedly at Doggett. She contended that she could deliver more as a member of the majority in Washington, and she criticized his inability to work across party lines. "I am a candidate that has access to the president and the leadership in Congress," she said. But her challenge never got seriously off the ground. Doggett tweaked her bid for ethnicity by pulling out her "long forgotten maiden name" and cited his many local endorsements. He won 68%–31%. Klein carried Gonzales and Live Oak Counties, both heavily Republican. Doggett won Travis County 79%–19% and Hidalgo County 60%–40%.

The Austin political cognoscenti had wrung their hands that redistricting might leave them without a local congressman. But now they have two, Doggett and Republican Michael McCaul, who won in the Austin-to-Houston 10th District.

TWENTY-SIXTH DISTRICT

Rep. Michael Burgess (R)

Elected 2002, 2d term; b. Dec. 23, 1950, Rochester, MN; home, Highland Village; N. TX St. U., B.S. 1972, M.S. 1976, U. of TX Med. Schl., M.D. 1977, U. of TX Dallas, M.S. 2000; Episcopalian; married (Laura).

Professional Career: Practicing obstetrician, 1981–2003.

DC Office: 1721 LHOB, 20515, 202-225-7772; Fax: 202-225-2919; Web site: www.house.gov/burgess/.

District Offices: Ft. Worth, 817-531-8454; Lewisville, 972-434-9700.

Committees: *Energy & Commerce* (30th of 31 R): Energy & Air Quality; Health; Oversight & Investigations.

Group Ratings

	ADA	ACLU	AFS	LCV	ITIC	NTU	COC	ACU	NTLC	CHC
2004	5	0	0	0	90	71	100	96	97	100
2003	5	—	0	5	—	69	100	92	—	—

National Journal Ratings

	2003 LIB	—	2003 CONS		2004 LIB	—	2004 CONS
Economic	31%	—	68%		17%	—	80%
Social	5%	—	87%		9%	—	85%
Foreign	11%	—	80%		23%	—	76%

Key Votes of the 108th Congress

1. Drilling in ANWR	Y	5. DC School Vouchers	Y	9. Ban Same-Sex Marriage	Y
2. Approve Bush Tax Cuts	Y	6. Ban Human Cloning	Y	10. Fund Iraq War	Y
3. Medicare/Rx Bill	Y	7. Restrict Gun Liability	Y	11. Bar Cuba Embargo Funds	N
4. Bar Overtime Pay Regs.	N	8. Ban Partial-Birth Abortion	Y	12. Intelligence Reorg.	Y

Election Results

2004 general	Michael Burgess (R)	180,519	(66%)	($817,015)
	Lico Reyes (D)	89,809	(33%)	($9,564)
	Other	4,211	(2%)	
2004 primary	Michael Burgess (R)	unopposed		
2002 general	Michael Burgess (R)	123,195	(75%)	($461,328)
	Paul William LeBon (D)	37,485	(23%)	($20,367)
	Other	3,998	(2%)	

The People		Race/Ethnic Origin	Ancestry		
Area size:	1,377 sq. mi.	66.1% White	German: 10.3%	Irish: 7.9%	
Urban population:	90.5%	15.5% Black	English: 7.5%		
Rural population:	9.5%	2.2% Asian	**2004 Presidential Vote**		
Pop. 2000:	651,619	0.5% Native Am.	Bush (R) 181,989	(65%)	
Median income:	$48,714	0.1% Hawaiian	Kerry (D) 99,633	(35%)	
Poverty status:	11.0%	1.3% Two+ races	**2000 Presidential Vote**		
Military veterans:	12.0%	0.1% Other	Bush (R) 134,189	(62%)	
		14.3% Hispanic Origin	Gore (D) 80,992	(38%)	
			Cook Partisan Voting Index: R +12		
Occupation	Blue collar: 22.1%	White collar: 64.5%	Gray collar: 13.4%		

Until the Texas Land and Immigration Company settled this portion of northeast Texas with a land grant from the Texas Congress in 1841, settlers were scarce and Indian raids were common. The area now known as Denton County takes its name from John Bunyan Denton, a Methodist pioneer preacher and lawyer killed in a skirmish with Indians. Today, this area on the northern edge of the Dallas-Fort Worth Metroplex is teeming with new arrivals: Denton County is part of one of America's fastest-growing metropolitan areas. It is booming and filled with young, well-educated, middle-class families. Its chief cities are Denton and Lewisville, Carrollton and Flower Mound, all north of the DFW Airport; truck-manufacturer Peterbilt Motors Company in Denton is among its largest private employers. And a quick look at the county map reveals that there is plenty more room for growth along the Interstate 35E and 35W corridors as they converge on the city of Denton in the heart of the county. The arrival of gas drilling rigs, protected by age-old Texas law on drilling rights, caused local controversy. Near Justin, in the southwest corner of Denton County, nearly 1 billion cubic feet of natural gas are produced daily. In 1940, there were 33,000 people in Denton County and they voted 88% Democratic for president. In 2000 there were 432,000 people in Denton County and they voted 70% Republican for president. In 2004 there were 530,000 and they voted 70% Republican again.

The 26th Congressional District of Texas is at the heart of the northern expansion of the Dallas-Fort Worth Metroplex. It includes three-quarters of suburban and exurban Denton County (but not Carrollton), most of rural Cooke County on the Oklahoma border, and a large slice of urban Tarrant County. The Tarrant County portion also includes booming new subdivisions north of Fort Worth and the Alliance Airport business parks, founded and operated by Ross Perot Jr., that employ about 20,000 people. It was changed significantly by the 2003 redistricting, in which the Republicans made it less significantly less Republican by removing suburban precincts and adding predominantly black precincts. Bush won 65%–35% here in 2004.

The congressman from the 26th District is Michael Burgess, a Republican first elected in 2002. He succeeded House Majority Leader Dick Armey. When Armey announced in December 2001 that he would not run again, there was no doubt that he would be succeeded by a Republican. But almost no one expected that the winner would be Michael Burgess. He grew up in Denton County and graduated from the University of North Texas and the University of Texas Medical School. He trained at Parkland Hospital in Dallas and set up an obstetrical-gynecological practice in Lewisville. After 21 years of practice, in which he delivered more than 3,000 babies, he decided to run for Congress—his first bid for elective office. He was so intimidated at his first campaign forum that he nearly walked out. The widespread expectation, in Texas and in Washington, was that the winner would be the majority leader's son Scott Armey, a former Denton County judge. He quickly made the rounds on Capitol Hill and among lobbyists: he was only 32 and it seemed likely he would be a congressman for many years to come. In the primary, Armey outspent Burgess by more than 6–1. But turnout was light, only 25,000 in a heavily Republican district with 456,000 voting age residents; there were no Republican primary contests at the top of the ticket and there didn't seem to be much suspense about the outcome of this race. Armey won 45% of the vote, not enough to avoid a runoff. Burgess won 23%, just 91 votes ahead of the third place finisher, a margin that presumably can be credited to parents of babies he had delivered or to the babies themselves.

Burgess said later that his initial goal in the four-week runoff campaign was to "not get embarrassed." But he benefited from a series of hard-hitting articles in the *Dallas Morning News* about Scott Armey's record as county judge. The paper reported that Armey had used his position to steer county jobs and contracts to close friends, including a $1.5 million transportation consulting contract. Burgess focused primarily on two issues—health care and taxes. A patient's rights advocate, he helped draft and pass the Texas Patients' Bill of Rights, and he vowed to do the same on a national level. Like Dick Armey, he is a supporter of a flat tax. Burgess's campaign was helped by the support of medical societies and local physicians who urged their patients to vote for him. Only 19,000 people turned out to vote in the April runoff and Burgess won 55%–45%. Armey carried Collin and Tarrant Counties, but lost 60%–40% in Denton County, where he was known best. After the runoff, Dick Armey spoke bitterly of the *Morning News's* "vicious unprofessionalism" and said they had conducted a vendetta against the Armey family. In the general election Burgess won 75%–23% over a Democrat whose son he had delivered.

In the House, Burgess had a reliably conservative voting record. As the only Texas Republican on the Transportation and Infrastructure Committee during his first term, he worked to change the funding formula so that Texas "receives its fair share." He chaired the health subcommittee of the Republican Policy Committee, and voiced caution about the safety risks of drug reimportation. He supported George W. Bush's call for limited federal funding of embryonic stem-cell research. In January 2005, his health-policy expertise helped him win a seat on the Energy and Commerce which other Texans had coveted. That assignment belied earlier speculation that Burgess would be a short-timer in the House, and a "place-holder" for his political ally, conservative state Senator Jane Nelson, who had encouraged him to run. In the redrawn district, he was reelected 66%–33% against an opponent who lost his 14th consecutive campaign.

TWENTY-SEVENTH DISTRICT

Rep. Solomon Ortiz (D)

Elected 1982, 12th term; b. June 3, 1937, Robstown; home, Corpus Christi; Del Mar Col., Natl. Sheriffs Training Inst., 1977; Methodist; divorced.

Military Career: Army, 1960–62.

Elected Office: Nueces Cnty. Constable, 1965–68, Commissioner, 1969–76, Sheriff, 1976–82.

DC Office: 2470 RHOB, 20515, 202-225-7742; Fax: 202-226-1134; Web site: www.house.gov/ortiz.

District Offices: Brownsville, 956-541-1242; Corpus Christi, 361-883-5868.

Committees: *Armed Services* (3d of 28 D): Readiness (RMM); Tactical Air & Land Forces. *Resources* (8th of 22 D): Energy & Mineral Resources; Fisheries & Oceans.

Group Ratings

	ADA	ACLU	AFS	LCV	ITIC	NTU	COC	ACU	NTLC	CHC
2004	55	36	100	55	67	10	47	28	6	54
2003	80	—	100	35	—	22	54	60	—	—

National Journal Ratings

	2003 LIB	—	2003 CONS	2004 LIB	—	2004 CONS
Economic	60%	—	39%	59%	—	41%
Social	56%	—	43%	57%	—	43%
Foreign	55%	—	44%	56%	—	44%

Key Votes of the 108th Congress

1. Drilling in ANWR	Y	5. DC School Vouchers	N	9. Ban Same-Sex Marriage	Y
2. Approve Bush Tax Cuts	N	6. Ban Human Cloning	*	10. Fund Iraq War	Y
3. Medicare/Rx Bill	N	7. Restrict Gun Liability	Y	11. Bar Cuba Embargo Funds	N
4. Bar Overtime Pay Regs.	Y	8. Ban Partial-Birth Abortion	Y	12. Intelligence Reorg.	*

Election Results

2004 general	Solomon Ortiz (D)	112,081	(63%)	($654,660)
	Willie Vaden (R)	61,955	(35%)	($51,228)
	Other	3,500	(2%)	
2004 primary	Solomon Ortiz (D)	unopposed		
2002 general	Solomon Ortiz (D)	68,559	(61%)	($539,401)
	Pat Ahumada (R)	41,004	(37%)	($19,648)
	Other	2,646	(2%)	

Prior Winning Percentages: 2000 (63%); 1998 (63%); 1996 (65%); 1994 (59%); 1992 (56%); 1990 (100%); 1988 (100%); 1986 (100%); 1984 (64%); 1982 (64%)

The People		Race/Ethnic Origin	Ancestry	
Area size:	6,319 sq. mi.	27.6% White	German: 5.7%	Irish: 3.9%
Urban population:	88.6%	2.5% Black	English: 3.6%	
Rural population:	11.4%	0.8% Asian	**2004 Presidential Vote**	
Pop. 2000:	651,619	0.2% Native Am.	Bush (R) 99,087	(55%)
Median income:	$31,327	0.0% Hawaiian	Kerry (D) 81,201	(45%)
Poverty status:	25.3%	0.7% Two+ races	**2000 Presidential Vote**	
Military veterans:	11.6%	0.1% Other	Gore (D) 81,454	(50%)
		68.1% Hispanic Origin	Bush (R) 80,755	(50%)
			Cook Partisan Voting Index: R + 1	

Occupation   Blue collar: 25.4%   White collar: 55.1%   Gray collar: 19.5%

South from Corpus Christi to the Rio Grande and the Mexican border are two Texas versions of dreamland. One, fronting the Gulf of Mexico, is the sand spit of Padre Island, for most of its 80-mile length a barrier reef island and national seashore, at the southern tip of which is a high-rise resort to which college students throng for spring break and where developers have built 5,500 rental units. Remains of a 1554 Spanish shipwreck have been found offshore, and Portuguese settlers began cattle ranching here not long after. The other, inland from the Laguna Madre in Kleberg County, is the vast grazing and oil lands of the 825,000-acre (that's 1,289 square miles) King Ranch. This still seemingly vacant land between the Nueces River and the Rio Grande was the territory in contention in the Mexican-American War. The United States won that war and declared its sovereignty. But today most people here are of Mexican ancestry, some from families who have lived for generations on this side of the border, some recent immigrants. The culture here is *Tejano*, proudly American but with Mexican flair and vitality.

The 27th Congressional District of Texas includes this land from Corpus Christi south to the Rio Grande. Its population is concentrated at the northern and southern ends of the district. In the north Corpus Christi and surrounding Nueces County, with a 56% Hispanic population, is the southernmost natural port on Texas's Gulf Coast and the nation's fifth largest in trading volume with big petrochemical plants and plans for a container cargo terminal; the bayfront, lined with palm trees, is a popular recreational spot. At the southern end is Cameron County, which includes South Padre Island; the population here is 84% Hispanic. The biggest city is Brownsville, on the Lower Rio Grande opposite Matamoros, Mexico, one of the major border crossings in Texas; not far away is the colonia of Cameron Park, where people live in trailers or makeshift structures without water or sewage service, rated by the Census Bureau as one of the poorest places in the nation. NAFTA has lifted the economy in parts of this area, and there has been a boom in commercial construction. The 2003 redistricting produced only small changes in the boundaries: a chunk of Cameron County was placed in the 15th District and territory north of Corpus Christi and west of Kingsville was added. Politically, the 27th District is Democratic, but not so Democratic as one might expect. In 1998 the 27th District gave a majority of its votes for Governor George W. Bush. In the 2000 presidential campaign, Bush just barely lost the district to Al Gore, and in 2004 he carried it with 55% of the vote. This was one of four Democratic-held districts in Texas that Bush won in 2004, three of which have Hispanic majorities.

The congressman from the 27th District is Solomon Ortiz, a Democrat and the only representative for this district since its creation in the 1982 redistricting. He grew up inland from Corpus in the Canta Ranas (singing frogs) neighborhood of Robstown, which is known for its political activism. His father died when he was 14, leaving him the eldest of four children who scratched out a living as migrant farm workers, sometimes working as far away as Colorado and Michigan. Ortiz worked as an Army investigator and translator, using his Spanish to learn French, took a correspondence course in police work and returned home to run for constable. In 1976 he was the first Hispanic elected Nueces County sheriff. In his first run for Congress, he got only 26% in the primary, but he made a propitious alliance with Democratic leaders in the Brownsville area and won the runoff with 52%. He has not been seriously challenged since then.

Ortiz's voting record has leaned toward the conservative end of House Democrats. As the third-ranking Democrat on the Armed Services Committee, he watches out for the four military installations in the Coastal Bend region around Corpus Christi; they emerged from the 1995 base-closing review with more jobs than before. As ranking Democrat on the Readiness Subcommittee, he remains an advocate of depot maintenance and adamantly opposed additional rounds of base closings; the House-Senate conference committee on the defense-spending bill in 2004 stripped his House-passed amendment to delay the new round from 2005 to 2007. Ortiz had good reason for trying to thwart the 2005 round: the Coastal Bend region, it turned out, was hit hard by the Pentagon's May 2005 recommendations. Naval Station Ingleside, which has supported the Navy's fleet of minehunters and minesweepers, was slated for closure with a net loss of 2,200 civilian and military employees; Naval Air Station Corpus Christi was to be realigned, with a net loss of 1,000 jobs. Corpus Christi Army Depot, a helicopter repair facility, was another realignment target: 92 lost civilian jobs there.

In 2001, five months after the Port of Corpus Christi dedicated its new conference center in his name, the *San Antonio Express-News* reported that Ortiz got favored treatment when the Port awarded a contract to provide security to a firm that he owned even though it was not the low bidder. Ortiz defended the contract as awarded in open competition and his supporters said that the original low bidder was unqualified. But more questions were raised when he enthusiastically supported the U.S. free trade agreement with Singapore; his business provides security guards to a subsidiary of a Singapore-owned firm doing business in Brownsville. In 2003, he agreed to sell his business. Separately, local news reports detailed Ortiz's support for projects represented by the lobbying firm of Randy DeLay, brother of the Majority Leader Tom DeLay; with encouragement from Ortiz, Randy DeLay also was defending local facilities from base-closing.

Ortiz is a sturdy internationalist: an enthusiastic supporter of NAFTA and normal trade relations with China, and one of 21 Democrats to vote for trade promotion authority in 2001, though he voted against it in 2002. He expressed reservations about George W. Bush's guest worker program as serving corporate interests, and preferred to focus on family reunification. He opposed the Bush administration's "catch and release" program for illegal immigrants caught along the border for whom there were insufficient detention centers.

In 2000 and 2002 Ortiz's Republican opponent was former Brownsville Mayor Pat Ahumada, who tried to take advantage of the controversy over the Port's contract with Ortiz; Ortiz won with 63% and 61% of the vote. In 2004, he won 63%–35% against Ingleside Mayor Willie Vaden, who refused to take large campaign contributions in order to draw a contrast with Ortiz. Ortiz reportedly is grooming his son Solomon Ortiz Jr., chairman of the Nueces County Democratic Party, as his successor.

TWENTY-EIGHTH DISTRICT

Rep. Henry Cuellar (D)

Elected 2004, 1st term; b. Sept. 19, 1955, Laredo; home, Laredo; Georgetown U., B.S. 1976, U. of TX, J.D. 1981, Ph.D. 1998, TX A&M U., M.A. 1982; Catholic; married (Imelda).

Elected Office: TX House of Reps., 1986–2000; TX Secy. of State, 2001.

Professional Career: Practicing atty., 1981–2004.

DC Office: 1404 LHOB, 20515, 202-225-1640; Fax: 202-225-1641; Web site: www.house.gov/cuellar.

District Offices: Laredo, 956-725-0639; San Antonio, 210-271-2851; San Marcos, 512-392-2364.

Committees: *Agriculture* (12th of 21 D): Conservation, Credit, Rural Development & Research; Department Operations, Oversight, Nutrition & Forestry; Specialty Crops & Foreign Agriculture Programs. *Budget* (15th of 17 D).

Group Ratings and Key Votes: Newly Elected

Election Results

2004 general	Henry Cuellar (D)	106,323	(59%)	($1,372,833)
	Jim Hopson (R)	69,538	(39%)	($43,581)
	Other	4,305	(2%)	
2004 primary	Henry Cuellar (D)	24,651	(50%)	
	Ciro Rodriguez (D)	24,448	(50%)	
2002 general	Ciro Rodriguez (D)	71,393	(71%)	($409,446)
	Gabriel Perales (R)	26,973	(27%)	($39,889)
	Other	2,054	(2%)	

The People		Race/Ethnic Origin	Ancestry	
Area size:	10,264 sq. mi.	27.9% White	German: 7.7%	Irish: 3.5%
Urban population:	75.9%	6.0% Black	USA: 3.1%	
Rural population:	24.1%	0.5% Asian	**2004 Presidential Vote**	
Pop. 2000:	651,620	0.2% Native Am.	Bush (R) 97,183	(53%)
Median income:	$31,355	0.0% Hawaiian	Kerry (D) 87,811	(47%)
Poverty status:	22.6%	0.7% Two+ races	**2000 Presidential Vote**	
Military veterans:	11.9%	0.1% Other	Gore (D) 77,647	(51%)
		64.5% Hispanic Origin	Bush (R) 74,042	(49%)
			Cook Partisan Voting Index: D + 1	

Occupation   Blue collar: 30.7%   White collar: 50.0%   Gray collar: 19.3%

The Mexican-American tradition in the part of South Texas radiating from San Antonio is anchored in two culturally conservative but adaptive institutions, the Catholic Church and the United States military. Both are a major presence in San Antonio, just 150 miles north of the border, which for many years had the largest Mexican-American population of any American city, where Spanish has long been widely spoken and political refugees from Mexico's revolution could be sure of freedom. The church in San Antonio was led for years by liberal bishops who also ran St. Mary's University, which educated many Hispanic politicians and leaders, including two longtime House Democratic committee chairmen, Henry B. Gonzalez and Kika de la Garza—and also Republican Senator John Cornyn, who graduated from St. Mary's law school. Just as visible a presence in San Antonio are the Army and Air Force, with huge Fort Sam Houston, Lackland Air Force Base, Randolph Air Force Base, and the Brooks City Base, all in or near the city limits. At the site of the former Brooks Air Force Base, Toyota is building a plant to manufacture Tundra pickup trucks; it will employ about 2,000 directly and many more from suppliers and related businesses. Mexican-Americans have long volunteered for military service in numbers higher than most ethnic groups, and for many years Mexican-Americans in San Antonio worked in civilian jobs for the military service: Uncle Sam has long been an equal opportunity employer.

San Antonio's Mexican-American community has produced many politicians who are liberal on economic issues, civil rights and civil liberties. But it has not produced many who are hostile to the military or to traditional religious and cultural values.

Hard by the Mexican border is a different kind of place, one where singer Johnny Cash, in "Streets of Laredo", summoned up images of lonely cowboys on dusty streets outside a row of saloons in a tiny town. But this is not the Laredo of today. Laredo, on the Rio Grande 150 miles south of San Antonio, is the main border crossing for U.S.-Mexico trade. Some 9,000 trucks and 1,200 rail cars cross its three bridges (one 17 miles upriver) every day, with merchandise worth upward of $100 billion a year, more than through all the other border crossings combined. Laredo was America's second fastest-growing city in the 1990s, with more warehouse space than San Antonio and Austin combined; its old downtown streets with their bargain stores are still filled with Mexicans who cross the border on foot, but those with cars head up the freeway to malls, and the Wal-Mart here is said to be the chain's top producer per square foot. Incomes and housing prices in Laredo (population 310,000 in 2000) are low by U.S. standards, but far above those of Nuevo Laredo (population 500,000 in 2000) across the Rio Grande, and there is money to be made here. Laredo's Tony Sanchez, proprietor of a family oil and gas business and owner of International Bank of Commerce, became rich enough to spend $60 million on his campaign for governor of Texas in 2002.

The border country along the Rio Grande is in some ways a zone all its own, a mixture of the U.S. and Mexico, where many people have roots on both sides of the border. As Laredo Mayor Betty Flores says, "The river for us is more like some street that we cross; it's really not a border." Webb County, almost all of whose people live in Laredo, had a population that was 94% Hispanic in 2000, and fast food restaurants here feature enchiladas more than hamburgers. Los Dos Laredos share a minor league baseball team. Yet the predictions that Latinos would Mexicanize the United States don't seem to be panning out. Years ago, movements like La Raza Unida—which got its beginnings here in 1969 when Hispanic youngsters wanted to elect high school cheerleaders in Crystal City—wanted the border country to become more like Mexico, with its union and party apparatchiks. More recently, Mexico, with its economic reforms and NAFTA, and with the election of President Vicente Fox in July 2000, has been trying to become more like the United States, and particularly like Texas, with open markets and privatized companies, less controlled by political or labor bosses.

The 28th Congressional District of Texas stretches from the southern half of San Antonio to the Mexican border. Some 44% of its people are in Bexar County, anchored by Hispanics on the south side of San Antonio and a smaller number of blacks on the east side. Brooks City Base (slated for closure under the Pentagon's May 2005 recommendations) is here, but the other military installations are located in the neighboring 20th and 21st Districts. The district extends south, through thinly settled ranch and oil well country, to the Rio Grande. The 2003 Republican redistricting plan added Anglo-majority Guadalupe and Wilson Counties and San Marcos in Hays County, all east of San Antonio, adjusted the boundaries in Bexar County, removed five heavily Hispanic counties on the border and just to the north and added half of Laredo's Webb County. Laredo has had a tumultuous politics in recent years. When local businessman Tony Sanchez was the Democratic candidate for governor in 2002, turnout in Webb County surged from 16,000 in 1998 to 39,000 in 2002, and the outpouring of Democratic votes almost enabled an upset of 23d District Republican Henry Bonilla. Republicans were obviously trying to shore Bonilla up by removing half the county from his district, but they also changed the political balance in the district.

The congressman from the 28th District is Henry Cuellar, a Democrat elected in 2004 after a bitter primary contest. Cuellar was the oldest of eight children of migrant workers who had only elementary education. He graduated from Georgetown University and the University of Texas law school, and he later got a Ph.D. in government from UT. From his base in Laredo, he served 14 years in Texas House from 1986 to 2000, where he helped to author the Texas Grant college-aid program. In December 2000 Governor Rick Perry appointed him secretary of state even though he was a Democrat. Cuellar resigned in January 2002 to run against Henry Bonilla in the 23d District. He was helped when Bonilla said he didn't need Laredo to win; the Webb

County Republican chairman endorsed Cuellar. Cuellar attacked Bonilla for his votes against funding the CHIP program, passage of the Family and Medical Leave Act, funding Pell grants, student loans, work study and classroom construction. And he accused him of being insufficiently Hispanic. Bonilla had the money advantage, but Tony Sanchez's turnout operation in Webb County almost beat him. Cuellar carried Webb County 84%–15%, with a 26,000 popular vote margin; only when the Bexar County votes were finally counted a few days later was it clear that Bonilla won by 52%–47%.

The 2003 redistricting strengthened Bonilla but gave Cuellar an opportunity to run in the 28th District against incumbent Ciro Rodriguez of San Antonio, who had the most liberal voting record of Texas's six Hispanic congressmen and was the chairman of the Hispanic Caucus. When Cuellar announced, Rodriguez had a hard time believing that a friend and former legislative colleague for whom he had raised money in 2002 would run against him. The ambitious Cuellar, on the other hand, explained his primary bid as a common political occurrence in South Texas. Besides, he told a local reporter, "nobody died and made [Rodriguez] king. . . . Democrats run against Democrats all the time, and that's what it's all about." Rodriguez had little time to get acquainted with the new district, since the March primary took place just five months after passage of the new map. He had the support of the Hispanic Caucus in Washington, but that delivered few votes in Texas. Cuellar criticized Rodriguez for voting against the Medicare/prescription drug bill. Rodriguez said that Cuellar sided with Republicans after he was appointed secretary of state by Governor Rick Perry. The initial vote count showed Rodriguez ahead by 145 votes. But Cuellar demanded a recount. Officials in Zapata County, the border county just south of Webb County, found 177 additional votes for Cuellar and none for Rodriguez, which put Cuellar ahead by 203 votes. After a lawsuit, a second recount, and a state appellate court ruling in July, Cuellar was declared the Democratic nominee by 58 votes out of 49,000 cast.

But if Zapata County put Cuellar over the top, the election was really decided in Webb County. It cast 31% of the primary votes, partly because of other local contests; Cuellar won there 84%–16%, and got more than half of his total votes in a county with only 15% of the total population. Rodriguez carried his base of Bexar County 80%–20%, but the turnout was smaller than in Webb even though the local population was nearly three times as large. Rodriguez carried six counties in the northern part of the district, and Cuellar carried the three that bordered Webb County. The recounts along the border were especially controversial. When the state appeals court dismissed Rodriguez's case, the five Republicans sided with Cuellar and the two Democrats with Rodriguez. After the July decision the state's Democratic congressional delegation reluctantly rallied behind Cuellar, lest he lose the seat to the Republican nominee. Cuellar won in November 59%–39%, with 68% of the vote in Bexar County and 90% in Webb County.

The likelihood is that there will be another contested primary in 2006. Even before he left office, Rodriguez said that he would challenge Cuellar, and state Representative Richard Raymond of Laredo also expressed interest in running; in spring 2005 both were raising money. In Washington, some House Democrats said that they did not trust Cuellar and there was speculation that he might switch parties. Cuellar said that he will always be a Democrat but, "I don't want anybody to take my vote for granted."

TWENTY-NINTH DISTRICT

Rep. Gene Green (D)

Elected 1992, 7th term; b. Oct. 17, 1947, Houston; home, Houston; U. of Houston, B.A., 1971, Bates Col. of Law at U. of Houston, 1973–77; Methodist; married (Helen).

Elected Office: TX House of Reps., 1972–84; TX Senate, 1985–92.

Professional Career: Practicing atty., 1977–92.

DC Office: 2335 RHOB, 20515, 202-225-1688; Fax: 202-225-9903; Web site: www.house.gov/green.

District Offices: Houston, 713-330-0761; Houston, 281-999-5879.

Committees: *Energy & Commerce* (14th of 26 D): Commerce, Trade & Consumer Protection; Energy & Air Quality; Environment & Hazardous Materials; Health. *Standards of Official Conduct* (3d of 5 D).

Group Ratings

	ADA	ACLU	AFS	LCV	ITIC	NTU	COC	ACU	NTLC	CHC
2004	85	60	100	73	50	12	45	20	6	30
2003	85	—	100	55	—	22	43	32	—	—

National Journal Ratings

	2003 LIB	—	2003 CONS		2004 LIB	—	2004 CONS
Economic	61%	—	39%		67%	—	33%
Social	61%	—	38%		65%	—	35%
Foreign	75%	—	21%		59%	—	40%

Key Votes of the 108th Congress

1. Drilling in ANWR	Y	5. DC School Vouchers	N	9. Ban Same-Sex Marriage	N
2. Approve Bush Tax Cuts	N	6. Ban Human Cloning	N	10. Fund Iraq War	Y
3. Medicare/Rx Bill	N	7. Restrict Gun Liability	Y	11. Bar Cuba Embargo Funds	N
4. Bar Overtime Pay Regs.	Y	8. Ban Partial-Birth Abortion	N	12. Intelligence Reorg.	N

Election Results

2004 general	Gene Green (D)	78,256	(94%)	($684,970)
	Clifford Messina (Lib)	4,868	(6%)	
2004 primary	Gene Green (D)	unopposed		
2002 general	Gene Green (D)	55,760	(95%)	($549,217)
	Paul Hansen (Lib)	2,833	(5%)	

Prior Winning Percentages: 2000 (73%); 1998 (93%); 1996 (68%); 1994 (73%); 1992 (65%)

The People		Race/Ethnic Origin	Ancestry	
Area size:	249 sq. mi.	21.9% White	USA: 4.1%	German: 3.1%
Urban population:	99.4%	9.7% Black	Irish: 2.8%	
Rural population:	0.6%	1.3% Asian	**2004 Presidential Vote**	
Pop. 2000:	651,619	0.2% Native Am.	Kerry (D) 59,897	(56%)
Median income:	$31,751	0.0% Hawaiian	Bush (R) 47,734	(44%)
Poverty status:	21.9%	0.7% Two+ races	**2000 Presidential Vote**	
Military veterans:	7.2%	0.1% Other	Gore (D) 61,303	(57%)
		66.1% Hispanic Origin	Bush (R) 45,626	(43%)
			Cook Partisan Voting Index: D + 8	
Occupation	Blue collar: 43.1%	White collar: 40.3%	Gray collar: 16.6%	

"What built Houston," wrote John Gunther in *Inside U.S.A.*, "was a combination of cotton, oil, and the ship canal." The cotton and oil were gifts of nature, though they required much human effort and ingenuity to produce in commercial quantities; the 54-mile Houston Ship Channel, by contrast, was almost totally man's creation. After the sand spit port of Galveston was destroyed by a hurricane and tidal wave in 1900, Houston's elders decided to dredge out Buffalo Bayou and make their inland city a seaport. And so a sluggish, 6-foot-deep creek became a 40-foot-deep channel—recently deepened to 45 feet, and widened from 400 feet to 530 feet—and Houston turned into one of the nation's biggest ports, with more than 400 vessels daily generating 205,000 jobs and $7.7 billion a year for the local economy; about 60% of the big ships are tankers, with a capacity of 800,000 barrels of crude oil. On the west side of town, Houston—a world-class metropolis of 5.2 million people—seems entirely a white-collar, office-bound city. But on the east and north, around the turning basin in the port and through the maze of refinery towers and tubing, Houston remains vibrant and blue collar, with blacks, Mexican-Americans and large numbers of whites from the rural South and even Michigan and California, who have come here to move up in the world.

The 29th Congressional District of Texas covers much of the Ship Channel area and working-class Houston—like a rough-edged wrench on the east side of the city. Included is much of the area on Houston's Northside, between the Eastex and North Freeways almost out to George Bush Intercontinental Airport and FM 1960, and blue-collar neighborhoods in northeast Houston. The 2003 redistricting removed some territory further north and some black precincts in northeast Houston and added territory to the east along the Ship Channel to heavily industrial Baytown. Redistricting increased the Hispanic percentage from 62% to 66% and reduced the black percentage from 15% to 10%. This part of Houston has always been considered heavily Democratic, but in 2004 Bush lost it by only a 56%–44% margin. "The civil rights movement isn't part of their culture," a local Democratic consultant said of these voters. "It's as simple as, 'This president appointed Alberto Gonzalez to be Attorney General. That sounds good to me.' "

The congressman from the 29th District is Gene Green, a Democrat first elected in 1992. Green grew up in the largely Hispanic Lindale section of north Houston, worked as a printer's apprentice and was admitted to the bar at age 30; he was elected to the state House in 1972, at 25, and to the state Senate in a special election in 1985. He has been a faithful union and trial lawyer man in Austin and Washington, and also an opponent of gun control, a politician whose natural political base is Texas' small, unionized blue-collar class. He is a compulsive campaigner who goes door to door, with lawn signs and a hammer in his trunk; and a good thing, for him anyway, since otherwise he never would have won in the 29th. In the 1992 primary he faced Ben Reyes, a tempestuous Houston councilman who once protested official inaction by demolishing a crack house. In the primary, Reyes led 34%–28% over Green. In the runoff, Green came out ahead by 180 votes out of 31,508 cast. Reyes went to court and charged that Republican voters had illegally crossed over and voted in the runoff. That got him a July re-runoff, but to no avail. This time Green won with 52%; he won the general election with 65%.

In the House, Green has had a relatively moderate voting record for a member in a heavily minority urban district. After a spirited fight with other Texas Democrats in 1997, he won a seat on the Energy and Commerce Committee. He opposed trade promotion authority but voted for the use of force in Iraq. With Heather Wilson, he won House passage of a bill to give regulators and Internet service providers more authority to restrict unwanted spam. With Chip Pickering, he sponsored a bill to more strictly enforce the licenses of satellite radio companies to assure that they do not endanger local stations.

Since 1996, no other Democrat has challenged him and he has been reelected easily. At a time when national and state Hispanic leaders are pressing for more Hispanic members, the 29th remains an inviting opportunity for an ambitious Hispanic politician. Perhaps in anticipation, Green organized a Spanish class for members of Congress. He survived the 2001 and 2003 redistrictings and had no major party opposition in 2002 and 2004.

THIRTIETH DISTRICT

Rep. Eddie Bernice Johnson (D)

Elected 1992, 7th term; b. Dec. 3, 1935, Waco; home, Dallas; St. Mary's at Notre Dame, B.A. 1955, TX Christian U., B.S. 1967, S. Methodist U., M.B.A. 1976; Baptist; divorced.

Elected Office: TX House of Reps., 1972–1977; TX Senate, 1986–92.

Professional Career: Registered nurse; Regional Dir., U.S. Dept. of HEW, 1977–80; Mgmt. consultant, Sammons Corp., 1979–81; Owner, Eddie Bernice Johnson & Assoc., 1981–present.

DC Office: 1511 LHOB, 20515, 202-225-8885; Fax: 202-226-1477; Web site: www.house.gov/ebjohnson.

District Offices: Dallas, 214-922-8885; Dallas, 214-324-0080.

Committees: *Science* (3d of 20 D): Energy; Research. *Transportation & Infrastructure* (10th of 34 D): Aviation; Railroads; Water Resources & Environment (RMM).

Group Ratings

	ADA	ACLU	AFS	LCV	ITIC	NTU	COC	ACU	NTLC	CHC
2004	100	90	88	100	60	13	63	17	0	7
2003	95	—	100	90	—	22	34	16	—	—

National Journal Ratings

	2003 LIB	—	2003 CONS		2004 LIB	—	2004 CONS
Economic	77%	—	23%		69%	—	30%
Social	81%	—	18%		82%	—	18%
Foreign	93%	—	6%		75%	—	24%

Key Votes of the 108th Congress

1. Drilling in ANWR	N	5. DC School Vouchers	N	9. Ban Same-Sex Marriage	N
2. Approve Bush Tax Cuts	N	6. Ban Human Cloning	N	10. Fund Iraq War	N
3. Medicare/Rx Bill	N	7. Restrict Gun Liability	N	11. Bar Cuba Embargo Funds	Y
4. Bar Overtime Pay Regs.	Y	8. Ban Partial-Birth Abortion	N	12. Intelligence Reorg.	N

Election Results

2004 general	Eddie Bernice Johnson (D)	144,513	(93%)	($405,453)
	John Davis (Lib)	10,821	(7%)	
2004 primary	Eddie Bernice Johnson (D)	unopposed		
2002 general	Eddie Bernice Johnson (D)	88,980	(74%)	($462,419)
	Ron Bush (R)	28,981	(24%)	($1,973)
	Other	1,856	(2%)	

Prior Winning Percentages: 2000 (92%); 1998 (72%); 1996 (55%); 1994 (73%); 1992 (72%)

The People		Race/Ethnic Origin	Ancestry	
Area size:	319 sq. mi.	21.9% White	German: 3.2%	USA: 3.1%
Urban population:	98.8%	41.4% Black	Irish: 2.9%	
Rural population:	1.2%	1.3% Asian	**2004 Presidential Vote**	
Pop. 2000:	651,620	0.3% Native Am.	Kerry (D) 136,116	(75%)
Median income:	$33,505	0.0% Hawaiian	Bush (R) 45,148	(25%)
Poverty status:	21.4%	0.9% Two+ races	**2000 Presidential Vote**	
Military veterans:	8.4%	0.1% Other	Gore (D) 113,747	(74%)
		34.2% Hispanic Origin	Bush (R) 39,468	(26%)
			Cook Partisan Voting Index: D +26	

Occupation	Blue collar: 30.7%	White collar: 52.1%	Gray collar: 17.2%

Dallas is, among other things, the westernmost city of the Deep South. Cotton was originally the major crop in this part of Texas, and many of Dallas's first enterprising businessmen, when the railroad reached the Trinity River here in the 1870s, were cotton brokers. Railroads made Dallas rich and helped it to grow. Geographically, Dallas is directly west of the Black Belt of Alabama and the Mississippi Delta, both heavy cotton-producing areas in the days before the boll weevil.

Many blacks and whites came west on U.S. 80—and now Interstate 20—to the Dallas-Fort Worth Metroplex, now the largest metro area in the South. The south side of Dallas, not much visited by tourists, is predominately black. But the Trinity River Corridor project, which has been talked about for decades, could change many features of Dallas with its ambitious plans for flood control, recreational features and transportation improvements, including three new bridges.

The 30th Congressional District of Texas, designed to be the Dallas-Fort Worth Metroplex's black-majority district, includes most of Dallas's predominantly black neighborhoods. Its creation in 1991 was insisted on by the then-chairman of the Texas Senate's redistricting committee (details to follow), and the result was one of the most grotesquely shaped districts in the country: Attached to the central body in south and east Dallas, were tentacles that appeared as complex and attenuated as a series of DNA molecules. A lawsuit was filed, claiming racial gerrymandering, and the Supreme Court ruled the 30th and two Houston districts unconstitutional. In 1996, a three-judge federal court drew new lines. In 2001, another three-judge federal court drew new lines for all of the state's 32 districts and in the process smoothed out the lines even more. The Republicans' redistricting in 2003 made them smoother still, though their higher priority was to assure that this would become the only Metroplex district that would elect a Democrat. Today the 30th District includes two compact geographic units centered in downtown Dallas. One consists of most of the south side of Dallas; the other runs northwest out Stemmons Freeway. In between is the "mixmaster," where three busy interstates—I-30, 35E and 45—come together within a square mile, surrounding many of the prominent sites in Dallas. The district's population is 41% black and 34% Hispanic. In 2004, George W. Bush lost here 75%–25%, his worst performance in Texas.

The congresswoman from the 30th District is Eddie Bernice Johnson, who created the district in 1991. She grew up in Texas and graduated from Texas Christian University as a registered nurse. She worked at St. Paul Hospital and was chief psychiatric nurse at the VA Hospital in Dallas. In 1972 she was elected to the Texas House—the first black woman elected to anything in Dallas. She became a regional HEW director in the Carter administration and was elected to the state Senate in 1986; in 1991 she was chairman of the Senate Redistricting Committee. She won the 1992 Democratic primary with 92% of the vote and has never had effective opposition.

In the House, Johnson has a mostly liberal voting record, but she has been attentive to business interests in Dallas. Though she once pledged to unions to oppose NAFTA, she changed her mind and voted for it; Dallas probably exports more to Mexico than any other American city, and many jobs depend on those exports. Johnson also sided with business on normal trade relations with China, but she later opposed trade promotion authority. On the Science Committee, where she was ranking Democrat on the Research Subcommittee, she shared credit for passing the Networking and Information Research and Development Act to double federal information research spending. She also sought to double spending for the National Science Foundation. As a health care professional, Johnson has taken an interest in minorities' health care problems. In 2001–2002, she chaired the Congressional Black Caucus. In 2004 she called for the United Nations to monitor the presidential election in Florida. "Too often, this country is rightly seen internationally as one who writes the rules and enforces them, but refuses to abide by them," she wrote on her Web site.

On the Transportation and Infrastructure Committee, she got a seat on the Aviation Subcommittee, of great importance here: The 30th District is not far from Dallas-Fort Worth International Airport and includes three others, Love Field, Dallas Executive Airport and Lancaster Airport. As one of her top priorities, she has worked to secure funds in the highway bill for construction of the I-30 suspension bridge over the Trinity River. In 2005, she became ranking Democrat on the Water Resources and Environment Subcommittee.

Johnson supported Nancy Pelosi for minority leader over her Metroplex neighbor Martin Frost, with whom Johnson had a difficult relationship, including on redistricting fights. "We respect each other. But when it comes to redistricting. . . . he's always worried about one person, and that's himself. And he doesn't care what happens to anybody else," she told the *Dallas Morning News*, explaining why she hired her own lawyer in the 2003 redistricting fight. She termed the final map that year offensive because it "packed" more minorities into her district than she needed. "It would definitely diminish minority impact."

THIRTY-FIRST DISTRICT

Rep. John Carter (R)

Elected 2002, 2d term; b. Nov. 6, 1941, Houston; home, Round Rock; TX Tech. U., B.A. 1964, U. of TX, J.D. 1969; Christian; married (Erika).

Elected Office: Dist. Ct. judge, 1982–2001.

Professional Career: Practicing atty., 1969–81.

DC Office: 408 CHOB, 20515, 202-225-3864; Fax: 202-225-5886; Web site: www.house.gov/carter/.

District Offices: Belton, 254-933-1392; Round Rock, 512-246-1600.

Committees: *Appropriations* (36th of 37 R): Foreign Operations, Export Financing & Related Programs; Homeland Security; Military Quality of Life & Veterans Affairs & Related Agencies.

Group Ratings

	ADA	ACLU	AFS	LCV	ITIC	NTU	COC	ACU	NTLC	CHC
2004	0	0	0	0	90	69	100	96	89	92
2003	5	—	0	5	—	65	100	92	—	—

National Journal Ratings

	2003 LIB	—	2003 CONS		2004 LIB	—	2004 CONS
Economic	21%	—	75%		5%	—	93%
Social	0%	—	95%		9%	—	85%
Foreign	0%	—	89%		10%	—	86%

Key Votes of the 108th Congress

1. Drilling in ANWR	Y	5. DC School Vouchers	Y	9. Ban Same-Sex Marriage	Y
2. Approve Bush Tax Cuts	Y	6. Ban Human Cloning	Y	10. Fund Iraq War	Y
3. Medicare/Rx Bill	Y	7. Restrict Gun Liability	Y	11. Bar Cuba Embargo Funds	N
4. Bar Overtime Pay Regs.	N	8. Ban Partial-Birth Abortion	Y	12. Intelligence Reorg.	Y

Election Results

2004 general	John Carter (R)	160,247	(65%)	($899,885)
	Jon Porter (D)	80,292	(32%)	($15,618)
	Other	6,888	(3%)	
2004 primary	John Carter (R)	25,293	(70%)	
	Wes Riddle (R)	8,215	(23%)	
	Dirk Armbrust (R)	2,868	(8%)	
2002 general	John Carter (R)	111,556	(69%)	($811,681)
	David Bagley (D)	44,183	(27%)	($23,763)
	Other	5,745	(4%)	

The People		Race/Ethnic Origin	Ancestry	
Area size:	7,194 sq. mi.	66.1% White	German: 12.6% Irish: 7.6%	
Urban population:	77.9%	13.0% Black	English: 6.8%	
Rural population:	22.1%	2.1% Asian	**2004 Presidential Vote**	
Pop. 2000:	651,619	0.4% Native Am.	Bush (R)	170,234 (67%)
Median income:	$43,381	0.2% Hawaiian	Kerry (D)	85,574 (33%)
Poverty status:	9.6%	1.8% Two+ races	**2000 Presidential Vote**	
Military veterans:	16.4%	0.1% Other	Bush (R)	136,116 (69%)
		16.3% Hispanic Origin	Gore (D)	62,493 (31%)
			Cook Partisan Voting Index: R +16	

Occupation	Blue collar: 22.7%	White collar: 62.6%	Gray collar: 14.7%

Williamson County, Texas, long a rural backwater almost no one elsewhere had ever heard of, has become a major population and business center deep in the heart of Texas. Its population has virtually doubled in every recent decade: 37,000 in 1970, 77,000 in 1980, 140,000 in 1990, 250,000 in 2000, 317,000 in 2004. From 2000 to 2004 it was the nation's 15th fastest-growing county. Williamson County is just north of Austin, and much of this growth has been generated by the Austin area's high tech boom; hugely successful Dell Computer is headquartered here in Round Rock. But Williamson County's growth continued, even accelerated, after the high-tech bust of 2000. And more growth will probably be generated by Texas 130, a 49-mile toll road under construction in empty farmland a few miles east of congested I-35. Local officials worried that the result will be more sprawl and inadequate local services: Most of the area served by the tollway has been outside the jurisdiction of local cities, and there have been complaints that Texas officials have not given the counties adequate planning and management tools. Bell and Coryell Counties, just north of Williamson County, are the site of Fort Hood, the largest U.S. military base in the world and the largest employer in Texas. The base is home to 42,000 Army soldiers and the only post in the United States that is capable of supporting two full armored divisions. Established in 1942 as a tank destroyer tactical and firing center, it uprooted on short notice 300 farming and ranching families who had been living a quiet life; now, this land serves a Texas-sized facility that covers 218,000 acres (that's 340 square miles, partner). Toward the end of World War II, about 4,000 German prisoners of war were interned at Hood. The primary mission of Fort Hood has become maintaining readiness for combat missions, including training Army Reservists in urban combat. Members of its 4th Infantry Division captured Saddam Hussein in a "spider hole" in the Iraq countryside. East of Fort Hood is Temple, a rail center and the only city in the area with a downtown business district. Decades ago, the freight carried from its rail yards was mostly cotton; now, it serves a variety of industries, including plastics manufacturers.

The 31st Congressional District of Texas, newly created in the 2001 court redistricting and sharply altered in the 2003 Republican legislative redistricting, is dominated by Williamson, Bell and Coryell Counties, which include 86% of its population. The district also includes two smaller counties north of Coryell County and two counties and part of another east of Williamson and Bell Counties. Historically this was solidly Democratic country for many years, devoted to the party of first the Confederacy and then the New Deal, full of cotton farmers who distrusted Wall Street and railroads and trusted in politicians like Sam Rayburn and Lyndon Johnson. As late as 1990 the district voted for Democratic Governor Ann Richards and Senator Lloyd Bentsen. But people here have cottoned on to George W. Bush's brand of Republicanism. In 2004 he carried the district 67%–33%.

The congressman from the 31st District is John Carter, a Republican first elected in 2002. He grew up in Houston and graduated from Texas Tech and the University of Texas law school. He practiced law in Williamson County and served as a municipal judge in Round Rock. He was appointed a district judge in 1981 by Governor Bill Clements and in 1982 stood for election; judicial elections are partisan in Texas, and he was the first Republican judge elected in Williamson County. Other Republicans started sweeping county offices as well, and Carter became known as the father of the county Republican party.

In 2001, a three-judge district court drew Texas's new congressional district lines, creating a new Republican 31st District stretching from Williamson County to Houston. Carter retired from the bench and started running for Congress. The real contest in this district was among the eight candidates for the Republican nomination. Carter's main rivals were Peter Wareing, the son-in-law of Texas oilman Jack Blanton, who was runner-up for the Republican nomination in the 7th District in Harris County in 2000, and Brad Barton, son of 6th District Congressman Joe Barton. In the primary, Wareing led with 37% to 26% for Carter and 16% for Barton. Wareing got 67% in his home base in Harris County; Carter got 58% in Williamson County. In the four-week runoff campaign Carter attacked Wareing as a liberal in disguise for his campaign contributions to Democrats like Congresswoman Sheila Jackson Lee. When Wareing proposed that each candidate sign a "clean campaign pledge," Carter offered what he called a "homestead pledge"—a ploy to highlight his charge that Wareing was a Houston carpetbagger who rented an apartment in the district for the sole purpose of running for office. Barton endorsed Carter as "the only true conservative in this race." Wareing out-spent Carter more than 2-to-1, but Carter won 57%–43%. He got 78% of the vote in Williamson County, which cast 33% of the vote; Wareing got 65% of the vote in Harris County, which cast 16% of the vote. Carter won the general election easily.

In the House, Carter became the freshman class representative on the Republican Steering Committee, which makes committee assignments. He is a social and fiscal conservative who opposes abortion rights, supports voluntary prayer in schools and promised to bring a faith-based family agenda to Washington. On the Judiciary Committee, he passed a bill to establish penalties for aggravated identity theft. He also won enactment of his proposal for a $29 million project in Williamson County to use recycled wastewater on large fields, to preserve limited and more expensive drinking water. Carter won House passage, 344–72, of his Terrorist Penalties Enhancement Act as an amendment to the intelligence reorganization bill.

In the October 2003 redistricting, the only territory carried over from the old 31st District to the new was Williamson County, which eliminated the possibility of competition from a Houston area candidate. Carter was reelected 65%–32% in 2004. In January 2005, with help from Majority Leader Tom DeLay, Carter became the fourth Texas Republican on the Appropriations Committee. His assignments included the reorganized Military Quality of Life Subcommittee, leaving him well-positioned—with ranking Democrat Chet Edwards of the next-door 17th District—to defend the interests of Fort Hood.

THIRTY-SECOND DISTRICT

Rep. Pete Sessions (R)

Elected 1996, 5th term; b. Mar. 22, 1955, Waco; home, Dallas; SW U., B.A. 1978; Methodist; married (Juanita).

Professional Career: District Mgr., SW Bell Telephone Co., 1978–93; V.P., Public Policy, Natl. Center for Policy Analysis, 1994–95.

DC Office: 1514 LHOB, 20515, 202-225-2231; Fax: 202-225-5878; Web site: sessions.house.gov.

District Office: Dallas, 972-392-0505.

Committees: *Budget* (15th of 22 R). *Rules* (4th of 9 R): Legislative & Budget Process (Vice Chmn.).

Group Ratings

	ADA	ACLU	AFS	LCV	ITIC	NTU	COC	ACU	NTLC	CHC
2004	0	0	0	0	100	73	100	100	100	92
2003	5	—	0	0	—	70	100	92	—	—

National Journal Ratings

	2003 LIB	—	2003 CONS		2004 LIB	—	2004 CONS
Economic	9%	—	84%		13%	—	85%
Social	5%	—	87%		9%	—	85%
Foreign	0%	—	89%		23%	—	76%

Key Votes of the 108th Congress

1. Drilling in ANWR	Y	5. DC School Vouchers	Y	9. Ban Same-Sex Marriage	Y
2. Approve Bush Tax Cuts	Y	6. Ban Human Cloning	Y	10. Fund Iraq War	Y
3. Medicare/Rx Bill	Y	7. Restrict Gun Liability	Y	11. Bar Cuba Embargo Funds	N
4. Bar Overtime Pay Regs.	N	8. Ban Partial-Birth Abortion	Y	12. Intelligence Reorg.	Y

Election Results

2004 general	Pete Sessions (R) 109,859	(54%)	($4,512,464)
	Martin Frost (D) 89,030	(44%)	($4,761,288)
	Other 3,347	(2%)	
2004 primary	Pete Sessions (R) .... unopposed		
2002 general	Pete Sessions (R) 100,226	(68%)	($530,671)
	Pauline Dixon (D) 44,886	(30%)	($10,578)
	Other 2,790	(2%)	

Prior Winning Percentages: 2000 (54%); 1998 (56%); 1996 (53%)

The People		Race/Ethnic Origin	Ancestry	
Area size:	161 sq. mi.	50.1% White	German: 7.7%	English: 7.5%
Urban population:	99.9%	7.7% Black	Irish: 6.1%	
Rural population:	0.1%	4.2% Asian	**2004 Presidential Vote**	
Pop. 2000:	651,620	0.4% Native Am.	Bush (R) 120,970	(60%)
Median income:	$45,725	0.0% Hawaiian	Kerry (D) 81,846	(40%)
Poverty status:	12.5%	1.3% Two+ races	**2000 Presidential Vote**	
Military veterans:	8.9%	0.1% Other	Bush (R) 118,257	(64%)
		36.2% Hispanic Origin	Gore (D) 66,003	(36%)
			Cook Partisan Voting Index: R +11	

Occupation	Blue collar: 21.3%	White collar: 65.9%	Gray collar: 12.8%

North Dallas has long been the home of the city's elite—indeed, of a good portion of the nation's elite. Early in the 20th century, Dallas's richest citizens started moving away from old neighborhoods next to downtown and out past Turtle Creek to the area around the suburbs of Highland Park and University Park—the Park Cities. Dallas grew lustily from mid-century on, and beyond the Park Cities miles of affluent neighborhoods were built, especially between the Central Expressway and the Dallas North Tollway. Galleries and office complexes followed; increasingly North Dallasites were working near where they lived. Not all of North Dallas is like that; there is an entertainment and singles apartment corridor along Greenville Avenue, working class black neighborhoods here and there, pockets of Latino neighborhoods near the freeways. But overall the tone has been set by the Dallas elite. In the 1960s and 1970s this was one of the politically most conservative parts of the country: people believed firmly in free markets, personal responsibility and the Republican party. Since 1992, North Dallas has moved, like elite areas in other big metropolitan areas, toward Democrats. Gun control is not much more popular here than in rural Texas, and the number of affluent women willing to vote Democratic on the abortion issue is much smaller than in similarly affluent quadrants of New York or Los Angeles; but there are some. A decade ago, both George W. Bush and Dick Cheney lived in North Dallas, in or near the Park Cities; Bush moved to Austin in January 1995 when he became governor and Cheney changed his residence to Wyoming in July 2000 so that he could be nominated vice president.

The 32d Congressional District of Texas includes pretty much all the area commonly thought of as North Dallas: the Park Cities and affluent North Dallas neighborhoods north to the Dallas County line. Most of the business and professional elite of Dallas live in this area. The district also includes affluent suburbs in Dallas County: parts of Richardson northeast of the city, Addison to the northwest and Irving to the west. The 2003 redistricting removed some suburban territory and added Irving and the heavily Latino Oak Cliff neighborhoods south of the Trinity River, where Lee Harvey Oswald was captured inside the old Texas Theater on November 22, 1963, shortly after he killed President John F. Kennedy. Redistricting raised the Hispanic percentage from 27% to 36%. As in the elite-heavy 7th District in Houston, Bush's percentage declined here in 2004, to 60%; an increase in Latino voters may also have contributed to this result.

The congressman from the 32d District is Pete Sessions, a Republican first elected in 1996. Sessions grew up in Waco, graduated from Southwestern University, then worked at Southwestern Bell in Dallas for 16 years; his father William Sessions, a federal judge, served as FBI director from 1987 to 1993. Sessions has shown he is willing to move around to different House districts. In 1991 he ran and finished sixth in the special election in the 3d District, which then included much of North Dallas. In 1993 he resigned from the phone company to run against Democratic incumbent John Bryant in the 5th District, which included much of the east side of Dallas and several rural counties to the south. The district had been designed to reelect Bryant, a liberal and active legislator. But Sessions ran a vigorous campaign, making a two-day, 12-city tour of the district's rural portions with a livestock trailer full of horse manure and a sign saying "the Clinton health care plan stinks worse than this trailer." This was a heavily Republican year and, although he outspent Sessions 2–1, Bryant won by just 50%–47%. In 1996 Bryant ran unsuccessfully for the Senate; Sessions ran again and won the primary. The district lines were changed by a federal court, and he faced Democrat John Pouland, a former regional GSA administrator. Sessions charged that Pouland was a big government liberal and would abandon U.S. military bases overseas; Pouland criticized subsidizing the foreign bases while pursuing Medicare "cuts." This was a seriously contested race; Sessions won 53%–47%.

In the House, Sessions has a voting record that has been among the more conservative in the Texas delegation. In 1999 he got a seat on the Rules Committee, a sure sign that he is regarded as a leadership loyalist. He sponsored the constitutional amendment to require a two-thirds vote to raise taxes and was a leading advocate of the Republican proposal to put Social Security and Medicare surpluses in a lockbox. He also joined with Democrats Charles Grassley, Ted Kennedy and Henry Waxman on a bill to permit families with disabled children to keep their Medicaid coverage even if their income rises; Sessions and his wife have a son with Down's syndrome. He was an early House supporter of George W. Bush's presidential candidacy. He wants to abolish the IRS and scrap the income tax code, and he talked about the need for private-sector actions to improve the quality of life and economic opportunities for all citizens, including local Hispanics.

Since winning office, Sessions has faced serious challenges in various districts. In 2000, Democrats spoke well of his challenger Regina Montoya Coggins, who was a Clinton White House liaison to local elected officials and whose husband was Clinton's U.S. attorney in the Dallas area; she was well known for her on-air work at KERA-TV in Dallas. In a strong Republican year in Texas, Sessions had a slightly smaller victory margin, 54%–44%. The federal court's redistricting plan, issued in November 2001, made the 5th District more Republican; the percentage in the newly created 32d District, which had no incumbent, was 64%. Sessions surprised almost everyone in the political world by leaving the 5th and running in the 32d, which included only 16% of his old district. He said he wanted to spend less time traveling around his district and that the new district was compatible with his pro-business philosophy; certainly the 32d has a stronger fundraising base. After Sessions's decision, state Representative Kenny Marchant abandoned his plan to run in the 32d; in 2004 Marchant was elected in the 24th District. Sessions had only token primary opposition in 2002 and won the general, 68%–30%.

In 2003, Sessions urged the legislature to order a new round of congressional redistricting to replace the "current partisan interim map," and he worked actively with Majority Leader Tom DeLay to make that happen. But in getting what he wished for, he found himself with a less Republican district and a reelection challenge from 13-term Democratic stalwart Martin Frost, whose 24th District had been shorn of its most Democratic precincts. Frost kept people guessing for several weeks which district he would run in and announced, shortly before the filing date, that he would run in the 32d. He chose the 32d because of the large Jewish population in the Park Cities and his view that Sessions was too conservative for the local establishment. From the start, Sessions voiced confidence that he would win by about 10 points, though he braced himself for negative attacks. Frost focused on his accomplishments, including national "AMBER Alert" legislation to protect missing children and his work on local issues to help the Dallas business community; he rarely mentioned John Kerry. This was the most expensive House campaign of 2004; Sessions spent $4.5 million and Frost $4.8 million; more was spent by party committees and independent groups. The candidates hurled charges at each other and tangential issues came into play. Frost criticized Sessions for having engaged in a streaking incident in college. Sessions criticized Frost for scheduling a fundraiser with Peter Yarrow, the Peter, Paul and Mary singer who had been convicted of "taking indecent liberties" with a 14-year-old girl in 1969.

Sessions kept his clothes on during the campaign and Frost canceled the fundraiser. Frost cited Sessions's vote, along with only eight other members, against a bill opposing establishment of new air passenger security rules after September 11, and ran an ad with images of the World Trade Center in flames and the message, "Protect America. Say No to Pete Sessions." Frost was endorsed by the *Dallas Morning News,* local police and firefighters groups, teachers' organizations, and the Sierra Club. Sessions had support from the Club for Growth and the National Federation of Independent Business.

Sessions won by 10 points, 54%–44%, as he had predicted, with more than 80% of the vote in some precincts in the Park Cities. Frost failed to get the higher turnout he needed in Oak Cliff. After the election, Frost made a serious bid to chair the Democratic National Committee, but dropped out a few days before the vote. On the Rules Committee, on which both served, Sessions filed and won unanimous support in the lame-duck session for his resolution paying tribute to Frost for his "honesty, integrity and a general willingness to work together with colleagues on a variety of important issues." Sessions has been mentioned as a possible statewide candidate in 2006, though that would be unlikely as he is contending to become chairman of the National Republican Congressional Committee for the 2008 election cycle.

★ UTAH ★

Utah is a triumph of man over nature, the creation of a productive and orderly civilization in a remote expanse of desert and mountain, arrayed around a desolate salt sea. Today's Utah and Mormonism have their roots in a very different landscape of more than 150 years ago, when a wave of religious enthusiasm, prophecy and utopianism swept across the "burnt-over district" of Upstate New York in the 1820s and 1830s. There Joseph Smith, a 14-year-old farmer, experienced a vision in which the angel Moroni appeared and told him where to unearth several golden tablets inscribed with hieroglyphic writings. With the aid of special spectacles, Smith translated the tablets and published them as the Book of Mormon in 1831. He later declared himself a prophet and founded the Church of Jesus Christ of Latter-day Saints.

The Mormons, as they were called, attracted thousands of converts and created their own communities; persecuted for their beliefs, they moved west to Ohio, Missouri and then Illinois. In 1844, the Mormon colony at Nauvoo, Illinois, had some 15,000 members living under the theocratic rule of Smith. It was here that Smith received a revelation sanctioning the practice of polygamy, which led to his death at the hands of a mob in 1844. After the murder, the new church president, Brigham Young, decided to move the faithful, "the saints," farther west into territory that was still part of Mexico and far beyond white settlement. In 1847 Young led a well-organized march across the Great Plains and into the Rocky Mountains on a path where Mormons reenacted the march 150 years later in 1997. In 1847, they stopped on the western slope of the Wasatch Range and, as Young gazed over the valley of the Great Salt Lake spread out below, he uttered the now famous words, "This is the place."

The place was Utah. Young was governor of the territory for many years, and it is the only state that largely continues to live by the teachings of a church. The early pioneers laid out towns foursquare to the points of the compass with huge city blocks, built sturdy houses and planted dozens of trees. Young's home still stands a block away from Temple Square, where the Temple, closed to non-Mormons, stands in gleaming marble, topped by the golden angel Moroni, across from the oval Mormon Tabernacle where its great choir sings. For 150 years this "Zion" has attracted thousands of converts from the Midwest, the north of England and Scandinavia. The object of religious fear and prejudice, Utah was not granted statehood until 1896, after the church renounced polygamy. Utah has grown steadily since then, and remains heavily Mormon, its basic character is stamped on the desert, mountain-shadowed, often surrealistic landscape that without the Mormons would probably have remained as unpopulated as Nevada without gambling.

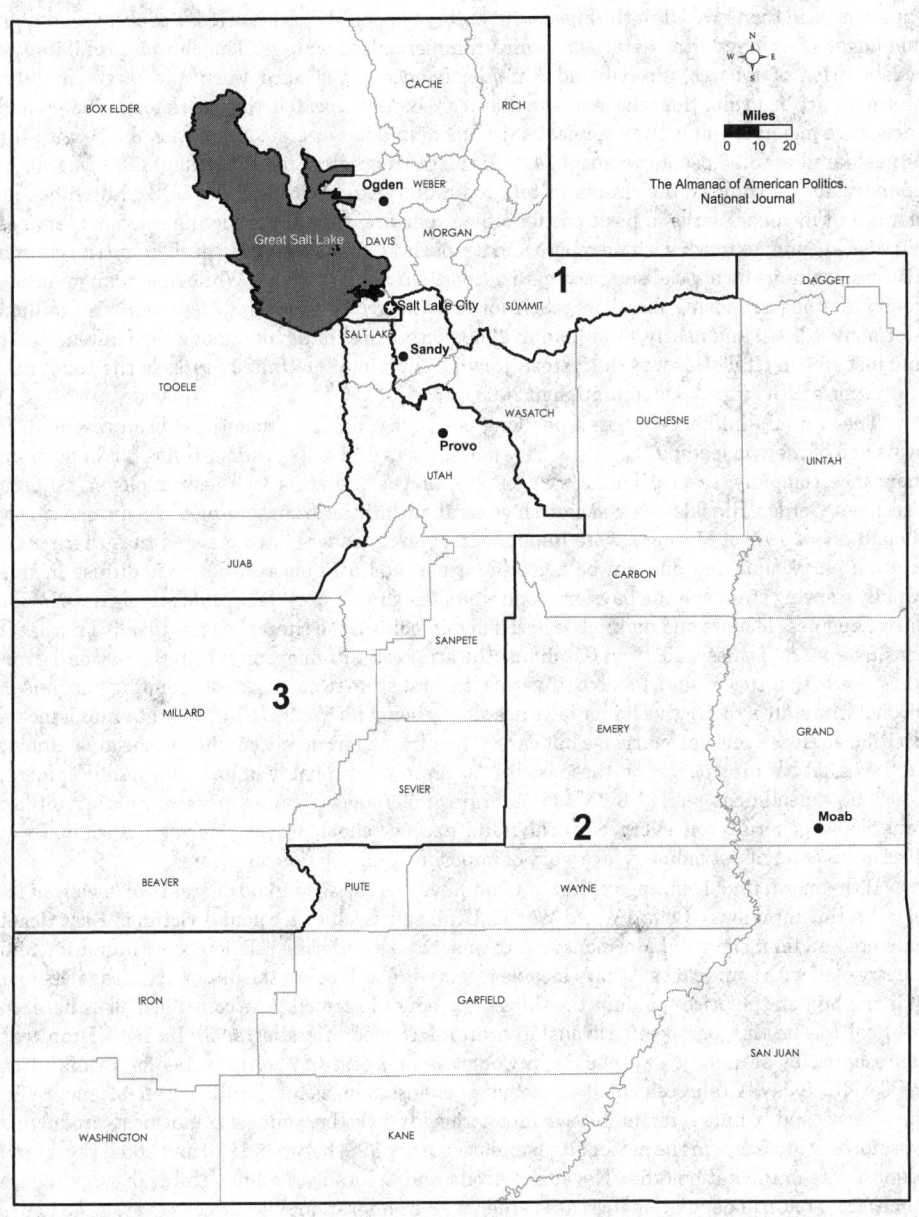

N

W ⊕ E

S

Miles
0 10 20

The Almanac of American Politics.
National Journal

BOX ELDER

CACHE

RICH

Ogden WEBER

Great Salt Lake DAVIS

MORGAN

Salt Lake City SUMMIT

1

DAGGETT

SALT LAKE

Sandy

TOOELE

WASATCH

DUCHESNE

UINTAH

Provo

UTAH

JUAB

CARBON

SANPETE

3

MILLARD

EMERY

GRAND

SEVIER

2

Moab

BEAVER

PIUTE

WAYNE

IRON

GARFIELD

SAN JUAN

WASHINGTON

KANE

Congressional district boundaries were first effective for 2002.

The LDS church remains distinctive in many ways. It cares deeply about its past: In caves in the mountains of Utah, the Church preserves America's most complete genealogical records in its Family History Library, which is also on the Internet. It tries to spread the faith: Young Mormons, 65,000 every year, spend missionary years in the United States and abroad, and their experiences in turn give Utah the biggest inventory of people with knowledge of obscure foreign languages of any state in the union, a nice commercial advantage. The church prohibits the consumption of tobacco, alcohol and caffeine; it encourages hard work and large families. Mormons are healthier than the average American; better educated, they work longer hours and earn more money. Utah is the youngest state (median age 27 versus the national 35), with the largest families (3.57 people versus 3.14) and the third greatest life expectancy (78.6 years). In an individualist country, the church fosters communitarian attitudes: The LDS Church has no clergy, but members serve in positions for which they are chosen, conducting religious services but also keeping in touch with members and counseling them when they need help. The church also maintains its own social service organizations. It evidently works: While American mainline denominations are losing members, the Mormon Church is growing. There were 2.9 million Mormons in 1970 and nearly 11 million in 2000, with more than half outside the United States and just 15% in Utah; this was the fastest-growing church in the United States in the 1990s and the nation's fifth largest denomination in 2003.

The church's influence in Utah has long been great and has sometimes been resented. It owns one of the two leading Salt Lake City newspapers and a TV station. It has holdings in an insurance company, several banks, real estate, and is the state's largest employer. Church President Gordon Hinckley barred church general authorities from serving on business boards; though about 70% of Mormons vote Republican, church leaders have insisted that there is no "church party" and that one can be a good Mormon and a Democrat. Power is diffuse in this rapidly growing state and the days are gone when the church president could sit down with four or five business leaders and make civic decisions. In politics the church weighs in only on what it considers moral issues—abortion (Utah has the strictest anti-abortion law in the nation), gambling (leave that to Nevada), tobacco (this was the first state to ban cigarette vending machines), alcohol (the state's restrictive liquor laws are slowly being liberalized). In 2004 the church took a position against same-sex marriage but carefully refrained from any opinion on the amendment on the ballot banning it. But on these issues the church is probably in line with public opinion; the 2004 amendment passed by a wide margin. Polls show Utahns more conservative than Americans generally on every cultural issue except school prayer; Mormons, originally a discriminated-against minority, are wary of imposing their religion on others.

If the moral underpinnings of life in Utah have not changed in 50 years, Utah's view of its place in the nation has. Before World War II, Utah saw itself as a colonial victim of East Coast bankers and financiers and Mormons saw themselves as suffering religious discrimination and bigotry—all with some cause. Utah's income levels were well below the national average, its cost of living higher, the prices paid for the things it produced seemed to be controlled elsewhere. In political terms, this perspective translated into a Democratic allegiance: In 1940 Utah was represented by staunch New Dealers in Congress and cast 62% of its votes for Franklin D. Roosevelt. Today, Utah sees itself as a busy generator of wealth, with a raft of successful businesses and a knack for high-tech innovation. It has the youngest and most productive workforce of any state in the nation. Its population grew 39% between 1990 and 2004, the fourth highest rate in the nation (after Nevada, Arizona and Colorado), and two-thirds of growth here comes from natural population increase rather than in-migration. Work weeks average 48 hours here, more than Japan and far more than anywhere else in America. It has had fast-rising incomes but not per capita incomes: all those children weigh those numbers down. Utah has the largest proportion of children of any state, by far, and low rates of divorce. Church doctrine discriminated against blacks until 1978, and Utah's population was only 1% black in 2000, but it was also 9% Hispanic, 2% Asian and 1% Pacific Islander. In many ways, Utah looks like the

America of the 1950s, but with 21st century high-tech: in 2000 it was the number one state in households with computers.

The fast-growing student population puts on pressure for high taxes to build new schools, and Utah politicians have bridled at George W. Bush's No Child Left Behind Act, arguing that Utah's testing process is better and that it makes no sense to test children by ethnic group. But politically, Utah's special characteristics have made it a heavily Republican state since the middle 1960s. The arithmetic is pretty simple: about 75% of voters are Mormon and about 70% of them usually vote Republican; that puts the Republicans over 50% without a single non-Mormon vote. This was not always so, just in the last 30 years, as traditional values thriving in Utah have come under attack elsewhere. Utahns, Mormons and gentiles alike, have made it arguably the most Republican of states—standing out in national statistics politically just as it does demographically. Interestingly, the Salt Lake City neighborhoods close to the church headquarters, with gracious old houses and a smaller street grid that attract academic and professional newcomers, have become the most heavily "gentile" and politically liberal parts of the state. As the Yankee hub of Boston filled up with Irish Catholic Democrats in the 1890s, so Salt Lake City is getting more than its share of secular liberal Democrats in the 1990s, people who cheer on the non-Church-owned *Salt Lake Tribune* when it runs stories attacking the church for converting a block of Main Street into a plaza with restrictions on speech, dress, and conduct. But for the most part, Democrats are competitive only if they seem consistent with Utah values and attitudes, and even then are in jeopardy.

The People		Race/Ethnic Origin			Military veterans: 161,351 (10.6%)	
Pop. 2004 (est):	2,389,039	1,904,265	85.3%	White	WWII: 21.0%	Korea: 13.9%
Pop. 2000:	2,233,169	16,137	0.7%	Black	Vietnam: 31.7%	Gulf War: 11.5%
Pop. 1990:	1,722,850	36,483	1.6%	Asian	**Most populous cities (2003):**	
Change 1990–2000:	Up 29.6%	26,663	1.2%	Native Am.	1. Salt Lake City	179,894
% of U.S. total:	0.8%	14,806	0.7%	Hawaiian	2. West Valley City	111,687
Pop. rank:	34th of 50	31,308	1.4%	Two+ races	3. Provo	105,410
Area size:	84,899 sq. mi.	1,948	0.1%	Other	4. Sandy	89,319
State Native:	62.9%	201,559	9.0%	Hisp. Origin	5. Orem	87,599
Non-citizen:	4.9%	**Ancestry**				
Language		English: 21.4%		German: 8.5%	Urban population: 88.3%	
English: 83.1%	Spanish: 9.1%	USA: 5.0%		Danish: 4.8%	Rural population: 11.7%	
Other Eur.: 4.5%		Irish: 4.3%				

Education		Work Sector		Utah	
H.S. Grad:	87.7%	Private: 78.2%	Govt: 15.7%	Senate	21 R 8 D
College Grad:	26.1%	Self: 5.8%	Family: 0.3%	House	56 R 19 D
Industry		Unemployment: 4.9%		Legislative Term Limits: No	
Agri: 1.9%	Con: 8.2%	**Household Income**		**Registered Voters**	
Fin: 6.8%	Info: 3.3%	<15k: 10.8%	15-35k: 25.1%	No party registration	
Mfg: 17.0%	Prof: 28.6%	35-50k: 19.0%	50-100k: 33.9%		
Public: 5.5%	Trade: 16.3%	100-150k: 7.5%	>150k: 3.7%		
Other: 12.4%		Median: $45,726			
Occupation		Poverty status: 9.4%			
Blue collar: 24.1%	White collar: 61.4%	**Home Value**			
Gray collar: 14.5%		<50k: 4.8% 50-100k: 15.9% 100-200k: 57.0% 200-300k: 14.3%			
		300-500k: 5.9% >500k: 2.0% Median: $142,600			

Presidential politics   Utah has been the most Republican state in six of the last eight presidential elections. As far back as 1960, Richard Nixon carried Utah with just 55% of the vote, but by 1972 he won with 68%. Ronald Reagan won 73% here in 1980 and 75% in 1984; George Bush won 66% here in 1988 and George W. Bush 67% in 2000 and 72% in 2004. In 1992, this was also the least Democratic state: Ross Perot finished ahead of Bill Clinton, 27% to 25%.

2004 Presidential Vote		
Bush (R)	663,742	(72%)
Kerry (D)	241,199	(26%)
Nader (NPA)	11,305	(1%)
Other	11,598	(1%)

2004 Democratic Presidential Primary		
Kerry (D)	19,232	(55%)
Edwards (D)	10,384	(30%)
Kucinich (D)	2,590	(7%)
Dean (D)	1,335	(4%)
Clark (D)	489	(1%)
Other	824	(2%)

2000 Presidential Vote		
Bush (R)	515,096	(67%)
Gore (D)	203,053	(26%)
Nader (Green)	35,850	(5%)
Other	16,755	(2%)

Governor Mike Leavitt spent much time and effort promoting a Western regional primary for the Friday following Southern Super Tuesday, March 10, 2000. But only Colorado and Wyoming (with a caucus, not a primary) adopted the date, and candidates paid little attention to western issues as Leavitt had hoped. Bill Bradley and John McCain pulled out of their races before March 10, and only 10% of Utah's registered voters bothered to vote. In 2004 Utah held a Democratic primary February 24; 35,000 people voted in a state of 2.3 million, and John Kerry led John Edwards 55%–30%.

Congressional districting   Utahns expected that the 2000 Census would give Utah a fourth seat in the House of Representatives. But, under the formula used for reapportionment, Utah fell 857 residents short of getting a new district; instead, North Carolina got an unexpected 13th seat. Utah did what comes naturally to Americans today: it sued, twice. The first lawsuit contended that if military personnel stationed abroad should be counted in their states of

109th Congress Lineup	
2 R	1 D

108th Congress Lineup	
2 R	1 D

residence, so should Mormon missionaries, who also can be accurately tracked and matched with their home states. As it happens, North Carolina had thousands of military personnel stationed abroad and only 107 attributable Mormon missionaries. Utah had fewer military personnel stationed abroad but 11,176 Mormon missionaries. In April 2001 a three-judge federal court threw out Utah's case, and one judge called its theory "wildly unfair." In late November 2001 the Supreme Court affirmed that ruling without opinion. Utah's other theory was that the Census Bureau violated the Constitution's injunction that it conduct an "actual enumeration" of the population when it employed what statisticians call "hot-deck imputation": when Census takers after repeated efforts cannot contact residents of one housing unit, they assume that it contains the same number of people in similar housing units nearby. Utah argued that this is "sampling," prohibited, the Supreme Court ruled in another case, by a 1957 statute. This argument did better in court: Utah lost by a 2–1 margin in a three-judge district court in early November 2001 and by 5–4 in the Supreme Court in June 2002. But the upshot was that North Carolina, not Utah, got the 435th district in the 2000 reapportionment.

Utah's legislature drew new congressional district lines in September 2001. Aware that the state was suing for another district, it adopted both three- and four-district plans. The large Republican majorities in the legislature argued that all districts should contain both urban and rural areas; this policy was followed when Utah had two congressional districts, but when it gained a third district in the 1980 Census, and then again after the 1990 Census, the legislature drew plans which had one district entirely inside Salt Lake County. This 2d District had had the temerity in 2000 to elect a Democratic congressman. The Republicans' principle, honored in the breach for the preceding 20 years, forced them to draw three districts which combined urban and rural areas and which increased the Bush 2000 percentage in the 2d District from 57% to 67%. At the same time, the Republican legislators drew a four-district plan, which would go into effect should Utah win one of its then two pending court cases. This plan included a new 4th District entirely within Salt Lake County but within the southern portion of the county, which is heavily Republican. Utah conducted its 2002 election with the three-district plan in place, and the Supreme Court decision narrowly rejecting the state's attack on "hot-deck imputation" came just five days before the June 2002 primary.

There is still some small prospect that Utah may get a fourth district before the 2010 Census. Virginia Republican Tom Davis has sponsored a bill that would award the District of Columbia one full member in the House and would award another to the state entitled under the reapportionment formula to the 436th district—Utah. This measure would have the advantage of giving the District congressional representation without, presumably, changing the current partisan balance of the House. Utah Democrats, however, have been worried that the chance to draw a new districting plan will endanger Matheson even more than the current three-district plan does. Republicans say they wouldn't do any such thing: a claim Democrats can't be blamed for doubting.

Governor

Jon Huntsman Jr. (R)

Elected 2004, term expires Jan. 2009, 1st term; b. Mar. 26, 1960, Palo Alto, CA; home, Salt Lake City; Attended U. of UT; U. of PA, B.A. 1987; Mormon; married (Mary Kaye).

Professional Career: Staff Asst., White House, 1982–83; Exec., Huntsman Corp., 1983–89; Dep. Asst. Sec. of Commerce, Trade Dev. Bureau, 1989–90; Dep. Asst. Sec. of Commerce for E. Asia & the Pacific, 1990–91; Amb. to Singapore, 1992–93; Pres., Huntsman Cancer Foundation, 1995–2001; U.S. trade amb., 2001–03; Chairman and CEO, Huntsman Family Holdings Co., 2003–04.

Office: East Office Building, Suite E220, PO Box 142220, Salt Lake City, 84114, 801-538-1000; Fax: 801-538-1528; Web site: www.utah.gov/governor.

Election Results

2004 general	Jon Huntsman Jr. (R)	531,190	(58%)
	Scott Matheson (D)	380,359	(41%)
	Other	8,411	(1%)
2004 primary	Jon Huntsman Jr. (R)	102,955	(66%)
	Nolan Karras (R)	52,048	(34%)
2000 general	Michael Leavitt (R)	424,837	(56%)
	Bill Orton (D)	321,979	(42%)
	Other	14,990	(2%)

Jon Huntsman Jr., a Republican, was elected governor of Utah in 2004. He was born in Palo Alto, California, the oldest of nine children, spent time in California and in Washington, D.C., where his father worked in the Nixon administration, then moved to Utah. He dropped out of high school to play keyboards in rock-and-roll bands; he attended the University of Utah briefly before leaving on a two-year Mormon mission to Taiwan. There he learned to speak fluent Mandarin Chinese. When he returned, he transferred to and graduated from the University of Pennsylvania. He is the son of billionaire philanthropist and industrialist Jon Huntsman, the wealthiest man in Utah (his company invented McDonald's Big Mac clamshell packaging), and the family owns a controlling interest in the Huntsman Corporation, a multinational petrochemical corporation headquartered in Salt Lake City. Jon Huntsman Jr. was a staff assistant to Ronald Reagan, served in the administration of George H.W. Bush as a deputy assistant secretary of Commerce and as ambassador to Singapore and was a deputy trade ambassador for George W. Bush. He also served as president of the Huntsman Cancer Foundation and as CEO of the Huntsman Family Holdings Co., the umbrella organization that holds the assets of the multibillion-dollar Huntsman chemical business.

Huntsman succeeded Republican Governor Olene Walker, who was the first woman to hold the position. A mother to seven children, grandmother to 25, and great-grandmother to four,

Walker was governor for 13 months; as lieutenant governor, she assumed office in November 2003 when Governor Mike Leavitt stepped down with one year remaining in his term to become administrator of the federal Environmental Protection Agency.

Walker would not say at first whether she planned to run for election in 2004, but she was no caretaker governor. She proposed 14 initiatives in the week of her inauguration, including some carryovers from the Leavitt administration; the list included a $30 million reading program, a Quality Growth Communities initiative, a program for transitioning foster children into adulthood and, later, an ambitious tax reform plan that called for a flat tax on income and lower sales tax rates. There were complaints from legislators who believed she had no mandate for her agenda since she had not been elected. After the 2004 legislative session, she vetoed a series of bills and then made the surprising announcement that she would run for a full term at age 74. Polls showed Walker was quite popular but she failed to get the 60% required to win the nomination outright at the state Republican convention in May and failed even to place among the top two candidates, thus preventing her from appearing on the June 22 primary ballot. Many convention delegates had been angered by her veto of a bill creating the Carson Smith Special Needs Scholarship Fund; the bill was favored by conservatives who saw it as a step toward offering tax breaks to families with students enrolled in private school.

Huntsman led in the polls from the start against former Speaker and Board of Regents Chairman Nolan Karras. The primary lacked much drama: the two candidates agreed on most issues, were unusually civil to each other and Huntsman kept the focus on his top issue, economic development. He outspent Karras $1.3 million to $1 million and won easily with 66%, carrying every county but one and winning populous Salt Lake County by a more than 2–1 margin.

The Democratic nominee was Scott Matheson, the son of the state's last Democratic governor, brother of 2nd District Congressman Jim Matheson, and a Rhodes Scholar who had managed his father's gubernatorial campaigns in 1976 and 1980. He served four years as U.S. Attorney for Utah and later became dean of the University of Utah law school. The tone of the general election campaign also was unusually civil. The two nominees shared similar views on many issues and even applauded each other during one debate. But they diverged on gay rights and school vouchers. Huntsman supported Amendment 3, a proposed state constitutional amendment that would ban same-sex marriage (a position held by the LDS Church, though it took no stand on the ballot measure itself; it passed in November with 66%), while Matheson opposed it. Huntsman advocated school choice, vouchers and a system of tuition tax credits; he claimed a vote for Matheson was a vote for the agenda of the state teachers' union, which had endorsed Matheson. Matheson emphasized the need to increase education spending.

Huntsman stayed focused on job creation and economic issues. He insisted that only an improved business climate would permit increased spending for highways and for the burgeoning public school system; revamping Utah's "dilapidated and anachronistic" tax system and phasing out the state sales tax on food was a necessary predicate. Huntsman closely aligned himself with the George W. Bush but parted company on two issues. Referring to the No Child Left Behind Act as an unfunded mandate, he argued that it "should be jettisoned out of the classroom"; the state has been a leader in the resistance to NCLB, with state officials arguing that the law is too rigid and a serious intrusion into Utah's right to control public schools. He also broke with the administration by suggesting he supported the importation of prescription drugs from Canada.

Huntsman outspent Matheson, $3.2 million to $2 million, loaning his campaign $275,000 but otherwise spent far less of his own money than other similarly situated candidates might have. He won all but four counties to win 58%–41%. Matheson carried Salt Lake County 51%–46%; Huntsman ran 14% behind George W. Bush there.

He began his term by breaking with tradition and delivering his first State of the State address in the historic statehouse in Fillmore, the territorial capital of Utah named in appreciation of President Millard Fillmore's decision to name Brigham Young as the first territorial governor. Huntsman proposed a phaseout of corporate income taxes and called for streamlining sales taxes. In his first legislative session as governor, he had a low-key style and got along well with legislators. He signed a bill banning Class B and C radioactive waste from Utah and vowed to prevent the shipment of mustard gas from Colorado to Utah for destruction. Broad tax reform was deferred but he raised salaries for state employees, got money for economic development and $18 million for tourism promotion. He also signed a measure to void undocumented immigrants' driver's licenses and replace them with a "driving privilege" card, which cannot be used as legal ID. He said he was open to relaxing the state's strict liquor laws. He called an April special session and then signed legislation limiting Utah's implementation of NCLB education requirements, despite warnings from the U.S. Education Department that the state eventually could lose millions in federal dollars.

Senior Senator

Orrin Hatch (R)

Elected 1976, seat up 2006, 5th term; b. Mar. 22, 1934, Pittsburgh, PA; home, Salt Lake City; Brigham Young U., B.S. 1959; U. of Pittsburgh, J.D. 1962; Mormon; married (Elaine).

Professional Career: Practicing atty., 1962–76.

DC Office: 104 HSOB, 20510, 202-224-5251; Fax: 202-224-6331; Web site: www.senate.gov/~hatch.

State Offices: Cedar City, 435-586-8435; Ogden, 801-625-5672; Provo, 801-375-7881; Salt Lake City, 801-524-4380; St. George, 435-634-1795.

Committees: *Finance*: Health Care (Chmn.); International Trade; Taxation & IRS Oversight. *Health, Education, Labor & Pensions*: Bioterrorism & Public Health Preparedness; Education & Early Childhood Development; Retirement Security & Aging. *Intelligence (Select)*. *Judiciary*: Antitrust, Competition Policy & Consumer Rights; Intellectual Property (Chmn.); Terrorism, Technology & Homeland Security. *Joint Committee on Taxation* (2d of 5 Sens.).

Group Ratings

	ADA	ACLU	AFS	LCV	ITIC	NTU	COC	ACU	NTLC	CHC
2004	10	0	0	0	100	72	100	96	90	100
2003	10	—	11	5	—	72	100	80	—	—

National Journal Ratings

	2003 LIB	—	2003 CONS		2004 LIB	—	2004 CONS
Economic	0%	—	82%		18%	—	78%
Social	0%	—	59%		0%	—	84%
Foreign	0%	—	78%		0%	—	67%

Key Votes of the 108th Congress

1. Ban Drilling in ANWR	N	5. Energy Bill	Y	9. Ban Same-Sex Marriage	Y
2. Approve Bush Tax Cuts	Y	6. Support Roe v. Wade	N	10. Ban Bunker-Buster Bomb	N
3. Medicare/Rx Bill	Y	7. Ban Partial-Birth Abortion	Y	11. Fund Iraq War	Y
4. Bar Overtime Pay Regs.	N	8. Assault Weapons Ban	N	12. Restrict Missile Defense	N

Election Results

2000 general	Orrin Hatch (R)	504,803	(66%)	($3,130,550)
	Scott N. Howell (D)	242,569	(31%)	($296,839)
	Other	22,332	(3%)	
2000 primary	Orrin Hatch (R)	unopposed		
1994 general	Orrin Hatch (R)	357,297	(69%)	($4,209,993)
	Pat Shea (D)	146,938	(28%)	($311,491)
	Other	15,088	(3%)	

Prior Winning Percentages: 1988 (67%); 1982 (58%); 1976 (54%)

Orrin Hatch, Utah's senior senator, was first elected to the Senate in 1976. Hatch grew up in Pittsburgh, where his father was a metal lather; he worked his way through Brigham Young University, then University of Pittsburgh law school, practiced law there and then moved to Salt

Lake City. For a time he was an amateur boxer and at one point he and his wife lived in a refurbished chicken coop. He got into the 1976 Senate race late; an endorsement from Ronald Reagan helped him win the Republican nomination, and in the general he upset three-term Democrat Frank Moss 54%–45%. His toughest re-election fight came in 1982, when he was opposed by Salt Lake City Mayor Ted Wilson; Hatch won 58%–41%.

Hatch's Senate career has been shaped by two impulses that are sometimes in tension with each other: a strong conservative philosophy and a sense of responsibility for the superintendency of legislation. He first attracted attention in a Senate dominated by Democrats when he successfully filibustered the AFL-CIO's labor law bill, which had been expected to pass. Then, after just four years, he became chairman of the Labor Committee after Republicans won a Senate majority in 1980. He worked to convert federal programs to block grants to states, but became a fan of some programs, like the Job Corps. But he remained a strong opponent of the striker replacement law sought by unions. On the Judiciary Committee, he fought abortion and a civil rights bill that produced racial quotas and preferences, and staunchly defended Supreme Court nominees Robert Bork and Clarence Thomas.

In 1993 Hatch switched from ranking Republican on Labor to the same post on Judiciary, when it was vacated by Strom Thurmond; in 1995 he became chairman of Judiciary and left Labor altogether. On Judiciary he worked on limiting tort liability and regulatory law and managed the balanced budget amendment to one-vote defeats in 1995 and 1997. He worked also on the flag amendment, which fell four votes short of passage in March 2000, the anti-terrorism law and the Religious Freedom Restoration Act. On judicial appointments, Hatch promised in 1995 to cooperate with the Clinton administration; by early 1997 some Democrats were charging that he was stalling approval of nominees, while some Republicans were complaining that he was allowing too many liberal, activist judges on the bench.

In 1997 Hatch again surprised some on both sides of the aisle when he joined Edward Kennedy in sponsoring a $24 billion program to get states to provide health insurance for children of low-income working parents who don't qualify for Medicaid. In 2000 he sponsored a number of bills which were signed into law—a law giving religious groups a federal remedy when their religious rights are violated by land use policies, an increase in the number of H1-B visas, funding for agents and training aimed at methamphetamines.

As chairman and, from June 2001 to January 2003, ranking minority member of Judiciary, Hatch defended the Bush Justice Department and judicial nominees against Democrats' attacks; he decried their refusal to hold hearings on many appointees when they were in the majority and their filibusters of judicial appointees after January 2003. In November 2003 he complained that Democrats "are treating these people just like dirt." But he initiated an investigation of a committee staffer who had accessed Democratic staffers' emails (which lacked the protection against partisan trespass available under the congressional system) and agreed on his dismissal, despite the objections of some conservatives. In 2005, though the Judiciary chairmanship had passed to Arlen Specter, Hatch continued aggressively to seek confirmation of filibustered appellate court nominees. After September 11, he was one of the framers of the USA Patriot Act, and in 2004 defended it against attempts to eliminate some provisions. "It seems to me that we should not make it any harder to go after suspected terrorists than after suspected drug dealers." He reintroduced the flag amendment but did not get another floor vote on it. He introduced another constitutional amendment to allow naturalized citizens to be eligible to serve as president and vice president 20 years after their naturalization. After the Supreme Judicial Court of Massachusetts ruled that its state constitution required legalization of same-sex marriages, Hatch proposed a constitutional amendment to would authorize states to refuse to recognize such marriages contracted in another state. But after same-sex couples in Massachusetts started obtaining marriage licenses, Hatch acquiesced in the amendment sponsored by Wayne Allard that would ban same-sex marriage altogether and supported it when it was brought to the floor, despite lack of action in the Judiciary Committee, in July 2004. Hatch has opposed federal gun control measures and in 2003 sponsored a bill to make it easier to carry handguns in the District of Columbia. In 2003, with Utah Congressman Chris Cannon, he sponsored a bill to allow children of illegal aliens to apply for conditional residency if they were in college, served in the military or performed 910 hours of community service; this would make them eligible for permanent residency and for in-state college tuition.

Hatch has also taken some surprising and bipartisan positions. He and Jeff Sessions sponsored a bill to increase the amount of crack cocaine required for an automatic five-year sentence from 5 grams to 20 grams. He sponsored a successful cyberterrorism amendment and co-sponsored with Joe Lieberman a bill to stimulate private sector development of medicines, vaccines and antidotes to combat bioterrorism. Despite his longstanding opposition to abortion, he has supported embryonic stem-cell research and argued that life is created in the womb, "not in a petri dish." In February 2003 the Senate passed his bill outlawing computer-enhanced child pornography, which the Supreme Court said was not covered by a previous law. He has sponsored bills to restrict class action lawsuits and to set limits on medical malpractice cases. In 2004 he gained wide acquiescence on setting up a trust fund to handle asbestos cases, but in 2005, when incoming Chairman Arlen Specter proposed a $140 billion trust fund, some businesses withdrew their support.

As Judiciary chairman and, since 2005, chairman of its Intellectual Property Subcommittee, Hatch has worked on the issue of protecting intellectual property in the face of technological advance. He supported the Digital Millennium Copyright Act of 1998 banning unlawful downloading of copyrighted music and movies and backed the record industry against the threat raised by Napster. In June 2004 the Senate passed his bill, co-sponsored with Patrick Leahy, to authorize the Justice Department to bring civil as well as criminal actions for illegal downloading. In June 2004 he drafted a bill barring technologies that were "intentionally inducing" copyright violations. Technology companies objected that this could make iPods illegal and on September 30 Hatch abandoned his markup and asked entertainment and technology representatives to come up with a mutually acceptable draft. He introduced his own version, with Leahy, Dianne Feinstein and John Cornyn in January 2005; it would also legalize movie filter technologies. Hatch and Leahy filed a friend of the court brief asking the Supreme Court to clarify some of the issues in the Grokster case.

Hatch's interest in these issues is not just theoretical. He has long written poetry and in 1995 began writing songs and has since written about 300. They have been recorded by a Utah firm, first in a 13-song album of Christmas music; some have been recorded by Gladys Knight, a convert to the LDS Church, and after Christian music publishers seemed uninterested in what Hatch has called his Latter-Day Sound, he began distributing his songs on www.hatchmusic.com. He wrote a song for Edward Kennedy on his fifth wedding anniversary—very moving, Kennedy said. He appeared in the movie *Traffic*, but criticized it for its frequent obscenities; one of his songs was used in the recent movie *Ocean's 12*.

Hatch and Utah colleague Bob Bennett have supported a permanent nuclear waste repository in Yucca Mountain, Nevada: better to have the waste transported over Utah than deposited there. He and Bennett have sought to prevent the Skull Valley Branch of the Goshute Indians' proposal to store radioactive waste on their reservation and to prevent the reclassification of waste from the Fernald and Niagara Falls sites in Ohio and New York to make it eligible for Skull Valley. He has also opposed transporting chemical weapons materials across state lines into Utah for destruction at the Dugway proving grounds.

Every senator, it sometimes seems, must run for president, and the time came for Hatch in June 1999. He admitted that it would take a "miracle" to win, but argued that he had more experience in federal office than the other candidates and could work with Democrats, and that he was not "beholden to the Republican establishment." At the August 1999 Iowa straw poll he came in last, with 2% of the votes. In the Iowa caucuses in January 2000 he won only 1% of the votes, fewer than John McCain, who did not campaign in the state. Two days later he withdrew from the race and endorsed George W. Bush.

Hatch's seat came up for election in 2000. He attracted competition for the Republican nomination, and was greeted with jeers as well as applause at the very conservative May 2000 state party convention. But he got 61% of the votes, just above the 60% required to win the nomination without a primary. For the fall campaign he spent $3.1 million; his opponent, for eight years the Democratic leader in the Utah Senate, spent $296,000. Hatch won 66%–31%, and became the first Utahn popularly elected five times to the Senate; the only other five-term senator in Utah history, Reed Smoot, who served from 1903 to 1933, was elected to his first term by the legislature. Hatch is widely expected to be reelected without difficulty in 2006.

Junior Senator

Robert Bennett (R)

Elected 1992, seat up 2010, 3d term; b. Sept. 18, 1933, Salt Lake City; home, Salt Lake City; U. of UT, B.S. 1957; Mormon; married (Joyce).

Military Career: Chaplain, Army Natl. Guard, 1957–60.

Professional Career: Staff Aide, U.S. Rep. Sherm Lloyd, 1962; Staff Aide, U.S. Sen. Wallace F. Bennett, 1963; Cong. Liaison, U.S. Dept. of Transp., 1969–70; Pres., Robert Mullen P.R., 1970–74; P.R. Dir., Summa Corp., 1974–78; Pres., Osmond Communications, 1978–79; Chmn., American Computers Corp., 1979–81; Pres., Microsonics Corp., 1981–84; CEO, Franklin Quest Co., 1984–91; Chmn., UT Educ. Strategic Plng. Comm., 1988.

DC Office: 431 DSOB, 20510, 202-224-5444; Fax: 202-228-1168; Web site: bennett.senate.gov.

State Offices: Cedar City, 435-865-1335; Ogden, 801-625-5676; Provo, 801-379-2525; Salt Lake City, 801-524-5933; St. George, 435-628-5514.

Committees: *Appropriations*: Agriculture, Rural Development & Related Agencies (Chmn.); Energy & Water; Homeland Security; Interior & Related Agencies; State, Foreign Operations & Related Programs; Transportation, Treasury, the Judiciary, HUD & Related Agencies. *Banking, Housing & Urban Affairs*: Financial Institutions (Chmn.); Housing & Transportation; Securities & Investment. *Homeland Security & Governmental Affairs*: Federal Financial Management, Govt. Information & International Security; Investigations (Permanent); Oversight of Govt. Management, the Federal Workforce & the District of Columbia. *Rules & Administration. Joint Economic Committee* (Vice Chmn.).

Group Ratings

	ADA	ACLU	AFS	LCV	ITIC	NTU	COC	ACU	NTLC	CHC
2004	20	11	0	0	100	70	100	88	93	100
2003	10	—	11	0	—	73	100	80	—	—

National Journal Ratings

	2003 LIB	—	2003 CONS		2004 LIB	—	2004 CONS
Economic	0%	—	82%		23%	—	76%
Social	0%	—	59%		34%	—	63%
Foreign	22%	—	68%		0%	—	67%

Key Votes of the 108th Congress

1. Ban Drilling in ANWR	N	5. Energy Bill	Y	9. Ban Same-Sex Marriage	Y
2. Approve Bush Tax Cuts	Y	6. Support Roe v. Wade	N	10. Ban Bunker-Buster Bomb	N
3. Medicare/Rx Bill	Y	7. Ban Partial-Birth Abortion	Y	11. Fund Iraq War	Y
4. Bar Overtime Pay Regs.	N	8. Assault Weapons Ban	N	12. Restrict Missile Defense	N

Election Results

2004 general	Robert Bennett (R)	626,640	(69%)	($2,649,234)
	Paul Van Dam (D)	258,955	(28%)	($116,959)
	Other	26,131	(3%)	
2004 primary	Robert Bennett (R)	unopposed		
1998 general	Robert Bennett (R)	316,652	(64%)	($1,546,219)
	Scott Leckman (D)	163,172	(33%)	($265,494)
	Other	15,085	(3%)	

Prior Winning Percentages: 1992 (55%)

Bob Bennett, Utah's junior senator, is a Republican who was first elected in 1992. He grew up in Salt Lake City, the grandchild of a president of the LDS Church (as is his wife). He was 17 when his father Wallace Bennett was elected in 1950 to the first of four terms in the Senate. He graduated from the University of Utah and worked as a congressional staffer and was the Transportation Department's chief lobbyist during the Nixon administration. He also headed the public relations firm (and CIA front) that employed Watergate burglar Howard Hunt, but was involved in no wrongdoing himself; some Watergate buffs believed that Bennett was Bob Woodward's "Deep Throat". After that, Bennett headed Microsonics Corporation, which makes audio discs for talking toys, for three years, then became head of Franklin Quest, which produces the Franklin day planners and organizers; he increased it from four to 700 employees and brought in sales of $80 million; he sold his interest in 1991 for a reported $25 million. He headed a commission that produced Utah's Strategic Plan for Education and wrote *Gaining Control*, a book on how to control your daily life.

In 1992, when Jake Garn retired from the Senate, Bennett decided to run for the seat his father once held. He was not the only millionaire in the race. The initial favorite was Republican Joseph Cannon, who had taken over the old Geneva Steel plant and made it profitable, and who spent $5 million of his own money. But Bennett spent $1.4 million of his own and effectively attacked Geneva's environmental record and won the primary 51%–49%. The Democratic nominee, Congressman Wayne Owens, was a familiar face, with a voting record that was moderate—but perhaps too liberal for Utah. Bennett won 55%–40%.

Bennett has had a moderate to conservative voting record and became chief deputy whip in January 2003. He has shown an interest in high-tech issues. He has worked on bills to protect the confidentiality of medical records, with uniform rules for access by researchers and law enforcement personnel. He has embraced some new technology himself: He drives a gasoline-electric hybrid 2000 Honda Insight that gets 61 miles per gallon. He has favored sales taxes on Internet transactions; in his mail order business, he says, he charged customers sales tax in every state and no one protested.

In the debate on homeland security, Bennett strongly supported the personnel provisions backed by the Bush administration. He cited his experiences at the then new Department of Transportation, where only the secretary's power to transfer personnel as needed enabled him to meld the congressional liaison offices of the FAA, Urban Mass Transit Authority, Coast Guard and Federal Highway Administration into a single responsive unit. Despite generally supporting the Bush administration, in 2001 he voted against the education bill, which has proved to be unpopular in Utah. He has been one of the few Republican senators voting against his Utah colleague Orrin Hatch's flag amendment. As chairman of the Joint Economic Committee in 2003 he called for rewriting the nation's tax laws, starting from scratch. In 2005, on Social Security, he called for progressively cutting future benefits and establishing personal retirement accounts. "You cannot solve the financial problems with personal accounts. But you cannot solve the long-term demographic problem without personal accounts."

Bennett has pressed for land exchanges between Utah and the federal government, to eliminate the checkerboard pattern of land ownership which prevents Utah from producing revenue for education from mining on state lands. In September 2000 he came out against the proposed nuclear waste depository on the lands of the Skull Valley Band of the Goshute Indians; in July 2002 he and Orrin Hatch supported the nuclear waste repository in Yucca Mountain, Nevada. In 1999 he urged federal regulators to allow Envirocare to get nuclear waste to store in its hazardous material dump in Tooele County. But in November 2003, after House appropriators included a provision reclassifying waste from the Fernald, Ohio, and Niagara Falls nuclear sites so that it could be sent to Envirocare, he joined Governor Olene Walker in opposing such a transfer, and the provision was dropped in conference. In June 2004 he got the Senate to approve an amendment blocking the moving of military excess mercury to the Utah Industrial Depot, formerly the Tooele Army Depot. In August 2004 he introduced a bill requiring input from Utah residents, radiation monitoring in Utah counties and advance notice before any testing of nuclear devices at the Nevada Test Site; Bennett emphasized that he has opposed new nuclear testing while backing development of new nuclear weapons. In April 2005 Bennett said that he might reconsider his support of Yucca Mountain if nuclear waste is deposited at Skull Valley.

On the Appropriations Committee Bennett got $18 million for the Natural History Museum at the University of Utah (75% of the collection is federally owned), $30 million for the TRAX

Utah / *1st District*

light rail medical center extension, $100,000 for streetscaping in the 9th and 9th neighborhood, $100,000 for the Shakespearean theater in Cedar City and $6 million for air quality and botanical research at the University of Utah. For years environmental groups have sought in vain a 9 million acre wilderness area in Utah; in 2004 Bennett said he favored gradual conversion of public lands to wilderness status.

In 1992 Bennett said he would run for only two terms, but in 1998 he said he would not rule out running again. He was re-elected 64%–33% that year against a Democrat who was a surgeon with an interest in the microloan programs in Bangladesh. In 2004 his Democratic opponent was former Attorney General Paul Van Dam, who rode around the state with his wife on a tandem bicycle. Bennett's campaign put up a series of billboards without the candidate's name: "Able. Articulate. Aerodynamic." "Big Heart. Big Ideas. Big Ears." "Better Looking than Abraham Lincoln. (Just Barely.)" He outspent Van Dam $2.4 million to $120,000 and won 69%–28%. He might be good for many more terms: his father lived to be 95.

FIRST DISTRICT

Rep. Rob Bishop (R)

Elected 2002, 2d term; b. July 13, 1951, Salt Lake City; home, Kaysville; U. of UT, B.A. 1974; Mormon; married (Jeralyn Hansen).

Elected Office: UT House of Reps., 1978–94; Speaker, 1993–94.

Professional Career: H.S. teacher, 1974–2002.

DC Office: 124 CHOB, 20515, 202-225-0453; Fax: 202-225-5857; Web site: www.house.gov/robbishop/.

District Office: Ogden, 801-625-0107.

Committees: *Rules* (8th of 9 R): Legislative & Budget Process.

Group Ratings

	ADA	ACLU	AFS	LCV	ITIC	NTU	COC	ACU	NTLC	CHC
2004	5	0	0	0	75	73	95	100	95	90
2003	0	—	0	5	—	65	100	92	—	—

National Journal Ratings

	2003 LIB	—	2003 CONS		2004 LIB	—	2004 CONS
Economic	0%	—	91%		24%	—	75%
Social	16%	—	83%		17%	—	81%
Foreign	0%	—	89%		22%	—	77%

Key Votes of the 108th Congress

1. Drilling in ANWR	Y	5. DC School Vouchers	Y	9. Ban Same-Sex Marriage	Y
2. Approve Bush Tax Cuts	Y	6. Ban Human Cloning	Y	10. Fund Iraq War	Y
3. Medicare/Rx Bill	Y	7. Restrict Gun Liability	Y	11. Bar Cuba Embargo Funds	N
4. Bar Overtime Pay Regs.	N	8. Ban Partial-Birth Abortion	Y	12. Intelligence Reorg.	Y

Election Results

2004 general	Rob Bishop (R)	199,615	(68%)	($435,494)
	Steven Thompson (D)	85,630	(29%)	
	Other	8,716	(3%)	
2004 primary	Rob Bishop (R)	unopposed		
2002 general	Rob Bishop (R)	109,265	(61%)	($670,302)
	Dave Thomas (D)	66,104	(37%)	($704,616)
	Other	4,043	(2%)	

The People		Race/Ethnic Origin	Ancestry	
Area size:	22,700 sq. mi.	83.3% White	English: 20.9%	German: 8.3%
Urban population:	88.7%	1.1% Black	USA: 5.0%	
Rural population:	11.3%	1.6% Asian	**2004 Presidential Vote**	
Pop. 2000:	744,389	0.7% Native Am.	Bush (R) 220,869	(73%)
Median income:	$45,058	0.6% Hawaiian	Kerry (D) 75,728	(25%)
Poverty status:	9.5%	1.4% Two+ races	Other 6,824	(2%)
Military veterans:	11.7%	0.1% Other	**2000 Presidential Vote**	
		11.1% Hispanic Origin	Bush (R) 167,716	(68%)
			Gore (D) 66,792	(27%)
			Other 13,415	(5%)
			Cook Partisan Voting Index: R +22	

Occupation	Blue collar: 26.2%	White collar: 58.7%	Gray collar: 15.1%

In May 1869, a motley crowd of Irish and Chinese laborers, teamsters, engineers, train crews, officials and guests from California and Salt Lake City gathered at Promontory Summit, Utah, to watch the opening of the transcontinental railroad. The Union Pacific train was late and Leland Stanford's raised hammer totally missed the golden spike, but an alert telegrapher mimicked the sound over the wire and a photographer recorded the scene for posterity: United at last were the civilized East and the mostly untamed West. Here, beyond sight of the snow-capped mountains crossed by Mormon pioneers, where the rail line was bypassed a century ago, the salt flats still stretch out endlessly.

In Salt Lake City, the center of the Mormon Church—and of Utah—is Temple Square, illuminated by 300,000 lights during Christmas week and nestled beneath the towering mountains that flank Salt Lake City. Here you can find the Mormon Tabernacle, home of the famous choir, and the Temple itself, crowned with the golden angel Moroni. This place has been the focal point of Utah since Brigham Young, looking down at this valley, said, "This is the place." Ironically, this part of Salt Lake City is the least Mormon and most cosmopolitan part of Utah, with the state university and businesses bringing in outsiders who, flouting Mormon strictures, keep purveyors of alcohol and caffeine in business. Salt Lake County voted 60% for George W. Bush in 2004, up from 55% in 2000, but still modest compared to the rest of the state.

The 1st Congressional District of Utah consists of the northern end of the state. It includes most of Salt Lake City's historic downtown, its distinctive Avenues District and the airport, but little of the fast-growing suburbia that stretches south of the city. More than half the people in the district live in the stretch of the Wasatch Front, between the mountains and the lake, just north of Salt Lake City, in Davis and Weber Counties. Davis County is suburban and fairly affluent; Ogden in Weber County is an old working class railroad town, an industrial center that depends on nearby Hill Air Force Base. Farther north in the Cache Valley is Logan, home of Utah State University. This is farming country and very heavily Mormon. Over the mountains to the east of Salt Lake City is Park City, the old mining town that is now an increasingly fashionable ski resort and home of the Sundance Film Festival. West of Salt Lake City are the Great Salt Lake, with a new 4,000 acre wetlands sanctuary, and the desolate Bonneville Salt Flats, where land speed records have been set. This land of stark beauty, much of it federally owned, has been used roughly by man: as a repository for hazardous wastes at civilian and military dumps in Tooele County and as a place for military experimentation on the Dugway Proving Ground, where scientists test defenses against chemical and biological agents, and the Wendover Range, where the designs of "Fat Man" and "Little Boy" were assessed before being dropped on Japan; new suburbs out Interstate 80 have made Tooele the state's second-fastest growing county. With the continuing delay in making Yucca Mountain in Nevada the nation's nuclear-waste repository, the Skull Valley temporary storage site—near Dugway—is beginning to look less and less temporary. Politically this is a heavily Republican area, with patches of Democratic strength. The district's portions of Salt Lake County are trendy and working class Democratic; they were kept out of the 2d District by Republican redistricters who wanted to beat a Democratic incumbent. Park City is on its way to becoming another Aspen, Democratic with leftist third party voters; farmers to the east of Park City complain that the county has given too much influence to the newcomers. The Cache Valley is very heavily Republican, though, and overall the district voted 68% for George W. Bush in 2000 and 73% in 2004.

The congressman from the 1st District is Rob Bishop, a Republican first elected in 2002. He grew up in Davis County and graduated from the University of Utah. He became a high school history and government teacher in Box Elder County. In 1978, at 27, he was elected to the state House; in 1993 and 1994 he was Speaker. He also served as state Republican chairman from 1997 to 2001. He continued working as a teacher after leaving the legislature and also worked as a lobbyist for state Republicans and for the National Rifle Association (though he does not own a gun). When Congressman Jim Hansen decided to retire after 22 years, Bishop ran and so did former House Majority Leader Kevin Garn. As a former state party chair, Bishop won 58% of the vote at the Republican nominating convention in May. The two had similar conservative views, and the difference came down to a contentious local issue in Utah, the ongoing battle between banks and credit unions. The credit union lobby endorsed Bishop who, as a lobbyist in 1999, helped defeat legislation to curtail the credit unions' tax-exempt status. Garn, as the wealthy chairman of a Layton bank, had the support of Utah bankers. The credit unions turned out to be the more valuable ally: They poured at least $100,000 in independent expenditures into an anti-Garn campaign, which helped even the financial balance since Garn outspent Bishop by 4–1. Bishop won the June primary 60%–40%. Democrats believed they had a chance in the general with the candidacy of Dave Thomas, a wealthy advertising executive and an anti-abortion Mormon bishop who presented himself as a fiscal conservative and "a regular guy" not tied to special interests. But Bishop won by a wider margin than expected, 61%–37%. Thomas carried Salt Lake County and Park City's Summit County, but they cast less than 15% of the votes.

In the House, Bishop has usually been a reliable conservative vote. With a few other House Republicans, he switched his vote under pressure from party leaders to help defeat an amendment that sought to deny funding to the Patriot Act provision authorizing access to library records. Although he voted for the constitutional amendment to bar same-sex marriages, he preferred a statute that would deny federal courts jurisdiction over state definitions of marriage. He worked on several local issues: He helped to enact a measure to adjust boundaries of the Mount Naomi Wilderness area. He sponsored a bill to block nuclear waste disposal on the Skull Valley Goshute Indian Reservation; he complained that the proposal was killed by members of the Nevada delegation, who were unhappy about support by the Utah delegation for the Yucca Mountain disposal site and opposed to the precedent of shipping the waste by rail to other parts of the Utah site. He sought to protect Hill Air Force Base from the base-closing review; it was not slated for closure under the Pentagon's May 2005 recommendations. He was criticized at home for supporting a change in federal law to permit Envirocare of Utah to dispose in Utah additional radioactive waste material from a bomb plant in Ohio; Envirocare, which was a client of his former lobbying firm, dropped the proposal after three months of controversy, including opposition from Utah Democrat Jim Matheson. Jim Hansen told the *Salt Lake Tribune* that Bishop had a sharp mind and a maverick streak. One example: Bishop, who is one of the few members of Congress who regularly plays on his office softball team, said, "I really get frustrated when they have votes on softball night." He was reelected easily in 2004, though he again lost Salt Lake and Summit Counties. In January 2005, Speaker Dennis Hastert signaled that Bishop had favorably impressed party insiders by giving him for a seat on the Rules Committee.

SECOND DISTRICT

Rep. Jim Matheson (D)

Elected 2000, 3d term; b. Mar. 21, 1960, Salt Lake City; home, Salt Lake City; Harvard U., B.A. 1982, U.C.L.A., M.B.A. 1987; Mormon; married (Amy).

Professional Career: Staff, Environmental Policy Inst., 1982–85; Project Dev. Mgr., Bonneville Pacific, 1987–91; Sr. Assoc., Energy Strategies Inc., 1992–98; Founder & Pres., The Matheson Group, 1998–99.

DC Office: 1222 LHOB, 20515, 202-225-3011; Fax: 202-225-5638; Web site: www.house.gov/matheson.

District Offices: Salt Lake City, 801-486-1236; St. George, 435-627-0880.

Committees: *Financial Services* (23d of 32 D): Capital Markets, Insurance & Government Sponsored Enterprises; Financial Institutions & Consumer Credit. *Science* (16th of 20 D): Energy; Environment, Technology & Standards. *Transportation & Infrastructure* (21st of 34 D): Aviation; Highways, Transit & Pipelines.

Group Ratings

	ADA	ACLU	AFS	LCV	ITIC	NTU	COC	ACU	NTLC	CHC
2004	70	35	75	55	100	29	86	48	28	61
2003	70	—	88	60	—	30	70	40	—	—

National Journal Ratings

	2003 LIB	—	2003 CONS		2004 LIB	—	2004 CONS
Economic	54%	—	45%		54%	—	46%
Social	59%	—	40%		53%	—	47%
Foreign	59%	—	39%		53%	—	46%

Key Votes of the 108th Congress

1. Drilling in ANWR	N	5. DC School Vouchers	N	9. Ban Same-Sex Marriage	Y
2. Approve Bush Tax Cuts	Y	6. Ban Human Cloning	Y	10. Fund Iraq War	Y
3. Medicare/Rx Bill	Y	7. Restrict Gun Liability	Y	11. Bar Cuba Embargo Funds	Y
4. Bar Overtime Pay Regs.	Y	8. Ban Partial-Birth Abortion	Y	12. Intelligence Reorg.	Y

Election Results

2004 general	Jim Matheson (D)	187,250	(55%)	($2,021,524)
	John Swallow (R)	147,778	(43%)	($1,471,198)
	Other	6,940	(2%)	
2004 primary	Jim Matheson (D)	unopposed		
2002 general	Jim Matheson (D)	110,764	(49%)	($1,405,199)
	John Swallow (R)	109,123	(49%)	($1,163,612)
	Other	4,211	(2%)	

Prior Winning Percentages: 2000 (56%)

The People		Race/Ethnic Origin	Ancestry	
Area size:	46,034 sq. mi.	88.0% White	English: 21.8%	German: 9.0%
Urban population:	84.9%	0.6% Black	Irish: 5.0%	
Rural population:	15.1%	1.5% Asian	**2004 Presidential Vote**	
Pop. 2000:	744,390	2.2% Native Am.	Bush (R) 227,668	(66%)
Median income:	$45,583	0.3% Hawaiian	Kerry (D) 108,286	(31%)
Poverty status:	9.0%	1.4% Two+ races	Other 8,434	(2%)
Military veterans:	11.3%	0.1% Other	**2000 Presidential Vote**	
		5.9% Hispanic Origin	Bush (R) 183,387	(67%)
			Gore (D) 84,266	(31%)
			Other 6,573	(2%)
			Cook Partisan Voting Index: R +17	

Occupation   Blue collar: 20.1%   White collar: 65.6%   Gray collar: 14.3%

Demographically, Utah is an urban state; geographically, it is not just rural but, over most of its acreage, scarcely inhabited. Three-quarters of its people live in the Wasatch Front, from Ogden south through Salt Lake City to Provo, between the Great Salt Lake and Utah Lake and the Wasatch Mountains. The scenery here has grandeur, but is surpassed by the landscape of much of southern Utah, most of it preserved in five national parks, five national monuments and a national recreation area. The terrain of southern Utah ranges from the soaring cliffs of Zion National Park to the popsicle-like outcroppings of Bryce Canyon National Park to the red-walled river cuts of Canyonlands National Park to the surreal moonscape of Arches National Park. Monument Valley, on Navajo land in far southeastern Utah, has become familiar to Americans as the site of countless car commercials, and the land around Moab and Springdale has become a major tourist destination. Land here is mostly owned by one agency or another of the federal government, and there have been bitter fights between locals dependent on mining and environmentalists who want to preserve scenery: you can see evidence of old uranium mines in some of the national parks. Bill Clinton's campaign-year creation of the Grand Staircase-Escalante National Monument in 1996, in a ceremony across the border in Arizona, enraged many Utahns, since it effectively removed 1.7 million acres from mineral development, much of it land owned by the state which used the proceeds for schools; local emotions remain raw over that action, as shown when local officials unhappy with federal restrictions removed 31 road signs and delivered them to the monument manager. Areas adjoining Dead Horse Point State Park and Arches National Park have been eyed for oil and gas projects by the Bush administration.

The 2d Congressional District of Utah includes these parts of the state, but 59% of its people live in Salt Lake County, east of a wobbling line between I-15 and the often dry Jordan River. This area includes most of the affluent neighborhoods in Salt Lake City and the suburbs of South Salt Lake, Murray (an old smelter city settled by southern and central Europeans), Midvale, Sandy and Draper. The 2d stretches to include the eastern part of the state and the southwest corner, including all the scenic territory described above.

The congressman from the 2d District is Jim Matheson, a Democrat first elected in 2000. Matheson grew up in Salt Lake City, graduated from Harvard and interned on Capitol Hill for Speaker Tip O'Neill. His father Scott Matheson, a Salt Lake City lawyer, was elected governor of Utah in 1976 and 1980. Jim Matheson worked for the Environmental Policy Institute, and then earned an M.B.A. from UCLA. He returned to Salt Lake City to join Bonneville Pacific, an energy development company, where he was a project development manager. He moved in 1992 to Energy Strategies, a consulting firm, where he was a senior associate. He served four years on the Salt Lake Public Utilities Board. In 1998, he started the Matheson Group to help businesses adapt to electricity deregulation, but he closed it a year later to run for the House.

Matheson ran in a district with a turbulent politics: From 1992 to 2000 it elected two Democrats and two Republicans to Congress. Much of the turbulence was caused by the volatile behavior of Congressman Merrill Cook. Elected in 1996, he became known for his temper tantrums, high staff turnover and his feud with Utah colleague Chris Cannon. He was challenged in the 2000 Republican primary by businessman Derek Smith; Cook charged him with financial misconduct and aides had to pull them apart after a 45-minute confrontation near the end of the campaign. Smith won the primary 59%–41%. In the general, Matheson played down his party affiliation and criticized Al Gore's prescription drug plan. Smith denounced Bill Clinton's creation of the Grand Staircase-Escalante National Monument, and charged that Matheson was trying to look like a Republican. Smith spent more than four times what Democrats spent on Matheson. But Matheson won 56%–41%.

In the House, Matheson has a voting record near the center of the House and has crossed party lines on many issues. He supported the 2001 tax cuts, trade promotion authority, the use of force in Iraq and was one of 16 Democrats who voted for the Medicare/prescription drug bill in November 2003. But he voted against a constitutional amendment on flag burning, oil drilling in the Alaska National Wildlife Refuge and making the Bush tax cuts permanent. He has opposed cost of living increases for members of Congress, but has failed to get a direct vote to stop them. He called for mandatory environmental reviews before any resumption of nuclear weapons testing in Nevada and opposed allowing additional nuclear waste to be disposed of by Envirocare in Tooele County. In 2005, he became a co-chairman of the Blue Dog Democrats.

Matheson has been a Republican target twice. In 2002 John Swallow, a three-term state legislator, won the Republican primary 52%–48% over venture capitalist Tim Bridgewater. Swallow emphasized his strong support for tax cuts and gun ownership rights, and reminded voters of Matheson's Democratic Party affiliation at every opportunity; he harshly criticized Matheson's vote against a partial-birth abortion ban. Matheson reminded rural voters of his family's local connections and said that Swallow would harm public schools by giving tax money to parents who send their kids to private schools (the 2d has the lowest private school enrollment in the nation). Both national parties spent lavishly. Matheson won by 1,641 votes—49.4%–48.7%; this was the narrowest percentage margin for any House incumbent that year. Swallow won most of the rural counties by huge margins, but lost 59%–39% in Salt Lake County, which cast 60% of the vote. Matheson also carried the old mining areas of Carbon County and Grand County, which includes the hip outdoorsmen of Moab (the county voted 15% for Ralph Nader in 2000). In 2004 Swallow ran again and had support from the Club for Growth; the House Republican campaign committee spent nearly $1 million on the contest. But Swallow's more strident negative campaign apparently backfired, and Matheson won 55%–43%, with a 2–1 margin in Salt Lake County. Matheson supported Wesley Clark for the Democratic presidential nomination in 2004, but did not attend the Democratic convention.

With the prospect of a serious challenge every two years in this seat, Matheson seems likely to run for statewide office. But he deferred to his brother, Scott Matheson, who ran for governor in 2004 and lost to Republican Jon Huntsman; in April 2005, he announced that he would not run against Senator Orrin Hatch in 2006.

THIRD DISTRICT

Rep. Chris Cannon (R)

Elected 1996, 5th term; b. Oct. 20, 1950, Salt Lake City; home, Mapleton; Brigham Young U., B.S. 1974, J.D. 1980; Mormon; married (Claudia).

Professional Career: Practicing atty., 1980–83; Asst. Assoc. Solicitor, Dept. of Interior, 1983–84, Assoc. Solicitor, 1984–86; Co-owner, Geneva Steel, 1987–90; Founder, Cannon Industries Inc., 1990–96.

DC Office: 2436 RHOB, 20515, 202-225-7751; Fax: 202-225-5629; Web site: chriscannon.house.gov.

District Offices: Provo, 801-379-2500; West Valley City, 801-955-3631.

Committees: *Government Reform* (11th of 23 R): Criminal Justice, Drug Policy & Human Resources; Regulatory Affairs. *Judiciary* (10th of 23 R): Commercial & Administrative Law (Chmn.); Courts, the Internet & Intellectual Property. *Resources* (11th of 27 R): Energy & Mineral Resources; Forests & Forest Health.

Group Ratings

	ADA	ACLU	AFS	LCV	ITIC	NTU	COC	ACU	NTLC	CHC
2004	0	0	0	0	100	73	100	100	97	84
2003	5	—	0	5	—	70	97	92	—	—

National Journal Ratings

	2003 LIB	—	2003 CONS		2004 LIB	—	2004 CONS
Economic	0%	—	91%		0%	—	95%
Social	0%	—	95%		34%	—	65%
Foreign	11%	—	80%		0%	—	96%

Key Votes of the 108th Congress

1. Drilling in ANWR	Y	5. DC School Vouchers	Y
2. Approve Bush Tax Cuts	Y	6. Ban Human Cloning	Y
3. Medicare/Rx Bill	Y	7. Restrict Gun Liability	Y
4. Bar Overtime Pay Regs.	*	8. Ban Partial-Birth Abortion	Y

9. Ban Same-Sex Marriage *
10. Fund Iraq War Y
11. Bar Cuba Embargo Funds *
12. Intelligence Reorg. Y

Election Results

2004 general	Chris Cannon (R)	173,010	(63%)	($634,195)
	Beau Babka (D)	88,748	(33%)	($35,111)
	Other	11,170	(4%)	
2004 primary	Chris Cannon (R)	27,663	(58%)	
	Matt Throckmorton (R)	19,672	(42%)	
2002 general	Chris Cannon (R)	103,598	(67%)	($345,073)
	Nancy Woodside (D)	44,533	(29%)	($66,491)
	Kitty Burton (Lib)	5,511	(4%)	

Prior Winning Percentages: 2000 (59%); 1998 (77%); 1996 (51%)

The People

Area size:	16,165 sq. mi.
Urban population:	91.2%
Rural population:	8.8%
Pop. 2000:	744,390
Median income:	$46,568
Poverty status:	9.7%
Military veterans:	8.8%

Race/Ethnic Origin
84.5% White
0.5% Black
1.7% Asian
0.7% Native Am.
1.1% Hawaiian
1.4% Two+ races
0.1% Other
10.0% Hispanic Origin

Ancestry
English: 21.5%   German: 8.2%
USA: 5.2%

2004 Presidential Vote
Bush (R) 215,205 (77%)
Kerry (D) 57,185 (20%)
Other 6,689 (2%)

2000 Presidential Vote
Bush (R) 163,983 (75%)
Gore (D) 51,878 (24%)
Other 4,002 (2%)

Cook Partisan Voting Index: R +26

Occupation   Blue collar: 26.2%   White collar: 59.7%   Gray collar: 14.1%

Part of the heartland of the Mormon Church in America is in a geographically isolated valley between 11,000-foot peaks of the Wasatch Range and the shores of Utah Lake. Here is Provo, the home of Brigham Young University, an institution long known for the conservative views of its faculty, the old-fashioned moral standards it encourages and its welcoming of technological innovation. The Mormon commonwealth, after all, started off with a terrific shortage of both labor and water and was eager to use technology to compensate and prosper in this fearsome terrain. Provo produced Philo Farnsworth, the inventor of television, and Harvey Fletcher, inventor of the hearing aid. This has become one of America's high-tech centers, the home of Novell and hundreds of other computer-related firms, some fleeing California's high taxes and cultural liberalism. Overseas missionary work has also bequeathed the area with unusual resources in foreign languages.

The 3d Congressional District of Utah includes all or part of seven counties in central and western Utah. Many of them are remote; during World War II, Japanese Americans were interned near Topaz in Millard County. But about 90% of its people live in Utah or Salt Lake Counties. The 3d includes the west side of Salt Lake City and the suburbs south of the city, including West Valley City (the state's second-largest city, home to many recent Mormon converts from Polynesia), West Jordan, South Jordan and Riverton. Kennecott, the old mining conglomerate that owns 90,000 acres in Salt Lake and Tooele Counties, has been rapidly unloading its landholdings to real estate developers, who have built many subdivisions and the unique Sunrise, a "walkable" community of 30,000 in South Jordan. The district includes almost all of Utah County, including Provo and the string of counties between high-jutting mountains and Utah Lake; in Utah County, Eagle Mountain and Saratoga Springs were created in the early 1990s and have grown rapidly. Politically, this is very much Republican country. Utah County is one of the most heavily Republican counties in the United States: Bill Clinton finished a poor third here in 1992 with 22% of the vote and lost 58%–29% to Bob Dole in 1996; George W. Bush carried the county 86%–12% in 2004. Overall the 3d District voted 77% for Bush in 2004, one of his half dozen best districts in the country.

3d District / Utah 1689

The congressman from the 3d District is Chris Cannon, a Republican first elected in 1996. Cannon is a great-grandson of Utah's first territorial delegate and counselor to Church President Brigham Young, George Q. Cannon, who had five wives and a lot of progeny. Chris Cannon grew up in Salt Lake City, graduated from Brigham Young and its law school and practiced law. From 1983 to 1986 he worked, sometimes controversially, in the Reagan Interior and Commerce departments, on surface coal mining and other issues. In 1987, with his older brother Joe, he purchased and reopened the Geneva Steel plant near Provo, restoring 2,500 jobs. During a family dispute over the business in 1990, Chris Cannon was bought out and set up his own venture capital investment firm. He was active in Republican politics, as was Joe, who ran for the Senate in 1992 and lost the primary 51%–49% to Bob Bennett. Since 2001, Joe Cannon has been Republican state chairman.

In 1996, Chris Cannon ran for the 3d District seat held by Democrat Bill Orton, a conservative Democrat who won it in 1990 after a fractious Republican primary. Cannon spent $1.8 million, $1.5 million of it his own money, against Orton's $709,000. He was helped when Bill Clinton in September, speaking in Arizona without consultation with Utah officials (including Orton), announced that he was establishing the 1.7 million-acre Grand Staircase-Escalante National Monument in southern Utah. This was heartily opposed in the area: much of the land was owned by a state school fund, which wanted to lease it for coal mining, and now would not get the revenue. Cannon ran an ad showing himself denim-clad, leading a horse, attacking Clinton, "I feel like I'm back in the 1850s again with the federal government encamped all around us." Orton said the designation was "a monumental blunder—pun intended." Cannon won 51%–47%.

In the House, Cannon usually had a solidly conservative voting record and continued to attack the national monument. He served on the Judiciary Committee during impeachment and was one of the House managers in the Senate trial, and was critical of Senate Republicans for short-circuiting the trial. He has chaired the Western Caucus, a group of more than 50 House members who advocate "rational, balanced and sound resource management." On Judiciary, Cannon worked to set up a regulatory framework for the Internet. In 2003, Cannon became chairman of the Judiciary Subcommittee on Commercial and Administrative Law, which handles bankruptcy and tort law; his efforts helped to reach the final agreement on the oft-stalled bankruptcy bill which George W. Bush signed in April 2005. Cannon served as a Mormon missionary in Guatemala, and he has taken an interest in immigration bills. In 2003 and 2004, he sponsored guest worker legislation, which would allow foreign nationals to come to work in the United States for willing employers who cannot find Americans to do their jobs and eventually achieve resident status. To charges that this amounts to amnesty for illegal immigrants, Cannon has said, "When you talk about amnesty, you can either put people in jail, fine them and throw them out of the country for 10 years, or you can give them a long term of duty and obligation. That seems to me to be a pretty substantial penalty for what they've done." In 2003 he sponsored a bill to allow states to charge in-state tuition to college students whose parents entered the country illegally. In 2003 he cosponsored the Central American Security Act, which would legalize the status of more than 250,000 Central American immigrants living in the U.S., who provide major economic benefits. The Farm Bureau and Chamber of Commerce have backed his "Agjobs" bill to streamline the seasonal foreign agricultural workers programs. Cannon backed Nevada's Yucca Mountain as a permanent nuclear waste repository in 2002, but after the unsuccessful move to ship nuclear waste to Envirocare in Tooele County and the continued efforts of the Skull Valley Band of Goshute Indians to store nuclear waste on their reservation, he reconsidered his support.

In 2004 Cannon faced a spirited primary challenge from former state Representative Matt Throckmorton, who attacked Cannon on immigration and was strongly backed by national anti-immigration and "pro-borders" groups. Cannon criticized the "terrifically nasty" campaign of outside groups. At the state party convention in May Cannon won 57% but fell short of the 60% required to avoid a primary. Throckmorton said that Cannon was ignoring the views of his constituents. Cannon won the primary 58%–42%—not an outstanding result for an incumbent. He won the general election 63%–33%. His seniority on three House committees has placed him in contention for influential subcommittee chairmanships.

★ VERMONT ★

Vermont is a mixture of the 19th and the 21st centuries—maple syrup and Ben & Jerry's Ice Cream, tiny clapboard villages and carefully zoned towns complete with unobtrusively signed outlet malls, covered bridges and civil unions—with much of the 20th, its factories and suburbs, skyscrapers and shopping malls, mostly left out. Not so long ago, Vermont seemed an entirely antique state, almost as carefully preserved as its Shelburne Museum, with a barn and jail, railroad station and blacksmith shop, covered bridge, and 37 buildings full of folk art. Yet it has been transformed by newcomers, who came here attracted to its antique look but have transformed its culture in their own image.

Vermont was first settled by flinty Yankees from Connecticut, and showed an independent streak from the beginning. After Ethan Allen's Green Mountain Boys repulsed the British in 1777, this was an independent republic for 14 years, claimed by New York and New Hampshire without avail. Allen conducted "international" negotiations with the British and tried to get George Washington to agree to make it a new state; two recent books argue that Vermont never voluntarily joined the United States. All this rugged independence paid off when when Vermont was admitted as the 14th state in 1791. The economy was almost entirely agricultural, as second sons and daughters from small New England farms struggled to scratch out livings from the rocky soil. In time, they quit struggling and raised dairy cows instead, producing milk for the masses of New York City. Vermont developed commerce as well. With its legendary thriftiness, it accumulated capital that, invested wisely, was used to build the solid stone office buildings and courthouses, the thick-timbered houses and gold-topped state Capitol that have remained long after ramshackle wooden buildings of the 19th century have crumbled into dust. Vermont made an economic asset of its maple trees and its quaintness; state government starting in the 1890s promoted it as a tourist destination and passed a law requiring Vermont maple syrup to be made only from the local trees (under a successor law, one sugar producer was recently sentenced to nearly four years in jail and fined $342,000 for adulterating his syrup with cane and beet sugar and then selling it as pure). But Vermont never developed labor-intensive industry, and so over the years it exported people, and it aged. From 1850 to the 1960s, as a result of continuous outmigration, Vermont's population hovered between 300,000 and 400,000. Today, millions of Americans have Vermont blood—far more than the 619,000 who live here now, many of whom have no Vermont roots at all. Two presidents were born here, but both made their careers elsewhere—Chester Arthur in New York, Calvin Coolidge in Massachusetts. Vermont made no visible impression on two great foreign writers who lived here for years—Rudyard Kipling and Aleksandr Solzhenitsyn.

Since then—perhaps the key date was 1963, when people first outnumbered cows—Vermont has changed rapidly. Its economy has boomed, led by leisure-time industries—ski resorts, summer homes—and IBM, with several big high-tech facilities around the Burlington area on the mostly undeveloped shores of glorious Lake Champlain. Here you can find big box retailers in Williston and ethnic diversity—Vietnamese, Bosnians, Koreans—in Winooski only 30 or 40 miles away from Sheldon, where 83% of residents are native Vermonters, the highest in the state, or tiny Buels Gore, a sliver of land left out when the first settlers drew town lines, whose population increased in the 1990s from 2 to 12. Homegrown firms started by Baby Boom rebels—Ben & Jerry's Ice Cream, founded in 1978, is the archetype—have flourished. "The merger between the old hardscrabble culture and the new earthy, crunchy ethic did not always take," novelist Paul Greenberg writes; but it often did, and the newcomers cherished what Greenberg calls "maple's homespun image." Vermont's population rose from 390,000 in 1960 to 511,000 in 1980 and 609,000 in 2000. It hasn't been random settlement: While next-door New Hampshire, trumpeting its low taxes and aversion to government, attracted right-leaning migrants from Massachusetts and elsewhere who were happy to live in spanking-new developments and ravenous for low taxes, Vermont, proclaiming its desire to preserve the environment and the past, attracted left-leaning migrants from New York and elsewhere who were willing to pay higher taxes and higher prices for the privilege of living in a seemingly pristine setting. The

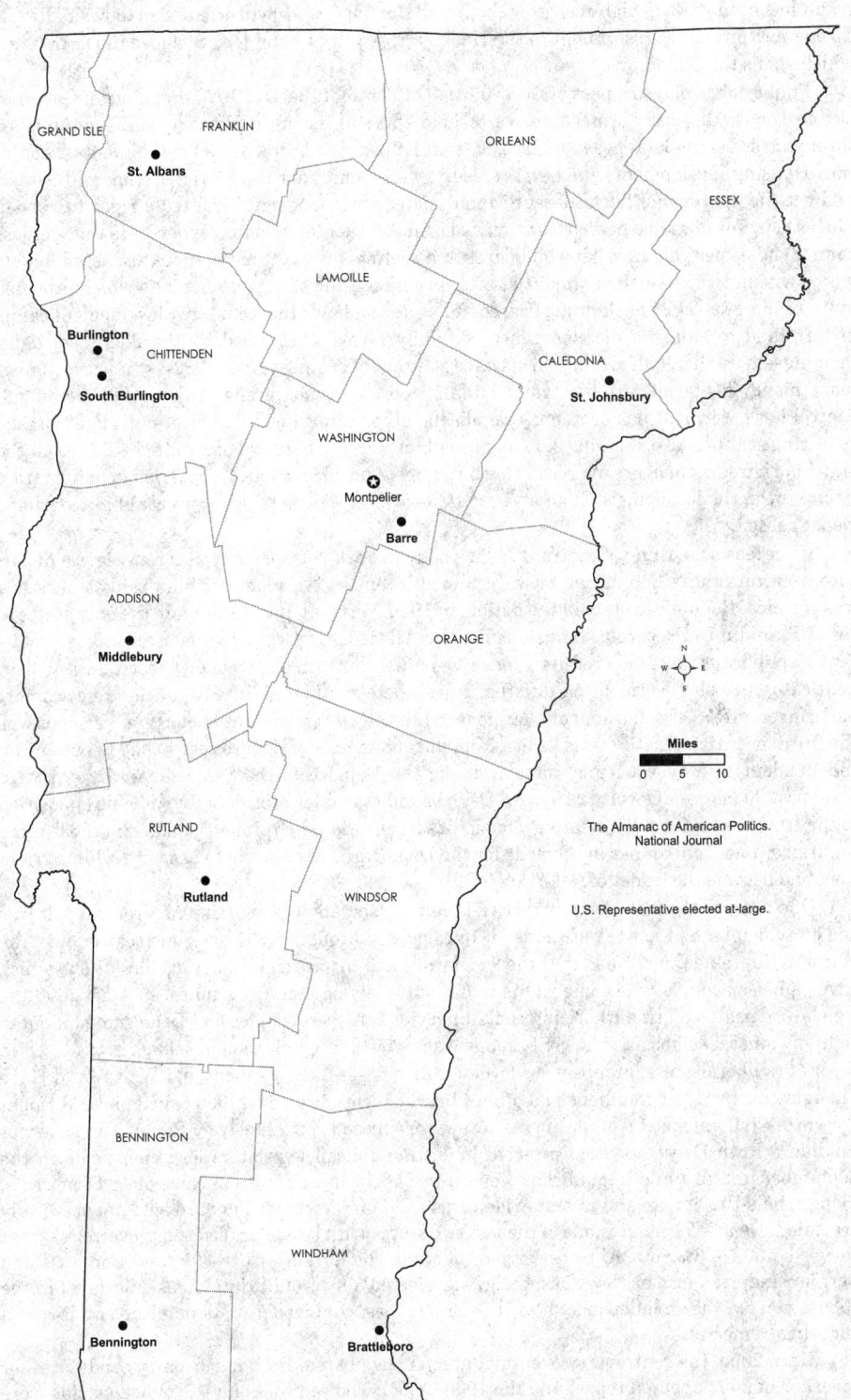

GRAND ISLE

FRANKLIN

ORLEANS

● St. Albans

ESSEX

LAMOILLE

Burlington
●   CHITTENDEN

CALEDONIA

● St. Johnsbury

South Burlington

WASHINGTON

✪
Montpelier
● Barre

ADDISON

ORANGE

● Middlebury

N
W ✦ E
S

Miles
0   5   10

RUTLAND

The Almanac of American Politics.
National Journal

● Rutland

WINDSOR

U.S. Representative elected at-large.

BENNINGTON

WINDHAM

● Bennington

Brattleboro ●

result has been growth, high-tech growth around Burlington, growth oriented to tourism. People throng not only to ski resorts but to the Haskell Free Library and Opera House in Derby Line, which spans the Canadian border.

Public policy played a part in the evolution of Vermont. Back in 1970, Republican Governor Deane Davis (the last Vermont native to hold the job), facing a primary challenge, pushed through a sweeping land use law (Act 250) that helped give Vermont its environmental reputation. Housing developments and new ski resorts were required to meet 10 environmental criteria and get the approval of five different commissions, with opponents granted a right to appeal. Since then, Vermont has passed its own Clean Air Act that levies a tax on new cars that get less than 20 miles per gallon. It bans billboards and rooftop air conditioning units. It passed Act 60, which attempted to equalize property taxes throughout the state, and Act 200, which provided state support for regional planning boards. It has a state land trust that buys development rights of farmland to stop the disappearance of family farms. Distressed by the demise of dairy farming—more than half of dairy farms have gone out of business since 1982—state government loans money for farmers to buy water buffalo to produce mozzarella. Although it has no gun control laws, Vermont has been busy regulating other things: banning clear-cutting of forests, requiring seat belt use, banning smoking in public places. There are now four Wal-Marts in the state, but three of them are in preexisting buildings. And when Home Depot tried to build a store in one town, the locals insisted on a vegetation-covered roof on which cows could graze: Home Depot passed.

If there is something of the Yankee busybody in such policies, they also represent a departure from the state's Republican past. In the 19th century, Vermont, with its Yankee heritage, was the most Republican state in the nation; in 1936, Vermont and Maine were the only states to resist Franklin D. Roosevelt's landslide. For three decades thereafter Vermont's Yankee Protestant Republicans outnumbered its French Canadian and Irish Catholic Democrats. But now, political issues slice Vermont on different lines—between liberal, highly educated newcomers and conservative, less educated old Vermonters. In the 2004 presidential election, Vermont was the third most Democratic state; its last Republican member of Congress switched to become an Independent in May 2001 and voted to make the Democrats the Senate majority party. In January 2003 former Governor Howard Dean set off to run for president; by July his opposition to the Iraq war (and not his relatively moderate fiscal record in Vermont) made him the leading fundraiser and frontrunner in the polls for the Democratic nomination. Vermont, valuing tradition, had become the leader of America's left.

One issue that made Dean attractive to left Democrats was civil unions. Ironically, it was one on which he had not taken the lead. In a lawsuit brought by three same-sex couples, the Vermont Supreme Court ruled that the legislature had to pass a gay marriage law or one which gave same-sex couples the same rights under state law as married couples. In April 2000 the legislature passed a law authorizing civil unions for same-sex couples and Dean signed it out of sight of cameras. Opposition to civil unions was fierce and vocal, though seldom articulated in the state's liberal press; groups were formed called Take Back Vermont and Who Would Have Thought. Backers of civil unions and other liberal policies formed a group called Move Vermont Forward. Civil unions and other liberal laws were opposed vociferously by Republican governor candidate Ruth Dwyer. Several pro-civil union Republican legislators lost their seats in the September primary, and Republicans won control of the state House in November. Democrats, though, held the Senate and in statewide races the Move Vermont Forward side unequivocally prevailed. Dean—Vermont is one of the last two states with two-year terms for governors—beat Dwyer by 50%–38% vote. Al Gore carried the state comfortably, 51%–41%, and Congressman Bernie Sanders, a former New Yorker who was elected mayor of Burlington as a Socialist in the 1980s, won 69% as an independent, to 18% for a transsexual moderate Republican and 5% for a left-wing Democrat.

Since 2000, the controversy over civil unions has abated. Both major party candidates for governor in 2002 opposed repeal and the 2000 Census showed that only 1% of households were same-sex unions. The 2004 exit poll showed that 40% favored same-sex marriage, 36% civil unions and only 21% neither. At the same time the state voted 59%–39% for John Kerry, his third highest percentage in the nation: Vermont was the only state in which George W. Bush won a smaller percentage of the vote in 2004 than in 2000. Vermont was also the only state whose entire congressional delegation voted against the $87 billion supplemental appropriation for Iraq in October 2003.

Yet at the same time Vermont has become somewhat less liberal on economic issues. Job losses at IBM and slow economic growth in what had been the booming Burlington area were accompanied by a questioning of the costs of Act 250 and Act 60. In the 2002 election for governor, longtime Republican officeholder Jim Douglas beat Lieutenant Governor Doug Racine by 45%–42%. Douglas's prime goal was revision of Act 250, and in May 2004 the Democratic Senate and Republican House voted for major changes. But Vermont's cultural liberalism persisted. Douglas was proud also of a law cleaning up Lake Champlain, and he let a medical marijuana bill become law without his signature. The political result was mixed. Republicans lost their majority in the state House in November 2004, but Douglas was reelected by a 59%–38% over Burlington Mayor Peter Clavelle.

The People		Race/Ethnic Origin			Military veterans: 62,809 (13.6%)	
Pop. 2004 (est):	621,394	585,431	96.2%	White	WWII: 19.4%	Korea: 14.3%
Pop. 2000:	608,827	2,921	0.5%	Black	Vietnam: 32.2%	Gulf War: 7.4%
Pop. 1990:	562,758	5,160	0.8%	Asian	**Most populous cities (2003):**	
Change 1990–2000:	Up 8.2%	2,325	0.4%	Native Am.	1. Burlington	39,148
% of U.S. total:	0.2%	120	0.0%	Hawaiian	2. Rutland	17,103
Pop. rank:	49th of 50	6,809	1.1%	Two+ races	3. South Burlington	16,285
Area size:	9,614 sq. mi.	557	0.1%	Other	4. Barre	9,166
State Native:	54.3%	5,504	0.9%	Hisp. Origin	5. Essex Junction	8,717
Non-citizen:	1.8%	**Ancestry**				
Language		English: 13.1%		Irish: 11.7%	Urban population: 38.2%	
English: 90.8%	Other Eur.: 6.8%	French: 10.3%		German: 6.5%	Rural population: 61.8%	
Spanish: 1.6%		Fr. Canadian: 6.3%				

Education		Work Sector		General Assembly	
H.S. Grad:	86.4%	Private: 75.3%	Govt: 14.2%	Senate	21 D 9 R
College Grad:	29.4%	Self: 10.3%	Family: 0.3%	House	83 D 60 R 7 I
Industry		Unemployment: 4.2%		Legislative Term Limits: No	
Agri: 3.0%	Con: 6.7%	**Household Income**		**Registered Voters**	
Fin: 4.7%	Info: 2.7%	<15k: 14.5%	15-35k: 27.9%	No party registration	
Mfg: 18.8%	Prof: 31.2%	35-50k: 18.6%	50-100k: 30.3%		
Public: 4.6%	Trade: 15.1%	100-150k: 5.7%	>150k: 3.0%		
Other: 13.3%		Median: $40,856			
Occupation		Poverty status: 9.4%			
Blue collar: 23.3%	White collar: 60.8%	**Home Value**			
Gray collar: 15.9%		<50k: 8.6%	50-100k: 33.8%	100-200k: 43.9%	200-300k: 8.8%
		300-500k: 3.6%	>500k: 1.5%	Median: $111,200	

Presidential politics   Vermont was the most Republican state in the 1936 presidential election, when Franklin Roosevelt's campaign manager had a good laugh updating an old adage to say, "As goes Maine, so goes Vermont." Times have changed. In the 2004 presidential election Vermont was the third most Democratic state. As a new granola Vermont has grown in the Green Mountain and maple syrup atmosphere of the old, Vermont has become solidly liberal on cultural and foreign issues and not very conservative on economics. The change was apparent as long ago as 1980, when Ronald Reagan got his seventh lowest percentage here and John Anderson, more Vermont's kind of Republican, his best, 15%.

In 2004 the big presidential story here was the candidacy of Howard Dean, headquartered in Burlington. In 2000, only 49,000 Vermonters voted in the Democratic presidential primary and 81,000 in the Republican contest, which was not yet decided; John McCain beat George W. Bush 60%–35%. Four years later things were

2004 Presidential Vote		
Kerry (D)	184,067	(59%)
Bush (R)	121,180	(39%)
Nader (I)	4,494	(1%)
Other	2,568	(1%)

2004 Democratic Presidential Primary		
Dean (D)	44,393	(54%)
Kerry (D)	26,171	(32%)
Edwards (D)	5,113	(6%)
Kucinich (D)	3,396	(4%)
Clark (D)	2,749	(3%)
Other	1,059	(1%)

2000 Presidential Vote		
Gore (D)	149,022	(51%)
Bush (R)	119,775	(41%)
Nader (Green)	20,374	(7%)
Other	5,137	(2%)

reversed. Although John Kerry clinched the Democratic nomination on March 2, 83,000 Vermonters voted in the Democratic primary a week later (it was the only primary Dean won in 2004), while only 27,000 voted in the (uncontested) Republican primary. In the fall this was the one state in which George W. Bush's percentage was lower than it had been in 2000.

The conflict between the old and new Vermonts is apparent in the NEP exit poll. In 2000, those without college degrees voted 48%–46% for Bush, but Gore carried college graduates 51%–36% and those with postgraduate degrees 62%–29%. The old divide between Protestants and Catholics has nearly vanished: in 2004, Bush carried Protestants 50%–47% and narrowly lost among Catholics 48%–52%. Kerry won those with no religion 82%–15%.

The Vermont presidential primary, abolished for 1992, reappeared in 1996, but has achieved little notice; all the action is next door in New Hampshire.

Governor

Jim Douglas (R)

Elected 2002, term expires Jan. 2007, 2d term; b. June 21, 1951, Springfield, MA; home, Middlebury; Middlebury Col., B.A. 1972; Congregationalist; married (Dorothy).

Elected Office: VT House of Reps., 1972–79; Maj. Ldr., 1977–79; VT Secy. of St., 1980–92; VT Treasurer, 1994–02.

Office: 109 State St., Montpelier, 05609, 802-828-3333; Fax: 802-828-3339; Web site: www.gov.state.vt.us.

Election Results

2004 general	Jim Douglas (R)	181,540	(59%)
	Peter Clavelle (D)	117,327	(38%)
	Other	10,418	(3%)
2004 primary	Jim Douglas (R)	unopposed	
2002 general	Jim Douglas (R)	103,436	(45%)
	Doug Racine (D)	97,565	(42%)
	Cornelius Hogan (I)	22,353	(10%)
	Other	6,807	(3%)

The key decision that led to Jim Douglas being elected governor of Vermont in 2002 may have been his decision 34 years earlier to attend Middlebury College. Douglas grew up in Longmeadow, Massachusetts, a political junkie and a strong Republican, passing out AuH2O stickers for Barry Goldwater in 1964, at 13. In 1968, he enrolled at Middlebury and almost immediately decided to live in the town; his wife is from Middlebury and they have lived there ever since. Douglas's college years were a time of campus protests against the Vietnam War, but he became an active Republican and organized a rally for President Richard Nixon in Middlebury in 1970. In 1972, the year he graduated, he ran for state representative from Middlebury and was elected; he was elected majority leader in 1977. In 1979, he lost a race for Speaker and became an aide to Republican Governor Richard Snelling. In between sessions of the legislature he worked as a radio announcer and became executive director of the local United Way. In 1980, he was elected secretary of state and served for 12 years. In 1992, he ran against Senator Patrick Leahy and lost 54%–43%—the closest race Leahy has had since 1980. In 1994, after working for the Porter Medical Center in Middlebury, he spotted an opening for state treasurer and was elected to the first of four terms. The Democratic party produces many gifted political entrepreneurs who win office even in unlikely years and districts; the Republican party has one in Douglas. He has been on the Vermont ballot every two years since 1972, and for most of that time has gotten up before 6 a.m. to commute over the Green Mountains to the tiny state capital of Montpelier.

His opening to run for governor came when Democratic Governor Howard Dean announced on September 5, 2001 that he would not run again. Returned to office every two years—Vermont and New Hampshire are the last two states with two-year gubernatorial terms—he advanced a number of innovative policies which, in the minds of many observers, entitled him to serious consideration as a candidate for president in 2004.

Most Vermonters responded positively to Dean's presidential candidacy, not so much because of his mixed moderate-and-liberal record on state issues as his loud stand against the Iraq war. But as Dean was preparing to leave Vermont politics, there was discontent with some of his policies. Not so much civil unions, which he embraced reluctantly (but which have become more popular as time goes on), but over the high property taxes engendered by Act 60, which levied a statewide property tax to provide each school district, the long delays in development caused by the environmental reviews under 30-year-old Act 250 and, most of all, by frequent news of job loss and a rising sense that Vermont has a reputation for being unfriendly to business. Douglas and his Democratic opponent, Lieutenant Governor Douglas Racine, agreed that Act 60 and Act 250 needed some changes; so did Con Hogan, former director of state human services, who started running for the Republican nomination but decided in February to run as an Independent. But there was a clear difference in emphasis. Douglas called for tax cuts, if spending cuts could be achieved, and promised to "create a more business-friendly environment." He advocated major modification in Act 60. He charged that despite its high spending on education, Vermont was still getting mediocre test scores. It was "time for a change," he said, in a state which had had Democratic governors 17 of the last 18 years.

Racine had run for the state Senate and lost in 1980, then won five terms; he lost the race for lieutenant governor in 1994 but won in 1996, 1998 and 2000. In the 2002 campaign, Racine said that as lieutenant governor he had helped fashion consensus on school funding, children's services and the budget. He called for conservation, environmental protection and broad access to health care. He conceded the need for simplifying Act 60 and speeding up Act 250.

The result was something of an upset. Douglas led Racine 45%–42%, with 10% for Hogan. Under Vermont law, if no candidate receives 50% of the vote, the governor is chosen by a combined vote of the two houses of the legislature. Republicans entered the campaign with a large majority of legislative seats; Racine announced that he would not take his candidacy to the legislature if he won under 50%, while Douglas said he would. Then, contrary to most expectations, Democrats made gains in the legislature and their majority in the Senate was larger than the Republicans' narrow margin in the House. But Racine kept his word and Douglas became governor.

Douglas's great success as governor was in getting the legislature to pass in April 2004 a bill revising Act 250—the first major change in 34 years. The five citizen approval boards were abolished and their powers given to a single Environmental Court; opponents of development were no longer given an automatic right to intervene; developers could pay for stormwater runoff by offsetting reductions elsewhere. Douglas did not get the legislature to act on Act 60. He did institute increased tax collection from out-of-state corporations, combined with a 14% cut in the corporate tax rate. Douglas sought state reimportation of prescription drugs from Canada; when the FDA denied that, Vermont in August 2004 became the first state to sue. On energy policy, Douglas said his plan was to "promote development and use of renewable energy by facilitating collaboration and market-based incentives that encourage employers and residents to install these alternatives." But that was not enough for legislative Democrats and environment group heads, who wanted to require greater percentages of renewable energy.

Douglas's opponent in the 2004 election was Peter Clavelle, longtime mayor of Burlington, who got his political start in 1982 as an appointee of Socialist Mayor Bernie Sanders, now Vermont's congressman-at-large. Clavelle was a longtime member of the left-wing Progressive party; deciding to run as a Democrat after Howard Dean announced his retirement, he arranged that the Progressive nomination would be won by an ally who would decline to run. Clavelle's major plank was health care. He proposed to use the $90 million the state spends on Medicaid on a universal health care insurance and said it could be paid for by greater efficiencies. To which Douglas said, "It's a $90 million plan that no one really understands, that its author can't explain and that they said is free. I think most Vermonters are pretty skeptical of that." He favored increasing competition by encouraging private insurers to reenter the state, health savings accounts and initiatives for chronic illness and encouraging healthy lifestyles in children. This issue, like renewable energy and smoking in bars (Clavelle favored a statewide ban, Douglas local option), was a clear-cut conflict between a Republican backing market incentives and a Democrat favoring government decisionmaking. Vermont, for all its leftism on issues like Iraq, seemed to be leaning more toward the market than government; as the campaign went on Clavelle said that voters should back him because of his opposition to the war in Iraq.

Douglas won 59%–38%, carrying all but one county. That looked like an endorsement of Douglas's market-based approach. But Democrats increased their margin in the state Senate and replaced a small Republican majority with a large Democratic majority in the House. That leaves Vermont, like Massachusetts and Rhode Island, the only states which gave John Kerry a higher percentage, with a Republican governor and large Democratic margins in the legislature.

Senior Senator

Patrick Leahy (D)

Elected 1974, seat up 2010, 6th term; b. Mar. 31, 1940, Montpelier; home, Burlington; St. Michael's Col., B.A. 1961, Georgetown U., J.D. 1964; Catholic; married (Marcelle).

Elected Office: VT St. Atty., Chittenden Cnty., 1966–74.

Professional Career: Practicing atty., 1964–74.

DC Office: 433 RSOB, 20510, 202-224-4242; Fax: 202-224-3479; Web site: leahy.senate.gov.

State Offices: Burlington, 802-863-2525; Montpelier, 802-229-0569.

Committees: *Agriculture, Nutrition & Forestry*: Forestry, Conservation & Rural Revitalization; Production & Price Competitiveness; Research, Nutrition & General Legislation (RMM). *Appropriations*: Commerce, Justice & Science; Defense; Homeland Security; Interior & Related Agencies; State, Foreign Operations & Related Programs (RMM); Transportation, Treasury, the Judiciary, HUD & Related Agencies. *Judiciary* (RMM): Antitrust, Competition Policy & Consumer Rights; Corrections & Rehabilitation; Intellectual Property (RMM).

Group Ratings

	ADA	ACLU	AFS	LCV	ITIC	NTU	COC	ACU	NTLC	CHC
2004	100	62	100	100	73	17	50	8	8	16
2003	85	—	100	100	—	18	35	16	—	—

National Journal Ratings

	2003 LIB	—	2003 CONS		2004 LIB	—	2004 CONS
Economic	81%	—	18%		76%	—	21%
Social	68%	—	26%		70%	—	26%
Foreign	79%	—	14%		92%	—	7%

Key Votes of the 108th Congress

1. Ban Drilling in ANWR	Y	5. Energy Bill	N	9. Ban Same-Sex Marriage	N
2. Approve Bush Tax Cuts	N	6. Support Roe v. Wade	Y	10. Ban Bunker-Buster Bomb	*
3. Medicare/Rx Bill	N	7. Ban Partial-Birth Abortion	Y	11. Fund Iraq War	N
4. Bar Overtime Pay Regs.	Y	8. Assault Weapons Ban	Y	12. Restrict Missile Defense	Y

Election Results

2004 general	Patrick Leahy (D)	216,972	(71%)	($1,531,833)
	Jack McMullen (R)	75,398	(25%)	($736,086)
	Other	14,838	(5%)	
2004 primary	Patrick Leahy (D)	27,459	(95%)	
	Craig Hill (D)	1,573	(5%)	
1998 general	Patrick Leahy (D)	154,567	(72%)	($1,014,751)
	Fred H. Tuttle (R)	48,051	(22%)	
	Other	11,418	(5%)	

Prior Winning Percentages: 1992 (54%); 1986 (63%); 1980 (50%); 1974 (50%)

Patrick Leahy, the only Democrat ever elected to the Senate in Vermont, has held public office for most of his adult life. He grew up in Burlington, went to Georgetown law school, then returned home to Burlington to practice law. He was elected Chittenden County state's attorney in 1966, at 26, and, after eight years in that post—and few public officials are scrutinized as closely as a local prosecutor—he was elected to the U.S. Senate at 34. Reelected in 2004, he is set to become the longest-serving senator in Vermont history in December 2008, when he will exceed his predecessor George Aiken's 33 years.

Leahy is the ranking Democrat on the Judiciary Committee and served as chairman from June 2001 to January 2003. He was also formerly chairman of the Agriculture Committee. Judiciary handles many of the cultural issues which have polarized the two parties and their constituencies—issues like abortion and gun control—and the committee has been sharply polarized at least since the hearings on the Supreme Court nomination of Judge Robert Bork in 1987. This was certainly true in the 1990s when Republicans were in the majority. Then, Leahy criticized Republicans for holding up Bill Clinton's judicial appointments and stoutly defended Clinton on impeachment. When Leahy became chairman, he began to hold up judicial nominations himself, as Republicans had done in the past. As chairman, he led the rejection by party line votes of two nominees for the Fifth Circuit and demanded from another nominee the memos he had written while working in the office of the solicitor general during the Clinton administration—something never before sought, and a demand denounced by all former solicitors general in administrations of both parties. As ranking minority member since January 2003, Leahy has also filibusters against 10 appeals court nominees—the first in history—which have been bitterly attacked by Republicans. Leahy points out that the large majority of nominees have been approved and cites statistics to argue that Democrats have been fairer to Bush appointees than Republicans were to Bill Clinton's. The key question heading into the 109th Congress was whether and to what extent Leahy and other Democrats will oppose any Bush nominees to the Supreme Court.

Judiciary had jurisdiction over much of the antiterrorism legislation brought forward after September 11. Leahy approached the task with some concern lest federal powers override individual rights. He and his staff worked with the Bush administration to hammer out the planks in the USA Patriot Act; it was essentially the Senate version, not the House version, which was passed in October 2001. It authorized roving wiretaps (to cover the target's cell phones and wireless communications devices as well as his home phone), imposed tougher penalties for terrorism, provided for tighter security on the U.S.-Canada border and toughened the laws against money laundering. But Leahy also criticized some of the Bush administration's actions and proposals. He opposed the administration's first proposal for broader powers to detain and deport immigrants suspected of terrorism without presenting evidence in court. In early 2004 he called for "a vigorous, bipartisan examination" of the Patriot Act when it comes up for reauthorization in 2005.

In September 2002, he said Justice should be required to disclose the number of U.S. citizens being spied on, the number of secret foreign intelligence wiretaps that had become part of criminal proceedings and the total number of persons targeted by foreign intelligence surveillance warrants. After the story broke on the Abu Ghraib prison scandal in April 2004 he sharply criticized the administration. He disagreed with Bush's declaration that the Geneva convention did not apply to unlawful combatants in Afghanistan and argued that methods authorized by Defense Secretary Donald Rumsfeld for Afghanistan prisoners in December 2002, though rescinded a month later, nonetheless migrated and were applied to prisoner in Iraq as well as in Afghanistan and at Guantanamo. "Somewhere in the upper reaches of the executive branch a process was set in motion that rolled forward until it produced this scandal."

Leahy was also harshly critical of the administration on DNA testing. In 2004 the House and the Senate Judiciary Committee passed by large bipartisan majorities a DNA testing bill sponsored by Leahy and Judiciary Chairman Orrin Hatch. But it was pulled from the calendar by the House Republican leadership with, he charged, the approval of the administration. By the end of October the bill was passed and became law.

Leahy is a gadgeteer and fine amateur photographer, and he was one of the first senators to go online in the 1990s; he has worked on various bills that affect high-tech and telecommunications. He co-sponsored with Hatch the Digital Millennium Copyright law, passed to comply with the WIPO treaty, and with Arizona Sen. Jon Kyl, the law making the theft of personal identification information a crime. More controversially, in 2004 he co-sponsored with Hatch and several others a bill to punish those who intentionally induce others to infringe copyrighted material. This was obviously aimed at the peer-to-peer software, like Grokster and Kazaa, which enables users to copy movies and recordings, and was strongly supported by Hollywood studios and the recording industry. But it was opposed by the high-tech industry and venture capitalists, as well as libertarians of the left and right. Over the summer and fall there were intense negotiations and numerous redraftings, but no bill was passed; this is an issue that will undoubtedly be revisited in the 109th Congress.

Another Leahy cause has been the elimination of land mines. Since 1989, he has been crusading against the export and use of land mines, which are easy and cheap to implant yet difficult and expensive to remove, and which injure thousands of civilians long after hostilities have ended. In 1994, he got the United Nations to approve unanimously their eventual elimination. Leahy continues to work to aid land mine victims and to deactivate the thousands of land mines still active in many parts of the world and to find alternatives for them. On foreign and defense issues, he tends to stand to the left of the Senate: He was one of three senators to vote against authorization of missile defense in March 1999 and has called for an end to the ban on travel to Cuba. He has been a staunch and outspoken critic of the Iraq war.

Leahy has long been one of the few members of the Senate Agriculture Committee not from a state with heavily subsidized crops like wheat, corn, soybeans or cotton. As ranking Democrat, he worked with Richard Lugar in the 1990s to phase out the old subsidy system. Their great success was the Freedom to Farm Act of 1996, but soon crop prices fell and Congress took to voting huge annual subsidies in the form of emergency relief; the 2002 farm bill largely rolled back the 1996 act. In that act, Leahy shaped the bill's conservation provisions and tried to save the Northeast Dairy Compact, to set milk prices in the six New England states; the Compact, however, expired in September 2001. Working with his adversary on the Northeast Dairy Compact, Wisconsin's Herb Kohl, he did obtain MILC provisions (Milk Income Loss Compensation Program), which have brought $45 million to Vermont dairy farmers. But his and Kohl's efforts to reauthorize MILC in October 2004, 11 months before its expiration, fell short.

Leahy serves on Appropriations and has procured funding for Vermont projects—$2.7 million for micromachine research at the Microtechnology Center at Burlington, an $800,000 Army research contract for Vermont Phototonics, $11.25 million for Vermont first responder agencies under the all-state minimum formula he wrote into the homeland security act (under that formula, Vermont ranked second among the states in fiscal 2004 per capita funding for first responders). Leahy is a strong partisan who usually expresses himself in a quiet, thoughtful way and sometimes with a puckish sense of humor, part of the Yankee heritage of Vermont, though his Irish and Italian ethnic origin is not standard Yankee. But his partisanship has rubbed some the wrong way. In a photo session in the Senate in June 2004, Leahy asked Vice President Dick Cheney whether he wasn't talking to Democrats; Cheney, nettled by what he considered criticism of his integrity in Leahy's frequent attacks on Halliburton, told the Vermonter to commit an impossible act.

The one close call Leahy has had with Vermont voters came in 1980, when he narrowly survived the Republican sweep. He beat popular Governor Richard Snelling 63%–35% in 1986, and in 1992, against Jim Douglas, then state treasurer and now governor, Leahy won 54%–43%. In 1998, he had an easier time against 77-year-old dairy farmer Fred Tuttle, winning 72%–22%. In 2004, against the man Tuttle upset in the Republican primary six years before, Leahy won by a nearly identical 71%–25%.

Junior Senator

James Jeffords (I)

Elected 1988, seat up 2006, 3d term; b. May 11, 1934, Rutland; home, Shrewsbury; Yale U., B.S. 1956, Harvard U., LL.B. 1962; Congregationalist; married (Elizabeth).

Military Career: Navy, 1956–59, Naval Reserves, 1959–90.

Elected Office: VT Senate, 1966–68; VT Atty. Gen., 1968–72; U.S. House of Reps. 1974–88.

Professional Career: Law clerk, 1962–63; Practicing atty., 1963–69, 1973–75; Shrewsbury Repub. Party Chmn., 1963–74; Town Agent, Grand Juror, 1964.

DC Office: 413 DSOB, 20510, 202-224-5141; Fax: 202-228-0776; Web site: jeffords.senate.gov.

State Offices: Burlington, 802-658-6001; Montpelier, 802-223-5273; Rutland, 802-773-3875.

Committees: *Aging (Special)*. *Environment & Public Works* (RMM). *Finance*: Health Care; Social Security & Family Policy; Taxation & IRS Oversight (RMM). *Health, Education, Labor & Pensions*: Education & Early Childhood Development; Employment & Workplace Safety; Retirement Security & Aging. *Veterans' Affairs*.

Group Ratings

	ADA	ACLU	AFS	LCV	ITIC	NTU	COC	ACU	NTLC	CHC
2004	85	78	86	100	75	23	59	4	5	0
2003	85	—	89	89	—	23	36	10	—	—

National Journal Ratings

	2003 LIB — 2003 CONS		2004 LIB — 2004 CONS	
Economic	58%	— 41%	69%	— 28%
Social	66%	— 33%	66%	— 33%
Foreign	74%	— 22%	85%	— 14%

Key Votes of the 108th Congress

1. Ban Drilling in ANWR	Y	5. Energy Bill	N	9. Ban Same-Sex Marriage	N
2. Approve Bush Tax Cuts	N	6. Support Roe v. Wade	Y	10. Ban Bunker-Buster Bomb	*
3. Medicare/Rx Bill	Y	7. Ban Partial-Birth Abortion	N	11. Fund Iraq War	N
4. Bar Overtime Pay Regs.	Y	8. Assault Weapons Ban	Y	12. Restrict Missile Defense	Y

Election Results

2000 general	James Jeffords (R)	189,133	(66%)	($1,889,243)
	Ed Flanagan (D)	73,352	(25%)	($1,054,977)
	Other	26,015	(9%)	
2000 primary	James Jeffords (R)	60,234	(78%)	
	Rick Hubbard (R)	15,991	(21%)	
	Other	1,204	(2%)	
1994 general	James Jeffords (R)	106,505	(50%)	($1,174,973)
	Jan Backus (D)	85,868	(41%)	($308,069)
	Gavin T. Mills (I)	12,465	(6%)	
	Other	6,834	(3%)	

Prior Winning Percentages: 1988 (70%); 1986 House (89%); 1984 House (65%); 1982 House (69%); 1980 House (79%); 1978 House (75%); 1976 House (67%); 1974 House (53%)

Jim Jeffords, the senator whose departure in May 2001 from the Republican Party gave the Democrats a majority in the Senate for 18 months, was first elected to the House in 1974 and to the Senate in 1988. He grew up in Rutland, the son of a Vermont chief justice, went to Yale, served in the Navy, went to Harvard Law School and then returned to Shrewsbury in the Green Mountains to practice law. He was elected state senator in 1966, at 32, and then state attorney general in 1968 and 1970. In 1974, he was elected to the House and in 1988, when Senator Robert

Stafford retired, to the Senate. For 27 years he had one of the most liberal voting records of any congressional Republican; since 2001 his voting record has been close to those of liberal Democrats.

In the 1990s, he was one of Bill Clinton's favorite Republicans. He voted for family and medical leave, motor voter, national service, the Brady bill and the 1994 crime package, despite Vermont's anti-gun control sentiment. In July 1993, he announced he was supporting the not-yet-written Clinton health care plan—the only Republican member of Congress who ever did. As chairman of the Health, Education, Labor, and Pensions Committee from 1997 to June 2001—a post he got with help from Majority Leader Trent Lott—he promised not to hold up legislation backed by all other Republicans, but otherwise mostly voted with ranking Democrat Edward Kennedy. He did, however, take the lead on the Republican bill to allow worker-management consultation, vehemently opposed by labor unions. His bill to allow import of prescription drugs from other countries passed 74–21 in July 2000 and was ultimately signed. He was the principal Republican co-sponsor of hate crimes legislation and of the bill to ban discrimination because of sexual orientation; he supported the Vermont civil unions law.

What prompted Jeffords to switch parties? He later said he had pondered doing so off and on for 20 years; he was obviously out of line with most other Republicans on many issues. He made his announcement on May 24, 2001, and said though he would call himself an Independent, he would caucus with the Democrats; the new organizing resolution giving Democrats the majority leadership and majorities on committees was not passed until June. Precipitating the issue was the Bush tax cut. Jeffords's refusal to support the $1.6 trillion Bush tax cut left it one vote short in the Senate; the result was a $1.3 trillion cut, which Jeffords voted for even as he announced he was leaving the Republican Party. In his negotiations with the White House, he says he asked for and got a commitment to a $180 billion increase over 10 years for special education, a program for which he has great affection. Bush aides said he asked for $1.5 billion in a meeting April 3 with Bush, and got it, and then evidently decided that wasn't enough and demanded more. He may have been more disturbed by conservative columnists' reports of further White House retaliation, including possible opposition to the Northeast Dairy Compact, set to expire in September 2001, which gave New England dairy farmers far higher prices than those in the Midwest. Certainly he was attracted by the offer from then-Democratic Whip Harry Reid of the chairmanship of the Environment and Public Works Committee. At the time it was widely thought that Democrats would get a majority if and when 98-year-old Strom Thurmond died and was replaced by a Democrat (as it happened, Thurmond lived to celebrate his 100th birthday in December 2002 in the Senate); a chairmanship would presumably not be on offer to a switcher who only added to a Democratic majority. Jeffords's account, at the time and in his 2001 book *My Declaration of Independence*, was that he "had to be true to what I thought was right, and leave the consequences to sort themselves out."

The consequences did not sort themselves out entirely favorably for him. The Northeast Dairy Compact expired in September 2001. Jeffords and colleague Patrick Leahy cobbled together a national dairy compact in December 2001, which would fix prices paid by milk processors and subsidize dairy farmers when prices fell below a certain level, but they were never able to reach agreement with critical colleagues from Wisconsin and no separate bill passed. The farm bill passed in spring 2002 did provide retroactive MILC payments to farmers, but the first didn't arrive until October 2002, and in Vermont some labeled them "welfare." Jeffords, Patrick Leahy and Wisconsin's Herb Kohl tried in October 2004 to extend MILC payments beyond their September 2005 expiration date, but were not successful.

On the Environment Committee, Jeffords pressed for environmental causes, with varying success. His bills in 2001 to scale back carbon emissions to 1990 levels, and in 2002 to scale back emissions of various substances went nowhere. Since 2002 he has waged a fight for documents regarding EPA's rescission of the Clinton's administration's 1997 New Source Review regulation. In October 2003 he and committee Democrats boycotted hearings on EPA administrator nominee Mike Leavitt, but Leavitt was confirmed later in the month. In January 2004 he charged that the departure of an EPA enforcement official was part of "an ongoing exodus" of officials uncomfortable with administration decisions. In April 2004 he held up nominees for four EPA positions because of what he called administration stonewalling on the New Source Review documents; committee chairman Jim Inhofe co-signed his letter expressing "our commonly held position that the agency is obligated to respond to requests from the chair and ranking member." In May 2004 Jeffords and nine other senators filed a legal brief arguing that the administration acted illegally on New Source Review.

Jeffords has opposed various versions of the Republicans' energy bill and, with Barbara Boxer, called for reinstatement of the tax on oil and chemical industries to finance Superfund cleanups. In June 2004 Jeffords's amendment to remove lead pipes from schools failed by 10–9 and was replaced by an amendment by Mike Crapo which provided $40 million grants to schools and $20 million to the District of Columbia, which, astonishingly, was shown to have a problem with lead contamination.

As an Independent who caucuses and mostly votes with Democrats, Jeffords is probably better off politically in Vermont than as a Republican. In 1994 he beat a Democratic state senator by only a 50%–41% margin. In 2000 he beat state Auditor Ed Flanagan 66%–25%. Since his party switch, Jeffords has been a star attraction at Democratic fundraisers; he has declined to campaign against incumbent Republican senators, but has campaigned for Democrats in open seats. Jeffords's seat comes up in 2006, and in April 2005 he announced he would not run for reelection. The early frontrunner to replace Jeffords was Congressman Bernie Sanders, an Independent who nevertheless had considerable support for his candidacy from Democrats. Governor Jim Douglas was considered the strongest possible Republican candidate but he declined to run. Other Republicans mentioned were Lieutenant Governor Brian Dubie; IDX Corp. CEO Richard Tarrant; Greg Parke, a retired Air Force pilot who twice lost to Sanders; and Jack McMullen, the party's nominee against Senator Pat Leahy in 2004.

Representative-At-Large

Bernie Sanders (I)

Elected 1990, 8th term; b. Sept. 8, 1941, New York, NY; home, Burlington; U. of Chicago, B.A. 1964; Jewish; married (Jane).

Elected Office: Burlington Mayor, 1981–89.

Professional Career: Writer; Dir., Amer. People's History Soc.; Lecturer, Harvard U., 1989; Prof., Hamilton Col., 1989–90.

DC Office: 2233 RHOB, 20515, 202-225-4115; Fax: 202-225-6790; Web site: www.bernie.house.gov.

District Offices: Brattleboro, 802-254-8732; Burlington, 802-862-0697.

Committees: *Financial Services* (1st of 1 I): Domestic and International Monetary Policy, Trade & Technology; Housing & Community Opportunity, Financial Institutions and Consumer Credit (RMM). *Government Reform* (1st of 1 I): Criminal Justice, Drug Policy & Human Resources; National Security, Emerging Threats & International Relations.

Group Ratings

	ADA	ACLU	AFS	LCV	ITIC	NTU	COC	ACU	NTLC	CHC
2004	95	100	100	91	10	12	30	4	0	7
2003	100	—	100	90	—	28	14	9	—	—

National Journal Ratings

	2003 LIB	—	2003 CONS		2004 LIB	—	2004 CONS
Economic	85%	—	14%		70%	—	29%
Social	69%	—	30%		88%	—	0%
Foreign	94%	—	0%		85%	—	14%

Key Votes of the 108th Congress

1. Drilling in ANWR	N	5. DC School Vouchers	N	9. Ban Same-Sex Marriage	N
2. Approve Bush Tax Cuts	N	6. Ban Human Cloning	Y	10. Fund Iraq War	N
3. Medicare/Rx Bill	N	7. Restrict Gun Liability	Y	11. Bar Cuba Embargo Funds	Y
4. Bar Overtime Pay Regs.	Y	8. Ban Partial-Birth Abortion	N	12. Intelligence Reorg.	N

Election Results

2004 general	Bernie Sanders (I)	205,774	(67%)	($810,050)
	Greg Parke (R)	74,271	(24%)	($670,350)
	Larry Drown (D)	21,684	(7%)	
	Other	3,279	(1%)	
2004 primary	Bernie Sanders (I)	unopposed		
2002 general	Bernie Sanders (I)	144,880	(64%)	($622,639)
	William Meub (R)	72,813	(32%)	($184,845)
	Other	7,783	(3%)	

Prior Winning Percentages: 2000 (69%); 1998 (63%); 1996 (55%); 1994 (50%); 1992 (58%); 1990 (56%)

Vermont's single House member is Bernie Sanders, a Socialist elected as an Independent since 1990 but treated as a Democrat in the House. Sanders grew up in Flatbush, Brooklyn, the son of a paint salesman who had emigrated from Poland. "I know what it's like to live in a family without any money. Lack of money was a constant stress on my parents' relationship and in our household." He became involved in radical politics at the University of Chicago, then came to Vermont as part of the hippie invasion of 1968. His rumpled, tieless, sincere persona helped him win election as mayor of Burlington in 1981 by 10 votes, after losing four statewide races. In 1988, when Congressman Jim Jeffords ran for the Senate, Sanders ran for the House and lost to Republican Peter Smith. Two years later he ran again and reversed the result by capitalizing on Smith's support of the 1990 budget summit agreement and his vote for the ban on semiautomatic weapons. The National Rifle Association came out against Smith, and Sanders' opposition to gun control helped this urban-based Socialist carry 227 of Vermont's 251 cities and towns, plus three gores and one grant. Sanders became only the third Socialist elected to the House, after Victor Berger of Milwaukee (1911–13, 1923–29) and Meyer London of Manhattan's Lower East Side (1915–23). His views haven't changed much since his first election.

At first, Democrats balked at accepting him in their caucus, but they granted him seniority as a Democrat when he arrived in 1991; he became ranking minority member on a subcommittee in 1997 over the objections of Elijah Cummings and, when a Banking subcommittee ranking position opened up in November 1997, he got that over the claims of Carolyn Maloney. Sanders adds to a heavily liberal voting record his own particular stamp. He formed a Progressive Caucus, with 52 members in the 108th Congress, with what was at the time a quixotic agenda: progressive tax reform, a Canadian-style single-payer health care system, a 50% cut in military spending over five years, a national energy policy and—a Vermont touch—support for family farms.

But Sanders has also been a practical and sometimes successful legislator, gaining Republican allies in targeting what they consider corporate welfare. With Chris Smith of New Jersey, for example, he passed an amendment barring spending for defense contractor mergers ("payoffs for layoffs"). In February 2001 he proposed a $300 per person income tax rebate; this quickly became Democratic party policy, and Republicans in assembling majorities for the Bush tax cuts included it in diluted form—a $300 rebate for income-tax-paying adults. Sanders and Democrats noted ruefully, and accurately, that Bush claimed credit for a tax cutting proposal which was initially theirs and which Republicans for a time resisted.

As much as any member of Congress, he has made the cost of prescription drugs a national issue. Since the 1980s, he has called for government programs to pay for prescription drugs, and was the first member of Congress to lead bus trips to Canada to buy drugs there. He has denounced "the insatiable greed that consumes this runaway industry," and added, "The simple truth is that the pharmaceutical industry lies a lot." To its claim that it costs $800 million to get FDA approval of a drug, Sanders replies that it is more like $200 million. He has objected consistently when Clinton HHS Secretary Donna Shalala and her Bush successor Tommy Thompson ruled that they could not certify that reimported Canadian drugs are safe. He argues that the safety threat is nonexistent and adds that "those who swear on the altar of free trade" are happy to let U.S. consumers eat imported fruits, vegetables and meat.

On trade issues, Sanders in October 2003 called for repeal of the 2000 Permanent Normal Trade Relations with China. "American workers should not be asked and forced to compete against Chinese workers who work for 30, 40, 50 cents an hour, who can't form unions, where there is no environmental protection." By December 2003 he had 15 Republicans as well as 42 Democrats as co-sponsors. Sanders wouldn't stop there. He has called for repeal of NAFTA as well as PNTR and for a moratorium on Free Trade Agreements. After a trip to Mexico, he reported to readers of *The Nation*, "We encountered horrendous poverty, environmental degradation and a lawless and corrupt environment." He argues that workers in both the United States and in foreign nations would be better off without free trade agreements. In 2004 Sanders sponsored an amendment to prohibit the ExImBank to lend to companies who laid off more workers at home than overseas, though an aide admitted there were no numbers available on foreign layoffs. He was more successful on a July 2004 amendment to prohibit the ExImBank from loaning to companies that move their headquarters to foreign countries; that passed the House by the impressive vote of 270–132.

Sanders has been a critic of the Patriot Act and has focused on Section 215 which permits government investigators to obtain business records including those of library and bookstore patrons after obtaining an order from an intelligence court. In July 2004 his amendment to repeal 215 was defeated on a tie vote only after the Republican leadership held the roll call open for 20 minutes and convinced 10 Republicans to change their votes. Sanders said he will pursue this cause when the Patriot Act comes up for reauthorization in 2005.

As Vermont's sole representative, Sanders was naturally the House's leading backer of the Northeast Dairy Compact, which propped up Northeast dairy prices. After the Compact expired in September 2001, his bill to establish a national dairy compact passed the House but was killed in conference committee when Vermonters were unable to come up with a version acceptable to Midwestern dairy states. Dismayed at conservative domination of talk radio, he started his own one-hour Monday talk show on WDEV in Waterbury in 2003, and he was interviewed for the movie "Outfoxed."

Just once has Sanders been seriously challenged for reelection. In 1994, after voting for the assault weapons ban and the crime bill with its gun control provisions, Sanders was opposed by the National Rifle Association-backed Vermont Sportsmen's Coalition. Sanders outspent state Senator John Carroll, but won by only 50%–47%. His Republican opponent in 2004 ran a radio ad calling him "Crazy Bernie" and saying, "Bernie loves long walks on the beach with child pornographers and pedophiles, candlelight dinners with illegal aliens and cozy evenings by the fire with al Qaeda terrorists." Republican Lieutenant Governor Brian Dubie denounced the ad and it ran for only one day. Sanders won 67%–24%, with 7% for a Democratic nominee who obviously had no support from Vermont's Democratic party.

Sanders twice gave serious consideration to running for Senate against Jeffords; when Jeffords announced in April 2005 that he would not run for another term in 2006, Sanders became the early frontrunner. By June, he had been endorsed by many Vermont Democrats, including former Governor Phil Hoff, Burlington Mayor Peter Clavelle, Senate President Pro Tempore Peter Welch and House Speaker Gaye Symington.

★ VIRGINIA ★

Traditions endure in Virginia. Through nearly 400 years of history, Virginians have honored, and sometimes been fixated by, traditions going back to the Revolution and before. For the last half-century, Virginia has been growing lustily, in the first years after World War II thanks mainly to government, in recent years thanks more to a vibrant private sector, but the first state in the nation to elect a black governor still hews to a course close to its roots. The first Virginia was a commonwealth ruled by a landed gentry that was, in the words of historian David Hackett Fischer, "elitist and libertarian." From the tobacco-growing counties emerged in the 1770s a group of leaders—George Washington, George Mason, Patrick Henry, Thomas Jefferson, Richard Henry Lee, James Madison—who in learning, wisdom and strength of character, equal any such group from any similarly sized polity since Periclean Athens or republican Rome. They were slaveholders who insisted on liberty, armed men living on the marches of civilization who insisted on the rule of law, believers in racial inequality who set forth principles of equality that would in time form the basis of a non-racist society. The Virginia they led into the American Revolution was not only the most populous and the richest of the 13 colonies, it also was the indispensable creator of the Republic and the Constitution that has held together the world's greatest democracy.

After the Revolutionary War, gentry control continued even as Virginia was eclipsed in population and wealth by Pennsylvania and New York and, its tobacco fields, all but exhausted, became a breeding ground for slavery. But Virginia had two more great heroes, Robert E. Lee and Stonewall Jackson, both of whom reluctantly and brilliantly fought for their state rather than their country. The state's leadership class was impoverished and embittered by the Civil War, so much of which was fought on Virginia soil. Industrialization was haphazard: Railroads were constructed to ship cotton up from the South and coal east to the seaports; textile mills were built in Southside towns and tobacco factories in Richmond; the giant Newport News Shipbuilding & Drydock Company was built by railroad magnate Collis Huntington. Politically, Virginia was ruled by a local gentry who worshipped their Revolutionary past and mourned their Lost Cause. They were pessimists, looking not for economic growth but for stability, bent on maintaining Virginia's segregation and content with its second-class economy. County courthouse organizations became the political machine of Harry Byrd, who ran Virginia politics from 1925, when he was elected governor, until 1965, when he retired from the Senate. In national politics, this machine lost battles more often than Lee lost on the battlefield, and less gallantly. For years the machine succeeded in keeping most vestiges of the welfare state and racial equality out of Virginia, to the point of closing public schools in the 1950s rather than obeying federal court desegregation orders.

This "massive resistance" collapsed in the late 1950s; Virginia's demographics changed and it went through a quarter-century of political flux. The government-employee filled northern Virginia suburbs of Washington D.C. and the industrial Tidewater region around Norfolk and Newport News, plus the enfranchisement of blacks, provided a political base for liberal Democrats. But they were never quite a majority. In the 1970s, conservatives who left the Democratic Party and ran as independents or Republicans held them at bay. In the 1980s, three moderate Democrats were elected governor—Charles Robb in 1981, Gerald Baliles in 1985, Douglas Wilder in 1989—because they no longer represented an attempt to impose a labor-liberal agenda on an unwilling Virginia, and because they argued they could use government effectively to improve education and build Virginia's economy. Wilder's election was a national breakthrough, a successful attempt by a black politician to campaign and govern on equal terms. His fiscal conservatism, which resulted in sharp spending cuts in the early 1990s, like his elegant manners and thick Richmond accent, echoes Virginia's elitist and libertarian tradition; his insistence on the rule of law helped him win election as Richmond's mayor in 2004.

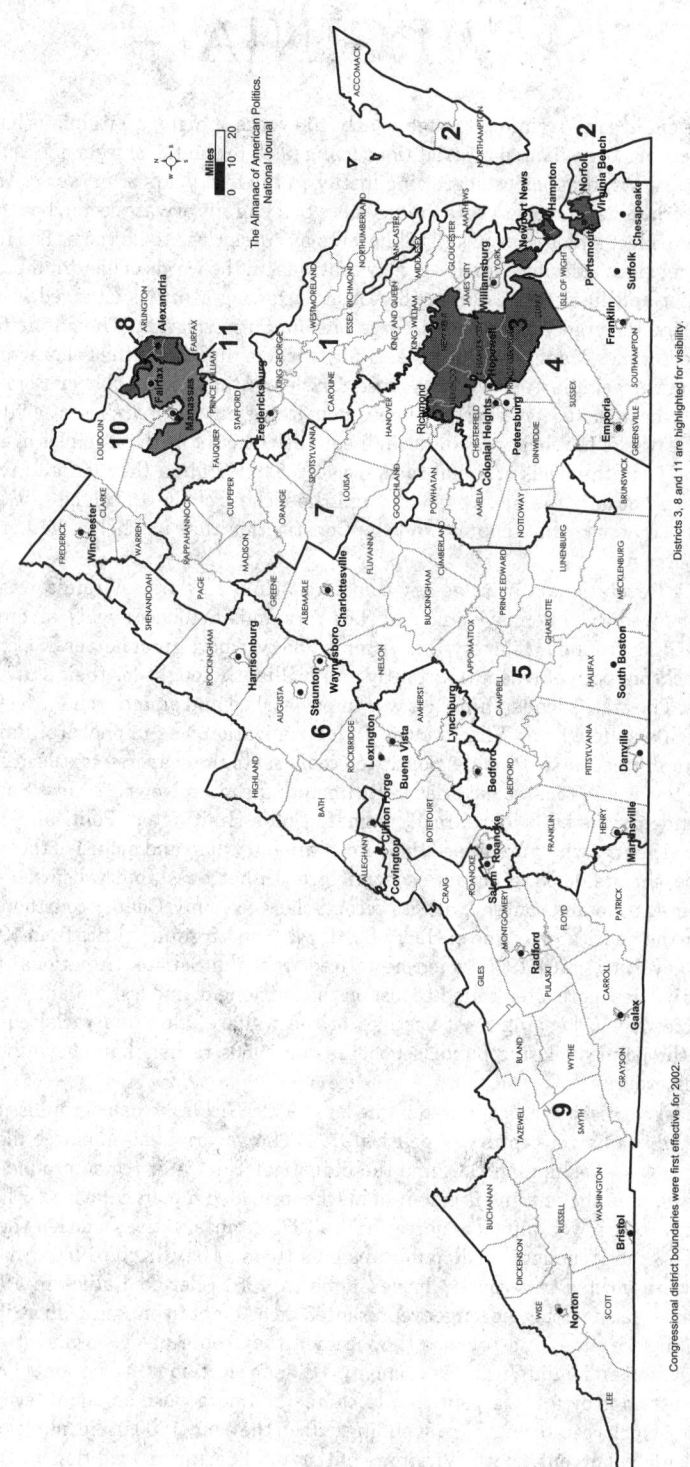

The Almanac of American Politics.
National Journal

Miles
0 10 20

Districts 3, 8 and 11 are highlighted for visibility.

Congressional district boundaries were first effective for 2002.

In the 1990s, Virginia developed ideological politics along party lines, and Republicans made historic strides by winning majorities with traditional party platforms. George Allen was elected governor by a wide margin in 1993 as a Republican who believed in lower taxes, traditional cultural values, longer prison terms, and teaching basic skills—he combined confrontational issue positions with a sunny temperament. In the 1997 contest for governor (Virginia is the last state which limits its governors to one term, another tradition that endures), Republican James Gilmore made his centerpiece issue the phasing out of the property tax on automobiles, and won a 56%–43% victory over Democrat Don Beyer. Republicans for the first time swept the top three statewide offices. In 1999 Gilmore led Republicans to legislative majorities in both chambers for the first time ever.

His successor was a Democrat, cell phone millionaire Mark Warner, who won in 2001 primarily due to an intensive 18-month campaign in rural Virginia—paying attention to the parts of the state not blessed by 1990s growth. This was not a victory for liberalism: Warner won 52%–47% and Democrat Timothy Kaine beat a very conservative Republican for lieutenant governor by 50%–48%, while Republican Jerry Kilgore was elected attorney general by 60%–40% and Republicans, helped by a partisan redistricting plan, swept to a 64–36 majority in the House of Delegates. In 2002 Warner cut state spending sharply; in 2004, he persuaded the Republican legislature to raise taxes by a record amount, yielding once again surpluses as the economic boom returned. In 2005 Virginia votes again for governor; the contenders are Kaine and Kilgore. The winner will preside in Thomas Jefferson's classic Capitol building, rewired for the Internet, in time to celebrate the 400th anniversary of the landing in Jamestown, and to celebrate that a state which was once rigidly segregated is now a multiethnic commonwealth.

The People

Pop. 2004 (est):	7,459,827			
Pop. 2000:	7,078,515			
Pop. 1990:	6,187,358			
Change 1990–2000:	Up 14.4%			
% of U.S. total:	2.5%			
Pop. rank:	12th of 50			
Area size:	42,774 sq. mi.			
State Native:	51.9%			
Non-citizen:	4.8%			

Race/Ethnic Origin

4,965,637	70.2%	White
1,376,378	19.4%	Black
259,277	3.7%	Asian
18,596	0.3%	Native Am.
3,380	0.0%	Hawaiian
114,022	1.6%	Two+ races
11,685	0.2%	Other
329,540	4.7%	Hisp. Origin

Military veterans: 786,359 (14.7%)

WWII: 14.1%	Korea: 10.5%
Vietnam: 35.4%	Gulf War: 16.8%

Most populous cities (2003):
1. Virginia Beach 439,467
2. Norfolk 241,727
3. Chesapeake 210,834
4. Richmond 194,729
5. Newport News 181,200

Language

English: 87.3%	Spanish: 5.2%
Other Eur.: 4.0%	

Ancestry

German: 9.5%	USA: 9.2%
English: 9.0%	Irish: 7.9%
Italian: 2.9%	

Urban population: 73.0%
Rural population: 27.0%

Education

H.S. Grad:	81.5%
College Grad:	29.5%

Industry

Agri: 1.3%		Con: 7.3%	
Fin: 6.6%		Info: 3.8%	
Mfg: 16.0%		Prof: 29.9%	
Public: 8.3%		Trade: 14.2%	
Other: 12.6%			

Occupation

Blue collar: 22.1%	White collar: 63.7%
Gray collar: 14.2%	

Work Sector

Private: 74.7%	Govt: 19.6%
Self: 5.5%	Family: 0.2%
Unemployment: 4.1%	

Household Income

<15k: 13.2%	15-35k: 23.5%
35-50k: 16.5%	50-100k: 31.7%
100-150k: 9.4%	>150k: 5.7%
Median: $46,677	
Poverty status: 9.6%	

Home Value

<50k: 10.6%	50-100k: 30.2%	100-200k: 37.4%	200-300k: 12.9%
300-500k: 6.7%	>500k: 2.3%	Median: $118,800	

General Assembly

Senate	24 R 16 D
House of Del.	60 R 38 D 2 I

Legislative Term Limits: No

Registered Voters
No party registration

Presidential politics   Virginia remains one of the more Republican states in presidential races, but not as solidly Republican as it once was. In 1996, Bill Clinton lost here by only 48%–46%. In 2000, George W. Bush won by 52%–44%. In 2004 Democrats, heartened by Mark Warner's victory in the 2001 governor election, targeted the state early; John Kerry spent $1 million in advertising here in the spring and early summer. But in August the polls showed Bush well ahead, and Virginia dropped off the target list. Bush carried the state by a seemingly comfortable margin, 54%–45%. But compared to 2000, he lost ground in Northern Virginia, which he lost 53%–46%, and failed to improve his margin in the Richmond area (55%–44%). He widened his margin in the Hampton Roads area (53%–46%) and, most impressively, in the rest of Virginia (60%–40%). Virginia could be a target state in the future. Until 2000, Virginia's national convention delegates were chosen at state conventions, but Republicans held an open primary in

2004 Presidential Vote		
Bush (R)	1,716,959	(54%)
Kerry (D)	1,454,742	(45%)
Badnarik (Lib)	11,032	(0%)
Other	15,634	(0%)

2004 Democratic Presidential Primary		
Kerry (D)	204,129	(52%)
Edwards (D)	105,489	(27%)
Clark (D)	36,566	(9%)
Dean (D)	27,634	(7%)
Sharpton (D)	12,863	(3%)
Other	9,500	(2%)

2000 Presidential Vote		
Bush (R)	1,437,490	(52%)
Gore (D)	1,217,290	(44%)
Nader (Green)	59,398	(2%)
Other	25,269	(1%)

2000, in which Bush took 53% of the vote to John McCain's 44%. In 2003, Virginia moved the presidential primary to February 2004, in order to gain the attention of presidential candidates and the national media; it was held February 10, two weeks after New Hampshire and on the same day as Tennessee. Wesley Clark concentrated on Tennessee and John Edwards spent time in Tennessee and southwest Virginia. They may have thought that Kerry had an insuperable lead in Northern Virginia; as it turned out Kerry carried every part of the state and won 52% of the votes, to 27% for Edwards and 9% for Clark.

Congressional districting   Republicans won control of both houses of the Virginia legislature in 1999 and, with Republican Jim Gilmore as governor, controlled the redistricting process in 2001 for the first time ever. Republican legislators promptly drew new lines, which made relatively minimal changes. They moved some black precincts from the 4th District to the 3d and increased its black majority while making the 4th more secure. They followed the wishes of the three Northern Virginia incumbents, two Republicans and one Democrat, who all strengthened themselves. They made the 9th District, held by Democrat Rick Boucher, a little more Republican, but it would have been difficult to do otherwise without drawing a geographical monstrosity. Bobby Scott of the black-majority 3d District raised questions about the 3d and 4th District lines, but the Justice Department approved the plan, and a lawsuit challenging the plan was dismissed in September 2004.

109th Congress Lineup	
8 R	3 D

108th Congress Lineup	
8 R	3 D

Governor

Mark Warner (D)

Elected 2001, term expires Jan. 2006, 1st term; b. Dec. 15, 1954, India-napolis, IN; home, Alexandria; George Washington U., B.A., 1977; Harvard U., J.D., 1980; Presbyterian; married (Lisa).

Professional Career: Fundraiser, DNC, 1980–82; Venture capitalist, 1982–89; Mng. Dir., Columbia Capital Corp., 1989–2001; Chairman, VA Democratic Party, 1993–95.

Office: State Capitol, Richmond, 23219, 804-786-2211; Fax: 804-371-6351; Web site: www.governor.state.va.us.

Election Results

2001 general	Mark Warner (D)	984,177	(52%)
	Mark Earley (R)	887,234	(47%)
2001 primary	Mark Warner (D)	unopposed	
1997 general	Jim Gilmore (R)	969,062	(56%)
	Don Beyer (D)	738,971	(43%)
	Sue Harris DeBauche (I)	25,777	(2%)

Mark Warner was elected governor of Virginia in 2001, the first Democrat to be elected since 1989, when Warner managed Douglas Wilder's successful campaign. Warner was born in India-napolis and moved to Hartford, Connecticut in the 8th grade. He was the first in his family to graduate from college, from George Washington University in 1977; then he graduated from Harvard Law School in 1980. After law school he worked in the fundraising office of the Democratic National Committee. There, former Congressman Tom McMillen told him about the potential of cell phone markets just as the Reagan administration was about to award almost 1,500 free licenses for metropolitan cell phone markets. Warner cobbled together investor groups and packaged their applications in exchange for a fee and a 5% ownership stake if they received the licenses. He made millions; his net worth in 2001 was estimated at $200 million.

In 1989, the same year he managed Wilder's campaign, Warner set up Columbia Capital, a venture capital fund which provided financing for more than 70 telecommunications and infor-mation technology firms, many of which went public; the best known is Nextel. From 1993 to 1995, he served as Virginia Democratic chairman. In 1996, he ran against Republican Senator John Warner (no relation) and spent $10 million of his own money on the campaign; he ran well throughout the state and held the Republican Warner to a 52%–47% margin, his closest since his first election in 1978. Over the next several years, Warner put millions into philanthropic efforts and set up four regional small business investment funds in Southwest Virginia, Southside Virginia, metro Richmond and Hampton Roads. By 1999, it was plain that Warner was going to run for governor in 2001. With no experience in elected office, he presented himself as an entrepreneur who could bring business methods to government.

Warner picked a good year to run. In 1993 and 1997, Republicans George Allen and Jim Gilmore had been elected governor by advancing popular proposals which their Democratic opponents opposed—Allen called for an end to parole and Gilmore for elimination of the car tax. In 2000, Allen was elected to the Senate, but Gilmore spent much of the year battling the Republican-controlled General Assembly over the budget; revenues were coming in lower than expected, and Gilmore wanted to keep phasing out the car tax. In 2000 and 2001, the two Republicans elected to downballot offices in 1997—Lieutenant Governor John Hager and Attor-ney General Mark Earley—were battling each other for the Republican nomination for governor. Against this background, Warner called for an end to old-style politics, regional divisions, partisan bickering and personal attacks. Earley won the June primary, but had little money and no clear campaign strategy—no bold proposal like Allen's in 1993 or Gilmore's in 1997. Warner had plenty of money: He ultimately spent $5 million of his own money on the campaign, but used his finely honed talents at fundraising to raise more in Virginia and around the nation.

Nor would Warner, who lives in a restored mansion in Alexandria's beautiful Old Town, be tabbed as an urban liberal. He called himself a "fiscal conservative" and pledged not to raise the income or sales taxes. Responding to complaints from traffic-choked Northern Virginia, he called for regional referendums on local sales tax increases: This pleased business interests and local legislators who feared congestion would stop growth and propitiated tax opponents who felt they would get a chance to vote no. He opposed any new gun control laws and wooed the National Rifle Association, which remained neutral—a victory for a Democrat. He ran ads featuring old pickup trucks and bluegrass music. He sponsored a NASCAR race truck. He traveled to all parts of rural Virginia, showing that this rich entrepreneur was in touch with folks and reminding them of his investment funds and his philanthropic initiatives. In October, Earley came out against the regional referendum, but this evidently hurt him with both sides: The businessmen and legislators were angry at him for opposing their project, while some tax opponents outside Northern Virginia thought it made a statewide tax increase more likely. Earley's ads were on hot-button issues like taxes and abortion, but Warner had inoculated himself on taxes and Earley's opposition to abortion put off some suburban Republicans.

The surprise is not that Warner won, but that he won by a small margin, 52%–47%, a reversal of the numbers in his 1996 Senate race. That time Warner had lost narrowly each of the major regions of the state; this time by narrow margins he carried them all. He carried Northern Virginia 54%–46% and the Hampton Roads region 53%–47%. He did well in the Richmond suburbs and carried metro Richmond 51%–48%. And in the part of Virginia outside the metro areas, he carried dozens of rural counties that national Democrats usually lose. Al Gore had won only 41% in this region the year before; Warner carried it 51%–48%, losing badly only in the Shenandoah Valley but carrying Southside and Southwest Virginia.

Once in office, Warner had to cope with unpleasant fiscal realities. Warner got the legislature to approve November 2002 transportation tax referenda in Northern Virginia and in Hampton Roads, but the House of Delegates killed his education initiative in March 2002. As the budget shortfall kept growing, Warner continued to rule out a tax increase, cut $858 million in spending and laid off 1,800 state employees. Meanwhile, opinion was moving against the tax increases in Northern Virginia and Hampton Roads. They were opposed by tax opponents who argued that the politicians would just shuffle the money around and by "smart growth" advocates, environmentally-minded activists who argued that more highways just meant more growth and more traffic congestion. In November 2002, Northern Virginia voted 55%–45% against the referendum and Hampton Roads rejected it by 62%–38%. These are not two insignificant areas: Together they cast a majority of the state's votes. Warner said the results showed a "sobering" mistrust of politicians. The prospect was for a battle for scarce highway dollars between the traffic-choked suburbs and rural areas. In 2003 Warner pushed through a budget balanced by one-time financial maneuvers that suggested that more fiscal troubles lay ahead.

In November 2003, after the legislative elections and when Virginia seemed to be in danger of losing its AAA bond rating, Warner presented his new fiscal plan, a $1 billion tax increase, with increases in the income, sales and cigarette taxes and reductions in taxes on those with lower incomes and in the car and food taxes. He argued that state government needed the revenue and that under his plan 65% of Virginians would pay less. In February this was rejected in the heavily Republican House of Delegates, which increased taxes by just $520 million and provided few spending increases. But the Republican state Senate, led by Finance Committee Chairman John Chichester, passed a $3.8 billion tax increase, with $1.7 billion in new spending for schools and $1.6 billion for transportation. Speaker William Howell was obdurate, but unable to hold his Republicans in line: 17 Republican delegates abandoned their anti-tax position. By April a conclusion was reached. The state Senate agreed to a $1.3 billion tax increase, more than Warner had requested, and the House went along. Warner had gotten his program through a Republican legislature.

By December 2004 the fiscal picture looked quite different. State government was facing a $1.2 billion surplus. Warner called for spending $32 million to offset state employees' health insurance premiums, $200 million more for Medicaid, $70 million to cover cost overruns in college construction; some $374 million of the $824 million in transportation spending was to come from the surplus. Howell called for a cut in the food tax and an end to accelerated collection of sales tax revenues. After his victory on taxes, Warner sought a bigger national profile. He became chairman of the National Governors Association, urged John Kerry's campaign to target Virginia and told other Democrats how he had managed to win support in rural areas and among voters with traditional values. In November 2004 he renewed his call, rejected by the legislature in February 2003, for a constitutional amendment to allow future governors to serve two terms.

Warner is ineligible to run for reelection. He has been mentioned as a possible presidential candidate on occasion, and more often as a possible opponent to Senator George Allen in 2006; in early 2005 he was giving no indication of whether he would run for either office.

Virginia votes for governor in November 2005, and the nominees were Democratic Lieutenant Governor Timothy Kaine, a former mayor of Richmond, who won 50%–48% in 2001, and Republican Attorney General Jerry Kilgore, a former federal and state prosecutor, who won 60%–40% in 2001. Kaine seemed primed to run on a platform of expanding educational and economic opportunities; he was prepared to run on Warner's record. Kilgore, from Scott County in Southwest Virginia, opposed tax increases during the 2004 controversy and argued they were unnecessary. He promised to use Kaine's positions on cultural issues against him and reminded voters that Kaine was an ACLU lawyer.

Senior Senator

John Warner (R)

Elected 1978, seat up 2008, 5th term; b. Feb. 18, 1927, Washington, D.C.; home, Alexandria; Washington & Lee U., B.S., 1949, U. of VA, LL.B. 1953; Episcopalian; married (Jeanne Vander Myde).

Military Career: Navy, 1944–46 (WWII), Marine Corps, 1950–52 (Korea).

Professional Career: Law Clerk, U.S. Court of Appeals, Chief Judge Barrett Prettyman, 1953–54; Practicing atty., 1954–56, 1960–69; Asst. U.S. Atty., 1956–60; U.S. Navy, Undersecy., 1969–72, U.S. Navy, Secy., 1972–74; Dir., Amer. Rev. Bicentennial Comm., 1974–76.

DC Office: 225 RSOB, 20510, 202-224-2023; Fax: 202-224-6295; Web site: warner.senate.gov.

State Offices: Abingdon, 276-628-8158; Midlothian, 804-739-0247; Norfolk, 757-441-3079; Roanoke, 540-857-2676.

Committees: *Armed Services* (Chmn.). *Environment & Public Works*: Fisheries, Wildlife & Water; Superfund & Waste Management; Transportation & Infrastructure. *Homeland Security & Governmental Affairs*: Federal Financial Management, Govt. Information & International Security; Investigations (Permanent); Oversight of Govt. Management, the Federal Workforce & the District of Columbia.

Group Ratings

	ADA	ACLU	AFS	LCV	ITIC	NTU	COC	ACU	NTLC	CHC
2004	25	11	0	0	100	68	100	72	93	83
2003	10	—	11	11	—	74	100	80	—	—

National Journal Ratings

	2003 LIB	—	2003 CONS		2004 LIB	—	2004 CONS
Economic	0%	—	82%		36%	—	63%
Social	44%	—	55%		52%	—	47%
Foreign	22%	—	68%		0%	—	67%

Key Votes of the 108th Congress

1. Ban Drilling in ANWR	N	5. Energy Bill	Y	9. Ban Same-Sex Marriage	Y
2. Approve Bush Tax Cuts	Y	6. Support Roe v. Wade	Y	10. Ban Bunker-Buster Bomb	N
3. Medicare/Rx Bill	Y	7. Ban Partial-Birth Abortion	Y	11. Fund Iraq War	Y
4. Bar Overtime Pay Regs.	N	8. Assault Weapons Ban	Y	12. Restrict Missile Defense	N

Election Results

2002 general	John Warner (R)	1,229,893	(83%)	($1,709,202)
	Nancy Spannaus (I)	145,102	(10%)	($61,984)
	Jacob Hornberger (I)	106,055	(7%)	($66,480)
2002 primary	John Warner (R)	unopposed		
1996 general	John Warner (R)	1,235,744	(52%)	($5,819,157)
	Mark Warner (D)	1,115,982	(47%)	($11,600,424)

Prior Winning Percentages: 1990 (81%); 1984 (70%); 1978 (50%)

John Warner, first elected in 1978, is the chairman of the Senate Armed Services Committee. He grew up in Washington, D.C., with Virginia roots; his grandparents lived in Amherst County, Virginia. His father was a field surgeon in World War I; a great-uncle served in the Confederate Army and lost his arm in the Battle of the Wilderness. Warner volunteered for both the Army and Navy in 1944, at 17; the Navy snapped him up first. (There are only five World War II veterans left in the Senate: Ted Stevens, Daniel Inouye, Daniel Akaka, Frank Lautenberg, John Warner; 45 of the 100 senators were born after World War II ended). Warner went to college at Washington & Lee and then interrupted his years at the University of Virginia law school when he volunteered to serve in the Marine Corps in Korea. He worked as an assistant U.S. attorney and then practiced law in Washington and had a house in the horse country in Middleburg, Virginia. During the Nixon administration, he was Secretary of the Navy and negotiated with the Soviets the Incidents at Sea Executive Agreement, still in effect and a model often imitated. From 1974 to 1976 he headed the American Revolution Bicentennial Commission. He ran for the Senate in 1978 with few political assets other than his then-wife, Elizabeth Taylor. Finishing second at the huge Republican state convention, he graciously supported winner Richard Obenshain; then, when Obenshain died in a plane crash, Republican leaders reluctantly named Warner to fill his place. Warner won the general over Democrat Andrew Miller by a 4,721-vote margin and was easily re-elected in 1984, 1990 and 2002. He had serious competition only in 1996 from now-Governor Mark Warner (no relation) and won 52%–47%.

Warner can be grandiloquent and showy, yet he works hard on important issues and has shown steadfastness in his beliefs. Warner has been chairman of the Armed Services Committee since January 1999, when the more senior Strom Thurmond stepped down, except for the 18 months when Democrats had a Senate majority. For years on the committee he had worked closely with Democratic chairman Sam Nunn; but he opposed Nunn and led the fight in 1991 for the Gulf War resolution, which passed by only 52–47. Warner made harsh criticisms of Clinton administration defense policy. He had supported previous rounds of base closings, but after Bill Clinton's politically-motivated tampering with the 1995 round of closings, he voted against another round in May 1999, saying, "Politics have destroyed the credibility of the process for closing bases." But in 2003 he foiled House Armed Services Chairman Duncan Hunter's attempt to postpone the 2005 base-closing round, and when asked to protect Virginia's Fort Monroe said, "There's nothing the law allows me to do. And I happen to be one who abides by the law. The concept of the BRAC process is to get Congress out—O-U-T—out of the business." In May 2005, Fort Monroe made the Pentagon's proposed closure list. Warner voted against the Comprehensive Test Ban Treaty in October 1999, arguing that it was impossible to monitor Russian compliance. He opposed NATO expansion and was wary of U.S. troop commitments in the Balkans.

Warner has shown some prescience about problems others did not discern. In 1999, he created a new Emerging Threats Subcommittee to focus on terrorism, chemical and biological warfare and cyberwarfare. He strongly backs missile defense and in June 2004 sponsored an amendment to require the Pentagon to develop criteria for real-life operational missile tests by February 2005 and to begin testing no later than October 2005. In a secret markup session in May 2000, he got approval of five new nuclear submarines of the Virginia class—a major increase in the submarine fleet. In June 2004, over the opposition of Appropriations Chairman Ted Stevens, he got reinstatement of $140 million for a future carrier and $110 million for a carrier refueling project. The evening of September 11 he appeared at a press conference with Defense Secretary Donald Rumsfeld and the Joint Chiefs at the Pentagon. Defense authorization bills usually pass with bipartisan support, but in May 2002 he voted against the bill because Democrats led by Chairman Carl Levin shifted $812 million away from missile defense; his opposition, plus a Bush veto threat, got the Democrats to back down. Shipbuilding is a major Warner interest, and much of it is done at Virginia's Newport News Shipbuilding & Drydock. Warner put into the 2002 defense bill $229 million to keep on schedule the $10 billion CVNX aircraft carrier to be built at Newport News; this is a transformational ship, with a new nuclear plant and electromagnetic catapults to hurl planes into flight. Warner sponsored the Iraq war resolution in October 2002. "We cannot let the United Nations think in any way that they can veto the authority of this president or the ability of this nation to defend itself." He continued to support the Iraq effort as others questioned it. After Richard Lugar and Chuck Hagel criticized Bush policy in September 2004, Warner said, "I looked at those remarks and I looked at what our president has done and what he is trying to do today, and I'm solidly in the Bush corner."

But Warner has not been uncritical of the military. In May 2004 he held widely publicized hearings on the Abu Ghraib prison scandal and put Rumsfeld under oath, despite criticism from Hunter ("the Senate has been mesmerized by cameras") and committee member Jim Inhofe. "This is as serious a problem of breakdown in discipline as I've ever observed," Warner said. Warner backed the administration plan to buy KC-767 refueling tankers from Boeing and, with Levin, in October 2003 proposed to lease 20 and buy 80, to solve a budgetary problem. But after Boeing was caught in scandal he and Levin withdrew their support in March 2004. In July 2004 Warner declared his flat-out opposition to a military draft and in December 2004, when many conservatives were attacking Rumsfeld, he said, "We should not at this point in time entertain any idea of changing those responsibilities in the Pentagon." Warner differed with the 9/11 Commission's conclusion that intelligence oversight was "dysfunctional" and fought unsuccessfully to limit the authority of the new national intelligence director over the military.

Warner's voting record is moderately conservative and sometimes liberal on cultural issues. He has voted for government funding of abortions in some cases, but favors parental consent laws and the partial-birth abortion ban. He voted for the Brady gun control bill; in February 2004 he co-sponsored renewal of the assault weapons ban and opposed the measure protecting gun manufacturers from lawsuits hold them responsible for crimes committed with their products. He put a hate crimes provision in the 2004 defense authorization. Representing a state that still has a large number of public employees, he favors higher federal pay and supported repeal of the Hatch Act. He led the bipartisan Virginia-Maryland delegation and in October 2000 raised the federal funding of the Woodrow Wilson Bridge across the Potomac to $1.5 billion and in October 2003 obtained $500 million to clean up military bases damaged by Hurricane Isabel. Warner owns a house in Cape Cod, near Edward Kennedy's, and in October 2004 sent a note to the Army Corps of Engineers expressing "concern" about the wind farms proposed on Nantucket Sound.

For a time in the 1990s, Warner seemed to be in a war with many Virginia Republicans. In 1993, he refused to endorse lieutenant governor candidate Michael Farris, the leader of the national home schooling movement, and in 1994 he announced he could not support Senate nominee Oliver North, whose conviction on Iran-Contra charges was overturned on the grounds of inadmissibility of some critical evidence. In the 1994 Senate race Warner backed independent (and twice Republican gubernatorial candidate) Marshall Coleman, and many blamed Warner for North's narrow loss to Charles Robb. Farris and North backers hoped to deny Warner renomination in 1996 at the gigantic Virginia Republican state convention. But Warner invoked a Virginia law that entitled him to insist on a primary. There he defeated James Miller, budget director under President Ronald Reagan and North's opponent at the 1994 convention, by 66%–34%. In the general election, against former Democratic state chairman and now-Governor Mark Warner, John Warner called himself a "common sense conservative" and, citing seniority, said, "Virginia's got an investment in me." Warner was reelected, but only narrowly, 52%–47%.

In 2002, by contrast, he had no serious opposition. Republicans had mostly forgotten Farris and North. Democrats were content not to run a candidate. Mark Warner, now governor, called John Warner "a great guy and a great senator." For his part, Senator Warner joined Governor Warner in campaigning for passage of the November 2002 transportation tax referenda in Northern Virginia and Hampton Roads. The referenda were defeated, but John Warner was reelected with 83% of the vote. In February 2004 he supported Governor Warner's proposed tax increase. "Politics be damned! Let's consider what's best for the men and women of this great state and their families and children."

Virginia has elected 51 men to the United States Senate, and Warner has served longer than all but one of them. He passed the record of Carter Glass in April 2005 and, if he is elected to another term, will pass Harry Byrd Sr. in September 2011.

Junior Senator

George Allen (R)

Elected 2000, seat up 2006, 1st term; b. Mar. 8, 1952, Whittier, CA; home, Earlysville; U. of VA, B.A. 1974, J.D. 1977; Presbyterian; married (Susan).

Elected Office: VA House of Delegates, 1982–91; U.S. House of Reps., 1991–92; VA Gov., 1993–97.

Professional Career: Practicing atty., 1977–91, 1998–99.

DC Office: 204 RSOB, 20510, 202-224-4024; Fax: 202-224-5432; Web site: allen.senate.gov.

State Offices: Abingdon, 276-676-2646; Herndon, 703-435-0039; Richmond, 804-771-2221; Roanoke, 540-772-4236; Virginia Beach, 757-518-1674.

Committees: *NRSC Chairman. Commerce, Science & Transportation*: Aviation; Consumer Affairs, Product Safety & Insurance (Chmn.); Science & Space; Surface Transportation & Merchant Marine; Technology, Innovation & Competitiveness; Trade, Tourism & Economic Development. *Energy & Natural Resources*: Energy; National Parks; Public Lands & Forests. *Foreign Relations*: East Asian & Pacific Affairs; European Affairs (Chmn.); International Operations & Terrorism; Western Hemisphere, Peace Corps & Narcotics Affairs. *Small Business & Entrepreneurship.*

Group Ratings

	ADA	ACLU	AFS	LCV	ITIC	NTU	COC	ACU	NTLC	CHC
2004	15	0	14	0	100	67	100	92	90	100
2003	5	—	0	0	—	76	100	85	—	—

National Journal Ratings

	2003 LIB	—	2003 CONS		2004 LIB	—	2004 CONS
Economic	0%	—	82%		31%	—	65%
Social	0%	—	59%		19%	—	71%
Foreign	0%	—	78%		0%	—	67%

Key Votes of the 108th Congress

1. Ban Drilling in ANWR	N	5. Energy Bill	Y	9. Ban Same-Sex Marriage	Y
2. Approve Bush Tax Cuts	Y	6. Support Roe v. Wade	N	10. Ban Bunker-Buster Bomb	N
3. Medicare/Rx Bill	Y	7. Ban Partial-Birth Abortion	Y	11. Fund Iraq War	Y
4. Bar Overtime Pay Regs.	N	8. Assault Weapons Ban	N	12. Restrict Missile Defense	N

Election Results

2000 general	George Allen (R)	1,420,460	(52%)	($9,995,980)
	Charles S. Robb (D)	1,296,093	(48%)	($6,610,252)
2000 primary	George Allen (R)	unopposed		
1994 general	Charles S. Robb (D)	938,376	(46%)	($5,501,697)
	Oliver L. (Ollie) North (R)	882,213	(43%)	($20,607,367)
	J. Marshall Coleman (I)	235,324	(11%)	($813,409)

Prior Winning Percentages: 1991 House (62%)

George Allen, a Republican elected in 2000, is one of only six Virginians to serve as governor and senator (the others were James Monroe, John Tyler, Claude Swanson, Harry Byrd Sr. and the man he beat, Charles Robb). Allen grew up in Illinois and California, graduating from high school in Palos Verdes. At that point his father had moved to Virginia to become the highly successful coach of the Washington Redskins ("Hit hard and good things will happen"), and he advised his son to go to college in the area. The younger George Allen graduated from college and law school at the University of Virginia. In 1977 he moved to a country home near Charlottesville and practiced law—wearing boots and chewing tobacco (he's a Copenhagen man). In 1982 he was elected to the Virginia House of Delegates, where he was a conservative backbencher while Robb was governor. In a 1991 special election he won a seat in the U.S. House, which the Democratic legislature promptly redistricted out from under him.

Out of office, he started running for governor in 1993. He maneuvered to get the support of religious conservatives at the 13,000-delegate June 1993 state convention, perhaps the largest legislative body in the history of democracy. The Democratic nominee, Attorney General Mary Sue Terry, was better known and had a moderate record on many issues, though she backed some forms of gun control and was pro-abortion rights. Democrats thought gun control and the religious right would hurt Republicans. But Allen won by a whopping 58%–41% margin.

Allen's term as governor (Virginia is the last state to limit governors to one term) was more successful than many had expected. His achievements included a more permissive concealed weapons law, abolition of parole (a big issue in the 1993 campaign), parental notification for abortions and welfare reform that required recipients to work after 90 days and cut off benefits after two years—which resulted in a big decline in welfare rolls. Allen was regarded by his foes as an intellectual lightweight, but his education reforms included Standards of Learning that were probably the toughest in the nation. But in 1995 the legislature rejected Allen's tax cut, and in elections that fall, despite a major effort by Allen, Republicans fell short of winning majorities in the legislature (they finally did so in 1999). Democrats disliked him for his partisanship and activist conservatism; he has a cheerful, sunny temperament but also a penchant for harsh conservative rhetoric. To the 1994 Republican state convention, he said, "My friends—and I say this figuratively—let's enjoy knocking their soft teeth down their whining throats." But he had 68% job approval when he left the governorship.

Out of office in 1998, Allen joined a Richmond law firm, but it was widely expected that he would run against Charles Robb in 2000. His record in the Senate was among the more conservative of Democrats, but he found himself in political trouble in 1994 because of scandal. In the Democratic primary Robb beat Delegate Virgil Goode (later, as congressman, an Independent and then a Republican) by the unimpressive margin of 58%–34% and in the general, against Oliver North, the epicenter of the Iran-contra scandal, who spent $20 million, Robb won by only 46%–43%. Robb continued to compile a moderate voting record and worked hard on military issues and on programs with appeal in rural areas, but Allen led in early polls. The centerpiece of Allen's campaign was a $1,000 per child tax credit for educational expenses for both public and private schools. Allen, a bit on the defensive on gun control, said he would vote to renew the assault weapons ban. In the last weeks of the campaign, Robb accused Allen of an "intolerable" and "appalling" record on racial issues; Democratic flyers attacked him for opposing a federal Martin Luther King Holiday, for displaying a Confederate flag in his house and for displaying a noose in his law office.

Allen won by a narrow 52%–48% margin. His votes tracked very closely with George W. Bush's. Robb, targeting the suburbs, carried Northern Virginia, but by only a 51%–49% margin. With his military credentials, he won in Tidewater Virginia, but by only 52%–48%. Allen carried the Richmond area 55%–45%, and won an even bigger margin, 57%–43%, in the one-third of the state outside these metropolitan areas. A bad sign for Democrats in the future: Robb, elected governor in 1981, carried voters 60 and older; Allen, elected governor in 1993, carried voters under 60, and by wider margins.

Allen has been active on technology issues. In 2003 he sponsored a bill with $3.7 billion for nanotechnology research and backed a CAN-Spam bill to regulate spam; both passed. He was the lead sponsor of extending the ban on Internet taxes to 2005, which became law in November 2001; in January 2003 he called for making the ban permanent, a measure opposed by many governors of both parties. Allen persisted and, after negotiations with John McCain, secured a four-year extension, with states allowed to continue existing taxes on DSL lines for two years and to continue existing Internet taxes levied before the first ban in 1998; Voice Over Internet Protocol could also be taxed. In 2001 he sponsored a bill to give citizenship to a Chinese scholar arrested while on vacation in Beijing; she later was prosecuted for passing information to the Chinese, but Allen said he didn't regret his action. Allen sponsored $1.25 billion in grants for computers and technology for historically black colleges and universities; it was blocked in the House. He also proposed that the Senate apologize for failing to enact anti-lynching laws in the 1930s and 1940s. He supported the tobacco buyout and voted for the Senate version even though it included FDA regulation of tobacco; the law eventually passed did not include that provision.

Although he said in his 2000 campaign he would support extension of the assault weapons ban, Allen changed his mind on 2004 and called it "a meaningless, toothless law that has virtually no impact on crime." His voting record was close to that of his Virginia colleague John Warner, but on that issue he took a stand opposite that of his Senate colleague, as he did when he voted for expanding healthcare benefits for Reserve and Guard soldiers on inactive status and when he voted against requiring seat belt use. He also differed on Virginia's taxes. While John Warner supported Governor Mark Warner's tax increase proposal in March 2004, Allen went to Richmond and, with former Democratic Governor Douglas Wilder, and argued against any increase and attacked Mark Warner as "unprincipled."

After the 2002 election, Allen was picked to succeed Bill Frist as head of the National Republican Senatorial Committee. The Democrats' campaign committee actually outraised Allen's during some reporting periods, but the NRSC was able to fund the races it wanted to. Some Republicans worried that divisive primaries would hurt their candidates in November; Allen cheerfully referred to them an "intrasquad scrimmages"—he is given to football metaphors—and said they led to stronger general election candidates. In the end most of the close races went Allen's way: Republicans picked up open Democratic seats in North Carolina, South Carolina, Georgia, Florida and Louisiana and beat Minority Leader Tom Daschle in South Dakota, while losing open seats in Illinois and Colorado. That changed the Republicans' majority in the Senate from a tenuous 51–49 to a more robust 55–45. "We exceeded all expectations," Allen said.

Allen has been mentioned as a possible presidential candidate in 2008, and his fundraising and travel as NRSC chairman would be assets in a national campaign. Allen waved aside questions about this. "My father always told his players, 'The future is now.' You pay attention to the task at hand. The future takes care of itself." The task at hand in early 2005 was preparing for the 2006 Senate race. The big unanswered question in early 2005 is whether Governor Mark Warner, ineligible to run for a second term in November 2005, would run against Allen in 2006.

FIRST DISTRICT

Rep. Jo Ann Davis (R)

Elected 2000, 3d term; b. June 29, 1950, Rowan Cnty., NC; home, Yorktown; Hampton Roads Bus. Col.; Assembly of God; married (Chuck).

Elected Office: VA House of Del., 1997–2000.

Professional Career: Real estate broker, 1984-present; Founder, Davis Mngmt. Co., 1988; Founder, Jo Ann Davis Realty, 1990.

DC Office: 1123 LHOB, 20515, 202-225-4261; Fax: 202-225-4382; Web site: www.house.gov/joanndavis.

District Offices: Fredericksburg, 540-548-1086; Tappahanock, 804-443-0668; Yorktown, 757-874-6687.

Committees: *Armed Services* (17th of 34 R): Military Personnel; Projection Forces. *International Relations* (15th of 27 R): Europe & Emerging Threats; Middle East & Central Asia. *Permanent Select Committee on Intelligence* (7th of 12 R): Intelligence Policy (Chmn.); Terrorism, Human Intelligence, Analysis & Counterintelligence.

Group Ratings

	ADA	ACLU	AFS	LCV	ITIC	NTU	COC	ACU	NTLC	CHC
2004	10	0	25	9	60	62	90	88	86	100
2003	15	—	13	5	—	60	80	84	—	—

National Journal Ratings

	2003 LIB	—	2003 CONS		2004 LIB	—	2004 CONS
Economic	33%	—	64%		43%	—	56%
Social	30%	—	65%		9%	—	85%
Foreign	38%	—	60%		22%	—	77%

Key Votes of the 108th Congress

1. Drilling in ANWR	Y	5. DC School Vouchers	Y
2. Approve Bush Tax Cuts	Y	6. Ban Human Cloning	Y
3. Medicare/Rx Bill	Y	7. Restrict Gun Liability	Y
4. Bar Overtime Pay Regs.	N	8. Ban Partial-Birth Abortion	Y

9. Ban Same-Sex Marriage Y
10. Fund Iraq War Y
11. Bar Cuba Embargo Funds N
12. Intelligence Reorg. Y

Election Results

2004 general	Jo Ann Davis (R)	225,071	(79%)	($375,339)
	William Lee (I)	57,434	(20%)	
	Other	4,029	(1%)	
2004 primary	Jo Ann Davis (R)	unopposed		
2002 general	Jo Ann Davis (R)	113,168	(96%)	($280,852)
	Other	4,829	(4%)	

Prior Winning Percentages: 2000 (58%)

The People
Area size: 4,612 sq. mi.
Urban population: 64.0%
Rural population: 36.0%
Pop. 2000: 643,514
Median income: $50,257
Poverty status: 6.7%
Military veterans: 17.7%

Race/Ethnic Origin
74.7% White
18.4% Black
1.7% Asian
0.4% Native Am.
0.1% Hawaiian
1.6% Two+ races
0.2% Other
3.0% Hispanic Origin

Ancestry
English: 10.7%   German: 10.4%
Irish: 8.8%
2004 Presidential Vote
Bush (R) 188,417 (60%)
Kerry (D) 122,771 (39%)
Other 2,255 (1%)
2000 Presidential Vote
Bush (R) 146,914 (58%)
Gore (D) 98,731 (39%)
Other 6,060 (2%)
Cook Partisan Voting Index: R + 9

Occupation   Blue collar: 22.1%   White collar: 62.8%   Gray collar: 15.0%

When English settlers first sailed up the estuaries that flow into the Chesapeake Bay, they were searching for gold, hoping to sail back soon with fortunes. But they couldn't help noticing that the spot where the James River feeds into the bay, now Hampton Roads, was a fine natural harbor, with calm, deep water and good anchorages. There they established a civilization whose elegance is recalled in the craftsmanship of restored Williamsburg and whose coarseness and brutality is brought to life by the story of Jamestown and the other beleaguered settlements. Tidewater Virginia brought slavery to America and tobacco to the world, and slave-raised tobacco was the center of its economy in the colonial era and in the years afterward, when its most talented sons left its depleted soil for better opportunities elsewhere.

Now the economy and tone of life in Tidewater Virginia are set by the American military. Six decades ago, as America faced world war, the Navy base at Norfolk and the shipbuilding centers in Newport News across Hampton Roads became the center of American naval might in the Atlantic. There were fewer than 370,000 people living then on both sides of Hampton Roads. Today there are nearly 1.6 million—a population collected from all over the country, making this a metropolitan area that is not so much Southern in atmosphere as it is, in the manner of military bases abroad, national.

The 1st Congressional District of Virginia contains much of this territory. The district ranges as far north from the Peninsula as rural Fauquier County, outside Washington, D.C., but the bulk of the population lives between the Potomac and James Rivers. Redistricting parceled most of the major Hampton Roads military installations into the surrounding congressional districts, but the 1st remains steeped in military culture, both past and present, and the Department of Defense continues to be a significant employer. Within the district lines, in 1781, George Washington's tattered and exhausted army at Yorktown finally pushed General Cornwallis to the sea where the French Navy waited: The final victory of the Revolutionary War. Today, historic Yorktown is adjacent to a Naval Weapons Station on the banks of the York River. To the north, in Caroline County, Fort A.P. Hill serves as a valuable training site for active and reserve-component units. Not far from there is Naval Surface Warfare Center Dahlgren, located on the Potomac River, originally established as the Navy's main proving ground for large-caliber guns. The 1st includes within its boundaries all of 13 counties and parts of five others; all of the cities of Fredericksburg and colonial Williamsburg; the Marine Corps Base at Quantico; the more populous and developed part of Spotsylvania County; and the Northern Neck between the Rappahannock and Potomac Rivers, where Robert "King" Carter, one of the great landowners of colonial Virginia, reigned, and where George Washington and Robert E. Lee were born. In the Hampton Roads area, the 1st includes parts of Hampton, Newport News, Poquoson, Williamsburg and York County—primarily north of Mercury Boulevard, once known as Military Highway but renamed to honor the Mercury 7 astronauts. About 45% of the district's votes are cast in the Hampton Roads area and about 40% in the metro Washington orbit. Ancestrally, much of this area was Democratic. But with a large military population drawn from across the country (and with heavily black precincts placed in the adjoining 3d District), the 1st District is now reliably Republican in most elections.

The congresswoman from the 1st District is Jo Ann Davis, a Republican first elected in 2000. She grew up in the Hampton Roads area; her father worked at a gas station and drove city buses in Hampton. She graduated from Hampton Roads Business College and went to work as an executive secretary for a real estate firm for several years before becoming a stay-at-home mom, then started a real estate career in 1988. Davis was elected to the House of Delegates in 1997, defeating a 15-year incumbent who outspent her 3-to-1. When 1st District Congressman Herb Bateman announced his retirement in January 2000, she jumped into the race three days later. She faced four other candidates for the Republican nomination, including real estate entrepreneur Paul Jost, who spent almost $1 million of his own money and won the endorsement of Governor James Gilmore. Davis, who spent less than one-tenth that sum, appealed to conservative activists, especially in the district's rural counties. She favored a Social Security lockbox, more flexibility to the states on education funding, elimination of the marriage penalty and estate taxes and protection of Second Amendment rights. Turnout was light and Davis won just 14,274 votes, but that was enough to defeat Jost 35%–30%. In the general, she faced Democrat Lawrence Davies, a Baptist minister and mayor of Fredericksburg for 20 years. The two biggest issues of the campaign were abortion rights—Davis against, Davies for—and the proposed King William reservoir, which many local officials said was necessary to meet the Peninsula's water demand: Davis considered it too expensive and Davies defended it as necessary for growth. Davis won 58%–37%.

In the House, Davis has been a strict conservative on cultural issues but toward the middle of House Republicans on economic and foreign policy. Not surprisingly, she got a seat on the Armed Services Committee. She reintroduced a bill to require the Navy to have no fewer than 375 vessels in active service, including 15 aircraft carrier battle groups and 15 amphibious ready groups; as of 2004, the Navy fleet had 294 ships. She defied Republican leaders by winning approval of her amendment to limit the Navy's ability to lease foreign-built ships. "When the Defense Department has a long-term need for ships," she said, "it ought to buy them from U.S. shipyards, or our industrial and skill capabilities will continue to erode." In October 2004, she got more than 50 House members to sign her letter urging Defense Secretary Donald Rumsfeld to reject a Navy plan to delay ship construction, including the new CVN-21 aircraft carrier, to be built at Newport News. She has secured funds to scrap several dozen ships from the "ghost fleet" that have been anchored on the James River. Davis defended the decision to invade Iraq as "a tough vote but the right one." Following a visit to the Mideast, she voiced doubt about President Bush's "roadmap" for peace between Israel and the Palestinians. "I'm not sure we have the right to be giving up any part of Jerusalem," she said. "That land belongs to the Lord." Davis won passage of a bill to assure that survivors of military personnel killed on duty receive the full additional life insurance benefit up to $250,000. In August 2004, Davis gave up her seat on the Government Reform Committee—and chairmanship of its Civil Service and Agency Organization Subcommittee—to join the Intelligence Committee. She voted against final approval of the intelligence bill because it did not include prohibitions on drivers' licenses to illegal aliens. At home, she backed six Indian tribes seeking federal recognition before the 400th anniversary of Jamestown.

Davis has been reelected without major-party opposition.

SECOND DISTRICT

Rep. Thelma Drake (R)

Elected 2004, 1st term; b. Nov. 20, 1949, Elyria, OH; home, Norfolk; Elyria H.S.; United Church of Christ; married (Ted).

Elected Office: VA House of Del., 1995–2004.

Professional Career: Real estate agent, 1975–2004.

DC Office: 1208 LHOB, 20515, 202-225-4215; Fax: 202-225-4218; Web site: www.drake.house.gov.

District Offices: Accomac, 757-787-7836; Virginia Beach, 757-497-6859.

Committees: *Armed Services* (30th of 34 R): Military Personnel; Projection Forces. *Education & the Workforce* (26th of 27 R): 21st Century Competitiveness; Workforce Protections. *Resources* (21st of 27 R): Energy & Mineral Resources; Fisheries & Oceans.

Group Ratings and Key Votes: Newly Elected

Election Results

2004 general	Thelma Drake (R)	132,946	(55%)	($828,185)
	David Ashe (D)	108,180	(45%)	($436,620)
2004 primary	Ed Schrock (R)	unopposed		
2002 general	Ed Schrock (R)	103,807	(83%)	($483,440)
	D.C. Amarasinghe (Green)	20,589	(16%)	($12,415)

The People		Race/Ethnic Origin	Ancestry	
Area size:	2,776 sq. mi.	67.4% White	German: 10.1% Irish: 9.1%	
Urban population:	91.7%	21.4% Black	English: 9.0%	
Rural population:	8.3%	4.0% Asian	**2004 Presidential Vote**	
Pop. 2000:	643,510	0.4% Native Am.	Bush (R)	141,097 (58%)
Median income:	$44,193	0.1% Hawaiian	Kerry (D)	101,576 (42%)
Poverty status:	8.7%	2.2% Two+ races	Other	1,896 (1%)
Military veterans:	20.3%	0.2% Other	**2000 Presidential Vote**	
		4.4% Hispanic Origin	Bush (R)	115,512 (55%)
			Gore (D)	90,256 (43%)
			Other	4,940 (2%)
			Cook Partisan Voting Index: R + 6	
Occupation	Blue collar: 21.1% White collar: 63.0% Gray collar: 15.9%			

The United States Navy Atlantic fleet berthed in its homeport of Norfolk is one of the great awe-inspiring sights in America, or anywhere. The aggregation of destructive power in the line of towering gray ships is probably greater than in any other single port in history. Several dozen ships are based here—aircraft carriers, cruisers, destroyers, large amphibious ships, submarines, supply and logistics ships—and many more aircraft. Norfolk has been a Navy port since 1801, and has long been recognized as one of the best natural harbors on the East Coast, one that never freezes, has a channel 50 feet deep and is within 750 miles of three-quarters of U.S. manufacturing capacity. The Norfolk Naval Station is now the world's largest naval station, situated on 4,300 acres on Sewells Point, and the Hampton Roads region is the world's largest naval base, where residents are always within minutes of one naval installation or another. Norfolk, once a small city, is now the center of a metro area with 1.6 million people. The local Navy community—retirees, dependents, active duty and civilian personnel, workers at the Newport News Shipbuilding & Drydock—is estimated at more than 300,000 and military spending pours over $11 billion annually into the local economy. The port also has become a major commercial hub for East Coast shippers and distributors, with imports of containerized retail cargo increasing more than 50% since 2000.

Next-door Virginia Beach, once a beach resort and acres of swamp, is the state's largest city, with more than 439,000 people. It began attracting tourists when rail service began in 1883; now it hosts the larger-than-life Williamsburg-style headquarters of Pat Robertson's Christian Broadcasting Network (the *700 Club* is produced here) and other Robertson operations. But like Norfolk, Virginia Beach is infused with military culture. It is home to four military installations—Oceana Naval Air Station is the city's largest employer—with 35,000 service and civilian employees and an annual payroll of over $1 billion. East Coast Navy SEAL teams are also based in Virginia Beach; these elite commandos endure punishing military training and have taken on some of the military's most secretive, daring and hazardous missions in Afghanistan and Iraq. They keep largely to themselves, deploying and returning quietly, and grieve amongst themselves when one of their own pays the ultimate price.

The 2d Congressional District of Virginia includes all of Virginia Beach. It also includes parts of Norfolk and Hampton with mostly white residents, including the Norfolk Navy base and Langley Air Force Base and, on a spit of land in the bay, Fort Monroe, where Jefferson Davis was confined after the Civil War. It also includes a more placid area, the two Virginia counties of the Delmarva Peninsula, Virginia's Eastern Shore, site of the annual roundup of wild Chincoteague ponies; these rural counties with their fishing villages are two of the state's poorest. Surrounded by water on three sides, far from markets, they are connected to Virginia Beach by the Chesapeake Bay Bridge-Tunnel with its $12 toll. Back in the 1960s and 1970s, most people in the 2d District were in Norfolk, and the district often voted Democratic. Now the overwhelming majority live in Virginia Beach, and the district is firmly Republican. George W. Bush carried it with 55% of the vote in 2000 and 58% in 2004.

The congresswoman from the 2d District is Thelma Drake, a Republican first elected in 2004. She has a unique biography and won the seat in an unusual set of circumstances. She grew up in Elyria, Ohio, got pregnant in high school and then married her Navy-bound high school boyfriend. They moved to Norfolk, where her husband soon divorced her and she was left to raise her child alone. Her experience as a single mother colors her outlook: "I always felt I was the only person responsible for myself. You don't turn to other people to help you." Drake declined to go on welfare and instead worked for 20 years as a real estate agent. In 1995, she defeated an incumbent to win a seat in the House of Delegates. She voted to hold a referendum in the Hampton Roads area in 2002 for a tax increase to pay for local transportation projects; it was rejected 62%–38%. In April 2004 she voted against Governor Mark Warner's tax increase package, which nonetheless passed when 17 Republican delegates and 15 Republican state senators supported it. Republican delegates were bitterly split over the issue, and local conservative activists were eager to defeat those who had supported the tax increase and to reward those who opposed it.

Drake had no plans to run for the House in 2004. Republican Ed Schrock, first elected in 2000, seemed likely to win reelection easily. Then on August 30, as the Republican National Convention was convening in New York, Schrock abruptly announced his retirement amid allegations that he had engaged in homosexual activity. The married lawmaker and retired Navy captain never confirmed or denied the allegations; his statement noted simply that the charges "called into question my ability to represent the citizens of Virginia's 2nd Congressional District." The next day, the 12-member Second Congressional District Republican Committee met to choose a new nominee. Drake ran, as did state Senator Nick Rerras, who voted for the Warner tax increase, and Virginia Beach Sheriff Paul Lanteigne. Drake won a majority of the votes in the secret ballot, in large part because of her stand against the tax increase.

The Republican turmoil gave unexpected life to the candidacy of Democrat David Ashe, a lawyer and Marine reservist who had recently returned from a two-year tour in the Middle East, including six months in Iraq, where he worked on restoring the judicial system. Ashe was a political newcomer but proved to be an active candidate, and national Democrats immediately elevated him on their priority list. He promised fiscal conservatism and reduction of the federal deficit. Drake attacked Ashe for "weakening the war on terror" because he supported John Kerry. But Democrats responded by highlighting Ashe's military credentials; the Democratic Congressional Campaign Committee ran ads urging voters to "send a Marine to Congress." Drake, in turn, promised to focus on military and national security issues and to vote to make the Bush tax cuts permanent. With help from national Republicans, she outraised Ashe by nearly 2–1 and won 55%–45%, carrying the four largest cities and counties by similar margins. As promised by Speaker Dennis Hastert, Drake got a seat on the Armed Services Committee.

Following the election, Schrock returned to Capitol Hill as a senior aide to the House Government Reform and Oversight Committee, chaired by Tom Davis of Northern Virginia.

THIRD DISTRICT

Rep. Bobby Scott (D)

Elected 1992, 7th term; b. Apr. 30, 1947, Washington, D.C.; home, Newport News; Harvard U., B.A. 1969, Boston Col., J.D. 1973; Episcopalian; single.

Military Career: Army Natl. Guard, 1970–73; Army Reserves, 1973–76.

Elected Office: VA House of Delegates, 1977–82; VA Senate, 1983–92.

Professional Career: Practicing atty., 1973–91.

DC Office: 1201 LHOB, 20515, 202-225-8351; Fax: 202-225-8354; Web site: www.house.gov/scott.

District Offices: Newport News, 757-380-1000; Richmond, 804-644-4845.

Committees: *Education & the Workforce* (6th of 22 D): 21st Century Competitiveness; Education Reform. *Judiciary* (5th of 17 D): Crime, Terrorism & Homeland Security (RMM); The Constitution.

Group Ratings

	ADA	ACLU	AFS	LCV	ITIC	NTU	COC	ACU	NTLC	CHC
2004	100	100	100	100	30	6	29	4	0	8
2003	100	—	100	95	—	20	23	8	—	—

National Journal Ratings

	2003 LIB	—	2003 CONS		2004 LIB	—	2004 CONS
Economic	87%	—	9%		97%	—	2%
Social	92%	—	0%		88%	—	0%
Foreign	93%	—	7%		91%	—	7%

Key Votes of the 108th Congress

1. Drilling in ANWR	N	5. DC School Vouchers	N	9. Ban Same-Sex Marriage	N
2. Approve Bush Tax Cuts	N	6. Ban Human Cloning	N	10. Fund Iraq War	N
3. Medicare/Rx Bill	N	7. Restrict Gun Liability	N	11. Bar Cuba Embargo Funds	Y
4. Bar Overtime Pay Regs.	Y	8. Ban Partial-Birth Abortion	N	12. Intelligence Reorg.	N

Election Results

2004 general	Bobby Scott (D)	159,373	(69%)	($482,504)
	Winsome Sears (R)	70,194	(31%)	($205,812)
2004 primary	Bobby Scott (D)	unopposed		
2002 general	Bobby Scott (D)	87,521	(96%)	($195,537)
	Other	3,552	(4%)	

Prior Winning Percentages: 2000 (100%); 1998 (76%); 1996 (82%); 1994 (79%); 1992 (79%)

The People		Race/Ethnic Origin	Ancestry	
Area size:	1,306 sq. mi.	37.7% White	English: 5.6%	USA: 5.3%
Urban population:	92.2%	56.0% Black	German: 5.3%	
Rural population:	7.8%	1.4% Asian	**2004 Presidential Vote**	
Pop. 2000:	643,476	0.5% Native Am.	Kerry (D) 158,561	(66%)
Median income:	$32,238	0.1% Hawaiian	Bush (R) 79,302	(33%)
Poverty status:	18.9%	1.6% Two+ races	Other 1,517	(1%)
Military veterans:	15.5%	0.2% Other	**2000 Presidential Vote**	
		2.6% Hispanic Origin	Gore (D) 134,020	(66%)
			Bush (R) 65,724	(32%)
			Other 3,603	(2%)
			Cook Partisan Voting Index: D +18	

Occupation   Blue collar: 25.8%   White collar: 55.4%   Gray collar: 18.7%

The history of African-American slavery literally began along the tidal expanse of the James River. In 1607, the first English colonists chose one of the marshiest, least healthy spots along the broad river as the site of their settlement at Jamestown. Only a dozen years later, the first slave ship sailed up the James and offloaded its human cargo, giving birth to the biracial society of the American South. In the 21st century, the great plantation houses of the Tidewater, entire communities once adorned by the most impressive architecture of the day and attended by hundreds of slaves, still dot the banks of the James. Charles City County—the site of William Byrd II's Westover, Benjamin Harrison III's Berkeley, and John Carter's Shirley—also was the birthplace of two successive presidents, William Henry Harrison and John Tyler. The county's population continues to be heavily black: The demography of the plantation remains.

The 3d Congressional District of Virginia is the descendant of a black-majority district formed in 1992, and redrawn twice in the 1990s after a federal court ruled it unconstitutional and then again after the 2000 Census. The district jumps back and forth across the James River to string together black precincts and communities in Norfolk, Hampton and Newport News, then upriver on the Peninsula past Jamestown and Charles City County all the way to Richmond and eastern suburban Henrico County. It includes the Army's Fort Eustis and all of the majority-black city of Portsmouth—a Navy port and industrial town with a charming old section. Politically, the 3d is the most Democratic district in Virginia and the only black-majority district. The economy of much of the district depends heavily on the Newport News Shipbuilding & Drydock Company (acquired by Northrop Grumman in 2001). The shipyard lies over the flat neighborhoods lining the baysides, with ships looming larger than life, their turrets and superstructures bristling with armored might. During the Cold War era, Newport News built two of the largest tankers ever made in the western hemisphere, in addition to its *Nimitz* class nuclear aircraft carriers and *Los Angeles* class nuclear attack submarines; the Navy plans to build its CVNX class nuclear carriers here. It is the largest industrial employer in Virginia.

The congressman from the 3d District is Bobby Scott, a Democrat first elected when the district was created in 1992. He grew up in Newport News, the son of a doctor, went to Harvard, where he was a classmate of Al Gore, and then to Boston College law school, where he preceded John Kerry. He served in the National Guard and Army Reserves, and returned home to practice law in 1973. In 1977, he was elected to the Virginia House of Delegates and in 1983 to the state Senate, representing a multi-racial district in a community where, because of the military tradition of integration, biracial politics came more naturally than in other places. In 1986 he ran a credible race for Congress and lost to Republican Herb Bateman, 56%–44%. In 1992, with his base in the Peninsula, and against two Richmond-based candidates, Scott won the crucial Democratic primary with 67% of the vote. He is the only black member of Congress elected from Virginia since Reconstruction.

Scott has a solidly liberal voting record, except on occasional economic and defense issues. He has become one of the House's most outspoken civil libertarians. He opposes the death penalty. When bipartisan coalitions passed legislation to permit states to display the Ten Commandments in schools or government buildings, he raised First Amendment objections, as he did to George W. Bush's plan to fund faith-based social programs. After September 11 he opposed the USA Patriot Act, arguing that it might promote racial profiling. He was one of three members to oppose condemnation of a federal court decision declaring unconstitutional the words "one nation under God" in the Pledge of Allegiance. "We ought to be standing up for unpopular decisions" and not voting for a resolution that "everyone knows is stupid, but it sounds popular." He unsuccessfully offered an amendment to prohibit religious discrimination by faith-based organizations receiving government funds for Head Start centers. Scott has had some success on civil liberties, as with enactment of the bipartisan Death in Custody Act requiring states to report deaths of prisoners. In September 2003, he attended a White House signing ceremony for a bill designed to eliminate rape inside the nation's prisons. Scott and other members of the Congressional Black Caucus met with George W. Bush in January 2005, and Bush included proposals to help children of offenders and to finance use of DNA evidence in death penalty appeals in his 2005 State of the Union address; on leaving the chamber he turned to Scott and said, "I heard what you said, Bobby."

On the Budget Committee, Republicans acknowledged that he is formidable in raising questions about the soaring budget deficit and big tax cuts. At the start of the Iraq war, he was one of 11 members to oppose a resolution supporting the effort. He said that President Bush had not stated a rationale, objected to clauses suggesting a link to the September 2001 terror attacks and said that the resolution was designed "to extract political advantage." One of his goals is affordable health care for all. Remembering how his father had been denied staff privileges in a Newport News hospital, he vowed that any health care bill would prohibit racial discrimination against patients and health care providers. At home, Scott supported restoration of the downtown train station in Richmond, which resulted in the return of Amtrak service. He clashed with former Governor Douglas Wilder and other Richmond officials over their plan to strengthen the office of mayor of that city; the Justice Department overrode Scott's civil rights objections and Wilder was elected in November 2004.

That year Scott faced his first Republican challenger since 1996, Winsome Sears, a former Marine and the first black Republican woman in the House of Delegates. Sears criticized Scott as "radical" on national security, education, gay rights and abortion; she called the war in Iraq a "battle for freedom". Scott focused on his record and criticized Republican policies, including an "overextended" military. In this strongly Democratic district, he won 69%–31%, carrying 81% of the vote in Richmond, 72% in Norfolk and 65% in Newport News.

FOURTH DISTRICT

Rep. Randy Forbes (R)

Elected June 2001, 2d full term; b. Feb. 17, 1952, Chesapeake; home, Chesapeake; Randolph-Macon Col., B.A. 1974, U. of VA, J.D. 1977; Baptist; married (Shirley).

Elected Office: VA House of Del., 1989–97; VA Senate, 1997–01.

Professional Career: Practicing atty., 1977-present.

DC Office: 307 CHOB, 20515, 202-225-6365; Fax: 202-226-1170; Web site: www.house.gov/forbes.

District Offices: Chesapeake, 757-382-0080; Colonial Heights, 804-526-4969; Emporia, 434-634-5575.

Committees: *Armed Services* (19th of 34 R): Readiness; Tactical Air & Land Forces. *Judiciary* (19th of 23 R): Commercial & Administrative Law; Courts, the Internet & Intellectual Property; Crime, Terrorism & Homeland Security. *Science* (15th of 24 R): Space & Aeronautics.

Group Ratings

	ADA	ACLU	AFS	LCV	ITIC	NTU	COC	ACU	NTLC	CHC
2004	5	0	0	0	90	66	100	100	89	100
2003	10	—	0	10	—	61	97	92	—	—

National Journal Ratings

	2003 LIB	—	2003 CONS		2004 LIB	—	2004 CONS
Economic	9%	—	84%		16%	—	84%
Social	30%	—	65%		24%	—	76%
Foreign	21%	—	77%		17%	—	78%

Key Votes of the 108th Congress

1. Drilling in ANWR	Y	5. DC School Vouchers	Y	9. Ban Same-Sex Marriage	Y
2. Approve Bush Tax Cuts	Y	6. Ban Human Cloning	Y	10. Fund Iraq War	Y
3. Medicare/Rx Bill	Y	7. Restrict Gun Liability	Y	11. Bar Cuba Embargo Funds	N
4. Bar Overtime Pay Regs.	N	8. Ban Partial-Birth Abortion	Y	12. Intelligence Reorg.	Y

Election Results

2004 general	Randy Forbes (R)	182,444	(64%)	($858,666)
	Jonathan Menefee (D)	100,413	(35%)	($30,215)
2004 primary	Randy Forbes (R)	unopposed		
2002 general	Randy Forbes (R)	108,733	(98%)	($1,668,314)
	Other	2,308	(2%)	

Prior Winning Percentages: 2001 (52%)

The People		Race/Ethnic Origin	Ancestry	
Area size:	4,575 sq. mi.	62.0% White	USA: 10.0%	English: 8.6%
Urban population:	70.9%	33.1% Black	German: 7.2%	
Rural population:	29.1%	1.3% Asian	**2004 Presidential Vote**	
Pop. 2000:	643,477	0.3% Native Am.	Bush (R) 166,689	(57%)
Median income:	$45,249	0.0% Hawaiian	Kerry (D) 125,164	(43%)
Poverty status:	9.5%	1.1% Two+ races	Other 1,713	(1%)
Military veterans:	16.2%	0.1% Other	**2000 Presidential Vote**	
		2.0% Hispanic Origin	Bush (R) 131,834	(54%)
			Gore (D) 107,553	(44%)
			Other 3,690	(2%)
			Cook Partisan Voting Index: R + 5	

Occupation	Blue collar: 27.6%	White collar: 57.8%	Gray collar: 14.6%

The clash of arms resounds through much of the history of Tidewater Virginia. The Tidewater was the scene of the final victory of the Revolutionary War and saw bitter fighting more than 80 years later in the Civil War, as Union troops invested the battlements of the small industrial city of Petersburg, 25 miles south of Richmond. Today, the Tidewater region boasts one of the densest concentrations of military power in the world: The Hampton Roads area has the nation's largest accumulation of Navy bases, while Fort Lee, the big Army base near Petersburg, has provided 6,800 local jobs and an estimated $686 million impact on the local economy.

The 4th Congressional District of Virginia includes much of the Tidewater south of the James River. About half its people are in the Hampton Roads area, mostly in the fast-growing suburbs of Chesapeake and Suffolk. In Chesapeake, which was named by *Money* magazine as among the best places to live in the country, residents cite their quality schools, open local government and ample green space. Suffolk's sandy loam soil is the eastern edge of Virginia's Peanut Belt, nearly all of which is in the 4th, where farmers begin planting in late April or early May and wait five months for the crop to reach maturity. The district also takes in the flat lands of Southside Virginia fanning south from the James River. These were tobacco lands after the English first settled them in the 17th century; today they also produce peanuts and Smithfield hams. The Great Dismal Swamp, which crosses into North Carolina, is a breathtaking national wildlife preserve that features long hikes into marshy woodland and the shallow Lake Drummond at its center; it was a sanctuary for runaway slaves. The district also includes all of Petersburg and Hopewell, with its Honeywell plant facing 18th century plantations. The 2001 redistricting removed majority-black Portsmouth from the district and added heavily white parts of suburban Chesterfield County outside Richmond; this reduced the 4th's black percentage from 39% to 33%.

The congressman from the 4th District is Randy Forbes, a Republican who won a June 2001 special election. Forbes grew up in Chesapeake, majored in government at Randolph-Macon, graduated from the University of Virginia Law School, and returned home to start a law firm which later merged with a larger Norfolk firm. His first job in politics was as an aide to the Democratic member of the House of Delegates from Chesapeake. When his boss retired in 1989, Forbes ran for and won the seat as a Republican. Four years later, when Republicans were still in the minority, he became the party's floor leader. In 1997 he was elected to the state Senate. Forbes was a classmate and friend of Governors George Allen and Jim Gilmore in law school, and in 1996 Allen made him Republican state chairman; he helped engineer the historic Republican 1997 sweep of all three statewide offices.

In early 2001, Forbes was a leading candidate for lieutenant governor. When 10-term Democratic Congressman Norman Sisisky died in March eight days after cancer surgery, national and state Republican leaders asked Forbes to run in what was then a competitive seat. The nominee was chosen at a convention, and Forbes won by forging unity in the delegations from Chesapeake and Portsmouth, then the district's two largest cities. He got a break when the strongest Democrat, Sisisky's son Mark, declined to run. Democrats chose state Senator Louise Lucas of Portsmouth, an African-American who held a majority-black seat. Lucas worked for 18 years at the Norfolk Naval Shipyard, where she became its first woman shipfitter. Both national parties and their interest-group allies spent heavily. Republicans attacked Lucas for opposing repeal of the sales tax on non-prescription drugs and for supporting a gasoline tax increase. Democrats criticized Forbes for backing "privatization" of Social Security. Forbes said that he favored George W. Bush's proposal to let younger workers invest some of their payroll taxes in individual investment accounts, but his ads emphasized that he would preserve current benefits—"every penny of it." Lucas carried Portsmouth 63%–37%. But Forbes more than overcame this by winning 61%–39% in more populous Chesapeake and majorities in seven of the 10 rural counties, for an overall win of 52%–48%.

In the House, Forbes has voted with conservatives and he sits on the Armed Services, Judiciary and Science committees. In a rare break with party leaders, he opposed the intelligence bill because it failed to address immigration problems. Forbes cosponsored the constitutional amendment to ban same-sex marriages, and spoke up for Representative Chris Smith's proposed Unborn Child Pain Awareness Act, which would require doctors to inform the mother of the pain that a fetus can feel from an abortion. He claimed credit for $50 million in housing and other base projects at Fort Lee, $7 million to replace two local bridges, and $200,000 to reimburse the Chesapeake police department for its expenses in the local trial of Washington Beltway sniper Lee Malvo. In 2005, he became co-chairman, with Susan Davis of California, of the Navy and Marine Corps Caucus.

After the Republicans' redistricting, Lucas decided against a rematch in 2002 and Forbes was unopposed. In 2004 Forbes won 64%–35%. And so a district held for 19 years by a Democrat has become safely Republican. As for Forbes, he wields influence as a political power broker in his hometown. He "continues to shape the future of Chesapeake even as his national political stature grows," the *Virginian Pilot* wrote in a profile. "By his own admission, he can't and won't let go of a place where his roots run so deep." That profile noted his interest in running for the Senate some day. As Forbes cited approvingly, Senator John Warner told an audience, "If I retire, there's nobody I know of that would be a better-suited replacement for me in the Senate than Randy Forbes."

FIFTH DISTRICT

Rep. Virgil Goode (R)

Elected 1996, 5th term; b. Oct. 17, 1946, Richmond; home, Rocky Mount; U. of Richmond, B.A. 1969, U. of VA, J.D. 1973; Baptist; married (Lucy).

Military Career: VA Natl. Guard, 1969–75.

Elected Office: VA Senate, 1973–96.

Professional Career: Practicing atty., 1973–96.

DC Office: 1520 LHOB, 20515, 202-225-4711; Fax: 202-225-5681; Web site: www.house.gov/goode.

District Offices: Charlottesville, 804-295-6372; Danville, 804-792-1280; Farmville, 804-392-8331; Rocky Mount, 540-484-1254.

Committees: *Appropriations* (25th of 37 R): Agriculture, Rural Development, FDA & Related Agencies; Science, State, Justice, Commerce & Related Agencies.

Group Ratings

	ADA	ACLU	AFS	LCV	ITIC	NTU	COC	ACU	NTLC	CHC
2004	10	0	25	9	50	65	90	96	86	100
2003	10	—	0	20	—	64	87	88	—	—

National Journal Ratings

	2003 LIB	—	2003 CONS		2004 LIB	—	2004 CONS
Economic	31%	—	68%		44%	—	56%
Social	0%	—	95%		0%	—	91%
Foreign	42%	—	57%		34%	—	63%

Key Votes of the 108th Congress

1. Drilling in ANWR	Y	5. DC School Vouchers	Y	9. Ban Same-Sex Marriage	Y
2. Approve Bush Tax Cuts	Y	6. Ban Human Cloning	Y	10. Fund Iraq War	Y
3. Medicare/Rx Bill	Y	7. Restrict Gun Liability	Y	11. Bar Cuba Embargo Funds	N
4. Bar Overtime Pay Regs.	N	8. Ban Partial-Birth Abortion	Y	12. Intelligence Reorg.	Y

Election Results

2004 general	Virgil Goode (R)	172,431	(64%)	($753,167)
	Al Weed (D)	98,237	(36%)	($481,071)
2004 primary	Virgil Goode (R)	unopposed		
2002 general	Virgil Goode (R)	95,360	(63%)	($707,704)
	Meredith Richards (D)	54,805	(36%)	($215,406)

Prior Winning Percentages: 2000 (67%); 1998 (100%); 1996 (61%)

The People		Race/Ethnic Origin	Ancestry	
Area size:	9,054 sq. mi.	72.4% White	USA: 14.7%	English: 9.0%
Urban population:	36.0%	23.9% Black	German: 6.6%	
Rural population:	64.0%	1.0% Asian	**2004 Presidential Vote**	
Pop. 2000:	643,497	0.2% Native Am.	Bush (R) 158,568	(56%)
Median income:	$35,739	0.0% Hawaiian	Kerry (D) 121,960	(43%)
Poverty status:	13.2%	0.8% Two+ races	Other 3,097	(1%)
Military veterans:	13.1%	0.1% Other	**2000 Presidential Vote**	
		1.6% Hispanic Origin	Bush (R) 137,223	(55%)
			Gore (D) 102,814	(41%)
			Other 8,907	(4%)
			Cook Partisan Voting Index: R + 6	

Occupation	Blue collar: 31.7%	White collar: 53.3%	Gray collar: 15.0%

Southside Virginia is a geographic name that for years was shorthand for a state of mind. Here is Appomattox Court House, in the serene little hamlet where Robert E. Lee surrendered to his onetime subordinate Ulysses S. Grant; here is Danville, where the tobacco auction originated in 1858; here also is Prince Edward County, where Harry Byrd's massive resistance shut down public schools in 1957 rather than obey a federal court desegregation order. This land north of the dividing line Colonel William Byrd surveyed in 1728 has some variety. Its eastern counties are flat and humid—frontier in the late colonial period, plantation country by 1800, now peanut fields and pine forests. Along U.S. 58, just north of Byrd's dividing line, are the vestiges of Virginia's Tobacco Road. In South Hill, the Tobacco Farm Life Museum pays tribute to that heritage, though only one of six tobacco warehouses is still in business. To the west, into the Piedmont, the land gradually gets more hilly. Here are the abandoned textile mills and furniture manufacturing centers of Danville and Martinsville, places that reminisce fondly about the last period of textile industry growth that peaked in 1973. Nearby is the D-Day Memorial in Bedford, which lost more men per capita, 23 of its 35 soldiers, in the Normandy invasion than any other town in the nation. Westward, nearer to the mountains, are more livestock and less tobacco, and the thick syrupy tones of the Southside Virginia accent turn to mountain twangs. Local officials have sought to add some of these areas to the federal map of Appalachia to make them eligible for anti-poverty funds.

The 5th District consists of much of Southside Virginia, west of metropolitan Richmond, and spreads as far north as the Blue Ridge Mountains. It includes all of liberal Charlottesville and surrounding Albemarle County and fast-growing Fluvanna County, but skirts around Lynchburg. Historically, politics here were Democratic, segregationist and conservative, run by chain-smoking local bankers and courthouse lawyers. Such Democrats are a rare breed these days, on the way to becoming extinct, and Southside is becoming part of the Republican heartland of Virginia.

The congressman from the 5th District is Virgil Goode (rhymes with mood), elected as a Democrat in 1996, an Independent for two years and officially a Republican since February 2002. Goode grew up in Franklin County, where his father was a prominent enough figure that part of U.S. 220 was named after him. He graduated from the University of Richmond and from the University of Virginia law school in 1973. That same year, he was elected to the Virginia Senate, at 27. In 1994, he ran against scandal-beleaguered Senator Charles Robb in the Democratic primary; Goode lost 58%–34%, but showed local strength. In 1995, his re-election in a Republican-leaning district enabled Democrats to hold control of the state Senate. In 1996, when conservative Democrat L.F. Payne retired, Goode seemed the only Democrat with a strong chance to win the district. He emphasized bipartisan cooperation with the slogan on the pencils and emery boards he handed out to voters: "Work together in Congress." Republicans ran George Landrith, a former Albemarle County school board member, who lost 53%–47% to Payne in 1994. Goode won by an impressive 61%–36%.

In his first years in the House, Goode had the most conservative voting record of any House Democrat. He passionately opposed one of the Clinton White House's favorite projects, the bill to curb tobacco consumption. He voted to impeach Bill Clinton, evidently not a close issue for him. "The party line says that lying under oath in a court proceeding is not an impeachable offense. I disagree with that." In January 2000, Goode announced that he would no longer be a member of the Democratic Caucus and would run for re-election as an Independent. He said that he would attend meetings of the House Republican Conference and contribute to their campaign committee. Republicans promptly gave him a seat on the Appropriations Committee. In his well-financed 2000 campaign, he attacked the Clinton administration for neglecting the woes of the Southside textile and apparel industries—Goode has voted against free trade agreements, including normal trade relations with for China and trade promotion authority—and campaigned with George Allen. Opposed by a Democrat who headed a black farmers' advocacy group, he won 67%–31%.

When Goode formalized his affiliation as a Republican, he offered a practical explanation: On certain voting machines, independents are listed "off-center," and "we had to do significant advertising" to alert voters. He said that the switch would not change his stand on issues. Some observers thought that redistricting was the reason Goode left the Democratic party; Republicans, who controlled the process, could have placed his Franklin County home into the 9th District represented by Democrat Rick Boucher. Instead, they made only minor adjustments to existing lines. As a Republican, Goode's voting record has become more conservative. He has won

House passage of amendments for the military to assist border security agents to prevent entry of terrorists, drug traffickers and illegal aliens. Pentagon officials opposed his proposal as unnecessary and potentially disruptive, and critics called the proposal "anti-immigrant." On the Appropriations Committee, he got funds for in-car cameras for local police cruisers, a program to bring broadband to the U.S. 58 corridor and a wildlife foundation in Halifax County. He was a leading advocate of the federal tobacco buyout, which was enacted in October 2004; Goode won a commitment for the measure from Republican leaders in exchange for his vote for the 2003 Medicare/prescription drug bill. He organized the Second Amendment Caucus to advocate for gun owners.

Goode was reelected by nearly 2–1 margins in 2002 and 2004, although he lost Charlottesville both times by better than 2–1.

SIXTH DISTRICT

Rep. Bob Goodlatte (R)

Elected 1992, 7th term; b. Sept. 22, 1952, Holyoke, MA; home, Roanoke; Bates Col., B.A. 1974, Washington & Lee Law Schl., J.D. 1977; Christian Scientist; married (Maryellen).

Professional Career: Dist. Dir., U.S. Rep. Caldwell Butler, 1977–79; Practicing atty., 1979–92.

DC Office: 2240 RHOB, 20515, 202-225-5431; Fax: 202-225-9681; Web site: www.house.gov/goodlatte.

District Offices: Harrisonburg, 540-432-2391; Lynchburg, 804-845-8306; Roanoke, 540-857-2672; Staunton, 540-885-3861.

Committees: *Agriculture* (Chmn. of 25 R). *Judiciary* (6th of 23 R): Courts, the Internet & Intellectual Property; Immigration, Border Security & Claims.

Group Ratings

	ADA	ACLU	AFS	LCV	ITIC	NTU	COC	ACU	NTLC	CHC
2004	0	0	0	0	100	67	100	100	86	100
2003	10	—	0	5	—	63	97	88	—	—

National Journal Ratings

	2003 LIB	—	2003 CONS		2004 LIB	—	2004 CONS
Economic	20%	—	79%		13%	—	85%
Social	24%	—	71%		0%	—	91%
Foreign	23%	—	71%		17%	—	78%

Key Votes of the 108th Congress

1. Drilling in ANWR	Y	5. DC School Vouchers	Y	9. Ban Same-Sex Marriage	Y
2. Approve Bush Tax Cuts	Y	6. Ban Human Cloning	Y	10. Fund Iraq War	Y
3. Medicare/Rx Bill	Y	7. Restrict Gun Liability	Y	11. Bar Cuba Embargo Funds	N
4. Bar Overtime Pay Regs.	N	8. Ban Partial-Birth Abortion	Y	12. Intelligence Reorg.	Y

Election Results

2004 general	Bob Goodlatte (R)	206,560	(97%)	($797,676)
	Other	7,088	(3%)	
2004 primary	Bob Goodlatte (R)	unopposed		
2002 general	Bob Goodlatte (R)	105,530	(97%)	($562,236)
	Other	3,202	(3%)	

Prior Winning Percentages: 2000 (100%); 1998 (69%); 1996 (67%); 1994 (100%); 1992 (60%)

The People		Race/Ethnic Origin	Ancestry	
Area size:	5,664 sq. mi.	84.8% White	USA: 13.4%	German: 11.9%
Urban population:	64.7%	10.9% Black	English: 8.9%	
Rural population:	35.3%	0.9% Asian	**2004 Presidential Vote**	
Pop. 2000:	643,504	0.2% Native Am.	Bush (R) 177,133	(63%)
Median income:	$37,773	0.0% Hawaiian	Kerry (D) 100,561	(36%)
Poverty status:	11.0%	1.0% Two+ races	Other 2,883	(1%)
Military veterans:	13.7%	0.1% Other	**2000 Presidential Vote**	
		2.0% Hispanic Origin	Bush (R) 147,961	(60%)
			Gore (D) 92,407	(37%)
			Other 6,984	(3%)
			Cook Partisan Voting Index: R +11	

Occupation   Blue collar: 28.5%   White collar: 55.9%   Gray collar: 15.6%

The sturdy men and women who settled the Valley of Virginia west of the Blue Ridge were quite different from the "second sons" of the European aristocracy who cleared the marshy forests of the Tidewater and built grand plantations there. Even before the Revolutionary War, Scots and Scots-Irish, German Protestants and Mennonites and Moravians—members of religious communities and fiercely independent farmers—poured down the great Wagon Road from Pennsylvania to the Valley. They were looking not for the flat, mahogany-brown land that eastern tobacco growers sought, but for fields, which could support wheat, corn and hay, crops that could be rotated, and that an individual farmer and his family could handle. That same independent spirit nurtured the growth of higher education here. In Lexington alone are Washington and Lee University, which Robert E. Lee headed, and the Virginia Military Institute, where Stonewall Jackson taught philosophy and artillery tactics, and which began admitting women in 1996 under order from the U.S. Supreme Court. A quartet of the South's most distinguished private women's colleges are only a short drive away: Mary Baldwin College at Staunton, Randolph-Macon Woman's College at Lynchburg, Sweet Briar College at Sweet Briar, and Hollins University at Roanoke, farther south in the Valley. A presidential library for Woodrow Wilson is planned for his birthplace of Staunton. Industry flourished here more than in most of Virginia east of the Blue Ridge. In the 19th century the Norfolk and Western Railway established its chief junction at Roanoke; as the years passed the city became the headquarters of the railroad, now Norfolk Southern, and many major companies have plants here. Now there is a proposal to build a parallel to Interstate 81, which links western Virginia as it runs through the Valley, solely for trucks.

The 6th Congressional District of Virginia covers the heart of the Valley of Virginia, from Strasburg south to Roanoke, and crosses over the Blue Ridge to take in Lynchburg, the home of Jerry Falwell's Thomas Road Baptist Church and Liberty University. Politically, this area has a Republican tradition hospitable to economic assistance for the little guy, and it fiercely opposed Harry Byrd Democrats. In recent decades the ancestral conservatism of Byrd Democrats and the feisty politics of the mountain rebels have melded into a single conservative Republicanism, more populist than elite in tone, as concerned with moral values as economic freedom, prickly about interference from Washington or even Richmond. In 2004 the 6th District voted 63% for George W. Bush, his highest percentage in a Virginia district.

The congressman from the 6th District is Bob Goodlatte, a Republican first elected in 1992, and now chairman of the House Agriculture Committee. Goodlatte grew up in Massachusetts, attended college in Maine and then law school at Washington & Lee, and went to work in Congressman Caldwell Butler's office in Roanoke. Goodlatte practiced law in Roanoke and stayed active in politics; in 1992, when Democrat Jim Olin retired, Goodlatte was nominated by convention and won the general 60%–40%.

Goodlatte has compiled a mostly conservative voting record. On the Judiciary Committee, he sponsored the House-passed bill to limit class-action lawsuits against tobacco companies, gun makers and other companies, and a separate bill to give federal courts jurisdiction over all class-action suits with claims exceeding $2 million. In response to conservatives' complaints over federal court decisions that cite legal rulings of other nations, he sponsored a bill stating that judicial decisions should not be based on foreign precedents. The Judiciary Committee approved his plan to eliminate the visa lottery program from the immigration law. The random program "poses a national security threat," Goodlatte warned.

With 9th District Democrat Rick Boucher, Goodlatte has been a leader among House members working on technology issues. He has chaired Speaker Dennis Hastert's High-Tech Working Group and co-chairs the Congressional Internet Caucus with Boucher, where they have encouraged open and non-taxed access to broadband technology. Goodlatte sponsored the Communications Decency Act, allowing censorship of obscene material on the Internet, which was overturned by the Supreme Court. To combat spyware software that tracks users' activities and identifying information, he won House passage of his "I-SPY Prevention Act" to criminalize the installation of such software without the owner's approval.

In January 2003, after the surprise retirement announcement of Larry Combest, Goodlatte became chairman of the Agriculture Committee. Combest's district in west Texas produces a lot of cotton; the agriculture in Goodlatte's district, as he notes, is "free-market oriented: poultry, livestock, orchards. It gives me a pretty free hand to work with all the different regions of the country." He is the first Agriculture chairman since 1967 from east of the Mississippi River. He joined ranking Democrat Charlie Stenholm in supporting the Bush administration's appeal of an April 2004 World Trade Organization ruling that U.S. cotton subsidies violated international trade rules. He worked to pass the Healthy Forests Initiative in 2003 and inserted into the 2003 omnibus appropriation a two-year postponement of the country of origin labeling provisions in the 2002 farm act. He worked with other tobacco state lawmakers to steer a perilous course in successfully attaching the tobacco buyout program—specifically, the end of Depression-era quotas and price supports—to the reform of corporate taxes, while rejecting Senate provisions to include FDA regulation of tobacco. "The tobacco program is a bad program, and we're glad to be rid of it." Also in October 2004, he passed a disaster-relief bill for victims of hurricanes in the Southeast and drought in the Midwest, which he coupled with a reduction in payments from the farm conservation program. But he met major protests, including some at home, when he refused to move a bill designed to stop the slaughter of horses; he argued that it would produce increased horse abuse and neglect, he said. The November 2004 omnibus appropriation contained a Goodlatte provision naming the oak as the national tree. The 2002 farm bill does not expire during the 109th Congress, but Goodlatte said he may start working on a new farm bill.

Goodlatte has been consistently reelected without difficulty. He has worked to fund projects in his district—$5 million for Roanoke River flood control, $14.2 million for airport runway reconstruction, $1 million for the Virginia Horse Center in Lexington—and has regularly donated his salary increases to local charities. No Democrat has run against him since 1998. Goodlatte encountered no problem when he abandoned in 2002 his self-imposed 12-year term limit.

SEVENTH DISTRICT

Rep. Eric Cantor (R)

Elected 2000, 3d term; b. June 6, 1963, Richmond; home, Richmond; George Washington U., B.A. 1985, Col. of William & Mary, J.D. 1988, Columbia U., M.S., 1989; Jewish; married (Diana).

Elected Office: VA House of Del., 1991–2000.

Professional Career: Practicing atty., 1990–2000.

DC Office: 329 CHOB, 20515, 202-225-2815; Fax: 202-225-0011; Web site: cantor.house.gov.

District Offices: Culpeper, 540-825-8960; Richmond, 804-747-4073.

Committees: *Chief Deputy Majority Whip. Ways & Means* (19th of 24 R): Oversight; Select Revenue Measures.

Group Ratings

	ADA	ACLU	AFS	LCV	ITIC	NTU	COC	ACU	NTLC	CHC
2004	0	0	0	0	100	69	100	100	89	92
2003	5	—	0	0	—	64	100	92	—	—

National Journal Ratings

	2003 LIB	—	2003 CONS		2004 LIB	—	2004 CONS
Economic	0%	—	91%		5%	—	93%
Social	5%	—	87%		20%	—	77%
Foreign	11%	—	80%		0%	—	96%

Key Votes of the 108th Congress

1. Drilling in ANWR	Y	5. DC School Vouchers	Y	9. Ban Same-Sex Marriage	Y
2. Approve Bush Tax Cuts	Y	6. Ban Human Cloning	Y	10. Fund Iraq War	Y
3. Medicare/Rx Bill	Y	7. Restrict Gun Liability	Y	11. Bar Cuba Embargo Funds	N
4. Bar Overtime Pay Regs.	N	8. Ban Partial-Birth Abortion	Y	12. Intelligence Reorg.	Y

Election Results

2004 general	Eric Cantor (R)	230,765	(75%)	($2,193,388)
	W. Brad Blanton (I)	74,325	(24%)	
2004 primary	Eric Cantor (R)	unopposed		
2002 general	Eric Cantor (R)	113,658	(69%)	($1,402,415)
	Ben "Cooter" Jones (D)	49,854	(30%)	($166,332)

Prior Winning Percentages: 2000 (67%)

The People		Race/Ethnic Origin	Ancestry	
Area size:	3,556 sq. mi.	78.2% White	English: 12.1% USA: 10.6%	
Urban population:	70.0%	16.1% Black	German: 10.2%	
Rural population:	30.0%	2.3% Asian	**2004 Presidential Vote**	
Pop. 2000:	643,499	0.3% Native Am.	Bush (R)	204,273 (61%)
Median income:	$50,990	0.0% Hawaiian	Kerry (D)	128,166 (38%)
Poverty status:	6.1%	1.1% Two+ races	Other	2,148 (1%)
Military veterans:	13.5%	0.1% Other	**2000 Presidential Vote**	
		2.0% Hispanic Origin	Bush (R)	172,425 (61%)
			Gore (D)	105,504 (37%)
			Other	6,261 (2%)
			Cook Partisan Voting Index: R +11	

Occupation Blue collar: 19.4% White collar: 68.4% Gray collar: 12.2%

In the center of Virginia, on a hill in downtown Richmond above the James River, is Thomas Jefferson's Capitol, one of the first classical-style buildings in North America, chaste and simple in the Jefferson style. A mile or so west is Monument Avenue, Richmond's grand 140-foot-wide boulevard, punctuated by circles, each with a statue of a Confederate hero—Robert E. Lee (62 feet tall, dedicated Memorial Day 1890), Jeb Stuart, Jefferson Davis, Stonewall Jackson, Matthew Fountain Maury, "the Pathfinder of the Sea." Richmond is a monument to Jefferson and to the Confederacy; its metro area is only the third largest in the state, but it still sets the tone for Virginia, and is the home of many of the state's great institutions—Dominion Resources, Main Street banks, big law firms, and the *Richmond Times-Dispatch*. Richmond's metro area has grown far past its city borders, covering almost all of suburban Henrico and Chesterfield Counties and spreading into what was until recently countryside. For many years Richmond was riven by sharp racial differences. It was from here that Virginia's leaders called for massive resistance to desegregation in the 1950s; when Richmond elected its first black-majority council in the 1970s, the outgoing council deeded the statue of Lee to the state for fear it would be torn down. Now Richmond has come to a better place. Blacks have been a majority in the city for two decades now, and in 1989 Virginia elected a black governor, Douglas Wilder, who grew up on Church Hill, in a segregated neighborhood overlooking the Capitol. In January 2005, Wilder made a triumphant return as mayor, elected by a biracial majority. The state's Martin Luther

King Jr. holiday pays homage to Confederate heroes and to the civil rights leader, and a statue of Richmond-born African-American tennis champion Arthur Ashe has been added to Monument Avenue. Richmond has been thriving economically with banking, securities, and health-care corporate offices and the Philip Morris headquarters. Politically, differences remain. Black-majority Richmond is solidly Democratic; Henrico, Chesterfield and the counties beyond are heavily Republican.

The 7th Congressional District of Virginia includes most of the area surrounding Richmond, but the black precincts in the city and Henrico County are mostly in the black-majority 3d District, which extends downriver along the James to Newport News and Norfolk. The district also extends past James Madison's home at Montpelier to fast-growing Spotsylvania and Culpeper Counties and as far north as Rappahannock County and the Blue Ridge Mountains. But 80% of the 7th's votes are cast in metro Richmond. This is one of the two most Republican districts in Virginia.

The congressman from the 7th District is Eric Cantor, a Republican first elected in 2000 and rapidly gaining influence in the House. He grew up in Henrico County, graduated from George Washington University and William and Mary law school and got a master's degree in real estate from Columbia University. He then began practicing law in his family's real-estate firm in Richmond. In 1991, he was elected to the first of five terms in Virginia's House of Delegates. In the legislature, he was a leading ally of business, sponsoring a bill to limit the liability of Philip Morris in a Florida court decree and opposing restrictions on telemarketers. When Congressman Tom Bliley announced his retirement in 2000, after six years as chairman of the Energy and Commerce Committee, Cantor entered the race. He had served as Bliley's campaign chairman for six years and had the backing of Bliley's political organization. He endorsed a $1,000 per child education tax credit, elimination of the marriage tax penalty, and an increase in the maximum IRA contribution. He faced a serious contest in the Republican primary from state Senator Stephen Martin, who emphasized his low-income background and had a solid base of social and religious conservatives. Their contest turned negative: Cantor attacked Martin for supporting a back-door pay raise for legislators; Martin questioned Cantor's business dealings. Cantor, who was well known in his Henrico County base, put on a substantial advertising campaign. Martin raised less than $200,000—a quarter of what Cantor spent in the primary. Cantor won the primary by only 263 votes. He got 74% of the vote in Henrico, while Martin got 77% in his Chesterfield County base. In the general election, Cantor won 67%–33%.

In the House, Cantor has been reliably conservative in the Richmond tradition. His first bill provided a tax credit of $1,000 per child for all parents with school-age children in public or private schools until they graduate from high school. With his knowledge of the Middle East and his strong support for Israel, Cantor, the only Jewish Republican in the House, chaired the Republican task force on terrorism and unconventional warfare; he praises George W. Bush as more committed to Israel than any other president. But his more significant activity was outside the public spotlight as a member of Tom DeLay's Whip team. His efforts to assure support for Republican initiatives impressed House leaders and led to a meteoric rise to leadership. In December 2002, incoming Majority Whip Roy Blunt unexpectedly named Cantor as his chief deputy whip, giving him a seat at the party's leadership table and handing him the often thankless task of tracking his colleagues' sentiments on pending legislation. As a party leader, he expanded his contacts with national Jewish groups and sought opportunities to draw favorable partisan comparisons for Republicans. Cantor also won a seat on the Ways and Means Committee, where he was a booster of the Medicare/prescription drug bill and health savings accounts.

Cantor was reelected in 2002 against Ben Jones, who served two terms in the House from Georgia before he lost a 1992 Democratic primary, but who remains better known for his "Cooter" character in *The Dukes of Hazzard*. Jones settled in Rappahannock County, where he opened two stores capitalizing on Cooter's popularity and joined a successful band. But Jones got little national Democratic support; Cantor mostly ignored him and won 69%–30%. The *Times-Dispatch* editorialized that Cantor's win showed he had become "indispensable" in Washington, as well as secure at home. His strong attacks on Democratic leaders in the 2004 campaign led the state Democratic chairman to call him "a Bush attack dog". He is among several Republicans mentioned as a possible contender if a Senate seat becomes open.

EIGHTH DISTRICT

Rep. Jim Moran (D)

Elected 1990, 8th term; b. May 16, 1945, Buffalo, NY; home, Alexandria; Col. of Holy Cross, B.A. 1967, City U. of NY, 1968, U. of Pittsburgh, M.P.A. 1970; Catholic; married (LuAnn).

Elected Office: Alexandria City Cncl., 1979–82; Alexandria Vice Mayor, 1982–84, Alexandria Mayor, 1985–90.

Professional Career: Budget analyst & auditor, U.S. Dept. of H.E.W., 1968–74; Fiscal policy spec., Library of Congress, 1974–76; Staff, U.S. Senate Approp. Cmte., 1976–80; Investment broker, 1980–88.

DC Office: 2239 RHOB, 20515, 202-225-4376; Fax: 202-225-0017; Web site: moran.house.gov.

District Offices: Alexandria, 703-971-4700; Reston, 703-481-4339.

Committees: *Appropriations* (12th of 29 D): Defense; Interior, Environment & Related Agencies.

Group Ratings

	ADA	ACLU	AFS	LCV	ITIC	NTU	COC	ACU	NTLC	CHC
2004	95	75	88	100	80	16	67	24	6	7
2003	95	—	100	95	—	27	54	24	—	—

National Journal Ratings

	2003 LIB	—	2003 CONS		2004 LIB	—	2004 CONS
Economic	66%	—	32%		63%	—	37%
Social	78%	—	20%		78%	—	19%
Foreign	68%	—	32%		87%	—	13%

Key Votes of the 108th Congress

1. Drilling in ANWR	N	5. DC School Vouchers	N	9. Ban Same-Sex Marriage	N
2. Approve Bush Tax Cuts	N	6. Ban Human Cloning	N	10. Fund Iraq War	N
3. Medicare/Rx Bill	N	7. Restrict Gun Liability	N	11. Bar Cuba Embargo Funds	Y
4. Bar Overtime Pay Regs.	Y	8. Ban Partial-Birth Abortion	N	12. Intelligence Reorg.	N

Election Results

2004 general	Jim Moran (D)	171,986	(60%)	($1,677,506)
	Lisa Marie Cheney (R)	106,231	(37%)	($337,580)
	Other	9,702	(3%)	
2004 primary	Jim Moran (D)	24,121	(59%)	
	Andrew Rosenberg (D)	17,067	(41%)	
2002 general	Jim Moran (D)	102,759	(60%)	($1,615,275)
	Scott Tate (R)	64,121	(37%)	($83,860)
	Other	4,919	(3%)	

Prior Winning Percentages: 2000 (63%); 1998 (67%); 1996 (66%); 1994 (59%); 1992 (56%); 1990 (52%)

The People		Race/Ethnic Origin	Ancestry	
Area size:	125 sq. mi.	57.1% White	German: 9.6%	Irish: 9.0%
Urban population:	100.0%	13.4% Black	English: 8.4%	
Rural population:	0.0%	9.5% Asian	**2004 Presidential Vote**	
Pop. 2000:	643,503	0.2% Native Am.	Kerry (D) 189,525	(64%)
Median income:	$63,430	0.1% Hawaiian	Bush (R) 104,298	(35%)
Poverty status:	7.5%	3.0% Two+ races	Other 2,782	(1%)
Military veterans:	11.3%	0.3% Other	**2000 Presidential Vote**	
		16.4% Hispanic Origin	Gore (D) 152,940	(57%)
			Bush (R) 101,788	(38%)
			Other 11,692	(4%)
			Cook Partisan Voting Index: D +14	

Occupation   Blue collar: 10.7%   White collar: 77.0%   Gray collar: 12.3%

More than two hundred years ago, when George Washington trod the brick sidewalks of Alexandria on his way to market or court or church, this was the largest city in Northern Virginia, far larger than Georgetown, Maryland, just up the Potomac River; what are now Capitol Hill and downtown Washington were hills above the river's mud flats. But Washington became the national capital, and as it grew Northern Virginia seemed left behind. In 1846, the District of Columbia retroceded its land south of the Potomac—now Alexandria and Arlington—to Virginia because it seemed obvious that the federal government would never need it, and it was 97 years before the first federal building was built on the Virginia side—the Pentagon; Franklin Roosevelt wondered out loud what they would do with all that space after the war. When the Pentagon was built, Alexandria and the rural countryside of Northern Virginia were represented in Congress by Judge Howard W. Smith, a Harry Byrd Democrat, who saw as his mission the maintenance of the standards of George Washington, Thomas Jefferson and Robert E. Lee. Yet by the 1960s, the area was changing around him. New subdivision dwellers with white-collar jobs and lots of children wanted schools with good academic programs—not the segregated schoolhouses Judge Smith's friends were willing to finance. The new generation wanted freeways, parks and recreation facilities. As Smith's district was moved farther out into the countryside, two-party politics came to the suburbs. The congressional seat here, though often bitterly contested, was held for 22 years by Republican Joel Broyhill, a real estate developer who ran a fine constituency service operation.

Now the onetime suburbs of Alexandria and Arlington have themselves become central cities of a sort—"edge cities," as Joel Garreau put it. Giant office developments sprang up from rail yards in Crystal City and from used car lots up-river in Rosslyn. Vietnamese and Salvadorans have moved into these neighborhoods, and one of America's biggest Vietnamese commercial districts is in Clarendon, about a mile from Arlington National Cemetery and Fort Myer. Politically, Alexandria and Arlington, once hotly contested, are now solidly Democratic, with gentrified older subdivisions and huge rental apartment complexes. Commuters find roads jammed, and there is a move to widen I-66 inside the Beltway, which was built with just four lanes as a compromise with opponents who didn't want the road at all.

The 8th Congressional District of Virginia consists of all of Arlington County and the cities of Alexandria and Falls Church. It takes in two separate parts of Fairfax County: A stretch of land from Tysons Corner west to Reston, and several areas south of Alexandria's Old Town—the gentle landscapes of Mount Vernon, lower-income Groveton along the old U.S. 1, suburban Springfield and the more rural areas around Fort Belvoir. The district now is solidly Democratic. Two local landmarks here were severely affected by the September 2001 attacks: The Pentagon was struck by American Airlines Flight 77 which caused a loss of 189 lives and nearly $1 billion in damage, and Ronald Reagan Washington National Airport was shut down because of security concerns for three weeks and did not return to nearly full operations for six months.

The congressman from the 8th District is Jim Moran, an oft-embattled Alexandria politician with traces in his accent of his Massachusetts roots. He graduated from Holy Cross and got a master's degree from the University of Pittsburgh, worked in Washington for HEW, the Library of Congress and the Senate Appropriations Committee. He was elected to the Alexandria City Council in 1979 and became vice mayor in 1982; in 1984 he pleaded no contest to a conflict of interest charge and resigned from the Council. The charges were later dropped, and in 1985 Moran was elected mayor. In 1990, he ran for Congress against Republican incumbent Stanford Parris. It was a nasty race: Parris said Moran was a supporter of Saddam Hussein; Moran said he wanted to "break [Parris's] nose," and called him "a deceitful, fatuous jerk." The major substantive issue was abortion, on which Moran ran a pro-choice ad portraying Lady Liberty behind bars. With a big margin in Alexandria, he won 52%–45%.

In the House, Moran has styled himself as a moderate among Democrats, though a bit more liberal on social issues. With Cal Dooley and Tim Roemer, he founded the New Democrat Coalition in 1997, made up of moderate Democrats to support alternatives to "traditional Democratic policies." Working with other New Democrats and with Virginians, he became a strong ally of the local high-tech industry. He criticized senior Democrat John Dingell for "doing the NRA's bidding" and harming Democrats on gun control legislation; Moran has called for a ban on the commercial sale of .50-caliber sniper rifles. On the Appropriations Committee, he worked to reverse the federal ban on adoptions by gay couples in the District. Also on Appropriations, he has been ranking Democrat on the Legislative Subcommittee, a strategic slot to distribute perks to colleagues. He strongly opposed the Republican initiative to rename Washington National Airport after Ronald Reagan.

Moran has been known for his short temper and quick tongue. He jousted—literally—with other Republicans, shoving Californian Duke Cunningham off the floor and out the House chamber doors in 1995 after Cunningham said that Moran had "turned his back on Desert Storm." He was strongly critical of Bill Clinton's conduct in the Lewinsky scandal and in September 1998 suggested the president should resign, but he voted against impeachment in December. At an anti-war forum in March 2003, Moran said, "If it were not for the strong support of the Jewish community for this war with Iraq we would not be doing this. . . . The leaders of the Jewish community are influential enough that they could change the direction of where this is going and I think they should." The furious reaction to his remarks led Moran to apologize; six Jewish Democratic members wrote to Minority Leader Nancy Pelosi that they "cannot and will not support" Moran's reelection in 2004. When Iraq Prime Minister Iyad Allawi spoke to a joint session of Congress in September 2004, Moran infuriated the Bush Administration with his reaction, "It sounded like the State Department wrote his speech."

His personal finances have raised frequent problems. He received negative headlines just before the 2000 election when the *Washington Post* reported that Maryland 8th District Democratic challenger—and pharmaceutical-company lobbyist—Terry Lierman gave his friend Moran a $25,000 loan on generous terms; Moran quickly agreed to repay the loan and suffered no apparent political damage. More trouble followed in 2002 with reports that he borrowed $50,000 from the founder of America Online, and that MBNA, the big credit-card company, had given him a favorable rate on a mortgage while Moran was arguing vehemently for the bankruptcy bill MBNA was strongly backing. Republican challenger Scott Tate attacked Moran's "twenty year history of self-inflicted ethical difficulties," but he raised little money. Moran won 60%–37%, a drop from his 63%–34% 2000 margin, despite running in a district that was slightly more Democratic. In 2004, several local officials threatened to challenge him in the Democratic primary but they never actually filed. His one primary opponent was Alexandria attorney Andrew Rosenberg, a political newcomer who criticized Moran's character and rhetoric, and ran as the more progressive candidate. Moran cited his legislative experience and his advocacy of district interests. He prevailed 59%–41%, with his largest margin in Alexandria. The general election against defense consultant Lisa Marie Cheney (whose husband is a distant relative of the Vice President) was never in serious doubt. She accused Moran of giving the district "a black eye and a bloody nose," and promised to "not embarrass us." Moran won 60%–37%.

NINTH DISTRICT

Rep. Rick Boucher (D)

Elected 1982, 12th term; b. Aug. 1, 1946, Abingdon; home, Abingdon; Roanoke Col., B.A. 1968, U. of VA, J.D. 1971; United Methodist; single.

Elected Office: VA Senate, 1975–1983.

Professional Career: Practicing atty., 1971–83.

DC Office: 2187 RHOB, 20515, 202-225-3861; Fax: 202-225-0442; Web site: www.house.gov/boucher.

District Offices: Abingdon, 540-628-1145; Big Stone Gap, 540-523-5450; Pulaski, 540-980-4310.

Committees: *Energy & Commerce* (4th of 26 D): Energy & Air Quality (RMM); Telecommunications & the Internet. *Judiciary* (3d of 17 D): Courts, the Internet & Intellectual Property.

Group Ratings

	ADA	ACLU	AFS	LCV	ITIC	NTU	COC	ACU	NTLC	CHC
2004	75	63	75	91	67	13	67	32	6	15
2003	90	—	88	75	—	23	53	24	—	—

National Journal Ratings

	2003 LIB — 2003 CONS	2004 LIB — 2004 CONS
Economic	58% — 41%	57% — 42%
Social	67% — 31%	57% — 43%
Foreign	81% — 17%	59% — 40%

Key Votes of the 108th Congress

1. Drilling in ANWR	N	5. DC School Vouchers	N	9. Ban Same-Sex Marriage	Y
2. Approve Bush Tax Cuts	N	6. Ban Human Cloning	N	10. Fund Iraq War	N
3. Medicare/Rx Bill	Y	7. Restrict Gun Liability	Y	11. Bar Cuba Embargo Funds	Y
4. Bar Overtime Pay Regs.	Y	8. Ban Partial-Birth Abortion	N	12. Intelligence Reorg.	Y

Election Results

2004 general	Rick Boucher (D)	150,039	(59%)	($1,628,026)
	Kevin Triplett (R)	98,499	(39%)	($646,669)
	Other	4,409	(2%)	
2004 primary	Rick Boucher (D)	unopposed		
2002 general	Rick Boucher (D)	100,075	(66%)	($1,085,883)
	Jay Katzen (R)	52,076	(34%)	($231,108)

Prior Winning Percentages: 2000 (70%); 1998 (61%); 1996 (65%); 1994 (59%); 1992 (63%); 1990 (97%); 1988 (63%); 1986 (99%); 1984 (52%); 1982 (50%)

The People		Race/Ethnic Origin	Ancestry	
Area size:	8,838 sq. mi.	93.3% White	USA: 20.0%	English: 7.7%
Urban population:	34.1%	3.8% Black	German: 7.7%	
Rural population:	65.9%	0.8% Asian	**2004 Presidential Vote**	
Pop. 2000:	643,514	0.1% Native Am.	Bush (R) 153,868	(59%)
Median income:	$29,783	0.0% Hawaiian	Kerry (D) 101,662	(39%)
Poverty status:	16.2%	0.7% Two+ races	Other 3,078	(1%)
Military veterans:	11.9%	0.1% Other	**2000 Presidential Vote**	
		1.1% Hispanic Origin	Bush (R) 129,110	(55%)
			Gore (D) 100,298	(42%)
			Other 7,011	(3%)
			Cook Partisan Voting Index: R + 7	
Occupation	Blue collar: 35.3%	White collar: 49.1%	Gray collar: 15.5%	

One of the first areas to be settled from the seacoast to the great American interior was what is now Southwest Virginia. As early as 1765, settlements were carved out of the great Valley of Virginia, which bends westward and south toward Tennessee and the Cumberland Gap. Most settlers were of Scot-Irish lineage, and the mountainous area where they moved developed almost apart from the rest of Virginia. The fiercely independent settlers were first farmers, later often coal miners, as in West Virginia, which wasn't a separate state until 1863. Politically, this virtually all-white area opposed slavery and was skeptical if not hostile to the Confederacy. Out of the crucible of struggle between secessionists and unionists, Southwest Virginia developed a robust two-party politics after the Civil War, with both parties resembling their national counterparts more closely than in the rest of Virginia. It is a long way here to plantation country: the state's extreme southwest corner is closer to the Mississippi River than to the Potomac.

The 9th Congressional District covers all of Southwest Virginia west of Roanoke. Over the years, the district became known as the "Fighting Ninth," because of its taste for raucous politics, culturally conservative and economically populist. Lately, it has become somewhat more like the rest of Virginia, as development has moved down Interstate 81 to, and even past, Blacksburg, home of Virginia Tech. It now includes Patrick County, the site of the R.J. Reynolds Homestead as well as annual peach and cabbage festivals. Mountain counties farther west continue to depend on coal and to lose population. It voted narrowly for Bill Clinton twice, and for 1996

Democratic Senate candidate Mark Warner, but by much wider margins, for George W. Bush in 2000 and 2004. No other Virginia district voted for that combination.

The congressman from the 9th District is Rick Boucher, a Democrat first elected in 1982. Boucher grew up in the antique town of Abingdon, went to Roanoke College and then the University of Virginia law school; he practiced law in Abingdon and was elected to the Virginia Senate in 1975, at 29. Politics runs in the family: His father was the Republican commonwealth's attorney in Washington County, while his mother was county Democratic chairwoman; his grandfather and great-grandfather were Democratic members of the House of Delegates. In 1982 Boucher ran for the House against veteran Representative William Wampler and won with big margins in coal counties on the Kentucky border. Boucher tends to vote with House Democrats but he sometimes strays, especially on economic issues.

Boucher has devoted much of his legislative time to technology issues. Back in 1988, he co-sponsored with then-Senator Al Gore a bill to allow phone companies to offer cable TV, and he sponsored the Satellite Home Viewers Act, so viewers without over-the-air network reception could subscribe to satellite services carrying network channels: The beginning of the now booming satellite TV business. Boucher sees new technologies, from satellite TV to the Internet, as a means for out-of-the-way places like the 9th to compete on an equal commercial basis with urban areas. On the 1996 Telecommunications Act, he helped write provisions intended to open up competition in the local telephone and cable TV markets. Boucher was a co-founder of the Congressional Internet Caucus and has been co-chairman with Bob Goodlatte of the next-door 6th District. He worked with Goodlatte on the Judiciary Subcommittee on Courts, the Internet and Intellectual Property to update copyright laws for the digital age and for a consensus on a National Information Infrastructure. He expressed concern that the recording industry's anti-piracy technology on CDs might override the consumer's ability to copy albums for personal use, as permitted by law, and he introduced a bill to permit circumventing such technology in digital content for "fair use."

His votes against the party line have caused Boucher some discomfort. In November 2003, he was one of 16 House Democrats who voted for the Medicare bill because of its prescription drug coverage. He worked actively for passage of the tobacco buyout bill. But he has voted with Democrats against tax cuts and the partial-birth abortion ban. Boucher has worked for binding arbitration to settle Superfund suits, for allowing state and local governments to engage in interstate shipment of municipal waste, and for electricity deregulation, which he hopes will benefit the coal industry and stimulate investment in mine facilities. He opposed normal trade relations with China and trade promotion authority, expressing concern about the impact on jobs in his district.

In this usually partisan district, Boucher conducts an active constituency service operation and has become highly popular despite his low-key style. His active encouragement and cheap local labor have helped his district to gain many telecom-support jobs, including telephone call centers, though they have been imperiled by out-sourcing overseas. His Commerce committee seat helps him to raise large sums of money and he usually wins comfortably. But he has faced spirited opposition. In 2004, his challenger was Kevin Triplett, a former NASCAR executive with significant support from national Republicans, including a Dick Cheney fundraiser. Triplett promised to bring more energy to local economic development and criticized Boucher for voting in 2003 against $87 billion for the war in Iraq; Boucher said that he opposed the reconstruction projects. He was supported by organized labor and the National Rifle Association and won 59%–39%, with Triplett narrowly leading in only two counties.

TENTH DISTRICT

Rep. Frank Wolf (R)

Elected 1980, 13th term; b. Jan. 30, 1939, Philadelphia, PA; home, Vienna; PA St. U., B.A. 1961, Georgetown U., LL.B. 1965; Presbyterian; married (Carolyn).

Military Career: Army, 1962–63, Army Reserves 1963–67.

Professional Career: Legis. Asst., U.S. Rep. Edward Biester, 1968–71; Asst., U.S. Interior Secy. Rogers Morton, 1971–74; Dep. Asst. Secy., U.S. Dept. of Interior, 1974–75; Practicing atty., 1975–80.

DC Office: 241 CHOB, 20515, 202-225-5136; Fax: 202-225-0437; Web site: www.house.gov/wolf.

District Offices: Herndon, 703-709-5800; Winchester, 540-667-0990.

Committees: *Appropriations* (5th of 37 R): Science, State, Justice, Commerce & Related Agencies (Chmn.); Transportation, Treasury, HUD, the Judiciary & District of Columbia.

Group Ratings

	ADA	ACLU	AFS	LCV	ITIC	NTU	COC	ACU	NTLC	CHC
2004	25	5	25	45	70	45	90	76	67	84
2003	15	—	13	5	—	57	83	84	—	—

National Journal Ratings

	2003 LIB	—	2003 CONS	2004 LIB	—	2004 CONS
Economic	33%	—	64%	46%	—	53%
Social	40%	—	58%	42%	—	57%
Foreign	11%	—	80%	25%	—	68%

Key Votes of the 108th Congress

1. Drilling in ANWR	Y	5. DC School Vouchers	Y	9. Ban Same-Sex Marriage	Y
2. Approve Bush Tax Cuts	Y	6. Ban Human Cloning	Y	10. Fund Iraq War	Y
3. Medicare/Rx Bill	Y	7. Restrict Gun Liability	Y	11. Bar Cuba Embargo Funds	N
4. Bar Overtime Pay Regs.	N	8. Ban Partial-Birth Abortion	Y	12. Intelligence Reorg.	Y

Election Results

2004 general	Frank Wolf (R)	205,982	(64%)	($1,611,149)
	James Socas (D)	116,654	(36%)	($921,094)
2004 primary	Frank Wolf (R)	unopposed		
2002 general	Frank Wolf (R)	115,917	(72%)	($691,008)
	John Stevens (D)	45,464	(28%)	($20,344)

Prior Winning Percentages: 2000 (84%); 1998 (72%); 1996 (72%); 1994 (87%); 1992 (64%); 1990 (62%); 1988 (68%); 1986 (60%); 1984 (63%); 1982 (53%); 1980 (51%)

The People		Race/Ethnic Origin	Ancestry	
Area size:	1,864 sq. mi.	77.2% White	German: 12.9% Irish: 10.5%	
Urban population:	83.3%	6.7% Black	English: 9.5%	
Rural population:	16.7%	6.6% Asian	**2004 Presidential Vote**	
Pop. 2000:	643,512	0.2% Native Am.	Bush (R)	182,210 (55%)
Median income:	$71,560	0.0% Hawaiian	Kerry (D)	145,741 (44%)
Poverty status:	4.4%	1.9% Two+ races	Other	2,736 (1%)
Military veterans:	13.5%	0.2% Other	**2000 Presidential Vote**	
		7.1% Hispanic Origin	Bush (R)	148,211 (56%)
			Gore (D)	109,063 (41%)
			Other	8,106 (3%)
			Cook Partisan Voting Index: R + 5	
Occupation	Blue collar: 15.9% White collar: 72.5% Gray collar: 11.6%			

When George Washington decided to place the new nation's capital on the Potomac just upriver from Mount Vernon, where the falls block navigation above the port of Georgetown, the land above the fall line on the Virginia side of the river—the rolling green Piedmont of northern

Virginia and the fertile mountain-bound lands of the Shenandoah Valley—was buzzing with new settlers. They came up the Potomac and the runs (a Virginia word for small rivers) that flow into it and into the Valley from the great Wagon Road south from Pennsylvania, moving onto lands speculated on by Washington and his peers. During the Civil War, this was some of the most heavily contested land on the continent; afterwards, the land was quiet: The frontier was very far to the west, and on these lands farmers quietly raised hay and grazed cattle and kept horses and hounds for fox hunting. During World War II and immediately after this was still open country: General George Marshall, driving from his office in the Pentagon to the old house he bought in the courthouse town of Leesburg 30 miles away, would pass a few gas stations and crossroads villages and hundreds of acres of farm fields. If he could make the trip today, he would see something very different. For metropolitan Washington has spread out into this bucolic land. There are still some horse farms in the Piedmont, long the first or second homes of some of the richest people in America, but they are increasingly flanked by subdivisions that sprout up in the fields overnight. Fairfax County, by many measures the highest-income county in the nation, had 98,000 people in 1950; the Census Bureau estimated its population in 2004 as 1,003,157. Loudoun County, just past Dulles Airport, was the fastest growing county in the United States from 2000 to 2004, from 170,000 to 239,000. Loudoun elected anti-growth supervisors in 1999 but voted them out in 2003. The Washington metropolitan area now extends past Fairfax and Loudoun and over the Blue Ridge into the Shenandoah Valley.

In the 1950s and 1960s, the Northern Virginia suburbs of Washington were just that: Bedroom communities where most workers headed into the District of Columbia and where one-third of them were employed by the federal government. Today Northern Virginia is an employment center and focus of innovation on its own. The Dulles Access Road, which ran through rural-looking territory 20 years ago, is now lined with office buildings holding high-tech firms and entrepreneurial startups. Along intersecting Route 28, crossing the Fairfax-Loudoun County line, are the headquarters of tech giants such as America Online and Telos Corp. The federal government is no longer the dominant employer here. Some of Northern Virginia's private sector is the spawn of government—"Beltway Bandits" and defense contractors—but this area has also become one of the nation's major centers of high-tech and telecommunications firms.

The 10th Congressional District covers much of Northern Virginia. It starts inside the Capital Beltway and includes most of McLean, home to much of Washington's political and lawyer-lobbyist elite, and goes beyond the Beltway to include woodsy Great Falls, Herndon and the Route 28 corridor around Dulles Airport. It includes Manassas, site of the Civil War's first battle and now of a spruced up Old Town, in Prince William County; all of Loudoun County, heavily built-up in the east with some still rural areas west of Leesburg; and the northern half of Fauquier County, which has limited development and is still mostly horse farms. It includes three counties in the northern end of the Shenandoah Valley, the country around Front Royal and Winchester. In 2004, 34% of the votes were cast in Fairfax County, 33% in Loudoun County, 11% in Prince William and Manassas, 5% in Fauquier and 18% in the Shenandoah Valley. The political leanings of parts of metro Washington reflect the government agencies that predominate there and the private economy that has grown up around them: Northern Virginia, with its defense and high-tech base, tends to be Republican, while Montgomery County, Maryland, with its health and biotech base, tends to be Democratic. The 10th District is a Republican district, though like other Northern Virginia districts it trended away from George W. Bush in 2004.

The congressman from the 10th District is Frank Wolf, first elected in 1980. Wolf grew up in Philadelphia, went to law school at Georgetown, worked as a staffer on Capitol Hill and as an Interior Department appointee in the Nixon and Ford administrations and practiced law. In 1976 he ran for Congress and lost the Republican primary. In 1978 he won the nomination to run against Joseph Fisher, a liberal who had won the district in 1974, and lost 53%–47%; in 1980 Wolf ran again and won 51%–49%. He started off, in the suburban Washington manner, maintaining an active constituency service operation and concentrating on issues affecting federal employees.

Over the years Wolf has come to specialize in three other areas—transportation, human rights and gambling. He used his seat on the Transportation Appropriations Subcommittee to work on projects in traffic-choked Northern Virginia. In October 2000, Wolf called for a study of a proposed "Techway" bridge over the Potomac linking Rockville and Dulles. But protests by homeowners in Great Falls and other areas convinced him to oppose the study in May 2001, and in May 2004 he withdrew a request for a study because of local opposition. He has also sought funding for a Metro rail link to Dulles Airport which, astonishingly, was not foreseen by the system's planners. Wolf has helped obtain funding for the project, $25 million in 2004 and $185 million in all; approval went ahead for preliminary engineering in July 2004. In June 2003 he and Tom Davis asked for an additional outbound lane on I-66 in Arlington. From 1995 to 2001, Wolf was chairman of the Transportation Appropriations subcommittee; he opposed earmarking proposals for specific congressmen, even as the chairman of the authorizing committee, Bud Shuster made the practice an art form; Wolf thus lost much of the appropriators' leverage. He used the subcommittee chairmanship to put through a national .08% blood alcohol limit for drunk driving and to promote truck safety. In January 2001, House Republicans' six-year limits on chairmanships caught up with both Wolf and Shuster: Shuster resigned from Congress, while Wolf took the chairmanship of the Commerce, Justice and State Subcommittee.

In that capacity he has worked since the September 11 attacks to change the culture of the FBI. He assisted Director Robert Mueller's reorganization and called for sharing information across international lines. In 2004 he sponsored a bill to allow the FBI to offer bonuses to hire and keep employees. In 2003 he obtained $5 million for a Response to Emergencies and Disasters Institute in Ashburn, in eastern Loudoun County. He opposed the bill to require destruction within 24 hours of gun buyer background checks because he thought the information should be available to terrorism investigators.

Wolf has been one of the House's leading crusaders for human rights and is co-chairman of the Congressional Human Rights Caucus. With Nancy Pelosi, he led the annual moves to withdraw normal trade relations with China because of human right violations; he strongly opposed normal trade relations in 2000, citing China's acts of jailing dissidents, killing Catholic priests, jailing evangelical pastors, persecuting Tibetan Buddhists and aiming missiles at the United States. In 2004 he, Joe Pitts and Senator Sam Brownback called on Trade Representative Robert Zoellick to accept the AFL-CIO's petition to impose sanctions on China because of its low wages. In 1998 he sponsored the law setting up a religious freedom office in the State Department and requiring annual reports on religious freedom throughout the world. He traveled to El Salvador in 1982, Sudan in 1989, Romania in 1990, East Timor and Tibet in 1997 (only the second time a congressman has been there since the Chinese takeover in 1959), Sierra Leone in 1999 and Ethiopia in 2003, where he saw starvation as ghastly as he had in 1984. He has made five visits to Sudan and reported on how the Sudanese government blocked food shipments, bombed civilians and supported slave raids. He has sought to track the trade in diamonds in West Africa, apparently utilized by Al Qaeda, and got money to put an FBI office there. Wolf and Chris Shays have been the only two members of the House to travel widely in Iraq without Defense Department escorts. Wolf has called for investigation of Department of Justice memos on interrogation and in December 2003, after an Iraq trip said, "I would urge the administration to be open to outside ideas and practice more humility."

Wolf is probably Congress's leading opponent of gambling. He first proposed the National Gambling Impact Study Commission, passed in 1997, but was not pleased by the appointees; he hailed its call in June 1999 for a pause in granting licenses for new casinos and for federal oversight of Indian and Internet gambling. He has opposed federal recognition of Indian tribes in Virginia, in contrast to Governor Mark Warner.

With his seat on Appropriations, Wolf has funded many projects in the 10th District, ranging from $100,000 for Belle Grove Plantation and Cedar Creek Battlefield Foundation to $2.65 million for local law enforcement to crack down on gangs to $100,000 for a common headquarters for Loudoun Cares, a group of local charities. He has generally been reelected by wide margins, and redistricting in 2001 was not a problem; he and Republican Tom Davis and Democrat Jim Moran agreed on boundaries for Northern Virginia, which were enacted by the Republican legislature. But in 2004 he had a more vocal challenger than usual. James Socas, a University of Virginia graduate who made a fortune as an investment banker in San Francisco in the tech boom, moved to the Washington area to work as a Senate staffer and then ran against Wolf. Socas spent $921,000 in all, $499,000 of it his own money, on radio ads harshly attacking Wolf. He charged that Wolf had failed to get Metro extended to Dulles and had not done enough to relieve traffic congestion. "He is a deep religious conservative. He legislates his faith," Socas said, and charged that Wolf was part of an "extremist" Christian group whose members "admire the strength and personal leadership" shown by Adolf Hitler, Vladimir Lenin, Ho Chi Minh and Osama bin Laden. Wolf spent $1.6 million on the race and pointed out that Socas had only recently moved to Northern Virginia and did not own a home in the district. "He doesn't understand the area. He's a millionaire who moved from California who's literally making an effort to buy a congressional seat here." He ran ads with surfing music (though Socas had lived in San Francisco, where there is little surfing). Wolf won 64%–36%, a lesser margin than his 72%–28% win in 2002, but still impressive; he carried every city and county.

ELEVENTH DISTRICT

Rep. Tom Davis (R)

Elected 1994, 6th term; b. Jan. 5, 1949, Minot, ND; home, Annandale; Amherst Col. B.A. 1971, U. of VA, J.D. 1975; Christian Scientist; married (Jeannemarie Devolites).

Military Career: Army, 1971–72; Army Reserves, 1972–79.

Elected Office: Fairfax Cnty. Bd. of Supervisors, 1979–94, Chmn., 1991–94.

Professional Career: Vice Pres. & Gen. Cnsl., PRC Inc., 1977–94.

DC Office: 2348 RHOB, 20515, 202-225-1492; Fax: 202-225-3071; Web site: tomdavis.house.gov.

District Offices: Annandale, 703-916-9610; Prince William, 703-590-4599.

Committees: *Government Reform* (Chmn. of 23 R): Federal Workforce & Agency Organization; Government Management, Finance & Accountability. *Homeland Security* (9th of 19 R): Economic Security, Infrastructure Protection & Cybersecurity; Management, Integration & Oversight.

Group Ratings

	ADA	ACLU	AFS	LCV	ITIC	NTU	COC	ACU	NTLC	CHC
2004	10	10	25	18	89	53	100	80	63	66
2003	5	—	0	30	—	58	93	72	—	—

National Journal Ratings

	2003 LIB	—	2003 CONS	2004 LIB	—	2004 CONS
Economic	36%	—	64%	25%	—	75%
Social	49%	—	50%	51%	—	48%
Foreign	43%	—	56%	37%	—	62%

Key Votes of the 108th Congress

1. Drilling in ANWR	Y	5. DC School Vouchers	Y	9. Ban Same-Sex Marriage	Y
2. Approve Bush Tax Cuts	Y	6. Ban Human Cloning	Y	10. Fund Iraq War	Y
3. Medicare/Rx Bill	Y	7. Restrict Gun Liability	Y	11. Bar Cuba Embargo Funds	N
4. Bar Overtime Pay Regs.	N	8. Ban Partial-Birth Abortion	Y	12. Intelligence Reorg.	Y

Election Results

2004 general	Tom Davis (R)	186,299	(60%)	($1,835,379)
	Ken Longmyer (D)	118,305	(38%)	($71,661)
	Other	4,629	(1%)	
2004 primary	Tom Davis (R)	unopposed		
2002 general	Tom Davis (R)	135,379	(83%)	($1,591,381)
	Frank Creel (CNP)	26,892	(16%)	($8,797)
	Other	1,027	(1%)	

Prior Winning Percentages: 2000 (62%); 1998 (82%); 1996 (64%); 1994 (53%)

The People		Race/Ethnic Origin	Ancestry		
Area size:	404 sq. mi.	66.8% White	German: 11.5%		Irish: 10.0%
Urban population:	95.9%	10.1% Black	English: 9.4%		
Rural population:	4.1%	10.9% Asian	**2004 Presidential Vote**		
Pop. 2000:	643,509	0.2% Native Am.	Bush (R) 161,104	(50%)	
Median income:	$80,397	0.1% Hawaiian	Kerry (D) 159,055	(49%)	
Poverty status:	3.8%	2.6% Two+ races	Other 2,561	(1%)	
Military veterans:	15.9%	0.2% Other	**2000 Presidential Vote**		
		9.1% Hispanic Origin	Bush (R) 140,961	(52%)	
			Gore (D) 123,702	(45%)	
			Other 8,087	(3%)	
			Cook Partisan Voting Index: R + 1		

Occupation	Blue collar: 11.7%	White collar: 76.5%	Gray collar: 11.8%

When author and *Washington Post* reporter Joel Garreau coined the term "edge city" to describe the autonomous urban centers developing on the rims of some of the nation's oldest municipalities, his prime example was Tysons Corner, Virginia. Rising on a hill west of Washington, Tysons Corner was a back-country intersection 50 years ago and a junction of several suburban roads 30 years ago; today it is home to the largest concentration of office space to be found anywhere between Washington and Atlanta, with a modern skyline and busy multi-lane avenues that serve as arteries to the Capital Beltway. Fairfax County, which includes all of Tysons Corner, has changed just as dramatically since the end of World War II. At first only a few District of Columbia residents seeking breathing room in the suburbs trickled into Northern Virginia; initially they went to Arlington and Alexandria. But that trickle became a rush as young marrieds with large families and whites avoiding the increasingly high-crime District pushed farther out into Fairfax. Now Fairfax County is no longer Washington's country cousin. By 2000 it had 969,000 residents, nearly twice D.C.'s 572,000; it reached 1 million by 2003. It had in 1999 the nation's highest median household income ($81,050), over half its residents have a bachelor's degree or more and 71% of its households have two or more vehicles. Fairfax County is taking on most of the aspects of a city, with new high-density cluster developments around Metro stops and plenty of immigrants, from Koreans and Vietnamese to Afghanis and Africans, and with growth slowing because most of its land has been developed. There is even faster growth to the west in Loudoun County and to the south in Prince William County, growth not only in housing but in jobs; in 2003–04, the number of jobs in Prince William grew 8%, the most of any county in the nation, and not far behind were Loudoun (5.5%) and Fairfax (4.2%). Prince William is growing more affluent too, as megahouse subdivisions spring up in the western part of the county its median household income rose to Fairfax's high level.

The 11th Congressional District of Virginia consists of much of Fairfax County and most of Prince William County. The district straddles the Capital Beltway and includes Tysons Corner. Inside the Beltway are Baileys Crossroads and Annandale; beyond are Vienna, Fairfax, much of Springfield, Burke, Clifton, Centreville, part of Mount Vernon. In Prince William County it includes Woodbridge and Dale City and stretches west to Haymarket. This is a cosmopolitan district: 10% black, 9% Hispanic, 11% Asian in 2000; some 25% of residents speak a language other than English at home. The district is made up largely of two-income families, many with at least one spouse employed in one of the many divisions of high-tech companies that dot Fairfax County. The district was first created in 1991, after Virginia got a new seat in the 1990 Census. It was originally designed to be equally divided between the parties, and within its 1991 boundaries it voted 43%–42% for George H.W. Bush in 1992, 49%–47% for Bill Clinton in 1996 and 49%–47% for Al Gore in 2000. In its post-redistricting 2002 form, the district voted 52%–45% for George W. Bush in 2000 but only 50%–49% for him in 2004.

The congressman from the 11th District is Tom Davis, a Republican first elected in 1994. Davis was born in Minot, North Dakota, grew up in Northern Virginia, and was always interested in politics; by seventh grade he could name every member of the House. He got a job as a Senate page and was president of his class at the Capitol Page School; he was a roommate of

David Eisenhower at Amherst College, where almost everyone else was a Democrat or something further left; he served on active duty in the Army before earning a law degree. He practiced law in Northern Virginia and was general counsel to computer services firm PRC. In 1979 he was elected to the Fairfax County Board of Supervisors, a high visibility position. In 1991 he was elected board chairman, something in the nature of a mayor.

In 1994 Davis ran for the 11th District seat against Democrat Leslie Byrne, who had won 50%–45% in 1992. Byrne had voted solidly for Clinton administration positions and called for discipline against members of the Democratic Caucus who did not; she had strong support from labor and feminist groups and spent $1.1 million. But Davis was able to raise and spend even more, $1.4 million. He won 53%–45%.

As soon as he arrived on Capitol Hill, Davis was handed by Speaker Newt Gingrich one of the hottest potatoes of the new Congress: Dealing with the affairs of the troubled District of Columbia government and its just re-elected mayor, Marion Barry. As chairman of the House Government Reform and Oversight Committee's D.C. Subcommittee, Davis first rejected Barry's request for massive federal aid, working closely with Gingrich and District Delegate Eleanor Holmes Norton to cut District spending. Together they passed in April 1995 a law establishing a five-member control board to oversee the D.C. government. He tended to oppose the appropriators' detailed policy prescription as micromanagement, but went along with the 1997 law taking power over nine agencies from Barry and giving it to the control board. In February 1999 Davis and Norton sponsored a bill restoring full management powers to the District and its new mayor, Anthony Williams; it was speedily passed. Davis and Norton also passed a bill suggested by *Washington Post* publisher Donald Graham to enable District students to attend Virginia and Maryland public colleges and universities at in-state tuition rates.

In 2003 Davis became chairman of the Government Reform Committee and abolished the D.C. subcommittee, allowing him to take the lead on District issues himself. The tuition program has grown beyond expectations, and Davis got a two-year extension in 2004 after objections from Senator Jeff Sessions to the treatment of private schools and historically black colleges and universities threatened to end it. In 2003 Davis also pushed through, against opposition from Norton and teachers' unions, but with the support of Mayor Williams and D.C. school board head Peggy Cooper Cafritz, a voucher program for the District of Columbia. Congress has the power to govern the District and change D.C. laws, but Davis managed to get the House to agree to eliminate riders to D.C. appropriations bills and let Government Reform oversee them; he opposed the House's symbolic repeal of the District's gun laws (the Senate didn't go along) as a "dangerous assault on home rule." He was less successful on his attempt to give the District voting representation in the House. His idea, floated in spring 2003, was to add two members, one for the District and the other for the state entitled under the statutory formula to the 436th seat in the House, which after the 2000 Census just happened to be Utah; that pretty much guaranteed that the District's Democrat would be balanced by a Utah Republican. But Speaker Dennis Hastert said, "Davis floats things from time to time," and Majority Leader Tom DeLay said, "It would require a constitutional amendment." Norton, in favor of full House and Senate representation, declined to endorse it, and Government Reform's ranking Democrat opposed it; he feared the Utah legislature would produce a redistricting that would threaten the state's single Democrat, Jim Matheson. In November 2004 Davis got a legal opinion from conservative scholars that the proposal was constitutional, and Matheson won reelection by a wide enough margin in a Republican-leaning district to suggest he was impervious to challenge; perhaps Davis will have more success with the proposal in the 109th Congress.

Davis is a political buff with a detailed knowledge of political statistics across the country. When the chairmanship of the NRCC became an elective post after the November 1998 election, in which Republicans lost seats, Davis ran against incumbent John Linder and won 130–77. He raised and spent $1 million on 1999 state legislative races in Virginia, in which Republicans captured both houses and won control of redistricting; within a few months conservative incumbent Congressman Virgil Goode left the Democratic Party and announced he would caucus with Republicans and conservative Democrat Owen Pickett retired—a quick two-seat gain. In the 1999–2000 cycle Davis early on spotted open seats which had long voted Democratic but where conservative non-economic issues helped Republicans—Pennsylvania's 4th, West Virginia's 2d, Missouri's 6th, Michigan's 8th, Virginia's 2d—and won them all. Against party-switcher Michael Forbes in New York's 1st, he spent money on billboards thanking him for his solid support of Newt Gingrich and the Contract With America; Forbes was upset in the September Democratic primary, and the seat went Republican in November. He spotted the weakness of 20-year incumbent Democrat Sam Gejdenson in Connecticut's 2d, which led to another gain. The Republican nomination in the open seat in Florida's 8th was not determined until the October runoff; but for two months before the NRCC spent heavily on ads attacking the Democratic nominee, who lost 51%–49%. Only four Republican incumbents lost, three in California and one in the Arkansas 4th District (the one district where a vote for impeachment hurt).

Davis was re-elected campaign committee chairman in November 2000. Republicans far outraised Democrats in the 2001–02 cycle, and once again Davis did a fine job of targeting vulnerable seats, but his most valuable work was on redistricting. Not since the death of California Democrat Phillip Burton in 1983 has a member of Congress with such a detailed knowledge of the political demography of the entire country taken such a lead role in redistricting. Davis and White House political strategist Karl Rove persuaded the chief Democratic redistricter in California, Michael Berman, brother of Congressman Howard Berman, to settle for a plan that gave the state's one new seat to Democrats but otherwise maintained the status quo. After Democrats put through an aggressively partisan redistricting plan in Georgia, Davis worked to see that Republicans in Pennsylvania put through a similarly aggressive plan. As a result, Republicans gained seats in a state that lost two seats while Democrats failed to achieve the gains they expected in a state that gained two seats. Davis urged the appointment of Ohio Democrat Tony Hall to the UN's FAO in Rome; redistricting made Hall's seat more Republican, and a Republican won it easily. Republicans picked up five seats—the second time in a row the party in the White House gained seats.

After the 2002 elections the Republican Steering Committee chose Davis to chair the Government Reform Committee, though he started the year off as only ninth in seniority. This was in part a reward for his work as campaign committee chairman and in part a recognition of his expertise on civil service law. He has long been attentive to federal employee issues; he opposed the Contract with America tax cut in 1995 because it would have required higher pension payments by federal employees. He and Maryland's Steny Hoyer got the House to pass a bill giving U.S. Park Police and the Secret Service Uniformed Division the same locality pay as other federal workers and Davis worked to see that they could buy back credit for military service to increase their retirement benefits. He has pushed successfully for civilian employees to get the same percentage pay increase as the military and to have better dental and vision benefits offered on federal employees' health insurance policies; when the Medicare prescription drug bill was pending, he sponsored a guarantee that federal retirees would get the same prescription drug benefits as federal employees. Against the opposition of federal employees unions, Davis has backed the Bush administration policies for competitive sourcing in the Defense and Homeland Security Departments, with access to the GAO's protest forums, but he accepted not having these procedures in the new national intelligence director's office. He has sponsored bills to set standards for Internet sites selling prescription drugs and, with Henry Waxman, to protect the security and privacy of government employees' computers from file sharing programs. In 2003 he passed an amendment allowing Richard Nixon's presidential papers to be transferred outside the Washington area; this enabled the Nixon Library in Yorba Linda, California, to become part of the National Archives system.

Davis has also been attentive to local issues. Over several years he worked on getting federal financing for the new Woodrow Wilson Bridge, which totaled $1.58 billion in federal aid, and with Frank Wolf called for an extra outbound lane on I-66 in Arlington. He has obtained money for widening Route 123 and an engineering study for extending Metro to Reston. He has paid attention to the growing immigrant population in Fairfax County and has worked for amnesty and refugee status for Vietnamese immigrants and their children.

Fairfax County has been trending Democratic, but Davis has not been in political trouble in the 11th District. In 2001, Davis, Wolf and Moran drew new district lines for Northern Virginia that helped all three. In November 2002, with no Democratic opponent, he won with 83% of the vote; in 2004, against an underfunded Democrat, he won 60%–38%, even as George W. Bush became the first Republican to lose Fairfax County since 1964. As Davis said, "The city is moving out to the suburbs. We all recognized that Fairfax was going to turn. How big it would turn was unclear." Davis has made no secret that he has statewide ambitions, and might run for the Senate if John Warner retires in 2008. They may have been complicated by his strong support in April 2004 for Governor Mark Warner's tax increases. A minority of House of Delegates Republicans as well as almost all Senate Republicans provided critical support for the increases; one of them was Davis's wife, state Senator Jeannemarie Devolites. Five of six Republican legislators who supported the tax increases beat back challenges from anti-tax candidates in the June 2005 primary; the outcome of those battles might be an indicator of the viability of Davis's statewide ambitions.

★ WASHINGTON ★

For a brief moment in the late 1990s, the eyes of the nation—and the world—were on Washington—Washington state, that is, not Washington, D.C. From Starbucks coffee to grunge music, from America's leading exporter, Boeing, to America's leading software maker, Microsoft, to America's most visible dot-com, amazon.com, Washington was a national trendsetter. An unusual environment and human creativity combined to produce these achievements: Seattle's cold misty air and 225 overcast days a year stimulate the appetite for strong aromatic coffee, and the shapeless blue jeans and sweatshirts worn year-round in this moist climate by professionals and teenagers alike created a trend made famous by Nirvana and Soundgarden and other grunge artists. Boeing's airframe business took off during World War II because the Pacific Northwest's abundant hydroelectric power made cheap aluminum possible, and the boom in air travel in the 1980s and 1990s kept Boeing's huge assembly lines humming. Microsoft, founded by the usually tie-less and tousle-haired Bill Gates and based in Redmond, across Lake Washington from Seattle, became one of America's great success stories as its software became embedded in the vast majority of the world's computers. With flannel shirts and umbrellas, blue-collar types working off hangovers as if in a Raymond Carver story, and professionals relaxing on woodsy acreage, Washington set a tone for the late 1990s, a style plainly Middle American but with attitude, an ordinariness so hip it is no longer ordinary. As the end of the century approached, Washington was a commonwealth of nearly 6 million people, economically booming, pleased to the point of smugness with its physical environment and lifestyle. But since that high point Washington has had its woes, and it is useful to see how it got there, and the strengths it has to approach another peak ahead.

For Washington is a state which is not much more than a century old, one which in the two decades after statehood in 1889 built a new civilization, as transcontinental railroads reached the great ports of Puget Sound, the wheat-processing city of Spokane inland, orchard towns and fishing ports and lumber settlements. Shielded from the storms of the Pacific by the Olympic Mountains and the Sound, Seattle quickly became a serious American city, a lusty town full of lumbermen and railroad workers. When gold was struck in the Klondike and Alaska, Seattle became a metropolis of miners, prospectors and get-rich-quick operators, the site of the original "Skid Road" (skid row is a corruption propagated by a 1937 magazine article), where logs were rolled downhill to the port; today it's the focus of the restored Pioneer Square area. Thriving young Seattle had a turbulent class-warfare politics in the years before World War I, pitting the Industrial Workers of the World (the IWW, or Wobblies) against city business and civic leaders; the businessmen, after some violence, prevailed. Adding to the area's distinctiveness was its large number of Scandinavian immigrants, with their favorable views of cooperative enterprises and government ownership.

Over time, Washington was transformed by a series of national decisions that set its course for decades. One was government development of hydroelectric power. The Columbia River and

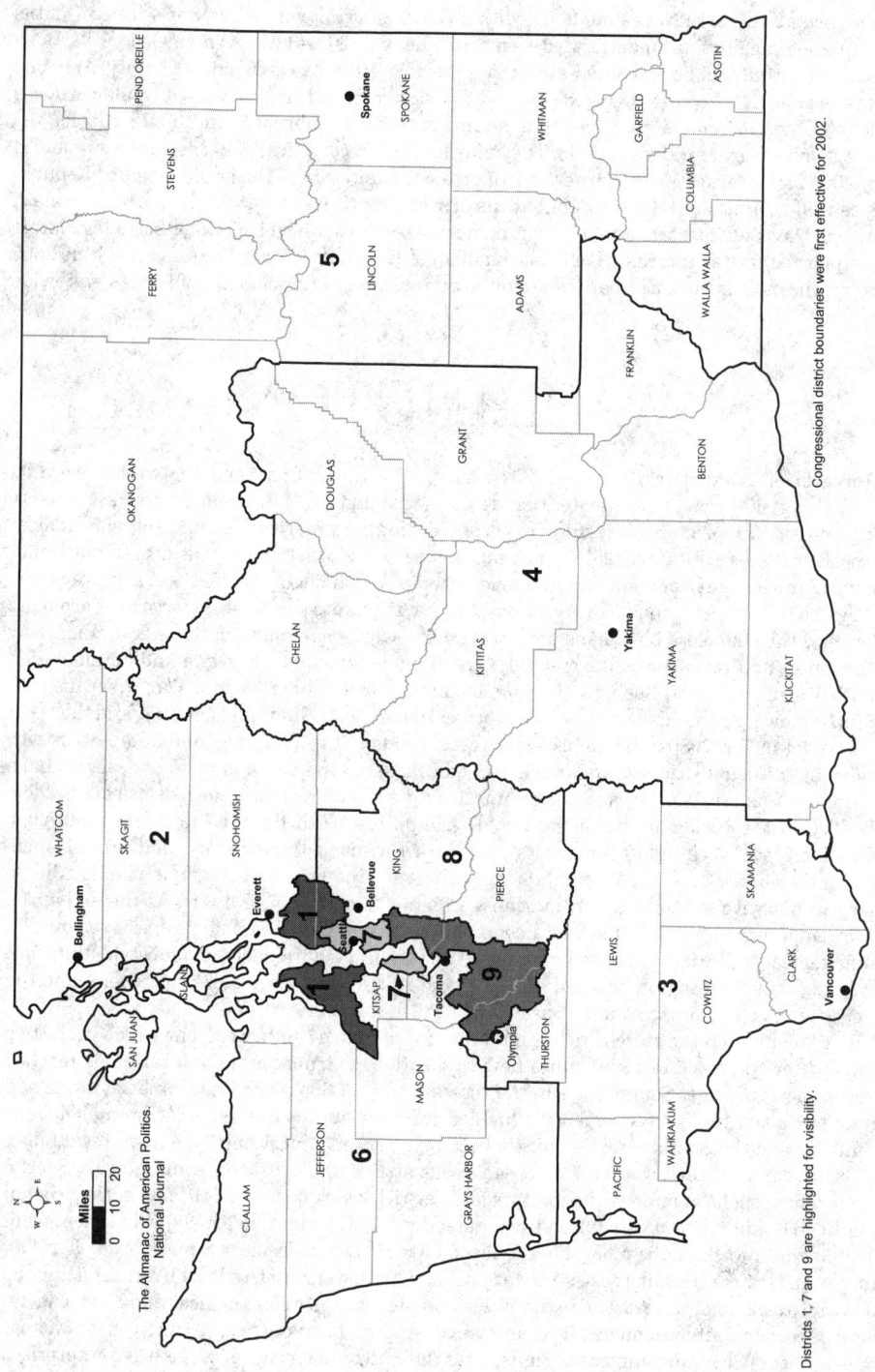

The Almanac of American Politics,
National Journal

Congressional district boundaries were first effective for 2002.

Districts 1, 7 and 9 are highlighted for visibility.

its tributary, the Snake, falling thousands of feet in a relatively short distance, had far greater hydroelectric potential than any other American river system, and Franklin D. Roosevelt, who grew up in a great river valley, was always interested in these river valley projects. In 1937 Bonneville Dam was completed on the lower Columbia; in 1940 Grand Coulee Dam, the largest man-made structure in the world at the time, was opened where the Columbia cuts through the arid, surrealistically contoured plains of eastern Washington. Washington proved hospitable to the industrial union movement of the 1930s and became one of the nation's most heavily unionized states. When war came, Washington's hydroelectric power—the cheapest electricity in the country—made it the natural site for huge aluminum production plants, which require vast amounts of electricity, and the Seattle area became the home not only of shipbuilders, but of what became the biggest aircraft manufacturer in the country, Boeing, founded in 1916 by William Boeing after he bought a shipyard on the Duwamish River and turned it into an airplane factory. After the war, the Hanford plant on the Columbia was one of the government's main nuclear weapons manufacturing sites. Cheap power, aluminum, aircraft, nuclear weapons and high unionized wages: these became Washington's economic foundations in the post-World War II years.

Today's Washington lives less off the brawn of hydroelectric power and rail and ship tonnage and more off the brains that made Boeing the world leader in aircraft and Microsoft the world leader in software. Yet since 1999 there has been trouble in this misty paradise. The turning point may have come in December 1999, when Seattle hosted a meeting of the World Trade Organization. This was supposed to be an occasion for the city to shine in the international spotlight. But 50,000 demonstrators took control of the streets, smashing Starbucks' windows and preventing leaders from Bill Clinton on down from attending meetings; Seattle's police chief and mayor did little to stop the violence, and even came out with statements, echoed by Clinton, expressing sympathy for the lawbreakers. Seattle became a symbol of mindless protest and lawless violence. The image was reinforced in the Mardi Gras riots in February 2001; voters responded, and Mayor Paul Schell carried only 22% of the vote in the September 2001 primary to become the first Seattle mayor in 45 years to lose a reelection bid. Washington was hurt also by the dot-com bust; the high-tech industry boomed as businesses retooled to avoid Y2K problems, then it suddenly became apparent that customers had all the high-tech they needed, the stock market started tanking in March 2000, takings thousands of dot-coms down. Microsoft was sued by the Justice Department's Antitrust Division in 1998; in March 2001, Boeing's chairman announced that the firm's headquarters would be moved out of Seattle, to Chicago. Then, after September 11, the airline industry was hard hit and cut back its orders; Boeing cut back its Seattle area employment from 102,000 in 1997 to 62,000 in 2002. Boeing continued to suffer from the airline recession, competition from Airbus and congressional opposition to the proposal to build KC-767 aerial refueling tankers. Recovery from the recession was slow: Washington's unemployment for a long time was the second highest in the nation, after Oregon's, and in early 2005 metro Seattle still had fewer jobs than it did at the end of 2000.

Amid this turbulence, the fundamentals undergirding Washington's affluent life seemed threatened. Light snowpacks threatened to reduce the supply of hydroelectric power even as demand from energy-starved California seemed likely to draw down supply. Proposals by Clinton administration officials to breach the dams on the Snake River threatened to reduce hydroelectric supply and to choke the agriculture of eastern Washington just as the court decision to protect the endangered spotted owl largely shut down Washington's logging industry in the early 1990s. The Hanford Nuclear Reservation, which produced plutonium for the military, for years leaked radioactive waste and now must be cleaned up at the cost of billions.

All these problems may turn out to be no more than footnotes to what is mainly a story of success. Look at a map that shows elevation of mountains and density of population. On both sides of the Pacific, vast numbers of people are squeezed into small margins of level land between steeply rising volcanic mountains and the sea, or tucked into valleys. These islands of settlement are surrounded by vast wildernesses—desert and mountains, open sea and Arctic lands. Yet the inhabitants of these pockets of the Pacific Rim in the last three decades have produced more economic growth than anywhere else in the world and, if there are occasional slumps, the Pacific

Rim (except for Japan) has always come surging back, as East Asia did in 1999. The question is whether Washington's laid-back tolerance can be so excessive as to undermine its impressive achievements.

Politically, Washington, with its Scandinavian and labor union heritage, was in the 1930s one of the most Democratic northern states: Franklin D. Roosevelt's campaign manager James Farley used to refer to "the 47 states and the Soviet of Washington." Its mainstream Democrats—notably Warren Magnuson and Henry Jackson, who represented the state in Congress for a total of 87 years—believed in an active and compassionate federal government that built dams, aluminum plants and the Hanford Works at home, and an internationalist, anti-Communist foreign policy abroad. Their political strength was built on a blue-collar base, augmented by the respect big businesses had for their political clout. Today, the fulcrum of the electorate has moved from blue collar to white collar, from economic class warfare to cultural wars. The balance favors the Democrats, but not necessarily by much. In presidential races, Washington leans Democratic. Washington's governor and both of its senators are all Democrats and all women, but Governor Christine Gregoire and Senator Maria Cantwell were elected by very narrow margins. Democrats hold six of Washington's nine U.S. House seats, and four different Democrats have held the governorship since 1984. But they almost lost it in 2004. The official count, after many shenanigans and legal challenges, declared that Gregoire had been elected governor by 129 votes. Republicans lost control of the state Senate in 2004 but gained the attorney general's office.

The political lines are fairly clear. The central city of Seattle is increasingly the liberal bastion, the upscale suburbs have been trending Democratic, while old blue-collar lumber country strongholds have soured on many Democrats. Seattle's King County, by a wide margin the most affluent county in the state, is also its liberal stronghold: 65% for John Kerry in 2004, with a popular vote margin of 279,000, the sixth highest of any county in the nation. Republicans run best in the arid country east of the Cascades with far lower income levels. This is a marchland between the culturally liberal Pacific Rim and the culturally conservative Rocky Mountains: it voted 60% for George W. Bush in 2004.

Washington had a tumultuous political year in 2004. Early on it was on both presidential candidates' lists of target states, but it had given Al Gore the best vote in 2000 of any of them and soon the Bush campaign stopped competing here. Nor did Republican Congressman George Nethercutt's challenge of Senator Patty Murray prove to be a serious threat. But the governor's race between Republican Dino Rossi and Democrat Christine Gregoire was close down to the wire—and after. Republicans did manage to hold two open House seats in which Democrats waged serious campaigns.

The People		Race/Ethnic Origin			Military veterans: 670,628 (15.3%)	
Pop. 2004 (est):	6,203,788	4,652,490	78.9%	White	WWII: 16.3%	Korea: 11.4%
Pop. 2000:	5,894,121	184,631	3.1%	Black	Vietnam: 35.9%	Gulf War: 12.2%
Pop. 1990:	4,866,692	319,401	5.4%	Asian	**Most populous cities (2003):**	
Change 1990–2000:	Up 21.1%	85,396	1.4%	Native Am.	1. Seattle	569,101
% of U.S. total:	2.1%	22,779	0.4%	Hawaiian	2. Tacoma	196,790
Pop. rank:	15th of 50	175,926	3.0%	Two+ races	3. Spokane	196,624
Area size:	71,300 sq. mi.	11,989	0.2%	Other	4. Vancouver	151,654
State Native:	47.2%	441,509	7.5%	Hisp. Origin	5. Bellevue	112,344
Non-citizen:	6.1%	**Ancestry**				
Language		German: 13.7%			Urban population: 82.0%	
English: 84.2%	Spanish: 6.1%	Irish: 8.3%		English: 8.8%	Rural population: 18.0%	
Asian: 4.6%		USA: 3.9%		Norwegian: 4.6%		

Education		Work Sector		Legislature	
H.S. Grad:	87.1%	Private: 76.1%	Govt: 16.5%	Senate	26 D 23 R
College Grad:	27.7%	Self: 7.2%	Family: 0.3%	House	55 D 43 R
Industry		Unemployment: 6.1%		Legislative Term Limits: No	
Agri: 2.5%	Con: 7.0%	**Household Income**		**Registered Voters**	
Fin: 6.1%	Info: 3.4%	<15k: 13.1%	15-35k: 24.2%	No party registration	
Mfg: 17.9%	Prof: 29.1%	35-50k: 17.1%	50-100k: 33.0%		
Public: 5.0%	Trade: 16.2%	100-150k: 8.3%	>150k: 4.3%		
Other: 12.8%		Median: $45,776			
Occupation		Poverty status: 10.6%			
Blue collar: 22.1%	White collar: 61.4%	**Home Value**			
Gray collar: 16.4%		<50k: 5.8%	50-100k: 15.2%	100-200k: 45.7%	200-300k: 19.3%
		300-500k: 10.1%	>500k: 3.9%	Median: $158,800	

Presidential politics   For three decades Washington was one of the most contrarian states in presidential politics, voting for losers Richard Nixon in 1960, Hubert Humphrey in 1968, Gerald Ford in 1976 and Michael Dukakis in 1988. In the 1990s it was in sync with the nation, voting for Bill Clinton twice, but now Washington seems contrarian once again. It gave Al Gore a 50%–45% victory in 2000 and John Kerry a victory by the wider margin of 53%–46% in 2004. Both times the winning margin and more came from just one of the state's nine congressional districts, the 7th District which includes all of Seattle and close-in suburbs to the north and south in King County. Gore carried the 7th District 72%–21%; Kerry

2004 Presidential Vote

Kerry (D)...................	1,510,201	(53%)
Bush (R)	1,304,894	(46%)
Nader (I)	23,283	(1%)
Other..........................	20,706	(1%)

2000 Presidential Vote

Gore (D).....................	1,247,652	(50%)
Bush (R)	1,108,864	(45%)
Nader (Green)	103,002	(4%)
Other..........................	27,915	(1%)

carried it 79%–19%. Politics in Washington was once almost class warfare, with union members favoring Democrats and more comfortable folk Republicans. No more. John Kerry ran better—a whopping 63%—among voters with incomes over $100,000 than those below, while voters in union households (27% of the total; in the 1960s it was more like 50%) gave Kerry only 55% of their votes. Kerry carried voters with college degrees; George W. Bush carried those without. Those who identified their religion as "other" or none were 25% of the electorate, an unusually high percentage, and they voted 72% for Kerry. A 53% majority of voters attend religious services never or only a few times a year, and they voted 65% for Kerry. Only 35% attend religious services weekly or more often, and they voted 64% for Bush.

Washington switched from a caucus system to primaries in 1992, after Pat Robertson won among Republicans and Jesse Jackson finished a solid second among Democrats in 1988. In April 1999 Washington, which has never seen much of presidential primary candidates, set its primary for leap-year day, February 29, 2000. For the Democrats, this was a "beauty contest," since under party rules delegates chosen within five weeks of New Hampshire were not entitled to seating at the convention. In 2000 Bill Bradley, without any other contests in which to pick up momentum, campaigned here for six days, to no avail; Al Gore won by about 2–1. George W. Bush beat John McCain by a razor-thin margin. In 2004 Washington's Democrats held caucuses February 7, which got little notice. But early in the cycle, in August 2003, Washington gave huge momentum to Howard Dean when he arrived in Seattle and addressed what *The Stranger*, a local alternative weekly, described as "8,000 screaming, hooting, Bush-hating liberals."

Congressional districting   In 1983 Washington voters approved a constitutional amendment which provided that congressional and legislative districts be drawn by a bipartisan commission; the lines can be changed by a two-thirds vote of the legislature. If the commission is deadlocked, the issue goes to the state Supreme Court. In 1991 the commission created four districts that were pretty evenly divided between the parties: only three of the nine districts were won by the same party in the five elections during which the lines were in effect. The problem was that even minor alterations in the closely divided districts—the 1st, 2d, 3d and 9th—can make changes that will turn out to be partisanly significant at some point in the next decade. But 6th District Democrat Norm Dicks and 8th District Republican Jennifer Dunn pressed the commissioners to compromise. Just before the constitutional deadline expired on January 1, 2002, they reached agreement. Attorney General Christine Gregoire pushed the legislature to change the statutory December 15 deadline to eliminate any question of the plan's legality; the legislators were happy to do so and made no changes in the plan. This 2002 plan followed pretty closely the lines drawn in 1991. The Washington plan has been lauded by many for taking partisanship out of redistricting and for creating more districts that both parties can win. But in Washington, where the commission is not bound by the mathematical requirements that in Iowa have resulted in districts not tailored to incumbents, incumbent protection has been the result. Only one district was seriously contested in 2002, the 2d. In 2004 there were serious contests, both in open seats where Republican incumbents were not running.

109th Congress Lineup
6 D   3 R
108th Congress Lineup
6 D   3 R

Governor

Christine Gregoire (D)

Elected 2004, term expires Jan. 2009, 1st term; b. March 24, 1947, Adrian, MI; home, Olympia; U. of WA, B.A. 1969; Gonzaga U., J.D. 1977; Catholic; married (Mike).

Elected Office: WA Atty. Gen., 1992–2004.

Professional Career: Dep. Atty. Gen., 1982–88; Dir., WA Dept. of Ecology, 1988–92.

Office: P.O. Box 40002, Olympia, 98504, 360-902-4111; Fax: 360-753-4110; Web site: www.governor.wa.gov.

Election Results

2004 general	Christine Gregoire (D)	1,373,361	(49%)
	Dino Rossi (R)	1,373,232	(49%)
	Other	63,465	(2%)
2004 primary	Christine Gregoire (D)	504,018	(66%)
	Ron Sims (D)	228,306	(30%)
	Other	35,742	(5%)
2000 general	Gary Locke (D)	1,441,973	(58%)
	John Eric Carlson (R)	980,060	(40%)
	Other	47,819	(2%)

Christine Gregoire is a Democrat elected governor in 2004 in the closest race in Washington history. She was born in Adrian, Michigan, but grew up on a small farm in Auburn, Washington, just south of Seattle. Her mother was a short-order cook who moved west to escape an abusive husband. Christine Gregoire graduated from the University of Washington and, unable to find a teaching position, took a job as a clerk-typist for the state parole board. She worked as a welfare caseworker, attended law school at Gonzaga University in eastern Washington, then worked for Republican Senator Slade Gorton in his Spokane office. There she drew the attention of another

Republican, Attorney General Ken Eikenberry, who hired her as a deputy attorney general in Olympia. In 1988, she was Democratic Governor Booth Gardner's unexpected choice to head the Department of Ecology. In 1992, nationally a good year for women candidates but especially good in Washington where Patty Murray was elected to the Senate and Maria Cantwell to the House, Gregoire ran as a Democrat and won election as attorney general.

She served three terms in that office and won national headlines as the lead negotiator in 1998 for the 46-state, $206 billion settlement with the tobacco industry. Though applauded by many, the deal still has its share of critics who contend that it ultimately strengthened the tobacco industry and made the states overly dependent on tobacco settlement money. But there is little doubt that Gregoire was the key player in putting together the agreement. After she assisted on the initial failed attempt to design a $368 billion settlement in 1997—the deal required congressional approval that was not forthcoming—Gregoire conscientiously worked with other state attorneys general to put together another settlement that did not require the approval of Congress. An agreement with the industry was reached in late 1998 and the money began to flow to the states a year later.

With high name recognition from her role in the tobacco settlement and three successful statewide races behind her, Gregoire came to be viewed as a governor-in-waiting. When Democrat Gary Locke, elected governor in 1996 and 2000, announced in 2003 that he would not run for a third term, Gregoire became the frontrunner to succeed him. But Gregoire almost didn't run. One week after announcing her candidacy in July 2003, her doctors told her she needed a mastectomy to remove an early form of breast cancer. She considered dropping out of the race, sought counsel from Janet Napolitano and Heidi Heitkamp, both former attorneys general and breast cancer survivors who had run for governor (Napolitano won in Arizona in 2002; Heitkamp lost in North Dakota in 2000), decided to have the surgery and then returned to the campaign trail a month later.

Gregoire figured to have tough primary opposition from former state senator and state Supreme Court Justice Phil Talmadge and from King County Executive Ron Sims in the September 14 primary. But Talmadge dropped out of the race in April for health reasons. That left Sims, who ran to Gregoire's left and whose political base was in the state's most populous county and biggest media market.

Washington's economy was hard-hit in the economic downturn; the industries that are central to the state economy—high-tech, aviation and natural resources—were slow to recover, leaving the state with the nation's second-highest unemployment rate in 2003. That made jobs, education, taxes and the environment the staples of the primary debate until August, when it was reported that Gregoire's sorority at the University of Washington excluded African-Americans. The Gregoire campaign charged that the Sims campaign was behind the story; Sims, who would have been the state's first African-American governor, denied being the source. Local black leaders harshly criticized Gregoire. The head of the Seattle NAACP said she took "an oath of white supremacy." She responded angrily to the charges of racism and claimed that she fought within the system to eliminate the sorority's exclusionary policy. Voters didn't seem to hold it against her: She defeated Sims 66%–30%, carrying every county in the state including Seattle's King County, which she won 59%–38%.

Republicans nominated state Senator Dino Rossi, a former Senate Ways and Means Committee chairman from the Seattle suburbs, who billed himself as a "fiscal conservative with a social conscience." He credited his outlook to a humble background: The grandson of an Italian immigrant coal miner, he grew up in a family that endured financial hardship while living through the alcoholism of his mother. Rossi, the only serious candidate in the Republican primary, had been personally lobbied to run by George W. Bush in 2003 when the state party was scrambling to come up with a viable candidate.

Rossi campaigned as a moderate and as an agent of change in a state where Republicans had not won the governorship since John Spellman's victory in 1980. He portrayed Gregoire as the representative of "a failed status quo." Business interests lined up with Rossi, a successful commercial real estate investor who said he wanted to change the culture in Olympia to a "free enterprise model" and promised to create a cabinet-level office of regulatory reform. Gregoire, who ran as a fiscal moderate, received strong support from the state's largest labor unions. Rossi's support for a constitutional amendment banning same-sex marriage and his opposition to abortion spurred abortion rights groups to donate heavily to Gregoire's campaign and led Democrats to characterize him as a right-wing extremist – the same tactic that worked against the last two Republican nominees. But as a youthful suburban legislator with four children who focused on economic, rather than social, issues, Rossi was not so easily caricatured.

The 2003 budget that he helped draft as Ways and Means chairman was a matter of contention. With the state facing a $2.6 billion deficit, Rossi won praise for brokering a deal with Locke that did not raise taxes or inflict severe cuts to social programs. Gregoire claimed the budget favored business interests over funding for social programs. Rossi framed it as a move designed to make the state more business-friendly. Each continued to take aim at the other's record in office, with Gregoire accusing Rossi of voting to cut health care benefits for children and Rossi lobbing charges about Gregoire's stewardship as attorney general.

By October, the race seemed to be moving in Gregoire's direction. She had built a double-digit lead in most public polls and national Republicans, who early in the campaign had high hopes for the ticket of Bush, Senate nominee George Nethercutt and Rossi, began to write off the state as a lost cause. But Rossi's change theme gained traction in the final weeks against Gregoire, a cautious candidate who had spent nearly her entire career in one government job or another.

Washington is one of just two states that allow absentee ballots to be postmarked as late as Election Day. So it took nearly three weeks for all the votes to be counted. Rossi was up by about 1,000 votes the morning after the election, but by evening Gregoire was ahead by 14,000. The lead see-sawed for days and in the ensuing weeks the election began to take on an eerie, Florida-like hue, replete with protesters, legal challenges, allegations of ballot fraud and the intervention of national parties. On November 12, the state Democratic Party sued the King County Elections Department over its handling of provisional ballots, seeking the names of those whose ballots were invalidated. Three days later, Seattle's King County, the state's Democratic stronghold, discovered 10,000 uncounted ballots and Gregoire took a 158-vote lead. Republicans sought a restraining order to stop the counting of provisional ballots; a King County judge denied the request. On November 17, after all counties had reported their results with the state, Dino Rossi was the winner by just 261 votes out of 2.8 million cast.

Washington state law requires a machine recount if the margin of victory is under 2,000 votes and half of one percent. Here the race was decided by 0.0093%. So a machine recount began and on November 24 Rossi was again the winner, this time by 42 votes. Rossi called on Gregoire to concede, but she refused; on November 29, he was certified as governor-elect. Gregoire still had another option for contesting the results. State election law allowed for a hand recount under the circumstances, provided that the party requesting it pays the costs. The state party wanted to do just that, but only in the counties where Gregoire stood to gain the most votes. This made it look as if Democrats were planning to cherry-pick only Democrat-friendly counties and Republicans were quick to criticize them for it. Gregoire would not go along with the party's plan; she said she would concede the race unless the party could raise enough to do a full statewide recount. State Democratic Chairman Paul Berendt responded, "That would be irrelevant. Concessions have no legal standing."

With leftover money contributed from Senator John Kerry's presidential campaign and with the financial assistance of MoveOn.org and the Democratic National Committee, enough money was raised to pay for a full, $730,000 statewide hand recount. But before it was finished, the state Democrats filed another lawsuit, this one requesting that county canvassing boards be ordered to reconsider thousands of ballots rejected in the first two vote counts; Gregoire denied any involvement with that suit. Rossi said she was trying to distance herself from a legal action that "left a bad taste in the public's mouth." The vote-counting slogged on through December as the action shifted back and forth between county election offices and the courts. King County suddenly discovered 561 wrongly-disqualified ballots on December 13. The next day, the state supreme court rejected the state Democratic party's request to order counties to reconsider rejected ballots. Then King County found even more uncounted ballots. Republicans filed suit in neighboring Pierce County, which they said was a fairer venue than King County, to prevent the counting of all the newfound ballots; a Pierce County judge found in their favor and kept the votes out. Democrats appealed to the state supreme court, which unanimously ruled that the disputed King County ballots could be counted. The votes were enough to put Gregoire over the top; on December 30, 58 days after Election Day, she was declared governor-elect by 129 votes. She won 48.8730% to Rossi's 48.8685%.

In January, just days before Gregoire's inauguration, Rossi and the Republican party filed suit in Chelan County Superior Court in central Washington asking that Gregoire's victory be nullified and a new election held. They presented evidence of allegedly improper votes including hundreds of votes cast by felons ineligible to vote, votes cast in the names of dead persons, votes cast by non-citizens and double votes. But on June 6 Chelan County Superior Court Judge John Bridges upheld Gregoire's election, finding that while there was evidence of 1,678 illegal votes, there was no evidence that Gregoire benefited from them and thus the standard for court intervention in the election was not met. Later that day, Rossi announced he would not file an appeal. "With today's decision, and because of the political makeup of the Washington state Supreme Court, which makes it almost impossible to overturn this ruling, I am ending this contest," he said.

In one of her first acts as governor, Gregoire created an election reform task force; in March 2005, the task force findings called for a statewide voter database, mandatory audits of local election systems by the Secretary of State and an earlier primary date.

Senior Senator

Patty Murray (D)

Elected 1992, seat up 2010, 3d term; b. Oct. 11, 1950, Seattle; home, Seattle; WA St. U., B.A. 1972; Catholic; married (Rob).

Elected Office: Shoreline Schl. Bd., 1985–89, Pres., 1985–86; WA Senate, 1988–92.

DC Office: 173 RSOB, 20510, 202-224-2621; Fax: 202-224-0238; Web site: murray.senate.gov.

State Offices: Everett, 425-259-6515; Seattle, 206-553-5545; Spokane, 509-624-9515; Tacoma, 253-572-3636; Vancouver, 360-696-7797; Yakima, 509-453-7462.

Committees: *Appropriations*: Commerce, Justice & Science; Energy & Water; Homeland Security; Labor, Health and Human Services, Education & Related Agencies; Military Construction & Veterans Affairs; Transportation, Treasury, the Judiciary, HUD & Related Agencies (RMM). *Budget. Health, Education, Labor & Pensions*: Bioterrorism & Public Health Preparedness; Education & Early Childhood Development; Employment & Workplace Safety (RMM). *Veterans' Affairs*.

Group Ratings

	ADA	ACLU	AFS	LCV	ITIC	NTU	COC	ACU	NTLC	CHC
2004	90	78	86	100	100	13	75	8	10	0
2003	90	—	100	95	—	16	43	10	—	—

National Journal Ratings

	2003 LIB	—	2003 CONS		2004 LIB	—	2004 CONS
Economic	70%	—	26%		57%	—	42%
Social	85%	—	0%		82%	—	0%
Foreign	70%	—	28%		71%	—	26%

Key Votes of the 108th Congress

1. Ban Drilling in ANWR	Y	5. Energy Bill	N	9. Ban Same-Sex Marriage	N
2. Approve Bush Tax Cuts	N	6. Support Roe v. Wade	Y	10. Ban Bunker-Buster Bomb	Y
3. Medicare/Rx Bill	N	7. Ban Partial-Birth Abortion	N	11. Fund Iraq War	Y
4. Bar Overtime Pay Regs.	Y	8. Assault Weapons Ban	Y	12. Restrict Missile Defense	Y

Election Results

2004 general	Patty Murray (D)	1,549,708	(55%)	($11,556,148)
	George Nethercutt (R)	1,204,584	(43%)	($7,726,296)
	Other	64,359	(2%)	
2004 primary	Patty Murray (D)	709,497	(92%)	
	Warren Hanson (D)	46,490	(6%)	
	Other	13,527	(2%)	
1998 general	Patty Murray (D)	1,103,184	(58%)	($5,600,592)
	Linda Smith (R)	785,377	(42%)	($5,159,527)

Prior Winning Percentages: 1992 (54%)

Patty Murray is the senior senator from Washington, first elected in 1992. Murray grew up in the Seattle suburb of Bothell, the daughter of a disabled veteran. She graduated from Washington State University in 1972, married and stayed home to raise her children. In 1980, when she was in Olympia trying to save from budget cuts a parent education class she was teaching at Shoreline Community College, a state legislator told her gruffly, "You're just a mom in tennis shoes; you can't make a difference." As she had said later, "Almost every woman I've ever met in politics got into it because she was mad about something." But like many committed public employees, she won her fight; then she ran for the Shoreline School District board, lost, was appointed and then elected, and served as president. In 1988 she challenged a Republican state senator, knocked on 17,000 doors and won the seat. Then in late 1991 she decided to run against U.S. Senator Brock Adams, who was under a cloud from charges of sexual harassment and later decided not to seek reelection.

Amid a crowd of better-known conventional male politicians, Murray, with her flat accent and "mom in tennis shoes" line, attracted most of the attention and most of the votes. In the all-party primary, her main Democratic opponent was former Congressman Don Bonker, who had narrowly lost a Senate nomination in 1988. But Murray won 28% of the total vote to Bonker's 19%. Meanwhile, three well-known Republicans vied: Congressman Rod Chandler won 20% to 16% for state Senator Leo Thorsness and 11% for King County Executive Tim Hill. Murray sprinted to a big lead in polls, and in November won 54%–46%.

In the Senate Murray has had a largely liberal voting record. In her first years she refused to see Washington industry lobbyists; in a scathing *Seattle Times* profile in 1996, Robert Nelson wrote of Murray, "Colleagues, lobbyists and former staff members view her as indifferent to issues that can't be explained through anecdotes about her family and neighbors." She got a seat on Appropriations and became involved in Washington issues. Murray defended Microsoft against the antitrust case brought by the Clinton Justice Department. Murray was one of the Senate's strongest proponents of normal trade relations with China—a position strongly backed by Boeing; she also favors relaxing export restrictions on encryption technology.

When Democrats gained their Senate majority in June 2001, Murray became chairman of the Transportation Appropriations Subcommittee. By December 2001 her appropriation had $190 million of projects for Washington, more than twice as much as in 2000. She has gotten money for a third runway at Sea-Tac Airport and a $500 million federal guarantee for Sound Transit light rail. In the transportation bill in 2003 she sought to quadruple spending for ferries to $150 million; Washington has an extensive ferry system used by 11 million vehicles a year. She opposed cuts in the Bush budget in Amtrak spending. She used her power to block a nominee to get the administration to back down on redirecting Operation Safe Cargo money away from the ports of Seattle and Tacoma. She worked to stop the closing of VA hospitals in Washington and block a Veterans Affairs nominee in 2004 when the department missed a deadline on a report on health care in north central Washington.

She has strongly backed the Air Force's controversial proposals to either lease or buy KC-767 aerial refueling tankers from Boeing. To proposals that Airbus be allowed to bid on the contract, she decried "the outsourcing of our national defense" and said, "As long as they are employing Europeans and taking over America's market share, they don't care. That's not competition. That's subsidized slaughter, and we have to wake up before it's too late for America's aerospace companies and workers." She and Richard Shelby took the lead in trying to keep

Mexican trucks from venturing into the U.S. beyond a 20-mile border zone, as provided by NAFTA. This was strongly supported by the Teamsters Union and opposed by the Bush administration. After much haggling over insurance and inspection provisions, the trucks were allowed in.

Murray has worked to remove restrictions on abortion, and has prevailed in the Senate on allowing abortions in military hospitals. She has sponsored bills for more benefits for National Guard and Reserve troops called up to active duty—permanent TRICARE, tax credits for employers who make up their lost pay, child care for their families. She sought unsuccessfully to eliminate what she called a loophole in the student loan program which guaranteed lenders profits. After an independent panel reporting to EPA recommended banning the use of asbestos in all products, Murray sponsored a bill to remove thousands of products from the market within two years.

In the 2002 cycle Murray chaired the Democratic Senatorial Campaign Committee. Murray nearly doubled the committee's fundraising and brought in $158 million during the cycle. She also did a fine job of recruiting candidates. But she did less well at the polls. Democrats took only one seat from Republicans and lost three to them—and the Senate majority. After the election Murray said, "We need to not feel we lost, as everyone likes to portray at this point. Had we not had those two plane crashes"—one which killed Democratic nominee Mel Carnahan in October 2000 and the other which killed incumbent Paul Wellstone in October 2002—"we would still be in the majority." But Carnahan's widow won the Senate seat and a Wellstone victory would have left Democrats one short of a majority.

Murray has won reelection twice by impressive margins. In 1998 she was opposed by Congresswoman Linda Smith, another mom in tennis shoes—a strong opponent of abortion, backer of campaign finance regulation and opponent of free trade, a favorite of Ross Perot who was mistrusted by the House Republican leadership. Murray campaigned as a public official who had addressed issues of importance to Washington voters—"apples to aerospace, high-tech to Hanford, saving salmon to educating kids." She raised far more money than Smith, who spent much of her money on direct mail rather than TV ads. On Election Day and before (about one-third of Washington's votes that year were cast by absentee ballot) Murray won 58%–42%.

In 2003 eastern Washington Congressman George Nethercutt announced he was running against Murray. But the "mom in tennis shoes" had become an excellent fundraiser. A Murray aide put out word to lobbyists that she would regard contributions to Nethercutt as hostile even if the contributor gave to her too. In the end she raised and spent $11.5 million—far more than Nethercutt who spent $7.7 million. Nethercutt campaigned vigorously, and big name Republicans came in for him. He tried to put his own stamp on one of Murray's issues. For years she has been trying to create a Wild Sky wilderness area in Snohomish County, west of the Cascades. Nethercutt had never supported this (it's outside his district), but in 2004 he sponsored the bill and persuaded Resources Chairman Richard Pombo, who had bottled it up, to allow a vote on it. But Pombo insisted on eliminating 13,000 acres of low-level forest, and leaders of environmental groups strenuously objected. At the end of September, Nethercutt started running a spot featuring Murray's controversial December 2002 comments on Osama bin Laden's good works; speculating about bin Laden's popularity in some corners of the world, Murray had been perhaps a bit too kind in crediting him with the building of local infrastructure, health care and day care facilities. At the end of the ad, Nethercutt said, "Winning a war on terror means fighting terrorists, not excusing them." Murray responded sharply. "George Nethercutt's ad is a lie, and he knows it. I have always said Osama bin Laden is an evil terrorist who is responsible for the deaths of thousands of Americans." The *Seattle Times* and other newspapers denounced the ad. Nethercutt responded, "I defy her to find a day care center that Osama bin Laden has built." But the ad did not seem to move votes, and he remained well behind in the polls.

Murray ran a series of attack ads, charging that Nethercutt had missed House votes, characterizing him as an extreme conservative, referring to his opposition to abortion by showing a woman being booked into jail on an abortion charge. Murray agreed to only two debates, one of which was broadcast only in eastern Washington, another in Seattle on the same night as a big baseball game. Eastern Washington casts only 20% of the state's votes, and no one from eastern

Washington has been elected to the Senate since 1928. The 2004 election did not break the string. Nethercutt reduced Murray's 1998 margin, but not by much: she won 55%–43%. It was almost as if the election were held in two states: Nethercutt carried every county east of the Cascades; Murray carried all but two counties to the west. Nethercutt's verdict: "There was an absolute protective network across the Puget Sound area that I don't think wanted to look at any other leadership options." In December 2004 incoming Minority Leader Harry Reid appointed Murray assistant floor leader, a position held by Richard Durbin, who stepped up to become minority whip.

Junior Senator

Maria Cantwell (D)

Elected 2000, seat up 2006, 1st term; b. Oct., 13, 1958, Indianapolis, IN; home, Edmonds; Miami U. (OH), B.A. 1981; Catholic; single.

Elected Office: WA House of Reps., 1986–92; U.S. House of Reps., 1992–94.

Professional Career: Owner, Cantwell & Assoc. PR firm, 1985–91; RealNetworks, 1995–2000.

DC Office: 717 HSOB, 20510, 202-224-3441; Fax: 202-228-0514; Web site: cantwell.senate.gov.

State Offices: Everett, 425-303-0114; Richland, 509-946-8106; Seattle, 206-220-6400; Spokane, 509-353-2507; Tacoma, 253-572-2281; Vancouver, 360-696-7838.

Committees: *Commerce, Science & Transportation*: Aviation; Disaster Prevention & Prediction; Fisheries & the Coast Guard (RMM); National Ocean Policy Study; Surface Transportation & Merchant Marine; Trade, Tourism & Economic Development. *Energy & Natural Resources*: Energy; Public Lands & Forests; Water & Power. *Indian Affairs. Small Business & Entrepreneurship.*

Group Ratings

	ADA	ACLU	AFS	LCV	ITIC	NTU	COC	ACU	NTLC	CHC
2004	95	78	86	100	100	17	65	8	18	0
2003	90	—	100	100	—	15	39	15	—	—

National Journal Ratings

	2003 LIB	—	2003 CONS		2004 LIB	—	2004 CONS
Economic	82%	—	10%		58%	—	39%
Social	78%	—	21%		77%	—	19%
Foreign	65%	—	32%		71%	—	26%

Key Votes of the 108th Congress

1. Ban Drilling in ANWR	Y	5. Energy Bill	N	9. Ban Same-Sex Marriage	N
2. Approve Bush Tax Cuts	N	6. Support Roe v. Wade	Y	10. Ban Bunker-Buster Bomb	Y
3. Medicare/Rx Bill	N	7. Ban Partial-Birth Abortion	N	11. Fund Iraq War	Y
4. Bar Overtime Pay Regs.	Y	8. Assault Weapons Ban	Y	12. Restrict Missile Defense	Y

Election Results

2000 general	Maria Cantwell (D)	1,199,437	(49%)	($11,533,295)
	Slade Gorton (R)	1,197,208	(49%)	($6,402,488)
	Other	64,734	(3%)	
2000 primary	Slade Gorton (R)	560,787	(44%)	
	Maria Cantwell (D)	472,609	(37%)	
	Deborah Senn (D)	168,110	(13%)	
	Other	85,732	(7%)	
1994 general	Slade Gorton (R)	947,821	(56%)	($4,792,764)
	Ron Sims (D)	752,352	(44%)	($1,228,098)

Prior Winning Percentages: 1992 House (55%)

Maria Cantwell is a Democrat elected in the closest Senate race of 2000. Cantwell grew up in Indianapolis, where her father, a construction worker, served as county commissioner, city councilman and state legislator. She graduated from Miami University (Ohio) in 1980—the first in her family to graduate from college—and worked in Ohio for Jerry Springer's 1982 campaign for governor. (In 2003, when Springer was considering running for senator in Ohio, she said, "I think people will be surprised by his intellect. There's much more to him than his TV show.") Then she worked for Senator Alan Cranston's presidential campaign and went to Seattle to set up a regional campaign office. The Cranston campaign went nowhere, and so did Cantwell: she loved the Pacific Northwest and decided to stay. She moved to Mountlake Terrace, a suburb in Snohomish County just north of Seattle, where she organized a coalition to build a new library. In 1986, at 28, she was elected to the Washington House.

In 1992 Cantwell ran for the U.S. House, for the just redrawn 1st District seat being vacated by Republican John Miller. She won a solid 55%–42% victory. In the House she supported the family and medical leave bill and the Clinton economic plan; she did not support the Clinton health care plan and supported NAFTA only at the last minute. She was a strong supporter of abortion rights and of stands backed by environmental advocacy groups. But by fall 1994 some of those positions had become unpopular. In November she lost 52%–48% to Republican nominee Rick White.

Back in the Seattle area, she joined a startup firm called Progressive Networks in 1995; five years later it had become RealNetworks, a leader in Internet-based audio and visual software. In late 1999 her stock was worth about $40 million, and she decided to run against Republican Senator Slade Gorton. A brainy and hard-working veteran of Washington politics, Gorton had an increasingly conservative record on environmental and economic issues; he was also Microsoft's leading advocate on Capitol Hill. Cantwell was an answer to Democrats' prayers; their well-known House members had declined to run, and Insurance Commissioner Deborah Senn, who was running, was widely considered too liberal to win. The real difference was money. Cantwell, who liquidated more than $5 million of her RealNetworks stock, spent freely, while Senn was on TV only during the last two weeks before the September all-party primary. Cantwell won 37% of the total vote, to only 13% for Senn; Gorton, with 44% of the vote, was ahead but short of a majority.

For the general Cantwell said she would spend "whatever it takes" to win. At the same time, she made her support of McCain-Feingold-type campaign finance regulation a major issue, and refused to take contributions from PACs or soft money from the Democratic Party (though it put $640,000 into the state before Cantwell won the primary). She charged that Gorton was beholden to special interest contributors, singling out his last-night amendment to open a cyanide-leach gold mine in Okanogan County. Gorton called Cantwell an old-style liberal Democrat who would have government meddling in health care, education and local environmental issues. Cantwell highlighted her experience in the high-tech private sector. Overall, Cantwell spent $11.5 million, $10.3 million of it her own money; Gorton spent $6.4 million.

Gorton led on election night, but not by much. Washington allows absentee voting, and 54% of the votes were cast absentee; two days after the election, one-quarter of the votes had yet to be counted. During the three weeks of counting, Gorton seemed to have the advantage. But the last two days' absentee ballots from heavily Democratic King County put Cantwell over the top by 1,953. A mandated recount left the margin at 2,229 for Cantwell, out of 2.4 million cast. Cantwell carried only five counties—King, Snohomish, Thurston (which includes the state capital of Olympia) and two small counties in the west. She won King County 59%–39%; she also carried the rest of western Washington 50%–47%. Gorton carried eastern Washington 61%–36%—a lot but not quite enough to win. Cantwell's victory created a tie in the Senate, until James Jeffords became an independent in May 2001 and gave Democrats a razor-thin majority. This race was a very big loss for the Republican Party.

In the Senate Cantwell worked hard on campaign finance in the March 2001 two-week session on the issue. After September 11, she put an amendment into the Patriot Act tripling the number of border guards on the Canadian border and another to require the administration to develop a form of biometric identification, perhaps by facial recognition software; she has pursued the subject and in 2004 she and Jeff Sessions sponsored a bill limiting the visa waiver program to countries which provide biometric passports. In June 2004 she criticized FERC for failing to obtain accounting records and tape transcripts that were evidence of Enron's electricity price manipulation. In March 2005 she continued: "The types of manipulation that took place during the Western energy crisis cannot be tolerated, and the performance of the federal agency charged with rooting out these types of market abuses was an abject failure." In October 2002 she voted for the Iraq war resolution, unlike her colleague Patty Murray. In May 2004 she tried to add to the corporate tax bill an extension of unemployment benefits. Republicans agreed to allow the vote on the amendment only if Democrats agreed to limit debate on the bill. Because of budget resolution rules, the amendment required 60 votes, but got only 59; John Kerry, who surely would have voted for it, was out campaigning for president. In March 2005 Cantwell offered the amendment to the budget resolution to bar oil drilling in the Arctic National Wildlife Refuge. It failed 51–49. Afterwards she said she was "prepared to use every tool at my disposal to stop drilling in the Arctic."

In February 2003 Cantwell and Kay Bailey Hutchison of Texas introduced a bill to allow taxpayers to deduct state sales taxes as well as state income taxes on their federal income tax forms; Texas like Washington has a sales tax but no income tax. That became law for two years as part of the corporate tax bill in November 2004; in 2005 she called for making it permanent. In January 2003 she moved off the strife-torn Judiciary Committee to Commerce, where she promised to look after Washington interests. In August 2003 she sponsored a bill to declare 20 miles of the White Salmon River near Mount Adams a wild and scenic river; a Bush administration official endorsed it in 2004. In September 2004 Congress passed the bill proposed by Cantwell and Republican Jennifer Dunn to add 800 acres to Mount Rainier National Park. When the FAA approved funding for research into advanced aircraft materials including composites in October 2003, Cantwell pressed the University of Washington to submit a proposal and said that it might help persuade Boeing to assemble the 7E7 in Washington state. In June 2004, after Lindsey Graham added to the defense authorization an amendment allowing reclassification of nuclear waste so that it could be kept in storage tanks in the Savannah River Site in his state, Cantwell offered a competing amendment. She said that Graham's measure might be a precedent for similar action in Washington, which has nuclear waste stored at the Hanford Site. Cantwell's amendment failed 48–48. In January 2005 she sponsored a bill with $35 million a year for tsunami detection and mapping of areas at risk in tsunamis, including Puget Sound. In September 2004 she held up an Energy Department appointment to try to get the department to continue the Former Hanford Workers Medical Screening Program, scheduled to be discontinued and replaced with a centralized support program accessible through an 800 number.

A strong supporter of campaign finance regulation, Cantwell had campaign finance problems of her own. To finance her 2000 campaign she had sold $5.6 million of her RealNetworks stock and had borrowed $3.8 million from a bank with RealNetworks stock as collateral. That enabled her to run the last minute ads that surely were essential to her victory. The FEC ruled in February 2004 that she violated the law by failing to disclose the terms of these decisive loans, but it evidently saw the offense as minor because it took no action against her. Paying off the loans should have been easy; Cantwell's net worth at one point was around $40 million. But RealNetworks, like so many high-tech firms, saw its stock price plummet, from $80 in spring 2000 to $6 in spring 2001. Suddenly she owed far more than the collateral was worth. She negotiated another loan due December 2001, guaranteed by the DSCC, which of course could use soft money to pay it off. And she began raising money, from committed Democrats and from Washington lobbyists. Between 2001 and 2004 she raised some $16.8 million; she broke her pledge on PAC money by accepting contributions from political and members' PACs. By the end of 2004 she had reduced the debt to $2.5 million. With $435,000 in cash she was in position to pay off the remaining $130,000 in bank loans; the rest of the money is owed to her, and she seemed uninterested in being repaid before the 2006 election.

Cantwell's narrow victory in 2000 naturally made her high on Republicans' target lists for 2006. Former Congressman George Nethercutt, who lost to Patty Murray 55%–43% in 2004, said he did not rule out a race, but many Washington Republicans seemed convinced a candidate from eastern Washington could not win. In January 2005 former Congressman Rick White, who beat Cantwell in 1994 for the House and lost himself in 1998, was exploring a race; he had been head of TechNet, a high-tech lobbying association, since 2001 and had planned to leave the position in summer 2005. Others mentioned as possible Republican candidates were former state Senator Dino Rossi, who lost to Governor Christine Gregoire by an officially reported 129 votes in 2004; state Senator Linda Evans Parlette; state Republican chairman and former legislator Chris Vance; T-Mobile Wireless President John Stanton; former prosecutor Diane Tebelius, who lost in the primary in the 8th District in 2004; and Safeco executive Mike McGavick.

FIRST DISTRICT

Rep. Jay Inslee (D)

Elected 1998, 4th term; b. Feb. 9, 1951, Seattle; home, Bainbridge Island; Stanford U., 1969–70, U. of WA, B.A. 1973, Willamette U., J.D. 1976.; Christian; married (Trudi).

Elected Office: WA House of Reps., 1988–92; U.S. House of Reps., 1992–94.

Professional Career: Practicing atty., 1976–92, 1995–96; Regional Dir., U.S. Dept. of H.H.S., 1997–98.

DC Office: 403 CHOB, 20515, 202-225-6311; Fax: 202-226-1606; Web site: www.house.gov/inslee.

District Offices: Mountlake Terrace, 425-640-0233; Poulsbo, 360-598-2342.

Committees: *Energy & Commerce* (24th of 26 D): Environment & Hazardous Materials; Oversight & Investigations; Telecommunications & the Internet. *Resources* (12th of 22 D): Forests & Forest Health.

Group Ratings

	ADA	ACLU	AFS	LCV	ITIC	NTU	COC	ACU	NTLC	CHC
2004	100	80	100	100	80	12	43	4	0	15
2003	100	—	100	100	—	24	37	16	—	—

National Journal Ratings

	2003 LIB — 2003 CONS		2004 LIB — 2004 CONS	
Economic	81%	— 18%	72%	— 28%
Social	75%	— 24%	73%	— 25%
Foreign	73%	— 25%	83%	— 16%

Key Votes of the 108th Congress

1. Drilling in ANWR	N	5. DC School Vouchers	N	9. Ban Same-Sex Marriage	N
2. Approve Bush Tax Cuts	N	6. Ban Human Cloning	N	10. Fund Iraq War	N
3. Medicare/Rx Bill	N	7. Restrict Gun Liability	N	11. Bar Cuba Embargo Funds	Y
4. Bar Overtime Pay Regs.	Y	8. Ban Partial-Birth Abortion	N	12. Intelligence Reorg.	N

Election Results

2004 general	Jay Inslee (D)	204,121	(62%)	($882,639)
	Randy Eastwood (R)	117,850	(36%)	($64,780)
	Other	5,798	(2%)	
2004 primary	Jay Inslee (D)	unopposed		
2002 general	Jay Inslee (D)	114,087	(56%)	($643,505)
	Joe Marine (R)	84,696	(41%)	($205,550)
	Other	6,251	(3%)	

Prior Winning Percentages: 2000 (55%); 1998 (50%); 1992 (51%)

The People		Race/Ethnic Origin	Ancestry	
Area size:	616 sq. mi.	81.6% White	German: 13.6%	English: 10.0%
Urban population:	95.4%	1.8% Black	Irish: 8.7%	
Rural population:	4.6%	7.9% Asian	**2004 Presidential Vote**	
Pop. 2000:	654,904	0.8% Native Am.	Kerry (D) 189,566	(56%)
Median income:	$58,565	0.3% Hawaiian	Bush (R) 143,146	(42%)
Poverty status:	5.6%	3.1% Two+ races	Other 4,414	(1%)
Military veterans:	14.5%	0.2% Other	**2000 Presidential Vote**	
		4.3% Hispanic Origin	Gore (D) 154,583	(53%)
			Bush (R) 123,879	(42%)
			Other 13,803	(5%)
			Cook Partisan Voting Index: D + 7	

Occupation	Blue collar: 18.0%	White collar: 69.4%	Gray collar: 12.6%

In the past 30 years, metropolitan Seattle spread out to the north and the east, as a growing wave of newcomers arrived seeking this area's distinctive blend of natural environmental beauty, freewheeling culture and briskly expanding economy. In the process some of the distinctiveness of the old Seattle is left behind. The fishy odor of its docks does not permeate the new subdivisions built on what were once vegetable fields or vineyards; the Scandinavian heritage of old neighborhoods like Ballard has been mixed into a Pacific Northwest blend.

The heart of this new Seattle is east of Lake Washington, in the edge city of Redmond. Here are the turquoise, pine-shaded, low-rise buildings of the Microsoft campus—a tranquil environment for a booming and boisterously aggressive company. With 56,000 employees in Washington (including those with subsidiaries and "contingent labor") the company expanded its 300-acre campus and made plans to build 2.2 million square feet of new office space in Redmond over the next 20 years. Not far away is the eastern shore of Lake Washington, home to many of the newly super-rich, where motorists on the causeway can make out from miles away the $60 million mansion that Bill and Melinda Gates took six years to complete—a 66,000-square-foot complex with a trampoline room with vaulted ceilings, video walls that can be electronically programmed with art from the world's great museums, and a garage large enough to hold 30 cars: Seattle's Xanadu.

The 1st Congressional District of Washington includes Redmond, Kirkland and other suburbs east of Seattle, plus Shoreline in the northwest corner of King County; it also includes suburban territory—Edmonds, Lynnwood, Bothell, Mukilteo—in Snohomish County to the north. Booming growth during the 1990s has been followed by some resistance to increased urbanization. Across Puget Sound it includes the northern tip of Kitsap County and Bainbridge Island, where you can commute by ferry to downtown Seattle each day and return home to what looks like the perfect American small town in the evening; the area's Metro has said that it might start ferry service. Politically, this area has been torn by forces of roughly equal strength, cultural liberalism and economic conservatism, though the former seems predominant. Most Seattle area residents appreciate, and want to preserve, the region's unique natural aura: the evergreen smell of a well-watered land; the subtle regional style that is plainly American yet distinct from most of the nation. But it is impossible not to recognize the spectacular success of market economics in the 1st District.

The congressman from the 1st District is Jay Inslee, a Democrat first elected here in 1998. Inslee grew up in north Seattle, the son of a high school biology teacher and football coach, and graduated from the University of Washington and Willamette School of Law. He moved to Selah, in Yakima County east of the Cascades, to practice law and served on the State Trial Lawyers board of directors. In 1988, at 37, he was elected to the state House over a former Yakima mayor. In 1992, when 4th District Congressman Sid Morrison ran for governor, Inslee won the general 51%–49% over Doc Hastings, a conservative supported by the Christian Coalition. In the House, Inslee voted for the Clinton budget and tax increase and for the crime bill with the assault weapons ban, despite promising to vote against gun control bills. In 1994 Hastings ran again and beat Inslee, 53%–47%. After his defeat, Inslee moved to Bainbridge Island and practiced law in

Seattle. In 1996 he ran for governor and finished fifth, with 10% of the total vote, in the all-party primary. Briefly he was a regional director of HHS.

In 1998, Inslee ran in the 1st District against Congressman Rick White. White was an economic conservative with liberal votes on some cultural issues, but he had problems. In April 1998 he was divorced, though he had portrayed himself as a family man in his first campaign in 1994. And Bruce Craswell, whose wife Ellen Craswell lost to Governor Gary Locke in 1996, decided to run on the line of the conservative American Heritage Party. Inslee attacked White for voting to reduce spending on education and the environment and for supporting electricity deregulation, claiming that White was "willing to sell our reasonably priced electricity to California." White tried to paint Inslee as an opportunist. To the carpetbagger charge, Inslee replied that he had grown up in the 1st District and had lived there more years than White. In the September all-party primary, White led 50%–44%; Craswell got 7%. By November, two issues changed the balance. One was White's divorce: Inslee's ad claimed that White intended to spend 10 years in the House and then be a lobbyist—a reference to a statement by his wife in the divorce papers. The second was impeachment: After White voted for the Clinton inquiry, Inslee ran an ad saying, "Rick White and Newt Gingrich shouldn't be dragging us through this. Enough is enough." In the acrimony, the primary numbers were reversed in November: Inslee won 50%–44%.

In the House, Inslee votes as a liberal-leaning Democrat and works on high-tech issues. He joined in protecting the privacy of consumer financial records—a cause that is important to Microsoft. When Congress passed the electronic signature bill, Inslee included an amendment to require that terms of consumer consent to receive electronic records be obvious and separate from other terms. He called for increased congressional oversight of the use of spyware by federal agencies. On other issues, he voted for normal trade relations with China but against trade promotion authority. He voted to override Bill Clinton's veto of the estate tax and marriage penalty repeal. He narrowly won House approval of his amendment to prohibit Bush officials from suspending or revising new mining regulations. After September 11 and the airline slowdown, he sought increased unemployment benefits for aerospace workers; later, he called for similar action to aid unemployed high-tech workers. On behalf of the Snohomish Public Utility District, he filed legislation to void its contract for power supply with the bankrupt Enron Corporation. After the devastating Indian Ocean tsunami in December 2004, he called for an expanded warning system. After earlier setbacks, he got a seat in 2005 on the Energy and Commerce Committee, where he planned to focus on financing of the Bonneville Power Administration, increasing renewable energy sources and ensuring the cleanup of the Hanford nuclear site.

In 2000 against former state Senate Republican leader Dan McDonald, Inslee won 55%–43%. His margins have grown wider since. He gave serious thought to running for governor in 2004, but decided against it. With the governor and two senators all Democrats, his statewide ambitions are on hold for now.

SECOND DISTRICT

Rep. Rick Larsen (D)

Elected 2000, 3d term; b. June 15, 1965, Arlington; home, Lake Stevens; Pacific Lutheran U., B.A. 1987, U. of MN, M.P.A. 1990; Methodist; married (Tiia).

Elected Office: Snohomish City Cncl., 1998–2000, Pres., 1999–2000.

Professional Career: Econ. Dev. Ofcl., Port of Everett, 1990–91; Dir., Pub. Affairs, WA St. Dental Assn., 1991–98.

DC Office: 107 CHOB, 20515, 202-225-2605; Fax: 202-225-4420; Web site: www.house.gov/larsen.

District Offices: Bellingham, 360-733-4500; Everett, 425-252-3188.

Committees: *Agriculture* (19th of 21 D): General Farm Commodities & Risk Management; Livestock & Horticulture. *Armed Services* (19th of 28 D): Strategic Forces; Terrorism, Unconventional Threats & Capabilities. *Transportation & Infrastructure* (23d of 34 D): Aviation; Highways, Transit & Pipelines.

Group Ratings

	ADA	ACLU	AFS	LCV	ITIC	NTU	COC	ACU	NTLC	CHC
2004	90	80	100	91	90	10	48	8	3	15
2003	95	—	100	95	—	27	50	28	—	—

National Journal Ratings

	2003 LIB	—	2003 CONS		2004 LIB	—	2004 CONS
Economic	66%	—	32%		68%	—	32%
Social	66%	—	34%		77%	—	22%
Foreign	61%	—	39%		73%	—	27%

Key Votes of the 108th Congress

1. Drilling in ANWR	N	5. DC School Vouchers	N	9. Ban Same-Sex Marriage	N
2. Approve Bush Tax Cuts	N	6. Ban Human Cloning	Y	10. Fund Iraq War	Y
3. Medicare/Rx Bill	N	7. Restrict Gun Liability	Y	11. Bar Cuba Embargo Funds	Y
4. Bar Overtime Pay Regs.	Y	8. Ban Partial-Birth Abortion	N	12. Intelligence Reorg.	N

Election Results

2004 general	Rick Larsen (D)	202,383	(64%)	($1,412,604)
	Suzanne Sinclair (R)	106,333	(34%)	($38,740)
	Other	7,966	(3%)	
2004 primary	Rick Larsen (D)	unopposed		
2002 general	Rick Larsen (D)	101,219	(50%)	($1,768,783)
	Norma Smith (R)	92,528	(46%)	($555,564)
	Other	8,403	(4%)	

Prior Winning Percentages: 2000 (50%)

The People		**Race/Ethnic Origin**	**Ancestry**	
Area size:	7,976 sq. mi.	85.6% White	German: 13.7%	English: 9.2%
Urban population:	69.4%	1.1% Black	Irish: 8.4%	
Rural population:	30.6%	2.8% Asian	**2004 Presidential Vote**	
Pop. 2000:	654,903	1.9% Native Am.	Kerry (D) 169,420	(51%)
Median income:	$45,441	0.2% Hawaiian	Bush (R) 156,632	(47%)
Poverty status:	10.0%	2.4% Two+ races	Other 5,904	(2%)
Military veterans:	16.3%	0.2% Other	**2000 Presidential Vote**	
		5.8% Hispanic Origin	Gore (D) 133,216	(48%)
			Bush (R) 129,027	(46%)
			Other 16,765	(6%)
			Cook Partisan Voting Index: D + 3	
Occupation	Blue collar: 27.6%	White collar: 55.1%	Gray collar: 17.3%	

The 172 San Juan Islands, in the waters of Puget Sound at the far northwest corner of Washington, were the last part of the continental United States to be turned over to this country; these waters were great whaling grounds and not until 1860 did the British relinquish them. Today, ferryboats ply the waters of the Sound, connecting the islands to mainland Washington, and to British Columbia directly to the west; the publicly operated Washington State Ferries system has about 25 million passengers annually. Whale watching is popular not only with tourists, but also among scientists on both sides of the border. This is some of the most beautiful land and water of North America, the steely blue Sound with green forested hills rising behind; it is wet country, shielded from the full force of Pacific rains by the Olympic Mountains, but still seldom dry. The little towns, on bits of level land between the water and mountains, have the look of pristine New England villages or Midwestern historic towns, but are better preserved than the originals; the stores are full of fresh produce and local seafood. Here the Seattle metropolitan area has marched north along the shore of Puget Sound, beyond the old lumber port and railroad terminus of Everett, with the huge Boeing plant—the largest building in the world—where 747s, 777s and the new 200-plus passenger 787s are built, amid intense competition with the French-

based Airbus. To the north are the small city of Bellingham and the town of Blaine on the 49th parallel, with America's most attractively landscaped border crossing and International Peace Arch, just south of British Columbia.

The 2d Congressional District of Washington includes the San Juan Islands, Whidbey Island and Puget Sound from Everett north, plus most of the margin of mainland along the Sound and the huge Cascade mountains, topped by snow-capped Mount Baker in northeast King County. The district has several military installations, including a relatively new and high-tech navy base at Everett and naval air station on Whidbey Island. This was the fastest-growing district in Washington during the 1990s. The political tradition in most of the lumbering and fishing areas here is Democratic, while the rich agricultural areas, like the flower-bulb-growing Skagit Valley, are more Republican. Everett tends to be Democratic, some of the nearby new suburban towns Republican. Overall, this is a nearly evenly balanced district that tends to vote close to the state average.

The congressman from the 2d District is Rick Larsen, a Democrat first elected in 2000. He grew up in Arlington, in Snohomish County, graduated from Pacific Lutheran University and got a masters degree at the University of Minnesota. He spent a year doing research on economic development for the Port of Everett. For six years he was director of public affairs for the Washington State Dental Association. In 1998 he won a seat on the Snohomish County Council and he later became its president. In 2000, Republican Jack Metcalf kept his promise to retire after three terms; he had won the formerly Democratic seat each time by a relatively narrow margin. The Democratic field was cleared for Larsen when a state legislator unpopular with labor leaders withdrew. The Republican field was cleared for conservative state Representative John Koster when a moderate legislator failed to raise much money and dropped out. In the September all-party primary, Koster unexpectedly led 49%–46%. The contest became a battle-ground for political action committees and one of the premier contests in the nation: anti-abortion groups and the National Rifle Association backed Koster, and unions and abortion rights groups fought for Larsen. Larsen said that the contest offered "a clear choice" on abortion, and he criticized Koster for referring to "our American holocaust." He won 50%–46%, improving his performance in each major county from the primary.

In the House, Larsen joined the New Democrat Coalition, leans toward the center in his voting record, and has seats on the Agriculture, Armed Services, and Transportation and Infra-structure committees. He voted for the Bush tax cuts in 2001. He voted against trade promotion authority in December 2001 but he was one of five Democrats who switched to vote for the conference agreement in July 2002. He voted against the Iraq war resolution. In 2004, he worked to secure funds for upgraded border security at Bellingham; on the highway bill, he has pushed for increased support for the Puget Sound ferries. He also has been an advocate for local dairy farmers in preventing the spread of mad cow disease. Larsen sponsored a proposal to expand the Wild Sky wilderness area in Snohomish County; this became an issue in the 2004 Senate campaign when Republican challenger George Nethercutt backed a version without 13,000 acres in low-level forest included in Larsen's proposal.

In 2002 Larsen was opposed by Norma Smith, a former top aide to Metcalf. Smith criticized Larsen's vote on Iraq and his vote against creation of the Homeland Security Department. She ran an ad that morphed the face of liberal Seattle Congressman Jim McDermott, who traveled to Baghdad that September and said that he believed Saddam Hussein more than George W. Bush, into Larsen's. Larsen spent three times as much money as Smith, who received no money from the national party. Larsen won 50%–46%, almost exactly the same as his margin in 2000. In 2004, Larsen won 64%–34%.

THIRD DISTRICT

Rep. Brian Baird (D)

Elected 1998, 4th term; b. Mar. 7, 1956, Chama, NM; home, Olympia; U. of UT, B.A. 1977, U. of WY, M.S. 1980, Ph.D. 1984; Protestant; married (Rachel).

Professional Career: Prof., Pacific Lutheran U., 1986–98.

DC Office: 1421 LHOB, 20515, 202-225-3536; Fax: 202-225-3478; Web site: www.house.gov/baird.

District Offices: Olympia, 360-352-9768; Vancouver, 360-695-6292.

Committees: *Budget* (8th of 17 D). *Science* (15th of 20 D): Environment, Technology & Standards; Research. *Transportation & Infrastructure* (19th of 34 D): Coast Guard & Maritime Transportation; Highways, Transit & Pipelines; Water Resources & Environment.

Group Ratings

	ADA	ACLU	AFS	LCV	ITIC	NTU	COC	ACU	NTLC	CHC
2004	90	75	100	100	70	13	53	17	6	7
2003	95	—	100	90	—	29	33	12	—	—

National Journal Ratings

	2003 LIB	—	2003 CONS		2004 LIB	—	2004 CONS
Economic	71%	—	27%		69%	—	31%
Social	72%	—	27%		70%	—	30%
Foreign	84%	—	14%		67%	—	33%

Key Votes of the 108th Congress

1. Drilling in ANWR	N	5. DC School Vouchers	N	9. Ban Same-Sex Marriage	N
2. Approve Bush Tax Cuts	N	6. Ban Human Cloning	N	10. Fund Iraq War	N
3. Medicare/Rx Bill	N	7. Restrict Gun Liability	Y	11. Bar Cuba Embargo Funds	*
4. Bar Overtime Pay Regs.	Y	8. Ban Partial-Birth Abortion	N	12. Intelligence Reorg.	N

Election Results

2004 general	Brian Baird (D)	193,626	(62%)	($850,014)
	Thomas Crowson (R)	119,027	(38%)	($55,727)
2004 primary	Brian Baird (D)	61,110	(85%)	
	Cheryl Crist (D)	10,518	(15%)	
2002 general	Brian Baird (D)	119,264	(62%)	($781,953)
	Joseph Zarelli (R)	74,065	(38%)	($198,886)

Prior Winning Percentages: 2000 (56%); 1998 (55%)

The People		Race/Ethnic Origin	Ancestry	
Area size:	7,961 sq. mi.	87.7% White	German: 14.3%	English: 8.9%
Urban population:	70.9%	1.2% Black	Irish: 8.3%	
Rural population:	29.1%	2.6% Asian	**2004 Presidential Vote**	
Pop. 2000:	654,898	1.0% Native Am.	Bush (R) 164,643	(50%)
Median income:	$44,426	0.3% Hawaiian	Kerry (D) 158,503	(48%)
Poverty status:	10.5%	2.5% Two+ races	Other 5,301	(2%)
Military veterans:	16.2%	0.1% Other	**2000 Presidential Vote**	
		4.6% Hispanic Origin	Bush (R) 131,958	(48%)
			Gore (D) 127,292	(46%)
			Other 15,732	(6%)
			Cook Partisan Voting Index: D + 0	
Occupation	Blue collar: 26.8%	White collar: 57.0%	Gray collar: 16.2%	

From the Pacific Ocean to the majestic row of active and inactive volcanoes from Mount Rainier to Mount St. Helens to Oregon's Mount Hood, southwest Washington was long one of America's most productive lumber areas. The moist air and almost constant rains blown in from the Pacific keep the trees on the coast growing rapidly; precipitation remains heavy in the valleys just past the Coast Range, and additional fast-growing forests. Then come the high mountains: The Cascades are a genuine divide, wrenching almost all precipitation out of the air so the climate eastward for a thousand miles is arid. Americans were reminded of the force of the volcanoes when Mount St. Helens, dormant for 123 years, erupted in 1980, killing 65 people, destroying its own peak and paving the land around with lava. Americans had long been taught that the lower 48 states had no active volcanoes; Mount St. Helens proved that wrong, and one of her sisters may do it again. In October 2004, a series of rumbles there punched a 200-foot hole in a glacier and attracted scientists and curious tourists, but the dome remained in place.

Lewis and Clark came here in 1805, down the Columbia River to a rainy and foggy winter by the ocean; for many years this part of Washington was sparsely settled, with lumber-mill and fishing-boat towns interspersed between mountains and water. It was flannel shirt country, Democratic since the New Deal days. In the early 1990s its resource-based economy was threatened by the environmental movement, which restricted fishing practices and got a court decision shutting down old growth forest logging to save spotted owl habitat. This roiled local politics and gave Republicans an opening. An important demographic shift has been the spread of two great metropolitan areas into these valleys. Clark County across the Columbia from Portland, Oregon, has filled up with new residents, eager to avoid Oregon's income tax and still able to make big purchases in Oregon free of sales tax; its population grew by 45% in the 1990s, the largest increase in the state. From the north, the Seattle-Tacoma conurbation has been moving past the small state capital of Olympia. This is one of America's great international trading areas, with big exports of logs and timber and vast imports on the docks of Portland and the Puget Sound.

The 3d Congressional District of Washington covers the land between the ocean and the Cascades, from Olympia on an inlet of Puget Sound, south to Vancouver, site of the Hudson Bay Company headquarters in the 19th century. Economic growth and diversification and the coming of many new residents with no roots in the old industries have made the 3d a politically marginal district; George W. Bush won here with 48% of the vote in 2000 and 50% in 2004.

The congressman from the 3d District is Brian Baird, a Democrat first elected in 1998. Baird grew up in northern New Mexico and western Colorado. He got a Ph.D. in clinical psychology from the University of Wyoming, and worked with veterans and families dealing with cancer, with juvenile delinquents in prison and with families of murder victims. He wrote a book called *Are We Having Fun Yet?* for couples on vacation. He moved to Washington in 1980 and was a professor at Pacific Lutheran University in Tacoma and living in Olympia when he ran for the House in 1996 against Republican incumbent Linda Smith, who had strong support from Christian conservatives. Baird led on election night and was pronounced the winner by an overeager media. But when the more than 40,000 absentee votes outstanding were counted, Smith won by 887 votes, 50.2%–49.8%. Taking a leave from his job, Baird never stopped running, while Smith ran unsuccessfully against Senator Patty Murray in 1998. Republicans nominated state Senator Don Benton, who called for a flat tax and respect for gun rights and property rights. Baird spent twice as much money and won 55%–45%.

In the House, Baird has a moderate voting record that trends liberal on foreign policy. He kept a campaign promise by sponsoring a bill to restore income tax deductibility for state sales taxes; with a big boost from the Texas delegation, a modified two-year version was passed in the 2004 corporate tax bill. He was among a handful of white Democrats who joined Black Caucus members in walking out of the Electoral College count to protest the Florida result in 2000. He proposed incentives for owners of gas-electric hybrid cars and owns one himself. He voted against Bush on trade promotion authority and the use of force in Iraq. He sought middle ground with a medical malpractice proposal with incentives for mediation and high caps on damages. On local issues, he helped to secure funds to deepen the Columbia River shipping channel to accommodate larger cargo ships. He sought more money to monitor volcanoes.

After September 11, Baird gained national attention when he focused on the issue of continuity of government—what would happen if many members of Congress were killed or incapacitated by an attack? He proposed a constitutional amendment providing that, if one-fourth of House seats became vacant, governors must appoint a successor within seven days. This would be quite a change; as House members like to note, under the Constitution no one has ever served in the House without winning an election. And Baird's amendment could result in a change of party balance. Baird argued that if many members were killed or incapacitated, the House might not be able to achieve the quorum of half the living members required to act. Many members thought that proposals from Baird and his allies were too radical; Congress usually moves cautiously on constitutional amendments, only 17 of which have been ratified since 1792. In July 2004, the House defeated his proposal, 63–353. But some members of both parties thought the problem should be addressed, and Republican Christopher Cox, working with Democrat Martin Frost, proposed modest rules changes to help the House adjust to such a catastrophe. When Baird objected to additional procedural changes to redefine a House "quorum," he lost on a party-line vote. Baird opposed House-passed legislation that would require special elections to fill House seats within 49 days following a catastrophe. On a separate internal issue, he made the novel suggestion that the House should enforce its three-day waiting period for consideration of major legislation.

Baird has been reelected easily. His 2002 opponent, state Senator Joseph Zarelli, was damaged when he acknowledged that he drew unemployment checks while serving in the legislature. Baird won 62%–38%. In 2004, he won by an identical margin even as George W. Bush was carrying the district a second time.

FOURTH DISTRICT

Rep. Doc Hastings (R)

Elected 1994, 6th term; b. Feb. 7, 1941, Spokane; home, Pasco; Columbia Basin Col., 1959–61, Central Washington U., 1963–64; Protestant; married (Claire).

Military Career: Army Reserves, 1964–69.

Elected Office: WA House of Reps., 1979–87.

Professional Career: Pres., Columbia Basin Paper & Supply, 1967–94.

DC Office: 1323 LHOB, 20515, 202-225-5816; Fax: 202-225-3251; Web site: www.house.gov/hastings.

District Offices: Pasco, 509-543-9396; Yakima, 509-452-3243.

Committees: *Rules* (3d of 9 R): Rules & Organization of the House (Chmn.). *Standards of Official Conduct* (Chmn. of 5 R).

Group Ratings

	ADA	ACLU	AFS	LCV	ITIC	NTU	COC	ACU	NTLC	CHC
2004	0	0	0	0	100	63	100	100	84	92
2003	10	—	0	0	—	60	97	92	—	—

National Journal Ratings

	2003 LIB	—	2003 CONS	2004 LIB	—	2004 CONS
Economic	9%	—	84%	8%	—	91%
Social	17%	—	79%	31%	—	67%
Foreign	23%	—	71%	0%	—	96%

Key Votes of the 108th Congress

1. Drilling in ANWR	Y	5. DC School Vouchers	Y	9. Ban Same-Sex Marriage	Y
2. Approve Bush Tax Cuts	Y	6. Ban Human Cloning	Y	10. Fund Iraq War	Y
3. Medicare/Rx Bill	Y	7. Restrict Gun Liability	Y	11. Bar Cuba Embargo Funds	N
4. Bar Overtime Pay Regs.	N	8. Ban Partial-Birth Abortion	Y	12. Intelligence Reorg.	Y

Election Results

2004 general	Doc Hastings (R)	154,627	(63%)	($557,536)
	Sandy Matheson (D)	92,486	(37%)	($404,802)
2004 primary	Doc Hastings (R)	unopposed		
2002 general	Doc Hastings (R)	108,257	(67%)	($250,574)
	Craig Mason (D)	53,572	(33%)	($37,657)

Prior Winning Percentages: 2000 (61%); 1998 (69%); 1996 (53%); 1994 (53%)

The People		Race/Ethnic Origin	Ancestry	
Area size:	19,430 sq. mi.	67.8% White	German: 13.1%	English: 7.8%
Urban population:	70.5%	0.8% Black	Irish: 6.9%	
Rural population:	29.5%	1.2% Asian	**2004 Presidential Vote**	
Pop. 2000:	654,901	1.9% Native Am.	Bush (R) 160,310	(63%)
Median income:	$37,764	0.1% Hawaiian	Kerry (D) 90,083	(35%)
Poverty status:	16.2%	1.7% Two+ races	Other 3,716	(1%)
Military veterans:	13.3%	0.1% Other	**2000 Presidential Vote**	
		26.4% Hispanic Origin	Bush (R) 141,891	(62%)
			Gore (D) 78,768	(34%)
			Other 8,629	(4%)
			Cook Partisan Voting Index: R +13	

Occupation   Blue collar: 23.7%   White collar: 52.8%   Gray collar: 23.5%

The rugged peaks of the Cascade Mountains divide Washington State into two starkly different climate zones and two almost as starkly different political cultures. West of the Cascades, Washington is moist, green, full of watery inlets; to the east it is barren and brown, except where irrigation ditches feed the waters of the Columbia River into thirsty valleys, or where mountaintop waters fall east, as they do to water the apple orchards in the Yakima Valley. The federal government has been a presence in the East-of-the-Cascades since the 1930s, when it began to build dams that provided cheap power and boosted economic development in this forbidding, often surreal, landscape. A giant bust of Franklin D. Roosevelt gazes from a bluff on the Columbia out over 550-foot-high Grand Coulee Dam, which Roosevelt initiated and which was one of his favorite projects. Other dams are strung along downriver, like beads on the necklace of the Columbia, most of the way to Bonneville Dam near Portland, where the river breaks through the Cascades.

The one exception is the Hanford Reach, the last undammed, undeveloped stretch of the upper Columbia River, near the 640-square mile Hanford Nuclear Reservation, north of the Tri-Cities of Richland, Kennewick and Pasco. Hanford was built by the Army to manufacture plutonium for the Manhattan Project and was where the Nagasaki bomb was constructed. After the war, the Hanford Works became the primary producer of materials for America's nuclear weapons and eastern Washington's largest employer. Then in 1989 Hanford's plutonium plant, which produced two-thirds of the nation's plutonium, was shut down because of hazardous leaks and contaminated waste; the spent fuel is scheduled to be shipped to Yucca Mountain in Nevada, when the nuclear waste repository there is completed. In 2004, workers completed the removal of millions of gallons of liquid radioactive waste from old tanks. Also that year, voters approved a referendum to prohibit the Energy Department from sending more radioactive waste into Washington until the existing sites have been cleaned up. A new plant is scheduled to convert million of gallons of nuclear waste to glass starting in 2007 at a cost of $4 billion. Total clean-up costs could exceed $50 billion and may take another three decades to complete.

The 4th Congressional District of Washington covers much of the center of the state east of the Cascades, running from Grand Coulee and the Columbia River through the Hanford Works down to the Dalles Dam and the Columbia River Gorge. One tends to think of this area as ethnically unvaried, but 26% of the district's residents, and 36% in Yakima County, are Hispanic: farm workers, in many cases, who have settled here permanently, or their children who have gone on to other things. Sentiment toward the federal government has soured in other parts of the district almost as much as around the Tri-Cities. Farmers in the Yakima Valley, which produces most of the nation's apples and many other crops, were enraged at environmental groups' proposals to breach the Snake River dams upriver to save salmon. Lumber towns in the Cascades responded angrily when those who wanted to preserve the spotted owl tried to shut down logging businesses. In an area once narrowly split between the parties and that as recently as 1992 elected a Democrat to Congress, opinion has shifted sharply, making this the most Republican district in the state and one where Democrats have little hope; the cultural liberalism of Seattle, an hour or two distant on I-90, seems very far away here. Said one Democrat when he looked at a party poll, "I don't know what Democrats did to these people, but it sure must have been bad."

The congressman from the 4th District is Doc Hastings, a Republican first elected in 1994. He got the nickname because an older brother could not pronounce his real name of Richard when they were kids. Hastings grew up in the Tri-Cities, went to college in Ellensburg and is one of the few members of Congress without a college degree. He served in the Army Reserves and for 27 years ran the Columbia Basin Paper and Supply Company in Pasco, where he was president of the chamber of commerce. In 1979 he was elected to the state House, served as a Republican leader, then retired in 1987. In 1992 he won the Republican nomination for Congress, but was beaten 51%–49% by Democrat Jay Inslee. But Inslee voted for the Clinton budget and tax package and the crime bill with its gun-control provisions—big liabilities when Hastings ran again in 1994. Hastings led with 50% in the all-party primary, to only 41% for Inslee. In November he won 53%–47%. Since then, Democrats have not seriously competed here and this has become a safe Republican seat.

In the House, Hastings has had a solidly conservative voting record and, with a seat on the Rules Committee, has usually been a leadership loyalist. Much of his time has been spent on Hanford. When George W. Bush proposed cuts in the Energy Department budget, Hastings warned that cuts in the cleanup program were not acceptable; within a few months, he secured sufficient funding for local projects to avoid an overall reduction. He created a House nuclear caucus to fight for Hanford funding. In 2004, Congress enacted his proposal for the Interior Department to study preservation of the Manhattan Project's historic sites at Hanford as part of the national park system. He strongly opposed environmental groups who sought to remove some of the 12 dams on the Snake and Columbia rivers.

In recent years, Hastings has become a prominent behind-the-scenes presence in Republican leadership circles. As chairman of the Investigating Subcommittee of the Ethics Committee, Hastings had the thankless task of reviewing the case against James Traficant, who was convicted of bribery in federal court in April 2002. The panel voted unanimously to expel him from the House, only the second such action since the Civil War; just before the House voted 420–1 for expulsion, Traficant called Hastings "a very fair man." He was part of the unanimous 10-member panel in 2004 that voted three admonishments of Majority Leader Tom DeLay, the mildest possible sanction. But many Republicans were incensed at the admonishments because the panel also ruled that DeLay had violated no House rules. Speaker Dennis Hastert removed Joel Hefley as chairman—after the usual four-year period, members said—and also removed two other Republicans from the committee; Hastings was named chairman. Republicans argued that he had earned a reputation for fairness: Hastert earlier delegated him to enforce Republican rules limiting members' committee assignments, and has often called on him to preside over the House during important debates, including what turned out to be the three-hour roll call on the Medicare/prescription drug bill in November 2003; Democrats have praised his evenhandedness. He rarely speaks on the House floor other than on the rules for debate and says he never called a press conference before he became Ethics chairman.

Yet Democrats decried Hastings's selection as chairman, and also complained when Republicans in January 2005 changed the House's ethics rules, requiring a majority vote on this one committee made up of equal numbers of members of both parties before an investigation could proceed. Democrats charged that this would give Republicans veto power over investigations and charged that Hefley's ouster was retaliation against the committee's treatment of DeLay. Hastings supported the rules changes and ousted the committee's top staffers, often a routine move for a new chairman. When the Democrats on the committee refused to attend committee meetings and prevented the establishment of a quorum there, Republicans agreed to restore the earlier rules. Hastings also got a big increase in committee funding to assist members with compliance. He and DeLay have not been close: Hastings voted against him for majority whip in 1994 and opposed his choice of Richard Pombo to chair the Resources Committee. The reputation for fairness that Hastings has won over many years seems likely to be tested in his new role as ethics chairman. On the Rules Committee, Hastings planned an ever-controversial review of the jurisdiction of House committees. If he credibly handles these tough assignments, this House insider can expect other leadership opportunities—perhaps the important Rules Committee chairmanship.

FIFTH DISTRICT

Rep. Cathy McMorris (R)

Elected 2004, 1st term; b. May 22, 1969, Salem, OR; home, Deer Lake; Pensacola Christian Col., B.A. 1990, U. of WA, M.B.A. 2002; Christian; single.

Elected Office: WA House of Reps., 1994–2004; Min. Ldr. 2002–04.

Professional Career: Owner-operator, Peachcrest Fruit Basket orchard, 1984–98; state legislative aide, 1990–94.

DC Office: 1708 LHOB, 20515, 202-225-2006; Fax: 202-225-3392; Web site: www.mcmorris.house.gov.

District Offices: Colville, 509-684-3481; Spokane, 509-353-2374; Walla Walla, 509-529-9358.

Committees: *Armed Services* (32d of 34 R): Readiness; Strategic Forces. *Education & the Workforce* (19th of 27 R): 21st Century Competitiveness; Select Education. *Resources* (23d of 27 R): Forests & Forest Health; Water & Power.

Group Ratings and Key Votes: Newly Elected

Election Results

2004 general	Cathy McMorris (R)	179,600	(60%)	($1,537,540)
	Don Barbieri (D)	121,333	(40%)	($1,628,666)
2004 primary	Cathy McMorris (R)	42,948	(50%)	
	Larry Sheahan (R)	23,593	(27%)	
	Shaun Cross (R)	19,878	(23%)	
2002 general	George Nethercutt (R)	126,757	(63%)	($857,642)
	Bart Haggin (D)	65,146	(32%)	($37,039)
	Rob Chase (Lib)	10,379	(5%)	($4,433)

The People		Race/Ethnic Origin	Ancestry	
Area size:	23,166 sq. mi.	87.7% White	German: 16.5% Irish: 9.0%	
Urban population:	71.9%	1.3% Black	English: 8.8%	
Rural population:	28.1%	1.7% Asian	**2004 Presidential Vote**	
Pop. 2000:	654,904	2.3% Native Am.	Bush (R)	177,311 (57%)
Median income:	$35,720	0.1% Hawaiian	Kerry (D)	127,162 (41%)
Poverty status:	14.4%	2.3% Two+ races	Other	5,705 (2%)
Military veterans:	16.2%	0.2% Other	**2000 Presidential Vote**	
		4.5% Hispanic Origin	Bush (R)	150,013 (56%)
			Gore (D)	106,610 (40%)
			Other	13,262 (5%)
			Cook Partisan Voting Index: R + 7	
Occupation	Blue collar: 21.1%	White collar: 60.0%	Gray collar: 18.9%	

Eastern Washington is a land of great rivers and bare parched land, where the Columbia, Spokane and Snake Rivers wind among vast plateaus, bringing water from the Rockies to the desert. Spokane grew up at the falls of the Spokane River when the railroads first came through, and became a major wheat, mining, electrical and railroad center early in the 20th century, the center of the so-called "Inland Empire"; it celebrated with the 1974 World's Fair and Exposition on the downtown riverfront. Nearby are some of the most fascinating landscapes in the United States: surreally undulating yellow wheat fields, the rolling ridges of the Palouse where the wheat-growing topsoil is 200 feet deep, the bare-rock coulees rising above dammed-up lakes and barren desert, the vast wilderness of Okanogan County that has long been gold country and where the locals have battled over whether to open a new mine. This is remote and inhospitable land: the summers can be blazing hot and winters bitter cold; many rivers run wildly. But much of it has been tamed by man, and the water from the Grand Coulee and other dams irrigates some of the richest farmland in the country.

The 5th Congressional District of Washington covers the easternmost part of the state. Two-thirds of the people here live in greater Spokane, a city whose voting habits have grown apart from the Washington west of the Cascades, especially on resource issues and the role of government. Several Spokane area politicians have called for creating a 51st state of Eastern Washington, with 60% of the current state's land and 22% of its population. Its political inclinations are Republican, but not as Republican as most of the nearby Rocky Mountain states. Spokane County voted for Bill Clinton in 1992 and 1996, but George W. Bush won the county 56%–44% in 2004 and won 57% in the entire 5th District.

The congresswoman from the 5th District is Cathy McMorris, a Republican elected in 2004. She spent much of her childhood in northern British Columbia, graduated from Pensacola Christian College and got an MBA from the University of Washington: a lot of moving around. The last time that eastern Washington elected a 35-year-old to Congress—Thomas Foley in 1964—he rose through the ranks and eventually became Speaker of the House. No one is yet predicting a similar ascent for Cathy McMorris, elected at 35, but her background suggests that she is likely to be on the leadership track. While working in the family-owned orchard and fruit stand in Kettle Falls, she was appointed then later elected to the state House, where she served for 10 years and chaired the Commerce and Labor Committee; she served her final two years as House Minority Leader, the first female House leader in state history. In 2004 George Nethercutt, who beat Foley in 1994, the first congressional candidate to defeat a Speaker since Charles Denison defeated Galusha Grow in 1862, ran for the Senate; McMorris and two other Republicans filed to compete for his seat in the Republican primary. McMorris was backed by the economic conservatives of the Club for Growth; that prompted the moderate Republican Main Street Partnership to launch a highly unusual direct-mail and radio attack on her, though it did not support either of her opponents. The three primary candidates agreed on most major issues. Each opposed abortion and favored a constitutional amendment banning same-sex marriage. All three supported tort law changes and making the Bush administration tax cuts permanent; all criticized the Endangered Species Act. McMorris won 50% of the vote in the primary to 27% for state senator Larry Sheahan and 23% for Spokane lawyer Shaun Cross; she led in nine of the 12 counties, losing only three small rural counties south of Spokane.

The Democratic nominee, Don Barbieri, a wealthy businessman, had a geographical edge over McMorris; he is from Spokane while she is from rural northeastern Washington. Barbieri also had a heavy financial advantage. He had no primary opposition and was well funded going in the general. The National Republican Congressional Committee spent heavily on McMorris's behalf. One NRCC-sponsored ad charged that Barbieri put "profits before jobs" when his hotel development company laid off workers following a merger with another company. McMorris highlighted her pro-business credentials and agricultural background as a farmer's daughter. That was enough to put her in by a comfortable margin, 60%–40%, another sign of how much has changed in Tom Foley's old district, where Democrats these days rarely win anything. She carried every county, with margins over 2–1 in many counties. She carried Spokane County 57%–43%.

Showing her political skill, she was elected the freshman representative to the Republican Steering Committee, which makes House committee assignments. She was placed on Armed Services and Resources, and became one of four freshmen named as an assistant whip.

SIXTH DISTRICT

Rep. Norm Dicks (D)

Elected 1976, 15th term; b. Dec. 16, 1940, Bremerton; home, Bremerton; U. of WA, B.A. 1963, J.D. 1968; Lutheran; married (Suzanne).

Professional Career: Legis. Asst., U.S. Sen. Warren Magnuson, 1968–73, A.A., 1973–76.

DC Office: 2467 RHOB, 20515, 202-225-5916; Fax: 202-226-1176; Web site: www.house.gov/dicks.

District Offices: Bremerton, 360-479-4011; Port Angeles, 360-452-3370; Tacoma, 253-593-6536.

Committees: *Appropriations* (3d of 29 D): Defense; Interior, Environment & Related Agencies (RMM). *Homeland Security* (4th of 15 D): Economic Security, Infrastructure Protection & Cybersecurity; Emergency Preparedness, Science & Technology; Prevention of Nuclear & Biological Attack.

Group Ratings

	ADA	ACLU	AFS	LCV	ITIC	NTU	COC	ACU	NTLC	CHC
2004	85	78	100	91	70	10	48	13	3	0
2003	90	—	100	95	—	22	38	24	—	—

National Journal Ratings

	2003 LIB	—	2003 CONS	2004 LIB	—	2004 CONS
Economic	66%	—	32%	64%	—	35%
Social	77%	—	22%	72%	—	27%
Foreign	57%	—	42%	78%	—	22%

Key Votes of the 108th Congress

1. Drilling in ANWR	N	5. DC School Vouchers	N	9. Ban Same-Sex Marriage	N
2. Approve Bush Tax Cuts	N	6. Ban Human Cloning	N	10. Fund Iraq War	Y
3. Medicare/Rx Bill	N	7. Restrict Gun Liability	N	11. Bar Cuba Embargo Funds	Y
4. Bar Overtime Pay Regs.	Y	8. Ban Partial-Birth Abortion	*	12. Intelligence Reorg.	N

Election Results

2004 general	Norm Dicks (D)	202,919	(69%)	($871,608)
	Doug Cloud (R)	91,228	(31%)	
2004 primary	Norm Dicks (D)	unopposed		
2002 general	Norm Dicks (D)	126,116	(64%)	($914,657)
	Bob Lawrence (R)	61,584	(31%)	($62,571)
	John Bennett (Lib)	8,744	(4%)	

Prior Winning Percentages: 2000 (65%); 1998 (68%); 1996 (66%); 1994 (58%); 1992 (64%); 1990 (61%); 1988 (68%); 1986 (71%); 1984 (66%); 1982 (63%); 1980 (54%); 1978 (61%); 1976 (74%)

The People		Race/Ethnic Origin	Ancestry	
Area size:	8,592 sq. mi.	77.7% White	German: 13.2% English: 8.5%	
Urban population:	78.8%	5.5% Black	Irish: 8.5%	
Rural population:	21.2%	4.4% Asian	**2004 Presidential Vote**	
Pop. 2000:	654,902	2.2% Native Am.	Kerry (D)	163,145 (53%)
Median income:	$39,205	0.7% Hawaiian	Bush (R)	137,891 (45%)
Poverty status:	13.2%	4.1% Two+ races	Other	5,365 (2%)
Military veterans:	19.8%	0.2% Other	**2000 Presidential Vote**	
		5.1% Hispanic Origin	Gore (D)	139,643 (52%)
			Bush (R)	115,736 (43%)
			Other	15,098 (6%)
			Cook Partisan Voting Index: D + 6	

Occupation	Blue collar: 25.3%	White collar: 54.8%	Gray collar: 19.8%

The rainiest part of the continental United States is at its far northwest corner, where the Olympic Mountains of Washington thrust into the Pacific Ocean. The waters of the Pacific evaporate, condense and then mist or rain down on the hills and mountains that jut up from the ocean and Puget Sound. The mountains here are always green, the trees that line the inlets towering, and during heavy rainfalls the rivers can rise six feet a day. This has long been lumbering and fishing country, where men go out to work at 6 a.m. in air cold enough to see your breath year-round, and where dependence on the vagaries of nature plus harsh environmental laws—like the ban on old-growth logging to protect the habitat of the spotted owl—have strengthened a traditional surly independence and suspicion of authority. Still, respect for the beauty of Nature endures at the 3,310 square mile Olympic Coast National Marine Sanctuary, which probes a vast underwater reserve.

The inlets of Puget Sound, winding sinuously through the mountains, are among America's most picturesque waterways and strategically among its most important. Here during World War II, shipyards built and sheltered much of the U.S. Navy's Pacific fleet, and here during the Cold War much of the nuclear submarine fleet anchored at the giant Bremerton Navy base, which has a new aircraft carrier pier. To the south is the Tacoma Straits Bridge, the replacement of the narrow span that, in a scene preserved on newsreel (and still viewed by civil engineering students), started vibrating on the wrong harmonic in high winds and collapsed in 1940. On the other side is Tacoma, long the second-ranking city on Puget Sound, with its massive docks, former pulp mills, pleasant hilly residential neighborhoods and the recent revival of a downtown streetcar line.

The 6th Congressional District of Washington includes the Olympic Peninsula, Bremerton and much of surrounding Kitsap County amid various inlets of Puget Sound, and most of Tacoma. Politically, the Olympic Peninsula and Bremerton are working-class Democratic. Tacoma also is traditionally Democratic. But as cultural issues have become more important, and as Seattle latte liberals come to symbolize the Democratic party, these areas have become trended a bit Republican. In 2004 the 6th District cast 45% of its votes for George W. Bush, far more than the 19% cast for him in Seattle's 7th District.

The congressman from the 6th District is Norm Dicks, a Democrat first elected in 1976. Dicks grew up in Bremerton, graduated from the University of Washington where he was on the football team. He became a top Appropriations Committee aide to Senator Warren Magnuson when his staff was one of the best on Capitol Hill. Dicks returned home to Bremerton to run for Congress in 1976, when the incumbent got a judgeship. He was elected easily that year and in every year since except 1980, when Magnuson lost. He has passed up several chances to run for the Senate. In his long tenure, Dicks has brought aggressiveness and political shrewdness, plus a hard-nosed interest in defense and intelligence reminiscent of Magnuson's colleague for 40 years, Henry "Scoop" Jackson. Before 1994 it never occurred to him that he would serve in the minority party, but he has adapted smoothly to that fate; he has been helped by the fact that on some issues, though not all, his goals are more congenial to Republicans than Democrats, and that most legislating on Appropriations is done on a bipartisan basis.

Dicks has a moderate voting record, especially on foreign issues, and has a seat on the Appropriations Committee and on its Defense Subcommittee—a vital post for Kitsap County, where most workers depend on Pentagon payrolls, and for Washington generally. In these posts Dicks has exerted pivotal influence on vital policies, usually operating behind the scenes. Quoting Jackson, he often says, "I'm not a hawk or a dove. I just don't want my country to be a pigeon." In the early 1980s Dicks took the lead in restoring Export-Import Bank loan authority—Boeing is America's biggest exporter and user of the loans—when the Reagan administration wanted to cut it, and led a campaign that switched 80 House votes overnight. During the post-Cold War downsizing of the Pentagon, he successfully looked out for the F-117 Stealth aircraft and especially for expanded production of the B-2 Stealth bomber. He was vindicated when the B-2 was used in the bombing of Serbia and Kosovo in 1999, Afghanistan in 2001 and Iraq in 2003, delivering weapons with pinpoint accuracy and sometimes flying halfway around the world to do so. Dicks was strong supporter of normal trade relations with China; Washington accounts for one-quarter of U.S. exports to China and in January 2005 China agreed to buy 60 Boeing 7E7s for $7.2 billion.

As ranking Democrat on the Interior Subcommittee, Dicks has used his Appropriations seat to help additional Washington communities, funneling money to lumber mill towns when logging in old-growth forests was banned, passing timber salvage riders to keep mills going, dealing with the cost of maintaining salmon runs in dammed rivers. Naturally, he looks after the interests of the Bremerton waterfront; he pushed for funding of a Tacoma waterfront development from which visitors can gaze upon Mount Rainier and see I-705, the last of the original interstate routes to be built. He was instrumental in defending Bill Clinton's "lands legacy" from attacks by Western Republicans, and in the bipartisan approval of billions of dollars for new conservation projects. He hammered out a deal with the Skokomish tribe and a Bellingham seafood company to end the dumping of salmon carcasses into Hood Canal, which suffered from algae growth. He is a booster of a tourist train from Tacoma to Mount Rainier.

Dicks had a long friendship with Al Gore that began when they entered the House in January 1977; they worked together on defense issues in the 1980s and on Northwest issues when Gore was Vice President. There was talk that Gore, if elected, would have given Dicks a prime national security job. Instead Dicks found himself meeting with George W. Bush to urge building more B-2s. During the slowdown in aircraft building in 2001, he successfully pushed for a $20 billion, 10-year lease of up to 100 Boeing 767s to replace aging KC-135 tankers. Opponents argued that was more expensive in the long run, but Dicks said, "We don't have the money to buy them." The future of the deal remained uncertain because of continuing turmoil, including the criminal conviction of a top Boeing official after he hired the Air Force's top procurement officer. Dicks worked quietly behind the scenes to build Democratic support for the Iraq war resolution even as his 7th District neighbor Jim McDermott went to Baghdad and said he found Saddam Hussein more credible than George W. Bush.

Dicks has been reelected easily since 1982.

SEVENTH DISTRICT

Rep. Jim McDermott (D)

Elected 1988, 9th term; b. Dec. 28, 1936, Chicago, IL; home, Seattle; Wheaton Col., B.S. 1958, U. of IL, M.D. 1963; Episcopalian; married (Therese Hansen).

Military Career: U.S. Navy Medical Corps., 1968–70.

Elected Office: WA House of Reps., 1970–72; WA Senate, 1974–87.

Professional Career: Asst. Prof., U. of WA, Practicing psychiatrist, 1970–83; Medical Officer, U.S. Foreign Svc., Zaire, 1987–88.

DC Office: 1035 LHOB, 20515, 202-225-3106; Fax: 202-225-6197; Web site: www.house.gov/mcdermott.

District Office: Seattle, 206-553-7170.

Committees: *Ways & Means* (5th of 17 D): Human Resources (RMM); Trade.

Group Ratings

	ADA	ACLU	AFS	LCV	ITIC	NTU	COC	ACU	NTLC	CHC
2004	95	100	100	82	44	15	15	0	0	7
2003	100	—	100	100	—	27	21	8	—	—

National Journal Ratings

	2003 LIB	—	2003 CONS		2004 LIB	—	2004 CONS
Economic	85%	—	14%		96%	—	4%
Social	92%	—	0%		88%	—	0%
Foreign	81%	—	17%		93%	—	7%

Key Votes of the 108th Congress

1. Drilling in ANWR	N	5. DC School Vouchers	N	9. Ban Same-Sex Marriage	N
2. Approve Bush Tax Cuts	N	6. Ban Human Cloning	N	10. Fund Iraq War	N
3. Medicare/Rx Bill	N	7. Restrict Gun Liability	N	11. Bar Cuba Embargo Funds	Y
4. Bar Overtime Pay Regs.	Y	8. Ban Partial-Birth Abortion	N	12. Intelligence Reorg.	N

Election Results

2004 general	Jim McDermott (D)	272,302	(81%)	($437,147)
	Carol Cassady (R)	65,226	(19%)	($23,632)
2004 primary	Jim McDermott (D)	unopposed		
2002 general	Jim McDermott (D)	156,300	(74%)	($436,384)
	Carol Cassady (R)	46,256	(22%)	($18,775)
	Stan Lippmann (Lib)	8,447	(4%)	

Prior Winning Percentages: 2000 (73%); 1998 (88%); 1996 (81%); 1994 (75%); 1992 (78%); 1990 (72%); 1988 (76%)

The People		Race/Ethnic Origin	Ancestry	
Area size:	246 sq. mi.	66.9% White	German: 11.1% Irish: 8.5%	
Urban population:	98.5%	8.3% Black	English: 8.2%	
Rural population:	1.5%	13.2% Asian	**2004 Presidential Vote**	
Pop. 2000:	654,902	0.9% Native Am.	Kerry (D)	288,161 (79%)
Median income:	$45,864	0.6% Hawaiian	Bush (R)	70,167 (19%)
Poverty status:	11.5%	3.9% Two+ races	Other	5,436 (1%)
Military veterans:	10.6%	0.3% Other	**2000 Presidential Vote**	
		5.8% Hispanic Origin	Gore (D)	228,988 (72%)
			Bush (R)	66,066 (21%)
			Other	23,952 (8%)
			Cook Partisan Voting Index: D +30	

Occupation	Blue collar: 14.7%	White collar: 70.9%	Gray collar: 14.4%

Seattle rises from the Puget Sound harbor of Elliott Bay on steep hills, once covered with 300-foot-high Douglas firs. Behind the hills and buildings you can see on a clear day, from almost anywhere, the nimbus of Mount Rainier. On the waterfront, below gleaming high-rises, is the Pike Place market, where you can get fresh salmon and Dungeness crabs; nearby is Pioneer Square, where stores and warehouses from the turn of the century have been restored; and Yesler Way, America's original "Skid Road," now has upscale shops but still some homeless people. Seattle's upper class, like San Francisco's, continues to be anchored downtown, with its upscale stores and busy sidewalks. Seattle first zoomed into the national consciousness with the 1897 Klondike gold strike, has been a major American city since around 1910 and hosted its own World's Fair in 1962. In the 1990s its combination of economic growth and creativity plus its physical beauty and distinctive style made it a national leader. Seattle still has old ethnic neighborhoods, like Scandinavian Ballard, and comfortable working-class frame houses on steep hillsides. But it also has a new ethnic mix, with thousands of Asian immigrants, and the Capitol Hill neighborhood with shoppers jamming busy stores and clubs. The dominant tone is set by highly educated, affluent, single professionals—the kind of people who have made the Victorian houses of Queen Anne overlooking the harbor or the 1940s houses lining the streets of Capitol Hill among the nation's highest priced residential real estate. There are still blue-collar workers on the south side of the city and in valleys; factories, warehouses and railroad yards are concentrated in a flat plain near Puget Sound and south of downtown. Boeing, long based in Seattle, is America's biggest exporter, but Seattle has exported other institutions: more than 150 Nordstrom department stores offer their famously polite service and fashionable goods. Seattle also is the headquarters of Starbucks coffee.

But as the 21st century dawned, all was not well in Seattle. In December 1999 rioters protesting globalism made a shambles of an international trade meeting at which Bill Clinton had hoped to chart new reductions in trade barriers. The city cancelled its New Year's Eve gala at the Space Needle because of terrorist threats. Then a federal judge back in the other Washington ruled that Microsoft was a monopoly. In perhaps the most stunning blow, Boeing chairman Phil

Condit announced in May 2001 that the company would relocate its corporate headquarters to Chicago. That decision followed a series of bitter labor disputes and less than hospitable treatment by Seattle area officials. The headquarters account for relatively few jobs, but top executives no longer feel the neighborly pressures to accommodate querulous workers and maintain economically marginal operations. Seattle's affinity for protest politics and unionism seemed, in post-September 11 America, an indulgence that could no longer be afforded. Even Seattle's leftish voters took notice: in September 2001 the dithering mayor finished third in the primary with only 22% of the vote. The city has expressed interest in hosting a national political convention, but the Republicans are certainly not going to come here and the Democrats probably won't either.

The 7th Congressional District of Washington includes nearly all of the city of Seattle, some industrial suburban fringe to the south and white collar suburban fringe to the north and rural looking Vashon Island in Puget Sound. This is the Seattle area's minority district: 13% Asian, 8% black and 6% Hispanic. Seattle shares more with San Francisco than hills and scenery: it is heavily populated by singles, gays, young professionals and elderly pensioners; it has one of the nation's lowest percentages of married couples and children. A generation ago, Seattle was roughly split between the parties; today, it is heavily Democratic and liberal. Al Gore carried this district 72%–21% and John Kerry carried it 79%–19%.

The congressman from the 7th District is Jim McDermott, one of the most liberal members of the House and its only (credentialed) psychiatrist, first elected in 1988. McDermott grew up in Chicago and was the first in his family to attend college; interestingly, he graduated from conservative religious Wheaton College, also the alma mater of Speaker Dennis Hastert. After service in the Navy and stints in New York and Illinois hospitals, he came to the University of Washington Hospital in Seattle. Almost immediately, he was elected to the state House in 1970, ran for governor in 1972 and finished third in the primary, and was elected to the state Senate in 1974. He ran for governor again in 1980, beat incumbent Dixy Lee Ray in the primary, then lost to Republican John Spellman; in 1984 he ran for governor a third time and lost the primary to Booth Gardner. In 1987 he retired from the legislature and went to Zaire (now Congo) as a medical officer in the Foreign Service. When the 7th District incumbent ran for the Senate in 1988, McDermott returned to Seattle and easily won his House seat, beating Norm Rice 38%–29% in the primary and taking 76% in the general.

In the House, McDermott's great cause has been health care but he has shared the frustration that many have met on the issue. He has long backed a single-payer, Canadian-style national health insurance program. In August 1994, as the Clinton health care plan was failing and Democratic leaders scrambled to come up with an alternative, McDermott urged Congress to abandon all health care bills for the year. He evidently expected a more favorable political environment after the election, and, like many, was surprised by the results. After Republicans took control, he said: "A lot of people around here have never been in the minority. I have. I know what to do: attack." He pushed another measure that first seemed quixotic, but it was enacted in 2000. This was the African Growth and Opportunity Act, which reduces import quotas and tariffs on African goods and includes investment funds. He was among the handful of Democrats who actively supported normal trade relations with China. But he opposed trade promotion authority in 2001 and 2002.

After the September 11 attacks, McDermott had trouble sleeping and believed that he was having symptoms of post-traumatic stress disorder. When George W. Bush ordered military strikes against Afghanistan, he was the first member to criticize him for acting too quickly. He continued to oppose the new foreign policy Bush propounded in speeches, and in late September 2002 went to Baghdad with former Minority Whip David Bonior and Mike Thompson of California. There, much to the astonishment of George Stephanopoulos, he told the audience of *This Week* that Bush was willing to "mislead the American people" and that he found Saddam Hussein more credible. This sparked harsh criticism from Republicans and dismay from those Democrats who sensed, probably accurately, that his comments hurt their party's chances in the November 2002 elections. "He combined the judgment of Neville Chamberlain before World War II and Jane Fonda in Hanoi," Texas Democrat Chet Edwards told *The New York Times*. McDermott retreated a bit and argued that Bush had failed to make the case for military action. He voted against the Iraq war resolution in October and joined five other Democrats in bringing a lawsuit to stop military action. He was one of 11 Democrats who voted against the resolution supporting the troops and the president at the start of the war in March 2003. In December 2003, McDermott regained the spotlight when he said on a Seattle radio talk show that U.S. military forces could have captured Saddam Hussein "a long time ago if they wanted." In April 2004, he omitted the words "under God" as he led the House in its daily pledge of allegiance to the flag. After leaders of both parties criticized him, he replied that his omission was not deliberate, but that the reaction "ain't fun" and was "a diversion from looking at real issues facing this country." He won praise from some liberals for his cameo appearance in Michael Moore's *Fahrenheit 9/11.* After a trip to Sudan in January 2005 with a bipartisan delegation, McDermott said that the United States should stop "sitting on the sidelines" while genocide continued.

In the meantime, McDermott was still dealing with another controversy that arose when he was ranking minority member on the ethics committee during its consideration of charges brought against Speaker Newt Gingrich. McDermott was angry that Republicans would not make public the report of special counsel James Cole before the House voted for speaker in January 1997. A few days later, the committee voted for a House reprimand and a $300,000 penalty. In the midst of the controversy, in December 1996 a Florida couple, both Democratic activists, happened to tape from a police scanner a conversation between Ohio's John Boehner, talking on a cell phone, and other House Republican leaders. They presented the tape to their congresswoman, Karen Thurman, who suggested they turn it over to McDermott. A few days later excerpts from the tape appeared in *The New York Times* and the *Atlanta Journal-Constitution.* Evidence suggested that McDermott was the source, and in 1998 Boehner sued him in federal court for invasion of privacy. The trial judge ruled that the suit would infringe McDermott's First Amendment rights, but the D.C. Circuit Court of Appeals reversed. The trial judge ruled in December 2002 that McDermott's conversations with a committee lawyer were not privileged. He approached Boehner in 2002 (they had not spoken in the 12 years they served together) and sought to settle the case. He agreed to one of Boehner's demands, that he apologize to the House, but would not agree to the other two, that he admit he was wrong and that he make a contribution to charity. On the eve of the 2004 election, the judge found McDermott guilty of violating the federal wiretapping law and ordered that he pay $60,000 in damages and $500,000 in attorneys' fees; he appealed the ruling, which friends in Seattle said they would help to pay. In November 2004, Boehner ally David Hobson filed an ethics complaint against McDermott.

McDermott considered running against Senator Slade Gorton in 2000, but backed away soon after he underwent open-heart surgery; he said that he didn't want to raise the $8 million that would be required. He has been reelected easily in this overwhelmingly Democratic district. His outspokenness may have hurt many Democrats elsewhere, but it has not hurt McDermott in Seattle.

EIGHTH DISTRICT

Rep. Dave Reichert (R)

Elected 2004, 1st term; b. Aug. 29, 1950, Detroit Lakes, MN; home, Auburn; Concordia Lutheran Col., A.A. 1970; Catholic; married (Julie).

Military Career: Air Force Reserve, 1971–76.

Elected Office: King Cnty. Sheriff, 1997–2004.

Professional Career: King Cnty. police officer, 1972–1997.

DC Office: 1223 LHOB, 20515, 202-225-7761; Fax: 202-225-4282; Web site: www.house.gov/reichert.

District Office: Mercer Island, 206-275-3438.

Committees: *Homeland Security* (17th of 19 R): Emergency Preparedness, Science & Technology; Intelligence, Information Sharing & Terrorism Risk Assessment; Management, Integration & Oversight. *Science* (19th of 24 R): Energy; Environment, Technology & Standards; Research. *Transportation & Infrastructure* (35th of 41 R): Coast Guard & Maritime Transportation; Highways, Transit & Pipelines.

Group Ratings and Key Votes: Newly Elected

Election Results

2004 general	Dave Reichert (R)	173,298	(52%)	($1,569,196)
	Dave Ross (D)	157,148	(47%)	($1,446,406)
	Other	6,053	(2%)	
2004 primary	Dave Reichert (R)	31,088	(43%)	
	Diane Tebelius (R)	16,468	(23%)	
	Luke Esser (R)	16,309	(23%)	
	Conrad Lee (R)	8,350	(12%)	
2002 general	Jennifer Dunn (R)	121,633	(60%)	($1,031,727)
	Heidi Behrens-Benedict (D)	75,931	(37%)	($120,333)
	Other	5,771	(3%)	

The People		Race/Ethnic Origin	Ancestry	
Area size:	2,621 sq. mi.	82.1% White	German: 14.0%	English: 9.4%
Urban population:	87.6%	2.0% Black	Irish: 8.3%	
Rural population:	12.4%	7.8% Asian	**2004 Presidential Vote**	
Pop. 2000:	654,905	0.8% Native Am.	Kerry (D) 177,601	(51%)
Median income:	$63,854	0.3% Hawaiian	Bush (R) 168,291	(48%)
Poverty status:	5.1%	2.8% Two+ races	Other 4,273	(1%)
Military veterans:	14.0%	0.2% Other	**2000 Presidential Vote**	
		4.0% Hispanic Origin	Gore (D) 140,387	(49%)
			Bush (R) 136,575	(47%)
			Other 11,838	(4%)
			Cook Partisan Voting Index: D + 2	

Occupation	Blue collar: 19.7%	White collar: 68.6%	Gray collar: 11.8%

The land east of Seattle's Lake Washington half a century ago was quiet countryside. Orchards and vineyards flourished in the rich, moist soil just below the rise of the Cascades Mountains, while farms and broad pasturelands spread toward 14,410-foot Mount Rainier like a living green quilt. But as Seattle has grown over the years, people have crossed the pontoon bridge across Mercer Island to Bellevue and have made this Eastside area one of the most vibrant parts of metropolitan Seattle. Bellevue now has 112,000 people and enough office space to make it an edge city; its population in 2000 was 17% Asian, the highest percentage in Washington's 15 largest cities. While downtown Seattle specialized in banks and law firms and trading companies, Bellevue and other communities in Overlake specialized in high-tech startups. Redmond, just to the north, is the headquarters of Microsoft, and there are dozens of other firms here that make this one of America's leading high-tech centers.

The 8th Congressional District of Washington includes most of the eastern edge of metro Seattle. It includes most of Bellevue, Mercer Island and the affluent suburbs on Lake Washington—Medina, Clyde Hill, Yarrow Point, Hunts Point, Beaux Arts—where Bill Gates has built his 66,000-square foot high-tech home (the 8th does not include Redmond, however). It also includes the suburbs to the south in King and Pierce Counties. It goes east to the crest of the Cascades Mountains and includes all of Mount Rainier, one of the nation's last inland old-growth rain forests, which Congress expanded in 2004 by 800 acres to improve access and permit more campsites. This is the most affluent district in Washington, rivaled only by the 1st; politically it is market-oriented on economics, more liberal on the environment and other cultural issues. Historically it is Republican, but George W. Bush lost this district twice, with 47% of the vote in 2000 and 48% in 2004.

The congressman from the 8th District is Dave Reichert, a Republican elected in 2004. Reichert was born in Detroit Lakes, Minnesota, but his family moved to the Seattle area a year later. He graduated from Concordia Lutheran College in Portland and then joined the Air Force

Reserves. He worked for 32 years in the King County sheriff's office and was elected sheriff in 1997; he was a national leader on gun-crime reduction and methamphetamine prevention. During the riots that accompanied the 1999 international trade meeting in Seattle, he criticized city leaders and the police force for inadequate preparation. He gained national attention for his prominent role in capturing Gary Ridgway, the "Green River Killer" who had terrorized the Seattle area with a two-decade spree in which he murdered 48 women. After Ridgway's capture in 2001, Reichert was featured on national television shows and documentaries, and he published a book about the experience during the campaign.

In January 2004 8th District Congresswoman Jennifer Dunn announced that she was retiring after 12 years in the House. Republicans actively recruited Reichert to run. He had three opponents in the September Republican primary. Two of them ran TV ads criticizing his call for harsher gun ownership requirements and for being too close to Democrats; he refused to appear with them in any public forum. He won the Republican nomination with 43% of the vote; state senator Luke Esser and former U.S. Attorney Diane Tebelius each got 23%. The leading Democrat in the race was Dave Ross, a New York native and longtime Seattle radio talk-show host. He continued his popular radio program after he announced in May; there were complaints by his opponents, Alex Alben, a self-financing retired RealNetworks executive who had been recruited by the Democratic Congressional Campaign Committee before Dunn retired, and Heidi Behrens-Benedict, who lost by wide margins in three previous races against Dunn. Ross stayed on the air until July, when he filed papers with the FEC. He won the September primary with 48% of the vote to 31% for Alben.

The general election thus featured two candidates who were widely known. Reichert argued that local law enforcement agencies should receive more money and equipment for homeland security. Sounding like a talk-show host, Ross said that he wanted to be the eyes and ears of the public "into what's going on, who's making the trades, where the money is going and whether it's being wisely spent." The national parties each swarmed in with well over $5 million in spending, visits by prominent leaders and ads to boost their respective nominees. Each candidate tried to portray the other as lacking in public policy experience and holding views too extreme for the swing district. A TV ad by the National Republican Congressional Committee suggested that Ross's opposition to the proposed missile defense system would "empower terrorists." On the other side, the DCCC ran an ad criticizing Reichert's opposition to abortion. Both Seattle newspapers, with strong liberal traditions, endorsed Ross for his greater familiarity with issues, and suggested that Reichert was too conservative for this district. This is the kind of district that Democrats must win to regain the majority, especially when it is an open seat. But Reichert retained it for the Republicans, 52%–47%.

Reichert got seats on the Homeland Security, Science, and Transportation and Infrastructure committees. He could be a prime target of Democrats in 2006; House Republican leaders placed him in their "Frontline" program of their 10 most vulnerable incumbents, making him a fundraising beneficiary.

NINTH DISTRICT

Rep. Adam Smith (D)

Elected 1996, 5th term; b. June 15, 1965, Washington, DC; home, Tacoma; Fordham U. B.A. 1987, U. of WA, J.D. 1990; Christian; married (Sara).

Elected Office: WA Senate, 1990–96.

Professional Career: Practicing atty., 1991–92; Seattle Prosecutor, 1992–95.

DC Office: 227 CHOB, 20515, 202-225-8901; Fax: 202-225-5893; Web site: www.house.gov/adamsmith.

District Office: Tacoma, 253-896-3775.

Committees: *Armed Services* (10th of 28 D): Tactical Air & Land Forces; Terrorism, Unconventional Threats & Capabilities. *International Relations* (20th of 23 D): Asia & the Pacific; Europe & Emerging Threats. *Judiciary* (16th of 17 D): Commercial & Administrative Law.

Group Ratings

	ADA	ACLU	AFS	LCV	ITIC	NTU	COC	ACU	NTLC	CHC
2004	90	69	100	91	88	17	55	17	18	10
2003	85	—	88	100	—	35	50	28	—	—

National Journal Ratings

	2003 LIB	—	2003 CONS		2004 LIB	—	2004 CONS
Economic	63%	—	37%		67%	—	33%
Social	70%	—	30%		69%	—	31%
Foreign	58%	—	41%		75%	—	24%

Key Votes of the 108th Congress

1. Drilling in ANWR	N	5. DC School Vouchers	N	9. Ban Same-Sex Marriage	N
2. Approve Bush Tax Cuts	N	6. Ban Human Cloning	N	10. Fund Iraq War	N
3. Medicare/Rx Bill	N	7. Restrict Gun Liability	Y	11. Bar Cuba Embargo Funds	Y
4. Bar Overtime Pay Regs.	Y	8. Ban Partial-Birth Abortion	*	12. Intelligence Reorg.	N

Election Results

2004 general	Adam Smith (D)	162,433	(63%)	($527,669)
	Paul Lord (R)	88,304	(34%)	($7,660)
	Other	5,934	(2%)	
2004 primary	Adam Smith (D)	unopposed		
2002 general	Adam Smith (D)	95,805	(59%)	($769,600)
	Sarah Casada (R)	63,146	(39%)	($61,073)
	Other	4,759	(3%)	

Prior Winning Percentages: 2000 (62%); 1998 (65%); 1996 (50%)

The People		Race/Ethnic Origin	Ancestry	
Area size:	691 sq. mi.	73.3% White	German: 13.2% Irish: 7.9%	
Urban population:	95.0%	6.3% Black	English: 7.7%	
Rural population:	5.0%	7.1% Asian	**2004 Presidential Vote**	
Pop. 2000:	654,902	1.1% Native Am.	Kerry (D)	146,494 (53%)
Median income:	$46,495	0.9% Hawaiian	Bush (R)	126,428 (46%)
Poverty status:	9.2%	4.2% Two+ races	Other	3,867 (1%)
Military veterans:	17.2%	0.3% Other	**2000 Presidential Vote**	
		6.7% Hispanic Origin	Gore (D)	128,076 (53%)
			Bush (R)	104,549 (43%)
			Other	10,874 (4%)
			Cook Partisan Voting Index: D+6	
Occupation	Blue collar: 24.7%	White collar: 59.4% Gray collar: 15.9%		

The misty shores of Puget Sound have seen some of America's most vibrant economic growth over the last two decades. It has spread south from Seattle, over the mixed suburban territory, south and west to the outskirts of the once industrial city of Tacoma. The subdivisions along the Sound, which have some of the loveliest views in America, tend to be high-income. But much of greater Seattle's prime industrial territory lies between the ridges that run north and south inland. Weyerhaeuser, the world's largest private owner of softwood timber, has its headquarters here in Federal Way. Boeing is a major presence in Renton, on the south end of Lake Washington; its aircraft and electronic components plants have made it America's number one exporter for many years. A host of smaller factories cluster near the rail lines that run from Minneapolis-St. Paul across the Great Plains to Puget Sound.

The 9th Congressional District of Washington covers much of this area. It includes Sea-Tac Airport, Burien and Renton, not far south of Seattle, and Kent, Des Moines, most of Auburn and Federal Way farther south in King County. It includes the recently expanded container port of Tacoma, though most of the rest of the city is in the 6th District; in surrounding Pierce County it includes Edgewood and Puyallup, Fort Lewis and McChord Air Force Base. It also includes a part of Thurston County outside the state capital Olympia. This district was created after the 1990 Census and politically was almost perfectly balanced in the mid-1990s: it elected a Democratic congressman in 1992, a Republican in 1994 and a Democrat in 1996. But as the Seattle area trended toward Democrats it has become more Democratic. George W. Bush won 43% of the vote here in 2000 and 46% in 2004.

The congressman from the 9th District is Adam Smith, a Democrat first elected in 1996. He grew up in the Sea-Tac area; his father, a baggage handler for United Airlines and active in the Machinists' Union, died when Smith was 17. The family went on welfare; Smith worked his way through Fordham driving trucks for UPS, then went to the University of Washington Law School. He worked as a lawyer, then as a Seattle prosecutor, handling drunk driving and domestic abuse cases. In 1990, at 25, he was elected to the state Senate, beating an incumbent Republican by doorbelling the district twice. In 1995, he decided to run against first-term Congressman Randy Tate. The two were born the same year, to families of modest backgrounds, were first elected to office at young ages and were firm believers in doorbelling. Tate, a religious conservative and strong supporter of Speaker Newt Gingrich, was a prime target of the AFL-CIO. Smith campaigned as a moderate Democrat, a supporter of the death penalty and three-strikes legislation. He attacked Tate for supporting Gingrich on 96% of House votes and for backing Medicare "cuts." Tate attacked Smith for opposition to channeling youthful offenders to adult courts and prisons and for voting for Governor Mike Lowry's $1.2 billion tax increase in 1993. This was one of the closest races in the country. In the September all-party primary, Smith led 49%–48%. In November, he won 50%–47%.

In the House, Smith won the locally useful assignment to the Armed Services Committee, joined the New Democrat Coalition, had a decidedly moderate voting record and was willing to take on established interests within his party. He voted for charter schools, but against school vouchers; he supported term limits and voted to allow concealed weapons permits to be transferred from state to state. He voted to authorize military action in Iraq, and sought to improve compensation and other quality of life benefits for military personnel. With Minnesota Republican Mark Kennedy, he co-sponsored a proposal to encourage innovative fee-based financing of new segments of the interstate highway system. In July 2004, he stirred controversy when he was one of only four House Democrats who opposed changes in the Patriot Act. A few days later, he told liberal activists that he should have voted the other way. On the Armed Services Committee, he urged speedy action on the recommendations of the 9/11 commission on intelligence reorganization. In 2005, he and Artur Davis and Ron Kind serve as co-chairmen of the House New Democrats.

Smith's independence has worked well for him back home. He has won reelection easily, and Republicans have quit targeting this district. In the 2004 campaign, he was one of the first congressional supporters of John Kerry and chaired his campaign in Washington; his centrist rhetoric occasionally offended supporters of Howard Dean and Dennis Kucinich.

★ WEST VIRGINIA ★

Almost heaven—that's what the song says about West Virginia. And indeed some things are looking up for this state, whose people have never lost their sense of hope or their affection for the hills and mountains that make this the most unhorizontal state in the nation. But West Virginia has had more than its share of tragedy and heartbreak. It was born out of the tragedy of the Civil War, when 55 mountain counties with few slaves seceded from Virginia, and it has made its living most of the years since on that cruelest of minerals, coal. West Virginia is laced with coal: there are coal seams in 53 of its 55 counties, and production even today, after many mines have closed, in 26. Coal kept the sons of large mountaineer families here for much of the 20th century, men who would otherwise have left for big cities; coal brought immigrants in, a few from odd corners of Europe, but more from adjacent areas of the South where the local farming economies were stagnant when West Virginia's coal economy was booming. Coal and local rock salt and brines brought the large concentration of chemical plants 50 years ago to the Kanawha Valley around Charleston; it built steel mills and glass factories in the panhandle and the Monongahela River valley, not far south of Pittsburgh.

But coal did not build a self-sustaining economy. When America was beleaguered abroad, demand for coal increased and energy prices rose, and West Virginia boomed, during World War II (the state reached its all-time population peak of two million in 1950) and the oil shocks of the 1970s. Coal changed the state's politics too. West Virginia's heritage from the Civil War days was Republican, though some counties tilted toward the Confederacy and the Democrats. But after John L. Lewis's United Mine Workers organized most of the West Virginia mines, the coal country shifted toward the New Deal Democrats, and West Virginia for more than half a century was one of the most Democratic states, deserting the national ticket only in Republican landslide years (1956, 1972, 1984) until George W. Bush carried it in 2000; its legislature has been controlled by Democrats since 1930. But neither Democratic administrations nor the pensions and medical benefits the UMW negotiated for retired miners were able to provide the economic growth to keep thousands of West Virginians from leaving their mountains to find work elsewhere—now more often south on I-77 to the booming Carolinas or over U.S. 33 to Columbus than farther north to the Great Lakes industrial cities. As underground miners were replaced by strip-mining machines, coal tonnage went way up but coal mine employment dropped from 22% of the state's work force in 1950 to 10% in 1980 and only 4% in the late 1990s; coal mines employed 126,000 West Virginians in 1948, 63,000 in 1978, 13,500 in 2002. The state's population, 2.0 million in 1950 and 1.95 million in 1980, fell to 1.8 million in 2000—the largest decrease, absolutely and in percentage terms, of any state. In the 2000 Census, West Virginia ranked 50th among states in household income, 50th in median value of housing (but first in percentage of home ownership), 48th in percentage of adults with a high school diploma and second in percentage living in poverty. Still, West Virginians have a strong attachment to this unique state, where the accent sounds Southern and the early 20th century factories and houses look Northern, where the landscape is rural and the economy industrial.

In the 1990s West Virginia was on the rebound, only to be threatened at the end of the decade with economic disaster. Population increased during the decade and the number of jobs rose by 8%. Unemployment since 2000 has been only slightly above and often below the national average, down to 4.8% in November 2004. Government has played a role. Senator Robert Byrd, as both chairman and ranking Democrat on the Appropriations Committee, achieved his career goal of channeling $1 billion of federal projects into West Virginia, and more. State tax breaks in the 1990s attracted investments from Georgia Pacific, Swearingen Aircraft, NGK Sparkplugs and Toyota; Lexus engines are produced in Buffalo, West Virginia. Forest products are replacing coal in rural counties, health care is growing as everywhere and telemarketing is growing as well. West Virginia has finally completed its interstate highway network and in a computer age it is no longer isolated. Still, West Virginia is losing young people. Even during the growing 1990s the number of people aged 25 to 34 fell by 33,000, while the number of those under 18 plunged by

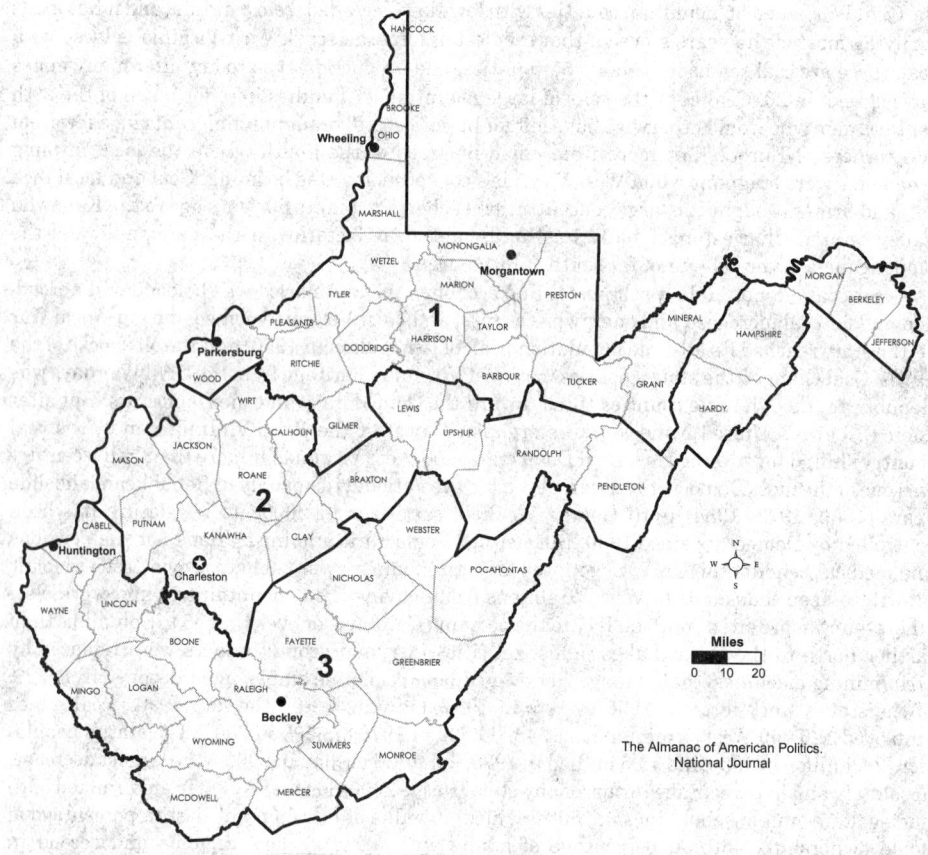

Congressional district boundaries were first effective for 2002.

41,000. The state's median age rose to 38.9, the highest in the nation, even above Florida's. Young people in close-packed Huntington and Wheeling are moving across the Ohio River to more spread-out subdivisions in Ohio.

One threat to West Virginia's economy came in October 1999 when, in a case brought by environmental groups, federal judge Charles Haden ruled that mountaintop mining violates federal environmental laws. Far fewer miners are needed for this work than in underground mining, but the pay is good and the jobs highly valued in counties which, in some cases, have half as many people as they did 50 years ago. Mining companies said that Judge Haden's decision would end coal mining in West Virginia. Senator Byrd threatened to overturn the decision in an appropriations bill; Bill Clinton said he would veto any such bill, and the provision was dropped. But the issue became important—arguably crucial—in the 2000 presidential race. In April 2000 the Clinton administration came out against a ban on mountaintop mining, but for stricter regulation; Al Gore was caught in the middle between environmentalists who supported it and West Virginia's all-Democratic congressional delegation which opposed it. George W. Bush, spotting an opening quickly, came out in favor of mountaintop mining and called for increased federal support of clean coal technology; he said that the Clinton administration "fears coal" and managed to mention coal in one of the presidential debates. Bush's support of coal and his opposition to gun control enabled him to carry West Virginia 52%–46%—a stunning upset in a state that hadn't voted for a Republican in an open presidential race since 1928. Its five electoral votes were crucial: Without them, it would not have mattered who won Florida. The environmental stands which helped Gore in large East and West Coast states proved fatal to his candidacy in West Virginia. In April 2001, the Fourth Circuit Court of Appeals reversed Judge Haden and ruled that under the 1977 Surface Mining Control and Reclamation Act, West Virginia's mining standards superseded federal standards.

As president, George W. Bush was attentive to coal. He got Congress to spend $2 billion on clean coal technology and from March 2002 to December 2003 slapped import quotas to help the steel industry, still a major coal user. All this helped Bush in the 2004 election. Democratic nominee John Kerry had voted against Byrd's amendment to save mountaintop mining and for air pollution control bills which would have cut coal usage by something like 40%. In October 2003 he said, "Where we see a beautiful mountaintop, George Bush sees a strip mine." Democrats who regarded Bush's victory here in 2000 as a fluke made West Virginia a target state. They hoped that economic dissatisfaction would give Kerry a victory. But by September 2004 it was apparent that Bush was well ahead, and West Virginia slipped off both candidates' target list. Bush ended up winning 46 of 55 counties on his way to a 56%–43% victory, and Republicans won surprise victories in races for secretary of state and state Supreme Court. Most West Virginia voters continue to identify as Democrats, but Bush's victory raises the question of whether West Virginia is going to follow other mountain states like Kentucky and Tennessee and become predominantly Republican.

The People		Race/Ethnic Origin			Military veterans: 201,701 (14.3%)	
Pop. 2004 (est):	1,815,354	1,709,966	94.6%	White	WWII: 21.4%	Korea: 14.9%
Pop. 2000:	1,808,344	56,825	3.1%	Black	Vietnam: 32.5%	Gulf War: 8.4%
Pop. 1990:	1,793,477	9,356	0.5%	Asian	**Most populous cities (2003):**	
Change 1990–2000:	Up 0.8%	3,456	0.2%	Native Am.	1. Charleston	51,394
% of U.S. total:	0.6%	335	0.0%	Hawaiian	2. Huntington	49,533
Pop. rank:	37th of 50	14,983	0.8%	Two+ races	3. Parkersburg	32,100
Area size:	24,230 sq. mi.	1,144	0.1%	Other	4. Wheeling	30,096
State Native:	74.2%	12,279	0.7%	Hisp. Origin	5. Morgantown	27,969
Non-citizen:	0.5%	**Ancestry**				
Language		USA: 14.8%		German: 11.0%	Urban population: 46.1%	
English: 95.5%	Other Eur.: 2.0%	Irish: 8.6%		English: 7.7%	Rural population: 53.9%	
Spanish: 1.8%		Italian: 3.0%				

Education		Work Sector		Legislature	
H.S. Grad:	75.2%	Private: 75.8%	Govt: 17.9%	Senate	21 D 13 R
College Grad:	14.8%	Self: 5.9%	Family: 0.4%	House of Del.	68 D 32 R
Industry		Unemployment: 7.3%		Legislative Term Limits: No	
Agri: 4.1%	Con: 7.0%	**Household Income**		**Registered Voters**	
Fin: 4.6%	Info: 2.2%	<15k: 25.4%	15-35k: 32.0%	D: 680,464	(58.2%)
Mfg: 17.9%	Prof: 29.7%	35-50k: 16.4%	50-100k: 21.2%	R: 349,193	(29.9%)
Public: 5.8%	Trade: 15.9%	100-150k: 3.3%	>150k: 1.8%	O: 139,037	(11.9%)
Other: 12.9%		Median: $29,696			
Occupation		Poverty status: 17.9%			
Blue collar: 28.7%	White collar: 54.0%	**Home Value**			
Gray collar: 17.3%		<50k: 35.4% 50-100k: 41.0% 100-200k: 19.0% 200-300k: 3.0% 300-500k: 1.0% >500k: 0.5% Median: $66,000			

Presidential politics　George W. Bush has now carried West Virginia twice, the first time since the 1920s that the state has voted Republican in two consecutive presidential elections. Between 1928 and 2000 the only Republican nominees it voted for were incumbents headed for landslide victories—Dwight Eisenhower in 1956, Richard Nixon in 1972, Ronald Reagan in 1984. In 2000 Bush cultivated the state assiduously, while Al Gore's campaign ignored it until the last weeks. In 2004 Democrats targeted the state early, and John Kerry made many appearances in the state; it was in Huntington, two weeks after he clinched the Democratic nomination, that he said, "I did actually vote for the $87 billion before I voted against it." But Kerry's record on coal issues and Bush's strong support from evangelical Christians and the National Rifle Association in a state in which 48% of voters are evangelical or born-again Christians and 71% are in gun-owning households put it far out of his reach. Bush won here 52%–46% here in 2000 and by a wider 56%–43% in 2004; turnout

2004 Presidential Vote		
Bush (R)	423,778	(56%)
Kerry (D)	326,541	(43%)
Nader (I)	4,063	(1%)
Other	1,504	(0%)

2004 Democratic Presidential Primary		
Kerry (D)	175,065	(69%)
Edwards (D)	33,950	(13%)
Lieberman (D)	13,881	(5%)
Dean (D)	10,576	(4%)
Clark (D)	9,170	(4%)
Other	10,197	(4%)

2000 Presidential Vote		
Bush (R)	336,475	(52%)
Gore (D)	295,497	(46%)
Nader (Green)	10,680	(2%)
Other	5,472	(1%)

was up 17% in a state with virtually no population growth. Bush carried every income group over $15,000, lost union households by only 53%–47% and carried 30% of self-identified Democrats. One possible glitch was South Charleston Mayor Richie Robb, a Republican elector who said he might not vote for Bush; but by Election Day he had changed his mind.

West Virginia's presidential primary, held in May, has not attracted much attention in years. But in 1960 it was the focus of the nation's attention when John F. Kennedy, reportedly fortified with large injections of cash from his father, took on Hubert Humphrey and beat him, proving that a Catholic could carry a virtually all-Protestant state.

Congressional districting　West Virginia's three congressional districts, created after the state lost one House seat in the 1990 Census, were not significantly altered in redistricting—even though the process was dominated by Democrats and the sole Republican, Shelley Moore Capito, who won an open seat narrowly in 2000, could have been harmed by a partisan redrawing of the lines. But one or both of the state's two Democratic incumbents might have been weakened, if not for the general election, then in a possible primary, by such a plan. One Democratic legislator suggested removing the eastern panhandle counties from Capito's 2d District, and her 2000 opponent, trial lawyer Jim Humphreys, called for a plan that removed

109th Congress Lineup	
2 D	1 R

108th Congress Lineup	
2 D	1 R

three Republican counties west of Charleston and substituted three heavily Democratic coal-mining counties to the south. But most legislators, preoccupied with redrawing their own districts, were content to please all three incumbents. In a September 2001 special session, the legislature with one dissenting vote removed Gilmer County from the 2d and placed it in the 1st and removed Nicholas County from the 2d and placed it in the 3d: Both are Democratic counties that had no significant impact on the 2002 results.

Governor

Joe Manchin (D)

Elected 2004, term expires Jan. 2009, 1st term; b. Aug. 24, 1947, Farmington; home, Charleston; WV U., B.S. 1970; Catholic; married (Gayle).

Elected Office: WV House, 1982–84; WV Senate 1986–96; WV Sec. of State, 2000–04.

Professional Career: Co-owner, Manchin's Carpet and Tile, 1968–82; Owner, Enersystems, 1989–2000.

Office: State Capitol, Charleston, 25305, 304-558-2000; Fax: 304-558-2722; Web site: www.state.wv.us/governor.

Election Results

2004 general	Joe Manchin (D)	472,758	(64%)
	Monty Warner (R)	253,131	(34%)
	Other	18,505	(2%)
2004 primary	Joe Manchin (D)	149,362	(53%)
	Lloyd Jackson (D)	77,052	(27%)
	Jim Lees (D)	40,161	(14%)
	Other	16,687	(6%)
2000 general	Robert Wise (D)	324,822	(50%)
	Cecil H. Underwood (R)	305,926	(47%)
	Other	17,299	(3%)

Joe Manchin, elected governor of West Virginia in 2004, comes from a family involved in politics for many years. Manchin grew up in Farmington, a few miles up Buffalo Creek from the industrial city of Fairmont on the Monongahela River. He remembers working in his grandfather's grocery store; he also worked in his father's carpet and furniture store, and took a semester off from college to rebuild it after a fire. His grandfather and father were elected mayor of Farmington; his uncle, A. James Manchin, was elected to the House of Delegates and, statewide, as secretary of state and state treasurer. After graduating from West Virginia University, Joe Manchin went to work in the carpet and furniture business, helping to send his four siblings to college. Then he started a coal brokerage company and eventually moved to Fairmont.

In 1982, at age 35, Joe Manchin was elected to the House of Delegates. In 1986 he was elected to the state Senate; a friend there was "Buffy" Warner, a Republican from next-door Monongalia County, the older brother of Manchin's 2004 Republican opponent Monty Warner. The family ties go back even further: Brud Warner, Buffy's and Monty's father, was a West Virginia University classmate of A. James Manchin and served with him in the House of Delegates. In 1996, after 10 years in the state Senate, Joe Manchin ran for governor. The Democratic primary was a riproaring contest between Manchin and legislator Charlotte Pritt, who had the support of organized labor. She attacked Manchin as the business candidate; unions opposed him because of his votes on workmen's comp. Pritt beat Manchin in the 11-candidate primary by 40%–32%. He declined to support her in the general election and attacked her in October; she lost to 74-year-old Republican Cecil Underwood, who had also been elected governor as a 34-year-old in 1956.

Manchin returned to Fairmont and seemed out of politics. But in 2000, when 86-year-old Secretary of State Ken Hechler ran for the U.S. House (where he had served from 1958 to 1976), Manchin ran for his office. So did Charlotte Pritt. This time Manchin beat her in the primary by 51%–29%. He worked with Republican U.S. attorneys to prevent vote fraud and was one of the few secretaries of state to comply with the federal requirement of a statewide voter registry. In May 2003, he announced he was challenging Democratic Governor Bob Wise in the 2004 primary. That seemed a daunting task, for Wise had already raised $1.2 million. But timing is everything: later in the month Wise announced that he had had an extramarital affair and would not seek reelection. In quick time eight Democrats and 10 Republicans joined the race.

In the 1996 governor's race, Manchin had been tagged as the business candidate. This time he worked successfully to get support from both labor and business. His stands on cultural issues were impeccably conservative: against abortion, gun control, same-sex marriage. But he emphasized economic issues, with a platform for concentrated state effort to spur economic development. It included "modernizing" taxes and workmen's comp, working with colleges to develop training programs, setting up large pools to buy drugs and purchase health insurance, and development of broadband and wireless technologies. He promised to seek more high-wage jobs in West Virginia's steel, polymer and chemical industries rather than lower-wage jobs in tourism.

The cast of characters in the May 2004 Democratic primary was not unfamiliar. Manchin's best financed opponent was former state Senator Lloyd Jackson, who had started running against him in 1996 and then bowed out; another was Charleston lawyer Jim Lees, who had also run in 1996. Jackson ran tough negative ads against Manchin, but they apparently didn't have much impact. Manchin won with 53% of the vote to 27% for Jackson and 14% for Lees. In the more fragmented Republican primary, Monty Warner, a retired Army colonel and Monongalia County developer, won with 23% of the vote, to 20% for big-spending former banker and auto dealer Dan Moore and 17% for former tax secretary Rob Capehart.

Manchin and Warner were old friends; Manchin substituted for the absent Buffy Warner at a family ceremony honoring Monty Warner on his retirement from the Army. They pledged to run a positive campaign, and mostly did. But the advantage was all with Manchin. He had far more money, and his implicitly low-tax platform undercut Warner's tax-cut, stop-lawsuit-abuse theme. Warner wasn't invited to appear on stage with George W. Bush during many of his frequent appearances in West Virginia, and Manchin's business support, plus the formation of a Republicans for Manchin group that included top Bush backers, helped convince the usually Republican *Daily Mail* to endorse him. The business community concentrated on an ultimately successful attempt to defeat Democratic state Supreme Court Justice Warren McGraw; his brother Attorney General Darrell McGraw was reelected by only a 50.4%–49.6% margin, while 90-year-old Ken Hechler lost his race for secretary of state 52%–48%. Republicans also made gains in state legislative races—a dividend, perhaps, of George W. Bush's 56%–43% victory in the state. But Manchin won by a wider margin, 64%–34%, carrying 52 of 55 counties.

Manchin entered office with the state budget in surplus but with a budget outlook in which expenditures seemed greater than revenues. His positions on some issues went against the grain of recent history—he said he wanted to slow school consolidation, in the face of complaints that high schools were too big. His plans to spur economic growth, which attracted support from both the Chamber of Commerce and the AFL-CIO, would now have to produce results. And the continuing battles over whether West Virginia courts unduly favor plaintiffs and trial lawyers would go on. West Virginia seems to have a consensus governor, but the state's problems remain daunting.

Senior Senator

Robert Byrd (D)

Elected 1958, seat up 2006, 8th term; b. Nov. 20, 1917, North Wilkesboro, NC; home, Sophia; American U., J.D. 1963; Baptist; married (Erma).

Elected Office: WV House of Delegates, 1946–50; WV Senate, 1950–52; U.S. House of Reps., 1952–58; U.S. Senate Majority Whip, 1971–76, Majority Ldr., 1977–80, 1987–88, Minority Ldr., 1981–86.

DC Office: 311 HSOB, 20510, 202-224-3954; Fax: 202-228-0002; Web site: byrd.senate.gov.

State Office: Charleston, 304-342-5855.

Committees: *Appropriations* (RMM): Defense; Energy & Water; Homeland Security (RMM); Interior & Related Agencies; Military Construction & Veterans Affairs; Transportation, Treasury, the Judiciary, HUD & Related Agencies. *Armed Services*: Emerging Threats & Capabilities; Readiness & Management Support; Strategic Forces. *Budget. Rules & Administration.*

Group Ratings

	ADA	ACLU	AFS	LCV	ITIC	NTU	COC	ACU	NTLC	CHC
2004	90	56	100	100	42	21	38	8	8	20
2003	95	—	100	68	—	19	29	30	—	—

National Journal Ratings

	2003 LIB	—	2003 CONS		2004 LIB	—	2004 CONS
Economic	74%	—	25%		93%	—	0%
Social	79%	—	15%		67%	—	31%
Foreign	69%	—	30%		61%	—	36%

Key Votes of the 108th Congress

1. Ban Drilling in ANWR	Y	5. Energy Bill	N	9. Ban Same-Sex Marriage	Y
2. Approve Bush Tax Cuts	N	6. Support Roe v. Wade	Y	10. Ban Bunker-Buster Bomb	Y
3. Medicare/Rx Bill	N	7. Ban Partial-Birth Abortion	Y	11. Fund Iraq War	N
4. Bar Overtime Pay Regs.	Y	8. Assault Weapons Ban	Y	12. Restrict Missile Defense	Y

Election Results

2000 general	Robert Byrd (D)..	469,215	(78%)	($1,045,993)
	David T. Gallaher (R).............................	121,635	(20%)	
	Other...	12,627	(2%)	
2000 primary	Robert Byrd (D)..................................	unopposed		
1994 general	Robert Byrd (D)..................................	290,495	(69%)	($1,550,354)
	Stan Klos (R)	130,441	(31%)	($267,165)

Prior Winning Percentages: 1988 (65%); 1982 (69%); 1976 (100%); 1970 (78%); 1964 (68%); 1958 (59%); 1956 House (57%); 1954 House (63%); 1952 House (56%)

Robert Byrd, the senior member of the United States Senate, may come closer to the kind of senator the Founding Fathers had in mind than any other. He comes from the humblest of beginnings, and when first elected to the Senate, as part of the large and talented Democratic class of 1958, he was scarcely noticed. Now he is the last member of that class still in the Senate, and an authentic power whether in majority or minority. He set the record for Senate votes at 12,134 in April 1990 and cast his 17,000th vote in March 2004. His erstwhile rival Edward Kennedy noted, "Every time Bob casts a vote, he sets a new record. It is not fair, though, that he counts the votes he cast in the Roman Senate too, but we love him anyway and we never stop learning from him." But Byrd is also capable of having a little fun. He played a Confederate general in the film *Gods and Generals*, shot in 2001, but eschewed a career in show business. "I haven't hired an agent and don't expect to be changing my day job any time soon."

Robert Byrd comes from a background as grindingly poor as that of any American politician. "I lived in a house without electricity," he lectured one Bush administration witness. "No running water, no telephone, little wooden outhouse." Son of a coal miner in southern West Virginia, he was a welder in wartime shipyards and a meat cutter in a coal company town when he won his seat in the House of Delegates in 1946; he campaigned in every hollow in the county, playing his fiddle and even going to the length of joining the Ku Klux Klan (which he quickly quit and has for many years regretted joining). He worked hard in the legislature, and won a U.S. House seat when the incumbent retired in 1952; he made such a name for himself in West Virginia that by 1958, when he was 40, he was elected to the Senate—even though the United Mine Workers initially opposed him and the coal companies never supported him.

In the Senate, he became a supporter of Majority Leader Lyndon B. Johnson and in return got a seat on Appropriations his first year. He backed Hubert Humphrey against John Kennedy in the 1960 West Virginia presidential primary not because he shared Humphrey's liberal politics—his voting record then was as conservative as any Southerner's and he opposed the Civil Rights Act of 1964—but because Johnson wanted to stop Kennedy. In his early years he took care to master the Senate's arcane rules; as he said in 2002, "Nobody has ever used the rules of the Senate more than I have." In the 1960s, Byrd's career took what in retrospect was a helpful detour. He became assistant majority whip, an unimportant position in 1965; in 1971, when Edward Kennedy neglected his duties as whip after Chappaquiddick, Byrd quietly lined up support and, with Richard Russell's deathbed vote, ousted Kennedy. There Byrd performed ably, managing Senate business and accommodating colleagues' needs, and when Majority Leader Mike Mansfield retired in 1976, Byrd easily won the job. All the while Byrd was working hard to keep in touch with West Virginians, to the point that he won 78% of the vote in 1970, becoming the first West Virginian in history to carry all 55 counties.

Byrd did not like being majority leader. Contrary to most people's assumptions, the post carries little power, because Senate rules requiring unanimous consent or supermajorities allow minorities and even individual senators to block action. Byrd was aware that his power came from meeting other senators' needs and did not have a national issues agenda of his own, though his voting record became notably less conservative. In 1987, with Democrats back in the majority after six years out of power, Byrd established some legislative priorities and then announced he would leave the post after the 1988 election.

In 1989, Byrd got the position he had been aiming for all along—chairman of the Appropriations Committee. He has been chairman or ranking minority member ever since. "I want to be West Virginia's billion dollar industry," he announced in 1990, and he has succeeded handsomely. An FBI office went to Clarksburg, Treasury and IRS offices to Parkersburg, a Fish and Wildlife Training Center to Harper's Ferry, a Bureau of Alcohol, Tobacco and Firearms office to Martinsburg, a NASA Research center to Wheeling. The December 2000 final appropriations included more than $1 billion of spending in West Virginia. Some of it represents the ordinary operations of government, but much of it is Byrd's work. Since 1990, he has attached more than $270 million to appropriations bills for the construction of one interstate highway alone. He boasts that when he was in the state House of Delegates in 1947, West Virginia had just four miles of divided, four-lane highway. Today, there are 1,087 miles. Byrd has worked hard to find funds for the depleted United Mine Workers health care program for retired miners and their widows. He has supported the state's coal mining industry, seeking funds for miners displaced by the Clean Air Act in 1990, co-sponsoring the 1997 resolution opposing the Kyoto Protocol so long as it excluded developing countries like China, and opposing EPA's 1999 proposed air quality standards. When a federal judge ruled in October 1999 that mountaintop mining violated federal environmental laws, Byrd tried to pass an appropriations rider reversing the decision; he was angry when the Clinton administration, at first agreeable, decided to oppose such a rider with a veto. The issue helped George W. Bush carry West Virginia in 2000; in April 2001, a federal appeals court reversed the decision and ruled that state laws governed mountaintop mining.

It should be added that Byrd's positions are not just parochial but are the product of serious study of the Constitution and of history. He always carries a copy of the Constitution in his left breast pocket. With the assistance of Senate historian Richard Baker, he wrote *The Senate 1789–1989*, a two-volume history, plus two volumes of classic speeches and statistics; based on impressive research, gracefully written, full of arresting anecdotes and sound insights, it surpasses any previous work on the subject. Byrd earned his law degree while in the Senate and had his diploma presented to him by President Kennedy at the 1963 American University commencement where Kennedy delivered his most important foreign policy speech. In 1994, he was awarded his B.A. summa cum laude by Marshall University, which he had attended for one semester 43 years before and could not afford to continue, and where he earned A's in all eight courses he took. Byrd has been educating himself as well, systematically reading the classics, and takes to quoting Shakespeare, Thucydides or Cato the Younger in debates on the balanced budget amendment and the line-item veto.

If Byrd is determined to uphold the prerogatives of the Senate, he is determined also to uphold the prerogatives of the Appropriations Committee. He sees the Senate as part of a separate and equal branch of government, and he believes strongly in the prerogatives of appropriators. The Appropriations Committee operates mostly on a bipartisan basis and appropriators have worked together for years and cooperate across party lines against institutional adversaries like OMB and the authorizing and Budget committees. Byrd has served on Appropriations with his predecessor and successor as chairman, Ted Stevens, since 1973. When the Republican takeover of the Senate in 2003 cost Byrd his position as President Pro Tempore and his first-floor office suite, his colleagues elected him President Pro Tempore Emeritus and appropriated money for a new office.

His relations with the previous five or six administrations have been strained. George W. Bush went out of his way to shake Byrd's hand at his first speech to a joint session of Congress; Byrd had not attended State of the Union addresses since 1994 out of distaste for Bill Clinton: "His lifestyle and mine were so different I didn't care about coming to hear him." But Byrd opposed Bush's tax cut as "sheer madness," arguing that it was based on inevitably untrustworthy economic forecasts and complaining that it would cut off funds for appropriators.

Byrd's insistence on maintaining what he regards as the Senate's constitutional prerogatives and his distaste for Bush administration policies led him to embark on two crusades in 2002 which may have helped lead to the Democrats' loss of their Senate majority in November. One was his opposition to the bill setting up the Department of Homeland Security. He insisted that the biggest reorganization of the federal government since the creation of the Department of Defense required more scrutiny, and he opposed giving the president authority to shift money between agencies without regard for congressional appropriators. His persistent speeches meant that the Senate, unlike the House, couldn't vote on it before the August recess or the September 11 anniversary that many senators had as a goal. In September, Byrd spoke frequently and at great length on the issue. He never used the word filibuster, but this was one in effect. It also gave government unions time to unite Democrats against the provisions for flexibility insisted on by Bush—a stand that hurt Democratic senators gravely in Georgia and Missouri on Election Day. In September, Byrd sought to require the president to get approval of the new department in three stages over the next year; that lost 70–28. After the election, Democrats realized it was in their political interest to pass the bill, and a motion to limit debate passed 65–29.

The other crusade was against military action in Iraq. In September, he accused Bush of political motivation, saying out loud what some other Democrats believed but were too politick to say. "All of a sudden the president was dropping in the polls, and the domestic situation was such that the administration was appearing to be much like the emperor who had no clothes. All of a sudden, bam! All of this war talk—the war fervor, the drums of war, the bugles of war, the clouds of war, this war hysteria—has blown in like a hurricane. And what has that done to the president's polls? Seventy percent." In October, he threatened to delay action on the Iraq war resolution by insisting on votes on individual clauses; he was foiled when Connecticut Sen. Joe Lieberman and Daschle made a change in wording that made his motion out of order. His attempt to filibuster lost 75–25, and the Senate passed the resolution 77–23. Byrd did not give up. In January 2003 he and Edward Kennedy sought to require Bush to get congressional approval again. In June 2003 he called Bush's landing on the carrier "flamboyant showmanship." In July 2004 he said Bush was "dangerous, reckless and arrogant." In September 2004 he drew on his knowledge of history and said, "The Roman Senate lost its nerve, lost its way and succumbed. That's what we are seeing here in our own country. Our own Senate lost its way when it voted for the Iraq resolution."

Byrd's umbrage at the Bush administration is clear. "I've never seen an administration so discourteous, so arrogant toward the legislative branch, as this one is. I've been here 51 years, so why shouldn't I speak out?" He opposed the Bush energy bill, even though it included money for clean coal research and utilization, and he referred during the first Bush term to "gargantuan tax cuts that are backloaded and will come due between 2007 and 2011 when Mr. Bush will be back on his ranch in Crawford, Texas, off the political stage." He fumed when a trade amendment he placed in a 2000 agricultural appropriation was found by the WTO to be in violation of international trade rules. Of the promoters of the Family Marriage Amendment, he said, "The people who put this out [are] taking West Virginians to be gullible, ignorant fools." Byrd attended the Democratic National Convention in 2004, his first since 1988, and plugged his just-published book *Losing America: Confronting a Reckless and Arrogant Presidency*.

In November 2000, Byrd was re-elected by a 78%–20% margin, his largest percentage margin ever, carrying all 55 counties for the third time. At a spirited rally at the end of the campaign he said, "West Virginia has always had four friends. God Almighty, Sears Roebuck, Carter's Liver Pills and Robert C. Byrd." He is the second senator to have been elected to eight six-year terms (the other was Strom Thurmond of South Carolina); he has served longer than any other senator but Thurmond and stands to beat his record in June 2006, on his 17,326th day in the Senate. He will turn 89 two weeks after the 2006 election, and some Republicans hope he will not run and that West Virginia, solidly for George W. Bush in 2004 despite Byrd's efforts, will elect a Republican senator for the first time since 1956. Yet even if Byrd does run, his reelection is unlikely to be as easy as in 2000. In spring 2005, national Republicans were hoping popular 2d District Congresswoman Shelley Moore Capito would challenge Byrd.

Junior Senator

Jay Rockefeller IV (D)

Elected 1984, seat up 2008, 4th term; b. June 18, 1937, New York, NY; home, Charleston; Harvard U., B.A. 1961, Intl. Christian U., Tokyo, Japan, 1957–60; Presbyterian; married (Sharon).

Elected Office: WV House of Delegates, 1966–68; WV Secy. of State, 1968–72; WV Gov., 1976–84.

Professional Career: Natl. Advisory Cncl., Peace Corps, 1961; Asst., Peace Corps Dir. Sargent Shriver, 1962–63; VISTA worker, 1964–66; Pres., WV Wesleyan Col., 1973–75.

DC Office: 531 HSOB, 20510, 202-224-6472; Fax: 202-224-7665; Web site: rockefeller.senate.gov.

State Offices: Beckley, 304-253-9704; Charleston, 304-347-5372; Fairmont, 304-367-0122; Martinsburg, 304-262-9285.

Committees: *Commerce, Science & Transportation*: Aviation (RMM); Science & Space; Surface Transportation & Merchant Marine; Technology, Innovation & Competitiveness; Trade, Tourism & Economic Development. *Finance*: Health Care (RMM); International Trade; Social Security & Family Policy. *Intelligence (Select)* (Vice Chmn.). *Veterans' Affairs. Joint Committee on Taxation* (5th of 5 Sens.).

Group Ratings

	ADA	ACLU	AFS	LCV	ITIC	NTU	COC	ACU	NTLC	CHC
2004	90	67	100	100	42	14	41	12	5	0
2003	100	—	100	79	—	18	30	15	—	—

National Journal Ratings

	2003 LIB	—	2003 CONS		2004 LIB	—	2004 CONS
Economic	93%	—	0%		93%	—	0%
Social	68%	—	26%		61%	—	38%
Foreign	68%	—	31%		67%	—	31%

Key Votes of the 108th Congress

1. Ban Drilling in ANWR	Y	5. Energy Bill	N	9. Ban Same-Sex Marriage	N
2. Approve Bush Tax Cuts	N	6. Support Roe v. Wade	Y	10. Ban Bunker-Buster Bomb	Y
3. Medicare/Rx Bill	N	7. Ban Partial-Birth Abortion	N	11. Fund Iraq War	Y
4. Bar Overtime Pay Regs.	Y	8. Assault Weapons Ban	Y	12. Restrict Missile Defense	Y

Election Results

2002 general	Jay Rockefeller IV (D)	275,281	(63%)	($2,299,519)
	Jay Wolfe (R)	160,902	(37%)	($136,935)
2002 primary	Jay Rockefeller IV (D)	198,327	(90%)	
	Bruce Barilla (D)	11,178	(5%)	
	William Galloway (D)	11,173	(5%)	
1996 general	Jay Rockefeller IV (D)	456,526	(77%)	($5,819,157)
	Betty A. Burks (R)	139,088	(23%)	

Prior Winning Percentages: 1990 (68%); 1984 (52%)

Jay Rockefeller's full name, John D. Rockefeller IV, has a familiar ring to those who remember his great-grandfather as the oil billionaire who was America's richest man, and his grandfather as the heir who had more than enough money to build New York's Rockefeller Center, restore Colonial Williamsburg, and found the Museum of Modern Art during the Depression of the 1930s. Jay Rockefeller's father and uncles were men of impressive achievement in different fields. One uncle, Winthrop Rockefeller, moved to an impoverished state in the southern hills—in his case Arkansas—and won two terms as governor, running an honest and reforming administration. Another, Nelson Rockefeller, became governor of the nation's then-biggest state and spent money expansively on generous welfare and gigantic monuments. Jay Rockefeller became governor of what turned out to be America's number one population-losing state of the 1980s, leaving behind a network of roads and highways and a progressive tax structure. Two of the Rockefellers—Nelson and Jay—were mentioned early in their political careers as presidential candidates: Nelson, never very shy about running, finally did so in 1964 at 56, and again in 1968, and served as Vice President from 1974 to 1977. Jay for years avoided projecting his name forward, then almost decided to run in the summer of 1991 at 54, but decided not to enter a contest in which he might have been nominated and elected.

The parallels stop here, for Jay Rockefeller lacks the aloof, imperial bearing of his Uncle Nelson; he is affable, full of self-deprecating humor, tall enough so that he stoops to get through doorways and uses hearing aids because of noise damage from frequent helicopter travel. He was careful to work his way up the political ladder. He grew up in New York, graduated from Harvard, and lived and studied in Japan for three years. He first came to West Virginia as a VISTA volunteer in Emmons in 1964. "Although I went to Emmons to help that community," he reminisced in 2002, "they helped me much more. My experience in Emmons set the course for the rest of my life." He was elected to the House of Delegates in Kanawha County in 1966 and as secretary of state in 1968, and then had the chastening experience of losing a 1972 race for governor to Republican Arch Moore. He served three years as president of West Virginia Wesleyan College in Buckhannon, and became more practical, dropping his opposition to strip mining. He was not shy about spending his own millions—his net worth was estimated at $200 million in 2004—and was elected governor in 1976 and, against Moore, reelected in 1980, after which the state was plunged into deep recession. In 1984, he ran for the U.S. Senate and beat Republican businessman John Raese by just 52%–48% after spending $12 million.

In his first years in the Senate, Rockefeller deferred to Robert Byrd and compiled a conventional liberal voting record, though somewhat more inclined to free trade because of his experience in East Asia. Then he began to concentrate on health care. With a seat on the Finance Committee, he got a place on the Pepper Commission on long-term health care. As chairman, he got majorities on the commission to back long-term care for all Americans regardless of age and, by 8–7, universal medical insurance coverage. But getting others to agree was harder. Rockefeller talked mostly about health care financing when he was mulling a presidential race, but he warmly endorsed Bill Clinton and applauded his emphasis on health care. He was motivated in part by anger at his mother's treatment during a long terminal illness—an experience that would be much worse for people of ordinary incomes, he thought—and he worked to increase the number of general practitioners, especially in states like West Virginia and Arkansas. Efforts at compromise came far too late, after voters had turned against a government takeover of health care, and the health care bill crashed and burned in September 1994. Rockefeller still would like a system-wide health care reform but recognizes that it cannot pass, and so he works on incremental changes, like the amendment he got passed unanimously in July 2002 to route $6 billion to Medicaid programs in the states.

Perhaps his biggest legislative achievement was his 1992 law, passed over furious opposition from Western coal states, which forced union and non-union coal companies and "reachback" companies that had gone out of the coal business to pay for the exploding cost of the United Mine Workers' health care trust funds; he has worked ever since to continue funding of this program for retired miners and their widows. In 2001, Rockefeller vehemently opposed the Bush tax cuts and argued that West Virginians, with the lowest incomes in the nation, received relatively little.

Steel has been a preoccupation of Rockefeller for a long time. He was one of those who helped Weirton Steel, now West Virginia's fourth largest employer, become employee-owned in 1984. In the late 1990s, he called for aid to steel makers in the face of what he regarded as a flood of subsidized steel imports, arguing that workers and companies that have "played by the book" should get government help to allow them to continue in their jobs and their homes. In 2002, he called for 40% tariffs for four years on steel imports. The Bush administration in March 2002 imposed a 24% tariff in the second year and 18% in the third; Rockefeller complained when the administration made exceptions and when it dropped the quotas. In December 2003, unhappy with a WTO ruling, he proposed setting up a panel of four former federal judges to review WTO decisions. Rockefeller has worked for several years to provide health care benefits to retired steelworkers whose former employers have gone out of business or filed for bankruptcy. He scaled down his original proposal to a $179 million refundable tax credit to cover 70% of health care costs. In May 2002, the Senate voted for this 56–40; not enough for approval, which required 60 votes. On the Aviation Subcommittee, Rockefeller passed a measure in 1999 increasing discretionary funding of small- and medium-sized airports; in May 2003 he got provisions for small airport aid in the FAA reauthorization. Included were $5.2 million in grants for Charleston's Yeager Airport, the 150th largest in the country. When the reauthorization bill was tied up in September 2003 over administration insistence on opening some air traffic controller jobs to private competition, Rockefeller worked to get a partial temporary reauthorization. In May 2004 he sponsored a bill for $700 million for better intelligence sharing, cargo security and air marshal programs. At home he worked with business leaders to set up the West Virginia Venture Connection Inc., a venture capital firm made possible by a law providing $25 million in EDA loans to such firms.

In January 2003 Rockefeller became vice chairman of the Intelligence Committee. The previous October he wrote to Pat Roberts, who became chairman, suggesting that if Democrats retained the majority he might fire all staff members and hire partisan staff. In July 2003 he argued that National Security Adviser Condoleezza Rice, and not just CIA Director George Tenet, should be blamed for the "sixteen words" about British intelligence in Africa in George W. Bush's 2003 State of the Union address. But at the same time he was criticized by some Democrats for not being a partisan "team player" and for not opposing Roberts's opposition to a far-ranging investigation of intelligence before September 11 and on Iraq. In June 2003, when John Kerry said Bush had "lied" about intelligence, Rockefeller said, "The Senator is running for president. And I think that Pat Roberts and I make a distinction between people who are running for president and therefore need to capture attention and what we on the Intelligence Committee have to do."

Later Roberts decided to hold hearings and in October 2003 he agreed with Rockefeller to include witnesses from the State and Defense Departments as well as the CIA. On November 4, radio talk show host Sean Hannity obtained a copy of a memo by Democratic committee staffers recommending that Democrats "pull the majority along" in extracting damaging disclosures from Democratic officials and then "pull the trigger" in 2004 to use the material to discredit Bush. Rockefeller said he never passed the memo along but declined to apologize for it, and approached Roberts with a letter promising not to let partisan motives affect the hearings. Roberts was not mollified. On November 12 he cancelled the committee's weekly assessment meeting and the next day he wrote in *The Washington Post*, "The Democrats planned to undermine the integrity of the committee by conducting a partisan attack, which threatens to destroy the credibility of an institution that has served the U.S. Senate and the nation well for nearly 30 years. I oppose them, and I make no apologies." Rockefeller responded, "One has to confront the very real possibility that this whole war was predetermined, so that the intelligence had to fit with the policymaking plans. So the Republicans just pounce on this little, pathetic stolen memo as the perfect opportunity to cover up whether there was White House manipulation of intelligence or whether there was [a] predetermined plan for war." In October 2002 Rockefeller had voted for the Iraq war resolution, so bitterly opposed by his West Virginia colleague Robert Byrd. In March 2004 he said, "If I had known then what I know now, I would have voted against it. I have admitted that my vote was wrong. . . . The decision got made before there was a whole bunch of intelligence. I think the intelligence was shaped. And I think the interpretation of the intelligence was shaped." Nonetheless, some comity was restored; the committee agreed unanimously in May 2004 to abolish the eight-year limit on committee service.

Rockefeller is in strong shape politically—strong enough that he no longer spends any of his own money and wins handsomely. He won by 63%–37% in 2002.

FIRST DISTRICT

Rep. Alan Mollohan (D)

Elected 1982, 12th term; b. May 14, 1943, Fairmont; home, Fairmont; Col. of William & Mary, A.B. 1966, WV U., J.D. 1970; Baptist; married (Barbara).

Military Career: Army, 1970, Army Reserves, 1970–83.

Professional Career: Practicing atty., 1970–82.

DC Office: 2302 RHOB, 20515, 202-225-4172; Fax: 202-225-7564; Web site: www.house.gov/mollohan.

District Offices: Clarksburg, 304-623-4422; Morgantown, 304-292-3019; Parkersburg, 304-428-0493; Wheeling, 304-232-5390.

Committees: *Appropriations* (6th of 29 D): Interior, Environment & Related Agencies; Science, State, Justice, Commerce & Related Agencies (RMM). *Standards of Official Conduct* (RMM of 5 D).

Group Ratings

	ADA	ACLU	AFS	LCV	ITIC	NTU	COC	ACU	NTLC	CHC
2004	65	70	86	64	30	15	37	24	8	61
2003	80	—	100	30	—	23	41	46	—	—

National Journal Ratings

	2003 LIB	—	2003 CONS	2004 LIB	—	2004 CONS
Economic	59%	—	41%	68%	—	31%
Social	57%	—	42%	59%	—	41%
Foreign	53%	—	46%	88%	—	12%

Key Votes of the 108th Congress

1. Drilling in ANWR	Y	5. DC School Vouchers	N	9. Ban Same-Sex Marriage	N
2. Approve Bush Tax Cuts	N	6. Ban Human Cloning	Y	10. Fund Iraq War	Y
3. Medicare/Rx Bill	N	7. Restrict Gun Liability	Y	11. Bar Cuba Embargo Funds	Y
4. Bar Overtime Pay Regs.	Y	8. Ban Partial-Birth Abortion	Y	12. Intelligence Reorg.	N

Election Results

2004 general	Alan Mollohan (D)	166,583	(68%)	($524,011)
	Alan Parks (R)	79,196	(32%)	
2004 primary	Alan Mollohan (D)	unopposed		
2002 general	Alan Mollohan (D)	unopposed		($326,462)

Prior Winning Percentages: 2000 (88%); 1998 (85%); 1996 (100%); 1994 (70%); 1992 (100%); 1990 (67%); 1988 (75%); 1986 (100%); 1984 (54%); 1982 (53%)

The People		Race/Ethnic Origin	Ancestry	
Area size:	6,344 sq. mi.	95.8% White	German: 14.1%	USA: 10.7%
Urban population:	53.7%	1.7% Black	Irish: 10.0%	
Rural population:	46.3%	0.7% Asian	**2004 Presidential Vote**	
Pop. 2000:	602,545	0.2% Native Am.	Bush (R) 150,052	(58%)
Median income:	$30,303	0.0% Hawaiian	Kerry (D) 107,904	(42%)
Poverty status:	17.0%	0.8% Two+ races	Other 2,062	(1%)
Military veterans:	14.8%	0.1% Other	**2000 Presidential Vote**	
		0.7% Hispanic Origin	Bush (R) 122,827	(54%)
			Gore (D) 97,432	(43%)
			Other 7,399	(3%)
			Cook Partisan Voting Index: R + 6	

Occupation	Blue collar: 28.5%	White collar: 54.0%	Gray collar: 17.5%

The northern part of West Virginia is in many ways an extension of the Pittsburgh metropolitan area. People here are Steelers and Pirates fans, they drink Iron City and Rolling Rock beer, they watch Pittsburgh TV, they live in the crevasses between hills cut by the Monongahela and Ohio rivers, on terrain that seems to forbid industrial and urban development. Yet this has been one of America's prime industrial areas; northern West Virginia is part of the same coal-and-steel economy that made Pittsburgh one of the nation's largest cities and filled the narrow bottomlands along the rivers with steel and glass factories, foundries and coal yards. These have been declining industries, or rather industries that have become far less labor-intensive; since 1980, the 12,000 mining jobs in this part of the state have dropped by more than two-thirds, with comparable fall-offs in manufacturing. Replacing these jobs are service jobs—West Virginia's largest employer now is Wal-Mart—and the government jobs brought in by Senator Robert Byrd (the largest employer in Harrison County is the U.S. Dept. of Justice), plus a congressionally-aided high-tech spurt that is projected to bring nearly 10,000 jobs to the Fairmont area.

The 1st Congressional District of West Virginia includes the northern third of the state. On the panhandle along the Ohio River are Victorian Wheeling, once one of the richest cities in the country with its steel and glass company investors and executives, and where the country music radio show "Jamboree U.S.A." has been broadcast every Saturday night for more than 50 years, and Weirton, a steel company town that is home to the nation's second-largest producer of tin-plated steel—an employee-owned company that has filed for bankruptcy. South of Pittsburgh on the Monongahela are Morgantown, site of West Virginia University and white-water rafting, plus Fairmont and Clarksburg. To the west, the district includes three lonely mountain counties—Doddridge, Ritchie and Tyler— that never heavily industrialized and have remained firmly Republican since the Civil War. West of these, on the Ohio River, is the former oil-refining and shipping center of Parkersburg, which has become a plastics and manufacturing hub. For most of the 20th century, most of this territory was solidly Democratic. But dissatisfaction with the Clinton-Gore policies on coal and the environment helped George W. Bush carry this district twice. Bush's March 2002 decision to limit steel imports, as unpopular as it was among free trade advocates, foreign steel producers and domestic steel users, was popular in northern West Virginia.

The congressman from the 1st District is Alan Mollohan, a Democrat elected in 1982. His father Robert Mollohan was elected congressman in 1952 and 1954, ran for governor and lost in 1956, and then won back the House seat a dozen years later when his Republican successor, Arch Moore, was elected governor. Alan Mollohan, a Washington lawyer for Consolidated Coal, among other clients, returned home in 1982 when his father retired and promptly won the seat. His one major challenge came in the 1992 primary, when he was redistricted into a seat with another congressman, Harley Staggers Jr., also the son of a congressman, and an ally of the National Rifle Association. Mollohan, who had represented more of the new district than Staggers, won 62%–38%. He has not been seriously challenged since then.

Mollohan's voting record has become increasingly centrist and he has concentrated on bringing projects to the district. A member of the Appropriations Committee, he is the ranking member on the Science, State, Justice, and Commerce Subcommittee. To the displeasure of Republican leaders, the culture of appropriators has remained bipartisan, so even in the minority and with cutbacks in the subcommittee's accounts, Mollohan has delivered the goods back home. He takes credit for the First District Federal Procurement Team, which was instrumental in bringing hundreds of jobs to the Institute for Scientific Research, as part of a 439-acre Fairmont industrial park. His earmarks include a $500,000 grant to researchers in Fairmont's high-tech corridor assisting police and national-security officers to battle steganography, the on-line transmission of secret messages. He has been memorialized with the Alan B. Mollohan Innovation Center, a computer software testing center in Fairmont. Other local accomplishments include a rapid-response training system to inform workers of the area's high-tech jobs, an SBA Business Information Center in Fairmont, plus an expansion of Morgantown's federal prison. His local successes also brought grumbling of favoritism from other House Democrats who have been the victim of partisan recriminations from Republican appropriators.

On national issues, Mollohan voted against the war in Iraq and strongly opposed the initial Bush tax cut. He supported Bush's steel import restrictions as a vital step against unfair competition from foreign steelmakers, but protested when the administration subsequently granted a series of waivers in response to pressure from domestic steel users complaining about price increases. He has fought successfully to continue loan guarantees for steel companies, which has helped to keep Weirton Steel alive despite its financial troubles.

Mollohan is the ranking minority member on the evenly-balanced House ethics committee. In September 2004 the committee unanimously voted to admonish—the weakest rebuke possible—House Majority Leader Tom DeLay for actions casting discredit on the House, though it found that he violated no House rules. Although Mollohan kept his customary low profile, he faced a no-win situation: Republicans complained about reports that he was sharing sensitive information with Democratic leaders; but when the committee later rebuked Texas Democrat Chris Bell for sloppy language in the complaint he filed against DeLay, Democrats privately charged Mollohan with seeking to protect West Virginia interests by cozying up to powerful Republicans. Locking arms with Chairman Joel Hefley, Mollohan defended the committee and criticized "erroneous" press reports.

Mollohan endorsed Howard Dean in late December 2003, his first-ever presidential-primary endorsement. "He's unafraid of engaging in vigorous debate about issues," he said, though he also welcomed Dean's pro-gun views. In 2004, against his first Republican opponent since 1994, Mollohan won 68% of the vote, and carried all 20 counties except for Grant in the eastern Panhandle. In the 2002 redistricting, he rebuffed Democrats who wanted a radical redrawing of West Virginia's district lines to disadvantage 2d District Republican Shelley Moore Capito. That would have meant relinquishing some Democratic counties and gaining Republican-leaning counties in the eastern panhandle that might have provided a base for opposition to Mollohan. The result protected his interests and his district, but have made it harder for Democrats to regain a majority in the House.

SECOND DISTRICT

Rep. Shelley Moore Capito (R)

Elected 2000, 3d term; b. Nov. 26, 1953, Glen Dale; home, Charleston; Duke U., B.S. 1975, U. of VA, M.Ed. 1976; Presbyterian; married (Charles).

Elected Office: WV House of Del., 1996–2000.

Professional Career: Career counselor, WV State Col., 1976–78; Dir., Educ. Info. Center, WV Board of Regents, 1978–81.

DC Office: 1431 LHOB, 20515, 202-225-2711; Fax: 202-225-7856; Web site: capito.house.gov.

District Offices: Charleston, 304-925-5964; Martinsburg, 304-264-8810.

Committees: *Rules* (6th of 9 R): Rules & Organization of the House.

Group Ratings

	ADA	ACLU	AFS	LCV	ITIC	NTU	COC	ACU	NTLC	CHC
2004	30	0	38	18	80	50	90	72	70	84
2003	15	—	25	25	—	55	87	72	—	—

National Journal Ratings

	2003 LIB	—	2003 CONS		2004 LIB	—	2004 CONS
Economic	41%	—	57%		50%	—	50%
Social	47%	—	52%		40%	—	59%
Foreign	40%	—	58%		25%	—	68%

Key Votes of the 108th Congress

1. Drilling in ANWR	Y	5. DC School Vouchers	Y	9. Ban Same-Sex Marriage	Y
2. Approve Bush Tax Cuts	Y	6. Ban Human Cloning	Y	10. Fund Iraq War	Y
3. Medicare/Rx Bill	Y	7. Restrict Gun Liability	Y	11. Bar Cuba Embargo Funds	N
4. Bar Overtime Pay Regs.	Y	8. Ban Partial-Birth Abortion	Y	12. Intelligence Reorg.	Y

Election Results

2004 general	Shelley Moore Capito (R)	147,676	(57%)	($1,654,898)
	Erik Wells (D)	106,131	(41%)	($77,410)
	Other	3,218	(1%)	
2004 primary	Shelley Moore Capito (R)	unopposed		
2002 general	Shelley Moore Capito (R)	98,276	(60%)	($2,530,078)
	Jim Humphreys (D)	65,400	(40%)	($8,150,237)

Prior Winning Percentages: 2000 (48%)

The People		Race/Ethnic Origin	Ancestry	
Area size:	8,512 sq. mi.	93.9% White	USA: 14.7%	German: 11.7%
Urban population:	46.2%	3.6% Black	Irish: 8.1%	
Rural population:	53.8%	0.5% Asian	**2004 Presidential Vote**	
Pop. 2000:	602,243	0.2% Native Am.	Bush (R) 151,019	(57%)
Median income:	$33,198	0.0% Hawaiian	Kerry (D) 112,418	(42%)
Poverty status:	14.8%	0.9% Two+ races	Other 1,738	(1%)
Military veterans:	14.8%	0.1% Other	**2000 Presidential Vote**	
		0.8% Hispanic Origin	Bush (R) 118,839	(54%)
			Gore (D) 96,524	(44%)
			Other 4,787	(2%)
			Cook Partisan Voting Index: R + 5	

Occupation	Blue collar: 28.9%	White collar: 55.1%	Gray collar: 16.1%

Not all of West Virginia has been coal country, not all of its valleys are industrial hollows choked with workingmen's homes and small factories, and not all of its hills are scarred with strip mining wounds or piled with tailings. It's true that for miles you can see gentle hills and rugged mountains, stands of green trees and vistas stretching to far horizons. Yet over another hill youmay find, amid scenery primeval and rural, sudden evidence of industrialization: a pulp mill or charcoal factory in a clearing scraped out of the forest; a small factory town, built close to a river in a cleft bordered with hills, its houses built in the same 1910s style as in the factory suburbs of Pittsburgh; the entrance to an underground coal mine or a mountaintop blasted open to allow surface mining. Large parts of this naturally beautiful state look as verdant and unchanged as they must have when George Washington was speculating in land here or taking the waters in Berkeley Springs, or when John Brown launched his assault on the federal arsenal at Harper's Ferry in 1859.

The 2d Congressional District of West Virginia is a central slice of the state, a belt of land from Berkeley Springs and Harper's Ferry in the Washington exurbs all the way west to the Ohio River town of Point Pleasant, where the Kanawha River (pronounced *kaNAW*) flows into the Ohio. It could easily take a full day to drive through this mountainous district that, if ironed out, would probably spread across the continent. The 2d District includes the few fast-growing parts of West Virginia—the eastern panhandle counties, which are part of the Washington, D.C., metro area and have become home to some city folks seeking a quieter life, plus chemical-producing Putnam County just west of Charleston, where Toyota built an engine plant. The major urban center here is Charleston, where on the banks of the Kanawha rises West Virginia's Capitol, built in 1932 and designed by Cass Gilbert with a dome higher than the U.S. Capitol and a chandelier with 10,000 pieces of cut glass. Charleston, with its two partisan newspapers, the Democratic *Gazette* and the Republican *Daily Mail*, is the center of the state's political culture. It also is a major industrial center, with coal in the hills all around and, downriver from the Capitol, huge petrochemical plants that convert coal tar into everyday products. This was a center of American high tech in the 1940s, when it produced all the nation's lucite, polyethylenes and nylon, as well as much of its artificial rubber and antifreeze. Today, the state boasts it is home to more polymer producers than any other place on the planet; the chemical industry makes products used in the manufacturing of cosmetics, detergents, shampoo, rubber, paints and coatings, fire retardants and agricultural products. Charleston is also West Virginia's professional center, with a few downtown skyscrapers and some affluent residential districts. But like much of the state, Kanawha County has continued to lose population since the 2000 Census. Politically, this is an ancestrally Democratic district now trending Republican in many, though not all, races; Berkeley County in the eastern panhandle votes like a Republican exurb. George W. Bush has carried the 2d District twice by comfortable margins, and it is the only district in the state to have elected a Republican House member in more than 20 years.

The congresswoman from the 2d District is Shelley Moore Capito, a Republican first elected in 2000. She grew up in northern West Virginia and in the Washington area, when her father, Arch Moore, served in the House from 1957–69. He was elected governor in 1968 and (over Jay Rockefeller) in 1972, and then again in 1984; later he was convicted and served three years in jail for fraud and extortion. Shelley Moore Capito graduated from Duke University and the University of Virginia, and is the first Cherry Blossom Princess elected to Congress. She worked for two years as a career counselor at West Virginia State College, and then was director of the state's Educational Information Center from 1978–81, when Rockefeller was governor. She served two terms in the West Virginia House of Delegates. Her opportunity to follow in her father's footsteps came when Bob Wise, a Democratic congressman first elected in 1982, ran for governor in 2000. She benefited from a divisive Democratic primary that was won by Jim Humphreys, a trial lawyer, former state senator and ally of labor unions, who made a fortune in asbestos litigation and spent $3 million of his own money to win the Democratic nomination. Capito, who supported abortion rights, started as the underdog but Humphreys, who spent another $6 million in the general, proved to be a poor candidate. One of the few beneficiaries of George W. Bush's coattails that year, she won 48%–46%, with big margins in the eastern panhandle counties.

In the House, Capito has received special attention from Republican leaders because of her precarious district. She was one of the few House Republicans to get a free pass to vote against trade promotion authority. Capito helped to make the case for her party's prescription drug plan for seniors and against the Democratic alternative. On the Transportation and Infrastructure Committee she won approval of $44 million—one of the largest earmarks in the 2004 highway bill—to begin the expansion of busy U.S. 35 west of Charleston. A firm Bush ally in the war on terror, she secured House commendation for Army Private Jessica Lynch, a district native who was rescued from captivity at the start of the war in Iraq. But the Bush administration rejected her proposal to distribute Iraqi assets to the former POWs.

At home, Capito has settled comfortably into her seat. In 2002, Democrats gave her a big break by again nominating Humphreys, who won another bruising and expensive primary. Discouraged national Democrats gritted their teeth; a new team of national consultants could not change Humphrey's approach, and his 2002 campaign was even more ineffective than in 2000. Capito won 60%–40%, and ran strongly across the district. In 2004, her Democratic opponent was former television anchorman Erik Wells, but national Democrats abandoned interest in the district. The United Mine Workers endorsed Capito after praising her for blocking a Labor Department bid to weaken regulations on coal dust, and for legislation to protect medical benefits for retired miners, including 15,000 in West Virginia. Her victory margin fell to a still comfortable 57%–41%, including a virtually dead-even result in Kanawha County. Capito has said she does not regard her district as safe. But she looks now to be a well-positioned incumbent, with some potential as a statewide candidate. In early 2005, national Republicans were hoping she would challenge Senator Robert Byrd in 2006; she said she would make a decision on the Senate race in the fall.

THIRD DISTRICT

Rep. Nick Rahall (D)

Elected 1976, 15th term; b. May 20, 1949, Beckley; home, Beckley; Duke U., B.A. 1971; Presbyterian; married (Melinda).

Professional Career: Civil Air Patrol, 1977–88; Staff Asst., U.S. Sen. Robert Byrd, 1971–74; Bd. of Dir., Rahall Communications Corp. 1974–76; Pres., Mountaineer Tour & Travel Agency, 1974–76; Pres., WV Broadcasting Corp. 1980–present.

DC Office: 2307 RHOB, 20515, 202-225-3452; Fax: 202-225-9061; Web site: www.house.gov/rahall.

District Offices: Beckley, 304-252-5000; Bluefield, 304-325-6222; Huntington, 304-522-6425; Logan, 304-752-4934.

Committees: *Resources* (RMM of 22 D). *Transportation & Infrastructure* (2d of 34 D): Aviation; Highways, Transit & Pipelines; Railroads; Water Resources & Environment.

Group Ratings

	ADA	ACLU	AFS	LCV	ITIC	NTU	COC	ACU	NTLC	CHC
2004	75	47	83	100	30	15	52	28	3	61
2003	85	—	100	85	—	25	30	40	—	—

National Journal Ratings

	2003 LIB	—	2003 CONS	2004 LIB	—	2004 CONS
Economic	66%	—	32%	59%	—	41%
Social	59%	—	41%	53%	—	47%
Foreign	70%	—	27%	89%	—	10%

Key Votes of the 108th Congress

1. Drilling in ANWR	N	5. DC School Vouchers	N	9. Ban Same-Sex Marriage	Y
2. Approve Bush Tax Cuts	N	6. Ban Human Cloning	Y	10. Fund Iraq War	N
3. Medicare/Rx Bill	N	7. Restrict Gun Liability	Y	11. Bar Cuba Embargo Funds	Y
4. Bar Overtime Pay Regs.	Y	8. Ban Partial-Birth Abortion	Y	12. Intelligence Reorg.	N

Election Results

2004 general	Nick Rahall (D)	142,682	(65%)	($930,079)
	Rick Snuffer (R)	76,170	(35%)	($89,312)
2004 primary	Nick Rahall (D)	unopposed		
2002 general	Nick Rahall (D)	87,783	(70%)	($374,850)
	Paul Chapman (R)	37,229	(30%)	

Prior Winning Percentages: 2000 (91%); 1998 (87%); 1996 (100%); 1994 (64%); 1992 (66%); 1990 (52%); 1988 (61%); 1986 (71%); 1984 (67%); 1982 (81%); 1980 (77%); 1978 (100%); 1976 (46%)

The People		Race/Ethnic Origin	Ancestry	
Area size:	9,375 sq. mi.	93.9% White	USA: 19.7%	Irish: 7.7%
Urban population:	38.4%	4.1% Black	English: 7.1%	
Rural population:	61.6%	0.4% Asian	**2004 Presidential Vote**	
Pop. 2000:	603,556	0.2% Native Am.	Bush (R) 122,707	(53%)
Median income:	$25,630	0.0% Hawaiian	Kerry (D) 106,219	(46%)
Poverty status:	21.9%	0.8% Two+ races	Other 1,668	(1%)
Military veterans:	13.5%	0.0% Other	**2000 Presidential Vote**	
		0.6% Hispanic Origin	Gore (D) 101,541	(51%)
			Bush (R) 94,809	(47%)
			Other 3,942	(2%)
			Cook Partisan Voting Index: D + 0	
Occupation	Blue collar: 28.8%	White collar: 52.6%	Gray collar: 18.5%	

Early in the 20th century, the coalfields of southern West Virginia were one of America's boom areas. Into rural farmland and hollows, inhabited by the same families since they first arrived at these mountains 100 years before, came coal company lawyers with mineral rights' leases to sign, coal company engineers to design and sink the mineshafts, and men from other mountain counties, as well as Europe, to work the mines. Company houses were built, company stores were stocked with goods as the company dictated and company paymasters kept close tabs on the finances of every employee. These conditions bred dull discontent, ignited into the fire of industrial unionism by the tongue of John L. Lewis, president of the United Mine Workers, who organized most of the mines in the 1930s. Lewis was not only a militant unionist, but also an isolationist, and during and after World War II he called out his coal miners on strikes, to the fury of Franklin Roosevelt and Harry Truman. The entire national war effort and postwar economic recovery seemed gravely threatened by these labor stoppages involving some 300,000 workers, centered in back corners of the country like southern West Virginia.

All that is history now. Coal is no longer central to the U.S. economy and there are only a few thousand coal miners left in southern West Virginia—and many are not UMW members anymore. Most of the old underground mines have been abandoned, leaving behind mineshafts and piles of tailings—and lives that were snuffed out by cave-ins or simple carelessness in America's deadliest industry. Manufacturing jobs in the area, which had been predominantly in the chemical industry, also have been reduced by more than half since 1980. There are few parts of the United States, apart from some central city neighborhoods and Great Plains farm counties, which have suffered such depopulation over the last half-century. But this region has still not hit bottom: Of seven counties in the nation with more than 20,000 residents that suffered more than 10% population loss in the 1990s, four—Logan, McDowell, Mingo and Wyoming—were in southern West Virginia, which has the oldest median age in the nation. To stem that tide, advocates of "clean coal" technology welcomed the Bush administration's 2004 unveiling of a $215 million project in Greenbrier County, which is designed to use waste coal to generate electric power with low pollution.

The 3d Congressional District of West Virginia includes most of the mountainous coal country in the southern part of the state that for years were among America's most heavily Democratic jurisdictions. Democratic voter registration is around 90% in Logan and McDowell Counties; nearby Mingo County—"Bloody Mingo," where coal company enforcers battled Matewan miners seeking to escape economic serfdom—is equally monolithic. But the coal mining counties now make up less than half of the 3d District. About a quarter of the population is in and around the industrial city of Huntington on the Ohio River, which includes Marshall University and continuing attempts at economic development; a possibly hopeful sign was a new Starbucks in nearby Barboursville, the first in a state that was last to get one. Another quarter is to the east, at the interstate junction at Beckley and in the farming uplands around the resorts of White Sulphur Springs where, at the Greenbrier Hotel resort, the government built a massive secret fallout shelter (code-named "Project Greek Island," the bunker was intended to house the entire U.S. Congress in the event of nuclear war) that was finally opened to the public in 1992. These two areas are much less Democratic than the coal counties.

The congressman from the 3d District is Nick Rahall, a Democrat first elected in 1976, at 27; he was the youngest member of the 95th Congress. He comes from the thin economic upper crust of the coal country; his family owned radio and TV stations in Beckley and in St. Petersburg, Florida. Rahall has concentrated on bringing public works projects and jobs to his district. He got seats on Transportation and Infrastructure, and Resources early on, and now is the ranking minority member on Resources and number two Democrat on Transportation. He was the chief House sponsor of the law requiring union and non-union coal operators to bail out the United Mine Workers health care funds. He has continued efforts to secure federal funds for retired mineworkers. When the Bush White House in 2004 threatened a veto of the highway bill approved by the Transportation Committee, he said, "These advisers need their heads examined."

Environmental activists were disappointed when Rahall in 2001 became ranking Democrat on the Resources Committee, because he had shown little support for their views. But, perhaps surprisingly, he has opposed oil drilling in the Arctic National Wildlife Refuge and favored expanding wilderness areas in the West. He opposed the Bush administration's energy package in 2003 for opening additional Western lands to coal producers without competitive bidding, and for "pay[ing] lip service to coal's role in our national energy mix." In 2004, he received the Wilderness Society's Ansel Adams award for being "forceful, energetic and wise in preventing special interests from exploiting places that Americans hold dear."

Rahall's family roots are in Lebanon, and he is often in the small minority of members voicing support for Arab causes and voting against Israel. He opposed military action in Iraq, saying, "I feel the Iraqis want to give peace a chance." When a former campaign contributor who is a founder of the American Muslim Council was arrested in September 2003 for allegedly illegal dealings with Libya, local Republicans called on Rahall to return all contributions from groups affiliated with the contributor.

Since his first election in 1976, Rahall has dropped below 61% of the vote only once. In October 2004, his Republican challenger said his polls showed him "neck and neck" with Rahall, and that voters wanted someone who "represents their interests ahead of his own." But perhaps he read the wrong line in the poll. George W. Bush carried the district—the first time a Republican presidential candidate has since 1972—but Rahall carried every county and won 65%–35%.

★ WISCONSIN ★

Wisconsin, tucked off north of the main east-west routes across the country and squeezed between Lake Michigan and the Mississippi River, was at the beginning of the 20th century one of America's premier "laboratories of reform," in Justice Louis Brandeis's phrase— and was again at the end of the 20th century: a state originating new public policies, seeing how they work, serving as an example for others. Wisconsin's first fame as a laboratory came during the Progressive era that began around 1900, and its primacy was due to an extraordinary governor, Robert LaFollette Sr., and to the state's unique history and German heritage. Wisconsin is the first state of that vast stretch of the United States reaching all the way to the Pacific, settled first by New England Yankees but even more by immigrants from Germany and Scandinavia. The German language is seldom heard now, the once plainly German beer brands now seem quintessentially American and few ties remain with the old country after two world wars, though in 2000 30% of Wisconsin residents said they were of German descent. But in the late 19th and early 20th centuries, Germans were among America's most numerous immigrants and until the 1890s probably the most distinct. They implanted, on the rolling dairyland of Wisconsin and the orderly streets of Milwaukee, their separate religions, often retaining their

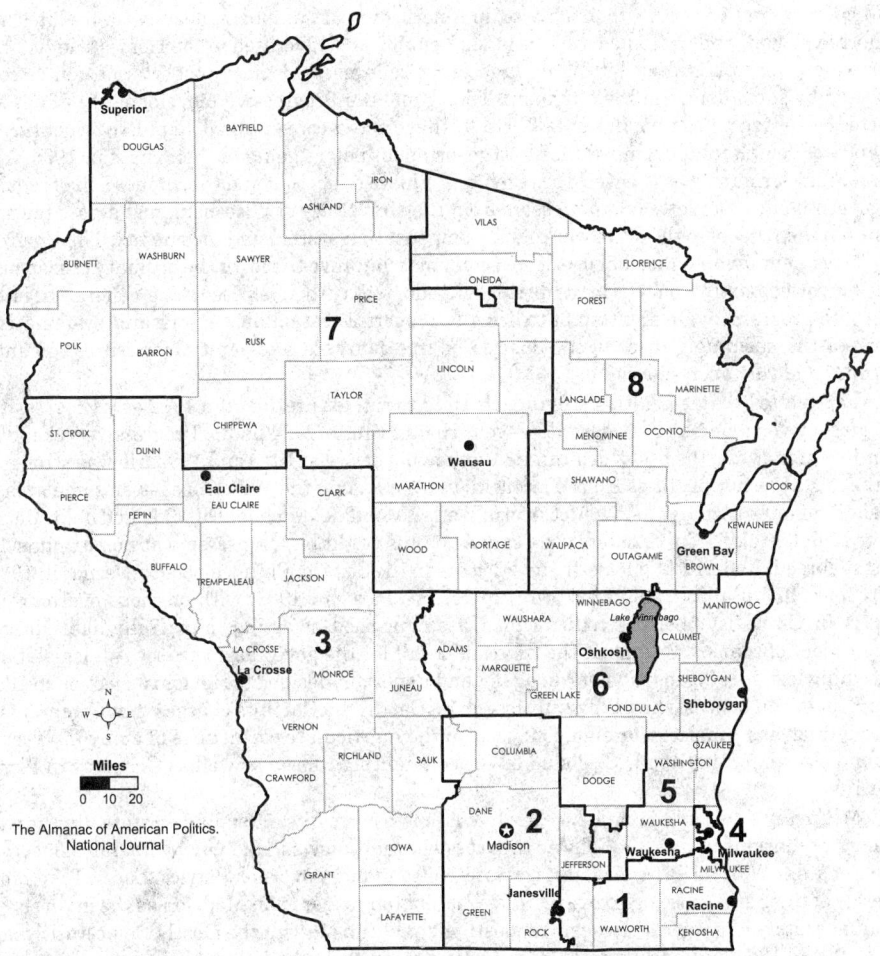

Congressional district boundaries were first effective for 2002.

language and maintaining old customs, from country weddings to drinking beer—a source of friction in temperance-minded America—to eating bratwurst.

Politically, the Germans were not monolithic. Their origins were diverse and they were spread too widely across the nation. But where they were concentrated, there was a distinctive politics, basically American, but with echoes of progressive ideas current in German-speaking countries in Europe. Nowhere was the politics of German-Americans more apparent than in Wisconsin. This is one of the two states that gave birth to the Republican Party in 1854 (the other is Michigan), and Germans, then arriving in America in vast numbers, heavily favored it. They abhorred slavery and welcomed the free lands Republicans advocated in the Homestead Act, the free education promised by setting up land grant colleges, and the transportation routes constructed by subsidizing railroad builders. Then came the Progressive movement of LaFollette, elected governor of Wisconsin in 1900. Up to that time a conventional Republican politician, LaFollette completely revamped the state government before going to the Senate in 1906. At a time when Germany was the world's leader in graduate education and the application of science to government, LaFollette had professors from the University of Wisconsin, just across town in Madison, help develop the state workmen's compensation system and income tax. The Progressive movement favored rational use of government to improve the lot of the ordinary citizen—an idea borrowed partly from German liberals and adopted by the New Dealers a generation later. All these programs were an attempt to bring bureaucratic rationality—Germanic systematization—to the seemingly disordered America of free markets and multiple cultures, gigantic fortunes and vast open spaces.

LaFollette became a national figure. He tried to run for president in 1912 as a Progressive, but was shoved aside by Theodore Roosevelt. He did run in 1924 on his Progressive ticket and won 18% of the vote, the best third-candidate showing between 1912 and 1992. He was strongest in the northern tier of states from Wisconsin west and along the West Coast—the same area of strength of later liberals George McGovern, Walter Mondale, Michael Dukakis and John Kerry. After LaFollette died in 1925, his sons carried on his tradition, progressive at home and isolationist abroad: Robert LaFollette Jr., for 22 years in the Senate; Philip, elected governor in 1930, 1934 and 1936. Philip created his own Progressive Party in 1934, with ominous overtones: a "Cross in Circle" symbol his critics called a circumcised swastika, huge rally-like parades reminiscent of some in Europe at the time and a call for the governor to propose all legislation. But Philip lost in 1938 and did not run again, and Robert Jr. decided to run for re-election in 1946 as a Republican but lost the primary to Joseph McCarthy. McCarthy's charges that Communists were influencing American foreign policy fed on the inarticulate convictions of many in Wisconsin and elsewhere that the U.S. should have been fighting Russia as well as Germany in World War II.

McCarthy's national prominence made Wisconsin seem like a Republican state. But he won by narrow margins and the LaFollette Progressive tradition was taken up by liberal Democrats like Senators William Proxmire and Gaylord Nelson, and Governor Patrick Lucey. Like most liberals of their era, these progressives saw Washington rather than Madison as the main site of their laboratory of reform. Wisconsin, a mostly Republican state in the mostly Democratic years from 1944 to 1964, became a mostly Democratic state in the mostly Republican years from 1968 to 1988.

In the 1990s Wisconsin moved in another direction, and was a laboratory for different reforms, for which the state's economy provided a favorable environment. Wisconsin's high-skill, precision manufacturing economy jumped into gear in the late 1980s, and helped lead the nation's export boom of the 1990s. Yet much of the political focus remains on the dwindling number of dairy farmers. Wisconsin ranks number two in milk production, number one in cheese, but thanks to improved productivity the number of dairy farms has declined from 105,000 in 1960 to 45,000 in 1980 and 21,000 in 2000. Waukesha County outside Milwaukee, once Cow County, U.S.A., now has only 67 dairy farms. The federal milk price fixing system is biased against Wisconsin, with prices higher the farther the farming operation is from Eau Claire; Wisconsin's members of Congress have spent much time and psychic energy trying to change this.

The motivating force for reform in the 1990s was, as in the early 1900s, a Republican governor, in this case Tommy Thompson, who beat a liberal Democrat in 1986. He cut taxes, sponsored a school choice program, and passed a series of welfare reforms—the nation's most thoroughgoing—which since 1987 cut caseloads by 93%. Across the nation other governors and leaders of the Republican Congress looked to learn from Wisconsin's experiments: it's a fair question whether the 1996 federal Welfare Reform Act would have passed without Wisconsin's example to give its backers confidence.

Thompson did not carry all before him and left some fiscal problems behind him, while Wisconsin, proud of its clean politics since the LaFollette era, was suddenly beset by political scandal. Neither party is dominant. Al Gore carried the state by 47.8%–47.6% in 2000, John Kerry by 49.7%–49.3% in 2004. Wisconsin has two Democratic U.S. senators, one elected twice by narrow margins; its U.S. House delegation is split 4–4. In 2002 it replaced Thompson's successor as governor, Scott McCallum, with Democrat Jim Doyle. But he won with less than a majority of the vote and Republicans gained control of the state Senate and made gains in the Assembly in 2002 and increased their margins in both in 2004. And squeaky clean Wisconsin has been touched by scandal. In 2001 and 2002 legislative leaders were swept aside when staffers were accused of running partisan campaigns from state offices and legislative leaders were charged with seeking contributions from lobbyists during discussions about legislation. In 2004 there was evidence of more serious vote fraud. In Milwaukee many people registered to vote without identification and failed to respond to inquiries sent out by clerks to their reported addresses. Wisconsin allows voters to register on Election Day and the *Milwaukee Journal Sentinel* found that more than 1,200 votes were cast from nonexistent addresses, 75% by people who registered on Election Day. Also the *Journal Sentinel* found that in Milwaukee 8,323 more people were recorded as voting than could be identified from the voter list. But Governor Doyle strongly resisted the efforts of Republican legislators to require photo identification of previously registered voters at the polls.

The People		Race/Ethnic Origin			Military veterans: 514,213 (12.9%)	
Pop. 2004 (est):	5,509,026	4,681,630	87.3%	White	WWII: 21.1%	Korea: 14.5%
Pop. 2000:	5,363,675	300,245	5.6%	Black	Vietnam: 30.6%	Gulf War: 8.3%
Pop. 1990:	4,891,769	87,995	1.6%	Asian	**Most populous cities (2003):**	
Change 1990–2000:	Up 9.6%	43,980	0.8%	Native Am.	1. Milwaukee	586,941
% of U.S. total:	1.9%	1,346	0.0%	Hawaiian	2. Madison	218,432
Pop. rank:	18th of 50	51,921	1.0%	Two+ races	3. Green Bay	101,467
Area size:	65,498 sq. mi.	3,637	0.1%	Other	4. Kenosha	92,871
State Native:	73.4%	192,921	3.6%	Hisp. Origin	5. Racine	80,266
Non-citizen:	2.2%	**Ancestry**				
Language		German: 29.9%		Irish: 7.6%	Urban population: 68.3%	
English: 90.5%	Spanish: 4.1%	Polish: 6.5%		Norwegian: 5.9%	Rural population: 31.7%	
Other Eur.: 3.9%		English: 4.5%				

Education		Work Sector			Legislature	
H.S. Grad:	85.1%	Private: 81.1%		Govt: 12.5%	Senate	19 R 14 D
College Grad:	22.4%	Self: 6.1%		Family: 0.3%	Assembly	60 R 39 D
Industry		Unemployment: 4.7%			Legislative Term Limits: No	
Agri: 2.8%	Con: 5.9%	**Household Income**			**Registered Voters**	
Fin: 6.1%	Info: 2.2%	<15k: 13.0%		15-35k: 25.9%	No state voter registration	
Mfg: 26.7%	Prof: 26.6%	35-50k: 18.1%		50-100k: 33.6%		
Public: 3.5%	Trade: 14.8%	100-150k: 6.4%		>150k: 3.0%		
Other: 11.3%		Median: $43,791				
Occupation		Poverty status: 8.7%				
Blue collar: 28.4%	White collar: 56.6%	**Home Value**				
Gray collar: 15.0%		<50k: 10.0%	50-100k: 33.8%	100-200k: 43.6%	200-300k: 8.7%	
		300-500k: 3.0%	>500k: 1.0%	Median: $109,900		

Presidential politics   Wisconsin has been seriously contested in seven of the last eight presidential elections, and has voted narrowly for the Democratic nominee in six of them. The margins have been exceedingly narrow in the last two: 5,708 votes for Al Gore in 2000, 11,384 for John Kerry in 2004. The state was inundated by ads and lawn signs in both campaigns, and was especially heavily contested in 2004; Kerry stumbled when he came to Green Bay September 1 and referred to "Lambert Field" (it's Lambeau Field, as any Cheesehead can tell you). But Kerry perhaps atoned by abjuring the Northeast Dairy Compact and by spending three days later that month doing debate preparation in Spring Green.

2004 Presidential Vote		
Kerry (D)	1,489,504	(50%)
Bush (R)	1,478,120	(49%)
Nader (I)	16,390	(1%)
Other	12,993	(0%)

2004 Democratic Presidential Primary		
Kerry (D)	327,438	(40%)
Edwards (D)	283,376	(34%)
Dean (D)	150,548	(18%)
Kucinich (D)	27,306	(3%)
Sharpton (D)	14,691	(2%)
Other	22,891	(3%)

2000 Presidential Vote		
Gore (D)	1,242,987	(48%)
Bush (R)	1,237,279	(48%)
Nader (Green)	94,070	(4%)
Other	22,375	(1%)

In both these races some historic patterns were reversed. Bush carried metro Milwaukee, which casts about one-third of the state's votes, by narrow margins both times, thanks to big margins in the suburbs; while he ran far behind his father's 1988 showings in the nations biggest metropolitan areas, he ran ahead in metro Milwaukee. But Gore and Kerry carried many historically Republican or marginal counties in western Wisconsin, just as they carried many rural counties across the Mississippi River in eastern Iowa. Indeed, this was the only rural part of the country where Gore and Kerry carried large numbers of counties and ran ahead of Democratic norms. Their biggest percentage margins were in Madison's Dane County and in Menominee County, which is an Indian reservation. Bush carried the Fox River Valley, and the eastern half of the state has become fairly solidly Republican. Western Wisconsin, with ailing dairy farms and an economy not so dynamic, has become the Democratic bastion of the state, with metro Madison providing the big Democratic majorities that metro Milwaukee no longer provides in the east. In 2000 Bush ran well ahead of Republican norms in the far north, as he did in the Upper Peninsula of Michigan and northern Minnesota. But in 2004 ancestral Democrats in this north country went back to Kerry, providing votes essential to keeping the state in the Democratic column. The Bush campaign in 2004 succeeded in increasing his popular vote margins in eastern Wisconsin, around Wausau and also in suburban Minneapolis-St. Paul. But Democrats held steady or better in western Wisconsin and increased their margins by 28,000 in Milwaukee County and 25,000 in Madison's Dane County. Those margins, perhaps augmented by vote fraud in Milwaukee, kept Wisconsin in the Democratic column.

Wisconsin once had one of the nation's most influential presidential primaries. It knocked Wendell Willkie out of the race in 1944, helped John F. Kennedy establish his lead over Hubert Humphrey in 1960, prompted Lyndon B. Johnson to withdraw as Eugene McCarthy was about to beat him here in 1968 and gave George McGovern his first victory in 1972. After that Wisconsin's primary, even after it was moved from April to March, tended to be ignored. So in 2003 the legislature moved the date up another month to February 17, 2004—the only primary held that day. Wisconsin saw heavier campaigning than it had in years, at least for a few days. It may have proved crucial. John Kerry led John Edwards 40%–34%, with Howard Dean in third place with only 18%. Kerry ran stronger among self-identified Democrats, Edwards better with Independents and Republicans, who made up 40% of primary voters; Wisconsin does not have party registration and few people bothered to vote in the uncontested Republican primary. Edwards carried only 12 of 72 counties (and tied in one other) and did not do as well as he might have hoped in rural areas but, evidently with help from Independents and Republicans, he did carry the Milwaukee suburbs. Wisconsin may have been the decisive primary. Dean went back to Vermont and ended his campaign, while Edwards failed to get the momentum an early victory here might have given him.

Congressional districting

109th Congress Lineup	
4 D	4 R

108th Congress Lineup	
4 D	4 R

Wisconsin lost a congressional district in the 2000 Census. Ordinarily that would trigger a fierce battle between a Republican governor and Assembly and Democratic state Senate. But in May 2001 5th District Democrat Tom Barrett announced he was running for governor. His north Milwaukee district had lost population and was easy to eliminate. The result was a consensus plan, approved by the House delegation, passed by both houses of the legislature and signed by the governor in March 2002. A lawsuit brought a year earlier was dismissed a day later. This is one state that produced a plan with regularly shaped districts with obvious communities of interest; it was also a plan that enabled all eight incumbents running to win reelection easily.

Governor

James Doyle (D)

Elected 2002, term expires Jan. 2007, 1st term; b. Nov. 23, 1945, Washington, DC; home, Maple Bluff; Attended Stanford U. 1963–66, U. of WI, B.A. 1967, Harvard U., J.D. 1972; Catholic; married (Jessica).

Elected Office: Dane Cnty. D.A., 1976–82; WI Atty. Gen. 1990–02.

Professional Career: Peace Corps, Tunisia, 1967–69; Atty., Navajo Indian Reservation (Chinle, AZ), 1972–75; Practicing atty., 1982–90.

Office: 115 E. State Capitol, Madison, 53707, 608-266-1212; Fax: 608-267-8983; Web site: www.wisgov.state.wi.us.

Election Results

2002 general	James Doyle (D)	800,515	(45%)
	Scott McCallum (R)	734,779	(41%)
	Ed Thompson (Lib)	185,455	(10%)
2002 primary	James Doyle (D)	212,066	(38%)
	Tom Barrett (D)	190,605	(34%)
	Kathleen Falk (D)	150,161	(27%)
1998 general	Tommy G.Thompson (R)	1,047,716	(60%)
	Ed Garvey (D)	679,553	(39%)
	Other	28,745	(2%)

James Doyle, a Democrat, was elected governor of Wisconsin in 2002. He grew up in Madison, in a political family. His parents were part of a group of Madison liberals in the rising Democratic party of the 1950s and the dominant Democratic party of the 1960s—Governor and Senator Gaylord Nelson, Senator William Proxmire, Governor Pat Lucey, Governor John Reynolds, *Capital Times* editor Miles McMillan. Doyle's mother was elected to the Wisconsin Assembly in 1948, only the second woman there, but the fourth generation of her family (the Bachhubers) to serve there. His father ran for governor in 1954 and lost the primary to Proxmire; in 1967 he became a federal judge, for years the only judge in the Western District of Wisconsin, and issued dozens of liberal rulings disallowing state and federal government actions. Jim Doyle was a star basketball player and top student in high school in Madison, went to Stanford for three years and then graduated from the University of Wisconsin. With his wife, a niece of Congressman and Defense Secretary Melvin Laird, he spent two years in the Peace Corps in Tunisia; back in the U.S. they marched in Washington in protest of the Vietnam War and then met Laird in his office in the Pentagon. Doyle graduated from Harvard Law School, then worked for three years as a lawyer on the Navajo Reservation in Arizona.

He returned to Madison in 1975 and in 1976 ran against Dane County District Attorney Humphrey Lynch, a Democrat, and beat him. He served for six years, then went into private practice in Madison. In 1990 he ran for attorney general and defeated the incumbent Republican. His best publicized accomplishment was the state's $6 billion tobacco settlement, but he was criticized for paying the state's lawyers $847 million; Ed Garvey, a Democrat who had run for governor, sued and got the fee blocked.

Governor Tommy Thompson, long the dominant figure in state politics and the author of the changes in welfare laws that became a model for the nation, left Madison in January 2001 after 14 years as governor to become Secretary of Health and Human Services, and Lieutenant Governor Scott McCallum became governor. He was faced with more serious budget problems than Thompson had faced in many years, and in January 2002 he proposed that the state cut $1 billion in aid to local governments over the next three years. The cut in local aid was unpopular and McCallum's job rating, hovering around 50% in fall 2001, fell to about 35% in spring 2002.

Four Democrats lined up to run against McCallum. Doyle set out a specific program; he would meet the state's budget problems by cutting the work force from 67,000 to 56,000, which is what it was when Thompson became governor in 1987, and would not increase taxes; he would tax business only on Wisconsin sales, not on Wisconsin payroll and property; he would continue current funding levels or more on education and health care. He was endorsed by former Governors Gaylord Nelson, Pat Lucey (who had managed his father's campaign for governor in 1954) and Martin Schreiber. But he was backed by few legislators, many of whom were angry at his prosecutorial attitude toward state Senate Majority Leader Chuck Chvala, who was in trouble because his staffers had been politicking in his state office. Doyle started off much better known than his Democratic rivals, none of whom had a statewide base. Milwaukee Congressman Tom Barrett was well known in his district and, from previous service in the state Senate and Assembly, popular among Democratic legislators, most of whom endorsed him. Dane County Executive Kathleen Falk ran as a candidate with executive experience and was relying on her Madison area base and EMILY's List. State Senator Gary George ran as the candidate with the most experience in state government and hoped to build on his base among teachers' unions and Milwaukee blacks. But Wisconsin's population is only 6% black (three-quarters of whom live in Milwaukee) and George was thrown off the ballot in July for invalid signatures.

The Democratic candidates avoided negative campaigning; the ads were mostly positive. Doyle's showed his two grown sons, who are adopted and of African-American descent, praising him. In the September primary Doyle ran pretty evenly statewide, in no county above 54% or below 30%; the others' support was mostly in their bases.

Doyle came out of primary night swinging at McCallum. "He's living proof that not all on-the-job training programs are successful," said Doyle. He continued to run on cutting $1 billion by reducing the number of state employees and attacked McCallum for spending the state's entire tobacco settlement on balancing one year's budget. McCallum, who emerged from the primary with three times as much money, ran an ad showing a messy desk and spilled coffee and attacked Doyle for missing deadlines while doing the state's legal business. McCallum said he would balance the budget through revenue growth and said Doyle had promised teachers' unions and other groups programs that would cost $2.7 billion on top of an anticipated $2.8 billion shortfall. Into the fray also stepped a third candidate, Libertarian nominee Ed Thompson, who ran the Tee-Pee Supper Club in Tomah and was elected mayor of the town. But the real reason Thompson attracted attention was because he is Tommy Thompson's brother. In public polls Doyle had the lead, but never took off, while McCallum never seemed to rise above his lackluster job rating and Thompson ran in the high single digits.

In November Doyle beat McCallum 45%–42%, with 11% for Ed Thompson; Thompson carried the county where he lived and the next-door county where he grew up. It was a narrow win for Doyle, and one accompanied by Republican gains in legislative races: Republicans won control of the state Senate 18–15 and enlarged their Assembly majority to 58–41. In many ways this was a different race in different media markets. In the Milwaukee market McCallum led 47%–44%, with Thompson at 7%; in the Fox River Valley McCallum led 47%–41%, with Thompson at 8%. This eastern part of Wisconsin, with 57% of votes, went Republican. Where Doyle won was in the Madison market, where he led 49%–30%, and Thompson got 17%, and in the Wausau and Eau Claire markets, where he led 44%–37%, and Thompson got 15%. These two areas cast

35% of the state's votes. In the farthest west counties, served by Twin Cities and Duluth TV, Thompson was not much of a factor, with just 5% of the votes; here Doyle led 50%–24%.

In office Doyle faced a $3.2 billion deficit but, working with Republican legislators, was able to balance the budget without increasing sales, income or corporate taxes. A tax on job creation was eliminated and a single-tax formula based on corporate sales established. So was a sales tax exemption for the cost of energy used in manufacturing. Doyle declared that taxes as a percentage of income were the lowest in Wisconsin in 34 years and said Republican legislators deserved some of the credit. They also cooperated on bills authorizing member-owned health insurance cooperatives, creating five regional health care purchasing alliances for farms and small businesses and establishing tax credits up to $50,000 for modernizing dairy farms. But Doyle clashed with Republicans on some issues. He called for no new prisons in four years. He vetoed bills establishing a right to carry concealed weapons, allowing local governments to hire private contractors without consent from unions, freezing property taxes and ending the Farmland Preservation Program. He sought to scale back or cut the school choice program in Milwaukee, long a target of teachers' unions. He resisted efforts to require voters to show identification at the polls; he cited his mother who had no driver's license of state ID. Republican legislators frustrated his attempts to raise the minimum wage.

In December 2004, he cut state employment by 1,500—a little below his goal. He sought to increase Wisconsin's trade with China (which is encouraging milk-drinking, despite its people's reputation for being lactose intolerant), Japan and Mexico. And in fact Wisconsin was gaining jobs, even manufacturing jobs, in 2003 and 2004, when job growth in nearby states like Michigan and Ohio was flagging.

In January 2005, facing a two-year projected deficit of $1.6 billion, Doyle again came out against a tax increase. He proposed to increase school aid by $850 million in order to hold down property tax increases (Republicans again wanted a freeze) and said he would not cut $930 million in aid to local governments. He called for $120 million in business tax credits and expansion of the Enterprise Development Zones authorized in 1995. He sought to expand the Badger Rx program for state employees and retirees and employees of participating companies. He called again for in-state college tuition for children of illegal immigrants who meet certain standards and for health care coverage for domestic partners of university and state employees.

Through all this Doyle was raising campaign funds for 2006 and in December 2004 had $2.25 million cash on hand. Republicans were busy running too. In January, Milwaukee County Executive Scott Walker, with a record that included freezing property taxes, said he would run. Green Bay Congressman Mark Green, who stumped for Assembly candidates all over the state in 2004 and in January 2005 transferred $1.3 million from his federal campaign fund to a state campaign treasury, announced in May 2005. Tommy Thompson, heading for the private sector in early 2005, refused to rule out a run for the office which he won in four of the last five elections.

Senior Senator

Herb Kohl (D)

Elected 1988, seat up 2006, 3d term; b. Feb. 7, 1935, Milwaukee; home, Milwaukee; U. of WI, B.A. 1956, Harvard U., M.B.A. 1958; Jewish; single.

Military Career: Army Reserves, 1958–64.

Professional Career: Businessman; Pres., Kohl Corp., 1970–79; Chmn., WI Dem. Party, 1975–77; Pres., Herbert Kohl Investments, 1979–88; Owner, Milwaukee Bucks pro basketball team, 1985–present.

DC Office: 330 HSOB, 20510, 202-224-5653; Fax: 202-224-9787; Web site: kohl.senate.gov.

State Offices: Appleton, 920-738-1640; Eau Claire, 715-832-8424; LaCrosse, 608-796-0045; Madison, 608-264-5338; Milwaukee, 414-297-4451.

Committees: *Aging (Special)* (RMM). *Appropriations*: Agriculture, Rural Development & Related Agencies (RMM); Commerce, Justice & Science; Homeland Security; Interior & Related Agencies; Labor, Health and Human Services, Education & Related Agencies; Transportation, Treasury, the Judiciary, HUD & Related Agencies. *Judiciary*: Antitrust, Competition Policy & Consumer Rights (RMM); Crime & Drugs; Intellectual Property; Terrorism, Technology & Homeland Security.

Group Ratings

	ADA	ACLU	AFS	LCV	ITIC	NTU	COC	ACU	NTLC	CHC
2004	100	78	100	100	36	18	44	4	5	0
2003	95	—	100	74	—	22	35	25	—	—

National Journal Ratings

	2003 LIB	—	2003 CONS		2004 LIB	—	2004 CONS
Economic	70%	—	26%		93%	—	0%
Social	63%	—	35%		76%	—	23%
Foreign	90%	—	0%		75%	—	19%

Key Votes of the 108th Congress

1. Ban Drilling in ANWR	Y	5. Energy Bill	N	9. Ban Same-Sex Marriage	N
2. Approve Bush Tax Cuts	N	6. Support Roe v. Wade	Y	10. Ban Bunker-Buster Bomb	Y
3. Medicare/Rx Bill	N	7. Ban Partial-Birth Abortion	N	11. Fund Iraq War	Y
4. Bar Overtime Pay Regs.	Y	8. Assault Weapons Ban	Y	12. Restrict Missile Defense	Y

Election Results

2000 general	Herb Kohl (D)	1,563,238	(62%)	($4,991,364)
	John Gillespie (R)	940,744	(37%)	($582,221)
	Other	35,199	(1%)	
2000 primary	Herb Kohl (D)	184,920	(90%)	
	Jim Sigl (D)	20,858	(10%)	
1994 general	Herb Kohl (D)	912,662	(58%)	($8,249,531)
	Robert T. Welch (R)	636,989	(41%)	($1,180,382)

Prior Winning Percentages: 1988 (52%)

Herb Kohl, Wisconsin's senior senator, is a Democrat first elected in 1988. He grew up in Milwaukee, where his parents immigrated from Russia and Poland in the 1920s and opened a food store, which became a Wisconsin supermarket and retail chain. He grew up in Milwaukee and graduated from the University of Wisconsin and Harvard Business School. He worked at Kohl's and was president in the 1970s; the firm was sold in 1979, and today is one of the fastest-expanding national retail chains. Kohl was a Democratic contributor and chairman of the Wisconsin Democratic party in the mid-1970s. In 1985 he became a local celebrity, in a city smarting from sports franchises with lousy records and eager to move elsewhere, when he spent $18 million to buy the Milwaukee Bucks basketball team to keep it from moving out of town; in January 2003 he said he was willing to sell, but only to those who would keep the team in Milwaukee (Forbes estimated the team was worth $168 million). In 1976 he bought a ranch near Jackson, Wyoming, from Senator Clifford Hansen, a Republican who says Kohl has been a "good steward of the land"; like the Bucks, the property is worth far more today than when he bought it. He is one of the richest members of Congress.

When Senator William Proxmire retired in 1988, Kohl decided to run for the Senate. He spent his own money liberally, running an extensive ad campaign with the theme, "Nobody's senator but yours." He won 47% in the primary to 38% for former Governor Tony Earl. In the general, against moderate Republican Susan Engeleiter, Kohl stressed his support of defense cuts—popular in dovish Wisconsin—and for requiring businesses to provide medical insurance; Engeleiter stressed her environmental stands, her legislative experience and her status as a wife and mother. This turned out to be one of the closest Senate races in the country, with Kohl winning 52%–48% after spending $7 million of his own money.

Kohl is a pleasant, shy, almost painfully earnest man, of transparent good will and seemingly little guile. He personally funds the Herb Kohl Educational Foundation, which has given more than $3.6 million in scholarships and grants to Wisconsin students, teachers and schools. He donated $25 million to the University of Wisconsin for the Kohl Center arena which opened in

1998. His voting record has been moderate to liberal; he dislikes the clash of partisan fighting. He opposed the Supercollider, the space station, and Trident II missiles, and has tried to keep defense spending increases down to Clinton budget levels. He was one of 12 Democratic senators who voted for the Bush tax cut in 2001 but he opposed the Bush tax cut in 2003. Four days after September 11 he was wary of military action. "We would take a tragic situation and make it infinitely worse if we just lash out." But in October 2002 he voted for the Iraq war resolution.

Kohl has supported gun control and wrote the 1990 law banning guns in schools that was overturned by the Supreme Court in 1995 (on the ground it had nothing to do with interstate commerce). Kohl and Ohio's Mike DeWine have run the Antitrust Subcommittee on a bipartisan basis in both the Clinton and Bush years. In 1997, a joint letter to FCC Chairman Reed Hundt prompted him to kill the proposed AT&T-SBC merger; subcommittee hearings in 1998 helped prevent the proposed American Airlines-British Airways merger. In 2001 they helped prevent the USAirways-United Airlines merger. As the only sports team owner in the Senate, he has recused himself on the issue of Major League Baseball's antitrust exemption. In June 2003 he and DeWine held hearings on the FCC ruling allowing media companies to own larger shares of local stations. That month they urged the FCC and Justice Department to scrutinize News Corporation's proposed purchase of DirectTV and in September they said regulators should press for concessions. In April 2004 they held a hearing on gasoline prices and co-sponsored a bill to make oil-producing and –exporting cartels illegal. In October 2004, after hearings on the subject, they co-sponsored a bill to give the government power to regulate the sale of medical products to hospitals. In March 2005 they co-sponsored a bill to allow the Justice Department to seek wiretaps on antitrust violators. That month Kohl said that consumers should not be limited to Baby Bell and cable TV companies for telecom services.

On the Judiciary Committee Kohl has joined other Democrats in opposing several appellate court nominees and threatening to filibuster them on the floor. As Republicans threatened to change the rules to prevent such filibusters, Kohl in March 2005 said, "The Democrats are saying there will be a price to pay for that. We're not trying to quantify in every detail, because different senators have different ideas of what this all means. But we're saying it's a serious, serious move. We've never said we're going to shut the place down, nor would I, Herb Kohl, be a part of that." He supported the class action bill in 2005 and voted against the confirmation of Alberto Gonzales as attorney general.

Kohl has pursued some issues prompted by events in Wisconsin. In 1997 he called for a national health care worker registry. He sought a criminal background check for nursing home workers in the Medicare/prescription drug act of 2003, which he voted against, and in 2005 got a $2.3 million pilot program to conduct criminal background checks on nursing homes in Wisconsin communities. Wisconsin has a large Hmong community, and in March 2004 Kohl asked Secretary of State Colin Powell to look into the treatment of the Hmong in Laos. In October 2004 he and Wisconsin colleague Russ Feingold put a halt to a routine trade measure by protesting the granting of non-discriminatory trade status to Laos because of their concern about the Hmong. In June 2004 he advanced a proposal by McNally Industries and the University of Wisconsin Center for Quick Response Manufacturing to create parts for aging military equipment by reverse engineering.

Kohl has fought with uncharacteristic fierceness to change what he considers the unfair treatment of Wisconsin dairy farmers. Since 1937, the Agriculture Department has fixed milk prices by a formula that allows higher prices the farther a farmer is from Eau Claire, Wisconsin. This increases prices to consumers, creates an oversupply of milk and reduces dairy prices in the Upper Midwest. Further aggravating the problem is the Northeast Dairy Compact set up in the 1980s, which allows the New England states to set even higher prices; other Northeastern states have sought to join. In debate on the 1996 Freedom to Farm Act, Kohl got the Senate to vote 50–46 to end the Northeast Dairy Compact, but in conference it was extended to 1999 and the Agriculture Secretary was ordered to set new milk marketing rules by then. In October 1999 New England senators inserted into an appropriations bill a two-year extension of the Northeast Dairy Compact and a rejection of Agriculture Secretary Dan Glickman's new rules; this was in part an effort to help then-Republican Jim Jeffords of Vermont, who was up for reelection in

2000. Kohl was outraged, and threatened to filibuster the bill and obstruct all business of the Senate. On November 18 and 19 he held the floor and filibustered. He was forced to desist, but got verbal support on the issue from party leaders Trent Lott and Tom Daschle and Agriculture Chairman Richard Lugar who promised the issue would be revisited. In 2001 he got 41 senators to sign a letter opposing the Northeast Dairy Compact, enough to threaten a filibuster if the issue was brought up, and on September 30 the compact expired. In its place Kohl helped to get in 2002 the Milk Loss Income Contract program, which pays dairy farmers if market prices fall. In its first three years it provided $2 billion to dairy farmers nationally, $413 million of that in Wisconsin. In October 2004 he attacked George W. Bush for inaction when House Republicans dropped renewal of MILC from the omnibus appropriation. In 2005 he and Republican Norm Coleman pushed for renewal of MILC with a double of the payment cap, and he was encouraged when the administration budget continued the program, though with a 5% decrease.

Kohl has been reelected easily. His sincere, unprepossessing demeanor has helped—and so has his money. He spent $6.5 million of his own money in 1994 (far more per voter, incidentally, than the much-ridiculed Michael Huffington was spending in California) and $5 million of his own money in 2000. His ability to self-finance has deterred many well-known Republicans from running against him. Kohl said in May 2003 that he would run for reelection in 2006, and in early 2005 no prominent Republican stepped forward to run against him. In December former Governor and HHS Secretary Tommy Thompson, when asked about making the race, said, "That's entirely possible. I happen to love politics. Why would I say no? There's a Senate seat open." But Republican insiders in Wisconsin seemed sure he would not run. As Milwaukee Republican consultant Todd Robert Murphy said, "No one credible would run against Kohl because Kohl could put $10 million" into his campaign tomorrow.

Junior Senator

Russell Feingold (D)

Elected 1992, seat up 2010, 3d term; b. Mar. 2, 1953, Janesville; home, Middleton; U. of WI, B.A. 1975, Rhodes Scholar, Oxford U., 1977, Harvard Law Schl., J.D. 1979; Jewish; divorced.

Elected Office: WI Senate, 1982–92.

Professional Career: Practicing atty., 1979–83; Prof., Beloit Col., 1985–93.

DC Office: 506 HSOB, 20510, 202-224-5323; Fax: 202-224-2725; Web site: feingold.senate.gov.

State Offices: Green Bay, 920-465-7508; LaCrosse, 608-782-5585; Middleton, 608-828-1200; Milwaukee, 414-276-7282; Wausau, 715-848-5660.

Committees: *Aging (Special). Budget. Foreign Relations*: African Affairs (RMM); East Asian & Pacific Affairs; European Affairs. *Judiciary*: Administrative Oversight & the Courts; Antitrust, Competition Policy & Consumer Rights; Constitution, Civil Rights & Property Rights (RMM); Corrections & Rehabilitation; Crime & Drugs; Immigration, Border Security & Citizenship; Terrorism, Technology & Homeland Security.

Group Ratings

	ADA	ACLU	AFS	LCV	ITIC	NTU	COC	ACU	NTLC	CHC
2004	100	89	100	100	42	22	35	8	13	0
2003	95	—	100	89	—	17	26	25	—	—

National Journal Ratings

	2003 LIB	—	2003 CONS		2004 LIB	—	2004 CONS
Economic	90%	—	7%		90%	—	7%
Social	79%	—	15%		67%	—	31%
Foreign	90%	—	0%		86%	—	8%

Key Votes of the 108th Congress

1. Ban Drilling in ANWR	Y	5. Energy Bill	N	9. Ban Same-Sex Marriage	N
2. Approve Bush Tax Cuts	N	6. Support Roe v. Wade	Y	10. Ban Bunker-Buster Bomb	Y
3. Medicare/Rx Bill	N	7. Ban Partial-Birth Abortion	N	11. Fund Iraq War	Y
4. Bar Overtime Pay Regs.	Y	8. Assault Weapons Ban	N	12. Restrict Missile Defense	Y

Election Results

2004 general	Russell Feingold (D)	1,632,697	(55%)	($9,239,908)
	Tim Michels (R)	1,301,183	(44%)	($5,542,087)
	Other	15,863	(1%)	
2004 primary	Russell Feingold (D)	unopposed		
1998 general	Russell Feingold (D)	890,059	(51%)	($3,846,089)
	Mark W. Neumann (R)	852,272	(48%)	($4,373,953)

Prior Winning Percentages: 1992 (53%)

Russ Feingold is a Democrat first elected to the Senate in 1992. He grew up in Janesville, where his father and Republican Congressman Paul Ryan's father practiced law in the same building. There was politics in his blood: his father ran for district attorney as a Progressive and once lost an election to the county board by one vote. In the second grade he cast the only vote in his class for John F. Kennedy and decided he wanted to be president and often said he wanted to be senator some day. He nurtured his ambition at the University of Wisconsin, as a Rhodes Scholar, and at Harvard Law School; he moved to Middleton, a not-so-academic suburb of Madison, and in 1982, at 29, beat an 83-year-old veteran state senator by 31 votes. Feingold has a flair for publicity, and for political reform issues and novel arguments. His great goal in the legislature was to ban the use of bovine growth hormones, an attempt to hold down the productivity of dairy cows, who have grown more productive even as Americans drink less milk than they did in the 1950s. Feingold decided to run in 1992 for the Senate seat held by Bob Kasten, a free-market conservative who had won by narrow margins in 1980 and 1986. In the Democratic primary, while Milwaukee businessman Joseph Checota and Congressman Jim Moody battered each other with negative ads, Feingold ran clever, humorous spots: one showing Elvis, alive and endorsing Feingold; another showing Feingold at home, opening up a closet and saying, "No skeletons." He also had detailed position papers, including an 82-point plan for reducing the deficit. Near primary day, Checota apologized for his ads and asked voters to vote for Feingold if they didn't vote for him. Feingold, already ahead in polls, zoomed to an astonishing 70% win in this three-way race. Feingold also bounced way ahead of Kasten, who ran his own Elvis ads attacking Feingold on issues; Feingold attacked Kasten's negativity and avoided engaging on specifics. The race narrowed, but Feingold won 53%–46%.

In the Senate, Feingold has had a liberal record on cultural and foreign issues, somewhat more moderate on economics. He attacked many spending programs and did not respond in lockstep with other Democrats on the Clinton scandals. In February 1997 he called for an independent counsel on the Clinton-Gore fundraising operations. In January 1999 he was the only Democrat to vote against Robert Byrd's motion to dismiss the charges against Clinton. He voted against removal in February.

Feingold has long said that the campaign finance system is "legalized bribery and influence-peddling"; democracy, he once said, "has been almost entirely corrupted in the last few years by soft money." In December 1995 he was surprised when John McCain called and asked if he would work with him against pork barrel spending. Out of this collaboration came the various versions of McCain-Feingold campaign finance bills, which were filibustered to death in July 1996 and in February 1998. The House passed one version in August 1998, but it was filibustered in the Senate in September. In October 1999 McCain-Feingold was again beaten, but McCain and Feingold did push through the bill requiring disclosure by Section 527 committees in June 2000. McCain's presidential campaign and his threats to bring up the issue at every turn forced Trent Lott to schedule two weeks of debate on campaign finance in March 2001. This time McCain and Feingold prevailed. They beat an amendment for lesser changes by Chuck Hagel by 60–40 and beat non-severability by 57–43, important because most senators considered at least some provisions constitutionally dubious. The bill passed 59–41 in April. In July it seemed about to come to the floor of the House, but the Republican leadership's rule was defeated and Speaker Dennis Hastert pulled it off the calendar. Then, after the Enron bankruptcy, pressure mounted. The bill's advocates got 218 signatures on a discharge petition and it was brought to the floor and passed. The Senate passed a final version in March. George W. Bush expressed doubts about the constitutionality of some provisions but signed it anyway, without ceremony and without inviting McCain and Feingold. Behind the scenes not all Democrats were happy; some thought it would hurt their party. The argument switched to the courts. In May 2003 a three-judge federal court, deeply divided, issued 1,700 pages of opinions and upheld some of the provisions but not others. The Supreme Court upheld most sections of the law in December 2003.

The campaign finance act had an impact, though not the expected impact, on the 2004 elections. Democrats, contrary to the expectations of many, were able to raise large sums, much of it over the Internet from voters who loathed Bush. And 527 organizations, not covered by the act, raised hundreds of millions, with most of the money going to anti-Bush efforts; three individuals, George Soros, Peter Lewis and Steve Bing contributed more than $60 million. Feingold and McCain asked the FEC to rule that the act covered 527s; it declined to do so. In September 2004 they called for amendments to cover the 527s; in January 2005 they and their co-sponsors Chris Shays and Marty Meehan in the House sponsored a bill to require 527s to register as political committees and use only hard money for any advertisements that mention federal candidates. It produced some interesting responses: left-leaning organizations like the Sierra Club and the League for Conservation Voters opposed it, other liberal organizations raised the question of whether 501(c) charitable organizations would be covered and Senate Rules Committee Chairman Trent Lott announced he was all for it and would shepherd it through his committee.

Feingold has pursued other ethics issues. He was one of the crusaders against lobbyists' gifts to lawmakers. He sought to prohibit members of Congress from using for personal travel frequent flier miles earned on business trips. He has tried to ban cost-of-living adjustments to congressional pay. He tried to attach repeal of the COLA to various measures and failed until he got a vote on it as an amendment to the homeland security bill in November 2002; it lost 58–36.

To the Patriot Act Feingold tried to offer amendments to limit secret searches, computer surveillance and roving wiretaps. Majority Leader Tom Daschle got them all tabled, and Feingold cast the sole vote against the bill. That is not an unusual posture for him: he voted against the 1996 anti-terrorism bill and he was the only Democrat to vote against Robert Byrd's $15 billion homeland security package in 2001. He was the only Democrat on the Budget Committee to join Republicans and vote for five-year caps on spending in 2002. He fought to apply "paygo" rules to the budget, requiring that all spending increases or tax cuts be compensated for by corresponding spending cuts or tax increases, and succeeded in the Senate in 2003 and 2004; this blocked the passage of a budget resolution, since the Republican House wouldn't accept paygo on taxes. When the *Portland Press Herald* criticized Republican Senator Susan Collins for being soft on paygo, Feingold called the editor and vouched for her support. He sought to block any co-payment on home health care and voted against the Medicare/prescription drug bill in November 2003; he sought to place a floor of $75,000 on homestead exemptions for those 62 and over in the bankruptcy bill.

Feingold has staked out some original positions on the Judiciary Committee. He has called for repeal of all federal death penalty statutes. He was one of eight Democrats who voted to confirm John Ashcroft; he argues that a president should be given great deference in Executive Branch appointments. But he voted against the confirmation of Alberto Gonzales in January 2005. He joined other Judiciary Democrats in opposing several Bush appellate judge appointees and threatening to filibuster them and opposed changing the rules on judicial filibusters.

On foreign policy, he was one of three Democratic senators in March 1999 to vote against air strikes in Serbia and Kosovo and in October 2002 he voted against the Iraq war resolution. He objected when the Bush administration abrogated the ABM Treaty and argued that it could do so only with the advice and consent of two-thirds of the Senate. As chairman of the Africa Subcommittee he traveled to Kenya, Tanzania and Mozambique in February 2002; his visa for Zimbabwe was revoked by the Mugabe government. He opposed the Australian Free Trade Agreement because it allowed some dairy exports into the United States and has opposed the Caribbean Area Free Trade Agreement as well. He and Herb Kohl held up a routine trade bill in October 2004 which provided non-discriminatory treatment of Laos, in protest of Laos's treatment of the Hmong.

Feingold has made it a practice to hold listening sessions in all 72 Wisconsin counties every year, speaking for five minutes and then taking all questions. And he has submitted voluntarily to some of the campaign restrictions he sought to place on all candidates. In 1998 he faced a strong opponent in Congressman Mark Neumann, a conservative elected in 1994. They agreed to limit their campaign spending, Feingold to $3.8 million, Neumann to $4.7 million (he actually spent $4.4 million), and to limit PAC money to 10% of donations and out-of-state contributions to 25% and to impose a $2,000 limit on candidate contributions (more of a handicap for Neumann, a self-made home-builder millionaire, who spent $700,000 of his own money on a losing race in 1992). Feingold's leads of 10% or so melted away by the fall and the race became about even. Neumann ran humorous ads attacking Feingold for sending dollars to Russia to study monkeys in space and for voting for a study of cow flatulence (the ad showed smock-clad scientists out in a field trying to isolate samples of cow gas). In one of the nation's closest Senate races, Feingold won 51%–48%.

In 2001 Feingold talked occasionally about running for president; in the fall he made a campus speaking tour. But he said it was unlikely and that he would decide by his 50th birthday in March 2003. He spent that evening at the Harmony Bar in Madison and, as he put it, "I turned to a couple of friends and family members and said, 'By the way, I'm not running for president in 2004.' They said, 'OK. Fine. Now listen to the band.'" All along he had said it was "extremely likely" that he would run for reelection in 2004. No well-known Republican was interested in running. The three serious candidates in their primary were state Senator Robert Welch, who lost 58%–41% to Herb Kohl in 1994, Milwaukee area car dealer Russ Darrow and businessman Tim Michels, a Waukesha County businessmen who served 12 years as an Army Airborne Ranger. Darrow spent $2.7 million and tried to capitalize on his familiarity from his dealership ads; Welch, banking on support from Republican insiders, spent only about $100,000; Michels campaigned as the most moderate of the candidates and spent $1.4 million. Michels got more for his money: he won the primary with 42% of the votes, to 30% for Darrow and 23% for Welch.

This time Feingold decided not to be outspent as he was in 1998. By August 2004 he had raised $9 million, and he started running his characteristically humorous ads nonstop in June, knowing that Wisconsin would be inundated with presidential advertising in the summer and fall. Michels argued that Feingold had spent too much time on campaign finance and not enough on health care and jobs, and he attacked Feingold for his vote against the Patriot Act. He said he had real life experience while Feingold had been a career politician for 22 years. But Michels did not make much headway, and before mid-October the NRSC cancelled plans to spend $1.2 million on ads against Feingold. Feingold's message that he was an independent vote and a candid voice seemed to have resonance. He won by a solid but not overwhelming 55%–45% margin and his 1,632,000 votes set an all-time Wisconsin record.

After the election Feingold once again showed interest in running for president. In November he went to play golf at the Robert Trent Jones Golf Trail near Greenville, Alabama, in Butler County, the "reddest spot" on the presidential map, he said—not quite, it had voted only 59% for George W. Bush, making it one of his weaker counties in the state. He talked to local voters amid the check cashing stores, trailer parks and "rundown" car lots. He wrote about this in salon.com: "And I can only wonder how many generations of central Alabamians will say 'yes' when the increasingly powerful Republican party asks them to be concerned about homosexuality but not about the security of their own health, about abortion but not about the economic futures of their own children." In January 2005 he told the Tiger Bay Club in Volusia County, Florida, that he would decide whether to run after "going around the country" and that he wanted to be "part of the process" of identifying a candidate; he conceded that Democrats were unlikely to win majorities in the Senate or House in 2006. In March 2005 he was in Alabama again, where he visited with a group of 65 residents in Shelby County (81% for Bush) and told the *Montgomery Advertiser*, "I think the Republicans are intoxicated with power. . . . They're against big government when they're out of power, but now that they're in power, deficits don't matter. Getting into the privacy of people's homes, even when it doesn't involve terrorism, doesn't matter."

FIRST DISTRICT

Rep. Paul Ryan (R)

Elected 1998, 4th term; b. Jan. 29, 1970, Janesville; home, Janesville; Miami U. of OH, B.A., 1992; Catholic; married (Janna).

Professional Career: Aide, U.S. Sen. Bob Kasten, 1992; Advisor & speechwriter, Empower America, 1993–95; Legis. Dir., U.S. Sen. Sam Brownback, 1995–97; Mktg. consultant., Ryan Inc. Central, 1997–98.

DC Office: 1113 LHOB, 20515, 202-225-3031; Fax: 202-225-3393; Web site: www.house.gov/ryan.

District Offices: Janesville, 608-752-4050; Kenosha, 262-654-1901; Racine, 262-637-0510.

Committees: *Budget* (16th of 22 R). *Ways & Means* (18th of 24 R): Social Security. *Joint Economic Committee.*

Group Ratings

	ADA	ACLU	AFS	LCV	ITIC	NTU	COC	ACU	NTLC	CHC
2004	20	6	0	18	90	78	90	92	97	91
2003	20	—	0	10	—	72	93	88	—	—

National Journal Ratings

	2003 LIB	—	2003 CONS		2004 LIB	—	2004 CONS
Economic	21%	—	75%		26%	—	74%
Social	30%	—	70%		20%	—	77%
Foreign	38%	—	60%		45%	—	54%

Key Votes of the 108th Congress

1. Drilling in ANWR	Y	5. DC School Vouchers	Y	9. Ban Same-Sex Marriage	Y
2. Approve Bush Tax Cuts	Y	6. Ban Human Cloning	Y	10. Fund Iraq War	Y
3. Medicare/Rx Bill	Y	7. Restrict Gun Liability	Y	11. Bar Cuba Embargo Funds	Y
4. Bar Overtime Pay Regs.	N	8. Ban Partial-Birth Abortion	*	12. Intelligence Reorg.	Y

Election Results

2004 general	Paul Ryan (R)	233,372	(65%)	($849,365)
	Jeffrey Thomas (D)	116,250	(33%)	($41,246)
	Other	7,354	(2%)	
2004 primary	Paul Ryan (R)	unopposed		
2002 general	Paul Ryan (R)	140,176	(67%)	($962,417)
	Jeffrey Thomas (D)	63,895	(31%)	($206,799)
	Other	4,542	(2%)	

Prior Winning Percentages: 2000 (67%); 1998 (57%)

The People		Race/Ethnic Origin		Ancestry	
Area size:	1,724 sq. mi.	87.4% White		German: 27.0%	Polish: 8.5%
Urban population:	84.4%	4.6% Black		Irish: 8.3%	
Rural population:	15.6%	1.0% Asian		**2004 Presidential Vote**	
Pop. 2000:	670,458	0.3% Native Am.		Bush (R)	197,970 (54%)
Median income:	$50,372	0.0% Hawaiian		Kerry (D)	170,371 (46%)
Poverty status:	6.3%	1.0% Two+ races		Other	1,618 (0%)
Military veterans:	13.2%	0.1% Other		**2000 Presidential Vote**	
		5.7% Hispanic Origin		Bush (R)	163,040 (51%)
				Gore (D)	144,138 (45%)
				Other	11,656 (4%)
				Cook Partisan Voting Index: R + 2	

Occupation	Blue collar: 29.4%	White collar: 57.4%	Gray collar: 13.2%

Rolling dairy country, blanketed by snow during most of the winter, gloriously green under sunny blue skies in summer, the southern tier of Wisconsin from Lake Michigan inland to the Rock River Valley, is some of America's prime industrial country. Settled by Yankee and German farmers 170 years ago, it was once primarily dairyland. By the early 20th century, the steady habits and high skills of the local dairy farmers provided a good labor pool for factories. Today there are still major plants here: the operations center for S. C. Johnson Wax (and its Frank Lloyd Wright-designed tower and Wingspread Center) in Racine, a DaimlerChrysler engine plant in Kenosha and a Chevrolet plant in Janesville. In between are lake resorts, most notably Lake Geneva, a favorite of wealthy Chicagoans; it also is the site of the Yerkes Observatory, one of the nation's largest centers for research in astronomy. Most of this area is becoming metropolitan, part of the almost continuously suburban zone where metro Milwaukee melds into metro Chicago. To the untrained eye, this part of southern Wisconsin looks much the same as nearby northern Illinois; politically, there is a vast difference. The dotted line on the map is the historic boundary between the once corruption-prone machine politics of Illinois and the once squeaky-clean progressive politics of Wisconsin.

This is the land of the 1st Congressional District of Wisconsin, from Lake Michigan west into Rock County. It includes all of Racine and Kenosha Counties on the lake and Walworth County, with Lake Geneva, inland. It includes the southern Milwaukee County suburbs of Oak Creek and Greenfield and the southern tier of townships in suburban Waukesha County. It extends west to Janesville in the middle of Rock County. Politically, it tilts a bit to the Republican side; Waukesha and Walworth Counties are heavily Republican. In this presidential battleground state, the district voted 51% for George W. Bush in 2000 and 54% in 2004.

The congressman from the 1st District is Paul Ryan, a Republican first elected in 1998. He grew up in Janesville, where in 1884 his great-grandfather started a family construction firm now run by his cousins. His father and Democratic Senator Russ Feingold's father had their law offices in the same building. Ryan got started in politics early, as a staffer for Senator Bob Kasten while attending college at Miami of Ohio; then he worked as a speechwriter for Jack Kemp and William Bennett at Empower America and was legislative director to Kansas Senator Sam Brownback. Ryan returned to the 1st District in anticipation of the Senate candidacy of Congressman Mark Neumann, who lost to Feingold in 1998. Ryan won the Republican primary with 81% of the vote. Democrats renominated Kenosha County official Lydia Spottswood, who had lost to Neumann in 1996. Ryan was for local control, against tax increases, in favor of gun ownership rights. This was a strenuously contested election, one of the Democrats' top 10 priorities in the nation. Spottswood spent $1.33 million, Ryan $1.24 million. But the final result was not that close. Ryan won 57%–43%.

In the House, Ryan became a mainstream Republican who was unafraid to occasionally challenge his party and who votes toward the center on foreign policy. He lost on the House floor when he pressed for language to require that any funds cut from appropriations bills be set aside to reduce total spending; appropriators in both parties objected that the provision would tie their hands. But as a leading voice of Republican fiscal conservatives, he continued to press for changes in the handling of the congressional budget to require more spending discipline. On the Ways and Means Committee, he advocated business tax cuts to spur economic growth and has been an ally of the Club for Growth in criticizing George W. Bush's tax cuts as too small. He pushed for increased competition in Medicare plans and was an eager proponent of personal retirement accounts in Social Security. With Senator John Sununu, he sponsored early in 2005 a comprehensive plan to create payroll-tax funded private retirement accounts that would be financed largely through spending cuts and new revenues predicted to result from the accounts. He complained that threatened retribution from Democratic leaders made it difficult for him to secure Democratic supporters: "I have been floating it to Democrats. Each of them replied to me, 'I like what you're doing, I like this bill, I think it's the right way to go, but my party leadership will break my back. The retribution they are promising against us is as great as I've ever seen, and I can't do it.'" Ryan supports tax changes, including a deferral of capital gains taxes on reinvested distributions for mutual fund investors. During the debate on the 1996 welfare act, he shaped legislation creating a "super-achiever" credit for Wisconsin that lowered the requirement for future welfare reduction because the state had already cut its caseload by 76% since 1995. On another issue with local appeal, he enacted in 2004 increased tariffs on imports of bow hunting equipment to assure prices equivalent to those of domestic manufacturers, who had been paying an excise tax.

Ryan has become entrenched with easy reelections in a district held by Democrats from 1970 to 1994. National conservatives have held up his success as an example for Republicans across the nation. Ryan has been mentioned as a candidate for the Senate but he has been unwilling to challenge either of his state's two Democratic incumbents. He has not ruled out the possibility of a statewide race some time in the future.

SECOND DISTRICT

Rep. Tammy Baldwin (D)

Elected 1998, 4th term; b. Feb. 11, 1962, Madison; home, Madison; Smith Col., A.B. 1984; U. of WI Law Schl., J.D. 1989; No religious affiliation; companion (Lauren Azar).

Elected Office: Dane Cnty. Bd. of Supervisors, 1986–94; WI Assembly, 1992–98.

Professional Career: Practicing atty, 1989–92.

DC Office: 1022 LHOB, 20515, 202-225-2906; Fax: 202-225-6942; Web site: www.tammybaldwin.house.gov.

District Offices: Beloit, 608-362-2800; Madison, 608-258-9800.

Committees: *Energy & Commerce* (25th of 26 D): Commerce, Trade & Consumer Protection; Environment & Hazardous Materials; Health; Oversight & Investigations.

Group Ratings

	ADA	ACLU	AFS	LCV	ITIC	NTU	COC	ACU	NTLC	CHC
2004	100	90	100	100	30	12	29	4	0	7
2003	100	—	100	100	—	26	23	8	—	—

National Journal Ratings

	2003 LIB	—	2003 CONS		2004 LIB	—	2004 CONS
Economic	87%	—	9%		87%	—	13%
Social	90%	—	8%		88%	—	0%
Foreign	89%	—	8%		89%	—	10%

Key Votes of the 108th Congress

1. Drilling in ANWR	N	5. DC School Vouchers	N	9. Ban Same-Sex Marriage	N
2. Approve Bush Tax Cuts	N	6. Ban Human Cloning	N	10. Fund Iraq War	N
3. Medicare/Rx Bill	N	7. Restrict Gun Liability	N	11. Bar Cuba Embargo Funds	Y
4. Bar Overtime Pay Regs.	Y	8. Ban Partial-Birth Abortion	N	12. Intelligence Reorg.	N

Election Results

2004 general	Tammy Baldwin (D)	251,637	(63%)	($1,448,889)
	Dave Magnum (R)	145,810	(37%)	($658,153)
2004 primary	Tammy Baldwin (D)	unopposed		
2002 general	Tammy Baldwin (D)	163,313	(66%)	($1,238,876)
	Ron Greer (R)	83,694	(34%)	($171,865)

Prior Winning Percentages: 2000 (51%); 1998 (53%)

The People		Race/Ethnic Origin	Ancestry		
Area size:	3,602 sq. mi.	89.0% White	German: 28.4%　　Irish: 9.4%		
Urban population:	75.6%	3.6% Black	Norwegian: 9.1%		
Rural population:	24.4%	2.4% Asian	**2004 Presidential Vote**		
Pop. 2000:	670,457	0.3% Native Am.	Kerry (D) 250,151	(62%)	
Median income:	$46,979	0.0% Hawaiian	Bush (R) 151,024	(37%)	
Poverty status:	8.7%	1.3% Two+ races	Other 3,303	(1%)	
Military veterans:	11.1%	0.1% Other	**2000 Presidential Vote**		
		3.4% Hispanic Origin	Gore (D) 201,738	(58%)	
			Bush (R) 125,442	(36%)	
			Other 19,398	(6%)	
			Cook Partisan Voting Index: D +13		

Occupation　　Blue collar: 22.3%　　White collar: 63.6%　　Gray collar: 14.1%

On a narrow isthmus between Lakes Mendota and Monona is the center of Madison and, in many ways, the center of Wisconsin. Here the state Capitol rises at one end of State Street; at the other end of several commercial blocks is the main campus of the University of Wisconsin, on a beautiful, parklike, sometimes windswept setting above Lake Mendota. For most of the 20th century, Wisconsin politics was dominated by the Madison-based LaFollettes and their liberal Democratic successors. And the traffic on State Street was two-way, with university faculty devoted to Bob LaFollette's "Wisconsin idea" of an apolitical bureaucracy, his Wisconsin Tax Commission and workmen's compensation law—both firsts in the nation. In recent years there was more division, with the liberal campus at odds with the welfare and school choice law enacted while Republican Tommy Thompson was governor and not entirely happy with the no-tax-increase policy of his Democratic successor Jim Doyle. But there is a steady debate carried on here between the very liberal Madison *Capital Times* and its more conservative rival, the *Wisconsin State Journal*; the two newspapers practice the kind of competitive journalism still seen in only a few major cities and state capitals. This is an urban capital set in the midst of farmland; the Dane County farmers' market is the largest in the nation.

Madison is the center of Wisconsin's 2d Congressional District, which includes surrounding Dane County and dairy and alfalfa country to the north and south, as well as several rural dairy counties that have traditionally been Republican; they include such picturesque scenes as the birthplace of the Ringling Brothers Circus in Baraboo, and the Swiss-settled town of New Glarus. With the largest indoor hydropark in the world, the Wisconsin Dells have become a popular year-round tourist destination. Madison spawned an activist and sometimes violent student movement (during the Vietnam War, a grad student was killed in a laboratory by a bomb set off by a protester) and a permanent postgraduate proletariat. In the 1990s, with double-digit job growth in both the public and private sectors, *Money* magazine rated Madison among the best places to live in America; but the industrial base has declined, including Schwinn Bicycle Company, which once employed thousands here but no longer makes bikes domestically. At the same time, the politics got more fluid: Dane County was open to Republicans like Thompson and to Republican Congressman Scott Klug, first elected in 1990. But in other elections the contrast between Madison's Dane County and the rural counties has faded, as Madison area liberals have moved into the countryside: a map of the 2004 presidential election results shows the rural areas south and west of Madison as a solid Democratic blue. This makes the 2d now a very Democratic district, 62%–37% for John Kerry in 2004.

The congresswoman from the 2d District is Tammy Baldwin, a Democrat elected in 1998. She grew up in Madison, where she was raised by her mother (a University of Wisconsin student when she was born) and her maternal grandparents, a UW biochemist and the theater department's head costume designer. She graduated first in her class at Madison West High School and went on to Smith College and UW law school. In 1986, at 24, while still in law school, she was elected to the Dane County Board of Supervisors. In 1992 she was elected to the Wisconsin Assembly from a heavily Democratic Madison seat.

In 1998, when moderate Republican Scott Klug honored his promise to serve only four terms, this seemed a good chance for Democrats to pick up an open seat. Four Democrats and six

Republicans ran. Baldwin had special advantages. As a woman with great political skills, she was supported by EMILY's List, which helped raised about one-quarter of her $1.5 million. And as a lesbian, she had support from national gay and lesbian organizations, which raised money from a large and affluent national constituency. With 86% of Democratic primary votes cast in Dane County, this was mostly a Madison contest. Baldwin won with 37% of the vote. Republicans nominated former state Insurance Commissioner Jo Musser. The primary results guaranteed that Wisconsin would elect its first woman member to Congress (the states that still have not are an odd bunch: Delaware, Iowa, Mississippi, New Hampshire and Vermont). Baldwin roused the enthusiasm of Madison liberals in a way not seen in years. She called for a single-payer health insurance system and suggested that Musser was dominated by cash from insurance companies; Musser, a nurse who founded the Madison Employers Health Care Alliance, argued that single-payer would reduce choices and create long waiting periods for elective surgery. Both sides were well-financed. Dane County went 57%–42% for Baldwin, and she won the district 53%–47%.

Baldwin thus became the first openly homosexual non-incumbent to win a seat in the House; the two other openly gay members of the House, Barney Frank and Jim Kolbe, revealed their sexual orientation after they had served several terms. Befitting Madison, she has a strongly liberal voting record, though she prefers to be called a progressive. She sponsored the Health Security for All Americans Act to guarantee universal coverage. At the Democratic convention in 2004, she cited four local anecdotes as she spoke from the podium about the urgency of addressing national health care issues. She has been a leader in urging additional federal support for embryonic stem-cell research, some of which has been done at UW. She strongly opposed the bankruptcy bill and twice enacted bills for short-term extension of special bankruptcy protections for farmers. Baldwin said that she did not want to be seen primarily as a lesbian congresswoman, but she was vocal—and visible—in her opposition to the constitutional amendment to bar same-sex marriages, and praised local jurisdictions that encouraged "people who have made lifelong, permanent commitments to one another." She sought to broaden hate crimes to include people targeted because of gender, sexual orientation or disability. Baldwin was an outspoken opponent of the Iraq war resolution; she said Iraq "poses no imminent threat."

In the 2000 campaign Baldwin faced Republican John Sharpless, whose ads in UW newspapers called him "our professor, our Congressman, our voice"; he had students in senior campaign positions. He said that Baldwin had sparse accomplishments, had ignored farmers and raised most of her campaign money out of state. Baldwin ran far behind Al Gore and won by only 51%–49%, a smaller margin than when she was first elected, a reversal of the usual pattern. Since then, she appears to have secured the seat. In 2002, Ron Greer, a black minister and firefighter who was suspended from the force for distributing what many considered anti-gay literature when he ran in the 1998 House Republican primary, complained that Republican officials abandoned him because "they find me too conservative." Baldwin won 66%–34%. In 2004, Portage radio station owner Dave Magnum won the primary over Greer; he spent $650,000 but got little national attention and Baldwin won 63%–37%. In January 2005, she got a seat on the Energy and Commerce Committee and its Health Subcommittee.

THIRD DISTRICT

Rep. Ron Kind (D)

Elected 1996, 5th term; b. Mar. 16, 1963, La Crosse; home, La Crosse; Harvard U., B.A. 1985, London Schl. of Econ., 1986, U. of MN, J.D. 1990; Lutheran; married (Tawni).

Professional Career: Practicing atty., 1990–92; Asst. St. Prosecutor, La Crosse Cnty., 1992–96.

DC Office: 1406 LHOB, 20515, 202-225-5506; Fax: 202-225-5739; Web site: www.house.gov/kind.

District Offices: Eau Claire, 715-831-9214; La Crosse, 608-782-2558.

Committees: *Chief Deputy Minority Whip. Budget* (16th of 17 D). *Education & the Workforce* (11th of 22 D): 21st Century Competitiveness; Education Reform. *Resources* (11th of 22 D): Fisheries & Oceans; National Parks.

Group Ratings

	ADA	ACLU	AFS	LCV	ITIC	NTU	COC	ACU	NTLC	CHC
2004	90	70	100	82	67	13	47	24	9	0
2003	95	—	100	95	—	31	38	16	—	—

National Journal Ratings

	2003 LIB	—	2003 CONS		2004 LIB	—	2004 CONS
Economic	71%	—	27%		66%	—	34%
Social	70%	—	30%		66%	—	33%
Foreign	66%	—	32%		61%	—	39%

Key Votes of the 108th Congress

1. Drilling in ANWR	N	5. DC School Vouchers	N	9. Ban Same-Sex Marriage	N
2. Approve Bush Tax Cuts	N	6. Ban Human Cloning	N	10. Fund Iraq War	Y
3. Medicare/Rx Bill	N	7. Restrict Gun Liability	Y	11. Bar Cuba Embargo Funds	Y
4. Bar Overtime Pay Regs.	Y	8. Ban Partial-Birth Abortion	N	12. Intelligence Reorg.	Y

Election Results

2004 general	Ron Kind (D)	204,856	(56%)	($1,186,471)
	Dale Schultz (R)	157,866	(43%)	($531,538)
2004 primary	Ron Kind (D)	unopposed		
2002 general	Ron Kind (D)	131,038	(63%)	($554,120)
	Bill Arndt (R)	69,955	(34%)	($12,325)
	Other	7,588	(3%)	

Prior Winning Percentages: 2000 (64%); 1998 (71%); 1996 (52%)

The People		Race/Ethnic Origin	Ancestry	
Area size:	13,849 sq. mi.	96.1% White	German: 29.7%	Norwegian: 14.1%
Urban population:	43.1%	0.5% Black	Irish: 8.5%	
Rural population:	56.9%	1.2% Asian	**2004 Presidential Vote**	
Pop. 2000:	670,462	0.5% Native Am.	Kerry (D) 192,297	(51%)
Median income:	$40,006	0.0% Hawaiian	Bush (R) 178,367	(48%)
Poverty status:	9.8%	0.7% Two+ races	Other 3,656	(1%)
Military veterans:	12.9%	0.0% Other	**2000 Presidential Vote**	
		0.9% Hispanic Origin	Gore (D) 155,832	(49%)
			Bush (R) 144,948	(46%)
			Other 16,626	(5%)
			Cook Partisan Voting Index: D + 3	

Occupation	Blue collar: 29.2%	White collar: 53.3%	Gray collar: 17.5%

On the rolling land of western Wisconsin, in the knobby hills just east of the Mississippi River, is some of the most beautiful river landscape in the country. This is where Laura Ingalls Wilder's family built the "little house in the big woods" in the 1870s, before the first railroad came steaming up the narrow floodplain alongside the Mississippi River. Today, it is hard to imagine the big woods: The trees have long since been cut and the hillsides are covered with grass grazed by placid dairy cattle. Where pioneers tried to scratch out diversified crops, farmers soon created America's premier dairy region, producing milk, butter and especially cheese. Some Amish communities from Pennsylvania have relocated here in recent years because land is less than half the price and there has been less modernity. But more than half of family dairy farmers have gone out of business since 1980. Cows are more productive, while demand for milk has decreased. And Wisconsin has trouble competing against the European Common Market's hugely subsidized cheese and butter. But other businesses have risen. Dodgeville in Iowa County (which is not on the Iowa border) is the headquarters of Lands' End, the catalog retailer. In the 1980s many communities here lost population, but since 1990 there has been growth, with very rapid growth in St. Croix County, which is part of the Minneapolis-St. Paul metro area.

The 3d Congressional District of Wisconsin follows the Mississippi and St. Croix River counties from the southern border of the state to St. Croix County, just east of St. Paul, and extends east two or three counties. This is the nation's number two dairy district, with 6,000 dairy farms, but it is very different in character than the number one district (California's 21st District), which has more milk cows concentrated on just 400 farms. It was settled largely by German and Scandinavian immigrants (Laura's Yankee family moved away as Swedes were moving into the area), and it once voted for LaFollette Progressives. More recently, it has been closely divided between Democrats and Republicans. Western Wisconsin was the one segment of rural America where Al Gore and John Kerry ran even with historic Democratic percentages, which was vital to the narrow victory that each won in this state; Gore carried the district 49%–46% and Kerry 51%–48%. It produced solid margins for other Democrats, Governor Jim Doyle in 2002 and Senator Russ Feingold in 2004. Cuba City, not far from the corner with Illinois and Iowa, calls itself the City of Presidents and features a separate shield for each president; a week before the 2004 election, George W. Bush was the first incumbent president who actually stopped in the tiny town.

The congressman from the 3d District is Ron Kind, a Democrat first elected in 1996. He grew up in a large family in La Crosse, the son of a telephone repairman and a secretary. He went to Harvard on scholarship and played quarterback, and worked as a summer intern for Senator William Proxmire, doing research for his Golden Fleece awards. He attended the London School of Economics and University of Minnesota law school, practiced law in a big firm in Milwaukee, then returned home to La Crosse to work as an assistant prosecutor on rape and sexual abuse cases. Kind started running for Congress soon after Republican Steve Gunderson announced during the 1994 campaign that he would not run again in 1996. Republican former state Senator Jim Harsdorf won the Republican primary after Gunderson rejected pleas to run again even though he was in line to become Agriculture Committee chairman. Harsdorf took hard-edged stands for the balanced budget and Governor Tommy Thompson's "Wisconsin Works" welfare program. Kind talked instead of campaign finance regulation and presented his own balanced budget proposal. Gunderson was neutral in the contest; he didn't agree with Harsdorf's views on civil and human rights and thought him too close to the Christian Coalition. Kind won 52%–48%.

In the House, Kind has compiled a moderate voting record. Like other Wisconsin members, he worked to reform the Federal Milk Marketing Order System, instituted in 1937; it pays higher prices the farther the farmer is from Eau Claire, which is in the northern part of the district, which means that 3d District dairy farmers get the lowest prices in the nation. In 2001, he sponsored the bipartisan amendment on the farm bill to shift $19 billion of commodity support dollars to environmental conservation of idle land. That was defeated 226–200. His Healthy Kids Bill would set aside $10 million for school districts to buy locally grown produce. In September 2004, he charged that the Bush administration was planning to impose a tax on dairy producers or cut price supports after the election; Agriculture officials issued denials.

Kind is a co-founder of the Upper Mississippi River Congressional Task Force. His own home is on the river and was flooded in 2001. With members from Illinois and Iowa, he got the House to pass a bill to establish a water quality monitoring network in the Upper Mississippi

River Basin. As co-chairman of the New Democrat Coalition, he said that he wanted to expand access to broadband in rural areas and to make his area "the Silicon Valley of agricultural research." After he voted for the use of force in Iraq, he was criticized by liberals back home; in October 2003, he offered an amendment to cut in half U.S. funding for reconstruction in Iraq and call for more contributions from other nations, but it was defeated 156–267. He sponsored a Library of Congress project for World War II veterans to record their oral histories and deliver personal memorabilia to the Smithsonian Institution.

Kind has been reelected easily since his first victory in 1996. Local union organizers have complained that he has not been sufficiently supportive on trade issues, but they have not put up a primary challenger. In 2004, he had a credible challenge from state senator Dale Schultz, a moderate in the legislature for more than two decades. Schultz ran on the unlikely Republican theme of criticizing Kind as a free trader who had been sending jobs overseas. Kind affirmed his support for trade agreements, but criticized the Bush administration for its failure to enforce their terms. Schultz backed Bush's handling of the war on terror and he promised to do more for agriculture, while Kind emphasized more support for education. Kind won, 56%–43%. He was considered a frontrunner for a seat on Ways and Means, but lost out in January 2005 to Rahm Emanuel of Illinois, who had leverage as the new chairman of the Democratic Congressional Campaign Committee.

FOURTH DISTRICT

Rep. Gwen Moore (D)

Elected 2004, 1st term; b. April 18, 1951, Racine; home, Milwaukee; Marquette U., B.A. 1978; Baptist; single.

Elected Office: WI Assembly, 1989–92; WI Senate, 1992–2004; Senate pres. pro tempore, 1997–98.

Professional Career: Housing and urban dev. specialist, 1985–89.

DC Office: 1408 LHOB, 20515, 202-225-4572; Fax: 202-225-8135; Web site: www.house.gov/gwenmoore.

District Office: Milwaukee, 414-297-1140.

Committees: *Financial Services* (32d of 32 D): Domestic and International Monetary Policy, Trade & Technology; Financial Institutions & Consumer Credit; Oversight & Investigations. *Small Business* (15th of 15 D).

Group Ratings and Key Votes: Newly Elected

Election Results

2004 general	Gwen Moore (D)	212,382	(70%)	($933,653)
	Gerald Boyle (R)	85,928	(28%)	($81,298)
	Other	6,832	(2%)	
2004 primary	Gwen Moore (D)	48,858	(64%)	
	Matt Flynn (D)	19,377	(25%)	
	Tim Carpenter (D)	7,801	(10%)	
2002 general	Jerry Kleczka (D)	122,031	(87%)	($478,091)
	Brian Verdin (Green)	18,324	(13%)	($1,593)

The People		Race/Ethnic Origin	Ancestry	
Area size:	113 sq. mi.	50.4% White	German: 18.3% Polish: 8.9%	
Urban population:	100.0%	33.0% Black	Irish: 5.4%	
Rural population:	0.0%	2.7% Asian	**2004 Presidential Vote**	
Pop. 2000:	670,458	0.7% Native Am.	Kerry (D) 219,636	(70%)
Median income:	$33,121	0.0% Hawaiian	Bush (R) 94,090	(30%)
Poverty status:	19.8%	1.8% Two+ races	**2000 Presidential Vote**	
Military veterans:	11.1%	0.2% Other	Gore (D) 183,810	(66%)
		11.2% Hispanic Origin	Bush (R) 84,823	(30%)
			Other 11,814	(4%)
			Cook Partisan Voting Index: D +20	

Occupation	Blue collar: 27.8%	White collar: 54.0%	Gray collar: 18.2%

Milwaukee is America's most German city, with an ethnic heritage noticeable not just in the names of its beers and its old German restaurants but in the solidness of its houses and the orderliness of its streets. Until World War I made this German character seem un-American, German was spoken on the streets and read in newspapers, German beer was produced in dozens of breweries and German cultural traditions breathed in churches, union halls and parlors. There was a German-type politics, with a Socialist mayor and an efficient, honest city government. The world's largest four-sided clock faces outward from all sides of the tower on the Allen-Bradley factory, looking out over the industrial city. It is an apt symbol, a piece of precision engineering, in this high-skill manufacturing town, with its skyline of smokestacks and church steeples, the closest thing in America to the factory cities of the Germany whence so many Milwaukeeans' ancestors came. Milwaukee has led the nation in industrial control equipment, mining gear, cranes and independent foundries. The work force, with German, Polish and Mitteleuropean work habits, is highly skilled and hard-working. Harley-Davidson began manufacturing on the West Side a century ago. Though some neighborhoods here are beset by crime and drug use, most of Milwaukee is solid and upstanding, and some of it—Brewers Hill near the old Schlitz brewery—is gentrifying. There is an Oktoberfest (as well as an Irish Fest, a huge musical Summerfest, etc.), and there are large and efficiently run factories that pay high wages to highly-skilled and well-disciplined workers. Residential development along the Milwaukee River recently has brought more people downtown, and there are plans to convert the 26 buildings of the long-vacant Pabst Brewery complex into an entertainment and residential mecca.

The 4th Congressional District of Wisconsin now covers the entire city of Milwaukee and a few of its suburbs. The 2002 redistricting eliminated the old 5th District in the northern half of Milwaukee, which had suffered significant population loss and moved its black and white neighborhoods to the 4th. Removed from the 4th were almost all of its suburbs in Waukesha and Milwaukee Counties; the only remaining suburbs are working class—St. Francis, Cudahy and South Milwaukee on Lake Michigan and West Milwaukee and part of West Allis west of the Allen-Bradley tower. This lowered the Bush 2000 percentage in the 4th District from 50% in 2000 to 30% in 2004, the biggest partisan shift of any district in the nation in the 2001–02 redistricting cycle. Both parties agreed on this change. For Republicans it was an easy call: the state was losing one seat and the Democrats would lose it. For Democrats it was an easy call as well: 5th District Democrat Tom Barrett was running for governor, and expanding the 5th would have made the 4th District more Republican.

The congresswoman from the 4th District is Gwen Moore, a Democrat elected in 2004. Moore was born in Racine, the eighth of nine children, and raised on the north side of Milwaukee. As an 18-year-old college freshman, she became a single mother who was forced to rely on welfare to help support her daughter. She graduated from Marquette University and worked as a housing and urban development specialist. She was elected to the state House in 1988 and to the state Senate in 1992, where she was the first black woman to serve.

In 2003, when old-style neighborhood 4th District Democrat Gerald Kleczka announced that he was retiring after 20 years in the House, Moore became the early frontrunner. But she had serious competition in the September 2004 Democratic primary. Moore faced two political veterans, state Senator Tim Carpenter and former state party chairman Matt Flynn, both white. The candidates agreed on most issues: all three supported abortion rights, focused on jobs and economic concerns, and called for eliminating the Bush administration's tax cuts for those making more than $200,000 a year. In the absence of significant ideological clashes, the fallout from Milwaukee's mayoral primary earlier in 2004 played a key role. The nonpartisan election in April featured former Congressman Tom Barrett, who is white, and acting Mayor Marvin Pratt, who sought to become the city's first black elected mayor. Barrett narrowly emerged as the winner in a vote that divided along racial lines and caused hard feelings in the black community. In the House race Moore took advantage of the energized black voter base, and she leveraged her financial support from national women's, teachers and other liberal groups. Flynn had chaired John Kerry's campaign in Wisconsin, was endorsed by Kleczka and boasted that he had backed Pratt for mayor; but he was damaged by his work as general counsel for the local Roman Catholic archdiocese in the sex abuse scandal. Carpenter was the only openly gay member of the Senate and had the support of national gay-rights groups. Moore won 64% of the vote to 25% for Flynn and 10% for Carpenter. Flynn won the five aldermanic districts and 49% of the vote on the south side, but Moore won about 80% of the vote north of I-94. She was helped by the efforts of America Coming Together, a 527 anti-Bush organization that used the September primary as a rehearsal of its November get-out-the-vote operation in black precincts. Although ACT did not endorse a candidate, Moore was the obvious beneficiary of its efforts.

In the general election Republican Gerald Boyle tried to win over Democrats disaffected with Moore. But he got no national money and Moore won, 70%–28%. In the House, she got seats on the Financial Services and Small Business committees. But the luster from Moore's victory was diminished when her 25-year-old son was one of five Kerry campaign employees charged in January 2005 with slashing the tires of more than 20 vans rented by Republicans to drive voters and monitors to the polls on Election Day; the vehicles were in a parking lot next to the Bush campaign office and the incident took place a few hours before voting started. Each of the five was charged with one felony count of criminal damage to property; in March, the judge scheduled the trial for July 2005.

FIFTH DISTRICT

Rep. Jim Sensenbrenner (R)

Elected 1978, 14th term; b. June 14, 1943, Chicago, IL; home, Menomonee Falls; Stanford U., A.B. 1965, U. of WI, J.D. 1968; Episcopalian; married (Cheryl).

Elected Office: WI Assembly, 1968–74; WI Senate, 1974–78.

Professional Career: Practicing atty., 1968–69; Staff asst., U.S. Rep. Arthur Younger, 1965.

DC Office: 2449 RHOB, 20515, 202-225-5101; Fax: 202-225-3190; Web site: www.house.gov/sensenbrenner.

District Office: Brookfield, 262-784-1111.

Committees: *Judiciary* (Chmn. of 23 R).

Group Ratings

	ADA	ACLU	AFS	LCV	ITIC	NTU	COC	ACU	NTLC	CHC
2004	20	0	13	18	60	83	86	92	95	76
2003	25	—	0	30	—	79	80	84	—	—

National Journal Ratings

	2003 LIB	—	2003 CONS		2004 LIB	—	2004 CONS
Economic	49%	—	51%		35%	—	64%
Social	24%	—	71%		17%	—	81%
Foreign	49%	—	51%		42%	—	57%

Key Votes of the 108th Congress

1. Drilling in ANWR	Y	5. DC School Vouchers	Y	9. Ban Same-Sex Marriage	Y
2. Approve Bush Tax Cuts	Y	6. Ban Human Cloning	Y	10. Fund Iraq War	Y
3. Medicare/Rx Bill	Y	7. Restrict Gun Liability	Y	11. Bar Cuba Embargo Funds	N
4. Bar Overtime Pay Regs.	N	8. Ban Partial-Birth Abortion	Y	12. Intelligence Reorg.	Y

Election Results

2004 general	Jim Sensenbrenner (R)	271,153	(67%)	($655,901)
	Bryan Kennedy (D)	129,384	(32%)	($267,814)
	Other	6,754	(2%)	
2004 primary	Jim Sensenbrenner (R)	unopposed		
2002 general	Jim Sensenbrenner (R)	191,224	(87%)	($493,305)
	Robert Raymond (I)	29,567	(13%)	

Prior Winning Percentages: 2000 (74%); 1998 (91%); 1996 (74%); 1994 (100%); 1992 (70%); 1990 (100%); 1988 (75%); 1986 (78%); 1984 (73%); 1982 (100%); 1980 (78%); 1978 (61%)

The People		Race/Ethnic Origin	Ancestry	
Area size:	1,301 sq. mi.	94.0% White	German: 34.6%	Irish: 8.8%
Urban population:	84.9%	1.3% Black	Polish: 7.7%	
Rural population:	15.1%	1.5% Asian	**2004 Presidential Vote**	
Pop. 2000:	670,458	0.2% Native Am.	Bush (R) 265,537	(63%)
Median income:	$58,594	0.0% Hawaiian	Kerry (D) 151,968	(36%)
Poverty status:	3.4%	0.7% Two+ races	Other 1,006	(0%)
Military veterans:	12.4%	0.1% Other	**2000 Presidential Vote**	
		2.2% Hispanic Origin	Bush (R) 233,005	(62%)
			Gore (D) 132,310	(35%)
			Other 13,080	(3%)
			Cook Partisan Voting Index: R +12	
Occupation	Blue collar: 21.3%	White collar: 68.2%	Gray collar: 10.5%	

For decades, the orderly, heavily German-American factory city of Milwaukee has been spreading slowly, mostly west and north, into Wisconsin dairy country. There are high-income enclaves here, like close-in Elm Grove and Oconomowoc spread out to the west around its lakes. There is office development in Brookfield; subdivisions spread out in Mequon and Menomonee Falls and farther, to reach small towns with roots deep in the 19th century. This is comfortable but not fancy territory, and the economy here is still based heavily on skilled manufacturing. Not far from Milwaukee are Port Washington, with Allen-Edmonds shoes; West Bend, with West Bend kitchen appliances; Pewaukee, with Quad/Graphics printing. In Ozaukee County is the tiny town of Waubeka where a schoolteacher in 1885 proclaimed America's first Flag Day. Closer to Milwaukee are its tonier suburbs along Lake Michigan—Shorewood, Whitefish Bay, and Fox Point—where wealthy neighborhoods are just a few miles from the poorest neighborhoods in the state on the other side of I-43.

The 5th Congressional District of Wisconsin, numbered the 9th before 2002 redistricting, includes most of the western, northwestern and northern suburbs of Milwaukee. It includes the close-in lakefront suburbs in Milwaukee County, Ozaukee County north of Milwaukee and Washington County to the west. It includes most of the Milwaukee County suburbs of Wauwatosa and West Allis and most of the northern three tiers of townships in Waukesha County just to the west. It also includes a part of Jefferson County further west. This is by far the most Republican district in the state; it voted 62% for George W. Bush in 2000 and 63% in 2004.

The congressman from the 5th District is Jim Sensenbrenner, a Republican first elected in 1978. Sensenbrenner grew up in the Milwaukee area, with strong Wisconsin roots; his great-grandfather was a founder of Kimberly-Clark. He graduated from Stanford and the University of

Wisconsin law school, and has spent most of his adult life in politics. He served briefly as a staffer in the House, then was elected to the Wisconsin Assembly in 1968 and the Wisconsin Senate in 1974. When incumbent Bob Kasten ran for governor in 1978, Sensenbrenner ran in this district and won the Republican primary by 589 votes. Of such narrow victories are long congressional careers made. He reports a net worth of $7.8 million, and *Roll Call* ranks him the 32d richest member of Congress; but that may be misleading, since Sensenbrenner lists his investments in detail and calculates his net worth with precision, while most wealthy members value their assets within broad categories. In December 1997 he won $250,000 in the District of Columbia lottery after buying two tickets while picking up some beer for an office party at a Capitol Hill liquor store.

Sensenbrenner has long been a stickler for ethics, and was one of the first to urge that Congress apply to itself the laws it imposes on the rest of the country. In the Clinton impeachment, he was one of the 13 House managers and was chosen by Hyde to start the managers' presentation to the Senate. From 1997 to 2001 Sensenbrenner was chairman of the Science Committee. He supported the space station and most manned space flight, but was persistently critical of the U.S.-Russia space agreement, particularly the condition of the Russian Mir spacecraft.

Sensenbrenner spent much of his long political career in the minority, but has been in the majority for more than a decade now and in January 2001 became chairman of the House Judiciary Committee. He immediately moved to rein in the number of hearings by subcommittee chairmen and he sought to protect the committee's jurisdiction from raids by other House committees, notably Energy and Commerce. He was proud of enacting the first congressional authorization of the Department of Justice in many years, citing the vital role that it gave his committee in improving oversight of the department. "I am a hawk on oversight," he said. "I don't back down because the president is in my party." After September 11, he pressed for a thorough congressional review of Attorney General John Ashcroft's call for additional law enforcement investigative powers. Concerned about possible violations of civil liberties, he insisted on a sunset provision under which the Patriot Act would expire in four years and objected in 2003 to extension of the sunset; in 2004 he said the law should be reexamined provision by provision in 2005. He passed a bill to split the Immigration and Naturalization Service into two different agencies; when they were placed in the new Homeland Security Department, Sensenbrenner expressed concern that longstanding internal problems would remain unresolved.

On some legislation he has worked for many years. He supported the bankruptcy bill passed by the House in 2002, but was frustrated when abortion opponents voted it down in November 2002 because of a provision inserted by Senator Charles Schumer, making non-dischargeable in bankruptcy fines and damages for violence or protest against abortion providers. In 2005, after Schumer's provision was rejected in the Senate, the bill passed. He has supported bills changing tort law on class actions, medical malpractice, asbestos cases and penalties for frivolous lawsuits. But he has not always followed the party line. In August 2003 he said he saw no need to amend the Constitution to ban same-sex marriages. Even after the Massachusetts Supreme Judicial Court ruled that such marriages were mandated by the state's constitution, he did not move forward on such an amendment; instead, the Republican leadership bypassed the committee and brought it to the floor in September 2004 where the vote was 227–186 in favor, well short of the required two-thirds. He opposed a bill, passed by a wide margin in committee, to allow law enforcement officers to carry concealed weapons in any state as a violation of federalism. He did bring forward a bill withdrawing federal courts' jurisdiction over cases challenging the constitutionality of the Pledge of Allegiance.

Sensenbrenner has taken the lead on some controversial matters. In March 2004 at the U.S. Judicial Conference he argued that federal courts have had a "decidedly mixed record" on internal discipline and have disregarded Congress's sentencing rules. He said the House "will begin assessing whether the disciplinary authority delegated to the judiciary has been responsibly exercised and ought to continue." He hailed the appointment in May by Chief Justice William Rehnquist of a commission headed by Justice Stephen Breyer to investigate the issue. He has resisted calls for a constitutional amendment permitting in case of a catastrophic attack the filling of House vacancies caused by death or incapacity by appointment. Instead he led the House in passing a bill requiring elections within 45 and, after states interposed objections, 49 days to fill vacancies. On the intelligence reorganization bill in 2004 he inserted immigration provisions setting national standards for driver's licenses (including denying them to illegal immigrants), prohibiting the use of Mexican *matricula consular* cards for identification, tightening standards for asylum and overriding state laws and regulations blocking border barriers. In November 2004 he joined Armed Services Chairman Duncan Hunter, who objected to the Senate version's chain of command provisions, in opposing the conference report, and Speaker Dennis Hastert pulled the bill from the floor. In December Hunter's objections were met and the bill went forward; Hastert promised that Sensenbrenner's immigration provisions would come to the floor in 2005 and be attached to the first must pass legislation. When the new Congress met, Sensenbrenner insisted on setting aside for later consideration the Bush administration's proposal for a guest worker system and the bill sponsored by David Dreier and Silvestre Reyes raising penalties on employers for hiring illegal immigrants, and the Sensenbrenner immigration provision were approved 261–161 in February.

Sensenbrenner has not had a serious electoral challenge since the 1978 primary. He reaches the end of House Republicans' six-year term limit on committee chairmen in January 2007.

SIXTH DISTRICT

Rep. Tom Petri (R)

Elected April 1979, 13th full term; b. May 28, 1940, Marinette; home, Fond du Lac; Harvard U., B.A. 1962, J.D. 1965; Lutheran; married (Anne).

Elected Office: WI Senate, 1972–79.

Professional Career: Peace Corps, Somalia, 1966–67; Law Clerk, Fed. Judge James Doyle, 1965–66; White House aide, 1969; Practicing atty., 1970–79.

DC Office: 2462 RHOB, 20515, 202-225-2476; Fax: 202-225-2356; Web site: www.house.gov/petri.

District Offices: Fond du Lac, 920-922-1180; Oshkosh, 920-231-6333.

Committees: *Education & the Workforce* (Vice Chmn. of 27 R): 21st Century Competitiveness. *Transportation & Infrastructure* (Vice Chmn. of 41 R): Aviation; Highways, Transit & Pipelines (Chmn.); Railroads.

Group Ratings

	ADA	ACLU	AFS	LCV	ITIC	NTU	COC	ACU	NTLC	CHC
2004	20	15	0	18	90	60	95	80	86	92
2003	20	—	0	50	—	70	77	84	—	—

National Journal Ratings

	2003 LIB	—	2003 CONS	2004 LIB	—	2004 CONS
Economic	49%	—	51%	42%	—	58%
Social	30%	—	65%	39%	—	60%
Foreign	50%	—	49%	43%	—	57%

Key Votes of the 108th Congress

1. Drilling in ANWR	N	5. DC School Vouchers	Y	9. Ban Same-Sex Marriage	Y
2. Approve Bush Tax Cuts	Y	6. Ban Human Cloning	Y	10. Fund Iraq War	Y
3. Medicare/Rx Bill	Y	7. Restrict Gun Liability	Y	11. Bar Cuba Embargo Funds	N
4. Bar Overtime Pay Regs.	N	8. Ban Partial-Birth Abortion	Y	12. Intelligence Reorg.	Y

Election Results

2004 general	Tom Petri (R)	238,620	(67%)	($478,540)
	Jef Hall (D)	107,209	(30%)	($4,333)
	Other	10,166	(3%)	
2004 primary	Tom Petri (R)	unopposed		
2002 general	Tom Petri (R)	unopposed		($344,870)

Prior Winning Percentages: 2000 (65%); 1998 (93%); 1996 (73%); 1994 (100%); 1992 (53%); 1990 (100%); 1988 (74%); 1986 (97%); 1984 (76%); 1982 (65%); 1980 (59%); 1979 (50%)

The People		Race/Ethnic Origin	Ancestry	
Area size:	5,816 sq. mi.	94.1% White	German: 38.8% Irish: 6.8%	
Urban population:	60.7%	1.0% Black	Polish: 5.4%	
Rural population:	39.3%	1.5% Asian	**2004 Presidential Vote**	
Pop. 2000:	670,440	0.4% Native Am.	Bush (R) 208,931	(56%)
Median income:	$44,242	0.0% Hawaiian	Kerry (D) 157,212	(43%)
Poverty status:	6.1%	0.7% Two+ races	Other 3,747	(1%)
Military veterans:	13.7%	0.0% Other	**2000 Presidential Vote**	
		2.3% Hispanic Origin	Bush (R) 170,134	(53%)
			Gore (D) 134,926	(42%)
			Other 13,499	(4%)
			Cook Partisan Voting Index: R + 5	

Occupation	Blue collar: 35.4%	White collar: 49.1%	Gray collar: 15.5%

Central Wisconsin is solid country, a producer of basic commodities—milk, butter and cheese, paper products, Mirro pots and pans, Mercury outboard motors, Oshkosh overalls and Kleenex. Settled first by Yankee Protestants, it was one of the birthplaces of the Republican Party in February 1854, when a group of Whigs, Free Soilers and Democrats met in a small white schoolhouse in Ripon, Wisconsin, and proclaimed themselves Republicans; Jackson, Michigan, also claims to be the birthplace of the party. Whichever, the party grew rapidly, winning a near-majority in the House in the 1854 elections. But Republican roots here are not just Yankee. The 1850s brought the first surge of German migration into the United States, and central Wisconsin was a favorite destination. Here they built the dairy farms and factory towns that seemed steadfastly prosperous 50 years ago, and developed a manufacturing economy that boomed in the 1990s. The German influence is still felt: Sheboygan, on Lake Michigan, is the Bratwurst Capital of the World, but it's also the home these days of 2,800 Hmong and 3,000 Hispanics. Here also was the testing ground, in Fond du Lac County, of Governor Tommy Thompson's W-2 welfare program; the welfare rolls there, never high, fell to zero after the program began in 1997.

The 6th Congressional District is a slice of central Wisconsin from Lake Michigan to the Wisconsin River. It has the highest percentage of residents of German ancestry (39%) in the nation and includes Sheboygan and Manitowoc on Lake Michigan, Oshkosh and Fond du Lac on Lake Winnebago in the Fox River Valley, and the towns of Menasha and Kimberly, just outside Appleton. It also includes most of five rural counties to the west and south. Politically, this has been mostly Republican territory since that first meeting in Ripon and remains so today, and it has elected Republican congressmen who have come up with thoughtful and original solutions to problems. One was William Steiger, first elected in 1966, who put on his staff a University of Wisconsin graduate student named Dick Cheney; Steiger's chief monuments are the all-volunteer military and the 1978 Steiger amendment cutting capital gains tax rates—considerable accomplishments for a member of the minority party, and for one who died at age 40 in 1978.

The congressman from the 6th District is Tom Petri, a Republican first elected in the 1979 contest to succeed Steiger. Petri grew up in Fond du Lac, graduated from Harvard, was a Peace Corps volunteer in Somalia and was elected to the state Senate in 1972, at 32. In 1974 he was the Republican nominee against Senator Gaylord Nelson; he walked across the state campaigning but in that Democratic year lost 62%–36%. When he ran for the House, Petri beat Tommy Thompson, then a state legislator, in the primary 35%–19% and then won the special with 50.4%.

Some of Petri's ideas have been adopted. He long boosted the Earned Income Tax Credit, which results in payments to low-income people who work, targeting aid to families much better than the minimum wage; the Clinton administration agreed and increased the EITC when Democrats were in control. Petri called for expanding the EITC concept with a $1,000 tax credit per child, in place of the current deduction; Congress and Bill Clinton agreed on a $500 per child credit, leaving the deduction in place. In 2003 he called for a commission to examine what he called the poverty trap—as low income people increase their earnings, they lose eligibility for the

EITC and other federal benefits and are in effect taxed at rates up to 100%. In 2004 he called for a $500 grant to all newborn children, to be held in an investment account and usable after age 18 for education or a first home.

Petri hoped to become chairman of the Education and the Workforce Committee after the 2000 elections. He was the most senior Republican on the committee, but the Republican Steering Committee passed over him and installed the fourth most senior Republican, John Boehner. Petri's office put out a statement saying this was part of a "purge of moderate Republicans," and Petri's voting record has been more liberal than it was before 2000. He was one of 13 Republicans to vote against repeal of the Clinton ergonomics rule in March 2001 and one of four Republicans to vote against the resolution backing Israel in May 2002. He voted with Democrats to urge budget negotiators to accept the Senate's "paygo" rules for tax cuts in the budget resolution in March 2004; the vote failed 209–209. He backed the Shays-Meehan campaign finance bill for some time and in July 2001 he was one of 19 Republicans to vote against the rule for debate on the bill; the rule failed, one of only two that did in the 107th Congress. He was urged by Shays-Meehan backers to sign the discharge petition to bring the bill to the floor, but hung back for several months. Then in January 2002, after the Enron bankruptcy, he was one of two Republicans who signed to provide the decisive 218th vote and brought the issue to the floor. He sponsored in 2004 a bill to prohibit video or audio monitoring of employees while changing clothing. With George Miller, he sponsored in March 2005 a $1,000 increase in Pell grants, to $5,050, which they said could be financed by savings from the expansion of the federal direct student loan program. He has worked with Senator Christopher Dodd to establish a national standard for electronic copies of textbooks so that they can easily be translated into Braille.

Since 1995 Petri has been chairman of the often renamed Highways, Transit and Pipelines Subcommittee, the key subcommittee of the largest congressional committee, Transportation and Infrastructure; after losing the Education chairmanship he has gotten waivers from the three-term limit on subcommittee chairmanships. He played a major role in shaping the 1998 TEA-21 transportation bill. The business before the subcommittee in the 108th Congress and in the 109th has been the reauthorization of TEA-21. Petri argued from the beginning for increases in transportation spending. In subcommittee and full committee, he pushed for a $375 billion bill, funded by a 5-cent gas tax increase; he also pressed for ending the 5.2 cent lower tax on ethanol, which was done away with in the corporate tax bill passed in October 2004. One reason for the high spending was the need to propitiate both donor states—those who get back less than 100% of their gas tax revenues and whose members insisted on getting 95 cent—and donee states, whose members wanted to avoid any cuts. Another reason was the need to fund hugely expensive special projects—Chicago rail consolidation, I-69, the Port to Plains highway. But the Bush administration threatened to veto any tax increase, and the House eventually passed a $283 billion bill. In fall 2004 the administration insisted it would accept no bill spending more than $256 billion, while the House bill stood at $283 billion and the Senate bill at $318 billion. Petri argues that the need is even greater. "Research has shown that every dollar of highway capital has a rate of return of 30 cents per year and highway capital investment has been responsible for 25% of our nation's gains in economic productivity. . . . While much attention has been placed on what level of transportation we can 'afford,' the real question is: How we can afford not to invest?"

Transportation is very much a bipartisan committee, and members look after their districts. In the 2004 bill Petri put in $199 million in earmarks for Wisconsin, $90 million of which were in the 6th District. They included widening Route 23 to four lanes between Plymouth and Fond du Lac and widening the highway between Oshkosh and Neenah to six lanes. He worked to prevent a $14.5 million loan guarantee to a company seeking to set up ferry service across Lake Michigan from Milwaukee to Muskegon, Michigan; it would compete with the existing unsubsidized line from Manitowoc to Ludington, Michigan.

Petri has been reelected easily, by a 67%–30% margin in 2004.

SEVENTH DISTRICT

Rep. David Obey (D)

Elected April 1969, 18th full term; b. Oct. 3, 1938, Okmulgee, OK; home, Wausau; U. of WI, B.S. 1960, M.A., 1962; Catholic; married (Joan).

Elected Office: WI Assembly, 1962–69.

Professional Career: Asst., family-run supper club & motel, 1962–68.

DC Office: 2314 RHOB, 20515, 202-225-3365; Web site: www.obey.house.gov.

District Offices: Superior, 715-398-4426; Wausau, 715-842-5606.

Committees: *Appropriations* (RMM of 29 D): Labor, Health and Human Services, Education & Related Agencies (RMM).

Group Ratings

	ADA	ACLU	AFS	LCV	ITIC	NTU	COC	ACU	NTLC	CHC
2004	90	74	100	100	0	15	25	4	6	27
2003	100	—	100	95	—	28	13	20	—	—

National Journal Ratings

	2003 LIB	—	2003 CONS		2004 LIB	—	2004 CONS
Economic	74%	—	25%		77%	—	22%
Social	74%	—	25%		72%	—	28%
Foreign	84%	—	16%		89%	—	10%

Key Votes of the 108th Congress

1. Drilling in ANWR	N	5. DC School Vouchers	N	9. Ban Same-Sex Marriage	N
2. Approve Bush Tax Cuts	N	6. Ban Human Cloning	N	10. Fund Iraq War	N
3. Medicare/Rx Bill	N	7. Restrict Gun Liability	Y	11. Bar Cuba Embargo Funds	Y
4. Bar Overtime Pay Regs.	Y	8. Ban Partial-Birth Abortion	Y	12. Intelligence Reorg.	N

Election Results

2004 general	David Obey (D)	241,306	(86%)	($775,009)
	Mike Miles (Green)	26,518	(9%)	
	Larry Oftedahl (CNP)	12,841	(5%)	
2004 primary	David Obey (D)	unopposed		
2002 general	David Obey (D)	146,364	(64%)	($860,378)
	Joe Rothbauer (R)	81,518	(36%)	($19,932)

Prior Winning Percentages: 2000 (63%); 1998 (61%); 1996 (57%); 1994 (54%); 1992 (64%); 1990 (62%); 1988 (62%); 1986 (62%); 1984 (61%); 1982 (68%); 1980 (65%); 1978 (62%); 1976 (73%); 1974 (71%); 1972 (63%); 1970 (68%); 1969 (52%)

The People		**Race/Ethnic Origin**	**Ancestry**	
Area size:	19,391 sq. mi.	95.1% White	German: 30.4%	Polish: 8.6%
Urban population:	42.0%	0.3% Black	Norwegian: 7.6%	
Rural population:	58.0%	1.5% Asian	**2004 Presidential Vote**	
Pop. 2000:	670,462	1.5% Native Am.	Kerry (D) 185,076	(50%)
Median income:	$39,026	0.0% Hawaiian	Bush (R) 179,963	(49%)
Poverty status:	8.6%	0.8% Two+ races	Other 3,987	(1%)
Military veterans:	14.5%	0.0% Other	**2000 Presidential Vote**	
		0.9% Hispanic Origin	Gore (D) 152,177	(47%)
			Bush (R) 150,068	(47%)
			Other 18,294	(6%)
			Cook Partisan Voting Index: D + 2	

Occupation　Blue collar: 31.8%　White collar: 51.5%　Gray collar: 16.7%

In the late 19th century, on the rail lines radiating northwest from Chicago and Milwaukee, came thousands of migrants whose descendants have made the northern reaches of Wisconsin the most thickly settled land this far north in the United States east of the Mississippi. What brought people up so far was not cropland—there are no industrial-sized wheat farms as in the Red River Valley of North Dakota—but trees, iron and cows. This was one of America's largest virgin timberlands, and the river towns are still dotted with paper mills. Farther north, iron brought Finns and Italians to the port of Superior, Wisconsin, right next to Duluth, Minnesota, and to smaller towns on the chilly lake, like Bayfield near the Apostle Islands. Then on the cleared forestlands came dairy farms. Dairy cattle, properly cared for, thrive in these northern uplands, and the sons of Wisconsin dairymen, many of them immigrants from Germany and Norway, moved their dairy herds even farther north. On this base small cities grew, some with big enterprises. Wausau has paper mills and Wausau Insurance, Wisconsin Rapids has Stora Enso, and Stevens Point has Sentry Insurance. While many rural areas have declined, the area around Wausau, Wisconsin Rapids and Stevens Point has generated new businesses and jobs and retained a high-skill work force. The number of dairy farmers is in sharp decline, but farmers are turning to potatoes, vegetables, cranberries and ginseng.

All these places are in Wisconsin's 7th Congressional District, which stretches from Stevens Point in the south to Lake Superior in the north. The politics of northern Wisconsin and the 7th District has a rough-hewn quality, a certain lumberjack populist flavor. Ancestrally Republican, this area favored the progressivism of the LaFollettes. Today, the Superior and Stevens Point areas are heavily Democratic; Wausau's Marathon County and many of the smaller counties have been more Republican. This was a closely divided district in the last two presidential elections: Al Gore carried it by 47.5%–46.8% and John Kerry by 50.1%–48.7%.

The congressman from the 7th District is David Obey, a Democrat first elected in April 1969. Obey was chairman of the Appropriations Committee from March 1994 to January 1995, and since then ranking minority member; he is one of the most capable and strongly motivated legislators on either side of the aisle. He grew up in Wausau, where his father worked in a roofing factory; he started off as a Republican, but was influenced by history teacher Arthur Henderson—who assigned papers on the politics of the 1920s and was attacked by McCarthyites—and between 1952 and 1956 Obey switched from supporting Dwight Eisenhower and Joe McCarthy to Adlai Stevenson and William Proxmire. Obey graduated from the University of Wisconsin and in 1962, when he was 24, he was elected to the Wisconsin Assembly even before he got his master's degree. When Melvin Laird resigned his House seat to become Richard Nixon's Defense secretary, Obey won an upset victory in the April 1969 special election.

In the state legislature, Obey was inspired by older New Deal Democrats who fought hard for the little guy; when he entered the House, the driving energy came from liberal Democrats opposed to the Vietnam War. Obey preserves something of the force of each group. He is not a sentimental liberal: He has a prickly personality and a vigorous temper and does not suffer gladly those he considers fools or knaves. But he can leaven that with humor: he likes to quote Archy the Cockroach, the supposed writer of Don Marquis's *Archy and Mehitabel*, and he is part of a band called The Capitol Offenses, which plays bluegrass music and gospel hymns. Even as he has moved to the top of the seniority ladder, Obey has retained his sense of outrage and his eagerness to fight for what he believes in—a quality that even some Democrats complain has been too intense. But he continues to display abundant energy and leadership on a host of fronts. He has had his disappointments. He lost the Budget Committee chairmanship to Oklahoma's Jim Jones in 1980 by 121–116. In 1984 he wanted to become Democratic Caucus chairman, but demurred when it became clear that Dick Gephardt had the votes. Even so, informally Obey became a key leader of liberal Democrats, in 1989 pushing Gephardt for majority leader when Jim Wright and Tony Coelho were resigning.

Obey remains a true believer in traditional liberalism, in Keynesian economics and economic redistribution. He thinks that government should provide economic security, create jobs and build infrastructure through public investment, that it should control health care costs and guarantee coverage and a choice of providers. He bucked the Clinton administration, vocally opposing NAFTA and, when Bill Clinton seemed to be backing away from universal health care coverage in July 1994, said "then I will walk away from the Clinton health care plan" and supported his real preference, a single-payer system. In June 1995, when Clinton accepted the Republicans' goal of a budget balanced in seven years, Obey immediately issued a written statement reading, "I think most of us learned some time ago that if you don't like the president's position on a particular issue you simply need to wait a few weeks." Obey also opposed some administration positions from the right. He has long opposed abortion, and has voted for the partial-birth abortion ban and other limits on abortion, but he is not for abolishing abortion rights. When former LaCrosse Archbishop Raymond Burke admonished Catholic officeholders who do not seek to outlaw abortion, Obey wrote in the Jesuit publication *America*, "While I detest abortion and agree with Catholic teaching that in most instances it is morally wrong, I decline to force my views into laws that, if adopted, would be unenforceable and would tear this society apart. That judgment may be wrong, but it is a judgment honestly arrived at, and one that I am obligated to make." Representing the north woods, Obey opposes gun control, and once pointed out that one of the guns singled out in the assault weapons ban was owned by 23,000 residents of the 7th District, including two sheriffs.

Obey is above all an appropriator, and takes some justifiable pride in his skill at this work. He first got his seat on Appropriations in August 1969, when he was just 30; when he became chairman in March 1994, he was the youngest person to hold the post since James Good of Iowa in 1919. Obey has shown great skill, plus a determination to get things done on time—which is not always how appropriating works. For years much of his work was on the Foreign Operations Subcommittee, which he chaired from 1985 to 1995. This panel handles rather small sums of money but deals with some very sensitive issues, and it was often rocked in disputes about aid to the Nicaraguan Contras, the pace of negotiations in the Middle East, the treatment of the liberated nations of Eastern Europe. Obey has not always gotten his way, but in each case he worked to move appropriations bills forward in an orderly manner. He passed separate foreign operations appropriation bills nine out of 10 years, something that had only been accomplished twice in 10 years by his predecessors. Similarly, when Obey became chairman of the full committee, all 13 appropriations bills were signed into law prior to the beginning of the new fiscal year for the first time in 47 years; it hasn't happened since.

Obey's climb to the chairmanship was sudden. In January 1993 Jamie Whitten, whose health was impaired, was voted out after 14 years as chairman. William Natcher, holder of the record for consecutive roll call votes, performed ably for a year, but then his health visibly failed in January 1994. When he died in March 1994, Obey challenged the next Democrat in line, 74-year-old Neal Smith of Iowa. Smith had the support of other cardinals (Appropriatese for subcommittee chairmen), but Obey had more from non-committee liberals and less senior members, and won in the Democratic Caucus 152–106. When Republicans took control in 1995, Obey and Chairman Bob Livingston managed to work together on numerous occasions, sometimes to reach agreement, often to frame disagreement in orderly choices for other members; he worked amicably with Livingston's successor Bill Young. He has opposed holding up appropriations on what he considers extraneous issues, but has on occasion offered partisan amendments. For the most part appropriators work on a bipartisan basis to get consensus on a bill under the limits set by budget resolutions or administration veto threats.

After September 11, Obey and other Appropriations leaders backed George W. Bush's emergency appropriation of $40 billion, but put restrictions on spending—the first $10 billion could be spent after consultation with congressional leaders, the next $10 billion only after giving Congress 15 days of notice in which members could make objections, the last $20 billion only with congressional approval. In October Bush asked for $20 billion more for homeland security; Obey, like Robert Byrd in the Senate, thought that more was needed. He delayed the measure for two days in November because the Republican leadership would not allow a vote on his amendment for $7 billion more; Obey argued that more was needed for, among other things, protecting nuclear sites, but the Republicans passed a rule 216–211 blocking the amendment.

Obey is ranking Democrat on the Labor-HHS Subcommittee, the focus of the appropriations process in fall 2002; the conservative Republican Study Committee was pressuring the leadership to bring up Labor-HHS and hold it to the Bush budget limits, while Obey and subcommittee

Chairman Ralph Regula, who have worked together harmoniously, argued that they would be forced to cut worthy programs. Obey asked Speaker Dennis Hastert to allow four alternatives on the floor, in vain, and all but the defense and military construction appropriations were delayed until after the election and not passed until February 2003. In June 2003, Obey proposed to restore $1 billion to military housing and to increase homeland security spending by $1 billion, to be financed by reducing the tax cut on those earning more than $1 million a year; this was brushed aside as an invasion of Ways and Means's prerogatives. In June 2004 the House leadership gave him a floor vote on a proposal to increase discretionary spending, largely education, homeland security and veterans' health care, by $14 billion and scaling back tax cuts. "This legislation will give the House, for the first time, a straight up-or-down vote—not a procedural vote—on our national priorities." It was defeated 184–230. But Obey did help facilitate the passage of other appropriations. When incoming Appropriations Chairman Jerry Lewis reduced the number of subcommittees from 13 to 10, Obey said Democrats "had no input whatsoever." "The result of this is you have not seen power this centralized since the days of Czar Cannon."

Obey is not one of those appropriators who load up their districts with earmarked projects, though he has supported some. But he has paid close attention to district interests. More important is the plight of Wisconsin dairy farmers; since 1937 the Agriculture Department has fixed milk prices by a formula that allows higher prices the farther a farm is from Eau Claire, Wisconsin. This increases prices to consumers, creates an oversupply of milk and reduces dairy prices in the Upper Midwest. Obey opposed the Northeast Dairy Compact, which allowed New England states to set higher prices, and it finally expired in September 2001. He voted against the farm bill in 2002; he supports its Milk Income Loss Contract provision but complained that it left in place unfair Federal Milk Marketing orders. In October 2004 he was miffed when House Republican leaders took the MILC program out of a drought and hurricane emergency appropriation and in January 2005 said that, despite George W. Bush's endorsement of the program, it would be hard to get an extension because of administration cuts in other farm programs.

Obey voted against the Iraq war resolution in October 2002 and has been harshly critical of administration actions in Iraq. In September 2003 he said that Donald Rumsfeld and Paul Wolfowitz should resign. "They had wildly romantic ideas about how easy it was going to be to turn Iraq into the second coming of New Hampshire in terms of democracy." He pressed Coalition Provisional Authority head Paul Bremer and other administration appointees for estimates of future costs in Iraq and for details on how funds have been spent. After revelations of the Abu Ghraib prison abuses he got the committee to adopt a ban on any Justice Department spending for legal justification of torture.

Obey is the third most senior member of the House and one of three who served in the 1960s. He has been reelected by wide margins, except in 1994, when he won 54%–46%. When rumors spread that he would retire in 2004, he said, "There isn't a snowball's chance in hell. Not a prayer." He said he planned to run at least through 2010, before the next round of redistricting. In July 2004 his Republican opponent dropped out of the race, and Obey was reelected with 86% of the vote.

EIGHTH DISTRICT

Rep. Mark Green (R)

Elected 1998, 4th term; b. June 1, 1960, Boston, MA; home, Hobart; U. of WI-Eau Claire, B.A. 1983, J.D. 1987; Catholic; married (Sue).

Elected Office: WI Assembly, 1992–98.

Professional Career: Teacher, Kenya, 1987–88; Practicing atty., 1988–98.

DC Office: 1314 LHOB, 20515, 202-225-5665; Fax: 202-225-5729; Web site: www.house.gov/markgreen.

District Offices: Appleton, 920-380-0061; Green Bay, 920-437-1954.

Committees: *International Relations* (16th of 27 R): Africa, Global Human Rights & International Operations; Oversight & Investigations. *Judiciary* (14th of 23 R): Commercial & Administrative Law; Crime, Terrorism & Homeland Security; The Constitution.

Group Ratings

	ADA	ACLU	AFS	LCV	ITIC	NTU	COC	ACU	NTLC	CHC
2004	20	0	13	18	70	71	86	88	84	92
2003	10	—	0	35	—	71	87	88	—	—

National Journal Ratings

	2003 LIB	—	2003 CONS		2004 LIB	—	2004 CONS
Economic	41%	—	57%		38%	—	61%
Social	24%	—	71%		20%	—	77%
Foreign	31%	—	65%		34%	—	63%

Key Votes of the 108th Congress

1. Drilling in ANWR	Y	5. DC School Vouchers	Y	9. Ban Same-Sex Marriage	Y
2. Approve Bush Tax Cuts	Y	6. Ban Human Cloning	Y	10. Fund Iraq War	Y
3. Medicare/Rx Bill	Y	7. Restrict Gun Liability	Y	11. Bar Cuba Embargo Funds	N
4. Bar Overtime Pay Regs.	N	8. Ban Partial-Birth Abortion	Y	12. Intelligence Reorg.	Y

Election Results

2004 general	Mark Green (R)	248,070	(70%)	($433,513)
	Dottie Le Clair (D)	105,513	(30%)	($11,160)
2004 primary	Mark Green (R)	unopposed		
2002 general	Mark Green (R)	152,745	(73%)	($428,296)
	Andrew Becker (D)	50,284	(24%)	
	Other	7,418	(4%)	

Prior Winning Percentages: 2000 (75%); 1998 (55%)

The People		Race/Ethnic Origin	Ancestry	
Area size:	10,118 sq. mi.	92.2% White	German: 30.8% Irish: 6.9%	
Urban population:	56.0%	0.6% Black	Polish: 6.5%	
Rural population:	44.0%	1.4% Asian	**2004 Presidential Vote**	
Pop. 2000:	670,480	2.6% Native Am.	Bush (R)	202,238 (55%)
Median income:	$43,274	0.0% Hawaiian	Kerry (D)	162,793 (44%)
Poverty status:	6.8%	0.9% Two+ races	Other	2,738 (1%)
Military veterans:	13.9%	0.0% Other	**2000 Presidential Vote**	
		2.2% Hispanic Origin	Bush (R)	165,819 (52%)
			Gore (D)	138,056 (43%)
			Other	13,974 (4%)
			Cook Partisan Voting Index: R + 4	
Occupation	Blue collar: 31.3%	White collar: 53.9% Gray collar: 14.8%		

In 1673, the French explorer and priest Father Marquette sailed from the open waters of Lake Michigan into what is now Green Bay. He had hoped to find the Northwest Passage to the Pacific.

He actually found the Fox River, which leads to Lake Winnebago and, after a not-too-difficult portage, the Wisconsin River, which flows into the Mississippi. Green Bay and the Fox River Valley remained mostly wilderness and Indian country for more than 150 years. But once settled by Europeans, they became, as Father Marquette would have liked, one of the most heavily Catholic parts of the United States, though Indians still remain a presence; there was a long dispute over Chippewa Indian spearfishing rights and Green Bay's best hotel is now next to the Oneida Indian casino. This has been a thriving area economically, with traditional paper mills joined by high-skill manufacturing in Green Bay and Appleton in the Fox River Valley; a creative local business found a way to make the small packets that are filled with sugar and sugar substitutes, and took the business away from a South Korean firm. Green Bay is known nationally as the home of pro football's Green Bay Packers, owned by 110,000 shareholding Wisconsinites and never likely to move (under the team's charter, if the Packers are ever sold, the proceeds would go to the local Sullivan-Wallen American Legion Post 11 "for the purposes of erecting a proper soldier's memorial"). In September 2004 John Kerry became the butt of jokes when he came to Green Bay and referred to Lambeau Field, home of the Packers, as "Lambert Field", perhaps confusing it with the airport in St. Louis. Appleton has produced a number of famous Americans—Senator Joseph McCarthy, novelist Edna Ferber and escape artist Harry Houdini—and has a growing Hispanic population.

The 8th Congressional District of Wisconsin includes Green Bay and the Fox River Valley south to Appleton. It also includes sprawling north woods and dairy counties inland, plus the Door County peninsula that juts out into Lake Michigan, a favorite summer vacation spot for Chicago and Milwaukee families. Politically, this has often been malleable country. Democrats can win here: John F. Kennedy, with enthusiasm from local Catholics, carried the Fox River Valley in the primary and general election in 1960, and Bill Clinton carried it in 1996. But the 8th District these days more often votes Republican; George W. Bush won 52% of the vote in 2000 and 55% in 2004.

The congressman from the 8th District is Mark Green, a Republican first elected in 1998, the only Republican to beat a Democratic incumbent that year. Green grew up in the Green Bay area; his father was from South Africa and his mother from Britain. In high school and college he was a champion swimmer; after graduating from the University of Wisconsin at Eau Claire and UW Law School in Madison, he and his wife spent a year in Kenya, working in a WorldTeach program. He practiced law and in 1992, at 32, was elected to the Wisconsin Assembly, where he became Republican Caucus chairman. In 1998 he challenged freshman Democratic Congressman Jay Johnson, a former TV news anchor. Green brought a conceptual framework to his campaign. He listed 55 issues on which he would vote differently from Johnson, one for each day between the primary and general election; they ranged from taxes and spending to abortion and defense. It was a solidly conservative platform, in opposition to Johnson's moderate-to-liberal voting record. Green called for "restoration of American values," an end to partial-birth abortions, scrapping the tax code, increasing local control of education and tougher crime laws. He carefully avoided any reference to the Clinton-Lewinsky scandal or to impeachment, saying that he had called for Clinton's resignation only to get the issue out of the way. The two candidates spent about the same amount of money, and Green won 55%–45%.

In the House, Green's voting record has leaned conservative but he has been more moderate on economic issues. He enacted a modified version of his two-strikes law, for mandatory life sentences for second-time child sex offenders. In 2003, Congress enacted as part of the "Amber alert" bill his proposal to expedite DNA testing with "rape kit" samples to eliminate the backlog of DNA evidence collected in sexual assault cases. Concerned about foreigners who overstay their visas, he sponsored a law to require states to have driver's licenses expire when the applicant's visa does, or earlier; in 2004, he opposed the intelligence reorganization because Senate opposition forced deletion of a similar provision. He would eliminate the capital gains tax on sales of farms to family members. In 2003, he was among the first House members to file legislation threatening huge tariffs on Chinese imports if China did not agree to float its currency. He complained to the Venezuela embassy about the high gasoline prices. With Marty Meehan, he proposed a bill to require that Internet sales of tobacco products comply with long-standing regulations of traditional retail sales, including state taxes; the Judiciary Committee approved the bill, but opposition from Indian tribes and delivery companies blocked House action.

Green has not been seriously challenged for reelection. In January 2005, he filed to run for governor in 2006 and transferred $1.3 million from his federal campaign treasury to a state fund. He appeared headed for a contest in the September primary with Milwaukee County Executive Scott Walker. Possible Republican candidates in the 8th District include Assembly Speaker John Gard, state Representatives Frank Lasee, Terri McCormick and Steve Wieckert. Possible Democratic candidates include state Senator Dave Hansen, Green Bay business consultant Jamie Wall and former Green Bay Mayor Paul Jadin.

★ WYOMING ★

Wyoming is "the land of the cowboy," as the *WPA Guide* called it more than 60 years ago. "Its mountains, plains, and valleys are essentially livestock country. A cowboy astride a bucking bronco greets the visitor from enameled license plates, from newspapers, magazines and painted signs." The cowboy is still on the license plates, and Wyoming remains the most western of states in spirit—largely unsettled, the least populous state, a thin veneer of civilization stretched over a forbidding and beautiful land.

But Wyoming's economy now depends not on cowboys and cattle but on mining and minerals. Wyoming boomed with oil prospectors during the energy price surge of the 1970s, but was hit hard by drops in oil prices in the early 1980s and again in the late 1990s. As the exploration for oil slumped, the production of other minerals has surged. The Clean Air Act put a premium on Wyoming's low-sulfur coal, and this is now the number one coal state, producing one-third of the nation's coal, more than West Virginia and Kentucky combined. In the Powder River Basin 30-story high machines blast away the topsoil and scoop out the coal; it is hauled away by 65 unit trains a day by the Burlington Northern and Union Pacific; the $1.4 billion Dakota, Minnesota & Eastern rail line is being built to the Mississippi River, the biggest U.S. rail construction project in a century. Wyoming is also the number seven oil and number four natural gas producer, and the nation's top producer of the mineral bentonite (used in oil drilling and cosmetics) and has the world's largest reserve of trona (used in glass and baking soda). Much of the natural gas is coal-bed methane, mixed with water next to coal seams; only in 1989 did engineers figure out how to separate the natural gas from the water. Now 200-foot drilling rigs are sinking wells as deep as 25,000 feet, and production has jumped enormously since 2000. And these capital-intensive industries produce relatively few jobs for young people: the coal operations employ only about 5,000. About one-quarter of people 25 to 34 left the state in the 1990s, and about two-thirds of the graduates of the University of Wyoming leave, which means that the state's population is getting older and less educated. Still, unemployment has been low and if the state economy did not boom in the 1990s, it did not go bust after 2000.

Wyoming's second industry is now tourism. Yellowstone National Park continues to draw millions, and Jackson Hole just to the south has become one of America's elite resort areas year-round; its airport is Wyoming's busiest and the only one that accommodates jets. There has been growth as well in the scenic and pastoral country on the eastern slope of the Big Horn Mountains around Buffalo and Sheridan. The third industry is agriculture: Wyoming is second in the nation in wool production, third in sheep inventory and also produces hay, sugar beets, barley, pinto beans and beef cattle. Drought hurt some farmers in 2002, but farm exports were sharply up.

Reliance on high-tech mineral extraction and high-end tourism may seem a contradiction of Wyoming's Old West heritage. But Wyoming has always depended on new technology to tame age-old nature. Cattle ranches after the open-range era were made possible only by the barbed wire that could fence in roaming herds, and the steam locomotives that could carry cattle to markets back east. This 19th century high tech was brought to Wyoming by large capitalist operators, some of them onetime Texas cowhands or second sons of English landed gentry, who

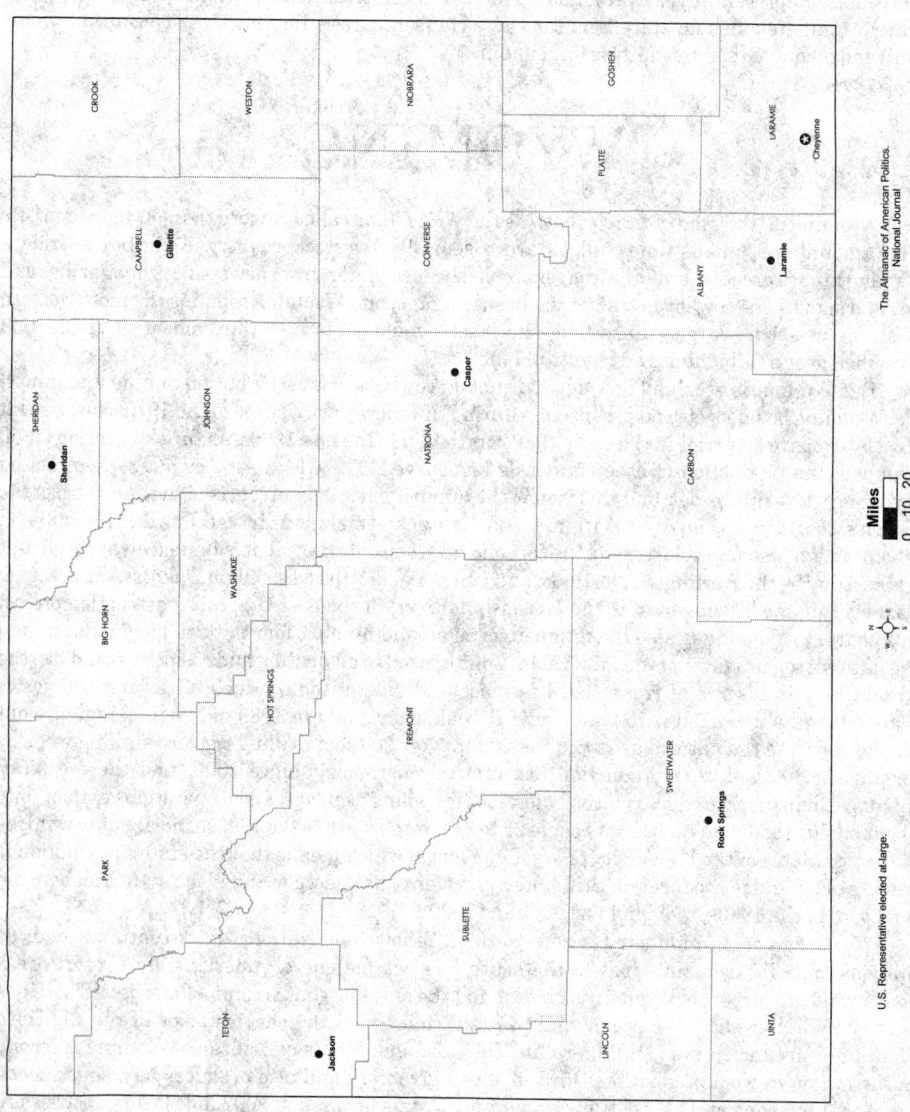

The Almanac of American Politics.
National Journal

Miles

0 10 20

U.S. Representative elected at-large.

CROOK

WESTON

NIOBRARA

GOSHEN

LARAMIE

Cheyenne

PLATTE

CAMPBELL
Gillette

CONVERSE

ALBANY

Laramie

SHERIDAN

Sheridan

JOHNSON

NATRONA

Casper

CARBON

BIG HORN

WASHAKIE

HOT SPRINGS

FREMONT

SWEETWATER

Rock Springs

PARK

SUBLETTE

TETON

Jackson

LINCOLN

UINTA

started the first big operations after the Civil War. And of course mining depends on high-tech machinery and responsiveness to markets that reward innovation and penalize stasis.

At the same time, Wyoming still is a kind of frontier: It was until recently one of the few states with more men than women—one reason it was the first part of the United States, when it was a territory in 1869, to give women the vote (exception: New Jersey allowed women with property to vote between 1776 and 1807, but there weren't many).

There is a settled part of Wyoming as well, in the medium-sized towns that are the state's largest cities, and among sheep and cattle ranches, sugar beet and malting barley farms and denizens of tiny settlements. This is a small state, a single community really, where people remember who played what position, when and how well, for what high-school football team; where because all locals know who your father's cousins married, you mostly live on the straight and narrow. The locals set the tone of life in Wyoming.

There was once a sharp economic and regional split traditionally reflected in partisan politics. The big economic interests—cattle ranchers, organized in the Wyoming Stock Growers' Association, and the Union Pacific Railroad management always favored the Republicans, as did the wildcatters, independent producers and oil company geologists. The main Democratic constituency had been the Union Pacific Railroad workers who built the first transcontinental line across southern Wyoming in the 1860s; the southern tier of counties, from Cheyenne through Laramie to Evanston, once voted Democratic. But now the Democrats are strongest in Teton County, the home of Jackson Hole, by far the wealthiest county in the state and the only one to vote for John Kerry in 2004. Wyoming has been one of the most Republican states since the 1970s; it hasn't elected a Democrat to the Senate since 1970 or the House since 1976, though it has had mostly Democratic governors over that time. In presidential elections it is solidly Republican—the most Republican state in the nation in 2000, when it voted for George W. Bush and native son Dick Cheney, a running back on the Natrona High School football team, by a 69%–28% margin.

Wyoming's Republican tendencies in the 1990s were strengthened by the Clinton administration's environmental policies—proposing grazing fee increases, the reintroduction of gray wolves into Yellowstone, proposing threatened species status on the black-tailed prairie dog, banning snowmobiles in national parks, the moratorium on road building in the national parks. But the policies of the Bush administration—removing endangered status from the gray wolves, opening the way to proving title to land currently controlled by the Bureau of Land Management—have removed some of these grievances. In a small state with not even half a million people—three-quarters the population of the average congressional district—Wyoming voters expect to talk person-to-person with their governors, senators and congressmen every so often. Personal campaigning is important, and Democrats have won six of the last eight races for governor. But party tends to trump personality when it comes to federal office.

The People		Race/Ethnic Origin			Military veterans: 57,860 (15.8%)	
Pop. 2004 (est):	506,529	438,799	88.9%	White	WWII: 16.8%	Korea: 12.3%
Pop. 2000:	493,782	3,504	0.7%	Black	Vietnam: 36.2%	Gulf War: 12.8%
Pop. 1990:	453,588	2,670	0.5%	Asian	**Most populous cities (2003):**	
Change 1990–2000:	Up 8.9%	10,238	2.1%	Native Am.	1. Cheyenne	54,374
% of U.S. total:	0.2%	264	0.1%	Hawaiian	2. Casper	50,632
Pop. rank:	50th of 50	6,164	1.2%	Two+ races	3. Laramie	26,956
Area size:	97,814 sq. mi.	474	0.1%	Other	4. Gillette	21,840
State Native:	42.5%	31,669	6.4%	Hisp. Origin	5. Rock Springs	18,400
Non-citizen:	1.2%	**Ancestry**			Urban population: 65.2%	
Language		German: 18.4%		English: 11.3%	Rural population: 34.8%	
English: 90.7%	Spanish: 5.7%	Irish: 9.4%		USA: 4.6%		
Other Eur.: 2.3%		Norwegian: 3.0%				

Education		Work Sector		Legislature	
H.S. Grad:	87.9%	Private: 70.2%	Govt: 20.4%	Senate	23 R 7 D
College Grad:	21.9%	Self: 8.9%	Family: 0.5%	House	46 R 14 D
Industry		Unemployment: 5.2%		Legislative Term Limits: No	
Agri: 10.7%	Con: 8.7%	**Household Income**		**Registered Voters**	
Fin: 4.7%	Info: 2.2%	<15k: 16.7%	15-35k: 29.2%	D: 62,385	(26.8%)
Mfg: 11.4%	Prof: 27.4%	35-50k: 18.3%	50-100k: 29.1%	R: 146,328	(63.0%)
Public: 6.3%	Trade: 14.1%	100-150k: 4.5%	>150k: 2.2%	O: 23,683	(10.2%)
Other: 14.5%		Median: $37,892			
Occupation		Poverty status: 11.4%			
Blue collar: 27.5%	White collar: 54.2%	**Home Value**			
Gray collar: 18.2%		<50k: 18.4%	50-100k: 39.0%	100-200k: 31.7%	200-300k: 6.0%
		300-500k: 2.5%	>500k: 2.4%	Median: $91,500	

Presidential politics   Wyoming is one of the least likely states in the nation to be seriously contested in presidential general elections: it is too Republican, too remote and has only three electoral votes. Candidates have seldom visited, except when Dick Cheney has gone to his home in Jackson. This was George W. Bush's number one state in 2000, when he carried it 69%–28%, and his number two state in 2004, when he carried it 69%–29%.

Wyoming holds presidential caucuses in early March. In 2004 the Democratic caucuses were held March 20, apparently with no members of the national press in attendance.

2004 Presidential Vote		
Bush (R)	167,629	(69%)
Kerry (D)	70,776	(29%)
Nader (I)	2,741	(1%)
Other	2,282	(1%)

2000 Presidential Vote		
Bush (R)	147,947	(69%)
Gore (D)	60,481	(28%)
Other	5,298	(2%)

Governor

Dave Freudenthal (D)

Elected 2002, term expires Jan. 2007, 1st term; b. Oct. 12, 1950, Thermopolis; home, Cheyenne; Amherst Col., B.A. 1973, U. of WY, J.D. 1980; Episcopalian; married (Nancy).

Professional Career: Practicing atty. 1980–94; U.S. Atty. for WY, 1994–2001

Office: State Capitol Bldg., Rm. 124, Cheyenne, 82002, 307-777-7434; Fax: 307-632-3909; Web site: www.state.wy.us.

Election Results

2002 general	Dave Freudenthal (D)	92,662	(50%)
	Eli Bebout (R)	88,873	(48%)
	Other	3,924	(2%)
2002 primary	Dave Freudenthal (D)	19,732	(54%)
	Paul Hickey (D)	13,793	(37%)
	Toby Simpson (D)	1,918	(5%)
	Kenneth Casner (D)	1,356	(4%)
1998 general	Jim Geringer (R)	97,235	(56%)
	John P. Vinich (D)	70,754	(40%)
	Other	6,899	(4%)

Dave Freudenthal, a Democrat, was elected governor of Wyoming in 2002. He grew up on a farm north of Thermopolis, the seventh of eight children. Freudenthal (pronounced *FREE-den-thal*) graduated from Amherst College and then returned to Wyoming to work for the state Department of Economic Planning and Development. Ed Herschler, a Democrat elected to the first of his three terms as governor in 1974, appointed him state planning coordinator in 1975 and administrative aide in 1978. In 1980 he graduated from the University of Wyoming Law School. From 1981 to 1993 he practiced law in Cheyenne; he also served on the Blueprint for Business Committee, the Wyoming Futures Project and the Economic Development and Stabilization Board and from 1981 to 1985 he was Wyoming Democratic chairman. In 1994 he was appointed U.S. Attorney for Wyoming and served until 2001. Then he started running for governor.

The incumbent, Republican Jim Geringer, was ineligible to run for a third term. Five Republicans and four Democrats got into the race. All agreed that economic development was a key concern. Freudenthal's chief competitor in the Democratic primary was Paul Hickey, son of Joseph Hickey, who was elected governor in 1958 and who was appointed to the Senate in January 1961. In the August primary Freudenthal beat Hickey 54%–37%. The winner in the Republican primary was state House Speaker Eli Bebout, with 49% of the vote. Bebout and his brother owned a mining business in Riverton that repaired cave-ins in old mines; he also had other mining investments. He had been elected to the state House in 1986 as a Democrat, but switched parties in 1994.

The two nominees had similar positions on many issues—for the death penalty, against gun control, for economic diversification, against a state income tax. Freudenthal called for a more efficient audit of oil and gas companies; he noted that the legislature insisted on auditing schools, but not the companies whose taxes furnished one-third of the state budget. Bebout claimed there were "huge differences" between him and Freudenthal and pointed out that, as U.S. Attorney, Freudenthal was a Clinton nominee. But his business interests caused him some problems. One of his primary opponents attacked him because a company on whose board he served had applied to build a temporary storage facility for spent nuclear rods. After the August primary the *Casper Star-Tribune* reported that SEC documents showed that he had not repaid a $468,000 loan made in 1983 by a company on whose board he served; Bebout presented the paper with a copy of the loan with "PAID" stamped on it. Polls showed many voters undecided, and on Election Day Freudenthal won 50%–48%. He won 59%–39% in the five counties in the southern end of the state—the traditionally Democratic Union Pacific counties.

Freudenthal entered office with state government in a good fiscal position. Increases in land values due to mining activity had produced surging increases in state revenue and the state budget was in surplus. But Republicans had majorities in the legislature big enough to override vetoes. He angered environmentalists with several early appointments, including one that put a mining executive in charge of the Department of Environmental Quality.

Higher natural gas and oil prices gave the state a projected $1.2 billion surplus as the 2004 legislative session convened. While most other states struggled with budget deficits, Wyoming was in the best fiscal shape of all; the only issue was how much to put into savings and how much to spend. In the final $2 billion budget bill–large by Wyoming standards–20% was directed into various reserve funds, with $100 million for the Permanent Mineral Trust Fund, the interest earnings of which helps pay the cost of state government and keep taxes low. School and prison construction got $462 million; $49 million went to raises and benefits for state and university employees. Freudenthal vetoed a provision that sent coal-lease funds into the Budget Reserve Account, arguing that the money should be in the school capital construction account where it would help convince the state supreme court, which had ruled in 2001 that capital outlays for school construction were inadequate, that the state was fully funding its 5-year school construction plan.

At an August 2004 press conference announcing that state revenues could be as much as $474 million more than expected due in large part to mineral severance tax revenues, Freudenthal said the state could be looking at years of strong economic performance—the increase suggested a plateau, rather than a spike in revenues. Some school districts in mineral-rich regions were collecting so much from high mineral prices and production that it skewed the state's attempts to equalize school funding. Under an earlier constitutional amendment, these districts were allowed to keep some of the excess money (rather than send it to the state for redistribution to less wealthy districts) when it gets above a certain amount per pupil; a proposed constitutional amendment in 2004 would have corrected this and repealed the limit on property tax revenues that could be taken from the "recapture districts." Freudenthal supported a constitutional amendment abolishing the limit on redistribution of property tax revenues, but the measure failed.

Another pressing issue, rising medical malpractice insurance costs, also appeared on the November ballot in two proposed constitutional amendments. A populist provision of the state constitution barred the legislature from setting limits on how much money people can collect in the instance of injury or death. In July, Freudenthal called a special session that sent to voters Constitutional Amendment D which allowed the legislature to debate and pass laws limiting the amount of non-economic damages plaintiffs could get in medical malpractice lawsuits. The proposed Constitutional Amendment C allowed legislative debate on a measure to require alternative dispute resolution or medical review panel approval before someone could file a lawsuit against a health-care provider. Freudenthal declined to take a position on Amendment D and backed Amendment C; the first failed 50.3%–49.7% and the second passed 53%–47%.

In 2005, again handed a surplus of close to $1 billion—an "astonishingly healthy state fiscal picture," he said—Freudenthal proposed $293 million of additional general fund spending for the second year of Wyoming's two-year budget. His wildlife trust fund proposal passed, though he got only $30 million in funding for it not the $75 million he sought. Money went to raises for teachers, a college scholarship endowment, a University of Wyoming library complex, and new four-lane highways; $76 million was allocated for a new prison in Torrington. Freudenthal also signed a suicide prevention bill in 2005; Wyoming has the highest rate in the country, about double the 11 per 100,000 national rate. All the while his approval ratings remained high—67% in 2005.

Senior Senator

Craig Thomas (R)

Elected 1994, seat up 2006, 2d term; b. Feb. 17, 1933, Cody; home, Casper; U. of WY, B.S. 1954, LaSalle U.; Methodist; married (Susan).

Military Career: Marine Corps, 1955–59.

Elected Office: WY House of Reps., 1984–89; U.S. House of Reps., 1989–94.

Professional Career: V.P., WY Farm Bureau, 1959–66; Legis. staff, Amer. Farm Bureau, 1966–75; Gen. Mgr., WY Rural Electric Assn., 1975–89.

DC Office: 307 DSOB, 20510, 202-224-6441; Fax: 202-224-1724; Web site: thomas.senate.gov.

State Offices: Casper, 307-261-6413; Cheyenne, 307-772-2451; Riverton, 307-856-6642; Rock Springs, 307-362-5012; Sheridan, 307-672-6456.

Committees: *Agriculture, Nutrition & Forestry*: Forestry, Conservation & Rural Revitalization; Marketing, Inspection & Product Promotion. *Energy & Natural Resources*: Energy; National Parks (Chmn.); Public Lands & Forests. *Ethics (Select)*. *Finance*: Health Care; International Trade (Chmn.); Taxation & IRS Oversight. *Indian Affairs*.

Group Ratings

	ADA	ACLU	AFS	LCV	ITIC	NTU	COC	ACU	NTLC	CHC
2004	5	0	0	0	100	78	100	100	93	100
2003	0	—	0	0	—	78	100	85	—	—

National Journal Ratings

	2003 LIB	—	2003 CONS	2004 LIB	—	2004 CONS
Economic	0%	—	82%	0%	—	98%
Social	0%	—	59%	0%	—	84%
Foreign	0%	—	78%	0%	—	67%

Key Votes of the 108th Congress

1. Ban Drilling in ANWR	N	5. Energy Bill	Y	9. Ban Same-Sex Marriage	Y
2. Approve Bush Tax Cuts	Y	6. Support Roe v. Wade	N	10. Ban Bunker-Buster Bomb	N
3. Medicare/Rx Bill	Y	7. Ban Partial-Birth Abortion	Y	11. Fund Iraq War	Y
4. Bar Overtime Pay Regs.	N	8. Assault Weapons Ban	N	12. Restrict Missile Defense	N

Election Results

2000 general	Craig Thomas (R)	157,622	(74%)	($762,833)
	Mel Logan (D)	47,087	(22%)	($4,187)
	Margaret Dawson (Lib)	8,950	(4%)	
2000 primary	Craig Thomas (R)	unopposed		
1994 general	Craig Thomas (R)	118,754	(59%)	($1,068,335)
	Mike Sullivan (D)	79,287	(39%)	($712,991)
	Other	3,669	(2%)	

Prior Winning Percentages: 1992 House (58%); 1990 House (55%); 1989 House (53%)

Craig Thomas, senior senator from Wyoming, grew up in Cody, where he knew Alan Simpson, later his colleague in the Senate. Thomas graduated from the University of Wyoming and served in the Marine Corps. For years he worked for the Wyoming Farm Bureau and the Wyoming Rural Electric Association, organizations with conservative political leanings that kept him in touch with hundreds of people active in their communities. In 1984 he was elected to the Wyoming House. In March 1989, when Congressman-at-Large Dick Cheney was appointed Secretary of Defense, Thomas ran for his seat. He had serious competition from veteran Democrat John Vinich, who had just run a close race against Senator Malcolm Wallop. Vinich noted that national Republicans were backing Thomas and said voters shouldn't let outsiders make decisions for Wyoming. Thomas rallied and won with 53%.

In the House Thomas concentrated on Wyoming issues and was reelected with 55% in 1990 and 58% in 1992. When Wallop retired in 1994, Thomas was the obvious Republican candidate and had no primary opposition. In the general, he faced Governor Mike Sullivan, personally popular and with a conservative record, but handicapped by his association with Bill Clinton, who asked him to run for the Senate. Thomas relentlessly attacked Sullivan as a "Friend of Bill" and ally of locally unpopular Interior Secretary Bruce Babbitt. Thomas won 59%–39%.

Thomas is the chairman of the National Parks Subcommittee. In 2004 he held a hearing and criticized the National Park Service for not meeting the goals of the 1998 act. He supported the Bush administration's reversal of the ban on logging in remote areas of the national forests, and challenged the Forest Service's 2004 decision to withhold oil and gas leasing in the Bridge-Teton National Forest. In 2004 he sponsored a bill to set guidelines for declaring national heritage areas; the whole state of Tennessee had been declared one in 1996. In 2005 he sponsored a law to bar federal government land purchases that would produce a net increase in federal land in any state where the government already owns 25%.

Thomas's proposal to trade state-owned land in Grand Teton National Park for mineral-producing federal land of equal value elsewhere in Wyoming, in order to generate state revenue for schools, shows how snarled federal lands bills can become. In October 2001 he got the Senate to pass this seemingly uncontroversial measure. But House Resources Chairman James Hansen wanted a bill to allow the Mormon Church to purchase from the government Martin's Cove in Wyoming, where nearly 150 Mormon pioneers died in a blizzard in 1856. This got attached to the Senate bill in the House, and the Senate passed it with those riders in November 2002. But too late: the House had already adjourned. Hansen retired in 2002 and in June 2003 both houses finally passed the bill. In 2005 Thomas sponsored a bill to return the royalty on soda ash production on federal land to 2%; soda ash is used in making glass and 90% of America's supply and 40% of the world's is produced in Wyoming. The royalty had been raised to 6% in the mid-1990s, when export growth was high. But exports declined as other countries established trade barriers. Thomas supported the Australian Free Trade Agreement, which eliminated a 5% tariff on soda ash; Australian imports of soda ash have been increasing due to high demand for wine bottles.

Starting in the 1990s Thomas has been trying to make changes in the Endangered Species Act. His various bills would require use of peer-reviewed scientific data open to the public, set minimum requirements for petitions rather than the current "postage stamp" petition, would give a more substantial role to states and local citizens and would make delisting species easier. He argues that the Fish and Wildlife Service emphasizes critical habitat over species recovery and that, as of 2004, only about 15 of 2,000 listed species have recovered. He points to the example of the Preble's Meadow Jumping Mouse, listed in Wyoming in the 1990s, though the Fish and Wildlife Service "admitted to uncertainties regarding taxonomic distinctions and ranges"—i.e., they weren't sure it was a separate species or where it lived. In January 2005 the Interior Department, relying on peer-reviewed scientists, said the mouse was not a separate species, and that within a year limitations imposed on 31,000 acres in Wyoming and Colorado would be removed. He has pointed out that Interagency Grizzly Bear Committee criteria for recovery of the species in the Yellowstone ecosystem have been met, but the bear has not been removed from the list. "The [Endangered Species Act] has become a clear example of good intentions gone astray and we need to inject some common sense into what has become a regulatory nightmare. We should start making the law more effective for local landowners, public land managers, communities and state governments who truly hold the key to any successful effort to conserve species."

Thomas played a key role in amending the electricity restructuring parts of the energy bill in March 2002. Over the opposition of Energy Chairman Jeff Bingaman, he got an amendment passed that would establish an industry-run organization, regulated by FERC, rather than run by FERC itself, to oversee power transmission access and conduct. And he got Bingaman to agree to a provision reducing FERC's authority to oversee mergers, regulate transmission construction and pass judgment on rates. With Charles Grassley and two Democrats he moved to bar meatpackers from owning livestock. He takes an interest in special education; his wife teaches special needs children in Northern Virginia.

Thomas had little trouble winning reelection in 2000. A backer of Lyndon LaRouche won the low-turnout Democratic primary, and Thomas, campaigning on rural health care, highway spending and expanding agricultural trade, won the general 74%–22%. In August 2001 he said he was thinking about running for governor, but in late September he said he would not do so. His seat comes up in 2006. In July 2004 he said, "I have made a decision, and that decision is to make that decision later on." No one doubts he will win if he runs.

Junior Senator

Michael Enzi (R)

Elected 1996, seat up 2008, 2d term; b. Feb. 1, 1944, Bremerton, WA; home, Gillette; George Washington U., B.S. 1966, Denver U., M.B.A. 1968; Presbyterian; married (Diana).

Military Career: WY Natl. Guard, 1967–73.

Elected Office: Gillette Mayor, 1975–82; WY House of Reps., 1986–90; WY Senate, 1990–96.

Professional Career: Owner, NZ Shoes, 1969–95; Dir. & Chmn., First WY Bank of Gillette, 1978–88; Accounting Mgr. & Computer Programmer, Dunbar Well Service, 1985–97; Educ. Comm. of States, 1989–93; Dir., Black Hills Corp., 1992–96; Western Interstate Comm. for Higher Educ., 1995–96.

DC Office: 379-A RSOB, 20510, 202-224-3424; Fax: 202-228-0359; Web site: enzi.senate.gov.

State Offices: Casper, 307-261-6572; Cheyenne, 307-772-2477; Cody, 307-527-9444; Gillette, 307-682-6268; Jackson, 307-739-9507.

Committees: *Banking, Housing & Urban Affairs*: Housing & Transportation; International Trade & Finance; Securities & Investment. *Budget. Health, Education, Labor & Pensions* (Chmn.). *Small Business & Entrepreneurship*.

Group Ratings

	ADA	ACLU	AFS	LCV	ITIC	NTU	COC	ACU	NTLC	CHC
2004	5	22	0	0	92	77	100	96	90	100
2003	5	—	0	0	—	76	100	80	—	—

National Journal Ratings

	2003 LIB — 2003 CONS		2004 LIB — 2004 CONS	
Economic	18%	77%	4%	95%
Social	0%	59%	0%	84%
Foreign	22%	68%	0%	67%

Key Votes of the 108th Congress

1. Ban Drilling in ANWR	N	5. Energy Bill	Y	9. Ban Same-Sex Marriage	Y
2. Approve Bush Tax Cuts	Y	6. Support Roe v. Wade	N	10. Ban Bunker-Buster Bomb	N
3. Medicare/Rx Bill	Y	7. Ban Partial-Birth Abortion	Y	11. Fund Iraq War	Y
4. Bar Overtime Pay Regs.	N	8. Assault Weapons Ban	N	12. Restrict Missile Defense	N

Election Results

2002 general	Michael Enzi (R)	133,710	(73%)	($884,114)
	Joyce Corcoran (D)	49,570	(27%)	($8,467)
2002 primary	Michael Enzi (R)	78,612	(86%)	
	Crosby Allen (R)	12,931	(14%)	
1996 general	Michael Enzi (R)	114,116	(54%)	($953,572)
	Kathy Karpan (D)	89,103	(42%)	($814,258)
	Other	7,858	(4%)	

Mike Enzi, the junior senator from Wyoming, was first elected in 1996 and is now chairman of the Health, Education, Labor and Pensions Committee (HELP). Enzi grew up in Thermopolis and Sheridan, the son of a shoe salesman, got degrees in accounting and marketing, moved to Gillette and became an oil well servicing company accountant and founded NZ Shoes. In the 1970s, at a Jaycees meeting, he met Senator Alan Simpson, who was impressed by his volunteerism and asked him to consider running for public office. In 1975 Enzi was elected mayor of Gillette, the center of Wyoming's coal belt and its fastest-growing town, and served eight years. In 1986 he was elected to the state House and in 1990 to the state Senate. After Simpson announced his retirement in December 1995, Enzi was one of nine Republicans and two Democrats to run for the seat. With support from a grass roots network of conservatives, Enzi finished first in a straw poll at the May 1996 Republican state convention; in second place was John Barrasso, an orthopedic surgeon from Casper who had appeared on statewide TV discussing health issues for 12 years. Their chief difference was on abortion; Barrasso supported and Enzi opposed abortion rights. Barrasso had more money, but Enzi won 32%–30%. The Democratic nominee was former Secretary of State Kathy Karpan, who opposed gun control and abortion. But she had the liabilities of having supported the presidential candidacies of Bill Clinton in 1992 and Bruce Babbitt (unpopular in Wyoming as Clinton's Interior Secretary) in 1988. Enzi led in polls all the way and won 54%–42%.

Enzi started off in the Senate by presiding for 100 hours in the chair by July and seeking permission to bring his laptop on the floor: a workhorse. The Rules Committee said no by a 6–1 vote; Enzi renewed his request in June 2002, noting that even the Senate is in a new century but the rule still stands. He has opposed meatpacker ownership of livestock and has pushed for country of origin labeling of meat.

In 2002, his sixth year in the Senate, Enzi was still little known in most of Washington, but he played a key role on a major piece of legislation. The issue was corporate accountability, and as the only accountant in the Senate Enzi could claim special expertise. In July 2000 he was one of 13 senators who signed a letter urging then-SEC Chairman Arthur Levitt to delay a decision on his proposal to bar accounting firms from doing auditing and consulting work for the same corporation. After the Enron bankruptcy in December 2001 raised questions about accounting, Enzi still urged caution and said he feared overregulation. Banking Chairman Paul Sarbanes held extensive hearings on the issue and Enzi, the fifth ranking Republican, paid close attention. The bill Sarbanes introduced to the committee did not go so far as the Levitt proposal, but did go farther than the bill passed by the House in April 2002. It included an accounting board independent of the SEC with power to set rules, investigate, punish violations and conduct regular inspections of accounting firms' work. Enzi worked closely with lobbyists for the big accounting firms but kept the perspective of a Wyoming small business accountant. He decided that some bill needed to be passed and Sarbanes, not wanting to report a bill supported only by Democrats, consulted him. On the evening of June 17, Enzi flew in from Wyoming and went to Sarbanes's office where they negotiated a compromise. Enzi got Sarbanes to agree that two of the four members of the board must be accountants, that the board could adopt rules favored by the accounting industry and that the board would not be financed by accountants. Disciplinary proceedings would be confidential. On June 18 in the office of Phil Gramm, the ranking Republican on the committee, Enzi told committee Republicans that he would vote for Sarbanes's bill. Others agreed: six of the 10 Republicans supported it. On June 26 the WorldCom accounting scam was made public. The Senate wanted to act, and Sarbanes could go to the floor with bipartisan support. On July 15 the Senate approved the bill 97–0. House negotiators got minor concessions from the Senate side in the conference committee, and the bill was passed and signed before the August recess.

In January 2005 Enzi became chairman of the HELP Committee; the last time a Wyoming senator chaired it was in the 1890s. It was not unprecedented that a relatively junior senator rose thanks to seniority to this chairmanship; Orrin Hatch did so after only four years in the Senate in 1981. Hatch was one of several former chairmen on the committee; the others were Judd Gregg (who left the chair to become chairman of Budget), James Jeffords and Edward Kennedy, now (as he was when Hatch became chairman 24 years before) ranking minority member. On the committee Enzi had become known as a hard worker, knowledgeable about the details of legislation and the views of those affected, not always following the lead of the Bush administration. As chairman, he worked to put together a reauthorization of the Carl Perkins vocational and technical education bill that passed the Senate 99–0 in March 2005. Enzi has argued that in an economy where workers will typically hold 14 jobs over a lifetime, 10 of them in careers that are not yet invented, lifelong education is crucial. The Carl Perkins act is one leg, he argued, of a three-legged stool; the others are his Workforce Investment Act, a version of which passed the Senate unanimously in 2004, and reauthorization of the Higher Education Act, a more controversial matter. He hoped to reauthorize Head Start, also a controversial matter since many Republicans want it to have a more academic approach. He called the 2005 Bush administration pension proposal a "starting point."

Enzi was a co-sponsor of the Genetic Nondiscrimination Act, which passed the Senate in February 2005 but faced serious opposition in the House. On health care issues says he has favored marked-oriented solutions with consumer choice and more information; an example is a bill funding state high risk pools. He has supported federal medical malpractice bills and funding states to test alternatives to current tort law. He has favored changes in FDA regulation of drugs and patient safety legislation. One of his priorities was to follow up the BioShield act to protect against bioterrorism by funding vaccines and treatments. He has sponsored worker safety legislation to provide for third party consultants to OSHA, certificates of compliance for employers, posting of sample material safety data sheets and hazard information. He has co-sponsored Judd Gregg's prescription drug reimportation bill; he says he wants to ensure the security of drugs and to allow imports to begin on a staggered basis.

Enzi did not have serious opposition in 2002. He won the Republican primary 86%–14% and the general election 73%–27%.

Representative-At-Large

Barbara Cubin (R)

Elected 1994, 6th term; b. Nov. 30, 1946, Salinas, CA; home, Casper; Creighton U., B.S. 1969; Episcopalian; married (Frederick).

Elected Office: WY House of Reps., 1986–92; WY Senate, 1992–94.

Professional Career: Office Mgr., Dr. Frederick Cubin, 1975–94.

DC Office: 1114 LHOB, 20515, 202-225-2311; Fax: 202-225-3057; Web site: www.house.gov/cubin.

District Offices: Casper, 307-261-6595; Cheyenne, 307-772-2595; Rock Springs, 307-362-4095.

Committees: *Energy & Commerce* (10th of 31 R): Commerce, Trade & Consumer Protection; Health; Telecommunications & the Internet. *Resources* (8th of 27 R): Energy & Mineral Resources; Water & Power.

Group Ratings

	ADA	ACLU	AFS	LCV	ITIC	NTU	COC	ACU	NTLC	CHC
2004	0	0	0	0	100	77	100	100	100	100
2003	5	—	0	5	—	67	96	91	—	—

National Journal Ratings

	2003 LIB	—	2003 CONS		2004 LIB	—	2004 CONS
Economic	0%	—	91%		5%	—	93%
Social	16%	—	83%		15%	—	84%
Foreign	20%	—	80%		41%	—	58%

Key Votes of the 108th Congress

1. Drilling in ANWR	Y	5. DC School Vouchers	Y	9. Ban Same-Sex Marriage	Y
2. Approve Bush Tax Cuts	Y	6. Ban Human Cloning	Y	10. Fund Iraq War	Y
3. Medicare/Rx Bill	Y	7. Restrict Gun Liability	Y	11. Bar Cuba Embargo Funds	N
4. Bar Overtime Pay Regs.	N	8. Ban Partial-Birth Abortion	Y	12. Intelligence Reorg.	Y

Election Results

2004 general	Barbara Cubin (R)	132,107	(55%)	($944,908)
	Ted Ladd (D)	99,989	(42%)	($373,436)
	Other	6,938	(3%)	
2004 primary	Barbara Cubin (R)	45,433	(55%)	
	Bruce Asay (R)	20,332	(25%)	
	Cale Case (R)	13,104	(16%)	
	Other	3,726	(5%)	
2002 general	Barbara Cubin (R)	110,229	(61%)	($635,271)
	Ron Akin (D)	65,961	(36%)	($19,154)
	Other	5,962	(3%)	

Prior Winning Percentages: 2000 (67%); 1998 (58%); 1996 (55%); 1994 (53%)

Wyoming, the nation's least populous state, has elected one congressman-at-large since it was admitted to the Union in 1890. The current incumbent is Barbara Cubin, a Republican first elected in 1994. The great-great-granddaughter of one of Wyoming's original homesteaders, she grew up in Casper, where she worked as a teacher, social worker, chemist and realtor; for 19 years she managed her husband's medical practice. She was divorced after an early first marriage, worked as a single mother, was subjected to sexual harassment, but insists: "I am not a feminist. I am not gender sensitive." She notes that Susan B. Anthony and all the early advocates of women's rights were opposed to abortion. In 1986 she was elected to the state House and in 1992 to the state Senate.

In 1994, when Congressman Craig Thomas ran for the Senate, Cubin was one of five Republicans and two Democrats to run for the House. She sharply attacked "the Clinton-Babbitt war on the West." In the Republican primary, she won with 39%. The Democratic nominee was

Bob Schuster, a law partner of high-profile Wyoming trial lawyer Gerry Spence. He spent $2.4 million, most of it his own money, on what was the third highest spending campaign in the country. Schuster's big issue was abortion; she called him a "a slick trial lawyer Clinton Democrat." Cubin won 53%–41%.

In the House Cubin has a solidly conservative voting record and became chairman of the Energy and Mineral Resources Subcommittee. She sponsored the successful bill to allow coal companies larger leases of federal lands. She decried the October 2000 decision to ban snowmobiling in national parks. In November 2000 she was elected Republican Conference Secretary, the number six position in the House leadership.

In April 2002 Cubin expressed interest in succeeding the retiring James Hansen as chairman of the Resources Committee. She was only the 12th Republican on the committee in seniority, but the most senior was James Saxton of New Jersey, who had voted against conservatives on many committee issues. She suggested reviving the old Merchant Marine and Fisheries Committee, abolished by Republicans in 1995, and making Saxton its chairman. She may have damaged her case in September 2002, when she sponsored a bill for $6 billion in drought relief; this was the position taken by Senate Democrats and opposed by the Bush administration and the House Republican leadership. The Republican Steering Committee interviewed Cubin and other candidates for the chairmanship in January 2003, and awarded it to Richard Pombo of California, who had been 11th in seniority.

Cubin endured personal difficulties in 2001 and 2002. Her husband had multiple surgeries for nonmalignant tumors and autoimmune disease; he and their two sons rallied to appear with her when she announced for reelection in April 2002. She considered not running again, but her husband persuaded her to run. Her Democratic opponent in 2002 criticized her for missing votes; she had missed the vote on Resources Chairman James Hansen's proposal to allow the Mormon Church to buy Martin's Cove in Wyoming, the site of the death of Mormon pioneers in a blizzard in 1856, a proposal opposed by the Wyoming delegation, because she had been caught in traffic returning from a doctor's appointment. She was reelected 61%–36% and said afterwards, "It's actually the first time I've felt pleasure in defeating someone. My husband's very life was hanging in the balance, and they tried to capitalize on that. It was pretty low." She did not seek reelection to the Conference Secretary position.

In 2003 Cubin got a waiver to serve one more term as chairman of the Energy and Mineral Resources Subcommittee; she did not get another in 2005, and questioned Pombo's realignment of subcommittee jurisdictions. She has worked on some issues that have turned out to be more controversial than might have been expected. With Senator Craig Thomas she supported in 2001 the trading of state lands in Grand Teton National Park with federal lands in other parts of the state that could generate revenue for schools; but in 2002 the bill was encumbered with outgoing Resources Chairman James Hansen's amendments, and did not pass until June 2003, after he retired. In 2004 Cubin joined with committee ranking Democrat Nick Joe Rahall on a bill to reauthorize the Abandoned Mine Reclamation Fund and continue payments to Wyoming and Rahall's West Virginia even though mine cleanups in Wyoming were complete. Cubin argued that the fund owed Wyoming $400 million in back payments and the bill removed the $70 million yearly cap on transfer of payments to retirees' health funds. "Many Western coal producers are frustrated that the interest on their [abandoned mine fund] fees is going to support retired miners they never employed in the first place, rather than moving dirt on actual reclamation projects. But unfortunately the health care and reclamation issues had a bit of a shotgun wedding in the early 1990s, and you can't just divorce the two and still get a bill with a broad bipartisan support."

Cubin's missed votes and her controversial stands on some issues have resulted in some difficulty at the polls. In 2002 she was reelected 61%–36%, but carried Natrona County, her home base, by exactly 1 vote. In 2004 she had two serious opponents in the primary, which she won with just 55% of the vote—less than an incumbent usually gets. In the general election she improved her showing in Natrona County but won statewide by just 55%–42%, running 14% behind George W. Bush.

PUERTO RICO, VIRGIN ISLANDS, ★ GUAM, AMERICAN SAMOA ★

Four American insular territories—Puerto Rico, Virgin Islands, Guam, American Samoa—are represented in Congress by elected delegates who, like the District of Columbia's delegate, have floor privileges and votes on committees but not votes on the floor (though House Democrats let them vote in committee of the whole proceedings in the 103d Congress). Each territory's status—its relationship to the United States—is different, governed by a separate law, and status is often the pivot around which territorial politics turn.

PUERTO RICO

Puerto Rico has a unique history. For four centuries, from Columbus's landing here in 1493 until the Spanish-American War of 1898, Puerto Rico was a Spanish colony, and the port of San Juan was the gathering place for its annual convoy of gold and silver from the Americas to Spain. Today, with 4 million people, it is the largest American territory—about the same population as South Carolina; and about 4 million people of Puerto Rican descent live on the mainland. Fifty years ago, it was "the poorhouse of the Caribbean," heavily populated, devoted almost entirely to sugar and coffee cultivation. Now it has a recognizably First World economy, with per capita incomes about half of those of the least affluent American states and among the highest in Latin America.

Puerto Rico has elected a resident commissioner to Congress since 1900 (the only member of Congress with a four-year term) and its residents have been American citizens since 1917, but it didn't elect its own governor until 1948. In the 1940s, 1950s and early 1960s, Puerto Rico was transformed by Governor Luis Munoz Marin and his Popular Democratic Party. Munoz initiated "Operation Bootstrap" (called "Operation Hands to Work" by Puerto Ricans) to lure businesses to Puerto Rico with promises of low-wage labor and government-built factories and tax exemptions. Munoz also developed Puerto Rico's commonwealth form of government—better understood in Spanish, Estado Libre Asociado (ELA): Free Associated State—approved by plebiscite in 1952. Under ELA, Puerto Rico is part of the United States for purposes of international trade, foreign policy and war, but has its own separate laws, taxes and representative government; it is not subject to federal income taxes and is not eligible for federal benefits (though some have been approved by Congress). Some 200,000 Puerto Ricans have served in the U.S. military; 2,000 died in service and four were awarded the Congressional Medal of Honor. Puerto Rico has also developed its own political parties: Munoz's Popular Democrats (the Spanish acronym is PPD), the New Progressives (PNP) who favor statehood, and two Independence parties.

The commonwealth solution, by its own terms, was open to amendment; ever since Munoz's voluntary retirement in 1964, the central issue in Puerto Rico's politics has been status: Should this island continue or modify ELA, should it seek statehood, or should it seek independence? For many years there was gradual movement toward statehood. In the July 1967 referendum, conducted when the Popular Democrats were in power, Puerto Ricans voted for ELA over statehood by 60%–39%; in the November 1993 referendum, conducted with PNP Governor Pedro Rossello in office, the vote was 48% for ELA, 46% for statehood. In March 1998 the U.S. House voted 209–208 for a referendum setting terms for statehood; this was a project of Speaker Newt Gingrich, who hoped to attract Hispanic votes, and of Resources Committee Chairman Don Young, who saw in statehood backers' demands echoes of Alaska's fight for statehood. But the bill went nowhere in the Senate. Rossello ordered a referendum on his terms (which are unlikely ever to be accepted in Congress) in December 1998; 47% voted for statehood and 50% for "none of the above," the option favored by the Popular Democrats. Independence has negligible support—4% in 1993, 3% in 1998—primarily from university students; nor are there many pro-independence abstentions, for voter turnout in the enthusiastic politics of Puerto Rico is the highest under the American flag, higher than in even the most affluent, long-settled suburbs of the mainland. Now, with the election of PPD Governor Sila Calderon in 2000 and Anibal Acevedo-Vila in 2004, the move toward statehood seems to have been halted. For years younger and more affluent voters have tilted toward statehood, but as they have aged and the island has grown more prosperous, support for statehood has stopped growing.

As Puerto Ricans were debating status in the 1990s, the island's economy was changing. In 1996 Congress voted to phase out over 10 years Section 936, the provision that shelters earnings of some Puerto Rico manufacturers from federal taxes and allows their products into the U.S. duty-free. Pharmaceutical companies in particular have set up highly visible plants in Puerto Rico—half of U.S. prescription drugs are manufactured in Puerto Rico—and ELA supporters claimed that the island's economy depended on the tax exemptions. But pharmaceutical companies have continued to invest in Puerto Rico after the phaseout of Section 936 began (it expires in January 2006). Fifteen of the top 20 pharmaceutical companies in the world are in Puerto Rico, which produces 16 of the 20 top value-added prescription drugs sold in the U.S. Abbott Laboratories chose Puerto Rico over Ireland and Singapore for a new $350 million plant in 2002, and Bristol-Myers Squibb and Amgen have made new investments. Unemployment continues to hover around 11% (it was 22% in the 1980s) but Puerto Rico is developing new jobs in services, tourism, trading and exports.

If Puerto Rico's economy has been changed by changes in federal law, it has also been changed over the last 10 years by its governors. Pedro Rossello, the PNP governor from 1992 to 2000, sold the government-owned Navieras shipping line and telephone company, privatized hospitals and the Aqueduct and Sewer Authority's facilities. He reduced the corporate tax rate, eliminated taxes on distributed dividends and started massive public works projects. Puerto Rico provides health insurance to the poor via *la tarjetita* (the little card) and Rossello instituted school vouchers and five minutes of daily reflection in schools. Sila Calderon, the PPD governor elected in 2000, halted privatizations. In August 2002 she announced that the government would invest $1 billion in the 700 poorest communities on the island, in infrastructure—water, electricity, roads—and education and health care programs.

One raging issue in Puerto Rico has been corruption; the other has been Vieques. The Vieques bombing range was established in 1941, and had long sparked protests from those who claimed the bombing jeopardized islanders' safety and polluted the environment; the Navy claimed that it was their most important training ground, the best place in the world for combined sea-land-air training exercises. For a year protesters streamed onto the range and prevented exercises, and many were arrested in protests after islanders were killed in 1999. Rossello and politicians of all parties demanded that the range be shut down. But the Navy got support in Senate Armed Services Committee hearings in December 1999, in which Chairman John Warner said that if the bombing range was closed, the Navy should abandon its Roosevelt Roads base in San Juan harbor. In January 2000 Rossello reached agreement with the Clinton White House. The Navy would set a date for a referendum in which voters in Vieques (population 9,300) would decide whether to end the bombing in May 2003 or allow it to continue, with $40 million of federal aid for the town; in the meantime, exercises would continue 90 days a year. In December 2000 the Navy announced the Vieques referendum would be held in November 2001.

Sila Calderon campaigned for an immediate end to the bombing on Vieques and made that and corruption her two top issues. In June 2001, George W. Bush announced that the Navy would halt all military exercises on Vieques by May 2003 and provide $40 million in local aid. Calderon engineered an advisory referendum in Vieques in July 2001; 68% voted for immediate closure, 30% for indefinite continuation of the bombing and 2% for closure in May 2003. September 11 obviously made military priorities seem more important, and in the December 2001 defense bill Congress barred the Navy from moving until an "equivalent or superior" site was found. In January 2002 at a bill signing, Bush assured Calderon that he would keep his word. In June 2002 the Navy turned over the western part of the island to the Interior Department. In January and February 2003 the Navy held its last military exercises there, and on May 1 the base was closed. In June people were buying up housing sites, and the Navy moved its training to various sites on the Atlantic coast with reportedly positive results. In Congress Defense Appropriations Subcommittee Chairman Jerry Lewis moved to close down Roosevelt Roads, whose work force had already been reduced and whose only mission was support of the Vieques bombing range. In March 2004 the Navy closed Roosevelt Roads, and the Naval Southern Command moved to Mayport, Florida; locals started trying to make the base a cruise ship port.

The 2004 campaign cycle was a time of angry charges and countercharges in Puerto Rico politics. Criminal trials of high officials in Pedro Rossello's administration sparked cries of corruption by PPD politicians; PNP politicians said their party was being persecuted to discredit the cause of statehood. The 2004 election resulted in the election of new leaders and was the first time Puerto Rico elected a split ticket: the PPD's Anibal Acevedo-Vila was elected governor over Rossello by a 48.4%–48.2% margin, after court battles over whether ballots should be counted on which voters marked the square for Anibal and the square for the pro-independence PIP party. But the PNP won a majority in the Senate, and one PNP member resigned to allow Rossello to become a member. And the PNP's Luis Fortuno was elected resident commissioner, Puerto Rico's non-voting member of the House, by a 48.5%–48.0% margin. Like Sila Calderon's election in 2000, Acevedo-Vila's election in 2004 probably keeps the status issue off the table for four years, at least so far as mainland politicians are concerned. The PNP's corruption problems seem likely to weaken the cause of statehood, and consensus on the terms of a referendum seems unlikely at best. Independence continues to be favored by only a splinter of the electorate. But there remains the question of whether the ties between the United States and Puerto Rico would be frayed or ruptured. The PPD champions Puerto Rico's separate identity, which has a popular resonance, as was apparent when the Puerto Rico basketball team beat the United States team 92–73 at the Athens Olympics in August 2004. And some Puerto Ricans still admire the nonagenarian Lolita Lebron, the nationalist who led the gunfire attack on the U.S. House of Representatives in March 1954.

At the same time, it appears that most Americans of Puerto Rican descent now live on the mainland. The huge Puerto Rican migration to New York City of the postwar period came to an end around 1960, when net flows between the island and the city evened out. But in the 1990s Puerto Rican immigration to other areas increased, and now there are large numbers of Puerto Ricans in the Boston, Hartford, northern New Jersey, Cleveland, Chicago, Houston, Orlando and Fort Lauderdale metro areas. As governor, Calderon led a voter registration drive among mainland Puerto Ricans from the 12 Puerto Rico Federal Affairs Administration offices in mainland cities which registered more than 100,000 voters. Puerto Ricans in New York have long voted heavily Democratic; in Florida it appears that many voted for George W. Bush, and his decision on Vieques may have helped him win that state by a comfortable margin. Puerto Rico also has the opportunity to play a unique role in regional affairs. Thirty years ago, as Puerto Rico was developing a First World economy, its Caribbean and Central American neighbors were still in the Third World, dependent on export of agricultural commodities, with tiny middle classes and ruling elites. Today they are moving ahead, with low-wage factory jobs that Puerto Rico, with its higher wages, can no longer compete for, and growing middle classes and electoral democracies. Passage of the Caribbean Free Trade Agreement could lead to greater trade and to a role for Puerto Rico as a helpful elder sister, with money to invest and expertise gained from its own economic development—and wisdom gained from its own political development.

Puerto Rico's ELA status is a compromise, often an uneasy one. But Munoz Marin's achievement, creating enthusiasm for a compromise, is an astonishing political feat. It is an example for others to ponder. Amid the noisy clash of the partisans of ELA and statehood and independence, the Puerto Rican people have developed a polity that is tolerant of divergence of opinion, determined to uphold personal liberty, increasingly intolerant of corruption and capable of fostering sustained economic growth. That is an achievement worthy of attention in Latin America and of respect on the mainland.

Presidential politics   One of the complaints of Puerto Rico's New Progressives is that it cannot vote for president, and in 2000 Governor Pedro Rossello tried to remedy that. On August 29, 2000, a federal judge in Puerto Rico ruled that Puerto Rican voters have a right to vote for president emanating from their U.S. citizenship and ordered that a vote be held and that

Congress count eight electoral votes for Puerto Ricans' choice (eight was the number of electoral votes Puerto Rico would have had under the 1990 Census if it were a state). This ruling went against precedent and the language of the Constitution, which gives votes only to states that have been admitted to the Union and, in an amendment, to the District of Columbia. But Rossello and the New Progressive legislature were happy to pass a law putting the presidential election on the November 7 ballot. On October 13, the First Circuit Court of Appeals predictably reversed the rules and ordered the presidential contest off the ballot. So no one knows for sure which candidate Puerto Rico would have preferred, George W. Bush (who nominally favored statehood, as Republican platforms long have) or Al Gore (who favored "self-determination" for Puerto Rico), although almost everyone assumes Gore would have won.

Puerto Rico does send delegates to the two mainland parties' national conventions. The Republicans, long identified with the New Progressives, though its two leading figures in 2000 identify with Democrats, held a primary in February in which the Spanish-speaking George W. Bush beat John McCain 93%-6%. That gave him 14 convention delegates, more than were elected by Vermont or Delaware and the same as Maine, Rhode Island and Hawaii. Al Gore won the March Democratic caucus, giving him 59 delegates, more than 24 states. In 2004, local Democrats canceled the June caucus. By then, John Kerry had no remaining opposition; all 58 delegates were designated as Kerry delegates.

Since Puerto Rico's Democratic delegates in the past have voted as a bloc, while Democratic rules require other states' delegates to be split proportionately, in a divided Democratic convention (if there ever is one again) Puerto Rico actually has more leverage than all but a half dozen or so states, as it did in the bitterly split convention in 1980.

Governor   Anibal Acevedo-Vila was elected governor of Puerto Rico in 2004. He is a former president of the Popular Democrats (PPD), was elected to a four-year term as Puerto Rico's Resident Commissioner—actually, non-voting delegate in the U.S. House—in 2000. He was born in San Juan and graduated from the University of Puerto Rico and Harvard Law School and was a law clerk in the Puerto Rico Supreme Court and the First Circuit Court of Appeals in Boston, which has jurisdiction over Puerto Rico. He returned to Puerto Rico to work on the staff of Governor Rafael Hernandez Colon from 1989 to 1992. In 1992 he was elected to the Puerto Rico House. In 2000 he was the PPD candidate for resident commissioner; his opponent was incumbent Carlos Romero Barcelo, who was elected mayor of San Juan in 1968 and 1972, governor in 1976 and 1980 and resident commissioner in 1992 and 1996. Romero was known for his pugnacious temperament and strong advocacy of statehood, and unlike many other New Progressives always identified with the mainland Democratic Party. Puerto Ricans tend to vote on straight party lines, and as the Popular Democrats' Sila Maria Calderon was winning the governorship 49%–46%, Acevedo-Vila was elected by a 50%–45% margin, with 5% for the Independence Party candidate.

In May 2003, Calderon unexpectedly announced she would not seek reelection in 2004; she immediately backed lawyer Jose Alfredo Hernandez Mayoral, son of the former three-term Governor Rafael Hernandez Colon, for the PPD nomination. But Hernandez Mayoral later withdrew from the race and the nomination went to Acevedo-Vila. Acevedo-Vila showed his independence of Calderon when in September 2003 he criticized her selection of Ferdinand Mercado as chief justice of the Puerto Rico Supreme Court. The PNP had a primary in November 2003 in which former Governor Pedro Rossello, elected in 1992 and 1996, defeated former Transportation Secretary Carlos Pesquera, the party's candidate in 2000. Rossello campaigned as a strong supporter of statehood and said he would bring a lawsuit against the federal government citing civil rights cases and seeking a decision declaring Puerto Rico a state—an unlikely prospect. Acevedo-Vila said he would let voters decide whether to call a constitutional convention on state to define options for a referendum or would ask Congress to authorize a plebiscite. He also frequently attacked Rossello for corruption in his administration; PNP supporters said the corruption prosecutions were a form of persecution of statehood advocates. Rossello led in the polls through much of the campaign. Acevedo-Vila urged supporters of the PIP independence party to make their ballots for the PIP and then for him. A PPD ballot was traditionally known as a *pavaso*, after the party symbol of the peasant's hat, or *pava*; a vote for the PIP and Acevedo became known as a *pivaso*.

The *pivasos* made all the difference. The initial count showed Acevedo leading by 3,880 votes, or 48.4%–48.2%, with 28,000 *pivasos*. Rossello said that *pivaso* ballots should not be counted for Acevedo; Acevedo said they should and that such ballots had been routinely counted in the past. Rossello sued and the Puerto Rico Supreme Court, most of whose members were PPD appointees, ruled that *pivasos* should be counted. Rossello went to federal court and Judge Daniel Dominguez, a PNP supporter, said that his court, not the Puerto Rico Supreme Court, had jurisdiction. Amid cries from both sides that the other was stealing the election, the PNP appealed to the First Circuit Court of Appeals in Boston, which ruled in late December that the Puerto Rico Supreme Court had jurisdiction. Acevedo was declared the winner and Rossello stopped contesting the election, but said, "We reaffirm that his certification is an illegitimate one." The PNP won a majority of seats in the Senate and elected its candidate Luis Fortuno as Resident Commissioner; this is the first time a governor of Puerto Rico has had to deal with a legislature and a representative in Congress of the opposite party. In April 2005 Acevedo vetoed a bill that would have called a referendum on whether to request the federal government honor any future decision by Puerto Rico to seek statehood.

Resident Commissioner

Luis Fortuno (R)

Elected 2004, 1st term; b. Oct. 31, 1960, San Juan; home, Guaynabo; Georgetown U., B.S.F.S. 1982; U. of VA, J.D. 1985; Catholic; married (Luce).

Professional Career: Practicing atty., 1985–2004; Sec., PR Dept. of Econ. Dev. and Comm., 1994–97.

DC Office: 126 CHOB, 20515, 202-225-2615; Fax: 202-225-2154; Web site: www.house.gov/fortuno.

District Office: Old San Juan, 787-723-6333.

Committees: *Education & the Workforce* (22d of 27 R): 21st Century Competitiveness; Select Education. *Resources* (22d of 27 R): Fisheries & Oceans; National Parks. *Transportation & Infrastructure* (38th of 41 R): Coast Guard & Maritime Transportation; Water Resources & Environment.

Luis Fortuno was elected Puerto Rico's resident commissioner in 2004, the first Puerto Rican to hold that office who identified with the Republican party in 100 years. Fortuno grew up in San Juan and graduated from Georgetown University and the University of Virginia law school. He practiced corporate law at a San Juan law firm until a gubernatorial appointment in 1993 as executive director of the Puerto Rico Tourism Company; in 1994 he became Puerto Rico's first Economic Development and Commerce Secretary. He returned to private practice in 1996 but in 2001 he became Puerto Rico's Republican National Committeeman and in 2003 he became the PNP nominee for resident commissioner; the incumbent PPD incumbent Anibal Acevedo Vila was running for governor and the PPD nominee was Senator Roberto Prats Palerm. This was the first Puerto Rico campaign in which the National Republican Congressional Committee and the Democratic Congressional Campaign Committee became involved. The previous PNP resident commissioner, Carlos Romero Barcelo, elected in 1992 and 1996, and former Governor Pedro Rossello, the PNP gubernatorial candidate again in 2004, identified with the Democratic party and were strong backers of Bill Clinton, while PPD officeholders have almost always identified with the Democratic party; an exception was former Governor Sila Calderon, who identified with neither mainland party and, after resolution of the Vieques issue, had good things to say about George W. Bush. Fortuno identified with the Republican party. "Hispanic values are Republican values, to a great degree," he said. "Family values are extremely important in our community. . . . I campaigned on a conservative platform of fiscal conservatism, family values, school vouchers, a five-minute moment of silence in the schools." He also campaigned in central Florida, which has a large Puerto Rican population, for George W. Bush, who carried or ran about even among non-Cuban Hispanics in that state. NRCC Chairman Tom Reynolds recruited Fortuno, and Illinois's Jerry Weller and Florida's Tom Feeney came to Puerto Rico to campaign for him. Fortuno spent $1.6 million and Prats $1.1 million.

Puerto Ricans tend to vote straight party tickets, and the result in this race was very close. Fortuno won 48.5% of the vote, 0.5% ahead of his party's losing candidate for governor; Prats won 48.0% of the vote, 0.4% behind his party's winning candidate for governor. That made Fortuno the first Republican to represent Puerto Rico in the House since Frederick Degetau, who served from 1901 to 1904. Fortuno was named vice president of the freshman class. This was the first time Puerto Rico has elected a split ticket: Governor Anibal Acevedo-Vila of the PPD backs some form of commonwealth status; Fortuno of the PNP favors statehood. Both pledged to work together.

VIRGIN ISLANDS

The United States's other insular territory in the Caribbean is the Virgin Islands, a very different sort of place from Puerto Rico, and the only place under the U.S. flag where people drive on the left. It is much smaller, with a resident population of only 110,000, mainly on the three islands of St. Thomas, St. John and St. Croix. They were settled not by Spaniards but by Dutch and Danes, and had a polyglot colonial society with one of the oldest Jewish communities in the Western Hemisphere; their most famous son is Alexander Hamilton, who grew up in St. Croix. Puerto Rico is multiracial and not self-conscious about it, but most Virgin Islanders are black and resent the clear divide between the races. While Puerto Rico has attracted all kinds of light industry, the Virgin Islands has lived primarily off tourism and refineries (the HOVENSA refinery on St. Croix is the largest refinery in the Western Hemisphere; it was built by Amerada Hess in the 1960s and is now half-owned by the Venezuela government oil company). These are industries that have produced high incomes for a few employees but have not provided the basis for a steady economy. Tourism, hurt by hurricanes in the 1990s, has recovered from September 11 and was up sharply in 2004, when the Virgin Islands were largely unscathed by the hurricanes that battered so much of the Caribbean and Florida. St. Thomas remains the number one cruise ship port in the world, with nearly 400 ships coming in each year, and in 2004 cruise ships returned to St. Croix after a two-year hiatus because of high crime. But unemployment has remained around 9%.

Nor does economic salvation seem likely to come from the investment businesses attracted to the Virgin Islands by tax breaks established by Congress and the Virgin Islands government. Individuals and businesses that qualify under the Economic Development Authority pay a maximum of 3.5% in income tax, which has yielded revenues of about $100 million a year to the island government. To qualify, you must live and do business in the Virgin Islands, under rules which Virgin Islands officials have asked the Treasury to clarify but which the Treasury says are clear. In 2002 and 2003 nearly 100 businesses were set up to qualify, but in 2004 the IRS started investigating whether investors really lived in the Virgin Islands; agents queried office and household staff on the location of their owners and how frequently they were in the islands. The first indictment came in February 2004 and the IRS in June said that lawyers and estate planners were making false claims. In October 2004 Congress passed a law that changed the rules which Virgin Islands Governor Charles Turnbull said could cost the Islands government between $42 and $63 million in revenue. In late 2004 the V.I. Economic Development Authority adopted an "informal policy" of limiting the number of partners in investment firms and requiring notices of new partners.

That could be a serious problem, because the Virgin Islands government has been running constant deficits on a budget of $608 million in 2004. One problem is the crushing burden of a $1 billion bond debt, which requires $45 million in debt service. Another is that the local government has largely ignored the recommendations of federal auditors; one agency had a 70% rate of delinquency on its loans. One-third of workers are employed by government. Virgin Island Delegate Donna Christensen, saying the government was on the brink of financial collapse, persuaded the U.S. House to pass in September 2004 a bill to establish a financial overseer with veto power over Virgin Islands government spending and renewable after five years by the federal government; the U.S. Senate did not act. Turnbull sharply opposed the measure. This was a dispute between Democrats, who have been the dominant party here; in recent elections Independents have run ahead of Republicans.

Governor   Charles Turnbull was born in St. Thomas, the son of immigrants from the British Virgin Islands. He earned undergraduate and graduate degrees from Hampton University and a doctorate in education from the University of Minnesota, then returned home to teach. As Virgin Islands's education commissioner, Turnbull upgraded the curriculum and built enough new schools to eliminate double school-day sessions. Promising a "grander vision" than offered by Independent Governor Roy Schneider—who focused on downsizing government, reducing spending and fighting drugs—Turnbull in 1998 defeated the one-term incumbent 59%–41%.

In April 1999, Turnbull said the government would be unable to pay its 10,000 workers because of $1 billion in debt from the previous administration. Turnbull tried to tackle this huge debt by cutting the government payroll through attrition and negotiated a memorandum of understanding with Interior Secretary Bruce Babbitt, promising to cut the budget, change the labor relations law and scrap five government holidays. But fiscal problems continued, and it appears that there has been no proper accounting of Virgin Islands government for many years. Nonetheless Turnbull was reelected on November 5, 2002, with 50.4% of the vote, just enough to avoid a runoff. In second place with 24% was Independent John deJongh, president of the chamber of commerce.

In his second term he has not been able to reduce government spending substantially and has faced a 15-member Senate in which his Democrats have a nominal majority but which has been dominated by a multiparty coalition. Despite the existing $1 billion bond debt, the Virgin Islands sold another $51 million of bonds in April 2004 to help HOVENSA finance a new crude processing plant; the company is the Virgin Islands's largest employer, with 2,000 employees. The Senate was unable to pass a budget in 2003 and went past the deadline to pass one in November 2004; Turnbull vetoed $10 million in pay raises and increased Senate spending. He strongly opposed Delegate Donna Christensen's bill, passed by the U.S. House in September 2004, to establish a financial overseer with the right to veto all Virgin Islands spending for at least five years. In October 2004 Turnbull signed a bill to create a constitutional convention, the Virgin Islands's fifth since 1964; the 1980 constitution draft was approved by the Senate but rejected by the voters in 1981. In November 2004 Turnbull vetoed three crime bills. One, aimed at dog fighting and perhaps cockfighting, would have made animal cruelty a felony, and allowed citizens to trespass on private property to protect animals; another would establish a police civilian review board (the police department had been under Justice Department review for possible civil rights violations); a third would have put fines for school vandalism into a school repair account.

Delegate

Donna Christensen (D)

Elected 1996, 5th term; b. Sept. 19, 1945, Teaneck, NJ; home, St. Croix; St. Mary's Col., B.S. 1966, George Washington U., M.D. 1970; Moravian; married (Christian).

Professional Career: Practicing physician, 1975–97; Territorial Asst., Commissioner of Health, 1988–94; Acting Commissioner of Health, 1994–95.

DC Office: 1510 LHOB, 20515, 202-225-1790; Fax: 202-225-5517; Web site: www.house.gov/christian-christensen.

District Offices: St. Croix, 340-778-5900; St. Thomas, 340-774-4408.

Committees: *Homeland Security* (12th of 15 D): Emergency Preparedness, Science & Technology; Management, Integration & Oversight; Prevention of Nuclear & Biological Attack. *Resources* (10th of 22 D): National Parks (RMM). *Small Business* (7th of 15 D): Regulatory Reform & Oversight.

The delegate from the Virgin Islands is Donna Christensen, first elected in 1996, when she beat Victor Frazer, a Republican who ran as an independent and was the upset winner in 1994. Christensen is from an old St. Croix family; her father was Virgin Islands Chief District Court Judge Almeric Christian. She graduated from St. Mary's College and George Washington Medical School; she practiced medicine for more than 20 years in the Virgin Islands, in a family practice and in several public positions. She was elected a Democratic national committeewoman in 1984 and ran one losing race for delegate in 1994. In 1996 she attacked Frazer, who after some hesitation caucused with the Democrats, for foreign travel (11 trips to four continents) and for inaction in opposing the welfare bill. Christensen led Frazer 38%–34% on November 5; in the runoff two weeks later she won 52%–48%. It was a regional race: Christensen won 69% on St. Croix, Frazer 64% on St. Thomas and St. John.

In the House, Christensen has forged alliances with the Congressional Black Caucus and, when it was in office, the Clinton administration to achieve her goals; she works on health issues for the Black Caucus. She opposed Bill Clinton's designation in January 2001 of 12,708 undersea acres as the U.S. Virgin Islands Coral Reef National Monument, arguing that it would hurt local fishermen. As ranking minority member of the Parks Subcommittee, she got a hearing on the issue in the Virgin Islands in July 2002.

Christensen has argued that the Virgin Islands government, with $1 billion in debt, is on the verge of bankruptcy. In October 2004 she persuaded the House to vote for her bill to establish a financial overseer with veto power over government spending for five years. On this she was strongly opposed by Governor Charles Turnbull. In August 2004 she advanced a constitutional amendment, co-sponsored by the delegates from Guam and American Samoa, allowing residents of U.S. territories overseas to vote for president. "Every conflict this country has been in, we have sent our young men and women to serve or to die in, per capita, some of the highest numbers you will find. While our nation is at war, and we're burying our soldiers just like everybody else, I think that maybe it's a timely point at which to introduce this."

Christensen was reelected by wide margins in 2002 and 2004.

GUAM

Some 3,800 miles west of Hawaii, 19 hours of flying time from Washington, D.C., is Guam, where America's day begins. Guam lies west of the International Date Line, and it is in the early hours of Tuesday there when the rest of us are just trying to get through Monday afternoon; the Interior Department came to Guam to see whether there were Y2K problems, as the clock struck midnight, January 1, 2000, while it was 9 a.m., December 31, in Washington. Geographically in the center of the Mariana Islands, Guam is legally separate: The Northern Marianas were administered by the U.S. as a United Nations trust territory until they became the Commonwealth of the Northern Marianas (CNMI) in 1978. Guam was ruled by Navy captains from 1898 to 1949, except for 32 months of Japanese occupation during World War II; in 1950 the Guam Organic Act made Guamanians U.S. citizens. Guam's first civilian governor, Carlton Skinner, who as a captain integrated the crew of his Navy ship in 1943, established the University of Guam and wrote its constitution; he died in June 2004. Guam elects its local government, but Congress still retains final power over the territory. It started electing a non-voting delegate to Congress in 1972.

Guam is 36 miles long by four to nine miles wide, with 168,000 people; 37% are Chamorro (descendants of the original islanders), 26% Filipino, 13% other Asian and 10% Caucasian; 85% of Guamanians are Catholic. The Catholic Church helped defeat a proposal for casino gambling 61%–39% in 2004, despite the competition for tourists from Japan and, it seems likely in future years, China from the Tinian Dynasty casino in the CNMI. Guam is tropical, but not an easy environment: in August 1993 it lived through an earthquake rated at 8.2 on the Richter scale, comparable to San Francisco in 1906; in December 2002, Supertyphoon Pongsona, with winds up to 184 miles per hour, cut off all electric power and caused hundreds of millions in damage. In July 2004 Typhoon Tingting pelted the island with 20 inches of rain in 48 hours.

Economically, Guam depends heavily on U.S. military bases; military bases occupy one-third of the land, 60% of income comes from the federal government and it makes for a pretty good living. Guam's gross domestic product per capita is the second highest in the Pacific, after Hawaii's. The slump in the Japanese economy hit Guam too: tourism was down from 1.3 million in 2000 to 1 million in 2002 and rose to just 1.15 million in 2004. Tourism seemed like the wave of the future when the military was being drawn down, from 30,000 personnel at the time of the Vietnam War to 5,000 after the end of the Cold War. Housing values plummeted and unemployment rose to as much as 15%. But September 11 changed that. Popular protests in South Korea and Japan against the U.S. military presence there, the threats of the North Korean government and the need to supply operations in South Asia have made Guam much more important militarily. Guam, 3,800 miles closer to Asia than Hawaii, reduces "the tyranny of distance" and is now a "power projection hub," in militaryspeak. And it has one additional advantage: as Air Force General William Begert put it, "Guam, first of all, is U.S. territory. I don't need overflight rights. I don't need landing rights. I always have permission to go to Guam. It might as well be California or New Jersey."

By 2004 military spending here was nearly double the levels of the mid-1990s. In fall 2002 two Los Angeles class submarines were stationed in Guam, and another followed in 2003. In February 2003 12 B-52s and 12 B-1s were stationed on Guam. The Navy spent $30 million dredging Apra Harbor and repairing World War II-era wharves; $500 million was spent on construction at Andersen Air Force Base, including a $32 million air-conditioned hangar for the humidity-sensitive B-2. Guam is a good site for training: the Marines rent typhoon-damaged structures for urban warfare exercises and the southern jungles, so thick that the last Japanese holdout was not flushed out until 1972, are good for rural warfare training. There are proposals to station a carrier group in Guam, which would bring in $423 million to the local economy and create 4,000 local jobs, and to station a flight wing there as well. Guam officials were delighted.

For much of the 1990s Guam sought a change in status, to give the Guam government control over immigration. Chamorros said they want to block others from coming in, establishing citizenship and making them a minority; another motive was to bring in guest workers as the surrounding Commonwealth of the Northern Marianas Islands has done, with local enforcement of labor laws. The first Bush administration rejected the bill as inconsistent with the constitutional provision giving Congress full powers over territories. For a time the Clinton administration seemed sympathetic and inclined to agree to "mutual consent." But the election of the Republican Congress abruptly changed the provision's prospects. Guamanians attempted to counter that in 1996 by showering the Democratic National Committee with $892,000 in contributions, the most per capita anywhere under the American flag. But in October 1997 a Clinton official said he saw no constitutional way to do what Guam wanted. There has been no revival of this issue since George W. Bush became president.

Instead Guam Delegate Robert Underwood sought increased Compact-Impact Aid and a War Reparations Commission. The latter, a goal of Guam delegates since 1972, was finally signed in December 2002, as Underwood was leaving office (he ran for governor and lost). It sets up a five-member commission to decide whether Guamanians who were victims of torture, forced labor, internment and deprivation during the Japanese occupation should get more than the $5,000 that was paid them under the 1940s Guam Meritorious Claims Act. The compact aid Guam has sought is compensating for the cost of absorbing immigrants from the Marshall Islands and Micronesia; the U.S. signed a compact with them in 1986, giving the U.S. full military access to their territory and in return allowing them to immigrate freely to the United States, including Guam, as 13,000 have. In 2003 Delegate Madeleine Bordallo and the Hawaii delegation sought a $35 million annual payment of compact aid, to be divided among Guam, Hawaii, the CNMI and American Samoa; the Bush administration offered $15 million, and eventually Congress voted $30 million. The Guam legislature in April 2004 voted to authorize $109 million in Compact Impact Grant Anticipation Notes, securitizing the expected funds and freeing money for immediate spending. Bordallo also sought forgiveness of $157 million in Guam's debt to federal agencies; the Bush administration denied the request in December 2004.

Guam votes for Democrats more often than Republicans, but politics here is a family matter. Governor Felix Camacho's father was also governor; his lieutenant governor, Kaleo Moylan, is the son of the elder Camacho's lieutenant governor. Robert Underwood ascribed his first victory as delegate to his large number of cousins; he was weakened in the 2002 governor race by primary competition from Geri Gutierrez, wife of term-limited Governor Carl Gutierrez. The 2002 Republican candidate for delegate, Joseph Ada, was elected governor in 1986 and 1990. His opponent in the latter race was Madeleine Bordallo, who beat him for delegate and whose husband Ricardo Bordallo was elected governor in 1974 and 1982. Bordallo won the 2002 Democratic nomination by beating Judith Won Pat, daughter of Antonio Borja Won Pat, Guam's first elected delegate who served from 1972 to 1984 and after whom Guam's civilian airport is named.

Guam of course does not cast any electoral votes for president, but has a part in presidential politics. It elects delegates to party national conventions—6 for Bush and 6 for Kerry in 2004. In November Guam has conducted a straw poll for president, and has voted for the winner every time since 1984. In 2000 George W. Bush beat Al Gore 52%–47%; in 2004, after the big military buildup, Bush beat John Kerry 65%–35%. That was a bigger increase in the Bush percentage he achieved in any state and, among congressional districts, was only equaled in the 9th District of New York.

Governor   Felix Camacho, a Republican, was elected governor of Guam in 2002. Camacho grew up in Guam and attended Catholic schools; his father Carlos Camacho was appointed governor in 1969 and elected to a single term in 1970. He graduated from Marquette University in Milwaukee and returned to Guam and worked for Pacific Financial Corporation and IBM. When he was 31, IBM proposed to transfer him off island, and he paused to set out his short-term and long-term goals; one of the long-term goals was "governor of Guam." Republican Joseph Ada was governor, and in March 1988 he appointed Camacho deputy chief of the Public Utility Agency, and in November 1988 he was appointed executive director of the Civil Service Commission. In 1992 he was elected to the Guam Legislature, where he was assistant majority leader.

In 2002 Carl Gutierrez was ineligible to run for a third term, and Camacho ran. In the Republican primary he defeated Tony Unpingco, the Speaker of the Guam Legislature, 54%–46%. In the Democratic primary, between Delegate Robert Underwood and Geri Gutierrez, Carl Gutierrez's wife, both Democrats spent more than $400,000 on this race, which got somewhat angry; Underwood won 64%–36%. Afterward there was talk that some Gutierrez backers were supporting Camacho in return for promises of jobs. The candidates debated in both English and Chamorro; Underwood spoke in Chamorro the whole time, while Camacho had to break into English. They disagreed on issues like casinos, waste treatment and return of military land. Camacho won 55%–45%, carrying some normally Democratic areas, but Democrats won a 9–6 majority in the Legislature.

Camacho urged Congress to include Guam in the Radiation Exposure Compensation Program because of the 67 nuclear tests conducted from 1946 to 1958 at the Marshall Islands atoll of Eniwetok. He sought disaster relief after Guam was hit by Typhoon Tingting in June 2004. In September 2004 Camacho vetoed the Legislature's $447 million budget, saying it would overspend revenue by $50 million; the Legislature partially overrode his veto. Perhaps his biggest achievement was the privatization of the Guam Telephone Authority, sold for $150 million in December 2004 to TeleGuam Holdings, part of a private investment fund of the Roy Disney family. Privatization of the Guam Water Authority continues to be debated; it has been cited by regulators for producing contaminated water.

Delegate

Madeleine Bordallo (D)

Elected 2002, 2nd term; b. May 31, 1933, Graceville, MN; home, Tamuning; St. Mary's Col. 1952, St. Katherine's Col., A.A. 1953; Catholic; widowed.

Elected Office: GU Senate, 1981–82, 1986–94; GU Lt. Gov., 1994–2002.

DC Office: 427 CHOB, 20515, 202-225-1188; Fax: 202-226-0341; Web site: www.house.gov/bordallo.

District Office: Hagatna, 671-477-4272.

Committees: *Armed Services* (23d of 28 D): Projection Forces; Readiness. *Resources* (18th of 22 D): Fisheries & Oceans; National Parks. *Small Business* (9th of 15 D): Regulatory Reform & Oversight (RMM).

Madeleine Bordallo, a Democrat, was elected delegate from Guam in 2002. She grew up in Minnesota and, from age 14, on Guam. She graduated from St. Katherine's College in St. Paul with a degree in vocal music and worked as a program director and program host on Guam radio stations. In 1953 she married Ricardo Bordallo, from a prominent Guam family, who owned an auto dealership and had many business interests and was well connected in island politics. Madeleine Bordallo became Guam's Democratic National Committeewoman in 1964 and has held that position ever since (she is the most senior member of the Democratic National Committee). Ricardo Bordallo was elected governor in 1974, defeated for reelection in 1978, then elected governor again in 1982. With her husband's encouragement, Madeleine Bordallo ran for the Guam Legislature and was elected in 1980, 1986, 1988, 1990 and 1992. In 1990 Ricardo Bordallo wrapped himself in the Guam flag, chained himself to the statue of Chief Quipuha and shot himself to avoid a prison term for bribery. Madeleine Bordallo was a candidate for governor that year, but lost 57%–43% to incumbent Joseph Ada. In 1994 she was elected lieutenant governor and was reelected in 1998.

In 2002, when Delegate Robert Underwood decided to run for governor, Bordallo ran for delegate. In the primary she faced Judith Won Pat, daughter of Guam's first delegate, Antonio Borja Won Pat, who served from 1974 to 1986. In this contest between longtime friends, Bordallo won 59%–41%. In the general she faced Joseph Ada, who beat her in 1990. This time she won by an impressive 65%–35% margin.

Bordallo got a seat on the Armed Services Committee and proceeded to lobby her colleagues there for more military deployments in Guam. "All I have to say is location, location, location." In 2003 she got an amendment passed defining U.S. territories and overseas possessions as part of the geographic United States; she had been miffed when a Chamorro State Department employee was denied reimbursement for his son's flight to attend the University of Guam on the grounds that it was not a U.S. school. She also got a bill signed in 2003 giving Guam and other insular areas the same access to guaranteed loans as the 50 states; this seemed likely to bring in $13.5 million, a significant chunk of money for GovGuam (the name for Guam's government).

She sought $157 million of debt relief for Guam but her request was denied by the Bush administration. Working closely with Senator Daniel Inouye, who she said was her mentor in Congress, she successfully got $30 million annual compact aid for 20 years, to be divided among Guam, Hawaii, the CNMI and American Samoa; this is to compensate Guam for the costs imposed by immigrants from Micronesia and the Marshall Islands, allowed in the United States by a 1986 compact which gave the U.S. military access to their territories. But she sought still more. "I still believe Guam should be compensated for past unreimbursed compact impact expenses."

The 2004 defense reauthorization included $90 million in military construction for Guam. It also included $250,000 for Bordallo's invasive species pilot project; Guam has been plagued by the voracious and repulsive brown tree snake, which has no natural enemies there.

Bordallo was unopposed for reelection in 2004.

AMERICAN SAMOA

American Samoa, the only American territory south of the Equator, has been relatively little influenced by Western settlers and remains almost as Polynesian today as it was when the United States took possession in 1900 at the request of tribal chiefs. These seven islands with a hot and rainy climate are 2,300 miles southwest of Hawaii, 1,600 miles northeast of New Zealand. American Samoa has 57,000 people, 90% of them on the island of Tutuila, 89% of them Polynesian, mostly Christian (50% Congregationalist, 20% Catholic); they are U.S. nationals but not U.S. citizens. An estimated 50,000 Samoans live on the U.S. mainland and 20,000 in Hawaii, including Honolulu Mayor Mufi Hannemann. Many keep the island in mind. After Cyclone Heta hit American Samoa in January 2004, Mufi Hannemann's brother Gus started organizing food relief in Honolulu, and Dwayne "The Rock" Johnson, actor and former pro wrestler, who is of Samoan descent, handed him a check for $10,000. American Samoa's population has doubled in the last 20 years, and fear that outsiders will change the culture has prompted some demands for stricter immigration standards. American Samoa is an unincorporated territory administered by the Interior Department since 1951; minimum wages are set for industries by the U.S. Department of Labor. American Samoa elects a governor and a two-house legislature known as the Fono. It is a bilingual society and government: Government is mostly conducted in English, Fono proceedings are in Samoan, and court sessions are conducted in English with each sentence then translated into Samoan.

The market economy has not made much progress here: American Samoa lives off the federal government, which spends some $23 million annually, plus varying amounts for construction (the Army in 2002 pitched in $1 million for a 55-year lease of six acres at Pago Pago Airport for a Reserve County), and two big tuna canneries, which employ 5,150 workers and provide one-third of all U.S. canned tuna. Another 4,000 work for the American Samoan government, most at $2.77 an hour. Residents are eligible for U.S. food stamps and welfare; local agriculture is minimal and sheltered (the territorial government in 2000 wanted to quadruple tariffs on bananas and taro). The bedrock of the local economy is the territorial government.

Tourism has been minimal: 2000 saw the opening of the first McDonalds, followed by a Kentucky Fried Chicken and a Quality Inn. Governor Togiola Tulafono says he hopes to develop "controlled tourism in a way that won't affect our fragile environment."

One cause celebre is the renaming of nearby Samoa, formerly British Samoa and Western Samoa. The single name suggests to many in American Samoa that they are regarded as not full Samoans, and the legislature threatened not to recognize Samoan passports—a problem, since 85% of the cannery work force is from Samoa. But Sunia, a nephew of the Samoan prime minister, promised to veto any such bill. But if American Samoans are proud Samoans, they are also proud Americans: On April 17, 2000, they celebrated the 100th anniversary of the American takeover, with a 60-foot American flag raised on Sogelau Hill, where the American flag was first raised; there was traditional singing and dancing at Veterans Stadium and a long boat race in Pago Pago Harbor, and a commemorative stamp was unveiled showing a Samoan alia (two-hull canoe) sailing in easterly winds near Suniatu Mountain in the Manu'a island group. And

Samoans have become devoted to one staple of American life: football. The island has six high school football teams and a 5,000-seat stadium where just about everyone comes to cheer. The style of play is aggressive, with lots of body contact. Of 900 boys who graduated from high school in 2002 and 2003, 97 left the island to play at four- or two-year colleges in the mainland; Penn State even sent its assistant coach to American Samoa to scout prospects.

American Samoa does not cast electoral votes for president, but does send delegates to the parties' national conventions. In February 2000, George W. Bush won four delegates in a caucus. In March 2000, Al Gore beat Bill Bradley by 21–4—those are not percentages, but the actual number of votes; Bradley got one convention vote split between four delegates. On March 8, 2004, John Kerry got 2.5 convention votes divided between 5 delegates and Dennis Kucinich got the remaining half-vote from the sixth delegate. The week before, Bush won all 6 Republican delegates.

Governor   Togiola T.A. Tulafono was sworn in as American Samoa's governor on April, 7, 2003, after the sudden death of Governor Tauese Sunia March 26. Togiola grew up in American Samoa and after high school graduated from Honolulu Police Academy and worked as a policeman for a year. He graduated from Chadron State College in Nebraska, worked in the American Samoan attorney general's office and graduated from the Washburn University law school in Topeka, Kansas, and National Judicial College in Reno, Nevada. He returned to American Samoa, where he practiced law for 20 years and served as a judge and a senator and in a variety of executive posts: administrative assistant to the Secretary of Samoan Affairs, Samoan Assistant to the Attorney General, the first chairman of the American Samoa Power Authority, and the first chairman of the Board of High Education. Togiola was elected lieutenant governor in 1996 and served under Tauese until his 2003 death. In April 2003, one of his first acts as governor was to appoint Treasurer Aitofele Toese Sunia, Tauese's brother, as lieutenant governor.

As governor, Togiola took action on a number of issues. In December 2003 he issued an order prohibiting shark finning, importing shark fins, prized by many Asians, without the entire shark carcass. In March 2004 he sponsored a statute criminalizing human trafficking, to complement the federal statute under which a Korean garment factory operator was prosecuted. In April 2004 he said he would appoint a commission to review American Samoa's relationship to the United States. In July 2004 he expressed concern that all the 200 Army reservists in American Samoa would be called to active duty at the same time. He wrote the Army "asking that they modify that policy to allow for partial deployments." In December 2004 56 were deployed, including his daughter Olita Tulafono. In September 2004 he expressed concern that foreign competition might result in the shutdown of the island's tuna canneries. In the November 2 election, Togiola won 48% of the vote to 39% for Afoa Moega Lutu and 12% for Senator Teo Fuavai. Togiola won the November 16 runoff with 56% of the vote.

Delegate

Eni F.H. Faleomavaega (D)

Elected 1988, 9th term; b. Aug. 15, 1943, Vailoatai; home, Pago Pago; Brigham Young U., B.A. 1972, U. of CA, LL.M. 1973; Mormon; married (Hinanui).

Military Career: Army, 1966–69 (Vietnam).

Elected Office: AS Lt. Gov., 1984–89.

Professional Career: A.A., U.S. Del. from AS, 1973–75; Cnsl., U.S. House Interior Cmte., 1975–81; AS Dpty. Atty. Gen., 1981–84.

DC Office: 2422 RHOB, 20515, 202-225-8577; Fax: 202-225-8757; Web site: www.house.gov/faleomavaega.

District Office: Pago Pago, 684-633-1372.

Committees: *International Relations* (4th of 23 D): Asia & the Pacific (RMM); Western Hemisphere. *Resources* (6th of 22 D): Energy & Mineral Resources; Fisheries & Oceans. *Small Business* (5th of 15 D): Regulatory Reform & Oversight; Tax, Finance & Exports.

American Samoa has elected a delegate to Congress since 1980. Delegate Eni F. H. Faleomavaega is a Democrat first elected in 1988. He went to high school in Hawaii, to Brigham Young University, then to law school in Houston and Berkeley; he served in Vietnam in the Army. In the 1970s he worked on the Natural Resources Insular subcommittee staff and for Utah Democrat Gunn McKay. In 1981 he became deputy attorney general of American Samoa, and in 1985 lieutenant governor.

Faleomavaega (he uses his last name in his press releases, rather than the first name used to refer to Samoan chiefs) serves on the Resources Committee, where he has been ranking Democrat on three subcommittees—Native Americans and Insular Affairs in January 1995; National Parks and Public Lands in January 1997; Fisheries, Conservation, Wildlife and Oceans in January 1999. He is also a member of International Affairs and ranking member on its East Asian and the Pacific Subcommittee. He led the congressional protest against the French nuclear tests in the Pacific, and was stopped by the French for approaching the French nuclear testing site at Mururoa Atoll and imprisoned in Tahiti in 1996.

With help from Senator Daniel Inouye and Pennsylvania Democrat John Murtha, Faleomavaega got into the October 1998 omnibus budget free transportation on military aircraft for veterans approved for VA health care in Hawaii; in July 2000 he complained that the VA was not cooperating and only one veteran had flown to Hawaii.

Faleomavaega has pressed for a bill to exempt interest on American Samoa bonds from state and local taxes—the same treatment enjoyed by bonds issued by Puerto Rico, Guam and the Virgin Islands. The House approved the measure by voice vote in September 2002 but the Senate did not act. He reintroduced the bill in 2003 and it passed the House in November 2003 and the Senate in September 2004 and was signed into law. When the Interior Department tightened conditions for funding capital improvement projects in the territories, Faleomavaega objected in March 2004. "What is the sense of having an elected governor if the deputy assistant secretary is going to be the one controlling the use of funds?" In October 2004, he called for an extension of Section 936 for tuna canneries; the provision, which provides favorable tax treatment, is sched-uled to expire in October 2006. He was concerned that tariffs on Ecuador's tuna exports might be rescinded in order to ease disputes between Ecuador and large U.S. companies operating there; he warned that Ecuador's tuna production capacity could "wipe out" American Samoa's economy. Also in October 2004 he urged the setting up of a confederation of Polynesian states, perhaps including Hawaii and the Maori of New Zealand, similar to the Melanesian Spearhead group and the Micronesian group.

American Samoa's election law provides for no primary contests and requires a runoff 14 days later if no candidate wins 50% of the vote in the November election. In 1996, 2000 and 2002, Faleomavaega was forced into runoffs. He protested that 14 days was not enough time to get ballots to and back from military personnel serving abroad. In 2002 this posed an additional problem: because of the infrequency of flights to and from American Samoa, Faleomavaega was not able to campaign and to return to Washington to vote in the November 14 Democratic Caucus where Bob Menendez defeated Rosa DeLauro for Caucus chairman by one vote (he would have voted for Menendez). In 2004 he sponsored a bill to abolish the runoff unless the Fono created a primary election for delegate. This passed the House and Senate unanimously and was signed into law October 30. It was moot for the November 2 election, since Faleomavaega had just one opponent, longtime Republican House staffer Aumua Amata Coleman, who also ran against him in 2000 and 2002. This time Faleomavaega won 53%–47%. Fewer votes are cast in American Samoa than in any other House race—11,502 in November 2004.

BY THE NUMBERS

THE 109th CONGRESS
(As of January 3, 2005)

House: 232R, 202D, 1I
Senate: 55R, 44D, 1I

Oldest member of the Senate:	Robert Byrd (born Nov. 20, 1917)
Youngest member of the Senate:	John Sununu (born Sept. 10, 1964)
Longest service in the Senate:	Robert Byrd (since Jan. 3, 1959)
Oldest member of the House:	Ralph Hall (born May 3, 1923)
Youngest member of the House:	Patrick McHenry (born Oct. 22, 1975)
Longest service in the House:	John Dingell (since Dec. 13, 1955)
Largest House delegation:	California (53 seats; 33D, 20R)
Female members of Congress:	65 (House) 14 (Senate)
Black members of Congress:	40 (House) 1 (Senate)
Hispanic members of Congress:	23 (House) 2 (Senate)

Top Ranked Congressional Districts

Largest (*excluding at-large districts*):	105,635 sq. miles	Nevada 2
Smallest:	12 sq. miles	New York 11
Rural:	78.7%	Kentucky 5
One-person households:	49.6%	New York 14
Graduate/professional degrees:	28.1%	Maryland 8
Government workers:	29.0%	Maryland 4
Military veterans:	21.7%	Florida 1
Black, non-Hispanic:	65.2%	Illinois 1
Asian, non-Hispanic:	53.6%	Hawaii 1
American Indian, non-Hispanic:	18.0%	Arizona 1
Hispanic:	77.7%	Texas 16
Social Security beneficiaries:	250,771	Florida 5

2004 PRESIDENTIAL ELECTION

George W. Bush (R)   50.7%
John Kerry (D)   48.3%

States carried by Bush	31	Congressional districts carried by Bush in 2004:	255	
States carried by Kerry	19	Democratic-held districts carried by Bush in 2004:	41	
Counties carried by Bush:	2,530			
Counties carried by Kerry:	583	Congressional districts carried by Kerry in 2004:	180	
Top Bush county:		Republican-held districts carried by Kerry in 2004:	18	
Ochiltree County, TX	92.0%			
Top Kerry county:		Districts carried by Bush in 2000 and Kerry in 2004:	2	
Shannon County, SD	84.6%	Districts carried by Gore in 2000 and Bush in 2004:	17	

Top 10 Best-Performing Bush Districts in 2004

District	Member	Bush %
TX 11	Conaway (R)	78.3
AL 6	Bachus (R)	77.9
TX 13	Thornberry (R)	77.7
TX 19	Neugebauer (R)	77.4
UT 3	Cannon (R)	77.1
GA 10	Deal (R)	76.7
GA 7	Linder (R)	75.6
NE 3	Osborne (R)	74.8
GA 8	Westmoreland (R)	73.5
UT 1	Bishop (R)	72.7

Top 10 Worst-Performing Bush Districts in 2004

District	Member	Bush %
NY 15	Rangel (D)	9.2
NY 16	Serrano (D)	10.1
PA 2	Fattah (D)	12.4
CA 9	Lee (D)	12.5
NY 11	Owens (D)	13.0
NY 10	Towns (D)	13.1
CA 8	Pelosi (D)	14.0
NY 6	Meeks (D)	14.9
PA 1	Brady (D)	15.4
CA 33	Watson (D)	15.9

Closest 2004 House Elections

		2004 %	2004 Bush % in District				2004 %	2004 Bush % in District
CO-7	Beauprez (R)	55	48		NE-1	Fortenberry (R)	54	63
FL-13	Harris (R)	55	56		NM-1	Wilson (R)	54	48
IA-1	Nussle (R)	55	46		TX-32	Sessions (R)	54	60
IA-3	Boswell (D)	55	50		CA-20	Costa (D)	53	48
KS-3	Moore (D)	55	55		IN-8	Hostettler (R)	53	62
LA-7	Boustany (R)	55	60		MO-3	Carnahan (D)	53	43
MO-5	Cleaver (D)	55	40		OR-5	Hooley (D)	53	50
NC-11	Taylor (R)	55	57		SD-AL	Herseth (D)	53	60
NV-3	Porter (R)	55	50		CT-4	Shays (R)	52	46
PA-8	Fitzpatrick (R)	55	48		GA-12	Barrow (D)	52	46
TN-4	Davis (D)	55	58		IL-8	Bean (D)	52	56
TX-22	DeLay (R)	55	64		WA-8	Reichert (R)	52	48
UT-2	Matheson (D)	55	66		CO-3	Salazar (D)	51	55
VA-2	Drake (R)	55	58		CO-4	Musgrave (R)	51	58
WY-AL	Cubin (R)	55	69		NY-27	Higgins (D)	51	45
CA-26	Dreier (R)	54	55		NY-29	Kuhl (R)	51	56
CA-2	Simmons (R)	54	44		PA-6	Gerlach (R)	51	48
IN-2	Chocola (R)	54	56		TX-17	Edwards (D)	51	70
IN-7	Carson (D)	54	42		LA-3	Melancon (D)	50	58
KY-4	Davis (R)	54	63		IN-9	Sodrel (R)	49	59
MN-6	Kennedy (R)	54	57					

Closest 2004 Senate Elections

	2004 %	2004 Bush % in State
Patty Murray (D-WA)	55	46
Jim DeMint (R-SC)	54	58
Tom Coburn (R-OK)	53	66
Arlen Specter (R-PA)	53	48
Richard Burr (R-NC)	52	56
Ken Salazar (D-CO)	51	52
Jim Bunning (R-KY)	51	60
David Vitter (R-LA)	51	57
John Thune (R-SD)	51	60
Lisa Murkowski (R-AK)	49	61
Mel Martinez (R-FL)	49	52

CONGRESSIONAL LEADERSHIP

U.S. SENATE

Republicans

Majority Leader	Bill Frist (TN)
Majority Whip	Mitch McConnell (KY)
President Pro Tempore	Ted Stevens (AK)
Conference Chairman	Rick Santorum (PA)
Conference Vice Chairman	Kay Bailey Hutchison (TX)
Policy Committee Chairman	Jon Kyl (AZ)
NRSC Chairman	Elizabeth Dole (NC)

Democrats

Minority Leader	Harry Reid (NV)
Minority Whip	Richard Durbin (IL)
Conference Secretary	Debbie Stabenow (MI)
Policy Committee Chairman	Byron Dorgan (ND)
Steering and Outreach Committee Chairman	Hillary Rodham Clinton (NY)
DSCC Chairman	Charles Schumer (NY)

U.S. HOUSE OF REPRESENTATIVES

Republicans

Speaker of the House	Dennis Hastert (IL-14)
Majority Leader	Tom DeLay (TX-22)
Majority Whip	Roy Blunt (MO-7)
Chief Deputy Whip	Eric Cantor (VA-7)
Conference Chairman	Deborah Pryce (OH-15)
Conference Vice Chairman	Jack Kingston (GA-1)
Conference Secretary	John Doolittle (CA-4)
Policy Committee Chairman	John Shadegg (AZ-3)
Chairman, Committee on Rules	David Dreier (CA-26)
NRCC Chairman	Tom Reynolds (NY-26)

Democrats

Minority Leader	Nancy Pelosi (CA-8)
Minority Whip	Steny Hoyer (MD-5)
Caucus Chairman	Robert Menendez (NJ-13)
Caucus Vice Chairman	James Clyburn (SC-6)
Assistant to the Democratic Leader	John Spratt (SC-5)
DCCC Chairman	Rahm Emanuel (IL-5)
Steering Committee Co-Chair	Rosa DeLauro (CT-3)
Steering Committee Co-Chair	George Miller (CA-7)
Senior Chief Deputy Whip	John Lewis (GA-5)
Chief Deputy Whip	Joe Crowley (NY-7)
Chief Deputy Whip	Diana DeGette (CO-1)
Chief Deputy Whip	Ron Kind (WI-3)
Chief Deputy Whip	Ed Pastor (AZ-4)
Chief Deputy Whip	Jan Schakowsky (IL-9)
Chief Deputy Whip	John Tanner (TN-8)
Chief Deputy Whip	Maxine Waters (CA-35)

FILING DEADLINES

STATE	CONGRESSIONAL FILING DEADLINE	CONGRESSIONAL PRIMARY DATE	RUNOFF DATE	ELECTIONS DIVISION PHONE NUMBER
Alabama	April 8, 2006	June 6, 2006	June 27, 2006	334-242-7210
Alaska	June 1, 2006	August 22, 2006		907-465-4611
Arizona	June 14, 2006	September 12, 2006		602-542-8683
Arkansas	April 4, 2006	May 23, 2006	June 13, 2006	501-682-1010
California	March 10, 2006	June 6, 2006		916-657-2166
Colorado	TBD	August 8, 2006		303-894-2200
Connecticut	May 23, 2006	August 8, 2006		860-509-6100
Delaware	July 28, 2006	September 9, 2006		302-739-4277
Florida	May 12, 2006	September 5, 2006		850-245-6200
Georgia	April 28, 2006	July 18, 2006	August 8, 2006	404-656-2871
Hawaii	July 25, 2006	September 23, 2006		808-453-8683
Idaho	March 17, 2006	May 23, 2006		208-334-2852
Illinois	December 19, 2005	March 21, 2006		217-782-4141
Indiana	February 17, 2006	May 2, 2006		317-232-3939
Iowa	March 17, 2006	June 6, 2006		515-281-0145
Kansas	June 12, 2006	August 1, 2006		785-296-4561
Kentucky	January 31, 2006	May 16, 2006		502-564-3490
Louisiana	August 11, 2006	November 7, 2006	Dec. 9, 2006	225-922-0900
Maine	March 15, 2006	June 13, 2006		207-624-7736
Maryland	July 3, 2006	September 12, 2006		410-269-2840
Massachusetts	June 6, 2006	September 19, 2006		617-727-2828
Michigan	May 16, 2006	August 8, 2006		517-373-2540
Minnesota	July 18, 2006	September 12, 2006		651-215-1440
Mississippi	March 1, 2006	June 6, 2006	June 27, 2006	601-576-2550
Missouri	March 28, 2006	August 8, 2006		573-751-2301
Montana	March 23, 2006	June 6, 2006		406-444-4732
Nebraska	March 1, 2006	May 9, 2006		402-471-2555
Nevada	May 19, 2006	August 15, 2006		775-684-5705
New Hampshire	June 16, 2006	September 12, 2006		603-271-3242
New Jersey	April 10, 2006	June 6, 2006		609-292-3760
New Mexico	February 14, 2006	June 6, 2006		505-827-3600
New York	TBD	TBD		518-474-6220
North Carolina	February 28, 2006	May 2, 2006	May 30, 2006	919-733-7173
North Dakota	April 17, 2006	June 13, 2006		701-328-4146
Ohio	February 16, 2006	May 2, 2006		614-466-2585
Oklahoma	June 7, 2006	July 7, 2006	August 24, 2006	405-521-2391
Oregon	March 7, 2006	May 16, 2006		503-986-1518
Pennsylvania	March 7, 2006	May 16, 2006		717-787-5280
Rhode Island	June 28, 2006	September 12, 2006		401-222-2345
South Carolina	March 30, 2006	June 13, 2006	June 27, 2006	803-734-9060
South Dakota	April 6, 2006	June 6, 2006	June 20, 2006	605-773-3537
Tennessee	April 6, 2006	August 3, 2006		615-741-7956
Texas	January 6, 2006	March 7, 2006	April 11, 2006	800-252-8683
Utah	March 17, 2006	June 27, 2006		801-538-1041
Vermont	July 17, 2006	September 12, 2006		802-828-2464
Virginia	April 19, 2006	June 13, 2006		804-864-8901
Washington	July 28, 2006	September 12, 2006		360-902-4180
West Virginia	January 28, 2006	May 9, 2006		304-558-6000
Wisconsin	July 11, 2006	September 12, 2006		608-266-8005
Wyoming	June 2, 2006	August 22, 2006		307-777-5860

TBD: To be determined

Compiled from information provided by state election offices; all dates and deadlines as of June 23, 2005.

SENATE SEATS

2006 ELECTION CYCLE

Republicans (15)	Previous %	Democrats (17)	Previous %
George Allen (VA)	52%	Daniel Akaka (HI)	73%
Conrad Burns (MT)	51%	Jeff Bingaman (NM)	62%
Lincoln Chafee (RI)	57%	Robert Byrd (WV)	78%
Mike DeWine (OH)	60%	Maria Cantwell (WA)	49%
John Ensign (NV)	55%	Thomas Carper (DE)	56%
Bill Frist (TN)*	65%	Hillary Rodham Clinton (NY)	55%
Orrin Hatch (UT)	66%	Kent Conrad (ND)	62%
Kay Bailey Hutchison (TX)	65%	Jon Corzine (NJ)**	50%
Jon Kyl (AZ)	79%	Mark Dayton (MN)*	49%
Trent Lott (MS)	66%	Dianne Feinstein (CA)	56%
Richard Lugar (IN)	67%	Edward Kennedy (MA)	73%
Rick Santorum (PA)	52%	Herb Kohl (WI)	62%
Olympia Snowe (ME)	69%	Joe Lieberman (CT)	63%
Jim Talent (MO)	50%	Bill Nelson (FL)	51%
Craig Thomas (WY)	74%	Ben Nelson (NE)	51%
		Paul Sarbanes (MD)*	63%
		Debbie Stabenow (MI)	49%

Independents (1)	Previous %
James Jeffords (VT)*	66%

Will not seek reelection in 2006.
**Democratic nominee for governor, 2005.*

2008 ELECTION CYCLE

Republicans (21)	Previous %	Democrats (12)	Previous %
Jeff Sessions (AL)	59%	Mark Pryor (AR)	54%
Ted Stevens (AK)	78%	Joseph Biden (DE)	58%
Wayne Allard (CO)	51%	Richard Durbin (IL)	60%
Saxby Chambliss (GA)	53%	Tom Harkin (IA)	54%
Larry Craig (ID)	65%	Mary Landrieu (LA)	52%
Pat Roberts (KS)	83%	John Kerry (MA)	80%
Mitch McConnell (KY)	65%	Carl Levin (MI)	61%
Susan Collins (ME)	58%	Max Baucus (MT)	63%
Norm Coleman (MN)	50%	Frank Lautenberg (NJ)	54%
Thad Cochran (MS)	85%	Jack Reed (RI)	78%
Chuck Hagel (NE)	83%	Tim Johnson (SD)	50%
John Sununu (NH)	51%	Jay Rockefeller IV (WV)	63%
Pete Domenici (NM)	65%		
Elizabeth Dole (NC)	54%		
James Inhofe (OK)	57%		
Gordon Smith (OR)	56%		
Lindsey Graham (SC)	54%		
Lamar Alexander (TN)	54%		
John Cornyn (TX)	55%		
John Warner (VA)	83%		
Michael Enzi (WY)	73%		

GOVERNORSHIPS

2005, 2 States

New Jersey (D)   **Virginia (D)**

2006, 36 States

Alabama (R)   Minnesota (R)
Alaska (R)   Nebraska (R)
Arizona (D)   **Nevada (R)**
Arkansas (R)   New Hampshire (D)*
California (R)   New Mexico (D)
Colorado (R)   New York (R)
Connecticut (R)   **Ohio (R)**
Florida (R)   Oklahoma (D)
Georgia (R)   Oregon (D)
Hawaii (R)   Pennsylvania (D)
Idaho (R)   Rhode Island (R)
Illinois (D)   South Carolina (R)
Iowa (D)   South Dakota (R)
Kansas (D)   Tennessee (D)
Maine (D)   Texas (R)
Maryland (R)   Vermont (R)*
Massachusetts (R)   Wisconsin (D)
Michigan (D)   Wyoming (D)

2007, 3 States

Kentucky (R)   Mississippi (R)
Louisiana (D)

2008, 11 States

Delaware (D)   North Dakota (R)
Indiana (R)   Utah (R)
Missouri (R)   Vermont*
Montana (D)   Washington (D)
New Hampshire*   West Virginia (D)
North Carolina (D)

Partisan control of governorships (as of July 12, 2005): 28 Republicans, 22 Democrats
*New Hampshire and Vermont have two-year terms. All others are four years.
Boldface indicates governors who cannot succeed themselves in the next election.

CAMPAIGN FINANCE

All data is derived from candidate and party reports as well as other official studies available from the Federal Election Commission. Individuals listed in italics were losing candidates in that election. Zip code analysis is compiled by The Center for Responsive Politics, as of June 7, 2005.

Top Donor Zip Codes for 2003-2004 Election Cycle

Rank	Zip Code	Location	Total Amount	Democrat	Republican
1.	10021	New York, NY	$20,750,096	71%	29%
2.	10022	New York, NY	8,981,776	67%	33%
3.	10024	New York, NY	7,093,704	90%	10%
4.	10028	New York, NY	6,727,838	75%	25%
5.	10023	New York, NY	6,720,610	86%	14%
6.	10128	New York, NY	6,384,543	76%	24%
7.	20007	Washington, DC	6,194,134	72%	28%
8.	90210	Beverly Hills, CA	6,109,790	65%	35%
9.	20008	Washington, DC	6,010,719	74%	26%
10.	22101	McLean, VA	5,492,488	37%	63%
11.	20016	Washington, DC	5,398,863	68%	32%
12.	20815	Chevy Chase, MD	5,293,672	77%	23%
13.	20854	Potomac, MD	4,962,710	55%	45%
14.	33480	Palm Beach, FL	4,891,715	42%	58%
15.	60611	Chicago, IL	4,856,884	69%	31%
16.	75202	Dallas, TX	4,702,123	26%	74%
17.	90049	Los Angeles, CA	4,695,589	72%	28%
18.	06830	Greenwich, CT	4,529,991	41%	59%
19.	60614	Chicago, IL	4,457,817	80%	20%
20.	10019	New York, NY	4,283,054	69%	31%
21.	06831	Greenwich, CT	4,062,199	43%	57%
22.	60093	Winnetka, IL	3,990,989	41%	59%
23.	10017	New York, NY	3,882,959	63%	37%
24.	60610	Chicago, IL	3,784,468	67%	33%
25.	77019	Houston, TX	3,744,542	31%	69%

U.S. SENATE

The following charts show the 15 top 2004 Senate candidates in terms of the highest total net receipts, net expenditures, political action committee (PAC) contributions, individual contributions, cash-on-hand and debts owed during the 2003-2004 election cycle as of June 7, 2005.

2004 Senate: Top Raisers		2004 Senate: Top Spenders	
1. *Blair Hull (D-IL)*	$29,079,128	1. *Blair Hull (D-IL)*	$28,968,436
2. *Tom Daschle (D-SD)*	$19,349,884	2. Arlen Specter (R-PA)	$20,307,099
3. John Thune (R-SD)	$16,253,147	3. *Tom Daschle (D-SD)*	*$19,991,369*
4. Barack Obama (D-IL)	$15,096,157	4. Charles Schumer (D-NY)	$15,467,530
5. Arlen Specter (R-PA)	$14,952,496	5. Barbara Boxer (D-CA)	$14,886,426
6. Barbara Boxer (D-CA)	$14,301,289	6. John Thune (R-SD)	$14,666,225
7. *Erskine Bowles (D-NC)*	$13,407,656	7. Barack Obama (D-IL)	$14,532,493
8. Richard Burr (R-NC)	$12,951,226	8. *Erskine Bowles (D-NC)*	$13,359,764
9. Mel Martinez (R-FL)	$12,857,498	9. Richard Burr (R-NC)	$12,853,110
10. Charles Schumer (D-NY)	$11,921,568	10. Mel Martinez (R-FL)	$12,836,836
11. *Betty Castor (D-FL)*	$11,645,379	11. Patty Murray (D-WA)	$11,556,148
12. Patty Murray (D-WA)	$11,081,050	12. *Betty Castor (D-FL)*	$11,472,071
13. Ken Salazar (D-CO)	$9,925,778	13. Ken Salazar (D-CO)	$9,886,551
14. Jim DeMint (R-SC)	$9,040,100	14. Russ Feingold (D-WI)	$9,239,908
15. Johnny Isakson (R-GA)	$8,577,130	15. Jim DeMint (R-SC)	$9,036,086

2004 Senate: Top PAC Recipients

1.	*Tom Daschle (D-SD)*	$2,823,761
2.	Richard Burr (R-NC)	$2,796,484
3.	Arlen Specter (R-PA)	$2,605,116
4.	Blanche Lincoln (D-AR)	$2,427,554
5.	Jim DeMint (R-SC)	$2,347,943
6.	Charles Grassley (R-IA)	$2,146,135
7.	Harry Reid (D-NV)	$2,103,980
8.	Christopher (Kit) Bond (R-MO)	$2,098,125
9.	Mel Martinez (R-FL)	$2,004,063
10.	Lisa Murkowski (R-AK)	$1,991,677
11.	Jim Bunning (R-KY)	$1,903,137
12.	Johnny Isakson (R-GA)	$1,713,570
13.	Patty Murray (D-WA)	$1,691,587
14.	George Voinovich (R-OH)	$1,670,976
15.	Judd Gregg (R-NH)	$1,654,297

2004 Senate: Top Cash-On-Hand

1.	Richard Shelby (R-AL)	$11,246,330
2.	Charles Schumer (D-NY)	$10,029,291
3.	Evan Bayh (D-IN)	$6,595,119
4.	Christopher Dodd (D-CT)	$2,342,800
5.	Ron Wyden (D-OR)	$2,025,980
6.	Charles Grassley (R-IA)	$1,961,481
7.	John Thune (R-SD)	$1,594,669
8.	Judd Gregg (R-NH)	$1,453,454
9.	Harry Reid (D-NV)	$1,321,048
10.	Michael Crapo (R-ID)	$1,315,358
11.	John McCain (R-AZ)	$1,283,451
12.	Daniel Inouye (D-HI)	$1,140,993
13.	Tom Coburn (R-OK)	$1,066,230
14.	Patrick Leahy (D-VT)	$975,487
15.	Christopher (Kit) Bond (R-MO)	$912,165

2004 Senate: Top Individual Contributions

1.	*Tom Daschle (D-SD)*	$16,005,216
2.	John Thune (R-SD)	$14,046,445
3.	Barack Obama (D-IL)	$13,611,700
4.	Arlen Specter (R-PA)	$11,850,246
5.	Barbara Boxer (D-CA)	$10,599,638
6.	*Betty Castor (D-FL)*	$10,191,365
7.	Mel Martinez (R-FL)	$9,804,686
8.	Charles Schumer (D-NY)	$9,613,625
9.	Patty Murray (D-WA)	$9,044,543
10.	*Erskine Bowles (D-NC)*	$8,505,712
11.	Ken Salazar (D-CO)	$7,838,762
12.	Russ Feingold (D-WI)	$7,586,404
13.	*Bill Jones (R-CA)*	$6,746,993
14.	Richard Burr (R-NC)	$6,735,312
15.	Jim DeMint (R-SC)	$6,245,121

2004 Senate: Top Debts Owed

1.	*Erskine Bowles (D-NC)*	$10,561,273
2.	*Blair Hull (D-IL)*	$7,258,890
3.	*James Oberweis (R-IL)*	$3,398,938
4.	*Andrew McKenna (R-IL)*	$2,358,000
5.	*E.J. Pipkin (R-MD)*	$1,591,057
6.	*Douglas Gallagher (R-FL)*	$1,516,325
7.	*Jack Orchulli (R-CT)*	$1,389,141
8.	Robert Bennett (R-UT)	$1,273,000
9.	*Pete Coors (R-CO)*	$1,213,657
10.	*Daniel Mongiardo (D-KY)*	$651,046
11.	David Vitter (R-LA)	$511,357
12.	Mel Martinez (R-FL)	$484,030
13.	*Joyce Washington (D-IL)*	$456,243
14.	*Larry Klayman (R-FL)*	$419,236
15.	*Bill Jones (R-CA)*	$350,083

U.S. HOUSE OF REPRESENTATIVES

The following charts show the 25 top 2004 House candidates in terms of the highest total net receipts, net expenditures, political action committee (PAC) contributions, individual contributions, cash-on-hand and debts owed during the 2003-2004 election cycle as of June 7, 2005.

2004 House: Top Raisers

1.	Dennis Hastert (R-IL)	$4,862,029
2.	*Martin Frost (D-TX)*	$4,623,104
3.	Allyson Schwartz (D-PA)	$4,597,032
4.	Pete Sessions (R-TX)	$4,520,880
5.	Stephanie Herseth (D-SD)	$4,031,986
6.	Robert Menendez (D-NJ)	$3,624,587
7.	*Ben Streusand (R-TX)*	$3,621,532
8.	Katherine Harris (R-FL)	$3,582,920
9.	Marilyn Musgrave (R-CO)	$3,422,482
10.	Heather Wilson (R-NM)	$3,415,781
11.	Anne Northup (R-KY)	$3,339,733
12.	*Jeanne Patterson (R-MO)*	$3,221,807
13.	Martin Meehan (D-MA)	$3,170,733
14.	Geoff Davis (R-KY)	$3,076,557
15.	Randy Neugebauer (R-TX)	$2,994,489
16.	Michael McCaul (R-TX)	$2,992,850
17.	Bob Beauprez (R-CO)	$2,967,373
18.	*Vernon Robinson (R-NC)*	$2,967,130
19.	Michael Ferguson (R-NJ)	$2,954,861
20.	Tom DeLay (R-TX)	$2,909,844
21.	Charles Boustany (R-LA)	$2,846,661
22.	Edward Markey (D-MA)	$2,840,650
23.	*Max Burns (R-GA)*	$2,799,984
24.	Jon Porter (R-NV)	$2,762,871
25.	Mark Kennedy (R-MN)	$2,691,038

2004 House: Top Spenders

1.	Dennis Hastert (R-IL)	$5,013,947
2.	*Martin Frost (D-TX)*	$4,761,288
3.	Allyson Schwartz (D-PA)	$4,572,500
4.	Pete Sessions (R-TX)	$4,512,464
5.	Stephanie Herseth (D-SD)	$4,026,661
6.	Robert Menendez (D-NJ)	$3,941,956
7.	*Ben Streusand (R-TX)*	$3,607,176
8.	Katherine Harris (R-FL)	$3,556,976
9.	Roy Blunt (R-MO)	$3,527,363
10.	Heather Wilson (R-NM)	$3,401,887
11.	Anne Northup (R-KY)	$3,339,760
12.	Marilyn Musgrave (R-CO)	$3,314,507
13.	Randy Neugebauer (R-TX)	$3,245,173
14.	*Jeanne Patterson (R-MO)*	$3,207,825
15.	Tom DeLay (R-TX)	$3,143,559
16.	Michael McCaul (R-TX)	$2,988,391
17.	Bob Beauprez (R-CO)	$2,970,799
18.	Geoff Davis (R-KY)	$2,959,526
19.	Michael Ferguson (R-NJ)	$2,847,822
20.	*Max Burns (R-GA)*	$2,798,725
21.	Charles Boustany (R-LA)	$2,785,524
22.	*Vernon Robinson (R-NC)*	$2,785,368
23.	David Wu (D-OR)	$2,752,272
24.	Chet Edwards (D-TX)	$2,664,661
25.	Jon Porter (R-NV)	$2,653,136

2004 House: Top PAC Recipients

1.	Dennis Hastert (R-IL)	$1,911,381
2.	Pete Sessions (R-TX)	$1,692,242
3.	Roy Blunt (R-MO)	$1,483,503
4.	Joe Barton (R-TX)	$1,474,272
5.	Tom DeLay (R-TX)	$1,420,263
6.	Earl Pomeroy (D-ND)	$1,352,690
7.	*Max Burns (R-GA)*	$1,336,297
8.	Stephanie Herseth (D-SD)	$1,302,247
9.	*Martin Frost (D-TX)*	$1,302,207
10.	Nancy Johnson (R-CT)	$1,288,755
11.	Heather Wilson (R-NM)	$1,285,215
12.	Bob Beauprez (R-CO)	$1,228,900
13.	Bill Thomas (R-CA)	$1,226,562
14.	Rick Renzi (R-AZ)	$1,205,645
15.	*Charlie Stenholm (D-TX)*	$1,189,208
16.	Mark Kennedy (R-MN)	$1,186,150
17.	Robert Simmons (R-CT)	$1,181,513
18.	Steny Hoyer (D-MD)	$1,173,105
19.	Eric Cantor (R-VA)	$1,167,034
20.	*Phil Crane (R-IL)*	$1,164,087
21.	Jon Porter (R-NV)	$1,145,916
22.	Chet Edwards (D-TX)	$1,141,103
23.	Jim Gerlach (R-PA)	$1,129,212
24.	Anne Northup (R-KY)	$1,115,393
25.	Michael Oxley (R-OH)	$1,100,917

2004 House: Top Cash-On-Hand

1.	Martin Meehan (D-MA)	$4,515,955
2.	David Dreier (R-CA)	$2,410,332
3.	Edward Markey (D-MA)	$2,398,146
4.	Rob Portman (R-OH)	$2,220,993
5.	Mark Foley (R-FL)	$2,122,042
6.	Sherrod Brown (D-OH)	$2,102,835
7.	Don Young (R-AK)	$1,898,567
8.	Cliff Stearns (R-FL)	$1,878,135
9.	Bill Delahunt (D-MA)	$1,874,620
10.	Lloyd Doggett (D-TX)	$1,736,706
11.	Robert Menendez (D-NJ)	$1,686,741
12.	Ed Royce (R-CA)	$1,523,707
13.	Ileana Ros-Lehtinen (R-FL)	$1,523,529
14.	Frank LoBiondo (R-NJ)	$1,430,989
15.	Robert Andrews (D-NJ)	$1,388,065
16.	Mark Green (R-WI)	$1,331,508
17.	Bud Cramer (D-AL)	$1,325,123
18.	Nick Rahall (D-WV)	$1,239,621
19.	Jerry Lewis (R-CA)	$1,228,761
20.	John Duncan (R-TN)	$1,228,554
21.	Richard Neal (D-MA)	$1,188,562
22.	Henry Bonilla (R-TX)	$1,176,717
23.	Jim Saxton (R-NJ)	$1,167,890
24.	Tom Reynolds (R-NY)	$1,149,060
25.	Nancy Johnson (R-CT)	$1,145,891

2004 House: Top Individual Contributions

1.	Allyson Schwartz (D-PA)	$3,908,881
2.	*Martin Frost (D-TX)*	$3,199,918
3.	Martin Meehan (D-MA)	$3,083,677
4.	Marilyn Musgrave (R-CO)	$2,951,635
5.	Dennis Hastert (R-IL)	$2,924,677
6.	*Vernon Robinson (R-NC)*	$2,861,840
7.	Katherine Harris (R-FL)	$2,821,194
8.	Stephanie Herseth (D-SD)	$2,649,324
9.	Robert Menendez (D-NJ)	$2,614,174
10.	Pete Sessions (R-TX)	$2,488,111
11.	*David Rogers (R-RI)*	$2,151,940
12.	Edward Markey (D-MA)	$2,136,776
13.	Tom Lantos (D-CA)	$1,918,915
14.	Bobby Jindal (R-LA)	$1,906,339
15.	*Goli Ameri (R-OR)*	$1,887,860
16.	Anne Northup (R-KY)	$1,869,198
17.	Heather Wilson (R-NM)	$1,804,890
18.	*Arlene Wohlgemuth (R-TX)*	$1,749,565
19.	Patrick Kennedy (D-RI)	$1,731,933
20.	Randy Neugebauer (R-TX)	$1,712,325
21.	Christopher Shays (R-CT)	$1,689,401
22.	*Richard Romero (D-NM)*	$1,642,367
23.	David Wu (D-OR)	$1,601,120
24.	Luis Fortuno (R-PR)	$1,576,763
25.	John Murtha (D-PA)	$1,547,392

2004 House: Top Debts Owed

1.	*Ben Streusand (R-TX)*	$3,489,000
2.	*Jeanne Patterson (R-MO)*	$2,845,058
3.	*Capri Cafaro (D-OH)*	$2,042,376
4.	Darrell Issa (R-CA)	$1,820,000
5.	*Melissa Brown (R-PA)*	$1,660,800
6.	*Janet Robert (D-MN)*	$1,517,100
7.	*Derek Smith (R-UT)*	$1,511,581
8.	Mike Sodrel (R-IN)	$1,331,798
9.	Charles Taylor (R-NC)	$900,000
10.	Michael McCaul (R-TX)	$618,504
11.	Chris Chocola (R-IN)	$611,744
12.	*Rick Murphy (R-AZ)*	$550,000
13.	*Robert Lamutt (R-GA)*	$529,587
14.	*Tim Bridgewater (R-UT)*	$521,185
15.	*Tom Gallagher (D-NV)*	$500,000
16.	Tom Price (R-GA)	$499,000
17.	Rahm Emanuel (D-IL)	$463,562
18.	*Gene DeRossett (R-MI)*	$445,500
19.	Rodney Frelinghuysen (R-NJ)	$441,079
20.	*Mike Crotts (R-GA)*	$436,500
21.	Mike Ferguson (R-NJ)	$420,000
22.	*Dave Phillips (R-TX)*	$418,461
23.	*Charles Broomfield (D-MO)*	$400,000
24.	*Dot Snyder (R-TX)*	$400,000
25.	*Mark Henry (R-TX)*	$396,000

SENATE COMMITTEE LEADERSHIP

	Due to Step Down		Due to Step Down
Aging (Special)		Finance	
Gordon Smith (OR)	2011	**Charles Grassley (IA)**	2009
RMM: Herb Kohl (WI)		RMM: Max Baucus (MT)	
Agriculture, Nutrition, & Forestry		Foreign Relations	
Saxby Chambliss (GA)	2011	**Richard Lugar (IN)**	2009
RMM: Tom Harkin (IA)		RMM: Joseph Biden (DE)	
Appropriations		Health, Education, Labor, & Pensions	
Thad Cochran (MS)	2011	**Mike Enzi (WY)**	2011
RMM: Robert Byrd (WV)		RMM: Edward Kennedy (MA)	
Armed Services		Homeland Security & Governmental Affairs	
John Warner (VA)	2007	**Susan Collins (ME)**	2009
RMM: Carl Levin (MI)		RMM: Joe Lieberman (CT)	
Banking, Housing, & Urban Affairs		Indian Affairs	
Richard Shelby (AL)	2009	**John McCain (AZ)**	2011
RMM: Paul Sarbanes (MD)		RMM: Byron Dorgan (ND)	
Budget		Intelligence (Select)	
Judd Gregg (NH)	2011	**Pat Roberts (KS)**	2009
RMM: Kent Conrad (ND)		RMM: Jay Rockefeller IV (WV)	
Commerce, Science & Transportation		Judiciary	
Ted Stevens (AK)	2011	**Arlen Specter (PA)**	2011
RMM: Daniel Inouye (HI)		RMM: Patrick Leahy (VT)	
Energy & Natural Resources		Rules & Administration	
Pete Domenici (NM)	2009	**Trent Lott (MS)**	2009
RMM: Jeff Bingaman (NM)		RMM: Christopher Dodd (CT)	
Environment & Public Works		Small Business & Entrepreneurship	
James Inhofe (OK)	2009	**Olympia Snowe (ME)**	2009
RMM: James Jeffords (VT)		RMM: John Kerry (MA)	
Ethics (Select)		Veterans' Affairs	
George Voinovich (OH)	2009	**Larry Craig (ID)**	2011
RMM: Tim Johnson (SD)		RMM: Daniel Akaka (HI)	

Committee chairmen are noted in boldface
RMM: Ranking Minority Member

SENATE COMMITTEES

Aging (Special)
aging.senate.gov

G-31 Dirksen
202–224–5364

Majority (R 11): Smith (OR), Chmn.; Shelby (AL), Collins (ME), Talent (MO), Dole (NC), Martinez (FL), Craig (ID), Santorum (PA), Burns (MT), Alexander (TN), DeMint (SC)
Minority (D 8): Kohl (WI), RMM; Feingold (WI), Wyden (OR), Lincoln (AR), Bayh (IN), Carper (DE), Nelson (FL), Clinton (NY)
Independent (1): Jeffords (I-VT)

NO SUBCOMMITTEES

Agriculture, Nutrition & Forestry
agriculture.senate.gov

328A Russell
202–224–2035

Majority (R 11): Chambliss (GA), Chmn.; Lugar (IN), Cochran (MS), McConnell (KY), Roberts (KS), Talent (MO), Thomas (WY), Santorum (PA), Coleman (MN), Crapo (ID), Grassley (IA)
Minority (D 9): Harkin (IA), RMM; Leahy (VT), Conrad (ND), Baucus (MT), Lincoln (AR), Stabenow (MI), Nelson (NE), Dayton (MN), Salazar (CO)

SUBCOMMITTEES

Forestry, Conservation & Rural Revitalization
Majority (R 6): Crapo, Chmn.; Lugar, Cochran, Talent, Thomas, Coleman
Minority (D 5): Lincoln, RMM; Leahy, Nelson, Dayton, Salazar

Marketing, Inspection & Product Promotion
Majority (R 6): Talent, Chmn.; McConnell, Thomas, Roberts, Grassley, Lugar
Minority (D 5): Baucus, RMM; Nelson, Salazar, Conrad, Stabenow

Production & Price Competitiveness
Majority (R 6): McConnell, Chmn.; Cochran, Roberts, Santorum, Coleman, Grassley
Minority (D 5): Conrad, RMM; Dayton, Baucus, Leahy, Lincoln

Research, Nutrition & General Legislation
Majority (R 6): Santorum, Chmn.; Lugar, Crapo, Cochran, McConnell, Roberts
Minority (D 5): Leahy, RMM; Stabenow, Lincoln, Baucus, Nelson

Appropriations
appropriations.senate.gov

S-128 The Capitol
202–224–7363

Majority (R 15): Cochran (MS), Chmn.; Stevens (AK), Specter (PA), Domenici (NM), Bond (MO), McConnell (KY), Burns (MT), Shelby (AL), Gregg (NH), Bennett (UT), Craig (ID), Hutchison (TX), DeWine (OH), Brownback (KS), Allard (CO)
Minority (D 13): Byrd (WV), RMM; Inouye (HI), Leahy (VT), Harkin (IA), Mikulski (MD), Reid (NV), Kohl (WI), Murray (WA), Dorgan (ND), Feinstein (CA), Durbin (IL), Johnson (SD), Landrieu (LA)

SUBCOMMITTEES

Agriculture, Rural Development & Related Agencies
Majority (R 8): Bennett, Chmn.; Cochran, Specter, Bond, McConnell, Burns, Craig, Brownback
Minority (D 7): Kohl, RMM; Harkin, Dorgan, Feinstein, Durbin, Johnson, Landrieu

Commerce, Justice & Science
Majority (R 8): Shelby, Chmn.; Gregg, Stevens, Domenici, McConnell, Hutchison, Brownback, Bond
Minority (D 7): Mikulski, RMM; Inouye, Leahy, Kohl, Murray, Harkin, Dorgan

Defense
Majority (R 10): Stevens, Chmn.; Cochran, Specter, Domenici, Bond, McConnell, Shelby, Gregg, Hutchison, Burns
Minority (D 9): Inouye, RMM; Byrd, Leahy, Harkin, Dorgan, Durbin, Reid, Feinstein, Mikulski

District of Columbia
Majority (R 3): Brownback, Chmn.; DeWine, Allard
Minority (D 2): Landrieu, RMM; Durbin

Energy & Water
Majority (R 9): Domenici, Chmn.; Cochran, McConnell, Bennett, Burns, Craig, Bond, Hutchison, Allard
Minority (D 8): Reid, RMM; Byrd, Murray, Dorgan, Feinstein, Johnson, Landrieu, Inouye

Homeland Security
Majority (R 9): Gregg, Chmn.; Cochran, Stevens, Specter, Domenici, Shelby, Craig, Bennett, Allard
Minority (D 8): Byrd, RMM; Inouye, Leahy, Mikulski, Kohl, Murray, Reid, Feinstein

Interior & Related Agencies
Majority (R 8): Burns, Chmn.; Stevens, Cochran, Domenici, Bennett, Gregg, Craig, Allard
Minority (D 7): Dorgan, Chmn.; Byrd, Leahy, Reid, Feinstein, Mikulski, Kohl

Labor, Health and Human Services, Education & Related Agencies
Majority (R 8): Specter, Chmn.; Cochran, Gregg, Craig, Hutchison, Stevens, DeWine, Shelby
Minority (D 7): Harkin, RMM; Inouye, Reid, Kohl, Murray, Landrieu, Durbin

Legislative Branch
Majority (R 3): Allard, Chmn.; Cochran, DeWine
Minority (D 2): Durbin, RMM; Johnson

Military Construction & Veterans Affairs
Majority (R 7): Hutchison, Chmn.; Burns, Craig, DeWine, Brownback, Allard, McConnell
Minority (D 6): Feinstein, RMM; Inouye, Johnson, Landrieu, Byrd, Murray

State, Foreign Operations & Related Programs
Majority (R 8): McConnell, Chmn.; Specter, Gregg, Shelby, Bennett, Bond, DeWine, Brownback
Minority (D 7): Leahy, RMM; Inouye, Harkin, Mikulski, Durbin, Johnson, Landrieu

Transportation, Treasury, the Judiciary, HUD & Related Agencies
Majority (R 10): Bond, Chmn.; Shelby, Specter, Bennett, Hutchison, DeWine, Brownback, Stevens, Domenici, Burns
Minority (D 9): Murray, RMM; Byrd, Mikulski, Reid, Kohl, Durbin, Dorgan, Leahy, Harkin

Armed Services
armed-services.senate.gov

228 Russell
202–224–3871

Majority (R 13): Warner (VA), Chmn.; McCain (AZ), Inhofe (OK), Roberts (KS), Sessions (AL), Collins (ME), Ensign (NV), Talent (MO), Chambliss (GA), Graham (SC), Dole (NC), Cornyn (TX), Thune (SD)
Minority (D 11): Levin (MI), RMM; Kennedy (MA), Byrd (WV), Lieberman (CT), Reed (RI), Akaka (HI), Nelson (FL), Nelson (NE), Dayton (MN), Bayh (IN), Clinton (NY)

SUBCOMMITTEES

Airland
Majority (R 8): McCain, Chmn.; Inhofe, Sessions, Ensign, Talent, Chambliss, Graham, Dole
Minority (D 7): Lieberman, RMM; Reed, Akaka, Nelson, Dayton, Bayh, Clinton

Emerging Threats & Capabilities
Majority (R 8): Cornyn, Chmn.; Roberts, Collins, Ensign, Talent, Graham, Dole, Thune
Minority (D 7): Reed, RMM; Kennedy, Byrd, Nelson (FL), Nelson, Bayh, Clinton

Personnel
Majority (R 5): Graham, Chmn.; McCain, Collins, Chambliss, Dole
Minority (D 4): Nelson (NE), RMM; Kennedy, Lieberman, Akaka

Readiness & Management Support
Majority (R 8): Ensign, Chmn.; McCain, Inhofe, Roberts, Sessions, Chambliss, Cornyn, Thune
Minority (D 7): Akaka, RMM; Byrd, Nelson (FL), Nelson (NE), Dayton, Bayh, Clinton

Seapower
Majority (R 4): Talent, Chmn.; McCain, Collins, Chambliss
Minority (D 3): Kennedy, RMM; Lieberman, Reed

Strategic Forces
Majority (R 6): Sessions, Chmn.; Inhofe, Roberts, Graham, Cornyn, Thune
Minority (D 5): Nelson (FL), RMM; Byrd, Reed, Nelson (NE), Dayton

Banking, Housing & Urban Affairs
banking.senate.gov

534 Dirksen
202–224–7391

Majority (R 11): Shelby (AL), Chmn.; Bennett (UT), Allard (CO), Enzi (WY), Hagel (NE), Santorum (PA), Bunning (KY), Crapo (ID), Sununu (NH), Dole (NC), Martinez (FL)
Minority (D 9): Sarbanes (MD), RMM; Dodd (CT), Johnson (SD), Reed (RI), Schumer (NY), Bayh (IN), Carper (DE), Stabenow (MI), Corzine (NJ)

SUBCOMMITTEES

Economic Policy
Majority (R 2): Bunning, Chmn.; Shelby
Minority (D 1): Schumer, RMM

Financial Institutions
Majority (R 8): Bennett, Chmn.; Allard, Santorum, Sununu, Martinez, Hagel, Bunning, Crapo
Minority (D 6): Johnson, RMM; Carper, Dodd, Reed, Stabenow, Bayh

Housing & Transportation
Majority (R 7): Allard, Chmn.; Santorum, Dole, Enzi, Bennett, Martinez, Shelby
Minority (D 6): Reed, RMM; Stabenow, Corzine, Dodd, Carper, Schumer

International Trade & Finance
Majority (R 5): Crapo, Chmn.; Hagel, Enzi, Sununu, Dole
Minority (D 3): Bayh, RMM; Johnson, Corzine

Securities & Investment
Majority (R 10): Hagel, Chmn.; Enzi, Sununu, Martinez, Bennett, Bunning, Crapo, Dole, Allard, Santorum
Minority (D 8): Dodd, RMM; Johnson, Reed, Schumer, Bayh, Stabenow, Corzine, Carper

Budget

624 Dirksen
budget.senate.gov
202–224–0642

Majority (R 12): Gregg (NH), Chmn.; Domenici (NM), Grassley (IA), Allard (CO), Enzi (WY), Sessions (AL), Bunning (KY), Crapo (ID), Ensign (NV), Cornyn (TX), Alexander (TN), Graham (SC)
Minority (D 10): Conrad (ND), RMM; Sarbanes (MD), Murray (WA), Wyden (OR), Feingold (WI), Johnson (SD), Byrd (WV), Nelson (FL), Stabenow (MI), Corzine (NJ)

NO SUBCOMMITTEES

Commerce, Science & Transportation

508 Dirksen
commerce.senate.gov
202–224–1251

Majority (R 12): Stevens (AK), Chmn.; McCain (AZ), Burns (MT), Lott (MS), Hutchison (TX), Snowe (ME), Smith (OR), Ensign (NV), Allen (VA), Sununu (NH), DeMint (SC), Vitter (LA)
Minority (D 10): Inouye (HI), RMM; Rockefeller (WV), Kerry (MA), Dorgan (ND), Boxer (CA), Nelson (FL), Cantwell (WA), Lautenberg (NJ), Nelson (NE), Pryor (AR)

SUBCOMMITTEES

Aviation
Majority (R 11): Burns, Chmn.; Stevens, McCain, Lott, Hutchison, Snowe, Smith, Ensign, Allen, Sununu, DeMint
Minority (D 9): Rockefeller, RMM; Inouye, Dorgan, Boxer, Cantwell, Lautenberg, Nelson (FL), Nelson (NE), Pryor

Consumer Affairs, Product Safety & Insurance
Majority (R 5): Allen, Chmn.; Stevens, Burns, DeMint, Vitter
Minority (D 2): Pryor, RMM; Boxer

Disaster Prevention & Prediction
Majority (R 4): DeMint, Chmn.; Stevens, Smith, Vitter
Minority (D 3): Nelson (NE), RMM; Cantwell, Nelson (FL)

Fisheries & the Coast Guard
Majority (R 6): Snowe, Chmn.; Stevens, Lott, Smith, Sununu, Vitter
Minority (D 4): Cantwell, RMM; Inouye, Kerry, Lautenberg

Global Climate Change & Impacts
Majority (R 4): Vitter, Chmn.; Stevens, McCain, Snowe
Minority (D 2): Lautenberg, RMM; Kerry

National Ocean Policy Study
Majority (R 8): Sununu, Chmn.; Stevens, Lott, Hutchison, Snowe, Smith, DeMint, Vitter
Minority (D 5): Boxer, RMM; Inouye, Kerry, Cantwell, Lautenberg

Science & Space
Majority (R 7): Hutchison, Chmn.; Stevens, Burns, Lott, Ensign, Allen, Sununu
Minority (D 5): Nelson (FL), RMM; Rockefeller, Dorgan, Nelson (NE), Pryor

Surface Transportation & Merchant Marine
Majority (R 10): Lott, Chmn.; Stevens, McCain, Burns, Hutchison, Snowe, Smith, Allen, Sununu, Vitter
Minority (D 8): Inouye, RMM; Rockefeller, Dorgan, Boxer, Cantwell, Lautenberg, Nelson, Pryor

Technology, Innovation & Competitiveness
Majority (R 8): Ensign, Chmn.; Stevens, Burns, Lott, Hutchison, Allen, Sununu, DeMint
Minority (D 5): Kerry, RMM; Rockefeller, Dorgan, Nelson, Pryor

Trade, Tourism & Economic Development
Majority (R 9): Smith, Chmn.; Stevens, McCain, Burns, Ensign, Allen, Sununu, DeMint, Vitter
Minority (D 8): Dorgan, RMM; Rockefeller, Kerry, Cantwell, Lautenberg, Nelson (FL), Nelson (NE), Pryor

Energy & Natural Resources

364 Dirksen
energy.senate.gov
202–224–4971

Majority (R 12): Domenici (NM), Chmn.; Craig (ID), Thomas (WY), Alexander (TN), Murkowski (AK), Burr (NC), Martinez (FL), Talent (MO), Burns (MT), Allen (VA), Smith (OR), Bunning (KY)
Minority (D 10): Bingaman (NM), RMM; Akaka (HI), Dorgan (ND), Wyden (OR), Johnson (SD), Landrieu (LA), Feinstein (CA), Cantwell (WA), Corzine (NJ), Salazar (CO)

SUBCOMMITTEES

Energy
Majority (R 10): Alexander, Chmn.; Burr, Martinez, Talent, Allen, Bunning, Murkowski, Craig, Thomas, Burns
Minority (D 8): Dorgan, RMM; Akaka, Johnson, Landrieu, Feinstein, Cantwell, Corzine, Salazar

National Parks
Majority (R 6): Thomas, Chmn.; Alexander, Allen, Burr, Martinez, Smith
Minority (D 5): Akaka, RMM; Wyden, Landrieu, Corzine, Salazar

Public Lands & Forests
Majority (R 8): Craig, Chmn.; Burns, Vice Chmn.; Thomas, Talent, Smith, Alexander, Murkowski, Allen
Minority (D 7): Wyden, RMM; Akaka, Dorgan, Johnson, Landrieu, Feinstein, Cantwell

Water & Power
Majority (R 8): Murkowski, Chmn.; Smith, Craig, Burr, Martinez, Burns, Bunning, Talent
Minority (D 7): Johnson, RMM; Dorgan, Wyden, Feinstein, Cantwell, Corzine, Salazar

Environment & Public Works
410 Dirksen
202–224–6176
epw.senate.gov
Majority (R 10): Inhofe (OK), Chmn.; Warner (VA), Bond (MO), Voinovich (OH), Chafee (RI), Murkowski (AK), Thune (SD), DeMint (SC), Isakson (GA), Vitter (LA)
Minority (D 7): Baucus (MT), Lieberman (CT), Boxer (CA), Carper (DE), Clinton (NY), Lautenberg (NJ), Obama (IL)
Independent (1): Jeffords (I-VT), RMM

SUBCOMMITTEES

Clean Air, Climate Change & Nuclear Safety
Majority (R 5): Voinovich, Chmn.; Bond, DeMint, Isakson, Vitter
Minority (D 4): Carper, RMM; Lieberman, Lautenberg, Obama

Fisheries, Wildlife & Water
Majority (R 5): Chafee, Chmn.; Warner, Murkowski, DeMint, Vitter
Minority (D 4): Clinton, RMM; Lieberman, Lautenberg, Obama

Superfund & Waste Management
Majority (R 4): Thune, Chmn.; Warner, Bond, Isakson
Minority (D 3): Boxer, RMM; Baucus, Lautenberg

Transportation & Infrastructure
Majority (R 6): Bond, Chmn.; Warner, Voinovich, Chafee, Murkowski, Thune
Minority (D 5): Baucus, Lieberman, Boxer, Carper, Clinton

Ethics (Select)
220 Hart
202–224–2981
ethics.senate.gov
Majority (R 3): Voinovich (OH), Chmn.; Roberts (KS), Thomas (WY)
Minority (D 3): Johnson (SD), RMM; Akaka (HI), Pryor (AR)

NO SUBCOMMITTEES

Finance
219 Dirksen
202–224–4515
finance.senate.gov
Majority (R 11): Grassley (IA), Chmn.; Hatch (UT), Lott (MS), Snowe (ME), Kyl (AZ), Thomas (WY), Santorum (PA), Frist (TN), Smith (OR), Bunning (KY), Crapo (ID)
Minority (D 8): Baucus (MT), RMM; Rockefeller (WV), Conrad (ND), Bingaman (NM), Kerry (MA), Lincoln (AR), Wyden (OR), Schumer (NY)
Independent (1): Jeffords (I-VT)

SUBCOMMITTEES

Health Care
Majority (R 7): Hatch, Chmn.; Snowe, Frist, Kyl, Thomas, Santorum, Bunning
Minority (D 4): Rockefeller, RMM; Bingaman, Kerry, Wyden
Independent (1): Jeffords (I)

International Trade
Majority (R 8): Thomas, Chmn.; Crapo, Lott, Smith, Bunning, Hatch, Snowe, Frist
Minority (D 6): Bingaman, Baucus, RMM; Rockefeller, Conrad, Wyden, Schumer

Long-Term Growth & Debt Reduction
Majority (R 2): Smith, Chmn.; Grassley
Minority (D 1): Kerry, RMM

Social Security & Family Policy
Majority (R 8): Santorum, Chmn.; Grassley, Bunning, Frist, Lott, Kyl, Smith, Crapo
Minority (D 5): Conrad, RMM; Rockefeller, Bingaman, Kerry, Lincoln
Independent (1): Jeffords (I)

Taxation & IRS Oversight
Majority (R 7): Kyl, Chmn.; Lott, Hatch, Snowe, Crapo, Thomas, Santorum
Minority (D 4): Baucus, Conrad, Lincoln, Schumer
Independent (1): Jeffords (I), RMM

Foreign Relations
450 Dirksen
202–224–4651
foreign.senate.gov
Majority (R 10): Lugar (IN), Chmn.; Hagel (NE), Chafee (RI), Allen (VA), Coleman (MN), Voinovich (OH), Alexander (TN), Sununu (NH), Murkowski (AK), Martinez (FL)
Minority (D 8): Biden (DE), RMM; Sarbanes (MD), Dodd (CT), Kerry (MA), Feingold (WI), Boxer (CA), Nelson (FL), Obama (IL)

SUBCOMMITTEES

African Affairs
Majority (R 5): Martinez, Chmn.; Alexander, Coleman, Sununu, Murkowski
Minority (D 4): Feingold, RMM; Sarbanes, Dodd, Obama

East Asian & Pacific Affairs
Majority (R 5): Murkowski, Chmn.; Alexander, Hagel, Chafee, Allen
Minority (D 4): Kerry, RMM; Biden, Feingold, Obama

European Affairs
Majority (R 5): Allen, Chmn.; Voinovich, Murkowski, Hagel, Chafee
Minority (D 4): Biden, RMM; Sarbanes, Dodd, Feingold

International Economic Policy, Export & Trade Promotion
Majority (R 5): Hagel, Chmn.; Alexander, Murkowski, Martinez, Voinovich
Minority (D 4): Sarbanes, RMM; Dodd, Kerry, Obama

International Operations & Terrorism
Majority (R 5): Sununu, Chmn.; Voinovich, Allen, Coleman, Alexander
Minority (D 4): Nelson, RMM; Biden, Kerry, Boxer

Near Eastern & South Asian Affairs
Majority (R 5): Chafee, Chmn.; Hagel, Coleman, Voinovich, Sununu
Minority (D 4): Boxer, RMM; Sarbanes, Nelson, Obama

Western Hemisphere, Peace Corps & Narcotics Affairs
Majority (R 5): Coleman, Chmn.; Chafee, Allen, Martinez, Sununu
Minority (D 4): Dodd, RMM; Kerry, Boxer, Nelson

Health, Education, Labor & Pensions
labor.senate.gov

428 Dirksen
202–224–5375

Majority (R 11): Enzi (WY), Chmn.; Gregg (NH), Frist (TN), Alexander (TN), Burr (NC), Isakson (GA), DeWine (OH), Ensign (NV), Hatch (UT), Sessions (AL), Roberts (KS)
Minority (D 9): Kennedy (MA), RMM; Dodd (CT), Harkin (IA), Mikulski (MD), Bingaman (NM), Murray (WA), Reed (RI), Clinton (NY)
Independent (1): Jeffords (I-VT)

SUBCOMMITTEES

Bioterrorism & Public Health Preparedness
Majority (R 8): Burr, Chmn.; Gregg, Frist, Alexander, DeWine, Ensign, Hatch, Roberts
Minority (D 7): Kennedy, RMM; Dodd, Harkin, Mikulski, Bingaman, Murray, Reed

Education & Early Childhood Development
Majority (R 8): Alexander, Chmn.; Gregg, Burr, Isakson, DeWine, Ensign, Hatch, Sessions
Minority (D 6): Dodd, RMM; Harkin, Bingaman, Murray, Reed, Clinton
Independent (1): Jeffords (I)

Employment & Workplace Safety
Majority (R 6): Isakson, Chmn.; Alexander, Burr, Ensign, Sessions, Roberts
Minority (D 4): Murray, RMM; Dodd, Harkin, Mikulski
Independent (1): Jeffords (I)

Retirement Security & Aging
Majority (R 5): DeWine, Chmn.; Isakson, Hatch, Sessions, Roberts
Minority (D 3): Mikulski, RMM; Bingaman, Clinton
Independent (1): Jeffords (I)

Homeland Security & Governmental Affairs
hsgac.senate.gov

340 Dirksen
202–224–4751

Majority (R 9): Collins (ME), Chmn.; Stevens (AK), Voinovich (OH), Coleman (MN), Coburn (OK), Chafee (RI), Bennett (UT), Domenici (NM), Warner (VA)
Minority (D 7): Lieberman (CT), RMM; Levin (MI), Akaka (HI), Carper (DE), Dayton (MN), Lautenberg (NJ), Pryor (AR)

SUBCOMMITTEES

Federal Financial Management, Govt. Information & International Security
Majority (R 7): Coburn, Chmn.; Stevens, Voinovich, Chafee, Bennett, Domenici, Warner
Minority (D 5): Carper, RMM; Levin, Akaka, Dayton, Lautenberg

Investigations (Permanent)
Majority (R 7): Coleman, Chmn.; Stevens, Coburn, Chafee, Bennett, Domenici, Warner
Minority (D 6): Levin, RMM; Akaka, Carper, Dayton, Lautenberg, Pryor

Oversight of Govt. Management, the Federal Workforce & the District of Columbia
Majority (R 8): Voinovich, Chmn.; Stevens, Coleman, Coburn, Chafee, Bennett, Domenici, Warner
Minority (D 6): Akaka, RMM; Levin, Carper, Dayton, Lautenberg, Pryor

Indian Affairs
indian.senate.gov

836 Hart
202–224–2251

Majority (R 8): McCain (AZ), Chmn.; Thomas (WY), Murkowski (AK), Coburn (OK), Domenici (NM), Smith (OR), Crapo (ID), Burr (NC)
Minority (D 6): Dorgan (ND), RMM; Inouye (HI), Conrad (ND), Akaka (HI), Johnson (SD), Cantwell (WA)
NO SUBCOMMITTEES

Intelligence (Select)
intelligence.senate.gov

211 Hart
202–224–1700

Majority (R 8): Roberts (KS), Chmn.; Hatch (UT), DeWine (OH), Bond (MO), Lott (MS), Snowe (ME), Hagel (NE), Chambliss (GA)
Minority (D 7): Rockefeller (WV), Vice Chmn.; Levin (MI), Feinstein (CA), Wyden (OR), Bayh (IN), Mikulski (MD), Corzine (NJ)

NO SUBCOMMITTEES

Judiciary
judiciary.senate.gov

224 Dirksen
202–224–5225

Majority (R 10): Specter (PA), Chmn.; Hatch (UT), Grassley (IA), Kyl (AZ), DeWine (OH), Sessions (AL), Graham (SC), Cornyn (TX), Brownback (KS), Coburn (OK)
Minority (D 8): Leahy (VT), RMM; Kennedy (MA), Biden (DE), Kohl (WI), Feinstein (CA), Feingold (WI), Schumer (NY), Durbin (IL)

SUBCOMMITTEES

Administrative Oversight & the Courts
Majority (R 4): Sessions, Chmn.; Specter, Grassley, Kyl
Minority (D 3): Schumer, RMM; Feinstein, Feingold

Antitrust, Competition Policy & Consumer Rights
Majority (R 6): DeWine, Chmn.; Specter, Hatch, Grassley, Graham, Brownback
Minority (D 5): Kohl, RMM; Leahy, Biden, Feingold, Schumer

Constitution, Civil Rights & Property Rights
Majority (R 5): Brownback, Chmn.; Specter, Graham, Cornyn, Coburn
Minority (D 4): Feingold, RMM; Kennedy, Feinstein, Durbin

Corrections & Rehabilitation
Majority (R 5): Coburn, Chmn.; Specter, Sessions, Cornyn, Brownback
Minority (D 4): Durbin, RMM; Leahy, Biden, Feingold

Crime & Drugs
Majority (R 6): Graham, Chmn.; Grassley, Kyl, DeWine, Sessions, Coburn
Minority (D 5): Biden, RMM; Kohl, Feinstein, Feingold, Schumer

Immigration, Border Security & Citizenship
Majority (R 7): Cornyn, Chmn.; Grassley, Kyl, DeWine, Sessions, Brownback, Coburn
Minority (D 6): Kennedy, RMM; Biden, Feinstein, Feingold, Schumer, Durbin

Intellectual Property
Majority (R 7): Hatch, Chmn.; Kyl, DeWine, Graham, Cornyn, Brownback, Coburn
Minority (D 6): Leahy, RMM; Kennedy, Biden, Feinstein, Kohl, Durbin

Terrorism, Technology & Homeland Security
Majority (R 7): Kyl, Chmn.; Hatch, Grassley, Cornyn, DeWine, Sessions, Graham
Minority (D 6): Feinstein, RMM; Kennedy, Biden, Kohl, Feingold, Durbin

Rules & Administration
rules.senate.gov

305 Russell
202–224–6352

Majority (R 10): Lott (MS), Chmn.; Stevens (AK), McConnell (KY), Cochran (MS), Santorum (PA), Hutchison (TX), Frist (TN), Chambliss (GA), Bennett (UT), Hagel (NE)
Minority (D 8): Dodd (CT), RMM; Byrd (WV), Inouye (HI), Feinstein (CA), Schumer (NY), Dayton (MN), Durbin (IL), Nelson (NE)

NO SUBCOMMITTEES

Small Business & Entrepreneurship
sbc.senate.gov

428A Russell
202–224–5175

Majority (R 10): Snowe (ME), Chmn.; Bond (MO), Burns (MT), Allen (VA), Coleman (MN), Thune (SD), Isakson (GA), Vitter (LA), Enzi (WY), Cornyn (TX)
Minority (D 8): Kerry (MA), RMM; Levin (MI), Harkin (IA), Lieberman (CT), Landrieu (LA), Cantwell (WA), Bayh (IN), Pryor (AR)

NO SUBCOMMITTEES

Veterans' Affairs
veterans.senate.gov

412 Russell
202–224–9126

Majority (R 8): Craig (ID), Chmn.; Specter (PA), Hutchison (TX), Graham (SC), Burr (NC), Ensign (NV), Thune (SD), Isakson (GA)
Minority (D 5): Akaka (HI), RMM; Rockefeller (WV), Murray (WA), Obama (IL), Salazar (CO)
Independent (1): Jeffords (I-VT)

NO SUBCOMMITTEES

HOUSE COMMITTEE LEADERSHIP

	Due to Step Down		Due to Step Down
Agriculture		International Relations	
Bob Goodlatte (VA-6)	2009	**Henry Hyde (IL-6)**	2007
RMM: Collin Peterson (MN-7)		RMM: Tom Lantos (CA-12)	
Appropriations		Judiciary	
Jerry Lewis (CA-41)	2011	**Jim Sensenbrenner (WI-5)**	2007
RMM: David Obey (WI-7)		RMM: John Conyers (MI-14)	
Armed Services		Resources	
Duncan Hunter (CA-52)	2009	**Richard Pombo (CA-11)**	2009
RMM: Ike Skelton (MO-4)		RMM: Nick Rahall (WV-3)	
Budget		Rules	
Jim Nussle (IA-1)	2007	**David Dreier (CA-26)**	*
RMM: John Spratt (SC-5)		RMM: Louise Slaughter (NY-28)	
Education & The Workforce		Science	
John Boehner (OH-8)	2007	**Sherwood Boehlert (NY-24)**	2007
RMM: George Miller (CA-7)		RMM: Bart Gordon (TN-6)	
Energy & Commerce		Small Business	
Joe Barton (TX-6)	2011	**Don Manzullo (IL-16)**	2007
RMM: John Dingell (MI-15)		RMM: Nydia Velazquez (NY-12)	
Financial Services		Standards of Official Conduct (Ethics)	
Michael Oxley (OH-4)	2007	**Doc Hastings (WA-4)**	2009
RMM: Barney Frank (MA-4)		RMM: Alan Mollohan (WV-1)	
Government Reform		Transportation & Infrastructure	
Tom Davis (VA-11)	2009	**Don Young (AK-AL)**	2007
RMM: Henry Waxman (CA-30)		RMM: James Oberstar (MN-8)	
Homeland Security		Veterans' Affairs	
Christopher Cox (CA-48)	2011**	**Steve Buyer (IN-4)**	2011
RMM: Bennie Thompson (MS-2)		RMM: Lane Evans (IL-17)	
House Administration		Ways & Means	
Bob Ney (OH-18)	2007	**Bill Thomas (CA-22)**	2007
RMM: Juanita Millender-McDonald (CA-37)		RMM: Charles Rangel (NY-15)	
Intelligence (Permanent Select)			
Pete Hoekstra (MI-2)	*		
RMM: Jane Harman (CA-36)			

Committee chairmen are noted in boldface
RMM: Ranking Minority Member

* Length of chairmanship is determined by the Speaker.
** On June 2, 2005, Cox was nominated by George W. Bush to be chairman of the Securities and Exchange Commission.

HOUSE COMMITTEES

Agriculture
agriculture.house.gov

1301 Longworth
202–225–2171

Majority (R 25): Goodlatte (VA), Chmn.; Boehner (OH), Vice Chmn.; Pombo (CA), Everett (AL), Lucas (OK), Moran (KS), Jenkins (TN), Gutknecht (MN), Hayes (NC), Johnson (IL), Osborne (NE), Pence (IN), Graves (MO), Bonner (AL), Rogers (AL), King (IA), Musgrave (CO), Neugebauer (TX), Boustany (LA), Schwarz (MI), Kuhl (NY), Foxx (NC), Conaway (TX), Fortenberry (NE), 1 vacancy

Minority (D 21): Peterson (MN), RMM; Holden (PA), McIntyre (NC), Etheridge (NC), Baca (CA), Case (HI), Cardoza (CA), Scott (GA), Marshall (GA), Herseth (SD), Butterfield (NC), Cuellar (TX), Melancon (LA), Costa (CA), Salazar (CO), Barrow (GA), Pomeroy (ND), Boswell (IA), Larsen (WA), Davis (TN), Chandler (KY)

SUBCOMMITTEES

Conservation, Credit, Rural Development & Research
Majority (R 9): Lucas, Chmn.; Moran, Osborne, Vice Chmn.; Graves, Rogers, King, Boustany, Schwarz, Fortenberry
Minority (D 8): Holden, RMM; Cuellar, McIntyre, Etheridge, Case, Davis, Herseth, Butterfield

Department Operations, Oversight, Nutrition & Forestry
Majority (R 7): Gutknecht, Chmn.; Pombo, Moran, Bonner, Foxx, Fortenberry, 1 vacancy
Minority (D 6): Baca, RMM; Cardoza, Butterfield, Holden, Cuellar, Costa

General Farm Commodities & Risk Management
Majority (R 15): Moran, Chmn.; Boehner, Everett, Lucas, Jenkins, Johnson, Pence, Graves, Bonner, King, Musgrave, Neugebauer, Boustany, Conaway, Fortenberry
Minority (D 13): Etheridge, RMM; Salazar, Marshall, Herseth, Butterfield, Melancon, Barrow, Pomeroy, Boswell, Larsen, Chandler, Scott, Costa

Livestock & Horticulture
Majority (R 12): Hayes, Chmn.; Boehner, Pombo, Osborne, Pence, Rogers, King, Neugebauer, Kuhl, Foxx, Conaway, 1 vacancy
Minority (D 10): Case, RMM; Scott, Herseth, Costa, Cardoza, Salazar, Boswell, Larsen, Pomeroy, Barrow

Specialty Crops & Foreign Agriculture Programs
Majority (R 8): Jenkins, Chmn.; Everett, Vice Chmn.; Gutknecht, Hayes, Rogers, Neugebauer, Schwarz, Foxx
Minority (D 7): McIntyre, RMM; Marshall, Melancon, Barrow, Scott, Chandler, Cuellar

Appropriations
www.house.gov/appropriations

H-218 The Capitol
202–225–2771

Majority (R 37): Lewis (CA), Chmn.; Young (FL), Regula (OH), Vice Chmn.; Rogers (KY), Wolf (VA), Kolbe (AZ), Walsh (NY), Taylor (NC), Hobson (OH), Istook (OK), Bonilla (TX), Knollenberg (MI), Kingston (GA), Frelinghuysen (NJ), Wicker (MS), Cunningham (CA), Tiahrt (KS), Wamp (TN), Latham (IA), Northup (KY), Aderholt (AL), Emerson (MO), Granger (TX), Peterson (PA), Goode (VA), Doolittle (CA), LaHood (IL), Sweeney (NY), Sherwood (PA), Weldon (FL), Simpson (ID), Culberson (TX), Kirk (IL), Crenshaw (FL), Rehberg (MT), Carter (TX), Alexander (LA)

Minority (D 29): Obey (WI), RMM; Murtha (PA), Dicks (WA), Sabo (MN), Hoyer (MD), Mollohan (WV), Kaptur (OH), Visclosky (IN), Lowey (NY), Serrano (NY), DeLauro (CT), Moran (VA), Olver (MA), Pastor (AZ), Price (NC), Edwards (TX), Cramer (AL), Kennedy (RI), Clyburn (SC), Hinchey (NY), Roybal-Allard (CA), Farr (CA), Jackson (IL), Kilpatrick (MI), Boyd (FL), Fattah (PA), Rothman (NJ), Bishop (GA), Berry (AR)

SUBCOMMITTEES

Agriculture, Rural Development, FDA & Related Agencies
Majority (R 8): Bonilla, Chmn.; Kingston, Latham, Emerson, Goode, LaHood, Vice Chmn.; Doolittle, Alexander
Minority (D 5): DeLauro, RMM; Hinchey, Farr, Boyd, Kaptur

Defense
Majority (R 9): Young, Chmn.; Hobson, Bonilla, Cunningham, Frelinghuysen, Vice Chmn.; Tiahrt, Wicker, Kingston, Granger
Minority (D 6): Murtha, RMM; Dicks, Sabo, Visclosky, Moran, Kaptur

Energy & Water Development & Related Agencies
Majority (R 8): Hobson, Chmn.; Frelinghuysen, Latham, Wamp, Emerson, Doolittle, Vice Chmn.; Simpson, Rehberg
Minority (D 5): Visclosky, RMM; Edwards, Pastor, Clyburn, Berry

Foreign Operations, Export Financing & Related Programs
Majority (R 8): Kolbe, Chmn.; Knollenberg, Kirk, Crenshaw, Sherwood, Vice Chmn.; Sweeney, Rehberg, Carter
Minority (D 5): Lowey, RMM; Jackson, Kilpatrick, Rothman, Fattah

Homeland Security
Majority (R 10): Rogers, Chmn.; Wamp, Latham, Emerson, Sweeney, Kolbe, Istook, Vice Chmn.; LaHood, Crenshaw, Carter
Minority (D 7): Sabo, RMM; Price, Serrano, Roybal-Allard, Bishop, Berry, Edwards

Interior, Environment & Related Agencies
Majority (R 8): Taylor, Chmn.; Wamp, Peterson, Sherwood, Istook, Aderholt, Doolittle, Simpson, Vice Chmn.
Minority (D 5): Dicks, RMM; Moran, Hinchey, Olver, Mollohan

Labor, Health and Human Services, Education & Related Agencies
Majority (R 10): Regula, Chmn.; Istook, Wicker, Northup, Vice Chmn.; Cunningham, Granger, Peterson, Sherwood, Weldon, Walsh
Minority (D 7): Obey, RMM; Hoyer, Lowey, DeLauro, Jackson, Kennedy, Roybal-Allard

Military Quality of Life & Veterans Affairs & Related Agencies
Majority (R 9): Walsh, Chmn.; Aderholt, Vice Chmn.; Northup, Simpson, Crenshaw, Young, Kirk, Rehberg, Carter
Minority (D 6): Edwards, RMM; Farr, Boyd, Bishop, Price, Cramer

Science, State, Justice, Commerce & Related Agencies
Majority (R 8): Wolf, Chmn.; Taylor, Kirk, Weldon, Vice Chmn.; Goode, LaHood, Culberson, Alexander
Minority (D 5): Mollohan, RMM; Serrano, Cramer, Kennedy, Fattah

Transportation, Treasury, HUD, the Judiciary & District of Columbia
Majority (R 9): Knollenberg, Chmn.; Wolf, Rogers, Tiahrt, Northup, Aderholt, Sweeney, Vice Chmn.; Culberson, Regula
Minority (D 6): Olver, RMM; Hoyer, Pastor, Kilpatrick, Clyburn, Rothman

Armed Services
www.house.gov/hasc

2120 Rayburn
202-225-4151

Majority (R 34): Hunter (CA), Chmn.; Weldon (PA), Vice Chmn.; Hefley (CO), Saxton (NJ), McHugh (NY), Everett (AL), Bartlett (MD), McKeon (CA), Thornberry (TX), Hostettler (IN), Jones (NC), Ryun (KS), Gibbons (NV), Hayes (NC), Calvert (CA), Simmons (CT), Davis (VA), Akin (MO), Forbes (VA), Miller (FL), Wilson (SC), LoBiondo (NJ), Bradley (NH), Turner (OH), Kline (MN), Miller (MI), Rogers (AL), Franks (AZ), Shuster (PA), Drake (VA), Schwarz (MI), McMorris (WA), Conaway (TX), Davis (KY)
Minority (D 28): Skelton (MO), RMM; Spratt (SC), Ortiz (TX), Evans (IL), Taylor (MS), Abercrombie (HI), Meehan (MA), Reyes (TX), Snyder (AR), Smith (WA), Sanchez (CA), McIntyre (NC), Tauscher (CA), Brady (PA), Andrews (NJ), Davis (CA), Langevin (RI), Israel (NY), Larsen (WA), Cooper (TN), Marshall (GA), Meek (FL), Bordallo (GU), Ryan (OH), Udall (CO), Butterfield (NC), McKinney (GA), Boren (OK)

SUBCOMMITTEES

Military Personnel
Majority (R 9): McHugh, Chmn.; Davis, Kline, Drake, Conaway, Saxton, Jones, Ryun, Hayes
Minority (D 7): Snyder, RMM; Meehan, Sanchez, Andrews, Davis, Udall, McKinney

Projection Forces
Majority (R 9): Bartlett, Chmn.; Simmons, Davis (VA), Miller (MI), Drake, Weldon, Saxton, Hostettler, Calvert
Minority (D 7): Taylor, RMM; Tauscher, Langevin, Israel, Marshall, Bordallo, Boren

Readiness
Majority (R 16): Hefley, Chmn.; Hostettler, Jones, Ryun, Forbes, Miller (FL), Rogers, Schwarz, McMorris, McHugh, McKeon, Hayes, Simmons, Bradley, Miller (MI), Franks
Minority (D 14): Ortiz, RMM; Evans, Taylor, Abercrombie, Reyes, Snyder, Brady, Davis (CA), Marshall, Meek, Bordallo, Ryan, Udall, Butterfield

Strategic Forces
Majority (R 8): Everett, Chmn.; Thornberry, Franks, Turner, Rogers, Schwarz, McMorris, Davis (KY)
Minority (D 6): Reyes, RMM; Spratt, Sanchez, Tauscher, Larsen, Cooper

Tactical Air & Land Forces
Majority (R 16): Weldon, Chmn.; McKeon, Gibbons, Calvert, LoBiondo, Bradley, Turner, Conaway, Everett, Bartlett, Jones, Ryun, Akin, Forbes, Wilson (SC), Shuster
Minority (D 14): Abercrombie, RMM; Skelton, Spratt, Ortiz, Evans, Smith, McIntyre, Brady, Israel, Cooper, Meek, Ryan, Butterfield, Boren

Terrorism, Unconventional Threats & Capabilities
Majority (R 12): Saxton, Chmn.; Hayes, Akin, Wilson (SC), Kline, Shuster, Davis (KY), Hefley, Thornberry, Gibbons, Miller (FL), LoBiondo
Minority (D 10): Meehan, RMM; Smith, McIntyre, Tauscher (CA), Andrews, Langevin, Larsen, Cooper, Marshall, McKinney

Budget
budget.house.gov

309 Cannon
202-226-7270

Majority (R 22): Nussle (IA), Chmn.; Ryun (KS), Crenshaw (FL), Putnam (FL), Wicker (MS), Hulshof (MO), Bonner (AL), Garrett (NJ), Barrett (SC), McCotter (MI), Diaz-Balart (FL), Hensarling (TX), Ros-Lehtinen (FL), Lungren (CA), Sessions (TX), Ryan (WI), Simpson (ID), Bradley (NH), McHenry (NC), Mack (FL), Conaway (TX), Chocola (IN)
Minority (D 17): Spratt (SC), RMM; Moore (KS), Neal (MA), DeLauro (CT), Edwards (TX), Ford (TN), Capps (CA), Baird (WA), Cooper (TN), Davis (AL), Jefferson (LA), Allen (ME), Case (HI), McKinney (GA), Cuellar (TX), Kind (WI), Schwartz (PA)

NO SUBCOMMITTEES

Education & the Workforce
2181 Rayburn
202–225–4527
edworkforce.house.gov

Majority (R 27): Boehner (OH), Chmn.; Petri (WI), Vice Chmn.; McKeon (CA), Castle (DE), Johnson (TX), Souder (IN), Norwood (GA), Ehlers (MI), Biggert (IL), Platts (PA), Tiberi (OH), Keller (FL), Osborne (NE), Wilson (SC), Porter (NV), Kline (MN), Musgrave (CO), Inglis (SC), McMorris (WA), Marchant (TX), Price (GA), Fortuno (PR), Jindal (LA), Boustany (LA), Foxx (NC), Drake (VA), Kuhl (NY)

Minority (D 22): Miller (CA), RMM; Kildee (MI), Owens (NY), Payne (NJ), Andrews (NJ), Scott (VA), Woolsey (CA), Hinojosa (TX), McCarthy (NY), Tierney (MA), Kind (WI), Kucinich (OH), Wu (OR), Holt (NJ), Davis (CA), McCollum (MN), Davis (IL), Grijalva (AZ), Van Hollen (MD), Ryan (OH), Bishop (NY), Barrow (GA)

SUBCOMMITTEES

21st Century Competitiveness
Majority (R 18): McKeon, Chmn.; Porter, Boehner, Petri, Castle, Johnson, Ehlers, Tiberi, Keller, Osborne, Inglis, McMorris, Price, Fortuno, Boustany, Foxx, Drake, Kuhl
Minority (D 15): Kildee, RMM; Payne, McCarthy, Tierney, Kind, Wu, Holt, McCollum, Van Hollen, Ryan, Scott, Davis, Bishop, Barrow, Owens

Education Reform
Majority (R 11): Castle, Chmn.; Osborne, Vice Chmn.; Souder, Ehlers, Biggert, Platts, Keller, Wilson, Musgrave, Jindal, Kuhl
Minority (D 9): Woolsey, RMM; Davis (IL), Grijalva, Andrews, Scott, Hinojosa, Kind, Kucinich, Davis (CA)

Employer-Employee Relations
Majority (R 12): Johnson, Chmn.; Kline, Boehner, McKeon, Platts, Tiberi, Wilson, Musgrave, Marchant, Jindal, Boustany, Foxx
Minority (D 9): Andrews, RMM; Kildee, Payne, McCarthy, Tierney, Wu, Holt, McCollum, Grijalva

Select Education
Majority (R 6): Tiberi, Chmn.; McMorris, Souder, Porter, Vice Chmn.; Inglis, Fortuno
Minority (D 4): Hinojosa, RMM; Davis, Van Hollen, Ryan

Workforce Protections
Majority (R 7): Norwood, Chmn.; Biggert, Vice Chmn.; Keller, Kline, Marchant, Price, Drake
Minority (D 5): Owens, RMM; Kucinich, Woolsey, Bishop, Barrow

Energy & Commerce
2125 Rayburn
202–225–2927
energycommerce.house.gov

Majority (R 31): Barton (TX), Chmn.; Hall (TX), Bilirakis (FL), Upton (MI), Stearns (FL), Gillmor (OH), Deal (GA), Whitfield (KY), Norwood (GA), Cubin (WY), Shimkus (IL), Wilson (NM), Shadegg (AZ), Pickering (MS), Vice Chmn.; Fossella (NY), Blunt (MO), Buyer (IN), Radanovich (CA), Bass (NH), Pitts (PA), Bono (CA), Walden (OR), Terry (NE), Ferguson (NJ), Rogers (MI), Otter (ID), Myrick (NC), Sullivan (OK), Murphy (PA), Burgess (TX), Blackburn (TN)

Minority (D 26): Dingell (MI), RMM; Waxman (CA), Markey (MA), Boucher (VA), Towns (NY), Pallone (NJ), Brown (OH), Gordon (TN), Rush (IL), Eshoo (CA), Stupak (MI), Engel (NY), Wynn (MD), Green (TX), Strickland (OH), DeGette (CO), Capps (CA), Doyle (PA), Allen (ME), Davis (FL), Schakowsky (IL), Solis (CA), Gonzalez (TX), Inslee (WA), Baldwin (WI), Ross (AR)

SUBCOMMITTEES

Commerce, Trade & Consumer Protection
Majority (R 14): Stearns, Chmn.; Upton, Deal, Cubin, Radanovich, Bass, Pitts, Bono, Terry, Ferguson, Rogers, Otter, Myrick, Murphy, Blackburn
Minority (D 12): Schakowsky, RMM; Ross, Markey, Towns, Brown, Rush, Green, Strickland, DeGette, Davis, Gonzalez, Baldwin

Energy & Air Quality
Majority (R 17): Hall, Chmn.; Bilirakis, Whitfield, Norwood, Shimkus, Wilson, Shadegg, Pickering, Fossella, Radanovich, Bono, Walden, Rogers, Otter, Sullivan, Murphy, Burgess
Minority (D 14): Boucher, RMM; Ross, Waxman, Markey, Engel, Wynn, Green, Strickland, Capps, Doyle, Allen, Davis, Solis, Gonzalez

Environment & Hazardous Materials
Majority (R 15): Gillmor, Chmn.; Hall, Deal, Wilson, Shadegg, Fossella, Bass, Pitts, Bono, Terry, Rogers, Otter, Myrick, Sullivan, Murphy
Minority (D 12): Solis, RMM; Pallone, Stupak, Wynn, Capps, Doyle, Allen, Schakowsky, Inslee, Green, Gonzalez, Baldwin

Health
Majority (R 17): Deal, Chmn.; Hall, Bilirakis, Upton, Gillmor, Norwood, Cubin, Shimkus, Shadegg, Pickering, Buyer, Pitts, Bono, Ferguson, Rogers, Myrick, Burgess
Minority (D 14): Brown, RMM; Waxman, Towns, Pallone, Gordon, Rush, Eshoo, Green, Strickland, DeGette, Capps, Allen, Davis, Baldwin

Oversight & Investigations
Majority (R 8): Whitfield, Chmn.; Stearns, Pickering, Bass, Walden, Ferguson, Burgess, Blackburn
Minority (D 6): Stupak, RMM; DeGette, Schakowsky, Inslee, Baldwin, Waxman

Telecommunications & the Internet
Majority (R 17): Upton, Chmn.; Bilirakis, Stearns, Gillmor, Whitfield, Cubin, Shimkus, Wilson, Pickering, Fossella, Radanovich, Bass, Walden, Terry, Ferguson, Sullivan, Blackburn
Minority (D 14): Markey, RMM; Engel, Wynn, Doyle, Gonzalez, Inslee, Boucher, Towns, Pallone, Brown, Gordon, Rush, Eshoo, Stupak

Financial Services
financialservices.house.gov

2129 Rayburn
202–225–7502

Majority (R 37): Oxley (OH), Chmn.; Leach (IA), Baker (LA), Pryce (OH), Bachus (AL), Castle (DE), King (NY), Royce (CA), Lucas (OK), Ney (OH), Kelly (NY), Vice Chmn.; Paul (TX), Gillmor (OH), Ryun (KS), LaTourette (OH), Manzullo (IL), Jones (NC), Biggert (IL), Shays (CT), Fossella (NY), Miller (CA), Tiberi (OH), Kennedy (MN), Feeney (FL), Hensarling (TX), Garrett (NJ), Brown-Waite (FL), Barrett (SC), Harris (FL), Renzi (AZ), Gerlach (PA), Pearce (NM), Neugebauer (TX), Price (GA), Fitzpatrick (PA), Davis (KY), McHenry (NC)
Minority (D 32): Frank (MA), RMM; Kanjorski (PA), Waters (CA), Maloney (NY), Gutierrez (IL), Velazquez (NY), Watt (NC), Ackerman (NY), Hooley (OR), Carson (IN), Sherman (CA), Meeks (NY), Lee (CA), Moore (KS), Capuano (MA), Ford (TN), Hinojosa (TX), Crowley (NY), Clay (MO), Israel (NY), McCarthy (NY), Baca (CA), Matheson (UT), Lynch (MA), Miller (NC), Scott (GA), Davis (AL), Green (TX), Cleaver (MO), Bean (IL), Wasserman Schultz (FL), Moore (WI)
Independent (1): Sanders (I-VT)

SUBCOMMITTEES

Capital Markets, Insurance & Government Sponsored Enterprises
Majority (R 26): Baker, Chmn.; Ryun, Vice Chmn.; Shays, Gillmor, Bachus, Castle, King, Lucas, Manzullo, Royce, Kelly, Ney, Fossella, Biggert, Miller, Kennedy, Tiberi, Barrett, Brown-Waite, Feeney, Gerlach, Harris, Hensarling, Renzi, Davis, Fitzpatrick
Minority (D 23): Kanjorski, RMM; Ackerman, Hooley, Sherman, Meeks, Moore, Capuano, Ford, Hinojosa, Crowley, Israel, Clay, McCarthy, Baca, Matheson, Lynch, Miller, Scott, Velazquez, Watt, Davis, Bean, Wasserman Schultz

Domestic and International Monetary Policy, Trade & Technology
Majority (R 14): Pryce, Chmn.; Biggert, Vice Chmn.; Leach, Castle, Lucas, Paul, LaTourette, Manzullo, Kennedy, Harris, Gerlach, Neugebauer, Price, McHenry
Minority (D 11): Maloney, RMM; Watt, Waters, Lee, Kanjorski, Sherman, Gutierrez, Bean, Wasserman Schultz, Moore, Crowley
Independent (1): Sanders (I)

Financial Institutions & Consumer Credit
Majority (R 25): Bachus, Chmn.; Jones, Vice Chmn.; Baker, Castle, Royce, Lucas, Kelly, Paul, Gillmor, Ryun, LaTourette, Biggert, Fossella, Miller, Tiberi, Feeney, Hensarling, Garrett, Brown-Waite, Barrett, Renzi, Pearce, Neugebauer, Price, McHenry
Minority (D 21): Maloney, Watt, Ackerman, Sherman, Meeks, Gutierrez, Moore (KS), Kanjorski, Waters, Hooley, Carson, Ford, Hinojosa, Crowley, Israel, McCarthy, Baca, Green, Moore (WI), Clay, Matheson, 1 vacancy
Sanders (I), RMM

Housing & Community Opportunity
Majority (R 14): Ney, Chmn.; Miller, Vice Chmn.; Baker, King, Jones, Shays, Tiberi, Brown-Waite, Harris, Renzi, Pearce, Neugebauer, Fitzpatrick, Davis
Minority (D 11): Waters, RMM; Velazquez, Carson, Lee, Capuano, Lynch, Miller, Scott, Davis, Cleaver, Green
Independent (1): Sanders (I)

Oversight & Investigations
Majority (R 11): Kelly, Chmn.; Paul, Vice Chmn.; Royce, LaTourette, Kennedy, Garrett, Barrett, Price, Fitzpatrick, Davis, McHenry
Minority (D 9): Gutierrez, RMM; Moore (KS), Maloney, Lynch, Davis, Cleaver, Scott, Wasserman Schultz, Moore (WI)

Government Reform
www.house.gov/reform

2157 Rayburn
202–225–5074

Majority (R 23): Davis (VA), Chmn.; Shays (CT), Vice Chmn.; Burton (IN), Ros-Lehtinen (FL), McHugh (NY), Mica (FL), Gutknecht (MN), Souder (IN), LaTourette (OH), Platts (PA), Cannon (UT), Duncan (TN), Miller (MI), Turner (OH), Issa (CA), Brown-Waite (FL), Porter (NV), Marchant (TX), Westmoreland (GA), McHenry (NC), Dent (PA), Foxx (NC), 1 vacancy
Minority (D 17): Waxman (CA), RMM; Lantos (CA), Owens (NY), Towns (NY), Kanjorski (PA), Maloney (NY), Cummings (MD), Kucinich (OH), Davis (IL), Clay (MO), Watson (CA), Lynch (MA), Van Hollen (MD), Sanchez (CA), Ruppersberger (MD), Higgins (NY), Norton (DC)
Independent (1): Sanders (I-VT)

SUBCOMMITTEES

Criminal Justice, Drug Policy & Human Resources
Majority (R 10): Souder, Chmn.; McHenry, Vice Chmn.; Burton, Mica, Gutknecht (MN), LaTourette, Cannon, Miller, Brown-Waite, Foxx
Minority (D 7): Cummings, RMM; Davis, Watson, Sanchez, Ruppersberger, Owens, 1 vacancy
Independent (1): Sanders (I)

Energy & Resources
Majority (R 6): Issa, Chmn.; Westmoreland, Vice Chmn.; Ros-Lehtinen, McHugh, McHenry, Marchant
Minority (D 4): Watson, RMM; Higgins, Lantos, Kucinich

Federal Workforce & Agency Organization
Majority (R 7): Porter, Chmn.; Mica, Vice Chmn.; Davis (VA), Issa, Marchant, McHenry, 1 vacancy
Minority (D 5): Davis (IL), RMM; Owens, Norton, Cummings, Van Hollen

Federalism & the Census
Majority (R 5): Turner, Chmn.; Dent, Vice Chmn.; Shays, Foxx, 1 vacancy
Minority (D 3): Clay, RMM; Kanjorski, Maloney

Government Management, Finance & Accountability
Majority (R 6): Platts, Chmn.; Foxx, Vice Chmn.; Davis, Gutknecht, Souder, Duncan
Minority (D 4): Towns, RMM; Owens, Kanjorski, Maloney

National Security, Emerging Threats & International Relations
Majority (R 11): Shays, Chmn.; Marchant, Vice Chmn.; Burton, Ros-Lehtinen, McHugh, LaTourette, Platts, Duncan, Turner, Porter, Dent
Minority (D 8): Kucinich, RMM; Lantos, Maloney, Van Hollen, Sanchez, Ruppersberger, Lynch, Higgins
Independent (1): Sanders (I)

Regulatory Affairs
Majority (R 6): Miller, Chmn.; Brown-Waite, Vice Chmn.; Souder, Cannon, Turner, Westmoreland
Minority (D 4): Lynch, RMM; Clay, Norton, Van Hollen

Homeland Security
433 Cannon
hsc.house.gov
202–226–8417
Majority (R 19): Cox (CA), Chmn.; Young (AK), Smith (TX), Weldon (PA), Shays (CT), King (NY), Linder (GA), Souder (IN), Davis (VA), Lungren (CA), Gibbons (NV), Simmons (CT), Rogers (AL), Pearce (NM), Harris (FL), Jindal (LA), Reichert (WA), McCaul (TX), Dent (PA)
Minority (D 15): Thompson (MS), RMM; Sanchez (CA), Markey (MA), Dicks (WA), Harman (CA), DeFazio (OR), Lowey (NY), Norton (DC), Lofgren (CA), Jackson Lee (TX), Pascrell (NJ), Christensen (VI), Etheridge (NC), Langevin (RI), Meek (FL)

SUBCOMMITTEES

Economic Security, Infrastructure Protection & Cybersecurity
Majority (R 10): Lungren, Chmn.; Young, Smith, Linder, Souder, Davis, Rogers, Pearce, Harris, Jindal
Minority (D 8): Sanchez, RMM; Markey, Dicks, DeFazio, Lofgren, Jackson Lee, Pascrell, Langevin

Emergency Preparedness, Science & Technology
Majority (R 10): King, Chmn.; Smith, Weldon, Simmons, Rogers, Pearce, Harris, Reichert, McCaul, Dent
Minority (D 8): Pascrell, RMM; Sanchez, Dicks, Harman, Lowey, Norton, Christensen, Etheridge

Intelligence, Information Sharing & Terrorism Risk Assessment
Majority (R 10): Simmons, Chmn.; Weldon, King, Souder, Lungren, Gibbons, Pearce, Jindal, Reichert, Dent
Minority (D 8): Lofgren, RMM; Sanchez, Harman, Lowey, Jackson Lee, Etheridge, Langevin, Meek

Management, Integration & Oversight
Majority (R 8): Rogers, Chmn.; Shays, Linder, Davis, Harris, Reichert, McCaul, Dent
Minority (D 6): Meek, RMM; Markey, Lofgren, Jackson Lee, Pascrell, Christensen

Prevention of Nuclear & Biological Attack
Majority (R 8): Linder, Chmn.; Young (AK), Shays, Lungren, Gibbons, Simmons, Jindal, McCaul
Minority (D 6): Langevin, RMM; Markey, Dicks, Harman, Norton, Christensen

House Administration
1309 Longworth
www.house.gov/cha
202–225–8281
Majority (R 6): Ney (OH), Chmn.; Ehlers (MI), Mica (FL), Doolittle (CA), Reynolds (NY), Miller (MI)
Minority (D 3): Millender-McDonald (CA), RMM; Brady (PA), Lofgren (CA)

NO SUBCOMMITTEES

International Relations
2170 Rayburn
www.house.gov/international_relations
202–225–5021
Majority (R 27): Hyde (IL), Chmn.; Leach (IA), Smith (NJ), Vice Chmn.; Burton (IN), Gallegly (CA), Ros-Lehtinen (FL), Rohrabacher (CA), Royce (CA), King (NY), Chabot (OH), Tancredo (CO), Paul (TX), Issa (CA), Flake (AZ), Davis (VA), Green (WI), Weller (IL), Pence (IN), McCotter (MI), Harris (FL), Wilson (SC), Boozman (AR), Barrett (SC), Mack (FL), Fortenberry (NE), McCaul (TX), Poe (TX)
Minority (D 23): Lantos (CA), RMM; Berman (CA), Ackerman (NY), Faleomavaega (AS), Payne (NJ), Menendez (NJ), Brown (OH), Sherman (CA), Wexler (FL), Engel (NY), Delahunt (MA), Meeks (NY), Lee (CA), Crowley (NY), Blumenauer (OR), Berkley (NV), Napolitano (CA), Schiff (CA), Watson (CA), Smith (WA), McCollum (MN), Chandler (KY), Cardoza (CA)

SUBCOMMITTEES

Africa, Global Human Rights & International Operations
Majority (R 7): Smith, Chmn.; Tancredo, Flake, Green, Boozman, Fortenberry, Royce, Vice Chmn.;
Minority (D 6): Payne, RMM; Lee, McCollum, Sherman, Meeks, Watson

Asia & the Pacific
Majority (R 7): Leach, Chmn.; Burton, Vice Chmn.; Gallegly, Rohrabacher, Chabot, Paul, Wilson
Minority (D 6): Faleomavaega, RMM; Brown, Blumenauer, Watson, Smith, Ackerman

Europe & Emerging Threats
Majority (R 7): Gallegly, Chmn.; Davis, King, Vice Chmn.; McCotter, Issa, Poe, Barrett
Minority (D 6): Wexler, RMM; Engel, Berkley, Napolitano, Smith, Chandler

International Terrorism & Nonproliferation
Majority (R 8): Royce, Chmn.; King, Tancredo, Issa (CA), Vice Chmn.; McCaul, Poe, Weller, Barrett
Minority (D 7): Sherman, RMM; Menendez, Wexler, Crowley, McCollum, Cardoza, Watson

Middle East & Central Asia
Majority (R 10): Ros-Lehtinen, Chmn.; Chabot, Vice Chmn.; McCotter, Boozman, Mack, Fortenberry, Davis, Pence, Harris, Issa
Minority (D 8): Ackerman, RMM; Berman, Engel, Crowley, Berkley, Schiff, Chandler, Cardoza

Oversight & Investigations
Majority (R 6): Rohrabacher, Chmn.; Royce, Flake, Vice Chmn.; Green, Pence, Wilson
Minority (D 4): Delahunt, RMM; Berman, Blumenauer, Schiff

Western Hemisphere
Majority (R 9): Burton, Chmn.; Paul, Weller, Vice Chmn.; Harris, Leach, Smith, Ros-Lehtinen, Mack, McCaul
Minority (D 7): Menendez, RMM; Napolitano, Meeks, Faleomavaega, Payne, Delahunt, Lee

Judiciary
www.house.gov/judiciary

2138 Rayburn
202–225–3951

Majority (R 23): Sensenbrenner (WI), Chmn.; Hyde (IL), Coble (NC), Smith (TX), Gallegly (CA), Goodlatte (VA), Chabot (OH), Lungren (CA), Jenkins (TN), Cannon (UT), Bachus (AL), Inglis (SC), Hostettler (IN), Green (WI), Keller (FL), Issa (CA), Flake (AZ), Pence (IN), Forbes (VA), King (IA), Feeney (FL), Franks (AZ), Gohmert (TX)
Minority (D 17): Conyers (MI), RMM; Berman (CA), Boucher (VA), Nadler (NY), Scott (VA), Watt (NC), Lofgren (CA), Jackson Lee (TX), Waters (CA), Meehan (MA), Delahunt (MA), Wexler (FL), Weiner (NY), Schiff (CA), Sanchez (CA), Smith (WA), Van Hollen (MD)

SUBCOMMITTEES

Commercial & Administrative Law
Majority (R 7): Cannon, Chmn.; Coble, Flake, Chabot, Green, Forbes, Gohmert
Minority (D 5): Watt, RMM; Delahunt, Smith, Van Hollen, Nadler

Courts, the Internet & Intellectual Property
Majority (R 12): Smith, Chmn.; Hyde, Gallegly, Goodlatte, Jenkins, Bachus, Inglis, Keller, Issa, Cannon, Pence, Forbes
Minority (D 10): Berman, RMM; Conyers, Boucher, Lofgren, Waters, Meehan, Wexler, Weiner, Schiff, Sanchez

Crime, Terrorism & Homeland Security
Majority (R 10): Coble, Chmn.; Lungren, Green, Feeney, Chabot, Keller, Flake, Pence, Forbes, Gohmert
Minority (D 6): Scott, RMM; Jackson Lee, Waters, Meehan, Delahunt, Weiner

Immigration, Border Security & Claims
Majority (R 10): Hostettler, Chmn.; King, Gohmert, Smith, Gallegly, Goodlatte, Lungren, Flake, Inglis, Issa
Minority (D 6): Jackson Lee, RMM; Berman, Lofgren, Sanchez, Waters, Meehan

The Constitution
Majority (R 8): Chabot, Chmn.; Franks, Jenkins, Bachus, Hostettler, Green, King, Feeney
Minority (D 5): Nadler, RMM; Conyers, Scott, Watt, Van Hollen

Permanent Select Committee on Intelligence
intelligence.house.gov

H-405 The Capitol
202–225–4121

Majority (R 12): Hoekstra (MI), Chmn.; LaHood (IL), Cunningham (CA), Everett (AL), Gallegly (CA), Wilson (NM), Davis (VA), Thornberry (TX), McHugh (NY), Tiahrt (KS), Rogers (MI), Renzi (AZ)
Minority (D 9): Harman (CA), RMM; Hastings (FL), Reyes (TX), Boswell (IA), Cramer (AL), Eshoo (CA), Holt (NJ), Ruppersberger (MD), Tierney (MA)

SUBCOMMITTEES

Intelligence Policy
Majority (R 5): Davis, Chmn.; Wilson, McHugh, Rogers, Renzi
Minority (D 3): Holt, RMM; Eshoo, Tierney

Oversight
Majority (R 7): Thornberry, Chmn.; LaHood, Everett, Wilson, Tiahrt, Rogers, Renzi
Minority (D 5): Cramer, RMM; Hastings, Reyes, Ruppersberger, Tierney

Technical & Tactical Intelligence
Majority (R 6): Wilson, Chmn.; Everett, Cunningham, Gallegly, Thornberry, McHugh
Minority (D 4): Eshoo, RMM; Cramer, Holt, Ruppersberger

Terrorism, Human Intelligence, Analysis & Counterintelligence
Majority (R 7): Cunningham, Chmn.; LaHood, Gallegly, Davis, McHugh, Tiahrt, Renzi
Minority (D 4): Boswell, RMM; Hastings, Reyes, Ruppersberger

Resources
1324 Longworth
202–225–2761
www.house.gov/resources
Majority (R 27): Pombo (CA), Chmn.; Young (AK), Saxton (NJ), Gallegly (CA), Duncan (TN), Gilchrest (MD), Calvert (CA), Cubin (WY), Radanovich (CA), Jones (NC), Cannon (UT), Peterson (PA), Gibbons (NV), Walden (OR), Tancredo (CO), Hayworth (AZ), Flake (AZ), Renzi (AZ), Pearce (NM), Brown (SC), Drake (VA), Fortuno (PR), McMorris (WA), Jindal (LA), Gohmert (TX), Musgrave (CO), 1 vacancy
Minority (D 22): Rahall (WV), RMM; Miller (CA), Markey (MA), Kildee (MI), DeFazio (OR), Faleomavaega (AS), Abercrombie (HI), Ortiz (TX), Pallone (NJ), Christensen (VI), Kind (WI), Inslee (WA), Napolitano (CA), Udall (NM), Udall (CO), Grijalva (AZ), Cardoza (CA), Bordallo (GU), Costa (CA), Melancon (LA), Boren (OK), Herseth (SD)

SUBCOMMITTEES

Energy & Mineral Resources
Majority (R 9): Gibbons, Chmn.; Young, Cubin, Cannon, Peterson, Pearce, Drake, Jindal, Gohmert
Minority (D 7): Grijalva, RMM; Faleomavaega, Ortiz, Costa, Melancon, Boren, Markey

Fisheries & Oceans
Majority (R 8): Gilchrest, Chmn.; Young, Saxton, Jones, Drake, Fortuno, Jindal, Musgrave
Minority (D 6): Pallone, RMM; Faleomavaega, Abercrombie, Ortiz, Kind, Bordallo

Forests & Forest Health
Majority (R 11): Walden, Chmn.; Duncan, Gilchrest, Cannon, Peterson, Tancredo, Hayworth, Flake, Renzi, Brown, McMorris
Minority (D 9): Udall (NM), RMM; Kildee, Abercrombie, Boren, DeFazio, Inslee, Udall (CO), Cardoza, Herseth

National Parks
Majority (R 9): Saxton, Gallegly, Duncan, Radanovich, Jones, Brown, Fortuno, Musgrave, 1 vacancy
Minority (D 7): Christensen, RMM; Kildee, Abercrombie, Kind, Udall (NM), Bordallo, Melancon

Water & Power
Majority (R 10): Radanovich, Chmn.; Calvert, Cubin, Walden, Tancredo, Hayworth, Pearce, McMorris, Gohmert, 1 vacancy
Minority (D 8): Napolitano, RMM; Grijalva, Costa, Miller, Udall (CO), Cardoza, 2 vacancies

Rules
H-312 The Capitol
202–225–9191
www.house.gov/rules
Majority (R 9): Dreier (CA), Chmn.; Diaz-Balart (FL), Hastings (WA), Sessions (TX), Putnam (FL), Capito (WV), Cole (OK), Bishop (UT), Gingrey (GA)
Minority (D 4): Slaughter (NY), RMM; McGovern (MA), Hastings (FL), Matsui (CA)

SUBCOMMITTEES

Legislative & Budget Process
Majority (R 5): Diaz-Balart, Chmn.; Sessions, Vice Chmn.; Bishop, Gingrey, Dreier
Minority (D 2): Hastings, RMM; Slaughter

Rules & Organization of the House
Majority (R 5): Hastings, Chmn.; Putnam, Vice Chmn.; Capito, Cole, Dreier
Minority (D 2): McGovern, RMM; Matsui

Science
2320 Rayburn
202–225–6371
www.house.gov/science
Majority (R 24): Boehlert (NY), Chmn.; Hall (TX), Smith (TX), Weldon (PA), Rohrabacher (CA), Calvert (CA), Bartlett (MD), Ehlers (MI), Gutknecht (MN), Lucas (OK), Biggert (IL), Gilchrest (MD), Akin (MO), Johnson (IL), Forbes (VA), Bonner (AL), Feeney (FL), Inglis (SC), Reichert (WA), Sodrel (IN), Schwarz (MI), McCaul (TX), 2 vacancies
Minority (D 20): Gordon (TN), RMM; Costello (IL), Johnson (TX), Woolsey (CA), Hooley (OR), Udall (CO), Wu (OR), Honda (CA), Miller (NC), Davis (TN), Carnahan (MO), Lipinski (IL), Jackson Lee (TX), Sherman (CA), Baird (WA), Matheson (UT), Costa (CA), Green (TX), Melancon (LA), 1 vacancy

SUBCOMMITTEES

Energy
Majority (R 12): Biggert, Chmn.; Hall, Weldon, Bartlett, Ehlers, Akin, Bonner, Inglis, Reichert, Sodrel, Schwarz, 1 vacancy
Minority (D 10): Honda, RMM; Woolsey, Davis, Costello, Johnson, Lipinski, Matheson, Jackson Lee, Sherman, Green

Environment, Technology & Standards
Majority (R 8): Ehlers, Chmn.; Gutknecht, Biggert, Gilchrest, Johnson (IL), Reichert, Schwarz, 1 vacancy
Minority (D 6): Wu, RMM; Miller, Udall, Davis, Baird, Matheson

Research
Majority (R 12): Inglis, Chmn.; Smith (TX), Weldon, Rohrabacher, Gutknecht, Lucas, Akin, Johnson (IL), Reichert, Sodrel, McCaul, 1 vacancy
Minority (D 10): Hooley, RMM; Carnahan, Lipinski, Baird, Melancon, Johnson (TX), 4 vacancies

Space & Aeronautics

Majority (R 11): Calvert, Chmn.; Hall, Smith (TX), Rohrabacher, Bartlett, Lucas, Forbes, Bonner, Feeney, McCaul, 1 vacancy

Minority (D 9): Udall, RMM; Wu, Honda, Miller, Jackson Lee, Sherman, Costa, Green, Melancon

Small Business
www.house.gov/smbiz

2361 Rayburn
202–225–5821

Majority (R 18): Manzullo (IL), Chmn.; Bartlett (MD), Kelly (NY), Chabot (OH), Graves (MO), Akin (MO), Shuster (PA), Musgrave (CO), Bradley (NH), King (IA), McCotter (MI), Keller (FL), Poe (TX), Sodrel (IN), Fortenberry (NE), Fitzpatrick (PA), Westmoreland (GA), Gohmert (TX)

Minority (D 15): Velazquez (NY), RMM; Millender-McDonald (CA), Udall (NM), Lipinski (IL), Faleomavaega (AS), Davis (IL), Christensen (VI), Case (HI), Bordallo (GU), Grijalva (AZ), Michaud (ME), Sanchez (CA), Barrow (GA), Bean (IL), Moore (WI)

SUBCOMMITTEES

Regulatory Reform & Oversight

Majority (R 7): Akin, Chmn.; Sodrel, Westmoreland, Gohmert, Kelly, King, Poe

Minority (D 6): Bordallo, RMM; Faleomavaega, Christensen, Case, 2 vacancies

Rural Enterprises, Agriculture & Technology

Majority (R 6): Graves, Chmn.; King, Bartlett, Sodrel, Fortenberry, Musgrave

Minority (D 5): Barrow, RMM; Udall, Case, Michaud, 1 vacancy

Tax, Finance & Exports

Majority (R 8): Bradley, Chmn.; Kelly, Chabot, McCotter, Keller, Poe, Fortenberry, Fitzpatrick

Minority (D 7): Millender-McDonald, RMM; Lipinski, Faleomavaega, Davis, Case, Michaud, Bean

Workforce, Empowerment & Government Programs

Majority (R 7): Musgrave, Chmn.; Bartlett, Shuster, Fitzpatrick, Westmoreland, McCotter, Bradley

Minority (D 6): Lipinski, RMM; Udall, Davis, Grijalva, Barrow, Bean

Standards of Official Conduct
www.house.gov/ethics

HT-2 The Capitol
202–225–7103

Majority (R 5): Hastings (WA), Chmn.; Biggert (IL), Smith (TX), Hart (PA), Cole (OK)

Minority (D 5): Mollohan (WV), RMM; Tubbs Jones (OH), Green (TX), Roybal-Allard (CA), Doyle (PA)

NO SUBCOMMITTEES

Transportation & Infrastructure
www.house.gov/transportation

2165 Rayburn
202–225–9446

Majority (R 41): Young (AK), Chmn.; Petri (WI), Vice Chmn.; Boehlert (NY), Coble (NC), Duncan (TN), Gilchrest (MD), Mica (FL), Hoekstra (MI), Ehlers (MI), Bachus (AL), LaTourette (OH), Kelly (NY), Baker (LA), Ney (OH), LoBiondo (NJ), Moran (KS), Miller (CA), Hayes (NC), Simmons (CT), Brown (SC), Johnson (IL), Platts (PA), Graves (MO), Kennedy (MN), Shuster (PA), Boozman (AR), Gerlach (PA), Diaz-Balart (FL), Porter (NV), Osborne (NE), Marchant (TX), Sodrel (IN), Dent (PA), Poe (TX), Reichert (WA), Mack (FL), Kuhl (NY), Fortuno (PR), Westmoreland (GA), Boustany (LA), 1 vacancy

Minority (D 34): Oberstar (MN), RMM; Rahall (WV), DeFazio (OR), Costello (IL), Norton (DC), Nadler (NY), Menendez (NJ), Brown (FL), Filner (CA), Johnson (TX), Taylor (MS), Millender-McDonald (CA), Cummings (MD), Blumenauer (OR), Tauscher (CA), Pascrell (NJ), Boswell (IA), Holden (PA), Baird (WA), Berkley (NV), Matheson (UT), Honda (CA), Larsen (WA), Capuano (MA), Weiner (NY), Carson (IN), Bishop (NY), Michaud (ME), Davis (TN), Chandler (KY), Higgins (NY), Carnahan (MO), Schwartz (PA), Salazar (CO)

SUBCOMMITTEES

Aviation

Majority (R 25): Mica, Chmn.; Petri, Coble, Duncan, Ehlers, Bachus, Kelly, Baker, Ney, LoBiondo, Moran, Hayes, Brown, Johnson, Graves, Kennedy, Boozman, Gerlach, Diaz-Balart, Porter, Dent, Poe, Kuhl, Westmoreland, 1 vacancy

Minority (D 21): Costello, RMM; Boswell, DeFazio, Norton, Brown, Johnson, Millender-McDonald, Tauscher, Pascrell, Holden, Berkley, Matheson, Honda, Larsen, Capuano, Weiner, Chandler, Carnahan, Salazar, Rahall, Filner

Coast Guard & Maritime Transportation

Majority (R 10): LoBiondo, Chmn.; Coble, Gilchrest, Hoekstra, Simmons, Diaz-Balart, Reichert, Mack, Fortuno, Boustany

Minority (D 8): Filner, RMM; Brown, Taylor, Millender-McDonald, Honda, Weiner, Higgins, Baird

Economic Development, Public Buildings & Emergency Management

Majority (R 5): Shuster, Chmn.; Gerlach, Marchant, Dent, Kuhl

Minority (D 4): Norton, RMM; Michaud, Davis, Carson

Highways, Transit & Pipelines

Majority (R 30): Petri, Chmn.; Boehlert, Coble, Duncan, Mica, Hoekstra, Bachus, LaTourette, Kelly, Baker, Ney, LoBiondo, Moran, Miller, Hayes, Simmons, Brown, Johnson, Platts, Graves, Kennedy, Shuster, Boozman, Diaz-Balart, Porter, Osborne, Marchant, Sodrel, Reichert, 1 vacancy

Minority (D 25): DeFazio, RMM; Rahall, Nadler, Taylor, Millender-McDonald, Cummings, Blumenauer, Tauscher, Pascrell, Holden, Baird, Berkley, Matheson, Honda, Larsen, Capuano, Weiner, Carson (IN), Bishop, Michaud, Davis, Chandler, Higgins, Carnahan, Schwartz

Railroads
Majority (R 14): LaTourette, Chmn.; Petri, Boehlert, Mica, Bachus, Moran, Miller, Simmons, Platts, Graves, Porter, Osborne, Sodrel, Westmoreland
Minority (D 12): Brown, RMM; Rahall, Nadler, Menendez, Filner, Cummings, Blumenauer, Boswell, Carson (IN), DeFazio, Costello, Johnson

Water Resources & Environment
Majority (R 19): Duncan, Chmn.; Boehlert, Gilchrest, Ehlers, LaTourette, Kelly, Baker, Ney, Miller, Brown, Shuster, Boozman, Gerlach, Osborne, Poe, Mack, Fortuno, Boustany, 1 vacancy
Minority (D 15): Johnson, RMM; Menendez, Salazar, Costello, Taylor, Baird, Bishop, Higgins, Schwartz, Blumenauer, Tauscher, Pascrell, Carnahan, Rahall, Norton

Veterans' Affairs
335 Cannon
veterans.house.gov
202–225–3527
Majority (R 16): Buyer (IN), Chmn.; Bilirakis (FL), Vice Chmn.; Everett (AL), Stearns (FL), Burton (IN), Moran (KS), Baker (LA), Brown (SC), Miller (FL), Boozman (AR), Bradley (NH), Brown-Waite (FL), Turner (OH), 3 vacancies
Minority (D 12): Evans (IL), RMM; Filner (CA), Gutierrez (IL), Brown (FL), Snyder (AR), Michaud (ME), Herseth (SD), Strickland (OH), Hooley (OR), Reyes (TX), Berkley (NV), Udall (NM)

SUBCOMMITTEES

Disability Assistance & Memorial Affairs
Majority (R 4): Miller, Chmn.; Moran, Vice Chmn.; Bradley, Brown-Waite
Minority (D 3): Berkley, RMM; Udall, Evans

Economic Opportunity
Majority (R 4): Boozman, Chmn.; Baker, Brown-Waite, Vice Chmn., 1 vacancy
Minority (D 3): Herseth, RMM; Hooley, Evans

Health
Majority (R 7): Brown, Chmn.; Stearns, Vice Chmn.; Baker, Moran, Miller, Turner, 1 vacancy
Minority (D 5): Michaud, RMM; Filner, Gutierrez, Brown, Snyder

Oversight & Investigations
Majority (R 4): Bilirakis, Chmn.; Everett, Boozman, Bradley
Minority (D 3): Strickland, RMM; Reyes, 1 vacancy

Ways & Means
1102 Longworth
waysandmeans.house.gov
202–225–3625
Majority (R 24): Thomas (CA), Chmn.; Shaw (FL), Johnson (CT), Herger (CA), McCrery (LA), Camp (MI), Ramstad (MN), Nussle (IA), Johnson (TX), English (PA), Hayworth (AZ), Weller (IL), Hulshof (MO), Lewis (KY), Foley (FL), Brady (TX), Reynolds (NY), Ryan (WI), Cantor (VA), Linder (GA), Beauprez (CO), Hart (PA), Chocola (IN), Nunes (CA)
Minority (D 17): Rangel (NY), RMM; Stark (CA), Levin (MI), Cardin (MD), McDermott (WA), Lewis (GA), Neal (MA), McNulty (NY), Jefferson (LA), Tanner (TN), Becerra (CA), Doggett (TX), Pomeroy (ND), Tubbs Jones (OH), Thompson (CA), Larson (CT), Emanuel (IL)

SUBCOMMITTEES

Health
Majority (R 8): Johnson (CT), Chmn.; McCrery, Johnson (TX), Camp, Ramstad, English, Hayworth, Hulshof
Minority (D 5): Stark, RMM; Lewis, Doggett, Thompson, Emanuel

Human Resources
Majority (R 8): Herger, Chmn.; Johnson (CT), Beauprez, Hart, McCrery, Camp, English, Nunes
Minority (D 5): McDermott, RMM; Cardin, Stark, Becerra, Emanuel

Oversight
Majority (R 8): Ramstad, Chmn.; Cantor, Beauprez, Linder, Shaw, Johnson (TX), Nunes, Hayworth
Minority (D 5): Lewis, RMM; Pomeroy, McNulty, Tanner, Rangel

Select Revenue Measures
Majority (R 8): Camp, Chmn.; Weller, Foley, Reynolds, Cantor, Linder, Hart, Chocola
Minority (D 5): McNulty, RMM; Doggett, Tubbs Jones, Thompson, Larson

Social Security
Majority (R 8): McCrery, Chmn.; Shaw, Johnson (TX), Hayworth, Hulshof, Lewis, Brady, Ryan
Minority (D 5): Levin, RMM; Pomeroy, Becerra, Tubbs Jones, Neal

Trade
Majority (R 9): Shaw, Chmn.; Herger, English, Nussle, Weller, Lewis, Foley, Brady, Reynolds
Minority (D 6): Cardin, RMM; Levin, Jefferson, Tanner, Larson, McDermott

JOINT COMMITTEES

Joint Committee on Taxation

www.house.gov/jct

1015 Longworth
202–225–3621

House (5): Thomas (CA), Chmn.; Shaw (FL), Johnson (CT), Rangel (NY), RMM; Stark (CA)
Senate (5): Grassley (IA), Vice Chmn.; Hatch (UT), Lott (MS), Baucus (MT), Rockefeller (WV)

Joint Economic Committee

www.house.gov/jec

G-01 Dirksen
202–224–5171

House (10): Saxton (NJ), Chmn.; Ryan (WI), English (PA), Paul (TX), Brady (TX), McCotter (MI), Maloney (NY), Hinchey (NY), Sanchez (CA), Cummings (MD)
Senate (10): Bennett (UT), Vice Chmn.; Brownback (KS), Sununu (NH), DeMint (SC), Sessions (AL), Cornyn (TX), Reed (RI), RMM; Kennedy (MA), Sarbanes (MD), Bingaman (NM)

Joint Committee on Printing

www.house.gov/jcp/

305 RSOB
202–224–3205

House (5): Ney (OH), Vice-Chmn.; Doolittle (CA), Reynolds (NY), Millender-McDonald (CA), Brady (PA)
Senate (5): Lott (MS), Chmn.; Cochran (MS), Chambliss (GA), Inouye (HI), Dayton (MN)

Joint Committee on the Library

1309 LHOB
202–225–8281

House (5): Ney (OH), Chmn.; Ehlers (MI), Miller (MI), Millender-McDonald (CA), Lofgren (CA)
Senate (5): Stevens (AK), Vice-Chmn.; Cochran (MS), Lott (MS), Dodd (CT), Schumer (MY)

Secretary of the Senate

S-312 The Capitol
202–224–3622

Emily Reynolds

Clerk of the House

H-154 The Capitol
202–225–7000

Jeff Trandahl

INDEX

The names of all the Governors, Senators and Representatives appear in boldface type. The number of the page that includes Members' corresponding biographical information also appears in bold.

THE AUTHORS

Michael Barone is a senior writer at *U.S. News & World Report* and a Fox News Channel contributor. The *Chicago Tribune* says, "Michael Barone is to politics what statistician-writer Bill James is to baseball, a mix of historian, social observer, and numbers cruncher who illuminates his subject with perspective and a touch of irreverence." His most recent book is *Hard America, Soft America*, published by Crown Forum in 2004.

Richard E. Cohen brings to the *Almanac* 28 years of experience covering Capitol Hill. He is the 1990 winner of the Everett McKinley Dirksen Award for distinguished reporting on Congress and *National Journal's* congressional correspondent since 1977. Cohen is the author of several books about Congress, including a biography of former Rep. Dan Rostenkowski.

THE PUBLISHER

"The nation's most respected, nonpartisan source of information about how Washington's policy-making machinery really works."

That's how *Newsweek* described *National Journal*. For more than 30 years, *National Journal* has reached subscribers with an award-winning weekly magazine noted for its dedication to "facts only" reporting. *National Journal* speaks to people who make it their business to know what's going on in the world's largest business—the United States Government.

Only *National Journal* is exclusively devoted to the coverage of what the government is doing today, what it's going to do tomorrow, and how its actions affect our lives.

This 2006 edition of *The Almanac of American Politics* marks the twelfth volume to be published by National Journal Group.

In addition to the *Almanac* and *National Journal*, National Journal Group publishes *Government Executive*, a monthly magazine for senior federal managers; *CongressDaily*, a twice-daily news service covering Congress; *The Hotline*, the premier daily publication on campaign politics; National Journal's *Technology Daily*, a twice-daily news service on information technology politics and policy; NationalJournal.com, the online source for political and policy professionals; *The Capital Source*, a semi-annual Washington directory; and the *National Journal Convention Daily*, a daily newspaper published at the Democratic and Republican Conventions.

600 New Hampshire Ave. NW, Washington, DC 20037 Telephone (202) 739-8400